Bloomsbury Thesaurus

Edited by
Fran Alexander

BLOOMSBURY

This edition published 1997

First published in 1993 by
Bloomsbury Publishing Plc
38 Soho Square
London W1V 5DF

A copy of the CIP entry for this book is available from the British Library

ISBN 07475 3261 3

10 9 8 7 6 5 4 3 2 1

Compiled and typeset by Market House Books Ltd, Aylesbury
Printed in Great Britain by Clays Ltd, St Ives plc

Contributors

Editor

Fran Alexander, BA

Contributors

Peter Blair, BA
Callum Brines, BA
Eve Daintith, BSc
John Daintith, BSc, PhD
Michael Durnin, BA
Rosalind Fergusson, BA
William Gould, BA
Robert Hine, BSc
Valerie Illingworth, MSc
Mandy Isaacs, BA
Pamela Kerr-Frost, BA
Jonathan Law, BA
Elizabeth Martin, MSc
David Pickering, MA
Megan Remmer, BA
Kathy Rooney, BA, MA, PhD
Mark Salad
Anne Stibbs, BA
John Wright, BA, PhD

Consultant Editors

Betty Kirkpatrick
Cecile Rheinhart Watters

Computer Systems

Anne Stibbs
Margaret Tuthill
Edmund Wright

Keyboarding

Elizabeth Bonham
Sandra McQueen
Jessica Scholes
Gwen Shaw
Linda Wells

Introduction

What is a Thesaurus?

The word 'thesaurus' comes from the Greek word for treasure and originally meant a place where treasure is stored. As with many words, the sense changed and thesaurus came to mean a book that served as a source or repository of information – a treasury of knowledge rather than of material wealth. In 1852, Peter Mark Roget published a new type of reference book, which he entitled *Thesaurus of English Words and Phrases, classified and arranged so as to facilitate the Expression of Ideas and assist in Literary Composition*. Roget arranged words not alphabetically, as in a dictionary or encyclopedia, but by concept. *Roget's Thesaurus* was immensely successful and 'Roget' has become a generic term for any book in which the words are arranged thematically rather than in A to Z form. With the development of computers and information technology, the term 'thesaurus' has been applied to any collection of words in a particular field, arranged or indexed for use in information processing.

Thesauruses are often contrasted with dictionaries. The user of a dictionary is seeking information about a particular word, usually its meaning. In a thesaurus, on the other hand, the user starts with an idea and is looking for a word to express it, or for the best word to use in a particular context. An author may wish to shun needless repetition and avoid Mark Twain's stricture '...that the writer's balance at the vocabulary bank has run dry and that he is too lazy to replenish it from the thesaurus'. Alternatively, the user may want a word that pinpoints a particular concept, for example an intense redness. A list that includes the word 'carmine' may be exactly what is needed.

A thesaurus, then, consists of sets of words connected in some way. The words 'idea–concept' and 'red–carmine' are synonyms. However, they are not exact synonyms. 'Carmine' is a less general word than 'red' and the two can be interchanged only in certain circumstances. One particular sense of the word 'idea' is fairly close in meaning to 'concept' but 'idea' has an additional range of such meanings as impression, belief, viewpoint, or plan.

A thesaurus is much more than a list of synonyms. It answers many questions. For instance, the user might want to be reminded of things that are typically red – blood, cherries, sunset, etc. The guide to connotation and allusion and the indication of possible metaphors is one of the most useful features of a thesaurus, extending not only the user's vocabulary but also their viewpoint. It opens up whole networks of references which lead, for example, from the synonyms for yellow through all the many types of yellow objects including precious stones and the Yellow Pages to the figurative uses of yellow in its connotations of cowardice.

In addition, a thesaurus provides information on words, such as musical instruments, chemical elements, breeds of cat, parts of a computer, sails of a ship, countries, types of fear, types of pasta, religious sects, great lovers, birthstones, the signs of the zodiac, or the seven deadly sins. Over 300 such lists, 126 in tabular form, have been included in the *Bloomsbury Thesaurus*.

The Bloomsbury Thesaurus

The aim in producing the *Bloomsbury Thesaurus* was to reflect the huge richness and variety of the English language today – as Roget had for his time. The classifications stem developed by Roget in the mid-nineteenth century was a magnificent creation, grouping words thematically into categories according to the ideas which they expressed. The classification focused on abstract ideas, listing words under general headings such as 'Relation', 'Quantity' and 'Order'.

The world has changed since 1852, and yet the numerous editors of later editions of *Roget's Thesaurus* have been forced to squeeze the thousands of new words, objects, concepts and phrases which have entered the language into the structure devised by Roget all those years ago. So even in the latest revision of Roget's original work, *computer* is listed under *abacus*.

The *Bloomsbury Thesaurus* was developed to provide a thematic classification of the English language which would be as useful to readers of the 1990s and beyond as the original *Roget* had been in the mid-nineteenth century.

It was a luxury to be able to start completely from scratch and work out a thematic organization which reflects the huge proliferation of language today. Each and every one of us is surrounded by language, written and spoken – from the latest hi-tech audio gizmos to the babble of TV advertising, from the proliferation of magazines to the latest paperback blockbuster, from job application forms to junk mail. In contrast to Roget's intellectual abstractions, the categories and lists in the *Bloomsbury Thesaurus* reflect the world of computers, of science and technology, of fashion and postmodern culture, of TV and video, of new medicine and drugs, of the boom in sports and leisure, of the worldwide spread of ethnic cuisines, of the earth as a global village. This edition of the *Bloomsbury Thesaurus* has been fully revised and updated so as to incorporate recent changes in the language such as the naming of new chemical elements but also the most current general terms like 'road rage', 'bad hair day', and 'alcopop'.

The book is divided into 815 categories in twenty three sections, which fall into three main groups. The first part of the book covers academic disciplines and major branches of knowledge, such subjects as anthropology, science, the arts, and so on, together with plants, animals, places, etc. This is more like the classification that would be used in an encyclopedia. The second part is a more traditional thesaurus division containing abstract ideas, such as time and space. The third group of sections cover human life, society, emotions, behaviour, etc. We believe that this approach creates a balanced book with a comprehensible arrangement: it has also allowed us to introduce a number of additional features:

Division of Categories: Each category is numbered and divided into sections corresponding to parts of speech – nouns, verbs, adjectives, etc. These sections are subdivided into numbered paragraphs corresponding to different aspects of the main idea. For example, under the noun section of *Hope* we have *hope, expectation, aspiration, comfort,* etc.

For clarity, each of these numbered paragraphs has a subheading in bold type. These subheadings should be regarded as key words indicating the general content of the paragraph. It is important to remember that the words in the paragraph are not necessarily synonyms of the key word, but they are all connected with it in some way.

Within a paragraph words are, as far as is possible, arranged in a logical order – for example, a range from a mild form of an emotion to an intense feeling. Informal words and phrases are usually placed at the end of the relevant paragraph.

Content: A thesaurus is simply a collection of words and phrases. It would not be practical in a book of this size to include all the possible words and phrases in the English language – inevitably – a selection has had to be made. We have based our selection on usage, frequency, and usefulness to the reader, focusing on the currency of contemporary English and avoiding for the most part the obsolete or archaic. We have tried to include good coverage of idiomatic English, to cover English as it is used throughout the world, and to include informal expression and slang. Where appropriate, labels indicate informal terms and those generally considered offensive.

As English is an international language, the book contains many expressions from America, Australia, and other parts of the English-speaking world. These are labelled as such. Foreign words and phrases that are used in English appear in italic type.

Lists of Words: A feature of the *Bloomsbury Thesaurus* is the inclusion of boxed tables of terms relevant to a particular subject. These tend to be quite specific items – countries, places, plants, animals, etc. – and many of them fall in the first section of the book. The criteria for inclusion of words in the lists is based on both importance and usage. We have included a certain amount of additional information where this may be helpful – for instance, capital cities of countries or symbols for chemical elements. We have not, however, encroached too far on the territory of an encyclopedia.

Cross-references: The book contains over 5000 cross-references to other entries in the book. The reference is to the main category number and title. The user will find other related information at these entries.

Quotations: The book contains a large number of quotations related to the categories. Many of these are a source of common phrases in the language. Others have been included for their general interest. As Doctor Johnson said, 'Every quotation contributes something to the stability or enlargement of the language'.

The Index: Roget said that most people who used his book start with the index. Unlike other thesauruses, which contain only selective indexes, the *Bloomsbury Thesaurus* indexes every occurrence of every word or phrase in the text, no matter how obscure the term.

It has been a rare privilege to compile, and subsequently revise, a completely new thesaurus. While following in the footsteps of Roget, we have tried to create a new classification that truly reflects the language of our times in a form which is easier for the reader to use – indeed, a treasury of language for the twenty-first century. We would like to thank the many people who have helped us, and in particular, mention Betsy Pitha, whose knowledge and experience were invaluable.

The Editors

Guide to the Thesaurus

The Main Text

The text is divided into numbered main categories. Each category contains words listed by *part of speech* (noun, verb, adjective, etc.). The categories are subdivided into *numbered paragraphs*, which group together words of similar meaning. These paragraphs each have a bold *subheading*. *Cross references* appear at the end of many paragraphs, indicating other related entries. *Quotations* appear at the beginning of many categories.
A large number of *lists* are also included in the text. These bring together specific groups of related words.

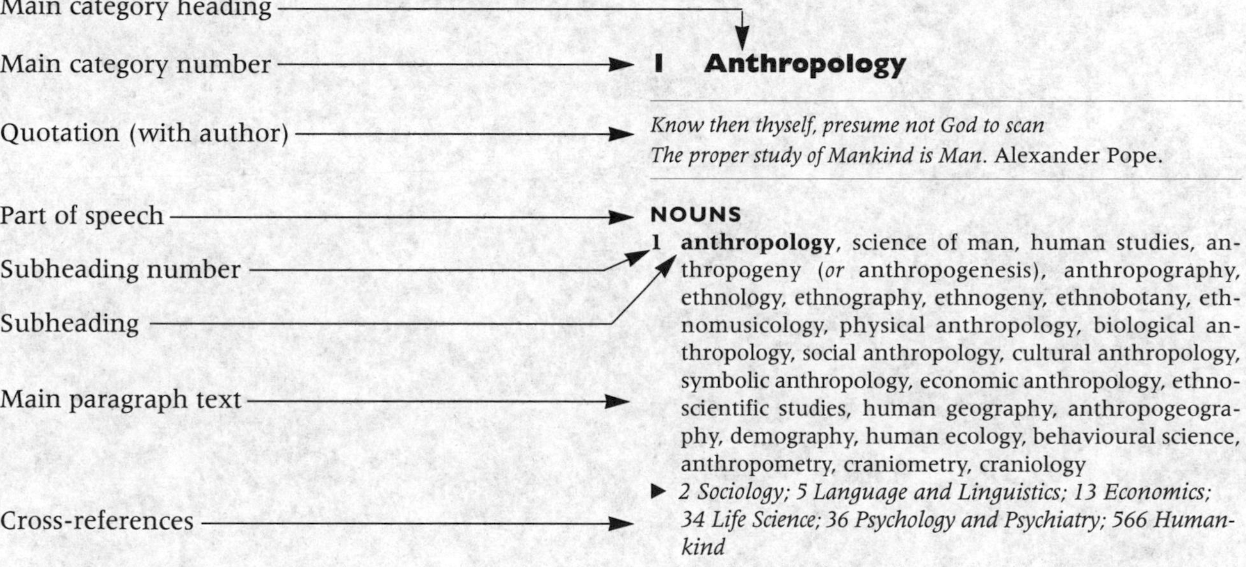
Main category heading
Main category number
Quotation (with author)
Part of speech
Subheading number
Subheading
Main paragraph text
Cross-references
1 Anthropology
Know then thyself, presume not God to scan
The proper study of Mankind is Man. Alexander Pope.
NOUNS
1 anthropology, science of man, human studies, anthropogeny (or anthropogenesis), anthropography, ethnology, ethnography, ethnogeny, ethnobotany, ethnomusicology, physical anthropology, biological anthropology, social anthropology, cultural anthropology, symbolic anthropology, economic anthropology, ethnoscientific studies, human geography, anthropogeography, demography, human ecology, behavioural science, anthropometry, craniometry, craniology
▶ 2 Sociology; 5 Language and Linguistics; 13 Economics; 34 Life Science; 36 Psychology and Psychiatry; 566 Humankind

The Index

The index contains all the category headings, subheadings, and words in the main paragraph text. The references are always to category numbers (not page numbers). Bold numbers are used to indicate main category headings. These come at the start of the entry. For example:

Anthropology is a main category, number 1. → **Anthropology 1**

anthropology is also a subheading at category 1, paragraph 1(i.e. 1.1). It also appears at 554.7 (*studies of life*) and 566.5 (*study of mankind*). → **anthropology 1.1**; 554.7 *studies of life*; 566.5 *study of mankind*

anthropometric appears at 1.11 (subheading *anthropological*) and at 26.16 (*micrometric*). → **anthropometric** 1.11 *anthropological*; 26.16 *micrometric*

Labels and Abbreviations used in the Thesaurus

Aus	Australian
Canad	Canadian
Dial	Dialect
Fr	French
Ger	German
Gk	Greek
Ir	Irish
Jap	Japanese
L	Latin
Lit	Literary, archaic, or formal
Naut	Nautical
NZ	New Zealand
S Afr	South African
Scot	Scottish
Sp	Spanish
US	United States
Inf	Informal or slang
™	Trademark
US	American

Other labels are unabbreviated.

Labels may appear in combination, e.g. (Aus and NZ inf).

List of Categories

Social and Human Studies

1 Anthropology
2 Sociology
3 History
4 Philosophy
5 Language and Linguistics
6 Education
7 Religion
8 Divinity
9 Worship
10 Ritual
11 Occultism
12 Government and Politics
13 Economics
14 Finance
15 Industrial Relations
16 Law

The Arts

17 Literature
18 Music
19 Painting and Sculpture
20 Architecture
21 Drama
22 Dancing
23 Furniture and Woodwork
24 Ceramics
25 Cookery

Science and Technology

26 Measurement
27 Mathematics
28 Physics
29 Astronomy
30 Earth Science
31 Meteorology and Climatology
32 Chemistry
33 Biochemistry
34 Life Science
35 Medicine
36 Psychology and Psychiatry
37 Pharmacology
38 Engineering
39 Electronics
40 Computers
41 Photography
42 Fabrics and Dyeing
43 Agriculture
44 Horticulture

Sports and Pastimes

45 Sport
46 American Football
47 Athletics
48 Baseball
49 Basketball
50 Boating Sports
51 Bowls
52 Combat Sports and Martial Arts
53 Cricket
54 Fencing
55 Fishing
56 Golf
57 Gymnastics
58 Hockey, Ice Hockey, and Lacrosse
59 Horse Riding and Racing
60 Hunting and Shooting
61 Motor Racing
62 Mountaineering and Climbing
63 Racquet Sports
64 Rugby Football
65 Snooker, Pool, and Billiards
66 Soccer
67 Swimming
68 Winter Sports
69 Games and Pastimes

Animals and Plants

70 Animals
71 Mammals
72 Birds
73 Reptiles and Amphibians
74 Fishes
75 Invertebrates
76 Insects and Arachnids
77 Plants
78 Flowers
79 Trees
80 Fruits
81 Grasses
82 Ferns and Mosses
83 Fungi
84 Algae and Lichens

Places

85 Countries
86 Regions
87 Cities, Towns, and Villages
88 Lakes
89 Mountains
90 Rivers
91 Seas
92 Other Geographical Features

Abstract Relations

93 Existence
94 Nonexistence
95 Reality
96 Unreality
97 Presence
98 Absence
99 Essence
100 Otherness
101 Unworldliness
102 Possibility
103 Impossibility
104 Probability
105 Improbability
106 Predetermination
107 Chance
108 Relatedness
109 Unrelatedness
110 Reciprocity
111 Sameness
112 Repetition
113 Opposition
114 Diversity
115 Similarity
116 Dissimilarity
117 Conformity
118 Nonconformity
119 Equality
120 Inequality
121 Superiority
122 Inferiority
123 Importance
124 Unimportance
125 Imitation
126 Originality
127 Inclusion
128 Exclusion
129 Precedence
130 Beginning
131 End
132 Consecutiveness
133 Discontinuity
134 Continuity
135 Requirement
136 Qualification
137 Class
138 Generality
139 Speciality
140 Rule

Spatial Relations

141 Space
142 Location
143 Situation
144 Displacement
145 Distance
146 Interval
147 Closeness
148 Length
149 Shortness
150 Broadness
151 Narrowness
152 Thickness
153 Thinness
154 Height
155 Lowness
156 Depth
157 Shallowness
158 Size

159 Smallness
160 Form
161 Shapelessness
162 Symmetry
163 Outline
164 Edge
165 Enclosure
166 Limit
167 Front
168 Back
169 Side
170 Surroundings
171 Outside
172 Inside
173 Centre
174 Top
175 Base
176 Angle
177 Curve
178 Straightness
179 Circularity
180 Convolution
181 Roundness
182 Convexity
183 Concavity
184 Wrinkle
185 Bulge
186 Verticality
187 Horizontality
188 Parallelism
189 Slantedness
190 Expansion
191 Contraction
192 Inversion
193 Interweaving

Number and Quantity

194 Number
195 Zero
196 Fraction
197 One
198 Two
199 Three
200 Four
201 Five and Over
202 Infinity
203 Quantity
204 Whole
205 Part
206 Few
207 Plurality
208 Multitude
209 Grading
210 Calculation
211 Addition
212 Subtraction
213 Increase
214 Decrease
215 Remainder
216 Average
217 Sufficiency
218 Insufficiency
219 Excess
220 List

Condition

221 State
222 Circumstances
223 Accompaniment
224 Change
225 Permanence
226 Stopping
227 Changeableness
228 Stability
229 Tendency
230 Perfection
231 Imperfection
232 Completeness
233 Incompleteness
234 Distortion
235 Worth
236 Worthlessness
237 Usefulness
238 Uselessness
239 Convenience
240 Inconvenience
241 Pleasantness
242 Unpleasantness
243 Preparation
244 Improvement
245 Deterioration
246 Success
247 Failure
248 Prosperity
249 Adversity
250 Freedom
251 Restraint
252 Safety
253 Security
254 Danger
255 Purity
256 Cleanness
257 Hygiene
258 Dirtiness
259 Health
260 Ill Health
261 Tiredness
262 Haste
263 Ease
264 Difficulty
265 Easiness
266 Obscurity
267 Stickiness
268 Slipperiness
269 Brevity
270 Vagueness
271 Simplicity
272 Ridiculousness
273 Accuracy
274 Error

Time

275 Time
276 Time Span
277 Duration
278 Transience
279 Eternity
280 Immediacy
281 Timekeeping
282 Present Time
283 Future Time
284 Past Time
285 Same Time
286 Different Time
287 Timeliness
288 Wrong Time
289 Succession
290 Daytime
291 Night-Time
292 Season
293 Earliness
294 Lateness
295 Newness
296 Oldness
297 Frequency
298 Regularity
299 Irregularity

Motion

300 Motion
301 Motionlessness
302 Forward Motion
303 Backward Motion
304 Ascent
305 Descent
306 Orbital Motion
307 Rotation
308 Opening
309 Closure
310 Convergence
311 Divergence
312 Arrival
313 Departure
314 Entry
315 Exit
316 Transfer
317 Way
318 Passage
319 Transport
320 Road Transport
321 Rail Transport
322 Aviation
323 Water Transport
324 Direction
325 Deviation
326 Oscillation
327 Agitation
328 Disturbance
329 Overstepping
330 Propulsion
331 Impulsion
332 Swiftness
333 Slowness

Power and Action

334 Power
335 Powerlessness
336 Strength
337 Weakness
338 Vigour
339 Inertness
340 Action
341 Inaction
342 Activity
343 Inactivity
344 Cause
345 Effect
346 Operation
347 Counteraction
348 Instrumentality
349 Use
350 Nonuse
351 Misuse
352 Means
353 Attempt
354 Undertaking
355 Relinquishment
356 Creation
357 Destruction
358 Obliteration
359 Preservation
360 Retention
361 Suspension
362 Traction
363 Attraction
364 Repulsion
365 Friction
366 Raising
367 Lowering
368 Insertion
369 Extraction
370 Admittance
371 Expulsion
372 Separation
373 Connection
374 Combination
375 Disintegration
376 Gathering
377 Dispersal
378 Obstruction
379 Trap
380 Violence

381 Attack
382 Killing
383 Resistance
384 Defence
385 Retaliation
386 Compulsion
387 Subjection
388 Submission
389 Escape
390 Deliverance
391 Liberation
392 Help
393 Repair
394 Remedy
395 Influence
396 Authority
397 Command
398 Delegate
399 Veto
400 Master
401 Servant

Substance and Structure

402 Material World
403 Structure
404 Texture
405 Component
406 Contents
407 Order
408 Disorder
409 Arrangement
410 Container
411 Layer
412 Mixture
413 Support
414 Heaviness
415 Lightness
416 Density
417 Sparseness
418 Hardness
419 Softness
420 Roughness
421 Smoothness
422 Elasticity
423 Toughness
424 Brittleness
425 Sharpness
426 Bluntness
427 Powderiness
428 Dryness
429 Moisture
430 Viscosity
431 Fluid
432 Gas
433 Water
434 Air
435 Materials
436 Provisions
437 Fuel
438 Tool
439 Store
440 Possessions
441 Waste

The Mind

442 Intellect
443 Thought
444 Reason
445 Intuition
446 Idea
447 Topic
448 Experiment
449 Discovery
450 Belief
451 Disbelief
452 Certainty
453 Uncertainty
454 Verification
455 Knowledge
456 Ignorance
457 Stupidity
458 Wisdom
459 Folly
460 Sanity
461 Insanity
462 Memory
463 Forgetfulness
464 Judgment
465 Misjudgment
466 Discrimination
467 Overestimation
468 Underestimation
469 Selection
470 Rejection
471 Attention
472 Inattention
473 Disinterestedness
474 Expectation
475 Prediction
476 Supposition
477 Imagination
478 Improvisation
479 Equivocation
480 Persuasion
481 Dissuasion
482 Intention
483 Motive
484 Plan
485 Skill
486 Unskilfulness
487 Unaccustomedness

Sensations

488 Sensation
489 Insensibility
490 Physical Pleasure
491 Physical Pain
492 Touch
493 Heat
494 Cold
495 Taste
496 Flavour
497 Blandness
498 Sweetness
499 Sourness
500 Smell
501 Odourlessness
502 Fragrance
503 Stench
504 Hearing
505 Deafness
506 Silence
507 Loudness
508 Sudden Sound
509 Repeated Sound
510 Resonance
511 Faintness
512 Hissing Sound
513 Harsh Sound
514 Human Cry
515 Animal Cry
516 Tunefulness
517 Dissonance
518 Vision
519 Blindness
520 Visibility
521 Invisibility
522 Light
523 Darkness
524 Dimness

Appearance

525 Appearance
526 Disappearance
527 Transparency
528 Opaqueness
529 Colour
530 Colourlessness
531 Whiteness
532 Blackness
533 Greyness
534 Brownness
535 Redness
536 Orangeness
537 Yellowness
538 Greenness
539 Blueness
540 Purpleness
541 Variegation
542 Decoration
543 Elegance
544 Inelegance
545 Beauty
546 Ugliness
547 Beautification
548 Blemish
549 Refinement
550 Covering
551 Dress
552 Undress
553 Fashion

Life and Society

554 Life
555 Youth
556 Age
557 Eating
558 Drinking
559 Secretion
560 Excretion
561 Reproduction
562 Fertility
563 Infertility
564 Inhabitant
565 Habitat
566 Humankind
567 Male
568 Female
569 Friendship
570 Marriage
571 Divorce and Widowhood
572 Celibacy
573 Aristocrat
574 Commoner
575 Title
576 Work
577 Workshop
578 Worker
579 Management
580 Leisure
581 Refreshment
582 Death
583 Burial
584 Military Affairs
585 War
586 Combatant
587 Weapon
588 Anarchy
589 Peace

Emotions

590 Feelings
591 Sensitivity
592 Insensitivity
593 Love
594 Hate
595 Liking
596 Dislike
597 Joy
598 Happiness

599 Humour
600 Rejoicing
601 Celebration
602 Sorrow
603 Lamentation
604 Disappointment
605 Resignation
606 Dissatisfaction
607 Annoyance and Aggravation
608 Relief
609 Satisfaction
610 Hope
611 Despair
612 Fear
613 Courage
614 Cowardice
615 Rashness
616 Caution
617 Desire
618 Indifference
619 Wonder
620 Boredom
621 Derision
622 Pride
623 Humility
624 Anger and Resentment
625 Grumpiness
626 Sullenness
627 Pity
628 Cruelty
629 Jealousy
630 Surprise

Character and Behaviour

631 Behaviour
632 Habit
633 Pursuit
634 Avoidance
635 Will
636 Willingness
637 Unwillingness
638 Resolution
639 Vacillation
640 Perseverance
641 Obstinacy
642 Frivolity
643 Solemnity
644 Curiosity
645 Cunning
646 Naivety
647 Severity
648 Leniency
649 Forgiveness
650 Benevolence
651 Malevolence
652 Philanthropy
653 Misanthropy
654 Sociability
655 Unsociability
656 Formality
657 Informality
658 Courtesy
659 Discourtesy
660 Insolence
661 Defiance
662 Disobedience
663 Obedience
664 Servility
665 Carefulness
666 Negligence
667 Respect
668 Disrespect
669 Approval
670 Disapproval
671 Gratitude
672 Ingratitude
673 Vanity
674 Modesty
675 Vulgarity
676 Affectation
677 Flattery
678 Scornfulness
679 Generosity
680 Thrift
681 Extravagance
682 Meanness
683 Selfishness
684 Self-Restraint
685 Moderation
686 Self-Indulgence
687 Fasting
688 Gluttony
689 Sobriety
690 Drunkenness
691 Drug-Taking

Communication

692 Communications
693 Information
694 Meaning
695 Intelligibility
696 Unintelligibility
697 Nonsense
698 Truth
699 Falsehood
700 Deception
701 Argument
702 Sophistry
703 Demonstration
704 Refutation
705 Question
706 Answer
707 Affirmation
708 Negation
709 Refusal
710 Request
711 Warning
712 Curse
713 Advice
714 Vindication
715 Accusation
716 Evidence
717 Representation
718 Misrepresentation
719 Interpretation
720 Misinterpretation
721 Description
722 Essay
723 Summary
724 Style
725 Clarity
726 Emphasis
727 Exaggeration
728 Understatement
729 Speech
730 Voicelessness
731 Talkativeness
732 Shyness
733 Address
734 Conversation
735 Soliloquy
736 Concealment
737 Secrecy
738 Display
739 Disclosure
740 Publication
741 News
742 Sign
743 Identification
744 Record
745 Maxim

Negotiations and Transactions

746 Negotiation
747 Cooperation
748 Mediation
749 Pacification
750 Agreement
751 Disagreement
752 Offer
753 Protest
754 Compromise
755 Contract
756 Promise
757 Permission
758 Exemption
759 Exchange
760 Conversion
761 Reversion
762 Substitution
763 Possession
764 Sharing
765 Profit
766 Loss
767 Disposal
768 Giving
769 Receiving
770 Allocation
771 Lending
772 Borrowing
773 Taking
774 Stealing
775 Giving Back
776 Trade
777 Purchase
778 Sale
779 Market
780 Money
781 Wealth
782 Poverty
783 Credit
784 Debt
785 Payment
786 Nonpayment
787 Expenditure
788 Receipt
789 Accounting
790 Price
791 Discount
792 Dearness
793 Cheapness
794 Prize

Morality

795 Morality
796 Immorality
797 Good
798 Evil
799 Honour
800 Dishonour
801 Right
802 Wrong
803 Virtue
804 Wickedness
805 Innocence
806 Guilt
807 Atonement
808 Remorse
809 Shamelessness
810 Duty
811 Reputation
812 Notoriety
813 Reward
814 Punishment
815 Prison

Alphabetical List of Categories

Absence 98
Accompaniment 223
Accounting 789
Accuracy 273
Accusation 715
Action 340
Activity 342
Addition 211
Address 733
Admittance 370
Adversity 249
Advice 713
Affectation 676
Affirmation 707
Age 556
Agitation 327
Agreement 750
Agriculture 43
Air 434
Algae and Lichens 84
Allocation 770
American Football 46
Anarchy 588
Anger and Resentment 624
Angle 176
Animal Cry 515
Animals 70
Annoyance and Aggravation 607
Answer 706
Anthropology 1
Appearance 525
Approval 669
Architecture 20
Argument 701
Aristocrat 573
Arrangement 409
Arrival 312
Ascent 304
Astronomy 29
Athletics 47
Atonement 807
Attack 381
Attempt 353
Attention 471
Attraction 363
Authority 396
Average 216
Aviation 322
Avoidance 634
Back 168
Backward Motion 303
Base 175
Baseball 48
Basketball 49
Beautification 547
Beauty 545
Beginning 130
Behaviour 631
Belief 450
Benevolence 650
Biochemistry 33
Birds 72
Blackness 532
Blandness 497
Blemish 548
Blindness 519
Blueness 539
Bluntness 426
Boating Sports 50
Boredom 620
Borrowing 772
Bowls 51
Brevity 269
Brittleness 424
Broadness 150
Brownness 534
Bulge 185
Burial 583
Calculation 210
Carefulness 665
Cause 344
Caution 616
Celebration 601
Celibacy 572
Centre 173
Ceramics 24
Certainty 452
Chance 107
Change 224
Changeableness 227
Cheapness 793
Chemistry 32
Circularity 179
Circumstances 222
Cities, Towns, and Villages 87
Clarity 725
Class 137
Cleanness 256
Closeness 147
Closure 309
Cold 494
Colour 529
Colourlessness 530
Combatant 586
Combat Sports and Martial Arts 52
Combination 374
Command 397
Commoner 574
Communications 692
Completeness 232
Component 405
Compromise 754
Compulsion 386
Computers 40
Concavity 183
Concealment 736
Conformity 117
Connection 373
Consecutiveness 132
Container 410
Contents 406
Continuity 134
Contract 755
Contraction 191
Convenience 239
Convergence 310
Conversation 734
Conversion 760
Convexity 182
Convolution 180
Cookery 25
Cooperation 747
Counteraction 347
Countries 85
Courage 613
Courtesy 658
Covering 550
Cowardice 614
Creation 356
Credit 783
Cricket 53
Cruelty 628
Cunning 645
Curiosity 644
Curse 712
Curve 177
Dancing 22
Danger 254
Darkness 523
Daytime 290
Deafness 505
Dearness 792
Death 582
Debt 784
Deception 700
Decoration 542
Decrease 214
Defence 384
Defiance 661
Delegate 398
Deliverance 390
Demonstration 703
Density 416
Departure 313
Depth 156
Derision 621
Descent 305
Description 721
Desire 617
Despair 611
Destruction 357
Deterioration 245
Deviation 325
Different Time 286
Difficulty 264
Dimness 524
Direction 324
Dirtiness 258
Disagreement 751
Disappearance 526
Disappointment 604
Disapproval 670
Disbelief 451
Disclosure 739
Discontinuity 133
Discount 791
Discourtesy 659
Discovery 449
Discrimination 466
Dishonour 800
Disintegration 375
Disinterestedness 473
Dislike 596
Disobedience 662
Disorder 408
Dispersal 377
Displacement 144
Display 738
Disposal 767
Disrespect 668
Dissatisfaction 606
Dissimilarity 116
Dissonance 517
Dissuasion 481
Distance 145
Distortion 234
Disturbance 328
Divergence 311
Diversity 114
Divinity 8
Divorce and Widowhood 571
Drama 21
Dress 551
Drinking 558
Drug-Taking 691
Drunkenness 690
Dryness 428
Duration 277
Duty 810
Earliness 293
Earth Science 30
Ease 263
Easiness 265
Eating 557
Economics 13
Edge 164
Education 6
Effect 345
Elasticity 422
Electronics 39
Elegance 543
Emphasis 726
Enclosure 165
End 131
Engineering 38
Entry 314
Equality 119
Equivocation 479
Error 274
Escape 389
Essay 722
Essence 99
Eternity 279
Evidence 716
Evil 798
Exaggeration 727
Excess 219
Exchange 759
Exclusion 128
Excretion 560
Exemption 758
Existence 93
Exit 315
Expansion 190
Expectation 474
Expenditure 787
Experiment 448
Expulsion 371
Extraction 369
Extravagance 681
Fabrics and Dyeing 42
Failure 247
Faintness 511
Falsehood 699
Fashion 553
Fasting 687
Fear 612
Feelings 590
Female 568
Fencing 54
Ferns and Mosses 82
Fertility 562
Few 206
Finance 14
Fishes 74
Fishing 55
Five and Over 201
Flattery 677
Flavour 496
Flowers 78
Fluid 431
Folly 459
Forgetfulness 463
Forgiveness 649
Form 160
Formality 656
Forward Motion 302
Four 200
Fraction 196
Fragrance 502
Freedom 250
Frequency 297
Friction 365
Friendship 569
Frivolity 642
Front 167
Fruits 80
Fuel 437
Fungi 83
Furniture and Woodwork 23
Future Time 283
Games and Pastimes 69
Gas 432
Gathering 376
Generality 138
Generosity 679
Giving 768
Giving Back 775
Gluttony 688
Golf 56
Good 797
Government and Politics 12
Grading 209
Grasses 81
Gratitude 671
Greenness 538
Greyness 533
Grumpiness 625
Guilt 806
Gymnastics 57
Habit 632
Habitat 565
Happiness 598
Hardness 418
Harsh Sound 513
Haste 262
Hate 594
Health 259
Hearing 504
Heat 493
Heaviness 414
Height 154
Help 392
Hissing Sound 512
History 3
Hockey, Ice Hockey, and Lacrosse 58
Honour 799
Hope 610
Horizontality 187
Horse Riding and Racing 59
Horticulture 44
Human Cry 514
Humankind 566
Humility 623
Humour 599
Hunting and Shooting 60
Hygiene 257
Idea 446
Identification 743
Ignorance 456
Ill Health 260
Imagination 477
Imitation 125
Immediacy 280
Immorality 796
Imperfection 231
Importance 123
Impossibility 103
Improbability 105
Improvement 244
Improvisation 478
Impulsion 331
Inaction 341
Inactivity 343
Inattention 472
Inclusion 127
Incompleteness 233
Inconvenience 240
Increase 213
Indifference 618
Industrial Relations 15
Inelegance 544
Inequality 120

Inertness 339
Inferiority 122
Infertility 563
Infinity 202
Influence 395
Informality 657
Information 693
Ingratitude 672
Inhabitant 564
Innocence 805
Insanity 461
Insects and Arachnids 76
Insensibility 489
Insensitivity 592
Insertion 368
Inside 172
Insolence 660
Instrumentality 348
Insufficiency 218
Intellect 442
Intelligibility 695
Intention 482
Interpretation 719
Interval 146
Interweaving 193
Intuition 445
Inversion 192
Invertebrates 75
Invisibility 521
Irregularity 299
Jealousy 629
Joy 597
Judgment 464
Killing 382
Knowledge 455
Lakes 88
Lamentation 603
Language and Linguistics 5
Lateness 294
Law 16
Layer 411
Leisure 580
Lending 771
Length 148
Leniency 648
Liberation 391
Life 554
Life Science 34
Light 522
Lightness 415
Liking 595
Limit 166
List 220
Literature 17
Location 142
Loss 766
Loudness 507
Love 593
Lowering 367
Lowness 155
Male 567
Malevolence 651
Mammals 71
Management 579
Market 779
Marriage 570
Master 400
Materials 435
Material World 402
Mathematics 27
Maxim 745
Meaning 694
Meanness 682
Means 352
Measurement 26
Mediation 748
Medicine 35
Memory 462
Meteorology and Climatology 31
Military Affairs 584
Misanthropy 653
Misinterpretation 720
Misjudgment 465
Misrepresentation 718
Misuse 351
Mixture 412
Moderation 685
Modesty 674
Moisture 429
Money 780
Morality 795
Motion 300
Motionlessness 301
Motive 483
Motor Racing 61
Mountaineering and Climbing 62
Mountains 89
Multitude 208
Music 18
Naivety 646
Narrowness 151
Negation 708
Negligence 666
Negotiation 746
Newness 295
News 741
Night-Time 291
Nonconformity 118
Nonexistence 94
Nonpayment 786
Nonsense 697
Nonuse 350
Notoriety 812
Number 194
Obedience 663
Obliteration 358
Obscurity 266
Obstinacy 641
Obstruction 378
Occultism 11
Odourlessness 501
Offer 752
Oldness 296
One 197
Opaqueness 528
Opening 308
Operation 346
Opposition 113
Orangeness 536
Orbital Motion 306
Order 407
Originality 126
Oscillation 326
Other Geographical Features 92
Otherness 100
Outline 163
Outside 171
Overestimation 467
Overstepping 329
Pacification 749
Painting and Sculpture 19
Parallelism 188
Part 205
Passage 318
Past Time 284
Payment 785
Peace 589
Perfection 230
Permanence 225
Permission 757
Perseverance 640
Persuasion 480
Pharmacology 37
Philanthropy 652
Philosophy 4
Photography 41
Physical Pain 491
Physical Pleasure 490
Physics 28
Pity 627
Plan 484
Plants 77
Pleasantness 241
Plurality 207
Possession 763
Possessions 440
Possibility 102
Poverty 782
Powderiness 427
Power 334
Powerlessness 335
Precedence 129
Predetermination 106
Prediction 475
Preparation 243
Presence 97
Present Time 282
Preservation 359
Price 790
Pride 622
Prison 815
Prize 794
Probability 104
Profit 765
Promise 756
Propulsion 330
Prosperity 248
Protest 753
Provisions 436
Psychology and Psychiatry 36
Publication 740
Punishment 814
Purchase 777
Purity 255
Purpleness 540
Pursuit 633
Qualification 136
Quantity 203
Question 705
Racquet Sports 63
Rail Transport 321
Raising 366
Rashness 615
Reality 95
Reason 444
Receipt 788
Receiving 769
Reciprocity 110
Record 744
Redness 535
Refinement 549
Refreshment 581
Refusal 709
Refutation 704
Regions 86
Regularity 298
Rejection 470
Rejoicing 600
Relatedness 108
Relief 608
Religion 7
Relinquishment 355
Remainder 215
Remedy 394
Remorse 808
Repair 393
Repeated Sound 509
Repetition 112
Representation 717
Reproduction 561
Reptiles and Amphibians 73
Repulsion 364
Reputation 811
Request 710
Requirement 135
Resignation 605
Resistance 383
Resolution 638
Resonance 510
Respect 667
Restraint 251
Retaliation 385
Retention 360
Reversion 761
Reward 813
Ridiculousness 272
Right 801
Ritual 10
Rivers 90
Road Transport 320
Rotation 307
Roughness 420
Roundness 181
Rugby Football 64
Rule 140
Safety 252
Sale 778
Sameness 111
Same Time 285
Sanity 460
Satisfaction 609
Scornfulness 678
Seas 91
Season 292
Secrecy 737
Secretion 559
Security 253
Selection 469
Self-Indulgence 686
Selfishness 683
Self-Restraint 684
Sensation 488
Sensitivity 591
Separation 372
Servant 401
Servility 664
Severity 647
Shallowness 157
Shamelessness 809
Shapelessness 161
Sharing 764
Sharpness 425
Shortness 149
Shyness 732
Side 169
Sign 742
Silence 506
Similarity 115
Simplicity 271
Situation 143
Size 158
Skill 485
Slantedness 189
Slipperiness 268
Slowness 333
Smallness 159
Smell 500
Smoothness 421
Snooker, Pool, and Billiards 65
Sobriety 689
Soccer 66
Sociability 654
Sociology 2
Softness 419
Solemnity 643
Soliloquy 735
Sophistry 702
Sorrow 602
Sourness 499
Space 141
Sparseness 417
Speciality 139
Speech 729
Sport 45
Stability 228
State 221
Stealing 774
Stench 503
Stickiness 267
Stopping 226
Store 439
Straightness 178
Strength 336
Structure 403
Stupidity 457
Style 724
Subjection 387
Submission 388
Substitution 762
Subtraction 212
Success 246
Succession 289
Sudden Sound 508
Sufficiency 217
Sullenness 626
Summary 723
Superiority 121
Support 413
Supposition 476
Surprise 630
Surroundings 170
Suspension 361
Sweetness 498
Swiftness 332
Swimming 67
Symmetry 162
Taking 773
Talkativeness 731
Taste 495
Tendency 229
Texture 404
Thickness 152
Thinness 153
Thought 443
Three 199
Thrift 680
Time 275
Timekeeping 281
Timeliness 287
Time Span 276
Tiredness 261
Title 575
Tool 438
Top 174
Topic 447
Touch 492
Toughness 423
Traction 362
Trade 776
Transfer 316
Transience 278
Transparency 527
Transport 319
Trap 379
Trees 79
Truth 698
Tunefulness 516
Two 198
Ugliness 546
Unaccustomedness 487
Uncertainty 453
Underestimation 468
Understatement 728
Undertaking 354
Undress 552
Unimportance 124
Unintelligibility 696
Unpleasantness 242
Unreality 96
Unrelatedness 109
Unskilfulness 486
Unsociability 655
Unwillingness 637
Unworldliness 101
Use 349
Usefulness 237
Uselessness 238
Vacillation 639
Vagueness 270
Vanity 673
Variegation 541
Verification 454
Verticality 186
Veto 399
Vigour 338
Vindication 714
Violence 380
Virtue 803
Viscosity 430
Visibility 520
Vision 518
Voicelessness 730
Vulgarity 675
War 585
Warning 711
Waste 441
Water 433
Water Transport 323
Way 317
Weakness 337
Wealth 781
Weapon 587
Whiteness 531
Whole 204
Wickedness 804
Will 635
Willingness 636
Winter Sports 68
Wisdom 458
Wonder 619
Work 576
Worker 578
Workshop 577
Worship 9
Worth 235
Worthlessness 236
Wrinkle 184
Wrong 802
Wrong Time 288
Yellowness 537
Youth 555
Zero 195

Social and Human Studies

1 Anthropology

Know then thyself, presume not God to scan
The proper study of Mankind is Man. Alexander Pope.

NOUNS

1 **anthropology**, science of man, human studies, anthropogeny (*or* anthropogenesis), anthropography, ethnology, ethnography, ethnogeny, ethnobotany, ethnomusicology, physical anthropology, biological anthropology, social anthropology, cultural anthropology, symbolic anthropology, economic anthropology, ethnoscientific studies, human geography, anthropogeography, demography, human ecology, behavioural science, anthropometry, craniometry, craniology

▶ *2 Sociology; 5 Language and Linguistics; 13 Economics; 34 Life Science; 36 Psychology and Psychiatry; 566 Humankind*

2 **palaeoanthropology**, prehistoric anthropology, archaeological anthropology, palaeoanthropography, palaeoethnography, palaeoethnology, palaeopsychology, Assyriology, Egyptology, Sumerology, epigraphy

▶ *3 History; 566 Humankind*

3 **anthropologist**, human scientist, ethnologist, ethnographer, ethnogenist, ethnomusicologist, anthropogeographer, demographer, human ecologist, behavioural scientist, anthropometrist, craniometrist, craniologer

▶ *2 Sociology; 5 Language and Linguistics; 36 Psychology and Psychiatry; 566 Humankind*

4 **palaeoanthropologist**, archaeological anthropologist, palaeoethnographer, palaeoethnologist, palaeopsychologist, Assyriologist, Egyptologist, Sumerologist, epigrapher, epigraphist

▶ *3 History; 566 Humankind*

5 **anthropological concept**, structuralism, functionalism, transactionalism, diffusionism, consanguinity, descent, kinship, age set, taboo

6 **race**, ethnic origin, colour, Caucasoid race, Caucasian, White, Nordic type, Alpine type, Aryan, Latino, Negroid race, Negro, Negrito, Negrillo, Nilotic type, Afro-Caribbean, African-American, Afro-American, Anglo-American, Anglo-African, Melanesian, Polynesian, Australasian, Mongoloid race, Oriental, Asian, Anglo-Indian, mixed race, mulatto, quadroon, octaroon, half-caste (Offensive), half-breed (Offensive), indigenous race, native people, native, aborigine, Indian, Amerindian, Amerasian, native American

▶ *85 Countries*

7 **society**, people, nation, nationality, population, folk, tribe, clan, culture, community, race, ethnic group, strain, stock

▶ *85 Countries; 108 Relatedness; 137 Class; 376 Gathering; 566 Humankind*

8 **tradition**, custom, habit, praxis, ritual, rite, symbol, taboo, ancient wisdom, ways of the fathers, common law, immemorial wisdom, Sunna, Talmud, Mishnah, myth, archetypal myth, mythology, legend, lore, folklore, folk tale, folk motif, folk art, folksong, folk history, oral tradition, archetype, racial memory, tribal memory, collective unconscious

▶ *7 Religion; 10 Ritual; 19 Painting and Sculpture; 36 Psychology and Psychiatry; 462 Memory; 570 Marriage; 583 Burial; 601 Celebration; 632 Habit*

9 **physical type**, build, physique, phthisic build, linear build, apoplectic build, stocky build, somatype, endomorphy, endomorph, mesomorphy, mesomorph, ectomorphy, ectomorph

10 **measurement**, anthrometry, anthroscopy, biometrics, craniometry, osteology, growth study, constitutional anthropology, height-weight ratio, Sheldon scale, skinfold, Bergmann's rule

ADJECTIVES

11 **anthropological**, anthropographical, ethnological, ethnographic, ethnogenic, anthropogenic, ethnoscientific, geographic, geographical, anthropogeographic, anthropogeographical, demographic, structuralist, functionalist, transactionalist, diffusionist, ecological, psychological, sociological, anatomical, anthropometric, anthropometrical, anthroposcopic, craniometric, craniometrical, craniological, osteometric

▶ *2 Sociology; 5 Language and Linguistics; 36 Psychology and Psychiatry; 566 Humankind*

12 **palaeoanthropological**, palaeoanthropographic, palaeoanthropographical, palaeoethnographic, palaeoethnological, palaeopsychological, epigraphic, epigraphical

▶ *3 History; 566 Humankind*

13 **racial**, ethnic, Caucasian, Caucasoid, White, Nordic, Alpine, Aryan, albinic, albinistic, albiniotic, Negroid, Black, Nilotic, Afro-Caribbean, African-American, Afro-American, Anglo-African, Melanesian, Polynesian, Aus-

tralasian, Mongoloid, Oriental, Asian, Anglo-Indian, mixed, mulatto, octaroon, quadroon, half-caste (Offensive), half-breed (Offensive), indigenous, native, aboriginal, Indian, Amerindian

▶ *85 Countries*

14 societal, communal, national, tribal, racial, ethnic, cultural, folk, established, time-honoured, immemorial, traditional, customary, received, handed down, unwritten, oral, mythological, legendary, heroic, archetypal

15 physical, stocky, apoplectic, lightly built, phthisic, endomorphic, mesomorphic, ectomorphic

ADVERBS

16 anthropologically, anthropographically, ethnologically, ethnographically, geographically, anthropogeographically, demographically, anthropometrically, craniometrically, craniologically

17 palaeoanthropologically, palaeoanthropographically, palaeoethnographically, palaeoethnologically, palaeopsychologically, epigraphically

18 societally, nationally, communally, tribally, racially, ethnically, culturally, traditionally, ritually, customarily, mythologically, mythically, archetypally

2 Sociology

Man is a social animal. Benedict Spinoza.

NOUNS

1 sociology, social science, behavioural science, social anthropology, rural sociology, urban sociology, sociobiology, political sociology, political behaviour, social psychology, macrosociology, comparative macrosociology, social morphology, sociology of knowledge, comparative sociology, human ecology, cultural ecology, applied sociology, pragmatic sociology, demography

▶ *1 Anthropology; 36 Psychology and Psychiatry; 455 Knowledge*

PEOPLES

African
- Afars
- Afrikaners
- Amhara
- Ashanti
- Azande
- Bantu
- Baqqarah
- Barotse
- Bemba
- Bushmen
- Dinka
- Edo
- Efik
- Ewe
- Fang
- Galla
- Ganda
- Hausa
- Herero
- Ibo
- Ik
- Issas
- Kabyle
- Khoikhoi
- Khoisan
- Kikuyu
- Lozi
- Lunda
- Luo
- Malinke
- Mandingo
- Masai
- Nguni
- Nyoro
- Pondo
- Pygmies (Twa)
- Rif
- Somali
- Sotho
- Swazi
- Teuso
- Xhosa
- Yoruba
- Zulu

European
- Achaeans
- Angles
- Anglo–Saxons
- Aryans
- Basque
- Belgians
- Bosnians
- Bretons
- Britons
- Bulgars
- Catalonians
- Celts
- Croatians
- Czechs
- Dorians
- Estonians
- Etruscans
- Flemings
- French
- Frisians
- Gauls
- Germans
- Ghegs
- Goths
- Gypsies (*or* Gipsies)
- Hellenes
- Iberians
- Jutes
- Lapps
- Lithuanians
- Magyars
- Picts
- Poles
- Saxons
- Scots
- Serbs
- Slavs
- Sorbs
- Tosks
- Visigoths
- Walloons

Middle Eastern
- Amalekites
- Amorites
- Arabs
- Armenians
- Babylonians
- Bakhtyari
- Bedouin
- Cumans
- Fulani
- Hittites
- Hurrians
- Israelis
- Jews
- Kassites
- Kazakh
- Kurds
- Palestinians
- Phoenicians
- Semites

Asian
- Ainu
- Andamanese
- Bashkir
- Bengalis
- Burmese
- Chinese
- Chukchi
- Cossacks
- Dards
- Georgians
- Hui
- Kaffirs
- Karen
- Khmer
- Maratha (*or* Mahratta)
- Mon
- Munda
- Pashtuns (*or* Pathans)
- Samoyed
- Sherpas
- Sinhalese
- Tai
- Talaing
- Tamils
- Tatars
- Turkmen

Australasian
- Aborigines
- Dayak
- Maoris
- Melanesians
- Polynesians
- Tagalog

Eskimo
- Aleut
- Inuit
- Yupik

North American Indian
- Algonquin
- Apache
- Arapaho
- Arikara
- Assiniboine
- Athapascan
- Bannock
- Blackfoot
- Caddo
- Cherokee
- Cheyenne
- Chickasaw
- Chinook
- Chippewa
- Chitimacha
- Choctaw
- Comanche
- Coushatla
- Cree
- Creek
- Crow
- Goshute
- Haida
- Hidatsa
- Hopi
- Hupa
- Huron
- Illinois
- Iowa
- Iroquois
- Karok
- Kickapoo
- Kiowa
- Kutenai
- Kwakiutl
- Lummi
- Maliseet
- Mandan
- Miccosukee
- Mohawk
- Mohican
- Narraganset
- Natchez
- Navaho
- Nez Percé
- Nootka
- Ojibwa
- Olmec
- Omaha
- Oneida
- Onondaga
- Osage
- Ottawa
- Paiute
- Papago
- Passamaquoddy
- Pawnee
- Penobscot
- Pequot
- Pima
- Potawatomi
- Powhatan
- Pueblo
- Quinault
- Seminole
- Seneca
- Shoshoni
- Siletz
- Sioux
- Tiwa
- Tlingit
- Tsimpshian
- Tunica–Biloxi
- Umatilla
- Ute
- Washoe
- Winnebago
- Yakima
- Yavapai
- Yurok
- Zuñi

Caribbean
- Arawaks
- Caribs

South American Indian
- Araucanians
- Aymara
- Aztec
- Cashinahua
- Chibcha
- Chimú
- Ge
- Guarani
- Inca
- Makuna
- Maya
- Mixtec
- Toltec
- Tupi
- Zapotec

2 **sociological research**, social survey, demographic research, demographic survey, demography, community study, population study, sociological theory, theory of social systems, role theory, locational theory, sociological method, sociometric technique, sociological model, sociological tool, questionnaire, survey, sociological analysis, structural-functionalism, sociological perspective, sociological jargon, sociologese

3 **social environment**, social relations, interaction, social interaction, interpersonal relations, intercourse, human interaction, human communications, social contact, socialization, friendship, marriage, symbolic interaction, human social behaviour, behavioural pattern, social trait, mores, values, value system, social role, sex role, gender, social order, social differences

4 **social organization**, family, group, community, religious organization, political organization, industrial organization, social system, belief system, community, *Gemeinschaft* (Ger), society, *Gesellschaft* (Ger)

► *4 Philosophy; 6 Education; 7 Religion; 12 Government and Politics; 123 Importance; 403 Structure; 407 Order; 408 Disorder; 409 Arrangement; 569 Friendship; 570 Marriage; 692 Communications; 742 Sign; 747 Cooperation; 810 Duty*

5 **society**, community, community relations, sense of community, social heterogeneity, homogeneity, collective adaptation, collectivity, mechanical solidarity, organic solidarity, rural sociology, rural society, folk society, rural sector, ruralism, rural-urban migration, urban society, urban sector, urban environment, urbanism, urbanization, suburbanization, urban planning, urban renewal, urban culture, industrialized society

► *142 Location; 564 Inhabitant; 565 Habitat*

6 **social group**, small group, primary group, family group, peer group, work group, ethnic group, racial group, age group, status group, group interaction, group behaviour, group solidarity

► *376 Gathering*

7 **social stratification**, social pyramid, hierarchy of authority, class boundary, social diversity, social status, prestige, social prestige, occupational prestige, economic status, economic power, educational status, employment status, earning status, class structure, social structure, social class system, social class, A, B, C1, C2, D, E, upper class, privileged class, ruling class, middle class, lower class, working class, class conflict, economic materialism, Marxism, social movement, mobility, social mobility, upward mobility, downward mobility

► *13 Economics; 137 Class; 144 Displacement; 227 Changeableness; 334 Power*

8 **human institution**, social institution, family, kinship, educational institution, school, religious institution, church, industrial institution, factory, political institution, political party, government institution, correctional institution

► *6 Education; 7 Religion; 12 Government and Politics; 15 Industrial Relations; 814 Punishment*

9 **social change**, social movement, social engineering, social control, social planning, social transformation, human development, social progress, social obligation, social action, social policy, social benefit

10 **social services**, social security, welfare, welfare organization, welfare state, poor relief, social work, good works, community service

11 **sociologist**, social scientist, empirical sociologist, sociobiologist, social psychologist, demographer, social worker, social reformer, economic determinist, Marxist

► *4 Philosophy; 13 Economics*

ADJECTIVES

12 **sociological**, societal, social, behavioural, interactive, symbolic, communal, educational, community-wide, religious, political, bureaucratic, military, environmental, sociobiological

13 **communal**, heterogeneous, collective, organic, rural, rural-urban, urban, urbanized, urbanizing, industrial, industrialized, industrializing governmental, correctional

14 **socioeconomic**, racial, occupational, economic, privileged, ruling, upper, middle, lower, working, Marxist, mobile, upward, downward, unequal, minority, communicative, communication, productive, territorial, demographic(al), locational, structural-functional

VERBS

15 **socialize**, interact, communicate, contact, organize, form a community, have a sense of community, participate, mingle, intermingle, join in, live side by side, work together, work from home, commute, employ, produce, improve living conditions, plan urban renewal, urbanize, industrialize, civilize, reform

ADVERBS

16 **sociologically**, socially, behaviourally, humanly, interactively, heterogeneously, collectively, symbolically, communally, educationally, religiously, politically, bureaucratically, governmentally, militarily, industrially, environmentally, sociobiologically, comparatively, culturally, pragmatically, ethnically, racially, economically, communicatively, socioeconomically, productively, territorially, demographically

3 History

The history of the world is but the biography of great men. Thomas Carlyle.

History is more or less bunk. Henry Ford.

NOUNS

1 **history**, historiography, philosophy of history, historical methodology, social history, economic history, religious history, political history, constitutional history, legal history, local history, history of ideas, history of science, counterfactual history, historical materialism, Marxist history, revisionist history, counterrevisionist history

2 **archaeology**, prehistoric archaeology, marine archaeology, fossilology, historical geology, Assyriology, Egyptology, Sumerology, palaeology, palaeohistology, palaeontography, palaeontology, human palaeontology, micropalaeontology, palaeogeography, palaeobiogeography, palaeolithy, palaeopotamology, palaeohydrography, palaeolimnology, palaeoeremology, palaeoceanography, palaeoecology, palaeobotany, palaeodendrology, palaeoglaciology, palaeoclimatology, palaeometeorology,

palaeocosmology, palaeobiology, palaeoherpetology, palaeomammology, palaeornithology, palaeozoology, palaeophytology, palaeophysiology, palaeophysiography, palaeopathology, palaeography, industrial archaeology

▶ *1 Anthropology; 5 Language and Linguistics; 30 Earth Science; 34 Life Science*

3 **historian**, recorder, biographer, archivist, historiographer

4 **archaeologist**, Assyriologist, Egyptologist, Sumerologist, palaeologist, palaeohistologist, palaeontographer, palaeontologist, micropalaeontologist, palaeogeographer, palaeobiogeographer, palaeopotamologist, palaeohydrographer, palaeolimnologist, palaeoecologist, palaeobotanist, palaeoclimatologist, palaeometeorologist, palaeocosmologist, palaeobiologist, palaeornithologist, palaeozoologist, palaeophytologist, palaeophysiologist, palaeopathologist, palaeographer, epigrapher

5 **chronicle**, history, account, record, diary, journal, log, logbook, recollection, report, reportage, documentary, documentation, recording, annals, archive, historical record, public record, minutes, minute book, notebook, notes, case notes, case history, track record, file, dossier, background, summary, information

6 **biography**, biographical record, autobiography, memoirs, life story, story, past, life, experiences, CV (*or* c.v.) (curriculum vitae), résumé (US)

7 **narrative**, narration, relation, description, tradition, place in history, legend, myth, folk tale, folk history

▶ *462 Memory; 554 Life; 693 Information; 741 News; 744 Record; 789 Accounting*

8 **past time**, history, the past, yesterday, yesteryear, good old days, days of yore, olden days, days of old, old times, foretime, former times, bygone days, bygones, days gone by, long ago, auld lang syne, ancient history, *ancien régime* (Fr), eld (Lit)

9 **distant past**, dim and distant past, remote age, antiquity, time immemorial, ancient times, way back (Inf), the year dot (Inf)

▶ *284 Past Time; 556 Age*

10 **past age**, ancient times, prehistory, protohistory, Stone Age, Heroic Age, Bronze Age, Iron Age, Classical Age, Hellenistic Age, Roman Republic, Roman Empire, Holy Roman Empire, Dark Ages, Middle Ages, Medieval times, Time of Troubles, Tudor times, Elizabethan Age, Renaissance, Enlightenment, Age of Reason, Victorian Age, Risorgimento, Reconstruction, Prohibition, the Roaring Twenties, the Swinging Sixties

▶ *284 Past Time; 556 Age*

11 **relic**, vestige, remains, ruin, remainder, archaism, antiquity, antique, museum piece, heirloom, ancient monument, eolith, neolith, microlith, megalith, monolith, cromlech, dolmen, menhir, earthwork, burial mound, barrow, fogou, cave painting, artefact, flint axe, flint tool, fossil, manuscript, scroll, Dead Sea Scrolls, Pipe rolls, epigraph, inscription, memento, memorabilia, Victoriana, souvenir

▶ *556 Age; 566 Humankind; 693 Information; 716 Evidence*

12 **historicism**, historical method, excavation, digging up the past, exhumation, medievalism, antiquarianism, archaism

13 **looking back**, remembrance, reminiscence, flashback, recalling, remembering, reviewing, harking-back, nostalgia, *déjà vu* (Fr)

▶ *462 Memory; 705 Question*

14 **historicalness**, historicity, reality, matter of fact, factualness, realness, actuality, genuineness, validity, fact, truth, event, deed, act, experience, incident, episode, happening

▶ *698 Truth*

ADJECTIVES

15 **historic**, ancient, old, ancestral, prehistoric, protohistoric, diachronic, before the Flood, antediluvian, pre-Christian, pre-classical, primordial, primal, aboriginal, antiquated, dated, archaic, former, prior, Classical, Hellenistic, Medieval, Elizabethan, Renaissance, Victorian, atavistic, vestigial, remaining, monumental

▶ *126 Originality; 284 Past Time; 556 Age*

16 **historical**, historiographical, prehistorical, protohistorical

17 **archaeological**, Assyriological, Egyptological, Sumerological, palaeological, palaeohistological, palaeontographical, palaeontological, micropalaeontological, palaeogeographical, palaeobiogeographical, palaeopotamological, palaeohydrographical, palaeolimnological, palaeoeremological, palaeoecological, palaeobotanical, palaeoclimatological, palaeometeorological, palaeocosmological, palaeobiological, palaeornithological, palaeozoological, palaeophysiological, palaeopathological, palaeographical, epigraphical

▶ *1 Anthropology; 5 Language and Linguistics; 30 Earth Science; 34 Life Science*

18 **in the past**, historical, over, finished, old hat, yesterday's news, old story, over and done with, no more, gone, dead and gone, dead and buried, dead as a dodo, extinct, ended, defunct, obsolete, expired, lapsed, passé, has-been, retroactive, bygone

▶ *131 End; 284 Past Time; 556 Age*

19 **chronicled**, recorded, logged, documented, minuted, filed, registered, archival, reported, described, descriptive, recollected, recalled, told, narrated, related, biographical, autobiographical, factual, true, real, actual, authentic, genuine, valid, verifiable, traditional, historical, legendary, famous, mythical

▶ *462 Memory; 693 Information; 698 Truth*

VERBS

20 **chronicle**, record, log, keep a diary, recollect, report, document, register, minute, file, summarize, inform, store information, narrate, relate, describe

▶ *462 Memory; 693 Information; 716 Evidence; 721 Description; 723 Summary*

21 **antiquarianize**, archaize, excavate, dig up the past, exhume, look back, trace back

22 **remember**, reminisce, recall, review, hark back, call to mind

23 **turn back time**, put the clock back, reconstruct, salvage

▶ *284 Past Time; 462 Memory*

ADVERBS

24 **historically**, prehistorically, protohistorically, ancestrally, diachronically, primordially, aboriginally, archaically, formerly, aforetime, of old, of yore, ago, long ago, long since, a long time ago, once, some time ago,

yesterday, yesteryear, in olden times, in the good old days, in the dim and distant past, in the mists of time, in days gone by, before now, hitherto, from time immemorial, time out of mind, yet, till now, until now, retrospectively, retroactively, with hindsight, from a historical perspective
▶ *126 Originality; 275 Time; 284 Past Time; 462 Memory; 556 Age*

25 reportedly, summarily, informatively, really, actually, genuinely, validly, vestigially, epigraphically, descriptively, biographically, autobiographically, reminiscently, nostalgically, memorially, monumentally, traditionally, mythically
▶ *554 Life ; 693 Information; 698 Truth; 741 News*

4 Philosophy

Do not all charms fly
At the mere touch of cold philosophy. John Keats.

Philosophy is not a theory but an activity. Ludwig Wittgenstein.

NOUNS

1 philosophy, viewpoint, point of view, view, outlook, attitude, opinion, doctrine, philosophical doctrine, feeling, sentiment, idea, thought, notion, conclusion, judgment, tenet, dogma, principle, canon, maxim, axiom, aphorism, statement, assertion, proposition, premise, assumption, precept, presupposition, thesis, postulate, supposition, conjecture, speculation, philosophical speculation, hypothesis, philosophical theory, concept, explanation, theory of knowledge, rationalization, justification
▶ *443 Thought; 444 Reason; 446 Idea; 450 Belief; 476 Supposition; 590 Feelings; 745 Maxim*

2 philosophical system, belief system, set of beliefs (*or* values), value system, value judgment, ethical system, ethos, morals, school of thought, code, moral code, code of practice, code of conduct, standards, principles, ideology, world view, *Weltanschauung* (Ger), teaching, creed, credo, stance, position, manifesto, metanarrative
▶ *7 Religion; 443 Thought; 446 Idea; 450 Belief; 464 Judgment; 476 Supposition; 590 Feelings; 795 Morality*

3 detachment, stoicism, sang-froid, control, self-control, self-possession, self-restraint, spartanism, dispassion, cool, coolness, cool-headedness, temperance, moderation, sobriety, calmness, inexcitability, imperturbability, aplomb, composure, level-headedness, reasonableness, common sense, rationality, lucidity, objectivity, equanimity, tolerance, balance, patience, thoughtfulness, even temper, good temper, peace of mind, tranquillity, ataraxia, serenity, quietude, placidity, passivity, resignation, horse sense (Inf)
▶ *343 Inactivity; 444 Reason; 473 Disinterestedness; 618 Indifference; 684 Self-Restraint; 685 Moderation; 689 Sobriety*

4 philosophical investigation, philosophical inquiry (*or* enquiry), examination, self-examination, introspection, analysis, consideration, scrutiny, investigation, investigation into first causes, search, survey, study, research, asking, challenge, questioning, elenchus, speculation, reflection, reasoning, ratiocination, concentration, contemplation, cogitation, excogitation, pondering, deliberation, musing, brainwork, conceptual thought, intuition, abstract thought, deduction, induction, inference, calculation, computation
▶ *443 Thought; 444 Reason; 476 Supposition; 619 Wonder; 705 Question*

5 philosophical argument, discussion, dialogue, symposium, conversation, colloquy, debate, dialectic, Hegelian dialectic, syllogism, thesis, antithesis, synthesis, interlocution, disputation, argument, logomachy, polemic, eristic, rhetoric, oratory
▶ *701 Argument; 702 Sophistry; 734 Conversation*

6 branch of philosophy, logic, formal logic, modal logic, deontic logic, axiomatic set theory, moral philosophy, ethics, metaethics, medical ethics, legal ethics, axiology, deontology, analytical philosophy, political philosophy, philosophy of mind, mental philosophy, metaphysics, ontology, epistemology, gnosiology, phenomenology, teleology, cosmology, natural philosophy, casuistry, aesthetics, philosophy of language, semantics, philosophy of signs, semiotics, philosophy of law, philosophy of history, philosophy of psychology, philosophy of commonsense, philosophy of science, quantum physics, quantum mathematics, propositional calculus, philosophy of religion, theology, ontotheology
▶ *5 Language and Linguistics; 7 Religion; 442 Intellect; 446 Idea; 795 Morality*

7 school of thought, Platonism, Neo-Platonism, Cambridge Platonism, Pythagoreanism, pre-Socratic philosophy, Eleaticism, euhemerism, eudaemonism, Socraticism, atomism, stoicism, scepticism, lyrenaic philosophy, cynicism, epicureanism, peripatetic philosophy, Aristotelian philosophy, Aristotelianism, Averroism, scholasticism, Thomism, Augustinian philosophy, vitalism, animism, panpsychism, pantheism, deism, theism, dynamism, mechanism, essentialism, holism, hylomorphism, hylozoism, Bergsonism, agnosticism, Gnosticism, Manichaeism, transcendentalism, idealism, mysticism, Sufism, Confucianism, Taoism, Buddhism, Zen Buddhism, Yoga, Vaisesika, Vijnanavada, Nyaya, Sankhya, satyagraha, Lokayata, mimamsa, ahimsa, naturalism, empiricism, Humism, Berkelianism, rationalism, materialism, dialectical materialism, physicalism, mentalism, sensationalism, instrumentalism, pragmatism, conceptualism, pluralism, dualism, monism, Cartesianism, phenomenalism, epiphenomenalism, functionalism, behaviourism, Kantianism (*or* Kantism), intuitionism, relativism, descriptivism, consequentialism, emotivism, boo-hurrah theory, utilitarianism, Benthamism, Nietzscheanism (*or* Nietzscheism), reductionism (*or* reductivism), determinism, fatalism, nihilism, solipsism, existentialism, Sartrism, subjectivism, objectivism, egoism, hedonism, altruism, humanism, Utopianism, collectivism, socialism, communism, Marxism, Frankfurt School, syndicalism, anarchism, anarcho-syndicalism, nationalism, Hobbism, Keyneseanism, monetarism, capitalism, aestheticism, structuralism, post-structuralism, deconstructionism, modernism, contextualism, isolationism, Hegelianism, apriorism, nominalism, individualism, realism, anti-realism, quasi-realism, logical empiricism, logical positivism, Vienna circle, positivism, chaos theory, game theory

▶ *7 Religion; 12 Government and Politics; 13 Economics; 450 Belief*

8 philosophical term, axiom, postulate, hypothesis, thesis, antithesis, synthesis, assertion sign, operator, function, reference, sense, quantifier, subaltern, major term (*or* premise), minor term (*or* premise), conjunction, disjunction, antecedent, conditional, biconditional, equivalence, identity, bivalence, categorical proposition, contingent truth, necessary truth, truth value, truth condition, truth function, truth table, verification principle, counterfactual, tautology, negation, dichotomy, counterexample, non sequitur, inference, deduction, salva veritate, argument ad hominem, reductio ad absurdum, argument a fortiori, argument a posteriori, argument a priori, argument from first principles, value judgment, imperative, utility principle, sense data, sensibilia, noumenon, syllogism, analogy, paradox, modality, probability, necessity, Gestalt, Hume's Law, Leibnitz's Law, Ockham's (*or* Occam's) razor

▶ *27 Mathematics*

9 philosophical problem, existence of god, a priori knowledge, nature of meaning, referential failure, (radical) indeterminacy of meaning, undistributed middle, anti-private language argument, speech-act theory, artificial intelligence, mental entities, mind-body problem, other minds, personal identity, free will, volition, predestination, categorical imperative, transcendental argument, weakness of will, akrasia, moral relativism, contract theory of morality, primary quality, secondary quality, category mistake, causal theory of perception, first cause, possible worlds, nature of time, beginning of time, end of time, time-travel paradox, Barber paradox, paradox of the unexpected hanging, Zeno's paradoxes, Russell's paradox, Richard's paradox, Schrödinger's cat

▶ *7 Religion; 27 Mathematics; 93 Existence; 101 Unworldliness; 443 Thought; 446 Idea; 619 Wonder; 705 Question; 795 Morality*

10 philosopher, thinker, academic, logician, dialectician, sophist, syllogist, metaphysician, cosmologist, moralist, theorist, theoretician, theorizer, speculator, hypothesizer, hypothesist, hypothecator, surmiser, investigator, researcher, analyst, inquirer (*or* enquirer), asker, seeker, searcher, dreamer, idealist, ideologue, visionary, doctrinarian, armchair critic

▶ *442 Intellect; 444 Reason; 458 Wisdom; 705 Question*

11 follower of a doctrine, Platonist, Neo-Platonist, Cambridge Platonist, Pythagorean, Eleatic, Euclidian (*or* Euclidean), Protagorean, sophist (*or* sophister), euhemerist, eudaemonist, Socratist, Democritean, Empedoclean, atomist, stoic, Senecan, sceptic, Heraclitean, Cyrenaic, Cynic, epicurean, Lucretian, Pyrrhonist, peripatetic, Aristotelian, Averroist, Thomist, Scholastic, Augustinian, vitalist, animist, panpsychist, pantheist, deist, theist, dynamist, mechanist, essentialist, Bergsonian, agnostic, transcendentalist, idealist, mystic, Sufi, Confucian, Taoist, Buddhist, naturalist, empiricist, Humist, Berkelian, Baconian, rationalist, materialist, physicalist, instrumentalist, conceptualist, pluralist, dualist, monist, Cartesian, compatibilist, phenomenalist, epiphenomenalist, functionalist, behaviourist, Kantian, relativist, descriptivist, axiologist, consequentialist, emotivist, utilitarian, Benthamite, Nietzschean, reductionist (*or* reductivist), determinist, fatalist, nihilist, solipsist, existentialist, Sartrist, subjectivist, objectivist, egoist, hedonist, altruist, humanist, Utopian, collectivist, socialist, communist, Marxist, syndicalist, anarchist, anarcho-syndicalist, nationalist, pacifist, Hobbist (*or* Hobbesian), Keynesian, monetarist, capitalist, Kierkegaardian, aesthetic, contextualist, structuralist, post-structuralist, deconstructionist, modernist, isolationist, Hegelian, Leibnitzian, Schellingian, Tregean, apriorist, nominalist, individualist, realist, anti-realist, quasi-realist, Chomskyan (*or* Chomskyite), logical empiricist, logical positivist, positivist, Wittgensteinian

▶ *7 Religion; 12 Government and Politics; 13 Economics; 450 Belief*

12 sage, wise man (*or* woman), savant, academic, intellectual, highbrow, pundit, expert, genius, authority, consultant, counsellor, adviser, mentor, teacher, tutor, guru, Socrates, Nestor, Solon, Solomon, boffin (Inf), egghead (Inf), nobody's fool (Inf), wise guy (Inf), know-all (Inf)

▶ *396 Authority; 442 Intellect; 458 Wisdom*

ADJECTIVES

13 of philosophy, theoretical, philosophical, notional, abstract, esoteric, ideological, moral, ethical, normative, prescriptive, nomothetic, descriptive, conceptual, conceptive, ideal, ideational, visionary, metaphysical, hypothetical, conjectural, speculative, unapplied, impractical, academic

▶ *442 Intellect; 443 Thought; 446 Idea; 476 Supposition*

14 of a philosophy, Platonic, Neo-Platonist, Pythagorean, Eleatic, Euclidian (*or* Euclidean), Protagorean, sophistical (*or* sophistic), euhemeristic, eudaemonistic (*or* eudaemonistical), Socratic, Democritean, Empedoclean, atomistic (*or* atomistical), stoic, Senecan, sceptical, Heraclitean, Cyrenaic, Cynic, epicurean, Lucretian, Pyrrhonist, peripatetic, Aristotelian, Averroist (*or* Averroistic), Thomist (*or* Thomistic *or* Thomistical), Augustinian, vitalist (*or* vitalistic), animistic, pantheistic (*or* pantheistical), deistic (*or* deistical), theistic (*or* theistical), dynamistic, mechanistic, essentialist, Bergsonian, agnostic, transcendentalist, idealistic, mystic (*or* mystical), Sufic, Confucian, Taoist (*or* Taoistic), Buddhist, naturalistic, empiricist, Berkelian, Baconian, rationalist, materialist (*or* materialistic), physicalist (*or* physicalistic), instrumentalist, conceptualistic, pluralist (*or* pluralistic), dualistic, monist (*or* monistic), Cartesian, compatibilist, phenomenalist, epiphenomenalist, functionalist, behaviourist (*or* behaviouristic), Kantian, Kierkegaardian, relativist, descriptivist, axiological, consequentialist, emotivist, utilitarian, Benthamite, Nietzschean, reductionist (*or* reductionistic), determinist (*or* deterministic), fatalistic, nihilist (*or* nihilistic), solipsist (*or* solipsistic), existentialist, subjectivistic, objectivist (*or* objectivistic), egoistic (*or* egoistical), hedonistic (*or* hedonic), altruistic, humanistic, utopian, collectivist (*or* collectivistic), socialist (*or* socialistic), communist, Marxist, syndicalist (*or* syndical *or* syndicalistic), anarchic, anarcho-syndicalist,

nationalist (*or* nationalistic), pacifist, Hobbist (*or* Hobbesian), Keynesian, monetarist, capitalist, aesthetic, contextualist, isolationist, Hegelian, Leibnitzian, Schellingian, nominalist, individualistic, realist, anti-realist, quasi-realist, Chomskyan (*or* Chomskyite), Fregean, positivist (*or* positivistic), Wittgensteinian
▶ *7 Religion; 12 Government and Politics; 13 Economics; 446 Idea; 450 Belief*

15 rational, reasoned, reasonable, philosophical, logical, objective, impartial, fair, unbiased, unprejudiced, sound, sensible, plausible, practical, pragmatic, down-to-earth, matter-of-fact, no-nonsense, common-sensical, realistic, ratiocinative, clear-headed, lucid, well-thought-out, well-reasoned, judicious, discriminating
▶ *442 Intellect; 444 Reason; 464 Judgment; 466 Discrimination*

16 dialectical, deictic, cogent, analytic, apodeictic, aporetic, elenctic, a priori, a posteriori, a fortiori, synthetic, dyadic, monadic, polyadic, heuristic

17 thoughtful, attentive, studious, studying, concentrated, concentrating, thinking, meditative, cogitative, contemplative, reflective, in a brown study, ruminant, ruminative, deliberative, speculative, musing, pensive, absorbed, lost in thought, introspective, dreaming, brooding, preoccupied, wistful
▶ *442 Intellect; 443 Thought; 446 Idea; 476 Supposition; 619 Wonder*

18 detached, unaffected, unemotional, unperturbed, imperturbable, undisturbed, unruffled, unshaken, unconcerned, dispassionate, unimpassioned, cool, cool-headed, pragmatic, sober, calm, collected, composed, level-headed, equable, equanimous, tolerant, controlled, temperate, moderate, self-controlled, self-possessed, self-restrained, restrained, stoical, resigned, patient, enduring, steady, even-tempered, good-tempered, serene, tranquil, placid, pacific
▶ *343 Inactivity; 473 Disinterestedness; 618 Indifference; 684 Self-Restraint; 685 Moderation; 689 Sobriety*

19 learned, wise, academic, intellectual, erudite, educated, scholarly, bookish, highbrow, profound, deep, sagacious, intelligent, knowledgeable, expert, skilled, accomplished, informed, well-read, well-versed, lettered, literate, enlightened, cultured, brainy (Inf)
▶ *156 Depth; 396 Authority; 442 Intellect; 458 Wisdom*

VERBS

20 philosophize, think about, speculate, conjecture, postulate, suppose, hypothesize, surmise, consider, conceptualize, visualize, contemplate, cogitate, excogitate, ratiocinate, ruminate, reflect, deliberate, ponder, muse, wonder, challenge, analyse, examine, explore, look into, scrutinize, observe, survey, study, research, investigate, question, query, inquire (*or* enquire), ask, seek, search, soul-search, introspect, brood, dream, idealize, have visions
▶ *442 Intellect; 443 Thought; 444 Reason; 446 Idea; 476 Supposition*

21 rationalize, philosophize, reason, think through, think out, logicize, logicalize, syllogize, intellectualize, interpret, construe, deduce, infer, work out, evaluate, unscramble, solve, resolve, figure out, calculate, compute, answer, fathom, understand, apprehend, realize, comprehend, follow, grasp, take to mean, take it that, read, define, expound, explicate, explain, elucidate, unfold, clarify, spell out, account for, clear up, make clear, illuminate, demonstrate, show, illustrate, exemplify, justify, vindicate, show sufficient grounds for
▶ *443 Thought; 464 Judgment; 476 Supposition; 694 Meaning; 706 Answer*

22 propound a philosophy, state, assert, put forward, propose, expound, aphorize, set forth, pose, posit, lay down, profess, pronounce, moralize, preach, sermonize, declare, proclaim, show, exhibit, demonstrate, espouse a theory, support, maintain, assume, presume, premise, suppose, postulate, judge, feel, conclude, deem, consider, tend to, be disposed to, opine, be of the opinion, hold an opinion, believe in, subscribe to, adhere to, follow, belong to a school of thought, view, take the attitude, look at in the light of
▶ *7 Religion; 443 Thought; 444 Reason; 450 Belief; 464 Judgment; 476 Supposition; 590 Feelings; 703 Demonstration*

23 discuss philosophically, debate, exchange ideas, colloquize, engage in dialectic, analyse, comment on, criticize, argue, logomachize, polemicize, contend, contest, dispute, dissent, refute, answer, respond, negate, contradict, deny, put forward a counterargument
▶ *464 Judgment; 701 Argument; 702 Sophistry; 705 Question*

ADVERBS

24 philosophically, intellectually, logically, analytically, deductively, dialectically, sophistically, metaphysically, argumentatively, polemically, rhetorically, epistemologically, axiologically, ontologically, phenomenologically, semantically, categorically

25 theoretically, notionally, ideally, academically, conceptually, abstractly, in the abstract, esoterically, idealistically, ideologically, morally, ethically, moralistically, proverbially, purportedly, as they say, supposedly, reputedly, seemingly, speculatively, hypothetically, ex hypothesi, assumptively, presumingly, presumptively, on the assumption that

26 rationally, philosophically, objectively, impartially, without prejudice, without bias, fairly, reasonably, logically, realistically, pragmatically, practically, sensibly, plausibly, lucidly, soundly, justifiably
▶ *444 Reason*

27 stoically, philosophically, dispassionately, imperturbably, restrainedly, moderately, temperately, soberly, coolly, calmly, composedly, unemotionally, equably, fairly, patiently, enduringly, resignedly, passively, quietly, serenely, placidly
▶ *618 Indifference; 685 Moderation*

28 thoughtfully, studiously, attentively, carefully, meditatively, ruminatively, cogitatingly, reflectively, contemplatively, deliberatively, introspectively, pensively, broodily, wistfully, dreamily

29 wisely, knowledgeably, expertly, authoritatively, advisably, advisedly, profoundly, deeply, inspirationally, inspiringly, discriminatingly, judiciously, judgmentally
▶ *442 Intellect; 458 Wisdom*

5 Language and Linguistics

In the beginning was the Word, and the Word was with God, and the Word was God. Bible: John.

I am always sorry when any language is lost, because languages are the pedigree of nations. Samuel Johnson.

NOUNS

1 **linguistics**, linguistic science, science of language, linguistic analysis, linguistic geography, linguistic distribution, syntactics, phonetics, pronunciation, phonology, phonography, phonemics, orthoepy, morphophonemics, morphology, morphophonology, lexicology, lexicography, lexicostatistics, philology, comparative grammar, grammatology, etymology, derivation of words, folk etymology, semantics, semasiology, meaning, graphemics, general linguistics, applied linguistics, comparative linguistics, contrastive linguistics, descriptive linguistics, structural linguistics, linguistic structure, structuralism, psycholinguistics, geolinguistics, linguistic typology, dialectology, onomastics (*or* onomasiology), nomenclature, sociolinguistics, philosophical linguistics, computational (*or* mathematical) linguistics, stylistics, areal linguistics, anthropological linguistics, theoretical linguistics, historical linguistics, diachronic linguistics, synchronic linguistics, comparative historical linguistics, glottochronology, palaeography, palaeology, *sprachgefühl* (Ger), foreign-language study, bilingualism, multilingualism, polyglottism, glossology (Lit)

▶ *4 Philosophy; 692 Communications; 693 Information; 694 Meaning; 727 Exaggeration; 729 Speech*

2 **linguist**, linguistician, linguistic scholar, linguistic scientist, linguistic analyst, linguistic geographer, grammarian, phonetician, phonetist, phonemicist, phonologist, orthoepist, morphologist, lexicologist, dictionary compiler, lexicographer, etymologist, semanticist, semasiologist, philologist (*or* philologer), grammatologist, structuralist, psycholinguist, geolinguist, dialectician, dialectologist, onomasiologist, sociolinguist, epigrammatist, palaeographer, epigraphist, language student, foreign-language student, classicist, bilingual, multilingual, polyglot, translator, interpreter, clarifier, expositor, exegete, orthographer, neologist, word-coiner, logophile, phrasemonger, phrasemaker, author, writer, poet, proverbialist, nomenclator, terminologist, namer, namegiver, christener, baptizer, namechild, roll-caller, glossologist (Lit)

▶ *10 Ritual; 17 Literature; 455 Knowledge; 477 Imagination; 721 Description*

3 **spoken language**, tongue, speech, vocalism, talk, parlance, *lingua* (L), *langue* (Fr), parole, living language, natural language, informal language, informal speech, English as she is spoken, vernacular, vernacular language, vernacularism, phraseology, colloquialism, conversationalism, idiom, idiomatic speech, common speech, slang, jargon, argot, patois, vulgate, vulgar tongue, vulgarism

▶ *657 Informality; 675 Vulgarity; 712 Curse; 729 Speech*

4 **parent language**, native language, native tongue, mother tongue, national language, regional language, dialect, basic English, lingo (Inf)

5 **nonstandard language**, personal language, gesture, body language, signal, code, parole, patter, idiolect, idioglossia, childish language, baby talk, empty phrase, empty words, empty talk, substandard language, substandard usage, uneducated speech, illiterate speech, barbarism, corruption, gobbledegook (*or* gobbledygook), language of confusion, confusion of tongues, polyglot medley, glossolalia, non-verbal glossolalia, vocalise semiotics, Babel, babble, jabber, gibberish, rhubarb (Inf), psychobabble (Inf)

▶ *412 Mixture; 456 Ignorance; 696 Unintelligibility; 697 Nonsense*

6 **official language**, standard language, standard usage, Received Pronunciation (RP), Received Standard (US), Queen's (*or* King's) English, BBC English, Oxford English, correct speech, formal language, written language, literary language, legalese

▶ *656 Formality*

7 **international language**, diplomatic language, business language, trade language, lingua franca, koine, International Scientific Vocabulary, Esperanto, metalanguage

8 **artificial language**, sign language, semaphore, Morse code, computer language, machine code, data processing language, assembly language

▶ *40 Computers; 742 Sign*

9 **ancient language**, classical language, dead language, lost language, archaism, archaic speech, Wardour Street English

▶ *3 History*

10 **language type**, inflected language, affixing language, analytic language, agglutinative language, polysynthetic language, monosyllabic language, polysyllabic language, symbolic language, tonal language, polytonic language, pidgin, creole

11 **family of languages**, language group, Proto-Indo-European, Indo-European, Indo-Germanic, Germanic, Teutonic, Anatolian, Anatolic, Aryan, Scandinavian, Celtic, Hellenic, Italic, Romance (*or* Romantic), Baltic, Slavonic, Balto-Slavic, Austric, Turkic, Indo-Iranian, Armenian, Tocharian, Turanian, Ural-Altaic, Finno-Ugric (*or* Finno-Ugrian), African, Afro-Asiatic, Paleo-Asiatic, Bushman, Bantu, Zulu-Kaffir, Fijian, Malay, Micronesian, Melanesian, Hamitic, Semitic, Hamito-Semitic, Assam-Burmese, Chinese-Siamese, Sino-Tibetan, Mongolic, Manchu, Dravidian, Austronesian, Malayo-Polynesian, Sabellian, Carib, Tagula, Tarapon, Uralian ndi

12 **translation**, rendering, literal translation, word-for-word translation, verbal translation, faithful translation, free translation, loose translation, paraphrase, rewording, restatement, edition, redaction, transliteration, abridgment, epitome, exegesis, Biblical interpretation, science of interpretation, hermeneutics, exegetics, epigraphy, palaeography, decipherment, decoding

▶ *7 Religion; 719 Interpretation*

13 **letter**, written letter, writing, lexigraphy, lettering, print, type, symbol, character, written character, grapheme, grammatic character, digraph, sign, ideogram, ideograph, pictogram, pictograph, cuneiform, hieroglyph, Chinese

character, Pinyin, Kanji, syllabic script, Devanagari, Nagari, rune, wen, initial, monogram, anagram, anagrammatism, acronym, acrostic

▶ *693 Information; 742 Sign*

14 alphabet, ABC, Roman alphabet, Cyrillic alphabet, Hebrew alphabet, Arabic alphabet, Cherokee alphabet, Greek alphabet, runic alphabet, runic letter, ogham (*or* ogam) alphabet, phonetic alphabet, phonetic symbol, futhark (*or* futharc), initial teaching alphabet (i.t.a. *or* ITA), International Phonetic Alphabet (IPA), syllabary

15 type style, face (*or* typeface), font, fount, bold type, italic type, sans serif type, cursive type, Gothic type, Old English type, Garamond type, Caslon type, big letter, capital letter, capital, cap., upper-case letter, majuscule, uncial, small letter, lower-case letter, minuscule

16 spoken letter, speech sound, phone, phonogram, phoneme, grapheme, syllable, vowel, consonant, voiced consonant, gutteral consonant, guttural, nasal, frictionless continuant, labial, labiodental, labionasal, liquid, spirant, sibilant, aspirate, glottal stop, fricative, sonant, polyphone, digraph, diphthong, stress, pitch, inflection (*or* inflexion)

▶ *726 Emphasis; 729 Speech*

17 word, written unit, spoken unit, *verbum* (L), Logos, term, name, meaning, glosseme, sememe (*or* semanteme), synonym, cognate word, cognate, paronym, metonym, antonym, homonym, homograph, homophone, tautonym, doublet, palindrome, root, etymon, false root, word form, back formation, clipped word, morphological unit, morpheme, stem, enclitic, pejorative, intensive, long word, polysyllable, sesquipedalian, short word, monosyllable, one-syllable word, easy word, new word, new term, neologism (*or* neology), coinage, unfamiliar word, newfangled expression, nonce word, loan word, borrowed word, imported word, loan translation, calque, hybrid expression, hybrid, ghost word, rhyming word, echoic word, onomatopoeic word, hard word, difficult word, jawbreaker (Inf)

▶ *126 Originality; 264 Difficulty; 265 Easiness; 295 Newness; 349 Use; 575 Title; 721 Description; 742 Sign*

18 slang, slang term, slang word, back slang, rhyming slang, cockney rhyming slang, dog Latin, pig Latin

19 swearword, taboo word, naughty word, bad word, rude word, vulgarism, vulgar language, low language, obscene language, blue language, coprolalia, billingsgate, scatology, expletive, four-letter word, the f-word, Anglo-Saxon (Inf)

▶ *675 Vulgarity; 712 Curse*

20 jargon word, jargon, Pentagonese (US), officialese, legalese, journalese, newspeak, telegraphese, technical word, technical term, technospeak, argot, cant, patter, lingo (Inf), technobabble (Inf), psychobabble (Inf)

21 catchword, portmanteau word, counterword, jingo, cliché, vogue word, catchphrase, well-worn phrase, commonplace saying, hackneyed expression, maxim, adage, moral, proverb, Biblical proverb, quotation, quote (Inf), slogan, motto, buzz word (Inf)

▶ *553 Fashion; 745 Maxim*

22 many words, pleonasm, wordiness, verbiage, stock of words, verbosity, loquacity, babbling, effusiveness, gushing, speechifying, rambling, equivocalness, double talk, tautology, repetition, incantation, rosary

▶ *479 Equivocation; 702 Sophistry; 731 Talkativeness*

23 phrase, noun phrase (*or* clause), verb phrase (*or* clause), adverbial phrase (*or* clause), adjectival phrase (*or* clause), prepositional phrase (*or* clause), conditional phrase (*or* clause), indirect question, indirect speech, reported speech, subject and predicate, protasis, apodasis, clause, sentence, collocation, frozen collocation, formula

24 phrasing, phraseology, choice of words, wording, surface structure, deep structure, rounded phrase, turn of phrase, well-turned phrase, choice of expression, turn of expression, fixed expression, set phrase, set terms, verbalism, locution, trope, metaphor, complimentary phrase, compliments, elegant phrase, elegance, roundabout phrase, circumlocution, periphrasis, diffuseness, paraphrase, translation, phraseogram, phrasegraph

▶ *17 Literature; 179 Circularity; 543 Elegance*

25 inscription, lapidary inscription, epitaph, obsequies, legend, corollary

▶ *19 Painting and Sculpture; 583 Burial; 723 Summary*

26 dialect, idiom, patois, regional pronunciation, local pronunciation, speech community, argot, isogloss, isophone, isolex, localism, regionism, provincialism, vernacularism, vernacular language, accent, guttural accent, clipped accent, brogue, broagh, burr, Africanism, Americanism, American accent, Southern accent, Boston accent, Brooklyn accent, Midwest accent, New England dialect, Cajun dialect, Texas accent, Mid-Atlantic accent, Briticism, Anglicism, British accent, Geordie dialect, Yorkshire accent, Birmingham (*or* Brummie) accent, Oxford accent, Cornish accent, Welsh accent, Scottish accent, Lallans (*or* Lallan), Scotticism, cockney accent, rhyming slang, Irishism, Hibernicism, Irish accent, Teutonism, Gallicism, French-Canadian dialect, dialectology, hybrid language, broken English, pidgin English, Estuary English, lingua franca, Strine, Franglais

▶ *412 Mixture*

27 spelling, orthography, orthographic convention, spelling bee, spelling game, spelling pronunciation, phonetic spelling, incorrect spelling, misspelling, cacography

▶ *140 Rule; 274 Error; 801 Right*

28 dictionary, lexicon, wordbook, general dictionary, unabridged dictionary, children's dictionary, illustrated dictionary, school dictionary, college dictionary, learner's dictionary, monolingual dictionary, foreign language dictionary, bilingual dictionary, multilingual dictionary, polyglot dictionary, concise dictionary, compact dictionary, desk dictionary, biographical dictionary, dictionary of (proper) names, dictionary of quotations, dictionary of slang, dictionary of dialects, rhyming dictionary, reverse word dictionary, Dr Johnson's Dictionary, *Oxford English Dictionary*, *Webster's Dictionary*, glossary, gloss, gradus, concordance, synonym dictionary, thesaurus, *Roget's Thesaurus*, *Bloomsbury Thesaurus*, lexicography, storehouse of words, treasury of words

▶ *740 Publication*

29 grammar, good grammar, good English, Standard English, correct English, correct style, grammatical rules, grammaticalness, formal language, formal usage, school grammar, structural linguistics, traditional grammar, de-

LANGUAGES AND GROUPS OF LANGUAGES

Abkhaz
Abnaki
Aborigine
Achinese
Adamawa
Adygei (*or* Adyghe)
Afghan (*or* Afghani)
African
Afrikaans
Afro–Asiatic
Ainu
Akan
Akkadian (*or* Accadian)
Albanian
Alemannic
Aleut
Algonquian (*or* Algonkian)
Algonquin (*or* Algonkin)
Altaic
American
Amharic
Anatolian
Ancient Greek
Anglo–French
Anglo–Irish
Anglo–Norman
Anglo–Saxon
Annamese
Apache
Arabic
Aramaic
Aranda
Arapaho
Araucanian
Arawakan
Armenian
Aryan
Assamese
Assiniboine
Assyrian
Athapascan (*or* Athapaskan *or* Athabascan *or* Athabaskan)
Australian
Austro–Asiatic
Austronesian
Avar
Avestan (*or* Avestic)
Aymara
Azerbaijani
Aztec
Babylonian
Bahasa Indonesia
Balinese
Baltic
Baluchi (*or* Balochi)
Bambara
Bantu
Barotse
Bashkir
Basque
Batan
Battak
Beach–la–Mar (*or* bêche–de–mer)
Belarussian (*or* Bielorussian *or* Byelorussian)
Bemba
Bengali
Benue–Congo
Berber
Bihari
Bikol
Blackfoot
Bohemian
Bokmål
Brahui
Breton
British
Brythonic
Bugi
Bulgarian
Burmese (*or* Burman)
Buryat (*or* Buriat)
Bushman
Caddoan
Canaanite
Canaanitic
Cantonese
Carib
Caroline
Castilian
Catalan
Catawba
Caucasian (*or* Caucasic)
Cayuga
Celtiberian
Celtic (*or* Keltic)
Chadic
Chaldee
Cham
Chamorro
Chari–Nile
Cheremiss (*or* Cheremis)
Cherokee
Chewa
Cheyenne
Chibchan
Chichewa
Chickasaw
Chin
Chinese
Chinook
Chinook Jargon
Choctaw
Chukchi (*or* Chukchee)
Chuvash
Circassian
Comanche
Coptic
Cornish
Cree
Creek
Crow
Cushitic
Cymric (*or* Kymric)
Czech
Dafia
Damara
Dani
Danish
Dardic
Delaware
Dinka
Divehi
Dravidian
Duala
Dutch
Dyak
Dyula
Dzongkha (*or* Dzongka)
East Germanic
Edo
Edomite
Efik
Egyptian
Elamite
English
Erie
Eskimo
Estonian (*or* Esthonian)
Ethiopian
Ethiopic
Etruscan (*or* Etrurian)
Evenki
Ewe
Faeroese (*or* Faroese)
Faliscan
Fang
Fanti
Farsi
Fijian
Finnic
Finnish
Finno–Tartar
Finno–Ugric (*or* Finno–Ugrian)
Flemish
Formosan
Fox
Franconian
Frankish
French
Frisian (*or* Friesian)
Friulian
Fula (*or* Fulah)
Fulani
Ga (*or* Gã)
Gadaba
Gaelic
Gagauzi
Galcha
Galibi
Galician
Galla
Gallo–Romance (*or* Gallo–Roman)
Ganda
Garo
Gaulish
Ge'ez
Georgian
German
Germanic
Gilbertese
Goidelic (*or* Goidhelic *or* Gadhelic)
Gondi
Gothic
Greek
Griqua (*or* Grikwa)
Guarani
Gujarati (*or* Gujerati)
Gur
Gurindji
Gurkhali
Gypsy
Haida
Haitian (*or* Haytian)
Hamitic
Hamito–Semitic
Hausa
Hawaiian
Hebrew
Hellenic
Herero
High German
Himyaritic
Hindi
Hindustani (*or* Hindoostani *or* Hindostani)
Hiri Motu
Hittite
Ho
Hopi
Hun
Hungarian
Huron
Hutu
Ibanag
Ibibio
Ibo (*or* Igbo)
Icelandic
Ido
Igorot
Illyrian
Ilokano
Inca
Indian
Indic
Indo–Chinese
Indo–European
Indo–Germanic
Indo–Hittite
Indo–Iranian
Indonesian
Indo–Pacific
Ingush
interlingua
Inuktitut
Iranian
Irish
Irish Gaelic
Iroquoian
Iroquois
Italian
Italic
Japanese
Javanese
Kabardian
Kaffir (*or* Kafir)
Kalmuck (*or* Kalmyk)
Kamasin
kamilaroi
Kanarese (*or* Canarese)
Kannada
Kara–Kalpak
Karelian
Karen
Kashmiri
Kasubian
Kavi
Kazakh (*or* Kazak)
Khalkha
Khasi
Khmer
Khoikoi
Khoisan
Khond
Kikuyu
Kingwana
Kirghiz (*or* Kirgiz)
Kirundi
Kodagu
Koibal
Komi
Kongo
Kordofanian
Korean
Korwa
Krio
Kriol
Kuki
Kurdish
Kurukh
Kwa
Kwakiutl
Kyrgyz
Ladino
Lahnda
Lampong
Lamut
Langobardic
Lao (*or* Laotian)
Lapp
Late Greek
Latin
Latvian
Lepcha
Lettish
Libyan
Lithuanian
Livonian
Low German
Lozi
Luba
Luganda
Luo
Lusatian
Lycian
Lydian
Macedonian
Madurese
Magyar
Mahican (*or* Mohican)
Mahon
Makassar
Malagasy
Malay
Malayalam (*or* Malayalaam)

scriptive grammar, structural grammar, surface structure, shallow structure, deep structure, underlying structure, systemic grammar, case grammar, phrase-structure grammar, transformational grammar, transformation-generative grammar, bad grammar, incorrect usage, solecism, malapropism, spoonerism, faulty syntax

▶ *274 Error; 802 Wrong*

30 syntax, word order, syntactic structure, syntactic meaning, syntactic analysis, immediate constituent (IC) analy-

LANGUAGES AND GROUPS OF LANGUAGES (CONT.)

- Malayo–Javanese
- Malayo–Polynesian
- Malinke (*or* Maninke)
- Maltese
- Manchu
- Mandarin Chinese (*or* Mandarin)
- Mande
- Manobo
- Manx
- Maori
- Marathi (*or* Mahratti)
- Masai
- Massachuset (*or* Massachusetts)
- Matabele
- Maya
- Mayan
- Medieval Greek
- Medieval Latin
- Melanesian
- Melano–Papuan
- Menomini (*or* Menominee)
- Messapian (*or* Messapic)
- Micmac
- Micronesian
- Middle Dutch
- Middle English
- Middle High German
- Middle Low German
- Mingrelian
- Mishmi
- Misima
- Mixtec
- Modern English
- Modern Greek
- Modern Hebrew
- Mohave (*or* Mojave)
- Mohawk
- Mon
- Mongol
- Mongolic
- Mon–Khmer
- Mordvin
- Moriori
- Moro
- Mossi
- Motu
- Mru
- Munda
- Muong
- Murmi
- Muskogean (*or* Muskhogean)
- Na–Dene (*or* Na–Déné)
- Naga
- Nahuatl
- Nama (*or* Namaqua)
- Narraganset (*or* Narragansett)
- Navaho (*or* Navajo)
- Ndebele
- Negrito
- Neo–Latin
- Neo–Melanesian
- Nepali
- Newara
- Nez Percé
- Nguni
- Niasese
- Nicobarese
- Niger–Congo
- Nilo–Saharan
- Nilotic
- Niue
- Nogai
- Nootka
- Norn
- Norse
- Northern Sotho
- North Germanic
- Norwegian
- Nuba
- Nupe
- Nuri
- Nyanja
- Nyoro
- Oceanic
- Ojibwa
- Okanagan
- Old Church Slavonic (*or* Slavic)
- Old Dutch
- Old English
- Old French
- Old Frisian
- Old High German
- Old Icelandic
- Old Irish
- Old Latin
- Old Norse
- Old Persian
- Old Prussian
- Old Slavonic (*or* Slavic)
- Oneida
- Onondaga
- Oraon
- Oriya
- Osage
- Oscan
- Osco–Umbrian
- Osmanli
- Ossetic (*or* Ossetian)
- Ostyak
- Ottoman (*or* Othman)
- Ovambo
- Pahari
- Pahlavi (*or* Pehlevi)
- Paiute (*or* Piute)
- Palau
- Palaung
- Pali
- Pama–Nyungan
- Pampango
- Pangasinan
- Papuan
- Pashto (*or* Pushto *or* Pushtu)
- Pawnee
- Pekingese (*or* Pekinese)
- Penutian
- Pequot
- Permian
- Persian
- Phoenician
- Phrygian
- Pictish
- Pintubi
- Pitjantjatjara (*or* Pitjantjara)
- Police Motu
- Polish
- Polynesian
- Pondo
- Portuguese
- Prakrit
- Proto–Germanic
- Proto–Indo–European
- Proto–Norse
- Protosemitic
- Provençal
- Punic
- Punjabi (*or* Panjabi)
- Quechua (*or* Kechua *or* Quichua)
- Rabbinic (*or* Rabbinical) Hebrew
- Rajasthani
- Rejang
- Rhaeto–Romanic
- Rhaetian
- Riksmål
- Romaic
- Romance
- Romanes
- Romanian (*or* Rumanian *or* Roumanian)
- Romansch (*or* Romansh)
- Romany (*or* Romani)
- Ronga
- Russian
- Rwanda
- Sabaean (*or* Sabean)
- Sabellian
- Sabine
- Sahaptin (*or* Sahaptan *or* Sahaptian)
- Saharan
- Sakai
- Salish (*or* Salishan)
- Samoan
- Samoyed
- San
- Sango
- Sanskrit
- Sanskritic
- Santali
- Sardinian
- Sassak
- Savara
- Scandinavian
- Scottish
- Scottish Gaelic
- Scythian
- Semang
- Semi–Bantu
- Seminole
- Semite
- Semitic (*or* Shemitic)
- Semito–Hamitic
- Seneca
- Serbo–Croat (*or* Serbo–Croatian *or* Croato–Serb)
- Sesotho
- Shan
- Shawnee
- Shelta
- Shilha
- Shina
- Shona
- Shoshone (*or* Shoshoni)
- Siamese
- Sindhi
- Sinhalese (*or* Singhalese)
- Sinitic
- Sino–Tibetan
- Siouan
- Sioux
- Slavonic (*or* Slavic)
- Slovak
- Slovene
- Sogdian
- Somali
- Songhai
- Sorbian
- Sotho
- Southron
- Soyot
- Spanish
- Sudanic
- Sumerian
- Susu
- Swahili
- Swazi
- Swedish
- Syriac
- Tadzhiki (*or* Tajik)
- Tagalog
- Tagula
- Tahitian
- Tahltan
- Taino
- Tamashek
- Tamil
- Tatar (*or* Tartar)
- Tavghi
- Teleut
- Telugu (*or* Telegu)
- Temne
- Teutonic
- Thai
- Thracian
- Thraco–Phrygian
- Tibetan
- Tibeto–Burman
- Tigré
- Tigrinya
- Tino
- Tipura
- Tiv
- Tlingit
- Tocharian (*or* Tokharian)
- Toda
- Tokelau
- Tonga
- Tongan
- Trans–New Guinea phylum
- Tshiluba
- Tsonga
- Tswana
- Tuamotuan
- Tulu
- Tungus
- Tungusic
- Tupi
- Tupi–Guarani
- Turanian
- Turkic
- Turkish
- Turkmen
- Turkoman (*or* Turkman)
- Tuscarora
- Twi
- Ugaritic
- Ugric
- Uigur (*or* Uighur)
- Ukrainian
- Umbrian
- Ural–Altaic
- Uralic (*or* Uralian)
- Urdu
- Ute
- Uto–Aztecan
- Uzbek
- Vedic
- Venda
- Venetic
- Veps
- Vietnamese
- Visayan
- Vogul
- Volapuk (*or* Volapük)
- Volscian
- Voltaic
- Vote
- Votyak
- Wa
- Wakashan
- Warlpiri
- Welsh
- Wendish
- West Atlantic
- West Germanic
- Winnebago
- Wolof
- Xhosa
- Yakut
- Yenisei
- Yiddish
- Yoruba
- Yuman
- Yurak
- Zapotec
- Zenaga
- Zulu
- Zuñi
- Zyrian

sis, agreement, number, gender, case, inflection, declension, conjugation, paradigm, mood, voice, tense, comparative grammar, philology, grammatical studies, grammatical analysis, parsing, construing, punctuation, accentuation, gradation, attraction, assimilation, dissimilation, conjunction, conjunction-reduction, hypotaxis, parataxis, syndeton, asyndeton, ellipsis, apposition

► *273 Accuracy; 403 Structure; 724 Style*

31 case, nominative, vocative, accusative, genitive, dative, ablative, locative

32 voice, active, middle, passive

33 mood, indicative, subjunctive, optative, imperative, jussive, infinitive

34 tense, present, future, future perfect, perfect, aorist, imperfect, pluperfect, conditional, historic present, past historic

35 part of speech, noun, common noun, proper noun, collective noun, substantive, pronoun, adjective, verb, predicate, reflexive verb, transitive verb, intransitive verb, participle, present participle, past participle, perfect participle, ablative absolute, adverb, preposition, copula, conjunction, subordinating conjunction, coordinate conjunction, interjection, subject, object, direct object, indirect object, complement, modifier, article, definite article, indefinite article, particle, affix, prefix, infix, suffix, inflection (*or* inflexion), formative, morpheme, semanteme, diminutive, intensive, augmentative, root, etymon, stem

► *140 Rule; 705 Question*

36 accent, diacritical mark, umlaut, diaeresis, ablaut, grave, acute, circumflex, breve, cedilla, macron, tilde, háček, ogonek, caron, alif, hamzah, horn, rude, ayn, apostrophe

37 linguistic theory, Grimm's law, Verner's law, bow-wow theory, ding-dong theory, pooh-pooh theory, Sapir-Whorf hypothesis, Great Vowel Shift

ADJECTIVES

38 linguistic, lingual, grammatical, comparative, descriptive, structural, analytic(al), syntactic(al), phonetic, pronounced, phonological, phonemic, orthoepic, orthographic, morphophonemic, morphological, diachronic, synchronic, Vernerian, lexicological, lexicographical, etymological, derivative, semantic, semasiological, glottological, glottochronological, lexicostatistical, philological, psycholingustic, geolinguistic, dialectological, onomastic, onomasiological, sociolinguistic, palaeographical, palaeological, bilingual, multilingual, polyglot, glossological (Lit)

39 of language, written, spoken, living, parent, native, mother, national, regional, Queen's (*or* King's), educated, pure, correct, standard, official, formal, literary, politically correct, informal, common, vernacular, colloquial, conversational, childish, holophrastic, personal, dialectal, guttural, burring, slang, slangy, jargonistic, jargonal, jargonish, journalistic, jingoistic, everyday, idiomatic, low, rude, vulgar, scatological, blasphemous, four-letter, obscene, nonstandard, substandard, uneducated, illiterate, ancient, classical, artificial, inflected, affixing, analytic, agglutinative, polysynthetic, monosyllabic, polysyllabic, symbolic, tonal, polytonic

40 translated, translating, rendering, literal, word-for-word, verbal, faithful, free, loose, paraphrased, paraphrasing, reworded, rewording, restated, restating, transliterated, abridged, edited, redacted, hermeneutic(al), exegetical, epigraphical, ciphered, deciphered, decoded, decoding

41 lettered, lettering, lexicographical, literal, graphic(al), printed, typed, symbolical, alphabetical, syllabic, Roman, Cyrillic, Arabic, Greek, runic, ogham (*or* ogam), phonogramic, phonographic, pictographic, ideographic, cuneiform, cuneal, hieroglyphic(al), large-lettered, capital, upper-case, majuscule, uncial, small-lettered, lower-case, minuscule, bold, italic, sans serif, cursive, Gothic, Old English, initial, monogrammatic(al), anagrammatic(al), acronymic, acronymous, acrostic, voiced, vocal, vocalic, consonantal, guttural, frictionless, liquid, labial, nasal, spirant, sibilant, fricative, sonant, polyphonic, polyphonous, digraphic

42 worded, wording, verbal, vocabular, lexical, glossarial, named, synonymic(al), cognate, paronymic (*or* paronymous), antonymous, homonymic (*or* homonymous), homographic, homophonic, tautonymic (*or* tautonymous), palindromic, root, back-formed, clipped, morphological, inflectional (*or* inflexional), meaningful, enclitic, pejorative, intensive, sesquipedalian, neologistical (*or* neological), newfangled, (newly) coined, rhyming, echoic, onomatopoeic, argotic, canting, cant, portmanteau, cliché, clichéd, proverbial, commonplace, well-worn, hackneyed, redundant, vogue, pleonastic, wordy, verbose, loquacious, equivocal, pretentious, archaic, obsolete, barbarous (*or* barbaric), corrupted, cacographic(al)

43 phrasal, phrased, phrasing, phraseological, clausal, sentential, collocated, collocating, surface, deep, rounded, well-turned, well-rounded, fixed, set, locutionary, metaphorical, complimentary, elegant, roundabout, circumlocutory, periphrastic, diffuse, paraphrastic, paraphrased, paraphrasing, translated, translating, translatable, phraseographic, inscribed, lapidary, epitaphic

44 grammatical, structural, descriptive, systemic, transformational, transformational-generative, syntactic, diacritical, substantive, pronominal, adjectival, verbal, predicate, copular, reflexive, transitive, intransitive, regular, irregular, heteroclite (*or* heteroclitic), participial, adverbial, prepositional, conjunctive, subordinating, coordinate, interjectional (*or* interjectory), objective, subjective, direct, indirect, complementary, modifying, definite, indefinite, inflectional (*or* inflexional), inflected, formative, morphemeic, diminutive, intensive, attributive, augmentative, comparative, superlative, masculine, feminine, neuter, singular, plural

VERBS

45 use language, communicate, write, speak, pronounce, utter, talk, state, verbalize, vocalize, voice, articulate, have the feel of a language, have a sense of idiom, turn a sentence, rhyme, phrase, express, formulate, anagrammatize, neologize, coin a word, colloquialize, vernacularize, jargonize, cant, patter, swear, blaspheme, curse

► *17 Literature; 729 Speech; 740 Publication*

46 translate, interpret, make a word-for-word translation, give a loose translation, paraphrase, reword, restate, abridge, edit, redact, decipher, decode, transliterate, transcribe, read, gloss

47 word, put into words, find words for, verbalize, define, syllabify, syllable, alphabetize, reword, rewrite, rephrase, letter, form letters, carve letters, initial, inscribe, mark, sign, spell, spell out, misspell

ADVERBS

48 linguistically, grammatically, comparatively, descriptively, structurally, analytically, syntactically, orthographically, lexicographically, etymologically, semantically, philologically, bilingually, multilingually, literarily, literally, word for word, letter for letter, verbatim, hermeneutically, exegetically, epigraphically, graphically, alphabetically, hieroglyphically, symbolically, monosyllabically, polysyllabically, anagrammatically, vocally, polyphonically, polyphonously, tonally, phonetically

49 **colloquially**, verbally, conversationally, informally, journalistically, idiomatically, obscenely, blasphemously, scatologically, illiterately

50 **lexically**, glossarially, morphologically, inflectionally (*or* inflexionally), meaningfully, pejoratively, intensively, pleonastically, wordily, verbosely, loquaciously, equivocally, pretentiously, neologistically (*or* neologically), archaically, obsoletely

51 **phraseologically**, in set phrases, in set terms, in round terms, in sentences, metaphorically, proverbially, obsequiously, elegantly, periphrastically

52 **grammatically**, syntactically, correctly, formally, descriptively, transitively, intransitively, regularly, irregularly, adverbially, prepositionally, conjunctively, subjunctively, objectively, subjectively, directly, indirectly, morphemically, attributively, comparatively, superlatively, singularly, plurally

6 Education

Education is simply the soul of a society as it passes from one generation to another. G. K. Chesterton.

NOUNS

1 **education**, teaching, schooling, pedagogy, tuition, coaching, guidance, catechization, private tuition, tutoring, tutelage, training, instruction, drilling, indoctrination, guidance, preparation, advice, illumination, enlightenment, edification, betterment, progress, amelioration, melioration, advancement, acculturation, cultivation, civilization, rearing, raising, upbringing, nurture

▶ *243 Preparation; 244 Improvement; 366 Raising; 713 Advice*

2 **educational system**, nursery education, pre-school education, primary education, Froebel system, Montessori system, secondary education, tertiary education, higher education, adult education, moral education, liberal education, remedial education, vocational training, job training, employment training, on-the-job training, in-service training, sandwich course, self-education, home learning, correspondence course, distance learning, autodidactics, recreational education, Open University, teacher training

3 **subject**, discipline, field, area, speciality, province, domain, branch, realm, sphere, department, faculty, curriculum, syllabus, course, module, timetable, core curriculum, National Curriculum, science subject, technical subject, language, humanities, arts, general studies, civics, RE (religious education), RI (religious instruction), PE (physical education), PT (physical training), vocational education, sex education, interdisciplinary education

▶ *136 Qualification*

4 **educator**, teacher, head teacher, headmaster, headmistress, principal, chancellor, vice chancellor, dean, don, professor, professor emeritus, doctor, lecturer, fellow, intern, reader, academic, preceptor, preceptress, tutor, instructor, governess, duenna, dominie (Scot), schoolman, school teacher, schoolmistress, schoolmaster, master, mistress, form teacher, student teacher, supply teacher, home tutor, private tutor, crammer, pedagogue, coach, trainer, mentor, adviser, authority, expert, pundit (*or* pandit), guru, mullah, maestro, docent (US), preacher, homilist

▶ *396 Authority; 400 Master; 458 Wisdom*

5 **educationalist**, educationist, educational psychologist, Educational Welfare Officer, School Attendance Officer, truancy officer, governor, board of governors, governing body, school board

6 **instructorship**, schoolmastery, tutorship, tutorage, tutelage, chair, professorship, professorhood, professorate, readership, lectureship, fellowship, research fellowship, staff, faculty

▶ *396 Authority; 400 Master*

7 **learner**, student, pupil, trainee, apprentice, novice, tiro (*or* tyro), beginner, rookie (Inf), recruit, initiate, neophyte, abecedarian, schoolboy, schoolgirl, classmate, sixth-former, freshman (*or* fresher), sophomore (US), undergraduate, undergrad (Inf), fellow student, tutorial partner, scholar, researcher, postgraduate, alumnus, alumna, autodidact, swot (Inf), bluestocking (Inf), bookworm (Inf), egghead (Inf)

▶ *130 Beginning; 295 Newness; 442 Intellect; 569 Friendship*

8 **learning**, study, acquisition of knowledge, scholarship, storing (*or* stocking) the mind, broadening the mind, absorption, contemplation, perusal, review, reading, brainwork (Inf), conning (Inf), cramming (Inf), swotting (Inf)

▶ *442 Intellect; 443 Thought; 455 Knowledge*

9 **learnedness**, studiousness, scholarliness, scholarship, intellectuality, literacy, bookishness, polymathy, erudition, savvy (Inf), nous (Inf)

10 **educability**, educatability, aptitude, aptness, quickness, cleverness, intelligence, brightness, readiness, willingness to learn, teachability, motivation, receptivity, curiosity, inquisitiveness, susceptibility, malleability, pliability, docility

▶ *442 Intellect; 483 Motive; 636 Willingness; 644 Curiosity*

11 **refinement**, education, taste, discernment, connoisseurship, discrimination, judgment, perception, perceptiveness, insight, acumen, sensitivity, sensibility, cultivation, sophistication, urbanity, suavity, elegance, breeding, background, savoir-faire

▶ *425 Sharpness; 442 Intellect; 445 Intuition; 464 Judgment; 466 Discrimination; 495 Taste; 543 Elegance; 549 Refinement; 591 Sensitivity*

12 **educational institution**, school, *école* (Fr), *scuola* (It), *Schule* (Ger), *escuela* (Sp), kindergarten, play school, playgroup, pre-school playgroup, crèche, nursery school, day nursery, day-care centre, first school, primary school, infant school, grade school (US), middle school, preparatory school, prep school, junior school, secondary school, junior high (US), high school, senior high (US), *lycée* (Fr), lyceum, day school, boarding school, public school, private school, independent school, grant-maintained

school, state school, comprehensive school, single-sex school, denominational school, special school, open-classroom school, summer school, night school, college, community college, sixth-form college, further education college, adult-education centre, institute, academy, seminary, finishing school, conservatory, choir school, schola cantorum, music school, ballet school, art college, drama college, riding school, military academy, officer-training school, graduate school, law school, medical school, library school, design school, film school, business school, secretarial college, Bible school, Sunday school, convent school, Talmud Torah, yeshiva, mesivta

13 **university**, polytechnic, college, redbrick university, Oxbridge, Ivy League (US), *Ecole Normale Supérieure* (Fr)

▶ *7 Religion; 137 Class*

14 **school book**, textbook, grammar, grammar book, dictionary, lexicon, encyclopedia, thesaurus, atlas, primer, abecedarium, crib, answer book, reader, notebook, copybook, exercise book, workbook, rough book, scratchpad (US), manual, handbook, database, literature, publication, examination paper, bibliography, prep book (Inf)

▶ *693 Information; 740 Publication*

15 **schoolroom**, classroom, formroom, staffroom, hall, lecture hall, assembly hall, auditorium, library, laboratory, language laboratory, workshop, music room, art room, dining room, common room, playground, schoolyard (US), gymnasium, sports field, playing field, sickroom, sanatorium, dormitory, hall of residence, fraternity house (US), sorority house (US), campus, schoolhouse

▶ *137 Class; 160 Form*

ADJECTIVES

16 **educational**, educatory, educative, instructive, instructional, informative, informational, revealing, illuminating, enlightening, edifying, improving, remedial, bettering, progressive, revelatory, eye-opening, communicative, helpful, guiding, advisory, authoritative, expert, academic, scholastic, pedagogical, preachy, schoolmarmish

▶ *244 Improvement; 396 Authority; 458 Wisdom; 692 Communications; 693 Information*

17 **educable**, educatable, teachable, trainable, schoolable, instructable, bright, clever, intelligent, quick, autodidactic, self-taught, apt, willing, motivated, ready, receptive, hungry (*or* thirsty) for knowledge, curious, inquisitive, susceptible, impressionable, malleable, pliable, docile, ESN (educationally subnormal)

▶ *483 Motive; 636 Willingness; 644 Curiosity; 663 Obedience; 705 Question*

18 **educated**, learned, erudite, literate, literary, numerate, well-read, academic, highbrow, intellectual, sagacious, wise, scholarly, scholastic, gnostic, book-wise, bookish, bibliophagic, polymathic, studious, absorbed, contemplative, clever, brainy, swotty (Inf)

▶ *400 Master; 442 Intellect; 443 Thought; 455 Knowledge; 458 Wisdom; 693 Information*

19 **knowledgeable**, educated, versed, well-versed, trained, well-trained, grounded, well-grounded, coached, guided, primed, briefed, cognizant, familiar, in the know, conversant with, *au fait* (Fr), at home with, strong in, experienced, practised, accomplished, qualified, skilled, skilful, enlightened, in touch, up-to-date, *au courant* (Fr), with it (Inf), hip (Inf), genned up (Inf), clued up (Inf), sussed (Inf), streetwise (Inf)

▶ *243 Preparation; 442 Intellect; 443 Thought; 455 Knowledge; 458 Wisdom; 485 Skill; 693 Information*

20 **refined**, educated, cultivated, cultured, civilized, discerning, critical, sensitive, sensible, discriminating, judicious, perceptive, insightful, shrewd, astute, sharp, polished, sophisticated, elegant, urbane, suave, soigné (*or* soignée), tasteful, advanced, nurtured, reared, raised, well-bred

▶ *425 Sharpness; 464 Judgment; 466 Discrimination; 495 Taste; 543 Elegance; 549 Refinement; 591 Sensitivity*

21 **curricular**, intramural, extramural, extracurricular, doctoral, graduate, postgraduate, collegiate, varsity, sixth-form, canonical, doctrinal, specialized, technical, classical, liberal

VERBS

22 **educate**, teach, tutor, train, instruct, school, coach, drill, discipline, indoctrinate, instil, inculcate, make ready, prepare, equip, brief, prime, ground, verse, acquaint, inform, tell, apprise, notify, impart, disclose, divulge, reveal, report, communicate, tip off, guide, advise, illuminate, enlighten, improve, further promote, develop, cultivate, civilize, refine, advance, encourage, mould, shape, form, foster, nurture, rear, raise, bring up

▶ *243 Preparation; 366 Raising; 455 Knowledge; 692 Communications; 693 Information; 713 Advice; 729 Speech*

23 **learn**, study, attend classes, go to school, take lessons, train, go into training, take part in a training scheme, serve an apprenticeship, be taught, be instructed, acquire knowledge, discover, research, find out, ascertain, become aware of, contemplate, broaden the mind, store (*or* stock) the mind, peruse, read, major (*or* minor) in, read up on, brush up, polish up, rub up, study up on, bone up (Inf), cram (Inf), con (Inf), swot (Inf)

▶ *449 Discovery; 455 Knowledge; 462 Memory; 644 Curiosity; 693 Information*

24 **know**, be informed, be up on, be grounded in, know by heart, know like a book, know backwards, know inside out, know the ropes, know the score, know what's what, know like the back of one's hand, command, master, get the hang of, be proficient in, understand, perceive, sense, judge, discern, discriminate

▶ *396 Authority; 455 Knowledge; 458 Wisdom; 464 Judgment; 466 Discrimination; 485 Skill; 591 Sensitivity*

ADVERBS

25 **educationally**, instructively, pedagogically, informatively, informedly, canonically, authoritatively, wisely, sagaciously, expertly, helpfully, advisedly, illuminatingly, revealingly, edifyingly, improvingly, remedially, progressively, encouragingly

▶ *244 Improvement; 396 Authority; 458 Wisdom; 485 Skill; 693 Information; 713 Advice*

26 **studiously**, academically, scholastically, brainily, bookishly, thoughtfully, contemplatively, intellectually, intelligently, aptly, quickly, cleverly, skilfully, technically, brightly, willingly, receptively, susceptibly, malleably, pliably, docilely

▶ *442 Intellect; 443 Thought; 485 Skill*

27 **discerningly**, tastefully, discriminatingly, judiciously,

judgmentally, insightfully, perceptively, sensitively, sophisticatedly, urbanely, suavely, elegantly

▶ *464 Judgment; 466 Discrimination; 495 Taste; 543 Elegance; 549 Refinement ; 591 Sensitivity*

7 Religion

Religion…is the opium of the people. Karl Marx.

Religion is love; in no case is it logic. Beatrice Webb.

NOUNS

1 religion, faith, belief, belief system, set of beliefs, creed, credo, dogma, doctrine, persuasion, superstition, conviction, religious group, religious movement, denomination, church, school, branch, movement, order, sect, cult, faction, chapter, way of life, attitude, outlook, morals, ethics, moral code, philosophy of life, point of view, perspective

▶ *4 Philosophy; 8 Divinity; 9 Worship; 10 Ritual; 11 Occultism; 443 Thought; 450 Belief; 452 Certainty; 480 Persuasion*

2 religiousness, piety, piousness, sanctimony, puja, reverence, honour, veneration, observance, strict observance, strictness, faithfulness, ritualism, deism, theism, mysticism, spirituality, chohan, prayerfulness, Kavannah, communion with God, trust in God, self-surrender, self-sacrifice, fear of God, theopathy, humility, prostration, dedication, devotion, adoration, unction, zeal, enthusiasm, fervour, speaking in tongues, glossolalia, sanctimoniousness, religiosity, overpiety, overorthodoxy, preachiness, churchiness, unctuousness, Bible-bashing (*or* thumping *or* punching), Bible-worship, bibliolatry, literalness, fundamentalism, salvationism, missionary spirit, fanaticism, witch-hunting, heresy-hunting, crusading, bigotry, persecution

▶ *10 Ritual; 273 Accuracy; 388 Submission; 663 Obedience*

3 religious person, religious, pietist, child of God, votary, saint, real saint, bodhisattva, marabout, martyr, pilgrim, palmer, hajji, mystic, charismatic, holyman, sadhu, sannyasi, bhikshu, fakir, man (*or* woman) of prayer, believer, worshipper, the faithful, convert, neophyte, catechumen, devotee, disciple, acolyte

▶ *255 Purity; 450 Belief; 623 Humility; 663 Obedience; 664 Servility; 667 Respect; 797 Good; 799 Honour; 803 Virtue*

4 religionist, zealot, iconoclast, formalist, precisian, inerrantist, Sabbatarian, bibliolater, preacher, pulpiteer, sermonizer, salvationist, missionary, fanatic, crusader, ghazi, witch-hunter, tyrant, bigot, persecutor

5 Christian, practising Christian, communicant, conformist, Catholic, Roman Catholic, papist (Offensive), Protestant, Anglo-Catholic, Anglican, Episcopalian, Unitarian, Trinitarian, Evangelical, born-again Christian, Nonconformist, Lutheran, Calvinist, Presbyterian, Wee Free (Offensive), Methodist, Wesleyan, Baptist, Congregationalist, Quaker, Friend, Puritan, Hussite, Huguenot, Lollard, Mormon, Latter-Day Saint, Mennonite, Jehovah's Witness, Christian Scientist, Moonie (Inf), Adventist, Seventh-Day Adventist, revivalist, evangelist, TV evangelist, televangelist, fundamentalist, militant Christian, hot gospeller (Inf), Jesus freak (Inf), the

CHRISTIAN MOVEMENTS

Abecedarianism
Abelianism (*or* Abelites)
Abode of Love
Abrahamites
Abstinents
Abyssinian Church
Acacianism
Adamites
Adiaphorism
Adoptionism
Adventism
African Methodism
African Orthodox Church
Agapemonites
Agnoetae
Agonizants
Albigensianism
Alogi
Alombrados
Amalricianism
Ambrosianism
American Orthodox Church
Amish
Amyraldianism
Anabaptism
Anglican Communion (*or* Anglicanism)
Anglo–Catholicism
Annihilationism
Anomoianism
Antipaedobaptism
Apollinarianism
Apostolic Brethren
Arianism
Arminianism
Artemonism
Assumptionism
Baptism
Barclayism
Basildeanism
Beguines
Biblicism
Bogomils
Bonosianism
Bosci
Bourignianism
Brinsers
Broad Church
Brownism
Brugglers
Buchanites
Calixtines
Calvinism
Cameronianism
Catharism
Catholicism
Cerdonianism
Chiliasm
Christian Science
Church of England
Church of Ireland
Church of Scotland
Congregationalism
Covenanters
Diggers
Docetism
Donatism
Dunkers
Dyophysites
Dyothelites
Eastern Orthodox Church
Encratites
Episcopal Church
Evangelicalism
Frankism
Free Church of Scotland
Fundamentalism
Generationism
Gideons
Greek Orthodox
Haugeanism
Hicksites
High Church
Huguenotism
Hussism (*or* Hussitism)
Illuminati
Infralapsarianism
Jacobites
Jansenism
Jehovah's Witnesses
Jumpers
Laestadianism
Latitudinarianism
Levellers
Lollardy (*or* Lollardry *or* Lollardism)
Low Church
Lullism
Lutheranism
Macedonianism
Mandeism
Maronism
Mar Thoma
Melchites
Melitianism
Mennonitism
Methodism
Montanism
Moral Rearmament
Moravian Church
Mormonism
Nestorian Church
Orthodox Church
Oxford Movement
Paulicianism
Pentecostalism
Plymouth Brethren
Presbyterianism
Protestantism
Puritanism
Quakerism
Redemptorism
Roman Catholicism
Russian Orthodox Church
Rosicrucianism
Salvation Army
Se–baptism
Shakers
Swedenborgianism
Syrian Orthodox
Taborites
Templars
Teutonic Knights
Theopaschites
Tractarianism
Trinitarianism
Tübingen School
Unification Church
Unitarianism

God squad (Inf), Bible-basher (*or* thumper *or* puncher) (Inf), creeping Jesus (Inf), holy roller (Inf)

6 **non-Christian**, Jew, Orthodox Jew, Zionist, Essene, Pharisee, Sadducee, Muslim, Mohammedan, Mussulman (Lit), infidel (Lit), Shiite, Sunnite, Sufi, Druse, Wahhabi, Black Muslim, fundamentalist, Baha'i, Hindu, Buddhist, Zen Buddhist, Sikh, Jain (*or* Jaina *or* Jainist), Rastafarian, Rasta (Inf)

7 **monk**, nun, prior, prioress, abbot, abbess, mother superior, reverend father, superioress, reverend mother, canoness, monastic, religious, sister, brother, kalogeros, trapa, talapoin, bo-san, shonin, bhikku, bhikkunis, bonze, fakir, dervish, caloyer, coenobite, conventual, hieromarch, mendicant, friar, pilgrim, palmer, stylite, pillarist, beadsman, hermit, abbacomes, anchorite, ascetic, novice, postulant, lay disciple, upasaka, upasika, koji, chela

▶ *401 Servant; 623 Humility; 663 Obedience; 687 Fasting; 797 Good; 803 Virtue*

8 **priest**, priestess, high priest, pope, papa, pontif, pontifex maximus, chief rabbi, hakam, Grand Lama, Dalai Lama, Panchen Lama, Dastur, Kalif (*or* Caliph), hierophant, Arch Druid, Arch Druidess, flamen, Brahman, Gosain, guru, pundit, purohita, cardinal, bishop, archbishop, primate, patriarch, hierarch, diocesan, suffragan, prelate, clergyman, clergywoman, ecclesiastic, ecclesiarch, churchman, cleric, clerk in holy orders, man (*or* woman) of the cloth, minister, ministress, pastor, pastoress, deacon, deaconess, ordinand, dean, canon, monsignor, parson, vicar, rector, curate, elder, father, confessor, chaplain, padre, rabbi (*or* rabbin), kohen (*or* cohen), maggid, koheleth, mullah, imam, ayatollah, qadi, sheikh, qasisha, mujtahid, darshan, rishi, dhammaduta, zen-ji, lama, poonghie, witch doctor, houngan, mamaloi, papaloi, haruspex, augur, churchwarden, almoner, verger, beadle, sexton, acolyte, thurifier, precentor, succentor, cantor, hazzan, muezzin, mukdam, maftir, Levite, scribe, Holy Joe (Inf), Sky Pilot (Inf)

▶ *396 Authority; 400 Master*

9 **priesthood**, priestship, hierocracy, ecclesiasticism (*or* ecclesiasticalism), clericalism, sacerdotalism, Brahmanism, the ministry, pastorate, pastorage, pastoral care, the Church, the clergy, the cloth, holy orders, ordination, ordainment, reading in, election, nomination, appointment, induction, institution, investiture, conferment, preferment, rabbinate, pontificate, papacy, popedom, cardinalship, primacy, prelature, abbacy, bishopric, bishopdom, episcopate, deanery, deanship, curacy, rectorship, rectorate, vicarship, vicariate, pastor-ship, deaconry, deaconship, chaplaincy, chaplainship, diocese, see, archdiocese, province, parish

▶ *10 Ritual*

10 **priestly dwelling**, vicarage, parsonage, rectory, deanery, manse, presbytery, archdeaconry, bishop's palace, Lambeth Palace, Vatican, ashram, retreat, hermitage, priory, friary, cloister, chapterhouse, monastery, convent, nunnery, lamasery

NON–CHRISTIAN RELIGIONS

Judaism
Ashkenazim, Assimilationism, Boethusian, Chazar, Conservative Judaism, Ebionite, Essenes, Falasha, Hasidism, Karaites, Messianic Judaism, Mizrachi, Nazarite, Orthodox Judaism, Pharisaism (*or* Phariseeism), Rabbinism, Reconstructionism, Reform Judaism, Sadduceeism, Sephardim, Zionism

Hinduism
Aghorapanthi, Ajivika, Arya Samaj, Brahmanism, Chaitanya Vaishnava, Dadu Panthis, Dakshincharin, Hare Krishna, Lingayata, Lokayata, Madhva, Pancharatra, Rama Krishna, Ramanandi, Saivism, Saktism, Sankar, Satnami, Sittar, Tantrism, Vamcharin, Vedantism, Yogism

Islam
Admadiya, Ahmadiya, Almohades, Almoravides, Babism, Bahaism, Black Muslims, Carmathian (*or* Karmathian), Druses, Ibadhi, Ja'alin, Malikite, Mohammedanism, Qadarite, Sanusi, Shiah, Sufism, Sunni, Wahhabiyah

Sikhism
Akali, Nirmalin, Udasin

Jainism
Sehanakavasi

Zoroastrianism (or Zoroastrism)
Mazdaism, Parsee (*or* Parsi), Yezidi

Buddhism
Adibuddhism, Hua–yen, Jodo, Kahdam–pa, Kegon, Koan, Lamaism, Mahayana, Maha Bodhi, Mokusho, Nichiren, Nyigma–pa, Obaku–shu, Sangha, Taoism, Tendai, Vajrayna, Won, Yogacara, Zen

Shinto
Fuso Kyo, Tenri Kyo

African religions
Bantu, Beninese, Hehe, Mtwaran, Voodoo, Xhosa, Yoruba

Nontheistic religions
Confucianism, Humanism, I Am, Spiritualism

Miscellaneous
Algonquin, Andamanese, Araucanian, Caodaism, Cargo Cult, Chuntokyo, Eskimo, Ghost Dance, Guarani, Navaho, Paressi, Peruvian, Pomo, Quiche, Rastafarianism, Sabaism, Scientology™, Sioux

Ancient religions
Adonism, Aegean, Ainu, Ammonite, Amorite, Ancestor Worship, Ancient and Mystical Order of Poahtun, Anglo–Saxon, Assyrian, Aztec, Babylonian, Bön (*or* Pon), Canaanite, Carthaginian, Celtic, Chaldean, Druidism, Eleusinianism, Etruscan, Germanic, Incan, Khond, Mammonism, Mayan, Mithraism, Naasene, Norse, Nubian, Ophian, Orphism, Oyomei, Paganism, Phoenician, Roman, Sankhya, Shamanism, Slavonic, Sumerian, Thag (*or* Thug), Totemism, Vedic

► *10 Ritual; 20 Architecture*

11 vestment, canonicals, regalia, habit, veil, robes, cloth, vesture, liturgical garment, ceremonial attire, pontificals, pontificalia, episcopal vestment, frock, mantle, gown, cloak, surplice, scapular, cassock, cope, pallium, amice, chasuble, alb, tunicle, tallith, ephod, apron, soutane, hood, capuche, clerical collar, fanon, headdress, wimple, cardinal's hat, mitre, tiara, triple crown, priest's cap, biretta, prayer cap, skullcap, yarmulke, turban, calotte, zucchetto, Salvation Army bonnet, stole, tippet, cingulum, maniple, crosier, crook, staff, episcopal ring, orphrey (*or* orfray), clericals (Inf), dog collar (Inf)

► *10 Ritual; 551 Dress; 632 Habit*

12 religious text, sacred text, scripture, sacred writings, sutra, shastra, word of God, canonical writings, canon, Christian text, Bible, Holy Bible, the Book, the Good Book, the Word, King James' Bible, Authorized Version, Revised Version, New English Bible, Geneva Bible, Breeches Bible, Jerusalem Bible, Good News Bible, Gideon Bible, Septuagint, Old Testament, New Testament, Gospels, Synoptic Gospels, Epistles, Apocrypha, Book of Mormon, Buddhist text, Pitaka, Tripitaka, Theravada, Dhamma, Dhammapada, Jataka, Apadana, Avadana, Lotus of the True Law, Nikaya, Dipavamsa, Mahavastu, Pali Canon, Confucian text, Lun-yu, Shinto text, Nihongi, Yengishiki, Jainist text, Agama, Hindu text, smriti, shruti, Upanishad, Bhagavad-Gita, Purana, Veda, Rigveda, Yajurveda, Samaveda, Atharvaveda, Aranyaka, Granth, Zoroastrian text, Avesta, Zend-Avesta, Islamic text, Koran, Quran, the Glorious Koran, Hadith, Sunna, Jewish text, Torah, Targum, Talmud, Mishnah, Gemara, Masorah, Bahir, Ancient Egyptian text, Book of the Dead

► *10 Ritual*

13 theology, divinity, dogmatic theology, philosophical theology, theological metaphysics, systematic theology, dialogical theology, patristic theology, patristics, natural theology, physicotheology, crisis theology, scholastic theology, existential theology, ontotheology, phenomenological theology, feminist theology, liberation theology, hierology, hierography, hagiology, hagiography, soteriology, Christology, Mariology, angelology, Buddhology, eschatology, theological hermeneutics, secularism, ecclesiology, doctrinism, doctrinalism, rationalism, apologetics, religious studies, religious education (RE), religious instruction (RI), scripture (Inf)

► *4 Philosophy; 694 Meaning; 719 Interpretation*

14 theologian, theologist, theologician, theologizer, theologer, theologue, divine, scholastic, canonist, hierologist, hagiologist, eschatologist, ecclesiologist

► *4 Philosophy; 719 Interpretation*

ADJECTIVES

15 religious, pious, devout, holy, godly, saintly, seraphic, cherubic, transcendent, spiritual, mystic, otherworldly, transcendent, churchgoing, practising, strict, faithful, believing, holding (*or* keeping) the faith, orthodox, pure, reverent, worshipful, prayerful, devoted, devotional, reverential, solemn, dedicated, God-fearing, theopathic, self-surrendering, humble, prostrate, self-sacrificing, monastic, anchoretic, ascetic, hermit-like, ardent, unctuous, zealous, overreligious, priest-ridden, formalistic,

MEMBERS OF RELIGIOUS ORDERS

Antonian	Crutched Friar	Maturine
Augustinian	Culdee	Minim
Austin Friar	Dominican	Minorite
Barnabite	Fontrevaut	Olivetan
Benedictine	Franciscan	Oratorian
Bernadine	Fratello	Poor Clare
Black Friar	Friar Preacher	Premonstratensian
Black Monk	Gilbertine	Recollect
Blue Nun	Grey Friar	Salesian
Bonhomin	Grey Nun	Servite
Brigittine	Hospitaller	Studite
Camaldolese Monk	Jacobin	Sylvestrine
	Jeronymite	Templar
Capuchin	Jesuit	Theatine
Carmelite	Loveltine	Trappist
Carthusian	Loyolite	Trinitarian
Cistercian	Marist	Ursuline
Cluniac	Maryknoll Sister	Visitandine
Crossed Friar	Maryknoll Father	White Friar

Pharisaic, overstrict, ritualistic, churchy, overdevout, overrighteous, holier-than-thou, self-righteous, sanctimonious, fervent, preachy, canting, Bible-worshipping, fundamentalist, evangelical, crusading, militant, missionary, fanatical, witch-hunting, bigoted, Bible-bashing (*or* thumping *or* punching) (Inf)

► *273 Accuracy; 388 Submission; 450 Belief; 623 Humility; 663 Obedience; 667 Respect; 797 Good; 803 Virtue*

16 denominational, sectarian, Christian, Catholic Roman, Roman Catholic, RC (Inf), popish, papish, papist (Offensive), Protestant, Anglican, C of E (Inf), High-Church, Low-Church, Episcopalian, Nonconformist, Orthodox, Jewish, Judaeo-Christian, Judaic (*or* Judaical), Hebrew, Reform, Conservative, Hasidic, Sephardic, Islamic, Muslim, fundamentalist, Hindu, Buddhist, Taoist

17 priestly, ecclesiastical, sacerdotal, hieratical, clerical, ministerial, churchly, pastoral, canonical, papal, pontifical, episcopal, rabbinic (*or* rabbinical), prelatic, presbyteral, hierophantic, druidic (*or* druidical), hierocratic, parochial, diocesan, ordained

► *396 Authority; 400 Master*

18 theological, religious, divine, patristic, physicotheological, ontotheological, hierological, hierographical, hagiological, hagiographical, soteriological, Christological, eschatological, doctrinal, ecclesiological, canonical, scriptural, metaphysical

► *4 Philosophy; 694 Meaning; 719 Interpretation*

VERBS

19 be religious, get religion, meet God, receive Christ, accept the Lord, enter the church, recant, repent, turn, convert, be converted, be saved, have a crisis of faith, hold (*or* keep) the faith, believe, have faith, recite the creed, go to church, receive communion, support the church, revere, venerate, honour, observe, trust in God, worship, adore, obey, devote oneself, prostrate oneself, humble oneself, surrender oneself, fear God, feel the spirit, be possessed by the spirit, go on a pilgrimage, perform the hajj

► *10 Ritual; 388 Submission; 450 Belief; 623 Humility; 663 Obedience; 667 Respect; 760 Conversion; 797 Good; 803 Virtue*

20 preach, spread the Word, spread the good news, fight the good fight, speak in tongues, sermonize, proselytize, evangelize, convert, convince, win for Christ, receive into the church, baptize, Christianize, Islamize, Judaize, depaganize, crusade, witch-hunt, heresy-hunt, persecute, preachify (Inf), Bible bash (*or* thump *or* punch) (Inf)

► *480 Persuasion*

21 ordain, consecrate, read in, elect, nominate, appoint, invest, frock, anoint, call, confer holy orders on, take holy orders, take vows, take the veil, wear the cloth

22 theologize, study theology, interpret the scriptures, study the Bible, ponder the nature of God, philosophize

► *4 Philosophy; 694 Meaning; 719 Interpretation*

ADVERBS

23 religiously, piously, spiritually, devoutly, strictly, worshipfully, faithfully, humbly, reverentially, solemnly, ardently, zealously, fanatically, theologically, doctrinally, rabbinically, canonically, ecclesiastically, by the book

► *273 Accuracy*

8 Divinity

God moves in a mysterious way
His wonders to perform. William Cowper.

NOUNS

1 divinity, divineness, godhood, godhead, deity, godship, godliness, numinousness, Brahmahood, Buddhahood, divine essence, divine principle, divine nature, perfection, sanctitude, sanctity, holiness, hallowedness, sacredness, sacrosanctity, transcendence, enlightenment, state of grace, blessed state, blessedness, nirvana, sublimity

► *7 Religion*

2 divine attribute, eternity, infinity, immortality, truth, love, mercy, wisdom, power, supremacy, sovereignty, majesty, Shekinah, omnipresence, omniscience, omnipotence, almightiness, theocracy

► *7 Religion; 97 Presence; 202 Infinity; 225 Permanence; 230 Perfection; 279 Eternity; 334 Power; 396 Authority; 797 Good*

3 God, Lord, the Lord, Providence, Jehovah, Yahweh (*or* Jahweh *or* Yahveh *or* Jahveh), Jah, Adonai, Elohim, Allah, Yuh-hwang-shangte, the Supreme Being, Almighty God, the Almighty, King of Kings, Lord of Lords, the Eternal, Alpha and Omega, the Maker, the Creator, the Father, God the Father, Everlasting Father, First Cause, Prime Mover, *primum mobile* (L), *Ens Entium* (L), Demiourgos, demiurge, the Mother, Great Mother, Mother Nature, the Holy Spirit, the Holy Ghost, Spirit of God, the Great Spirit, the Supreme Soul, oversoul, world soul, Atman, Paramatman, the Preserver, the Universal Self, the Blessed One, the Teacher, Buddha, Bodhisattva, Amida, Dai Nichi, Akshobhya, the Lord of Wisdom, the Wise One, the King of Light, Ahura Mazda (*or* Ormazd), the Trinity, Holy Trinity, Father, Son and Holy Ghost, Trimurti

► *7 Religion; 11 Occultism; 202 Infinity; 230 Perfection; 279 Eternity; 334 Power; 344 Cause; 396 Authority; 797 Good*

4 God the Son, Son of God, Jesus Christ, Christ, Jesus, Lord Jesus, King of the Jews, Messiah, Emmanuel (*or* Immanuel), The Saviour, The Redeemer, Lamb of God, Son of Man, the Good Shepherd, Prince of Peace, the Way, the Truth, and the Life, the Light of the World

5 deity, divinity, god, goddess, deva, devi, the gods, the immortals, the Olympians, fertility god, corn god, rain god, earth goddess, moon goddess, household gods, minor deity, demigod, spirit, guiding spirit, numen, daemon, genius, inspiration, muse, the Muses, animistic spirit, mana, manitou, huaca, nagual, pokunt, tamanoas, wakan, zemi, forest spirit, vegetation spirit, year daemon, faun, satyr, nymph, wood nymph, tree nymph, dryad, hamadryad, oread, water nymph, water spirit, naiad, undine, Anahita, sea nymph, Nereid, object of worship, idol, fetish, totem, supernatural being

► *10 Ritual; 11 Occultism*

6 angel, angelhood, archangel, archangelship, guardian angel, fairy godmother, seraph, cherub, putto, celestial, heavenly being, principality, messenger of God, heavenly host, angelic host, choir invisible, thrones, dominations, virtues, powers, ministering spirits, Amesha Spentas, Lha, angel of love, angel of light, Abdiel, Chamuel, Gabriel, Jophiel, Michael, Raphael, Uriel, Zadkiel, Haurvatat, Khshathra Vairya, Rashnu, Sraosha, Vohu Manah, angel of death, Azrael, Israfel, Aesma, fallen angel, Lucifer

► *392 Help; 797 Good*

7 devil, demon, demonkind, powers of darkness, evil spirit, namtar, kmukamtch, dybbuk, shedu, gyre, incubus, succubus, afreet, fiend, imp, lost soul, fallen angel, rebel angel, the Devil, Satan, Lucifer, the Evil One, the Enemy, the Common Enemy, Prince of Darkness, His Satanic Majesty, Lord of the Flies, Archfiend, Antichrist, The Tempter, Diabolus, Belial, Beelzebub, Mephisto, Mephistopheles, Shaitan, Eblis (*or* Iblis), Apollyon, Abaddon, Ahriman, Angra Mainyu, Sammael, Aeshma, Azidahaka, Pisacha, Putana, Ravana, Mara, Azazil, Tutivillus, Asmodeus, Set, Typhan, Loki, deil (Scot), *diable* (Fr), *diavolo* (It), *diablo* (Sp), *Teukl* (Ger), Old Nick (Inf), Old Harry (Inf), Old Scratchy (Inf), Old Hornie (Dial), Old Clootie (Dial)

► *11 Occultism; 651 Malevolence; 798 Evil; 804 Wickedness*

8 divine manifestation, epiphany, avatar, materialization, incarnation, embodiment, the Word, the Word made Flesh, appearance, apparition, visitation, vision, annunciation, theophany, angelophany, Christophany, divine revelation, Bat Kol, direct communication, direct intuition, mystical experience, meeting with God, mystical intuition, divination, clairvoyance

9 deification, apotheosis, divinization, immortalization, idolization, fetishization, canonization, beatification, sainting, santification, angelization, consecration, enshrinement, exaltation, adulation, glorification, elevation, assumption, dedication, dignification, ennoblement, magnification, lionization

► *669 Approval; 813 Reward*

10 deified person, saint, martyr, patron saint, beatified soul, canonized person, redeemed soul, soul in glory, soul in bliss, Madonna, Our Lady, Mother of God, Holy Mary, Queen of Heaven, Queen of Angels, the Blessed Virgin, the Virgin, the Virgin Mary, the Virgin Mother

▶ *7 Religion; 797 Good; 799 Honour; 803 Virtue*

11 heaven, sky, firmament, empyrean, welkin, happy hunting ground, the Land of the Leal, the happy land, the Pearly Gates, realm of light, Beulah, Holy City, Zion, New Jerusalem, Celestial City, throne of God, Kingdom of God, Kingdom come, celestial kingdom, telestial kingdom, Gimli, Raj, Tien, Dyu, Sattyaloka, Tushita, Alfardaws, Assama, Falak al Aflak, Dar-el-jannah, Svarog, Swarga, paradise, Bouyan, Sukhavati, Vaikuntha, Amaravati, nirvana, satori, devaloka, Kamavachara, Kamaloka, devachan, Elysium, Elysian fields, Isles of the Blest, Avalon, Kailasa, Valhalla, Abode of the Gods, Olympus, Asgard, Fensalir, Glashem, Vingolf, Valaskjalf, Noatun, Glitnir

▶ *174 Top; 279 Eternity; 463 Forgetfulness; 582 Death; 797 Good; 813 Reward*

12 hell, place of the dead, limbo, purgatory, Arat Duzzakh, lower world, underworld, nether world, Hades, Dis, Tartarus, Avernus, Erebus, Orcus, realm of Pluto, sheol, Abaddon, Annwn, Hel, Niflheim, Amenti, Duat (*or* Tuat), Apaya, Aralu, Laza, Naraka, Tophet, Gehenna, jahannan, avici, pit of Acheron, inferno, abyss, bottomless pit, lake of fire and brimstone, perdition, eternal damnation

▶ *582 Death; 712 Curse; 814 Punishment*

ADJECTIVES

13 divine, godly, godlike, deistic, theistic, Yahwistic (*or* Jahwistic *or* Yahvistic *or* Jahvistic), Elohistic, Christlike, Christly, messianic, incarnate, theomorphic, epiphanic, numinous, holy, hallowed, sacred, sacrosanct, transcendent, transcendental, enlightened, blessed, full of grace, sublime, perfect, supreme, sovereign, majestic, theocratic, providential, omnipresent, ubiquitous, all-seeing, all-knowing, prescient, omniscient, all-powerful, omnipotent, almighty, absolute, immortal, eternal, infinite, immeasurable, ineffable, mystical, oracular, supernatural, supramundane, extramundane, unearthly

▶ *202 Infinity; 225 Permanence; 230 Perfection; 279 Eternity; 334 Power; 396 Authority*

14 heavenly, celestial, empyrean, empyreal, on high, Elysian, paradisiac, paradisical, paradisiacal, Olympian, supernal, ethereal, angelic, angelical, archangelic, seraphic, cherubic, saintly

▶ *174 Top; 434 Air; 797 Good; 803 Virtue*

15 deified, divinized, immortalized, canonized, beatified, sanctified, angelized, haloed, glorified, saved, redeemed, martyred, consecrated, enshrined, elevated, dedicated, dignified, ennobled, magnified, exalted, adulated, idolized

▶ *7 Religion; 9 Worship; 10 Ritual; 669 Approval; 813 Reward*

16 devilish, devil-like, evil, satanic, diabolic, diabolical, demonic (*or* demonical), demoniac (*or* demoniacal), demon-like, Mephistophelean, fiendish, fiendlike, fallen, damned, hell-born, hellish, infernal, sulphurous, chthonian, chthonic, subterranean, pandemonic, Plutonian, Avernal, Tartarean, abysmal, purgatorial

▶ *491 Physical Pain; 651 Malevolence; 798 Evil; 804 Wickedness; 814 Punishment*

VERBS

17 deify, apotheosize, divinize, immortalize, canonize, bless, beatify, sanctify, angelize, consecrate, hallow, enshrine, elevate, dedicate, dignify, ennoble, magnify, exalt, adulate, glorify, idolize, go to heaven, ascend, transcend, sublimate, enlighten

▶ *7 Religion; 9 Worship; 10 Ritual; 11 Occultism; 669 Approval; 813 Reward*

18 devilize, diabolize, demonize, bedevil, possess, damn, condemn, curse

▶ *11 Occultism; 712 Curse*

ADVERBS

19 divinely, numinously, perfectly, sacredly, transcendently, transcendentally, sublimely, supremely, majestically, theocratically, providentially, ineffably, infinitely, absolutely, ubiquitously, omnisciently, almightily, omnipotently, eternally, supernaturally, spiritually, mystically, gracefully, angelically, seraphically, cherubically, celestially, messianically, theistically, Yahwistically, as God, by God's will, *Deo volente* (L), DV, by divine right

▶ *7 Religion; 10 Ritual; 202 Infinity; 225 Permanence; 230 Perfection; 334 Power; 396 Authority; 455 Knowledge*

20 devilishly, satanically, diabolically, demonically, fiendishly, infernally, hellishly, in hell, in hellfire, in torment, below, underground

▶ *11 Occultism ; 582 Death; 651 Malevolence; 712 Curse; 798 Evil; 804 Wickedness; 814 Punishment*

9 Worship

When two or three are gathered together in thy Name thou wilt grant their requests. The Book of Common Prayer.

NOUNS

1 worship, honour, reverence, devotion, devotedness, bhakti, dedication, veneration, adoration, adulation, esteem, dignification, glorification, exaltation, magnification, laudation, praise, extolment, celebration, thanksgiving, hymn-singing, psalm-singing, duty, obedience, homage, kneeling, genuflection, prostration, humility, humbling oneself, piety, holy fear, awe, propitiation, appeasement, confession, penitence, atonement, offering, oblation, sacrifice, muda, supplication, petition, praying, contemplation, meditation, communion with God, asceticism, fasting, pilgrimage, hajj, puja

▶ *7 Religion; 8 Divinity; 10 Ritual; 11 Occultism; 18 Music; 388 Submission; 516 Tunefulness; 601 Celebration; 623 Humility; 667 Respect; 669 Approval; 671 Gratitude; 710 Request; 752 Offer; 808 Remorse*

2 idolatry, idolism, idolization, iconolatry, superstition, cult, cargo cult, cultism, heathenism, heathenry, paganism, paganry, pagano-Christianism, totemism, fetishism (*or* fetichism), phallicism, priestcraft, bibliolatry, ecclesiolatry, obi (*or* obeah), obiism (*or* abeahism), allotheism, animism, animatism, anthropomorphism, animal worship, zoolatry, zoomorphism, theriolatry, snake worship, ophiolatry, sun worship, heliolatry, star worship, Sabaism, fire worship, pyrolatry, tree worship, dendrol-

DEITIES

Greek

- Aglaia
- Ananke
- Aphrodite
- Apollo
- Ares
- Artemis
- Asclepius
- Ate
- Athene
- Atropos
- Castor
- Clotho
- Cronos
- Demeter
- Dionysus
- Dis
- Eos
- Eris
- Eros
- Eumenides
- Euphrosyne
- Gaia (*or* Ge *or* Ga)
- Hades
- Hebe
- Hecate
- Helios
- Hephaestus
- Hera
- Hermes
- Hestia
- Hypnos
- Iris
- Lachesis
- Lyssa
- Nemesis
- Nike
- Ops
- Ouranos
- Pan
- Persephone
- Phoebe
- Pluto
- Plutus
- Pollux
- Poseidon
- Rhea
- Selene
- Thanatos
- Tuche
- Zeus

Roman

- Acca Larentia
- Aesculapius
- Apollo
- Aurora
- Bacchus
- Bellona
- Ceres
- Cupid
- Cybele
- Diana
- Faunus
- Fortuna
- Hyperion
- Iris
- Juno
- Jupiter (*or* Jove)
- Juventas
- Lares
- Luna
- Mars
- Mercury
- Minerva
- Mors
- Neptune
- Nox
- Penates
- Phoebus
- Pluto
- Pontus
- Proserpina
- Saturn
- Sol
- Somnus
- Tellus
- Uranus
- Venus
- Vertumnus
- Vesta
- Vulcan

Etruscan

- Cupra
- Feronia
- Fufluns
- Horta
- Ilythyia–Leucothea
- Losna
- Menrva
- Nortia
- Thalna
- Tina
- Voltumna

Norse

- Aegir
- Balder
- Bil
- Bragi
- Eir
- Forseti
- Frey (*or* Freya)
- Frigg (*or* Frigga)
- Gerda
- Heimdal
- Hel
- Hermod
- Hödur
- Idun
- Lofri
- Loki
- Nanna
- Nerthus
- Njord (*or* Njorth)
- Sif
- Skuld
- Surt
- Thor
- Tiw (*or* Tiu)
- Urd
- Vanir
- Verdandi
- Vidar
- Wotan (*or* Odin)

Germanic

- Eostre (*or* Estre)
- Forseti
- Frimla
- Hod
- Holle
- Hulda
- Khors

Celtic

- Adsullata
- Angus
- Anu
- Artio
- Badb
- Basso–juan (Basque)
- Benzozia (Basque)
- Bile
- Bormanus
- Borvo
- Briganta (British)
- Brigit
- Bussumanus
- Ceridwen (British)
- Cermait
- Cocidius
- Cyhiraeth
- Dagda
- Damona
- Danu
- Dirona
- Dylan
- Epona
- Fea
- Grannos
- Hesus (Gallic)
- Kelpie
- Leucetios
- Lir (Gaelic)
- Lug
- Macha
- Moccus
- Morrigu
- Murigen (Irish)
- Nemon
- Nodens (British)
- Orko (Basque)
- Segomo
- Shoney
- Teutates (Gallic)
- Thunar (British)
- Tuatha de Danann (Irish)

Egyptian

- Aaah–te–huti
- Ammon
- Amon–ra
- Andjeti
- Anhur
- Anit
- Anquet
- Anubis
- Apep
- Apet
- Atmu
- Aton
- Bast
- Bes
- Chnoumis
- Dua
- Geb
- Hapi
- Hathor
- Hequet
- Hershef
- Hey–tau
- Horus
- Imhotep
- Isis
- Khensu (*or* Khons)
- Khepera (*or* Khopri)
- Khnemu (*or* Khnum)
- Maat
- Mehueret
- Menthu
- Meshkenit
- Min
- Munt (*or* Mont)
- Mut
- Nekhebit
- Nekhen
- Neneh
- Nephthys
- Net
- Neter
- Nun
- Nut
- Osiris
- Ptah
- Ra (Re)
- Renpet
- Reret
- Seb
- Sebek
- Seker
- Sekhmet
- Sesheta
- Set (*or* Seth)
- Shu
- Tatumen
- Taueret
- Tefnut
- Thoth
- Upuaut

Babylonian

- Ashushu–Namir
- Baal Shamain
- Belit
- Anshar
- Kishar
- Anu
- Aruru
- Adad
- Allatu
- Damkina
- Ea
- Enki
- Enlil
- Enmesharra
- Enzu
- Ga–tum–dag
- Gibil
- Gula
- Haya
- Innana
- Kingu
- Lakhame
- Lakhmu
- Marduk
- Merodach
- Mylitta
- Nebo
- Nergal
- Ningal
- Ningirsu
- Ninib
- Nusku
- Oannes
- Samkhat
- Tammuz
- Yamm
- Zu

Middle Eastern

- Adad (Canaanite, Syrian)
- Adrammelech (Samaritan)
- Allat (Nabatean)
- Amor (Amorite)
- Anahita (Persian)
- Anthat (Ugarit)
- Asari (Syrian)
- Asheratian (Semitic)
- Ashirat (Canaanite)
- Ashur (Assyrian)
- Astarte (Semitic)
- Attar (Arabian)
- Atter (Semitic)
- Attis (Phrygian)
- Baal (Phoenician, Canaanite, Semitic)
- Baalat (Semitic)
- Babbar (Sumerian)
- Belet (Semitic)
- Belili (Sumerian)
- Berouth (Phoenician)
- Buriash (Kassitic)
- Cybele (Phrygian)
- Dagan (Assyrian)
- Dagon (Canaanite)
- El (Canaanite, Semitic)
- Elat (Semitic)
- Elegabalus (Syrian)
- Elioun (Phoenician)
- Enurta (Assyrian)
- Heres (Canaanite)
- Ilah (Semitic)
- Ilat (Arabian)
- Ilmagah (Semitic)
- Khoser–et–hasis (Phoenician)
- Ma (Turkish)
- Milcom (Ammonite)
- Molech (Semitic)
- Mot (Phoenician)
- Nana (Sumerian)
- Nannar (Chaldean)
- Nikkal (Sumerian)
- Ninella (Mesopotamian)
- Ninib (Assyrian)
- Nisroch (Ninnevan)

atry, devil worship, diabolism, demonism, Satanism, Mammonism, mammonolatry, ancestor worship, necrolatry, hero worship, anthropolatry

► *7 Religion; 8 Divinity; 10 Ritual; 11 Occultism*

3 idol, image, graven image, effigy, golden calf, god, deity, Baal, Juggernaut, joss, icon, maumet (Lit), fetish, symbol, yoni, lingam

► *8 Divinity; 11 Occultism*

4 idolized person, hero, heroine, celebrity, superstar, megastar, darling, pet, favourite

DEITIES (CONT.)

- Omicle (Phoenician)
- Pontus (Phoenician)
- Qadesh (Syrian)
- Rimman (Syrian)
- Sabazios (Phrygian)
- Samas (Semitic)
- Sinurc (Persian)
- Suwa (Arabian)
- Teshub (Hittite)
- Urbanus (Canaanite)
- Uzza (Arabian)
- Verethagna (Zoroastrian)
- Yaghuth (Arabian)

Hindu

- Aditya
- Agni
- Ahi
- Aiyanar
- Asura
- Bali
- Bhairava
- Brahma
- Devi
- Diti
- Ganesha
- Garuda
- Hanuman
- Ida
- Indra
- Jagannath (*or* Juggernaut)
- Jyestha
- Kali
- Kalki
- Kama
- Kamashi
- Kartikeya
- Krishna
- Kubera
- Kurma
- Lakshmi
- Mahadeva
- Mahadevi
- Matsya
- Nanda
- Narsinh
- Parvati
- Parshuram
- Pasupati
- Prajapati
- Prithivi
- Rama
- Rati
- Rudra
- Saranyu
- Sarasvati
- Savitri
- Sesha
- Sitala
- Siva (*or* Shiva)
- Sugriva
- Surya
- Uma
- Vaman
- Varah
- Varuna
- Vata
- Vayu
- Vishnu
- Visva–Karma
- Visvesvara
- Yama

Vedic

- Aditi
- Asvin
- Brihaspati
- Daksha
- Dhatri
- Dyaus
- Parjana
- Prithivi
- Pushan
- Sita
- Tvastri
- Ushas
- Vastosh–Pati
- Vayu

Far Eastern

- Aizen myo–o (Japanese)
- Amaterasu–omikami (Japanese)
- Amitayus (Tibetan)
- Benten (Japanese)
- Bimbo–gami (Japanese)
- Bishamon (Japanese)
- Daikoku (Japanese)
- Dakini (Buddhist)
- Ebisu (Japanese)
- Ema (Japanese)
- Fuchi (Japanese)
- Fudo (Japanese)
- Fukurokuju (Japanese)
- Futsunushi (Japanese)
- Hachiman (Japanese)
- Heu T'U (*or* Hau–Too) (Chinese)
- Hotei (Japanese)
- Hsuan–wu (Taoist)
- Inari (Shinto)
- Infoniwoo (Taiwanese)
- Itzanagi (Japanese)
- Itzanami (Japanese)
- Jade Emperor (Taoist)
- Jingo (Japanese)
- Jizo (Japanese)
- Jorojin (Japanese)
- Kagu–Tsuchi (Japanese)
- Kishi Bojin (Japanese)
- Komoku (Japanese)
- Kuan Yin (Chinese)
- Nat (Burmese)
- Raiden (Japanese)
- Sengen (Japanese)
- Susa–no–o (Shinto)
- Takemikadzuchi (Japanese)
- Tou Mu (Chinese)
- Tsuki–yumi (Japanese)
- W'en–ch'ung (Chinese)

African

- Agassou (Beninese)
- Amirini (Yoruban)
- Fa (Beninese)
- Gwalu (Yoruban)
- Huntin (Bantu)
- Jo–Uk (Sudanese)
- Legba (Beninese)
- Lissa (Beninese)
- Maahes (Nubian)
- Maou (Beninese)
- Mumbo Jumbo (Sudanese)
- Mwari (Mtwaran)
- Nguruhe (Hehe)
- Obatalla (Yoruban)
- Obi (West African)
- Olorun (Yoruban)
- Orishako (Yoruban)
- Quamta (Xhosan)
- Tanit (Carthaginian)
- Yemaja (Yoruban)

American Indian and Eskimo

- Akycha (Alaskan)
- Aningan (Eskimo)
- Angpetu Wi (Dakota)
- Anpao (Dakota)
- Anungite (Dakota)
- Apisirahts (Blackfoot)
- Arnaknagsak (Eskimo)
- Asaya–Gigagei (Cherokee)
- Ahsonnulti (Navajo)
- Aka–kanet (Araucanian)
- Awahili (Cherokee)
- Awahokshu (Pawnee)
- Awonawilona (Zuni)
- Begochiddi (Navajo)
- Chahuru (Pawnee)
- Chasca (Peruvian)
- Chia (Muscaya)
- Epunamun (Araucanian)
- Estanatlehi (Navajo)
- Gaoh (Iroquois)
- Geyaguga (Cherokee)
- Haokah (Sioux)
- Heloha (Choctaw)
- Hinun (Iroquois)
- Hisakitaimisi (Creek)
- Hitchi (Hitchiti)
- Hunthaca (Chibcha)
- Hurakan (Quiche)
- Jacy (Tupi–Guarani)
- Jurupari (Tupi–Guarani)
- Ka–ata–killa (Peruvian)
- Kanati (Cherokee)
- Katkochila (Wintun)
- Kitche Manitou (Algonquin)
- Ludjatako (Creek)
- Maiso (Paressi)
- Marumda (Pomo)
- Mixacoatl (Mexican)
- Monan (Tupi–Guarani)
- Nichant (Algonquin)
- Onnion (Huron)
- Oonawieh Unggi (Cherokee)
- Pautiwa (Hopi)
- Pilan (Araucanian)
- Quahootze (Nootka)
- Sedna (Eskimo)
- Selu (Cherokee)
- Sus'sistinnako (Sia)
- Tohi (Quiche)
- Tornarsuk (Eskimo)
- Uchtsiti (Acoma)
- Ukteni (Natchez)
- Winabojo (Chippewa)
- Xilonen (Mexican)
- Yanauluha (Zuni)

Polynesian

- Apu–matangi
- Apu–hau
- Io
- Kiho Tumi
- Maui
- Oro
- Sina
- Tangaloa
- Tawhiri
- Vari–ma–te–takere

Australian

- Awhiowhio
- B–lame
- Bun–jil
- Daramulum
- Nurrundere

Aztec

- Camaxtli
- Chacmool
- Chantico
- Cihuacoatl
- Cintzotl
- Citallinicue
- Coatlicue
- Huahuantli
- Huitzilopochtli
- Huixtocihuatl
- Ilamatecuhtli
- Itzlacoliuhqui
- Itzli
- Itzpapalotl
- Ixcuina
- Ixtlilton
- Macuilxochitl
- Metztli
- Mictlancihvatl
- Mictlantecuhtli
- Omacatl
- Omeciuatl
- Ometecuhtli
- Piltzintecuhtli
- Quetzalcoatl
- Tezcatlipoca
- Tlaloc
- Tlazolteotl
- Tloque Nahuaque
- Tonacatacuhtli
- Tonqtiuh
- Xipe
- Xiuhtecuhtli
- Xochiquetzal
- Yacatecutli

Mayan

- Algahom Naum
- Bacab
- Camazotz
- Cauac
- Itzamna
- Ix
- Ixazalvoh
- Kabul
- Kan
- Kinich–ahau
- Kukulcan
- Yum Kaax

Inca

- Ataquchu
- Huaca
- Mama Allpa
- Mama Cocha
- Punchau
- Supay
- Visacocha

Miscellaneous

- Asura (Aryan)
- Byelun (Slavonic)
- Czarnobog (Slavonic)
- Da–bog (Slavonic)
- Dyaus–Pitar (Aryan)
- Jah (Rastafarian)
- Meke Meke (Easter Island)
- Murugan (Tamil)
- Nemu (New Guinea)
- Pele (Hawaiian)
- Perchta (Slavonic)
- Perkunas (Finnish)
- Ras Tafari Makonnen (Rastafarian)
- Stribog (Slavonic)
- Vainamoinen (Finnish)
- Volos (Serbian)
- Zombi (Voodoo)

5 worshipper, venerator, adorer, praise-singer, celebrant, churchgoer, communicant, supplicant (*or* suppliant), petitioner, penitent, pilgrim, hajji, adherent, votary, follower, admirer, lionizer, idolizer, devotee, aficionado, hero-worshipper, fan, groupie (Inf)

► *7 Religion; 10 Ritual*

6 idolater, idolizer, iconolater, cultist, heathen, pagan, pagano-Christian, totemist, fetishist (*or* fetichist), phallicist, bibliolater, ecclesiolater, allotheist, animist, animatist, anthropomorphist, animal worshipper, zoolater, theriolater, zoomorphist, snake worshipper, ophiolater, sun worshipper, heliolater, star worshipper, Sabaist, fire worshipper, pyrolater, tree worshipper, dendrolater, devil worshipper, diabolist, Satanist, Mammonist, mammonolater, ancestor worshipper, necrolater

► *1 Anthropology; 7 Religion; 8 Divinity; 11 Occultism*

VERBS

7 **worship**, honour, respect, revere, reverence, venerate, hallow, esteem, dignify, adulate, adore, be devoted to, dedicate oneself to, glorify, exalt, magnify, laud, extol, praise, applaud, acclaim, sing (someone's) praises, sing hymns, celebrate, give thanks, pray, say prayers, meditate, contemplate, commune with God, pay homage to, kneel, genuflect, prostrate oneself, humble oneself, obey, fear God, propitiate, appease, atone, make amends, take communion, sacrifice, fast, go on a pilgrimage

► *7 Religion; 10 Ritual; 601 Celebration; 623 Humility; 669 Approval; 687 Fasting*

8 **idolatrize**, worship idols, fetishize, totemize, heathenize, paganize, anthropomorphize, idolize, put on a pedestal, idealize, apotheosize, lionize, admire, look up to, hero-worship, make an idol of, deify

ADJECTIVES

9 **worshipful**, worshipping, reverential, reverent, venerational, adoring, adorational, praising, full of praises, hero-worshipping, anthropolatrous, devoted, devotional, prostrate, humbled, humble, supplicatory, supplicating, supplicant, penitent, prayerful, dutiful, meditative, meditational, contemplative, ascetic

► *10 Ritual; 388 Submission; 443 Thought; 623 Humility; 669 Approval; 671 Gratitude*

10 **idolatrous**, iconolatrous, superstitious, cult, cultish, cultist, heathen, pagan, totemic, totemistic, fetishistic (*or* fetichistic), fetish-like (*or* fetich-like), phallic, bibliolatrous, ecclesiolatrous, allotheistic, animistic, animatistic, anthropomorphic, zoolatrous, animal-worshipping, zoomorphic, theriolatrous, snake-worshipping, ophiolatrous, sun-worshipping, heliolatrous, star-worshipping, Sabaic, fire-worshipping, pyrolatrous, tree-worshipping, dendrolatrous, devil-worshipping, diabolic, diabolical, demonic, Satanic, Mammonistic, mammonolatrous, necrolatrous, ancestor-worshipping

11 **worshipped**, honoured, revered, venerated, blessed, esteemed, adored, glorified, extolled, praised, admired, lionized, idolized

ADVERBS

12 **worshipfully**, honorifically, honourably, reverentially, adoringly, devotedly, idolatrously, devotionally, humbly, ascetically, penitentially, sacrificially, meditatively, contemplatively, mystically, mysteriously

10 Ritual

I think weddings is sadder than funerals, because they remind you of your own wedding. You can't be reminded of your own funeral because it hasn't happened. But weddings always make me cry. Brendan Behan.

NOUNS

1 **ritual**, procedure, established practice, custom, praxis, habit, convention, routine, usage, institution, formality, ceremony, ceremonial, ordinance, office, service, form, formula, formulary, duty, order, observance, religious observance, strict observance, solemnity, solemn observance, ritual practice, religious practice, rite, worship, form of worship, order of worship, prescribed form, liturgy, sacrament

► *7 Religion; 632 Habit; 656 Formality*

2 **ritualism**, rituality, ritualization, liturgism, liturgics, liturgology, formalism, ceremonialism, solemnization, symbolism, symbolics, cult, cultism, sacramentalism, sacramentarianism, Sabbatism, Sabbatarianism

► *11 Occultism*

3 **rite of worship**, honour, reverence, veneration, adoration, glorification, exaltation, magnification, laudation, praise, celebration, thanksgiving, blessing, benediction, hymn-singing, psalm-singing, confession, astiamnu, penitence, offering, oblation, alms-giving, chalukah, potlatch, sacrifice, asvamedha, muda, supplication, petition, praying, prayer, puja

► *7 Religion; 8 Divinity; 9 Worship; 18 Music; 516 Tunefulness; 601 Celebration; 710 Request; 752 Offer; 808 Remorse*

4 **public worship**, prayer meeting, prayers, abodah (*or* avodah), musaph, church service, divine service, divine office, form of worship, liturgy, morning service, morning prayers, matins, evening service, evening prayers, evensong, vespers, minchah, maarib, memorial service, yahrzeit, order of service, canonical hour, lauds, prime, terce, sext, nones, compline (*or* complin), call to prayer, azan, muezzin's cry

5 **Christian rite**, holy rite, sacrament, seven sacraments, baptism, christening, immersion, total immersion, affusion, aspersion, confirmation, first communion, penance, confession, propitiation, penitential rites, Eucharist, Mass, marriage, Holy Matrimony, marriage service, nuptial Mass, holy orders, ordination, anointing the sick, Chrism (*or* chrisom), unction, Requiem Mass, extreme unction, viaticum, last rites, burial of the dead, ritual act, sign of the Cross, laying on of hands, lustration, purification, cleansing, ablution, thurification, sprinkling, Asperges, recessional, kiss of peace, denunciation, excommunication, exorcism

► *7 Religion; 256 Cleanness; 570 Marriage; 582 Death; 583 Burial; 712 Curse; 808 Remorse*

6 **Eucharist**, Holy Communion, Lord's Supper, Mass, High Mass, *Missa solemnis* (L), Low Mass, *Missa bassa* (L), *Missa brevis* (L), Midnight Mass, order of service, introit, Kyries, Gloria, Lesson, Epistle, Gradual, Collects, Gospel, creed, credo, offertory, lavabo, biddings, thanksgiving, consecration, consecrated elements, bread and wine, breaking of bread, elevation of the Host, transubstantiation, real presence, intinction, consubstantiation, impanation, subpanation, body and blood of Christ, Communion, dismissal, blessing

7 **non-Christian ritual**, initiation rite, passage right (*or* rite of passage), bar mitzvah, bat (*or* bas) mitzvah, ritual mutilation, circumcision, milah, female circumcision, female genital mutilation, clitoridectomy, couvade, circumambulation, cleansing, taslich, oharai, hogahn, bathing, mikvah, abhiseka, fertility rite, rite of spring,

spring rounds, ambarvalia, ritual prostitution, dance of Siva, ghost dance, sun dance, potlatch, rain dance, war dance, fetishism, cannibalism, infanticide, suicide, hara-kiri

► *11 Occultism*

8 hymn, hymning, hymnology, hymnography, hymn-singing, psalm, psalm-singing, psalmody, psalter, chant, niggun, Gregorian chant, kalophonic chant, kontakion, kanon, plainsong, plainchant, Ambrosian chant, mantra, hymnal, hymnary, Rigveda, Samaveda, anthem, cherubicon, carol, exultet, cantata, motet, canticle, doxology, greater doxology, lesser doxology, antiphon, response, Gloria, Gloria Patri, Gloria in Excelsis, Gradual, Te Deum, Benedicite, Sanctus, Jubilate Deo, paean, Magnificat, gospel song, Homeric hymn, Vedic hymn, Alleluia, Hallelujah, Hosanna, maoz tzur, nusach, yigdal, zemitot

► *18 Music; 516 Tunefulness; 669 Approval*

9 prayer, orison, devotion, impetration, petition, request, petitionary prayer, bidding prayer, invocation, epidesis, nembutsu, gayatri, allocution, intercession, geullah, suffrage, prayer for the dead, anamnesis, vigils, special prayer, comprecation, supplication, intention, rogation, eulogia, blessing, motzi, kol nidre, benediction, nishmat, grace, benison, norito, litany, collect, secret (*or* secreta), Credo, Angelus, the Lord's Prayer, Paternoster, Our Father, rosary, Hail Mary, Ave, Ave Maria, Kyrie Eleison, Pax, Agnus Dei, Nunc Dimittis, Sursum Corda, mantra, alenu, dharani, om (*or* aum), berakah

► *623 Humility; 671 Gratitude; 705 Question; 752 Offer; 808 Remorse*

10 religious manual, prayer book, Book of Common Prayer, Alternative Prayer Book, breviary, missal, book of hours, farse, lectionary, pontifical, Virginal, ordinal, canon, rubric, church book, mass book, machzor, siddur, menaion

► *7 Religion*

11 place of worship, house of God, house of prayer, church, kirk, mission, meetinghouse, chapel, conventicle, chantry, Lady chapel, chapel of rest, abbey, cathedral, minster, *duomo* (It), basilica, oratory, oratorium, temple, tabernacle, synagogue, shul, mosque, masjid, wat, pantheon, ziggurat, pagoda, fane (Lit), shrine, cell

► *7 Religion*

12 church, nave, transept(s), chancel, choir, sanctuary, altar, pulpit, lectern, pew, stall, choir stall, confessional, cloister, aisle, clerestory, triforium, tribune gallery, font, rood screen, crypt, presbytery, sacristy, vestry

► *7 Religion; 20 Architecture*

13 shrine, chapel, sanctuary, sanctum, sanctum sanctorum, holy of holies, sacrarium, reliquary, tabernacle, dagoba, cella, naos, stupa, tope, sacred place, holy place, Jerusalem, Bethlehem, Wailing Wall, Mount Omei, Mount Tai, Butsuden, Chorten, Myoskinji, Sarnath, Angkor Wat, Shwe Dagon, Abhayagiri, Tashi Lumpo, Kumbum, Bayon, Adam's Peak, Badrinath, Gangotri, River Ganges, River Narbada, River Godavari, River Kistna, Golden Temple of Amritsar, Kaaba, Mecca, Benares, Zem-Zem, Blue Mosque, Fujiyama, Miya-zaki-jingu, Abydos, Mitla, marae, cromlech, Avebury, Stonehenge, Ayers Rock, Bethel

14 sacred object, relic, monstrance, ostensorium, eucharistial, pyx, ciborium, tabernacle, ark, Torah scrolls, aronha-kodesh, phylactery, tefillin, mezuzah, asterisk, crucifix, cross, rood, holy cross, black stone, Bo tree, Banyan tree, osculatory, icon, veronica, *bambino* (It), pietà, holy water, aspergillum, asperger, incense, thurible, censer, incensory, chrismal, scrobis, cruet, urceole, rosary beads, beadroll, prayerwheel, prayermat, prayer shawl, tallith, chaplet, candle, votive candle, paschal candle, vigil light, menorah, bugia, sanctus bell, sacring bell, chair of Saint Peter, Sangreal, Holy Grail, chalice, juju, totem, talisman, charm, amulet, fetish, totem pole, sacrificial knife

► *11 Occultism*

15 holy day, holiday, feast, feast day, fast day, Yob Tom, Lord's Day, Sabbath, Sunday, Saturday, All Hallows' Day, All Saints' Day, All Souls' Day, Lady Day, Purification, Assumption, Candlemas, Lammas, Epiphany, Twelfth Night, Septuagesima, Shrove Tuesday, Mardi Gras, Pancake Day, Ash Wednesday, Quadragesima, Palm Sunday, Maundy Thursday, Good Friday, Ascension Day, Whitsunday, Michaelmas, Martinmas, Shabuoth, Rosh Hashanah, Yom Kippur, Day of Atonement, Rosh Chodesh, summer solstice, winter solstice, autumnal equinox, vernal equinox

► *462 Memory; 600 Rejoicing; 601 Celebration; 603 Lamentation; 671 Gratitude*

16 religious festival, festival, fiesta, encaenia, festivity, feast, love feast, Agape, taanit, celebration, Advent, Christmas, Yuletide, Nativity, Noel, Carnival, Lent, Easter, Eastertide, Whitsun, Harvest Festival, Feast of the Annunciation, Pesach, Passover, Hannukah, Feast of the Dedication, Feast of Weeks, Feast of Tabernacles, Sukkoth, Purim, Feast of Circumcision, Fast of Av (*or* Ab), Eid-ul-Fitr, Eid-ul-Adha, Ramadan, Muharram, Zulhijyah, Baraim, Divali, Festival of Lights, Holi, Dasehra, Durga-puja, Chinese New Year, Beltane, Hallowe'en, Samhain, Saturnalia, Lupercalia, Floralia, Agrionia, Panathenea, Dionysia, Thesmophoria, Delia, Carneia, Anthesteria, Apaturia

► *462 Memory; 557 Eating; 600 Rejoicing; 601 Celebration; 603 Lamentation; 671 Gratitude*

17 worshipper, venerator, follower, communicant, celebrant, supplicant (*or* suppliant), petitioner, penitent, churchgoer(s), parishioner(s), chapelgoer(s), fold, flock, sheep, congregation, congress, assembly, gathering, concourse, sangha, minyn

► *7 Religion; 9 Worship; 376 Gathering*

VERBS

18 perform rites, ritualize, observe, celebrate, keep, solemnize, receive the sacrament, commune, oblate, give alms, confess, receive absolution, commune, minister, officiate, anoint, chrism, confirm, lay on hands, bless, baptize, christen, sprinkle, asperse, shrive, absolve, denounce, excommunicate, exorcise, curse

► *7 Religion; 11 Occultism; 160 Form; 396 Authority; 656 Formality; 712 Curse*

19 offer worship, honour, revere, reverence, venerate, adore, glorify, exalt, extol, magnify, laud, praise, celebrate, give thanks, sing hymns, say prayers, kneel, genuflect, bow, stoop, cross oneself, make the sign of the cross, sacrifice, propitiate

▶ *7 Religion; 9 Worship; 516 Tunefulness; 601 Celebration; 669 Approval*

20 pray, request, invoke, impetrate, petition, rogate, supplicate, implore, beseech, offer a prayer, say one's prayers, say 'Our Father', say the Lord's Prayer, say grace, invoke a blessing, give thanks, recite the rosary, count (*or* tell *or* say) one's beads, chant, incant

▶ *112 Repetition; 667 Respect; 669 Approval; 710 Request*

ADJECTIVES

21 ritualistic, ceremonial, festive, festal, formulaic, official, ordained, impetrational, petitionary, invocational, supplicatory, liturgical, hymnological, hymnographical, comminatory, anthemic, celebratory, laudational, doxological, glorified, glorious, extolled, dignified, consecrated, sacramental, sacral, oblational, libational, libationary, chrismal, sacrificial, nuptial, matrimonial, penitential, funereal, baptismal, symbolic, eucharistic (*or* eucharistical), transubstantial, totemistic, fetishistic, cannibalistic, exorcised, excommunicated, cursed

▶ *7 Religion; 8 Divinity; 11 Occultism; 112 Repetition; 160 Form; 407 Order; 570 Marriage; 583 Burial; 601 Celebration; 603 Lamentation; 656 Formality; 705 Question; 810 Duty*

22 worshipping, reverent, devout, pious, observant, religious, devotional, prayerful, dutiful, solemn, congregational, parochial

▶ *7 Religion; 9 Worship*

ADVERBS

23 ritually, ritualistically, observantly, officially, solemnly, dutifully, devoutly, worshipfully, sacramentally, prayerfully, liturgically, doxologically, processionally, festally, communally, congregationally, symbolically

11 Occultism

From ghoulies and ghosties and long-leggety beasties
And things that go bump in the night
Good Lord, deliver us! Cornish prayer.

There are more things in Heaven and Earth, Horatio
Than are dreamt of in your philosophy. William Shakespeare.

NOUNS

1 occultism, esoterics, esotericism, supernaturalism, supranaturalism, preternaturalism, mystery, mystification, mysticism, shamanism, spiritism, animism, Rosicrucianism, hermetics, hermetism, hermeticism, symbolics, symbolism, anagogics, cabbalism (*or* cabalism), cabbala, voodooism, witchcraft, magic, transcendentalism, yoga, yogism, reincarnationism, metaphysics, hyperphysics, transphysical science, psychism, psychics, psychic research, metapsychism, parapsychology, psychosophy, theosophy, anthroposophy, scientology, pseudopsychology, spiritualism, mediumism, poltergeistism, mesmerism, hypnotism, autohypnotism, alchemy, astrology, divination, prophecy, fortune-telling, extrasensory perception (ESP), telepathy, telepathic transmission, telergy, thought transference, mind reading, faith healing, astral projection, telekinesis, psychokinesis, fork bending, telaesthesia, teleportation, levitation, pyramidology, ufology, phrenology, Kirlian photography, psychorrhagy, psychography, automatism, automatic writing, spirit writing, trance speaking, ghost dance, spirit rapping (Inf), table tapping (Inf)

▶ *10 Ritual; 101 Unworldliness; 736 Concealment; 737 Secrecy*

2 the occult, the paranormal, the supernatural, the supersensible, supernature, supranature, spirit world, astral plane, esoterica, enigma, arcanum, cabbala, sealed book, code, cipher (*or* cypher), occultness, obscurity, secrecy, mystery, mysteriousness, miraculousness, supernaturalness, supernaturality, supernormalness, supersensitiveness, superphysicalness, superhumanity, unearthliness, unworldliness, otherworldiness, spirituality, eeriness, ghostliness, numinousness

▶ *101 Unworldliness; 266 Obscurity; 334 Power; 736 Concealment; 737 Secrecy*

3 witchcraft, witchery, bewitchery, witchwork, Wicca, coven, witches' Sabbath (*or* Sabbat), Walpurgis Night, Hallowe'en, witching hour, sorcery, wizardry, necromancy, spellcraft, spellbinding, spellcasting, enchantment, bedevilment, possession, voodooism, voodoo, hoodoo, wanga, jujuism, obi (*or* obeah), obiism (*or* obeahism), shamanism, magism, magianism, totemism, fetishism (*or* fetichism), vampirism, magic, sortilege, theurgy, gramyre (Lit), thaumaturgy, thaumaturgia, thaumaturgics, alchemy, natural magic, sympathetic magic, white magic, chaos magic, black magic, black art, diablerie

▶ *7 Religion; 9 Worship; 334 Power; 395 Influence; 798 Evil*

4 witch, witchwoman, witchman, witch master, witch doctor, obeah (*or* obi) doctor, voodooist, wangateur, medicine man, isangoma, mundunugu, shaman, shamaness, shamanist, sorcerer, sorceress, magician, mage, magus, Merlin, necromancer, wizard, warlock, theurgist, thaumaturge, thaumaturgist, lamia, bewitcher, charmer, enchanter, enchantress, spellbinder, siren, mermaid, lorelei, water witch, white witch, weird sister, Witch of Endor, Hecate, Circe, Medusa, Medea, Stheno, Euryale

▶ *7 Religion; 334 Power; 395 Influence; 458 Wisdom*

5 spell, magic spell, charm, love charm, love potion, philtre, rune, glamour (Lit), weird (Scot), wanga, evil eye, hex, jinx, whammy (US inf), conjuration, conjurement, evocation, invocation, magic words, incantation, chant, hocus-pocus, mumbo jumbo, abracadabra, paternoster, open sesame, abraxas, fee faw fum, glossolalia, pentagram (*or* pentacle)

▶ *266 Obscurity; 334 Power; 696 Unintelligibility; 712 Curse*

6 talisman, charm, mascot, amulet, periapt, phylactery (Lit), fetish, totem, juju, obi (*or* obeah), mojo, tiki, medallion, relic, St Christopher (medal), symbol, emblem, mandala, ankh, scarab (*or* scarabaeus), swastika, fylfot, gammadion, lucky charm, crucifix, good-luck charm, luck piece, lucky bean, four-leaf clover, shamrock, horseshoe, rabbit's foot, black cat, antidote, garlic, silver bullet, bell, book, and candle, witch's broomstick, wizard's cap, familiar, familiar spirit, black cat, magic circle, magic ring, ring of invisibility, magic belt, magic sword, magic carpet, seven-league boots, cap of darkness, wishbone, wishing well, wishing stone, fairy ring

► *10 Ritual; 737 Secrecy; 742 Sign*

7 spirit, soul, geist, atman, mind, inner mind, inner being, psyche, pneuma, animus, anima, the unconscious, the subconscious, id, ego, superego, third eye, astral body, linga sharira, design body, bliss body, Buddhic body, karmic body, kamarupa, mental body, causal body, subtle body, vital body, spiritual body, etheric body, soul body

► *101 Unworldliness; 554 Life*

8 psychic power, sixth sense, inner sense, intuition, feyness, second sight, psi faculty, third eye, precognition, premonition, clairvoyance, clairaudience, clairsentience, insight, foresight, crystal vision, psychometry, telepathy, telekinesis, metapsychosis, cosmic consciousness

► *334 Power; 455 Knowledge; 518 Vision*

9 divination, divining, prophecy, soothsaying, clairvoyance, prediction, premonition, precognition, forecasting, fortune-telling, tea-leaf reading, Tarot-reading, Tarot cards, dowsing, water-divining, divining rods, dowsing rods, hydromancy, radiaesthesia, augury, sortilege, haruspication, haruspicy, ichthyomancy, ophiomancy, pythonism, mantology, palmistry, palm-reading, chiromancy, chirognomy, crystal-gazing, crystal ball, astrology, horoscopy, sideromancy, astrodiagnosis, astromancy, horoscope, star chart, birth (*or* natal) chart, numerology, arithmomancy, logomancy, dream interpretation, oneiromancy, I Ching, psephomancy, capnomancy, pyromancy, metereomancy, geomancy, hieromancy, hieroscopy, theomancy, necromancy, psychomancy

► *445 Intuition; 475 Prediction*

10 psychic phenomenon, illusion, hallucination, telepathic hallucination, *déjà vu* (Fr), telepathic dream, premonition, maya, trance, yoga trance, dharana, dhyana, samadhi, hypnosis, hypnotic trance, mediumistic trance, spirit-raising, seance, sitting, Ouija (board)™, planchette, ectoplasm, bioplasma, exteriorized protoplasm, aura, emanation, ectoplasy, effluvium, biofeedback, cosmic vibration, synchronicity, out-of-body experience (Oobe), crop circle, UFO sighting, alien encounter

► *10 Ritual; 101 Unworldliness; 376 Gathering; 763 Possession*

11 ghost, spirit, ghoul, phantom, apparition, manifestation, materialization, poltergeist, shade, manes, lemures, spectre, spook (Inf), phantasm, wraith, presence, undead, vampire, zombie (*or* zombi), fetch, demon, jinni (*or* genie), familiar spirit, elemental spirit, will-o'-the-wisp, fairy, fay, sylph, Mab, Titania, Befana, genius, elf, pixie, piskie (Lit), Puck, alfar, brownie, gnome, dwarf, troll, trow, kobold, orc, werewolf, werecat, goblin, imp, sprite, hobgoblin, leprechaun, changeling, cluricaune, gremlin, little green men (LGM), alien, extraterrestrial (ET), Martian, cosmic being

► *97 Presence; 525 Appearance*

12 occultist, psychic, esoteric, mystic, mystagogue, cabbalist (*or* cabalist), Rosicrucian, druid, druidess, houngan, supernaturalist, telepathist, mind reader, thought reader, telekinetic, fork bender, telaesthetic, panpsychist, metaphysician, metaphysicist, metapsychist, transcendentalist, spiritualist, spiritist, medium, ecstatic, automatist, psychographist, alchemist, hypnotist, faith healer, psychometer, psychometrist, anthroposophist, theosophist, psychist, psychicist, parapsychologist, pyramidologist, ufologist, phrenologist, adept, mahatma, yogi, fakir, exorcist, exorcizer, unspeller, spirit rapper (Inf), table tapper (Inf), ghostbuster (Inf)

► *7 Religion; 36 Psychology and Psychiatry; 101 Unworldliness; 445 Intuition; 736 Concealment; 737 Secrecy*

13 diviner, dowser, predictor, foreteller, forecaster, psychic, clairvoyant, clairaudient, clairsentient, seer, prophet, soothsayer, *vates* (L), augur, auspex, haruspex, weather prophet, astrologer, fortune teller, tea-leaf reader, Tarot reader, crystal gazer, palmist, palmreader, chiromancer, gypsy, romany, wise woman, sibyl, pythoness, oracle, geomancer, necromancer, psychomancer, icthyomancer, ophiomancer, pythonist, sideromancer, astromancer, numerologist, dream interpreter, oneiromancer, pyromancer, capnomancer, psephomancer, hieromancer, theomancer

► *445 Intuition; 455 Knowledge; 458 Wisdom; 475 Prediction; 742 Sign*

ADJECTIVES

14 occult, cryptic, paranormal, supersensible, superphysical, supernatural, supranatural, supernormal, preternatural, hermetic, symbolic, anagogic(al), latent, covert, enigmatic, arcane, esoteric, obscure, secret, mysterious, encoded, cabbalistic (*or* cabalistic), runic, Rosicrucian

► *266 Obscurity; 719 Interpretation; 736 Concealment; 737 Secrecy*

15 witchlike, wizard-like, wizardly, sorcerous, necromantic, alchemic(al), alchemistic, druidic, shamanic, talismanic, Circean, bewitching, magical, enchanting, charming, spellbinding, entrancing, fascinating, invocational, conjural, incantational, incantatory, hypnotic, autohypnotic, voodooistic, totemistic, totemic, fetishistic (*or* fetichistic), diabolic, diabolical, demonic, demonic(al), fiendish, devilish, Satanic, hellish, undead, vampiric, vampirish

► *8 Divinity; 334 Power; 619 Wonder; 712 Curse; 798 Evil*

16 psychic, psychical, unconscious, subconscious, transcendental, cosmic, telepathic, telekinetic, psychokinetic, telergic, telaesthetic, radiaesthetic, extrasensory, spiritualistic, mediumistic, psychosensory, transphysical, hyperphysical, metapsychic, metapsychical, panpsychic, parapsychological, theosophical, psychosophical, anthroposophical, scientological, pseudopsychological

► *334 Power; 395 Influence*

17 divinatory, prophetic, clairvoyant, clairaudient, clairsentient, predictive, predictable, predicted, premonitory, precognitive, augural, haruspical, sibylline, oracular, astrological

► *445 Intuition; 475 Prediction*

18 spiritual, immaterial, nonmaterial, incorporeal, insubstantial, intangible, unembodied, disembodied, unphysical, nonphysical, ethereal, airy, elemental, fairy, fey, ghostly, spectral, shadowy, phantom, phantasmic, phantasmal, wraithy, wraithlike, unearthly, otherworldly, astral, alien, extraterrestrial, ufological, extramundane, supramundane, transmundane, unworldly, eerie, weird, eldritch, uncanny, strange, creepy (Inf), spooky (Inf)

▶ *521 Invisibility; 527 Transparency; 582 Death*

19 bewitched, enchanted, charmed, spellbound, entranced, fascinated, hypnotized, mesmerized, hag-ridden, obsessed, possessed, bedevilled, cursed, hexed, jinxed, haunted, ghost-ridden, spooked (Inf)

▶ *712 Curse; 763 Possession*

VERBS

20 occult, hide, obscure, veil, cloak, mystify, symbolize, encode, spiritualize, dematerialize, immaterialize, etherealize

▶ *101 Unworldliness; 266 Obscurity; 521 Invisibility; 524 Dimness; 736 Concealment; 737 Secrecy; 742 Sign*

21 bewitch, enchant, incant, charm, mesmerize, hypnotize, practise witchcraft, cast spells, spellbind, say magic words, wave a wand, ride a broomstick, put the evil eye on, hex, jinx, curse, sorcerize, theurgize, thaumaturgize, shamanize, diabolize, demonize, bedevil, possess

▶ *10 Ritual; 334 Power; 395 Influence; 712 Curse*

22 conjure, conjure up, invoke, evoke, raise ghosts, wake the dead, practise spiritualism, call up spirits, summon spirits, hold a séance (*or* sitting)

23 divine, prophesy, soothsay, predict, forecast, foretell, foresee, intuit, tell fortunes, read tea leaves, read (*or* consult) the Tarot, read palms, crystal-gaze, cast nativities, draw up birth (*or* natal) charts, plot horoscopes, cast the I Ching, interpret dreams, dowse, water-divine, read signs

▶ *334 Power; 445 Intuition; 475 Prediction; 591 Sensitivity*

24 experience psychic phenomena, see signs, see auras, sense vibrations, hallucinate, transmit thoughts, transfer thoughts, read minds, bend forks, leave one's body, astral-project, travel in the astral plane, levitate, teleport, faith-heal, go into a trance, see the little people, communicate with aliens, encounter aliens

▶ *101 Unworldliness; 477 Imagination*

ADVERBS

25 occultly, obscurely, mystically, mysteriously, secretly, secretively, enigmatically, arcanely, cabbalistically, esoterically, metaphysically, transcendentally, spiritually, supernaturally, paranormally, psychically, parapsychologically, telepathically, mesmerically, hypnotically, prophetically, clairvoyantly, astrologically, consciously, subconsciously

26 magically, eerily, spookily, weirdly, ghoulishly, necromantically, thaumaturgically, theurgically, superstitiously, diabolically, demonically

12 Government and Politics

Every country has the government it deserves. Joseph de Maistre.

That government of the people, by the people, and for the people, shall not perish from the earth. Abraham Lincoln.

NOUNS

1 government, direction, management, administration, executive, local government, national government, international government, world government, form of government, state system, political system, hierarchy, political organization, polity, political rule, political authority, political administration, politicking, tribal system, tribalism, feudalism, feudality, physiocracy, Poujadism, benevolent despotism, paternalism, squirearchy, clan system, patriarchy, matriarchy, matriarchate, gynaecocracy, gynarchy, gynocracy, constitutional government, constitutionalism, legal government, rule of law, legality, Senatus Populusque Romanus (SPQR), church government, theocracy, thearchy, priestly government, papal rule, hierocracy, clericalism, ecclesiasticism, medieval government, government by estates, monarchy, monarchical absolutism, constitutional monarchy, monarchical government, kingship (*or* queenship), republicanism, federalism, aristocracy, meritocracy, oligarchy, minority rule, elitism, gerontocracy, senatorial government, duumvirate, triumvirate, rule of wealth, plutocracy, representative government, parliamentary government, government by the ballot box, party system, democracy, independence, people's choice, egalitarianism, democracy unlimited, popular will, public opinion, vox populi, majority rule, one man one vote, proportional representation, isocracy, pantisocracy, pluralism, collectivism, proletarianism, dictatorship of the proletariat, communism, Leninism, Marxism-Leninism, Maoism, Titoism, party rule, Bolshevism, totalitarian dictatorship, totalitarianism, Fascism, Nazism, National Socialism, demagogy, demagoguery, puppet government, instrument, committee rule, sovietism, quangocracy (Inf), imperium in imperio, stratocracy, army rule, military government, martial law, ochlocracy, mobocracy, mob rule, mob law, anarchy, misgovernment, syndicalism, socialism, guild socialism, Fabianism, statism, bureaucracy, technocracy, self-government, autocracy, autarchy, self-rule, autonomy, home rule, caretaker government, regency, interregnum, sphere of influence, mandate, mandated territory

▶ *250 Freedom; 348 Instrumentality; 469 Selection; 588 Anarchy*

2 politics, political science, public affairs, civil affairs, statecraft, statesmanship, diplomacy

3 governance, rule, sway, iron sway, governmental power, reins of government, direction, command, absolute command, directorship, control, supreme control, hold, grip, clutches, domination, mastery, whip hand, effective control, reach, long arm, ascendancy, dominion, joint dominion, joint rule, condominium, sovereignty, suzerainty, raj, overlordship, presidency, supremacy, superiority, reign, regnancy, regency, dynasty, self-rule, autonomy, foreign rule, occupational power, heteronomy, empery, empire, rod of empire, subjection, imperialism, colonialism, neocolonialism, white supremacy, Black Power, regime, regiment, regimen, state control, statism, dirigisme, paternalism, bureaucracy, apparat, civil service, petty officialdom, officialism, beadledom, bumbledom, Parkinson's law, expansion, red tape, bumph (*or* bumf) (Inf)

▶ *121 Superiority; 190 Expansion; 251 Restraint; 360 Retention; 396 Authority; 579 Management*

4 governing body, Parliament, British government, Mother of Parliaments, Westminster, House of Commons, Lower House, Lower Chamber, House of Lords,

Upper House, Upper Chamber, House of Peers, Lords Spiritual, Lords Temporal, Scottish Grand Committee, Welsh Grand Committee, US government, Congress, Capitol Hill, Senate, Upper House, Upper Chamber, House of Representatives, House, Lower House, Lower Chamber, Irish government, Oireachtas, Dáil Éireann, Seanad Éireann

▶ *579 Management*

5 political organization, body politic, state, nation state, commonwealth, country, realm, kingdom, republic, city state, Athens, Sparta, Rome, city, free city, polis, temple state, federation, confederation, principality, duchy, archduchy, dukedom, palatinate, empire, dominion, colony, dependency, protectorate, mandate, mandated territory, territory, free world, communist bloc, developing world, Third World, superpower, buffer state, county, region, province, district, corporative state, social state, welfare state, laws, constitution, banana republic (Inf)

▶ *16 Law; 86 Regions; 121 Superiority; 122 Inferiority*

6 political party, right, left, centre, Conservative Party, Tories, Labour Party, New Labour (Inf), Labourite, Liberal Democrat Party, Social Democratic Party (SDP), Social and Liberal Democratic Party, Ulster Democratic Unionist Party (UDUP), Democratic Party (US), Republican Party (US), Grand Old Party (GOP) (US), Fine Gael (Ireland), Fianna Fáil (Ireland), Progressive Democrats (Ireland), Scottish National Party (SNP), Plaid Cymru (Wales), Ulster Unionist Party (Northern Ireland), Social Democratic and Labour Party (SDLP) (Northern Ireland), Sinn Féin (Northern Ireland), Green Party, Ecologists, National Front (NF), Liberals, Radicals, Whigs, Socialists, Nationalists, Social Democratic Party (Germany), Christian Democratic Union (Germany), New Democratic Party (Canada), Progressive Conservative Party (Canada), Popular Coalition (Spain), Democratic Social Centre (Spain), Christian Democratic Party (Italy), People's Party (Austria), Women's Alliance (Iceland), Workers' Revolutionary Party, International Socialists, Trotskyists, Marxists, Communists, Bolsheviks, Mensheviks, Fascists, Nazis, Falangists, Blackshirts, Brownshirts, Jacobins, Girondists, coalition, popular front, bloc, comrade, tovarisch, Fabian, syndicalist, anarchist, anarcho-syndicalist, revolter, right-winger, rightist, Tory, reactionary, hardliner, left-winger, leftist, leftie, pinko (US), populist, democrat, centrist, moderate, Eurosceptic, Europhile, communautaire, party member, party worker, canvasser, Red (Inf), commie (Inf), Trot (Inf), dry (Inf), wet (Inf)

7 governor, controller, legislator, lawgiver, lawmaker, statesman, stateswoman, president, vice president, prime minister, premier, chancellor, governor general

▶ *400 Master; 579 Management*

8 politician, member of parliament (MP), Parliamentarian, backbencher, peer, life peer, member of Congress (US), Senator (US), Congressman (*or* Congresswoman) (US), Representative (US), Senate majority leader (US), House majority leader (US), leader of the House of Commons, Father of the House, Senate minority leader (US), House minority leader (US), leader of the Opposition, cabinet minister, cabinet member (US), secretary, minister, undersecretary, junior minister, party chairman, party manager, whip, party whip, majority whip (US), minority whip (US), chief whip, politico (US inf), pol (US inf)

▶ *400 Master; 579 Management*

ADJECTIVES

9 governmental, political, presidential, gubernatorial (US), parliamentary, democratic, republican, independent, constitutional, federal, state, public, civil, civic, administrative, executive, ministerial, senatorial, official, bureaucratic, centralized, technocratic, matriarchal, patriarchal, theocratic, monarchical, feudal, aristocratic, meritocratic, oligarchic, plutocratic, dictatorial, totalitarian, popular, classless, self-governing, self-ruling, autonomous, autarchic, anarchic, Marxist, Leninist, Fascist, Nazi, Socialist, socialistic, Communist, communistic, Conservative, Labour, Liberal, Green

▶ *250 Freedom; 579 Management; 588 Anarchy*

10 governing, ruling, leading, commanding, controlling, dictating, in charge, in power, holding the reins of government, acting, titular, reigning, regnant, regnal, sovereign, holding the sceptre, on the throne, royal, regal, majestic, monarchical, kinglike, kingly, queenlike, queenly, princely, lordly, dynastic, imperial, magisterial

▶ *396 Authority; 400 Master; 573 Aristocrat; 579 Management*

VERBS

11 govern, rule, command, control, lead, be in charge, hold sway, reign, reign supreme, sit on the throne, wear the crown, wield the sceptre, direct, manage, hold the reins, hold office, have a place, occupy a post, fill a post, be in power, occupy 10 Downing Street, occupy the White House (US), have power, have authority, wield power, exert authority, use one's authority, rule absolutely, tyrannize, oppress, dictate, lay down the law, give laws to, legislate for, divide and rule, Balkanize, keep law and order, police

▶ *16 Law; 334 Power; 396 Authority; 397 Command; 579 Management; 647 Severity*

12 take authority, assume authority, seize power, gain power, take control, take command, assume command, take office, take over, take over the reins, form a government, make appointments, mount the throne, ascend the throne, accede to the throne, succeed to the throne, get the power into one's hands, get a hold on, get the whip hand, stage a coup d'état, usurp, usurp the throne

▶ *396 Authority; 400 Master*

13 be governed, owe allegiance, owe fealty, owe loyalty, owe obedience, have laws, have a constitution, be under authority

▶ *251 Restraint*

ADVERBS

14 politically, presidentially, governmentally, democratically, constitutionally, administratively, ministerially, bureaucratically, dictatorially, by law, by authority, in the name of, *de par le Roi* (Fr), by warrant of, in virtue of one's authority

13 Economics

Respectable Professors of the Dismal Science. Thomas Carlyle.

NOUNS

1 economics, economic policy, fiscal policy, monetary policy, welfare economics, economic growth, economic theory, microeconomics, macroeconomics, Keynesian economics, economic system, private enterprise economy, private sector, private enterprise, privatization, denationalization, centrally planned economy, public sector, public utilities, public enterprise, nationalization, public ownership, state-owned industry, mixed economy, fair trade laws (US), interstate commerce (US)

2 economy, free-market economy, private sector, personal sector, corporate sector, financial sector, public sector, foreign sector, manufacturing, wholesaling, retailing, selling, marketing, trading, exporting, importing, purchasing power, price controls, goods, producer goods, capital goods, consumer goods, economic upturn, boom, boom/bust cycle, economic downturn, recession, depression, slump, stagflation, inflation, deflation, disinflation, stagnation, deficit financing, deficit spending, black market, black economy

▶ *14 Finance; 356 Creation; 776 Trade; 778 Sale; 779 Market; 790 Price*

3 economic statistics, econometrics, regression analysis, gross national product (GNP), gross domestic product (GDP), price index, retail price index (RPI), cost of living, economic productivity, prices, vital statistics, economic analysis, supply-side economics, national debt, budget deficit, inflation

4 economic development, economic growth, industrialization, natural resources, labour force, developed countries, the West, underdeveloped countries, Third World, International Finance Corporation (IFC), International Development Association, International Bank for Reconstruction and Development (IBRD), World Bank, International Monetary Fund (IMF), capital accumulation, capital investment, public debt, improved technology, improved productivity, restructuring of industry, demographic transition, population growth

▶ *244 Improvement*

5 international trade, free trade, free-trade zone, economic zone, commerce, trade agreement, General Agreement on Tariffs and Trade (GATT), World Trade Organization (WTO), restrictive trade agreement, restraint of trade, economic union, trade integration, Exchange Rate Mechanism (ERM), European Free Trade Association (EFTA), European Economic Community (EEC), European Union (EU), Euromarket, Organization of Petroleum-Exporting Countries (OPEC), Benelux, Council for Mutual Economic Assistance (COMECON), Group of Seven (G7), Club of Paris, Caribbean Community and Common Market (CARICOM), Latin American Integration Association (LAIA), visible trade, invisible trade, balance of trade, balance of payments

▶ *776 Trade*

6 economic factors, capital, market, buyers' market, sellers' market, bear market, bull market, supply and demand, competition, monopoly, cartel, cooperative, revenue, sales revenue, pricing, profit, profit motive, profit margin, research and development (R and D), technology, automation, commodity, goods, dry goods, durable goods, durables, perishable goods, perishables, productivity, production, production costs, production efficiency, rationalization, distribution, fiscal policy, taxation, progressive taxation, regressive taxation, proportional taxation, income tax, taxable income, standard rate of taxation, tax evasion, tax avoidance, individual retirement account (IRA) (US), Inland Revenue, Internal Revenue (US), sales tax, value-added tax (VAT), excise duty, tariff duty, import duty, protectionism, embargo, sanction, economic sanction, tariff, trade barrier, customs barrier, tariff barrier, protection quota, intervention, free duty, free goods, free port, public expenditure, services, employment, unemployment, wages, real wages, pay increases, business cycle, inflation, inflationary spiral, price-wage spiral, deflation, balance of payments, money supply, exchange rate, standard of living, income, financial security, consumer confidence, price support, subsidy, capitalism, private enterprise, mercantile system, *laissez faire* (Fr), physiocratic school, industrial revolution

▶ *12 Government and Politics; 14 Finance; 356 Creation; 579 Management; 779 Market*

7 corporation, firm, company, limited company (Ltd), public limited company (plc), incorporated company (Inc) (US), specialized company, costs, fixed costs, marginal costs, indirect costs, budget, budgetary control, budget surplus, budget deficit, profit-and-loss account, balance sheet, profit, gross profit, net profit, excess profit, assets, fixed assets, general audit, liquidation, receivership, takeover, takeover bid, friendly takeover, hostile takeover, buy-out, leveraged buyout, management buyout, merger, business affairs, business association, chamber of commerce, junior chamber of commerce (US)

▶ *579 Management; 789 Accounting*

8 industrial relations, labour force, workforce, casual labour, labor union (US), trade union, closed shop, labour costs, wages and salaries, working hours, flexitime, industrial safety, working conditions, strike, general strike, go-slow, work-to-rule, lockout, pension, retirement benefits, workmen's compensation, unemployment insurance, International Labour Organisation, American Federation of Labor and Congress of Industrial Organizations (AFL-CIO) (US), Trades Union Congress (TUC), Advisory Conciliation and Arbitration Services (ACAS), labour law, the dole (Inf)

▶ *15 Industrial Relations*

9 economist, economic expert, businessman (*or* businesswoman), profiteer, merchant, merchandiser, dealer, trader, seller, barterer, importer, exporter, supplier, employer, chamber of commerce member, junior chamber of commerce member (US), Jaycee (US), liveryman, trade unionist, labor union member (US), spender, consumer, buyer, purchaser, customer, patron, client, clientele

▶ *579 Management; 776 Trade; 777 Purchase; 778 Sale*

VERBS

10 trade with, open a trade, traffic in, export, import, market, merchandise, offer for sale, have on offer, sell at a profit, make a profit, realize one's capital, encash, commercialize, corner the market, monopolize, nationalize, privatize

► *776 Trade; 778 Sale; 779 Market*

11 **deal**, negotiate, barter, drive a hard bargain, make a bid, raise the bid, take over, act as a white knight, finance, underwrite, bankroll (US inf)

► *14 Finance; 746 Negotiation*

12 **cheat**, gazump, gazunder, sell a pig in a poke, cook the books, evade tax, con (Inf), swindle (Inf), fiddle (Inf), rip off (Inf)

ADJECTIVES

13 **economic**, fiscal, monetary, pecuniary, financial, budgetary, inflationary, deflationary, mercantile, commercial, commercialistic, marketable, profitable, taxable, wholesale, retail, export, import, nationalized, privatized

ADVERBS

14 **economically**, fiscally, financially, commercially, profitably

14 Finance

If possible, honestly, if not, somehow, make money. Horace.

NOUNS

1 **finance**, world of finance, high finance, international finance, International Monetary Fund (IMF), banking, telebanking, accounting, financial accounting, financial control, money power, purse strings, power of the purse, money dealings, cash transaction, financial affairs, budget, money management, investment, money market, foreign exchange market, Eurodollar market, European Monetary System (EMS), Exchange Rate Mechanism (ERM), European Currency Unit (ECU), green pound, foreign currency reserves, exchange rate, exchange premium, interest rate, bank rate, minimum lending rate, effective rate, valuta, parity, par, equality, agio, agiotage, snake, floating currency, devaluation, depreciation, falling exchange rate, deterioration, rising exchange rate, strong currency, rallying, improvement, bimetallism, gold standard, managed currency, equalization fund, sinking fund, revolving fund, deficit finance, inflation, inflationary spiral, disinflation, deflation, stagflation, reflation, financial year

► *13 Economics; 244 Improvement; 245 Deterioration; 776 Trade; 780 Money; 787 Expenditure; 789 Accounting*

2 **stock exchange**, exchange, stock market, bull market, bear market, market, Big Bang, Dow Jones Industrial Index (US), Dow (Jones) Industrials (US), the Dow (US), Financial Times Ordinary Share Index (FT Index), Financial Times-Stock Exchange 100 Index (FT-SE 100 Index), Hang Seng Index, Nikkei Dow Index, issue, issue price, bid price, dividends, earnings per share, Footsie (Inf)

► *779 Market*

3 **stockbroker**, broker, market maker, stock-jobber, financial adviser, speculator, bull, bear, investor, bidder, backer, financier, banker, capitalist, plutocrat

► *780 Money; 785 Payment*

4 **personal finance**, savings, deposit, bank account, building society account, TESSA (Tax Exempt Special Savings Account), PEP (Personal Equity Plan), pension, something for a rainy day

► *780 Money; 781 Wealth; 783 Credit*

VERBS

5 **invest**, venture, risk, speculate, put one's money to work, sink one's capital in, invest in, fund, finance, go on the stock exchange, float, buy shares, play the stock exchange, play the futures market, deal in futures, bull, bear, stag, bid for, hold the purse strings

► *785 Payment*

ADJECTIVES

6 **financial**, monetary, fiscal, economic, rising, bull, falling, bear, devaluated, depreciated, managed, floating, inflationary, deflationary, disinflationary, reflationary

► *13 Economics*

15 Industrial Relations

The most conservative man in the world is the British Trade Unionist when you want to change him. Ernest Bevin.

NOUNS

1 **industrial relations**, employee relations, employer-employee relations, management-employee relations, labour relations, union-management relations, work relations, workforce relations, on-the-job relations, employment relationships, social charter, employee rights, employer rights, employee jurisdiction, employer jurisdiction, employers' organization, employer's association, Confederation of British Industry (CBI), work (*or* working) practices, custom and practice, terms and conditions, employment laws, contract of employment, employment contract, employment rules, workplace rules, joint regulations, unfair labour practices, featherbedding, industrial unionism, unionism, (free) collective bargaining, company-wide bargaining, association bargaining, negotiation, salary negotiations, industrial tribunal, collective agreement, the common rule, no strike – no lockout agreement, multiemployer agreement, piecemeal agreement, management practices, employee practices, management demands, employee demands, management, line management, labour-management body, wage council, works council, labour, union labour, nonunion labour, workforce, labour force, work group

► *397 Command; 576 Work; 579 Management; 750 Agreement; 776 Trade*

2 **industrial negotiations**, negotiating rights, negotiated points, union recognition, employment standards, conditions of employment, employer's liability, modernization, automation, computerization, seniority, pay differential, wage rates, minimum wages, sliding-scale rates, cost-of-living adjustment, systematic wage structure, method of payment, bonuses, benefits, profit-sharing, nonwage demands, fringe adjustments, training and education, induction training, on-the-job (*or* in-service) training, hours worked, working hours, minimum hours, make-work rules (US), overtime work, night-shift work, work measurement, work efficiency, work achievement, sports and recreation, promotion, hiring practices, probationary period, contractual obligations, violation of

TRADE UNIONS

Amalgamated Engineering and Electrical Union (AEEU)
Associated Metalworkers' Union (AMU)
Associated Society of Locomotive Engineers and Firemen (ASLEF)
Association of First Division Civil Servants
Association of Magisterial Officers
Association of University Teachers
Bakers, Food and Allied Workers' Union
Banking, Insurance and Finance Union
British Actors' Equity Association
British Air Line Pilots Association
British Association of Colliery Management
Broadcasting, Entertainment, Cinematograph, and Theatre Union (BECTU)
Card Setting Machine Tenters' Society
Ceramic and Allied Trades Union
Chartered Society of Physiotherapy
Civil and Public Services Association
Communication Managers' Association
Communication Workers' Union
Confederation of Health Service Employees (COHSE; now part of UNISON)
Educational Institute of Scotland
Engineering and Fasteners Trade Union
Engineers' and Managers' Association
Fire Brigades Union
General Union of Associations of Loom Overlookers
GMB (formerly General, Municipal, Boilermakers and Allied Trade Union)
Graphical, Paper and Media Union (GPMU)
Hospital Consultants and Specialists Association
Inland Revenue Staff Federation
Institute of Professionals, Managers and Specialists
Iron and Steel Trades Confederation
Manufacturing, Science and Finance Union (MSF)
Military and Orchestral Musical Instrument Makers' Trade Society
Musicians' Union (MU)
NATFHE (University and College Lecturers' Union)
National and Local Government Officers' Association (NALGO; now part of UNISON)
National Association of Colliery Overmen, Deputies and Shotfirers
National Association of Co–operative Officials
National Association of Licensed House Managers
National Association of Probation Officers
National Association of Schoolmasters and Union of Women Teachers (NAS/UWT)
National League of the Blind and Disabled
National Union of Civil and Public Servants (NUCPS)
National Union of Domestic Appliances and General Operatives
National Union of Insurance Workers
National Union of Journalists (NUJ)
National Union of Knitwear, Footwear and Apparel Trades
National Union of Lock and Metal Workers
National Union of Marine, Aviation and Shipping Transport Officers
National Union of Mineworkers (NUM)
National Union of Public Employees (NUPE; now part of UNISON)
National Union of Rail, Martime and Transport Workers (RMT)
National Union of Teachers (NUT)
Northern Carpet Trades' Union
Power Loom Carpet Weavers' and Textile Workers' Union
Prison Officers' Association
Professional Footballers Association
Public Services, Tax and Commerce Union
Rossendale Union of Boot, Shoe and Slipper Operatives
Scottish Prison Officers' Association
Scottish Union of Power–Loom Overlookers
Sheffield Wool Shear Workers Union
Society of Radiographers
Society of Telecom Executives
Transport and General Workers' Union (TGWU)
Transport Salaried Staffs' Association
Union of Construction, Allied Trades and Technicians (UCATT)
Union of Shop, Distributive and Allied Workers (USDAW)
Union of Textile Workers
UNISON
United Road Transport Union
Writers' Guild of Great Britain

contract, disciplinary procedure, discipline, worker participation, work demarcation, allocation of work, job description, job flexibility, flexitime (*or* flextime), safety and health, accident prevention, sick leave, holidays, vacation time (US), transfers, grounds for dismissal, dismissal, laying off, sacking, firing, lay-offs, redundancy, guarantee payments, workman's compensation, retraining, retirement, voluntary retirement, early retirement, pension programme

▶ *98 Absence; 252 Safety; 275 Time; 295 Newness; 780 Money; 785 Payment*

3 **organized labour**, trade union, labour union, international union organization, World Federation of Trade Unions (WFTU), International Confederation of Free Trade Unions (ICFTU), International Federation of Christian Trade Unions (IFCTU), national union organization, TUC (Trades Union Congress), AFL-CIO (American Federation of Labor-Congress of Industrial Organizations), independent union, general union, craft union, guild, industrial union, in-company union, white-collar union, blue-collar union, public sector union, union shop, union branch, union demands, union dues, union subscriptions, closed shop, open shop, chapel

4 **industrial dispute**, labour dispute, industrial conflict, industrial strife, employee claim, claim, grievance, complaint, whipsaw tactics (US), political action, industrial action, unofficial action, action, work-to-rule, go-slow, slow-down, work stoppage, stopping work, walkout, sit-in, sit-down strike, stay-in strike, work-in, lightning strike, picketing, picket, picket line, secondary picketing, flying picket, striking, union strike, strike notice, called strike, organized strike, general strike, mass strike, industry-wide strike, official strike, approved strike, sympathy strike, unofficial strike, wildcat strike, spontaneous strike, overtime ban, boycott, management lock-out, sympathy lock-out, strike-breaking, crossing the picket lines, strike settlement, pattern settlement, disputes procedure, grievance procedure, joint consultation committee, negotiations, breakdown in negotiations, arbitration, arbitration of rights, arbitration of interests, voluntary arbitration, compulsory arbitration, arbitration tribunal, arbitration court, arbitration award, Advisory Conciliation and Arbitration Service (ACAS), mediation, conciliation, injunction, turnout (Lit)

▶ *226 Stopping; 480 Persuasion; 734 Conversation*

5 **labour law**, industrial law, uniform labour law policy, right-to-work law (US), Labour Management Relations (*or* Taft-Hartley) Act (US), National Labor Relations Act (NLRA) (US), Shops Act, National Labor Relations Board (NLRB) (US), Industrial Relations Act, Social Chapter, open shop, closed shop

▶ *16 Law*

6 **employer**, manager, employment manager, director, managing director, boss (Inf), executive, overseer, head

of department, training officer, education officer, welfare officer, personnel manager, personnel officer, line manager, production manager, supervisor, arbitrator, mediator, counsellor, conciliator, umpire

► *400 Master*

7 **employee**, wage earner, breadwinner, wage worker (US), taxpayer, staff member, white-collar worker, nonmanual worker, skilled worker, semiskilled worker, unskilled worker, blue-collar worker, manual worker, part-time worker, workplace representative, union member, trade union official, national official, district official, elected representative, staff representative, shop steward, father (*or* mother) of the chapel, councillor, convener, health and safety representative, striker, strike-breaker, scab, blackleg

► *578 Worker*

ADJECTIVES

8 **industrial**, commercial, professional, employer, employee, labour, work, employment, employed, employing, employable, contractual, contracting, contracted, regulatory, collective, piecemeal, managerial, managed, managing, supervised, supervising, working, worked, wage-earning, staff, manual, nonmanual, skilled, semiskilled, unskilled

9 **negotiated**, negotiating, negotiable, modernized, modernizing, automated, automatic, computerized, sliding-scale, systematic, profit-sharing, fringe, on-the-job, make-work (US), featherbedded, featherbedding, overtime, hiring, hired, probationary, promotional, promoted, disiplinary, disciplining, disciplined, dismissed, laid off, redundant, fired, sacked, retraining, retrained, retiring, retired

10 **unionized**, union, organized, independent, public sector, white-collar, blue-collar, closed, open, work-to-rule, slow-down, sit-in, sit-down, stay-in, work-in, picketed, picketing, striking, industry-wide, official, unofficial, wildcat, lightning, spontaneous, boycotted, boycotting, strike-breaking, arbitrated, arbitrating, mediated, mediating, conciliatory, injunctive

VERBS

11 **conduct industrial relations**, hire, lay down conditions of employment, train, educate, provide on-the-job (*or* in-service) training, promote, work overtime, work the night shift, work on flexitime (*or* flextime), meet contractual obligations, featherbed, modernize, automate, computerize, discipline, demote, dismiss, fire, sack, lay off, make redundant, become redundant, retrain

12 **have an industrial dispute**, complain, take industrial action, take action, work to rule, go slow, slow down, stop work, walk out, sit in, sit down, strike, call a strike, call out, boycott, lock out, cross the picket lines, settle a strike, negotiate, arbitrate, mediate

ADVERBS

13 **industrially**, commercially, contractually, under contract, collectively, together, managerially, under supervision, with supervision, manually, with one's hands, through negotiations, on the job, independently, officially, unofficially, spontaneously, through arbitration, conciliatorily

16 Law

'If the law supposes that,' said Mr Bumble…, 'the law is a ass – a idiot.' Charles Dickens.

Laws grind the poor, and rich men rule the law. Oliver Goldsmith.

NOUNS

1 **the law**, law, body of law, corpus juris, law and equity, constitution, written constitution, unwritten constitution, charter, institution, codification, codified law, statute book, legal code, pandect, Ten Commandments, Decalogue, Pentateuch, Twelve Tables, Corpus Juris Civilis, Digest, Pandects of Justinian, Corpus Juris Canonici, penal code, civil code, Magna Carta, Napoleonic code, written law, lex scripta, statute law, common law, unwritten law, lex non scripta, natural law, jus naturale (Roman Law), equity law, personal law, private law, canon law, jus canonicum, ecclesiastical law, international law, European Community law, EEC law, law of nations, jus gentium (Roman Law), law of the sea, law of the air, law of commerce, commercial law, business law, lex mercatoria, law of contract, law of crime, criminal law, civil law, constitutional law, law of the land, long arm of the law

2 **jurisdiction**, portfolio, function, judicature, magistracy, commission of the peace, mayoralty, shrievalty, bumbledom, competence, legal competence, authority, legal authority, cognizance, mandate, administration of justice, legal administration, Home Office, Justice Department, local jurisdiction, local authority, corporation, municipality, council, town council, city council, board of aldermen (US), aldermanic board (US), county commission (US), county board, county council, regional council, district council, parish council, community council, bailiwick, vigilance committee, watch committee, tribunal, office, bureau, secretariat, workshop

► *86 Regions; 396 Authority*

3 **law**, bylaw, statute, decree, ordinance, edict, order, standing order, canon, rule, rescript, precept

4 **bad law**, legal flaw, loophole, let-out, contradictory law, antinomy, error of law, mistake of law, overruled verdict, overturned verdict, bad judgment, misjudgment, miscarriage of justice, injustice, false arrest, wrong verdict, wrong conviction, wrong execution

5 **litigation**, legal action, legal case, legal dispute, legal issue, legal remedy, action, case, cause, dispute, quarrel, issue, contest, lawsuit, suit at law, suit, seeking legal protection, seeking a verdict, seeking justice, going to law, litigiousness, quarrelsomeness, matter for judgment, case for decision, test case, prosecution, arraignment, impeachment, charge, accusation, claim, counterclaim, plea, petition, request, pleading, objection, demurrer, affirmation, affidavit, written statement, averment, assertion

► *751 Disagreement*

6 **legal process**, proceedings, legal proceedings, legal procedure, due process, course of law, (long) arm of the law, jurisdiction, citation, subpoena, summons, warrant,

search warrant, apprehension, arrest, recitation of rights, detention, questioning, committal, restraint, habeas corpus, bail, surety, security, recognizance, personal recognizance, injunction, stay, order, writ, certiorari, mandamus, nisi prius

7 **legal trial**, trial, fair trial, justice seen to be done, trial by law, trial by jury, trial by one's peers, trial at the bar, trial in court, television trial (US), assize, court sessions, sessions, court sitting, court of law, law court, military court, military justice, inquest, inquisition, inquiry, hearing, prosecution, defence, setting of court date, settlement out of court, plea-bargaining, questioning of potential jurors, empanelling a jury, evidence, circumstantial evidence, hearing of evidence, taking of evidence, recording of evidence, insufficient evidence, examination, cross-examination, re-examination, objection sustained, objection overruled, testimony, pleadings, arguments, reasoning, counterargument, rebutter, rebuttal, rejoinder, proof, demonstration, disproof, confutation, final arguments, summing up, charge to the jury, charge to the jury, sequestering of the jury, ruling, finding, decision, judgment, verdict, majority verdict, unanimous verdict, hung jury, reading of the verdict, favourable verdict, not guilty, acquittal, unfavourable verdict, guilty, condemnation, execution of judgment, sentence, prison term, execution, appeal, retrial, precedent, case law, law reports, cause list, case record, dossier, record

▶ *701 Argument; 716 Evidence*

8 **litigant**, litigator, libellant, party, party to a suit, suitor, petitioner, suer claimant, plaintiff, pursuer, defendant, appellant, libellee, respondent, objector, intervener, accused, accused person, prisoner before the court, prisoner at the bar, litigious person, prosecutor, accuser, common informer, informer

▶ *693 Information; 715 Accusation*

9 **lawmaker**, lawgiver, legislator, Supreme Court Justice (US), Law Lord, Chief Justice of the United States (US), associate justice of the Supreme Court (US)

10 **law officer**, legal administrator, public prosecutor, judge advocate, district attorney, Crown Attorney (Canada), judge, mayor, city manager (US), provost general, sheriff, justice of the peace (JP), court officer, clerk of the court, bailiff, procurator fiscal, summoner, process-server, macebearer, official, apparitor, beadle

11 **British law officer**, Lord Chancellor, Attorney General, Solicitor General, Lord Advocate, King's (*or* Queen's) Proctor, Crown Counsel, Crown Prosecution Service (CPS), lord mayor, lord provost, tipstaff, catchpoll, Bow Street runner

12 **US law officer**, Attorney General, Solicitor General, federal marshal, state attorney general, state prosecuting attorney, state prosecutor, district attorney (DA)

13 **lawyer**, solicitor, barrister, attorney (US), attorney-at-law (US), counsel, Queen's (*or* King's) counsel, legal adviser, legal representative, advocate, member of the legal profession, jurist, legal practitioner, judge, recorder, magistrate, jury, trial jury, legal beagle (Inf), legal eagle (Inf), brief (Inf)

14 **police**, police force, the force, forces of law and order, (the long arm of) the law, the boys in blue, constabulary, gendarmerie, military police (MP), shore patrol (US), airport police, mounted police, Royal Canadian Mounted Police (RCMP), Mounties (Inf), international police, Interpol, the fuzz (Inf), Old Bill (Inf), the pigs (Inf), the filth (Inf)

15 **British police**, Metropolitan Police, Scotland Yard, Special Branch, special patrol group (SPG), flying squad, Serious Crime Squad, fraud squad, drugs squad, community police

16 **US police**, Federal Bureau of Investigation (FBI), city police, county sheriff, state highway patrol, special patrol, shotgun patrol

17 **police officer**, policeman (*or* policewoman), law-enforcer, constable, special constable, patrolman (*or* patrolwoman), police sergeant, desk sergeant, police lieutenant, police inspector, police superintendent, chief constable, chief of police (US), commissioner of police, police commissioner, provost marshal, watch, neighbourhood watch, posse (US), posse comitatus (US), detective, plain-clothes officer, private detective (*or* investigator), private police, security officer, copper (Inf), cop (Inf), traffic cop (Inf), bobby (Inf), bizzy (Inf), bull (US inf), flatfoot (Inf), rozzer (Inf), pig (Inf), Smokey (the) Bear (*or* Smokey *or* bear) (US inf), *flic* (Fr inf), Mountie (*or* Mounty) (Inf), dick (US inf), fly dick (*or* ball) (US inf), private eye (Inf)

18 **tribunal**, seat of justice, judgment seat, woolsack, throne, bar, bar of justice, court of conscience, tribunal of penance, confessional, Judgment Day, forum, ecclesia, wardmote, council, public opinion, vox populi, electorate, judicatory, bench, board, bench of judges, panel of judges, judge and jury, judicial assembly, Areopagus, commission of the peace

19 **law court**, court, open court, court of law, court of justice, high court, criminal court, civil court, appellate court, county court, probate court, divorce court, court of equity, court of arbitration, court of session, assizes, police court, juvenile court, children's court, small claims court, coroner's court, court of record, sheriff court, feudal court, manorial court, court martial, drumhead court martial, summary court martial, summary court, kangaroo court, sessions, quarter sessions, petty sessions

20 **British court**, House of Lords, Supreme Court of Judicature, Court of Appeal, High Court (of Justice), King's (*or* Queen's) Bench (Division), Lord Chancellor's Court, Chancery Division (*or* chancery), Admiralty Division (*or* admiralty), crown court, High Court of Justiciary, sheriff court, Central Criminal Court, Old Bailey, magistrates' court, Court of Session, Court of Common Pleas, Court of Exchequer (*or* Exchequer), court of oyer and terminer, assizes, Star Chamber, (court) leet, Eyre of Justice

21 **US court**, US Supreme Court, Federal Court, District Court, state supreme court, court of claims, court of appeals, circuit court of appeals, circuit court, municipal court, night court, family court, court of common pleas, court of chancery, court of oyer and terminer

22 **ecclesiastical court**, Papal Court, Curia, Court of Arches, Inquisition, Holy Office

23 **judge**, justice, justiceship, your Lordship, your Honour, his (*or* her) Honour, his (*or* her) Worship, my lud (*or* m'lud), justiciary, verderer, military judge, judge advo-

cate general, chief justice, county court judge, recorder, sessions judge, subordinate judge, magistrate, district magistrate, city magistrate, police magistrate, coroner, justice of the peace (JP), bench, judiciary, magistracy, hanging judge, Judge Jeffreys, Judge Roy Bean (US), the Law West of the Pecos (US), umpire, referee, arbiter, arbitrator, ombudsman, assessor, estimator, recorder, Recording Angel, Solomon, Rhadamanthus, Daniel come to judgment, the beak (Inf), his (*or* her) nibs (Inf)

24 US judge, Chief Justice of the United States, federal judge, district judge, circuit judge, state Supreme Court Justice, municipal court judge, night court judge, family court judge, associate justice of the Supreme Court

25 British judge, Lord Chancellor, Lord Chief Justice, Master of the Rolls, Lord of Appeal, crown court judge, sheriff, assize judge

26 jury, assize, twelve good men and true, twelve just men, twelve men in a box, grand jury, special jury, common jury, petit jury, trial jury, jury panel, juror's panel, jury list, juror, juryman, jurywoman, jurist, jurat, foreman of the jury

27 courtroom, courthouse, law courts, bench, jury box, judgment seat, woolsack, mercy seat, dock, bar, witness box

28 legality, lawfulness, licitness, legitimacy, legitimateness, validity, justice, right, keeping within the law, adherence to the law, adherence to the letter of the law, legalism, respect for the law, respect for legal principles

▶ *801 Right*

29 legalization, legitimization, decriminalization, authorization, sanction, permission, authority, licence, warrant

▶ *757 Permission*

30 legitimacy, rightfulness, genuineness, authenticity

31 legislation, nomology, lawmaking, lawgiving, becoming law, passing into law, codification, ratification, enactment, enacting, validation, confirmation, affirmation, regulation, regulation by law, regulation by statute, constitutionality, constitutionalism, legislature, legislatorship

32 jurisprudence, nomology, science of law, knowledge of law, legal learning, law consultancy, legal advice

33 litigation, justice, justice under the law, judgment, judgment according to the law, due process of law, jurisdiction, legal process, lawsuit, legal action, writ, summons, trial, verdict, sentence, punishment

▶ *464 Judgment*

34 legal formality, formality, form of law, form, formula, rite, procedure, workings of the law, letter of the law, four corners of the law

35 illegality, illegitimacy, illicitness, unlawfulness, ban, proscription, veto, prohibition, impermissibility, unauthorization, irregularity

36 stolen property, contraband, black-market goods, haul, hot item (Inf), swag (Inf)

37 criminology, penology, criminal statistics, criminologist

38 lawbreaking, trespass, transgression, violation, breach, infringement, encroachment, contravention, overstepping, sin, vice, fraud, wickedness, villainy, guilt, culpability, criminality, delinquency, dishonesty, improbity, crookedness (Inf), shadiness (Inf)

▶ *800 Dishonour*

39 crime, capital crime, felony, offence, criminal offence, indictable offence, punishable offence, misdemeanour, misdeed, wrong, wrongdoing, criminality, foul play, criminal activity, malpractice, trespass, tort, civil wrong, malfeasance, misfeasance, theft, robbery, burglary, driveby shooting, assault, rape, manslaughter, homicide, justifiable homicide, murder, fraud, corruption, champerty, maintenance, misprision, victimless crime

40 lawbreaker, criminal, felon, offender, wrongdoer, miscreant, malefactor, villain, delinquent, culprit, convict, recidivist, thief, car thief, robber, bank robber, burglar, housebreaker, rapist, murderer, crook (Inf), mugger (Inf), jailbird (Inf), lag (Inf)

▶ *651 Malevolence; 802 Wrong*

41 lawlessness, anarchy, chaos, antinomianism, riot, rioting, hooliganism, ruffianism, rebellion, revolt, sedition, mutiny, insurgence, coup d'état, usurpation, arrogation, outlawry, breakdown of law and order, crime wave, gang rule, mob law, lynch law, vigilantism, kangaroo court

42 acquittal, favourable verdict, verdict of not guilty, verdict of not proven, benefit of the doubt, innocence, clearance, exoneration, exculpation, absolution, discharge, release, let-off, thumbs up, liberation, deliverance, freedom, justification, compurgation, vindication, successful defence, defeat of the prosecution, nonsuit, case dismissed, thrown-out case, dismissal for lack of evidence, no case, withdrawal of the charge, quashing, quietus, reprieve, pardon, forgiveness, nonprosecution, exemption, impunity, nonliability

▶ *649 Forgiveness; 714 Vindication; 758 Exemption; 805 Innocence*

43 conviction, condemnation, verdict of guilty, unfavourable verdict, hostile verdict, hostile jury, unsuccessful defence, successful prosecution, judgment, sentence, punishment, fine, court costs, prison sentence, going down, death sentence, death warrant, black cap, thumbs down, condemned cell, death row (US), death house (US), execution chamber, electric chair, gas chamber, firing squad, outlawry, proscription, blacklisting, attainder, price on one's head

▶ *670 Disapproval; 806 Guilt; 814 Punishment*

ADJECTIVES

44 legal, lawful, licit, legitimate, valid, just, right, proper, within the law, sanctioned, allowable, permissible, permitted, authorized, licensed, warranted, legalized, legitimized, legitimatized, decriminalized, brought within the law, according to law, by right, de jure, legit (Inf)

▶ *757 Permission; 801 Right*

45 legislative, nomothetic, lawmaking, lawgiving, legislatorial, legislational, decretal, nomological, jurisprudential, learned in the law

46 legislated, made law, put into legal effect, enacted, passed, voted, decreed, ordained, ordered, codified, ratified, constitutional, statutory, legally sound, good in law

47 liable to law, amenable to law, fit for legislation, justiciable, cognizable, triable, actionable, accusable

▶ *715 Accusation*

48 jurisdictional, jurisdictive, judicatory, judicatorial, municipal, regional, executive, administrative, administrational, directive, directing, justiciary, judiciary, juridical, justiciable, subject to jurisdiction, liable to the law

▶ *579 Management*

49 judicatory, judicatorial, judicial, judicative, jurisdictional, jurisdictive, jural, jurisprudential, justiciary, curial, inquisitional, forensic, Rhadamanthine, original, appellate, tribunal, magisterial, judicious, critical

50 law-abiding, honest, upright, obedient, authorized, licensed, competent

▶ *663 Obedience*

51 legitimate, rightful, genuine, authentic, real, true

52 legalistic, litigious, disputatious, contentious, quibbling

53 litigating, litigant, suing, accusing, bringing legal action against, at law with, going to law, appearing in court, appearing before the judge, claiming, contesting, objecting, disputing, arguing, quarrelling, litigious, quarrelsome, argumentative

▶ *16 Law; 701 Argument; 715 Accusation; 751 Disagreement*

54 litigated, on trial, up for trial, brought before the court (*or* judge), hauled before the court (*or* judge), *coram judice* (L), *coram populo* (L), argued, disputed, contested, claimed, submitted for judgment, offered for arbitration, sub judice, on the cause list, down for hearing, ready for hearing, litigable, actionable, justiciable, disputable, arguable, suable, accusable, up before the beak (Inf)

55 illegal, not legal, illegitimate, illicit, unlawful, outlawed, banned, proscribed, prohibited, forbidden, *verboten* (Ger), impermissible, contrary to law, against the law, not according to law, outside the law, outwith the law (Scot), on the wrong side of the law, exceeding the law, out of bounds

▶ *774 Stealing*

56 unauthorized, without authority, unlicensed, unofficial, informal, irregular, unconstitutional, unstatutory, unlegislated, unchartered, unwarranted, injudicial, extrajudicial, unknown to law, not covered by law, without legal backing, having no legal protection

57 null, null and void, nullified, annulled, abrogated, suspended, superseded, no longer law

58 unjust, unwarrantable, wrongful, wrong, tortious, justiciable, cognizable, triable, actionable, accusable, punishable

▶ *715 Accusation; 798 Evil; 802 Wrong*

59 stolen, contraband, smuggled, black market, nicked (Inf), pinched (Inf), filched (Inf), hot (Inf), too hot to handle (Inf), bent (Inf), off the back of a lorry (Inf)

60 offending, breaking the law, trespassing, transgressing, violating, breaching, infringing, encroaching, sinning, bad, wicked, nefarious, heinous, villainous, guilty, culpable, criminal, felonious, dishonest, fraudulent, corrupt, crooked (Inf), shady (Inf), bent (Inf)

▶ *329 Overstepping; 800 Dishonour; 804 Wickedness; 806 Guilt*

61 lawless, without law, anarchic, antinomian, chaotic, ungovernable, licentious, riotous, rebellious, seditious, mutinous, insurgent, violent

▶ *588 Anarchy; 660 Insolence; 662 Disobedience*

62 above the law, acting as a law unto oneself, despotic, tyrannical, dictatorial, oppressive, overmighty

▶ *647 Severity*

63 acquitted, not guilty, not proven, guiltless, innocent, clear, cleared, in the clear, exonerated, exculpated, absolved, vindicated, without a stain on one's character, uncondemned, unpunished, unchastised, let off, let go, let off the hook, discharged, released, liberated, free, reprieved, pardoned, forgiven, recommended for leniency, recommended for mercy, immune, exempted, exempt, nonliable

64 convicted, condemned, guilty, blameworthy, liable, self-convicted, confessing, without a case, having no case, without a leg to stand on, nonsuited, sentenced, sentenced to death, proscribed, outlawed, with a price on one's head, disapproved, lost, damned, in hell, burning in hell, frying in hell (Inf)

VERBS

65 make legal, legalize, legitimize, legitimatize, decriminalize, bring within the law, validate, sanction, allow, permit, authorize, license, warrant

66 be legal, come within the law, stand up in law (*or* in court)

67 follow the law, abide by the law, respect the law, follow the letter of the law, keep within the law, stay on the right side of the law

68 legislate, make laws, give laws, enact, pass, vote, decree, ordain, order, codify, ratify, confirm, affirm, formalize, endorse, vest, establish

69 have jurisdiction over, hold court, administer justice, sit on the bench, sit in judgment, judge, hear a complaint, hear a cause, hear a case, try a case, take cognizance, take judicial notice

70 litigate, bring legal action, start an action, bring a lawsuit, bring a suit, file a suit, seek legal protection, seek a verdict, seek justice, go to law, appeal to law, set the law in motion, institute legal proceedings, petition, request, prepare a case, prepare a brief, file a brief, brief counsel, claim, file a claim, contest at law, have the law on, take to court, bring before the court (*or* judge), haul before the court (*or* judge), have up, sue, implead, arraign, impeach, accuse, charge, prefer charges, press charges, indict, cite, summon, serve notice on, prosecute, try, put on trial, bring to trial, bring to justice, bring to the bar, argue one's case (before the jury), take the stand, go to the witness box, swear to tell the truth, advocate, plead, call evidence; argue

▶ *701 Argument; 715 Accusation*

71 try a case, take cognizance, put down for hearing, commit for trial, empanel a jury, question potential jurors, hear a case, hear a cause, call witnesses, examine, cross-examine, object, take statements, sit in judgment, rule, find, decide, adjudicate, judge, close the pleadings, close the proceedings, sum up, charge the jury, sequester the jury, bring in a verdict, have the verdict read, pronounce sentence

72 stand trial, come before (the court), come up for trial, be on trial, stand in the dock, give evidence, plead guilty, plead not guilty, plead nolo contendere, plead to the charge, ask to be tried, defend an action, put in one's defence, make one's defence, submit to judgment, hear sentence

73 be illegal, break the law, violate the law, circumvent the law, bend the law, twist the law, torture the law, defy the law, drive a coach and horses through the law, do wrong, offend, commit a crime

▶ *802 Wrong*

74 **be lawless**, have no law, know no law, take the law into one's own hands, please oneself, exceed one's authority, stand above the law, stand outside the law

▶ *588 Anarchy*

75 **make illegal**, outlaw, criminalize, illegalize, ban, proscribe, veto, prohibit, forbid, punish, bastardize, illegitimize

▶ *399 Veto; 814 Punishment*

76 **judge**, administer justice, exercise judgment, adjudge, adjudicate, hold court, hold the scales, sit on the bench, sit in judgment, preside, hear a case, give a hearing, try (a case), conduct a trial, agree on a verdict, return a verdict, bring in a verdict, pass judgment, decide, pass sentence, pronounce, decree

77 **annul**, nullify, make null and void, abrogate, suspend, cancel

78 **acquit**, find (*or* pronounce) not guilty, find for, prove innocent, find the case not proven, give the benefit of the doubt, find there is a lack of evidence, find there is no case to answer, clear, exonerate, exculpate, absolve, vindicate, let off, let go, let off the hook, get off, discharge, dismiss charges, release, liberate, free, reprieve, respite, grant a respite, pardon, forgive, not press charges, not prosecute, set aside the sentence, quash, quash the conviction, remit the penalty, reduce the fine, recommend for leniency, recommend for mercy, justify, allow a dismissal, allow an appeal, abrogate, make immune, exempt, make exempt

▶ *391 Liberation; 649 Forgiveness; 714 Vindication; 758 Exemption*

79 **convict**, condemn, find guilty, pronounce guilty, find against, bring in an unfavourable verdict, reject one's defence, prove guilty, bring home the charge, find liable, sentence, give a prison sentence, sentence to death, put on the black cap, sign one's death warrant, reject one's appeal, reject, attaint (Lit), outlaw, bar, proscribe, make illegal, blacklist, attaint (Lit), put a price on one's head, disapprove, damn, curse, excommunicate

80 **convict oneself**, confess, sign a confession, plead guilty, stand condemned out of one's own mouth, be verballed (Inf)

▶ *470 Rejection; 670 Disapproval*

ADVERBS

81 **legally**, lawfully, judicially, judgingly, jurally, jurisdictionally, jurisprudently, juristically, licitly, legitimately, validly, justly, rightly, properly, within the law, by law, according to law, by right, de jure, by order, through the legislative process, through the courts, in court, before the bench (*or* bar *or* court), in the eyes of the law

82 **illegally**, illicitly, illegitimately, unlawfully, criminally, wrongly, against the law, contrary to law, without authority, without legal backing

83 **dishonestly**, fraudulently, on the black market, under the counter (*or* table)

84 **lawlessly**, anarchically, riotously, rebelliously, violently

85 **summarily**, arbitrarily, despotically, tyrannically, dictatorially

86 **jurisdictionally**, municipally, regionally, parochially, communally, administratively, executively, on the council, at the bar, legally, lawfully

87 **in litigation**, at law, in court, before the judge, *coram judice* (L), *coram populo* (L), sub judice, pendente lite, litigiously

88 **forgivingly**, mercifully, leniently, freely, guiltlessly, innocently, pardonably

89 **guiltily**, culpably, wickedly, illegally, unlawfully, against the law

The Arts

17 Literature

Literature and butterflies are the two sweetest passions known to man. Vladimir Nabokov.

Great Literature is simply language charged with meaning to the utmost possible degree. Ezra Pound.

NOUNS

1 **literature**, writing(s), letters, belles-lettres, *literae humaniores* (L), republic of letters, polite literature, serious literature, underground literature, popular literature, folk literature, oral literature, wisdom literature, the classics, the arts, the humanities, learning, erudition, culture, lore, civilization

2 **fiction**, prose fiction, narrative fiction, novel, novella, *nouvelle* (Fr), novelette, story, short story, vignette, sketch, *roman* (Fr), thriller, psychological thriller, *roman à clef* (Fr), *roman fleuve* (Fr), novel sequence, stream-of-consciousness novel, psychological novel, *nouveau roman* (Fr), antinovel, metafiction, picaresque novel, Gothic novel, epistolary novel, epic novel, novel of sensibility, regional novel, erotic novel, pornographic novel, *Bildungsroman* (Ger), *Künstlerroman* (Ger), autobiographical novel, fictional biography, historical novel, social novel, thesis novel, *roman à thèse* (Fr), novel of ideas, problem novel, campus novel, love story, Mills & Boon, adventure story, western, science-fiction novel, sci-fi (Inf), cyberpunk novel, fantasy novel, Utopia, dystopia, Gothic horror, horror story, splatterpunk novel, crime story, spy story, detective story, mystery story, ghost story, supernatural tale, fairy tale, *Märchen* (Ger), legend, myth, mythology, mythopoeia, folk tale, folk story, fable, urban myth, *fabliau* (Fr), beast fable, parable, *conte* (Fr), geste, romance, whodunit (Inf), cliffhanger (Inf), bodice ripper (Inf), pulp fiction (Inf), shopping and fucking novel (Inf), s and f (Inf), sword and sorcery novel (Inf), blockbuster (Inf), penny dreadful (Inf)

3 **aspect of fiction**, story, storyline, narrative, plot, subplot, scenario, argument, plan, scheme, subject, theme, motif, leitmotiv (*or* leitmotif), development, structure, architecture, continuity, action, incident, episode, complication, turning point, denouement, peripeteia, recognition, anagnorisis, device, contrivance, coincidence, atmosphere, tone, mood, background, description, symbolism, local colour, characterization, dramatic irony, comic relief, catharsis, stream of consciousness, digression, interior monologue, metanarrative, first-person narrative, third-person narrative, point of view, omniscient narrator, unreliable narrator, narrative voice, narratology

4 **nonfiction**, descriptive writing, travel writing, travelogue, history, annals, chronicle, record, life story, life, journal, diary, memoir, confessions, kiss-and-tell confession, profile, biographical sketch, curriculum vitae, autobiography, biography, hagiography, historiography, homily, polemic, anatomy, apology, treatise, discourse, thesis, dissertation, essay, study, commentary, critique, criticism, review

5 **prose**, prose fiction, expository prose, prose style, prose rhythm, prose poetry, poetic prose, polyphonic prose

LITERARY GROUPS AND MOVEMENTS

absurdism	Crepuscular school	Harlem Renaissance	modernism	Pylon Poets	socialist realism
Acmeism	Dadaism	hermeticism	naturalism	realism	Spasmodic School
Aesthetic movement	decadence	Imagism	neoclassicism	Renaissance humanism	structuralism
Alliterative Revival	Encyclopédistes	Kailyard School	neorealism	Romanticism	Sturm und Drang (Ger)
Angry Young Men	Euphuism	kitchen–sink drama	Parnassians	Russian Formalists	surrealism
Augustans	existentialism	Lake poets	Philosophes	Scottish Chaucerians	Symbolism
Beat Generation	expressionism	Liverpool poets	Pléiade, la	Scottish Enlightenment	Transcendentalism
Bloomsbury group	Futurism	magic realism	postmodernism	sentimentalism	tremendismo (Sp)
Cavalier Poets	Georgian poetry	mannerism	post–structuralism	social realism	verismo (It)
Celtic Twilight	Gongorism	Martian poets	Pre–Raphaelitism		Vorticism
Classicism	graveyard poetry	medievalism	preromanticism		Wertherism
	Group, the	minimalism	primitivism		

6 **poetry**, poesy, verse, rhyme, song, numbers (Lit), balladry, versification, poetics, lyric poetry, epic poetry, epos, elegiac poetry, narrative poetry, heroic poetry, mock-heroic poetry, dramatic poetry, pastoral poetry, metaphysical poetry, erotic poetry, didactic poetry, confessional poetry, topographical poetry, satirical poetry, comic poetry, light verse, occasional verse, *vers de société* (Fr), concrete poetry, pattern poetry, nonsense poetry, folk poetry, runic verse, performance poetry, dub poetry, rap poetry, doggerel, lame verse, Hudibrastic verse, jingles, ditties, macaronics

7 **poem**, verse, rhyme, ballade, ballad, epic, epos, lay, saga, dithyramb, epigram, cento, limerick, clerihew, lyric, madrigal, nursery rhyme, ode, epode, choric ode, Pindaric ode, Sapphic ode, Horatian ode, palinode, narrative poem, dramatic monologue, conversation poem, verse epistle, complaint, encomium, satire, sonnet, sonnet sequence, Shakespearean sonnet, English sonnet, Petrarchan sonnet, Italian sonnet, sestina, chanson, tenzone, rondeau, rondel, roundel, roundelay, alba, aubade, reverdie, virelay, triolet, eclogue, idyll, pastoral, georgic, bucolic, prothalamion, epithalamium, elegy, threnody, elegiac poem, pastoral elegy, monody, dirge, song, vilanelle, troubadour poem, hymn, psalm, haiku, tanka

8 **part of poem**, verse, stanza, stave, measure, strain, strophe, antistrophe, epode, line, half line, foot, hemistich, monostich, distich, tristich, tetrastich, pentastich, hexastich, heptastich, octastich, rhyming couplet, closed couplet, couplet, triplet, tercet, quatrain, sestet, septet, octet, octave, verse paragraph, refrain, chorus, envoi, burden, book, canto, fit, bob and wheel

9 **metre**, metrics, measure, numbers (Lit), rhythm, scansion, prosody, quantitative metre, syllabic metre, accentual metre, accentual-syllabic metre, duple metre, triple metre, accent, accentuation, stress, beat, emphasis, quantity, metrical unit, foot, dipody, iamb, spondee, trochee, dactyl, anapaest (*or* anapest), pyrrhic, tribrach, amphibrach, amphimacer, cretic, ionic, paeon, choriamb, dimeter, trimeter, tetrameter, pentameter, hexameter, heptameter, octameter, iambic pentameter, elegiac pentameter, Alexandrine, dactylic hexameter, heroic couplet, elegiac couplet, elegiac distich, distich, sprung rhythm, counterpoint, anacrusis, catalexis, caesura, diaeresis

10 **verse form**, fixed form, ballade, *chant royal* (Fr), rondeau, sestina, triolet, vilanelle, sonnet, terza rima, ottava rima, rhyme royal, Chaucerian stanza, Spenserian stanza, Burns stanza, Sapphics, Anacreontics, Alcaics, alliterative verse, free verse, blank verse

11 **rhyme**, masculine rhyme, feminine rhyme, single rhyme, double rhyme, end rhyme, tail rhyme, eye rhyme, broken rhyme, half rhyme, near rhyme, pararhyme, consonance, internal rhyme, initial rhyme, rhyme scheme, blank verse, unrhymed poetry

12 **poetic language**, poetic diction, poeticism, archaicism, decorum, the grand style, aureate diction, alliteration, repetition, anaphora, epistrophe, assonance, consonance, onomatopoeia, euphony, elision, inversion, chiasmus, peraphrasis, figurative language, imagery, conceit, trope, metaphor, simile, Homeric simile, epic simile, Homeric epithet, compound epithet, transferred epithet, kenning, personification, prosopopoeia, apostrophe, metonymy, synecdoche, antonomasia, paronomasia, parallelism, synaesthesia, pathetic fallacy, poetic licence, pseudo-statement, irony, pun

13 **poetic genius**, inspiration, afflatus, poesy, creative imagination, Muse, the Muses, Apollo, Parnassus, Helicon, Hippocrene, Castilian Spring, Pierian Spring, Pegasus

14 **author**, writer, fiction writer, storyteller, novelist, short-story writer, crime writer, fabler, fabulist, mythologist, allegorist, romancer, novelettist, diarist, chronicler, historian, historiographer, biographer, autobiographer, annalist, poet, poetess, major poet, minor poet, poet laureate, minnesinger, Meistersinger, rhapsodist (*or* rhapsode), dithyrambist, elegist, satirist, sonneteer, symbolist, lyric poet, epic poet, pastoral poet, metaphysical poet, lake poet, romantic poet, modern poet, modernist, beat poet, rap poet, librettist, lyricist, vers-librist, rhymer, rhymester, versemonger, versifier, versesmith, verse-maker, poetaster, ballad monger, ballad maker, balladeer, bard, minstrel, jongleur, trouvère, troubadour, scop, skald, comic poet, tragic poet, dramatic poet, playwright, dramatist, dramaturge, screenwriter, wordsmith (Inf), penman (Inf), scribe (Inf)

15 **literary person**, woman of letters, man of letters, belletrist, literary scholar, educator, student of literature, literary critic, Leavisite, New Critic, structuralist, post-structuralist, deconstructor, book reviewer, cultural commentator, the clerisy

ADJECTIVES

16 **literary**, written, humanistic, belletristic, polished, learned, lettered, formal, scholarly, erudite, well-read, critical, interpretive, intertextual, classical, romantic, surrealistic, realistic, futuristic, decadent, postmodern, naturalistic, metaphysical

17 **fictional**, fictionalized, mythical, mythological, legendary, fabulous, allegorical, romantic

18 **descriptive**, well-drawn, graphic, depictive, illustrative, vivid, expressive

SHAKESPEARE'S PLAYS

Henry VI Part 1
Henry VI Part 2
Henry VI Part 3
Richard III
Love's Labour's Lost
The Two Gentlemen of Verona
The Taming of the Shrew
A Midsummer Night's Dream
The Merchant of Venice
Much Ado About Nothing
Twelfth Night
As You Like It
Romeo and Juliet
Richard II
Julius Caesar
Henry IV Part 1
Henry IV Part 2
Hamlet
Othello
King Lear
Macbeth
The Winter's Tale
The Tempest
The Comedy of Errors
Titus Andronicus
King John
Henry V
Henry VIII
The Merry Wives of Windsor
Antony and Cleopatra
Coriolanus
Troilus and Cressida
Measure for Measure
All's Well That Ends Well
Timon of Athens
Pericles
Cymbeline

19 narrative, storified, biographical, autobiographical, historiographical, poetic, poetical, Parnassian, Homeric, Dantesque, Miltonic, Pindaric, Sapphic, Horatian, Virgilian, Augustan, Shakespearean, Petrarchan, Spenserian, dramatic, epic, heroic, mock-heroic, elegiac, lyrical, pastoral, bucolic, idyllic, rhapsodic, tragic, comic, doggerel

20 metrical, rhythmical, measured, accentual, scanning, scanned, iambic, octosyllabic, hendecasyllabic, trochaic, spondaic, dactylic, anapaestic, catalectic, rhyming, assonant, alliterative, onomatopoeic, dimetic

VERBS

21 write, compose, dramatize, make into a play, make into a novel, poetize, versify, compose, poetry, elegize, rhyme, put into verse, compose an epic, write a lyric, write a sonnet, prosify, prose, describe, portray, represent, express, delineate, characterize

ADVERBS

22 poetically, lyrically, rhythmically, metrically, elegiacally

23 descriptively, expressively, vividly, dramatically

► *21 Drama*

MUSICAL INSTRUMENTS

accordion
acoustic guitar
adenkum (stamping tube)
aeolian harp
alboka (hornpipe)
alghaita (shawm)
alphorn (or alpenhorn)
altohorn
angel chimes
angle harp
anklung (rattle)
arghul (clarinet)
arpanetta (zither)
atumpan (kettledrum)
auloi (shawm)
autoharp
bagana (lyre)
bagpipe
balalaika (lute)
banana drum
bandoura (lute)
bandurria (lute)
banjo
banjolele
barrel drum
barrel organ
baryton (viol)
bassanello (double reed)
bass drum
bass guitar
basset horn
bass horn
bassonore (bassoon)
bassoon
bata (drum)
bell cittern
bells
bhaya (kettledrum)
bible regal (organ)
bicitrabin (vina)
bin (vina)
biniou (bagpipe)
bird scarer
bivalve bell
biwa (lute)
bladder pipe
board zither
bodhran (drum)
bombarde (shawm)
bombardon (tuba)
bongo drums
bonnang (gong)
bouzouki (lute)
bow harp
bowl lyre
box lyre
buccina (trumpet)
bugle
buisine (trumpet)
bullroarer
bumbass
bumpa (clarinet)
buzz disk
calliope (mechanical organ)
carillon
carnyx (trumpet)
castanets
celeste
cello
chakay (zither)
chalumeau (clarinet)
chang (dulcimer)
changko (drum)
cha pei (lute)
chengcheng (cymbals)
chime
chime bar
ch'in (zither)
Chinese wood block
chitarra battente (guitar)
chitarrone (lute)
cimbalom (dulcimer)
cipactli (flute)
cittern
clapper bell
clappers
clarinet
clarinet d'amore
classical guitar
clave
clavichord
clavicor (brass family)
clavicytherium (harpsichord)
claviorgan
claw bell
cobza (lute)
cocktail drums
cog rattle
colascione (lute)
componium (mechanical organ)
contrabass (double bass)
contrabassoon
cor anglais
cornemuse (bagpipe)
cornet
cornett
cornopean (brass family)
cornu (trumpet)
courtaut (double reed)
cowbell
crecelle (cog rattle)
crook horn
crotals (percussion)
crumhorn (double reed)
crwth (lyre)
curtal (double reed)
cylindrical drums
cymbals
cythara anglica (harp)
da–daiko (drum)
daibyoshi (drum)
darabukke (drum)
darbuk (drum)
dauli (drum)
deutsche schalmei (double reed)
dhola (drum)
didgeridoo
diplice (clarinet)
diplo–kithara (zither)
djunadjan (zither)
dobro (guitar)
double bass
double bassoon (contrabassoon)
drum
dudelsack (bagpipes)
dugdugi (drum)
dulcimer
dvojachka (flute)
dvoynice (flute)
electric guitar
enzenze (zither)
erh–hu (fiddle)
euphonium (brass family)
fandur (fiddle)
fiddle
fidel (fiddle)
fidla (zither)
fife
fipple flute
fithele (fiddle)
flageolet (flute)
flexatone (percussion)
flugelhorn
flute
french horn
fujara (flute)
fuye (flute)
gadulka (fiddle)
gaita (bagpipe)
gajdy (bagpipe)
gambang kaya (xylophone)
gansa gambang (metallophone)
gansa jongkok (metallophone)
geigenwerk (mechanical harpsichord)
gekkin (lute)
gender (metallophone)
gittern
gling–bu (flute)
glockenspiel (metallophone)
gong
gong ageng
gong chimes
gong drum
gongue (percussion)
grand piano
guitar
guitar–banjo
guitar–violin
gusle (fiddle)
hackbrett (dulcimer)
handbell
hand horn
handle drum
hand trumpet
hardangerfele (fiddle)
harmonica
harmonium
harp
harpsichord
hawkbell
heckelclarina (clarinet)
heckelphone (oboe)
helicon
hi–hat cymbals
horn
hu ch'in (fiddle)
hula ipu (percussion)
hummel (zither)
hurdy–gurdy
huruk (drum)
hydraulis (organ)
ingungu (drum)
isigubu (drum)
jew's harp
jingling Johnny
kachapi (zither)
kakko (drum)
kalungu (talking drum)
kamanje (fiddle)
kantele (zither)
kanteleharpe (lyre)
kanun (qanun)
kayakeum (zither)
kazoo (mirliton)
kelontong (drum)
kemanak (clappers)
kena (quena)
kenong (gong)
kerar (lyre)
kettledrum
khen (mouth organ)
khumbgwe (flute)
kissar (lyre)
kit (fiddle)
kithara (lyre)
koboro (drum)
ko–kiu (fiddle)
komungo (zither)
könighorn (brass family)
koto (zither)
langleik (zither)
langspil (zither)
lap organ (melodeon)
launeddas (clarinet)
lira (fiddle)
lirica (fiddle)
lirone (fiddle)
lithophone (percussion)
lituus (trumpet)
lontar (clappers)
lur (horn)
lute
lyra (lyre)
lyre

18 Music

The English may not like music – but they absolutely love the noise it makes. Thomas Beecham.

Music has charms to soothe a savage breast. William Congreve.

If music be the food of love, play on,
Give me excess of it, that, surfeiting,
The appetite may sicken and so die. William Shakespeare.

NOUNS

1 **music**, harmony, melody, musicality, tunefulness, melodiousness, musicalness, musicianship
2 **music making**, playing, performance, improvisation, orchestration, instrumentation, composing, composition, jamming (Inf)
3 **classical music**, romantic music, impressionist music, twelve-tone (*or* dodecaphonic) music, musique concrète, minimalist music, chamber music, contrapuntal music, choral music, operatic music, organ music, modern

MUSICAL INSTRUMENTS (CONT.)

machete (lute)
mandobass (lute)
mandocello (lute)
mandola (lute)
mandolin (lute)
mandolinetto (ukulele)
mandolone (lute)
maracas (percussion)
marimba (percussion)
masenqo (fiddle)
mayuri (lute)
mbila (xylophone)
mellophone (horn)
melodeon
melodica
metallophone (percussion)
migyaun (zither)
mirliton (kazoo)
mokugyo (drum)
Moog™ synthesizer
morin–chur (fiddle)
moropi (drum)
moshupiane (drum)
mouth organ
mridanga (drum)
murumbu (drum)
musette (bagpipe)
musette (shawm)
mu yü (drum)
mvet (zither)
nakers (drums)
naqara (drums)
ngoma (drum)
nguru (flute)
ntenga (drum)
nyckelharpa
oboe
obukano (lyre)
ocarina (flute)
octavin (wind)
o–daiko (drum)
okedo (drum)
oliphant (horn)
ombgwe (flute)
ophicleide (brass family)
organ
orpharion (cittern)
orphica (piano)
o–tsuzumi (drum)
ottavino (virginal)
oud (ud)
outi (lute)
p'ai hsiao (panpipe)
paimensarvi (horn)
p'ai pan (clappers)
pandora (cittern)
panhuéhuetl (drum)
panpipe
peacock sitar (lute)
penorcon (cittern)
pianino
piano
pianoforte
pianola
pibcorn (hornpipe)
piccolo
picco pipe (flute)
pien ch'ing (lithophone)
piffaro (shawm)
pi nai (shawm)
p'i p'a (lute)
pipe
pochette (kit)
pommer (shawm)
psaltery (zither)
pu–ilu (clappers)
putorino (trumpet)
qanun (zither)
quena (flute)
quinton (viol)
racket (double reed)
ramkie (lute)
ranasringa (horn)
raspa (scraper)
rattle
rauschpfeife (double reed)
rebab (fiddle)
rebec (fiddle)
recorder
reshoto (drum)
rinchik (cymbals)
rkan–dung (trumpet)
rkan–ling (horn)
rommelpot (drum)
ronéat–ek (xylophone)
rote (lyre)
ruan (lute)
sackbut (trombone)
salpinx (trumpet)
samisen (lute)
san hsien (lute)
sansa
santir (dulcimer)
santoor (dulcimer)
sarangi (fiddle)
sarinda (fiddle)
saron demong (metallophone)
saron (metallophone)
sarrusophone (brass)
savernake horn
saw–thai (fiddle)
saxhorn
saxophone
saxotromba
saxtuba
saz (lute)
schrillpfeife (flute)
serpent
shaing (horn)
shaker
shakuhachi (flute)
shanai (shawm)
shawm
sheng (mouth organ)
shield (percussion)
shiwaya (flute)
shô (mouth organ)
shofar (horn)
shoulder harp
side drum
sistrum (rattle)
sitar (lute)
sleigh bells
slide trombone
slit drum
sona (shawm)
sonajero (rattle)
sopile (shawm)
sordine (kit)
sordone (double reed)
sousaphone
spagane (clappers)
spike fiddle
spinet
spitzharfe (zither)
spoons (clappers)
sralay (shawm)
sringara (fiddle)
stock–and–horn (hornpipe)
strumento di porco (zither)
stylophone
surbahar (lute)
surnaj (shawm)
switch (percussion)
symphonium (mouth organ)
synthesizer
syrinx (panpipe)
tabla (drum)
tabor (drum)
taiko (drum)
talambas (drum)
tallharpa (lyre)
tam âm la (gong)
tambourine
tambura (lute)
tam–tam (gong)
tar (drum; lute)
tarabuka (drum)
tarogato (clarinet; shawm)
teponaztli (drum)
terbang (drum)
theorbo (lute)
theorbo–lute
thumb piano (jew's harp)
tibia (shawm)
tiktiri (clarinet)
timbales (drum)
timpani
tin whistle
tiple (shawm)
tippoo's tiger (organ)
ti–tzu (flute)
tlapanhuéhuetl (drum)
tlapiztali (flute)
tom–tom (drum)
totombito (zither)
triangle
triccaballacca (clappers)
tro–khmer (fiddle)
trombone
tro–u (fiddle)
trumpet
tsuri daiko (drum)
tsuzumi (drum)
tuba
tuba–dupré
tubular bells
tudum (drum)
tumyr (drum)
tupan (drum)
turkish crescent (jingling Johnny)
txistu (flute)
tympani
uchiwa daiko (drum)
ud (lute)
ujusini (flute)
ukulele (*or* uke)
urua (clarinet)
uti (lute)
valiha (zither)
vibraphone
vibra slap™ (percussion)
vielle (fiddle)
vihuela (guitar)
vina (stringed instrument related to sitar)
viol
viola
viola bastarda (viol)
viola da gamba (viol)
viola d'amore (viol)
violetta (viol)
violin
violoncello
violone (viol)
virginal
whip (percussion)
whistle
whistle flute
wood block
Wurlitzer
xylophone
xylorimba (xylophone)
yangchin (dulcimer)
yangum (dulcimer)
yü (scraper)
yueh ch'in (lute)
yun lo (gong)
yun ngao (gong)
zampogna (bagpipe)
zither
zobo (mirliton)
zummara (clarinet)
zurla (shawm)
zurna (shawm)

music, symphonic music, orchestral music, romantic music, madrigal, sonata

4 **opera**, grand opera, *opera seria* (It), *opera semiseria* (It), *opera buffa* (It), *opéra bouffe* (Fr), *opéra comique* (Fr), operetta, music drama, pasticcio, *Singspiel* (Ger), aria, recitative, leitmotiv, Sprechgesang, bel canto, sinfonia, overture, prelude, intermezzo, surtitle, libretto

5 **sacred music**, church music, liturgical music, hymn, hymn tune, psalm, chorale, anthem, motet, oratorio, passion, mass, Requiem Mass, requiem, offertory, cantata, church parable, doxology, introit, canticle, recessional, spiritual, negro spiritual, gospel music, gospel, hymnody, psalmody, hymnology

6 **campanology**, bell-ringing, change ringing, peal, change, Bob Major, Grandsire Triple, handbell, carillon

7 **dance music**, ballet music, ballroom music, modern dance music, disco, euro-disco

8 **jazz**, mainstream jazz, progressive jazz, avant-garde jazz, modern jazz, third-stream jazz, cool jazz, acid jazz, fusion, blue note, blues, traditional jazz, trad, Dixieland, syncopation, ragtime, swing, jive, doowop, bebop, Afro-Cuban, bop, boogie-woogie

9 **popular music**, pop music, pop, light music, easy-listening, popular song, pop song, hit, hit tune, charts, top twenty, Karaoke, torch song, rock, rock 'n' roll, hard rock, soft rock, acid rock, folk rock, country rock, prog rock, rhythm 'n' blues (R and B), AOR (adult-orientated rock), industrial rock (*or* dance), hardcore, death metal, heavy metal, thrash metal, soft metal, punk rock, thrash punk, New Wave, indie, britpop, ska, rap, gangsta rap, ragamuffin, ragga, reggae, dancehall, soul, jazz-funk, fusion, electro, hip-hop, grebo, grunge, garage, house, house music, acid house, hard house, techno, jungle, drum 'n' bass, trip-hop, trance, ambient

10 **world music**, soul, ska, reggae, bhangra, ethnic music, kwela, mbaqanga, township jive, township jazz, marabi, rai, zydeco, son, salsa, merengue, zouk, qawwali, macumba, marabenta, soca, calypso

11 **folk music**, folksong, folk ballad, folk rock, border ballad, country music, hillbilly music, country and western, bluegrass, skiffle

12 **Tin Pan Alley**, Nashville, Broadway

13 **melody**, tune, air, aria, strain, song, line, hook, riff, lick, descant, harmony, concord, condordance, concert, attunement, chime, diapason, synchronization, unison, euphony, homophony, monody, resolution, cadence, perfect cadence, two- (*or* three-, *or* four-) part harmony, theme, subject, coda

▶ *516 Tunefulness*

14 **harmonics**, melodics, rhythmics, music theory, musicology, musicography

15 **composition**, opus, piece, arrangement, adaptation, setting, transcription, accompaniment

16 **musical note**, note, pitch, keys, keyboard, ivories (Inf), manual, pedal point, black notes, white notes, sharp, flat, double flat, double sharp, accidental, natural, tone, semitone, keynote, fundamental note, partial, overtone, harmonic, tonic, supertonic, mediant, subdominant, dominant, submediant, subtonic, leading note, interval, major (*or* minor) interval, second, third, fourth, fifth, sixth, seventh, octave, ninth, diatessaron, diapason, gamut, scale, chord, common chord, broken chord, primary chord, secondary chord, tertiary chord, triad, tetrachord, arpeggio, grace note, grace, ornament, crush note, appoggiatura, acciaccatura, mordent, turn, shake, trill, tremolo, vibrato, cadenza

17 **notation**, musical note, tonic sol-fa, solfeggio, solfege, solmization, signature, time signature, key signature, clef, treble clef, bass clef, tenor clef, alto clef, bar, measure (US), staff, stave, line, ledger (*or* leger) line, space, brace, rest, pause, interval, breve, semibreve, minim, crotchet, quarter note (US), quaver, eighth note (US), semiquaver, sixteenth note (US), demisemiquaver, thirty-second note (US), hemidemisemiquaver, sixty-fourth note (US)

18 **written music**, sheet music, score, notation, proportional notation, chart (Inf), paper (Inf)

19 **tempo**, time, beat, rhythm, prosody, measure, pulse, metre, timing, syncopation, counterpoint, counterpoint rhythm, upbeat, downbeat, short note, suspension, suspended note, long note, prolonged note, tempo rubato, rallentando, andante, adagio, metronome, back beat (Inf)

20 **key**, signature, clef, bass clef, C clef, treble clef, modulation, transposition, running changes (Inf), major key, minor key, scale, major scale, gamut, minor scale, harmonic minor scale, diatonic scale, modal scale, chromatic scale, harmonic scale, melodic scale, enharmonic scale, twelve-tone scale, series, tone row, mode, Lydian mode, Phrygian mode, Dorian mode, Doric mode, Gregorian mode, mixolydian, Ionian mode, Aeolian mode, Locrian mode, Indian mode, raga

21 **tone**, tonality, register, pitch, concert pitch, high pitch, low pitch, absolute pitch, relative pitch, perfect pitch, high note, stridor, low note, resonance, undertone, overtone, harmonic, upper partial, sustained note, monotone, drone, key centre

22 **phrase**, flourish, sennet, tune, bugle call, call

23 **singer**, songster, vocalist, lead vocalist, backing vocalist, crooner, torch singer, belter (Inf)

24 **musician**, player, instrumentalist, performer, artiste, soloist, virtuoso, singer, songster, vocalist, prima donna, bard, minstrel, troubadour, street musician, busker, composer, scorer, arranger, orchestrator, songwriter, librettist, lyricist, balladeer, hymn writer, psalmist, musical director, MD, conductor, maestro, kappelmeister, choir master, chorus master, bandleader, bandmaster, repetiteur, music teacher, music master, syncopator, jazzman, swinger (Inf), cat (Inf), bluesman (Inf), popster (Inf), funkster (Inf)

25 **musical instrument**, aerophone, idiophone, membranophone, chordophone, woodwind, brass, percussion, timpani, strings, mechanical instrument, keyboard instrument, electronic instrument, synthesizer, sequencer, sampler

26 **musical group**, orchestra, symphony orchestra, chamber group, chamber orchestra, sinfonietta, duo, trio, quartet, string quartet, quintet, sextet, septet, octet, nonet, ensemble, band, string band, jazz band, ragtime band, brass band, military band, marching band,

MUSICAL TERMS

a battuta – return to strict time
accelerando – accelerating
adagietto – quite slow
adagio – slow
ad lib – at will
affettuoso – tender
affrettando – hurrying
agitato – agitated; rapid tempo
al fine – to the end
alla caccia – in hunting style
alla cappella – in church style
allargando – broadening; more dignified
allegretto – quite lively, brisk
allegro – lively, brisk
al segno – as far as the sign
amoroso – loving, emotional
animato – spirited
a piacere – as you please
assai – very
attacca – attack; continue without a pause
bewegt – agitated
bis – repeat
bisbigliando – whispering
brillant – brilliant
buffo – comic
calando – ebbing; lessening of tempo
cantabile – in a singing fashion
cantilena – lyrical, flowing
chiuso – stopped (of a note); closed
coda – final part of a movement
codetta – small coda; to conclude a passage
col canto (*or* colla voce) – accompaniment to follow solo line
col legno – to strike strings with stick of the bow
con brio – with vigour
con fuoco – fiery; vigorous
da capo – from the beginning
dal segno – from the sign
dehors – outside; prominent
dim – becoming softer
diminuendo – becoming softer
divisi – divided
dolce – sweet
dolente – sorrowful
doppio – double
estinto – extremely softly, almost without tone
f – loud
facile – easy, fluent
ff – very loud
fioritura – decoration of a melody
forte – loud
fortissimo – very loud
giocoso – merry; playful
glissando – sliding scale played on instrument (*or* sung)
in modo di – in the manner of
largo – very slow
legato – bound, tied (of notes), smoothly
leggeramente – lightly
lento – slowly
maestoso – majestic
marcato – accented
marcia – march
meno mosso – slower pace
mesto – sad, mournful
mezza voce – at half power
mezzo – half
mezzoforte – half loud
mf – half loud
minacciando – menacing
moderato – moderately
molto – very much
morbido – soft, delicate
mosso – moving, fast
moto – motion
niente – nothing
nobile – noble
nobilmente – nobly
obbligato – not to be omitted
p – soft
ped – pedal
perdendosi – dying away gradually
pesante – heavily, firmly
pianissimo – very soft
piano – soft
più – more
piuttosto – somewhat
piz – plucked
pizzicato – plucked
portamento – carrying one note into the next
portando – carrying one note into the next
pp – very soft
quasi – almost, as if
rall – slowing down
rallentando – slowing down
ravvivando – quickening
retenu – held back
rfz – accentuated
rinforzando – accentuated
rit – slowing down, holding back
ritardando – slowing down, holding back
ritenuto – slower, held back
scherzando – joking; playing
schleppend – dragging; deviating from correct speed (Ger)
schnell – fast (Ger)
schneller – faster (Ger)
scorrevole – gliding; fluent
segno – sign
sempre – always, still
senza – without
sf – strongly accented
sfogato – effortless; in a free manner
sforzando – strongly accented
sfz – strongly accented
sin'al fine – up to the end
sino – up to; until
slentando – slowing down
soave – sweet; gentle
sordino – mute
sostenuto – sustained
sotto voce – quiet subdued tone
sourdine – mute (Fr)
staccato – detached
stark – strong, loud (Ger)
stretto – accelerating or intensifying; overlapping of entries of fugue
stringendo – tightening; intensification
subito – immediately
tacet – instrument is silent
tanto – so much
tempo – the speed of a composition
ten – held
tenuto – held
tief – deep; low (Ger)
tutti – all
via – remove mutes
vif – lively (Fr)
vivement – lively (Fr)
zoppa – in syncopated rhythm

mounted band, pipe band, skiffle group, steel band, rock band (*or* group), punk band (*or* group), pop group, one-man band
27 performance, concert, recital, promenade concert, prom, show, gig (Inf)
28 concert hall, opera house, salon, venue

ADJECTIVES

29 musical, music loving, musicophile, musicianly, virtuoso, philharmonic
30 harmonic, harmonizing, tuneful, attuned, in tune, tonal, symphonious, synchronous, homophonic, harmonious, melodious, melifluous, mellow, lyric, dulcet, agogic, singable, catchy
31 composed, compositional, orchestrated, scored, arranged, formulated, modulated, improvised
32 instrumental, vocal, choral, operatic, liturgical, hymnal, psalmic, psalmodic, romantic, impressionist, twelve-tone, concrete, minimalist, contrapuntal, heroic, dramatic, bass, baritone, alto, tenor, soprano, treble, falsetto, castrato
33 jazz, syncopated, avant-garde, cool, mainstream, traditional, trad, Dixieland, blue, pop, swinging, punk, folk, folksy, country, soul

VERBS

34 harmonize, melodize, attune, assonate, tune, tune up
35 compose, write, orchestrate, instrumentate, set to music, score, adapt, arrange, transcribe, transpose
36 play, make music, strike up, perform, render, interpret, play by ear, improvise
37 syncopate, swing, jam (Inf), riff (Inf), rock
38 sound, blow, toot, whistle, lip, tongue, double-tongue, triple-tongue, trumpet, bow, fiddle, pluck, strum, pick, twang, beat, thrum, pound, clash, ring, tinkle the ivories
39 sing, break into song, vocalize, croon, carol, warble, quaver, trill, pipe, flute, intone, chant, descant, sing together, chorus, harmonize, belt out (Inf)
40 conduct, direct, lead, wield (*or* take) the baton

ADVERBS

41 in tune, in key, in time, in tempo
42 musically, melodically, melodiously, harmoniously, tunefully, dulcetly, rhythmically, instrumentally, harmonically

19 Painting and Sculpture

I paint objects as I think them, not as I see them. Pablo Picasso.

My business is to paint not what I know, but what I see. Joseph Turner.

NOUNS

1 art, the arts, the visual arts, fine arts, applied arts, *beaux arts* (Fr), plastic art, graphic arts, decorative arts, decoration, design, arts of design, industrial design, industrial art, commercial art, kinetic art, craft, handicraft, arts and crafts, painting, sculpture, engraving, etching, calligraphy, batik, screen printing, silk-screen printing, embroidery, tapestry, woodcarving, metalwork, enamelling, mosiacs, ceramics, stained glass, photography, lithography

▶ *24 Ceramics; 41 Photography; 42 Fabrics and Dyeing*

2 painting, colouring, colourizing, the brush (Lit), the pencil (Lit), daubing, washing, underpainting, overpainting, tinting, touching up, illumination, composition, scene painting, sign painting, action painting, finger painting

▶ *529 Colour; 549 Refinement*

3 drawing, sketching, drafting, delineating, delineation, limning, outlining, freehand drawing, mechanical drawing, technical drawing, draughtsmanship, tracing, copying, doodling

▶ *125 Imitation; 163 Outline; 717 Representation*

4 treatment, tone, values, form, colour, local colour, shadow, shading, *sfumato* (It), *chiaroscuro* (It), scumbling, marbling, ambience, atmosphere, line, composition, balance, arrangement, grouping, design, golden section, golden mean, perspective, scientific perspective, geometric perspective, Renaissance perspective, optical perspective, linear perspective, aerial perspective, foreshortening, vanishing point, illusionism, trompe l'oeil technique, draughtsmanship, brushwork, painterliness, painterly values, tactile values, significant form

▶ *160 Form; 162 Symmetry; 403 Structure; 404 Texture; 409 Arrangement; 484 Plan; 485 Skill; 522 Light; 529 Colour; 724 Style*

5 artistry, art, artistic skill, artistic flair, artistic technique, talent, genius, mastery, invention, artistic invention, artistic quality, artistic taste, virtu, connoisseurship, craftsmanship, artisanship, artistic temperament, artiness, arty-craftiness (Inf), artsy-craftiness (Inf), artsy-fartsiness (Inf)

▶ *126 Originality; 446 Idea; 466 Discrimination; 477 Imagination; 485 Skill; 549 Refinement*

6 work of art, artwork, work, *objet d'art* (Fr), art object, artistic production, artistic creation, composition, design, study, piece, masterpiece, masterwork, *chef-d'oeuvre* (Fr), article of virtu, object of virtu, piece of virtu, museum piece, old master

7 picture, pictorial equivalent, likeness, image, representation, illustration, painting, drawing, engraving, miniature, tableau, illumination, mosaic, tapestry, stained-glass window, reproduction, copy, plate, print, colour print, block-print, photoprint, photogravure, woodcut, aquatint, poster, picture postcard, montage, photomontage, collage, brass rubbing, frottage

▶ *41 Photography; 42 Fabrics and Dyeing; 115 Similarity; 125 Imitation; 717 Representation*

8 painting, canvas, daub, easel painting, cabinet painting, miniature, wall painting, fresco, mural, icon, altarpiece, diptych, triptych, reredos, retable, cave painting, rock

WESTERN ART STYLES AND MOVEMENTS

abstract art
abstract expression
action art
action painting
aestheticism
analytical cubism
Anglo–Saxon art
Archaic art
art brut (Fr)
Art Deco
arte povera (It)
art informel (Fr)
Art Nouveau
arts and crafts movement
baroque
Biedermeier
body art
Bohemian art
Bolognese school
Burgundian school
Byzantine art
Carolingian art
Celtic art
Classical Greek art
classicism
cloisonnisme
Cologne school
conceptual art
concrete art
constructivism
cubism
Dada
Danube school
divisionism
Dutch genre painting
Early Christian art
Early Renaissance art
earth art
eclecticism
environmental art
Etruscan art
expressionism
expressive abstraction
Fauvism
Ferrarese school
figurative art
Florentine school
folk art
Fontainebleau school
futurism
geometrical abstraction
Gothic art
Graeco–Roman art
Grand Manner
Hadrianic art
Hague school
Hellenistic art
high baroque
High Renaissance art
impressionism
International Gothic
intimisme
Jugendstil
junk art
kinetic art
kitsch
land art
lyrical abstraction
magic realism
mannerism
medieval art
metaphysical painting
minimal art
mozarabic art
naive art
naturalism
neoclassicism
neoexpressionism
neoimpressionism
neoromanticism
Neue Sachlichkeit (Ger)
New York school
nonrepresentational art
op art
orphism
performance art
Pergamene school
photorealism
plein air painting
pointillism
Pompeian art
pop art
postimpressionism
postmodernism
post–painterly abstraction
precisionism
pre–Raphaelitism
primitive art
purism
quattrocento (It)
rayonism
realism
regionalism
Renaissance art
representational art
rococo art
romanesque art
Roman school
romanticism
School of Paris
Sienese school
socialist realism
social realism
spatialism
superrealism
suprematism
surrealism
Symbolism
synchronism
synthetic cubism
synthetism
tachisme
transavantgarde, the
trecento (It)
Tuscan school
Venetian school
verism
vorticism

painting, action painting, finger painting, spray-can painting, oil painting, oil, airbrush painting, acrylic, watercolour, water, gouache, aquarelle, wash, pastel, tempera, impasto, encaustic, grisaille, monochrome, polychrome

► *7 Religion; 20 Architecture; 23 Furniture and Woodwork*

9 drawing, line drawing, delineation, black-and-white, sketch, draft, rough draft, outline, rough outline, rough copy, study, design, vignette, thumbnail sketch, lightning sketch, silhouette, doodle, scribble, graffito, caricature, cartoon, comic strip, comic, animated cartoon, amimation, pen-and-ink, pencil drawing, charcoal drawing, charcoal, crayon, pastel drawing, silverpoint drawing, diagram, graph, tracing

► *163 Outline; 243 Preparation; 717 Representation; 740 Publication*

10 art subject, portrait, profile, head, full-face portrait, *profil perdu* (Fr), full-length portrait, half-length portrait, three-quarter-length portrait, nude, landscape, seascape, marine painting, riverscape, skyscape, cloudscape, scene, townscape, prospect, panorama, view, bird's-eye view, pastoral, nocturne, nightpiece, interior, exterior, historical painting, battle painting, genre painting, *fête champêtre* (Fr), conversation piece, animal painting, equestrian painting, still-life, flower painting, crucifixion, pietà, nativity, annunciation, maestà, vanitas

11 artist's materials, pen, pencil, drawing pencil, ink, chalk, charcoal, crayon, pastel, paintbrush, palette, palette knife, spatula, maulstick, mahlstick, spraygun, airbrush, paintbox, paint tube, paints, pigments, oil paint, oils, watercolours, gouache, gesso, tempera, distemper, ground, medium, solvent, thinner, turpentine, white spirit, siccative, fixative, size, varnish, paper, art paper, drawing paper, sketchpad, scratchpad (US), sketchbook, easel, stretcher, drawing frame, camera obscura, camera lucida, Claude glass, studio, atelier, model, sitter, subject, picture frame, picture gallery, salon, art museum

► *41 Photography; 435 Materials; 438 Tool; 529 Colour*

12 sculpture, plastic art, sculpturing, figuring, modelling, carving, stone-carving, pointing, direct carving, stone-cutting, statuary, monumental sculpture, architectural sculpture, statue, statuette, figure, figurine, bust, head, torso, group, caryatid, telemon, atlantes, herm, garden sculpture, portrait sculpture, funerary sculpture, abstract sculpture, stone sculpture, metal sculpture, wire sculpture, paper sculpture, glass sculpture, clay sculpture, earth art, mobile, stabile, kinetic sculpture, minimal sculpture, marble, bronze, terracotta, woodcarving, ivory-carving, bone-carving, whittling, scrimshaw, rock-carving, petroglyph, wax modelling, model, maquette, moulding, ceroplastics, casting, sand casting, plaster casting, cast, plaster cast, *cire-perdue* (Fr), lost-wax casting, waxwork, ready-made, *objet trouvé* (Fr), found object, environment, installation, assemblage

► *20 Architecture*

13 relief-carving, relief, rilievo (*or* relievo), low relief, bas-relief, *basso rilievo* (It), half relief, *mezzo rilievo* (It), high relief, *alto relievo* (It), *stiacciato* (It), intaglio, *intaglio rilievo* (It), glyph, anaglyph, anaglyptics, anaglyptography, cameo, medallion, medal, embossment, boss, embossing, engraving, chasing

SCHOOLS AND GROUPS OF ARTISTS

Abstraction–Création	Group Zero
Allied Artists Association	Gutai group
American Abstract Artists' Group	Heidelberg school
Ancients	Hudson River school
Antwerp Mannerists	Jeune Peinture Belge
Ashcan school	Luminists
Automatistes, Les	Nabis
Bamboccianati	Nazarenes
Barbizon school	New English Art Club
Bauhaus	Norwich school
Blaue Reiter	Novecento Italiano
Blaue Vier	Novembergruppe
Bloomsbury group	Painters Eleven
Brotherhood of Ruralists	Plasticiens
Brücke	Pont–Aven school
Camden Town Group	Pre–Raphaelite Brotherhood
Cobra	Rocky Mountain School
the Eight	Scottish Colourists
Euston Road school	Section d'Or
Fronte Nuovo delle Arti	De Stijl
Glasgow Boys	Unit One
Group of Seven	Les Vingt
Groupe de Recherche d'Art Visuel (GRAV)	Wanderers
	World of Art group

14 sculptor's materials, mallet, chisel, claw chisel, burin, modelling tool, point, spatula, drill, punch, pointing machine, welding torch, cutting torch, soldering iron, armature, modelling clay, sculptor's wax, wax, Plasticine™, plaster, solder, marble, Pathian marble, granite, bronze, terracotta, stucco

► *160 Form; 435 Materials; 438 Tool*

15 engraving, line engraving, plate engraving, etching, woodcut, drypoint, metal engraving, steel engraving, copper engraving, chalcography, zincography, wood engraving, xylography, lignography, linocut, lithograph, cerography, gem engraving, glyptography, chasing, aquatint, mezzotint, stone, block, wood block, plate, steel plate, copperplate, chisel, burin, bur-chisel, graver, needle, style, point, etching point

16 artist, visual artist, graphic artist, designer, industrial artist, commercial artist, industrial designer, craftsman, artisan, painter, colourist, dauber, easel-painter, action painter, oil painter, watercolour, painter, aquarellist, pastellist, mural painter, icon painter, portrait painter, portraitist, landscape painter, marine painter, historical painter, genre painter, still-life painter, flower painter, animal painter, equestrian painter, religious painter, scene painter, sign painter, pavement artist, drawer, draughtsman, sketcher, limner (Lit), delineator, illustrator, copyist, illuminator, miniaturist, poster artist, cartoonist, political cartoonist, caricaturist, animator, comic-strip artist, doodler, finger painter, enameller, fashion artist, architectural artist, master, old master, modern master, academician, RA, Sunday painter (Inf)

► *24 Ceramics; 126 Originality; 477 Imagination; 553 Fashion*

17 sculptor, stone-carver, carver, statuary, monumental sculptor, monumental mason, architectural sculptor, fig-

NON–WESTERN ART

Prehistoric Art
Palaeolithic art
cave painting
rock painting

African Art
African tribal art
Benin bronzes

Middle Eastern Art
Islamic art
Sumerian art
Assyrian art
Babylonian art
Mesopotamian art
Ottoman art

Indian art
art of the Indus valley
Gandharan art
Mogul art
Tamil art

Ancient Egyptian Art
Old Kingdom art
New Kingdom art

Oceanic Art
Melanesian art

Pre-Columbian Art
Mesoamerican art
Aztec art
Tultec art

Mediterranean Cultures
Cycladic art
Minoan art
Mycenean art

Chinese Art
Chinese calligraphy
Han dynasty art
Song dynasty art
Tang dynasty art
Yuan dynasty art
Ming dynasty art
Ch'ing dynasty art

Japanese Art
Japanese scroll painting
Japanese woodblocks
Fujiwara style
Heian style
Ukiyo–e
floating world

urist, modeller, wax modeller, moulder, caster, metal sculptor, abstract sculptor

▶ *20 Architecture*

18 engraver, etcher, metal engraver, wood engraver, aquatinter, chaser, gem engraver, lapidary, type-cutter, typographer, printer

▶ *740 Publication*

VERBS

19 paint, colour, colourize, tint, coat, brush, tone, overpaint, underpaint, scumble, wash, shade, daub, illuminate, ink in, touch up

▶ *529 Colour; 542 Decoration*

20 draw, sketch, draft, pencil, chalk, limn, outline, doodle, cartoon, caricature, represent, portray, depict, copy, trace, stencil, silhouette, hatch, cross-hatch

▶ *125 Imitation; 163 Outline; 717 Representation*

21 sculpt, carve, cut, chisel, chip, whittle, shape, cast, model, mould, form

22 engrave, grave, incise, etch, chase, scrape, bite, impress, emboss, aquatint, print

23 design, create, visualize, put onto paper, lay out, compose, plan, arrange, group, balance, foreshorten

▶ *126 Originality; 162 Symmetry; 409 Arrangement; 484 Plan; 518 Vision*

ADJECTIVES

24 pictorial, pictographic, graphic, calligraphic, geometric(al), linear, optical, illusionist, aerial, atmosphere, photographic, iconic, mosaic

25 sculptural, marmoreal, monumental, graven, moulded, ceramic, tactile, plastic, glyptic, anaglyptic, ceroplastic, toreutic

▶ *525 Appearance*

26 artistic, painterly, imaginative, illustrative, stylized, decorative, baroque, picturesque, aesthetic, scenic, statuesque, arty (Inf), arty-crafty (Inf), arty-farty (Inf)

▶ *545 Beauty*

27 painted, coloured, washed, daubed, tinted, shaded, illuminated, inked, drawn, sketched, drafted, delineated, outlined, designed, foreshortened, traced, copied

28 sculpted, sculptured, carved, modelled, moulded, embossed, engraved, *repoussé* (Fr)

29 realist, naturalist, photorealist, verist, socialist realist, social realist, regionalist, precisionist, purist, classical, neoclassical, romantic, neoromantic, impressionist, neoimpressionist, postimpressionist, pointillist, divisionist, minimalist, primitive, naive, Fauvist, vorticist, concrete, constructivist, cubist, expressionist, neoexpressionist, figurative, symbolist, Dadaist, abstract, eclectric, mannerist, postmodernist, rayonist, Orphistic, suprematist, synchronic, synthetic, analytic, Renaissance, baroque, rococo, Gothic, Hellenistic, Etruscan, Celtic, Byzantine, Bohemian

ADVERBS

30 pictorially, optically, visually, graphically, sculpturally, photographically, geometrically, realistically, naturalistically, impressionistically, minimally, primitively, concretely, expressionistically, figuratively, symbolically, abstractly, eclectically, in oils, in water colours, in pencil, in pastels, in relief

31 artistically, imaginatively, creatively, conceptually, illustratively, decoratively, picturesquely, aesthetically, scenically, atmospherically

20 Architecture

Architecture in general is frozen music. Friedrich Wilhelm Joseph von Schelling.

NOUNS

1 architecture, architectonics, tectonics, architectural design, building design, building style, architectural engineering, domestic architecture, civil architecture, governmental architecture, civic architecture, religious architecture, military architecture, industrial architecture, recreational architecture, landscape architecture, rendering, drawing, perspective, skiagraphy

2 architect, civil architect, domestic architect, designer, architectural engineer, military architect, industrial architect, landscape architect, master builder, builder, mason, master mason, stone mason

3 building, structure, erection, pile, listed building, castle, ranch house (US), colonial home (US), town house, detached house, semidetached house (*or* semi), terraced house, row house (US), cottage, thatched cottage, country cottage, single-storey building, multistorey building, high-rise building (*or* high-rise), skyscraper, tower, low-rise building (*or* low-rise), half-timbered building, architectural monstrosity, eyesore, carbuncle

▶ *38 Engineering*

4 building material, stone, building stone, granite, marble, sandstone, brownstone (US), Cotswold stone, slate, brick, rustic brick, engineering brick, brickwork, building block, breeze block, concrete, reinforced concrete, ferroconcrete, prestressed concrete, glass, ferrovitreous construction, aluminium, girder, steel

5 arch, rounded arch, lancet arch, parabolic arch, segmental arch, false arch, Norman arch, semicircular arch,

ARCHITECTURAL DECORATION

abacus
acanthus
accolade
acroter
annulet
antefix
anthemion
apophyge
architrave
astragal
atlantes
atlas
baguette (*or* baguet)
band
banderole (*or* banderol *or* bannerol)
bas-relief (*or* basso rilievo)
bay leaf
bead
beak
bezant (*or* bezzant *or* byzant)
billet
boss
calotte
canephorae
capstone
cartouche (*or* cartouch)
caryatid
cavetto
chevron
cinquefoil
congé
console
coping stone (*or* copestone)
cordon
cornice
corona
cove (*or* coving)
crocket (*or* crochet)
crown (*or* crownpiece)
cusp
cyma
cyma recta
cyma reversa
cymatium
dentil
dogtooth
echinus
ectype
egg and dart (*or* egg and tongue *or* egg and anchor)
epistyle
facet
fascia
festoon
fillet
finial
flute
foil
foliation
fret
frieze
frontispiece
gadroon (*or* godroon)
gorgerin
guilloche
gutta
head
head mould
head moulding
headpiece
helix
herms
hood mould
hypophyge
label
lierne
list
listel
medallion
metope
modillion
moulding
mullion
mutule
necking
neckmould
ogee
ovolo
pendant
polychromy
poppy head
pulvinate frieze
putto
quadrega
quarter round
quatrefoil
quirk
quoin
reed
reeding
reglet
relief (*or* relievo *or* rilievo)
respond
rustication
scotia
scroll
scrolling
splay
stria
strigil
stucco
taenia
talon
telemon
term (*or* terminal *or* terminus)
thumb
topping
torus (*or* tore)
tracery
transome
trefoil
triglyph
tympanum (*or* tympan)
vaulting boss
vignette
volute
zigzag

ogee arch, Tudor arch, *anse de panier* (Fr), basket arch, horseshoe arch, two centred arch, four centred arch, catenary arch, elliptical arch, corbel arch, depressed arch, lancet arch, keel arch, raking arch, rampant arch, rowlack arch, shouldered arch, skew arch, stilted arch, strainer arch, arcuation

6 **roof**, flat roof, pitch roof, pitched roof, hip roof, hipped roof, gambrel roof (*or* gambrel), imbricated roof (*or* imbricate), mansard roof (*or* mansard), dome, saucer dome, pendentive dome (*or* pendentive), geodesic dome (*or* geodesic)

7 **vault**, vaulting, barrel (*or* tunnel) vault, rib vault, groin vault, fan vault, fan vaulting, lierne vault, parabolic vault, segmental vault, quadripartite vault, intersecting vault, domical vault, voussoir, sexpartite vault, tierceron ridge rib, transverse ridge rib

8 **column**, support, pillar, post, pier, pilaster, buttress, flying buttress, abutment, monolithic column, engaged column, Salomonic column, coupled column, demi-column, columniation, intercolumniation, colonnade, stylobate, diastyle, hexastyle, peristyle, pedestal, shaft, drum, fluting, flute, entasis, capital, chapiter, cap, entab-

ARCHITECTURAL STYLES

academic
American
Art Deco
Art Nouveau
baroque
Bauhaus
beaux arts
brutalist
Byzantine
Carolingian
Christian
churrigueresque (*or* churrigueresco)
cinquecento
classical
colonial
colossal
Corinthian
Cyclopean
Deconstructionism
Decorated
De Stijl
Doric
Early Christian
Early English
Early Renaissance
Edwardian
Egyptian
Elizabethan
Empire
English
Federation
flamboyant
French
functional
Georgian
German
Gothic
Gothic Revival
Graeco–Roman (*or* Greco–Roman)
Grecian (*or* Greek)
Greek Revival
High Renaissance
international
Ionic
Islamic
Italian
Jacobean
Louis Quatorze
Louis Quinze
Louis Seize
Louis Treize
mannerist
medieval (*or* mediaeval)
Mesopotamian
modern
moderne
modernist
Moorish
Moresque
Mozarabic
Mudéjar
neoclassical
Neo–Gothic
new–brutalist
Norman
Palladian
Perpendicular
Persian
postmodernist (*or* post–modern)
Queen–Anne
Regency
Renaissance
rococo
Roman
Romanesque
romantic classical
Saracen
Spanish
transitional (*or* transition)
Tudor
Tuscan
vernacular
Victorian

NOTED BUILDINGS

Acropolis (Athens)
Battersea Power Station (London)
Blenheim Palace (Woodstock, England)
Blue Mosque (Istanbul)
Bourges Cathedral (France)
British Museum (London)
Buckingham Palace (London)
Casa Milá (Barcelona)
Central Station (Milan)
Chartres Cathedral (France)
Chongqing Tower (Chongqing, China)
Church of the Madeleine (Paris)
Cologne Cathedral
Colosseum (Rome)
Crystal Palace (London)
Edinburgh Castle
Eiffel Tower (Paris)
Empire State Building (New York)
Erectheum (Athens)
Flat Iron Building (New York)
Florence Cathedral
Galleria Vittorio Emanuele II (Milan)
Golden Temple (Amritsar, India)
Guggenheim Museum (New York)
Hagia Sophia (Istanbul)
Hermitage (Saint Petersburg)
Houses of Parliament (London)
Jefferson Memorial (Washington)
John Hancock Center (Chicago)
J. Paul Getty Museum (Malibu, California)
King's College Chapel (Cambridge, England)
Law Courts (London)
Leaning Tower of Pisa
Louvre (Paris)
Notre Dame Cathedral (Paris)
Opéra (Paris)
Pagoda (Kew, England)
Pantheon (Rome)
Parliament House (Vienna)
Parthenon (Athens)
Pennsylvania Station (New York)
Petronas Towers (Kuala Lumpur)
Pompidou Centre (Paris)
Pyramids (Egypt)
Reims Cathedral (France)
Royal Crescent (Bath, England)
Royal Pavilion (Brighton)
Saint Basil's Cathedral (Moscow)
Sainte-Chapelle (Paris)
Saint Mark's Cathedral (Venice)
Saint Patrick's Cathedral (New York)
Saint Paul's Cathedral (London)
Saint Peter's (Rome)
Sears Tower (Chicago)
Staatsgalerie (Stuttgart)
Stratosphere Tower (Las Vegas)
Sun Temple (Konarak, India)
Taj Mahal (Agra, India)
Temple of Apollo Epicurius (Bassae, Greece)
Tower of London
Transamerica Pyramid (San Francisco)
Trans World Airways Terminal (New York)
US Capitol (Washington)
Versailles (Paris)
Westminster Abbey (London)
Westminster Cathedral (London)
White House (Washington)
World Trade Center (New York)

lature, impost, Doric order, Tuscan order, Ionic order, Corinthian order, Composite order

9 **miscellaneous architectural features**, abacus, ambulatory, ancon (*or* ancone), anta, arcade, articulation, ashlar, astylar, attic, balcony, base, beak, bolster, bow, cantilever, case, casement, cella, centering, coin (*or* quoin), concha, corbel, cordon, cupola, fenestrated cupola, lantern cupola, dado, die, drip, dripstone, extrados, fantail, fascia (*or* facia), fenestella, fenestra, filler, frieze, frustum, gable, gable end, groin, haunch (*or* hance), headstone, hip, imperia, impost, intrados, invert, lantern, lintel, loggia, louvre, module, naos, neck, pace, pier, podium, portico, propylaeum, prostyle, re-entrant corner, respond, reveal, rib, rotunda, rustication, shafting, spandrel, springer, squint, squinch, string, stringer, table, tailpiece, tail beam, tambour, trumeau, truss, verge, vestibule, voussoir, wall, curtain wall, cheek wall, load-bearing wall, nonbearing wall, window, lancet window (*or* lancet), lunette, Oriel window

10 **church architecture**, cuniform church, Greek cross plan, Latin cross plan, crossing, conch, ambulatory, apse, semicircular apse, transept, liturgical east end, chancel, westwork, vestibule, narthex, dome, flèche, spirelet, chevet, triforium, clerestory (*or* clearstory), blindstorey (*or* blindstory), basilica, tribune gallery, flying buttress, galilee porch

► *19 Painting and Sculpture*

ADJECTIVES

11 **architectural**, edificial, architectonic, tectonic, designed, architecturally designed, architecturally engineered

12 **structural**, erected, listed, designed, colonial (US), detached, semidetached, terraced, single-storey, multistorey, high-rise, low-rise

13 **arched**, arcuated, arcuate, rounded, lancet, parabolic, segmental

14 **roofed**, pitched, hipped, imbricate, domed, pendentive

15 **vaulted**, ribbed, fanned

16 **columned**, columnated, columnar, supported, pilastered, buttressed, fluted, Doric, Tuscan, Corinthian, Composite

17 **structured**, formed, decorated, ornamented, ornamental, abutting, arcuated, articulated, bossed, embossed, corniced, crowned, cuniform, fascial, fenestrated, ferrovitreous, geodesic, intersecting, moulded, parabolic, pendentive, re-entrant, ribbed, rusticated, segmental, scrolled, triglyphic

VERBS

18 **be an architect**, design buildings, design houses, design, draw blueprints, build houses, build buildings, build, construct, structure, erect, prefabricate, package, select building materials, brick, glass

19 **decorate**, ornament, dome, arch, vault, rib, abut, buttress, cantilever, coffer, articulate, flute, mould, boss, fret, crown, cornice, stucco, rusticate

ADVERBS

20 **architecturally**, with an architect, architectonically, tectonically, constructionally, by design, domestically, civilly, industrially, ornamentally, decoratively, structurally

21 Drama

Theatre director: a person engaged by the management to conceal the fact that the players cannot act. James Agate.

Don't put your daughter on the stage, Mrs Worthington. Noël Coward.

NOUNS

1 **drama**, the theatre, the stage, the play, the scenes (Lit), traffic of the state, dramatic entertainment, dramatics, amateur dramatics, dramaticism, theatrics, theatricals, histrionics, histrionism, dramatic art, histrionic art, Thes-

pian art, Thespis, cinema, television, stagedom, playland, the West End, Broadway, off-Broadway, off-off-Broadway, the Fringe, fringe theatre, repertory, live theatre, legitimate theatre, straight drama, alternative theatre, street theatre, pub theatre, experimental theatre, rep (Inf), legit (Inf), the boards (Inf), the footlights (Inf), greasepaint (Inf)

▶ *17 Literature; 703 Demonstration; 738 Display*

2 **play**, stage play, drama, dramatic representation, dramatic entertainment, dramatic recital, show, work, piece, vehicle, script, text, lines, libretto, book, book of words, prompt book, monologue, dramatic monologue, monodrama, one-man show, one-woman show, duologue, duodrama, two-hander, dialogue, skit, sketch, playlet, *divertissement* (Fr), charade, burlesque, curtain-raiser, curtain-lifter, intermezzo, entr'acte, double bill, one-act play, five-act play, trilogy, tetralogy, dramatic cycle, Greek drama, *fabula* (L), *Nō* play, *Kyōgen* (Jap), *Kabuki* (Jap), mystery play, morality play, miracle play, passion play, Oberammergau, liturgical drama, folk play, mummers' play, swordplay, *commedia dell'arte* (It), farce, harlequinade, pantomime, mime, dumbshow, masque, antimasque, pastoral, interlude, verse drama, poetic drama, closet drama, melodrama, heroic drama, Grand Guignol, drama of suspense, well-made play, *pièce bien faite* (Fr), problem play, sociodrama, psychodrama, psychological drama, slice of life, kitchen-sink drama, docudrama, documentary drama, drama-documentary, rockumentary, community drama, collective creation, improvised drama, improvisation, happening, broadcast drama, radio drama, radio play, television drama, television play, teleplay, screenplay, biopic, scenario, shooting script, serial, soap opera, soap (Inf)

3 **films**, movies, pictures, the silver screen, Hollywood, Bollywood, flicks (Inf)

4 **musical drama**, opera, operetta, musical, Broadway musical, show, musical comedy, comic opera, *opera buffa* (It), *opera seria* (It), ballad opera, rock opera, *Singspiel* (Ger), ballet, Gilbert and Sullivan, cabaret

▶ *18 Music; 22 Dancing*

5 **show business**, entertainment industry, vaudeville, variety, burlesque, music hall, song and dance, striptease, the stage, the boards, Broadway, off-Broadway, off-off-Broadway, West End, Hollywood, the big top, showbiz (Inf), straw hat (US inf)

6 **cinema**, cinematography, film directing, screenwriting, Academy Awards, Oscars (Inf)

▶ *41 Photography*

7 **show**, stage show, live show, spectacle, extravaganza, variety show, vaudeville show, burlesque show, cabaret, song and dance, revue, review, intimate review, late-night review, minstrel show, music hall, repertory show, Follies, floor show, strip show, striptease, peepshow, sex show, *tableau vivant* (Fr), tableau, hootchy-kootchy show, raree show, medicine show, road show, magic show, puppet show, puppetry, Punch-and-Judy show, marionette show, *fantoccini* (It), shadow play, shadow show, *ombres chinoises* (Fr), slide show, light show, laser show, *son et lumière* (Fr), circus, travelling circus, the Big Top, the ring, rodeo, ice show, carnival, pageant, sideshow, flea circus, game show, quiz show, panel show, lecture, rep show (Inf), girly show (Inf), leg show (Inf), nudie show (Inf), flesh show (Inf)

▶ *552 Undress; 601 Celebration; 703 Demonstration; 738 Display*

8 **scene**, act, speech, monologue, soliloquy, episode, item, piece, number, routine, sketch, turn, bill, top of the bill, bottom of the bill, curtain-music, overture, curtain-raiser, curtain-lifter, rising of the curtain, prologue, introduction, opening scene, expository scene, chorus, interval, intermission, break, intermezzo, entr'acte, interlude, *divertimento* (It), *divertissement* (Fr), climax, catastrophe, denouement, resolution, exposure scene, recognition scene, *deus ex machina* (L), battle scene, alarums and excursions, love scene, sex scene, transformation scene, set piece, finale, curtain, drop of the curtain, final curtain, curtain call, blackout, epilogue, encore, exode, exodus, afterpiece, jig, applause, ovation, standing ovation, chaser (Inf)

9 **dramaturgy**, dramatic structure, dramatic form, play construction, stagecraft, theatre craft, theatrical convention, dramatic convention, dramatic unities, the unities, dramatic irony, dramatic conflict, *agon* (Gk), dramatic tension, alienation effect, a-effect, *Verfremdungseffekt* (Ger), play writing, script writing, plot, subplot, characterization, story, *stichomythia* (Gk), staging, choreography, action, movement, gesture, theatricality, theatrics, sensationalism, blood and thunder, *Sturm und Drang* (Ger), Grand Guignol, dramatic coup, dramatic stroke, *coup de théâtre* (Fr), spectacle, showmanship, ham (Inf)

▶ *17 Literature; 447 Topic; 485 Skill; 488 Sensation; 518 Vision*

10 **theatre movements**, activism, *Aktie Tomaat* (Dutch), Angry Young Men, community theatre, constructivism, *Décentralisation Dramatique* (Fr), documentary theatre, epic theatre, expressionism, feminist theatre, formalism, kitchen-sink drama, naturalism, New Drama, realism, ritual drama, *Sturm und Drang* (Ger), *théâtre du quotidien* (Fr), theatre of the absurd, theatre of cruelty, theatre of fact, theatre of silence, *théâtre total* (Fr), total theatre, *verismo* (It), *Vormingstoneel* (Dutch)

11 **tragedy**, tragic drama, high tragedy, classical tragedy, Greek tragedy, Aeschylean tragedy, Euripidean tragedy, Sophoclean tragedy, Senecan tragedy, Renaissance tragedy, Shakespearean tragedy, Elizabethan tragedy, Jacobean tragedy, revenge tragedy, domestic tragedy, drama of fate, romantic tragedy, melodrama, tragicomedy, tragic muse, Melpomene, cothurnus, buskin, tragic flaw, *hamartia* (Gk), hubris, catharsis

▶ *593 Love; 602 Sorrow*

12 **comedy**, high comedy, low comedy, broad comedy, light comedy, romantic comedy, sentimental comedy, *comédie larmoyante* (Fr), comedy of manners, comedy of ideas, comedy of humours, comedy of intrigue, comedy of morals, comedy of character, comedy of situation, situation comedy, sitcom (Inf), sex comedy, black comedy, dark comedy, bitter comedy, *comédie rosse* (Fr), tragicomedy, satire, satirical comedy, farce, knockabout farce, stand-up comedy, bedroom farce, Feydeau farce, Whitehall farce, French farce, slapstick, burlesque, burletta, high camp, low camp, alternative comedy, satyr play,

Aristophanean comedy, Old Comedy, Middle Comedy, New Comedy, Roman comedy, *commedia dell'arte* (It), *commedia a soggetto* (It), *commedia erudita* (It), *burla* (It), *lazzo* (It), interlude, Shakespearean comedy, Jonsonian comedy, Restoration comedy, *comédie-ballet* (Fr), drawing-room comedy, comic relief, light relief, comic business, comic muse, Thalia, motley, sock, cap and bells, coxcomb, bladder

▶ *593 Love; 599 Humour*

13 theatrical performance, show, production, stage presentation, presentment, exhibition, bill, premiere performance, premiere, preview, first night, gala night, debut, farewell performance, personal appearance, command performance, bespeak performance (Lit), benefit, charity gala, matinée, first house, second house, successful production, success, critical success, sell-out, full house, hit, box-office hit, smash hit (Inf), long run, failure, short run, flop (Inf), turkey (Inf), bomb (US inf)

▶ *246 Success; 247 Failure; 738 Display*

14 production, direction, staging, mounting, putting on, stage management, *mise-en-scène* (Fr), audition, casting, rehearsal, readthrough, walkthrough, run-through, blocking, dress rehearsal, technical rehearsal, new production, revival, modern production, modern-dress production

▶ *243 Preparation; 356 Creation*

15 engagement, theatrical engagement, playing engagement, booking, date, gig, stand, one-night stand, run, tour, circuit, variety circuit, club circuit, pub circuit, vaudeville circuit, repertory circuit, rep (Inf), strawhat circuit (US inf), borscht belt (US inf), scampi-and-chips circuit (Inf), chicken-in-a-basket circuit (Inf), rubber-chicken circuit (Inf)

16 theatre, venue, playhouse, house, hall, hippodrome, auditorium, arena, amphitheatre, stadium, circus, Greek theatre, odeum, odeon, Elizabethan theatre, spectacle theatre, open-air theatre, outdoor theatre, theatre-in-the-round, circle theatre, arena theatre, little theatre, variety theatre, vaudeville theatre, vaudeville house, burlesque theatre, burlesque house, cabaret, music hall, opera house, opera, concert hall, cinema, movie theatre, picture house, nightclub, club, nightspot, *boîte de nuit* (Fr), *boîte* (Fr), booth, showboat, big top, pavilion, end of the pier, toy theatre, *ediophusikon* (Gk), fleapit (Inf)

▶ *20 Architecture*

17 stage, the boards, performing area, acting area, playing area, proscenium stage, proscenium, proscenium arch, bridge, picture-frame stage, apron stage, apron, forestage, thrust stage, segment stage, wagon stage, slip stage, revolving stage, trap, stage left, stage L, stage right, stage R, upstage, downstage, centrestage, frontstage, above, below, orchestra pit, orchestra, pit, bandstand, podium, rostrum, dais, soapbox, wings, backstage, dressing room, greenroom, stage door, flies, fly floor, fly gallery, gridiron, grid, lightboard, switchboard, board, sounddesk, prompter's box, scene dock, scene bay

▶ *18 Music; 23 Furniture and Woodwork*

18 auditorium, seating, parquet (US), parquet circle (US), stalls, orchestra stalls, front stalls, back stalls, pit, front rows, fauteuil, parterre, loge, box, box seat, stage box, parterre box, proscenium box, royal box, circle, upper circle, dress circle, balcony, gallery, mezzanine, standing room, front of house, foyer, box office, the gods (Inf), heaven (US inf), paradise (US inf), peanut gallery (US inf)

19 stage set, stage setting, setting, set, box set, scenery, scene, *mise-en-scène* (Fr), decor, flat, side scene, cyclorama, stage screw, wing, wingcut, border, tormentor, teaser, flipper, batten, drop, drop curtain, drop scene, cloth, backdrop, backcloth, hanging, gauze, scrim, transparency, transformation scene, curtain, drape, house curtain, act curtain, act drop, tabs, safety curtain, fire curtain, advertisement curtain, rag (Inf)

20 stage lighting, lights, footlights, limelight, floodlight, flood, spotlight, arc light, arc, bunch light, battens, house lights, klieg light, colour filter, colour wheel, medium, gelatin, gel (Inf), gobo, diaphragm, iris diaphragm, iris, projector, sciopticon (US), stroboscope, lightboard, lighting board, lighting desk, lighting plot, Varilite™, foots (Inf), spot (Inf), following spot (Inf), strobe (Inf)

▶ *522 Light; 529 Colour*

21 stage requisite, stage property, property, prop, handprop, theatrical costume, costume, wardrobe, theatrical make-up, make-up, theatrical cosmetics, greasepaint, spirit gum, whiteface, blackface, clown face

▶ *542 Decoration; 553 Fashion*

22 acting, play-acting, playing, role-playing, taking a role, taking a part, creating a role, creating a part, impersonation, personation, portrayal, representation, characterization, interpretation, projection, performing, performance, enactment, mimesis, mimicry, mimicking, miming, pantomiming, character acting, method acting, the Method, improvisation, improvising, histrionics, overacting, barnstorming, business, stage business, byplay, stage whisper, aside, entrance, exit, cue, theatrical technique, stage presence, showmanship, star quality, stage fever, first-night nerves, stage fright, ham acting (Inf), hamming (Inf), hamming it up (Inf), camping it up (Inf), hoking it up (US inf), hoking (US inf), mummery (Inf)

▶ *125 Imitation; 185 Bulge; 525 Appearance; 612 Fear; 717 Representation; 719 Interpretation; 727 Exaggeration; 738 Display*

23 role, part, character, person, personage, dramatis personae, title role, title part, name part, starring role, leading role, lead role, lead, chief part, good part, principal character, hero, heroine, antihero, villain, protagonist, antagonist, supporting character, deuteragonist, supporting part, supporting role, minor role, bit part, speaking part, walk-on part, walking part, straight part, straight man, cameo, vignette, comic relief, chorus, Greek chorus, stock part, stock character, stereotype, central casting, ingenue, soubrette, juvenile lead, *jeune première* (Fr), love interest, confidante, heavy father, heavy woman, walking lady, walking gentleman, supernumerary, merry widow, injured husband, breeches part, *miles gloriosus* (L), buffoon, fool, stage villain, stage Irishman, stage drunk, Harlequin, Columbine, Pantaloon, Pierrot, Scaramouch, principal boy, principal girl, pantomime dame, heavy (Inf), bad guy (Inf), fat part (Inf), juicy part (Inf), bit (Inf), feeder (Inf), feed (Inf)

24 actor, actress, play-actor, player, stage player, strolling player, Thespian, trouper, stage performer, repertory player, Roscius (Lit), barnstormer, actor-manager, tragedian, tragedienne, comedian, comedienne, comedy actor, comedy actress, light comedian, low comedian, farcer, character actor, character actress, method actor, improviser, film actor, film actress, film star, star, superstar, starlet, star of stage and screen, matinée idol, idol, icon, leading man, leading lady, lead, juvenile lead, *jeune premier (or première)* (Fr), supporting actor, support, body double, understudy, stand-in, standby, lookalike, substitute, extra, bit player, spear-carrier, supernumerary, super, pantomimist, opera singer, diva, prima donna, prologue, presenter, narrator, speaker, ham (Inf), mummer (Inf), darling (Inf), lovie (Inf)

25 cast, characters, dramatis personae, persons of the drama, chorus, ladies (*or* gentlemen) of the chorus, supporting cast, cast of thousands, ensemble, company, repertory company, stock company, touring company, outfit, troupe, circus troupe, *corps de ballet* (Fr)

▶ *376 Gathering*

26 dramatist, dramaturge, dramatizer, playwright, play writer, scenario writer, scenarioist, scenarist, screenwriter, script writer, librettist, radio dramatist, television dramatist, *farceur* (Fr), *farceuse* (Fr), joke writer, tragedian, comedian, tragic poet, comic poet, melodramatist, choreographer, mimographer, play doctor (US inf), play fixer (US inf), jokesmith (Inf), gag man (Inf), gag writer (Inf)

▶ *17 Literature; 126 Originality; 477 Imagination*

27 producer, director, auteur, stage manager, manager, actor-manager, impresario, exhibitor, promoter, showman, master of ceremonies, ringmaster, choreographer, *regisseur* (Fr), *choragus* (Gk), designer, set designer, costume designer, *costumier* (Fr), *costumière* (Fr), business manager, publicity manager, publicity man, publicity woman, press officer, press agent, booking agent, ticket agent, agent, theatrical agent, advance agent, advance man, playbroker, patron, backer, angel (Inf), ten-per-cent man (US inf), ten-per-center (US inf), MC (Inf), emcee (Inf), SM (Inf)

▶ *356 Creation; 392 Help; 396 Authority*

28 stagehand, stage technician, state crew, electrician, sound recordist, sound man, lighting man, machinist (Lit), stage carpenter, scene painter, scene shifter, flyman, special effects man, dresser, wardrobe mistress, make-up artist, make-up man, wig maker, callboy, prompter, ticket collector, programme-seller, usher, usherette, doorman, front-of-house staff, box-office staff

29 entertainer, public entertainer, artiste, artist, performer, act, vaudeville artist, vaudevillian, variety artist, song and dance man, quick-change artist, drag artist, female impersonator, impersonator, impressionist, mimic, ventriloquist, reciter, monologist, diseuse, diseur, conjuror, magician, mountebank, prestidigitator, sleight-of-hand artist, hypnotist, escapologist, escape artist, mind reader, memory artist, comedian, comedienne, comic, stand-up comic, humorist, straight man, minstrel, troubadour, goliard (Lit), jongleur (Lit), busker, street performer, show girl, chorus girl, chorus boy, striptease artist, presenter, host, game-show host, quiz-show host, chat show host, radio personality, television personality, burlesque queen (Inf), stripper (Inf), stooge (Inf), foil (Inf), feed (Inf)

▶ *125 Imitation; 552 Undress; 705 Question; 735 Soliloquy; 738 Display*

30 dancer, ballet dancer, ballerina, prima ballerina, *danseur* (Fr), *danseuse* (Fr), coryphée, figurante, figurant, Terpsichorean, dancing girl, show girl, chorus girl, cancan dancer, tap dancer, belly dancer, disco dancer, go-go dancer, nautch-girl, geisha girl, geisha, striptease artist, exotic dancer, erotic dancer, ecdysiast, stripper (Inf), hoofer (Inf)

▶ *22 Dancing; 552 Undress*

31 circus performer, circus artist, tightrope walker, rope-walker, slack-rope artist, high-wire artist, equilibrist, trapeze artist, tumbler, acrobat, *saltimbanco* (It), contortionist, juggler, strongman, stunt man, human cannonball, fire-eater, snake charmer, lion tamer, bareback rider, ringmaster, equestrian director, clown, barker, spiel man (Inf)

▶ *57 Gymnastics; 599 Humour*

32 clown, fool, jester, buffoon, *buffo* (Inf), zany, cap and bells, motley, slapstick comedian, slapstick, Punch, Punchinello, Pulcinella, Polichinelle, Harlequin, Columbine, Pantaloon, Pantalone, Scaramouch, Pierrot, Pedrolino, Pasquino, merry-andrew (Lit), pickle-herring (Lit), jack-pudding (Lit)

▶ *599 Humour*

33 theatregoer, playgoer, operagoer, filmgoer, balletgoer, spectator, fan, enthusiast, opera buff, buff, balletomane, audience, house, full house, packed house, thin house, stalls, pit, circle, boxes, gallery, balcony, promenader, standee (US), groundling (Lit), pittite (Lit), *claque* (Fr), *claqueur* (Fr), pass holder, critic, reviewer, talent spotter, first-nighter (Inf), stage-door Johnny (Inf), deadhead (Inf), plant (Inf)

VERBS

34 act, perform, enact, play, play-act, appear, project, enter, make an entrance, take the stage, tread the boards, face the cameras, play the lead, support, co-star, understudy, see one's name in lights, mimic, mime, imitate, represent, personify, impersonate, take off (Inf), exit, take a bow

▶ *125 Imitation; 185 Bulge; 314 Entry; 315 Exit; 738 Display*

35 overact, send up, overplay, rant, roar, play to the gallery, upstage, barnstorm, steal the show, play the fool, improvise, ad-lib, wing it (Inf), chew up the scenery (Inf), milk it (Inf), ham (Inf), ham (*or* camp) it up (Inf)

▶ *219 Excess; 329 Overstepping; 514 Human Cry; 727 Exaggeration*

36 underact, walk on, have a cameo role, miss one's cue, fluff, dry up, go blank, throw away (Inf)

▶ *274 Error; 728 Understatement*

37 rehearse, con, learn one's lines, mug up, memorize, recite, run through, read through, walk through, block, interpret the part, get into character, method act

▶ *243 Preparation*

38 dramatize, melodramatize, theatricalize, adapt for the stage, write, script, produce, put on, direct, cue, prompt, stage-manage, cast, bill, star, feature, typecast, present, release, preview, premiere, open, raise the curtain

► *17 Literature; 126 Originality; 308 Opening; 356 Creation; 396 Authority*

ADJECTIVES

39 **dramatic**, dramaturgic, melodramatic, spectacular, theatrical, mimetic, musical, operatic, choral, balletic, choreographic, Terpsichorean, histrionic, Thespian, stagy, staged, enacted, performed, interpreted, characterized, scripted, prompted, directed, improvised, protagonistic, antagonistic

40 **tragic**, tragicomic, buskined, romantic, cathartic, comic, vaudevillian, slapstick, burlesque, farcical, knockabout, sensational, stereotypical, typecast, miscast, hammy (Inf), hammed up (Inf)

41 **stagestruck**, starstruck, all-star, top of the bill, starring, featuring, showing, running

42 **activist**, constructivist, expressionist, formalist, naturalist, realist, Restoration

ADVERBS

43 **on stage**, in the spotlight (*or* limelight), stage left, stage right, upstage, downstage, centrestage, frontstage, offstage, in the wings, backstage, behind the scenes

44 **dramatically**, melodramatically, histrionically, theatrically, tragically, comically, romantically, protagonistically, antagonistically, choreographically, chorally, stereotypically, realistically

22 Dancing

Can't act. Can't sing. Can dance a little. Anonymous (Report on Fred Astaire's first screen test).

Ladies and gentleman, it takes more than one to make a ballet. Ninette de Valois.

NOUNS

1 **dancing**, dance, promenade (US), ball, *bal masqué* (Fr), masked ball, masquerade, *bal costumé* (Fr), costume ball, fancy dress dance, *thé dansant* (Fr), tea dance, cotillion (*or* cotillon) (US), ceilidh, barn dance, square dance (US), disco, disco dancing, breakdancing, bodypopping, robot dancing, robotics, tap dancing, clog dancing, folk dancing, country dancing, Scottish country dancing, Highland dancing, Irish dancing, morris dancing, old-time dancing, sequence dancing, ballroom dancing, ballet dancing, modern dance, choreography, eurhythmics (*or* eurythmics), aerobics, muse of dancing, Terpsichore, prom (US inf), hop (Inf), bop (Inf), jam session (Inf), shindig (Inf), knees-up (Inf), rave (Inf)

2 **dance**, ballroom dance, shuffle, soft-shoe shuffle, cakewalk, Castle walk, solo dance, pas seul, clog dance, step dance, tap dance, toe dance, sand dance, fan dance, dance of the seven veils, hula-hula, hula, high kicks, cancan, belly dance, polka, waltz, *valse* (Fr), last waltz, Viennese waltz, hesitation waltz, St Bernard, valeta, Lancers, excuse-me dance, Paul Jones, snowball, foxtrot, slow foxtrot, fast foxtrot, turkey trot, quickstep, Charleston, black bottom, blues, one-step, English one-step, two-step, Boston two-step, English waltz, military two-step, paso doble, peabody, tango, rumba, samba, mambo, bossanova, habanera, beguine, conga, conga line, bunny hop, cha-cha-cha (*or* cha-cha), boomps-a-daisy, hokey cokey, Lambeth Walk, Palais Glide, the big apple, stomp, bop, bebop, shimmy, jive, Lindy-hop, jitterbug, rock and roll (*or* rock'n'roll), twist, mashed potato, jerk, hitch-hike, bogle, lambada

3 **ballroom dance steps**, chassé, waltz, balance, pivot, walking steps, running steps, syncopated steps

4 **historic dancing**, animal dance, totem dance, hunting dance, trance dance, curative dance, devil dance, agricultural dance, rain dance, harvest dance, courtship dance, fandango, fertility dance, wedding dance, funeral dance, medieval dance, court dance, sword dance, sailor's dance, hornpipe, keel row, war dance, pyrrhic (dance), meke, haka, ritual dance, corroboree (Aus), sacred dance, Indian temple dance, Gypsy dance, flamenco, country dance, morris dance, rapper, long sword, jig, gigue, Irish jig, Walls of Limerick, fling, Highland fling, reel, eightsome reel, foursome reel, Virginia reel, Sir Roger de Coverley, Scottish reel, Strathspey, Gay Gordons, Duke of Perth, Strip the Willow, Dashing White Sergeant, hay (*or* hey), saraband (*or* sarabande), set dance, barn dance, military schottische (US), square dance (US), hoedown (US), rigadoon (*or* rigaudon), folk dance, dionysiac (*or* bacchic) dance, Russian dance, Cossack dance, farandole, maypole dance, nautch (*or* nauch), tarantella, bolero, polka, mazurka, polonaise, czardas, dramatic dance, *Kabuki* (Jap), social dance, *danse basse* (Fr), waltz, galliard, courante, gavotte, contredanse (*or* contradance), quadrille, pavane (*or* pavan), minuet, scherzo, écossaise, galop (*or* gallopade), volta, allemande, cotillion (*or* cotillon)

5 **dancer**, tap dancer, clog dancer, classical dancer, high-kicker, Radio City Rockettes (US), cancan dancer, go-go dancer, entertainer, waltzer, foxtrotter, shuffler, jiver, jitterbug, bebopper, disco dancer, jumper, choreographer, hoofer (Inf)

6 **famous dancers**, Irene and Vernon Castle, Fred Astaire and Ginger Rogers, Jack Buchanan, Gene Kelly,

► *21 Drama*

7 **dance hall**, ballroom, palais de danse, discotheque, disco, dance floor

8 **ballet**, dance, ballet dancing, dancing, classical ballet, Russian ballet, romantic ballet, modern ballet, modern dance, toe dance, solo, choreography

► *21 Drama*

9 **ballet steps**, attitude, chassé, glissade, bourrée, arabesque, arabesque penchée, pirouette, petit allegro, soubresauté, changement, pas de chat, brisé volé, temps de poisson, batterie, cabriole, entrechat, jeté, deboulé, ballong, fouetté, fouetté en tournant, tours en l'air, pas de deux

10 **positions at the barre**, plié, tendus, glissées, ronds de jambes à terre, battement, fondus, ronds de jambes en l'air, développés, petits battements, grands battements

11 **classical ballets**, Swan Lake, The Sleeping Beauty, The Nutcracker, Coppelia, Giselle, Les Sylphides

12 **ballet companies**, Bolshoi Ballet, Kirov Ballet, Paris Opera Ballet, Royal Ballet, Ballet Rambert, Sadler's Wells Ballet, Royal Festival Ballet, New York City Ballet, American Ballet, Royal Danish Ballet

13 ballet dancer, *danseur* (Fr), ballerina, *danseuse* (Fr), prima ballerina, *corps de ballet* (Fr)

14 famous ballet dancers, Anna Pavlova, Vaslav Nijinsky, Maria Taglioni, Galina Ulanova, Maya Plisetskaya, George Balanchine, Maria Tallchief, Martha Graham, Edward Villella, Alicia Markova, Ninette de Valois, Marie Rambert, Rudolf Nureyev, Margot Fonteyn, Robert Helpmann, Frederick Ashton, Merle Park, Peter Schaufuss, Mikhail Baryshnikov

► *21 Drama*

VERBS

15 dance, join the dance, go dancing, choreograph, tap-dance, waltz, foxtrot, quickstep, Charleston, tango, rumba, jive, jitterbug, stomp, bop, twist, rock, rock and roll (*or* rock'n'roll), disco-dance, breakdance, bodypop, whirl, rotate, cavort, gambol, frolic, prance, caper, jig, jig about, bob up and down, shuffle, trip, tread a measure, trip the light fantastic (toe), skip, hop, leap, hoof it (Inf)

► *307 Rotation*

23 Furniture and Woodwork

I make no secret of the fact that I would rather lie on a sofa than sweep beneath it. Shirley Conran.

NOUNS

1 furniture, furnishings, home furnishings, pine furniture, wood furniture, laminated furniture, veneer furniture, veneering, lacquered furniture, lacquering, painted furniture, painting, trompe l'oeil, chinoiserie, japanning, inlaid decoration, marquetried furniture, marquetry, parquetried furniture, parquetry, metal furniture, plastic furniture, tubular furniture, upholstery, soft furnishings, built-in furniture, built-in cupboard, unit furniture, furniture-designing, furniture-making, cabinet-making, furniture factory, furniture store, cabinet shop

► *411 Layer; 435 Materials; 440 Possessions; 550 Covering; 577 Workshop; 779 Market*

2 chair, wooden chair, bentwood chair, captain's chair, cane chair, box chair, barrel chair, straight chair, Shaker chair, ladder-back chair, wheel-back chair, panel-back chair, rocking chair, Boston rocker, nursing chair, bucket seat, dining chair, upholstered chair, leather chair, armchair, easy chair, Morris chair, Queen-Anne chair, Sheraton chair, Windsor chair, wing chair, club chair, reclining chair, recliner, lounge chair, side chair, carver chair, folding chair, swivel chair, deck chair, highchair, camp chair (*or* seat), stool, milking stool, bar stool, stall, choir stall, bench, settle, couch, studio couch, Grecian couch, sofa, chesterfield, chaise longue, settee, divan, love seat

► *413 Support*

3 chair leg, scroll leg, twist-turned leg, ball-and-claw leg, cabriole leg, sabre leg

4 table, dining table, side table, end table, pier table, drop-leaf table, coffee table, tea table, Pembroke table, gate-leg table, console table (*or* console), bedside table, dressing table, pedestal table, card table, gaming table, worktable, kitchen table, writing table, library table, desk, writing desk, escritoire, secretaire (*or* secretary), davenport, roll-top desk, slant-top (*or* slope-top) desk, knee-hole desk, bureau, reading desk, lectern, board (Lit)

► *17 Literature*

5 cabinet, dresser, Welsh dresser, double (or triple) dresser, mirror cabinet, chest, chest of drawers, cassone, tallboy, highboy, lowboy, bottom drawer, hope chest (US), commode, wardrobe, china cabinet, drinks cabinet, liquor cabinet (US), sideboard, canterbury, cupboard, corner cupboard, press, bookcase, shelves, bookshelf, whatnot

► *410 Container*

6 bed, single bed, double bed, twin bed, king-size bed, queen-size bed, panelled bed, four-poster bed, feather bed, Colonial bed, canopied bed, Empire bed, day bed, chaise longue, convertible sofa, sofa bed, futon, divan, davenport (US), bunk bed, crib, cot, cradle, berth, hammock, foldaway bed, zed (*or* Z) bed, camp bed, truckle (*or* trundle) bed, water bed, bedstead, headboard, footboard

► *413 Support*

7 furniture style, Louis Quatorze, Louis Quinze, Louis Seize, Tudor, Elizabethan, Jacobean, Queen-Anne, Chippendale, Adam Hepplewhite, rococo, Georgian, William and Mary, French provincial, colonial, Early American, Early Federal, Shaker, Empire, Sheraton, Regency, chinoiserie, boulle, Gothic, baroque, Biedermeier, Victorian, (William) Morris, Art Nouveau, Bauhaus, Scandinavian, modern

► *20 Architecture; 724 Style*

8 woodwork, woodworking, woodcraft, timberwork, carpentry, joinery, cabinet-making, carving, woodcarving, wood turning, wood sculpting, wood sculpture, treen (*or* treenware), whittling, wood-burning, pyrography, xylopyrography, woodenware, woodcut, cut, black-line woodcut, white-line woodcut, woodcut illustration, wood block, wood-block printing, relief printing, xylography, lignography, wood engraving, woodprint, xylograph, pyrogravure

► *19 Painting and Sculpture*

9 decorative woodwork, wood inlay, Certosina work, intarsia, horn inlay, mother-of-pearl inlay, tortoiseshell inlay, brass inlay, metal inlay, silver inlay, gold-sheet inlay, true inlay, marquetry, boulle (*or* boullework), floral marquetry, seaweed marquetry, oysterwood marquetry, oyster pieces, brass on shell, *première partie* (Fr), shell on brass, *contre partie* (Fr)

► *542 Decoration*

10 carpenter's term, joint, bevel, mitre joint (*or* mitre), timber joint, housed joint, lap joint, fish joint, scarf joint, flitched joint, tusk tenon joint, birdsmouth joint, tenon, mortise, mortise and tenon, dovetailing, cogging, trimming, framing, joist, trimmed joist, strut, strutting, herringbone strutting, truss, king-post truss, queen-post truss, laths, studs, studwork

► *267 Stickiness; 403 Structure*

11 woodworking tool, lathe, saw, tenon saw, rip saw, crosscut saw, panel saw, plane, smoothing plane, jack plane, drawknife (*or* drawshave), spokeshave, adze, band saw, jigsaw, circular saw, power-driven saw, radial-arm saw, planer (*or* surfacer), jointer, shaper, router, sander, belt sander, disk sander, spindle sander, drum-bed sander, mortiser, hollow-chisel mortiser, chain-saw mortiser, tenoner, single tenoner, double tenoner, boring machine, borer, drill, wood-engraving tool, chisel, router, burin, graver, tint tool, velo, lamina, sandpaper

▶ *438 Tool*

12 wood, timber, lumber, softwood, hardwood, heartwood, sapwood, beam, rafter, joist, board, boarding, plank, planking, deal, red deal, white deal, stick, stave, pole, post, two-by-four, slab, puncheon, slat, splat, lath, lathing, lathwork, timbering, timberwork, sheeting, panelling, panelboard, panelwork, plywood, sheathing, sheathing board, siding, weatherboard, clapboard, hardboard, blockboard, chipboard, shingle, shake, log, cordwood, woodgrain, wood texture, end-grain wood

▶ *79 Trees; 150 Broadness; 404 Texture*

13 carpenter, joiner, cabinet-maker, furniture-maker, coach-builder, wheelwright, turner, sawyer, cooper, carver, woodcarver, woodcraftsman, wood engraver, marquetry worker, *ébéniste* (Fr), *marqueteur* (Ger), woodcutter, form engraver, *Formschneider* (Ger), xylographer, xylopyrographer, pyrographer, chippie (Inf)

▶ *19 Painting and Sculpture; 578 Worker*

ADJECTIVES

14 wooden, lacquered, painted, inlaid, marquetried, parquetried, upholstered, built-in, straight, ladder-back, panel-back, rocking, reclining, folding, drop-leaf, gateleg, roll-top, slant-top (*or* slope-top), knee-hole, panelled, canopied, convertible, foldaway

15 woodcrafted, carved, woodcarved, wood-turned, wood-sculpted, whittled, woodburned, woodcut, blackline, white-line, wood-engraved, wood-blocked, woodprinted, xylographic(al), xylopyrographic(al), pyrographic(al)

16 joined, joining, jointed, mitred, timbered, housed, flitched, mortised, dovetailed, dovetailing, cogged, cogging, trimmed, trimming, framed, framing, joisted, herringbone, beamed, boarded, boarding, two-by-four, slatted

VERBS

17 carpenter, mitre, mortise, dovetail, cog, trim, frame, joist, strut, truss, lathe, saw, cut, crosscut, rip, drill, screw, plane, shape, sand, tenon, bore, chisel, fit a beam, raise a rafter, board, plank, post, slat, lath, timber, sheet, panel, shingle

18 work wood, laminate, veneer, lacquer, paint, inlay, build in, upholster, carve, turn wood, sculpt wood, whittle

24 Ceramics

'Who is the Potter, pray, and who the Pot?' Edward Fitzgerald.

NOUNS

1 ceramics, ceramic ware, ceramic decoration, sgraffito, ornamental ware, pottery, art pottery, whiteware, redware, stoneware, black stoneware (*or* blackware), lustreware, agateware, basaltware, marbled ware, slipware, refractory ware, crackle (*or* crackleware), glazed ware, porous pottery, earthenware, ironstone (*or* ironstone china), unglazed earthenware, coarse pottery, ovenware, terracotta, tin-glazed earthenware, clayware, faience, creamware, blue and white ware, spongeware, crouch ware, translucent ceramics, porcelain, fired porcelain, biscuit (*or* bisque) ware, soft-paste (*or* soft) porcelain, hard-paste (*or* hard) porcelain, salt-glazed porcelain, eggshell porcelain, porcelain enamel, enamelware, tin-enamelled ware, stanniferous ware, china, chinaware, crockery, fine china, bone china, English bone china, American household china, glassware, decorative glass, cameo glass, French art nouveau glass, American art glass, Tiffany glass, brown glass, bottle glass, lead crystal, photochromic glass

▶ *19 Painting and Sculpture; 410 Container; 418 Hardness; 419 Softness; 742 Sign*

2 raw material, potter's clay, clay, primary clay, secondary clay, argil, potter's earth, adobe, porcelain clay, refractory clay, lean clay, fat clay, pipeclay, marl, kaolin, china clay (*or* stone), pegmatite, calcareous clay, slip, engobe, china stone, petuntse (*or* petuntze), ball clay, blue ball clay, feldspar, silica, Cornish stone, flint, flint pebbles, gypsum, bone ash

3 glaze, transparent glaze, opaque white glaze, eggshell glaze, smear glaze, soft glaze, matt (*or* matte *or* mat)

TYPES OF CERAMICS

Albion ware	Doulton ware	Lowestoft ware	Satsuma porcelain
Alcora ware	Dresden china	majolica (*or* maiolica)	Seto ware
Allervale pottery	gombroon	Meissen ware	Sèvres (*or* Sèvres porcelain)
Arita ware	Hirado ware	Mennecy ware	Spode ware
Belleek ware	Hispano–Moresque ware	Mezza–Maiolica (It)	Staffordshire ware
Berlin ware	Hizen porcelain	Ming ware	Steingut (Ger)
Bonnin and Morris porcelain	Imari ware	Nabeshima ware	Sung ware
Castleford ware	istoriato ware	Nanking ware	Talavera ware
Castor ware	Jackfield ware	Neiderviller ware	Tang ware
champlevé (Fr)	jasper (*or* jasper ware)	Old Worcester ware	Ting ware
Chantilly ware	Kakiemon ware	Palissy ware	Toft ware
Chelsea porcelain	Kinkozan ware	Parian porcelain	Tucker porcelain
Ching (*or* Ch'ing) porcelain	Ko–Kutani ware	Pennsylvania Dutch ware	Vincennes ware
cloisonné (*or* cloisonné enamel)	Kubachi ware	Queensware	Wedgwood ware
Coalport	Leeds pottery	Rockingham ware	Worcester porcelain
Crown Derby porcelain	Limoges (*or* Limoges ware)	Rockwood pottery	
Delft (*or* delftware)	Lladro	Royal Doulton porcelain	

glaze, semiopaque glaze, raw glaze, fritted glaze, salt-glaze, coloured glaze, underglaze, underglaze decoration, overglaze, overglaze decoration, hare's fur glaze, crackle, crazing, slip, body slip, transfer printing, decalcomania, hand-painted decorations, gold decoration, gilded decoration

► *542 Decoration*

4 porcelain mark, earthenware mark, Meissen's crossed swords, Sèvres' royal monogram, factory mark, monogram, seal, trademark

5 ceramic process, grinding, plastic mixing, blunging, ball milling, pugging, screening, magnetic separating, filter pressing, de-airing, wedging, throwing, wheel throwing, slip casting, luting, collaring, steaming, smoking, drying chamber, glazing, firing, glaze firing, hard firing, soft firing, biscuit (*or* bisque) firing, ghost firing, raku firing, soaking, fettling, slab method

► *493 Heat*

6 ceramic workshop, potter's workplace, pottery factory, pottery, potter's wheel, wheel, slow wheel, hand-turned wheel, kick wheel, pedal wheel, power wheel, electrical wheel, jigger, blunger, dolly (*or* dolly peg), pug, pug mill, jolly (*or* jolley), kiln, glaze kiln, acid kiln, brick kiln, cement kiln, enamel kiln, muffle kiln, limekiln, bottle kiln, beehive kiln, tunnel kiln, down-drawn kiln, raku kiln, reverberatory, reverberatory kiln, kiln furniture, ribs, oven, stove, furnace, open hearth, converter, smelter, ore roaster, pyrometer, pyrometric cone, Seger cone, mixing tank, filter press, filter cloth

► *577 Workshop*

7 potter, ceramist (*or* ceramicist), turner, firer, glazer, pyroglazer, china decorator, china painter, tile painter, majolica painter, enamellist (*or* enameller)

8 ceramic object, urn, vase, bowl, jar, amphora, jug, toby jug, mug, vessel, ampulla, pipkin, cruse, crock, pot, pitcher, ewer, plate, cup, saucer, figurine, clock case, tile, decorative tile, encaustic tile, inlaid tile, tiling, mosaic, tessera

► *410 Container*

9 industrial ceramics, porcelain insulation, electrical porcelain, brick, sun-dried brick, adobe, firebrick, refractory brick, mud brick, cement, natural cement, Portland cement, hydrolic cement, concrete, terracotta, drain tile, hollow tile, architectural tile, quarry tile, roofing tile, pantile, wall tile, floor tile, china plumbing ware, chemical porcelain, glass, crystallized glass, devitrified glass, structural glass, window glass, plate glass, safety glass, laminated glass, optical glass, photosensitive glass, glass fibre, foam glass, light bulb, fluorescent tube, lens, television tube, electronic tube

► *435 Materials; 522 Light*

ADJECTIVES

10 ceramic, enamelled, tin-enamelled, enamelling, stanniferous, ornamental, unglazed, glazed, tin-glazed, salt-glazed, underglazed, underglazing, overglazed, overglazing, glazing, translucent, fired, soft-paste, soft, hard-paste, hard, fine, encaustic, refractory, transparent, opaque, mat (*or* matte *or* matt), semiopaque, hand-painted, gilded, blunged, blunging, pugging, screened, screening, hand-turned, jolly (*or* jolley), wedged, thrown, down-drawn, reverberatory, pyrometric(al), industrial, bricking, sun-dried, crystallized, devitrified, optical, photosensitive

VERBS

11 make ceramics, pot, grind, mix, blunge, pug, screen, filter, de-air, lute, shape, mould clay, mould, cast, wedge, throw, throw a pot, turn a pot, turn, hand-turn, jigger, jolly (*or* jolley) a cup, roll a slab, dry, fire, bake, glaze, pyroglaze, glaze-fire, hard-fire, soft-fire, ghost-fire, draw a kiln, underglaze, overglaze, tin-glaze, fettle, enamel, tin-enamel, decorate china, paint china, hand-paint, decorate pottery, paint tile, paint majolica, gild, transfer a decal, mark, monogram, seal, tile, insulate, brick, cement, concrete, glass, devitrify, crystallize, laminate

ADVERBS

12 ornamentally, translucently, encaustically, refractorily, transparently, opaquely, semiopaquely, by hand, pyrometrically, industrially, optically

25 Cookery

Kissing don't last: cookery do! George Meredith.

NOUNS

1 cookery, cooking, microwave cooking, pressure cooking, baking, food preparation, food processing, home economics, domestic science, style of cooking, gastronomy, cuisine, haute cuisine, *nouvelle cuisine* (Fr), lean cuisine, catering, provisioning, recipe, cookbook (US), cookery book

► *436 Provisions; 581 Refreshment*

2 cook, chef, sous chef, commis chef, apprentice chef, cuisinier, cordon bleu chef, fast-food chef, short-order cook (US), baker, caterer, barbecue cook, ranch-house cook (US), chuck-wagon cook (US), cookie (US), cook's helper

3 kitchen, cookhouse, bakehouse, bakery, galley, pantry, larder, buttery, still room, cellar

4 kitchen container, bread bin, cake tin, biscuit barrel, meat safe, meat compartment, cold store, larder, larder-fridge, refrigerator, freezer, deepfreeze, icebox (US), fridge (Inf)

► *410 Container; 439 Store*

5 cooker, stove, hob, hotplate, grill, griddle, kitchen range, (conventional) oven, fan oven, kettle, toaster, waffle iron (US), sandwich-maker, barbecue, spit, microwave, Dutch oven, gas ring, Aga™

6 kitchen equipment, *batterie de cuisine* (Fr), cooking utensil, pan, saucepan, frying pan, skillet (US), frier, deep frier, roasting pan, omelette pan, crêpe pan, cooking pot, stew pan, casserole, cocotte, wok, tajine, pressure cooker, ovenproof dish, gratin dish, pie plate, flan dish, flan ring, cake tin, baking sheet, mould, soufflé dish, preserving pan, skimmer, steamer, poacher, mixing bowl, pudding basin, measuring jug, scales, rolling pin, pastry bag, forcing bag (US), pastry cutter, flour dredger, chopping board, larding needle, trussing needle, vegetable peeler, grater, colander, whisk, beater, hand beater, rotary beater, food mixer, electric mixer, food processor, blender, liquidizer, mincer, grinder (US), coffee grinder, kilner jar, vegetable mill, spatula, wooden spoon, ladle,

CHEESES

Beaufort	Dorset Vinney	mozarella
Bel Paese	Double Gloucester	Neufchâtel
blue	Dunlop	New York
blue cheese	Edam	Oka
Blue Stilton	Emmental (*or* Emmentaler)	Oxfordshire
blue Vinney	Fontainebleu	Parmesan
Boursin™	fromage frais	Port Salut
Brie	Gloucester	pot cheese
Brillat Savarin	Gorgonzola	processed cheese
Buxton blue	Gouda	Red Leicester
Caerphilly	Grana	Red Windsor
Camembert	grated cheese	Reggiano
Cheddar	Gruyère	Roquefort
Cheshire	Lancashire	Sage Derby
chèvre	Leicester	Stilton
Colby	Limburger	Tilamook
cottage cheese	Livarot	vegetarian cheese
cream cheese	Lymeswold	Vermont Sage
curd cheese	Mascarpone	Vignotte
Danish Blue	Monterey	Wensleydale
Derby	Monterey Jack	White Stilton
Dolcelatte		Windsor

can (*or* tin) opener, lemon squeezer, juicer, greaseproof paper, waxed paper, aluminium foil, self-adhesive film, Clingfilm™, plastic wrap, oven gloves

7 **basic ingredient**, flour, plain flour, self-raising flour, meal, wheatmeal, wholemeal, cornmeal, cornflour, yeast, leaven, baking powder, fat, butter, margarine, shortening, lard, ghee, suet, grease, dripping, oil, olive oil, vegetable oil, sunflower oil, eggs, sugar, granulated sugar, caster sugar, icing sugar, brown sugar, demerara sugar, salt, cooking salt, table salt, sea salt, pepper, seasoning, vinegar, malt vinegar, wine vinegar, aspic, gelatine, bicarbonate of soda, balsam, herb, spice

▶ *498 Sweetness*

8 **cooking technique**, boiling, parboiling, simmering, poaching, steaming, bain marie, coddling, scrambling, casseroling, baking, roasting, oven-roasting, spit-roasting, pot-roasting, broiling, charbroiling, grilling, barbecuing, toasting, sautéeing, frying, deep frying, stir-frying, curing, smoking, pickling

9 **dish**, course, hors d'oeuvres, savouries, first course, starter, soup, fish course, entrée, remove, main course, side-dish, salad, cheese, fruit, entremets, dessert, sweet, pudding, pud (Inf), afters (Inf), speciality, speciality of the house, *spécialité de la maison* (Fr), special, *pièce de résistance* (Fr), culinary masterpiece, dish fit for a king (*or* queen), dish of the day, *plat du jour* (Fr), soup of the day

10 **snack**, nibbles, crisps, potato chips (US), nuts, peanuts, salted nuts, cheese straws, pretzels, twiglets™, olives

11 **sandwich**, club sandwich, double-decker, finger sandwich, open sandwich, roast-beef sandwich, barbecue sandwich (US), bacon, lettuce, and tomato sandwich (BLT) (US), pastrami sandwich (US), cheese (and pickle) sandwich, ham sandwich, ham and cheese sandwich, turkey sandwich, chicken sandwich, salmon sandwich, tuna sandwich, cucumber sandwich, jam sandwich, peanut butter and jelly sandwich (US), Dagwood sandwich (US), French dip sandwich (US), hero (US), hoagie (US), poor-boy (US), po-boy (US), muffuletta (US), oyster loaf (US), shrimp loaf (US), grinder (US), hamburger, cheeseburger, quarter-pounder, Big Mac™, hot dog, Reuben sandwich (US), toasted sandwich, butty (Inf), sarnie (Inf)

12 **hors d'oeuvre**, appetizer, starter, antipasto, smorgasbord, prawn cocktail, cold cuts, pâté, taramasalata, hummus, raitha, mezze, vol-au-vent, canapé, blini, samosa, pakora

13 **soup**, cream soup, clear soup, broth, Scotch broth, *potage* (Fr), consommé, stock, bouillon, julienne, bisque, lobster bisque, chowder (US), clam chowder, purée, vichysoisse, cock-a-leekie, mulligatawny, minestrone, borscht, gazpacho, fish soup, bouillabaisse, gumbo (US), onion soup, mushroom soup, celery soup, asparagus soup, tomato soup, chicken soup, vegetable soup, oxtail soup, bird's-nest soup

14 **salad**, side salad, tossed salad, green salad, mixed salad, chef's salad (US), potato salad, Russian salad, Waldorf salad (US), Caesar salad, salad niçoise, coleslaw, macedoine

15 **sauce**, tomato sauce, tomato ketchup, catsup, brown sauce, Worcester sauce, soy sauce, Tabasco sauce, tartare sauce, cranberry sauce, apple sauce, mint sauce, horseradish sauce, mayonnaise, salad cream, salad dressing, French dressing, aïoli, vinaigrette, Thousand Island dressing, dip, cheese dip, garlic dip, fondue, bolognese sauce, milanese sauce, barbecue sauce, béarnaise sauce, bordelaise sauce, bourguignonne, sauce espagnole, pesto, sauce suprême, hollandaise sauce, béchamel sauce, white sauce, cheese sauce, onion sauce, bread sauce, roux, velouté, demi-glace, chaudfroid, gravy

16 **fish dish**, fresh fish, fried fish, boiled fish, poached fish, fishcake, fish finger, fish pie, fish ball, fish stick, fish and chips, quenelle, gefilte fish, kedgeree, soft roe, hard roe, caviar, Beluga caviar, black caviar, red caviar, lumpfish caviar, taramasalata, jellied eel, smoked fish, smoked haddock, finnan haddock (*or* haddie), smoked mackerel, smoked salmon, smoked trout, kippered fish, kippered herring, kipper, smoky, Arbroath smokey, bloater, cured fish, lox, gravadlax (*or* gravlax), pickled herring, rollmop

17 **freshwater fish**, game fish, salmon, Atlantic salmon, Pacific salmon, trout, brown trout, rainbow trout, sea trout, salmon trout, grayling, coarse fish, eel, carp, perch, pike, bass, catfish

▶ *74 Fishes*

18 **sea fish**, saltwater fish, flatfish, dab, flounder, plaice, lemon sole, Dover sole, coalfish, coley, dogfish, rock salmon , whiting, cod, skate, hake, halibut, haddock (*or* haddie), turbot, brill, mullet, mackerel, herring, sprat, whitebait, sardine, bristling, sild, pilchard, tuna, kingfish, swordfish, hoki, Bombay duck, octopus, squid, calamari

▶ *74 Fishes*

19 **shellfish**, seafood, oyster, bluepoint, scallop, cockle, mussel, winkle, whelk, shrimp, prawn, kingprawn, Dublin bay prawn, crab, lobster, crayfish, crawfish (US), crawdad (US), *écrevisse* (Fr), sping lobster, *langouste* (Fr), snail, *escargot* (Fr)

▶ *74 Fishes*

20 **meat**, flesh, red meat, white meat, beef, pork, mutton, lamb, veal, goat, poultry, chicken, turkey, goose, duck,

game, rabbit, hare, venison, pheasant, grouse, partridge, pigeon, squab, woodcock, snipe, plover, quail, minced meat, mince, ground meat, meatballs, faggots, rissoles, hamburger, beefburger

21 meat substitute, soya, TVP (textured vegetable protein), Quorn™, tofu, bean curd, nut protein

22 beef (British): neck, chuck, blade, fore rib, thick rib, thin rib, rolled ribs, T-bone, sirloin, rump, silverside, topside, leg, flank, brisket, shin, filet steak, undercut steak

23 beef (US): chuck, rib, back rib, short loin, Porterhouse steak, tenderloin, sirloin, round, boneless rump roast, round steak, hind shank, short plate, brisket, fore shank

24 pork (British): spare rib, blade, loin, leg fillet, hock, belly, hand, trotter

25 pork (US): blade shoulder, loin, tenderloin, leg, side, spare rib, shoulder, hock

26 lamb (British): scrag end, middle neck, shoulder, best end of neck, loin, chump, chump chops, leg, breast

27 lamb (US): shoulder, neck slice, rib, loin, loin chop, leg, hind shank, breast, riblets, fore shank

28 poultry, white meat, dark meat, breast, leg, drumstick, wing, parson's nose, wishbone

29 sausage, sausagemeat, pork sausage, beef sausage, banger (Inf), chipolata, cocktail sausage, saveloy, wiener (US), *Wienerwurst* (Ger), wienie (US inf), weenie (US inf), Cumberland sausage, herb sausage, frankfurter, Vienna sausage, liver sausage, garlic sausage, salami, bologna sausage, polony, boloney, *Knackwurst* (*or Knockwurst*) (Ger), *Bratwurst* (Ger), black pudding, blood sausage, blood pudding, haggis, pâté, *pâté de foie gras* (Fr)

30 bacon, smoked bacon, unsmoked bacon, green bacon, streaky bacon, back bacon, middle cut, belly pork, sowbelly (US), rasher, side of bacon, flitch, bacon joint, gammon, salt pork, Danish bacon, Canadian bacon, ham, boiled ham

31 offal, variety meat, liver, lamb's liver, calf's liver, chicken liver, kidney, steak and kidney, heart, tongue, ox tongue, ox cheek, pig's head, Bath chap, calf's head, brains, brawn, chitterlings, pig's fry, sweetbread, melts, stomach sweetbread, neck sweetbread, pig's feet, pig's knuckles, trotters, cowheel, tripe, thick seam, cow's udder, elder (Dial), oxtail

32 meat dish, roast, pot roast, grill, mixed grill, pie, pasty, hash, fricassée, rissole, casserole, stew, goulash, haggis

33 vegetable, root vegetable, tuber, green vegetable, greens, spring greens, salad vegetable, pulse, legume, brassica, mushroom, field mushroom, horse mushroom, button mushroom, puffball mushroom, Chinese mushroom, *champignon* (Fr), cep, chanterelle, morel, blewit, boletus, horn of plenty, truffle, earthnut, seaweed, laver, laver bread, samphire, chick pea

► *77 Plants; 83 Fungi*

34 vegetarian dish, vegetable curry, vegetable chilli, vegetable casserole, vegetable flan, nut cutlet, nut roast, cauliflower cheese, macaroni cheese, omelette, aubergine roll, aubergine and tomato pie, stuffed marrow (*or* peppers *or* vine leaves), fondue, pease pudding, chilladas, hummus

► *557 Eating*

35 dessert, sweet, pudding, cake, pie, jelly, blancmange, custard, floating island (US), ice cream, dairy ice cream, sorbet, granita, water ice, knickerbocker glory, Mississippi mud pie, marquise, crême caramel, yoghurt, fool, mousse, soufflé, sundae, banana split, peach melba, trifle, rice pudding, semolina, tapioca, bread-and-butter pudding, steamed pudding, suet pudding, Christmas pudding, plum pudding, summer pudding, brown betty (US), betty (US), roly-poly, spotted dick, Black Forest gateau, pavlova, fruit flan, fruit cup (US), crumble, charlotte, charlotte russe, stewed fruit, compote, fruit salad, fresh fruit, cheese and biscuits, cheese board

► *80 Fruits; 498 Sweetness*

36 cake, gateau, birthday cake, wedding cake, Christmas cake, yule log, chocolate cake, chocolate gateau, devil's food cake, German chocolate cake (US), coffee cake, fudge cake, brownies (US), angel cake, sponge cake, maids of honour, madeleine, Swiss roll, upside-down cake (US), carrot cake, fruitcake, spice cake, seed cake, lardy cake, Dundee cake, gingerbread, parkin, Madeira cake, cupcake (US), cheesecake, torte, apple pie, black bottom (US), lemon meringue pie, Boston cream pie (US), coconut pie (US), pumpkin pie (US), sweet potato pie (US), pecan pie (US), chess pie (US), Bakewell tart, blackberry cobbler (US), peach cobbler (US), turnover, flan, tart, jam tart, mince pie, eclair, macaroon, fritter, apple fritter, Danish pastry, Danish, Eccles cake, sweet roll (US), cinnamon roll (US), Chelsea bun, Bath bun, doughnut, jam doughnut, doughnut hole (US), sinker (US inf)

37 pastry, shortcrust pastry, flaky pastry, puff pastry, rough puff pastry, suet crust pastry, hot-water crust pastry, choux pastry, fleur pastry, Genoese pastry, cheese pastry, filo pastry

38 bread, dough, crust, crumb, sliced bread, white bread, enriched bread, soda bread, sourdough bread (US), brown bread, wholemeal bread, malt bread, granary bread, black bread, potato bread, Boston brown bread (US), rye bread, pumpernickel, corn bread (US), corn

TYPES OF PASTA

agnolotti	fettuccine	penne rigate
annellini	fidelini	pennette rigate
bavette	filini	pipette
bigoli	fusilli	ravioli
bucatini	gramigna	rigatoni
cannelloni	lasagne (*or* lasagna)	risoni
capelli		rotelle
capellini	lasagnette	sedani
cappelletti	linguini	sedanini
chifferi	lumache	spaghetti
chifferoni	macaroni (*or* maccheroni)	stelline
conchiglie		tagliatelle
conchigliette	maccheroncini	tempesta
cravattine	manicotti	tortelli
ditali	mezza	tortellini
ditalini	noodles	tortiglioni
ditalini rigati	orecchiette	trenette
ditaloni	paglia e fieno	tuffoli
eliche	pappardelle	vermicelli
farfalle	penne	vermicellini
farfalline	penne lisce	zita

pone (US), hush puppies (US), spoon bread (US), fried bread, beer bread, banana-nut bread, nut bread, raisin bread, pumpkin bread (US), pitta bread, poppadom, puri, nan, chapatti, toast, toastie (Inf), cinnamon toast, Melba toast, French toast, rusk, crouton

39 **loaf**, pan loaf, pan, cottage loaf, cob, tin, split tin, farmhouse, bloomer, plait, French bread, baguette, French stick, bread stick, roll, breakfast roll, bridge roll, bap, barm cake, pikelet, bagel, croissant, brioche, bun, currant bun, teacake, English muffin (US), crumpet, muffin, popover (US), blueberry muffin (US), biscuit (US), buttermilk biscuit (US), sourdough biscuit (US), soda biscuit (US), scone, drop scone, pancake, battercake (US), flapjack (US), buttermilk pancake (US), blueberry pancake (US), *crêpe* (Fr), waffle, wafer, biscuit, cookie (US), digestive biscuit, shortbread, flapjack, farl, cracker, soda cracker (US), creamcracker, crispbread, water biscuit, oatcake, bannock (Scot)

40 **breakfast cereal**, cornflakes, bran flakes, bran, wheat germ, muesli, oatmeal, porridge, gruel, skilly, brewis (Dial), brose (Scot), grits (US), mush (US), polenta

41 **sweet**, sweetmeat, bonbon, comfit, confectionary, toffee, taffy, boiled sweet, barley sugar, butterscotch, caramel, chocolate, chocolate bar, fondant, fudge, gobstopper, gum, gumdrop, jelly bean, jujube, liquorice, liquorice allsort, lollipop, marshmallow, marzipan, peppermint, praline, crystallized fruit, toffee apple, sweetie (Inf)

► *498 Sweetness*

42 **preserve**, jam, jelly, marmalade, conserve, bottled fruit, pickle, chutney, dried fruit, currant, raisin, sultana, prune

► *80 Fruits*

43 **US dish**, New England clam chowder, Waldorf salad, chef's salad, porterhouse steak, barbecued spare ribs, Maine lobster, clam chowder, oysters Rockefeller, Southern fried chicken, jambalaya, stuffed Idaho potato, succotash, corn bread, grits, red beans with rice, pancakes and maple syrup, soul food, ham-bone soup, cow-pea soup, crackling biscuit, fried catfish, scrambled pork brains, blackplate, Kentucky Fried Chicken™, eggs Benedict

44 **British dish**, cock-a-leekie, English breakfast, Yorkshire pudding, Lancashire hotpot, Welsh rarebit (*or* rabbit), Irish stew, porridge, Scotch broth, fish and chips, Dover sole, smoked salmon, kippers, eel pie and mash, bangers and mash, roast beef, mutton, Aylesbury duck, haggis, ploughman's lunch, mixed grill, toad-in-the-hole, bubble and squeak, devilled kidneys, shepherd's pie, cottage pie

45 **French dish**, onion soup, quiche, quiche Lorraine, soufflé, pâté, pressed duck, chateaubriand, steak tartare, fondue, escargots, frogs legs, petits pois, ratatouille, cassoulet, crêpes suzette, rillettes, coq au vin, steak au poivre, boeuf bourgignon, lobster thermidor

46 **German dish**, Gemusesuppe, Wiener Schnitzel, Rehschnitzel, Sauerbraten, Sauerkraut, Apfelstrudel, Pfannkuchen, Bratwurst, Rotkohl, Kalbshaxe, Gebratene Huhnerleber

47 **Italian dish**, minestrone, pasta, antipasto, pizza, risotto, zabaglione, tiramisu

48 **Chinese dish**, egg drop soup, egg roll, chow mein, chop suey, won ton, dim sum, sweet and sour pork, beef congee, lemon chicken, Peking duck, stir-fry, egg fu yung, shrimp balls, fried noodles, fried rice, spring roll

49 **Indian dish**, pakora, samosa, bhaji, dhal, raitha, biryani, curry, tikka, tandoori, chicken tikka masala, vindaloo, madras, korma, malaya, mughlai, butter chicken, kashmiri, dansak, rogan josh, bhuna, pathia, dopiaza, masala dosa, spiced green bananas, rice pancake, poppadom, nan bread, keema nan, chapatti, paratha, bombay mix, puri, pilau rice, kulfi, lassi

50 **Central American dish**, black bean soup, taco, tostada, tortilla, tamale, burrito, empanada, enchilada, nacho, guacamole, Montezeuma pie, olla podrida, mole poblano, chilli con carne, monteria

51 **West Indian dish**, asapao, calalou, chiquetaille, féroce, macadam, pasteles, piononos, stoba

52 **Greek dish**, meze, kefta, moussaka, dolmades, calamari, hummus, tzatziki, taramasalata, spinakoturikopita, souvlaki, baklava, stuffed vine leaves, Greek salad

53 **African dish**, aitiou, canari, cosidou, dou louf, foutou, gari, nkui, pepe supi, placali, putu, yassa, zegeni

54 **other dishes**, paella (Spanish), tapas (Spanish), Hungarian goulash, kebabs (Turkish), shish kebab, donner kebab, balti (Pakistani), sushi (Japanese), musi-yaki (Japanese), couscous (Algerian), halvah (Middle East and Asian)

VERBS

55 **cook**, prepare a meal, put in the oven, bake, put in the microwave (oven), microwave, pressure-cook, heat, heat up, warm through, reheat, roast, spit-roast, pot-roast, brown, toast, grill, charcoal-grill, barbecue, spatchcock, griddle, devil, curry, fry, deep-fry, shallow-fry, sauté, stir-fry, fry sunny side up, fry over lightly (US), double-fry, scramble, coddle, boil, parboil, blanch, scald, seethe, simmer, steam, poach, casserole, stew, braise, baste, lard, bard, flip, whip, whisk, beat, blend, knead, mix, fold in, liquidize, stir, draw, gut, bone, fillet, stuff, dress, garnish, cut, chop, dice, shred, grind, mince, grate, sauce, flavour, spice, season, whip something up (Inf), throw something together (Inf)

► *372 Separation; 412 Mixture*

ADJECTIVES

56 **culinary**, gastronomic, epicurean, mensal, prandial, preprandial, postprandial, after-dinner, mealtime, dressed, oven-ready, prepared, ready-to-cook, made-up, ready-to-serve, cooked, done, well-done, overcooked, burnt, al dente, underdone, undercooked, red, rare, raw, roasted, browned, toasted, grilled, barbecued, devilled, curried, fried, deep-fried, sautéed, stir-fried, scrambled, coddled, boiled, steamed, poached, stewed, braised, beaten, stuffed, chopped, ground, minced, au gratin, au naturel, à la mode, à la carte, table d'hôte

ADVERBS

57 **culinarily**, gastronomically, palatably, succulently, nutritiously, nutritionally

INTERJECTIONS

58 **grub's on!**, grub's up!, come and get it!, chow down!, soup's on!, *bon appetit!*(Fr)

Science and Technology

26 Measurement

To measure is to know. Ernst von Siemens.

NOUNS

1 **measurement**, mensuration, measure, measuring, admeasurement, metage, quantification, quantitation, gauging, calibration, reading, readout, calculation, computation, reckoning, metrology, assessment, valuation, rating, evaluation, appraisal, appraisement, estimation, estimate, approximation, rough measure, determination, survey, surveying, triangulation, geodesy, geodetics, topography, cartography, oceanography

► *141 Space; 148 Length; 154 Height; 203 Quantity; 210 Calculation*

2 **micrometry**, telemetry, tacheometry, tachymetry, odometry, cyclometry, photogrammetry, dilatometry, planimetry, goniometry, clinometry, altimetry, hypsometry, bathometry, bathymetry, stereometry, volumetry, densimetry, hydrometry, viscometry, plastometry, acidimetry, alkalimetry, stoichiometry, oxidimetry, iodometry, saccharimetry, salinometry, salimetry, atmometry, aerometry, hygrometry, colorimetry, thermometry, tasimetry, calorimetry, cryometry, pyrometry, photometry, spectrophotometry, spectrometry, sensitometry, refractometry, fluorometry, polarimetry, bolometry, actinometry, dosimetry, radiometry, anemometry, barometry, piezometry, manometry, dynamometry, chronometry, tachometry, magnetometry, coulometry, galvanometry, potentiometry, electrometry, interferometry, astrometry, heliometry, biometry, biometrics, zoometry, anthropometry, cephalometry, craniometry, optometry, spirometry, pneumatometry, rheometry, psychometry, dolorimetry, algometry, audiometry, tonometry

3 **measurability**, mensurability, quantifiability, determinability

4 **size**, magnitude, height, altitude, depth, length, distance, range, scope, breadth, width, volume, capacity, weight, quantity, amount, dosage, degree, extent, value, coordinates, ordinate, abscissa, latitude, longitude, azimuth, right ascension, declination

► *158 Size*

5 **measuring system**, metric system, imperial system, Système International d'Unités (SI), apothecaries' measure, apothecaries' weight, troy weight, avoirdupois weight

6 **measuring instrument**, measuring rod, yardstick, foot rule, feeler gauge, line, plumb line, lead, chain, Gunter's chain, rule, ruler, tape measure, steel rule, scale, graduated scale, calibrated scale, vernier, dividers, callipers, set square, try square, T-square, protractor, quadrant, sextant, octant, astrolabe, log, echo sounder, dipstick, watermark, water line, tidemark, high-water mark, Plimsoll line, load line, milestone

7 **standard**, norm, yardstick, touchstone, benchmark, criterion, rule of thumb, canon, test, check, type, model, pattern, prototype, weighing machine, weighbridge, scales, balance

8 **meter**, gauge, dial gauge, indicator, chart recorder, micrometer, micrometer gauge, micrometer calliper, telemeter, tellurometer, tacheometer, tachymeter,

SI UNITS

Base and Supplementary Units
metre (m, length)
kilogram (kg, mass)
second (s, time)
ampere (A, electric current)
kelvin (K, thermodynamic temperature)
candela (cd, luminous intensity)
mole (mol, amount of substance)
radian (rad, plane angle)
steradian (sr, solid angle)

Derived Units
hertz (Hz, frequency)
joule (J, energy)
newton (N, force)
watt (W, power)
pascal (Pa, pressure)
coulomb (C, electric charge)
volt (V, electric potential difference)
ohm (W, electric resistance)
siemens (S, electric conductance)
farad (F, electric capacitance)
weber (Wb, magnetic flux)
henry (H, inductance)
tesla (T, magnetic flux density *or* magnetic induction)
lumen (lm, luminous flux)
lux (lx, illuminance)
gray (Gy, absorbed dose)
becquerel (Bq, activity)
sievert (Sv, dose equivalent)

Decimal Prefixes
deci (d, 10^{-1})
centi (c, 10^{-2})
milli (m, 10^{-3})
micro (m, 10^{-6})
nano (n, 10^{-9})
pico (p, 10^{-12})
femto (f, 10^{-15})
atto (a, 10^{-18})
deca (da, 10)
hecto (h, 10^{2})
kilo (k, 10^{3})
mega (M, 10^{6})
giga (G, 10^{9})
tera (T, 10^{12})
peta (P, 10^{15})
exa (E, 10^{18})

theodolite, alidade, pedometer, mileometer, odometer, cyclometer, dilatometer, planimeter, goniometer, clinometer, altimeter, hypsometer, bathometer, volumeter, densimeter, densitometer, hydrometer, viscometer, plastometer, acidimeter, alkalimeter, nitrometer, saccharimeter, saccharometer, salinometer, salimeter, alcoholometer, vaporimeter, atmometer, evaporimeter, tensimeter, tensiometer, aerometer, hygrometer, colorimeter, tintometer, thermometer, tasimeter, calorimeter, cryometer, pyrometer, photometer, spectrophotometer, spectrometer, sensitometer, refractometer, fluorometer, polarimeter, solarimeter, pyranometer, bolometer, thermopile, actinometer, dosimeter, Geiger counter, radiometer, anemometer, wind gauge, barometer, pressure gauge, thermobarometer, piezometer, manometer, dynamometer, seismometer, chronometer, tachometer, speedometer, rev counter, accelerometer, decelerometer, magnetometer, variometer, voltmeter, ammeter, voltammeter, voltameter, coulometer, galvanometer, potentiometer, electrometer, interferometer, heliometer, cephalometer, craniometer, optometer, spirometer, pneumatometer, rheometer, pulsimeter, algometer, audiometer, tonometer, phonometer, water meter, gas meter, electricity meter

9 **measurer**, researcher, scientist, gauger, assessor, valuer, valuator, appraiser, estimator, surveyor, geodesist, topographer, cartographer, oceanographer, timekeeper, quantifier, actuary

▶ *27 Mathematics*

VERBS

10 **measure**, measure up, take the measurements of, admeasure, quantify, meter, gauge, calibrate, grade, graduate, calculate, compute, count, reckon, assess, value, cost, rate, evaluate, appraise, estimate, determine, survey, triangulate, plumb, sound, fathom, probe, assay, weigh, time, size up, measure off, measure out, mark off, pace off

11 **measure out**, mete out, weigh out, dole out, share, share out, apportion, allot

ADJECTIVES

12 **metrical**, metric, imperial, avoirdupois, SI, linear, cubic, measuring, mensural, mensurational, mensurative, quantitative, metrological, geodetic, topographic, cartographic, oceanographic

13 **measured**, admeasured, quantified, metered, gauged, calibrated, graduated, reckoned, assessed, valued, rated, estimated, determined, surveyed, triangulated, plotted, mapped

14 **measurable**, mensurable, quantifiable, meterable, gaugeable, calculable, computable, assessable, appraisable, estimable, determinable, perceptible, fathomable

15 **deliberate**, unhurried, leisurely, slow, studied, planned, calculated

16 **micrometric**, telemetric, tacheometric, tachymetric, photogrammetric, dilatometric, planimetric, goniometric, clinometric, altimetric, hypsometric, bathometric, bathymetric, stereometric, volumetric, densimetric, densitometric, hydrometric, viscometric, plastometric, acidimetric, alkalimetric, stoichiometric, oxidimetric, iodometric, nitrometric, salinometric, salimetric, aerometric, hygrometric, colorimetric, thermometric, tasimetric, calorimetric, pyrometric, photometric, spectrophotometric, spectrometric, refractometric, fluorometric, polarimetric, bolometric, actinometric, dosimetric, radiometric, anemometric, barometric, piezometric, manometric, dynamometric, chronometric, tachometric, magnetometric, voltametric, coulometric, galvanometric, electrometric, interferometric, astrometric, heliometric, biometric, zoometric, anthropometric, cephalometric,

SCIENTIFIC AND TECHNICAL UNITS

abampere
abcoulomb
abfarad
abhenry
abohm
abvolt
abwatt
ampere
ampere–hour
ampere–turn
amu
angstrom
astronomical unit
atmosphere
atomic mass
atomic mass unit
barn
barye
baud
becquerel
bel
bit
Board of Trade Unit
British thermal unit
bucket
byte
calorie (*or* calory)
Calorie
candela
candle
centimetre–gram–second
centimetre–gram–second
centimorgan
centner
chronon
circular mil
coulomb
curie
cusec (flow rate)
cycle
dalton
daraf
darcy
decibel
degree–day
dioptre (*or* diopter)
dyne
epoch
erg
farad
faraday
fathom
fermi
foot–candle
foot–lambert
foot–pound
foot–poundal
foot–ton
fresnel
gal
gallon
gamma
gauge (*or* gage)
gauss
gigahertz
gilbert
grade
gram (*or* gramme)
gram atom (*or* gram–atomic weight)
gram calorie
gram molecule (*or* gram–molecular weight)
grav
gray
henry
hertz
international candle
jansky
joule
kelvin
kilocycle
kilogram (*or* kilogramme)
kilogram calorie
kiloton
kilowatt–hour
light year
line
lumen
Mach number
magneton (*or* Bohr magneton)
maxwell
measurement ton
megaton
metre
mho
micrometre
micromicron
micron
mil
millibar
millimicron
mmHg
mole
neper
nit
oersted
ohm
okta (*or* octa)
parsec
pascal
perceived noise decibel
phon
phot
poise
poundal
rad
radian
roentgen (*or* röntgen)
rutherford
sabin
shed
siemens
sievert
slug
small calorie
standard candle
steradian
stilb
stokes (*or* stoke)
tesla
therm
torr
unit pole
var
volt
volt–ampere
watt–hour
weber
x–unit

GENERAL UNITS

acre
acre–foot
acre–inch
air mile
are
bar
barleycorn
barrel
board foot
board rule
bushel
butt (US)
cable
carat
cental
centiare (*or* centare)
chain
column inch
cord (wood)
cup
degree
denier
DIN (photography)
em (printing)
en (printing)
fathom
firkin
fluid dram
fluid ounce
foot
freight ton
furlong
gallon
gallonage
geographical mile
gill
grain
gross ton
Gunter's chain
hank (cloth)
hogshead
Hoppus foot (wood)
horsepower
horsepower–hour
hundredweight (*or* long hundredweight)
inch
international nautical mile
kilderkin
kilo
kip
knot
last (weight *or* capacity)
lea (length of yarn)
league
link (length)
man–hour
metric ton
mile (*or* statute mile)
milline (advertising)
minim
minute
nail (length of cloth)
nautical mile
net ton
noggin
ounce
peck (dry measure)
pennyweight
perch
pica (printing)
pint
pipe
point (printing)
point (jewellery, weight)
pole
pound
puncheon
quart
quarter
quartern
quintal
rod (length, area)
rood
scruple
sea mile
second
short hundredweight
short ton
shot (length)
span (length)
stere (volume of timber)
stone
surveyor's chain
tog (insulation)
ton
tonne
yard

Some Foreign Units

archine (Russia, length)
ardeb (Middle East, dry measure)
arpent (former French, length *or* area)
arroba (Spain, weight, volume)
congius (ancient Rome, liquid)
drachma (ancient Greece, weight)
lepton (Greek)
li (Chinese, length)
libra (ancient Rome, weight)
maund (Asia, weight)
mina (Asia Minor, weight)
morgen (South Africa, area)
morgen (formerly Prussia, area)
mutchkin (Scottish, liquids)
obolus (Greek, weight)
oka *or* oke (Turkey, liquids)
Olympiad (ancient Greece, time)
omer (ancient Hebrew, dry measure)
parasang (Persia, distance)
picul (Far East, weight)
pood (Russia, weight)
reed (ancient Hebrew, length)
Roman mile
Roman pace
rotl (Muslim countries, weight)
ser *or* seer (India, weight)
Swedish mile
tael (Far East, weight)
talent (ancient world, weight)
tical (Thailand, weight)
tola (India, weight)
vara (Spain, length)
verst (Russia, length)

craniometric, optometric, spirometric, rheometric, psychometric, audiometric, tonometric, phonometric

ADVERBS

17 **measurably**, with precise measurements, perceptibly, noticeably, metrically, quantitatively, metrologically, geodetically, topographically, cartographically, oceanographically

27 Mathematics

As far as the laws of mathematics refer to reality, they are not certain, and as far as they are certain, they do not refer to reality. Albert Einstein.

Let no one ignorant of mathematics enter here. Plato.

NOUNS

1 **mathematics**, maths (Inf), math (US inf), pure mathematics, classical mathematics, new mathematics, higher mathematics, branch, field, study, theory, arithmetic, algebra, calculus, geometry, trigonometry, analysis, numerical analysis, systems analysis, statistics, mathematical logic (*or* symbolic logic), metamathematics, numeracy, calculation, computation, reckoning, numbers, figures, sums

2 **mathematician**, arithmetician, algebraist, geometrician (*or* geometer), numerical analyst, systems analyst, statistician

3 **applied mathematics**, mathematical biology, mathematical biophysics, mathematical computing, mathematical ecology, mathematical geography, mathematical physics

► *28 Physics; 38 Engineering; 40 Computers*

4 **simple arithmetic**, number work, sums, number theory, higher arithmetic, modular arithmetic

5 **number**, signed number, directed number, positive number, negative number, non-negative number, even number, odd number, prime number (or prime), composite number, perfect number

► *194 Number*

6 **complex number**, real part, imaginary part, modulus, absolute value, argument, complex conjugate, real number, real, imaginary number, rational number, rational, irrational number, irrational, integer, whole number, fraction, mixed number, algebraic number, transcendental number

7 **natural number**, cardinal number, cardinal, ordinal number, ordinal, finite number, infinite number, transfinite number, random number

8 **number system**, counting system, positional notation, place-value notation, decimal notation, decimal system, binary notation, binary system, octal notation, hexadecimal (*or* hex) notation, duodecimal notation, decimal number, binary number, base, radix point, decimal point, units place, tens place, hundreds place, significant digits, significant figures, fixed-point notation, floating-point notation, precision, accuracy

9 **numeral**, Arabic numeral, Roman numeral, digit, figure,

MATHEMATICAL THEORIES AND CONCEPTS

Theories
catastrophe theory
chaos theory
game theory
group theory
knot theory
number theory
queuing theory
set theory

Theorems and Laws
associative law
binomial theorem
commutative law
distributive law
four–colour theorem
mean–value theorem
midpoint theorem
remainder theorem

Named Concepts
Abelian group
Agnesi, witch of
Apollonius' theorem
Argand diagram
Banach space
Bayes's theorem
Bernoulli trial
Bessel functions
Boolean algebra
Briggsian logarithms
Cantor set
Cartesian coordinates
Cauchy sequence
Chinese remainder theorem
de Moivre's formula
Diophantine equation
Dirichlet series
Eratosthenes, sieve of
Euclidean geometry
Euclid's axioms
Euler's constant
Euler's formula
Fermat's last theorem
French curve
Fibonacci numbers
Fourier analysis
Fourier series
Galois group
Gaussian distribution
Gauss's theorem
Gödel numbers
Green's theorem
Gregory's series
Hanoi, towers of
Heron's (*or* Hero's) formula
Hilbert's problems
Hilbert space
Julia set
Klein bottle
Lagrange's theorem
Laplace operator (*or* Laplacian)
Legendre polynomials
Leibnitz's theorem
L'Hospital's rule
Lie group
Lobachevskian geometry
Maclaurin series
Markovian chain
Mandelbrot set
Mersenne numbers
Mersenne prime
Möbius strip
Monte Carlo method
Napierian logarithm
Newton's method
Pascal's triangle
Poisson distribution
Pythagoras's theorem
Riemannian geometry
Russell's paradox
Simpson's rule
Stokes's theorem
Taylor series
Venn diagram

zero, one, two, three, four, five, six, seven, eight, nine, binary digit, bit

10 zero, nought, nothing, nill, cypher (Lit), infinitesimal number

11 infinity, infinite number, transfinite number, infinitude

12 numeration, enumeration, quantification, numbering, counting, reckoning, figuring, quantifying, computation, calculation, mental arithmetic, measurement, count, census, tally, score, whole

13 mathematical symbol, plus sign, minus sign, multiplication sign, division sign, equal (*or* equals) sign, square root sign, radical sign, integral sign, implication sign, operator, operand, arithmetic operator, relational operator, logical operator

14 operation, arithmetic operation, algebraic operation, logical operation, associative operation, commutative operation, distributive operation, relation, relationship, formula, solution, result, results, value

15 addition, summation, sum, aggregate, total, addend, augend

16 subtraction, difference, subtrahend, minuend

17 multiplication, product, multiplier, multiplicand, multiple, lowest (*or* least) common multiple (LCM), factor, submultiple, highest (*or* greatest) common factor (HCF, GCF), prime factor, power, square, cube, fourth power, exponent, index, square root, cube root, surd, root mean square (rms), factorial, factorization, exponentiation, extraction of roots, multiplication tables

18 division, long division, short division, divisibility, quotient, ratio, proportion, percentage, quota, rate, reciprocal, inverse, dividend, divisor, aliquot part, remainder, residue, fraction, numerator, denominator, common denominator, decimal fraction, decimal, recurring decimal, repeated decimal, circular decimal, truncated decimal, vulgar fraction, simple fraction, proper fraction, common fraction, compound fraction, complex fraction, partial fraction, continued fraction, truncation, rounding up, rounding down

19 logarithm, log, common logarithm, natural logarithm, base, mantissa, characteristic, antilogarithm, logarithmic scale, logarithm tables, log tables, Napierian (*or* Naperian) logarithm, natural logarithm

20 sequence, progression, finite sequence, infinite sequence, arithmetic progression, geometric progression, harmonic progression, series, convergent series, divergent series, arithmetic series, geometric series, binomial series, exponential series, logarithmic series, power series, Fourier series

21 set, finite set, infinite set, null set, empty set, universal set, complement, union, intersection, set difference, closure, disjoint sets, ordered set, *n*-tuple, subset, combination, unordered arrangement, permutation, ordered arrangement, element, member, identity element, identity, inverse, bound, upper bound, lower bound, class, group, ring, field

22 matrix, row, column, order, square matrix, diagonal matrix, identity matrix, null matrix, inverse, transpose, determinant

23 algebra, linear algebra, abstract algebra, set algebra, algebra of propositions, Boolean algebra, set, poset, ring, field, group

24 evaluation, simplification, manipulation, expansion, substitution, cross-multiplication, reduction, elimination, cancellation

25 algebraic expression, expression, binomial expression, binomial, polynomial expression, polynomial, term, variable, unknown quantity, unknown, coefficient, numerical coefficient, constant, invariant, parameter, brackets, parentheses, square brackets, braces, angle brackets, vinculum, root sign

26 equality, inequality, identity, equivalence, conditional

27 equation, root, solution, solution set, degree, linear equation, quadratic equation, cubic equation, differential equation, integral equation, functional equation, simultaneous equations

28 algorithm, recursive procedure, step-by-step procedure, effective procedure, iteration, recursion, fractal

29 mathematical function, function, mapping, transformation, domain, codomain, range, image, dependent variable, independent variable, argument, limit, continuous function, step function, inverse function, composite function, composition, trigonometric function, logarithmic function, exponential function, periodic function, gamma function, beta function, functional

30 calculus, infinitesimal calculus, differential calculus, integral calculus, calculus of variations, variational calculus, analysis, real analysis, complex analysis, functional analysis

31 differentiation, integration, differential, increment, decrement, derivative, first derivative, second derivative, partial derivative, rate of change, fluxion, integral, indefinite integral, definite integral, limit, upper limit, lower limit, line integral, surface integral, double integral, convolution, differential equation, ordinary differential equation, partial differential equation, integral equation

32 graph, chart, plot, graphic representation, curve, bar graph, bar chart, histogram, pie chart, scatter diagram, scattergram, axis, *x*-axis, *y*-axis, *z*-axis, linear scale, logarithmic scale, origin, intercept, graph paper, logarithmic paper, log paper

33 coordinates, coordinate system, Cartesian coordinates, polar coordinates, spherical coordinates, cylindrical coordinates, rectangular coordinates, *x*-coordinate, *y*-coordinate, *z*-coordinate, abscissa, ordinate, frame of reference

34 geometry, plane geometry, solid geometry, coordinate geometry, analytic geometry, algebraic geometry, projective geometry, differential geometry, spherical geometry, Euclidean geometry, non-Euclidean geometry

35 space, three-dimensional space, four-dimensional space (*or* space–time continuum), *n*-space, n-dimensional space, hyperspace, hypercube, hypersphere, Euclidean space, Cartesian space, enclosed space, interior, inside, exterior, outside, spatial extension, extent, dimension, dimensions, size, area, volume, capacity

36 point, fixed point, reference point, variable point, midpoint, set of points, coordinates (of a point), position, location, point of inflection, stationary point, fiducial point, point at infinity, locus (of a point), path

37 line, straight line, curved line, line segment, edge, side, boundary, curve, arc, contour, diagonal, diameter, chord, transversal (*or* transverse), bisector, ray, tangent, asymptote, perpendicular, normal, geodesic, slope (of a line), gradient, parallel lines, intersecting lines, converging lines, diverging lines, skew lines, perpendicular lines, orientation, direction, linear measurement, linear extent, length, width, breadth, height, depth, altitude, radius, perimeter, circumference, linearity, curvature

38 surface, flat surface, plane surface, plane, inclined plane, two-dimensional figure, curved surface, concave surface, convex surface, anticlastic surface, synclastic surface, closed surface, solid surface, lamina, face, side, surface measurement, surface area, superficial area, area, extent, flatness, curvature, concavity, convexity, sphericity

39 angle, vertex, apex, corner, cusp, node, plane angle, solid angle, dihedral angle, right angle, oblique angle, acute angle, obtuse angle, reflex angle, complementary angle, round angle (*or* perigon), straight angle, interior angle, exterior angle, re-entrant (*or* re-entering) angle, salient angle, conjugate angles, supplementary angles, alternate angles, opposite angles, vertical angles, angle of elevation, angle of depression, angle subtended, angular measurement, angular distance, angular direction, bearing, bearings, latitude, longitude

40 curve, sine curve, sinusoid, spiral, Archimedes spiral, logarithmic spiral, hyperbolic spiral, helix, catenary, cardioid, cissoid, cruciform, cycloid, epicycloid, hypocycloid, folium, lemniscate, logistic, trochoid, involute, evolute, trajectory, family (of curves)

41 geometric figure, figure, geometric shape, configuration, solid, bounded volume, closed figure, plane figure, solid figure, simplex, fractal, segment, sector, section, cross section, inscribed figure, circumscribed figure, escribed figure, symmetric(al) figure, symmetry, rotational symmetry, mirror symmetry, line (*or* axis) of symmetry, plane of symmetry, centre of symmetry

42 circle, annulus, ring, disc, great circle, small circle, circumcircle, incircle, concentric circles, eccentric circles, semicircle, quadrant, sector, crescent, lune, meniscus, circumference, arc, radius, diameter, chord, ellipse, oval, major axis, minor axis, parabola, hyperbola, conic section (or conic), focus, directrix, eccentricity

43 triangle, trigon (Lit), right-angled triangle, right triangle, acute-angled triangle, obtuse-angled triangle, equilateral triangle, isosceles triangle, scalene triangle, median triangle, circular triangle, spherical triangle, congruent triangles, similar triangles, equivalent triangles, adjacent, opposite, hypotenuse, base, altitude, median, centroid, orthocentre

44 polygon, triangle, square, rectangle, oblong, parallelogram, rhombus, rhomb, diamond, lozenge, rhomboid, quadrilateral, quadrangle, tetragon, trapezoid, trapezium, golden rectangle, golden mean, golden section, pentagon, hexagon, heptagon, octagon, nonagon, decagon, regular polygon, quadrangle, star-shaped figure, pentagram, pentangle, pentacle, hexagram, polyline

45 curved surface, closed surface, surface of revolution, solid of revolution, sphere, spheroid, ellipsoid, paraboloid, hyperboloid, cylinder, cone, truncated cone, frustum, torus, anchor ring, toroid, zone

46 polyhedron, tetrahedron, pentahedron, hexahedron, cube, cuboid, parallelepiped, octahedron, dodecahedron, icosahedron, pyramid, truncated pyramid, frustum, prism, wedge, prismatoid, prismoid, rhombohedron, regular polyhedron, Platonic solid, irregular polyhedron

47 topology, algebraic topology, analysis situs (Lit), continuous distortion, stretching, knotting, knot, Möbius (*or* Moebius) strip, torus, Klein bottle, manifold

48 transformation, affine transformation, translation, reflection, rotation, glide reflection, dilation, dilatation, homothety, similitude, congruence, shear, projection, perspective projection, orthogonal projection, isometric projection, mirror image, enantiomorphic figure

49 geometric construction, construction, drawing, geometric instrument, compass, compasses, pair of compasses, dividers, ruler, rule, straightedge, protractor, set square, T-square, squaring the circle

50 scalar quantity, scalar, vector quantity, vector, magnitude, direction, absolute value, unit vector, position vector, radius vector, component, resultant, parallelogram of forces, vector sum, scalar product, dot product, inner product, vector product, cross product, outer product, differential operator, nabla, del, gradient, divergence, curl, tensor

51 trigonometry, trig (Inf), plane trigonometry, spherical trigonometry, triangulation, sine rule, cosine rule, tangent rule

52 trigonometric function, circular function, hyperbolic function, inverse trigonometric function, sine (sin), cosine (cos), tangent (tan), cosecant (cosec), secant (sec), cotangent (cot), hyperbolic sine (sinh), hyperbolic cosine (cosh), hyperbolic tangent (tanh), inverse sine (arc-sine), inverse cosine (arc-cosine), inverse tangent (arc-tangent)

53 statistics, descriptive statistics, statistical inference, statistical analysis, probability theory, vital statistics, parametric statistics, nonparametric statistics

54 hypothesis testing, null hypothesis, alternative hypothesis, test statistic, significance level, significance test, one-tailed test, two-tailed test, goodness-of-fit test

55 statistical methods, analysis of variance, regression analysis, multivariate analysis, cluster analysis, factor analysis, principle component analysis

56 nonparametric methods, ordering, ranking, nominal scale, ordinal scale, interval scale, ratio scale, rank, order number

57 population, sample, random sample, biased sample, sample size, data collection, sampling, random sampling, systematic sampling, bias, crude data, data summarization, statistic, sample statistic, random variable, stochastic variable, stochastic process

58 frequency distribution, frequency, absolute frequency, relative frequency, event, occurrence, particular instance, success, histogram

59 probability distribution, discrete distribution, continuous distribution, normal distribution, Gaussian distribution, binomial distribution, Poisson distribution, exponential distribution, gamma distribution, chi-square distribution, t-distribution, skew distribution, bimodal distribution, skewness, kurtosis, frequency function, probability density function, cumulative distribution function

60 parameter, characteristic, average, average value, typical value, expected value, mean, median, mode, arithmetic mean, geometric mean, weighted mean, weighting, variation, spread, dispersion, standard deviation, standard error, mean deviation, covariance, range, interquartile range, percentile, probable error, mean error, confidence level, confidence limits

61 correlation, positive correlation, negative correlation, association, correlation coefficient, significance

62 probability, chance, mathematical probability, empirical probability, conditional probability, certainty, impossibility, possible outcome, favourable outcome, likelihood, maximum likelihood

63 mathematical logic, symbolic logic, formal logic, propositional calculus, predicate calculus, functional calculus, logical proposition, proposition, statement, premise (*or* premiss), assertion, affirmation, denial, logical expression, logical formula, well-formed formula, logical operation, logical connective, operator, logical operator, relational operator, negation, conjunction, logical product, disjunction, alternation, logical sum, implication, equivalence, conditional, relation, relationship, equivalence relation, ordering relation, transitive relation, reflexive relation, irreflexive relation, symmetric relation, antisymmetric relation, asymmetric relation, truth value, logical value, truth, falsity, truth table, universal quantifier, existential quantifier

64 reasoning, mathematical reasoning, logical reasoning, argument, inference, deduction, induction, derivation, premise (*or* premiss), rules of inference, valid argument, sound argument, invalid argument, unsound argument, conclusion, indication, heuristic solution, validation, verification, validity, soundness, rigour, correctness, truth, completeness, consistency, compatibility, sufficiency, invalidity, falsity, inconsistency, incompatibility, insufficiency, condition, restriction, contingency, necessary and sufficient condition, tautology, contradiction, converse, paradox

65 theory, mathematical model, theoretical framework, simulation, generalization, abstraction, idealization, law, general principle, principle, criterion, rule, theorem, hypothesis, general proposition, proposition, lemma, corollary, formal expression, formula, equation, postulate, supposition, presupposition, premise (*or* premiss), conjecture, axiom, first principles

66 proof, rigorous proof, direct proof, indirect proof, QED (quod erat demonstrandum), demonstration, test, procedure, method, evaluation, estimation, approximation, extrapolation, interpolation, error

67 calculator, computer, adding machine, abacus, Napier's bones, tally stick, score card, cash register

► *40 Computers*

ADJECTIVES

68 mathematical, arithmetical, algebraic, geometrical, trigonometrical, analytic(al), topological, statistical

69 theoretical, abstract, analytic(al), formal, theorematic, theoremic, hypothetical, propositional, axiomatic, self-evident, empirical, observational, experiential, heuristic

70 universal, general, fundamental, basic, simple, standard, normal, canonical, uniform, continuous, discrete, noncontinuous, distinct, unique

71 numerical, signed, positive, negative, non-negative, unsigned, even, odd, integral, whole, digital, fractional, decimal, denary, binary, ternary

72 complex, real, imaginary, rational, irrational, transcendental, infinitesimal, finite, infinite

73 numerable, enumerable, denumerable, countable, quantifiable, measurable, mensurable, calculable, computable, soluble, solvable, insoluble, insolvable, unsolvable, decidable, undecidable

74 divisible, indivisible, prime, composite, compound, reciprocal, inverse, in proportion, proportional, percentile, rational, commensurable, irrational, incommensurable

75 equal, identical, unequal, ordinal, ordered, partially ordered, ranked, cardinal, first, second, third, fourth, fifth, sixth, seventh, eighth, ninth, tenth, zeroth, maximal, greatest, largest, highest, minimal, least, lowest, smallest, upper, higher, greater, lower, lesser

76 functional, relational, exponential, logarithmic, linear, quadratic, cubic, binomial, trinomial, multinomial, polynomial, differential, integral, one-one, one-to-one, one-many, many-one

77 given, assumed, known, stipulated, explicit, implicit, characteristic, dependent, variable, variate, independent, invariable, constant, parametric

78 pictorial, diagrammatic, graphic, tabular

79 spatial, flat, planar, plane, two-dimensional, coplanar, superficial, three-dimensional, solid, symmetrical, regular, asymmetric, asymmetrical, irregular, distorted

80 linear, lineal, straight, straight-lined, straight-edged, rectilinear, horizontal, flat, vertical, upright, oblique, sloping, slanted, at an angle, tangential, asymptotic, parallel, perpendicular, normal, orthogonal, orthographic, angular, angled, pointed, intersecting, convergent, divergent, skew, collinear, equidistant, equilateral

81 curvilinear, curved, arcuate, convex, concave, round, rounded, circular, annular, ringlike, ring-shaped, spiral, helical, semicircular, quadrantal, crescent-shaped, lunate, lenticular, elliptical, elliptic, oval, parabolic, hyperbolic, central, focal, concentric, confocal, eccentric, radial, diametral, diametric, antipodal

82 polygonal, multiangular, triangular, wedge-shaped, three-sided, square, rectangular, oblong, rhombic, rhomboidal, diamond-shaped, quadrilateral, four-sided, tetragonal, pentagonal, fivc-sided, hexagonal, six-sided, heptagonal, seven-sided, octagonal, eight-sided

83 spherical, ellipsoidal, oval, ovoid, oblate, prolate, spheroidal, parabaloid(al), hyperboloid(al), cylindrical, disc-shaped, disclike, rod-shaped, conical, cone-shaped, toric, toroidal

84 cubic, cubiform, cuboid, oblong, hexahedral, octahedral, pyramidal, prismatic, wedge-shaped, polyhedral, multifacial

85 cyclic, periodic, harmonic, sinusoidal

86 logical, deductive, inductive, inferential, valid, sound, correct, true, invalid, unsound, incorrect, false, equivalent, complete, consistent, compatible, necessary, sufficient, inconsistent, incomplete, incompatible, contingent, conditional, tautological, contradictory, converse, paradoxical

ADVERBS

87 mathematically, theoretically, analytically, generally, logically, fundamentally, basically, continuously, uniformly, discretely, numerically, positively, negatively, digitally, per cent, infinitesimally, finitely, infinitely, equally, approximately, almost, about, unequally, functionally, exponentially, logarithmically, trigonometrically, spatially, linearly, spherically

PREPOSITIONS

88 equal to, not equal to, approximately equal to, proportional to, inversely proportional to, directly proportional to, less than, less than or equal to, much less than, greater than, greater than or equal to, much greater than, plus, minus, divided by, divided into, multiplied by, times

VERBS

89 theorize, hypothesize, postulate, presuppose, assume, analyse, reason, deduce, infer, conclude, derive, generalize, prove, validate, demonstrate, satisfy, disprove, invalidate

90 enumerate, count, number, reckon up, quantify, measure, compute, calculate, determine, solve, evaluate, resolve

91 add, add up, sum, aggregate, subtract, take away, multiply, multiply out, cross multiply, times, raise (to a power), square, cube, extract a root, take the square root, factorize, borrow, carry, divide, subdivide, proportion, decimalize, truncate, round up, round down

92 manipulate, simplify, expand, cancel, eliminate, substitute

93 equate, equalize, equal, approximate, estimate, sample, extrapolate, interpolate, correct for, correlate

94 order, rank, maximize, minimize, vary, approach (a limit), tend to, vanish, standardize, normalize

95 evaluate, differentiate, integrate

96 represent, draw, configure, construct, generate, plot, graph, project, transform, translate, rotate, reflect

97 align, line up, extend, produce (a line), converge, diverge, intersect, disect, bisect, slope, subtend (an angle), curve, circle, encircle, circumscribe, inscribe

28 Physics

Classical physics has been superseded by quantum theory: quantum theory is verified by experiments. Experiments must be described in terms of classical physics. C. F. von Weizsäcker.

NOUNS

1 physics, physical science, exact science, natural science, natural philosophy, physicist

2 classical physics, classical mechanics, Newtonian mechanics, dynamics, statics, kinematics, fluid mechanics, hydrodynamics, aerodynamics, sound, acoustics, ultrasonics, phonetics, optics, geometric optics, physical optics, heat, thermodynamics, electricity, magnetism, magnetics, electroacoustics, electrodynamics, electromagnetism, electro-optics

3 modern physics, quantum theory, quantum mechanics, wave mechanics, matrix mechanics, quantum statistics, statistical mechanics, atomic physics, nuclear physics, particle physics, statistical physics, spectroscopy, solid-state physics, crystallography, low-temperature physics, cryogenics, plasma physics, magnetohydrodynamics, radiation physics, relativity theory, relativistic quantum mechanics, quantum gravity, quantum electrothermodynamics

4 experimental physics, theoretical physics, pure physics, applied physics, medical physics, geophysics, meteorology, oceanography, astrophysics, cosmology, physical chemistry, chemical physics, biophysics

► *27 Mathematics; 30 Earth Science; 32 Chemistry*

5 theory, kinetic theory, wave theory of light, electromagnetic theory, quantum theory, quantum field theory, special theory of relativity, general theory of relativity

6 **law**, principle, laws of motion, laws of thermodynamics, laws of reflection, laws of refraction, uncertainty principle, rule, criterion, equation, equation of state, effect, model, atmospheric model, cosmological model, hypothesis, proposition, theorem, premise, thesis, statement, axiom

7 **space**, position, space coordinates, coordinates, length, breadth, height, altitude, thickness, radius, diameter, area, volume, angle, plane angle, solid angle, vacuum, free space, four-dimensional space, four-dimensional continuum, space-time, space-time continuum

► *27 Mathematics; 141 Space*

8 **time**, period, interval, frequency, angular frequency, phase, motion, linear motion, circular motion, simple harmonic motion, flow, steady flow, turbulence, speed, velocity, relative velocity, angular velocity, acceleration, angular acceleration, acceleration due to gravity (*or* of free fall)

► *275 Time; 300 Motion*

9 **mass**, amount of substance, density, relative density, specific gravity, momentum, angular momentum, inertia, moment of inertia, centre of mass, centre of gravity, conservation of mass

10 **force**, weight, gravitational force, centripetal force, centrifugal force, couple, moment, torque, torsion, equilibrium, stable equilibrium, unstable equilibrium, metastable equilibrium, buoyancy, field of force, field, flux, flux density, pressure, atmospheric pressure, vapour pressure, stress, strain, elasticity, viscosity, friction, static friction, dynamic friction, rolling friction, abrasion, erosion, osmosis, surface tension

11 **energy**, potential energy, kinetic energy, chemical energy, solar energy, electrical energy, nuclear energy, conservation of energy, conservation of mass and energy, work, machine, engine, power, power station, nuclear power, fission energy, fusion energy, renewable energy, solar energy, wave power, wind power, tidal power, geothermal energy

12 **wave**, vibration, oscillation, transient disturbance, undulation, wave motion, longitudinal wave, transverse wave, torsional wave, travelling wave, standing wave, node, antinode, wave propagation, radiation

► *326 Oscillation*

13 **electromagnetic radiation**, radio waves, microwaves, television, radio, radar, infrared (IR) radiation, near infrared, far infrared, light, visible radiation, ultraviolet (UV) radiation, near ultraviolet, far ultraviolet, UVA, UVB, X-rays, gamma rays, electromagnetic spectrum, visible spectrum, radio spectrum, particle–wave (*or* wave–particle) duality, photon

► *692 Communications*

14 **sound wave**, acoustic wave, ultrasonic wave, water wave, ripple, tsunami (*or* tidal wave), seismic wave, bow wave, shock wave, electrical oscillation, mechanical oscillation, vibration, oscillating current, vibrating string, forced vibration, resonance, resonant frequency

15 **wave property**, transmission, attenuation, absorption, dissipation, deflection, diffusion, reflection, refraction,

NAMED LAWS, EFFECTS, AND EQUATIONS

Amagat's experiments
Ampère–Laplace law
Ampère's law
Andrews' experiments
Archimedes' principle
Aragadro's hypothesis
Balmer series
Barkhausen effect
Bernouilli effect
Biot–Savart law
Bitter pattern
Bloch wall
Bohr atom
Boltzmann constant
Bose–Einstein statistics
Boyle's law
Boy's experiment
Bragg's law
Brewster angle
Bunsen cell
Callendar and Barnes' experiment
Carnot's principle
Cavendish's experiment
Charles' law
Clark cell
Cockroft–Walton accelerator
Compton effect
Coulomb's law
Curie's law
Curie–Weiss law
Dalton's law
Daniell cell
de Broglie principle
Dewar flask
Dirac's equation
Doppler effect
Dulong and Petit's law
Faraday effect
Faraday's laws
Fermat's principle
Fermi level
Fraunhofer diffraction
Fraunhofer lines
Fresnel's biprism
Fresnel diffraction
Fresnel lens
Gay–Lussac's law
Geiger counter
Geiger–Müller counter
Gibbs function
Hall effect
Heisenberg uncertainty principle
Helmholtz coils
Helmholtz function
Hooke's law
Joly steam calorimeter
Joule–Kelvin (or Joule Thomson) effect
Joule's laws
Kepler's laws
Kerr effect
Kirchoff's laws
Lambert's law
Leclanché cell
Lees' disk
Lenz's law
Leslie's cube
Leyden jar
Linde process
Lissajous' figures
Lloyd's mirror
Lorentz–Fitzgerald contraction
Lyman series
Mach number
Maxwell–Boltzmann statistics
Maxwell distribution
Maxwell's equation
Meissner effect
Michelson–Morley experiment
Moseley's law
Néel temperature
Nernst calorimeter
Neumann's law
Newton's law of cooling
Newton's laws of motion
Newton's law of gravitation
Newton's rings
Nicol prism
Ohm's law
Otto cycle
Paschen series
Peltier effect
Planck's radiation law
Poisson ratio
Poynting vector
Prévost's theory of exchanges
Rayleigh scattering
Regnault's apparatus
Reynolds number
Rochon prism
Roentgen rays
Rydberg constant
Searle's bar
Seebeck effect
Stefan's law
Schrödinger's cat
Schrödinger's wave equation
Thomson effect
Van de Graaff generator
van der Waals equation
Weston standard (*or* cadmium) cell
Wheatstone bridge
Wien's displacement law
Wimshurst machine
Wollaston prism
Young's experiment

dispersion, scattering, interference, diffraction, polarization, plane polarization, circular polarization

16 waveform, waveshape, sine wave, sinusoidal wave, nonsinusoidal wave, pulse, rectangular pulse, square wave, pulse train, wavelength, wave number, frequency, frequency band, frequency spectrum, amplitude, hertz, wave crest, wave trough, wave speed, phase speed, speed of light, speed of sound

► *692 Communications*

17 sound, noise, white noise, music, ultrasound, infrasound, ear, audibility, inaudibility, loudness

► *18 Music; 504 Hearing*

18 source of sound, sound generator, musical instrument, amplifier, public-address system (PA), megaphone, loudspeaker, speaker, hearing aid

► *18 Music; 39 Electronics; 504 Hearing; 740 Publication*

19 sound propagation, speed of sound, subsonic speed, supersonic speed, Mach number, Mach 1, sonic boom, sound (*or* sonic) barrier, audiofrequency, ultrasonic frequency, sound level, sound-pressure level, sound-power level, loudness level, decibel

20 musical note, tone, fundamental, overtone, harmonic, partial, pitch, musical interval, musical scale

► *18 Music*

21 architectural acoustics, auditorium, echo, reverberation, reverberation time, reverberation (*or* echo) chamber, dead room, anechoic chamber, sound insulation, soundproofing

22 sounding, echo sounding, depth sounding, sonar, ultrasonic imaging (*or* ultrasonography), ultrasonic cleaning, ultrasonic welding

23 light, daylight, sunlight, moonlight, electric light, gaslight, candlelight, vision, colour vision, visual acuity, eye, visibility, brightness, clarity, contrast

► *518 Vision; 522 Light*

24 light emission, incandescence, luminescence, bioluminescence, thermoluminescence, fluorescence, phosphorescence, radioluminescence, illumination, shadow, umbra, penumbra, light beam, ray of light, pencil of light, luminous intensity, luminous flux, luminous efficiency, luminous efficacy, illuminance (*or* illumination), luminance

25 light source, lamp, light, lighting, incandescent lamp, filament lamp, tungsten lamp, quartz–iodine lamp, light bulb, filament, fluorescent light, strip light, fluorescent tube, mercury-vapour lamp, neon lamp, gas-discharge tube, light-emitting diode (LED)

► *522 Light*

26 laser (light amplification by stimulated emission of radiation), gas laser, helium-neon laser, carbon dioxide laser, ruby laser, neodymium-glass laser, YAG (yttrium aluminium garnet) laser, semiconductor laser, tunable laser, dye laser, monochromatic radiation, coherent radiation, stimulated emission, population inversion, maser (microwave amplification by stimulated emission of radiation)

27 polarized light, plane-polarized light, circularly polarized light, elliptically polarized light, birefringence, Polaroid™

28 colour, pure colour, spectral colour, rainbow, red, orange, yellow, green, blue, indigo, violet, high saturation, low saturation, hue, tint, shade, interference pattern, iridescence, white light, primary colours, secondary colours, red, green, blue, cyan, magenta, yellow, complementary colours, additive process, subtractive process, pigment, paint, dye, lake, colour printing, colour television, colour photography

► *529 Colour*

29 optical element, mirror, plane mirror, convex mirror, concave mirror, paraboloid (*or* parabolic) mirror, silver coating, aluminium coating, front-surfaced, back surfaced, hand mirror, full-length mirror, shaving mirror, rear-view mirror, wing mirror, lens, converging lens, diverging lens, convex lens, biconvex lens, planoconvex lens, concave lens, spherical lens, cylindrical lens, toric lens, achromatic lens (*or* achromat), antireflection coating, coated lens, bloomed lens, spectacles, glasses, bifocals, dark glasses, sunglasses, photochromic lenses, contact lenses, prism, diffraction grating, grating, reflection grating, optical fibre, light pipe, light guide, reflection, total internal reflection, refraction, refractivity, refractive index, diffraction

► *518 Vision*

30 lens system, compound lens, mirror system, catadioptric system, eyepiece, objective, condenser, camera lens

► *41 Photography*

31 lens element, focal length, focal plane, focal point, focus, circle of least confusion, caustic, lens aperture, mirror aperture, f-number (*or* F-number), relative aperture, object distance, image distance, real image, virtual image, optic axis, axial ray, paraxial ray, aberration, optical aberration, spherical aberration, coma, astigmatism, chromatic aberration

32 optical instrument, camera, telescope, binoculars, field glasses, opera glasses, microscope, periscope, electrophotometer, spectrophotometer, spectrometer, photometer, sextant, theodolite, interferometer, focusing, magnification, magnifying power, resolution, resolving power, aperture stop, field stop, field of view, depth of field, depth of focus

► *29 Astronomy; 41 Photography; 518 Vision*

33 photosensitivity, photosensitive material, light-sensitive material, photoelectric effect, photoconductivity, photovoltaic effect, electro-optical effect, optical activity, optical rotation

34 photometry, photography, photolithography, fibre optics, fibre-optics transmission

35 heat, quantity of heat, warmth, hotness, hot body, hot substance, heating device, heater, heating system, furnace, cooker, combustion, burning, fuel, cold, cold body, cold substance, cooling system, refrigeration, refrigerator, freezer

► *493 Heat; 494 Cold*

36 heat flow, heat transfer, conduction, convection, radiation, heat flow rate, heat exchange, thermal equilibrium, thermal conductivity, heat capacity, specific heat capacity, molar heat capacity

37 temperature, temperature scale, phase change, transition, freezing, fusion, melting, boiling, ebullition, liquefaction, vaporization, evaporation, sublimation, transition temperature, freezing point, melting point, boiling point, sublimation point, triple point

38 thermodynamics, first law, second law, third law, thermodynamic temperature, absolute zero, triple point of water, volume, pressure, entropy, internal energy, enthalpy, Gibbs function, Helmholtz function, work, external work, latent heat, specific latent heat, standard temperature and pressure (STP), normal temperature and pressure (NTP), standard atmosphere, equation of state, van der Waals equation, critical state, critical temperature, Carnot cycle, Diesel cycle, Otto cycle, Wankel cycle

39 expansion, expansion coefficient, compression, compressibility, adiabatic change, isothermal change

40 heating effect, incandescence, thermionic emission, thermoelectricity, thermoelectric effect, thermal radiation, black-body radiation, black body, full radiator

41 thermometry, pyrometry, thermal imaging

42 electricity, current electricity, static electricity (*or* static), frictional electricity, atmospheric electricity, thermoelectricity, photoelectricity, bioelectricity

43 electrical conduction, conduction of electricity, conductivity, conducting medium, conductor, metal conductor, liquid conductor, electrolytic conductor, semiconductor, insulator, electrolyte, electrode, anode, cathode, electrolysis, electrolytic cell, primary cell, secondary cell, battery, fuel cell

▶ *32 Chemistry*

44 semiconductor, n-type semiconductor, p-type semiconductor, charge carrier, electron, hole, electron conduction, hole conduction, n-type conductivity, p-type conductivity, p–n junction, energy band, conduction band, valence band, energy gap, impurity atom, acceptor impurity, donor impurity, doping, semiconductor device, diode, transistor

▶ *39 Electronics*

45 superconductivity, superconductor, transition temperature, high-temperature superconductor, superconducting magnet

46 electric discharge, gas discharge, arc discharge, electric arc, arc, glow discharge, transient discharge, spark discharge, spark, gas-discharge tube

47 electric storm, thunderstorm, lightning, lightning conductor (*or* rod), lightning arrester

▶ *30 Earth Science*

48 insulation, insulator, nonconductor, dielectric, dielectric constant, dielectric coefficient, dielectric polarization, breakdown voltage

49 electromagnetic induction, electrostatic induction, thermoelectric effect, photoelectric effect, photovoltaic effect, photoconductivity, piezoelectric effect, electrostriction

50 electric charge, quantity of electricity, charge, positive charge, negative charge, charged particle, electron, proton, ion, charged body, charged substance, charge attraction, charge repulsion, conservation of charge, dipole, dipole moment, quadrupole, charge density, electric constant

51 electric current, current, flow of electricity, direct current (d.c.), alternating current (a.c.), transient current, pulse, frequency, phase, conduction current, displacement current, induced current, eddy current, current density, juice (Inf)

52 electric potential, potential, potential difference (p.d.), voltage, electromotive force (e.m.f.), back e.m.f., ground, earth, live, neutral

53 resistance, reactance, impedance, resistivity, conductivity, capacitance, inductance, mutual inductance, self-inductance, conductance, mutual conductance

54 electric field, electric field strength, electric flux, displacement, permittivity, relative permittivity

55 circuit, electronic circuit, electric circuit, network, interconnected circuits, circuit element, electronic component, electronic device, resistor, capacitor, inductor, diode, transistor, rectifier, amplifier, oscillator, filter, transformer, transducer

▶ *39 Electronics*

56 electrical energy, electric power, generator, electric motor, power station, power supply

57 magnetism, magnetic attaction, magnetic repulsion, electromagnetism

58 geomagnetism, earth's magnetism, terrestrial magnetism, magnetosphere, magnetic North, magnetic South, magnetic North Pole, magnetic South Pole, magnetic equator, magnetic meridian, magnetic declination (*or* magnetic variation), magnetic dip (*or* magnetic inclination, angle of dip), (geo)magnetic storm, palaeomagnetism, magnetic reversal, magnetic epoch

▶ *30 Earth Science*

59 ferromagnetism, ferromagnetic material, iron, nickel, cobalt, magnetic alloy, domain, Permalloy™, Mu metal™, paramagnetism, diamagnetism, antiferromagnetism, ferrimagnetism

60 magnet, permanent magnet, bar magnet, horseshoe magnet, pot magnet, keeper, electromagnet, solenoid, magnetizing coil, coil, ferromagnetic core, superconducting magnet, magnetite, magnetic iron ore, lodestone, ferrite, magnetic monopole

61 magnetic quantity, magnetic variable, magnetomotive force, magnetic potential difference, magnetic field, magnetic field strength, magnetic flux, magnetic induction (*or* magnetic flux density), magnetization, permeability, relative permeability, magnetic dipole moment, magnetic moment, magneton, magnetic constant

62 electromagnetic radiation, electromagnetic wave, electromagnetic spectrum

63 magnetic phenomenon, magnetic hysteresis, hysteresis, residual magnetization, remanence, electromagnetic induction, mutual induction, self-induction, magnetostriction, magneto-optical effect, magnetic damping, magnetic deflection, magnetic focusing, magnetic lens, magnetic mirror, magnetic levitation (*or* maglev)

64 magnetic recording, magnetic tape, video tape, magnetic track, magnetic storage, magnetic memory, magnetic disk, hard disk, floppy disk, magnetic ink character recognition (MICR), magnetic ink, magnetic card, credit card, smart card, phonecard, magnetic stripe, magnetic resonance imaging (MRI)

65 atom, atomic structure, nucleus, proton, neutron, nucleon, binding energy, electron, electron configuration, electron shell, subshell, s-electron, p-electron, d-electron, f-electron, atomic orbital, energy level

66 ion, positive ion, cation, negative ion, anion, charge number, ionization, ionization energy, ionization potential

► *32 Chemistry*

67 excited atom, excited state, ground state, metastable state, excitation, transition, quantum jump, excitation energy

68 emission, absorption, emission spectrum, absorption spectrum, continuous spectrum, line spectrum, band spectrum, optical spectrum, infrared spectrum, ultraviolet spectrum, microwave spectrum, X-ray spectrum

69 isotope, nuclide, atomic mass, atomic mass constant, relative atomic mass, atomic weight, atomic number, proton number, mass number, nucleon number, neutron number

70 radioactivity, radioactive decay, decay, alpha decay, beta decay, radioactive substance, radioisotope, radionuclide, alpha emitter, beta emitter, parent nuclide, daughter nuclide, daughter product, alpha particle, beta particle, alpha rays, beta rays, gamma rays, radioactive series, half-life, mean life, decay constant, activity, energy imparted, absorbed dose, dose equivalent, ionizing radiation, high-energy radiation, X-rays, particulate radiation, cosmic rays, radiometric dating, radiocarbon dating, potassium–argon dating, radiography, radiology, radiotherapy

► *30 Earth Science; 35 Medicine*

71 nuclear reaction, disintegration, transmutation, collision, scattering, elastic scattering, inelastic scattering, cross section

72 nuclear fission, fission reaction, fission, chain reaction, splitting the atom, atom-smashing, fissionable nuclide, fissile nuclide, fertile nuclide, fission product, critical mass, nuclear fusion, fusion reaction, fusion, thermonuclear fusion, controlled nuclear fusion, cold fusion, nuclear energy, atomic energy, nuclear power, nuclear power station, nuclear engineering, nucleonics

73 nuclear reactor, reactor, atomic pile, thermal reactor, gas-cooled reactor (GCR), advanced gas-cooled reactor (AGR), high-temperature gas-cooled reactor (HTR), pressurized-water reactor (PWR), boiling-water reactor (BWR), magnox reactor, fast reactor, breeder reactor, fast-breeder reactor, reactor core, core, nuclear fuel, uranium, enriched uranium, plutonium, fuel assembly, fuel element, fuel rod, coolant, moderator, control rods, biological shield, shield

74 nuclear waste, radioactive waste, high-level waste, low-level waste, intermediate-level waste, waste disposal, waste processing

75 nuclear accident, meltdown, fallout, nuclear contamination, decontamination, radiation exposure, Chernobyl, Three Mile Island

76 fusion reactor, thermonuclear reactor, tokamak, plasma, plasma containment, plasma confinement

77 elementary particle, fundamental particle, subatomic particle, particle, lepton, electron, muon, tauon, neutrino, quark, quark flavour, quark colour, hadron, baryon, meson, proton, neutron, nucleon, pion, pi meson, kaon, K meson, fermion, boson, antiparticle, antiproton, antineutron, positron, antielectron, antiquark

78 quantum, quantum of radiation, photon, quantized property, quantum number, charge, spin, isospin, parity, strangeness, charm, beauty, up, down, left, right

79 fundamental interaction, gravitational interaction, electromagnetic interaction, nuclear interaction, strong interaction, strong nuclear interaction, weak interaction, weak nuclear interaction, electroweak interaction, exchange force, unified field theory, string, superstring, theory of everything

80 quantum theory, quantum mechanics, wave mechanics, matrix mechanics, Dirac notation, wave–particle duality, Copenhagen interpretation, quantum electrodynamics, quantum chromodynamics, Schrödinger's cat, Bell's inequality, Aspect experiment, quantum uncertainty, quantum jump, quantum leap

81 causality, cause and effect, causal law, deterministic law, determinism, unpredictability, chaos theory, probability, indeterminacy, uncertainty principle, Heisenberg uncertainty principle

82 measuring instrument, instrument, instrumentation, measuring device, gauge, meter, digital meter, indicating instrument, recording instrument, recording device, measurement, observation, recording, measured quantity, measured value, indicated value, meter reading, reading, readout, scale, graduated scale, pointer, needle, digital readout, digital reading

83 sensitivity, response, linear response, frequency response, calibration, accuracy, precision, error, systematic error, observational error, personal error, probable error, standard error, standard deviation, estimated value, computed value, specified value

84 altimeter, callipers, micrometer, vernier scale, compass, gyroscope, gyrostat, gyrocompass, sextant, theodolite

85 microscope, optical microscope, simple microscope, compound microscope, stereomicroscope, phase-contrast microscope, ultramicroscope, polarizing microscope, electron microscope, scanning electron microscope, scanning transmission electron microscope, atomic-force microscope, field-emission microscope (FEM), field-ion microscope (FIM), telescope, optical telescope, radio telescope, radio interferometer

86 weighing instrument, balance, spring balance, scales, steelyard, torsion balance

87 clock, atomic clock, caesiumX clock, chronometer, quartz clock, digital clock, analogue clock, pendulum

► *275 Time*

88 barometer, aneroid barometer, mercury barometer, pressure gauge, vacuum gauge, strain gauge, flowmeter, hygrometer, hydrometer

89 thermometer, mercury thermometer, alcohol thermometer, maximum and minimun thermometer, clinical thermometer, gas thermometer, platinum resistance thermometer, thermocouple, thermopile, pyrometer, calorimeter

90 ammeter, galvanometer, voltmeter, potentiometer, electrometer, wattmeter, bridge, oscilloscope, stroboscope, magnetometer

91 spectrometer, spectrograph, spectroscope, spectrophotometer, monochromator, mass spectrometer, mass spectrograph

92 light meter, photometer, radiometer, bolometer, interferometer, polarimeter, colorimeter

93 radiation detector, particle detector, particle counter, Geiger counter, Geiger–Müller counter, ionization chamber, scintillation counter, electron multiplier

94 particle accelerator, accelerator, collider, particle collider, cyclotron, Beratron, betatron, synchrotron, proton synchrotron, linear accelerator, Van de Graaff accelerator, Joint European Torus (JET)

95 mensuration, metrology, telemetry, remote sensing

96 microscopy, thermometry, pyrometry, spectrometry, spectroscopy, photometry, interferometry

97 fundamental constant, physical constant, universal constant, speed of light (in vacuum) gravitational constant, Planck constant, permeability of vacuum (*or* magnetic constant), permittivity of vacuum (*or* electric constant), elementary charge, electron mass, proton mass, Boltzmann constant, Stefan–Boltzmann constant, fine-structure constant, Rydberg constant, Bohr radius, Avogadro constant, Faraday constant, molar gas constant

ADJECTIVES

98 physical, classical, mechanical, dynamic, static, kinetic, kinematic, hydrodynamic, aerodynamic, acoustic(al), ultrasonic, subsonic, optic, optical, thermal, calorific, thermodynamic, cryogenic, electric, electrical, magnetic, electrodynamic, atomic, crystallographic, solid-state, spectroscopic, spectrometric, monochrome, polychrome, magnetohydrodynamic, nonclassical, quantum, quantum mechanical, quantized, statistical, relativistic

99 theoretical, hypothetical, mathematical, experimental, pure, applied

VERBS

100 physically, classically, mechanically, dynamically, statically, kinetically, kinematically, hydrodynamically, aerodynamically, acoustically, ultrasonically, subsonically, optically, thermally, calorifically, thermodynamically, cryogenically, electrically, magnetically, electrodynamically, crystallographically, spectroscopically, spectrometrically, magnetohydrodynamically, nonclassically, quantum mechanically, statistically, relativistically

29 Astronomy

In my studies of astronomy and philosophy I hold this opinion about the universe, that the Sun remains fixed in the centre of the circle of heavenly bodies, without changing its place; and the Earth, turning upon itself, moves round the Sun. Galileo Galilei.

NOUNS

1 astronomy, stargazing, star watching, optical astronomy, observational astronomy, radio astronomy, infrared astronomy, X-ray astronomy, ultraviolet astronomy, gamma-ray astronomy, radar astronomy, astrophysics, cosmology, cosmogeny, uranography, astrometry, celestial mechanics, astrodynamics, stellar statistics, astrochemistry, cosmochemistry, astrobiology, exobiology, astrobotany, astrogeology, astrophotography

2 astronomer, observer, astrophysicist, cosmologist, cosmogenist, uranographer, cosmochemist, astronomer royal, stargazer

3 universe, cosmos, macrocosm, totality, world, heavens, firmament, space, deep space, outer space, sky, empyrean, welkin, vault of heaven

► *8 Divinity; 141 Space*

4 cosmological model, Ptolemaic universe, Copernican universe, Einstein universe, general relativity, big bang, steady state, expanding universe, inflationary universe, oscillating universe, open universe, closed universe, flat universe, primordial fireball, cosmic background, microwave background, dark matter, gravitational force, gravitational constant

5 celestial sphere, celestial equator, celestial poles, ecliptic, horizon, meridian, zenith, nadir, equinox, vernal equinox, autumnal equinox, solstice, galactic latitude, galactic longitude, celestial latitude, celestial longitude, right ascension, declination, hour angle, altitude, azimuth

6 star catalogue, star atlas, sky survey, Messier Catalogue, New General Catalogue (NGC), ephemeris

7 galaxy, island universe, galactic nebula, anagalactic nebula, elliptical galaxy, spiral galaxy, barred spiral galaxy, irregular galaxy, lenticular galaxy, Hubble classification, supergiant elliptical, giant elliptical, giant spiral, dwarf elliptical, cluster, Local Group, supercluster, active galaxy, quasar, radio galaxy, Seyfert galaxy, starburst galaxy, filament, void, galactic centre, nucleus, disc, arm, halo, gravitational redshift, Hubble constant

GALAXIES

Andromeda	Small Magellanic Cloud (Nubecular Minor)
Large Magellanic Cloud (Nubecular Major)	Sombrero Galaxy
Maffei 1	Triangulum Spiral
Maffei 2	Whirlpool Galaxy
Milky Way System	

CLUSTERS

Beehive (Praesepe)	Hyadese
Gould Belt	Jewel Box
Great Cluster in Hercules	Sword Handle

NEBULAE

Nebula (Constellation *or* Direction)	
Coalsack (Crux)	North American Nebula (Cygnus)
Crab Nebula (Taurus)	Omega *or* Swan Nebula (Sagittarius)
Dumbbell Nebula (Vulpecula)	Ophiuchus Nebula
Great Looped *or* Loop *or* Tarantula Nebula (Dorado)	Owl Nebula (Ursa Major)
Great Nebula in Orion	Ring Nebula (Lyra)
Helix Nebula (Aquarius)	Rosette Nebula (Monoceros)
Hind's Nebula (Taurus)	Saturn Nebula (Aquarius)
Horsehead Nebula (Orion)	Swan *or* Omega Nebula (Sagittarius)
Hubble Nebula (Monoceros)	Tarantula *or* Great Looped *or* Loop Nebula (Dorado)
Keyhole Nebula (Carinus)	Trifid Nebula (Sagittarius)
Lagoon Nebula (Sagittarius)	Veil Nebula (Cygnus)
Loop *or* Great Looped *or* Tarantula Nebula (Dorado)	

THE CONSTELLATIONS (TECHNICAL NAMES)

Technical Name (Common Name)

Andromeda
Antlia (Air Pump *or* Pump)
Apus (Bird of Paradise)
Aquarius (Water Bearer)
Aquila (Eagle)
Ara (Altar)
Aries (Ram)
Auriga (Charioteer)
Boötes (Herdsman)
Caelum (Chisel)
Camelopardalis (Giraffe)
Cancer (Crab, Moon Child (US)
Canes Venatici (Hunting Dogs)
Canis Major (Great Dog)
Canis Minor (Little Dog)
Capricornus *or* Capricorn (Sea Goat *or* Goat)
Carina (Keel)
Cassiopeia
Centaurus (Centaur)
Cepheus
Cetus (Whale)
Chameleon
Circinus (Compasses)
Columba (Dove)
Coma Berenices (Bernice's Hair)
Corona Australis (Southern Crown)
Corona Borealis (Northern Crown)
Corvus (Crow)
Crater (Cup)
Crux (*or* Crux Australis) (Southern Cross)
Cygnus (Swan)
Delphinus (Dolphin)
Dorado (Swordfish)
Draco (Dragon)
Equuleus (Little Horse)
Eridanus (River)
Fornax (Furnace)
Gemini (Twins)
Grus (Crane)
Hercules
Horologium (Clock)
Hydra (Monster *or* Sea Serpent)
Hydrus (Water Snake)
Indus (Indian)
Lacerta (Lizard)
Leo (Lion)
Leo Minor (Little Lion)
Lepus (Hare)
Libra (Balance *or* Scales)
Lupus (Wolf)
Lynx
Lyra (Lyre)
Mensa (Table Mountain)
Microscopium (Microscope)
Monoceros (Unicorn)
Musca (Fly)
Norma (Rule *or* Level)
Octans (Octant)
Ophiuchus (Serpent Bearer)
Orion
Pavo (Peacock)
Pegasus
Perseus
Phoenix
Pictor (Painter)
Pisces (Fishes)
Piscis Austrinus (Southern Fish)
Piscis Volans *or* Volans (Flying Fish)
Puppis (Poop *or* Stern)
Pyxis (Mariner's Compass)
Reticulum (Net)
Sagitta (Arrow)
Sagittarius (Archer)
Scorpius (Scorpion)
Sculptor
Scutum (Shield)
Serpens (Serpent)
Sextans (Sextant)
Taurus (Bull)
Telescopium (Telescope)
Triangulum (Triangle)
Triangulum Australe (Southern Triangle)
Tucana (Toucan)
Ursa Major (Great Bear)
Ursa Minor (Little Bear)
Vela (Sails)
Virgo (Virgin *or* Maiden)
Volans *or* Piscis Volans (Flying Fish)
Vulpecula (Fox)

THE CONSTELLATIONS (COMMON NAMES)

Common Name (Technical Name)

Air Pump or Pump (Antlia)
Altar (Ara)
Andromeda
Archer (Sagittarius)
Arrow (Sagitta)
Balance *or* Scales (Libra)
Bernice's Hair (Coma Berenices)
Bird of Paradise (Apus)
Bull (Taurus)
Cassiopeia
Centaur (Centaurus)
Cepheus
Chameleon
Charioteer (Auriga)
Chisel (Caelum)
Clock (Horologium)
Compasses (Circinus)
Crab *or* Moon Child (US) (Cancer)
Crane (Grus)
Crow (Corvus)
Cup (Crater)
Dolphin (Delphinus)
Dove (Columba)
Dragon (Draco)
Eagle (Aquila)
Fishes (Pisces)
Fly (Musca)
Flying Fish (Volans *or* Pisces Volans)
Fox (Vulpecula)
Furnace (Fornax)
Giraffe (Camelopardalis)
Goat *or* Sea Goat (Capricornus *or* Capricorn)
Great Bear (Ursa Major)
Great Dog (Canis Major)
Hare (Lepus)
Hercules
Herdsman (Boötes)
Hunting Dogs (Canes Venatici)
Indian (Indus)
Keel (Carina)
Level *or* Rule (Norma)
Lion (Leo)
Little Bear (Ursa Minor)
Little Dog (Canis Minor)
Little Horse (Equuleus)
Little Lion (Leo Minor)
Lizard (Lacerta)
Lynx
Lyre (Lyra)
Maiden *or* Virgin (Virgo)
Mariner's Compass (Pyxis)
Microscope (Microscopium)
Monster *or* Sea Serpent (Hydra)
Moon Child (US) *or* Crab (Cancer)
Net (Reticulum)
Northern Crown (Corona Borealis)
Octant (Octans)
Orion
Painter (Pictor)
Peacock (Pavo)
Pegasus
Perseus
Phoenix
Poop *or* Stern (Puppis)
Pump *or* Air Pump (Antlia)
Ram (Aries)
River (Eridanus)
Rule *or* Level (Norma)
Sails (Vela)
Scales *or* Balance (Libra)
Scorpion (Scorpius)
Sculptor
Sea Goat *or* Goat (Capricornus)
Serpent (Serpens)
Serpent Bearer (Ophiuchus)
Sextant (Sextans)
Shield (Scutum)
Southern Cross (Crux *or* Crux Australis)
Southern Crown (Corona Australis)
Southern Fish (Piscis Austrinus)
Southern Triangle (Triangulum Australe)
Stern or Poop (Puppis)
Swan (Cygnus)
Swordfish (Dorado)
Table Mountain (Mensa)
Telescope (Telescopium)
Toucan (Tucana)
Triangulum (Triangle)
Twins (Gemini)
Unicorn (Monoceros)
Virgin *or* Maiden (Virgo)
Water Bearer (Aquarius)
Water Snake (Hydrus)
Whale (Ceta)
Wolf (Lupus)

8 interstellar medium, cosmic dust, interstellar dust, interstellar gas, interstellar molecule, HI region, HII region, nebula, emission nebula, reflection nebula, bright nebula, absorption nebula, dark nebula, gaseous nebula, diffuse nebula, planetary nebula, ring nebula, Orion nebula, Crab nebula, Horsehead nebula, Coalsack, cosmic rays

9 constellation, zodiac, stellar cluster, globular cluster, open cluster, stellar group, stellar association, stellar population, double star, optical double, binary star, visual binary, eclipsing binary, spectroscopic binary, close binary, X-ray binary, multiple star

10 star, luminary, orb, sphere, heavenly body, celestial body, fixed star, evening star, Hesperus, Vesper, morning

NAMED STARS

Star (Constellation)
Achernar (Eridanus)
Acrux *or* Alpha Crucis (Crux)
Adhara (Canis Major)
Albireo (Cygnus)
Alcaid *or* Alkaid *or* Benatnasch (Ursa Major)
Alcor (Ursa Major)
Alcyone (Taurus)
Aldebaran (Taurus)
Algeiba (Leo)
Algenib (Pegasus)
Algol (Perseus)
Alioth (Ursa Major)
Alkaid *or* Alcaid *or* Benatnasch (Ursa Major)
Almach (Andromeda)
Alpha Centauri *or* Rigil Kent (Centaurus)
Alpha Crucis *or* Acrux (Crux)
Alphard (Hydra)
Alpheratz (Andromeda)
Altair (Aquila)
Antares (Scorpius)
Arcturus (Boötes)
Barnard's Star (Ophiuchus)
Bellatrix (Orion)
Beta Centauri *or* Hadar (Centaurus)
Beta Crucis *or* Mimosa (Crux)
Betelgeuse (Orion)
Canopus (Carina)
Capella (Auriga)
Castor (Gemini)
Cor Caroli (Canes Venatici)
61 Cygni (Cygnus)
Deneb (Cygnus)
Denebola (Leo)
Dog Star *or* Sirius (Canis Major)
Dubhe (Ursa Major)
El Nath (Taurus)
Epsilon Eridani (Eridanus)
Epsilon Indi (Indus)
Fomalhaut (Piscis Austrinus)
Garnet star (Cepheus)
Hadar *or* Beta Centauri (Centaurus)
Kepler's star (Ophiuchus)
Kruger
Lalande
Luyten
Markab (Pegasus)
Merak (Ursa Major)
Mimosa *or* Beta Crucis (Crux)
Mira (Orion)
Mirach (Andromeda)
Mirfak (Perseus)
Mirzam (Canis Major)
Naos (Puppis)
North Star *or* Polaris (Ursa Minor)
Phecda *or* Phekda (Ursa Major)
Polaris *or* North Star (Ursa Minor)
Pollux (Gemini)
Porrima (Virgo)
Procyon (Canis Minor)
Proxima Centauri (Centaurus)
Ras Algethi (Hercules)
Regulus (Leo)
Rigel (Orion)
Rigil Kent *or* Alpha Centauri (Centaurus)
Ross
Saiph (Orion)
Scheat (Pegasus)
Schedar *or* Shedir (Cassiopeia)
Shaula (Scorpius)
Shedir *or* Schedar (Cassiopeia)
Sirius *or* Dog Star (Canis Major)
Spica (Virgo)
Tau Ceti (Cetus)
Thuban (Draco)
Trapezium (Orion)
Tycho's star (Cassiopeia)
Vega (Lyra)
Wolf
Zeta Aurigae (Auriga)

star, Lucifer, circumpolar star, nebulous star, variable star

11 **stellar birth**, protostar, molecular cloud, stellar evolution, main sequence, gravitational collapse, dying star, red giant, white dwarf, supernova, supernova remnant, neutron star, pulsar, black hole, event horizon, singularity, white hole

12 **variable star**, Algol variable, pulsating variable, Cepheid variable, Mira variable, RR Lyrae star, cataclysmic variable, nova, recurrent nova, flare star

13 **luminosity**, magnitude, apparent magnitude, absolute magnitude, proper motion, radial velocity, parallax, precession, spectral type, O star, B star, A star, F star, G star, K star, M star, luminosity class, supergiant, giant star, giant, subgiant, main-sequence star, Hertzsprung–Russell diagram

14 **solar system**, planetary system, Kepler's laws, interplanetary space, solar wind, zodiacal light, gegenschein, earthshine, the old moon in the new moon's arms

15 **sun**, daystar, Sol, Helios, Hyperion, sunlight, sunshine, midnight sun, solar eclipse, corona, chromosphere, photosphere, solar activity, active sun, quiet sun, solar cycle, sunspot cycle, 11-year cycle, butterfly diagram, solar flare, prominence, sunspot, facula, filament, granule, solar spectrum, Fraunhofer lines

16 **planet**, major planet, Mercury, Venus, Earth, Mars (*or* Red Planet), Jupiter, Saturn, Uranus, Neptune, Pluto, giant planet, Jovian planet, terrestrial planet, inferior planet, superior planet, wandering star, minor planet, asteroid, asteroid belt, planetoid, earthgrazer, opposition, conjunction, greatest elongation, syzygy, albedo, planetary atmosphere, aurora, radiation belt, Van Allen belts, magnetosphere

17 **moon**, moonlight, phase, new moon, full moon, harvest moon, hunter's moon, crescent moon, horned moon, first quarter, last quarter, half-moon, gibbous moon, waxing moon, waning moon, terminator, libration, lunar month, lunar eclipse, crater, mare (*pl.* maria), sea, basin, highlands, rille, mascon, queen of night, Sister Moon, Selene, Diana, Cynthia, Artemis, man in the moon

18 **satellite**, natural satellite, moon, Galilean satellite

19 **comet**, cometary nucleus, coma, tail, dirty snowball, Oort cloud

20 **meteor**, shooting star, falling star, fireball, bolide, meteor shower, meteor swarm, radiant, meteorite, iron meteorite (*or* iron), stony meteorite (*or* stone), aerolite, siderite, siderolite, chondrite, carbonaceous chondrite,

OTHER GROUPS OF STARS

Diamond of Virgo
False Cross (Carina, Vela)
Great Square of Pegasus
Orion's Belt
Orion's Sword
Pleiades *or* Seven Sisters
Plough *or* Big Dipper (US) (Ursa Major)
Pointers (Ursa Major)
Sickle of Leo

PLANETS AND THEIR SATELLITES

Planet (Named Satellites)
Mercury
Venus
Earth (Moon)
Mars (Phobos, Deimos)
Jupiter (Metis, Adastea, Amalthea, Thebe, Io, Europa, Ganymede, Callisto, Leda, Milalia, Lysithea, Elara, Ananke, Carme, Pasiphae, Sinope)
Saturn (Mimas, Enceladus, Tethys, Dione, Rhea, Titan, Hyperion, Iapetus, Phoebe, Janus)
Uranus (Miranda, Ariel, Umbriel, Titania, Oberon)
Neptune (Triton, Nereid)
Pluto (Charon)

Minor Planets
Achilles
Adonis
Amor
Apollo
Astraea
Aten
Ceres
Chiron
Eros
Eunomia
Euphrosyne
Hebe
Hermes
Hidalgo
Hygiea
Icarus
Iris
Juno
Pallas
Vesta

LUNAR FEATURES

Craters
Aitken
Alphonsus
Archimedes
Aristarchus
Aristillus
Arzarchel
Autolycus
Bailly
Clavius
Cleomedes
Copernicus
Cyrillas
Eratosthenes
Gassendi
Giordano Bruno
Grimaldi
Jules Verne
Kepler
Langrenus
Plato
Proclus
Ptolemaeus
Reiner
Schickard
Schiller
Stevinus
Theophilus
Tsiolkovsky
Tycho
Wargentin
Van de Graaff

Mountains
Alps
Altai Scarp
Apennines
Apollonius
Aristarchus Plateau
Carpathians
Caucasus
Cordillera
Haemus
Harbinger
La Hire
Marius Hills
Piton
Pyrenees
Riphaeus
Rook
Rümker Hills
Spitzbergen
Straight
Taurus
Tenerife

Rills and Valleys
Alpine Valley
Aridaeus
Byrgius
Cauchy Fault
Hadley
Hyginus
Lee Lincoln Scarp
Posidonius
Rheita Valley
Schröter's Valley
Schrödinger Canyon
Sirsalis
Straight Wall

Seas (Maria)
Oceanus Procellarum (Ocean of Storms)
Mare Imbrium (Sea of Rains)
Mare Serenitatis (Sea of Serenity)
Mare Fecunditatis (Sea of Fertility)
Mare Tranquillitatis (Sea of Tranquillity)
Mare Crisium (Sea of Crises)
Mare Humorum (Sea of Moisture)
Mare Nectaris (Sea of Nectar)
Mare Frigoris (Sea of Cold)
Mare Orientale (Eastern Sea)
Mare Australe (Southern Sea)
Mare Cognitum (Sea of Knowledge)
Mare Nubium (Sea of Clouds)
Mare Marginis (Border Sea)
Mare Smythii (Smyth's Sea)
Mare Spumans (Foaming Sea)
Mare Undarum (Sea of Waves)
Mare Humboldtianum (Humboldt's Sea)
Mare Moscoviense (Sea of Moscow)
Mare Ingenii (Sea of Ingenuity)
Mare Anguis (Serpent Sea)
Mare Vaporum (Sea of Vapours)
Sinus Medii (Central Bay)
Sinus Aestuum (Bay of Heats)
Sinus Roris (Bay of Dews)
Sinus Amoris (Bay of Love)
Sinus Iridum (Bay of Rainbows)
Palus Putredinis (Marsh of Decay)
Palus Somnii (Marsh of Sleep)
Palus Epidemiarum (Marsh of Epidemics)
Palus Nebularum (Marsh of Mists)
Lacus Mortis (Lake of Death)
Lacus Somniorum (Lake of Dreams)
Lacus Veris (Lake of Spring)
Lacus Autumni (Lake of Autumn)

achondrite, find, fall, meteorite crater, tektite, meteoroid, micrometeorite

21 orbit, elliptical orbit, revolution, trajectory, orbital period, eccentricity, inclination, semimajor axis, perihelion, aphelion, parabolic orbit, hyperbolic orbit, rotation, rotational axis, rotational period, precession, eclipse, transit, occultation, twinkling, scintillation, zenith, nadir, fiducial point, reddening, redshift, blueshift

22 astronomical unit, light year, parsec, solar mass

23 observatory, astronomical observatory, ground-based observatory, optical observatory, infrared observatory, Royal Greenwich Observatory (RGO), Royal Observatory Edinburgh (ROE), Mauna Kea Observatory, Palomar Observatory, Hale Observatories, Kitt Peak National Observatory (KPNO), Anglo-Australian Observatory, European Southern Observatory (ESO), dome, observation, seeing, light pollution, radio observatory, Jodrell Bank, planetarium, planisphere, astrolabe, orrery

24 telescope, astronomical telescope, optical telescope, reflector (*or* reflecting telescope), William Herschel Telescope, Anglo-Australian Telescope, Hale Telescope, Hubble Space Telescope, Cassegrain telescope, Newtonian telescope, Schmidt telescope, Dobsonian telescope, refractor (*or* refracting telescope), Galilean telescope, Keplerian telescope, infrared telescope, flux collector, solar telescope, heliostat

25 mounting, equatorial mounting, altazimuth mounting, guide telescope, finder, setting circle, draw tube, collimation, primary mirror, objective lens, eyepiece, spherical aberration, coma, astigmatism, chromatic aberration

26 radio telescope, radio dish, antenna, receiver, array, radio interferometer, Very Large Array (VLA), aperture synthesis, very long baseline interferometry (VLBI), X-ray telescope, grazing-incidence telescope

27 imaging, wide-angle photography, spectrometry, photometry, interferometry, blink comparator, detector, recording system, imaging system, spectrometer, spectrograph, photometer, radiometer

28 resolution, angular resolution, resolving power, aperture, light-gathering power, limiting magnitude, field of view

29 astronautics, cosmonautics, space (*or* aerospace) engineering, space (*or* aerospace) technology, space (*or* aerospace) research, space (*or* aerospace) science, space navigation, space exploration, space (*or* aerospace) medicine, bioastronautics

30 spacecraft, space capsule, space probe, module, lunar module, space station, Mir, Salyut, Skylab, space shuttle, shuttle, Columbia, Challenger, 496 Discovery, Atlantis, space laboratory, spacelab, space platform, spaceship

31 space travel, trip to the moon, manned flight, spaceflight, space age, NASA (National Aeronautics and Space Administration), ESA (European Space Agency), Vostok, Apollo, Soyuz, astronaut, cosmonaut, spaceman, spacewoman, weightlessness, free fall, microgravity, spacesuit, space helmet, spacewalk, extravehicular activity (EVA), space port, lunar base, moon base

COMETS

Arend–Roland	Faye	Pons–Brooks
Bennett	Giacobini–Zinner	Pons–Winnecke
Biela	Grigg–Skiellerup	Schaumasse
Borrelly	Hale–Bopp	Shoemaker–Levy
Bronsen–Metcalf	Halley	Stephan–Oterma
Comas Solá	Kohoutek	Tuttle
Crommelin	Kopff	West
Daylight Comet	Lexell	Westphal
Encke	Olbers	Whipple

32 **satellite**, artificial satellite, earth satellite, unmanned satellite, Sputnik, research satellite, astronomical satellite, X-ray satellite, space observatory, orbiting observatory, geophysical satellite, communications satellite, Telstar™, geostationary orbit, geosynchronous orbit, meteorological satellite, weather satellite, navigational satellite, spy satellite, solar cell, solar panel, telemetry, data transmission, satellite tracking, tracking station, relay station

33 **planetary probe**, orbiter, lander, Mariner, Pioneer, Viking, Voyager, Venera

34 **SETI (search for extraterrestrial intelligence)**, flying saucer, UFO (unidentified flying object), alien, LGM (Little Green Man)

35 **rocketry**, rocket propulsion, engine, booster, propellant, liquid fuel, solid fuel, burn, thrust, launch vehicle, launcher, Ariane, Saturn V, Delta, multistage rocket, payload, retrorocket, solid rocket booster (SRB), escape velocity, orbit, earth orbit, perigee, apogee, parking orbit, transfer orbit, insertion, injection, trajectory, flyby, rendezvous, docking, re-entry, splashdown, soft landing, hard landing

ADJECTIVES

36 **astronomical**, astrophysical, cosmological, uranographic(al), cosmic, celestial, heavenly, universal, infinite, boundless, galactic, intergalactic, extragalactic, interstellar, stellar, sidereal, starry, astral, star-studded, solar, heliacal, interplanetary, planetary, Mercurian, Venusian, Martian, Jovian, Saturnian, Neptunian, Uranian, Plutonian, extraterrestrial, extramundane, terrestrial, telluric, tellurian, synodic, lunar, asteroidal, cometary, meteoric, meteoritic, heliocentric, geocentric, telescopic, spectrometric, photometric, astronautic(al)

VERBS

37 **observe**, orbit, revolve, rotate, eclipse, transit, radiate, shine, twinkle, emit, absorb

38 **launch**, enter orbit, travel in space

ADVERBS

39 **astronomically**, astrophysically, cosmologically, cosmically, celestially, universally, infinitely, boundlessly, galactically, intergalactically, extragalactically, sidereally, extraterrestrially, terrestrially, meteorically, heliocentrically

METEOR SHOWERS

Australids	Ophiuchids
Capricornids	Orionids
Cepheids	Perseids
Cygnids	Phoenicids
Geminids	Quadrantids
Leonids	Taurids
Lyrids	Ursids

30 Earth Science

We are living beyond our means. As a people we have developed a life-style that is draining the earth of its priceless and irreplaceable resources without regard for the future of our children and people all around the world. Margaret Mead.

NOUNS

1 **earth science**, geoscience, geology, physical geology, structural geology, mineralogy, petrology, hydrology, geochemistry, tectonics, volcanology, marine geology, glaciology, geomorphology, physiography, pedology, geodesy, historical geology, stratigraphy, palaeontology, palaeogeography, palaeoclimatology, geochronology, economic geology, geopolitics, planetology, astrogeology, geography, human geography, physical geography

2 **geophysics**, geomagnetism, geomagnetics, gravity geophysics, gravimetry, solid-earth geophysics, seismology, seismography, volcanology, plate tectonics, physical oceanography, climatology, meteorology

► *28 Physics; 31 Meteorology and Climatology*

3 **geologist**, mineralogist, petrologist, hydrologist, geochemist, volcanologist, glaciologist, geomorphologist, physiographer, pedologist, geodesist, stratigrapher (*or* stratigraphist), palaeogeographer, palaeoclimatologist, palaeontologist, geochronologist, planetologist

4 **geophysicist**, geomagnetist, seismologist, volcanologist, oceanographer, climatologist, meteorologist

5 **earth**, planet earth, the world, the globe, earth's surface, surface, atmosphere, hydrosphere, waters of the earth, geosphere, biosphere, ecosphere, asthenosphere, geoid, mother earth, Gaia

6 **continent**, subcontinent, continental shelf, continental margin, continental drift, land, mainland, landmass, dry land, ground, topography, relief, elevation, terrain, landscape

7 **landform**, surface feature, natural feature, geomorphic feature, geographical feature, basin, plain, coastal plain, flood plain, shield, valley, rift valley, V-shaped valley, U-shaped valley, glacial valley, fjord, hanging valley, cirque, cwm, valley floor, canyon, gorge, ravine, hill, plateau, scarp (*or* escarpment), mountain, arrête

► *89 Mountains; 92 Other Geographical Features*

8 **drainage**, drainage system, river network, drainage channel, stream course, drainage pattern, drainage basin, catchment area, watershed, divide, continental divide

9 **groundwater**, subsurface water, subterranean water, underground water, water table, aquifer, artesian basin, artesian spring

10 **water cycle**, hydrological cycle, evaporation, transpiration, precipitation, runoff, percolation

► *31 Meteorology and Climatology; 88 Lakes; 90 Rivers; 91 Seas; 92 Other Geographical Features*

11 **coast**, coastline, shore, shoreline, seaside, cliff, stack, beach, shingle, sand dune, sand bar, bar, spit, sandbank, sand wave, barrier island, barrier reef, lagoon, peninsula

12 ocean, deep ocean, ocean depths, coastal waters, sea water, ocean water, salinity, sea level

13 ocean current, surface current, wind-induced current, tidal current, density current (*or* subsurface current), circulation pattern, lateral movement, vertical movement, gyre, up-welling, down-welling, Gulf Stream

14 wave, seawave, ocean wave, swell, roller, breaker, surf, spume, white horses, whitecap, white foam, storm wave, seiche, tsunami, seismic seawave, tidal wave

15 tide, spring tide, neap tide, high tide, low tide, tidal range, intertidal zone

16 ocean floor, ocean basin, sea floor, continental margin, continental shelf, continental slope, continental rise, submarine canyon, land bridge, abyssal plain, abyssal hill, midoceanic (*or* midocean) ridge, oceanic ridge, Mid-Atlantic Ridge, oceanic trench, Mariana Trench, Tonga Trench, Kuril Trench, volcanic island, seamount, guyot, atoll

17 ocean research vessel, drilling vessel, submersible, bathysphere, bathyscaph (*or* bathyscape), deep-sea drilling, echo sounding, sub-bottom profiling, bathymetry, hydrography

18 earth's crust, crust, continental crust, oceanic crust, mantle, core, bedding plane, discontinuity, Mohorovičić discontinuity (*or* Moho *or* M discontinuity), lithosphere, asthenosphere, isostacy, isostatic equilibrium, sial, sima

19 plate tectonics, plate, lithospheric plate, plate margin, plate boundary, divergence zone, convergence zone, subduction zone, midoceanic ridge, oceanic trench, transform fault, seafloor spreading, continental drift, Gondwana, Laurasia, Pangaea

20 earth movement, crustal movement, diastrophism, tectonic forces, deformation, strain, folding, fracture, faulting, cleavage, jointing, uplift, subsidence, fold, upright fold, inclined fold, overturned fold, recumbent fold, fold-hinge, anticline, syncline, fault, normal fault, block fault, reverse fault, thrust fault, Moine Thrust, slip-strike fault, joint, fault line, San Andreas fault, mobile belt, mountain belt, island arc

21 mountain building, orogenesis, orogeny, fold mountain, fold-belt mountain, alpine chain, fault-block mountain, oceanic ridge, oceanic rise, volcanic mountain

► *89 Mountains; 92 Other Geographical Features*

22 seismic activity, seismicity, earthquake, seism, seismic event, temblor (US), quake, macroseism, major earthquake, microseism, minor earthquake, earth tremor, shock, foreshock, main shock, aftershock, focus, epicentre, earthquake magnitude, Richter scale, earthquake zone

23 seismic wave, body wave, primary wave (*or* P wave), secondary wave (*or* S wave), surface wave, seismograph

24 volcanic activity, volcanism (*or* vulcanism), volcano, active volcano, inactive volcano, shield volcano, volcanic cone, composite volcano (*or* stratovolcano), crater, caldera, vent, fissure, magma chamber, magma, melt

25 eruption, lava, ejecta, tephra, pyroclastic material, ash, pumice, volcanic gas, lava flow, aa, pahoehoe (*or* ropy lava), pillow lava, fumurole, gas vent, geyser, hot spring, thermal spring

► *92 Other Geographical Features*

26 mass movement, landslide, slide, glide, slump, mudflow, debris flow, earthflow, plastic flow, lahar, creep, rock fall, avalanche

27 sediment, mud, deposit, organic sediment, inorganic sediment, oceanic sediment, pelagic ooze, ooze, alluvial deposit, delta, lake sediment, glacial deposit, rock, boulder, stone, gravel, granules, pebbles, shingle, chesil, sand, grain of sand, silt, clay, loess, bedrock

28 rock, mineral aggregate, stone, igneous rock, sedimentary rock, metamorphic rock, rock formation, texture, crystalline texture, coarse-grained texture, medium-grained texture, fine-grained texture, porphyritic texture, aphanitic texture, cleavage, slaty cleavage, fabric, facies, rock-forming mineral, xenolith, batholith, laccolith, lopolith

29 petrogenesis, lithification, sedimentation, consolidation, cementation, crystallization, magmatism, metamorphosis, recrystallization, foliation, intrusion, extrusion

30 igneous rock, magmatic rock, plutonic rock, plutonic intrusion, hypabyssal intrusion, dyke, sill, batholith, laccolith, pluton, volcanic rock, extrusive rock, pyroclastic rock, glassy rock, acid rock, intermediate rock, basic rock, ultrabasic rock, mafic rock, felsic rock, ultramafite, peridotite, perknite, picrite

31 sedimentary rock, lithified sediment, stratified rock, clastic rock, nonclastic rock, stratum (*pl.* strata), bed, bedding, breccia

32 metamorphism, regional metamorphism, contact metamorphism, thermal metamorphism, dynamic metamorphism, dislocation metamorphism, metamorphic grade, cataclasis, retrograde metamorphism, autometamorphism

33 metamorphic rock, parent rock, low-grade rock, high-grade rock, primary character, secondary character, foliated rock, schistosity, ultrametamorphic rock

34 mineral, crystalline mineral, noncrystalline mineral, amorphous mineral, rock-forming mineral, silicate, neosilicate, sorosilicate, cyclosilicate, inosilicate, phyllosilicate, tectosilicate, feldspar, alkali feldspar, chromite, magmatite, pegmatite, mica, orthoclase, oligoclase, pla-

COMMON ROCKS

Igneous Rocks		
andesite	rhyolite	oolite
anorthosite	serpentine	sandstone
aplite	syenite	shale
appinite	trachyte	siltstone
basalt	**Sedimentary Rocks**	**Metamorphic Rocks**
breccia	argillite	epidiorite
diorite	breccia	gneiss
dolerite	chalk	granulite
gabbro	chert	hornblende
granite	claystone	hornfels
monzonite	coal	marble
obsidian	conglomerate	mylorite
pegmatite	flint	phyllite
peridotite	limestone	quartzite
porphyrite	marl	schist
porphyry	mudstone	slate

MINERALS

actinolite	bornite	diamond	hawk's-eye	monzonite	rhodonite	thorianite
albite	braunite	diaspore	hematite	mullite	rutile	thorite
allanite	brookite	diopside	hemimorphite	muscovite	samarskite	tiemannite
allophane	calaverite	dioptase	hessite	natrolite	saponite	topaz
alunite	calcite	diorite	heulandite	natron	sapphirine	torbernite
amblygonite	carnallite	dolomite	hiddenite	nepheline	scapolite	tourmaline
analcite	carnotite	dumortierite	hornblende	nephrite	scheelite	tremolite
anatase	cassiterite	emery	hyacinth	niccolite	scolecite	triphylite
andalusite	celestite	enstatite	hypersthene	olivenite	senarmontite	trona
andesine	cerargyrite	epidote	illite	opal	serpentine	troostite
andradite	cerussite	erythrite	ilmenite	orpiment	siderite	tungstite
anglesite	chabazite	euxenite	jadeite	ozocerite	siderolite	turgite
anhydrite	chalcanthite	fayalite	jarosite	pentlandite	sillimanite	turquoise
ankerite	chalcocite	fluorapatite	kainite	periclase	smaltite	uralite
annabergite	chalcopyrite	fluorspar	kaolinite	perovskite	smaragdite	uraninite
anorthite	Chile saltpetre	fool's gold	kernite	petuntse	smectite	vanadinite
apatite	chlorite	forsterite	kieserite	phenacite	smithsonite	variscite
apophyllite	chromite	franklinite	kunzite	phosgenite	sodalite	vermiculite
aragonite	chrysoberyl	fulgurite	lapis lazuli	phosphorite	sperrylite	vesuvian
argentite	chrysotile	gadolinite	lazulite	piedmontite	sphalerite	vesuvianite
arsenopyrite	cinnabar	gahnite	leucite	pinite	sphene	water sapphire
asbestos	cleveite	galena	limonite	pitchblende	spherulite	wavellite
augite	cobaltite	garnet	magnesite	pollucite	spodumene	wernerite
autunite	colemanite	garnierite	magnetite	polybasite	stannite	white alkali
axinite	columbite	gehlenite	malachite	proustite	staurolite	willemite
azurite	coprolite	germanite	manganite	psilomelane	stibnite	witherite
baddeleyite	cordierite	geyserite	marcasite	pyrargyrite	stilbite	wolframite
barytes	corundum	gibbsite	margarite	pyrite	strontianite	wollastonite
bastnaesite	cristobalite	glance	massicot	pyrolusite	sylvanite	wulfenite
beryl	crocidolite	glauconite	meerschaum	pyromorphite	sylvite	zeolite
biotite	crocoite	goethite	microcline	pyrophyllite	talc	zincite
bismuthinite	cryolite	greenockite	millerite	pyroxenite	tantalite	zinkenite
blackjack	cuprite	gummite	mimetite	pyrrhotite	tenorite	zircon
Boehmite	cyanite	gypsum	molybdenite	quartz	tetradymite	zoisite
boracite	datolite	halite	monazite	realgar	tetrahedrite	
borax	diallage	harmotome	montmorillonite	rhodochrosite	thenardite	

gioclase, olivine, chrysolite, pyroxene, orthopyroxene, clinopyroxene, amphibole, spinel, clay mineral

▶ *32 Chemistry*

35 weathering, mechanical weathering, chemical weathering, erosion, wind erosion, wave erosion, rain erosion, river erosion, ice erosion, glacial erosion, denudation, deposition, sedimentation, abrasion, striation

▶ *31 Meteorology and Climatology*

36 soil, earth, topsoil, subsoil, regolith, soil profile, soil horizon, A horizon, B horizon, C horizon, soil texture, gravel, sand, loam, silt, clay, soil structure, alluvium, pedalfer, podzol, pedocal, lateritic soil, soil erosion

▶ *44 Horticulture*

37 dune, sand dune, coastal dune, desert dune, longitudinal dune, seif, crescent dune, barchan, transverse dune

38 glacier, alpine glacier, valley glacier, cirque glacier, continental glacier, continental ice sheet, ice sheet, icecap, ice field, crevasse, icefall, sérac, ice shelf, ice tongue, snout, moraine, till, boulder clay, drift, erratic, meltwater, glacier milk

39 iceberg, berg, growler, calf, sea ice, ice floe, floe, pack ice, ice pack, ice raft

40 glaciation, glacial advance, glacial surge, glacial period, ice age, glacial maximum, stadial, interglacial, deglaciation, glacial recession (*or* retreat)

41 geological time, geological time scale, geological time unit, geochronological unit, eon, olam, era, period, subperiod, epoch, chronostratigraphic unit, time-rock unit, rock division, eonothem, erathem, system, series, stage, relative age, absolute age, uniformitarianism

42 dating, radioactive dating, radiometric dating, uranium–lead dating, potassium–argon dating, rubidium–strontium dating, radiocarbon dating, carbon-14 dating, dendrochronology

43 fossil, fossil record, fossil man, hominid, fossil animal, fossil plant, ammonite, trilobite, graptolite, coprolite, petrified wood, coal, index fossil, zone fossil, mineralized bone, mineralized shell, cast, mould, fossil track, fossil footprint, fossilization, mineralization, petrification

▶ *70 Animals*

44 geomagnetism, terrestrial magnetism, geomagnetic field, magnetosphere, magnetopause, magnetic anomaly, magnetic storm, palaeomagnetism, polarity reversal, magnetic reversal

45 magnetic pole, geomagnetic pole, north magnetic pole, south magnetic pole, magnetic equator, aclinic line, agonic line, declination, dip, inclination, polar wandering

46 aurora, polar lights, auroral display, aurora borealis, northern lights, aurora australis, southern lights

47 **radiation belt**, Van Allen belts, ozonosphere, ozone layer

ADJECTIVES

48 **geological**, mineralogical, petrological, hydrological, geochemical, volcanological, glaciological, geomorphological, pedological, geodetic, stratigraphical, palaeontological, geochronological, geopolitical

49 **geophysical**, geomagnetic, palaeomagnetic, gravimetric, seismological, seismographic, seismometric, oceanographic, bathymetric, hydrographic, climatological, meteorological

► *31 Meteorology and Climatology*

50 **terrestrial**, global, surficial, atmospheric, hydrospheric, geospheric, continental, topographical, subsurface, subterranean, underground

51 **oceanic**, deep-sea, marine, maritime, undersea, submarine, suboceanic, thalassic, pelagic, benthic, bathymal, abyssal, hadal, terrigenous

52 **coastal**, littoral, neritic, tidal, intertidal, riverine, alluvial

53 **solid-earth**, crustal, lithospheric, sialic, isostatic

54 **tectonic**, deformational, diastrophic, orogenic, epeirogenic

55 **volcanic**, eruptive, seismic, pyroclastic, molten, laval

56 **petrographic**, petrographical, petrological, petrogenic, lithic, consolidated, unconsolidated, igneous, magmatic, volcanic, plutonic, pyroclastic, intrusive, extrusive, sedimentary, stratified, clastic, detrital, metamorphic, foliated

57 **chalky**, flinty, shaly, slaty, basaltic, granitic, gneissic, gneissoid, gneissose, schistose, calcareous

58 **earthy**, rocky, stony, gravelly, pebbly, sandy, loamy, silty, clayey

59 **weathered**, eroded, abraded, scoured, gouged, striated

60 **glaciated**, glacial, interglacial, postglacial, morainal, morainic

61 **fossilized**, petrified, mineralized, fossiliferous

VERBS

62 **lithify**, crystallize, recrystallize, mineralize, fossilize, petrify, consolidate, cement

63 **ebb**, flow, drain, run off, percolate, well up, spring up, evaporate, transpire, precipitate, ooze, settle

64 **fold**, fracture, strain, cleave, subside, quake, tremble, shake

65 **map**, chart, plan, survey, explore, mine, quarry

ADVERBS

66 **geographically**, geologically, geomorphologically, geodetically, palaeogeographically, topographically, seismologically, petrographically, petrologically, mineralogically, tidally, bathymetrically, hydrologically, meteorologically, continentally, volcanically, on the coast, under the ground

31 Meteorology and Climatology

The work is going well, but it looks like the end of the world.
Frank Rowland, about his research into the destruction of the ozone layer.

NOUNS

1 **meteorology**, aerology, weather science, synoptic meteorology, weather forecasting, micrometeorology, macrometeorology, agricultural meteorology, aviation meteorology, maritime meteorology, atmospheric physics, hydrometeorology, hyetography, nephology, nephanalysis, anemology, climatology, planetary meteorology

2 **meteorologist**, climatologist, weather forecaster, weatherman, weatherwoman, weather observer, weather prophet

3 **weather**, weather situation, pattern, conditions, the elements, period, interval, spell, weather lore, St Swithin's day, Groundhog Day, dog days, halcyon days, blackthorn winter, Indian summer

4 **weather forecast**, forecast, report, bulletin, regional forecast, outlook, general outlook, travel report, road report, short-term forecast, medium-term forecast, long-term forecast, long-range forecast, numerical forecast, shipping forecast, general synopsis, sea area, hurricane (*or* storm *or* gale) warning, tornado watch, weather map, synoptic map (*or* chart), weather symbols, isobar, isotherm, weather bureau, US Weather Bureau, Meteorological Office (*or* Met. Office)

5 **weather station**, land station, ground station, field station, coastal station, weather ship, automatic buoy, weather satellite, weather balloon, radiosonde

6 **weather data**, elements, air pressure, pressure gradient, pressure tendency, rising pressure, falling pressure, air temperature, dew point, humidity, relative humidity, absolute humidity, damp, dampness, moisture, air density, air movement, wind speed, wind strength, chill factor, wind-chill factor, anemogram

7 **weather instruments**, barometer, aneroid barometer, barograph, mercury barometer, glass, weatherglass, storm glass, thermometer, thermograph, hygrometer, psychrometer, hygrograph, Stevenson screen, wind gauge, anemometer, cup anemometer, anemograph, windsock, wind cone, wind sleeve, drogue, weather vane, weathercock, wind rose, rain gauge, pluviometer, udometer, weather radar, sunshine recorder

► *28 Physics*

8 **atmosphere**, earth's atmosphere, air, atmospheric layer, troposphere, stratosphere, upper atmosphere, ionosphere, ozone layer, ozonosphere, exosphere, tropopause, stratopause, atmospheric water vapour, clean dry air, condensation nuclei, atmospheric dust, pollution, pollutant, CFC (chlorofluorocarbon)

► *28 Physics*

9 **atmospheric process**, radiation balance, energy balance, absorption, reflection, scattering, heat transfer, heat transport, convection, radiation, advection, adiabatic process, adiabatic cooling, adiabatic lapse rate, water balance, evaporation, condensation, sublimation, saturation, supercooling, Coriolis force, geostrophic force

10 **air movement**, atmospheric circulation, air current, air flow, air stream, jetstream, convection cell, thermal, downdraught, updraught, air mass, cold air, warm air, moist air, dry air, polar air, tropical air, front, polar front, cold front, warm front, occlusion, occluded front, warm occlusion, cold occlusion

11 **weather system**, pressure system, frontal system, depression, area of low pressure, low, cyclone, shallow de-

pression, deepening depression, deep depression, filling depression, stationary depression, warm sector, area of high pressure, high, anticyclone, stationary high, blocking high, Azores high, Icelandic low, trough (*or* trough of low pressure), ridge (*or* ridge of high pressure)

12 wind, breeze, zephyr, surface wind, sea breeze, land breeze, onshore wind, offshore wind, local wind, katabatic wind, anabatic wind, mountain wind, valley wind, gust, scud, squall, wind storm, dust storm, sandstorm, upper wind, high-altitude wind, gradient wind, geostrophic wind

13 wind strength, wind force, wind speed, Beaufort scale, calm, light air, breeze, light breeze, gentle breeze, moderate breeze, fresh breeze, strong breeze, near gale, gale, strong gale, storm, violent storm, hurricane, variable wind, wind-chill, wind-chill factor

14 windiness, gustiness, breeziness, puff of wind, breath of wind, zephyr, fresh wind, brisk wind, high wind, strong wind, stiff wind, blow, blast, spanking wind, force eight, force nine, force ten, storm force ten, howling gale, tempest, full gale, half a gale (Inf)

15 wind direction, north wind, Boreas (Lit), northerly, norther (US), northeast wind, northeasterly, northeaster, east wind, Eurus (Lit), easterly, southeast wind, southeasterly, southeaster, south wind, Auster (Lit), southerly, southwest wind, southwesterly, southwester, west wind, Zephyr (Lit), westerly, northwest wind, northwesterly, northwester, prevailing wind, headwind, crosswind, tailwind, following wind, favourable wind, wind shift, backing, veering

16 wind vortex, eddy, rotating air mass, tropical revolving storm (TRS), tropical storm, cyclone (Indian Ocean), typhoon (N Pacific), hurricane (US and West Indies), Mauritius hurricane (Indian Ocean), South Seas hurricane (S Pacific), baguio (Philippines), willy-willy (Aus), eye of the storm, waterspout, tornado, whirlwind, dust devil, sand column, twister (US inf)

17 wind system, trade winds (*or* trades), northeast trades, southeast trades, intertropical convergence zone (ITCZ), doldrums, horse latitudes, roaring forties, antitrade winds (*or* antitrades), monsoon, summer monsoon, winter monsoon

18 cloud, high cloud, low cloud, cloud base, ice cloud, water cloud, mixed cloud, cirrus, cirrocumulus, altostratus, cirrostratus, altocumulus, nimbostratus, stratocumulus (*or* cumulostratus), stratus, cumulus, cumulonimbus, rain cloud, rain-bearing cloud, nimbus, scud, storm cloud, thundercloud, anvil cloud, dark cloud, noctilucent cloud

19 cloud cover, cloudiness, thin cloud, patchy cloud, broken cloud, thick cloud, dense cloud, widespread cloud, overcast sky

20 cloud appearance, filamentary cloud, wispy cloud, billowy cloud, fleecy cloud, feathery cloud, cottony cloud (US), wisp (*or* billow *or* patch) of cloud, mare's-tail, heaped cloud, globular cloud, lumpy cloud, band of cloud, belt of cloud, bank of cloud, roll of cloud, sheet of cloud, layer cloud, veil of cloud, cloud tower, cloud street, lenticular cloud, lee-wave cloud, iridescent cloud, mackerel sky, buttermilk sky (US)

21 thunderstorm, thunder, thunderclap, clap of thunder, lightning, lightning flash (*or* stroke), track, fork (*or* forked) lightning, sheet lightning, ball lightning, summer lightning, thunderbolt, bolt of lightning, electric storm, lightning strike, lightning conductor

22 sun, sunshine, strong sun, weak sun, recorded sunshine, clear sky, cloudless sky, blue sky, solar radiation, sunlight, ultraviolet radiation (UV), UVA, UVB, direct radiation, indirect radiation, halo, corona, parhelic circle, parhelion (*or* mock sun *or* sundog), anthelion (*or* countersun), solar power (*or* energy), sunbathing, sun worshipper, sunstroke, sunburn, suntan, suntanning, suntan lotion (*or* cream), barrier cream

23 heat, hot weather, hot spell, heat wave, Indian summer, humidness, humidity, muggy weather, muggy spell, warm weather, warm spell, sunny weather, sunny period (*or* interval), sunny spell, scorcher (Inf), sizzler (Inf)

24 precipitation, rain, hail, sleet, snow, rainfall, snowfall, rain day, raindrop, hailstone, snowflake, ice crystal, hydrometeor

25 rain, rainfall, rainwater, fine rain, drizzle, light rain, shower, light shower, flurry, smir (*or* smirr *or* smur) (Scot), outbreak of rain, occasional showers (*or* rain), intermittent showers (*or* rain), scattered showers, April showers, thundery shower, steady drizzle, persistent rain, rainstorm, torrential rain, driving rain, drenching rain, sheet of rain, stream of rain, downfall, deluge, downpour, cloudburst, spate, belt of rain (*or* rain belt)

26 raininess, showeriness, pluviosity, wetness, rainy season, wet season, monsoon season, the rains, the wet (Aus), rain damage, flood, acid rain, rainmaking, rain dance, cloud-seeding

27 rainbow, double rainbow, primary rainbow, secondary rainbow, fogbow (*or* white rainbow *or* fogdog *or* seadog), rainbow's end

28 dryness, drought, dry spell

29 hail, soft hail (*or* graupel), hailstorm, sleet, freezing rain, glaze ice, glazed frost, silver frost, hoar frost

WINDS

berg wind (South Africa)
bise (Switzerland, France, Italy)
bora (E Adriatic coast)
buran (Central Asia)
Cape doctor (South Africa)
chinook (*or* snow eater) (Rocky Mountains)
el Niño (E Pacific)
etesian (E Mediterranean)
Föhn (*or* Foehn) (Alps)
ghibli (*or* gibli) (N Africa)
gregale (*or* euroclydon *or* euroaquilo) (Malta)
harmattan (W African coast)
khamsin (*or* kamsin *or* kamseen) (Egypt)
levanter (W Mediterranean)
libeccio (*or* libecchio) (Corsica)
meltemi (Mediterranean)
mistral (S France, Mediterranean coast)
monsoon (S Asia)
nor'wester (New Zealand)
simoom (*or* samiel) (Arabia, N Africa)
sirocco (N Africa, S Europe)
southerly buster (SE Australia)
tramontane (*or* tramontana) (Italy and W Mediterranean)
wet chinook (US, Washington and Oregon coasts)
williwaw (US and Canada)

30 snow, snowfall, snow shower, flurry, snowstorm, blizzard, drifting snow, driven snow, white-out, snow cover, mantle of snow, blanket of snow, bank of snow, snowdrift, snow bed, wet snow (*or* papp), powdery snow, granular snow, spindrift, consolidated snow (*or* firn *or* neve), melt, meltage, meltwater, slush, avalanche

31 coldness, cold, chill, chilliness, coolness, cold weather (*or* spell), cold snap, cold wave, chill (*or* nip) in the air, wintriness (*or* winteriness *or* winterliness), hard winter, brass monkey weather (Inf)

32 freeze, big freeze, hard freeze, freeze-up, ice, black ice, glacier

33 fog, ground fog, hill fog, lake fog, river fog, coastal fog, sea fog, radiation fog, advection fog, dense fog, thick fog, fog bank, pea soup (Inf), peasouper (Inf), freezing fog, smog

34 mist, mountain mist, hill mist, fret (*or* haar *or* roke) (Dial), thick mist, Scotch mist, brume, haze, heat haze

35 visibility, good visibility, poor visibility, fogginess, haziness, mistiness, har (Scot)

36 frost, touch of frost, moderate frost, severe frost, hard frost, sharp frost, ground frost, air frost, radiation frost, advection frost, hoar frost, hoar, white frost, rime, frost hollow, permafrost, frost damage, Jack Frost (Inf)

37 dew, fog drip, false dew, dewdrop, dew point

38 climate, local climate, microclimate, regional climate, macroclimate, maritime (*or* marine) climate, Mediterranean climate, oceanic climate, continental climate, mountain climate, desert climate, tundra climate, rainforest climate, snow-forest climate, dry climate, arid climate, semiarid climate, humid climate, semihumid climate, hot climate, tropical climate, subtropical climate, temperate climate, moderate climate, cool climate, cold climate, polar climate (*or* arctic climate)

39 climatic zone, tropics, equatorial rainy zone, tropical summer rainy zone (*or* marginal tropics), subtropics, subtropical dry zone, subtropical winter rainy zone, temperate zone, continental zone, subpolar zone, polar zone, tundra

40 climatic change, climatic variation, climatic trend, ice age, glaciation, interglaciation, interglacial, postglaciation, postglacial, global warming, greenhouse effect, desertification, climate modification

► *28 Physics; 30 Earth Science*

ADJECTIVES

41 meteorologic, meteorological, synoptic, elemental, climatic, climatological

42 barometric, barographic, isobaric, thermometric, thermographic, isothermal, hygrometric, hygrographic, psychrometric, anemometric, anemographic, pluviometric, udometric

43 atmospheric, tropospheric, stratospheric, ionospheric, geostrophic, radiative, thermal, convective, advective, adiabatic, isothermal, evaporated, condensed, sublimated, saturated, supercooled

44 frontal, cyclonic, anticyclonic

45 fine, fair, bright, sunny, dry, rainless, calm, windless, clear, cloudless, brighter, milder, sunnier, drier, settled, fresh, bracing, brisk, crisp, invigorating

46 seasonal, springlike, summery, autumnal, wintry (*or* wintery), unseasonal, changeable, unsettled, deteriorating

47 windy, breezy, blowy, cooling, windier, fresh, brisk, gusty, blustery, squally, keen, piercing, sharp, biting, cold, freezing, raw, bitter, icy, strong, high, gale-force, storm-force, hurricane-force, northerly, boreal, northeasterly, easterly, southeasterly, southerly, southwesterly, westerly, favonian, northwesterly, prevailing, aeolian, anemological

48 stormy, cyclonic, inclement, violent, rough, tempestuous, raging, foul, ugly, dirty, thundery

49 cloudy, cloud-flecked, cloud-crossed, cloud-laden, cloud-covered, overcast, overclouded, cloud-capped, cloud-topped, dull, dreich (Scot), gloomy, dark, grey, heavy, cirrose (*or* cirrous), cirriform, cumuliform, cumulous, cirrocumuliform, cirrocumulous, altocumuliform, altocumulous, stratous, stratiform, altostratous, cirrostratous, nimbostratous, cumulonimbiform, nephological

50 warm, mild, moderate, temperate, pleasant, balmy, warmer, hotter

51 hot, overwarm, overhot, sweltering, sweltry, sizzling, blistering, torrid, boiling (Inf)

52 humid, muggy, damp, close, heavy, oppressive, sticky, sweaty

53 rainy, showery, wet, drizzly, drizzling, rainier, wetter, steady, persistent, heavy, torrential, driving, streaming, pouring, pelting, drumming, blinding, raining cats and dogs (Inf), coming down in buckets (*or* torrents *or* sheets *or* stair-rods) (Inf), pissing down (Inf)

54 pluvial, pluvious (*or* pluviose), hydrometeorologic(al), hyetographic(al)

55 cool, chilly, chill, coldish, nippy, cooler, colder, cold, bitterly cold, raw, frigid, frosty, frosted, frost-covered, freezing, icy, below zero, snowy, snow-covered, snow-clad, slushy, sludgy, sleety, bleak, arctic, Siberian, boreal, parky (Inf), perishing (Inf)

56 foggy, thick, fogbound, enshrouded, smoggy, misty, hazy, nebulous

VERBS

57 forecast, predict

58 blow, stir, sigh, sough, whisper, murmur, hum, freshen, blow up, get up, whistle, moan, gust, buffet, bluster, roar, howl, screech, wail, scream, shriek, back, veer

59 storm, gather, brew, set in, blow a gale, blow a hurricane, thunder, lightning

60 cloud, cloud over, darken, grow dark, roll, scud, break, thin

61 shine, radiate, glimmer, shimmer, blaze, burn, glare, shine brightly, brighten, lighten, clear

62 rain, precipitate, fall, shower, drizzle, mizzle (Dial), patter, spatter, splatter, plash, pour, pelt, teem, stream, drum, spit (Inf), bucket down (Inf), come down (Inf), come down in buckets (*or* torrents *or* sheets *or* stair-rods) (Inf), rain cats and dogs (Inf), piss down (Inf)

63 snow, blizzard, sleet, hail, frost, ice, ice over, freeze, thaw, melt

64 fog, befog, enshroud, mist, bemist, enmist, haze

ADVERBS

65 meteorologically, synoptically, climatologically, climatically, windily, stormily, cloudily, warmly, mildly, hotly, swelteringly, humidly, rainily, wetly, moistly, coolingly, coldly, frostily, snowily, foggily, mistily, hazily

32 Chemistry

NOUNS

1 **chemistry**, organic chemistry, inorganic chemistry, physical chemistry, chemical physics, theoretical chemistry, quantum chemistry, quantum mechanics, thermodynamics, thermochemistry, statistical mechanics, analytical chemistry, analysis, synthesis, kinetics, crystallography, catalysis, photochemistry, radiochemistry, geochemistry, astrochemistry, polymer chemistry, metallurgy, industrial chemistry, chemical engineering, nuclear chemistry, zymurgy, zoochemy, chemurgy, iatrochemistry, biochemistry, alchemy (Lit)

► *33 Biochemistry*

2 **chemist**, organic chemist, inorganic chemist, physical chemist, physiochemist, theoretical chemist, statistical mechanic, analytical chemist, analyst, synthetic chemist, kineticist, crystallographer, photochemist, electrochemist, radiochemist, geochemist, astrochemist, polymer chemist, metallurgist, chemical engineer, chemiatrist, alchemist (Lit)

3 **phase**, solid, liquid, melt, gas vapour, phase change, phase diagram, boiling, condensation, melting, freezing, evaporation, sublimation, solution, concentrated solution, dilute solution, saturated solution, unsaturated solution, supersaturated solution, solvent, solute, polar solvent, nonpolar solvent, precipitation, precipitate, flocculent precipitate, colloid, colloidal solution, lyophobic colloid, lyophilic colloid, hydrophobic colloid, hydrophilic colloid, disperse phase, continuous phase, stabilizer, destabilizer, sol, gel, emulsion, hydrosol, aerosol, mist, smoke, fog, thixotropy, colligative property, mixture, eutectic

► *30 Earth Science; 402 Material World; 431 Fluid; 432 Gas*

4 **crystal**, amorphous substance, glass, single crystal, microcrystal, crystallite, crystal boundary, crystallization, supernatant liquid, growth, form, structure, habit, crystal system, lattice, cubic crystal, face-centred-cubic (f.c.c.) crystal, body-centred-cubic (b.c.c.) crystal, cubic close packing, tetragonal crystal, rhombic (*or* orthorhombic) crystal, hexagonal crystal, hexagonal close packing, trigonal crystal, monoclinic crystal, triclinic crystal, crystallography, X-ray crystallography, Bragg's law

5 **process**, precipitation, crystallization, fractional crystallization, filtration, vacuum filtration, separation, distillation, fractional distillation, refluxing, chromatography, saponification, adsorption

6 **chemical element**, element, metal, heavy metal, nonmetal, semimetal, metalloid, noble gas, inert gas, rare gas, alkali metal, alkaline-earth element, chalconide, halogen, transition element, rare-earth element, lanthanoid (*or* lanthanon *or* lanthanide), actinoid (*or* actinon *or* actinide), transuranic element, superheavy element, coinage metal, platinum metal, periodic table, Döbereiner's triads, Newland's octaves, diagonal relationship, period, short period, long period, group, s-block, p-block, d-block, f-block

7 **chemical compound**, compound, organic compound, inorganic compound, organometallic compound, covalent compound, ionic compound, coordination compound, interstitial compound, lamellar compound, intercallation compound, clathrate, eutectic, cryohydrate, intermetallic compound, alloy, amalgam, ceramic, refractory, stoichiometric compound, nonstoichiometric compound, polar compound, nonpolar compound, saturated compound, unsaturated compound, electron-

CHEMICAL ELEMENTS AND COMMON ALLOTROPES

actinium (Ac)
aluminium (Al)
americium (Am)
antimony (Sb)
argon (Ar)
arsenic (As)
*grey arsenic
astatine (At)
barium (Ba)
berkelium (Bk)
beryllium (Be) (formerly glucinum *or* glucinium)
bismuth (Bi)
bohrium (Bh)
boron (B)
bromine (Br)
cadmium (Cd)
caesium (Cs)
calcium (Ca)
californium (Cf)
carbon (C)
*graphite
*diamond
cerium (Ce)
chlorine (Cl)
chromium (Cr)
cobalt (Co)
copper (Cu)
curium (Cm)
dubnium (Db)
dysprosium (Dy)
einsteinium (Es)
erbium (Er)
europium (Eu)
fermium (Fm)
fluorine (F)
francium (Fr)
gadolinium (Gd)
gallium (Ga)
germanium (Ge)
gold (Au)
hafnium (Hf)
hahnium (Ha)
hassium (Hs)
helium (He)
holmium (Ho)
hydrogen (H)
*dihydrogen
*orthohydrogen
*parahydrogen
*nascent hydrogen
indium (In)
iodine (I)
iridium (Ir)
iron (Fe)
krypton (Kr)
lanthanum (La)
lawrencium (Lr)
lead (Pb)
lithium (Li)
lutetium (Lu)
magnesium (Mg)
manganese (Mn)
meitnerium (Mt)
mendelevium (Md)
mercury (Hg)
molybdenum (Mo)
neodymium (Nd)
neon (Ne)
neptunium (Np)
nickel (Ni)
niobium (Nb)
nitrogen (N)
nobelium (Nb)
osmium (Os)
oxygen (O)
*dioxygen
*ozone
*trioxygen
palladium (Pd)
phosphorus (P)
*red phosphorus
*white phosphorus
platinum (Pt)
plutonium (Pu)
polonium (Po)
potassium (K)
praseodymium (Pr)
promethium (Pm)
protactinium (Pa)
radium (Ra)
radon (Rn)
rhenium (Re)
rhodium (Rh)
rubidium (Rb)
ruthenium (Ru)
rutherfordium (Rf) *or* kurchatovium (Ku)
samarium (Sm)
scandium (Sc)
seaborgium (Sg)
selenium (Se)
silicon (Si)
silver (Ag)
sodium (Na)
strontium (Sr)
sulphur *or* sulfur (US) (S)
tantalum (Ta)
technetium (Tc)
tellurium (Te)
terbium (Tb)
thallium (Tl)
thorium (Th)
thulium (Tm)
tin (Sn)
titanium (Ti)
tungsten *or* wolfram (W)
uranium (U)
vanadium (V)
xenon (Xe)
ytterbium (Yb)
yttrium (Y)
zinc (Zn)
zirconium (Zr)

*common allotrope

deficient compound, cyclic compound, acyclic compound, heterocyclic, homocyclic, aromatic, aliphatic, alicyclic, pseudoaromatic, nonbenzenoid aromatic, complex, coordination complex, ammine, chelate, sandwich compound, binary compound, ternary compound

8 **acid**, mineral acid, organic acid, carboxylic acid, protonic acid, Lewis acid, Lowry–Brønsted acid, strong acid, weak acid, monobasic acid, dibasic acid, tribasic acid

9 **base**, alkali, inorganic base, organic base, quaternary base, Lewis base, Lowry–Brønsted base, strong alkali, weak alkali, monoacidic base, diacidic base, triacidic base, amphoteric compound

TYPES OF COMPOUNDS

acetal
acid anhydride
acyl halide
alcohol
aldehyde
aldohexose
aldol
aldopentose
aldose
alkaloid
alkane
alkene
alkyne
alkoxide
alkyl halide
alkyne
aluminate
amide
amine
amino acid
azide
azine
azo compound
bicarbonate
borane
borate
boride
boron hydride
borosilicate
carbide
carbohydrate
carbonate
carbonyl
carboxylic acid
chlorate
chloride
chlorite
chlorofluorocarbon (CFC)
chromate
cresol
cyanide
detergent
diazonium salt
diol
enzyme
epoxide
ester
ether
fluoride
fluorocarbon
furanose
halide
haloalkane
haloform
hexose
hydrogencarbonate
imine
iodide
ketal
ketohexose
ketone
ketopentose
ketose
lactam
lactate
lactone
mercaptan
metallocene
nitrile
nitrite
nitro compound
oxime
ozonide
paraffin
peptide
permanganate
peroxide
petrochemical
phenol
polymer
protein
pseudohalogen
quaternary compound
saccharide
Schiff's base
semicarbazone
silane
silicate
silicide
silicone
siloxane
soap
stearate
suboxide
sugar
sulphate
sulphide
sulphite
sulphonamide
sulphonic acid
superoxide
tartrate
terpene
thio alcohol
thio ether
thiosulphate
triol
tungstate
zeolite
zincate

COMMON CHEMICAL COMPOUNDS

acetaldehyde (ethanal)
acetamide
acetic acid (ethanoic acid)
acetone
acetylene (ethene)
alcohol (ethanol)
alum (potash alum)
alumina (aluminium oxide)
ammonia
baking soda (sodium hydrogencarbonate)
bicarbonate of soda (sodium hydrogencarbonate)
blanc fixe (barium sulphate)
bleaching powder
blue vitriol (copper sulphate)
boracic acid (boric acid)
bromoform (tribromomethane)
butadiene
caliche (sodium nitrate)
calomel (mercurous chloride)
carbolic acid (phenol)
carbon dioxide
carbon moxoxide
carbon tetrachloride (tetrachloromethane)
carborundum (silicon carbide)
chloral (trichloroethanal)
chloral hydrate
Chile saltpetre (sodium nitrate)
chloroform (trichloroethane)
chrome alum
cinnabar (mercuric chloride)
citric acid
common salt (sodium chloride)
corundum (aluminium oxide)
cryalite (sodium hexafluoroaluminate)
cyanamide (calcium cyanamide)
cyanide (sodium cyanide)
cyanogen
cyclohexane
diethylene glycol
Epsom salt (magnesium sulphate)
ethane
ethanol
ethyl alcohol (ethanol)
ethylene (ethene)
firedamp (methane)
folic acid
formaldehyde (methanal)
formic acid (methanoic acid)
fumaric acid (butenedioic acid)
galena (plumbous sulphide)
gallium arsenide
Glauber's salt (sodium sulphate)
glycerine (glycerol)
gypsum (calcium sulphate)
hexane
hydrazine
hydrochloric acid (hydrogen chloride)
hydrogen peroxide
hydrogen sulphide
jeweller's rouge
killed spirits (zinc chloride)
laughing gas (dinitrogen monoxide)
lithia (lithium hydroxide)
magnesia (magnesium oxide)
malic acid
marsh gas (methane)
naphthalene
nitric acid
nitric oxide (nitrogen monoxide)
nitrous acid
nitrous oxide (dinitrogen monoxide)
octane
oil of vitriol (sulphuric acid)
paraldehyde
pentane
perchloric acid
phosphine
plaster of Paris (calcium sulphate)
plumbane (lead hydride)
potassium permanganate
potassium chloride
propane
propylene (propene)
pyridine
quicklime (calcium oxide)
red lead (lead oxide)
saltpetre (potassium nitrate)
silica (silicon dioxide)
soda (sodium carbonate)
sodamide
sodium bicarbonate (sodium hydrogencarbonate)
stannane (tin hydride)
strontia (strontium oxide)
sulphur dioxide
sulphuric acid
sulphurous acid
tetraethyl lead
tetrahydrofuran
washing soda (sodium carbonate)
xylene (dimethylbenzene)

10 salt, acid salt, basic salt, double salt, alum, hydrate, monohydrate, dihydrate, trihydrate, quadrihydrate, pentahydrate, hexahydrate, heptahydrate, octahydrate, nonahydrate, decahydrate, undecahydrate, dodecahydrate, hemihydrate, sesquihydrate, anhydride, anhydrous salt

11 chemical bond, valence bond, ionic bond, electrovalent bond, covalent bond, coordinate bond, ligand, dative bond, donor, acceptor, polar bond, heteropolar bond, homopolar bond, semipolar bond, intermediate bond, pair bond, lone pair, metallic bond, electron-deficient bond, multicentre bond, bent bond, banana bond, dipole–dipole interaction, hydrogen bond, dispersion force, van der Waals force, bond energy, bond strength, bond angle, dissociation energy

12 valence, valency, valence-bond (*or* VB) theory, molecular-orbital (*or* MO) theory, orbital, molecular orbital, bonding orbital, antibonding orbital, overlap integral, hybridization, hybrid orbital

13 structure, formula, chemical formula, empiracle formula, molecular formula, structural formula, stereochemistry, steric effect, steric hindrance, isomerism, isomer, structural isomer(ism), stereoisomer(ism), cis–trans isomer(ism), syn–anti isomer(ism), optical isomer(ism), epimerism, epimer, anomerism, anomer, asymmetric centre, chiral centre, chirality, optical activity, optical rotation, dextro form, *d*-form, laevo form, *l*-form, meso-form, racemate, racemic mixture, D-form, L-form, R-form, S-form, CORN rule, resolution, racemization, inversion, invert sugar, polarimetry, ORD (optical rotary dispersion)

14 chemical reaction, process, reactant, product, reagent, fast reaction, slow reaction, irreversible reaction, reversible reaction, equilibrium, equilibrium constant, main reaction, side reaction, fission reaction, heterolysis, heterolytic fission, ionization, homolytic fission, homolysis, addition, condensation, substitution, elimination, displacement, disproportionation, rearrangement, ring closure, cyclization, aromatization, ring opening, polymerization, pyrolysis, neutralization, electrophilic reaction, electrophile, nucleophilic reaction, nucleophile, kinetics, unimolecular reaction, bimolecular reaction, reaction order, mechanism, step, rate-determining step, absolute rate theory, collision theory, transition state, activated complex, rate constant, activation energy, isotope effect, photochemical reaction, radiochemical reaction, chain reaction

15 catalysis, catalyst, homogeneous catalysis, heterogeneous catalysis, acid–base catalysis, autocatalysis, deactivation, accelerator, stabilizer, poison, substrate, platinum black, Raney nickel, enzyme

16 synthesis, synthetic compound, synthetic, stoichiometric synthesis, by-product, biosynthesis, biotechnology

17 analysis, qualitative analysis, quantitative analysis, spectrographic analysis, spectrometry, spectrograph, spectometer, spectrum, mass spectrometry, ultraviolet (*or* UV) spectrometry, infrared (*or* IR) spectrometry, X-ray spectroscopy, microwave spectroscopy, electron spectroscopy, PES (photoelectron spectroscopy), UPS (ultraviolet photoelectron spectroscopy), XPS (X-ray photoelectron spectroscopy), NHR (nuclear magnetic resonance), ESR (electron-spin resonance), ENDOR (electron-nuclear double resonance), polarography, polarogram, chromatography, chromatogram, column chromatography, GLC (gas–liquid chromatography), GSC (gas–solid chromatography), TLC (thin-layer chromatography), paper chromatography, electrophoresis, electro-osmosis, gel filtration, ion-exchange chromatography, HPLC (high-performance liquid chromatography), stationary phase, mobile phase, carrier, elution, eluent, solvent front

18 gravimetric analysis, gravimetry, volumetric analysis, titration, titre, indicator, litmus, litmus paper, phenolphthalein, methyl orange, methyl red, mixed indicator, universal indicator, absorption indicator, conduc-

TYPES OF CHEMICAL REACTION

acetylation	chlorination	halogenation	ozonolysis
acylation	deuteration	hydration	reduction
benzoylation	diazotization	hydrogenation	saponification
bromination	esterification	hydrolysis	solvation
calcination	fermentation	neutralization	solvolysis
carbonation	fixation	nitration	sulphonation
carburization	fluorination	oxidation	tritiation

NAMED REACTIONS, PROCESSES, AND CONCEPTS

Acheson process	Faraday's laws	Kjeldahl's method	Sachse reaction
Arrhenius equation	Fehling's solution	Kolbe electrolysis	Schiff's base
Beckmann thermometer	Fischer–Tropsch process	Leblanc process	Schiff's reagent
Born–Haber cycle	Fittig reaction	Le Châtelier's principle	Schoffen–Baumann reagent
Bosch process	Friedel–Crafts reaction	Lowry–Brønsted theory	Strecker synthesis
Brin process	Gay–Lussac's law	Markovnikoff's rules	Tollen's reagent
Brownian movement	Gibbs function	Mendius reaction	van der Waals force
Cannizzaro reaction	Graham's law	Moseley's law	van't Hoff factor
Corius method	Haber process	Natta process	Victor Meyer's method
Carnot cycle	Hell–Volard–Zelinsky reaction	Newland's law	Wacker process
Claisen condensation	Helmholtz function	Ostwald's dilution law	Walden universion
Dewar structure	Henry's law	Pauli exclusion principle	Williamson's process
Dow process	Hesse's law	Phillip's process	Williamson's synthesis
Downs process	Hofmann degradation	Raney nickel	Wöhler's synthesis
Dulong and Petit's law	Hofmann's method	Raoult's law	Wurtz reaction
Dumas' method	Kekulé structure	Rashig process	Zeisel reaction
Fajan's rules	Kipp's apparatus	Regnault's method	Ziegler process

ALLOYS

admiralty metal	bush metal	ferrochromium	manganese bronze	pig iron	stainless steel
alloy steel	carbon steel	ferromanganese	misch metal	pig lead	steel
Alnico™	cast iron	ferromolybdenum	Monel metal™	pinchbeck	Stellite™
aluminium bronze	chrome steel	ferronickel	Muntz metal	platiniridium	sterling silver
amalgam	chromel	ferrosilicon	Nichrome™	red brass	tombac
babbitt metal	coinage metal	fusible alloy	nickel bronze	Rose's metal	type metal
bearing metal	constantan	German silver	nickel silver	silicon bronze	white gold
bell bronze	cupronickel	gunmetal	osmiridium	silicon steel	white metal
bell metal	damask	high–speed steel	permalloy	silver solder	Wood's metal
brass	Duralumin™	invar	perminvar	solder	wrought iron
Britannia metal	electrum	magnolia metal	pewter	speculum metal	yellow brass
bronze	elinvar	magnox	phosphor bronze	spiegeleisen	zircalloy

tiometric titration, equivalence point, end point, standard solution, standardization, gas analysis

19 electrochemistry, cell, anode, cathode, electrolyte, concentration cell, half cell, electrode potential, electrochemical series, electromotive series, electrolysis, electrolytic cell, electrodeposition, electroplating, electrolytic refining, electrolytic forming, anode sludge, voltaic cell, battery, wet cell, dry cell, polarization, overpotential, Leclanché cell, Daniell cell, Bunsen cell, Weston cell, NIFE cell, fuel cell, electrolytic corrosion, rusting, sacrificial anode, pH, hydrogen electrode, glass electrode

20 surface chemistry, absorption, adsorption, chemisorption, physisorption, sorption, desorption, degassing, outgassing, flash desorption, field desorption, vacuum, high vacuum, low vacuum, hard vacuum, soft vacuum, uhv (ultra-high vacuum), vacuum pump, filter pump, rotary pump, diffusion pump, ion pump, sputtering, sputter-ion pump, gettering, getter-ion pump, cryogenic pump, vacuum gauge, monometer, McLeod gauge, Pirani gauge, ion (*or* ionization) gauge, Bayerd–Alpert gauge, leak detector, RGA (residual-gas analyser), Tesla coil

21 polymer, polymerization, monomer, macromolecule, addition polymer(ization), condensation polymer(ization), chain, cross linking, homopolymer(ization), copolymer(ization), stereospecific polymerization, stereoregular polymer, atactic polymer, isotactic polymer, syndiotactic polymer, Bakelite™, PVC (polyvinyl chloride *or* polychloroethene), uPVC (ultra-hard PVC), polythene (*or* polyethylene *or* polyethene), polypropylene (*or* polypropene), polyester, nylon, polycarbonate, polyurethane, epoxide resin, polystyrene, expanded polystyrene, PTFE (polytetrafluoroethylene), Teflon™, polymethylmethacrylate, Perspex™, Plexiglass™, vulcanite, isoprene rubber, chloroprene rubber, resin, plasticizer, stabilizer, plastic, thermosetting plastic, thermoplastic material

► *422 Elasticity*

22 industrial chemistry, chemical engineering, refining, oil refining, refinery, cracking, cat-cracking reforming, steam reforming, fractionation, fractional distillation, fraction, petrochemicals, plastics, fibres, dyestuffs, fertilizers, explosives, fine chemicals, pharmaceuticals

23 metallurgy, metal, metalloid, alloy extractive metallurgy, production metallurgy, extraction, blast furnace, electrolytic extraction, refining, froth flotation, electrorefining, electroplating

24 ore, deposit, vein, lode, lodestuff, placer, gangue

VERBS

25 solidify, liquefy, vaporize, condense, melt, freeze, evaporate, concentrate, dilute, dissolve, saturate, supersaturate, precipitate, disperse, stabilize, destabilize, flocculate, gel, emulsify, separate, filter, distil, steam-distil, vacuum-distil, fractionate, refine, crystallize, crystallize out

26 react, bond, coordinate, add, substitute, condense, eliminate, transfer, rearrange, dissociate, ionize, heterolyse, neutralize, acidify, cyclize, pyrolyse, irradiate, polymerize, racemize, invert, catalyse, activate, promote, poison, acetylate, acylate, benzoylate, brominate, calcine, calcify, carbonate, carburize, chlorinate, deuterate, diazotize, esterify, ferment, fluormate, fluoridate, halogenate, hydrate, hydrogenate, hydrolyse, nitrate, oxidize, ozonize, reduce, saponify, solvate, sulphonate, sulphurize, tritiate

27 synthesize, analyse, degrade

28 electrolyse, electrodeposit, electroplate, electroform

29 absorb, adsorb, physisorb, chemisorb, sorb, desorb, degass, outgas, getter, sputter, field desorb, field ionize

30 extract, win, concentrate, purify, refine, sinter, alloy, anneal, case-harden, work harden, temper

ADJECTIVES

31 chemical, physiochemical, organic, inorganic, theoretical, thermodynamic, statistico-mechanical, analytic(al), synthetic, kinetic, crystallographic, catalytic, photo-

COMMON METAL ORES

Ore (Metal)	
anglesite (lead)	haematite (iron)
argentite (silver)	ironstone (iron)
arsenopyrite (iron, arsenic)	limonite (iron)
bauxite (aluminium)	litharge (lead)
carnotite (uranium)	lodestone (iron)
cassiterite (tin)	magnetite (iron)
cerrusite (lead)	mispickel (iron, arsenic)
chalcocite (copper)	pitchblende (uranium)
chalcopyrite (copper)	siderite (iron)
chromite (chromium)	smithsonite (zinc)
copper pyrites (copper)	stibnite (antimony)
cinnabar (mercury)	tinstone (tin)
galena (lead)	zinc blende (zinc)
	zincite (zinc)

chemical, radiochemical, biochemical, astrochemical, metallurgical, zymurgic, alchemic(al) (Lit)

32 **solid**, liquid, gaseous, vapourous, condensed, melted, molten, frozen, evaporated, concentrated, dilute, saturated, unsaturated, supersaturated, flocculent colloidal, lyophobic, lyophilic, hydrophobic, hydrophilic, disperse, continuous, stabilized, destabilized, gelled, emulsoid, thixotropic, colligative, eutectic, precipitated, filtered, distilled, pure, refined

33 **crystalline**, microcrystalline, crystallized, crystalloid, noncrystalline, amorphous, irregular, supernatant, structural, cubic, tetragonal, rhombic, orthorhombic, hexagonal, trigonal, monclinic, triclinic, face-centred, body-centred, close-packed, cubic close packed, hexagonal close packed

34 **elemental**, native, uncombined, metallic, metalloid, inert, transuranic, superheavy, aluminous, aluminiferous, antimonous, antimonic, arsenous, arsenious, arsenic, bismuthous, bismuthic, bismuthyl, bromous, bromic, brominated, calciferous, carbonic, carboniferous, graphitic, cerous, ceric, chlorous, chloric, chlorinated, chromous, chromic, chromyl, cobaltous, cobaltic, cuprous, cupric, cupriferous, fluoric, fluorinated, fluoridated, germanous, germanic, aurous, auric, auriferous, hydrogenous, iodous, iodic, iridous, iridic, ferrous, ferric, ferrosoferric, ferriferous plumbous, plumbic, plumbiferous, manganous, manganic, mercurous, mercuric, molybdous, molybdenous, molybdic, nickelous, nickelic, nickeliferous, niobous, niobic, columbous, columbic, nitrogenous, osmous, osmious, osmic, oxygenated, oxygenized, phosphorous, phosphoric, platinous, platinic, platinized, platinoid, platiniferous, rhodic, rhodous, scandic, selenous, selenious, selenic, silicic, argentous, argentic, argentiferous, sulphurous, sulphuric, sulphonous, sulphonic, sulphuryl, sulphuretted, tantalous, tantalic, tellurous, telluric, thallous, thallic, stannous, stannic, stanniferous, titanic, titanous, tungstous, tungstic, uranous, uranic, uranyl, vanadous, vanadic, zinciferous

35 **combined**, organic, inorganic, organometallic, covalent, electrovalent, ionic, univalent, monovalent, divalent, bivalent, trivalent, tervalent, tetravalent, quadrivalent, pentavalent, quinquevalent, hexavalent, sexivalent, heptavalent, septivalent, octavalent, nonstoichiometric, polar, nonpolar, saturated, unsaturated, delocalized, electron-deficient, cyclic, acyclic, heterocyclic, homocyclic, carbocyclic, aromatic, aliphatic, alicyclic, pseudoaromatic, binary, ternary, molecular, monatomic, diatomic, triatomic, polyatomic, complex, transient, metastable

36 **acid**, acidic, basic, alkaline, weak, strong, monobasic, dibasic, tribasic, monoacidic, diacidic, triacidic, protonic, amphoteric, neutral, saline, hydrated, anhydrous

37 **structural**, steric, conformational, isomeric, stereoisomeric, epimeric, anomeric, asymmetric, chiral, racemized

38 **reactive**, unreactive, inactive, deactivated, passive, fast, slow, reversible, irreversible, equilibrated, homolytic, heterolytic, additive, substitutional, cyclic, electrophilic, nucleophilic, polymeric, monomolecular, bimolecular, first-order, second-order, third-order

39 **catalytic**, autocatalytic, activated, deactivated, poison

40 **synthetic**, synthesized, separative, naturally-occurring

41 **analytic**, quantitative, spectroscopic, spectrographic, polarographic, chromatographic, electrophoretic, stationary, mobile, reversed-phase, gravimetric, volumetric, standardized, neutralized, equivalent

42 **electrochemical**, electrolytic, electromotive, electrovoltaic, electrodeposited, electroplated, electroformed, anodic, cathodic

43 **absorbed**, adsorbed, physisorbed, chemisorbed, sorbed, desorbed, outgassed, degassed

44 **polymeric**, monomeric, copolymeric, stereospecific, stereoregular, atactic, tactic, isotactic, syndiotactic

45 **metallurgical**, extractive, alloyed

ADVERBS

46 **chemically**, practically, theoretically, thermodynamically, catalytically, photochemically, metallurgically, synthetically, analytically, colloidally, amorphously, covalently, ionically, electrovalently

33 Biochemistry

NOUNS

1 **biochemistry**, biosynthesis, bioenergetics, biomolecule, biochemical taxonomy, biotechnology, enzymology, endocrinology

► *34 Life Science*

2 **biochemist**, plant biochemist, enzymologist, endocrinologist

3 **carbohydrate**, saccharide, sugar, monosaccharide, simple sugar, triose, tetrose, pentose, hexose, heptose, octose, aldose, ketose, aldotriose, aldotetrose, aldopentose, aldohexose, aldoheptose, aldooctose, ketotriose, ketotetrose, ketopentose, ketohexose, hetoheptose, ketooctose, hemiacetal, pyranose, hemiketal, furanose, complex sugar, disaccharide, trisaccharide, tetrasaccharide, oligosaccharide, sugar alcohol, sorbitol, mannitol, glycerol, glycerine, inositol, sugar acid, aldonic acid, aldaric acid, saccharic acid, uronic acid, sugar derivative, glycoside, glucoside, cardiac glycoside, digitalin

► *37 Pharmacology*

4 **polysaccharide**, glycan, homopolysaccharide, heteropolysaccharide, storage polysaccharide, starch, amylose, amylopectin, inulin, animal starch, glycogen, dextran, fructan, arabinan, xylon, mannan, structural polysaccharide, cellulose, hemicellulose, pectic substance, pectin, extensin, lignin, agar, gum arabic, chitin, mucopolysaccharide, glycosaminoglycan (GAG)

5 **sugar test**, alpha-naphthol test, Barfoed's test, Benedict's test, Fehling's test, Molisch's test, Schiff's reagent, Seliwanoff's test, Tollen's reagent

6 **lipid**, complex lipid, saponifiable lipid, fat, oil, wax, glycolipid, cerebroside, phospholipid, phosphatide, phosphoglyceride, glycerophosphatide, lecithin (*or* phosphatidylcholine), cephalin (*or* phosphatidylethanolamine), sphingolipid, sphingomyelin, lipoprotein, simple lipid, nonsaponifiable lipid, terpene, steroid, sterol, cholesterol, bile acid

7 **fat**, fatty-acid ester, glyceride, acylglycerol, simple glyceride, mixed glyceride, monoglyceride, diglyceride, triglyceride, fatty acid, carboxylic acid, essential fatty

COMMON FATTY ACIDS

Traditional name (Systematic name)	
formic (methanoic)	lauric (dodecanoic)
acetic (ethanoic)	myristic (tetradecanoic)
propionic (propanoic)	palmitic (hexadecanoic)
butyric (butanoic)	stearic (octadecanoic)
valeric (pentanoic)	lactic (hydroxypropanoic)
caproic (hexanoic)	acrylic (propenoic)
oenanthic (heptanoic)	crotonic (trans–buteneoic)
caprylic (octanoic)	malic (hydroxybutanedioic)
pelargonic (nonanoic)	fumaric (trans–butenedioic)
capric (decanoic)	maleic (cis–butenedioic)
	oxalic (ethanedioic)
	citric

AMINO ACIDS

Acid (Abbreviation)	
alanine (ala)	methionine (met)*
arginine (arg)*	phenylalanine (phe)*
asparagine (asn)	proline (pro)
aspartic acid (asp)	serine (ser)
cysteine (cys)	threonine (thr)*
glutamic acid (glu)	tryptophan (trp)*
glutamine (gln)	tyrosine (tyr)
glycine (gly)	valine (val)*
histidine (his)*	ornithine
isoleucine (ile)*	citrulline
leucine (leu)*	
lycine (lys)*	*essential amino acid

acid, saturated fat, unsaturated fat, monounsaturated fat, polyunsaturated fat, lipolysis, saponification

8 amino acid, essential amino acid, nonessential amino acid, imino acid, peptide, peptide bond, disulphide bond, cystine, kinin, bradykinin, kalidin, dipeptide, tripeptide, oligopeptide, polypeptide, amino-acid residue

9 protein, protein structure, primary structure, secondary structure, tertiary structure, quaternary structure, oligomeric protein, protomer, globular protein, globulin, fibrous protein, alpha-helix, conjugated protein, nucleoprotein, lipoprotein, glycoprotein, proteoglycan, mucoprotein, mucin, peptidoglycan, phosphoprotein, haemoprotein, flavoprotein, metalloprotein, scleroprotein, sclerotization, prion, prosthetic group, biuret test, denaturization, albumin, albumen, casein, collagen, fibrin, gelatin (*or* gelatine), gluten, histone, immunoglobulin, insulin, interferon, keratin, myoglobin

10 nucleoside, nitrogenous base, purine base, adesnine, guanine, pyrimidine base, thymine, cytosine, uracil, nucleotide, deoxynucleotide, ribonucleotide, nucleic acid, DNA (deoxyribonucleic acid), double helix, RNA (ribonucleic acid), mRNA (messenger RNA), tRNA (transfer RNA)

▶ *34 Life Science*

11 enzyme, substrate, active site, apoenzyme, cofactor, coenzyme, prosthetic group, holoenzyme, inhibition, feedback inhibition, enzyme class, oxidoreductase, transferase, hydrolase, lyase, isomerase, ligase, amylase, diastase, dehydrogenase, gastrin, lactase, lipase, lysozyme, papain, protease, peptidase, proteolytic enzyme, proteolysis, pepsin, trypsin, rennin, restriction enzyme, restriction endonuclease, transaminase, zymogen

12 coenzyme, CoA (coenzyme A), CoQ (coenzyme Q), NAD (nicotinamide adenine dinucleotide), NADP (nicotinamide adenine dinucleotide phosphate), FAD (flavin adenine dinucleotide), flavoprotein, thiamin (*or* thiamine), pyrophosphate, lipoamide, biocytin, pyridoxal phosphate

13 vitamin, vitamin A (retinol), vitamin B complex, vitamin B_1 (thiamin *or* thiamine), vitamin B_2 (riboflavin), vitamin B_6 (pyridoxine), vitamin B_{12} (cyanocobalamin), nicotinic acid, pantothenic acid, folic acid, biotin, lipoic acid, choline, vitamin C (ascorbic acid), vitamin D_2 (ergocalciferol *or* calciferol), vitamin D_3 (cholecalciferol), vitamin E (tocopherol), vitamin K

14 vitamin deficiency disease, night blindness, xerophthalmia, beriberi, pernicious anaemia, scurvy, rickets, osteomalacia

▶ *260 Ill Health*

15 essential element, major element, macronutrient, carbon, hydrogen, oxygen, nitrogen, calcium, phosphorus, potassium, sodium, chlorine, sulphur, magnesium, trace element, micronutrient, iron, manganese, zinc, copper, iodine, cobalt, selenium, molybdenum, chromium, silicon

16 hormone, neurohormone, releasing hormone, neurohumour, catecholamine, dopamine, steroid hormone, sex hormone, androgen, anabolic steroid, oestrogen, oral contraceptive, corticosteroid, mineralocorticoid, glucocorticoid, gonadotrophin, gonadotrophic hormone, externally acting hormone, ectohormone, pheromone, hormone-like substance, prostaglandin, chemical messenger (Inf)

▶ *37 Pharmacology; 559 Secretion*

17 plant hormone, phytohormone, growth substance, auxin, giberellin, ethylene (*or* ethene), abscisic acid, IAA (indolacetic acid), 2,4-D (2,4-dichlorophenoxyacetic acid), 2,4,5-T (2,4,5-trichlorophenoxyacetic acid), cytokinin (*or* kinin), zeatin

18 pigment, plant pigment, flavonoid, flavonol, flavone, anthocyanin, phytochrome, photosynthetic pigment, chlorophyll, phycobilin, carotenoid, carotene, xanthophyll, fucoxanthin, respiratory pigment, haemoglobin, bile pigment, bilirubin, biliverdin

▶ *529 Colour*

19 alkaloid, morphine, cocaine, atropine, quinine, caffeine, aconite, papaverine, strychnine, coniine, colchicine

▶ *37 Pharmacology*

20 terpene, isoprene unit, monoterpene, sesquiterpene, diterpene, triterpene, tetraterpene, geraniol, limonene, menthol, pinene, camphor, carvone, farnesol, phytol, carotenoid, squalene, vitamin A, vitamin E, vitamin K

21 metabolism, catabolism, anabolism, metabolic pathway, metabolite

▶ *34 Life Science*

22 bioenergetics, ATP (adenosine triphosphate), ADP (adenosine diphosphate), AMP (adenosine monophosphate), phosphorylation, phosphate bond, energy-rich bond, phosphagen, creatine phosphate, ATP cycle

23 photosynthesis, light reaction, dark reaction, chloro-

HORMONES

ACTH (*or* adrenocorticotropic hormone *or* adrenocorticotrophin *or* corticotrophin)
adrenalin(e), epinephrine (US)
aldosterone
androgen
androsterone
angiotensin
antidiuretic hormone (ADH *or* vasopressin *or* pitressin)
bovine somatotrophin (BST)
calcitonin (*or* thyrocalcitonin)
cholecystokinin
chorionic gonadotrophin
corticoid
corticosterone
corticotrophin
cortisol
cortisone
deoxycorticosterone
ecdysone (moulting hormone)
enterogastrone
erythropoietin
follicle–stimulating hormone (FSH)
glucagon
growth hormone
hydrocortisone
insulin
intermedin (*or* melanocyte–stimulating hormone)
interstitial–cell– stimulating hormone (ICSH)
juvenile hormone
lactogenic hormone
lipotrophin
luteinizing hormone (LH)
luteotrophic hormone (*or* luteotrophin)
melanocyte–stimulating hormone (MSH *or* intermedia)
melatonin
noradrenalin, norepinephrine (US)
oestradiol
oestriol
oestrogen
oestrone
oxytocin
pancreozymin
parathyroid hormone (*or* parathormone)
pitressin
progesterone
progestogen (*or* progestin)
prolactin (*or* lactogenic hormone *or* luteotrophic hormone *or* luteotrophin)
relaxin
secretin
somatotrophin
testosterone
thyrocalcitonin (*or* calcitonin)
thyroglobulin
thyroid hormone
thyroid–stimulating hormone (TSH *or* thyrotrophin)
thyroxine
triiodothyronine
vasotocin
vasopressin (*or* antidiuretic hormone)

phyll a, chlorophyll b, photophosphorylation, Calvin cycle

▶ *34 Life Science; 77 Plants*

24 **respiration**, aerobic respiration, anaerobic respiration, photorespiration, external respiration, internal respiration, cell respiration, haemoglobin, myoglobin, haem, glycolysis, Embden–Meyerhof pathway, Krebs cycle, citric acid cycle, TCA cycle (tricarboxylic acid cycle), respiratory chain, electron-transport chain

▶ *34 Life Science; 434 Air*

VERBS

25 **metabolize**, photosynthesize, synthesize, catalyse

ADJECTIVES

26 **biochemical**, biosynthetic, biomolecular, enzymic, hormonal, metabolic, catabolic, anabolic, bioenergetic, photosynthetic, glycolytic

ADVERBS

27 **biochemically**, biosynthetically, photosynthetically, enzymically, hormonally, metabolically, catabolically, anabolically

34 Life Science

Natural science does not simply describe and explain nature, it is part of the interplay between nature and ourselves. Werner Heisenberg.

NOUNS

1 **life science**, biological science, natural science, biology, zoology, botany, palaeobotany, dendrology, pomology, phytochemistry, phytoecology, phytobiology, phytography, phytology, vegetable (*or* plant) pathology, vegetable (*or* plant) physiology, microbiology, algology, bryology, fungology, epidemiology, bacteriology, virology, gnotobiotics, parasitology, anatomy, morphology, physiology, biochemistry (*or* biochemy *or* biochemics), enzymology, endocrinology, neuroscience, immunology, histology, cell biology, cytology, molecular biology, genetics, biogenetics, genetic engineering, biotechnology, developmental biology, embryology, evolution, palaeontology, taxonomy, systematics, natural history, marine biology, ecology, bioecology, bionomics, biophysics, biometry (*or* biometrics), bionics, cybernetics, cryobiology, electrobiology, radiobiology, space biology, astrobiology, exobiology, xenobiology, ethnobiology, sociobiology

▶ *1 Anthropology; 2 Sociology; 30 Earth Science; 33 Biochemistry; 35 Medicine; 43 Agriculture; 44 Horticulture; 70 Animals; 77 Plants*

2 **living world**, natural world, nature, plant and animal life, flora and fauna, biota, biosphere, ecosphere

▶ *554 Life*

3 **organism**, living organism, being, living being, organic being, living thing, creature, entity, body, individual, animal, plant, eukaryote (*or* eucaryote), prokaryote (*or* procaryote), aerobe, anaerobe, microorganism, microbe, animalcule, microphyte, protist, monad, germ, bacterium, coccus, bacillus, spirillum, rickettsia, mycoplasma, virus, filtrable virus, bacteriophage, phage, retrovirus, virion, viroid, plasmid, provirus, organic remains, fossil

▶ *70 Animals; 75 Invertebrates; 77 Plants; 260 Ill Health*

4 **anatomy**, form, structure, gross structure, morphology, comparative anatomy, dissection, zootomy, tissue structure, histology

▶ *172 Inside; 403 Structure; 431 Fluid*

5 **physiology**, vital functions, nutrition, absorption, respiration, photosynthesis, metabolism, anabolism, catabolism, transpiration, guttation, osmoregulation, secretion, excretion, sensation, reproduction, growth, locomotion

▶ *300 Motion; 434 Air; 488 Sensation; 557 Eating; 559 Secretion; 560 Excretion; 561 Reproduction*

6 **cell biology**, cytology, cell structure, ultrastructure, mi-

croscopical examination, light microscopy, electron microscopy, phase-contrast microscopy, fixation, sectioning, staining, counterstaining, cytochemistry, histochemistry, tissue culture, histology, cytological test, smear test, cell physiology, biochemistry, internal respiration, aerobic respiration, anaerobic respiration, glycolysis, Krebs cycle

► *33 Biochemistry; 35 Medicine*

7 **cell**, prokaryotic (*or* procaryotic) cell, eukaryotic (*or* eucaryotic) cell, plant cell, animal cell, bacterial cell, protoplast, cellule, germ cell, germen, reproductive cell, gamete, spore, somatic cell, blood cell, corpuscle, muscle cell, bone cell, pigment cell, unicellular organism, unicell, cell membrane, plasma membrane, plasmalemma, microvillus, cell wall, cellulose, lignin, chitin, cell plate, middle lamella, plasmodesma, cellular tissue, protoplasm, cytoplasm, bioplasm, cytosome, hyaloplasm, energid, trophoplasm, ectoplasm, endoplasm, reticulum, coenocyte, syncytium, idioplasm, germ plasm

► *561 Reproduction*

8 **cell organ**, organelle, nucleus, mitochondrion, chondriosome, Golgi apparatus, Golgi body, Golgi vesicle, Golgi complex, cisternum, microtubule, endoplasmic reticulum (ER), rough endoplasmic reticulum, smooth endoplasmic reticulum, microsome, mesosome, microfibril, ribosome, polysome (*or* polyribosome), spherosome, centrosome, centrosphere, central body, microcentrum, centriole, basal body, kinetosome, flagellum, cilium, pilum, lysosome, peroxisome, plastid, chromatophore, chromoplast, chloroplast, leucoplast, plastosome, vacuole, tonoplast

9 **cell nucleus**, macronucleus, meganucleus, micronucleus, nucleolus, plasmosome, nuclear membrane, nuclear envelope, nuclear pore, nucleoplasm, karyoplasm, nuclear sap, chromatin, chromatin strands, karyotin, karyosome, nucleosome, basichromatin, heterochromatin, oxychromatin, nucleoprotein, nucleopeptide, nucleic acid, DNA (deoxyribonucleic acid), RNA (ribonucleic acid)

10 **cell division**, cell cycle, mitosis, meiosis, reduction division, amitosis, endomitosis, metamitosis, eumitosis, promitosis, haplomitosis, mesomitosis, karyomitosis, karyokinesis, apoptosis, interphase, prophase, metaphase, anaphase, telophase, diaster, cytokinesis, spindle, equator, centrosome, centromere, aster, spindle fibres, linkage, crossing over

11 **genetics**, classical genetics, Mendelian genetics (*or* Mendelism), Mendel's laws, heredity, inheritance, hereditary character, factor, gene, chromosome, dominance, recessiveness, double recessiveness, genetic constitution, genotype, biotype, phenotype, population genetics, genecology, gene flow, gene frequency, gene pool, genetic drift, gene complex, cytogenetics, molecular genetics, biochemical genetics, microbial genetics, genetic engineering, eugenics

► *35 Medicine*

12 **molecular biology**, biological molecule, macromolecule, protein, nucleic acid, macromolecular structure, protein structure, polypeptide chain, amino-acid sequence, protein sequencing, nucleic-acid structure, DNA double helix, nitrogenous base, adenosine, cytosine, guanine, thymine, uracil, nucleoside, nucleotide, polynucleotide, molecular genetics, gene structure, gene sequencing, genetic mapping, recombinant DNA technology, biotechnology, genetic engineering, genetic (*or* DNA) fingerprinting, gene (*or* DNA) probe, restriction enzyme, gene cloning, cloning vector, gene splicing, designer gene, genotype, phenotype

► *33 Biochemistry*

13 **genetic material**, DNA, RNA, genetic element, gene, factor, allele, operon, structural gene, regulator gene, operator gene, gene complement, genome, genetic code, codon, anticodon, messenger RNA (mRNA), transfer RNA (tRNA), ribosomal RNA, protein synthesis, extrachromosomal genetic element, plasmagene, plasmid, transposon, gene mutation, gene sequence, exon, intron, gene splicing

14 **chromosome**, heterosome, autosome, heterochromosome, allerome, idiochromosome, sex chromosome, W chromosome, X chromosome, Y chromosome, Z chromosome, euchromosome, homologous chromosome, univalent chromosome, chromatid, centromere, kinetochore, chromomere, chromonema, gene string, chromatin, chromosome, complement, chromosome number, diploid number, haploid number, diploidy, haploidy, polyploidy, autopolyploidy, allopolyploidy, chromosome mutation

15 **developmental biology**, embryology, ontogeny, embryogenesis, embryogeny, germination, cleavage, blastulation, gastrulation, induction, evocation, embryo, germ, primordium, rudiment, zygote, oosperm, morula, blastomere, blastula, blastocyst, gastrula, germ layer, ectoderm, endoderm, mesoderm, fetus (*or* foetus), extraembryonic membrane, amnion, chorion, allantois, juvenile, larva, nymph, pupa, chrysalis, metamorphosis, paedogenesis, neoteny

► *73 Reptiles and Amphibians; 76 Insects and Arachnids*

16 **evolution**, phylogeny, speciation, convergent evolution, parallel evolution, natural selection, survival of the fittest, Darwinism, Weismannism, continuity of germ plasm, neo-Darwinism, Lamarckism, inheritance of acquired characteristics, neo-Lamarckism, Lysenkoism, uniformitarianism, catastrophism, palaeontology, fossil record, recapitulation, Haeckel's law

17 **taxonomy**, systematics, biological classification, classical taxonomy, cytotaxonomy, numerical taxonomy, experimental taxonomy, biosystematics, cladistics, cladism, clade, taxonomic group, taxon, kingdom, subkingdom, division, subdivision, phylum, subphylum, superclass, class, subclass, order, suborder, superfamily, family, subfamily, tribe, subtribe, genus, section, series, species, subspecies, variety, cultivar, race, form, binomial nomenclature, Linnaean system

18 **ecology**, synecology, autecology, plant ecology, phytoecology, animal ecology, zooecology, ecosystem, ecotype, community, population, niche, ecophysiology, food chain, food web, food pyramid, producer, primary producer, consumer, primary consumer, secondary consumer, parasitism, parasite, host, mutualism, symbiosis, symbiont, symbiote (US), commensalism, commensal, biodiversity, competition, succession, sere, climax, human ecology, conservation, pollution, biohazard

▶ *70 Animals*

19 **life scientist**, biologist, natural scientist, zoologist, botanist, microbiologist, bacteriologist, virologist, parasitologist, anatomist, morphologist, physiologist, biochemist, endocrinologist, immunologist, histologist, cell biologist, cytologist, molecular biologist, geneticist, developmental biologist, embryologist, palaeontologist, evolutionist, Darwinist, neo-Darwinist, taxonomist, cladist, naturalist, marine biologist, ecologist, biophysicist, biometrist, cryobiologist, space biologist, ethnobiologist, sociobiologist

ADJECTIVES

20 **biological**, zoological, botanical, microbiological, bacteriological, virological, gnotobiotic, parasitological, anatomical, morphological, physiological, biochemical, endocrinological, endocrine, immunological, histological, cytological, genetic, biotechnological, embryological, evolutionary, palaeontological, taxonomic, systematic, ecological, bionomic, biophysical, biometric, bionic, cryobiological, ethnobiological, sociobiological

21 **living**, live, alive, animate, vital, viable, organic, natural, biotic, plant, animal, microbial, bacterial, rickettsial, viral

▶ *554 Life*

22 **physiological**, metabolic, anabolic, catabolic, alimentary, respiratory, aerobic, anaerobic, photosynthetic, secretory, excretory, reproductive, locomotory

▶ *300 Motion; 434 Air; 488 Sensation; 557 Eating; 559 Secretion; 560 Excretion; 561 Reproduction*

23 **cellular**, cell, cellulus, prokaryotic (*or* procaryotic), eukaryotic (*or* eucaryotic), multicellular, unicellular, single-celled, acellular, plasmic, protoplasmic, cytoplasmic, ectoplasmic, endoplasmic, reticular, coenocytic, syncytial, mitochondrial, ribosomal

24 **nuclear**, nucleal, nucleary, nucleic, nucleate, uninucleate, multinucleate, nucleolar, nucleolate(d)

25 **genetic**, genotypic(al), genomic, gene, genic, factorial, hereditary, Mendelian, dominant, recessive, mutant, mutational, chromosomal, mitotic, meiotic, haploid, diploid, polyploid

26 **developmental**, ontogenic (*or* ontogenetic), developing, primordial, rudimentary, germ, germinal, germinating, germinant, germinative, in the bud, embryonic, ectodermal (*or* ectodermic), endodermal (*or* endodermic), mesodermal (*or* mesodermic), fetal (*or* foetal), amniotic, chorionic, allantoic, juvenile, larval, pupal, neotenous, paedogenetic (*or* paedogenic)

27 **evolutionary**, phylogenetic (*or* phyletic), Darwinian, neo-Darwinian, Lamarckian, neo-Lamarckian, uniformitarian

28 **taxonomic**, systematic, biosystematic, cladistic, generic, specific, subspecific

ADVERBS

29 **biologically**, zoologically, botanically, anatomically, morphologically, physiologically, biochemically, immunologically, histologically, cytologically, genetically, embryologically, taxonomically, generically, systematically, specifically, ecologically

35 Medicine

The art of medicine is generally a question of time. Ovid.

Formerly, when religion was strong and science weak, men mistook magic for medicine, now, when science is strong and religion weak, men mistake medicine for magic. Thomas Szasz.

As long as men are liable to die and are desirous to live, a physician will be made fun of, but he will be well paid. Jean de La Bruyère.

NOUNS

1 **medicine**, medical practice, medical profession, medical ethics, Hippocratic oath, medical jurisprudence, orthodox medicine, allopathic medicine, conventional medicine, general medicine, internal medicine, tropical medicine, industrial medicine, occupational medicine, community medicine, public-health medicine, preventive medicine, medical care, health care, primary health (*or* medical) care, general practice, group practice, practice, fund-holding, National Health Service, Medicare (US), Medicaid (US), private medicine, medical insurance, BUPA (British United Provident Association), Blue Cross™ (US), Blue Shield (US trademark)

▶ *36 Psychology and Psychiatry; 260 Ill Health*

2 **natural medicine**, traditional medicine, folk medicine, old wives' medicine, healing, faith healing, holistic medicine, alternative medicine, complementary medicine, supplementary medicine, unorthodox medicine, unconventional medicine, fringe medicine, herbalism, homeopathy, naturopathy, osteopathy, chiropractic, acupuncture, acupressure, shiatsu, aromatherapy, reflexology, ayurveda, ayurvedic medicine

▶ *394 Remedy*

3 **medical specialty**, clinical medicine, internal medicine, surgery, anaesthetics, anaesthesiology, gynaecology, obstetrics, paediatrics, teratology, embryology, geriatrics, gerontology, nostology, orthopaedics, rheumatology, physical medicine, osteology, gastroenterology, nephrology, urology, venereology, genitourinary medicine, dermatology, neurology, ophthalmology, otology, ENT (ear, nose, and throat), otorhinolaryngology, otolaryngology, eye, ear, nose, and throat (US), nuclear medicine, cardiology, nuclear cardiology, oncology, radiology, haematology, serology, medical science, immunology, endocrinology, biochemistry, medical genetics, eugenics, bacteriology, microbiology, virology, parasitology, toxicology, epidemiology, posology, nosology, aetiology, symptomatology, semeiology, pathology, forensic medicine, space medicine, biomedicine, psychiatry

▶ *16 Law; 34 Life Science; 36 Psychology and Psychiatry; 37 Pharmacology*

4 **dentistry**, dental surgery, oral surgery, exodontics, endodontics, orthodontics, prosthetic dentistry, prosthodontics, periodontics, periodontology, oral pathology, fillings, root canal work, crowning, capping, scaling, polishing, extraction, fissure sealing

5 **veterinary medicine**, veterinary practice, small-animal

practice, large-animal practice, veterinary clinic, veterinary surgery, animal welfare

► *43 Agriculture; 70 Animals*

6 **health care**, health promotion, health education, community medicine, public-health medicine, preventive medicine, prophylaxis, immunization, inoculation, vaccination, fluoridation, nutrition, dietetics, hygiene, genetic counselling, midwifery, chiropody, podiatry, medical consultation, call-out, home visit, medical history, case history, medical examination, medical, check-up (Inf), physical examination, physical, internal examination, second opinion, referral, prognosis, follow-up

► *33 Biochemistry; 257 Hygiene; 259 Health; 394 Remedy*

7 **diagnosis**, diagnostics, differential diagnosis, prognosis, diagnostic test, test, medical test, laboratory test, screening test, screening, mass screening, genetic screening, battery of tests, eye test, hearing test, blood test, serotest, sputum test, skin test, patch test, sample, blood sample, stool sample, urine sample, semen sample, tissue sample, biopsy, puncture, lumbar puncture, smear test, cervical smear, Pap test, pregnancy test, prenatal diagnosis, amniocentesis, chorionic villus sampling (CVS), fetoscopy, diagnostic procedure, electrocardiography, ECG (electrocardiogram), electroencephalogy, EEG (electroencephalogram), radiography, diagnostic radiology, barium meal, barium enema, radiograph, X-ray, mass X-ray, chest X-ray, arteriography, angiography, angiogram, lymphography, lymphogram, venography, venogram, thermography, mammothermography, mammography, mammogram, pyelography, pyelogram, intravenous (IV) pyelogram, scanning, scan, ultrasound scan, body scan, Grain scan, tomography, tomogram, CT (*or* CAT) scan, PET scan, MUGA scan, thallium scan, MRI (magnetic resonance imaging), NMR (nuclear magnetic resonance) scan, endoscopy, bronchoscopy, laparoscopy, gastroscopy, colposcopy, ureteroscopy, cystoscopy, diagnostic instrument, stethoscope, ophthalmoscope, auriscope, otoscope, endoscope, fibrescope, fetoscope, bronchoscope, gastroscope, laparoscope, colposcope, ureteroscope, cystoscope, postmortem (examination) (PM), autopsy

8 **treatment**, therapy, therapeutics, medical treatment, medical care, intensive therapy (*or* care), nursing care, nursing, medical intervention, clinical treatment, allopathy, conservative (*or* palliative) treatment, radical treatment, active treatment, drug treatment, medication, prescription, hormone replacement therapy, naturopathy, homeopathy, herbalism, chemotherapy, immunotherapy, radiotherapy, therapeutic radiology, gene therapy, gene replacement therapy, dialysis, surgical treatment, surgery, manipulative treatment, physiotherapy, orthontics, osteopathy, chiropractic, speech therapy, occupational therapy, rehabilitation, aftercare

► *37 Pharmacology; 394 Remedy*

9 **surgery**, surgical treatment, surgical intervention, general surgery, heart surgery, open-heart surgery, bypass surgery, brain surgery, neurosurgery, plastic surgery, dental surgery, psychosurgery, major surgery, minor surgery, keyhole surgery, laser surgery, surgical operation, operation, op (Inf), premedication, premed (Inf), sedation, induction, anaesthesia, acupuncture, incision, section, resection, division, excision, amputation, advancement, transplantation, grafting, transfusion, perfusion, suture

► *36 Psychology and Psychiatry; 37 Pharmacology; 394 Remedy*

10 **hospital**, general hospital, teaching hospital, university hospital (US), women's hospital, maternity hospital, children's hospital, day hospital, community hospital, cottage hospital, county hospital (US), cooperative hospital (US), NHS hospital, private hospital, NHS trust hospital, municipal hospital, city hospital, voluntary hospital, infirmary, sanatorium, nursing home, convalescent home, rest home, hospice, hospital ward, ward, isolation ward, operating theatre, intensive therapy (*or* care) unit (ITU *or* ICU), dispensary, clinic, polyclinic, out-patient clinic, antenatal clinic, prenatal clinic (US), well-woman clinic, child-health clinic, well-baby clinic, health centre, surgery, consulting room

► *394 Remedy*

11 **doctor**, physician, surgeon, medical doctor (MD), medical practitioner, general practitioner (GP), family doctor, fund-holder, family practitioner (US), locum (*or* locum tenens), medical student, hospital doctor, intern, resident, houseman, house physician, house surgeon, senior house officer, registrar, medical registrar, surgical registrar, senior registrar, consultant, medical officer (MO), health officer, community physician, public-health physician, psychiatrist, doc (Inf), medic (*or* medico) (Inf), quack (Inf), sawbones (Inf), trick cyclist (Inf), leech (Lit)

► *36 Psychology and Psychiatry; 394 Remedy*

12 **healer**, therapist, faith healer, alternative practitioner, acupuncturist, homeopath, naturopath, aromatherapist, reflexologist, osteopath, chiropractor, bonesetter, herbalist, hakim

13 **medical specialist**, specialist, consultant, clinician, diagnostician, surgeon, general surgeon, heart surgeon, brain surgeon, neurosurgeon, plastic surgeon, radiotherapist, anaesthetist, anaesthesiologist (US), gynaecologist, obstetrician, paediatrician, teratologist, embryologist, geriatrician, gerontologist, nostologist, orthopaedist, rheumatologist, osteologist, gastroenterologist, nephrologist, urologist, venereologist, dermatologist, neurologist, ophthalmologist, otologist, aurist, otorhinolaryngologist, otolaryngologist, cardiologist, oncologist, radiologist, haematologist, serologist, immunologist, endocrinologist, bacteriologist, microbiologist, virologist, parasitologist, toxicologist, epidemiologist, nosologist, posologist, pathologist, forensic pathologist, medical examiner (US)

14 **dentist**, dental surgeon, oral surgeon, children's dentist, exodontist, endodontist, orthodontist, prosthodontist, periodontist, periodontologist, oral pathologist

15 **veterinarian**, veterinary, vet (Inf), veterinary practitioner, veterinary surgeon, veterinary student, veterinary nurse, veterinary technician (US), animal doctor, horse doctor (Inf), horseleech (Lit)

16 **nurse**, male nurse, student nurse, trainee nurse (US), probationer (nurse), staff nurse, head nurse (US), charge nurse, sister, night sister, ward sister, theatre sister, head nurse (US), nursing officer, senior nursing officer, principal nursing officer, matron, Licensed Practical Nurse

SURGICAL OPERATIONS

Surgical Incision
amniotomy (amniotic membranes)
arteriotomy (artery)
arthrotomy (joint capsule)
capsulotomy (lens capsule of eye)
cardiomyotomy (stomach opening)
cholecystotomy (gall bladder)
choledochotomy (bile duct)
colpotomy (vagina)
cordotomy (part of spinal cord)
craniotomy (skull)
cystotomy (bladder)
embryotomy (fetus)
enterotomy (intestine)
episiotomy (vaginal opening)
gastrotomy (stomach)
goniotomy, trabeculotomy (duct in eye)
hymenotomy (hymen)
hysterotomy (womb)
iridotomy (iris)
jejunotomy (jejunum)
keratotomy (cornea)
laparotomy (abdomen)
laryngotomy (larynx)
leucotomy (nerve fibres in brain)
lithotomy, lithonephrotomy, nephrolithotomy, pyelolithotomy (kidney stone)
lobotomy, prefrontal leucotomy (nerve fibres from frontal lobe of brain)
mastoidotomy (mastoid bone)
myotomy (muscle)
myringotomy, tympanotomy (eardrum)
nephrotomy (kidney)
neurotomy (nerve)
oesophagotomy (gullet)
ophthalmotomy (eye)
orbitotomy (bone around eye)
orchidotomy (testis)
osteotomy (bone)
ovariotomy (ovary)
pancreatotomy (pancreas)
papillotomy (part of bile duct)
pericardiotomy, pericardotomy (membrane around heart)
phlebotomy (vein)
pleurotomy (pleural membrane)
proctotomy (rectum *or* anus)
pubiotomy (pubic bone)
pyelotomy (pelvis of kidney)
pyloromyotomy (stomach outlet)
rachiotomy (backbone)
rhizotomy (nerve roots)
sclerotomy (white of eye)
scrototomy (scrotum)
sphincterotomy (sphincter muscle)
sternotomy (breastbone)
symphysiotomy (front of pelvis)
tenotomy (tendon)
thalamotomy (part of brain)
thoracotomy (chest cavity)
thyrotomy (thyroid gland)
tonsillotomy (tonsil)
tracheotomy (windpipe)
ureterotomy (ureter)
urethrotomy (urethra)
vagotomy (vagus nerve)
valvotomy, valvulotomy (heart valve)
varicotomy (varicose vein)
vasotomy (sperm duct)

Surgical Opening *or* Surgical Joining (of two organs)
antrostomy (bone cavity)
appendicostomy (appendix)
caecostomy (caecum)
cholecystenterostomy (gall bladder and small intestine)
cholecystoduodenostomy (gall bladder and duodenum)
cholecystogastrostomy (gall bladder and stomach)
colostomy (colon)
cystostomy, vesicostomy (bladder)
dacryocystorhinostomy (tear sac and nose)
duodenostomy (duodenum)
enterostomy (small intestine)
epididymovasostomy (sperm ducts)
gastroduodenostomy (stomach and duodenum)
gastroenterostomy (stomach and small intestine)
gastrojejunostomy (stomach and jejunum)
gastro–oesophagostomy (stomach and gullet)
gastrostomy (stomach)
hepaticostomy (liver)
ileocolostomy (ileum and colon)
ileoproctostomy (ileum and rectum)
ileostomy (ileum)
jejunoileostomy (jejunum and ileum)
jejunostomy (jejunum)
nephrostomy (kidney)
oesophagostomy (gullet)
pericardiostomy (membrane around heart)
salpingostomy (fallopian tube)
tracheostomy (wind pipe)
transuretero–ureterostomy (one ureter to the other)
ureteroenterostomy (ureter and bowel)
ureteroneocystostomy (ureter and bladder)
ureterosigmoidostomy (ureter and part of bowel)
ureterostomy (ureter)
urethrostomy (urethra)
vaso–epididymostomy (sperm ducts)
vasovasostomy (rejoining of severed sperm duct)
ventriculostomy (cavity of brain)

Surgical Removal
adenoidectomy (adenoids)
antrectomy (part of stomach)

(LPN) (US), Registered Nurse (RN) (US), private nurse (US), visiting nurse (US), Enrolled Nurse, Registered General Nurse (RGN), State Enrolled Nurse (SEN), State Registered Nurse (SRN), special nurse, children's nurse, school nurse, day nurse, night nurse, district nurse, home nurse, health visitor, occupational-health nurse, nurse practitioner, midwife, domiciliary midwife, Florence Nightingale, lady with a lamp, ministering angel, angel of mercy

17 **paramedic**, paramedical, crash team, anaesthetist (US), radiographer, physiotherapist, occupational therapist, speech therapist, dental therapist, dietician, nutritionist, chiropodist, hygienist, dental (*or* oral) hygienist, medical attendant, nurse, midwife, carer, care attendant, ambulanceman, stretcher-bearer, medical assistant, surgical assistant, dresser, dental surgery assistant, medical auxiliary, dental auxiliary, nursing auxiliary, orderly, ward orderly, medical technician, dental technician, hospital social worker, hospital administrator

► *394 Remedy*

18 **patient**, in-patient, out-patient, client, case, terminal case, invalid, sick person

► *260 Ill Health*

VERBS

19 **practise medicine**, hold surgery, attend, advise, examine, refer, seek a second opinion, consult, diagnose, prognosticate, immunize, inoculate, vaccinate, test for, screen (for), X-ray, scan, treat, doctor, prescribe, medicate, administer, inject, care for, look after, minister to, nurse, tend, support, relieve, ease, palliate, restore, cure, heal, rehabilitate, follow up, make a house call, be called out

► *37 Pharmacology; 257 Hygiene; 394 Remedy; 608 Relief*

20 **practise surgery**, prepare for surgery, prep (Inf), sedate, anaesthetize, operate, induce, maintain, make an incision, incise, divide, excise, amputate, transfuse, perfuse, suture, dialyse, transplant

► *394 Remedy*

21 **practise dentistry**, treat teeth, descale, polish, fill, stop, crown, extract, pull (Inf)

SURGICAL OPERATIONS (CONT.)

apicectomy (root of tooth)
appendicectomy, appendectomy (US)
arteriectomy (artery)
arthrectomy (joint)
cholecystectomy (gall bladder)
cingulectomy (part of brain)
clitoridectomy (clitoris)
colectomy (colon)
cordectomy (vocal cord)
cystectomy (bladder)
embolectomy (embolus, blood clot)
endarterectomy (inner wall of artery)
enterectomy (intestine)
epididymectomy (sperm duct)
fraenectomy (tissue beneath tongue)
gastrectomy (stomach)
gingivectomy (gum tissue)
glossectomy (tongue)
haemorrhoidectomy (haemorrhoids)
hemicolectomy (part of colon)
hepatectomy (liver)
hypophysectomy (pituitary gland)
hysterectomy (womb)
ileectomy (ileum)
incudectomy (middle ear osside)
iridectomy (iris)
jejunectomy (jejunum)
keratectomy (cornea)
laryngectomy (larynx)
lobectomy (lobe of an organ)
lumpectomy (breast tumour)
lymphadenectomy (lymph node)
mastectomy (breast)
mastoidectomy (mastoid)
meniscectomy (knee cartilage)
myectomy (muscle)
myomectomy (fibroids)
nephrectomy (kidney)
nephroureterectomy, ureteronephrectomy (kidney and ureter)
neurectomy (nerve)
omentectomy (peritoneum of stomach)
oophorectomy, ovariectomy (ovary)
ophthalmectomy (eye)
orchidectomy (testis)
ostectomy (bone)
pallidectomy (part of brain)
pancreatectomy (pancreas)
parathyroidectomy (parathyroid gland)
pericardiectomy, pericardectomy (membrane around heart)
phalangectomy (finger *or* toe bones)
pharyngectomy (pharynx)
phlebectomy (vein)
phrenicectomy (phrenic nerve)
pleurectomy (pleural membrane)
pneumonectomy (lung)
polypectomy (polyp)
proctectomy (rectum)
proctocolectomy (rectum and colon)
prostatectomy (prostate gland)
pylorectomy (part of stomach)
salpingectomy (fallopian tube)
sclerectomy (white of eye)
sequestrectomy (dead bone)
sigmoidectomy (part of colon)
sphincterectomy (sphincter muscle)
splenectomy (spleen)
stapedectomy (third ear ossicle)
staphylectomy, uvulectomy (uvula)
sympathectomy (sympathetic nerve)
synovectomy (membrane around joint)
tarsectomy (ankle bones *or* eyelid tissue)
thoracectomy (rib *or* ribs)
thrombectomy (blood clot)
thymectomy (thymus gland)
thyroidectomy (thyroid gland)
tonsillectomy (tonsils)
topectomy (part of brain)
trabeculectomy (part of eye)
turbinectomy (bone in nose)
ureterectomy (ureter)
varicectomy (varicose veins)
vasectomy (sperm duct)
vesiculectomy (seminal vesicle)
vitrectomy (vitreus humour)
vulvectomy (vulva)

Surgical Repair
angioplasty (blood vessel)
arterioplasty (artery)
arthroplasty (joint)
blepharoplasty, tarsoplasty (eyelid)
colpoperineoplasty (vaginal opening)
cystoplasty (bladder)
dermatoplasty (skin)
gastroplasty (stomach)
genioplasty (chin)
helcoplasty (skin ulcers)
hernioplasty (hernia)
keratoplasty (cornea)
labioplasty, cheiloplasty (lips)
mammoplasty (breast)
myoplasty (muscle)
myringoplasty, tympanoplasty (eardrum)
neuronoplasty (nerves)
otoplasty (ear)
palatoplasty (cleft palate)
perineoplasty (vaginal opening)
phalloplasty (penis)
pyeloplasty (pelvis of kidney)
pyloroplasty (stomach outlet)
rhinoplasty (nose)
stricturoplasty (stricture)
tenoplasty (tendon)
thoracoplasty (chest cavity)
ureteroplasty (ureter)
urethroplasty (urethra)
vaginoplasty, colpoplasty (vagina)

ADJECTIVES

22 medical, iatric, Hippocratic, clinical, allopathic, homeopathic, surgical, osteopathic, gynaecological, obstetric, paediatric, geriatric, neurological, dermatological, urological, genitourinary, ophthalmological, cardiac, radiological, epidemiological, forensic, pathological, veterinary

► *394 Remedy*

23 dental, oral, orthodontic, exodontic, endodontic, prosthodontic, periodontic, periodontal

24 diagnostic, symptomatological, symptomatic, prognostic, indicative

25 therapeutic, medicinal, preventive (*or* preventative), prophylactic, remedial, curative, healing, nursing, tending

► *394 Remedy; 608 Relief*

ADVERBS

26 medically, clinically, surgically

36 Psychology and Psychiatry

What progress we are making. In the Middle Ages they would have burned me. Now they are content with burning my books.
Sigmund Freud.

NOUNS

1 psychology, science of the mind, science of human and animal behaviour, abnormal psychology, academic psychology, Freudian psychology, psychoanalysis, Freudianism, psychoanalytic theory, Jungian psychology, analytic(al) psychology, Adlerian psychology, individual psychology, apperceptionism, applied psychology, associationism, association psychology, mental chemistry, animal psychology, ethology, animal behaviour, behavioural psychology, behaviourism, stimulus-response psychology, Skinnerian psychology, Watsonian psychology, Pavlovian psychology, Lacanian psychology, clinical psychology, child psychology, cognitive psychology, comparative psychology, constitutional psychology, criminal psychology, depth psychology, developmental psychology, dianetics, differential psychology, dynamic psychology, ecological psychology, educational psychology, empirical psychology, existential psychology, experimental psychology, faculty psychology, folk psychology, functional psychology, genetic psychology, Gestaltism, Gestalt psychology, Gestalt theory, configurationism, group psychology, hedontics, hormic psychology, Horneyan psychology, humanistic psychology, industrial psychology, introspection psychology, metaphysics, metapsychology, morbid psychology, neuropsychology, object-relations theory, objective psychology, phenomenological psychology, physiological psychology, popular psychology, psychic determinism, psychoacoustics, psychobiochemistry, psychobiology, psychodynamics, psychogenesis, psychogenetics, psychognosis, psychography, psycholinguistics, psychologism, psychometrics, psychometry, psychoneurosis, psychopathology, psychopharmacology, psychophysics, psychophysiology, psychosociology, psychosomatics, psychotechnics, psychotechnology, psychological warfare, psychosexuality, psychosexual development, race psychology, rational psychology, reactology, reflexology, Reichian psychology, orgone theory, self psychology, social psychology, structuralism, structural psychology, parapsychology, psychokinesis (PK)

► *11 Occultism; 35 Medicine*

2 **psychiatry**, medicopsychology, prophylactic psychiatry, psychodiagnostics, psychodiagnosis, antipsychiatry, neuropsychiatry, orthopsychiatry, psychogeriatrics, psychological medicine, psychosocial medicine, psychosomatic medicine

► *35 Medicine*

3 **psychiatric treatment**, psychiatric care, drug treatment, psychotropic drug, psychosurgery, leucotomy, prefrontal leucotomy (*or* lobotomy), cingulectomy, amygdalectomy, stereotaxy, psychoanalysis, analysis, ego analysis, Freudian analysis, psychoanalytic method, the couch, James-Lange theory, transactional analysis (TA), assertiveness training, psychotherapeutics, psychotherapy, behaviour modification, behaviour therapy, New Consciousness, bioenergetics, autosuggestion, biofeedback, client-centred therapy, aversion therapy, confrontation therapy, desensitization, conditioning, relaxation therapy, counselling, psychological counselling, pastoral counselling, directive therapy, ego therapy, est (Erhard seminars training), existential therapy, evocative psychotherapy, Gestalt therapy, group psychotherapy, group dynamics, marathon group, family therapy, family training, conjoint therapy, co-counselling, encounter group, consciousness raising, sensitivity training, sensitivity training group (*or* T-group), group relations training, sensory awareness training (SAT), marriage encounter, marriage guidance, humanistic therapy, logotherapy, mind cure, modelling, nondirective therapy, occupational therapy, play therapy, recreational therapy, primal therapy, regression therapy, scream therapy, psychodrama, drama therapy, radical therapy, feminist therapy, rational-emotive therapy, reality therapy, release therapy, abreaction, catharsis, psychocatharsis, reminiscence therapy, Rogerian therapy, role-playing, sex therapy, supportive theory, token economy, transcendental meditation (TM), transpersonal theory, Arica movement, vocational therapy, suggestion therapy, suggestionism, hypnotherapy, hypnotic suggestion, posthypnotic suggestion, narcohypnosis, autohypnosis, self-hypnosis, sleep treatment, sleep therapy, narcotherapy, pentothal interview, narcoanalysis, shock treatment, shock therapy, convulsive therapy, electroconvulsive therapy (ECT), electroconvulsive shock therapy (EST), electroshock, electroshock therapy, electronarcosis, metrazol shock therapy, hypoglycaemic shock therapy, insulin shock therapy, nonconvulsive electric treatment

► *35 Medicine; 37 Pharmacology; 394 Remedy*

4 **psychometrics**, psychometry, intelligence testing, mental test, psychological screening, psychography, psychogram, psychometer, lie detector, polygraph, psychogalvanometer, psychogalvanic skin response, psychogalvanic response (PGR), IQ meter (Inf)

5 **psychological test**, mental test, aptitude test, intelligence test, general aptitude test battery (GATB), Allport-Vernon draw-a-person test, Allport-Vernon study of values, association test, word-association test, controlled-association test, free-association test, personality test, personality adjustment test, personality inventory, personality research form, Bernreuter personality inventory, Brown personality inventory, Minnesota multiphasic personality inventory (MMPI), Candle problem, frustration test, Gesell's development schedule, graduated reciprocation in tension reduction (GRIT), group test, inkblot test, Rorschach test, Holtzman inkblot technique, Lüscher colour test, individual test, Oseretsky test, projective test, Szondi test, house-tree-person (HTP) projective test, Rogers' process scale, Rotter incomplete sentences blank, scientific aptitude test, strong vocational interest test, thematic apperception test (TAT)

6 **intelligence test**, intelligence quotient (IQ), IQ test, Army General Classification Test (AGCT), alpha test, beta test, Army Alpha test, Army Beta test, Weschler-Bellvue intelligence test, Weschler intelligence scale for children (WISC), Weschler Adult Intelligence Scale (WAIS), Stanford-Binet Intelligence Scale, Stanford revision, Stanford-Binet test, Binet (*or* Binet-Simon) test, Babcock-Levy test, Cattell's Infant Intelligence Scale, Minnesota pre-school scale, Goldstein-Sheerer test, Kent mental test

7 **personality type**, personality tendency, introvert, introversion, introvertedness, ingoingness, extrovert, extroversion, extrovertedness, outgoingness, other-directedness, syntone, syntony, ambivert, ambiversion, choleric, melancholic, sanguine, phlegmatic, ectomorph, ectomorphy, ectomorphism, endomorph, endomorphy, endomorphism, mesomorph, mesomorphism, mesomorphy

► *461 Insanity*

8 **disordered personality**, personality disorder, neurotic personality, neurotic, neuropath, psychoneurotic, disturbed person, emotionally disturbed person, unstable person, hysterical personality, weak personality, inferior personality, immature personality, antisocial personality, sociopath, shut-in personality, escapist, mentally defective personality, maladjusted personality, hostile personality, perverse personality, paranoid personality, schizoid, schizoid personality, dual personality, double personality, multiple personality, split personality, alternating personality, schizothyme, schyzothymia, schizothymic personality, cyclothyme, cyclothymic personality, cyclothymia, cycloid, cycloid personality, psychopath, psychopathic personality, psychotic, psychotic personality, lunatic, loony (Inf), schizo (Inf), psycho (Inf), wacko (Inf)

9 **psychological disorder**, mental disorder, nervous disorder, psychogenic disorder, functional nervous disorder, neurosis, psychosis, mental subnormality, intellectual subnormality

► *457 Stupidity; 461 Insanity*

10 **neurosis**, psychoneurosis, neuroticism, neurotic disorder, accident neurosis, anxiety neurosis, anxiety reaction, neurotic-depressive reaction, deviation, blast neurosis, compensation neurosis, conversion neurosis, expectation neurosis, dissociation reaction, fixation neurosis, fright neurosis, flight reaction, homosexual neurosis, hypochondria, depression, melancholia, hysteria, occupational neurosis, pathoneurosis, regression neurosis, traumatic neurosis, transference neurosis, compulsion neurosis, obsessional neurosis, obsessive-compulsive neurosis (*or* reaction), phobia, reactive neurosis, situational neurosis, combat neurosis, battle fatigue, shell shock, psychopathia martialis, breakdown, nervous breakdown, mental breakdown

► *612 Fear*

11 **psychosis**, psychopathy, organic psychosis, functional psychosis, affective psychosis, schizoaffective psychosis, cycloid psychosis, manic-depressive psychosis, onecroid psychosis, puerperal psychosis, schizophrenia, dementia praecox, hebephrenia, catatonia, cyclothymia, alcoholic psychosis, Korsakoff's psychosis

► *461 Insanity*

12 **stress**, mental stress, psychological stress, pre-menstrual syndrome, emotional strain (*or* tension), stress reaction, anxiety, panic attack, psychalgia, anxiety state, anxiety equivalent, free-floating anxiety, hysteria, anxiety hysteria, conversion hysteria, dissociative hysteria, hysterics, trauma, traumatism, shock, shock reaction, post-traumatic stress disorder, frustration, conflict, ambivalence (of impulse), mental (*or* emotional) shock, decompensation, nervous tic, nerves (Inf)

► *612 Fear*

13 **depression**, clinical depression, melancholia, involutional melancholia, endogenous depression, reactive depression, depressive reaction, SAD syndrome (seasonal affective disorder), agitated depression, dejection, detachment, alienation, withdrawal, abstraction, preoccupation, apathy, lethargy, indifference, unresponsiveness, insensibility, stupor, catatonic stupor

► *602 Sorrow*

14 **trance**, stupor, daze, hypnotic trance, catatonic trance, hysterical trance, trance state, catalepsy, cataplexy, dream state, reverie, daydreaming, sleepwalking, somnambulism, fugue, fugue state, amnesia, meditation, religious ecstasy, aphonia, aphasia

15 **compulsion**, urge, craving, addiction, bulimia nervosa, anorexia nervosa, dipsomania, passion, obsession, impulsion, craze, mania, megalomania, monomania, egomania, paranoia, nymphomania, satyriasis

► *461 Insanity; 632 Habit*

16 **dissociation**, disconnection, dissociation of personality, disintegration of personality, schizoidism, schizoid personality, double personality, split personality, multiple personality, alternating personality, knight's-move thought, schizothymia, schizophrenia, depersonalization, paranoia, paranoid personality

17 **fixation**, libido fixation, libido arrest, arrested development, fixation of affect, infantile fixation, Freudian fixation, parent fixation, mother fixation, father fixation

18 **complex**, inferiority complex, superiority complex, parent complex, Oedipus complex, mother complex, Electra complex, father complex, Diana complex, persecution complex, castration complex, compulsion complex

19 **defence mechanism**, defence reaction, censor, repression, suppression, inhibition, block, blocking, blockage, resistance, avoidance, denial, negation, rejection, reaction formation, splitting, rigid control, suppressed desire, sublimation, regression, reversion, projection, identification, fantasy, escapism, flight, withdrawal, isolation, negativism, alienation, dreamlike thinking, wishful thinking, autism, dereism, compensation, overcompensation, decompensation, substitution, blame-shifting, displacement, rationalization

20 **conditioning**, Pavlovian conditioning, classical conditioning, operant conditioning, psychogogy, re-education, reorientation, conditioned reflex, reinforcement, positive reinforcement, negative reinforcement, simple reflex, unconditioned reflex, reflex, suggestion, counterconditioning, avoidance conditioning

21 **psyche**, psychic apparatus, self, psychological me, mind, pneuma, soul, personality, preconscious, foreconscious, stream of consciousness, coconscious, subconscious, unconscious, subliminal, subliminal self, unconscious mind, primitive self, id, conscious mind, conscious self, ego, ethical self, superego, ego ideal, ego-id conflict, anima, animus, persona, inner child, collective unconscious, racial unconscious

22 **libido**, sex(ual) drive, life instinct, Eros, vital force, motive force, psychic energy, sex instinct, libidinal energy, libidinal (*or* libido) object, libido analogue, erotic desire, eroticism, pleasure principle, death instinct, death wish, Thanatos

23 **memory**, engram, recall, reproduction, recognition, recollection, retention, memory trace, unconscious memory, forgetting

24 **symbolism**, symbolization, symbol, universal symbol, father symbol, mother symbol, phallic symbol, fertility symbol, dream-symbol interpretation, imago, image, archetype, archetypal image (*or* symbol), father (*or* mother *or* child) image

25 **surrogate**, substitute, parent surrogate, father figure, mother figure, father (*or* mother) image, mother surrogate

26 **gestalt**, pattern, figure, form, perceptual concept, configuration, sensory pattern, figure-ground

27 **association of ideas**, association, linking, reinforce-

ment, controlled association, free association, association by contiguity, word association, association by sound, clang association, stream of consciousness, transference, negative transference, synaesthesia

28 **cathexis**, cathection, desire concentration, charge, energy charge, cathectic energy, anticathexis, countercathexis, counterinvestment, hypercathexis, overcharge

29 **psychologist**, psychologue, clinical psychologist, clinician, child psychologist, psychiatrist, psychotherapist, therapist, psychoanalyst, analyst, psychopathologist, psychotechnologist, industrial psychologist, psychobiologist, psychochemist, psychophysiologist, psychophysicist, psychographer, psychosociologist, Freud, Jung, Adler, Horney, James, Janrt, Lange, Pavlov, Reich, Skinner, Watson, Laing, Lacan, Klein, Piaget

30 **psychiatrist**, mental specialist, neuropsychiatrist, psychogeriatrician, clinical psychologist, alienist, analyst, psychotherapist, psychotherapeutist, hypnotherapist, narcotherapist, dramatherapist, behaviour therapist, psychiatric social worker, counsellor, mad doctor, shrink (Inf), headshrinker (Inf), trick cyclist (Inf), men in white coats (Inf), barred-window boys (Inf)

▶ *461 Insanity*

31 **psychiatric hospital**, psychiatric unit, psychiatric ward, special hospital, mental hospital

▶ *394 Remedy; 461 Insanity*

ADJECTIVES

32 **psychological**, psychiatric, neuropsychiatric, psychotherapeutic, hypnotherapeutic, psychoanalytical, psychodiagnostic, psychometric, psychopathological, psychosocial, psychosomatic, psychophysical, psychobiological, psychoneurological, psychosexual, psychogenic, psychogenetic, psychotechnical, psychogeriatric, psychopharmacological

33 **Freudian**, Jungian, Adlerian, Horneyan, Pavlovian, Reichian, Skinnerian, Watsonian, Lacanian, Laingian, Kleinian

34 **introverted**, introvert, introversive, ingoing, indirected, withdrawn, isolated

▶ *655 Unsociability*

35 **extroverted**, extrovert, extroversive, outgoing, outdirected

▶ *654 Sociability*

36 **psychologically disturbed**, neurotic, disturbed, nervous, traumatized, emotional, schizoid, sociopathic, psychopathic, psychotic, hypochondriacal, paranoid, dissociated, disconnected

37 **subconscious**, subliminal, unconscious, coconscious, repressed, suppressed, inhibited, restrained, blocked, controlled

VERBS

38 **psychologize**, psychoanalyse, analyse, counsel, condition

ADVERBS

39 **psychologically**, psychiatrically, unconsciously, subconsciously, subliminally, neurotically, hysterically, inhibitedly, depressively

37 Pharmacology

A drug is that substance which, when injected into a rat, will produce a scientific report. Anonymous.

Half the modern drugs could well be thrown out the window except that the birds might eat them. Martin H. Fischer.

NOUNS

1 **pharmacology**, pharmacy, pharmaceutics, pharmacodynamics, pharmacokinetics, pharmocognosy, therapeutics, chemotherapy, pharmacopoeia, materia medica, posology, dosology

▶ *35 Medicine; 394 Remedy*

2 **pharmacologist**, pharmacist, pharmaceutist, chemist, druggist (US), dispenser, drug store (US)

3 **drug**, medicine, medication, medicinal, preparation, potion, dose, draught, tonic, healing agent, pharmaceutical, generic name, proprietary name, brand name, ethical drug, prescription (*or* prescribed) drug, nonprescription drug, over-the-counter drug, premedication, broad-spectrum drug, wonder drug, panacea, cure-all, catholicon, elixir, placebo, tolerance, side effect, drug dependence

▶ *394 Remedy; 691 Drug-Taking*

4 **drug type**, abortifacient, alkaloid, alkylating agent, anabolic steroid, androgen, antiviral drug, antipsychotic drug, anaesthetic, painkiller, analeptic, analgesic, antihydrotic, anodyne, antacid, anthelmintic, antibiotic, anticholinergic drug, anticoagulant, anticonvulsant, antidepressant, antidote, antiemetic, antifebrile, antifungal drug, antihistamine, anti-inflammatory, antimalarial drug, antimetabolite, antimycotic, antipyretic, antipruritic, antiseptic, antiserum, antispasmodic, antispastic, antithrombin, antitussive, antivenene (*or* antivenin), aperient, astringent, bactericide, bacteriostatic, barbiturate, beta blocker, bromide, bronchoconstrictor, bronchodilator, carminative, cathartic, caustic, choleretic, coagulant, collyrium, corticosteroid, counterirritant, cytoxic drug, decongestant, demulcent, deobstruent, deodorant, depilatory, depressant, diaphoretic, dilator, disinfectant, diuretic, emetic, epispastic, expectorant, febrifuge, fungicide, germicide, hallucinogen, hidrotic, humectant, hydragogue, hypnotic, immunosuppressive, inhibitor, insecticide, lachrymator, lactifuge, laxative, lithagogue, MAO inhibitor, muscle relaxant, narcotic, natriuretic, neuroleptic, opiate, oral contraceptive, palliative, parasiticide, parasympatholytic, parasympathomimetic, paregoric, pediculicide, penicillin, pressor, prophylactic, psychedelic drug, pulicide, purgative, pyrogen, relaxant, rubefacient, scabicide, sedative, somnifacient, sleeping pill, soporific, spasmolytic, spermicide, sporicide, sternutator, steroid, sulpha drug, sulphonamide, sulphone, sympatholytic, sympathomimetic, taeniacide, tetracycline, tonic, tranquillizer, vasoconstrictor, vasodilator, vasopressor, vermicide, vermifuge, vesicant

5 **prescription**, formula, dose, effective dose, course, active principle, essence, vehicle, excipient, galenical, confection, antagonist

MEDICATION

Antiseptics and Disinfectants
ABC powder
aminacrine
benzalkonium
benzelthonium
benzoic acid
borax
boracic acid
calomel
cetrimide
chloramine
chlorhexidine
chlorocresol
chlorooxylenol
clotrimazole
cresol
Dettol™
dequalinium
diiodohydroxyquinoline
diloxanide
domiphen
formaldehyde
hexachlorophane
hexamine
hydrogen peroxide
iodochlorhydroxyquin
iodoform
lye
peroxide
sodium hypochlorite
thimeracol
trimethroprim

Antipyretics
acetanilide
aspirin
benorylate
mepacrine
phenacetin
phenazone

Antihistamines
antazoline
bromodiphenylhydraine
bromopheniramine
buclizine
carbinoxamine
chlorcyclizine
chloropyrilene
chlorpheniramine
chlorphenoxamine
clemizole
cyclizine
cyproheptadine
dimenhydrinate
dimethothiazine
diphenhydramine
hydroxyzine
meclozine
mepyramine
methapyrilene
pheniramine
promethazine
trimeprazine

Antidepressants
amitriptyline
clomipramine
desipramine
dipenzepin
doxepin
imipramine
iprindole
iproniazid
maprotiline
mianserin
nialamide
nortryptyline
phenelzine
protriptyline
pulvule
tranylcypromine
trimipramine

Antibiotics
actinomycin
amphotericin
ampicillin
basitracin
benthazine penicillin
benzyl penicillin
bleomycin
capreomycin
carbenicillin
carbomycin
cephalexin
cephaloglycin
cephaloridine
cephalosporin
cephalothin sodium
chloramphenicol
chlortetracycline
clindamycin
cloxacillin sodium
colistin
co–trimoxazole
cycloserine
dimethylchlortetracycline
dihydrostreptomycin
doxorubicin
doxycycline
erythromycin
fradicin
framycetin
gentamycin
griseofulvin
hydrargaphen
hydroxystilbamidine
kanamycin
lincomycin
methicillin
mithramycin
mycomycin
nalidixic acid
neomycin
nifuratel
nitrofurantoin
novobiocin
oleandomycin
oxacillin
oxolinic acid
oxytetracycline
paromomycin
penicillin
phenethicillin
phenoxymethylpenicillin
podophylline
polymixin
procaine penicillin
pyocyanase
pyocyanin
rifampicin
rifamycin
spectinomycin
subtilin
streptomycin
tetracycline
tylocin
tyrothrycin
vanomycin
viomycin

Sulpha Drugs (Sulphonamides)
sulphacetamide
sulphadiazine
sulphadidimine
sulphadoxine
sulphafurazole
sulphaquanidine
sulphamethizole
sulphamethoxazole
sulphisoxazole

Analgesics
acetanilide
aloxiprin
anileridine
aspirin
barbitone
benorylate
carisprodol
chlormezanone
choline salicylate
codeine
dextromoramide
dextropropoxyphene
diamorphine *or* heroin (narcotic)
dihydrocodeine
dipipanone
fenoprofen
flufenamic acid
heroin *or* diamorphine (narcotic)
indomethacin
ketoprofen
levorphanol (narcotic)
mefanamic acid
meperidine
methadone (narcotic)
morphine (narcotic)
naproxen
opium (narcotic)
oxyphenbutazone
papaveretum
paracetamol
pentazocine
pethidine
phenacetin
phenazocine
phenazopyridine
phenylbutazone
salicylamide

Anaesthetics
ACE mixture
amethocaine
benzocaine (local)
bupivacaine (local)
butacaine (local)
CE mixture
chloroform
cinchocaine (local)
cocaine (local)
cyclomethycaine
cyclopropane
dibucaine
ethychloride (local)
ethylene
halocaine
halothane
hydroflumethiazide
laughing gas
lignocaine (local)
nitrous oxide
oxythiazine (local)
piperocaine
prilocaine
procaine (local)
propanidid
tetracaine
tribromoethanol (local)
trichloromethane
urethane
vinyl ether

Vasodilators
aminophylline
azapetine
buphenine
cyclandelate
erythritol
glycerine trinitrate
isoxuprine
nicotinyl
pentaerythritol
phenoxybenzamine
phentolamine
prenylamine
tetrahydrozoline
thymoxamine
tolazoline

Tranquillizers
amobarbital
amylobarbitone
benzodiazepine
carisprodol
chlordiazepoxide
chlormezanone
chlorpromazine

MEDICATION (CONT.)

chlorprothixene
chlorazepate potassium
diazepam
doxepin
fluphenazine
fluspirilene
haloperidol
hyoscine
lorazepam
meprobamate
methotrimeprazine
oxazepam
oxypertine
perphenazine
phenothiazine
pimozide
prochlorperazine
promazine
prothipendyl
thiopropazate
thioridazine
trifluoperazine

Stimulants
amphetamine
colcynth
cyclopentamine
dexamphetamine
methylamphetamine
nikethamide
nux vomica
oubain
picrotoxin
strychnine

Sedatives
barbitone
buclizine
butobarbitone
carbromal
chloral
chloral hydrate
chlordiazepoxide
chlorhexadol
chlormethiazole
cyclobarbitone
dichloralphenazone
ethinamate
flurazepam
hydroxyzine
methaqualone
methyprylone
prothipendyl
thalidomide (formerly)
thiopentone (oral)
triclofos

Laxatives
aloes
bisacodyl
calomel
cascara
castor oil
colcynth
Epsom salt
Glauber's salt
jalap
liquid paraffin
magnesium sulphate
methylcellulose
phenolphthalein
Rochelle salt
Seidlitz powder
senna
sodium sulphate

Antacids
Alka Seltzer™
bicarbonate of soda
Bromo Seltzer™
magnesium carbonate
magnesium hydroxide
Milk of Magnesia™
seltzer water
sodium bicarbonate

Diuretics
acetazolamide
amiloride
aminophylline
bendrofluazide
chlorothiazide
chlorthalidone
clopamide
clorexolone
cyclopenthiazide
dichlorophenamide
ethacrynic acid
frusemide
hydrochlorothiazide
mannitol
metolazone
theobromine
triamterene
trometamol

Steroids
allylestrenol
chlorotrianisene
cortisone
cyproterone
dienoestrol
diethylstilbesterol
dimethisterone
drostanolone
dydrogesterone
ethinyloestradiol
ethisterone
ethyloestrenol
ethynodiol
fludrocortisone
hydrocortisone
hydroxyprogesterone
liothyronine
lynoestrenol
medroxyprogesterone
megestrol
mestranol
methanderione
methandrione
methenolone
methyltestosterone
nadrolone
norethandrolone
norethisterone
oestrogen
oxymesterone
progestogen
stanolone
stilboestrol

Hallucinogens
dimethyltriptomine
jimson weed
LSD (lysergic acid diethylamide)
mescal
mescaline
psilocybin

Depressants
aconite
biperiden
bromide

Treatment of Gout
allopurinol
colchicine
ethebenecid
probenecid
sulphinpyrazole

Treatment of High Blood Pressure
alprenolol
bethanidine
clonidine
debrisoquine
deserpidine
dihydralazine
guanethidine
hydrallazine
mecamylamine
methoserpidine
methyldopa
metoprolol
oxprenadol
propanolol
sotalol

Cancer Treatments
bisulphan (leukaemia)
chlorambucil (leukaemia)
cyclophosphamide
cytarabine (leukaemia)
etoglucid
fluoxuridine
hydroxyurea (leukaemia)
laetrile
mannomustine
melphalan
mercaptopurine
methotrexate
mitrobronitol
mustine
nitrogen mustard
procarbazine
thioguanine
triaziquone
uramustine
urethane
vinblastine
vincristine

Anticonvulsants
barbitone *or* barbital
beclamide
carbamazepine
clonazepam
ethosuximide
ethotoin
methoin
paraldehyde
paramethadione
pheneturide
phensuximide
phenetoin
primidone
sulthiame
troxidone
valproic acid

Balms
balm of Gilead
balsam
blue ointment
glycerine *or* glycerin
melissa
olive oil
petrolatum

Miscellaneous Drugs
acetohexamide (diabetes mellitus)
acetylcysteine (respiratory diseases)
amantadine (influenza, parkinsonism)
amodiaquine (malaria)
amyl nitrite (angina pectoris)
Antabuse™ (alcoholism)
apomorphine (emetic)
azathioprine (immunosuppressive)
beclomethasone (skin disorders)
benzhexol (parkinsonism)
betamethasone (rheumatic diseases)
candicidin (fungicide)
carbachol (glaucoma)
carbimazole (hyperthyroidism)
chlorbutanol (fungicide)
chlordantoin (fungicide)
chlorphentermine (appetite suppressor)
chlorpropamide (diabetes)
choline theophyllinate (asthma, bronchitis)
clofibrate (reduces cholesterol level)
clorindole (anticoagulant)

MEDICATION (CONT.)

cromolyn sodium (asthma, bronchitis)
crotamiton (skin infections)
cyclopentolate (eye infections)
dapsone (leprosy, dermatitis)
dexamethasone (allergies, inflammatory conditions)
dextromethorphan (antitussive)
dextrothyroxine (reduces cholesterol level)
dichlorophen (anthelmintic)
dicoumarol (anticoagulant)
diethylpropion (appetite suppressor)
digitalis (heart failure)
digitoxin (heart failure)
digoxin (heart failure)
dihydrocodeine (antitussive)
dihydroergotamine (migraine)
dimethylsulphoxide *or* DMSO (skin disorders)
diphenoxylate (diarrhoea)
diprophylline (bronchodilator)
disopyramide (heart conditions)
disulfiram (alcoholism)
dithiazinine (anthelmintic)
dithranol (skin disorders)
dopa (parkinsonism)
emetine (liver and gut infections)
ethambutol (tuberculosis)
ethionamide (tuberculosis)
ethyl biscoumacetate (anticoagulant)
fenfluridine (obesity)
gallamine (muscle relaxant)
glibenclamide (diabetes)
glucagon (diabetic hypoglycaemia)
glutethimidine (insomnia)
glymidine (diabetes)
guaiphenesin (expectorant)
heparin (anticoagulant)
heptabarbitone (insomnia)
hexobarbitone (insomnia)
hirudin (anticoagulant)
hydroxyamphetamine (decongestant)
hyoscyamine (muscle spasm)
ichthammol (skin diseases)
idoxuridine (antiviral agent)
insulin (diabetes mellitus)
ipecacuanha (expectorant)
isoniazid (tuberculosis)
isoprenaline (bronchial conditions)
L–dopa *or* levodopa (parkinsonism)
lithium carbonate (schizophrenia)
menthol (cold relief)
mephenesin (muscle relaxant)
metformin (diabetes)
mathimazole (reduces thyroid activity)
mazindol (appetite suppressor)
methoxamine (low blood pressure)
methoxyphenamine (asthma)
methylene blue (urinary infections)
methysergide (migraine)
Mogadon™, insomnia)
naphazoline (decongestant)
nitrazapam (insomnia)
orciprenaline (asthma, bronchitis)
orphenadrine (muscle spasm)
papaverine (muscle relaxant, asthma)
para–aminosalicylic acid (tuberculosis)
paraformaldehyde (skin disorders)
penicillamine (rheumatoid arthritis)
pentobarbitone (insomnia)
phenindione (anticoagulant)
phenmetrazine (appetite suppressor)
phentermine (appetite suppressor)
phenylephrine (vasoconstrictor, decongestant)
phenylpropanolamine (asthma, allergies)
pholcodine (antitussive)
phthalylsulphathiazole (bowel infections)
physostigmine (constricts eye pupil)
philocarpine (constricts eye pupil)
piperazine (anthelmintic)
piperidolate (colic)
prednisolone (rheumatic diseases, inflammatory conditions)
prednisone (rheumatic diseases, inflammatory conditions)
primaquine (malaria)
procyclidine (muscle relaxant, parkinsonism)
proquanil (malaria)
propantheline (heart conditions)
prothionamide (tuberculosis)
pyrazinamide (tuberculosis)
quinidine (heart conditions)
quinine (malaria)
resorcinol (acne, dandruff)
rimiterol (asthma, bronchitis)
salbutamol (asthma, bronchitis)
salicylic acid (skin disorders)
suramin (sleeping sickness)
terbutaline (bronchodilator)
tetrahydrozoline (decongestant)
theophylline (asthma)
thiacetazone (leprosy, tuberculosis)
thyrocalcitonin (hypercalcaemia)
tolazamide (diabetes)
triamcinolone (inflammation)
tryparsamide (sleeping sickness)
vasopressin (diabetes insipidus)
warfarin (thrombosis)
xylometazoline (decongestant)

6 pill, tablet, capsule, cachet, lozenge, pastille, dragée, troche, powder, gel

7 ointment, salve, cream, balm, balsam, lotion, ungent, embrocation, paint, poultice, fomentation, unguent, unction, oil, liniment, emollient, demulcent, abirritant, arquebusade

8 drops, guttae, ear drops, nose drops, eye drops, eyewash, dropper

9 pessary, suppository

10 inhalant, spray, atomizer, nebulizer, aerosol

11 linctus, gargle, mouthwash, wash, eyebath, undine, douche

12 injection, intracutaneous injection, intradermal injection, subcutaneous injection, intramuscular injection, intravenous injection, venoclysis, intubation, drip, implant, pellet, translumbar injection, transdermal injection, patch, epidural

13 administration, topical administration, inhalation, oral administration, enteral administration, peroral administration, rectal administration, parenteral administration, infusion

ADJECTIVES

14 counteracting, suppressing, inhibiting, destroying, antipsychotic, anaesthetic, analgesic, antihydrotic, antacid, anthelmintic, vermicidal, vermifugal, antibiotic, antibacterial, antifungal, antimycotic, antiviral, bacteriostatic, bacteriocidal, fungicidal, germicidal, antiseptic, disinfectant, anticholinergic, anticoagulant, antidepressant, antidotal, antiemetic, anti-inflammatory, antimalarial, antimitotic, cytotoxic, antipruritic, antipyretic, febrifugal, antispasmodic, spasmolytic, antispastic, antitussive, counterirritant, decongestant, immunosuppressive, lactifugal, parasympatholytic, sympatholytic, spermicidal, antiscorbutic

15 sedative, calmative, depressant, soporific, hypnotic, tranquillizing, neuroleptic, narcotic

16 soothing, relieving, anodyne, demulcent, emollient, balsamic

17 stimulating, enhancing, tonic, invigorating, astringent, anabolic, analeptic, aperient, purging, purgative, cathartic, laxative, choleretic, diaphoretic, sudorific, diuretic, natriuretic, uricosumic, emetic, expectorant, hallucinogenic, psychedelic, hidrotic, parasympathomimetic, sympathomimetic, rubefacient, abortifacient

18 pharmacological, pharmaceutical, pharmacodynamic, pharmacokinetic, pharmacognostic, therapeutic

► *35 Medicine; 394 Remedy*

VERBS

19 administer, inject, inoculate, instil, infuse, perfuse, apply, anoint, insert, implant, take in, inhale, ingest, swallow

38 Engineering

NOUNS

1 **engineering**, civil engineering, mechanical engineering, aeronautical engineering, automotive engineering, naval engineering, agricultural engineering, electrical engineering, electronics engineering, chemical engineering, mining engineering, metallurgical engineering, metallurgy, nuclear engineering, production engineering, environmental engineering, engineering geology, engineering design, engineering drawing, CAE (computer-aided engineering), CAD (computer-aided design), management engineering, bioengineering

2 **engineer**, mechanical engineer, civil engineer, electrical engineer, chartered engineer

► *28 Physics; 30 Earth Science; 32 Chemistry; 39 Electronics; 319 Transport*

3 **mechanical engineering**, machine-design engineering, industrial engineering, automotive engineering, aeronautical engineering, marine engineering

► *319 Transport*

4 **mechanical engineer**, mechanic, technician, fitter

5 **dynamic structure**, dynamic system, machinery, mechanical device, machine, engine, motor, mechanism, tool, servomechanism

6 **simple machine**, lever, wheel and axle, pulley, block and tackle, inclined plane, wedge, screw, gear drive, hydraulic press

7 **gear**, spur gear, rack and pinion, helical gear, bevel gear, skew gear, worm gear, gear train, pinion, internal gear, external gear, gear tooth, diametral pitch, pitch diameter

8 **machine element**, machine part, wheel, gear, gearwheel, pulley, shaft, crank, rod, axle, hub, cam, belt, coupling, bearing, ball bearing, roller bearing, journal, bush, differential

9 **machine tool**, horizontal machine, vertical machine, drill, drilling machine, press drill, boring machine, lathe, engine lathe, turret lathe, capstan lathe, milling machine, broaching machine, grinder, planer, shaper, saw, circular saw, band saw, single-point tool, multipoint tool, speed, feed, cutting fluid, cooling fluid, coolant, high-speed steel

► *438 Tool*

10 **work**, useful work, efficiency, load, effort, mechanical advantage, velocity ratio, erg

11 **engine**, internal-combustion engine, Wankel engine, external-combustion engine, reciprocating engine, steam engine, petrol engine, car engine, automotive engine, diesel engine, aero engine, jet engine, rocket engine, Stirling engine, piston, cylinder, crank, crankshaft, prime mover, governor

► *39 Electronics*

12 **turbine**, water turbine, steam turbine, gas turbine, impulse turbine, reaction turbine, impulse-reaction turbine

13 **engine cycle**, heat-engine cycle, four-stroke cycle, two-stroke cycle, Carnot cycle, Otto cycle, Diesel cycle, Rankine cycle, thermal efficiency

► *32 Chemistry*

14 **load**, applied load, static load, dynamic load, live load, dead load, transverse load, stress, normal stress, tension, compression, shear stress, strain, longitudinal strain, linear strain, volume strain, bulk strain, shear strain, elastic strain, inelastic strain, plastic strain, structural loading, forces, stability, centre of gravity

15 **strength of materials**, cohesive strength, yield strength, ultimate tensile strength, resistance to compaction, resistance to sliding, stiffness, elasticity, modulus of elasticity, bending moment

16 **deformation**, distortion, elongation, compression, bending, sliding, angular deformation, torsion, plastic deformation, creep, instability, failure, rupture, fracture, metal fatigue, corrosion

► *28 Physics*

17 **civil engineering**, structural engineering, transportation engineering, highway engineering, railway engineering, airport engineering, traffic engineering, river engineering, coastal engineering, water-supply engineering, geotechnical engineering, rock mechanics, soil mechanics, construction engineering, construction, architectural engineering, urban planning, community planning, land-use planning, photogrammetry, surveying, theodolite, level, clinometer, alidade, topographic surveying, mapping, photoelastic modelling

18 **civil engineer**, structural engineer, surveyor, quantity surveyor, contractor

19 **structure**, construction, building, bridge, tunnel, tunnelling, dam, retaining wall, embankment, bulkhead, road, railway, runway, pylon

► *319 Transport*

20 **building**, public building, auditorium, church, theatre, stadium, institutional building, hospital, school, prison, residential building, house, apartment building (*or* complex *or* block) (US), block of flats, hotel, commercial building, store, shop, department store, factory, office building, storage building, garage, warehouse, multistorey building, high-rise building, tower block, skyscraper

► *20 Architecture; 565 Habitat; 776 Trade*

21 **bridge**, road bridge, railway bridge, flyover, overpass, humpback bridge, viaduct, aqueduct, canal bridge, causeway, ford, toll bridge, footbridge, pedestrian bridge, walkway, catwalk, rope bridge, stepping stones, duckboard, gangway, gangplank, fixed bridge, beam bridge, girder bridge, box-girder bridge, plate-girder bridge, truss bridge, arch bridge, suspension bridge, cantilever bridge, cable-stayed bridge, concrete bridge, movable bridge, lift bridge, vertical-lift bridge, swing bridge, bascule bridge, drawbridge, ferry bridge, transporter bridge, Bailey bridge, pontoon bridge, trestle bridge, deck bridge, through bridge, square bridge, skewed bridge, span, single span, multiple span, deck, flooring, pier, abutment

22 **tunnel**, road tunnel, railway (*or* rail) tunnel, cut-and-cover tunnel, bored tunnel, subway, underpass, channel, culvert, drain, sewer, cloaca

23 **dam**, concrete dam, arch dam, buttress dam, gravity dam, earth dam, reservoir, impoundment, weir, barrage, embankment

24 **water system**, water-supply system, drainage system, sewage system, irrigation system, flood-control system, sea wall, barrage, floodgate, sluicegate, breakwater, mole,

groyne, canal, lock, harbour, port, dock, wharf, pier, quay, jetty

► *30 Earth Science*

25 **construction material**, structural material, building material, stone, brick, steel, rolled steel, sheet steel, plate steel, cast steel, stainless steel, cast iron, wrought iron, aluminium alloy, magnesium alloy, concrete, reinforced concrete, prestressed concrete, precast concrete, cement, mortar, wood, timber, lumber (US), plywood, glulam (glued-laminated) timber, plastic, reinforced plastic, carbon fibre, glass fibre, composite, Tarmac™ (*or* tarmacadam), asphalt, bitumen, hardcore

► *23 Furniture and Woodwork; 32 Chemistry; 79 Trees*

26 **masonry**, stonework, brickwork, building stone, stone, limestone, sandstone, granite, marble, brick, bricklaying, header, stretcher, bond, stretcher bond, English bond, Flemish bond, breeze block, tile, slate, mortar, grout, plaster, cement, Portland cement, gravel, sand, clay, terracotta, pavior

27 **superstructure**, structural framework, skeletal frame, frame, space frame, truss, structural member, supporting member, horizontal member, vertical member, strut, tie, beam, girder, stringer, joist, boom, cantilever, RSJ (rolled steel joist), plate girder, I-beam, H-beam, T-beam, continuous beam, concrete slab, column, pillar, pier, tower, rib, spar, abutment, buttress, arch, vault, dome, shell, bearing, bearing plate, flange, shoe, structural connection, rivet, bolt, weld, web connection, seat connection, pin connection, geodesic dome

28 **substructure**, foundation, foundations, spread foundation, footing, mat, raft, slab, pile, caisson, cofferdam, underpinning, fill, backfill

29 **construction equipment**, excavator, digger, trenching machine, trencher, power shovel, front-end loader, backhoe, dragline, clamshell, grab bucket, belt loader, dredge, dredger, JCB™, bulldozer, dozer (Inf), scraper, hauler, earthmover, dump truck, rear-dump truck, pile-driver, pile hammer, auger, compactor, hoist, crane, mobile crane, tower crane, derrick, guy derrick, cableway, elevator, conveyor, excavation, hauling, drilling, hoisting, grading, paving

VERBS

30 **engineer**, construct, build, erect, plan, design, survey, map, excavate, dig, dredge, drill, tunnel, blast, lay, haul, hoist

31 **load**, stress, strain, deform, bend, slide, fail, fracture, rupture, shear

ADJECTIVES

32 **structural**, constructional, edificial, architectural, architectonic, skeletal, superstructural, substructural, foundational, mechanical, fabricated, precast, prestressed

ADVERBS

33 **structurally**, mechanically, architecturally, architectonically, constructionally

39 Electronics

NOUNS

1 **electronics**, microelectronics, computer electronics, optoelectronics, telecommunications, electronics engineering, electrical engineering, electrotechnology, electrotechnics

2 **electronics engineer**, electrical engineer, electrotechnician, electrician

► *40 Computers; 692 Communications*

3 **electricity**, current electricity, static electricity, static electrical conduction, conduction, conductivity, conducting medium, conductor, metallic conductor, copper, aluminium, liquid conductor, electrolyte

4 **semiconductor**, silicon, germanium, gallium arsenide, n-type semiconductor, p-type semiconductor, charge carrier, electron, hole, electron conduction, hole conduction, n-type conductivity, p-type conductivity, p–n junction, impurity atom, acceptor impurity, donor impurity, doping, dopant

5 **electrolytic conduction**, electrolyte, electrode, anode, cathode, ion, anion, cation, electrolytic cell, cell, primary cell, voltaic cell, secondary cell, battery

► *32 Chemistry*

6 **electric discharge**, gas discharge, arc discharge, arc, glow discharge, corona discharge, silent discharge, transient discharge, spark discharge, spark, disruptive discharge, gas-discharge tube

7 **nonconductor**, insulator, dielectric, dielectric constant, insulating material, insulation

8 **electric charge**, charge, charge density, charge carrier

► *28 Physics*

9 **electric current**, current, direct current (d.c.), alternating current (a.c.), instantaneous current, frequency, phase, phase difference, phase angle, induced current, eddy current, current density, juice (Inf)

10 **electric potential**, potential, potential difference (p.d.), voltage, alternating voltage, instantaneous voltage, bias voltage, bias, electromotive force (e.m.f.), back e.m.f., earth (*or* (esp. US) ground) potential, earth, earthed conductor, live conductor, live circuit

11 **electric field**, field strength, flux, displacement, permittivity, relative permittivity

12 **resistance**, internal resistance, reactance, impedance, input impedance, characteristic impedance, resistivity, conductivity, capacitance, capacity, stray capacitance, inductance, mutual inductance, self-inductance, conductance, mutual conductance

13 **circuit**, electronic circuit, electric circuit, network, printed circuit, printed circuit board (*or* card), microcircuit, chip, microchip, silicon chip, integrated circuit (IC), LSI (large-scale integration), VLSI (very large-scale integration), equivalent circuit, closed circuit, open circuit, short circuit (*or* short), linear circuit, nonlinear circuit, digital circuit, logic circuit, gate, bistable circuit, flip-flop, resonant circuit, tuned circuit, resonant (*or* resonance) frequency, coupling circuit, switching circuit, bridge, Wheatstone bridge, circuit diagram, circuit design, circuitry, electronics

14 **terminal**, input terminal, output terminal, signal, waveform, pulse train, input signal, output signal, input (*or* output) voltage (*or* power *or* current), load, noise, spurious signal, signal-to-noise ratio, distortion

15 **circuit function**, amplification, gain, feedback, negative feedback, oscillation, positive feedback, negative resistance, rectification, switching, filtering

16 circuit element, component, discrete component, electronic device, semiconductor device, solid-state device, series connection, parallel connection

17 resistor, variable resistor, rheostat, potentiometer (*or* pot), capacitor, condenser, ceramic capacitor, mica capacitor, electrolytic capacitor, inductor, induction coil, winding, choke

18 diode, p–n junction diode, photodiode, light-emitting diode (LED), Zener diode, Schottky diode, diode rectifier

19 transistor, bipolar transistor, pnp transistor, npn transistor, base, base electrode, emitter, emitter electrode, collector, collector electrode, FET (field-effect transistor), MOS (metal–oxide–silicon) transistor, MOSFET, source, source electrode, drain, drain electrode, gate, gate electrode, channel, transistor amplifier, transistor switch, power transistor

20 electron tube, gas-discharge tube, fluorescent lamp, mercury-vapour lamp, glow lamp, CRT (cathode-ray tube), television receiver, VDU, microwave generator, klystron, magnetron, thermionic valve, valve, triode, tetrode, pentode, anode, cathode, grid, neon light

21 rectifier, full-wave rectifier, half-wave rectifier, amplifier, voltage amplifier, power amplifier, audio amplifier, radio amplifier, microwave amplifier, maser, oscillator, radio oscillator, microwave oscillator, piezoelectric oscillator, crystal oscillator, crystal-controlled oscillator, quartz oscillator

22 transformer, primary coil, secondary coil, step-up transformer, step-down transformer, voltage transformer, current transformer, instrument transformer, transducer, electroacoustic transducer, pickup, microphone, loudspeaker, filter, band-pass filter, low-pass filter, high-pass filter, band-stop filter

23 electrical instrument, ammeter, galvanometer, voltmeter, potentiometer, electrometer, wattmeter, oscilloscope

24 electron emission, thermionic emission, thermionic cathode, electron lens, electron gun, electron tube, electron multiplier, photoelectric effect, photoelectric emission, photoelectron, photocathode, photomultiplier, secondary emission, secondary electron, field emission

25 photoconductivity, photocurrent, photodetector, photocell, photodiode, photovoltaic effect, photovoltaic cell, solar cell

26 electrical energy, electric power, apparent power, active power, reactive power, power factor

27 wire, multistranded wire, lead, flex, cord (US), electric filament, electric cable, coaxial cable (*or* coax), paired cable, twin cable, twisted pair, bus, waveguide, cordless appliance

28 plug, socket, power point, fuse, circuit breaker, switch, trip switch, dimmer, dimming switch, termination, interface

29 power source, cell, primary cell, secondary cell, dry cell, wet cell, battery, dry battery, alkaline battery, accumulator, storage battery, secondary battery, rechargable battery, battery charger, fuel cell, solar cell, solar battery, solar panel, solar energy

30 generator, a.c. generator, alternator, oscillator, dynamo, magneto, armature, windings, electrostatic generator, Van de Graaff generator, wind-driven generator, thermoelectric generator

31 electric motor, induction motor, stator, rotor, cage rotor, slip-ring rotor, synchronous motor, synchronous-induction motor, asynchronous motor, universal motor, commutator, vibrator

32 power station, generating station, powerhouse, thermal power station, nuclear power station, hydroelectric power station, geothermal power station, power generation, power production, power plant, generator, turbine

33 power distribution, distribution network, national grid, a.c. (alternating current) transmission, high-voltage a.c. transmission, extra-high-voltage a.c. transmission, d.c. (direct current) transmission, high-voltage d.c. transmission, power line, transmission line, overhead wire, underground cable, feeder, pylon (*or* tower), substation

34 power supply, mains supply (*or* mains), three-phase supply, two-phase supply, single-phase supply, power conversion, power regulation, voltage regulator, transformer, rectifier, filter, converter, inverter, power pack, peak load, power cut, electric meter, watt-hour meter, domestic wiring, ring main, off-peak supply, white meter, blackout, brownout (Inf)

VERBS

35 conduct, insulate, earth, ground, charge, discharge, amplify, oscillate, connect, disconnect, switch (*or* turn) on (*or* off), plug in, wire (*or* wire up), fuse, input, output, electrocute, generate, transmit

ADJECTIVES

36 electronic, electric, electrical, photoelectric, thermoelectric, piezoelectric, hydroelectric, electrodynamic, electrolytic, electromagnetic, electromechanical, electromotive, electrostatic, negative, positive, neutral, live, resistive, capacitive, inductive, rechargeable, cordless, solid-state

ADVERBS

37 electronically, electrically, photoelectrically, thermoelectrically, electrodynamically, electrolytically, electromagnetically, electromechanically, electrostatically, negatively, positively, in series, in parallel

40 Computers

The most participatory form of mass speech yet developed.....A never ending worldwide conversation. US Federal Court, referring to the Internet.

NOUNS

1 computing, computer science, systems analysis, programming, DP (data processing), EDP (electronic data processing), data entry, information technology (IT), DTP (desk-top publishing), CIM (computer-integrated manufacture), CMI (computer-managed instruction), CAD (computer-aided design), CAM (computer-aided manufacturing), CAI (computer-aided instruction), CAT (computer-aided testing), CAL (computer-assisted learning), CBL (computer-based learning), cybernetics, robotics

2 operator, programmer, DP manager, systems analyst, hacker, liveware

3 **computer**, digital computer, hybrid computer, supercomputer, parallel computer, mainframe, minicomputer, mini, microcomputer, micro, PC (personal computer), home computer, games computer, laptop, palmtop, personal organizer, calculator, programmable calculator, machine, electronic computer, smart card, electronic brain, ABC (Atanasoff–Berry computer), Turing machine, Analytical Engine, ACE (Automatic Computing Engine), ATLAS, ENIAC, UNIVAC, Cray, ERNIE, adding machine, calculating machine, abacus, Napier's bones

4 **computer part**, hardware, architecture, processor, memory, peripheral, software

5 **processor**, central processor, CPU (central processing unit), ALU (arithmetic and logic unit), CU (control unit), microprocessor, math co-processor

6 **memory**, store, storage, main memory, primary memory, register, cache, semiconductor memory, core store, solid-state memory, cryogenic memory, backing store, auxiliary (*or* secondary) memory, bulk memory, bubble memory, buffer, scratchpad, volatile memory, nonvolatile memory, dynamic memory, RAM (random access memory), DRAM (dynamic RAM), ROM (read-only memory), EAROM (electrically alterable read-only memory), CD-ROM (compact-disk ROM), Diskman™

7 **peripheral**, backing store, disk, disk pack, disk reader, hard disk, Winchester, floppy disk, floppy, diskette, microfloppy, microdiskette, minifloppy, minidiskette, optical disk, CD-ROM, MTU (magnetic-tape unit), tape streamer, ATU (automatic tape unit) tape, cartridge, cassette, VDU (visual display unit), flat screen, keyboard, console, terminal, monitor, card punch, punched card, tape punch, paper tape, reader, input-output device, I/O device, port, printer, band printer, belt printer, barrel printer, drum printer, chain printer, letter-quality printer, daisywheel printer, dot-matrix printer, electrophotographic printer, electrostatic printer, golfball printer, impact printer, ink-jet printer, bubble-jet printer, thermal ink jet printer, serial printer, ionographic printer, laser printer, line printer, matrix printer, colour printer, plotter, flat-bed plotter, x-y plotter, printout, pretty printing, scanner, wand, bar-code reader, light pen, digitizer, data tablet, joystick, mouse, tailless mouse, modem, acoustic coupler, voice synthesizer, vocoder, tonepad

8 **software**, operating system (OS), UNIX™, DOS™ (disk operating system), MSDOS™ (Microsoft DOS), OS/2™, CP/M™, program, programming language, language, compiler, interpreter, driver, filter, pipe, analyser, parser, applications program, package, shareware

9 **programming language**, language, machine code, high-level language, low-level language, compiled language, interpreted language, source code, object code, syntax, semantics, trace program, JCL (job-control language), DML (data manipulation language), query language, pseudolanguage, Turbo language™

10 **character**, alphanumeric character, code, character set, ASCII (American standard code for information interchange), EBSIDIC (extended binary-coded decimal interchange code), ISO-7 (International Standards Organization 7-bit code), printable character, nonprintable character, control character, escape character, escape sequence, CR (carriage return), graphic character, binary code, hexadecimal code, decimal code, octal code

11 **application**, word processing (*or* word processor) (WP), text editor, editor, Wordstar™, WordPerfect™, Word™, spelling checker, dictionary, thesaurus, database, hierarchical database, network database, relational database, database management system (DBMS), data manipulation language (DML), dBase™, spreadsheet, Visicalc™, Supercalc™, Lotus-123™, DTP (desktop publishing), Ventura™, Pagemaker™, QuarkXPress™, TEX, window, window manager, wimp (windows icons menus pointers), Windows™, MIDI (musical instrument digital interface)

12 **electronic office**, paperless office, ACU (automatic calling unit), facsimile, fax, electronic mail (*or* e-mail), bulletin board, mailbox, teleconferencing, videoconferencing, EFTS (electronic funds transfer system), EPOS (electronic point of sale), ATM (automatic teller machine), PIN (personal identification number), smart card, modem

13 **character recognition**, scanner, OCR (optical character reader *or* recognition), ICR (intelligent character recognition), MICR (magnetic ink character recognition)

14 **data transfer**, multiplexing, modem (modulator and demodulator), codec (coder–decoder), acoustic coupler, telecommunications, EDI (electronic data interchange), packet switching, handshake, protocol, acknowledgment, ACK, NCK, fibre optics, ISDN (Integrated Services Digital Network), electronic superhighway, information superhighway

15 **network**, network architecture, ring, star, bus, server, node, LAN (local-area network), Ethernet, Euronet, Arpanet (Advanced Research Projects Agency Network), BITNET, JANET (Joint Academic Network), SOSENET (Social Security Network), Telenet, bridge, gateway, Internetworking, teleworking, telecommuting, file server, multitasking, fax

16 **Internet,** the Net, World Wide Web, the Web, web site, web page, home page, hypertext link, bookmark, HTML (hypertext mark-up language), URL (uniform resource locator), http (hypertext transfer protocol), FTP (file transfer protocol), search engine, browser, Netscape™, Yahoo™, Internet Explorer™, gopher, cookie, MIME (multipurpose Internet mail extension), Usenet, newsgroup, Sysop, FAQ (frequently asked question), webspeak, netiquette (Inf), surfing (Inf), flaming (Inf)

PROGRAMMING LANGUAGES

Ada	CIS–COBOL	HOPE	PARLOG
AED	Clear	IAL	Pascal
Algol	Cobol	ICON	Pascal–Plus
APL	COMAL	JAVA	PL/I (*or* PL/1)
B	Common Lisp	JOVIAL	POP
Babbage		Logo	POPLOG
Basic	CORAL	Maclisp	Prolog
BCPL	CPL	MIRANDA	SCHEME
C	Forth	ML	SIMULA
C–plus	Fortran	Modula	Smalltalk
CHILL	Franzlisp	OBERON	SNOBOL

17 artificial intelligence (AI), game-playing, perceptual computing, natural-language understanding, theorem proving, means-ends analysis, semantic net, game theory, expert system, cybernetics, robotics, neurocomputer, neural computer, neural net (*or* network), fuzzy logic

18 virtual reality, artificial reality, cyberspace

▶ *96 Unreality*

19 computing terms: access, address, algorithm, archive, backup, batch processing, band rate, baud rate, benchmark, bisection search, bit, bit map, block, bootstrap, branch, bug, byte, carriage return (CR), channel, chip, clock, clock rate, command, compatibility, controller, counter, crash, cross talk, cursor, data, debugging, diagnostics, direct access, directory, display, download, downsize, downtime, dump, emulator, field, file, flip-flop, floating point operation, flops, format, function, gateway, gigabyte, goto, handshake, hard return, hard sector, header, help, icon, input, interface, job, kilobyte, leader, logic bomb, login, logon, logout, logoff, loop, megabyte, menu, Michelangelo virus, middleware, millenium virus, multiplexing, nagware, nesting, nibble, output, packet, parallel access, parity, password, patch, pixel, protocol, queue, random access, raster, real time, record, scanner, sector, sequential access, soft return, soft sector, sortkey, sprite, suite of programs, time sharing, toolbox, Trojan horse, turnkey operation, virus, write ring, wysiwyg (what you see is what you get)

VERBS

20 abort, access, address, archive, back up, bootstrap, boot, branch, compile, copy, crash, debug, decode, decompile, delete, downgrade, download, dump, emulate, erase, format, hardwire, input, interface, load, login, logon, logoff, logout, loop, output, patch, read, scroll, spool, upgrade, write

ADJECTIVES

21 on-line, off-line, digital, graphic, virtual, robotic, cybernetic, user-friendly, erasable, rewritable, read-only, write-enabled

ADVERBS

22 on-line, off-line, digitally, graphically, robotically, cybernetically

41 Photography

In a portrait, I'm looking for the silence in somebody. Henri Cartier-Bresson.

NOUNS

1 photography, picture taking, colour photography, black-and-white photography, aerial photography, astrophotography, landscape photography, architectural photography, underwater photography, wildlife photography, documentary photography, fashion photography, portraiture, photojournalism, time-lapse photography, telephotography, macrophotography, microphotography, flash photography, infrared photography, cine photography, cinematography, stereophotography, holography, phototopography, radiography

2 photoreproduction, photocopying, Xerography, photogrammetry, photolithography, photogravure, photointaglio

3 photograph, photo, picture, image, shot, snapshot, take, daguerreotype, colour photo(graph), black-and-white, monotone, half-tone, transparency, slide, radiograph, X-ray, shadowgraph, photograph album, snap (Inf)

4 portrait, close-up, long shot, medium shot, pin-up, Photofit™, mug shot (Inf), beefcake (Inf), cheesecake (Inf), group photograph, rogues' gallery, photobiography, landscape, cloudscape, silhouette, action shot, studio photograph, still-life, abstract, split image, multiple image, action sequence, photomontage, photomural

5 stereoscopic image, holographic image, hologram, colour hologram, reflection hologram

6 microphotograph, microcopy, microfilm, microfiche

7 photocopy, Photostat™, Xerox™, photomicrograph, PMT (photo mechanical transfer)

8 composition, framing, perspective, colour balance, contrast, highlights, tonal range, high key, low key, sharpness, focus, depth of field, image blur, acutance, overexposure, underexposure, colourcast, flare, fog, red-eye

9 film, photographic plate, photographic paper, bromide paper, roll film, black-and-white film, colour film, panchromatic film, chromogenic film, Polaroid™ film, X-ray film, infrared film, spool, reel, cassette, cartridge

10 graininess, fine grain, coarse grain, film speed, fast film, slow film, sensitivity, photosensitivity, ISO rating, ASA number, DIN number, DX code, hypersensitization, photographic density, transmission density, opacity, characteristic curve, H-D (Hurter-Driffield) curve, dynamic range, gamma, reciprocity failure, saturation level, fog level

11 emulsion, silver halide, gelatin, backing, latent image

12 development, processing, colour processing, printing, enlargement, darkroom, safelight, enlarger, developer, acid stop, stop bath, fixing solution, fixer, hypo, frame, exposure, negative, colour negative, print, colour print, slide, transparency, diapositive, sepia, lanternslide, contact print, silver print, gum print, sun print, enprint, enlargement, blow-up, reprint, gloss finish, matt finish, semimatt finish, slide projector, overhead projector, slide carrier, screen, magic lantern

13 framing, cropping, bracketing, soft focusing, differential focusing, controlled blur, panning, pulling, pushing (*or* uprating), solarization

14 cine film, Super-8, home movie, cine camera, projector, screen, camcorder

15 lighting, light source, daylight, natural light, ambient light, white light, soft light, hard light, backlighting, textured lighting, artificial light (*or* lighting), tungsten light (*or* lighting), studio lighting, studio flash, spotlight (*or* spot), photoflood, bounced light, fill-in light, diffuser, reflector, floodlight, colour temperature, guide number

16 camera, single-lens reflex (SLR), twin-lens reflex, large-format camera, box Brownie, automatic camera, compact camera, miniature camera, disc camera, disposable camera, plate camera, camera obscura, cine camera, pinhole camera, video camera, camcorder, TV camera, security camera, film camera, gamma camera, digital camera, Instamatic™, Polaroid™, photo booth

17 lens, lens system, standard (*or* normal) lens, fixed-focus lens, long-focus lens, telephoto lens, mirror lens, reflex lens, catadioptric lens, zoom lens, short zoom (*or* wide-angle zoom), mid-range zoom, telephoto zoom, wide-angle lens, ultrawide lens, shift lens, fisheye lens, macro lens, focal length, focus, angle of view, prism, pentaprism, lens mount, lens attachment, lens cap, lens cover, lens hood

18 exposure time, shutter, shutter release, cable release, shutter speed, B setting, self-timer, motordrive, aperture, diaphragm, iris diaphragm, aperture setting, f-stop (*or* F-stop), f-number (*or* F-number), viewfinder, rangefinder, infinity, vanishing point, hyperfocal distance, light meter, TTL (through-the-lens) meter, CdS meter, selenium meter, spot meter, autofocus, autoexposure, aperture priority, shutter priority, film advance, film rewind, take-up spool, film plane, focusing screen, depth of focus, tripod

19 flash, electronic flash, synchronized flash, flashgun, flashbulb, flash cube, hot-shoe, slave unit

20 filter, colour-balancing filter, colour-correcting (*or* compensating) filter, UV (*or* haze) filter, skylight filter, polarizing (PL) filter, neutral-density (ND) filter, diffusing filter

VERBS

21 photograph, shoot, take a photograph (*or* photo *or* picture), focus, stop down, open up, zoom in, zoom out, pan, expose, develop, process, print, enlarge, blow up, reduce, project, video, photo (Inf), snap (Inf), vid (Inf)

ADJECTIVES

22 photographic, photogenic, camera-shy, photosensitive

ADVERBS

23 photographically, photogenically, cinematographically, holographically

42 Fabrics and Dyeing

NOUNS

1 fibre, thread, filament, yarn, natural fibre, synthetic fibre, braided fibre, monofilament, denier

NATURAL FABRICS

alpaca (wool)
astrakhan (wool)
baize (wool)
balbriggan (cotton)
batiste (cotton)
brocade
brocatelle
buckram (cotton, linen)
bunting (cotton)
burlap (jute, hemp)
calico (cotton)
cambric (cotton, linen)
camel hair *or* camel's hair
Canton crepe
canvas (cotton, hemp, jute)
cashmere *or* Kashmir (wool)
cassimere *or* casimere (wool)
castor (beaver fur)
challis (wool, cotton)
chambray (cotton, linen)
cheesecloth (cotton)
chenille (silk, wool)
cheviot (wool)
chiffon
chinchilla (wool)
chino (cotton)
chintz (cotton)
cord
corduroy (cotton)
cotton
crash (cotton, linen)
crepe (cotton, silk)
crepe de Chine
cretonne (cotton, linen)
crinoline
damask (silk, linen)
denim (cotton)
dimity (cotton)
doeskin
Donegal tweed
drill (cotton)
drugget
duck (cotton)
duffel (wool)
dungaree (cotton)
duvetine *or* duvetyne *or* duvetyn
faille (silk, rayon, taffeta)
felt (wool, hair)
flannel (wool, cotton)
flannelette (cotton)
fleece
foulard (silk, rayon)
frieze (wool)
fustian (cotton/wool)
gaberdine *or* gabardine (cotton, rayon)
gauze
Georgette crepe
gingham (cotton)
gossamer (silk)
grenadine
grogram
grosgrain (silk, rayon)
gunny (jute)
haircloth
Harris tweed
herringbone
hessian (jute)
homespun
hopsacking *or* hopsack (wool, cotton)
horsehair
huck *or* huckaback (linen, cotton)
Jacquard *or* Jacquard weave
jean (cotton)
jersey
lamé (silk, cotton, wool)
lawn (linen, cotton)
linen
linsey–woolsey (linen–wool)
lisle (cotton)
loden (wool)
longcloth (cotton)
mackinaw (US)
mackintosh
madras (cotton, silk)
malines *or* maline (silk)
marquisette
marseille *or* marseilles (cotton)
matting
melton (wool)
messaline (silk)
mohair (wool)
moiré (silk)
moleskin (cotton)
moquette
mousseline (rayon, silk)
mousseline de laine (wool)
mousseline de soie (rayon, silk)
muslin (cotton)
nainsook (cotton)
nankeen (cotton)
net
netting
oil silk
organdy *or* organdie (cotton)
organza
paisley (wool)
panne velvet
percale (cotton)
piqué (cotton, silk, rayon)
plaid
plush
pongee (silk)
poplin (cotton)
rep
russet
sackcloth
sacking
sailcloth
samite (silk)
sarcenet *or* sarsenet (silk)
sateen (linen, cotton)
satin
say (wool)
scrim
seersucker (cotton, linen)
serge
shalloon (wool)
shantung (silk, cotton, rayon)
sharkskin (acetate rayon)
sheer
shoddy (wool)
shot silk
silk
stammel (wool)
stockinet *or* stockinette
suede *or* suede leather
swan's–down *or* swansdown (wool, cotton)
tabaret (silk)
tabby (silk, taffeta)
tapestry
tarpaulin
terry
ticking *or* tick (cotton)
toile (linen, cotton)
towelling
tricot (rayon, nylon)
tricotine (wool)
tulle (silk, rayon)
tussore (silk)
tweed (wool)
twill
velours *or* velour
velure
velvet
velveteen (cotton)
vicuna (wool)
webbing (hemp, cotton, jute)
wool
worsted (wool)

SYNTHETIC FIBRES AND FABRICS

acetate	Dacron™	polyamide
acetate rayon	Leatherette™	PVC (polyvinyl chloride)
acrylic	Lycra™	polyester
artificial silk	microfibre	rayon
Acrilan™	nylon	Terylene™
Celanese™	Orlon™	viscose (rayon)
Crimplene™	polyacetate	

2 **spinning**, twining, intertwining, braiding, interbraiding, braid, plaiting, plait, spinning wheel, spinning mule, spinning jenny, spinner, extrusion, extruder, spinerette

3 **fabric**, cloth, textile, material, drapery, rag, natural fabric, synthetic fabric, synthetic, woven fabric, knitted fabric, soft furnishing, print, screen print, carpet, carpeting, Axminster, Wilton, broadcloth, broadloom

4 **weaving**, weave, plain weave, twill weave, warp, weft (*or* woof), selvage (*or* selvedge), list, web, webbing, lace, lacing, interweaving, shoot, weaving frame, loom, hand loom, machine loom, Jacquard loom, shuttle, bobbin, weaver, texture, nap, pattern

5 **knitting**, stitch, interlock stitch, plain stitch, purl stitch, cable stitch, moss stitch, stocking stitch, knit, machine knitting, knitting machine, pattern, needle, gauge

► *551 Dress; 553 Fashion*

6 **dye**, colourant, dyestuff, natural dye, vegetable dye, mineral dye, synthetic dye, chemical dye, acid dye, basic dye, vat dye, direct dye, mordant, lake, soluble dye, fast dye, absorption, chromophore, acridine dye, alizarin dye, aniline dye, azo dye, phthalocyanine dye, rhodamine dye, xanthine dye, crocein, eosin, fuchsine, madder, mauveine (*or* Perkin's mauve), Tyrian purple, woad, bleach, chromotrope, garance, lake naphthol, pincoffin

7 **dyeing**, colouring, staining, patterning, printing, screen printing, tie-dyeing, batik (*or* battik)

8 **fabric treatment**, cleaning, washing, laundering, dry-cleaning, stain removal, bleaching, flameproofing, preshrinking, Sanforizing™, wrinkleproofing, waterproofing, vulcanizing

ADJECTIVES

9 **spun**, twisted, braided, twined, plaited, extrudable, extruded

10 **woven**, knitted, cloth, fabric, fine, sheer, coarse, netted, fine-weave, open-weave, ikat weave, twill, felted, brushed, napped, looped, uncut, cut

11 **treated**, washed, bleached, dyed, coloured, dyed-in-the-wool, dyed-in-the-yarn, tie-dyed, coated, flameproof, preshrunk, Sanforized™, waterproof (*or* waterproofed), showerproof (*or* showerproofed), drip-dry, crease-resistant, rubberized, vulcanized

12 **natural**, wool, woollen, woolly, silk, silky, silken, cotton, linen, rayon

VERBS

13 **spin**, twist, braid, plait, extrude

14 **weave**, knit, felt, mat, brush, nap

15 **treat**, wash, bleach, dye, tie-dye, flameproof, preshrink, Sanforize™, waterproof, showerproof, rubberize, vulcanize

43 Agriculture

We plough the fields, and scatter
The good seed on the land,
But it is fed and watered
By God's Almighty Hand. Jane Montgomery Campbell.

NOUNS

1 **agriculture**, farming, husbandry, intensive farming, factory farming, extensive farming, subsistence farming, mixed farming, share farming, sharecropping, arable farming, livestock farming, organic farming, ecofarming,

BREEDS OF CATTLE

Aberdeen Angus	Brahman	German Red Pied	Longhorn	Red Steppe
Africander	Bangus (hybrid)	German Yellow	Luing	Red Welsh
Ala–Tau	British White	Gir	Maine Anjou	Romagnola
Andalusian	Brown Swiss	Groningen Whiteheaded	Marchigiana	Salers
Angeln	Canadian Charbray	Guernsey	Meuse–Rhine–Ijssel	Santa Gertrudis
Ankole	Charollais	Hereford	Miranda	Shetland
Aubrac	Chianina	Highland	Mongolian	Shorthorn
Australian Illawarra Shorthorn	Danish Red	Holstein–Friesian (*or* Holstein)	Murray Grey	Simmental
Ayrshire	Devon	Irish Moiled	N'Dama	South Devon
Bapedi	Dexter	Jamaica Hope	Nguni	Sussex
Barrosã	Drakensberger	Jersey	Normandy	Swedish Red–and–White
Beefalo (hybrid)	Droughtmaster	Kankre	Old Gloucestershire	Tarentaise
Beef Shorthorn	Durham	Kerry	Pembroke	Telemark
Belgian Blue	Dutch Belted	Khillari	Piemontese	Texas Longhorn
Belted Galloway	Fighting Bull	Kholmogor	Pinzgauer	Tharparkar
Belted Welsh	Finncattle	Kuri	Polled Hereford	Welsh Black
Blacksided Trondheim and Nordland	Finnish Ayrshire	Kyloe	Polled Welsh Black	West Highland
Blonde d'Aquitaine	Friesian	Limousin	Red–and–White Friesian	White Galloway
Blue Albian	Fulani	Line–Backed Welsh	Red Poll	White Fulani
Boran	Galician Blond	Lincoln Red	Red Sindhu	White Park
	Galloway		Red Ruby Devon	White Welsh
	Gascony			

BREEDS OF SHEEP

Awassi
Baalwen
Beulah Speckled Face
Blackface
Blackhead Persian
Black Welsh Mountain
Bluefaced Leicester (Hexham Leicester)
Boreray
Border Leicester
Brecknock Hill Cheviot
British Bleu du Maine
British Charolais
British Friesland
British Milksheep
British Oldenburg
British Texel
Cambridge
Cannock Chase Cardy
Castlemilk Moorit
Cheviot
Chios
Clun Forest
Colbred
Columbia
Corriedale
Cotswold
Dalesbred
Dartmoor
Derbyshire Gritstone
Devon Closewool
Devon and Cornwall Longwool
Dorset Down
Dorset Horn
English Longwool
Exmoor Horn
Galway
Gritstone
Hampshire Down
Hebridean
Herdwick
Hill Radnor
Ile de France
Jacob
Karakul
Kerry Hill
Lacaune
Leicester Longwool
Lincoln
Llanwenog
Lleyn
Lonk
Manx Loghtan
Merino
Norfolk Horn
North Country Cheviot
North Ronaldsay
Oxford Down
Panama
Polled Dorset
Polwarth
Portland
Radnor
Rambouillet
Rhiw Hill
Romanov
Romeldale
Romney Marsh
Rough Fell
Ryeland
Scottish Blackface
Shetland
Shropshire
Soay
Southdown
South Devon
South Wales Mountain
Suffolk
Swaledale
Targhee
Teeswater
Texel
Torddu
Torwen
Vendeen
Welsh Hill Speckled Face
Welsh Mountain – Badger Faced (Rare breed)
Welsh Mountain – Hill Flock
Welsh Mountain
Wensleydale
Whiteface Dartmoor
Whiteface Woodlands
Wicklow Cheviot
Wiltshire Horn

biodynamic farming, agroecology, agroecosystem, agricultural science, agroscience (*or* agriscience), agronomy, agrology, agrobiology, agrogeology, agroforestry, geoponics, agronomics, rural economics, agrarianism, estate management, agribusiness, farm business, agricultural sale, Smithfield, farm-gate sale

▶ *44 Horticulture; 79 Trees*

2 **Common Agricultural Policy (CAP)**, green pound, quota, subsidy, grant, premium, marketing board, levy, set-aside, butter mountain, beef mountain, wine (*or* milk) lake

3 **livestock farming**, herding, stock rearing, ranching, dairy farming, dairying, beef farming, sheep farming, grazing, strip grazing, paddock grazing, zero grazing, folding, pig farming, poultry farming, chicken farming, fish farming, pisciculture, rabbit farming, mink farming, duck farming, animal husbandry, animal breeding, artificial insemination (AI), thremmatology, zootechnics, gnotobiotics, animal nutrition, animal health, animal production

4 **arable farming**, grain farming, dry farming, dirt farming (US inf), Green Revolution, crop rotation, monoculture, monocropping, slash-and-burn, crop husbandry, plant breeding, hydroponics, tank farming, fruit farming, truck farming (US), market gardening, tree farming, forestry

▶ *44 Horticulture; 79 Trees*

5 **cultivation**, culture, tillage, tilth, ploughing, harrowing, sowing, planting, hedge-laying, hedging, pleaching, plashing, heathering, ethering, irrigation, fertilizing, muckraking, muckspreading, dunging, weeding, crop-spraying, insurance spraying, harvesting, haymaking, turning, bale-carting, straw-burning, silaging

▶ *44 Horticulture; 79 Trees*

6 **farm**, mixed farm, family farm, factory farm, organic farm, state farm, collective farm, kolkhoz, kibbutz, livestock farm, stock farm, dairy farm, poultry farm, chicken farm, beef farm, sheep farm, deer farm, fish farm, trout farm, ranch, rancho (US), spread (US), station (Aus), sheep ranch, cattle ranch, beef ranch, dude ranch, hacienda, hill farm, arable farm, grain farm, fruit farm, tree farm, mushroom farm, truck farm (US), plantation, tea plantation, coffee plantation, estate, tea estate, coffee estate, holding, smallholding, croft, farmstead, homestead, steading, toft (Lit), demesne, home farm, farmtoun, city farm

7 **farm building**, grange, farmhouse, yard, covered yard, farmyard, barton (Lit), barnyard, barn, granary, smokehouse, oast house, cowshed, dairy, milking parlour, hayloft, haybarn, Dutch barn, collecting yard, stable, pen, loosebox, box, stall, cubicle, byre, feedlot (US), piggery, pigsty, sty, pigpen (US), farrowing crate, farrowing house, pig ark, fattening house, lambing house, fold, sheepfold, pinfold, corral, henhouse, chicken house, broiler house, hutch, coop, hen coop, battery house, deep-litter house, aviary, chicken run, hen run, tractor shed, silo, grain elevator, workshop, farm office

▶ *165 Enclosure*

8 **livestock**, stock, beasts, fatstock, cattle, cow, heifer, calf, stirk, fatling, veal calf, yearling, milker, dry cow, suckler cow, milch cow, nurse cow, barren cow, bull, steer, bullock, store, store cattle, fat cattle, bull beef, barley beef, suckler beef, sheep, ewe, lamb, hogget, hogg, teg, ram, wether, tup, fat lamb, pig, hog, swine, sow, piglet, weaner, gilt, boar, porker, baconer, cutter, heavy hog, barrow (US), goat, nanny goat, billy goat, kid, poultry, chick, poult, pullet, chicken, hen, battery hen (*or*

BREEDS OF PIG

Berkshire
British Lop
British Saddleback
Chester White
Duroc
Gloucester Old Spot
Hampshire
Hereford
"Iron Age" pig
Landrace
Large Black
Large White
Mangalitsa
Meishan
Middle White
Oxford Sandy–and–Black
Pietrain
Poland–China
Tamworth
Vietnamese Pot–Bellied
Welsh

BREEDS OF FOWL

Large Fowl
Ancona
Andalusian
Araucana
Aseel
Australorp
Barnevelder
Brahma
Bresse
Campine
Cochin
Creve–coeur
Croad Langshan
Dorking
Faverolle
Frizzle
Hamburgh
Houdan
Indian Game
Jubilee Indian Game
Ixworth
Jersey Giant
La Fleche
Lakenfelder
Leghorn
Malay
Malines
Marans
Marsh Daisy
Minorca
Modern Game
Modern Langshan
New Hampshire Red
Norfolk Grey
North Holland Blue
Old English Game
Old English Pheasant Fowl
Orloff
Orpington
Phoenix
Plymouth Rock
Poland
Redcap
Rhode Island Red
Scots Dumpy
Scots Grey
Sicilian Buttercup
Silkie
Spanish
Sultan
Sumatra Game
Sussex
Transylvanian Naked Necks
Welsummer
Wyandotte
Yokohama

Bantam
Belgian, Barbu d'Anvers
Belgian, Barbu d'Uccles
Booted
Frizzles
Japanese
Nankin
Old English Game
Pekin (*or* Cochin)
Rosecomb
Rumpless
Sebright

Guinea Fowl
Lavender
Pearl Grey
White

Ducks
Aylesbury
Black East Indian
Cayuga
Crested
Decoy
Indian Runner
Khaki Campbell
Magpie
Muscovy
Orpington
Pekin
Rouen
Welsh Harlequin
Whalesbury

Geese
African
Brecon Buff
Chinese
Embden
Pilgrim
Roman
Sebastopol
Toulouse

Turkeys
Arnewood International Double AA
Arnewood International Treble CCC
Beltsville
Black Norfolk
Bourbon Red
Broad–Breasted Bronze
Broad–Breasted White
Cambridge Bronze
Mammoth Bronze
Narragansett
Nicholas
White Austrian
White Holland

chicken), free-range hen (*or* chicken), fowl, laying hen, layer, broiler, boiler, roaster, cock, capon, rooster, goose, gander, gosling, duck, drake, duckling

► *59 Horse Riding and Racing; 71 Mammals; 72 Birds*

9 **animal feedstuff**, feed, ration, fodder, roughage, hay, haylage, silage, grass silage, maize silage, bale, big-bale silage, dried grass, straw, barley straw, wheat straw, oat straw, sugar-beet pulp, molasses, brewers' grains, malt culms, brewers' yeast, flaked maize, bran, coconut meal, groundnut meal, cottonseed cake, linseed meal, palm-kernel meal, soyabean meal, sunflower-seed meal, fish-meal, whey, meat-and-bone meal

10 **farm tool**, farm implement, farm machinery, deadstock, tractor, trailer, drill, corn drill, seed drill, plough, chisel plough, harrows, spring-tine harrows, chain harrows, draw harrows, disc harrows, power harrow, roll, flat roll, Cambridge roll, disc, cultivator, breaker (US), Rotavator™, subsoiler, potato planter, beet planter, ridger, sprayer, harvester, combine harvester, combine, potato harvester, beet harvester, pea viner, scythe, sickle, reaping hook, swather, binder, baler, bale sledge, bale carrier, bale wrapper, mower, mowing machine, flail mower, rotary mower, conditioner, topper, forage harvester, hay turner, tedder, haywain, haystack, hayrick, rick, haycock, stook, buckrake, transport box, front-end loader, telescopic loader, all-terrain vehicle (ATV), farm bike, fertilizer spreader, muckspreader, pitchfork, pikle (Inf), muckfork, shovel, scubbin, slurry tanker, slurry tank, slurry pit, muckheap, midden, manure heap, slurry scraper, silage clamp, irrigator, hedgecutter, plasher, electric fencer, trough, feeder, drinker, water bowl, feedbin, feedstore, grain bin, grain drier, hayrack, crush, race, milking machine, milk tank, bulk tank, churn

► *438 Tool*

11 **farmland**, arable land, arable, glebe (Lit), farm belt, corn belt, wheat belt, cotton belt, tobacco belt, black belt, fruit belt, citrus belt, plot (*or* piece) of land, acreage (US), field, hedgerow, hedge, quick, quickset, plot, piece, patch, parcel, paddock, strip, clearing, terrace, paddy, paddy field, rice paddy, potato field, cornfield, wheatfield, hayfield, grassland, meadow, mead (Lit), lea, pasture, grazing, rough grazing, enclosed land, enclosure, fence, hurdle, electric fence, barbed wire, post, stake, rail, gate, five-barred gate, wicket gate, wire netting, pig netting, sheep netting, ploughed land, cultivated land, furrow, drill, row, ridge, seedbed, tramline, headland, swathe, windrow, stubble

► *81 Grasses; 165 Enclosure*

12 **crop**, cash crop, catch crop, break crop, cover crop, cereal crop, corn, winter wheat, spring wheat, barley, winter barley, spring barley, oats, winter oats, spring oats, rye, triticale, millet, maize, rice, sorghum, root crop, fodder crop, green manure, turnips, swedes, fodder beet, sugar beet, mangels (*or* mangolds), potatoes, early potatoes, earlies, first early, second early, maincrop potatoes, peas, fodder peas, field peas, beans, field beans, black beans, soyabeans (*or* soybeans), groundnuts, peanuts, kale, cabbage, rape, oilseed rape, fodder rape, linseed, mustard, clover, red clover, white clover, alfalfa, lucerne, lupin, sainfoin, vetch, flax, okra, tobacco, cotton, fescue, ryegrass, Italian ryegrass, timothy, cocksfoot

► *25 Cookery; 44 Horticulture; 81 Grasses*

13 **fertilizer**, manure, muck, dung, slurry, effluent, farmyard manure, green manure, organic manure, dried-blood meal, hoof-and-horn meal, meat-and-bone meal, fishmeal, bonemeal, seaweed meal, compost, sewage, sludge, compound fertilizer, straight fertilizer, nitrate, phosphate, potash, granule, prill, dust, lime, limestone, quicklime, slaked lime, basic slag, bagmuck (Inf)

14 **pest control**, rat trap, mousetrap, mole trap, snare, gintrap, hang, scarecrow, bird scarer, gas gun, sheep-dip, pesticide, rodenticide, rat poison, insecticide, contact

insecticide, residual insecticide, molluscicide, slug pellet, fungicide, contact herbicide, systemic herbicide, spray, wetting agent, herbicide, weedkiller, agrochemicals, DDT, aldrin, dieldrin, parathion, warfarin, Paraquat™, 2,4-D

15 **agriculturist**, agriculturalist, agronomist, agrologist, agrobiologist, agrogeologist, agroecologist, rural economist, farmer, yeoman, granger, husbandman, tiller, tiller of the soil, gentleman farmer, tenant farmer, peasant farmer, hill farmer, crofter, smallholder, kibbutznik, livestock farmer, stock farmer, dairy farmer, beef farmer, poultry farmer, pig farmer, sheep farmer, stockkeeper (Aus), stock raiser, stockbreeder, breeder, cattle breeder, sheep breeder, pig breeder, cattleman, grazier, rancher, ranchman, ranchero (US), arable farmer, grower, raiser, cultivator, sharecropper, tank farmer, dirt farmer, dry farmer, truck farmer (US), fruit farmer, planter, tea planter, coffee planter, barley baron

16 **farm worker**, farm manager, bailiff, farm agent, (migrant) farm labourer, farmhand, farmboy, stockman, stockperson, cowman, cowherd, cowboy, cowgirl, cowpuncher, puncher, herdsman, herd manager, cowhand, dairyhand, milkmaid, dairymaid, pigman, swineherd, shepherd, shepherdess, goatherd, bronco-buster (US), buckaroo (US), gaucho, wrangler (US), groom, ostler, hostler, stableboy, stableman, herder, drover, gooseboy, goosegirl, swanherd, tractor driver, ploughman, potato picker, hop picker, fruit picker, crew (US)

VERBS

17 **farm**, work the land, cultivate, grow, sharecrop, till, till the soil, plough, rotavate, dig, delve, spade, harrow, rake, plant, sow, drill, direct drill, scatter seed, broadcast, top-dress, fertilize, muck, manure, dung, mulch, irrigate, spray, weed, hoe, mow, cut, harvest, reap, glean, gather, swathe, turn, crop, bale

► *44 Horticulture*

18 **practise livestock farming**, ranch, raise, rear, grow, breed, feed, nurture, suckle, wean, fatten, run, graze, fodder, water, muck out, bed, drench, worm, groom, comb, rub down, castrate, dehorn, brand, milk, handmilk, machine-milk, dry off, calve, lamb, harness, bridle, yoke, hitch, drive, herd, tend, drove, punch cattle, wrangle (US), round up, corral, shepherd, stable, pen

ADJECTIVES

19 **agricultural**, agrarian, agronomic, agrological, agroecological, agrobiological, geoponic, farm, farming, farmhouse, rustic, rural, pastoral, peasant, bucolic, agrestic, praedial (*or* predial), georgic (Lit)

20 **farmable**, arable, cultivable, ploughable, tillable, fertile, productive, fruitful, farmed, cropped, ploughed, broken down, tilled, grazed, fallow, undersown

21 **domesticated**, domestic, broken in, reared, raised, bred, milked, dry, fat, bought-in, purebred, cross-bred, thoroughbred, half-bred, inbred

ADVERBS

22 **agriculturally**, hydroponically, pisciculturally, gnotobiotically, organically, ecologically, rurally, pastorally, rustically, bucolically, productively, fruitfully, down on the farm

44 Horticulture

To get the best results you must talk to your vegetables. Charles, Prince of Wales.

NOUNS

1 **horticulture**, gardening, landscape gardening, landscape architecture, flower growing, floriculture, rose growing, market gardening, truck farming (*or* gardening) (US), vegetable growing, mushroom growing, fruit growing, soft-fruit growing, pomiculture, citriculture, fruitage, viticulture, viniculture, indoor gardening, arboriculture, silviculture

► *43 Agriculture; 79 Trees; 80 Fruits*

2 **garden**, pleasure garden, formal garden, flower garden, ornamental garden, rock garden, alpine garden, rose garden, water garden, knot garden, parterre, Japanese garden, sunken garden, indoor garden, winter garden, bottle garden, hanging garden, bonsai, herb garden, garden centre, garden shop, vegetable garden, kitchen garden, allotment, cabbage patch, market garden, truck garden (*or* farm) (US), fruit farm, orchard, hop garden, lemon grove, olive grove, orange grove, vineyard, arboretum, tea garden, beer garden, roof garden, civic garden, municipal garden, public garden, zoological garden, botanical garden, garden city, garden suburb, victory garden, garden of remembrance, garden of rest, Hanging Gardens of Babylon, Garden of the Hesperides, Garden of Eden, Kew Gardens

► *79 Trees*

3 **ornamental garden**, flower garden, bed, flowerbed, rose bed, rosery (*or* rosary), rosarium, herbaceous border, border, rockery, lawn, pond, lily pond, fountain, birdbath, bird table, garden gnome, bench, garden seat, garden chair, sun lounger, shrubbery, hedge, topiary, fence, trellis, rustic fence, lap fence, bower, arbour, grotto, summer house, gazebo, pergola, belvedere, ha-ha (*or* haw-haw), water butt, garden path, paving, crazy paving, patio, terrace, hanging basket, window box, patio set, barbecue, barbie (Inf)

4 **nursery**, glasshouse, greenhouse, conservatory, orangery, garden shed, potting shed, polytunnel, hothouse, coolhouse, forcing house, forcing bed, hotbed, frame, cold frame, propagator, cloche, module, seed tray, grow bag, compost heap, flowerpot, planter, jardinière

5 **gardening**, growing plants, green fingers, repotting, potting on, bedding out, pruning, pinching out, cutting back, hard pruning, feeding, watering, weeding, composting, aquiculture, hydroponics, propagation, planting, grafting, budding, layering, stooling, graft, rootstock, stock, scion, graft union, cutting, stem cutting, leaf cutting, offset, budstick, maiden, whip, sucker, runner, plant breeding, variety, strain, cultivar, diploid, triploid, polyploid

6 **garden tool**, spade, fork, hoe, Dutch hoe, draw hoe, Canterbury hoe, onion hoe, rake, lawn rake, trowel, handfork, dibble, dibber, drill, seed drill, lopper, pruner, secateurs, lawn mower, cylinder mower, power mower, rotary mower, hover mower, Strimmer™, edger, edging tool, cultivator, Rotavator™, distributor, spreader, flame gun, garden line, shears, hedge trimmer, sprinkler, hose,

leaf sweeper, roller, sprayer, knapsack sprayer, nozzle, lance, trug, watering can, rose, wheelbarrow, stake, tie, rabbit guard, beanpole, peastick

7 fertilizer, manure, compost, potting compost, mulch, peat, fishmeal, foliar feed

8 weedkiller, herbicide, moss killer, fungicide, systemic fungicide, Bordeaux mixture, pesticide, spray, slug pellet, insecticide, pyrethrum, derris, benzene hexachloride (BHC), Malathion™, primicarb, dimethoate, dinitro ortho cresol (DNOC)

9 garden plant, seedling, cutting, bulb, corm, rhizome, tuber, rock plant, alpine, bedding plant, annual, biennial, perennial, herb, flower, succulent, creeper, ground cover, turf, climber, climbing plant, rambler, woody plant, shrub, tree, specimen shrub, specimen tree

► *77 Plants; 78 Flowers; 79 Trees*

10 fruit tree, bush tree, dwarf bush tree, cordon, dwarf pyramid, fan-trained tree, espalier, half standard, standard, fruit, soft fruit, stone fruit, citrus fruit

► *80 Fruits*

11 vegetable, green vegetable, brassica, salad vegetable, root vegetable, root, tuber, legume, bean, pulse, dried vegetable, herb, culinary herb, sweet herb, potherb, mushroom

► *25 Cookery; 83 Fungi*

12 pests and diseases, beetle, wireworm, asparagus beetle, flea beetle, raspberry beetle, thrips, weevil, apple blossom weevil, scale insect, leaf-hopper, leaf miner, aphid, apple aphid, cabbage aphid, root aphid, greenfly, whitefly, blackfly, black bean aphid, woolly aphid, raspberry midge, blackcurrant midge, cabbage fly, carrot fly, celery fly, onion fly, caterpillar, cutworm, leatherjacket, Colorado beetle, cabbage white, pea moth, codling moth (*or* codlin moth), apple sawfly, plum sawfly, gooseberry sawfly, red spider mite, big bud mite, mealy bug, eelworm, slug, snail, earwig, club root, mildew, powdery mildew, downy mildew, blight, brown rot, canker, damping-off, sooty mould, grey mould, botrytis, leaf curl, leaf mould, leaf spot, ring spot, honey fungus, rust, scab, silver leaf, root rot, wilt, crown rot, stem rot, crown gall, fireblight, heart rot, blackleg, soft rot, chlorosis, scald, bitter pit, dieback, mosaic, yellow edge, crinkle, spotted wilt, fruit drop

► *83 Fungi*

13 horticulturist, gardener, plantsman, landscape gardener, landscapist, topiarist, landscape architect, floriculturist, flower grower, rose grower, rosarian, seedsman, nurseryman (*or* -woman), market gardener, truck gardener (*or* farmer) (US), fruit grower, fruiter, fruit farmer, pomologist, orchardist, vine grower, viniculturist, *vigneron* (Fr), vegetable grower, mushroom grower, hop grower, fruit picker, hop picker, under-gardener, arboriculturist

► *78 Flowers; 79 Trees*

VERBS

14 practise horticulture, garden, landscape, cultivate, grow fruit, grow vegetables, market garden, truck garden (*or* farm) (US)

15 cultivate, plant, pot, sow, seed, put in, set, drill, heel in, dib, dibble, puddle in, transplant, pot on, prick out, plant out, bed out, dig, double-dig, trench, bastard-trench, delve, spade, fork, rotavate, hoe, rake, weed, thin, thin out, train, tie in, stake, prune, cut, mow, strim, crop, top, lop, deadhead, debud, deblossom, mulch, muck, dung, manure, straw, top-dress, fertilize, compost, sprinkle, water, spray, dust, propagate, breed, pollinate, graft, bud, take cuttings, layer

► *43 Agriculture*

ADJECTIVES

16 horticultural, floricultural, floral, flowery, florescent, efflorescent, in bloom, uniflorous, multiflorous, herbaceous, herbal, vegetable, vegetal, vegetative, leguminous, cereal, farinaceous, arboricultural, arboreal, arborical, dendroid, sylvan, silvicultural, pomological, viticultural, vinicultural, aquicultural, hydroponic

VEGETABLES

adzuki bean	calabrese	cucumber	Jerusalem artichoke	pak–choi cabbage	red pepper	string bean
asparagus	capsicum	curly kale	kale	parsnip	romaine lettuce	succory
aubergine	cardoon	dishcloth gourd	kidney bean	pea	runner bean	succotash
avocado pear	carrot	eggplant (US)	kohlrabi	pea bean	rutabaga (US)	sugar pea
bamboo shoots	cassava	elephant garlic	lady's fingers	pepper	salsify	Swiss chard
bean	cauliflower	elephant's ear	lentil	petit pois	savoy cabbage	swede
beansprout	celeriac	endive	lettuce	pe–tsai cabbage	scallion (US)	sweet corn
beef tomato	celery	fennel	lima bean (US)	pimiento	scarlet runner	sweet potato
beet	chard	finocchio	lotus root	pinto bean	sea kale	taro
beetroot	chayote	flageolet	mangetout	plum tomato	shallot	tomato
bhindi	cherry tomato	French bean	manioc	potato, spud (Inf), murphy (Inf), tattie (*or* tatty) (Scot)	silver beet	tonka bean
black–eyed pea	chervil	garlic	marrow	potherb	skillet	turnip
bok choy	chick pea	gherkin	marrow squash	pumpkin	sorrel	vegetable marrow
broad bean	chicory	gibbon (Dial)	mung bean	radish	soya bean	water chestnut
broccoli	Chinese cabbage	globe artichoke	mustard and cress	red bean	spinach	watercress
Brussels sprout	Chinese leaves	gourd	neep (Scot)	red beet (US)	spinach beet	wax bean (US)
butter bean	collard	gumbo	okra	red cabbage	split pea	white cabbage
butternut pumpkin	corn on the cob	green cabbage	onion		spring cabbage	yam
cabbage	courgette	green pepper	oyster plant		spring onion	yellow pepper
cabbage lettuce	cos lettuce	haricot bean			sprout	zucchini (US)
	cress	horse bean			squash	

17 botanical, annual, biennial, perennial, hardy, half-hardy, succulent, verdant, verdurous, mossy, grassy, bushy, fruity, woody, shrubby, scrubby, mildewy, rotten, mouldy, blighted, wilting, weed-choked, bug-infested, gone to seed

18 herbicidal, pesticidal, fungicidal, insecticidal

19 ornamental, alpine, exotic, tropical, subtropical, landscaped, cultivated, cultured, forced, trained, pruned, grafted, cut, watered, hoed, raked

ADVERBS

20 horticulturally, hydroponically, pomologically, florally, botanically, annually, biennially, perennially, succulently, verdantly, ornamentally, exotically, tropically, subtropically

Sports and Pastimes

45 Sport

The game isn't over till it's over. Yogi Berra.

Exercise is bunk. If you are healthy, you don't need it: if you are sick, you shouldn't take it. Henry Ford.

NOUNS

1 **sport**, game, contest, match, event, meeting, meet, bout, round, set, tournament, knockout, league, division
2 **sportsground**, venue, stadium, field, track, ground, course, links, court, ring, arena, green, alley
3 **sportsman**, sportswoman, player, competitor, contender, defender, challenger, opponent, team member, athlete, sporty type
4 **sporting activity**, indoor sport, outdoor sport, participator sport, spectator sport, contact sport, blood sport

ADJECTIVES

5 **sporting**, competitive, agonistic, sportive, sporty, athletic, gymnastic, acrobatic

VERBS

6 **participate**, take part, compete, contend, join in, enter, play

ADVERBS

7 **sportingly**, athletically, gymnastically, acrobatically, competitively

46 American Football

NOUNS

1 **football**, football game, professional football, NFL (National Football League), AFC (American Football Conference), NFC (National Football Conference), exhibition game, playoff game, bowl game, Pro Bowl, Super Bowl, World Bowl, college football, Rose Bowl, Sugar Bowl, Cotton Bowl, Orange Bowl, high-school football, tag football, touch football, pigskin (Inf)
2 **football player**, All-Pro, All-American, varsity player, captain, redshirt, rookie, draft pick, free agent, substitute, sub, coach, head coach, assistant coach, offensive coordinator, defensive coordinator, referee, umpire, head linesman, field judge, back judge, line judge, side judge, zebra (Inf), side-line crew, chain gang (Inf)
3 **uniform**, jersey, helmet, nose guard, flak jacket, facemask, mouthguard, pads
4 **stadium**, bowl, field, Astroturf™, artificial grass, rug (Inf), carpet (Inf), gridiron, goal posts, crossbar, uprights, press box, scoreboard, scoreboard clock, 30-second clock, midfield stripe, goal line, end line, end zone, sideline, restraining line, hash mark, yard marker, chains
5 **game time**, quarter, half, half-time, time-out, officials' time-out, television (*or* commercial) time out, two-minute warning, overtime, sudden death
6 **scoring**, touchdown, extra point, PAT (point after touchdown), conversion, two-point conversion, field goal, safety
7 **offence**, possession, offensive team, offensive drive, forward progress, offensive formation, I-formation, T-formation, shotgun formation, spread formation, slot formation, single-wing formation, double-wing formation, strong side, weak side, balanced line, unbalanced line, two-minute offence, two-minute drill, hurry-up offence, run-and-shoot offence, offensive backfield, offensive backs, quarterback, signal-caller (Inf), field general (Inf), passer, fullback, halfback, running back, runner, up back, wingback, blocker, offensive line, offensive lineman, centre, guard, tackle, receiver, wide receiver, flanker
8 **huddle**, set, shift, signals, line call, read, audible, snap count, quick count, snap
9 **play**, trick play, gadget play, ground game, running game, run, quarterback sneak, option run, pitchout, bootleg, keeper, lateral, draw, cutback, sweep, power sweep, rollout, reverse, end around, inside run, outside run, misdirection, trap, handoff, play-action, play fake, fumble, turnover, passing game, pocket, pass, complete pass, pass reception, incomplete pass, intercepted pass, protection, option pass, screen pass, flare pass, spot pass, square-out pass, square-in pass, hook pass, curl pass, slant-in pass, bomb, hail-Mary, flea-flicker, fly pattern, post pattern, Z pattern, block, cross block, lead block, scissors block, isolation block
10 **defence**, defensive team, defensive formation, zone defence, nickel defence, dime defence, flex defence, 4-3 defence, 3-4 defence, prevent defence, man-to-man defence, single coverage, double coverage, zone coverage, overshift, undershift, slant, stunt, pinch, penetration, defensive backfield, secondary, defensive backs, linebacker, cornerback, safety, strong safety, defensive line,

defensive lineman, defensive end, defensive tackle, the front four, the Fearsome Foursome (Inf)

11 defensive huddle, pass rush, rush, blitz, dog, sack, bump and run

12 special team, specialty team, kicking team, receiving team, kicker, field-goal kicker, place kicker, quick-kicker, holder, kicking tee, kickoff, onside kick, squib kick, quick kick, free kick, fake kick, punt, hang time, catch, fair catch, touchback, run back, return

13 penalty, 5-yard penalty, 10-yard penalty, 15-yard penalty, penalty marker, penalty flag, offensive foul, defensive foul, dead-ball foul, spot of enforcement, delay

SPORTING ACTIVITIES

Air Sports
aerobatics
air racing
ballooning
freefalling
gliding
hang–gliding
helicopter flying
kiting
parachuting
paragliding
parascending
skydiving

Angling
big–game fishing
coarse fishing
fly–fishing
game fishing
match fishing
sea fishing

Animal Sports
dressage
falconry
greyhound racing
gymkhana
harness horseracing
horseracing
pato
pigeon racing
point–to–point
polo
puissance
rodeo
showjumping
sled–dog racing
steeplechasing
three–day eventing
trotting

Athletics
caber tossing
cross–country running
decathlon
discus throwing
fell running
hammer throwing
heptathlon
high jumping
hurdling
javelin throwing
long–distance running
long jumping
marathon running
middle–distance running
modern pentathlon
mountain running
pole-vaulting
relay racing
shot-putting
sprinting
steeplechasing
triathlon
triple jump
tug of war
walking events

Blood Sports
beagling
bullfighting
coursing
deerstalking
ferreting
fox-hunting
grouse shooting
mink hunting
otter hunting
pheasant shooting
pigeon shooting
wildfowling

Combat Sports
aikido
boxing
fencing
haphido
judo
karate
kendo
kenipo
kick boxing
kung fu
tae kwon do
tang soo do
Thai boxing
wrestling

Court Games
aeroball
badminton
court handball
jai alai (pelota)
lawn tennis
racquetball
rugby fives
short tennis
squash
table tennis (ping–pong)
tennis
volleyball

Gymnastics
asymmetric bars
beam
floor exercises
horizontal bar (high bar)
parallel bars
pommel horse
rings
rhythmic gymnastics
sports aerobics
trampolining
tumbling
vault

Target Sports
airgun shooting
clay pigeon shooting
cross bow archery
darts
darts cricket
darts football
down–the–line shooting
field archery
free pistol shooting
horseshoe pitching
Olympic French shooting
pistol shooting
rapid–fire pistol shooting
rifle shooting
rough shooting
running game target shooting
sharpshooting
skeet shooting
target archery
trapshooting

Target Ball Games
boules (boccie)
bowling
Canadian 5–pin bowling
carom billiards
croquet
crown–green bowls
curling
English billiards
flat–green bowls
golf
pool
skittles
snooker
tenpin bowling

Team Games
American football
Australian rules football
bandy
baseball
basketball
Canadian football
cricket
field hockey
French cricket
Gaelic football
hurling
ice hockey
kabaddi
korfball
lacrosse
netball
roller hockey
rounders
rugby league
rugby union
sepak takrow
shinty
soccer (Association Football)
softball
speedball
stoolball
team handball
volleyball

Water Sports
Canadian canoe racing
canoe polo
canoe sailing
canoe slalom racing
canoe sprint racing
diving
jet skiing
kayaking
laser sailing
offshore yacht racing
Olympic yacht classes
powerboat racing
rowing
sailplaning
scuba diving
sculling
short board sailing
snorkelling
surfing
swimming
synchronized swimming
underwater diving
water polo
water skiing
white water rafting
wild water racing
windsurfing
yacht racing

Wheel Sports
autocross
cycle racing
drag racing
karting
motorcycle racing
motor racing
mountain biking
rally cross
roller blading
roller derby
roller hockey
roller skating
roller skiing
sidecar racing
skateboarding
stock–car racing

Winter Sports
Alpine combined event
Alpine skiing
biathlon
bobsleigh racing
cross–country (Nordic)
downhill racing
figure skating
freestyle skiing
giant slalom
ice–dancing
langlauf
luge
Nordic combined event
off–piste skiing
short–track speed skating
skibob racing
ski-jumping
ski-mountaineering
slalom
speed-skating
super–G
tobogganing

Other
alpine climbing
bunji jumping
caving
hiking
ice climbing
mountaineering
orienteering
parascending
potholing
rock climbing
spelunking
weightlifting

of game, offside, encroachment, holding, faceguarding, clipping, chucking, crackback block, illegal motion, false start, personal foul, unsportsmanlike conduct, ineligible receiver, pass interference, intentional grounding, illegal use of hands, roughing the passer, roughing the kicker, piling on (Inf)

14 miscellaneous terms, cheerleader, coin-toss, game plan, pep rally, pep squad, spike, training camp, transfer, yardage, waiver

VERBS

15 play offence, quarterback, be the field general, call signals, run the offence, run the hurry-up offence, call the plays, be in the shotgun, pass, have possession, lateral, fake, sweep, sneak, run the quarterback sneak, call a draw, call an audible, read the defence, throw a completion, hit a receiver, throw a pass, stick to the ground game, trap, handoff, option, pitchout, bootleg, keep, rollout, leave the pocket, get sacked, score, convert, run a pattern, protect, block, cross block, lead block, centre, cutback, run the power sweep

16 play defence, have coverage, overshift, undershift, slant, stunt, pinch, penetrate, rush the passer, red-dog, pass rush, rush, blitz, dog, sack, bump and run, play back

17 kick, place kick, quick-kick, split the uprights, hit the crossbar, kick off, quick kick, be awarded a free kick, have good hang time, call for a fair catch, make a fair catch, have a touchback, run back, return, be on the special team

18 be penalized, be offside, have encroachment, hold, faceguard, clip, chuck, throw a crackback block, have illegal motion, have a false start, draw a personal foul, commit unsportsmanlike conduct, throw to an ineligible receiver, interfere, ground intentionally, rough the passer, rough the kicker, pile on, have illegal use of hands, facemask, take too much time, illegally ground the ball

ADJECTIVES

19 varsity, collegiate, professional, offensive, defensive, specialist, kicking

47 Athletics

I think we'll find in the next decade that women athletes will finally get the attention they deserve. Billie Jean King.

NOUNS

1 track events, indoor track events, race, racing, run, running, heat, preliminary race, semi-final race, final, starting position, set position, start, false start, disqualification, acceleration, curve running, full stride, finishing, finish tape, lane, leg, sprinting, sprint, sprint racing, sprint race, 50-yard dash (US), 50m race, 100m race, 200m race, middle-distance running, middle-distance racing, middle-distance race, 400m race, 800m race, 1500m race, one-mile race, women's 3000m race, 5000m race, long-distance running, long-distance racing, long-distance race, marathon racing, marathon race, relay racing, relay race, 400m relay race (*or* 4 × 100m relay race), 1600m relay race (*or* 4 × 400m relay race), medley relay race, baton, baton change, baton changing, changeover, upsweep method, downsweep method, takeover zone, relay box, hurdles, women's 80m hurdles, women's 100m hurdles race, 110m hurdles race, women's 200m hurdles, 400m hurdles, hurdle, barrier, obstacle, steeplechase, 3000m steeplechase, water jump, cross-country racing, 10000m race, racewalking, walking race, walking, walk, 20km walk, 50km walk

▶ *300 Motion; 331 Impulsion*

2 field events, jump, jumping, high jump, high jumping, back-layout style, flop, Fosbury flop, straddle style, scissors style, Eastern cut-off style, Western roll style, long jump, long jumping, broad jump (US), broad jumping (US), scratch line, run-up, approach, eight-step approach, plant, takeoff point, takeoff, clearance, landing, landing area, sand pit, hitchkick technique, hang technique, triple jump, triple jumping, hop, step, and jump, 10-step approach, bounding, hopping, running hop, pole-vault, pole-vaulting, take-off point, rockback, pole, fibre pole, vaulting pit, crossbar (*or* bar), shot, shot put, 16lb shot-put, shot-putting, shot velocity, discus, discus throw, discus throwing, preliminary swing, transition, swingback, turn, release, drive-foot landing, hammer, hammer throw, hammer throwing, hammer glove, circle, lift, early lift, late lift, single-support phase, rotation, acceleration path, javelin, javelin throw, javelin throwing, javelin carrying, measuring tape, pentathlon, decathlon, heptathlon

▶ *145 Distance; 148 Length; 154 Height; 304 Ascent; 330 Propulsion*

3 athlete, amateur athlete, Olympic athlete, competitor, champion, medallist, gold medallist, silver medallist, bronze medallist, runner, racer, sprinter, middle-distance runner, long-distance runner, miler, marathon runner, marathoner, steeplechaser, cross-country runner, harrier, hurdler, racewalker, walker, starter, timekeeper, vaulter, jumper, high jumper, long jumper, broad jumper (US), triple jumper, pole-vaulter, thrower, shot-putter, discus thrower, hammer-thrower, javelin thrower, pentathlete, decathlete, heptathlete, coach, judge, field judge

4 sports equipment, running shoes, spiked shoes, spikes, starting blocks, blocks, starting pistol, running shorts, running vest, tracksuit, jogging suit, shell suit, athletic support, jockstrap (Inf)

5 competition, games, World Games, European Games, Pan-American Games, Commonwealth Games, Olympic Games, record, title, medal, gold medal, silver medal, bronze medal, drug test, anabolic steroid, sex test

VERBS

6 compete in track and field, take part, contest, contend, vie, come first, win, set (*or* break) a record, win in record-breaking time

7 race, start, fire the starting gun, make a false start, get off to a fast start, run, run full stride, sprint, accelerate, stay in one's lane, lead, lap, finish first, hit the finish tape, hand over the baton, make a changeover, hurdle (a barrier), knock down a hurdle

8 jump, leap, spring, bound, do the Fosbury flop, hop, step, and jump, (pole) vault, land, clear the crossbar, hit the crossbar

ADJECTIVES

9 track, track and field, field, Olympic, gold, silver, bronze, record-breaking, racing, sprinting, 50-yard (US), one-mile, middle-distance, long-distance, marathon, relay, medley relay, baton, hurdles, cross-country, walking, jumping, back-layout, takeoff, triple, hopping, landing

ADVERBS

10 **fast**, (at) full stride, with a sprint, at a good pace, rhythmically, with velocity, far, high

48 Baseball

NOUNS

1 **baseball**, the great American game, America's national sport, baseball game, professional baseball, major league baseball, National League, American League, World Series, All-Star Game, pennant winner, world champions, minor league baseball, Triple-A league, Double-A league, farm club, college baseball, NCCA Baseball Championship, Little League baseball, Little League World Series, National Baseball Hall of Fame and Museum, baseball stadium, stands, bleachers, baseball field, diamond, infield, batter's box, catcher's box, pitcher's plate, pitcher's mound, home base, first base, second base, third base, foul line, outfield, left field centre field, right field, outfield fence, fair territory, foul territory, dugout, bullpen, on-deck circle, inning, top of the inning, bottom of the inning, extra innings

2 **baseball player**, the battery, middle position, pitcher, relief pitcher, catcher, fielder, infielder, keystone combination, first-baseman, second-baseman, short stop, third-baseman, outfielder, left fielder, centre fielder, right fielder, batter, hitter, long-distance hitter, home-run hitter, power hitter, left-handed hitter, right-handed hitter, lead-off man, clean-up man, base runner, runner, designated runner, starter, substitute, pinch hitter, designated hitter, batting champion, home-run leader, runs-batted-in leader, RBI leader, earned-run-average leader, All-Star, All-American, Rookie of the Year, manager, head coach, pitching coach, batting coach, home-plate umpire, first-base umpire, third-base umpire, official scorer

3 **baseball equipment**, baseball, baseball bat, bat, Louisville slugger, baseball uniform, stockings, baseball shoes, cap, sliding pads, catcher's glove, catcher's mitt, first-baseman's glove, infielder's glove, outfielder's glove, catcher's mask, umpire's mask, chest protectors, shin guards, batter's helmet, horsehide (Inf), apple (Inf)

4 **pitching terms**, catcher's sign, strike zone, strike, ball, wind-up, hard pitch, soft pitch, curveball, reverse curve, fast ball, knuckle ball, change-up, change-of-pace, slider, breaker, fadeaway, screwball, spitball, brushing off the batter, brush-off, dusting off the batter, dust-off, strike-out, wild pitch, balk, intentional pass, base on balls, loading the bases, walking a man in, forcing a run, shut-out, perfect game, earned-run average (ERA), win, save, Annie Oakley (Inf)

5 **batting terms**, hit, single, line drive, one you can hang the wash on, pop single, double, triple, home run, inside-the-park home run, grand-slam home run, grand-slammer, fair ball, foul ball, foul tip, ground ball, up-the-middle hit, grounder, bounder, hopper, dribbler, fly ball, fly, pop up, bunt, squeeze play, suicide squeeze, sacrifice fly, perfect sacrifice, sacrifice, hit-and-run play, interference, being hit by a pitched ball, missed third strike, runs batted in (RBI), batting average, Texas Leaguer (Inf), Texas League single (Inf), murderers' row (Inf)

6 **fielding terms**, out, double play, triple play, going around the corner, put-out, throw-out, force play, run-down, tag-out, forced out, infield fly, infield fly rule, stolen base, pickup, fly-out, hot corner

VERBS

7 **play baseball**, take the field, come to bat, pitch, throw a fast ball, throw a curve, throw a slider, throw a wild pitch, balk, brush off the batter, hit the batter, load the bases, give an intentional walk, pitch a shut-out, pitch a perfect game, have a conference on the mound, be relieved, call for a relief pitcher, swing, strike at, foul off, foul, hit, hit a fly, hit a grounder, hit a home run, hit a grand-slam home run, hit a grand-slammer, ground out, hit into a double play, force out, fly out, pop up, bunt, sacrifice, squeeze, strike out, walk, be walked, be intentionally walked, be hit by a pitched ball, be brushed off, bat in a run, leave a runner stranded, run bases, slide home, score a run, score, catch a fly, throw out, catch in a run-down, make a double play, take a trip to the showers (Inf)

49 Basketball

NOUNS

1 **basketball**, basketball game, professional basketball, National Basketball Association (NBA), NBA Championship, college basketball, NCCA Basketball Championship, NIT Championship, Basketball Hall of Fame, basketball arena, basketball gymnasium, basketball gym, playing court, centre court, centre line, ten-second line, back court, front court, free-throw lane, quarter, half, half-time, two-minute warning, overtime, sudden death

2 **basketball player**, centre, forward, guard, pivot man, shooter, foul shooter, scorer, passer, blocker, rebounder, All-American, All-Pro, varsity player, first-team player, captain, rookie, draft pick, substitute, draft player, draft, NBA Most Valuable Player, NBA Rookie of the Year, coach, head coach, assistant coach, official, referee, umpire, timer, sub (Inf)

3 **basketball equipment**, basketball, basket, net, rim, backboard, rectangular backboard, fan-shaped backboard, scoring desk, timer's desk, shot-clock, uniform, jersey, shorts, gym shoes, sneakers, knee guard, round ball (Inf), apple (Inf), rock (Inf)

4 **playing terms**, dribbling, shooting, dunking, passing, holding, freezing, rebounding, pivoting, screening, blocking, guarding, dribble, shot, two-pointer, three-pointer, foul, personal foul, technical foul, double foul, free throw, free shot, foul shot, penalty shot, one-pointer, hook shot, jump shot, bank shot, lay up, dunk, over-the-rim shot, one-hand shot, two-hand shot, set shot, goal, field goal, tip-in, pass, bounce pass, hook pass, baseball pass, behind-the-back pass, rebound, screen, block, loose ball, live ball, held ball, dead ball, jump ball, possession, fast break offence, running offence, shoot-and-run offence, ball-control offence, possession ball, high post, low post, man-to-man defence, zone defence, five-man

defence, pressing defence, the press, air ball (Inf), hanger (Inf), whish (Inf)

5 **penalties**, running with the ball, travelling, walking, double-dribbling, kicking the ball, tripping, hacking, three-second lane violation, ten-second backcourt violation, goal-tending, stepping over foul line during free throw, stepping over end line on throw-in, technical foul

VERBS

6 **play basketball**, dribble, shoot, tip in, dunk, slam dunk, pass, hold the ball, freeze the ball, rebound, pivot, screen, block, guard, drive, cut, foul, foul out, travel, walk, double-dribble, trip, hack, goal-tend, press, can a shot (Inf), knock the bottom out (Inf), shoot an air ball (Inf)

50 Boating Sports

All rowed fast but none so fast as stroke. Desmond Coke.

NOUNS

1 **sailing**, yachting, international sailing, sailing techniques, beating, bearing off (*or* away), reefing, reaching, fine reaching, close reaching, beam reaching, broad reaching, bottom turn, close hauling, sheeting in, sheeting out, gybe, duck gybe, clew gybe, slam gybe, scissor gybe, flare gybe, stop gybe, tacking, port tacking, starboard tacking, tack, duck tack, clew tack, heading up, luffing, wearing, taking up, competitive sailing, team dinghy racing, regatta, yacht racing, Grand Prix yacht racing, yacht race, handicap race, Cowes regatta, Admiral's Cup series, offshore racing, ocean racing, Sydney to Hobart Race, Fastnet Race, Bermuda Race, single-handed racing, dinghy racing, cruiser racing, multihull racing, transatlantic racing, Single-handed Transatlantic Race, the Atlantic Race for Cruisers (ARC), the Whitbread Round the World Race, World Team Racing Championship, sailing trophy, the America's Cup, Congressional Cup, Wilson Trophy, Hinman Cup, tall-ship racing, yachting association, International Yacht Racing Union (IYRU), Intercollegiate Yacht Racing Association (IYRA) (US), the United States Yacht Racing Union (USYRU), Royal Yachting Association (RYA), sailing wind, true wind, apparent wind, anabatic wind, katabatic wind, land breeze, sea breeze, course, wake course

► *433 Water; 434 Air*

2 **sailing boat**, yacht, cruising yacht, ocean-cruising yacht, ocean-racing yacht, yacht class, Formula 40 class, half-tonner class, 50-foot class, Olympic class, Soling class, Star class, Tornado class, Flying Dutchman (FD) class, 470 class, Finn class, Europe class, Sailboard class, yacht tender, keelboat, two-man keelboat, three-man keelboat, planing keelboat, dinghy, single-handed dinghy, two-man dinghy, catamaran, cruiser, single-masted boat, cutter, sloop, masthead sloop, two-masted boat, two-man trapeze boat, schooner, kedge, yawl, double-ender, square-rigger, lugger, one-design boat, committee boat, stiff boat, tender boat, tide-rode boat, wind-rode boat

3 **parts of a sailing boat**, helm, tiller, wheel, deck, deckhead, bow, prow, stem, pulpit, beam, quarter, amidships, afterpart, stern, transom, pushpit, rudder, rudderpost, cockpit, companionway, hull, carvel-built hull, clinker-built hull, moulded hull, GRP (glass-reinforced plastic) hull, centreboard, daggerboard, keel, fin keel, leeboards, sidelight, rig, Bermudan rig, Marconi rig, gaff rig, gunter rig, jury rig, rigging, running rigging, standing rigging, tackle, Cunningham tackle, Cunningham hole, purchase, downhaul, uphaul, bulkhead, bulwarks, sail, jib, mainsail, trysail, foresail, Genoa, headsail, spinnaker, gaffsail, fore-and-aft sail, lugsail (*or* lug), loose-footed sail, gaff, forestay, backstay, staysail, bilge, bitts, block, snatch block, sheave, spar, sprit, yard, mast, forward mast, mainmast, aft mast, mizzenmast, deck-stepped mast, keep-stepped mast, boom, boom preventer, vang, boom vang, kicking strap, rope, bolt rope, sheet, shock cord, halyard, hawser, lanyard, warp, outhaul, heaving line, breast line, ratline, reef point, painter, lifeline, mooring line, spring, shroud, lift, topping lift, guy, ballast, chainplates, clew, gasket, fairlead, barber hauler, gooseneck, battens, drogue, cleat, jamming cleat, claw ring, gimbal, hank, cross-tree, sheet winch, bosun's chair, flag, ensign, pennant, burgee, coffee grinder (Inf)

► *323 Water Transport*

4 **rowing**, amateur rowing, single-oar rowing, fixed-seat rowing, sweep rowing, sculling, double-oar rowing, single sculling, double sculling, quadruple sculling, competitive rowing, racing, scull racing, skiff racing, regatta, the Henley Royal Regatta, Royal Canadian Henley, Olympic rowing, Olympic regatta, the World Championships, intercollegiate rowing, the boat race, Oxford-Cambridge race, Harvard-Yale race, rowing race, bumping race, open event, pairs, fours, eights, sprint race, sweep (US), racing boat, rowboat, dinghy, skiff, outrigger, coxed fours, coxswainless fours, quadruple sculls, coxed pairs, coxswainless pairs, sculls, double sculls, single sculls, parts of a racing boat, seat, sliding seat, fixed seat, stroke side, bow side, oar, racing oar, spade oar, spoon oar, scull, handle, blade, loom, collar, button, rowlock, notch, tholepin, gunwale (*or* gunnel), swivel, thwart, stretcher, rowing technique, catch, stroke, English stroke, American stroke, recovery, feathering, finish, squaring, balance, diving, striking, rate of striking, paddling, blade slip, rowing association, Fédération Internationale des Sociétés d'Aviron (FISA), American Rowing Association, catching a crab (Inf)

► *331 Impulsion*

5 **Henley trophies**, the Grand Challenge Cup (eights), Thames Cup (eights), Ladies Plate (college and school eights), Princess Elizabeth Cup (schoolboy eights), Prince Philip Cup (coxed fours), Britannia Cup (coxed fours), Stewards' Cup (fours), Visitors' Cup (college and school fours), Wyfold Cup (fours), Silver Goblets (pairs), Diamond Sculls, Double Sculls

► *794 Prize*

6 **canoeing**, recreational canoeing, wild-water canoeing, white-water running, shooting the rapids, competitive canoeing, single-paddle canoeing, double-paddle canoeing, birchbark canoe, dugout canoe, open canoe, Canadian canoe, foldboat, faltboat, paddling canoe, racing canoe, cruising canoe, sailing canoe, outrigger, catamaran, international 10 square metre canoe, V-bottom, war canoe, kayak, decked kayak, folding canoe, paddle,

single-bladed paddle, double-bladed paddle, double-ended paddle, softwood paddle, hardwood paddle, parts of a canoe, bow, stern, keel, gunwale (*or* gunnel), seat, sliding outrigger seat, thwart, centreboard, deck, well, cockpit, canoe techniques, stroke, cruising stroke, bow stroke, forward bow stroke, cruising hook, J stroke, draw stroke, turning stroke, pushover stroke, sweep stroke, jamming stroke, stopping stroke, locking the blade, keel lock, Eskimo roll, shaking out, canoe racing, slalom racing, Olympic canoeing, canoe race, one-man (C-1) canoe race, two-man (C-2) canoe race, single kayak (K-1) race, double kayak (K-2) race, four-man kayak (K-4) race, single-blade race, double-blade race, tandem race, open cruising race, decked-canoe race, watercourse, gate, canoe trophy, International Challenge Cup, canoe association, International Canoe Federation (ICF), British Canoe Union, Royal Canoe Club, British Schools Canoeing Association, American Canoe Association (ACA)

► *183 Concavity; 550 Covering; 585 War*

7 windsurfing, boardsurfing, sailing, free sailing, freestyle sailing, displacement sailing, windsurf racing, slalom racing, one-design racing, open-class racing, ins and outs, wavesailing, wave riding, wave jumping, ice surfing, sailboard, parts of a sailboard, board, custom board, customs, GRP (glass-reinforced plastic) board, flatboard, displacement board, roundboard, pop-out board, funboard, gun, floater, sinker, marginal, tandem, tridem, rail, fin, skeg, wing, sail, funboard storm sail, rotational sail, RAF (rotating asymmetrical foil), powerhead, fathead, universal joint, boom, wishbone boom, footstrap, harness, harness line, ding, hull, V-shape hull, daggerboard, bowline, bumper, rocker, downhaul line, camber inducer, cleat, clew, windsurfing classes, Division I, Division II, Division III, slalom course, drysuit, windsurfing terms, centre of effort (CE), centre of lateral resistance (CLR), cavatation, railing, spinning out, spin-out, wiping out, wipe out, windsurfing techniques, Le Mans start, water start, foot steering, planing, pumping, off-the-lip turn

► *148 Length; 175 Base; 187 Horizontality*

8 punting, pleasure punting, double punting, one-arm punting, punt-racing, competitive punting, Professional Punting Championship, canoe poling, punt, pleasure punt, family punt, racing punt, two-foot punt, Thames punt, *Stocherkahn* (Ger), *trajinera* (Sp), *punter* (Dutch), punt pole, racing pole, parts of a punt, saloon, huff, sheer, swim, knee, tread, grating, rounds, floors, till, locker, deck, counter, shoe, mud shoe, sprit, box, after back rest, punting techniques, climbing the pole, levering, pinching, running, reaching, windmill stroke, shove, C-shape shove, half-shove, after-shove, back-shove, stop-up, throw, d drop, recovery, crossover recovery, the bucket, picking up, pole-body-foot movement, trailing

9 sailor, yachtsman, helmsman, captain, skipper, crewman, sailing boat designer, yacht designer, rower, oarsman, bow, number one, number two, number three, number four, number five, number six, stroke, sculler, coxswain (*or* cox), Henley stewart, windsurfer, boardsurfer, ice surfer, punter, waterman, sitter

ADJECTIVES

10 sailing, yachting, tacking, handicap, offshore, single-handed, multihull, transatlantic, anabatic, katabatic, cruising, half-tonner, 50-foot, Olympic, two-man, three-man, planing, two-masted, square-rigged, one-design, tide-rode, wind-rode, carvel-built, clinker-built, moulded, GRP, jury, Cunningham, fore and aft, forward, aft, deck-stepped, keel-stepped, heaving, mooring, goosenecked, jamming, abeam, adrift, aloft, aweigh, close-hauled, roller-reefed, Bermudan-rigged, Marconi-rigged, gaff-rigged, gunter-rigged, head-to-wind, off-wind, in irons, loose-footed, quartering, stiff, tender, clew, slam, scissor, flare, stop, luffing

11 rowing, single-oar, single, fixed-seat, sweep (US), double-oar, double, quadruple, intercollegiate, coxed, coxswainless, recovering, feathering, finished, squared, squaring, balanced, balancing, diving, striking, paddling

12 canoeing, V-bottom, decked, paddled, single-bladed, double-bladed, double-ended, pushover, sweep, jamming, stopping

13 windsurfing, freestyle, pop-out, marginal, tandem, tridem, rotational, universal, wishbone, V-shape, downhaul, planing, sub-planing, hooked-in, pumping, off-the-lip

14 punting, one-arm, levered, pinched, running, reaching, trailing, C-shape, crossover, pole-body-foot

VERBS

15 sail, captain, skipper, crew, launch, cast off, shake, slip anchor, sail close-hauled, steer, sail close to the wind, harden up, luff up, reach, fetch, sail downwind, goosewing, go about, go astern, heel, careen, miss stays, rig, jury-rig, set a sail, furl a sail, roll a sail, reef a sail, back a sail, tighten, take up, let fly, maintain course, stand on, hitch, bear off (*or* away), bear down, turn head-to-wind, pitchpole, plane, tack, beat, broach to, slew, sail by the lee, run, sail on a run, close-haul, ease out a line, pay out, loose a rope, ride out a storm, lie a sailboat, fix a position, make a dead reckoning, gybe, duck gybe, clew gybe, slam gybe, scissor gybe, flare gybe, stop gybe, port tack, starboard tack, duck tack, clew tack, head up, sheet in, sheet out, wear, bring up, make fast, heave to, come to anchor, sound the depth, lay up a sailboat, splice ropes, quarter (of the wind)

16 row, cox, scull, race, skiff-race, stroke, catch, feather, recover, finish, square, balance, dive, strike, paddle, swing, slide, lift an oar, drop an oar, cover a blade, run level, clear the water, lurch, steer, catch a crab (Inf)

17 canoe, shoot the rapids, paddle, single paddle, double paddle, kayak, lock the blade, shake out

18 windsurf, boardsurf, free sail, sail, wavesail, ride a wave, wave-ride, jump a wave, wave-jump, ice surf, sailboard, cavatate, rail, spin out, wipe out, steer with the foot, plane, sub-plane, pump, hook in, tip the board

19 punt, double punt, shove, half-shove, run a punt, walk a punt, prick a punt, race a punt, punt-race, pole a canoe, climb the pole, lever, pinch, reach, stop up, throw, drop, recover, pick up, trail

ADVERBS

20 offshore, on the rail, on the nose, on the tail, inside the boom, back to sail, to leeward, about, astern, athwart, a-hull, aback, abaft, abeam, adrift, aloft, by the head, by the stern, by the lee, windward, on the quarter, broadside-on

INTERJECTIONS

21 avast!, belay!, paddle!, give her ten!, easy!, stroke!

51 Bowls

There is plenty of time to win this game, and to thrash the Spaniards too. Francis Drake.

NOUNS

1 green bowling, bowling, lawn bowls, bowls, level-green bowls, crown-green bowls, bowls match, singles match (*or* singles), pairs match (*or* pairs), triples match (*or* triples), three-on-a-side match, fours match (*or* fours), end, green, bowling green, slow green, fast green, bowling rink, boundary, backboard, ditch, bank, rolling the jack, wood, bowl, bias, jack, kitty, mat, bowling side, rink

2 grip, forehand grip, backhand grip, the claw, the palm, aiming point, delivery, smooth delivery, wobble, head, plant, weight, whip, shot, path, grass, green, backhand shot, controlled shot, yard-on, running shot, reaching shot, wrestling shot, upshot, onshot, run-through shot, trail shot, block shot, draw shot (*or* draw), drive, firing shot, cant, tilt, follow-through, front bowls, shot bowl, dead bowl, live bowl, dead jack, live jack, backwood bowl, backest bowl, toucher, wrestling toucher, chalk mark, hit, direct hit, dead end, burnt end (US), shots up, shots down, foot fault

3 bowls player, leader, second, third (*or* vice-skip), skip (*or* captain), marker, measurer, umpire

4 bowling, tenpin bowling (*or* tenpins), line of tenpins, game of tenpins, ninepins, skittles, duckpins (US), candlepins (US), frame, bowling lane, foul line, gutter, rear cushion, pit, 1–3 strike pocket, ball return, automatic pin-setter, rangefinder, bowling ball, bowling pin (*or* pin), head pin (*or* no. 1 pin), pin spot, bowling shoes, bowling bag

5 bowling delivery, four-step delivery, straight-line delivery, hook, curve, backup, follow-through, strike, spare, split, converted split, triple, turkey, error, gutter shot, gutter ball

6 bowler, tenpin bowler, professional bowler

VERBS

7 bowl, roll the jack, fire a shot, draw a shot, draw close to jack, go for the jack, go short and wide, lay a block, tilt the bowl, drive with the bowl, take more grass, take out

8 bowl, play a frame, release the ball, bowl a hook ball, knock down pins, make a strike, score a strike, score a spare, split, score a perfect game, score 300

ADJECTIVES

9 bowls, level-green, crown-green, singles, pairs, triples, three-on-a-side, fours, slow, fast, forehand, backhand, aiming, smooth, controlled, yard-on, running, reaching, wrestling, run-through, block, draw, firing, follow-through, front, dead, live, backest, jack-high, draw-weight

10 bowling, tenpin, foul, head, split, converted, gutter, four-step, straight-line, hooked, curved, backup, follow-through

52 Combat Sports and Martial Arts

Float like a butterfly
Sting like a bee. Muhammad Ali.

NOUNS

1 combat sports, combative sport, fighting sport, fighting skill, fighting, boxing, professional boxing, wrestling, professional wrestling, martial art, self-defence, judo, karate, tae kwon do, aikido

2 boxing, fighting, prizefighting, pugilism, noble art of self-defence, shadow boxing, fisticuffs, sparring, jabbing, socking, slugging, pummelling, boxing match, prizefight, fight, championship fight, fixed fight, throwing a fight, boxing purse, receipts, boxing rules, Marquess of Queensberry rules, point system, boxing ring, corner, ropes, bell, round, boxing gloves, boxing scorecard, decision, boxing shorts, mouthpiece, sparring helmet, boxing technique, stance, footwork, dancing, bobbing, bob, feinting, feint, parrying, parry, blocking, block, boxing punch, left jab, left hook, right hook, right cross, straight punch, straight left, left uppercut, right uppercut, swing, knockdown punch, knockdown, knockout punch, knockout (KO), count, technical knockout (TKO), foul, hitting below the belt, butting, butt, rabbit punch, boxing association, International Boxing Federation, European Boxing Union, World Boxing Association (WBA) (US), British Boxing Board of Control (BBBC)

3 boxing weight divisions, light-flyweight, flyweight, bantamweight, featherweight, junior-lightweight, lightweight, light-welterweight, welterweight, light-middleweight, middleweight, light-heavyweight, cruiserweight, heavyweight

4 boxer, professional boxer, amateur boxer, Olympic boxer, fighter, prizefighter, pugilist, flyweight, bantamweight, featherweight, welterweight, middleweight, cruiserweight, heavyweight, slugger, puncher, jabber, sparring partner, champion, heavyweight champion, world champion, titleholder, challenger, second, manager, trainer, referee, champ (Inf), southpaw (Inf), pug (Inf)

5 wrestling, professional wrestling, amateur wrestling, Graeco-Roman wrestling, Olympic wrestling, wrestling weight divisions, 106 pounds, 115 pounds, 126 pounds, 137 pounds, 150 pounds, 163 pounds, 181 pounds, 198 pounds, 220 pounds, 286 pounds, freestyle wrestling, all-in wrestling, catch-as-catch-can wrestling, no-holds-barred wrestling, tag-team wrestling, wrestle, grapple, wrestling match, round, wrestling ring, corner, rope, wrestling hold, full nelson, half-nelson, flying mare, headlock, armlock, body slam, fall, pin, illegal hold, choking, choke, strangling, stranglehold, kicking, kick, gouging, gouge, hair-pulling

6 wrestler, professional wrestler, amateur wrestler, Olympic wrestler, freestyle wrestler, Graeco-Roman wrestler, NCAA (National Collegiate Athletic Association) wrestler (US), grappler, referee, grunt-and-groaner (US inf)

7 **judo**, the way of gentleness, women's judo, junior judo, judo kata, judo grade, Kyu grade, 1st Kyu, brown belt, Dan grade, black belt, judo technique, nage-waza (throwing techniques), tachi-waza (standing), te-waza (hand), koshi-waza (hip), ashi-waza (foot and leg), sutemi-waza (sacrifice), katame-waza (groundwork), shime-waza (strangle), judo mat, judo club, dojo (practice hall), judo practitioner, judoist, judoka (judo player), tori (attacker), uka (defender), judo match, competition judo, judo referee, corner judge, timekeeper, recorder

8 **karate**, the way of the empty hand, sport karate, recreational karate, karate styles, Shotokan, Shukokai, Wado Kyu, Kyokushinkai, Shotokai, karate grade, Dan grade, beginner (red belt), 8th Kyu (white), 7th Kyu (yellow), 6th Kyu (orange), 5th Kyu (green), 4th–1st Kyu (brown), 3rd Dan (black), karate technique, jun-zuki (punching), gyaku-zuki (punching), kin-geri (kicking), mae-geri (kicking), mawashi-geri (kicking), yoko-geri (kicking), jodan-uke (blocking), gedan-barai (blocking), uchi-ude-uke (blocking), soto-ude-uke (blocking), karate mat, karate club, dojo (practice hall), karate expert, karate combatant, karate referee, judge, arbitrator, timekeeper, scorekeeper

9 **tae kwon do**, the way of the foot and fist, tae kwon do grade, 10th kup (white belt), 8th kup (yellow), 6th kup (green), 4th kup (blue), 2nd kup (red), 1st Dan (black), tae kwon do technique, lunge punch, reverse punch, jab, front kick, turning kick, side kick, back kick, axe kick, crescent kick, flying kick, flying back kick, flying reverse crescent kick, blocking techniques, evasion, block, deflection, blocking with wrist and hand, x-block, knife block, inner block, outer block, blocking kick, tae kwon do combinations, tae kwon do patterns, competitive tae kwon do, competitor, referee, judge, jury

10 **aikido**, the way of harmony of the spirit, aikido grade, 5th Kyu (yellow belt), 4th Kyu (orange), 3rd Kyu (green), 2nd Kyu (blue), 1st Kyu (brown), aikido technique, immobilization techniques, ikkyo, omote, ura, nikkyo, sankyo, yonkyo, aikido throws, shiho nage, kote gaeshi, irimi nage, tenchi nage, kaiten nage, techniques of the bokken (wooden practice sword), ken no kamae, ken suburi, kumi tachi, tachi dori, techniques of the aiki jo (wooden stave), jo suburi, jo kata, kumi jo, competition aikido, tori (thrower), uke (attacker)

VERBS

11 **fight**, box, spar, prizefight, practise self-defence, shadow box, engage in fisticuffs, fight as a heavyweight, land a blow, jab, sock, slug, stun, pummel, hold a boxing match, have a prizefight, fix a fight, throw a fight, enter the ring, go to one's corner, have someone on the ropes, save by the bell, box a round, dance about, bob, feint, parry, block, jab throw a left hook, swing, knock down, knock out, win by a TKO, foul, hit below the belt, butt, land a rabbit punch

12 **wrestle**, wrestle freestyle, grapple, hold a wrestling match, last a round, have a full nelson on, secure a fall, pin someone, pin someone's shoulders, choke, strangle, kick, gouge, pull hair

13 **practise judo**, earn a black belt, become a karate expert, practise tae kwon do, make a flying kick, deflect, block, make a blocking kick, use aikido techniques, immobilize

ADJECTIVES

14 **combat**, combative, fighting, professional, amateur, pugilistic, self-defensive, sparring, jabbed, jabbing, slugged, slugging, hit, hitting, knocked out, dancing, bobbing, feinting, parrying, blocking, mixing it up, left, right, straight, knockdown, knockout, light-flyweight, flyweight, bantamweight, featherweight, junior-lightweight, lightweight, light-welterweight, welterweight, light-middleweight, middleweight, light-heavyweight, cruiserweight, heavyweight, Olympic, champion, world champion

15 **wrestling**, freestyle, Graeco-Roman, all-in, catch-as-catch-can, tag-team, no-holds-barred, grunt-and-groan (US inf), judo, all-red, red-and-white, black, recreational, punching, kicking, blocking, crescent, competitive, immobilized, wooden

ADVERBS

16 **professionally**, competitively, in the ring, in self-defence, below the belt, squarely, on the nose, on the chin, for the count, freestyle, evasively

53 Cricket

I have always looked upon cricket as organised loafing. William Temple.

NOUNS

1 **cricket match**, test match, first-class cricket, county cricket, minor-counties cricket, league cricket, village cricket, limited-over match, innings, end of play, rain stopped play, match abandoned

2 **ground**, square, wicket, sight screen, scoreboard, pavilion, Lord's, the Oval, MCC (Marylebone Cricket Club)

3 **official**, umpire, square-leg umpire, scorer

4 **team**, side, eleven, cricketer, player, batting side, all-rounder, batter, batsman (*or* batswoman), opening batsman, opener, first wicket down, striker, runner, night watchman, fielding side, bowler, opening bowler, change bowler, fast bowler, pace bowler, medium-pace bowler, seam bowler, seamer, swing bowler, slow bowler, spin bowler, spinner, fieldsman, fielder, wicketkeeper, keeper, stumper, stumpie (Inf), the slips, slip, first slip, second slip, third slip, gully, square, point, silly point, mid on, silly mid on, third man, the covers, cover, long on, long off, mid off, square leg, deep square, leg slip, on-side fielder, off-side fielder, longstop

5 **wicket**, stump, bail, crease, popping crease, batting crease, sticky wicket, fast wicket, slow wicket, greentop

6 **pad**, glove, cap, helmet, faceguard, elbow protector, boot, box, whites, ducks

7 **bat**, willow, spline, ball, new ball, shine, old ball, seam, stitching, raised seam

8 **delivery**, fast delivery, pace, bounce, swing, lift, seamer, inswinger, outswinger, yorker, long hop, full toss, bodyline bowling, leg theory, leg trap, bouncer, donkey dropper, beamer, slow delivery, spin, flight, leg break, off break, googly, bosie, chinaman, flipper, shooter, cutter,

leg cutter, off cutter, daisycutter, over, no-ball, wide, maiden over, maiden, wicket maiden, hat trick, split hat trick

9 **stroke**, defensive stroke, block, stonewalling, attacking stroke, edge, snick, glide, leg glide, glance, leg glance, cut, square cut, drive, on drive, off drive, hook, sweep, reverse sweep

10 **score**, run, one, two, three, boundary, four, six, leg bye, bye, extra, no-ball, wide, overthrow, fifty, century, duck, pair, king pair, nelson

11 **dismissal**, bowling, catch, stumping, lbw (leg before wicket), obstruction, hit wicket, run out

ADJECTIVES

12 **cricketing**, fielding, batting, bowling, in, out

13 **bowling**, fast, pacey, slow, swing, off-break, leg-break, underarm, overarm

14 **positioned**, on, off, onside, offside, square, leg, mid, silly

VERBS

15 **play**, take the field, go in (to bat), end play, leave the field, draw stumps

16 **field**, keep wicket, change the field

17 **bat**, go out to the middle, take guard, take stance, receive, pad, pad up to, play, block, stonewall, edge, snick, guide, force, cut, square cut, drive, glide, glance, sweep, loft, hook, slog, knock the cover off, score

18 **bowl**, run in, swing, seam, york, bounce, cut, spin, turn, flight, polish, shine, pick the seam

19 **dismiss**, bowl, stump, run out, catch, appeal

ADVERBS

20 **in**, out, to leg, to off, on the up

INTERJECTIONS

21 **how's that!**, howzat!, owzat!

54 Fencing

NOUNS

1 **fencing**, foil fencing, épée fencing, sabre fencing, fencing bout, fencing assault, swordplay, *escrime* (Fr), *scherma* (It), duelling, historic fencing, singlestick, quarterstaff, cane, kendo, *Schläger-Mensur* (Ger), bayonet fencing, fencing area, piste, fencing association, Fédération Internationale d'Escrime (FIE)

2 **fencing equipment**, fencing weapon, foil, electrical foil, foil button, foil guard, foil grip, duelling sword, épée, electrical épée, épée prongs, sabre, blade, fencing clothes, wire-mesh mask, chest protector, sailcloth jacket, padded gloves, elbow guard, body cord

▶ *551 Dress; 587 Weapon*

3 **fencing movements**, on guard, *en garde* (Fr), attack, composite attack, straight thrust (*or* cut), lunge, bind, envelopment, jump, march, running attack, flèche, glide, cutover, *coupé* (Fr), line of attack, high-outside, high-inside, low-outside, low-inside, parry, composite parry, redoublement, disengage, false attack, feint, counter (*or* circular) parry, semicircle, *mezzocerchio* (It), beat, counterattack, riposte (*or* ripost), counter-riposte (*or* counter-ripost), stop thrust, remise, time thrust (*or* cut), closing in, *corps à corps* (Fr), clinch, guard, first guard (*or* parry), second guard (*or* parry), third guard (*or* parry), fourth guard (*or* parry), fifth guard (*or* parry), sixth guard (*or* parry), seventh guard (*or* parry), eighth guard (*or* parry), pronation, supination, hit, touch

▶ *381 Attack; 384 Defence; 385 Retaliation*

4 **fencer**, foilsman, épéeist, dueller (*or* duellist)

▶ *586 Combatant*

VERBS

5 **fence**, duel, foil-fence, épée-fence, sabre-fence, bayonet-fence, have a fencing bout, swordplay, be on guard, attack, have a line of attack, thrust, make a straight thrust, lunge, recover from the lunge, recover, make a false attack, use footwork, jump forward, march, make a running attack, glide, parry, avoid a parry, block an attack, feint, make a feint, counterattack, disengage, riposte (*or* ripost), clinch, guard, hit, touch, pronate, supinate

ADJECTIVES

6 **fencing**, foil, épée, sabre, electrical, padded, wire-mesh, attacking, lunging, running, cutover, high-outside, high-inside, low-outside, low-inside, parried, parrying, disengaged, false, feinting, countered, countering, composite, counterattacking, pronated, supinated

ADVERBS

7 **on guard**, with swordplay, with footwork, by parrying, by counterattacking, high-outside, high-inside, low-outside, low-inside

55 Fishing

Fly fishing may be a very pleasant amusement; but angling or float fishing I can only compare to a stick and a string, with a worm at one end and a fool at the other. Samuel Johnson.

Angling is somewhat like poetry, men are to be born so. Izaak Walton.

NOUNS

1 **angling**, fishing, game fishing, still fishing, bait fishing, fishing with bait, freshwater bait fishing, trolling, float fishing, trotting, ledgering, coarse (*or* bottom) fishing, casting, spinning, bait casting (US), spin-casting (US), fly-fishing, dapping, natural fly-fishing, natural fly, mayfly, artificial fly-fishing, wet-fly fishing, dry-fly fishing, fishing the water, fishing to the rise, bait, worm, insect, minnow, maggot, bread, ground bait, rubby-dubby, chum (US), catch, bite, strike, take, ice fishing, ice hole, ice bar, ice spoon, surf fishing, beach-casting, saltwater fishing, saltwater bait fishing, saltwater trolling, deep-sea fishing, deep-sea trolling, strip-casting, mooching, big-game fishing, fighting seat, turntable chair, chair socket, harness, throwout level, braided line, sea swivel, competitive fishing, competitive casting, tournament casting, skish, distance event, accuracy event, American Casting Association, International Casting Federation, match fishing, National Anglers Council

2 **artificial fly**, tied fly, dressed fly, lure, artificial lure, jig, streamer, plug, surface plug, floating plug, floating diver, popper, underwater plug, sinking plug, deep diver, jointed plugs, spoon, fly spoon, barspoon, spinner, wagtail, mackerel spinner, artificial minnow, Devon minnow

3 **fishing tackle**, fishing rod (*or* rod), double-handed rod,

single-handed rod, telescopic rod, float rod, ledger rod, spinning rod, fishing pole (*or* pole), bamboo pole, fly rod, casting rod, handgrip, butt guide, ferrule, tip top, reel, centre-pin reel, single-action reel, multiplier reel, fixed-spool (*or* spinning) reel, closed-face (*or* spin-casting) reel, open-face reel, float tackle, float, line, nylon line, sunk line, bobber, sinker, lead sinker, lead, coffin lead, barleycorn lead, plummet lead, fish-hook (*or* hook), eye, shank, bend, point, double hook, treble hook, shot, split-shot, gaff, cork, bobbin, keepnet, forcep, disgorger

4 **American game fish**, salmon, Atlantic salmon, Pacific salmon, chinook salmon, silver salmon, trout, lake trout, brook trout (*or* speckled trout), rainbow trout, smallmouth black bass, largemouth black bass, yellow perch, northern pike, muskellunge, walleye, arctic char, sailfish, marlin, blue marlin, swordfish, tuna, tarpon, bonefish, striped bass, bluefish, yellowtail, channel bass, snook, bonito, flounder, sea trout, barracuda, snapper, shark, mackerel, Spanish mackerel

5 **British game fish**, salmon, trout, sea trout, pike, perch, roach, rudd, chub, carp, barbel, tench, bream, eel, grayling, European sea bass, mackerel, grey mullet, skate, plaice, pollack, blue shark, conger eel

6 **angler**, compleat angler, fisher, fly-fisher, fisherman, saltwater fisherman, sea angler, big-game fisherman, deep-sea fisherman, trawlerman (*or* trawler)

VERBS

7 **angle**, cast, spin-cast, fish, fish the water, fish with bait, fish to the rise, fish with a rod, fish with a pole, fly-fish, entangle one's line, use bait, bait the hook, anchor bait, cast bait, cast a lure, cock the float, pump a fish, watch the float, catch fish, have a bite, hook, reel in, haul in, net, tie a fly, dress a fly, troll, ice fish, deep-sea fish

ADJECTIVES

8 **angling**, fishing, fished, piscatorial (*or* piscatory), coarse, bottom, wet-fly, dry-fly, ground, baited, baiting, casting, cast, trolling, trolled, tied, dressed, artificial, natural, sinking, jointed, double-handed, single-handed, single-action, centre-pin, fixed-spool, spinning, closed-face, open-face

ADVERBS

9 **on the water**, on the surface, by casting, by trolling, underwater, naturally, artificially, piscatorially, competitively

56 Golf

Golf may be played on Sunday, not being a game within the view of the law, but being a form of moral effort. Stephen Leacock.

Golf is a good walk spoiled. Mark Twain.

NOUNS

1 **golf**, golfing, golf game, game of golf, golf match, stroke play, medal play, match play, best-ball match, single, threesome, three-ball match, foursome, four-ball match, mixed foursome, golf course, eighteen-hole course, nine-hole course, links, teeing ground, fairway, through the green, approach, pitch-and-run approach, pitch, loose impediments, obstruction, bunker, face, water hazard, lateral water hazard, casual water, sand trap, rough, blind, green, putting green, bent grass, hole, dogleg hole, rub of the green, out of bounds, ground under repair, golf bodies, the Royal and Ancient Golf Club (R and A), Professional Golfers Association (PGA), the United States Golf Association (USGA), United States Professional Golfers Association (USPGA), major championships, the Grand Slam, the (British) Open, the US Open, the Masters, the US PGA, major golf courses, St Andrews', Augusta

2 **golfing terms**, golf ball, dead ball, tee, hole, cup, flag, flagstick, pin, lie of the ball, hole-high ball, hanging ball, divot, par, bogey, birdie, eagle, albatross, score card, Nassau scoring, defaulted match, odd, gross score, net score, handicap score, handicap, halved hole, conceded hole, stroke play, like stroke, square match, all square match, up side, down side, dormie side, bye holes, golf rules, honour system, "Fore!", nineteenth hole

3 **golf shots**, wood shot, iron shot, approaching shot, sand shot, putting, addressing the ball, grounding the club, downswing, backswing, upswing, follow-through, teeing off, driving off, honour, pivot, stance, stroke, carry, line, penalty stroke, handicap stroke, bisque, long game, lofted shot, recovery shot, bunker shot, putt, spot putt, curve putt, gobble, pull, slice, fade, hook, draw, dubbed shot, sclaff, chip, backspin, sidespin, ace, hole in one, hole out

4 **golf club**, wood club, wood, driver, brassie, spoon, baffy, iron club, iron, driving iron, cleek, midiron, mid mashie, mashie iron, mashie, spade mashie, spade, mashie niblick, pitching niblick, niblick, wedge, putter, golf club part, cap, grip, shaft, hosel, neck, face, head, heel, sole, toe

5 **golf ball**, feather ball, special, Gourlay, guttapercha ball, gutta, OK, Clan, Agrippa, Heley, White Brand, A1, bouncing billy

6 **golfer**, linksman, scratch player, caddie, outside agency, referee, marker, forecaddie, observer, duffer (Inf), dub (US inf)

VERBS

7 **golf**, play golf, have a foursome, tee off, drive, pitch, putt, spot putt, use backspin, pull, slice, fade, hook, chip, sclaff, recover, shoot par, have a birdie, have a bogey, shoot an eagle, hole, ace, have a hole in one, have a penalty stroke, concede a hole, sign one's score card

57 Gymnastics

O, he flies through the air with the greatest of ease,
This daring young man on the flying trapeze. George Leybourne.

NOUNS

1 **gymnastics**, Swedish gymnastics, free exercises, rhythmic gymnastics, artistic gymnastics, German gymnastics, strength exercises, balancing exercises, competitive gymnastics, Olympic gymnastics, gold medal, silver medal, bronze medal, prescribed exercise, optional exercise, gymnastic routine, gymnastic scoring, fluency,

correctness, execution, difficulty, originality, gymnasium (*or* gym)

▶ *300 Motion; 336 Strength*

2 **gymnastic clothing**, leotard, tracksuit, wrist bandage, handstrap, gymnastic (*or* gym) shoes, training shoes (*or* trainers), sneakers (US)

▶ *551 Dress; 553 Fashion*

3 **gymnastic apparatus**, gymnastic mat, springboard, horizontal bar, parallel bars, horse, rings

4 **gymnastic organization**, gymnastics club, gymnastics association, Amateur Athletic Union of the United States (AUU), British Amateur Gymnastics Association, Fédération Internationale de Gymnastique

5 **horizontal bar**, parallel bars, balance, steel poles, guy wires, swinging, swing, backward swing, vaulting, vault, turn, full turn, pirouette, upstarts, back and front, giant circles, handstand position, handstand, inverted grip, dislocated grip, changed grip, straddle, forward somersault, backward somersault, finish, landing

6 **pommel horse**, side horse, pommel, saddle, neck, croup, single-leg circle, double-leg circle, scissors, turn, Moore turn, vaulting (*or* long) horse, vault, elastic board, springboard, run, rebound, straddled-leg vault, squatting vault, stooping vault, handspring, pivot cartwheel, giant cartwheel vault, beam, balance beam, vaulting, jump, jumping, turning, sitting, lying, steps, running, held position, scale, front scale, horizontal scale

7 **stationary rings**, strap, handstand, lever, upstart, forward upstart, backward upstart, uprise, forward uprise, backward uprise, cross, cross hang, hang, straight hang, inverted hang, L position, dislocate circle, forward dislocate circle, backward dislocate circle, uneven parallel bars, swinging, swing, balance movement, cross handstand

8 **floor exercises**, callisthenics, canvas, movement, combined movement, tumbling, handspring, cartwheel, somersault, forward somersault, backward somersault, halfturn, round-off, jump, jumping, holding, splits, backbend, balance, rhythm, harmony

9 **gymnasts**, competitive gymnast, all-round gymnast, vaulter, gymnastics judge, gymnastics coach

VERBS

10 **compete in gymnastics**, exercise, do a prescribed exercise, do an optional exercise, perform a gymnastic routine, execute a gymnastic movement, swing on the horizontal bar, pirouette, do a handstand, somersault, perform a somersault, finish, land, balance, vault, do a cartwheel vault, rebound, jump, turn, sit, lie, hold a position, hang, hold, hold the L position, perform a combined movement, tumble, do a handspring, do a backward somersault, round-off, do the splits

ADJECTIVES

11 **gymnastic**, Swedish, free, rhythmic, artistic, German, balancing, competitive, Olympic, prescribed, optional, training, horizontal, parallel, inverted, dislocated, forward, backward, single-leg, double-leg, vaulting, long, straddled-leg, squatting, stooping, turning, stationary, cross, combined, all-around

ADVERBS

12 **competitively**, optionally, correctly, with balance, forwards, backwards, with rhythm, in the L position

58 Hockey, Ice Hockey, and Lacrosse

NOUNS

1 **hockey**, field hockey (US), indoor hockey, Olympic hockey, hockey stick, hockey ball, goal, striking circle, shooting circle, penalty spot, hockey technique, stroke, push stroke, pushing, flick stroke, flicking, scoop stroke, scooping, pass, passing, dribble, dribbling, strike, striking, push-in, hit-in, hitting, passing back, pass-back, penalty plays, hook, hooking, hold, holding, interference, high-sticking, tripping, charging, penalty award, penalty corner, corner, penalty stroke, free hit, hockey clothing, goalkeeper's protective clothing, shin guard, glove, pads, abdominal protector, helmet, hockey association, Fédération Internationale de Hockey (FIH), International Hockey Board, All England Women's Hockey Association (AEWHA)

2 **hockey player**, striker, forward, centre forward, back, halfback, centre half, wing half, fullback, goalkeeper, goaltender, goalie (Inf)

▶ *586 Combatant*

3 **ice hockey**, ice hockey stick, hockey stick, left stick, right stick, neutral stick, goalkeeper's stick, ice hockey skates, goal, puck, ice rink, rink, barrier board, sideboards, endboards, red goal line, goal crease, blue line, centre line, centre spot, face-off circle, red face-off spot, zone, defence zone, neutral zone, centre zone, attacking zone, slot, face-off, point, ice hockey tactics, carrying the puck, rushing the puck, puck possession, stealing the puck, triangular offence, three-man combination attack, two-one-two system, power play, check, checking, stickchecking, stickcheck, forechecking, forecheck, pokechecking, pokecheck, assisting, assist, passing, pass, drop-passing, drop pass, headmanning the puck, drawing, draw, faking, fake, deke, backchecking, backcheck, backhand shot, breakout play, peel-off, give and go, man-to-man assignment, one-on-one assignment, screening, dribbling, dribble, delayed dribbling, delayed dribble, playing short-handed, dead puck, goal, garbage goal, pulling the goalie, penalty plays, offsides, offside pass, icing, charging, bodychecking, boarding, cross-checking, kneeing, elbowing, highsticking, holding, roughing, hooking, tripping, spearing, slashing, butt-ending, interference, fighting, penalty award, five-minute penalty, penalty shot, misconduct penalty, ten-minute penalty, abusive language, penalty box, ice hockey clothing, knee pad, elbow pad, shin guard, protective shoulder, pad, padded glove, helmet, goalkeeper's protective clothing, catching glove, stick glove, face-mask, leather leg-guard, shoulder-guard, arm-guard, chest protector, ice hockey association, International Ice Hockey Federation, professional ice hockey, professional team, National Hockey League (NHL) (US), Stanley Cup, sin-bin (Inf)

4 **ice hockey player**, hockey player, forward, centre, winger, left wing, right wing, defender, left defence, right defence, linesman, forechecker, backchecker, puck-carrier, goalminder, goalkeeper, goaltender, goalie (Inf)

5 **lacrosse**, lacrosse stick, crosse, lacrosse ball, helmet, faceguard, shoulder pad, arm pad, glove, goal, goal crease, goal area, wing area, centre line, lacrosse tech-

niques, passing, bodychecking, facing the ball, penalty play, offside, interference, throwing the crosse, entering the crease area, foul, technical foul, personal foul, tripping, pushing, slashing, illegal bodycheck, unnecessary roughness, penalty award, free play, free position, thirty-second suspension, one-minute suspension, three-minute suspension, loss of ball, lacrosse association, United States Intercollegiate Lacrosse Association, United States Women's Lacrosse Association

6 **lacrosse player**, attack player, midfield player, defence player, point, cover point, first defence, right wing, centre, left wing, first attack, inside home, outside home, referee, judge

7 **hurling**, *iomáin* (Gael), Irish hockey, hurling stick, hurley, *camán* (Gael), hurling ball, *sliotar* (Gael), boss, goal, crossbar, hurling association, Gaelic Athletic Association, shinty, *camanachd* (Gael), Scottish hockey, shinty stick, *camán* (Gael)

ADJECTIVES

8 **hockey**, field, indoor, Olympic, pushed, flicked, scooped, passed, dribbled, struck, push-in, hit-in, pass-back, hooked, hooking, held, holding, interfered, interfering, tripped, tripping, charged, face-off, two-one-two, checked, checking, assisting, drop-passing, headmanning, drawn, faked, deked, deking, crosschecked, crosschecking, bodychecked, bodychecking, boarded, boarding, backchecked, backchecking, backhand, breakout, peel-off, man-to-man, one-on-one, screened, screening, short-handed, dead, garbage, offside, iced, icing, kneed, kneeing, elbowed, elbowing, highsticked, highsticking, roughed, roughing, speared, spearing, slashed, slashing, butt-ended, butt-ending

VERBS

9 **play hockey**, play field hockey (US), stroke, push, flick, scoop, pass, pass back, dribble, strike, push in, hit in, hit, draw a penalty, hook, hold, interfere, highstick, trip, charge, hit from the penalty corner, have a corner, face-off, hit the puck, carry the puck, rush the puck, keep possession of the puck, steal the puck, check, stickcheck, forecheck, pokecheck, assist, drop-pass, headman, draw, fake, deke, backcheck, peel off, give and go, go one-on-one, screen, pull the goalie out, go offsides, ice the puck, bodycheck, board, crosscheck, knee, elbow, rough, spear, slash, butt end, fight, face the ball, throw the crosse, foul, draw a technical foul, draw a personal foul, lose the ball

ADVERBS

10 **on the field**, defensively, roughly, in the crease area

59 Horse Riding and Racing

They say princes learn no art truly, but the art of horsemanship. The reason is, the brave beast is no flatterer. He will throw a prince as soon as his groom. Ben Jonson.

NOUNS

1 **horse**, equine species, quadruped, horseflesh, dobbin, pony, mount, steed, trusty steed, stallion, gelding, mare, sire, dam, foal, colt, yearling, filly, wild horse, untamed horse, bronco, brumby (Aus), outlaw, trail horse, range horse, winter horse, untrainable horse, horse lacking quality, unsound horse, nag, jade, hack, old horse, Rosinante, plug (US), studhorse, stud, brood mare, stable horse, packhorse, beast of burden, circus horse, liberty horse, roan, strawberry roan, grey, dapple-grey, bay, chestnut, sorrel, black, piebald, skewbald, pinto, mustang, dun, bayo coyote, bangtail, quarter horse, Indian horse, cayuse, palomino, cob, montura, hackney, hunter, light horse, winged horse, Pegasus, legendary horse, Al Borak, Bayard, Black Bess, Houyhnhnm, fictional horse, Black Beauty, film horse, Trigger, Champion, Silver, Velvet, gee-gee (Inf), owlhead (Inf), skate (Inf), screw (Inf)

► *71 Mammals*

2 **thoroughbred**, purebred, bloodstock, English thoroughbred, blood-horse, pacer, stepper, high-stepper, trotter, courser, racehorse, racer, goer, stayer, sprinter, speeder, steeplechaser, hurdler, fencer, jumper, hunter, fox-hunter, draught horse, plough horse, carthorse, drayhorse, shaft horse, trace horse, carriage horse, coach horse, post horse, pit pony, punch, hackney

3 **warhorse**, cavalry horse, charger, courser, steed, remount, destrier (Lit), Bucephalus, Copenhagen, Marengo

4 **saddle horse**, riding horse, cow pony, (cow-)cutting horse, mustang, bronco, stockhorse (Aus), mount, roadster, ambler, jennet, palfrey (Lit), hack, jade, nag, pad (Dial), pad-nag (Dial)

5 **pony**, cob, galloway, garron, sheltie, fell pony, dell pony, polo pony, riding pony

6 **horsemanship**, horsewomanship, equitation, equestrianism, riding, horse riding, classical riding, *haute école* (Fr), high school, manège, dressage, horse show, showjumping, eventing, gymkhana, racing, horseracing, steeplechasing, point-to-point racing, polo, bareback riding, pony trekking

► *485 Skill*

7 **horseracing**, racing, sport of kings, flat racing, steeplechasing, hurdle racing, two-horse race, walkover, maiden race, race meeting, meet, mixed meeting, post, start, finish, form, handicap, penalty, odds, evens, price, betting, antepost betting, bet, totalizator, perfecta, exacta, win, place, show (US), each-way bet, double, dividend, weight allowance, weight cloth, weights, weigh in, the field, entry, runner, scratch, favourite, co-favourite, odds-on bet, certainty, dark horse, outsider, maiden, sprinter, stayer, mudder (US), pacemaker, also-ran, starter's orders, dead heat, photo finish, objection, weigh out, winner's enclosure, turf, the Turf, racecourse, racing track, dirt track, bush track (US), training tracks (Aus), weighing room, paddock, English Classics, the Derby, the Oaks, the 1,000 Guineas, the 2,000 Guineas, the St Leger, American Triple Crown, Kentucky Derby, Preakness, Belmont Stakes, race card, silks, point-to-point racing, steeplechase, National Hunt racing, Grand National, Maryland Hunt Cup (US), hurdles, fences, jumps, sticks, leap, the Jockey Club, tote(Inf), sure thing (Inf), sleeper (US inf), ringer (US inf)

► *107 Chance; 300 Motion*

8 **hunting**, hunt, fox-hunting, fox hunt, meet, lawn meet, opening meet, hunter trials, hunter, scent, draghunt, drag, hound, foxhound, foxdog, draghound, hunt terrier,

BREEDS OF HORSE AND PONY

Akhal Teke
Albino
Alter–Réal
American quarter horse
American saddle horse
American Shetland pony
American thoroughbred
Andalusian
Anglo–Arab
Anglo–Kabardin
Anglo–Norman
Anglo–Persian
Appaloosa
Arab
Ardennes (*or* Ardennais)
Assateague
Australian pony
Auxois
Avelignese
Balearic
Bali pony
Barb
Barbary
Bashkirsky
Basuto
Batak
Bavarian Warmblood
Belgian Ardennes
Belgian Heavy Draught, Brabant
Bhutia
Bokhara
Bosnian
Boulonnais
Brabant, Belgian Heavy Draught
Brandenburg
Breton
Breton Heavy Draught
Brumby
Budyonny
Burma pony, Shan
Calabrese
Camargue
Campolino
Canadian Cutting Horse
Carthusian
Caspian
Charollais Half–bred
Charro
Chincoteague
Cleveland Bay
Clydesdale
Comtois
Connemara
Corlay
Corsican pony
Criollo
Crioulu Braziliero
Curraleiro
Dales pony
Danubian
Dartmoor pony
Demi–Sang, French Trotter
Dølehest
Don
Dongola
Dosanko
Dülmen
Dutch Draught
Dutch Warmblood
East Bulgarian
East Friesian
Einsiedler
Exmoor pony
Falabella
Faxaflói
Fell
Finnish Horse
Fjord
Frederiksborg
Freiberger
French Saddle Horse
French Trotter, Demi–Sang
Friesian
Furioso
Galiceño
Garranos, Minho
Gayoe
Gelderland
German Trotter
Gidran
Groningen
Guarapuavano
Hackney
Hackney pony
Haflinger
Hanoverian
Highland pony
Hispano Arab
Holstein
Huçul
Hunter
Iceland Pony
Iomud
Irish Draught
Irish Hunter
Isabella
Italian Heavy Draught
Jutland
Kabardin
Karabair
Karabakh
Karadagh
Kathiawari
Kazakh
Kiso
Kladrub
Knabstrup
Kustanair
Landais Pony
Latvian Harness Horse
Limousin Half–bred
Lippizaner
Lithuanian Heavy Draught
Llanero
Lokai
Lundy Island
Lusitano
Mangalarga
Manipur pony
Maremmana, Maremma
Marwari
Masuren
Mecklenburg
Mérens pony
Métis Trotter
Mierzyn
Mimoseano
Minho, Garranos
Morgan
Muraköz
Murgese
Mustang
Nanfan, Tibetan Pony
New Forest pony
New Kirgiz, Novokirghiz
Nonius
Norfold Roadster
Norman
Northlands Pony
North Swedish
Norwegian Racing Trotter
Novokirghiz, New Kirgiz
Oldenburg
Orlov Trotter
Pahlavan
Palomino
Partbred Arabian
Paso Fino
Pechorsky
Percheron
Persian Arab
Peruvian Stepping Horse
Pinkafelder
Pinto
Pinzgauer Noriker
Plateau Persian
Pleven
Poitevin
Polo Pony
Pony of the Americas
Przevalski's Horse
Quarter Horse
Rhineland Heavy Draught
Rottaler
Russ
Russian Heavy Draught
Russian Trotter
Sable Island
Saddlebred
Salerno
Sandalwood Pony
Sardinian
Schleswig
Schwarzwald Heavy Horse
Sertanejo
Shagya
Shan, Belgian pony
Shetland pony
Shire Horse
Skyros pony
Sorraia
Soviet Heavy Draught
Spiti
Standardbred
Suffold Punch
Swedish Half–bred
Swedish Warmblood
Tarpan
Tartar Pony
Tchenaran
Tennessee Walking Horse
Tersky
Thessalian
Thoroughbred
Tibetan Pony, Nanfan
Timor
Toric
Trait du Nord
Trakehner
Turkoman
Viatka
Vladimir Heavy Draught
Voronezh Harness Horse
Waler
Welsh Cob
Welsh Mountain Pony
Welsh Pony
Wielkopolski
Windsor Grey
Württemberg
Yakut
Zemaituka

fox, Charley, cry, halloa, baying, tongue, music, hunt master, stale line, country, earth, hunting horn, hunt livery, hunting cap, stock, hunt button, stag hunting, hare hunting

▶ *382 Killing; 633 Pursuit*

9 jumping, showjumping, show arena, course, circuit, jumping lane, fence, straight fence, spread fence, gate, wall, parallel bars, triple bar, planks, post and rails, hog's back, water jump, wing, obstacle, combination obstacle, double, treble, clear round, fault, refusal, time allowed, time limit, against-the-clock competition, jump-off, shying, running out, barrage, international show jumping, Prix des Nations

▶ *366 Raising; 378 Obstruction*

10 dressage, dressage movement, quadrille, passage, piaffe, pirouette, caracole, curvet, renvers, travers, volte, half volte, serpenting, two track, turn on the forehand, gait, freestyle, kur, Lippizaner stallion, Spanish Riding School, habit

11 eventing, three-day event, one-day event, course, cross-country, circuit, fence, straight fence, parallel bars, dressage, speed and endurance, showjumping, Badminton, Burghley, Hickstead, Pan-American Three-Day Event (US)

▶ *366 Raising*

12 rodeo, standard event, calf-roping, saddle-bronc-riding, bareback-(bronc-)riding, bull-riding, steer-wrestling, bull-dogging, barrel-racing, camp-drafting (Aus), All-Around Champion, All-Around Cow Horse, cow horse, calf horse, rope horse, Cheyenne Frontier Days, Pendleton Round Up, Denver Stock Show, Oklahoma City All-American Finals, ground money, mount money

13 breeding, conformation, pedigree, bloodline, dam, sire, stud, studbook, bred horse, blooded horse, purebred, Orientale, Anglais, thoroughbred

14 horse-riding terms, riding school, horse box, horsecloth, horsehair, horseshoe, horsewhip, horse-trading, grooming, grooming kit, currycomb, tack, reins, bit, blinkers, bridle, noseband, neckstrap, cavesson (US), numnah (*or* numdah), tail guard, sweat scraper, saddle, American saddle, English saddle, racing saddle, side saddle, stock saddle (Aus), farriery, livery stable, mucking out, skepping out, stable management, pancake (Inf)

15 horse person, breeder, owner, rider, horse rider, horseman (*or* horsewoman), equestrian, equestrienne, postilion, postboy, courier, mounted police, mounted troops, mounted rifles, cavalry regiment, horse, light horse, horse artillery, horse soldier, cavalryman, yeoman, trooper, sowar, hussar, lancer, dragoon, light dragoon, heavy dragoon, Ironsides, Cossack, rough-rider, chivalry, cavalier, knight, knight errant, hunt, hunt master, joint-master, huntsman, hunter, hunt secretary, hunt servant, whipper-in, kennel huntsman, kennel man, racing steward, jockey, jump jockey, steeplechaser, bookmaker, turf accountant, tipster, better, punter, showjumper, eventer, trainer, breaker, rough-rider, bareback rider, broncobuster, buckaroo, cowboy, cowgirl, cowpuncher, rep, drover (Aus), gaucho, rodeo rider, saddler, black saddler, loriner, farrier, blacksmith, vet, veterinarian, horse doctor, ostler (Lit), groom, stud groom, stableboy, stable lad, Mountie (*or* Mounty) (Inf), jockette (Inf), bookie (Inf)

▶ *586 Combatant; 633 Pursuit*

VERBS

16 ride, ride bareback, ride side-saddle, saddle, mount, trot, canter, gallop, break in, train, race, steeplechase, hunt, jump, groom, curry, muck out

ADJECTIVES

17 equine, equestrian, cross-country, mounted, thoroughbred, purebred

60 Hunting and Shooting

Detested sport,
That owes its pleasures to another's pain. William Cowper.

Hunting people tend to be church-goers on a higher level than ordinary folk. One has a religious experience in the field. Christopher Seal.

NOUNS

1 target shooting, pistol shooting, rifle shooting, air-rifle shooting, air-pistol shooting, clay pigeon shooting, skeet shooting, trapshooting

2 hunting, game shooting, shoot, field sports, gunning, small-game hunting, hunt, rough shooting, grouse shooting, pheasant shooting, waterfowl shooting, rabbit hunting, squirrel hunting, duck hunting, hare hunting, beagling, big-game hunting, bear hunting, bear hunt, deer hunting, deer hunt, stag hunting, stag hunt, tracking, stalking, woodland stalking, deerstalking, still hunting (US), night lamping, killing, culling, driving, beating, dogging, sitting, calling, sighting-in, shooting party, hunting party (US), hunting season, open season, closed season, hunting limit, bag limit, field trial, hunting lodge, shooting box (*or* lodge), game licence, hunting licence (US), shooting association, hunting association (US), The British Association for Shooting and Conservation (BASC), The British Field Sports Society, The National Rifle Association (US), Ducks Unlimited (US), hunting at force (Lit)

▶ *382 Killing; 633 Pursuit*

3 hunting equipment, sporting rifle, hunting rifle (US), high-powered rifle, level-action rifle, bolt-action rifle, auto-loading rifle, single-shot rifle, .22 rimfire rifle, .22 centrefire rifle, shotgun, ammunition round, ammunition, shooting kit, hunting accessories, decoy, telescopic sight, knife, scope sight, shooting stick, stalking stick, binoculars, rifle sling, hunting clothes, hunting jacket, hunting boots

▶ *551 Dress; 587 Weapon*

4 hunter, huntress, shooter, sportsman, sportswoman, sportsperson, deer hunter, duck hunter, big-game hunter, dogger (Aus), stalker, deerstalker, tracker, beater, poacher, Diana, Nimrod

5 game, quarry, prey, beast of prey, small game, big game, deer, red deer, American elk, moose, antelope, caribou, bear, mountain lion, wild boar, rabbit, game birds, ring-necked pheasant, grouse, partridge, quail, duck, goose, turkey

▶ *71 Mammals; 72 Birds*

6 sporting dog, hunting dog, gundog, pointer, English setter, Brittany spaniel, German short-haired pointer, Irish setter, English springer, retriever, golden retriever, flatcoat retriever, Labrador, Chesapeake Bay retriever, Irish water spaniel, American water spaniel

▶ *71 Mammals*

VERBS

7 shoot, go shooting, hunt, go hunting, hunt for, go big-game hunting, stalk, deer-stalk, track, trail, follow the scent, scent out, dog, kill, cull, drive, beat, flush, poach, join a shooting party, sight quarry, scent game, point, retrieve, aim at, draw a bead on, sight in, zero (a rifle), fire (at), pull the trigger, squeeze the trigger

ADJECTIVES

8 shooting, hunting, tracking, stalking, killed, culled, high-powered, level-action, single-shot, auto-loading

ADVERBS

9 on the trail, on the track, on the scent, hot on the trail, in hot pursuit

61 Motor Racing

There's no secret. You just press the accelerator to the floor and steer left. Bill Vukovich.

NOUNS

1 motor racing, auto (*or* automobile) racing (US), motor sport, sports car racing, road racing, endurance racing, speedway racing, international racing, Grand Prix Formula One Class, Formula 1 (F1) racing, Grand Prix (GP) racing, Grand Prix World Championship, World Championship points, points table, Formula Super Vee racing, Formula 2 (F2) racing, Formula 3, Formula 3000, Formula Vauxhall Lotus, IndyCar racing, production car racing, stock-car racing, drag racing, midget-car racing, hot-rod racing, rallying, hill climbing, karting, Go-Karting™, vintage-car racing, racetrack, raceway, race, motor race, automobile race (US), road race, sports-car race, speedway race, stock-car race, drag race, midget-car race, hot-rod race, Formula 1 race, Grand Prix race, hill climb, Pikes Peak climb, motor rally, automobile rally (US), Monte Carlo rally, East African Safari rally, endurance event, maximum-speed event, maximum-acceleration event, sprint, motor trial, automobile trial (US), reliability trial, Scottish Six-Days trial, grasstrack racing, autocross, Formula 1 car, F1 car, Grand Prix car, racing tyre, racing circuit, banger racing (Inf)

► *300 Motion*

2 **Formula 1 race**, Grand Prix (GP), *grandes épreuves* (Fr), United States GP at Phoenix, Brazilian GP at Interlagos, San Marino GP at Imola, Italy, Monaco GP at Monte Carlo, Mexican GP at Mexico City, Canadian GP at Montreal, French GP at Bandol, British GP at Silverstone, German GP at Hockenheim, Hungarian GP at Hungaroring, Belgian GP at Spa Francorchamps, Italian GP at Monza, Portuguese GP at Estoril, Spanish GP at Jerez, Japanese GP at Suzuka, Australian GP at Adelaide

3 **sports-car race**, Le Mans 24-hour race, Sebring 12-hour race, Monza 1,000 kilometres, Targa Florio

4 **motor rally**, Monte Carlo, East African Safari, the Alpine, the Acropolis, the San Remo Rally of the Flowers, the Swedish Midnight Sun, the Netherlands' Tulip Rally

5 **motorcycle racing**, motorbike racing, dirt-track racing, motocross, rally cross, scrambling, dirt-track race, motorcycle race, motorbike race, Grand Prix (GP) race, Race of the Year, 500 Italian Grand Prix, Daytona 200, TT (Tourist Trophy) race, Isle of Man TT, Dutch TT, Gran Premio de Barcelona, Macau Grand Prix, motorcycle class, 50 cc, 125 cc, 250 cc, 350 cc (junior), 500 cc (senior), 750 cc, unlimited class, sidecar class, motorcycle, motorbike, superbike, six-wheeler

6 **motor-racing terms**, grid, pole position, scrambling, roughriding, ride height, tyre stagger, active(-ride) suspension system, passive suspension system, setup, slipstreaming, sliding off, hooking off, clipping, jetting, hacking, gearing, bottom gear, clutch-slip, changing down, cranking over, peeling off, tucking in, spinning out, spin-out, spoiling, straight-lining, T-boning, run-and-bump tactic, outbraking, sweeping, funnelling, mixed set, ground clearance, wheelie, carburation, powerband, down-force, G-force loading, track, road circuit, circuit, oval, long circuit, short circuit, banked circuit, mountain circuit, ripple, apex, lap, flying lap, starting grid, start, warm-up lap, restart, pit, pit lane, pit wall, pit stop, fuel stop, *parc fermé* (Fr), straight, six-gear straight, corner, off-camber corner, bend, S-bend, right-hander, left-hander, right-hand kink, left-hand kink, hairpin, sweeper, chicane, safety barrier, Armco™, chequered flag, skidpan, hoicking back (Inf), over-rev (Inf), rev limiter (Inf)

► *130 Beginning; 179 Circularity*

7 **racing governing body**, Fédération Internationale de l'Automobile (FIA), United States Automobile Club (USAC), National Association for Stock Car Auto Racing (NASCAR) (US), National Hot Rod Association (NHRA) (US), Sports Car Club of America, Royal Automobile Club (RAC), British Racing Drivers' Club (BRDC), motorcycling association, Fédération Internationale Motocycliste (FIM), Auto-Cycle Union, American Motorcycle Association

8 **driver**, Grand Prix driver, Formula 1 driver, number-one driver, number-two driver, racer, Grand Prix racer, Formula 1 racer, motor racer, automobile (*or* auto) racer (US), drag racer, pit mechanic, cornerman, motorcyclist, motorcycle racer, motocrosser

► *319 Transport; 586 Combatant*

VERBS

9 **race**, motor race, auto race (US), road-race, drag-race, scramble, start, restart, roughride, set up, slipstream, slide off, hook off, clip the apex, clip, jet, hack, gear, clutch-slip, change down, crank over, peel off, tuck in, spin out, spoil, straight-line, T-bone, outbrake, sweep, funnel, have ground clearance, do a wheelie, have G-force loading, lap, make a pit stop, make a fuel stop, change the tyres, hit a straight, hoick back (Inf), over-rev (Inf)

ADJECTIVES

10 **racing**, maximum-acceleration, speedway, international, unlimited, active-ride, banked, run-and-bump, T-boned, T-boning, lapped, lapping, spun-out, six-gear, off-camber, right-hand, left-hand

ADVERBS

11 **in a race**, at the starting grid, in the pits, in pole position, on the track, at maximum speed, internationally

62 Mountaineering and Climbing

NOUNS

1 **mountaineering**, mountain climbing, alpinism, climbing mountains, climbing, hill climbing, fell walking, rock climbing, bouldering, serious climbing, strenuous climbing, sustained climbing, thin climbing, balance climbing, bold climbing, free climbing, clean climbing, aid climbing, snow and ice climbing, winter climbing, climb, up-climb, climbing expedition, camp, base camp, advance camp, bivouac, route, air route, bolt route, classic route, artificial route

► *89 Mountains; 304 Ascent*

2 **climbing dangers**, bad weather, frostbite, mountain hypothermia, altitude sickness, avalanche, loose rocks, falling rocks, friable rock, greasy rock, thin ice, concealed crevasse, lack of oxygen

► *254 Danger*

3 **climbing technique**, back and knee, back and foot, back rope, ascent, ascending, soloing, cleaning, gardening, prusiking, moving together, committing move, delicate move, desperate move, layaway move, laybacking, bridging, step-cutting, jamming, scrambling, smearing, glissading, top roping, heel-hook, swinging, yo-yoing, front-pointing, pendule, pendulum, stomach traverse,

toe traverse, tension traverse, Tyrolean traverse, descent, descending, reverse, descending *en rappel* (Fr), abseiling down, abseil, classic abseil, rappel, roping off, belaying, direct belay, dynamic belay, deadman belay, belay braking, waist belay, snow bollard belay, boot-axe belay, running belay, Italian friction hitch, edging, cheating, frigging, chimneying, blind move, combined tactics

► *305 Descent*

4 **climbing equipment**, climbing gear, rack of equipment, metal spike, piton, knifeblade piton, RURP (realized ultimate reality piton), bong, peg, metal clip, karabiner (*or* krab), locking karabiner, snaplink, screwgate, skyhook, harness, waist belt, body harness, sit-harness, sit-sling, snap ring, anchor, runner, nut, wedge-shaped nut (*or* wedge), nut key, prodder, hexentric nut (*or* hex), chock, bolt, belay anchor, camming device, hammer, peg hammer, ice hammer, axe, ice axe, adze, knife, ascender, belay brake (*or* plate), sticht plate, rope, kernmantel rope, live rope, static rope, safety rope, accessory cord, tape, nylon webbing, microwire, extension sling, extender, étrier, stirrup (US), descender, willow wands, aneroid barometer, compass, map, oxygen tank, walkie-talkie, torch, chalk, chalk bag, rucksack, shoulder sling, bandoleer, portable radio, waterproof matchbox, cooking equipment, tent, sleeping bag, climbing boots, cleated boots, kletterschuh (*or* klett), sticky boots, crampons, skis, goggles, sunglasses, snowglasses, heavy clothing, windproof clothing, parka, thermal underwear, helmet, mittens, heavy socks, sun-block cream, cow's tail (Inf)

► *252 Safety; 438 Tool; 551 Dress*

5 **rock face**, wall, ridge, slab, glacis, pitch, ledge, terrace, mantelshelf, ramp, stance, hold, pocket hold, polished hold, fixing point, air point, foothold, corner, groove, shallow groove, V-groove, crack, off-width crack, niche, scoop, cave, amphitheatre, gully, couloir, crevasse, bergschrund, rimaye, chimney, capstone, glacier, neve, firn, flake, spike, arête, knob, bollard, block, pillar, rib, crag, knife edge, outcrop, overhang, roof, prow, bulge, nose, chockstone, gritstone, buttress, sérac, mountain-top, peak, pinnacle, summit

► *156 Depth; 174 Top; 186 Verticality; 187 Horizontality; 361 Suspension*

6 **mountaineering association**, Union Internationale des Associations d'Alpinisme (UIAA), climbing club, British Mountaineering Council (BMC), Scottish Mountaineering Club (SMC), Alpine Club, American Alpine Club, Alpine Club of Canada

7 **mountaineer**, alpinist, climber, rock climber, ascender, upclimber, cragsman (*or* cragswoman), fell walker, guide, Sherpa guide, porter

ADJECTIVES

8 **mountaineering**, boldering, bold, free, clean, aid, climbed, climbing, soloing, cleaning, gardening, prusiking, layaway, laybacking, step-cutting, scrambling, glissading, front-pointing, Tyrolean, deadman, belay, belayed, belaying, boot-axe, blind, bolt, aneroid, goggled, crevassed, gullied, wedge-shaped, hexentric, camming, peg, live, static, safety, cleated, ridged, ledged, terraced, ramped, polished, fixing, off-width, outcropping, overhanging

VERBS

9 **mountaineer**, go mountaineering, mountain-climb, solo, go fell walking, rock-climb, upclimb, ascend, get a foothold, clean, garden, prusik, move together, bridge, step-cut, jam, scramble, smear, glissade, top rope, heel-hook, swing, yo-yo, front-point, traverse, scale a peak, descend, reverse, descend *en rappel* (Fr), abseil, rappel, rope off, belay, edge, cheat, frig, chimney

ADVERBS

10 **on a climb**, under bad weather, with the back-and-knee technique, with the back-and-foot technique, with cleated boots, by a classic route, by an artificial route

63 Racquet Sports

Anyone for tennis? Anonymous.

NOUNS

1 **tennis**, lawn tennis, real tennis, royal tennis, table tennis, ping pong, *jeu de paume* (Fr), Wimbledon, All-England Championships, Davis Cup, US Open, French Open, Wightman Cup

2 **tennis strokes**, service, serve, ace, slice service, American twist service, reverse twist, drive, forehand drive, backhand drive, ground drive, swing, follow-through, ground stroke, volley, forehand volley, backhand volley, smash, overhead smash, hitting it on the fly, lob

3 **tennis equipment**, tennis racket, tennis ball, net, strap, band, posts, tennis court, singles court, doubles court, umpire's chair, linesman's chair

4 **tennis terms**, singles, doubles, pair, delivery, net position, service line, baseline, tramlines, game, set, match, love deuce, advantage, van, rally, foot fault, fault, let, in, out

5 **real tennis**, tennis, royal tennis, court, net (line), first gallery, door, second gallery, last (winning) gallery, service line, service side, hazard side, main wall, grille penthouse, dedans penthouse, side penthouse, service penthouse, marker's box, net, net post, game terms, grille, tambour, dedans, rough, smooth, server, striker-out, volley, half-volley, not up, chase

6 **tennis player**, singles player, doubles player, net player, server, receiver, volleyer, umpire, linesman, ball boy

7 **famous tennis players**, Bill Tilden, Fred Perry, Rod Laver, John Newcombe, Jimmy Connors, Arthur Ashe, Björn Borg, John McEnroe, Boris Becker, Ivan Lendl, Andre Agassi, Pete Sampras, Maureen Connolly, Margaret Smith, Billie Jean King, Chris Evert, Virginia Wade, Martina Navratilova, Steffi Graf, Monica Seles, Martina Hingis

8 **squash**, squash rackets, squash (US), board, telltale, back wall, service line, service court line, squash court, doubles court

9 **squash terms**, service box, hand in, hand-out, in-play wall, out-of-play wall, eight all, set two, sudden death, squash equipment, squash racket, squash ball

10 **badminton**, shuttlecock, battledore, Poona, International Badminton Federation (IBF), Thomas Cup, Uber Cup

11 **badminton equipment**, racket, shuttlecock, shuttle, plastic shuttle, bird, feathers, net posts, badminton court

12 **badminton terms**, shot, clear shot, smash, drop-shot, drive, in side, out side, server, receiver, fault, let, short service line, side boundary line, tramlines, back boundary line, centre line

VERBS

13 **serve**, receive, drive, volley, smash, lob

ADJECTIVES

14 **forehand**, backhand, overhead, singles, doubles

64 Rugby Football

I wanted a play that would paint the full face of sensuality, rebellion and revivalism. In South Wales these three phenomena have played second fiddle only to the Rugby Union which is a distillation of all three. Gwyn Thomas.

NOUNS

1 **rugger**, rugby, rugby football, Rugby Union, RFU (Rugby Football Union), Rugby League, RFC (Rugby Football Club), rugby side, rugby pack, rugby match, rugby ball, rugby stadium, Twickenham, rugby ground, rugby pitch, goal, goal posts, crossbar, goal line, in-goal area, corner flag, half-way line, 22 metre line, 5 metre line, sideline, touch, touchline, touch-in-goal line, dead-ball line

2 **championship**, five-nations championship, triple crown, Calcutta Cup, Rugby World Cup

3 **rugby play**, possession, put-in, scrum (*or* scrummage), set scrum (*or* scrummage), tight scrum, loose scrum, collapsing scrum, formation, 3-4-1 formation, 3-3-2 formation, pile-up, shove, eight-man shove, ruck, maul, line-out, run, running, dummying, looping, peeling off, grounding the ball, heeling, pass, passing, close-passing, throw-forward, catch, fair catch, interception, rebound, cover, kick, kickoff, kick-ahead, drop kick, dropout, place kick, clearance kick, free kick, penalty kick, penalty goal, dropped goal, kick at goal, conversion goal, tackle, tackling, fielding (the ball), knock-on, try, ball in touch, touch down, defence, cover defence, penalty, offside, high tackle, lying on the ball, not playing the ball, handling the ball in a scrum, illegal hooking, tripping, intentional knock-on, penalty try

4 **rugby player**, forward, loose forward, prop forward, prop, scrum half, stand-off half (*or* fly-half), halfback, fullback, three-quarter back, right wing three-quarter, left wing three-quarter, right centre three-quarter, left centre three-quarter, flanker, hooker, blocker, jumper, front row, back row, second row, second-row forward, lock, No. 8, ball-carrier, attacker, try scorer, support player, defender, rugby coach, rugby referee

VERBS

5 **play rugby**, attack, pack a scrum, win a scrum, heel the ball, win the ball, score a try, score, convert a try, kick, take a penalty kick, peel off, ruck, maul, jump, throw in, drop kick the ball, tackle, take out a tackler, get one's head in, bend, bind, drive, shove, play the ball, block, protect the ball, go offside, make a high tackle, lie on the ball, not play the ball, handle the ball, trip

ADJECTIVES

6 **rugger**, in-goal, halfway, dead ball, set, tight, loose, eight-man, collapsing, in touch, running, dummying, looping, peeling, grounding, heeling, passing, dropped, converted, tackled, offside

65 Snooker, Pool, and Billiards

It was remarked to me by the late Mr Charles Roupell…that to play billiards well was a sign of an ill-spent youth. Herbert Spencer.

NOUNS

1 **billiards**, pool (*or* pocket billiards), English billiards, French billiards, break, inning (US), billiard table, centre spot, cushion, top cushion, pocket, billiard cloth, baize, triangle, rack (US), pool ball, numbered ball, white cue ball, cue stick (*or* cue), cue rest, triangle, chalk, billiards club, pool hall

2 **billiards play**, run-through, safety, coup, scratch (US), bank shot, cannon, carom (US), dead ball, side, English (US), massé shot (*or* massé), touching ball, frozen ball (US), full-ball aim, spot stroke, half-ball stroke, screw, hazard, long loser, long in-off, long on-off (US), stun and stab, miscue, miss, pocketing the ball

3 **English billiards**, cue, long-butt cue, half-butt cue, rest, half-butt rest, six-pocket table, pocket, top pocket, centre pocket, bottom pocket, the spot, billiard spot, pyramid spot, centre spot, centre line, baulk-line spot, baulk line, baulk cushion, the D, white ball, spot white ball (*or* spot), red ball, plain, cue ball, object ball, break, making a break, stroke, foul stroke, push stroke, string, playing from hand, playing up the table, playing down the table, losing hazard (*or* loser), winning hazard (*or* pot), cannon, direct cannon, indirect cannon, in-off

4 **carom**, French billiards, pocketless table, head cushion, side rail, diamond, centre spot, head spot, foot spot, foot string, centre string, head string, three-cushion billiards, red ball, white ball, white object ball, first object ball, striking the cushion, lagging, break shot, carom, carom count, carom score, safety, foul, kiss shot, push shot, shove shot, double stroke, straight-rail billiards, baulk-line, baulk-line game, anchor space

5 **snooker**, volunteer snooker, frame, pocket billiard table, snooker table, baulk, baulk line, baulk spot, billiard spot, pyramid spot, the spot, centre spot, D area, bottom cushion, bottom pocket, centre pocket, top pocket, free ball, nominated ball, cue ball, white ball, red ball, colours, black ball, pink ball, blue ball, brown ball, green ball, yellow ball, potting a ball, stringing, respotting a ball

6 **pool**, American pocket billiards, 15-ball pocket billiards, open table, eight ball, line-up, forty-one, one and nine balls, pool table, foot spot, long string, head spot, head string, break ball, jumped ball, solid-coloured ball, striped ball, called ball, calling the ball, called pocket, calling the pocket, bumper pool (*or* bumpers), bumper, breaking violation, lag, scratch

7 **billiards player**, pool player, snooker player, striker, referee, marker

VERBS

8 **play billiards**, turn at the table, break, make a break, chalk a stick, make a bank shot, cannon, carom (US), put

side on the ball, put English on the ball (US), drive out of baulk, miscue, miss, pocket the ball, spot the ball, make a kiss shot, pot a ball, repot a ball, call a ball, call a pocket

ADJECTIVES

9 **billiard**, numbered, miscued, missed, stroked, spotted, pocketed, centred, straight-rail, baulk-line, free, nominated, called, snookered, crotched, in baulk, full-ball, half-ball

66 Soccer

Football...causeth fighting, brawling, contention, quarrel picking, murder, homicide and great effusion of bloode, as daily experience teacheth. Philip Stubbes.

NOUNS

1 **soccer**, Association Football, football, soccer football (US), professional football, football match, football game (US), League match, friendly match, Football League, football team, football side, football, football club, football ground, football stadium (US), football pitch, football field (US), goal, goal area, goal post, crossbar, net, stanchion, scoreboard, perimeter, touchline (*or* by-line), penalty area, penalty spot, six-yard box, eighteen-yard box, half-way line, centre circle, goal line, corner area, corner flag, football kit, football uniform (US), shorts, boots, shinpads, gloves, football championship, World Cup, European Cup, European Cup Winners' Cup, Football Association Challenge Cup (*or* FA Cup), football organization, Football Association (FA), US Soccer Football Association, Fédération Internationale de Football Association (FIFA)

2 **football play**, kickoff, kick, kicking, pass, passing, back pass, wall pass, one-two, head, heading, foul, fouling, advantage, trip, shoot, shooting, save, miss, tackle, tackling, dribbling, nutmeg, trapping, parrying, handball, throw-in, goal kick, corner kick (*or* corner), drop ball, scoring, score, penalty, handling, deliberate kicking, deliberate tripping, pushing, violent charging, striking, holding, offside, onside, free kick, direct free kick, indirect free kick

3 **football player**, professional footballer, Footballer of the Year, captain, goalkeeper (*or* goalie), defender, fullback, centre back, centre half, centre forward, wing half, right half, left half, outside left, outside right, inside left, inside right, winger, striker, midfield striker, sweeper, goalscorer, playmaker, substitute (*or* sub), reserve, football manager, football coach, football trainer, football referee, linesman, football fan

VERBS

4 **play soccer**, kick off, kick, pass, make a pass, head, throw in, shoot, save, miss, tackle, score, foul, trip, push, hold, go offside, go onside, have a free kick, have a goal kick, take a corner, trap, dive, strike, parry, flick, stab, smother, chip

ADJECTIVES

5 **soccer**, halfway, six-yard, eighteen-yard, passed, headed, fouled, tripped, missed, tackled, dribbled, trapped, scored, handled, offside, onside, direct, indirect, midfield

67 Swimming

NOUNS

1 **swimming**, natation (Lit), recreational swimming, competitive swimming, swimming team, freestyle event, relay event, medley race, lap, turn, open-water swimming, long-distance swimming, swimming the English Channel, cross-Channel swimming, synchronized swimming, swimming stroke, stroke, breaststroke, sidestroke, backstroke, back crawl, crawl, front crawl, Australian crawl, butterfly, paddling, paddle, doggy-paddling, dog-paddle, treading water, buoyancy, bobbing, head bobbing, floating, back floating, supine floating, float, dead-man's float, swimming under water, underwater swimming, subaqua swimming, skin diving, scuba (self-contained underwater breathing apparatus) diving, snorkeling, swimming equipment, underwater mask, underwater breathing tube, snorkel, fin, flipper

2 **swimming technique**, breath control, alternate breathing, swimming movements, arm stroke, dolphin-butterfly stroke, recovery stroke, single overarm, double-arm movement, double overarm, single-rhythm crawl, trudgen stroke, four-beat trudgen crawl, six-beat crawl, eight-beat crawl, ten-beat crawl, kick, scissors kick, wide scissors kick, upkick, downkick, frog kick, wedge kick, whip kick, fishtail kick, dolphin kick, flutter kick, crossover kick

► *485 Skill*

3 **survival swimming**, drown-proofing (US), swimming in clothes, survival device, floating device, float, inner tube, water wings, armband, rubber ring, life preserver (US), life belt, life jacket, life vest (US), life buoy, swimming rescue, lifeguarding, life-saving, swim-and-tow, artificial respiration, resuscitation, mouth-to-mouth resuscitation, kiss of life, Mae West (Inf)

► *252 Safety; 392 Help*

4 **swimmer**, competitive swimmer, long-distance swimmer, underwater swimmer, subaqua swimmer, skin-diver, scuba-diver, snorkeler, lifeguard, life-saver

5 **swimming association**, International Swimming Federation (FINA), NCAA (National Collegiate Athletic Association) swimming (US), Amateur Swimming Association (ASA)

6 **diving**, recreational diving, competitive diving, springboard diving, platform diving, high diving, dive, takeoff, entry dive, entry, swallow dive, duck dive, forward dive, header forward straight, header forward with tuck, tuck dive, backward dive, reverse dive, inward dive, twisting dive, handstand dive, plain jump, tuck jump, somersault, double somersault, diving position, straight position, pike position, tuck position, diving board, springboard, one-metre springboard, three-metre springboard, platform, five-metre platform, ten-metre platform, competitive diving marks, form, execution, difficulty of the dive, variety diving (Lit), fancy diving (Lit)

► *305 Descent*

7 **swimming pool**, outdoor swimming pool, indoor swimming pool, natatorium, swimming bath, short-course pool, long-course pool, Olympic-size(d) pool, wading pool, children's swimming pool, swimming area,

swimming lake, swimming hole (US), pond, river, beach, swimming beach, leisure pool, wave pool, heated pool

► *88 Lakes*

8 **swimwear**, swimsuit, bathing suit (US), swimming (*or* bathing) costume, one-piece swimsuit, two-piece swimsuit, bikini, monokini, swimming trunks, trunks, bathers (Aus), bathing cap, goggles, diving mask, flippers

► *551 Dress*

VERBS

9 **swim**, take a dip, dog-paddle, tread water, float, bob, swim under water, snorkel

10 **dive**, plunge, skin-dive, scuba-dive, cannonball, belly flop, jump in

ADJECTIVES

11 **swimming**, swim, bathing, natatory (*or* natatorial), natational (Lit), recreational, competitive, freestyle, relay, medley, open-water, long-distance, cross-Channel, synchronized, paddling, dog-paddling, buoyant, floated, floating, underwater, subaqua, recovery, double, double-arm, trudgen, frog, wedge, whip, fishtail, dolphin, flutter, crossover, survival, drown-proofed, drown-proofing, mouth-to-mouth, entry, swallow, duck, tuck, backward, reverse, inward, twisting, handstand, plain, pike, springboard, platform, outdoor, indoor, short-course, long-course, Olympic-size(d), wading, one-piece, two-piece, variety (Lit), fancy (Lit)

ADVERBS

12 **by swimming**, for recreation, competitively, in competition, in the open water, with synchronization, underwater

68 Winter Sports

It is unbecoming for a cardinal to ski badly. Pope John Paul II.

NOUNS

1 **skiing**, snow-skiing (US), alpine skiing, competitive skiing, Olympic skiing, biathlon, freestyle skiing, acrobatic skiing, ballet-skiing, stunt-skiing, mogul skiing, hot-dogging, somersaulting, helicopter skiing (*or* heli-skiing), off-piste skiing, birdsnesting, skiing on ice, nordic skiing, mountain skiing, cross-country skiing, touring, *Langlauf* (Ger), *ski du Fond* (Fr), ski-jumping, jump, ski jump, acrobatic jump, aerial, ski-mountaineering, speed-skiing, grass-skiing, ski run, downhill ski run, *Abfahrt* (Ger), *descente* (Fr), ski trail, marked trail, piste, moguled piste, motorway, gunbarrel, loipe, ski slope, slope, artificial slope, nursery slope, run, green run, blue run, black run, straight run, *Schuss* (Ger), *Steilhang* (Ger), fall-line, wall, couloir, compression, skiing snow, good piste, hard-surface snow, breakable crust, powder snow, soft damp snow, heavy wet snow, wind crust, windslab, porridge, ice, slush, frozen corn snow, bump, mogul, rut, tramline, ridge, washboard, ledge, season skiing ticket, *abonnement* (Fr), ski-tow, lift, ski lift, gondola lift, bubble, bucket, drag lift, T-bar lift, button, poma, cable car, cabin lift, *Luftseilbahn* (Ger), *téléphérique* (Fr), chair lift, *Sesselbahn* (Ger), *télésiège* (Fr), funicular, ski teaching method, GLM (graduated length method) (US), skiing association, Fédération Internationale de Ski, British Ski Federation, Canadian Ski Association

2 **cross-country skiing**, *Langlauf* (Ger), ski touring, mountain ski touring, touring, off-track touring, ski rambling, biathlon race, biathlon, biathlon relay race, sprinting race, marathon, American Birkebeiner, Canadian *Coureur des Bois* (Fr), cross-country technique, two-phase walk, two-phase glide, diagonal stride, diagonal stride with pole planting, star turn, kick turn, sidestep, stepping a curve, diagonal sidestep, double-pole, double-pole with leg kick, swing, herringbone, direct descent, traverse downhill, snowplough glide, snowplough turn, stem turn, parallel turn, telemark, tacking, two-phase uphill, swing to the hill, snowplough brake, cross-country championships, World Grand Prix of Cross-country Skiers, Giant's Ridge International Classic Marathon, *Internationaler Deutscher Skimarathon in Hirschau* (Ger), cross-country equipment, touring ski, racing ski

3 **ski racing**, ski race, racing, race, alpine racing, alpine race, downhill racing, downhill race, slalom racing, slalom race, giant slalom racing, giant slalom race, super giant slalom racing, super giant slalom race, super G race, giant slalom in one run, (ski) skating, single-sided skating, double-sided skating, ski orienteering (*or* Ski-O), ski championship, the World Championship, the World Cup, the Winter Olympic gold medal, slalom pole, rapid slalom pole, gate, open gate, vertical gate, verticale, flush gate, diagonal gate, hairpin, closed gate

4 **skiing technique**, compensation technique, skiing posture, schussing position, tuck, unweighting, up-unweighting, down-unweighting, ski move, snow-ploughing, snowplough (*or* wedge), reverse snowplough, herringbone, pole plant, ski turn, christiania, christie, parallel christie, stem christie, uphill christie, cornering, stemming, stem turn, step turn, star turn, weldel, basic swing, parallel swing, telemarking, telemark, scissors turn, pressure turn, compression turn, jet turn, rotation turn, inner ski turn, down-motion turn, racing-step turn, snowplough turn (*or* crab), snowplough wedeln, jump turn, kick turn, carved turn, jet, *avalement* (Fr), *projection circulaire* (Fr), edging, sidecutting, sidecut, sideslipping, sideslip, sidestepping, sidestep, traversing, climbing, hockey stop

5 **ski equipment**, ski, downhill ski, cross-country ski, alpine ski, touring ski, outside ski, uphill ski, inside ski, short ski, compact ski, soft ski, long ski, stiff ski, slalom ski, giant slalom ski, RS-ski, I-ski, instructional ski, wooden ski, metal ski, plastic ski, parablock, safety strap, ski pole, ski stick, safety ski stick, basket, boot, binding, gaiter, slipper pad, toe piece, anti-friction pad, brake, ski stopper, ski wax, klister wax, ski clothes, quilted clothing, anorak, skisuit, racing suit, ski pants, ski jacket, gloves, sunglasses, goggles

6 **ice-skating**, figure-skating, free-skating, pair-skating, pairs, shadow skating, competitive ice-skating, Olympic skating, compulsory figure, three, paragraph double three, loop, change loop, paragraph loop, bracket, paragraph bracket, rocker, counter, free-skating movement, jump, loop jump, salchow jump, axel jump, toe jump, split jump, spin, camel spin, lay-back spin, one-foot up-

right spin, sit spin, cross-foot spin, pair-skating movement, death spiral, pairs sit spin, catch-waist camel spin, lift, axel lift, lasso lift, split lutz lift, twist lift, flying axel, throw axel, double throw axel, throw salchow, skating association, International Skating 135 Union, skating equipment, skate, MK skates™, skating boot, Stanzione™

7 ice-dancing, dancing on ice, competitive ice-dancing, Olympic ice-dancing, compulsory dancing, set pattern dancing, free-dancing, ice-dancing move, dance step, arabesque, pivot, pirouette, hold, killian hold, reverse killian hold, waltz hold, turn, three turn, dropped three, dropped mohawk, dance lift, ice-dance music, Viennese waltz, Yankee polka, the blues, Westminster waltz, paso doble, rumba, starlight waltz, killian, tango romantica, Ravensburger waltz, quickstep, Argentine tango, competitive scoring, originality, variety, difficulty, timing, selection of music

8 speed-skating, sprint-skating, long-distance racing, middle-distance racing, short-distance racing, short-track racing, speed-skating race, 500-metre race, 1,500-metre race, 5,000-metre race, 10,000-metre race, speed-skating circuit, speed-skating track

9 bobsledding (*or* bobsledging *or* bobsleighing), bobsled (*or* bobsledge *or* bobsleigh), bob, two-man bobsled, four-man bobsled, luge, one-seater toboggan, two-seater toboggan, skeleton, parts of a toboggan, hood, runner, axle, cable, brake, cowling, toboggan racing, toboggan race, luge racing, lugeing, competitive lugeing, Olympic lugeing, European Luge Championships, luge race, luge techniques, steering, lifting, dragging, run, bobrun, toboggan chute, toboggan run, Cresta Run at St. Moritz, Fédération Internationale de Bobsleigh et Tobogganing, International Luge Federation, St. Moritz Tobogganing Club

10 curling, curling match, points game, bonspiel, spiel, curling rink, house, hog line, centre line, foot line, tee line, back line, hack, crampit, curling stone, loofie, kuting stone, heavy, light, guard, in-wick, lose handle, narrow, wick, wide, freeze, shot, pad-lid (*or* pot-lid), cup, arridge (*or* arris), curling broom, besom, curling tee, button, dolly, curling ice, dour ice, drug ice, swingy ice, bunker, curling technique, curl, sweeping, sooping, running a stone, borrowing, quacking, rubbing, take-out, double take-out, double, hack weight, in-handle turn (*or* in-turn), out-handle turn (*or* out-turn), curling championship, the Silver Broom, the World Curling Championship, the Uniroyal World Junior Championship, the Ladies' World Championship, curling association, Royal Caledonian Curling Club, United States Curling Association, Canadian Curling Association, kuting (Lit), cockee (Lit), gogsee (Lit), the roaring game (Inf)

11 skier, ski racer, slalom racer, slalomer, individualist, ice-skater, ice-dancer, speed-skater, curling player, skip, lead, tobogganist, bobsledder (*or* bobsledger *or* bobsleigher), bobsled captain, oversman (Lit)

ADJECTIVES

12 ski, skiing, alpine, nordic, Olympic, freestyle, acrobatic, ballet, stunt, mogul, moguled, hot-dogging, somersaulting, off-piste, aerial, downhill, hard-surface, breakable, rutted, ridged, ledged, T-bar, touring, off-track, biathlon, sprinting, two-phase, diagonal, double-pole, direct, traverse, snowplough, snowploughing, single-sided, double-sided, open, vertical, flush, hairpin, closed, schussing, tucked, tucking, unweighting, sidecutting, sideslipping, sidestepping, anti-friction, klister, quilted

13 ice-skating, figure, free, pair, compulsory, catch-waist, lifted, lifting, twist, ice-dance, dropped, killian, original, varied, timed, selected, long-distance, middle-distance, short-distance, short-track, lugeing, steering, dragging, in-wick, hack

VERBS

14 ski, snow ski (US), alpine ski, hot-dog, somersault, birdsnest, ski-jump, double-pole, swing, snowplough, turn, tack, swing to the hill, schuss, do a christie, corner, stem, swing, telemark, sideslip, sidestep, traverse, climb, wax a ski

15 ice-skate, figure-skate, free-skate, shadow-skate, jump, spin, pivot, pirouette, speed-skate, sprint-skate

16 bobsled, bobsledge, bobsleigh, luge, toboggan, steer, lift, drag, make a run, sweep, loop, run a stone, burn a stone, chip a stone, bury a stone, blank an end, chap and lie, out-wick, fill the port, in turn, out turn, break an egg (Inf)

ADVERBS

17 on a ski run, downhill, acrobatically, artificially, diagonally, vertically

INTERJECTIONS

18 danger!, look out!, *Achtung!* (Ger), *Piste!* (Fr), *Pista!* (It)

69 Games and Pastimes

Life's too short for chess. Henry James Byron.

Gamesmanship or The Art of Winning Games Without Actually Cheating. Stephen Potter.

NOUNS

1 game, ball game, board game, card game, darts game, dice game, billiards game, word game, children's game, gambling game, computer game, video game, indoor game, outdoor game, war game

2 contest, bout, round, match, session, hand (of cards), competition

▶ *45 Sport*

3 card game terms, cards, card game, pack, playing card, heart, club, diamond, spade, picture card, face card, court card, one eye, one-eyed jack, ace, deuce, joker, wildcard, canasta pack, piquet pack, cut, shuffle, deal, shoe, misdeal, hand, banker, pot, ante, limit, raise, cull, kicker, hold, stack, pair, three of a kind, trey, prial, four of a kind, full house, dead man's hand, flush, run, straight, running flush, royal flush, trump, bid, no bid,

BOARD GAMES

backgammon	draughts	Monopoly™
checkers (US)	go	Scrabble™
chess	halma	snakes and ladders
Chinese checkers	ludo	Talisman™
Cluedo™	Mah Jong	Trivial Pursuit™

pass, fold, pre-emptive bid, underbid, undertrick, finesse, contract, rubber, slam, small slam, Yarborough, grand slam

4 chess terms, board, square, piece, chess piece, chessman, pawn, castle, rook, knight, bishop, king, queen, opening, fork, pin, castling, check, end game, checkmate, mate

5 dice, die, spots, throw, double, snake eyes, craps, liar dice, poker dice, Yahtzee™

6 darts, arrow, flight, board, single, double, treble, twenty-five, bull (*or* bull's eye), top, double top, treble top, one hundred and eighty, throw, oche, out, three hundred and one (301), five hundred and one (501), round the clock, shanghai, killer

7 other games, dominoes, roulette, skittles, ninepins, paintball

8 pastime, hobby, activity, recreation, amusement, entertainment

ADJECTIVES

9 recreational, fun, entertaining, amusing, competitive

VERBS

10 play, compete, gamble, join in, throw, shuffle, cut, deal, misdeal, bank, up the ante, raise, call, hold, pass, stack, throw in, fold, bid, double, pre-empt, ruff, finesse, open, move, castle, queen, crown

ADVERBS

11 recreationally, entertainingly

CHILDREN'S GAMES AND PARTY GAMES

blind man's buff	hide-and-seek	pass the parcel
catch	hopscotch	pig (*or* piggy) in the middle
charades	I-spy	pin the tail on the donkey
Chinese whispers	jacks (*or* jackstones)	postman's knock
consequences	jackstraws	sardines
cowboys and Indians	kickean	Simon says
crambo	leapfrog	snakes and ladders
dumb crambo	ludo	spin the bottle
doctors and nurses	marbles	ticktacktoe
fivestones	murder in the dark	tiddlywinks
fox and geese	musical chairs	tig (*or* tag)
grandmother's footsteps	noughts and crosses	tipcat
hangman		wink murder

HOBBIES AND PASTIMES

aerobics	beachcombing	coin collecting	flower pressing	lampshade making	patchwork	spinning
amateur dramatics	beekeeping	collage	fossil hunting	lapidary	philately	stamp collecting
antique collecting	beer making	collecting	fretwork	lepidoptery	photography	stencilling
appliqué	birdwatching	cookery	gardening	macramé	pokerwork	tapestry
autograph hunting	book binding	crochet	genealogy	marquetry	pottery	tatting
bark rubbing	brass rubbing	crosswords	glass engraving	model making	quilting	topiary
basketry	butterfly collecting	découpage	home brewing	model railways	raffia work	train spotting
batik	calligraphy	dressmaking	keep fit	mosaics	reading	upholstery
	candlemaking	embroidery	kite flying	origami	rug making	weaving
	canework	enamelling	knitting	painting	screen printing	wine making
		flower arranging	lace making		shell collecting	woodwork

CARD GAMES

all fours	clubs	find-the-lady	matrimony	pontoon	snipsnapsnorum
auction bridge	connections	fish	monte	Pope Joan	solitaire
baccarat	contract bridge	five hundred	nap (*or* napoleon)	primero	solo whist (*or* solo)
banker	cooncan (*or* conquian)	flinch	Newmarket	quadrille	speculation
beggar my neighbour	cribbage (*or* crib)	fright	nine-card brag	quinze	straight poker
bezique	draw poker	frog	old maid	reverse	strip Jack naked
blackjack	duplicate bridge	gin rummy (*or* gin)	ombre	rouge et noir	strip poker
black maria	Earl of Coventry	go fish	pairs	rubber bridge	stud poker
blind poker	écarté	hearts	patience	rummy	tarak
Boston	eight-five-three	high low	pelmanism	Russian brag	three-card brag
brag	euchre	keno (*or* kino)	penny ante	seven-card brag	three-card monte
bridge	fan-tan	knockout whist	pinochle	seven up	twenty-one
canasta	faro	lansquenet	piquet	skat	vingt-et-un
chemin de fer		loo	poker	snap	whist

Animals and Plants

70 Animals

And God said, Let the earth bring forth the living creature after his kind, cattle, and creeping thing, and beast of the earth after his kind: and it was so. Bible: Genesis.

There are two things for which animals are to be envied: they know nothing of future evils, or of what people say about them. Voltaire.

NOUNS

1 **animals**, animal life, animal kingdom, Animalia, fauna, the bird, beast, and fish, the beasts of the field, the fowl of the air, and the fish of the sea, wildlife, endangered species, game, big game, small game
▶ *34 Life Science*

2 **animal**, creature, beast, brute, dumb animal, dumb friend, furry friend, four-legged friend, creeping thing, varmint (Inf), critter (US)

3 **domesticated animal**, beast of burden, pack animal, draught animal, farm animal, livestock, stock, circus animal, experimental animal, laboratory animal, tame animal, pet animal, pet, house pet
▶ *43 Agriculture; 71 Mammals*

4 **type of animal**, invertebrate, animalcule, zooid, protist, protozoan, worm, mollusc, gastropod, arthropod, insect, chordate, vertebrate, fish, amphibian, reptile, bird, mammal, biped, quadruped, herbivore, browser, grazer, filter-feeder, scavenger, omnivore, carnivore, flesh-eater, meat-eater, insectivore, predator, prey, parasite, bloodsucker, ectoparasite, endoparasite, host, intermediate host, vector, symbiont, commensal
▶ *71 Mammals; 72 Birds; 73 Reptiles and Amphibians; 74 Fishes; 75 Invertebrates*

5 **aquatic animal**, marine animal, marine mammal, cetacean, whale, dolphin, seal, fish, starfish, echinoderm, cuttlefish, cephalopod, octopus, shellfish, bivalve, jellyfish, coelenterate, coral, sponge, plankton, zooplankton, nekton, benthos (*or* benthon), fry, krill, larva
▶ *71 Mammals; 74 Fishes; 75 Invertebrates*

6 **flying animal**, flier, bird, flying insect, fly, butterfly, flying fish, flying mammal, flying fox, bat
▶ *71 Mammals; 72 Birds; 74 Fishes; 76 Insects and Arachnids*

7 **legendary beast**, unicorn, Pegasus, Cerberus, dragon, drake (Lit), firedrake (*or* firedragon), griffin (*or* griffon *or* gryphon), chimera, banshee, siren, lamia, harpy, manticore, behemoth, centaur, minotaur, cyclops, elf, gnome, goblin, orc, troll, jinn, hippogriff (*or* hippogryph), wyvern, cockatrice, basilisk, phoenix, roc, snark, kraken, Loch Ness monster, Sasquatch, Bigfoot, Yeti, Abominable Snowman, zoomorphism, therianthropism, bestiary
▶ *11 Occultism; 72 Birds*

8 **animal welfare**, animal health, veterinary science, animal breeding, zootechnics, thremmatology, animal conservation, zoological garden, zoo, safari park, wildlife park, game reserve (*or* preserve), dolphinarium, animal protection, Royal Society for the Prevention of Cruelty to Animals (RSPCA), animal rights movement, animal liberation, Animal Liberation Front (ALF)
▶ *35 Medicine; 43 Agriculture*

9 **animal science(s)**, zoology, animal taxonomy, systematic zoology, zoography, zoometry, animal anatomy, comparative anatomy, zootomy, animal physiology, zoonomy, embryology, animal biochemistry, zoochemistry, animal ecology, parasitology, marine biology, animal behaviour, animal psychology, ethology, sociobiology, zoogeography, animal pathology, zoopathology, palaeozoology, palaeontology, vertebrate zoology, mammology, ornithology, herpetology, ichthyology, invertebrate zoology, entomology, malacology, helminthology, protozoology
▶ *30 Earth Science; 34 Life Science; 36 Psychology and Psychiatry; 71 Mammals; 72 Birds; 73 Reptiles and Amphibians; 74 Fishes; 75 Invertebrates; 76 Insects and Arachnids*

10 **animal welfarist**, veterinarian, vet (Inf), thremmatologist, conservationist, zoo-keeper, game warden, animal lover, zoophile, pet owner, dog lover, cat lover, antivivisectionist, animal-rights activist, animal liberationist, hunt saboteur, hunt sab (Inf)

11 **zoologist**, animal taxonomist, systematic zoologist, zoographer, zoometrist, comparative anatomist, zootomist, animal physiologist, zoonomist, embryologist, zoochemist, animal ecologist, paransitologist, marine biologist, ethologist, behaviourist zoographer, zoopathologist, palaeozoologist, vertebrate zoologist, mammologist, ornithologist, herpetologist, ichthyologist, invertebrate zoologist, entomologist, malacologist, helminthologist, protozoologist

▶ *30 Earth Science; 34 Life Science; 36 Psychology and Psychiatry; 71 Mammals; 72 Birds; 73 Reptiles and Amphibians; 74 Fishes; 75 Invertebrates; 76 Insects and Arachnids*

12 **zoophilism**, zoophilia, bestiality, animality, animalism

▶ *593 Love*

13 **fear of animals**, zoophobia

▶ *612 Fear*

ADJECTIVES

14 **animalian**, animal, animalic, animalistic, zoic, brutish, subhuman, dumb, brutal, bestial, beastly, beastlike, animal-like, zoomorphic, therianthropic, theriomorphic (*or* theriomorphous)

▶ *380 Violence*

15 **of animals**, invertebrate, animalcular, zooidal, chordate, vertebrate, bipedal, quadrupedal, domesticated, tamed, feral, wild, solitary, social, colonial, terrestrial, arboreal, aquatic, marine, planktonic, benthic, pelagic, littoral, diurnal, nocturnal, carnivorous, herbivorous, omnivorous, insectivorous, predacious, parasitic, bloodsucking, ectoparasitic, endoparasitic, symbiotic, commensal

16 **zoological**, zoographic(al), zoometric(al), zoonomic(al), zoogeographic(al), zoochemical, embryological, ethological, zoopathological, palaeozoological

17 **animal-loving**, zoophilic

18 **animal-fearing**, zoophobic

71 Mammals

Dogs, like horses, are quadrupeds. That is to say, they have four rupeds, one at each corner, on which they walk. Frank Muir.

NOUNS

1 **mammal**, Mammalia, warm-blooded animal, homoiotherm, study of mammals, mammology

2 **mammalian characteristic**, mammary gland, mamilla, mamma, udder, dug, nipple, teat, pap, papilla, milk, colostrum, beestings, sweat gland, sebaceous gland, scent gland, musk gland, hair, spine, bristle, whisker, vibrissa, wool, fur, pelage

3 **egg-laying mammal**, prototherian, Prototheria, monotreme, Monotremata (platypus *or* duck-billed platypus *or* duckbill, echidna *or* spiny anteater)

4 **pouched mammal**, metatherian, Metatheria, marsupial, Marsupialia, marsupial characteristic, marsupium, pouch

5 **placental mammal**, eutherian, Eutheria, eutherian characteristic, placenta, uterus

6 **insect-eating mammal**, insectivore, Insectivora (hedgehogs, shrews, moles, *etc.*), anteater, scaly anteater, pangolin, pholidote, spiny anteater, echidna, ant bear, aardvark, tubulidentate

7 **flying mammal**, chiropteran (*or* chiropter), Chiroptera (bats), dermopteran, Dermoptera (flying lemur)

8 **flesh-eating mammal**, carnivore, Carnivora, canine, canid, Canidae (dogs, wolves, foxes, jackals, *etc.*), ursid, Ursidae (bears), mustelid, Mustelidae (weasels, otters, badgers, *etc.*), procyonid, Procyonidae (raccoons), viverrid, Viverridae (mongooses, civets, *etc.*), hyaenid, Hyaenidae (hyenas *or* hyaenas), feline, felid, Felidae (cats)

9 **dog**, canine, bitch, whelp, pup, puppy, puppy-dog, mongrel, cross-breed, lurcher, cur, tyke, pariah dog, pi-dog, hound, hunting dog, gundog, working dog, guard dog, watchdog, police dog, tracker dog, sniffer dog, guide

BREEDS OF DOGS

Aberdeen (*or* Scottish) terrier
affenpinscher
Afghan hound
Airedale terrier
Alaskan malamute
Alsatian, German shepherd
American cocker spaniel
Australian terrier
basenji
basset hound
beagle
Bedlington terrier
Belgian shepherd dog
Bernese mountain dog
Blenheim spaniel
bloodhound
Border collie
Border terrier
borzoi
Boston terrier
Bouvier des Flandres
boxer
briard
bulldog
bull mastiff
bull terrier
Cairn terrier
chihuahua
chow (*or* chow chow)
clumber spaniel
cocker spaniel
collie
coonhound
corgi
dachshund
Dalmatian, carriage (*or* coach) dog
Dandie Dinmont terrier
deerhound
Doberman pinscher
elkhound
English setter
Eskimo dog, husky
field spaniel
Finnish spitz
foxhound
fox terrier
French bulldog
German shepherd, Alsatian
golden retriever
Gordon setter
Great Dane
greyhound
griffon
Groenendael
harrier
Hungarian puli
Hungarian vizsla
husky, Eskimo dog
Ibizan hound
Irish setter
Irish terrier
Irish wolfhound
Jack Russell terrier
Japanese chin
keeshond
kelpie
Kerry blue terrier
King Charles spaniel
Komondor
Kuvasz
Labrador retriever
Lakeland terrier
Large Munsterlander
Lhasa apso
Löwchen
Maltese
Manchester terrier
mastiff
Mexican hairless
Newfoundland
Norfolk terrier
Norwich terrier
Old English sheepdog
otterhound
papillon
pekingese
pharaoh hound
pit bull terrier
pointer
Pomeranian
poodle
pug
puli
Pyrennean mountain dog
retriever
Rhodesian ridgeback
Rottweiler
Saluki
Samoyed
schipperke
schnauzer
Scottish (*or* Aberdeen) terrier
Sealyham terrier
setter
Shetland sheepdog, sheltie
shih tzu
silky terrier
Skye terrier
spaniel
spitz
springer spaniel
Staffordshire bull terrier
staghound
St Bernard
terrier
vizsla
Weimaraner
Welsh corgi
Welsh terrier
West Highland white terrier
whippet
wire–haired pointing griffon
Yorkshire terrier

BREEDS OF CATS

Abyssinian	cream	rex
Birman	Devon rex	Russian blue
blue Burmese	domestic	seal–pointed
blue cream	long–hair	Siamese
blue–pointed	domestic tabby	Siamese
Siamese	Havana	silver tabby
British blue	lilac–pointed	smoke
brown Burmese	Siamese	tabby
brown tabby	long–haired blue	tabby–pointed
Burmese	Manx	Siamese
chestnut brown	Persian	tortoiseshell
chinchilla	red Abyssinian	tortoiseshell and
chocolate–pointed	red–pointed	white
Siamese	Siamese	tortoiseshell–
colourpoint	red self	pointed Siamese
Cornish rex	red tabby	Turkish

dog, sheepdog, show dog, toy dog, lapdog, man's best friend, Fido, bow-wow (Inf), mutt (Inf), pooch (US inf)

10 cat, feline, wildcat, big cat, domestic cat, mouser, ratter, house cat, tom (*or* tomcat), gib, queen, grimalkin, kitten, kit (*or* kitty) (Inf), puss (*or* pussy *or* pussycat) (Inf), mog (*or* moggy) (Inf)

11 marine mammal, cetacean, Cetacea (whales, dolphins, porpoises), pinniped, Pinnipedia (seals, phocids, sealions, walrus), sirenian, Sirenia (dugong, sea cow, manatee)

12 gnawing mammal, rodent, Rodentia, sciuromorphs (beavers, squirrels, chipmunks, *etc.*), myomorphs (murids, rats, mice, lemmings, gerbils, voles, *etc.*), histricomorphs (porcupines, cavies, *etc.*), lagomorph, Lagomorpha (pika (*or* cony), leporids, rabbits, hares)

13 toothless mammal, edentate, Edentata (anteaters, sloths, armadillos)

14 pachyderm, subungulate, proboscidean, Proboscidea (elephant, Jumbo, mastodon, mammoth), rhinoceros, hippopotamus, river horse (Inf)

15 hoofed mammal, ungulate, ungulant, odd-toed ungulate, perissodactyl, Perissodactyla (equines, equids, Equidae (horses), tapirs, rhinoceroses), even-toed ungulate, artiodactyl, Artiodactyla, suid, Suidae (pigs, hogs, swine), hippopotamus, ruminant, cud-chewer, Ruminantia, camelid, Camelidae (camels, llamas, *etc.*), cervid, Cervidae (deer), giraffe, camelopard (Lit), okapi, bovid, bovine, Bovidae (cattle, antelopes, gazelles, goats, ovines, sheep, *etc.*), hyracoid, Hyracoidea (hyraxes *or* conies)

▶ *43 Agriculture; 59 Horse Riding and Racing*

16 primate, Primates, prosimians (lemurs, lorises, bushbabies, tarsiers, *etc.*), anthropoids, monkeys, New World monkeys (capuchins, howlers, marmosets, tamarins, *etc.*), Old World monkeys (macaques, baboons, *etc.*), apes, anthropoid apes, pongids, Pongidae (gibbons, great apes, orangutan, chimpanzee, gorilla), hominids, Hominidae (man, *Homo sapiens*, human, human being), study of primates, primatology

▶ *566 Humankind*

17 male mammal, dog (dog, wolf, fox, coyote), buck (reindeer, antelope, hare, rabbit, kangaroo), stag (deer, caribou), hart (deer, red deer), stallion (horse, zebra), colt (horse), bull (buffalo, camel, cattle, elephant, giraffe, moose, elk, ox, rhinoceros, seal, walrus, whale), boar (pig, badger, bear, weasel), ram (sheep, impala), tom (cat, bobcat, cougar), billy goat (goat), roebuck (roe deer), jackass (ass, donkey), jack (ferret)

18 female mammal, bitch (dog, wolf), doe (deer, antelope, hare, rabbit, kangaroo), hind (deer, red deer), mare (horse, zebra), filly (horse), cow (buffalo, camel, cattle, elephant, giraffe, moose, elk, ox, rhinoceros, weasel, seal, walrus, whale), heifer (cattle), sow (pig, badger, bear), gilt (pig), ewe (sheep, impala), vixen (fox), tigress (tiger), leopardess (leopard), lioness (lion), nanny goat (goat), jenny (ass, donkey), queen (cat), jill (ferret)

▶ *568 Female*

19 young mammal, kitten (cat, bobcat, beaver, rabbit, skunk), kit (weasel), pup (*or* puppy) (dog), whelp (wolf, dog), cub (bear, fox, lion, tiger, leopard, badger), calf (cattle, buffalo, camel, elephant, elk, giraffe, rhinoceros, seal, whale), dogie (US), weaner (any weaned animal), foal (horse, zebra), colt (horse), filly (horse), piglet (pig), lamb (sheep), lambkin (sheep), kid (goat, antelope, roe deer), yeanling (goat, sheep), fawn (deer, caribou, reindeer), leveret (hare), joey (kangaroo)

20 abode of mammals, lair, den, covert, form, burrow, earth, sett (*or* set), lodge, couch, run, drey, sty, pen, pound, cage, corral, stable, stall, hutch

21 assemblage of mammals, pack, herd, drove, train, troop, team, flock, school (porpoises), bevy (roedeer), leap, pride (lions)

22 mammologist, primatologist, zoologist

23 mammal hunting, big-game hunting, fox-hunting, stag hunting, deerstalking, chase, chivy (*or* chevy), venery, hare coursing, beagling, otter hunting, pigsticking, boar hunting, bear-baiting, bullfighting, dog-fighting, whaling, trapping, ratting, ferreting, rabbiting, mole-catching

24 hunter, big-game hunter, white hunter, fox-hunter, deerstalker, trapper, rat-catcher, rodent operative

ADJECTIVES

25 mammalian, mammal-like, warm-blooded, homoiothermic, prototherian, monotrematous, metatherian, marsupial, marsupialian (*or* marsupian), eutherian, placental (*or* placentate)

26 insectivorous, anteating, pholidote, tubulidentate, edentate, toothless

27 chiropteran, dermopteran, winged, flying

28 carnivorous, flesh-eating, clawed, unguiculate, canine, doglike, doggy, doggish, puppyish, foxy, foxlike, vulpine,

MARSUPIALS

bandicoot	marsupial rat	sminthopsis
cuscus	mouse opossum	Tasmanian devil
dasyure	numbat	thylacine,
Diprotodon*	opossum, possum	Tasmanian wolf
flying phalanger	(Inf)	tree kangaroo
hare wallaby	pademelon	wallaby
honey mouse (*or*	phalanger	wallaroo
honey phalanger)	planigale	wombat
kangaroo	quokka	yapok
koala	rat kangaroo	
marsupial mole	rat opossum	*extinct
marsupial mouse	rock wallaby	marsupial

PLACENTAL MAMMALS

aardvark, ant bear
aardwolf
acouchi
addax
African elephant
agouti
ai
alpaca
angwantibo
anoa
ant bear, aardvark
anteater
antelope
aoudad
ape
Arctic fox
Arctic hare
argali
armadillo
ass
aurochs, urus
axis deer
aye–aye
babirusa
baboon
Bactrian camel
badger
Baluchitherium*
bamboo rat
banteng
Barbary ape
barbastelle
barking deer, muntjac
bat
bear
beaver
bettong
bighorn
binturong
bison, buffalo (US)
black bear
blackbuck
blesbok
blue fox
blue whale

boar, wild boar
bobcat
bongo
bontebok
bottlenose
Brontotherium*
brown bear
buffalo
bushbaby
bushbuck
cachalot
cacomistle
camel
camelopard (Arch)
cane rat
Cape buffalo
capuchin monkey
capybara
caracal
carcajou (US), wolverine, glutton
caribou
cat
catamount (*or* catamountain)
cattle
cavy
chamois
cheetah
chevrotain, mouse deer
chickaree, American red squirrel
chigetai
chimpanzee
chinchilla
Chinese water deer
chipmunk
chiru
chital
cinnamon bear
civet
clouded leopard
coati (*or* coatimundi)
colobus
colugo

cony
cottontail
cougar, puma, mountain lion
cow
coyote
coypu
crabeater seal
creodont*
deer
deer mouse
desert rat
desman
dhole
dik–dik
dingo
dog
dolphin
donkey
Dorcas gazelle
dormouse
douroucouli
drill
dromedary
Dryopithecus*
dugong
duiker
eland
elephant
elephant seal (*or* sea elephant)
elk
entellus
eohippus*
ermine
eyra
fallow deer
fennec
ferret
fieldmouse
fisher
flying fox
flying lemur
flying squirrel
fossa

foumart, polecat
fox
fruit bat
galago
gaur
gayal
gazelle
gelada
gemsbok
genet
gerbil
gerenuk
gibbon
giraffe, camelopard (Arch)
glutton, wolverine
Glyptodon*
gnu
goat
goat antelope
golden cat
golden mole
gopher
goral
gorilla
grampus
grass monkey
grey squirrel
grey wolf
grison
grizzly bear
groundhog
ground squirrel
guanaco
guenon
guinea pig
gymnure, hairy hedgehog
hamadryas
hamster
harbour seal
hare
hartebeest
harvest mouse
hedgehog
hinny
Hipparion*

hippopotamus, hippo (Inf)
hog
honey badger, ratel
honey bear
hooded seal
horse
horseshoe bat
howler monkey
humpback whale
hutia
hyena (*or* hyaena)
hyrax
ibex
impala
Indian elephant
indri
Irish elk*
jackal
jackrabbit
jaguar
jaguarundi
jerboa
jumping mouse
kangaroo rat
kiang
killer whale
kinkajou
kit fox (*or* swift fox)
klipspringer
kob
Kodiak bear
kudu
langur
lemming
lemur
leopard
leopard seal
liger
linsang
lion
llama
loris
lynx
macaque
mammoth*

vulpecular, wolflike, wolfish, lupine, bearish, bearlike, ursine, weaselly, musteline, viverrine, feline, catlike, cattish, catty, kittenish, leonine, lion-like, tigerish, tiger-like

29 cetacean, cetaceous, whalelike, pinniped, pinnipedian, seal-like, sirenian

30 rodent-like, rodentian, gnawing, murine, ratlike, rattish, ratty, mouselike, mousy (*or* mousey), squirrel-like, sciurine

31 rabbit-like, rabbity, harelike, lagomorphic, lagomorphous, leporid, leporine

32 pachydermatous, subungulate, proboscidean (*or* proboscidian), elephantine, elephantoid, rhinocerotic

33 ungulate, hoofed, unguligrade, cloven-hoofed, perissodactyl, odd-toed, equine, horselike, horsy (*or* horsey), asinine, mulish, artiodactyl, artiodactylous, even-toed, piglike, piggy, piggish, porcine, hoggish, swinish, ruminant, cud-chewing, camel-like, camelid, deerlike, cervid, cervine, oxlike, bovid, bovine, cowlike, cowish, bull-like, bullish, taurine, sheep-like, ovine, goatlike, caprine, hircine, cavicorn, hyrax-like, hyracoid

34 primate, primatial, prosimian, anthropoid, simian, simious, pongid, hominid

VERBS

35 give birth, drop, farrow, lamb, foal, calve, cub, pup, whelp, kitten, litter, kindle

36 lactate, milk, nurse, suckle, breast-feed

37 graze, ruminate, chew the cud, browse, grass

ADVERBS

38 warmly, homoiothermically, insectivorously, carnivorously, doggily, cattily, foxily, wolfishly, bullishly, sheepishly

PLACENTAL MAMMALS (CONT.)

manatee
mandrill
mangabey
mara
margay
markhor
marmoset
marmot
marten
mastodon*
meerkat
Megaloceros*
Megatherium*
mink
mole
mole rat
mona monkey
mongoose
monkey
moon rat
moose
mouflon
mountain beaver
mountain cat
mountain goat (*or* Rocky Mountain goat)
mountain lion, puma, cougar
mountain sheep
mouse
mouse deer, chevrotain
mule
mule deer
muntjac, barking deer
musk deer
musk ox
muskrat, musquash
Mylodon*
narwhal
New World monkey
nilgai
noctule
nyala
ocelot
okapi
Old World monkey
olingo
onager
orang–utan
oribi
oryx
otter
otter shrew
ounce, snow leopard
ox
paca
pack (*or* wood rat)
Pallas's cat
palm civet
pampas cat
panda
pangolin, scaly anteater
panther
patas monkey
peccary
Père David's deer
pig
pika
pilot whale
pine marten
pipistrelle
pocket gopher
pocket mouse
polar bear
polecat, foumart
porcupine
porpoise
potto
pouched rat
prairie dog (*or* prairie marmot)
prairie wolf
proboscis monkey
Proconsul*
pronghorn (*or* pronghorn antelope)
puma, cougar, mountain lion
pygmy hippopotamus
quagga*
rabbit
raccoon
raccoon dog
rat
ratel, honey badger
red deer
red fox
red squirrel
reedbuck
reindeer
rhesus monkey
rhinoceros, rhino (Inf)
right whale
roan antelope
Rocky Mountain goat (*or* mountain goat)
roe deer
rorqual
royal antelope
sable
sable antelope
sabre–toothed tiger (*or* cat), Smilodon*
saiga
saki
sambar (*or* sambur)
scaly anteater, pangolin
scaly–tailed squirrel
sea cow
sea elephant (*or* elephant seal)
seal
sea lion
sea otter
sei whale
serotine bat
serow
serval
sheep
shrew
siamang
sifaka
sika
silver fox
sitatunga
skunk
sloth
sloth bear
Smilodon, sabre–toothed tiger*
snow leopard, ounce
snowshoe hare (*or* snowshoe rabbit)
solenodon
souslik (*or* suslik)
spectacled bear
sperm whale
spider monkey
spiny dormouse
springbok
springhaas
squirrel
squirrel monkey
Stegodon*
steinbok
stoat
stone marten
sun bear
suslik (*or* souslik)
swine
tahr
takin
talapoin
tamandua
tamarin
tamarou
tapir
tarpan*
tarsier
tatouay
tayra
tenrec
tiger
tigon
timber wolf
titanothere*
titi
tucotuco
tree shrew
unau
urus, aurochs
vampire bat
vervet
vicuna
Virginia (*or* white–tailed deer)
viscacha
vole
walrus
wapiti
warthog
waterbuck
water buffalo
water rat
water shrew
water vole
weasel
whale
white rhinoceros
white whale
wild boar
wildcat
wild dog
wildebeest
wisent, European bison
wolf
wolverine, glutton, carcajou (US)
woodchuck
wood (*or* pack) rat
woolly monkey
woolly rhinoceros
woolly spider monkey
yak
zebra
zebu
zorilla

*extinct mammal

72 Birds

All the birds of the air
Fell a-sighing and a-sobbing,
When they heard the bell toll
For poor Cock Robin. Nursery rhyme.

NOUNS

1 birds, birdlife, avifauna, Aves, wildfowl, fowl of the air, fowl, birdie (Inf), feathered friend, bird of peace, dove, bird of passage, migratory bird, migrant

2 flightless bird, ratite, ostrich, rhea, cassowary, emu, kiwi, takahe, penguin

3 water bird, seabird, oceanic bird, gull, seagull, shag, tern, skua, puffin, auk, albatross, petrel, fulmar, shearwater, frigate bird, gannet, cormorant, fishing bird, pelican, kingfisher, diving bird, diver, loon, grebe, wading bird, wader, marsh bird, mud hen, shore bird, plover, sandpiper, lapwing, curlew, snipe, avocet, oystercatcher, crane, rail, crake, coot, heron, bittern, stork, flamingo, spoonbill, ibis, waterfowl, duck, dabbling duck, diving duck, perching duck, whistling duck, sea duck, swan, goose

4 table bird, game bird, game fowl, pheasant, partridge, grouse, quail, snipe, woodcock, guinea fowl, pigeon, turkey, domestic fowl

► *25 Cookery; 43 Agriculture*

5 bird of prey, raptor, falcon, hawk, goshawk, eagle, osprey, kestrel, harrier, kite, vulture, condor, buzzard, owl, barn owl, screech owl, hoot owl, horned owl

6 songbird, passerine (bird), perching bird, lark, wren, warbler, flycatcher, thrush, tit, shrike, wagtail, pipit, bunting, finch, Darwin's (*or* Galapagos) finches, weaver-

BIRDS

accentor
adjutant stork
Aepyornis, elephant bird*
albatross
American (*or* bald) eagle
antbird
apteryx, kiwi
Archaeopteryx*
Arctic tern
auk
auklet
avadavat (*or* amadavat)
avocet
babbler
bald (*or* American) eagle
Baltimore oriole
barbet
barnacle goose
barn owl
bateleur
bearded tit, reedling
bearded vulture, lammergeier
bee–eater
bird of paradise
bittern
blackbird
blackcap
black grouse
black swan
bluebill (US), scaup
bluebird
bluetit
boatbill
bobolink
bobwhite (*or* bobwhite quail)
booby
bowerbird
brambling
brent goose, brent, brant (US)
broadbill
brush turkey
budgerigar, budgie (Inf)
bulbul
bullfinch
bunting
burrowing owl
bushtit
bush wren
bustard
butcherbird
button quail
buzzard
Canada goose
canary
canvasback (*or* canvasback duck)
capercaillie
caracara
cardinal (*or* cardinal bird)
carrion crow
cassowary
catbird
chaffinch
chat
chickadee
chiffchaff
chipping sparrow
chough
coal tit
cockatiel
cockatoo
coly
condor
coot
cormorant
corncrake
courser
cowbird
crake
crane
creeper (US), treecreeper
crested tit
crocodile bird
crossbill
crow
cuckoo
cuckoo–shrike
curassow
curlew
currawong
dabchick
darter
demoiselle crane
diamondbird
dipper
diver
dodo*
dotterel
dove
drongo
duck
dunlin
dunnock, hedge sparrow
eagle
eagle owl
egret
eider (*or* eider duck)
elephant bird, Aepyornis*
emperor penguin
emu
emu wren
erne (*or* ern), sea eagle
fairy bluebird
fairy penguin
falcon
fantail
fieldfare
finch
finfoot
firecrest
fish hawk, osprey
fish owl
flamingo
flicker
flowerpecker
flycatcher
francolin
friarbird
frigate bird, man–of–war (*or* man–o'–war) bird
frogmouth
fulmar
gadwall
gallinule
gannet, solan goose (Arch)
garganey
gnatcatcher
goatsucker (US), nightjar
godwit
goldcrest
golden eagle
goldeneye
golden pheasant
goldfinch
goose
goosander
goshawk
grackle
grassfinch
great crested grebe
great tit
grebe
greenfinch
greenshank
greylag goose
griffon vulture
grosbeak
guillemot
guinea fowl
gull, seagull, mew, sea mew
gyrfalcon
hammerhead
harlequin duck
harpy eagle
harrier
Hawaiian goose
hawfinch
hawk
hawk owl
hedge sparrow, dunnock
heron
herring gull
Hesperornis*
hill mynah
hoatzin
hobby
honeycreeper
honeyeater
honey guide
hooded crow
hoopoe
hoot owl
hornbill
horned owl
house martin
house sparrow
huia
hummingbird
ibis
Ichthyornis*
ivory–billed woodpecker
jabiru
jacamar
jacana
jackdaw
jay
junco
jungle fowl
kagu
kakapo
kea
kestrel
killdeer
kingbird
kingfisher
kinglet
kite
kittiwake
kiwi, apteryx
knot
kookaburra
lammergeier, bearded vulture
lanner falcon
lapwing, peewit
lark
laughing jackass
laughing owl
linnet
little owl
long–tailed tit
lory
lovebird
lyrebird
macaw
magpie
mallard

bird, sparrow, starling, oriole, crow, magpie, jackdaw, rook, raven, nightingale

7 cagebird, canary, songster, talking bird, parrot, parakeet, budgerigar, budgie (Inf), mynah bird, cockatoo

8 extinct bird, fossil bird, Archaeopteryx, Aepyornis, elephant bird, moa, dodo, great auk, passenger pigeon

9 fabulous bird, mythological bird, phoenix, roc, garuda, senmurv, simurg, cockatrice, griffin (*or* griffon *or* gryphon), harpy, bird god, Horus, heraldic bird, martlet

10 male bird, cock, cockerel, chanticleer, rooster, tom turkey, turkey cock, gobbler (Inf), bubby-jock (Scot), peacock, guinea cock, drake, gander, cob, blackcock, heathcock, cock-sparrow, cock-robin

11 female bird, hen, peahen, pen, greyhen, heath hen, goose, duck

12 young bird, chick, poult, pullet, eaglet, owlet, cygnet, duckling, gosling, eyas, squab, nestling, fledgling, clutch, hatch, brood

13 assemblage of birds, flock, flight, gaggle (geese), skein (geese), covey (grouse, partridge), covert (coots), wing, charm, exaltation (larks), murder (crows)

14 nest, perch, roost, eyrie, aerie (US), rookery, covert, mew, lek, nest site, nestbox, bird box, birdhouse (US), hatchery, nest building, nidification

15 eggs, hatch, clutch, egg, shell, eggshell, white, yolk, vitelline membrane, chalaza

16 avian anatomy, bill, beak, feathers, wings, talons, syrinx, carina, keel, wishbone, crop, gizzard, webbed feet

17 plumage, feathers, ruff, crest, plume, frill, feather, contour feather, quill, vane, rachis, barbule, barbicel, aftershaft, down feathers, plumulae, down, eiderdown, swan's-down, flight feather, wing feather, primary, secondary, tail feather, rectrix (*pl.* rectrices), remex (*pl.* remiges), alula, bastard wing, filoplume, covert, tectrix (*pl.* tectrices), pteryla, apterium

18 bird song, bird call, dawn chorus, chirp, chirrup, cheep, peep, tweet, twitter, warble, hoot, cock-a-doodle-doo
► *515 Animal Cry*

19 ornithology, birdwatching, ringing, birdbanding (US),

BIRDS (CONT.)

mallee fowl
manakin
mandarin duck
mannikin
man–of–war (*or* man–o'–war) bird, frigate bird
marabou (*or* marabou stork)
marsh harrier
martin
mavis (Dial), song thrush
meadowlark
megapode
merganser
merlin
mew, mew gull, sea mew
minivet
mistle (*or* missel) thrush
moa*
mockingbird
moorhen
Mother Carey's chicken, storm (*or* stormy) petrel
motmot
mourning dove
mousebird
murre
Muscovy duck
mute swan
muttonbird
mynah (*or* myna), mynah (*or* myna) bird
night hawk
night heron
nightingale
nightjar, goatsucker (US)
noddy
nutcracker
nuthatch
oilbird
oriole
ortolan
osprey, fish hawk
ostrich
ouzel
ovenbird
owl
owlet frogmouth
oxpecker
oystercatcher
parakeet
parrot
partridge
passenger pigeon*
peacock
peafowl
peewee (*or* pewee)
peewit, lapwing
pelican
penguin
peregrine falcon
petrel
pewee (*or* peewee)
phalarope
pheasant
Philippine eagle
phoebe
pigeon
pigeon hawk
pintail
pipit, titlark
plains–wanderer
plover
pochard
pratincole
prion
ptarmigan
puffin
pygmy owl
quail
quelea
quetzal
rail
raven
razorbill
red grouse
redhead
redpoll
redshank
redstart
redwing
reedbird
reedling, bearded tit
reed warbler
rhea
ricebird
riflebird
rifleman
ringdove
ring–necked pheasant
ring ouzel
roadrunner
robin
rock dove
roller
rook
rosella
ruddy duck
ruff
ruffed grouse
sacred ibis
saddleback
sage grouse
sanderling
sandgrouse
sand martin
sandpiper
sapsucker
scaup, bluebill (US)
scops owl
screamer
screech owl
scrub bird
sea eagle, erne (*or* ern)
seagull, gull, sea mew
secretary bird
seriema
serin
shag
shearwater
sheathbill
shelduck
shoebill
shoveler duck
shrike
siskin
skimmer
skua
skylark
smew
snakebird
snipe
snow bunting (*or* snowbird)
snow goose
snowy owl
solan *or* solan goose (Arch), gannet
song thrush, mavis (Dial)
sparrow
sparrowhawk
spoonbill
standardwing
starling
stilt
stonechat
stone curlew
stork
storm (*or* stormy) petrel, Mother Carey's chicken
sunbird
sun bittern
swallow
swan
swiftlet
tailorbird
takahe
tanager
tawny owl
teal
tern
thickhead
thornbill
thrasher
thrush
tinamou
tit, titmouse
titlark, pipit
toucan
touraco (*or* turaco)
towhee
tragopan
tree creeper, creeper (US)
trogon
tropic bird
trumpeter
tui
turaco (*or* touraco)
turkey
turkey buzzard (*or* turkey vulture)
turnstone
turtledove
tyrant flycatcher
umbrella bird
vulture
wagtail
wallcreeper
warbler
waxbill
waxwing
weaverbird (*or* weaver)
weaverfinch
wheatear
whidah (*or* whydah)
whimbrel
whinchat
whipbird
whippoorwill
whistler
white–eye
whitethroat
whooping crane
whydah (*or* whidah)
wigeon (*or* widgeon)
willet
willow warbler
woodchat
woodcock
woodcreeper
wood duck
woodpecker
wood pigeon
wren
wren babbler
wrybill
wryneck thers
yellowhammer
yellowlegs
zebra finch

*extinct *or* fossil bird

aviculture, aviary, swannery, bird sanctuary, bird reserve, birdhouse, birdcage, dovecote, pigeon loft, columbarium, nestbox, bird box, hatchery

20 ornithologist, aviculturist, fancier, pigeon fancier, ringer, birdwatcher, birder (Inf), twitcher (Inf)

ADJECTIVES

21 avian, birdlike, birdy, flightless, ratite, ostrich-like, struthious, struthioniform, gooselike, goosy, anserine (*or* anserous), anseriform, fowl-like, gallinaceous, galliform, rasorial, dovelike, pigeon-like, columbine, columbiform, parrot-like, psittacine, psittaciform, cuckoo-like, cuculiform, raptorial, predatory, hawkish, aquiline, vulturine, owl-like, owlish, strigiform, swallow-like, hirundine, perching, passerine, passeriform, singing, oscine, finchlike, fringilline (*or* fringillid), thrushlike, turdine, crowlike, corvine

22 newly hatched, unfledged, altricial, newly fledged, precocial, nidicolous, nidifugous

23 ornithological, avicultural

VERBS

24 nest, nidify, brood, hatch, perch, peck, preen

► *561 Reproduction*

25 fly, take wing, wing, soar, hover

► *300 Motion; 304 Ascent; 319 Transport*

26 sing, warble, chirp, chirrup, cheep, peep, tweet, twitter, hoot

73 Reptiles and Amphibians

Eye of newt, and toe of frog,
Wool of bat, and tongue of dog,
Adder's fork, and blind-worm's sting,
Lizard's leg, and howlet's wing… William Shakespeare.

NOUNS

1 reptile, reptilian, cold-blooded animal, poikilotherm, Reptilia, Squamata (lizards and snakes), Rhynocephalia (tuatara), Crocodilia (crocodilians)

2 lizard, saurian, lacertilian (*or* lacertian), Sauria, Lacertilia, iguana, chameleon, gecko, skink, monitor, glass snake, Komodo dragon, basilisk, legless lizard, slow-worm, lizard-like reptile, rhynocephalian, tuatara

3 snake, serpent, ophidian, Serpentes, Ophidia, nonvenomous snake, constrictor, boa, python, anaconda, venomous snake, viper, asp, cobra, mamba, rattlesnake, rattler (US inf), legendary serpent, basilisk, cockatrice

4 chelonian, chelonid, tortoise, turtle, terrapin

5 crocodilian, crocodile, alligator, cayman, croc (Inf), gator (US inf)

6 extinct reptile, fossil reptile, giant reptile, terrestrial reptile, dinosaur, ornithischian, ornithopod, saurischian, sauropod, marine reptile, ichthyopterygian, ichthyosaur, sauropterygian, plesiosaur, nothosaur, mosasaur, flying reptile, pterosaur, mammal-like reptile, therapsid

7 amphibian, batrachian, Amphibia, limbless amphibian, caecilian, apodan, Apoda (*or* Gymnophiona), tailed amphibian, urodele, caudate, Urodela *or* Caudata (salamanders, newts), tailless amphibian, salientian, anuran, Salienta *or* Anura (frogs, toads), paddock (Dial)

8 young amphibian, frogspawn, tadpole, polliwog, froglet, toadlet, metamorphosis, immature amphibian, neotenous amphibian, axolotl, neoteny, paedogenesis

9 herpetology, ophiology, reptile house, reptilarium, reptiliary

10 herpetologist, ophiologist, snake charmer

ADJECTIVES

11 reptilian, reptilelike, reptiliform, reptiloid, apodal (*or* apodous), cold-blooded, poikilothermic, creeping, slithering, reptant, lizard-like, saurian, lacertilian, snakelike, ophidian, turtlelike, chelonian, crocodilian, scaly, squamous

12 snakelike, snaky, serpentine, serpentiform, sinuous, twisting, ophidian, ophiomorphic, colubrine, colubriform, anguine, viper-like, viperish, viperous (*or* viperine), hissing

13 amphibian, batrachian, apodan, salamandrian, newt-like, caudate, neotenous, frog-like, froggy, toadlike, toadish, anuran, salientian

14 herpetological, herpetology, ophiological

VERBS

15 live as a reptile, creep, crawl, glide, twist, hiss

► *325 Deviation; 512 Hissing Sound*

16 live as an amphibian, creep, crawl, hop, croak, grunt

► *333 Slowness; 513 Harsh Sound; 515 Animal Cry*

AMPHIBIANS

arrow–poison frog
axolotl
bullfrog
caecilian
clawed frog, Xenopus
congo eel (*or* congo snake)
eft (Dial)
fire salamander
frog
goliath frog
hairy frog
hellbender
labyrinthodont*
midwife toad
mudpuppy
natterjack (*or* natterjack toad)
newt, eft (Dial)
olm
pipa, Surinam toad
salamander
siren
spadefoot toad
Surinam toad, pipa toad
tree frog
Xenopus, clawed frog
*extinct amphibian

REPTILES

adder
agama
alligator
amphisbaena
anaconda
anole
asp
basilisk
bearded lizard
black snake
blind snake
blindworm
boa
boa constrictor
boomslang
box turtle
bull snake
bushmaster
cayman
chameleon
chuckwalla
cobra
constrictor
copperhead
coral snake
cottonmouth, water moccasin
crocodile
diamondback (rattlesnake *or* terrapin)
fer–de–lance
flying lizard (*or* flying dragon)
flying snake
frilled lizard
gaboon viper
Galápagos giant tortoise
garter snake
gavial (*or* gharial)
gecko
Gila monster
glass snake
grass snake
green turtle
hamadryad, king cobra
harlequin snake
hawksbill turtle
hognose snake
horned toad (*or* horned lizard)
horned viper
iguana
jacaré
king cobra, hamadryad
king snake
Komodo dragon
krait
leatherback (*or* leatherback turtle)
lizard
loggerhead (*or* loggerhead turtle)
mamba
mangrove snake
matamata, snake–necked turtle
milk snake
moccasin, water moccasin, cottonmouth
moloch
monitor lizard
mugger
pit viper
pond turtle
puff adder
python
racer
rat snake
rattlesnake, rattler (US inf)
ringhals
Russell's viper
sand lizard
sea snake
sidewinder
skink
slow–worm
smooth snake
snake
snake–necked turtle, matamata
snapping turtle
soft–shelled turtle
sphenodon, tuatara
taipan
terrapin
tokay
tortoise
tree snake
tuatara, sphenodon
turtle
vine snake
viper
wart snake
water moccasin, cottonmouth
water snake
whip snake
worm lizard

Fossil Reptiles

allosaur, Allosaurus
ankylosaur, Ankylosaurus
apatosaur, Apatosaurus
atlantosaur, Atlantosaurus
brachiosaur, Brachiosaurus
brontosaur, Brontosaurus
cotylosaur
dicynodon(t), Dicynodon
Dimetrodon
Diplodocus
elasmosaur
hadrosaur, Hadrosaurus
ichthyosaur, Ichthyosaurus
iguanodon(t), Iguanodon
megalosaur, Megalosaurus
Mesosaurus
mosasaur, Mosasaurus
nothosaur, Nothosaurus
Ornitholestes
pelycosaur
phytosaur
plesiosaur, Plesiosaurus
pliosaur, Pliosaurus
Protoceratops
pteranodon(t), Pteranodon
pterosaur (*or* pterodactyl)
stegodon(t), Stegodon
stegosaur, Stegosaurus
titanosaur
Triceratops
tyrannosaur, Tyrannosaurus

74 Fishes

3RD FISHERMAN: *Master, I marvel how the fishes live in the sea.*
1ST FISHERMAN: *Why, as men do a-land – the great ones eat up the little ones.* William Shakespeare.

NOUNS

1 fishes, fish, Pisces, sea fish(es), saltwater fish(es), marine fish(es), shoal, school, freshwater fish(es)

2 fish, jawless fish, cyclostome, cartilaginous fish, Chondrichthyes, elasmobranch, selachian, holocephalan, bony fish, lobe-finned fish, crossopterygian, dipnoan, ray-finned fish, teleost fish, flying fish, mouthbrooder, flatfish, food fish, game fish, aquarium fish, tropical fish

3 young fish, fry, elver, alevin, fingerling, parr, smolt, grilse

4 fossil fish, placoderm, arthrodire, ostracoderm, Pteraspis, crossopterygian, Osteolepis, living fossil, coelacanth

5 fish anatomy, fin, pectoral fin, pelvic fin, dorsal fin, anal fin, caudal fin, tail fin, scale, placoid scale, ganoid scale, cosmoid scale, gill, gill cover, operculum, gill slit, spiracle, swim bladder, air bladder, lateral line, roe, soft roe, hard roe

6 study of fish, ichthyology, fish breeding, fish farm, aquarium, fishpond, fishtank, fishbowl

7 fishing, piscatology, fishability, angling, game fishing, coarse fishing, fly-fishing, sea fishing, big-game fishing, deep-sea fishing, shark fishing, whaling, fish farming, pisciculture, fishery, fishing bank, fishing ground, piscary, fishing fleet, trawler, shrimper, fish-finder, fish-hold, fishing line, fish line (US), fishnet, trawl, drift net, seine, catch, tonnara, eel basket, fishgig, fishtrap, fish weir, fish ladder, fish way (US), gill net, shark net, fish-hook

FISHES

- albacore
- alewife
- amberjack
- anchovy
- anemone fish
- angelfish
- anglerfish
- archer fish
- barbel
- barracuda
- barramunda
- basking shark
- bass
- batfish
- beluga
- bichir
- black bass
- blackfish
- bleak
- blenny
- blindfish
- blowfish, puffer
- bluefish
- blue shark
- Bombay duck
- bonito
- bonefish
- bowfin
- boxfish, trunkfish
- bream
- brill
- brisling
- brook trout
- brotulid
- brown trout
- buffalo fish
- bullhead
- burbot
- butterfish
- butterfly fish
- candlefish
- capelin
- carp
- catfish
- cave fish
- char
- characin
- chimera
- Chinook salmon
- chub
- cichlid
- cisco
- climbing perch
- clingfish
- cobia
- cod (*or* codfish)
- coelacanth, Latimeria
- conger eel
- cornetfish
- crappie
- croaker
- cutlass fish
- dab
- dace
- damselfish
- danio
- darter
- dealfish
- devil ray (*or* fish), manta ray
- dogfish
- Dolly Varden (trout)
- dorado
- dory
- dragonet
- dragonfish
- drumfish
- eel
- eelpout
- electric eel
- electric ray
- fighting fish
- filefish
- flatfish
- flathead
- flounder
- fluke
- flying fish
- flying gurnard
- four–eyed fish
- frogfish
- gar (*or* garfish *or* garpike)
- ghost shark
- glassfish
- globefish
- goblin shark
- goby
- goldfish
- goosefish
- gourami
- grayling
- Greenland shark
- grenadier
- grey mullet
- grouper
- grunion
- grunt
- gudgeon
- guitar fish
- gunnel
- guppy
- gurnard
- haddock
- hagfish
- hake
- halfbeak
- halibut
- hammerhead shark
- hatchetfish
- herring
- hippocampus, sea horse
- hogfish
- horse mackerel
- icefish
- ide
- jewfish
- John Dory
- killifish
- kingfish
- labyrinth fish
- lake trout
- lamprey
- lancet fish
- lantern fish
- Latimeria, coelacanth
- lemon sole
- ling
- lizard fish
- loach
- lumpsucker
- lungfish
- mackerel
- mackerel shark, porbeagle
- mako shark
- man–eating shark
- manta ray, devil ray (*or* fish)
- marlin
- menhaden
- midshipman
- miller's thumb
- minnow
- molly
- monkfish
- moonfish
- Moorish idol
- moray eel
- mudfish
- mudskipper
- mullet
- Murray cod
- muskellunge
- needlefish
- nurse shark
- oarfish
- opah
- orfe
- paddlefish
- parrot fish
- pearlfish
- perch
- pickerel
- pike
- pikeperch
- pilchard
- pilot fish
- pink salmon
- pipefish
- piranha
- plaice
- pollack
- pompano
- porbeagle, mackerel shark
- porcupine fish
- porgy
- powan
- puffer, blowfish
- rabbitfish
- rainbow trout
- ratfish
- ray
- redfin
- redfish
- red mullet
- red (*or* sockeye) salmon
- remora, suckerfish
- requiem shark
- ribbonfish
- roach
- rock bass
- rudd
- sailfish
- saithe
- salmon
- salmon trout
- sardine
- saury
- sawfish
- scorpion fish
- sculpin
- scup
- sea bass
- sea bream
- sea horse, hippocampus
- sea perch
- sea robin
- sea trout
- sergeant fish
- shad
- shark
- shovelhead
- shovelnose
- silverside
- skate
- skipjack (*or* skipjack tuna)
- smelt
- snapper
- snook
- sockeye (*or* red salmon)
- sole
- sprat
- stargazer
- steelhead (*or* steelhead trout)
- stickleback
- stingray
- stone bass
- stonefish
- sturgeon
- sucker
- suckerfish, remora
- sunfish
- surgeonfish
- swamp eel
- swordfish
- swordtail
- tarpon
- tautog
- tench
- tetra
- thornback (*or* thornback ray)
- threadfin
- thresher (*or* thresher shark)
- tigerfish
- tiger shark
- toadfish
- tooth carp
- tope
- top minnow
- torpedo fish
- triggerfish
- trout
- trunkfish, boxfish
- tuna, tunny
- turbot
- wahoo
- walleye (*or* walleyed pike)
- weakfish
- weever
- wels
- whale shark
- whitebait
- whitefish
- white shark
- whiting
- wolf fish
- wrasse
- wreckfish
- yellowfin tuna
- yellowtail
- zebra fish

► *55 Fishing*

8 **food fish**, cod, haddock, mackerel, herring, whitebait, sprat, sardine, flatfish, plaice, sole, halibut, turbot, game fish, salmon, trout, wet fish, pan fish, preserved fish, smoked fish, kipper, bloater, brisling, smoked haddock, finnan haddock (*or* haddie), stockfish, jellied eel, rollmop

9 **fish product**, fish roe, herring roe, caviar, fish-liver oil, cod-liver oil, fishmeal, fish glue, isinglass

► *25 Cookery; 55 Fishing*

10 **fisher**, angler, whaler, fisherman, trawlerman, piscator, fisherfolk, fish farmer, pisciculturalist, fish seller, fishmonger, fishman, fishwife

11 **fishing animal**, otter, sea otter, polar bear, fishing cat, fish eagle (*or* hawk), osprey, kingfisher

12 **ichthyologist**, aquarist, fish lover, ichthyophile

ADJECTIVES

13 **fishlike**, fishy, cold-blooded, poikilothermic, piscine, pisciform, piscatorial (*or* piscatory), ichthyic, ichthyoid(al), ichthyomorphic, sharklike, sharkish, selachian, herring-like, clupeoid, codlike, gadoid, perchlike, percoid, carplike, cyprinoid, eel-like, anguilliform

14 **ichthyological**, piscicultural, piscatorial (*or* piscatory), scaly, squamous

VERBS

15 **fish**, angle, fly-fish, trawl, net, shrimp, seine

► *55 Fishing; 633 Pursuit*

75 Invertebrates

The cut worm forgives the plough. William Blake.

NOUNS

1 **invertebrate**, lower animal, invertebrate chordate, protochordate, many-celled invertebrate, metazoan, Metazoa, nonchordate invertebrate, mesozoan, parazoan, single-celled invertebrate, protozoan, protist

2 **protochordate**, hemichordate, Hemichordata, acorn worm, chordate, Chordata, urochordate, Urochordata, tunicate, ascidian, sea squirt, salp, cephalochordate, Cephalochordata (*or* Acrania), lancelet, amphioxus, craniate, Craniata (vertebrates)

► *71 Mammals; 72 Birds; 73 Reptiles and Amphibians; 74 Fishes*

3 **echinoderm**, Echinodermata, crinoid, sea lily, feather star, asteroid (*or* asteroidean), starfish, crown-of-thorns, sea star, ophiuroid, brittle star, echinoid, sea urchin, heart urchin, sand dollar, sea biscuit, holothurian, sea cucumber, trepang, bêche-de-mer

4 **arthropod**, Arthropoda, extinct arthropod, trilobite, eurypterid, living fossil, horseshoe (*or* king) crab, limulus, arachnid, Arachnida (scorpions, spiders, ticks, mites, *etc.*), insect, Insecta, pycnogonid, Pycnogonida (sea spiders), crustacean, Crustacea, branchiopod, fairy shrimp, brine shrimp, tadpole shrimp, water flea, daphnia, ostracod, mussel shrimp, seed shrimp, copepod, cyclops, branchiuran, fish louse, cirripede, barnacle, acorn barnacle, stalked barnacle, goose barnacle, malacostracan, amphipod, mantis shrimp, Tasmanian shrimp, opossum shrimp, sand hopper (*or* beach hopper *or* sand flea *or* beach flea), skeleton shrimp, whale louse, isopod, water louse, woodlouse, pill bug, sow bug (US), slater (Aus), gribble, shrimp, prawn, crab, hermit crab, robber (*or* coconut) crab, fiddler crab, pea crab, spider crab, land crab, lobster, crayfish, spiny lobster, crawfish (US), shellfish, seafood, myriapod, Myriapoda, diplopod, Diplopoda (millipedes), thousand-leggers (Inf), chilopod, Chilopoda (centipedes), pauropod, symphylan, arthropod-like invertebrate, tardigrade, water bear, Tardigrada, pentastomid, Pentastomida, onychophoran, Onychophora

► *25 Cookery; 76 Insects and Arachnids*

5 **mollusc**, Mollusca, amphineuran, Amphineura (chitons), gastropod (*or* gasteropod), Gastropoda (limpets, snails, slugs, *etc.*), bivalve, lamellibranch, Bivalvia *or* Lamellibranchia (shellfish, clams, mussels, scallops, oysters, *etc.*), scaphopod, Scaphopoda (tusk shells), cephalopod, Cephalopoda (cuttlefish, squids, octopods, octopuses, *etc.*), mollusc-like invertebrate, lampshell, brachiopod, Brachiopoda

► *25 Cookery*

6 **worm**, parasitic worm, helminth, flatworm, platyhelminth, Platyhelminthes, free-living flatworm, planarian, turbellarian, Turbellaria, parasitic flatworm, fluke, liver fluke, blood fluke, trematode, Trematoda, tapeworm, cestode, Cestoda, ribbonworm, nemertean (*or* nemertine), Nemertea (*or* Nemertina), aschelminth, roundworm, nematode, Nematoda, horsehair worm, nematomorph, Nematomorpha, wheel animacule (*or* worm), rotifer (*or* rotiferan), Rotifera, kinorhynch, Kinorhyncha, gastrotrich, Gastrotricha, spiny-headed worm, acanthocephalan, Acanthocephala, segmented worm, annelid worm, Annelida, bristle worm, polychaete, Polychaeta, earthworm, oligochaete, Oligochaeta, leech, medicinal leech, hirudinean, Hirudinea,

MOLLUSCS

abalone	cockle	helmet shell	paper nautilus	sea slug	top shell
ammonite*	conch	keyhole limpet	pearly nautilus	shipworm	triton shell
argonaut	cone shell	limpet	periwinkle (or winkle)	slipper shell	tusk shell
ark shell	cowrie	mitre shell		slit shell	venus clam
auger shell	cuttlefish	money cowrie	piddock	slug	volute
belemnite*	elephant's–tusk shell	murex	quahog, hard–shell clam	snail	wentletrap
bleeding tooth		mussel		soft–shell clam	whelk
chiton, coat–of–mail shell	geoduck	nautilus	razor shell	spider conch	winkle (or periwinkle)
	giant clam	nudibranch	scallop	squid	
clam	hard–shell (or hard–shell clam), quahog	octopus	sea butterfly	teredo	worm shell
coat–of–mail shell, chiton		olive shell	sea hare	tiger cowrie	
		oyster	sea lemon	tooth shell	*extinct mollusc

WORMS

annelid worm	guinea worm	platyhelminth
arrow worm	hairworm	pogonophoran
Ascaris	heartworm	proboscis worm
bamboo worm	hookworm	ragworm
beard worm	horsehair worm	ribbonworm
blood fluke	kidney worm	roundworm
bootlace worm	leech	scaleworm
bristle worm	liver fluke	schistosome
Cestoda	lugworm	sea mouse
cone worm	lungworm	serpulid
earthworm	nematode	sipunculid
eelworm	Nemertina	tapeworm
eyeworm	paddleworm	threadworm
fanworm	palolo worm	Trematoda
Fasciola	parchment worm	tubifex
feather duster	peacock worm	vinegar eel
filaria	peanut worm	whipworm
flatworm	pinworm	
fluke	planarian	

wormlike invertebrate, peanut worm, sipunculid, Sipunculida, beard worm, pogonophoran, Pogonophora, peripatus, phoronid, Phoronida, onychophoran, Onychophora, arrow worm, chaetognath, Chaetognatha, acorn worm, hemichordate, insect, glow-worm, bookworm, insect larva, woodworm, wireworm, caterpillar, silkworm

► *76 Insects and Arachnids*

7 coelenterate, cnidarian, Cnidaria, polyp, medusa, hydrozoan, Hydrozoa (sea fir, *Hydra*, Portuguese man-of-war, *etc.*), scyphozoan, Scyphozoa (jellyfish, box jellyfish, sea wasp, *etc.*), anthozoan, Anthozoa (coral, organ-pipe coral, dead-men's fingers, sea fan, sea pen, sea pansy, sea anemone, *etc.*), ctenophore (*or* ctenophoran), comb jelly, Ctenophora (sea gooseberry, Venus's girdle, *etc.*), polypoid invertebrate, bryozoan, Bryozoa, ectoproct, Ectoprocta (sea mats, moss animals), entoproct, Entoprocta

8 sponge, bath sponge, Venus's flower basket, poriferan, Porifera, parazoan, Parazoa

9 protozoan, protozoon, Protozoa, flagellate protozoan, flagellate, mastigophoran, Mastigophora (*Euglena*, *Chlamydomonas*, *Volvox*, dinoflagellate, trypanosome, trichomonad, *etc.*), amoeboid protozoan, Sarcodina (amoeba, foraminiferan, radiolarian, heliozoan), spore-producing protozoan, sporozoan, Sporozoa (malaria parasite, *Plasmodium*, *etc.*), ciliate protozoan, ciliate, Ciliata (*Paramecium*, *etc.*)

10 parasite, fish louse, whale louse, sand hopper, helminth, fluke, blood fluke, liver fluke, tapeworm, pinworm, guinea worm, hookworm, protozoan, entamoeba, trypanosome, piroplasm, leishmania, giardia, toxoplasma, bloodsucker, leech

11 helminthic disease, fascioliasis, schistosomiasis, hookworm disease, ascariasis, filariasis, dirofilariasis, onchocerciasis, river blindness, toxocariasis

► *260 Ill Health*

12 protozoal disease, amoebiasis, amoebic dysentery, sleeping sickness, trypanosomiasis, leishmaniasis, trichomoniasis, giardiasis, coccidiosis, malaria, babesiosis, piroplasmosis, theileriosis, toxoplasmosis

► *260 Ill Health*

13 invertebrate larva, tornaria, nauplius, trochophore, veliger, microfilaria, redia, cercaria, miracidium, hydatid, cysticercus, caenurus, onchosphere, hexacanth

► *76 Insects and Arachnids*

14 invertebrate zoology, arachnology, entomology, malacology, conchology, helminthology, protozoology, parasitology

► *76 Insects and Arachnids*

15 invertebrate zoologist, arachnologist, entomologist, malacologist, conchologist, helminthologist, protozoologist, parasitologist

► *76 Insects and Arachnids*

ADJECTIVES

16 invertebrate, protochordate, hemichordate, urochordate, cephalochordate, acraniate, coelomate, pseudocoelomate, acoelomate, metazoan, mesozoan, protozoan

17 echinodermal, echinodermatous, crinoidal, asteroid (*or* asteroidal), ophiuroid, echinoid, holothurian

18 arthropodous, arthropodial, jointed, chelicerate, arachnidan, arachnoid, spider-like, spidery, insect-like, insectile, crustacean, crustaceous, shrimplike, crablike, arachnological, entomological

► *76 Insects and Arachnids*

19 molluscan, gastropodan, gastropodous, snail-like, univalve(d), sluglike, bivalve(d), bivalvular, clamlike, oyster-like, cephalopodic, cephalopodous, cephalopodan, octopod, malcological, conchological

20 wormlike, vermicular, vermiform, helminthic, helminthoid, platyhelminthic, fluky, cestoid, annelid, annelidan, segmented, polychaetous, oligochaetous, lumbricoid, hirudinean, leechlike, helminthological

21 coelenterate, hydroid, polypoid, medusoid, hydrozoan, scyphozoan, anthrozoan, coralline, coralloid, ctenophoran

22 spongelike, poriferan, poriferous, spongy, fibrous, calcareous

23 protozoan, protozoic, amoebic, amoeboid, flagellate, ciliate, sporozoan, protozoological

76 Insects and Arachnids

'Will you walk into my parlour?' said a spider to a fly: ''Tis the prettiest little parlour that ever you did spy.' Mary Howitt.

NOUNS

1 insect, Insecta, Hexapoda, winged insect, fly, gnat, midge, mosquito, cranefly, dragonfly, caddis fly, butterfly, moth, bee, wasp, ant, beetle, cockroach, earwig, stick insect, mantis, hopper, grasshopper, locust, leaf-hopper, creepy-crawly (Inf), roach (US inf), skeeter (US inf), mozzy (Aus inf), daddy longlegs (Inf)

2 arachnid, Arachnida, scorpion, pseudo-scorpion, false scorpion, spider, black widow, tarantula, phalangid, opilionid, harvestman, acarid (*or* acardian), mite, tick, hard tick, soft tick

3 pest, parasite, vermin, cockroach, weevil, boll weevil, grain weevil, borer, woodborer, corn borer, deathwatch beetle, woodworm, bookworm, wireworm, cutworm, screwworm, chafer, cockchafer, corn chafer, scale insect, scale, locust, seventeen-year locust, bug, plant bug, aphid, greenfly, blackfly, louse, head louse, nit, body louse, crab louse, crab, flea, rat flea, dog flea, cat flea, human flea, sand flea, chigoe, chigger, red bug (US), jigger, mite, harvest mite, itch mite, bloodsucker, bedbug, tick, sheep tick, dog tick, wood tick, mosquito, midge, cootie (US inf)

4 **social insect**, bee, honeybee, wasp, yellow jacket (US), ant, emmet (Dial), pismire (Dial), red ant, army ant, white ant, termite, caste, reproductive, queen, queen bee, drone, king (termite), worker, soldier, soldier ant, hive, beehive, apiary, beeswax, honey, wasps' nest, vespiary, anthill, antheap, termite colony, termitarium, swarm, army, plague

► *376 Gathering*

5 **larva**, grub, maggot, nest, nidus, spiderling, caterpillar, woolly bear, looper, army worm, bagworm, silkworm, cutworm, antlion, doodlebug (US), leatherjacket, caddis worm, bloodworm, glow-worm, mealworm, wireworm, screwworm, nymph, pupa, chrysalis, cocoon, metamorphosis, imago

INSECTS

- aedes (mosquito)
- alderfly
- Amazon ant
- ambrosia beetle
- anopheles (mosquito)
- ant
- antlion
- aphid
- army ant
- army worm
- assassin bug
- backswimmer
- bagworm moth
- bark beetle
- bedbug
- bee
- bee fly
- beetle
- black beetle
- black fly, buffalo gnat
- blackfly
- blister beetle
- bloodworm
- blowfly, bluebottle
- body louse, cootie (US inf)
- boll weevil
- bombardier beetle
- booklouse
- bookworm
- borer
- botfly
- brimstone butterfly
- bristletail
- buffalo gnat, black fly
- bug
- bumblebee
- burying (*or* sexton) beetle
- bush cricket
- cabbage root fly
- cabbage white butterfly
- Cactoblastis (moth)
- cactus moth
- caddis fly
- Camberwell beauty
- capsid
- carpenter bee
- carpet beetle
- cat flea
- cecropia moth
- chafer
- chigoe, chigger, jigger, sand flea
- chinch bug
- cicada
- cinnabar moth
- clearwing moth
- click beetle
- clothes moth
- cockchafer
- cockroach, roach (US inf)
- codling moth
- Colorado potato beetle
- cootie (US inf), body louse
- corn borer
- corn chafer
- cotton stainer
- crab (louse)
- cranefly, daddy longlegs (Inf)
- cricket
- croton bug
- cuckoo–spit insect
- culex (mosquito)
- cutworm
- daddy longlegs (Inf), cranefly
- damselfly
- darkling beetle
- death's–head moth
- deathwatch beetle
- deer fly
- devil's coach horse
- digger wasp
- diving beetle
- dobsonfly
- dog flea
- dor beetle
- dragonfly
- driver ant
- drosophila (fruit fly)
- dung beetle
- earwig
- elm bark beetle
- emperor moth
- fire ant
- firebrat
- firefly
- flea
- flea beetle
- fly
- foot–spinner (*or* webspinner)
- fritillary
- froghopper
- fruit fly
- gad fly
- gall midge
- gall wasp
- geometrid moth
- giant water bug
- glow worm
- goat moth
- goliath beetle
- grain weevil
- grasshopper
- greenbottle (fly)
- greenfly
- ground beetle
- ground bug
- gypsy moth
- hairstreak
- harlequin bug
- hawk moth
- head louse
- hercules beetle
- hercules moth
- honey ant
- honeybee
- hornet
- horntail
- horse fly
- housefly
- hoverfly
- ichneumon
- io moth
- jigger, sand flea
- June beetle (*or* bug)
- katydid
- kissing bug
- lacewing
- lac insect
- ladybird beetle
- lantern fly
- leaf beetle
- leafcutter ant
- leafcutter bee
- leaf–hopper
- leaf insect
- leatherjacket
- locust
- louse
- luna moth
- mantis, praying mantis
- mason bee
- mayfly
- mealworm
- mealy bug
- midge
- milkweed butterfly
- miller (moth)
- mole cricket
- monarch butterfly
- mosquito, skeeter (US inf), mozzy (Aus inf)
- noctuid moth
- nymphalid butterfly
- oil beetle
- owlet moth
- painted lady
- papilionid butterfly
- peacock butterfly
- peppered moth
- phylloxera
- plant bug
- plant hopper
- pond skater
- potato beetle
- potter wasp
- praying mantis
- puss moth
- pyralid moth
- red admiral
- red ant
- red bug (US)
- rhinoceros beetle
- ringlet (butterfly)
- roach (US inf), cockroach
- robber fly
- rove beetle
- sand flea, jigger, chigoe, chigger
- sandfly
- saturniid moth
- satyrid butterfly
- sawfly
- scale insect
- scarab beetle
- scorpion fly
- screwworm
- seventeen–year locust
- sexton (*or* burying) beetle
- sheep ked
- shield bug
- silkworm moth
- silverfish
- skipper (butterfly)
- slave–making ant
- snakefly
- snout beetle, weevil
- soldier beetle
- Spanish fly
- spider wasp
- spittlebug
- springtail
- squash bug
- stag beetle
- stick insect, walking stick (US)
- stink bug
- stonefly
- stylops
- swallowtail butterfly
- swift moth
- termite, white ant
- thrips
- tiger beetle
- tiger moth
- tineid moth
- tortoise beetle
- tortoiseshell butterfly
- treehopper
- tsetse fly
- tussock moth
- underwing moth
- walking stick (US), stick insect
- warble fly
- wasp
- water beetle
- water boatman
- water bug
- water scorpion
- water strider
- wax moth
- webspinner (*or* foot–spinner)
- weevil, snout beetle
- whirligig
- white ant, termite
- whitefly
- wireworm
- woodborer
- woodwasp
- woodworm
- yellow jacket (US), wasp

ORDERS OF INSECTS

Thysanura (bristletails), thysanuran
Diplura (bristletails), dipluran
Collembola (springtails), collembolan
Protura, proturan
Ephemeroptera (mayflies), ephemerid (*or* ephemeropteran)
Odonata (dragonflies)
Plecoptera (stoneflies), plecopteran
Orthoptera (grasshoppers), orthopteran (*or* orthopteron)
Phasmida (stick insects), phasmid
Dermaptera (earwigs), dermapteran
Embioptera (foot–spinners *or* webspinners), embiopteran
Dictyoptera (cockroaches and mantids), dictyopteran
Isoptera (termites), isopteran
Psocoptera (book lice), psocopteran
Mallophaga (biting lice), mallophagan
Anoplura (sucking lice), anopluran
Hemiptera (bugs), hemipteran (*or* hemipteron)
Thysanoptera (thrips), thysanopteran
Grylloblatodea, grylloblatodean
Zoraptera, zorapteran
Neuroptera (lacewings), neuropteran (*or* neuropteron)
Megaloptera (alderflies), megalopteran
Mecoptera (scorpion flies), mecopteran
Lepidoptera (butterflies and moths), lepidopteran (*or* lepidopteron)
Trichoptera (caddis flies), trichopteran
Diptera (flies), dipteran (*or* dipteron)
Siphonaptera (fleas), siphonapteran
Hymenoptera (ants, bees, and wasps), hymenopteran (*or* hymenopteron)
Coleoptera (beetles), coleopteran (*or* coleopteron)
Strepsiptera (stylops), strepsipteran

ARACHNIDS

bird spider
black widow
chigger, harvest mite
daddy longlegs (US inf), harvestman
dog tick
false scorpion, pseudoscorpion
follicle mite
fowl tick
funnel weaver
harvestman, daddy longlegs (US inf)
harvest mite, scrub mite, chigger
hunting spider, wolf spider
itch mite
microwhip scorpion
mite
money spider
orb weaver
pseudoscorpion, false scorpion
red mite
scorpion
scorpion spider
scrubmite, harvest mite
sheep tick
spider
spider mite
sun spider (*or* sun scorpion)
tarantula
tick
trap–door spider
water spider
whip scorpion
wind scorpion
wolf spider, hunting spider
wood tick

6 spinner, spider, silkworm, silk, silk gland, spinneret, cocoon, web, spider's web, cobweb

7 study, entomology, beekeeping, sericulture, arachnology, acarology

8 entomologist, lepidopterist, bug hunter, beekeeper, apiarist, sericulturalist

9 arachnologist, acarologist

ADJECTIVES

10 insectan (*or* **insectean**), insectile, insectiform, insectlike, thysanuran, dipluran, collembolan, proturan, ephemeropteran, plecopteran, orthopteran (*or* orthopterous), phasmid, dermapteran, embiopteran, dictyopteran, isopteran, psocopteran, mallophagan, anopluran, hemipteran (*or* hemipterous), homopteran, heteropteran, thysanopteran, grylloblatodean, zorapteran, neuropteran (*or* neuropterous), megalopteran, mecopteran, lepidopteran (*or* lepidopterous), trichopteran, dipteran (*or* dipterous), siphonapteran, hymenopteran (*or* hymenopterous), coleopteran (*or* coleopterous), strepsipteran

11 arachnidan, spider-like, spidery, arachnoid, mitelike, ticklike, acarid (*or* acaridan), acaroid

12 verminous, infested, buggy, weevilly, maggoty, grubby, lousy, flea-bitten, mothy, moth-eaten, flyblown

13 immature, larval, pupal, chrysalid (*or* chrysalidal)

► *555 Youth*

14 entomological, apiarian, sericultural

15 arachnological, acarological

VERBS

16 infest, invade, swarm, buzz, drone, plague, sting, bite, parasitize, swarm with, crawl with, teem with, contaminate, flyblow

► *258 Dirtiness; 381 Attack*

17 develop, hatch, pupate, metamorphose

77 Plants

When he has learnt that bottinney means a knowledge of plants, he goes and knows 'em. That's our system, Nickleby; what do you think of it? Charles Dickens.

NOUNS

1 plants, plant life, flora, plant kingdom, Plantae, vegetable kingdom, vegetable life, vegetation, green plants, growth, herbage, verdure, greenery, forest, jungle, grassland, savanna (*or* savannah), steppe, scrub, chaparral

► *79 Trees; 81 Grasses; 538 Greenness*

2 plant, green plant, vascular plant, herbaceous plant, seedling, herb, flower, wild flower, weed, escape, cultivated plant, garden plant, house plant, pot plant, hothouse plant, exotic, food plant, cereal, vegetable, potherb, culinary herb, medicinal plant, medicinal herb, wort, succulent (plant), cactus, xerophyte, aquatic (plant), hydrophyte, air plant, epiphyte, parasite, ephemeral, annual, biennial, perennial, herbaceous perennial, woody perennial, woody plant, tree, sapling, shrub, bush, evergreen, climber, twiner, vine, liana

► *25 Cookery; 44 Horticulture; 78 Flowers; 79 Trees; 394 Remedy*

3 seed plant, spermatophyte, Spermatophyta, phanerogam, gymnosperm, Gymnospermae (conifers, softwoods, cycads, gnetums, welwitschia, *etc.*), flowering plant, angiosperm, Angiospermae, monocotyledon (*or* monocot), Monocotyledonae, palms, grasses, cereals, reeds, sedge family (Cyperaceae), rush family (Juncaceae), orchids, lily family (Liliaceae), pineapple family (Bromeliaceae, bromeliads, *etc.*), dicotyledon (*or* dicot), Dicotyledonae (hardwoods), rose family (Rosaceae), daisy family (Compositae, composites), buttercup family (Ranunculaceae), mustard family (Cruciferae, Brassicaceae, crucifers, brassicas), parsley family (Umbelliferae, umbellifers), nettle family (Labiatae, labiates), pea family (Leguminosae, legumes), goosefoot family (Chenopodiaceae, chenopods, *etc.*)

► *78 Flowers; 79 Trees; 81 Grasses*

4 **lower plant**, nonseed-bearing plant, cryptogam, pteridophyte, Pteridophyta (ferns, horsetails, clubmosses, *etc.*), bryophyte, Bryophyta (mosses, liverworts), thallophyte, Thallophyta, fungus, saprophyte, parasite, lichen, alga, seaweed

► *82 Ferns and Mosses; 83 Fungi; 84 Algae and Lichens*

5 **stem**, axis, caulis, caudex, trunk, caulid, shoot, sprout, plumule, internode, node, axil, offshoot, scion, branch, twig, spray, stalk, stipe, seta, leafstalk, petiole, rachis, rachilla, flower stalk, peduncle, pedicel, seed stalk, funicle (*or* funiculus), underground stem (*or* shoot), rhizome, runner, stolon, sucker, rootstock, stock, corm, bulb, tuber, stem tuber, stem tissue, epidermis, cortex, pith, medulla, cambium, vascular bundle, xylem, phloem

► *79 Trees; 81 Grasses*

6 **leaf**, leaflet, needle, frond, megaphyll, microphyll, leaf blade, lamina, vein, leafstalk, petiole, leaves, foliage, greenery, leaflike part, bract, bracteole, cladode, phylloclade, phyllode, involucre, scale leaf, ligule, stipule, modified leaf, tendril, spine, floral leaf, petal, sepal, seed leaf, cotyledon, leaf tissue, palisade, mesophyll, stoma (*pl.* stomata), guard cell, leaf fall, abscission

► *78 Flowers; 81 Grasses; 538 Greenness*

7 **root**, radix, rootlet, radicle, taproot, lateral root, fibrous root, prop root, buttress root, stilt root, adventitious root, aerial root, tuberous root, root tuber, tuber, root cap, calyptra, root hair, root nodule, rootlike part, rootstock, rhizoid, rhizomorph

8 **bud**, burgeon, leaf bud, foliage bud, flower bud, apical bud, terminal bud, axillary bud, lateral bud, adventitious bud, winter bud, resting bud, dormancy, gemma, gemmule, budding, gemmation, gemmulation

► *343 Inactivity; 561 Reproduction; 562 Fertility*

9 **seed**, grain, kernel, pip, hayseed, rapeseed, flaxseed, linseed, cottonseed, birdseed, seedcase, seed capsule, seed pod, seed coat, testa, micropyle, hilum, seed stalk, funicle (*or* funiculus), seed leaf, cotyledon, embryo, ovule, endosperm, germinating seed, germination, seedling, shoot, bamboo shoot, mustard and cress, plumule, acrospire, coleoptile, radicle, coleorhiza

► *80 Fruits; 561 Reproduction; 562 Fertility*

10 **plant science(s)**, botany, phytology, plant taxonomy, phytography, plant biochemistry, phytochemistry, phytogenesis, plant anatomy, plant physiology, plant cytology, plant ecology, phytosociology, plant geography, phytogeography, plant pathology, phytopathology, palaeobotany, palynology, pollen analysis, palaeoethnobotany, ethnobotany, pteridology, bryology, mycology, phycology, algology, lichenology, dendrology, economic botany, arboriculture, silviculture, horticulture, forestry, pomology, crop husbandry, agrobiology

► *34 Life Science; 43 Agriculture; 44 Horticulture; 78 Flowers; 79 Trees; 83 Fungi; 84 Algae and Lichens*

11 **herbarium**, hortus siccus, botanic garden, seed bank, flora, florilegium, herbal

12 **plant scientist**, botanist, plant hunter, herbalist, naturalist, phytologist, phytographer, phytochemist, phytogeneticist, phytogeographer, phytopathologist, ethnobotanist, phytosociologist, palaeobotanist, agrobiologist, dendrologist, pomologist, pteridologist, bryologist, mycologist, phycologist, algologist, lichenologist

► *34 Life Science*

ADJECTIVES

13 **plantlike**, vegetable, vegetal, vegetative, herbal, herbaceous, green, grassy, leafy, verdant, flourishing, planted, plant-covered, wooded, forested, growing, luxuriant, lush, dense, overgrown, rank, weedy, unweeded, weed-choked, gone to seed

► *79 Trees; 81 Grasses*

14 **of plants**, green, herbaceous, ephemeral, annual, biennial, perennial, bulbous, cormous, tuberous, woody, deciduous, evergreen, leafy, foliate, branched, succulent, xerophytic, aquatic, hydrophytic, terrestrial, land, creeping, prostrate, erect, twining, climbing, epiphytic, parasitic, saprophytic, insectivorous, carnivorous, photosynthetic

15 **wild**, native, indigenous, cultivated, alien, exotic, introduced, escaped, naturalized, hardy, half-hardy

16 **taxonomic**, vascular, seed-bearing, phanerogamic, cone-bearing, coniferous, flowering, monocotyledonous, cyperaceous, juncaceous, orchidaceous, liliaceous, bromeliaceous, dicotyledonous, rosaceous, composite, ranunculaceous, cruciferous, brassicaceous, umbelliferous, labiate, leguminous, chenopodiaceous, nonseed-bearing, cryptogamic, thallophytic

17 **of stems**, axial, cauline, rachial (*or* rachidial), axillary

18 **of leaves**, simple, entire, ovate, lanceolate, linear, orbicular, cordate, lobed, toothed, serrate, dentate, crenate, hastate, sagittate, stalked, unstalked, sessile, peltate, compound, trifoliate, palmate, pinnate, bipinnate

19 **of roots**, radical, radicular, rooted, fibrous-rooted, tuberous-rooted, rootlike, rhizoid

20 **botanical**, botanic, plant, phytological, phytographic(al), phytochemical, phytogeographic(al), phytopathological, ethnobotanical, phytosociological

► *34 Life Science; 43 Agriculture; 44 Horticulture; 78 Flowers; 79 Trees; 82 Ferns and Mosses; 83 Fungi; 84 Algae and Lichens*

VERBS

21 **vegetate**, grow, germinate, root, take root, sprout, sprout up, shoot, shoot up, bud, gemmate, unfold, leaf, flower, flourish, burgeon, overgrow, overrun, run to seed, shed seeds, dehisce, photosynthesize

► *213 Increase*

22 **be dormant**, shed leaves, abscise, wilt, wither, suspend growth, overwinter, perennate, survive, exist, rest, vegetate

► *343 Inactivity*

23 **study plants**, collect plants, botanize, be a botanist

ADVERBS

24 herbaceously, exotically, succulently, ephemerally, annually, biennially, perennially, xerophytically, epiphytically, saprophytically, photosynthetically

25 botanically, phytologically, horticulturally, ecologically, phytogenetically, phytosociologically, algologically, dendrologically

78 Flowers

Gather the flowers, but spare the buds. Andrew Marvell.

Say it with flowers. Patrick O'Keefe.

NOUNS

1 flower, floweret, floret, bloom, blossom, blow (Lit), flowers, may blossom, apple blossom, orange blossom, cherry blossom, wild flower, garden flower, pot plant, flower arrangement, spray, cut flowers, posy, bouquet, garland, wreath, nosegay, daisy chain, buttonhole, boutonniere, dried flower, everlasting flower, pressed flower

► *542 Decoration*

2 flowering plant, flowerer, bloomer, annual, biennial, ephemeral, perennial, bulb, corm, angiosperm

► *77 Plants*

3 flower part, sepal, calyx, petal, nectary, corolla, perianth, floral envelope, epicalyx, involucre (*or* involucrum), bract, whorl, spathe, stamen, filament, anther, androecium, pollen, pollen grain, stigma, style, ovary, carpel, gynoecium, pistil, pollen tube, ovule, micropyle, receptacle, floral diagram, floral formula

► *77 Plants; 80 Fruits*

4 flower head, flower cluster, inflorescence, racemose

FLOWERS AND FLOWERING PLANTS

Aaron's rod	bird's–nest orchid	charlock	deadly nightshade	germander
acacia	bishop's weed	chickweed	deadnettle	gillyflower
acanthus	bistort	Chinese lantern plant	delphinium	gladdon
aconite	bittersweet	Christmas cactus	dianthus	gladiolus, glad (*or* gladdie) (Inf)
Adam's–needle	blackberry lily	Christmas rose	dock	
aechmea	black–eyed Susan	chrysanthemum	dogbane	glasswort
African violet	black nightshade	cineraria	dog rose	globe flower
agapanthus	bladderwort	cinquefoil	dog's–tooth violet	globe thistle
agave	bleeding heart	clarkia	dog violet	gloxinia
agrimony	bluebell	cleavers	Dutchman's breeches	goatsbeard
alfalfa	bluets	clematis	Dutchman's pipe	golden bell
alkanet	bougainvillea	clianthus	dyer's broom	goldenrod
allamanda	briar (*or* briar rose)	clove pink	edelweiss	goosefoot
allium	bridal wreath	clover	eglantine	goosegrass
althaea	broom	cocklebur	enchanter's nightshade	gorse
alsike	broomrape	cockscomb	epiphyllum	goutweed
amaranthus	bryony	coleus	erica	granadilla
amaryllis	buddleia	coltsfoot	eucharis	grape hyacinth
Amazon lily	bugloss	columbine	euphorbia	grass of Parnassus
anchusa	burdock	coneflower	eyebright	ground elder
anemone	busy Lizzie	convolvulus	fig marigold	groundsel
anthurium	buttercup	corncockle	figwort	guelder rose
antirrhinum	butterwort	cornflower	firethorn	gypsophila
aquilegia	cabbage rose	corn poppy	fireweed	harebell
arrowroot	cactus	corydalis	flag	hawkbit
arum lily	calceolaria	cosmos	flax	hawkweed
asphodel	calendula	cow parsley	fleabane	heath
aspidistra	California lilac	cowpea	fleawort	heather
aster	calla lily	cowslip	flowering currant	hedgehog cactus
astilbe	calypso orchid	cranesbill	flowering quince	heliotrope
aubrietia	camellia	creeping Jenny	forget–me–not	hellebore
auricula	camomile (*or* chamomile)	crocus	forsythia	helleborine
autumn crocus	campanula	crowfoot	foxglove	hemlock
avens	campion	crown-of-thorns	frangipani	henbane
azalea	candytuft	cuckoopint	freesia	henequen
baby's–breath	canna	cyclamen	fritillary	herb Paris
bachelor's– button	Canterbury bell	cymbidium	frog–bit	herb Robert
bedstraw	cardinal flower	daffodil, daff (Inf)	fuchsia	hibiscus
begonia	carnation	dahlia	fumitory	hollyhock
belladonna	carrion flower	daisy	furze	honesty
belladonna lily	catbrier	damask rose	gaillardia	honeysuckle
bellflower	catmint	dandelion	gardenia	horehound
bergenia	ceanothus	darnel	garlic mustard	houseleek
bindweed	celandine	datura	gentian	hoya
bird–of–paradise flower	century plant	day lily	geranium	hyacinth

FLOWERS AND FLOWERING PLANTS (CONT.)				
hydrangea	meadow saffron	pennyroyal	sanicle	syringa
hypericum	meadowsweet	peony	saxifrage	tea rose
hyssop	mecanopsis	periwinkle	scabious	teasel
ice plant	medick	petrea	sea lavender	thistle
impatiens	mesembryanthemum	petunia	sedum	thorn apple
Indian paintbrush	Michaelmas daisy	peyote	self heal	thrift
iris	mignonette	philadelphus	shamrock	thunbergia
jack–by–the–hedge	milfoil	phlox	shrimp plant	tiger lily
jack–in–the– pulpit	milkweed	pigweed	slipper orchid	toad lily
japonica	milkwort	pimpernel	slipperwort	tormentil
jimson weed	mimosa	pink	snakeroot	touch–me–not
jonquil	moccasin flower	plantain	snake's head	townhall clock
kalanchoe	mock orange	plumbago	snapdragon	tradescantia
kangaroo paw	moneywort	poinsettia	snowdrop	traveller's joy
kingcup	monkeyflower	polyanthus	snow–on–the–mountain	trefoil
knapweed	monkshood	pontentilla		trumpet creeper
knotweed	montbretia	poppy	soapwort	tuberose
laburnum	moonflower	portulaca	Solomon's seal	tulip
lady's slipper	morning glory	pot marigold	sorrel	Turk's–cap lily
lady's smock	moschatel	prickly pear	sow thistle	valerian
larkspur	moss pink	prickly poppy	speedwell	Venus flytrap
lavender	moss rose	primrose	spider flower	verbena
leopard lily	motherwort	primula	spider plant	veronica
lilac	mullein	protea	spiderwort	vervain
lily	musk rose	pyracantha	spikenard	vetch
lily–of–the–valley	narcissus	pyrethrum	spiraea	viburnum
lobelia	nasturtium	Queen Anne's lace	spurge	viola
London pride	nemesia	ragged robin	spurrey	violet
lords–and–ladies	nettle	ragwort	squill	wallflower
lotus	nicotiana	ranunculus	star of Bethlehem	water lily
love–in–a–mist	night–scented stock	rape	stephanotis	waxplant
love–lies– bleeding	old man cactus	red–hot poker	stitchwort	Welsh poppy
lungwort	old man's beard	rhododendron, rhodie (Inf)	St John's wort	wichuraiana (rose)
lupin	oleander		stock	willowherb
Madonna lily	opium poppy	rock rose	stonecrop	winter aconite
magnolia	opuntia	rose	strawflower	winter jasmine
mallow	orchid	rose of China	strelitzia	wisteria
marguerite	organ–pipe cactus	rose of Jericho	streptocarpus	witchweed
marigold	orpine	rose of Sharon	sundew	wolfsbane
marsh mallow	oxeye daisy	rudbeckia	sunflower	wood sorrel
marsh marigold	oxlip	safflower	sun rose	wormwood
martagon (*or* martagon lily)	pansy	saguaro	sweet briar	woundwort
	passionflower	sainfoin	sweet flag	yarrow
marvel–of–Peru	patchouli	salvia	sweet pea	yucca
may (*or* mayflower)	pelargonium	samphire	sweet william	zinnia

inflorescence, raceme, panicle, corymb, spadix, spike, spikelet, catkin, ament, umbel, capitulum, ray floret, disc floret, cyme, cymose inflorescence, monochasium, monochasial cyme, dichasium, dichasial cyme, thyrse, verticillaster

5 **flowering**, florescence, efflorescence, blossoming, blooming, flowerage, unfolding, anthesis, blowing, blow, full blow, full bloom

6 **pollination**, cross-pollination, self-pollination, selfing

▶ *561 Reproduction*

7 **flower culture**, floriculture, flower growing, flower selling, floristics, floriculturist, flower grower, florist, flower seller, flower girl

▶ *44 Horticulture*

8 **flower product**, nectar, rose water, attar of roses, rose (*or* primrose) oil, lavender water, oil of lavender, camomile tea, elderflower (*or* dandelion) wine, crystallized (*or* jellied) rose petals

▶ *502 Fragrance; 558 Drinking*

9 **figurative usage**, floral dance, flower child, flower power, daisycutter, daisywheel, Poppy Day, primrose path, rose window, rosette, Sunflower State, bed of roses, shrinking violet (Inf)

ADJECTIVES

10 **floral**, flowered, flowery, bloomy, floristic, flower-like, fragrant, florid, ornate, floreate, floriate(d)

▶ *502 Fragrance; 542 Decoration*

11 **flowering**, in flower, in bloom, in full bloom, in full blow, in blossom, blossoming, blooming, flourishing, florescent, inflorescent, efflorescent

▶ *248 Prosperity*

12 **of flowers**, staminate, male, pistillate, female, imperfect, perfect, monoecious, dioecious, regular, irregular,

synsepalous, synpetalous, synandrous, aposepalous, apopetalous, apoandrous, hypogynous, epigynous, perigynous, racemose, cymose, corymbose, umbelliferous

▶ *77 Plants*

VERBS

13 flower, bud, bloom, blossom, blow, be in flower, be in bloom, effloresce, flourish

▶ *248 Prosperity*

ADVERBS

14 florally, floristically, floridly, fragrantly

79 Trees

I think that I shall never see
A poem lovely as a tree. Alfred Joyce Kilmer.

NOUNS

1 tree, shrub, bush, sapling, coniferous tree, conifer, evergreen (tree), deciduous tree, broadleaf, broadleaved tree, palm (tree), fan palm, feather palm, tree fern, tree mallow, shade tree, timber tree, softwood (tree), hardwood (tree), tropical hardwood, amenity tree, ornamental (tree), Christmas tree, fruit tree, fruiter, bonsai tree, dwarf tree, hedgerow tree, specimen tree, standard, maiden, pollard, coppice, stool

2 tree part, trunk, collar, bole, gnarl, knot, burl, burr, crutch, fork, crown, limb, branch, bough, twig, spur, leader, leaf, palm leaf, palm frond, needle, pine needle, cone, pine cone, fir cone, tree stump, stump, snag (US)

▶ *77 Plants*

3 timber, wood, lumber (US), cordwood, cord, cordage, log, pole, flitch, faggot, brushwood, firewood, kindling, pulpwood, sapwood, alburum, wetwood, heartwood, duramen, reaction wood, tension wood, compression wood, spring wood, summer wood, autumn wood, early wood, late wood, trunkwood, branchwood, woody tissue, bark, cork, phellem, lignin, tree ring, annual ring, growth ring, tree-ring dating, dendrochronology

▶ *418 Hardness*

4 trees, tree line (*or* zone), timber line, forest, rainforest, tropical forest, jungle, thorn forest, cloud forest, gallery forest, virgin forest, primeval forest, coniferous forest, taiga, woodland, woods, ancient woodland, chaparral, brush, bocage, wood, greenwood, copse, spinney, coppice, thicket, clearing, glade, bower, arbour, underwood, undergrowth, tree litter, leaf litter, leaf mould, beech mast, brake, covert, bosket (*or* bosquet), bosk, holt (Lit), hurst (Lit), shelter belt, plantation, stand, timberland (US), wood lot, bush lot (Canad), tree farm, arboretum, pinetum, pinery, tree nursery, orchard, orangery

▶ *44 Horticulture*

5 forestry, tree farming, agroforestry, tree planting, afforestation, reforestation, deforestation, conservation, dendrology, arboriculture, silviculture, woodcraft (US), treen, treenware, cabinet-making

▶ *23 Furniture and Woodwork; 43 Agriculture*

6 tree management, beating up, brashing, thinning, pruning, lopping, topping, drop-crotching, coppicing, pollarding, tree surgery, tapping, rubber tapping, felling, tree felling, logging, lumbering (US), felling licence

7 timber production, timber yard, lumber yard (US), saw, chain saw, power-saw, bowsaw, felling saw, axe, hatchet, billhook, wedge, splitter, chipper, sawmill, sawbench, circular saw, band saw, skidder, forwarder, grapple

▶ *438 Tool*

8 forester, forest manager, ranger, forest ranger, verderer, woodlander, woodcutter, lumberjack, timberman, woodsman, woodman, logger, lumberer (US), tapper, tapster, tree farmer, tree surgeon, arboriculturist, arborist, silviculturist, dendrologist

9 tree product, wood alcohol, wood coal, wood pitch, wood spirit, wood sugar, wood tar, pine tar, wood vinegar, gum turpentine, oil, pinewood oil, palm oil, resin, gum, wax, rubber, fruit, nuts

▶ *25 Cookery; 37 Pharmacology; 80 Fruits; 394 Remedy; 421 Smoothness; 422 Elasticity; 430 Viscosity*

10 tree disease, defoliation, mosaic, mottle, ring spot, leaf curl, dieback, witches' broom, soft rot, wilt, canker, butt rot, blight, mildew, rust, heart rot, pocket rot, leaf cast, needle cast, crown gall, oak apple, oak gall, Dutch elm disease

▶ *44 Horticulture; 83 Fungi*

11 tree-related animal, tree creeper, tree frog, treehopper, tree kangaroo, tree shrew, tree snake, tree sparrow, wood ant, woodborer, wood duck, woodcock, woodchat, woodgrouse, woodchuck, woodlark, woodlouse, woodpecker, wood pigeon, wood rat, wood warbler, woodwasp, woodworm, pine marten, willow grouse, willow tit, willow warbler

▶ *71 Mammals; 72 Birds; 76 Insects and Arachnids*

12 figurative usage, family tree, genealogical tree, shoetree, axeltree, manteltree, rooftree, ridgetree, summer tree, saddletree, swingletree, whippletree (*or* whiffletree), cross-tree, trestletree, olive branch

13 tree mythology, tree of knowledge, tree of life, tree of Jesse, Yggdrasil, Bo tree, wood nymph, tree nymph, dryad, hamadryad, Daphne

▶ *23 Furniture and Woodwork; 59 Horse Riding and Racing*

ADJECTIVES

14 treelike, arboreal, arboraceous, arborescent, dendritic, dendroid (*or* dendroidal), dendriform, palmate, palmaceous, branching, slender, willowy, shrubby, bushy, gnarled, coniferous, evergreen, piny, resinous

15 woody, wood, ligneous, ligniform, hardwood, softwood,

TREE PRODUCTS

acaroid gum	canella	gamboge	rauwolfia
animé	carnauba	guttapercha	rubber
annatto	cascara	haematoxylin	sassafras
araroba	cassia bark	henna	sassafras oil
balm of Gilead	catechu	kapok	senna pods
	chicle	kermes	storax
balsam	cinchona	kino	tacamahac
benzoin	copalm	latex	tolu
borneol	dragon's blood	mastic	tragacanth
cajuput		myrrh	tung oil
calisaya	frankincense	ouabain	turpentine
camphor	fustic	pereira bark	yohimbine

TREES AND SHRUBS

Conifers and Related Trees

- alerce
- araucaria
- arbor vitae
- bald cypress
- balsam fir
- big tree
- black pine
- black spruce
- blue spruce
- bristlecone pine
- bunya
- cade
- cedar
- cedar of Lebanon
- celery pine
- cryptomeria
- cupressus
- cypress
- cypress pine
- dawn redwood
- deodar
- Douglas fir
- fir
- ginkgo
- hemlock (*or* hemlock spruce)
- hoop pine
- Huon pine
- incense cedar
- jack pine
- Japanese cedar
- juniper
- kahikatea
- kauri (*or* kauri pine)
- larch
- lignum vitae
- loblolly
- longleaf pine
- macrocarpa
- maidenhair tree
- matai
- monkey puzzle
- Norway spruce
- nut pine
- Paraná pine
- pencil cedar
- pinaster
- pine
- radiata pine
- red cedar
- red fir
- red pine
- redwood
- sandarac
- savin
- Scots pine
- sequoia
- silver fir
- sitka spruce
- spruce
- spruce pine
- stone pine
- sugar pine
- swamp cypress
- tamarack
- thuja
- totara
- umbrella pine
- wellingtonia
- western hemlock
- western red cedar
- white cedar
- white pine
- white spruce
- yew

Palms

- babassu
- betel palm
- cabbage palm
- coco de mer
- coconut palm
- coquito
- date palm
- doum palm
- gomuti
- ivory palm
- nikau (*or* nikau palm)
- nipa
- oil palm
- palmyra
- sago palm
- talipot (*or* talipot palm)
- Washington palm
- wax palm
- wine palm

Hardwoods, Ornamentals, and Others

- acacia
- acer
- ailanthus
- alder
- almond
- ambatch
- amboyna
- apple
- apple box
- arbutus
- ash
- aspen
- assegai
- axe–breaker
- balata
- balsa
- balsam poplar
- banak
- banksia
- banyan
- baobab
- basswood
- bayberry
- bay rum tree
- bay (*or* bay tree)
- baywood
- bean tree
- beech
- bebeeru
- beefwood
- belah
- ben
- birch, birk (Scot)
- black bean
- blackjack
- black walnut
- blackthorn
- blackwood
- bladdernut
- blue gum
- bo tree
- bottlebrush
- bottle tree
- box (*or* boxwood)
- box elder
- bulletwood
- butcher's broom
- butternut
- buttonball
- buttonwood
- cabbage tree
- cacao
- calabash
- camphor tree
- camwood
- candleberry (*or* candle–tree)
- candlewood
- canoewood
- cassia
- casuarina
- catalpa
- champac (*or* champak)
- chaste tree
- chaulmoogra
- chestnut
- chinaberry (*or* China tree)
- coachwood
- cockspur
- cocuswood
- coffee tree
- coolabah
- coral tree
- cork oak
- corkwood
- cornel
- cottonwood
- courbaril
- cow tree
- crabwood
- croton
- cucumber tree
- cudgerie
- daphne
- desert oak
- dhak
- divi–divi
- dogwood
- dragon tree
- durmast (*or* durmast oak)
- Dutch elm
- eaglewood
- ebony
- elder
- elm
- eucalyptus
- eucryphia
- euonymus
- false acacia
- fever tree
- flame–of–the–forest
- flame tree
- flowering ash
- fringe tree
- gaboon
- gean
- ghost gum
- gidgee
- greasewood
- greenheart
- guaiacum
- guayule
- gum (*or* gum tree)
- gympie
- haematoxylon
- hakea
- hawthorn
- hazel
- Hercules'–club
- hevea
- hickory
- holly
- holm oak (*or* holly oak)
- honey locust
- hop–hornbeam
- hornbeam
- horse chestnut
- Indian mulberry
- inkberry
- iroko
- ironwood
- ivorywood
- jacaranda
- Japanese maple
- jarrah
- jelutong
- jojoba
- Joshua tree
- Judas tree
- kaffirboom
- kalmia
- kamala
- karri
- kawakawa
- Kentucky coffee tree
- kiaat
- kingwood
- koa
- kowhai
- kurrajong
- lacquer tree
- lancewood
- lantana
- laurel
- lemonwood
- lilly–pilly
- lime
- linden
- liquidambar
- liriodendron
- locust
- logwood
- Lombardy poplar
- madroña
- mahogany
- mako
- mallee tree
- manchineel
- mangrove
- manna
- manuka
- maple
- marblewood
- marmalade tree
- maté
- may tree
- mazzard
- melaleuca
- mesquite
- mountain ash
- myrtle
- needle bush
- neem
- ngaio
- Norway maple
- nux vomica
- oak
- ocotillo
- osier
- pagoda tree
- paper mulberry
- partridge–wood
- paulownia
- pedunculate oak
- peepul
- pepper tree
- plane (*or* plane tree), platan
- pohutukawa
- poinciana
- poison oak
- poison sumac
- poplar
- prickly ash
- privet
- puriri
- pussy willow
- pyinkado
- quassia
- quebracho
- rain tree
- rangiora
- redbud
- red gum
- red oak
- rewa–rewa
- ribbonwood
- robinia
- roble
- rosewood
- rowan
- royal poinciana
- rubber plant
- rubber tree
- sallee
- sallow
- sandalwood
- sandbox tree
- sapele
- sappan (*or* sappanwood)
- saskatoon
- sassafras
- sassy (*or* sasswood *or* sassy wood)
- satin walnut
- satinwood
- screw pine
- seringa
- serviceberry
- service tree
- shagbark
- shea
- silk–cotton tree
- silky oak
- silver birch
- silver maple
- simarouba
- slippery elm
- smoke tree
- sneezewood
- snowball tree
- snowdrop tree
- soapbark
- sorb
- sorrel tree
- sour gum
- sourwood
- Spanish cedar
- spindle tree
- spotted gum
- stinkwood
- strawberry bush
- strawberry tree
- styrax
- sugar gum
- sugar maple
- sumach (*or* sumac)
- sweet bay
- sweet gum
- sycamine
- sycamore
- tallow wood
- tamarind
- tamarisk
- tawa
- teak
- tea tree
- terebinth
- thorn tree
- toon
- toothache tree
- tree of heaven
- tuart
- tulip tree
- tupelo
- Turkey oak
- turpentine tree
- umbrella tree
- upas
- varnish tree
- wahoo
- walnut
- wandoo
- wattle
- wax tree
- wayfaring tree
- weeping willow
- whitebeam
- white oak
- white poplar
- wilga
- willow
- witch hazel
- wych–elm
- yarran
- yaupon
- yellow poplar
- yellowwood
- ylang–ylang
- yucca
- zanthoxylum
- zebrawood

hard-grained, soft-grained, wooden, treen, oaken, beechen, ashen, solid, massive

16 wooded, forested, forestal, timbered, afforested, reafforested, planted, tree-covered, arboreous, woodland, sylvan (*or* silvan), sylvatic, sylvestral, shaded, shady, bosky, copsy, braky, woodsy (US inf)

17 arboricultural, silvicultural, silvical (US), dendrologic(al), dendrologous

VERBS

18 manage trees, practise forestry, thin, prune, grub, lop, top, pollard, coppice, tap, cut timber, fell, clear, log, lumber (US), build a tree house

19 grow, spread, bloom, flower, leaf out, lose (*or* drop *or* shed) leaves, branch out, provide shade, (produce) fruit, whisper (aspen), weep (willow)

ADVERBS

20 arboriculturally, silviculturally, dendrologically

80 Fruits

An apple a day keeps the doctor away. Proverb.

NOUNS

1 fruits, fruits of the earth, produce, crop, yield, soft fruit, stone fruit, citrus fruit, dried fruit, nuts, kernels, grain, seeds, pulses, vegetables, legumes, root vegetables, roots, tubers, green vegetables, salad vegetables

► *25 Cookery; 43 Agriculture; 44 Horticulture; 81 Grasses; 562 Fertility*

2 botanical fruit, simple fruit, true fruit, composite fruit, aggregate fruit, multiple fruit, false fruit, succulent fruit, citrus fruit, drupe, berry, pome, pepo, sorosis, syconus, hesperidium, dry fruit, dehiscent fruit, legume, pod, capsule, follicle, siliqua, silicula, pyxidium, indehiscent fruit, nut, achene, samara, caryopsis, cypsela, schizocarpic fruit, schizocarp, carcerulus, cremocarp, lomentum, regma, fruiting body

► *77 Plants; 83 Fungi*

3 fruit structure, fruit wall, pericarp, exocarp (*or* epicarp), skin, rind, peel, shell, shuck, husk, seed pod, seed capsule, mesocarp, endocarp, flesh, pulp, meat, pith, stone, pit (US), nutlet, seed, pip, kernel, grain

► *77 Plants; 561 Reproduction*

4 fruit eating, fruit-eater, fruit-eating animal, fruit bat, frugivore, fruit-eating person, fruitarian, vegetarian, vegan, frugivorousness, fruitarianism, vegetarianism, fruit growing, market gardening, truck farming (*or* gardening) (US), fruit selling, fruit seller, fruiterer, greengrocer

► *44 Horticulture; 557 Eating; 778 Sale*

5 figurative usage, forbidden fruit, apple of one's eye, Adam's apple, apple of discord, lotus-eater, cherry picker, strawberry mark, grapevine (Inf), raspberry (Inf), peanuts (Inf), banana skin (Inf), lemon (Inf), melon (Inf), limey (US inf), apples (*or* apples and pears) (Inf),

FRUITS

- ackee (*or* akee)
- alligator pear
- amarelle (cherry)
- ananas
- anchovy pear
- apple
- apricot
- Asian pear
- assai
- avocado
- babaco
- bael
- bakeapple
- banana
- barberry
- bayberry
- beach plum
- bearberry
- bergamot
- bilberry
- blackberry
- blackcurrant
- blackheart (cherry)
- blaeberry
- Blenheim (apple)
- blueberry
- boysenberry
- Bramley (*or* Bramley's seedling) (apple)
- breadfruit
- bullace
- calamondin
- canistel
- cantaloupe (melon)
- capulin
- carambola
- carob
- casaba
- chayote
- chempaduk
- cherimoya
- cherry
- cherry plum
- chinaberry
- Chinese gooseberry (kiwi fruit)
- chokeberry
- chokecherry
- choko
- citron
- clementine
- clingstone (peach)
- coconut
- Concord (grape)
- Conference (pear)
- costard
- Cox's Orange Pippin (apple)
- crab apple
- cranberry
- crowberry
- currant
- custard apple
- damson
- date
- Delaware (grape)
- dewberry
- durian (*or* durion)
- elderberry
- feijoa
- fig
- fox grape
- geebung
- genipap (*or* genip)
- gingerbread plum
- Golden Delicious (apple)
- gooseberry, goosegog (Inf)
- gourd
- granadilla
- grape
- grapefruit
- greengage
- guava
- hackberry (*or* hagberry)
- hanepoot (grape)
- hautboy (strawberry)
- honeydew (melon)
- huckleberry
- icaco plum
- imbu
- jaboticaba
- jackfruit
- Jaffa (orange)
- Japanese quince
- Japanese persimmon
- Jerusalem cherry
- jujube
- kaki
- kiwi fruit
- kumquat (*or* cumquat)
- lemon
- lime
- lingonberry
- litchi (*or* lichee *or* lichi *or* lychee)
- loganberry
- longan (*or* lungan)
- loquat
- love apple (Arch)
- mammee apple
- mandarin
- mango
- mangosteen
- manzanilla
- marang
- marasca (cherry)
- May apple
- medlar
- melon
- minneola
- mombin
- morello (cherry)
- mulberry
- muscadine (grape)
- muscat (*or* muscatel) (grape)
- muskmelon
- myrobalan
- nashi
- navel orange
- nectarine
- nipa
- olive
- orange
- Osage orange
- papaw
- papaya
- passion fruit
- peach
- pear
- Persian melon
- persimmon
- pineapple
- pippin
- plantain
- plum
- pomegranate
- pomelo
- prickly pear
- quandong (*or* quandang *or* quantong)
- queen olive
- quince
- rambutan
- raspberry
- redcurrant
- rhubarb
- rose apple
- russet (apple)
- salmonberry
- sapodilla
- satsuma
- serviceberry
- Seville orange
- sharon fruit
- sloe
- sorb apple
- sour cherry
- sour gourd
- soursop
- spiceberry
- star–apple
- star fruit
- strawberry
- sweet cherry
- sweetsop
- tamarillo
- tamarind
- tangelo
- tangerine
- tayberry
- tomato, love apple (Arch)
- tree tomato
- ugli fruit
- watermelon
- whitecurrant
- whortleberry
- Williams (pear)
- winter melon
- youngberry

NUTS

acorn	coconut	marron (Fr)
almond	coffee nut	mockernut
areca	cola (*or* kola) nut	monkey nut
beechnut	conker	palm nut
betel nut	coquilla nut	peanut
bitternut	double coconut	pecan
black walnut	dwarf chestnut	pignut
brazil (*or* brasil) nut	earthnut	pili nut
breadnut	filbert	pine nut (*or* piñon)
burrawang nut	groundnut	pistachio
butternut	grugru nut	Queensland nut
candlenut	gum nut	sal nut
cashew	hazelnut	souari nut
chestnut	hickory	sweet (*or* Spanish) chestnut
chinquapin (*or* chincapin *or* chinkapin)	hognut	walnut
cob (*or* cobnut)	horse chestnut	water chestnut (*or* caltrop)
coco de mer	ivory nut	water chinquapin
	kola nut	white walnut
	litchi nut	
	macadamia nut	

apple sauce (US inf), apple polisher (US inf), banana republic (Inf), Banana bender (Aus inf), lemon squeezer (NZ inf), cherry (Inf)

ADJECTIVES

6 **fruiting**, fruit-bearing, fructiferous, pomiferous, leguminous, fructuous, fruitful, productive, fertile

► *562 Fertility*

7 **fruitlike**, fruity, citrus, citrous, citric, citrine

8 **fruit-eating**, frugivorous, vegetarian

9 **of a fruit**, fleshy, succulent, ripe, unripe, indehiscent, dehiscent, monocarpellary, bicarpellary, polycarpellary, syncarpous, apocarpous, monocarpic, schizocarpic, parthenocarpic

VERBS

10 **fruit**, bear fruit, fructify, ripen, be fruitful, yield, release seeds, dehisce

► *248 Prosperity; 561 Reproduction; 562 Fertility*

ADVERBS

11 **fructiferously**, fruitily, fructuously, succulently, fruitfully, productively

81 Grasses

NOUNS

1 **grass**, true grass, grass family, Gramineae, Poaceae, graminaceous plant, ornamental grass, mowing grass, lawn grass, fodder grass, meadow grass, pasture grass, ley grass, cereal grass, grasslike plant, rush, sedge

2 **grassland**, meadow, field, meadow land, mead (Lit), lea (Lit), pasture land, permanent pasture, pasturage, herbage, verdure, ley, grazing, plain, range (US), pampas (South America), savanna (*or* savannah) (Africa), llano (South America), campo (Brazil), veld (*or* veldt) (South Africa), prairie (US), steppe (Russia), champaign (France), campagna (Italy), common, moor, moorland, heath, downs, downland, wold (Lit), park, parkland, lawn, green, sward (Lit), greensward (Lit), turf, grass, sod, divot, clump, tussock, tuft, hassock

► *43 Agriculture; 538 Greenness*

3 **grass plant**, stem, culm, haulm, cane, reed, straw, spear, spire, blade, blade of grass, leaf, sheath, ligule, auricle, grass flower, spike, panicle, spikelet, glume, rachilla, lemma, palea (*or* pale), awn, lodicule, tassel

4 **cereal grass**, cereal, grain, ear, ear of corn, cob, corncob, barleycorn, husk, bran, chaff, stubble, straw

► *25 Cookery; 43 Agriculture; 80 Fruits*

5 **grass cutter**, mower, mowing machine, lawn mower, scythe, reed cutter, thatcher

► *43 Agriculture; 44 Horticulture; 438 Tool*

6 **grass eater**, browser, grazer, graminivore, herbivore

7 **figurative usage**, Bamboo Curtain, grass roots, grass widow, broken reed (Inf)

ADJECTIVES

8 **grasslike**, gramineous, graminaceous, poaceous, graminiferous, farinaceous, wheaten, oaten

9 **grassy**, verdant, green, grass-green, grass-covered, verdured, meadowy, swardy, turfy, reedy, rushy, sedgy

► *77 Plants; 538 Greenness*

GRASSES

True grasses		
bamboo	gama grass	sheep's fescue
barley	grama grass	sorghum
beach grass (US)	hair grass	spelt
beard grass	hare's–tail	squirrel–tail grass
bent (*or* bent grass)	herd's grass (US)	sugar cane
Bermuda grass	Indian corn	switch grass
black bent	Indian rice	sword grass
bluegrass	Italian ryegrass	timothy (*or* timothy grass)
bog hair grass	Japanese (*or* Korean) lawn grass	tufted hair grass
bristle grass	Kentucky bluegrass	twitch grass
brome (*or* brome grass)	lesser quaking grass	vernal grass
broomcorn	lovegrass	wheat
buckwheat	lyme grass	wild oat
buffalo grass	maize	wild rice
bunch grass (US)	marram grass	wild rye
canary grass	meadow fescue	wire grass
cane	meadow foxtail	wood meadow grass
cat's–tail	meadow grass	Yorkshire fog
China grass	melick	zoysia
citronella	millet	
cocksfoot	oat grass	**Grasslike Plants**
cockspur	oats	bulrush
cordgrass	orchard grass	Dutch rush
corn	paddy	eelgrass
cotton grass	pampas grass	elephant grass
couch (*or* couch grass)	quack grass	goosegrass
crab grass	quaking grass	grass of Parnassus
creeping bent	quitch grass	grass tree
cut–grass	rattan	horsetail
darnel	redtop (US)	paper reed
dog's–tail	reed	papyrus
durra	reed grass	reedmace
emmer	rice	rush
English ryegrass	rye	scouring rush
feather grass	rye–brome	sedge
fescue	ryegrass	spear grass
fiorin	scutch (*or* scutch grass)	star grass
finger grass		tape grass
foxtail		woodrush
		worm grass

10 grass-eating, graminivorous, herbivorous, grazing, browsing

VERBS

11 eat grass, graze, browse, crop, forage, pasture, ruminate, chew the cud, put out to grass (*or* pasture), forage, fodder

12 manage grassland, cut, mow, scythe, top, grass, grass over, turf, sod, seed, sow seed, fertilize, feed, water, weed, top-dress, spray, roll

ADVERBS

13 herbivorously, verdantly

82 Ferns and Mosses

NOUNS

1 fern, true fern, pteridophyte, filicopsid, Filicinae, Filicopsida, bracken, brake, tropical fern, tree fern, fern ally, sphenopsid, horsetail, equisetum, Dutch rush, calamite, lycopsid, clubmoss, lycopodium, lycopod, ground pine, quillwort, fernlike plant, asparagus fern, seed fern, pteridosperm, cycad, cycad fern

► *77 Plants*

2 fern plant, stem, rachis, leaf, frond, leaflet, pinna, plant body, sporophyte, fern seed, spore, spore case, sporangium, sorus, indusium, prothallus, reproductive organ, archegonium, antheridium, study of ferns, pteridology, pteridologist

3 moss, true moss, bryophyte, Musci, Bryopsida, bryopsid, peat moss, bog moss, sphagnum, granite moss, wall moss, wood moss, hair moss, tree moss, moss ally, liverwort, Hepaticae, Hepaticopsida, leafy liverwort, thallose liverwort, horned liverwort, hornwort, mosslike plant, lichen, Spanish moss, long moss, reindeer moss, oak moss, alga, Irish moss

► *84 Algae and Lichens*

4 moss plant, plant body, gametophyte, root, rhizoid, spore capsule, seta, stalk, calyptra, cap, elater, foot, propagation, gemma, gemma cup, reproductive organ, archegonium, venter, antheridium, study of mosses, bryology, bryologist

FERNS

- adder's–tongue
- beech fern
- bird's–nest fern
- bladder fern
- Boston fern
- bracken
- buckler fern
- cliffbrake
- dryopteris
- grape fern (US)
- hard fern
- hart's–tongue
- holly fern
- lady fern
- maidenhair fern
- male fern
- marsh fern
- moonwort
- oak fern
- osmunda
- pepperwort
- pillwort
- polypody
- ponga
- rock brake
- royal fern
- shield fern
- spleenwort
- staghorn
- tree fern
- walking fern (US)
- wall rue
- woodsia

ADJECTIVES

5 fernlike, ferny, pteridophyte, pteridophytic, pteridophytous, pteridological

6 mosslike, mossy, moss-covered, moss-grown, bryophyte, bryophytic, hepatic, bryological

83 Fungi

Life is too short to stuff a mushroom. Shirley Conran.

NOUNS

1 fungus, fungosity, mould, must, mildew, rot, dry rot, wet rot, blight, canker

2 mushroom, toadstool, *champignon* (Fr), cultivated mushroom, button mushroom, wild mushroom, field mushroom, fairy ring, magic mushroom, mushroom cloud

► *25 Cookery; 44 Horticulture*

3 fungi, Fungi (*or* Mycota), true fungi, Eumycota, basidiomycetes, Basidiomycotina, agarics, bracket fungi, pore fungi, tooth fungi, club fungi, skin fungi, jelly fungi, rusts, smuts, ascomycetes, Ascomycotina, sac fungi, cup fungi, flask fungi, deuteromycetes, imperfect fungi, Deuteromycotina (*or* Fungi Imperfecta), phycomycetes, Mastigomycotina, Zygomycotina, myxomycetes, Myxomycota, slime moulds, cellular slime moulds

FUNGI

Mushrooms, Toadstools, etc.

- agaric
- agrocybe
- amanita
- ascomycetes
- beefsteak fungus
- bird's–nest fungus
- blewits
- blusher
- boletus
- bootlace fungus
- bracket fungus
- brain fungus
- cep
- chanterelle
- collybia
- coprinus
- cortinarius
- death cap
- destroying angel
- earth ball
- earthstar
- earth tongue
- elf–cup
- entoloma
- fairy–ring mushroom (*or* champignon)
- false morel
- field mushroom
- fly agaric
- funnel cap
- hare's ear
- helvella
- honey fungus (*or* agaric)
- horn of plenty
- horsehair toadstool (*or* fungus)
- horse mushroom
- hydnum
- hydrocybe
- ink cap
- inocybe
- jew's ear
- lactarius
- lepista
- leptonia
- liberty cap
- meadow mushroom
- milk cap
- miller
- morel
- orange–peel fungus
- oyster mushroom
- panaeolus
- panther cap
- parasol mushroom
- pluteus
- polypore
- psilocybe
- psathyrella
- puffball
- russula
- St George's mushroom
- Satan's (*or* devil's) boletus
- shaggy inkcap
- stag's–horn fungus
- stinkhorn
- truffle
- tuckahoe
- velvet shank
- verdigris toadstool
- wax cap
- witches' butter
- wood hedgehog
- wood woollyfoot

Moulds, Mildews, and Pathogens

- aspergillus
- black rust (of wheat)
- blue (*or* green) mould
- botrytis
- bread mould
- brewers' (*or* bakers') yeast
- brown rot (of apples)
- bunt
- candida
- corn smut
- cramp ball
- downy mildew
- ergot
- mucor
- penicillium
- pin mould
- potato blight
- powdery mildew
- rhizopus
- rust
- smut
- sooty mould
- stinking smut
- streptomyces
- verticillium
- water mould
- yeast

4 **fungal body**, thallus, mycelium, hypha, haustorium, rhizoid, rhizomorph, plasmodium, reproductive body, carpophore, fruiting body, mushroom, cap, pileus, gill, lamella, stalk, stipe, veil, volva, annulus, bracket, conk, sporophore, basidiocarp, basidium, sterigma, hymenium, ascocarp, ascus, spore, basidiospore, ascospore, conidium

5 **fungal association**, symbiosis, mycorrhiza, ectotrophic mycorrhiza, endotrophic mycorrhiza, lichen, symbiotic fungus, mycobiont, parasitism, parasitic fungus, parasite, dermatophyte, saprophyte, pathogen, fungal disease, mycosis, dermatophytosis, ringworm, tinea, athlete's foot, dhobi itch, favus, thrush, candidiasis, moniliasis, phycomycosis, aspergillosis, ergotism, histoplasmosis, farmer's lung, mycetoma, Madura foot, blastomycosis, coccidioidomycosis, plant disease, damping-off, dieback, Dutch elm disease

▶ *43 Agriculture; 44 Horticulture; 79 Trees; 84 Algae and Lichens; 260 Ill Health*

6 **fungal antibiotic**, penicillin, streptomycin, actinomycin, neomycin, chloramphenical

▶ *37 Pharmacology*

7 **antifungal agent**, fungicide, fungistat, antimycotic

▶ *382 Killing; 394 Remedy*

8 **study of fungi**, mycology, mycologist, mushroom grower, mushroom farmer, mushroom farm, truffle hunter, mushroom eating, mycophagy, mycophagist

ADJECTIVES

9 **fungal**, fungous, fungoid, fungiform, mildewed, mildewy, mouldy, musty, rotten, blighted, cankered, yeasty, fermented

10 **of fungi**, saprophytic, parasitic, homothallic, heterothallic, mycelial, hyphal, ascogenous, mycotic, mycologic(al), coprophilous, decurrent, epigeal, deliquescent, adnate, adnexed, alveolate, amyloid, aeriolate, bulbous, cespitose, fusiform, reticulate, sessile

VERBS

11 **moulder**, mildew, rot, putrefy, decompose, ferment, deliquesce

▶ *245 Deterioration*

12 **mushroom**, germinate, spring up, flourish, burgeon, proliferate, multiply

▶ *158 Size; 213 Increase*

ADVERBS

13 **saprophytically**, parasitically, symbiotically

84 Algae and Lichens

Is ditchwater dull? Naturalists with microscopes have told me that it teems with quiet fun. G. K. Chesterton.

NOUNS

1 **alga**, thallophyte, seaweed, wrack, kelp, phytoplankton, algal bloom, eutrophication, red tide, mat, pond scum, frog spit, symbiotic alga, phycobiont, lichen

ALGAE

anabaena	conferva	kelp	sargassum
badderlocks	desmid	laminaria	sea lace
bladderwrack	diatom	laver	sea lettuce
bull kelp	dinoflagellate	nostoc	sea tangle
carrageen (*or* carragheen, *or* carageen)	dulse	nullipore	seaware
	euglena	oarweed	sea wrack
	fucoid	peacock's tail	spirogyra
Ceylon moss	fucus	redware	stonewort
chlorella	gulfweed	rockweed	wrack

2 **algae**, blue-green algae, cyanobacteria, Cyanophyta, golden-brown algae, Chrysophyta, chrysophyte, yellow-green algae, Xanthophyta, xanthophyte, green algae, Chlorophyta, chlorophyte, isokont, brown algae (*or* seaweeds), Phaeophyta, phaeophyte, red algae (*or* seaweeds), Rhodophyta, rhodophyte, study of algae, algology, phycology, algologist, phycologist

3 **plant body**, thallus, frond, holdfast, hapteron, stem, stipe, branch, branchlet, lamina, blade, float, air bladder, thread, rhizoid, protonema, frustule, theca, epitheca, hypotheca, algal pigment, chlorophyll, carotene, xanthophyll, fucoxanthin, phycocyanin, phycoerythrin, eyespot, stigma, blepharoplast, food store, pyrenoid, starch, paramylum

4 **reproductive body**, zoospore, aplanospore, hypnospore, autospore, cyst, propagule, hormogonium, coenobium, sexual reproduction, isogamy, anisogamy, oogamy, gamete, spermatozoid, antherozoid, oosphere, gonidium, antheridium, oogonium, manubrium, conceptacle, spermatangium, spermatium, carpogonium, carpospore

5 **algal product**, agar, algin, alginate, laver bread, miru (Jap), kombu (Jap), fossil algae, diatomaceous earth, stromatolite

6 **lichen**, reindeer moss, rock tripe, oak moss, Spanish moss, crustose lichen, foliose lichen, fruticose lichen, symbiosis, fungal constituent, mycobiont, algal constituent, phycobiont, root, rhizine, propagation, podetium, isidium, soredium, study of lichens, lichenology, lichenometry, lichenologist

▶ *82 Ferns and Mosses; 83 Fungi*

ADJECTIVES

7 **algal**, algoid, diatomaceous, conferval, confervoid, fucoid, unicellular, colonial, coenobial, filamentous, thalloid, siphonaceous, palmelloid, dendroid, sessile, motile, symbiotic, epiphytic, epilithic, flagellate, uniflagellate, biflagellate, multiflagellate, parenchymatous, pseudoparenchymatous, algological, phycological

8 **lichenoid**, lichenous, lichenose, lichened, lichenized, licheniform, crustose, foliose, fruticose, corticolous, saxicolous, lichenological

ADVERBS

9 **algologically**, colonially, epiphytically, symbiotically

Places

85 Countries

The day of small nations has long passed away. The day of Empires has come. Joseph Chamberlain.

NOUNS

1 **country**, nation, nationhood, state, statehood, land, body politic, sovereign state (*or* nation), sovereignty, self-governing state, independent state, free country (*or* nation), self-determination, democracy, parliamentary democracy, dictatorship, oligarchy, monarchy, republic, people's republic, capitalist country, socialist country, communist country, Iron Curtain country, power, superpower, Western nation, third-world country, nonaligned (*or* unaligned) country, neutral nation, isolationist nation

2 **union of nations**, federation, confederation, commonwealth, commonweal, British Commonwealth, EU (European Union), CIS (Commonwealth of Independent States), UN (United Nations), Western bloc, Eastern bloc, Soviet bloc

▶ *12 Government and Politics; 86 Regions*

3 **dominion**, domain, realm, kingdom, principality, principate, duchy, dukedom, grand duchy, archduchy, archdukedom, earldom, palatinate, sultanate, chieftaincy, toparchy, empire, British Empire, Roman Empire, Holy Roman Empire, Ottoman Empire, Mogul Empire, province, territory, occupied country, colony, settlement, protectorate, mandate, mandated territory (*or* mandate), mandatory, captive nation, Lebensraum, buffer state, ally, satellite nation, statelet, puppet regime, sphere of influence, imperialism, colonialism

▶ *140 Rule; 334 Power; 387 Subjection; 396 Authority; 397 Command*

4 **nationalism**, nationality, ultranationalism, national consciousness, patriotism, chauvinism, jingoism, isolationism, protectionism, xenophobia, racism, gung-ho nationalism (Inf)

▶ *622 Pride*

5 **internationalism**, internationality, global outlook, universality, universalism, cosmopolitanism

6 **native land**, native soil, country of origin, mother country, motherland, fatherland, *Vaterland* (Ger), *patria* (L), the old country, one's native ground, birthplace, cradle, home, homeland, home ground, God's (own) country (Inf)

▶ *130 Beginning; 565 Habitat*

7 **United States (US)**, United States of America (USA), America, the States, Stateside, Columbia, Land of Liberty, the Land of the Free, the Americans, Americanism, Americana, Americanization, American eagle, Stars and Stripes, Yankee (Doodle), the Melting Pot (Inf), Uncle Sugar (US inf), Yank (Inf), US of A (Inf), Uncle Sam (Inf)

8 **Great Britain**, the British Isles, United Kingdom (UK), Britain, (Perfidious) Albion (Lit), Britannia, Britishism, Briticism, the British, Briton, Brit (Inf), British bulldog (Inf), Limeyland (US inf)

9 **England**, (Perfidious) Albion (Lit), the English, Englishman (*or* woman), Northerner, Southerner, Englishness, Anglicization, Anglicism, Anglophile, Anglophobe, John Bull

10 **Ireland**, the Emerald Isle, Erin (Lit), Hibernia (Lit), Eire, the Republic of Ireland, the Republic, the South, Northern Ireland, Ulster, the Six Counties, the North, the Irish, the Northern Irish, Irishman (*or* woman), Irishness, Irishism

11 **Scotland**, Caledonia (Lit), the Highlands, the Lowlands, the Scottish, Scotsman (*or* woman), Scot, Caledonian, Highlander, Lowlander, Scottishness

12 **Wales**, *Cymru* (Welsh), *Cambria* (L), the Principality, North Wales, South Wales, the Welsh, North Walian, South Walian, Welshman, Welshwoman, Welshness

13 **native**, countryman, countrywoman, citizen, national, local

▶ *564 Inhabitant*

14 **nationalist**, ultranationalist, colonialist, patriot, jingoist, isolationist, protectionist, xenophobe, racist

15 **internationalist**, universalist, cosmopolitan, citizen of the world

ADJECTIVES

16 **national**, federal, state, sovereign, self-governing, independent, self-determining, democratic, republican, welfare, socialist, socialistic, communist, communistic, nonaligned (*or* unaligned), international, imperialistic, colonial, mandated, buffer, satellite, puppet, nationalistic, ultranational, ultranationalistic, chauvinistic, jingoistic, gung-ho (Inf)

VERBS

17 **become a nation**, become independent, declare inde-

COUNTRIES (WITH CAPITALS)

Afghanistan (Kabul)
Albania (Tirana)
Algeria (Algiers)
Angola (Luanda)
Antigua and Barbuda (St John's)
Argentina (Buenos Aires)
Armenia (Yerevan)
Australia (Canberra)
Austria (Vienna)
Azerbaijan (Baku)
Bahamas, The (Nassau)
Bahrain (Manama)
Bangladesh (Dhaka)
Barbados (Bridgetown)
Belarus (Minsk)
Belau *or* Palau (Koror)
Belgium (Brussels)
Belize (Belmopan)
Benin (Porto Novo)
Bhutan (Thimphu)
Bolivia (La Paz)
Bosnia–Hercegovina (Sarajevo)
Botswana (Gaborone)
Brazil (Brasilia)
Brunei (Bandar Seri Begawan)
Bulgaria (Sofia)
Burkina Faso (Ouagadougou)
Burma *or* Myanmar (Rangoon *or* Yangon)
Burundi (Bujumbura)
Byelorussia *or* Belarus (Minsk)
Cambodia (Phnom Penh)
Cameroon (Yaoundé)
Canada (Ottawa)
Cape Verde (Praia)
Central African Republic (Bangui)
Chad (Ndjamena)
Chile (Santiago)
China (Beijing *or* Peking)
Colombia (Bogota)
Comoros (Moroni)
Congo (Brazzaville)
Congo, Democratic Republic of (formerly Zaïre) (Kinshasa)
Costa Rica (San José)
Croatia (Zagreb)
Cuba (Havana)
Cyprus (Nicosia *or* Lefkosia)
Czech Republic (Prague)
Denmark (Copenhagen)
Djibouti (Djibouti)
Dominica (Roseau)
Dominican Republic (Santo Domingo)
Ecuador (Quito)
Egypt (Cairo)
El Salvador (San Salvador)
Equatorial Guinea (Malabo)
Eritrea (Asmara)
Estonia (Tallinn)
Ethiopia (Addis Ababa)
Fiji (Suva)
Finland (Helsinki)
France (Paris)
Gabon (Libreville)
Gambia, The (Banjul)
Georgia (Tbilisi)
Germany (Bonn)
Ghana (Accra)
Greece (Athens)
Grenada (St George's)
Guatemala (Guatemala City)
Guinea (Conakry)
Guinea–Bissau (Bissau)
Guyana (Georgetown)
Haiti (Port–au–Prince)
Honduras (Tegucigalpa)
Hungary (Budapest)
Iceland (Reykjavik)
India (New Delhi)
Indonesia (Jakarta)
Iran (Tehran)
Iraq (Baghdad)
Ireland (Dublin)
Israel (Jerusalem)
Italy (Rome)
Jamaica (Kingston)
Japan (Tokyo)
Jordan (Amman)
Kazakhstan (Alma–Ata; to transfer to Akmola in 2000)
Kenya (Nairobi)
Kirghizia *or* Kyrgyzstan (Bishkek *or* Pishpek)
Korea, North (Pyongyang)
Korea, South (Seoul)
Kuwait (Kuwait)
Kyrgyzstan *or* Kirghizia (Bishkek *or* Pishpek)
Laos (Vientiane)
Latvia (Riga)
Lebanon (Beirut)
Lesotho (Maseru)
Liberia (Monrovia)
Libya (Tripoli)
Liechtenstein (Vaduz)
Lithuania (Vilnius)
Luxembourg (Luxembourg)
Madagascar (Antananarivo)
Malawi (Lilongwe)
Malaysia (Kuala Lumpur)
Maldives (Malé)
Mali (Bamako)
Malta (Valletta)
Mauritania (Nouakchott)
Mauritius (Port Louis)
Mexico (Mexico City)
Moldova (Kishinev *or* Chisinau)
Monaco (Monaco–Ville)
Mongolia (Ulan Bator)
Morocco (Rabat)
Mozambique (Maputo)
Myanmar *or* Burma (Yangon *or* Rangoon)
Namibia (Windhoek)
Nauru (Yaren)
Nepal (Kathmandu)
Netherlands, The (Amsterdam)
New Zealand (Wellington)
Nicaragua (Managua)
Niger (Niamey)
Nigeria (Abuja)
Norway (Oslo)
Oman (Muscat)
Pakistan (Islamabad)
Panama (Panama City)
Papua New Guinea (Port Moresby)
Paraguay (Asunción)
Peru (Lima)
Philippines (Manila)
Poland (Warsaw)
Portugal (Lisbon)
Qatar (Doha)
Romania (Bucharest)
Russia (Moscow)
Rwanda (Kigali)
St Christopher and Nevis *or* St Kitts–Nevis (Basseterre)
St Lucia (Castries)
St Vincent and the Grenadines (Kingstown)
San Marino (San Marino)
São Tomé e Principe (São Tomé)
Saudi Arabia (Riyadh)
Senegal (Dakar)
Serbia (Belgrade)
Seychelles (Victoria)
Sierra Leone (Freetown)
Singapore (Singapore)
Slovakia (Bratislava)
Slovenia (Ljubljana)
Solomon Islands (Honiara)
Somalia (Mogadishu)
South Africa (Pretoria)
Spain (Madrid)
Sri Lanka (Colombo)
Sudan (Khartoum)
Surinam(e) (Paramaribo)
Swaziland (Mbabane)
Sweden (Stockholm)
Syria (Damascus)
Tadzhikistan *or* Tajikistan (Dushanbe)
Taiwan (Taipei)
Tanzania (Dodoma)
Thailand (Bangkok)
Togo (Lomé)
Tonga (Nuku'alofa)
Trinidad and Tobago (Port of Spain)
Tunisia (Tunis)
Turkey (Ankara)
Turkmenistan (Ashkhabad *or* Ashgabat)
Uganda (Kampala)
Ukraine (Kiev)
United Arab Emirates (Abu Dhabi)
United Kingdom (London)
United States of America (Washington)
Uruguay (Montevideo)
Uzbekistan (Tashkent)
Vanuatu (Vila)
Venezuela (Caracas)
Vietnam (Hanoi)
Western Samoa (Apia)
Yemen (Sana'a)
Zaïre (now called Democratic Republic of Congo) (Kinshasa)
Zambia (Lusaka)
Zimbabwe (Harare)

pendence, become self-governing, become autonomous, gain self-determination, have sovereignty, democratize, socialize, communize

18 exert sovereignty, rule, occupy, colonize, settle, mandate, Americanize, Anglicize

▶ *140 Rule*

ADVERBS

19 nationally, federally, independently, democratically, socialistically, communistically, internationally, imperialistically, colonially, nationalistically, patriotically, in a patriotic way, chauvinistically, jingoistically

86 Regions

He was imperfect, unfinished, inartistic; he was worse than provincial – he was parochial. Henry James.

NOUNS

1 region, area, territory, terrain, zone, belt, section, sector, place, space, ground, geographical unit, land, landmass, continent, peninsula, island, islet

2 geographical region, zone, longitude, meridian, prime

meridian, latitude, parallel, equator, the Line, tropic, tropics, subtropics, horse latitudes, roaring forties

3 **regional boundary**, boundary, outer limit, bounds, pale, confines, marches, shore, territorial limits, territorial waters, continental shelf, offshore rights, 3-mile limit, 12-mile limit, 200-mile limit, exclusion zone, airspace, economic zone

4 **territorial division**, political entity, nation, nation state, sovereign state, power, superpower, territory, country, state, republic, democratic republic, people's republic, kingdom, realm, domain, principality, sultanate, dominion, protectorate, mandate, possession, colony, dependency, commonwealth, union of nations, empire, homeland, fatherland, land of our fathers, motherland,

COUNTIES

English Counties and Former Counties (with Administrative Centres)

Avon* (Bristol)
Bedfordshire (Bedford)
Berkshire (Reading)
Buckinghamshire (Aylesbury)
Cambridgeshire (Cambridge)
Cheshire (Chester)
Cleveland* (Middlesbrough)
Cornwall (Truro)
Cumberland* (Carlisle)
Cumbria (Carlisle)
Derbyshire (Matlock)
Devon (*or* Devonshire) (Exeter)
Dorset (Dorchester)
Durham (Durham)
East Riding of Yorkshire (Beverley)
East Sussex (Lewes)
Essex (Chelmsford)
Gloucestershire (Gloucester)
Greater London*
Greater Manchester*
Hampshire (Winchester)
Hereford and Worcester* (Worcester)
Herefordshire* (Hereford)
Hertfordshire (Hertford)
Humberside* (Beverley)
Huntingdonshire* (Huntingdon)
Kent (Maidstone)
Lancashire (Preston)
Leicestershire (Leicester)
Lincolnshire (Lincoln)
Merseyside* (Liverpool)
Norfolk (Norwich)
Northamptonshire (Northampton)
North Riding of Yorkshire* (Middlesbrough)
Northumberland (Morpeth)
North Tyneside (Wallsend)
North Yorkshire (Northallerton)
Northumberland (Morpeth)
Nottinghamshire (Nottingham)
Oxfordshire (Oxford)
Rutland (Oakham)
Shropshire *or* Salop (Shrewsbury)
Somerset (Taunton)
South Tyneside (South Shields)
South Yorkshire* (Barnsley)
Staffordshire (Stafford)
Suffolk (Ipswich)
Surrey (Kingston upon Thames)
Thamesdown (Swindon)
Tyne and Wear* (Newcastle–Upon–Tyne)
Warwickshire (Warwick)
West Midlands* (Birmingham)
Westmorland* (Kendal)
West Riding of Yorkshire* (Wakefield)
West Sussex (Chichester)
West Yorkshire* (Wakefield)
Wight, Isle of (Newport)
Wiltshire (Trowbridge)
Wirral (Birkenhead)
Worcestershire* (Worcester)

*Former *or* Metropolitan County

Welsh Counties and Selected Local Authorities (with Administrative Centres)

Anglesey (Llangefni)
Blaenau Gwent (Ebbw Vale)
Breconshire* (Brecon)
Caernarfonshire* (Caernarfon)
Cardiganshire* (Aberystwyth)
Carmarthenshire (Carmarthen)
Ceredigion (Aberaeron)
Clwyd* (Mold)
Conwy (Bodlondeb)
Denbighshire (Ruthin)
Dyfed* (Carmarthen)
Flintshire (Mold)
Glamorgan* (Cardiff)
Gwent* (Cwmbran)
Gwynedd (Caernarfon)
Merionethshire* (Dolgellau)
Mid Glamorgan* (Cardiff)
Monmouthshire (Cwmbran)
Montgomeryshire* (Welshpool)
Neath–Port Talbot (Port Talbot)
Pembrokeshire (Haverfordwest)
Powys (Llandrindod Wells)
Radnorshire* (Llandrindod Wells)
Rhondda–Cynon–Taff (Clydach Vale)
South Glamorgan* (Cardiff)
Swansea
Torfaen (Pontypool)
Vale of Glamorgan (Barry)
West Glamorgan* (Swansea)
Wrexham

*Former County

Scottish Local Authorities (with Administrative Centres)

Aberdeenshire (Aberdeen)
Angus (Forfar)
Argyll and Bute (Lochgilphead)
Argyll* (Lochgilphead)
Ayrshire* (Ayr)
Banff* (Banff)
Berwick* (Duns)
Borders (Newton St Boswells)
Bute* (Rothesay)
Caithness* (Wick)
Central* (Stirling)
Clackmannanshire (Alloa)
Dumfries* (Dumfries)
Dumfries and Galloway (Dumfries)
Dunbartonshire* (Dumbarton)
East Ayrshire (Kilmarnock)
East Dunbartonshire (Kirkintilloch)
East Lothian (Haddington)
East Renfrewshire (Giffnock)
Fife (Glenrothes)
Grampian* (Aberdeen)
Highland* (Inverness)
Inverclyde (Greenock)
Inverness(-shire)* (Inverness)
Kincardineshire* (Stonehaven)
Kinross* (Kinross)
Kirkcudbright* (Kirkcudbright)
Lanarkshire* (Hamilton)
Lothian* (Edinburgh)
Midlothian (Dalkeith)
Moray (Elgin)
Nairn* (Nairn)
North Ayrshire (Irvine)
North Lanarkshire (Motherwell)
Orkney (Kirkwall)
Peebles* (Peebles)
Perth and Kinross (Perth)
Perthshire* (Perth)
Renfrewshire (Paisley)
Ross and Cromarty* (Dingwall)
Roxburgh* (Newtown St Boswells)
Scottish Borders (Newtown St Boswells)
Selkirk* (Selkirk)
Shetland (formerly Zetland) (Lerwick)
South Ayrshire (Ayr)
South Lanarkshire (Hamilton)
Stirling (Stirling)
Strathclyde (Glasgow)
Sutherland* (Golspie)
Tayside (Dundee)
West Dunbartonshire (Dumbarton)
Western Isles (Lewis)
West Lothian (Livingston)
Wigtownshire* (Stranraer)

* Former Region *or* County

Northern Ireland Historic Counties (with County Towns)

Antrim (Belfast)
Armagh (Armagh)
Down (Downpatrick)
Fermanagh (Enniskillen)
Londonderry (Londonderry)
Tyrone (Omagh)

REPUBLIC OF IRELAND

Provinces

Connacht (*or* Connaught)
Leinster
Munster
Ulster

Counties (with County Towns)

Carlow (Carlow)
Cavan (Cavan)
Clare (Ennis)
Cork (Cork)
Donegal (Lifford)
Dublin (Dublin)
Galway (Galway)
Kerry (Tralee)
Kildare (Naas)
Kilkenny (Kilkenny)
Laois (Portlaoise)
Leitrim (Carrick–on–Shannon)
Limerick (Limerick)
Longford (Longford)
Louth (Dundalk)
Mayo (Castlebar)
Meath (Trim)
Monaghan (Monaghan)
Offaly (Tullamore)
Roscommon (Roscommon)
Sligo (Sligo)
Tipperary (Clonmel)
Waterford (Waterford)
Westmeath (Mullingar)
Wexford (Wexford)
Wicklow (Wicklow)

AMERICAN STATES

State (Capital)
Alabama (Montgomery)
Alaska (Juneau)
Arizona (Phoenix)
Arkansas (Little Rock)
California (Sacramento)
Colorado (Denver)
Connecticut (Hartford)
Delaware (Dover)
Florida (Tallahassee)
Georgia (Atlanta)
Hawaii (Honolulu)
Idaho (Boise)
Illinois (Springfield)
Indiana (Indianapolis)
Iowa (Des Moines)
Kansas (Topeka)
Kentucky (Frankfort)
Louisiana (Baton Rouge)
Maine (Augusta)
Maryland (Annapolis)
Massachusetts (Boston)
Michigan (Lansing)
Minnesota (St Paul)
Mississippi (Jackson)
Missouri (Jefferson City)
Montana (Helena)
Nebraska (Lincoln)
Nevada (Carson City)
New Hampshire (Concord)
New Jersey (Trenton)
New Mexico (Santa Fe)
New York (Albany)
North Carolina (Raleigh)
North Dakota (Bismarck)
Ohio (Columbus)
Oklahoma (Oklahoma City)
Oregon (Salem)
Pennsylvania (Harrisburg)
Rhode Island (Providence)
South Carolina (Columbia)
South Dakota (Pierre)
Tennessee (Nashville)
Texas (Austin)
Utah (Salt Lake City)
Vermont (Montpelier)
Virginia (Richmond)
Washington (Olympia)
West Virginia (Charleston)
Wisconsin (Madison)
Wyoming (Cheyenne)

mother country, native land, country of origin, old country
▶ *12 Government and Politics; 85 Countries*

5 state, territory, overseas territory, enclave, exclave, province, region, administrative area, council area, county, shire, metropolitan district, division, district, regional council, canton, duchy, *département* (Fr), *Kreis* (Ger), borough, ward, enumeration district, riding, bailiwick, hundred, wapentake, soke, eparchy, congressional district, electoral district, constituency, electorate, precinct, diocese, archdiocese, bishopric, archbishopric, parish, sheading, tithing, barony (Ireland), *arondissement* (Fr), *départment* (Fr), *oblast* (Russia), *fylker* (Norway), *Land* (Germany), *Län* (Sweden)
▶ *7 Religion*

6 regions, highlands, lowlands, borders, borderland, march, panhandle (US), corridor, rural area, country, countryside, green belt, hinterland, heartland, backcountry, provinces, outback, bush, brush, back-woods, backwater, outpost, back of beyond, wilderness, virgin territory, wasteland, the sticks (Inf), boondocks (US inf), boonies (US inf), yokeldom (Inf), hickdom (Inf)

7 regions of the world, Old World, New World, East and West, North and South, North-South divide, Western Hemisphere, Occident, Eastern Hemisphere, Orient, Middle East, Far East, Antipodes, down under (Inf), Third World, developed world, undeveloped world, underdeveloped world, developing nations
▶ *85 Countries*

8 regions of the US, Wild West, the Coast, Middle West (*or* Midwest), Dixie, Dixieland, Sunbelt, Silicon Valley, Yankeeland (Inf)

9 regions of Britain, Home Counties, Midlands, the Highlands, the North, the South, north of Watford, Fens, Broads, Marches, Borders, West Country

10 urban area, built-up area, urban sprawl, city, metropolitan area, megalopolis, metropolis, capital city, cathedral city, new city, garden city, inner city, city centre, central business district (CBD), precinct, uptown, downtown, ghetto, no-go area, slums, skid row (US inf), nowhere city (Inf), wrong side of the tracks (US inf), burg (US inf), big smoke (Aus inf), New York, Big Apple (Inf), Gotham (Inf), London, the Smoke (Inf)
▶ *87 Cities, Towns, and Villages*

11 settlement, village, hamlet, town, township, municipality, market town, county town, new town, dormitory town (*or* village), boom town, ghost town, shanty town, small town, one-horse town (Inf), suburbs, suburbia, outskirts, stockbroker belt (Inf), exurbia (US), gin and Jaguar belt (Inf)

12 plot, plot of land, parcel of land, enclosure, patch, lot, acreage, block, section, tract, allotment, holding, claim
▶ *165 Enclosure; 763 Possession*

13 locality, locale, neighbourhood, vicinity, area, haunt, circuit, beat, round, orbit, walk, environs, back yard (Inf), neck of the woods (Inf), stamping ground (Inf), turf (Inf), manor (Inf), patch (Inf)
▶ *142 Location; 170 Surroundings*

14 sphere, field, arena, province, ambit, theatre, territory,

CANADIAN PROVINCES AND TERRITORIES

Province/Territory (Capital)
Alberta (Edmonton)
British Colombia (Victoria)
Manitoba (Winnipeg)
New Brunswick (Fredericton)
Newfoundland (St John's)
Northwest Territories (Yellowknife)
Nova Scotia (Halifax)
Ontario (Toronto)
Prince Edward Island (Charlottetown)
Quebec (Quebec)
Saskatchewan (Regina)
Yukon Territory (Whitehouse)

AUSTRALIAN STATES AND TERRITORIES

State/Territory (Capital)
New South Wales (Sydney)
Queensland (Brisbane)
South Australia (Adelaide)
Tasmania (Hobart)
The Australian Capital Territory (Canberra)
The Northern Territory (Darwin)
Victoria (Melbourne)
Western Australia (Perth)

pale, jurisdiction, scope, realm, domain, bailiwick, interest, line, discipline, forte, métier, pigeon (Inf)

15 regionalism, provincialism, parochialism, nationalism, patriotism

▶ *12 Government and Politics*

ADJECTIVES

16 regional, areal, spatial (*or* spacial), geographical, topographic (*or* topographical), territorial, zonal, longitudinal, latitudinal, meridian, highland, lowland, peninsular, insular, tropical, subtropical, continental, eastern, western, northern, southern, Occidental, Oriental, antipodean

17 national, state, provincial, sectional, divisional, district, municipal, urban, metropolitan, suburban, rural, up-country, colonial, dependent, republican, democratic, patriotic

18 local, localized, next-door, neighbouring, nearby, provincial, parochial, diocesan, insular, confined, limited, back-country, back-woods, small-town, uptown, downtown, ghettoized, slummy

ADVERBS

19 geographically, spatially, longitudinally, latitudinally, regionally, territorially, continentally, equatorially, tropically, subtropically

20 nationally, internationally, divisionally, provincially, municipally, locally, nearby, colonially, politically, democratically, nationalistically, patriotically

87 Cities, Towns, and Villages

The first Care in building of Cities, is to make them airy and well perflated; infectious Distempers must necessarily be propagated amongst Mankind living close together. John Arbuthnot.

NOUNS

1 city, municipality, metropolis, metropolitan area, greater city, megalopolis, conurbation, urban complex, urban spread (*or* sprawl), seat of government, capital, industrial city, commercial city, twinned city, sister city (US), town, country town, holiday town, community, village, hamlet, urbanization, gentrification, suburbanization, countrification

▶ *159 Smallness; 205 Part; 565 Habitat*

2 American cities, state capital, county seat, New York, Chicago, Los Angeles, Hollywood, San Francisco, Philadelphia, Pittsburgh, Boston, Miami, Atlanta, New Orleans, Houston, Dallas, St Louis, Seattle, Detroit, Washington, Denver, Nashville, Las Vegas

3 New York, the Big Apple, Gotham, Manhattan, the Bronx, Queens, Brooklyn, Richmond (*or* Staten Island), Central Park, the Bowery, Harlem, Greenwich Village, Wall Street, East Side, West Side, Chinatown, Little Italy, the Bowry, Hell's Kitchen, Times Square, Greater New York

4 British cities, garden city, cathedral city, county town, shire town, London, Birmingham, Manchester, Leeds, Liverpool, Plymouth, Portsmouth, Canterbury, Oxford, Lincoln, Newcastle-upon-Tyne, York, Edinburgh, Glasgow, Aberdeen, Inverness, Cardiff, Swansea, Belfast

5 London, the Smoke, the Great Wen, East End, West End, Mayfair, Soho, Docklands, the Isle of Dogs, the City, the Square Mile, Hyde Park, Regent's Park, Knightsbridge, Paddington, Kensington, South Kensington, Holborn, Barbican, Earl's Court, Belgravia, Westminster, Hampstead, Highgate, Hackney, Lambeth, Southwark, Greater London

6 other cities, Paris, Rome, Madrid, Lisbon, Ankara, Athens, Moscow, Vienna, Budapest, Prague, Belgrade, Beijing (*or* Peking), Cairo, Calcutta, Mexico City, Rio de Janeiro, Tokyo, Hong Kong, Berlin, Quebec, Toronto, Sydney, Melbourne, Pretoria

7 city district, district, quarter, precinct, voting precinct (US), shopping precinct, ward, central city, city centre, inner city, high street, main street (US), block, square, marketplace, market square, market, mart, forum, plaza, piazza, uptown (US), midtown (US), downtown (US), shopping area, shopping centre, shopping arcade, shopping mall, financial district, business district, business (*or* commercial) zone (US), residential area, residential zone (US), tenement district, housing estate, ghetto, Black ghetto, niggertown (Offensive), Jewish ghetto, Jewtown (Offensive), barrio (US), slum (*or* slums), blighted area, blighted neighbourhood, no-go area, Tenderloin (US), red-light district, skid row (*or* road) (US inf), the other side of the tracks (US inf)

▶ *12 Government and Politics; 123 Importance; 173 Centre; 779 Market; 782 Poverty*

8 suburb, suburbia, subtopia, outskirts, built-up area, exurb (US), exurbia (US), green belt, dormitory suburb (*or* town), bedroom suburb (US), garden suburb, stockbroker belt (Inf)

▶ *164 Edge; 170 Surroundings; 179 Circularity*

9 town, township, community, country town, market town, new town, county town, county seat (US), boom town, ghost town (US), borough, burgh (Scot), burg (US inf)

10 village, country village, rural village, hamlet, tanktown (US), crossroads (US), whistle stop (US), wide place in the road (US), jumping-off place (US), village green, one-horse town (Inf), hick town (US inf), jerkwater town(US inf), rube town (US inf)

11 urbanite, urban dweller, city dweller, burgher, burgess, freeman, downtowner (US), uptowner (US), city father, city manager (US), slum-dweller, suburbanite, suburban dweller, commuter, townsman (*or* townswoman), local, oppidan, villager, parishioner, city slicker (Inf), townee (Inf)

12 rural dweller, countryman (*or* countrywoman), country bumpkin, rustic, yokel, hayseed (US inf), rube (US inf)

▶ *564 Inhabitant*

13 municipal building, city hall, town hall, fire station, firehouse (US), police station (*or* headquarters), precinct station (US), courthouse, county courthouse (US), community centre, county building

ADJECTIVES

14 urban, interurban, metropolitan, civic, municipal, city, citified, financial, business, residential, suburbanized, gentrified, blighted, no-go, suburban, subtopian, exurban (US), oppidan, town, high-street, main street (US), downtown (US), midtown (US), uptown (US), village,

CITIES, TOWNS, AND VILLAGES

Afghanistan
Herat
Kabul
Kandahar

Albania
Durrës
Tirana

Algeria
Algiers
Constantine
El Djazair
Qacentina
Oran
Wahran

Angola
Lobito
Luanda

Argentina
Buenos Aires
Córdoba
La Plata
Mendoza
Rosario

Armenia
Kirovakan
Yerevan

Australia
Adelaide
Alice Springs
Brisbane
Canberra
Darwin
Hobart
Melbourne
Newcastle
Perth
Sydney
Wollongong

Austria
Graz
Innsbruck
Salzburg
Vienna

Azerbaijan
Baku
Kirovabad

Bahamas, The
Nassau
New Providence

Bangladesh
Chittagong
Dhaka
Khulna

Belarus
Brest
Minsk
Pinsk

Belgium
Antwerp
Bruges
Brussels
Ghent
Liège
Namur
Ostend
Ypres
Zeebrugge

Bolivia
Cochabamba
La Paz
Santa Cruz

Bosnia-Hercegovina
Banja Luka
Sarajevo
Zenica

Brazil
Brasilia
Fortaleza
Porto Alegre
Recife
Rio de Janeiro
São Paulo

Bulgaria
Plovdiv
Sofia
Varna

Burma (*or* Myanmar)
Mandalay
Moulmein
Rangoon (*or* Yangon)

Cambodia
Batambang
Phnom Penh

Cameroon
Douala
Yaoundé

Canada
Calgary
Charlottetown
Edmonton
Fredericton
Halifax
Hamilton
Kingston
Montreal
Moose Jaw
Niagara Falls
Ottawa
Quebec
Regina
St John's
Saskatoon
Thunder Bay
Toronto
Vancouver
Victoria
Whitehouse
Windsor
Winnipeg
Yellowknife

Chile
Concepción
Santiago
Valparaíso

China
Anshan
Beijing (*or* Peking)
Canton
Changchun
Chengdu
Chongqing
Fushun
Harbin
Jinan
Kunming
Lanchow
Lüda
Lüshun
Nanjing
Shanghai
Shenyang
Taiyuan
Tianjin
Wuhan
Xi An

Colombia
Barranquilla
Bogotá
Cali
Cartagena
Medellin

Congo
Brazzaville
Pointe–Noire

Congo, Democratic Republic of (Zaïre)
Kananga
Kinshasa
Lubumbashi

Costa Rica
San José

Croatia
Split
Zagreb

Cuba
Guantánamo
Havana
Santiago de Cuba

Cyprus
Nicosia (*or* Lefkosia)

Czech Republic
Brno
Ceské Budějovice
Ostrava
Prague

Denmark
Aalborg (*or* Ålborg)
Copenhagen
Esbjerg

Dominican Republic
Santo Domingo

Ecuador
Guayaquil
Quito

Egypt
Alexandria
Aswan
Cairo
El Giza
Ismailia
Luxor
Port Said
Suez
Thebes

El Salvador
San Salvador
Santa Ana

England
Arundel
Aylesbury
Barnsley
Bath
Bedford
Berwick–on–Tweed
Beverley
Birmingham
Blackburn
Blackpool
Bournemouth
Bradford
Brighton
Bristol
Buckingham
Cambridge
Canterbury
Carlisle
Cheltenham
Chester
Chesterfield
Chichester
Colchester
Coventry
Cowes
Crewe
Darlington
Dartmouth
Deal
Derby
Devizes
Doncaster
Dorchester
Douglas
Dover
Durham
Exeter
Folkestone
Gloucester
Great Yarmouth
Grimsby
Halifax
Harrogate
Harwich
Hastings
Hereford
Hertford
Huddersfield
Hull
Ipswich
King's Lynn
Lancaster
Leeds
Leicester
Lincoln
Liverpool
London
Luton
Maidenhead
Maidstone
Manchester
Matlock
Middlesbrough
Milton Keynes
Morpeth
Newark
Newcastle–upon–Tyne
Newmarket
Newport
Northampton
Norwich
Nottingham
Oldham
Oxford
Penzance
Peterborough
Plymouth
Poole
Portsmouth
Preston
Reading
Richmond
Rugby
St Ives
Salisbury
Scarborough
Sheffield
Shrewsbury
Southampton
Southport
Stafford
Stoke–on–Trent
Stratford–on–Avon
Sunderland
Swindon
Taunton
Torquay
Trowbridge
Truro
Tunbridge Wells
Wakefield
Warrington
Warwick
Wells
Weymouth
Whitby
Wigan
Winchester
Windsor
Wolverhampton
Worcester
York

Eritrea
Asmara

Estonia
Tallinn (*or* Tallin)
Tartu

Ethiopia
Addis Ababa

Finland
Helsinki
Tampere
Turku

France
Abbeville
Aix–en–Provence
Alençon
Amiens
Avignon
Bayeux
Bayonne
Biarritz
Bordeaux
Boulogne
Brest
Caen
Calais
Cannes
Chartres
Cherbourg
Cluny
Dieppe
Dijon
Dunkirk (*or* Dunkerque)
Grenoble
Le Havre
Le Mans
Lille
Limoges
Lourdes
Lyons (*or* Lyon)
Mâcon
Marseilles (*or* Marseille)
Metz
Montélimar
Montpellier
Nancy
Nîmes
Nantes
Nice
Orléans
Paris
Perpignan
Reims (*or* Rheims)
Rouen
St Étienne
St Malo
St Tropez
Strasbourg
Toulon
Toulouse
Tours
Verdun
Versailles
Vichy

Georgia
Sukhumi
Tbilisi

Germany
Aachen
Augsburg
Baden–Baden
Berlin
Bonn
Brandenburg
Bremen
Brunswick
Cologne (*or* Köln)
Darmstadt
Dortmund
Dresden
Düsseldorf
Erfurt
Essen
Frankfurt am Main
Frankfurt an der Oder
Halle
Hamburg
Hanover (*or* Hannover)
Heidelberg
Homburg
Ingolstadt
Kassel
Kiel
Koblenz
Leipzig
Lübeck
Magdeburg
Mainz
Mannheim
Meissen
Munich (*or* München)
Neuburg an der Donau
Nuremberg (*or* Nürnberg)
Potsdam
Rostock
Saarbrücken
Spandau
Stuttgart
Wiesbaden
Worms

Ghana
Accra
Kumasi

Greece
Athens
Canea
Corinth
Kavála
Patras
Peristerion
Piraeus
Salonika (*or* Thessaloníki)

Guatemala
Guatemala City
Quezaltenango

Haiti
Port–au–Prince

CITIES, TOWNS, AND VILLAGES (CONT.)

Honduras
San Pedro Sula
Tegucigalpa

Hungary
Budapest
Debrecen
Miskolc
Pécs

Iceland
Reykjavik

India
Agartala
Agra
Ahmedabad
Ajmer
Allahabad
Amritsar
Bangalore
Bhopal
Bhubaneswar
Bombay (*or* Mumbai)
Calcutta
Chandigarh
Darjeeling
Gwalior
Howrah
Hyderabad
Imphal
Indore
Jaipur
Jamshedpur
Jhansi
Jodhpur
Kanpur
Kohima
Lucknow
Madras (*or* Chennai)
Meerut
Mysore
Nagpur
New Delhi
Old Delhi
Patna
Poona (*or* Pune)
Rampur
Shillong
Simla
Srinagar
Trivandrum
Vadodara
Varanasi

Indonesia
Bandung
Jakarta
Medan
Palembang
Semarang
Surabaya

Iran
Abadan
Shiraz
Tabriz
Tehran

Iraq
Baghdad
Basra
Kirkuk
Mosul

Ireland
Balla
Ballymurphy
Blarney
Carlow
Carrick–on–Shannon
Castlebar
Cavan
Clare
Clonmel
Connemara
Cork
Dublin
Dundalk
Ennis
Galway
Kells
Kildare
Kilkenny
Killarney
Lifford
Limerick
Longford
Monaghan
Mullingar
Naas
Portlaoise
Roscommon
Shannon
Shillelagh
Sligo
Tipperary
Tralee
Trim
Tullamore
Waterford
Wexford
Wicklow

Israel
Beersheba
Bethlehem
Gaza
Haifa
Jaffa
Jerusalem
Tel Aviv

Italy
Agrigento
Bologna
Brindisi
Florence
Genoa
Messina
Milan
Naples
Padua
Palermo
Parma
Pisa
Ravenna
Reggio di Calabria
Rome
Salerno
San Remo
Siena
Syracuse
Trento (*or* Trent)
Trieste
Turin
Venice
Verona

Jamaica
Kingston

Japan
Fukuoka
Hiroshima
Kawasaki
Kitakyushu
Kobe
Kyoto
Nagasaki
Nagoya
Osaka
Sapporo
Sendai
Tokyo
Yokohama

Jordan
Amman
Az–Zargu

Kazakhstan
Akmola
Alma–Ata
Karaganda

Kenya
Mombasa
Nairobi

Korea, North
Pyongyang
Wônsan

Korea, South
Pusan
Seoul
Taegu

Kuwait
Kuwait

Latvia
Daugavpils
Riga

Lebanon
Beirut
Tripoli

Liberia
Monrovia

Libya
Benghazi
Tobruk
Tripoli

Lithuania
Kaunas
Vilnius

Luxembourg
Luxembourg

Madagascar
Antananarivo

Malawi
Blantyre–Limbe
Lilongwe

Malaysia
Kuala Lumpur

Mali
Bamako
Timbuktu

Malta
Valletta

Mauritania
Nouakchott

Mauritius
Port Louis

Mexico
Acapulco
Guadalajara
Juárez
Matamoros
Mérida
Mexico City
Monterrey
Puebla
Tampico
Tijuana
Veracruz

Monaco
Monaco–Ville
Monte Carlo

Mongolia
Ulan Bator

Morocco
Casablanca
Marrakech (*or* Marrakesh)
Rabat
Tangier

Mozambique
Maputo

Netherlands, The
Amsterdam
Arnhem
Dordrecht (*or* Dort)
Eindhoven
Hague, The
Leiden (*or* Leyden)
Maastricht
Rotterdam
Utrecht

New Zealand
Auckland
Christchurch
Dunedin
Manukau
Napier
Nelson
Wellington

Nicaragua
Managua

Nigeria
Abuja
Enugu
Ibadan
Kano
Lagos

Northern Ireland
Antrim
Armagh
Ballymena
Belfast
Coleraine
Downpatrick
Dunmore
Enniskillen
Kilconnell
Larne
Lisburn
Londonderry (*or* Derry)
Lurgan
Newcastle
Newry
Newtownabbey
Omagh
Portadown
Portrush
Strabane
Trillick

Norway
Bergen
Oslo
Trondheim

Oman
Muscat

Pakistan
Faisalabad
Hyderabad
Islamabad
Karachi
Lahore
Peshawar
Quetta
Rawalpindi

Panama
Panama City

Peru
Arequipa
Callao
Cuzco (*or* Cusco)
Lima

Philippines, The
Cebu
Davao
Manila
Quezon City

Poland
Cracow
Gdansk (*or* Danzig)
Lodz
Lublin
Poznań
Przemyśl
Warsaw
Wroclaw

Portugal
Coimbra
Lisbon
Oporto

Romania
Braşov
Bucharest
Constanţa

Russia
Astrakhan
Gorky
Irkutsk
Kalinin
Kaliningrad
Moscow
Novgorod
Omsk
Pskov
St Petersburg (formerly Leningrad)
Smolensk
Sverdlovsk
Volgograd
Yakutsk

Saudi Arabia
Jidda
Mecca
Medina
Riyadh

Scotland
Aberdeen
Ayr
Banff
Bannockburn
Bonar Bridge
Braemar
Coldstream
Douglas
Dumbarton
Dumfries
Dunbar
Dundee
Dunfermline
Dunoon
Duns
East Kilbride
Edinburgh
Falkirk
Forfar
Fort William
Galashiels
Glasgow
Glencoe
Glenrothes
Greenock
Hamilton
Hawick
Inverness
Islay
John o'Groats
Kelso
Kilmarnock
Kinross
Kirkcaldy
Kirkcudbright
Kirkwall
Lanark
Lerwick
Lockerbie
Lossiemouth
Montrose
Motherwell
Newton St Boswells
Newport
Oban
Paisley
Perth
Ronaldsay
St Andrews
Selkirk
Stirling
Stornoway
Strathblane
Thurso
Troon
Wick

Senegal
Dakar
Kaolack

Serbia
Belgrade
Kruevac

Sierra Leone
Freetown

Singapore
Singapore

Slovakia
Bratislava
Košice

Slovenia
Ljubljana
Maribor

Somalia
Mogadishu

South Africa
Bloemfontein
Cape Town
Durban
Johannesburg
Kimberley
Ladysmith
Mafikeng (formerly Mafeking)
Pietermaritzburg
Port Elizabeth
Pretoria
Sharpeville
Soweto
Springbok

Spain
Alicante
Barcelona
Bilbao

CITIES, TOWNS, AND VILLAGES (CONT.)

Cádiz
Córdoba
Granada
Madrid
Málaga
Pamplona
San Sebastián
Santiago de Compostela
Saragossa (*or* Zaragoza)
Seville
Toledo
Valencia

Sri Lanka
Colombo
Kandy
Trincomalee

Sudan
Dongola
Khartoum
Omdurman
Port Sudan

Swaziland
Lavumisa
Mbabane
Stegi

Sweden
Boden
Göteborg (*or* Gothenburg)
Hälsingborg
Linköping
Malmö
Örebro
Stockholm
Uppsala

Switzerland
Basel (*or* Basle)
Bern
Geneva
Lausanne
Lucerne
Lugano
St Moritz
Zürich

Syria
Aleppo
Damascus
Homs (*or* Hums)
Palmyra

Taiwan
Kaohsiung
Taipei

Tanzania
Dar es Salaam
Dodoma
Zanzibar

Thailand
Bangkok
Chumphon
Lampang

Togo
Lomé
Mango

Trinidad and Tobago
Plymouth
Port of Spain

Tunisia
Tunis

Turkey
Ankara
Erzurum
Istanbul
Izmir
Tarsus

Uganda
Entebbe
Kampala

United Arab Emirates
Abu Dhabi

USA
Abilene
Akron
Albany
Albuquerque
Amarillo
Anaheim
Anchorage
Annapolis
Ann Arbor
Appomattox
Arlington
Atlantic City
Atlanta
Augusta
Aurora
Austin
Baltimore
Bangor
Baton Rouge
Berkeley
Bethlehem
Beverly Hills
Biloxi
Birmingham
Bismarck
Boise
Boston
Boulder
Brooklyn
Buffalo
Butte
Cambridge
Camden
Canton
Carson
Cedar Rapids
Champaign
Charleston
Charlotte
Chattanooga
Cheyenne
Chicago
Cincinnati
Cleveland
Colorado Springs
Columbia
Columbus
Concord
Corpus Christi
Dallas
Dayton
Dearborn
Denver
Des Moines
Detroit
Dover
Duluth
El Paso
Eugene
Evansville
Fairbanks
Fayetteville
Flint
Fort Lauderdale
Fort Wayne
Fort Worth
Frankfurt
Fresno
Galveston
Garland
Gary
Gettysburg
Grand Rapids
Green Bay
Greensboro
Greenville
Hampton
Hannibal
Harrisburg
Hartford
Helena
Hoboken
Hollywood
Honolulu
Houston
Huntingdon Beach
Huntsville
Independence
Indianapolis
Jackson
Jacksonville
Jefferson City
Jersey City
Johnstown
Juneau
Kalamazoo
Kansas City
Key West
Knoxville
Lancaster
Lansing
Las Vegas
Lexington
Lima
Lincoln
Little Rock
Long Beach
Los Angeles
Louisville
Lowell
Lubbock
Madison
Memphis
Mesa
Miami
Milwaukee
Minneapolis
Mobile
Modesto
Montgomery
Montpelier
Nashville
Nassau
Newark
New Bedford
New Brunswick
New Haven
New London
New Orleans
Newport News
New York
Niagara Falls
Norfolk
Oakland
Oak Ridge
Oklahoma City
Olympia
Omaha
Orlando
Oxnard
Ozark
Palm Springs
Palo Alto
Pasadena
Peoria
Philadelphia
Phoenix
Pierre
Pittsburgh
Portland
Poughkeepsie
Princeton
Providence
Raleigh
Reading
Reno
Richmond
Riverside
Roanoke
Rochester
Sacramento
Saginaw
St Louis
St Paul
St Petersburg
Salem
Salt Lake City
San Antonio
San Diego
San Francisco
San Jose
Santa Ana
Santa Barbara
Santa Fe
Savannah
Schenectady
Seattle
Selma
Shreveport
Spokane
Springfield
Stamford
Stockton
Syracuse
Tacoma
Tallahassee
Tampa
Toledo
Tombstone
Topeka
Trenton
Troy
Tucson
Tulsa
Tuscaloosa
Urbana
Utica
Virginia Beach
Waco
Washington
Waterbury
Wheeling
Wichita
Worcester
Yonkers
Youngstown

Ukraine
Chernobyl
Chernovtsy
Donetsk
Kharkov
Kiev
Krivoy Rog
Lvov
Odessa
Sevastopol (*or* Sebastopol)
Yalta

Uruguay
Maldonado
Montevideo
Salto

Uzbekistan
Samarkand
Tashkent

Venezuela
Caracas
Maracaibo
San Cristóbal

Vietnam
Dien Bien Phu
Haiphong
Hanoi
Ho Chi Minh City
My Lai

Wales
Aberdare
Abergavenny
Aberystwyth
Bala
Bangor
Barry
Brecon
Bridgend
Caernarfon (*or* Caernarvon)
Cardiff
Cardigan
Carmarthen
Colwyn Bay
Cwmbran
Ebbw Vale
Fishguard
Flint
Haverfordwest
Holyhead
Holywell
Llandudno
Llanelly
Llandrindod Wells
Llangollen
Maesteg
Merthyr Tydfil
Monmouth
Montgomery
Newport
Newtown
Pembroke
Pontypool
Pontypridd
Port Talbot
Pwllheli
Rhondda
Rhyl
Swansea
Tenby
Towyn
Treorchy
Usk
Welshpool
Wrexham

Yemen
Aden
Hodeida
Sana'a (*or* Sanaa)

Zambia
Kitwe
Lusaka
Ndola

Zimbabwe
Bulawayo
Harare
Hwange

village-like, community, communal, county, parochial, country, countrified, rural, local, public, civil, hick (US inf), jerkwater (US inf), skid-row (US inf)

VERBS

15 **urbanize**, citify, gentrify, suburbanize, commute, countrify

ADVERBS

16 **municipally**, communally, parochially, rurally, locally, publicly, civically

88 Lakes

NOUNS

1 **lake**, loch (Scot), lough (Ir), llyn (Welsh), natural lake, artificial lake, man-made lake, reservoir, freshwater lake, mountain lake, tarn, volcanic lake, glacial lake, oxbow lake, broad, flash (Dial), sea loch, salt lake, salina, lagoon, inland sea, the Dead Sea, the Great Salt Lake

2 **small lake**, lakelet, pool, linn (Scot), tidal pool, clear

pool, muddy pool, pond, millpond, farm pond, village pond, fishpond, dew pond, water hole, swimming hole (US), swimming pool, swimming bath, landlocked water, standing water, backwater, water pocket, still water, stagnant water, dead water, bayou, wash, marsh, mere

► *30 Earth Science; 31 Meteorology and Climatology; 433 Water*

3 **US lakes**, the Great Lakes, Erie, Superior, Huron, Michigan, Ontario, Great Salt Lake, Tahoe, Bear, Yellowstone

4 **British lakes**, English lakes, the Lake District (*or* Lakeland), Windermere, Grasmere, Hawes Water, Coniston Water, Wast Water, Derwent Water, Rydal Water, Ullswater, Buttermere, Thirlmere, Bassenthwaite, Rutland Water, Breydon Water, the Broads, Hickling Broad, Oulton Broad, The Serpentine, Bala, Vyrnwy, Loch Lomond, Loch Ness, Loch Rannoch, Loch Leven, Loch Tay, Lough Neagh, Strangford Lough, Lower Lough Erne, Upper Lough Erne

5 **other major lakes**, Manitoba, Caspian Sea, Aral Sea, Tanganyika, Baykal, Great Bear, Malawi, Great Slave, Winnipeg, Balkhash, Ladoga, Chad, Maracaibo, Onega, Eyre, Volta, Titicaca, Nicaragua, Athabasca, Albert, Kariba, Nipigon, Urmia, Victoria

6 **lake dweller**, lakeside dweller, lacustrine dweller, lacustrian, pile dweller, pile builder, laker

7 **lake dwelling**, lacustrine dwelling, lake house, lakeside house, lake lodge, lakeside village, pile house, stilt house, Cajun cabin (US), crannog (Scot), stilt village, kampong

8 **limnology**, limnologist, limnometer, limnograph, limnetic zone

ADJECTIVES

9 **lakelike**, pondlike, landlocked, tidal, clear, muddy, standing, still, stagnant, marshy, lacustrine, lacustrian, lacustral, lacuscular, limnologic(al), limnophilous

ADVERBS

10 **limnologically**, stagnantly, muddily, clearly

89 Mountains

Mountains are the beginning and the end of all natural scenery.
John Ruskin.

NOUNS

1 **mountain**, mount, alp, snow-capped mountain, mountain range, range, chain, sierra, cordillera, massif, high-

LAKES

Albert (Uganda, Congo (Zaïre))
Athabasca (Canada)
Awe (Scotland)
Baikal (Russia)
Balaton (Hungary)
Bala (Wales)
Balkhash (Kazakhstan)
Bangweulu (Zambia)
Bassenthwaite (England)
Bear (USA)
Becharof (USA)
Breydon (England)
Buttermere (England)
Celyn (Wales)
Central Park Lake (USA)
Chad (Chad, Niger, Nigeria, Cameroon)
Champlain (USA)
Chiemsee (Germany)
Clark (USA)
Clywedog (Wales)
Como (Italy)
Coniston (England)
Constance (Germany)
Cwellyn (Wales)
Dall (USA)
Derwent Water (England)
Dongting (*or* Tungting) (China)
Edward (Uganda, Congo (Zaïre))
Ennerdale (England)
Ericht (Scotland)
Erie (Canada, USA)
Erne (Northern Ireland)
Esthwaite (England)
Eyre (Australia)
Flathead (USA)
Foyle (Ireland)
Garda (Italy)
Geneva (Switzerland, France)
Grasmere (England)
Great Lake (USA, Canada; Australia)
Great Bear (Canada)
Great Salt Lake (USA)
Great Slave (Canada)
Hawes Water (England)
Hickling Broad (England)
Huron (USA, Canada)
Ijsselmeer (*or* Ysselmeer) (Netherlands)
Iliamna (USA)
Issyk–kul (Kyrgyzstan)
Kariba (Zambia, Zimbabwe)
Katrine (Scotland)
Kivu (Congo (Zaïre), Rwanda)
Kyoga (*or* Kioga) (Uganda)
Ladoga (Russia)
Lake of the Woods (Canada)
Leech (USA)
Léman (Switzerland, France)
Leven (Scotland)
Lochy (Scotland)
Lomond (Scotland)
Lop Nur (*or* Lop Nor) (China)
Lucerne (Switzerland)
Maggiore (Italy, Switzerland)
Malawi (Malawi, Tanzania, Mozambique)
Manitoba (Canada)
Maracaibo (Venezuela)
Maree (Scotland)
Martin (USA)
Menindee (Australia)
Michigan (USA)
Mille Lacs (USA)
Mobutu (Uganda, Congo (Zaïre))
Moosehead (USA)
Naknek (USA)
Nasser (Egypt)
Natron (Tanzania)
Neagh (Northern Ireland)
Nemi (Italy)
Ness (Scotland)
Neusiedl (Austria, Hungary)
Nicaragua (Nicaragua)
Nipigon (Canada)
Nu Jiang (China, Burma (Myanmar))
Nyasa (*or* Nyassa) (Malawi, Tanzania, Mozambique)
Okeechobee (USA)
Onega (Russia)
Ontario (Canada, USA)
Oulton Broad (England)
Padarn (Wales)
Pend Oreille (USA)
Peipus (Russia, Estonia)
Pontchartrain (USA)
Poyang (*or* P'o–yang) (China)
Pyramid (USA)
Qinghai Hu (*or* Koko Nor) (China)
Rainy (USA)
Rannoch (Scotland)
Red Tarn (England)
Reindeer (Canada)
Rudolf (Kenya, Ethiopia)
Rutland (England)
Rydal Water (England)
Saimaa (Finland)
St Clair (USA, Canada)
St James's Park Lake (England)
Salton Sea (USA)
Serpentine, The (England)
Superior (USA, Canada)
Tahoe (USA)
Tana (*or* Tsana) (Ethiopia)
Tanganyika (Congo (Zaïre), Burundi, Tanzania, Zambia)
Taupo (New Zealand)
Tay (Scotland)
Tegid (Wales)
Teshekpuk (USA)
Thirlmere (England)
Titicaca (Peru, Bolivia)
Tonle Sap (Cambodia)
Torrens (Australia)
Trasimeno (Italy)
Tungting (*or* Tung–t'ing) (China)
Turkana (Kenya, Ethiopia)
Tustumena (USA)
Ugashik (USA)
Ullswater (England)
Upper Klamath (USA)
Urmia (Iran)
Utah (USA)
Vänern (Sweden)
Van (Turkey)
Victoria (Uganda, Tanzania, Kenya)
Vierwaldstättersee (Switzerland)
Volta (Ghana)
Vyrnwy (Wales)
Wast Water (England)
Windermere (England)
Winnebago (USA)
Winnibigoshish (USA)
Winnipeg (Canada)
Yellowstone (USA)

MOUNTAINS, MOUNTAIN RANGES, AND HILLS

Aconcagua (Mt) (Argentina)
Adirondack (Mts) (USA)
Allegheny (Mts) (USA)
Alps (Range) (France, Switzerland, Italy, Austria)
Altai (Mts) (Russia, China, Mongolia)
Andes (Range) (South America)
Annapurna (Mt) (Nepal)
An Teallach (Mt) (Scotland)
Apennine (Hills) (Italy)
Appalachian (Mts) (USA)
Ararat (Mt) (Turkey)
Aso (Mt) (Japan)
Athos (Mt) (Greece)
Atlas (Mts) (Morocco, Algeria)
Balkan (Mts) (Bulgaria)
Bernese Alps (*or* Oberland) (Range) (Switzerland)
Bernina (Mt) (Switzerland)
Black (Mts) (Wales)
Blanc (Mt) (France, Italy)
Blue (Mts) (Australia)
Blue Ridge (Mts) (USA)
Boundary Peak (Mt) (USA)
Brecon Beacons (Mts) (Wales)
Brocken (Mt) (Germany)
Cader Idris (Mt) (Wales)
Cairngorm (Mts) (Scotland)
Cambrian (Mts) (Wales)
Cantabrian (Mts) (Spain)
Carmel (Mt) (Israel)
Carnedd Llywelyn (Mt) (Wales)
Carpathian (Mts) (Slovakia, Poland, Romania, Ukraine)
Carrantuohill (Mt) (Ireland)
Caucasus (Mts) (Russia, Georgia, Azerbaijan)
Cévennes (Range) (France)
Cheviot (Hills) (England, Scotland)
Chianti (Range) (Italy)
Chiltern (Hills) (England)
Chimborazo (Mt) (Ecuador)
Citlaltépetl (Mt) (Mexico)
Coast (Mts) (Canada)
Cook (Mt) (New Zealand)
Cotopaxi (Mt) (Ecuador)
Cotswold (Hills) (*or* Cotswolds) (England)
Cumbrian (Mts) (England)
Dolomites (Mts) (Italy)
Drakensberg (Mts) (South Africa)
Dunsinane (Hill) (Scotland)
Egmont (Mt) (New Zealand)
Eiger (Mt) (Switzerland)
Elbert (Mt) (USA)
Elbrus (Mt) (Russia)
Elgon (Mt) (Uganda, Kenya)
Etna (Mt) (Sicily)
Everest (Mt) (Nepal, China (Tibet))
Finsteraarhorn (Mt) (Switzerland)
Flinders (Range) (Australia)
Fujiyama (*or* Fuji) (Mt) (Japan)
Ghats (Range) (India)
Godwin Austen (*or* K2) (Mt) (India)
Golan Heights (Hills) (Israel)
Grampian (Mts) (Scotland)
Granite Peak (Mt) (USA)
Gran Paradiso (Mt) (Italy)
Hamersley (Range) (Australia)
Harz (Mts) (Germany)
Helvellyn (Mt) (England)
Hermon (Mt) (Syria, Lebanon)
Himalayas (Range) (Central Asia)
Hindu Kush (Range) (Afghanistan, Pakistan)
Hoggar (*or* Ahaggar) (Mts) (Algeria)
Hood (Mt) (USA)
Humphreys Peak (Mt) (USA)
Hymettus (Mt) (Greece)
Ida (Mt) (Turkey, Greece)
Ingleborough (Mt) (England)
Jungfrau (Switzerland)
Jura (Mts) (France, Switzerland)
Kaikoura (Ranges) (New Zealand)
Kamet (Mt) (India)
Kanchenjunga (Mt) (Nepal, India)
Karakoram (Range) (China, India)
Kenya (Mt) (Kenya)
Kilimanjaro (Mt) (Tanzania)
Kings Peak (Mt) (USA)
Kosciusko (Mt) (Australia)
Kunlun (Range) (China)
Ladakh (Range) (India)
Lammermuir (Hills) (Scotland)
Lenin (Peak) (Tadzhikistan)
Logan, Ben (Mt) (Canada)
Lomond, Ben (Mt) (Scotland)
Macdonnell (Ranges) (Australia)
McKinley (Mt) (USA)
Malvern (Hills) (England)
Matopo (Hills) (Zimbabwe)
Matterhorn (Mt) (Switzerland, Italy)
Mauna Kea (Mt) (USA)
Mendip (Hills) (England)
Middleback (Range) (Australia)
Moelwyn (Mts) (Wales)
Montserrat (Range) (Spain)
Mount Elbert (Mt) (USA)
Mourne (Mts) (Northern Ireland)
Musgrave (Ranges) (Australia)
Nevis, Ben (Mt) (Scotland)
North West Highlands (Mts) (Scotland)
Ojos del Salado (Mt) (Argentina, Chile)
Olives (Mt of) (Israel)
Olympic (Mts) (USA)
Olympus (Mt) (Greece, USA)
Ossa (Mt) (Australia)
Palomar (Mt) (USA)
Pamirs (Range) (Tadzhikistan, China, Afghanistan)
Parnassus (Mt) (Greece)
Peak District (Hills) (England)
Pennines (Hills) (England)
Pikes Peak (Mt) (USA)
Pindus (Mts) (Greece, Albania)
Popocatepetl (Mt) (Mexico)
Pyrenees (Mts) (France, Spain)
Rainier (Mt) (USA)
Rhinog Fawr (Mt) (Wales)
Rigi (Mt) (Switzerland)
Rocky (Mts) (*or* Rockies) (USA, Canada)
St Elias (Mts) (Alaska, Canada)
Sayan (Mts) (Russia)
Scafell Pike (Mt) (England)
Shropshire (Hills) (England)
Siding Spring (Mt) (Australia)
Sierra Madre (Range) (Mexico)
Sierra Morena (Range) (Spain)
Sierra Nevada (Range) (USA, Spain)
Smoky (Mts) (*or* Smokies) (USA)
Snowdon (Mt) (Wales)
Snowy (Mts) (Australia)
Taurus (Mts) (Turkey)
Tian Shan (Central Asia)
Ural (Mts) (Russia)
Vesuvius (Mt) (Italy)
Vosges (Range) (France)
Wheeler Peak (Mt) (USA)
Whitney (Mt) (USA)
Wilson (Mt) (USA)
Zagros (Mts) (Iran)
Zugspitze (Peak) (Germany)

lands, heights, mountaintop, precipice, summit, peak, ben (Scot), cloud-capped peak, snow-clad peak, pike (Dial), tor, crag, pinnacle, crest, ridge, saddle, spur, hill, brae (Scot), hillock, hummock, downs, hilltop, fell, monticule, foothill, steepness, climb, mountaineering, mountain climbing, rock climbing

► *154 Height; 174 Top; 185 Bulge; 187 Horizontality; 189 Slantedness*

2 **orology**, orometer, orologist

► *30 Earth Science*

3 **mountaineer**, mountain climber, rock climber, alpinist, mountain-dweller, mountain man, hill-dweller, hillbilly (US), Abominable Snowman, yeti, Bigfoot, Sasquatch, Brocken Spectre

► *565 Habitat*

4 **US mountains**, Wheeler Peak, Rocky Mountains, Sierra Nevada Mountains, Cascade Range, Olympic Mountains, Appalachian Mountains, Smoky Mountains, Adirondack Mountains, Allegheny Mountains, Bighorn Mountains, Mount McKinley, Mount Whitney, Mount Wilson, Mount Palomar, Pikes Peak

5 **British mountains**, Scottish mountains, Grampian Mountains, Monadhliath Mountains, North West Highlands, Cairngorm Mountains, Ben Nevis, Ben Lomond, Welsh mountains, Snowdonia, Brecon Beacons, Molewyn Mountains, Cambrian Mountains, Snowdon, Cader Idris, English mountains, Pennines, Cumbrian Mountains, Cheviot Hills, Shropshire Hills, Malvern Hills, Cotswolds, Mendip Hills, Peak District, Helvellyn

6 **other major mountains and ranges**, Himalayas, Alps, Pyrenees, Caucasus, Andes Mountains, Everest, K2 (*or* Godwin Austen), Annapurna, Matterhorn, Mont Blanc, Eiger, Ararat, Kilimanjaro, Mount Logan, Mount Cook, Mount Olympus, Aconcagua, Atlas Mountains

► *30 Earth Science*

ADJECTIVES

7 **mountainous**, mountained, alpine, alpestrine, alpigene, subalpine, Himalayan, Olympian, mountain-dwelling, altitudinous, elevated, mounting, ascending, towering, soaring, lofty, topping, monumental, highest, topmost, cloud-capped, snow-capped, snow-clad, high, highland, hilly, upland, rolling, monticulous, hill-dwelling

8 orogenic, orographic, orogenetic, orological, orometric

► *154 Height*

VERBS

9 tower, soar, spire, rise, rise above (*or* over), tower above (*or* over), overtop, top, surmount, overlook, look down upon, command, dominate, overshadow

10 climb a mountain, mountaineer, climb, mount, scale, conquer a mountain, dwell (*or* live) on a mountain

ADVERBS

11 on the mountain, on the summit, on the peak, on the crest, on the pinnacle, atop, on high, high up, high, aloft, straight up, above, in the clouds, on (*or* at the) top of the world

90 Rivers

I have seen the Mississippi. That is muddy water. I have seen the St Lawrence. That is crystal water. But the Thames is liquid history. John Burns.

NOUNS

1 river, flowing river, meandering river, lazy river, racing river, navigable river, river running to the sea, braided river, freshet (*or* fresh), running water, polluted river, open sewer, watercourse, waterway, canal, cut (Dial), stream, mountain stream, small stream, streamlet, rivulet, freshet, millstream, rillet, brook, babbling brook, bourn (*or* bourne), burn (Scot), runnel (*or* runlet), run (US), rill, gill (Dial), kill (US), beck, arroyo (US), brooklet, creek, crick (US), sike (Dial), wadi, underground (*or* subterranean) river, tributary, confluent stream, confluent, confluence, bayou (US), branch, feeder, affluent, distributary, fork, effluent, anabranch, billabong (Aus), river system, water system

► *30 Earth Science; 300 Motion*

2 channel, midchannel, midstream, sandbank, (river) bend, meander, (river) bank, embankment, levee (US), riverside, waterside, water's edge, source of a river, headwaters, headstream, head, riverhead, fountainhead, backwater, waterfall, falls (*or* fall), cataract, linn (Scot), cascade, force, rapids, chute, shoot, nappe, sault (US), spillway (*or* spill), overflow, sluiceway (*or* sluice), bore, tidal bore, river's end, river's mouth, delta, river crossing, ford, bridge, ferry

► *30 Earth Science; 319 Transport*

3 US rivers, Mississippi, Missouri, Rio Grande, Alabama, Colorado, Columbia, Hudson, Potomac, Red, Tennessee, Yukon, Old Man River (Inf)

4 British rivers, Thames, Severn, Mersey, Avon, Ouse, Trent, Tees, Humber, Cam, Isis, Old Father Thames (Inf), Conwy, Clwyd, Taff, Forth, Clyde, Dee, Spey

5 other major rivers, Seine, Danube, Rhine, Rhône, St Lawrence, Nile, Amazon, Congo (Zaïre), Elbe, Po, Moselle, Tiber, Shannon, Jordan, Ganges, Tigris, Euphrates, Don, Volga, Yellow (*or* Huang He), Chang Jiang, Mackenzie, Mekong, Niger, Oxus, Styx

RIVERS

Adige (Italy)
Ain (France)
Aire (England, France)
Aisne (France)
Alabama (USA)
Allier (France)
Amazon (Peru, Brazil)
Amu Darya (Turkmenistan, Uzbekistan)
Amur (Mongolia, Russia, China)
Angara (Russia)
Annan (Scotland)
Arkansas (USA)
Arno (Italy)
Assiniboine (Canada)
Athabasca (Canada)
Aube (France)
Avon (England)
Beas (India)
Bermejo (Argentina)
Bío-Bío (Chile)
Brahmaputra (China (Tibet), India)
Bug (Ukraine, Poland, Germany)
Bure (England)
Cam (England)
Canadian (USA)
Cauvery (India)
Charente (France)
Chari (Central African Republic, Cameroon, Chad)
Chenab (Pakistan)
Churchill (Canada)
Clutha (New Zealand)
Clwyd (Wales)
Clyde (Scotland, Canada)
Colorado (USA)
Columbia (USA)
Congo (Congo, Congo (Zaïre))
Connecticut (USA)
Conwy (Wales)
Cooper (Australia)
Coppermine (Canada)
Crouch (England)
Damodar (India)
Danube (Germany, Austria, Romania, Hungary, Slovakia, Serbia, Bulgaria)
Darling (Australia)
Dart (England)
Dee (Scotland, Wales, England)
Demerara (Guyana)
Derwent (England)
Dnieper (*or* Dnepr) (Ukraine)
Dniester (*or* Dnestr) (Ukraine)
Don (Russia; Scotland; England; France; Australia)
Doon (Scotland)
Dordogne (France)
Doubs (France, Switzerland)
Douro (*or* Duero) (Spain, Portugal)
Dove (England)
Dovey (Wales)
Drava (Italy, Austria, Croatia, Hungary)
Ebro (Spain)
Elbe (Germany)
Ems (Germany, Netherlands)
Esk (Australia)
Essequibo (Guyana)
Euphrates (Iraq)
Exe (England)
Fal (England)
Forth (Scotland)
Fraser (Canada)
Frome (Australia)
Gambia (The Gambia, Senegal)
Ganges (India)
Garonne (France)
Gironde (France)
Glomma (Norway)
Godavari (India)
Great Ouse (England)
Han (China)
Hawkesbury (Australia)
Hooghly (India)
Hsi Chiang (China)
Hudson (USA)
Humber (England)
Hunter (Australia)
Illinois (USA)
Indus (India, Pakistan, China)
Irrawaddy (Burma)
Irtysh (China, Russia, Kazakhstan)
Isis (England)
Itchen (England)
James (USA; Australia)
Jordan (Israel, Jordan)
Juba (Ethiopia, Somalia)
Jumna (India)
Juruá (Brazil)
Kama (Russia)
Kasai (Angola, Congo (Zaïre))
Kolyma (Russia)
Kuban (Russia)
Kura (Turkey, Georgia, Azerbaijan)
Lachlan (Australia)
Lea (England)
Lena (Russia)
Liffey (Ireland)
Limpopo (South Africa, Zimbabwe, Mozambique)
Lippe (Germany)

RIVERS (CONT.)

Loire (France)
Lualaba (Congo (Zaïre))
Lune (England)
Lüne (Germany)
Maas (Netherlands)
Mackenzie (Australia)
Madeira (Brazil)
Magdalena (Colombia)
Main (Germany; Northern Ireland)
Manawatu (New Zealand)
Maritsa (Bulgaria, Turkey)
Marne (France)
Medina (USA)
Medway (England)
Mekong (Laos, China, Vietnam)
Menderes (Turkey)
Mersey (England)
Meuse (France, Belgium)
Miño (*or* Minho) (Spain, Portugal)
Mississippi (USA)
Missouri (USA)
Moselle (*or* Mosel) (France, Germany)
Murray (Australia; Canada)
Murrumbidgee (Australia)
Neckar (Germany)
Neisse (Poland, Czech Republic, Germany)
Niger (Nigeria, Mali, Guinea)
Nile (Sudan, Egypt)
Ob (Russia)
Oder (Germany, Czech Republic, Poland)
Ohio (USA)
Oise (France)
Orange (South Africa)
Orontes (Syria, Turkey)
Ouachita (USA)
Ouse (England)
Paraguay (Paraguay)
Paraná (Brazil)
Pecos (USA)
Peel (Australia, USA)
Piave (Italy)
Platte (USA)
Po (Italy)
Potomac (USA)
Ravi (India, Pakistan)
Rede (England)
Red (USA)
Rhine (Switzerland, France, Germany, Netherlands)
Ribble (England)
Río de la Plata (Argentina, Uruguay)
Rio Grande (*or* Río Bravo) (USA, Mexico)
Ruhr (Germany)
Saar (Germany, France)
St John (Canada, USA)
St Lawrence (USA)
Saskatchewan (Canada)
Savannah (USA)
Seine (France)
Severn (England)
Shannon (Ireland)
Shenandoah (USA)
Slave (Canada)
Snake (USA)
Somme (France)
Songhua (*or* Sungari) (China)
Spey (Scotland)
Stour (England)
Susquehanna (USA)
Suwannee (*or* Swanee) (USA)
Swale (England)
Taff (Wales)
Tagus (*or* Tajo *or* Tejo) (Portugal, Spain)
Tallahatchie (USA)
Tamar (England)
Tawe (Wales)
Tay (Scotland)
Tees (England)
Teifi (Wales)
Tennessee (USA)
Test (England)
Thames (England)
Tiber (Italy)
Tigris (Iraq, Turkey)
Trent (England)
Tunguska (Russia)
Tweed (England, Scotland)
Tyne (England)
Ural (Russia, Kazakhstan)
Ure (England)
Uruguay (Uruguay, Brazil, Argentina)
Usk (Wales, England)
Vistula (Poland)
Volga (Russia)
Volta (Ghana)
Volturno (Italy)
Wabash (USA)
Waikato (New Zealand)
Wear (England)
Weaver (England)
Weser (Germany)
Windrush (England)
Witham (England)
Wye (Wales, England)
Yangtze (China)
Yare (England)
Yellow (*or* Huang Ho) (China, USA)
Yellowstone (USA)
Yenisei (Russia)
Yeo (England)
Yukon (USA)
Zambezi (Zambia, Angola, Zimbabwe, Mozambique)

6 **river flow**, water flow, water power, stream, millstream, millrace, coure, onward course, current, undercurrent, undertow, eddy, whirlpool, whirl, swirl, twirl, gulf, vortex, maelstrom, Maelstrom, Charybdis, flowing, flowage, flux, fluency, afflux, drift, driftage, ripple, riffle (US), washing, wash, wake, splash, plash, slosh, lapping, lap, inflow, ingress, affluence, flowing together, confluence, convergence, concourse, conflux, outflow, egress, effluence, crossflow, crosscurrent, counterflow, countercurrent, counterflux, backflow, ebb, reflux, refluence, backwash, back stream, profluence, surge, gush, rush, onrush, spate, race, run, rapids, torrent, mountain torrent, freshet (*or* fresh), flood, flash flood, deluge, overflow, overflowing, overrunning, spillage, spillover (US), washout, flush, inundation, engulfment, submersion, alluvium, cataclysm, the Flood, the Deluge

► *30 Earth Science; 31 Meteorology and Climatology; 180 Convolution*

VERBS

7 **flow**, meander, race, braid, run, course, channel, pour, stream, drift, glide, slide, flow over, babble, bubble, burble, gurgle, purl, trill, murmur, trickle, dribble, eddy, rotate, whirl, swirl, twirl, engulf, ripple, riffle (US), wash, swash, splash, plash, slosh, lap, flow together, converge, flow in, surge, gush, rush, flood, overflow, overrun, spill (over), cascade, fall, flush, inundate, submerge, swamp, flow out, flow back, ebb

8 **cause to flow**, open the sluice gates, drain, divert a river, irrigate

9 **stop the flow**, stem the flow, staunch, obstruct a river, dam (up), build a breakwater

ADJECTIVES

10 **fluvial**, fluviomarine, flowing, fluent, effluent, profluent, affluent, confluent, convergent, streaming, running, coursing, winding, meandering, sluggish, snaking, serpentine, rippling, ripply, purling, racing, gushing, rushing, surging, torrential, dam-breaking, vortical, inundant (*or* inundatory), falling, ebbing, refluent

11 **flooded**, deluged, inundated, engulfed, swamped, drowned, afloat, awash, washed, in (*or* at) flood, in spate

12 **hydrological**, hydrologic, hydrospheric, hydrostatic, fluvioterrestrial

ADVERBS

13 **fluently**, affluently, convergently, sluggishly, torrentially, like a torrent, in (*or* at) flood, vortically, inundatorily, cataclysmically, hydrologically

91 Seas

For all at last return to the sea – to Oceanus, the ocean river, like the ever-flowing stream of time, the beginning and the end.
Rachel Carson.

NOUNS

1 **sea**, ocean, deep sea, deep blue sea, seven seas, the deep, high seas, ocean blue, the blue, main, bounding main, the billow, sea water, salt water, brine, salt sea,

OCEANS AND SEAS

Adriatic (Sea)	Black (Sea)	Ligurian (Sea)
Aegean (Sea)	Caribbean (Sea)	Marmara (Sea of)
Amundsen (Sea)	Caspian (Sea)	Mediterranean (Sea)
Andaman (Sea)	China (Sea)	North (Sea)
Antarctic (Ocean)	Coral (Sea)	Okhotsk (Sea of)
Arabian (Sea)	Dead (Sea)	Pacific (Ocean)
Arafura (Sea)	East China (Sea)	Philippine (Sea)
Aral (Sea) (*or* Lake Aral)	Galilee (Sea of) (*or* Tiberias Lake)	Red (Sea)
Arctic (Ocean)	Greenland (Sea)	Ross (Sea)
Atlantic (Ocean)	Indian (Ocean)	Sargasso (Sea)
Azov (Sea of)	Inland (*or* Seto Naikai) (Sea)	South China (*or* Nanhai) (Sea)
Baltic (Sea)	Ionian (Sea)	Tasman (Sea)
Banda (Sea)	Irish (Sea)	Timor (Sea)
Barents (Sea)	Japan (Sea of)	Weddell (Sea)
Beaufort (Sea)	Java (Sea)	White (Sea)
Bellingshausen (Sea)	Kara (Sea)	Yellow (*or* Huang Hai) (Sea)
Bering (Sea)	Laptev (Sea)	

blue water, tide, wave, ocean depths, ocean floor, sea bed, sea bottom, benthos, Davy Jones's locker, Mariana Trench, sea lane, shipping lane, the briny (Inf), the briny deep (Inf), the (big) drink (Inf), watery waste (Inf), great waters (Inf), herring pond (Inf)

▶ *319 Transport*

2 tide, tidal current, tidal flow, tidal flood, tidal stream, tide race, tidewater, tideway, tide gate, riptide (*or* tide-rip *or* rip), direct tide, opposite tide, high tide, high water, full tide, lunar tide, solar tide, flood tide, spring tide, equinoctial tide, ebb tide (*or* ebb), rising tide, flux, flow, flood, low tide, low water, neap tide (*or* neap), reflux, refluence, tidal rise and fall, ebb and flow, flux and reflux, tidal range, tide chart, tidal table, tide gauge, thalassometer, tidal power, tideland (US)

▶ *300 Motion; 302 Forward Motion; 303 Backward Motion; 366 Raising; 367 Lowering*

3 wave, billow, swell, heavy swell, surge, heave, undulation, waviness, rise, trough, wavelet, ripple, riffle (US), spume, foam, froth, surf, breaker, comber (US), roller, roll, peak, wave crest, whitecap, white horses, broken water, rough water, rough sea, heavy sea, choppy sea, choppiness, turbulent sea, overfall, angry sea, (tidal) bore, eagre (*or* eager), rogue wave, tidal wave, tsunami, undertow, undercurrent

▶ *326 Oscillation*

4 sea god, Neptune, Triton, Oceanus, Poseidon, Nereus, Varuna, merman, sea nymph, Oceanid, Nereid, siren, Amphitrite, Thetis, Dylan, Calypso, undine, mermaid, water sprite, water spirit, sea serpent

▶ *7 Religion*

5 oceanography, thalassography, hydrography, bathymetry, marine biology, aquaculture (*or* aquiculture), sea survey, Admiralty chart, diving bell, bathysphere, diving vessel, bathyscaph (*or* bathyscaphe), bathythermograph

▶ *30 Earth Science; 31 Meteorology and Climatology*

6 oceanographer, thalassographer, hydrographer, marine biologist, deep-sea diver, underwater explorer, Jacques Cousteau

ADJECTIVES

7 oceanic, nautical, tidal, sea, salty, briny, equinoctial, lunar, solar, ebb, ebbing, neap, billowing, swelling, surging, breaking, rolling, choppy, heavy, turbulent, angry, dirty, marine, maritime, ocean-going, sea-going, seaworthy, seafaring, undersea, underwater, deep, deep-sea, submarine, subaqueous, subaquatic, subaqua, thalassic, pelagic, pelagian, benthic, estuarine, littoral, sublittoral, intertidal, abyssal, terrigenous

8 oceanographic(al), thalassographic(al), hydrographic(al), bathymetric(al)

VERBS

9 sail the high seas, sail the ocean (blue), go over the bounding main, conduct a sea survey, explore underwater, descend in a diving bell, plumb the ocean depths

10 billow, swell, surge, heave, toss, popple, become choppy, become turbulent, undulate, rise, peak, draw to a peak, scend (*or* send), ripple, riffle (US), wave, foam, froth, break, dash, crash, comb (US), roll, flow in, flow out, surge back, ebb, rise and fall, ebb and flow

ADVERBS

11 nautically, at sea, on the sea, on the high seas, afloat, by sea, by water, over the water, across the sea, oversea, overseas, beyond seas, oceanwards (*or* oceanward), seawards (*or* seaward), offshore, off soundings, out of soundings, in blue water, tidally

12 oceanographically, hydrographically, bathymetrically

92 Other Geographical Features

The desert, the abode of enforced sterility, the dehydrated sea of infertility, the post-menopausal part of the earth. Angela Carter.

NOUNS

1 continent, America, Africa, Europe, Asia, Antarctica, landmass, North America, South America, Eurasia, Oceania, Australasia, subcontinent, India

▶ *30 Earth Science; 86 Regions*

DESERTS

Arabian (Egypt)	Negev (Israel)
Atacama (Chile)	Nubian (Sudan)
Australian (Australia)	Painted (USA)
Betpak–Dala (Kazakhstan)	Patagonian (Argentina)
Black Rock (USA)	Rub' al Khali (Saudi Arabia, Oman, Yemen, United Arab Emirates)
Chihuahuan (USA, Mexico)	Sahara (North Africa)
Colorado (USA)	Simpson (Australia)
Death Valley (USA)	Sonotan (USA, Mexico)
Gibson (Australia)	Sturt Stony (Australia)
Gobi (Mongolia, China)	Syrian (Syria, Iraq, Jordan, Saudi Arabia)
Great Salt Lake (USA)	Taklimakan (China)
Great Sandy (Australia)	Thar (*or* Indian *or* Great Indian) (India, Pakistan)
Great Victoria (Australia)	Turfan Depression (China)
Kalahari (South Africa, Namibia, Botswana)	Ustyurt (*or* Ust Urt) (Kazakhstan)
Kara Kum (Turkmenistan)	
Mojave (USA)	
Namib (Namibia)	
Nefud (Saudi Arabia)	

2 **island**, isle, islet, river island, holm (Dial), ait (*or* eyot) (Dial), inch (Scot), skerry (Scot), coral island, lagoon, island, atoll, reef, coral reef, Great Barrier Reef, cay, key, Key West, sandbank (*or* bank), sand bar (*or* bar), floating island, iceberg, ice floe, island continent, continental island, archipelago, island group, island chain

▶ *86 Regions*

3 **marsh**, marshland, wetlands, fen, fenland, flat, mud flat, salt flat, salt marsh, saltpan, salina, playa, bog, peat bog, moss, moor, carr, swamp, swampland, the Everglades, swamp-forest, bayou (US), morass, quag, quagmire, quicksand, mudhole, mud, mire, ooze, wallow, slough, sudd, mangrove sudd, (river) delta

▶ *429 Moisture; 433 Water*

4 **coast**, coastline, shoreline, coastland, rocky coast, ironbound coast, sea wall, sea cliff, beach, shore, ocean shore, seashore, seaboard, seaside, strand, sand, pebbles, shingle, submerged coast, continental shelf, coastal plain, the Riviera, Costa Brava, Costa del Sol

▶ *164 Edge; 166 Limit*

5 **peninsula**, point of land, point, tongue, neck, spit, sandspit, hook, spur, cape, promontory, bill, foreland, headland, head, mull (Scot), chersonese (Lit), projection, isthmus, land bridge, Hook of Holland, Cape of Good Hope, Cape Horn, Portland Bill

▶ *185 Bulge*

6 **lowland**, flat country, flats, level, meadow, field, mead (Lit), weald (Lit), lea, water meadow, bottom land (US), plain, the plains, alluvial plain, flood plain, polder, vale, strath (Scot), open country, wide-open spaces, range, heath, grassland, prairie, pampas, llano, veld (*or* veldt), savanna (*or* savannah), campos, steppe (*or* steppes), moor, moorland, grouse moor, inch (Scot)

▶ *155 Lowness; 187 Horizontality*

7 **upland**, high country, highland, heights, wold (Lit), plateau, mesa, tableland, undulating land, downs, downland

▶ *89 Mountains*

8 **valley**, vale, dale, dell, dingle, dip, coomb (*or* combe *or* comb), cirque, corrie (Scot), cwm (Welsh), glen, ravine, gorge, canyon, gully, crevasse, chimney, ditch, chine, clough, couloir, Grand Canyon

▶ *183 Concavity; 308 Opening*

9 **inlet**, bay, gulf, arm of the sea, natural harbour, port, bight, fleet (Dial), cove, fiord (*or* fjord), firth (Scot), sound, backwater, bayou (US), outlet, estuary, mouth, delta, channel, gut, straits, Bay of Biscay, Persian Gulf, Great Australian Bight, Bay of Bengal, Firth of Forth, Kyle of Lochalsh, Plymouth Sound, Strait of Messina, Dardanelles, Hellespont, Bight of Benin, Chesapeake Bay, Gulf of Mexico, Gulf of California, Gulf of Saint Lawrence, Gulf of Alaska, Hudson Bay, Gulf of Campeche, Gulf of Guinea

▶ *91 Seas*

10 **miscellaneous**, desert, desert sands, sands, geyser, Old Faithful, hot spring, warm spring, thermal spring, thermae, fault, San Andreas fault, volcano

▶ *371 Expulsion; 380 Violence; 493 Heat*

ADJECTIVES

11 **continental**, subcontinental, insular, islander, isleted,

ISLANDS

Alderney (UK)
Australia
Baffin (Canada)
Bali (Indonesia)
Banks (Canada)
Barbados
Bermuda (UK)
Borneo (Indonesia, Malaysia, Brunei)
Bougainville (Papua New Guinea)
Cape Breton (Canada)
Cebú (Philippines)
Corfu (Greece)
Corsica (France)
Crete (Greece)
Cuba
Curaçao (The Netherlands)
Cyprus
Devon (Canada)
Dominica
Ellesmere (Canada)
Flores (Indonesia)
Gotland (Sweden)
Great Britain
Greenland (Denmark)
Grenada
Guadalcanal (Solomon Islands)
Guam (USA)
Guernsey (UK)
Hainan (China)
Haiti
Halmahera (Indonesia)
Hawaii (USA)
Hispaniola (Haiti, Dominican Republic)
Hokkaido (Japan)
Hong Kong (China)
Honshu (Japan)
Iceland
Ireland (Ireland, UK)
Isle of Man
Isle of Wight (UK)
Isle of Youth (Cuba)
Jamaica
Java (Indonesia)
Jersey (UK)
Key West (USA)
Kodiak (USA)
Kyushu (*or* Kiushu) (Japan)
Leyte (Philippines)
Long Island (USA)
Luzon (Philippines)
Madagascar
Madeira (Portugal)
Madura (Indonesia)
Majorca (Spain)
Malta
Manhattan (USA)
Martha's Vineyard (USA)
Martinique (France)
Mauritius
Melville (Canada)
Mindanao (Philippines)
Mindoro (Philippines)
Nantucket (USA)
Negros (Philippines)
New Britain (Papua New Guinea)
New Caledonia (France)
Newfoundland (Canada)
New Guinea (Indonesia, Papua New Guinea)
New Ireland (Papua New Guinea)
New Zealand
Novaya Zemlya (Russia)
Oahu (USA)
Okinawa (Japan)
Palawan (Philippines)
Panay (Philippines)
Penang (Malaysia)
Prince Edward Island (Canada)
Prince of Wales (Canada)
Puerto Rico (USA)
Rhodes (Greece)
St Lucia
St Vincent (St Vincent and the Grenadines)
Sakhalin (*or* Saghalien) (Russia)
Samar (Philippines)
Santa Catalina (USA)
Sardinia (Italy)
Sark (UK)
Seram (*or* Ceram) (Indonesia)
Shikoku (Japan)
Sicily (Italy)
Singapore
Skye (UK)
Somerset (Canada)
Southampton (Canada)
South Georgia (UK)
Spitsbergen (Norway)
Sri Lanka
Sulawesi (Indonesia)
Sumatra (Indonesia)
Tahiti (France)
Taiwan (China)
Tasmania (Australia)
Tenerife (Spain)
Tierra del Fuego
Timor (Indonesia)
Trinidad (Trinidad and Tobago)
Unalaska (USA)
Vancouver (Canada)
Victoria (Canada)
Viti Levu (Fiji)
Wrangel (Russia)
Zanzibar (Tanzania)

archipelagic, marooned, ashore, submerged, estuarial, coastal, littoral, ashore, sandy, pebbled, shingled, swampy, boggy, marshy, paludal, deltaic, soggy, poached, squashy, squishy, spongy, oozy, quaggy, undrained, waterlogged, muddy, alluvial, miry, flat, plain, rocky, peninsular, isthmian, promontory, downland, lowland, rolling, open, campestral, moorish, fenny, upland, highland, volcanic, thermal

VERBS

12 **be marooned**, become stranded on an island, hit a sandbar, hit a reef, hit an iceberg, fall into quicksand, become stuck in a quagmire, wallow in the mud, sight a coastline, land on a beach, round a cape, cross a land bridge, cross an isthmus, farm bottom land (US), start a prairie fire, fall into a gorge, dock at a port

ADVERBS

13 **continentally**, on land, ashore, adrift, subcontinentally, insularly, with insularity, soggily, muddily, with mud, rockily, with rocks, openly, volcanically, like a volcano, thermally, with heat

Abstract Relations

93 Existence

I know perfectly well that I don't want to do anything; to do something is to create existence – and there's quite enough existence as it is. Jean-Paul Sartre.

Cogito, ergo sum. (I think, therefore I am.) René Descartes.

NOUNS

1 **existence**, being, life, subsistence, coexistence, entity, ens, esse, occurrence, presence, metaphysics, metaphysics of presence, monadism, existentialism

▶ *4 Philosophy; 97 Presence; 554 Life*

2 **thing**, something, entity, being, body, object, substance, item, monad, phenomenon, happening

3 **nature**, fundamental nature, essential nature, essence, quiddity, innateness, ontology, materiality, substantiality

▶ *99 Essence*

4 **demonstrable existence**, reality, actuality, factuality, truth, authenticity, necessity, historicity, the real thing, facticity (Inf)

▶ *95 Reality; 693 Information; 698 Truth*

5 **fact**, fact (*or* truth) of the matter, matter of fact, *fait accompli* (Fr), the case, the basic fact(s), the basics, the realities, the specifics, the fundamentals, the essentials, what's what (Inf), the whole story (Inf), the picture (Inf), the gen (Inf), nitty-gritty (Inf), brass tacks (Inf), nuts and bolts (Inf), the dope (Inf), the scoop (Inf), the score (Inf), the dirt (Inf)

6 **continuing existence**, duration, endurance, persistence, continuance, survival, perpetuity

7 **self-existence**, aseity, uncreated being, deity, divinity

▶ *7 Religion*

8 **creation**, coming into being, materialization, actualization, birth, evolution, big-bang theory, ontogeny

▶ *130 Beginning; 344 Cause*

9 **mere existence**, vegetable existence, vegetation, stagnation, inertia, indolence, sloth, torpor, PVS (persistent vegetative state *or* syndrome)

▶ *339 Inertness*

ADJECTIVES

10 **existing**, existent, being, living, subsistent, coexistent, occurring, present, prevalent, current, extant, manifest, necessary, obvious, in force, in effect

11 **intrinsic**, innate, inherent, essential, basic, fundamental, natural, material, substantial, substantive, concrete, ontological

12 **lasting**, enduring, persisting, persistent, abiding, continual, continuous, surviving, perpetual

13 **real**, actual, factual, de facto, true, authentic, veritable, undeniable, indisputable, positive, provable, empirical, historical, phenomenal, well-known, honest-to-God (Inf), for real (Inf)

14 **self-existent**, self-existing, uncreated, godlike, divine

15 **created**, materialized, made, actualized, evolved

16 **vegetating**, stagnating, stagnant, inert, torpid, indolent, slothful

VERBS

17 **exist**, be, live, breathe, coexist, subsist, live in, inhabit, dwell, occur, be there, be found, be true

18 **come to be**, become, materialize, take shape (*or* form), be born, evolve, arise, come about, grow, develop, unfold

19 **continue to be**, endure, last, persist, continue, survive, prevail, live on, stand, hold, remain, stay

20 **bring into being**, create, make, form, make up, compose, devise, invent, cause, realize, actualize, factualize, reify

21 **merely exist**, vegetate, stagnate

ADVERBS

22 **really**, actually, basically, fundamentally, necessarily, essentially, existentially, inherently, truly, demonstrably, manifestly, positively, in fact, as a matter of fact, in point of fact, ipso facto, de facto, to all intents and purposes, as it happens, no ifs or buts (Inf)

23 **now**, at the moment, currently, presently, immediately

▶ *275 Time*

94 Nonexistence

As I was going up the stair
I met a man who wasn't there.
He wasn't there again to-day.
I wish, I wish he'd stay away. Hughes Mearns.

NOUNS

1 **nonexistence**, nonbeing, nonentity, unbeing, nonsubsistence, nonoccurrence, nonhappening

2 **nothingness**, nullity, nihility, nothing, nil, nought, zero,

love, naught, nowt (Dial), nothing whatever, nothing at all, nothing on earth (*or* under the sun), *nada* (Sp), *niente* (It), no such thing, zilch (Inf), sweet Fanny Adams (*or* sweet FA) (Inf)

3 negativeness, negativity, negation, denial, refusal, *via negativa* (L)

▶ *704 Refutation; 708 Negation*

4 emptiness, vacuity, vacancy, vacuum, void, limbo, blank, hole, gap, break, lacuna, interval, space

▶ *141 Space; 146 Interval*

5 nonreality, unreality, imagination, fantasy, fiction, make-believe

▶ *96 Unreality; 477 Imagination*

6 absence, none, no-one, nobody, not a one, never a one, ne'er a one, nary a one (Dial), not a blessed one (Inf)

▶ *98 Absence*

7 not any, not a bit, not a whit, not a hint, not a speck, not a mite, not a particle, not an iota, not a jot, not a scrap, not a trace, not a suspicion, not a shadow of a suspicion (*or* doubt), neither hide nor hair, not a lick (Inf), not a lick or smell (Inf), not a smidgen (Inf)

8 extinction, obliteration, annihilation, obsolescence, oblivion, death

▶ *358 Obliteration; 463 Forgetfulness*

ADJECTIVES

9 nonexistent, absent, missing, minus, negative, null, void, vacant, empty, blank, devoid, lacking

10 unreal, imaginary, illusory, fanciful, fantastical, delusory, hallucinatory

11 no more, extinct, died out, vanished, dead, passed away, dead and gone, lost, all over, all over and done with, defunct, obsolete, dead as a dodo, past, finished, ended, annihilated, obliterated, destroyed, wiped out, kaput (Inf)

▶ *3 History; 384 Past Time; 357 Destruction; 358 Obliteration; 582 Death*

VERBS

12 cease to exist, vanish, disappear, end, leave no trace, sink without trace, melt, dissolve, evaporate, melt into thin air, go up in a puff of smoke, die, expire, pass away, die out, die away, peter out, fade away, turn to nothing, pass out of the picture (Inf), snuff it (Inf), kick the bucket (Inf)

13 cause not to exist, annihilate, destroy, exterminate, eradicate, wipe out, stamp out, extinguish, snuff out, kill, slay, murder, abort, miscarry, cancel, invalidate, annul, negate, end, veto, vaporize, nuke (Inf)

▶ *382 Killing*

ADVERBS

14 not at all, by no means, absolutely not, to no extent, on no account, under no circumstances, not by any stretch of the imagination, in no way, no way (Inf)

15 not ever, never, at no time, not at any time, not in a million years (Inf)

16 nowhere, in no place, neither here nor there, not on this earth

95 Reality

Human kind
Cannot bear very much reality. T. S. Eliot.

NOUNS

1 reality, objective existence, actuality, occurrence, presence, entelechy, material existence, materiality, corporeality, substance, matter, thing, solidity, substantiality, tangibility, substantivity, validity, fact, factuality, matter of fact, historicity, the here and now, practicality

▶ *93 Existence; 452 Certainty*

2 real world, universe, cosmos, physical world, natural world, earth matter

▶ *402 Material World*

3 realism, real life, naturalism, authenticity, pragmatism, verisimilitude, documentary, cinema vérité, kitchen-sink drama, slice of life

▶ *273 Accuracy; 698 Truth*

4 realist, pragmatist

5 realities, basics, fundamentals, facts of life, home truths, bottom line (Inf), crunch (Inf)

ADJECTIVES

6 real, actual, occurring, existing, entelechial, true, factual, valid, historical, material, corporeal, tangible, solid, substantial, substantive

7 realistic, natural, naturalistic, lifelike, real-life, true-to-life, truthful, authentic, genuine, faithful, graphic

8 practical, realistic, pragmatic, expedient, sensible, matter-of-fact, no-nonsense, no frills, down-to-earth, businesslike, hard-headed, level-headed, sound, functional, utilitarian, usable, serviceable, workable, in working order, operative

9 realizable, achievable, attainable, practicable, plausible, feasible, possible, probable, likely

VERBS

10 be real, exist, occur, loom large, happen

11 make real, actualize, materialize, factualize, realize, reify, visualize

12 establish reality, validate, authenticate, verify, prove, demonstrate, establish, settle the matter, set at rest, prove one's point, nail down, ascertain, substantiate, corroborate, bear out, confirm, attest, uphold, certify, sustain, reinforce, back up, ratify, endorse, clinch (Inf)

ADVERBS

13 really, actually, in reality, in fact, de facto, in effect, in actuality, in practice, in all likelihood, when it comes to the crunch (Inf), when the chips are down (Inf), when the push comes to the shove (Inf)

14 certainly, indeed, truly, honestly, in truth, undoubtedly, indubitably, no buts about it, nothing else but, really-truly (Inf), honest to God (Inf)

96 Unreality

Never being, but always at the edge of Being. Stephen Spender.

NOUNS

1 unreality, nonexistence, unactuality, subjective existence, subjectivity, unsubstantiality, intangibility, impalpability, incorporeality, ethereality, immateriality, immaterialism

2 **illusion**, fantasy, chimera, phantasmagoria, fancy, flight of fancy, figment, castle in the air (*or* Spain), pipe dream, daydream, dream, nightmare, hallucination, mirage, Fata Morgana, will-o'-the-wisp, jack-o'-lantern, ignis fatuus, vision, appearance, phantasm, phantom, ghost, spectre, spirit, wraith, shade, shadow, fetch, doppelgänger, simulacrum (Lit), spook (Inf)

▶ *477 Imagination*

3 **delusion**, misconception, self-deception, fallacy, false impression, optical illusion, trompe l'oeil, trick of the light, sleight of hand, illusionism, magic, conjuring, trick

▶ *274 Error; 700 Deception*

4 **theorization**, theory, hypothesis, assumption, speculation, conjecture, guesswork, fiction, empty talk, empty promises, fool's paradise, false dawn, wishful thinking, idealism, Utopianism, pie in the sky (Inf), hot air (Inf), wind (Inf), gas (Inf)

▶ *476 Supposition*

5 **insubstantial person**, a nobody, a nothing, nonperson, unperson, nonentity, hollow man, straw man (US), man of straw, broken reed, paper tiger, puppet, dummy, jack-straw, windbag (Inf), dud (Inf)

6 **unrealistic person**, speculator, theorizer, idealist, romantic, visionary, dreamer

7 **artificiality**, imitation, simulation, artificial reality, virtual reality, shadow, image, fake, sham, artifact

▶ *699 Falsehood*

ADJECTIVES

8 **unreal**, nonexistent, incorporeal, intangible, impalpable, insubstantial, unsubstantial, ethereal, elusive, fugitive, fleeting, obscure, nebulous, tenuous, vague, flimsy, hollow, airy, hazy, indeterminate, indefinite, undefined, blurred, shadowy, ghostly, spectral, phantasmal

9 **illusory**, imaginary, subjective, fantastic, dreamlike, chimerical, phantasmagorical, fanciful, fancied, hallucinatory, figmental, visional, delusory

10 **theoretical**, hypothetical, abstract, ideal, speculative, assumed, putative, mythical, fanciful, imaginary, fictional, fictitious, made-up, make-believe

11 **unrealistic**, idealistic, utopian, visionary, romantic

12 **artificial**, synthetic, man-made, simulated, imitation, virtual, mock, pretend, pretended, dummy, sham, fake, false, spurious, specious, phony, bogus, counterfeit, so-called, put-on, quasi, pseudo (Inf)

VERBS

13 **imagine**, fantasize, conjure up, dream, daydream, hallucinate, hear things, see things

14 **theorize**, hypothesize, conceptualize, conjecture, guess

15 **idealize**, romanticize, see through rose-coloured glasses (Inf), build castles in the air (Inf)

16 **delude**, deceive, mislead, give a wrong idea (*or* impression), misrepresent, belie, distort, pervert, twist, fudge, embroider, embellish, gild, varnish, whitewash, spin a yarn (Inf), waffle (Inf)

17 **fabricate**, manufacture, simulate, imitate, make up, invent, hatch, concoct, cook up (Inf)

ADVERBS

18 **ideally**, in theory, theoretically, hypothetically, perfectly

19 **apparently**, to all appearances, seemingly, ostensibly, allegedly, putatively, purportedly, professedly, avowedly, superficially, in name only

97 Presence

A certain person may have, as you say, a wonderful presence: I do not know. What I do know is that he has a perfectly delightful absence. Idries Shah.

NOUNS

1 **presence**, physical presence, bodily presence, existence, being, manifestation, manifestness, reality, actuality, materialness, materiality, solidity, ontology, metaphysics of presence, thusness (Inf)

▶ *93 Existence; 95 Reality; 99 Essence; 402 Material World*

2 **omnipresence**, ubiquitousness, ubiquity, all-presence, pervasiveness, pervasion, permeation, diffusion, diffusiveness, attendance, personal attendance, appearance, frequenting, visiting, participation, accompaniment, company, companionship, society, association

▶ *8 Divinity; 202 Infinity; 270 Vagueness; 525 Appearance*

3 **residence**, occupancy, inhabitance, habitation

▶ *564 Inhabitant; 565 Habitat*

4 **availability**, plenty, sufficiency, accessibility, readiness, handiness, convenience, proximity, nearness, immediacy, propinquity, vicinity, neighbourhood, immediate circle

▶ *142 Location; 143 Situation; 170 Surroundings; 217 Sufficiency*

5 **someone present**, participant, spectator, audience, theatregoer, cinemagoer, bystander, onlooker, looker-on, witness, eyewitness, watcher, observer, beholder, viewer, passer-by, attender, attendee, visitor, patron, frequenter, haunter, habitué, regular customer, regular (Inf)

▶ *21 Drama*

6 **ghostly presence**, presence, ghost, apparition, manifestation, spectre, phantom, vision, spook (Inf)

▶ *11 Occultism; 518 Vision*

ADJECTIVES

7 **present**, existent, existing, extant, in being, real, actual, material, solid, manifest, omnipresent, all-present, all-over, present throughout, ubiquitous, infinite, everywhere, pervasive, all-pervasive, pervading, diffusive, penetrating, permeating, permeative, suffusive, suffusing, ghostly, spectral, haunted

▶ *93 Existence; 275 Time; 698 Truth*

8 **attendant**, in attendance, on hand, participating, watching, witnessed, associated, accompanying, concomitant, companionable, sociable, regular, habituated

▶ *223 Accompaniment; 654 Sociability*

9 **resident**, residential, in residence, on the premises, on the spot, occupying, in occupation, live-in, in-house, at home

10 **available**, plenty, sufficient, accessible, at hand, on, on tap, ready, handy, convenient, within reach (*or* sight *or* call), to hand, near, nearby, nearest, close, closest, immediate, in view, at one's fingertips (*or* elbow), under one's nose, before one's eyes

VERBS

11 be present, be, exist, occur, live, breathe, be here, be there, be everywhere, pervade, permeate, penetrate, suffuse, diffuse, imbue, impregnate, fill, soak, saturate, leave no space (*or* void), run through, filter through, infiltrate, overrun, overswarm, meet one at every turn, appear, materialize, solidify

12 attend, be present at, be there in person, sit in on, be on hand, make one's presence felt, participate, take part, join in, stand by, spectate, look on, witness, see, watch, observe, view, visit, appear, turn up, show up, put in an appearance, show one's face, look in on, grace the occasion, honour with one's presence, present oneself, report, report for duty, be all present and correct (*or* all present and accounted for), frequent, haunt, hang around (Inf), hang out (Inf)

▶ *185 Bulge; 654 Sociability*

13 reside, be in residence, occupy, inhabit, live in, dwell

ADVERBS

14 in person, personally, live, in existence, really, actually, solidly, materially, bodily, *in propria persona* (L), in the flesh (Inf)

15 here, there, where, everywhere, somewhere, anywhere

16 on the spot, on the ground, on location, on site, *in situ* (L), in place, to hand, near at hand, within reach, on call, on tap, before one's very eyes, under one's nose, in the face of, in the presence of, before

17 at home, in residence, on the premises, in

98 Absence

Absence makes the heart grow fonder. Thomas Haynes Bayly.

Absence is to love what wind is to fire; it extinguishes the small, it inflames the great. Bussy-Rabutin.

NOUNS

1 absence, nonpresence, nonentity, nonbeing, unbeing, inexistence, nonexistence, unreality, nonoccurrence, nullity, nihility

▶ *94 Nonexistence; 96 Unreality; 101 Unworldliness*

2 disappearance, dematerialization, vanishment, departure, loss, lack, want, deficiency, shortage, scarcity, dearth, insufficiency, paucity, scantiness

▶ *218 Insufficiency; 526 Disappearance; 766 Loss*

3 emptiness, voidness, vacancy, vacuity, bareness, blankness, hollowness, barrenness, nothingness, void, gap, vacuum, nothing, empty space, empty shell, husk, clean sheet, clean slate, blank paper, blank slate, *tabula rasa* (L)

▶ *141 Space*

4 absenteeism, absentation, nonappearance, nonattendance, truantism, truancy, desertion, defection, French leave, unauthorized absence, AWOL (absence without leave), hooky (*or* hookey) (Inf), cut (Inf), bunk (Inf)

▶ *313 Departure; 372 Separation; 389 Escape*

5 leave of absence, leave, holiday, vacation, furlough, break, time off, day off, compassionate leave, sabbatical, sabbatical leave, sick leave, sickie (Aus inf)

▶ *601 Celebration*

6 absentee, nonperson, missing person, defector, deserter, truant, runaway, no-show (Inf), skiver (Inf)

7 nobody, no-one, no man, no woman, nobody present, nobody there, not one, not a soul, not a single person, not a living thing

ADJECTIVES

8 absent, not present, nonattendant, unavailable, nonexistent, inexistent, unreal, nonoccurrent, null, void

9 away, out, no longer among us, gone, departed, dematerialized, out of sight, missing, lost, nowhere to be found, disappeared, vanished, absconded, flown, fled, vamoosed (Inf), off (Inf)

10 nonresident, not resident, not in residence, away from home, not at home, out of town, on tour, on the road, on location, on leave, on holiday, on vacation, on furlough, on sabbatical, not at work, on sick leave, on compassionate leave

▶ *582 Death*

11 truant, absentee, defected, deserted, jumped ship, AWOL (absent without leave)

12 missing, lacking, wanting, wanted, deficient, minus, short, taken away, deleted, subtracted, omitted, mislaid, excluded, left out, not included

13 vacant, vacuous, void, devoid, empty, without content, hollow, barren, bare, blank, clean, clear, featureless, characterless

14 unoccupied, empty, vacant, available, unfilled, unlived-in, uninhabited, untenanted, unpeopled, unsettled, unmanned, unstaffed, depopulated, deserted, abandoned, forsaken, godforsaken

VERBS

15 be absent, keep away, stay away, take no part in, not come, fail to appear, not turn up, not show up, be conspicuous by one's absence, vote with one's feet, turn up missing (Inf), stay away in droves (Inf)

16 absent oneself, take one's leave, leave, take leave, withdraw, retire, retreat, depart, exit, leave the scene, bow out, vacate, slip away, slip out, sneak out (Inf), make oneself scarce (Inf)

▶ *315 Exit*

17 take leave of absence, go on leave, go on vacation, go on holiday, go on furlough, go on sabbatical, take time off, take a day off, go out of town, go on location

18 abscond, decamp, disappear, vanish, dematerialize, go missing, fly the nest, escape, fly, flee, run away, desert, defect, jump ship, go AWOL (absent without leave), take French leave, play truant, bunk off (Inf), do a bunk (Inf), vamoose (US inf), skive off (Inf), cut (Inf), skip (Inf), play hooky (*or* hookey) (Inf)

19 leave empty, evacuate, vacate, desert, depopulate, abandon, forsake

ADVERBS

20 absently, vacantly, vacuously, emptily, hollowly, blankly, in one's absence, behind one's back, in absentia

21 away, elsewhere, not here, out of house, off the premises, on tour, on location, on leave, on vacation, on holiday, on furlough, on sabbatical, out of town, somewhere else, not there, neither here nor there, nowhere, no place

99 Essence

A good book is the purest essence of a human soul. Thomas Carlyle.

NOUNS

1 **essence**, quiddity, quid, subject, substance, structure, stuff, material, matter, fabric, medium, building blocks

▶ *403 Structure*

2 **essential content**, basis, core, kernel, gist, meat, heart, backbone, nub, nucleus, marrow, pith, sap, lifeblood, crux, subject matter, principle, issue, gravamen, highlight, high point, centre, focus, pivot, keystone, cornerstone, landmark, benchmark, milestone, nuts and bolts (Inf), nitty-gritty (Inf), name of the game (Inf), bottom line (Inf)

3 **quintessence**, embodiment, incarnation, personification, epitome, archetype, soul, spirit, entelechy, flower, elixir, extract, concentrate, distillate, distillation

4 **nature**, distinguishing feature(s), character, suchness, make-up, constitution, composition, complexion, temperament, disposition, mould, pattern, stamp, type, breed, strain, stripe, humour, mood, trait, hue, quality, attribute, property, nature of the beast (Inf), thusness (Inf)

▶ *525 Appearance*

ADJECTIVES

5 **essential**, crucial, vital, necessary, paramount, indispensable, of the essence, prerequisite, requisite, obligatory, mandatory, compulsory, imperative, inalienable, unalienable, uninfringeable, unquestionable

▶ *123 Importance*

6 **intrinsic**, inherent, basic, primary, fundamental, immanent, innate, inborn, inbred, deep-seated, deep-rooted, ingrained, bred-in-the-bone

7 **integral**, inseparable, ineradicable, built-in, component, constituent, indivisible, integrated

8 **quintessential**, constitutional, structural, organic, peerless, singular, unique, consummate, archetypical (*or* archetypal)

9 **characteristic**, distinctive, distinguishing, typical, specific, particular, peculiar, defining, discriminating, idiosyncratic

VERBS

10 **be essential**, be central to, be part and parcel of

11 **characterize**, stamp, inform, mark, identify, depict, portray, represent, delineate, designate, distinguish, differentiate, demarcate

12 **embody**, incarnate, personify, epitomize, constitute, comprise, incorporate, assimilate, include, embrace, encompass

ADVERBS

13 **in essence**, essentially, intrinsically, per se, primarily, in the main, substantially, materially, by and large, mainly, mostly, chiefly, effectually, for the most part, almost entirely, for all practical purposes, necessarily

14 **at heart**, basically, at bottom, *au fond* (Fr), fundamentally, radically, at the core, in substance

100 Otherness

NOUNS

1 **extraneousness**, irrelevance, irrelevancy, immateriality, inessentiality, superfluity, pleonasm, superficiality, redundancy, pointlessness, inapplicability, incidentalness, secondariness, insignificance, triviality, lack of importance

▶ *124 Unimportance; 211 Addition; 372 Separation*

2 **foreignness**, alienism, alienage, unrelatedness, unconnectedness, disconnectedness, difference, otherness, exoticness, strangeness, the unknown

3 **separateness**, segregation, dissociation, disaffiliation, nonassimilation, discreteness, apartheid, isolation, insularity, detachment, noninvolvement, independence, nonconformity

▶ *118 Nonconformity; 128 Exclusion*

4 **externality**, extrinsicality, exteriority, coming from without, outside, outwardness, surface, periphery, circumference, the external, foreign product, importation, incoming, invasion, infringement, interloping, intrusion, trespassing, gate-crashing, externalization, projection, the supernatural, the paranormal

▶ *314 Entry; 381 Attack*

5 **nonconformist**, rebel, maverick, anarchist, outlaw, gypsy, nomad, eccentric, Bohemian, hippie, New-Age traveller, beatnik, crank (Inf), weirdo (Inf)

6 **outsider**, alien, stranger, foreigner, outlander, ultramontane, tramontane (*or* transmontane), extraterrestrial (being), E.T., space invader, Martian, man from Mars, cosmic being, little green man

▶ *145 Distance*

7 **new arrival**, newcomer, exile, refugee, emigrant, émigré, displaced person (DP), the Wandering Jew, Diaspora, settler, new resident, expatriate, guest worker, *Gastarbeiter* (Ger), migrant worker, economic migrant, political refugee, homeless person, stateless person, immigrant, new face, new boy, new kid on the block (US), tenderfoot, greenhorn

8 **intruder**, gate-crasher, interloper, trespasser, squatter, uninvited guest, stowaway, cuckoo in the nest,

▶ *12 Government and Politics; 43 Agriculture; 295 Newness*

ADJECTIVES

9 **extraneous**, irrelevant, irrelative, immaterial, inessential, unessential, superfluous, extra, superficial, redundant, pleonastic, pointless, inapplicable, unrelated, disrelated, unconnected, disconnected, incidental, adventitious, secondary, insignificant, trivial

10 **foreign**, alien, unrelated, other, continental, overseas, transatlantic, ultramontane, tramontane (*or* transmontane), strange, different, deviating, outlandish, unknown, exotic, barbaric, barbarian, wandering, travelling, rambling, roaming, nomadic, gypsy, migrant, homeless, stateless

11 **separate**, separated, apart, dissociated, unaffiliated, disaffiliated, nonassimilated, segregated, removed, isolated, discrete, detached, independent, nonconforming, anarchic, anarchistic, rebellious

12 **external**, extrinsic, exterior, extraterrestrial, not of this world, distant, outward, outer, outside, ulterior, peripheral, superficial, foreign-made, imported, importing, in-

coming, invading, invasive, infringing, interloping, intrusive, trespassing, gate-crashing, externalizing, externalized, projecting, projected, supernatural, paranormal

VERBS

13 be extraneous, be irrelevant, miss the point, not come to the point, digress, talk off the subject, ramble, go off at (*or* on) a tangent, beat about the bush, beat around the bush (US), have no point, have no relevance, have no relation to, not relate, not apply, not fit

14 be foreign, come from another country, live in another land, emigrate, immigrate, flee one's homeland, travel, wander, ramble, roam, live on the road

15 separate, keep apart, segregate, isolate, remove, detach, divide

16 be external, come from without, exist outside, import, invade, infringe, interlope, squat, intrude, trespass, stowaway, gate-crash, externalize, project, delve into the supernatural

17 not conform, be different, be independent, live one's own life, do one's own thing (Inf)

ADVERBS

18 extraneously, irrelevantly, immaterially, superfluously, superficially, prima facie, pointlessly, beside the point, neither here nor there, inapplicably, without application, incidentally, adventitiously, secondarily, insignificantly, without significance, trivially, strangely, in a strange way, differently, outlandishly, exotically, nomadically, like a nomad, discretely, separately, independently, externally, extrinsically, distantly, from a distance, on one's travels, abroad, in a foreign country, in foreign lands, in foreign parts, overseas, from outer space, outwardly, on the outside, away from, apart, peripherally, intrusively, with an intrusive manner, supernaturally

101 Unworldliness

NOUNS

1 nonmaterial world, nonphysical world, metaphysical world, ethereal world, other world, another world, imaginary world, heaven, heavenly kingdom, Elysium (*or* Elysian Fields), Valhalla, Olympus, happy hunting ground, hell, lower world, nether world, nether regions, place of the damned, underworld, other place, Hades, eternity, eternal life, afterlife, life after death, perpetuity, hereafter

► *7 Religion; 8 Divinity; 96 Unreality; 279 Eternity; 477 Imagination; 582 Death*

2 unworldliness, otherworldliness, unearthliness, spiritualness, spiritualization, spirituality, religion, immateriality, immaterialness, immaterialism, unreality, incorporeity (*or* incorporeality), incorporealness, insubstantiality (*or* unsubstantiality), unsubstantialness, intangibility, disembodiment, disincarnation, dematerialization, impalpability, imponderability, shadowiness, ghostliness

► *582 Death*

3 spiritual world, spirit world, world of spirits, the other side, occult phenomena, the occult, spiritualism (*or* spiritism), supernaturalism, animism, animatism, astral plane, astral body, spirit, ghost, phantom, ESP (extrasensory perception), sixth sense

4 parapsychology, psychokinesis, precognition, clairvoyance, telepathy, psychic phenomena, psychic(al) research

► *11 Occultism*

5 idealism, philosophical idealism, metaphysical idealism, absolute idealism, transcendental idealism, transcendentalism, Platonism, Neo-Platonism, Hegelianism, Kantianism

► *4 Philosophy; 442 Intellect; 443 Thought; 446 Idea*

6 internal world, nonexternality, subjectivity, solipsism, selfhood, consciousness, the conscious, myself, me, yours truly, self, ego, superego, subconscious, unconsciousness, the unconscious, id, psyche, spirit, soul, mind, intellect, psychoanalysis

► *36 Psychology and Psychiatry*

7 believer in a nonmaterial world, spiritualist, medium, supernaturalist, psychic, occultist, animist, parapsychologist, clairvoyant, crystal gazer, fortune teller, mind reader, telepathist, solipsist, idealist, religious believer, philosopher, Platonist, Neo-Platonist, Hegelian, Kantian, psychoanalyst

► *7 Religion; 11 Occultism*

ADJECTIVES

8 nonmaterial, nonphysical, unphysical, metaphysical, imaginary, illusory, ethereal, heavenly, eternal, perpetual, unworldly, otherworldly, other, unearthly, transcendent, transmundane, extramundane, spiritual, celestial, supernal (Lit), religious, higher, psychic, psychical, immaterial, immaterialist, immaterialistic, unreal, incorporeal, incorporate (Lit), insubstantial (*or* unsubstantial), intangible, airy, without mass, disincarnated, disembodied, unembodied, bodiless, without body, unfleshly, dematerializing, dematerialized, impalpable, imponderable, shadowy, ghostly

9 parapsychological, extrasensory, supersensible (*or* supersensory), precognitive, clairvoyant, telepathic, psychokinetic, psychic(al), occult, spiritual, spiritualist, spiritualistic (*or* spiritistic), supernatural, animist, animistic, astral, phantom

10 idealistic, idealist, Platonic, Neo-Platonic, Hegelian, Kantian

11 internal, nonexternal, subjective, personal, solipsist, solipsistic, conscious, subconscious, unconscious, psychoanalytic, mental, abstract

VERBS

12 enter a nonmaterial world, go to heaven, go to hell, spiritualize (*or* spiritize), dematerialize, immaterialize, disembody, disincarnate, insubstantialize (*or* unsubstantialize), practise one's religion, dabble in occultism, psychoanalyse

ADVERBS

13 metaphysically, illusorily, like an illusion, ethereally, eternally, for eternity, perpetually, forever, transcendently, spiritually, celestially, religiously, immaterially, incorporeally, insubstantially (*or* unsubstantially), intangibly, airily, impalpably, imponderably, occultly, supernaturally, clairvoyantly, telepathically, psychically

14 subjectively, personally, internally, within, nonexternally, psychoanalytically, mentally, consciously, unconsciously, abstractly, idealistically, with idealism, Platonically, Neo-Platonically

102 Possibility

The grand Perhaps! Robert Browning.

Your If is the only peace-maker; much virtue in If. William Shakespeare.

NOUNS

1 **possibility**, potential, potentiality, plausibility, likelihood, prospect, promise, chance, odds, opportunity, virtuality, eventuality, contingency

▶ *104 Probability; 107 Chance*

2 **possibleness**, the realms of possibility, conceivability, conceivableness, credibility, feasibility, viableness, practicability, practicality, workability, operability, accessibility, admissibility, flexibility, approachability, availability, aptitude, ability, capacity, facility

▶ *93 Existence; 95 Reality; 340 Action; 342 Activity; 443 Thought*

3 **strong possibility**, good chance, sporting chance, best chance, even chance, half a chance, opening, luck, good opportunity, sure bet, evens, odds-on, sure thing (Inf)

▶ *104 Probability; 283 Future Time*

4 **remote possibility**, hope, faint hope, outside hope, small chance, off chance, slim chance, poor prospect, long odds, long shot, outside chance (Inf)

▶ *105 Improbability; 107 Chance; 610 Hope*

ADJECTIVES

5 **possible**, potential, conceivable, imaginable, thinkable, credible, believable, feasible, admissible, viable, tenable, reasonable, practical, practicable, doable, workable, performable, operable, achievable, attainable, realizable, likely, accessible, approachable, reachable, available, flexible, able, capable, apt

▶ *104 Probability*

6 **potential**, possible, promising, undeveloped, future, prospective, eventual, virtual, dormant

VERBS

7 **make possible**, enable, empower, permit, allow, clear the way for, give a chance to, take a chance, gamble, hope

▶ *317 Way; 334 Power*

8 **be possible**, could be, might be, stand a chance, stand a good chance

ADVERBS

9 **possibly**, perhaps, perchance, peradventure (Lit), haply, maybe, for all one knows, if possible, by chance, on the off chance, by any means

10 **practically**, workably, tenably, reasonably, within reach, within sight, within one's power

▶ *104 Probability*

11 **potentially**, virtually, conceivably, imaginably, credibly, believably, feasibly, plausibly, prospectively, eventually, in all likelihood, somehow

103 Impossibility

I believe because it is impossible. Tertullian.

In two words: im - possible. Samuel Goldwyn.

ADJECTIVES

1 **impossible**, not possible, beyond the bounds of possibility, inconceivable, unthinkable, not to be thought of, unimaginable, out of the question, unquestionable, unreasonable, contrary to reason, absurd, ridiculous, preposterous, illogical, irrational, paradoxical, self-contradictory, self-defeating

▶ *94 Nonexistence; 272 Ridiculousness; 696 Unintelligibility; 704 Refutation; 708 Negation*

2 **unbelievable**, incredible, counterintuitive, beyond belief, fantastic, miraculous, fabulous, bizarre, weird, ineffable, mysterious, mystical

▶ *96 Unreality; 451 Disbelief*

3 **hopeless**, impractical, unfeasible, unworkable, unachievable, untenable, irrecoverable, unviable, inoperable, broken, irreparable, irrevocable, unattainable, insurmountable, insuperable, inaccessible, unaccessible, unapproachable, unreachable, impenetrable, impervious, unobtainable, unavailable, out, away, over, finished, gone

▶ *3 History; 131 End; 226 Stopping; 238 Uselessness; 249 Adversity; 264 Difficulty; 766 Loss*

4 **forbidden**, prohibited, denied, disallowed, blocked, barred, banned, stopped, cancelled, ruled out

▶ *128 Exclusion; 399 Veto*

NOUNS

5 **impossibility**, impossibleness, inconceivability, unthinkability, unimaginability, nonexistence, unreality, self-contradiction, absurdity, paradox, logical impossibility, illogicality, what cannot be

▶ *94 Nonexistence; 96 Unreality; 105 Improbability; 451 Disbelief; 696 Unintelligibility; 697 Nonsense; 704 Refutation; 708 Negation*

6 **hopelessness**, impossibility, impracticality, impracticability, unfeasibility, unworkability, inoperability, unattainability, insuperability, insurmountability, inaccessibility, unaccessibility, impenetrability, imperviousness, unobtainability, unavailability

▶ *335 Powerlessness; 611 Despair*

7 **obstacle**, prohibition, no-go area, deadlock, block, impasse, barrier, problem, Sisyphean task, no-no (Inf)

▶ *249 Adversity; 264 Difficulty; 399 Veto*

VERBS

8 **make impossible**, prohibit, block, bar, ban, forbid, rule out, disqualify, exclude, deny, withhold, negate, disenable, disable, put out of reach, make things difficult, scupper (Inf), put (*or* throw) a spanner in the works (Inf)

9 **be impossible**, fly in the face of reason, be a waste of time, not stand a chance

10 **attempt the impossible**, waste time, cry for the moon, try for a miracle, look for a needle in a haystack, seek the end of the rainbow, teach an old dog new tricks, make the leopard change its spots, turn back time, turn back

the tide, stop the world from turning, make hell freeze over, make rivers run uphill, make a silk purse from a sow's ear, fetch water in a sieve, walk on water, catch the wind, draw blood from a stone

► *272 Ridiculousness*

ADVERBS

11 impossibly, inconceivably, unthinkably, unimaginably, unquestionably, incredibly, illogically, irrationally, absurdly, ridiculously, paradoxically

12 hopelessly, impractically, unworkably, inoperably, irreparably, irrecoverably, irrevocably, unattainably, insurmountably, insuperably, unapproachably

INTERJECTIONS

13 impossible!, no way! (Inf), no fear! (Inf), no can do! (Inf), not on your life! (Inf), not on your nelly! (Inf), no chance! (Inf), not a hope in hell! (Inf)

104 Probability

NOUNS

1 probability, likelihood, likeliness, chance, odds, liability, liableness, proneness, predictability, prospect, forecast, outlook, expectation, presumption, anticipation, prognosis, prediction

► *107 Chance; 229 Tendency; 283 Future Time; 474 Expectation; 475 Prediction*

2 tendency, propensity, trend, drift, tenor, tone, swing, bearing, tending, general tendency, the way it looks

► *134 Continuity; 229 Tendency; 317 Way*

3 plausibility, probability, possibility, reasonability, credibility, verisimilitude

► *102 Possibility; 115 Similarity; 444 Reason; 450 Belief*

4 chance, good chance, sporting chance, main chance, even chance, strong possibility, odds-on chance, best bet, well-grounded hope, fair expectation, favourable prospect

► *102 Possibility; 107 Chance; 474 Expectation; 610 Hope*

5 probability theory, mathematical probability, statistical probability, empirical probability, subjective probability, probability distribution, probability function, probability density function, probability curve, uncertainty principle, law of averages, probabilism

► *27 Mathematics; 210 Calculation*

ADJECTIVES

6 probable, likely, expected, undoubted, indubitable, unquestionable, apparent, ostensible, evident, presumable, presumed, presumptive, predictive, predictable, prone, liable, apt, anticipated, prospective, tending, drifting, on the cards

► *229 Tendency; 474 Expectation*

7 plausible, probable, possible, reasonable, credible, believable, persuasive

► *102 Possibility; 444 Reason; 450 Belief; 525 Appearance*

VERBS

8 be probable, seem likely, lead one to expect, promise, show a tendency, show signs of, have the makings of, be on the cards, stand a good chance, be in the running, bid fair to, stand a fair chance, impend, come as no surprise, be bound to happen (Inf)

► *229 Tendency; 283 Future Time; 756 Promise*

9 make probable, smooth the way for, make likely, increase the odds, increase the chances

► *317 Way; 392 Help*

10 think likely, expect, anticipate, presume, suppose, dare say, predict, prognosticate, foresee, look for, count on, reckon, take for granted, risk, gamble, bet on, bet one's bottom dollar on, take a chance, not put it past (Inf)

► *107 Chance; 450 Belief; 474 Expectation; 475 Prediction; 476 Supposition; 610 Hope*

ADVERBS

11 probably, in all probability, in all likelihood, likely, most likely, as likely as not, doubtless (*or* doubtlessly), indubitably, unquestionably, to all intents and purposes, all things considered, ten to one, presumably, apparently, ostensibly, predictably, expectedly, to be expected, as expected, as usual, on average, in anticipation

► *111 Sameness ; 216 Average; 474 Expectation; 632 Habit*

105 Improbability

Faith may be defined briefly as an illogical belief in the occurrence of the improbable. H. L. Mencken.

ADJECTIVES

1 improbable, unlikely, uncertain, doubtful, dubious, dubitable, unpromising, inauspicious, scarcely to be expected, unrealistic, remote, far-fetched, unexpected

► *453 Uncertainty*

2 questionable, implausible, unbelievable, fanciful, extraordinary, exceptional, wild, too good to be true, hard to believe, incredible, beyond belief, hard to swallow (Inf)

► *451 Disbelief*

3 unexpected, unforeseeable, unpredictable, unanticipated, unguessed, unpredicted, unforeseen, fortuitous, rare, accidental, freakish, chance, fluky (Inf)

► *107 Chance*

NOUNS

4 improbability, unlikeliness, unlikelihood, uncertainty, doubt, doubtfulness, poor prospect, remote possibility, foolish hope, castle in the air (*or* in Spain), pipe dream, small chance, hardly a chance, outside chance, ghost of a chance, slim chance, long shot, long odds, a chance in a million, million-to-one chance (*or* shot), hundred-to-one chance (*or* shot), fat chance (Inf)

► *103 Impossibility; 453 Uncertainty; 611 Despair*

5 unexpectedness, unforeseeableness, unpredictability, miraculousness, rarity, oddity, the unforeseen, the last thing one would expect, more than one bargained for, freak accident, miracle, prodigy, wonder, surprise, lucky shot, fluke, chance

► *107 Chance; 630 Surprise*

6 implausibility, incredibility, unbelievability, questionableness, tall story, fib, lie, porky (Inf), whopper (Inf)

► *451 Disbelief*

VERBS

7 be improbable, go beyond belief, strain one's credulity, go beyond the bounds of reason, be economical with the truth, build castles in the air (*or* in Spain), dream, fib, lie, spin a yarn, tell tales

▶ *451 Disbelief; 699 Falsehood*

ADVERBS

8 **improbably**, incredibly, unbelievably, questionably, doubtfully, dubiously, uncertainly

9 **unexpectedly**, unpredictably, unforeseeably, contrary to expectation, by accident, without warning, out of the blue, never in a month of Sundays

10 **rarely**, exceptionally, seldom if ever, once in a blue moon, once in a lifetime, hardly ever, uncommonly, uniquely

11 **luckily**, happily, fortuitously, by chance, by accident

106 Predetermination

VERBS

1 **predetermine**, destine, predestine, predestinate, appoint, foreordain, preordain, decree, intend

▶ *283 Future Time; 482 Intention*

2 **premeditate**, preconceive, decide beforehand, resolve beforehand, plan, plan beforehand, preset, prearrange, arrange, contrive, agree beforehand, preconcert, ensure a result, contrive a result, pack a jury, prime a witness, stack the cards, load the dice, fix (Inf), set up (Inf), frame (Inf)

▶ *344 Cause; 409 Arrangement; 484 Plan; 699 Falsehood*

ADJECTIVES

3 **predetermined**, destined, predestined, fated, doomed, appointed, foreordained, preordained, ordained, decreed, on the cards (Inf), cut-and-dried (Inf)

▶ *283 Future Time*

4 **deliberate**, intentional, willed, premeditated, aforethought, prepense, with a motive, planned, preplanned, considered, measured, weighed, calculated, designed, prearranged, preset, pre-established, fixed, set, controlled, studied, advised, devised, contrived, packed, primed, stacked, loaded, put-up (Inf), setup (Inf), framed (Inf)

▶ *409 Arrangement; 482 Intention; 484 Plan*

NOUNS

5 **predetermination**, predestination, foreordination, preordination, destiny, fate, doom, lot, karma, kismet, will, decree, self-fulfilling prophecy

▶ *635 Will*

6 **premeditation**, predeliberation, resolve, project, plan, intention, prearrangement, preparation, order of the day, order paper, agenda, plot, packed jury, primed witness, preconceived opinion, *parti pris* (Fr), closed mind, foregone conclusion, agreed result, ready-made verdict, closed book, open-and-shut case, frame-up (Inf), put-up job (Inf)

▶ *243 Preparation; 482 Intention; 484 Plan*

107 Chance

Of all the gin joints in all the towns in all the world, she walks into mine! Humphrey Bogart, in *Casablanca*.

Fortune, that favours fools. Ben Jonson.

NOUNS

1 **chance**, blind chance, randomness, random chance, whatever happens, unpredictability, fortuitousness, fortuity, indeterminacy, indetermination, uncertainty, unaccountability, inexplicability, casualness, coincidence, accident, contingency, hazard, risk, gamble, jeopardy

▶ *453 Uncertainty*

2 **luck**, blind luck, fortune, providence, wheel of fortune, lady luck, luck of the draw, whatever comes, destiny, fate, lot, one's lot, good luck, good fortune, luck on one's side, run of good luck, bad luck, ill fortune, tough luck, rotten luck, worst luck, run of bad luck, bit of luck, fluke, lucky shot, lucky strike, chance hit, chance meeting, chance encounter, chance discovery, serendipity, the way the ball bounces (Inf), the way the cookie crumbles (US inf), potluck (Inf), a good hand (Inf)

▶ *248 Prosperity; 249 Adversity; 449 Discovery; 630 Surprise*

3 **equal chance**, even chance, fifty-fifty, odds-on, toss-up, flip (*or* spin) of the coin, throw of the dice, turn of the card, spin of the wheel, random sample, game of chance, gambling, gaming, lottery, state lottery (US), raffle, draw, bingo, lucky dip, tombola, sweepstake, sweep, premium bond

▶ *119 Equality*

4 **fair chance**, decent chance, sporting chance, fighting chance, gambling chance, (distinct) possibility

▶ *102 Possibility*

5 **good chance**, best chance, main chance, favourable chance, opportunity, occasion, good odds, long odds, odds-on, probability, likelihood, small risk, safe bet, sure thing, certainty, dead cert (Inf)

▶ *104 Probability; 287 Timeliness; 452 Certainty*

6 **poor chance**, small chance, rare chance, half a chance, long shot, shot in the dark, chance in a million, one in a hundred, improbability, impossibility, no chance (at all), snowball's chance in hell, fat chance (Inf)

▶ *103 Impossibility; 105 Improbability*

7 **calculation of chance**, probability, mathematical probability, the probabilities, theory of probabilities, aleatorics, statistics, stochastics, doctrine of chance, actuarial calculation, insurance, assurance, underwriting, risk-taking, speculation, gambling, bookmaking

▶ *27 Mathematics; 252 Safety; 254 Danger; 448 Experiment*

ADJECTIVES

8 **chance**, random, unpredictable, unforeseeable, fortuitous, indeterminable, incalculable, uncertain, stochastic, aleatoric, haphazard, hit-or-miss, sink or swim, catch-as-catch-can (US), casual, aleatory, serendipitous, accidental, adventitious, contingent, unexpected, unforeseen, noncausal, epiphenomenal, incidental, coincidental, lucky, fortunate, unlucky, unfortunate, risky, chancy (Inf), fluky (Inf), dicey (Inf), iffy (Inf)

9 **causeless**, groundless, uncaused, unmotivated, undesigned, unplanned, unpremeditated, unmeant, unintended, unintentional, inadvertent, unexplainable, unaccountable, inexplicable

VERBS

10 chance, happen, just happen, so happen, occur, turn up, pop up, crop up, fall to one's lot, befall, betide

▶ *282 Present Time*

11 chance upon, encounter by chance, encounter unexpectedly, meet by accident (*or* chance), run into, run across, come upon, light upon, hit upon, stumble upon, blunder upon, bump into (Inf)

▶ *449 Discovery*

12 take a chance, chance it, chance, chance one's arm, take a risk, risk it, risk, hazard, venture, go out on a limb, leave it to chance, leave it to fate, try one's luck, gamble, cast the die, speculate, bet, wager, have luck, be lucky, have a chance, have small chance

▶ *254 Danger*

ADVERBS

13 by chance, by accident, accidentally, inadvertently, unintentionally, casually, fortuitously, coincidentally, by coincidence, randomly, at random, haphazardly, unpredictably, unexpectedly, unaccountably, inexplicably, serendipitously, luckily, as (good) luck would have it, fortunately, unluckily, as ill luck would have it, unfortunately

14 perchance, perhaps, for all one knows, possibly, according to chance, as it may happen, as the case may be, as it may be, as it may chance, whatever happens, in any event

INTERJECTIONS

15 hard luck!, better luck next time!, hard lines!, hard cheese!, shame!

16 fluke!, lucky dog!, jammy swine!

108 Relatedness

NOUNS

1 relatedness, relation, relationship, relevance, pertinence, germaneness, bearing, appositeness, connectedness, connection, affinity, friendship, propinquity, kinship, bond, tie, rapport, family relationship, blood relationship, consanguinity, partnership, marriage relationship, link, tie-up, involvement, implication, casual relationship, merger, association, affiliation, alliance, linkage, liaison, interconnection, mutuality, combination, correspondence, agreement, similarity, something in common, parallel, comparison, reference, cross-reference, analogy, correlation, homology, addition, adjunct, attachment, appendix, accompaniment

▶ *111 Sameness; 115 Similarity; 117 Conformity; 123 Importance; 373 Connection; 569 Friendship; 570 Marriage; 694 Meaning*

2 interrelatedness, similar relation, similarity, equality, comparability, homology, correlation, reciprocity, reciprocation, interdependence, cross-reference, reference, citation, complementarity, interconnection, association, mutuality, relativity, proportionality, interlocking, interlinkage, interalliance, interassociation, covariation, interaction, interplaying, interworking, intercourse, intercommunication, interweaving, intertwining, interlacing, interpenetration, interchanging, interchange, tit for tat, blow for blow, engagement, intermeshing, mesh, alternation, seesaw, relativeness, ratio, proportion, scale, direct ratio, inverse ratio, direct proportion, inverse proportion, contrast

▶ *110 Reciprocity; 119 Equality; 747 Cooperation*

3 relative position, rank, class, classification, order, degree, echelon, rating, status, level

▶ *209 Grading; 409 Arrangement*

ADJECTIVES

4 related, relevant, pertinent, germane, apposite, connected, associated, affiliated, allied, linked, bonded, kindred, cognate, agnate, akin to, consanguineous, consanguine, wedded, bound, joined, tied, tied up with, twinned, paired, involved, implicated, merged, combined, added, attached, accompanied, spliced (Inf)

5 interrelated, correlated, reciprocal, interdependent, complementary, interconnected, associated, mutual, relative, proportional, interlocked, interlinked, interallied, interassociated, interwoven, intertwined, interchanged, interacting, interworking, engaged, intermeshed, cross-referred, corresponding, agreed, similar, parallel, comparable, analogous, equal, homologous, relational, commensurate, opposite

6 ranked, classed, classified, ordered, graded, rated, given status

▶ *137 Class*

VERBS

7 relate to, relate, have a relationship, stand in relation to, have relevance, apply to, apply, bear upon, pertain to, pertain, appertain, affect, interest, have to do with, have a bearing on, refer to, make a reference to, touch upon, touch, associate, connect, establish a connection, put in its context, juxtapose, bracket, bracket together, couple, tie up, tie together, tie, bring to bear upon, reconcile, contrast, cross-refer, answer to, have a connection with, liaise with, deal with, pair up with, belong to, link with, tie in with, tie into, become a factor, have a point, support an analogy, serve as an example, sketch in, provide a background, come to the point, stick to the point, address the question, get down to the nitty-gritty (Inf), get down to brass tacks (Inf)

8 be proportionate to, correspond to, correlate, compare, have a mutual relationship, interconnect, interlock, interpenetrate, interlink, interassociate, interact, interplay, interwork, balance, liken, parallel, draw a parallel with (*or* between), equalize, proportion, symmetrize, match, equate, accord, fit, tally

9 have a relative position, have a classification, hold a certain position, rank, rate, belong to a class, have certain status, fit into a category (*or* pigeonhole)

ADVERBS

10 relevantly, pertinently, germanely, concerning, touching, regarding, as to, as regards, in regard to, in relation to, appositely, mutually, equally, on equal terms, reciprocally, interdependently, respectively, correspondingly, proportionally, proportionately, in proportion to, to scale, similarly, comparably, comparatively, in (*or* by) comparison, analogously, commensurately, consanguineously, consanguinely, in a context, in some degree, to some extent, oppositely, in contrast

109 Unrelatedness

The poet and the dreamer are distinct,
Diverse, sheer opposite, antipodes.
The one pours out a balm upon the world,
The other vexes it. John Keats.

NOUNS

1 **unrelatedness**, irrelation, irrelevance, irrelevancy, pointlessness, inappositeness, extraneousness, randomness, arbitrariness, coincidence, illogicality, inapplicability, inaptitude, inaptness, inappropriateness, unconnectedness, difference, heterogeneity, disconnection, disassociation, disjuncture, foreignness, separateness, independence, nonconformity, singularity, unilateralism, neutrality, individuality, freedom, homelessness, no fixed abode, rootlessness, divorce, insularity, isolation, isolationism

▶ *114 Diversity; 116 Dissimilarity; 124 Unimportance; 250 Freedom; 325 Deviation; 372 Separation*

2 **unrelated thing**, non sequitur, fish out of water, square peg in a round hole, cuckoo in the nest, red herring

3 **unconnected person**, hermit, recluse, dropout, misfit, stranger, alien, foreigner, draft dodger (US), displaced person (DP), expatriate, refugee, tenderfoot, uninvited guest, gate-crasher, gooseberry, stowaway

4 **distortion**, disparity, imbalance, asymmetry, disproportion, dissimilarity, inequality

▶ *118 Nonconformity; 120 Inequality; 234 Distortion; 408 Disorder*

5 **misconnection**, no connection, bad connection, misrelation, no relation, wrong association, misalliance, mésalliance, misapplication, misreference, wrong reference

▶ *274 Error*

ADJECTIVES

6 **unrelated**, irrelevant, inapposite, inapplicable, inapt, inappropriate, unconnected, separate, separated, unilateral, disconnected, disassociated, extraneous, difference, heterogenous, independent, singular, individual, unallied, unaffiliated, disrelated, detached, reclusive, discrete, disjunct, removed, segregated, apart, other, floating, uninvolved, divorced, foreign, alien, strange, exotic, owing nothing to, free, rootless, homeless, carefree, fancy-free

7 **illogical**, improbable, impractical, immaterial, incommensurable, beside the point, off the subject, nothing to do with, something else, nonessential, extrinsic, aleatoric, neither here nor there, unimportant, random, arbitrary, coincidental, incidental, remote, far-fetched, distant, out-of-the-way, strained, laboured, forced

8 **distorted**, disproportionate, out of (all) proportion, imbalanced, asymmetrical, dissimilar, unequal, discordant, incongruent

9 **misconnected**, not connected, not related, unrelated, not associated, not allied, misapplied, misreferred

VERBS

10 **be unrelated**, not concern, not involve, not relate to, not connect with, become irrelevant, have no bearing on, go off the point, stray from the topic, digress, get sidetracked, lose the thread, ramble, wander, miss the point, avoid the issue, cloud the issue, draw a red herring, throw dust in one's eyes, strain, labour

11 **be unconcerned**, have no concern with (*or* for), have no interest in, have nothing to do with, owe nothing to, disown, not be one's business, not give (*or* care) a toss (Inf), not give a monkey's (Inf)

ADVERBS

12 **irrelevantly**, without relevance, irrelatively, without reference, without regard, inapplicably, inaptly, inappositely, inappropriately, extraneously, incidentally, coincidentally, by the way, beside the point, off the point, separately, independently, with an independent manner, freely, singularly, individually, as an individual, strangely, exotically

13 **disproportionately**, asymmetrically, dissimilarly, without similarities, unequally, discordantly, incongruently

110 Reciprocity

Scratch my back and I'll scratch yours. Proverb.

NOUNS

1 **interchange**, interchangeability, reciprocation, interplay, interaction, interacting, give and take, compromise, exchange, equal exchange, fair exchange, balance, justice, change, bartering, barter, swap, trade-off, alternation, turn and turn about, compensation, retaliation, payment in kind, tit for tat, an eye for an eye, blow for blow, measure for measure, quid pro quo, *tu quoque* (L), return, retort, reaction, requital, counteraction, recoil, counterstroke, comeback (Inf)

▶ *224 Change; 326 Oscillation; 347 Counteraction; 385 Retaliation; 754 Compromise; 759 Exchange; 776 Trade*

2 **interconnection**, interrelationship (*or* interrelation), interdependence, mutual relationship (*or* relation), mutual dependence, mutual influence, mutuality, mutualism, mutualization, symbiosis, cooperation, partnership, sharing, each other, one another, opposite number, complement, counterpart, alter ego

▶ *373 Connection; 747 Cooperation; 750 Agreement*

3 **correlation**, correlativity, correspondence, similarity, parallelism, comparability, comparison, analogy, analogue, allegory, equivalence, symmetry, proportionality, proportion, proportionment, pattern, tally, match, identity

▶ *111 Sameness; 115 Similarity; 119 Equality; 162 Symmetry; 743 Identification*

ADJECTIVES

4 **reciprocal**, reciprocative, reciprocatory, reciprocating, interacting, interchangeable, interchanged, interplaying, give-and-take, compromising, exchanged, exchangeable, changed, bartered, swapped, trade-off, alternative, alternate, alternating, balancing, seesaw, compensatory, retaliatory, tit-for-tat, eye-for-eye, blow-for-blow, reacting, recoiling, requited, requitable, counteracting, counteractive

5 **interconnected**, interrelated, interlocking, interlinked, interdependent, mutual, symbiotic, cooperative, two-way, bilateral, complementary, complemental, opposite

6 **correlative**, correlational, correlating, correlated, correspondent, corresponding, comparable, analogous, allegorical, parallel, symmetrical, proportional, proportionate, proportioned, patterned, matching, equivalent, similar, identical

VERBS

7 **reciprocate**, interchange, interplay, interact, give and take, compromise, exchange, give an equal exchange, change, give in exchange, counterchange, barter, swap, trade off, trade, alternate, compensate, balance, seesaw, take turn and turn about, take turns, retaliate, pay in kind, give tit for tat, take an eye for an eye, give blow for blow, react, counteract, recoil, counterstrike, requite, return, retort

8 **interrelate**, establish an interrelationship, interconnect, interlock, interlink, interdepend, interassociate, neutralize, cooperate, partner, pair, twin, participate, share, complement, act as a foil to

► *193 Interweaving*

9 **correlate**, correspond, identify with, parallel, parallelize, compare, proportion, tally, answer, match, resemble, equalize

► *706 Answer*

ADVERBS

10 **reciprocally**, interchangeably, compromisingly, proportionally, proportionately, in (mutual) exchange, alternatively, to and fro, by turns, turn and turn about, first one and then the other, interdependently, mutually, equally, bilaterally, cooperatively, symbiotically, contrariwise, vice versa, complementally, oppositely

11 **correlatively**, correspondingly, comparably, analogously, allegorically, symmetrically, proportionally, proportionately, equivalently, similarly, identically

111 Sameness

NOUNS

1 **sameness**, the same, the very same, the exact same, *idem* (L), very thing, actual thing, selfsameness, one and the same, no other, none other, uniformity, identicalness, isotrophy, indistinguishability, no difference, oneness, oneness with, unity, solidarity, mergence, coalescence, assimilation, agreement, repetition, redundancy, tautology, the very words, *ipsissima verba* (L), verbatim, homoousia, consubstantiality, consubstantiation, birds of a feather

► *7 Religion; 10 Ritual; 112 Repetition; 117 Conformity; 197 One; 370 Admittance; 743 Identification; 750 Agreement*

2 **equivalence**, equivalent, correspondence, concordance, accordance, harmony, agreement, congruence (*or* congruency), equipollence, interchangeability, reciprocation, equal exchange, representation, similarity, homoiousia, parallelism, coincidence, synchronicity, synonymousness, synonymy, synonymity, homogeneity, homonym, homograph, homophone, analogy, analogue, analog (US), simile, metaphor, reflection, shadow

► *5 Language and Linguistics; 110 Reciprocity; 115 Similarity; 188 Parallelism; 285 Same Time; 694 Meaning; 750 Agreement*

3 **lookalike**, double, doppelgänger, alter ego, other self, ka, ba, twin, Siamese twin, family resemblance, homophyly, very image, (exact) counterpart, reflection, two of a kind, two peas in a pod, Tweedledum and Tweedledee, pair, match, suit, portrait, clone, chip off the old block (Inf), spit (Inf), dead spit (Inf), spitting image (Inf), picture of (Inf), living image (Inf), dead ringer (Inf)

► *198 Two; 525 Appearance; 553 Fashion; 743 Identification*

4 **duplicate**, duplication, triplicate, imitation, copy, carbon copy, photocopy, Xerox™, Photostat™, Mimeograph™, hectograph copy, microcopy, facsimile, fax, photograph, positive, negative, enlargement, print, contact print, PMT (photomechanical transfer), reprint, offprint, separate (US), second printing, second edition, reproduction, impression, hologram, replication, replica, representation, model, mould, moulding, stamp, seal, ditto (Inf), dupe (US inf)

► *19 Painting and Sculpture; 41 Photography; 125 Imitation; 356 Creation; 561 Reproduction; 717 Representation*

5 **equality**, coequality, parity, symmetry, balance, equilibration, equiponderance, equal standing, equal rights, equal opportunity, impartiality, justice, equal value, even money, six of one and half a dozen of the other, six and two threes, nothing to choose between, nothing in it, par, tie, draw, drawn match, tied game, love-all score, deuce, stalemate, deadlock, dead heat, neck-and-neck race, half-and-half split, fifty-fifty split (Inf), level pegging (Inf), quits (Inf), even break (Inf)

► *119 Equality*

6 **regularity**, clockwork regularity, routine, daily routine, daily round, constancy, changelessness, smoothness, even pace, evenness, levelness, equilibrium, homeostasis (*or* homoeostasis), homogeneity, consistency, invariability, unvariableness (*or* invariableness), invariant, no change, uniformity, standardization, conformity, conformance, monotonousness, monotony, repetition, flatness, treadmill, mass production, assembly line, automation, regimentation, same old thing, same old story

► *134 Continuity; 140 Rule; 187 Horizontality; 216 Average; 225 Permanence; 228 Stability; 298 Regularity; 310 Convergence; 407 Order; 412 Mixture; 421 Smoothness; 452 Certainty; 620 Boredom; 632 Habit*

VERBS

7 **be the same**, be identical, be as like as two peas in a pod, correspond, agree, harmonize, merge, coalesce, coincide, match, tally, answer, interchange, reciprocate, imitate, look alike, shadow, reflect, repeat, quote, tell the same (old) story

8 **make the same**, unify, unite, join, merge, homogenize, coalesce, assimilate, synthesize, synchronize, consubstantiate, parallel, equate, pair, twin, symmetrize, balance, harmonize, smooth, level, flatten, even up, stereotype, standardize, regulate, regularize, phase, mass-produce, automate, clone

► *117 Conformity; 412 Mixture*

9 **duplicate**, triplicate, copy, imitate, ape, photocopy, Xerox™, Photostat™, Mimeograph™, fax, photograph, shoot, enlarge, print, reprint, offprint, run a second edition, reproduce, make an impression, replicate, mould, stamp, ditto (Inf)

10 **be equal**, equal, match, balance, measure up to, equalize, equiponderate, equilibrate, draw a match, tie a game, stalemate, deadlock, come to the same thing, break even, race neck-and-neck, split half-and-half, go fifty-fifty (Inf)

11 be regular, continue the same, fall into a routine, repeat, iterate, persist, drag on, harp on, hum, drone, keep an even pace, typify, conform, toe the line, get in a rut

▶ *225 Permanence; 640 Perseverance*

ADJECTIVES

12 same, *idem* (L), selfsame, one and the same, identical, isotrophic (*or* isotropous), indistinguishable, undifferentiated, repetitious, repetitive, unvarying, repeated, redundant, tautological (*or* tautologous), verbatim, united, solid, all the same, one, all one, homogeneous, merging, merged, of that ilk, absorbed, coalescent, coalesced, assimilated, agreed, consubstantial, homoousian, of the same kidney, tarred with the same brush

13 equivalent, corresponding, concordant, accordant, harmonious, agreeing, agreeable, congruent, equipollent, interchangeable, reciprocal, representative, parallel, similar, homoiousian, coincidental, synchronous, synonymous, homogeneous, homographic, homonymic (*or* homonymous), homophonic (*or* homophonous), analogous, metaphorical, reflective, shadowing

14 lookalike, twin, homophyllic, matching, matched, like, alike, paired, like two peas in a pod, cloned

15 duplicate, triplicate, copied, photocopied, xeroxed, photostated, mimeographed, microcopied, faxed, photographic, photographed, positive, negative, printed, reprinted, offprinted, reproduced, holographic, replicated, moulded, cast out of the same mould, stamped

16 equal, coequal, symmetrical, balanced, equiponderant, equidistant, on equal terms, on the same footing, as good as, no better and no worse, neither more nor less, level, impartial, par, on par, on a par, tied, drawn, love-all, stalemated, deadlocked, neck-and-neck, half-and-half, fifty-fifty (Inf), level pegging (Inf), quits (Inf)

17 regular, clockwork, routine, hourly, daily, weekly, monthly, yearly, annual, constant, smooth, steady, even, level, changeless, homeostatic (*or* homoeostatic), homogenous, consistent, unvariable, unvarying, unvaried, unaltered, invariant, invariable, always the same, unchanging, unchanged, unchangeable, undeviating, undiversified, uniform, flat, standardized, conforming, mundane, repetitive, repetitious, monotonous, automative, automated, regimented

▶ *275 Time; 281 Timekeeping*

ADVERBS

18 identically, alike, just the same, in the same way, in the same place, ibid, *ibidem* (L), at the same time, coincidentally, synchronously, again, ditto, likewise, isotrophically, indistinguishably, repetitiously, repetitively, in duplicate, in triplicate, tautologically, homogenously, consubstantially, equivalently, correspondently, correspondingly, congruently, agreeably, concordantly, harmoniously, synonymously, analogously, metaphorically, reflectively, imitatively, holographically, photographically

19 equally, coequally, on equal terms, on the same footing, levelly, impartially, in par, on a par, neck and neck, fifty-fifty (Inf)

20 regularly, routinely, like clockwork, hourly, daily, weekly, monthly, yearly, annually, days, mornings, afternoons, evenings, nights, constantly, smoothly, steadily, in phase, evenly, levelly, on a level, unvariably, invariably, changelessly, always, without exception, uniformly, monotonously, flatly, repetitively, in a rut, in a groove

112 Repetition

Only constant repetition will finally succeed in imprinting an idea on the memory of the crowd. Adolf Hitler.

NOUNS

1 repetition, repeating, doing again, rehearsal, practice, practising, recital, duplication, reduplication, doubling, redoubling, reproduction, replication, recurrence, imitation, copying, plagiarism, echo, echolalia, re-echo, ditto, anaphora, epistrophe

▶ *125 Imitation; 198 Two; 561 Reproduction*

2 iteration, reiteration, repeating, saying again, relating, relation, recounting, retelling, recapitulation, going over again, review, résumé, summary, summing up, peroration, restatement, tautology, redundancy, padding, filling, quotation, plagiarism, recap (Inf), waffle (Inf)

▶ *270 Vagueness; 723 Summary*

3 repetitiveness, repetitiousness, repetition, stale repetition, monotony, tedium, uniformity, regularity, invariability, familiarity, daily grind, same old round, humdrum, rut, routine, habit, cliché, same old story, old joke, (old) chestnut (Inf)

▶ *228 Stability; 632 Habit*

4 return, reappearance, comeback, renewal, starting again, beginning again, starting afresh, reprise, recurrence, rebirth, reincarnation, renaissance, revival, restoration, recycling, cycle, round, eternal return

5 repeat, repetition, repeat performance, encore, curtain call, rerun, reshowing, replay, replaying, return match, repeat order, second helping, reprint, offprint, reissue, new edition, remake, rehash (Inf)

6 reverberation, echo, re-echo, resonance, vibration, oscillation, rhythm, beat, pulse, pulsation, throb, throbbing, drumming, hammering, rhyme, alliteration, assonance

▶ *509 Repeated Sound; 510 Resonance*

7 replica, double, duplicate, copy, carbon copy, photocopy, print

▶ *111 Sameness*

8 creature of habit, copycat, parrot, mimic, automaton, robot

▶ *125 Imitation; 632 Habit*

ADJECTIVES

9 repeated, duplicated, reduplicated, doubled, redoubled, reproduced, replicated, echoed, re-echoed, mirrored, imitative, parrot-like, plagiarized

▶ *125 Imitation; 561 Reproduction*

10 iterated, reiterated, said again, retold, twice-told, said before, recounted, related, restated, quoted, cited

11 reprinted, reissued, remade, replayed, reshown, revived, restored, renewed, reborn, reincarnated, reheated, warmed up, recycled, reprocessed, rehashed (Inf)

12 repetitious, repetitive, repetitional, repeating, duplicative, reproductive, doubling, redoubling, echoing, reechoing, iterative, reiterative, reiterant, tautological, redundant, otiose, pleonastic, recapitulative, harping, stuck-in-a-groove, wordy, prolix
► *270 Vagueness*
13 monotonous, tedious, boring, uniform, invariable, changeless, monotone, singsong, familiar, habitual, humdrum, mundane, routine, stale, cliché-ridden, clichéd, hackneyed, trite, yawn-making (Inf)
► *228 Stability; 620 Boredom; 632 Habit*
14 recurrent, regular, periodic, cyclical, returning, recurring, reoccurring, reappearing, ubiquitous, haunting, continual, continuous, constant, nonstop, incessant, ceaseless, unremitting
► *134 Continuity; 225 Permanence*
15 reverberatory, resonant, vibrational, oscillatory, rhythmical, rhythmic, beating, pulsing, pulsating, throbbing, drumming, hammering, chiming, chanting, rhymed, rhyming, alliterative, alliterating, assonant
► *509 Repeated Sound; 510 Resonance*

VERBS
16 repeat, redo, do again, do a repeat, rehearse, practise, duplicate, reduplicate, double, redouble, reproduce, replicate, plagiarize, copy, echo, mirror, parrot, imitate, mimic
► *125 Imitation; 198 Two; 561 Reproduction*
17 iterate, reiterate, repeat, say again, say over again, relate, recite, recount, retell, recapitulate, perorate, go over again, review, resume, summarize, sum up, restate, reemphasize, quote, cite, quote oneself, repeat oneself, go over the same ground, give an encore, recap (Inf)
► *723 Summary*
18 harp, harp on, go on about, plug, labour, belabour, go on at, hammer away at, churn out, trot out, sing the same old song, play the same old record, tell the same old story, go over again and again, say over and over, hammer into, din (*or* drum) into, nag, go on and on, never hear the last of
► *270 Vagueness*
19 return to, go back, retrace one's steps, go over the same ground, relapse, regress, revert, remember, recall
► *462 Memory*
20 renew, resume, restart, start again, begin again, start afresh, go back to the beginning, come back, stage a comeback, revive, restore, recycle, reprocess, reheat, warm up, reprint, reissue, rerun, replay, play back, remake, rehash (Inf)
21 be repeated, recur, reoccur, happen again, return, reappear, pop up, crop up, show up again, keep coming, come again and again, turn up like a bad penny
22 resound, reverberate, echo, re-echo, vibrate, oscillate, beat, pulse, pulsate, throb, drum, thrum, hammer, pound, rhyme, alliterate
► *509 Repeated Sound; 510 Resonance*

ADVERBS
23 repeatedly, reiteratively, repetitively, repetitiously, monotonously, recurrently, frequently, often, continually, incessantly, again and again, over and over, over and over again, time after time, time and again, many times over, day after day, year after year, day in day out, year in year out, ad nauseam
24 again, once more, once again, encore, *bis* (L), da capo, from the beginning, afresh, anew, twice over, ditto

113 Opposition

I have spent many years of my life in opposition and I rather like the role. Eleanor Roosevelt.

NOUNS
1 opposition, hostility, antagonism, antipathy, dislike, hate, hatred, aversion, repugnance, repugnancy, disapproval, disapprobation, unfriendliness, stiff opposition, resistance
► *383 Resistance; 594 Hate; 596 Dislike; 670 Disapproval*
2 oppositeness, opposite side, other side, opposing side, opposition, opposite number, contraposition, opposure, antithesis, contrariety, contraries, contradiction, contrariness, confrontment, contrast, reverse, reversal, inverse, inversion, obverse, converse, back, rear, polarity, polarization, polar opposition, opposite pole, counterpole, poles apart, antipodes, antipodal points, extremes, other side of the fence, other side of the coin, other side of the picture
► *167 Front; 168 Back; 192 Inversion*
3 opposites, east and west, north and south, night and day, black and white, good and evil, high and low, rich and poor, hill and dale, great and small, hot and cold, sweet and sour, fair and foul, laughter and tears, land and sea, Yin and Yang, ancient and modern, feast and famine, heads and tails, man and beast, Jekyll and Hyde, chalk and cheese, oil and water, sheep and goats, beauty and the beast, the lion and the lamb, the hare and the tortoise, cat and mouse, Tom and Jerry, the prince and the pauper, Dives and Lazarus, the lady and the tramp, Socrates and the fool, saints and sinners, cops and robbers, cowboys and Indians, goodies and baddies (Inf)
4 objection, complaint, fuss, clamour, demurral, demur, remonstration, expostulation, protest, dissent, dissidence, controversy, disputation, disagreement, argument, contradiction, contravention, challenge, impugnation, impugnment, rebuttal, refutation, controversion, denial, refusal, rejection, defiance
► *470 Rejection; 661 Defiance; 751 Disagreement; 753 Protest*
5 conflict, friction, disaccord, dissension, crosscurrent, undercurrent, collision, clashing, confrontation, strife, discord, rivalry, vying, competition, emulation, contention, fighting, fight, battle, war, warfare, attack, defence, bad blood, enmity
► *381 Attack; 384 Defence; 585 War*
6 uncooperativeness, unhelpfulness, negativeness, negativity, unwillingness, nonacceptance, dissociation, noncooperation, obstructiveness, obstruction, prevention, foot-dragging, bloody-mindedness (Inf)
► *378 Obstruction; 637 Unwillingness*
7 contrariness, perverseness, perversity, oppugnancy, stubbornness, obstinacy, disobedience, fractiousness, refractoriness, recalcitrance, reaction

▶ *641 Obstinacy; 662 Disobedience*

8 **contrariety**, oppositeness, disagreement, difference, discrepancy, inconsistency, disparity, contrast, contradistinction, antithesis, polarity, contraposition

▶ *118 Nonconformity*

9 **countermeasure**, counterargument, counterproposal, countercheck, countermove, counterattack, counterwork, counteraction

▶ *347 Counteraction*

10 **the opposition**, the other side, opposing party, opposing force, opposite camp, the enemy, the field, all-comers, faction, minority (party *or* group), opposition party, cross-benches, Her Majesty's Loyal Opposition

▶ *12 Government and Politics*

11 **opposer**, oppositionist, objector, protester, dissenter, dissentient, dissident, agitator, heckler, disputant, litigant, plaintiff, defendant, radical, rebel, revolutionary, counter-revolutionary, resister, intransigent, die-hard, reactionary, conservative, true blue, obstructionist, filibusterer, obstructive, negativist, naysayer (US), gainsayer, anti (Inf), bitter-ender (US inf), last-ditcher (Inf)

▶ *708 Negation*

12 **competitor**, contestant, contender, player, rival, emulator, corrival

13 **opponent**, adversary, antagonist, combatant, enemy, foe

▶ *586 Combatant*

VERBS

14 **oppose**, stand against, act against, go (*or* act) in opposition, traverse, protest against (*or* at *or* about), fight against, strive against, resist

▶ *383 Resistance; 753 Protest*

15 **be opposite**, oppose, stand on the opposite side, take the opposing side, lie opposite, set against (*or* over), polarize, subtend, face, traverse, run counter, counteract, contradict, contrapose, contrast, reverse, invert, confront, meet head-on, meet a crosscurrent, meet a headwind

16 **be contrary**, go against, work against, militate against, counter, run counter to, conflict with

17 **be against**, discountenance, disapprove of, disagree with, not support, vote against, object to, not hold with, not abide, not tolerate, not put up with, dissociate oneself from, not have anything to do with, set one's face (*or* oneself) against, reject, dislike, hate

▶ *470 Rejection; 594 Hate; 596 Dislike; 670 Disapproval; 751 Disagreement*

18 **object**, complain, demur, raise (*or* make) objections, make a fuss, gripe, grouse, moan, take exception, protest, remonstrate, expostulate, speak out, deprecate, dissent, express disapproval, assail, criticize, disagree, take issue, beg to differ, call into question, dispute, oppugn, contradict, contravene, belie, rebut, refute, negate, deny, controvert, gainsay, counter, retaliate, defend, defy, challenge, impugn, combat, fight, attack, litigate, kick (Inf)

▶ *381 Attack; 384 Defence; 661 Defiance; 670 Disapproval; 751 Disagreement; 753 Protest*

19 **confront**, front, face, breast, stem, meet head-on, take on, conflict, clash, come into conflict, join battle, grapple with, contest with, contend, compete with (*or* against), vie with, rival, emulate, set against, pit against, match against

20 **withstand**, stand firm (*or* fast), stand up to, hold one's own, breast the storm, stem the tide (*or* wind), hold out, resist, obstruct, make difficulties, hinder, check, block, bar, dig one's heels in, refuse to budge, stand one's ground, defy, disobey, refuse

▶ *251 Restraint; 378 Obstruction; 383 Resistance; 661 Defiance; 662 Disobedience*

21 **counteract**, antagonize, countervail, work against, act against, countercheck, counterattack, countermine, frustrate, cross, thwart, foil, prevent, counterbalance, match, offset, set off against, set in opposition, contrast, compare

▶ *347 Counteraction*

ADJECTIVES

22 **oppositional**, opposing, opposed, hostile, antagonistic, inimical, unfriendly, unfavourable, unpropitious, adverse, contrary, counteractive, counteracting, counter, cross, antipathetic(al), unsympathetic, averse, disapproving, alien, repugnant

▶ *347 Counteraction; 596 Dislike*

23 **opposite**, opposing, opposed, oppositional, diametrically opposite (*or* opposed), diametrical, other, contrapositive, antithetical, antipodal (*or* antipodean), contrary, contrariwise, contrasting, reverse, reversed, inverse, inverted, obverse, converse, subcontrary, confronting, oncoming, facing, face-to-face, polarized

24 **discordant**, disagreeing, contentious, dissentient, dissenting, dissident, different, conflicting, clashing, adversarial, confronting, face to face, eyeball to eyeball, head-on, challenging, defiant, rival, competitive, competing, contending, in opposition, at odds, at cross purposes, at variance, at issue, anti (Inf)

▶ *661 Defiance; 751 Disagreement*

25 **contrary**, contrasting, contrasted, opposite, reverse, inconsistent, incompatible, contradictory, repugnant, antithetical, diametric(al), diametrically opposed, adversative, irreconcilable, polarized, con (Inf)

26 **uncooperative**, unhelpful, negative, noncooperative, unwilling, obstructive, hindering, contrary, perverse, oppugnant, stubborn, obstinate, disobedient, fractious, refractory, recalcitrant, reactionary, reactionist, conservative, true-blue, resistant, bloody-minded (Inf)

▶ *378 Obstruction; 383 Resistance; 637 Unwillingness; 641 Obstinacy; 662 Disobedience*

ADVERBS

27 **opposingly**, antagonistically, inimically, adversely, antipathetically, defiantly, competitively, contrastingly, contradictorily, antithetically, uncooperatively, perversely, unhelpfully, stubbornly

28 **in opposition**, contrastively, inversely, obversely, conversely, diametrically, on the other side, of the opposing party, of the opposite camp

29 **at odds**, at cross purposes, at variance, at issue, in confrontation, face to face, eyeball to eyeball, up in arms, at daggers drawn

30 **contrariwise**, against the tide (*or* stream *or* wind), counter, *au contraire* (Fr)

PREPOSITIONS

31 **opposed to**, in opposition to, in contrast to, in conflict

with, against, versus, despite, in spite of, in the face of, counter to, at variance with, contrary to, agin (Inf)

114 Diversity

If we cannot now end our differences, at least we can help make the world safe for diversity. John Fitzgerald Kennedy.

NOUNS

1 **diversity**, difference, variety, multiplicity, heterogeneity, miscellany, diversification, variation, versatility, dissimilarity, contrast, disorder, deviation, variousness, divergence, variegation, incongruity, nonconformity, exception, exception to the rule, special case, odd man out, nonuniformity, inconsistency, inequality, discontinuity, variability, unevenness, bumpiness, raggedness, irregularity, changeability, instability, unpredictability, haphazardness, fitfulness, modifiability, alterability, abnormality, mutation, individuality, uniqueness, freak, one-off (Inf)

► *116 Dissimilarity; 118 Nonconformity; 133 Discontinuity; 227 Changeableness; 299 Irregularity; 325 Deviation; 408 Disorder; 541 Variegation*

2 **assortment**, mixture, medley, miscellany, *e pluribus unum* (L), all shapes and sizes, all sorts and conditions, hotchpotch, hodgepodge (US), odds and ends, motley, variegation, dappleness, multiplicity, multiformity, omnifariousness, allotropy (*or* allotropism), heteromorphism, Proteus, all colours of the rainbow, everything but the kitchen sink

► *412 Mixture*

3 **diverse thing**, motley collection, miscellanea, ragbag, lucky dip, grab bag (US), mosaic, stained-glass window, crazy paving, patchwork quilt, coat of many colours, rainbow, kaleidoscope, chequered career, mixed bag (Inf)

4 **dissension**, disagreement, controversy, discordance, different opinions, various opinions, many voices

ADJECTIVES

5 **diverse**, varied, variable, nonuniform, heterogeneous, dissimilar, contrasting, deviant, diverging, diversiform, different, manifold, incongruous, variegated, chequered, exceptional, abnormal, freakish, unique, individual, unusual, inconsistent, changeable, unstable, uneven, bumpy, versatile, all-round, all-around (US), unpredictable, spasmodic, sporadic, erratic, haphazard, fitful, inconstant, never the same, out of step

6 **assorted**, mixed, chequered, miscellaneous, motley, dapple, omnifarious, multifarious, allotropic, kaleidoscopic, sundry, all and sundry, various, multipurpose, multifaceted, multiform, diversiform, polymorphous, heteromorphous, of many kinds, of all sorts, multicoloured, divers (Lit)

7 **dissenting**, disagreeing, controversial, discordant, of different opinions

VERBS

8 **be diverse**, diverge, branch out, differ, variegate, deviate, mutate, make diverse, differentiate, vary, contrast, chequer, diversify, mix, stir, jumble, shake up, shuffle, scramble, tangle, blend, intermix, intersperse, interleave, ring the changes, have many irons in the fire, have many strings to one's bow, spread one's wings

9 **dissent**, disagree, have discord, vote against, hold opposite opinions, have different opinions

ADVERBS

10 **diversely**, differently, variably, nonuniformly, heterogeneously, miscellaneously, omnifariously, kaleidoscopically, variously, in different ways, dissimilarly, dissentingly, out of step, differently, exceptionally, individually, abnormally, freakishly, uniquely, unusually, untidily, changeably, unequally, unevenly, bumpily, versatilely, unpredictably, inconsistently, without consistency, inconstantly, unsteadily

11 **irregularly**, spasmodically, sporadically, erratically, haphazardly, fitfully, chaotically, without order, in turmoil, in confusion, all over the place (*or* shop), here, there, and everywhere, in all manner of ways, willy-nilly, helter-skelter, harum-scarum, huggermugger, topsy-turvy, every which way (US inf), at sixes and sevens (Inf), higgledy-piggledy (Inf)

115 Similarity

Birds of a feather flock together. Proverb.

Great minds think alike. Proverb.

NOUNS

1 **similarity**, sameness, resemblance, synonymy, homonymy, likeness, alikeness, similitude, affinity, kinship, seeming, analogy, correspondence, equivalence, comparability, common feature, point in common, parallel, parallelism, uniformity, conformity, parity, equality, proportionality, accordance, agreement, nearness, approximation, near likeness, closeness, close likeness, similar look, family resemblance, family likeness, genetic likeness, good likeness, faithful likeness, faint resemblance, the like(s) of, suchlike, duplication, similation, imitation, semblance, assimilation, simile, metaphor, parable, allegory, portrayal, copying, aping, mimicking

► *108 Relatedness; 112 Repetition; 119 Equality; 125 Imitation; 162 Symmetry; 273 Accuracy; 525 Appearance; 717 Representation; 750 Agreement*

2 **copy**, photocopy, facsimile (*or* fax) (copy), stencil, duplicate, Mimeograph™, photomechanical transfer (PMT), reproduction, imitation, close imitation, pirated record, twin, clone, trend, style, fashion, fad, bootleg copy (Inf)

► *117 Conformity; 553 Fashion*

3 **copier**, photocopier, facsimile (*or* fax) machine, duplicator, stenciller, press, printer, computer printer, laser printer, camera, video cassette recorder (VCR) (*or* video), camcorder, tape recorder, Xerox™ machine, Photostat™

► *40 Computers*

4 **person who copies**, copyist, transcriber, forger, counterfeiter, plagiarist, mimic, impersonator, imitator, painter, sketcher, printer, photographer, record pirate, follower of fashion, clotheshorse (Inf), fashion victim (Inf), copycat (Inf)

► *700 Deception*

5 **counterpart**, equivalent, correspondent, pendant, reciprocal, coordinate, twin, copy, clone, alter ego, kindred spirit, soul mate, second self, doppelgänger, image, living image, another edition, brother (*or* sister) under the skin, blood brother, double, lookalike, reflection, shadow, understudy, stunt man (*or* woman), better half, other half, other, fellow, mate, companion, ka, chip off the old block (Inf), spitting image (Inf), spit (Inf), (dead) ringer (Inf)

6 **couple**, pair, twins, matched pair, matching set, two of a kind, two peas in a pod, birds of a feather, Tweedledum and Tweedledee

ADJECTIVES

7 **similar**, same, synonymous, symmetrical, akin, like, alike, something like, not unlike, resembling, allied, connected, related, matching, corresponding, analogous, equivalent, comparable, commensurable, parallel, identical, of a piece, uniform with, duplicated, approximate, approximating, near, close, much the same, nearly the same, quasi, bracketed with, connatural, homogeneous, assonant, alliterative, rhyming, much of a muchness, favouring, following, pretty much the same, damned little difference (Inf)

8 **simulated**, artificial, false, imitation, imitative, cultured, ersatz, synthetic, aped, mimicked, imitated, mocked, mock, phoney, counterfeit, copied, duplicated, duplicate, replicated, spurious, pseudo (Inf)

9 **lifelike**, realistic, photographic, exact, faithful, true-to-life, true-to-nature, true-to-type, graphic, vivid, eidetic, natural, living, breathing, speaking

VERBS

10 **be similar**, be like, resemble, bear resemblance, correspond, coincide, agree, accord, tally, compare, take after, favour, suggest, evoke, put one in mind of, bring to mind, call to mind, seem like, smack of, savour of, have all the signs of, have all the appearances (*or* features) of, have all the earmarks of, have all the hallmarks of, reflect, mirror, echo, match, parallel

11 **make similar**, equalize, homogenize, assimilate, compare, liken, draw a parallel between, compare with, approximate to, not tell apart, not tell one from the other, see no difference

12 **imitate**, emulate, copy, reproduce, duplicate, Mimeograph™, Photostat™, Xerox™, fax, clone, simulate, camouflage, portray, make like, ape, mimic, counterfeit, replicate, alliterate, rhyme

ADVERBS

13 **similarly**, in a similar situation, likewise, in like manner, like, by the same token, as, just as, as if, as it were, so to speak, so, correspondingly, metaphorically, in a way, in the same category, in the same boat, as in a mirror, like father like son, like a chip off the old block (Inf), like the spitting image (Inf)

14 **comparably**, synonymously, symmetrically, correspondingly, at the same time, in the same way, analogously, equivalently, equally, with equal measures, identically, approximately, nearly, almost the same way, closely, homogeneously, alliteratively, realistically, photographically, like a photograph, exactly, with the exact touch, faithfully, graphically, vividly, eidetically, naturally, with a natural look, artificially, falsely, imitatively, synthetically, spuriously

116 Dissimilarity

What is food to one man is bitter poison to others. Lucretius.

NOUNS

1 **dissimilarity**, dissimilitude, difference, disparity, diversity, discrepancy, divergence, unsimilarity, extraneousness, nonuniformity, differentiation, variation, multiformity, discrimination, distinction, variance, variety, contrast, heterogeneity

2 **unlikeness**, unrelatedness, incongruity, incompatibility, contrast, asymmetry, incommensurability, no comparison, nothing in common, a different kettle of fish, another matter, another story, no common ground, no match, not a pair, misfit, odd man out, odd bod (Inf)

► *109 Unrelatedness; 114 Diversity*

3 **disguise**, camouflage, caricature, bad likeness, concealment, misrepresentation, poor imitation, copy, counterfeit, make up, cosmetic (*or* plastic) surgery

► *234 Distortion; 699 Falsehood; 718 Misrepresentation; 736 Concealment*

ADJECTIVES

4 **dissimilar**, different, disparate, divergent, diverse, various, multiform, unequal, asymmetrical, nonuniform, not true to life, unresembling, unlike, unalike, unidentical, nothing like, incongruous, incompatible, contrasting, poles apart, strange, unrealistic, scarcely like, hardly like, discrepant, far from it, way off, a mile off, no such thing, distinctive, unusual, peculiar, out of the ordinary, original, singular, unrelated, far above, superior, far below, inferior, new, unique, peerless, matchless, nonpareil, untypical, atypical, unprecedented, incomparable, incommensurate, incommensurable, novel, cast in a different mould, a far cry from, not a bit alike, not a bit of it, nothing of the sort (*or* kind), something else, quite another thing, way out (Inf)

VERBS

5 **be dissimilar**, be unlike, differ, not resemble, bear no resemblance, have nothing in common, have little in common, diverge, deviate, depart from, contrast, conflict, not look like, not compare with, look superior, look inferior, stand out, stand out in a crowd, stick out like a sore thumb

6 **differentiate**, make unlike, distinguish, discriminate, split hairs, innovate, vary, modify, change, convert, distort, caricature, misrepresent, dissemble, disguise, deceive, conceal, camouflage, tell the men from the boys, separate the sheep from the goats, nit-pick (Inf)

ADVERBS

7 **dissimilarly**, differently, discordantly, contrastingly, variously, at different times, disparately, divergently, in different directions, diversely, unequally, without equal, incongruously, incompatibly, strangely, in a strange way, unrealistically, distinctively, unusually, peculiarly, singularly, incomparably, without comparison, incommensurately

117 Conformity

When in Rome, live as the Romans do: when elsewhere, live as they live elsewhere. St Ambrose.

NOUNS

1 **conformity**, conformance, conformation, accord, accordance, agreement, harmony, compatibility, consistency, uniformity, congruity, correspondence, concurrence, line, keeping, similarity, likeness, imitation, emulation, parrotry

► *115 Similarity; 125 Imitation; 750 Agreement*

2 **compliance**, obedience, observance, respect, abidance, acquiescence, submission, subordination

► *388 Submission; 663 Obedience*

3 **pliancy**, flexibility, malleability, plasticity, softness, adaptability, adaption, adaptation, accommodation, adjustment, assimilation, naturalization, acclimatization, rehabilitation

► *419 Softness; 760 Conversion*

4 **conventionalism**, conservatism, conformism, orthodoxy, traditionalism, Babbittry, bourgeois ethic, etiquette, formality, formalism, strictness, severity, primness, prudery

► *647 Severity; 656 Formality*

5 **convention**, practice, form, done thing, order of the day, received idea, party line, policy, rule, tradition, custom, fashion, trend, vogue, style

► *140 Rule; 632 Habit*

6 **conformist**, conformer, traditionalist, conventionalist, formalist, pedant, precisian, prude, bourgeois, burgher, Babbitt, Philistine, Mrs Grundy, Middle American, herd, sheep, company man, organization man, follower, loyalist, party hack, running dog, trimmer, lapdog, time-server, yes-man, flatterer, parrot, copycat, imitator, square (Inf), stick-in-the-mud (Inf), square John (Inf), grey (Inf), do-right man (Inf)

► *7 Religion; 125 Imitation; 664 Servility; 677 Flattery; 810 Duty*

VERBS

7 **conform**, conform to, accord, agree, concur, correspond, match, tally, fit, square with, harmonize, suit, meet, run true to form

► *750 Agreement*

8 **comply**, comply with, adapt, adapt oneself, adjust, accommodate oneself, fit in, fall in with, go along with, play the game, submit, yield, acquiesce, accede, consent, agree, go by, abide by, follow, observe, respect, obey, obey regulations, stick to the rules, toe the line (*or* mark), stay in line, keep in step, follow suit, go with the flow, go with the stream (*or* current *or* tide), swim with the stream (*or* tide), run with the pack (*or* herd), follow the beaten path, imitate, emulate, copy, do as others do, do as the Romans do, follow the fashion, follow the trend, keep up with the Joneses, jump on the bandwagon

► *125 Imitation; 388 Submission; 663 Obedience*

9 **make conform**, conform, accommodate, adjust, straighten, align, bring into line, fit, fit in, trim, cut (*or* trim) down to size, form, shape, mould, force into a mould, press, standardize, stereotype

10 **assimilate**, naturalize, acclimatize, rehabilitate, re-educate, indoctrinate, brainwash, imbue, instil, implant, drill, school, teach, train, coach, instruct, correct, discipline, knock (*or* lick) into shape

ADJECTIVES

11 **conformable**, adaptable, adaptive, adjustable, flexible, pliant, malleable, soft, plastic

12 **conforming**, accordant, concordant, harmonious, compatible, consistent, consonant, congruous, congruent, corresponding, agreeing, in agreement, in accord, in keeping, in line, in step

13 **compliant**, willing, obedient, acquiescent, submissive, yielding, sheep-like, lemming-like, tractable, complaisant, accommodating, agreeable, passive

14 **conformist**, orthodox, kosher, conservative, law-abiding, conventional, traditional, traditionalist, traditionalistic, bourgeois, provincial, correct, proper, pedantic, formal, old-fashioned, staid, strait-laced, prim, prudish, square (Inf), stuffy (Inf), stodgy (Inf), grey (Inf), uptight (Inf)

► *632 Habit*

15 **everyday**, quotidian, ordinary, unexceptional, common, commonplace, common or garden, familiar, household, typical, stock, standard, general, usual, identikit, stereotyped, average, median, middling, normal, straight

ADVERBS

16 **adaptably**, conformably, pliantly, malleably, flexibly, willingly, yieldingly, complaisantly, submissively, compliantly, obediently, passively

17 **conformingly**, harmoniously, compatibly, consistently, congruously, in harmony, in accord, in keeping, in line, in place, in accordance

18 **as usual**, as a matter of course, of course, as always, as before

19 **according to rule**, by the book, conventionally, traditionally, by the numbers (Inf)

118 Nonconformity

Nonconformity and lust stalking hand in hand through the country, wasting and ravaging. Evelyn Waugh.

The young always have the same problem – how to rebel and conform at the same time. They have now solved this by defying their parents and copying one another. Quentin Crisp.

NOUNS

1 **nonconformity**, unconformity, nonconformance, discord, disaccordance, disagreement, inconsistency, incongruity, incompatibility, disparity, contrast, difference, diversity

► *114 Diversity; 116 Dissimilarity; 751 Disagreement*

2 **dissent**, nonconcurrence, disagreement, dissidence, noncompliance, infringement, infraction, nonobservance, disobedience, recalcitrance, contrariety, contumely, protest, recusance, revolt, rebellion, breaking away

► *662 Disobedience; 753 Protest*

3 **nonconformism**, unorthodoxy, heterodoxy, heresy,

iconoclasm, schism, revisionism, deviationism, unconventionality, unconventional behaviour, eccentricity, Bohemianism, hippiedom

4 unusualness, uncommonness, exceptionality, extraordinariness, uniqueness, rareness, rarity, individuality, singularity, originality, oddity, queerness, curiosity, peculiarity, strangeness, bizarreness, weirdness, outlandishness, freakishness, quirkiness, grotesqueness, grotesquerie, monstrousness

5 idiosyncrasy, quirk, peculiar trait, peculiarity, mannerism, kink

6 deviation, deviance, aberration, vagary, abnormality, anomaly, anomalousness, unnaturalness, mutation, perversion, variant, exception, special case

▶ *114 Diversity*

7 nonconformist, nonconformer, maverick, unconventionalist, *enfant terrible* (Fr), Bohemian, free spirit, dropout, hippie, beatnik, flower child, traveller, New-Age traveller, tramp, vagrant, hobo, gentleman of the road, bag lady, independent, free-thinker, outsider, odd man out, misfit, fish out of water, square peg in a round hole

▶ *250 Freedom*

8 dissenter, dissentient, dissident, protester, radical, revolutionary, zealot, fanatic, crank, iconoclast, schismatic, apostate, heretic, recusant, rebel, anarchist, renegade, young Turk, angry young man, punk, outlaw

9 hermit, loner, lone wolf, solitary, solitudinarian, solitaire, eremite, anchorite, marabout, ascetic, stylite, recluse, isolationist, seclusionist

10 eccentric, character, natural, original, oddity, odd fellow, odd customer, odd stick, queer specimen, freak, deviant, mutant, monster, wacko (Inf), weirdo (Inf), crackpot (Inf), rum one (*or* customer) (Inf), odd (*or* queer) fish (Inf), odd bod (Inf), oddball (Inf), screwball (US inf), one-off (Inf), card (Inf), case (Inf), headcase (Inf), nutcase (Inf), basketcase (Inf), loony (Inf), nut (Inf), fruitcake (Inf)

▶ *461 Insanity*

ADJECTIVES

11 nonconforming, unconformable, inconsistent, incongruous, incompatible, contrasting, different

▶ *100 Otherness*

12 nonconformist, unorthodox, heterodox, heretical, iconoclastic, schismatic, schismatical, dissident, dissenting, dissentient, contumacious, recusant, radical, revolutionary, rebellious, anarchic, renegade, uncompliant, unsubmissive, recalcitrant, contrary, defiant

▶ *661 Defiance; 662 Disobedience*

13 unconventional, maverick, independent, free-thinking, Bohemian, fringe, beat, hippie, wandering, nomadic, travelling, off the wall (Inf)

14 eccentric, offbeat, idiosyncratic, quirky, individual, individualistic, singular, original, rare, unusual, exotic, unique, exceptional, far out, way out, extraordinary, out of the ordinary, out of this world, out of the common, out on a limb, odd, queer, curious, peculiar, strange, bizarre, outlandish, weird, freakish, grotesque, monstrous, oddball (Inf), freaky (Inf), wacko (Inf), kooky (Inf), funny (Inf), rum (Inf), dolally (Inf)

▶ *461 Insanity; 619 Wonder*

15 irregular, nonstandard, against the rules, not done, out of place, out of line, out of step, out of tune, out of one's element, misplaced, displaced, stray, not cricket (Inf)

▶ *802 Wrong*

16 solitary, standoffish, unsociable, antisocial, lone, reclusive, isolated, aloof

17 abnormal, anomalous, unnatural, deviant, aberrant, mutant, variant

VERBS

18 not conform, dissent, protest, rebel, revolt, kick over the traces, get out of line, rock the boat, make waves

▶ *753 Protest*

19 be independent, break away, break step, break bounds, drop out, opt out, go one's own way, do one's own thing, go against the grain, swim against the tide, go out on a limb, buck the trend, march to a different drum, leave the beaten path, go off the beaten track, deviate, break with custom, break the habit, break the mould, not fit in, stick out like a sore thumb

20 infringe a law, break a law, commit crime, violate, disobey, break the rules, transgress

▶ *662 Disobedience*

ADVERBS

21 unconformably, inconsistently, incongruously, rebelliously, unconventionally, unusually, uncommonly, singularly, unnaturally, abnormally, queerly, peculiarly, strangely, oddly, outlandishly

22 out of step, out of keeping, out of line, out on a limb, independently, off the beaten track, out of the way

119 Equality

Equality may perhaps be a right, but no power on Earth can turn it into a fact. Honoré de Balzac.

All animals are equal but some animals are more equal than others. George Orwell.

NOUNS

1 equality, equivalence, equivalency, sameness, equal footing, same quantity, same degree, correspondence, parallelism, coequality, sharing, going halves, likeness, equiponderance, egalitarianism, fairness, democracy, equal rights, equal opportunity, justice, evenness, levelness, parity, par, even money, nothing in it, nothing to choose between, six of one and half a dozen of the other, quits (Inf), level pegging (Inf), going Dutch (Inf), an eye for an eye

▶ *115 Similarity; 188 Parallelism; 750 Agreement; 759 Exchange*

2 equilibrium, balance, poise, counterpoise, equipoise, even keel, evenness, steadiness, stable state, steady state, balance of power, balance of terror, mutually assured destruction, homeostasis, symmetry, proportion, stability, the same, status quo, stop, stasis, stalemate, deadlock, standstill, log jam (US), hung jury, hung parliament, tie, tied score, knotted score, tied game, draw, drawn game, drawn match, drawn battle, dead heat, photo finish, neck-and-neck race, nip-and-tuck race (US), ding-dong race, cliffhanger, touch and go, Greek meets Greek, deuce (Tennis), love-all (Tennis), a distinction without a difference, even break (Inf), fair shake (US inf)

3 **equalization**, equation, equilibration, balancing, weighing, adjustment, readjustment, weighing up, levelling up (*or* down), evening up (*or* down), rounding up (*or* down), compensation, positive discrimination, affirmative action, counteraction, offset, exchange, interchange, interchangeability, equipollence (*or* equipollency), isotropy, synonymity, synonym, reciprocation, fair exchange, barter, trade-off, exchange value, fair value, value, fair price, just price

► *393 Repair; 776 Trade; 790 Price*

4 **equilizer**, counterweight, ballast, makeweight, stopgap, counterpoise, stabilizer, rudder, fin, aileron, spoiler

5 **equal**, peer, twin, match, mate, fellow, counterpart, opposite number, coequal, compeer, comrade, companion, brother, sister, shadow, competitor, parallel, oppo (Inf)

► *569 Friendship*

ADJECTIVES

6 **equal**, equalized, same, similar, parallel, convertible, identical, equivalent, corresponding, coequal, egalitarian, democratic, equitable, just, fair, impartial, sharing, co-sharing, homologous, congruent, coextensive, equilateral, equidistant, coordinate, coincident, symmetrical, equable, stable, static, homeostatic, self-regulating, steady, balanced, fixed, round, rounded, square, squared, flush, even-sided, regular, well-ordered, commensurate, tantamount, equipollent, correspondent, proportionate, uniform, unvarying, monotonous, much the same, as broad as long, neither more no less, Dutch (Inf)

7 **dividing line**, radius, diameter, coordinate, equator, bisector, longitudinal line, latitudinal line

8 **on equal terms**, equally divided, even, par, on a par, at par, level, one-to-one, on the same level, on the same plane, on the same footing, half-and-half, neck-and-neck, nip-and-tuck (US), ding-dong, abreast, all one, all the same, drawn, tied, parallel, well-matched, evenly matched, matched, Greek meeting Greek, fifty-fifty (Inf), level pegged (Inf)

9 **adequate**, capable, fit, able, competent, suitable, apt, appropriate, up to, up to the mark

VERBS

10 **be equal**, be equal to, correspond to, accord with, agree with, coincide with, tie, draw, measure up to, come up to, match up with, parallel, break even, hold one's own, keep up with, keep in step with, keep pace with, keep abreast with, cope with, run abreast, run neck and neck, run nip and tuck (US), run level, make it all square, go shares, go halves, go Dutch (Inf), stack up with (Inf)

11 **equalize**, synchronize, even, redress the balance, balance, tally, make good, set off, accommodate, adjust, readjust, even up (*or* down), level, level up (*or* down), round, round up (*or* down), square (up), equate, strike a balance, poise, counterpoise, counterbalance, countervail, offset, cancel out, coordinate, integrate, proportion, fit, smooth, stabilize, compensate, come to the same thing, add up to the same thing, add nothing, detract nothing, leave no remainder, make no difference, right oneself, hold the road, rob Peter to pay Paul

ADVERBS

12 **equally**, on equal terms, similarly, coequally, correspondingly, equivalently, evenly, as good as, other things being equal, *ceteris paribus* (L), by the same token, identically, to all intents and purposes, as much as to say, to the same degree, *ad eundem* (L), at the same rate, *pari passu* (L), abreast, neck and neck, nip and tuck (US), in equilibrium, on an even keel

13 **equitably**, justly, with justice, fairly, in a fair way, impartially, without prejudice, democratically, congruently, coextensively, equidistantly, coincidentally, symmetrically, equably, stably, steadily, with a steady pace, roundly, squarely, regularly, uniformly, monotonously

120 Inequality

Men are by nature unequal. It is vain, therefore, to treat them as if they were equal. J. A. Froude.

NOUNS

1 **inequality**, disparity, difference, difference of degree, discrepancy, disproportion, heterogeneity, imparity, unlikeness, dissimilarity, nonuniformity, diversity, variability, patchiness, overbalance, overcompensation, addition, subtraction, imbalance, unbalance, odds, overload, overkill, top-heaviness, extra, shortage, shortfall, deficiency, inclination of balance, tilt, camber, list, superiority, inferiority, unevenness, oddness, odd number, casting (*or* deciding) vote, distortion, roughness, irregularity, asymmetry, lopsidedness, skewness, obliquity, disequilibrium, dizziness, the staggers, tilting of the scales, preponderance, overweight, underweight, lightness, insufficiency, insufficience, defect, disadvantage, handicap, loaded dice

► *114 Diversity; 116 Dissimilarity; 121 Superiority; 122 Inferiority; 211 Addition; 212 Subtraction; 218 Insufficiency; 234 Distortion; 414 Heaviness; 415 Lightness*

2 **injustice**, inequity, discrimination, prejudice, bias, partiality, lack of fairness, lack of democracy

► *465 Misjudgment*

ADJECTIVES

3 **unequal**, disparate, different, disproportionate, disproportioned, incongruent, dissimilar, diverse, disagreeing, unlike, uneven, odd, asymmetrical, distorted, irregular, scalene, unique, unequalled, at an advantage, at a disadvantage, inferior, below par, unequable, variable, variegated, deficient, defective, patchy, inadequate, insufficient, falling short, mismatched, ill-matched, ill-sorted, unbalanced, ill-balanced, lopsided, unwieldy, listing, leaning, canting, heeling, off balance, overbalanced, top-heavy, overweight, underweight, overloaded, underloaded, overshot, undershot, askew, awry, in disequilibrium, swinging, swaying, rocking, unstable, untrimmed, unballasted, uncompensated, losing balance, dizzy, giddy, toppling, falling, skewwhiff (Inf)

4 **unjust**, unfair, inequitable, discriminatory, prejudiced, biased, partial, undemocratic

VERBS

5 **be unequal**, not match, not equate, not balance, disagree, have the advantage, have superiority, prepon-

derate, outclass, outstrip, outrank, outvote, outweigh, outdo, surpass, play below par, overtop, give points to, have the disadvantage, not suffice, fall short, play above par, disadvantage, handicap, tip the scales, throw the casting vote, cast the deciding vote, throw off (*or* out of) balance, unbalance, disbalance, overbalance, unequalize, leave a remainder, make disproportionate, disproportion, skew, destabilize, upset, list, tilt, lean, heel, rock, swing, sway, lilt, fluctuate, vary, change, capsize, miss, overcompensate, overshoot, undershoot

6 **be unjust**, lack fairness, discriminate, be prejudiced, show prejudice, be biased, show bias, show partiality, be undemocratic

ADVERBS

7 **unequally**, disparately, differently, disproportionately, dissimilarly, diversely, nonuniformly, unevenly, off balance, off-centre, all at sea, asymmetrically, irregularly, variously, uniquely, variably, on the heavy side, at (*or* with) an advantage, out in front, at (*or* with) a disadvantage, on the light side, up against it, from behind, from the rear, deficiently, defectively, inadequately, insufficiently, with a handicap, with the odds stacked against one

8 **unjustly**, without justice, unfairly, without fairness, inequitably, discriminatorily, prejudicially, undemocratically

121 Superiority

My parents just didn't have that sense of innate superiority that the successful parents had. Michael Palin.

NOUNS

1 **superiority**, precedence, eminence, pre-eminence, primacy, greatness, preponderance, predominance, predomination, prepotence, prepotency, transcendence, transcendency, prestige, ascendancy, loftiness, altitude, sublimity, pride of place, first place, priority, seniority, influence, leverage, say, effectiveness, excellence, quality, perfection, high calibre, virtuosity, inimitability, incomparability, majority, supremacy, paramountcy, prominence, success, domination, privilege, right, prerogative, be-all and end-all (Inf), clout (Inf), pull (Inf)

► *129 Precedence; 230 Perfection; 246 Success*

2 **leadership**, authority, jurisdiction, power, authorization, rule, sway, control, hegemony, sovereignty, kingship, imperium, dominion, lordship, command, generalship, captaincy, directorship, management, prime ministership (*or* prime ministry), presidency, premiership, headship, mastership, top, spot (Inf)

► *12 Government and Politics; 396 Authority; 579 Management*

3 **advantage**, vantage, odds, points, handicap, edge, lead, commanding lead, being ahead, start, head start, running start, flying start, upper hand, whip hand, trump hand, something in hand, vantage point, vantage ground, coign of vantage, favour, lion's share, seeded position, winning position, pole position, inside track (Inf), bulge (Inf), drop (US), something extra, something in reserve, second wind, one-upmanship (Inf), card up one's sleeve (Inf), ace in the hole (Inf), jump (Inf)

4 **summit**, top, top of the pyramid, height, the heights, high ground, lofty ground, acme, zenith, pinnacle, peak, Everest, Nob Hill (US), climax, crest, crest of the wave, new high, record high, top rung of the ladder

► *154 Height; 174 Top*

5 **superior**, master, prophet, leader, chief, chief executive officer (CEO) (US), executive, manager, head, superintendent, foreman, commander, general, captain, ruler, king, emperor, sheik, sultan, prime minister, president, premier, governor, mayor, bishop, archbishop, cardinal, pope, rabbi, imam, elder, senior, principal, VIP (very important person), fugleman, headmaster, headmistress, head boy (*or* girl), first among equals, *primus inter pares* (L), boss (Inf), gaffer (Inf), Mr Big (Inf), the main man (Inf), the big cheese (Inf), the big enchilada (Inf), higher-up (Inf), brass hat (Inf), top dog (Inf), cock of the walk (Inf), Triton among the minnows (Inf), big fish (*or* frog) in a small pond (Inf), bigwig (Inf), big gun (Inf), big cheese (Inf), big noise (Inf), big enchilada (US inf), head honcho (Inf)

► *123 Importance; 400 Master*

6 **paragon**, genius, prodigy, nonpareil, virtuoso, prima donna, diva, first lady, expert, specialist, laureate, poet laureate, high-flier, mastermind, superman, superwoman, wonder woman, champion, victor, star, superstar, celebrity, winner, prizewinner, world-beater, record-holder, cup-holder, record-breaker, ace (Inf), whiz kid (Inf), pop star (Inf), chart-topper (Inf), the greatest (Inf), number one (Inf), numero uno (US inf), the most (US inf), the biz (Inf)

► *458 Wisdom; 485 Skill*

7 **the best people**, the best, the elite, top people, nobility, aristocracy, cream, cream of the crop (US), upper class, one's (elders and) betters, chosen few, select few, happy few, *crème de la crème* (Fr), the brightest and best, the pick of the bunch, the ruling class, the Establishment, the power structure, upper crust (Inf), the brass (Inf), top brass (Inf), big boys (Inf), top drawer (Inf), nobs (Inf), aristos (Inf)

► *2 Sociology; 573 Aristocrat*

VERBS

8 **be superior**, excel, exceed, predominate, transcend, prevail, better, get the better of, surpass, go one better, have it over one, get ahead of, shoot ahead of, win, triumph, defeat, overcome, best, beat, take command, rise above, tower above (*or* over), prove too much for, steal the show, come to the front, steal a march on, have the edge on (*or* over), beat the record, set a record, set a new record, improve on, reach new heights, reach a new high, rise to a peak, peak, culminate, climax, pass, outdistance, top, trump, overtrump, overplay, overstep, override, overjump, overleap, overtop, overlook, overshadow, eclipse, throw into the shade, extinguish, carry the day, batter, thrash, trounce, put to shame, have the whip hand, have the last laugh, carry off the laurels, wear the crown, bear the palm, win the prize, win the championship, win the blue ribbon, win the cup, hold all the cards, hold all the aces, steal someone's thunder, out-Herod Herod, cap (Inf), cap it all (Inf), hammer

(Inf), lick (Inf), beat (*or* lick) someone hollow (Inf), run rings (*or* circles) around, clobber (Inf), get (*or* have) the jump on (Inf), make mincemeat of someone (Inf)

▶ *329 Overstepping*

9 outdo, outplay, outrank, outvie, outbid, outshine, outstrip, outwit, outgo, outtrump, outrace, outpace, outmarch, outrun, outride, outjump, outleap, outstep, outrange, outdistance, outreach, outperform, outmanoeuvre

10 lead, take the lead, hold (*or* have) the lead, hold (*or* have) a healthy lead, head, direct, manage, run, front, spearhead, captain, take precedence, come first, rank first, rank, lead the dance, play the lead, star

11 get ahead, be ahead, hold (*or* have) an advantage, hold (*or* have) the edge, get a head start, get a running start, get off to a flying start, hold the upper hand, hold the whip hand, hold the trump hand, have something in hand, have a vantage point, have the lion's share, have the pole position, get the drop on someone (US), have something extra, have something in reserve, get a second wind, have the inside track (Inf), have a card up one's sleeve (Inf), have an ace in the hole (Inf), get the jump on someone (Inf)

ADJECTIVES

12 superior, greater, better, finer, higher, over, super, above, surpassing, eclipsing, overtopping, arch, exceeding, leading, outclassing, more than a match for, ahead, in a different class, more so, (always) one step ahead, above average, head-and-shoulders above, ascendant, in the ascendant, in ascendancy, preferred, favourite, top-drawer, cut above (Inf), one-up (on) (Inf), capping (Inf), streets ahead (Inf)

13 dominant, dominating, dictatorial, magisterial, authoritative, in authority, ruling, overruling, overriding, governing, ordering, imperial, sovereign, royal

14 best, best ever, greatest, supreme, superlative, crowning, cardinal, capital, matchless, unmatched, unmatchable, peerless, unparalleled, unrivalled, unequalled, unapproachable, unsurpassed, unsurpassable, unexcelled, inimitable, incomparable, beyond compare, beyond criticism, unique, without equal, *sans pareil* (Fr), *nulli secundus* (L), unbeatable, invincible, perfect, highest, maximal, maximum, max, most, uppermost, utmost, top, topmost, tiptop, prime, primary, dominant, predominant, preponderant, hegemonic, prevailing, paramount, foremost, headmost, main, chief, principal, central, focal, first, record, record-breaking, top-ranking, top-ranked, champion, gold-medal, victorious, winning, triumphant, world-beating, record-holding, A1, number-one, pre-eminent, supereminent, supernormal, immortal, ultimate, transcendent, transcending, transcendental, the last word in, upmost (Inf), topnotch (Inf), chart-topping (Inf), chart-busting (Inf), out of this world (Inf)

15 excellent, major, first-rate, first-class, top-flight, prestigious, elder, senior, master, superb, upper, prominent, eminent, important, distinguished, singular, outstanding, banner (US), star, blue-chip, rare, classic, marked, chosen, of choice, not like the rest, every inch a king (*or* queen)

ADVERBS

16 superiorly, with superiority, superlatively, surpassingly, exceedingly, dominantly, dominatingly, with a dominating manner, dictatorially, magisterially, authoritatively, with authority, royally, predominantly, preponderantly, mainly, in the main, chiefly, primarily, principally, paramountly, centrally, victoriously, triumphantly, eminently, transcendently, transcendentally, excellently, prestigiously, masterly, superbly, prominently, extremely, importantly, outstandingly, above average, above par, especially, rarely, advantageously, with an advantage, favourably, out of the common run, out of the top drawer

17 supremely, superlatively, *par excellence* (Fr), incomparably, without comparison, inimitably, peerlessly, unmatchably, matchlessly, unsurpassedly, unsurpassably, at the top of the scale, on the crest, at the peak, at the zenith, above all, to crown all, to the highest degree, far and away, by far, the most, even more, all the more, still more, more than ever, uniquely, first of all, second to none, *nulli secundus* (L), invincibly, out of this world, singularly, perfectly, in a perfect way

122 Inferiority

No one can make you feel inferior without your consent.
Eleanor Roosevelt.

NOUNS

1 inferiority, secondariness, supporting role, second rank, second class, lower class, inferior standing, inferior status, subordinate position, second best, ordinariness, obscurity, lowliness, baseness, subordination, abasement, dependence, humbleness, humility, subservience, insignificance, unimportance, back seat (Inf), second fiddle (Inf), second eleven (Inf), second string (US inf)

▶ *124 Unimportance; 623 Humility*

2 deficiency, disadvantage, handicap, impairment, stain, blemish, defect, fault, faultiness, imperfection, failure, failing, decline, worsening, deterioration, reversion, insufficiency, shortfall, poverty, beggarliness

▶ *214 Decrease; 218 Insufficiency; 245 Deterioration; 247 Failure*

3 inferior numbers, minority, fewness, littleness, smallness, meanness, meagreness, inadequacy

▶ *155 Lowness; 206 Few*

4 poor quality, badness, cheapness, shoddiness, worthlessness, shabbiness, vulgarity, bad taste, kitsch

▶ *236 Worthlessness; 675 Vulgarity*

5 inferior state, reduced circumstances, straitened circumstances, low point, low ebb, low, record low, all-time low, nadir, lowest point, minimum, floor, base, bottom, rock bottom, trough, depression, lowness, level, plain, flatness, sameness, mediocrity

6 inferior, younger, minor, junior, subordinate, subaltern, assistant, satellite, vassal, tributary, underling, henchman, menial, servant, retainer, subject, slave, hireling, agent, subsidiary, deputy, dupe, pawn, flunky, tool, instrument, dependant, follower, camp follower, supporter, backbencher, nonentity, poor relation, private, other ranks, lower classes, hoi polloi, lower orders, lowlife, criminal classes, scum, the masses, the mob, rabble, *canaille* (Fr), lesser creation, beasts of the field, beast, worm, serpent, loser, second, poor second, poor third, also-ran, second-stringer, second-rater, third-rater, reject, failure, lowest of the low, small fry (Inf), small beer (Inf), small potatoes (US inf), sidekick (Inf), no-hoper (Inf), groupie (Inf), gofer (US inf)

▶ *388 Submission; 401 Servant; 574 Commoner*

7 **inferior thing**, sweepings, leavings, remains, leftovers, crumbs, (load of) rubbish, seconds, rejects, B-movie, one-horse town (Inf), hick town (US inf), jerkwater town (US inf), lemon (Inf), (old) clunker (US inf), clinker (US inf), (load of) crap (Inf), (load of) cobblers (*or* old cobblers) (Inf)

VERBS

8 **be inferior**, fail, fall short, come short of, fall below, not come up to, not come up to scratch, not come up to the mark, not come up to standard, lag, trail, fall behind, drag one's feet, not make the grade, not pass, not pass the test, not be up to it (Inf)

9 **yield to**, give in to, cede to, concede the victory to, have to hand it to, hand to on a plate, bow to, knuckle under, submit, lose face, lose the upper hand, not hold a candle to (Inf), have (got) nothing on (Inf)

10 **follow**, take (*or* play) a supporting role, withdraw into the background, sink into obscurity, lapse into oblivion, be dependent upon, play second fiddle (Inf), take a back seat (Inf)

11 **become inferior**, get worse, worsen, go from bad to worse, lack, want, deteriorate, decline, diminish, descend, plunge, sink, sink low, sink without trace, plumb the depths, touch rock bottom, reach one's nadir, hit the skids (Inf), have the skids put under one (Inf)

ADJECTIVES

12 **inferior**, lesser, least, lower, lowest, bottommost, low-grade, not up to much, low-class, below the salt, second-best, second-rate, third-rate, low-caste, secondary, second-class, third-class, unworthy, nothing special, nothing to shout about, nothing out of the ordinary, nothing to write home about (Inf)

13 **insignificant**, minimal, minimum, small, inconsiderable, smaller, smallest, diminished, small-time, unimportant, lightweight, small-town, one-horse (Inf), hick (US inf), jerkwater (US inf)

14 **poor**, worthless, bad, shoddy, poor-quality, substandard, subnormal, tatty, cheap, scratch, makeshift, jerry-built, patchy, crummy (Inf), crappy (Inf), duff (Inf)

15 **subordinate**, minor, junior, dependent, subsidiary, subject, subservient, humble, tributary, ancillary, auxiliary, untouchable, criminal, lowlife

16 **ordinary**, middling, mediocre, common, vulgar, base, plebeian

17 **defective**, deficient, marred, spoilt, shopsoiled, shopworn (US), like the curate's egg, failed, failing, faulty, imperfect, weak, slight, feeble, unsound, underweight, not up to snuff (*or* scratch) (Inf)

18 **outclassed**, outshone, bested, worsted, trounced, beaten, defeated, humiliated, humbled, ruined, on one's beam-ends, not fit to hold a candle to (Inf), not in the same league (Inf), not a patch on (Inf)

ADVERBS

19 **inferiorly**, in an inferior state, in an inferior place, minimally, at a low ebb, in the lowest position, at one's lowest ebb, below standard, below the mark, under par, short of, less, less than, minus, beneath, under, below

20 **insignificantly**, inconsiderably, unimportantly, worthlessly, commonly, ordinarily, middlingly

21 **badly**, shoddily, unsoundly, cheaply, defectively, deficiently, imperfectly, weakly, slightly, feebly, poorly, subnormally

22 **basely**, subordinately, dependently, subserviently, humbly, unworthily

123 Importance

In heaven an angel is nobody in particular. George Bernard Shaw.

Art and religion first; then philosophy; lastly science. That is the order of the great subjects of life, that's their order of importance. Muriel Spark.

NOUNS

1 **importance**, first importance, primacy, pre-eminence, priority, urgency, precedence, prominence, distinction, eminence, reputation, repute, paramountcy, supremacy, superiority, essentiality, irreplaceability, import, consequence, significance, weight, weightiness, gravity, seriousness, solemnity, materiality, materialness, substance, pith, moment, substantiality, interest, consideration, concern, business, matter, account, note, notability, noteworthiness, memorability, mark, influence, prestige, size, magnitude, greatness, degree, rank, rating, standing, status, high standing, high approval, value, worth, excellence, merit, use, usefulness, strategic importance, utility, power, stress, emphasis, insistence, affirmation

▶ *95 Reality; 121 Superiority; 129 Precedence; 158 Size; 209 Grading; 235 Worth; 237 Usefulness; 334 Power; 395 Influence; 707 Affirmation*

2 **important matter**, vital concern, grave affair, crucial moment, turning point, crisis, breath of life, matter of life and death, no joke, no laughing matter, key point, notable point, memorandum, reminder, news, big news, great news, exploit, deed, great doings, big deal, important occasion, landmark, milestone, red-letter day, big day, great day, special day, the crunch (Inf), be-all and end-all (Inf), nothing to sneeze at (Inf), not peanuts (Inf), not chickenfeed (Inf), heavy scene (Inf)

▶ *287 Timeliness; 340 Action; 462 Memory; 601 Celebration; 741 News*

3 **chief thing**, what matters, the thing, great thing, main thing, issue, supreme issue, crux of the matter, crux, main topic, fundamentals, basics, grass roots, bedrock, core, hard facts, reality, essential, *sine qua non* (L), requirement, priority, first priority, choice, first choice, highlight, main attraction, main feature, best part, cream, *crème de la crème* (Fr), pick, elite, gist, meaning, substance, essence, essential part, sum and substance, heart, heart of the matter, kernel, nucleus, nub, nitty-gritty (Inf), nuts and bolts (Inf), centre, hub, nexus, fulcrum,

pivot, keynote, cornerstone, mainstay, linchpin, kingpin, head, spearhead, cardinal point, main point, salient point, half the battle, main part, chief hope, secret weapon, trump card, ace in the hole, big play, main chance, high spot (Inf)

► *95 Reality; 99 Essence; 135 Requirement; 173 Centre; 235 Worth; 469 Selection; 694 Meaning*

4 **bigwig**, important person, influential person, powerful person, personage, notable, notability, personality, captain of industry, magnate, mogul, tycoon, MD (managing director), lord of the manor, local worthy, pillar of the community, pillar of society, grandee, noble, aristocrat, member of the establishment, great man (*or* woman), top person, very important person, VIP, His (*or* Her) Highness, big name, high muck-a-muck, grand panjandrum, mandarin, leading light, master spirit, sage, kingpin, key person, expert, prima donna, star, lion, catch, great catch, favourite, uncrowned king (*or* queen), head, chief, leader, godfather, Big Brother, superior, superior person, the greatest, heavyweight (Inf), somebody (Inf), salt of the earth (Inf), top brass (Inf), brass hat (Inf), his (*or* her) nibs (Inf), biggie (US inf), big guy (US inf), big gun (Inf), big shot (Inf), big dooley (US inf), big noise (Inf), big wheel (Inf), big cheese (Inf), big enchilada (US inf), big fish (Inf), big but (Inf), big white Chief (Inf), big Chief (Inf), big Daddy (Inf), Mr Big (Inf), big-time operator (BTO) (Inf), wheeler-dealer (Inf), macher (US inf), big timer (Inf), big man (Inf), big man on campus (BMOC) (US inf), the man (US inf), Big John (US inf), first fiddle (Inf), superman (*or* superwoman) (Inf)

► *121 Superiority; 235 Worth; 334 Power; 395 Influence; 458 Wisdom; 485 Skill; 573 Aristocrat; 579 Management*

ADJECTIVES

5 **important**, primary, pre-eminent, urgent, imperative, prominent, distinct, eminent, weighty, grave, solemn, serious, pregnant, heavy, big, of consequence, consequential, significant, of importance, of weight, of concern, of consideration, considerable, worth considering, world-shattering, earth-shaking, momentous, critical, crucial, fateful, chief, cardinal, capital, staple, major, main, top, topmost, paramount, supreme, prime, foremost, leading, overriding, overruling, uppermost, most important, superior, essential, material, to the point, relevant, pivotal, central, basic, fundamental, bedrock, radical, going to the root, grass roots, worthwhile, to be taken seriously, not to be despised, not to be overlooked, valuable, necessary, vital, indispensable, irreplaceable, key, required, helpful, useful, telling, trenchant, meaningful, taking precedence, high-priority, high-level, top-level, summit, top-secret, secret, confidential, high, grand, noble, great, not to be sneezed at (Inf), hush-hush (Inf)

► *108 Relatedness; 121 Superiority; 129 Precedence; 135 Requirement; 158 Size; 173 Centre; 174 Top; 235 Worth; 237 Usefulness; 287 Timeliness; 694 Meaning; 737 Secrecy*

6 **notable**, noteworthy, remarkable, of mark, egregious (Lit), memorable, unforgettable, signal, first-rate, A1, gold-medal, silver-medal, bronze-medal, outstanding, sterling, excellent, superior, top-rank, top-ten, top-flight, ranking, high-ranking, prestigious, conspicuous, prominent, eminent, distinguished, exalted, august, dignified, imposing, leading, commanding, impressive, formidable, powerful, influential, newsworthy, front-page, eventful, stirring, breathtaking, shattering, monumental, world-shattering, seismic, earth-shaking, epoch-making

► *121 Superiority; 235 Worth; 334 Power; 395 Influence; 462 Memory*

VERBS

7 **be important**, matter, bulk large, weigh, carry, carry weight, tell, count, make an impression, make someone sit up and notice, attract attention, cast a long shadow, influence, motivates, signify, represent, import, mean, concern, interest, affect, have priority, take precedence, precede, come before, come first, predominate, take the lead, command respect, take the limelight, deserve notice, make a stir, create a sensation, make it big, make waves (Inf), cut a figure (Inf), cut a dash (Inf)

► *108 Relatedness; 121 Superiority; 129 Precedence; 395 Influence; 471 Attention; 480 Persuasion; 667 Respect; 694 Meaning*

8 **make important**, build up, give weight to, attach (*or* ascribe) importance to, seize on, fasten on, bring to the fore, place in the foreground, enhance, highlight, stress, emphasize, underline, labour, publicize, promote, advertise, put in bright lights, put in capital letters, headline, splash, bring to notice, bring to attention, put on the map, proclaim, announce, write in letters of gold, celebrate, lionize, honour, glorify, exalt, show respect, respect, value, esteem, regard, consider, take seriously, make a fuss about, make a stir, make much ado, make much of, put (*or* set) store by, think everything of, magnify, enlarge, exaggerate, overestimate, overrate

► *190 Expansion; 467 Overestimation; 601 Celebration; 667 Respect; 707 Affirmation; 727 Exaggeration; 740 Publication*

ADVERBS

9 **importantly**, primarily, pre-eminently, urgently, prominently, eminently, seriously, consequentially, significantly, materially, considerably, critically, crucially, largely, mainly, in the main, above all, to crown all, supremely, *par excellence* (Fr), notably, remarkably, memorably

124 Unimportance

ADJECTIVES

1 **unimportant**, without importance, insignificant, immaterial, circumstantial, not related, not apropos, off the point, irrelevant, ineffectual, uninfluential, forgettable, inconsequential, of no consequence, of no great weight, insubstantial, inessential, nonessential, not vital, unnecessary, dispensable, expendable, small, little, slight, light, inconsiderable, negligible, forgivable, venial, nondescript, inappreciable, not worth considering, not worth worrying about, of little value, out of the running

► *96 Unreality; 109 Unrelatedness*

2 **obscure**, disregarded, overlooked, neglected, not considered, beneath notice, beneath contempt, contemptible, good-for-nothing, wretched, miserable, measly, paltry, pitiful, pitiable, pathetic, impoverished, poor, mean, lowly, humble, sorry, scruffy, shabby, weak,

powerless, impotent, puny, no-account (US inf), no-count (US inf)

▶ *335 Powerlessness; 666 Negligence; 668 Disrespect; 782 Poverty*

3 **secondary**, minor, incidental, by-side, subsidiary, peripheral, low-level, of second rank

4 **trivial**, petty, trifling, nugatory, piffling, piddling, peddling (US), fiddling, niggling, technical, pettifogging, frivolous, puerile, childish, featherbrained, featherheaded, foolish, windy, airy, frothy, flimsy, insubstantial, superficial, shallow, not worth a second thought, small, tiny, teeny, teeny-weeny, teensy-weensy, toy, token, nominal, symbolic, small-time, lightweight, cheap, low-priced, five-and-dime (US), twopenny, twopenny-halfpenny, inferior, bad, poor, poor-quality, shoddy, jerry-built, tawdry, rubbishy, trashy, trumpery, catchpenny, pinchbeck, gimcrack, potboiling, pulp, worthless, valueless, useless, second-rate, third-rate, mediocre, commonplace, ordinary, usual, limited, parochial, parish-pump, uneventful, nit-picking (Inf), footling (Inf), grotty (Inf), dinky (US inf), rinky-dink (Inf), ricky-tick (US inf), two-bit (US inf), Mickey Mouse (Inf), no great shakes (Inf), one-horse (Inf), jerkwater (US inf)

▶ *157 Shallowness; 236 Worthlessness; 238 Uselessness; 459 Folly; 793 Cheapness*

NOUNS

5 **unimportance**, insignificance, immateriality, unrelatedness, irrelevance, irrelevancy, inconsequence, inessentiality, dispensability, expendability, lack of substance, insubstantiality, nothingness, nullity, vacancy, emptiness, secondariness

▶ *96 Unreality; 109 Unrelatedness*

6 **obscurity**, contemptibility, wretchedness, paltriness, meanness, weakness, powerlessness, impotence

▶ *335 Powerlessness; 668 Disrespect*

7 **triviality**, pettiness, lack of seriousness, frivolousness, frivolity, flippancy, snap of the fingers, superficiality, shallowness, smallness, cheapness, inferiority, worthlessness, uselessness, inutility, mediocrity

▶ *157 Shallowness; 236 Worthlessness; 238 Uselessness; 793 Cheapness*

8 **trifle**, insignificant matter, inessential, nonessential, triviality, technicality, detail, more detail, petty detail, details, trifles, minutiae, trivia, nothing, mere nothing, bagatelle, little bit, least bit, whit, jot, iota, tittle, trickle, dab, drop, drop in the bucket, drop in the ocean, damn, tinker's damn (*or* cuss), straw, rush, chaff, pin, button, feather, dust, cobweb, gossamer, tithe, fraction, small change, doit, cent (US), dime (US), twopence (*or* tuppence), fleabite, pinprick, scratch, child's play, nothing to it, taking candy from a baby, jest, joke, harmless joke, practical joke, farce, amusement, trifling fault, petty sin, venial sin, peccadillo, no matter, no great matter, accessory, secondary matter, sideshow, diversion, red herring, nothing of note, nothing in particular, matter of indifference, ordinary matter, nothing to boast of, nothing to write home about, nothing to speak of, nothing to worry about, not the end of the world, a mountain out of a molehill, a storm in a teacup, no great shakes (Inf), brass farthing (Inf), plugged nickel (US inf), bawbee (Scot inf), peanuts (Inf), chickenfeed (Inf), small beer (Inf), small potatoes (US inf)

▶ *265 Easiness; 467 Overestimation; 697 Nonsense*

9 **bauble**, toy, plaything, small toy, rattle, trinket, novelty, gewgaw, geegaw (US), gimcrack, knick-knack (*or* nick-nack), bibelot, bric-a-brac, doodah, bagatelle, tinsel, trumpery, frippery, froth, foam, trash

▶ *793 Cheapness*

10 **nonentity**, nobody, unimportant person, obscure person, unknown, nonperson, man of straw, figurehead, cipher, zero, nothing, sleeping partner, fribbler, trifler, beachcomber, smatterer, jack of all trades and master of none, mediocrity, lightweight, small fry, small change, small game, other ranks, commonalty, inferior, subordinate, underling, understrapper, second fiddle, servant, puppet, pawn, pawn in the game, piece on the board, instrument, Cinderella, poor relation, weak person, pipsqueak, scorned person, object of scorn, scum, scum of the earth, trash (US), poor White trash (US), small beer (Inf), small potatoes (US inf), stooge (Inf), squirt (Inf), creep (Inf), wimp (Inf), twerp (*or* twirp) (Inf), squit (Inf), slum hustler (US inf)

▶ *122 Inferiority; 401 Servant; 574 Commoner; 668 Disrespect*

VERBS

11 **be unimportant**, not matter, weigh light upon, have no weight, carry no weight, not weigh, not count, count for nothing, have no clout, have no pull, make no impression, mean little, signify little, cut no ice (Inf)

▶ *697 Nonsense*

12 **think unimportant**, disregard, overlook, pass over, underrate, underestimate, pejorate, shrug off, snap one's fingers at, hold cheap

13 **make unimportant**, trivialize, belittle, degrade, denigrate, demote, relegate, reduce one's importance, deflate one's ego, trim (*or* cut) down to size, knock down a few rungs, humiliate, disparage, mock, scorn, put down (Inf)

▶ *623 Humility; 660 Insolence*

ADVERBS

14 **unimportantly**, insignificantly, circumstantially, irrelevantly, ineffectually, inconsequentially, unnecessarily, negligibly, secondarily, incidentally, trivially, superficially

INTERJECTIONS

15 **no matter!**, never mind!, so what!, too bad!, *tant pis* (Fr)!, who cares?, who gives a shit (*or* toss *or* fuck) (Inf)?

125 Imitation

Imitation is the sincerest form of flattery. Charles Caleb Colton.

It is an infallible sign of the second-rate in nature and intellect to make use of everything and everyone. Ada Beddington Leverson.

NOUNS

1 **imitation**, copying, simulation, repetition, mimesis, parody, onomatopoeia, emulation, impersonation, imposture, the sincerest form of flattery, conformity, slav-

ishness, slavish, literalism, representation, reflection, mirror, echo, canon, fugue, mirroring, following

► *112 Repetition; 117 Conformity; 717 Representation*

2 **copy**, reproduction, image, likeness, replica, model, working model, duplication, duplicate, imitation, dummy, mock-up, facsimile, photocopy, picture, portrait, pastiche (*or* pasticcio), fair copy, faithful copy, carbon copy, clone, doppelgänger, simulation, fake, forgery, sham, bootleg, counterfeit, plagiarism, disguise, camouflage, crib (Inf), pony (US inf), phoney (Inf), rip-off (Inf)

► *115 Similarity; 561 Reproduction*

3 **mockery**, mimicry, pantomime, mime, satire, caricature, travesty, burlesque, impersonation, parody, apery, parrotry, spoof (Inf), takeoff (Inf), send-up (Inf), wind-up (Inf)

► *599 Humour; 719 Interpretation*

4 **camouflage**, protective colouration, mimicry, simulation, cosmetics, make-up, disguise, dissimulation, playing possum, playing dead

► *234 Distortion; 699 Falsehood; 718 Misrepresentation; 736 Concealment*

5 **duplicate**, photocopy, Xerox™, Mimeograph™, Photostat™, pantograph, graph, stencil, facsimile, fax, carbon copy, replica, model, tracing, rubbing, transfer, transcript, video recording, tape recording, print, offprint, photograph, negative, enlargement

6 **photocopier**, copier, duplicator, facsimile (*or* fax) machine, telex machine, stenciller, computer printer, camera, camcorder, video cassette recorder (VCR) (*or* video), tape recorder

7 **imitator**, ventriloquist, impersonator, female impersonator, mimic, imposter, poseur, charlatan, mountebank, hypocrite, Tartuffe, illusionist, follower, disciple, slave to fashion, sheep, ape, parrot, phoney (Inf), drag artist (Inf)

8 **copier**, copyist, plagiarist, counterfeiter, record pirate, forger, faker, painter, sketcher, printer, photographer, bootlegger

VERBS

9 **imitate**, emulate, follow, model oneself upon, ape, parrot, flatter, mirror, repeat, echo, reflect, copy after, model after, take after, take as a model, pattern after, take a leaf out of one's book, mimic, mock, caricature, satirize, burlesque, parody, travesty, impersonate, mime, spoof (Inf), take off (Inf), send up (Inf)

10 **copy**, reproduce, duplicate, clone, photocopy, Mimeograph™, stencil, plagiarize, borrow, replicate, counterfeit, fake, forge, pirate, crib (Inf)

11 **emulate**, follow, follow on, follow in the (foot)steps of, walk in the shoes of, follow in the wake of, follow the example of, follow suit, follow the herd, follow like sheep, play follow-my-leader, play follow-the-leader, climb (*or* jump) on the bandwagon

ADJECTIVES

12 **imitative**, imitated, derivative, unoriginal, parodied, transcribed, mimetic, onomatopoeic, emulating, echoing, aping, parrot-like, parroting, following, posing, apish, echoic, fugal

13 **imitation**, mock, sham, fake, forged, plagiarized, copied, counterfeit, ersatz, artificial, synthetic, cultured, man-made, pseudo (Inf), phoney (Inf), so-called, copycat (Inf), hokey (US inf)

ADVERBS

14 **imitatively**, apishly, like an ape, mockingly, onomatopoeically, onomatopoetically, unoriginally, artificially, synthetically, derivatively, quasi, verbatim, word for word, ditto, parrot-fashion, like a parrot, to the life, truly, to the letter, letter for letter, literally, literatim

126 Originality

An original writer is not one who imitates nobody, but one whom nobody can imitate. Vicomte de Chateaubriand.

NOUNS

1 **originality**, creativity, creativeness, creation, nonimitation, dissimilarity, genuineness, authenticity, inventiveness, innovation, initiation, imagination, original thought, individuality, independence, idiosyncrasy, eccentricity, novelty, newness, uniqueness, freshness, the one and only, new departure, precedence, beginning, something new, all my own work, a poor thing but my own

► *109 Unrelatedness; 116 Dissimilarity; 250 Freedom; 295 Newness; 477 Imagination*

2 **original**, autograph, holograph, signature, one's own hand, manuscript, first edition, source, model, paradigm, blueprint, pattern, mould, prototype, archetype, test case, precedent, pilot (film), invention, patented invention, trademarked product, copyrighted work, the real thing, the real article, the genuine article, it (Inf), absolutely it (Inf), the real McCoy (Inf)

► *99 Essence*

3 **originator**, inventor, creator, innovator, deviser, source, creative writer, composer, designer

► *139 Speciality*

ADJECTIVES

4 **original**, creative, inventive, imaginative, innovative, unimitated, first, first-hand, first in the field, pioneering, seminal, prototypal, archetypal

5 **novel**, unique, different, personal, individual, one-off, one and only, one of a kind, unparalleled, unprecedented, unheard of, offbeat, sui generis, inimitable, incomparable, new, fresh, avant-garde, revolutionary, transcendent, unmatched, out of reach

6 **authentic**, genuine, real, *echt* (Ger), bona fide, verified, unimitated, true, natural, sincere, unadulterated, uncopied, unduplicated, patented, copyrighted, trademarked

VERBS

7 **originate**, invent, innovate, create, devise, design, imagine, dream up, conceive, generate, pioneer, start, initiate, begin, auspicate (Lit), revolutionize, patent, blueprint, copyright, trademark

ADVERBS

8 **originally**, seminally, first, innovatively, conceptually, creatively, inventively, newly, freshly, imaginatively, with imagination, individually, personally, uniquely, differently, with a difference, inimitably, incomparably, without comparison, naturally, sincerely, truly, honestly

127 Inclusion

For years I have been known for saying 'Include me out'; but today I am giving it up for ever. Samuel Goldwyn.

NOUNS

1 **inclusion**, enclosure, encirclement, encapsulation, containment, comprisal, comprehension, involvement, implication, concern, reception, admission, admittance, admissibility, elegibility, participation, membership, presence, accommodation, room, space, capacity, volume, inclusiveness, inclusive language, coverage, full coverage, blanket coverage, wall-to-wall coverage, global approach, universality, generality, versatility, comprehensiveness, no exception, no omission, nothing left out, set, full set, complete set, package, package deal, complement, full complement, full quota, allowance, comprising, composition, composing, construction, make-up, constitution, constituting, incorporation, integration, embodiment

▶ *97 Presence; 138 Generality; 141 Space; 165 Enclosure; 204 Whole; 232 Completeness; 356 Creation; 370 Admittance*

2 **thing included**, inclusion, enclosure, ingredient, constituent, factor, additive, appurtenance, feature, component, component part, item, element, part, piece, bit, contents

3 **person included**, insider, participant, member, brother, sister, one of us, co-worker, staff member, staff, crew member, crew, team, workforce, complement, company, personnel, citizen

▶ *205 Part; 211 Addition; 405 Component; 406 Contents; 578 Worker*

VERBS

4 **include**, contain, hold, have, enclose, encircle, envelop, encapsulate, comprehend, involve, implicate, embrace, cover, encompass, take in, receive, admit, find room for, find space for, accommodate, count, number, boast, take into account, take into consideration, allow for, take account of, take cognizance of, recognize, allow (of), admit of, consist of, comprise, compose, be made up of, incorporate, integrate, embody, constitute, mean

▶ *165 Enclosure; 204 Whole; 232 Completeness; 370 Admittance; 376 Gathering; 410 Container; 763 Possession; 769 Receiving*

5 **be included**, be one of, be part of, make up, belong, enter into, become involved with, be mixed up in, be implicated in, participate, take part, share, merge, belong to, appertain to, pertain to, relate to

▶ *108 Relatedness; 763 Possession; 764 Sharing*

6 **subsume**, place under, count with, reckon among, number with, enumerate with, class with, classify as, categorize as (*or* with), enter, list, enter as, put in, put among, arrange in, add to

▶ *137 Class; 211 Addition; 368 Insertion; 407 Order; 409 Arrangement*

ADJECTIVES

7 **including**, inclusive, containing, holding, accommodating, having, allowing, considering, counting, consisting of, comprising, composed of, made up of, incorporating, incorporative, all-in, all-inclusive, all-embracing, comprehensive, wholesale, blanket, extensive, widespread, across-the-board, wall-to-wall, sweeping, global, worldwide, universal, expansive, broad-based, covering, umbrella, overall, general, encyclopedic, nonexclusive, nondiscriminatory, without exception, without omission

▶ *138 Generality; 204 Whole; 232 Completeness*

8 **included**, built-in, integrated, unsegregated, unseparated, constituent, component, part of, part and parcel of, inherent, intrinsic, belonging, pertinent, pertaining, appurtenant, admissible, admitted, allowed, eligible, in the same class, in the same league, classed with, classified with, related, akin, congenerous, congeneric, entered, listed, on the list, noted, recorded, added, linked, joined, combined, merged, inner, interior

▶ *99 Essence; 108 Relatedness; 137 Class; 172 Inside; 211 Addition; 220 List; 370 Admittance; 374 Combination; 405 Component; 744 Record; 763 Possession*

ADVERBS

9 **inclusively**, inherently, intrinsically, pertinently, as well as, comprehensively, universally, globally, generally, from A to Z, alpha to omega, et cetera, etc., and so on, and so forth, inside, within

▶ *172 Inside; 406 Contents*

128 Exclusion

To be an Englishman is to belong to the most exclusive club there is. Ogden Nash.

NOUNS

1 **exclusion**, noninclusion, omission, suppression, rejection, refusal, denial, forbiddance, prohibition, veto, proscription, interdiction, ban, taboo, embargo, bar, exception, an exception in favour of, exemption, special case, dispensation, special dispensation, relegation, exclusion order, lockout, picket line, closed door, no entry, nonadmission, shunning, blacklisting, blacklist, blackball, limitation, circumscription, segregation, sequestration, seclusion, ghettoization, discrimination, boycott, ostracism, preclusion, pre-emption, prevention

▶ *166 Limit; 255 Purity; 399 Veto; 465 Misjudgment; 470 Rejection; 709 Refusal; 758 Exemption*

2 **ejection**, eviction, expulsion, dismissal, redundancy, firing, suspension, disqualification, disbarment, removal, riddance, deletion, cancellation, elimination, obliteration, censorship, bowdlerization, expurgation, eradication, excommunication, deportation, extradition, banishment, exile, expatriation, the sack (Inf), sacking (Inf), the heave-ho (Inf), the elbow (Inf), the big E (Inf), the push (Inf), the shove (Inf), the boot (Inf)

▶ *358 Obliteration; 371 Expulsion*

3 **exclusion zone**, ghetto, no-go area, no-man's-land, outer darkness, the outside, pale, enclosure, dam, cofferdam, wall, fence, partition, screen, curtain, Iron Curtain, Bamboo Curtain, barricade, defensive wall, ditch, moat, rampart, barrier, customs barrier, tariff wall, economic zone, quarantine, isolation

▶ *165 Enclosure; 171 Outside*

4 **exclusiveness**, exclusivity, restrictiveness, closed shop, private club, clique, inner circle, members only, possessiveness, sole rights, monopoly, dog-in-the-manger policy, social discrimination, apartheid, colour bar, racial discrimination, xenophobia, sexual discrimination, speciesism

▶ *465 Misjudgment; 466 Discrimination; 683 Selfishness*

5 **excluded person**, nonmember, victim of discrimination, outsider, alien, odd man out, forgotten man, exile, outcast, pariah, outlaw, incomer, intruder, interloper, trespasser, burglar, invader, besieger

6 **thing excluded**, foreign body, contaminant, impurity, reject

▶ *100 Otherness*

VERBS

7 **exclude**, leave out, count out, not include, omit, miss, miss out, disregard, ignore, pass over, exempt, excuse, except, make an exception (of), treat as a special case, keep out, warn off, forbid, prohibit, disallow, veto, proscribe, interdict, ban, taboo, embargo, place under an embargo, put an embargo on, bar, suppress, stifle, relegate, put (*or* lay) aside, leave, give up, abandon, reject, refuse, deny, vote against, vote out, vote down, shut out, shut the door on, deny entry, spurn, blacklist, blackball, rule out, draw the line at, limit, circumscribe, enclose, wall off, fence off, screen off, curtain off, box off, segregate, discriminate against, sequester, quarantine, isolate, seclude, ghettoize, boycott, shun, cold-shoulder, send to Coventry, ostracize, preclude, forestall, pre-empt, prevent, not entertain (the possibility of), count out (Inf), include out (Inf)

▶ *165 Enclosure; 166 Limit; 255 Purity; 399 Veto; 470 Rejection; 709 Refusal; 758 Exemption*

8 **eject**, evict, expel, throw out, cast out, dismiss, make redundant, suspend, disqualify, disbar, unfrock, defrock, strike off, remove, dispense with, oust, thrust out, get rid of, take out, delete, cross out, strike out, rub out, blot out, cancel, eliminate, obliterate, censor, edit out, blue-pencil, bowdlerize, expurgate, eradicate, uproot, excommunicate, deport, extradite, banish, exile, outlaw, expatriate, sack (Inf), fire (Inf), send packing (Inf), kick out (Inf), give the elbow (*or* boot *or* push *or* shove) (Inf), give the big E (*or* heave-ho) (Inf)

▶ *358 Obliteration; 371 Expulsion*

9 **be excluded**, not belong, stay out, stay outside, go into exile, go into voluntary exile

▶ *171 Outside*

ADJECTIVES

10 **excluding**, exclusive, exclusionary, exclusory, close, closed, close-knit, clannish, cliquish, cliquey, narrow, restrictive, xenophobic, racist, sexist, restricted, limited, private, elite, select, choice, unique, sole, exemptive, interdictory, prohibitive, preventive, preclusive, pre-emptive, silent about

▶ *139 Speciality; 399 Veto; 469 Selection*

11 **excluded**, not included, absent, missing, not counted, left out, omitted, missed out, excepted, excused, exempt, exempted, barred, banned, embargoed, forbidden, taboo, prohibited, rejected, deleted, dismissed, evicted, expelled, shut out, shunned, blackballed, blacklisted, disbarred, struck off, outcast, exiled, untold, unsaid, unrecounted, unreported, inadmissible, beyond the pale, peripheral, extra, extraneous, foreign, not considered, disregarded, out of account, not in contention, outclassed, not in the same league, out in left field (US), out in the cold, precluded, pre-empted, forestalled, prevented

▶ *98 Absence; 100 Otherness; 399 Veto; 758 Exemption*

ADVERBS

12 **exclusively**, narrowly, with reservations, with restrictions, outside, excluding, exclusive of, except, excepting, except for, with the exception of, bar, barring, save, not counting, ignoring, omitting, outside of, short of, apart from, let alone

129 Precedence

Sir, there is no settling the point of precedency between a louse and a flea. Samuel Johnson.

NOUNS

1 **precedence**, antecedence, antecedency, preceding, going before, coming before, precession, anteriority, anteposition, taking precedence, pre-emption

▶ *130 Beginning; 293 Earliness*

2 **priority**, primacy, supremacy, dominion, pre-eminence, superiority, higher position, higher rank, seniority, prerogative, privilege, front, front position, forefront, vanguard, front of the queue, pole position, first place, the lead, pride of place, top of the tree, top priority, urgency, importance, preference, first concern

▶ *121 Superiority; 123 Importance; 167 Front*

3 **preparation**, groundwork, foundation, development, exploration, pioneering, innovation, avant-gardism, breakthrough, discovery, leap

▶ *243 Preparation; 449 Discovery*

4 **precedent**, antecedent, lead, example, standard, prototype, model, pattern, paradigm, yardstick, criterion

5 **preface**, foreword, proem, prologue, frontispiece, introduction, opening, opener, preliminaries, prelims, front matter, prelude, overture, curtain-raiser, apéritif, appetizer, hors d'oeuvre

▶ *130 Beginning*

6 **preview**, trailer, foretaste, taster, premonition, omen, warning

▶ *475 Prediction; 711 Warning*

7 **prefix**, prefixion, prefixation, prothesis

8 **precursor**, forerunner, foregoer, herald, harbinger, messenger, announcer, crier, frontrunner, lead runner, leader, vanguard, scout, reconnaissance party, guide, pilot, explorer, pathfinder, trailblazer, avant-garde, avant-gardist, groundbreaker, pioneer, frontiersman, founding father, trendsetter, innovator, inventor, discoverer

▶ *167 Front; 295 Newness; 396 Authority; 449 Discovery; 740 Publication*

9 **predecessor**, forebear, forefather, foremother, ancestor, firstborn, eldest, senior

ADJECTIVES

10 **preceding**, precedent, antecedent, anterior, precessional, leading, first, pre-emptive, earliest

▶ *167 Front*

11 prior, former, ex, late, erstwhile, one-time, previous, last, earlier, foregoing, above, above-mentioned, aforementioned, beforementioned, aforenamed, forenamed, aforesaid

▶ *284 Past Time; 293 Earliness*

12 primary, senior, superior, supreme, leading, preeminent, first, foremost, headmost, chief, elder

▶ *121 Superiority; 123 Importance; 396 Authority; 579 Management*

13 precursory, preliminary, initial, initiatory, introductory, elementary, basic, inaugural, baptismal, prefatory, prefatorial, proemial

▶ *130 Beginning*

14 preparatory, foundational, developmental, leading, guiding, piloting, exploratory, reconnoitring, founding, discovering, innovatory, innovative, avant-garde, pioneering, trailblazing, ground-breaking

▶ *243 Preparation; 295 Newness; 449 Discovery*

VERBS

15 precede, antecede, predate, antedate, come before, go before, lead, go first, go ahead of, guide, pilot, indicate, show (*or* lead) the way, point the way, head, spearhead, stand at the head, front, head up (Inf)

▶ *167 Front; 579 Management*

16 take precedence, have precedence, outrank, be superior, have priority, take priority, pre-empt

▶ *121 Superiority; 123 Importance*

17 give priority, put first, prioritize

18 forerun, pioneer, explore, reconnoitre, discover, invent, found, inaugurate, initiate, innovate, blaze a trail, set a trend, set the fashion, lead the dance, set the example, influence, pave the way, map out

▶ *130 Beginning; 295 Newness; 395 Influence; 449 Discovery*

19 forecast, foretell, presage, introduce, herald, usher in, ring in, predict, warn

▶ *11 Occultism; 475 Prediction*

ADVERBS

20 before, prior to, formerly, previously, earlier, beforehand

21 first, first and foremost, ahead, in front, in advance

22 in anticipation, in preparation, preparatorily, as a prelude, as a preliminary

23 primarily, supremely, pre-eminently, first, preemptively

130 Beginning

The distance doesn't matter; it is only the first step that is difficult. Marquise du Deffand.

NOUNS

1 beginning, start, commencement, opening, launch, onset, outset, outbreak, day one, square one

▶ *129 Precedence; 167 Front*

2 creation, the Creation, genesis, origin, origination, emergence, appearance, arrival, first beginnings, dawn, daybreak, break of day, morning

▶ *290 Daytime; 312 Arrival; 525 Appearance*

3 source, origin, provenance, fountainhead, wellspring, root, seed, seedbed, bud, germ, embryo, egg, nucleus, primordial soup, protoplasm, nest, womb, cradle

▶ *344 Cause*

4 conception, pregnancy, birth, nativity, delivery, parturition, pullulation, babyhood, cradle, infancy, first steps, childhood, youth

▶ *555 Youth; 561 Reproduction*

5 invention, discovery, formation, creation, origin, origination, conception, innovation, coinage

▶ *126 Originality; 449 Discovery*

6 inauguration, inception, inchoation, incipience, foundation, institution, establishment, setting up, installation, instigation, setting in motion, launch, embarkation

▶ *300 Motion; 449 Discovery*

7 rudiments, basics, elements, principles, first principles, preparation, groundwork, spadework (Inf)

▶ *99 Essence; 243 Preparation*

8 enrolment, investiture, induction, ordination, installation, initiation, initiation ceremony, christening, baptism, baptism of fire, honeymoon, house-warming

▶ *314 Entry*

9 premiere, first night, first time, first appearance, debut, coming out, curtain rise, curtain-raiser, maiden speech, inaugural address, presentation, launch, launching, flotation, opening, opening ceremony, unveiling, cutting the ribbon, laying the first stone, maiden voyage

▶ *308 Opening*

10 introduction, gambit, opening gambit, opener, opening line, lead-in, prelude, preamble, exordium, preface, foreword, front matter, preliminaries, prelims, title page, frontispiece

▶ *129 Precedence*

11 starting point, point of departure, starting post, starting block, starting pistol, zero hour, blastoff, opening, initiative, kickoff, bully off, jump-off, start, flying start, false start, square one (Inf)

▶ *313 Departure*

12 first move, commencing (*or* opening) move, first step, first base, first lap, first round, first stage, first leg, first innings, early stages, early days, first course, starter

▶ *25 Cookery; 129 Precedence; 293 Earliness*

13 new beginnings, fresh start, new departure, new tack, fresh fields, pastures new, new leaf, new page, new chapter

▶ *224 Change; 295 Newness*

14 beginner, starter, novice, learner, trainee, student, pupil, apprentice, probationer, recruit, raw recruit, tenderfoot, initiate, new boy, new girl, freshman, fresher, neophyte, tyro, debutante, greenhorn (Inf), rookie (Inf), deb (Inf)

15 baby, newborn, infant, fledgling, nestling, babe in arms, rugrat (Inf), ankle-biter (Inf), sprog (Inf)

▶ *555 Youth*

16 originator, initiator, maker, creator, inventor, architect, prime mover, the Creator, God

▶ *356 Creation*

VERBS

17 begin, start, commence, open, originate, initiate, establish

▶ *308 Opening*
18 make a beginning, make a start, get started, debut, set to work, put one's hand to the plough, go to it, go at it, embark on, set to (*or* about), turn to, fall to, go ahead, tackle, broach, face, get off to a good start, kick off, bully off, tee off, blast off, fire away (Inf), blast away (Inf), take the plunge (Inf), get one's feet wet (Inf), plunge into (Inf), head into (Inf), dive in (Inf), pitch in (Inf), get going (Inf), get weaving (Inf), get cracking (Inf), pull one's finger out (Inf), get the show on the road (Inf), put one's shoulder to the wheel (Inf)
▶ *340 Action; 342 Activity; 576 Work*
19 start off, start out, set off (*or* out), sally forth, make a move, get moving, get under way, set sail, take off, get on the road, hit the road (Inf)
▶ *313 Departure*
20 activate, start up, start going, turn on, switch on, set in motion, prompt, provoke, spark off, trigger off, apply the match, light the fuse, launch, set the ball rolling, kick-start, boot (*or* boot up)
▶ *344 Cause*
21 pioneer, explore, guide, pilot, lead, lead the way, set a precedent, head, spearhead, break new ground, open up, blaze a trail, trailblaze, take the first step, take the initiative, make the first move, break the ice
▶ *129 Precedence; 579 Management*
22 invent, discover, innovate, form, create, dream up, call into being, originate, generate, conceive, think of, coin, come up with, sow the seeds
▶ *356 Creation; 449 Discovery*
23 inaugurate, initiate, auspicate (Lit), establish, found, institute, set up, start up, install, induct, instigate, cause, commission, launch, float, present, be a founder member, be in at the beginning, be in on the ground floor
▶ *344 Cause*
24 open, unveil, cut the ribbon, declare open, lay the foundation stone, lay the first stone, cut the first turf
25 enrol, invest, crown, induct, ordain, install, institute, initiate, blood, baptize, christen
26 produce, give birth, bear, mother, father, sire, engender, bring into being, bring into the world, pullulate, breed, teem, bud, germinate
▶ *561 Reproduction*
27 emerge, appear, arrive, originate, arise, issue, issue forth, burst forth, erupt, spring, spring up, crop up, sprout, germinate, be born, come into the world, come into being, come into existence, come to be, come forth, see the light of day, dawn, come out, make one's debut
▶ *312 Arrival; 315 Exit; 525 Appearance*
28 begin again, recommence, make a fresh start, start afresh, start anew, turn over a new leaf, go back to square one, go back to the drawing board, return to go (Inf)
▶ *224 Change; 295 Newness*

ADJECTIVES

29 beginning, starting, commencing, opening, first, primary, initial, initiatory, initiative, maiden, early, formative
▶ *293 Earliness; 308 Opening*
30 front, frontal, leading, foremost, head
31 prime, primal, primordial, primeval, primitive, aboriginal, earliest, original, pristine
▶ *293 Earliness*
32 embryonic, budding, in the bud, nascent, germinal, inchoate, developing, fetal, pregnant, gestatory, parturient, dawning, emergent, new, fresh, raw, newborn, baby, infant, unfledged, young
▶ *295 Newness; 555 Youth; 561 Reproduction*
33 inventive, innovative, creative, original, conceptional, conceptive
34 inaugural, inauguratory, incipient, inceptive, inchoative, inchoate, foundational, institutionary, establishing, instigatory, instigative
35 rudimentary, rudimental, basic, elementary, fundamental
▶ *99 Essence*
36 introductory, preliminary, preparatory, precursory, initiatory, baptismal, prefatory, proemial, preludial, prepositive, prefixed
▶ *129 Precedence*
37 enrolled, installed, initiated, baptized, christened, premiered, inaugurated, presented, launched, opened, newly opened, unveiled

ADVERBS

38 in the beginning, at the beginning, at the first, at the very start, originally, initially
39 from the beginning, from the first, from the foundations, from its inception, from its birth, *ab ovo* (L), *ab initio* (L), *ab origine* (L), from scratch (Inf), from the word go (Inf)
40 first, firstly, primarily, at first, first thing, in the first place, first of all, first and foremost, before everything, for a start, as a start, for a beginning, for starters (Inf), for a kick-off (Inf)
41 in the bud, in embryo, in its infancy
42 principally, primarily, mainly, chiefly, basically, fundamentally

131 End

This is the way the world ends
Not with a bang but a whimper. T. S. Eliot.

NOUNS

1 end, ending, conclusion, finish, close, finis, finale, completion, wind-up (Inf)
2 cessation, ceasing, expiry, expiration, termination, stop, stoppage, halt, abrogation, cancellation, annulment
▶ *226 Stopping*
3 death, demise, decease, expiration, passing, departure, exit, release, quietus, last gasp, last breath, last words, swan song, end of the line, curtains (Inf)
▶ *582 Death*
4 annihilation, destruction, extermination, extinction, elimination, dissolution, liquidation, ruin
▶ *357 Destruction; 358 Obliteration*
5 fate, destiny, doom, doomsday, crack of doom, end of time, end of the world, eschatology, last judgment, Day of Judgment, apocalypse, twilight of the gods, Götterdämmerung

6 **end point**, terminus, terminal, end of the line, last stop, journey's end, destination

7 **limit**, boundary, frontier, border, rim, edge, fringe, verge, extent, extreme, extremity, pole, point, tip, peak, cusp, summit, zenith, top, last frontier, ends of the earth, where the rainbow ends

▶ *164 Edge; 166 Limit; 174 Top*

8 **tail**, tail end, butt, butt end, fag end, scrag end, bin end, bitter end, last penny, last cent, bottom dollar, dregs, lees, bottom of the barrel (Inf)

▶ *168 Back*

9 **close**, closing stages, last stage, final stage, last lap, home stretch, last round, last innings, last ball, last over, end of the day, evening, dusk, twilight, decline, end of the road, beginning of the end

▶ *245 Deterioration; 291 Night-Time*

10 **ending**, finale, finish, last act, climax, culmination, crowning glory, denouement, catastrophe, final curtain, epilogue, envoy (*or* envoi), coda, postscript (PS), end matter, back matter, appendix, suffix, last word, last laugh, punch line, sting in the tail, parting shot, Parthian shot

11 **finality**, deadline, time up, closing time, close of play, last orders, throwing (*or* chucking) out time, stop tap (Inf)

12 **end result**, result, effect, consequence, issue, outcome, upshot, payoff (Inf)

▶ *345 Effect*

13 **ender**, stopper, finisher, clincher, settler, crusher, knockout, knockout blow, deathblow, mortal blow, death stroke, finishing stroke, *coup de grâce* (Fr), the end (Inf), the limit (Inf), the last straw (Inf), the final blow (Inf)

14 **aim**, intent, intention, aspiration, goal, target, object, objective, purpose, reason, drift

▶ *482 Intention*

VERBS

15 **end**, conclude, finish, close, achieve, complete, finalize, resolve, decide, settle, finish off, round off, culminate, consummate, crown, cap, wind up (Inf), wrap up (Inf), be done with (Inf)

16 **cease**, stop, halt, terminate, discontinue, put an end to, put a stop to, scotch, bring to an end, call a halt, close down, shut down, shut up shop, ring down (*or* drop) the curtain, make an end of, finish off, kill off, polish off, dispose of, abort, annul, cancel, abrogate, put paid to, scrap (Inf), scratch (Inf), put the (tin) lid on (Inf), fold up (Inf), pull the plug on (Inf), put the stoppers on (Inf), draw stumps (Inf)

▶ *133 Discontinuity; 226 Stopping*

17 **kill**, extinguish, annihilate, destroy, exterminate, eliminate, dissolve, liquidate, wipe out, knock out, shoot down, kayo (*or* KO) (Inf), shoot down in flames (Inf), zap (Inf)

▶ *357 Destruction; 358 Obliteration; 382 Killing*

18 **come to an end**, draw to a close, go out, run out, run out of time, be over, be no more, fade out, fade away, peter out, fizzle out, tail off, die away, come to the end of the road

▶ *526 Disappearance*

19 **expire**, pass away, pass on, give up the ghost, draw one's last breath, die, die out, become extinct, end it all, commit suicide, come to a sticky end (Inf)

▶ *582 Death*

ADJECTIVES

20 **ending**, last, final, ultimate, terminal, concluding, conclusive, completing, completive, closing, finishing, definitive, culminating, culminative, consummative, consummatory, crowning, capping, apocalyptic, catastrophic, eschatological

21 **ended**, at an end, finished, complete, finalized, terminated, concluded, decided, settled, done, done with, through, over, all over, over and done with, dead and buried, all up (Inf), wound up (Inf), washed up (Inf), all over bar the shouting (Inf)

▶ *226 Stopping*

22 **cancelled**, off, all off, played out, called off, scrapped

23 **annihilated**, destroyed, exterminated, eliminated, dissolved, liquidated, ruined, doomed, fated, destined

▶ *357 Destruction*

24 **limiting**, boundary, frontier, bordering, fringing, furthest, extreme, polar, eventual, last

25 **hindmost**, rear, back, tail, end, endmost

▶ *168 Back*

ADVERBS

26 **finally**, lastly, in conclusion, eventually, ultimately, at last, at long last, in the end, at the end of the day, when all is said and done, in the final analysis, in the long run, when the chips are down (Inf)

27 **to the end**, to the bitter end, to the last gasp, for always, to the end of the road, till hell freezes over (Inf)

28 **conclusively**, definitively, once and for all, for good, for good and all, never again

132 Consecutiveness

NOUNS

1 **consecutiveness**, successiveness, succession, progression, queue, line-up, procession

▶ *289 Succession*

2 **consecution**, sequence, series, nexus, run, course, turn, one thing after another, order, ascending order, descending order, chronological order, list, catenation, concatenation, chain, chaining, train, file, line, queue, string, thread, ladder, stairs, staircase, steps, colonnade, scale, arpeggio, gamut, spectrum, rainbow, suite, suit of cards

▶ *407 Order*

3 **line**, lineage, bloodline, descent, pedigree, dynasty, family tree, genealogy

▶ *108 Relatedness; 129 Precedence*

4 **repercussion**, result, consequence, effect, causality, cause and effect, domino theory, knock-on effect, snowball effect, chain reaction, aftermath, backlash, reverberation

▶ *344 Cause; 345 Effect; 347 Counteraction*

5 **continuity**, continuousness, continualness, continuance, uninterruption, unbrokenness, uniformity, sameness, undifferentiation, monotony, endlessness, ceaselessness, incessancy, constancy, constant flow

▶ *111 Sameness; 134 Continuity; 279 Eternity*

6 **continuum**, continuous motion, cycle, circle, round,

endless round, rotation, periodicity, recurrence, assembly line, conveyor belt, treadmill, vicious circle (*or* cycle), endless band, Möbius strip (*or* band), Klein bottle

► *112 Repetition; 179 Circularity; 307 Rotation*

7 stability, steadiness, steady state, equilibrium, balance, routine, rut, flow, trend

► *228 Stability; 632 Habit*

8 procession, parade, pageant, promenade, march past, cortege, funeral procession, cavalcade, motorcade, caravan, train, line, column, file, crocodile, stream, steady stream, queue, traffic jam, tailback, gridlock

► *10 Ritual*

ADJECTIVES

9 consecutive, successive, succeeding, following, serial, seriate, sequential, in order, running, ongoing, progressive, chronological, catenary, ordinal, linear, lineal

► *289 Succession; 407 Order*

10 repercussive, causal, resultant, knock-on, consequential, reverberatory

► *344 Cause; 345 Effect*

11 continuous, continual, constant, incessant, perpetual, nonstop, endless, unending, never-ending, ceaseless, unremitting, interminable, unrelieved, unbroken, solid, smooth, serried, seamless, uninterrupted, uniform, undifferentiated, featureless, monotonous

► *111 Sameness; 134 Continuity; 279 Eternity*

12 cyclical, periodic, rhythmic, recurrent, repetitive

► *112 Repetition; 179 Circularity*

VERBS

13 be consecutive, succeed, come after, follow on, follow in a series, run on, progress

► *289 Succession*

14 continue, be continuous, not stop, extend, run, run and run, go on (and on), carry on

► *134 Continuity*

15 concatenate, catenate, connect, connect up, join, link, string, string together, thread, chain

► *373 Connection*

16 arrange consecutively, arrange in succession, array, range, rank, line, line up, align, string out

► *407 Order; 409 Arrangement*

17 line up, get in line, fall in, form a line, queue, queue up, form a queue, form a crocodile, parade, promenade, march past, file, file past, stream past

ADVERBS

18 consecutively, successively, in succession, serially, in a series, sequentially, in order, chronologically, progressively, on the run, one after another, one after the other, one behind the other, in turn, turn and turn about, on the trot (Inf)

19 continuously, continually, constantly, incessantly, perpetually, nonstop, without stopping, at one go, endlessly, ceaselessly, day in day out, round the clock, night and day

20 in a line, in a row (*or* queue), in file, in single file, in Indian file, in a crocodile, end to end, bumper to bumper, nose to tail

133 Discontinuity

The irregular side of nature, the discontinuous and erratic side – these have been puzzles to science, or worse, monstrosities. James Gleick.

NOUNS

1 discontinuity, discontinuousness, discontinuation, discontinuance, lack of continuity, disconnectedness, disconnection, disjunction, disjointedness, irregularity, intermittence, brokenness, fitfulness, spasmodicalness, sporadicalness, disorder, incoherence, confusion, nonuniformity, unevenness, roughness, jerkiness, bumpiness, joltiness, choppiness

► *114 Diversity; 299 Irregularity; 372 Separation; 408 Disorder*

2 cessation, cease, ceasing, end, stop, halt, termination, finish

► *131 End; 226 Stopping*

3 interval, interim, intermission, lull, pause, pause for thought, time-out, break, rest, stopover, time lag, time warp, jump in time, let-up (Inf)

► *146 Interval*

4 interruption, break, suspension, breach, gap, fissure, crevasse, fault, split, crack, fracture, cut, wound

► *146 Interval; 328 Disturbance*

5 caesura, hiatus, lacuna, diaeresis, ellipsis, pause, rest, fermata

6 intervention, interruption, interjection, interpolation, disturbance, disruption

► *328 Disturbance*

7 broken thread, broken train of thought, digression, non sequitur, parenthesis, nonseriality, nonlinearity, missing link, lost connection

ADJECTIVES

8 discontinuous, noncontinuous, unsuccessive, disconnected, disjointed, disunited, discrete, fragmented, broken, unjoined, unconnected, irregular, intermittent, fitful, spasmodic, sporadic, erratic, random, desultory, episodic, periodic, alternate, alternating, stop-go, on-off, gappy, incoherent, confused, nonuniform, uneven, rough, choppy, jerky, snatchy, bumpy, jolty, scrappy, bitty, patchy, spotty, dotted

► *114 Diversity; 299 Irregularity; 372 Separation; 696 Unintelligibility*

9 discontinued, nonrecurrent, unrepeated, ended, ceased, stopped, halted, terminated, finished, given up, no longer made

► *131 End; 226 Stopping*

10 interrupted, disturbed, disrupted, broken off, suspended

11 digressive, parenthetic, nonserial, nonlinear, nonsequential

VERBS

12 discontinue, end, put an end to, cease, stop, halt, terminate, finish, quit, give up, suspend, break off, cut off, cut short, leave off, refrain from, drop, call it a day (Inf), pack it in (Inf), call it quits (Inf)

► *131 End; 226 Stopping*

13 pause, pause for thought, take time out, take a sabbatical (*or* vacation *or* holiday), rest, have a break, lay over, stop over, let up, take five (Inf)

14 **disconnect**, break the connection, break (off), disjoin, disunite, separate, sever, cut

15 **lose one's train of thought**, digress, stray (from the subject), ramble, go off at a tangent, wander, go off the point

16 **interrupt**, disturb, disrupt, break one's chain of thought, intervene, interject, interpolate, interpose, put between, chip in (Inf), chime in (Inf), butt in (Inf), cut in (Inf), barge in on (Inf), put one's oar in (Inf)

▶ *328 Disturbance*

ADVERBS

17 **discontinuously**, periodically, at intervals, intermittently, fitfully, spasmodically, sporadically, irregularly, occasionally, infrequently, once in a while, now and then, off and on, by fits, in fits and starts, by degrees, here and there, *passim* (L), in spots, in dribs and drabs (Inf)

18 **disconnectedly**, disjointedly, brokenly, desultorily, by catches, by jerks, by skips, by fits and starts

134 Continuity

For men may come and men may go
But I go on for ever. Alfred, Lord Tennyson.

NOUNS

1 **continuity**, continuance, continuation, continuousness, constancy, progression, progress, succession, sequence, supplement, sequel, follow-up, postscript, repetition, recurrence, regular recurrence, flow, run, uninterrupted course, connectedness, connection, interconnection, interrelatedness, interrelation, cohesion, preservation, maintenance, sustenance, support

▶ *112 Repetition; 132 Consecutiveness; 225 Permanence; 228 Stability; 302 Forward Motion*

2 **protraction**, prolongation, long duration, extension, addition, furtherance, perpetuation, perpetuity, endurance, persistence, perseverance, survival, pursuit, resumption, recommencement, return

▶ *277 Duration; 640 Perseverance*

VERBS

3 **continue**, not stop, proceed, advance, make progress, progress, succeed, recur, repeat, connect, interconnect, interrelate, add, supplement, cohere, flow, run on, go on, follow through, maintain, keep up, sustain, support, uphold, preserve, harp on, keep on, keep alive, keep going, keep things moving, keep the ball rolling, keep the ball in play, keep the pot boiling, not interfere, let nature take its course, let things take their course, let sleeping dogs lie, let (*or* leave) alone, let be, keep on keeping on (US inf)

4 **protract**, prolong, further, extend, draw out, spin out, maintain, perpetuate, persist, persist in, persevere, pursue, pursue one's course, resume, follow up, pick up, take up again, continue, recommence, restart, return to, pick up where one left off, last, endure, remain, abide, live on, survive, stay, stay on, haunt, frequent, carry on, keep on, march on, roll on, plod on, keep at it, peg away, stick at it, stick to, go on for a long time, stand the test of time, live out one's time (*or* life), see the end of, hang on, hang on in there (US inf), stick it out to the bitter end (Inf), sit it out (Inf), carry one's bat (Inf)

ADJECTIVES

5 **continual**, continuous, continuing, in progress, ongoing, constant, steady, incessant, progressive, sequent, sequential, additional, supplemental, repetitive, recurrent, flowing, running, connected, unbroken, undivided, uninterrupted, interconnected, interrelated, cohesive, sustained, supported, not out (Inf)

6 **protracted**, prolonged, extended, lengthened, drawn out, interminable, unvarying, unending, unceasing, undying, unstoppable, unremitting, unrelenting, persistent, unfailing, inexhaustible, without respite, with no letup, nonstop, endless, enduring, lasting, everlasting, eternal, perpetual

ADVERBS

7 **continually**, continuously, constantly, repeatedly, endlessly, steadily, incessantly, progressively, sequentially, additionally, supplementally, repetitively, recurrently, without interruption, protractedly, interminably, unendingly, unceasingly, unremittingly, unrelentingly, persistently, inexhaustibly, enduringly, lastingly, everlastingly, eternally, perpetually, without respite, with no letup, nonstop, all the time, always, forever, on and on

INTERJECTIONS

8 **go on!,** carry on!, drive on!, keep it up!, keep going!, keep up the good work!, keep moving!, stick with it!, never say die!, onward and upward!

135 Requirement

NOUNS

1 **requirement**, essential, *sine qua non* (L), necessity, necessary, a must, desideratum, bare essentials, needs, necessities, necessaries, shopping list, order, indent, requisition, stipulation, specification, requisite, prerequisite, precondition, prior conditions, condition, proviso, provision, conditions, standards, request, ultimatum, injunction, command

▶ *397 Command; 617 Desire; 710 Request; 746 Negotiation*

2 **need**, want, lack, insufficiency, shortage, shortfall, slippage, gap, lacuna, gap in the market, demand, consumer demand, call, call for, run on, sellers' market, consumption, consumer consumption, input, intake, balance due, what is owing, debt, claim

▶ *98 Absence; 218 Insufficiency; 779 Market; 784 Debt*

3 **needfulness**, case of need, occasion, need for, necessity, essentiality, indispensability, desirability, necessitousness, neediness, want, pinch, poverty, poverty level, subsistence level, breadline, poverty trap, predicament, urgency, exigency, emergency, crisis, vitalness, matter of life and death, obligation, duty, bare minimum, the least one can do, face-saving measures, Queer Street (Inf)

▶ *123 Importance; 782 Poverty*

ADJECTIVES

4 **required**, essential, necessary, needed, needful, vital, indispensable, not to be spared, compulsory, obligatory, requisite, prerequisite, demanded, ordered, requested,

desired, wanted, in demand, called for, on call, earmarked, reserved, booked, on order, lacking, missing, absent

► *98 Absence; 218 Insufficiency; 386 Compulsion; 617 Desire; 710 Request*

5 **necessitous**, needy, in need, in want, poor, pinched, feeling the pinch, penniless, without a penny, bankrupt, destitute, on the breadline, at poverty level, below the poverty line, in the poverty trap, lacking, deprived of, needing, craving, longing for, hungry, starving, deprived, disadvantaged, bust (Inf), broke (Inf), dead (*or* stony) broke (Inf), stony (Inf), flat broke (Inf), in hock (US inf), down on one's uppers (Inf), skint (Inf), brassick (Inf)

► *218 Insufficiency; 617 Desire; 782 Poverty*

6 **demanding**, crying out for, calling for, imperative, urgent, exigent, exacting, crying, pressing, squeezing, pinching

VERBS

7 **require**, need, have need of, want, lack, not have, be without, stand in need of, feel the need for, have occasion for, have a vacancy for

► *98 Absence; 218 Insufficiency*

8 **miss**, long for, desire, desiderate, crave, need badly, ask for, call for, cry out for, clamour for, claim, put in a claim for, apply for

► *617 Desire*

9 **find necessary**, find indispensable, be unable to do without, must have, use, consume, take, use up

► *349 Use*

10 **necessitate**, render necessary, involve, create a need, oblige, compel, set requirements, make demands, demand, request, stipulate, dictate, order, send an order for, order by telephone, requisition, indent, reserve, book, earmark, set aside

► *386 Compulsion; 397 Command; 710 Request*

11 **be needy**, live in poverty, live on a pittance, live from hand to mouth, live on (*or* below) the breadline, be broke (Inf)

► *782 Poverty*

ADVERBS

12 **in need**, in want, necessarily, essentially, vitally, indispensably, *sine qua non* (L), of necessity, urgently, imperatively, in a pinch

136 Qualification

People at the top of the tree are those without qualifications to detain them at the bottom. Peter Ustinov.

NOUNS

1 **qualification**, qualifiedness, eligibility, suitability, suitableness, suitedness, acceptability, appropriateness, propriety, fitness, fittedness, preparedness, readiness, adequacy, sufficiency, efficacy, appositeness, relevance, applicability, aptness, aptitude, ability, ableness, capability, capableness, worthiness, deservedness, meritedness, dueness, entitlement, competence, efficiency, proficiency, potentiality, equipment

► *102 Possibility; 217 Sufficiency; 235 Worth; 237 Usefulness; 243 Preparation; 334 Power; 485 Skill; 801 Right*

2 **ability**, facility, faculty, capability, capacity, quality, mastery, attribute, tendency, endowment, natural power, innate ability, talent, skill, genius, flair, gift, bent, knack, what it takes (Inf), green fingers (Inf), know-how (Inf)

► *229 Tendency; 455 Knowledge; 458 Wisdom; 485 Skill; 693 Information*

3 **qualifications**, authorization, permit, licence, documentation, certification, certificate, diploma, degree, licentiate, baccalaureate, examinations, skills, expertise, experience, record, background, history, references, credentials, testimonial

► *3 History; 6 Education; 396 Authority; 485 Skill; 757 Permission*

4 **permission**, authorization, empowerment, enablement, investment, endowment, equipment

► *334 Power; 396 Authority; 669 Approval; 750 Agreement; 757 Permission; 768 Giving*

5 **modification**, qualification, adjustment, adaptation, alteration, change, variation, modulation, coordination, regulation, attunement, improvement, reconciliation, palliation, mitigation, softening, allowance, extenuating circumstances

► *244 Improvement; 549 Refinement; 750 Agreement*

6 **specification**, qualification, frame of reference, terms of reference, definition, determination, limitation, restriction, circumscription, bounding, confinement, control, check, demarcation, delimitation, prescription, proscription, mandate, bounds, conditions

► *165 Enclosure; 166 Limit; 755 Contract*

7 **condition**, qualification, grounds, reservation, parameter, stipulation, obligation, requisite, prerequisite, provision, proviso, *sine qua non* (L), limiting condition, boundary condition, escape clause, saving clause, small print

► *135 Requirement; 165 Enclosure; 166 Limit; 436 Provisions; 755 Contract*

8 **qualified person**, graduate, postgraduate, specialist, professor, expert, professional, ace, doctor, technician, skilled worker, consultant, adviser, boffin, connoisseur, virtuoso, perfect candidate, right person for the job (Inf), old hand (Inf)

► *455 Knowledge; 458 Wisdom; 485 Skill*

ADJECTIVES

9 **qualified**, capable, able, eligible, suitable, suited, well-adapted, acceptable, appropriate, fit, fitting, fitted, prepared, ready, apt, worthy, deserved, merited, competent, efficient, professional, businesslike, proficient, equipped, endowed, talented, gifted, masterful, expert, skilled, skilful, experienced, practised, versed, tried and tested, cut out for (Inf)

10 **authorized**, certified, empowered, enabled, permitted, licensed, entitled, allowed, documented

11 **modified**, adjusted, adapted, altered, changed, varied, variational, modulated, coordinated, conditioned, regulated, attuned, improved, reconciled, palliative, palliated, mitigatory, mitigated, softened, moderated

12 **conditional**, qualificatory, reserved, stipulatory, stipulated, parametric, obligatory, requisitional, provisional, provisory, specified, defined, definitional, mandatory, determined, limiting, limited, restricted, restrictive, circumscribed, contingent, bound, confined, controlled,

EDUCATIONAL QUALIFICATIONS

Advanced level (A level)
Advanced Ordinary level (AO level)
Advanced Supplementary level (AS level)
Associate of Arts (AA)
Bachelor of Arts (BA, AB)
Bachelor of Divinity (BD)
Bachelor of Education (BEd)
Bachelor of Laws (LLB)
Bachelor of Medicine (MB)
Bachelor of Music (BMus)
Bachelor of Science (BS, SB, BSc)
Certificate of the Business and Technician Education Council (BTEC)
Certificate of Prevocational Education (CPVE)
Certificate of Secondary Education (CSE)
Certificate of Sixth Year Studies (CSYS)
City and Guilds Diploma of Vocational Education
Diploma in Education (DipEd)
Diploma in Higher Education (DipHE)
Doctor of Divinity (DD)
Doctor of Education (DEd, EdD)
Doctor of Jurisprudence (JD)
Doctor of Letters (LittD, DLitt)
Doctor of Laws (LLD)
Doctor of Medicine (MD)
Doctor of Music (MusD, DMus)
Doctor of Philosophy (PhD, DPhil)
General Certificate of Secondary Education (GCSE)
General Diploma
General National Vocational Qualification (GNVQ)
Higher National Certificate (HNC)
Higher National Diploma (HND)
Higher Grade (*or* Highers)
International Baccalaureate
Master of Arts (AM, MA)
Master of Business Administration (MBA)
Master of Divinity (MDiv)
Master of Fine Arts (MFA)
Master of Library Science (MLS)
Master of Philosophy (MPhil)
Master of Science (MS, MSc)
National Certificate
National Vocational Qualification (NVQ)
Ordinary level (O level)
Postgraduate Certificate (PG Cert)
Postgraduate Certificate of Education (PGCE)
Scottish Certificate of Education (SCE)
Sixth Year Studies
Special (*or* Scholarship) level (S level)
Standard grade

checked, curbed, demarcated, delimited, prescribed, prescriptive, proscribed, proscriptive

VERBS

13 **qualify**, permit, authorize, empower, enable, invest, endow, equip, license, certify, pass, get into the final, get through

▶ *246 Success*

14 **be qualified**, suit, fit, suffice, apply, deserve, merit, know how, know one's job, have the knack, be trained (in)

15 **modify**, qualify, adjust, adapt, alter, change, vary, colour, modulate, coordinate, regulate, attune, improve, reconcile, temper, palliate, tone down, mitigate, moderate, soften, allow, extenuate, make allowances, make exception, set apart, split hairs

16 **specify**, qualify, frame, define, determine, limit, restrain, restrict, circumscribe, bind, confine, control, check, demarcate, delimit, prescribe, proscribe, stipulate, reserve, oblige, require, state terms, propose conditions

ADVERBS

17 **capably**, ably, masterfully, competently, efficiently, proficiently, professionally, skilfully, acceptably, aptly, appropriately, properly, fittingly, readily, worthily, deservedly

18 **with qualification**, conditionally, provisionally, contingently, restrictively, proscriptively, prescriptively, with the proviso, with strings attached

137 Class

All the world over, I will back the masses against the classes. William Ewart Gladstone.

The history of all hitherto existing society is the history of class struggles. Karl Marx.

NOUNS

1 **classification**, categorization, grouping, ordering, ranking, grading, hierarchy, taxonomy

2 **class**, subclass, category, subcategory, division, subdivision, bracket, set, subset, slot, niche, pigeonhole, compartment, pocket, section, subsection, group, subgroup, grouping, head, heading, list, listing, order, branch, department

▶ *205 Part; 220 List; 376 Gathering; 407 Order; 410 Container*

3 **kingdom**, subkingdom, phylum, subphylum, branch, subbranch, class, subclass, order, suborder, family, subfamily, genus, subgenus, species, subspecies, variety, subvariety, sex, gender

▶ *70 Animals; 77 Plants*

4 **type**, sort, kind, genre, variety, version, style, ilk, strain, species, genus, league, realm, domain, sphere, brand, make, mark, marque, label, shape, cast, form, mould, frame, stripe, feather, line, grain, kidney, stamp, colour, complexion, hue, character, nature, manner, persuasion, the like (*or* likes) of (Inf)

▶ *115 Similarity; 160 Form*

5 **social class**, social status, standing, station, position, grade, rating, pecking order, rank, tier, level, stratum, band, league, order, sphere, caste, group, set, clique, coterie

▶ *2 Sociology; 376 Gathering*

6 **students**, class, pupils, grade, form, year, track, year-group, subject-group, stream, discussion group

7 **lecture**, class, seminar, lesson, presentation, discussion

▶ *6 Education*

8 **genealogy**, line, lineage, birth, descent, ancestry, extraction, stock, strain, breed, pedigree, blood, kin, ilk, family, clan, tribe, race, religion, denomination, sect

▶ *7 Religion; 108 Relatedness*

9 **distinction**, prestige, merit, excellence, presence, bearing, breeding, style, chic

▶ *235 Worth; 549 Refinement*

ADJECTIVES

10 **classificatory**, classificational, categorical, hierarchical, taxonomic(al), indexical, tabular

11 **typical**, characteristic, representative, generic, stereotypical, special, specific, particular, peculiar, distinctive, defining, definitive

► *139 Speciality*

12 classed, classified, categorized, grouped, ranked, graded, rated, sorted, ordered, placed, pigeonholed

VERBS

13 class, classify, categorize, group, type, place, pigeonhole, catalogue, designate, fix, assign, dispose, distribute, label, brand

► *743 Identification*

14 sort, organize, assort, arrange, range, order, grade, rank, rate, divide, subdivide, analyse, tabulate, index, codify

► *372 Separation; 407 Order; 409 Arrangement*

15 be in a class of one's own, stand out, shine, be head and shoulders above the rest

ADVERBS

16 taxonomically, hierarchically, categorically, characteristically, typically, generically, specifically, distinctively, definitively

138 Generality

All generalizations are dangerous, even this one. Alexandre Dumas, fils.

NOUNS

1 generality, universality, general applicability, comprehensiveness, inclusiveness, globality, cosmopolitanism, internationalism

► *127 Inclusion*

2 catholicity, catholicism, ecumenicalism, ecumenicism, ecumenicity, Broad Church, eclecticism

3 nonspecificness, broadness, sweepingness, looseness, imprecision, inexactitude, broad canvas, broad spectrum, blanket coverage, dragnet, catch-all, open house, open letter, circular

► *150 Broadness; 274 Error*

4 widespreadness, extensiveness, rifeness, rampantness, pervasiveness, ubiquity, omnipresence

► *97 Presence*

5 averageness, ordinariness, standardness, rule, general rule, commonness, commonality, routineness, routine, habitualness, habit, usualness

► *117 Conformity; 140 Rule; 216 Average; 632 Habit*

6 average, run-of-the-mill, run, general run, ordinary run, common run, ruck, lowest common denominator

7 global view, world view, panorama, bird's-eye view, overview, overall picture

► *204 Whole; 518 Vision*

8 generalization, general idea, abstract, abstraction, sweeping (*or* loose *or* vague) statement, cliché, platitude, trite (*or* hackneyed *or* jaded) expression

► *745 Maxim*

9 everyman, everywoman, common man (*or* woman), common type, Mr (*or* Mrs) Average, man (*or* woman) in the street, man (*or* woman) on the Clapham omnibus, Joe Bloggs, Joe Public, John Q. Public, ordinary Joe, Joe Six-Pack (US), John Doe (US), girl (*or* boy) next door, little man

► *566 Humankind; 574 Commoner*

10 everyone, everybody, everything, all, one and all, all hands, the long, the short, and the tall, all and sundry, each one, each and every one, every mother's son, every man Jack, every Tom, Dick, and Harry, all the world and his wife (*or* brother), the whole world, *tout le monde* (Fr), everybody under the sun, Uncle Tom Cobbley and all, all and then some, the whole kit and caboodle (Inf), the whole shooting match (Inf), the whole shebang (Inf)

► *204 Whole; 232 Completeness*

11 general public, populace, common people, grass roots, rank and file, masses, multitude, hoi polloi, vox populi, rabble, mob, the great unwashed (Inf)

► *208 Multitude; 376 Gathering; 574 Commoner*

12 any, anything, anyone, anybody

13 whoever, whosoever, whomever, whomsoever, no matter who

14 whatever, whatsoever, what, which, what have you, what you will, no matter what (*or* which)

ADJECTIVES

15 general, universal, whole, comprehensive, fully comprehensive, inclusive, all-inclusive, nonexclusive, all-embracing, all-encompassing, all-covering, all-comprehending, all-pervading, overall, synoptic, heterogenous, diversified, miscellaneous, eclectic, liberal, catholic, ecumenical, cosmopolitan, broad-based, encyclopedic, blanket, extensive, sweeping, wide, broad, across-the-board, panoramic, bird's-eye

► *127 Inclusion; 150 Broadness; 204 Whole; 412 Mixture*

16 universal, cosmic, galactic, planetary, worldwide, global, international, cosmopolitan, national, nationwide, countrywide

17 widespread, extensive, rife, rampant, pervasive, ubiquitous, omnipresent, endemic, epidemic, pandemic

► *97 Presence*

18 far-reaching, wide-reaching, far-ranging, extensive, wide-ranging, far-flung

► *145 Distance*

19 prevailing, prevalent, widespread, common, popular, accepted, predominant, dominant, predominating, public, communal, community, unrestricted

20 generalized, nonspecific, unspecific, generic, approximate, inexact, imprecise, indefinite, indeterminate, undetermined, unspecified, ill-defined, broad, loose, vague, sweeping, abstract, nebulous

► *150 Broadness; 274 Error*

21 common, regular, standard, normal, usual, ordinary, average, unexceptional, run-of-the-mill, customary, habitual, routine, everyday, equotidian, familiar, accustomed, middlebrow, middle-of-the-road, conventional, pedestrian, vernacular, vulgar, down-market, plebeian

► *117 Conformity; 574 Commoner; 632 Habit*

22 commonplace, trite, platitudinous, hackneyed, uninspired, unimaginative, jaded, overused, overworked, stereotyped, stereotypical, common or garden

► *745 Maxim*

VERBS

23 generalize, universalize, globalize, catholicize, ecumenicize

24 broaden, widen, spread, expand, extend

► *150 Broadness; 190 Expansion*

25 broadcast, diffuse, disperse, disseminate, sow

► *377 Dispersal*

26 popularize, vulgarize, take to the masses

27 make a generalization, make a sweeping statement, generalize, deal in generalities, paint with a broad brush

28 prevail, predominate, dominate, obtain, reign, rule, be the rule, have currency, be the rage (Inf), be in (Inf), be the in thing (Inf)

▶ *334 Power; 396 Authority; 553 Fashion*

ADVERBS

29 generally, in general, generally speaking, broadly, broadly speaking, loosely, approximately

30 usually, as a rule, almost always, normally, ordinarily, typically, invariably, routinely, habitually, as a matter of course, in the usual course, without exception

▶ *632 Habit*

31 overall, on balance, on average, all things considered, all in all, on the whole, as a whole, in the long run, for the most part, in the main, mainly, mostly, largely, wholly

▶ *204 Whole; 205 Part*

32 universally, cosmically, internationally, nationally, widely, extensively, commonly, predominantly, invariably, everywhere, the world over

139 Speciality

NOUNS

1 speciality, specialness, specific quality, specificity, particularity, individuality, originality, uniqueness, distinctiveness, differentness, differentiation

▶ *126 Originality; 197 One; 743 Identification*

2 personality, character, nature, temperament, identity, persona, psyche, make-up

▶ *99 Essence*

3 characteristic, feature, distinctive feature, singularity, attribute, quality, property, trait, quirk, mannerism, peculiarity, idiosyncrasy, eccentricity, trick, mark, earmark, hallmark, trademark, stamp, seal, brand, cachet, token, mould, cut, shape, figure, configuration, taste, flavour, savour, smell, odour, aroma, touch, feel

▶ *160 Form; 495 Taste; 500 Smell*

4 specifications, conditions, qualifications, particulars, details, minutiae, essentials, essential facts, fundamentals, specs (Inf), nitty-gritty (Inf), fine print (Inf), nuts and bolts (Inf), ins and outs (Inf)

▶ *136 Qualification*

5 the special, the specific, the particular, the individual, the unique

▶ *197 One*

6 exception, exception to the rule, isolated instance, special case, anomaly, irregularity, peculiarity, departure, one-off

▶ *118 Nonconformity; 299 Irregularity*

7 special skill, expertise, métier, forte, strong point, genius, gift, talent, aptitude, skill

▶ *485 Skill*

8 specialization, special study, particularization, concentration, special interest, pursuit, line, field, area, sphere, school, subject, pet subject, special subject, major (US), vocation, trade, craft, bag (Inf), scene (Inf), thing (Inf), cup of tea (Inf), baby (Inf), claim to fame (Inf)

▶ *576 Work*

9 special, speciality of the house, *spécialité de la maison* (Fr), chef's special, dish of the day, feature, main feature, leader, leading item

10 specialized language, technical language, code, jargon, idiom, dialect, patois, idiolect, argot, technobabble (Inf), psychobabble (Inf)

▶ *5 Language and Linguistics*

11 identity, id, ego, self, oneself, real self, inner self, inner man (*or* woman), true self, subliminal self, subconscious self, hidden self, other self, alter ego, outward self, outer self, psyche, soul, spirit

12 I, me, myself, I myself, my humble self, we, I and I, us, ourselves, yourself, yourselves, himself, herself, itself, themselves, yours truly (Inf), number one (Inf)

13 person, character, individual, being

▶ *197 One; 566 Humankind*

14 specialist, authority, consultant, expert, master, connoisseur, professional, scholar

▶ *455 Knowledge; 485 Skill*

ADJECTIVES

15 special, especial, specific, particular, express, precise, individual, respective, individualistic, original, unique, quintessential, intrinsic, single, singular, distinct, distinctive, different

▶ *99 Essence; 126 Originality; 197 One; 273 Accuracy; 725 Clarity*

16 characteristic, distinguishing, personal, peculiar, idiosyncratic, idiomatic, unusual, out of the ordinary, extraordinary, uncommon, curious, marked, quirky, eccentric, typical, in character, true to form

▶ *118 Nonconformity; 743 Identification*

17 exceptional, special, one of a kind, unique, sui generis, inimitable, distinguished, remarkable, notable, noteworthy, esoteric, exotic, ageneric, way out

18 subjective, individualistic, solipsistic, egotistical, self-centred, selfish

▶ *683 Selfishness*

19 personal, private, intimate, inner

▶ *99 Essence*

20 personalized, individualized, custom-built, made-to-measure, bespoke, one-off

21 specialized, technical, specialist, expert, authoritative, knowledgeable, professional, scholarly

▶ *455 Knowledge; 485 Skill*

VERBS

22 characterize, distinguish, mark, differentiate, identify, brand, label, earmark, set apart, select, single out, pick out, point out, highlight, pinpoint, put one's finger on (Inf)

▶ *469 Selection; 726 Emphasis; 743 Identification*

23 particularize, descend to particulars, give details of, treat in detail, go into detail, spell out, come to the point, get down to brass tacks (Inf), get down to the nitty-gritty (Inf)

24 specify, stipulate, designate, determine, fix, set, assign, pin down, define, describe, delineate, depict, enumerate, quantify, itemize, list, denominate, name, signify, name names, point to (*or* out), mention, cite, quote

▶ *220 List; 721 Description*

25 excel, stand out, shine, in a class of one's own

► *121 Superiority; 235 Worth*

26 **personalize**, individualize, make one's own, put one's mark upon

27 **specialize**, specialize in, pursue, follow, study, major in (US), go in for, be into (Inf)

ADVERBS

28 **specially**, especially, specifically, particularly, expressly, exactly, precisely, distinctly, in particular, to be specific

29 **personally**, privately, individually, for one's own part, as far as one is concerned, in person, in the flesh

30 **characteristically**, peculiarly, uniquely, singularly, distinctively, markedly, exceptionally, remarkably, like no other, in its own way

31 **namely**, that is to say, *videlicet* (L), viz, to wit, i.e., e.g., *scilicet* (L), scil., sc

32 **severally**, each, apiece, respectively, singly, one by one, in turn, in detail, bit by bit

140 Rule

The exception proves the rule. Proverb.

Rules and models destroy genius and art. William Hazlitt.

NOUNS

1 **rule**, regulation, law, directive, ruling, injunction, statute, bylaw, order, prescription, standing order, decree, edict, ukase, fiat, commandment, act, covenant, ordinance, enactment

► *16 Law; 397 Command*

2 **canon**, code, rulebook, statute book, constitution, charter, jurisprudence

3 **rule** (*or* **law**) **of nature**, law of the jungle, sod's law, Murphy's law, Parkinson's law, law of averages, rule of thumb, natural (*or* universal) law, Procrustean law

4 **guide**, guideline, direction, instruction, prescription, precept, principle, tenet, keynote, axiom, maxim, canon, norm, standard, criterion, firm principle, hard and fast rule, condition

► *745 Maxim*

5 **precedent**, forerunner, example, model, pattern, prototype, formula

► *117 Conformity*

6 **custom**, habit, convention, tradition, wont, praxis, way, method, system, practice, procedure, routine, drill, rut, groove, policy, form, done thing, way of things, order of things, way things are

► *117 Conformity; 317 Way; 632 Habit*

7 **uniformity**, constancy, consistency, regularity, harmony

► *298 Regularity*

8 **authority**, command, direction, management, administration, influence, control, sway, dominion, domination, power, supremacy, mastery, reign, sovereignty

► *334 Power; 395 Influence; 396 Authority; 579 Management*

ADJECTIVES

9 **legal**, statutory, mandatory, compulsory, obligatory, *de rigueur* (Fr), regulatory, injunctive, prescriptive, procedural, administrative, official

► *16 Law*

10 **customary**, habitual, accustomed, wonted, conventional, traditional, regulation, standard, routine, usual, normal, typical, copybook, regulated, methodical, systematic, orderly

► *632 Habit*

11 **uniform**, constant, consistent, regular, harmonious

► *298 Regularity*

12 **ruling**, authoritative, commanding, influential, controlling, powerful, dominant, supreme, masterful, reigning, sovereign

VERBS

13 **rule**, ordain, decree, prescribe, lay down, lay down the law, make a ruling, decide, determine, adjudicate, judge, deem, find, resolve, settle, hand down a judgment, pronounce, declare, establish

► *464 Judgment*

14 **regulate**, standardize, normalize, systematize, organize, order, bring into line

► *407 Order; 409 Arrangement*

15 **be the rule**, hold sway, prevail, predominate

16 **direct**, guide, steer, control, regulate, lead, administer, manage, run, preside over, superintend, supervise, oversee, govern, rule, rule over, hold sway over, dominate, command, be in power, reign, wear the crown, sit on the throne, wield the sceptre, rule the roost

► *334 Power; 395 Influence; 396 Authority; 579 Management*

17 **obey orders**, follow the party line, go by the book (*or* rulebook), stick to the rules, watch one's step, stay (*or* keep) on the straight and narrow, mind one's p's and q's, toe the line (Inf), keep one's nose clean (Inf)

► *663 Obedience*

ADVERBS

18 **as a rule**, habitually, customarily, normally, ordinarily, usually, generally, as is one's wont, on the whole, for the most part, mostly, more often than not, mainly, in the main, chiefly, commonly

19 **to rule**, according to the rules, by the book, methodically, systematically

Spatial Relations

141 Space

Nature abhors a vacuum. François Rabelais.

Outer space is no place for a person of breeding. Violet Bonham Carter.

NOUNS

1 space, expanse, expansion, extent, extension, spatial extension, measure, dimensions, proportions, size, length, breadth, width, height, depth, depth of space, surface, area, diameter, circumference, tract, volume, cubic content, capacity

▶ *26 Measurement; 145 Distance; 148 Length; 156 Depth; 190 Expansion; 203 Quantity*

2 empty space, emptiness, void, nothingness, infinite space, infinity, unlimited space, sky, heavens, aerospace, airspace, outer space, interplanetary space, interstellar space, intergalactic space, space the final frontier (Inf)

▶ *29 Astronomy; 101 Unworldliness; 202 Infinity; 463 Forgetfulness*

3 geographical space, region, open space, clear space, clearing, glade, open country, wide-open space, wide horizons, expanse, stretch, tract, reach, green belt, hinterland, grassland, prairie, steppe, veld, plain, upland, moorland, back-country, outback (Aus), wild, wilderness, waste, desert, back of beyond

▶ *30 Earth Science; 86 Regions; 142 Location*

4 spaciousness, roominess, extensiveness, expansiveness, capaciousness, voluminousness, vastness, immensity

▶ *158 Size*

5 reserved space, room, accommodation, capacity, stowage, storage, storage space, seating capacity, seating, standing room, berthage, place, seat, berth, parking space

6 available space, room, latitude, leeway, scope, swing, play, margin, clearance, windage, amplitude, headroom, room overhead, headway, elbowroom, legroom, room to spare, sea room, seaway, airspace, breathing space, living space, Lebensraum, turning space, room to manoeuvre, room to swing a cat (Inf)

▶ *410 Container*

7 range, reach, coverage, scope, compass, radius, sweep, stretch, grasp, sphere, field, area, gamut, spectrum, array

▶ *166 Limit*

8 intervening space, distance, interval, gap, remove, break, hiatus, lacuna, blank, pause, interruption, intermission, lapse, time lapse, while, duration, span, spell, stretch, period, turn, go (Inf), trick (Inf)

▶ *145 Distance; 146 Interval; 275 Time; 276 Time Span; 277 Duration; 372 Separation*

9 fourth dimension, space-time, time-space, space-time continuum, continuum, relativity, Einstein theory, general theory of relativity

▶ *28 Physics; 275 Time*

10 spaceman, spacewoman, space traveller, astronaut, cosmonaut, rocket pilot, astronavigator, rocket man (Inf)

▶ *29 Astronomy*

ADJECTIVES

11 spatial, spacial, space, dimensional, proportional, two-dimensional, surface, radial, superficial, flat, three-dimensional (3-D), cubic, volumetric, stereoscopic, fourth-dimensional, space-time, spatiotemporal

12 extensive, regional, widespread, global, far-flung, far-reaching, wide-ranging, worldwide, interstellar, intergalactic, universal, boundless, infinite, unconfined, uncircumscribed, unrestricted

13 spacious, roomy, airy, lofty, capacious, voluminous, commodious, cavernous, sizeable, ample, vast, great, immense, enormous, outsized, oversized, expansive, extended, long, broad, wide, deep, high, amplitudinous

▶ *158 Size; 434 Air*

ADVERBS

14 spatially, three-dimensionally, spatiotemporally

15 spaciously, sizeably, amply, voluminously, capaciously, immensely, vastly, deeply, expansively, spatially, spatiotemporally, three-dimensionally

16 extensively, widely, everywhere, globally, universally, intergalactically, here there and everywhere, in every place, in all places, in every quarter, in all lands, in all areas, the (whole) world over, throughout the world, on the face of the earth, under the sun, high and low, upstairs and downstairs, near and far, far and wide, inside and out, no stone unturned, in every nook and cranny, all round the globe, all around, all over, all over the map (Inf), all over the shop (Inf), all over hell (Inf), every which way (Inf), hell west and crooked (Inf), six ways from Sunday (Inf)

17 from end to end, from pole to pole, from coast to coast, from top to bottom, from north to south, from

Land's End to John O'Groats (Inf), from here to the back of beyond (Inf), from hell to breakfast (Inf), from here to eternity (Inf), from here until kingdom come (Inf)

18 from everywhere, from the four corners of the earth (*or* world), from every place, from the furthest corners of the earth (*or* world), from all points of the compass

19 to all places, to the four winds, to the ends of the earth (*or* world), to hell and back

VERBS

20 extend, expand, lengthen, widen, dilate, distend, deepen, raise, spread out, spread, range, sweep, reach, stretch, cover, encompass, span, straddle, enclose, surround, environ, contain, hold

▶ *165 Enclosure*

21 space, space out, spread out, place at intervals, organize, empty, make room for, order, rank, array, lay out, set out, measure out, proportion, time, mark time, pause, wait, break, lapse, omit, leave out

▶ *407 Order; 409 Arrangement*

142 Location

A place for everything, and everything in its place. Samuel Smiles.

NOUNS

1 location, locality, situation, place, site, position, whereabouts, locale, spot, setting, environs, environment, habitat, parts, haunt, patch, pitch, beat, territory, seat, station, post, base, neck of the woods (Inf), stamping ground (Inf), hole (Inf), turf (Inf), manor (Inf)

▶ *143 Situation; 170 Surroundings; 565 Habitat*

2 exact location, spot, point, pinpoint, dot, benchmark, grid reference, map reference, coordinates, bearings, compass direction, eastings and northings, latitude and longitude, declination, chart, map, plan, address, postal address, postal district, postcode, zip code (US)

▶ *30 Earth Science; 484 Plan; 733 Address*

3 locating, pinpointing, finding the spot (*or* place), homing in on, finding, discovering, detecting, unearthing, running to earth, laying one's hands (*or* fingers) on, turning up, tracking down, pinning down, coming across, chancing upon, hitting on

▶ *449 Discovery*

4 placing, locating, situating, siting, placement, emplacement, establishment, installation, settling, fixation, fixing, posting, stationing

5 topography, geography, cartography, chorography, surveying, triangulation, navigation, orienteering, geodesy

▶ *26 Measurement; 30 Earth Science; 86 Regions*

ADJECTIVES

6 located, situated, placed, positioned, sited, set, stationed, posted, established, installed, settled, fixed, emplaced, planted, ensconced

7 found, located, locatable, discovered, pinpointed, detected, unearthed, tracked down, pinned down

8 locational, situated, positional, topographical, geographical, cartographical, navigational, geodetic, surveyed

VERBS

9 locate, situate, place, site, position, emplace, put, put in place, install (*or* instal), establish, set up, plant, ensconce, station, post, billet, quarter, base, fix, spot (Inf), stick (Inf)

10 settle, take up residence, establish residence, move in, ensconce oneself, stay at, inhabit, dwell, reside in, locate (Inf), relocate, change address, move, move house

▶ *144 Displacement; 564 Inhabitant*

11 find, find the spot, pinpoint, zero in on, home in on, discover, detect, unearth, run to earth, lay one's hands (*or* fingers) on, turn up, track down, pin down, come across, chance upon (*or* on), hit upon (*or* on), get a fix, get a bearing, calculate (*or* fix) one's position, navigate, survey, triangulate

▶ *210 Calculation*

ADVERBS

12 where, whereabouts, whither, here, hereat, hereabouts, just here, on this spot, at this point, in this vicinity (*or* neighbourhood), in place, *in situ* (L), *in loco* (L), on location, on site, on the spot, there, thereat, in that place, thereabouts, thither, to that place, here and there, in places, in spots, *passim* (L)

13 topographically, geographically, cartographically, geodetically

143 Situation

Whose Finger do you want on the Trigger When the World Situation Is So Delicate? Headline from the *Daily Mirror.*

NOUNS

1 situation, position, orientation, direction, bearings, latitude, longitude, aspect, side, frontage, altitude, topography, geography, location, site, setting, place, spot, point, seat, venue, scene, scenery, locale, locality

▶ *142 Location*

2 circumstances, setting, ground, background, footing, basis, stand, standing, standpoint, viewpoint, position, place, context, factor, contingency, condition, juncture, case, state, state of affairs, status quo, climate, atmosphere, scene, scenario, lay of the land, the way of the world, how things stand, how it is, outfit, layout (Inf), ball game (Inf), kettle of fish (Inf), setup (Inf), picture (Inf), whole picture (Inf), the size of it (Inf)

▶ *170 Surroundings; 221 State; 222 Circumstances*

3 difficult circumstances, tricky situation, plight, predicament, fix, jam, trouble, pickle (Inf), hot water (Inf)

▶ *249 Adversity; 264 Difficulty*

4 employment, post, position, job, service, station, office, place, livelihood, occupation, situations vacant, sitvac column (Inf), berth (Inf), billet (Inf)

▶ *576 Work*

5 rank, sphere, status, standing, station, position, position in society, estate

▶ *407 Order*

ADJECTIVES

6 situated, positioned, located, set, placed, sited, seated, stationed, orientated, directed towards, pointed, appointed, posted, employed, occupational

7 **situational**, directional, topographical, geographical, local

8 **circumstantial**, contextual, contingent, grounded, based, climatic, atmospheric, surrounding, troublesome, difficult

VERBS

9 **be situated**, be located, be, lie, stand, rest, sit, take up a position

▶ *93 Existence*

10 **situate**, place in a situation (*or* position *or* location), place, position, locate, site, put, install (*or* instal), stand, fix, set, set up, station, post, deploy, direct, orientate

ADVERBS

11 **geographically**, topographically, locally, round about, around, round here, in place, in position, on site, *in situ* (L), on location

12 **circumstantially**, contingently, contextually, as it stands, under the circumstances

144 Displacement

Now, here, *you see, it takes all the running* you *can do, to keep in the same place. If you want to get somewhere else, you must run at least twice as fast as that!* Lewis Carroll.

NOUNS

1 **displacement**, dislocation, dislodgment, disturbance, disarrangement, derangement, derailment, shift, shunt, move, movement, motion, removal, relocation, translocation, transference, transshipment, switch, swerve, veer, deflection, knocking off course (*or* out of place), aberration, perturbation

▶ *325 Deviation; 328 Disturbance*

2 **removal**, extraction, extrication, taking away, uprooting, ripping out, tearing out, pulling up, plucking out, pulling out by the roots

▶ *212 Subtraction; 369 Extraction*

3 **replacement**, substitution, supplantation, transfer, relocation, removal, forcible removal, overthrow, coup, deposition (*or* deposal), unseating, takeover, evacuation, ejection, banishment, expulsion, eviction, deportation, diaspora, enforced repatriation, ethnic cleansing

▶ *224 Change; 364 Repulsion; 371 Expulsion; 381 Attack; 762 Substitution*

4 **relegation**, demotion, downgrading, dismissal, discharge, lay-off, redundancy, marching orders, the sack, the boot (Inf), one's cards (Inf), the elbow (Inf), the big E (Inf), the (old) heave-ho (Inf), the bounce (Inf), boot-out (Inf), kicking downstairs (Inf), kicking upstairs (Inf)

▶ *313 Departure; 470 Rejection; 767 Disposal*

5 **disconnection**, separation, detachment, unhinging, disjointedness, dislocation, putting out of joint, disarticulation, disengagement, luxation, dismemberment

▶ *372 Separation; 375 Disintegration*

6 **misplacement**, mislaying, mislocation, misputting, losing, wrong place

7 **displaced person**, refugee, evacuee, exile, deportee, outcast, stateless person, homeless person, waif, stray, fish out of water, square peg in a round hole

▶ *371 Expulsion*

ADJECTIVES

8 **displaced**, dislocated, dislodged, disturbed, disarranged, deranged, derailed, shifted, shunted, moved, removed, relocated, transferred, switched, swerved, veered, deflected, knocked off course (*or* out of place), disturbing, shifting, moving, swerving, veering

9 **removed**, extracted, extricated, uprooted, ripped, torn, wrested, pulled, drawn, plucked, pulled out by the roots

10 **replaced**, overthrown, deposed, substitute, supplanted, transferred, removed, relocated, banished, thrown out, expelled, deported, exiled, ostracized, stateless, outcast, refugee, evicted, evacuated, unhoused, unharboured, houseless, homeless, rootless, of no fixed abode, of no fixed address, out of place, in the wrong place, like a fish out of water, like a square peg in a round hole, out of one's element

11 **relegated**, demoted, downgraded, dismissed, discharged, laid off, sacked, out of a job, booted out (Inf), out on one's ear (Inf), out on one's arse (Inf)

12 **disconnected**, disjointed, out of joint, disarticulated, dislocated, unhinged, disengaged, dismembered, detached, separated

13 **misplaced**, mislaid, misput, mislocated, lost, missing, gone missing (*or* astray)

VERBS

14 **displace**, dislodge, dislocate, unseat, upset, disturb, disarrange, disorder, disorganize, disrupt, derail, knock (*or* throw) off course, throw out of gear, switch, swerve, veer, deflect, shift, move, shunt, transfer, transport, relocate, move lock, stock, and barrel, translocate, transship

15 **remove**, extract, extricate, draw out, pull out, pull up, uproot, root out (*or* up), pull up by the roots, rip out, tear out, pluck out

16 **replace**, substitute, supplant, overthrow, dethrone, unseat, depose, oust, usurp, stage a coup, take over, banish, expel, exile, ostracize, deport, cast out, turn out, evict, eject, boot out (Inf), boot out on one's ear (*or* arse) (Inf)

17 **relegate**, demote, downgrade, discharge, dismiss, let go, make redundant, lay off, sack, fire, kick downstairs (Inf), kick upstairs (Inf), kick out (Inf), boot (Inf), give the (old) heave-ho (Inf), give the elbow (Inf), give the big E (Inf), give one's cards (Inf), give the brown envelope (Inf), give one's walking papers (Inf), give one's marching orders (Inf), show the door (Inf)

18 **disconnect**, unhinge, undo, disjoint, put out of joint, disarticulate, dislocate, luxate, pull apart, fracture, shatter, dismember, separate, detach

19 **misplace**, mislay, misput, mislocate, put in the wrong place, lose, lose track of

ADVERBS

20 **out of place**, in the wrong place, on the move, in transit, on the run, instead, in place of, in lieu, as an alternative

21 **disconnectedly**, disjointedly, detachedly, separately, fragmentedly

145 Distance

The distance doesn't matter; it is only the first step that is difficult. Marquise du Deffand.

NOUNS

1 **distance**, farness, remoteness, inaccessibility, aloofness, removal, separation, divergence, deviation, dispersion, perspective, long range, astronomical distance, deep space, depths of space, light years, infinity

▶ *141 Space; 146 Interval; 148 Length; 311 Divergence; 372 Separation*

2 **great distance**, step, long way, great way, good way, fair way, long run, long haul, long trail, day's march, marathon, far cry, tidy step (Inf), miles away (Inf), long chalk (Inf)

3 **distant place**, background, periphery, circumference, horizon, skyline, offing, vanishing point, where the earth meets the sky, godforsaken place, the back of beyond, back o'Bourke (Aus), outback, outskirts, outpost, antipodes, pole, the North Pole, the South Pole, Thule, ultima Thule, Pillars of Hercules, Timbuktu, Outer Mongolia, Darkest Africa, Siberia, Pago Pago, the Great Divide, Far East, Far West, four corners of the earth, ends of the earth, world's end, end of the rainbow, outer space, the moon, the middle of nowhere (Inf), God knows where (Inf), the sticks (Inf), the boondocks (US inf), the boonies (US inf)

▶ *163 Outline; 166 Limit; 168 Back*

4 **reserve**, aloofness, standoffishness, shyness, coldness, coolness

▶ *634 Avoidance; 655 Unsociability*

VERBS

5 **be distant**, outlie, outrange, outdistance, stand far away, lie out of the way, stretch to the ends of the earth

6 **keep away**, keep off, keep one's distance, keep at a distance, remain at a distance, stand off, stand away, stand aloof, stand back, distance onself, keep away from, keep out of the way of, keep a safe distance from, keep clear of, stand clear of, steer clear of, give a wide berth to, keep at arm's length, keep apart, separate, space out

7 **reach**, stretch, extend, go, carry, reach out, stretch out, outreach, outstretch, reach to, stretch to, extend to, go to, lead to, run to, carry to, get to, come to

ADJECTIVES

8 **distant**, far, far off, far away, far-flung, remote, yonder, yon (Dial), ulterior, farther, further, outlying, offshore, inaccessible, out-of-the-way, godforsaken, exotic, antipodean, hyperborean, overseas, transatlantic, transpacific, transoceanic, transmarine, ultramarine, transcontinental, transalpine, transmontane, tramontane, ultramontane, transpolar, transpontine, transmundane, ultramundane, out of this world, away, apart, asunder, separated, distal, peripheral, long-distance, long-range, out of sight, out of range, out of reach, farthest, farthermost, furthest, furthermost, ultimate, extreme, terminal, unget-at-able (Inf)

9 **reserved**, aloof, standoffish, unapproachable, untouchable, shy, cold, cool

ADVERBS

10 **distantly**, remotely, far, afar, far off, far away, a long way off, a long way away, over the hills and far away, overseas, abroad, afield, far afield, far and wide, far and near, widely, broadly, to the ends of the earth, out of this world, in the distance, yonder, yon (Dial), in the background, in the offing, on the horizon, as far as the eye can see, out of sight, out of hearing, out of earshot, out of range, out of reach, beyond reach, out of bounds, too far, further, farther, ahead, in front, behind, way behind, way in front, away, off, at a distance, at arm's length, apart, asunder, aloof, aside, astray, clear, wide, wide of the mark, in the back of beyond, out of the way, in the sticks (Inf), in the boondocks (US inf), in the boonies (US inf)

11 **reservedly**, aloofly, standoffishly, in a standoffish mood, shyly, coldly, coolly, with an unapproachable manner

146 Interval

I sometimes wonder which would be nicer – an opera without an interval, or an interval without an opera. Ernest Newman.

NOUNS

1 **interval**, gap, space, distance, room, margin, clearance, headroom, leeway, freeboard, distance between, space between, intervening space, interspace, spacing, single space, double space, half space, en space, em space, thin space, hair space, interruption, daylight, firebreak, passage, separation, time interval, discontinuity, hiatus, lacuna, caesura, jump, leap

▶ *18 Music; 133 Discontinuity; 141 Space; 275 Time; 308 Opening; 372 Separation*

2 **crack**, crevice, cleft, fissure, scissure, interstice, chink, cranny, check, flaw, hairline crack, notch, nick, cut, incision, gash, slit, split, rift, fault, rupture, rent, tear, break, fracture, breach, hole, opening, aperture, orifice, cavity, groove, slot, furrow, trench, ditch, dyke, moat, haha

▶ *156 Depth*

3 **gulf**, abyss, chasm, void, gape, gorge, ravine, canyon, box canyon, crevasse, chimney, gully, gulch, ghat, pass, defile, col, couloir, coulee (US), flume, kloof (S Africa), donga (Aus and NZ), draw, clough (Dial), valley, dell, cwm (Welsh)

▶ *183 Concavity; 318 Passage*

VERBS

4 **space**, space out, interspace, separate, break up, part, set apart, keep apart, place at intervals, make a space, make room, clear

5 **crack**, cleave, check, notch, nick, cut, incise, gash, slit, split, split apart, rive, rupture, rend, tear, break, fracture, breach, open, gape, groove, slot, furrow, trench, ditch

ADJECTIVES

6 **spaced**, spaced-out, interspaced, interspatial, interstitial, separate, separated, parted, set apart, removed, placed at intervals, intervallic, discontinuous

7 **cracked**, cleft, cloven, fissured, fissile, cut, slit, split, riven, ruptured, rent, torn, broken, fractured, open, gaping, gappy, grooved, furrowed, rimose, dehiscent

ADVERBS

8 **apart**, separately, discontinuously, at intervals, with a break, with an intermission, with an interval, off and on, now and then, now and again, every so often, interspatially, interstitially

147 Closeness

NOUNS

1 **nearness**, closeness, proximity, propinquity, immediacy, intimacy, inseparability, handiness, convenience, accessibility, approximation, approach, convergence, juncture, collision course, conjunction, syzygy, appulse, perigee, perihelion

▶ *97 Presence; 280 Immediacy; 310 Convergence*

2 **short distance**, no distance, little way, short way, short cut, step, stone's throw, spitting distance, striking distance, earshot, gunshot, bowshot, close range, close quarters, brink, verge, hair's-breadth, fingerbreadth, finger's-breadth, finger's width, inch, millimetre, ace, near miss, photo finish, near thing (Inf), narrow squeak (Inf), level pegging (Inf)

▶ *164 Edge*

3 **juxtaposition**, apposition, adjacency, nearness, closeness, contiguity, contiguousness, abuttal, abutment, tangency, touching, touch, contact, continuity, junction, joining, connection, union, bordering, border, borderland, frontier, buffer state

▶ *132 Consecutiveness; 147 Closeness; 164 Edge; 166 Limit; 267 Stickiness; 492 Touch*

4 **meeting**, encounter, confrontation, interface, intercommunication, impingement, touch, nudge, brush, graze, glance

5 **near place**, vicinity, vicinage, neighbourhood, locality, precinct, environs, surroundings, purlieus, confines, approaches, foreground, front, ringside seat

▶ *170 Surroundings*

6 **neighbour**, next-door neighbour, bystander, onlooker

7 **interface**, place of contact, meeting point, adjoining section, threshold, battlefront, division line, shared frontier, common boundary, common border, political border, Iron Curtain, Bamboo Curtain, forty-ninth parallel, Mason-Dixon Line, Berlin Wall, Hadrian's Wall, Antonine Wall, Maginot Line, Siegfried Line

▶ *113 Opposition; 147 Closeness; 166 Limit; 310 Convergence; 384 Defence; 492 Touch*

8 **interaction**, common ground, cooperation, compatibility, working together, permeation, interpenetration, blend, dovetail, fitting together

▶ *267 Stickiness*

ADJECTIVES

9 **near**, nigh, close, proximate, proximal, side-by-side, shoulder-to-shoulder, cheek-by-jowl, hand-in-hand, arm-in-arm, intimate, elbow-to-elbow, bumper-to-bumper, inseparable, neck-and-neck, close-run, nearby, in the vicinity, in the neighbourhood, local, home, wayside, roadside, inshore, neighbouring, vicinal, next-door, next, adjoining, contiguous, immediate, nearest, closest, on the spot, to hand, at hand, handy, convenient, accessible, at one's fingertips, nearer, closer, approximate, approximating, nearing, approaching, converging, convergent, forthcoming, warm (Inf), hot (Inf), level pegging (Inf), get-at-able (Inf)

10 **juxtaposed**, juxtapositional, juxtapositive, adjacent, near, close, tangent, tangential, contiguous, adjoining, abutting, touching, in contact, continuous, joined, connecting, intercommunicating, linking, bordering, conterminous, coterminous, side-by-side, cheek-by-jowl, face-to-face, nose-to-nose, eyeball-to-eyeball, end-to-end, elbow-to-elbow, bumper-to-bumper, nose-to-tail

11 **meeting**, impinging, rubbing, brushing, grazing, glancing

ADVERBS

12 **near**, nigh (Lit), close, closely, at close quarters, at close range, not far, nearby, close by, hard by, fast by, in the vicinity, in the neighbourhood, locally, next-door, hereabouts, thereabouts, about, around, around and about, at hand, near at hand, close at hand, at one's fingertips, at one's elbow, at one's side, at one's feet, under one's nose, within reach, within range, within earshot, within hearing, within call, within sight, a stone's throw away, only a step, just around the corner, on one's doorstep, in one's own back yard, in spitting distance, as near as makes no difference, verging on, on the verge of, on the brink of, by a hair's-breadth, by the skin of one's teeth, by a whisker, on the tip of one's tongue

13 **nearly**, almost, well-nigh, not quite, just about, all but, as good as, near enough, virtually, practically, for all practical purposes, to all intents and purposes, more or less, give or take a little, approximately, roughly, in round numbers, generally speaking, say

14 **beside**, alongside, in juxtaposition, adjacently, tangentially, in contact, contiguously, continuously, side by side, cheek by jowl, face to face, nose to nose, eyeball to eyeball, end to end, elbow to elbow, bumper to bumper, nose to tail

VERBS

15 **be near**, stand close to, lie in the vicinity of, lie in the neighbourhood of

16 **near**, come near, get near, get close, move close, bring near, draw near, draw nigh, approach, converge, verge on, close up, move up, get warm (Inf), get hot (Inf)

17 **stay near**, keep close to, follow, shadow, dog, sit on the tail of, tread on the heels of, breathe down the neck of, hover over, tailgate, go with, hang around, hang about, stick to, cling to, hug, embrace, skirt, tail (Inf)

18 **juxtapose**, appose, adjoin, abut, butt, touch, make contact, come into contact, bring into contact, join, connect, border, neighbour, be next to, be beside, be side by side, place side by side

19 **meet**, encounter, confront, interface, intercommunicate, impinge, hit, nudge, jostle, elbow, rub, brush, kiss, graze, scrape, shave, skim, glance, rub shoulders (*or* elbows) with (Inf)

148 Length

A line is length without breadth. Euclid.

ADJECTIVES

1 **long**, lengthy, tall, high, lengthened, extended, pro-

longed, protracted, drawn out, long-drawn-out, dragged out, stretched, outstretched, stretched out, spun out, strung out, straggling, overlong, extensive, far-reaching, far, sustained, polysyllabic, sesquipedalian, sesquipedal, interminable, endless, no end to, without end, long-winded, verbose, as long as one's arm, a mile long, shoulder-length, waist-length, knee-length, ankle-length, full-length, unabridged

► *145 Distance; 154 Height; 156 Depth; 158 Size; 190 Expansion; 232 Completeness; 270 Vagueness; 277 Duration; 731 Talkativeness*

2 **elongated**, oblong, rectangular, elliptical

► *178 Straightness*

3 **longitudinal**, lengthways (*or* lengthwise), longways (*or* longwise), endways (*or* endwise), linear

NOUNS

4 **length**, longitude, longness, overall length, lengthiness, tallness, height, distance, measure, mileage, yardage, footage, extent, reach, span, stretch, duration, stretching out, spinning out, stringing out, drawing out, dragging out, lengthening, elongation, extension, prolongation, protraction, sesquipedalianism, infinity, interminability, endlessness, full length

5 **piece**, portion, section, measure, roll, bolt, coil, run, strip, band, stripe, bar, streak, line, string, queue, crocodile (Inf), single file

6 **oblong**, rectangle, ellipse

7 **measure of length**, inch, foot, yard, mile, nautical mile, knot, millimetre, centimetre, metre, kilometre, light year, parsec

► *26 Measurement*

8 **measure of time**, millisecond, second, minute, hour, day, week, month, year, decade, lifetime, century, millenium

VERBS

9 **be long**, extend, stretch, stretch out, outstretch, reach out, outreach, spread-eagle, stretch oneself, crane, crane one's neck, stand on tiptoe

10 **lengthen**, extend, stretch, produce, continue, increase, elongate, unroll, uncoil, unfurl, unfold, drop, let down, take up time, prolong, protract, draw, draw out, drag out, spin out, string out

ADVERBS

11 **lengthily**, extensively, in length, end to end, stem to stern, at (full) length, *in extenso* (L), interminably, endlessly, without end, ad infinitum

12 **longitudinally**, lengthways (*or* lengthwise), longways (*or* longwise), endways (*or* endwise), along, in a line, in single file, in tandem, one behind the other

149 Shortness

I will make you shorter by a head. Elizabeth I.

NOUNS

1 **shortness**, diminutiveness, littleness, stubbiness, stumpiness, stockiness, dumpiness, lowness, squatness, stuntedness, snubness, transience, briefness, brevity, skimpiness, scantiness, curtness, terseness, conciseness, succinctness, compendiousness

► *147 Closeness; 155 Lowness; 159 Smallness; 269 Brevity; 278 Transience*

2 **shortening**, abbreviation, abridgment, compression, capsulization, encapsulation, epitomization, elision, aphaeresis, syncope, apocope, foreshortening, cutting, truncation, curtailment, retrenchment, reduction, cut, cutback, docking, clipping, trimming, pruning, mowing, shearing, shaving, decapitation, beheading

► *191 Contraction; 212 Subtraction; 214 Decrease; 814 Punishment*

3 **shortened version**, synopsis, summary, precis, résumé, conspectus, compendium, abbreviation, digest, abridgment, abstract, capsule, outline, epitome, ellipsis

► *723 Summary*

4 **short thing**, short cut, shorts, short legs, miniskirt, crew cut, February, shorthand, one-hit wonder, nine-day wonder, flash in the pan

► *278 Transience*

5 **short person**, dwarf, midget, midge, pygmy, elf, gnome, brownie, bantam, small fry, runt, Lilliputian, Tom Thumb, Thumbelina, banty (US inf), shorty (Inf), short stuff (Inf), squirt (Inf), shrimp (Inf), tiddler (Inf), titch (Inf), peewee (Inf), half-pint (Inf)

6 **abruptness**, curtness, brusqueness, gruffness, rudeness, irascibility

► *625 Grumpiness; 659 Discourtesy*

ADJECTIVES

7 **short**, diminutive, little, stubby, stumpy, thickset, stocky, dumpy, squat, stunted, low, snub, turned-up, retroussé, snub-nosed, pug-nosed, short and sweet, transient, brief, skimpy, scanty, curt, terse, concise, succinct, synoptic, summary, compendious

8 **shortened**, abbreviated, abridged, condensed, compressed, digested, abstracted, capsulized, encapsulated, epitomized, elliptical, elided, foreshortened, cut, sawn-off, truncated, cut short, curtailed, curtal, curtate, docked, bobbed, clipped, trimmed, cropped, pruned, mown, mowed, sheared, shorn, shaved, shaven, polled, decapitated, beheaded

9 **abrupt**, curt, brusque, gruff, rude, irascible, short-tempered

VERBS

10 **shorten**, abbreviate, abridge, condense, compress, digest, abstract, boil down, capsulize, encapsulate, epitomize, synopsize (US), summarize, sum up, elide, telescope, foreshorten, truncate, cut, cut short, curtail, retrench, reduce, cut back, cut down, cut off, dock, bob, clip, trim, crop, reap, prune, lop, mow, shear, shave, poll, decapitate, behead, axe, slash, stunt, skimp, take up, turn up

11 **cut short**, take a short cut, cut across, cut through, cut a corner, go as the crow flies

ADVERBS

12 **short**, shortly, briefly, abruptly, suddenly, all of a sudden, in short, in brief, in a word, in a nutshell, to summarize, curtly, tersely, concisely, succinctly, elliptically, diminutively

150 Broadness

ADJECTIVES

1 **broad**, wide, wide-set, wide-spaced, splayed, splay, patulous, transverse, extensive, expansive, roomy, ample, deep, widespread, wide-ranging, spread-out, beamy, broadcast, open, wide-open, full, baggy, wide-cut, flared, bell-bottomed, wide-angle, wide-screen, broad-gauge, broad-gauged, broadloom, as wide as a barn door, as wide as a truck (US)

▶ *145 Distance; 152 Thickness; 190 Expansion*

2 **broad-shaped**, broad-faced, broad-based, broad-bottomed, wide-bottomed, broad in the beam (Inf), broad-beamed, wide-hipped, broad-tailed, wide-bodied, broad-brimmed, broad-leaved, broad-billed, wide-billed, broad-toothed, broad-lipped, wide-mouthed, wide-eyed, broad-nosed, broad-headed, broad-backed, broad-shouldered, broad-chested, broad-breasted, broad-winged

3 **broad-minded**, open-minded, liberal, open, unprejudiced, unbiased, impartial, disinterested, unbigoted, freethinking, free, direct, frank, candid, explicit

NOUNS

4 **breadth**, broadness, width, wideness, span, wingspan, gauge, radius, diameter, bore, calibre, handbreadth, range, scope, beam, latitude, extent, extensiveness, catholicity, expanse, expansiveness, spaciousness, roominess, amplitude, ampleness, bagginess, fullness, flare, splay, openness, opening, dilation

5 **broad** (*or* **wide**) **thing**, wide screen, Cinemascope™, Cinerama™, broad gauge, broadsword, broadcloth, broadleaf, broadbill, crossbeam, ocean, Pacific Ocean, desert, Sahara

6 **broad-mindedness**, open-mindedness, liberality, openness, lack of prejudice, impartiality, freedom, freethinker, directness, explicitness

ADVERBS

7 **broadly**, widely, extensively, generally, by and large, on the whole, openly, freely, obscenely, in an explicit way

8 **breadthwise**, breadthways, broadwise, broadways, widthwise, widthways, across, athwart, transversely, crosswise, crossways, sideways, broadside, through, from one side to the other, all the way across, clear across

VERBS

9 **be broad** (*or* **wide**), extend, flare, splay

10 **span**, straddle, bestride, cross, link

11 **broaden**, widen, expand, enlarge, spread, diverge, open, dilate

12 **be broad-minded**, keep an open mind, be unbiased, lack prejudice, speak directly

151 Narrowness

It created in me a yearning for all that is wide and open and expansive. Something that will never allow me to fit in in my own country, with its narrow towns and narrow roads and narrow kindnesses and narrow reprimands. Anthony Hopkins.

ADJECTIVES

1 **narrow**, slender, thin, close, tight, strait, clinging, cramped, pinched, compressed, contracted, pent, pent-up, close-fitting, figure-hugging, limited, restricted, straitened, confined, constricted, circumscribed, incommodious

▶ *153 Thinness; 191 Contraction*

2 **fine**, finespun, fine-drawn, wire-drawn, threadlike, hairlike, filamentous, filiform, spindle-shaped, spindling, spindly, bacillary, bacilliform, spidery, wispy, scanty, tenuous, exiguous, delicate, fragile

3 **tapered**, tapering, convergent, attenuated, attenuate, pointed, peaked, conical, cone-shaped, wedge-shaped, fusiform

4 **narrow-leaved**, angustifoliate, stenophyllous, leptophyllous, narrow-petalled, stenopetalous, narrow-beaked, angustirostrate, narrow-nosed, leptorrhine, catarrhine, narrow-skulled, leptocephalic, narrow-gauge, narrow-gauged, single-track, isthmian

NOUNS

5 **narrowness**, slenderness, thinness, closeness, tightness, straitness, limitation, restriction, confinement, constriction, circumspection, incommodiousness

6 **narrow place**, confined space, small gap, tight squeeze, chink, crack, narrows, strait, straits, channel, slip (US), tunnel, passage, corridor, bottleneck, bridge, ridge, pass, ford, defile, ravine, gully, ditch, isthmus, peninsula, spit

7 **fineness**, spideriness, wispiness, tenuity, exiguity, fragility

8 **narrow thing**, neck, waist, fingers, strip, band, stripe, taper, spindle, stick, rod, pipe, tube, wire, thread, strand, hair, filament, splinter, wisp, streak, line, knife edge, razor's edge, point, peak, spire, cone, wedge, narrow gauge, single track

9 **narrowing**, shrinking, tapering, taper, convergence, contraction, stricture, attenuation, stenosis

VERBS

10 **narrow**, tighten, cramp, pinch, compress, contract, limit, restrict, straiten, confine, constrict, circumscribe, taper, converge, attenuate, draw, stretch

VERBS

11 **narrowly**, tightly, closely, nearly, only just, barely, hardly, by the skin of one's teeth, by a hair's-breadth, by a whisker

152 Thickness

Blood is thicker than water. Proverb.

ADJECTIVES

1 **thick**, broad, wide, deep, massive, substantial, bulky, ample, chunky, heavy, stout, buxom, endomorphic, fat, corpulent, obese, overweight, well-fed, plump, portly, round, rotund, flabby, chubby, podgy, tubby, potbellied, fat as a pig (*or* hog), big as a house, like the back of a bus (Inf), solid, padded, swollen, incrassate, stocky, sturdy, thick-bodied, thickset, barrel-chested, thick-necked, bull-necked, thickheaded, thick-lipped, thick-jawed, thick-legged, thick-ankled, thick-fingered, thick-wristed, thick-leaved, thick-stemmed, thick-stalked, thick-ribbed, thick-barked, pachydermatous, thick-skinned, thick-coated, thick-walled

▶ *150 Broadness; 158 Size*

2 **dense**, full-bodied, semiliquid, viscous, condensed, congealed, coagulated, clotted, thickened, intensified, boiled-down, reduced, thick with, crowded, abundant, packed, swarming, teeming, jammed, chock-a-block, impenetrable

▶ *416 Density; 430 Viscosity*

3 **thick-witted**, slow-witted, dull-witted, dull, dense, stupid, obtuse, dim, dumb, boneheaded (Inf), thick (Inf)

▶ *459 Folly*

4 **thick-skinned**, callous, insensitive, hard, coarse

NOUNS

5 **thickness**, breadth, width, depth, mass, massiveness, bulk, bulkiness, chunkiness, heaviness, stoutness, buxomness, fatness, corpulence, obesity, plumpness, portliness, roundness, rotundity, flabbiness, chubbiness, podginess, tubbiness, potbelly, fat, blubber, padding, upholstery, solidity, body, fullness, viscosity, density, slab, thick slice, doorstep (Inf)

6 **denseness**, density, viscosity, condensation, congealment, coagulation, thickening, intensity, abundance, impenetrability, closeness, friendship

VERBS

7 **thicken**, congeal, condense, coagulate, clot, boil down, reduce, gel, set, solidify, harden, firm up, intensify, compress, crowd, swarm

8 **fatten**, coarsen, thicken, fill out, put on weight, pad, upholster

ADVERBS

9 **thick**, thickly, densely, coarsely

153 Thinness

As lene was his hors as is a rake. Geoffrey Chaucer.

One can never be too thin or too rich. Duchess of Windsor.

ADJECTIVES

1 **thin**, slender, slim, svelte, gracile, sylphlike, sylphic, willowy, twiggy, slight, slightly built, small-framed, leptosomic, ectomorphic, narrow-waisted, wasp-waisted, flat-chested, girlish, boyish, lean-limbed, thin-legged, spindle-legged (*or* spindle-shanked), hatchet-faced, thin-faced, lantern-jawed, lean, spare, wiry, bony, rawboned, rangy, lanky, gawky, underweight, skinny, scrawny, scraggy, puny, gangling (*or* gangly), weedy (Inf)

▶ *151 Narrowness; 687 Fasting*

2 **emaciated**, malnourished, undernourished, underfed, starved, starving, anorexic (*or* anorectic), wizened, shrivelled, withered, wasted, peaked, tabescent, wasting away, tabetic, marasmic, gaunt, haggard, hollow-cheeked, hollow-eyed, sunken-eyed, drawn, pinched, cadaverous, corpse-like, skeletal, skin-and-bone, frail, wraithlike, thin as a lath (rake, *or* rail), worn to a shadow

3 **slimming**, dieting, reducing, slenderizing, weight-watching, calorie-counting

4 **fine**, delicate, light, insubstantial, flimsy, sheer, diaphanous, gossamer, gauzy, lacy, papery, wafer-thin

▶ *411 Layer*

5 **thinned**, diluted, watered-down, watery, runny, weak, attenuated, attenuate, rarefied, rare, flattened, pressed, rolled out

6 **scant**, scanty, sparse, meagre, few in number, few, thin on the ground

NOUNS

7 **thinness**, slenderness, slimness, gracility, willowiness, twigginess, slightness, slight build, small frame, hourglass figure, narrow waist, wasp waist, flat chest, girlish figure, boyish figure, hatchet face, lantern jaws, leanness, spareness, wiriness, boniness, ranginess, lankiness, gawkiness, skinniness, scrawniness, scragginess, puniness, gangliness, weediness (Inf)

8 **emaciation**, malnutrition, starvation, anorexia nervosa, anorexia, wasting, atrophy, tabescence, tabes, marasmus, gauntness, haggardness, hollow cheeks, hollow eyes, sunken eyes, cadaverousness, boniness, frailty, lean and hungry look

9 **thin person**, slip, sylph, leptosome, ectomorph, spindlelegs (*or* spindleshanks), weakling, runt, slimmer, dieter, weight watcher, calorie counter, anorexic (*or* anorectic), wraith, shadow, bag of bones (Inf), skeleton (Inf), walking skeleton (Inf), beanpole (Inf), long drink of water (Inf), broomstick (Inf), scarecrow (Inf)

10 **diet**, dieting, slimming, weight-watching, watching one's figure, calorie-counting, crash-dieting, slimming pills, diet plan, diet programme

11 **fineness**, delicacy, lightness, insubstantiality, flimsiness, sheerness, diaphanousness, gauziness, laciness, paperiness, gossamer, gauze, muslin, lace, paper, tissue, wafer, lath, slat, shaving, film

12 **thinning**, dilution, watering down, wateriness, runniness, weakness, rarefaction, attenuation, meagreness, paucity, scantiness, sparseness, fewness

13 **thinner**, diluter, solvent

VERBS

14 **become thin**, slim, slim down, slenderize, reduce, diet, watch one's weight, lose weight, count the calories

15 **be emaciated**, starve, undereat, waste away

16 **make thin**, thin, thin down, thin out, dilute, water down, weaken, rarefy, attenuate, flatten, press, roll out

ADVERBS

17 **thin**, thinly, meagrely, scantily, sparsely

154 Height

O ye'll tak' the high road, and I'll tak' the low road,
And I'll be in Scotland afore ye. Anonymous.

NOUNS

1 **height**, altitude, highness, tallness, stature, lankiness, ranginess, pitch, loftiness, elevation, rise, lift, uprise, uplift, exaltation, eminence, prominence, sublimity

▶ *158 Size*

2 **heights**, highlands, upland(s), moorland, moor(s), downs, wold, fell, foothills, rising ground, acclivity, incline, escarpment, climb, zenith, acme, apex, pinnacle, summit, peak, top, mountaintop, hilltop, knap, tableland, plateau, mesa

▶ *174 Top; 189 Slantedness*

3 **mountain**, mount, alp, tor, ben, Olympus, Everest,

Matterhorn, Mont Blanc, McKinley, Ben Nevis, hill, brae, pike, butte, cliff, bluff, crag, scar, precipice, hillock, hummock, monticule, knoll, kop, kopje, inselberg, roche moutonnée, drumlin, knob, hump, dune, sand dune, mound, tump, barrow, tumulus, motte

4 **mountain range**, massif, sierra, chain, cordillera, Himalayas, Alps, Andes, Rockies, Urals, Caucasus, Snowdonia, ridge, arête, chine, spur, kame, esker, os, moraine, col, saddleback, hogback, hog's back, watershed, divide, Continental Divide, Great Divide, bank, bench, crest, spine, comb, saddle

► *30 Earth Science; 92 Other Geographical Features*

5 **height measure**, relief, topography, orography, hypsography, hypsometry, altimetry, altimeter, hypsometer

6 **tall thing**, telegraph pole, streetlight, steeple, spire, flèche, tower, turret, bell tower, campanile, belfry, watchtower, barbican, Martello tower, water tower, observation tower, Eiffel Tower, minaret, pagoda, ziggurat, lighthouse, windmill, pile, skyscraper, Empire State Building, tower block, office block, high-rise flats, multistorey car park, mast, radio mast, chimney, smokestack, pillar, column, shaft, pilaster, pole, telegraph pole, maypole, flagstaff, post, lamppost, pylon, crane, derrick, obelisk, Cleopatra's Needle, monument, sequoia, redwood, giraffe, elephant

7 **tall person**, six-footer, seven-footer, basketball player, giant, Goliath, colossus, Amazon, beanpole (Inf), longlegs (*or* longshanks) (Inf), long drink of water (Inf)

8 **high thing**, ceiling, roof, vault, cupola, dome, lantern, attic, garret, loft, cockloft, mansard, penthouse, top floor, clerestory, weathercock, weather vane, topmast, topgallant mast, masthead, crow's nest, eyrie, vantage point, viewpoint, triangulation station, sky, heaven, heavens, ether, stratosphere, mesosphere, thermosphere, exosphere, highchair, ladder, steps, stilts, high heels, platform soles, high tide, high water, flood, flood tide, spring tide, equinoctial tide, tidal wave, tsunami, trig point (Inf)

ADJECTIVES

9 **high**, tall, altitudinal, altitudinous, high up, sky-high, lofty, elevated, uplifted, upreared, upraised, high-rise, multistorey, towering, skyscraping, ascending, rising, uprising, mounting, aspiring, soaring, flying, hovering, topping, overtopping, overlooking, dominating, overshadowing, overhanging, beetling, cloud-topped, cloud-capped, aerial, supernal, ethereal, airy, as high as a steeple, vertiginous, dizzy, giddy

10 **higher**, taller, highest, tallest, superior, upper, upmost, uppermost, topmost, nearest the top

11 **exalted**, elevated, eminent, prominent, sublime, supreme, superlative

12 **tall**, lanky, rangy, leggy, long-legged, long-limbed, long-necked, giant, gigantic, colossal, statuesque, monumental, Amazonian, Olympian, as tall as a maypole, knee-high, thigh-high, waist-high, chest-high, shoulder-high, gangling (Inf), gangly (Inf)

13 **mountainous**, hilly, rolling, undulating, hillocky, hummocky, orogenic, orogenetic, alpine, alpestrine, subalpine, Himalayan, Andean, mountain-dwelling, hill-dwelling

14 **altimetric**, topographic, orographic, hypsometric, hypsographic

VERBS

15 **be high**, tower, tower above, spire, aspire, soar, fly, hover over, top, overtop, clear, surmount, overlook, look down on, dominate, command, overshadow, overarch, bestride, overhang, beetle

16 **rise**, rise up, uprise, climb, ascend, mount, rear, rear up, uprear, stand on tiptoe, grow, shoot up, culminate, peak

► *304 Ascent*

17 **raise**, heighten, elevate, hoist, lift, lift up, uplift, exalt, hold up

► *366 Raising*

18 **erect**, construct, build, put up

ADVERBS

19 **high**, high up, on high, aloft, above, over, overhead, above one's head, in the air, in the clouds, in orbit, at the top, on top, upstairs, above stairs, as high as a kite, toweringly, sublimely, on stilts, on tiptoe, up to the knees, up to the waist, up to the shoulders

20 **higher**, up, straight up, vertically, upwards, skyward(s), heavenward(s)

155 Lowness

Holland…lies so low they're only saved by being dammed.
Thomas Hood.

NOUNS

1 **lowness**, shortness, squatness, stumpiness, stuntedness, shallowness, lowering, flattening, lying down, prostration, proneness, supineness, recumbency, reclining, subordination, inferiority

► *149 Shortness*

2 **lowlands**, foothills, hillock, hummock, molehill, nursery slope, plain, flats, level ground, flatness, sea level, depression, hollow, valley

► *156 Depth; 175 Base; 187 Horizontality*

3 **lowest point**, lowest level, nadir, low tide, low water, ebb, ebb tide, neap tide

4 **low thing**, nether regions, subjacency, subscript, subcortex, submucosa, hypolimnion, underlay, underfelt, substratum, subsoil, undersoil, bedrock, floor, bottom, foot, base, subbase, subfloor, subgrade, basement, cellar, underneath, underside, undersurface, underbelly, underpart, underbody, undercarriage, bungalow, coffee table, low-cut neckline, décolletage, dachshund, low heels, flats, flatties (Inf)

► *122 Inferiority*

ADJECTIVES

5 **low**, short, squat, stumpy, stunted, shallow, ankle-high, knee-high, lowered, low-slung, flattened, laid low, knocked down, knocked over, knocked flat, lying down, prostrate, prone, supine, recumbent, reclining, couchant, crouched, crouching, stooped, stooping, low-level, low-set, low-hung, low-heeled, low-necked, low-cut, décolleté, low-built, low-rise, single-storey, knee-high to a grasshopper (Inf)

6 **lower**, lowest, inferior, nether, bottom, bottommost, undermost, subjacent, underlying, underlaid, subscript, subcutaneous, hypodermic, subcartilaginous, subcranial,

subcortical, suborbital, subauricular, submental, subglottal, subclavian, subscapular, subaxillary, infracostal, subdorsal, subabdominal, hypogastric

7 lowland, subalpine, submontane, piedmont, low-lying, flat, at sea level, below sea level, submerged, sunken, depressed

VERBS

8 be low, bottom out, underlie, underlay, look up to, lie down, prostrate oneself, recline, couch, crouch, squat, stoop, slouch, bend, bow, crawl, creep, grovel, lie low, go below

▶ *305 Descent*

9 lower, flatten, depress, lay low, knock down, knock over, knock flat, squash flat

▶ *367 Lowering*

ADVERBS

10 low, low down, under, below, underneath, beneath, neath, down, downwards, down below, downstairs, underground, underfoot, at the bottom, at the foot

156 Depth

I'll break my staff,
Bury it certain fathoms in the earth,
And deeper than did ever plummet sound
I'll drown my book. William Shakespeare.

NOUNS

1 depth, deepness, drop, fall, bottomlessness, unfathomableness, fathomlessness, soundlessness, cavernousness, deepening, lowering, sinking, sinkage, diving, deep-sea diving, submersion, immersion, excavation, spelunking, potholing, digging, burial, interment, mining, drilling, tunnelling, subterraneity

▶ *155 Lowness; 175 Base*

2 intensity, strength, extent, measure, deep-seatedness, deep-rootedness

3 profundity, profoundness, understanding, wisdom, sagacity, insight, perspicacity, penetration, acuity, discernment, astuteness

▶ *458 Wisdom*

4 deep thing, the deeps, the depths, lower depths, pit, mine, shaft, well, hole, basin, cavity, crater, pothole, crevasse, valley, ravine, coombe, corrie, cwm, cirque, chasm, gulf, abyss, subway, underpass, underground, tunnel, grave, vault, crypt, hypogeum, catacomb, dungeon, underworld, hell, bowels of the earth, bottomless pit, nadir, bottom of the sea, sea bed, sea bottom, sea floor, ocean bottom, ocean floor, ocean depths, deep water, deep sea, benthos, Davy Jones's locker, Mariana Trench, submarine, submersible, bathysphere, bathyscaph, diving bell, benthoscope, bathometer, depth sounder, echo sounder, Fathometer™, lead, lead line, plumb, plumb line, sounding line, sound, probe, sounder, fathomer

5 submariner, deep-sea diver, spelunker, potholer, miner

6 bathymetry, bathometry, oceanography, sounding, depth sounding, probing, echo sounding, sonar, echolocation, draught, displacement

7 deep thinking, profundity, wisdom, wise man, wise woman, sage, intellectual

ADJECTIVES

8 deep, bottomless, unfathomable, fathomless, unfathomed, unsoundable, soundless, unsounded, unplumbed, abysmal, abyssal, cavernous, plunging, yawning, gaping, as deep as the ocean (*or* the sea), as deep as a well, as deep as hell, ankle-deep, knee-deep, waist-deep, deep-down, deep-lying, deep-laid, deep-set, sunken, deep-reaching, engraved, incised, deep-cut, deep-dish, deep-pan

9 deep-seated, deep-rooted, intense, extreme, sincere, profound, serious, heartfelt, earnest

10 deeper, deepest, deepmost, lowest, bottom, rock-bottom

11 wise, profound, deep, understanding, knowledgeable, perspicacious, acute, astute, discerning

12 under, underground, subterranean, subterraneous, subterrestrial, hypogeal, hypogeous, hypogene, buried, sunk, submerged, immersed, underwater, subaqua, subaquatic, subaqueous, undersea, submarine, suboceanic, deep-sea, deep-water, bathyal, bathypelagic, benthic, benthal, benthonic

13 bathymetric, bathometric, oceanographic, sounding, depth-sounding, probing, echolocating

VERBS

14 deepen, lower, go lower, drop, fall, sink, founder, descend, dive, plunge, yawn, gape, submerge, immerse, excavate, dig, bury, inter, mine, drill, tunnel, fathom, sound, take soundings, heave the lead, plumb, plumb the depths, probe, touch bottom, reach the bottom, sink to the bottom

15 be profound, understand, have deep understanding, be wise, be knowledgeable

ADVERBS

16 deep, deeply, deep down, out of one's depth, up to one's eyes (*or* ears), at the lowest point, at rock bottom

17 profoundly, deeply, in depth, in detail, extensively, thoroughly, exhaustively, comprehensively

157 Shallowness

ADJECTIVES

1 shallow, not deep, shoal, shoaly, reefy, unnavigable, ankle-deep, knee-deep, waist-deep, shallow-bottomed, shallow-rooted

2 superficial, surface, one-dimensional, cursory, hasty, slight, light, skin-deep, epidermal, thin, flat, low, trivial, trifling, lightweight, unimportant, petty, meaningless, empty, flimsy, frivolous, foolish, idle, silly

▶ *124 Unimportance*

NOUNS

3 shallowness, lack of depth, shoaliness, superficiality, triviality, cursoriness, slightness, lightness, surface, sprinkling, dusting, superficies (Lit)

4 shallow thing, skin, epidermis, cuticle, veneer, film, shallows, shallow, shoal, shoals, ford, shallow water, low water, low tide, puddle, pool, wetlands, swamp, shelf, reef, coral reef, bank, sandbank, mudbank, bar, sand bar, flat, flats, mud flat, tidal flats, pool, puddle, shallow-bottomed boat, shallow cut, superficial wound, scratch, graze, abrasion, pinprick

▶ *153 Thinness; 155 Lowness; 156 Depth; 171 Outside; 411 Layer*

5 **shallow person**, man of straw, lightweight, mediocrity, nonentity, nobody

VERBS

6 **be shallow**, skim, skim over, touch, touch the surface, scratch the surface, scrape, graze

7 **make shallow**, shallow, shoal, silt up

ADVERBS

8 **shallowly**, near the surface, within one's depth, on the surface, superficially, cursorily, lightly, once-over, with a lick and a promise

158 Size

I don't pretend to understand the Universe – it's a great deal bigger than I am. Thomas Carlyle.

NOUNS

1 **size**, magnitude, order of magnitude, amplitude, dimension(s), proportion(s), measurement(s), measure, gauge, scale, extent, extension, scope, range, reach, limit, expanse, spread, coverage, area, length, breadth, width, height, depth, radius, diameter, calibre, scantling, girth, circumference, mass, bulk, volume, capacity, cubature, cubage, content, room, space, accommodation, stowage, tonnage, displacement, burden, tankage

▶ *141 Space; 148 Length; 152 Thickness; 154 Height; 156 Depth; 163 Outline; 273 Accuracy; 414 Heaviness*

2 **bigness**, largeness, greatness, full size, full growth, life size, sizableness, ampleness, generousness, voluminousness, bagginess, capaciousness, spaciousness, roominess, hugeness, enormity, immenseness, immensity, massiveness, grandness, grandeur, prodigiousness, tallness, bulkiness, unwieldiness, cumbersomeness, broadness, wideness, comprehensiveness, expansiveness, extensiveness, vastness

▶ *204 Whole; 232 Completeness*

3 **large scale**, good size, fair size, large size, family size, economy size, king-size, queen-size, giant size, record size, outsize, oversize, overgrowth

4 **gigantism**, giantism, hypertrophy, hyperplasia, acromegaly, elephantiasis

5 **fatness**, obesity, overweight, corpulence, portliness, rotundity, roundness, endomorphy, grossness, fleshiness, flabbiness, bloatedness, puffiness, fullness, plumpness, fattishness, paunchiness, buxomness, bustiness, plumpishness, podginess, tubbiness, chubbiness, adiposity, stoutness, *embonpoint* (Fr)

6 **squatness**, dumpiness, stockiness, squareness, heavy build, burliness, brawniness, beefiness, meatiness, chunkiness, heaviness, heftiness, hulkiness, lumpishness, lumpiness

7 **mass**, lump, chunk, hunk, block, clump, cluster, wad, heap, mountain, clod, cake, glob, gob, wodge (Inf), gobs (Inf), dollop (Inf)

8 **fat**, cellulite, double chin, potbelly, paunch, flab (Inf), blubber (Inf), lard (Inf), corporation (Inf), beer belly (Inf), spare tyre (Inf)

9 **big thing**, giant, monster, whale, dinosaur, mammoth, mastodon, elephant, hippopotamus, leviathan, behemoth, King Kong, Empire State Building, redwood tree, whopper (Inf), spanker (Inf), lunker (US inf), jumbo (Inf), humdinger (Inf)

10 **big person**, hulk, man mountain, monster man, giant, giantess, ogre, ogress, Titan, Titaness, colossus, Amazon, Goliath, Brobdingnagian, Gargantua, Pantagruel, Cyclops, Polyphemus, Atlas, Hercules, Typhon, heavy (Inf)

11 **tall person**, six-footer, colossus, giant, longlegs (Inf), highpockets (Inf), beanpole (Inf), long drink of water (Inf)

12 **fat person**, roly-poly, heavyweight, Falstaff, fatty (Inf), tub of lard (Inf), dumpling (Inf), blimp (Inf), hippo (Inf), fatso (Inf)

ADJECTIVES

13 **this size**, about this size, so big, this big, about this big, of that order

14 **medium**, medium-size(d), average, average-size(d), standard, regular

15 **big**, large, great, full-size(d), full-grown, full-blown, full-scale, life-size(d), large as life, sizable, good-size(d), fair-size(d), large-size(d), large-scale, considerable, substantial, goodly, bumper, ample, generous, voluminous, baggy, capacious, spacious, roomy, family-size(d), economy-size(d), man-size(d), king-size(d), queen-size(d), giant-size(d), record-size(d), huge, enormous, immense, massive, massy, gigantic, gigantesque, colossal, titanic, monstrous, great big, larger than life, mammoth, giant, monster, Gargantuan, Brobdingnagian, Cyclopean, towering, monumental, grand, imposing, Homeric, epic, tremendous, stupendous, prodigious, mountainous, megalithic, macroscopic, astronomical, outsize, extra large, oversized, too big, overlarge, overgrown, bulky, mighty, broad, wide, comprehensive, expansive, extensive, vast, limitless, infinite, tidy (Inf), healthy (Inf), jumbo (Inf), almighty (Inf), whopping (Inf), walloping (Inf), whacking (Inf), spanking (Inf), thumping (Inf), thundering (Inf), mega (Inf), ginormous (Inf), humongous (Inf)

16 **fat**, obese, overweight, endomorphic, gross, fleshy, flabby, bloated, puffy, swollen, distended, full, plump, podgy, tubby, chubby, bonny, adipose, stout, corpulent, portly, rotund, round, roly-poly, well-fed, overfed, fat as a pig, plump as a dumpling, plump as a partridge, squab, dumpy, round-faced, moon-faced, full-faced, chubby-faced, chubby-cheeked, double-chinned, big-bellied, full-bellied, potbellied, paunchy, abdominous, big-bottomed, buxom, busty, bosomy, full-bosomed, well-endowed, top-heavy, steatopygic, steatopygous, hippy (Inf), broad in the beam (Inf), well-upholstered (Inf), fat-arsed (Inf)

17 **stocky**, stout, thickset, heavyset, squat, square, well-built, heavily built, burly, strapping, lusty, brawny, beefy, meaty, heavy, chunky, hefty, hulking, hulky, lumbering, lumpish, lumpy, elephantine

VERBS

18 **measure**, gauge, size, grade, group, rank, sort, match, graduate, adjust, proportion, enlarge

19 **be big**, bulk, loom, loom large, fill space, tower, soar

ADVERBS

20 **largely**, on a large scale, in the large, greatly, considerably, substantially, amply, generously, voluminously, baggily, capaciously, spaciously, hugely, in a big way, enormously, immensely, massively, monstrously, mightily, limitlessly, infinitely, as can be, fatly, obesely, plumply, stoutly, roundly, buxomly

159 Smallness

It has long been an axiom of mine that the little things are infinitely the most important. Arthur Conan Doyle.

NOUNS

1 **littleness**, smallness, smallishness, diminutiveness, shortness, petiteness, squatness, dumpiness, dwarfishness, daintiness, dinkiness, small scale, compactness, handiness, portability, tininess, minuteness, fineness, thinness, slightness, exiguity, tenuousness, imperceptibility, intangibility, impalpability, imponderability, inappreciability, invisibility, undersize, stuntedness, puniness, runtiness, shrunkenness, scrubbiness, scrawniness, scragginess, meagreness, scantness, scantiness, skimpiness, pokiness, snugness, cosiness, paltriness, pettiness, miniaturization, microminiaturization, microscopy, micrography, microscope, micrometer

2 **little thing**, particle, grain, grain of sand, seed, mustard seed, granule, corpuscle, molecule, cell, nucleus, monad, atom, subatomic particle, ion, electron, proton, neutron, neutrino, parton, meson, muon, quark, point, pinpoint, pinhead, dot, microdot, pixel, microbe, bacterium, virus, germ, bacillus, microorganism, animalcule, protozoan, zoospore, microphyte, amoeba, euglena, plankton, miniature, mini, baby, toy, doll, puppet, model, microcosm, microphotograph, microfilm, microfiche, thumbnail sketch, pocket edition, Elzevir edition, duodecimo, twelvemo, chip, silicon chip, microchip, integrated circuit

3 **little piece**, bit, fragment, sliver, shaving, filing, jot, tittle, iota, speck, fleck, mote, scrap, crumb, morsel, snippet, minutia, minim, drop, droplet

4 **little person**, dwarf, midget, pygmy, manikin, homunculus, Hop-o'-my-thumb, Tom Thumb, Thumbelina, Pinocchio, Alberich, Nibelung, hobbit, elf, gnome, fairy, sprite, brownie, leprechaun, halfling, runt, weakling, shrimp (Inf), minnow (Inf), tiddler (Inf), squirt (Inf), squit (Inf), fingerling, slip, chit, wisp, snip (US inf), small fry, titch (Inf), half-pint (Inf), pipsqueak (Inf), peewee (Inf), bantam, lightweight, featherweight, mouse, tot, mite

5 **little space**, hole, pigeonhole, cubbyhole, doll's house, tight squeeze, tight spot, pinch

VERBS

6 **be little**, be small, take up no room, fit on the head of a pin

ADJECTIVES

7 **little**, small, smallish, diminutive, short, petite, squat, dumpy, dwarfish, dwarfed, elfin, dainty, dinky, pint-size(d) (Inf), knee-high (to a grasshopper), Lilliputian, miniature, subminiature, mini, dwarf, midget, pygmy, bantam, baby, model, small-scale, miniaturized, microcosmic, compact, handy, portable, pocket-size(d), pocket, vest-pocket (US), duodecimo, twelvemo, tiny, minute, minuscule, infinitesimal, microscopic, ultramicroscopic, rudimentary, rudimental, incipient, embryonic, germinal, fine, thin, slight, exiguous, tenuous, imperceptible, intangible, impalpable, imponderable, inappreciable, negligible, indiscernible, invisible, undersize(d), stunted, puny, runty, pindling (US inf), shrunk, contracted, shrunken, wizened, shrivelled, scrubby, scrawny, scraggy, meagre, scant, scanty, skimpy, inadequate, poky, cramped, limited, restricted, no room to swing a cat, snug, cosy, bijou, two-by-four (Inf), one-horse (Inf), piddling (Inf), paltry, petty, trifling, trivial, inconsiderable, insignificant, unimportant, minimal, granular, corpuscular, molecular, atomic, subatomic, microbic, microbial, bacterial, animalcular, protozoan, amoebic, amoeboid, wee (Inf), teeny (Inf), weeny (Inf), teeny-weeny (Inf), titchy (Inf), tiddly (Inf), bitsy (Inf), itsy-bitsy (Inf), itty-bitty (Inf)

ADVERBS

8 **in a small way**, on a small scale, in a nutshell, in miniature, diminutively, daintily, slightly, minimally, tinily, minutely, punily, finely, tenuously, inappreciably, negligibly, inconsiderably, insignificantly, unimportantly

9 **microscopically**, microcosmically, atomically, subatomically, infinitesimally, indiscernibly, imperceptibly, invisibly, intangibly, impalpably, imponderably

160 Form

It would follow that 'significant form' was form behind which we catch a sense of ultimate reality. Clive Bell.

NOUNS

1 **form**, structure, order, system, formation, forming, conformation, format, configuration, construction, composition, composure, gestalt, Gestalt whole, shape, shaping, figure, profile, contour, frame, lines, outline, silhouette, relief, pattern, patterning, arrangement, design, designing, significant form, inner form, essence, substance, nominalism, Platonism, Platonic form, idea, morphology, isomorphism

► *95 Reality; 99 Essence; 163 Outline; 204 Whole; 298 Regularity; 356 Creation; 403 Structure; 407 Order; 409 Arrangement; 525 Appearance*

2 **prototype**, form, formula, format, model, dummy, mould, example, paradigm, pattern, jig, template, stencil, matrix, frame, blank, punch, stamp, cast, die, blueprint

► *126 Originality; 243 Preparation; 484 Plan*

3 **kind**, form, type, sort, variety, character, order, genre, art form, inscape, verse form, word form, sonata form

► *17 Literature; 18 Music; 19 Painting and Sculpture; 137 Class; 407 Order; 724 Style*

4 **forming**, formulation, creation, morphogenesis, construction, production, expression, fashioning, modelling, moulding, tailoring, knitting, weaving, shaping, setup, make-up, composition

► *356 Creation; 435 Materials; 576 Work*

5 **formality**, good form, decorum, etiquette, protocol, behaviour, conduct, practice, routine, habit, fashion, trend, style, custom, tradition, convention, procedure, form of law, litigation, ceremony, ritual, solemnity

► *10 Ritual; 117 Conformity; 553 Fashion; 631 Behaviour; 632 Habit; 656 Formality; 658 Courtesy; 724 Style; 750 Agreement*

6 **nature**, health, fitness, condition, shape, fettle, soundness, character, attitude, turn, appearance, features, lineament, face, expression, look, mein, aspect, demeanour, cast, set, physiognomy, physique, anatomy, body, build, ectomorph, endomorph, mesomorph, figure, trim, posture, stance, cut, cut of one's jib (Inf), get-up (Inf)

► *167 Front; 259 Health; 525 Appearance; 724 Style*

VERBS

7 **form**, structure, order, systematize, formalize, arrange, pattern, figure, design, draft, sketch, formulate, draw, format, lay out, rough out, block out, shape, turn, round, square, frame, outline, silhouette, cut out, cut, whittle, hew, rough-hew, carve, chisel, sculpt (*or* sculpture), mould, model, knead, throw (pots), blow (glass), cast, coin, mint, stamp, found, hammer out, punch out, forge, smith, fashion, work up, work, build, construct, create, bring into being, make, produce, express, verbalize, put into words, put into shape, knock into shape, lick into shape (Inf)

8 **be formal**, conform, comply, toe the line, stick to the rules, follow protocol, practise etiquette, behave well, mind one's manners, mind one's p's and q's, maintain tradition, stand on ceremony, observe a ritual, solemnize

ADJECTIVES

9 **formed**, formative, formal, orderly, systematic, conformable, configurational, configurative, creative, created, made, constructed, produced, shaped, sculptured, carved, moulded, modelled, tailored, thrown (pot), blown (glass), turned, rounded, squared, fashioned, setup, composed, styled, stylized, stylish, expressive, morphologic (*or* morphological), morphogenic (*or* morphogenetic), isomorphic, isomorphous, Platonic, concrete, solid, plastic, fictile

10 **prototypical**, original, exemplary, dummy, paradigmatic, generic, model, custom-built, ready-made, off-the-rack, off-the-peg, tailor-made, designer

11 **formal**, conventional, procedural, protocol, decorous, behavioural, traditional, ceremonial, solemn, ritual, customary, routine, habitual, litigious, ritualistic, fashionable, trendy, stylish

12 **on form**, in shape, in good condition, fit, able, capable, healthy, salubrious, hale, in fine fettle, hearty, in the pink, in good nick (Inf)

ADVERBS

13 **formatively**, formally, systematically, by design, conformably, configurationally, concretely, solidly, plastically, stylishly, creatively, constructively, productively, prototypically, originally, paradigmatically, generically, healthily, heartily, expressively, morphologically, Platonically

14 **conventionally**, procedurally, routinely, habitually, traditionally, fashionably, stylishly, ceremonially, solemnly, litigiously, ritually

161 Shapelessness

And formless ruin of oblivion. William Shakespeare.

NOUNS

1 **shapelessness**, formlessness, featurelessness, amorphousness, amorphism, undevelopment, incompleteness, incompletion, rawness, lack of definition, obscurity, vagueness, obscureness, unclearness, fuzziness, blurriness, haziness, mistiness, fog, fogginess, chaos

► *234 Distortion; 408 Disorder; 524 Dimness*

2 **shapeless thing**, diamond in the rough, old pillow, sack dress, sloppy sweater, blob, amoeba, jellyfish

VERBS

3 **make shapeless**, deform, distort, misform, unform, misshape, unshape, unmake, knock out of shape, twist, bend, leave undeveloped, keep incomplete, remain raw, lack definition, be vague, obscure, be unclear, blur, fog

4 **disorder**, put into disorder, cause chaos, muddle, jumble, obfuscate

► *328 Disturbance; 357 Destruction; 412 Mixture*

ADJECTIVES

5 **shapeless**, unshaped, formless, unformed, amorphous, unfinished, undefined, lacking definition, indefinite, undeveloped, underdeveloped, incomplete, raw, uncut, unhewn, unlicked, vague, obscure, unclear, shadowed, fuzzy, blurred, hazy, misty, ill-defined, featureless

ADVERBS

6 **shapelessly**, formlessly, amorphously, indefinitely, obscurely, unclearly, fuzzily, hazily, mistily, foggily

162 Symmetry

Symmetry is tedious, and tedium is the very basis of mourning. Victor Hugo.

NOUNS

1 **symmetry**, symmetricalness, uniformity, balance, balance of form, bilateral symmetry, proportion, proportionality, rhyme, harmony, chiasmus, counterbalance, equality, equilibrium, equipose, even sides, congruence, congruity, correspondence, parallelism, correlation, coordinateness, interrelation, interconnectedness, interdependence, interaction, reciprocity, reciprocation

► *119 Equality; 188 Parallelism; 750 Agreement*

2 **symmetry operation**, reflection, rotation, inversion, translation, symmetry element, mirror plane, axis of symmetry, glide plane, rotational symmetry, bilateral symmetry

► *32 Chemistry*

3 **evenness**, regularity, conformity, regular features, consistency, uniformity, eurhythmy, harmony, beauty, shapeliness

► *117 Conformity; 545 Beauty*

ADJECTIVES

4 **symmetrical**, symmetric, uniform, balanced, well-balanced, proportional, proportionate, well-proportioned, proportioned, harmonious, counterbalanced, equal, equilateral, even-sided, bisymmetric(al), isosceles, congruent, correspondent, corresponding, correlational,

coordinate, interdependent, interacting, reciprocal, enantiomorphic, chiastic

5 **even**, even-sided, regular, consistent, uniform, eurhythmic, eurhythmical, harmonious, beautiful, shapely

VERBS

6 **symmetrize**, make uniform, balance, proportion, harmonize, counterbalance, equalize, equilibrate, correlate, coordinate, even, even up, regularize, make consistent

ADVERBS

7 **symmetrically**, uniformly, proportionally, equilaterally, proportionately, correspondingly

8 **equally**, evenly, even-sidedly, reciprocally, on the one hand and on the other, even Stevens (Inf)

163 Outline

NOUNS

1 **outline**, plan, summary, synopsis, abstract, epitome, precis, notes, class notes, brief impression, single aspect, bare essentials, frame, profile, projection, ground plan, layout, blueprint, representation, limning, emblem, sample, representative sample, random sample, survey, contour line, contour, brief description, illustration, etching, engraving, delineation, depiction, chart, graph, line graph, bar graph, diagram, portrayal, picture, simple picture, sketch, thumbnail sketch, tracing, cartoon, stick figure, matchstick man, skeleton, bare bones, reduction, abridgment, digest, condensation, contraction, abbreviation, long story made short

► *19 Painting and Sculpture; 160 Form; 484 Plan; 525 Appearance; 721 Description*

2 **shadow**, silhouette, shape, form, relief, profile, contour, figure, frame, framework

► *169 Side; 403 Structure*

3 **edge**, upper edge, horizon, skyline, coastline, outside edge, perimeter, border, fringe, flange, margin, circumference, surround, rim, circumscription

► *164 Edge; 179 Circularity*

4 **map**, road map, world map, city map, town plan, A to Z, treasure map, sketch map, relief map, political map, historical map, projection map, Mercator projection, Peters' projection, globe, atlas, cartography

► *717 Representation*

VERBS

5 **outline**, plan, sketch out, rough out, block out, summarize, synopsize (US), abstract, epitomize, precis, present the main points, note, frame, profile, project, lay out, blueprint, draw an outline, picture, portray, sketch, limn, represent, sample, survey, describe briefly, boil down, illustrate, etch, engrave, delineate, depict, chart, graph, diagram, make a thumbnail sketch, trace, reduce, abridge, digest, condense, contract, abbreviate, cut a long story short

ADJECTIVES

6 **outlined**, in outline, summarized, synopsized (US), brief, impressionistic, representative, emblematic, sample, random, descriptive, delineative, depictive, thumbnail, skeletal, abridged, abbreviated, circumscriptive, projectional, peripheral, marginal

ADVERBS

7 **essentially**, skeletally, depictively, in outline, in brief, marginally, peripherally

164 Edge

We stand today on the edge of a new frontier. John Fitzgerald Kennedy.

NOUNS

1 **edge**, border, rim, brim, margin, limit, periphery, lip, skirt, fringe, brink, verge, extremity, bounds, confines, limits, frontier, boundary, water's edge, shoreline, shore, seaside, coast, tideline, waterfront, littoral, strand, beach, riverside, waterside, bank, verge, hard shoulder, soft shoulder, roadside, wayside, sideline, kerb, ragged edge

► *131 End; 163 Outline; 166 Limit; 319 Transport; 433 Water*

2 **edging**, hem, hemline, border, selvage (*or* selvedge), fringe, flounce, piping, trimming, valance, furbelow, gimp (*or* guimpe), crenellation

► *553 Fashion*

3 **cutting edge**, sharp edge, knife edge, razor's edge, blade, sharpness, steel, point of action

► *342 Activity; 425 Sharpness*

4 **advantage**, upper hand, whip hand, little something extra, head start, flying (*or* running) start, the jump (Inf), inside track (Inf), ace in the hole (Inf)

► *121 Superiority; 334 Power; 395 Influence; 442 Intellect*

VERBS

5 **border**, verge, rim, be limiting, skirt, be at the brink, verge on, bind, confine, be on the beach, be on the sideline

6 **edge**, border, hem, fringe, pipe, trim, furbelow, decorate, crenellate, marginalize

7 **have an advantage**, be ahead, outwit, outthink, outmanoeuvre, outstrip, outshine, have a head start, have a flying (*or* running) start, have that little extra something (Inf), have the jump on (Inf), have the inside track (Inf), have an ace in the hole (Inf)

ADJECTIVES

8 **edging**, edged, bordered, marginal, extreme, seaside, waterfront, coastal, littoral, beach, riverside, waterside, roadside, wayside, sideline, peripheral

9 **skirting**, skirted, edged, fringed, valanced

10 **advantaged**, ahead, keen, sharp, acute, biting, pungent, effective, forceful, incisive, powerful

ADVERBS

11 **marginally**, peripherally, on the edge, at the limit, on the border, at the extreme, extremely, on the threshold

12 **at an advantage**, powerfully, forcefully, incisively, effectively, acutely, keenly, sharply, pungently

165 Enclosure

NOUNS

1 **enclosure** (*or* **inclosure**), enclosing, closing in, ringing round, circumvallation, circumscription, envelopment, encirclement, appropriation of land

▶ *163 Outline; 179 Circularity; 410 Container; 550 Covering*

2 **enclosed place**, enclosure, confine, precinct, close, pen, pigpen, pigsty, paddock, field, corral (US), reserve, enclave, special area, compound, fold, pound, quadrangle, quad, courtyard, walled garden, royal enclosure, reserved section, holy of holies, sanctum sanctorum, high table, cloister, monastery, convent, back yard, yard, park, patio, stockade, prison, palisade, harbour, marina

▶ *7 Religion; 142 Location; 309 Closure; 736 Concealment*

3 **enclosing thing**, wall, fence, post and rail, railing, paling, pale, moat, trench, hedge, hedgerow, mole, ditch, dyke, fosse, ha-ha, balustrade, barrier

▶ *378 Obstruction; 384 Defence*

4 **wrapper**, wrapping, bandage, cast, wrapping paper, Cellophane™, clingfilm™, bubblewrap, foil, scarf, wrapround skirt, sheath, net, dustsheet, dust cover, container, envelope, folder, dust jacket, frame, framework

▶ *17 Literature*

VERBS

5 **enclose**, surround, close, close in, fence, fence in, wall, wall in, rail, pale, moat, dyke, shut, shut in, hem in, build in, pen, pen up, paddock, corral (US), reserve, cloister, confine, imprison

6 **wrap**, bandage, bind, sheath, net, contain, envelop, enfold, encompass, circumscribe, frame

ADJECTIVES

7 **enclosed**, closed-in, fenced-in, walled-in, shut-in, hemmed-in, built-in, penned, pent-up, indoor, cloistered, monastic, conventual, intramural, confined, imprisoned, claustrophobic

ADVERBS

8 **confinedly**, cloisteredly, intramurally, monastically, claustrophobically

166 Limit

In order to draw a limit to thinking, we should have to be able to think both sides of this limit. Ludwig Wittgenstein.

NOUNS

1 **limitation**, limit, restriction, proscription, circumscription, demarcation, definition, moderation, mitigation, exclusion, restraint, constraint, control, containment, inhibition

2 **limiting factor**, upper limit, lower limit, self-control, self-restraint, check, prohibition, restricted area, no-go area, off-limits area (US), specification, ceiling, speed limit, high-water mark, bottom, threshold, failing grade, low-water mark, hindrance, brake, drag, repression, censorship, narrow outlook, veto, ban, stricture, rationing, price freeze, curtailment, curb, curfew, restrictive practice, closed shop, trading ring, monopoly, cartel, trust, quota, embargo, tariff, allotment, finite quantity, extent, measure, dose, lot, copyright, patent

▶ *136 Qualification; 226 Stopping; 251 Restraint; 387 Subjection; 709 Refusal; 770 Allocation*

3 **furthest point**, extremity, farness, boundary, verge, margin, edge, outside edge, brink, three-mile limit, frontier, outpost, last outpost, back of beyond

▶ *131 End; 145 Distance; 164 Edge*

4 **boundary marker**, boundary stone, partition wall, fence, stone wall, hedge, river, checkpoint, line, line in the sand, time zone, international date line, longitude, latitude

ADJECTIVES

5 **limited**, restricted, restrictive, proscripted, prohibitive, repressive, inhibiting, no-go, off-limits (US), exclusive, definite, under control, under restraint, held back, in check, confined, frozen, under curfew, curtailed, finite, narrow, cramped, hidebound, copyrighted, patented, tight (US)

6 **furthest**, extreme, far, verging, on the brink, at the three-mile limit, boundary, border, bordering, longitudinal, latitudinal

VERBS

7 **limit**, restrict, proscribe, circumscribe, demarcate, draw the line at, define, moderate, be exclusive, exclude, restrain, constrain, control, lay down guidelines, mitigate, be inhibited, inhibit, have self-control, have self-restraint, check, hamper, hold in, confine, prohibit, specify, set parameters, limit one's speed, reach one's threshold, hinder, brake, drag, repress, put a stop to, curb, bottle up, censor, have a narrow outlook, veto, ban, place strictures on, ration, freeze prices, curtail, set a curfew, contain, hold one back, monopolize, set a quota, embargo, allot, measure out, copyright, patent

ADVERBS

8 **within limits**, under control, under restrictions, when forbidden, to a certain extent, off-limits, out of bounds

167 Front

Take that black box away. I can't act in front of it. Herbert Beerbohm Tree.

NOUNS

1 **front**, forefront, fore, frontage, front elevation, façade, foreground, front door, entrance, main entrance, entrance hall, foyer, vestibule, lobby, forecourt, antechamber, anteroom, proscenium, seafront, waterfront, shore, marina, promenade, esplanade, strand, front line, forward line, battlefront, battleground, theatre of war, first, beginning, introduction, preliminaries, prefix, preface, foreword, frontispiece, front page, front matter, prelims, prologue, avant-garde, advance guard, vanguard, spearhead, figurehead, prow, bowsprit, forecastle (*or* fo'c'sle), foredeck, foremast

▶ *129 Precedence; 308 Opening; 381 Attack*

2 **face**, visage, façade, physiognomy, countenance, profile, full-face picture, head-and-shoulders shot, mug shot (Inf), mug (Inf), pan (Inf), puss (Inf), kisser (Inf), phiz (Inf), clock (Inf), dial (Inf), index (US inf)

▶ *174 Top; 525 Appearance*

3 **show**, surface show, outward appearance, projected image, persona, mask, façade, display

4 **assurance**, self-assurance, confidence, self-confidence, composure, equanimity, authority

5 **boldness**, cheek, nerve, audacity, brazenness, brassi-

ness, arrogance, sauce, effrontery, brass neck (Inf), front (Inf), sass (US inf), bottle (Inf), chutzpah (US inf)

ADJECTIVES

6 **front**, fore, foreground, frontal, fronting, entrance, obverse, anterior, preceding, forward, physiognomic, physiognomical, full-faced, head-and-shoulders, full-frontal (Inf)

7 **outward**, surface, facial, superficial, displayed, projected, assumed

8 **assured**, self-assured, self-confident, composed, authoritative

9 **arrogant**, overconfident, bold, brazen, sassy (US inf)

VERBS

10 **be in front,** stand in front, front, come to the front, come forward, be ahead of, be first, be in the vanguard (or van), put up front, put in advance, ante, take the lead, lead, take the helm, head, introduce, prefix, preface, prelude, spearhead, challenge, face, confront, face up to, front up to

ADVERBS

11 **in front**, up front, to the fore, forward, ahead, before, in advance, in the lead, in the vanguard (*or* van)

168 Back

He led his regiment from behind
He found it less exciting. W. S. Gilbert.

NOUNS

1 **rear**, behind, background, hinterland, backstage, rear part, back part, rear entrance, back door, postern, tradesman's entrance, back end, afterpart, wake, train, tail end, tailpiece, pigtail, heel, heel piece, coda, endpiece, back matter, end matter, colophon, afterword, verso, afterpiece, epilogue, afterthought, postscript (PS), continuation, appendix, supplement, suffix, stern, afterquarters, poop deck, mizzenmast (*or* mizenmast), rear mast

▶ *17 Literature; 18 Music; 131 End; 132 Consecutiveness*

2 **rear end**, end, rump, behind, stern, bottom, anus, posterior, backside, buttocks, back, lower back, fundament, lumbar region, dorsal region, hindquarters, haunches, hunkers, tail, latter end, derriere, sitter (Inf), sit-upon (Inf), tush (*or* tushie) (US inf), cheeks (Inf), butt (US inf), back passage (Inf), fanny (US inf), rusty-dusty (US inf), arse (Inf), bum (Inf), keister (*or* keester) (US inf), Gary Glitter (Inf)

3 **rearing up**, rising up, leaning backwards, going backwards, elevating oneself, going up on hind legs, lifting front legs

▶ *154 Height; 213 Increase; 243 Preparation*

ADJECTIVES

4 **rear**, rearward, back, hind, hindmost, postern, posterior, mizzen (*or* mizen), dorsal, lumbar, tail, end, continued, supplemental, anal, caudal, latter, lower

5 **bred**, well-bred, fattened-up, grown

VERBS

6 **be in the rear**, be behind, trail, tag along, lag behind, drop behind, follow, follow in the wake, bring up the rear, be last

7 **rear up**, rise up, lean backwards, go backwards, elevate oneself, go up on hind legs, lift front legs

8 **nurture**, raise children, bring up children, rear, raise, breed, stock, incubate, fatten up, farm, grow plants

ADVERBS

9 **in the rear**, to the rear, at the end, rearward, behind, behind the scenes, in back of, in the background, after, aftermost, sternmost, aft, backward

169 Side

Do not on any account attempt to write on both sides of the paper at once. W. C. Sellar.

NOUNS

1 **side**, laterality, edge, side entrance, side door, siding, side elevation, hillside, flank, right hand, dexter side, starboard, left hand, sinister side, port, ribs, hip, side of the face, cheek, jowl, temple, jaw, side whiskers, sideboards, profile, side view

▶ *164 Edge; 189 Slantedness*

2 **surface**, facing, front, façade, back, top, bottom, far side of the moon, side of a coin, exterior, interior

3 **side direction**, windward side, right-hand side, left-hand side, lee side, south side, east side, west side, north side, right side, left side, other side, farside, nearside, offside

▶ *324 Direction*

4 **aspect**, feature, facet, element, bright side, funny side, dark side, cruel side

▶ *525 Appearance*

5 **team**, group, circle, camp, coterie, home side, away side, visiting side, our side, opposing side, opposite side

▶ *376 Gathering*

ADJECTIVES

6 **side**, sidelong, oblique, lateral, flanking, skirting, facing, southern, eastern, western, northern, right, left, far, near, two-sided, many-sided, multifaceted, bilateral, trilateral, quadrilateral, collateral

VERBS

7 **be alongside**, side, side up to, edge, flank, be next to, stand side by side, skirt, face

8 **move sideways**, go sideways, step aside, sidestep, sidle, make a side move, avoid, deviate

▶ *325 Deviation*

9 **side with**, side, support, back, take sides, be partisan, conspire with

ADVERBS

10 **laterally**, sideways, sidewards, obliquely, to one side, to the side, sidewise, alongside, side-by-side, hand-in-hand

170 Surroundings

President Robbins was so well adjusted to his environment that sometimes you could not tell which was the environment and which was President Robbins. Randall Jarrell.

NOUNS

1 **surroundings**, environment, environs, area, neigh-

bourhood, confines, locale, background, backdrop, setting, arena, stage, scene, scenery, outskirts, outposts, perimeter, periphery, precincts, vicinity, suburb, green belt

▶ *163 Outline; 165 Enclosure; 171 Outside*

2 **encirclement**, envelopment, enfoldment, encompassment, circumambience (*or* circumambiency)

3 **atmosphere**, ambience, milieu, aura, feeling, tone, overtone, undertone, situation, vibrations (Inf), vibes (Inf)

▶ *143 Situation*

ADJECTIVES

4 **surrounding**, environmental, neighbourhood, background, outlying, perimetric (*or* perimetrical), peripheral, suburban

5 **surrounded**, encircled, enveloped, wrapped, enfolded, encompassed, girded, circumscribed, circumambient, on all sides, roundabout, round and about, hemmed-in, enclosed

6 **atmospheric**, ambient, in the air, aural, situational

VERBS

7 **surround**, lie around, environ, outlie, encircle, circle, go round, envelop, enfold, encompass, surround, be around, enclose, contain, keep in, edge, border, frame

ADVERBS

8 **round**, about, round about, on all sides, right and left, all round, in the neighbourhood, in the vicinity

171 Outside

NOUNS

1 **exterior**, exteriority, external, externality, externalness, surface, outer side, façade, front, face, outer face, facet, shell, rind, pod, crust, covering, coating, outer wall, envelope, integument, superstratum, superficies, outer layer, skin, epidermis, cuticle, exoskeleton, cortex, hull, husk, periphery, circumference, outline, fringe, surroundings, border

▶ *167 Front; 170 Surroundings; 550 Covering*

2 **outside**, outwardness, out of doors, the great outdoors, open air, the open, hinterland, outland, outback (Aus)

▶ *145 Distance*

3 **appearance**, surface appearance, outward appearance, apparentness, aspect, image, mien, impression, public persona, guise, seemingness, superficiality, shallowness

▶ *525 Appearance*

4 **externalization**, exteriorization, projection, openness, outwardness, extroversion, extrovert

5 **extraneousness**, foreignness, strangeness, otherworldliness, the other side, others, outsiders, strangers, foreigners

▶ *100 Otherness*

ADJECTIVES

6 **exterior**, external, surface, outer, front, facing, faceted, shelly, podded, crusty, crusted, covered, enveloped, integumental, epidermal, epidermic, epidermoid, cuticular, exoskeletal

7 **outside**, outward, out-of-doors, outdoor, open, open-air, alfresco, outermost, outlying, extramural

8 **apparent**, surface, outward, ostensible, superficial, shallow, seeming, imaginal, imaginary, impressional

9 **externalized**, exteriorized, projected, open, outward, extroverted

10 **extraneous**, foreign, alien, exotic, strange, otherworldly

VERBS

11 **be exterior**, cover, surface, overlie, front, face, encrust, skin over, envelop, outline, fringe, surround, border

12 **be outside**, be out-of-doors, enjoy the open air, dine alfresco, picnic, take to the road

13 **appear outwardly**, appear, seem, look, give an impression

14 **externalize**, exteriorize, project, reveal, bring out, bring into the open

ADVERBS

15 **externally**, outwardly, outwards, outside, on the outside, in the open air, in the open, out of doors, without, alfresco, on the surface, on the face of it, apparently, to all appearances, seemingly, superficially

172 Inside

'Good grief,' said Arthur, 'is this really the interior of a flying saucer?' Douglas Adams.

NOUNS

1 **interior**, interiority, internal, internality, internalness, inwardness, centrality, inner surface, inner layer, inner side, inner wall, undersurface, endodermis, endoderm, subcortex, substratum, subsoil, depth, cave, pothole

▶ *156 Depth; 165 Enclosure; 175 Base*

2 **inside**, indoors, home, room, confinement, cell, prison, jail, solitary confinement, inner part, centre, middle, heart, core, depths, recesses, secret place, seclusion, retreat, sanctuary

▶ *173 Centre*

3 **inland**, inlands, the interior, hinterland, heartland, upstate, upcountry, the Midwest (US), the Midlands

▶ *30 Earth Science; 31 Meteorology and Climatology*

4 **insides**, contents, internal organs, bodily organs, vital organs, the vitals, viscera, gland, heart, lung, liver, kidney, spleen, abdomen, stomach, belly, paunch, womb, uterus, entrails, intestines, duodenum, jejunum, colon, rectum, offal, tripe, tummy (Inf), innards (Inf), guts (Inf)

▶ *35 Medicine*

5 **inner nature**, inner life, intrinsicality, inner person, inner man (*or* woman), innermost being, heart, soul, animus, anima, core, marrow, pith, nitty-gritty (Inf)

▶ *99 Essence*

6 **internalization**, secretiveness, secrecy, privacy, inwardness, self-absorption, engrossment, egocentrism, introversion, introvert

▶ *736 Concealment; 737 Secrecy*

ADJECTIVES

7 **interior**, internal, central, inside, inward, inner, undersurfaced, enclosed, endemic, endodermal, endodermic, subcutaneous, subcortical, intravenous, substrative (*or* substratal), deep

8 **internal**, inward, indoor, homelike, homy, home, in-

house, domestic, local, civil, national
9 **inland**, interior, landlocked, central, upstate, upcountry, midland, continental
10 **visceral**, internal, bodily, vital, splanchnic, glandular, cardiac, pulmonary, cardiovascular, renal, intestinal, enteric, gastric, duodenal, jejunal, uterine, intrauterine, abdominal, colonic, rectal
11 **intrinsic**, innate, inherent, innermost, fundamental, radical, constitutional
12 **internalized**, intimate, personal, private, secret, hidden, veiled, inmost, inward, self-absorbed, engrossed, egocentric, secretive, introverted

VERBS

13 **be interior**, lie within, lie beneath, underlie, lie below the surface, be at the bottom of
14 **go inside**, enter, retreat into, take refuge, seclude oneself, home
15 **keep inside**, internalize, bottle up, contain, absorb, hold within, hide, conceal, confine, imprison, jail

ADVERBS

16 **inwardly**, internally, inside, deeply, intimately, secretively, innately, intrinsically

173 Centre

We know what happens to people who stay in the middle of the road. They get run over. Aneurin Bevan.

NOUNS

1 **centre**, dead centre, centre point, centre of gravity, middle, mean, median, midpoint, focal point, focus, epicentre, centroid, nucleus, heart, core, hub, nub, pivot, fulcrum, axis, kernel, pith, backbone, marrow, omphalos
▶ *99 Essence; 172 Inside; 416 Density*
2 **central thing**, centrepiece, sun, centrosphere, eye of the hurricane, nave, bull's-eye, gold, bull, pupil, midriff, navel, belly button, umbilical cord
3 **centrality**, centricity, centralness, centralization, centralism, centring, concentricity, focusing, focalization, focalizing, convergence, confluence, concentration, pinpointing, locating
4 **centre of activity**, hotbed, main place, place of pilgrimage, holy place, Jerusalem, Lourdes, Mecca, capital city, capital, town centre, Piccadilly Circus, Times Square, shopping centre, mall, shopping mall, medical centre, civic centre, market town, marketplace, mart, forum, airport, train station, depot, central office, main office, nerve centre, headquarters (HQ), general headquarters (GHQ), where the action is (Inf), where it's at (Inf)
▶ *142 Location; 779 Market*
5 **focus**, focal point, main interest, centre of interest, centre of attention (*or* attraction), star, cynosure, personality, chief, head, principal, key figure, primary source
▶ *334 Power*

ADJECTIVES

6 **central**, middle, mean, median, average, midmost, midpoint, epicentral, geocentric, heliocentric, centripetal, nuclear, nucleate, umbilical, pivotal, key, axial, omphalic
7 **centralized**, centred, centric, centrical, concentric, homocentric, focalized, convergent, converging, confluent, concentrated, pinpointed, pinpointing
8 **focal**, cynosural, favourite, chief, head, principal, main, key, primary, crucial

VERBS

9 **centre**, centralize, nucleate, focus, bring into focus, focalize, centre on, converge, converge on, flow together, concentrate, concentrate on, pivot on, zero in on, home in on, come to a point, pinpoint, focus on, locate, headquarter (US)

ADVERBS

10 **centrally**, in the centre of, in the middle of, in the midst of, at the core, at the heart of

174 Top

As far as I knew, he had never taken a photograph before, and the summit of Everest was hardly the place to show him how. Edmund Hillary.

NOUNS

1 **summit**, top, mountaintop, hilltop, peak, pinnacle, acme, zenith, meridian, pole, apogee, climax, culmination, maximum, limit, apex, vertex, cusp, point, tip, extremity, crest, brow, ridge, pitch, highest point, highest level, upper extremity, utmost height, tiptop, very top, top of the world, crest of the wave, upper regions, exosphere, sky, heaven, heavens, seventh heaven, cloud nine (Inf)
▶ *154 Height*
2 **head**, crown, cap, topknot, pinhead, heading, headpiece, crownpiece, masthead, topmast, topgallant, topgallant mast, topsail, topgallant sail, spire, treetop
3 **architectural summit**, capital, chapiter, necking, gorgerin, abacus, architrave, epistyle, taenia, entablature, cornice, cymatium, finial, fastigium, headstone, keystone, quoin, capstone, copestone, coping stone, coping, cope, gable, pediment, frontispiece, tympanum, lintel, frieze, picture rail, ceiling, roof, rooftop, housetop, ridgepole, top floor, top storey, penthouse, stairhead, landing
▶ *550 Covering*
4 **top layer**, topping, icing, frosting, superstratum, topsoil, top dressing, topside, upper side, upside, surface, top surface, upper surface

ADJECTIVES

5 **top**, tiptop, topmost, upmost, uppermost, highest, ultimate, maximum, maximal, consummate, climactic, culminating, crowning, meridian, meridional, polar, head, leading, chief, capital, supreme, paramount, summital, zenithal, apical, vertical
6 **topped**, capped, crowned, tipped, crested, headed, covered, roofed, iced, frosted

VERBS

7 **top**, top off, top out, cap, crown, head, lead, peak, culminate, climax, surmount, overtop, overarch, cover, roof, ice, frost

ADVERBS

8 **on top**, on the top, at the top, at the summit, at the highest level, tiptop, on top of the world, on the crest of

the wave, at the top of the ladder (*or* tree), in seventh heaven, on cloud nine (Inf)

175 Base

One sees great things from the valley; only small things from the peak. G. K. Chesterton.

NOUNS

1 **base**, bottom, fundus, fundament, foundation, support, basis, root, footing, ground, earth, sea level, lowest point, lowest level, nadir, floor, bed, bedrock, hardpan, rock bottom, river bed, sea bed, sea floor, ocean floor, substratum, underlayer, deck, pavement, paving, flagstone, concrete, Tarmac™, flooring, floor covering, rug, carpet, parquet, tile, linoleum

▶ *99 Essence; 155 Lowness; 156 Depth*

2 **foot**, sole, toe, heel, footnote, baseboard, skirting board, mopboard (US), baseplate, keel, chassis, undercarriage, frame, substructure, infrastructure, stand, plinth, pedestal, sill, threshold, dampcourse, wainscot, dado, ground floor, first floor (US), underneath, underside, undersurface, lower ground floor, basement, cellar, lower deck, hold, bilge, sump

▶ *413 Support*

ADJECTIVES

3 **base**, ground, ground-level, supporting, underlying, basal, basilar, basilary, bottom, rock-bottom, bottommost, undermost, nethermost, lowest, basic, fundamental, essential, inherent, radical, rudimentary, vestigial

VERBS

4 **base**, found, build, establish, anchor, fix, root, ground, underlie, support, underpin

ADVERBS

5 **basically**, fundamentally, essentially

176 Angle

What is algebra exactly; is it those three-cornered things? J. M. Barrie.

NOUNS

1 **angle**, bend, fork, corner, sharp corner, intersection, junction, zigzag, obtuse angle, oblique angle, acute angle, right angle, circumflex angle, perpendicular, A-frame, V-shape, T-shape, U-shape, chevron, V-sign, hairpin bend, dogleg, angle iron, elbow-joint, knee-joint, gonion, mitre joint

▶ *27 Mathematics; 182 Convexity; 193 Interweaving*

2 **obliquity**, skewness, bias slope, bevel, cant, bezel, edge, wedge, slant, ramp, hill, slope, tilt, declivity, steepness, escarpment, scarp, tangent

▶ *189 Slantedness*

3 **angled figure**, triangle, equilateral triangle, isosceles triangle, scalene triangle, right-angled triangle, quadrangle, quadrilateral, square, rectangle, parallelogram, tetragon, rhombus, lozenge, rhomboid, pentagon, hexagon, hexagram, heptagon, octagon, decagon, decahedron, duodecahedron, polyhedron, prism, pyramid, diamond

4 **angular measurement**, trigonometry, goniometry, geometry, goniometer, protractor, sextant, sundial, bevel square, set square, T-square, theodolite, quadrant, astrological angle, semi-sextile, sextile, biquintile, square, quintile, trine, quincunx, opposition

5 **viewpoint**, aspect, standpoint, stand, view, impression, slant, bias, premise, theory

▶ *4 Philosophy; 450 Belief; 455 Knowledge*

6 **motive**, personal motive, purpose, angle (Inf)

▶ *483 Motive; 683 Selfishness*

ADJECTIVES

7 **angular**, cornered, pointed, sharp-cornered, bent, hooked, jointed, forked, bifurcate, V-shaped, A-framed, doglegged, mitred

8 **oblique**, skew, skewed, sloping, bevelled, slanting, hilly, sloped, inclined, tilted, steep, tangential, diagonal, transverse, thwart, skewwhiff (Inf)

9 **angled**, acute-angled, oblique-angled, obtuse-angled, scalene, triangular, square, right-angled, perpendicular, rectangular, quadrilateral, quadrangular, polygonal, pentagonal, rhomboidal, hexagonal, heptagonal, hexagrammoid, octagonal, decagonal, trilateral, cuneate, cuneiform, decahedral, polyhedral, prismatic, pyramidal, faceted, diamond

10 **biased**, slanted, angled toward

VERBS

11 **angle**, fork, intersect, zigzag, bend, hook over, tip, tilt, slope, lean, cant, bevel, bank, mitre, incline, careen, twist, warp, camber, go off on (*or* at) a tangent

ADVERBS

12 **askew**, aslant, obliquely, diagonally, at an angle, (off) on (*or* at) a tangent, on the bias

177 Curve

NOUNS

1 **curvature**, incurvature, concavity, convexity, bending, arching, circularity, circularness, curliness, curvilinearity, sinuousity

▶ *180 Convolution; 182 Convexity; 183 Concavity*

2 **bend**, camber, turn, U-turn, S-curve, detour, curl, arc, arch, crescent, coil, loop, spiral, circuit, circle, oval, rondure, semicircle, meniscus, parabola, hyperbola, roundness, wave, undulation

▶ *179 Circularity*

3 **curved things**, horseshoe, dome, half-moon, archer's bow, figure (of) eight, bend in the road, rainbow, horizon, earth's orbit, sine wave

ADJECTIVES

4 **curved**, curving, cambered, curviform, curvilinear, bent, concave, convex, turning, sloping, sloped, stooped, bowed, vaulted, arciform, arched, archiform, spiraled, curled, coiled, looped, round, oval, semicircular, circular, crescentic, lunar, meniscal, parabolic, hyperbolic, domical, sinusoidal

5 **well-rounded**, rounded, curvy, wavy, undulatory, pear-shaped, sinuous, curvaceous

VERBS

6 **curve**, bend, loop, arc, arch, turn, detour, curl, coil, spiral, bow, circle, twine, entwine

ADVERBS

7 **curvedly**, curvilinearly, sinuously, sinusoidally, convexly, concavely, parabolically, hyperbolically, circularly, circuitously, roundly, curvaceously, wavily

178 Straightness

Second to the right, and straight on till morning. J. M. Barrie.

ADJECTIVES

1 **straight**, linear, rectilinear, straight-lined, perpendicular, horizontal, vertical, true, right, plumb, rigid, dead straight, straightened, straightened out, uncurled, unbent, direct, as the crow flies, straight as an arrow

2 **straightforward**, simple, direct, plain, clear, uncomplicated, easy to understand

3 **continuous**, straight through, uninterrupted, nonstop, one-hop (Inf)

4 **traditional**, conventional, conservative, moderate, old-fashioned, cautious, heterosexual, not using drugs, square (Inf)

5 **honourable**, straightforward, candid, plain, frank, open, overt, manifest, direct, unambiguous, truthful, trustworthy, fair and square, as good as one's word, honest, straight down the line (Inf), straight up (Inf), upfront (Inf)

NOUNS

6 **straightness**, directness, linearity, rectilinearity, perpendicularity

► *148 Length*

7 **straight line**, beeline, vertical line, horizontal line, unbroken line, plumb line, perpendicular, ascending order, descending order, row, colonnade

► *186 Verticality; 187 Horizontality*

8 **directness**, plainness, plain speaking, straight talking, truth, honesty, straightforwardness, simplicity, clarity, fairness, scrupulousness, fair dealing, truthfulness, candour

9 **straight person**, conservative, moderate, heterosexual, nonuser of drugs, straight-shooter (US inf)

► *117 Conformity; 799 Honour*

VERBS

10 **straighten**, make straight, unravel, iron out, flatten out, straighten out, uncurl, unbend, unroll, unfurl, untangle, unfold, disentangle, comb out, uncoil, untwist, smooth out, unscramble, tidy up, neaten, make shipshape

11 **be straight**, talk straight, talk plainly, speak the truth, stick to the truth, speak one's mind, give it to someone straight, make a clean breast of, mean what one says, keep to the point, not deviate

ADVERBS

12 **straight**, straightly, horizontally, vertically, directly, unswervingly, as the crow flies, on the beam (Inf)

13 **straightforwardly**, honourably, honestly, directly, plainly, truthfully, frankly, openly

179 Circularity

The wheel is come full circle. William Shakespeare.

NOUNS

1 **circularity**, roundness, orbicularity, sphericalness, curvedness, rotundity, annularity

► *177 Curve; 181 Roundness*

2 **circle**, full circle, circumference, ambit, curve, orb, sphere, cycle, full cycle, orbit, epicycle, annulus, semicircle, half circle, oval, zodiac, mandala, circular path, circular road, circuit, annulation, loop, ring, figure of eight, roundabout, roundabout way, circuitous route, racecourse, detour, bypass, arc, round trip, lap

► *319 Transport*

3 **circular thing**, headband, hairband, crown, coronet, collar, neckband, dog collar, necklace, choker, belt, waistband, cummerbund, sash, girdle, bracelet, wristband, anklet, discus, plate, saucer, disc, ring, hoop, band, tyre, wheel, noose, wreath, equator, halo, corona

4 **parts of a circle**, centre, circumference, radius, diameter, quadrant, sextant, sector, segment, chord, crescent, arc

ADJECTIVES

5 **circular**, annular, annulate, discoid, spherical, orbital, orbicular, spheric, spherelike, spheroidal, rounded, round, ring-shaped, semicircular, cyclic, elliptic, ovate, oval, ovoid, egg-shaped, rotund, circulatory, circumferential

VERBS

6 **circle**, encircle, surround, go round, travel in a circle, make a round trip, make a circle, circulate, circumambulate, circumnavigate, lap, take a turn, orbit, go into orbit, revolve, rotate, detour, make a detour, bypass, skirt around

7 **make circular**, circularize, draw a circle, arrange in a circle, make round, girdle, encompass, round, turn

ADVERBS

8 **circularly**, circuitously, circumferentially, cyclically, orbitally, orbicularly, annularly, elliptically, ovately, ovally, spherically, spheroidally, roundly, rotundly

180 Convolution

Before the Roman came to Rye or out to Severn strode,
The rolling English drunkard made the rolling English road.
G. K. Chesterton.

NOUNS

1 **convolution**, convolutedness, involution, circumvolution, circling upon itself, intricacy, intricateness, twistedness, sinuousness, undulation, anfractuosity

► *179 Circularity; 325 Deviation; 408 Disorder*

2 **coil**, turn, twist, twirl, intricacy, spiral, turbination, screwthread, corkscrew, spring, whorl, (double) helix, curl, curlicue, ringlet, loop, meandering, squiggle, kink, corrugation, squirm, shimmy, wriggle

► *177 Curve*

3 **convoluted thing**, snail shell, ammonite, nautilus, scallop (*or* scollop) shell, snake, whirlpool, vortex, tornado,

twister (US inf), labyrinth, maze, braid, intestines, cochlea

ADJECTIVES

4 **convolutional**, convoluted, winding, twisted, involutional, circumlocutory, sinuous, undulatory, intricate, braided, wavy, twirled, entwined, corrugated, tortuous, meandering, labyrinthine, like a maze, serpentine, vermiform, wriggling, squirming, squiggly, coiled, spiral, helical, cochleate, whorled, turbinate

5 **ambiguous**, equivocal, difficult to comprehend, involved, complicated, complex, contorted

▶ *479 Equivocation; 702 Sophistry*

VERBS

6 **convolute**, convolve, circle upon itself, wind together, twist together, weave together, enlace, twine, entwine, coil, roll, braid, corkscrew, spiral, twirl, curl, wave, undulate, corrugate, scallop (*or* scollop), distort, meander, loop, snake, twist, turn, twist and turn, wriggle, writhe, squirm, squiggle, shimmy

7 **be ambiguous**, equivocate, complicate, make complex

ADVERBS

8 **circularly**, circuitously, all around the houses, ambiguously, equivocally, complexly, intricately, tortuously, spirally, helically, sinuously, wavily

181 Roundness

NOUNS

1 **roundness**, rotundity, orbicularity, sphericity, sphericalness, globosity, globularity, gibbousness, convexity, cylindricality

▶ *179 Circularity; 182 Convexity*

2 **round body**, well-rounded shape, shapeliness, pear shape, fatness, corpulence, obesity, fleshiness, stoutness, plumpness, portliness, paunchiness, podginess, tubbiness, chubbiness, potbelly, curvaceousness

▶ *158 Size*

3 **round thing**, circle, circuit, orbit, sphere, globe, orb, egg, spheroid, hemisphere, ball, bubble, balloon, marble, pellet, bead, pill, pea, bulb, globule, drop, droplet, dewdrop

4 **cylinder**, roller, rod, rung, tube, cigar, pipe, stalk, trunk, bole, column, rolling pin

▶ *308 Opening*

5 **cone**, cornet, horn, trumpet, bell shape, top, spinning top

6 **round**, turn, bowl, lap, round trip, circuit, chukker, daily round, orbit, ambit, circumambulation, circumnavigation, groove, rut

7 **round**, part song, madrigal, quodlibet

8 **round**, live ammunition, shot, bullets

ADJECTIVES

9 **round**, rotund, orbicular, gibbous, spherical, globose, globous, globular, convex, egg-shaped, ovoid, cylindrical, tubular, conical, conic, bell-shaped, bulbous, spherelike, spheric, hemispherical, round as a ball

10 **well-rounded**, rounded out, round, pear-shaped, shapely, well-proportioned, well-turned, fleshy, fat, overweight, obese, corpulent, stout, plump, portly, paunchy, podgy, tubby, chubby, potbellied, curvaceous

VERBS

11 **make round**, roll, smooth, turn, make spherical, balloon out, ball up, coil up, roll up, ball, round off, round out, fill out

12 **move round**, orbit, circle, circulate, circumambulate, circumnavigate, lap, complete a circuit

ADVERBS

13 **roundly**, rotundly, orbicularly, spherically, globosely, globularly, convexly, cylindrically, conically, bulbously, curvaceously

182 Convexity

And the winds and sunbeams with their convex gleams
Build up the blue dome of air. Percy Bysshe Shelley.

NOUNS

1 **convexity**, convexness, bulbousness, bulginess, bulging, swelling, gibbousness, billowing, distention, protrusion, protuberance, prominence, excrescence, tumescence, meniscus, camber

▶ *177 Curve; 181 Roundness; 185 Bulge*

2 **bulge**, hump, lens, arc, bubble, knob, button, boss, bud, nose, bump, wart, knot, oedema, swelling, erection, bubo, carbuncle, boil, blister, corn, bunion, tumour, cyst, pregnancy, beergut, muscle, biceps, pectoral, pecks (Inf), nipple, papilla, mamilla, bosom, breast, bust, boobs (Inf), knockers (Inf), tits (Inf), testicles, balls (Inf), rocks (Inf), bollocks (Inf)

▶ *158 Size; 260 Ill Health*

3 **dome**, cupola, vault, arc, arch, beehive, barrow, mound, hillock, hummock, hump (Dial)

▶ *154 Height; 550 Covering*

ADJECTIVES

4 **convex**, bulbous, bulgy, bulging, swelling, gibbous, billowing, protruding, distended, humped, prominent, excrescent, tumescent, swollen, meniscoid, arcuated, bowed out, arched, vaulted, lenticular, lentiform

VERBS

5 **be convex**, arcuate, arch, curve, camber, bow, protrude, bulge, stick out, swell out, swell, hump, balloon out, round out, distend, billow

ADVERBS

6 **convexly**, bulbously, bulgingly, protuberantly, prominently, excrescently

183 Concavity

In a hole in the ground there lived a hobbit. J. R. R. Tolkien.

NOUNS

1 **concavity**, hollowness, curving inwards, sinking, incurvation, indentation, indention, depression, impression

▶ *98 Absence; 156 Depth; 177 Curve*

2 **concave land**, hollow, cove, dip, hole, pothole, borehole, foxhole, crater, valley, vale, dell, glen, dingle, col, combe, gap, pass, ravine, gorge, abyss, crevasse, canyon, gully, den, burrow, warren, cave, cavern, trough, sap, tunnel, tube, trench, fosse (*or* foss), moat, grave, quarry,

pit, mine, coalmine, colliery, gold mine, diamond mine, cutting, excavation, canal, inlet, gulf
► *30 Earth Science; 31 Meteorology and Climatology*
3 **cavity**, dent, nook, cranny, niche, recess, alcove, basin, trough, bowl, cup, sump, socket, footprint, dimple, honeycomb, pockmark (*or* pock)
► *308 Opening; 410 Container*
4 **notch**, indentation, nick, nock, hack, cut, incision, incisure, dent, groove, cleft, slit, split, gash, gouge, tooth, score, kerf, serration, serrulation, crenel (*or* crenelle), crenation, crenulation, crenature
► *146 Interval; 183 Concavity; 384 Defence; 425 Sharpness*
5 **digger**, miner, excavator, quarryman, tunneller, burrower, grave digger, sapper, archaeologist, driller, borer, dredger, dredge

ADJECTIVES

6 **concave**, hollow, curved inwards, incurvate, depressed, sunken, cavernous, indented, cup-shaped, bowl-shaped, dented, dimpled, pocked, pockmarked, pitted, full of holes, porous, spongy
7 **notched**, notchy, indented, crenate, crenated, cut, slit, split, toothed, cogged, dentate, scalloped, pinked, jagged, jaggy, incisural, sawlike, saw-toothed, serrated, serriform, zigzag, zigzagged, uneven

VERBS

8 **be concave**, curve inwards, sink, cave in, collapse, settle
9 **make concave**, hollow, press (*or* push) inwards, press, impress, imprint, indent, punch in, depress, dent, stamp, stave in, excavate, delve into, tunnel, burrow, bore, bore into, dig out, scoop out, gouge out, hollow out, dig, spade, mine, sink a shaft, pockmark, honeycomb
10 **notch**, indent, nick, nock, cog, hack, cut, incise, dent, slit, split, gash, gouge, score, kerf, serrate, pink, crenellate

ADVERBS

11 **concavely**, hollowly, cavernously
12 **jaggedly**, crenately, dentately, denticulately, unevenly

184 Wrinkle

NOUNS

1 **wrinkle**, ruck, rumple, crinkle, pucker, crow's foot, laugh (*or* laughter) line, crumple, crimp, crease, fold, bend, turn, overlap, layer, roll, furl, coil, doubling, doubling over, dog-ear, plication, plicature, plica, flexure, flection, buckling, geological fold, anticline, syncline
► *176 Angle; 167 Front; 550 Covering; 556 Age*
2 **furrow**, trench, trough, scratch, seam, groove, wheel-track, slot, fissure, chink, cut, slit, channel, conduit, rut, ditch, gutter, canal, flute, score, corrugation
► *150 Broadness; 183 Concavity; 372 Separation; 433 Water; 744 Record*
3 **pleat**, plait, accordion pleat, knife pleat, box pleat, crease, pucker, tuck, gather, ruche (*or* rouche), ruffle, shirr, flounce, ripple, furrow, corrugation
► *180 Convolution; 328 Disturbance*
4 **wrinkled thing**, knitted brow, scrunchie, crushed velvet, turtle's neck, crêpe paper, corduroy material, pleated dress, washboard, corrugated paper, corrugated iron, ploughed field, rippled lake, choppy sea
5 **enfoldment**, envelopment, enclosure, wrapping, swathing, entwining, hug, embrace, clasp
► *165 Enclosure*

ADJECTIVES

6 **wrinkly**, wrinkled, crinkly, crinkled, crumply, crumpled, scrumpled, rumpled, scrunched, crushed, screwed-up, creased, puckered, lined, seamed, knitted, furrowed, scratched, grooved, wheel-tracked, slotted, chinky, rutty, rutted, rimose, fluted, scored, corrugated, etched, engraved, ploughed
7 **folded**, folded over, bent, pleated, plicate, plical, flexuous, flectional, doubled over, turned over (*or* down), dog-eared, rolled, creased, creasy, rucked up, ruched, flexed

VERBS

8 **wrinkle**, crinkle, crease, scrunch, scrumple, crumple, rumple, screw up, pucker, line, knit, furrow, trench, trough, scratch, seam, groove, track, slot, fissure, chink (US), cut, etch, engrave, slit, channel, rut, plough, ditch, gutter, canal, flute, score, corrugate
9 **fold**, fold up, fold over, fold around, lap, double, double over (*or* under), turn over (*or* under), turn up (*or* down), dog-ear, bend, buckle, overlap, layer, roll, roll up, furl, coil
10 **pleat**, crease, pucker, tuck, tuck up, gather, ruffle, shirr, flounce, ruck, crimp, ripple, furrow, corrugate
11 **enfold**, envelop, enclose, wrap, swathe, entwine, intertwine, hug, embrace, clasp

ADVERBS

12 **doubly**, in two, plicately, flexuously, ripplingly, ruttily, rimosely

185 Bulge

NOUNS

1 **prominence**, eminence, distinction, importance, salience, mark, repute, esteem, prestige, kudos, cachet, glory, position, impressiveness, exaltedness, primacy, clout (Inf)
► *667 Respect; 669 Approval; 783 Credit*
2 **projection**, spit, headland, promontory, cape, cliff, ness, point, peninsula, island, breakwater, mole, jetty, pier, mountain, foothill, peak, fortification, projection, overhang, outcrop, shelf, ledge, balcony
► *176 Angle*
3 **protuberance**, bump, swelling, protrusion, prominent feature, face, forehead, brow, proboscis, trunk, antenna, beak, nose, snout (Inf), snoot (Inf), conk (Inf), hooter (Inf), bugle (Inf), schnozzle (*or* schnozz) (US inf)
► *167 Front; 182 Convexity*
4 **conspicuousness**, obviousness, distinctness, clear visibility, clearness, clarity
► *520 Visibility*

ADJECTIVES

5 **protuberant**, protrudent, swelling, sticking out, proud, standing out, poking out, jutting out, bumpy, beaked, beaky
6 **eminent**, prominent, distinctive, important, salient,

reputable, esteemed, glorious, impressive, exalted, primary

7 **conspicuous**, distinct, clearly visible, plainly visible, easily seen, well-defined, unblurred, clear-cut, obvious, eye-catching

VERBS

8 **protrude**, swell, stick out, stick out like a sore thumb, stand out, poke out, project, jut out, overhang, have a prominent feature, be conspicuous, catch one's eye

9 **be prominent**, have distinction, be exalted, have clout (Inf)

ADVERBS

10 **protuberantly**, juttingly, conspicuously, visibly, obviously, distinctly

11 **eminently**, prominently, importantly, exaltedly, distinctively, impressively, proudly, gloriously

186 Verticality

Let us honour if we can
The vertical man
Though we value none
But the horizontal one. W. H. Auden.

NOUNS

1 **verticality**, verticalness, uprightness, erectness, erection, straightness, perpendicularity, squareness, sheerness, precipitousness, steepness, fall, drop, plunge, dive

▶ *178 Straightness*

2 **making vertical**, upending, standing up, straightening, rearing, uprearing, rising, uprising, raising, upraising, elevating, elevation, building, erecting, erection

▶ *361 Suspension; 366 Raising; 413 Support*

3 **vertical thing**, upright, post, newel post, newel, pole, pillar, pylon, column, lighthouse, stake, palisade, wall, skyscraper, face, cliff, precipice, scarp, escarpment, scar, crag, bluff, stack, stalagmite, stalactite, vertical line, vertical axis, vertical, plumb, perpendicular, right angle, normal

4 **plumb line**, plumb, square, set square, try square, T-square

VERBS

5 **be vertical**, stand, stand up, stand upright, stand erect, stand up straight, hold oneself straight, stand to attention, rear, rear up, uprear, rise, rise up, get up, arise, uprise, rise (*or* get) to one's feet, be upstanding, straighten up, sit up

6 **make vertical**, erect, build, elevate, raise, raise up, upraise, stick up, cock up, prick up, bristle, pitch (camp), set up, upend, stand on end, straighten, plumb, square

7 **fall vertically**, drop, drop like a stone, plummet, plunge, dive

ADJECTIVES

8 **vertical**, upright, erect, upended, standing, standing up, upstanding, straight, bolt upright, up-and-down, straight-up-and-down, straight up, straight down, plumb, sheer, precipitous, plunging, very steep

9 **unbowed**, rampant, rearing, reared, upreared, raising, raised, upraised, cocked up, pricked up

10 **perpendicular**, orthogonal, right-angled, square, normal, rectangular

ADVERBS

11 **vertically**, upright, uprightly, erectly, straight, up, on end, endways, endwise, bolt upright, on one's feet, on its hindlegs, on top of each other

12 **perpendicularly**, at (*or* with) right angles, up and down, straight up and down, up, down, plumb, sheer, very steeply

187 Horizontality

An adult is one who has ceased to grow vertically but not horizontally. Anonymous.

NOUNS

1 **horizontality**, horizontalness, flatness, levelness, planeness, plainness, smoothness, evenness, flushness, lying, reclining, reclination, recumbency, decumbency, accumbency, prostration, proneness, supineness, sprawling, sprawl

▶ *155 Lowness; 263 Ease; 421 Smoothness*

2 **horizontal surface**, horizontal, flat, level, plane, plane surface, homaloid, horizontal line, horizontal axis, water level, sea level, horizontal angle, azimuth

3 **flat thing**, disc, slab, layer, stratum, tablet, pancake, flatfish, flounder, flatware, saucer, plate, platter, tray, gridiron, flat tyre, flat surface, flat land, level ground, flats, plain, prairie, pampas, steppe, green, bowling green, bedding plane, bed, esplanade, plateau, tableland, terrace, ledge, platform, table, billiard table, floor, ceiling, horizon, skyline

4 **flattener**, plane, press, trouser press, iron, flatiron, steam iron, mangle, rolling pin, roller, garden roller, steamroller, bulldozer

5 **planometer**, planimeter, spirit level, ruler, rule

VERBS

6 **be horizontal**, recline, lie, lie down, lie flat, lie on one's back (*or* face), sprawl, spread-eagle, prostrate oneself, grovel

7 **make horizontal**, level, level out, flatten, grade, plane, flush, even, equalize, smooth, smoothen, smooth out, smooth down, iron, press, roll, roll out, beat flat, squash flat, tread flat, trample down, lay, lay down, spread, knock down, knock flat, prostrate, fell, raze, raze to the ground

ADJECTIVES

8 **horizontal**, flat, level, plane, plain, planar, two-dimensional, tabular, homaloidal, even, smooth, unwrinkled, flush, flat as a pancake (*or* board, flounder, fluke, billiard table, bowling green)

9 **flattened**, levelled, smoothed, smoothened, pressed, ironed, rolled, consolidated, beaten flat, squashed flat, well-trodden, trodden flat, trampled down, spread

10 **lying**, lying down, lying flat, flat out, recumbent, decumbent, accumbent, prostrate, procumbent, prone, face down, supine, couchant, reclining, sprawling, sprawled, spreadeagled, knocked down, knocked flat, razed to the ground

ADVERBS

11 **horizontally**, flat, flat on one's back (*or* face), flatly, flatways, flatwise, lengthways, lengthwise, on its side, level, plane, evenly, smoothly, flush

188 Parallelism

Even parallel lines, reaching into infinity, meet somewhere yonder. Pearl Buck.

NOUNS

1 **parallelism**, parallel, equidistance, concentricity, coextension, collimation, nonconvergence, nondivergence, correlation, correspondence, balance, alignment, equality, uniformity, harmony

► *115 Similarity; 119 Equality*

2 **parallel thing**, parallelogram, parallelepiped, parallel bars, railway tracks, aligned wheels, dual carriageway, World Trade Center twin towers (US)

ADJECTIVES

3 **parallel**, equidistant, concentric, coextensive, nonconvergent, nondivergent, antiparallel

4 **correlated**, correlative, correspondent, corresponding, balanced, aligned, equal, uniform, harmonious

VERBS

5 **parallel**, lie parallel, run parallel, run abreast, coextend, collimate

6 **correlate**, correspond, balance, align, equal, harmonize

ADVERBS

7 **in parallel**, abreast, alongside, side by side, collaterally, coextensively

189 Slantedness

NOUNS

1 **obliqueness**, obliquity, deviation, divergence, skewness, diagonal, deflection, indirection, indirectness, transverseness, crookedness, convolution, digression, meandering, twist, turn, veer, bend, bias, swerve, zigzag, inclination, leaning, curvature, slope, grade, slant, cant, bank, ramp, slide, camber, pitch, tip, tilt, list, tangent

► *154 Height; 176 Angle; 177 Curve; 186 Verticality; 325 Deviation*

2 **oblique line**, diagonal, slash, oblique, solidus, separatrix, stroke, virgule, bevelled edge, oblique angle, rakish angle, rhomboid, hairpin curve, dogleg, slide, ski jump, Tower of Pisa

3 **deviousness**, circumlocution, periphrasis, circuitousness, indirection, furtiveness, backhandedness, evasion, equivocation, prevarication, hedging, deception, distortion, dissemblance, euphemism, fraudulence, spuriousness, shadiness (Inf), fishiness (Inf)

► *234 Distortion; 479 Equivocation*

ADJECTIVES

4 **oblique**, deviating, divergent, skewed, askew, diagonal, on the diagonal, deflected, deflective, indirect, sidelong, transverse, sideways, crosswise (*or* crossways), cater-cornered (*or* cater-corner) (US), kitty-cornered (*or* kitty-corner) (US), crooked, convoluted, digressive, meandering, tangent, bevelled, twisted, turning, bending, zigzag, zigzagged, inclining, inclined, inclinational, sloping, sloped, on the slope, slanting, slanted, pitched, tilting, atilt, on the tilt, leaning, listing, off course, off-target, skewwhiff (Inf)

5 **devious**, deviant, circumlocutory, periphrastic, circuitous, roundabout, indirect, sidelong, furtive, backhand, backhanded, evasive, deceptive, equivocal, hedging, distorted, distortive, euphemistic, dissembling, fraudulent, spurious, shady (Inf), fishy (Inf)

VERBS

6 **be oblique**, oblique, transect, deviate, diverge, bear off, angle off, skew, deflect, crook, digress, meander, twist, turn, veer, bend, swerve, zigzag, wind in and out, incline, camber, curve, slope, slant, cant, bank, pitch, tip, tilt, lean, list, tip to one side

7 **deviate**, circumlocute, evade, equivocate, prevaricate, hedge, deceive, distort, dissemble, bend the truth

ADVERBS

8 **obliquely**, diagonally, at an angle, askew, askance, transversely, sideways, crosswise (*or* crossways), across, on the bias, cater-cornered (*or* cater-corner) (US), kitty-cornered (*or* kitty-corner) (US), off course, off-target

9 **deviously**, circuitously, periphrastically, indirectly, euphemistically, sidelong, furtively, equivocally, spuriously

190 Expansion

Great oaks from little acorns grow. Proverb.

NOUNS

1 **growth**, enlargement, increase in size, extension, lengthening, drawing out, stretch, stretching, stretching out, outstretching, spread, spreading, spreading out, outspreading, sprawl, sprawling, splay, splaying, branching, ramification, fanning, fanning out, dispersion, expansion, widening, broadening, flare, flaring, dilation, dilatation, diastole, opening, unfolding, distension, distention, swell, swelling, swollenness, bloat, bloating, bloatedness, tumefaction, tumescence, intumescence, tumidity, tumidness, turgescence, turgidity, turgidness, dropsy, oedema, puffiness, inflation, reflation, blowing up, bulging, bulbousness, stuffing, padding, fattening, increase, building, build-up, augmentation, addition, heightening, rising, raising, elevation, hiking, magnification, aggrandizement, amplification, development, overdevelopment, hypertrophy, overgrowth, waxing, crescendo, germination, budding, shooting, sprouting, vegetation, burgeoning, blossoming, blooming, flowering, maturation, flourishing, thriving, multiplication, reproduction, procreation, breeding, pullulation

2 **enlargeability**, extendability, extendibility, extensibility, extensibleness, stretch, stretchability, elasticity, spreadability, expansibility, dilatability, dilatableness, distensibility

3 **enlarged thing**, enlargement, extension, swelling, tumour, bulge, balloon, bubble, inflatable

4 **enlarger**, extensor, lengthener, stretcher, spreader, disperser, expander, widener, broadener, dilater, dilator, distender, stuffing, padding, inflater, inflator, pump, increaser, augmenter, augmentor, developer

VERBS

5 **make bigger**, make larger, enlarge, increase in size, extend, lengthen, draw out, stretch, stretch out, outstretch, spread, spread out, outspread, sprawl, splay, ramify, fan, fan out, disperse, expand, widen, broaden, flare, dilate, open, distend, swell, bloat, puff up, inflate, blow up, pump, pump up, stuff, pad, fatten, fat, plump, plump up, increase, build, build up, augment, add to, heighten, raise, elevate, hike, hike up, up, magnify, aggrandize, amplify, develop, overdevelop, hypertrophy

6 **become bigger**, become larger, grow, enlarge, increase in size, extend, lengthen, draw out, stretch, stretch out, spread, spread out, outspread, sprawl, splay, branch, branch out, ramify, fan, fan out, disperse, expand, widen, broaden, flare, dilate, open up, unfold, distend, swell, bloat, tumify, puff up, inflate, balloon, belly, bulge, fatten, fat, plump, plump out, fill out, get fat, gain weight, put on weight, become overweight, increase, build, build up, augment, mushroom, snowball, overdevelop, hypertrophy, outgrow, overgrow, grow like a weed, spread like wildfire, magnify, amplify, develop, wax, greaten, crescendo, gather, brew, rise, grow up, shoot up, spring up, upspring, sprout up, germinate, bud, shoot, sprout, vegetate, burgeon, blossom, bloom, flower, flourish, thrive, multiply, reproduce, procreate, breed, pullulate

ADJECTIVES

7 **bigger**, larger, enlarged, extended, lengthened, drawn out, stretched, stretched out, outstretched, spread, spread-out, outspread, widespread, splayed, fanned, fanned out, dispersed, expanded, widened, broadened, flared, dilated, open, wide-open, unfolded, distended, swelled, swollen, bloated, tumid, turgid, incrassate, dropsical, oedematous, puffed up, puffy, inflated, blown-up, pumped-up, stuffed, padded, fatter, fattened, fatted, overweight, increased, built-up, augmented, heightened, raised, elevated, magnified, amplified, developed, mature, grown, full-grown, fully grown, full-fledged, fully fledged, full-blown, fully developed, overdeveloped, hypertrophied, overgrown

8 **growing**, crescent, extending, lengthening, stretching, spreading, sprawling, sprawly, splaying, patulous, branching, fanning, fanlike, fan-shaped, flabellate, flabelliform, deltoid, expanding, widening, broadening, flaring, dilating, opening, unfolding, swelling, tumescent, turgescent, bulging, bulbous, increasing, waxing, gathering, brewing, mushrooming, snowballing, heightening, rising, developing, germinating, budding, shooting, sprouting, burgeoning, blossoming, blooming, flowering, flourishing, thriving, multiplying, pullulating

9 **enlargeable**, extendable, extendible, extensible, extensive, extensile, extensional, stretchable, stretchy, elastic, spreadable, dispersive, expandable, expansible, expansive, expansile, expansionary, dilatable, dilational, dilatant, dilative, distensible, distensive, inflatable, inflationary, augmentative, elevatory, multipliable, magnifiable, amplifiable, developable

ADVERBS

10 **largely**, broadly, widely, extensively, expansively, increasingly, additionally, reproductively, procreatively, bulbously, puffily, turgidly, tumidly

191 Contraction

Anyone informed that the universe is expanding and contracting in pulsations of eighty billion years has a right to ask, 'What's in it for me?' Peter De Vries.

NOUNS

1 **contraction**, decrease in size, systole, syneresis, synizesis, shrinking, shrinkage, shrunkenness, preshrinking, preshrinkage, constringency, astringency, astringence, compression, compaction, compactedness, condensation, concentration, miniaturization, scaling-down, squeeze, squeezing, tightening, tightness, pressing, pressure, crush, crushing, pinch, pinching, clenching, clamping, cramping, constriction, coarctation, limitation, restriction, circumscription, strangling, strangulation, stenosis, deflation, flattening, flatness, implosion, collapse, cave-in, shortening, abbreviation, elision, curtailment, abridgment, pruning, trimming, clipping, shearing shaving, filing, grinding, narrowing, drawing in, drawing together, closing up, taking in, gathering, puckering, puckering up, pursing, knitting, wrinkling, shrivelling, withering, searing, wasting, consumption, tabescence, atrophy, marasmus, emaciation, thinning, slimming, losing weight, decrease, reduction, lessening, diminuendo, wane, waning, levelling off, bottoming out

2 **contractibility**, contractility, shrinkability, compressibility, compactability, condensibility, crushability, limitability, circumscribability, deflatability, collapsibility

3 **contracted thing**, epitome, compendium, digest, bottleneck, neck, isthmus, hourglass, hourglass figure, wasp waist

4 **contractor**, astringent, styptic, compressor, compacter, condenser, tourniquet, squeezer, press, crusher, foller, mangle, clamp, vice, corset, straitjacket, constrictor, trimmer, grinder

VERBS

5 **make smaller**, contract, decrease in size, shrink, preshrink, Sanforize™, constringe, compress, compact, condense, concentrate, boil down, miniaturize, scale down, squeeze, tighten, press, crush, pinch, cram, jam, roll up, rool up into a ball, clench, clamp, cramp, constrict, limit, restrict, circumscribe, strangle, strangulate, deflate, flatten, implode, collapse, telescope, shorten, abbreviate, curtail, abridge, stunt, prune, trim, clip, shear, shave, whittle away, file, grind, narrow, draw, draw in, draw together, close up, take in, gather, smock, tuck, pucker, pucker up, purse, knit, wrinkle, shrivel, sear, waste, emaciate, thin, slim, decrease, reduce, lessen

6 **become smaller**, contract, shrink, condense, concentrate, boil down, tighten, roll up, rool up into a ball, curl up, huddle, crowd together, deflate, go down, implode, collapse, cave in, fall in, fold up, telescope, shorten, narrow, draw in, close up, pucker, pucker up, knit, wrinkle, shrivel, shrivel up, wither, wizen, waste, waste away, emaciate, thin, slim, diet, lose weight, decrease, reduce, lessen, wane level off, bottom out

ADJECTIVES

7 **smaller**, contracted, shrunk, shrunken, preshrunk, Sanforized™, compressed, compact, compacted, condensed,

concentrated, boiled-down, miniaturized, scaled-down, squeezed, tight, tightened, pressed, crushed, pinched, rolled-up, curled-up, huddled, clenched, cramped, constricted, coarctate, limited, restricted, circumscribed, strangled, strangulated, deflated, flat, collapsed, telescoped, shortened, abbreviated, curtailed, abridged, stunted, pruned, trimmed, clipped, shorn, narrow, narrowed, drawn-in, drawntogether, closed-up, gathered, smocked, tucked, puckered, puckered up, pursed, knitted, wrinkled, shrivelled, shrivelled-up, withered, wizen, wizened, sear, seared, wasted, consumptive, emaciated, thin, slim, decreased, reduced

8 **contracting**, contractive, contractional, shrinking, constringent, astringent, styptic, compressive, tightening, crushing, pinching, cramping, constricting, constrictive, limiting, restricting, restrictive, circumscriptive, strangling, deflationary, implosive, collapsing, shortening, stunting, narrowing, gathering, puckering, pursing, shrivelling, searing, wasting, tabescent, emaciating, thinning, slimming, decreasing, reducing, lessening, waning

9 **contractible**, contractile, shrinkable, compressible, compactable, condensible, crushable, limitable, circumscribable, deflatable, collapsible, foldable, telescopic

192 Inversion

Fish die belly-upward and rise to the surface; it is their way of falling. André Gide.

NOUNS

1 **inversion**, reversion, reversal, reverse, converse, transposition, inverted order, contrary, opposite, antithesis, turning upside down, turning inside out, turning back to front, turning backwards, introversion, retroversion, evagination, invagination, capsizing, overturning, upset, spill, cartwheel, somersault, handspring, headstand, undermining, palindrome, counterpoint, other side of the coin

► *187 Horizontality; 303 Backward Motion; 759 Exchange; 761 Reversion*

ADJECTIVES

2 **inverted**, reversed, transpositional, in inverted order, inside-out and back-to-front, inside-out, back-to-front, upside-down, head-over-heels, bottom-up, topsy-turvy, wrong way in, wrong way out, capsized, capsizing, arsy-versy (Inf)

VERBS

3 **invert**, reverse, transpose, put in inverted order, turn upside down, turn inside out, turn back to front, turn backwards, introvert, retrovert, evaginate, invaginate, capsize, overturn, upset, spill, cartwheel, somersault, handspring, stand on one's head, undermine, turn the tables, put the cart before the horse, try to run before one can walk

ADVERBS

4 **inversely**, conversely, backwards, the other way around, turned around, topsy-turvy, upside-down, head over heels, contrariwise, vice versa, in reverse, arsy-versy (Inf), arse over tit (Inf), ass backwards (US inf)

193 Interweaving

The web of our life is of a mingled yarn, good and ill together. William Shakespeare.

NOUNS

1 **interweaving**, weaving, crisscross, interlacing, interlacement, intertexture, interwork, lacing, intertwining, intertwinement, twining, entanglement, webbing, braiding, plaiting, pleaching (*or* plashing), interlocking, intercommunication, interfusion, interlineation, interdigitation, reticulation, interpenetration

► *180 Convolution; 408 Disorder; 412 Mixture*

2 **braid**, plait, pigtail, wreath, arabesque, filigree, cat's cradle, web, skein, network, webbing, netting, net, fishnet, mesh, spider's web, wickerwork, trellis, espalier, lattice, wattle, grid, tracery, fretwork, knitting, tatting, macramé, crochet, lace, laciness, lace making, lacework, knotting

3 **weaving**, loom, hand loom, warp, weft, woof, shuttle, distaff, spinning wheel, sewing machine, weaver, knitter, spinner, spider, weaverbird

4 **textile**, woven cloth, cloth, material, fabric, broadcloth, suiting, sacking, sackcloth, jute, linen, cheesecloth, muslin, towelling, flannel, flannelette, wool, mohair, cashmere, tweed, vicuna, alpaca, merino, angora, cotton, khaddar (*or* khadi), homespun, drill, twill, moleskin, denim, voile, poplin, madras, seersucker, chintz, cotton jersey, silk, satin, tussore, taffeta, shantung, chiffon, velvet, velveteen, corduroy, lace, chenille

► *42 Fabrics and Dyeing*

5 **crossroads**, crossing, intersection, interchange, road junction, cloverleaf, spaghetti junction

► *318 Passage; 319 Transport*

ADJECTIVES

6 **interwoven**, woven, handwoven, crisscross, interlaced, laced, lacy, intertwined, twined, webbed, webby, interdigitated, braided, plaited, pleached, wreathed, reticulate (*or* reticular), loomed, woollen, woolly, tweedy

7 **crossing**, intersecting, interchanging, interconnecting, intersectional

VERBS

8 **interweave**, inweave, weave, crisscross, enlace, interlace, lace, intertwine, entwine (*or* intwine), twine, entangle, web, braid, plait, pleach (*or* plash), interlock, interdigitate, reticulate, filigree, net, mesh, mesh together, knit, tat, macramé, crochet, knot, twist, warp, shuttle, spin, sew, intercrop, espalier, interfile, interfuse, intermingle, interlay, interline, interpenetrate

9 **cross**, intersect, interchange, come to a junction

ADVERBS

10 **interlacedly**, interlinearly, interlineally, interspatially, intertwiningly, interpenetratively, interchangeably

Number and Quantity

194 Number

Numbers constitute the only universal language. Nathaniel West.

Round numbers are always false. Samuel Johnson.

NOUNS

1 **number**, numeral, no. (*or* n.), figure, digit, cipher, character, decimal, symbol, sign, constant, variable, notation, Arabic numeral, Roman numeral, decimal system, binary system

2 **kind of number**, whole number, integer, odd number, even number, prime number, complex number, imaginary number, real number, rational number, irrational number, transcendental number, algebraic number, cardinal number, ordinal number

3 **large number**, astronomical number, million, milliard, billion, trillion, quadrillion, quintillion, sextillion, septillion, octillion, nonillion, decillion, undecillion, duodecillion, tredecillion, quattuordecillion, quindecillion, sexdecillion, septendecillion, octodecillion, novemdecillion, vigintillion, centrillion, googol, googolplex, infinity, umpteen (Inf), zillion (Inf), jillion (Inf), squillion (Inf)

► *201 Five and Over; 202 Infinity; 208 Multitude*

4 **mathematical result**, sum, summation, total, running total, score, reckoning, tally, bill, aggregate, whole, amount, quantity, difference, residual, remainder, product, factor

► *204 Whole; 210 Calculation; 215 Remainder*

5 **ratio**, proportion, percentage, per cent, fraction, proper fraction, improper fraction, simple fraction, vulgar fraction, common fraction, compound fraction, numerator, denominator, decimal fraction, decimal

► *196 Fraction; 205 Part*

6 **power**, exponent, index, root, square root, cube root, surd, logarithm, common logarithm, log, natural logarithm, mantissa, antilogarithm, antilog

► *27 Mathematics*

ADJECTIVES

7 **numerical**, numeric, numerary, numerative, numerate, digital, figurate, figural

8 **odd**, impair, even, pair, cardinal, ordinal, imaginary, real, rational, irrational, arithmetical, geometric(al), algorithmic (*or* algorismic), digital, round, whole, prime, positive, negative

9 **fractional**, decimal, exponential, logarithmic, logometric, differential, integral, surd, radical, finite, infinite, aliquot

VERBS

10 **number**, enumerate, count, tell, reckon, tally, notch up, tot up, sum up, add, tote up (Inf), tick off (Inf), figure out (Inf), dope out (US inf)

11 **total**, come to, make, equal, amount to

► *210 Calculation*

ADVERBS

12 **numerically**, in numerical order, arithmetically, geometrically, digitally

195 Zero

Nothing will come of nothing. Speak again. William Shakespeare.

NOUNS

1 **zero**, nought, 0, cipher, nothing, none, nil, love, duck, no score, absolute zero, blob (Inf), goose egg (US inf)

2 **nothing**, naught, aught, *nihil* (L), *nada* (Sp), *nichts* (Ger), nothing at all, not any, none, not a one, nobody, no-one, not a soul, not a mite, not an iota, not a jot, not a whit, not a blessed one (Inf), not a lick (Inf), not a smell (Inf), not a sausage (Inf), zilch (Inf), nix (Inf), damn all (Inf), bugger all (Inf), sod all (Inf), fuck all (Inf), sweet fuck all (Inf), sweet FA (Inf), sweet Fanny Adams (Inf), Jack shit (Inf)

3 **nothingness**, nullity, nonexistence, nonbeing, nihility, floccinaucinihilipilification (Lit)

► *94 Nonexistence*

4 **zero level**, nadir, rock bottom, lowest point, last moment, zero hour, crisis point

► *175 Base*

5 **nonentity**, anonymity, nobody, unknown, unperson, nothing (Inf)

ADJECTIVES

6 **zero**, nil, no, not one, not any, infinitesimal, all gone

7 **null**, void, nonexistent, missing, lacking, gone, vanished

VERBS

8 **not exist**, not occur, be absent, be fictitious, vanish, disappear
9 **annihilate**, eradicate, nullify, wipe out, put an end to
10 **hit rock bottom**, reach an all-time low

ADVERBS

11 **none**, no, not at all, in no way
12 **absently**, anonymously, by proxy

196 Fraction

The only way I can distinguish proper from improper fractions
Is by their actions. Ogden Nash.

NOUNS

1 **fraction**, simple fraction, common fraction, vulgar fraction, compound fraction, proper fraction, improper fraction, decimal fraction, decimal
► *194 Number*
2 **fractional part**, part, percentage, proportion, portion, share, piece, section, segment, division, subdivision, ration
► *205 Part*
3 **fragment**, particle, chip, shard, sherd, splinter, sliver, scrap, shred, bit, speck, morsel, crumb, atom, iota, whit, jot, tittle
4 **less than one**, half, third, two-thirds, quarter, fourth, three-quarters, fifth, sixth, seventh, eighth, ninth, tenth, eleventh, twelfth, thirteenth, fourteenth, fifteenth, sixteenth, seventeenth, eighteenth, nineteenth, twentieth, thirtieth, fortieth, fiftieth, sixtieth, seventieth, eightieth, ninetieth, hundredth, thousandth, millionth, billionth, thou (Inf), mil (Inf)

ADJECTIVES

5 **fractional**, half, quarter, three-quarter, part, partial, fragmentary, incomplete, proportional, sectional, segmental, divisional, subdivisional
► *205 Part; 233 Incompleteness*
6 **small**, tiny, infinitesimal, insignificant

ADVERBS

7 **fractionally**, partially, partly, part, half, three-quarters, two-thirds, slightly, marginally

VERBS

8 **divide**, subdivide, split, part, share, fragment
► *372 Separation; 770 Allocation*

197 One

One is one and all alone
And ever more shall be so. Anonymous.

NOUNS

1 **one**, unity, unit, integer, ace, entity, singleton, single, monad, atom, point, item, article, module, individual, person, persona, soul, one and only, no other, nothing else, naught beside, nobody else
2 **item**, detail, bit, piece, single instance, isolated instance, isolated case, only exception
3 **oneness**, singleness, wholeness, integrality, unity, union, undividedness, indivisibility, solidarity, solidity, indissolubility, coherence, integrity
► *204 Whole*
4 **singularity**, individuality, uniqueness, specialness, speciality, particularity, identity, distinctiveness
5 **aloneness**, loneness, solitude, solitariness, isolation, apartness, separateness, separatism, isolationism, unilateralism, aloofness, detachment, insularity, privacy, seclusion, loneliness, lonesomeness, friendlessness
► *655 Unsociability*
6 **singleness**, celibacy, divorce, separation, widowhood, chastity
► *571 Divorce and Widowhood; 572 Celibacy*
7 **single person**, single, unmarried man, bachelor, unmarried woman, bachelor girl, spinster, maiden aunt, single parent, divorcée, divorcé, widow, widower
8 **loner**, lone wolf, only child, solitary, hermit, eremite, anchorite, marabout, stylite, ascetic, recluse, isolationist, seclusionist
► *118 Nonconformity*
9 **soloist**, one-man band, one-man show, one-woman show, solo effort, solo, monologue, soliloquy, monologist, soliloquist
► *735 Soliloquy*
10 **single thing**, unicycle, uniped, monocle, monohull, singleton, solitaire, patience, single ticket, single file, single cream, single track, single decker

ADJECTIVES

11 **one**, single, solo, mono, monadic, atomic, individual, solitary, sole, lone, only, one and the same, first, primary
12 **one-sided**, unilateral, uniplanar, one-way, unidirectional, one-size, one-piece, unisex, unisexual, unicellular, unipolar, unicameral, monolingual, monochromatic
13 **whole**, entire, complete, integral, unified, united, joined, rolled into one, undivided, indivisible, inseparable, indissoluble, solid, unanimous
► *204 Whole; 232 Completeness*
14 **singular**, individual, special, particular, distinct, unique, one and only, only-begotten, first and last, unrepeated, one-off, once-in-a-lifetime
15 **solo**, one-man, one-woman, independent, single-handed, on one's own, alone, unaided, unassisted, unabetted, unsupported, unaccompanied, unescorted, unchaperoned
16 **alone**, lone, solitary, isolated, apart, separate, separated, separatist, isolationist, unilateralist, detached, aloof, insular, withdrawn, reclusive, lonely, lonesome, friendless, companionless, deserted, abandoned, forsaken
► *655 Unsociability*
17 **single**, unmarried, unwedded, divorced, separated, widowed, chaste, celibate
► *571 Divorce and Widowhood; 572 Celibacy*

VERBS

18 **be one**, stand alone, stand by oneself, stand on one's own two feet, go solo, stand apart, stand aloof, isolate oneself, withdraw, retreat, plough a lonely furrow, go it alone (Inf), go one's own sweet way (Inf), do one's own thing (Inf), paddle one's own canoe (Inf), hoe one's own row (Inf), roll one's own (Inf), look after number one (Inf), take care of number one (Inf)

19 become one, make one, unite, unify, integrate, cohere, merge, combine, fuse, join, blend
▶ *204 Whole; 374 Combination*
20 single out, pick out, isolate, separate, detach
▶ *372 Separation; 469 Selection*

ADVERBS

21 alone, on its own, uniquely, by itself, per se, on one's own, by oneself, all by oneself, independently, solo, single-handedly, under one's own steam, on one's lonesome (Inf), on one's Jack (Inf), on one's tod (Inf)
22 one by one, one at a time, singly, individually, separately, apart, in the singular
23 wholly, completely, integrally, indivisibly, unanimously, as one
24 once, once only, just once, just this once, never again, once and for all, only, solely, exclusively, simply, purely

198 Two

Tea for Two, and Two for Tea. Otto Harback.

NOUNS

1 two, deuce, twain (Lit), set of two, pair, couple, brace, span, yoke, team, double harness, duet, duo, twosome, Darby and Joan, dyad, power of two, square, squared, me and you (Inf)
2 double, doublet, couplet, distich, duet, two-hander, diptych, double-decker, tandem, two-seater, two-wheeler, bicycle, biplane, catamaran, two-piece, duplex, bivalve, biped, bipod, binoculars, biathlon
3 duality, doubleness, dualism, duplexity, bilingualism, bisexuality, ambidexterity, ambiguity, double meaning, double entendre, irony, ambivalence, dual personality, split personality, Jekyll and Hyde, double life, double agent, two-facedness, double-dealing, double-crossing, double-sidedness, duplicity, Janus
▶ *479 Equivocation*
4 doubling, pairing, twinning, gemination, cloning, duplication, reproduction, repetition, double exposure
▶ *112 Repetition; 561 Reproduction*
5 twin, double, lookalike, doppelgänger, clone, duplicate, copy, carbon copy, photocopy, counterpart, ringer (Inf), dead ringer (Inf), spitting image (Inf), dead spit (Inf)
▶ *111 Sameness; 115 Similarity; 125 Imitation*
6 twins, identical twins, fraternal twins, Siamese twins, Tweedledum and Tweedledee, Castor and Pollux, Gemini, Twin Stars
7 halving, dichotomy, bisection, bipartition, dividing by two, splitting (*or* cutting) in two, splitting (*or* cutting) in half, bifurcation, forking, ramification, branching
▶ *372 Separation*
8 half, fifty percent, moiety, hemisphere, semicircle, diameter, equator, great circle, bisector, fork, swallowtail, branch, prong
▶ *205 Part*

ADJECTIVES

9 two, dual, dualistic, double, duple, duplex, binary, dyadic, twofold, bifold, paired, coupled, yoked, bracketed, twinned, matched, mated, doubled, squared, two by two, two abreast, in pairs, in twos, *à deux* (Fr), both, the two, second, secondary
10 two-sided, double-sided, two-way, two-ply, dual-purpose, two-stroke, two-storey, two-level, two-dimensional, biennial, biannual, biform, bipartite, bifurcate, biped, bipedal, binocular, bifocal, bilateral, bicameral, bilingual, ambidextrous, bisexual, AC/DC (Inf)
11 double-edged, double-barrelled, ambiguous, ironic, ambivalent, duplicitous, two-faced, hypocritical, double-faced, double-dealing, double-crossing, Janus-like, two-timing (Inf)
▶ *479 Equivocation*
12 double, twin, duplicate, geminate, repeat, second, duplicated, geminated, copied, photocopied, repeated, cloned
▶ *111 Sameness; 112 Repetition; 115 Similarity; 125 Imitation; 561 Reproduction*
13 half, halved, bisected, divided by two, split in half, split two ways, dichotomous, dichotomic, bifurcated, forked, ramified, branched, cloven, cleft, halfway, mid, middle, midway
▶ *372 Separation*

VERBS

14 pair, couple, bracket, yoke, span, double-harness, twin, match, mate, matchmake, pair off, couple up, team (up)
15 double, multiply by two, square, duplicate, replicate, clone, twin, geminate, copy, mirror, echo, repeat
▶ *112 Repetition; 561 Reproduction*
16 halve, bisect, transect, divide in half, divide by two, split (*or* cut) in half, split (*or* cut) in two, cleave, sunder, dichotomize, bifurcate, fork, ramify, branch
▶ *372 Separation*
17 go halves, go fifty-fifty, share, split two ways, split down the middle, go Dutch (Inf)
▶ *770 Allocation*
18 have it both ways, have the best of both worlds, have one's cake and eat it (Inf)

ADVERBS

19 twice, twofold, doubly, dually, twice as much, as much again, twice over, two times, once more, again, over again, yet again, encore, *bis* (Fr)
20 two by two, two abreast, in pairs, in twos
21 second, secondly, in the second place, secondarily
22 in half, in halves, in two, in twain (Lit), down the middle, half, fifty percent, half-and-half (Inf), fifty-fifty (Inf)

199 Three

Chi Wen Tzu always thought three times before taking action. Twice would have been quite enough. Confucius.

NOUNS

1 three, trey, set of three, trio, threesome, triad, trinity, trine, triune, triple, treble, power of three, cube
2 trident, tripod, trivet, tricorn, triangle, trihedron, three-wheeler, tricycle, trimaran, three-decker, three-hander, triumvirate, trihebdomadary, troika, triennial, triennium, trimester, trinomial, trilogy, triptych, trimeter, tristich, triplet, trefoil, shamrock, *ménage à trois* (Fr), hat trick

3 threeness, triality, trimorphism, triplicity, tripleness, trebleness, threefoldness
4 triplication, tripling, triplicating, trebling, multiplying by three
5 trisection, tripartition, trichotomy, trifurcation, dividing by three, splitting in three
► *372 Separation*
6 third, tierce, third part, one third, *tertium quid* (L), third party, third person, third power, major third, minor third, Third World, third age, third eye, third degree

ADJECTIVES
7 three, triple, triplex, triadic, trinal, trine, triform, trimorphic, ternary, trinary, triune, treble, triplicate, threefold, trifold, three times as much, cubed, third, tertiary
8 three-sided, triangular, triangulate, trigonal, trilateral, trihedral, deltoid, fan-shaped, three-pointed, three-pronged, trident, tridentate, three-cornered, tricorn, tricornered, three-leaved, trifoliate, three-legged, three-footed, tripedal, tripodic, three-ply, three-way, three-dimensional (3-D), tridimensional, trilingual, trimetric, triennial, trimestrial
9 trisected, tripartite, three-part, three-parted, triparted, trichotomous, trifid, trifurcated

VERBS
10 triple, triplicate, treble, multiply by three, increase threefold, cube
11 trisect, divide by three, split (*or* cut) in three, trichotomize, trifurcate, split three ways (Inf)

ADVERBS
12 thrice, threefold, three times, trebly, triply, trinely, in triplicate
13 in threes, three by three, three abreast
14 third, thirdly, in the third place

200 Four

Whatever a man prays for, he prays for a miracle. Every prayer reduces itself to this: 'Great God grant that twice two be not four.' Ivan Turgenev.

NOUNS
1 four, quatre, set of four, quartet, foursome, tetrad, quaternity, quadruple, quadruplet, quad
2 quadrilateral, tetragon, quadrangle, square, rectangle, oblong, parallelogram, rhombus, trapezium, trapezoid, tetrahedron
3 foursome, quadruped, tetrapod, tetradactyl, quadrennium, quadrennial, quadrille, square dance, quatrefoil, four-leaf (*or* four-leaved) clover, four-in-hand, four-poster, four winds, four seasons, four corners of the earth, tetrameter, quatrain, tetragram, tetragrammation, tetralogy, four-letter word
4 quadruplication, quadruplicature, quadrupling, quadruplicating, quadruplicity, fourfoldness
5 quadrisection, quadripartition, quartering, dividing by four, splitting in four
6 quarter, fourth, fourth part, one fourth, twenty-five percent, quadrant

ADJECTIVES
7 four, quaternary, quadratic, quadruple, quadruplex, quadruplicate, fourfold, fourth
8 quadrilateral, four-sided, square, rectangular, quadrate, tetrahedral, foursquare
9 tetramerous, quadruped, four-legged, four-footed, quadraphonic, quadrennial, tetravalent, quadrivalent
10 quartered, quadrisected, quadripartite, four-part, four-parted, four-handed, four-stroke, quarterly, quadrifid

VERBS
11 quadruple, quadruplicate, multiply by four, increase fourfold, quadrate
12 quadrisect, quarter, divide by four, divide into four, split four ways (Inf)

ADVERBS
13 four times, fourfold, quadruply, quadrennially, quarterly, squarely, foursquare
14 in fours, four by four, on all fours
15 fourth, fourthly, in the fourth place

201 Five and Over

'Why only twelve?' 'That's the original number.' 'Well, go out and get thousands.' Samuel Goldwyn.

NOUNS
1 five, cinque, quintet, fivesome, quintuplicate, quintuple, quintuplet, quin, fifth, fifth part, one fifth, pentagon, pentahedron, pentagram, pentacle, pentameter, pentastich, Pentateuch, pentarchy, pentathlon, pentachord, quint, quinquereme, quincunx, cinquefoil, five-finger, quinquennium, quinquennial, pentathlon, five-a-side, five-by-five, fivestones, a bunch of fives, five-dollar bill (US), five-pound note, fiver (Inf), five-spot (US inf), fin (US inf)
2 six, half-a-dozen, hexad, sextet, sextuplicate, sextuple, sextuplet, sixth, sixth part, one sixth, sextile, hexagon, hexahedron, hexagram, hexameter, sixain, Hexateuch, hexachord, hexapod, sixth sense, six-footer, six-shooter, sixth-form (*or* year), sixer (Inf), Captain Hicks (Inf), Jimmy Hix (Inf)
3 seven, heptad, septet, septenary, septuplicate, septuple, septuplet, seventh, seventh part, one seventh, heptagon, heptahedron, heptameter, Heptateuch, seven deadly sins, Seven Wonders of the World, diminished seventh, seven days, week, sevener (Inf), God's in heaven (Inf)
4 eight, octad, octet, octonary, octuple, octuplet, octagon, octahedron, octave, Octateuch, octopus, octarchy, octavo (8vo), figure of eight, piece of eight, eighth, eighth part, one eighth, one over the eight (Inf), eighter (Inf), eighter from Decatur (US inf), garden gate (Inf), Harry Tate (Inf)
5 nine, ennead, nonet, nonary, novena, nonuplet, nonagon, enneagon, enneahedron, ninth, ninth part, one ninth, nine-days wonder, niner (Inf), Nina from Carolina (US inf)
6 ten, decade, decennium, decagon, decahedron, decapod, decagram, decathlon, Decalogue, Ten Command-

ments, tenth, tenth part, one tenth, tithe, tenner (Inf), big Dick (Inf), cock and hen (Inf), Downing Street (Inf)

7 **double figures**, eleven, undecagon, hendecagon, hendecahedron, twelve, dozen, dodecagon, dodecahedron, duodecimal, duodecimo, twelfth man, Twelfth Night, Twelfth Day, twelvemonth, teens, teenager, thirteen, baker's dozen, long dozen, fourteen, two weeks, fortnight, fifteen, quindecaplet, quindecagon, quindecennial, sixteen, hexadecimal, legs eleven (Inf), boxcar (Inf), monkey's cousin (Inf)

8 **twenty and over**, score, twenty-four, four and twenty, two dozen, twenty-five, five and twenty, pony, silver jubilee, forty, twoscore, quadragenarian, fifty, half a hundred, half century, jubilee, quinquagenarian, sixty, threescore, sexagenary, sexagenarian, seventy, threescore and ten, septuagenarian, eighty, fourscore, octogenarian, ninety, fourscore and ten, nonagenarian

9 **treble figures**, hundred, one hundred, century, one hundredfold, centuple, centuplicate, hundred percent, centennial, centenary, centennium, centenarian, centurion, centimetre, centigrade, hundredweight (cwt), centipede, the hundred days, hundred and twenty, great (*or* long) hundred, hundred and forty-four, gross, two-hundred, bicentennial, bicentenary, three hundred, tercentennial, tercentenary, four hundred, quatercentenary, five hundred, five centuries, quincentenary, six centuries, sexcentenary, seven centuries, eight centuries, octocentenary, nine centuries, ten centuries, millennium, hundreds and hundreds, hundreds and thousands, one C (Inf), ton (Inf), five C's (Inf), monkey (Inf)

10 **thousand**, K, chiliad, millennium, millenary, milligram, millilitre, millimetre, kilometre, kilogram, kilo, kilobyte, gigabyte, millipede, ten thousand, myriad, hundred thousand, lakh, G (Inf), grand (Inf), yard (Inf), archer (Inf)

11 **million**, ten million, crore, thousand million, billion, milliard, million million, trillion, quadrillion, quintillion, sextillion, septillion, octillion, nonillion, decillion, undecillion, duodecillion, tredecillion, quattuordecillion, quindecillion, sexdecillion, septendecillion, octodecillion, novemdecillion, vigintillion, centrillion, googol, googolplex, multimillion, millionaire, multimillionaire, billionaire, milliardaire, zillion (Inf), jillion (Inf), squillion (Inf)

► *40 Computers; 208 Multitude*

ADJECTIVES

12 **fifth**, five, fivefold, quintuple, quintuplicate, quinary, quinquennial, quintic, quinquepartite, pentadic, pentagonal, pentangular, pentahedral, pentatonic

13 **sixth**, six, sixfold, sextuple, sextuplicate, sexennial, sexpartite, hexadic, hexagonal, hexangular, hexahedral, hexatonic

14 **seventh**, seven, sevenfold, septuple, septuplicate, septenary, septennial, heptadic, heptagonal, heptangular, heptahedral, heptatonic

15 **eighth**, eight, eightfold, octuple, octonary, octennial, octadic, octagonal, octangular, octahedral, octatonic

16 **ninth**, nine, ninefold, nonuple, novenary, nonary, enneadic, nonagonal, enneagonal, enneahedral

17 **tenth**, ten, tenfold, decuple, decimal, denary, decennial, decagonal, decahedral

18 **eleventh**, undecennial, hendecagonal, twelfth, duodenary, duodecimal, thirteenth, fourteenth, fifteenth, quindecagonal, quindecennial, sixteenth, hexadecimal, in one's teens, umpteenth

19 **twentieth**, vigesimal, vicenary, vicennial, thirtieth, fortieth, fiftieth, sixtieth, seventieth, eightieth, ninetieth

20 **hundredth**, centesimal, centennial, centenary, centenarian, hundredfold, centuple, centuplicate

21 **thousandth**, millenary, millenarian, millenial, thousandfold, four-figure, five-figure, six-figure

22 **millionth**, billionth, trillionth

VERBS

23 **quintuple**, quintuplicate, sextuple, sextuplicate, septuple, octuple, centuple, centuplicate, decimalize, decimate

ADVERBS

24 **fivefold**, fifth, fifthly, quinquennially, sixfold, sixth, sixthly, sexennially, sevenfold, seventh, seventhly, septennially, tenfold, tenth, tenthly, decennially, hundredfold, centennially

202 Infinity

I cannot help it; – in spite of myself, infinity torments me. Alfred de Musset.

ADJECTIVES

1 **infinite**, boundless, limitless, unlimited, without limit (*or* end), illimitable, bottomless, endless, interminable, recurring

2 **immeasurable**, measureless, vast, immense, enormous, astronomical, incalculable, uncountable, countless, innumerable, myriad, numberless, unnumbered, without number, beyond reckoning, untold, indeterminable, inestimable, unfathomable, incomprehensible, beyond comprehension, transcendent, mind-boggling (Inf)

► *208 Multitude*

3 **eternal**, perpetual, everlasting, immortal, undying, forever, ceaseless, endless, unending, never-ending, constant, continual, continuous, unremitting, open-ended, without beginning or end, no end of

► *225 Permanence; 279 Eternity*

NOUNS

4 **infinity**, infiniteness, infinitude, boundlessness, limitlessness, illimitability, endlessness, interminability, infinite supply, bottomless pit

5 **immeasurability**, measurelessness, incalculability, countlessness, innumerability, numberlessness, indeterminableness, incomprehensibility

► *208 Multitude*

6 **vastness**, immenseness, immensity, space, outer space, infinite space

7 **eternity**, perpetuity, forever, everlastingness, immortality, perpetual motion

► *225 Permanence; 279 Eternity*

VERBS

8 **have no limit**, have no bounds, know no limit (*or* bounds *or* end)

9 **be infinite**, last forever, never end, go on and on, never

die, never cease, recur, perpetuate, continue, be eternal, gain immortality, discover the secret of eternal life

ADVERBS

10 **infinitely**, boundlessly, limitlessly, illimitably, endlessly, interminably, indefinitely, without end, without limit, to infinity, ad infinitum

11 **immeasurably**, measurelessly, vastly, immensely, astronomically, incalculably, innumerably, indeterminably, inestimably

12 **eternally**, perpetually, constantly, immortally, forever, in perpetuity, until the end of time, until the rivers run uphill, until all the seas run dry, until the sun ceases to shine, for keeps (Inf), till hell freezes over (Inf), till the cows come home (Inf)

203 Quantity

NOUNS

1 **quantity**, amount, measurement, measure, measured quantity, measuring, extent, dimension, proportions, size, space, area, magnitude, multitude, amplitude, length, width, breadth, thickness, thinness, height, altitude, depth, deepness, capacity, volume, weighing, weight, mass, matter, substance, body, bulk, gravity, heaviness, lightness

► *26 Measurement; 141 Space; 148 Length; 150 Broadness; 154 Height; 156 Depth; 158 Size; 204 Whole; 232 Completeness; 414 Heaviness; 415 Lightness*

2 **certain amount**, portion, piece, share, lot, load, batch, bunch, pack, packet, parcel, part, mess, limit, stint, quota, quorum, dosage, dose, ration, quantum, upper limit, ceiling, lower limit, floor, great quantity, large amount, mass, mountain, lake, chunk, hunk, majority, increase, addition, extension, more, most, small quantity, small amount, some, somewhat, few, fewness, pittance, dribble, fraction, minority, decrease, subtraction, less, least, heap (Inf), gob (Inf), whack (Inf)

► *166 Limit; 194 Number; 206 Few; 208 Multitude; 211 Addition; 212 Subtraction; 213 Increase; 214 Decrease; 406 Contents*

3 **container(ful)**, armful, handful, mouthful, pocketful, spoon(ful), teaspoon(ful), tablespoon(ful), cup(ful), glass(ful), bottle(ful), jar(ful), pitcher(ful), bowl(ful), pot(ful), plate(ful), bag(ful), sack(ful), basket(ful), box(ful), carton(ful), case(ful), can(ful), bin(ful), crate(ful), barrel(ful), bucket(ful), shovel(ful), roomful, lorryload, truckload

► *410 Container*

4 **total**, whole, all, lock, stock, and barrel, totality, entirety, aggregate, sum, count, number, nett (total), gross (total), the whole thing, the whole caboodle (Inf)

► *204 Whole; 232 Completeness*

5 **numbers**, integers, variable, plurality, zero, infinity, mean, average

► *27 Mathematics; 194 Number; 195 Zero; 197 One; 198 Two; 199 Three; 200 Four; 201 Five and Over; 202 Infinity; 207 Plurality; 208 Multitude; 210 Calculation; 216 Average*

ADJECTIVES

6 **quantitative**, quantified, quantized, measured, measuring, weighed, weighing, counted, sized, ample, high, deep, long, wide, massive, voluminous, thick, thin, heavy, light, bunched, packed, sparse, mountainous, increased, added, extended, greater, majority, most, many, so many, so much, any, about, approximate, more or less, plural, infinite, all, total, whole, entire, enough, small, some, certain, limited, rationed, finite, few, smaller, least, numbered, fractional, variable, average

► *26 Measurement; 27 Mathematics; 158 Size; 194 Number; 197 One; 202 Infinity; 207 Plurality; 208 Multitude; 217 Sufficiency; 452 Certainty*

ADVERBS

7 **quantitatively**, to such an extent, finitely, about, approximately, some, nearly, as much as, more or less, wholely, entirely, totally, infinitely, amply, highly, deeply, widely, massively, hugely, enormously, voluminously, thickly, heavily, variably, fractionally, slightly, thinly, sparsely, lightly, mathematically, to the tune of (Inf), all of (Inf)

VERBS

8 **quantify**, quantize, measure, weigh, count, number, rate, fix, size, piece, portion, apportion, allot, allocate, divide, share, pack, parcel, limit, set a quota, take a dose, ration, set an upper limit, set a ceiling, set a lower limit, set a floor, increase, add, extend, decrease, reduce, subtract

► *166 Limit; 190 Expansion; 191 Contraction; 194 Number; 211 Addition; 212 Subtraction; 213 Increase; 214 Decrease; 770 Allocation*

204 Whole

Now a whole is that which has a beginning, a middle, and an end. Aristotle.

NOUNS

1 **whole**, wholeness, totality, integrality, integrity, integration, fullness, completeness, indivisibility, oneness, unity, universality, generality, holism, holistic approach, comprehensiveness, inclusiveness, generalization

► *138 Generality; 232 Completeness*

2 **whole thing**, entity, whole number, integer, unit, entirety, Gestalt, totality, sum, total sum, sum total, summation, total, aggregate, corpus, complete works, complex, ensemble, system, four corners of the Earth, world, globe, universe, cosmos, macrocosm, microcosm, Lebensraum, life space

► *197 One; 374 Combination*

3 **whole situation**, grand design, full view, grand view, panorama, bird's-eye view, overview, survey, conspectus, synopsis, world view, world picture, full course, circuit, lap, round

► *306 Orbital Motion; 518 Vision*

4 **all**, everything, everybody, everyone, one and all, everyone and everything, everything but the kitchen sink, the world, the whole world, all the world, the world and his wife, the whole, the aggregate, the total, the lot, the whole lot, *le tout ensemble* (Fr), the gross amount, one hundred per cent, Alpha and Omega, be-all and end-all, the rough with the smooth, the length and breadth, the sum and substance

▶ *138 Generality; 208 Multitude; 376 Gathering*

5 **unit**, family, ensemble, set, complete set, series, pack, kit, outfit, inventory, full list, complete list, whole list, rind, pips, and all, the whole caboodle (Inf), the whole kit and caboodle (Inf), the whole bang shoot (Inf), the whole shooting match (Inf), the whole shebang (Inf)

▶ *220 List; 374 Combination*

ADJECTIVES

6 **whole**, integral, total, holistic, general, universal, complete, full, integrated, unified, all, every, any, each, individual, single, one, in one piece, all of a piece, all-inclusive, comprehensive, fully comprehensive, gross, all-embracing, across-the-board, global, worldwide, international

▶ *127 Inclusion; 138 Generality; 197 One; 232 Completeness*

7 **uncut**, entire, unabridged, unexpurgated, undivided, undiminished, unbroken, intact, unharmed, unscathed, unhurt, uninjured, undamaged, unimpaired, unspoiled, unadulterated, uncontaminated, untouched, inviolate, virgin, pure, faultless, flawless, perfect

▶ *230 Perfection; 232 Completeness; 255 Purity*

8 **sound**, sound in wind and limb, able-bodied, strong, fit, well, healthy, in good health, hale, hale and hearty, in fine fettle, recovered, fully restored, better

▶ *259 Health; 393 Repair*

VERBS

9 **be whole**, form a whole, unite, unify, integrate, total, sum up, add up to, amount to, come to, number, comprise, embrace, encompass

▶ *194 Number*

10 **complete**, fulfil, succeed, accomplish, reach one's goal, achieve (one's purpose), leave no loose ends, bring to a head, culminate, climax, take to the limit, carry through, finish (off), polish off (Inf), round off, end, finalize, perfect, put the finishing touches on, put the icing on the cake

ADVERBS

11 **wholly**, entirely, integrally, holistically, completely, body and soul, heart and soul, totally, utterly, absolutely, fully, every bit, every inch, pound for pound, in every respect, without exception, without exemption, one hundred per cent, universally, *in toto* (L), hook, line, and sinker, lock, stock, and barrel, root and branch, rind, pips, and all

12 **one and all**, as a whole, as a team, as a group, as a unit, comprehensively, collectively, all together, corporately, bodily, and all, in sum, altogether, in the aggregate, in the mass, in bulk, *en masse* (Fr), *en bloc* (Fr)

13 **on the whole**, generally, in general, all in all, by and large, as a rule, predominantly, mostly, for the most part, mainly, in the main, largely, taking everything into consideration, all things considered, when all is said and done, in all truth, essentially, in essence, altogether, quite, substantially, in substance, virtually, practically, almost, nearly, all but, to all intents and purposes, as far as one can tell, in effect, effectively, as good as

▶ *99 Essence; 138 Generality; 147 Closeness*

205 Part

My anatomy is only part of an infinitely complex organisation, my self. Angela Carter.

NOUNS

1 **part**, fragment, small fragment, particle, portion, proportion, certain proportion, majority, minority, fraction, half, moiety, third, quarter, eighth, tenth, tithe, percentage, aliquot, aliquant, divisor, factor, quotient, dividend, share, whack (Inf), quota, remainder, balance, surplus, element, better element, worse element, faction, class, subclass, category, subcategory, group, subgroup, family, subfamily, genus, subgenus, species, subspecies, phylum, division, subdivision, segment, sector, arc, curve, semicircle, hemisphere, partition, compartment, department, ward, community, parish, district, county, region, area

▶ *86 Regions; 137 Class; 196 Fraction; 215 Remainder; 372 Separation; 376 Gathering; 409 Arrangement; 770 Allocation*

2 **particular**, detail, item, article, chapter, episode, instalment, fascicule (*or* fascicle), part, number, issue, edition, canto, verse, section, subsection, paragraph, sentence, clause, coordinate clause, subordinate clause, phrase, word, part of speech, page, folio, sheet, leaf, volume, passage, quotation, citation, sound bite, gobbet, extract, text, part payment, down payment, deposit, tranche, advance, earnest, earnest of good faith, foretaste, preview, appetizer, sample, example, quote (Inf)

▶ *740 Publication; 785 Payment*

3 **stage**, phase, leg, lap, round, heat

▶ *276 Time Span*

4 **component**, constituent, ingredient, particle, element, molecule, member, appendage, organ, feeler, antenna, limb, hindlimb, leg, foot, forelimb, hand, arm, forearm, wing, flipper, fin, privates, private parts

▶ *405 Component*

5 **largest part**, principal part, main part, main body, the main, chief part, greater part, major part, ninety-nine per cent, bulk, mass, majority, vast majority, lion's share, biggest slice of the cake, essential part, the essentials, bare essentials, nuts and bolts, gist, summary, almost all, nearly all, all but, all but the kitchen sink, best part, best bit, nitty-gritty (Inf), the long and the short of it (Inf)

▶ *99 Essence; 123 Importance; 208 Multitude; 723 Summary*

6 **branch**, subbranch, offshoot, ramification, flower head, petal, sepal, stamen, anther, calyx, tendril, leaf, leaflet, shoot, switch, scion, sucker, sprig, spray, slip, foliage, bough, limb, spur, twig, stem, stalk, trunk, bole, stump, torso

7 **piece**, bit, segment, section, patch, insertion, interpolation, addition, length, roll, swatch, scrap, offcut, rag, shred, wisp, speck, morsel, bite, crust, crumb, sliver, splinter, snip, snippet, chip, cut, slice, tranche, wedge, finger, rasher, cutlet, collop, chop, steak, gobbet, chunk, hunk, lump, slab, bar, block, mass, heap, tump (Dial), clod, sod, turf, divot, shard, sherd, potsherd, flake, scale, drop, dose, portion, helping, piece of land, allotment, parcel, wodge (Inf), dollop (Inf), smidgen (Inf)

▶ *153 Thinness; 211 Addition; 368 Insertion; 411 Layer; 770 Allocation*

8 **bits and pieces**, bits and bobs, miscellanea, oddments, flotsam and jetsam, *disjecta membra* (L), bin ends, shavings, filings, swarf, clippings, parings, peelings, leavings, rubble, trash, detritus, moraine, debris, rags, tatters, odds and ends, odds and sods (Inf)

▶ *215 Remainder; 441 Waste*

9 **participation**, role, character, duty, responsibility, function

▶ *21 Drama; 810 Duty*

VERBS

10 **part**, divide, subdivide, share, apportion, cut up, dissect, segment, sectionalize, compartmentalize, partition, separate, split, bisect, sever, fragment, dismantle, break, break up

▶ *372 Separation; 375 Disintegration; 770 Allocation*

ADJECTIVES

11 **partial**, part, not whole, broken, fragmented, fragmentary, in bits, in pieces, in smithereens, brashy, crumbly, incomplete, with bits missing, armless, legless, limbless, headless, imperfect, inadequate, insufficient, scrappy, bitty, piecemeal, unfinished, half-finished, fractional, aliquot, proportional, proportionate, partitive, segmental, sectional, compartmental, departmental, divided, molecular, atomic, elemental, departmentalized, compartmentalized, sectionalized, sliced, diced, minced, ground, shredded, wispy

▶ *196 Fraction; 218 Insufficiency; 231 Imperfection; 233 Incompleteness; 372 Separation*

ADVERBS

12 **partly**, in part, in some measure, to some extent, to a certain extent, to a (*or* some) degree, a little, a bit, somewhat, quasi, slightly, moderately, partially, half, half and half, fractionally, not wholly, not fully, incompletely, inadequately, scrappily, piecemeal, part by part, bit by bit, little by little, a little at a time, in (*or* by) instalments, in dribs and drabs, by fits and starts, drop by drop, by degrees, gradually, in parts, in detail, in lots, part for part, proportionally, proportionately, pro rata

206 Few

Never in the field of human conflict was so much owed by so many to so few. Winston Churchill.

We few, we happy few, we band of brothers. William Shakespeare.

NOUNS

1 **few**, a few, only a few, just a few, not many, some, small number, one or two, two or three, couple, handful, mere handful, almost none, too few to mention, not enough to count (*or* matter), low turnout, poor turnout, low attendance, scattering, sprinkling, trickle, small quantity, small amount, little, a little, *soupçon* (Fr), derisory amount, dash, hint, suspicion, smidgen (Inf)

▶ *194 Number*

2 **least**, minimum, less, minority, the minority, minority group

3 **fewness**, sparsity, sparseness, scarcity, scarceness, scantiness, exiguity, paucity, dearth, lack, deficiency, skimpiness, meagreness, shortage, undersupply, underpopulation, skeleton staff

▶ *218 Insufficiency*

4 **rarity**, rareness, infrequency, intermittence, sporadicness

ADJECTIVES

5 **few**, a few, some, not many, hardly any, scarcely any, precious few, too few, little, a little, not much, precious little, to be counted on one's fingers, to be counted on the fingers of one hand, soon counted

6 **sparse**, scant, scanty, light, thin, little, minimal, meagre, exiguous, measly, niggardly, infrequent, occasional, sporadic, intermittent, rare, seldom seen, seldom met with, uncommon, near extinction, scarce, thin on the ground, few and far between, strung out, spread-out, widely spaced, at great intervals, dispersed, scattered, sprinkled, dotted about, underpopulated, low-density, understaffed, undermanned

▶ *218 Insufficiency*

7 **fewer**, less, reduced, diminished, diminishing, least, minimum, minimal, minority, in a minority, too few, inquorate

VERBS

8 **reduce**, diminish, rarefy, thin, thin out, weed out, eliminate, decimate, pare (*or* cut) down, scale down, downsize (US), cut back, prune, trim, rationalize, underman, understaff

9 **scatter**, sprinkle, dot, dot about, string out, space out, spread out, disperse

ADVERBS

10 **in ones and twos**, in twos and threes, here and there, in places, in spots, in a trickle, in dribs and drabs (Inf)

11 **sparsely**, scantily, lightly, thinly, meagrely, exiguously, little, rarely, infrequently, seldom, occasionally, scarcely, hardly, barely

207 Plurality

There is safety in numbers. Proverb.

NOUNS

1 **plurality**, pluralness, the plural, plural number, many, several, some, a number, a few, a couple, a handful, more than one, (the odd) one or two, two or three, more, a greater number

2 **multiplicity**, multitude, numerousness, multitudinousness, multifariousness, variety, diversity, compositeness, multiformity, many-sidedness, polygon, polyhedron, multilateralism, polygamy, polygyny, polyandry, polytheism, pluralism, multiple personality

▶ *114 Diversity; 208 Multitude*

3 **majority**, greater number, more, greatest number, most, more than half, greater (*or* best) part, greater proportion, bulk, mass, preponderance, lion's share

▶ *205 Part*

4 **multiplication**, proliferation, increase, multiple, product, multiplier, multiplicand, multiplication table

▶ *210 Calculation; 213 Increase*

5 **pluralist**, all-rounder, polymath, Renaissance man (*or* woman), polyglot, multilateralist, polygamist, polytheist

ADJECTIVES

6 **plural**, in the plural, not singular, more than one, multiple, nonsingle, many, several, some, certain, few, upwards of, more, most, majority, numerous, multitudinous

▶ *205 Part; 208 Multitude*

7 **various**, divers, diverse, sundry, multifarious, multiform, composite, multilateral, polygonal, many-sided, multifaceted, versatile, multipurpose, multirole, polymorphous (*or* polymorphic), multinational, multiracial, multilingual, polyglot

▶ *114 Diversity*

8 **multiplicative**, multiplied, multiple, manifold, multifold, increasing, increased, proliferative, proliferating, proliferated

▶ *213 Increase*

VERBS

9 **pluralize**, plurify, multiply, proliferate, increase, propagate, replicate, clone

▶ *213 Increase*

ADVERBS

10 **plurally**, severally, multitudinously, multiply, variously, diversely, multifariously, multilaterally

11 **in majority**, in the majority, more, most

12 **et cetera**, etc., and so on, *et al.* (L), and others, and the rest

208 Multitude

I am one of the unpraised, unrewarded millions without whom Statistics would be a bankrupt science. It is we who are born, who marry, who die, in constant ratios. Logan Pearsall Smith.

NOUNS

1 **multiplicity**, multitudinousness, numerousness, multifoldness, countlessness, innumerability, infinity

▶ *202 Infinity*

2 **multitude**, many, great number, large numbers, quite a few, a lot, lots, large amount, tidy sum, dozens, scores, hundreds, hundreds and thousands, thousands, tens of thousands, hundreds of thousands, millions, billions, trillions, myriads, umpteen (Inf), zillions (Inf), jillions (Inf), big bucks (Inf), telephone numbers (Inf), scads (Inf), wads (Inf)

▶ *194 Number; 201 Five and Over; 207 Plurality*

3 **profuseness**, profusion, rifeness, abundance, plenty, tons (Inf), oodles (Inf), bags (Inf), barrels (Inf), heaps (Inf), loads (Inf), heck of a lot (Inf), hell of a lot (Inf), devil of a lot (Inf)

▶ *217 Sufficiency; 219 Excess*

4 **throng**, multitude, mass, mob, crowd, congregation, horde, host, army, troop, legion, fleet, high turnout, large turnout, rout, ruck, jam, clutter, press, crush, swarm, flock, flight, cloud, hail, bevy, covey, shoal, hive, colony, nest, brood, pack, bunch, drove, array, galaxy, mass of, masses of, sea of, world of, worlds of, forest of

▶ *376 Gathering*

ADJECTIVES

5 **multitudinous**, multitudinal, numerous, legion, multiple, multifold, multifarious, manifold

6 **many**, a good few, not a few, a good many, very many, ever so many, considerable, umpteen (Inf), quite some (Inf)

7 **myriad**, hundred, a hundred and one, thousand, a thousand and one, million, billion, trillion, zillion (Inf), jillion (Inf)

▶ *194 Number; 201 Five and Over; 207 Plurality*

8 **numberless**, innumerable, countless, uncountable, incalculable, immeasurable, measureless, beyond measure, unnumbered, uncounted, untold, infinite, endless, without end, limitless, without limit, boundless, inexhaustible, countless as the stars (*or* sand on the seashore), countless as the hairs on one's head, no end of (Inf), more than you can shake a stick at (Inf)

▶ *202 Infinity; 279 Eternity*

9 **ample**, abundant, superabundant, profuse, rife, plentiful, plenteous, copious, bumper, thick on the ground, in abundance, in plenty, in profusion, galore (Inf)

▶ *217 Sufficiency; 219 Excess*

10 **crowded**, thronged, mobbed, congested, massed, packed, jammed, jam-packed, high-density, pressed, crushed, packed like sardines in a can (*or* tin), cluttered, overcrowded, overpopulated, overmanned, overstaffed, overrun

VERBS

11 **crowd**, throng, mob, mass, congregate, pack, jam, press, crush, swarm, teem, crawl, pullulate, hum, buzz, bristle, seethe, mill, troop, flock, pour, stream, flood, brim, overflow, burst, swarm like flies, swarm like ants, swarm like bees around a honey-pot

▶ *376 Gathering*

12 **overcrowd**, overpopulate, overman, overstaff, outnumber, overrun, infest, swamp, overwhelm, snow under

▶ *219 Excess*

ADVERBS

13 **numerously**, aplenty, multitudinously, multiply, multifariously, innumerably, countlessly, incalculably, immeasurably, beyond measure, beyond count, infinitely, no end (Inf), by leaps and bounds (Inf)

14 **in crowds**, in swarms, in masses, *en masse* (Fr), in heaps, in loads, thick and fast

209 Grading

We boil at different degrees. Ralph Waldo Emerson.

NOUNS

1 **degree**, extent, measure, amount, frequency, intensity, rate, amplitude, magnitude, value, calibre, quantity, depth, height, altitude, size, breadth, speed, gradualism, gradualness, slowness, scope, range, duration, reach, compass, limitation, stint, scale, pitch, tenor, register, key

► *18 Music; 26 Measurement; 150 Broadness; 154 Height; 156 Depth; 158 Size; 166 Limit; 203 Quantity; 277 Duration; 300 Motion; 333 Slowness; 516 Tunefulness*

2 rank, level, hierarchy, grading, grade, echelon, precedence, order, place, position, power structure, station, circumstance, footing, standing, status, social rank, class, caste, authority, military rank, generalship, leadership, ecclesiastical rank

► *7 Religion; 137 Class; 222 Circumstances; 396 Authority; 586 Combatant; 770 Allocation*

3 gradation, graduation, measurement, calibration, valuation, differentiation, differential, degree of difference, classification, rating, ranking, remove, relativeness, relative quantity, comparison, ratio, proportion, ration, standard, grading, shading, notation, bar, line, mark, notch, peg, score

► *26 Measurement; 108 Relatedness; 205 Part*

4 interval, period, time, stint, shift, portion, part, shade, shadow, nuance, majority, minority, point, place, step, rung, tread, stair, stage, plane, level, plateau, space, stepping stone, milestone, turning point, juncture, crisis

► *141 Space; 146 Interval; 304 Ascent*

VERBS

5 measure, classify, evaluate, rate, rank, order, class, grade, sort, mark, peg, score, scale, shade, graduate, place, position, estimate, quantify, calibrate, calculate, clock speed, compare, differentiate, precede, lead

6 change gradually, lower, taper off, shade off, cut back, trim, pare, whittle down, abate, die away, melt away, fade out, fade, diminish, decrease, wane, dissolve, evolve, melt into, increase, augment, build up, crescendo, grow, expand, inflate, swell, wax, unfold

► *190 Expansion; 191 Contraction; 211 Addition; 212 Subtraction; 213 Increase; 214 Decrease*

ADJECTIVES

7 gradational, graduated, graded, measured, rated, scaled, in scale, calibrated, classified, valued, sized, sorted, differentiated, differential, relative, comparative, comparable, proportional, proportionable, portioned, standard, within the bounds of, encompassing, limited, majority, minority, level, regular, frequent, extensive, progressive, gradual, slow-ranging, slow-changing, growing, increasing, waxing, reaching, waning, shading off, tapering, fading, fading out, diminishing

8 ranked, hierarchic, hierarchical, leading, preceding, authoritative, ecclesiastical

ADVERBS

9 differentially, relatively, comparatively, by comparison, comparably, proportionally, levelly, regularly, routinely, frequently, often, extensively, hierarchically, authoritatively

10 by degrees, progressively, gradually, slowly, by inches, inchmeal, piecemeal, slowly but surely, a little at a time, in slight measure, inch by inch, just a bit, bit by bit, little by little, by stages, step by step, drop by drop, however little, however much, increasingly, more and more, decreasingly, less and less

11 to a degree, to (*or* in) some degree, to some extent, in a way, in a measure, in some measure, somewhat, sort of, kind of, fairly, quite, rather, to a great degree, extremely, very, to a small degree, scarcely, slightly, a little, a bit, pretty (Inf)

210 Calculation

NOUNS

1 calculation, computation, numeration, enumeration, reckoning, figuring, determining, estimation, assessment, figure work, number work, sums, addition, subtraction, multiplication, division, algebra, geometry, trigonometry, calculus, differentiation, integration, analysis, extraction of roots, reduction, inversion, involution, evolution, convolution, approximation, interpolation, extrapolation, permutation, transformation, equation, algorithm, logarithm

► *26 Measurement; 27 Mathematics; 194 Number; 211 Addition; 212 Subtraction; 464 Judgment*

2 statistics, figures, vital statistics, indexes (*or* indices), tables, averages, psephology

3 count, tally, census, poll, opinion poll, head count, inventory, stocktaking, numbering, counting, accounting, telling, tallying, calculating, ciphering, reckoning, adding, totalling, yan tan tethera, one-two-three

4 computing, computation, data processing (DP), electronic data processing, computer technology, information technology (IT), information processing, information retrieval, numbercrunching (Inf)

► *40 Computers*

5 computer, calculator, pocket calculator, Comptometer™, adding machine, cash register, till, abacus, ready reckoner, table, multiplication table, log table, rule, ruler, slide rule, Napier's bones (*or* rods), tabulator, tape measure, yardstick, gauge, dividers, compass, difference machine, suan pan, totalizer, numbercruncher (Inf)

► *26 Measurement*

6 calculator, computer, counter, teller, enumerator, census-taker, pollster, reckoner, estimator, abacist, computer operator, computer programmer, systems analyst, liveware

► *40 Computers*

7 mathematician, arithmetician, algebraist, geometrician, geometer, trigonometrician, geodesist, surveyor, statistician, actuary, pollster, psephologist, accountant, book-keeper

► *789 Accounting*

VERBS

8 calculate, compute, work out, solve, cipher, reckon, figure, determine, estimate, tally, notch up, score, keep the score, count, keep a count, figure out (Inf), dope out (US inf), guesstimate (Inf)

► *194 Number*

9 add, add up, sum, sum up, tot up, totalize, subtract, take away, deduct, multiply, divide, square, cube, extract roots, integrate, differentiate, extrapolate, interpolate

10 total, aggregate, add up to, tot up to, amount to, come to, make, equal

11 number, numerate, enumerate, count, count up, tell, tally, poll, count heads, count hands, count noses, call the roll, take stock, inventory, list, quantify, quantize, measure, gauge

► *26 Measurement; 220 List*

12 **check**, verify, audit, balance, balance the books, account, keep accounts

► *789 Accounting*

ADJECTIVES

13 **calculative**, computative, numerative, enumerative, estimative, calculating, computing, computational, numerical, quantifying, statistical, actuarial, psephological

14 **calculable**, computable, reckonable, estimable, countable, numerable, measurable, mensurable, quantifiable

15 **mathematical**, arithmetical, algebraic(al), geometric(al), logarithmic, algorithmic, trigonometrical, differential, integral, analytic(al)

ADVERBS

16 **mathematically**, arithmetically, algebraically, geometrically, trigonometrically, numerically, calculably, computably, estimably, measurably, quantifiably, logarithmically, exponentially

211 Addition

We used to think that if we knew one, we knew two, because one and one are two. We are finding that we must learn a great deal more about 'and'. Arthur Eddington.

NOUNS

1 **addition**, adding, joining, annexation, admixture, agglutination, superaddition, load, extra load, encumbrance, burden, imposition, superimposition, superposition, interjection, interposition, supervention, insertion, inclusion, attachment, affixture, prefixion, suffixion, supplementation, augmentation, accession, accrual, accretion, increase, increment, supplement, complement, enlargement, extension, addendum, accessory, appurtenance, appendage, appanage, reinforcement, continuation, prolongation

► *100 Otherness; 190 Expansion; 213 Increase; 219 Excess; 368 Insertion; 378 Obstruction*

2 **mathematical addition**, arithmetic, adding-up, summation, computation, calculation, totalling, counting-up, ringing-up, total, toll, tally

► *210 Calculation*

3 **additional item**, addition, add-on (US), adjunct, augmentation, augment, inflection, affix, prefix, suffix, infix, adjective, adverb, additive, attachment, addendum, additament, carry-over, leftover, contribution, reinforcement, patch, padding, stuffing, lining, tail, tailpiece, coda, appendix, postscript, PS, PPS, ending, epilogue, envoy, codicil, rider, annotation, footnote, marginal note, marginalia, interpolation, interlineation, interlude, intermezzo, ingredient, component, flap, lapel, tag, tab, ticket, lappet, frill, fringe, edging, border, decoration, ornamentation, garnish, garnishing, seasoning, flavouring, sauce, dressing, trimmings, all the trimmings, all that goes with it, accoutrements, furnishings, trappings, finish, finishing touch, icing on the cake, conclusion, corollary, side effect, side issue, additional part, aftereffect, annexe, wing, ell, outhouse, shed, the works (Inf)

► *25 Cookery; 232 Completeness; 277 Duration; 550 Covering*

4 **extra**, little extra, added extra, peripheral (computer), by-product, interest, gain, benefit, bonus, plus, perquisite, tip, gratuity, lagniappe (US), graft, free gift, giveaway (US), windfall, find, lucky find, serendipity, supernumerary, surplus, superfluity, superaddition, extras, sundries, reserves, reserve equipment, spare parts, spares, provisions, items, oddment, odd items, odds and ends, extra help, auxiliaries, auxiliary forces, reinforcements, extra time, injury time, sudden death, extra innings, odds and sods (Inf), golden handshake (Inf), bit on the side (Inf), perk (Inf), freebie (US inf)

5 **extra person**, extra pair of hands, substitute, relief, auxiliary, reinforcement, backup, stand-in, locum, extra mouth to feed, the other man (*or* woman), co-respondent (Lit)

► *16 Law; 21 Drama*

VERBS

6 **add**, add up, count, count up, calculate, total, total up, sum, sum up, do sums, do (the) addition, compute, carry, carry over, add to, append, annex, subjoin, attach, pin to, staple to, clip to, stick to, stick onto (*or* on), glue onto, tag, tag on, tack on, hitch to, hitch up to, hook up to, yoke to, join, tie to, unite to, conjoin, glue together, agglutinate, accrete, preface, prefix, affix, suffix, infix, interpolate, insert, stick in, introduce, interject, interpose, engraft, let in, bring to, contribute to, make one's contribution, add one's share, add (*or* put in) one's two penn'orth (Inf), swell, augment, expand, extend, supplement, crown, complete, put the finishing touch(es) to, make up the shortfall, fill a space, fill the gap, lay on, place on, put upon, impose, burden, load, overload, saddle with, burden (*or* load) with, heap on, pile on, superadd, superimpose, overlay, paint, paint over, coat, plaster, decorate, ornament, embellish, garnish, season, spice, flavour, mix with, mix in, take to oneself, take in, encompass, absorb, include, add value, accrue, bear interest, tote up (Inf), tot up (Inf)

7 **support**, add one's support, adhere to, combine with, mix with, join, make an addition to, make one more, reinforce, recruit, make up the numbers, swell the ranks

► *336 Strength; 376 Gathering*

ADJECTIVES

8 **additional**, added, included, interpolated, lined, inclusive, annexed, loaded, reinforced, additive, cumulative, adjunctive, adjunct, conjunctive, attached, adjoined, joined, subjoined, inserted, prefixed, adscititious, adventitious, supplemental (*or* supplementary), complementary, accretive, accretionary, agglutinative, subsidiary, incremental, auxiliary, collateral, contributory, another, yet another, further, more

9 **extra**, new, fresh, supererogatory, supernumerary, surplus, spare, superfluous, decorative, ornamental, padded, stuffed, dressed-up

ADVERBS

10 **additionally**, in addition (to), plus, and, extra, cumulatively, adjunctly, supplementarily, collaterally, superfluously, et cetera (*or* etc.), and so on, and so forth, more, over and above, on top of, as a tip, as a lagniappe (US), with interest, with a vengeance, also, as well (as), too, to boot, into the bargain, not to mention, let alone, not forgetting, moreover, furthermore, further, (or) else,

besides, on the side, apart from, together with, along with, conjointly, jointly, at the same time, in collaboration, in conjunction with, coupled with, including, inclusive of, even with, despite, in spite of, for all that, beside (Lit), with (brass) knobs on (Inf)

212 Subtraction

The big print giveth and the fine print taketh away. J. Fulton Sheen.

NOUNS

1 **subtraction**, deduction, taking away, minus, discounting, detraction, devaluation, diminution, decrease, cut, cutting, cutting back, retrenchment, shrinkage, decimation, price cutting, discount, offset, exception, abstraction, exclusion, withdrawal, elimination, expulsion, ejection, extraction, precipitation, sedimentation, removal, alleviation, relief, erosion, corrosion, wear and tear, rubbing out, deletion, erasure, obliteration, eradication, editing, bowdlerization, expurgation, striking out, extirpation, chopping, lopping, mutilation, cutting off, amputation, beheading, decapitation, severance, excision, circumcision, docking, curtailment, condensation, abridgment, abbreviation, shortening, castration, emasculation, fixing (Inf), altering (US inf)

► *128 Exclusion; 144 Displacement; 149 Shortness; 214 Decrease; 369 Extraction; 371 Expulsion; 469 Selection; 561 Reproduction; 740 Publication; 741 News; 773 Taking; 791 Discount*

2 **subtracted item**, thing deducted, decrement, subtrahend, minuend, allowance, remission, discount, price cut, refund, rebate, cut, cutback, limitation, restriction, drawback, shortfall, loss, forfeit, sacrifice, clawback (Inf), rake-off (Inf)

► *194 Number*

VERBS

3 **subtract**, deduct, take away, do subtraction, detract from, devalue, diminish, decrease, condense, abbreviate, abridge, decimate, cut, cut prices, discount, allow, set off, offset, leave out, take out, except, make an exception, abstract, exclude, omit, eliminate, withdraw, throw out, expel, eject, remove, unload, alleviate, relieve, shift, draw off, drain, empty, void, file down, corrode, erode, rub out, cross out, cancel, delete, erase, obliterate, cull, eradicate, thin, thin out, weed, uproot, pull up by the roots, extirpate, pull out, root out, rip out, hoick out (Inf), extract, precipitate, pick, pick out, hand-pick, pick a pocket, put on one side, censor, blue-pencil, bowdlerize, expurgate, garble, mutilate

4 **take off**, sever, cut off, amputate, behead, decapitate, excise, chop off, lop, prune, dock, curtail, shorten, circumcise, castrate, geld, caponize, emasculate, unman, spay, uncover, strip, strip off (*or* away), doff, denude, divest, skin, peel, pluck, fleece, kill (Inf), knock off (Inf), fix (Inf), alter (US inf), de-ball (US inf)

► *774 Stealing*

ADJECTIVES

5 **subtracted**, taken away, removed, deducted, excepted, abstracted, withdrawn, extracted, excluded, expelled, ejected, eliminated, eradicated, deleted, rubbed out, erased, obliterated

6 **subtractive**, reductive, extirpative, deductive, abstract, removable, eradicable

7 **reduced**, decreased, minus, curtailed, mutilated, headless, beheaded, decapitated, tailless, docked, chopped, lopped, severed, limbless, short, shortened, condensed, abridged, abbreviated, cut-price, cut-rate (US), discounted, devalued, diminished, lessened, decimated, eroded, corroded, worn

ADVERBS

8 **by subtraction**, at a discount, deductively, in deduction, less, short of, minus, without, bar, barring, save, exclusive of, excluding, except, excepting, with the exception of, save and except (Lit)

9 **decreasingly**, diminishingly, less and less, in a downward curve (*or* spiral), deductively, corrosively, removably, eradicably

213 Increase

From fairest creatures we desire increase,
That thereby beauty's rose might never die. William Shakespeare.

NOUNS

1 **increase**, addition, increment, augmentation, enlargement, growth, development, progress, advancement, advance, accumulation, cumulativeness, cumulative effect, build-up, accretion, snowballing effect, gain, waxing, bulging, swelling, dilation, expansion, fattening, thickening, broadening, widening, deepening, improvement, prosperity, profitability, appreciation, excess, overenlargement, magnification, doubling, redoubling, duplication, trebling, triplication, quadruplication, multiplication, reproduction, propagation, proliferation, amplification, extension, prolongation, protraction, intensification, escalation, acceleration, speeding, stepping up, concentration, condensation, enrichment, supplement, added contribution, accrual, heightening, enhancement, exaltation, elevation, aggrandizement, glorification, exaggeration, reinforcement, invigoration, stimulation, stimulus, spur, aggravation, exacerbation, culmination, climax

► *190 Expansion; 198 Two; 211 Addition; 302 Forward Motion; 356 Creation; 561 Reproduction; 562 Fertility; 727 Exaggeration*

2 **spread**, spiral, upswing, upturn, upward curve, upward trend, upsurge, uprush, push, swell, swelling, intumescence, surge, gush, boost, boom, rise, climb, crescendo, leap, jump, takeoff

► *152 Thickness; 154 Height; 304 Ascent; 366 Raising*

3 **increasing thing**, snowball, spring tide, flood tide, rising tide, waxing moon, bull market, inflation, interest, simple interest, compound interest, rising price

VERBS

4 **increase**, grow, gain, develop, escalate, wax, bulge, swell, dilate, distend, expand, fill, fill out, fatten, thicken, broaden, become larger, grow larger, put on weight, bud, sprout, burgeon, blossom, flower, flourish, thrive,

breed, swarm, spawn, proliferate, mushroom, multiply, spread, swell, intumesce, grow up, shoot up, spring up, grow by leaps and bounds, climb, spiral, mount, rise, soar, accumulate, snowball, take off, take off in a big way, rocket, flare up, gain strength, improve, grow rich, prosper, profit, be profitable, earn interest, gain in value, appreciate, rise in price, boom, surge, exceed, rise to a peak, rise to a maximum, crescendo, progress, gain ground, advance, hit the roof (Inf), go through the roof (*or* ceiling) (Inf), skyrocket (Inf)

5 **make bigger**, make more, augment, supplement, add to, contribute to, bring to, increase, increase numbers, enlist, recruit, enlarge, magnify, double, triple, quadruple, redouble, multiply, duplicate, square, cube, raise to the power of, reproduce, propagate, breed, grow, rear, raise from seed, raise from cuttings, develop, build up, fill up, fill in, fill out, pad out, expand, amplify, extend, prolong, stretch, lengthen, broaden, thicken, concentrate, condense, deepen, enrich, accrue to, repay with interest, widen, inflate, blow up, heighten, enhance, raise, exalt, erect, elevate, aggrandize, glorify, overrate, exaggerate, raise one's sights, set one's sights higher, raise the stakes, spur on, speed up, accelerate, intensify, escalate, step up, energize, stimulate, invigorate, reinforce, boost, give a boost to, maximize, stoke, fuel, add fuel to, aggravate, exacerbate, bring to the boil, bring to a head, culminate, climax, heat up (Inf), hot up (Inf), hike up (Inf), jack up (Inf), bump up (Inf), beef up (Inf), hop up (Inf), jazz up (Inf)

ADJECTIVES

6 **increasing**, progressive, progressing, expanding, growing, spreading, spreading like wildfire, escalating, bigger and better, crescent, waxing, filling, on the up and up, on the increase, ever-increasing, cumulative, snowballing, augmentative, prolific, additional, supplementary

7 **increased**, enlarged, magnified, accelerated, swollen, bloated, expanded, extended, stretched, intensified, heightened, enhanced, augmented, supplemented, hiked (Inf), jazzed up (Inf)

ADVERBS

8 **increasingly**, to an increasing extent, additionally, in addition, progressively, more and more, all the more, more so, even more so, greater and greater, bigger and bigger, bigger and better, cumulatively, prolifically, supplementarily

214 Decrease

Less is more. Ludwig Mies Van Der Rohe.

O mighty Caesar! dost thou lie so low?
Are all thy conquests, glories, triumphs, spoils,
Shrunk to this little measure? William Shakespeare.

NOUNS

1 **decrease**, deduction, subtraction, lessening, decrement, regression, de-escalation, abatement, slackening, moderation, growing soft, diminuendo, decrescendo, dimming, fading, fade-out, evanescence, diminution, waning, shrinking, shrinkage, contraction, detumescence, dwindling, ebb, drain, wasting away, degeneration, atrophy, failure, subsidence, loss of value, depreciation, enfeeblement, weakening, impoverishment, shortage, scarcity, exhaustion, diminishing returns, slow-down, deceleration, retardation, weight loss, reduction, disappearance, evaporation, deliquescence, erosion, attrition, wear, wear and tear, decay, dilapidation, damage, wastage, waste, leakage, loss, extinction, consumption, limitation, restriction, curtailment, downsizing, squeeze, compression, retrenchment, rationalization, cutback, rollback (US), economization, economizing, shortening, abbreviation, abridgment, precis, mitigation, extenuation, belittlement, underestimation, undervaluation

▶ *155 Lowness; 191 Contraction; 206 Few; 212 Subtraction; 218 Insufficiency; 303 Backward Motion; 305 Descent; 766 Loss; 782 Poverty*

2 **decline**, downturn, downward trend, downward curve, fall, drop, falling off, sinking, plunge, collapse, slump, downward spiral, deflation, depression, levelling off, levelling out, bottoming out, nose dive (Inf), tailspin (Inf)

▶ *14 Finance; 155 Lowness; 305 Descent; 791 Discount*

3 **decreasing thing**, punctured tyre, ebb tide, neap tide, waning moon, bear market, deflation, recession, slump, crash, falling price

VERBS

4 **decrease**, grow less, lessen, de-escalate, ease, abate, slacken, moderate, die down, fade, fade away, evanesce, grow soft, grow dim, grow smaller, wane, wither, shrink, contract, shrivel, diminish, dwindle, ebb, ebb away, drain, drain away, dry up, waste away, wear away, eat away, corrode, run down, run low, fail, degenerate, atrophy, die away, tail off, taper off, peter out, decline, drop (off), fall (off), subside, sink, go down, come down, take a turn for the worse, plunge, collapse, slump, spiral, downwards, go into recession, depreciate, not increase, not grow, level off, level out, bottom out, slow down, decelerate, lose, shed, cast off, cast away, lose one's voice, become invisible, fade from sight (*or* view), disappear, evaporate, melt away, become scarce, thin out, thin, detumesce, become endangered, become extinct, die out, pass away, pass into history, pass into oblivion, take a nosedive (Inf), go into a tailspin (Inf)

5 **make smaller**, make less, decrease, whittle, pare down, scrape, shave, trim, prune, dock, clip, slash, reduce, lose weight, become anorexic, cut, cut down, thin out, weed out, rid oneself of, run down, impoverish, cut back, roll back (US), limit, restrict, curtail, scale down, downsize, squeeze, compress, contract, retrench, economize, rationalize, shorten, abbreviate, abridge, condense, precis, edit down, slow down, reduce speed, decelerate, retard, depress, lower, hush, quieten, turn down, weaken, enfeeble, debilitate, dilute, water down, extenuate, mitigate, alleviate, belittle, minimize, undervalue, underestimate, degrade, downgrade, play down

ADJECTIVES

6 **decreasing**, declining, falling, dwindling, waning, wasting away, fading, evanescent, abating, moderation, softening, diminuendo, decrescendo, sinking, going down, subsiding, detumescent, ebbing, decaying, diminished, decreased, belittled, on the slide (Inf), on a downer (Inf)

7 **decrescent**, declinate, reductive, depressive, debilitative, deflationary, deflationist, depreciatory, depreciative, loss-making, regressive, corrosive, deliquescent, decompressive, decadent, decayable, declinable, deductible, depreciable (US)

ADVERBS

8 **decreasingly**, diminishingly, in decline, on the wane, at low ebb, less and less, less so, ever less, even less, in descending order, downwards, down and down, on a declining scale, at a lower rate, at a lower price

215 Remainder

He intended, he said, to devote the rest of his life to learning the remaining twenty-two letters of the alphabet. George Orwell.

NOUNS

1 **remainder**, remains, rest, relic, relict, remnant, frustum, piece, chunk, shard (*or* sherd), shell, empty shell, husk, stump, rump, stub, plug, dottle (*or* dottel), cigarette end, butt, cigarette butt, butt end, fag end, roach (Inf), scrag end, body, torso, trunk, corpse, mortal remains, skeleton, bones, fossil, fragments, bits, debris, wreckage, ruins, all that is left, record, vestige, trace, track, trail, wake, footprint, fingerprint, afterglow, memory, tribal memory, memorabilia, souvenir, reminder, remembrance, survival, effect, aftereffect, result

► *3 History; 131 End; 149 Shortness; 205 Part; 206 Few; 210 Calculation; 219 Excess; 357 Destruction; 583 Burial; 744 Record*

2 **residue**, deposit, sediment, silt, precipitate, alluvium, moraine, loess, detritus, residual, residuum (Lit), leavings, leftovers, grounds, dregs, lees, dross, heeltaps, skimmings, offscourings, scum, slag, ashes, cinders, scoria, sludge, bilge, powder, sawdust, shavings, filings, scrapings, crumbs, husks, bran, chaff, stubble, scourings, sweepings, peelings, peel, skin, slough, scurf, dandruff, combings, clippings, trimmings, remnants, castoffs, offcuts, scraps, oddments, odds and ends, bits and pieces, bits and bobs, lumber, jumble, junk, rubbish, trash (US), rejects, refuse, litter, dirt, waste, excrement, sewage

3 **difference**, discrepancy, surplus, margin, amount (*or* sum) outstanding, (net) balance, balance carried forward, carry-over, credit, profit, excess, loss, deficit, debit

► *13 Economics; 14 Finance*

4 **surplus**, excess, overgrowth, abundance, superabundance, overabundance, oversupply, redundancy, pleonasm, surfeit, superfluity, overload, glut, leftovers, extras, spares, bonus, dividend, something for a rainy day (Inf)

► *211 Addition*

5 **estate**, effects, hereditament, acquest, bequest, inheritance, patrimony

► *258 Dirtiness; 345 Effect; 427 Powderiness; 470 Rejection; 560 Excretion*

6 **person remaining**, person left, survivor, sole survivor, last one out, heir, inheritor, successor, widow, widower, orphan, descendant, offspring, line, lineage

► *561 Reproduction; 582 Death*

VERBS

7 **be left**, be left over, remain, survive, result, continue, subsist, stay, rest

8 **leave**, leave over, owe, leave behind, deposit, bequeath, leave out, exclude, reject, abandon, discard, cast off, cast away, except, not choose

ADJECTIVES

9 **remaining**, residual, residuary, resultant, resting, left, hereditary, patrimonial, left behind, vestigial, precipitated, deposited, sedimentary, surviving, bereft, widowed, orphan, orphaned, abandoned, discarded, rejected, cast-off

10 **surplus**, net, unused, unspent, unexpired, unconsumed, outcast, on the shelf, over, leftover, passed over, unwanted, odd, still remaining, outstanding, owed, carried over, extra, spare, to spare, excess, excessive, overabundant, superabundant, overloaded, redundant, superfluous, pleonastic, otiose

ADVERBS

11 **residually**, vestigially, memorably, discrepantly, excessively, superfluously, abundantly, overabundantly, superabundantly, pleonastically, redundantly

12 **with a remainder**, with the rest, among those remaining, in arrears, in default, outstandingly, sparely, redundantly, superfluously, like a relic, like a fossil, on the shelf

216 Average

Most people are such fools that it is really no great compliment to say that a man is above the average. W. Somerset Maugham.

ADJECTIVES

1 **average**, usual, normal, par, typical, general, common, prevailing, current, popular, prevalent, predominant, across-the-board, sweeping, universal, generic, representative, characteristic, ordinary, everyday, familiar, household, common or garden, routine, habitual, customary, accustomed, wonted, traditional, accepted, conventional, middlebrow, standard, stock, set, established, regular, regulation, regulated, classic, orthodox, normative, prescriptive

► *117 Conformity; 138 Generality; 298 Regularity*

2 **medium**, median, medial, mesial, mesiad, mean, average, middle, middling, mid-, midmost, middlemost, midway, intermediate, intermediary, balanced, halfway, half and half, fifty-fifty, central, middle-of-the-road, sitting on the fence, moderate, nonextremist

► *173 Centre; 685 Moderation*

3 **mediocre**, average, passable, fair, fairish, fair to middling, middling, moderate, tolerable, adequate, not bad, neither good nor bad, alright, indifferent, lukewarm, unremarkable, undistinguished, unexceptional, unnoteworthy, unspectacular, commonplace, pedestrian, prosaic, second-class, second-best, second-division, second-rate, inferior, down-market, banal, grey, dull, run-of-the-mill, *comme ci comme ça* (Fr), *così-così* (It), so-so (Inf), okay (OK) (Inf), nothing to write home about (Inf), no great shakes (Inf), small-time (Inf)

▶ *117 Conformity; 122 Inferiority; 124 Unimportance*

NOUNS

4 **average**, norm, standard, par, rule, measure, criterion, yardstick, model, type, class, category, run, averageness, generality, commonness, commonality, prevalence, popularity, predominance, universality, ordinariness, familiarity, normality, normalcy, common or garden variety, conventionality, conformity, standardness, regularity, the usual, the ordinary, the common lot, the way things are, the way of the world

▶ *117 Conformity; 138 Generality; 298 Regularity*

5 **medium**, happy medium, intermedium, average, mean, golden mean, *juste milieu* (Fr), balance, middle, mid (Lit), midpoint, median, halfway point, halfway house, centre, midsection, middle ground, midterm, middle term, middle course, *via media* (L), moderation, moderateness

▶ *27 Mathematics; 173 Centre; 685 Moderation*

6 **mediocrity**, mediocreness, averageness, fairishness, passableness, tolerableness, adequacy, mixed blessing, half-measure, indifference, unremarkableness, second best, second division, beta minus, C grade, inferiority, small change, small fry, small potatoes (US inf), small beer (Inf), nothing to boast (*or* brag) about (Inf), nothing special (Inf), nothing to write home about (Inf), no oil painting (Inf)

▶ *122 Inferiority; 124 Unimportance; 217 Sufficiency*

7 **average person**, Mr (*or* Mrs) Average, commoner, boy (*or* girl) next door, man (*or* woman) in (*or* on) the street, man (*or* woman) on the Clapham omnibus, ordinary Joe, plain Jane, Joe Soap, Joe Bloggs, GI Joe, Joe Public, John Q. Public, everyman, everywoman, Tom, Dick, or Harry, Brown, Jones, and Robinson, Uncle Tom Cobbley and all, rank and file, masses, ruck, common folk, common (Lit), people, hoi polloi, the great unwashed (Offensive), proletariat, working classes, second-rater, unskilled worker, semiskilled worker, manual worker, labourer

▶ *137 Class; 208 Multitude; 574 Commoner; 578 Worker*

8 **middle classes**, bourgeois, bourgeoisie, Babbitt (US), Pooter, burgher, burgherdom, respectability, suburb, suburbia, suburbanite, villadom, small town, Middle America, Home Counties, commuter, commuter belt, dormitory town, semidetached house, family car, middle-income earner, white-collar worker, skilled worker, C1, C2, semiprofessional, professional, middle manager, nonextremist, moderate, middle-of-the-roader

▶ *117 Conformity; 137 Class*

VERBS

9 **be average**, be the norm, prevail, predominate, be about right, suffice, be enough, get by, make do, be moderate, sit on the fence, not cause a stir, conform, go with the crowd, go unnoticed, blend with the crowd, blur, take a back seat, stay in the background, be a nobody, play second fiddle

▶ *122 Inferiority; 138 Generality; 217 Sufficiency*

10 **make average**, even out (*or* up), average out, level, level up (*or* down), normalize, generalize, conventionalize, standardize, equalize, equate, balance, balance out, strike a balance, symmetrize, regularize, proportion, smooth out, share out, distribute, allocate, divide, take the mean, establish a mean, split down the middle, split the difference, halve, bisect, make it all square, go shares, go fifty-fifty, go halves, go halfway, go Dutch (Inf)

▶ *27 Mathematics; 173 Centre; 210 Calculation; 298 Regularity; 764 Sharing; 770 Allocation*

ADVERBS

11 **on average**, chiefly, mainly, commonly, generally, in general, generally speaking, broadly, broadly speaking, as a rule, roughly, roughly speaking, at a guess, as an approximation, as a general rule, about, round about, just about, more or less, mostly, for the most part, on the whole, as a whole, by and large, altogether, taking all things together, all things considered, all things being equal, on balance, in the long run, all in all, overall, prevailingly, predominantly, usually, normally, ordinarily, typically, habitually, routinely, as a matter of course, to be expected, as per usual (Inf)

▶ *117 Conformity; 138 Generality; 298 Regularity*

12 **mediumly**, medianly, medially, intermediately, centrally, midway, halfway, half and half, midmost, middlemost, in the middle, moderately, neither here nor there, in between, betwixt and between (Inf)

▶ *173 Centre*

217 Sufficiency

ADJECTIVES

1 **sufficient**, enough, adequate, satisfactory, acceptable, sufficing, all-sufficing, complete, self-sufficient, enough to go round, competent, equal, equal to, a match for, fitting, suitable, satisfying, contenting, measured, commensurate, up to the mark, just right, not too much, not too little, barely sufficient, only just enough, hand-to-mouth, makeshift, provisional, up to snuff (Inf), filling the bill (Inf)

▶ *119 Equality; 218 Insufficiency; 232 Completeness; 436 Provisions; 609 Satisfaction; 762 Substitution*

2 **plentiful**, plenteous, ample, enough and to spare, more than enough, beyond expectations, superfluous, redundant, open-handed, generous, bountiful, lavish, liberal, extravagant, prodigal, wholesale, without stint, unsparing, unmeasured, endless, inexhaustible, bottomless, great, luxuriant, luxuriating, riotous, lush, rank, fat, fertile, prolific, profuse, abundant, copious, overflowing, superabundant, rich, opulent, affluent

▶ *219 Excess; 562 Fertility; 679 Generosity; 681 Extravagance; 781 Wealth*

3 **filled**, well-filled, full, full up, chock-full, chock-a-block, flush, replete, sated, satiated, stuffed, glutted, bloated, ready to burst, satisfied, contented, content, well-provided, well-provisioned, well-stocked, well-furnished, rich in, teeming, crawling, overflowing, up to one's neck (*or* eyes) in, multitudinous, chocker (Aus inf), up to one's ass in (Inf)

▶ *208 Multitude; 232 Completeness; 436 Provisions; 609 Satisfaction*

VERBS

4 **suffice**, be enough, prove adequate, prove acceptable, satisfy, content, do, answer, quench, just do, do and no more, work, get the job done, get one by, serve, serve as a makeshift, qualify, reach, make the grade, pass, pass

muster, measure up to, meet requirements, withstand testing, do all that is possible, rise to the occasion, stand, stand up to, take the strain, support, do what is required, fulfil, carry out, fill, refill, replenish, fill up, top up, more than satisfy, sate, satiate, overeat, stuff oneself, glut oneself, gorge, have a bellyful, overdo it, provide for, make adequate provision, wash (Inf), fill the bill (Inf)
► *239 Convenience; 246 Success; 413 Support; 436 Provisions*
5 **about**, be plentiful, proliferate, teem, swarm, bristle with, crawl with, exuberate, riot, luxuriate, grow in profusion, pour, flow, stream, shower, rain, snow, brim, overflow, flow with milk and honey, superabound, rain cats and dogs (Inf), roll in (Inf), wallow in (Inf), swim in (Inf), stink of (Inf)
► *208 Multitude; 219 Excess; 562 Fertility; 781 Wealth*
6 **have enough**, eat one's fill, drink one's fill, have had enough, have had more than enough, have had it up to here, have had a bellyful, be fed up, afford, have the means
► *25 Cookery; 606 Dissatisfaction; 609 Satisfaction; 781 Wealth*

NOUNS

7 **sufficiency**, enough, adequacy, adequate amount, satisfaction, satisfactory amount, right amount, required number, quorum, right qualities, qualification, requirement, pass, pass marks, assets, competence, adequate income, living wage, enough to live on, enough to get by, enough to keep body and soul together, subsistence farming, autarky, self-sufficiency, exact amount, no surplus, minimum, bare minimum, no less, least one can do, minimum requirement, acceptability, the possible, all that is possible, all that could be desired, content, contentment, full measure, fulfilment, completion, repletion, one's fill, bellyful, satiety
► *102 Possibility; 609 Satisfaction*
8 **plenty**, plentifulness, plenteousness, God's plenty, seven years of plenty, horn of plenty, cornucopia, abundance, proliferation, profusion, outpouring, shower, flood, spate, stream, great quantity, lots, galore, fullness, copiousness, amplitude, plenitude, affluence, riches, wealth, richness, fat, fat of the land, loaded table, groaning board, feast, banquet, orgy, riot, prodigality, extravagance, luxury, fertility, fecundity, productivity, productiveness, prolificacy, prolificness, luxuriance, lushness, rich harvest, vintage harvest, bumper crop, foison (Lit), rich vein, bonanza (US), bountiful supply, endless supply, more where it came from, more than enough, more that one can eat, too much, superabundance, glut, *embarras de richesses* (Fr), superfluity, excess, surplus, lashings(Inf), oodles (Inf), boo koos (US inf)
► *25 Cookery; 219 Excess; 232 Completeness; 439 Store; 562 Fertility; 681 Extravagance; 781 Wealth*

ADVERBS

9 **enough**, just enough, exactly enough, more than enough, sufficiently, adequately, satisfactorily, acceptably, tolerably, to the full, to one's heart's content, ad libitum, ad lib, on tap, on demand, abundantly, plentifully, plenteously, amply, inexhaustibly, interminably, endlessly, luxuriantly, prolifically, profusely, copiously, on the nose (Inf), flat out (Inf)

218 Insufficiency

ADJECTIVES

1 **insufficient**, not sufficient, inadequate, not enough, too little, too few, unsatisfactory, not satisfying, disappointing, unacceptable, insubstantial, too small, limited, cramped, slender, meagre, skimpy, scanty, scant, sketchy, deficient, incomplete, lacking, light on, low on, wanting, found wanting, poor, inferior, incompetent, incapable, unequal to, not up to it, weak, weak as a kitten, weak as a baby, thin, watery, wersh (Scot), jejune, undernourished, underfed, niggardly, miserly, mean, stingy, parsimonious, not up to snuff (Inf), unable to hack it (US inf)
► *96 Unreality; 122 Inferiority; 233 Incompleteness; 337 Weakness; 486 Unskilfulness; 604 Disappointment; 606 Dissatisfaction; 682 Meanness*
2 **unprovided**, unsupplied, unfurnished, ill-furnished, ill-supplied, ill-equipped, absent, vacant, bare, empty, unstocked, unfilled, unreplenished, empty-handed, with empty pockets, unsuccessful, unsatisfied, discontented, unfulfilled, unprovided for, unaccommodated, insatiable, greedy, unsated, stinted, rationed, skimped, starved of, lacking, needing, hindered, hard up, scraping by, poor, undercapitalized, underfinanced, underpaid, underfunded, understaffed, undermanned, short-handed, under strength
► *98 Absence; 247 Failure; 378 Obstruction; 606 Dissatisfaction; 617 Desire; 782 Poverty*
3 **underfed**, undernourished, half-fed, half-starved, on short commons, hungry, hungry as a bear, famished, famine-stricken, unfed, starved, starving, voracious, ravenous, ravening, fasting, emaciated, macerated, thin, thin as a rail, lean, spare, skinny, skin-and-bone, wasting, anorexic, starveling, scurvy, scraggy, stunted
► *153 Thinness; 687 Fasting*
4 **scarce**, rare, infrequent, sparse, few, few and far between, short, in short supply, at a premium, hard to get, hard to come by, not to be had, not to be had at any price, not to be had for love or money, scarce (*or* rare) as hen's teeth, thin on the ground, unavailable, unobtainable, unprocurable, nonexistent, out of season, out of stock, sold out, out, off the market, out of print, off the menu, off
► *206 Few*

VERBS

5 **be insufficient**, not suffice, not meet requirements, not meet expectations, cramp one's style, hinder, restrain, restrict, limit, lack, need, want, require, leave a gap, leave a lacuna, fail, disappoint, fall below, fall short, come short, default, run out, dry up, take half measures, tinker, fill in the gaps, paper over the cracks
► *135 Requirement; 231 Imperfection; 233 Incompleteness; 251 Restraint; 604 Disappointment; 606 Dissatisfaction*
6 **be unsatisfied**, ask for more, beg for more, come back, come again, take a second helping, still feel hungry, feel hungry, feel dissatisfied, feel cheated, increase one's demands, reject an offer, laugh at an offer, want, desire, desiderate, long for, yearn for, miss, feel unfulfilled, feel the lack, stand in need of, feel something is missing, need, require

▶ *135 Requirement; 470 Rejection; 606 Dissatisfaction; 617 Desire; 687 Fasting; 688 Gluttony*

7 **make insufficient**, demand too much, ask too much, expect too much, overtax, overextend, overwork, overcrop, overgraze, overfish, impoverish, damage, impair, exhaust, drain, deplete, run down, squander, waste, hold back, begrudge, grudge, stint, skimp, ration, put on half rations, put on short commons, deprive, disinherit, cut off without a penny, cut off without a dime (US), cut off with a shilling

▶ *441 Waste; 682 Meanness; 773 Taking*

NOUNS

8 **insufficiency**, inadequacy, not enough, too little, too few, nonsatisfaction, lack of satisfaction, disappointment, discontent, small amount, small quantity, little few, drop in the bucket, drop in the ocean, meagreness, skimpiness, scantiness, scantness, deficiency, deficit, shortfall, slippage, no quorum, not a full team, not a full deck, incompleteness, incompetence, inferiority, imperfection, defect, nonfulfilment, noncompletion, temporary substitute, makeshift, half measures, stopgap measures, tinkering, failure, weakness, bankruptcy, insolvency, bare subsistence, subsistence level, poverty level, stinginess, meanness, parsimony, low pay, pittance, dole, mite, minimum allowance, short allowance, short commons, iron rations, starvation rations, half rations, austerity, belt-tightening, Lenten fare, Spartan fare, starvation diet, bread and water, fast, fasting, asceticism, anorexia, anorexia nervosa, malnutrition, anaemia, vitamin deficiency

▶ *206 Few; 231 Imperfection; 233 Incompleteness; 604 Disappointment; 606 Dissatisfaction; 682 Meanness; 687 Fasting; 782 Poverty; 786 Nonpayment*

9 **scarcity**, scarceness, paucity, dearth, shortage, leanness, seven lean years, drought, famine, starvation, infertility, unproductiveness, power cut, oil crisis, energy crisis, decrease, diminution, nothing (*or* none) to spare, short supply, sellers' market, bearish market, deprivation, poverty, lack, want, need, ebb, low water, shallowness, (a case of) the shorts (US inf)

▶ *135 Requirement; 157 Shallowness; 206 Few; 214 Decrease; 563 Infertility; 782 Poverty*

ADVERBS

10 **insufficiently**, inadequately, not enough, less than somewhat, unsatisfactorily, disappointingly, unacceptably, insubstantially, skimpily, scantly, scantily, sketchily, poorly, incompetently, stingily, parsimoniously, scarcely, rarely, infrequently, sparsely, in default, failing, for want of, at a low ebb

219 Excess

The road of excess leads to the palace of Wisdom. William Blake.

NOUNS

1 **excess**, redundance, redundancy, overspill, overflow, inundation, flood, outflow, deluge, abundance, superabundance, glut, exuberance, luxuriance, riot, profusion, plenty, richness, *embarras de richesses* (Fr), bonanza (US), more than is fair, lion's share, most, main part, increase, upsurge, uprush, avalanche, spate, great quantity, too many, plethora, congestion, mob, crowd, overpopulation, saturation, supersaturation, saturation point, all the market can bear, plenitude, waste, excessiveness, nimiety, exorbitance, extreme, extremes, too much, exaggeration

▶ *213 Increase; 217 Sufficiency; 232 Completeness; 315 Exit; 439 Store; 441 Waste; 727 Exaggeration*

2 **overdoing it**, overstretching oneself, overextension, overexpression, too much on one's plate, too many irons in the fire, overactivity, overpoliteness, officiousness, excessive bureaucracy, red tape, overpraise, effusiveness, overoptimism, overestimation, overmeasure, overpayment, overweight, burden, load, overload, last straw, overindulgence, intemperance, immoderation, overeating, overfeeding, gluttony, overdrinking, drunkenness, engorgement, satiety, more than enough, one too many, bellyful, sufficiency, fat, fattiness, obesity, overdose, OD (Inf), overjolt (US inf), OJ (US inf)

▶ *158 Size; 217 Sufficiency; 342 Activity; 414 Heaviness; 467 Overestimation; 686 Self-Indulgence; 688 Gluttony; 690 Drunkenness*

3 **superfluity**, superfluousness, more than is needed, luxury, luxury article, luxury car, luxury hotel, luxury flat, luxuriousness, nonessential, extra, frill, perquisite, overfulfilment, overkill, duplication, supererogation, something over, something extra, lagniappe (US), bonus, spare cash, money to burn, margin, overlap, surplus, leftovers, overplus, surplusage, balance, remainder, spare, accessory, spare tyre, spare wheel, fifth wheel, excrescence, parasite, uselessness, inutility, expletive, pleonasm, rambling speech, padded text, circuitous writing, diffuseness, tautology, redundancy, inactivity, overemployment, overmanning, too much of a good thing, *embarras de richesses* (Fr), glut, oversupply, product dumping, inflation, surfeit, satiety, perk (Inf)

▶ *215 Remainder; 238 Uselessness; 270 Vagueness; 342 Activity; 343 Inactivity*

VERBS

4 **be excessive**, have excess, overspill, overflow, brim over, well over, inundate, flood, engulf, flow out, flow, stream, deluge, overwhelm, burst its banks, burst at the seams, ooze at every pore, abound, superabound, luxuriate, riot, run riot, overproduce, overpopulate, bristle with, teem with, swarm with, crawl with, outnumber, meet one at every turn, extend, know no bounds, spread far and wide, reach to the far ends of the earth, reach to the four corners of the earth, overextend, overexpand, overstep, overlap, soak, saturate, drench, stuff, cram, fill, congest, choke, suffocate, oversatisfy, glut, cloy, satiate, sate, sicken, overfeed, gorge, overeat, overdrink, pamper oneself, overindulge oneself, overdose, overfulfil, oversubscribe, do more than enough, go overboard, oversell, flood the market, dump on the market, overstock, pile up, overdo, overplay, overact, overstep the mark, talk too much, pile it on, lay it on thick, lay it on with a trowel, exaggerate, overpraise, overload, overburden, bite off more than one can chew, have too much on one's plate, have too many irons in the fire, overcharge, surcharge, overspend, make a splash, lavish, lav-

ish upon, overindulge, pamper, spoil, run one's mouth (US inf), roll in (Inf), wallow in (Inf), swim in (Inf), stink of (Inf), OD (Inf), overjolt (US inf), OJ (US inf), go over the top (Inf)

► *141 Space; 208 Multitude; 217 Sufficiency; 232 Completeness; 232 Completeness; 315 Exit; 329 Overstepping; 429 Moisture; 562 Fertility; 679 Generosity; 681 Extravagance; 686 Self-Indulgence; 688 Gluttony; 727 Exaggeration*

5 **be superfluous**, go begging (*or* a-begging), remain on one's hands, have on one's hands, do twice over, duplicate, carry coals to Newcastle, gild the lily, teach one's grandmother to suck eggs, labour the obvious, take a sledgehammer to crack a nut, flog a dead horse, exceed requirements, have no use

► *215 Remainder; 238 Uselessness; 343 Inactivity*

ADJECTIVES

6 **excessive**, redundant, overflowing, filled to overflowing, brimming over, running over, full, overfull, flooding, streaming, flowing, overwhelming, overwhelmed, saturated, supersaturated, drenched, soaked, abundant, superabundant, exuberant, luxuriant, riotous, profuse, plentiful, too many, one too many, plethoric, overpopulated, bristling, teeming, swarming, crawling, outnumbered, too much, overmuch, immoderate, exorbitant, extreme, inordinate, disproportionate, cloying, satiating, nauseating, sickening, cloyed, satiated, sated, replete, overfed, gorged, crammed, stuffed, bloated, congested, ready to burst, bursting, overstretched, overburdened, overloaded, overcharged, exaggerated, overdone, overplayed, overacted, effusive, gushing, overpolite, overexcited, one over the eight (Inf), over-the-top (OTT) (Inf), over the moon (Inf)

► *208 Multitude; 217 Sufficiency; 429 Moisture; 620 Boredom; 686 Self-Indulgence; 688 Gluttony; 727 Exaggeration*

7 **superfluous**, supererogatory, excess, extra, spare, surplus, leftover, remaining, nonessential, luxury, unnecessary, needless, diffuse, rambling, circuitous, tautologous, tautological, otiose, pleonastic, redundant, overemployed, overmanned, overstaffed

► *135 Requirement; 215 Remainder; 238 Uselessness; 270 Vagueness*

ADVERBS

8 **excessively**, redundantly, abundantly, immoderately, over and above, too much, overmuch, overly, unnecessarily, needlessly, beyond measure, to excess, in excess of requirements, superfluously, enough and to spare, above expectations

220 List

I would sooner read a time-table or a catalogue than nothing at all. They are much more entertaining than half the novels that are written. W. Somerset Maugham.

NOUNS

1 **list**, listing, enumeration, series, items, itemization, inventory, tally, stock, repertory, register, registry, table, chart, checklist

► *744 Record*

2 **table**, table of contents, contents, index, card index, file, filing system, catalogue, reference list, bibliography, book list, reading list, syllabus, filmography, discography, publisher's catalogue (*or* list), computer listing, menu, window, database, spreadsheet, website

► *40 Computers; 407 Order; 409 Arrangement*

3 **dictionary**, lexicon, glossary, word list, vocabulary, terminology, nomenclature, thesaurus, gazetteer, atlas, encyclopedia, almanac, yearbook, reference book, directory, guidebook, who's who, telephone directory, phone book, Yellow Pages, address book

► *5 Language and Linguistics*

4 **bill**, invoice, account, itemized account, statement, ledger, books, account books, daybook, journal, bill of lading, manifest, docket, price list, tariff, bill of fare, menu, carte, wine list, shopping list

► *25 Cookery; 789 Accounting; 790 Price*

5 **list of appointments**, diary, engagement diary, engagement book, daybook, Filofax™, calendar, agenda, order of business, docket (US), programme, timetable, schedule, itinerary, prospectus, syllabus, curriculum, synopsis, compendium

► *723 Summary*

6 **list of names**, roll, register, rota, roster, scroll, panel, census, poll, head count, roll call, muster roll, tax roll, electoral roll, electorate, voting list, property roll, cadaster, payroll, active list, retired list, civil list, waiting list, sick list, shortlist, blacklist, cast list, dramatis personae, credits, line-up

7 **listing**, enumeration, itemization, registration, filing, indexing, cataloguing, tabulation, charting, classification, taxonomy

VERBS

8 **list**, make a list, enumerate, itemize, inventory, register, record, note, write down, put down, set down, chronicle, enter, book, post, file, pigeonhole, classify, catalogue, index, tabulate, chart, diarize, timetable, schedule, bill, invoice, shortlist, blacklist

► *137 Class; 744 Record*

9 **enlist**, enrol, matriculate, sign up, join, volunteer, engage, participate

10 **score**, keep score, tally, keep a tally of, enumerate, keep count

► *194 Number*

ADJECTIVES

11 **listed**, enumerated, itemized, inventoried, registered, recorded, entered, noted, filed, catalogued, taxonomic, classificatory, indexed, tabulated, charted, scheduled, programmed, timetabled

12 **inventorial**, glossarial, cadastral, tabular, schematic, diagrammatic, alphabetical

ADVERBS

13 **inventorially**, glossarially, tabularly, terminologically, encyclopedically, taxonomically, alphabetically, numerically, in order, in series, in sequence

Condition

221 State

Alas, O Lord, to what a state dost Thou bring those who love Thee! St Teresa of Ávila.

NOUNS

1 **state**, condition, situation, circumstances, lot, fettle, form, order, repair, estate, social position, position, station in life, role, status, standing, rank, ranking, place, posture, footing, walk of life, class, echelon, category, structure, aspect, guise, shape, phase, light, mode, manner, way, style, lifestyle, fashion, complexion, appearance, tone, modality, modus vivendi, modus operandi, trend, stamp, fit, mould, street credibility, cred (Inf)

▶ *12 Government and Politics; 99 Essence; 143 Situation; 160 Form; 222 Circumstances; 229 Tendency; 403 Structure; 525 Appearance; 707 Affirmation; 729 Speech; 738 Display*

2 **predicament**, problem, dilemma, plight, trouble, difficulties, hot water (Inf), jam (Inf), fix (Inf), pickle (Inf)

▶ *113 Opposition; 264 Difficulty; 378 Obstruction*

3 **state of affairs**, the nature of things, the shape of things, the way things shape up, the way things are, how things stand, the way of the world, the lie of the land, the lay of the land (US), how it is (Inf), where it's at (Inf), the size of it (Inf), how things stack up (Inf)

4 **state of mind**, frame of mind, mood, humour, disposition, temper, temperament, attitude, vein, morale, fettle, fine fettle, spirits, good spirits, high spirits, good humour, bad spirits, low spirits, bad humour

▶ *598 Happiness*

5 **physical state**, state of health, physical form, physical condition, shape, good condition (*or* shape), bad (*or* poor) condition (*or* shape), trim, kilter (*or* kelter), fettle, fine fettle, fig (Inf)

▶ *259 Health*

VERBS

6 **be in a state of**, be so, have a standing, stand, maintain a certain footing, maintain one's status, lie, sit, occupy (*or* enjoy) a certain social position, occupy (*or* enjoy) a certain standing, occupy a certain walk of life, have a station in life, play a role, fare, manage, do well, do poorly, get on (*or* along), come on (*or* along), live a certain way, follow a trend, fit a mould, come through, turn out, come out, make out (Inf), get by (Inf), shape up (Inf), stack up (Inf)

7 **be in a predicament**, have a predicament, have a problem, have a dilemma, run into trouble, have difficulties, labour under, need help, see no way out, get into a jam (Inf), get into a fix (Inf), be up shit creek (without a paddle) (Inf)

ADJECTIVES

8 **in a state of**, in a certain state, on form, in form, in good form, in bad form, conditional, modal, ranking, ranked, placed, situated, classed, in fine fettle, in good spirits, in a good mood, high-spirited, good-humoured, in bad spirits, low-spirited, in a bad mood, bad-humoured, temperamental, in condition, in order, in good condition (*or* shape), in bad condition (*or* shape), out of order, out of sorts, out of kilter (*or* kelter), stylish, fashionable, trendy, cred (Inf)

ADVERBS

9 **conditionally**, as it is, as it stands, in a state of, in a certain state, such being the case, as things are, as the matter stands, in the circumstances, in the present case, in fine fettle, in good form, in good spirits, good-humouredly, in bad form, in bad spirits, bad-humouredly, temperamentally, provisionally, contingently, stylishly, in style, fashionable, in fashion, trendily

222 Circumstances

Myth deals in false universals, to dull the pain of particular circumstances. Angela Carter.

NOUNS

1 **circumstances**, conditions, condition, relative condition, situation, total situation, existing conditions, environment, surroundings, setting, milieu, background, the times, context, the whole picture, the picture, status quo, status, state of affairs, state of play, position, means, resources, state, posture, attitude, terms, footing, standing, lie of the land, lay of the land (US), full particulars, ins and outs, story so far, the way it is, contingency, eventuality, setup (Inf), how it goes (Inf), the score (Inf)

▶ *108 Relatedness; 129 Precedence; 143 Situation; 170 Surroundings; 221 State; 407 Order*

2 **occurrence**, event, episode, incident, case, happening, occasion, instance, juncture, conjuncture, stage, point,

milestone, moment, hour, right time, opportunity, stepping stone

► *275 Timeliness*

3 **critical moment**, hour of decision, crossroads, turning point, match point, point of no return, Rubicon

► *224 Change; 278 Transience*

4 **difficult circumstances**, awkward situation, trouble, catch-22, plight, dilemma, predicament, crisis, emergency, exigency, quandary, pretty pass, pinch, corner, hole, jam (Inf), fix (Inf), pickle (Inf), time when the chips are down (Inf)

► *254 Danger; 264 Difficulty; 378 Obstruction; 782 Poverty*

5 **comfortable circumstances**, comfort, ease, security, well-being, prosperity, success, luck, luckiness, good fortune, life of ease, the good life, lap of luxury, halcyon days, golden age

► *107 Chance; 248 Prosperity; 252 Safety; 609 Satisfaction; 781 Wealth*

6 **aspect**, element, factor, fact, facet, datum, detail, minor detail, minutia, incidental, item, particular, point, thing

► *698 Truth*

ADJECTIVES

7 **circumstantial**, dependent on circumstances, relative, given, contingent, conditional, indirect, inferential, hearsay, conjectural, presumed, implied, provisional, fitting the circumstances, adventitious, situational, surrounding, environmental, background, situated, placed, contextual, changeful, variable, transient, incidental, eventual, eventful

8 **difficult**, awkward, critical, crucial, pivotal, decisive, troublesome, exigent, in a jam (Inf), in a fix (Inf), in a pickle (Inf), up shit creek (without a paddle) (Inf)

9 **comfortable**, easy, secure, well, prosperous, lucky, opportune, suitable, auspicious, favourable

10 **detailed**, meticulous, elaborate, minute, incidental, particular, full, precise, exact, specific, special, fussy, finicky, pernickety, nit-picking (Inf)

VERBS

11 **circumstantiate**, itemize, specify, particularize, substantiate, put in context, see the whole picture, get the lie of the land, get the lay of the land (US), get the full particulars, detail, go (*or* enter) into detail, cite, instance, adduce, document, spell out, quote chapter and verse, atomize, anatomize, know the ins and outs, see how it goes (Inf)

12 **come to a juncture**, come to a crossroads, reach a stage, reach the turning point, reach a milestone, play match point, come to the point of no return, cross one's Rubicon

13 **get into difficulties**, get into trouble, be in a catch-22 situation, reach a crisis, have an emergency, get into a jam (Inf), get into a fix (Inf), get into hot water (Inf), get in a pickle (Inf), find oneself up shit creek (without a paddle) (Inf)

14 **be comfortable**, prosper, enjoy good fortune, get lucky, live a life of ease, live in the lap of luxury, be smiled on by fate, fare well, succeed, flourish

ADVERBS

15 **under the circumstances**, according to circumstances, circumstantially, accordingly, as it is, as it happened, as things stand, as it turns out, as matters stand, as the winds blow, as the case may be, that (*or* such) being the case, in that case, in this way, that (*or* it) being so, given that, from that angle, at that rate, taking it that, and so, thus, so, in the event, in the case, if, if so, provided that, supposing, assuming, granting, allowing, as it may happen, as things may fall, like this, like that, should it so happen, should it be that, by the same token, equally, similarly, consequently, if not, unless, except, without, like so (Inf)

16 **relatively**, in a relative way, conditionally, under certain conditions, provisionally, with provisions, indirectly, inferentially, conjecturally, adventitiously, environmentally, contextually, changefully, with many changes, variably, incidentally, contingently, eventually

17 **difficultly**, awkwardly, critically, crucially, at a crucial time, at a crucial point, exigently, when the chips are down (Inf)

18 **comfortably**, easily, safely, securely, prosperously, luckily, opportunely, suitably, auspiciously, favourably

19 **meticulously**, with a fine-tooth (*or* fine-toothed) comb, elaborately, in an elaborate manner, minutely, incidentally, particularly, fully, in full, precisely, exactly, just so, specifically, specially, fussily, sedulously, assiduously

223 Accompaniment

SEAGOON: *I want you to accompany me on the safari.*
BLOODNOCK: *Gad sir, I'm sorry, I've never played one.* Spike Milligan.

NOUNS

1 **accompaniment**, concomitance, coexistence, symbiosis, cohabitation, combination, conjunction, association, union, coagency, convoy

► *374 Combination*

2 **synchronism**, simultaneity, contemporaneity, coincidence, concurrence, conjunction, co-occurrence

► *285 Same Time*

3 **companionship**, company, togetherness, fellowship, friendship, partnership, consortship, cohabitation, marriage, society, community, mateyness (Inf)

► *569 Friendship; 570 Marriage; 654 Sociability*

4 **concomitant**, attribute, feature, fixture, accessory, appendage, adjunct, appurtenance, ornament, attendant, corollary, symptom, syndrome, indication, sign, background, context

► *99 Essence; 211 Addition; 742 Sign*

5 **side-dish**, salad, vegetables, condiments, sauce, dressing, drinks

► *25 Cookery*

6 **accompanier**, accompanist, repetiteur, backing band (*or* group), backing vocalists (*or* singers), rhythm section, string (*or* brass *or* wind) section, *Nebenstimme* (Ger)

► *18 Music*

7 **attendant**, squire, cavalier, escort, outrider, chaperon (*or* chaperone), duenna, protector, keeper, guard, bodyguard, minder (Inf), heavy (Inf), muscle (Inf)

► *252 Safety*

8 **usher**, shepherd, marshal, conductor, leader, guide, pilot

▶ *579 Management*

9 follower, shadow, tail, satellite, dependant, hanger-on, parasite, sycophant, camp follower, groupie (Inf)

▶ *401 Servant*

10 attendance, cortege, retinue, following, entourage, court, suite, retainers

11 companion, colleague, partner, associate, co-worker, fellow, classmate, flatmate, comrade, friend, best friend, travelling companion, fellow traveller, mate (Inf), buddy (Inf)

▶ *569 Friendship; 747 Cooperation*

12 partner, constant companion, escort, date, girlfriend, boyfriend, lover, consort, cohabitant, cohabitee, live-in lover, common-law spouse, spouse, husband, wife, better half, hubbie (Inf), trouble and strife (Inf)

▶ *570 Marriage; 593 Love*

VERBS

13 accompany, go together, go with, belong with, complement, go together with, come with, be linked with, go hand in hand with, go hand in glove with, concur, coincide, synchronize, keep time with

14 keep company with, travel with, run with, work with, partner, escort, go out with, date (US), consort with, associate with, frequent, befriend, socialize, club together, team up, gang up, pair up, couple, live together, live with, cohabit, hobnob (Inf), hang around with (Inf), hang out with (Inf)

▶ *569 Friendship; 654 Sociability; 747 Cooperation*

15 escort, squire, chaperone, protect, guard, safeguard, guide, lead, pilot, usher, shepherd, marshal, conduct, convoy, bring (*or* take) in tow, mind (Inf)

▶ *252 Safety; 579 Management*

16 attend, dance attendance on, wait on, follow, tag along, attach oneself to, dog the footsteps of, shadow, tail, track

▶ *401 Servant*

ADJECTIVES

17 accompanying, concomitant, attending, attendant, belonging, complementary, accessory, collateral, incidental, background, contextual

18 concurrent, concurring, coincident, coinciding, simultaneous, contemporary, contemporaneous, parallel, correlative, coexistent, coexisting, symbiotic, cohabiting

19 associated, partnered, coupled, paired, wedded, married, combined, joined, inseparable, thick as thieves, hand-in-glove

▶ *374 Combination*

20 accompanied, attended, escorted, chaperoned, protected, guarded, ushered, shepherded, marshalled, guided, led, conducted, minded (Inf)

ADVERBS

21 together, in a body, all together, in unison, collectively, inseparably, unitedly, in convoy, in a crocodile, in tow, in someone's wake

22 hand in hand, arm in arm, side by side, cheek by jowl, hand in glove

23 concurrently, simultaneously, contemporaneously, symbiotically

PREPOSITIONS

24 with, together with, along with, in company with, in association with, coupled with, paired with, partnered with, in tandem with, in conjunction with

224 Change

Plus ça change, plus c'est la même chose. (The more things change, the more they stay the same.) Alphonse Karr.

NOUNS

1 change, variation, variety, mutability, alteration, difference, diversity, fluctuation, vicissitude, inconsistency, inconstancy, waxing and waning, modification, adjustment, qualification, variegation, process, activation, fermentation, leavening, modulation, inflection, declension, change of course, change of direction, deviation, diversion, detour, turn, U-turn, reversal, shift, eversion, inversion, change of position, change of scenery, change of place, relocation, passage, transference, transition, translation, interpretation, adaptation, transcription, sea change, sudden change, violent change, revolution, revolt, coup, subversion, reformation, break with the past, break, change for the better, invention, innovation, diversification, modernization, renewal, redecoration, rearrangement, reorganization, restructuring, reordering, remoulding, reshaping, restyling, remodelling, revision, emendation, amendment, improvement, betterment, restoration, revival, repairing, repair, amelioration, change for the worse, adulteration, dilution, distortion, deterioration, degeneration, perversion

▶ *136 Qualification; 227 Changeableness; 244 Improvement; 245 Deterioration; 295 Newness; 303 Backward Motion; 318 Passage; 325 Deviation; 719 Interpretation*

2 change of mind, change of opinion, change of belief, change of stance, change of heart, conversion, tergiversation, desultoriness, vacillation, fickleness, capriciousness, caprice, whimsicality, flip-flop

▶ *479 Equivocation; 760 Conversion*

3 transformation, mutation, transmutation, transfiguration, transubstantiation, metamorphosis, transmogrification, transmigration of souls, metempsychosis, metabolism, conversion

▶ *760 Conversion*

4 exchange, interchange, trade, substitution, commutability, permutation, transposition, alternation, replacement, exchange of gifts, exchange of goods, barter, swap, change of clothes, displacement

▶ *759 Exchange*

5 changer, modifier, kaleidoscope, activator, converter, transformer, agent, catalytic agent, catalytic converter, catalyst, enzyme, yeast, ferment, leaven, leavening agent, adapter

6 editor, reviser, censor, bowdlerizer, innovator, alterer, tailor, dressmaker, decorator, chemist, alchemist, magician, conjurer, sorcerer, good influence, restorer, reformer, revolutionary, improver, destroyer, bad influence, bad apple

VERBS

7 be changed, change, become different, undergo a change, reform, adapt, vary, alter, wax and wane, modify, reorganize, modernize, diversify, adjust, fluctuate, turn, shift, change course, divert, deviate, detour, change position, relocate, change places, change direction, do a U-turn, turn back, reverse, revert, revolt, change one's mind, change one's opinion, change one's belief, change one's stance, change one's heart, change for the worse, deteriorate, degenerate, change for the better, improve, get better, pass the crisis, get over the worst, turn the corner, better oneself, be converted, convert, vacillate, tergiversate, flip-flop, blow hot and cold, change one's expression, change one's tune, sing a different tune, break with the past, make a break, move with the times, turn over a new leaf

8 **cause change**, make a change, effect a change, work a change, make different, convert, influence, cause, affect, alter, diversify, divert, reform, innovate, invent, modify, inflect (a word), decline (a word), activate, ferment, leaven, qualify, modulate, commute, modernize, renew, remodel, restyle, reorganize, restructure, redecorate, rearrange, reorder, remould, reshape, bring in new blood, turn upside down, subvert, revolt, revolutionize, evert, turn inside out, invert, adapt, shift, move, transfer, arrange, change round, translate, interpret, perform magic, conjure, dabble in sorcery, variegate, adjust, influence in a good way, better, change for the better, make better, improve, ameliorate, process, edit, revise, censor, bowdlerize, amend, revamp, rehash, influence in a bad way, change for the worse, worsen, impair, wreck, destroy, pervert, spoil, mark, interfere with, tamper with, meddle with, tinker with, mess with, adulterate, doctor, dilute, weaken, warp, distort, discolour, change back, repair, reset, restore, revive, turn back, ring the changes, chop and change, fiddle with (Inf)

9 **transform**, transmute, transfigure, transubstantiate, transmogrify, mutate, metamorphose, metabolize

10 **exchange**, interchange, trade, substitute, commute, transpose, change round, permute, shuffle the cards, alternate, replace, exchange gifts, exchange goods, barter, swap, change one's clothes, displace

ADJECTIVES

11 **changeable**, changeful, mutable, variable, alterable, different, diverse, fluctuating, vacillating, wavering, inconsistent, inconstant, shifty, shifting, waxing and waning, kaleidoscopic, deviatory, turning, reverse, transitional, transitory, transient, revolutionary, subversive, reformative, reformational, inventive, innovative, innovational, ameliorative, better, worse, perverse, desultory, indecisive, fickle, capricious, ever-changing, whimsical, flip-flop

12 **changed**, varied, altered, modified, qualified, diversified, modernized, renewed, redecorated, rearranged, reorganized, restructured, reordered, restyled, remodelled, remoulded, reshaped, revised, emended, amended, improved, repaired, restored, revived, deteriorated, degenerated

13 **transformative**, mutative, transmutative, transubstantial, metabolic, metamorphic, metamorphous, convertive

14 **exchangeable**, interchangeable, tradeable, substitutable, commutable, permutable, transpositional, replaceable

ADVERBS

15 **changeably**, mutably, variably, alterably, differently, diversely, vacillatingly, inconsistently, inconstantly, shiftily, kaleidoscopically, transitionally, subversively, inventively, innovatively, desultorily, indecisively, capriciously, whimsically, back and forth, off and on, on and off, in and out, *mutatis mutandis* (L), with amendments, with emendations

225 Permanence

The British love permanence more than they love beauty. Hugh Casson.

NOUNS

1 **permanence**, permanency, continuance, continuity, no change, the status quo, everlastingness, perpetuity, establishment, entrenchment, persistence, perseverance, dependability, steadfastness, reliability, endurance, abidance, durability, survival, subsistence, conservation, conservancy, preservation, environmentalism, indestructibility, imperishability, immortality, changelessness, eternity, constancy, immutability, finality, fixedness, fixity, firmness, solidity, steadiness, stability, immobility, rigidity

▶ *134 Continuity; 228 Stability; 277 Duration; 279 Eternity; 296 Oldness; 301 Motionlessness; 359 Preservation*

2 **conservatism**, conservative attitude, conservative politics, right-wing politics, the political right, rightism, the right wing, the hard right, the Conservative Party, stubbornness, obstinacy

▶ *641 Obstinacy*

3 **conservative person**, conservative, traditionalist, Conservative, Tory, Republican (US), right-winger, true blue, obstinate person, hardliner, reactionary, die-hard, dyed-in-the-wool conservative, dry (Inf), stick-in-the-mud (Inf)

4 **conservationist**, conservator, environmentalist, ecologist, green, Green Party member

VERBS

5 **be permanent**, last, continue, persist, persevere, stand fast, stand firm, stand pat (US), stand one's ground, resist change, be the same as ever, be always the same, remain the same, look as young as ever, not look a day older, endure, abide, survive, subsist, outlive, be here for good, last forever, last an eternity, be here for the duration, stay, be here to stay, come to stay, set in, take root, remain unchanged, remain at rest, refuse to budge, dig in one's heels (*or* toes)

6 **make permanent**, perpetuate, conserve, preserve, maintain the status quo, oppose change, sustain, keep, keep up, immortalize, fix, finalize, establish, stabilize, immobilize, let (*or* leave) be, let (*or* leave) alone, let well enough alone, let sleeping dogs lie, live and let live

ADJECTIVES

7 **permanent**, lasting, unchanging, unchangeable, everlasting, long-lasting, perpetual, persistent, persisting, persevering, continuing, continuous, constant, changeless, invariable, unalterable, immutable, unfailing, dependable, reliable, steadfast, sustained, perennial, evergreen, abiding, enduring, surviving, subsisting, durable, stable, standing, fixed, established, well-established, entrenched, longstanding, still standing, indestructible, conserved, preserved, well-preserved, imperishable, un-

breakable, inviolable, immortal, undying, eternal, sempiternal, unfading, firm, solid, steady, rock-steady, rock-like, immobile, immovable, rigid, static, stationary, part of the furniture

8 **conservative**, traditional, traditionalist, right-wing, rightist, hard-right, true-blue, reactionary, obstinate, stubborn, old-fashioned, unprogressive, die-hard, dyed-in-the-wool, stick-in-the-mud (Inf)

ADVERBS

9 **permanently**, lastingly, changelessly, *in statu quo* (L), as is, as usual, as ever, still the same, as before, persistently, perseveringly, continuously, constantly, invariably, unalterably, immutably, unfailingly, reliably, steadfastly, perennially, abidingly, enduringly, firmly, solidly, steadily, rigidly, fixedly, at a standstill, indestructibly, imperishably, inviolably, immortally, undyingly, perpetually, eternally, sempiternally, forever, for ever and ever, everlastingly, always, for good, for good and all, once and for all

10 **conservatively**, traditionally, reactionarily, obstinately, stubbornly, old-fashionedly, unprogressively

226 Stopping

And time, that takes survey of all the world,
Must have a stop. William Shakespeare.

NOUNS

1 **cessation**, termination, ceasing, stopping, closing, desistance, discontinuance, discontinuation, discontinuity, relinquishment, withdrawal, abandonment, breakoff, death

2 **stop**, dead stop, halt, holdup, standstill, standoff, deadlock, stalemate, draw, checkmate, defeat, failure, breakdown, shutting down, shutdown, closing down, closedown, stoppage, temporary stoppage, blockage, log jam (US), gridlock (US), interruption, stay, check, hitch, technical hitch, hindrance, work stoppage, retirement, resignation, dismissal, lay-off, strike, general strike, industrial action, walkout, lockout, permanent stoppage, end, ending, finish, conclusion, hanging up, ringing off, breaking off, breaking off of negotiations, closure, closure of debate, cloture (US), guillotine, firing (Inf), sacking (Inf), shutting up (Inf), piping down (Inf), glitch (Inf)

▶ *247 Failure; 301 Motionlessness; 309 Closure; 343 Inactivity; 378 Obstruction; 383 Resistance; 605 Resignation; 751 Disagreement*

3 **pause**, break, lull, let-up, respite, rest, sleep, nap, interruption, lacuna, gap, breathing space, interim, interim period, cooling-off period, interlude, interval, fermata, caesura, time-out (US), time off, day off, holiday, vacation, leisure, leisure time, close (*or* closed) season, delay, truce, moratorium, suspension, suspension of hostilities, cease-fire, armistice, breather (Inf)

▶ *146 Interval; 580 Leisure; 581 Refreshment*

4 **stopping place**, stop, bus stop, request stop, station, railway station, train station, taxi rank, halt, railway halt, tube station, bus station, service station, petrol station, lay-by, motorway services, highway restaurant (US), port, port of call, harbour, terminal, terminus, ferry terminal, air terminal, airport, waiting room

▶ *312 Arrival*

5 **resting place**, bed, bedroom couch, hospital, nursing home, retirement home, lodging, hotel, motel, billet, prison, prison cell, jail, final resting place, cemetery, graveyard, grave

▶ *131 End*

VERBS

6 **cease**, stop, come to a stop, halt, come to a halt, stop abruptly, stop dead, stop short, stop in one's tracks, freeze in one's tracks, grind to a halt, brake, put on the brake, pull up, draw up, come to a standstill, stall, stick, jam, discontinue, break down, quit, hold up, refrain from, desist, relinquish, give up, give in, admit defeat, leave off, disappear, fade out, fade away, blow over, run out, run down, peter out, let up, slacken off, tail off (*or* away), die off, die away, end, come to an end, finish, conclude, terminate, break off, break off negotiations, stop talking, hang up, ring off, put the phone down, be quiet, be silent, stop breathing, die, shut up (Inf), pipe down (Inf), fold (Inf), fold up (Inf), give over (Inf), call it a day (Inf), call it quits (Inf), run out of gas (US inf)

7 **stop working**, stop work, leave one's job, retire, resign, stand down, be laid off, be made redundant, strike, go on strike, come out on strike, call a strike, stage a strike, walk out, vote with one's feet, close down, close, shut up shop, put up the shutters, shut down, cease trading, go out of business, ring down the curtain, wind up, fail, collapse, go bankrupt, go into liquidation, go into receivership, call in the receiver, be sacked (Inf), be fired (Inf), go belly up (US inf)

8 **cause to cease**, put a stop to, stay, freeze, call a halt, cancel, call off, cut short, interrupt, bring to a standstill, catch, hinder, thwart, block, check, stem, arrest, restrain, hold, hold up, stalemate, checkmate, defeat, closure, cloture (US), guillotine, shut down, quieten down, close down, lock out, dismiss, lay off, make redundant, exhaust, use up, bring to an end, end, disconnect, break off, see the last of, cut off, cut someone off in his (*or* her) prime, kill, murder, shut up (Inf), fire (Inf), sack (Inf), see off (Inf)

9 **pause**, pause for breath, relax, rest, fall asleep, sleep, nap, interrupt, suspend, stay, adjourn, recess, break, take a break, take five (*or* ten) (US), call time-out (US), take a day off, take a holiday, holiday, take a vacation, vacation, let up, cool off, hold up, hold back, hang fire, stay one's hand, call a truce, suspend hostilities, cease fire, make peace, hold one's horses, rest on one's oars, rest on one's laurels, hang loose (US inf), take a breather (Inf)

ADJECTIVES

10 **finished**, ended, at an end, stopped, over, complete, closed, in recess, adjourned, interrupted, pending, on hold, on ice, redundant, fired (Inf), sacked (Inf)

ADVERBS

11 **finally**, in the end, at the end, at the finish, in his (*or* her) prime, when all is said and done

INTERJECTIONS

12 **stop!**, whoa!, enough!, that's enough!, stop it!, quit it!, that's it!, stop thief!, break it up!, leave off!, get off!, come off it!, drop it!, forget it!, let up! (Inf), lay off! (Inf), give over! (Inf), shut up! (Inf), shut your face!

(Inf), can it! (US inf), knock it off! (Inf), cut it out! (Inf), uncle! (US inf), pack it in! (Inf), chuck it! (Inf), cool it (Inf), stow it! (Inf), shut your trap! (Inf), naff off! (Inf)

227 Changeableness

Everything flows and nothing stays. Heraclitus.

NOUNS

1 **changeableness**, changeability, changefulness, mutability, mobility, flexibility, versatility, variety, variegation, iridescence, inconsistency, inconstancy, variability, irregularity, imbalance, disequilibrium, plasticity, pliancy, softness, suppleness, fluidity, flux, fluctuation, alternation, turning, veering, oscillation, uncertainty, unreliability, unpredictability, vicissitude, unsteadiness, instability, wobbliness, rockiness, shakiness, impermanence, transience, metamorphosis

2 **irresolution**, vacillation, uncertainty, tergiversation, wavering, hesitation, procrastination, fickleness, whim, whimsicality, moodiness, capriciousness, caprice, desultoriness, flightiness, light-mindedness, volatility, erraticism, restlessness, agitation, fitfulness, disquiet, inquietude, fidgeting, chopping and changing, bobbing and weaving, ducking and diving, darting, shiftiness, equivocation, slipperiness, disloyalty, infidelity, treacherousness

► *114 Diversity; 120 Inequality; 224 Change; 278 Transience; 299 Irregularity; 300 Motion; 326 Oscillation; 327 Agitation; 419 Softness; 431 Fluid; 472 Inattention; 479 Equivocation; 541 Variegation; 639 Vacillation; 642 Frivolity*

3 **changeable thing**, moon, phases of the moon, chameleon, kaleidoscope, changing scene, shifting sands, mercury, quicksilver, wind, wind of change, weathercock, weather vane, luck, chance, fortune, wheel of fortune, variable, random number, ERNIE (Electronic Random Number Indicator Equipment), April shower, proteus, free radical

► *194 Number*

4 **editor**, amender, corrector, reformer, revisionist, revolutionary, swapper, dealer, exchanger, trader, replacer, chemist, alchemist, magician

► *759 Exchange*

5 **changeable person**, moody person, temperamental person, Doctor Jekyll and Mister Hyde, manic-depressive, schizophrenic

6 **fickle person**, ladies' man, philanderer, adulterer, two-timer, double-dealer, hypocrite, turncoat, traitor, counterspy, Vicar of Bray

7 **person who moves around**, wanderer, traveller, New-Age traveller, vagrant, tramp, hobo, explorer, adventurer, voyager, tourist

8 **person who changes costume**, actor, actress, mimic, quick-change artist, impersonator, female impersonator

9 **person who changes sex**, transsexual

10 **person who is exchanged**, changeling, hostage

VERBS

11 **be changeable**, change, metamorphose, vary, fluctuate, alternate, oscillate, show variety, show phases, go through phases, ring the changes, flash, flicker, twinkle, gutter, wave, wave in the wind, flutter, whiffle, flap, falter, stagger, teeter, totter, sway, reel, rock, tremble, vibrate, shake, wobble, swing, shuttle, pitch, roll, yaw, tack, turn, veer, back, ebb and flow, wax and wane, have as many phases as the moon

12 **be irresolute**, tergiversate, vacillate, seesaw, blow hot and cold, waver, hesitate, hover, drift, float, chop and change, dodge about, dart, duck and dive, bob and weave, flit, flitter, fidget, shillyshally, play fast and loose, change one's mind, change the rules, move the goalposts

ADJECTIVES

13 **changeable**, changeful, mutable, alterable, mobile, versatile, varied, variant, variegated, protean, kaleidoscopic, iridescent, inconsistent, inconstant, variable, irregular, imbalanced, plastic, pliant, soft, supple, flowing, melting, fluid, fluctuating, in a state of flux, ever-changing, never the same, alternating, tidal, vibrating, oscillating, uncertain, unreliable, unpredictable, unstable, unsteady, floating, loose, unattached, labile, wobbly, rocky, shaky, swaying, tottering, teetering, built on sand, built on weak foundations, unsettled, impermanent, transient, rootless, homeless, of no fixed abode, vagrant, rambling, wandering, roving, precarious, touch and go, fitful, shifting, ephemeral, spasmodic, flickering, wavering

14 **irresolute**, hesitating, vacillating, seesawing, fickle, whimsical, moody, wayward, capricious, desultory, malleable, impressionable, yielding, flighty, dizzy, giddy, scatterbrained, light-headed, light-minded, volatile, mercurial, restless, tossing and turning, fidgety, shifty, disloyal, unfaithful, traitorous, like putty in someone's hands, scatty (Inf)

ADVERBS

15 **changeably**, alterably, back and forth, to and fro, in and out, inconsistently, off and on, on and off, inconstantly, variably, irregularly, iridescently, pliantly, softly, fluidly, alternatively, now this, now that, uncertainly, unreliably, unpredictably, unsteadily, shakily, precariously, fitfully, impermanently, now here, now there, waveringly, ephemerally, spasmodically, irresolutely, round and round, whimsically, moodily, waywardly, capriciously, desultorily, impressionably, dizzily, shiftily, disloyally, unfaithfully, traitorously

228 Stability

NOUNS

1 **stability**, stabilization, steadiness, steadfastness, rootedness, fixedness, fixity, solidity, soundness, secureness, strength, durability, permanence, consistency, reliability, constancy, rest, quietude, quiet, calm, immobilization, immobility, immovability, hardening, stiffening, stiffness, firmness, firming up, inflexibility, steady state, stable equilibrium, homeostasis, balance, equality, stasis, immutability, unchangeableness, unchangeability, changelessness, invariability, irreversibility, indestructibility, deathlessness

► *119 Equality; 225 Permanence; 277 Duration; 279 Eternity; 301 Motionlessness; 416 Density; 418 Hardness*

2 **determination**, resolution, resolve, nerve, nerves of steel, iron nerve, iron will, inflexibility, toughness, hard-

ness, steeliness, obstinacy, stubbornness, obduracy, aplomb, imperturbability, coolness (Inf)

▶ *452 Certainty; 638 Resolution; 641 Obstinacy*

3 **stabilizer**, keel, centreboard, fin, aerofoil, wing flap, spoiler, counterbalance, counterweight, ballast, support, prop, buttress, beam, crossbeam, joist, buttress, aileron

▶ *413 Support*

4 **stable thing**, perpetual motion, the Establishment, fixture, firm fixture, firm foundation, strong foundation, solid foundations, solid footing, cornerstone, rock, bedrock, pillar, tower, pyramid, granite rock, mountain, constant, invariable, invariable quantity, immutable law, the Code of Hammurabi, law of the Medes and the Persians, Ten Commandments, Twelve Tables, Justinian's Code, written constitution, US Constitution, the Bill of Rights (US), prescriptive right, rights under law, droit de seigneur, indelible ink, fast colour, engraving

▶ *140 Rule*

5 **stable person**, born leader, a man of his word, pillar of society, pillar of the community, pillar of the church, tower of strength, Rock of Gibraltar, Victorian, Darby and Joan, square (Inf), straight (Inf)

VERBS

6 **be stable**, not change, stay in one place, stick fast, hold, remain fixed, adhere, stand, stand up well, hold up, stand firm, stay put, harden, stiffen, stabilize, keep one's balance, set in, settle in, settle down, stay, take root, strike root, quieten down, rest, keep one's cool (Inf)

7 **make stable**, stabilize, steady, transfix, freeze, balance, equalize, fix, establish, confirm, validate, ratify, make sure, ensure, secure, firm up, set up, set on its feet, found, erect, build on a rock, build on a firm foundation, support, buttress, engrave, stamp, print, stereotype, set, set in stone, set in concrete, set in granite, keep stable, bind, make fast, root, entrench, tie, fasten down, batten down (the hatches), put at rest, quieten, quieten down

8 **show determination**, persist, persevere, stand firm, stand pat (US), stiffen, not budge, show stubbornness, hold out, hold out to the bitter end, stay with it, stick with it, stick fast, hold the road, stand (*or* hold) one's ground, hang on by one's teeth (Inf), weather the storm (Inf), not bat an eyelid (Inf), put one's foot down (Inf), stick it out (Inf), stick to one's guns (Inf)

ADJECTIVES

9 **stable**, steady, steadfast, solid, sound, firm, stiff, secure, strong, durable, permanent, consistent, reliable, constant, dependable, predictable, unchangeable, unchanging, unvarying, inalterable, irrevocable, irreversible, restful, quiet, calm, immobile, immovable, held, at rest, at anchor, riding at anchor, aground, stuck fast, high and dry, written in stone, well-founded, frozen, frozen like a statue, hard, inflexible, unshakable, incontrovertible, indisputable, indefeasible, equal, homeostatic, immutable, changeless, invariable, incommutable, intransmutable, indissoluble, imperishable, inextinguishable, invulnerable, indestructible, ineradicable, indelible, perennial, evergreen, enduring, long-lasting, deathless, perpetual, rocklike, steady as a rock, like the Rock of Gibraltar

10 **stabilized**, unchanged, unaltered, settled, transfixed, stereotyped, fixed, anchored, moored, tethered, tied, chained, grounded, stranded, pinned down, rooted, rooted to the spot, deep-rooted, well-rooted, established, well-established, ingrained, entrenched, engraved, balanced

11 **determined**, resolute, resolved, certain, sure, nerved, iron-nerved, iron-willed, inflexible, unwavering, tough, hard, steely, obstinate, stubborn, obdurate, imperturbable, cool (Inf)

ADVERBS

12 **stably**, unalterably, steadily, steadfastly, solidly, soundly, securely, strongly, permanently, consistently, reliably, constantly, dependably, predictably, irrevocably, irreversibly, restfully, quietly, calmly, stiffly, firmly, on a firm basis, on a firm footing, on a strong foundation, inflexibly, unshakably, indisputably, equally, immutably, indissolubly, imperishably, invulnerably, indestructibly, indelibly, perennially, enduringly, perpetually

13 **determinedly**, with determination, resolutely, in a resolute manner, inflexibly, unwaveringly, toughly, obstinately, stubbornly, obdurately, imperturbably, coolly (Inf)

229 Tendency

NOUNS

1 **tendency**, tenor, drift, trend, course, current, stream, fashion, taste, the way things are going, sign of the times, spirit of the age, *Zeitgeist* (Ger), turn, cast, climate, climate of opinion, influence, contribution

▶ *324 Direction; 363 Attraction; 750 Agreement*

2 **attitude**, cast of mind, turn of mind, mind set, disposition, predisposition, proclivity, susceptibility, affinity, attraction, liability, probability, proneness, bent, inclination, gravitation, leaning, bias, prejudice, partiality, weakness, readiness, preparedness, propensity, predilection, liking, penchant, humour, mood, vein, grain, strain, tincture, tone, quality, character, genius, idiosyncrasy

▶ *104 Probability; 243 Preparation; 482 Intention*

3 **aptitude**, ability, talent, natural talent, gift, instinct

▶ *485 Skill*

VERBS

4 **tend**, have a tendency, show a tendency, show a trend, bend, have a bent, develop an attitude, incline, lean, have a leaning, like, show an affinity, have a propensity, have an aptitude, have a genius for, show talent, have natural talent, have a gift, have an instinct, be biased, show prejudice, have a predisposition, be disposed, gravitate towards, incline towards, lean towards, prepare, approach, affect, contribute, redound, influence, turn to, point to, lead to, conduce to, bid fair, bode well

ADJECTIVES

5 **tending to**, trending, leading, leading to, inclined towards, inclining towards, inclining, leaning, leaning towards, intending, working towards, aiming at, pointing to, conducive to, calculated, calculated to, prejudiced, prejudicial, partial, biased, tendentious, probable, likely, liable to, apt to, prone to, ready, ready to, about to, prepared

ADVERBS

6 **probably**, readily, with a strong tendency, prejudicially, tendentiously, from a biased standpoint

230 Perfection

The pursuit of perfection, then, is the pursuit of sweetness and light…He who works for sweetness and light united, works to make reason and the will of God prevail. Matthew Arnold.

Perfection has one grave defect; it is apt to be dull. W. Somerset Maugham.

ADJECTIVES

1 **perfect**, perfected, brought to perfection, finished, completed, fulfilled, polished, ripened, ripe, fully ripe, ready, matured, mature, fully mature, exact, just right, just so, ideal, best, flawless, unflawed, faultless, impeccable, infallible, indefectible, without defect, correct, precise, accurate, spot on, irreproachable, immaculate, without a stain, unstained, unspotted, spotless, unblemished, blemish-free, without blemish, unmarked, uncontaminated, untainted, pure, unmixed, unalloyed, blameless, exemplary, guiltless, innocent, impeccant, sinless, godly, saintly, sound, unbroken, uncracked, sound as a bell, right as right can be, right as rain, in perfect condition, undamaged, unmarred, unspoiled (*or* unspoilt), safe and sound, unhurt, unscathed, scatheless (Lit), unscarred, unscratched, no harm done, tight, airtight, vacuum-packed, watertight, seaworthy, intact, whole, entire, complete, absolute, utter, total, one hundred per cent, undiminished, unreduced, without loss, full, excellent, sublime, superb, dazzling, brilliant, masterly, expert, proficient, skilled, skilful, consummate, supreme, transcendent, unsurpassable, unequalled, unmatched, unrivalled, peerless, top, number-one, champion, at the peak of perfection, pattern, standard, model, archetypal, classic, classical, Augustan, in perfect health, in the pink, right as a trivet (Inf), A-OK (Inf), A1 (Inf)

▶ *121 Superiority; 204 Whole; 232 Completeness; 235 Worth; 255 Purity; 259 Health; 485 Skill; 805 Innocence*

2 **perfectionist**, purist, pedantic, precise, punctilious, meticulous, fastidious, scrupulous, particular, exacting, demanding, fussy

NOUNS

3 **perfection**, sheer perfection, perfectness, finish, completion, consummation, polish, ripeness, readiness, maturity, exactness, idealness, the ideal, flawlessness, faultlessness, impeccability, infallibility, indefectability, correctness, correctitude, preciseness, accuracy, irreproachability, immaculacy, immaculateness, spotlessness, purity, blamelessness, guiltlessness, innocence, impeccancy, soundness, perfect condition, wholeness, completeness, excellence, brilliance, mint condition, mastery, expertise, proficiency, skill, superiority, transcendence, essence, quintessence, peak, top, zenith, acme, summit, pinnacle, capstone, height (*or* pitch) of perfection, acme of perfection, peak of perfection, pattern, standard, model, archetype, paragon, *ne plus ultra* (L), ultimate, extreme, last word, crowning achievement, masterpiece, *chef-d'oeuvre* (Fr), flawless performance, ten out of ten, one hundred per cent

4 **perfectionist**, purist, pedant, stickler, perfecter, expert, master, expert mechanic, master painter, master thief, maestro, prima ballerina, *premier danseur* (*or première danseuse*) (Fr)

▶ *485 Skill*

VERBS

5 **perfect**, finish, complete, fulfil, realize, accomplish, achieve, execute, carry out, ripen, mature, bring to perfection, consummate, correct, rectify, improve, ameliorate, elaborate, polish, refine, put on the finishing touch, crown

6 **be perfect**, leave nothing to be desired, give a flawless performance, score ten out of ten, score one hundred per cent

ADVERBS

7 **perfectly**, flawlessly, faultlessly, impeccably, exactly, precisely, irreproachably, immaculately, spotlessly, excellently, consummately, to perfection, to just the right degree, to a turn, just as one would wish, verbatim, word for word, to the letter, literally

8 **completely**, wholly, entirely, absolutely, utterly, totally, quite, thoroughly, unequivocally, unambiguously, purely

231 Imperfection

ADJECTIVES

1 **imperfect**, flawed, faulty, defective, dysfunctional, not perfect, not (quiet), right, less than perfect, capable of perfection, perfectible, fallible, peccable, irregular, uneven, good and bad, patchy, good in parts, like the curate's egg, unsteady, wobbly, shaky, rickety, weak, vulnerable, bungled, botched, damaged, broken, cracked, leaky, not airtight, not waterproof, unsound, soiled, shopsoiled, stained, spotted, marked, scratched, chipped, blemished, tainted, corked, stale, overripe, past its sell-by date, past its prime, bad, off, off-colour, not in the pink, below par, off form, off stride, unfit, unhealthy, not good enough, unsatisfactory, unacceptable, not up to expectations, not up to the mark, second-best, second-class, third-class, second-rate, third-rate, inferior, poor, unimpressive, worthless, flubbed (US inf), dodgy (Inf)

▶ *122 Inferiority; 236 Worthlessness; 245 Deterioration; 260 Ill Health; 337 Weakness; 486 Unskilfulness; 548 Blemish*

2 **incomplete**, deficient, wanting, lacking, inadequate, insufficient, perfunctory, cursory, unthorough, careless, not entire, partial, fragmentary, unfilled, half-filled, unequipped, undermanned, short-staffed, short-handed, below strength, unfinished, half-finished, makeshift, jerry-built, rough and ready, provisional, raw, crude, untrained, scratch, immature, undeveloped, unpolished, unrefined, overwrought, overelaborated, overdone, exaggerated

▶ *218 Insufficiency; 233 Incompleteness; 472 Inattention*

3 **deformed**, distorted, warped, twisted, handicapped, disabled, blind, deaf, dumb, mute, deaf and dumb, deaf-mute, mutilated, maimed, armless, legless, lame, halt (Lit), crippled

4 **ordinary**, middling, average, median, everyday, commonplace, mediocre, much of a muchness, middle-of-

the-road, moderate, unheroic, only passable, tolerable, bearable, better than nothing, so-so (Inf), wet (Inf)

▶ *216 Average*

NOUNS

5 **imperfection**, imperfectness, faultiness, defectiveness, room for improvement, possibility of perfection, perfectibility, fallibility, peccability, erroneousness, error, peccadillo, bungle, botch, irregularity, unevenness, patchiness, curate's egg, adulteration, weakness, vulnerability, frailty, failure, damage, unsoundness, staleness, overripeness, unfitness, infirmity, ill health, inferiority, worthlessness, second class, third class, low standard, minimum requirement, passing grade, incompleteness, deficiency, want, lack, need, requirement, shortfall, inadequacy, insufficiency, perfunctoriness, cursoriness, lack of thoroughness, carelessness, underachievement, immaturity, unripeness, rawness, crudeness, undevelopment, underdevelopment, Third World, deformity, distortion, blindness, deafness, lameness

▶ *122 Inferiority; 218 Insufficiency; 233 Incompleteness; 234 Distortion; 236 Worthlessness; 260 Ill Health; 274 Error*

6 **imperfect item**, second, reject, misshape, shopsoiled item, not one's best, second best, poor effort, weak effort, inferior version, poor relation, missing link, incomplete set, broken set, makeshift, stopgap, *pis aller* (Fr), consolation, substitute

7 **defect**, fault, flaw, blemish, mark, taint, stain, blot, spot, smudge, scratch, chip, tear, mistake, error, rift, leak, loophole, crack, chink, lacuna, gap, deficiency, lack, limitation, shortfall, kink, quirk, idiosyncrasy, eccentricity, foible, failing, shortcoming, weakness, weak point, weak link in the chain, blind spot, soft spot, soft underbelly, tragic flaw, feet of clay, vulnerable point, chink in one's armour, Achilles' heel, soft heart, disability, handicap, disadvantage, difficulty, drawback, catch, snag, hindrance, obstacle, hang-up (Inf), fly in the ointment, loose screw (Inf)

▶ *146 Interval; 274 Error; 378 Obstruction; 461 Insanity; 548 Blemish*

8 **ordinariness**, averageness, mediocrity, nothing to speak of, nothing to write home about, nothing earthshattering (Inf), no great shakes (Inf)

▶ *216 Average*

VERBS

9 **be imperfect**, have a fault, fall short, fall short of perfection, not live up to expectations, not impress, not bear inspection, not pass muster, fail, fail the test, not make the grade, dissatisfy, not suffice, barely pass, scrape through, have a chink in one's armour, show one's Achilles' heel, have feet of clay, have a crack, not hold water, leak

▶ *218 Insufficiency; 548 Blemish; 606 Dissatisfaction*

10 **leave imperfect**, finish halfway, leave unfinished, make a weak effort

ADVERBS

11 **imperfectly**, defectively, below par, irregularly, unevenly, incompletely, insufficiently, to a limited extent, barely, scarcely, almost, not quite, all but, with all its faults

232 Completeness

We have finished the job, what shall we do with the tools? Haile Selassie.

NOUNS

1 **completeness**, finished state, nothing lacking, nothing missing, nothing to add, sufficiency, self-sufficiency, entirety, totality, wholeness, unity, integrality, universality, comprehensiveness, solidarity, solidity, balance, harmony, concord, fulfilment, consummation, finishing touch, final touch, last touch, icing on the cake, finish, the end, the limit, *ne plus ultra* (L), the utmost, summit, peak, zenith, culmination, ideal, perfection, the whole hog (Inf)

▶ *131 End; 174 Top; 204 Whole; 217 Sufficiency; 230 Perfection; 750 Agreement*

2 **fullness**, plenitude, pregnancy, capacity, full capacity, full size, full length, full extent, full volume, full value, maximum, saturation, saturation point, satiety, repletion, filling, refilling, replenishment, refill, filling up, brimming, overfilling, overflowing, overflow, overfulfilment, full complement, full crew, requisite number, quorum, quota, full quota, full house, full load, full measure, bumper, brimmer, bellyful, skinful (Inf), makeweight, complement, supplement, fill-up, compensation

▶ *211 Addition; 217 Sufficiency; 219 Excess*

3 **completion**, completing, end, ending, finish, finishing, finishing off, finalization, close, conclusion, termination, expiration, culmination, attainment, accomplishment, achievement, fulfilment, consummation, realization, fruition, topping-out ceremony

▶ *131 End*

VERBS

4 **complete**, make complete, make into a whole, integrate, unite, join, make whole, complement, supplement, eke out, fill a gap, fill a need, fill in, fill out, build up, make up, construct, piece together, compose, do, perform, execute, discharge, fulfil, realize, accomplish, achieve, do thoroughly, leave nothing out (*or* undone), have nothing to add, leave nothing to chance, carry through, carry out, carry out to the full, carry out to the letter, crown, cap, overfulfil, overdo, put the icing on the cake, put the finishing touch (*or* touches) to, finalize, perfect, finish, end, terminate, close, conclude, round off, wrap up (Inf)

▶ *131 End; 230 Perfection; 340 Action; 356 Creation; 374 Combination*

5 **be complete**, make a whole, have everything, have it all, say it all, reach (*or* touch) perfection, climax, culminate, come to an end, come to a close, end, finish, close, terminate, have enough, want (*or* lack) nothing, become complete, fill out, develop fully, reach full growth, become grown-up, become adult, reach maturity, realize one's potential, be full (*or* filled), brim with, overflow, run over, slop over, bulge, swell, have one's fill, eat (*or* drink) one's fill

▶ *131 End; 190 Expansion; 217 Sufficiency; 219 Excess*

6 **fill**, refill, replenish, fill up, top up, top off, satisfy, sate, saturate, overfill, soak, drench, overwhelm, swamp,

drown, pervade, suffuse, fill to capacity, cram, jam, stuff, bloat, pack in, pile in, pile on, ram in, ram down, squeeze in, pack, stow, load, charge, lade, freight, stock, supply, fill a space (*or* gap), cover, occupy, line, spread over, extend (*or* reach) to, overrun

► *97 Presence; 368 Insertion; 406 Contents; 436 Provisions; 550 Covering; 609 Satisfaction*

ADJECTIVES

7 complete, entire, integral, intact, unbroken, unimpaired, undivided, individual, united, self-contained, self-sufficient, whole, plenary, quorate, sufficient, adequate, effective, effectual, lacking nothing, all there, unexpurgated, unabridged, uncut, unabbreviated, all-in, all-inclusive, all-embracing, comprehensive, absolute, utter, total, exhaustive, full-scale, detailed, thorough, thoroughgoing, all-out, wholesale, sweeping, unconfined, unrestricted, unlimited, unqualified, plain, plumb, downright, pure, unadulterated, out-and-out, unmitigating, unmitigated, dyed-in-the-wool, consummate, full-blown, full-grown, fully grown, full-fledged, fully fledged, mature, perfect, faultless, perfected, finished, accomplished, achieved, compleat (Lit), crowning, culminating, supplementary, complementary, finalized, ended, concluded, closed, terminated, over, done

► *197 One; 204 Whole; 217 Sufficiency; 230 Perfection; 255 Purity*

8 full, filled, refilled, replenished, replete, satisfied, topped up, topped off, full up, filled up, well-filled, well-stocked, well-lined, bulging, brimming, brimful, full to the brim, level with, flush, overfilled, overfull, overflowing, full to overflowing, running over, slopping over, oozing, leaking, swamped, overwhelmed, drowned, saturated, coming out of one's ears, full to bursting, bursting at the seams, stuffed, gorged, sickened with, up to here with, sated, satiated, chock-full, chock-a-block, no room to spare, no room to turn round, no room to swing a cat, crowded, congested, solid, crop-full, cram-full, crammed, packed, packed like sardines, jammed, jam-packed, tight, jammed tight, loaded, laden, fully laden, overloaded, heavy-laden, freighted, fraught, fully charged, all seats taken, standing room only, sold out, full of, stiff with, seething with, teeming with, jumping with, alive with, lousy with, crawling with, infested, overrun, rolling in, dripping with, fit to bust (Inf)

► *208 Multitude; 217 Sufficiency; 219 Excess*

ADVERBS

9 completely, entirely, wholly, totally, absolutely, utterly, quite, thoroughly, clean, plain, plumb, downright, perfectly, in every way, in all, in all respects, on all counts, outright, stark, hollow, unequivocally, unconditionally, root and branch, neck and crop, all round, all around, all the way, heart and soul, body and soul, head over heels, solidly, *en masse* (Fr), *en bloc* (Fr), all in all, *in toto* (L), all told, from wall to wall, from A to Z, from first to last, throughout, from beginning to end, from end to end, from one end to the other, the length and breadth of, from sea to sea, from sea to shining sea, from coast to coast, from Land's End to John o' Groats, from the four points of the compass, from the four corners of the world, from far and near, (from) far and wide, high and low, fore and aft, from stem to stern, from top to bottom, from top to toe, from head to foot, altogether, hook, line, and sinker, lock, stock, and barrel, rind, pips, and all, warts and all

► *145 Distance; 150 Broadness; 204 Whole*

10 fully, in full, every inch, every whit, to capacity, to the maximum, as … as can be, as … as possible, to the utmost, to the top of one's bent, (up) to the hilt, up to the neck, up to the ears, up to the eyes, to the full, to the brim, to the top, over the top, with knobs on, with a vengeance, with all the trimmings, and then some, through and through, to the heart, to the marrow, to the core, (down) to the quick, (down) to the ground, full out, at full stretch, through thick and thin, to the last breath, to the last man, for good, for good and all, forever, to the end, to the bitter end, to the end of the chapter, to the end of the road, to the end of the line

233 Incompleteness

One never notices what has been done; one can only see what remains to be done. Marie Curie.

I read part of it all the way through. Samuel Goldwyn.

NOUNS

1 incompleteness, partialness, partiality, defectiveness, deficiency, falling short, insufficiency, poverty, scantness, scantiness, inadequacy, lack, want, need, ineffectiveness, ineffectuality, imperfection, unfinished state, interrupted state, unpreparedness, unreadiness, underdevelopment, unripeness, immaturity, rawness, roughness, sketchiness, scrappiness, bittiness, hollowness, superficiality, insubstantiality, perfunctoriness, halfheartedness, negligence, default, arrears, noncompletion, nonfulfilment, broken state, mutilation, impairment, nonsatisfaction, dissatisfaction

► *205 Part; 218 Insufficiency; 231 Imperfection; 606 Dissatisfaction*

2 omission, gap, lacuna, void, interval, break, breakage, missing link, loss, deficit, lack, want, need, deficiency, insufficiency, shortfall, slippage, ullage, defalcation, arrears, default, part missing, screw loose, a few sandwiches short of a picnic (Inf), not sixteen ounces to the pound (Inf), not the full pound (*or* shilling) note (Inf)

► *128 Exclusion; 133 Discontinuity; 146 Interval; 218 Insufficiency; 231 Imperfection; 766 Loss*

3 incomplete thing, part, fraction, proportion, part payment instalment, sketch, draft, rough, embryo

► *205 Part; 785 Payment*

ADJECTIVES

4 incomplete, defective, deficient, scant, scanty, skimpy, short, insufficient, inadequate, ineffective, ineffectual, like Hamlet without the Prince, missing, omitting, lacking, wanting, needing, in need of, requiring, short of, shy of, shortened, abbreviated, abridged, truncated, curtailed, cropped, docked, lopped, maimed, mutilated, mangled, lame, limping, halting, marred, spoiled, impaired, garbled, broken, fragmentary, eyeless, legless, armless, limbless, one-armed, one-legged, one-eyed, unsatisfactory, blemished, stained, flawed, imperfect, half, partial, unfinished, not finished, going on, continuing, developing, in progress, in the pipeline, on the stocks, begun, in embryo, in preparation, left unfinished, half-finished, half-done, neglected, uncompleted, underdeveloped, undeveloped, unprepared, unready, unripe, immature, raw, underdone, undercooked, rude, rough, crude, rough-hewn, sketchy, scrappy, bitty, thin, poor, meagre, hollow, superficial, insubstantial, perfunctory, half-hearted, left hanging, left in the air, interrupted, omitted, lost, missed, *manqué* (Fr), in default, defaulting in arrears, not up to date, not all there

▶ *135 Requirement; 149 Shortness; 205 Part; 218 Insufficiency; 231 Imperfection; 666 Negligence; 786 Nonpayment*

VERBS

5 **be incomplete**, need, want, be wanting, lack, be lacking, miss, fall short, skimp on, give a lick and a promise (Inf), fail to fulfil, default, leave undone, begin, sketch, draft, rough (out), leave unfinished, not complete, interrupt, leave hanging, leave dangling, leave in the air, neglect, omit, miss out, exclude

▶ *128 Exclusion; 130 Beginning; 218 Insufficiency; 231 Imperfection; 243 Preparation; 666 Negligence*

ADVERBS

6 **incompletely**, partially, partly, in part, in (*or* by) instalments, by halves, half, insufficiently, poorly, inadequately, ineffectually, ineffectively, deficiently, insubstantially, scantily, roughly, embryonically, sketchily, superficially, scrappily, crudely, improperly, in default, negligently, neglectfully, in arrears, without, minus

234 Distortion

NOUNS

1 **distortion**, asymmetry, disproportion, lopsidedness, imbalance, difference, irregularity, crookedness, warp, strain, stress, contortion, bias, skewness, twist, torsion, twistedness

▶ *120 Inequality; 189 Slantedness; 299 Irregularity*

2 **facial distortion**, contortion, grimace, girn (Dial), scowl, frown, snarl, sneer, leer, pout, *moue* (Fr), rictus, tic, squint

3 **deformity**, malformation, hunchback, club foot, cleft palate, mutation, misshapenness, ugliness, hideousness, disfigurement, grotesquerie, defacement, imperfection, scar, cicatrix, spot, stain, mark, welt, weal, pockmark, blemish, pimple, zit (Inf)

▶ *118 Nonconformity; 546 Ugliness; 548 Blemish*

4 **distortion of the truth**, exaggeration, misrepresentation, perversion, misconstruction, false reading, fiction, deception, fabrication, falsity, spuriousness, perfidy, mendacity, deceitfulness, misinformation, disinformation, brainwashing, whitewashing, untruthfulness, lie, falsehood, travesty, burlesque, parody, propaganda, economy with the truth, terminological inexactitude, selective facts, imaginative journalism, poetic truth, pork pie (Inf), porky (Inf), cock-and-bull story (Inf), bull (Inf), bullshit (Inf), tall story (Inf)

5 **defacer**, spoiler, distorter, propagandist, spin doctor, hypocrite, liar, vandal, hooligan, thug, pervert, bullshitter (Inf)

▶ *699 Falsehood; 702 Sophistry; 720 Misinterpretation; 727 Exaggeration*

ADJECTIVES

6 **distorted**, asymmetric, unsymmetrical, unbalanced, out of balance, out of kilter, out of true alignment, out of shape, misshapen, irregular, lopsided, crooked, askew, disproportionate, unequal, out of context, off-target, off-centre, skewwhiff (Inf), cockeyed (Inf)

7 **deformed**, malformed, hunchbacked, clubfooted, disfigured, imperfect, ugly, hideous, grotesque, defaced, scarred, marked, pockmarked, spotty, pitted, blemished, ill-made, zitty (Inf)

8 **exaggerated**, false, perfidious, evasive, fake, misrepresented, perverted, fictitious, deceptive, fabricated, spurious, misinformed, misguided, misleading, untruthful, deceitful, deceiving, mendacious, lying, economical with the truth, burlesqued, parodied, creative (Inf), bullshitting (Inf)

VERBS

9 **distort**, warp, twist, strain, stress, contort, bias, disproportion, imbalance, misshape, knock out of true alignment, put out of kilter

10 **make faces**, grimace, girn (Dial), leer, scowl, frown, snarl, sneer, pout, contort

11 **deform**, malform, disfigure, deface, damage, impair, stain, spot, mark, welt, weal, pit, pockmark, warp, cicatrize, blemish

12 **distort the truth**, exaggerate, reshape, deform, misrepresent, pervert, misconceive, misconstrue, give a false reading, twist words, read something into it, falsify, fabricate, dissemble, embroider, fake, deceive, dress up, forge, concoct, rig, misinform, mislead, misguide, be false, lie, brainwash, whitewash, propagandize, be economical with the truth, translate the truth, stretch the truth, take out of context, tell porkies (Inf), tell a cock-and-bull story (Inf), bullshit (Inf), speak with forked tongue (Inf), lead up the garden path (Inf)

ADVERBS

13 **asymmetrically**, unsymmetrically, differently, irregularly, disproportionately, lopsidedly, crookedly, contortedly, misshapenly, hideously, grotesquely, imperfectly

14 **distortedly**, evasively, deceptively, hypocritically, falsely, spuriously, deceitfully, untruthfully, mendaciously, perfidiously, perversely

235 Worth

If a job's worth doing, it's worth doing well. Proverb.

ADJECTIVES

1 **worthy**, praiseworthy, laudable, meritorious, deserving, admired, esteemed, respected, valued, admirable, estimable, creditable, approved, excellent, fine, braw (Scot), noble, exemplary, worth imitating, good, good as gold, good as one's word, virtuous, above par, preferable, better, superior, very good, first-class, first-rate, first-string, capital, prime, quality, good quality, superfine, most desirable, rare, vintage, classic, outstanding, superlative, in a class by itself, all-star, all-American (US), topnotch, top-flight, of the first water, flawless, perfect,

choice, select, picked, hand-picked, exquisite, recherché, chosen, selected, tested, exclusive, restricted, pure, unmixed, famous, great, noteworthy, notable, eminent, distinguished, glorious, dazzling, splendid, splendiferous, brilliant, magnificent, marvellous, sensational, terrific, wonderful, superb, *couleur de rose* (Fr), grand, fantastic, fabulous, amazing, prodigious, gorgeous, lovely, heavenly, delicious, fab (Inf), super (Inf), super-duper (Inf), superfly (US inf), out of this world (Inf), dynamite (Inf), deadly (Inf), def (Inf), magic (Inf), way out (Inf), radical (Inf), rad (US inf), way-rad (US inf), out of sight (Inf), ace (Inf), A1 (Inf), A-OK (Inf), alpha plus (Inf), stunning (Inf), famous (Inf), massive (US inf), (a) mean (Inf), bad (US inf), smashing (Inf), corking (Inf), spiffy (Inf), spiffing (Inf), topping (Inf), ripping (Inf), real George (US inf), George (US inf), swell (Inf), swell-elegant (Inf), dandy (Inf), classy (Inf), neat (US inf), cool (Inf), hunky-dory (Inf), groovy (Inf), bully (Inf), brill (Inf), cosmic (Inf), wizard (Inf), boffo (US inf), bang-up (Inf), bang-on (Inf), delish (Inf), scrumptious (Inf), juicy (Inf), plum (Inf), peachy (keen) (Inf), plummy (Inf), jammy (Inf), crackerjack (Inf), copacetic (*or* copasetic) (US inf), God's own (Inf), God's answer to (Inf)

▶ *121 Superiority; 230 Perfection; 669 Approval; 797 Good; 803 Virtue*

2 **best**, very best, optimum, champion, grand-champion, winning, blue-ribbon, gold-medal, platinum (record), tiptop, nothing like it, first, first-class, first-rate, second to none, supreme, incomparable, unequalled, unbeaten, unbeatable, unmatched, matchless, unparalleled, peerless, unsurpassed, unsurpassable, perfect, record, record-breaking, world-beating, best-selling, chart-topping, number-one, crowning, principal, capital, cardinal, important, topnotch, top-hole, tops (Inf), ace (Inf), A1 (Inf), crack (Inf), a cut above (Inf), best ever (Inf), all-time (Inf)

▶ *121 Superiority; 123 Importance; 230 Perfection*

3 **valuable**, of value, invaluable, inestimable, priceless, above price, beyond price, costly, expensive, rich, irreplaceable, unique, rare, precious, prized, valued, treasured, golden, worth its weight in gold, worth a king's ransom, worth a mint, worth a million, sterling, gilt-edged, blue-chip, sound, solid

▶ *790 Price; 792 Dearness*

4 **worthwhile**, profitable, useful, advantageous, beneficial, wholesome, healthy, salutary, sound, good (for), salubrious, refreshing, edifying, favourable, kind, propitious, harmless, hurtless, inoffensive, innocuous, innocent, like water off a duck's back

▶ *237 Usefulness; 257 Hygiene; 765 Profit; 805 Innocence*

5 **not bad**, tolerable, adequate, sufficient, fair, satisfactory, good enough, passable, respectable, standard, up to the mark, in good condition, in fair condition, nice, decent, pretty good, all right, unexceptionable, unobjectionable, indifferent, yes-and-no, middle-of-the-road, middling, fair to middling, neither good nor bad, mediocre, ordinary, average, median, sound, fresh, unspoiled, fifty-fifty (Inf), so-so (Inf), up to snuff (Inf), okay (Inf), OK (Inf), oke (Inf), okey-doke (*or* okey-dokey) (Inf)

▶ *216 Average; 217 Sufficiency*

NOUNS

6 **worth**, worthiness, praiseworthiness, merit, desert, admiration, esteem, respect, credit, value, price, cost, pricelessness, costliness, rarity, excellence, greatness, goodness, virtue, quality, good quality, classic quality, vintage, soundness, health, virtuosity, skill, forte, strong point, good point, redeeming feature, likable trait, claim to fame, title to fame, eminence, pre-eminence, supereminence, superiority, flawlessness, perfection, essence, distilled essence, quintessence, beneficence, benevolence, nobility, brilliance, magnificence, strong suit (Inf), long suit (Inf), best foot (Inf), best side (Inf)

▶ *121 Superiority; 123 Importance; 230 Perfection; 237 Usefulness; 790 Price; 792 Dearness; 797 Good; 803 Virtue*

7 **elite**, chosen few, chosen people, the elect, the saints, prime, flower, cream, *crème de la crème* (Fr), salt of the earth, pick, pick of the bunch, *corps d'élite* (Fr), SAS, Special Forces (US), best people, top people, meritocracy, meritocrat, aristocracy, aristocrat, gentry, nobility, upper class, charmed circle, top drawer, *haut monde* (Fr), jet set, Brahman (*or* Brahmin), Sloane Ranger, Valley Girl (US), choice bit, titbit, prime cut, *pièce de résistance* (Fr), plum, prize, trophy, crack troops (Inf), upper crust (Inf)

▶ *121 Superiority; 123 Importance; 794 Prize*

8 **exceller**, nonpareil, nonesuch (Lit), champion, top seed, titleholder, world-beater, prizewinner, winner, victor, prodigy, gifted child, genius, paragon, hero, star, film star, pop star, celebrity, idol, toast of the town, toast from coast to coast (US), beauty, charmer, wonder, wonder of the world, Miss Universe, Miss America, May Queen, homecoming queen (US), Admirable Crichton, grand fellow, one of the best, one in a thousand, one in a million, treasure, perfect treasure, favourite, jewel, gem, gem of the first water, pearl, pearl of price, ruby, diamond, gold, pure gold, refined gold, masterpiece, *chef-d'oeuvre* (Fr), *pièce de résistance* (Fr), collector's item, collector's piece, museum piece, record-breaker, best-seller, chart-topper, top of the pops, the greatest show on earth, best ever, best thing since sliced bread, best of its kind, *ne plus ultra* (L), last word (in), superhero (Inf), superman (*or* superwoman) (Inf), superjock (US inf), supermom (US inf), wonder woman (Inf), the goods (Inf), winner (Inf), corker (Inf), humdinger (Inf), lollapalooza (US inf), wow (Inf), knockout (Inf), hit (Inf), smash hit (Inf), smasher (Inf), the tops (Inf), the greatest (Inf), bee's knees (Inf), cat's pyjamas (Inf), cat's whiskers (Inf), cat's meow (Inf), topnotcher (Inf), top banana (US inf), top brass (Inf), top dog (Inf), first-rater (Inf), cock of the walk (Inf)

▶ *123 Importance; 230 Perfection; 246 Success; 545 Beauty*

VERBS

9 **be worthy**, have merit, have quality, merit, deserve, qualify, stand the test, pass, pass muster, suffice, bear (*or* stand) comparison, contend, vie, rival, equal, equal the best, excel, surpass, transcend, overtop, take the prize, walk off with all the prizes, sweep the board

▶ *119 Equality; 121 Superiority; 217 Sufficiency*

10 **do good**, benefit, have a good effect, improve, make better, edify, do a world of good, work wonders, be the making of, make a man of, help, favour, do a good turn, confer an obligation, put in one's debt, do no harm, cause no problems, not hurt, break no bones

ADVERBS

11 **worthily**, laudably, admirably, excellently, nobly, well, famously, greatly, notably, gloriously, splendidly, brilliantly, OK, all right, profitably, beneficially

INTERJECTIONS

12 **fantastic!**, great!, well done!, all right! (Inf)

236 Worthlessness

What do the ravages of time not injure? Our parents' age (worse than our grandparents') has produced us, more worthless still, who will soon give rise to a yet more vicious generation. Horace.

ADJECTIVES

1 **worthless**, valueless, of little value, unimportant, insignificant, paltry, useless, futile, not worth the effort, not worth a second thought, not worth powder and shot, not worth the paper it's written on, not worth a light, not worth a hill of beans (Inf), not worth a bean (*or* button) (Inf), not worth a piss in the snow (Inf), not worth a plugged nickel (US inf), not worth a bucket of warm spit (US inf), not worth a bumper (Aus inf)

▶ *124 Unimportance; 238 Uselessness*

2 **inferior**, no good, low-quality, low-grade, of poor quality, low-standard, faulty, flawed, imperfect, defective, substandard, badly made, shoddy, punk, tawdry, trashy, rubbishy, cheap, second-class, third-class, second-rate, third-rate, not good enough, unsatisfactory, bad, incompetent, inefficient, unskilled, clumsy, badly done, bungled, botched, mangled, spoiled, ruined, nowhere (US inf), crummy (Inf), pathetic (Inf), tacky (Inf), naff (Inf), junky (US inf), schlocky (US inf), crappy (Inf), ropy (*or* ropey) (Inf), klutzy (US inf)

▶ *122 Inferiority; 231 Imperfection; 486 Unskilfulness; 606 Dissatisfaction*

3 **bad**, nasty, obnoxious, noxious, noisome, objectionable, unpleasant, disagreeable, unlikable, not nice, horrible, horrid, evil, base, gross, black, utterly bad, irredeemable, as bad as (bad) can be, execrable, unspeakable, abdominable, awful, horrific, horrendous, terrible, dreadful, perfectly dreadful, gruesome, grim, unendurable, intolerable, too bad, onerous, burdensome, tedious, fatiguing, annoying, distressing, vicious, villainous, wicked, heinous, depraved, immoral, accursed, sinful, dishonest, illegal, criminal, wrong, wrongful, unjust, ghastly (Inf), beastly (Inf), crooked (Inf)

▶ *242 Unpleasantness; 798 Evil; 800 Dishonour; 802 Wrong; 804 Wickedness*

4 **poor**, mean, wretched, miserable, sad, woeful, melancholy, pitiful, pitiable, grievous, sore, lamentable, deplorable, abject, contemptible, despicable, disreputable, scruffy, shabby, mangy, sordid, sleazy, squalid, grubby, dirty, filthy, sickening, nauseating, nauseous, revolting, disgusting, loathsome, detestable, hateful, low, indecent, improper, coarse, vulgar, pornographic, obscene, X-rated, shocking, scandalous, reprehensible, disgraceful, unworthy, undeserving, discreditable, shameful, rotten, rotten to the core, decaying, decayed, decomposed, putrefying, putrid, rank, stinking, stinky (US), foul, noisome, fetid, corrupt, peccant, gone bad, off, not fresh, stale, mouldy, tainted, affected, unsound, disordered, morbid, diseased, infected, septic, poisoned, envenomed, incurable, irremediable, measly (Inf), lousy (Inf), grotty (Inf), sleazo (US inf), sleazoid (US inf), gungy (Inf), grungy (US inf), scrungy (Inf), gunky (US inf), manky (Inf), pukey (Inf), pukish (US inf), yucky (Inf), plaguy (*or* plaguey) (Inf)

▶ *245 Deterioration; 258 Dirtiness; 260 Ill Health; 682 Meanness; 782 Poverty; 812 Notoriety*

5 **harmful**, hurtful, injurious, damaging, deleterious, detrimental, prejudicial, disadvantageous, destructive, corrosive, wasting, consuming, pernicious, deadly, fatal, killing, virulent, disastrous, ruinous, calamitous, like the end of the world, adverse, degenerative, noxious, noisome, malignant, unhealthy, unwholesome, infectious, insalubrious, contaminating, venomous, poisonous, toxic, miasmal, polluting, acid, radioactive, dangerous, unsafe, risky, evil, sinister, ominous, dire, dreadful, baleful, baneful, accursed, devilish, mischievous, spiteful, snide, vindictive, malign, malicious, malevolent, ill-disposed, malefic, mischief-making, puckish, impish, cruel, bloody, bloodthirsty, inhuman, violent, furious, rough, harsh, intolerant, persecuting, oppressive, monstrous, outrageous, bitchy (Inf), full of the devil (Inf), full of Old Nick (Inf)

▶ *249 Adversity; 254 Danger; 357 Destruction; 382 Killing; 647 Severity; 651 Malevolence; 798 Evil*

6 **damnable**, damned, darned, blasted, confounded, bothersome, execrable, accursed, cursed, diabolic, diabolical, bloody (Inf), dad-blamed (US inf), dad-blasted (US inf), blinking (Inf), dratted (Inf), blankety-blank (Inf), bleeping (*or* blipping) (US inf), infernal (Inf), devilish (Inf), hellish (Inf)

NOUNS

7 **worthlessness**, lack of value, unimportance, insignificance, uselessness, futility

▶ *124 Unimportance; 238 Uselessness*

8 **inferiority**, poor quality, low quality, low grade, low standard, faultiness, fault, flaw, defect, imperfection, shoddiness, tawdriness, trashiness, trash, rubbish, cheapness, badness, incompetence, inefficiency, lack of skill, unskilfulness, clumsiness, bungle, botch, hiccup (Inf), glitch (Inf), blip (Inf), queeb (US inf), crumminess (Inf), tackiness (Inf), junk (Inf), schlock (US inf), crap (Inf), klutziness (US inf)

▶ *122 Inferiority; 231 Imperfection; 486 Unskilfulness*

9 **badness**, bad, nastiness, obnoxiousness, unpleasantness, horridness, evilness, evil, vileness, baseness, grossness, blackness, irredeemability, execrableness, abomination, awfulness, horror, dreadfulness, grimness, onerousness, tediousness, annoyance, distress, viciousness, villainousness, villainy, wickedness, heinousness, depravity, immorality, sinfulness, sin, vice, dishonesty, illegality, crime, wrong, wrongfulness, injustice, ghastliness (Inf), beastliness (Inf), crookedness (Inf)

▶ *242 Unpleasantness; 798 Evil; 800 Dishonour; 802 Wrong; 804 Wickedness*

10 **poverty**, meanness, wretchedness, misery, sadness, woe, melancholy, pitifulness, abjectness, contemptible-

ness, despicableness, disreputability, scruffiness, shabbiness, sordidness, sleaziness, squalidness, squalor, grubbiness, dirtiness, dirt, filthiness, filth, sewer, lowness, indecency, impropriety, coarseness, vulgarity, pornography, obscenity, disgrace, scandal, slur, unworthiness, shame, rottenness, decay, decomposition, putrefaction, putridness, rankness, stink, foulness, fetor, corruption, peccancy, staleness, mouldiness, taint, unsoundness, disorder, morbidity, disease, sickness, cancer, canker, blight, bane, plague, pestilence, scourge, infection, contamination, poison, venom, lousiness (Inf), grottiness (Inf), sleaze (Inf)

► *245 Deterioration; 258 Dirtiness; 260 Ill Health; 682 Meanness; 782 Poverty; 812 Notoriety*

11 harmfulness, harm, hurtfulness, hurt, injury, ill, damage, detriment, destruction, consumption, perniciousness, deadliness, virulence, disaster, ruin, calamity, the end of the world, adversity, noxiousness, malignancy, unhealthiness, insalubrity, venomousness, poisonousness, toxicity, miasma, pollution, danger, risk, balefulness, banefulness, mischievousness, mischief, spite, spitefulness, vindictiveness, malignity, malice, malevolence, hostility, unkindness, bitterness, rancour, gall, wormwood, suffering, anguish, angst, anxiety, agony, painfulness, pain, sting, ache, pang, cruelty, bloodthirstiness, inhumanity, violence, harshness, severity, intolerance, persecution, oppression, subjection, tyranny, harassment, sexual harassment, maltreatment, ill-treatment, abuse, sexual abuse, child abuse, molestation, child molestation, libel, slander, spell, curse, malediction, the evil eye, jinx, mojo, voodoo, voodoo doll, witchcraft, sorcery, black magic, bad omen, ill wind, evil star, poltergeist, gremlin, dog howling at night (US), hoodoo (Inf)

► *357 Destruction; 491 Physical Pain; 647 Severity; 651 Malevolence*

12 bad person, bad character, bad influence, troublemaker, evildoer, evil genius, evil spirit, demon, devil, Satan, Hitler, Stalin, Simon Legree, wicked stepmother, bad fairy, wicked witch, snake in the grass (Inf)

VERBS

13 be worthless, have no value, do no good, be in vain, bungle, botch, do badly, make badly, spoil, ruin, hurt, injure, damage, impair, do one a mischief, scathe (Lit), rot, decay, pollute, contaminate, infect, corrupt, pervert, deprave, do evil, work evil, do wrong, torment, plague, vex, harass, trouble, land one in trouble, spite, thwart, queer one's pitch (Inf), do for (Inf)

► *231 Imperfection; 238 Uselessness; 486 Unskilfulness; 651 Malevolence*

14 ill-treat, mistreat, maltreat, mishandle, misuse, ill-use, burden, overburden, put upon, tyrannize, oppress, bear down on, tread on, trample (on), trample underfoot, crush, squash, victimize, harass, persecute, abuse, molest, prey upon, hold prisoner, hold as hostage, wrong, aggrieve, distress, torment, torture, agonize, rack, crucify, force, outrage, violate, rape, wound, savage, maul, bite, scratch, tear, stab, pierce, strike, hit, slap, buffet, bruise, batter, spite, take out one's spite on, walk over, wipe one's feet on, wreak one's malice on, libel, slander, ruin, defeat, destroy, dump on (Inf)

► *351 Misuse; 491 Physical Pain*

ADVERBS

15 worthlessly, badly, ill, wrongly, amiss, nastily, unpleasantly, abominably, wickedly, awfully, cruelly, spitefully, in (*or* with) malice, disgracefully, shamefully, abjectly, contemptibly

237 Usefulness

ADJECTIVES

1 useful, of use, handy, helpful, of help, of service, for everyday use, utilitarian, pragmatic, practical, applied, functional, practicable, commodious, convenient, advisable, sensible, suitable, expedient, applicable, versatile, multipurpose, all-purpose, for all ages, of all work, adaptable, disposable, throwaway, ready, rough and ready, at hand, available, on call, ready for use, operative, up, on-line, on-stream, on tap (Inf)

► *239 Convenience; 349 Use; 392 Help*

2 usable, serviceable, fit (for), good (for), fit for use, approved for use, reusable, recyclable, employable, workable, good, valid, current

3 instrumental, subsidiary, subservient, able, competent, efficacious, effective, effectual, efficient, powerful, conducive, tending, adequate, sufficient

► *217 Sufficiency; 334 Power*

4 profitable, making a profit, remunerative, lucrative, paying, gainful, productive, fruitful, beneficial, advantageous, salutary, for one's benefit, to one's advantage, good, edifying, worthwhile, worth one's salt, worth one's keep, worth one's weight in gold, worth a mint, worth a million, valuable, invaluable, priceless

► *235 Worth; 356 Creation; 765 Profit; 797 Good*

NOUNS

5 usefulness, use, purpose, point, utility, handiness, helpfulness, help, aid, service, avail, good stead, good, utilitarianism, practicality, application, functionalism, commodity, convenience, suitability, expediency, applicability, versatility, adaptability, readiness, availability, usage, utilization, employment

► *239 Convenience; 349 Use; 392 Help*

6 usability, serviceability, employability, workability, value, worth, merit, good, virtue, function, capacity

► *235 Worth; 797 Good*

7 instrumentality, ability, competence, efficacy, efficiency, power, potency, clout, influence, adequacy, sufficiency

► *217 Sufficiency; 334 Power*

8 benefit, advantage, gain, profit, profitability, return, earning capacity, productivity, productiveness, fruitfulness, general benefit, public benefit, public good, public utility, commonweal

► *356 Creation; 765 Profit*

VERBS

9 be useful, come in handy, help, aid, advance, promote, prove helpful, avail, serve, do service, suit one's purpose, further one's purpose, have some use, perform a function, function, work, operate, perform do, answer, suffice, make oneself useful, subserve, serve one's turn, fill the bill (Inf)

► *217 Sufficiency; 349 Use; 392 Help*

10 **benefit**, advantage, be to one's advantage, serve one well, stand one in good stead, bestead (Lit), do good, bring results, bear fruit, profit, gain, pay, pay off

► *235 Worth; 765 Profit; 797 Good*

11 **find useful**, have a use for, find a use for, use, utilize, employ, make use of, take advantage of, turn to good account, capitalize on, make capital out of, profit by, gain from, reap the profit from, reap the benefit of, be the better for

► *244 Improvement; 349 Use; 765 Profit*

ADVERBS

12 **usefully**, handily, helpfully, practically, conveniently, usably, serviceably, efficiently, advantageously, profitably, *pro bono publico* (L), for the public good, *cui bono?* (L), to whose advantage?, for what purpose?

238 Uselessness

All Art is quite useless. Oscar Wilde.

A useless life is an early death. Goethe.

ADJECTIVES

1 **useless**, not useful, of no use, inutile, futile, unhelpful, unfit, unapt, inapt, unsuitable, inapplicable, inconvenient, inexpedient, impractical, impracticable, unworkable, unpractical, nonfunctional, functionless, ornamental, redundant, superfluous, extra, excessive, unnecessary, not needed, unneeded, unwanted, expendable, dispensable, disposable, throwaway, unusable, unserviceable, fit for nothing, good-for-nothing, unemployable, unqualified, unskilled, unskilful, unable, incompetent, inept, inefficient, ineffective, ineffectual, feckless, impotent, powerless, inadequate, nonfunctioning, inoperative, not working, out of order, down, broken down, worn out, spent, effete, *hors de combat* (Fr), no good, invalid, void, null, null and void, abrogated, obsolete, outmoded, old-fashioned, antiquated, worthless, valueless, rubbishy, trashy, unsaleable, not worth the paper it's written on, naff (Inf), no-go (US inf), screwed-up (Inf), fucked-up (Inf), dud (Inf), kaput (Inf), no bloody good (Inf), out of action (Inf), past it (Inf), over the hill (Inf), Mickey Mouse (Inf), crappy (Inf), shitty (Inf)

► *219 Excess; 236 Worthlessness; 240 Inconvenience; 296 Oldness; 335 Powerlessness; 378 Obstruction; 486 Unskilfulness; 542 Decoration*

2 **futile**, purposeless, pointless, Sisyphean, hopeless, vain, in vain, idle, unavailing, abortive, unsuccessful, profitless, bootless, not worthwhile, offering no advantage, offering no benefit, unprofitable, not paying, lossmaking, uneconomic, unproductive, fruitless, barren, sterile, wasteful, ill-spent, wasted, squandered, timewasting, effort-wasting, not worth the effort, unrewarding, unrewarded, thankless

► *247 Failure; 441 Waste; 563 Infertility; 766 Loss*

3 **uselessness**, lack of use, inutility, futility, unhelpfulness, disservice, unfitness, unaptness, inaptitude, unsuitability, inapplicability, inconvenience, inexpedience, inexpediency, impracticality, impracticability, unworkability, lack of function, redundancy, superfluousness, superfluity, expendability, dispensability, disposability, unserviceableness, unemployability, unskilfulness, lack of skill, inability, incompetence, ineptitude, inefficiency, ineffectiveness, inefficacy, ineffectualness, fecklessness, impotence, powerlessness, inadequacy, effeteness, worthlessness, unsaleability

► *219 Excess; 236 Worthlessness; 240 Inconvenience; 335 Powerlessness; 378 Obstruction; 486 Unskilfulness*

4 **futility**, purposelessness, lack of purpose, pointlessness, hopelessness, vanity, vanity of vanities, idleness, failure, loss, unprofitability, profitlessness, bootlessness, lack of advantage, lack of benefit, unproductiveness, fruitlessness, barrenness, sterility, waste, wastefulness, thanklessness

► *247 Failure; 563 Infertility; 766 Loss*

5 **waste of effort**, wasted effort, wasted labour, lost labour, waste of time, waste of breath, waste of space, false scent, red herring, wild-goose chase, fool's errand, fool's gold, labour of Sisyphus, Penelope's web, half measures, tinkering, futilitarianism, dead loss (Inf), blind alley (Inf), nigger-rigging (US inf)

► *441 Waste*

6 **refuse**, rubbish, trash (US), junk, litter, scrap, throwaway, disposable, cast-off, reject, leftovers, leavings, scraps, lumber, stuff, spoilage, wastage, bilge, load of old rubbish, discarded matter, waste, waste product, mullock (Aus), wastepaper, scourings, offscourings, sweepings, shavings, chaff, husks, stubble, bran, seeds, cotton seeds, bits, crumbs, offal, carrion, debris, muck, dirt, dush, ash, cinder, clinker, dross, slag, scoria, scum, peel, apple peel, orange peel, banana skin, leaves, weeds, dead wood, old newspaper, tares, odds and ends, bits and pieces, rags and bones, old clothes, empty bottle, can, tin, compost, compost heap, dump, refuse dump, rubbish dump, rubbish pile, trash dump (US), rubbish heap, midden (Lit), landfill, tip, sump, drain, cesspool, septic tank, sewage works (*or* farm), dustheap, slag heap, dustbin

► *215 Remainder; 258 Dirtiness; 441 Waste*

VERBS

7 **be useless**, have no use, have no purpose, not help, hinder, achieve nothing, be in vain, have no chance, fail, not work, not function, malfunction, go wrong, not go, break down, fall by the wayside, go to waste, go begging

► *219 Excess; 247 Failure; 378 Obstruction*

8 **make useless**, disqualify, disable, render unfit, unfit, unman, disarm, unarm, render harmless, cripple, make lame, lame, dismantle, disassemble, undo, take to pieces, break up, break down, unmount, dismast, unrig, decommission, put out of commission, lay up, deactivate, make inactive, sabotage, put a spoke in one's wheel, obstruct, abrogate, withdraw from currency, devalue, cheapen, impair, deface, pollute, contaminate, destroy, obliterate, lay waste, make barren, sterilize, castrate, emasculate, exhaust, use up, overwork, overfish, take the sting out of (Inf), clip one's wings (Inf), let the air out of one's tyres (Inf), throw a wrench in one's plans (US inf), throw a spanner in the works (Inf), cramp one's style (Inf)

▶ *335 Powerlessness; 343 Inactivity; 357 Destruction; 358 Obliteration; 793 Cheapness*

9 **waste effort**, labour the obvious, waste one's breath, waste (one's) time, go round in circles, accomplish nothing, get nowhere, labour in vain, sweat for nothing, attempt the impossible, tinker, leave unfinished, spin one's wheels (Inf), talk to a brick wall (Inf), beat one's head against a brick wall (Inf), rearrange the deckchairs on the Titanic (Inf), preach to the converted (Inf), carry coals to Newcastle (Inf), flog (*or* beat) a dead horse (Inf), beat the air (Inf), tilt at windmills (Inf), cry for the moon (Inf), search for the end of the rainbow (Inf), paper over the cracks (Inf), spoil the ship for a ha'p'orth of tar (Inf)

▶ *103 Impossibility; 441 Waste*

ADVERBS

10 **uselessly**, unhelpfully, inconveniently, impractically, incompetently, ineffectively, ineffectually, to no purpose, in vain, to no avail, unsuccessfully, unprofitably, on a wild-goose chase, until one is blue in the face, on a hiding to nothing (Inf)

239 Convenience

The fundamental tendency in the modern view of life is always to seek what is more convenient. Rudolf Steiner.

ADJECTIVES

1 **convenient**, handy, helpful, practical, pragmatic, practicable, usable, workable, effective, effectual, qualified, adapted to, cut out for, applicable, to the purpose, suitable, commodious, appropriate, fit, fitting, befitting, seemly, proper, right, expedient, expediential, advantageous, to one's advantage, beneficial, profitable, useful, prudent, politic, judicious, wise, advisable, commendable, desirable, worthwhile, acceptable, approved, owing, due, *in loco* (L), timely, well-timed, auspicious, opportune, seasonable, right up one's alley (Inf), right up one's street (Inf)

▶ *237 Usefulness; 287 Timeliness; 458 Wisdom; 669 Approval; 801 Right*

2 **nearby**, next-door, accessible, available, ready, close, adjacent, neighbouring, touching, bordering on

▶ *147 Closeness*

NOUNS

3 **convenience**, handiness, helpfulness, practicality, pragmatism, practicability, practicableness, usability, workability, qualification, adaptation, application, suitability, fitness, propriety, expedience, expediency, contrivance, utilitarianism, opportunism, rule of expediency, time-serving, profit, advantage, benefit, usefulness, utility, prudence, good policy, advisability, desirability, dueness, timeliness, auspiciousness, opportunity, proper time, right time, right time and place, high time (Inf), due time (Inf)

4 **nearness**, proximity, closeness, juxtaposition, adjacency, accessibility, availability

5 **convenience**, facilities, means, expedient, last resort, *pis aller* (Fr)

VERBS

6 **be convenient**, come in handy, come in useful, fit, befit, suit, suit the occasion, not come amiss, not go amiss, serve the time, expedite one's end, bring about, help, aid, promote, advance, forward, answer, have the desired effect, produce results, do, serve, prove itself, be better than nothing, succeed achieve one's aim, qualify for, correspond with, accord, profit, benefit, give an advantage, advantage, do good, hit the spot (Inf), wash (Inf), deliver the goods (Inf), fill the bill (Inf)

▶ *217 Sufficiency; 237 Usefulness; 246 Success; 392 Help; 750 Agreement; 797 Good*

ADVERBS

7 **conveniently**, handily, practically, fittingly, expediently, opportunely, accessibly, within reach, in the right place at the right time, to fill (*or* fit) the bill (Inf)

8 **nearby**, close by, next to, at hand, in the vicinity (*or* neighbourhood), within reach, at one's fingertips, on the tip of one's tongue

240 Inconvenience

No one wants the truth if it is inconvenient. Arthur Miller.

ADJECTIVES

1 **inconvenient**, discommodious, incommodious, disadvantageous, detrimental, hurtful, harmful, inexpedient, inadvisable, unadvisable, undesirable, uncommendable, not recommended, ill-advised, ill-considered, impolitic, imprudent, injudicious, unwise, inappropriate, unfitting, misapplied, malapropos, out of place, improper, unseemly, undue, not right, objectionable, offensive, wrong, unfit, unsuitable, ineligible, unqualified, inadmissible, unfortunate, unhappy, infelicitous, sad, inept, unapt, inopportune, unseasonable, untimely, ill-timed, poorly timed, wrongly timed, disruptive, disrupting, disturbing, unsettling, useless, unprofitable, unhelpful, hindering, untoward, adverse, unprofessional, ill-contrived, ill-planned, awkward, clumsy, cumbersome, lumbering, hulking, unwieldy, burdensome, onerous, troublesome, bothersome, annoying, irritating, irksome, boring, tiresome, vexatious, tedious

▶ *238 Uselessness; 328 Disturbance; 378 Obstruction; 459 Folly; 670 Disapproval; 802 Wrong*

2 **distant**, remote, out-of-the-way, innaccessible, unapproachable, unavailable

▶ *145 Distance*

NOUNS

3 **inconvenience**, disadvantage, drawback, detriment, hurt, harm, inexpedience, inexpediency, mixed blessing, Pyrrhic victory, two-edged sword, inadvisability, undesirability, bad policy, imprudence, inappropriateness, unfittingness, impropriety, lack of protocol, unseemliness, undueness, lack of planning, poor timing, wrongness, wrong, error, unfitness, unsuitability, inaptitude, inopportuneness, untimeliness, disruption, disturbance, disability, handicap, impediment, obstacle, hindrance, nuisance, bother, trouble, upset, discomfort, incommodiousness, pain, difficulty, annoyance, irritation, vexation, awkwardness, burden, cumbersomeness, troublesomeness, unwieldiness

► *238 Uselessness; 328 Disturbance; 378 Obstruction; 802 Wrong*

4 **distance**, remoteness, inaccessibility, unapproachability, unavailability

VERBS

5 **be inconvenient**, come amiss, go amiss, not do, not fit, not help, inconvenience, trouble, bother, disturb, disrupt, upset, put to inconvenience, put to trouble, discommode, incommode, put out, annoy, irritate, vex, irk, embarrass, hinder, obstruct, handicap, disadvantage, penalize, work against, militate against, hurt, harm, pester, make a nuisance of oneself, hassle (Inf)

ADVERBS

6 **inconveniently**, discommodiously, incommodiously, inexpediently, inadvisably, injudiciously, improperly, inopportunely, disruptively, uselessly, unhelpfully, awkwardly, clumsily, annoyingly, irritatingly, boringly, tediously, tiresomely, vexatiously

241 Pleasantness

Pleasant words are as an honeycomb, sweet to the soul, and health to the bones. Bible: Proverbs.

ADJECTIVES

1 **pleasant**, pleasing, nice, enjoyable, pleasurable, agreeable, acceptable, gratifying, satisfying, tasteful, inviting, welcome, charming, appealing, sweet, lovely, delightful, idyllic, heavenly, divine, Elysian (Lit), sublime, blissful, out of this world (Inf)

2 **likable**, amiable, affable, friendly, cordial, compatible, congenial, genial, engaging, good-natured, easy-going, amusing, bright, sunny, attractive, kind, kindly, courteous, polite, well-mannered, chivalrous, civil, civilized

3 **comfortable**, soothing, relaxing, restful, dulcet, mellow, emollient, easy, cosy, snug, comfy (Inf)

4 **tasty**, palatable, appetizing, tempting, savoury, flavourful, mouthwatering, delicious, delectable, luscious, juicy, succulent

5 **pleasure-loving**, pleasure-seeking, hedonistic, epicurean, gourmet, gourmand, voluptuous, self-indulgent

► *490 Physical Pleasure; 686 Self-Indulgence*

NOUNS

6 **pleasantness**, pleasurableness, niceness, agreeableness, charm, appeal, loveliness, delightfulness, heaven, bliss

7 **pleasure**, enjoyment, satisfaction, ease, comfort, luxury, creature comforts, hedonism, self-indulgence, epicureanism, voluptuousness, entertainment, amusement, diversion

8 **amiability**, affability, friendliness, cordiality, compatibility, congeniality, geniality, good company, attractiveness, kindliness, courtesy, chivalry, politeness, civility

9 **tastiness**, palatability, deliciousness, delectability, lusciousness

10 **pleasant thing**, treat, delicacy, luxury, holiday, honeymoon, pleasant remark, pleasantry, compliment, praise, tribute, honour, flattery

► *599 Humour; 677 Flattery*

11 **pleasant person**, charmer, delight, pleasure, joy

12 **pleasure-loving person**, hedonist, epicurean, voluptuary

VERBS

13 **give pleasure**, please, gratify, satisfy, comfort, soothe, agree with, charm, delight, brighten one's day

14 **like**, appreciate, delight in, enjoy, relish, savour

ADVERBS

15 **pleasantly**, agreeably, with pleasure, with good grace, cordially, genially, politely

242 Unpleasantness

ADJECTIVES

1 **unpleasant**, displeasing, unpleasing, disagreeable, unacceptable, rebarbative, uncomfortable, painful, discomfiting, discordant, unharmonious, trying, annoying, irksome, invidious, unwelcome, uninviting, disliked, distasteful, unpalatable, unsavoury, nasty, horrible, hateful, horrid, disgusting, offensive, odious, repulsive, loathsome, revolting, sickening, nauseating

► *364 Repulsion; 517 Dissonance; 594 Hate*

2 **objectionable**, awkward, unattractive, ungracious, discomforting, impolite, uncivil, discourteous, unchivalrous, unkind, uncouth, impertinent, rude, boorish, mean, cantankerous, obnoxious, quarrelsome, crabbed, crabby, quarrelling, aggressive, bellicose, beastly (Inf), bloody-minded (Inf), like a bear with a sore head (Inf)

► *381 Attack; 607 Annoyance and Aggravation; 701 Argument*

3 **unpalatable**, unappetizing, uneatable, inedible, acid, bitter, sour, rancid, off, turned

► *495 Taste; 499 Sourness*

4 **painful**, sore, tender, aching, smarting, stinging

► *491 Physical Pain*

NOUNS

5 **unpleasantness**, disagreeableness, pain, discomfort, discomfiture, affront, offence, umbrage, distastefulness, unpalatability, nastiness, offensiveness, repulsiveness

6 **objectionability**, awkwardness, unattractiveness, ungraciousness, impoliteness, incivility, discourtesy, unkindness, impertinence, rudeness, bad manners, boorishness, meanness, cantankerousness, aggressiveness, beastliness

7 **dissension**, disagreement, disharmony, bad feeling, friction, disunity, discord, discordance, aggravation, antagonism, squabbling, fighting, bickering

► *381 Attack; 517 Dissonance; 607 Annoyance and Aggravation*

8 **quarrel**, argument, difference of opinion, squabble, scuffle, clash, scrap, wrangle, brawl, fisticuffs, altercation, row, conflict, strife, chastisement, vendetta, feud, set-to (Inf), tiff (Inf), bother (Inf), stick (Inf), aggro (Inf), spot of bother (Inf)

9 **unpleasant person**, pest, nuisance, boor, oaf, lout, cad, shrew, troublemaker, mischief-maker, quarreller, wrangler, aggressor, fighter, hooligan, beast (Inf), pain (Inf), pain in the neck (Inf), pain in the arse (Inf), shit (Inf), shitbag (Inf)

VERBS

10 **displease**, put off, discomfit, discomfort, embarrass, en-

rage, offend, repel, appal, disgust, revolt, horrify, sicken, nauseate, stick in one's throat (Inf), get up one's nose (Inf)

11 quarrel, disagree, dissent, argue, nag, have differences with, take umbrage, insult, offend, take liberties with, squabble, wrangle, scrap, bicker, brawl, fight, cross swords with, clash, conflict, feud, wind up (Inf)

12 be painful, hurt, ache, throb, smart, sting

ADVERBS

13 unpleasantly, disagreeably, nastily, distastefully, offensively, repulsively, discourteously, aggressively

243 Preparation

When I think of all the books I have read, and of the wise words I have heard spoken, and of the anxiety I have given to parents and grandparents, and of the hopes that I have had, all life weighed in the scales of my own life seems to me preparation for something that never happens. W. B. Yeats.

VERBS

1 prepare, make preparations, get ready, make ready, take steps, take measures, pioneer, pave the way, lead the way, show the way, go before, scout the territory, see the lay of the land, bridge, build a bridge, make contact, introduce, lead up to

► *129 Precedence*

2 do the groundwork, lay the foundations, found, establish, provide the basis, prepare the ground, sow the seed, set the stage, predispose, incline, soften up, set to work on, address oneself to, begin, make basic plans, research, document, gather notes, outline, draft, sketch, make a rough sketch, cut out, block out, rough-hew, blueprint, plan, organize, plot, contrive, concert, prearrange, predetermine, improvise, rustle up (Inf)

► *106 Predetermination; 130 Beginning; 484 Plan*

3 be prepared, prepare for, forearm, guard against, insure, take precautions, save, put something aside, hoard supplies, prepare for a rainy day, anticipate, look for, wait for, expect

► *252 Safety; 436 Provisions; 474 Expectation; 680 Thrift*

4 prepare for action, ready, make ready, finish one's preparations, have ready, set in order, put in readiness, mobilize, put on alert, make operational, commission, put in commission, put in working order, fix, adjust, focus, tune, tune up, wind, wind up, screw up, gear up, arrange, array, order, put together, assemble, count down, prepare for blastoff (US), prepare for takeoff, fasten (*or* buckle) one's seatbelt, prepare to dive, batten down the hatches, stow, stow away, pack, store, shuffle the cards, tee up, set the alarm, whet the knife, load the gun, prime, cock, raise steam, heat the boiler, stoke up, warm up, crank, crank up, rev up, get into gear, bring up to scratch (Inf), bring up to snuff (Inf), clear the decks (Inf)

► *393 Repair; 407 Order; 409 Arrangement; 439 Store*

5 equip, fit, fit out, outfit, furnish, provide, supply, kit out (*or* up), rig out, dress, arm, provide with arms, provide firepower, crew, man, provide with teeth (Inf)

► *436 Provisions*

6 brief, inform, bring up to date, instruct, teach, educate, train, coach, groom, drill, exercise, rehearse, lick into shape (Inf)

► *6 Education; 693 Information*

7 develop, mature, mellow, ripen, bring to fruition, force, bring on, bring to a head, cook, stew, brew, gestate, hatch, incubate, breed, grow, farm, cultivate, fledge, nurse, nurture, raise, make, produce, concoct, elaborate, work out, carry through, cure, smoke, salt, dry, age, season, weather, temper, harden, inure, acclimatize

► *25 Cookery; 43 Agriculture; 230 Perfection; 356 Creation; 418 Hardness; 561 Reproduction; 632 Habit*

8 prepare oneself, ready oneself, get ready, compose oneself, brace oneself, study, educate oneself, brief oneself, do one's homework, serve an apprenticeship, train, exercise, rehearse, practise, limber up, warm up, gear oneself up, gird up one's loins, roll up one's sleeves, flex one's muscles, buckle on one's armour, take sword in hand, shoulder arms, get ready for action, be prepared, stand ready, stand by, be on stand-by, be on call, hold oneself in readiness, order one's life, put one's house in order, psych oneself up (Inf), keep one's powder dry (Inf)

NOUNS

9 preparation, preparing, getting ready, making ready, taking steps, taking measures, pioneering, mobilization, battening down the hatches, tuning, priming, loading, cocking, planning, organization, prearrangement, premeditation, predetermination, consultation, preconsultation, forethought, anticipation, foresight, promotion, inauguration, flotation, launching

► *106 Predetermination; 129 Precedence; 130 Beginning; 713 Advice*

10 preparations, preliminaries, measures, steps, preliminary step, preliminary course, trial run, trial, experiment, practice, rehearsal, dress rehearsal, preparatory work, study, homework, spadework, groundwork, foundation, basis, framework, frame, scaffold, scaffolding, sketch, draft, rough sketch, first draft, rough, outline, plan, blueprint, original model, prototype, pilot scheme, arrangement, arrangements, savings, reserves, store, bottom drawer, nest egg

► *130 Beginning; 175 Base; 409 Arrangement; 413 Support; 439 Store; 484 Plan; 576 Work*

11 fitting out, provisioning, furnishing, provision, supply, appointment, commission, equipment, kit, gear, outfit, marshalling, array, armament, logistics

12 briefing, instruction, education, training, drill, exercise, practice, apprenticeship, novitiate, probationary period

13 development, maturation, ripening, seasoning, hardening, inurement, acclimatization, brewing, gestation, hatching, incubation, nursing, nurture, cultivation, tillage, sowing, planting, blooming, flowering, florescence, efflorescence, fruition, fructification, making, production, manufacture

► *43 Agriculture; 356 Creation; 561 Reproduction*

14 preparedness, readiness, maturity, ripeness, mellowness, puberty, nubility, fitness, prime condition, top condition, shipshape condition, peak, pitch of perfection

► *230 Perfection; 556 Age*

15 preparer, teacher, tutor, coach, trainer, drillmaster, drill sergeant, torchbearer, trailblazer, pioneer, bridge-builder, paver, paviour, loader, packer, stevedore, fitter, equipper, provisioner, provider, cultivator, grower, farmer, agriculturalist, ploughman, sower, planter, cook, brewer

ADJECTIVES

16 preparatory, preparative, preparing, preliminary, introductory, basic, elementary, provisional, stopgap, makeshift, precautionary

► *129 Precedence; 130 Beginning; 252 Safety; 478 Improvisation; 762 Substitution*

17 developing, maturing, cooking, stewing, brewing, marinating, brooding, hatching, incubating, in the embryonic stage, in embryo, in preparation, in progress, afoot, on foot, on the stocks, on the anvil, on the drawing board, in the offing, forthcoming, impending, being discussed, under consideration, at the committee stage, agitated for, mooted, planned, learning, under training, probationary, on probation

► *283 Future Time*

18 prepared, ready, alert, vigilant, made ready, readied, in readiness, at the ready, mobilized, standing by, on call, set, all set, ready to go, raring to go, teed up, keyed up, spoiling for, trained, fully trained, qualified, well-prepared, experienced, practised, well-rehearsed, organized, in practice, tuned, primed, on one's marks, briefed, instructed, tutored, warned, forewarned, forearmed, saddled, in the saddle, in harness, armed, in armour, fully armed, armed to the teeth, armed at all points, rigged, rigged out, equipped, furnished, fully furnished, well-appointed, groomed, accoutred, dressed, fully dressed, psyched up (Inf), in one's best bib and tucker (Inf), in full war-paint (Inf)

► *551 Dress*

19 in hand, in store, ready to hand, ready for use, ready for anything, ready to go, primed, fit for use, in working order, operational

20 developed, matured, ripened, mature, ripe, mellow, seasoned, weathered, hardened, veteran, adult, grown, grown up, full-grown, fledged, fully fledged (*or* full-fledged), blooming, flowering, in flower, florescent, fruiting, overripe, overmature, well-cooked, well-done, elaborate, wrought, highly wrought, overwrought, overdone, worked up, laboured, deep-laid, completed, perfected

21 ready-made, ready-mixed, cut-and-dried, ready to use, ready-to-wear, off-the-peg, ready-formed, prefabricated, ready-furnished, processed, convenience, oven-ready, ready-to-cook, precooked, ready-to-serve, instant, predigested

► *25 Cookery*

ADVERBS

22 in preparation, in hand, under way, under construction, on the stocks, under consideration, in anticipation, vigilantly, in readiness, readily, willingly

23 preparatorily, preparatively, preliminarily, introductorily, provisionally

244 Improvement

He so improved the city that he justly boasted that he found it brick and left it marble. Augustus.

VERBS

1 improve, make better, better, ameliorate, meliorate, reform, change for the better, make improvements, improve upon, polish, perfect, elaborate, enrich, enhance, improve out of all recognition, work miracles with, transform, transfigure, convert, redeem, rehabilitate, make, be the making of, have a good influence on, leaven, raise, uplift, regenerate, refine, upgrade, elevate, sublimate, purify, civilize, socialize, teach manners, mend, repair, straighten, straighten out, rectify, make healthy, restore, cure, recruit, revive, infuse new (*or* fresh) blood into, refresh, soften, lessen, alleviate, mitigate, palliate, moderate, forward, further, advance, promote, market, hype, foster, encourage, bring to fruition, mature, profit from, make the most of, get the best out of, take advantage of, use, exploit, develop, open up, reclaim, till, weed, dress, water, cultivate, arrange, tidy, tidy up, make shipshape, make neat, neaten, spruce up, smarten up, freshen up, clean, clean up, do up, vamp up, shape up, tone up, touch up, patch up, fix up (US), rationalize, renovate, refurbish, recondition, renew, bring up to date, modernize, give a face-lift to, beautify, improve on nature, gild the lily, dress up, make up, titivate, prink, primp, embellish, adorn, ornament, decorate, add frills

► *224 Change; 235 Worth; 255 Purity; 393 Repair; 394 Remedy; 395 Influence; 547 Beautification; 581 Refreshment; 685 Moderation; 760 Conversion*

2 get better, grow better, improve, mend, take a turn for the better, turn the corner, pick up, rally, revive, recover, recuperate, get over the worst, pass the crisis, convalesce, make a comeback, feel like a new man (*or* woman), make progress, make headway, advance, develop, evolve, progress, mellow, ripen, mature, fructify, bear fruit, increase, rise, ascend, graduate, succeed, rise in the world, better oneself, be upwardly mobile, climb the ladder of success, make one's way, make out like a bandit (US), do well, prosper, mend one's ways, reform, turn over a new leaf, improve oneself, learn, study, learn by experience, take advantage of, make capital out of, cash in on, profit by, make the grade (Inf), make good (Inf), make it (Inf), make it big (Inf), go straight (Inf), straighten up and fly right (Inf)

► *213 Increase; 246 Success; 248 Prosperity; 259 Health; 304 Ascent*

3 rectify, put right, set right, remedy, make good, straighten, straighten out, adjust, repair, mend, patch, fix, correct, make corrections, make improvements, make clear, make concise, blue-pencil, proofread, remove errors, revise, redact, edit, copy-edit, subedit, amend, emend, alter, rewrite, redraft, retell, recast, remould, refashion, remodel, recreate, reform, reorganize, regularize, fine-tune, streamline, rationalize, review, reexamine

► *393 Repair; 394 Remedy*

4 reconsider, redo, take back to the drawing board, go back to square one, stop in time, stop and think, think again, think better of, have second thoughts, have cold feet (Inf)

NOUNS

5 **improvement**, betterment, amelioration, melioration, change for the better, turn for the better, sea change, transfiguration, transformation, conversion, redemption, rehabilitation, reform, reformation, radical reform, penitence, new leaf, new resolution, good influence, the making of, polish, perfection, elaboration, enrichment, enhancement, rise, ascent, increase, lift, uplift, upturn, upswing, upward mobility, graduation, success, prosperity, self-improvement, regeneration, refinement, upgrading, elevation, sublimation, purification, cleansing, civilization, socialization, education, repair, rectification, remedy, restoration, cure, recruitment, revival, recovery, recuperation, convalescence, refreshment, alleviation, mitigation, palliation, moderation, furtherance, advancement, advance, onward march, progress, headway, progression, promotion, tidying, cleaning, rationalization, renovation, refurbishment, reconditioning, renewal, modernization, face-lift, beautification, titivation, adornment, embellishment, ornament, ornamentation, decoration, finishing touch, final touch, icing on the cake, last word, completion, perfectionism, fussiness, kick upstairs (Inf)

6 **rectification**, putting right, making good, straightening out, adjustment, repair, mending, correction, blue pencil, proofreading, revision, revise, revisal, recension, redaction, edition, editing, copy editing, subediting, amendment, emendation, alteration, reorganization, shake-up (Inf)

7 **reconsideration**, re-examination, review, further reflection

8 **better thing**, better choice, better idea, new idea, another idea, better thought, second thought, updated model, revised edition, new edition, updated version, improved version, corrected copy, corrected proof, sequel

9 **physical improvement**, exercise, aerobics, callisthenics, eurhythmics, jogging, yoga

10 **reformatory**, reform school, house of correction, youth custody centre, borstal, juvenile detention centre, juvenile home (US)

11 **reformism**, humanism, meliorism, perfectionism, idealism, Utopianism, millenarianism, chiliasm, liberalism, socialism, progressivism, gradualism, Fabianism, New Deal (US), radicalism, extremism, revolution, communism, Marxism, integration (US), assimilationism, social change, feminism, womanism, suffragism, suffragettism, antiracism, Black Consciousness, Black Power, antifascism, class war, prohibitionism, Prohibition (US), peace movement, Campaign for Nuclear Disarmament (CND), ecology, the environmental movement, Greenpeace, Friends of the Earth

► *652 Philanthropy*

12 **reformer**, reformist, humanist, meliorist, perfectionist, idealist, Utopian, millenarian, chiliast, visionary, liberal, egalitarian, Leveller, socialist, progressive, progressivist, progressionist, gradualist, Fabian, New Dealer (US), moderate, radical, extremist, revolutionary, communist, Marxist, Red, agitator, integrationist (US), assimilationist, antiracist, antifascist, social worker, philanthropist, feminist, womanist, suffragist, suffragette, prohibitionist, Prohibitionist (US), peace advocate, CND member, peacenik (US), ecologist, environmentalist, ecowarrior (Inf)

► *652 Philanthropy*

13 **reviser**, improver, repairer, restorer, mender, amender, emender, corrector, rewriter, editor, copy editor, subeditor, proofreader

► *393 Repair; 740 Publication*

ADJECTIVES

14 **improved**, better, superior, bettered, enhanced, touched up, beautified, reformed, transformed, revised, edited, rewritten, repaired, restored, renovated, modernized, better off, all the better for, recovering, recuperating, looking up, on the mend, rising, increasing, better advised, wiser

► *121 Superiority*

15 **improvable**, perfectible, ameliorable, meliorable, reformable, corrigible, curable

16 **improving**, advancing, ameliorative, meliorative, remedial, restorative, reformative, reformatory, reforming, reformist, progressive, radical, extreme, extremist, civilizing, cultural, idealistic, perfectionist, Utopian, millenarian, chiliastic, ecological, environmental

► *393 Repair*

ADVERBS

17 **better**, for the better, improvably, remedially, restoratively, progressively, radically, idealistically

245 Deterioration

America is the only nation in history which miraculously has gone directly from barbarism to degeneration without the usual interval of civilization. Georges Clemenceau.

VERBS

1 **deteriorate**, worsen, get worse, not improve, get no better, take a turn for the worse, go from bad to worse, go to the devil, go to rack and ruin, slip, slide, go downhill, lose ground, not maintain one's position, have seen better days, be a shadow of one's former self, fall, fall off, slump, decline, decrease, decelerate, slow down, wane, ebb, sink, fail, totter, droop, stoop, slip back, retrograde, retrogress, regress, revert, lapse, relapse, tergiversate, degenerate, let oneself go, take it easy, tread the primrose path, go to ruin, go to pieces, self-destruct, ruin oneself, go (*or* run) to seed, go (to the) bad, lose control, disintegrate, crumble, collapse, break down, come apart, fall apart, contract, shrink, wear out, age, grow old, become obsolete, lose value, depreciate, fade, wither, wilt, shrivel (up), wrinkle, perish, become dilapidated, fray, become threadbare, become shabby, weaken, lose health, sicken, fall ill, do worse, jump from the frying pan into the fire, go farther and fare worse, go to pot (Inf), go to the dogs (Inf), hit the skids (Inf), flop (Inf)

► *191 Contraction; 214 Decrease; 260 Ill Health; 305 Descent; 337 Weakness; 357 Destruction; 375 Disintegration; 556 Age*

2 **decay**, decompose, rot, putrefy, moulder, mildew, grow moss, weather, rust, corrode, spoil; go bad, go off, go

sour, become rancid, turn, stale, go stale, grow stale, lose taste, lose flavour, go flat, corrupt, rankle, fester, suppurate, go septic, gangrene, smell, stink, pong (Inf)

▶ *503 Stench*

3 **make worse**, worsen, deteriorate, make things worse, aggravate, exacerbate, irritate, embitter, adulterate, corrupt, sophisticate, alloy, debase, denature, infect, contaminate, taint, poison, envenom, ulcerate, canker, pollute, foul, dirty, make unclean, defile, desecrate, profane

▶ *258 Dirtiness; 412 Mixture; 607 Annoyance and Aggravation*

4 **impair**, damage, make inoperative (*or* inoperable), put out of action, deactivate, make inactive, dismantle, dismast, spoil, mar, maul, ruin, destroy, play havoc with, mess up, untidy, jumble, derange, disorganize, bungle, botch, touch, tinker, tamper, trifle with, meddle, wreck, vandalize, ravage, rape, plunder, waste, lay waste, scorch, overthrow, crush, crumble, pulverize, muck up (Inf), fuck up (Inf), bugger up (Inf), screw up (Inf), cock up (Inf), balls up (Inf), make a balls-up of (Inf), bollocks up (Inf), pull a boner (US inf), pull a bonehead play (US inf), monkey with (Inf), fool (around) with (Inf), screw around with (Inf), fuck (around) with (Inf)

▶ *328 Disturbance; 343 Inactivity; 357 Destruction; 486 Unskilfulness*

5 **hurt**, harm, injure, wound, weaken, damnify, scathe (Lit), not improve, do no good, waste one's efforts, kill with kindness, mutilate, maim, lame, cripple, hamstring, disable, scotch (Lit), pinion, clip the wings of, cramp, hamper, hinder, castrate, unman, undermine, mine, sap, demoralize, take the starch out of, take the wind out of someone's sails, shake, honeycomb, fret, bore, gnaw, gnaw at the roots, eat away, erode, corrode, rust, rot, decay, decompose, mildew, blight, blast, plague, overrun, invade, blacken, soil, stain, spot, blot, mark, blemish, deface, disfigure, scar, wrinkle, uglify, make ugly, dilapidate, fray, frazzle, wear out, reduce to rags, drain, deplete, exhaust, consume, use up, reduce, make small, trim back, cut back, shorten, truncate, dock, curtail, censor, cut out, expurgate, eviscerate, bowdlerize, cream (off), skim (off), asset-strip, take the heart out of, put the skids under (*or* to) (Inf), cramp one's style (Inf), de-ball (Inf), beat (*or* whip) with an ugly stick (US inf)

▶ *149 Shortness; 191 Contraction; 214 Decrease; 335 Powerlessness; 337 Weakness; 378 Obstruction; 491 Physical Pain; 546 Ugliness; 548 Blemish*

6 **pervert**, deform, warp, twist, distort, abuse, misuse, prostitute, deprave, debauch, ruin, vitiate, corrupt, subvert, lower, degrade, debase, abase, treat cruelly, brutalize, dehumanize, barbarize, denature, denaturalize, denationalize, detribalize, propagandize, brainwash, misteach, vulgarize, coarsen, make coarse, drag down to one's level, devalue, cheapen

▶ *234 Distortion; 351 Misuse; 367 Lowering; 793 Cheapness; 796 Immorality; 804 Wickedness*

NOUNS

7 **deterioration**, worsening, lack of improvement, lack of betterment, turn for the worse, losing ground, retrogradation, retrogression, regression, reversion to type, throwback, slipping back, backsliding, recidivism, lapse, relapse, tergiversation, setback, descent, downward course, primrose path, falling off, slump, downturn, downtrend, decline, depression, recession, decrease, depreciation, impoverishment, poverty, law of diminishing returns, bad money driving out good money, Gresham's law, exhaustion of supplies, Malthusianism, deceleration, slowing down, wane, ebb, twilight, fading, dimness, tragedy, misfortune, bad ending, the skids (Inf), the road to hell (Inf), going to hell in a basket (*or* handbasket) (Inf), bad news (Inf), bad scene (Inf)

▶ *214 Decrease; 305 Descent; 524 Dimness; 782 Poverty*

8 **perversion**, deformation, distortion, abuse, misuse, prostitution, depravation, depravity, immorality, degeneration, degeneracy, degenerateness, addiction, indulgence, drunkenness, intoxication, promiscuity, impureness, impurity, decadence, ruin, vitiation, corruption, subversion, degradation, debasement, abasement, brutalization, dehumanization, barbarism, vulgarization, coarsening, devaluation, cheapening

▶ *234 Distortion; 351 Misuse; 793 Cheapness; 796 Immorality; 804 Wickedness*

9 **dilapidation**, collapse, disintegration, breakdown, ruination, destruction, ruin, rack and ruin, lack of repair, disrepair, lack of maintenance, neglect, negligence, shabbiness, slum, backstreet, urban blight, inner-city ghetto, wreck, mere wreck, perfect wreck, physical wreck, rambling wreck (US), shadow of one's former self, wear and tear, erosion, corrosion, oxidization, rustiness, rust, moth and rust, rot, rottenness, decay, decomposition, putrefaction, gangrene, corruption, mould, mouldiness, mildew, blight, canker, cancer, discoloration, weathering, bleaching, patina, verdigris, decrepitude, old age, senility, ravages of time, Father Time, one foot in the grave, hardening of the arteries, marasmus, atrophy, disease, illness, walking disaster (Inf), rat trap (US inf), fleapit (Inf), tired bones (Inf)

▶ *260 Ill Health; 357 Destruction; 375 Disintegration; 556 Age; 666 Negligence*

10 **impairment**, detriment, damage, spoiling, spoilage, waste, loss, ruination, devastation, havoc, demolition, destruction, attack, assault, insult, outrage, sabotage, terrorism, disorganization, derangement, aggravation, exacerbation, adulteration, sophistication, mixture, debasement, watering down, infection, contagion, contagious disease, contamination, poisoning, intoxication, autointoxication, autotoxaemia, ulceration, pollution, acid rain, dirtiness, uncleanness, defilement

▶ *258 Dirtiness; 328 Disturbance; 357 Destruction; 381 Attack; 412 Mixture; 607 Annoyance and Aggravation*

11 **hurt**, harm, mischief, injuriousness, injury, pain, sprain, strain, dislocation, pulled muscle, wound, mutilation, lameness, crippling, hobbling, disabling, disablement, weakening, weakness, demoralization, loss of morale, draining, depletion, exhaustion, nobbling (Inf)

▶ *335 Powerlessness; 337 Weakness; 491 Physical Pain*

ADJECTIVES

12 **deteriorated**, worsened, worse, getting worse, worse and worse, the worse for, gone from bad to worse, not improved, no better, exacerbated, aggravated, deteriorating, worsening, failing, going downhill, in a bad way, past one's best, decreasing, declining, in decline, on the decline, falling off, in recession, impoverished, poor,

falling, slipping, sliding, nodding, tottering, senile, senescent, ageing (*or* aging), spoilt, bad, gone bad, gone off, off, rotten, corked, stale, flat, bland, tasteless, impaired, damaged, hurt, harmed, injured, ruined, destroyed, harmful, injurious, effete, worn out, exhausted, tired, overtired, drained, run-down, worthless, useless, descending, on the downgrade, on the downward path, downfallen (US), fallen by the wayside, weakened, undermined, honeycombed, sapped, shaken, faded, discoloured, decaying, decayed, decomposed, withered, sere (Lit), wasting away, ebbing, at low ebb, retrogressive, regressive, retrograde, unprogressive, unimproved, undeveloped, backward, old-fashioned, outdated, lapsed, relapsed, recidivist, tergiversating, degenerate, degenerative, depraved, corrupt, going to pot (Inf), past it (Inf), far gone (Inf), done in (Inf), done for (Inf), on the way out (Inf)

► *214 Decrease; 236 Worthlessness; 238 Uselessness; 261 Tiredness; 305 Descent; 375 Disintegration; 497 Blandness; 607 Annoyance and Aggravation; 782 Poverty*

13 **dilapidated**, in disrepair, the worse for wear, falling apart, falling to pieces, in ruins, in shreds, in bits and pieces, beyond repair, cracked, broken, leaking, battered, weather-beaten, storm-tossed, decrepit, rickety, tottery, shaky, unsteady, not functioning, not working, out of order, not in proper condition, out of kilter, ruinous, ramshackle, derelict, tumbledown, run-down, on its last legs, about to go, exhausted, weakened, ruined, slummy, condemned, rat-infested, worn, well-worn, shopsoiled, frayed, shabby, tatty, unkempt, dingy, holey, in holes, in tatters, in rags, worn out, worn to a frazzle, worn to a fritter (US), worn to a shadow, worn to the threads, seedy, down-at-heel, down-and-out, rusty, mildewed, mouldering, moth-eaten, worm-eaten, dog-eared, kaput (Inf), wonky (Inf), out of whack (US inf), on the fritz (US inf), flea-bitten (Inf)

ADVERBS

14 **worse**, for the worse, down, downhill, down in the world, badly, poorly

246 Success

One's religion is whatever he is most interested in, and yours is Success. J. M. Barrie.

To succeed in the world, we do everything we can to appear successful. Duc de la Rochefoucauld.

NOUNS

1 **success**, achievement, accomplishment, attainment, feat, great success, triumphant success, runaway success, sweet smell of success, sensation, overnight sensation, breakthrough, mastery, ascendancy, fame and fortune, fame, famousness, success story, stardom, celebrity, name up in lights, name recognition, name, place in history, happiness, thriving, plenty, luxury, prosperity, fortune, wealth, riches, affluence, the big time (Inf), luck, lucky break, lucky stroke, beginner's luck, run of luck, favourable outcome, happy ending, fairy-tale ending, landing on one's feet, celebration, momentary success, flash in the pan, feather in one's cap, coming up roses (Inf), roaring success (Inf), howling success (Inf), hit (Inf), big hit (Inf), smash hit (Inf), smash (Inf), killing (Inf)

► *121 Superiority; 248 Prosperity; 484 Plan; 601 Celebration; 781 Wealth*

2 **victory**, triumph, conquest, win, beating, whipping, thrashing, hiding, trouncing, runaway victory, crushing victory, landslide victory, knockout, winning by a mile, love game, overrunning, successful attack, taking by storm, rout, game, set, and match, extra-time victory, overtime victory (US), sudden-death victory, military victory, successful battle, defeat of the enemy, narrow victory, Pyrrhic victory, licking (Inf), pushover (Inf), walkover (Inf), piece of cake (Inf), KO (Inf), skunk (US inf)

► *265 Easiness; 302 Forward Motion; 340 Action; 357 Destruction; 381 Attack; 452 Certainty; 485 Skill*

3 **successful thing**, best-seller, chart-topper, blockbuster, box-office success, rave reviews, number-one ranking (*or* rating), good move, checkmate, hole in one, ace, good shot, score, touchdown (TD) (soccer, American football), try (Rugby), goal, field goal (Basketball, American football), home run (Baseball), six (Cricket), hit (Baseball), bull's-eye, grand slam, triple crown, hat trick, championship, league championship, division championship, conference championship (US), exam success, sell-out (Inf), box-office hit (Inf), number one (Inf), homer (US inf), KO (Inf), wow (Inf)

4 **successful person**, success, winner, hero, heroine, self-made man (*or* woman), achiever, high flyer, superman, superwoman, man (*or* woman) of the year, record-breaker, star, star in the firmament, starlet, celebrity, top of the class, whiz kid, graduate, honour graduate, valedictorian (US), talk of the town, first-rater, VIP (very important person), man of the match, MVP (most valuable player) (US), *crème de la crème* (Fr), rising star, up-and-coming star, comer (Inf), surefire winner (Inf), hit (Inf), number one (Inf), the tops (Inf), wow (Inf), corker (Inf)

5 **victorious person**, victor, winner, conqueror, champion, reigning champion, Olympic champion, world champion, world-beater, titleholder, medallist, prizewinner, first-place finisher, first, victorious general, defeater, vanquisher, subjugator, subduer, sure winner, champ (Inf), shoo-in (US inf)

VERBS

6 **be successful**, succeed, have success, enjoy success, meet with success, score a success, make a success of, prosper, thrive, flourish, flower, blossom, accomplish, effect, achieve, compass, get results, show results, come off well, become a self-made man (*or* woman), do well, do oneself proud, pass, qualify, graduate, get on, get there, get ahead, get promoted, advance, progress, rise in the world, make good, make one's mark, gain one's goal, gain one's end, secure one's object, obtain one's objective, arrive, go over, earn a standing ovation, reap the harvest, reap the fruits, make money, get rich, break the bank, bring it off, bring off, pull it off, pull off, hit it off, hit it, carry off, work miracles, make the grade, do wonders, work wonders, not put a foot wrong, get lucky,

win one's spurs, top the charts, write a bestseller, come off with flying colours, pull oneself up by one's bootstraps, work one's way up the ladder, have the world at one's feet, set the world on fire, ring the bell, hit the mark, make a go of (Inf), make a killing (Inf), hit the jackpot (Inf), make the big time (Inf), make a hit (Inf), bring home the bacon (Inf), make it (Inf), click (Inf), go great guns (Inf), go over big (Inf)

7 **overcome obstacles**, brush obstacles aside, overcome difficulties, sweep problems out of the way, manage, prevail, persevere, escape, surmount, get over the (*or* a) hump, get over a snag, avoid defeat, rise to the occasion, make headway against, muddle through, stem the tide, weather the storm, not know the meaning of failure, find a loophole, find a way out, find a way round, cut the Gordian knot, not know when one is beaten, come right in the end, turn out well, turn up trumps, land on one's feet, come up smiling, come up smelling like roses

▶ *378 Obstruction; 389 Escape; 638 Resolution*

8 **be effective**, be efficacious, work, go, do, answer the purpose, answer, show results, turn out well, do the job, do wonders, work like magic, act like a charm, pay dividends, pay off, bear fruit, come off (Inf), do the trick (Inf), ring the bell (Inf), fill the bill (Inf)

9 **be victorious**, be triumphant, triumph (over), conquer, win, win a victory, win by a landslide, win the game, win the match, beat, beat all comers, become champion, take the prize, take the cup, take the championship, win the race, win the battle, achieve victory, claim a victory, win the last battle, force a surrender, defeat, defeat the enemy, vanquish, prevail, quell, subdue, carry the day, carry, take, storm, take by storm, sweep the boards, put down, crush, capture, subject, suppress, subjugate, win on points, win a (*or* the) point, win on moves, checkmate, check, put in check, wear the crown, wear the laurel wreath, wear the laurels, have the best of it, celebrate a victory, only just win, scrape through, scrape home, do for (Inf), win by a whisker (Inf), pip at the post (Inf)

10 **defeat heavily**, defeat easily, rout, put to flight, scatter, win hands down, win going away, romp home, storm home, win in straight sets, sweep the board, sweep, carry all before one, wipe out, break, bankrupt, drive to the wall, destroy, have it all one's way, walk off with, thrash, whip, trounce, overwhelm, crush, drub, give a drubbing, whitewash, trample underfoot, knock out, put out for the count, knock the stuffing out of, knock (*or* beat) the shit out of (Inf), flatten (Inf), lick (Inf), waltz away with (Inf), wipe the floor with (Inf), beat to a pulp (Inf), cook somone's goose (Inf), KO (Inf)

11 **overmaster**, beat, master, overpower, overcome, overthrow, overturn, override, outclass, outplay, outpoint, trump, carry a point, score a point, come off best, pass with flying colours, come through with flying colours, outflank, outmanoeuvre, break through

12 **succeed to**, succeed, inherit, come into, be left, take one's heritage

ADJECTIVES

13 **successful**, succeeding, winning, crowned with success, wealthy, prosperous, fruitful, thriving, flourishing, favourable, famous, renown, efficacious, effective, masterly, best-selling, chart-topping, best ever, lucky, fortunate, never-failing, surefire, sure-footed, certain, rising, on the up and up, crowning, sitting pretty (Inf), home and dry (Inf), home free (US inf)

14 **rewarding**, financially rewarding, profitable, lucrative, paying, gainful, remunerative, advantageous, worthwhile

15 **victorious**, winning, triumphant, triumphal, flushed with victory, match-winning, game-winning (US), prizewinning, the best, on top, top of the league, top of the division, world-beating, always victorious, ever-victorious, undefeated, unbeaten, unbowed, unvanquished, unbeatable, unconquerable, invincible, crushing, quelling, on top of the heap (Inf)

ADVERBS

16 **successfully**, victoriously, triumphantly, in triumph, with flying colours, prosperously, rewardingly, fruitfully, profitably, lucratively, gainfully, advantageously, favourably, efficaciously, effectively, invincibly, luckily, fortunately, beyond all expectation, beyond one's fondest dreams, well, marvellously, swimmingly, to some purpose, to good purpose, with good results, with good effect

247 Failure

She knows there's no success like failure
And that failure's no success at all. Bob Dylan.

NOUNS

1 **failure**, nonfulfilment, lack of success, negative result, hopeless failure, fallibility, inability, inefficiency, ineffectiveness, weakness, unproductiveness, barrenness, nonperformance, noncompletion, discontinuation, dereliction, withdrawal, setback, error, mistake, mess, complete failure, collapse, debacle, fiasco, botch (*or* botch-up), bungle, bungling, blunder, omission, neglect, negligence, default, miss, near miss, vain attempt, futile effort, futility, frustration, disappointment, no luck, misfortune, uselessness, lost labour, no result, no answer, no progress, discontinuance, stoppage, shutdown, nonresumption, closure, stalling, stall, breakdown, dead stop, halt, fall, crash, decline, decline in health, failing health, deterioration, failing, ailing, downfall, comedown, letdown, shortage, shortfall, incapacity, insufficiency, insolvency, inability to pay, failure to pay, bankruptcy, ruin, nail in one's coffin, the pits (Inf)

▶ *226 Stopping; 238 Uselessness; 249 Adversity; 274 Error; 305 Descent; 335 Powerlessness; 337 Weakness; 378 Obstruction; 486 Unskilfulness; 563 Infertility; 604 Disappointment; 786 Nonpayment*

2 **defeat**, loss, collapse, reversal, retreat, total defeat, trashing, utter defeat, rout, beating, drubbing, hiding, thrashing, trouncing, subjugation, submission, deathblow, narrow defeat, final defeat, military defeat, lost battle, Waterloo, lost war, lost cause, losing move, fatal move, losing game, licking (Inf)

▶ *357 Destruction; 388 Submission; 766 Loss*

3 **personal fault**, foible, failing, weakness, weakness of

the flesh, disloyalty, unfaithfulness, promiscuity, peccadillo, vice, mortal sin, sin
► *231 Imperfection; 686 Self-Indulgence*

4 unsuccessful thing, bankruptcy, bad idea, lost election, abortion, lost bet, wasted day, wild-goose chase, miscarriage, bad hair day, engine failure, electrical fault, computer fault, mechanical malfunction, crop failure, damp squib, faux pas, dud (Inf), nonstarter (Inf), washout (Inf), wipeout (Inf), flop (Inf), slip-up (Inf), boo-boo (Inf), boob (Inf), lemon (Inf), turkey (US inf), bomb (US inf)

5 failing person, failure, losing person, loser, defeated player, losing general, unsuccessful candidate, unsuccessful competitor, unsuccessful applicant, unsuccessful challenger, deposed champion, nonpaying person, nonpayer, debtor, insolvent, bankrupt, underachiever, slow learner, born loser, misfit, bungler, reject, second-rater, underling, underdog, unfortunate, victim, dupe, dropout (Inf), dud (Inf), hopeless case (Inf), also-ran (Inf), flop (Inf), nonstarter (Inf), washout (Inf), has-been (Inf), fly-by-night (Inf), no-hoper (Inf), wuss (Inf), patsy (US inf), lemon (Inf)

VERBS

6 fail, not succeed, lose out, come to nothing, get no results, not pass, do badly, make a bad move, blunder, bungle, collapse, discontinue, shut down, close up, wind up, come to the end of the line, bite the dust, spoil one's reputation, fail in one's duties, let someone down, disappoint, disillusion, dash someone's hopes, fall short, not come up to expectations, fall by the wayside, fall, miss the boat, miss an opportunity, miss, have bad luck, draw a blank, back the wrong horse, return empty-handed, tire, have fatigue, droop, sink, flag, fail in health, ail, decline, take a turn for the worse, make a loss, become insolvent, go bankrupt, go to the wall, go on the rocks, not make the grade (Inf), flop (Inf), fold (Inf), go bust (Inf), go to the dogs (Inf), slip up (Inf), fizzle out (Inf), not come off (Inf), come a cropper (Inf), not come up to scratch (Inf), not come up with the goods (Inf), drop a clanger (Inf), make a hash of (Inf), blot one's copybook (Inf), flunk (out) (US inf), plough (Inf), balls up (Inf), ball up (US inf), bollocks up (Inf), bollix up (US inf), poop (US inf), go belly up (US inf)

7 be defeated, suffer defeat, lose, lose the game, lose the match, lose the vote, lose the election, lose the battle, lose the war, retreat, run away, surrender, lose the race, come off second best, lose out, lose badly, lose hands down, take a beating, take a drubbing, come in last, fail to score, be eliminated, get the worse of it, concede defeat, lose by a whisker, just miss, get pipped at the post (Inf)

8 miscarry, abort, go wrong, go amiss, go awry, not go well, not come off, come to nothing, come to naught (Lit), come to grief, go by the board, end in futility, prove a fiasco, fall flat, go (*or* end) up in smoke

9 malfunction, not start, not work, stop running, stop, come to a dead stop, come to a halt, fail, stall, misfire, jam, seize up, overheat, lose power, go wrong, break, fall to pieces, crash, conk out (Inf), go kaput (Inf)

ADJECTIVES

10 failed, failing, unsuccessful, ineffective, ineffectual, inefficacious, insufficient, unproductive, hopeless, insolvent, bankrupt, negligent, neglectful, unlucky, unfortunate, empty, miscarried, miscarrying, bungled, bungling, blundered, blundering, stillborn, abortive, aborted, shutdown, closed, weak, ailing, fruitless, bootless, profitless, useless, futile, of no effect, on the rocks, on one's beam-ends, washed up (US inf), dud (Inf), flunked (US inf), ploughed (Inf), kaput (Inf)

11 defeated, beaten, bested, lost, outmanoeuvred, outclassed, outmatched, outgunned, outplayed, outshone, outvoted, outwitted, thrashed, on the losing team (*or* side), out of the running, in retreat, put to flight, routed, captured, overthrown, knocked out, licked (Inf), among the also-rans (Inf), pipped (Inf), wiped out (Inf), KO'd (Inf)

ADVERBS

12 unsuccessfully, without success, to little purpose, to no purpose, in vain, fruitlessly, bootlessly, ineffectually, ineffectively, inefficaciously, insufficiently, unproductively, hopelessly, insolvently, negligently, neglectfully, unluckily, unfortunately, emptily, blunderingly, abortively, weakly, futilely, uselessly

248 Prosperity

The rich are the scum of the earth in every country. G. K. Chesterton.

With the great part of rich people, the chief employment of riches consists in the parade of riches. Adam Smith.

NOUNS

1 prosperity, prosperousness, well-being, welfare, wealth, success, fame, fame and fortune, fortune, health and wealth, luxury, lap of luxury, comfort, ease, life of ease, the good life, having it good, thriving, security, plenty, economic prosperity, high standard of living, affluent society, affluence, boom, bull (*or* bullish) market, booming economy, expanding economy, roaring trade, prestige, glory, honour and glory, happiness, felicity, blessedness, blessings, milk and honey, fat of the land, fleshpots, bed of roses, life of Riley, place in the sun, weal (Lit), land-office business (US inf), living in clover (Inf), clover (Inf), Easy Street (Inf), lap of luxury (Inf)
► *217 Sufficiency; 246 Success; 490 Physical Pleasure; 589 Peace; 597 Joy; 781 Wealth*

2 good fortune, happy fortune, fortune, smiles of fortune, luck, good luck, piece of good luck, run of luck, streak of luck, winning streak, bonanza, lucky shot, lucky strike, luck of the draw, auspiciousness, favour, blessings, Midas touch, break (Inf), good break (Inf), lucky break (Inf), the breaks (Inf)

3 time of plenty, good times, golden days, golden age, golden time, halcyon days, palmy days, salad days, heyday, honeymoon period, easy times, holiday, summer, prime, youth, *Saturnia regna* (L), age of Aquarius

4 prosperous person, rich person, successful person, success, self-made man (*or* woman), man (*or* woman) of property, man (*or* woman) of means, man (*or* woman) of substance, person of repute, VIP (very important person), parvenu, nouveau riche, capitalist, plutocrat, tycoon, millionaire, multimillionaire, billionaire, the haves, the upwardly mobile, lucky fellow, lucky devil, child of fortune, fortune's favourite, favourite of the gods, lucky dog (Inf), yuppie (Inf), Sloane Ranger (*or* Sloane) (Inf), fat cat (US inf)

VERBS

5 **be prosperous**, prosper, enjoy prosperity, do well, succeed, live well, get on well, get on swimmingly, fare well, make good, make one's mark, rise in the world, get on (*or* go up) in the world, have everything going one's way, do all right by oneself, get going, progress, advance, arrive, go far, thrive, flourish, blossom, flower, bloom, profit, make a profit, make one's fortune, make money, make a fortune, get rich, grow rich, strike it rich, feather one's nest, line one's pockets, get fat, grow fat, have a good time of it, strike it lucky, rise to fame, become famous, win fame, win glory, win fame and glory, have it easy, live a life of ease, live the life of Riley, live in the lap of luxury, bask in the sunshine, ride on the crest of a wave, live on the fat of the land, make it (Inf), have it made (Inf), make one's pile (Inf), be rolling in it (Inf), hit the big time (Inf), have a lucky break (Inf), live in clover (Inf), lie on velvet (Inf), live high on the hog (Inf), live on Easy Street (Inf)

6 **be fortunate**, be lucky, have luck, have all the luck, have a stroke of luck, have a lucky break, have a run of good luck, hit a streak of luck, strike it lucky, strike it rich, come into money, come into an inheritance, be on to a good thing, fall on one's feet, lead a charmed life, be born under a lucky star, be born with a silver spoon in one's mouth, strike oil (Inf), strike a rich vein (Inf), get a break (Inf), get on the gravy train (Inf)

7 **be auspicious**, bode well, promise well, augur well, favour, look kindly on, smile on, shine on, bless, shed blessings on

ADJECTIVES

8 **prosperous**, prospering, successful, thriving, flourishing, booming, doing well, well-to-do, well-off, rising, up-and-coming, on the up and up, upwardly mobile, up in the world, profiteering, famous, affluent, rich, opulent, wealthy, luxurious, in luxury, fat, comfortable, comfortably off, comfortably situated, cosy, at ease, bullish, fortunate, lucky, in luck, happy, felicitous, palmy, balmy, halcyon, golden, rosy, blissful, in bliss, blessed, favourable, promising, auspicious, propitious, cloudless, born with a silver spoon in one's mouth, born under a lucky star, on the make (Inf), in the money (Inf), well-heeled (Inf), rolling in it (Inf), high on the hog (Inf), in clover (Inf), on velvet (Inf), on Easy Street (Inf)

ADVERBS

9 **prosperously**, successfully, swimmingly, in the swim, famously, affluently, richly, opulently, luxuriously, comfortably, in comfort, cosily, bullishly, fortunately, luckily, with luck, propitiously, happily, felicitously, blissfully, in a blissful manner, blessedly, favourably, promisingly, auspiciously, high on the hog (Inf), in clover (Inf), on velvet (Inf), on Easy Street (Inf)

INTERJECTIONS

10 **good luck!**, lots of luck!, bless you!, all the best!, live it up!, have a good time!, have fun!

249 Adversity

For of fortunes sharp adversitee
The worst kinde of infortune is this,
A man to have ben in prosperitee,
And it remembren, what is passed is. Geoffrey Chaucer.

NOUNS

1 **adversity**, difficulty, opposition, struggle, trials, travail, hardship, hard life, adverse circumstances, decline, fall, comedown, trials and tribulations, troubles, pack of troubles, predicament, emergency, misadventure, mishap, casualty, accident, injury, hard blow, plight, misfortune, affliction, wretchedness, misery, bleakness, gloom and doom, pressure, suffering, sorrow, sadness, dejection, despondency, distress, worry, worries, cares, trouble ahead, threat, ill wind, gathering clouds, storm clouds, dark clouds, deterioration, humiliation, downfall, defeat, rebuff, unrequited love, lost love, lost game, lost match, lost battle, lost war, retreat, poor health, decline in health, setback, illness, terminal illness, cancer, pain, evil, death, bitter cup, cup of sorrows, bitter pill, bane, load, burden, cross to bear, coldness, cold wind, darkness, curse, infection, visitation, blight, scourge, plague, disaster, natural disaster, desolation, destitution, homelessness, ruin, calamity, catastrophe, the worst, hell (Inf), living hell (Inf), raw deal (Inf), downer (Inf), bad news (Inf), the pits (Inf)

► *113 Opposition; 245 Deterioration; 247 Failure; 264 Difficulty; 357 Destruction; 491 Physical Pain; 494 Cold; 523 Darkness; 602 Sorrow*

2 **economic adversity**, financial setback, financial reverse, financial disaster, financial ruin, mortgage arrears, rent arrears, negative equity, cash-flow problems, need, want, poverty, no money, lost fortune, lost inheritance, (personal) bankruptcy, stock market decline, bear market, slumping market, slump, recession, depression, unemployment

► *779 Market; 782 Poverty*

3 **bad fortune**, ill fortune, misfortune, frowns of fortune, bad luck, hard luck, no luck, no success, malign influence, evil star, hard fate, mischance, missed chance, rotten luck (Inf)

► *107 Chance*

4 **time of adversity**, time of sorrow, bad times, hard times, lean period, rough patch, tough time, bad patch, bad spell, winter of discontent, winter, cold day, gloomy day, rainy day

5 **person in adversity**, poor person, bankrupt, homeless person, destitute, poor wretch, sufferer, unfortunate, loser, born loser, underdog, weakling, lame duck, tramp, down-and-out, bag lady, poor risk, unlucky person, plaything of the gods, victim of fate, victim, dupe, scapegoat, prey, martyr, no-hoper (Inf), sad sack (US inf)

ADJECTIVES

6 **adverse**, contrary, conflicting, opposed, opposing, in opposition, hostile, antagonistic, troublesome, difficult, hard, bleak, cold, detrimental, dreadful, dire, inauspicious, ominous, unpropitious, unfavourable, bad, harm-

ful, sinister, disadvantageous, disastrous, destructive, ruinous, tragic, doomed, unsuccessful, miserable, gloomy, not doing well, in trouble, in difficulties, up against it, in a bad way, in poor shape, in poor health, ill, unwell, on one's last legs, declining, on the wane, on the downgrade, on the slippery slope

7 unprosperous, badly off, in adverse circumstances, poor, penurious, impecunious, poverty-stricken, penniless, bankrupt, in dire straits, homeless, down-and-out, with one's back to the wall, on the road to ruin, on one's beam-ends, broke (Inf), flat broke (Inf), hard up (Inf), stone-broke (Inf), stony-broke (Inf), stony (Inf), skint (Inf), belly up (US inf)

8 unlucky, not lucky, out of luck, down on one's luck, luckless, hapless, accident-prone, unfortunate, unblessed, ill-fated, ill-starred, star-crossed, accursed, under a cloud, born under an evil star, born under a bad sign, washed up (Inf)

VERBS

9 be in trouble, have trouble, meet adversity, have a bad time, have a hard time of it, have difficulties, hit a bad patch, fall foul of, bear the brunt, bear more than one's share, not know which way to turn, fail, lose, lose the game, lose the match, lose the battle, lose the war, lose out on love, miscarry, endure hardship, fall on hard times, fall on bad days, have seen better days, have no luck, be unlucky, run out of luck, suffer misfortune, have a mishap, have an accident, sink, founder, decline, go down in the world, go downhill, slip, fall from grace, have a comedown, hit rock bottom, run aground, go on the rocks, go to rack and ruin, come to a bad end, come to grief, grieve, sorrow, regret, suffer humiliation, be ill, have an illness, suffer from poor health, suffer, feel pain, deteriorate, degenerate, go to pot, die, stew in one's own juice, go to the dogs (Inf), be on (*or* hit) the skids (Inf)

10 need money, have no money, have a financial setback, have a financial reverse, suffer a financial disaster, come to financial ruin, want, fall below the poverty line, lose one's fortune, lose one's inheritance, have a cheque bounce, be overdrawn, go bankrupt, become insolvent, feel the pinch, feel the draught, have the wolf at one's door, go belly up (US inf)

11 cause adversity, cause grief, cause trouble, trouble, create a controversy, create problems, defeat, injure, oppress, sink, humiliate, make ill, burden, overburden, overload, weigh down, cause an accident, cause a death, bring bad luck, jinx, put the jinx on, put the evil eye on, put the skids under, voodoo (*or* hoodoo) (Inf), hex (US inf), put the (*or* a) whammy on (Inf), put the (*or* a) double whammy on (Inf)

ADVERBS

12 in adversity, adversely, in adverse circumstances, if worst comes to worst, from bad to worse, from the frying pan into the fire, sadly, unhappily, unfortunately, unluckily, as ill (*or* bad) luck would have it, conflictingly, contrarily, antagonistically, bleakly, unfavourably, detrimentally, dreadfully, grievously, inauspiciously, ominously, unpropitiously, harmfully, sinisterly, disastrously, tragically, accidentally, by accident, by mischance, by misadventure, unsuccessfully, miserably, poorly

INTERJECTIONS

13 too bad!, bad luck!, what rotten luck!, terrible!, dreadful!, alas!, woe is me! (Lit)

250 Freedom

Those who deny freedom to others, deserve it not for themselves. Abraham Lincoln.

The liberty of the individual must be thus far limited; he must not make himself a nuisance to other people. John Stuart Mill.

'O liberté! O liberté! Que de crimes on commet en ton nom!' (Oh liberty! Oh liberty! What crimes are committed in thy name!) Madame Roland.

Man was born free and everywhere he is in chains. Jean Jacques Rousseau.

NOUNS

1 freedom, freedom of action, liberty, personal liberty, lack of confinement, freedom of movement, being at large, lack of restraint, unrestraint, noncoercion, nonintimidation, option, choice, freedom of choice, freedom of thought, prerogative, discretion, free will, own free will, own account, initiative, own initiative, personal initiative, own responsibility, own volition, liberation, women's liberation, gay liberation, licence, artistic licence, poetic licence, privilege, exemption, nonliability, exception, immunity, diplomatic immunity, discharge, release, deliverance, emancipation, Emancipation Proclamation (US), broad-mindedness, open-mindedness, toleration, tolerance, liberalism, libertarianism, latitudinarianism, free thinking, liberated mind, Bohemianism, nonconformity, noninterference, nonintervention, *laissez faire* (Fr), free enterprise, free trade, free-trade area, free port, high seas, self-regulating market, open market, free market, capitalism, noninvolvement, seclusion, nonalignment, neutrality, isolationism, say-so (Inf), women's lib (Inf)

2 free speech, freedom of religion, freedom of the press, lack of censorship, academic freedom, the Four Freedoms, freedom of speech and expression, freedom of worship, freedom from want, freedom from fear (US), rights, the Bill of Rights (US), First Amendment, constitutional rights, legal rights, human rights, inalienable (*or* unalienable) rights, right to bear arms (US), equal rights, civil rights, civil liberties

3 independence, own authority, own way, being in control, self-determination, the Magna Carta (*or* Magna Carta), Declaration of Independence (US), Statue of Liberty (US), Liberty Bell (US), individualism, self-expression, individuality, self-reliance, self-sufficiency, independent means, private means, wealth, no allegiance, unmarried state, bachelorhood, maidenhood, franchisement, enfranchisement, citizenship, authority, statehood, nationhood, national status, unilaterality, autonomy, autarky (*or* autarchy), self-rule, self-government, independent rule, home rule, states' rights (US)

4 informality, ease, familiarity, frankness, candidness, relaxation, friendliness, casualness, candour, openness, unconstraint

5 **scope**, free scope, full scope, play, free play, full play, full opportunity, wide range, free range, manoeuvrability, room, living room, Lebensraum, living space, elbow-room, wide berth, leverage, leeway, wide margin, latitude, clearance

6 **liberality**, carte blanche, blank cheque, free hand, laxness, laxity, licence, excess, excess of freedom, libertinism, immoderation, uninhibitedness, intemperance, incontinence, free love, illicit love, lack of discipline, unruliness, abandon, abandonment, no holds barred, free fight, licentiousness, wantonness, permissiveness, permissive society, nothing in one's way, one's own way, one's own devices, the run of, plenty of rope, enough rope to hang oneself, room to swing a cat, Liberty Hall (Inf), free-for-all (Inf)

7 **free person**, citizen, free citizen, freeman, freewoman, voter, burgher, burgess, bourgeois, freedman, freedwoman, ex-slave, ex-convict, released prisoner, escapee, free agent, freelancer (*or* freelance), free spirit, individualist, rugged individualist, independent, cross-bencher, mugwump, independent voter, undecided voter, floating voter, states' righter (US), isolationist, nonpartisan, neutral, moderate, liberal, free-trader, capitalist, women's libber (Inf), liberated woman (Inf), new man (Inf), undecided (Inf), don't-know (Inf), ex-con (Inf)

8 **free-thinker**, rationalist, humanist, atheist, nonbeliever, latitudinarian, libertarian, Bohemian, hippie, libertine, eccentric, nonconformist, loner (Inf), lone wolf (Inf)

ADJECTIVES

9 **free**, freeborn, emancipated, liberated, franchised, enfranchised, authorized, constitutional, inalienable (*or* unalienable), national, unilateral, autonomous, self-governing, self-determining, self-ruling, autarkic (*or* autarchic), unconfined, unrestrained, unregulated, unhindered, unimpeded, unshackled, unfettered, unbridled, uncurbed, unbound, unchained, unmuzzled, unchecked, ungoverned, acquitted, on the loose, at large, escaped, discharged, released, freed, scot-free, privileged, exempt, nonliable, excepted, immune, noninvolved, secluded, nonaligned, nonpartisan, neutral, isolationist, noninterventional, self-regulating, self-regulatory, open, capitalistic, broad-minded, open-minded, unbiased, unprejudiced, uninfluenceable, uninfluenced, cross-bench, undecided, floating, moderate, just, tolerant, liberal, libertarian

10 **independent**, individual, self-employed, one's own boss, freelance, wildcat, free-minded, free-spirited, one's own man (*or* woman), maverick, individualistic, self-reliant, self-sufficient, self-contained, self-supporting, self-motivated, inner-directed, one's own master, unsubjected, unwedded (*or* unwed), unmarried, footloose, fancy-free, footloose and fancy free, freewheeling, free as air, free as the wind, free as a bird, left to one's own devices, ungoverned, ungovernable, anarchic, uncontrolled, uncompelled, uninfluenced, unattached, detached, indifferent, free to choose, enjoying liberty, unconventional, breakaway, dissenting, free-thinking, rationalist, rationalistic, humanist, humanistic, atheistic(al), nonbelieving, latitudinarian, Bohemian, nonconforming, eccentric, nonconformist, cowboy (Inf)

11 **ranging**, travelling, ranging freely, free-range, having full play, unconfined, untethered, unfettered, manoeuvrable

12 **unconditional**, unconditioned, unrestricted, unlimited, without strings, no strings attached, catch-as-catch-can (US), no-holds-barred, anything goes, absolute, discretionary, arbitrary, liberated, lax, excess, excessive, immoderate, loose, uninhibited, unbridled, intemperate, incontinent, unruly, abandoned, licentious, wanton, impure, permissive, wide-open (US inf), no catch (Inf), free-for-all (Inf)

13 **informal**, relaxed, casual, easy, easy-going, at ease, free-and-easy, at leisure, at home, out of harness, retired, familiar, frank, candid, open, self-expressive, free-speaking, plain-spoken, plain, uninhibited, unconstrained, spontaneous, willing, degage, unbuttoned (Inf)

VERBS

14 **be free**, go free, get free, sample freedom, breathe the air of freedom, escape, enjoy liberty, move freely, lack restraint, take French leave, have a free mind, speak freely, worship freely, publish freely, have artistic licence, have no censorship, teach freely, have freedom of choice, keep an open mind, have a liberated mind, tolerate, think freely, have free will, support human rights, support equal rights, support civil rights, support women's liberation, have a say-so (Inf)

15 **set free**, emancipate, manumit, enfranchise, franchise, liberate, release, let go, let off, excuse, grant immunity, give diplomatic immunity, exempt, except, loose, unchain, unfetter, unbind, untie, rescue, deliver, extricate, give scope, allow initiative, give one his head, allow full play, give the run of, give someone carte blanche, give someone a blank cheque, facilitate, give a free hand, give the freedom of, give one leeway, give free rein to, allow enough rope, leave one to his own devices, leave to one's own choice, live and let live, keep hands off, not interfere, not tamper, not meddle, not butt in, let sleeping dogs lie, not cramp one's style (Inf)

16 **be independent**, have a will of one's own, go one's own way, have one's way, have (*or* do) it one's own way, use one's own initiative, fend for oneself, shift for oneself, become a free agent, freelance, stand alone, stand up for one's rights, stand on one's own two feet, stay in control, have the ball at one's feet, have authority, have self-reliance, have independent means, stay unmarried, ask no favours, call no man master, suit oneself, please oneself, do as one pleases, do as one chooses, do what one likes, vote independent, remain neutral, do one's own thing, follow one's bent, roam, stray, drift, drop out, paddle one's own canoe, act eccentrically, live in a bohemian way, go it alone (Inf)

17 **be informal**, take it easy, feel at home, make oneself at home, feel free, feel at liberty, let one's hair down, show candour

18 **have scope**, have the run of, have the freedom of, range, have room to breathe, have play, have a free hand, have elbowroom, have one's head, have plenty of rope, have enough rope to hang oneself

19 **liberalize**, live immoderately, have a free hand, have

carte blanche, have a blank cheque, lack restraint, let oneself go, let go, permit oneself, make bold to, take liberties, presume, make free with, cut loose, run wild, sow one's wild oats, have one's fling, let one's hair down, go too far, pull out all the stops, lack discipline, support free love, go all out (Inf), go flat out (Inf), let it all hang out (Inf)

ADVERBS

20 **freely**, free, with immunity, autonomously, independently, alone, by oneself, individually, individualistically, on one's own initiative, on one's own account, of one's own accord, of one's own volition, of one's own free will, at one's own discretion, on one's own responsibility, with self-reliance, with selfmotivation, free-mindedly, broad-mindedly, open-mindedly, tolerantly, moderately, neutrally, justly, without affiliation, indifferently, with an indifferent attitude, rationalistically, atheistically, eccentrically, on one's own say-so (Inf), all on one's lonesome (Inf)

21 **excessively**, with excess, with full play, unconditionally, with no holds barred, with no strings attached, arbitrarily, immoderately, loosely, without control, without restraint, without stint, unreservedly, with abandon, intemperately, incontinently, licentiously, wantonly, impurely, permissively

22 **informally**, in an informal way, casually, easily, familiarly, frankly, candidly, with candour, freely, openly, plainly, spontaneously, willingly

251 Restraint

The workers have nothing to lose but their chains. Karl Marx.

NOUNS

1 **restraint**, constraint, suppression, repression, strictness, coercion, hindrance, impediment, obstacle, stumbling block, retardation, deceleration, slowness, slowing down, stopping, prevention, control, strict control, curb, check, veto, ban, bar, blackball, prohibition, restriction, restraint, legal restraint, injunction, interdict, Official Secrets Act, D-notice, press laws, severity, discipline, penalty, fine, punishment, authority, duress, pressure, censorship, subdual, putting down, quelling, quashing, suppressant, squelching, smothering, stifling, throttling, crushing, smashing, crackdown, limitation, allotment, stipulation, qualification, requirement, limiting factor, limit, speed limit, limitations, retrenchment, constriction, squeeze, cuts, curtailment, circumscription, exclusive rights, exclusivity, copyright, circle, charmed circle, demarcation, restricted area, no-go area, off-limits area (US), cramping one's style (Inf)

► *128 Exclusion; 166 Limit; 191 Contraction; 226 Stopping; 358 Obliteration; 378 Obstruction; 387 Subjection; 396 Authority; 399 Veto; 647 Severity; 663 Obedience; 693 Information; 740 Publication; 814 Punishment*

2 **economic restraint**, economic pressure, rationing, ration, freeze, price freeze, pay freeze, price control, credit squeeze, rate-capping, restrictive practice, restraint of trade, monopoly, cartel, closed shop, intervention, interventionism, protectionism, price-fixing, protection racket, mercantilism, mercantile system tariff, protective tariff, tariff wall, embargo, Anti-Trust laws (US)

► *13 Economics; 14 Finance*

3 **self-restraint**, self-control, self-discipline, discipline, temperance, continence, abstinence, abstemiousness, asceticism, ascesis, spartanism, moderation, inhibition, introversion, formality, reserved nature, reserve, modesty, shyness, quietness, embarrassment, stiffness

► *674 Modesty; 684 Self-Restraint; 685 Moderation; 730 Voicelessness*

4 **detention**, quarantine, blockade, siege, starving out, guarding, care, custodianship, charge, ward, custody, protective custody, impoundment, restriction on movement, curfew, remand, refusal of bail, arrest, house arrest, sentence, incarceration, imprisonment, internment, confinement, solitary confinement, captivity, kidnapping, bondage, slavery, servitude, durance (Lit), immurement (Lit), time (Inf), BOT (balance of time) (US inf), stretch (Inf), porridge (Inf), lag (Inf), bird (Inf)

► *381 Attack; 815 Prison*

5 **means of restraint**, diet, fast, ban, veto, damper, governor, drag, cramp, clamp, restraining hand, gag, muzzle, leash, lead, tether, hobble, reins, bridle, bit, halter, harness, collar, yoke, corset, girdle, straitjacket, fetters, bonds, irons, chains, shackles, ball and chain, handcuffs, manacles, trammels, bilboes, stocks, pillory, cuffs (Inf), bracelets (Inf)

6 **lawmaker**, legislator, judge, member of parliament (MP), District Attorney (DA), policeman (*or* policewoman), enforcer, censor, monopolist, protectionist, restrictionist, disciplinarian, dictator, tyrant, kidnapper, ascetic, Spartan, interventionalist, mercantilist, monetarist, warder, warden (US), jailer, prison guard, screw (Inf)

► *16 Law*

7 **charge**, ward, patient, shut-in, hostage, prisoner, jailbird, inmate, convict, con (Inf), old lag (Inf)

► *35 Medicine*

VERBS

8 **restrain**, constrain, suppress, repress, hold back, hold down, oppress, close down, coerce, hinder, impede, bottle up, clog up, retard, decelerate, slow, stop, put a stop to, vote down, veto, blackball, brake, put the brakes on, act as a brake, prevent, pull back, control, curb, check, hold in check, ban, bar, prohibit, restrict, put a damper on, damper, drag, cramp, clamp down on, clamp, issue an injunction, interdict, regulate, discipline, keep order, police, patrol, impose a fine, punish, pressure, censor, black out, subdue, put down, crack down, quell, quash, squelch, smother, stifle, throttle, crush, smash, allot, stipulate, require qualifications, list requirements, limit, enforce a speed limit, retrench, constrict, squeeze, cut, curtail, demarcate, draw the line, circumscribe, keep within bounds, stop from spreading, hem in, box in, hold at bay, localize, hold exclusive rights, copyright, join a charmed circle, exclude, keep out, rope out, sit on (Inf), put the lid on (Inf), cramp one's style (Inf)

9 **economize**, ration, freeze prices, control prices, freeze pay, squeeze credit, cap rates, restrain trade, monopolize, form a cartel, operate a closed shop, intervene, restrict

supplies, restrict consumption, hold down inflation, protect, restrict imports, impose a tariff, impose an embargo

10 **restrain oneself**, show self-restraint, control oneself, demonstrate self-control, deny oneself, hold oneself back, hold back, diet, slim, fast, stay within one's limits, know when to stop, keep calm, keep quiet, say nothing, abstain, take the pledge, live in a spartan way, live like a monk (*or* nun), take a cold bath (*or* shower), go on the wagon (Inf), keep one's wool (Inf), keep a stiff upper lip (Inf), keep one's shirt on (Inf), keep one's hair on (Inf), keep one's cool (Inf), stay cool (Inf), cool out (US inf)

11 **detain**, quarantine, put into quarantine, blockade, block, siege, besiege, starve out, guard, take custody of, protect, impound, restrict one's movement, impose a curfew, remand, refuse bail, arrest, make an arrest, put under arrest, take into custody, apprehend, seize, sentence, incarcerate, imprison, send to prison, throw in prison, take prisoner, intern, confine, keep under lock and key, keep behind bars, make captive, kidnap, take hostage, hold in captivity, hold incommunicado, hold, put in bondage, nab (Inf), collar (Inf), haul in (Inf), run in (Inf), serve time (Inf), serve a stretch (Inf), do porridge (Inf), lag (Inf), do bird (Inf), pinch (Inf), nick (Inf), send up the river (US inf), go to the big house (US inf)

12 **gag**, muzzle, silence, interdict, shout down, leash, lead, tether, hobble, rein in, keep a tight rein on, put a ball and chain on, harness, collar, yoke, girdle, straitjacket, fetter, bind, tie up (*or* down), tie hand and foot, tie, throw in irons, chain up (*or* down), chain, shackle, handcuff, manacle

ADJECTIVES

13 **restraining**, restrained, under restraint, constrained, kept under constraint, under the thumb, suppressive, suppressing, oppressive, suppressed, strict, coercive, slow, preventive, controllable, controlling, controlled, under control, under remission, strictly controlled, prohibitive, prohibited, conditional, restrictive, restricting, restricted, tied down, with strings attached, in check, injunctive, interdictive, severe, disciplined, punished, authoritative, pressurized, censorial, censorious, censoring, censored, banned, stifling, limiting, limited, required, constrictive, narrow, cramped, kept on a lead, circumscriptive, exclusive, copyrighted, rationed, frozen, rate-capped, monopolistic, interventional, protective, embargoed

14 **self-restrained**, temperate, self-disciplined, self-controlled, dieting, fasting, continent, abstinent, abstemious, ascetic, Spartan, moderate, inhibiting, inhibited, introversive, formal, reserved, quiet, modest, shy, embarrassing, embarrassed, pent-up, stiff, uptight (Inf), cool (Inf), ultracool (US inf)

15 **detained**, quarantined, shut-in, confined to bed, housebound, snowbound, fogbound, besieged, custodial, arrested, under arrest, under house arrest, sentenced, incarcerated, imprisoned, in custody, on remand, confined, captive, in captivity, kidnapped, enslaved, gagged, muzzled, in bonds, in irons, serving a sentence, doing time (Inf), doing porridge (Inf), up the river (US inf), in the big house (US inf)

ADVERBS

16 **under restraints**, strictly, coercively, slowly, preventively, controllably, with controls, under controls, prohibitively, conditionally, with conditions, restrictively, under restrictions, interdictively, severely, authoritatively, censorial, censoriously, circumscriptively, within limits, within bounds, exclusively, protectively, while confined to bed, while in captivity

17 **with self-restraint**, temperately, abstemiously, by abstaining, moderately, in moderation, formally, as a formality, modestly, shyly, embarrassingly, to one's embarrassment, to one's chagrin, stiffly

252 Safety

Out of this nettle, danger, we pluck this flower, safety. William Shakespeare.

NOUNS

1 **safety**, safeness, security, protection, invulnerability, impregnability, immunity, lack of danger, charmed life, lack of risk, harmlessness, safety in numbers, safe place, safe distance, wide berth, avoidance, regained safety, danger past, all clear, coast clear, storm blown over, safe job, secure position, permanent post, social security, welfare, welfare state, Medicaid (US), Medicare (US), National Health Service, guarantee, warranty, warrant, certainty, sense of security, assurance, confidence, faith, means of escape, back door, opt-out clause, escape clause, rescue, negotiated release, deliverance, nanny state (Inf), safety valve (Inf)

► *2 Sociology; 389 Escape; 390 Deliverance; 452 Certainty; 634 Avoidance*

2 **protection**, safeguard, precaution, security system, electronic surveillance, alarm system, burglar alarm, preventive measure, security check, vetting, positive vetting, Big Brother, surveillance, safe conduct, passport, pass, permit, escort, convoy, guard, armed force, defence, defences, sure defence, bulwark, bastion, tower of strength, moat, ditch, palisade, stockade, haven, sanctuary, asylum, refuge, safe house, shelter, battered women's shelter, homeless shelter, orphan's home, orphanage, care, keeping, custody, charge, safe hands, safekeeping, grasp, grip, embrace, ward, watch and ward (US), patronage, support, aid, sponsorship, good offices, auspices, aegis, fatherly eye, tutelage, protectorate, guardianship, wardship, wardenship (US), custodianship, protective custody, surrogacy, anchor, sheet anchor, shield, breastplate, panoply, armour plate, armour, means of protection, deterrent, weapon, sanitary precaution, hygiene, immunization, vaccination, inoculation, prophylaxis, contraception, *cordon sanitaire* (Fr), quarantine, isolation, segregation, seclusion, trade tariff, insurance, life insurance, life assurance, fire insurance, car insurance, household insurance, surety, buffer, cushion, screen, cover, umbrella, shelter, savings, savings account, collateral, nest egg, something for a rainy day, provision, store

► *165 Enclosure; 257 Hygiene; 359 Preservation; 360 Retention; 384 Defence; 392 Help; 436 Provisions; 587 Weapon; 616 Caution; 665 Carefulness; 680 Thrift*

3 **protector**, protectress, guardian, mentor, tutor, guardian angel, patron saint, tutelary god (*or* goddess), liege lord, feudal lord, patron, patroness, benefactor, benefactress, fairy godmother, champion, knight in shining armour, white knight, chaperon (*or* chaperone), governess, duenna, nurse, nursemaid, nanny, mammy (US), sitter, baby-sitter, child-minder, companion, keeper, defender, preserver, shepherd, coastguard, lifeguard, lifesaver, bodyguard, minder, Secret Service (US), doorman, vigilante, Guardian Angels (US), Neighbourhood Watch, conservator, custodian, curator, warden, warder, watcher, surveillant, lookout, watch, watchman, night watchman, guard, security guard, security man (*or* woman), sentry, sentinel, garrison, picket, armed guard, vanguard, security forces, Home Guard, Territorial Army, Territorial, militia, customs official, park keeper, gamekeeper, forester, (forest) ranger (US), firewatcher, fire fighter, fireman, police, policeman, policewoman, police officer, police constable, PC, WPC, police sergeant, detective, patrol, patrolman, riot policeman, sheriff, drug enforcement officer, vice squad member, private investigator, private detective, watchdog, guard dog, sniffer dog, police dog, Cerberus, Argus, strong-arm man (Inf), bouncer (Inf), copper (Inf), cop (Inf), bobby (Inf), private eye (Inf), weekend warrior (US inf)

► *359 Preservation; 384 Defence*

4 safety device, means of safety, safeguard, protection, precautionary steps, precautions, alarm, burglar alarm, crowd control methods, crush barrier, police barrier, crash barrier, guardrail, railing, pilot (US), cowcatcher (US), mail, chain mail, armour, bulletproof vest, bulletproof car, bulletproof glass, shatterproof glass, toughened glass, fail-safe device, fail-safe system, deterrent, Star Wars, Strategic Defense Initiative (SDI), respirator, oxygen tent, mask, gas mask, safety goggles, earmuffs, ear plugs, safety chain, dead man's handle (*or* pedal), safety catch, safety lock, bolt, dead bolt, deadlock, safety valve, safety pin, safety razor, safety match, lightning conductor, fuse, circuit breaker, earth, fire alarm, smoke alarm, fire extinguisher, fire blanket, sprinkler system, fire escape, fire door, fire wall, crash helmet, safety helmet, football helmet (US), protective clothing, seat belt, safety belt, safety harness, shoulder harness, air bag, ejector seat, escape hatch, means of escape, parachute, safety net, lifeboat, rubber dinghy, life raft, life buoy, lifeline, preserver, life belt, life vest (US), life jacket, buoyancy jacket, buoyancy aid, Mae West, water wings, breeches buoy, rope, plank, anchor, sheet anchor, kedge, grapnel, grappling iron, killick (*or* killock), drogue, lead, reins, brake, fetter, bar, lock, key, stopper, ballast, mole, breakwater, groyne, embankment, sea wall, lighthouse, lightship, jury mast, jury rig, emergency part, spare part, spare, extra

► *309 Closure; 384 Defence; 551 Dress; 587 Weapon*

5 refuge, sanctuary, asylum, retreat, safe retreat, safe place, place of safety, traffic island, pedestrian crossing, safety zone (US), zebra crossing, pelican crossing, resort, recourse, last resort, hole, foxhole, dugout, pit, bolt hole, trench, underground shelter, concrete shelter, (nuclear) bunker, blockhouse, bomb shelter, air-raid shelter, Anderson shelter, fallout (*or* nuclear) shelter, burrow, hideout, hiding place, priest hole, cache, secret place, lap, bed, bedroom, hearth, home, private space, inviolable place, privacy, sanctum, chamber, monastery, nunnery, cloister, cell, hermitage, ivory tower, sanctum sanctorum, holy of holies, temple, ark, acropolis, citadel, wall, rampart, bulwark, parapet, battlement, fortification, bastion, stronghold, fortress, fastness, fort, keep, ward, rock, Rock of Gibraltar, Rock of Ages, pillar, tower, tower of strength, mainstay, buttress, prop, support, funk hole (Inf), hidy-hole (*or* hidey-hole) (Inf)

► *384 Defence; 413 Support; 565 Habitat; 736 Concealment; 815 Prison*

ADJECTIVES

6 safe, secure, protected, guarded, defended, not in danger, not at risk, assured, sure, certain, sound, safe and sound, safe as houses, snug, spared, preserved, intact, undamaged, unharmed, uninjured, unhurt, unscathed, with a whole skin, whole, garrisoned, well-defended, insured, covered, immunized, vaccinated, inoculated, disinfected, salubrious, hygienic, in safety, in security, under guard, on the safe side, on sure ground, on home ground, on the home stretch, on terra firma, in harbour, in port, at anchor, above water, out of danger, out of the wood, out of harm's way, clear, in the clear, unaccused, unthreatened, unmolested, unexposed, under shelter, sheltered, shielded, screened, patronized, under the protection of, under the wing of, in safe hands, in safe keeping, held, in custody, behind bars, under lock and key, imprisoned, reliable, dependable, trustworthy, guaranteed, under warrant, warranted, benign, innocent, innocent as a lamb, tame, harmless, innocuous, unthreatening, not dangerous, without risk, risk-free, unhazardous, nonflammable, nontoxic, unpolluted, edible, eatable, drinkable, potable, good, home free (US inf), home and dry (Inf), home and hosed (Aus inf), in the clink (Inf), in the hoosegow (US inf)

► *257 Hygiene; 359 Preservation; 452 Certainty; 797 Good; 799 Honour; 815 Prison*

7 invulnerable, immune, impregnable, sacrosanct, inexpugnable, unassailable, unattackable, ungettable (*or* ungetable), unbreakable, unchallengeable, made in heaven, founded on a rock, built like a fortress, defensible, tenable, strong, proof, foolproof, fail-safe, mothproof, childproof, weatherproof, waterproof, showerproof, leakproof, rustproof, gasproof, shatterproof, fireproof, bulletproof, bombproof, armoured, steel-clad, panoplied, snug, tight, seaworthy, airworthy, shrink-wrapped, vacuum-packed, vacuum-sealed, hermetically sealed, freeze-dried, frozen

► *336 Strength*

8 tutelary, protective, custodial, guardian, surrogate, shepherdlike, watchful, vigilant, keeping, guarding, protecting, preserving, prophylactic, antiseptic, disinfectant, hygienic

► *257 Hygiene; 359 Preservation; 665 Carefulness*

VERBS

9 be safe, be out of danger, protect oneself, defend oneself, take precautions, play safe, be on the safe side, hedge one's bets, take no chances, demand assurances, seek safety, find safety, reach safety, come through, survive, save one's skin, keep a whole skin, live to fight another day, escape, run away, land on one's feet, keep one's head above water, weather the storm, ride it out, see it through, be saved by the bell, bear (*or* live) a charmed life, have nine lives, stay at home, be (*or* stay) under cover, have a roof over one's head, take refuge, hide, lie low, go underground, keep a safe distance, give a wide berth, shy away, avoid, save one's ass (Inf), save one's bacon, go on the lam (US inf), cut and run (Inf), do a runner (Inf), beat a retreat (Inf), skedaddle (Inf), shorten sail (Inf), run for port (Inf)

▶ *389 Escape; 634 Avoidance; 736 Concealment*

10 protect, safeguard, keep safe, guard, defend, spare, show mercy, support, champion, stand up for, vouch for, stand surety for, go bail for, cover up for, provide an alibi for, shield, harbour, rescue, save, deliver, patronize, grant (political) asylum, afford sanctuary, keep, conserve, preserve, treasure, hoard, store, lock away (*or* up), hide away, hide, conceal, put in a safe place, keep under cover, warehouse, garage, take in, house, shelter, imprison, keep in custody, keep behind bars, keep locked up, ward, watch over, care for, look after, mind, mother, take under one's wing, nurse, tend, foster, cherish, have charge of, take charge of, keep an eye on, monitor, chaperon (*or* chaperone), immunize, inoculate, vaccinate, pasteurize, chlorinate, fluoridate, fluorinate, disinfect, sanitate, sanitize, assure, give assurances, promise, give vows, warrant, guarantee, make certain, cushion, buffer, ensconce, enfold, embrace, envelop, cocoon, wrap, enclose, insulate, earth, cover, shroud, cloak, shade, screen, make safe, secure, fortify, strengthen, entrench, fence in, fence round, arm, armour, armour-plate, convoy, escort, shepherd, flank, garrison, mount guard, keep order, police, patrol, honcho (US inf), ride shotgun (US inf)

▶ *165 Enclosure; 257 Hygiene; 336 Strength; 359 Preservation; 384 Defence; 390 Deliverance; 392 Help; 436 Provisions; 452 Certainty; 627 Pity; 665 Carefulness; 736 Concealment*

ADVERBS

11 safely, securely, in safety, with impunity, without risk, out of danger, out of harm's way, under cover, in the lee of, under the aegis of, under lock and key, invulnerably, impregnably, protectively, watchfully, hygienically

253 Security

Probably the only place where a man can feel really secure is in a maximum security prison, except for the imminent threat of release. Germaine Greer.

NOUNS

1 protection, safety, safeness, safekeeping, invulnerability, impregnability, immunity, secure position, asylum, sanctuary, shelter, refuge, cover, mainstay, anchor, support, hope, pillar of strength, defence, safeguard, shield, security system, alarm system, deterrent, sense of security, reliance, faith, confidence, courage, national insurance, health insurance, BUPA, Blue Cross (US), National Health Service (NHS), Medicare (US), unemployment benefits, old-age security, social security, welfare, welfare state, retirement benefits, the dole (Inf)

▶ *252 Safety; 359 Preservation; 384 Defence; 613 Courage; 616 Caution; 665 Carefulness*

2 promise, pledge, word, word of honour, assurance, insurance, credit, honour, recognizance, warrant, warranty, guarantee, underwriting, certificate, bond, coupon, passport, visa, permit, authority, authorization, title deed, gilt-edged security, share, debenture, mortgage, deed, insurance policy, will, last will and testament, collateral, indemnity, covenant, receipt, IOU, counterfoil, stub, cheque stub, ticket stub, ticket, pawn ticket, docket, proof of purchase, acquittance, quittance, authentication, verification, endorsement, stamp, seal, signature

▶ *716 Evidence; 744 Record; 755 Contract; 756 Promise; 785 Payment*

3 security officer, protector, sentinel, sentry, watchman, night watchman, watch, warner, bodyguard, lifeguard, policeman, policewoman, police officer, police constable, special constable, highway patrolman (US), bobby (Inf), copper (Inf), cop (Inf), pig (Inf), Smokey (the bear) (US inf), bear (US inf), rozzer (Inf), flatfoot (Inf), Old Bill (*or* the Bill) (Inf), the fuzz (Inf), bizzy (Inf), ploddy (Inf)

4 security forces, national defence, armed forces, army, navy, air force, marines, police force, private security company, Securicor™, Brinks™ (US), Neighbourhood Watch

▶ *586 Combatant*

5 safe, safety deposit box, wall safe, lockbox, vault, bank vault

ADJECTIVES

6 secure, safe, sure, without risk, safe and sound, protective, protected, sheltered, invulnerable, impregnable, locked away, locked up, immune, safeguarded, shielded, deterrent, safe as houses (Inf), safe as the Bank of England (Inf)

7 guaranteed, warranted, under warranty, certified, authenticated, assured, certain, reliant, unshaken, gilt-edged, covered, insured, mortgaged, on mortgage, guaranteed, covenanted, pledged, promised, pawned, in hock (US inf), hocked (US inf)

8 accomplished, done, won, completed, sewn up (Inf), under one's belt (Inf), in the bag (Inf)

▶ *246 Success*

9 fast, fixed, sound, steadfast, stable, steady, immovable, irremovable

▶ *228 Stability*

VERBS

10 secure, make safe, protect, keep order, police, patrol, guard, safekeep, keep safe and sound, lock away, lock up, keep under lock and key, offer refuge, offer shelter, anchor, support, defend, safeguard, shield, give a sense of security

11 promise, pledge, give one's word (of honour), give one's IOU, assure, insure, give personal recognizance, warrant, guarantee, act as guarantor, act as security, stand (*or* go) surety, stand (*or* go) bail, vouch for, endorse, seal, stamp, countersign, indemnify, underwrite, safeguard, make certain

12 certify, authenticate, cover, insure, mortgage, pledge, promise, verify, offer collateral, give security

13 secure one's objective, accomplish, reach one's goal, win through, win, succeed, complete, pull it off, bring it off, sew up (Inf), have under one's belt (Inf), have in the bag (Inf)

14 make fast, make firm, fortify, stabilize, steady, strengthen, fix to, secure to, nail down, screw down, make sound, make steadfast, make immovable

15 reserve, make a reservation, book, order, pay in advance, leave a deposit

▶ *744 Record*

ADVERBS

16 surely, safely, in a safe manner, without risk, safe and sound, protectively, invulnerably, impregnably, reliably, assuredly, verifiably, with assurance

17 fastly, fixedly, in a fixed position, soundly, steadfastly, immovably, without moving

254 Danger

Dangers by being despised grow great. Edmund Burke.

Believe me! The secret of reaping the greatest fruitfulness and the greatest enjoyment from life is to live dangerously! Friedrich Wilhelm Nietzsche.

ADJECTIVES

1 dangerous, perilous, treacherous, hazardous, risky, beset with perils, fraught with danger, unknown, uncertain, unlit, venturous, venturesome, difficult, chancy, tricky, snaggy, speculative, crucial, critical, serious, nasty, ugly, menacing, threatening, ominous, foreboding, alarming, frightening, at the boiling point, at the flash point, at stake, in question, inflammable, flammable, explosive, radioactive, toxic, poisonous, life-threatening, deadly, harmful, unhealthy, infectious, unhygienic, sticky (Inf), dicey (Inf), dodgy (Inf), iffy (Inf), hairy (Inf), clutch (US inf)

▶ *107 Chance; 453 Uncertainty; 612 Fear*

2 unsafe, not safe, treacherous, untrustworthy, unreliable, doubtful, shaky, slippery, insecure, unsecure, unsound, precarious, unbalanced, unsteady, unstable, tottering, top-heavy, tumbledown, ramshackle, dilapidated, rickety, frail, falling to pieces, crumbling, condemned, jerry-built, shoddy, gimcrack, crazy, weak, built on sand, on shaky foundations, leaky, waterlogged, critical, delicate, ticklish, risky, heart-stopping, nerve-racking, touch and go, hanging by a thread, trembling in the balance, teetering on the edge, on the edge, on the brink, on the verge, last-second, last-minute, dicey, dicky (*or* dickey) (Inf)

▶ *245 Deterioration; 337 Weakness; 453 Uncertainty*

3 vulnerable, unprotected, undefended, not secure, in danger, not immune, liable, susceptible, open to, wide-open, exposed, naked, bare, uncovered, unarmoured, unfortified, expugnable, pregnable, helpless, at the whim of, at the mercy of, defenceless, unarmed, isolated, deserted, abandoned, stranded, left high and dry, out on a limb, unsupported, unshielded, shelterless, guideless, unattended, unguarded, unescorted, unshepherded, unflanked, unwarned, unaware, naive, not on guard, off one's guard, unprepared, unready

▶ *102 Possibility; 335 Powerlessness; 337 Weakness; 552 Undress*

4 endangered, in danger, in peril, at risk, in jeopardy, in double jeopardy (US), slipping, drifting, on the rocks, in shallow water, on dangerous ground, on slippery ground, on thin ice, in a bad way, in a tight corner, in a bind, surrounded, trapped, at bay, cornered, with one's back to the wall, under siege, under fire, in the lion's den, thrown to the lions, on the razor's edge, in a catch-22 situation, caught both ways, between two fires, between two chairs, between the devil and the deep blue sea, between a rock and a hard place (US), between Scylla and Charybdis, on the run, not out of the wood, at the last stand, reduced to the last extremity, facing death, facing the firing squad, under sentence, condemned, with a noose round one's neck, awaiting execution, on death row (US), in a jam (Inf), in the soup (Inf), in the hot seat (Inf)

NOUNS

5 danger, peril, jeopardy, risk, hazard, dangerousness, perilousness, riskiness, hazardousness, treacherousness, treachery, dangerous situation, unhealthy situation, biohazard, desperate situation, perilous state, parlous state (Lit), shadow of death, jaws of death, lion's mouth, dragon's lair, dire straits, predicament, emergency, urgency, crisis, insecurity, unsoundness, ticklishness, ticklish business, precariousness, slipperiness, shakiness, unsteadiness, uncertainty, acute dilemma, razor's edge, black spot, deathtrap, snag, pitfall, trap, surprise attack, ambush, endangerment, imperilment, hazarding, venturesomeness, daring, overdaring, rashness, gambling, venture, risky venture, dangerous course, leap in the dark, throw of the dice, spin of the wheel, turn of a card, slippery slope, road to ruin, impending disaster, sword of Damocles, menace, threat, sense of danger, apprehension, anxiety, nervousness, fear, narrow escape, hairbreadth escape, near tragedy, near miss, near thing (Inf), close shave (Inf)

▶ *107 Chance; 264 Difficulty; 354 Undertaking; 379 Trap; 381 Attack; 389 Escape; 453 Uncertainty; 612 Fear; 615 Rashness; 736 Concealment*

6 danger signal, cause for alarm, night sounds, strange noise, gunshot, scream, sudden pain, snarling dog, ticking parcel, rocks ahead, breakers ahead, storm brewing, gathering storm, gathering clouds, thick fog, rising river, cloud on the horizon

▶ *711 Warning*

7 vulnerability, liability, susceptibility, nonimmunity, openness, exposure, nakedness, pregnability, helplessness, defencelessness, lack of protection, naivety, innocence, instability, insecurity, easy target, sitting target, exposed part, exposed flank, vulnerable point, undefended part, breach in the wall, chink in the armour, Achilles' heel, weakness, tender spot, soft spot, soft underbelly, unsoundness, failing, flaw, defect, imperfection, defect of character, human failing, feet of clay, tragic flaw, fatal flaw, sitting duck (*or* target) (Inf)

▶ *231 Imperfection; 335 Powerlessness; 337 Weakness; 419 Softness*

VERBS

8 be in danger, run the risk of, run into danger, enter the lion's den, put one's head in the lion's mouth, ride a tiger, walk into a trap, tread on dangerous ground, be on slippery ground, skate on thin ice, be out of one's depth, sail close (*or* near) to the wind, play with fire, feel the ground slip away, feel the ground give way, be up against it, have to run for it, hang by a thread, tremble in the balance, hover on the brink, teeter on the edge, totter, slip, slide, tumble, fall, get lost, wander away, stray, go astray, play with dynamite (Inf), sit on a powder keg (Inf), sleep on a volcano (Inf), lean on a broken reed (Inf)

▶ *305 Descent; 325 Deviation*

9 face danger, face death, take one's life in one's hands, expose oneself, lay oneself open to, stand in the breach, risk, defy, look danger in the face, look down a gun barrel, face heavy odds, have the odds (stacked) against one, have the deck (*or* cards) stacked against one, have one's back to the wall, engage in a forlorn hope, challenge fate, tempt fate, tempt providence, court disaster, take a tiger by the tail, put one's head in the lion's mouth, play Russian roulette, dice with death, run the gauntlet, come under fire, venture, dare, hazard, gamble, take a chance, take a flier (US), stick one's neck out

▶ *107 Chance; 613 Courage; 615 Rashness; 661 Defiance*

10 endanger, expose to danger, put in danger, put at risk, put in jeopardy, put in double jeopardy (US), jeopardize, imperil, compromise, hazard, risk, stake, gamble, venture, drive headlong, run on the rocks, drive dangerously, drive recklessly, drive without due care and attention, put someone in fear of his (*or* her) life, threaten one's life, threaten danger, loom, forebode, bode ill, menace, intimidate, threaten, hold over one's head, run one hard, overtake, outdo

▶ *107 Chance; 612 Fear*

ADVERBS

11 dangerously, treacherously, perilously, hazardously, riskily, precariously, in the face of death, on the brink, naively, unawares, recklessly, rashly, ominously, threateningly, menacingly, vulnerably, helplessly, defencelessly

255 Purity

I'm as pure as the driven slush. Tallulah Bankhead.

NOUNS

1 purity, pureness, cleanness, cleanliness, freshness, clearness, clarity, spotlessness, immaculacy, stainlessness, sinlessness, innocence, faultlessness, flawlessness, perfection, moral purity, morals, morality, high moral tone, high-mindedness, moral rectitude, virtue, decency, honesty, honour, integrity, piety, virginity, chastity, delicacy, propriety, good taste, simplicity, modesty, pudency, false modesty, primness, priggishness, prudery, prudishness, censorship, bowdlerization, expurgation, euphemism, coyness, sanctimoniousness, sanctimony, Puritanism, Grundyism, Victorian values

▶ *230 Perfection; 256 Cleanness; 549 Refinement; 674 Modesty; 684 Self-Restraint; 795 Morality; 803 Virtue; 805 Innocence*

2 purification, cleansing, cleaning, washing, lustration, Asperges, purgation, washing out, flushing, dialysis, purging, clearance, riddance, expulsion, elimination, ventilation, airing, fumigation, deodorization, antisepsis, disinfection, sterilization, decontamination, disinfestation, delousing, sanitation

▶ *257 Hygiene; 560 Excretion*

3 purifier, cleanser, cleaner, cleansing agent, soda, washing soda, carbolic acid, detergent, washing powder, soapflakes, washing-up liquid, dishwashing liquid (US), soap, soap and water, water, hot water, shampoo, mouthwash, gargle, toothpaste, dentifrice, lotion, hand lotion, hand cream, cleansing cream, cold cream, vanishing cream, disinfectant, deodorant, air freshener, filter, water filter, strainer

4 purgative, purgative agent, purge, cathartic, enema, diuretic, nauseant, emetic, laxative, aperient, evacuant

5 pure person, saint, virgin, maid, maiden, virgo intacta, vestal, vestal virgin, spinster, old maid, religious celibate, monk, nun, Puritan, Quaker, paragon, paragon of virtue, Lancelot, knight in shining armour, angel (Inf), goody-goody (Inf), wowser (Aus and NZ inf)

▶ *7 Religion*

6 prude, prig, Victorian, moral guardian, Mrs Grundy, Mary Whitehouse, censor, Watch Committee

▶ *670 Disapproval; 795 Morality*

7 purebred, thoroughbred, pedigree

8 simplicity, simpleness, homogeneity, uniformity, oneness, absoluteness, bedrock, indivisibility, essence, no mixture, no dilution

VERBS

9 be pure, have no sin, have no faults, live purely, live honourably, keep a high moral tone, have morals, have integrity, have (*or* lead a life of) virtue, stay virtuous, stay innocent, live like a monk, live like a nun, live like a Puritan, resist temptation, control oneself, keep to (*or* on) the straight and narrow (path)

10 purify, clean, cleanse, purge, wash, lave, lustrate, purify oneself, wash clean, wipe clean, freshen, fumigate, deodorize, edulcorate, ventilate, desalinate, decontaminate, disinfect, chlorinate, pasteurize, sanitize, sanitate, sterilize, free from impurities, refine, sublimate, distil, strain, filter, percolate, leach, lixiviate, sift, sieve, winnow, depurate, clarify, clear, skim, scum, despumate, rack, decarbonize, decoke, elutriate, flush, dialyse, catheterize, wash out, drain, flush out, clean out, censor, expurgate, blue-pencil, bowdlerize

11 simplify, make simple, make uniform, unify, make one, reduce to its constituent parts, reduce to its elements, not mix, not dilute, unscramble, unravel, sort out, weed out, eliminate, get rid of, expel, eject, clear out, exclude

ADJECTIVES

12 morally pure, pure, virtuous, righteous, decent, moral, chaste, virginal, faithful, high-minded, unerring, perfect, noble, spotless, sinless, innocent, uncorrupt, uncorrupted, honourable, angelic, modest, prudish, prim, priggish, coy, euphemistic, Christian, sanctimonious, Puritanical, Victorian, on the side of the angels

13 pure, purified, cleansed, clean, cleanly, spotless, stainless, unblemished, immaculate, unmuddied, unsullied, untarnished, unspoilt, unpolluted, uncontaminated, unadulterated, undiluted, neat, unfortified, unmedicated, unflavoured, unfragranced, unspiced, unseasoned, uncoloured, undyed, untinged, free from, clear, clarified, refined, blank, purebred, thoroughbred, pedigreed

14 purified, cleansed, cleaned, clean, spick-and-span, shining, shiny, polished, scrubbed, snowy, white, snow-white, pure as the driven snow, dainty, nice, fresh, fresh as a daisy, bright (*or* clean) as a new pin, bright, deodorized, disinfected, aseptic, antiseptic, sterilized, sterile, ritually clean, kosher (Judaism), halal

15 purifying, cleansing, purificatory, lustral, hygienic, sterilizing, germicidal, sanitary, disinfectant, detergent, purging, purgative, purgatory, ablutionary

16 simple, one, single, homogeneous, unified, all of a piece, monolithic, uniform, undifferentiated, indivisible, elemental, entire, nothing but, unadulterated, undefiled, unalloyed, uncompounded, uncombined, unblended, mere, sheer, utter, irreducible, basic, fundamental, elementary, intrinsic, simplified, unmixed, unmingled, pure and simple, no frills, unravelled, disentangled, intelligible, comprehensible

17 direct, unsophisticated, simplistic, homespun, straight, straight from the shoulder, unqualified, unmitigated, wholehearted, single-minded, downright, sincere, unpretentious, honest, honourable, unaffected, undisguised, naked, bare

ADVERBS

18 virtuously, righteously, decently, morally, chastely, virginally, faithfully, with faith, high-mindedly, unerringly, perfectly, in a perfect way, nobly, innocently, in all innocence, uncorruptibly, honourably, angelically, modestly, prudishly, primly, priggishly, coyly, sanctimoniously, Puritanically, like a Puritan

19 purely, cleanly, spotlessly, without a spot, immaculately, aseptically, antiseptically, sterilely, hygienically, purgatively

20 homogenously, irreducibly, fundamentally, intrinsically, directly, in a direct fashion, simplistically, wholeheartedly, with all one's heart, single-mindedly, sincerely, unpretentiously, without pretence, honestly, honourably

256 Cleanness

NOUNS

1 cleanness, keeping clean, freedom from dirt, absence of dirt, immaculateness, spotlessness, freshness, dewiness, purity, whiteness, shine, polish, cleanliness, daintiness, fastidiousness, spit and polish (Inf)

► *255 Purity; 531 Whiteness*

2 cleaning, spring-cleaning, housecleaning (US), cleaning up, clearing up, tidying, washing-up, wiping up, mopping-up, scrubbing, dusting, sweeping, vacuuming, hoovering, polishing, washing, laundry, dry-cleaning, washing out, flushing out, dialysis, cleansing, purification, purging, defecation, excretion, purgative, laxative, aperient, enema, freshening, ventilation, airing, deodorization, fumigation, desalination, decontamination, disinfestation, delousing, disinfection, sterilization, antisepsis, asepsis, chlorination, pasteurization, refining, distillation, clarification, filtration, percolation, hygiene, sanitation, drainage, plumbing, sewerage

► *257 Hygiene; 258 Dirtiness; 560 Excretion*

3 religious cleansing, purification, baptism, Asperges, sprinkling of water, lustration, purgation, Purgatory

► *10 Ritual*

4 censorship, expurgation, bowdlerization, blue-pencilling, editing, cleaning up

5 ablutions, washing, wash, toilet, hygiene, oral hygiene, lavage, lavation (Lit), lick (and a promise), bathing, dipping, dip, plunge, rinsing, soaking, soaping, lathering, shampoo

6 bath, hot bath, hot tub, cold bath, bubble bath, steam bath, vapour bath, Turkish bath, sauna, Jacuzzi™, sponge bath, blanket bath, footbath, shower, hot shower, cold shower, douche, bath, bathtub (US), tub (US), hip bath, plunge bath, bidet, basin, washbasin, washbowl, washstand, basin and pitcher, basin and ewer, bathroom, washroom, baths, public baths, Turkish baths, thermae, sudatorium, swimming bath(s), swimming pool, natatorium

7 washer, washing machine, twin-tub, washer-drier, washtub, washboard, dolly (Dial), copper, boiler, laundrette, dishwasher, car wash

8 laundry, wash, washing, dirty clothes, dirty linen, dirty dishes, washing-up

9 cleaning agent, cleansing agent, cleaner, cleanser, purifier, antiseptic, disinfectant, carbolic acid, phenol, bleach, freshener, air freshener, room freshener, deodorant, soda, washing soda, baking soda (US), detergent, washing powder, soap, scented soap, toilet soap, guest soap, soapflakes, soap powder, washing-up liquid, soap and water, water, hot water, shampoo, bubble bath, shower gel, cleansing cream, body lotion, hand lotion, face cream, cold cream, mouthwash, gargle, toothpaste, dentifrice, dental powder, abrasive, pumice, pumice stone, hearthstone, holystone, scouring powder, scouring pad, soap pad, polish, furniture polish, floor polish, shoe polish, boot polish, blacking, whiting, wax, varnish, whitewash, paint, graphite, black lead

10 cleaning object, broom, besom, mop, sponge, swab, scourer, strigil, dishcloth gourd, loofah, duster, feather duster, whisk, brush, scrubbing brush, shoe brush, clothes brush, lint remover, nailbrush, toothbrush, toothpick, dental floss, hairbrush, comb, pocket comb, dog brush, dustpan and brush, carpet sweeper, vacuum cleaner, Hoover™, roadsweeper, snowplough, bin, dustbin, rubbish bin, litter bin, waste disposal unit, compactor, poop-scoop, doormat, boot-scraper, squeegee, squilgee, pipe cleaner, pull through, reamer, windscreen wiper, screen, sieve, riddle, strainer, filter, air filter, oil filter, fuel filter, water filter, blotter, eraser, rubber, rake, hoe, sprinkler, waterworks, sewer, drainpipe, waste pipe

11 cleaning cloth, duster, dishcloth, dishclout (Dial), dishrag (US), J-cloth™, tea towel, chamois (leather), shammy (leather), leather, flannel, face flannel, facecloth, towel, bath towel, hand towel, handkerchief, paper handkerchief, tissue, Kleenex™, toilet paper, toilet tissue, toilet roll, lavatory paper, apron, bib, (table) napkin, serviette, placemat, tablemat, doily (*or* doyley), tablecloth, mat, drugget, cover, chair cover, dust cover, dustsheet, bog roll (Inf), pinny (Inf)

12 cleaner, dry-cleaner, launderer, laundress, laundryman (*or* -woman), washerman, washwoman, washerwoman, dhobi, scrubber, swabber, washer-up, dishwasher, scullion (Lit), charwoman, charlady, housecleaner (US), housemaid, maid, domestic servant, domestic help, domestic, help, daily help, daily, home help, scavenger, street cleaner, sweeper, dustman, refuse collector, dustman, lavatory attendant, sanitary engineer, chimney sweep (*or* sweeper), window cleaner, bootblack, shoeblack, shoeshiner (US), shoeshine boy (US), barber, hairdresser, beautician, gleaner, picker, beachcomber, scavenger bird, crow, vulture, turkey buzzard, buzzard, char (Inf), Mrs Mop (Inf)

VERBS

13 **clean**, make clean, keep clean, remove the dirt, make immaculate, make fresh, freshen, freshen up, disinfect, phenolate, carbolize, spring-clean, clean up, clean out, clear, clear up, clear out, spruce, spruce up, groom, valet, make neat, neaten, tidy, make tidy, trim, shave, wash, wash clean, wash up, wash off, wash out, wash down, wipe, wipe clean, wipe up, wipe off (*or* away), sponge, sponge off, mop, mop up, swab, scrub, scour, do the cleaning, dust, whisk, sweep, sweep up, beat, vacuum, hoover, brush, brush up, brush off, comb, polish, shine, buff, black, black lead, whiten, whitewash, bleach, launder, do the washing, do the laundry, starch, iron, dry-clean, erase, rub out, obliterate, strip, strip clean, pick clean, rake out, muck out, make a clean sweep, flush, flush out, sandblast, holystone, scrape, rub, dry, drip-dry, tumble-dry, wring, wring out, mangle

▶ *358 Obliteration; 409 Arrangement; 522 Light; 531 Whiteness*

14 **bathe**, take a bath, have a bath, dip, dunk, rinse, soak, steep, soap, lather, shampoo, shower, take a shower, have a shower, douche, sluice, swill (out), drench

▶ *429 Moisture; 433 Water*

15 **purify**, purge, censor, expurgate, bowdlerize, edit out, blue-pencil, clean up, sublimate, elevate, cleanse, wash, lave (Lit), lustrate, purify oneself, wash one's hands of, freshen, air, ventilate, fan, deodorize, fumigate, edulcorate, desalt, desalinate, desalinize, disinfect, decontaminate, sterilize, antisepticize, chlorinate, pasteurize, sanitize, free from impurities, depurate, refine, distil, clarify, rack, skim, scum, despumate, decarbonize, elutriate, decant, strain, filter, percolate, lixiviate, leach, sift, sieve, eliminate, sort out, weed out, flush out, dialyse, catheterize, clean out, wash out, drain

▶ *255 Purity; 257 Hygiene*

ADJECTIVES

16 **clean**, not dirty, dirt-free, unsoiled, unsullied, undefiled, virginal, untainted, unmuddied, untarnished, unstained, immaculate, spotless, stainless, blank, perfect, cleanly, dainty, nice, fastidious, fresh, dewy, pure, unmixed, unadulterated, unpolluted, uncontaminated, hygienic, sanitary, sterile, aseptic, antiseptic, salubrious, spruce, dapper, well-groomed, neat, tidy, spick-and-span, orderly, bright, shining, white, snowy, kosher, ritually clean, ritually prepared, untouched, clean as a whistle, fresh as a daisy, bright as a new pin, bright as silver, white as snow, natty (Inf)

▶ *230 Perfection; 255 Purity; 257 Hygiene; 522 Light; 531 Whiteness*

17 **cleaned**, freshened, disinfected, cleaned up, cleaned out, trimmed, shaven, washed, scrubbed, scoured, swept, brushed, polished, whitened, bleached, laundered, starched, ironed, cleansed, purified, purged, expurgated, decontaminated, sterilized, pasteurized, refined, distilled, filtered

18 **cleansing**, lustral, purificatory, disinfectant, hygienic, sanitary, purgative, purgatory, cleaning, detergent, abstergent, ablutionary, balneal

ADVERBS

19 **cleanly**, spotlessly, hygienically, neatly, tidily

20 **clean**, altogether, wholly, entirely, totally, completely, utterly, absolutely, quite

257 Hygiene

NOUNS

1 **hygiene**, sanitation, cleanliness, cleanness, asepsis, antisepsis, disinfection, sterilization, chlorination, pasteurization, preventive medicine, prophylaxis, prophylactic, quarantine, isolation, *cordon sanitaire* (Fr), protection, immunity, immunization, inoculation, vaccination, disease prevention, fumigation, decontamination, purification, sanatorium, health spa, spa, hot springs, thermae, health resort, health farm, health club (US), keeping healthy, keeping fit, exercise, sport, working-out, swimming, running, jogging, walking, constitutional, hygienics

▶ *35 Medicine; 252 Safety; 256 Cleanness; 394 Remedy*

2 **salubrity**, salubriousness, healthiness, health, state of health, well-being, fitness, healthfulness, wholesomeness, nutritiousness, good nutrition, healthy diet, health food, wholefood, smokeless area, no-smoking section, ventilation, fresh air, open air, sea air, outdoors, out-of-doors, good climate, congenial climate

▶ *259 Health; 434 Air*

3 **hygienist**, sanitarian, sanitary inspector, environmental health officer, health inspector, public-health inspector, sanitary engineer, medical officer, nutritionist, dietician (*or* dietitian), fresh-air fiend (Inf)

ADJECTIVES

4 **hygienic**, sanitary, disinfected, chlorinated, pasteurized, sterilized, sterile, clean, pure, aseptic, antiseptic, germ-free, sanative, prophylactic, immunizing, protective, remedial, salubrious, healthy, healthful, health-giving, ventilated, well-ventilated, refreshing, restorative, salutary, what the doctor ordered, beneficial, wholesome, nutritious, nourishing, high-fibre, low-fat, low-salt, body-building, noninjurious, harmless, benign, nonmalignant, uninfectious, noninfectious, innoxious, innocuous, immune, immunized, vaccinated, inoculated, protected, invulnerable

▶ *252 Safety; 256 Cleanness; 259 Health; 393 Repair; 394 Remedy*

VERBS

5 **by hygienic**, practise hygiene, prevent disease, keep fit, agree with one, do one good

6 **make hygienic**, sanitate, sanitize, disinfect, chlorinate, pasteurize, boil, sterilize, antisepticize, immunize, inoculate, vaccinate, quarantine, put in quarantine, isolate,

ventilate, aerate, freshen, fumigate, decontaminate, purify, cleanse, clean, drain, dry, conserve, preserve
► *255 Purity; 256 Cleanness; 359 Preservation*

ADVERBS

7 **hygienically**, sanitarily, antiseptically, aseptically, salubriously, healthily, healthfully, wholesomely

258 Dirtiness

There was no need to do any housework at all. After the first four years the dirt doesn't get any worse. Quentin Crisp.

NOUNS

1 **dirtiness**, uncleanness, soiling, defilement, muckiness, grubbiness, griminess, filthiness, duskness, pollution, foulness, squalidity, squalidness, squalor, sleaze, sleaziness, slumminess, untidiness, slovenliness, sluttishness, blackness, dinginess, messiness, muddiness, sliminess, miriness, encrustation, turbidity, cloudiness, mustiness, mouldiness
► *800 Dishonour*

2 **uncleanness**, unholiness, profanity, corruption, impurity, coarseness, sepsis, infection, contamination, foulness, abomination, stink, stench, fetor, excretion, dirty habits, beastliness, wallowing, scruffiness, shabbiness, pediculosis, phthiriasis, rot, decomposition, putrefaction, putrescence, taint
► *503 Stench; 560 Excretion*

3 **obscenity**, rudeness, indecency, ribaldry, smuttiness, scatology, pornography, dirty joke, dirty book, dirty magazine, dirty film, salaciousness, prurience, lewdness, lasciviousness, licentiousness, porn (Inf)
► *796 Immorality*

4 **dirt**, muck, grime, filth, stain, mark, patch, spot, blot, smudge, smear, mud, mire, quagmire, bog, soil, earth, clay, loam, dung, manure, ordure, faeces, excrement, stool, night soil, droppings, guano, mucus, nasal mucus, snot, pus, matter, dust, mote, smut, soot, smoke, grounds, grouts, dregs, lees, draff, sweepings, scourings, offscourings, shavings, leavings, leftovers, residue, residuum, sediment, sedimentation, deposit, sludge, slime, ooze, goo, mullock (Aus), precipitate, fur, scum, froth, dross, scoria, ash, cinder, clinker, slag, cast-off, cast-off skin, exuviae, slough, dandruff, scurf, scales, tartar, plaque, feculence, litter, rubbish, garbage (US), trash (US), refuse, rot, dry rot, wet rot, rust, mildew, mould, fungus, decay, carrion, offal, vermin, flea, nit, louse, cobweb, shit (Inf), crap (Inf), crud (Inf), gunk (Inf), grunge (US inf), gunge (Inf), yuck (Inf)
► *441 Waste; 560 Excretion*

5 **swill**, pigswill, slops, hogwash, bilge water, bilge, dishwater, ditchwater, stagnant water, dirty water, sewage, sewerage, drainage, wallow, hog-wallow, slough, slosh

6 **dirty person**, chimney sweep, coalman, car mechanic, mud-wrestler, slut, sloven, slattern, drab (Lit), litterbug, litter lout, ragamuffin, urchin, street Arab, street urchin (US), scavenger, beachcomber, beggar, homeless person, vagrant, tramp, hobo (US), bog lady, beast, pig, wallower, obscene person, dirty old man, purveyor of filth, teller of dirty jokes, slammock (Lit), draggletail (Inf), mudlark (Inf), bum (US inf)

ADJECTIVES

7 **dirty**, not clean, unclean, uncleaned, soiled, defiled, mucky, grubby, grimy, filthy, dusty, sooty, smoky, polluted, unwashed, unwiped, unscrubbed, unscoured, unrinsed, unswept, littered, foul, fouled, befouled, squalid, sleazy, slummy, untidy, unkempt, bedraggled, frowzy, slatternly, slovenly, sluttish, black, dingy, unpolished, unburnished, tarnished, stained, spotted, smudged, besmirched, besmeared, messy, greasy, oily, muddy, slimy, miry, begrimed, clotted, caked, matted, encrusted, dirt-encrusted, mud-dried, thick, turbid, cloudy, murky, furred up, clogged, scummy, musty, mouldy, fusty, cobwebby
► *800 Dishonour*

8 **unclean**, unhallowed, unholy, profane, corrupt, impure, coarse, unrefined, unpurified, septic, festering, poisonous, toxic, unsterilized, nonsterile, insanitary, unhygienic, infectious, contaminated, insalubrious, unhealthy, offensive, foul, nasty, abominable, disgusting, repulsive, noisome, nauseous, nauseating, malodorous, stinking, stinky, fetid, uncleanly, unfastidious, beastly, hoggish, sordid, squalid, scruffy, shabby, scurfy, leprous, scabby, mangy, pediculous, crawling, faecal, dungy, stercoraceous, excremental, excrementitious, carious, rotting, rotted, tainted, flyblown, maggoty, carrion, grotty (Inf), manky (Inf), yuck (Inf), yucky (*or* yukky) (Inf), ponging (Inf), pongy (Inf), flea-bitten (Inf), lousy (Inf)
► *503 Stench; 560 Excretion*

9 **obscene**, dirty, filthy, rude, indecent, risqué, ribald, smutty, scatological, pornographic, blue, adult, near the knuckle, salacious, prurient, lewd, lascivious, licentious, scabrous
► *796 Immorality*

VERBS

10 **be dirty**, get dirty, collect dust, foul up, clog, rust, mildew, moulder, fester, have gangrene, gangrene, mortify, putrefy, decay, rot, go bad, go off, addle, grow rank, smell, stink, wallow, roll in the dirt (*or* mud)

11 **dirty**, make dirty, make unclean, soil, defile, foul, befoul, grime, begrime, cover with dust, stain, spot, patch, maculate (Lit), blot, sully, tarnish, blacken, untidy, make a mess (of), mess up, daub, smear, besmear, smirch, besmirch, smudge, blur, streak, grease, cake, clot, clog, muddy, bemire, beslime, roil, rile, draggle, bedraggle, drabble, spatter, bespatter, splash, slobber, slaver, poison, taint, corrupt, pollute, contaminate, infect, profane, desecrate, unhallow, much up (Inf)

ADVERBS

12 **dirtily**, grubbily, untidily, sluttishly, messily, mustily, uncleanly, coarsely, offensively, sordidly, obscenely, rudely, indecently, salaciously, pruriently, lewdly, lasciviously

259 Health

ADJECTIVES

1 **healthy**, fit, well, fine, sound, in health, in good health, bursting with health, fighting fit, eupeptic, fresh, thriv-

ing, flourishing, blooming, glowing, ruddy, rosy, rosy-cheeked, florid, hale, hearty, hale and hearty, bouncing, bonny, lusty, energetic, full of vitality, vigorous, of good constitution, never ill, strong, strong as a horse, strong as an ox, strapping, robust, hardy, sturdy, stalwart, fit and ready, in condition, in good condition, in good shape, in good heart, in peak condition, in tip-top condition, in A1 condition, in the pink, in fine fettle, on form, in fine form, in trim, in fine trim, in fine (*or* high) feather, feeling well, feeling fine, feeling good, feeling great, feeling like a million dollars (US), fit as a fiddle, sound in wind and limb, sound as a bell, fresh as a daisy, a picture of health, getting well, convalescent, on the mend, on the up-grade, on the up and up, on one's legs, up and about, cured, healed, restored to health, pretty good, not bad, in fair health, fair to middling, no worse, comfortable, holding one's own, as well as can be expected, safe and sound, unharmed, full of beans (Inf), full of steam (Inf), all steamed up (Inf), in good nick (Inf)

▶ *336 Strength; 338 Vigour; 393 Repair; 394 Remedy*

2 **healthful**, health-giving, wholesome, good for one, nutritious, nourishing, tonic, bracing, invigorating, hygienic, sanitary, salubrious, salutary, beneficial

▶ *257 Hygiene*

NOUNS

3 **health**, good health, glowing health, robust health, rude health, healthiness, fitness, well-being, physical well-being, soundness, trim, form, condition, good condition, tip-top condition, pink of condition, heartiness, constitution, good constitution, iron constitution, strength, vigour, health and strength, energy, vitality, robustness, bloom, ruddy complexion, rosiness, rosy cheeks, apple cheeks, eupepsia, haleness, *mens sana in corpore sano* (L), incorruption, incorruptibility, long life, longevity, ripe old age, shape, tone, fettle, state, healthy state, clean bill of health, goddess of health, Hygeia, recuperation, convalescence

▶ *336 Strength; 338 Vigour; 393 Repair; 394 Remedy*

4 **healthfulness**, wholesomeness, goodness, nutritiousness, hygiene, salubriousness, salubrity

▶ *257 Hygiene*

VERBS

5 **be healthy**, mind one's health, look after oneself, take care of oneself, feel well, feel fine, feel good, feel great, feel like a million dollars (US), have never felt better, look young, wear well, be well-preserved, bloom, thrive, flourish, have a clean bill of health, enjoy good health, brim with good health, be in the pink, keep (up) one's health, keep fit, keep well, keep body and soul together, keep on one's legs

6 **get healthy**, get well, recover, recover one's health, return to health, recuperate, feel (*or* look) like oneself again, get the colour back in one's cheeks, respond to treatment, mend, convalesce, become convalescent, get back on one's feet, take a fresh (*or* new) lease on (*or* of) life, become a new man (*or* woman), bounce back (Inf)

▶ *244 Improvement*

7 **make healthy**, make well, treat, cure, heal, revive, restore, restore to health, put the colour back in one's cheeks

▶ *35 Medicine; 393 Repair; 394 Remedy*

ADVERBS

8 **healthily**, heartily, healthfully, nutritiously, hygienically, salubriously

260 Ill Health

NOUNS

1 **ill health**, bad health, poor health, delicate health, failing health, unhealthiness, delicacy, weak constitution, lack of fitness, lack of strength, weakness, weakliness, infirmity, debility, diathesis, sickiness, loss of condition, manginess, morbidity, illness, sickness, indisposition, cachexia, chronic illness, chronic complaint, allergy, hay fever, catarrh, chronic ill health, invalidism, valetudinarianism, hypochondria, nerves, neurosis, seediness (Inf)

▶ *245 Deterioration; 261 Tiredness; 337 Weakness; 461 Insanity*

2 **illness**, disease, disorder, sickness, ailment, indisposition, malady, distemper, affliction, complaint, disability, handicap, infirmity, weakness, condition, history of illness, bout of sickness, visitation, attack, acute attack, spasm, stroke, seizure, apoplexy, fit, shock, virus, poisoning, blood poisoning, food poisoning, metal poisoning, lead poisoning, complication, terminal illness, terminal disease, fatal illness, coma, death, sickbed, deathbed, bug (Inf)

▶ *582 Death*

3 **symptom**, sign, sign of illness, indication, syndrome, rash, spots, sore, blister, discharge, congestion, breathing difficulty, hoarseness, sore throat, cough, lack of appetite, weight loss, weakness, fatigue, malaise, depression, numbness, diarrhoea, nausea, waves of nausea, queasiness, queasy stomach, vomiting, inflammation, swelling, lump, growth, tumour, carcinoma, temperature, high temperature, feverishness, fever, calenture, pyrexia, hyperpyrexia, hyperthermia, hyperthermy, delirium, ague, chill, hypothermia, shivers, shakes, spasm, pain, headache, splitting headache, migraine, dizziness, fainting, loss of consciousness, breakdown, collapse, unconsciousness, insensibility, prostration, stiffness, paralysis, bleeding, high blood pressure, hypertension, low blood pressure, hypotension

▶ *261 Tiredness; 489 Insensibility; 491 Physical Pain*

4 **disease**, notifiable disease, epidemic disease, endemic disease, congenital disease, infectious disease, contagious disease, communicable disease, tropical disease, deficiency disease, malnutrition, anorexia nervosa, bulimia nervosa, avitaminosis, kwashiorkor, beriberi, pellagra, rickets, scurvy, degenerative disease, debilitating disease, wasting disease, musuclar dystrophy, marasmus, atrophy, killer disease, AIDS (acquired immune deficiency syndrome), cancer, neoplastic disease, traumatic disease, trauma, organic disease, goitre, functional disease, circulatory disease, neurological disease, nervous disease, epilepsy, falling sickness, brain disease, mental disorder, musculoskeletal disease, cardiovascular disease, cardiopulmonary disease, heart disease, cardiac disease, coronary thrombosis, fibrosis, haematopoietic disease, endocrine disease, hyperthyroidism, diabetes,

urogenital disease, venereal disease, sexually transmitted disease (STD), syphilis, gonorrhoea, herpes simplex, dermatological disease, skin cancer, respiratory disease, asthma, gastrointestinal disease, gastroenteritis, virus disease, influenza, lentivirus disease, retrovirus disease, leukaemia, blood disease, anaemia, thalassaemia, bacterial disease, diarrhoea, waterborne disease, typhoid fever, febrile disease, febrile seizure, sweating sickness, hydrocele, dropsy, occupational disease, alcoholism, alcohol abuse, drug addiction, unknown disease, the crud (Inf)

► *461 Insanity*

5 **plague**, pest, scourge, bane, pestilence, infection, contagion, epidemic, pandemic, pneumonic plague, bubonic plague, Black Death

6 **infection**, contagion, pollution, miasma, taint, infectiousness, contagiousness, toxicity, toxin, poisonousness, poisoning, poison, sepsis, purulence, suppuration, festering, gangrene, plague spot, trouble spot, hotbed, vector, host, carrier, germ-carrier, parasite, worm, toxocariasis, virus, lentivirus, retrovirus, HIV (human immunodeficiency virus), bacillus, bacterium, bacteria, germ, pathogen, blood poisoning, toxaemia, septicaemia, pyaemia, food poisoning, ptomaine poisoning, botulism, gastroenteritis, cholera, cold, common cold, influenza, diphtheria, pneumonia, viral pneumonia, infective hepatitis, tuberculosis (TB), consumption, measles, German measles, rubella, rubeola, roseola, whooping cough, pertussis, mumps, chickenpox, smallpox, variola, scarlet fever, scarlatina, fever, malarial fever, malaria, typhus, jail fever, trench fever, typhoid, paratyphoid, glandular fever, infectious mononucleosis, mono, poliomyelitis, polio, meningitis, ME (myalgic encephalomyelitis), encephalitis, encephalitis lethargica, sleeping sickness, tetanus, lockjaw, rabies, hydrophobia, flu (Inf), kissing disease (Inf)

7 **tropical disease**, fever, malarial fever, malaria, ague, cholera, Asiatic cholera, yellow fever, blackwater fever, miliary fever, sweating sickness, breakbone fever, dengue, Lassa fever, green monkey disease, kala-azar, visceral leishmaniasis, trypanosomiasis, (South) American trypanosomiasis, Chagas' disease, (African) sleeping sickness, sleepy sickness, encephalitis lethargica, schistosomiasis, bilharziasis, ascariasis, ancylostomiasis, hookworm disease, ebola virus, trachoma, glaucoma, onchocerciasis, river blindness, framboesia, yaws, leprosy, dhobi itch, Hansen's disease, beriberi, kwashiorkor

8 **indigestion**, gastralgia, upset stomach, stomach ache, cramp, colic, gripes, acidity, hyperacidity, acidosis, heartburn, pyrosis, cardialgia, dyspepsia, liverishness, biliousness, nausea, vomiting, retching, stomach ulcer, peptic ulcer, gastric ulcer, duodenal ulcer, stomach cancer, bowel cancer, gastritis, enteritis, regional enteritis, Crohn's disease, colitis, duodenitis, dysentery, cholera, food poisoning, ptomaine poisoning, botulism, flatulence, flatus, gas, defecation, diarrhoea, constipation, stomach flu (Inf), bellyache (Inf), collywobbles (Inf), butterflies (Inf), wind (Inf), the trots (Inf), the runs (Inf), Montezuma's revenge (Inf), gyppy (*or* gippy) tummy (Inf)

► *371 Expulsion; 560 Excretion*

9 **respiratory disease**, cough, smoker's cough, cold, common cold, head cold, runny nose, watering eyes, catarrh, coryza, rhinitis, rhinorrhoea, sinusitis, glue ear, influenza, sore throat, swollen adenoids, tonsillitis, pharyngitis, laryngitis, tracheitis, croup, bronchitis, asthma, emphysema, pleurisy, pneumonia, bronchopneumonia, legionnaire's disease, diphtheria, whooping cough, pertussis, lung cancer, asbestosis, silicosis, pneumoconiosis, anthracosis, black lung (disease), cystic fibrosis, tuberculosis (TB), pulmonary phthisis, consumption, flu (Inf), crying cold (Inf)

10 **cardiovascular disease**, heart disease, heart condition, heart trouble, bad heart, weak heart, coronary heart disease, rheumatic heart disease, cardiac disease, carditis, endocarditis, myocarditis, pericarditis, angina pectoris, angina, chest-pain, chest-spasm, breast-pang, brachycardia, tachycardia, galloping (*or* gallop) rhythm, arrhythmia, palpitation, dyspnoea, vulvulitis, valvular lesion, mitral stenosis, cardiac hypertrophy, enlarged heart, athlete's heart, fatty degeneration of the heart, cardiac arrest, heart attack, heart failure, coronary thrombosis, coronary, myocardial infarction, stroke, blood pressure, high blood pressure, hypertension, low blood pressure, hypotension, vascular disease, atheroma, aneurysm (*or* aneurism), hardening of the arteries, arteriosclerosis, arteritis, phlebitis, varicose veins, thrombosis, clot, blood clot, embolism, infarction

11 **blood disease**, anaemia, aplastic anaemia, haemolytic anaemia, anaemia, pernicious anaemia, sickle-cell anaemia, sickle-cell disease (US), thalassaemia, leukaemia, lymphoma, Hodgkin's disease, haemophilia, bleeding, internal bleeding, haemorrhage, bleeder's disease (Inf)

12 **cancer**, neoplasm, growth, cancerous growth, primary growth, secondary growth, tumour, benign tumour, innocent tumour, malignant tumour, cancerous tumour, carcinoma, sarcoma, epithelioma, melanoma, skin cancer, breast cancer, throat cancer, lung cancer, stomach cancer, bone cancer, brain cancer, cervical cancer, prostate cancer, cancer of the pancreas, leukaemia, the big C (Inf)

13 **skin disease**, dermatitis, cutaneous disease, skin lesion, scabies, erythema, leucoderma, vitiligo, albinism, lupus, yaws, framboesia, leprosy, eczema, mange, miliaria, heat rash, prickly heat, erysipelas, St Anthony's fire, impetigo, herpes, herpes zoster, shingles, serpigo, ringworm, prurigo, pruritis, itch, dhobi itch, formication, urticaria, hives, nettle rash, rash, eruption, breaking out, athlete's foot, acne, spot, pimple, blackhead, pustule, cyst, blister, wart, verruca, swelling, blemish, macula, mole, freckle, birthmark, pockmark, variola, smallpox, chickenpox, cowpox, melanoma, skin cancer, tetter (Inf)

► *182 Convexity; 492 Touch; 548 Blemish*

14 **venereal disease**, VD, sexual disease, sexually transmitted disease (STD), social disease, AIDS (acquired immune deficiency syndrome), AIDS-related complex, syphilis, gonorrhoea, NSU (nonspecific urethritis), herpes, herpes simplex, venereal ulcer, chancre, syphilitic sore, the French disease (Inf), (the) clap (Inf), (the) scrud (US inf), dose (Inf), crabs (Inf), lobstertails (US inf)

15 ulcer, ulceration, gathering, festering, purulence, inflammation, sore, abscess, boil, carbuncle, fistula, cyst, blain, chilblain, kibe (Lit), corn, hard corn, soft corn, swelling, gangrene, rot, decay, discharge, pus, matter

▶ *375 Disintegration*

16 rheumatism, rheumatics, rheumatic fever, muscular rheumatism, myalgia, fibrositis, tennis elbow, bursitis, frozen shoulder, prepatella bursitis, housemaid's knee, RSI (repetitive strain injury), arthritis, rheumatoid arthritis, gout, osteoarthritis, degenerative joint disease, lumbago, slipped disc, pulled muscle

17 nervous disorder, nervous breakdown, neuralgia, sciatica, neurilemma, seizure, paralysis, general paralysis, quadriplegia, tetraplegia, hemiplegia, diplegia, bilateral paralysis, paraplegia, atrophy, numbness, insensibility, partial paralysis, general paresis, paresis, palsy, cerebral palsy, tic, tic douloureux, trigeminal neuralgia, twitch, tremor, spasm, petit mal, grand mal, epilepsy, falling sickness, infantile paralysis, poliomyelitis, polio, spina bifida, paralysis agitans, Parkinson's disease, chorea, Huntingdon's chorea, St Vitus's dance, multiple sclerosis (MS), disseminated sclerosis, muscular dystrophy, myasthenia gravis, myasthenia, motor neurone disease, CJD, Creutzfeld-Jakob disease

▶ *327 Agitation; 489 Insensibility*

18 veterinary disease, mange, rabies, distemper, canine distemper, hard pad, equine distemper, strangles, BSE (bovine spongiform encephalopathy), mad-cow disease, scrapie, foot-and-mouth disease, hoof-and-mouth disease, swine fever, swinepox, variola porcina, myxomatosis, rinderpest, murrain, anthrax, blackleg, sheeprot, bloat, liver fluke, worms, megrims, staggers, glanders, farcy, sweeny, spavin, thrust, parrot fever, psittacosis

19 sick person, invalid, patient, hospital patient, nursing home patient, paediatric patient, geriatric patient, inpatient, out-patient, shut-in (US), sufferer, case, stretcher case, hospital case, mental case, chronic invalid, valetudinarian, hypochondriac, malingerer, martyr to ill health, weakling, consumptive, asthmatic, bronchitic, dyspeptic, diabetic, haemophiliac, bleeder, insomniac, neuropath, addict, drug addict, alcoholic, spastic, arthritic, paralytic, paraplegic, quadriplegic, hemiplegic, disabled person, cripple, (old) crock (Inf)

▶ *337 Weakness; 461 Insanity*

20 pathology, forensic pathology, diagnosis, prognosis, etiology, nosology, epidemiology, bacteriology, parasitology, therapy

▶ *35 Medicine; 394 Remedy*

ADJECTIVES

21 unhealthy, ill, unfit, unsound, sickly, infirm, decrepit, weakly, weak, tired, fatigued, exhausted, run down, delicate, of weak constitution, prone to sickness, liable to illness, chronically ill, chronically sick, always ill, invalid, valetudinarian, hypochondriac, mangy, undernourished, underfed, anorexic, malnourished, emaciated, sallow, wan, pale, white, pale as a ghost, white as a sheet, peaked, peaky, anaemic, colourless, jaundiced, yellow, bilious, green

▶ *261 Tiredness; 337 Weakness; 530 Colourlessness; 591 Sensitivity*

22 sick, ill, unwell, not well, not in good health, in bad health, in poor health, in poor condition, in poor shape, in a bad way, bad, poorly, peaky, below par, indisposed, out of sorts, off-colour, drooping, flagging, pining, languishing, wasting away, in a decline, squeamish, queer, queasy, nauseated, ailing, showing signs of, showing symptoms of, coming down with, off one's food, refusing to eat, feverish, headachy, confined, quarantined, shut in, bedridden, (flat) on one's back, prostrate, in bed, taking it easy, in hospital, hospitalized, on the sick list, invalided, seized, taken ill, taken bad, collapsed, comatose, in a coma, on the danger list, in intensive care, in ICU, not allowed visitors, serious, critical, chronic, incurable, terminal, inoperable, mortally ill, dying, near death, moribund, crummy (Inf), shitty (Inf), like death warmed up (Inf), in bad nick (Inf), out of kilter (Inf), under the weather (Inf), seedy (Inf), groggy (Inf), grotty (Inf), green around the gills (Inf), laid up (Inf)

▶ *245 Deterioration*

23 diseased, infected, contaminated, tainted, affected, stricken, plague-stricken, distempered, disordered, pathological, pathogenic, morbid, morbific, peccant, insalubrious, unhygienic, iatrogenic, psychosomatic, vitiated, rotten, rotting, gangrenous, decaying, decomposed, infectious, contagious, poisonous, toxic, festering, purulent, degenerative, consumptive, phthistic, tuberculous, tubercular, diabetic, dropsical, hydrocephalic, hydrocephalous, anaemic, bloodless, leukaemic, haemophilic, arthritic, rheumatic, rheumatoid, rheumaticky, rickety, palsied, paralysed, paralytic, spastic, epileptic, leprous, carninomatous, carcinomatoid, cancerous, cankerous, oncogenic, oncogenous, carcinogenic, syphilitic, venereal, swollen, oedematous (*or* oedematose), gouty, bronchial, bronchitic, throaty, croupy, sniffly, snuffly, asthmatic, allergic, pyretic, febrile, fevered, feverish, delirious, shivering, aguish, sore, tender, painful, ulcerous, ulcerated, inflamed, rashy, spotty, erysipelatous, spavined, mangy

▶ *375 Disintegration; 491 Physical Pain*

VERBS

24 be unhealthy, be ill, have poor health, ail, suffer, labour under, undergo treatment for, have a complaint, have an affliction, not feel well, feel ill, feel bad, feel rotten, come over all queer, complain of, feel sick, vomit, sicken, fall sick, fall ill, catch, catch an infection, contract a disease, go down with, break out in, have an attack, have a heart attack, have a stroke, collapse, faint, take to one's bed, go to hospital, be hospitalized, become a patient, become an in-patient, become an out-patient, go off sick, be invalided out, languish, pine, peak, droop, go into a decline, lose strength, weaken, grow weak, fail, flag, drop, sink, fade away, deteriorate, get worse, feel like hell (Inf), be laid up (Inf), waste away (Inf)

▶ *245 Deterioration; 337 Weakness; 371 Expulsion*

ADVERBS

25 unhealthily, weakly, chronically, morbidly, pathologically, in sickness, with suffering, in hospital, under the doctor, under doctor's orders, in the doctor's hands, under treatment, on the sick list

261 Tiredness

I haven't got time to be tired. Wilhelm I.

ADJECTIVES

1 **fatigued**, tired, weary, wearied, sleepy, drowsy, nodding, yawning, ready to rest, ready for bed, ready for sleep, half-awake, dozy, half-asleep, asleep on one's feet, fit to drop, dropping, exhausted, tired out, worn out, tired to death, dead tired, faint, spent, weak, drained, dull, stale, strained, overworked, overtired, overfatigued, overstrained, overwrought, burned out, weakened, enervated, fainting, swooning, flat, prostrate, more dead than alive, stiff, aching, sore, footsore, footweary, walked off one's feet, travel-weary, jet-lagged, wayworn, tired-looking, tired-eyed, heavy-eyed, heavy-lidded, hollow-eyed, haggard, worn, pale, drooping, flagging, languid, languorous, listless, lethargic, forever tired, still tired, unrefreshed, unrested, dopey (Inf), travelled out (Inf), dog-tired (Inf), dog-weary (Inf), dead to the world (Inf), out of it (Inf), beat (Inf), dead beat (Inf), half-dead (Inf), done for (Inf), done in (Inf), done up (Inf), pooped (US inf), fagged (Inf), fagged out (Inf), knocked up (Inf), washed up (*or* out) (Inf), clapped out (Inf), tuckered out (US inf), worn to a frazzle (Inf), stupid with fatigue (Inf), all in (Inf), on one's last legs (Inf), bushed (Inf), whacked (Inf), knackered (Inf), flaked out (Inf), sacked out (Inf), flat out (Inf)

▶ *337 Weakness; 343 Inactivity*

2 **bored**, bored, tired, weary, jaded, satiated, sated, sick and tired of (Inf), sick of (Inf), fed up with (Inf), cheesed off (Inf), pissed (*or* fucked) off (Inf)

▶ *217 Sufficiency; 620 Boredom*

3 **panting**, puffing, blowing, puffing and blowing, out of breath, short of breath, breathless, gasping for breath, wheezing, snorting, winded, broken-winded

4 **fatiguing**, tiring, exhausting, laborious, tiresome, wearisome, wearying, wearing, gruelling, punishing, exacting, tough, demanding, physically demanding, irksome, vexatious, annoying, trying, tedious, boring, monotonous

VERBS

5 **be fatigued**, be tired, tire, become weary, flag, droop, languish, fail, sink, stagger, faint, swoon, feel dizzy, feel giddy, yawn, nod, drowse, sleep, succumb, drop, collapse, beg for sleep, cry out for rest, have no strength left, have nothing left to give, can do no more, tire oneself out, overdo it, overtax one's strength, overwork, overexert, ache in every muscle (*or* limb), gasp, pant, puff, blow, grunt, breathe heavily, get stale, need a rest, need a change, need a break, need a holiday, need a vacation (US), flake out (Inf), crack up (Inf), crock up (Inf), pack up (Inf)

▶ *337 Weakness; 343 Inactivity; 434 Air*

6 **fatigue**, exhaust, tire, tire out, tire to death, wear, wear out, weary, prostrate, double up, wind, work, drive, task, tax, strain, demand too much (of), make extra demands, overwork, overdrive, overtask, overtax, overburden, overload, overstrain, burn out, weaken, debilitate, enervate, drain, take it out of, distress, trouble, bother, harass, annoy, irritate, irk, vex, exasperate, jade, bore, bore to tears, put (*or* send) to sleep, keep from sleep, deprive of sleep, allow no rest, do up (Inf), do in (Inf), fag (Inf), fag out (Inf), whack (Inf), knock up (Inf), crock up (Inf)

NOUNS

7 **fatigue**, tiredness, weariness, sleepiness, drowsiness, exhaustion, lassitude, languor, listlessness, lethargy, dullness, staleness, jadedness, boredom, physical fatigue, aching muscles, mental fatigue, tired brain, mental and physical distress, limit of endurance, total exhaustion, collapse, prostration, strain, exertion, work, overtiredness, overexertion, overwork, overdoing it, shortness of breath, hard breathing, laboured breathing, panting, gasping, palpitations, heart pain, languishment, weakness, enervation, debilitation, faintness, fainting, faint, swoon, blackout, insensibility, loss of consciousness

▶ *263 Ease; 337 Weakness; 434 Air; 489 Insensibility; 576 Work*

ADVERBS

8 **tiredly**, wearily, sleepily, drowsily, weakly, listlessly, lethargically, dozily, dopily (Inf)

9 **tiringly**, exhaustingly, laboriously, wearisomely, annoyingly, tediously, monotonously

262 Haste

'Will you walk a little faster?' said a whiting to a snail,
'There's a porpoise close behind us, and he's treading on my tail.' Lewis Carroll.

In skating over thin ice, our safety is in our speed. Ralph Waldo Emerson.

If it were done when 'tis done, then 'twere well
It were done quickly. William Shakespeare.

VERBS

1 **hasten**, speed up, accelerate, quicken, precipitate, hurry, rush, expedite, dispatch, urge, impel, propel, drive, stampede, spur, goad, whip, lash, flog, incite, hustle, hustle away, bundle out (*or* off), rush along, allow no time, push, press, push forward, brook no delay, railroad (Inf), breathe down someone's neck (Inf)

2 **make haste**, hasten, move fast, go fast, speed, rush, spurt, sprint, dash, bolt, race, fly, run, rush headlong, run helter-skelter, run pell-mell, go like a rocket, scurry, scuttle, scamper, decamp, hasten away, dash off, rush off, tear off, cut and run, make up for lost time, hurry, catch up, overtake, outrun, outstrip, whirl by, zoom past, make a forced march, accelerate, speed up, go faster, pick up the pace, hustle, bustle, fret, fume, fidget, rush to and fro, dart to and fro, have no time to spare, have no time to lose, ignore formalities, act without ceremony, brush aside, cut short the preliminaries, rush through, dash through, cut corners, rush one's fences, make short work of, bolt down one's meal, be pressed for time, work against time, work to a deadline, meet a deadline, be behind time, be late, miss one's deadline, work under pressure, think on one's feet, do at the last moment, lose no time, lose not a moment, make every second count, skedaddle (Inf), run like hell (Inf), run like the devil

(Inf), fly like a bat out of hell (Inf), pick them up and lay them down (Inf), burn up the track (Inf), go into overdrive (Inf), make oneself scarce (Inf), make tracks (US inf), scat (Inf), show one's heels (Inf), make someone eat dust (Inf)

▶ *294 Lateness; 313 Departure; 342 Activity; 615 Rashness*

ADJECTIVES

3 **hasty**, done in haste, rushed, speedy, prompt, brisk, quick, presto, allegro, swift, rapid, fast, fleet, expeditious, impetuous, impulsive, precipitant, precipitate, headlong, overhasty, reckless, heedless, rash, hotheaded, feverish, impatient, all impatience, thoughtless, unthinking, ill-considered, ardent, fervent, rushing, scampering, pushing, shoving, elbowing, uncontrolled, boisterous, furious, violent, breathless, breakneck, without delay, urgent, immediate, in haste, in all haste, hotfoot, running, racing, hastening, speeding, in a hurry, in a rush, unable to wait, pressed for time, hard-pressed, driven, hurried, haphazard, slapdash, careless, negligent, cursory, perfunctory, superficial, fleeting, brief, rush, last-minute, rough and tumble, rough and ready, unprepared, forced, rushed into, stampeded, allowing no time, brooking no delay, pushed through, railroaded (Inf)

▶ *380 Violence; 590 Feelings; 615 Rashness; 666 Negligence*

NOUNS

4 **haste**, hurry, rush, speed, promptness, briskness, quickness, swiftness, rapidity, alacrity, celerity, expeditiousness, urge, impulsion, drive, stampede, push, spur, goad, whip, activity, scurry, hurry-scurry, hustle, bustle, hassle, flurry, whirl, scramble, flutter, fidget, fuss, agitation, distress, panic, last-minute rush, rush job, job due yesterday, nonpreparation, feverish haste, deadline, pressure, race against a deadline, race against time, no time to lose, lateness, urgency, immediacy, importance, expedition, dispatch, velocity, hastening, acceleration, dash, spurt, forced march, tearing hurry (Inf), flap (Inf), skedaddle (Inf)

▶ *123 Importance; 294 Lateness; 327 Agitation; 342 Activity*

5 **hastiness**, overhaste, precipitance, precipitateness, impetuosity, impetuousness, impulsiveness, recklessness, rashness, inability to wait, impatience, thoughtlessness, carelessness, negligence

ADVERBS

6 **hastily**, hurriedly, precipitantly, precipitately, helter-skelter, pell-mell, feverishly, posthaste, hotfoot, apace, quickly, swiftly, rapidly, fast, promptly, speedily, with all haste, like a rocket, like a bat out of hell, in a flash, before you can say Jack Robinson, at short notice, on the spur of the moment, immediately, without delay, straight away, right away, urgently, with urgency, under pressure, against the clock, by forced march, with not a moment to lose (*or* spare), pronto (Inf), like greased lightning (Inf), lickety-split (US inf), p.d.q. (pretty damned quick) (Inf), ASAP (as soon as possible) (Inf)

7 **rashly**, recklessly, impetuously, impulsively, impatiently, heedlessly, thoughtlessly, overhastily

▶ *615 Rashness*

INTERJECTIONS

8 **hurry up!**, faster!, quick!, be quick!, get a move on!, step on it!, at (*or* on) the double!, catch up!, speed up!, right now!, move it! (Inf)

263 Ease

What e'r he did was done with so much ease,
In him alone, 'twas Natural to please. John Dryden.

NOUNS

1 **ease**, relaxation, repose, rest, rest from one's labours, inactivity, idleness, stillness, restfulness, comfort, well-being, content, contentment, eudaemonia, peace, quiet, peace and quiet, tranquillity, serenity, quiescence, sleep, nap, catnap, sweet sleep, sweet dreams, happy dreams, refreshment, breathing space (*or* room), break, tea (*or* coffee) break, pause, respite, lull, recess, interval, interim, leave, holiday, vacation, furlough, time off, day off, sabbatical (year), leisure, free time, spare time, spare hours, day of rest, Sabbath, Lord's day, bank holiday, final rest, eternal peace, the peace that passeth all understanding, nirvana, death, let-up (Inf), breather (Inf), snooze (Inf), forty winks (Inf), shut-eye (Inf)

▶ *226 Stopping; 248 Prosperity; 265 Easiness; 275 Time; 301 Motionlessness; 343 Inactivity; 490 Physical Pleasure; 580 Leisure; 581 Refreshment; 608 Relief*

VERBS

2 **take it easy**, take one's ease, relax, repose, rest, take a rest, have a rest, rest from one's labours, find peace and quiet, come to rest, perch, roost, sit down, sit back, put one's feet up, recline, lie down, lie back, loll, lounge, laze, sprawl, couch, go to bed, bed down, go to sleep, sleep, doze, drowse, nap, take a nap, have a catnap, unwind, unbend, slow down, let up, slack off, forget one's problems, forget work, put on one's robe and slippers, rest and be thankful, rest on one's laurels, rest on one's oars, take time off (*or* out), take a holiday, go on vacation (US), go on leave, go on a furlough, kip down (Inf), catch some Zs (US inf), have forty winks (Inf), get some shuteye (Inf), snooze (Inf), take a breather (Inf), take five (Inf), chill (out) (Inf)

▶ *187 Horizontality; 265 Easiness; 301 Motionlessness; 343 Inactivity; 367 Lowering; 581 Refreshment*

3 **ease**, loosen, slacken, moderate, reduce, relieve, alleviate, comfort

▶ *214 Decrease; 608 Relief; 685 Moderation*

ADJECTIVES

4 **at ease**, easy, easeful, relaxed, relaxing, reposeful, resting, restful, robed, slippered, unbuttoned, in one's shirt-sleeves, casual, carefree, laid-back, content, eudaemonic, cushioned, pillowed, snug, comfortable, peaceful, quiet, still, quiescent, tranquil, leisured, idle, lazy, sluggish, slow, leisurely, unhurried, sabbatical, holiday, vacation, postprandial, after-dinner

▶ *301 Motionlessness; 490 Physical Pleasure; 580 Leisure; 609 Satisfaction*

5 **labour-saving**, back-saving, time-saving, restful, reposeful, easy on, thirst-quenching, like a breath of fresh air

ADVERBS

6 **with ease**, easily, at rest, restfully, reposefully, quietly,

peacefully, casually, in a carefree manner, on leave, on holiday, on vacation, on sabbatical, on furlough

264 Difficulty

A difficulty for every solution. Herbert Samuel.

NOUNS

1 **difficulty**, hardness, complexity, complication, intricacy, knottiness, technicality, abstruseness, convolution, reconditeness, obscurity, unintelligibility, effort, arduousness, laboriousness, strenuousness, strain, severity, toughness, ruggedness
▶ *266 Obscurity; 408 Disorder; 576 Work; 647 Severity; 696 Unintelligibility*
2 **awkwardness**, clumsiness, unwieldiness, lack of ease, lack of grace, lack of skill, ham-fistedness (Inf)
▶ *486 Unskilfulness*
3 **difficult task**, hard task, hard work, labour, toil, struggle, trial, tribulation, tough assignment, tough proposition, no easy task, tall order, large order (US), big undertaking, hard graft, hard row to hoe, tough lineup to buck (US), hard row of stumps (US), hard furrow to plough, hard pull (US), heavy sledding (US), hard going, rough going, rough ground, difficult terrain, rough terrain, hard road to travel, the hard way, uphill task, uphill struggle, Herculean task, superhuman task, brutal task, handful (Inf), no picnic (Inf), backbreaker (Inf), ballbuster (US inf), bitch (Inf), bastard (Inf), bugger (Inf), sod (Inf), real bitch (Inf), real bastard (Inf), real bugger (Inf), real sod (Inf)
▶ *576 Work*
4 **problem**, worry, anxiety, quandary, dilemma, conundrum, brain-teaser, brain-twister, teaser, poser, nonplus, nodus, crux, maze, puzzle, perplexity, imbroglio, thorny problem, knotty problem, hard nut to crack, Gordian knot, can of worms, vexed question, headache (Inf)
▶ *408 Disorder; 696 Unintelligibility*
5 **predicament**, plight, situation, tangle, mess, muddle, tricky situation, tricky spot, ticklish spot, hot water, cleft stick, difficult position, nice predicament, fine mess, unholy mess, fine kettle of fish, pig in a poke, sorry plight, pretty pass, pretty pickle, no-win situation, catch-22 (situation), pickle (Inf), fix (Inf), jam (Inf), scrape (Inf), hobble (US inf), hole (Inf), spot (Inf), squeeze (Inf), clutch (US inf), bind (Inf), pinch (Inf), how-do-you-do (Inf), snarl (Inf), snarl-up (Inf), snafu (Inf)
6 **critical situation**, tight corner, tight spot, tight squeeze, nowhere to turn, desperate (*or* dire *or* parlous) straits, emergency, exigency, hard times, hard life, hardship, adversity, danger, slippery slope, quagmire, quicksand, swamp, morass, the crunch (Inf)
▶ *249 Adversity; 254 Danger*
7 **awkward situation**, awkward position, delicate situation, diplomatic incident, embarrassing situation, embarrassing position, financial embarrassment, bother, spot of bother, spot of trouble, bad patch, hard times, dispute, disagreement, tail in a gate (US inf), tit in the wringer (US inf), sticky wicket (Inf), shtook (Inf)
▶ *751 Disagreement*
8 **snag**, hitch, catch, drawback, pitfall, teething troubles, complication, aggravation, annoyance, inconvenience, obstacle, hurdle, obstruction, hindrance, impasse, stalemate, deadlock, standstill, log jam, halt, stop, stoppage, cul-de-sac, blind alley, dead end, blank wall, no-go area
▶ *103 Impossibility; 378 Obstruction*
9 **difficult person**, troublemaker, malcontent, problem child, (juvenile) delinquent, criminal, outlaw, disruptive pupil, fussy eater, all one can manage, thorn in one's flesh, *bête noire* (Fr), handful (Inf)

ADJECTIVES

10 **difficult**, hard, not easy, arduous, strenuous, laborious, toilsome, demanding, exacting, challenging, tough, heavy, hefty, onerous, burdensome, effortful, physically demanding, requiring effort, wearisome, backbreaking, gruelling, punishing, exhausting, fatiguing, uphill, oppressive, severe, formidable, superhuman, Herculean, impossible, impracticable, easier said than done, steep (Inf), stiff (Inf)
▶ *103 Impossibility; 261 Tiredness; 576 Work*
11 **rough**, rugged, craggy, rough-going, heavy-going, impenetrable, impassable, unnavigable
12 **problematic**, puzzling, baffling, confusing, perplexing, troubling, obfuscating, demanding, exacting, challenging, tough, complex, complicated, intricate, delicate, convoluted, involved, confused, labyrinthine, skilled, specialized, technical, overspecialized, overtechnical, abstruse, recondite, esoteric, impenetrable, obscure, unclear, unintelligible, illegible, indecipherable, garbled, jumbled, scrambled, jawbreaking, knotty (Inf), tricky (Inf), thorny (Inf), ticklish (Inf), sticky (Inf), hairy (Inf), pernickety (Inf), crabbed (Inf), cramped (Inf)
▶ *266 Obscurity; 408 Disorder; 485 Skill; 696 Unintelligibility*
13 **inconvenient**, awkward, troublesome, bothersome, irksome, vexatious, vexing, annoying, aggravating, exasperating, tedious, tiresome, boring, trying, worrying, worrisome, troubling, plaguey (Inf)
▶ *327 Agitation; 328 Disturbance; 620 Boredom*
14 **troublesome**, demanding, contrary, perverse, wayward, unmanageable, out of hand, beyond control, stubborn, obstinate, obdurate, headstrong, intractable, refractory, difficult to handle, ill-behaved, badly behaved, naughty, disobedient, disruptive, obstreperous, critical, overcritical, hypercritical, fault-finding, censorious, disapproving, grudging, discontented, hard to please, hard to satisfy, fussy, fastidious, finicky, particular, difficult to live with, bloody-minded (Inf), stroppy (Inf), moody (Inf), nitpicking (Inf), pedantic, pernickety (Inf)
▶ *631 Behaviour; 641 Obstinacy; 662 Disobedience; 670 Disapproval*
15 **clumsy**, cumbersome, unwieldy, awkward, ungainly, hulking, ponderous, bulky, lumbering
▶ *158 Size*
16 **troubled**, beset, worried, anxious, perturbed, bothered, vexed, annoyed, puzzled, confused, baffled, perplexed, bewildered, mystified, nonplussed, inconvenienced, put out, harassed, plagued, distressed, embarrassed, in a predicament, in a mess, in a tangle, at a loss, at a standstill, at an impasse, deadlocked, at one's wits' end, at the end of one's tether, in a quandary, in a dilemma, between two stools, on the horns of a dilemma, between

the devil and the deep blue sea, between Scylla and Charybdis, in trouble, in a tight spot, in a corner, snookered, behind the eight ball (US), on the spot, out of one's depth, in deep water, in hot water, in the soup, out on a limb, on a tightrope, in difficulties, stumped (Inf), stuck (Inf), in a scrape (Inf), in a jam (Inf), in a pickle (Inf), in a fix (Inf), up a tree (US inf), in Dutch (Inf), on Queer Street (Inf)
▶ *327 Agitation; 696 Unintelligibility*

VERBS

17 **be difficult**, present difficulties, present problems, pose problems, take some doing, require some effort, set one a problem, give one trouble, pester, hassle (Inf)

18 **find difficult**, struggle with, get all tangled up, get all snarled up, make heavy weather of, not see the wood for the trees

19 **have difficulty**, have trouble, struggle, flounder, be hard put (to), have one's work cut out, let oneself in for, labour under difficulties, labour under a disadvantage, have one hand tied behind one's back, do it the hard way, swim against the current, swim upstream, walk (*or* tread) on hot coals, come unstuck, invite difficulties, make it hard on oneself
▶ *576 Work*

20 **be in difficulty**, have a problem, face difficulties, get into difficulties, run into trouble, get in a mess, strike a bad patch, hit hard times, have a hard time of it, feel the pinch, paint oneself into a corner, put oneself in a spot, tread carefully, pick one's way, tread on (*or* walk among) eggs (US), have one's hands full, bite off more than one can chew, have more than enough, be at a loss, be at one's wits' end, be at the end of one's tether, come to a standstill, have one's back to the wall, not know which way to turn, bear the brunt, go under, go to the wall, be out of one's depth, flounder, get one's ass in a bind (US inf)

21 **get into trouble**, get into hot water, be asking for trouble, fish in troubled waters, burn one's fingers, bring down on one's head (*or* around one's ears), cop it (Inf), catch it (Inf), catch a packet (Inf)

22 **cause trouble**, give trouble, irk, annoy, aggravate, exasperate, bedevil, try one's patience, lead one a merry dance, stir up a hornet's nest, have a tiger by the tail, have a wolf by the ears, open Pandora's box, raise the roof, raise the devil, raise Cain, raise (merry) hell, play (merry) hell, sow the wind and reap the whirlwind, raise hob (US inf), play hob (US inf)
▶ *607 Annoyance and Aggravation; 631 Behaviour*

23 **cause difficulties**, trouble, raise difficulties, find problems, find fault, criticize, carp, disrupt, put out, disturb, worry, bother, perturb, baffle, perplex, nonplus, puzzle, mystify, confuse, bewilder, inconvenience, discommode, obstruct, hamper, hinder, embarrass, corner, box in, trap, snooker, put to a lot of trouble, make things awkward, make things (*or* matters) worse, complicate matters, put to it, give one a hard (*or* bad) time, make it tough for, put one's foot in it, force (*or* push *or* drive) to the wall, stump (Inf), tree (US inf), drop one in it (Inf)
▶ *328 Disturbance; 378 Obstruction; 408 Disorder; 696 Unintelligibility*

24 **create difficulties**, raise difficulties, make things difficult, criticize, carp, find fault, find problems
▶ *670 Disapproval*

ADVERBS

25 **difficultly**, hardly, ill, with difficulty, at a pinch, in spite of, in the teeth of, with much ado, the hard way, against the stream, against the wind, uphill

26 **arduously**, strenuously, laboriously, punishingly, formidably

27 **problematically**, intricately, delicately, obscurely, unintelligibly

28 **awkwardly**, clumsily, ponderously, unwieldily, unmanageably, inconveniently, annoyingly, tediously

29 **perversely**, waywardly, stubbornly, obstinately, disobediently, disruptively, critically, censoriously, disapprovingly

265 Easiness

'Why Sir, it is much easier to say what it is not. We all know *what light is; but it is not easy to* tell *what it is.'* Samuel Johnson.

NOUNS

1 **easiness**, ease, facility, effortlessness, comfort, proficiency, competence, dexterity, fluency, ability, capability, talent, aptitude, skill, skilfulness, speed, efficiency, readiness
▶ *263 Ease; 485 Skill*

2 **simplicity**, simpleness, plainness, uncomplicatedness, unambiguousness, preciseness, precision, comprehensibility, understandability, clarity, intelligibility, lucidity, facileness, glibness, superficiality
▶ *271 Simplicity; 695 Intelligibility; 725 Clarity*

3 **wieldiness**, manageability, handiness, manoeuvrability, convenience, practicality, feasibility, practicableness, possibility, workability, flexibility, pliability, pliancy, adaptability

4 **ease of manner**, poise, nonchalance, polish, insouciance, sang-froid, calmness, confidence
▶ *618 Indifference*

5 **smoothness**, freedom, lack of hindrance, help, assistance
▶ *392 Help*

6 **easy thing**, simple twist of the wrist, soft option, sinecure, plain sailing, easy ride, clear course (US), clear coast (US), clear road, smooth road, royal road, the high road, easy meat, soft touch, sitting duck, easy target, no trouble, a pleasure, cinch (Inf), snap (Inf), doddle (Inf), breeze (Inf), picnic (Inf), setup (US inf), pie (US inf), velvet (US inf), pushover (Inf), walkover (Inf), child's play (Inf), kid's stuff (Inf), piece of cake (Inf), duck soup (US inf), cushy number (Inf), dead cert (Inf), sure thing (Inf), no sweat (Inf)

7 **easing**, facilitation, smoothing, expediting, hastening, speeding, quickening, streamlining, simplifying, simplification, clarification
▶ *262 Haste*

8 **disentanglement**, disembarrassment, disinvolvement, extrication, disengagement, freeing, clearing, disen-

cumberment, uncluttering, disburdenment, unburdening, unscrambling, unsnarling
▶ *407 Order; 409 Arrangement*

ADJECTIVES

9 **easy**, facile, not difficult, not hard, undemanding, effortless, painless, light, moderate, unburdensome, smooth, uncomplicated, simple, uninvolved, straightforward, plain, clear, intelligible, elementary, glib, superficial, dead easy, dead simple, easy as pie, easy as falling off a log, nothing to it, simple as ABC, like shooting fish in a barrel (US), like taking candy from a baby (US), with the current (*or* tide), with the crowd, downstream, downhill, downhill all the way, no sooner said than done, cushy (Inf), Mickey Mouse (Inf), easy as winking (Inf), easy-peasy (Inf)
▶ *271 Simplicity; 695 Intelligibility; 725 Clarity*

10 **feasible**, practicable, workable, practical, possible, facilitating, helpful, useful, labour-saving
▶ *102 Possibility; 237 Usefulness; 392 Help*

11 **made easy**, made easier, facilitated, simplified, user-friendly, accessible, comprehensive, comprehensible, in plain English (*or* language) (Inf)

12 **wieldy**, wieldable, manageable, manoeuvrable, tractable, flexible, pliable, pliant, malleable, ductile, yielding, handy, convenient, foolproof, untroublesome, practical, adaptable, smooth-running, easy-running (US), easy-flowing (US), frictionless, lubricated, well-oiled, well-greased

13 **easy-going**, undemanding, lenient, tolerant, permissive, indulgent, tractable, docile, relaxed, calm, serene, acquiescent, compliant, submissive, biddable
▶ *388 Submission; 648 Leniency*

14 **relaxed**, comfortable, painfree, troublefree, carefree, easy in one's mind, leisurely, unhurried, gentle
▶ *263 Ease; 333 Slowness*

VERBS

15 **be easy**, present no difficulties, give no trouble, make no demands, be one's for the asking, be had for the asking, have a simple answer, come out easily, be easy as pie

16 **make easy**, make easier, facilitate, ease, assist, aid, help, help on, help along, smooth, grease, oil, lubricate, iron out, pave the way, smooth the way, prepare the way, grease the ways (US), soap the ways (US), grease the wheels, clear, unclog, unblock, unjam, unbar, free, loose, open up, clear the ground, clear the way, make way for, not stand in the way of, make all clear for (US), open the door to, bridge the gap, allow, permit, enable, make possible, promote, advance, further, forward, hasten, speed, accelerate, expedite, pioneer, give scope, make clear, explain, clarify, simplify, gloss, popularize, vulgarize, interpret, translate
▶ *262 Haste; 268 Slipperiness; 271 Simplicity; 392 Help; 725 Clarity; 757 Permission*

17 **do easily**, make light (*or* little) of, make light work of, make short work of, think nothing of, do with both eyes shut, do with one hand tied behind one's back, do standing on one's head, take in one's stride, take to like a duck to water, be in one's element, be quite at home, have it easy, have it soft (US), have it all one's own way, have the game in one's hands, carry all before one, have it in the bag, hold all the trumps, freewheel, coast, coast home, sail home, breeze in, walk over the course (US), win in a walk (US), win hands down, win at a canter, have a walkover
▶ *246 Success*

18 **disentangle**, disembarrass, disinvolve, extricate, disengage, free, clear, disencumber, lighten, unload, unclutter, disburden, unburden, alleviate, obviate, cut free, untie, unravel, liberate, unscramble, unsnarl, untangle
▶ *407 Order; 409 Arrangement*

19 **go easily**, go smoothly, run smoothly, go (*or* run) like clockwork, work like a machine (US), work well, flow, glide, roll, slide, coast, freewheel, sweep, sail, go (*or* run) on oiled wheels

20 **take it easy**, swim with the stream, drift with the current, go with the tide, save oneself the trouble, take the easy way out, take the line of least resistance, look for a short cut, go easy, put one's feet up (Inf), cool it (Inf), easy does it (Inf)
▶ *263 Ease*

ADVERBS

21 **easily**, effortlessly, comfortably, facilely, simplistically, superficially, without difficulty, readily, simply, without ado, no problem, like nothing (US), just like that, at the flick of a switch, with one's eyes closed, with one hand tied behind one's back, hands down, freely, smoothly, without let or hindrance, without a hitch, like clockwork, swingingly (Inf), no sweat (Inf)

266 Obscurity

NOUNS

1 **obscurity**, obscuration, lack of clarity, obfuscation, unintelligibility, incomprehensibility, opacity, lack of transparency, cloudiness, obsidian, fogginess, fuzziness, murkiness, muddiness, difficulty, hard words, Johnsonese, ornament, purple prose, tortuousness, convolution, involved style, complexity, muddle, gobbledegook, confusion, indistinctness, vagueness, uncertainty, imprecision, impreciseness, inexactness, inaccuracy, indefiniteness, abstraction, indirectness, allusion, ambiguity, equivocalness, shapelessness, amorphousness, convolution, mysteriousness, enigma, abstruseness, profundity, depth, overcompression, ellipsis, flood of words, verbiage, diffuseness, jibberish, mumbo jumbo, inelegance, lack of naturalness, stiffness
▶ *124 Unimportance; 156 Depth; 264 Difficulty; 269 Brevity; 270 Vagueness; 274 Error; 408 Disorder; 453 Uncertainty; 456 Ignorance; 523 Darkness; 524 Dimness; 528 Opaqueness; 542 Decoration; 544 Inelegance; 696 Unintelligibility; 736 Concealment*

ADJECTIVES

2 **obscure**, unclear, obfuscatory, unintelligible, incomprehensible, opaque, not transparent, cloudy, foggy, fuzzy, murky, muddy, as clear as mud, hard, obsidian, difficult, full of difficult words, Johnsonian, ornamental, purple, tortuous, convoluted, involved, complex, confused, gnostic, muddled, indistinct, vague, uncertain, imprecise, inexact, inaccurate, indefinite, abstract, indirect, allusive, ambiguous, Cimmerian, cabalistic, equivocal, shapeless, amorphous, mysterious, enigmatic, cryptic, abstruse, esoteric, arcane, recondite, profound, deep,

overcompressed, elliptical, diffuse, jibbering, mumbo-jumbo, inelegant, not natural, stiff, crabbed

► *124 Unimportance; 156 Depth; 264 Difficulty; 269 Brevity; 270 Vagueness; 274 Error; 408 Disorder; 453 Uncertainty; 456 Ignorance; 523 Darkness; 524 Dimness; 528 Opaqueness; 542 Decoration; 544 Inelegance; 696 Unintelligibility; 736 Concealment*

VERBS

3 **make obscure**, obscure, obfuscate, make abstruse, complicate, confound, muddy, confuse, muddle, mix up, use gobbledegook

ADVERBS

4 **obscurely**, unintelligibly, incomprehensibly, fuzzily, murkily, ornamentally, tortuously, indistinctly, vaguely, imprecisely, inexactly, inaccurately, indefinitely, indirectly, allusively, ambiguously, equivocally, mysteriously, enigmatically, cryptically, abstrusely, profoundly, elliptically, inelegantly, stiffly

267 Stickiness

NOUNS

1 **adhesion**, adhesiveness, holding together, sticking (together), cohesion, cohesiveness, attachment, bonding, connection, connectedness, linkage, continuity, coherence, unity, stickiness, cementation, agglutination, conglutination, soldering, welding, agglomeration, conglomeration, consolidation, congealment, condensation, concentration, compaction, inseparability, indivisibility, birds of a feather

► *132 Consecutiveness; 373 Connection; 374 Combination; 376 Gathering; 416 Density*

2 **tenacity**, tenaciousness, pertinacious, perseverance, persistence, determination, endurance, stubbornness, obstinacy, headstrongness, bull-headedness, holding on, attachment, adherence, loyalty, fidelity, stick-to-itiveness (US inf)

► *360 Retention; 423 Toughness*

3 **adhesive**, glue, superglue, fish glue, gum, birdlime, lime, epoxy resin, fixative, paste, size, clay, lute (*or* luting), cement, putty, mortar, plaster, grout, sealing wax, solder, flypaper, sticky tape, masking tape, Scotch™ tape, Sellotape™, Blu-tack™, sticking plaster, adhesive tape (US), Elastoplast™, Band-Aid™ (US), magnet

4 **adherent**, sticky label, decal, stamp, barnacle, limpet, remora, leech, parasite, bur, brier, bramble, clinging vine, gum, chewing gum, toffee, taffy (US), treacle, molasses (US)

5 **follower**, disciple, apostle, adherent, supporter, suitor, fan, satellite, dependent, parasite, hanger-on, clinger, sycophant, sucker (Isnf), sponger (Inf), clinging vine (US inf), groupie (Inf)

VERBS

6 **adhere**, cohere, hang together, hold together, grow together, hold, hold fast, bunch, bunch up, bunch together, close ranks, stand side by side, stand shoulder to shoulder, sit cheek by jowl, stick, stick close(ly), stick together, grip, clasp, grasp, take hold of, hug, embrace, squeeze, cling to, twine around, close with, grapple with, clinch, fit, fit tight(ly), fit like a glove, mould the figure, stick like glue, stick onto, cleave to, come (*or* rub) off on, freeze onto, stick like a leech, stick like a limpet, cling like ivy, condense, coagulate, solidify, consolidate, agglomerate, conglomerate, freeze

7 **cause to adhere**, stick, stick to, affix to, stick together, hold together, gum, glue, superglue, agglutinate, conglutinate, paste, lute, cement, weld, solder, braze, unite, join

8 **be tenacious**, persevere, adhere, hold on, hang on, stick to, cling to, attach oneself to, hold on like a bulldog, show loyalty to

ADJECTIVES

9 **adhesive**, adherent, coherent, cohesive, connective, sessile, sticky, gummy, tacky, gluey, viscous, viscid, colloidal, dense, condensed, concentrated, compact, solid, congealed, coagulated, concrete, indivisible, infrangible, inseparable, inextricable, linked, bonded, cemented, close, side-by-side, shoulder-to-shoulder, cheek-by-jowl, close-fitting, close-packed, continuous, tight, clinging, figure-hugging, moulding, skintight

10 **tenacious**, pertinacious, persevering, persistent, determined, enduring, stubborn, obstinate, bull-headed, attached, loyal, faithful, supportive, stick-to-itive (US inf), dependent, parasitic, sycophantic, clingy (Inf)

ADVERBS

11 **cohesively**, unitedly, in unison, coherently, indivisibly, solidly, compactly, densely, concretely, inseparably, inextricably, tightly, side by side, closely, shoulder to shoulder, cheek by jowl, stickily, viscously, like a limpet, like ivy

12 **tenaciously**, pertinaciously, persistently, determinedly, enduringly, stubbornly, obstinately, loyally, faithfully, parasitically, sycophantically

268 Slipperiness

NOUNS

1 **slipperiness**, slitheriness, lubrication, nonfriction, lubricating, lubrification (Lit), smoothness, slickness, sleekness, lubricity, grease job (Inf), lube (Inf)

► *421 Smoothness*

2 **runniness**, liquid, liquidity, fluidity, looseness, bagginess, floppiness, uncondensed state, wateriness, sliminess

► *133 Discontinuity; 372 Separation; 377 Dispersal; 431 Fluid*

3 **oiliness**, greasiness, waxiness, unctuousness, unctuosity, soapiness, saponacity (*or* saponaceousness), fattiness, fatness, pinguidity

4 **anointment**, unction, oiling, inunction, chrismation

► *10 Ritual*

5 **lubricant**, lubricator, lubricating oil, lubricating agent, anti-friction, graphite, plumbago, black lead, silicone, glycerine (*or* glycerin), wax, grease, tallow, cart grease, motor oil, oil, *oleum* (L), soap, lather, mucilage, mucus, synovia, saliva, spit, spittle

► *431 Fluid*

6 **ointment**, salve, balm, lotion, cream, unguent, unguentum, inunction, inunctum, unction, chrism, emollient, lenitive, soothing syrup, embrocation, demulcent, spikenard, nard, balsam, macassar

▶ *394 Remedy*

7 **pomade**, pomatum, brilliantine, hair conditioner, setting lotion, styling mousse, styling gel, cleanser, cold cream, face cream, hand lotion (*or* cream), lanolin, eye lotion, eyewash, collyrium, eyebath

▶ *547 Beautification*

8 **lubricator**, oilcan, grease gun

▶ *438 Tool*

9 **duplicity**, trickiness, slyness, craft, cunning

▶ *645 Cunning; 700 Deception*

ADJECTIVES

10 **slippery**, slippy, nonstick, unconsolidated, loose, undone, friable, smooth, crumbly, slithery, slidy, slimy, sleek, slick, skiddy (Inf), glassy, like grains of sand, free, wide-ranging, lax, slack, relaxed, streaming, running, runny, watery, liquid, fluid

11 **lubricated**, oiled, well-oiled, well-greased, smooth-running, not rusty, silent

12 **lubricant**, lubricative, lubricating, lubricatory, lubricational, lenitive, emollient, soothing

13 **slippery**, slithery, sliding, unctuous, unctional, unguinous, oleaginous, oleic, fat, fatty, adipose, pinguid, pinguidinous, pinguescent, lardy, lardaceous, blubbery, tallowy, suety, sebaceous, oily, greasy, waxy, rich, buttery, butyraceous, soapy, saponaceous, mucoid

14 **unguent**, unguentary, unguentous, chrismal, chrismatory

15 **crafty**, deceptive, sly, duplicitous, untrustworthy

VERBS

16 **slip**, slither, slide, skate, skid, skidder, glide, glissade

17 **liquefy**, melt, thaw, run, become runny, unstick, unglue, peel off, unpeel, pull off, pull apart, detach, undo, free, loose, loosen, separate

18 **lubricate**, lubrify (Lit), lubricitate, oil, grease, wax, beeswax, soap, lather, grease leather, butter, lard, glycerolate, glycerinate, glycerinize

19 **anoint**, salve, unguent, embrocate, dress, pour oil (*or* balm) upon, smear, daub, cream, pomade, lard

20 **ease**, smooth over, smooth the way, oil (*or* grease) the wheels, pour oil on troubled waters, soap the ways

21 **cheat**, double-deal, double-cross, smooth talk, con (Inf)

ADVERBS

22 **slimily**, snakily, runnily, fluidly

23 **oilily**, greasily, soapily, slickly, unctuously

24 **duplicitously**, slyly, cunningly

269 Brevity

I strive to be brief, and I become obscure. Horace.

NOUNS

1 **conciseness**, concision, brevity, briefness, shortness, succinctness, pithiness, pithy saying, crispness, compactness, terseness, curtness, brusqueness, taciturnity, monosyllabism, words of one syllable, laconism, laconicism, briskness, exactness, incisiveness, pointedness, nutshell, the long and the short of it, the heart of the matter, witticism, soul of wit, brachylogy, concise style, economy of words, no words wasted, few words, clipped speech, portmanteau word, compression, telegraphese, ellipsis, elision, syncope, apocope, abbreviation, contraction, truncation, shortening, compendiousness, sententiousness, abridgment

▶ *149 Shortness; 659 Discourtesy; 732 Shyness*

2 **outline**, summary, synopsis, precis, résumé, brief sketch, compendium, condensation, monostich, haiku, epitome, maxim, aphorism, epigram, clerihew

▶ *723 Summary; 745 Maxim*

ADJECTIVES

3 **concise**, brief, short, succinct, pithy, crisp, compact, terse, curt, brusque, taciturn, monosyllabic, laconic, sparing of words, brisk, exact, incisive, trenchant, pointed, to the point, in a nutshell, short and sweet, brachylogous, concisely styled, economically worded, tight-knit, portmanteau, compressed, telegraphic, elliptic, syncopal, clipped, abbreviated, contracted, truncated, shortened, compendious, epitomical, aphoristic, epigrammatic, sententious, outlined, summarized, summary, condensed, abridged, cut, not long in the telling

▶ *149 Shortness; 659 Discourtesy; 732 Shyness*

VERBS

4 **be concise**, waste no words, need few words, put in a nutshell, express pithily, cut a long story short, put it bluntly, not beat about the bush, come (straight) to the point, telescope, compress, compact, condense, abridge, cut, abbreviate, truncate, clip, shorten, contract, outline, sketch, epitomize, synopsize (US), sum up, summarize, abstract, precis, cut short, cut off, epigrammatize, pull no punches, talk turkey (US inf), give it straight (Inf), tell it like it is, cut the cackle (Inf), get down to brass tacks (Inf), get down to the nuts and bolts (*or* nitty-gritty) (Inf)

▶ *149 Shortness; 723 Summary*

ADVERBS

5 **concisely**, briefly, succinctly, pithily, crisply, compactly, tersely, curtly, brusquely, laconically, briskly, exactly, incisively, trenchantly, pointedly, telegraphically, elliptically, compendiously, sententiously, summarily, with few words, without wasting words, in brief, in short, in a word, in a nutshell, to the point, in outline, to sum up, to put it succinctly, to cut a long story short, in words of one syllable

270 Vagueness

He really deserves some sort of decoration…a medal inscribed 'For Vaguery in the Field'. John Osborne.

NOUNS

1 **diffuseness**, diffusion, diffusiveness, profuseness, copiousness, abundance, superabundance, amplitude, amplification, elaboration, expansion, extension, protraction, enlargement, expatiation, filler, expletive, padding, extra, circumstantiality, minuteness, detail, detailed account, blow-by-blow account, superfluity, repetitiveness, repetition, reiterativeness, reiteration, twice-told tales, redundancy, redundance, tautology, pleonasm, excess, richness, rich vocabulary, fertility, output, productivity, productiveness, vein, flow, outpouring, exuberance, gush, effusiveness, effusion, verboseness, verbosity,

loquacity, talkativeness, nonstop talking, wordiness, verbiage, long-windedness, waffle, prolixity, cloud of words, epic length, tedium, rigmarole, empty talk, rhetoric, oration, tirade, sermon, disquisition, dissertation, logorrhoea, verbal diarrhoea (Inf), blah (Inf)

▶ *112 Repetition; 148 Length; 190 Expansion; 219 Excess; 277 Duration; 562 Fertility; 620 Boredom; 722 Essay; 729 Speech; 731 Talkativeness*

2 **circumlocution**, circuitous writing, periphrasis, ambage (Lit), roundabout phrase, digression, deviation, discursion, excursion, excursus, rambling, wandering, indirectness, irrelevance, pointlessness, aimlessness, sidetrack, departure, beating about the bush, equivocalness

▶ *109 Unrelatedness; 211 Addition; 325 Deviation; 408 Disorder; 479 Equivocation*

ADJECTIVES

3 **diffuse**, diffusive, profuse, prolific, copious, abundant, superabundant, detailed, minute, amplified, expanded, extended, protracted, drawn out, long-drawn-out, spun out, padded out, padded, long, loose-knit, lengthy, never-ending, nonstop, going on and on, repetitive, reiterative, epic, repeated, tautologous, tautological, redundant, pleonastic, superfluous, excessive, talkative, verbose, loquacious, fluent, gushing, effuse, effusive, inspired, wordy, exuberant, rich, fertile, flowing, overflowing, polysyllabic, sesquipedalian, waffling, prosy, prolix, long-winded, windy, fustian, flatulent, pretentious, empty, incoherent, ornate, rhetorical, magniloquent, bombastic, turgid, voluminous, tedious, boring, in love with one's own voice, of many words

▶ *112 Repetition; 148 Length; 190 Expansion; 219 Excess; 277 Duration; 542 Decoration; 562 Fertility; 620 Boredom; 722 Essay; 729 Speech; 731 Talkativeness*

4 **circumlocutory**, circuitous, periphrastic, ambagious (Lit), roundabout, deviating, digressive, discursive, excursive, rambling, wandering, oblique, indirect, irrelevant, pointless, aimless, sidetracked

▶ *109 Unrelatedness; 211 Addition; 325 Deviation; 408 Disorder*

VERBS

5 **be diffuse**, amplify, enlarge upon, expatiate, dilate, expand, extend, lengthen, protract, draw out, spin out, pad out, pad, repeat, repeat oneself, reiterate, tautologize, gush, flow, overflow, pour out, let oneself go, wax eloquent, elaborate, particularize, detail, go into detail, go on and on, never end, discourse at length, waffle, orate, harangue, rant, rant and rave, use long words, bore, spin a long tale, ramble on, blether on, rabbit on (Inf)

▶ *112 Repetition; 148 Length; 190 Expansion; 620 Boredom; 722 Essay; 729 Speech; 731 Talkativeness*

6 **be circuitous**, digress, diverge, deviate, ramble, maunder, wander, make no point, not come to the point, beat about the bush, get sidetracked, get off the subject, go off on (*or* at) a tangent

▶ *109 Unrelatedness; 325 Deviation*

ADVERBS

7 **diffusely**, diffusively, profusely, prolifically, copiously, abundantly, minutely, in detail, repetitively, tautologously, tautologically, verbosely, loquaciously, effusively, in full, long-windedly, bombastically, turgidly, with many words, at length, at great length, on and on, ad nauseam, *in extenso* (L)

8 **circuitously**, periphrastically, in a roundabout way, digressively, discursively, obliquely, indirectly, on (*or* at) a tangent

271 Simplicity

A child of five would understand this. Send somebody to fetch a child of five. Groucho Marx.

Our life is frittered away by detail...Simplify, simplify. Henry David Thoreau.

ADJECTIVES

1 **simple**, plain, basic, ordinary, common, commonplace, common-variety, garden-variety, everyday, workaday, homy, homely, homespun, humble, lowly, austere, severe, Spartan, spare, ascetic, stark, bald, bare, naked, classic, neat, uncluttered, stripped-down, clear, clean, pure, unadulterated, unmixed, uninvolved, uncomplicated, unpretentious, unaffected, unassuming, modest, chaste, uninflated, played-down, unemphatic, undramatic, unsensational, restrained, sober, serious, dry, stodgy, tedious, boring, humdrum, mundane, usual, vernacular, matter-of-fact, prosaic, quotidian, mundane, unimaginative, uninspired, unpoetical, common or garden

▶ *138 Generality; 140 Rule; 255 Purity; 256 Cleanness; 265 Easiness; 543 Elegance; 552 Undress; 574 Commoner; 620 Boredom; 623 Humility; 632 Habit; 674 Modesty; 675 Vulgarity; 695 Intelligibility; 725 Clarity; 728 Understatement*

2 **unadorned**, unembellished, undecorated, unornamented, untrimmed, ungarnished, unpainted, uncoloured, unvarnished

3 **natural**, artless, simple-hearted, candid, frank, blunt, open, guileless, ingenuous, honest, veracious, direct, straightforward, plain-speaking, forthright, unpretentious, unaffected, unassuming, unfeigning, unsophisticated

▶ *646 Naivety; 698 Truth*

NOUNS

4 **simplicity**, unadorned simplicity, simpleness, plainness, ordinariness, commonness, homeyness, homeliness, humbleness, lowliness, austerity, severity, spareness, asceticism, ascesis, starkness, baldness, bareness, nakedness, neatness, clarity, cleanness, cleanliness, purity, unpretentiousness, modesty, chastity, restraint, soberness, seriousness, dryness, stodginess, tediousness, boredom, usualness, matter-of-factness, mundaneness, common speech, everyday speech, idiom, natural idiom, vernacular, prose, plain prose, plain words, plain English, household words, intelligibility

▶ *255 Purity; 256 Cleanness; 552 Undress; 620 Boredom; 623 Humility; 632 Habit; 674 Modesty; 675 Vulgarity; 695 Intelligibility; 725 Clarity*

5 **unadornment**, unembellishment, lack of decoration, lack of ornamentation, lack of colour

6 **naturalness**, artlessness, candidness, candour, frankness, bluntness, openness, honesty, veracity, directness, straightforwardness, unpretentiousness, unaffectedness, plain speech, plain speaking, home truth, speaking straight from the shoulder, mincing no words

▶ *646 Naivety; 698 Truth*

VERBS

7 **be simple**, make simple, simplify, use common speech, use plain English, speak plainly, speak simply, come to the point, say outright, call a spade a spade, speak straight from the shoulder, mince no words, make no bones about it, tell it like it is, tell one straight to his (*or* her) face, get down to brass tacks (Inf), talk turkey (US inf)

▶ *695 Intelligibility; 698 Truth; 719 Interpretation; 725 Clarity*

ADVERBS

8 **simply**, plainly, basically, starkly, baldly, purely, unpretentiously, undramatically, candidly, frankly, bluntly, openly, directly, point-blank, intelligibly, clearly, matter-of-factly, prosaically, in the vernacular, in plain words, in common parlance, in prose, not to put too fine a point upon it, in words of one syllable

272 Ridiculousness

The sublime and the ridiculous are often so nearly related that it is difficult to class them separately. One step above the sublime makes the ridiculous; and one step above the ridiculous makes the sublime again. Thomas Paine.

NOUNS

1 **ludicrousness**, daftness, absurdity, laughableness, foolishness, comicality, drollery, eccentricity, clowning, buffoonery, whimsicality, zaniness, bizarreness, bathos, folly, senselessness, fatuity, fatuousness, nuttiness (Inf)

2 **slapstick comedy**, farce, burlesque, knockabout, custard pie

3 **object of ridicule**, idiot, fool, clown, eccentric, buffoon, figure of fun, stooge, fall guy, straight man, twit (Inf), nut (Inf)

▶ *621 Derision*

4 **joke**, malapropism, spoonerism, piece of nonsense, drollery, clowning, howler, mistake, boob (Inf), booboo (Inf)

ADJECTIVES

5 **ridiculous**, preposterous, far-fetched, daft, nutty (Inf), laughable, priceless, absurd, asinine, foolish, funny, comical, clownish, droll, eccentric, bizarre, Pythonesque, zany, humourous, witty, comic, farcical, slapstick, clownish, hilarious, wacky (Inf), rib-tickling (Inf), side-splitting (Inf), risible, fatuous, burlesque, knockabout, derisory, funny ha-ha (Inf), rum (Inf)

VERBS

6 **be ridiculous**, play the fool, go from the sublime to the ridiculous, arse about (Inf)

7 **make one laugh**, have them rolling in the aisles, be funny, be hilarious, tickle one's fancy (Inf), set one off (Inf), give one the giggles (Inf)

ADVERBS

8 **ridiculously**, preposterously, hilariously, absurdly, laughably, comically

273 Accuracy

NOUNS

1 **accuracy**, precision, preciseness, exactness, exactitude, meticulousness, fastidiousness, scrupulousness, subtlety, nicety, refinement, strictness, rigidity, pedantry, rigour, rigorousness, acuity, attention to detail, hair-splitting, pinpoint accuracy, mathematical precision, clockwork precision, perfect pitch, fine tuning

▶ *656 Formality*

2 **correctness**, attention to fact, truth, literalness, literalism, the literal truth, the letter, faithfulness, fidelity, high fidelity, realism, naturalism

▶ *95 Reality; 698 Truth*

3 **accurate thing**, precise measurement, precision instrument, fine adjustment, dead centre, micrometer, metronome, atomic clock, fine detail, finer points, fine distinction, nice distinction, quibble, legal quibble, fine line, *mot juste* (Fr), proven fact, documented fact, photographic memory, bull's-eye (Inf), hole in one (Inf)

▶ *28 Physics; 281 Timekeeping*

4 **accurate person**, pedant, hair-splitter, quibbler, nitpicker (Inf)

▶ *702 Sophistry*

ADJECTIVES

5 **accurate**, precise, exact, perfect, pinpoint, detailed, meticulous, scrupulous, rigorous, pedantic, hair-splitting, subtle, nice, point-blank, dead right (Inf), spot on (Inf), on the button (Inf), bang-on (Inf), nit-picking (Inf)

6 **correct**, factual, truthful, literal, true-to-the-letter, word-perfect, true-to-life, unerring, verbatim, faithful, lifelike, high-fidelity, realistic, naturalistic, photographic

VERBS

7 **be accurate**, go into details, go into particulars, particularize, refine, hone, split hairs, stick to the facts, stick to the letter, go by the book (Inf), dot the i's and cross the t's (Inf), hit the nail on the head (Inf), score a bull's-eye (Inf)

ADVERBS

8 **accurately**, precisely, exactly, just, just so, dead, squarely, on the mark, right, to a nicety, correctly, literally, faithfully, verbatim, word for word, letter by letter, by the book, (according) to the letter, to the nth degree, plumb (Inf), plumb on (Inf), to a hair (Inf), to a T (Inf)

274 Error

It is the true nature of mankind to learn from mistakes not from example. Fred Hoyle.

NOUNS

1 **mistake**, error, fault, miscalculation, misconstruction, misconception, misinterpretation, misjudgment, misapprehension, misunderstanding, false conclusion, wrong turning, false move, bad move, false step

2 **inaccuracy**, imprecision, inexactness, inexactitude, looseness, sloppiness, carelessness, laxity, negligence, approximation, guesswork, speculation, generalization, randomness, shooting in the dark (Inf), hit or miss (*or* hit and miss) (Inf)
3 **erroneousness**, wrongness, untrueness, untruth, falsity, falseness, incorrectness, fallaciousness, fallacy
► *699 Falsehood*
4 **faulty reasoning**, fallacy, sophistry, flawed logic, circular argument, inconsistency, self-contradiction, sloppy thinking, choplogic
► *4 Philosophy*
5 **misrepresentation**, distortion, falsification, misquotation, misstatement, travesty, parody, caricature
6 **fallibility**, human error, subjectivity, prejudice, bias, self-deception, wishful thinking, delusion, illusion, hallucination, false impression, popular misconception, superstition, old wives' tale
► *450 Belief*
7 **errancy**, wrongdoing, culpability, guiltiness, aberrancy, deviancy, perversion, heresy, heterodoxy, unorthodoxy
► *802 Wrong*
8 **moral error**, transgression, misdeed, sin, offence, crime
► *796 Immorality*
9 **trivial error**, slip, slip-up, lapse, oversight, omission, slip of the tongue, *lapsus linguae* (L), slip of the pen, *lapsus calami* (L), Freudian slip, miscue (Inf)
10 **blunder**, bungle, gaffe, faux pas, glaring error, bloomer (Inf), blooper (Inf), clanger (Inf), boner (Inf), howler (Inf), screamer (Inf), boob (Inf), boo-boo (Inf), muff (Inf), fluff (Inf), goof (Inf), banana skin (Inf), botch-up (Inf), balls-up (*or* ball up) (Inf), foul-up (Inf), louse-up (Inf), cockup (Inf), screw-up (Inf), fuck-up (Inf)
11 **grammatical error**, solecism, spelling mistake, misspelling, dropping one's aitches, mispronunciation, bad grammar, incorrect usage, faulty syntax, misusage, abuse of language, abuse of terms, cacology, barbarism, spoonerism, malapropism, Goldwynism, bull, Irish bull, ambiguity, tautology, double negative, split infinitive, dangling participle, folk etymology, anacoluthia (Lit), catachresis (Lit), murdering the Queen's English (Inf)
12 **typing error**, typographical error, literal, printing error, misprint, erratum, corrigendum, clerical error, typo (Inf)
13 **sporting error**, miss, mishit, miscue, no-ball, own goal, wide, dropped catch, hit wicket, double fault
14 **technical error**, bug, glitch, hitch, virus, gremlins (Inf)

ADJECTIVES

15 **erroneous**, wrong, untrue, incorrect, false, fallacious, illogical, faulty, flawed, falsified, inaccurate, inexact, loose, inconsistent, self-contradictory, distorted
16 **errant**, erring, fallible, culpable, guilty, sinful, aberrant, deviant, perverse, perverted, heretical, unorthodox
17 **mistaken**, in error, at fault, wrong, all wrong, self-contradicting, prejudiced, biased, deluded, wide of the mark (Inf), way off the mark (Inf), off the track (*or* rails) (Inf)

VERBS

18 **be in error**, misunderstand, misapprehend, get it wrong, labour under a false impression, bark up the wrong tree (Inf), back the wrong horse (Inf), have another thing coming (Inf)
19 **make a mistake**, err, miscalculate, misconstrue, misinterpret, misjudge, misrepresent, distort, parody, caricature, falsify, misstate, misquote, overlook, omit, misspell, mispronounce, misprint, mishit, misfield, miscue, slip, slip up, lapse, bungle, blunder, boob (Inf), muff (Inf), botch up (Inf), balls up (*or* ball up) (Inf), foul up (Inf), louse up (Inf), cock up (Inf), screw up (Inf), fuck up (Inf)
20 **transgress**, err, sin, deviate, lapse, fall

ADVERBS

21 **erroneously**, in error, mistakenly, by mistake
22 **wrongly**, incorrectly, badly, faultily, awry, amiss, inaccurately, approximately, imprecisely, out of true, inexactly, loosely, carelessly, without thinking

275 Time

Except Time all other things are created. Time is the creator; and Time has no limit, neither top nor bottom. The Persian Rivayat.

Men talk of killing time, while time quietly kills them. Dion Boucicault.

O aching time! O moments big as years! John Keats.

NOUNS

1 time, space-time, space-time continuum, the fourth dimension, arrow of time, time warp, time travel, time machine, timeslip, chronon, tachyon, ontological time, psychological time, sense of time

► *28 Physics*

2 passage of time, lapse of time, ravages of time, time and tide, (Old) Father Time, time's winged chariot, time the enemy, time the great healer, the sands of time

3 duration, continuation, extent, time span, span, allotted span, life span, threescore years and ten, course, course of time, stretch, space, spell, period, limited period, fixed term, stint, reign, office, tenure, tenancy, tour of duty, shift, a bit, a while, a short while

4 term, semester, quarter, cycle, season, year, month, calendar month, lunar month, fortnight, week, day, hour, minute, second, millisecond, microsecond, nanosecond, aeon, millennium, century, decade, olympiad, epoch, era, geological period

► *30 Earth Science*

5 indefinite period, indefinite time, some time, age, aeon, ages, days, a while, heyday, palmy days, salad days

6 interval, interlude, lull, break, tea (*or* coffee) break, breather, respite, pause, interim, interregnum, meantime, breathing space, interim period, pause for breath, time-out

7 time measurement, clock time, real time, right time, exact time, chronology, chronography

8 dating, radiometric dating, carbon dating, thermoluminescent dating, tree-ring dating, dendrochronology

9 time zone, local time, daylight saving, International Date Line, sidereal time, solar time, ephemeris time, equation of time, Greenwich Mean Time, British Summer Time, Double Summer Time, Central European Time, Atlantic Standard Time, Atlantic Daylight Time, Eastern Standard Time, Eastern Daylight Time, Central Standard Time, Central Daylight Time, Mountain Standard Time, Mountain Daylight Time, Pacific Standard Time, Pacific Daylight Time, Yukon Standard Time, Yukon Daylight Time, Alaska–Hawaii Standard Time, Alaska–Hawaii Daylight Time, Bering Standard Time, Bering Daylight Time

10 chronometry, chronoscopy, horology, timekeeping, watchmaking, clockmaking

11 date, day, Calends, Nones, Ides, birthday, name day, saint's day, anniversary, occasion, red-letter day, moment, instant, juncture, point, appointed day, fixed day, right time, right moment, zero hour, H-hour, D-day

12 musical time, rhythm, metre, beat, tempo, polyrhythm, pulse, syncopation, time signature

► *18 Music*

13 timer, counter, timing device, time clock, timepiece, clock, watch, chronometer, horologe, chronograph, chronogram, calendar, Julian calendar, Gregorian calendar, perpetual calendar, diary, daybook

14 timekeeper, chronologist, chronographer, chronicler, annalist, diarist, calendar-maker, calendarist, horologist, clockmaker, watchmaker, clock watcher

VERBS

15 pass, pass by, elapse, roll by, roll on, flow, flow by, flow onwards, drag, drag by, drag on, fly, fly by, intervene

16 time, keep time, measure time, clock, monitor, record, count, judge, set, set a date for, set a time for, settle on a date, settle on a time, schedule, timetable, time it right, mark time, beat time

17 date, calendar, chronologize, assign a date to, be dated, carry (*or* bear) a date

18 adjust the clock, synchronize, synchronize watches, set the alarm, the hands of the clock, put the clocks forward, put the clocks back

19 clock on, clock off, clock in (*or* out), watch the clock, clockwatch, count the hours (*or* minutes)

ADJECTIVES

20 temporal, time-based, time-related, temporary

21 lasting through time, long-lasting, constant, chronic, eternal, perpetual, everlasting, immemorial, time-honoured, horological, pending, throughout

22 periodic, periodical, cyclic, repetitive, annual, yearly, biannual, biennial, monthly, weekly, daily, hourly

23 occasional, sporadic, intermittent, infrequent
24 between times, interim, intermediate, intercalary, intercalated, intervallic, interwar, interglacial, interlunar
25 of known date, dated, in date order, chronological, chronometric, chronographic, chronogrammatic, calendrical, annalistic

ADVERBS

26 all the time, while, whilst, between whiles, during, in the course of, all along, all through, so long as, till, until, for now, for the time being, in the meantime, meanwhile, in the interim, for the interim, for a time, for a season, for the duration, the whole time, always, ever, forever, day by day, from day to day, day in day out, week in week out
27 at what time, when, at the time, then, whereupon, at that moment, now, at this moment, at this moment in time, yesterday, today, tonight, tomorrow, this morning, this afternoon, this evening, sometime, someday, any day, any time
28 sometimes, often, now and then, now and again, on and off, occasionally, infrequently, sporadically, intermittently, from time to time, once in a while
29 one day, once upon a time, in the days (*or* time) of, in the year of, AD (Anno Domini), BC (Before Christ), AC (Ante Christum), AH (Anno Hegirae *or* Anno Hebraico), AUC (Anno urbis conditae), CE (Common Era), BCE (before the Common Era)
30 chronologically, temporally, annually, biannually, perennially, perpetually, eternally, forever, for always
▶ *279 Eternity*

276 Time Span

Decades have a delusive edge to them. They are not, of course, really periods at all, except as any other ten years would be. But we, looking at them, are caught by the different name each bears, and give them different attributes, and tie labels on them, as if they were flowers in a border. Rose Macaulay.

NOUNS

1 period, interval, span, time, time span, term, stretch, space, fit, spell, break, pause, breather (Inf)
▶ *275 Time*
2 time period, era, aeon, age, generation, epoch, millennium, chiliad, century, decade, decennium, quinquennium, year, quarter, month, fortnight, week, day, weekday, hour, minute, second, moment, instant, millisecond, microsecond, nanosecond
3 geological period, era, epoch, eon, olam
▶ *30 Earth Science*
4 period of activity, stint, spell, phase, turn, watch, session, shift, work shift, overtime, half-time, working day, man-hour, tour, tour of duty, term, school term, academic year, semester, tenure, term (*or* tenure) of office, fiscal (*or* financial) year, term of imprisonment, sentence, bout, innings, inning (US), go (Inf), whack (Inf)
5 recurrent period, series, season, cycle, iteration, periodic function, recurrent pattern, menstrual cycle, menstruation, biorhythm, circadian rhythm, biological clock, photoperiodism

GEOLOGICAL TIME INTERVALS

Archaean	Lower Triassic	Pliocene
Cambrian	Mesozoic	Precambrian
Carboniferous	Middle Jurassic	Proterozoic
Cenozoic	Middle Triassic	Quaternary
Cretaceous	Miocene	Recent
Devonian	Neogene	Silurian
Eocene	Oligocene	Tertiary
Holocene	Ordovician	Triassic
Jurassic	Palaeocene	Upper Carboniferous
Lower Carboniferous	Palaeogene	Upper Cretaceous
Lower Cretaceous	Palaeozoic	Upper Jurassic
Lower Jurassic	Permian	Upper Triassic
	Phanerozoic	
	Pleistocene	

▶ *292 Season*
6 periodicity, recurrence, return, repetition, repetitiveness, regularity
7 periodical, periodical publication, magazine, journal, learned journal, academic journal, newsletter, bulletin, weekly, monthly, annual

ADJECTIVES

8 periodical, regular, repetitive, repetitious, iterative, returning, recurrent, quinquennial, millennial, millenary (*or* millenarian), cyclic, seasonal, yearly, annual, biannual, biennial, monthly, weekly, daily
▶ *298 Regularity*
9 periodic, intermittent, sporadic, discontinuous, fitful, irregular
▶ *299 Irregularity*

VERBS

10 be periodical, recur, reappear, repeat, iterate, reiterate, return, come round again
11 make periodical, regulate, regularize, modulate

ADVERBS

12 periodically, regularly, recurrently, repeatedly, repetitively, repetitiously
13 for specified periods, quinquennially, biennially, biannually, yearly, annually, quarterly, monthly, weekly, daily, hourly
14 for short periods, on occasion, occasionally, at odd times, now and again, now and then, fitfully, irregularly, off and on, on and off, by fits and starts

277 Duration

NOUNS

1 duration, period, term, course, course of time
2 time, length of time, passage of time, lapse of time, march of time, river of time, tide of time, flow of time, time flies, *tempus fugit* (L)
3 continuity, continuation, continuousness, progress, progression, process, due process (of law)
4 long-lastingness, endurance, permanence, fixity, permanency, constancy, durableness, durability, perdurability (Lit), stability, staying power, survival, will to live
5 long duration, a long time, an age, ages, aeons, generations, a lifetime, a life sentence, a long stretch, an eter-

nity, days, years, years on end, a month of Sundays, time immemorial, donkey's years (Inf), yonks (Inf)

VERBS

6 **last**, endure, stay, stay the course, stand, stand the test of time, abide, remain, last out, hold out, survive, outlive, outlast, hang on, hang on in there (Inf)

7 **go on**, move on, continue, progress, proceed, run, run its course, elapse, pass

ADJECTIVES

8 **lasting**, durable, enduring, long-lasting, long-lived, abiding, continuing, continuous, continual, longstanding, evergreen, long-term, lifelong

9 **permanent**, unceasing, incessant, everlasting, eternal, perpetual, perennial, undying, immortal

ADVERBS

10 **for the duration**, to the end, to (*or* till) the bitter end, forever, for evermore, for good, for good and all

11 **long**, for long, for a long time, till the cows come home (Inf), till one is blue in the face (Inf)

12 **everlastingly**, permanently, perennially, without end, eternally, without stopping, without pausing for breath, incessantly, continually, continuously

278 Transience

Faith, Sir, we are here to-day, and gone tomorrow. Aphra Behn.

Not to hope for things to last for ever, is what the year teaches and even the hour which snatches a nice day away. Horace.

NOUNS

1 **transience**, transitoriness, impermanence, fugacity (Lit), momentariness, suddenness, quickness, brevity, ephemerality, instability, evanescence, volatility

2 **transient thing**, passing fashion, nine-days wonder, flash in the pan, shooting star, meteor, bird of passage, brief encounter, a ship that passes in the night, *sic transit gloria mundi* (L)

3 **short duration**, brief span, short time, short space of time, moment, instant, a second or two, a minute or two, just a minute, just a second, just a tick (Inf), half a mo (Inf)

VERBS

4 **be transient**, pass, pass away, flit, fly, fly away, be fleeting, melt, melt away, decay, rot, turn to ashes, come to dust, fade, evanesce, evaporate, vanish, vanish into thin air, disappear, disappear in a puff of smoke, burst like a bubble, burst like a balloon, crumble away, fall to pieces, fall apart, shatter

5 **make transient**, shorten the life of, cut off, curtail, make disappear, bring to an end, put an end to, shatter the dreams of, burst someone's bubble (*or* balloon)

ADJECTIVES

6 **transient**, fleeting, flying, fugitive, fugacious (Lit), quick, ephemeral, perishable, unstable, brief, short, short-term, shortlived, evanescent, volatile, disappearing, fading, decaying, passing, transitory, meteoric, momentary, sudden, here today and gone tomorrow

7 **impermanent**, temporary, one-off, single-use, throw-away, biodegradable, nondurable, brittle, fragile, mortal

ADVERBS

8 **transiently**, transitorily, ephemerally, quickly, fleetingly, temporarily, impermanently, not long, briefly, shortly, momentarily, for a moment, in a moment, suddenly, in an instant, in a trice, in a twinkling, in the twinkling of an eye

9 **for the time being**, meantime, in the meantime, meanwhile, between whiles, for the nonce (Lit)

279 Eternity

Eternity's a terrible thought. I mean, where's it going to end? Tom Stoppard.

NOUNS

1 **eternity**, endlessness, infinity, infinitude, everlastingness, time without end, forever and a day, timelessness, perpetuity, sempiternity (Lit), permanence, continuity, changelessness, perpetuity, incorruptibility, imperishability

► *275 Timelessness*

2 **a long time**, age, aeon, epoch, olam, millennium, donkey's years

► *275 Time; 276 Time Span*

3 **life without end**, life everlasting, deathlessness, immortality, heaven, paradise, the hereafter, the afterlife, the next world, eternal rest (*or* rest eternal)

4 **eternalization**, perpetuation, memorialization, remembrance

VERBS

5 **be eternal**, last forever, outlast, outlive, remain forever, endure forever, go on forever, continue forever, never cease, be permanent, have no end

6 **eternalize**, perpetuate, preserve, maintain, immortalize, memorialize, remember forever

7 **make permanent**, establish, set up, continue, preserve, maintain

ADJECTIVES

8 **eternal**, everlasting, never-ending, unending, infinite, perpetual, timeless, sempiternal (Lit), permanent, enduring, durable, incorruptible, imperishable, immortal, undying, deathless, unchanging, immutable, evergreen

9 **agelong**, aeonian, millennial, immemorial

10 **continuing forever**, ceaseless, unceasing, continuous, constant, unending, nonstop, interminable, incessant, going on and on, lasting, everlasting, changeless

ADVERBS

11 **eternally**, throughout eternity, forever, for always, for aye (Lit), evermore, for evermore, for ever and ever, for ever and a day, until the end of time, till the crack of doom, till doomsday, to infinity, until the twelfth of never, until the Greek Calends (Lit), until hell freezes over, without end, on and on, through thick and thin, for better or worse, from age to age, from generation to generation, world without end, for good, for good and all, for keeps (Inf)

280 Immediacy

Carpe diem. (Seize the day.) Horace.

NOUNS

1 **immediacy**, immediateness, lack of delay, instantaneousness, instantaneity, directness, urgency, emergency, exigency, promptness, promptitude

2 **closeness**, nearness, proximity, contiguity

3 **instant**, second, split second, a sec, half a sec, moment, twinkling, twinkling of an eye, flash, jiffy (Inf), mo (Inf), half a mo (Inf), tick (Inf), half a tick (Inf)

4 **point in time**, point, moment, juncture, occasion, instant

ADJECTIVES

5 **immediate**, instantaneous, instant, prompt, quick, fast, rapid, swifty, speedy, direct, split-second, urgent, on-the-spot

6 **allowing no delay**, demanding, importunate, burning, imperative, exigent, urgent

7 **prepared for immediate use**, ready-to-wear, off-the-peg, ready-to-eat, fast (of food), convenience (of food), precooked

ADVERBS

8 **immediately**, instantaneously, instantly, without delay, at once, now, right now, on the spot, swiftly, speedily, rapidly, quick, as quick as lightning, as quick as a flash, promptly, right away, straight away, forthwith, before one knows it, before you can say Jack Robinson (Inf), like greased lightning (Inf), in two shakes of a lamb's tail (Inf), yesterday (Inf)

9 **in the shortest possible time**, in no time, in an instant, in the same breath, in a twinkling, in the twinkling of an eye, in a trice, in a flash, on the instant, ASAP (as soon as possible), posthaste

281 Timekeeping

I am a sundial, and I make a botch
Of what is done far better by a watch. Hilaire Belloc.

NOUNS

1 **timekeeping**, timing, dating, scheduling, timetabling, calendar-making

► *275 Time; 276 Time Span; 277 Duration; 407 Order; 409 Arrangement*

2 **timetable**, calendar, schedule, diary, journal, order of the day, order of service, programme, course, curriculum, list

► *220 List; 409 Arrangement; 484 Plan*

3 **chronology**, chronography, dendrochronology (*or* tree-ring dating), radiocarbon dating, thermoluminescence, calendar, Julian calendar, Gregorian calendar, era, epoch, date, date line, International Date Line, time zone, clock time, local time, civil time, astronomical time, solar time, sidereal time, Universal Time (UT), the time now, the exact time, time of day, time of night, hour, summertime, daylight saving time, 12-hour clock, 24-hour clock

► *275 Time*

4 **horology**, clockmaking, watchmaking

5 **timekeeper**, timepiece, horologe, chronometer

6 **clock**, grandfather clock, grandmother clock, longcase clock, carriage clock, travelling clock, wall clock, bracket clock, electric clock, quartz clock, digital clock, alarm clock, clock radio, cuckoo clock, water clock, clepsydra, speaking clock, Tim (Inf), atomic clock, caesium clock, body clock, biological clock

7 **watch**, wristwatch, analogue watch, digital watch, quartz watch, pocket watch, fob, turnip, hunter, half-hunter, repeater, clip watch

8 **face**, clockface, watchface, dial, analog dial, hands, gnomon, digital display, chronogram

9 **hourglass**, sandglass, egg timer, sundial, chronograph, chronoscope

10 **signal**, time signal, hooter, siren, four-minute warning, gong, bell, minute gun, starting gun, stopwatch, timer, timing device, time switch, time-fuse, time bomb

► *742 Sign*

11 **person keeping time**, timekeeper, referee, time beater, conductor, bandleader

12 **chronologist**, chronologer, chronographer, calendrist, calendar-maker, clockmaker, watchmaker, horologist

13 **chronicler**, diarist, annalist, historian, historiographer, scribe, recorder

► *3 History; 744 Record*

VERBS

14 **keep time**, clock, time, monitor, set a date for, set a time for, fix the time, fix the date, fix the day, schedule, timetable, slate, adjust the hands of the clock, put the clock forward, put the clock back, set the alarm, synchronize watches

15 **chronologize**, calendar, date, be dated, carry a date, bear a date, record, chronicle, diarize, keep a journal

16 **measure time**, count the hours, count the minutes, mark time, beat time, keep time, watch the clock, clock in (*or* clock on), clock out (*or* clock off)

ADJECTIVES

17 **timekeeping**, horological, chronometric, chrono-

TIMEPIECES AND TIMERS

alarm clock (*or* watch)	Caesium clock	gnomon	marine chronometer	stemwinder (watch)
Albert (watch)	clepystra (*or* water clock)	grandfather clock	metronome	stopwatch
ammonia clock	clock radio	grandmother clock	pendulum clock	sundial
analogue clock (*or* watch)	cuckoo clock	half–hunter (watch)	pocket watch	travelling clock
astronomical clock	digital clock (*or* watch)	hourglass	quartz (*or* quartz–crystal) clock	wall clock
atomic clock	egg timer	hunter (watch)		water clock
box chronometer	electric clock	isochronon	repeater	wristwatch (*or* wristlet watch)
calendar clock	electronic clock	journeyman (watch)	sandglass	

graphic, chronologic, chronological, annalistic, diaristic, calendrical, chronogrammatic, temporal

ADVERBS

18 horologically, by the clock, chronologically, chronographically, annalistically, at this hour, at that hour, at this time, at that time, o'clock, a.m., p.m.

282 Present Time

No time like the present. Proverb.

The now, the here, through which all future plunges to the past. James Joyce.

NOUNS

1 present time, the present, the here and now, the present moment, this moment, this moment in time, this very minute, this second, this instant, this hour, this very day, today, tonight, this morning, this afternoon, this evening

▶ *280 Immediacy*

2 the present day, the time being, this time, the nonce (Lit), this day, this day and age, the present time, the present situation, the current situation, contemporary life, the modern day, our day, our own day, the present generation, modern times, the modern world, the world of today, the contemporary world, one's contemporaries

▶ *285 Same Time*

3 actuality, happening, existence, present tense

4 up-to-dateness, modernity, modernism, currency, topicality, the height of fashion

▶ *295 Newness*

VERBS

5 be present, exist, be, live, not be absent, be now, live in the present, live for today, live for the day, *carpe diem* (L), live in the modern world, be modern, modernize

ADJECTIVES

6 present, current, existent, existing, extant, of today, of this date, of today's date, topical, actual, contemporary, contemporaneous, modern, fashionable, in fashion, up-to-date, bang up-to-date, instant

▶ *280 Immediacy; 285 Same Time*

7 occasional, temporary, provisional, interim, passing, pro tem (*or pro tempore*)

8 available, at hand, to hand, ready, ready to hand, here, there, in attendance, nearby, close by, standing by, accounted for, present and correct

ADVERBS

9 at present, at this moment, now, at this time, at this moment in time, right now, just now, presently, today, tonight, nowadays, these days

10 for the present, for the moment, for a while, meanwhile, in the meantime, in the interim, for this occasion, for the occasion, for the time being, for the nonce, not for long, provisionally, temporarily

283 Future Time

FUTURE, *That period of time in which our affairs prosper, our friends are true and our happiness is assured.* Ambrose Bierce.

NOUNS

1 future time, future, the future, futurity, time to come, days and years to come, the years ahead, the time ahead, future years, the near future, tomorrow, *mañana* (Sp), tomorrow morning, tomorrow afternoon, tomorrow evening, tomorrow night, the day after tomorrow, next week, next month, next year, the far future, the distant future, the remote future, the long run, the long term, after ages, the womb of time, the morrow (Lit), by-and-by (US), sweet by-and-by (US inf)

▶ *145 Distance; 147 Closeness*

2 future generation, descendants, heirs, inheritors, successors, posterity

3 future condition, future state, what the future brings, what the future holds, better days, jam tomorrow, uncertain future, fate, destiny, coming events, what fate has in store, latter days, doomsday, the crack of doom, the end of the world, the end of time, the millennium, Judgment Day, Day of Judgment, Last Judgment, postexistence, good time coming, life after death, life to come, the hereafter, the next world, kingdom come, paradise, nirvana, heaven, damnation, the underworld, hell, hellfire, eternal fire

▶ *7 Religion; 8 Divinity*

4 looking to the future, eschatology, teleology, looking ahead, waiting, expectancy, expectation, great expectations, anticipation, foresight, foreknowledge, prescience, preparation, prospect, prospects, likelihood, outlook, forecast, prediction, prophecy, premonition, astrology, horoscope, fortune-telling, crystal-ball gazing, crystal-gazing, second sight

5 predictor, forecaster, prophet, prophetess, soothsayer, oracle, seer, diviner, augur, geomancer, astrologer, fortune teller, crystal gazer

▶ *11 Occultism; 243 Preparation; 474 Expectation; 475 Prediction*

6 future event, forthcoming event, scheduled event, advent, coming, approach of time

▶ *302 Forward Motion*

VERBS

7 be in the future, be to come, lie ahead, lie in the future, lie just around the corner, draw near, approach, come soon, overhang, threaten, stare one in the face, cast a shadow before, draw nigh (Lit)

8 intend, have every intention to, be about to, plan to, have in mind to, have an eye to, mean to, shall, will

9 look ahead, look forward, think of the future, hope for, foresee, predict, presage, prophesy, have a premonition, divine, foretell, augur, look into a crystal, read tea leaves, cast bones, haruspicate

10 expect, await, wait for, see it coming, prepare for, have prospects, put by for a rainy day, anticipate, forestall, forewarn, take thought for tomorrow, take the long view, take the long-term view

ADJECTIVES

11 **future**, forthcoming, upcoming (US), coming, to come, yet to come, to be, yet to be, eventual, later, ahead, near, at hand, near at hand, close at hand, just round the corner, approaching, oncoming, due, fated, destined, imminent, threatening, overhanging, impending, pending, waiting, waiting in the wings, nigh (Lit)

12 **predictable**, foreseeable, probable, possible, potential, likely, certain, sure

13 **foreseen**, foretold, predicted, expected, anticipated, awaited, looked for, hoped for, promised

ADVERBS

14 **in the future**, in future, tomorrow, next week, next month, next year, someday, one fine day, some other time, not now, soon, imminently, just round the corner, in the offing, in the wind, on the horizon, getting on for, heading for, at the right time, in the fullness of time, eventually, later, later on, ultimately, when the time is right, when the time is ripe, by and by, in due course, on the morrow (Lit)

15 **after**, afterwards, hereafter, hereinafter (Lit), henceforth, henceforward, from this time forth, from now on, from this moment on

16 **predictably**, probably, possibly, potentially, likely, in the stars

284 Past Time

Even God cannot change the past. Agathon.

Study the past, if you would divine the future. Confucius.

The past is a foreign country: they do things differently there. L. P. Hartley.

NOUNS

1 **past time**, past times, the past, times past, times gone by, former times, recent past, yesterday, yesterday morning, yesterday afternoon, yesterday evening, last night, the day before yesterday, last week, last month, last year, yesteryear (Lit), years gone by, the far past, prehistory, protohistory, history, the remote past, ancient times, antiquity, high antiquity, remote ages, time immemorial, a bygone age, bygone days, days of old, good old days, days of yore, olden days, auld lang syne (Scot), golden age, the ancient world

▶ *3 History; 296 Oldness*

2 **retrospection**, retrospective, remembrance, reminiscence, review, reprise, looking back

▶ *462 Memory*

3 **geological period**, geological epoch, Precambrian era, Palaeozoic era, Mesozoic era, Cenozoic era, Cambrian period, Ordovician period, Silurian period, Devonian period, Carboniferous period, Permian period, Triassic period, Jurassic period, Cretaceous period, Tertiary period, Palaeocene period, Eocene period, Oligocene period, Miocene period, Pliocene period, Quaternary period, Plistocene period, Holocene period, the age of amphibians, the age of reptiles, glacial period, ice age

▶ *276 Time Span*

4 **prehistoric age**, Stone Age, Palaeolithic period, Mesolithic period, Neolithic period, Chalcolithic period, Bronze Age, Iron Age

5 **historical period**, heroic age, Classical Age, Dark Ages, Middle Ages, Renaissance, Age of Reason, Age of Enlightenment, *ancien régime* (Fr), Industrial Revolution

6 **people of the past**, people of antiquity, prehistoric people, cave dweller, caveman, Neanderthal man, Neanderthaler, Peking man, Cro-Magnon man, the ancients, Egyptians, Babylonians, Sumerians, Ethiopians, Phoenicians, Persians, ancient Greeks, ancient Romans, Etruscans, Parthians, Huns, Incas, Mayas, Toltecs, Aztecs, Picts, Vandals, Goths, Visigoths, Saxons, Angles, Caribs, Arawaks, Maori, Aborigines, American Indians

▶ *1 Anthropology; 3 History*

7 **thing of the past**, survival, remainder, museum piece, antique, relic, relict, remains, vestiges, fossilized remains, monument, ancient monument, ruin, ancient ruin, artefact (*or* artifact), megalith, dolmen, cromlech, menhir, standing stone(s), Stonehenge, ancient flint, arrowhead, eolith, microlith, earthwork, barrow, burial chamber, tholos, beehive tomb, fogou, pyramid, ziggurat, King Tutankhamen's tomb, dinosaur

▶ *3 History; 20 Architecture; 215 Remainder; 583 Burial; 742 Sign*

8 **excavation**, archaeological dig (Inf), dig (Inf)

▶ *449 Discovery*

9 **antiquarianism**, classicism, medievalism, archaeology, industrial archaeology, palaeontology, palaeozoology, palaeoanthropology, palaeogeography, palaeontography, palaeography, palaeethnology, palaeoclimatology, palaeometeorology, prehistoric anthropology, prehistoric archaeology

▶ *3 History*

10 **fossilization**, petrification, petrified forest, fossil, ammonite, trilobite, dinosaur, mammoth, fossil record, amber, fossil fuel, coal, coal measures, brown coal, peat, oil, petroleum

11 **antiquarian**, antiquary, palaeontologist, archaeologist, Egyptologist, Assyriologist, Hebraist, Arabist, classicist, medievalist, palaeozoologist, palaeoanthropologist, palaeogeographer, palaeontographer, palaeographer, palaeethnologist, palaeoclimatologist, palaeometeorologist, prehistoric anthropologist, prehistoric archaeologist

▶ *3 History*

12 **genealogy**, lineage, ancient lineage, pedigree, family history, family tree

▶ *132 Consecutiveness; 289 Succession*

VERBS

13 **be past**, be over, be over and done with, have expired, have had one's day, be in the past, be history, be lost and gone, have gone out with the Ark (Inf)

14 **pass**, pass away, pass into history, finish, end, elapse, expire, become extinct, die out, run out, run its course

15 **look back**, trace back, remember, reminisce, review, reprise, regress, antiquarianize, put the clock back, turn back the clock, turn back time, archaize, return to the past, go back to the past, hark back, relive, live in the past, look over one's shoulder, cast one's eyes backwards

16 excavate, excavate the past, unearth the past, exhume, unearth, dig up the past, archaeologize, conduct a dig (Inf)

ADJECTIVES

17 past, historical, historic, old, olden, prehistoric, prehistorical, protohistoric, ancient, early, earlier, elder, primitive, primal, primeval

18 over, over and done with, gone, gone for good, gone forever, lost forever, lost and gone, completely past, past and gone, bygone, finished, exhausted, ended, done, spent, completed, irrecoverable, dead, dead and gone, dead and buried, extinct, dead as a dodo

▶ *582 Death*

19 antiquarian, ancestral, antecedent, preceding, foregoing, out of date, outdated, outworn, outmoded, old hat, behind the times, anachronistic, belonging to the past, antiquated, fossilized, old-fashioned, obsolete, passé, past its sell-by date, long past, stale, moth-eaten

20 former, late, quondam, sometime, obsolescent, retired, emeritus, superannuated, deceased, no longer present, no longer serving, ex (Inf)

21 retrospective, retroactive, diachronic, remembering, reminiscing, looking back, backward-looking, retro (Inf)

ADVERBS

22 in the past, during the past, in past times, in times gone by, formerly, of old, in days of yore, ago, long ago, long since, once upon a time, years ago, ages ago, some time ago, a while ago, a while back, some while back, far back in the past, in the mists of time, at (*or* from) the dawn of time, from time immemorial, time out of mind, lately, recently, yesterday, yesterday evening, yestreen (Scot), the day before yesterday, last week, last month, last season, last year, yesteryear, within living memory, only yesterday, the other day, aforetime (Lit)

23 before now, hitherto, heretofore, yet, as yet, until now, till now, up to now, up to this moment, up to this time, *ex post facto* (L), already, no longer, not any more

24 retrospectively, historically, with hindsight, with the wisdom of hindsight, from experience, from past experience

285 Same Time

NOUNS

1 same time, same date, same day, simultaneity, contemporaneousness, contemporaneity, contemporariness, coevality, accompaniment, coexistence, existing together, concomitance, concurrence, coincidence, photo finish

2 present time, present age, present day, present moment, today, now

▶ *282 Present Time*

3 synchronism, synchronization, isochronism, sync (Inf), lip-sync (Inf)

4 equal race, dead heat, tie, draw, neck-and-neck, nip-and-tuck (US), level pegging (Inf), lock step (US)

5 contemporary, coeval, compeer, friend, classmate, one of the boys, one of the girls, one's contemporaries, one's peers, one's own generation, brother, sister, men (*or* women) of today, people of today, peer group, one of the lads, one of the lasses, one of the gang, age group, class, class of (a certain year)

VERBS

6 be simultaneous, exist simultaneously, be contemporary, happen at the same time, live at the same time, coexist, exist together, accompany, concur, coincide, encounter

7 synchronize, keep the same beat, keep in time, keep time with, stay in time, keep in step, keep in step with, keep pace with, march in lock step (US), go hand in hand, say together, sing together, chorus, sync (Inf)

8 run equally, run a dead heat, tie, draw, run neck and neck, run nip and tuck (US), be level pegging (Inf)

ADJECTIVES

9 simultaneous, coeval, contemporary, contemporaneous, coexistent, coexisting, coeternal, concomitant, coincident, coincidental, concurrent, accompanying, of the same generation, of the same year, of the same age, matched in age, twinned, of the same vintage

10 synchronized, synchronous, isochronal, isochronous, timed, phased, on (*or* with) the beat, in time, in step, in lock step (US), in sync (Inf)

11 equal, level, dead heat, tied, neck-and-neck, nip-and-tuck (US), nothing in it, on a par with, level pegging (Inf)

ADVERBS

12 simultaneously, at the same time, together, all together, coevally, contemporarily, contemporaneously, coeternally, concomitantly, concomitant with, coincidentally, concurrently, concurrent with

13 synchronously, isochronally, isochronously, in time, in step, *pari passu* (L), on (*or* with) the beat, in unison, in chorus, in concert, at one time, with one voice, as one man, as one, in sync (Inf)

14 equal with, level with, in a dead heat, neck and neck, nip and tuck(US), level pegged (Inf)

15 as, just as, even as, as soon as, at the moment of, just when, in the very moment that, in the same breath as, while (*or* whilst)

286 Different Time

Time present and time past
Are both perhaps present in time future
And time future contained in time past. T. S. Eliot.

NOUNS

1 different time, another time, asynchronism, archaism, some other time, other times, distant time, better time, more convenient time, any time but this (*or* now), the past, past time, former time, future time, the future, later time, wrong time, mistiming, wrong date, misdating, chronological error, anachronism, parachronism, prochronism, time shift, time warp, time traveller

▶ *288 Wrong Time*

ADJECTIVES

2 occurring at a different time, asynchronous, unsynchronized, off beat, off tempo, out of sync (Inf), out of time, of (*or* from) another time, of (*or* from) another age, unmodern, behind the times, retrogressive, out of date, archaic, ahead of the times, avant-garde, mistimed, misdated, anachronistic, anachronic, retro (Inf)

ADVERBS

3 **another time**, asynchronously, some other time, not now, not today, not at the moment, not just this minute, sometime, someday, sooner or later, any (old) time, tomorrow, in the future, later, soon, one of these days, *mañana* (Sp), yesterday, in the past, previously, earlier, then, once upon a time, anachronistically, anachronically

VERBS

4 **mistime**, misdate, live in the past, miss the moment, miss the beat

287 Timeliness

Liberality lies less in giving liberally than in the timeliness of the gift. Jean de La Bruyère.

NOUNS

1 **timeliness**, opportuneness, providence, providentiality, suitability, convenience, appropriateness, propitiousness, auspiciousness, favourableness, aptness, fitness, right time, right moment, just the time, perfect moment, readiness, ripeness, maturity, proper time, auspicious moment, good occasion, happy coincidence

▶ *239 Convenience*

2 **opportunity**, good opportunity, fine opportunity, favourable opportunity, golden opportunity, chance, good chance, happy chance, best chance, only chance, luck, good luck, opening, break, lucky break, piece of luck, stroke of luck, elbowroom, clear field, clear run, clear view, scope, stepping stone, look-in (Inf)

▶ *107 Chance*

3 **critical time**, critical moment, crucial time, crucial moment, critical juncture, crisis, key point, turning point, pivotal point, nexus, pinch, rub, crux, moment of truth, decisive moment, point of no return, pregnant moment, emergency, eleventh hour, last minute, nick of time

▶ *264 Difficulty; 294 Lateness*

VERBS

4 **be timely**, suit the occasion, fit the occasion, come at the right time (*or* moment), befit the occasion, befit the time, offer an opportunity, provide a chance

5 **take the opportunity**, profit by, cash in on, capitalize on, turn to good account, exploit, improve the occasion, take time by the forelock, *carpe diem* (L), take one's chance, seize one's chance, seize one's opportunity, grab one's opportunity, seize the day, create an opening for oneself, make hay while the sun shines, strike while the iron is hot, not be caught flatfooted (Inf)

ADJECTIVES

6 **timely**, opportune, seasonable, providential, propitious, auspicious, appropriate, apropos, suitable, suited, befitting, fitting, fit, convenient, apt, for the occasion, heaven-sent, welcome, favourable, fortunate, lucky, happy, felicitous

7 **critical**, crucial, decisive, momentous, pivotal, key, vital to the occasion

8 **in time**, on time, punctual, within the time limit, well-timed, well-judged, eleventh-hour, last-minute, deathbed

ADVERBS

9 **opportunely**, seasonably, providentially, propitiously, auspiciously, appropriate, apropos, suitably, befittingly, fittingly, fitly, conveniently, aptly, for the occasion, favourably, fortunately, luckily, happily, as (good) luck would have it

10 **critically**, crucially, decisively, momentously, pivotally

11 **in time**, on time, punctually, within the time limit, just in time, in the nick of time, at the last minute, at the eleventh hour, on one's deathbed

288 Wrong Time

The rule is, jam tomorrow and jam yesterday – but never jam today. Lewis Carroll.

NOUNS

1 **wrong time**, wrong date, wrong day, mix-up in dates, misdating, dating error, mistiming, untimeliness, anticipation, prolepsis, chronological error, anachronism, parachronism, metachronism, prochronism

▶ *274 Error*

2 **untimeliness**, mistiming, inopportuneness, inauspiciousness, unpropitiousness, unfavourableness, unseasonableness, ominousness, immaturity, unripeness, poor timing, bad timing, bad time, wrong time, unsuitable time, prematurity, pre-emption, earliness, lateness, tardiness, unpunctuality, bad time of the month, inopportune moment, untimely occurrence, awkward occurrence, untimely action, inexpedience, inappropriateness, unsuitableness, awkwardness, inconvenience, intrusion, interruption, disturbance, disruption

▶ *240 Inconvenience; 288 Wrong Time; 293 Earliness; 294 Lateness*

3 **lost chance**, lost opportunity, missed opportunity, misfortune, ill fortune, ill luck, bad luck, hard luck, mischance, misjudgment, mistake, error, blunder, bungle, boo-boo (Inf), boob (Inf)

▶ *247 Failure; 465 Misjudgment; 486 Unskilfulness; 666 Negligence*

4 **mishap**, misadventure, contretemps, accident, disaster, calamity, death

▶ *249 Adversity*

VERBS

5 **mistime**, antedate, anticipate, jump the gun, pre-empt, go off at half cock, (of clocks) gain, be fast, postdate, lag behind, take no note of time, (of clocks) lose, be slow

6 **take untimely action**, mistime, time badly, arrive at the wrong time, arrive early, arrive late, lose time, waste time, be late, misjudge, intrude, disturb, disrupt, interrupt, break in upon, bust in on, butt in, find engaged, shut the stable door after the horse has bolted

7 **lose one's chance**, be unlucky, lose an opportunity, waste an opportunity, spoil one's chances, wreck one's chances, throw away an opportunity, throw it all away, let an opportunity slip, let slip through one's fingers, allow the occasion to go by, miss the boat, miss the bus, blow one's chance (Inf), blow it (Inf)

8 **be busy**, be engaged, have a prior engagement, not

have time, have other things to do, have other fish to fry (Inf)

9 **make a mistake**, err, misjudge, blunder, bungle, put one's foot in it (Inf), put one's foot in one's mouth (US inf), drop a clanger (Inf), make a boo-boo (Inf), boob (Inf)

ADJECTIVES

10 **mistimed**, untimely, misdated, wrongly dated, undated, anachronistic, metachronistic

11 **too early**, antedated, previous, ahead of time, precipitate, overhasty, ahead of one's time, prochronistic, pre-emptive, proleptic

► *293 Earliness*

12 **too late**, tardy, overdue, unpunctual, behind time, post-dated, out of date, behind the times, parachronistic

► *294 Lateness*

13 **untimely**, ill-timed, inopportune, inauspicious, unpropitious, unfavourable, unseasonable, immature, unripe, ill-starred, ill-omened, ominous, not in time, unpunctual, out of turn, out of order, inexpedient, inappropriate, malapropos, unsuited, inapt, unsuitable, unbefitting, awkward, inconvenient, intrusive, interrupting, disturbing, disrupting

14 **anachronistic**, misdated, parachronistic, prochronistic, out of season

15 **busy**, engaged, having a prior engagement, not having time, having other things to do, having other fish to fry (Inf)

16 **mistaken**, erroneous, mistaking, erring, misjudging, blundering, bungling

17 **accidental**, unlucky, unfortunate, infelicitous, disastrous, calamitous

ADVERBS

18 **out of chronological order**, out of sequence, anachronistically, metachronistically, too soon, too early, ahead of time, ahead of one's time, pre-emptively, prochronistically, too late, behind time, unpunctually, behind the times, out of fashion, out of date, parachronistically

19 **at the wrong time**, at just the wrong time, inopportunely, inauspiciously, unpropitiously, unfavourably, unseasonably, ominously, inexpediently, inappropriately, malapropos, unsuitably, unbefittingly, awkwardly, inconveniently, intrusively, disturbingly, disruptively

20 **anachronistically**, parachronistically, prochronistically

21 **mistakenly**, erroneously, accidentally, unluckily, unfortunately, blunderingly, disastrously, calamitously

289 Succession

NOUNS

1 **succession**, sequence, order, arrangement, cycle, rota, list, turn, hierarchy, pecking order, Buggins's turn, queue, line (US), tailback, series, run, chain, train, retinue, entourage, suite, wake, following, subsequence, procession, process, progression, flow, flux, continuation, course, progress, forward movement, forward motion, successiveness

► *132 Consecutiveness; 134 Continuity; 300 Motion; 407 Order; 409 Arrangement*

2 **descent**, line of descent, lineage, family, family tree, tribe, race

3 **subordination**, inferiority, lesser importance, lower merit, no priority, little worth, second place, second class, second eleven, second division, last place

4 **accession**, takeover, inauguration, assumption, assumption of office, entry upon, entry into office, taking up the post of, taking over, transfer, changeover, elevation, promotion, inheritance

► *126 Originality; 130 Beginning; 215 Remainder*

5 **successor**, descendant, inheritor, heir, heir apparent, heir presumptive, heiress, beneficiary, replacement, substitute, next in line, next man in, new boy, new broom, new arrival, new kid on the block, new blood, fresh blood, newcomer

6 **posterity**, the unborn, later generations, future generations

► *283 Future Time; 561 Reproduction*

7 **subordinate**, inferior, the person in second place, assistant, right-hand man, subaltern, second fiddle, always the bridesmaid but never the bride

► *122 Inferiority*

8 **follower**, camp follower, groupie (Inf), hanger-on, sycophant, dependant, dependent relative, poor relation, last in the field, latecomer, incomer, upstart, last man in, no-hoper, also-ran

► *108 Relatedness; 215 Remainder; 223 Accompaniment; 294 Lateness*

9 **sequel**, continuation, development, follow-up, conclusion, end, result, net result, denouement, consequence, outcome, upshot, aftermath, postmortem, afterword, postlude, coda, epilogue, postscript, payoff (Inf), the way things pan out (Inf), the way the cookie crumbles (Inf)

VERBS

10 **succeed**, follow, follow in sequence, come next, come after, come last, bring up the rear, be subsequent to, be consequent upon, result, result from, ensue, proceed, supervene

11 **follow in office**, follow in the position of, accede to, succeed, succeed to, assume, assume office, assume the mantle, embark upon office, take over, take over the mantle, take over the reins, take the helm, replace, supplant, supersede, take up, enter upon, come into, become possessed of, come into possession of, come into ownership of

ADJECTIVES

12 **succeeding**, successive, successional, following, next, proximate, close, near, sequential, consecutive, ordered, arranged, second, another, every, every other, every second, alternate, subsequent, consequent, ensuing, pursuant, late, later, latter, last, latest

13 **subordinate**, inferior, less important, second-class, second-division

ADVERBS

14 **in succession**, successively, one after the other, one after another, one behind the other, in line, in a row, in sequence, in order, consecutively, running, on the trot (Inf)

15 **as follows**, secondly, in second place, in the second place, lastly, last

290 Daytime

'Tis always morning somewhere in the world. Richard Henry Horne.

NOUNS

1 **morning**, morning time, forenoon, a.m. (ante meridiem), dawn, false dawn, waking time, daybreak, break of day, crack of dawn, sunrise, sunup, morning light, first light, daylight, matins, prime, terce (*or* tierce), cockcrow, dawn chorus, rosy-fingered dawn, Aurora, Eos, morn (Lit), morrow (Lit)

▶ *293 Earliness; 522 Light*

2 **morning thing**, morning star, Venus, morning glory, morning sickness, crowing cock, early bird, breakfast, rush hour, elevenses

3 **noon**, 12 noon, 12 o'clock, 1200 hours, noonday, noontime, high noon, noontide, mid-day, middle of the day, eight bells, meridian (Lit)

4 **afternoon**, p.m. (post meridiem), matinée, five o'clock, afternoon tea, siesta, after (Inf)

ADJECTIVES

5 **morning**, matin, matinal, matutinal, forenoon, dawn, dawning, early, fresh, morning-fresh, dewy, antemeridian, auroral (Lit)

6 **noon**, high-noon, midday, meridian

7 **afternoon**, postmeridian

ADVERBS

8 **in the morning**, of a morning, at sunrise, at sunup, at dawn, at the crack of dawn, by the dawn's early light, at daybreak, at first light, at break of day, at the dawning of the day, at cockcrow, with the sun, with the lark, ante meridiem, every morning, mornings, aurorally (Lit)

291 Night-Time

The darkest hour is just before the dawn. Proverb.

NOUNS

1 **evening**, evening time, eve, early evening, p.m. (post meridiem), vespers, sunset, sundown, setting of the sun, going down of the sun, lighting-up time, dusk, twilight, evening twilight, gloaming (Scot), nightfall, close of day, day's end, moonrise, moonset, darkfall, eventide, evensong

▶ *294 Lateness; 524 Dimness*

2 **night**, night-time, bedtime, the cloak of night, (the) dark, darktime, darkness, the dark of night, blackness

▶ *532 Blackness*

3 **midnight**, 12 midnight, 12 o'clock, 24:00 hours, the witching hour, the dead of night, night watch, small hours, wee small hours

4 **evening thing**, sunset, evening star, Venus, Hesperus, evening news, evening class, evening primrose, rush hour, afternoon tea, dogwatch, soirée

5 **night thing**, owl, night shift, night school, nightlife, nightclub, dinner, sleep, dreams, nightmare

ADJECTIVES

6 **evening**, afternoon, postmeridian, vesperine, vesperal, twilight, dusky, crepuscular, nocturnal, dark, nightly, night-time, benighted (Lit)

ADVERBS

7 **evening**, every evening, in the evening, during the evening, afternoon, in the afternoon, every afternoon, post meridiem, every night, at night, after dark, nocturnally, in the dead of night, through the night, all through the night, overnight, by night, nightly, late, late at night, in the small hours, in the wee small hours, evenings, nights

292 Season

Four seasons fill the measure of the year;
There are four seasons in the mind of men. John Keats.

NOUNS

1 **season**, season of the year, time of year, time, period, annual period, quarterly period, spell, term, interval, dry season, rainy season, snow season, social season, the season, the English season, the New York season, tourist season, football season, baseball season (US), cricket season, basketball season, hunting season, shooting season, open season, duck season, deer season, grouse season, pheasant season, fishing season, close (*or* closed) season, ecclesiastical season, Easter season, Advent season, the Season (Christmas), silly season

▶ *275 Time; 276 Time Span; 654 Sociability*

2 **spring**, springtime, spring tide, vernal season, vernal equinox, point of Aries, seedtime, Easter, Eastertide, blossom time, budtime, Maytime, the merry month of May, the month of Maying, May Day, first cuckoo, rustle of spring

3 **summer**, summertime, good old summertime, summertide, growing season, Whitsuntide, Whitsun, midsummer, Midsummer (*or* Midsummer's) Day, summer solstice, high summer, dog days, haymaking, Indian summer, St Martin's summer, aestivation

▶ *493 Heat*

4 **autumn**, fall (US), fall of the leaf, back end (Dial), harvest, harvest time, harvest moon, hunter's moon, autumnal equinox, point of Libra, Michaelmas

▶ *43 Agriculture; 294 Lateness*

5 **winter**, wintertime, wintertide, midwinter, winter solstice, Christmas, Christmas time, the Season, yuletide, yule (Lit), hibernation

▶ *7 Religion; 9 Worship; 10 Ritual; 494 Cold*

VERBS

6 **spend the season**, summer, spend the summer, pass the summer aestivate, winter, overwinter, spend the winter, pass the winter, hibernate, have a long winter's sleep, celebrate Christmas, celebrate the yuletide, send Season's greetings

7 **season**, harden, anneal, inure, discipline, toughen, mature, acclimatize, acclimate, accustom

8 **mitigate**, temper, leaven, mollify, moderate

ADJECTIVES

9 **seasonal**, in season, out of season, equinoctial, solstitial

10 **spring**, vernal, springlike, flowery, sappy, juicy, young

11 **summer**, summery, summerlike, aestival, midsummer

12 autumn, autumnal, autumnlike, golden
13 winter, wintry, wintery, hibernal, winterlike, midwinter, hiemal, brumal
14 seasonable, suited to the weather, appropriate, suitable, convenient, timely, well-timed, welcome, providential, opportune
15 seasoned, hardened, toughened, matured, inured, accustomed
16 mitigated, tempered, leavened, mollified, moderated
17 in season, in (*or* on) heat, oestrous, rutting, lusting, leching (Inf)

ADVERBS

18 seasonally, equinoctially, vernally, in spring, summerly, in summer, autumnally, in autumn, wintrily, in winter

293 Earliness

Not to be abed after midnight is to be up betimes. William Shakespeare.

Early to rise and early to bed makes a male healthy and wealthy and dead. James Thurber.

NOUNS

1 earliness, promptness, promptitude, punctuality, punctualness, immediacy, dispatch, expedition, early start, head start, time to spare, readiness, alacrity, quickness, hastiness, haste, hurriedness, hurry, timeliness
▶ *262 Haste; 280 Immediacy; 287 Timeliness*
2 early hour, early time, early morning, unearthly hour, sunrise, sunup (US), dawn, first crack of dawn, first crack, daybreak, the small hours, the wee small hours
▶ *290 Daytime*
3 early stage, earliest stage, advanced stage, first step, early warning, early warning system, primeval stage, primitive stage, primitiveness, early history, ancient history, early man, beginning, very beginning, creation, big bang
▶ *130 Beginning; 284 Past Time*
4 early comer, early arrival, first arrival, advance man (US), premature baby, early riser, precursor, predecessor, ancestor, forefather, prophet, earliest inhabitant, primitive, aborigine, Aborigine (*or* Aboriginal) (Aus), American Indian, earliest settler, colonist, scout, explorer, discoverer, early bird (Inf), Johnny on the spot (Inf)
▶ *449 Discovery*
5 prematurity, prematureness, precipitance, prevenience, preparation, foresight, anticipation, expectation, impetuosity, haste, hastiness, early maturity, precociousness, precocity, pre-emption
▶ *243 Preparation*
6 getting ahead, getting in early, getting in on the ground floor, seizing one's chance, seizing the moment, seizing the occasion, taking the opportunity, jumping at the chance, moving with the times
▶ *129 Precedence*

VERBS

7 be early, arrive early, arrive first, arrive ahead of time, arrive ahead of schedule, get there early, get there ahead of time, get there first, start early, start too soon, jump the gun, pre-empt, anticipate, get a head start, gain a flying start, rise at the crack of dawn, gain time, be fast (of clocks), have time to spare, be ready and waiting, show readiness, hasten, hurry, dispatch, expedite
8 precede, precede in time, predate, get ahead of, go before, colonize, settle, scout ahead, explore, discover
9 prepare, precipitate, reserve, order, book, book in advance, engage, anticipate, expect, foresee, pre-empt, forestall, nip in the bud, prevent, catch napping, steal a march on, take the words out of one's mouth, step on someone's lines (US)
10 hasten, lose no time, jump to it (Inf), hop to it (Inf), get one's finger out (Inf), get a wiggle on (Inf), go off half-cocked (*or* at half-cock) (Inf), be half-baked (Inf), jump the gun (Inf)
11 get ahead, get in early, get in on the ground floor, seize one's chance, seize the moment, seize the occasion, take the opportunity, jump at the chance, move with the times

ADJECTIVES

12 early, first, earliest, prompt, punctual, on time, timely, immediate, expeditious, ready, ahead of time, ahead of schedule, advanced, alacritous, fast (of clocks), quick, hurried, hasty, summary, good and early (Inf), bright and early (Inf)
13 imminent, forthcoming, impending, looming, expected soon, at hand, near at hand, just round the corner
14 primeval, primitive, ancient
15 precursory, precursive, preceding, ancestral, aboriginal, indigenous, colonial, exploratory
16 premature, precipitate, precipitative, precipitous, precocious, forward, ahead of one's time, beforehand, forehand, too early, prevenient, preparatory, prophetic, foresighted, anticipatory, anticipative, expectative, impetuous, hasty, overhasty, too soon, pre-emptive, half-cocked (Inf), half-baked (Inf)

ADVERBS

17 early, at an early time, at the earliest, firstly, first, as soon as possible, soon, promptly, punctually, immediately, without delay, forthwith, directly, right away, expeditiously, readily, in advance, ahead of time, ahead of schedule, ahead of oneself, first thing, at the first opportunity, before time, forehand, ahead of its time, in the small hours, in the wee small hours, in time, in good time, on time, on schedule, to the minute, to the second, with plenty of time, with time to spare, quickly, hurriedly, hastily, summarily, before the ink was dry, betimes (Lit), anon (Lit), good and early (Inf), bright and early (Inf)
18 soon, presently, shortly, directly, imminently, before long, in a short time, in a while, in a short while, by and by, at short notice, suddenly, without notice, at the drop of a hat (Inf)
▶ *147 Closeness*
19 primevally, primitively, anciently, aboriginally, indigenously, colonially, ancestrally
20 prematurely, precipitately, precipitously, precociously, forwardly, ahead of one's time, beforehand, forehand, too early, preveniently, preparatorily, prophetically, foresightedly, anticipatorily, anticipatively, hastily, impetuously, overhastily, too soon

294 Lateness

'Twenty-three and a quarter minutes past', Uncle Matthew was saying furiously, 'in precisely six and three-quarter minutes the damned fella will be late.' Nancy Mitford.

Ah! the clock is always slow;
It is later than you think. Robert William Service.

NOUNS

1 **lateness**, unpunctuality, belatedness, tardiness, late arrival, last arrival, slowness, retardation, lag, time lag, lagging, delay, unreadiness, unpreparedness, slow development

► *333 Slowness*

2 **late hour**, the lateness of the hour, advanced hour, small hours, wee small hours, day's end, sunset, nighttime, last minute, eleventh hour, high time (Inf)

3 **delayed action**, delay, wait, delayed reaction, last-minute preparations, dilatoriness, procrastination, *mañana* (Sp), putting off, putting on hold, pigeonholing, tabling, postponement, deferment, deferral, adjournment, prorogation, prolongation, extension, protraction, filibuster, stonewalling, delaying tactics, prevention, hindrance, obstruction, jam, log jam (US), suspension, hold-up, red tape, blockage, block, restraint, detention, remand, moratorium, halt, pause, cooling-off period, truce, cease-fire, lull, respite, rest and recreation (R & R) (US), days of grace, stay of execution, stay, reprieve, last-ditch stand, last word, afterthought, esprit d'escalier, mothballing, putting on ice (Inf), putting in cold storage (Inf), putting on the back burner (Inf)

► *226 Stopping; 277 Duration; 343 Inactivity; 378 Obstruction*

4 **latecomer**, late arriver, last arriver, Johnny-come-lately, laggard, late developer, late bloomer, slow starter, slow learner, late riser, slugabed, sluggard, idler, delayer, slowpoke (US inf), slowcoach (Inf)

5 **delayer**, procrastinator, filibusterer, stonewaller, bureaucrat

VERBS

6 **be late**, arrive late, arrive last, stay up late, sit up late, stay out late, keep late hours, burn the candle at both ends, burn the midnight oil, awake late, oversleep, lag, lag behind, be behindhand, develop late, lose time, be slow (of clocks), drag one's feet, take one's time, take ages, drag on

7 **wait**, pause, stop, stay, tarry, linger, dawdle, waste time, loiter, hang around, hang about, await, be kept waiting, kick one's heels, cool one's heels, delay, dally, dilly-dally, hang fire, hang back, miss the boat, lose (*or* miss) one's chance

8 **delay**, stall, retard, set back, hold back, hold up, obstruct, jam, create a logjam (US), suspend, halt, block, stonewall, prevent, hinder, restrain, remand, detain, hold over, put off, postpone, reprieve, stay, adjourn, prorogue, defer, gain time, buy time, play for time, play the waiting game, filibuster, prolong, extend, protract, spin out, procrastinate, temporize, sleep on it, hold one's horses, bide one's time, wait and see, reserve, keep for later, have the last word, keep (*or* save) for a rainy day, withhold, file, shelve, pigeonhole, table, lay on the table, hold, hold on, hold the line, make a last-ditch stand, hang on, stand by, put on hold, mothball, put on ice (Inf), put in cold storage (Inf), put on the back burner (Inf)

ADJECTIVES

9 **late**, belated, happening late, delayed, not on time, never on time, overdue, unpunctual, dilatory, unready, unprepared, tardy, behind schedule, behind time, behindhand, slow, sluggish

10 **held up**, postponed, deferred, adjourned, prorogued, prolonged, extended, protracted, stonewalled, hindered, obstructed, suspended, blocked, tabled, stalled, restrained, detained, remanded, halted, jammed, logjammed (US), bogged down, on hold, mothballed, on ice (Inf), in cold storage (Inf), on the back burner (Inf)

11 **late in the day**, last-minute, eleventh-hour, deathbed

12 **delaying**, slowing, procrastinating, obstructive, obstructing, hindering, retarding, blocking, restraining, detaining, lagging, lagging behind, late-running, following, coming later

13 **later**, future, distant, upcoming

14 **dead**, deceased, late, late lamented, former, previous, past, erstwhile, sometime, old, posthumous

ADVERBS

15 **late**, lately, belatedly, unpunctually, dilatorily, unreadily, unpreparedly, tardily, behind schedule, behind time, behindhand, slowly, leisurely, at one's leisure, sluggishly, extendedly, protractedly, obstructively

16 **at a late hour**, at such a late hour, none too soon, at the last minute, at the eleventh hour, at last, at long last, on one's deathbed, too late

17 **later**, later on, much later on, in the future, at a later time, in time, in due course, in a while, after a while

18 **formerly**, lately, posthumously

295 Newness

He that will not apply new remedies must expect new evils: for time is the greatest innovator. Francis Bacon.

NOUNS

1 **newness**, recentness, recency, recent occurrence, contemporaneity, topicality, currency, up-to-dateness, new production, mint condition, state of the art, modernism, modernity, innovation, invention, originality, usualness, unfamiliarity, unknownness, newfangledness, gimmickry, novelty, neology, neologism, neophilia, new (*or* latest) wrinkle (Inf)

► *126 Originality; 282 Present Time*

2 **trendiness**, the latest craze, the latest fashion, fad (Inf), high fashion, artistic movement, modernism, postmodernism, New Wave, *Nouvelle Vague* (Fr), New Look, New Age, New Thought (US), futurism, *nouvelle cuisine* (Fr), the rage (Inf), the last word (Inf), the latest thing (Inf), the in thing (Inf), what's in (Inf)

► *553 Fashion; 724 Style*

3 **immaturity**, inexperience, youth, virginity, dewiness,

callowness, greenness, rawness, naivety, ingenuousness, innocence, freshness, cleanness, cleanliness

▶ *256 Cleanness; 555 Youth*

4 **beginning**, birth, start, inception, commencement, inauguration, initiation, generating, generation, opening, auspication, grand opening, house-warming, unveiling, launching, maiden voyage, first night, premiere

▶ *130 Beginning*

5 **fresh start**, new start, clean slate, *tabula rasa* (L), renewal, regeneration, renovation, restoration, refurbishment, rejuvenation, repainting, resurrection, revival, revivification, remake, change, reconstruction, rebuilding, restructure, redesign, reorganization, alteration, modernization, updating, upgrading, revisal, new look, new leaf, addition, extra, supplement, doing up (Inf)

▶ *393 Repair*

6 **avant-garde**, advance guard, vanguard, van, fashionable set, in-group, in-set, in-crowd, jet set, beautiful people, trendsetting group, younger generation, young generation, new generation, next generation

7 **new thing**, trend, gimmick, new wrinkle, new moon, new town, new maths, New Year, New Deal (US), New American Bible (US)

8 **new arrival**, newborn baby, newcomer, beginner, fledgling, amateur, novice, tyro, greenhorn, raw recruit, new recruit, new member, freshman, fresher, new convert, neophyte, new boy, new kid on the block (US), new broom, debutante, latecomer, upstart, parvenu, nouveau riche, incomer, immigrant, foreigner, alien, illegal alien, *novus homo* (L), Johnny-come-lately (Inf), rookie (Inf)

9 **modern person**, modern man (*or* woman), new man (*or* woman), trendsetter, avant-garde artist, avant-gardist, modernist, ultramodernist, postmodernist, futurist, advanced thinker, bright young thing, yuppie, faddist, neophiliac, neologist, neoteric

ADJECTIVES

10 **new**, brand new, newly, recent, contemporary, topical, current, up-to-date, modern, modernistic, futuristic, ultramodern, postmodern, innovative, revolutionary, inventive, advanced, original, first, latest, most recent, state-of-the-art, newly produced, just out, new-made, oven-fresh, mint condition, trendy, gimmicky, neological, neologistic, neologistical, neophytic, brand spanking new (Inf), bang up-to-date (Inf), hot off the press (Inf), in (Inf), faddish (Inf)

11 **unfamiliar**, unknown, not seen before, unheard of, unprecedented, unused, untried, untested, untrodden, unbeaten, unexplored, out of the ordinary, newfangled, novel, nontraditional, mould-breaking

12 **immature**, inexperienced, budding, aspiring, upstart, parvenu (*or* parvenue), nouveau riche, amateurish, amateur, novice, apprentice, new to the job, embryonic, inchoate, newborn, young, youthful, virginal, virgin, maiden, dewy, callow, green, raw, naive, naïf, ingenuous, innocent, fresh, fresh as a daisy, fresh as paint, clean, clean as a new pin, spick-and-span, rookie (Inf)

13 **inaugurated**, initiated, opened, unveiled, launched, premiered, premiere

14 **renewed**, renovated, restored, refurbished, regenerated, rejuvenated, refreshed, freshened up, touched up, repainted, resurrected, revived, revivified, remade, good as new, changed, reconstructed, rebuilt, restructured, redesigned, reorganized, altered, modernized, new look, updated, upgraded, revised, added, additional, extra, supplementary, done up (Inf)

15 **renewable**, restorable, reconstructible, rebuildable, redesignable, alterable, updateable, upgradeable, revisable

16 **avant-garde**, advanced, advance, trendsetting, trendy, fashionable, modish, à la mode, all the rage, with it (Inf)

VERBS

17 **become new**, begin again, start anew, start from the beginning, renew oneself, get up to date, start afresh, have a fresh start, have a new start, wipe the slate clean, reform, have a new look, turn over a new leaf

18 **be trendy**, follow the trend, try the latest craze, move with the times, get the new look, go contemporary, go modern, innovate, invent, originate, set a trend, try something new, get with it (Inf)

19 **begin**, give birth to, commence, generate, inaugurate, initiate, open, have a grand opening, have a house-warming, unveil, launch, take a maiden voyage, premiere

20 **make new**, renew, renovate, restore, refresh, freshen up, touch up, refurbish, rejuvenate, regenerate, repaint, resurrect, give a new lease of life, revive, revivify, remake, change, reconstruct, rebuild, restructure, redesign, reorganize, alter, modernize, update, bring up to date, upgrade, revise, add on, supplement, gentrify, trendify (Inf), yuppify (Inf), do up (Inf)

ADVERBS

21 **newly**, like new, as new, new, lately, latterly, of late, only yesterday, not long ago, a short time ago, just, just now, recently, contemporarily, topically, currently, modernistically, futuristically, innovatively, revolutionarily, inventively, originally, first, firstly, nontraditionally, unusually, neologically, neologistically

22 **again**, anew, afresh, once more, from the top, from the ground up, from the start, from the beginning, all over again, from scratch

23 **trendily**, fashionably, in fashion, modishly, in the current mode

24 **immaturely**, aspiringly, amateurishly, youthfully, virginally, maidenly, dewily, rawly, freshly, fresh, cleanly, clean

296 Oldness

I love everything that's old: old friends, old times, old manners, old books, old wine. Oliver Goldsmith.

NOUNS

1 **oldness**, elderliness, age, hoary age, old age, ripe old age, mellowness, venerableness, maturity, seniority, dotage, senility, decrepitude, the autumn of one's life, the burden of years, retirement

2 **old people**, the elderly, elders, elders and betters, older generation, grandparents, ancestors, forebears, senior citizens, pensioners, wrinklies (Inf), crumblies (Inf), Methuselah, Nestor, Sibyl of Cumae, Tithonus, Father Time

► *556 Age*

3 **antiquity**, primitiveness, ancientness, *ancien régime* (Fr), dust of antiquity, cobwebs of antiquity, rust, decay, olden days, olden times, ancient times, distant past, time out of mind, time immemorial

4 **antiquarianism**, classicism, medievalism, archaism, archaeology

► *284 Past Time; 556 Age*

5 **old thing**, thing of the past, archaism, antique, Victoriana, heirloom, museum piece, artefact (*or* artifact), relic, relic of the past, ancient monument, Stonehenge, ancient manuscript, Dead Sea Scrolls, historic building, listed building, Historic District (US), fossil, petrified wood, dinosaur

6 **tradition**, custom, common law, lore, folklore, legend, myth, mythology, ancient wisdom, ancient tale

► *3 History*

7 **ancient people**, prehistoric man, primitive man, early man, humanoid, protohuman, apeman, hominid, Homo erectus, Homo sapiens, caveman, cave dweller, Australopithecus, Pithecanthropus, Neanderthal man, Cro-Magnon man, Heidelberg man, Java man, Peking man, Stone-Age man, Bronze-Age man, Iron-Age man

8 **prehistoric animal**, woolly mammoth, mastodon, sabre-toothed tiger (*or* cat), dinosaur, brontosaurus, tyrannosaurus, ichthyosaurus, pterodactyl, giant sloth, ammonite, trilobite

9 **antiquarian**, antiquary, classicist, medievalist, archaeologist, archaist, antique dealer, antique collector

10 **staleness**, sourness, rottenness, overripeness, rankness, spoilage

ADJECTIVES

11 **old**, older, elderly, elder, aged, full of years, venerable, veteran, senior, patriarchal, of advanced years, advanced in years, getting on, getting on in years, mature, mellow, ripe, grey, old and grey, grey-haired, white-haired, grizzled, hoary, decrepit, senile, senescent, past one's prime, past one's best, doddering, past it (Inf), over the hill (Inf)

12 **olden**, antiquarian, antique, antiqued, ancient, time-worn, archaic, archaistic, antiquated, outdated, outmoded, moth-eaten, musty, crumbling, mouldering, mouldy, stale, time-honoured, rooted, established, long established, longstanding, traditional, age-old, ancestral, immemorial, antediluvian, from before the Flood, out of the Ark, as old as the hills, as old as time, as old as Adam, adamic, as old as Methuselah, old-world, olde-worlde (Lit), ye olde (Lit), prewar, antebellum, venerable, inveterate, vintage, classic, classical

13 **former**, previous, prior, erstwhile, one-time, sometime, quondam, retired, emeritus

14 **historic**, historical, of historical interest, heroic, Helladic, Hellenic, classical, Hellenistic, Roman, Etruscan, Ottoman, Persian, Byzantine, medieval, Saxon, Norman, feudal, Romanesque, Gothic, Tudor, Elizabethan, Jacobean, Georgian, Hanoverian, Colonial, Victorian, Edwardian

15 **primal**, primordial, primitive, primeval, early, antediluvian, prelapsarian, Precambrian Palaeozoic, Mesozoic, Cenozoic, preglacial, glacial, prehistoric, Palaeolithic, Mesolithic, Neolithic, Chalcolithic, Stone-Age, Bronze-Age, Iron-Age

VERBS

16 **be old**, belong to the past, survive from the past, go back a long way, go back in time

17 **grow old**, age, decline, deteriorate, fade, burn out, decay, rot, spoil, wither, moulder, decompose, rust, crumble, crumble into dust, become obsolete, go out of style, lose currency, dodder

ADVERBS

18 **venerably**, patriarchally, maturely, mellowly, ripely, mustily, stalely, greyly, decrepitly, senilely

19 **anciently**, in ancient times, in olden days, in the good old days, of old, of yore, since long ago, since days of yore, ages ago, way back when, since the big bang, since the world was young, since the world was new, since before the Flood, since the year one, since God knows when (Inf), since Adam was a lad (Inf)

20 **formerly**, previously, earlier, before, before now

21 **archaically**, ancestrally, immemorially, old-worldly, inveterately, venerably, classically, historically, primordially, primitively, primevally, primarily, originally, early

297 Frequency

'Do you come here often?'
'Only in the mating season.' Spike Milligan.

ADVERBS

1 **frequently**, often, many a time, repeatedly, repetitively, recurrently, regularly, periodically, cyclically, commonly, usually, generally, constantly, continually, consecutively, perpetually, ordinarily, routinely, habitually, incessantly, persistently, sustainingly, steadily, numerously, crowdedly, multitudinously, prevalently, assidously, hauntingly, without ceasing, without stopping, without stop, thick and fast, all the time, times without number, as often as one likes, daily, hourly, every hour, every minute, every second, morning, noon, and night, day and night, night and day, day in day out, day after day, as often as not, more often than not, in quick succession, in rapid succession, time after time, time and again, again and again, over and over, many times, many a time, oft (Lit), oftentimes (Lit), many a time and oft (Lit), ever and anon (Lit)

► *112 Repetition; 132 Consecutiveness; 134 Continuity; 208 Multitude; 298 Regularity*

2 **sometimes**, occasionally, from time to time, every so often, now and again, every now and again, now and then, once in a while

ADJECTIVES

3 **frequent**, recurrent, recurring, repetitive, repeated, repetitious, regular, periodic, cyclic, cyclical, continual, consecutive, persistent, sustained, steady, constant, non-stop, incessant, common, of common occurrence, run-of-the-mill, many, numerous, crowded, multitudinous, prevalent, often encountered, assiduous, habitual, haunting

NOUNS

4 **frequency**, frequence, frequentness, oftenness, recur-

rence, repetition, periodicity, continuity, consecutiveness, constancy, persistence, sustainment, steadiness, commonness, numerousness, crowdedness, multitudinousness, incessancy, prevalence, regularity, assiduity, assiduousness, habitualness, frequent occurrence, regular occurrence, common occurrence, cycle, speed, pulse, everyday occurrence

5 **frequenting**, patronizing, visiting often, coming to often, attending regularly, being a regular customer, hanging out, haunting

▶ *654 Sociability*

6 **radio frequency**, radio-frequency band, frequency band, citizens band (CB), frequency spectrum, long wave (LW), medium wave (MW), short wave (SW), very high frequency (VHF), ultrahigh frequency (UHF), frequency modulation (FM), amplitude modulation (AM), wavelength, wave, cycles per second, hertz (Hz), kilohertz (kHz), megahertz (MHz)

VERBS

7 **be frequent**, happen often, recur, reoccur, repeat itself, happen every day, occur regularly, occur periodically, have continuity, continue, go on, prevail, repeat oneself, do habitually, do nothing but

8 **frequent**, be often seen at, be found at, visit often, come to often, attend regularly, be a regular customer of, patronize, haunt, hang out at (Inf)

298 Regularity

NOUNS

1 **regularity**, frequency, recurrence, regular recurrence, regular occurrence, clockwork regularity, periodicity, repetition, repetitiveness, return, serialization, timing, phasing, pattern, symmetry, alternation, reciprocity, tidal flow, ebb and flow, wave motion, wave frequency, oscillation, to-and-fro movement, pendulum movement, piston movement, shuttle movement, undulating motion, undulation, simple harmonic motion, swing, rhythm, tempo, meassure, beat, pulsation, throb, tick

▶ *112 Repetition; 132 Consecutiveness; 326 Oscillation; 509 Repeated Sound*

2 **cycle**, return, circular return, revolution, rotation, orbital motion, regular return, life cycle, yearly cycle, biorhythm, alpha rhythm, alpha wave, circadian rhythm, menstrual cycle, oestrous cycle, menstruation, menses, period, routine, daily round, round, beat, wheel of life, orbit, circuit, lap, shift, relay, turn, go, rota

▶ *276 Time Span; 306 Orbital Motion; 307 Rotation*

3 **anniversary**, commemoration, annual occurrence, centenary (*or* centennial), sesquicentennial (*or* sesquicentenary), bicentenary (*or* bicentennial), tricentenary (*or* tricentennial *or* tercentenary *or* tercentennial), millennium

4 **orderliness**, regularity, balance, uniformity, evenness, steadiness, levelness, flatness, ordinariness, continuity, continuousness, constance, constancy, consistency, normality, regulation, rule, order, law, custom, tradition, routine

▶ *407 Order; 632 Habit*

5 **regular thing**, death and taxes, pendulum, metronome, metre, rhythm, beat, tempo, drumbeat, heartbeat, pulsebeat, pulse, breathing, alternating current (AC), shuttle service, comet, Halley's Comet, tide, spring tide, neap tide, incoming tide, ebb tide, Old Faithful (US), serial, holiday, vacation, annual vacation, summer holiday, bank holiday, day and night, sunrise and sunset, calendar, days of the week, months of the year, leap year, seasons of the year, spring, summer, winter, autumn, fall (US)

▶ *275 Time; 290 Daytime; 291 Night-Time; 292 Season*

6 **annually celebrated day**, wedding anniversary, silver wedding anniversary, ruby wedding anniversary, golden wedding anniversary, birthday, saint's day, holy day, jubilee, silver jubilee, diamond jubilee, New Year's Day, Australia Day (Australia), St. Valentine's Day, Easter, April Fools' Day (*or* All Fools' Day), May Day, V-E Day, Mother's Day, Father's Day, Memorial Day (US), D-day, Canada Day, Fourth of July (US), Independence Day (US), Bastille Day (France), V-J Day, Labor Day (US), Hallowe'en, Guy Fawkes Day, Remembrance Sunday (*or* Day), Poppy Day, Thanksgiving Day (US), Christmas, Boxing Day

VERBS

7 **be regular**, recur, reoccur, reoccur constantly, repeat, be in order, run on in order, succeed, follow a pattern, intermit, reciprocate, alternate, take one's turn, work a shift, have a turn, have a go, beat time, tick, throb, pulse, pulsate, have a rapid (*or* slow) heartbeat, breathe regularly, undulate, oscillate, swing, sway, swing and sway, go to and fro, come and go, ebb and flow, go back and forth, ply, commute, shuttle, holiday, vacation, take a summer holiday

8 **be cyclic**, cycle, circle, orbit, cycle round, come again, go and return, come round again, return once again, return, walk one's beat, make one's daily round, run a lap, turn, spin, revolve, rotate, occur monthly, menstruate, have one's period, occur annually, happen yearly

9 **commemorate**, celebrate Christmas, have an anniversary, celebrate an anniversary, have a birthday, celebrate a birthday, honour the dead, burn the guy

10 **make regular**, regularize, make consistent, make uniform, balance, make routine, regulate, time, adjust, set (a clock), order, impose order upon, bring order out of chaos, rule, make ordinary, normalize, rationalize, systematize, steady, serialize, make continual, make constant, level, level out, make even, flatten, flatten out

ADJECTIVES

11 **regular**, frequent, periodic, periodical, recurrent, recurring, repeating, repetitive, tidal, reciprocal, alternating, alternate, alternative, to-and-fro, oscillatory, oscillating, revolving, returning, timed, isochronal, isochronous, phasic, phaseal, phased, serial, serialized, rhythmic, rhythmical, measured, swinging, steady, stable, clockwork, beating, ticking, throbbing, pulsating, pulsatory, pulsatile, undulating, constant, even, symmetric, symmetrical, consistent, level, flat, featureless

12 **cyclic**, cyclical, circular, circling, orbital, revolving, rotational, rotative, rotating, routine, hourly, daily, diurnal, quotidian, nightly, tertian, semiweekly, weekly, hebdomadary, hebdomadal, biweekly, fortnightly, semimonthly, monthly, bimonthly, seasonal, semiannual,

biannual, annual, yearly, perennial, bissextile, biennial, Metonic cycle, biorhythmic, menstrual, oestrous

13 **anniversary**, commemorative, annual, yearly, centenary (*or* centennial), sesquicentennial (*or* sesquicentenary), bicentenary (*or* bicentennial), tricentenary (*or* tricentennial *or* tercentenary *or* tercentennial), Metonic, millennial, secular

14 **orderly**, regular, balanced, uniform, even, steady, level, flat, ordinary, everyday, typical, routine, continual, constant, methodical, metrical, consistent, normal, legal, customary, traditional

ADVERBS

15 **regularly**, frequently, periodically, at regular intervals, at fixed intervals, at stated times, at specified times, at fixed periods, repeatedly, repetitiously, reciprocally, alternately, alternatively, by turns, turn and turn about, in a swinging motion, up and down, from side to side, to and fro, serially, rhythmically, steadily, like clockwork, pulsatingly, undulatingly, constantly, evenly, symmetrically, consistently, flatly

16 **cyclically**, circularly, orbitally, round and round, routinely, hourly, hour by hour, daily, every day, day by day, diurnally, per diem, nightly, every night, every other day, every other night, semiweekly, twice a week, weekly, every week, biweekly, every other week, fortnightly, semimonthly, twice a month, monthly, every month, bimonthly, every other month, seasonally, semiannually, biannually, twice a year, annually, yearly, per annum, every year, perennially, biennially, every other year, centennially, sesquicentennially, bicentennially, tricentennially, tercentennially, millennially, secularly, commemoratively

17 **orderly**, regularly, uniformly, evenly, steadily, flatly, ordinarily, routinely, in an everyday manner, continually, constantly, consistently, normally, legally, according to law, according to order, customarily, by custom, according to rule, traditionally, according to tradition

299 Irregularity

NOUNS

1 **irregularity**, unregularity, nonuniformity, unequalness, inequality, asymmetry, unevenness, roughness, choppiness, spottiness, patchiness, brokenness, disconnection, discontinuation, discontinuity, sporadicalness, infrequency, intermittence, fluctuation, changeableness, change, waver, wavering, variability, variableness, variety, diversity, inconsistency, inconstancy, unpredictability, randomness, randomness of recurrence, fitfulness, fits and starts, capriciousness, caprice, restlessness, desultoriness, unmethodicalness, haphazardness, disorder, instability, unsteadiness, oscillation, wobbliness, shakiness, jerkiness, flickering, staggering, lurching, careening, veering, bumping, wobble, shake, jerk, flicker, stagger, lurch, careen, veer, bump

► *114 Diversity; 120 Inequality; 133 Discontinuity; 224 Change; 227 Changeableness; 326 Oscillation; 327 Agitation; 408 Disorder; 642 Frivolity*

2 **unusualness**, uncommonness, exceptionalness, anomalousness, incongruousness, aberrance, aberration, abnormality, eccentricity, nonconformity, unconventionality, unorthodoxy, oddness, peculiarity, whimsicality, whimsy, moodiness

3 **irregular thing**, unpaved road, mountain range, stormy sea, British weather, stock exchange, gambling, crooked teeth

► *118 Nonconformity*

ADJECTIVES

4 **irregular**, unregular, nonuniform, unequal, asymmetric, asymmetrical, unsymmetrical, uneven, rough, choppy, spotty, patchy, broken, disconnected, discontinuous, sporadic, spasmodic, halting, off and on, on and off, on-again-off-again, stop and go, stop-go, infrequent, intermittent, fluctuating, changeable, changeful, wavering, variable, varying, diverse, inconsistent, erratic, inconstant, unpredictable, random, fitful, capricious, restless, desultory, unmethodical, unsystematic, unsystematical, unrhythmic, unrhythmical, haphazard, disorderly, disordered, unstable, unsteady, oscillatory, oscillating, wobbly, wobbling, shaky, shaking, jerky, jerking, flickering, staggering, lurching, careening, veering, bumpy, bumping, herky-jerky (US inf)

5 **unusual**, uncommon, exceptional, anomalous, incongruous, incoherent, aberrant, erratic, abnormal, eccentric, idiosyncratic, unique, individual, nonconforming, unconventional, unorthodox, odd, peculiar, whimsical, moody

VERBS

6 **be irregular**, lack regularity, intermit, break, disconnect, fluctuate, change, change directions, change speed, vary, waver, oscillate, wobble, shake, jerk, go by fits and starts, flicker, stagger, lurch, careen, veer, bump

7 **be unusual**, be eccentric, differ, stand out, surprise, amaze, act erratically, act oddly

ADVERBS

8 **irregularly**, unregularly, unequally, asymmetrically, unevenly, roughly, discontinuously, spasmodically, sporadically, in spots, haltingly, off and on, on and off, on again off again, stop and go, infrequently, once in a while, now and then, every now and again, intermittently, changeably, waveringly, variably, inconsistently, erratically, in a disorderly manner, inconstantly, unpredictably, randomly, at random, fitfully, by fits and starts, unrhythmically, capriciously, restlessly, desultorily, unmethodically, unsystematically, haphazardly, unsteadily, shakily, jerkily, flickeringly, bumpily

9 **unusually**, uncommonly, exceptionally, anomalously, abnormally, eccentrically, unconventionally, oddly, peculiarly, whimsically, moodily

Motion

300 Motion

For my part, I travel not to go anywhere, but to go. I travel for travel's sake. The great affair is to move. Robert Louis Stevenson.

NOUNS

1 motion, movement, moving, change of position, migration, movability, movableness, mobility, motility, locomotion, walking, perambulation, pedestrianism, going, running, rushing, marching, kinetic energy, motivity, actuation, motive power, laws of motion, kinetics, dynamics, kinesis, kinematics, kinesiatrics, kinesipathy, kinesitherapy
▶ *28 Physics*

2 momentum, propulsion, impulsion, mobilization, motivation, actuation, impetus, stir, stirring, restlessness, unrest, action, activity, agitation, bustle, course, passage, set, trend, career, stream, flow, flux, flight, current, rush, onrush, run, drift, driftage, transit, traffic, flow of traffic, transport, transportation, travel, riding, equitation, land travel, water travel, air travel
▶ *316 Transfer; 327 Agitation; 330 Propulsion; 331 Impulsion; 340 Action*

3 motion towards, advance, approach, arrival, progress, progression, headway, evolution, motion into, ingress
▶ *302 Forward Motion; 312 Arrival; 314 Entry*

4 backward motion, regression, backing, backflowing, reflowing, refluence, reflux, retreat, withdrawal, departure, exit, motion out of, egress, sternway, recession
▶ *303 Backward Motion; 313 Departure; 315 Exit*

5 circuition, motion round, circumnavigation, rotation, axial motion, radial motion, oscillation, fluctuation, vibration, gyration, agitation, to-and-fro movement, irregular motion, sideward (*or* sideways) motion, oblique motion, angular motion, random motion, Brownian movement
▶ *306 Orbital Motion; 307 Rotation; 325 Deviation; 326 Oscillation; 327 Agitation*

6 descending motion, descent, downward motion, subsiding motion, sinking, plunging
▶ *305 Descent*

7 ascending motion, upward motion, ascent, ascending, rising, soaring, mounting, climbing
▶ *304 Ascent*

8 rapid motion, rapidity, speed, velocity
▶ *332 Swiftness*

9 slow motion, slowness, pottering
▶ *333 Slowness*

10 regular movement, recurring movement, rhythm, uniform movement, continual movement, motion in front, precession, motion after, following, pursuit
▶ *112 Repetition; 298 Regularity*

11 bodily movement, exercise, athletics, gymnastics, aerobics, gesticulation, wave, gesture, thumbs up, V-sign

12 gait, walk, carriage, bearing, tread, pace, step, stride, stroll, saunter, tramp, stamp, run, lope, jog, jog trot, dogtrot, trot, amble, dance step, hop, skip, jump, leap, waddle, swagger, shuffle, creep, stalk, strut, goosestep, march, quick march, scamper, scramble, canter, gallop, clip (Inf), lick (Inf)
▶ *22 Dancing*

VERBS

13 be in motion, move, have mobility, change position, stir, budge, go, flow, drift, stream, progress, advance, develop, drive forward, evolve, make one's way, proceed, gather way, keep going, go on, pick (*or* fight) one's way, wade through, back, back up, regress, retrogress, subside, ebb, wane, change direction, deviate, soar, mount, rise, ascend, climb, descend, sink, plunge, oscillate, go sidewards (*or* sideways), gyrate, go round, rotate, spin, whirl, move over, get over, shift, change, change place
▶ *302 Forward Motion; 303 Backward Motion; 304 Ascent; 305 Descent; 307 Rotation; 311 Divergence; 326 Oscillation*

14 set in motion, move, actuate, push, nudge, shove, drive, hustle, motivate, pull, tug, draw, haul, propel, impel, throw, mobilize, send, dispatch, scatter, disperse, bring together, gather, transfer, transport, convey, transpose, displace
▶ *316 Transfer; 330 Propulsion; 331 Impulsion; 362 Traction*

15 walk, march, stride, tramp, lope, tread, trip, amble, jog, stroll, saunter, shuffle, waddle, dance, leap, toddle, patter, potter, strut, stagger, mince, stalk, run, rush, gallop, hare, fly, dash, dart, roll, cruise, freewheel, coast, trundle, taxi, chug, stream, travel, roam, wander, drift, stray, shift, dodge, duck, weave, tack, manoeuvre, make a move, change (places), interchange, move over, move house, remove, change one's address, motion, gesture, gesticulate, wave

▶ *332 Swiftness; 333 Slowness*

ADJECTIVES

16 **moving**, having motion, in motion, motive, motory, motor, motile, motional, movable, mobile, motivational, locomotive, automotive, self-propelled, shifting, impelling, propelling, propellant, driving, travelling, riding, running, rushing, going, passing, fluent, flowing, streaming, flying, transitional, fleeting, mercurial, restless, active, agitated, bustling, scurrying, stirring, wandering, drifting, nomadic, peripatetic, ambulant, erratic, runaway

17 **directional**, advancing, advance, progressive, progressing, backward, regressive, retrogressive, back, backtracking, backflowing, refluent, reflowing, downward, sinking, plunging, descending, subsiding, upward, ascending, rising, soaring, mounting, climbing, rapid, speedy, speeding, slow, toddling, pottering, regular, recurring, rhythmic, periodic, uniform, continuous, continual, circuitous, rotary, rotatory, rotational, centripetal, centrifugal, axial, radial, oscillating, fluctuating, vibrating, agitating, irregular, sideward (*or* sideways), oblique, angular, random, to-and-fro, Brownian, gyratory, gyrational, gyrating, kinetic, kinesodic, dynamic, kinematic, kinesipathic

ADVERBS

18 **in motion**, kinetically, dynamically, on the move, on the go, up and about, astir, on the march, on the run, on the wing, on the hop (Inf), under way, on the road, en route, in transit, under sail, from pillar to post, transitionally, movably, motivationally, progressively, regressively, automotively, mercurially, restlessly, actively, nomadically, peripatetically, rapidly, slowly, circuitously, centripetally, centrifugally

INTERJECTIONS

19 **go!**, move it!, faster!, forward!, advance!, retreat!, step on it!

301 Motionlessness

Be still then, and know that I am God. Bible: Psalms.

NOUNS

1 **motionlessness**, immobility, stillness, inactivity, inaction, fixity, fixation, rigidity, stiffness, standstill, stand, stop, halt, pause, dead stop (*or* stand), full stop, lock, dead set, stability, equilibrium, poise, equipoise, balance, stasis, steadiness, inertness, inertia, dormancy, passiveness, passivity, apathy, latency, torpor, indifference, indolence, lotus-eating, languor, stagnancy, vegetation, coma, deathliness, deadliness, numbness, trance, catalepsy, catatonia, suspension, cessation, stagnation, deadlock, gridlock (US), stalemate, truce, lull, suspense, abeyance, stoppage, embargo, freeze, strike

▶ *119 Equality; 226 Stopping; 341 Inaction; 343 Inactivity; 618 Indifference*

2 **repose**, rest, sleep, slumber, insensibility, silken repose, eternal rest, death, quiescence, quiescency, silence, quietness, quiet, quietude, placidity, placidness, tranquillity, serenity, peace, composure, quietism, contemplation, satori, nirvana, ataraxia, calmness, calm, restfulness, peacefulness, imperturbability, stillness, still, hush, lull, calm (*or* lull) before the storm, dead (*or* flat) calm, deathlike calm, windlessness, doldrums, eye of the hurricane, horse latitudes, anticyclone, not a breath of air, airlessness, nothing stirring, not a mouse stirring

▶ *506 Silence; 582 Death; 589 Peace*

3 **resting place**, refuge, shelter, journey's end, home, haven, quarters, bivouac, bed, pillow, hammock, final resting place, last rest, grave, tomb, mausoleum, cemetery, graveyard, burial ground, heaven, paradise, happy hunting ground (US)

▶ *583 Burial*

ADJECTIVES

4 **motionless**, immobile, still, inactive, unmoving, immotive, static, stationary, stagnant, standing, steady, poised, balanced, immovable, unmovable, fixed, stiff, stuck, paralysed, unmoved, petrified, transfixed, rooted to the spot, sedentary, stock-still, spellbound, frozen, still as a statue, quiet as a mouse, still as death, airless, windless, becalmed, at anchor

▶ *343 Inactivity*

5 **sedentary**, stay-at-home, housebound, shut-in (US), home-loving, domesticated, supine, bedridden, disabled, on one's back, untravelled, stick-in-the-mud, idle, unemployed, out of commission, inert, dormant, passive, latent, languid, languorous, apathetic, indifferent, indolent, phlegmatic, sluggish, vegetating, unaroused, suspended, abeyant, sleeping, slumbering, smouldering, groggy, heavy, leaden, dull, flat, slack, tame, dead, lifeless, catatonic, cataleptic, numb, dopey (Inf)

▶ *341 Inaction; 582 Death; 618 Indifference*

6 **quiescent**, silent, quiet, still, hushed, insensible, soundless, placid, tranquil, calm, serene, easy-going, peaceful, restful, composed, contemplative, smooth, unruffled, untroubled, unperturbed, unagitated, unhurried, unmoved, unstirring, stolid, stoic, impassive, calm as a mill pond, quiet as death, inexcitable, imperturbable, cool, cool as a cucumber, pacific, halcyon, undisturbed, sequestered, leisured, at rest, resting, reposing, reposeful, sleepy

▶ *506 Silence; 589 Peace; 618 Indifference*

7 **sedentary person**, shut-in (US), stick-in-the-mud, sluggard, couch potato (US inf)

VERBS

8 **be motionless**, stand still, stand, not budge, freeze, remain, abide, stay, stay put, sit, sit down, sit tight, remain seated, remain *in situ* (L), perch, land, alight, mark time, wait, stand firm, stand like a post, not stir (a step), not breathe, hold one's breath, tread water, coast, cease, stop, halt, stop short, stop in one's tracks, slow down, decelerate, pull up, check, brake, come to a standstill, come to a halt, come to journey's end, stand fast, stick fast, remain at anchor, subside, settle, settle down, die down, come to rest, pause, rest, tarry, relax, rest on one's oars, keep still, keep quiet, rest and be thankful, stagnate, vegetate, idle, hang fire, sleep, slumber, repose, retire, go to bed, stay at home, stay indoors, not go out, die, go to one's eternal rest, go to the happy hunting ground, take a breather (Inf), doss down (Inf), cool it (Inf)

9 make motionless, bring to a standstill, immobilize, suspend, stalemate, call a truce, lock, jam, catch, stick, lodge, put a stop to, embargo, lay an embargo on, prohibit, freeze, soothe, lull, calm (down), tranquillize, pacify, assuage, becalm, take the wind out of someone's sails

ADVERBS

10 motionlessly, fixedly, stationarily, inertly, inactively, statically, dormantly, passively, latently, stagnantly, calmly, quietly, still, tranquilly, peacefully, placidly, restfully, smoothly, unperturbedly, languidly, languorously, sluggishly, heavily, lifelessly, apathetically, coldly, phlegmatically, stoically, stolidly, impassively, in repose, at a halt, at a stand, far from the madding crowd, after death, posthumously, after life's fitful fever, stilly (Lit)

INTERJECTIONS

11 stop!, stay!, halt!, whoa!, hold!, hold hard!, hold it!, don't move!, lay off! (Inf), pipe down! (Inf), no way! (Inf), cool it! (Inf)

302 Forward Motion

Take a step forward, lads. It will be easier that way. Erskine Childers.

VERBS

1 go forward, proceed, progress, make progress, advance, go (*or* move) forward, step forward, pass on, move, be in motion, travel, get along, come along, roll, roll on, make headway (Inf)

▶ *300 Motion*

2 start, make a good start, make initial progress, make good progress, break the back of

▶ *130 Beginning*

3 press on, push, press forward, drive on, keep on, make leeway, make (rapid) strides, push on, gain ground, cover ground, gather way, forge (*or* shoot) ahead, go ahead, climb, gain height, rise, rise higher

▶ *304 Ascent; 366 Raising*

4 make good time, make the best of one's way, make up for lost time, make up leeway, recover lost ground, recoup, gain time

▶ *275 Time*

5 develop, evolve, move with the times, show promise, come on, get on, do well, prosper

▶ *248 Prosperity*

6 march on, rub (*or* run) on, jog on, roll on, flow, flow on, drift along, go (*or* move) with the stream

7 make one's way, work one's way, weave (*or* worm *or* thread) one's way, inch forward, muddle through, carve (*or* force *or* fight) one's way, further oneself, get somewhere, climb, reach towards, reach out, raise one's sights

8 further, bring on, foster, contribute to, advance, aid, raise, lift, elevate, bounce up, promote, upgrade, improve, better, forward, hasten, modernize, bring forward, push, force, develop, grow, augment, step up, accelerate, put ahead, put in front, put forward, propose, favour, make for, conduce

9 maintain progress, never look back, hold one's lead, overtake, gain on, distance, outdistance, outstrip, leave behind, move fast, go fast, go ahead, get a move on, get ahead, advance by leaps and bounds

NOUNS

10 forward motion, going forward, progress, steady progress, progression, progressiveness, advance, headway, arithmetic progression, geometric progression, forward march, forwarding, forwardal, roll, rolling on, travel

▶ *300 Motion*

11 course, march, passage, way, ongoing, career, march (*or* passage *or* course) of time, tide, current, flood, onward course, ongo, go ahead, way forward

▶ *275 Time*

12 advance, advancement, promotion, preferment, leg-up, furtherance, furthering, rise, raise, lift, ascent, elevation, gain, ground gained, enterprise, success, achievement, economic progress, prosperity, go-getting (Inf)

▶ *304 Ascent; 366 Raising*

13 step, stride, jump, leap, spurt, sudden progress, leaps and bounds, step on the ladder

14 development, growth, evolution, furtherance, next step

15 improvement, betterment, reform, perfectibility, majestic progress, irreversibility, irresistible progress, getting ahead, overtaking, overstepping, encroachment

▶ *244 Improvement; 329 Overstepping*

16 progressive person, progressive, improver, reformer, coming man (*or* woman), made man (*or* woman), upstart, man (*or* woman) of action, doer, hustler, bustler, go-getter (Inf), ball of fire (Inf), live wire (Inf), whiz kid (Inf)

ADJECTIVES

17 forward, progressive, progressing, advanced, advancing, go-ahead, forward-looking, up-to-date, abreast of the times, enterprising, reformist, go-getting (Inf)

18 ongoing, continuing, inexorable, irreversible, onward, oncoming, proceeding, moving, profluent, flowing on, unbroken

ADVERBS

19 forward, forwards, onward, onwards, forth, on, along, ahead, forrard (Dial), on the way to, on the road, en route to (*or* for), on one's way

20 in progress, in mid-progress, in transit, going on, progressively, by leaps and bounds, under way, in sight of

303 Backward Motion

I'm walking backwards till Christmas. Spike Milligan.

VERBS

1 go backwards, regress, return, revert, relapse, backslide, slip back, lose ground, slide down the slippery slope, lapse, fall off, decline, recidivate, retrogress, retrograde, retroflex, retrocede, go down the tubes (*or* chute *or* drain), go back to the drawing board

▶ *245 Deterioration; 761 Reversion*

2 retreat, withdraw, retire, sound (*or* beat) a retreat, pull back, pull out, advance to the rear, disengage, fall back, fall behind, draw back, run back, move back, stand back,

back out, back out of, back down, give way, give ground, give place, run away, resign, recede into the distance, back into a corner
▶ *388 Submission*
3 **reverse**, back, turn, backtrack, take the backtrack, back up, go into reverse, back off, back-pedal, back away, back trail, countermarch, reverse one's field, retrace one's steps, double back, take the reciprocal course, back water, run back, flow back, ebb, regurgitate, crawfish (US inf)
4 **slip back**, ebb, fall, drop, decline, descend
▶ *305 Descent*
5 **turn back**, put back, double, double back, retrace one's steps, turn, return, go (*or* come) back, go (*or* come) home, remigrate
6 **shrink back**, avoid, shy, shy away, shrink, jib
▶ *634 Avoidance*
7 **recoil**, bounce back, come back to where one started, box the compass
▶ *347 Counteraction*
8 **look back**, look over one's shoulder, hark back, reminisce
▶ *3 History; 284 Past Time*
9 **turn round**, turn around (*or* about), face about, about-face (US), about-turn, volte-face, right-about-face, turn on one's heel, turn one's back, come (*or* go *or* fetch) about, make a U-turn, turn tail, double, wheel, turn on a dime (US), veer, veer around, swivel, pivot, swing round, crane one's neck

NOUNS

10 **backward motion**, going back, regression, regress, recession, infinite regress, reverse direction, backward step (*or* motion), retroflexion (*or* retroflection), retrocession, retrogression, retrogradation, retroaction
▶ *761 Reversion*
11 **retreat**, motion from, recess, withdrawal, *reculade* (Fr), retirement, fallback, pullout, pullback, pulling (*or* falling or drawing) back, advance to the rear, disengagement, resigning, resignation
▶ *388 Submission*
12 **reversal**, reverse, reversing, reversion, inversion, backing, backing up (*or* off *or* out), backup, regurgitation, voidance, re-entrance, re-entry, turn of the tide, reflux, refluence, ebb
▶ *761 Reversion*
13 **about-turn**, about-face (US), volte-face, right-about, right-about-face, U-turn, turnaround, turnabout, swing around, backtrack, backtracking, back trail
14 **decline**, fall off, ebb, falling away, drop, fall, slump, downturn, downward trend, deterioration
▶ *245 Deterioration*
15 **looking back**, reminiscing, harking-back, reminiscence, nostalgia
16 **countermotion**, counteraction, countermovement, countermarching, reversion, turn, turning point
17 **resilience**, reflex, elasticity, recoil, return to base (*or* starting point), circular argument
▶ *179 Circularity*
18 **setback**, backset, throwback, rollback
19 **backsliding**, lapse, relapse, recidivism, recidivation, sliding down the slippery slope, going down the tubes (*or* chute *or* drain *or* pan) (Inf)
20 **return**, homecoming, homeward journey
21 **backslider**, tergiversator, recidivist, failure, no-hoper (Inf)
▶ *247 Failure*

ADJECTIVES

22 **backward**, retrograde, retrogressive, retrocessive
23 **receding**, recessive, retreating, retractile, regressive, declining, ebbing, refluent, backsliding, lapsing, relapsing
24 **retroactive**, nostalgic, reactionary, backward-looking, retrospective
25 **reversed**, reverse, reversible, reflex, turned around, wrong way, wrong way round, counter, recoiling, counterclockwise (US), anticlockwise
26 **resilient**, elastic, reflexive
27 **returning**, homing, homeward-bound, remigrating

ADVERBS

28 **backwards**, hindward(s), in reverse, rearward(s), retrally, arear, astern, reflexively, back to where one started
29 **in reverse**, counterclockwise (US), anticlockwise, withershins (*or* widdershins) (Dial), against the grain, *à rebours* (Fr),

304 Ascent

Per ardua ad astra. (Through endeavour to the stars.)
Anonymous.

NOUNS

1 **ascent**, ascension, rise, rising, levitation, assumption, uprise, uprising, uprisal, upward motion, uphill, upslope, upgo, upgoing, upcoming, upping, upgang (Dial), gaining height, defying gravity, surfacing, breaking surface, floating up
▶ *67 Swimming; 186 Verticality; 366 Raising*
2 **upturn**, upsurge, surge, spurt, gush, jet, spout, fountain, upsurgence, uptrend, upswing, upsweep, upbend, upcurve, upcast, upgrowth, upgrade, upleap, upshoot, uprush, updraught, increase, spiral, uplift, elevation, rising air, rising current, upthrow, gradient, incline, slope, hill, ramp, rising ground, high land
▶ *174 Top; 177 Curve; 330 Propulsion*
3 **sunrise**, sunup, dawn, first light, morning, morn, moonrise, star-rise
▶ *290 Daytime; 291 Night-Time*
4 **taking off**, leaving ground, takeoff, liftoff, departure, flying up, soaring, gaining altitude, zoom, zooming up, spiralling up, gyring up, shooting up, rocketing up, mushrooming
▶ *29 Astronomy; 313 Departure*
5 **jump**, vault, leap, bound, leapfrog, quantum leap (*or* jump), spring, handspring, saltation, bounce, hop, skip, hop, skip, and jump, high jump, pole-vault, pole-jump, recoil, hurdle, hurdling, steeplechase, steeplechasing, standing (*or* running *or* flying) jump, ski-jump
▶ *22 Dancing*
6 **mounting**, mount, upclimb, climb, climbing, scaling, scaling the heights, clamber, ladder climbing, hill climb-

ing, mountaineering, alpinism, anabasis, going up, skylarking, attack, culmination
► *154 Height*
7 means of ascent, stairway, stairs, staircase, *escalier* (Fr), steps, treads and risers, flight of stairs (*or* steps), spiral (*or* winding) staircase, companionway, companion, backstairs, perron, fire escape, landing, landing stage
► *23 Furniture and Woodwork*
8 lift, escalator, elevator, ski lift, chair lift, cable car, funicular (railway), springboard, vault, trampoline
► *57 Gymnastics; 366 Raising*
9 ladder, scale, stepladder, folding ladder, loft ladder, extension ladder, roof ladder, companion ladder, accommodation ladder, side ladder, gangway ladder, quarter ladder, stern ladder, rope ladder, Jacob's ladder, ratline, ratlin
10 step, stair, footstep, rest, footrest, rung, rundle, round, spoke, stave, scale, doorstep, tread, riser, bridgeboard, string, stepstool, kickstool, stepping stone
11 ascender, rocket, skylark, laverock (Dial), skyrocket, lark, eagle, soarer, climber, upclimber, mountaineer, mountain climber, alpinist, rock climber, cragsman, excelsior figure, steeplejack, stegophilist, foretopman
► *62 Mountaineering and Climbing; 72 Birds*
12 geyser, gusher, fountain, spouter

VERBS

13 ascend, climb, lift, rise, rise up, arise, uprise, mount, levitate, soar, spiral, spire, aspire, curl upwards, upwind, upspin, upgo, go up, upsurge, surge, upstream, upheave, swarm up, upswarm, sweep up, upgrow, grow up, reach the top, reach the zenith, culminate
► *174 Top*
14 climb, upclimb, mount, walk up, struggle up, climb hand over fist, shin up, shinny up, monkey up, scale, escalade, scale the heights, top, breast, clear, hurdle, clamber, clamber up, scramble, scrabble up, claw one's way up, ramp, work one's way up, climb over, surmount, skylark, go over the top, go OTT (Inf)
15 mount, get on, climb on, back, bestride, climb into the saddle, bestraddle, board, go aboard, go on board, hop in, pile in, hop aboard, jump in, go upstairs
16 stand up, get up, rise to one's feet, vacate one's seat, rear, rear up, ramp
17 spring up, surface, float up, break water, shoot up, jump up, leap up, vault up, start up, fly up, pop up, bob up, upshoot, upspring, upstart, upleap, spurt, gush, jet, spout, fountain, play, dance, flow out, blow up, explode
18 jump, spring, leap, vault, hurdle, bound, bounce, hop, skip, push up, grow up, upheave
19 take off, lift off, rocket, skyrocket, leave the ground, leave the earth, launch, gain altitude, gain height, claw skyward, become airborne, soar, zoom, fly, plane, kite, fly aloft, spire, gyre upward
20 hover, levitate, float, hang, poise, float in the air, tower, loom, loom over
► *361 Suspension*
21 upturn, turn up, take an upturn, improve, get better, trend upwards, slope up, upcast, upsweep, upbend, upcurve, steepen
► *244 Improvement*

ADJECTIVES

22 ascending, upward, uphill, uphillward, in the ascendant, climbing, scansorial, scandent, steep, upgrade (US), uparching, upwith (Dial), upturned, upcast, uplifted, turned-up, retroussé
23 rising, mounting, buoyant, rampant, rearing, on the up and up, bullish, escalating, uprising, upgoing, upcoming, ascendant, ascensional, ascentive, anabatic, soaring, zooming, rocketing, lifting, gaining height, light, floating, airborne
► *13 Economics; 415 Lightness*
24 leaping, springing, vaulting, jumping, hopping, saltatory, saltant, saltatorial, skipping, prancing, bounding, bouncing, spiralling, skyrocketing
25 ladder-like, scalar, scalariform, scalable, climbable, stepped

ADVERBS

26 up, upwards, upwith (Dial), upstairs, uphill, uphillward, upstream, upstreamward, uplong, upalong, uptown, up north, excelsior, ever higher, skyward, heavenward, hand over fist, onward and upward
► *186 Verticality; 324 Direction*

INTERJECTIONS

27 alley-oop!, upsy-daisy!, lift off!

305 Descent

I started at the top and worked my way down. Orson Welles.

NOUNS

1 descent, going down, descension, descending, lowering, declension, decline, declination, downcome, comedown, way down, down, downturn, downcurve, downbend, downdraught, downthrow, demotion, contraction, downer (Inf)
► *30 Earth Science; 177 Curve; 214 Decrease; 317 Way; 367 Lowering*
2 sinkage, decline, decrease, lowering, downward trend, depression, subsidence, droop, drooping, sag, sagging, catenary, slump, immersion, drowning, submergence, lapse, decurrence, cadence, gravitation, downgrade
► *183 Concavity; 229 Tendency; 245 Deterioration; 414 Heaviness*
3 downflow, downrush, pour, downpour, shower, rain, cascade, nappe, waterfall, rapids, cataract, chute, precipice, defluxion, landslide, landslip, subsidence, avalanche, snowslide, snowslip
► *30 Earth Science; 164 Edge; 433 Water*
4 fall, falling, dropping, plummeting, plunging, swooping, dipping, tumble, overturning, stumble, stumbling, titubation, trip, *culbute* (Fr), sprawl, crash, flop, spill, header, fate of Icarus, downfall, collapse, debacle, failure, comedown, demotion, humiliation, ruin, end, nightfall, sunset, curtains (Inf), pratfall (US inf)
► *131 End; 247 Failure; 274 Error; 291 Night-Time; 357 Destruction; 358 Obliteration; 523 Darkness; 623 Humility*
5 dive, duck, stoop, dip, plunge, swoop, pounce, header, belly flop, nose dive, power dive, drop, fall, *chute* (Fr), landing, touchdown, forced landing, crash-landing, crash

▶ *29 Astronomy; 67 Swimming*

6 **slide**, sliding, slip, slippage, slither, slid, glide, coast, glissade, glissando, inclination, declivity, hill, slope, tilt, dip, acclivity, precipice, sheer drop

7 **tunnelling**, boring, mining, burrowing, caving, speleology, digging, excavation, potholing, sapping, undermining

▶ *38 Engineering; 156 Depth*

8 **descender**, faller, free-faller, parachutist, paratrooper, aeronaut, sky-diver, hang-glider, diver, frogman, submariner, submarine, diving bell, bathysphere, underwater swimmer, diving bird, merganser, kingfisher

▶ *67 Swimming; 72 Birds*

VERBS

9 **descend**, come (*or* go) down, down, dip down, lose height (*or* altitude), gravitate, lower, get lower, get lower and lower, decrease, decline, abate, ebb, fall off, drop off, tread downward, go downhill, sink, sink down, seep, seep down, soak in, subside, settle, set, submerge, go under, drown, founder, go under water, dive, reach a lower level, alight, get down, get off, climb down, abseil, rappel, dismount

10 **droop**, sag, slouch, swag, slump, slump down, sit down, flop, flop down, plump, plop, plump down, plop down, come down a peg, hang down, prolapse, collapse, cave, cave in, crash, give way, fail, fall down, fall in, touch depth, reach the depths, touch bottom, sink to the bottom, reach one's nadir

11 **trip**, fall, fall over, fall down, take a fall (*or* spill), slip, slip up, totter, career, pitch, topple, topple over, overbalance, overturn, capsize, tumble, take a tumble, stumble, stagger, lurch, sprawl, spread-eagle, fall headlong, fall flat on one's face, take a header, take a nosedive, measure one's length, fall prostrate, miss one's footing, take a running jump, crash, bite the dust, go for a burton (Inf)

12 **drop**, fall, fall (*or* drop) down, plummet, pitch, toss, roll, plunge, swoop, dip, bow down, titubate, flutter down, spiral, spiral down, dive, drop, drop from the sky, fall through the air, parachute, skydive, fly down, pounce, duck, belly flop, nose dive, power dive, prang, drop on, dump upon, hit (*or* strike) upon, land, light upon, alight upon, come down on, settle on, descend on, perch, touch down, get down, crashland, crash

13 **drip**, drizzle, patter, shower, cascade, flow down, pour, pour down, rain, rain cats and dogs, precipitate, snow, avalanche, overflow

14 **slide**, slide down, slip, slither, slidder (Dial), skid, glide, skim, coast, glissade, toboggan, incline, sideslip, slope, tilt, dip, list, be oblique

15 **tunnel**, bore, mine, burrow, excavate, go underground, dig down, sink into the earth, sap, undermine

ADJECTIVES

16 **descending**, descendant, on the descendant, down, downward, downhill, decurrent, declivitous, deciduous, downflowing, pouring, downrushing, downturning, sinking, declining, bearish, decreasing, lowering, subsiding, slumping, drowning, foundering, tottering, tumbling, crashing, collapsing, tumbledown, submersible, sinkable

▶ *13 Economics*

17 **drooping**, droopy, sagging, on the downgrade, depressed, downcast, demoted, down at heart, down in the mouth (Inf)

▶ *602 Sorrow*

18 **falling**, tumbling, stumbling, titubant, tripping, sprawling, flopping, spilling, lurching, plunging, plummeting, diving, dipping, nose-diving, dropping, falling, swooping, stooping, ducking, sliding, slipping, slithering, skidding, gliding, coasting

ADVERBS

19 **down**, downwards, down with (Dial), adown, down below, downright, downhill, downstairs, downstream, downstreet, downtown, down south, downgrade, nose-down

▶ *324 Direction*

306 Orbital Motion

All things from eternity are of like forms and come round in a circle. Marcus Aurelius.

NOUNS

1 **orbital motion**, orbiting, wheeling, circling, rounding, orbit, circularity, rotation, turning, spiralling, spiral, gyre, gyring, helix, coil, ellipse, revolution, circulation, circumnavigation, circumambulation, circumambience (*or* circumambiency), circumflexion, circummigration

▶ *177 Curve; 307 Rotation; 744 Record*

2 **circuitousness**, circuitry, circuition, circulation, roundaboutness, indirection, meandering, deviance, deviation, digression, circumlocution, excursion, circumbendibus, ambages (Lit), turning, cornering, turn, U-turn

▶ *179 Circularity; 180 Convolution; 311 Divergence; 325 Deviation*

3 **orbit**, cycle, circle, full circle, wheel, circuit, ambit, round trip, lap, loop, walk, turn, rounds, beat, tour

▶ *170 Surroundings*

4 **orbiting body**, satellite, moon, planet, sun, star, asteroid, planetesimal, planetoid, Sputnik, spaceship

▶ *29 Astronomy; 141 Space; 307 Rotation*

5 **ringroad**, orbital, bypass, M25, *péripherique* (Fr), detour, roundabout way, scenic route, tourist route, long way round, country route, the pretty way (Inf)

▶ *317 Way; 318 Passage; 325 Deviation*

VERBS

6 **orbit**, go into orbit, circuit, revolve, turn, make a circuit, describe (*or* move in) a circle, circulate, go around, go about, spiral, gyre, wheel, come full circle, make a round trip, return to the starting point, go round in circles, chase one's tail, U-turn

7 **ring**, circle, encircle, compass, encompass, surround, skirt, gird, girdle, loop, bend, curve, flank, go the round, make one's rounds, lap, circumvent, circumambulate, circummigrate, circumnavigate, girdle the earth

▶ *30 Earth Science; 165 Enclosure; 166 Limit; 177 Curve*

8 **detour**, make a detour, turn a corner, go the long way round, go all round the houses, go out of one's way, go the pretty way, deviate, bypass, digress, meander, circumlocute, beat about the bush, wander off the point

▶ *180 Convolution; 702 Sophistry*

ADJECTIVES

9 **orbital**, rotatory, rotary, revolutionary, circuitous, circulatory, turning, roundabout, indirect, oblique, meandering, ambagious (Lit), deviating, circumnavigable, circumambient, circumlocutory

10 **circular**, round, O-shaped, wheel-shaped, curved, spiral, heliacal, elliptical, cyclical, gyratory, coiled, looped

► *179 Circularity*

11 **orbiting**, wheeling, circling, spiralling, turning, spinning, gyring, gyrating

ADVERBS

12 **circuitously**, indirectly, roundabout, in a roundabout way, deviously, obliquely, by a side door (*or* wind), circlewise, wheelwise

307 Rotation

Because I do not hope to turn again
Because I do not hope
Because I do not hope to turn. T. S. Eliot.

NOUNS

1 **rotation**, rotational motion, revolution, revolutions, revs (Inf), revolutions per minute (rpm), revolving, volution, orbit, orbiting, orbital motion, cycle, full circle, circulation, turbination, circumference, circumrotation, circumnutation, circumvolution, gyration, spin, spinning motion, axial motion, angular motion (*or* momentum *or* velocity), dizziness, giddiness, vertigo

► *179 Circularity; 180 Convolution; 306 Orbital Motion*

2 **turning**, whirling, swirling, twirling, spinning, pivoting, pirouetting, wheeling, whir, whirring, reeling, centrifugation, rolling, bowling, trolling, trundling, volutation, spiral, spiralling, twisting, torsion, torque

3 **reel**, pirouette, turn, roll, whirl, wheel, swirl, twirl, spin, dance, whirlabout, round, dizzy round, rat race

► *22 Dancing*

4 **vortex**, whirl, whirlwind, whirlblast, maelstrom, charybdis, cyclone, tornado, whirlpool, eddy, swirl, surge, gurge, waterspout, twister (US inf),

► *30 Earth Science; 90 Rivers; 91 Seas; 433 Water; 434 Air*

5 **axle**, axis, shaft, axle shaft, spindle, axle spindle, axlebar, axle-true, axlebox, journal, journal box, hotbox, swivel, pivot, gudgeon, trunnion, pole, radiant, fulcrum, pin, pintle, hinge, hingle, rowlock, oarlock, hub, nave, distaff, mandrel, gimbal, bearing, ball bearing, roller bearing, thrust bearing, needle bearing, bevel bearing, bushing, jewel, headstock

► *38 Engineering*

6 **rotator**, wheel, cartwheel, wagon wheel, steering wheel, drive wheel, gearwheel, gear, spur wheel (*or* gear), worm gear (*or* wheel), cog, cogwheel, pinwheel, flywheel, ratchet wheel, idler wheel, crown wheel, balance wheel, escape wheel, sprocket wheel, mill wheel, paddle wheel, water wheel, spinning wheel, charka, spinning jenny, potter's wheel, buffing wheel, roulette wheel, Catherine wheel, Ferris wheel, prayerwheel, wheel of fortune, Ixion's wheel, top, spinning top, peg top, humming top, bobbin, spindle, spool, drill, rotary drill, Archimedes' screw, rotor, circular saw, gyro, gyroscope, gyrocompass, gyrostabilizer, gyroplane, autogyro, spin-dryer, centrifuge, ultracentrifuge, impeller, turbine, propeller, prop, screw, airscrew, winder, capstan, extractor fan, turntable, gramophone record, disc (*or* disk), compact disk, floppy disk, windmill, treadmill, spit, turnspit, whisk, egg whisk, eggbeater, food processor, revolving door, rolling pin

► *23 Furniture and Woodwork; 25 Cookery; 29 Astronomy; 38 Engineering; 330 Propulsion*

7 **science of rotation**, science of rotatory motion, gyrostatics, trochilics

► *28 Physics; 38 Engineering*

VERBS

8 **rotate**, revolve, spin, turn, orbit, go round, circle, circulate, circuit, turn right round, chase one's own tail, spin (like a top), spin like a teetotum, twirl, pirouette, gyre, gyrate, swing, waltz, circumnutate, circumvolve, circumvolute, swing round, spin round, whirl, whirl like a dervish, go into orbit, wheel, pivot, swivel, hinge

► *22 Dancing; 29 Astronomy*

9 **roll**, wind, roll up, fold, scroll, furl, reel, spin, spin yarn, twist, screw, crank, yarn, wamble, roll along, bowl, trundle, troll, trill, set rolling

10 **swirl**, eddy, whirlpool, surge, gurge, seethe, mill around (*or* about), stir, roil, moil, mix, flounder, wallow, roll about in, welter, grovel, roll, tumble

► *328 Disturbance; 412 Mixture; 623 Humility*

ADJECTIVES

11 **rotating**, revolving, gyrating, turning, orbiting, swivelling, pivoting, whirling, spinning, swirling, twirling, reeling, wheeling, rolling, trolling, bowling

12 **rotary**, rotational, rotatory, rotative, orbital, pivotal, trochilic, circumrotatory, circumgyratory, gyratory, gyrational, gyroscopic, gyrostatic, centrifugal, centripetal, circling, cyclic, cyclical, circulatory, torsional, vortical, vorticose, vorticular, cyclonic, turbinated, vertiginous, dizzy, giddy, tornadic, whirlwindy, whirlwindish

ADVERBS

13 **round**, around, in a circle, round and round, in circles, in a whirl, in a spin, head over heels, heels over head, like a horse in a mill, clockwise, anticlockwise, counterclockwise, widdershins

308 Opening

I declare this thing open – whatever it is. Prince Philip.

NOUNS

1 **opening**, gap, hole, hollow, cavity, aperture, orifice, gape, duct, passageway, passage, space, open space, interval, slot, split, crack, hairline crack, crevice, chasm, pass, fault, flaw, breach, break, fracture, rupture, cut, tear, cleft, fissure, perforation, piercing, pricking, puncture, bore

► *141 Space; 146 Interval; 183 Concavity; 190 Expansion; 318 Passage; 410 Container; 587 Weapon*

2 **opener**, key, master key, skeleton key, passkey, key card, smart card, password, open sesame, tin-opener, bottle-opener, corkscrew, drill, brace and bit, reamer, awl, needle, hypodermic needle, pin, bodkin, punch,

leather punch, auger, bit, probe, pick, pickaxe, axe, saw, trephine, trepan, lance, lancet, bayonet, knife

3 **person who opens**, locksmith, doorman, warder, excavator, tunneller, digger, miner, plumber, carpenter, surgeon, wine steward, Pandora

4 **body orifice**, pore, sweat gland, aural cavity, ear, nasal cavity, nostril, nose, anus, cloaca, urethra, vagina, oral cavity, mouth, maw, trap (Inf), kisser (Inf), gob (Inf), lug (Inf), arse (Inf), arsehole (Inf)

5 **hole**, keyhole, peephole, knothole, eyehole, eyelet, eye, buttonhole, pinhole, porthole, borehole, blowhole, airhole, shaft, well, mine, mineshaft, excavation, cavern, cave, volcano

6 **porous thing**, sponge, sieve, colander, teabag, honeycomb, screen, mosquito net, nylon stockings, lattice, grate, grille, filter

7 **passageway**, gangway, hallway, corridor, aisle, entrance, exit, doorway, postern, pass, gorge, defile, window, skylight, dormer, fanlight, arch, gate, porch, portal, manhole, tunnel, underpass, tube, mousehole, rabbithole, molehole, foxhole, conduit, funnel, hose, sewer, drain, pipe, pipeline, windpipe, throat, oesophagus, artery, vein, colon, intestines, alimentary canal, anal canal, ureter, sperm duct, stoma, vent, flue, chimney, chimneystack, smokestack, smokehole

▶ *35 Medicine; 314 Entry; 315 Exit*

8 **open space**, open country, open sea, clearing, meadow, beach, desert, court, yard, glade, stage

9 **openness**, opening up, frankness, bluntness, explicitness, plain words, candour, honesty, sincerity, artlessness, open heart, open face, ingenuousness, naivety

10 **opportunity**, opening, open door, toe (*or* foot) in the door, toehold, foothold, chance, possibility, golden opportunity, occasion, available post, vacancy, position, job, lucky break, break (Inf)

11 **beginning**, start, commencement, initiation, inception, dawn, birth, inauguration, launch, debut

▶ *130 Beginning*

ADJECTIVES

12 **open**, wide-open, pushed open, pulled open, unclosed, uncovered, unwrapped, unfolded, exposed, visible, ajar, punched open, cut open, split, torn, cracked, creviced, cleft, fissured, breached, gaping, open-mouthed, agape, hacked, hewn, cut, sawed (*or* sawn), broken, fractured, ruptured

▶ *739 Disclosure*

13 **opened up**, unblocked, unlocked, unbolted, unbarred, unlatched, unfastened, unsealed, uncovered, uncorked, unstopped, unobstructed, patent, clear, evident, obvious, apparent, manifest, free, unimpeded, unhindered, unhampered, unrestricted, accessible, open door, available, vacant, public, unenclosed, unfenced, unprotected, unshielded, extended, extensive, bare, open-plan

14 **holed**, perforated, porous, permeated, riddled with holes, punched full of holes, filled with holes, sievelike, cribriform, honeycombed, spongy, leaky, injected, penetrated, probed, pierced, pricked, punctured, lanced, bayoneted, knifed, stabbed, stuck, slashed, gashed, shot, peppered with shot, bored, hollowed, drilled, reamed, dug, burrowed, tunnelled, sunk, excavated, cavernous, spacial, volcanic

15 **providing passage**, gated, draining, arterial, venous, colonic, intestinal, alimentary, anal

16 **open**, frank, blunt, explicit, plain, candid, unreserved, open-hearted, open-faced, honest, sincere, ingenuous, naive, artless

17 **beginning**, starting, commencing, dawning, initial, inceptive, inaugural, introductory, first, newborn, debut

VERBS

18 **open**, push open, pull open, open up, open out, unclose, uncover, unwrap, unfold, expose, disclose, reveal, show, leave ajar, punch open, cut open, split, tear, crack, cleave, breach, hack, hew, cut, saw, break, fracture, rupture, burst open, gape, erupt, explode

19 **open up**, unblock, unlock, unbolt, unbar, unlatch, unfasten, unseal, uncover, uncork, unstop, not obstruct, clear, free, gain access, access, not enclose, extend, spread

20 **hole**, make porous, perforate, permeate, riddle with holes, punch full of holes, fill with holes, honeycomb, fissure, slot, break the skin, trephine, trepan, inject, penetrate, probe, pierce, prick, puncture, lance, bayonet, knife, stab, run through, stick, slash, gash, shoot, pepper with shot, bore, hollow, drill, ream, dig a hole, burrow, tunnel, sink a mineshaft, excavate

21 **provide passage for**, drain, pipe, funnel, vent, sieve, screen

22 **be open**, have openness, open up, speak straight from the shoulder, use plain words, open one's heart

23 **find an opening**, gain a foothold, be in the right place at the right time, get a (lucky) break (Inf)

24 **begin**, start, commence, initiate, dawn, inaugurate, launch, debut

ADVERBS

25 **obviously**, apparently, manifestly, visibly, patently, clearly, evidently, plainly, in the open, publicly, availably, accessibly, extensively, widely

26 **openly**, candidly, bluntly, plainly, explicitly, frankly, sincerely, honestly, straight from the shoulder, in plain words, ingenuously, naively, artlessly, vacantly, blankly

27 **cavernously**, gapingly, porously, volcanically, intestinally, arterially, venously, anally

309 Closure

I went to New Zealand but it was closed. Anonymous.

NOUNS

1 **closure**, closing, closing up, closing down, close-down, shutdown, finish, cessation, discontinuance, stop, stoppage, conclusion, resolution, fulfilment, completion, termination, end, foreclosure, imperviousness, impermeability, impenetrability, impassability, obstruction, occlusion, contraction, constriction, congestion, strangulation, blockage, constipation, blockade, block, chock, barrier, bar, hindrance, let, impasse, sealing off, standstill, deadlock, stalemate

▶ *166 Limit; 191 Contraction; 226 Stopping; 378 Obstruction*

2 **stopper**, stop, cap, lid, top, cork, covering, cover, seal, plug, bandage, tourniquet, bung, peg, pin, spigot, valve, tap, faucet, stopcock, wad, wadding, stuffing, tampion,

wedge, blood clot, thrombus, embolus, infarct, tampon, damper, choke, trip switch, cutout switch, piston
▶ *373 Connection; 550 Covering*
3 **restrainer**, lock, padlock, latch, bolt, bar, clamp, clasp, hasp, catch, safety catch, straitjacket, handcuffs, chain, rope, leash, lead, muzzle
▶ *252 Safety*
4 **closed place**, enclosed place, dead end, cul-de-sac, blind alley, roadblock, enclosure, courtyard, quadrangle, reserve, sanctuary, zoo, walled garden, pen, hutch, cage, kennel, coop, pigsty, corral, paddock, fold, ghetto, grave, tomb, sepulchre, trap, prison, jail, dungeon, cell, oubliette, reformatory, borstal, can (Inf), clink (Inf), nick (Inf), cooler (Inf), slammer (Inf), the big house (US inf)
▶ *165 Enclosure; 815 Prison*
5 **person who closes**, doorman, doorkeeper, porter, concierge, gatekeeper, commissionaire, warder, turnkey, jailer, caretaker, sentry, sentinel, night watchman, screw (Inf)
6 **closed-in person**, prisoner, inmate, detainee, internee, miner, submariner, shut-in (US)

VERBS

7 **close**, close up, shut, shut up, seal, fasten, secure, lock, lock up, bolt, bar, latch, padlock, do up, button, button up, zip up, seal off, batten down, batten down the hatches, put the lid on, cover, contain
8 **stop**, stopper, plug, cap, top, cork, dam, staunch, bandage, tampon, stop up, bar, stay, block, block up, clog, clog up, bung, bung up, obstruct, occlude, constipate, contract, constrict, congest, strangle, throttle, choke, blockade, hinder
9 **close down**, close up, shut down, finish, cease, discontinue, terminate, end, foreclose, conclude, resolve, fulfil, complete, wind up
10 **enclose**, confine, keep in, lock up (*or* in), shut up (*or* in), imprison, jail, cage, impound, pen, hutch, kennel, coop, corral, fold, intern, immure, incarcerate, bury, entomb, throw in the slammer (Inf), bang up (Inf), send down (Inf), send to the big house (US inf)
11 **restrain**, handcuff, chain, shackle, rope, bind, tie, leash, muzzle, straitjacket

ADJECTIVES

12 **closed**, unopened, shut, shut up, locked, bolted, barred, latched, padlocked, burglar-proof, fastened, secured, buttoned, buttoned-up, zipped up, sealed, hermetically sealed, airtight, vacuum-packed, watertight, waterproof, lightproof, nonporous, impermeable, impervious
13 **stopped**, stopped up, plugged, capped, corked, dammed, staunched, bandaged, blocked, obstructed, occluded, blocked up, clogged, clogged up, impenetrable, impassable, bunged up, stuffed up, constipated, costive, constricted, congested, choked, choked up, full, stuffed, packed, jammed
14 **closed down**, closed-up, shut down, wound up, finished, resolved, completed, ended
15 **enclosed**, closed-in, shut up, jailed, imprisoned, confined

ADVERBS

16 **impermeably**, imperviously, impenetrably, impassably, nonporously, hermetically, costively
17 **finally**, at last, in the end, completely, over, over (and done) with

310 Convergence

NOUNS

1 **convergence**, converging, confluence, conflux, concurrence, concourse, collision, mutual approach, concentration, meeting, coming together
▶ *750 Agreement*
2 **approach**, advance, confrontation, collision course, narrowing gap
3 **convergent view**, perspective, vanishing point (*or* line *or* plane)
4 **meeting place**, congress, congregation, assembly, union, junction, crossing
▶ *376 Gathering*
5 **focus**, centre, hub, pivot, centring, coming to the point, concentralization, focalization, asymptote, converging line, radius, tangent, spokes
6 **narrowing**, narrowing gap, taper, tapering, funnel, bottleneck
▶ *151 Narrowness*

ADJECTIVES

7 **convergent**, converging, confluent, uniting, concurrent, meeting, focal, focusing, focused, confocal, centrolineal, centripetal, asymptotic(al), radial, radiating, tangent, tangential, centring, pointed, tapering, narrowing, conical, pyramidal, knock-kneed
8 **advancing**, oncoming, approaching, mutually approaching, connivent

VERBS

9 **converge**, close in, approach, draw near, intersect, be on a collision course, narrow the gap, close with, close, close up, funnel, taper, pinch, nip
▶ *151 Narrowness; 302 Forward Motion*
10 **come together**, assemble, congregate, concentrate, gather, cluster, run together, meet, unite, fall in with, get together, roll up, roll in, pour in
11 **focus**, bring into focus, centre, home in, zero in, centralize, taper, concentralize, concentre, come to a focus, concentrate, corradiate, come to the point

ADVERBS

12 **convergently**, confluently, concurrently, congruently, mutually, together

311 Divergence

Two roads diverged in a wood, and I –
I took the one less traveled by,
And that has made all the difference. Robert Frost.

NOUNS

1 **divergence**, divergency, divarication, aberration, declination, deviation, difference, contradiction, contrariety
▶ *116 Dissimilarity; 325 Deviation; 704 Refutation*
2 **parting**, moving (*or* going) apart, drifting apart, spread, spreading out, splaying, fanning, fanning out, deployment, separation, centrifugence, division, decentralization

▶ *372 Separation*

3 **radiation**, ray, radius, spoke, radiance, scattering, diffusion, dispersion, emanation

▶ *377 Dispersal*

4 **branching**, branching out, ramification, arborescence, arborization, treelikeness, forking, furcation, bifurcation, biforking, trifurcation, triforking, parting of the ways, intersection, crossroads, crossing

5 **fork**, prong, trident, branch, Y-shape, V-shape, stem, offshoot, fan, delta, groin, inguen, furcula, furculum, wishbone

ADJECTIVES

6 **divergent**, diverging, divaricate, separated, separate, aberrant, different, contradictory, centrifugal, deviating

▶ *116 Dissimilarity; 325 Deviation; 372 Separation*

7 **radiating**, radial, radiate(d), radiant, rayed, spoked

▶ *377 Dispersal*

8 **fanlike**, fan-shaped, deltoid(al), delta-like, delta-shaped, palmate(d), splayed, spreadeagled

9 **branched**, branching, arborescent, arboreal, arboriform, treelike, tree-shaped, dendriform, dendritic, branchlike, ramose, ramous, Y-shaped, V-shaped, forking, forked, furcate, forklike, biforked, bifurcated, trifurcated, pronged, trident-like

VERBS

10 **diverge**, divaricate, aberrate, deviate

11 **move apart**, part, spread, spread out (*or* apart), outspread, fan, fan out, deploy, go off (*or* away)

12 **separate**, divide, splay, splay apart, go separate ways, split, split off, part company, be disjoined

▶ *372 Separation*

13 **radiate**, ray, diffuse, emanate, disperse, scatter

▶ *377 Dispersal*

14 **branch**, stem, ramify, branch off (*or* out), spread-eagle, straddle, step wide, fork, furcate, bifurcate, trifurcate

15 **change direction**, switch, fly (*or* go) off at a tangent, glance, fly off

ADVERBS

16 **divergently**, apart, radiantly, radially, diffusely, ramosely, ramously, aberrantly, differently, separately

312 Arrival

He travelled in order to come home. William Trevor.

VERBS

1 **arrive**, appear, come, make (*or* put in) an appearance, be present, be found, turn up, show up (Inf), roll up (Inf), drop in (Inf), blow in (Inf), pop up (Inf), bob up (Inf), hit (Inf), hit town (Inf)

▶ *525 Appearance*

2 **reach**, reach there, get there, get to, come to, fetch, fetch up in (*or* at), end up in (*or* at), make it, reach one's destination (*or* goal), come to one's journey's end, find, discover, arrive at (*or* upon), come upon, strike upon, hit upon, fall upon, light upon, pitch upon, stumble upon (*or* on), come to rest, finish the race, breast the tape, be in at the death, be received

▶ *449 Discovery*

3 **approach**, draw up, sight, stand at the door, be on the threshold, knock at the door, look for a welcome

4 **land**, make port, put into port, dock, beach, berth, moor, tie up, drop anchor, ground, run aground, make a landfall, set foot on dry land, step (*or* go) ashore, disembark, debark, unboat, alight, touch down, disemplane, deplane, get off, detrain, debus, dismount, get down, unharness, unhitch, quit the saddle, emerge, surrender one's ticket, home, return, come (*or* get *or* return) home, perch, discharge, unload

5 **get in**, come in, set foot in, enter, burst upon, make an entrance, check in, clock in, punch in, ring in, sign in

▶ *314 Entry*

6 **stop at**, visit, put in, pull in, stop over, stop off, break one's journey, pause

7 **be brought**, be delivered, come to hand

8 **meet**, join, rejoin, see again, go (*or* come) to meet, be at the station, keep a date, rendezvous, come upon (*or* across), encounter, come into contact, run into (*or* across), bump into, meet by chance, butt into, knock into, collide with, gather, assemble, congregate

▶ *376 Gathering*

9 **achieve**, accomplish, attain, gain, succeed, be successful, prosper, get to the top, reach the top, get ahead, make good, make it (Inf), make the grade (Inf), get somewhere (Inf), get there (Inf)

▶ *246 Success; 248 Prosperity*

NOUNS

10 **arrival**, coming, advent, approach, onset, advance, appearance, entrance, emergence, presence, debut, beginning

▶ *130 Beginning; 314 Entry*

11 **landing**, landfall, docking, touchdown, mooring, disembarkation, disembarkment, debarkation, coming (*or* going) ashore, tying up, dropping (*or* weighing) anchor

12 **reception**, hospitality, welcome, greeting, handshake, aloha, hello

▶ *654 Sociability*

13 **return**, homecoming, coming back, recursion, reentrance, re-entry, prodigal's return

14 **meeting**, encounter, recounter, rejoining, rendezvous, meeting place

15 **destination**, goal, objective, bourn (Lit), terra firma, harbour, haven, home, end, stop, last stop, terminal point, point of arrival, journey's end, end of the line, terminus, terminal, stopping place, arrival at the winning post, finish, close finish, photo finish, last lap, port, aerodrome, airport, heliport, air terminal, depot, junction, railway station

▶ *131 End*

16 **stopover**, stage, halt, billet, shelter, dock, port in a storm, dry dock, berth, stable

17 **achievement**, accomplishment, attainment, accession, fulfilment, reaching, making

▶ *246 Success*

ADJECTIVES

18 **arriving**, incoming, immigrant, entering, emerging, appearing

▶ *314 Entry; 525 Appearance*

19 **approaching**, impending, imminent, oncoming, ad-

vancing, coming, incoming, inbound, inwardbound, homeward, homeward-bound, nearing, terminal

▶ *130 Beginning*

20 attainable, achievable, approachable, accessible, get-at-able (Inf)

21 welcoming, inviting, hospitable

▶ *654 Sociability*

ADVERBS

22 on arrival, on the doorstep (*or* threshold), at the door, here, home, back home, home again, aground, ashore, at journey's end

INTERJECTIONS

23 hello!, hail!, hi!, hiya!, *ciao!* (It), *salut!* (Fr), how do you do?, how are you?, alright? (Inf)

24 welcome!, greetings!, (do) come in!, make yourself at home!, have a seat!, help yourself!

313 Departure

A journey of a thousand leagues begins with a single step. Chinese Proverb.

Once I leave, I leave. I am not going to speak to the man on the bridge, and I am not going to spit on the deck. Stanley Baldwin.

VERBS

1 depart, leave, take (*or* make) one's leave, take (*or* make) one's departure, go, go away, get away (*or* off), get (*or* go) along, make tracks, go (*or* get) on, toddle along, trot along, stagger along, gang along (Scot), walk away, slink off, slope off, flounce off (*or* out), fling off (*or* out), leave in high dudgeon, stamp off, storm out, up and go (Inf), mosey along (Inf), push off (Inf), clear off (Inf), buzz off (Inf), piss off (Inf), fuck off (Inf), bugger off (Inf), sod (*or* bog *or* mog) off (Inf)

2 withdraw, retreat, beat a retreat, turn back, turn one's back on, pull out, exit, make one's exit, leave the stage, bow out, leave work, clock out, punch out, cease work, retire, receive a golden handshake, resign, sign off, sign out, check out, vacate, evacuate, abandon, relinquish, die, depart this life, pass away, pass over

▶ *226 Stopping; 303 Backward Motion; 315 Exit; 355 Relinquishment; 582 Death; 605 Resignation*

3 quit, quit the scene, leave the country, emigrate, expatriate, move house, remove, relocate, leave home, leave the nest, leave the neighbourhood, disappear, vanish, leave no trace, take wing, slip away, elope, escape, give someone the slip, abscond, absent oneself, march out, debouch, decamp, break camp, strike camp (*or* tent), up sticks, pull up stakes, sling one's hook (Inf), flit (Inf), do a moonlight flit (Inf)

▶ *98 Absence; 389 Escape; 526 Disappearance*

4 hurry off, move fast, take off, make off, run away, run off, flee, bolt, take flight (*or* wing), take to one's heels, run for one's life, cut and run, decamp, absquatulate, rush off, hasten off, scamper away, skip, skip off, dash, dash off, nip, nip off, whip off, whiz off, tear off (*or* out), cut, cut away, make oneself scarce, beetle off (Inf), vamoose (Inf), skedaddle (Inf), scarper (Inf), beat it (Inf), scram (Inf), hightail (Inf), split (Inf), lam (US inf), take it on the lam (US inf), take a powder (US inf)

▶ *262 Haste*

5 set out, set forth (*or* forward), put (*or* go) forth, be off, be on one's way, emerge, sally forth, issue, issue forth, start, start out (*or* off), strike out, get off, move off, march off, march away, embark, board, entrain, embus, enplane, emplane, go aboard (*or* on board), jump on, hop on, mount, set sail, spread sail, spread canvas, hoist the Blue Peter, weigh anchor, unmoor, cast off, drop the pilot, push off, put to sea, get under way, leave land behind, take off, pull out of the station, hit the road (Inf)

▶ *130 Beginning; 315 Exit; 319 Transport; 371 Expulsion*

6 part, separate, part company, take (*or* break) oneself off, tear oneself away, take one's leave, say farewell, bid farewell, bid (*or* say) goodbye (*or* goodnight *or* Godspeed), make one's adieus, wave goodbye, speed the parting guest, give someone a good sendoff, have one for the road

NOUNS

7 departure, leaving, going, going away, exit, egress, exodus, emigration, migration, Hegira (*or* Hejira), flight, escape, getaway, flit, moonlight flit, elopement, decampment, abandonment, withdrawal, retreat, retirement, evacuation, pulling out, remigration, going back, return

▶ *303 Backward Motion; 315 Exit; 389 Escape*

8 start, outset, embarkation, embarkment, boarding, going on board, entrainment, enplanement, emplanement, takeoff, ascent, liftoff, blastoff, zero hour

▶ *130 Beginning; 319 Transport*

9 parting, separation, leavetaking, leave, congé, farewell, goodbye, goodnight, adieu, one's adieus, parting shot, valediction, valedictory, valedictory address, farewell address, last words, funeral oration, obituary, epitaph, last post, last handshake, golden handshake, dismissal, viaticum, one for the road, nightcap, stirrup cup, deoch-an-doruis (*or* doch-an-doris) (Scot), sendoff (Inf)

10 place of departure, port, dock, place of embarkation, airport, gate, station, railway station, departure platform, bus station, bus stop, starting point, outset, base, springboard, jumping-off point

▶ *319 Transport*

ADJECTIVES

11 departing, leaving, farewell, valedictory, parting, leave-taking, last, final

12 departed, gone, gone away, gone off, left

13 outgoing, outward-bound, emigratory

INTERJECTIONS

14 goodbye!, goodnight!, farewell!, adieu!, *au revoir!* (Fr), *auf Wiedersehn!* (Ger), *ciao!* (It), *adios!* (Sp), so long!, bye-bye!, bye!, cheerio!, see you!, see you later!, have a nice day!, bon voyage!, cheers!

15 go!, go away!, begone!, never darken my door again!, get thee hence! (Lit), get out!, clear out!, shoo! (Inf), get lost! (Inf), get going! (Inf), shove off! (Inf), push off! (Inf), clear off! (Inf), buzz off! (Inf), piss off! (Inf), naff off! (Inf), sod off! (Inf), bog off! (Inf), bugger off! (Inf), fuck off! (Inf), beat it! (Inf), scram! (Inf), vamoose! (Inf), get! (Inf), git! (Inf)

314 Entry

For all men have one entrance into life, and the like going out. Bible: Wisdom.

1 **entry**, entrance, ingress, ingression, intergression, entrée, access, incoming, ingoing, import, input, re-entry, re-entrance, admission, reception, enrolment, enlistment, induction, initiation, introduction, debut, appearance, arrival
▶ *312 Arrival; 316 Transfer; 370 Admittance; 525 Appearance*
2 **influx**, inflow, flood, inflooding, stream, indraught, inhalation, indrawing, indrawal, intake, inrush, inrun, afflux, affluxion, affluence
3 **inroad**, encroachment, insertion, penetration, interpenetration, insinuation, infiltration, percolation, seepage, leakage, intrusion, invasion, forced entry, raid, irruption, incursion, attack, illegal entry, trespassing, housebreaking, breaking and entering, burglary
▶ *328 Disturbance; 368 Insertion; 381 Attack*
4 **right of entry**, non-restriction, admission, admittance, access, permission, permit, ticket, pass, passport, visa, immigration, inmigration, foreign influx, importation, importing, trade, free trade, free port, open-door policy, free market, expansionism
▶ *370 Admittance; 757 Permission; 776 Trade; 779 Market*
5 **entrance**, way in, entry, access, inlet, ingress, approach, adit, mouth, opening, orifice, conduit, channel, passage
▶ *308 Opening; 317 Way; 318 Passage*
6 **means of entry** (*or* **access**), porch, propylaeum, portico, portal, porte-cochere, doorway, threshold, lintel, doorpost (*or* -jamb), door, front door, side door, French door (*or* window), patio door, back door, postern, storm door, cellar door, trap door, hatch, hatchway, scuttle, gate, gateway, gate post, lychgate, archway, tollgate, turnstile, turnpike, stile, lobby, vestibule, foyer
7 **entrant**, incomer, comer, arrival, visitor, visitant, caller, guest, immigrant, inmigrant, newcomer, new face, new member, new boy, new girl, intake, beginner, debutante, settler, colonist, competitor, contender, ticketholder, cardholder, audience, house
▶ *130 Beginning; 654 Sociability*
8 **intruder**, invader, raider, attacker, gate-crasher, unwelcome guest, trespasser, burglar, housebreaker, picklock, thief
▶ *328 Disturbance; 774 Stealing*

VERBS

9 **enter**, go in (*or* into), come in (*or* into), get in (*or* into), gain admittance, be admitted, open the door, let oneself in, cross the threshold, set foot in, arrive, make an entrance, visit, call, call in, look in, pop in, find one's way into, have an in, turn into, put in (*or* into), board, embark, go aboard, mount
▶ *312 Arrival; 370 Admittance; 654 Sociability*
10 **invade**, irrupt, raid, attack, storm, escalade, encroach, trespass, gate-crash, barge in, rush in, burst in, storm in, butt in, interrupt, muscle in, horn in, outstay one's welcome, put one's foot in it, break in, break and enter, pick the lock, burgle
▶ *328 Disturbance*
11 **infiltrate**, permeate, percolate, filter in, soak in, leak in, seep, drip, work (*or* worm) one's way into, insinuate, creep in, slip in, sneak in, slink in, penetrate, interpenetrate, break through, get (*or* pass *or* go) through, bore in, pierce, puncture, insert, bite into, eat into, cut into
▶ *368 Insertion*
12 **flood in**, inflood, flow in, inflow, rush in, inrush, pour in, swarm in, pack in, crowd in, throng in, press in, cram in, squeeze in, wedge in, jam in, congregate
▶ *376 Gathering*
13 **fall into**, drop into, plunge into, dive into, sink into
▶ *305 Descent; 367 Lowering*
14 **enrol**, join, admit, take in, enlist, inscribe, sign on, enter for, contend, induct, initiate, introduce, immigrate, settle, settle in, colonize
▶ *130 Beginning*

ADJECTIVES

15 **entering**, ingressive, inward, incoming, ingoing, inbound, immigrant, imported, allowed in, homing
16 **invasive**, incursive, intrusive, trespassing, attacking, penetrating, irruptive, ingrowing, inflowing, inflooding, inpouring, inrushing

ADVERBS

17 **in**, inward, inwards, inwardly, invasively, intrusively, incursively

PREPOSITIONS

18 **into**, in, to

315 Exit

Few men of action have been able to make a graceful exit at the appropriate time. Malcolm Muggeridge.

NOUNS

1 **exit**, egress, egression, going out, outgoing, outgo, coming out, outcoming, outcome, emergence, emerging, emersion, issue, issuance, extrusion, exodus, departure, walkout, walk-off, evacuation, outbreak, breakout, eruption, proruption, outburst
▶ *313 Departure; 369 Extraction; 371 Expulsion*
2 **outflow**, outflowing, outpouring, outpour, flood, inundation, spill, waste, effluence, effusion, outflux, efflux, effluxion, defluxion, outfall, waterfall, gush, gushing, stream, streaming, jet, fountain, well, spring, gusher, exhaust, emission, discharge, emanation, exudation, secretion, voidance, excretion, evaporation, perspiration, sweating, sweat, transudation, diaphoresis, running sore, streaming eyes, runny nose, haemorrhage
▶ *441 Waste; 560 Excretion*
3 **leakage**, leak, leaking, seepage, seep, seeping, drip, dripping, dribble, dribbling, trickle, trickling, filtration, filtering, exfiltration, straining, percolation, percolating, leaching, lixiviation, effusion, extravasation, ooze, oozing, weep, weeping
4 **emigration**, outmigration, migration, expatriation, deportation, exile, expulsion, dismissal
▶ *371 Expulsion*
5 **export**, exporting, exportation, transference, outgoings, outlay, expenditure, spending, loss

▶ *316 Transfer; 766 Loss; 776 Trade; 787 Expenditure*

6 **way out**, exit, egress, door, back door, gate, outgate, port, emergency exit, fire escape, escape hatch, escape route, path, avenue, channel, loophole

▶ *317 Way; 389 Escape*

7 **outlet**, outfall, chute, spout, tap, drain, drainpipe, gutter, conduit, gargoyle, overflow, flume, sluice, weir, floodgate, opening, orifice, vent, ventage, venthole, pore, blowhole, spiracle, anus

▶ *308 Opening; 318 Passage*

8 **outgoer**, goer, leaver, departer, emigrant, émigré, outmigrant, migrant, colonist, settler, expellee, exile, expatriate, remittance man

VERBS

9 **exit**, make an (*or* one's) exit, egress, go, leave, depart, withdraw, go out, pass out, get out, walk out, run out, pop out, march out, bow out, walk off, die, pass over

▶ *313 Departure; 582 Death*

10 **emerge**, come out, issue, issue forth, debouch, sally, sally forth, emanate, effuse, come out in the open, appear, surface, arise, erupt, break out, break forth, project, protrude, jut, break cover, burst out, escape, evacuate, bale out, jump out

▶ *304 Ascent; 389 Escape; 525 Appearance*

11 **run out**, drain, drain out, flow out, outflow, flood, flood out, inundate, pour, outpour, pour out, disembogue, surge, well out (*or* up *or* over), gush, gush out, jet, spurt, spurt out, spout, spout out, vomit, spew, spew out, blow out, overflow, spill, spill over, slop, slop over

12 **leak**, leak out, drip, dribble, trickle, seep, seep out, weep, ooze, ooze out, extravasate, filter, filtrate, exfiltrate, strain, percolate, leach, lixiviate, effuse, drivel, drool, slaver, slobber, salivate, water at the mouth, emanate, exude, emit, discharge, secrete, excrete, exudate, perspire, sweat, exhale, breathe out

▶ *560 Excretion*

13 **emigrate**, outmigrate, migrate, expatriate, deport, exile, expel, dismiss, export, send abroad

▶ *371 Expulsion*

14 **be dismissed**, leave, resign, retire, walk out, get the boot (Inf), get the sack (Inf), get fired (Inf), get the bird (Inf)

▶ *371 Expulsion*

ADJECTIVES

15 **outgoing**, outbound, outward-bound, going, departing, leaving, forthcoming, issuing, egressive, emerging, emergent, coming out, arising, surfacing, erupting, eruptive, volcanic, explosive, expulsive, emanating, emanent, emanative, transeunt, transient

▶ *278 Transience*

16 **outflowing**, outpouring, effluent, effusive, effused, extravasated, expended, spent

17 **leaky**, oozy, weeping, runny, excretory, porous, permeable, exudative, transudative

ADVERBS

18 **forth**, out, outwards, outward, apart, away, outwardly, effusively, eruptively, explosively

PREPOSITIONS

19 **out of**, from

316 Transfer

NOUNS

1 **transfer**, transference, transferral (US), translocation, transmittal, transmittance, transposition, metathesis, transposal, transplacement, transmigration (of souls), metempsychosis, transplantation, removal, relocation, moving, movement, removement, displacement, delocalization, deportation, expulsion, extradition, relegation, shift, shifting, transition, mutual transfer, interchange, trade, exchange, barter, swap

▶ *300 Motion; 776 Trade*

2 **transportation**, transport, conveyance, transshipment, dispatch, sending, posting, mailing (US), export, exportation, import, importation, transit, transition, bridge, passage, vection, vectitation, vecture, carriage, delivery, hand over, haulage, hauling, cartage, carry, portage, porterage, waft, waftage, truckage, waggonage, drayage, ferriage, lighterage, telpherage, freightage, freight, expressage, railway express, air express, air freight, airlift, shipment, shipping, asportation (Lit), humping (Inf)

▶ *319 Transport*

3 **transmission**, conduction, convection, osmosis, transpiration, throughput, electromagnetic conduction, diapedesis, transduction, transfusion, perfusion, decantation, dispersal, transmission of disease, contagion, infection, contamination, communication, contact, dissemination, spread, spreading, diffusion, metastasis, dispersion

▶ *260 Ill Health*

4 **translation**, transcription, literary conversion, transumption, transliteration, copying, photocopying, plagiarism

5 **means of transport**, conveyance, public transport, rail transport, road transport, sea transport, air transport, car, automobile, vehicle, truck, lorry, juggernaut, trailer, bus, postbus, taxi, tram, carriage, van, delivery van, train, goods train, freight train (US), Pullman, cargo vessel, freighter, tramp steamer, (oil) tanker, bicycle, motorcycle, conveyor belt, escalator, travolator, moving pavement, lift, sleigh, sledge, sled (US), trolley, stretcher, litter, roller (*or* ice) skates, rollerblades, skateboard

▶ *319 Transport*

6 **beast of burden**, pack (*or* draught) animal, packhorse, draughthorse, pack mule, ass, donkey, cuddy (Scot), burro, ox, coach horse, sledge dog, husky, malamute, reindeer, llama, camel, dromedary, elephant, sumpter (Lit), moke (Inf)

7 **transferor** (*or* **transferrer**), testator, conveyor (*or* conveyer), conveyancer, carrier, transporter, hauler, carter, drayman, common carrier, trucker, driver, truck driver, bus driver (*or* busman), taxi driver, tram driver, chauffeur, waggoner, boatman, gondolier, ferryman, importer, exporter, freighter, stevedore, cargo handler, bearer, porter, retainer, redcap (US), skycap (US), bellboy, page, bus boy (US), litter bearer, coolie, stretcher-bearer, shield-bearer, gunbearer, cupbearer, Ganymede, water carrier (*or* bearer), Aquarius, the Water Carrier, water boy, caddy, pallbearer

8 **messenger**, letter carrier, mail carrier (US), Royal Mail, Pony Express, postman, mailman (US), expressman,

courier, carrier pigeon, homing pigeon, winged messenger, Mercury, Hermes, Iris

▶ *692 Communications*

9 **disease carrier**, sick person, infectious person, vector, transmitter, diffuser, contaminator

▶ *260 Ill Health*

10 **transferred thing**, passenger, fare, freight, freightage, consignment, shipment, goods, load, cargo, cargo load, payload, baggage, luggage, impedimenta, personal belongings, everything but the kitchen sink, container, pack, backpack, knapsack, rucksack, carrier bag, shopping bag, handbag, message, post, mail (US), letters, card, postcard, telegram, telegraph, gift, security, trust, legacy, bequest, pledge, driftwood, flotsam, jetsam, sediment, silt, drift, alluvium, alluvion, loess, moraine, scree, sinter, detritus, debris, infectious disease, contagious disease

▶ *406 Contents; 410 Container*

VERBS

11 **transfer**, transmit, translocate, transpose, metathesize, transplant, consign, assign, turn over, hand over, make over, conduct, convect, radiate, transpire, transfuse, diffuse, perfuse, spread, disseminate, disperse, metastasize, infect, contaminate, strain, decant, siphon, tap, funnel, channel, interchange, exchange, barter, swap, switch, shuffle, castle

12 **transport**, take, convey, freight, dispatch, send, send off (*or* away), send forth, remit, consign, transmit, forward, expedite, ship, import, export, carry, deliver, hand over, bear, haul, cart, heave, pack, tote, lug, manhandle, push, propel, lift, waft, whisk, wing, fly, send flying, airlift, truck, bus, ship, ferry, raft, boat, barge, sledge, sled (US), hump (Inf), schlep (US inf)

13 **post**, mail (US), airmail, forward, drop a line to, express, air-express, send by hand, fax, telex, address, readdress

14 **bring back**, fetch, get, bring, go and get, go after, go for, pick up, call for, procure, obtain, secure, retain, retrieve, chase, chase after, run after, fetch and carry, disperse, bequeath, commit, assign, leave, entrust, hand on (*or* down), pass on, scatter, deport, expel, eject, extradite, send

15 **take away**, cart away, carry off (*or* away), manhandle, set aside, lay (*or* put) aside, side, relegate, remove, relocate, move, displace, ladle, scoop, dip, bail, bucket, dish, spoon (out), shovel, spade, fork, dig, dislodge, unload, shift, shunt

16 **translate**, transcribe, transliterate, copy, make a copy, photocopy, plagiarize

▶ *5 Language and Linguistics; 125 Imitation*

ADJECTIVES

17 **transferable**, transmittable, transmissible, transmissive, communicable, contagious, infectious, transfusable, importable, metastatic(al), metathetic(al), shifting, conveyable, mailable, consignable, conductive, conductional, interchangeable, exchangeable, negotiable, removable, movable, portable, portative, transportable, transportative, transportive, transposable, displaceable, carriageable, roadworthy, airworthy, seaworthy

ADVERBS

18 **in transit**, en route, on (*or* along) the way, on the (high) road, on the (high) sea, on the wing, as one goes, in passing, *en passant* (Fr), in mid-stream, by hand, *per manus* (L), by transfer, from door to door, by express, by rail, by special delivery, by remittance, from hand to hand, from pillar to post, conductively, interchangeably, exchangeably, contagiously, infectiously, communicably, metastatically

317 Way

All roads lead to Rome. Proverb.

The Great White Way. Albert Bigelow Paine.

NOUNS

1 **way**, ways and means, mode, manner, wise (Lit), means, form, method, methodology, system, technique, procedure, process, proceeding, modus operandi, line, line of action, order, mode of operation (MO), manner of working, way of doing things, modus vivendi, practice, skill, conduct, algorithm, approach, tack, line of attack, tactics, routine, the how, the drill, the way of, operation, working arrangement, usual way, fashion, style, tone, guise, progress, progression, way of life, behaviour, know-how (Inf)

▶ *352 Means; 407 Order*

2 **route**, itinerary, course, track, trail, direction, way to, way in, way out, way through, way over, line, march, beaten track, beat, road, run, trajectory, orbit, lane, traffic lane, flight lane, sea lane, sea path, primrose path, path of least resistance, line of advance, line of retreat, detour, roundabout way, short cut, bypass, circumlocution, circumbendibus, circumference, circuit, access, means of access, right of way, approach, direct approach, doorway, door, entrance, side entrance, back door, side door, tradesman's entrance, adit, drive, path, garden path, hall, hallway, lobby, porch, vestibule, corridor, gangway, gangplank, passage, aisle, staircase, flight of stairs, step, tread, stepladder, ladder, fireman's ladder

▶ *319 Transport*

3 **road**, high road, roadway, main road, A road, carriageway, thoroughfare, arterial road, artery, highway (US), King's (*or* Queen's) highway, royal road, highways and by-ways, trunk road, motorway, freeway (US), superhighway (US), interstate highway (US), expressway (US), *Autobahn* (Ger), *autostrada* (It), *autoroute* (Fr), state highway (US), throughway (US), parkway (US), dual carriageway, controlled access highway, toll road, turnpike (*or* pike) (US), ringroad, beltway (*or* belt) (US), clearway, overpass, causeway, underpass, flyover, cloverleaf, spaghetti junction, (road) junction, crossroads, intersection, roundabout, traffic circle (US), secondary road, local road, B road, private road, country road, byway, driveway, dirt road, gravel road, paved road, *pavé* (Fr), plank road, corduroy road, street, through street, arterial street, one-way street, high street, main street (US), drive, avenue, boulevard, crescent, circus, close, place, court, row, terrace, lane, alley, blind alley, alleyway, side street, cul-de-sac, dead end, mews, wynd (Scot)

4 **road surface**, surface, Tarmac™, Tarmacadam™, bitu-

men, asphalt, blacktop (US), cement, concrete, road metal, paving stone, flagstone (*or* flag), tile, brick, stone, cobblestone (*or* cobble), causey (Scot), kerb, kerbstone

5 crossing, pedestrian crossing, zebra crossing, pelican crossing, panda crossing, main drag (US inf)

► *38 Engineering; 319 Transport*

6 path, pathway, footpath, footway, pavement, sidewalk (US), bypath, towpath, side-path, bridle path, bicycle (*or* cycle) path, track, racing track, athletics track, racecourse, trail, hiking trail, rut, groove, berm, sea path, sea lane, shipping lane

► *318 Passage*

7 arcade, colonnade, covered way, gallery, portico, aisle, cloister, triforium, nave, loggia, ambulatory, (shopping) mall, promenade, esplanade, parade, *prado* (Sp), seafront

8 tunnel, underpass, way under, subway, underground, tube, *métro* (Fr), railway (*or* railroad) tunnel, Channel Tunnel, Chunnel (Inf)

9 bridge, span, viaduct, aqueduct, overpass, overcrossing, way over, footbridge, overbridge, suspension bridge, cantilever bridge, humpback bridge, arched bridge, railway bridge, floating bridge, pontoon bridge, Bailey bridge, drawbridge, stepping stones, catwalk, rope bridge, toll bridge, Bifrost

► *38 Engineering*

10 railway, railroad, track, line, railway (*or* railroad) line, tram (*or* tramcar), streetcar (US), tramline, streetcar line (US), trolley line, street railway, elevated railway, underground, subway (US), tube, metro, *métro* (Fr), electric railway, horse railway, cog railway, rack railway, rack-and-pinion railway, cable (*or* rope) railway, gravity-operated railway, light railway, main line, branch line (*or* branch), trunk line (*or* trunk), feeder line (*or* feeder), turnout, switchback, gauge, standard gauge, junction, turntable, level crossing, grade crossing (US), embankment, trestle, cutting, siding, sidetrack (US), marshalling yard, shunting yard, railroad yard (US), stop, station, platform, whistle, signal, signal box, rails, points, switch (US), sleeper, tie (US), tracks, roadbed, terminus (*or* terminal), end of the line, el (*or* L) (US inf)

11 channel, canal, conduit, aisle, alley, lane, inlet, exit, outlet, gulf, culvert, strait, sound, dike (*or* dyke), ditch, sewer, waterway, watercourse, river, navigable river, estuary, delta, stream, lock

12 cableway, wire ropeway, wireway, cable (*or* rope) railway, funicular (railway), monorail, telpher (railway), telpher way, telpher line, ski lift, chair lift, gondola

13 flight path, flight lane, airlane, air route, skyway, air corridor, path, landing field, runway, taxiway, airstrip, flight strip, take-off strip, launching site, blastoff, trajectory, orbit, earth orbit, parking orbit, docking, re-entry, splashdown

VERBS

14 find one's way, find a way, make a way, have a method, do things the usual way, enter, use the side entrance, use the tradesman's entrance, have a route, draw up an itinerary, approach, take the high road, take to the road, come to a crossroads, detour, take a short cut, bypass, go round, go up a blind alley, cross the street, use a pedestrian crossing, use a footpath, bridge a river, take the train, take a plane, fly, blast off, orbit, splash down, come to the end of the line, reach one's destination

ADJECTIVES

15 accessible, through, connecting, connected, communicating, linked, bridged, flyover, spanned, arched, main, arterial, trunk, paved, cobbled, well-paved, well-laid, smooth, skid-proof, signposted, marked, signalled, well-lit, lit, floodlit, well-used, busy, crowded, overcrowded, jammed, beaten, trodden, bumper-to-bumper

ADVERBS

16 how, in this way, after this fashion, along these lines, on the lines of, thus, so, as, like, anyway, anyhow, anywise, by any (manner of) means, in any event, in any case, at any rate, nevertheless, nonetheless, however, regardless, irregardless, at all, somehow, in some way (or other), by some means, somehow or other (*or* another), in one way or another, after a fashion, no matter how, by hook or (by) crook, by fair means or foul

17 via, by way of, through, by, passing by (*or* through), over, around, round about, here and there, all through, towards, in the direction of, to, up, on, over against, on the way to, on the (high) road, in transit to, en route to (*or* for), on route to, in passage to

318 Passage

This world nis but a thurghfare ful of wo,
And we ben pilgrimes, passinge to and fro;
Deeth is an ende of every worldly sore. Geoffrey Chaucer.

NOUNS

1 passage, passing, passing through, movement, transit, transmission, transference, transduction, transfusion, crossing, traversing, traverse, transcursion, journey, voyage, trip, perambulation, patrol, round, beat

► *300 Motion; 316 Transfer*

2 passing along, walking, driving, riding, cycling, sailing, flying, progress, thoroughfare, road, highway, clearway, motorway, airlane, sea lane, route, course, track, path, orbit, traffic, circulation, traffic flow, traffic pattern, traffic load, traffic jam, loading, unloading, waiting, parking, kerbside parking, offstreet parking, lay-by, parking place (*or* area *or* zone), car park, diversion, alternative route

► *319 Transport*

3 passage into, entrance, entry, ingress, penetration, interpenetration, intervention, infiltration, transudation, permeation, percolation, osmosis, endosmosis

► *314 Entry*

4 access, approach, road, right of way, path, pathway, footpath, bridle path, stepping stones, pass, channel, passageway

► *317 Way*

5 crossing point, crossing, intercrossing, intersection, junction, crossroads, roundabout, cloverleaf, spaghetti Junction, overcrossing, overpass, flyover, bridge, pontoon, viaduct, undercrossing, underpass, tunnel, level crossing, ford, pedestrian crossing, zebra crossing, pelican crossing, traffic lights, Belisha beacon, island, central reservation, frontier post, checkpoint

▶ *38 Engineering; 193 Interweaving*

6 **passport**, visa, pass, safe conduct, *laissez passer* (Fr), ID, clearance, clearance papers, papers, documentation, permit

7 **traffic controller**, air-traffic controller, traffic police, road patrol, traffic engineer, traffic warden, metermaid, traffic cop (Inf)

VERBS

8 **pass**, pass by, flash by, overtake, get past, leave on one side, skirt, pass through, get through, move through, shoot through, come out the other side

9 **proceed**, go, move along, travel, journey, voyage, circulate, patrol, do the rounds, join the traffic, weave

▶ *300 Motion*

10 **enter**, penetrate, infiltrate, permeate, percolate, osmose, soak through, open a way, force a passage, elbow through, worm one's way in, clear the ground, progress

▶ *314 Entry; 317 Way*

11 **cross**, traverse, transit, negotiate, go across, cross over, make a crossing, reach the other side, ford, wade across, step over, bridge, straddle, bestride, span, overfly, traject, transmit, carry across, move across, transport, convey, hand over, transfer, translate

▶ *316 Transfer; 319 Transport*

ADJECTIVES

12 **passing**, overtaking, moving, proceeding, transferring, transducing, crossing, traversing, transitional, transilient

13 **penetrating**, infiltrating, transudating, permeating, percolating, osmotic, intervening

ADVERBS

14 **by the way**, *en passant* (Fr), via, by way of, en route, in transit, transitionally, through, across

319 Transport

They change their clime, not their frame of mind, who rush across the sea. We work hard at doing nothing: we look for happiness in boats and carriage rides. What you are looking for is here, is at Ulubrae, if only peace of mind doesn't desert you. Horace.

NOUNS

1 **transport**, transportation, transport system, passenger transport, commuting, personal transport, commercial transport, freight carriage, carriage, haulage, hauling freightage, portage, shipment, transshipment, cartage, carting, distribution, forwarding, sending, loading, unloading, off-loading, intermodal transportation, containerization, palletization, road, rail, air, water

▶ *144 Displacement; 300 Motion; 316 Transfer; 318 Passage*

2 **thing transported**, cargo, freight, goods, load, payload, consignment, shipment, contents, mail, luggage, baggage, container, pallet

3 **transporter**, shipper, conveyor, distributer, carrier, consignee, courier, loader, unloader, docker, stevedore

VERBS

4 **transport**, transport goods, transport door-to-door, haul, freight (US), portage, ship, cart, convey, consign, carry, act as a freight carrier, distribute, deliver, forward, dispatch, export, send, move, remove, load, unload, offload (US), handle cargo, handle a consignment, transship, reship, bus, fly, commute, ride

ADJECTIVES

5 **transportable**, transported, transporting, movable, portable, roadworthy, airworthy, seaworthy, transport, transportation (US), door-to-door, urban, commercial, shipped, shipping, freight, private, forwarded, forwarding, loaded, loading, unloaded, unloading, bussed, bussing, commuting, road, rail, air, water, biking, biked, main, rural, farm (US), motorway, interstate (US), lorry, truck (US), railway, passenger, express, goods, piggyback, elevated (US), monorail, air-cargo, aeroplane, short-range, medium-range, long-range, jumbo, supersonic, waterborne, towed, towing, river, navigational, navigated, navigable, inland, canal, ocean, ocean-going, merchant, dry-cargo, container, oil, piped, piping, pumped, pumping, pack, consigned

ADVERBS

6 **commercially**, as freight, door to door, hand to hand, by road, by motorway, by lorry, by bus, by rail, by train, with British Rail, by air, by aeroplane, supersonically, by water, by sea, by ship, by tanker, with the merchant navy, by pipeline, in the pipeline, in transit, en route, on the way

320 Road Transport

The car has become the carapace, the protective and aggressive shell, of urban and suburban man. Marshall McLuhan.

NOUNS

1 **road transport**, road transportation, foot transport, horse transport, cycling, motorcycling, motor transport, driving, trucking, motor haulage

2 **road**, road system, route, highway, Queen's highway, main road, trunk road, A road, clearway, urban clearway, motorway, freeway (US), interstate highway (US),

CARRIAGES AND CARTS

barouche	dogcart	randem
brake	drag	ratha
britzka	dray	rickshaw
brougham	droshky	rig
buckboard	equipage	rockaway
buggy	fiacre	spider phaeton
cab	fly	stagecoach
cabriolet	four–in–hand	sulky
calash	gharry	surrey
Cape cart	gig	tarantass
cariole	Gladstone	tilbury
carriage	hackney	trap
carryall	hansom	trishaw
cart	haywain	tumbrel (*or* tumbril)
chaise	herdic	
chariot	jaunting car	victoria
clarence	landau	vis–à–vis
coach	one–horse carriage	voiturette
Conestoga wagon	oxcart	wagon
coupé	phaeton	wagonette
covered wagon	post chaise	wain
curricle	prairie schooner	whim

MOTOR VEHICLES

ambulance
amphibian
armoured car
articulated lorry
automatic
automobile
autorickshaw
beach buggy
bloodmobile (US)
bookmobile (US)
bowser
breakdown van (*or* truck)
bubble car
buggy
bulldozer
bumper car
bus
camper
car
carryall
car transporter
caterpillar
coach
convertible
coupé
crash wagon (*or* waggon) (US)
crawler tractor
delivery truck
digger
Dormobile™
dragster
dray
duck
dune buggy
dustcart
electric car
estate car
farm tractor
fastback
fire engine
float
fork–lift truck
four–wheel drive
garbage truck (US)
go–kart (*or* go–cart)
golf cart
gritter
half–track
hardtop
hatchback
hearse
HGV
hot rod
JCB
Jeep™
jigger (NZ)
juggernaut
kart
landau
Land Rover™
limousine
lorry
loudspeaker van
low–loader
mammy wagon (*or* waggon) (W Africa)
milk float
Mini™
mobile home
mobile library
motor caravan
moving van
phaeton
postbus
PSV (public service vehicle)
racing car
rally car
refrigerator (*or* refrigerated) van
removal van
roadroller
rocket car
runabout
RV (recreational vehicle) (US)
saloon
scout car
sedan
semitrailer
shooting brake
snowmobile
snowplough
sports car
steamroller
stock-car
streetcar
swamp buggy
taxi
tourer
tracklayer
tractor
trailer
tram
transporter
trolley
trolleybus
truck
van
wagon (*or* waggon)
weasel

superhighway (US), expressway (US), *Autobahn* (Ger), *autoroute* (Fr), *autopista* (Sp), *autostrada* (It), toll road, turnpike (US), side road, B road, single track, rural road, farm road (US), farm track, beef road (Aus), dirt road (*or* track), rat run (Inf)

3 carriageway, lane, single lane, dual carriageway, slow lane, fast lane, hard shoulder, soft shoulder, crawler lane, escape lane, corner, bend, S-bend, hairpin bend, chicane, camber, intersection, T-junction, crossroads, box junction, roundabout, traffic circle (US), cloverleaf (*or* cloverleaf junction), spaghetti junction, slip road, feeder road, filter, one-way system, lights, traffic lights, crossing, pedestrian crossing, zebra crossing, panda crossing, pelican crossing, Belisha beacon

4 personal transport, walking, shanks's pony, people mover, driverless car, moving pavement, travolator (*or* travelator), lift, elevator (US), paternoster

5 pack, carrier, saddlebag, pannier, backpack, bearer

6 litter, stretcher, pallet, bier, sedan (*or* sedan chair), dooly (*or* doolie) (East Indies), jainpan (India), muncheel (India), norimon (Japan), palanquin (*or* palankeen) (Orient), tonjon (Sri Lanka), horse litter, camel litter

7 handcart, cart, pushcart, dumpcart (US), barrow, handbarrow, wheelbarrow, coster's barrow, push car, trolley, bag trolley, luggage trolley, shopping trolley, tea trolley, dolly

8 baby carriage, pram, perambulator, go cart (US), baby walker, baby buggy, pushchair, stroller, carrycot

9 animal transport, horse, riding, pack animal, packhorse, mule train, dispatch rider, pony express, wagon train, draught animal, carthorse, draught horse, carriage, dray

10 sled, sledge, sleigh, toboggan, luge, snowboard, bobsled (*or* bobsleigh *or* bob), jumper, pung (US), scoot (US), drag, dray, dogsled, troika, motorized sled, snowmobile, bombardier, Sno-Cat, Skimobile, weasel, cat-train (Canada)

11 bicycle part, frame, fork, crossbar, mixte frame, wheel, spoke, disc wheel, brake, hub brake, brake block, rod brake, cable brake, caliper brake, cantilever brake, crank, pedal, rat trap, toeclip, bicycle chain, chainguard, gear, clanger, hub gear, derailleur, handlebars, drop handlebars, racing handlebars, straight handlebars, saddle, saddlebag, pannier, kickstand, mudguard, mud flap, bicycle pump, bicycle clips

12 bicycle, bike, cycle, push-bike, wheel (US), racing bicycle, roadster, sit-up-and-beg, minibike, trailbike, BMX (bicycle motocross), mountain bike, chopper, ATB (all-terrain bike), hobbyhorse (*or* hobby), velocipede, boneshaker, penny-farthing, safety bicycle, tandem, bicycle-made-for-two, tricycle, trike, fairy cycle, quadricycle, monocycle, unicycle, folding cycle, trick cycle, bicycle rickshaw, trishaw, iron horse (Inf)

13 motorcycle, motorbike, bike, motorbicycle, motorscooter, scooter, moped, autocycle, motorbike and sidecar, combination, autorickshaw, superbike

14 cyclist, bicyclist, motorcyclist, bike rider, motorcycle courier, bicycle courier, motocross racer, biker (Inf), bikie (Aus inf), rocker (Inf), greaser (Inf), easy rider (Inf)

15 motor transport, driving, motoring, bussing, road transport, road haulage

16 car, motorcar, (motor) vehicle, automobile, auto, private car, family car, runabout, tourer, roadster, saloon, hatchback, coupé, fixed-head coupé, drophead coupé, estate (*or* estate car), station wagon, shooting brake, sports car, convertible, limousine, limo (Inf), stretch limo (Inf), buggy (Inf), motor (Inf), wheels (Inf), jalopy (Inf), tin lizzie (Inf), crate (Inf), bomb (US inf), heap (Inf), banger (*or* old banger) (Inf), put put (Inf), rattletrap (Inf)

17 police car, patrol car, squad car, prowl car, panda car, unmarked car, police van, wagon (*or* waggon), Black Maria, paddy wagon (*or* waggon) (Inf), jam sandwich (Inf)

18 cab, taxi, taxicab, minicab, hackney cab (*or* hackney), hack (US), hire car (*or* hired car)

19 bus, omnibus, single decker, double decker, coach, motor coach, luxury coach, charabanc, trolleybus (*or* trolley)

20 truck, lorry, wagon (*or* waggon), cart, transporter, articulated vehicle, tractor, trailer, van

MOTOR VEHICLE PARTS

- ABS brake
- accelerator
- air bag
- alternator
- antidazzle mirror
- antilock brake
- anti–roll bar
- anti–theft device
- automatic choke
- automatic transmission
- axle
- bench seat
- bezel
- blinker
- bodywork
- bonnet
- boot
- brake
- brake drum
- brake light
- bucket seat
- bumper
- camshaft
- carburettor (*or* carburetter)
- catalytic converter (cat)
- central locking
- chassis
- clutch
- connecting rod
- courtesy light
- cowl
- crank
- crankcase
- cruise control
- cylinder
- cylinder head
- dashboard (*or* dash)
- death seat
- differential gear
- dimmer
- disc brake
- distributor
- driving wheel
- drum brake
- emergency light
- fender (US)
- fifth gear
- fifth wheel
- filler cap
- flasher
- fluid drive
- flywheel
- fog light
- four–wheel drive
- freewheel
- gate
- gauge (*or* gage)
- gear
- gearbox
- gear lever (*or* gearshift)
- generator
- grille (*or* grill)
- hazard warning light
- headlight (*or* headlamp)
- headrest
- hood (US)
- horn
- hydraulic brake
- hydraulic suspension
- hypoid gear
- ignition
- ignition key
- indicator
- jump leads
- jump seat
- license plate (US)
- kingpin
- manifold
- mileometer (*or* milometer)
- monocoque
- motive power
- muffler
- numberplate
- odometer (US)
- oil gauge
- overrider
- overrun brake
- parking light (*or* lamp)
- pintle
- piston
- pneumatic tyre
- power brakes
- power steering
- propeller shaft
- rack and pinion
- radial tyre
- radiator
- radius rod (*or* arm)
- reach
- rear light (*or* lamp)
- rear–view mirror
- reflector
- reverse
- reversing light
- roof rack
- rumble seat
- running board
- seat belt
- shaft
- shift
- shock absorber
- sidelight
- side mirror
- silencer
- solenoid
- spare tyre
- spare wheel
- spark plug (*or* sparking plug)
- speedometer
- splashboard
- sprag
- starter
- starter motor
- steering column
- steering gear
- steering wheel
- stick
- stick shift (US)
- stop light
- sun roof
- suspension
- tachograph (*or* tacho)
- tail light
- tailpipe
- tail wheel
- top gear
- towbar
- track rod
- trafficator
- transmission
- tyre
- wheel
- windscreen
- windshield
- winker
- wing

21 miscellaneous motoring terms, antilock braking system (ABS), antiroad protester, autocade, aquaplaning, automobilia, automotive engineering, body shop, brake-fade, bump start, carnet, carsickness, coach building, *concours d'élégance*, cornering, crash barrier, crashworthiness, deathtrap, double declutch, double parking, driving licence, endorsement, fade, garage, garaging, gas, grab, green card, gridlock (US), gritter, gritting, handbrake turn, hard standing, hit-and-run accident, hitchhiker, hitchhiking, hot-wiring, jack, jaws of life, jerrycan, judder, knock-for-knock, lighting-up time, lock, logbook, lubritorium, mechanic, mileage (*or* milage), misfiring, MOT, motel, motion sickness, motorcade, nearside, no-claims bonus, offside, overdrive, oversteer, overtaking, panel beater, parking, parking meter, parking space, pile-up, piston slap, pit, pull in, rack and pinion, registration, registration document, registration number, road-fund licence, roadholding, road rage, road tax, road test, shimmy, shunt, side- impact bar, sideslip, skid, skidpan, slip, speed limit, speed trap, stall, tailskid, tailspin, tax disc, test drive, three-point turn, tow, traction, trade plate, traffic, traffic calming, traffic jam, triptyque, turning circle, underseal, understeer, U-turn, weighbridge, wheelbase, wheel wobble

321 Rail Transport

Ever since childhood, when I lived within earshot of the Boston and Maine, I have seldom heard a train go by and not wished I was on it. Paul Theroux.

NOUNS

1 railway, railroad (US), railway system, main-line railway, overground railway, light railway, tramway, tramcar, tram, cog railway, rack railway, inclined railway, cable railway, cable car, funicular, monorail, telpher (*or* telfer *or* telpherage *or* telferage), scenic railway, elevated railway, elevated (US), el (US inf), underground railway, underground, tube, subway (US), metro, metritis, rapid-transit system (RTS)

2 track, main line, up line, down line, section, branch line, spur (*or* spur track), loop, siding, sidetrack (US), switch (US), lay-by, cutting, embankment, gradient, gradient post, crossing, level crossing, gated crossing, manned crossing, unmanned crossing, signal, lights, semaphore, signal box, fog signal, highball (US), torpedo (US), water tower, water trough

3 rail, rails, metals, gauge, narrow gauge, standard gauge, broad gauge, roadbed, permanent way, ballast, sleeper, tie (US), fish joint, fishplate, frog, points, catch points, switch (US), crossover, turntable, buffer, end of steel

4 locomotive, engine, diesel locomotive, diesel-electric, electric locomotive, steam locomotive, steamer, iron horse, tank engine, tanker, shunting engine, shunter, light engine, wildcat (US), jerkwater engine (US), jigger (NZ), loco (Inf), choo choo (Inf), chuffer (Inf), chuff chuff (Inf), puffer (Inf), puff puff (Inf)

5 locomotive part, traction unit, motorcar, pantograph, dead man's handle, boiler, tank, side tank, saddle tank, tender, footplate, firebox, funnel, piston, sandbox

6 rolling stock, car, carriage, railcar, observation car, *coupé* (Fr), parlor car (US), dog box (Aus), dining car, restaurant car, sleeping car, sleeper, roomette (US), *couchette* (Fr), *wagon lit* (Fr), luggage van, baggage car (US), caboose (US), guard's van, mailcoach, mail van, Pullman (*or* Pullman car), freight car, freightliner, wagon (*or* waggon), truck, van, gondola, low-loader, hoppercar (*or* hopper), tank wagon (*or* waggon)

7 train, passenger train, express, slow train, stopping train, milk train, mail train, night mail, freight train, goods train, rake (NZ), double header, twin bill, bogie, coupling, drawbar, draw gear, king bolt (*or* king rod)

8 railway station, rail station, station, terminus, railhead, end of the line, main-line station, halt, whistle stop (US), platform, bay, booking office, waiting room, left-luggage office (*or* locker), barrier, depot, shed, yard, marshalling yard, switch yard (US), snow shed (US)

9 **railway worker**, railwayman (*or* woman), engine driver, engineer (US), motorman, fireman, conductor (US), guard, inspector (*or* ticket inspector), plate-layer, lengthman, trackman (US), pointsman, signalman, station manager, stationmaster, porter, gandy dancer (Inf)

10 **miscellaneous**, British Rail (BR), Amtrak, Canadian Pacific, Trans-Siberian Railway, APT (advanced passenger train), TGV (*train à grande vitesse*) (Fr), Bullet Train (Japan), Orient Express, Brighton Belle, Stephenson's Rocket, Locomotion, Puffing Billy, train spotting, train spotter, gricer (Inf)

322 Aviation

The airplane stays up because it doesn't have the time to fall.
Orville Wright.

NOUNS

1 **aviation**, flying, flight, gliding, piloting, pilotage, aerial reconnaissance, air transport, air travel, scheduled flight, sortie, air route, air corridor, air freight, air cargo, airmail (*or* air mail), payload, airlift, airdrop, paradrop, mercy flight, flying doctor, flying circus, aerobatics, crop dusting, skywriting, skyjack, jet lag

2 **aeronautics**, aeronautical engineering, aircraft design, avionics, aerothermodynamics, aeroballistics, aerooptics, bioaeronautics

3 **aircraft personnel**, aviator, flyer, pilot, airline pilot, glider pilot, test pilot, aircrew, crew, captain, co-pilot, first officer, flight engineer, navigator, observer, pathfinder, purser, steward, stewardess, air hostess, groundcrew, aircraftsman (*or* aircraftswoman), ground engineer, air-traffic controller, groundling

4 **airport**, airfield, airbase, air station, aerodrome, airstrip, landing strip, landing field, terminal, apron, hard standing, hangar, control tower, taxiway, runway, clearway, flight line, airside, landside

5 **flight**, takeoff, climb, flight level, flight formation, airspeed, groundspeed, heading, headwind, tailwind, terminal velocity, ceiling, aeropause, absolute ceiling, service ceiling, descent, approach, flare, glide path, landing, touchdown, belly landing, pancake landing, three-point landing, ground run, overflight, overshoot, undershoot, crash-landing, manoeuvre, bank, banking, barrel roll, buffeting, bunting, chandelle, crab, dive, crash-dive, figure of eight (*or* figure eight), flat spin, flutter, hunting, hedgehopping, low-level flying, Immelann turn, loop, looping the loop, nose dive, pitching, rolling, stall, stalling, shock stall, sideslip, skidding, snap roll, soaring, spin, spiral, turn, roll, vectoring, VIFF (vector in flight), victory roll, wingover, whipstall, yawing, zooming

6 **flight control**, ground control, air-traffic control, AEW (airborne early warning), ASDE (airport surface detection equipment), fly-by-light, fly-by-wire, landing beam, loran, navar, radar beacon, SBA (standard beam approach), shortan, talk down, Teleran™, traffic pattern, stack, stacking

7 **miscellaneous aviation terms**, aerotowing, air flow, air miss, air pocket, airsickness, angle of bank, angle of incidence, anhedral, bird strike, boarding card, dihedral, dip, downwash, drag, drift, driftage, feathering, flameout, flypast, footprint, gremlin, hook-up, icing, load factor, loading, parasite drag, rake, reheating, slipstream, spread, STOL (short take-off and landing), sweepback, trim, turbulence, clear-air turbulence, VTOL (vertical take-off and landing), washin, wind shear, wind tunnel, wing loading, wingspan

8 **aircraft**, heavier-than-air craft, airplane, aeroplane, air-

TYPES OF AIRCRAFT

aerodyne	flying wing	multiplane
amphibian	freighter	night fighter
autogiro	gyrocopter	pusher
bomber	gyrodyne	ramjet
canard	interceptor	rotaplane
coleopter	jet plane (*or* jet)	seaplane
convertiplane	jumbo jet	swing wing
cyclogiro	jump jet	taxiplane
dive bomber	lifting body	turbofan
drone	microlite	turbojet
fighter	MRCA (multirole combat aircraft)	turboprop
fighter-bomber		

AIRCRAFT PARTS

aerodynamic brake	arrester	bypass ratio	dive brake	frame	main plane	seat belt
aero engine	artificial horizon	cabin	drogue	fuselage	monocoque	slinger ring
aeroplane cloth	astrocompass	canopy	drop tank	galley	nacelle	spinner
aerostructure	astrodome	cantilever	ejector seat	gull wing	nose	spoiler
afterburner	automatic pilot	chassis	electronic flight information system	head–up display	nose wheel	stabilizer
aileron	auxilliary power unit	clamshell	elevator	hold	plane	tailplane
air brake	backwash	cockpit	elevon	horn balance	pod	tailskid
air dam	barostat	control column	empennage	inclinometer	pressure cabin	tail wheel
airframe	bay	control stick	engine pod	jet engine	prop	trim tab
air intake	black box	control surface	fairing	jet pipe	propeller	turbofan
air scoop	blister	cowling (*or* cowl)	flap	joystick	pusher	turbojet engine
all–flying tail	bombsight	dashboard (*or* dash)	flight deck	kymograph (*or* cymograph)	pylon	undercarriage
altimeter	bucket seat	de–icer	flight recorder	longeron	ram–air turbine	windmill
anti–icer	bulkhead			Machmeter	ramjet	wing
					rudder	winglet

liner, kite (Inf), glider, hang-glider, rogallo, helicopter, copter (Inf), chopper (Inf), eggbeater (Inf), lighter-than-air craft, balloon, hot-air balloon, helium balloon, dirigible, aerostat, blimp, Zeppelin

ADJECTIVES

9 **aeronautical**, aerobatic, avionic, aerodynamic

VERBS

10 **fly**, glide, soar, ride a thermal, cruise, take off, land, bank, loop, spin, spiral, hedgehop, buzz (Inf)

ADVERBS

11 **aeronautically**, aerobatically, avionically, aerodynamically, up and away

323 Water Transport

There is nothing – absolutely nothing – half so much worth doing as simply messing about in boats. Kenneth Grahame.

NOUNS

1 **water travel**, shipping, boating, sailing, rowing, sea travel, seafaring, cruising, sea trip, boat trip, life on the ocean wave, voyage, voyaging, passage, crossing, river travel, canal travel, inland navigation, navigation, circumnavigation

► *584 Military Affairs*

2 **waterway**, navigable water, sea lane, seaway, ocean track, steamer route, crossing, ferry crossing, inland waterway, river, lake, canal, cut

3 **vessel**, ship, boat, craft, rowing boat, rowboat, skull, sailing boat, sailboat, pleasure boat, yacht, steamship, steamboat, passenger ship, liner, ferry, canal boat, narrow boat, barge, merchant ship, merchantman, freighter, tanker, fishing boat, trawler, drifter, whaler, warship

4 **shipbuilding**, ship design, naval architecture, naval engineering, ship materials, wood, steel, medium steel, high-tensile steel, special-treatment steel, aluminium alloy, reinforced concrete, shipbuilding skill, ship specifications, structural design, structural model, structural test, launching, launching ceremony, christening, shipbuilding contract, shipbuilding yard

SAILING SHIPS AND BOATS

- barque (*or* bark)
- barquentine (*or* barquantine)
- brig
- brigantine
- caïque
- caravel (*or* carvel)
- carrack
- cat
- catamaran
- catboat
- clipper
- corsair
- corvette
- cutter
- dhow
- dragon
- dromond (*or* dromon)
- felucca
- four–master
- frigate
- gabert
- galiot (*or* galliot)
- galleon
- hermaphrodite brig
- hooker
- jolly boat
- junk
- keelboat
- ketch
- lateen
- longboat
- longship
- lugger
- monohull
- multihull
- nuggar
- ocean racer
- outrigger
- pink
- pinnace
- piragua
- pirogue
- polacre
- proa (*or* prau)
- púcán
- razee
- rigger
- sabot
- sailboard
- sailer
- sailing boat (*or* sailboat)
- sailing dinghy
- schooner
- scow
- shallop
- skiff
- skipjack
- sloop
- sloop of war
- smack
- square-rigger
- tall ship
- tartan
- tea clipper
- trimaran
- windjammer
- xebec (*or* zebec *or* zebeck)
- yacht
- yawl

► *160 Form; 403 Structure*

5 **navigation**, celestial navigation, astronavigation, inertial navigation, compass reading, piloting, pilotage, pilotship, helmsmanship, seamanship, steering, plane sailing, plain sailing, spherical sailing, great-circle sailing, parallel sailing, dead reckoning, dead-reckoning position, estimated position, plotting, navigational aid, sailing aid, navigational instrument, marine sextant, sextant, quadrant, angular measure, traverse table, log, ship's log, towed log, submerged log, compass, ship's compass, magnetic compass, gyrocompass (*or* gyroscopic compass), astrocompass, needle, magnetic needle, card, compass card (*or* rose), binnacle, chronometer, ship's chronometer, ship's timekeeper, chart, Admiralty chart, nautical almanac, ephemeris, directional reference, bearings, sea mark, buoy, lighthouse, pharos, lightship, lead,

SHIPS AND BOATS

- amphibious landing craft
- ark
- banana boat
- barge
- bateau
- battleship
- boatel (*or* botel)
- bulk carrier
- bumboat
- cabin cruiser
- cable ship
- caïque
- canal boat
- canoe
- cargo boat
- catamaran
- catboat
- cockleboat
- cockleshell
- collier
- coracle
- crabber
- cruiser
- currach (*or* curagh)
- cutter
- dinghy
- dory
- dredger
- drifter
- DUKW (duck)
- E–boat
- factory ship
- faltboat
- fishing boat
- flagship
- flatboat
- flotel (*or* floatel)
- freighter
- galley
- gig
- gondola
- hooker
- houseboat
- hovercraft
- hydrofoil
- icebreaker
- Indiaman
- inflatable
- jet–boat
- jolly boat
- kayak (*or* kaiak)
- keelboat
- launch
- liberty ship
- lifeboat
- lighter
- lightship (*or* light vessel)
- longboat
- lugger
- mail boat
- merchantman
- mosquito boat
- motorboat
- narrow boat
- nuggar
- oiler
- outboard
- outrigger
- oyster crab
- packet
- paddle boat (*or* steamer)
- pearler
- pilot (*or* pilot boat)
- pinnace
- pontoon
- post boat
- powerboat
- PT boat
- punt
- Q–ship
- racing shell
- randan
- refrigeration ship
- revenue cutter
- roll–on/roll–off
- rowing boat (*or* rowboat)
- runabout
- sabot
- sailing boat (*or* sailboat)
- sailing ship
- sampan
- school ship
- scow
- scull
- sealer
- shallop
- shell
- ship's boat
- slaver
- slave ship
- steamboat
- steamer
- steamship
- supertanker
- surfboat
- swamp boat
- tanker
- tender
- torpedo boat
- towboat
- tramp steamer
- trawler
- trimaran
- troop carrier
- tug (*or* tugboat)
- umiak (*or* oomiak)
- weather ship
- whaleboat
- wherry
- yawl

SAILS

Bermuda rig
canvas
course
foreroyal
foresail
forestaysail
foretop
fore–topgallant
fore–topsail
Genoa
headsail
jenny
jib
jigger
kite
lateen sail
lugsail
main course
mainsail
maintopsail
mizzen
moonraker
rig
royal
skysail
spanker
spinnaker
spritsail
square sail
staysail
studdingsail
topgallant
topsail
trysail

Rigging
arm
backstay
bibb
bitt
boom
bull's–eye
burton
cable
clamp
clinch
club
club foot
crosshead
crossjack
crowfoot
eye
fall
foremast
fore–topmast
fox
gaff
garland
gasket
gooseneck
gripe
hank
horse
hound
jack
jigger
lanyard (*or* laniard)
lead
leader (*or* fairlead)
mainstay
martingale
mizzenmast (*or* mizenmast)
messenger
moorings
mouse (*or* mousing)
pendant (*or* pennant)
pole
preventer
service
shroud
sling
snub
spider
spring
stick
stirrup
stop
tabernacle
thimble
topmast
traveller
truck
truss
warp
whelp
yolk

line, lead line, shore direction-finding (DF) station, radiobeacon station, automatic direction finder, single-loop goniometer, crossed-loop goniometer, loran (long range navigation) system, loran-A system, loran-B system, decca system, decca phasemeter, consol system, radar, navigational radar, sonar, navigational satellite, Transit system, NAVSTAR Global Positioning System (GPS), ship's steering, helm, wheel, tiller, rudder, steering oar, navigation laws, rules of the sea

► *325 Deviation; 693 Information*

6 nautical speed, ship's speed, knot, log-line knot, nautical mile per hour

7 nautical person, navy man, naval man (*or* woman), naval officer, admiral, Sea Lord, Admiral of the Fleet, Fleet Admiral (US), sailor, sailorman, seaman, able-bodied seaman (AB), able seaman, coastguardsman, marine, seafarer, seafaring man (*or* woman), Wren, Wran (Aus), mariner, master mariner, master, ship's master, sailing master, quartermaster, captain, skipper, navigator, pilot, helmsman, steersman, wheelman, man at the wheel, circumnavigator, ship's steward, boatswain (*or* bosun), bosun's mate, coxswain (*or* cox), shipmate (*or* mate), deckhand (*or* hand), leadsman, lookout man, foretopman, reefer, cabin boy, (ship's) crew, (ship's) complement, watch, fisherman, deep-sea fisherman, trawler, whaler, sea scout, sea cadet, bad sailor, fair-weather sailor, salt, old salt, sea dog, pirate, piratess, privateer, buccaneer, sea king, Viking, mythical seaman, argonaut, Jason, Ancient Mariner, Flying Dutchman, Captain Ahab, Sinbad the Sailor, sea god, Neptune, Poseidon, sea rover (Lit), hearty (Inf), tar (Inf), Jack Tar (Inf), matelot (Inf), swabbie (*or* swab) (US inf), marine scientist, shipbuilder, ship designer, naval architect

8 boatman, waterman, yachtsman (*or* yachtswoman), canoeist, paddler, rower, oarsman (*or* oar), sculler, galley slave, punter, gondolier, ferryman, Charon, wherryman, bargee, bargeman (US)

PARTS OF A SHIP

accommodation ladder
after deck
berth
bilge
bitt
board
boat deck
boiler room
bollard
bow
bridge
brig
bulkhead
bull's–eye
bulwarks
cabin
capstan
carling (*or* carline)
cathead
cat hole
centreboard
chain locker
chart room
cleat
companion ladder
companionway
counter
crow's nest
daggerboard
davit
engine room
false keel
figurehead
fin keel
flight deck
forecastle (*or* fo'c'sle)
freeboard
futtock
galley
gangplank
gangway
glory hole
gudgeon
gun deck
gunwale (*or* gunnel)
half deck
hatch
hatchway
hawsehole
head
hold
keel
keelson
larboard
lazaretto (*or* lazaret *or* lazarette)
leeward
limber
limber hole
lower deck
main deck
maintop
middle deck
mizzentop
monkey rail
oar
orlop (*or* orlop deck)
outboard
outrigger
paddle wheel
painter
paint locker
pilot house
pintle
planking
Plimsoll line
poop
poop deck
port
porthole
portside
promenade deck
propeller
propeller shaft
prow
quarters
radio room
rail
riding lamp
rigger
round house
rowlock
rudder
rudderpost
scupper
sea ladder
skeg
stabilizer
stack
stanchion
starboard
stateroom
stern
sternpost
strake
strecher
stringer
superstructure
thole
tiller
top deck
transom
turtleback
wardroom
washboard
water line
weatherboard
weather deck
wheel
winch
windlass
windward

VERBS

9 **navigate**, circumnavigate, use dead reckoning, plot, use a sextant, use a compass, chart, find one's bearings, travel by water, take on a pilot, pilot a ship, steer, hold the helm, man a ship, crew, ship out, sail, set sail, hoist sail, trim the sails, square (away), spread canvas, launch, push off, cast off, boom off, unmoor, get under way, weigh anchor, get up steam, raise steam, put to sea, set a course, steer for, make for, head for, make way, gather way, carry sail, read the chart, go by the card, take soundings, heave the lead, bring into the wind, sail close to the wind, haul, beat to windward, run before the wind, run before a gale, scud, put the helm up, fall to leeward, luff, pay off, put the helm down, head into the wind, change course, turn round, veer, back, go astern, regress, crab, put about, tack, weather, back and fill, wear, gybe, yaw, race, cross one's bows, outmanoeuvre, gain the weather gauge, foul, collide

10 **sail**, set sail, heave to, lie to, lay to, bring to rest, surface, break water, flood the tanks, dive, plunge, run for port, weather the storm, ride out the storm, ride, ride on an even keel, take the wind out of one's sails, keep afloat, list, overturn, capsize, heel over, keel over, careen, turn turtle, ground, run aground, wreck, be cast away, sight land, make a landfall, land, make port, drop anchor, cast anchor, wedge, clubhaul, warp, draw, moor, tie up, dock, disembark, get one's sea legs (Inf)

ADJECTIVES

11 **nautical**, naval, marine, seafaring, seaworthy, sea-going, ocean-going, at the helm, on board, at sea, on the high seas, seaborne, floating, afloat, launched, waterborne, salty, sailing, steaming, plying, ferrying, coasting, rolling, pitching, tossing, wallowing, yawing, aquatic, sailorly, seaman-like, able-bodied, able, amphibious, amphibian, natatory (*or* natatorial), swimming, buoyant

ADVERBS

12 **nautically**, at sea, on the high seas, afloat, like a sailor, amphibiously, under way, under sail, under canvas, under steam, before the mast, on board, on deck, on the bridge, on the quarterdeck, at the helm, at the wheel

324 Direction

He did not care in which direction the car was travelling, so long as he remained in the driver's seat. Lord Beaverbrook.

NOUNS

1 **direction**, bearing, bearings, location, situation, position, lie of the land, set, quarter, line, line of direction, aim, goal, target, objective, steering, steerage, navigation, piloting, helmsmanship

▶ *142 Location*

2 **bearing**, heading, trend, tendency, run, set, inclination, bent, tenor, drift, thrust, course, route, line, track, path, way, lay, lie, short cut, beeline, line of sight, compass direction, compass bearing (*or* heading), relative bearing (*or* heading), true bearing (*or* heading), relative (*or* true) course, tack, vector

▶ *229 Tendency; 317 Way*

3 **orientation**, bearings, collimation, adaptation, adjustment, alignment, accommodation, direction finder (D/F), compass, signpost, map, tracking device, rangefinder, gauge, degrees, compass rose, compass card, lubber line, rhumb line, azimuth

▶ *742 Sign*

4 **compass point**, cardinal point, half-point, north (N), magnetic North, northward, nor', south (S), southward, east (E), eastward, the Orient, sunrise, west (W), westward, the Occident, sunset, southeast, southwest, northeast, northwest, easting, westing, northing, southing

5 **directions**, direction, pointing (out), guiding, leading, guidance, instruction, education, supervising, managing

▶ *6 Education; 579 Management; 713 Advice*

VERBS

6 **direct**, direct to, give directions, point (*or* show) the way, indicate, guide, signpost, steer, point, aim, determine, set, fix, present, point to (*or* at), point out to, push in the right direction, lead, conduct, steer towards, put on the right track, set straight (*or* right), put right

7 **take a direction**, bear, aim, navigate, collimate, set one's sights on, fix on, train upon, sight on, aim at, point, turn, head, lead, go, hold a heading, direct (*or* align) oneself, incline, tend, tend to go, trend, set, dispose, verge, head for, go for, bear for, hit for, steer for, make for, put for, set out (*or* off) for, strike out for, take off for, lay for, bear up to (*or* for), set in towards, set one's course for, direct one's course for, set one's compass for, sail for, align one's march, dash for, make a break for, run for, go straight, go directly, head straight on, follow one's nose, make a beeline for, get straight to the point, steer a straight course, hold steady, cleave to the line, keep pointed, take the airline (US), stay on the beam, hold the line, keep the nose down

8 **orient** (*or* **orientate**), orient onself, take (*or* get) one's bearings, get the lay (*or* lie) of the land, see which way the wind blows, see which way the land lies, adapt, adjust, accommodate, box the compass, take (*or* shoot) the sun, check one's course

ADVERBS

9 **directly**, direct, straight, point-blank, straightly, straightforward (*or* straightforwards), full tilt, unswervingly, undeviatingly, unveeringly, due, due north, right, forthright, in a direct (*or* straight) line, in line with, in a beeline, as the crow flies, straight as a dye, straight as an arrow, straight across, on course, on the right track, squarely, square, dead right, dead ahead, dead, straight ahead, full, flush, exactly, precisely, kerplunk (Inf), plop, plumb (Inf), plump (Inf), plunk (Inf), smack (Inf), smack-dab (Inf), spang (US inf)

▶ *178 Straightness; 302 Forward Motion*

10 **clockwise**, anticlockwise, counterclockwise, withershins (*or* widdershins) (Scot), leftward (*or* leftwards), rightward (*or* rightwards), homeward, landward, seaward, leeward, earthward, heavenward, windward

▶ *307 Rotation*

11 **in all directions**, in every direction, in all manner of ways, every way, everywhere, every which way, in all directions at once, in every quarter, on every side, around, all round, round and about, from every quarter, from (*or* to) the four corners of the earth, from (*or* to) the four

winds, upstream, downstream, upwind, downwind, before the wind, close to the wind, near the wind, against the wind, in the wind's eye, close-hauled, downtown (US), uptown (US)

12 north, northerly, northwards, northwardly, south, southerly, southwards, southwardly, east, easterly, eastwards, eastwardly, west, westerly, westernly, westwards, westwardly, northeast, northeasterly, northeastwards, north-northeast, northeast by east, northeast by north, northwest, northwesterly, northwestwards, northwestwardly, north-northwest, northwest by west, northwest by north, southeast, southeasterly, southeastwards, southeastwardly, south-southeast, southeast by east, southeast by south, southwest, southwesterly, southwestwards, southwestwardly, south-southwest, southwest by west, southwest by south

ADJECTIVES

13 directional, northern, north, northward, northerly, northernmost, northbound, arctic, boreal, hyperborean, southern, south, southward, southerly, southernmost, southbound, meridional, antarctic, austral, eastern, east, eastward, easterly, easternmost, eastbound, Oriental, western, west, westward, westerly, westernmost, westbound, Occidental, northeastern, northeast, northeasterly, southeastern, southeast, southeasterly, northwestern, northwest, northwesterly, southwestern, southwest, southwesterly

14 directed, directable, steerable, guidable, dirigible, leadable, aligned, parallel, oblique, axial, cross-country, downwind, upwind, downtown (US), uptown (US), orientated towards, directed towards, pointed for, headed for, bound for, set, signposted, aimed, well-aimed, well-directed, on the mark, on the nose (US inf), on the money (US inf)

15 direct, immediate, straight, straightforward, straight away, undeviating, unswerving, unveering, uninterrupted, unbroken, one-way, unidirectional, irreversible

16 directing, directive, guiding, steering, leading, instructing, educating

325 Deviation

VERBS

1 deviate, diverge, divert, divaricate, vary, depart from, digress, branch, branch out, tralineate, detour, go off at a tangent, sheer, curve, heel, trend, bear off, filter, swerve, turn a corner, leave the straight and narrow, turn (*or* go) out of one's way, alter (*or* depart) from one's course, change direction, tack, yaw, veer, back, navigate

2 divert, change course (*or* the course of), put rudder on, pull (*or* push *or* draw) aside, put screw on, slice, pull, hook, glance, bowl wide

3 go astray, stray, get lost, lose (*or* miss) one's way, lose one's bearings, lose one's sense of direction, take a wrong turn (*or* the wrong turning), foul the line, go adrift, drift, get sidetracked, err, ramble, wander, rove, straggle, excurse, pererrate, divagate

4 lose track of, lose the thread, blunder, be inattentive, miss the point, daydream

5 twist, turn, bend, meander, wind, weave, twine, snake, curve, twist and turn, zigzag, hairpin, pull, crook, dogleg

6 distort, warp, bias, twist, skew, screw

7 misdirect, put off the scent, divert, avert, mislead, misaddress, misinform

8 sidestep, sidetrack, turn (*or* move *or* draw *or* step) aside (*or* to one side), side, sidle, make way for, avoid, turn away, shy, shy off, jib, avert, avoid, gee, haw, be oblique, steer clear of, get out of the way of, go (*or* bear *or* sheer *or* veer *or* ease *or* edge) off, fly off, passage

9 shove aside, sidetrack, shunt, switch, shuffle, put on one side

10 slide, slip, sideslip, skid, swing, wobble, oscillate

11 turn round, turn about, about-turn, wheel, face about, face the other way, reverse, reverse direction, return, revert, turn back, go back

12 deflect, diffract, bend, diverge, scatter, disperse, diffuse, refract

NOUNS

13 deviation, deviance, deviancy, deviousness, disorientation, misdirection, aberration, aberrancy, nonconformism, eccentricity, exorbitation, wrong course (*or* turning), digression, excursion, departure, declension, tangent, diversion, deflection, divergence, divarication, curvature, branching off, aside, parenthesis, divagation, declination, variation, indirection, obliqueness, obliquity, skew, slant, bias

▶ *118 Nonconformity; 177 Curve; 189 Slantedness; 311 Divergence*

14 deviating course, curve, turn, flexure, double, declension, bend, corner, hairpin bend, dogleg, zigzag, slope, slant, sheer, sweep, pitch, tack, indirect course, detour, diversion, bypass, bypath, long way round, winding course, slalom course

▶ *324 Direction*

15 deviating motion, indirect motion, swerve, swerving, veering, skid, sideslip, sidestep, crabwalk, shift, drift, leeway, roll, pitch, yaw, swing, break, leg break, off break, knight's-move

16 wandering, drifting, circuitousness, circumlocution, circumbendibus, rambling, digression, discursion, discursiveness, excursus, straying, errantry, pererration, vagrancy, lapse, error, wandering mind, abstractedness

17 torsion, twisting, torque, distortion, warp

▶ *234 Distortion*

18 diffraction, scatter, refraction, reflection, diffusion, dispersion, diaspora, fanning out

▶ *28 Physics; 377 Dispersal*

19 deviant person, deviant, deviate, deviationist, nonconformist, unconformist, Bohemian, dropout, misfit, oddity, freak, square peg in a round hole, fish out of water, ugly duckling, black swan, odd man out, joker in the pack, one in a million, character, eccentric, dissident, dissenter, heretic, tergiversator, rebel, marginal, renegade, outsider, outcast, pariah, outlaw, criminal, hermit, lone wolf, loner, solitary, extremist, fanatic, lunatic fringe, blackleg, scab, sexual deviant, pervert, queer fish (Inf), crank (Inf), weirdo (Inf), oddball (Inf)

▶ *118 Nonconformity; 796 Immorality*

ADJECTIVES

20 deviant, deviative, deviatory, deviating, misdirected,

nonconformist, aberrant, aberrational, eccentric, off-centre, out of orbit, exorbitant
▶ *118 Nonconformity*
21 indirect, turning, curving, roundabout, winding, bending, meandering, snaking, serpentine, labyrinthine, mazy, shifting, swerving, deflected, deflective, twisting, veering, zigzag, crooked, out-of-the-way, off course, off the beam, off-target, off the mark, wide, wide of the mark, lost, stray, astray, off the fairway, in the rough
▶ *324 Direction*
22 undirected, unguided, random
▶ *107 Chance*
23 oblique, skewed, biased, slanted, distorted, twisted
▶ *189 Slantedness; 234 Distortion*
24 diverging, divaricating, branching, divergent, once (*or* twice) removed
▶ *311 Divergence*
25 wandering, drifting, digressive, circuitous, devious, divagatory, rambling, digressing, discursive, straying, errant, erratic, desultory, abstracted, inattentive, off the point, off the subject, vagrant, loose, footloose, footloose and fancy free
26 diffractive, refractive, refractile, refrangible, refracted, diffracted, scattered, reflected, diffuse, diffused, dispersed
▶ *28 Physics; 377 Dispersal*

ADVERBS

27 astray, adrift, off the mark, wide of the mark, round about, discursively
28 indirectly, obliquely, sideways, diagonally, at one remove, at a tangent
29 erratically, eccentrically, oddly, strangely

326 Oscillation

The pendulum of the mind oscillates between sense and nonsense, not between right and wrong. Carl Gustav Jung.

NOUNS

1 oscillation, fluctuation, alternation, (simple) harmonic motion, pendular motion, swing, swing of the pendulum, pendulation, lunar motion, libration, nutation, reciprocation, periodicity, frequency, coming and going, toing and froing, shuttle service, ebb and flow, *va-et-vien* (Fr), ups and downs, boom and bust, wax and wane, flux and reflux, systole and diastole, night and day
▶ *110 Reciprocity; 188 Parallelism; 297 Frequency; 298 Regularity; 306 Orbital Motion*
2 vibration, vibratility, vibrancy, resonance, pulsation, rhythm, tempo, pulse, throb, beat, heartbeat, heartthrob, beating, throbbing, staccato, rat-a-tat, rataplan, drumming, flickering, shaking, quivering, shivering, palpitation, flutter, tremor, agitation, pitter-patter, pitapat, arrhythmia
▶ *260 Ill Health; 327 Agitation; 509 Repeated Sound; 510 Resonance; 612 Fear*
3 vacillation, wavering, equivocation, indecision, hesitation, irresolution, dubiety, mental fluctuation
▶ *453 Uncertainty; 479 Equivocation; 639 Vacillation*
4 rock, roll, reel, lurch, careen, pitch, shake, dance, swing, swinging, sway, swag, wag, waggle, wave, waver, waving, wave motion, undulation, undulancy, brandishing, flourishing, shaking, flaunting
▶ *22 Dancing; 300 Motion; 306 Orbital Motion; 307 Rotation; 738 Display*
5 wave, ray, transverse wave, longitudinal wave, electromagnetic wave (*or* radiation), light, radio wave, sky wave, mechanical wave, radiation, heat wave, acoustic wave, sound wave, sawtooth wave, square wave, sine wave, seismic wave, seismicity, earthquake, shock wave, groundwork, tremor, de Broglie wave, diffracted wave, guided wave, one- (*or* two- *or* three-)dimensional wave, node, antinode, surface wave, tidal wave, tsunami, amplitude, crest, trough, wavelength, frequency, frequency band, frequency spectrum, resonance, resonant (*or* resonance) frequency, period, wave number, diffraction, reinforcement, interference, beat, in phase, out of phase, wave equation, Schrödinger equation, Huygens' principle
▶ *27 Mathematics; 28 Physics; 30 Earth Science*
6 measuring instrument, oscilloscope, oscillograph, oscillometer, harmonograph, vibroscope, vibrograph, kymograph, seismoscope, seismograph, seismometer
▶ *28 Physics*
7 oscillator, bob, pendulum, vibrator, pendulum wheel, metronome, swing, teeter, teeter-totter, teeterboard, teetery-bender, rocker, rocking chair, rocking stone, logan stone, seesaw, cradle, shuttle, shuttlecock
▶ *18 Music; 23 Furniture and Woodwork; 281 Timekeeping*

VERBS

8 oscillate, fluctuate, alternate, vary, swing, sway, move to and fro, pendulate, nutate, reciprocate, come and go, ebb and flow, wax and wane, ride and tie, hitch and hike, back and fill, seesaw, teeter, teeter-totter, shuttle, shuttlecock, wigwag, wibble-wobble, zigzag, pass and repass, leapfrog
▶ *110 Reciprocity; 297 Frequency; 298 Regularity*
9 vibrate, resonate, pulsate, pulse, beat, beat time, drum, tick, ticktock, throb, flutter, agitate, shake, quiver, rattle, shiver, flicker, tremble, palpitate, pant, heave, go pitapat
▶ *281 Timekeeping; 300 Motion; 327 Agitation; 509 Repeated Sound; 612 Fear*
10 vacillate, waver, hesitate, fluctuate, dither
▶ *453 Uncertainty; 639 Vacillation*
11 rock, roll, reel, lurch, careen, pitch, shake, dance, stagger, totter, tumble, swing, sway, swag, waggle, waddle, wave, waver, dangle, nod, flutter, bob, bob up and down, bounce
▶ *22 Dancing; 300 Motion*
12 wave, undulate, brandish, flourish, shake, wield, float, fly, flutter, flap, wag, wave to and fro, wave up and down, wallow, flounder
▶ *330 Propulsion; 738 Display*

ADJECTIVES

13 oscillating, oscillatory, swinging, fluctuating, fluctuant, alternating, alternate, alternative, reciprocal, reciprocative, back-and-forth, to-and-fro, up-and-down, seesaw, periodical, harmonic, libratory, nutational
14 vibrating, vibratory, vibratile, resonant, pulsating, pulsatory, pulsatile, pulsing, pulsative, beating, throbbing, staccato, rhythmic, rhythmical, flickering, quivering, shivering, shaking, agitating, palpitating, palpitant

15 vacillating, vacillatory, wavering, hesitant, dithering
16 rocking, rolling, reeling, lurching, careening, pitching, shaking, dancing, tossing, staggering, swaying
17 waving, undulating, undulatory, undulant, sinusoidal, sinuous, shaking, tremulous, seismic, seismatical, seismological, seismographic, seismometric, successive, succussatory, sussultatory, earth-shaking

ADVERBS

18 to and fro, back and forth, backwards and forwards, in and out, up and down, side to side, left to right, right to left, zigzag, seesaw, wibble-wobble, shuttlewise, like a bucket in a well, from pillar to post, ride and tie, hitch and hike, round and round
▶ *179 Circularity ; 306 Orbital Motion; 307 Rotation*

327 Agitation

Miss Bolo rose from the table considerably agitated, and went straight home, in a flood of tears and a Sedan chair. Charles Dickens.

NOUNS

1 agitation, perturbation, mental agitation, conturbation (Lit), embarrassment, discomposure, disquiet, disquietude, inquietude, unease, nervousness, jerkiness, jumpiness, edginess, nerviness, nervosity, twitter, dither, flap, upset, unsteadiness, fits and starts, the channels (Inf), jitters (Inf), butterflies (Inf), heebie-jeebies (Inf), collywobbles (Inf)
▶ *264 Difficulty; 326 Oscillation; 342 Activity; 453 Uncertainty; 612 Fear; 639 Vacillation*
2 tumult, turmoil, commotion, racket, din, confusion, stir, bustle, moil, tumultation, disturbance, hubbub, hurly-burly, rout, rush, furore, frenzy, fever, excitement, maelstrom, disorder, bobbery (Inf), brouhaha (Inf)
▶ *328 Disturbance; 408 Disorder; 507 Loudness; 585 War; 588 Anarchy; 701 Argument; 751 Disagreement*
3 turbulence, turbidity, ferment, fermentation, effervescence, seethe, seething, swell, squall, swirl, choppiness, changeableness, pitching, rolling, joltiness, bumpiness, stir, churn, ebullition, boil, boiling, embroilment, roil, fume
▶ *30 Earth Science; 91 Seas; 328 Disturbance; 412 Mixture; 433 Water*
4 fuss, bother, fluster, bluster, flap, flurry, flutteration, bustle, row, song and dance, to-do, tizz (Inf), tizzy (Inf), tiz-woz (Inf)
5 restlessness, unrest, fever, feverishness, the fidgets, fidgetiness, hopping, twitchiness, itchiness, tossing and turning, jactation, jactitation, formication, pruritus, itching
▶ *36 Psychology and Psychiatry; 227 Changeableness; 260 Ill Health; 620 Boredom*
6 shaking, vibrating, quaking, quivering, quavering, shivering, shuddering, juddering, faltering, dancing, throbbing, trembling, aspen (Lit), tremulousness, vibration, succussion
▶ *510 Resonance*
7 shake, tremor, quiver, wriggle, squirm, wag, waggle, wiggle, shudder, judder, falter, throb, the shakes, delirium tremens (DTs), shivers, cold shivers, rigor, ague, chorea, St Vitus's dance, trembling palsy, uncontrollable tremor, shaking palsy, parkinsonism
▶ *260 Ill Health*
8 spasm, orgasm, ejaculation, climax, cramp, convulsion, paroxysm, fit, seizure, throes, twitch, tic, nervous tic, rictus, vellication, attack, pang, access, grip, the jerks, falling sickness, epilepsy, catalepsy, tarantism, megrims, frenzy, staggers, stroke, apoplexy, eclampsia
▶ *260 Ill Health; 461 Insanity*
9 jolt, jar, knock, tremor, shock, throb, jerk, jump, sudden motion, start, judder, bump, nudge, dig, jog, joggle, jostle, jounce, bounce, bob, bobbing, jig, jigget (Inf)
▶ *508 Sudden Sound*
10 beat, beating, throb, throbbing, thrill, *frisson* (Fr), palpitation, flutter, pitapat, pitter-patter
▶ *112 Repetition; 508 Sudden Sound; 509 Repeated Sound*
11 stagger, stumble, totter, falter, flounder, flounce, rock, roll, lurch, careen, swing, sway, pitch, toss, tumble, plunge, wallow, welter, volution
12 flicker, flutter, twinkle, flash, flit, waver, quiver, sputter
▶ *326 Oscillation*
13 tempest, storm, swell, ground swell, squall, heavy sea, magnetic storm, vortex, whirlwind, disturbance, atmospherics
▶ *30 Earth Science*
14 agitator, shaker, vibrator, beater, jiggler, paddle, whisk, eggbeater, food processor, churn
▶ *307 Rotation*

ADJECTIVES

15 agitated, perturbed, troubled, disturbed, discomposed, embarrassed, nervous, nervy, edgy, uneasy, jittery, upset, unsteady, confused, ruffled, flurried, flustered, shaken, shaken up, shocked, stirred up, worked up, in a lather, troublous (Lit), hopping, leaping, aspen
16 restless, feverish, fevered, fidgety, itchy, unquiet, unpeaceful, twitchy, all of a tizz, all of a flutter, excited, flustered, fussing, fluttering, fluttery, hot and bothered, in a flap, panting, breathless, giddy, in a spin
17 turbulent, choppy, rough, bumpy, bouncy, pitching, rolling, stormy, tempestuous, boiling, seething, fuming, effervescent
18 shaky, shaking, quaky, quaking, quivery, quivering, quavery, quavering, unsteady, doddering, shivery, shivering, aguey, shuddering, juddering, joggling, wriggling, squirming, wiggling, wriggly, squirmy, wiggly, faltering, trembling, tremulous, wobbly, successive, succussatory, vibratory, vibrating, pulsating, throbbing
19 convulsive, jerky, jolting, jarring, jolty, twitchy, twitchety, jumping, jumpy, palsied, fitful, spasmodic, paroxysmic, eclamptic, spastic, vellicative, orgasmic, saltatory, choreic, choreal, epileptic, cataleptic
20 flickering, flickery, sputtering, spluttering, guttering, sputtery, wavery

VERBS

21 be agitated, fuss, flap, flutter, twitter, dither, bustle, rush, mill around, jerk, jump, jump about, hop about, bounce, dance, ripple, effervesce, be in turmoil, bubble, ferment, foam at the mouth, spit tacks, seethe, simmer, boil, boil over, throw a fit, convulse, writhe, squirm,

thresh, toss and turn, jactitate, thrash about, rampage, be angry
▶ *342 Activity; 607 Annoyance and Aggravation; 625 Grumpiness*
22 agitate, shake, wag, waggle, wave, flourish, brandish, fly a flag, flutter, fluster, perturb, disturb, perturbate, discompose, upset, untidy, disquiet, worry, stir, ruffle, rumple, move, trouble, swirl, churn, whip, whisk, beat, paddle, mix, stir up, rile, work up, roil, beat up, churn up, whip up, excite, muddy the waters
23 jolt, judder, shudder, shock, jar, jerk, twitch, bump, jog, joggle, jostle, jounce, bounce, bob, hustle, jump
▶ *330 Propulsion; 331 Impulsion*
24 shake, vibrate, quake, quiver, quaver, shiver, falter, shudder, judder, throb, drum, beat, pulse, thrill, pulsate, palpitate, tremble, go pitapat, twitter, didder, fidget, twitch, jerk, itch, vellicate, jig, jiggle, jigger, shake in one's shoes (*or* boots), tremble like an aspen leaf, shake like a leaf, have an ague, wriggle, squirm, wiggle, twist and turn, have ants in one's pants (Inf), jigget (Inf)
25 pitch, rock, wobble, waggle, totter, teeter, dither, stagger, swing, sway, lurch, swag, roll, reel, careen, plunge, toss and turn, toss and tumble, pitch and plunge, be the sport of wind and waves, flounder, founder, flounce, wallow, welter, stumble, falter, blunder, wallop, struggle, labour, thrash about
26 flicker, flutter, twinkle, flash, splutter, sputter, spatter, spit, flick, gutter, bicker, wave, waver, dance

ADVERBS

27 agitatedly, restlessly, uneasily, troublously (Lit), unquietly, unpeacefully, nervously, feverishly, in a dither, in a tizzy (Inf)
28 shakily, quiveringly, tremulously, quakily, tremblingly, unsteadily, waveringly, all of a twitter
29 jerkily, convulsively, spasmodically, in fits, in spasms, by fits and starts, with a hop, skip, and a jump, by snatches, saltatorily, like a cat on hot bricks, like a cat on a hot tin roof

328 Disturbance

NOUNS

1 disturbance, perturbation, agitation, convulsion, upheaval, upset, disconcertedness, disquiet, discomfiture, discomposure, worry, anxiety, annoyance, bother, nuisance
▶ *327 Agitation*
2 disarrangement, derangement, disorder, disorganization, muddle, confusion
▶ *408 Disorder*
3 dispersion, displacement, dislodgment, dislocation, disorientation, derailment
▶ *144 Displacement; 377 Dispersal*
4 disruption, disturbance, interruption, intrusion, interference, intervention, molestation, perversion, sabotage, hindrance, obstruction, inconvenience, untimeliness, distraction
▶ *240 Inconvenience; 378 Obstruction*
5 commotion, disturbance, disorder, breach of the peace, tumult, turmoil, ferment, furore, outcry, outburst, clamour, uproar, fuss, rumpus, bedlam, hubbub, hurly-burly, hullabaloo (*or* hullaballoo), brouhaha, to-do, ado, racket, din, noise, bother, trouble, scuffle, fracas, fray, riot, ruction (Inf), shemozzle (Inf), spot of bother (Inf)
▶ *408 Disorder; 507 Loudness*
6 derangement, mental derangement, mental disorder, insanity, madness, instability, screw loose (Inf)
▶ *461 Insanity*

VERBS

7 disturb, perturb, agitate, stir, convulse, upset, distress, unsettle, disconcert, disquiet, discomfit, discompose, throw into confusion, fluster, ruffle, shake, rattle, alarm, concern, worry, trouble, bother, pester, harass, annoy, irritate, vex, irk, throw into a tizzy (Inf), hassle (Inf), spook (Inf), bug (Inf)
▶ *327 Agitation; 602 Sorrow; 612 Fear*
8 disarrange, derange, disorder, throw into disorder, disorganize, muddle, confuse, put out of gear, roil (the waters)
▶ *264 Difficulty; 408 Disorder*
9 disperse, displace, dislodge, dislocate, disorient, derail
▶ *144 Displacement; 377 Dispersal*
10 disrupt, interrupt, intrude, butt in on, break in on, interfere, intervene, molest, pervert, tamper with, sabotage, hinder, obstruct, inconvenience, put out, distract, put off
▶ *240 Inconvenience; 378 Obstruction*
11 derange, unhinge, unbalance, drive insane, drive mad, enrage, drive round the bend (*or* the twist) (Inf), drive up the wall (Inf)
▶ *461 Insanity*

ADJECTIVES

12 disturbed, perturbed, agitated, convulsed, upset, distressed, unsettled, disconcerted, disquieted, discomfited, discomposed, uncomfortable, uneasy, confused, flustered, ruffled, shaken, rattled, alarmed, concerned, worried, anxious, troubled, bothered, annoyed, irritated, vexed, in a tizzy (Inf), bugged (Inf)
▶ *327 Agitation; 602 Sorrow; 612 Fear*
13 disarranged, deranged, disordered, disorganized, muddled, confused, roiled
▶ *408 Disorder*
14 dispersed, displaced, dislodged, dislocated, disorientated, derailed
▶ *144 Displacement; 377 Dispersal*
15 disrupted, interrupted, interfered with, molested, sabotaged, hindered, obstructed, inconvenienced, distracted
▶ *240 Inconvenience; 378 Obstruction*
16 deranged, mentally deranged, disordered, unhinged, unbalanced, maladjusted, disturbed, demented, neurotic, psychotic, unstable, mad, insane, hung-up (Inf), gaga (Inf), off one's head (*or* trolley *or* rocker *or* box) (Inf), round the bend (*or* twist) (Inf), out to lunch (Inf)
▶ *461 Insanity*
17 disturbing, upsetting, distressing, unsettling, disconcerting, alarming, worrying, bothersome, annoying, vexatious, muddling, disruptive, distracting, off-putting (Inf)

ADVERBS

18 disturbingly, disconcertingly, confusingly, alarmingly, disquietingly, worryingly, annoyingly, irritatingly, inconveniently, disruptively, intrusively, obstructively, perversely, off the rails, on the wrong track, off course

19 distractedly, uneasily, anxiously, nervously, neurotically, crazily, insanely, psychotically

329 Overstepping

It is the overtakers who keep the undertakers busy. William Ewart Pitts.

VERBS

1 overstep, overrun, overpass, overreach, overgrow, overgo, overstride, overleap, leapfrog, overjump, go beyond, go too far, overstep the mark (*or* bounds), aim too high, overspread, overflow, irrupt, flood, spill over, brim over

▶ *190 Expansion; 213 Increase; 219 Excess*

2 cross, cross over, cross the border, cross the Rubicon, pass the point of no return

▶ *164 Edge; 166 Limit*

3 exceed, surpass, outdo, outclass, excel, transcend, surmount, rise above, sow above, outrival, overbid, outbid, outmanoeuvre, outflank, outstrip, steal a march on, make the running, outdistance, outride, outrun, overtake, come in front, shoot ahead, lap, leave standing, leave behind, race, beat hollow

▶ *121 Superiority; 129 Precedence; 145 Distance; 244 Improvement; 246 Success; 262 Haste; 300 Motion; 302 Forward Motion; 633 Pursuit*

4 exaggerate, overdo, superabound, overrate, overestimate, strain, stretch, stretch a point, go over the limit, overbid, overcall one's hand, overact, overplay, overindulge, go over the top, go OTT (Inf)

▶ *467 Overestimation; 686 Self-Indulgence; 727 Exaggeration*

5 transgress, trespass, infringe, encroach, entrench, impinge, violate, breach, usurp, squat, poach, break bounds, make inroads, barge in, intrude, invade, overrun, impair, infest

▶ *380 Violence; 773 Taking; 774 Stealing*

NOUNS

6 overstepping, overrunning, overrun, overpassing, overtaking, overgrowth, overspreading, inundation, overflowing, irruption, flooding, flood

7 crossing, transcursion, transilience, transcendence, leapfrog, jump, excursion, extravagation

8 transgression, trespass, incursion, infringement, infraction, encroachment, intrusion, invasion, breach, infestation, plague, violation, usurpation, taking liberties

9 excessiveness, exaggeration, overplaying, overacting, overestimation, overrating, arrogation, hyperbole, excess, overfulfilment, surplus, redundance, overindulgence, intemperance, greed

▶ *219 Excess; 686 Self-Indulgence; 727 Exaggeration*

10 expansionism, overextension, ribbon development, empire building, imperialism

▶ *190 Expansion*

ADJECTIVES

11 overrun, overspread, overgrown, overflowing, brimming, flooding, flooded, inundated, infested, beset, teeming, swarming, plagued, encroaching, trespassing, intrusive, invasive

12 excessive, unwarranted, overreaching, undue, uncalled-for, exorbitant, surplus

13 exaggerated, overdone, pretentious, affected, hyperbolic, overrated, overindulgent, overambitious, strained, far-fetched, grandiose, grandiloquent, bombastic, over-the-top (OTT) (Inf)

14 surpassing, overextended, overlong, one up on, in the lead, overtaken, outclassed, outdone, outbid, transcended, surmounted, outmanoeuvred

15 out of reach, unreachable, far away, cut off, secluded, out of bounds, forbidden

ADVERBS

16 excessively, overindulgently, hyperbolically, greedily, intrusively, invasively

17 ahead, in front, in the lead, across the line, over the border, on the other side, over the hills and far away

▶ *145 Distance*

330 Propulsion

NOUNS

1 propulsion, impulsion, pulsion, propelling, propelment, drive, driving (*or* propulsive *or* propelling) force, momentum, motive power, thrust, impetus, push, shove, butt, bunt, shunt, kick, jaculation

▶ *331 Impulsion*

2 method of propulsion, steam propulsion, gas propulsion, petrol propulsion, diesel propulsion, diesel-electric propulsion, jet propulsion, turbojet propulsion, turboprop propulsion, rocket propulsion, pulsejet propulsion, plasmajet propulsion, ramjet propulsion, resojet propulsion, reaction propulsion, wind propulsion

▶ *319 Transport*

3 throwing, projection, trajection, jaculation, flinging, slinging, pelting, stone-throwing, precipitation, pitching, casting, hurling, lobbing, heaving, chucking (Inf)

4 ejection, expulsion, ejector seat, defenestration

5 throw, toss, pitch, pitch and toss, cast, bowl, fling, sling, swipe, shy, cockshy, hurl, chuck, chunk, lob, heave, flip, knock, peg (Inf), put, shot-put, pass, forward (*or* lateral) pass, kick, punt, dribble, throw-in, full toss (*or* pitch), yorker, stroke, drive, fast ball, curve, upcurve, downcurve, sinker, slider, knuckle ball, spitball, spitter, service, return, volley, smash, rally, kill, slice, pull

▶ *45 Sport*

6 shooting, gunnery, ballistics, artillery, firing, musketry, trapshooting, skeet, skeet shooting, archery, toxophily

7 shot, discharge, shooting, gunfire, gunshot, potshot, volley, fusillade, salvo, bombardment, cannonade, tattoo, spray, ejection, detonation, bowshot, stoneshot

▶ *381 Attack*

8 missile, projectile, weapon, ballistic missile, shot, small shot, grapeshot, grape, ball, pellet, bullet, slug, shell, mortar, cannon, cannonball, torpedo, Exocet™, Scud (Inf), heat-seeking missile, rocket, trajectile, ejector, ejectamenta, arrow, dart, shaft, bolt, slingstone, slingshot, brickbat, stone

9 firearm, gun, shotgun, rifle, musket, blunderbuss, double-barrelled shotgun, elephant gun, revolver, six-shooter, pistol, shooter (Inf), toy gun, pop gun, water gun (*or* pistol), blowpipe, peashooter, catapult, sling, mangonel, bow, longbow, crossbow

▶ *587 Weapon*

10 ball, tennis ball, hockey ball, golf ball, cricket ball, football, rugby ball, floater, bowl, wood, puck, curling stone, discus, shot, javelin, dart, arrow, quarrel, quoit, hammer, caber, snowball

11 propeller, prop, pedal, lever, oar, turbo, turbine, booster, thruster, propellant, propulsor, driver, screw, blade, wheel, paddle wheel, screw propeller, twin screws, fan, impeller, rotor, piston

12 propellant, driving force, energy, thrust, charge, explosive device, detonator, jet, steam, tailwind, following wind

13 fuel, coal, wood, peat, petrol, gas, oil, diesel, electricity, dynamite, cordite, guncotton, gunpowder, solid fuel, rocket fuel, nuclear fuel, hydrogen, helium

14 thrower, pitcher, hurler, heaver, tosser, flinger, slinger, bowler, shot-putter, javelin thrower, discus thrower, discobolus, snowballer, knife-thrower, server, striker, curler, stone-slinger, chucker (Inf)

15 shooter, marksman, markswoman, target shooter, shot, crack shot, good shot, dead shot, deadeye (Inf), gun, gunner, gunman, sniper, rifleman, musketeer, pistoleer, carabineer, cannoneer, artillery man, trapshooter

16 archer, toxophilite (Lit), bowman, hunter, Nimrod, Artemis, Sagittarius

ADJECTIVES

17 propulsive, propellant, propulsory, pulsive, propelling, motive, driving, shoving, pushing

18 projectile, trajectile, jaculatory, ejective, ballistic, missile, expulsive, explosive

19 propelled, petrol-propelled, diesel-propelled, jet-propelled, steam-propelled, gas-propelled, wind-propelled, self-propelled

VERBS

20 propel, push, shove, thrust, impel, launch, move, traject, project, jaculate, drive, kick, pedal, row, pole, treadle, wheel

21 move forward, advance, sweep, sweep before one, move on, hustle, drive, drive like leaves, put to flight, butt, bunt, shunt

22 roll, bowl, bowl a hoop, trundle, troll

23 throw, toss, pitch, cast, hurl, fling, sling, lob, heave, shy, york, catapult, pelt, lapidate, stone, shower, snowball, jerk, flip, snap, pass, serve, return, volley, slice, smash, put, put the shot, dart, lance, throw the javelin, tilt, chuck (Inf), peg (Inf), bung (Inf)

24 push, shove, send flying, send headlong, shoulder, ease along, fork, pitchfork, pitch forward

25 eject, expel, defenestrate

26 bat, slam, slog, drive, loft, cut, pull, glance, shank, slice, strike

27 kick, dribble, punt, pass

28 shoot, discharge, explode, fire, fire at, open fire, fire off, loose off, volley, fire a volley, volley and thunder, bombard, cannonade, detonate, let off, let fly, send off, gun, gun down, gun for (Inf), pistol, shoot at, pull the trigger, strike, hit, shoot down, fell, drop, blast, blow away, puff away, stop in one's tracks, draw a bead on, shower with arrows, plug (Inf)

▶ *381 Attack*

29 riddle, pepper, pelt, pump (*or* blast) full of lead (Inf)

30 blow up, fulminate, put dynamite under

31 snipe, pick off, pot, potshoot, potshot, take a pot shot, torpedo

32 load, prime, charge, cock, send off

33 start, start off (*or* up), give a start, set (*or* put) in motion, launch, set going, start going, set out on foot, start the ball rolling, kick off, bully off, bundle, bundle off, set afloat, float

ADVERBS

34 forward, onward, progressively, impulsively, forcefully, powerfully, thrustingly, pushily, explosively, ballistically

331 Impulsion

VERBS

1 impel, give an impetus to, import momentum, accelerate, drive, propel, compel, motivate, incite, urge, spur, start, run, set going, set in motion, move, animate, actuate, galvanize, power, goad, drive on (*or* forward), project, traject, thrust, press, stress, push, shove, heave, prod, poke, dig, jostle, push around, jolt, jog, tug, wrench, joggle, jerk, elbow, shoulder, hustle, butt, thwack, press on, bear, bear upon, bring pressure to bear on, throw out, run out, push out of the way, expel, eject, frogmarch

▶ *300 Motion; 330 Propulsion; 334 Power*

2 collide, impact, crash, crash into, bump into, smash, impinge upon, crunch, crump, clash, cannon into, carom into (US), jolt, nudge, bump, meet, encounter, confront, charge, attack, converge, careen, bang, percuss, concuss, foul, run foul of, hurtle, smash up, cross swords, fence, run one's head against, run up against a brick wall, knock heads together, ram, ram down, tamp, hammer, bulldoze, sledgehammer, pile-drive, shoulder, butt, bash, slam into, brunt (Lit), pile up (Inf), whomp (US inf)

3 hit, strike, stroke, rap, punch, thwack, pound, slam, bang, smack, swipe, dash, belt, clout, swat, swing, buffet, hit over the head, box, box someone's ears, jab, knock, bat, poke, thump, pelt, biff, sock, cut, slog, slug, bash, bonk, dent, aim a blow, deal a blow, strike at, clip round the ear, dint (Lit), let have it (Inf), knock cold (Inf), plunk (Inf), whop (Inf), bop (Inf), deck (Inf), coldcock (Inf), clobber (Inf), paste (Inf)

▶ *381 Attack*

4 throw, throw stones at, fling, hurl, toss, launch, propel, pitch, cast, hurtle, heave, lob, fire, catapult, let fly (Inf)

5 beat, trounce, leather, hammer, spank, pound, pummel, rain blows down on, give a good hiding, whip, flog, flail, thrash, cut, lash, stripe, cane, baste, lambaste, batter, pulverize, beat up (Inf), wallop (Inf), lick (Inf), dust off (US inf)

6 tap, rap, touch, chuck (under the chin), tip, pat, dab, flick, flip, peck, pick, brush, whisk

7 kick, boot, drop kick, penalty kick, place kick, punt, knee, stamp, clump, clop, drub, trample, tread on, stamp on, kneel on, ride roughshod over, stomp (Inf)

8 club, cudgel, blackjack, sandbag, cosh, hit over the head, crown, concuss, assail, attack

9 fight, go at it hammer and tongs, cut and thrust, box, knock out, knock down, give someone a bloody nose, give someone a black eye, leave senseless (Inf)

10 bat, strike a ball, drive, hit, lift, smash, volley, slice, cut, pull

NOUNS

11 impulsion, impulse, impellent, impelling force, impetus, momentum, moment, moment of force, force, irresistible force, driving force, power, motive power, propulsion, compulsion, incentive, incitement, science of forces, mechanics, dynamics, transmission (mechanics)

12 collision, head-on collision, meeting, encounter, charge, attack, convergence, multiple collision, pile-up, smash-up, percussion, concussion, scrape, friction, crash, impact, shock, smash, crunch, cannon, carom (US), jolt, nudge, bump, ramming, hammering, drumming, rapping, tapping, beating, thrusting, bulling, bulldozing, shouldering, smashing, sledgehammering, butting, bashing, spanking, trouncing, leathering, paddling, pummelling, raining (of blows), hiding, whipping, flogging, corporal punishment, thrashing, assault, assault and battery, grievous bodily harm (GBH), attack, exchange of blows, fisticuffs, boxing, hammer and tongs, cut and thrust, dusting off (US inf), licking (Inf)

13 blow, hit, strike, stroke, rap, punch, thwack, pound, slam, bang, butt, smack, swipe, dash, belt, clout, swat, swing, buffet, blow on the ears, body blow, jab, knock, poke, thump, pelt, cut, slog, slug, bash, bonk, dent, thrust, press, stress, pressure, pressing, push, shove, heave, prod, nudge, dig, biff, jostle, jolt, jog, joggle, hustle, tap, touch, chuck, tip, pat, dab, flick, flip, fillip, peck, brush, whisk, slap, spank, cuff, box, whip, lash, stripe, kick, boot, drop kick, penalty kick, place kick, punt, stamp, clump, clop, drub, dint (Lit), brunt (Lit), plunk (Inf), whop (Inf), stomp (Inf)

14 sporting hit, boxing blow, hook, jab, punch, left, right uppercut, swing, backhand, backhander, backstroke, sidewinder, short-arm blow, round-arm blow, round house, Long Melford, bolopunch, knockout punch, haymaker, straight left, body blow, batting hit, drive, on (*or* off) drive, straight drive, hit, cut, pull, slice, bunt, line drive, home run

▶ *45 Sport*

15 ram, rammer, ramrod, battering ram, bulldozer, piledriver, monkey, tamper, tamp, tamping iron, pusher, shover, cue, billiard cue, hammer, sledge, sledgehammer (*or* sledge), hammerhead, peen, hammerstone, punch, puncher, knocker, door knocker, carpet-beater, tapper, bat, mallet, hockey stick, baseball bat, rounders bat, tennis racket

16 weapons, cudgel, mace, truncheon, whip, flail, cosh, knuckle-duster, brass knuckles (US), bicycle chain, boxing glove

ADJECTIVES

17 impelling, impellent, impulsive, pulsive, dynamic, motive, moving, thrusting, thrustful, driving, ramming, smashing, thrashing, flogging

ADVERBS

18 dynamically, impulsively, with momentum, with power, percussively, forcefully, violently, shockingly

332 Swiftness

Wisely and slow; they stumble that run fast. William Shakespeare.

ADJECTIVES

1 swift, swift-moving, fast, quick, rapid, fleet, speedy, speeding, high-speed, high-velocity, darting, dashing, snappy, round, smart, wasting no time, expeditious, hustling, hurrying, hurried, hasty, double-quick, rapid-fire, alacritous, prompt, sudden, early, immediate, instantaneous, express, meteoric, jet-propelled, faster than sound, supersonic, hypersonic, ultrasonic, electric, high-geared, high-velocity, high-speed, adapted for speed, streamlined, running, runaway, charging, racing, galloping, cantering, fleet of foot, light-footed, nimble-footed, nimble, agile, volant (Lit), quick-footed, wing-footed, winged, eagle-winged, like an eagle, like a bird, flying, hurtling, whirling, rattling, headlong, tempestuous, pelting, breakneck, precipitate, precipitous, expeditious, darting, flashing, quick as lightning, quick as a wink, quick as a flash, quick as the wind, faster than a speeding bullet, quick on the draw (Inf), quick on the trigger (Inf), hair-trigger (Inf), like greased lightning (Inf), nifty (Inf), zippy (Inf), whizzing (Inf), spanking (Inf), all-out (Inf), flat-out (Inf), wide-open (Inf), barrelling (Inf), go-go (US inf), ton-up (Inf), scorching, souped-up (Inf), hotted-up (Inf), hopped-up (US inf)

▶ *262 Haste; 280 Immediacy; 300 Motion; 330 Propulsion; 331 Impulsion*

2 mentally quick, quick-thinking, nimble-witted, quick-witted, bright, lively, brisk, vigorous, mercurial, quicksilver, reckless, rash

▶ *442 Intellect; 615 Rashness*

3 accelerating, accelerated, quickening, speeding-up, getaway, overtaking, passing, passed, lapping, lapped

▶ *389 Escape*

VERBS

4 be swift, move fast, really move, drive quickly, speed, run, lope, race, chase, hurtle, bowl along, tear along, sweep along, scoot, scamper, scuttle, scurry, rush, dash, whisk, skirr, scour (territory), charge, stampede, ride hard, gallop, canter, trot, expedite, precipitate, hasten, hurry, career, careen, break the speed limit, fly, wing, move at the speed of sound, break the sound barrier, move at the speed of light, travel at maximum speed, go full tilt, go full pelt, go full steam, storm along, thunder along, rattle along, streak, dark, flit, zoom, zip, zing, whizz, hustle, expedite, lunge, spring, bound, leap, jump, pounce, swoop, dive, plunge, show a clean pair of heels, hie (Lit), skedaddle (Inf), get a move on (Inf), get cracking (Inf), get (*or* pull) one's finger out (Inf), step on it (Inf), hotfoot it (Inf), cut and run (Inf), go all out (Inf), make tracks (Inf), tear up the road (Inf), burn up the miles (Inf), rip along (Inf), nip along (Inf), barrel along (US inf), hare off (*or* after) (Inf), vroom (Inf), burn rubber (Inf), grayhound (US inf), put the hammer down (US inf), go full bat (Inf), zap along (Inf), shift (Inf), scorch (Inf), shag ass (US inf), haul ass (US inf)

▶ *262 Haste*

5 **run like a shot**, run like the wind, run like a hare, run like a scared rabbit, run like wildfire, run like (*or* in) a flash, run like lightning, run like a streak of lightning, run like a streak, run like the devil, run like a bat out of hell, run like a blue-streak (US inf), run like greased lightning (Inf), run like the clappers (Inf), run like a house on fire (*or* afire) (Inf), run like sixty (US inf), run like mad (Inf), run like crazy (Inf), run like sin (Inf), run to beat the band (US inf), pour it on (US inf), highball it (US inf), ball the jack (US inf)

6 **accelerate**, quicken, quicken one's speed, gather speed, speed up, pick up speed, put on speed, spurt, sprint, burst ahead, have a burst of speed, have a burst of energy, gather momentum, impart momentum, step up the pace, raise the tempo, open the throttle, thrust ahead, flash by, run away, dash forward, dash off, dart off, tear off (*or* away *or* out), set off at a run, get off to a flying start, make up time, make up for lost time, bolt, jump ahead, spring forward, spring, bound forward, dash, scamper, run, leave standing, leave at the starting post, gain on, overtake, overhaul, catch up (with), make the running, pass, lap, shake off, lose someone, outdistance, outrun, outpace, outstrip, outmarch, outsail, outdrive, outclass, outdo, leave behind, romp home, win the race, get a move on (Inf), step on it (Inf), let it rip (Inf), step on the gas (Inf), put one's foot down (Inf), put on one's running shoes (Inf), open up (Inf), whizz by (Inf)

7 **hurry someone up**, hasten, urge on, urge forward, drive, spur, chivy (*or* chivvy) along, lend wings to, put dynamite under (Inf), put a bomb under (Inf)

▶ *262 Haste*

NOUNS

8 **speed**, velocity, speediness, swiftness, quickness, fastness, fleetness, promptness, promptitude, rapidity, celerity, quick pace, round pace, smart pace, snappy pace, briskness, rattling pace, rapid tempo, fast rate, fast motion, speeding, driving, hard driving, racing, bowling along, dispatch, expedition, expeditiousness, precipitation, hastiness, haste, hurry, flurry, no loss of time, instantaneity, instantaneousness, agility, nimbleness, rashness, career, full career, full pelt, full sail, press of sail, great speed, speed of light, speed of sound, sonic speed, sound barrier, supersonic speed, ultrasonic speed, hypersonic speed, express speed, utmost speed, full speed, top speed, maximum speed, lightning speed, excessive speed, dangerous speed, breakneck speed, reckless speed, illegal speed, speed trap, radar trap, rate of speed (*or* speed-rate), airspeed, groundspeed, miles per hour (mph), kilometres per hour (kph), rpm (revolutions per minute), knot, Mach number, speed measurement, tachometer, speedometer, mileometer, odometer (US), accelerometer, cyclometer, gauge, wind gauge, anemometer, log, chip log, flat-out speed (Inf), wide-open speed (Inf), pickup (US inf), good (*or* fair) clip (Inf), nifty pace (Inf), full lick (Inf), blue streak (Inf), spanking rate (Inf), making tracks (Inf), barrelling (along) (US inf), burning rubber (Inf), bat (Inf), burn-up (Inf), scorching (Inf)

9 **acceleration**, quickening, speed up, spurt, burst, burst of speed, burst of energy, thrust, drive, impetus, impulse, jump, spring, bound, pounce, leap, swoop, swoosh, vroom, zip, zoom, dive, power dive, flying start, getaway, rush, headlong rush, headlong plunge, dash, scamper, run, sprint, canter, gallop, tantivy, overtaking, passing, lapping, whizz (Inf), zing (Inf), zap (Inf)

10 **quickness of mind**, quick-wittedness, speed of thought, alacrity, mental quickness, mental agility, brightness, liveliness

▶ *442 Intellect*

11 **swift thing**, lightning, lightning flash, streak of lightning, hurricane, gale, tempest, torrent, arrow, express, pony express, express train, racing car, sports car, speedboat, clipper, jet, jet flight, supersonic flight, rocket, missile, bullet, cannonball, electricity, telegraph, telephone, magic carpet, seven-league boots, race, forced march, quick march, double march, quick retreat, greased lightning (Inf)

12 **swift animal**, racehorse, racer, thoroughbred, galloper, courser, greyhound, cheetah, hare, scared rabbit, fox, deer, doe, gazelle, antelope, ostrich, eagle, swallow, swift, roadrunner, bat out of hell (Inf)

▶ *59 Horse Riding and Racing*

13 **swift person**, runner, sprinter, harrier, speeder, racer, racing driver, Jehu, hustler, courser, courier, messenger, express messenger, messenger of the gods, Mercury, Hermes, Iris, Ariel, speed maniac (Inf), speed demon (Inf), speed freak (US inf), hell-driver (US inf), scorcher (Inf)

ADVERBS

14 **swiftly**, quickly, rapidly, fleetly, apace, speedily, snappily, allegro, at express speed, headlong, with all speed, at full speed, prestissimo, at full throttle, full speed ahead, at one's top speed, at full tilt, at full blast, in full sail, under press of sail, in full career, in high gear, under full steam, for all one is worth, in full gallop, *ventre à terre* (Fr), with whip and spur, with giant strides, with giant leaps, on eagle's wings, roundly, smartly, on (*or* at) the double, double-quick, in double-quick time, in double-time, accelerando, in no time, by leaps and bounds, helter-skelter, expeditiously, posthaste, hurryingly, hastily, presto, quick-wittedly, promptly, suddenly, immediately, instantaneously, meteorically, supersonically, hypersonically, ultrasonically, in high gear, in high, nimbly, agilely, as fast as one's legs would carry one, before one could (*or* can) say Jack Robinson, amain (Lit), niftily (Inf), lickety-split (US inf), all out (Inf), flat out (Inf), in nothing flat (Inf), at a good (*or* fair) slip (Inf), at a rate of knots (Inf), pronto (Inf), hell for leather (Inf), p.d.q. (pretty damn quick) (Inf), ASAP (as soon as possible) (Inf)

333 Slowness

Slow and steady wins the race. Robert Lloyd.

VERBS

1 **move slowly**, walk slowly, barely move, go slow, go at a snail's pace, amble, saunter, march in slow-time, take it easy, stroll, get nowhere fast, laze, creep, crawl, inch along, ease along, trickle, ooze, drip, idle, go dead slow, shuffle along, stagger along, poke along, wobble, totter along, toddle along, scuff, take short steps, mince, plod, trudge, shamble, peg away, plod along, chug on, stump along, jog-trot, dogtrot, limp, hobble, hirple, traipse (Inf), mosey along (*or* on) (Inf), plug along (*or* away) (Inf), mooch around (Inf)

2 hesitate, barely move, grope (*or* feel) one's way, show caution, speak slowly, drawl, pause, falter, flag, dawdle, linger, loiter, tarry, hover, hang over, delay, dally, waste time, lag, drag, drag one's feet, take one's time, run out of steam, go lame, trail, halt, not get started, dilly-dally (Inf), shillyshally (Inf), lollygag (*or* lallygag) (US inf), goof off (US inf)

▶ *453 Uncertainty; 616 Caution; 639 Vacillation*

3 slow down, slow up, slow, let up, ease off (*or* up), slacken (*or* slack) off, relax, moderate, lose speed, reduce speed, lose momentum, decelerate, retard, delay, detain, impede, arrest, obstruct, hinder, stay, check, curb, hold back, keep back, set back, hold in check, rein in, draw rein, throttle down, take one's foot off the gas (US), brake, put on the drag, reef, take in sail, shorten sail, back water, back-pedal, lose ground, clip the wings, reverse, regress

▶ *251 Restraint; 378 Obstruction*

ADJECTIVES

4 slow, slow-moving, slow-paced, slow-footed, slow-running, ambling, strolling, sauntering, lumbering, easy-paced, snail-paced, snail-like, faltering, flagging, slow-as-slow, slow as death, creeping, crawling, walking, dragging, waddling, slouching, shuffling, plodding, clumsy, limping, halting, hobbling, shambling, tottering, staggering, poking, poky (US inf)

▶ *339 Inertness; 343 Inactivity*

5 unhurried, leisurely, sluggish, languorous, lethargic, inert, slack, slothful, languid, lazy, indolent, sluggardly, listless, idle, apathetic, phlegmatic, methodical, patient, deliberate, circumspect, gradual, Fabian, meticulous, restrained, easy, moderate, gentle, relaxed, taking one's time, imperceptible, stealthy

▶ *453 Uncertainty; 616 Caution*

6 hesitant, tentative, softly-softly, cautious, reluctant, lagging, dawdling, drawling, procrastinating, unwilling, slow off the mark, groping, foot-dragging (Inf)

7 delayed, held up, detained, checked, arrested, obstructed, impeded, set back, slowed down, retarded, restrained, slack, backward, behind, late, tardy, tardigrade, hysteretic, dilatory, lingering, dawdling, loitering, dallying, dilly-dallying (Inf), shillyshallying (Inf), lollygagging (*or* lallygagging) (US inf)

NOUNS

8 slowness, leisureliness, unhurriedness, lack of haste, no hurry, sluggishness, languor, lethargy, inertia, slackness, sloth, laziness, indolence, inertness, lentitude, dilatoriness, wasting time, methodicalness, patience, deliberation, deliberateness, circumspection, *festina lente* (L), gradualism, Fabianism, leisurely progress, meticulousness, restraint, time to spare, easy stages

9 deceleration, brake, curb, restraint, friction, retardation, retardment, slackening, flagging, slowing down (*or* up), easing off (*or* up), negative (*or* minus) acceleration

10 slow motion, leisurely gait, walk, amble, stroll, saunter, dawdle, low gear, piaffer, dragging, lumbering, creeping, snail's pace, tortoise's pace, creep, crawl, pace, trudge, waddle, slouch, shuffle, plod, limp, hobble, shamble, trot, dogtrot, jog trot, jog, single-foot, rack, mincing steps

▶ *251 Restraint*

11 lingering, lagging, dawdling, loitering, dallying, dalliance, dilly-dallying (Inf), shillyshallying (Inf), lollygagging (*or* lallygagging) (US inf), goofing off (US inf)

12 hesitation, tentativeness, caution, cautiousness, reluctance, drawling, tardiness, procrastination, unwillingness, standing start, slow start, delay, holdup, go-slow, slow-down (US), work-to-rule, detention, setback, check, arrest, obstruction, hysteresis, foot-dragging (Inf)

▶ *616 Caution*

13 slow thing, slow clock, funeral march, funeral procession, fugue, slow train, stopping train

14 slow creature, sloth, tortoise, slug, snail, creepy-crawly (Inf)

▶ *73 Reptiles and Amphibians; 76 Insects and Arachnids*

15 slow person, plodder, slow-goer, lingerer, loiterer, sloth, tortoise, snail, dawdler, dawdle, laggard, sloucher, slacker, idler, procrastinator, slug, sluggard, stick-in-the-mud, drone, slow starter, slowcoach (Inf), slowpoke (US inf), sleepyhead (Inf), foot-dragger (Inf), stick-in-the-mud (Inf), goof-off (US inf), gold brick (US inf)

ADVERBS

16 slowly, slow, leisurely, unhurriedly, patiently, easily, moderately, gently, adagio, largo, larghetto, andante, languidly, sluggishly, languorously, lazily, idly, indolently, lingeringly, dilatorily, loiteringly, haltingly, falteringly, cautiously, deliberately, circumspectly, tentatively, reluctantly, gradually, by degrees, inch by inch, little by little, step by step, bit by bit, by easy stages

17 in slow motion, creepingly, crawlingly, pokingly, pokily, softly-softly, at a slow pace, at a snail's pace, at a funeral pace, in low gear, at half speed, allargando, ritenuto, ritardando

Power and Action

334 Power

Power tends to corrupt, and absolute power corrupts absolutely. Great men are almost always bad men…There is no worse heresy than that the office sanctifies the holder of it. Lord Acton.

NOUNS

1 **power**, powerfulness, potency, forcefulness, might, mightiness, greatness, puissance (Lit), omnipotence, governance, government, authority, sovereignty, hegemony, control, sway, superiority, ascendancy, prevalence, predominance, influence, persuasion, charisma, mana, special power, special gift, occult power, magical power, magic, witchcraft, sorcery, staying power, endurance, stamina, force, driving force, main force, virility, muscle, brute force, strength, brute strength, effort, exertion, right arm, right hand, endeavour, stress, strain, gravitation, gravity, weight, weight of numbers, manpower, staff, personnel, position of power, position of strength, strong position, vantage ground, high ground, truth, validity, cogency, emphasis, accent, additional power, extra power, overdrive

▶ *11 Occultism; 121 Superiority; 208 Multitude; 228 Stability; 336 Strength; 395 Influence; 396 Authority; 480 Persuasion; 578 Worker; 707 Affirmation*

2 **ability**, potentiality, potential, capability, competence, effectuality, effectiveness, efficiency, efficacy, proficiency, capacity, faculty, property, virtue, attribute, endowment, gift, flair, native wit, talent, skill, qualification, aptitude, fitness, scope, range, reach, compass, grasp, what it takes, know-how (Inf), the real stuff (Inf), the right stuff (Inf), street smarts (US inf)

▶ *102 Possibility; 485 Skill*

3 **vitality**, dynamism, vigour, energy, vivacity, animation, verve, liveliness, drive, spirit, get-up-and-go (Inf), spunk (Inf), pep (Inf), zip (Inf)

4 **energy**, internal energy, chemical energy, mass energy, rest energy, potential energy, work, binding energy, kinetic energy, heat, electrical energy, radiant energy, atomic energy, nuclear energy, mechanical energy, muscle power, pedal power, engine power, horsepower, manpower, electric power, hydroelectric power, hydraulic power, water power, steam power, nuclear power, atomic power, force of inertia, resistance, friction, force, field of force, force of gravity, centrifugal force, buoyancy, compression, spring, springiness, elasticity, pressure, head, steam pressure, full head of steam, electricity, magnetism, magnetic force, magnetic field, attraction, repulsion, polarity, electromagnetism, electromagnetic field, charge, electromotive force, potential, electrical potential, tension, high tension, potential difference, motive power, pulling power, traction, pushing power, thrust, jet, jet propulsion, momentum, angular momentum, impetus, suction, expulsion

▶ *330 Propulsion; 363 Attraction; 364 Repulsion*

5 **unit of work**, erg, joule, calorie, foot-pound, poundal, unit of electrical power, voltage, volt, wattage, watt, kilowatt, megawatt, ohm, amperage, ampere, amp

▶ *28 Physics*

6 **source of energy**, fossil fuel, coal, gas, natural gas, oil, nuclear fuel, nuclear power, renewable energy source, wind power, solar power, solar energy, geothermal power, hydroelectricity, wave power, tidal power, powerhouse, power plant, power station, generating station, electricity substation, pumped storage scheme, hydroelectric station, waterfall, tidal barrage, water wheel, windmill, wind farm, solar cell, solar battery, solar panel, heat exchanger, heater, generator, motor, oscillator, alternator, commutator, magneto, dynamo, turbine, turbocharger, turbosupercharger

▶ *307 Rotation; 326 Oscillation; 437 Fuel; 493 Heat; 494 Cold; 522 Light*

7 **electrical power**, electricity, electric light, induced electricity, photoelectricity, thermoelectricity, piezoelectricity, voltaic electricity, galvanic electricity, static electricity, lightning, electrodynamics, electrostatics, induction, inductance, capacitance, resistance, conduction, conductivity, superconductivity, oscillation, frequency, pulse, electric charge, electric shock, electrocution, electric current, direct current, alternating current, circuit, closed circuit, short circuit, electrode, positive electrode, positive, anode, negative electrode, negative, cathode, electrolysis, conductor, semiconductor, superconductor, nonconductor, insulator, lightning conductor, earth, ground (US), live wire, electrification, electricity supply, power line, lead, flex, cord (US), power cord (US), cable, distributor, junction box, pylon, grid, national grid, transformer, power pack, battery, storage battery, accumulator, cell, wet cell, dry cell, fuel cell, photoelectric cell, photocell, valve, tube, vacuum tube, cathode-ray tube, transistor

► *39 Electronics*

8 **nuclear power**, atomic power, nucleonics, nuclear physics, thermonuclear reaction, chain reaction, fission, fusion, atom smasher, particle accelerator, linear accelerator, cyclotron, synchrotron, ZETA (Zero-Energy Thermonuclear Apparatus), JET (Joint European Torus), CERN (Conceil européen pour la recherche nucléaire), European Organization for Nuclear Research, International Atomic Energy Agency (IAEA), Nuclear Regulatory Commission (US), Energy Information Administration (US), superconductor, supercollider, atomic pile, nuclear reactor, fast-breeder reactor, advanced gas-cooled reactor (AGR), light water reactor (LWR), pressurized-water reactor (PWR), coolant, fuel rod, moderator, radioactivity, fallout, radioactive waste, waste reprocessing, nuclear weapon, nuclear warhead, nuclear missile, atomic bomb, hydrogen bomb, fusion bomb, neutron bomb

► *28 Physics; 587 Weapon*

9 **electronics**, electron physics, optics, light, electromagnetic radiation, laser, integrated circuit, microprocessor, microelectronics, microcircuit, computerization, computing, data processing, word processing, desktop publishing (DTP), telecommunications, telegraph, telephone, radio, television, automation

► *28 Physics; 39 Electronics; 254 Danger; 692 Communications*

VERBS

10 **be powerful**, have power, be able, lie in one's power, have it in one's power, be capable of, have the talent for, measure up to, exercise power, govern, have authority, manage, control, maintain control, have sway, dominate, compel, use force, force, use brute force, use one's brute strength, exert energy, endeavour, stress, strain, enjoy the power of, win power, come into power, gain power, ascend, prevail, predominate, influence, exert influence, show potential, have a gift, have a flair, have charisma, show talent, have aptitude, qualify, be fit for, have vitality, have stamina, have drive, have staying power, possess spirit, possess special power, possess magical power, practise witchcraft, have what it takes, have know-how (Inf), be made of the right stuff (Inf), muscle in (Inf)

11 **give power**, empower, enable, authorize, invest with power, vest power in, endow, endow with power, give teeth, arm, strengthen, energize, animate, electrify, charge, transistorize, magnetize, plug in, switch on, turn on, power up, charge up, power, drive, go into overdrive, step on it (Inf), step on the gas (US inf), give it some welly (Inf), give it the gun (Inf), put the hammer down (US inf), soup up (Inf)

12 **generate power**, produce power, power, fuel, pump, radiate, heat, cool, light, transform energy, amplify, store energy, compute

ADJECTIVES

13 **powerful**, potent, mighty, virile, strong, puissant (Lit), great, prevailing, prevalent, predominant, superior, influential, omnipotent, almighty, irresistible, in full control, empowered, endowed, authoritative, sovereign, hegemonic, with full powers, plenipotentiary, at the height of one's powers, potential, virtual, possible, competent, capable, fit, adequate, able, gifted, talented, qualified, equal to, up to, more than a match for, effectual, effective, efficacious, efficient, proficient, forceful, compelling, charismatic, compulsive, cogent, forcible, violent

14 **operative**, working, switched on, workable, armed, having teeth, in force, valid, established

15 **full of energy**, energetic, dynamic, vigorous, lively, vivacious, animated, spirited, attractive, drawing, pulling, impelling, propulsive, moving, motive, locomotive, kinetic, driven, automated, powered up, on-line, proactive, on-stream, live

16 **charged**, supercharged, high-tension, magnetic, polarized, mechanized, mechanical, electric, electrical, electronic, souped-up (Inf)

17 **powered**, electrical, atomic, nuclear, thermonuclear, geothermal, hydroelectric, wave-powered, solar, wind-powered, wind-driven, steam-powered, steam-operated

ADVERBS

18 **powerfully**, potently, strongly, mightily, with telling effect, with might and main, with all one's might, by dint of, by virtue of, prevailingly, prevalently, predominantly, influentially, omnipotently, irresistibly, authoritatively, potentially, virtually, possibly, competently, adequately, effectually, effectively, efficaciously, efficiently, proficiently, forcefully, compellingly, compulsively, cogently, forcibly, by force, by force of arms, violently

19 **energetically**, dynamically, vigorously, magnetically, electrically, electronically

335 Powerlessness

I have more flesh than another man, and therefore more frailty.
William Shakespeare.

NOUNS

1 **powerlessness**, lack of power, absence of power, lack of authority, ineffectiveness, ineffectuality, inefficiency, impotence, inability, incapacity, incompetence, emptiness, barrenness, sterility, sterilization, vasectomy, futility, uselessness, inutility, incapability, ineptitude, unfitness, disqualification, invalidation, decrepitude, frailty, fragility, power vacuum, power failure, energy depletion, neutralization, disarmament, demilitarization

► *238 Uselessness; 247 Failure; 251 Restraint; 337 Weakness; 486 Unskilfulness*

2 **futile effort**, futile exploit, labour of Sisyphus, dead letter, empty threats, bluster, impotent fury, frustration, all talk and no action

3 **helplessness**, defencelessness, lack of protection, vulnerability, harmlessness, innocence, babyhood, infancy, weakness, softness, meekness

► *254 Danger; 555 Youth; 805 Innocence*

4 **disability**, physical weakness, invalidity, weakness, mental handicap, physical handicap, physical disability, sexual impotence, sterility, infertility, prostration, exhaustion, tiredness, fatigue, collapse, breakdown, faint, dead faint, swoon, loss of consciousness, unconsciousness, coma, catatonic fit, catatonia, narcosis, stroke, heart attack, apoplexy, debilitating illness, paralysis, hemiplegia, paraplegia, quadriplegia, tetraplegia, atrophy, ataxia,

loss of control, incontinence, mental decay, hardening of the arteries, softening of the brain, dementia, senile dementia, senility, Alzheimer's disease

▶ *245 Deterioration; 260 Ill Health; 261 Tiredness; 461 Insanity; 556 Age*

5 **powerless person**, unauthorized person, figurehead, titular head, invalid, sick (*or* sickly) person, hermaphrodite, man of straw (*or* straw man), broken reed, shut-in (US), pushover (Inf), easy mark (US inf), easy meat (Inf), patsy (US inf), schnook (US inf)

VERBS

6 **be powerless**, be impotent, stand defenceless, cannot, not work, not operate, not do, not help, be of no help, not change anything, not alter things, avail nothing, be of no avail, strive in vain, fail, have no power, have no influence, have no say, have no control, get nowhere, have no resistance, feel helpless, wring one's hands, stamp one's feet, gnash one's teeth, do nothing, look on, stand by, have a hopeless case, have no chance, become unconscious, lose consciousness, lapse into unconsciousness, faint, pass out, collapse, not have a leg to stand on, be like putty in someone's hands, not make the grade (Inf), cut no ice (Inf), not be able to cut the mustard (US inf)

7 **remove power from**, remove authority from, deprive of power, deprive of authority, invalidate, incapacitate, disable, disempower, disqualify, abrogate, disarm, demilitarize, neutralize, weaken, emaciate, debilitate, sap, undermine, consume, exhaust, use up

8 **overpower**, disarm, put out of action, knock down, prostrate, bowl over, wind, knock out, tie up, tie hand and foot, numb, benumb, paralyse, cripple, lame, maim, hobble, hamstring, stifle, smother, choke, throttle, suffocate, strangle, garrotte (*or* garrote), kill, deaden, muzzle, silence, spike someone's guns, put a spoke in someone's wheel, deflate, power down, switch off, put out of commission, take the wind out of someone's sails, throw a spanner in the works (Inf), throw a monkey wrench into (US inf), KO (Inf), nobble (Inf), put the kibosh on (Inf)

▶ *387 Subjection*

9 **make impotent**, sterilize, make barren, vasectomize, castrate, geld, spay, neuter, unsex, emasculate, evirate, effeminize, unman, unnerve, enervate, devitalize, fix (Inf), de-ball (US inf), de-nut (US inf)

ADJECTIVES

10 **powerless**, unable, not able, not enabled, incapable, not empowered, unauthorized, invalid, invalidated, null and void, not lawful, illegal, disfranchised (*or* disenfranchised), inoperative, unemployed, deactivated, not working, switched off, suspended, out of action, out of order, in abeyance, mothballed, out of circulation, broken, broken down, deposed, disqualified, unqualified, unfit, inept, good-for-nothing, unworkable, worthless, useless, ineffective, ineffectual, inefficacious, inefficient, incompetent, unpowered, without a leg to stand on, dud (Inf), duff (Inf), laid up (Inf), kaput (Inf), buggered (Inf), fucked (Inf), fucked-up (Inf)

11 **unprotected**, undefended, unguarded, defenceless, indefensible, ill-equipped, weaponless, unarmed, disarmed, unfortified, exposed, pregnable, untenable, dependent, subject, without resource, orphaned, friendless, vulnerable, harmless, innocent, meek

12 **impotent**, weak, feeble, frail, debilitated, etiolated, tired, fatigued, worn out, tired out, exhausted, used up, decrepit, senile, paraplegic, hemiplegic, paralytic, unconscious, comatose, catatonic, drugged, insensible, incapacitated, disabled, paralysed, quadriplegic, crippled, incontinent, lacking self-control, prostrate, supine, irresolute, spineless, nerveless, unnerved, demoralized, shell-shocked, *hors de combat* (Fr), out of the running, helpless, out of control, drifting, rudderless, swamped, waterlogged, on one's beam-ends, grounded, on one's back, all in (Inf), done in (*or* up) (Inf), beat (Inf), dead beat (Inf), clapped out (Inf), fixed (Inf), belly up (US inf), zonked (Inf)

13 **unsexed**, sterilized, sterile, barren, infertile, vasectomized, emasculated, castrated, gelded, neutered, spayed, caponized, unmanned, effete, sexless, de-balled (US inf), de-nutted (US inf)

ADVERBS

14 **powerlessly**, illegally, without authority, ineptly, worthlessly, uselessly, ineffectively, ineffectually, inefficiently, incompetently, beyond one, beyond one's power, above one's head, too much for, defencelessly, indefensibly, dependently, harmlessly, innocently, impotently, weakly, feebly, irresolutely, helplessly, in over one's head, out of one's league (US inf)

336 Strength

This is the Law of the Yukon, that only the strong shall thrive;
That surely the weak shall perish, and only the Fit survive.
Robert William Service.

NOUNS

1 **strength**, power, potency, might, force, mechanical strength, load-bearing capacity, tensile strength, compressive strengh, torsional strength, physical strength, athleticism, physical force, brute force, assertiveness, aggressiveness, aggression, bellicosity, brute strength, virility, manliness, musculature, muscularity, muscle, biceps, triceps, pectorals, laterals, sinews, thews, brawn, burliness, greatness, superiority, effectuality, effectiveness, firmness, steadfastness, determination, stability, durability, endurance, survivability, staying power, stamina, resourcefulness, resolution, stout-heartedness, backbone, courage, pluck, grit, nerve, bravery, toughness, tenacity, resilience, resistance, fortification, protection, impregnability, impenetrability, inviolability, invincibility, invulnerability, unassailability, beefiness (Inf), spunk (Inf), guts (Inf)

▶ *28 Physics; 158 Size; 252 Safety; 334 Power; 338 Vigour; 418 Hardness; 423 Toughness; 585 War; 613 Courage; 638 Resolution; 647 Severity*

2 **healthiness**, soundness, fitness, physical fitness, vitality, liveliness, energy, enthusiasm, zeal, compulsion, vehemence, vim, vigour, youth, acuity, keenness, dedication

▶ *259 Health; 554 Life; 555 Youth; 598 Happiness*

3 **intensity**, concentration, depth, emphasis, stress, urgency, rashness, cogency, weight, pressure, severity

▶ *615 Rashness*

4 **strengthening**, toughening, tempering, reinforcing, hardening, stiffening, fortifying, protecting, invigorating, restoring, convalescing, refreshing, reviving, revivifying, revival, reinforcement, invigoration, restoration, refreshment, tonic, revivification, convalescence

▶ *259 Health; 393 Repair; 581 Refreshment*

5 **athlete**, sportsman (*or* sportswoman), sporty person, amateur athlete, letterman (US), professional athlete, footballer, football player (US), baseball player (US), all-American (US), cricketer, all-round player, all-rounder, gymnast, tumbler, circus performer, acrobat, contortionist, funambulist, tightrope walker, trapeze artist, bareback rider, strongman, weightlifter, boxer, wrestler, sumo wrestler, runner, sprinter, marathon runner, high jumper, pole-vaulter, contender, champion, gold medallist, runner-up, silver medallist, bronze medallist, challenger

▶ *47 Athletics*

6 **muscleman**, bodybuilder, Mr Universe, superhero, Superman, Supergirl, Batman and Robin, Captain America, Wonder Woman, Tarzan, Rambo, mythical hero, Atlas, Hercules, Titan, Biblical strong men, Samson, Goliath, giant, strong woman, Amazon, virago (Lit), tower of strength, bully, bullyboy, bruiser, he-man (Inf), strong-arm man (Inf), tough guy (Inf), heavy (Inf), hunk of a man (Inf), hunk (Inf), hulk (Inf), beefcake (Inf), meathead (Inf), bouncer (Inf), chucker-out (Inf)

VERBS

7 **be strong**, possess strength, have what it takes, come in force, overwhelm, overpower, outmatch, be more than a match for, overmaster, become stronger, rally, recover, revive, convalesce, not weaken, hold out, hold up, bear up, gird (up) one's loins, never say die (Inf), come down (on) like a ton of bricks (Inf), pack a punch (Inf)

8 **strengthen**, make strong, give strength to, lend force to, confirm, underline, underscore, emphasize, stress, reinforce, fortify, protect, entrench, pad, stuff, buttress, prop up, sustain, support, brace, toughen, harden, case-harden, temper, energize, animate, quicken, enliven, invigorate, boost, revive, revivify, reinvigorate, refresh, set someone up properly, set someone on his (*or* her) feet (*or* legs), build up, tune up, strengthen oneself, steel oneself, temper oneself, nerve oneself, screw up one's courage, stiffen, stiffen one's resolve, stiffen the sinews, put life into, put body into, put one's back into, use force, use muscle, beef up (Inf), soup up (Inf)

ADJECTIVES

9 **physically strong**, strong, powerful, athletic, muscular, sinewy, burly, brawny, virile, manly, Herculean, Amazonian, strapping, healthy, hale, hale and hearty, robust, able-bodied, abled, sound, sound in wind and limb, sound as a bell, fit, fit as a fiddle, fit as a flea, in fine fettle, in good health, in good shape, in the pink (of health), hardy, lusty, feisty, vigorous, sturdy, tough, stalwart, stout, strong as a horse, strong as a bull, strong as an ox, strong as a lion, beefy (Inf), red-blooded (Inf), in good nick (Inf)

10 **potent**, forceful, powerful, puissant (Lit), mighty, redoubtable, formidable, great, high-powered, overpowering, overwhelming, superior, compelling, convincing, persuasive, effective, cogent, telling, trenchant, weighty, clear, clear-cut, distinct, marked, unmistakable, urgent, pressing, severe, intense, vehement, extreme, drastic, Draconian, thoroughgoing, deep-rooted, well-established, well-founded, firm, staunch, fervent, fervid, fierce

11 **strong in spirit**, firm, steadfast, determined, resolute, stout-hearted, courageous, plucky, resilient, resourceful, acute, keen, dedicated, enthusiastic, energetic, zealous, eager, tough, tenacious, unyielding, brave, assertive, self-assertive, aggressive, bellicose, warlike

12 **strong to the senses**, striking, bold, daring, stark, brilliant, bright, dazzling, glaring, loud, strong-smelling, strong-tasting, biting, mordant, sharp, pungent, piquant, spicy, highly flavoured, highly seasoned, hot, concentrated, undiluted, pure, neat, intoxicating, heady

13 **strengthened**, toughened, reinforced, fortified, armed, well-armed, well-protected, protective, hard-wearing, heavy-duty, on a firm footing, on a firm foundation, well-built, stout, substantial, durable, tough, resistant, restored, revived, braced, buttressed

ADVERBS

14 **strongly**, powerfully, energetically, forcefully, forcibly, by force, by sheer force, in force, with might and main, soundly, hardily, sturdily, stoutly, robustly, ruggedly, fiercely, courageously, tenaciously, bravely, assertively, aggressively, boldly, invulnerably, unyieldingly

15 **acutely**, keenly, enthusiastically, energetically, vigorously, zealously, lustily, resolutely, eagerly, heartily, firmly, fervently, urgently, compulsively, by compulsion, intensely, extremely, drastically, brilliantly, brightly, loudly, sharply, pungently, potently, compellingly, convincingly, persuasively, effectively, distinctly, unmistakably

337 Weakness

Oh, your precious 'lame ducks'! John Galsworthy.

NOUNS

1 **weakness**, lack of strength, feebleness, impotence, enfeeblement, softness, limpness, flaccidity, floppiness, slackness, looseness, weak foundation, dilapidation, impairment, damage, decay, rust, wear, deactivation, neutralization, adulteration, dilution, feet of clay, instability, fragility, delicateness, delicacy, puniness, smallness, helplessness, innocence, harmlessness, vulnerability, defencelessness, defect, Achilles' heel

▶ *124 Unimportance; 231 Imperfection; 245 Deterioration; 249 Adversity; 335 Powerlessness; 415 Lightness; 419 Softness; 555 Youth*

2 **indecisiveness**, indecision, irresolution, hesitance, doubtfulness, pusillanimity, ineffectuality, slowness, sheepishness, spinelessness, nervelessness, nervousness, timorousness, cowardliness, cowardice, gutlessness (Inf)

▶ *227 Changeableness; 453 Uncertainty; 614 Cowardice; 639 Vacillation*

3 **poor health**, sickliness, debility, frailty, infirmity, weak-

liness, faintness, paleness, anaemia, asthenia, thinness, anorexia, anorexia nervosa, senility, caducity, decrepitude, dizziness, giddiness, vertigo, shakiness, lameness, blindness, deafness, loss of strength, weakened state, enervation, deflation, depletion, dissipation, impoverishment, burnout, failure, waning, flagging, weariness, exhaustion, fatigue, tiredness

► *153 Thinness; 260 Ill Health; 261 Tiredness; 556 Age*

4 **weakling**, seven-stone weakling, ninety-pound weakling (US), broken reed, small fry, dupe, victim, milksop, namby-pamby, hypochondriac, invalid, sick person, poor dab (Welsh), lame duck, lame dog, kitten, infant, baby, babe in arms, big baby, cry-baby, coward, teacher's pet, mummy's boy, man of straw, straw man (US), easy mark (US inf), easy meat (Inf), weed (Inf), softy (Inf), pushover (Inf), doormat (Inf), drip (Inf), lightweight (Inf), jellyfish (Inf), (poor) fish (Inf), wimp (Inf), twit (Inf), wet (Inf), patsy (US inf), sissy (Inf), pansy (Inf), nerd (US inf), chicken (Inf)

5 **weak thing**, flimsy item, insubstantial thing, reed, cobweb, gossamer, thread, gossamer thread, sand castle, house built on sand, house of cards, castle in the air, castle in Spain, fragile item, paper, tissue paper, matchstick, matchwood, glass, china, eggshell, water, thin gruel, watered-down soup, dishwater, milk and water, slops (Inf)

VERBS

6 **be weak**, be ill, grow weak, weaken, sicken, faint, languish, flag, fail, fall, drop, droop, flop, wilt, fade, decrease, diminish, decline, dwindle, crumble, wear, wear out, wear thin, yield, sag, give way, break, split, come apart at the seams, fall apart at the seams, shake, tremble, totter, teeter, stagger, dodder, go lame, limp, halt

7 **weaken**, make weak, enfeeble, debilitate, enervate, unnerve, rattle, alarm, shake, relax, slacken, loosen, deflate, diminish, reduce, reduce in number, decimate, extenuate, thin, thin out, lessen, deplete, drain, impoverish, starve, deprive, rob, sap, undermine, impair, damage, invalidate, spoil, mar, disarm, disable, strain, sprain, lame, maim, cripple, hurt, harm, injure, wound, strip, strip bare, denude, expose, adulterate, dilute, water down, shake up, soften up, soften, muffle, mute

ADJECTIVES

8 **weak**, lacking strength, not strong, impotent, powerless, feeble, deprived of strength, enfeebled, unhardened, untempered, soft, limp, flaccid, floppy, drooping, hanging, sagging, unstrung, slack, loose, relaxed, gimcrack, shoddy, jerry-built, rickety, tottery, tottering, teetering, wobbly, creaky, run down, seedy, breakable, brittle, fragile, delicate, puny, small, lightweight, ineffectual, helpless, defenceless, unsafe, unprotected, unguarded, unfortified, untenable, wonky (Inf)

9 **dilapidated**, broken, broken down, tumbledown, weather-beaten, laid bare, worn, worn out, the worse for wear, on its last legs, rotten, decayed, rusted, withered, diminished, deflated, wasted, depleted, drained, spent, used up, laid up

10 **ill**, sickly, faint, pale, pallid, bloodless, white as a sheet, anaemic, asthenic, groggy, below par, languid, feeble, weakly, weak as a child, weak as a baby, weak as a kitten, weak as water, wasted, thin, skinny, emaciated, skin-and-bone, skeletal, anorexic, frail, decrepit, infirm, crippled, lame, game, limping, hobbling, shaky, unsteady, unsound, feeble-minded, imbecile, slow, dim-witted (Inf), poorly (Inf), under the weather (Inf), green about the gills (Inf), gammy (Inf), gimpy (US inf)

11 **weakened**, debilitated, enervated, dissipated, burnt out, sapped, wearied, exhausted, fatigued, tired, laid low, weary, worn out, on one's last legs, on the wane, failed, impoverished

12 **weak-willed**, indecisive, irresolute, wavering, dithering, pusillanimous, vacillating, hesitant, doubtful, half-hearted, nerveless, unnerved, nervous, timid, timorous, cowardly, sheepish, effete, mealy-mouthed, spineless, lily-livered, chicken-hearted, sissy, namby-pamby, limp-wristed, weak-kneed, scared, yellow (Inf), gutless (Inf), chicken (Inf)

13 **insufficient**, inadequate, insubstantial, inconclusive, invalid, unconvincing, unsatisfactory, lacking, wanting, deficient, flimsy, slight, small, little, thin, light, shallow, hollow, faulty, substandard, poor, pathetic, under strength, below par, imperceptible, inaudible, invisible, faint, low, distant, muffled, soft, muted, quiet, diluted, runny, tasteless, insipid, watery, milk-and-water, wishy-washy (Inf)

ADVERBS

14 **weakly**, impotently, softly, ineffectually, without effect, helplessly, unsafely, faintly, languidly, feebly, weakly, unsteadily, while ill, on one's last legs, unsoundly, indecisively, irresolutely, half-heartedly, nervously, timidly, cowardly, in a cowardly way, sheepishly, insufficiently, inadequately, inconclusively, unsatisfactorily, slightly, thinly, lightly, poorly, pathetically, imperceptibly, inaudibly, quietly, tastelessly, insipidly

338 Vigour

Energy is Eternal Delight. William Blake.

NOUNS

1 **vigour**, energy, physical energy, exertion, effort, activity, excitement, enthusiasm, stimulation, inspiration, dynamism, strength, power, robustness, force, forcefulness, life, animation, exhilaration, spirit, pluck, mettle, liveliness, intensity, impetus, dash, élan, éclat, vitality, health, invigoration, refreshment, revitalization, freshness, zest, verve, sparkle, drive, keenness, lustiness, gusto, pep (Inf), spunk (Inf), guts (Inf), kick (Inf), pepper (US inf), punch (Inf), snap (Inf), pizzazz (*or* pizazz) (Inf), zip (Inf), go (Inf), get-up-and-go (Inf), wallop (Inf), welly (Inf), vim (Inf), oomph (Inf), piss and vinegar (Inf), balls (Inf)

► *262 Haste; 327 Agitation; 334 Power; 336 Strength; 342 Activity; 380 Violence; 597 Joy; 613 Courage; 638 Resolution; 640 Perseverance; 726 Emphasis*

VERBS

2 **be full of vigour**, thrive, have zest, enjoy life, enthuse, burst with energy, burst with health, never stop, rush around, be up and doing, exert oneself, drive, push, raise the pressure, put on a spurt, pull out all the stops, strike hard, hit hard, tell upon, make an impression,

rush around like a chicken with its head cut off, steam away (Inf), get up a good head of steam (Inf), give it some welly (Inf), have a lot of pizzazz (*or* pizazz) (Inf), have a lot of get-up-and-go (Inf), give it the gun (Inf), go like a bat out of hell (Inf), go like gangbusters (US inf), be full of piss and vinegar (Inf), have balls (Inf)

3 **invigorate**, activate, energize, galvanize, exhilarate, electrify, intensify, double, redouble, rouse, kindle, inflame, excite, stimulate, enliven, put life into, pep up, ginger up, boost, fire up, hike up, step up, wind up, act like a tonic, give heart to, hearten, put heart into, egg on, cheer on, inspire, intoxicate, freshen, refresh, revive, restore, reinvigorate, revitalize, give an edge to, sharpen, make glow, fertilize, bump up (Inf), psych up (Inf), root for (Inf), pep up (Inf), step on the gas (Inf), turn up the juice (Inf), soup up (Inf)

ADJECTIVES

4 **vigorous**, energetic, active, dynamic, powerful, strong, forceful, forcible, strenuous, vehement, intense, animated, spirited, vibrant, brisk, lively, vital, healthy, spry, hale, hale and hearty, hardy, zestful, lusty, feisty, mettlesome, strapping, virile, extrovert, extroverted, outgoing, robust, effective, efficient, enterprising, go-ahead, thrusting, aggressive, keen, enthusiastic, flourishing, growing, red-blooded (Inf), full of beans (Inf), full of pep (Inf), peppy (Inf), nippy (Inf), spunky (Inf), snappy (Inf), punchy (Inf), zippy (Inf), pushy (Inf), go-getting (Inf)

5 **invigorating**, healthy, bouncy, bouncing, fresh, exhilarating, rousing, stimulating, inspiring, exciting, bracing, strengthening, reinvigorating, reviving, revivifying, restoring, rejuvenating, refreshing, revitalizing

ADVERBS

6 **with vigour**, vigorously, energetically, forcefully, forcibly, with telling effect, straight from the shoulder, con brio, lustily, zestfully, hard, at full tilt, all out, hammer and tongs, firing on all cylinders, with the throttle wide open, full pelt, with a vengeance, with a will, like a chicken with its head cut off, flat out (Inf), full steam ahead (Inf), like mad (Inf), like crazy (Inf), like hell (Inf), like a bat out of hell (Inf), like gangbusters (US inf)

339 Inertness

NOUNS

1 **inertness**, inertia, inactivity, inaction, stillness, motionlessness, indolence, idleness, lifelessness, deathliness, languor, torpor, torpidity, paralysis, insensibility, numbness, vegetation, stagnation, quiescence, dormancy, latency, fallowness, apathy, indifference, dullness, sloth, slowness, sluggishness, laziness, sleepiness, hibernation, laxity, slackness, passivity, passiveness, peacefulness, impassivity, immobility, stolidity, inexcitability, indecisiveness, indecision, irresolution, gutlessness (Inf)

► *301 Motionlessness; 333 Slowness; 335 Powerlessness; 337 Weakness; 341 Inaction; 343 Inactivity; 489 Insensibility; 563 Infertility; 589 Peace; 592 Insensitivity; 618 Indifference; 639 Vacillation*

2 **inert person**, heavy sleeper, dolt, dullard, comatose patient, vegetable (Inf), cabbage (Inf)

3 **inert thing**, extinct volcano, dormant volcano, inanimate object, sailboat on calm waters, flag on a windless day, broken clock, ghost town, unexploded bomb, dud (Inf)

VERBS

4 **be inert**, sleep, slumber, doze, laze around, lie, lie still, lie idle, lie in wait, lurk, smoulder, hang fire, hold one's fire, hold one's breath, hold one's horses, stagnate, vegetate, just sit there, just stand there, just lie there, not stir, freeze, snooze (Inf), have (*or* take) forty winks (Inf), nod off (Inf), lie doggo (Inf)

ADJECTIVES

5 **inert**, inactive, passive, impassive, apathetic, indifferent, unexcitable, pacific, unaggressive, unwarlike, peaceful, unreactive, indecisive, irresolute, unresponsive, stolid, idle, lazy, indolent, slack, lax, limp, flaccid, heavy, slothful, lumpish, doltish, sluggish, slow, slumberous (Lit), dull, numb, dormant, smouldering, latent, dead, lifeless, languid, torpid, insensible, hibernating, sleepy, immobile, unmoving, motionless, still, static, stagnant, stagnating, vegetating, paralysed, quiet, quiescent, fallow, gutless (Inf)

6 **suspended**, pending, in abeyance, switched off, on hold, on ice, in reserve, abrogated, off the active list, deactivated, uninfluential, powerless

ADVERBS

7 **inertly**, inactively, passively, impassively, apathetically, indifferently, peacefully, idly, lazily, indolently, limply, sluggishly, slowly, numbly, latently, lifelessly, languidly, insensibly, sleepily, motionlessly, quietly, at rest, in suspense, in abeyance, on hold, on ice, in reserve, in cold storage (Inf), in the deepfreeze (Inf)

340 Action

Suit the action to the word, the word to the action; with this special observance, that you o'erstep not the modesty of nature.
William Shakespeare.

NOUNS

1 **action**, doing, happening, performance, execution, steps, measures, move, enactment, policy, transaction, commission, perpetration, dispatch, accomplishment, achievement, effectuation, completion, proceeding, process, procedure, routine, custom, praxis, practice, behaviour, conduct, movement, play, swing, motion, operation, functioning, working, interaction, evolution, agency, force, pressure, sway, control, influence, effect, power, work, labour, exertion, effort, attempt, endeavour, campaign, programme, crusade, battle, war, militancy, activism, activeness, activity, drama, occupation, business, manufacture, production, employment, use, implementation, putting into effect, administration, handling, management, direction, legal action, legal proceeding, lawsuit

► *300 Motion; 334 Power; 342 Activity; 349 Use; 353 Attempt; 356 Creation; 395 Influence; 484 Plan; 576 Work; 579 Management; 585 War; 632 Habit*

2 **deed**, act, overt act, action, exploit, feat, achievement, accomplishment, gesture, useless gesture, meaningless act, *beau geste* (Fr), good deed, bad deed, wrongdoing,

criminal act, crime, foul play, stunt, *tour de force* (Fr), special effort, stroke of genius, pretence, dissimulation, posture, affectation, gesticulation, measure, step, move, policy, manoeuvre, evolution, tactics, sudden action, stroke, blow, coup, *coup de main* (Fr), *coup de grâce* (Fr), coup d'état, overthrow, job, task, work, operation, exercise, undertaking, proceeding, transaction, deal, doings, actions, dealings, affairs, handiwork, handicraft, workmanship, craftsmanship, skill, *pièce de résistance* (Fr), *chef-d'œuvre* (Fr), masterpiece, drama, play, scene, narrative

▶ *21 Drama; 354 Undertaking; 484 Plan; 485 Skill; 613 Courage; 700 Deception; 721 Description*

3 **doer**, man (*or* woman) of action, self-starter, busy person, activist, political activist, lobbyist, active supporter, campaigner, crusader, militant, practical person, realist, finisher, achiever, high achiever, high-flier (*or* high-flyer), hero, heroine, good role model, benefactor, brave person, practitioner, professional, expert, stunt man (*or* woman), player, performer, actor, actress, creative person, creative worker, artistic person, artist, executant, perpetrator, committer, offender, criminal, gangster, evildoer, malefactor, mover, mover and shaker (US), canvasser, controller, manipulator, motivator, operator, agent, contractor, undertaker, entrepreneur, executor, executive, chief executive, administrator, manager, general manager, managing director, director, hand, worker, manual worker, workman, operative, craftsman (*or* woman), handicraftsman (*or* woman), handicraft worker, artisan, go-getter (Inf), live wire (Inf), whiz kid (Inf), street-fighter (Inf), do-gooder (Inf)

▶ *19 Painting and Sculpture; 21 Drama; 342 Activity; 485 Skill; 578 Worker; 579 Management; 613 Courage; 651 Malevolence*

VERBS

4 **act**, do, happen, perform, carry out, execute, take action, take steps, take measures, enact, legislate, commission, dispatch, accomplish, achieve, complete, carry through, get in on the act, be in on the action, take effect, come into operation, operate, function, militate for, militate against, act upon, sway, influence, manipulate, motivate, use tactics, twist, turn, manoeuvre, proceed, proceed with, get on with, push on with, get going, get cracking (Inf), move, do something, make an (*or* the) effort, lift a finger, raise a finger, try, attempt, tackle, take on, shoulder, undertake, do the deed, perpetrate, commit, do what is required (*or* needed), do the needful, take care of, implement, fulfil, put into practice, put into use, solemnize, observe, do great deeds, make history, win renown, become celebrated, become famous, acquire a reputation, practise, exercise, carry on, discharge, prosecute, pursue, wage, ply, ply one's trade, employ oneself, occupy oneself, busy oneself, do business, transact, deal, officiate, direct, be in charge, administer, administrate, manage, control, have to do with, deal with, work, labour, sweat, campaign, canvass, use, exploit, take advantage of, make the most of, intervene, come between, work for, strike a blow for, help, aid, have a hand in, be active in, take part in, play a part in, have a finger in (Inf), participate, interfere, deal in, get mixed up in, meddle, conduct oneself, indulge in, behave, play about, frolic about, lark around, skylark (Inf), fool around, stunt, perform a stunt, show off, pretend, feign, dissemble

▶ *342 Activity; 346 Operation; 353 Attempt; 354 Undertaking; 395 Influence; 480 Persuasion; 645 Cunning*

ADJECTIVES

5 **acting**, doing, happening, performing, enacting, working, at work, occupational, in action, red-handed, in operation, in harness, operative, up and doing, industrious, busy, active, interactive, creative, artistic, dramatic, militant, crusading, brave, heroic

▶ *342 Activity; 576 Work*

6 **effective**, forceful, powerful, productive, useful, direct, influential, functional, operational, procedural, professional, managerial, executive, administrative, tactical

▶ *334 Power; 345 Effect; 576 Work*

ADVERBS

7 **actively**, overtly, in the act, red-handed, in flagrante delicto, in the midst of, in the thick of, by enactment, by custom, with a stroke

8 **effectively**, forcefully, powerfully, productively, usefully, directly, influentially, functionally

341 Inaction

NOUNS

1 **inaction**, lack of action, nonaction, nothing happening, inertia, inertness, inability to act, impotence, refusal to act, failure to act, neglect, negligence, abstinence from action, abstention, refraining, avoidance, passive resistance, *laissez* (or *laisser*) *aller* (Fr), *laissez* (or *laisser*) *faire* (Fr), suspension, abeyance, dormancy, inactivity, nonuse, deadlock, stalemate, log jam (US), stop, standstill, lack of progress, bogging down, immobility, motionlessness, paralysis, impassivity, insensibility, passivity, apathy, stagnation, vegetation, doldrums, stillness, quiet, quietness, calm, calmness, tranquillity, quiescence, all the time in the world, time on one's hands, time to kill, idle hours, *dolce far niente* (It), leisure, rest, repose, relaxing, relaxation, lack of ambition, laziness, loafing, idleness, indolence, watching (*or* letting) the world go by, twiddling one's thumbs, unemployment, nonemployment, underemployment, joblessness, redundancy, no work, easy work, sinecure, Fabianism, Fabian policy, do-nothingism, delay, putting off till tomorrow, procrastination, noninterference, nonintervention, hands off, defeatism, hopelessness, no courage, cowardice, indifference, head in the sand

▶ *226 Stopping; 263 Ease; 294 Lateness; 301 Motionlessness; 335 Powerlessness; 339 Inertness; 343 Inactivity; 350 Nonuse; 489 Insensibility; 614 Cowardice; 618 Indifference; 634 Avoidance; 666 Negligence*

2 **nonacting person**, idler, idle rich, leisured classes, loafer, layabout, lazybones, shirker, sleeper, dreamer, daydreamer, waverer, ditherer, hesitator, nihilist, solipsist, pessimist, fatalist, defeatist, non interventionist, abstainer, killjoy, wallflower, party-pooper (Inf), coward, chicken (Inf)

▶ *339 Inertness; 343 Inactivity*

ADJECTIVES

3 inactive, nonactive, inert, unable to act, impotent, powerless, negligent, neglectful, abstaining, abstentious, suspended, in abeyance, dormant, inoperative, deadlocked, stalemated, at a standstill, stationary, immobile, motionless, still, calm, becalmed, tranquil, quiet, quiescent, stagnant, not stirring, hardly breathing, half-dead, half-gone, without a sign of life, gone, dead, extinct, benumbed, cold, frozen, paralysed, impassive, insensible, passive, apathetic, phlegmatic, dull, sluggish, leisured, leisurely, relaxed, lazy, indolent, idle, fallow, unoccupied, unemployed, without employment, underemployed, laid off, redundant, jobless, without a job, out of work, collecting unemployment (US), do-nothing, wait-and-see, unprogressive, ostrich-like, Fabian, refraining, delaying, procrastinating, cunctative, defeatist, cowardly, indifferent, neutral, hands off, tolerant, unseeing, unhearing, blind, deaf, on the dole (Inf), signing on (Inf), collecting (US inf)

▶ *263 Ease; 294 Lateness; 301 Motionlessness; 335 Powerlessness; 339 Inertness; 343 Inactivity; 489 Insensibility; 580 Leisure; 582 Death; 614 Cowardice; 618 Indifference; 666 Negligence*

VERBS

4 not act, do nothing, fail to act, refuse to act, be inactive, be inert, suffer from inertia, refrain, avoid, abstain, pass up, stand by, look on, watch, have no ambition, loaf, idle, watch the world go by, let the world go by, watch and wait, wait and see, bide one's time, wait, sit tight, delay, procrastinate, put off (till tomorrow), defer, live and let live, let the good times roll, let things take their course, let things take care of themselves, leave alone, let alone, let sleeping dogs lie, let well (enough) alone, hold no brief for, wash one's hands of, keep out of, stay neutral, sit on the fence, tolerate, pretend not to see, disregard, ignore, let pass, not react, not move, not budge, not stir, not bat an eye (*or* eyelid), show no sign of life, not raise (*or* lift) a finger, stagnate, vegetate, rest on one's laurels, rest on one's oars, relax one's efforts, tread water, drift, glide, slide, coast, freewheel, abandon hope, have no hope, give up, despair, neglect, stay still, keep quiet, keep mum, sit back, relax, unwind, rest, repose, have no function, be redundant, be superfluous, be useless, have free time, have nothing to do, kill time, kick one's heels, twiddle one's thumbs, look out the window, sit on one's hands, stop, pause, desist, quit, cease, rust, gather dust, lie idle, lie fallow, stay on the shelf, stay packed away, have no life, be lifeless, lie dead, die, hang fire (US inf), pass the buck (Inf), turn a blind eye (Inf), turn a deaf ear (Inf), button (up) one's lip (*or* mouth) (Inf)

▶ *226 Stopping; 238 Uselessness; 263 Ease; 294 Lateness; 339 Inertness; 343 Inactivity; 580 Leisure; 582 Death; 611 Despair; 618 Indifference*

ADVERBS

5 without action, without movement, with one's hands in one's pockets, with folded arms, inertly, powerlessly, negligently, impassively, apathetically, lazily, idly, indifferently, calmly, quietly, tranquilly, at rest

342 Activity

No-wher so bisy a man as he ther nas,
And yet he semed bisier than he was. Geoffrey Chaucer.

NOUNS

1 activity, action, activeness, movement, motion, life, stirring, stir, agitation, excitation, stimulation, ado, much ado, to-do, great doings, drama, commotion, racket, disturbance, row, quarrel, squabble, brawl, fray, tumult, turmoil, frenzy, whirl, maelstrom, vortex, midst of things, thick of things, thick of the action, kick (Inf), buzz (Inf), eye of the hurricane (*or* storm) (Inf)

▶ *300 Motion; 307 Rotation; 327 Agitation; 340 Action; 408 Disorder; 701 Argument*

2 social activity, group activity, interaction, person-to-person interaction, participation, active participation, volunteering, volunteerism, sociability, mingling, mixing, interest, special interest, active interest, hobby, pastime, pursuit, occupation, enterprise, undertaking, venture, a piece of the action (Inf)

▶ *340 Action; 354 Undertaking; 576 Work; 580 Leisure; 654 Sociability; 764 Sharing*

3 nimbleness, briskness, alacrity, promptitude, willingness, readiness, punctuality, quickness, speed, velocity, haste, dispatch, expedition, scramble, mad scramble, race, mad race, rat race, dash, mad dash, wild dash, burst, spurt, fit, spasm, overhaste, frantic haste, hurry, flurry, hurry-scurry, hustle, bustle, hustle and bustle, fuss, bother, fuss and bother, nuisance, botheration (Inf), hassle (Inf)

▶ *262 Haste; 293 Earliness; 636 Willingness*

4 energy, ceaseless energy, dynamic energy, dynamism, vigour, vigorousness, abandon, frenzy, vitality, vivacity, vivaciousness, life, liveliness, animation, spirit, high spirits, pep, eagerness, enthusiasm, ardour, fervour, vehemence, strong feeling, warm feeling, activation, motive, reason, cause, aggressiveness, enterprise, initiative, drive, push, ambition, go (Inf), get-up-and-go (Inf), moxie (US inf)

5 activism, political activism, militancy, militant scene, mass movement, popular movement, political movement, uprising, sedition

▶ *338 Vigour; 554 Life; 590 Feelings*

6 business, industry, call on one's time, imposition on one's time, press of business, pressure of work, pressure of deadlines, no sinecure, plenty to do, busyness, no break, no rest for the wicked, hive of activity, hive of industry, hive, beehive, high street, marketplace, workshop, hum of activity, hum, press, crush, jostling crowd, seething mob, hoi polloi, madding crowd (Lit), crush of shoppers, heavy traffic, a full plate (Inf), several (*or* many) irons in the fire (Inf)

▶ *576 Work; 577 Workshop*

7 restlessness, aimlessness, aimless activity, randomness, desultoriness, lack of concentration, inattention, dawdling, puttering (US), pottering, fiddling, fidgetiness, the fidgets, wanderlust, unrest, unease, unquietness, unquiet, jumpiness, nervousness, nerves, agitation, excitability, fever, fret, sleeplessness, insomnia, wakefulness, watchfulness, itchy feet (Inf)

► *472 Inattention; 665 Carefulness*

8 **assiduity**, application, concentration, intentness, attention, diligence, sedulity, industriousness, industry, hard work, laboriousness, monotonous work, drudgery, labour, determination, resolution, earnestness, *empressement* (Fr), tirelessness, indefatigability, perseverance, stamina, stickability (US), studiousness, painstaking, perfectionism, attention to detail, devotedness, wholeheartedness, gung-ho attitude, stick-to-itiveness (*or* stick-at-itiveness) (US inf)

► *471 Attention; 576 Work; 638 Resolution; 640 Perseverance*

9 **overactivity**, hyperactivity, overextension, overexpansion, overdiversification, overambition, oversupply, excess, redundancy, Parkinson's law, displacement activity, useless work, futile activity, wild-goose chase, chasing one's own tail, lost labour, wasted effort, useless exercise, hyperthyroidism, overexertion, petty officialdom, petty bureaucracy, red tape, officiousness, beadledom, meddlesomeness, interference, intrusiveness, interruption, meddling, interfering, sticking one's nose in, a finger in every pie, tampering, intrigue, conspiracy, secret plot, plot, song and dance (Inf)

► *219 Excess; 238 Uselessness; 327 Agitation; 484 Plan*

10 **busy person**, active person, fully occupied person, socially active person, jet-setter, socialite, energetic person, bustler, hustler, wheeler-dealer, someone in a hurry, fidget, hyperactive child, person of active habits, man (*or* woman) of action, activist, militant, doer, participator, volunteer, sharp fellow, sharpie (US inf), careerist, pusher, thruster, yuppie, enthusiast, zealot, fanatic, devotee, toiler, slogger, no slouch, hard worker, tireless worker, fanatical worker, high-pressure worker, Stakhanovite, demon for work, glutton for work, workaholic, new broom, worker, factotum, handyman, jack of all trades, maid of all work, drudge, Trojan, live wire (Inf), dynamo (Inf), human dynamo (Inf), powerhouse (Inf), whiz kid (Inf), whiz (Inf), go-getter (Inf), buff (Inf), glutton for punishment (Inf), gofer (US inf), dogsbody (Inf), fag (Inf), slave (Inf), galley slave (Inf), horse (Inf), workhorse (Inf), willing horse (Inf), mule (Inf), beaver (Inf), ant (Inf), bee (Inf), busy bee (Inf), eager beaver (Inf)

► *340 Action; 578 Worker; 641 Obstinacy*

11 **meddler**, meddling person, prying person, busybody, interferer, intermeddler, dabbler, stirrer, troublemaker, officious person, inquisitive person, tamperer, intriguer, planner, adviser, nuisance, fuss-budget (US inf), fusspot (Inf), spoilsport (Inf), nosy parker (Inf), kibitzer (US inf), back-seat driver (Inf)

► *484 Plan; 644 Curiosity; 713 Advice*

VERBS

12 **be active**, act, do, wake up, rouse oneself, bestir oneself, rub the sleep from one's eyes, rise and shine, rise, get up, be up and doing, move, stir, agitate, squabble, start a row, run riot, rampage, have one's fling, roar, rage, bluster, blow, explode, burst, spurt, flow, surge, rush, dash, race, fly, run, move fast, hasten, hurry, scurry, scramble, have no time to lose, come and go, rush to and fro, hustle, bustle, fuss, bother, fret, fume, drum one's fingers, stamp with impatience, have other things to do, have other fish to fry (Inf), stir one's stumps (Inf), get the lead out (Inf), get one's ass in gear (Inf), kick up a shindy (Inf), raise the dust (Inf), go at it nineteen to the dozen (Inf)

► *262 Haste; 300 Motion; 327 Agitation; 340 Action; 380 Violence; 408 Disorder*

13 **be busy**, busy oneself, keep busy, prosper, thrive, hum, make progress, progress, keep moving, keep on the go, keep on, have several irons in the fire, have one's hands full, be rushed off one's feet, not have a moment to spare (*or* to call one's own), live in a whirl, join the rat race, go all ways at once, not know which way to turn, not know which way is up, waste effort, rise early, go to bed late, burn the midnight oil, burn the candle at both ends, make hay while the sun shines, not let the grass grow under one's feet, keep on keeping on (US inf), keep the pot boiling (Inf), have one's plate full (Inf), spread oneself thin (Inf), run round in circles (Inf), chase one's own tail (Inf)

► *238 Uselessness; 246 Success; 302 Forward Motion*

14 **push**, shove, thrust, drive, impel, elbow one's way, thrust oneself forward, assert oneself, seize the opportunity, take one's chance, take the bull by the horns, profit by, protest, demonstrate, defy, react, react sharply, show fight, be up in arms, not take it lying down, be willing, show willingness, jump to it, show zeal, burn with zeal, not sleep, wake, watch, be on one's toes, be alert, respond, anticipate

► *331 Impulsion; 338 Vigour; 636 Willingness; 661 Defiance; 753 Protest*

15 **try**, attempt, try hard, take pains, make an effort, exert oneself, strain oneself, do one's best, rise to the occasion, dispatch, make short work of, work wonders, concentrate, put one's mind to, buckle down, put one's shoulder to the wheel, put one's hand to the tiller, persist, persevere, beaver away, work, slave, slog, overwork, overdo it, make work, never stop, plug away (Inf), do one's damnedest (Inf), polish off (Inf), go the whole hog (Inf), make the sparks fly (Inf), make things hum (Inf)

► *353 Attempt; 471 Attention; 576 Work; 640 Perseverance*

16 **be sociable**, interact, mingle, circulate, mix, join in, participate actively, participate, volunteer, have an active interest, show interest, interest oneself in, get a piece of the action (Inf)

► *654 Sociability; 764 Sharing*

17 **meddle**, intermeddle, interpose, intervene, interfere, be officious, have a finger in every pie, not mind one's own business, pry, poke one's nose in, spy, put one's oar in, put one's two cents in (US), butt in, interrupt, intrude, pester, bother, dun, importune, annoy, irritate, trouble, harass, boss, boss around, bully, persecute, tyrannize, oppress, tinker, tamper, fiddle, touch, impair, hassle (Inf)

► *242 Unpleasantness; 314 Entry; 644 Curiosity; 647 Severity*

ADJECTIVES

18 **active**, interactive, sociable, activated, moving, going, running, working, operative, in action, incessant, unceasing, expeditious, businesslike, able, able-bodied, strong, quick, fast, speedy, brisk, spry, nimble, agile, smart, keen, gleg (Scot), light-footed, lightsome, tripping, vigorous, strenuous, energetic, forceful, dynamic, thrust-

ful, thrusting, stirring, pushing, up-and-coming, enterprising, lively, sprightly, frisky, coltish, dashing, spirited, mettlesome, live, alive, alive and kicking, full of vitality, animated, vivacious, eager, ardent, fervent, perfervid, fierce, desperate, resolute, determined, enthusiastic, fanatical, zealous, prompt, instant, ready, willing, alert, on one's toes, awake, wakeful, watchful, careful, on the alert, vigilant, sleepless, restless, feverish, fretful, tossing, dancing, fidgety, nervous, nervy, jumpy, agitated, tense, fussy, like a cat on a hot tin roof, like a cat on hot bricks, like a long-tailed cat in a room full of rocking chairs (US), like a hen on a hot griddle, frenzied, frenetic, frantic, manic, demonic, hyperactive, overactive, overwrought, excitable, involved, actively involved, deeply involved, *engagé* or *engagée* (Fr), aggressive, militant, up in arms, warlike, nippy (Inf), go-getting (Inf), full of beans (Inf), into (Inf), hyper (Inf)

► *134 Continuity; 262 Haste; 300 Motion; 327 Agitation; 336 Strength; 338 Vigour; 340 Action; 354 Undertaking; 585 War; 590 Feelings; 636 Willingness; 638 Resolution; 665 Carefulness*

19 busy, active, bustling, hustling, humming, hectic, lively, eventful, in full swing, coming and going, rushing to and fro, puttering (US), pottering, doing chores, up and doing, stirring, astir, afoot, on the move, on the go, employed, in harness, at work, at one's desk, engaged, occupied, fully occupied, fully engaged, hard at work, hard at it, slogging, overworked, overemployed, rushed off one's feet, up to one's eyes, up to one's ears, up to one's neck, working oneself into the grave, fussing like a hen with chickens, busy as a bee, busy as a beaver, on the trot (Inf), on the make (Inf), up to one's ass (Inf), up to one's neck (*or* eyes *or* elbows) (Inf)

20 industrious, sedulous, diligent, assiduous, studious, persevering, hard-working, workaholic, plodding, slogging, labouring, laborious, unflagging, unwearied, tireless, indefatigable, full of stamina, energetic, unsleeping, keeping long hours, burning the midnight oil, burning the candle at both ends, never-tiring, never-resting, never-slacking, never-sleeping, efficient, workmanlike, businesslike, professional, stick-to-itive (*or* stick-at-itive) (US inf)

► *576 Work; 640 Perseverance*

21 meddling, overbusy, officious, interfering, meddlesome, intrusive, nosy, prying, irritating, annoying, troublesome, tyrannical, intriguing, dabbling, fiddling, participating, taking part, in the business, pushy (Inf)

► *314 Entry; 644 Curiosity*

ADVERBS

22 actively, fast, nimbly, vigorously, forcefully, eagerly, enthusiastically, promptly, restlessly, busily, industriously, on the go, on one's toes, full tilt, on all cylinders, with haste, with might and main, for all one is worth, for dear life, as if one's life depended on it, like a bomb (Inf)

INTERJECTIONS

23 rise and shine!, wakey wakey!, up you get!, shake a leg!, get going!, get a move on!, buckle down!, get the lead out! (Inf)

343 Inactivity

The Commons, faithful to their system, remained in a wise and masterly inactivity. James Mackintosh.

ADJECTIVES

1 inactive, quiescent, still, quiet, motionless, immobile, stationary, static, sedentary, stagnant, inert, passive, extinct, lifeless, inanimate

► *301 Motionlessness; 339 Inertness; 341 Inaction; 506 Silence*

2 not working (*or* **operating**), unemployed, unengaged, laid off, redundant, on strike, out, out of work, between jobs, jobless, signing on (Inf), off work, off duty, resting, free, available, at a loose end, laid up, out of action, out of commission, off, at a standstill, broken down, unused, fallow, idle, disengaged, unoccupied, vacant, empty

3 not participating, lazy, idle, indolent, slothful, work-shy, bone idle, loafing, lolling, parasitic, slack, lax, slow, dilatory, dawdling, tardy, procrastinating, laggard, sluggish, lethargic, languid, dull, listless, torpid, apathetic, indifferent, uninterested, phlegmatic, impassive

4 not awake, somnolent, drowsy, dozy, sleepy, soporific, heavy-eyed, slumberous, nodding off, yawning, dozing, resting, dopey, half-asleep, drugged, sedated, narcotized, anaesthetized, hypnotized, sleeping, asleep, dormant, torpid, hibernating, aestivating, dreaming, fast asleep, sound asleep, dead to the world, unconscious, insensible, out cold, comatose, doped (Inf), flaked out (Inf)

NOUNS

5 inactivity, quiescence, stillness, quietness, quiet, silence, immobility, inaction, inertia, passivity, inertness, lull, suspension, cessation, extinction, lifelessness

6 unemployment, shutdown, lay-off, slump, recession, depression, redundancy

7 idleness, laziness, indolence, sloth, slothfulness, absenteeism, slowness, slow progress, dawdling, delay, procrastination, sluggishness, lethargy, languor, dullness, listlessness, torpor, apathy, indifference, phlegm, impassivity

8 nonworker, idler, shirker, slacker, dawdler, skiver, sluggard, *fainéant* (Fr), clock watcher, passenger, dummy, sinecurist, sleeping partner, absentee landlord, *rentier* (Fr), idle rich, leisured classes, dreamer, lotus-eater, drifter, vagrant, tramp, hobo (US), beggar, drone, leech, parasite, layabout, *flâneur* (Fr), loafer, lounger, cadger, sponger, scrounger, freeloader (Inf), free-rider (US inf), couch potato (Inf), bum (Inf)

► *580 Leisure*

9 sleep, sleepiness, somnolence, doziness, drowsiness, heaviness, oscitancy, slumber, rest, repose, land of Nod, Morpheus, dreamland, sandman, heavy sleep, dormancy, hibernation, aestivation, unconsciousness, coma, stupor, trance, catalepsy, hypnosis, oblivion, insensibility, light sleep, nap, catnap, snooze, doze, siesta, forty winks (Inf), shut-eye (Inf), bye-byes (Inf), kip (Inf)

10 soporific, somnifacient, sleeping pill (*or* draught), nightcap, sedative, barbiturate, narcotic, opiate, poppy, opium, morphine, nepenthe, anaesthetic

11 sleeper, slumberer, dozer, drowser, hibernator, dormouse, Rip van Winkle, Sleeping Beauty, lie-abed (Inf), sleepyhead (Inf), Weary Willie (Inf)

VERBS

12 be inactive, stagnate, vegetate, do nothing, idle, laze, skive, loaf, lounge, cadge, sponge, slouch, mooch, kill time, kick one's heels (Inf), waste time, hang about, lie around, delay, procrastinate, hang fire, dawdle, drift

13 sleep, snooze, doze, drowse, yawn, nod off, nap, catnap, rest, slumber, sleep like a log (*or* top), lie dormant, hibernate, aestivate, kip (Inf), have forty winks (Inf), get one's head down (Inf)

14 make inactive, inactivate, dismantle, defuse, neutralize, extinguish, shut down, suspend, lay up, lay off, dismiss, fire, sack, sack, demobilize, immobilize, incapacitate, disable, deaden, drug, dope, sedate, narcotize, knock out, anaesthetize hypnotize

ADVERBS

15 inactively, motionlessly, statically, at a standstill, at rest, inertly, passively, lifelessly, inanimately

16 impassively, indifferently, apathetically, listlessly, dully, languidly, lethargically, sluggishly, slothfully, indolently, lazily

17 sleepily, somnolently, soporifically, dozily, dopily, drowsily, insensibly, unconsciously

344 Cause

NOUNS

1 cause, causation, causality, formal cause, underlying cause, motivation, initiation, instigation, determinant, creation, authorship, attribution, origination, occasion, invention, derivation, production, propagation, cultivation, generation, evocation, provocation, compulsion, temptation, impulsion, stimulation, inspiration, fomentation, encouragement, force, spark, etiology, etymology

► *126 Originality; 130 Beginning; 386 Compulsion; 483 Motive*

2 source, spring, wellspring, mainspring, wellhead, fountainhead, fountain, fount, *fons et origo* (L), headwaters, mine, quarry, home, birthplace, breeding ground, genitalia, womb, fertile soil, grow bag, growing medium, greenhouse, hothouse, propagator, seedbed, hotbed, incubator, hatchery, cradle, nursery

► *555 Youth; 565 Habitat*

3 rudiment, principle, first principle, element, first step, first thing, hypothesis, raw material, nucleus, germ, spore, seed, sperm, egg, embryo, fetus, larva, chrysalis, pupa, cocoon, bud, stem, stock, rootstock, root, taproot, bulb, tuber, radical, radix, etymon, base, basis, foundation, bedrock, fundamentals, basics, building blocks, beginnings, groundwork, spadework, the nitty-gritty (Inf), nuts and bolts (Inf)

4 contributing factor, contributory cause, contribution, agent, leaven, stimulus, factor, hidden cause, influence, planetary influence, stars, astrological influence, destiny, fate

► *480 Persuasion*

5 reason, reason why, reason behind, idea behind, the why, the why and wherefore, key, explanation, answer, basis, ground, grounds, rationale, idea, *raison d'être* (Fr), occasion, motive, object, purpose, aim, opportunity, excuse, pretext

► *706 Answer*

6 undertaking, enterprise, attempt, action, case, subject, matter, topic, purpose, principle, ideal, worthy cause

7 Prime Mover, God, Father, Maker, the Creator, Divine Creator, the Deity, deity, Supreme Being, *primum mobile* (L), producer, begetter, only begetter, sire, father, mother, parent, ancestor, progenitor, propagator, instigator, originator, author, founder, inventor, motivator, inspirer

► *8 Divinity*

8 contributor, accessory, abettor, helper, aider, fomenter, agent, astrologer, power behind the throne, boys in the back-room

VERBS

9 be the cause of, cause, create, originate, be the author of, author, beget, propagate, father, bring into the world, bring into being, make, produce, invent, derive, cultivate, generate, lie at the bottom of, make or mar, result in, bring about, bring off, bring to pass, make happen, effect, effectuate, have the effect of, lead to, give rise to, occasion, give occasion for

10 awaken, stimulate, tempt, excite, kindle, inspire, encourage, motivate, influence, impel, compel, force, make, foment, provoke, incite, set off, touch off, trigger off, spark off, evoke, bring on, bring out, draw out, induce, precipitate, hasten, elicit, plan, contrive, procure, find means, find the means, engineer, manage

11 inaugurate, initiate, start, begin, launch, instigate, institute, found, lay the foundations, erect, establish, open, broach, set up, set going, set on foot, set afloat, set in motion, sow the seeds of, open the door to, be an open sesame to

12 determine, decide, decide the result, decide the outcome, decide the issue, turn (*or* tip) the scale, have the casting vote, come down on one side or the other, come (*or* climb) down off the fence, help decide, contribute to, have a hand in, have a large part in, have an effect, promote, advance, foster, aid, abet, help

ADJECTIVES

13 causal, causative, etiological, explanatory, creative, inventive, original, aboriginal, primary, primal, primordial, primitive, basic, fundamental, intrinsic, foundational, elemental, elementary, ultimate, radical, effectual, effective, pivotal, determinant, decisive, crucial, central, significant, productive, genetic, generative, germinal, seminal, embryonic, inceptive, rudimentary, formative, initiatory, suggestive, inspiring, inspirational, influential, impelling, compelling, responsible, answerable, blameworthy, at the bottom of, behind the scenes

ADVERBS

14 causally, because, by reason of, causatively, creatively, inventively, originally, primarily, primordially, primitively, basically, fundamentally, intrinsically, ultimately, radically, effectually, effectively, pivotally, decisively, crucially, centrally, significantly, productively, genetically, inceptively, suggestively, inspiringly, inspirationally, influentially, compelling, responsibly, answerably, behind the scenes, in the background

345 Effect

NOUNS

1 **effect**, outcome, logical outcome, counteraction, reaction, action, event, happening, achievement, issue, end, denouement, result, final result, net result, end result, upshot, termination, completion, conclusion, aftermath, aftereffect, culmination, consequence, impact, product, by-product, repercussion, side effect, spin-off, sequel, corollary, inference, derivation, derivative, precipitate, remainder, residue, payoff (Inf)

► *215 Remainder; 260 Ill Health; 340 Action; 744 Record*

2 **visible effect**, handiwork, print, imprint, impress, mark, trace, side effect, fingerprint, footprint, backwash, wake, legacy, inheritance, hereditament, property, belongings, effects, personal effects

3 **growth**, development, expansion, increase, swelling, outgrowth, bud, blossom, florescence, flower, fruit, ear, crop, harvest, produce, gain, profit, malignant growth, lump, carcinoma, cancer

► *213 Increase; 765 Profit*

4 **significance**, import, meaning, purport, sense, tendency, trend, drift

VERBS

5 **show an effect**, affect, have an effect, have a side effect, have consequence, have impact, impact upon, counteract, react, act, happen, achieve, effect, accomplish, issue, end in, result in, eventuate in, terminate, complete, conclude, culminate, produce, precipitate, spin off, pay off

6 **have a visible effect**, print, imprint, impress upon, mark, leave a trace, have a side effect, leave a footprint, leave a fingerprint, inherit

7 **follow from**, follow on from, follow, ensure, supervene, result, result from, spin off from, be the result of, be due to, owe everything to, borrow from, derive from, be derived from, inherit, descend from, have its roots in, originate in (*or* from), come of, come out of, emanate from, emerge, proceed from, issue from, begin from, arise from, spring from, flow from, unfold, evolve, develop, bear the stamp of, depend on, hang upon, turn on, pivot on, centre on, be subject to

8 **grow**, grow from, accrue, develop, develop from, expand, increase, swell, sprout, germinate, bud, blossom, flower, bear fruit, harvest, produce, gain, profit, have a malignant growth, have cancer

9 **take effect**, come into effect, become law, come about, transpire, arise, happen, occur, take place, end up, turn out, fall out, come to pass, work out, come off (Inf), crop up (Inf), pan out (Inf)

ADJECTIVES

10 **caused**, caused by, effected by, effected, reacting to, reacting, resulting from, resulting, resultant, ensuing, following from, following, coming from, due to, owing to, developing from, developed, deriving from, derived, derivative, evolving from, evolved, arising from, descending from, descended, inheriting from, inherited, hereditary, genetic, depending on, dependent on, dependent, attributed to, attributable to, consequent, consequent upon, consequential, contingent, contingent upon, subject to, subsequent, sequential, secondary, second-generation, next-generation, unoriginal, emergent, eventual, born of, out of, by

11 **growing**, developing, expanding, increasing, swelling, budding, blossoming, flowering, fruit-bearing

ADVERBS

12 **with the effect of**, in consequence, as a consequence, consequently, consequentially, derivatively, dependently, attributively, contingently, secondarily, unoriginally, subsequently, eventually, because of, as a result, with the result that, necessarily, naturally, accordingly, of course, and so, and there, ergo, hence, following upon, it follows that

346 Operation

Our doctor would never really operate unless it was necessary. He was just that way. If he didn't need the money, he wouldn't lay a hand on you. Herb Shriner.

NOUNS

1 **operation**, implementation, execution, action, performance, exercise, treatment, work, working, doing, course of action, course, procedure, measure, process, movement, motion, power, force, stress, strain, swing, play

► *338 Vigour; 340 Action; 342 Activity*

2 **joint operation**, joint venture, cooperation, coordination, interaction, takeover, merger, buy-out

3 **business**, office, production, undertaking, venture, matter, cause, affair, task, work, job, position, post

► *356 Creation*

4 **management**, responsibility, effectiveness, effectuality, efficiency, direction, handling, manipulation, manoeuvring, maintenance, service, support

► *395 Influence*

5 **operator**, dealer, trader, handler, speculator, agent, worker, employee, co-worker, skilled worker, driver, mechanic, technician, computer operator, telephone operator, telephonist, conductor, manager, director, administrator, executive

6 **operative**, labourer, hand, unskilled worker, semiskilled worker, machinist

VERBS

7 **be operational**, be in action, operate, work, go, run, act, play, be in play, do, idle, tick over, serve, perform, function, do one's job, come into operation, come into effect, take effect, be in force, do one's thing (Inf), do one's stuff (Inf)

8 **activate**, actuate, bring into action, bring into operation, make operational, make operate, make work, bring into effect, bring into force, bring into play, make happen, effectuate, influence, stimulate, motivate, wind up, plug in, turn on, switch on, flip the switch, press the button, set going, start up, rev up

9 **take action**, use, handle, deal with, manage, manipulate, manoeuvre, wield, process, treat, employ, implement, execute, move, power, drive, cause, act upon, work upon, bear upon, play upon, maintain, service, sustain, support, crew, man, procure, get done

► *349 Use*

ADJECTIVES

10 **operational**, operating, in operation, functional, functioning, going, working, in working order, usable, running, in running order, in play, in use, up and going, up and doing, active, on the active list

11 **workable**, operable, doable, manageable, manipulatable, manoeuvrable, negotiable, practicable, practical, useful, viable

12 **operative**, in force, carrying force, relevant, significant, important, crucial, critical, key, influential, efficacious, efficient, effective, effectual

ADVERBS

13 **operationally**, functionally, actively, in an active manner, usefully, readily, efficaciously, efficiently, with efficiency, effectively, effectually, practically, relevantly, significantly, importantly, crucially, critically, influentially

347 Counteraction

NOUNS

1 **counteraction**, opposing action (*or* cause), polarity, polarization, opposition, prevention, remedy, compensation, contravention, reaction, counter, retroaction, return action, repercussion, kickback, boomerang effect, backlash, backfire, recoil, kick, recalcitrance, conflict, clash, antagonism, antipathy, hostility, resistance, opposing force, countermove, counterintelligence, counteroffensive, counterattack, counterpunch, counterblast, deterrent, defence, defensive measure, inhibitor, preventive, preventative, friction, drag, check, block, hindrance, obstruction, obstacle, barrier, frustration, interference, counterpressure, repression, intolerance, persecution, suppression, restraint, moderation, neutralization, derestriction, deregulation, decriminalization, demagnetization, deactivation, invalidation, cancellation, abrogation, negation, nullification, veto, offset, counterweight, counterpoise, counterbalance, counterirritant, neutralizer, countermeasure, countercharm, counterspell

► *113 Opposition; 331 Impulsion; 378 Obstruction; 384 Defence; 387 Subjection; 399 Veto*

2 **counteracting thing**, headwind, crosscurrent, crossfire, antidote, antitoxin, antivenin, antivenom, cure, remedy, degausser (US), burglar alarm, Mace, defender, protection, prophylactic, contraceptive, condom

VERBS

3 **counteract**, counter, run counter to, obviate, contravene, oppose, cause opposition, polarize, react against, go against, militate against, agitate against, work against, cross, traverse, thwart, hinder, inhibit, prevent, prohibit, drag, block, check, obstruct, not be conducive to, frustrate, interfere with, repress, persecute, suppress, restrain, resist, fight against, defend against, withstand, conflict with, antagonize, clash, react, recoil, backfire, boomerang, countervail, counterbalance, counterpoise, compensate for, kick back, cancel out, cancel, annul, undo, invalidate, negate, nullify, veto, abrogate, decontrol, derestrict, deregulate, decriminalize, deactivate, demagnetize, degauss, neutralize, moderate, cure, find a remedy, recover, get back, retrieve, find a way round

ADJECTIVES

4 **counteracting**, counteractive, counter, oppositional, opposing, contravening, opposed to, polarized, contrary, conflicting, clashing, antipathetic, antagonistic, inimical, hostile, resistant, resisting, recalcitrant, intractable, reactionary, retroactive, reactive, frictional, restraining, frustrating, interfering, repressive, suppressive, intolerant, obstructive, preventive, preventative, antidotal, contraceptive, remedial, corrective, balancing, offsetting, moderating, neutralizing, invalidating, nullifying, compensatory

ADVERBS

5 **counter**, counteractively, contrarily, contrary to, counter to, against, conflictingly, antipathetically, antagonistically, inimically, hostilely, resistantly, resistingly, in opposition to, in contrast, in spite of, despite, although, notwithstanding, intractably, retroactively, reactively, repressively, intolerantly, preventively, antidotally, remedially, correctively

348 Instrumentality

The state is an instrument in the hands of the ruling class for suppressing the resistance of its class enemies. Joseph Stalin.

NOUNS

1 **instrumentality**, agency, operation, occasion, opportunity, responsibility, cause, effect, result, influence, significance, power, weight, effectiveness, efficacy, performance, achievement, functionality, function, service, promotion, advancement, aid, assistance, support, help, midwifery, intermediacy, intermediateness, intervention, interposition, intercession, mediation, interference, pressure, cooperation, subordination, subservience, employment, use, medium, means, mechanical means, electronic means, use of machinery, instrumentation, mechanization, computerization, automation, application, practicality, serviceability, utility, usefulness, handiness

► *237 Usefulness; 334 Power; 342 Activity; 344 Cause; 345 Effect; 352 Means; 392 Help; 663 Obedience; 747 Cooperation; 748 Mediation*

2 **instrument**, means, medium, catalyst, vehicle, agency, influence, mechanism, force, factor, organ, implement, device, tool, machine, apparatus, appliance, equipment, gadget, contrivance, expedient, compromise, contraption (Inf), gizmo (*or* gismo) (US inf)

► *18 Music; 203 Quantity; 275 Time; 281 Timekeeping; 319 Transport; 438 Tool*

3 **assistant**, helper, help, aide, hand, man (*or* girl) Friday, the hand of God, agent, amanuensis, midwife, handmaid, servant, lackey, slave, slave of the lamp, genie of the lamp, intermediary, mediator, go-between, pander, pimp, procurer, puppet, creature, cat's-paw, pawn

► *401 Servant*

VERBS

4 **be an instrument**, be instrumental, function, operate, work, act, perform, do, serve, be useful, work for, lend oneself to, minister to, pander to, pander, pimp, procure, help, assist, aid, support, cooperate, promote, advance,

have a hand in, cause, control, be responsible for, bridge, channel, interpose, intervene, intercede for, intermediate, mediate, compromise, influence, use one's influence, use one's good offices, pressure, pull strings, implement, effect, bring into effect, carry into effect, carry through, carry out, expedite, achieve, save someone's bacon (Inf), pull someone's chestnuts out of the fire (Inf)

5 **find means**, find a way, obtain assistance, use one's connections, network, get by hook or (by) crook

ADJECTIVES

6 **instrumental**, useful, applicable, employable, utilizable, handy, helping, helpful, assisting, cooperative, advancing, promoting, promotive, promotional, aiding, supportive, subordinate, subservient, effective, efficient, effectual, efficacious, performance-oriented

7 **causal**, responsible, instrumental, central, powerful, weighty, significant, telling, influential, mediative, intermediate, intervening, interventional, intercessional, interfering, pressuring, maieutic, Socratic, agential

8 **practical**, applied, servicing, serviceable, general-purpose, working, functioning, functional, operating, operational, operative, hand-operated, manual, mechanical, automatic, automated, electronic, computerized, pushbutton

ADVERBS

9 **instrumentally**, through the instrumentality of, by means of, by virtue of, usefully, handily, helpfully, with the help of, with the aid of, by way of, by, via, thanks to, with, herewith (Lit), through, per, cooperatively, supportively, subserviently, effectively, efficiently, effectually, efficaciously, powerfully, significantly, influentially, by (*or* through) the good offices of, manually, by the hand of, at the hands of, mechanically, automatically, electronically

349 Use

What is the use of a new-born child? Benjamin Franklin.

VERBS

1 **use**, make use of, put to use, utilize, employ, exercise, practise, put into practice, put into operation, take up, adopt, apply try out, try, bring to bear, administer, spend on, give to, devote to, consecrate to, dedicate to, assign to, allot, use up, exhaust, wear out, wear, go through, spend, expend, absorb, consume, waste, squander, handle, finger, touch, tread, follow, beat (a path), work, drive, manipulate, manoeuvre, operate, wield, ply, brandish, treat, overwork, tax, task, fatigue, prepare for use, work on, work up, mould, form

▶ *160 Form; 261 Tiredness; 441 Waste; 492 Touch; 632 Habit; 729 Speech*

2 **frequent**, be a (regular) customer of, shop at, use the services of, avail oneself of

▶ *777 Purchase*

3 **exploit**, exhaust the possibilities of, make the most of, use to the full (*or* fullest), maximize, milk, drain, extract, convert to use, convert, reuse, recycle, reclaim, get mileage out of, get the best out of, get one's money's worth, find useful, put to good use, turn to account, capitalize on, make capital out of, use to advantage, make hay of (US), profit by, take advantage of, make play with, play on, trade on, cash in on, play off, play off against, use people, make a tool (*or* handle) of, make a pawn of, make a cat's paw of, befool, make a fool of, abuse, misuse, run into the ground (Inf), make a patsy of (US inf)

▶ *237 Usefulness; 351 Misuse; 369 Extraction; 700 Deception; 765 Profit*

4 **resort to**, have recourse to, fall back on, rely on, run to, turn to, draw on, impose on, presume on, ask favours of, press into service, enlist in one's service, pick someone's brains

5 **dispose of**, have at one's disposal, control, command, have at one's command, call the tune, do what one likes with, assign, allot, allocate, apportion, requisition, call into play, call in, set in motion, set in action, set going, deploy, motivate, ejoy, have the use of, have the usufruct, possess, consume, expend, use up, go through, make do with, make shift with, get by on, do what one can with, make the most (*or* best) of, spare, have to spare, call the shots (Inf)

▶ *480 Persuasion; 763 Possession; 770 Allocation*

NOUNS

6 **use**, usage, utilization, exploitation, employment, exercise, practice, operation, disposal, enjoyment, usufruct, possession, conversion to use, conversion, application, appliance, deployment, resort, recourse, control, management, mode of use, treatment, handling, normal use, good usage, proper treatment, carefulness, ill-treatment, hard usage, wrong use, misuse, abuse, effect of use, depreciation, wear, wear and tear, dilapidation, exhaustion, consumption, conspicuous consumption, waste, reuse, recycling, reclamation, usefulness, advantage, benefit, good, profit, service, serviceability, practicality, convertibility, applicability, utility, function, purpose, point, avail, functioning, power, long use, wont, habit, demand, need

▶ *135 Requirement; 237 Usefulness; 245 Deterioration; 351 Misuse; 441 Waste; 632 Habit; 665 Carefulness; 763 Possession*

7 **reused product**, recycled substance, blackboard, palimpsest, milk bottles, used car, second-hand clothes, reclaimed land

8 **user**, customer, shopper, client, driver, operator, consumer, owner, exploiter, abuser

▶ *777 Purchase*

ADJECTIVES

9 **used**, put to use, utilized, employed, exercised, in service, in use, occupied, in constant use, in everyday use, in practice, used up, exhausted, consumed, spent, worn, worn out, threadbare, shabby, down-at-heel, dilapidated, second-hand, previously owned, pre-owned, cast-off, reused, recycled, reclaimed, well-used, well-thumbed, dog-eared, well-worn, shopsoiled, beaten, well-trodden, well-known, known, hackneyed, stale, pragmatic, practical, utilitarian, everyday, ordinary, convenient, makeshift, provisional, exploited, subservient, like putty in one's hands, instrumental, hand-me-down (Inf)

▶ *237 Usefulness; 239 Convenience; 245 Deterioration; 455 Knowledge*

10 **usable**, utilizable, employable, exploitable, convertible, applicable, available, at one's service, functioning, working, in operation, useful, profitable, advantageous, consumable, disposable, throwaway, takeaway, reusable, recyclale

▶ *237 Usefulness*

ADVERBS

11 **usefully**, usably, practically, pragmatically, instrumentally, conveniently, profitably, advantageously, beneficially, powerfully, convertibly, reusably

350 Nonuse

ADJECTIVES

1 **unused**, not used, not utilized, not activated, out of order, out of service, inoperational, not available, absent, unusable, unemployable, useless, impractical, lacking application, unapplied, unconverted, nonconvertible, nonreturnable, undisposed of, in hand, in reserve, reserved, saved, stored, spare, extra, unspent, unconsumed, preserved, idle, fallow, untried, unessayed, unexercised, in abeyance, suspended, deferred, pigeonholed, left to rot, wasted, kaput (Inf), on the blink (Inf), on the fritz (US inf)

▶ *98 Absence; 238 Uselessness; 240 Inconvenience; 359 Preservation; 439 Store; 441 Waste*

2 **new**, clean, pure, blank, fresh, unopened, untilled, virgin, unexploited, untapped, undeveloped, untrodden, unbeaten, untouched, unhandled, ungathered, unplucked, unharvested, unreaped

3 **not wanted**, unwanted, not required, unrequired, unneeded, unnecessary, unsold, unbought, remaindered, remaining, leftover, superfluous, redundant, otiose, vacant, free, dispensed with, waived, shunned, underused, unemployed, jobless, out of work, dismissed, discharged, laid off, redundant, superannuated, retired, resting, idle, inactive, fired (Inf), sacked (Inf)

▶ *343 Inactivity; 618 Indifference*

4 **disused**, derelict, abandoned, discarded, cast-off, jettisoned, scrapped, laid up, mothballed, out of commission, decommissioned, frozen, rusting, in limbo, neglected, done with, used up, run down, worn out, on the shelf, retired, out of use, supplanted, superseded, superannuated, discontinued, discredited, obsolete, old-fashioned, antiquated, archaic, junked (Inf), written off (Inf)

▶ *245 Deterioration; 666 Negligence*

VERBS

5 **not use**, not utilize, have no use for, not activate, hold in abeyance, not touch, leave alone, abstain, forbear, hold off, do without, avoid, dispense with, waive, not proceed with, overlook, disregard, ignore, neglect, underuse, underutilize, waste, fail to take advantage of, keep, spare, save, reserve, store, have in reserve, keep in reserve, have on the side, keep in hand, keep stored away, not accept, decline, refuse, reject

▶ *355 Relinquishment; 439 Store; 470 Rejection; 634 Avoidance; 666 Negligence*

6 **stop using**, disuse, turn off, leave off, ban, stop, cease, leave, lay up, put in mothballs, mothball, put out of commission, decommission, freeze, take apart, dismantle, be finished with, have done with, lay aside, put aside, set aside, put on the shelf, put in reserve, store away, stockpile, pack away, hang up, discard, dump, ditch, scrap, jettison, throw away, throw overboard, eject, slough, cast off, doff, take off, give up, relinquish, put in limbo, suspend, withdraw, cancel, abrogate, drop, supersede, replace, substitute, be unused, lie idle, lie fallow, deteriorate, squirrel away (Inf), sock away (US inf), junk (Inf), write off (Inf)

▶ *226 Stopping; 238 Uselessness; 245 Deterioration; 355 Relinquishment; 371 Expulsion; 439 Store; 552 Undress; 762 Substitution; 767 Disposal*

7 **stop work**, quit work, resign, retire, relinquish control, be dismissed, dismiss, discharge, lay off, pay off, make redundant, pension off, put out to grass, hang it up (US inf), hang up one's spikes (US inf), fire (Inf), sack (Inf)

▶ *371 Expulsion; 576 Work; 605 Resignation*

NOUNS

8 **nonuse**, lack of use, abeyance, suspension, abstinence, forbearance, avoidance, neglect, negligence, underuse, underutilization, superfluity, unemployment, redundancy, reserve, store, storage

▶ *439 Store; 470 Rejection; 634 Avoidance; 666 Negligence*

9 **newness**, cleanness, blankness, purity, freshness, virginity, mint condition

▶ *126 Originality; 295 Newness; 555 Youth*

10 **disuse**, desuetude, dereliction, abandonment, rejection, limbo, inactivity, idleness, disposal, discarding, dumping, scrapping, dismissal, discharge, resignation, retirement, superannuation, obsolescence, obsoleteness

▶ *245 Deterioration; 371 Expulsion; 605 Resignation*

11 **unused thing**, spare, extra, store, savings, stockpile, remainder, remains, reject, castoffs, discard

▶ *215 Remainder; 439 Store; 470 Rejection*

ADVERBS

12 **out of use**, idly, out of operation, aside, unusably, uselessly, impractically, superfluously, redundantly, obsolescently, obsoletely

13 **newly**, cleanly, blankly, purely, freshly

351 Misuse

The greater the power, the more dangerous the abuse. Edmund Burke.

VERBS

1 **misuse**, abuse, use wrongly, misemploy, put to bad use, misdirect, divert, misappropriate, expropriate, embezzle, defraud, violate, desecrate, defile, take in vain, profane, prostitute, pervert, distort, abuse the environment, pollute, spoil, make unclean, ill-use, ill-treat, maltreat, mistreat, molest, do violence to, harm, injure, manhandle, beat, batter, knock about, attack, force, strain, take advantage of, exploit, oppress, overwork, overtask, overtax, fatigue, work hard, wear out, impair, damage, misuse power, abuse power, misgovern, misrule, mismanage, maladminister, mishandle, bungle, misuse words, commit a malapropism, squander (away), fritter (away), waste, misapply, misjudge, overreact, use a sledge-

hammer to crack a nut, waste effort, overuse, overgraze, overfish, screw up (Inf), fuck up (Inf)

► *234 Distortion; 236 Worthlessness; 238 Uselessness; 245 Deterioration; 258 Dirtiness; 261 Tiredness; 349 Use; 380 Violence; 441 Waste; 486 Unskilfulness; 647 Severity; 678 Scornfulness; 774 Stealing*

NOUNS

2 **misuse**, abuse, wrong use, misemployment, bad use, manipulation, misdirection, diversion, misappropriation, embezzlement, peculation, fraud, violation, desecration, profanation, defilement, impiety, prostitution, perversion, distortion, environmental abuse, pollution, mistreatment, molestation, maltreatment, ill-treatment, ill-use, violence, force, outrage, assault, battery, injury, harm, evil, exploitation, power abuse, oppression, misrule, mismanagement, maladministration, malpractice, mishandling, bungling, misuse of words, malapropism, solecism, barbarism, overuse, overgrazing, overcropping, overfishing, extravagance, waste, misapplication, misjudgment

► *234 Distortion; 236 Worthlessness; 245 Deterioration; 258 Dirtiness; 274 Error; 349 Use; 380 Violence; 441 Waste; 486 Unskilfulness; 647 Severity; 678 Scornfulness; 774 Stealing*

3 **abuser**, child abuser, wife-beater, violent person, polluter, desecrator, dishonest politician, loudmouth (Inf), thug (Inf)

ADJECTIVES

4 **misused**, abused, misemployed, misdirected, diverted, misappropriated, violated, desecrated, defiled, perverted, distorted, polluted, spoilt, unclean, ill-treated, maltreated, beaten, battered, exploited, used, oppressed, mishandled, bungled, wasted

► *234 Distortion; 258 Dirtiness; 349 Use; 380 Violence; 441 Waste*

5 **abusive**, violent, harmful, injurious, forceful, offensive, damaging, evil, exploitative, oppressive, fraudulent, extravagant, wasteful, barbarous, solecistic, outrageous, impious, profane

ADVERBS

6 **abusively**, badly, wrongly, evilly, profanely, impiously, outrageously, pervertedly, distortedly, forcefully, offensively, violently, harmfully, injuriously, exploitatively, oppressively, fraudulently, extravagantly, wastefully, barbarously, solecistically

352 Means

The end justifies the means. Proverb.

NOUNS

1 **means**, way, manner, mode, method, methods, measure, measures, steps, course, ways and means, methods and resources, the wherewithal, the basics, power, capacity, ability, capability, strong hand, trumps, trump, trump card, ace, tool, instrument, vehicle, medium, agency, conveniences, facilities, appliances, tools, tools of the trade, tricks of the trade, bag of tricks, technology, new technology, high technology, high tech, knowledge, technique, knack, skill, process, approach, resort, recourse, expedient, device, contrivance, makeshift, ad hoc measure, substitute, let-out, means of escape, remedy, cure, desperate remedy, last resort, last hope, last gasp, last throw, alternative, choice, freedom of choice, know-how (Inf), lost shot (Inf)

► *107 Chance; 317 Way; 334 Power; 389 Escape; 394 Remedy; 438 Tool; 455 Knowledge; 469 Selection; 484 Plan; 485 Skill*

2 **supplies**, basic supplies, vital supplies, provisions, stock, material, materials, working materials, equipment, machinery, munitions, ammunition, resources, natural resources, raw material, nuts and bolts (Inf)

► *435 Materials; 436 Provisions; 438 Tool*

3 **human resources**, labour resources, pool of labour, workforce, manpower, personnel, staff, workers

► *578 Worker*

4 **financial resources**, finances, funds, wealth, money, substance, liquidity, cash, cash flow, capital, start-up capital, investment capital, working capital, assets, stock-in-trade, premises, property, stocks and shares, stocks and bonds, investments, investment portfolio, revenue, income, receipts, credits, credit, overdraft, borrowing capacity, credit limit, line of credit, credit rating, credit-worthiness, backing, support, sponsorship, subsidy, readies (Inf)

► *413 Support; 440 Possessions; 780 Money; 781 Wealth; 783 Credit; 788 Receipt*

5 **reserves**, reserve, store, something in reserve, backup, emergency funds, nest egg, standby, card up one's sleeve, two strings to one's bow, safeguard

► *252 Safety; 439 Store*

VERBS

6 **find means**, find a way, develop a method, provide the wherewithal, enable, facilitate, secure the basics, find, supply, furnish, provide, equip, buy supplies, fit out, make ready, prepare, hire personnel, staff, finance, fund, raise money, promote, sponsor, float, subsidize, have the means, be able, plan, contrive, think laterally, get by any means, beg, borrow, or steal, get by hook or (by) crook, get by fair means or foul, acquire

► *243 Preparation; 334 Power; 436 Provisions; 484 Plan; 765 Profit*

ADVERBS

7 **by means of**, with, wherewith, by, by use of, using, through, with the aid of, by resorting to, with recourse to, by dint of, by hook or (by) crook, by fair means or foul, somehow

353 Attempt

If at first you don't succeed, try, try again. Then quit. No use being a damn fool about it. W. C. Fields.

VERBS

1 **attempt**, try, essay, seek, seek to, aim, aim to, make it one's aim, bid, offer, make a bid, make an attempt, make shift to, do something about, make the effort, not just stand there, not let the grass grow under one's feet, try one's hand at, have a go, give it a try, give it a go, give it

a whirl (Inf), have a shot at (Inf), have a crack at (Inf), have a stab at (Inf)

▶ *482 Intention; 705 Question*

2 try hard, endeavour, struggle, strive, give it one's all, try and try again, do one's best, double (*or* redouble) one's efforts, go all out, exert oneself, work, labour, pull hard, push hard, strain, sweat, do one's damnedest (Inf), go flat out (Inf), give it one's best shot (Inf), go for broke (Inf)

▶ *576 Work; 638 Resolution*

3 tackle, take on, undertake, get down to, get to grips with, take the bull by the horns, take a chance, try one's luck, tempt providence, tempt fate, venture, speculate, gamble, attempt too much, bite off more than one can chew, have too much on one's plate, die in the attempt, chance one's arm (Inf)

▶ *107 Chance; 247 Failure; 354 Undertaking*

4 test, experiment, put out a feeler, dip a toe in the water, hold a finger to the wind, make a trial of, launch a trial balloon, launch a balloon d'essai, fly a kite

▶ *448 Experiment; 616 Caution*

NOUNS

5 attempt, try, essay, bid, move, step, gambit, endeavour, effort, struggle, strain, tackle, good try, stout try, brave try, valiant effort, best one can do, best effort, determined effort, set, dead set, half-hearted attempt, catch-as-catch-can (US), first attempt, debut, final attempt, last try, swan song, last bid, last challenge, go (Inf), run (Inf), leap (Inf), shot (Inf), stab (Inf), jab (Inf), whirl (Inf), crack (Inf), whack (Inf), bash (Inf), best shot (Inf), one's level best (Inf), first go (Inf), last shot (Inf)

▶ *130 Beginning; 131 End; 638 Resolution*

6 venture, adventure, quest, speculation, trial (run), experiment, operation, exercise, undertaking, seeking, aiming, aim, goal, objective, intention, worthy aim, high endeavour, perfectionism

▶ *230 Perfection; 354 Undertaking; 448 Experiment; 482 Intention*

7 attempter, trier, essayer, bidder, volunteer, adventurer, adventurous person, tackler, tester, experimenter, researcher, searcher, quester, inquirer, striver, struggler, contestant, contender, fighter, challenger, idealist, perfectionist, lobbyist, activist, reformer, undertaker (US), contractor, entrepreneur

▶ *230 Perfection; 244 Improvement; 705 Question*

ADJECTIVES

8 attempting, trying, essaying, seeking, striving, doing one's best, game, nothing daunted, daring, venturesome, ambitious, enterprising

9 tentative, experimental, trial, pilot, testing, searching, inquiring, probationary, on approval, on appro(Inf)

▶ *636 Willingness; 638 Resolution*

ADVERBS

10 ambitiously, out for (*or* to), as far as one can, with all one's might, valiantly, adventurously, experimentally, tentatively, speculatively, on the make (Inf)

INTERJECTIONS

11 here goes!, give it a (*or* your best) shot!, have a go!, go for it!, nothing ventured, nothing gained!

354 Undertaking

The love of life is necessary to the vigorous prosecution of any undertaking. Samuel Johnson.

VERBS

1 undertake, engage in, devote oneself to, apply oneself to, address oneself to, get one's mind into, take up, go in for, venture on, do, tackle, confront, try, attempt, endeavour, go about, take in hand, turn (*or* put *or* set) one's hand to, set forward, set going, start, launch, initiate, begin, set about, embark on, launch into, plunge into, proceed to, fall to, set to, buckle to, get one's head down, put one's best foot forward, set one's shoulder to the wheel, set one's hand to the plough, get one's teeth into, come to grips with, take the bull by the horns, grasp the nettle, assume, take on, assume (*or* accept) responsibility, take charge of, direct, manage, execute, carry out, set up shop, have fish to fry, have irons in the fire, busy oneself, shoulder, take on one's shoulders, take upon oneself, assume an obligation, volunteer, agree, promise, contract, pledge, vow, engage, commit oneself, sign up, get involved, let oneself in for, take on too much, bite off more than one can chew, have too much on one's plate, have too many irons in the fire, show enterprise, pioneer, venture, adventure, dare, challenge, apprentice oneself, prepare oneself, take a crack at (Inf), take a shot at (Inf), take a whack at (Inf), get down (US inf)

▶ *130 Beginning; 243 Preparation; 254 Danger; 340 Action; 342 Activity; 353 Attempt; 579 Management; 613 Courage; 636 Willingness; 756 Promise; 810 Duty*

NOUNS

2 undertaking, engagement, venture, affair, business, occupation, matter in hand, job, task, assignment, project, enterprise, campaign, mission, self-imposed task, labour of love, mission, pilgrimage, voluntary work, operation, exercise, programme, plan, design, planned event, big undertaking, a lot to ask, hard task, emprise (Lit), quest, adventure, search, inquiry, speculation, gambling, try, attempt, struggle, effort, endeavour, work, feat, tall order (Inf)

▶ *264 Difficulty; 340 Action; 353 Attempt; 484 Plan; 576 Work; 636 Willingness; 705 Question*

3 contract, agreement, signed agreement, gentlemen's (*or* gentleman's) agreement, promise, pledge, vow, assurance, guarantee, obligation, engagement, commitment

▶ *756 Promise*

4 volunteer, adventurer, speculator, innovator, pioneer, hard worker, workaholic, entrepreneur, enterprising businessman (*or* businesswoman), go-getter (Inf)

▶ *576 Work*

ADJECTIVES

5 undertaken, done, executed, incurred, assumed, self-imposed, assigned, promised, with obligations, contractual

6 enterprising, resourceful, innovative, pioneering, adventurous, venturesome, speculative, daring, courageous, go-ahead, progressive, opportunist, alive to opportunity, with an eye to the main chance, ambitious, responsible, managerial, taking on responsibility, shouldering responsibility

▶ *295 Newness; 613 Courage; 617 Desire*

7 **overambitious**, rash, overloaded, overextended, snowed under (Inf)

▶ *615 Rashness*

ADVERBS

8 **responsibly**, under obligation, contractually, as agreed

9 **enterprisingly**, innovatively, adventurously, ambitiously, progressively, courageously, daringly, as never before, overambitiously, rashly

355 Relinquishment

If you resolve to give up smoking, drinking and loving, you don't actually live longer; it just seems longer. Clement Freud.

VERBS

1 **relinquish**, give up, surrender, drop, loosen one's grip, quit one's hold, unclench, let go of, release, loose, resign, abdicate, back down, lower one's sights, yield, waive, forgo, cede, transfer, hand over, assign, forfeit, lose, renounce, swear off, abnegate, recant, change one's mind, tergiversate, not proceed with, drop the idea, give up the idea, forget it, drop it, wean oneself, disaccustom, forswear, deny oneself, abstain, avoid, shed, slough, slough off, cast off, divest, doff, repudiate, discard, get rid of, tear up, shred, put through the shredder, jettison, throw away, scrap, stop using, lose interest, have other (*or* bigger) fish to fry, leave hold of (Inf), cough up (Inf), kick (the habit) (Inf), go cold turkey (Inf), junk (Inf), write off (Inf)

▶ *350 Nonuse; 463 Forgetfulness; 479 Equivocation; 487 Unaccustomedness; 552 Undress; 618 Indifference; 623 Humility; 634 Avoidance; 766 Loss; 767 Disposal; 775 Giving Back*

2 **withdraw**, decline, remove one's name from, scratch, retire, abdicate, resign, stand down, drop out, throw in the sponge (*or* towel), throw up the game, throw in one's hand, give up, give in, submit, go, depart, leave, quit, vacate, evacuate, move out, abandon, forsake, run out on, leave stranded, desert, forsake one's duties, quit one's post, go absent without leave, go AWOL, play truant, strike, down tools, stop, cease, come out, walk out, secede, divide, schismatize, change allegiances, change sides, go over, sell out, apostatize, break off a relationship, break (it) off, end an affair, go back on one's word, jilt, abandon discussion, stop negotiations, waste no more time, pass on to the next, postpone, put off, shelve, table, invalidate, annul, void, cancel, abolish, abrogate, seek seclusion, turn one's back on the world, jack (*or* pack) it in (Inf), cut out (US inf), cop out (Inf), dump (Inf), chuck (Inf), play hooky (US inf), rat (Inf), throw over (Inf), ditch (Inf)

▶ *98 Absence; 294 Lateness; 313 Departure; 479 Equivocation; 605 Resignation*

NOUNS

3 **relinquishment**, giving up, surrender, resignation, retirement, abdication, yielding, waiving, waiver, forgoing, transfer, handing over, cession, forfeit, abnegation, renunciation, recantation, abandonment, desertion, going, departure, leaving, evacuation, dereliction, defection, absence, truancy, withdrawal, secession, schism, strike, walkout, lack of commitment, abstinence, avoidance, disuse, nonuse, discontinuance, desuetude, cancellation, abolition, annulment, abrogation, reclusion, seclusion, hooky (US inf), cop-out (Inf)

▶ *98 Absence; 226 Stopping; 313 Departure; 350 Nonuse; 605 Resignation; 634 Avoidance; 655 Unsociability; 767 Disposal; 775 Giving Back*

4 **deserter**, runaway, jilter, truant, dropout, hermit, castaway, striker, retiree (US), abdicator, abdicating monarch, abolitionist, abstainer, abnegator, recanter, yielder, defector, turncoat, cop-out (Inf), rat (Inf)

ADJECTIVES

5 **relinquished**, surrendered, dropped, waived, forgone, scrapped, jettisoned, cast-off, castaway, forsaken, apostatical, abandoned, derelict, deserted, stranded, jilted, cancelled, void, invalid, discontinued, abolished

▶ *767 Disposal*

6 **apathetic**, indifferent, noncommittal, resigned, retired, withdrawn, aloof, absent, distant

▶ *343 Inactivity; 605 Resignation; 618 Indifference*

7 **on hold**, on a back burner, in abeyance, off the agenda, on the shelf, on the scrap heap, forsakenly, invalidly

8 **apathetically**, indifferently, resignedly, absently, distantly, apostatically, delinquently

INTERJECTIONS

9 **forget it!**, drop it!, let go!, quit!, all out!

356 Creation

The art of creation
is older than the art of killing. Andrei Voznesensky.

NOUNS

1 **production**, making, producing, preparation, creation, invention, innovation, origination, original work, originality, creative impulse, creative urge, inspiration, discovery, doing, productivity, productiveness, output, throughput, turnout, effort, endeavour, attempt, try, undertaking, project, enterprise, performance, execution, accomplishment, achievement, art, painting, sculpture, writing, composition, musicianship, musical composition, authorship, literary composition, literary work, assembly of materials, cogitation, conception, formulation, concoction, brewing, fermenting, moulding, forming, shaping, casting, technology, workmanship, skill, handiwork, craftsmanship, design, planning, organization, structure

▶ *295 Newness; 340 Action; 353 Attempt; 485 Skill; 562 Fertility; 576 Work*

2 **manufacture**, manufacturing, making, fabrication, construction, building, engineering, civil engineering, tectonics, architecture, erection, setting up, establishment, business, industry, heavy industry, light industry, sunrise industry, processing, process, treatment, machining, assembly, machine, machinery, plant, conveyor belt, assembly line, production line, workshop, factory, work-

shop practice, technology, low technology, intermediate technology, ecodevelopment, industrialization, increased output, mass production, automation, high technology, new technology, computerization, robotics, development, growth, agriculture, growing, market gardening, farming, factory farming, stockbreeding, animal husbandry

► *20 Architecture; 38 Engineering; 43 Agriculture; 366 Raising; 561 Reproduction; 577 Workshop*

3 **product**, manufacture, artefact (*or* artifact), article, finished article, item, manufactured item, thing, object, creation, creature, result, consequence, effect, outcome, issue, output, turnout, extract, essence, decoction, concoction, confection, compound, end-product, by-product, spin-off, offshoot, waste product, waste, slag, leavings, fallout

4 **mental product**, brainchild, brainwave, figment, figment of the imagination, fiction, idea

5 **work of art**, production, performance, work, *oeuvre* (Fr), composition, piece, musical composition, opus, sonata, symphony, concerto, ballet, opera, literary composition, literary work, work of literature, piece of writing, book, pamphlet, article, poem, work of fiction, story, short story, short novel, novella, novel, full-length novel, theatrical production, play, sketch, film, movie, short, feature film, B-feature, B-movie, travelogue

6 **great work**, magnum opus, *chef-d'oeuvre* (Fr), masterwork, masterpiece, crowning achievement

► *17 Literature; 18 Music; 19 Painting and Sculpture; 21 Drama; 22 Dancing; 345 Effect; 576 Work*

7 **produce**, goods and services, gross national product (GNP), gross domestic product (GDP), goods, merchandise, wares, commodity, pottery, earthenware, porcelain, china, stoneware, ironware, kitchenware, hardware, ironmongery, brown goods, fabric, cloth, textile, drapery, white goods, hosiery, animal products, meat, dairy products, milk, butter, cheese, cream, yoghurt, eggs, skin, fur, leather, hide, plant products, fruit, flower, blossom, berry, stalk, leaf, heart, head, crop, harvest, vintage, yield, interest, return, increase, dividend, gain, profit, revenue, income, offspring, baby, child, young, egg, seed, spawn, young creature

► *24 Ceramics; 25 Cookery; 42 Fabrics and Dyeing; 213 Increase; 555 Youth; 561 Reproduction; 765 Profit; 785 Payment*

8 **construction**, structure, building, edifice, piece of architecture, pile, dome, tower, high-rise building, skyscraper, office block, block of flats, apartment building, church, chapel, cathedral, temple, mausoleum, tomb, cenotaph, monument, ancient monument, pyramid, ziggurat, acropolis, Colosseum, Coliseum, theatre, hospital, college, school, hall, habitation, house, great house, mansion, stately home, palace, castle, fort, fortress, folly, stonework, brickwork, bricks and mortar, timbering, half-timbering, wattle and daub

► *7 Religion; 384 Defence; 403 Structure; 565 Habitat; 583 Burial*

9 **producer**, maker, creator, God, Nature, Mother Nature, originator, inventor, discoverer, prime mover, instigator, innovator, founder, founding father, founder member, establisher, begetter, onlie begetter (Lit), father, mother, parent, creative artist, author, writer, poet, playwright, dramatist, artist, painter, sculptor, composer, musician, director, stage director, film director, television director, play producer, film producer, programme-maker, radio producer, television producer, designer, planner, developer, builder, constructor, contractor, architect, engineer, fabricator, manufacturer, industrialist, entrepreneur, business executive, businessman, businesswoman, worker, labourer, artificer, artisan, craftsman, craftswoman, craftworker, planter, grower, cultivator, gardener, plantsman, plantswoman, farmer, stockbreeder, sheep farmer, rancher (US), grazier (Aus), miner, prospector

► *43 Agriculture; 130 Beginning; 344 Cause; 483 Motive; 561 Reproduction; 578 Worker; 579 Management*

VERBS

10 **produce**, make, create, originate, invent, innovate, fabricate, engineer, manufacture, output, mine, quarry, extract, exploit, process, industrialize, develop industrially, mechanize, automate, computerize, mass-produce, synthesize, blend, concoct, combine, put together, cobble together, make up, assemble, build, construct, erect, set up, establish, found, institute, constitute, organize, structure, arrange, stage, direct, bring about, set in motion, cause, beget, bear, give birth to, spawn, bring into the world, bring into being, bring into existence, generate, engender, breed, hatch, sow, grow, farm, cultivate, raise, rear, bring up, educate, train, develop, evolve, cogitate, cogitate upon, think of, imagine, think up, conceive, dream up, plan, devise, formulate, do, perform, achieve, accomplish, implement, carry out, execute, effect, yield, supply, provide, furnish, give, present, bring out, take out, show, reveal, unfold, uncover, find, discover, write, author (US), compose, paint, shape, form, mould, fashion, frame, design, spin, weave, knit, sew, run up, carve, chisel, sculpt, forge, cast, coin, mint, mill, machine, prefabricate, turn out, knock out, churn out, multiply, reproduce, propagate, make by hand, craft, custom-build, customize, bash out (Inf), get up (Inf)

► *17 Literature; 18 Music; 19 Painting and Sculpture; 344 Cause; 403 Structure; 409 Arrangement; 436 Provisions; 443 Thought; 477 Imagination; 561 Reproduction; 768 Giving*

ADJECTIVES

11 **productive**, creative, innovative, inventive, original, formative, structural, constructive, architectonic, manufacturing, industrial, industrialized, developed, mechanized, automated, high-technology, computerized, robotic, postindustrial, nonindustrial, underdeveloped, developing, low-technology, agricultural, fertile, fruitful, fecund, prolific, rich, profitable, remunerative, lucrative, paying, high-yielding, interest-bearing, worthwhile, high-tech (Inf), low-tech (Inf)

► *213 Increase; 219 Excess; 235 Worth; 436 Provisions; 562 Fertility; 765 Profit*

12 **produced**, created, made, man-made, synthetic, artificial, manufactured, processed, ready-made, machine-made, untouched by human hand, mass-produced, factory-made, handmade, done by hand, home-made, homespun, tailor-made, architect-designed, craftsman-built, custom-built, invented, thought of, dreamed-up, imagined, devised, worked out, discovered, begotten, born, bred, hatched, sown, grown, raised, reared, brought up, educated

ADVERBS

13 **productively**, creatively, innovatively, inventively, fruitfully, prolifically, profitably, remuneratively

357 Destruction

It takes twenty years or more of peace to make a man, it takes only twenty seconds of war to destroy him. Baudouin I.

Carthage must be destroyed. Cato the Elder.

NOUNS

1 **destruction**, unmaking, undoing, nullification, annihilation, obliteration, deletion, erasure, liquidation, elimination, extermination, extinction, abolition, abolishment, repression, suppression, silencing, stifling, smothering, suffocation, threatening, insidiousness, subversion, overturning, overthrow, prostration, precipitation

▶ *94 Nonexistence; 251 Restraint; 358 Obliteration*

2 **destroying**, demolition, demolishment, flattening, razing, knocking down, decomposition, dissolution, breaking up, disruption, shattering, crushing, grinding, pulverization, disintegration, shredding, incineration, defoliation, eradication, uprooting, deracination, extirpation, decimation, slaughter, massacre, genocide, mass murder, mass destruction, killing, murder, hatchet job (Inf)

▶ *375 Disintegration; 382 Killing; 427 Powderiness; 493 Heat*

3 **destructiveness**, wanton destructiveness, wanton destruction, vandalism, sabotage, arson, fire-raising, iconoclasm

4 **ruin**, downfall, someone's undoing, crushing blow, knockout blow, knockout punch, fatal blow, ruination, perdition, disaster, calamity, catastrophe, act of God, collapse, debacle, upheaval, cataclysm, breakdown, irretrievable breakdown, crack-up, failure, utter failure, meltdown, China syndrome, breakup, crash, smash, smash-up, write-off, wreck, shipwreck, sinking, wreckage, ruins, ancient ruins, dilapidation, wrack, rack and ruin, loss, total loss, Waterloo, bankruptcy, insolvency, road to ruin, slippery slope, the beginning of the end, *coup de grâce* (Fr), end, end of the world, apocalypse, doom, doomsday, crack of doom, knell, death knell

▶ *131 End; 247 Failure; 367 Lowering; 372 Separation; 766 Loss*

5 **havoc**, damage, turmoil, confusion, mayhem, chaos, devastation, laying waste, raid, raiding, despoiling, spoliation, pillage, looting, rape, rapine, depredation, explosion, blitz, nuclear blast, nuclear winter, desolation, scene of desolation, scene of destruction, disaster area, wasteland, desert, desert waste, wilderness, scorched earth, shambles, carnage, slaughterhouse, holocaust, hecatomb

▶ *408 Disorder*

6 **destroyer**, wrecker, spoiler, despoiler, raider, ravager, pillager, looter, arsonist, pyromaniac, demolisher, leveller, Luddite, iconoclast, destructionist, annihilationist, nihilist, anarchist, revolutionary, revolutionist, saboteur, vandal, defacer, eraser, rubber, extinguisher, liquidator, exterminator, killer, murderer, assassin, executioner, hangman, barbarian, Hun, Vandal, Viking, berserker, death, the grim reaper, the angel of death, time, the scythe of time, time's scythe, the hand of time, hatchet man (Inf), hit man (Inf)

▶ *382 Killing; 582 Death; 588 Anarchy*

7 **agent of destruction**, plague, pestilence, disease, bubonic plague, the Black Death, cholera, AIDS, locusts, moth, woodworm, dry rot, wet rot, rust, mildew, blight, potato blight, wear, wear and tear, erosion, decay, corrosion, corrosive, acid, poison, pesticide, defoliant, Agent Orange, radiation, nuclear fallout, natural disaster, landslide, landslip, avalanche, earthquake, fire, flood, inundation, storm, the Four Horsemen of the Apocalypse (conquest, war, famine, disease), Fury, avenging angel, weapon, dagger, sword, bow and arrow, crossbow, longbow, slingshot, catapult, gun, cannon, machine gun, explosive, gunpowder, dynamite, blasting powder, nitroglycerine, TNT, Semtex™, bomb, nuclear missile, nuclear warhead, nuclear weapon, blockbuster, bulldozer, battering ram, juggernaut

▶ *245 Deterioration; 260 Ill Health; 587 Weapon*

VERBS

8 **destroy**, unmake, undo, bankrupt, destruct, annihilate, liquidate, terminate, end, put an end to, exterminate, put down, put out of his (*or* her) misery, put away, do away with, make away with, get rid of, dispose of, dispatch, decimate, massacre, slaughter, kill, murder, quell, extinguish, quench, put out, snuff out, blow out, blow away, stamp out, extirpate, eradicate, deracinate, uproot, root up, abolish, axe, invalidate, tear up, revoke, abrogate, cancel, obliterate, efface, expunge, wipe out, wipe off the map, erase, rub out, blot out, strike out, delete, scratch out, nullify, annul, quash, squash, suppress, repress, sit on, keep down, clamp down on, silence, muzzle, muffle, blanket, stifle, smother, suffocate, strangle, drown, submerge, overturn, subvert, overthrow, throw out, precipitate, scatter, disperse, dispel, dissipate, dissolve, vaporize, evaporate, lose, sacrifice, neutralize, counteract, negate, zap (Inf), do in (Inf), do for (Inf), chuck out (Inf)

▶ *94 Nonexistence; 347 Counteraction; 358 Obliteration; 377 Dispersal; 382 Killing; 708 Negation*

9 **demolish**, dismantle, take apart, take to pieces, take to bits, tear apart, rend asunder, tear (*or* rend) to pieces, tear (*or* rend) to bits, tear to rags, tear to shreds, tear limb from limb, pick (*or* pluck) to pieces, pull to pieces, pull apart, unbuild, break, break down, break up, blow away, carry away, blow down, knock down, fell, cut down, pull down, tear down, throw down, bulldoze, steamroller, flatten, level, raze, raze to the ground, lay in the dust, mow down, cut to pieces, butcher, slaughter, knock over, topple, kick over, overturn, upset, overthrow, subvert, cause the downfall of, turn upside down, invert, sap (*or* undermine) the foundations of, mine, blast, explode, dynamite, blow up, blow to bits, blow to smithereens, blow to kingdom come, bombard, bomb, blitz, shatter,

smash, smash up, shiver, smash to matchwood, smash to smithereens, wreck, pulp, crush, crush to pieces, grind, grind (*or* turn) to dust, grind to powder, pulverize, shred, grind into the dust, trample underfoot, grind underfoot, grind under one's heel, atomize, make mincemeat of, shake to pieces, batter, beat down, ram

▶ *187 Horizontality; 372 Separation; 375 Disintegration; 380 Violence; 427 Powderiness*

10 lay waste, devastate, waste, desolate, defoliate, deforest, denude, strip, strip bare, gut, damage, vandalize, run amok, bring destruction, deal destruction, wreak havoc, cause a shambles, lay waste with fire and the sword, lay in ruins, lay in ashes, make a wilderness and call it peace, despoil, depopulate, put to the sword, raid, sack, ransack, pillage, rape, ravage, violate, loot, plunder

11 ruin, bring to ruin, spoil, mar, bedevil, play hell with, play merry hell with, play the devil with, wreck, shipwreck, sink, scupper, torpedo, shoot down in flames, mutilate, deface, knock out, knock flat, floor, flatten, make short work of, make mincemeat of, defeat comprehensively, trounce, hamstring, hobble, nip in the bud, abort, cut off, cut short, KO (Inf), put the kibosh on (Inf), put the skids under (Inf), dish (Inf), spifflicate (Inf), clobber (Inf)

▶ *247 Failure*

12 consume, eat up, gobble up, devour, swallow up, engulf, envelop, drown, swamp, overwhelm, burn, burn up, incinerate, waste, squander, throw away, fling to the four winds, run through, play ducks and drakes with, throw to the dogs, cast pearls before swine

▶ *349 Use; 441 Waste; 681 Extravagance*

13 be destroyed, self-destruct, go to waste, perish, go down, go under, plunge, sink, sink without trace, disappear, fail, founder, go on the rocks, disintegrate, split, break up, go to pieces, crumple up, turn to dust, end, come to an end, come to a sticky end, have had it, fall, fall into ruin, go to rack and ruin, tumble, tumble down, crumble, crumble away, crumble to dust, go to the dogs, go to the wall, go downhill, go downhill fast, go to pot, bite the dust, go to blazes (Inf), go to hell (Inf), have bought it (Inf), have bought the farm (Inf), go west (Inf)

▶ *131 End; 245 Deterioration; 247 Failure; 375 Disintegration; 526 Disappearance*

ADJECTIVES

14 destructive, destroying, devastating, ruinous, internecine, cutthroat, annihilating, consuming, all-consuming, raging, rampaging, suicidal, sacrificial, mortal, life-threatening, deadly, lethal, fatal, disastrous, catastrophic, apocalyptic, cataclysmic, overwhelming, subversive, revolutionary, anarchistic, incendiary, mischievous, threatening, insidious, pernicious, noxious, harmful, injurious, baneful, negative, adverse, unfavourable

▶ *678 Scornfulness*

15 destroyed, wiped out, ruined, devastated, undone, fallen, crushed, ground, pulverized, pulped, shredded, broken up, broken, disintegrated, shattered, wrecked, torpedoed, sunk, done for, dished, in tatters, in ruins, crumbling, dilapidated, falling down, falling apart, tumbledown, coming apart at the seams, failing, not long for this world, sinking fast, doomed, for the chop, heading for the scrap heap, marked out for destruction, due for demolition, on the way to the breaker's yard, bankrupt, bust, in liquidation, in receivership, in the hands of the receiver, down-and-out, up the chute (Inf), buggered (Inf), fucked (Inf), kaput (Inf)

▶ *94 Nonexistence*

ADVERBS

16 destructively, fatally, lethally, ruinously, devastatingly, catastrophically, disastrously, with crushing effect, with a sledge hammer, with one blow, at a stroke, root and branch

358 Obliteration

It became necessary to destroy the town of Ben Tre to save it.
Anonymous US Major, in Vietnam.

VERBS

1 obliterate, erase, expunge, eliminate, delete, dele, take out, remove, efface, deface, write over, print over, overprint, paint over, make illegible, scribble out, cover up, cover, conceal, remove any trace, scratch out, scratch through, score out, score through, strike out, strike through, cross out, cross through, rule out, rub out, rub off, sponge off, sponge out, wash out, wash off, wipe out, wipe off, blot, blot out, black out, white out, brush off, cancel, annul, abrogate, edit out, blue-pencil, censor, take out of print, leave on the cutting-room floor, destroy, eradicate, extirpate, annihilate, demolish, raze, burn to the ground, liquidate, exterminate, purge, leave no survivors, leave no trace, vaporize, wipe off the map, bury, force into oblivion, submerge, sink without trace, drown, silence, scrub (Inf)

▶ *256 Cleanness; 357 Destruction; 365 Friction; 382 Killing; 506 Silence; 526 Disappearance; 550 Covering; 583 Burial; 736 Concealment*

2 forget, have a mental block, block out, repress, suppress

▶ *462 Memory; 463 Forgetfulness*

NOUNS

3 obliteration, erasure, erasing, expunction, elimination, deletion, dele, removal, effacement, defacement, writing over, printing over, overprinting, painting over, illegibility, covering up, cover, concealment, crossing out, rubbing out, cancellation, annulment, abrogation, cessation, amnesty, editorial change, editing, blue pencil, censorship, destruction, eradication, extirpation, annihilation, demolition, liquidation, extermination, purge, interment, burial, oblivion

4 eraser, rubber, correction fluid, cleanser, abrasive, paint-stripper, duster, sponge, clean slate, *tabula rasa* (L)

▶ *256 Cleanness; 258 Dirtiness*

5 forgetfulness, forgetting, amnesia, loss of memory, memory gap, absent-mindedness, mental block, repression, suppression

▶ *462 Memory; 463 Forgetfulness*

ADJECTIVES

6 obliterated, erased, expunged, eliminated, deleted, effaced, illegible, scribbled out, covered, concealed, crossed out, rubbed out, vaporized, liquidated, extirpated, cancelled, edited, censored, out of print, destroyed, eradicated, annihilated, demolished, razed to the ground, exterminated, buried, forgotten, unrecorded, unregistered, unwritten, intestate

► *357 Destruction; 463 Forgetfulness ; 550 Covering; 736 Concealment*

359 Preservation

What destroys one man preserves another. Pierre Corneille.

He was gifted with the sly, sharp instinct for self-preservation that passes for wisdom among the rich. Evelyn Waugh.

NOUNS

1 **preservation**, protection, safekeeping, keeping alive, perpetuation, continuation, prolongation, conservation, conservancy, permanence, ecology, environmental movement, green movement, Greenpeace, Friends of the Earth, conservation area, protected area, (wild) bird sanctuary, (wild) animal sanctuary, game reserve, nature reserve, reservation, park, saving, salvation, redemption, deliverance, retention, keep, maintenance, support, provision, self-preservation, selfishness, frugality, economy, thrift, saving up, insulation, heat retention, storage, keeping fresh, cold storage, freezing, deep-freezing, freeze-drying, refrigeration, boiling, pickling, marination, curing, smoking, dehydration, desiccation, drying, sun-drying, ultra heat treatment (UHT), canning, tinning, processing, packaging, packing, irradiation, sterilization, hygiene, preventive medicine, quarantine, *cordon sanitaire* (Fr), upkeep, service, servicing, valeting, cleansing, painting, varnishing, waterproofing, embalming, mummification, taxidermy

► *225 Permanence; 252 Safety; 257 Hygiene; 390 Deliverance; 428 Dryness; 436 Provisions; 439 Store; 494 Cold; 554 Life; 583 Burial; 680 Thrift; 683 Selfishness*

2 **preserver**, preservative, formaldehyde, alcohol, camphor, mothball, amber, plastic, salt, brine, spice, pickle, marinade, aspic, pectin, jelly, ice, freezer, refrigerator, vacuum flask, Thermos™ (flask), Dewar (flask), jar, pot, bottle, can, tin, paint, varnish, whitewash, creosote, rescue device, lifeline, life belt, life jacket, safety device, seat belt, safety belt, air bag, gas mask, incubator, respirator, iron lung, life-support system, good-luck charm, charm, amulet, mascot, talisman, silo, cannery, canning factory, bottling plant, conservation campaign, preservation order, fridge (Inf)

► *25 Cookery; 252 Safety; 494 Cold*

3 **preserved thing**, protected building, registered historic building (US), listed building, protected species, endangered species, mummy, fossil, stuffed animal, frozen food, freeze-dried food, vacuum-packed food, long-life food, long-life milk, dehydrated food, dried food, dried milk, processed food, canned food, tinned food, preserves, jam, jelly, marmalade, conserve, pickles, bottled fruit

► *25 Cookery*

4 **preservationist**, conservationist, conservator, environmentalist, ecologist, green, Greenpeace member (*or* supporter), Friends of the Earth member (*or* supporter), lifeguard, life-saver, saviour, rescuer, deliverer, embalmer, mummifier, bottler, canner, tinner, forester, (forest) ranger (US)

► *390 Deliverance*

VERBS

5 **preserve**, protect, guard, keep safe, keep alive, perpetuate, continue, prolong, uphold, defend, conserve, keep fresh, freeze, freeze-dry, keep on ice, refrigerate, irradiate, pickle, salt, souse, marinate, cure, smoke, kipper, dehydrate, dry, sun-dry, pot, bottle, can, tin, process, season, paint, varnish, whitewash, creosote, waterproof, embalm, mummify, stuff, maintain, service, keep up, keep running, keep in good repair, support, prop up, shore up, bolster, sustain, feed, provision, provide, supply, keep going, safeguard, shelter, keep under cover, warehouse, garage, keep, store, reserve, save, save up, bottle up, withhold, nurse, mother, foster, tend, cherish, treasure, look after, hold, retain, not let go, grasp, hug, hide, spare, rescue, deliver

► *252 Safety; 360 Retention; 390 Deliverance; 393 Repair; 394 Remedy; 413 Support; 428 Dryness; 436 Provisions; 439 Store; 494 Cold; 554 Life; 665 Carefulness; 680 Thrift*

ADJECTIVES

6 **preserving**, preservative, conserving, conservative, protecting, protective, prophylactic, preventive, preventative, salubrious, hygienic, redemptive, energy-saving, ecological, environment-friendly, environmental, conservational, green

7 **preserved**, well-preserved, kept, well-kept, alive, fresh, undecayed, intact, whole, perfect, dehydrated, desiccated, dried, sun-dried, freeze-dried, frozen, iced, on ice, in the freezer, in the refrigerator, pickled, marinated, salted, corned, soused, smoked, cured, canned, tinned, potted, bottled, mummified, embalmed, stuffed, laid up in lavender, mothballed, stored, conserved, protected, saved, safe, treasured, cherished

► *25 Cookery; 230 Perfection; 252 Safety; 439 Store*

ADVERBS

8 **preservatively**, conservatively, protectively, prophylactically, preventively, ecologically, environmentally

360 Retention

I am a kind of burr; I shall stick. William Shakespeare.

NOUNS

1 **retention**, retainment, keeping, holding (on), grabbing, prehension, prehensility, adhesion, stickiness, viscidity, hanging on, clinging on (*or* to), tenaciousness, tenacity, persistence, handhold, foothold, footing, toehold, clutch, clamp, clinch, clench, grasp, hug, bear hug, embrace, clasp, cuddle, squeeze, compression, hold, firm hold, seizure, grip, tight grip, iron grip, grip of iron, grip of steel, vicelike grip, death grip, stranglehold, lock, headlock, hammerlock, full nelson, half-nelson

► *191 Contraction; 251 Restraint; 267 Stickiness; 373 Connection; 413 Support; 492 Touch*

2 **detention**, suppression, repression, containment, envelopment, enclosing, pincer movement, keeping in, imprisoning, holding in, bottling up, plug, stop, stopper,

cork, locking in, holding back, saving, cherishing, maintenance, preservation

▶ *309 Closure; 359 Preservation; 378 Obstruction; 439 Store; 709 Refusal; 736 Concealment*

3 **tools for gripping**, pliers, wrench, spanner, tongs, fire tongs, sugar tongs, tweezers, pincers, nippers, vice, clamp, grip, forceps, grapnel, grappling iron, hook, anchor, fastening, staple, stapler, glue, gum, paste, adhesive, clasp, clip, paperclip, tie clasp (*or* clip), finger, fingers, fist, clenched fist, hand, paw, claw, talon, fingernails, nails, tooth, teeth, fangs, tentacle, tendril, feeler, dukes (Inf), hooks (Inf), meathooks (Inf), mitts (Inf), bunch of fives (Inf)

▶ *438 Tool*

4 **wall**, stone wall, brick wall, retaining wall, bulwark, embankment, abutment, buttress, flying buttress, fence, picket fence, barbed wire, chicken wire

▶ *165 Enclosure*

5 **retentiveness**, retention, constipation, remembrance, good memory, photographic memory, recalling, recall, recollection, memorizing, memorization, not forgetting

▶ *462 Memory*

VERBS

6 **retain**, keep, hold (on to), take hold of, buttonhole, get a firm hold, maintain one's hold, hold tight (*or* fast), cleave to, not let go, grab, stick to, adhere (to), agglutinate, hang on (to), staple, glue, gum, paste, fasten on, cling on (*or* to), show tenaciousness, have tenacity, have persistence, get a foothold, get one's footing, get a toehold, clutch, clamp, clinch, clench, grasp, hug, give a bear hug, embrace, grapple, clasp, cuddle, squeeze, compress, seize, grip, get a tight grip, have an iron grip, have a grip of iron, have a grip of steel, have a vicelike grip, get a stranglehold on, get a half-nelson on, have by the throat, throttle, strangle, lock, get a headlock on, tighten one's grip, fix one's teeth into, dig one's toes (*or* teeth *or* nails) into, never let go, hang on with all one's might, hang on for dear life, hold on like a bulldog, hold on like a snapping turtle (*or* snapper) (US), stick like a leech, gripe (Lit)

7 **detain**, suppress, repress, restrain, imprison, hold (*or* pin) down, get (*or* keep) a firm hold on, catch, steady, support, contain, draw the line, envelop, enclose, keep in, hold in, wall in, fence in, bottle up, plug, stop, cork, clog, constipate, lock in, keep secret, keep (*or* hold) back, hold up, keep to one side, keep to oneself, keep in one's own hands, keep in hand, keep, have in hand, hold on to, keep a tight hold (*or* rein) on, retain, withhold, refuse, monopolize, save, maintain, preserve, cherish, take to one's bosom, not part with, not dispose of, store

8 **remember**, have a good memory, have a photographic memory, not forget, recall, recollect, memorize, hold in one's mind

ADJECTIVES

9 **retentive**, retaining, tenacious, cohesive, adhesive, costive, constipated, clogged, indissoluble, firm, sticky, gluelike, gluey, gummy, prehensile, tightfisted, parsimonious, grasping, gripping, clinging, clasping, vicelike, strangling, throttling, restraining, gooey (Inf)

10 **retained**, stuck firm (*or* fast), fast, held, bound, glued, gummed, grasped, gripped, in the grip of, clasped, clutched, pinioned, pinned, stapled, strangled, detained, imprisoned, penned, kept in, held in, walled-in, fenced-in, contained, circumscribed, saved, kept (back), withheld, refused, preserved

ADVERBS

11 **tenaciously**, with resolution, cohesively, adhesively, like glue, indissolubly, stickily, parsimoniously, with a tight fist, firmly, in a firm grip, like a vice, for keeps, to keep, for good, for good and all, forever, for always

361 Suspension

It's better like that, if you want to kill a picture all you have to do is to hang it beautifully on a nail and soon you will see nothing of it but the frame. When it's out of place you see it better. Pablo Picasso.

NOUNS

1 **suspension**, suspendibility, suspensiveness, hanging, dangling, pendency, pendulousness, pensileness, hang, swing, dangle, drape, droop, sag

▶ *326 Oscillation; 373 Connection; 422 Elasticity*

2 **projection**, projecting part, overhang, overlie, protruberance

▶ *185 Bulge*

3 **suspended object**, hanging object, pendulum, pendant, plumb bob, tassel, curtain, pigtail, ponytail, earring, bell rope, icicle, chandelier, picture, coat-tail, fringe, suspended cymbal, hammock, trapeze, swing, suspension bridge

4 **hanger**, suspender, hook, peg, clothes peg, nail, knob, coat hanger, hat rack, clothesline, clotheshorse, picture hook, curtain rod, braces, suspender belt, gallows, gibbet, crane

5 **projecting object**, diving board, balcony, mantelpiece, hat brim, nose, pier, buttress, gable, cantilever

▶ *20 Architecture*

6 **interruption**, pause, postponement, suspension, deferment, adjournment, moratorium, cooling-off period, shelving, tabling, delay, procrastination, putting off, stopping, withholding, stay, discontinuance, abeyance, dormancy

▶ *133 Discontinuity; 226 Stopping; 294 Lateness; 341 Inaction; 371 Expulsion*

ADJECTIVES

7 **suspended**, hanging, hung, dangling, swinging, sagging, pendulous, pendent, pensile, suspendible (*or* suspensible), suspensive

8 **projecting**, overhanging, jutting, sticking out, beetling, beetle-browed

9 **interrupted**, postponed, delayed, suspended, deferred, adjourned, put off, shelved, tabled, withheld, stopped, stayed, discontinued, abeyant, dormant, pending

VERBS

10 **suspend**, hang, hang up, hook up, fasten (up), put up, drape, hang down, dangle, swing, swing from, droop, trail, bungee jump, hang glide

11 **project**, overhang, hang over, overlie, jut, beetle, stick out over, hover

12 **interrupt**, postpone, suspend, defer, adjourn, shelve,

table, delay, procrastinate, hold up, pause, put off, withhold, stop, discontinue, stay, arrest, put on hold (Inf)

ADVERBS

13 **pendulously**, pendently, suspensively, on a string, in mid air, in suspense

362 Traction

Everyone is dragged on by their favourite pleasure. Virgil.

NOUNS

1 **traction**, pulling, draught, drawing, heaving, tugging, pulling (*or* tractive) power, pulling back, retractiveness, retraction, retractility, retractability, towage, towing, haulage, hauling, drayage

▶ *316 Transfer; 319 Transport*

2 **pull**, tug, tow, heave, draw, draught, haul, lug, drag, strain, trawl, tug of war, rowing

▶ *334 Power*

3 **jerk**, yerk (Dial), yank, twitch, sudden pull, tweak, pluck, wrench, snatch, hitch, start, bob, flip, flick, flirt, flounce, jig, jiggle, jolt, jog, joggle

▶ *327 Agitation*

4 **friction**, drag, grip, purchase, adhesion, adhesiveness, clinginess, stickiness

▶ *267 Stickiness*

5 **magnetism**, attraction, pulling towards, drawing power, charisma

▶ *363 Attraction*

6 **towline**, towrope, drawer, puller, tower, hauler, haulier, dragnet, windlass, tugboat, tractor, traction engine, locomotive

7 **magnet**, magnetizer, lodestone (*or* loadstone), electromagnet

▶ *28 Physics*

ADJECTIVES

8 **tractional**, tractive, pulling, drawing, hauling, tugging, towing, pulling back, attracting, drawn, horse-drawn

9 **retractive**, retractable, retractile, ductile

10 **magnetic**, attractive, charismatic

VERBS

11 **pull**, haul, draw, heave, tow, take in tow, hale, lug, tug, trail, train, trice, warp, kedge

12 **drag**, trawl, dredge, winch, reel in, wind in, wind up, lift, tug, draggle, snake, troll, rake, rake in, rake out, drag up, elevate, drag down

13 **pull at**, pull out, tug, yank, jerk, tweak, yerk (Dial), twitch, pluck, snatch, snatch at, wrench, hitch, flip, flick, flirt, flounce, jig, jiggle, jolt, joggle, jog

14 **draw in**, draw back, retract, withdraw, sheathe, pull back, pull in

15 **pull towards**, attract, magnetize, spellbind

▶ *11 Occultism*

ADVERBS

16 **magnetically**, charismatically, attractively, adhesively, retractably

363 Attraction

If you would hit the mark, you must aim a little above it; Every arrow that flies feels the attraction of earth. Henry Wadsworth Longfellow.

NOUNS

1 **attraction**, attractiveness, attractivity, attractance, attractancy, mutual attraction, pull, draw, drag, tug, itch, desire, affinity, sympathy

▶ *362 Traction; 617 Desire*

2 **pulling power**, magnetism, magnetization, gravity, force of gravity, centripetal force, capillarity, capillary attraction, adhesion, cohesion, adduction, inducement, hypnotism, mesmerism

3 **magnet**, bar magnet, horseshoe magnet, coil magnet, electromagnet, field magnet, artificial magnet, solenoid, paramagnet, magnetic needle, lodestone (*or* loadstone), lodestar, pole star, magnetite, siderite, magnetized iron

▶ *28 Physics; 30 Earth Science*

4 **allurement**, allure, fascination, charm, charisma, seduction, seductiveness, temptation, appeal, enticement, sex appeal, animal magnetism (Inf), come-on (Inf), pull (Inf)

5 **lure**, bait, decoy, charm, siren, siren song, snare

6 **charmer**, temptress, seductress, seducer, enchantress, enchanter, vamp, *femme fatale* (Fr), Lothario, ladies' man, Don Juan, Casanova, favourite, siren, Circe, Adonis, sex symbol, screen idol, teen idol, man-eater (Inf), foxy lady (US inf), stud (Inf), hunk (Inf)

7 **centre of attraction**, centre of attention, focal point, cynosure, focus, centre

▶ *185 Bulge*

ADJECTIVES

8 **attracting**, pulling, drawing, dragging, tugging, adductive, associative, adducent

9 **attractive**, seductive, enticing, tempting, charming, fascinating, captivating, charismatic, irresistible, alluring, fetching, appealing, good-looking, sexually attractive, sexy (Inf), dishy (Inf), hunky (Inf)

▶ *545 Beauty; 617 Desire*

10 **magnetic**, magnetized, gravitational, centripetal, convergent, inductive, influential

VERBS

11 **attract**, pull, draw, adduct, drag, tug, have an attraction, draw towards, influence, persuade, magnetize, be magnetic, exercise a pull, pull towards, appeal, charm, move, pluck at one's heartstrings, induce

▶ *395 Influence*

12 **lure**, allure, draw in, coax, bait, ensnare, seduce, decoy, lead on, tempt, entice, tantalize, fascinate, captivate, enthral, hypnotize, mesmerize

ADVERBS

13 **attractionally**, attractively, centripetally, adhesively, cohesively, inductively, magnetically, mesmerically, hypnotically, irresistibly

14 **attractively**, influentially, sympathetically, appealingly, charismatically, charmingly, enchantingly, seductively, sexily (Inf)

364 Repulsion

VERBS

1 **repel**, drive (*or* push *or* put) away, head off, repulse, turn back, drive (*or* push *or* thrust) back, chase off (*or* away), reject, rebuff, snub, cold-shoulder, slight, cut, spurn, refuse, say no to, reject someone's advances, show someone the door, give someone the bird, make someone keep his (*or* her) distance, brush off (Inf)

▶ *470 Rejection*

2 **eject**, expel, throw out, send packing, pack off, send someone about his (*or* her) business, give someone his (*or* her) marching (*or* walking) orders, dismiss, sack (Inf), boot out (Inf)

▶ *371 Expulsion*

3 **fend off**, deflect, ward off, keep at bay, put off, head off, parry, keep at arm's length, beat (*or* fight) off, make unwelcome, send someone off with a flea in his (*or* her) ear

▶ *347 Counteraction*

4 **be repulsive**, disgust, revolt, sicken, nauseate, repel, upset, offend, appal, turn one's stomach, make one's gorge rise

▶ *242 Unpleasantness*

NOUNS

5 **repulsion**, repellence, repellency, repelling, ugliness, repellent quality, repulsiveness, recoil, mutual repulsion, repulsive force, centrifugal force, polarization, disaffinity, magnetic repulsion, diamagnetism, antigravity

▶ *28 Physics; 546 Ugliness*

6 **repulse**, rebuff, dismissal, snub, cut, cold shoulder, spurning, refusal, rejection, ejection, expulsion, brush-off (Inf), the big E (Inf)

▶ *371 Expulsion; 470 Rejection*

7 **deflection**, defence, foil, counterstroke, parry, counterattack, resistance

▶ *383 Resistance; 384 Defence*

ADJECTIVES

8 **repulsive**, repellent, repugnant, offensive, noisome, off-putting, antipathetic, ugly, abhorrent, obnoxious, disgusting, nauseating, sickening, foul, loathsome, horrible, appalling, hideous, obscene

▶ *242 Unpleasantness; 546 Ugliness*

9 **abducent**, abductive, centrifugal, repelling, diamagnetic, of opposite polarity

▶ *28 Physics*

10 **defensive**, resistant, hostile, dismissive

▶ *383 Resistance; 384 Defence; 470 Rejection*

ADVERBS

11 **repulsively**, repellently, repugnantly, offensively, antipathetically, abhorrently, noisomely, obnoxiously, horribly, hideously, obscenely

12 **defensively**, resistantly, dismissively, against

365 Friction

NOUNS

1 **friction**, rubbing, drag, force, resistance, viscosity, static friction, rolling friction, internal friction, sliding friction, slip friction, coefficient of friction, skin friction, roughness, rub, affriction, frottage, frication (Lit), confrication (Lit), perfrication (Lit)

▶ *28 Physics; 383 Resistance*

2 **wearing away**, attrition, abrasion, rubbing against, rubbing together, erosion, wear, corrosion, detrition, ablation, collision, rubbing out (*or* off *or* away), erasure, obliteration, sandblasting

▶ *357 Destruction; 358 Obliteration; 427 Powderiness*

3 **grinding**, filing, rasping, fretting, limation, chafing, galling, chafe, levigation

▶ *427 Powderiness*

4 **scraping**, scratching, grazing, scuffing, scrub, scrubbing, scouring, scrape, scratch, scuff

5 **polishing**, rubbing, burnishing, sanding, smoothing, buffing, shining, dressing, elbow grease

6 **massage**, massaging, massotherapy, stroking, rubdown, kneading, facial massage, facial, shampoo, whirlpool bath, Jacuzzi™, vibrator

▶ *547 Beautification*

7 **eraser**, rubber, scraper, sander, sanding disc, sandpaper, glasspaper, emery paper, emery board, nailfile, file, rasp, pumice (pumice stone), facemask, facial scrub

▶ *438 Tool*

8 **masseur**, masseuse, massotherapist, shampooer, beautician

▶ *547 Beautification*

9 **irritation**, grating, prickliness, irascibility, tension

▶ *327 Agitation; 625 Grumpiness*

ADJECTIVES

10 **frictional**, friction, abrasive, anatriptic, irritant, rubbing, attritive, erosive, ablative, gnawing

11 **rough**, rasping, grating, grinding, chafing, fretting, galling

VERBS

12 **rub**, rub up, smooth, polish, wax, levigate, burnish, furbish, buff, scour, scrub, sandpaper, sand, sandblast, dress, brush, curry, currycomb

13 **abrade**, frictionize, abrase, rub against, scrape, scuff, graze, raze, bark, scratch, gnaw, gnaw away, strike (a match)

14 **erode**, corrode, wear, wear away, fray, frazzle, skin, erase, rub out (*or* away *or* off), obliterate

▶ *358 Obliteration*

15 **grind**, rasp, file, plane, grate, catch, stick, chafe, gall, fret, irritate, rub up the wrong way

16 **massage**, knead, rub down, pulverize, shampoo, rub gently, smooth, iron out, iron, stroke, caress, pet

ADVERBS

17 **abrasively**, roughly, raspingly, irritatingly, harshly

366 Raising

VERBS

1 **raise**, erect, build, up, put up, upraise, raise up, set up, lift, levitate, uplift, lift up, hoist, heist, hike, hoick, heft, heave, upheave, uphoist, upthrow, upcast, lever, jack up, prop up, shoulder, boost, hold up, uphold, stick up, support, prevent from falling, perk up, buoy up, upbuoy, help up, put on, mount

► *154 Height; 304 Ascent; 413 Support*

2 **send up**, throw in the air, lob, loft, knock up, flight, sky, shoot up, propel, blow up, puff up, swell, increase, escalate

► *213 Increase; 244 Improvement; 300 Motion; 304 Ascent; 330 Propulsion; 331 Impulsion*

3 **promote**, heighten, give a lift, give a leg-up, aid, perk, perk up, elevate, enshrine, put on a pedestal, exalt, enhance, apotheosize, lionize, deify, beatify, canonize, sublimate, chair, shoulder, crown

► *8 Divinity; 174 Top; 185 Bulge; 244 Improvement; 392 Help*

4 **gather up**, pick up, pluck up, take up, draw up, fish up, haul up, drag up, dredge up, weigh, trip (anchor)

5 **arise**, rise, rise up, rear, uprear, lift oneself, stand up, be upstanding, get up, jump up, jump to one's feet, leap up, leap (*or* spring) to one's feet, pull oneself up, hold oneself up, hold one's head up, draw oneself to one's full height, stand on tiptoe, be vertical

► *186 Verticality*

NOUNS

6 **raising**, elevation, lifting, erection, escalation, rearing, uprearing, uplifting, upbuoying, uptrending, uplift, levitation, hoist, heave, upheaval, sublevation, upthrow, upcast, upthrust, picking up, ascent, defiance of gravity, antigravity

7 **lift**, boost, upswinging, upgrading, aid, leg-up (Inf), promotion, exaltation, apotheosis, god-making, deification, canonization, beatification, enshrinement, assumption, bodily assumption, *sursum corda* (L), lionization

8 **height**, eminence, sublimity, loftiness, prominence

► *154 Height; 174 Top*

9 **lifter**, crane, dredger, derrick, hoist, gantry crane, lever, jack, jackscrew, crab, lift, hydraulic lift, forklift, hydraulic tailgate, windlass, winch, tackle, capstan, jeer capstan, purchase, rope and pulley, block and tackle, luff-tackle, jeers

► *38 Engineering; 62 Mountaineering and Climbing; 438 Tool*

10 **elevator**, lift, escalator, moving staircase, dumb waiter, spring, springboard, trampoline, ski lift, funicular, chair lift, conveyor, hot-air balloon, helium balloon, barrage balloon, hydrogen balloon, hot air, gas, hydrogen, helium, raising agent, yeast, leven, raiser, lightener, fermentation

► *304 Ascent*

ADJECTIVES

11 **raised**, lifted, upraised, elevated, levitated, erected, erectile, set up, escalated, upreared, uplifted, upcast, upbuoyed, attollent, supportive, upstanding, vertical, hoisted, heaved, mounted, lobbed, thrown, shot up, blown up, swollen

► *413 Support*

12 **exalted**, eminent, prominent, promoted, upgraded, lofty, sublime, high-flown, elevated, enshrined, on high, deified, canonized, lionized, beatified, apotheosized

ADVERBS

13 **highly**, sublimely, on stilts, on tiptoe, on one's hind legs, on high, aloft, on the shoulders of, on the back of

367 Lowering

VERBS

1 **lower**, depress, deflate, let down, take down, lay down, set down, put down, reduce, decrease, deteriorate, worsen

► *155 Lowness; 214 Decrease; 218 Insufficiency; 245 Deterioration; 305 Descent*

2 **flatten**, level, demolish, rase, raze, raze to the ground, fell, cut down, hew, chop, hew down, chop down, wack down, mow down, lumber, ground, fetch down, down, pull down, tear down, dash down, pull down about one's ears, trample in the dust, dent, crush, stave in, hollow

► *131 End; 183 Concavity; 357 Destruction; 358 Obliteration; 585 War*

3 **bring down**, overthrow, overturn, shoot down, shoot down in flames, couch, pull down, take down, overset, upset, topple, subvert, floor, send headlong, deck, lay out, bowl over, spread-eagle, torpedo, scuttle, sink, submerge, drown, duck, souse, douse, dip, plunge, send to the bottom

► *192 Inversion; 585 War*

4 **debase**, abase, degrade, downgrade, lower standards, demote, put down, humble, reduce to the ranks, cashier, humiliate, snub, deflate, debunk, take the wind out of one's sails, take the rise out of, water down, dilute, adulterate

► *122 Inferiority; 337 Weakness; 623 Humility*

5 **bear down on**, downbear, push down, thrust down, weigh on, press, press on, suppress, keep down, keep under, hold down, squash, detrude, put a lid on

6 **throw down**, throw, cast down, fling, fling down, blow over, blow down, pitch, throw overboard, drop over the side, let fall, drop, let drop, shed, let go, let slip (*or* slide), slip (*or* slide) through one's fingers, scatter, dust, sow, broadcast, disperse, pour out, pour, decant, void, spill, slop, moisten, sprinkle, shower

► *377 Dispersal; 429 Moisture*

7 **lean**, incline, lean over backwards, lean forwards, bend forwards, bend backwards, bend over, trip, topple, tumble, fall headlong, capsize, roll over, tip, tilt

► *303 Backward Motion*

8 **sit**, sit down, seat oneself, be seated, park oneself, perch, alight, squat, get down on one's haunches (*or* hunkers), crouch, hunch, stoop, bend, duck, get down, hunch down, scrooch (*or* scrunch) down, prostrate, supinate, lie down, prone, flatten oneself, couch, recline, drape oneself, spread-eagle

► *343 Inactivity*

9 **bow**, bend, genuflect, make a bow, bow low, bow down, kneel, kowtow, salaam, kiss hands, revere, pay respects, do reverence, curtsy, bob, duck, nod, incline one's head, make obeisance, prostrate oneself, grovel, cower, cringe, wallow, welter

► *623 Humility; 663 Obedience; 664 Servility*

10 **lower the flag**, lower the standard, haul down, half-mast, strike

► *584 Military Affairs*

NOUNS

11 **lowering**, depression, deflation, sinking, levelling, de-

molition, reduction, decrease, deterioration, worsening, de-escalation, diminution, descent, drop, downfall, rainfall, shower, fall, trip, tumble, spillage

▶ *30 Earth Science; 305 Descent; 433 Water*

12 **downthrow**, downcast, flattening, levelling, grounding, overthrow, overturn, overset, upset, toppling, subversion, revolution, overturning, precipitation, defenestration

13 **submergence**, sinking, ducking, sousing, pushing under, thrusting under, pushing down, detrusion, plunging, keeping down, keeping under, suppression, oppression

14 **depression**, indentation, hollow, cavity, concavity, dip, dent, sinkhole, well

15 **debasement**, degradation, downgrading, demotion, deterioration, humiliation, bowing and scraping, grovelling, Uriah Heep

16 **courtesy**, courteous act, deference, respect, comity, bow, genuflect, kneeling, kowtow, salaam, kissing hands, reverence, obeisance, curtsy, bob, duck, nod, crouch, hunch, stoop, bend, squat, prostration, supination

ADJECTIVES

17 **lowered**, depressed, deflated, flattened, grounded, levelled, demolished, reduced, decreased, deteriorated, worse

▶ *214 Decrease; 245 Deterioration*

18 **lowering**, descendent, descending, depressing, humiliating, demeaning, debasing, low, at a low ebb

19 **fallen**, sunk, sunken, soused, submerged, downcast, downthrown, defenestrated

20 **falling**, toppling, tumbling, tripping, showering, sprinkling, scattering, spilling, dropping, precipitous

21 **degraded**, debased, downgraded, demoted, humiliated, cast down, downcast, depressed, depressive, kowtowing, kneeling, grovelling, courteous, deferential

22 **overthrown**, cast down, overturned, overset, upset, toppled, subverted, suppressed, oppressed, subversive, revolutionary

▶ *387 Subjection*

23 **sedentary**, sitting, crouching, stooping, squatting, hunched, bent, bent double, prostrate, supine

ADVERBS

24 **down**, downwards, to the ground, decreasingly, reductively, subversively, oppressively, on the ground, on the floor, in the dirt, on the bottom, at rock bottom, in Davy Jones' locker, at a low ebb, at half-mast

▶ *91 Seas; 156 Depth; 175 Base*

25 **courteously**, humbly, degradingly, on one's knees, on one's back

368 Insertion

VERBS

1 **insert**, put in, stick in, introduce, introject, insinuate, add, interject, interpolate, intercalate, put between, intromit, include, drag in, import, bring in, drop in, pot, hole, put in the slot

▶ *127 Inclusion; 211 Addition*

2 **inject**, inoculate, vaccinate, implant, impregnate, enter, penetrate, pierce, poke in, squirt in, introduce, pop in, infuse, instil, imbue, perfuse, transfuse, pour in, decant, shoot (Inf)

▶ *314 Entry*

3 **impact**, thrust in, drive in, plunge in, run in, push in, force in, hammer in, knock in, pound in, ram in, jam in, cram in, press in, squeeze in, crowd in, stuff in, pack in

▶ *406 Contents; 410 Container*

4 **immerse**, immerge (Lit), submerge, dip, plunge, dunk, duck, baptize, steep, souse, drench, flood, bury, inter, immerse oneself in, bury oneself in

▶ *367 Lowering; 583 Burial*

5 **inset**, set in, inlay, slip in, slide in, ease in, wedge in, infix, dovetail, embed, bed in, encapsulate, ensheathe, sheathe, encase, case, box, cover, mount, frame, circumscribe

▶ *170 Surroundings; 550 Covering*

6 **plant**, implant, transplant, plant out, bed out, graft, engraft, ingraft, imp, bud

▶ *43 Agriculture*

7 **install**, instate, inaugurate, initiate, invest, ordain, induct, enrol, enlist, sign up, sign on, admit

▶ *370 Admittance*

NOUNS

8 **insertion**, introduction, introjection, insinuation, addition, interjection, interpolation, intercalation, intromission, embolism, parenthesis, import, importation, infixion, impaction, impactment, planting, implantation, transplantation, transplant, graft, grafting, embedment, tessellation

9 **injection**, inoculation, vaccination, implantation, impregnation, entry, ingress, penetration, infusion, perfusion, transfusion, shot (Inf)

10 **immersion**, submersion, submergence, dip, plunge, bath, ducking, baptism, interment, burial, burial at sea

11 **thing inserted**, insert, insertion, inset, inlay, inclusion, supplement, filling, stuffing, syringe, tampon, tampion, suppository, enema, clyster

ADJECTIVES

12 **inserted**, introduced, introjected, insinuated, added, interpolated, intercalated, interpolative, intercalative, parenthetical, by-the-by, imported, infixed, impacted, planted, transplanted, grafted, embedded, tessellated, inlaid, included

13 **injected**, inoculated, vaccinated, implanted, impregnated, infused, perfused

14 **immersed**, submersed, submerged, baptized, interred, buried

ADVERBS

15 **in**, inside, parenthetically, in parenthesis, in brackets

369 Extraction

Whoso pulleth out this sword of this stone and anvil is rightwise King born of all England. Sir Thomas Mallory.

NOUNS

1 **extraction**, removal, withdrawal, pull, pulling out, drawing, drawing out, tug, tugging out, wrench, wrenching out, wresting out, evulsion, avulsion, ripping out, tearing out, rooting out, uprooting, deracina-

tion, eradication, elimination, dredging, fishing, extrication, disengagement, liberation

▶ *357 Destruction; 358 Obliteration; 362 Traction; 390 Deliverance; 391 Liberation*

2 **displacement**, dislodgment, expulsion, expression, squeezing out, pruning, thinning, thinning out, weeding, deforestation

▶ *144 Displacement; 371 Expulsion*

3 **digging out**, digging up, unearthing, disinterment, exhumation, disentombment, grave-robbing, cutting out, excision, exsection, excavation, mining, quarrying, drilling

▶ *183 Concavity; 372 Separation*

4 **sucking**, sucking out, suction, exsuction, drawing, drawing off, draught, vacuuming, aspiration, pumping, siphoning, tapping, milking, pipetting, broaching, emptying, draining, cupping, bleeding, blood-letting, phlebotomy, venesection, evisceration, gutting, disembowelment, shelling

5 **drawing out**, bringing forth, elicitation, evocation, eduction, calling forth, arousal, stimulation, obtaining, derivation

▶ *765 Profit*

6 **extorsion**, wresting, wrenching, wringing, tearing, ripping, wrest, wrench, wring, exaction, demand, claim

▶ *773 Taking*

7 **obtaining an extract**, extraction, separation, refinement, purification, distillation, sublimation, condensation, vaporization, decoction, infusion, squeezing, pressing, expressing, rendering, rendition, steeping, soaking, marinating, concentration

8 **extract**, essence, quintessence, spirit, elixir, decoction, infusion, distillate, sublimate, concentrate, juice

▶ *99 Essence; 205 Part*

9 **extractor**, separator, siphon, pump, syringe, pipette, aspirator, vacuum pump, press, wringer, mangle, lemon squeezer, juice extractor, cherry stoner, apple corer

10 **excavator**, miner, quarrier, digger, mechanical digger, JCB™, shovel, pick, pickaxe, toothpick, rake, dredge, dredger, shadoof, Persian wheel, scoop, spoon, lever, crowbar, wrench, corkscrew, screwdriver, forceps, pliers, tweezers, pincers

▶ *438 Tool*

VERBS

11 **extract**, remove, withdraw, pull out, draw out, take out, get out, tug out, wrench out, wrest out, evulse, avulse, rip out, tear out, root out, uproot, deracinate, eradicate, eliminate, pluck out, pick out, rake out, dredge, fish, fish out, grub out, winkle out, extricate, disengage, free, liberate

▶ *362 Traction; 390 Deliverance; 391 Liberation; 469 Selection*

12 **displace**, dislodge, lever out, smoke out, expel, express, squeeze out, wring out, prune, thin, thin out, weed out, deforest

▶ *144 Displacement; 371 Expulsion*

13 **dig out**, dig up, unearth, disinter, exhume, disentomb, gouge out, cut out, excise, excavate, mine, quarry, drill

▶ *183 Concavity; 372 Separation*

14 **suck**, suck out, draw, draw off, aspirate, vacuum, pump, pump out, siphon, siphon off, tap, milk, pipette, broach, empty, drain, cup, bleed, eviscerate, gut, disembowel, shell

15 **draw out**, bring forth, elicit, evoke, educe, worm out, bring to light, summon up, call up, rouse, arouse, stimulate, obtain, get, procure, secure, derive, induce, deduce, glean

▶ *765 Profit*

16 **extort**, wrest, wrench, wring, force out, tear out, rip out, exact, demand, claim

▶ *773 Taking*

17 **obtain an extract**, separate, refine, purify, cream off, distil, condense, vaporize, decoct, infuse, squeeze, press, melt down, render, steep, soak, marinate, concentrate, essentialize

ADJECTIVES

18 **extractive**, eductive, educible, eradicative, eradicable, removable, uprooting, elicitory, evocative, arousing, stimulating

19 **dislodged**, displaced, uprooted, deracinated, extricated, disengaged, liberated, eliminated, extracted

20 **exacting**, exactive, extortionate, extortionary, extortive

ADVERBS

21 **away**, apart, asunder, removably, exactingly, exigently

22 **expressively**, evocatively, stimulatingly

370 Admittance

He is not a proper person to be admitted into respectable society, being the most perverse and malevolent creature that ill-luck has thrown my way. William Wordsworth.

NOUNS

1 **admittance**, admission, readmission, taking in, receipt, receiving, reception, acceptance, import, importing, importation, introception, immission, intromission, insertion, interjection, invitation, inclusion, interjacence

▶ *127 Inclusion; 368 Insertion; 769 Receiving*

2 **receptivity**, receptiveness, openness, recipience, recipiency, hospitality, welcome, welcoming, effusive welcome, welcoming with open arms, refuge, sanctuary, asylum, shelter, protection, open door, access, entrance, entrée, entry

▶ *252 Safety; 314 Entry; 654 Sociability*

3 **introduction**, bringing in, initiation, baptism, rite of passage, enrolment, investiture, ordination, induction, registration, enlistment, instatement, installation, inauguration, naturalization, admissibility, acceptability

▶ *130 Beginning*

4 **intake**, indrawal, indraught, engulfing, engulfment, ingestion, consumption, eating, drinking, fluid intake, imbibition, ingurgitation, engorgement, swallow, swallowing, gulp, gulping, suck, sucking, suction, aspiration, respiration, breathing in, inspiration, inhalement, inhalation, sniff, sniffing, snuff, snuffle, sniffle, slurp (Inf), slurping (Inf)

▶ *495 Taste; 500 Smell; 557 Eating; 558 Drinking*

5 **absorption**, adsorption, sorption, chemisorption, resorption, digestion, engrossment, assimilation, incorporation, absorbency, resorbence, sponging, blotting, seeping, percolation, osmosis, endosmosis, exosmosis

6 **sponge**, blotter, blotting paper, chromatography paper, absorbent, adsorbent

VERBS

7 **admit**, receive, take in, include, readmit, let in, allow in, allow access, give a ticket (*or* pass) to, give admittance (*or* entrance) to, intromit, open the door to, open the hatches, insert, import, bring in

▶ *127 Inclusion; 368 Insertion; 769 Receiving*

8 **show in**, usher, usher in, introduce, go before, come before, send in

▶ *129 Precedence*

9 **welcome**, embrace, adopt, accept, fling wide the gates, welcome with open arms, put the flags out, invite, call in, give refuge to, give sanctuary to, grant asylum, naturalize, shelter, accommodate, protect, safeguard

▶ *252 Safety; 654 Sociability*

10 **introduce**, bring in, initiate, baptize, register, inscribe, enlist, take on, install, inaugurate, enrol, invest, ordain, show the ropes (Inf)

11 **ingest**, eat, imbibe, drink, drink up (*or* in), lap up, engulf, engorge, ingurgitate, swallow, gulp, gulp down, wolf down, gobble, slurp (Inf)

▶ *495 Taste; 557 Eating; 558 Drinking*

12 **draw in**, suck, suck in (*or* up), suckle, aspirate, respire, inhale, inspire, breathe in, sniff, sniffle, snuff, snuffle, smell, scent, scent (*or* smell) out, detect

▶ *500 Smell*

13 **absorb**, adsorb, sorb, chemisorb, digest, incorporate, assimilate, internalize, engross, take up, blot, blot up, soak, soak up, sponge, osmose, soak in, seep in, permeate, percolate, infiltrate, reabsorb, resorb

ADJECTIVES

14 **admissive**, admissory, admissible, acceptable, suitable, receivable, receptible, introceptive, intromissive, intromittent

15 **receptive**, recipient, open, accessible, welcoming, hospitable, inviting, invitatory

16 **introductory**, introductive, initiatory, initiative, baptismal

17 **absorbent**, absorptive, adsorbent, sorbent, chemisorptive, assimilative, digestive, ingestive, imbibitory, bibulous, soaking, blotting, spongy, spongeous, osmotic, endosmotic, exosmotic

ADVERBS

18 **receptively**, welcomingly, hospitably, invitingly, with open arms

371 Expulsion

VERBS

1 **expel**, eject, put out, turn out, throw out, cast out, toss out, heave out, hustle out, show someone the door, bounce (Inf), chuck out (Inf), turf out (Inf), kick out (Inf), boot out (Inf), give the bum's rush (US inf), give the old heave-ho (Inf), throw out on one's ear (Inf)

▶ *330 Propulsion*

2 **dismiss**, discharge, disemploy, suspend, lay off, furlough (US), make redundant, drop, let go, release, let out, retire, superannuate, pension off, sack (Inf), give the sack (Inf), fire (Inf), give one's marching orders (*or* walking papers) (Inf), kick out (Inf), boot out (Inf), give the boot (Inf), give the hook (US inf), axe (Inf), give the axe (Inf), kick upstairs (Inf)

3 **disbar**, excommunicate, unfrock, defrock, strip, deplume, displume, disqualify, strike off, strike off the roll, drum out, cashier, depose, dethrone, expel, suspend, send down, rusticate, demote, degrade, downgrade, relegate, bust (US), kick downstairs (Inf)

▶ *814 Punishment*

4 **ostracize**, exclude, seclude, blackball, spurn, snub, cut, send to Coventry, give the silent treatment, brush off, give the cold shoulder, make unwelcome, outlaw, fugitate, ban, proscribe, prohibit, banish, rusticate, exile, expatriate, repatriate, deport, transport, extradite, send away

▶ *128 Exclusion; 470 Rejection; 655 Unsociability*

5 **take the place of**, usurp, supplant, supersede, substitute, replace, displace

▶ *144 Displacement; 762 Substitution*

6 **send away**, send off, see off, order off (*or* away), turn away, bundle away, bundle off, pack off, send about one's business, send to the showers, shake off, shoo off (*or* away), send away with a flea in one's ear (Inf), send packing (Inf)

7 **drive out**, drum out, chase out, rout out, push out, force out, hunt out, smoke out, freeze out, drive into the open, run out of town, ride on a rail

8 **evict**, oust, remove, dispossess, repossess, expropriate, deprive, dislodge, extirpate, uproot, put out, turn out, turn out of doors, turn out of house and home, turn (*or* put) out bag and baggage, unhouse, unkennel

▶ *773 Taking*

9 **depopulate**, unpeople, depeople, dispeople, desolate, devastate

▶ *382 Killing*

10 **exterminate**, do away with, purge, liquidate, dispel, eradicate, root out, deracinate, eliminate, get rid of, reject, throw off, cast off, fling off, shake off, shed, destroy, rub out, erase, obliterate, exorcise

▶ *358 Obliteration; 470 Rejection*

11 **void**, evacuate, eliminate, remove, deplete, exhaust, empty, empty out, vent, drain, drink up, drain to the dregs, siphon off, pump out, clear out, clean out, curette, purge, gut, disembowel, eviscerate, draw, bone, fillet, unclog, unfoul, blow, blow out, clear off, clear away, sweep out, make a clean sweep, clear the decks

12 **unload**, unburden, disburden, off-load, unlade, unpack, discharge, dump, unship

13 **throw away**, throw out, jettison, throw overboard, discard, scrap, precipitate, defenestrate, get rid of, rid oneself of, junk (Inf), bin (Inf), get shot (*or* shut) of (Inf)

▶ *767 Disposal*

14 **let out**, give out (*or* off), emit, send out, radiate, emit rays, perfume, scent, exhaust, give vent to, exhale, expire, respire, breathe (out), let one's breath out, blow, puff, fume, smoke, reek, steam, vaporize, stream, turn on the tap, open the floodgates, open the sluice gates, disgorge, debouch, disembogue, discharge, ejaculate, cast forth, cast out, send forth, extrude, detrude, obtrude, erupt, eruct, blow out, pour out, outpour, spew, spout, jet, spurt, squirt, sputter, splutter, extravasate, bleed,

defecate, urinate, excrete, egest, secrete, sweat, perspire, ooze, suppurate, dribble, drool, slaver, slobber

▶ *315 Exit; 330 Propulsion; 560 Excretion*

15 vomit, spew, regurgitate, spit, spit out, bring up, be sick, retch, heave, gag, puke (Inf), barf (US inf), throw up (Inf), sick up (Inf), chuck up (Inf), upchuck (Inf), shoot (*or* toss) one's cookies (US inf), shoot a cat (Inf), cat (Inf), cry (*or* call for) Hughie (*or* Ralph) (Inf), talk on the big white telephone (Inf), chunder (Inf)

16 belch, hiccup, eruct, eructate, fart, break wind, blow a raspberry, burp (Inf), gurk (Inf), drop one (Inf), drop one's guts (Inf), blow off (Inf), let rip (Inf)

NOUNS

17 expulsion, ejection, ejectment, throwing out, rejection, propulsion, kicking out (Inf), booting out (Inf), the push (Inf), the bounce (Inf), the chuck (Inf), the boot (Inf), the bum's rush (US inf), the old heave-ho (Inf)

18 dismissal, discharge, congé, suspension, laying off, furlough (US), redundancy, drumming out, cashiering, demotion, degradation, relegation, stripping, depluming, displuming, externment, exclusion, excommunication, unfrocking, defrocking, disqualification, disfellowship, striking off, the sack (Inf), sacking (Inf), firing (Inf), axing (Inf), the axe (Inf), the boot (Inf), the gate (Inf), one's marching orders (Inf), one's walking papers (Inf), one's cards (Inf), pink slip (US inf)

19 ostracism, ostracization, exclusion, seclusion, blackballing, sending to Coventry, the cold shoulder, the brushoff, outlawing, outlawry, fugitation, banning, proscription, banishment, rustication, exile, exilement, expatriation, repatriation, deportation, transportation, extradition

20 eviction, ousting, removal, dispossession, repossession, expropriation, deprivation, dislodgment, throwing overboard, jettison, precipitation, defenestration, unloading, off-loading

21 removal, elimination, evacuation, voidance, voiding, clearance, clearing, clearage, cleaning out, scouring out, purging, purgation, catharsis, unfouling, emptying, depletion, exhaustion, draining, drainage, egress

22 disgorgement, disemboguement, ejaculation, extrusion, detrusion, obtrusion, eruption, eruptiveness, blowout, outburst, outpour, effusion, jet, spout, spurt, squirt, excretion, secretion, extravasation, blood-letting, cupping, bleeding, venesection, phlebotomy, paracentesis, tapping, spilling, shedding, libation, oblation

23 vomiting, vomition, vomit, sickness, sick, regurgitation, egestion, emesis, heaving, retching, gagging, nausea, puking (Inf), puke (Inf), multicolour (*or* technicolour) yawn (Inf), pavement pizza (Inf), tactical vom (Inf)

24 belch, belching, hiccup, ructation, eructation, wind, gas, flatulence, flatulency, flatuosity, flatus, fart, farting, breaking wind

25 emission, emissivity, radioactivity, radiation, fallout

26 ejector, expeller, ouster, evictor, dispossessor, depriver, taker, displacer, supplanter, superseder, substitute, cuckoo, cuckoo in the nest, bouncer (Inf), chucker-out (Inf)

27 expellee, deportee, refugee, outlaw, outcast, outcaste

28 propellant, explosive, emitter, radiator, ejecting mechanism, ejector seat, volcano, emetic, aperient, purgative, laxative

ADJECTIVES

29 expulsive, expellent, ejective, ejaculative, eliminant, explosive, eruptive, radiating, emitting, emissive, secretory, sweaty, sudatory, sudorific, salivary, salivant, sickening, emetic, purgative, laxative, cathartic, emetocathartic, sialagogue, emmenagogic

30 vomiting, sick, sickened, nauseated, seasick, airsick, carsick, travel-sick, vomitive, vomitory, pukey (Inf)

31 eructative, flatulent, flatulous, belching

ADVERBS

32 expulsively, explosively, eruptively, emetically, cathartically

INTERJECTIONS

33 go away!, begone!, get thee hence!, get you gone!, run along!, away!, away with you!, off with you!, off you go!, be off!, on your way!, get out!, get out of here!, get the hell out of here!, clear out!, clear off!, buzz off! (Inf), push off! (Inf), shove off! (Inf), bug off! (Inf), bugger off! (Inf), piss off! (Inf), naff off! (Inf), fuck off! (Inf), beat it! (Inf), scram! (Inf), vamoose! (Inf), skidoo! (Inf), skedaddle! (Inf), get lost! (Inf), walk! (Inf), take a walk! (Inf), take a running jump! (Inf), go chase yourself! (Inf), cheese it! (Inf), take a powder! (Inf), blow! (Inf)

▶ *313 Departure*

372 Separation

Absence from whom we love is worse than death. William Cowper.

Every parting gives a foretaste of death; every coming together again a foretaste of the resurrection. Arthur Schopenhauer.

NOUNS

1 separation, disconnection, disunion, disunity, discontinuity, disjunction, disjuncture, dislocation, separability, disintegration, breakage, breakup, dispersion, dispersal, scattering, dissolution, decomposition, breakdown, dissection, analysis, resolution, resolving power, high resolution, low resolution, disruption, fragmentation, shattering, splitting, fission, nuclear fission, separating, parting, severance, uncoupling, divorce, divorcement, moving apart, growing apart, divergence, spreading, spread, deviation, split, schism, detachment, unfastening, undoing, untying, unbuttoning, unthreading, unravelling, loosening, loosing, liberating, freeing

▶ *133 Discontinuity; 245 Deterioration; 268 Slipperiness; 375 Disintegration; 377 Dispersal; 391 Liberation; 571 Divorce and Widowhood; 751 Disagreement*

2 setting apart, setting aside, ejection, expulsion, exception, exemption, rejection, boycott, avoidance, exclusion, selection, choice, division, severance, discrimination, apartheid, segregation, zoning, zone, compartment, no-go area, off-limits area (US), ghetto, box, cage, prison, isolation, loneliness, seclusion, quarantine, putting aside, keeping to one side, conservation, preservation, reservation, taking away, deprivation, expropriation, removal, withdrawal, resignation, retirement, nonattachment, nonalignment, insularity

► *128 Exclusion; 212 Subtraction; 371 Expulsion; 469 Selection; 605 Resignation; 634 Avoidance; 655 Unsociability*

3 separateness, separability, immiscibility, oil and water, severalty, separatism, nationalism, isolationism, difference, dichotomy, division, subdivision, segmentation, partition, cutting, scission, section, break, tear, laceration, dilaceration, tearing apart, rip, rent, fissure, split, gap, breach, rift, crack, cleft, chasm, cleavage, slit, slot, gash, incision, hole, rupture, opening, ladder, run(US), abscission, offcut, decapitation, beheading, amputation, castration, circumcision, docking, curtailment, retrenchment, cutting away, resection

4 disunity, disagreement, lack of unity, lack of harmony, dissension, opposition, hostility, no common ground, poles apart

5 separator, dividing line, caesura, comma, slash, solidus, dash, hyphen, partition, diaeresis, umlaut, full stop, period (US)

6 boundary, fence, hedge, wall, ha-ha, screen, curtain, limit, frontier, border, barrier, barricade, Berlin Wall, Iron Curtain, Mason-Dixon Line (US)

7 separates, coordinates, accessories, peripherals, add-ons (US)

8 person who separates, surgeon, judge, Moses, Solomon, critic, selector, chemist, separatist, segregationist, isolationist

VERBS

9 separate, part, sever, break, fracture, chip, crack, rupture, snap, break in two, split up, disunite, dissociate, disassociate, divorce, unhitch, uncouple, disconnect, unplug, disengage, displace, wrench, dislocate, throw out of gear, detach, unseat, unhorse, dismount, throw, unstick, untie, unfasten, undo, unbutton, unlace, unhook, unclasp, unzip, unstring, unlock, unlatch, unchain, unbind, unfetter, sever ties, cut the knot, cut the ties that bind, break the link, disentangle, unravel, unstitch, unpick, ladder, run (US), loosen, slacken, relax, loose, set free, liberate, release, eject, expel, dispel, scatter, disband, demobilize, disperse, disintegrate, break up, break down, come undone, come unstuck, spring apart, fall apart, come apart, come (*or* fall) to pieces (*or* bits), take to pieces (*or* bits), take apart, cannibalize, slit, split, rive, cleave, rend, tear, tear apart, rip, tear (*or* rip) to bits (*or* pieces), lacerate, dilacerate, hack, hew, cut, chop, stab, slash, gash, cut through, saw, slice, shred, mince, mash, grind, crunch, bite, bite into, bite through, gnaw, carve, carve up, disassemble, dismantle, disjoin, dissolve, unmake, decompose, decay, degrade, blow up, blow to pieces (*or* bits), smash, shatter, shiver, splinter, crumble, cave in, pulverize, destroy, sunder (Lit)

10 set apart, set aside, put aside, lay up, store, conserve, preserve, reserve, mark out, select, sort, tick off, check off (US), pick out, single out, distinguish, differentiate, discern, resolve (images), discriminate, exclude, except, boycott, ban, bar, blacklist, blackball, banish, ostracize, send to Coventry, isolate, insulate, cut off, hive off, remove, take away, detract, subtract, deduct, strip, strip bare, denude, peel, pare, flake, skin, flay, fleece, shear, clip, pluck, behead, decapitate, amputate, curtail, dock, lop, prune

11 divide, divide up, subdivide, sectionalize, separate the sheep from the goats, separate the wheat from the chaff, segment, fragment, fractionalize, fractionate, fractionize, factorize, analyse, cut up, anatomize, dissect, bisect, halve, apportion, share out, dismember, disembowel, quarter, partition, screen off, compartmentalize, circumscribe, keep apart, segregate, sequester, seclude, quarantine, maroon, keep (*or* hold) apart, set against, estrange, alienate, divorce, make enemies, become enemies

12 disagree, lack unity, lack harmony, have dissention, dissent, oppose, show hostility, find no common ground, stand poles apart

13 diverge, go away, go separate (*or* different) ways, follow separate paths, depart, scatter, disperse, deviate, bifurcate, part, part company, cast adrift, set (*or* cut) adrift, cut loose, get loose, get free, free oneself, get away, break away, fall away, escape, quit, leave, relinquish, abandon, wash one's hands of, get shot of

14 come between, step between, put asunder, divide, keep (*or* hold) apart, interpose, flow between, drive apart, drive a wedge between, sunder (Lit)

ADJECTIVES

15 separate, separated, disunited, disjointed, disjunctive, dislocated, divorced, broken up, disconnected, unplugged, unstuck, untied, undone, unzipped, unloosed, loosened, loose, liberated, released, expelled, ejected, unfettered, unchained, free, open, discontinuous, interrupted, partitioned, bipartite, multipartite, dichotomous, dividing, divided, subdivided, halved, quartered, dismembered, disembowelled, cut, torn, severed, ruptured

16 apart, in pieces (*or* bits), asunder, broken, shattered, split, schizoid, cut up, cut to pieces (*or* bits), shot to pieces, rent, riven, cloven, cleft, dispersed, scattered, fugitive, divergent, radiating, sundered (Lit)

17 unjoined, unfastened, adrift, detached, unattached, nonattached, nonaligned, neutral, unfixed, unconnected, discrete, distinct, distinctive, differentiated, separative, hived off, excluded, excepted, exempt, abstracted, absent-minded, withdrawn, uninvolved, unmixed, immiscible, unassimilated, unassimilable, not belonging, unrelated, alien, foreign, external, extrinsic, self-sufficient, insular, isolated, secluded, lonely, alone, cast off, cast out, left, abandoned, rejected, selective, picked out, set apart, reclusive

18 disagreeable, disagreeing, unharmonious, dissenting, hostile, adverse, opposed, opposite, antipathetic, inimical

19 separable, severable, partiable, divisible, fissionable, fissile, scissile, tearable, breakable, biodegradable, dissolvable, dissoluble, resolvable (image), high-resolution, low-resolution, discernible, distinguishable

ADVERBS

20 separately, severally, singly, one at a time, one by one, piecemeal, piece by piece, bit by bit, in bits, in pieces, in halves, in two, dichotomously, discontinuously, disjunctively, loosely, freely, in twain (Lit)

21 apart, asunder, divergently, brokenly, in pieces, in bits, to bits, to smithereens, to shreds, to tatters, to matchwood, limb from limb, never the twain shall meet

22 in isolation, in splendid isolation, aloof, apart, away, adrift, separatively, distinctly, distinctively, discretely, self-sufficiently, neutrally, abstractly, absent-mindedly, externally, in an alien way, extrinsically, selectively, diagnostically

23 disagreeably, antipathetically, inimically, hostilely, with hostility, unharmoniously, with dissent, adversely, oppositely

373 Connection

Only connect! E. M. Forster.

NOUNS

1 connection, union, merger, conjunction, interconnection, attachment, graft, linking, joining, coupling, fastening, meeting, cohesion, adhesion, involvement, entanglement

▶ *267 Stickiness; 309 Closure*

2 association, relationship, relation, liaison, nexus, network, intercourse, commerce, communication network, communication, intercommunication, satellite link

▶ *692 Communications*

3 associate, business associate, contact, ally, friend, kith, relation, relative, family member, kin, kinsman, blood kin, clan, tribe

▶ *108 Relatedness; 413 Support; 569 Friendship; 654 Sociability*

4 means of connection, bond, chain, fetter, shackle, tie, band, hoop, yoke, link, junction, arch, joint, hinge, ramification, branching, branch, nexus, connective, bonding agent, intermedium, tie beam, beam, girder, stay, stretcher, strut, interconnection, stairway, stairs, ladder, stepladder, steps, stepping stone, canal, isthmus, neck, col, ridge, copula, punctuation mark, hyphen, dash, slash, solidus, parenthesis, bracket, square bracket, angle bracket, brace, zeugma, en rule

▶ *5 Language and Linguistics; 251 Restraint*

5 road, main road, arterial road, A road, motorway, highway (US), interstate (highway) (US), expressway (US), freeway (US), turnpike (US), toll road, toll bridge, bridge, span, causeway, access road, exit, slip road, service road (US), interchange, highway ramp (US), cloverleaf, spaghetti junction, intersecting road, flyover (*or* overpass), underpass, bypass, street, main street, lane, path, track

▶ *319 Transport*

6 line, cable, hawser, cord, whipcord, rope, painter, moorings, guy, guy rope, guest rope, towline, towrope, lifeline, umbilical cord, communication cord, ripcord, string, wire, tape, adhesive tape, twine, binder, binding twine, fibre, ligature, connective tissue, ligament, tendon, muscle, withe (*or* withy), raffia, bast (*or* bass), osier, lashing, binding, thread, band, ribband, bandage, tourniquet, roller bandage, braid, plait, thong, drawstring, lace, shoelace, bootlace, tag, tie, cravat, stock, knot, granny knot, slipknot, stitch

7 tackle, chain, anchor chain, rope, cordage, rig, rigging, sheets, ratline, shroud, clew line, stay, guy, garnet, halyard (*or* halliard), bowline, harness, lanyard

8 fastening, fastener, zip (fastener), zipper (US), button, buttonhole, eyelet, loop, frog, toggle, hook, hook and eye, stud, press stud, snaps (US), stitch, basting, Velcro, collar stud, cufflink, tiepin, suspender, garter (US), braces, suspenders (US), brooch, clasp, clip, tie clasp (*or* clip), grip, hairgrip, bobby pin (US), (hair) slide, barrette (US), curlers, rollers, hairpin, hatpin, skewer, spit, brochette, drawing pin, pushpin (US), thumbtack (US), tack, safety pin, straight pin (US), toggle pin, cotter pin, linchpin, kingpin (*or* swivel pin), peg, dowel, nail, treenail, brad, holdfast, staple, brace, batten, clamp, cramp, nut, bolt, rivet, screw, buckle, hasp, hinge, catch, safety catch, spring catch, latch, lock, lock and key, combination lock, mortise lock, Yale lock, Yale key, padlock, manacles, handcuffs, ring, cleat, bollard, post, stake, pile, pale, bar, popper (Inf), bracelets (Inf)

▶ *253 Security; 267 Stickiness; 553 Fashion*

9 yoke, coupling, coupler, traces, drawbar, hook, claw, grapple, grappling iron, anchor, sheet anchor, harness, reins, ribbons, halter, collar, lead, leash, tether, lasso, lariat (US), noose, loop

10 band, girdle, belt, strap, waistband, cummerbund, bellyband, girth, cinch, sash, shoulder belt, bandoleer (*or* bandolier), Sam Brown belt, collar, neckband, headband, fillet, ribbon

VERBS

11 connect, link, join, conjoin, unite, unify, merge, couple, fasten, attach, interconnect, interweave, entwine, entangle, lace, braid, plait, knot, lash, bind, ligate, bandage, tie, stitch, sew, tack, zip (up), snap (US), button (up), buckle, hook, clip, pin, nail, staple, peg, rivet, screw, skewer, bolt, hinge, stick, bond, glue, tape, bracket, bridge, graft

12 bind, tie, chain, fetter, shackle, yoke, harness, leash,

KNOTS

becket knot
bend
Blackwall hitch
blood knot
bow
bowknot
bowline
bowline on the bight
builder's knot
carrick bend
cat's–paw
clove hitch
diamond knot
Englishman's tie (*or* knot)
figure of eight (*or* figure eight)
fisherman's bend
fisherman's knot
flat knot
French knot
granny knot (*or* granny's knot)
half hitch
hangman's knot
harness hitch
hawser bend
hitch
Hunter's bend
loop knot
love knot
magnus hitch
Matthew Walker
mesh knot
overhand knot
prusik
reef knot
rolling hitch
round turn and two half hitches
running bowline
sheepshank
sheet bend
shroud knot
slipknot
square knot
stevedore's knot
surgeon's knot
sword knot
thumb knot
tie
timber hitch
truelove knot (*or* true–lover's knot)
Turk's–head
wall knot
weaver's knot
Windsor knot

tether, lasso, manacle, handcuff, secure, lock, bolt, latch, padlock, batten, clamp, clasp, grip, moor, anchor

13 intercommunicate, communicate, contact, meet, liaise, network, interface, associate, relate, cohere, adhere, stick together, involve, entangle, form an alliance, pair up, match

ADJECTIVES

14 connective, conjunctive, cohesive, adhesive, sticky, interconnective, communicative, in contact, liaising, associated, related, joint, coherent

15 connected, tied, linked, joined, united, merged, coupled, interfaced, fastened, attached, interconnected, interwoven, entangled, laced, braided, plaited, knotted, lashed, bound, stitched, sewn, tacked, zipped (up), buttoned (up), buckled, hooked, wired (up), pinned, nailed, stapled, pegged, riveted, screwed, hinged, stuck, bonded, glued, bracketed, hyphenated, bridged

16 bound, tied, chained, fettered, shackled, yoked, harnessed, leashed, tethered, lassoed, manacled, handcuffed, secured, locked, bolted, latched, padlocked, battened, clamped, clasped, gripped

ADVERBS

17 in connection with, connectively, in relation to (*or* with), jointly, conjunctively, cohesively, adhesively, with a rope, with a hook, with a pin, with a lock, securely

374 Combination

We must indeed all hang together, or most assuredly, we shall all hang separately. Benjamin Franklin.

NOUNS

1 combination, combining, joining together, growing together, symphysis, symbiosis, synthesis, bringing together, composition, fusion, coalescence, conflation, blending, blend, mingling, mixing, mixture, mix, syncretism, amalgamation, merger, unification, uniting, assimilation, absorption, digestion, integration, embodiment, incorporation, centralization, coincidence, concurrence, conjunction, synchronicity

▶ *412 Mixture*

2 cooperation, collaboration, concurrence, conjunction, synchronization, union, coagency, alliance, league, marriage, federation, confederation, confederacy, association, plot, conspiracy, cabal, agreement, unity, concord, harmony, chord, counterpoint, music, orchestration, jigsaw, mosaic, tessellation, collage, patchwork

▶ *18 Music; 285 Same Time; 484 Plan; 747 Cooperation; 750 Agreement*

3 assembly, assemblage, collection, set, compendium, anthology, aggregation, aggregate, agglomeration, conglomeration, conglomerate, combine, syndicate, consortium, bloc, corporation, company, society, association, club, party, force, army, regiment, brigade, division, squadron, air squadron, wing, flotilla, fleet, team, group, grouping, pressure group, rock group, pop group, band, wind band, brass band, orchestra, symphony orchestra, chamber orchestra, duo, dynamic duo, duet, trio, quartet, string quartet, quintet, sextet, septet, octet, nonet, chorus, choir, congregation, audience

▶ *18 Music; 376 Gathering; 409 Arrangement; 584 Military Affairs; 723 Summary*

4 compound, mixture, suspension, solution, blend, alloy, amalgam, composite, make-up, hybrid, cocktail, portmanteau word

▶ *412 Mixture*

VERBS

5 combine, join together, unite, fit together, put together, assemble, make up, compose, synthesize, integrate, fuse, merge, coalesce, consolidate, grow together, run together, converge, have an affinity, blend, mingle, commingle, mix, mix together, syncretize, mix with water, add water, dilute, hydrate, interweave, intertwine, network, connect, join, conjoin, link, conjugate, yoke, centralize, unify, incorporate, embody, impregnate, imbue, infuse, instil, inoculate, inculcate, absorb, digest, assimilate, soak up, take in with one's mother's milk, amalgamate, pool, collect, heap up, lay up, store, aggregate, congregate, compound, lump together, bracket together, group, regroup, rally, bring together

▶ *211 Addition; 368 Insertion; 412 Mixture*

6 come together, band together, brigade, associate, partner, go into partnership with, league with, federate, confederate, join hands, join forces with, team up with, cooperate, come to an agreement, agree, concur, make a pact, make an alliance, ally, collaborate, act together, harmonize, synchronize, make friends with, fraternize, bond, cement a relationship, marry, wed, mate, couple, copulate, put heads together, conspire, plot

▶ *376 Gathering; 484 Plan; 561 Reproduction; 569 Friendship; 570 Marriage; 654 Sociability; 747 Cooperation*

ADJECTIVES

7 combined, combinatory, combinative, integrated, fused, composed, blended, mingled, mixed, syncretic, harmonized, interwoven, intertwined, networked, connected, joined, joint, conjugate, conjoined, conjoint, yoked, linked, united, unified, centralized, incorporated, embodied, bred into, bred-in-the-bone, inbred, ingrained, impregnated, absorbed, digested, coalescent, symphystic

8 cooperative, symbiotic, in agreement, in harmony, harmonious, on the same wavelength, associated, in association, orchestrated, leagued, in league, conspiratorial, cabbalistic, in partnership, allied, federated, confederate, coagent, concurrent, synchronized, synchronous, coincident, conjunctive

9 assembled, collected, heaped up, congregated, aggregated, amalgamated, merged, collective, aggregate, conglomerate, associative, congregational

▶ *376 Gathering*

ADVERBS

10 in combination, in concert, in league (with), in partnership (with), jointly, cooperatively, harmoniously, conspiratorially, cabbalistically, collectively, associatively, congregationally, concurrently, coincidentally, synchronously, symbiotically, syncretically, together, as one

375 Disintegration

NOUNS

1 disintegration, breakup, disorder, chaos, disturbance, derangement, explosion, collapse, wear, wear and tear, erosion, death, decomposition, corruption, corrosion, rust, decay, mould, mouldering, fungus, rot, rotting, compost, putrefaction, mortification, necrosis, gangrene, caries, adipocere, grave-wax, carrion

► *245 Deterioration; 328 Disturbance; 408 Disorder; 582 Death*

2 deconstruction, demolition, destruction, breakdown, taking apart, dismantling, decentralization, devolution, delegation, demerging, demerger, regionalization, compartmentation, compartmentalization, division, partition, disunion, separation, dispersal, scattering, dissolution, melting, liquefaction, deliquescence, reduction, simplification, resolution, analysis, parsing, syllabification, dissection, dismemberment, anatomization, electrolysis, hydrolysis, catalysis, photolysis, catabolism, atom-smashing, fission, nuclear fission, atomization

► *5 Language and Linguistics; 28 Physics; 32 Chemistry; 357 Destruction; 372 Separation; 377 Dispersal*

VERBS

3 disintegrate, come apart, come to pieces, break up, break down, collapse, fall apart, fall to pieces, go to pieces, explode, blow up, smash to pieces, shatter, splinter, crumble, decompose, corrupt, corrode, rust, perish, decay, moulder, rot, rot down, putrefy, mortify, gangrene, necrose, consume, waste away, erode, wear away, wear out

► *245 Deterioration; 372 Separation*

4 deconstruct, demolish, pull down, wreck, smash, break up, destroy, unsettle, disorder, cause chaos, disturb, derange, pull apart, pull to pieces, take apart, take to pieces, dismantle, disband, decentralize, devolve, delegate, demerge, regionalize, compartmentalize, partition, divide, disperse, scatter, dissolve, melt, liquefy, deliquesce, reduce, simplify, unscramble, resolve, decompound, separate, separate out, break down, analyse, parse, syllabify, dissect, dismember, electrolyse, hydrolyse, catalyse, split, fission, atomize

► *5 Language and Linguistics; 28 Physics; 32 Chemistry; 328 Disturbance; 357 Destruction; 372 Separation; 377 Dispersal; 408 Disorder*

ADJECTIVES

5 disintegrated, in pieces, in bits, smashed, shattered, destroyed, demolished, uncombined, chaotic, disordered, broken down, dissolved, melted, molten, liquefied, separated, curdled, decomposed, deconstructed, high, well hung, bad, off, rotted, rotten, putrid, rancid, sour, gangrenous, corrupted, decayed, composted, mouldering, rusty, corroded, dilapidated, ruined, in ruins, decomposable, compostable, biodegradable, recyclable, disposable

► *245 Deterioration; 357 Destruction; 372 Separation*

6 disintegrating, crumbling, falling apart, tumbledown, dilapidated, decomposing, rotting, decaying, melting, deliquescent, catabolic, gangrenous, necrotic, rusty, corroding

ADVERBS

7 to pieces, to bits, to smithereens, in parts, partitively, analytically, on (*or* by) analysis, electrolytically, hydrolytically, catalytically, photolytically, catabolically

8 destructively, divisively, separately, reductively, explosively, corrosively, chaotically, disturbingly, necrotically, gangrenously, putridly

376 Gathering

Kings govern by means of popular assemblies only when they cannot do without them. Charles James Fox.

NOUNS

1 assembly, party, group, body, band, company, set, bunch, gang, crowd, corps, assemblage, bringing together, coming together, convergence, confluence, collection, collecting, gathering, ingathering, forgathering, grouping, congregation, mobilization, muster, rally, call-up, combination, joining together, junction, collocation, colligation

► *373 Connection; 374 Combination*

2 herding, whipping in, roundup, shepherding, driving, corralling, marshalling, rodeo

3 meeting, assembly, gathering, meet, concourse, turnout, congregation, convocation

4 rally, mass meeting, demonstration, protest meeting, sit-in, demo (Inf)

► *703 Demonstration; 753 Protest*

5 conference, symposium, convention, convocation, congregation, congress, caucus, synod, diet, council, legislature, conclave

► *12 Government and Politics*

6 sitting, session, board meeting, business meeting, discussion group

7 committee, commission, council, panel, board, cabinet, body, inner circle, consortium

8 rendezvous, tryst, assignation, date, appointment

9 social gathering, get-together, reunion, gathering of the clans, party, celebration, festival, fiesta, festivity, social, reception, function, gala, shindig, wedding breakfast, wedding reception, stag party, hen party, at home, soirée, house-warming, do (Inf), bash (Inf), thrash (Inf), shindig (Inf), shindy (Inf), beanfeast (Inf), beano (Inf), bunfight (Inf), blowout (Inf)

► *601 Celebration; 654 Sociability*

10 dance, ball, hunt ball, charity ball, prom (US), disco, acid-house party, rave, hop, barn dance, ceilidh, knees-up (Inf), bop (Inf)

► *22 Dancing*

11 group, grouping, party, company, body, band, gang, pack, ring, circle, posse, bevy, bunch (Inf), crowd (Inf)

12 team, squad, crew, force, outfit, complement, corps, troupe, cast, company, orchestra, band, rock group, pop group

► *18 Music; 21 Drama*

13 workforce, staff, personnel, manpower, crew, factory floor, shop floor

► *578 Worker*

14 force, armed force, army, navy, air force, troop, squadron, squad, platoon, unit, regiment, corps, battalion, division, brigade, legion, fleet

► *584 Military Affairs; 586 Combatant*

15 association, alliance, partnership, organization, society, corporation, federation, cartel, conglomerate, club,

COLLECTIVE NAMES FOR BIRDS AND ANIMALS

bask (crocodiles)
bevy (roe deer, quails, larks, pheasants)
bloat (hippopotami)
brood (chickens)
bury (rabbits)
busyness (ferrets)
charm (finches, goldfinches)
chattering (choughs)
clowder (cats)
covey (partridges)
crash (rhinoceros)
descent (woodpeckers)
desert (lapwings)
dout (wild cats)
down (hares)
doylt (swine)
drove (horses, ponies, bullocks)
flock (sheep)
fluther (jellyfish)
gaggle (geese on land)
gam (whales)
gang (elk)
gulp (swallows)
herd (cattle, elephants, bison)
hive (bees)
hover (trout)
kennel (dogs)
labour (moles)
leap (leopards)
lepe (leopards)
litter (kittens, pigs)
murder (crows)
murmuration (starlings)
muster (peacocks, penguins)
mute (hares)
obstinacy (buffalo)
pack (hounds, dogs, grouse)
paddling (ducks on water)
pandemonium (parrots)
parade (elephants)
parcel (penguins)
parliament (owls)
pod (seals)
pride (lions)
rafter (turkeys)
rookery (rooks, seals)
safe (ducks)
sawt (lions)
school (whales, porpoises, dolphins)
serge (herons)
shoal (fish)
skein (geese in flight)
skulk (foxes)
sloth (bears)
smack (jellyfish)
sowse (lions)
span (mules)
spring (teal)
stare (owls)
string (horses)
stud (mares)
swarm (flies, locusts, bees)
tittering (magpies)
tribe (goats)
turmoil (porpoises)
turn (turtles)
unkindness (ravens)
watch (nightingales)
zeal (zebras)

COLLECTIVE NAMES BY ANIMAL

bears (sloth)
bees (hive, swarm)
bison (herd)
buffalo (obstinacy)
bullocks (drove)
cats (clowder)
cattle (herd)
chickens (brood)
choughs (chattering)
crocodiles (bask)
crows (murder)
dogs (kennel, pack)
dolphins (school)
ducks (paddling, safe)
elephants (herd, parade)
elk (gang)
ferrets (busyness)
finches (charm)
fish (shoal)
flies (swarm)
foxes (skulk)
geese (gaggle, skein)
goats (tribe)
goldfinches (charm)
grouse (pack)
hares (down, mute)
herons (serge)
hippopotami (bloat)
horses (drove)
hounds (pack)
jellyfish (smack, fluther)
kittens (litter)
larks (bevy)
lapwings (desert)
leopards (leap, lepe)
lions (pride, sawt, sowse)
locusts (swarm)
magpies (tittering)
mares (stud)
moles (labour)
mules (span)
owls (parliament, stare)
parrots (pandemonium)
partridges (covey)
peacocks (muster)
penguins (muster)
pheasants (bevy)
pigs (litter)
ponies (drove)
porpoises (school, turmoil)
quails (bevy)
rabbits (bury)
ravens (unkindness)
rhinoceros (crash)
roe deer (bevy)
rooks (rookery)
seals (pod, rookery)
sheep (flock)
starlings (murmuration)
swallows (gulp)
swine (doylt)
teal (spring)
trout (hover)
turkeys (rafter)
turtles (turn)
woodpeckers (descent)
wildcats (dout)
whales (school, gam)
zebras (zeal)

union, trade union, guild, syndicate, fellowship, brotherhood, fraternity, confraternity, sisterhood, sorority

▶ *654 Sociability*

16 party, faction, movement, wing, junta, cabal, cell, unit, cadre, bloc, caucus, quango

▶ *205 Part*

17 family, nuclear family, extended family, household, kith and kin, folks (Inf), relatives, social group, peer group, community, class, clan, tribe, speech community, people

▶ *2 Sociology; 108 Relatedness; 137 Class*

18 generation, age group, peer group, cohort (US), compeers

19 clique, circle, set, coterie, in-crowd, in-group, them and us, club, lodge, house

20 crowd, mob, mass, throng, multitude, horde, host, swarm, ruck, rabble, the masses, the hoi polloi, all and then some, all the world and his wife (Inf), the great unwashed (Inf), every mother's son (Inf), every Tom, Dick, and Harry (Inf)

▶ *138 Generality; 208 Multitude; 566 Humankind*

21 scrum, scrummage (*or* scrimmage), huddle, crush, squeeze, jam, press

22 flood, deluge, spate, surge, stream, volley, shower, hail, storm

▶ *219 Excess*

23 flock, herd, pack, kennel, drove, drive, stable, string, colony, set, host, troop, army, swarm, school, shoal

24 brace, pair, clutch, batch, litter, brood

▶ *198 Two; 561 Reproduction*

25 assemblage, collection, set, batch, group, accumulation, congeries, agglomeration, conglomeration, aggregation, hoard, store, stockpile, food mountain, fund, holdings

▶ *219 Excess; 374 Combination; 439 Store*

26 mass, heap, pile, stack, mound, mountain, embankment, bank, sandbank, dune, drift, snowdrift, deposit, sediment

▶ *215 Remainder*

27 bundle, wad, batch, clump, cluster, bunch, knot, parcel, package, bale, truss, rick, hayrick, haystack, roll, bolt, quiver, sheaf, skein, hank, tussock, hassock, crop

28 cluster, galaxy, constellation, nebula, star system

▶ *29 Astronomy*

29 bunch, bouquet, posy, nosegay, spray

▶ *78 Flowers*

30 compilation, collection, corpus, compendium, anthology, composition, roundup (Inf)

▶ *412 Mixture*

31 exhibition, show, display, collection, gallery, museum, library, zoo, menagerie, aviary, aquarium
32 miscellany, miscellanea, collectanea, chrestomathy (Lit), medley, assortment, mixture, mixed bag, mixed lot, potpourri, smorgasbord, jumble, hotchpotch (*or* hodgepodge), sundries, oddments, bits and pieces, odds and ends, bits and bobs (Inf)
► *412 Mixture*
33 putting together, assembly, assemblage, collage, montage, construction, erection, connection, fitting (*or* joining *or* piecing) together, manufacture, fabrication, assembly line, production line
► *356 Creation; 373 Connection*
34 assembler, convener (*or* convenor), whip, whipper-in, herdsman, shepherd, sheepdog
35 collector, accumulator, gatherer, gleaner, beachcomber, harvester, reaper, tax collector, rent collector, debt collector, stamp collector, philatelist, coin collector, numismatist
► *43 Agriculture; 785 Payment*
36 hoarder, squirrel, magpie, miser, penny-pincher, niggard, Scrooge
► *439 Store; 682 Meanness*

VERBS

37 assemble, collect, gather, bring together, draw together, group, group together, accumulate, agglomerate, aggregate, mass, amass, hoard, store, stockpile, heap, pile, stack, build up, mound, bank, bank up
► *439 Store*
38 group, batch, clump, cluster, bunch, bundle, parcel, package, wrap, bale, truss, bind
39 come together, collect together, gather together, forgather, meet, rendezvous, congregate, group, flock together, gather round, rally round, huddle, go into a huddle, cluster, bunch
40 crowd, mass, throng, pack, cram, mill, mill around, seethe, teem, crawl, swarm, horde, troop, flood, stream, pour, surge, sweep, flow, rush
► *208 Multitude*
41 band together, get together, join forces, unite, team up, join up, link up, gang up, fall in, swell the ranks
► *747 Cooperation*
42 call together, convene, convoke, summon, call a meeting, hold a meeting, muster, marshal, rally, mobilize, call up
43 herd, shepherd, round up, corral, drive, drive together, whip in, call in
44 put together, compose, compile, colligate, connect, join, unite, combine, fit (*or* join *or* piece) together, construct, erect, fabricate, manufacture, make
► *356 Creation; 373 Connection; 374 Combination*
45 reassemble, rejoin, put back together

ADJECTIVES

46 assembled, gathered, congregate, congregated, convened, summoned, mobilized, called up, herded, mustered, shepherded, rounded up
47 collected, amassed, massed, accumulated, hoarded, stockpiled, heaped, piled, stacked, put together
48 cumulate, glomerate, conglomerate, agglomerate, aggregate, convergent, confluent, collective, combined, joined, united, connected
49 grouped, clumped, clustered, bunched, bundled, packaged, baled, trussed, wrapped, parcelled, wrapped up, fascicled, fascicular, congressional, congregational, factional, cabalistic
50 crowded, packed, crammed, congested, dense, close, serried, swarming, seething, teeming, bristling, milling, crawling, jam-packed (Inf), chock-a-block (Inf), thick as flies (Inf), thick on the ground (Inf)

ADVERBS

51 together, unitedly, collectively, all together, *en masse* (Fr), in a mass, in a body, as one

377 Dispersal

Lord Ronald said nothing; he flung himself from the room, flung himself upon his horse and rode madly off in all directions.
Stephen Leacock.

NOUNS

1 dispersion, dispersal, diffusion, distribution, dissemination, sowing, strewing, casting, seeding, scattering, scatterment, circulation, publication, broadcast, broadcasting, spread, deployment, propagation, issuance, giving out, dispensation
► *740 Publication; 770 Allocation*
2 disbandment, dissolution, demobilization, deactivation, dismissal, sending home, going home, demob (Inf)
► *313 Departure*
3 dilution, watering down, attenuation, liquefaction, deliquescence, evaporation, boiling away, vaporization, volatilization, dissipation, disappearance
► *526 Disappearance*
4 sprinkling, spraying, spattering, splattering, smattering, dusting, powdering, peppering, circumfusion, studding, spotting, dotting, speckling, freckling
5 divergence, radiation, branching, branching out, ramification, fanning out, splaying, deflection, diffraction, disintegration, fragmentation, decomposition, breakup, separation, parting, split-up (Inf)
► *311 Divergence; 372 Separation; 375 Disintegration*
6 decentralization, deconcentration, regionalization, localization, federalization, subsidiarity
7 sprawl, urban sprawl, ribbon development, dispersed population, population drift, diaspora, emigration
8 driftwood, flotsam and jetsam

VERBS

9 be dispersed, disperse, scatter, separate, part, break up, split up, part company, go one's separate ways, move apart, drift apart, drift off, stray, straggle, spread, spread out, sprawl
► *313 Departure; 372 Separation*
10 diverge, fork, branch out (*or* off), ramify, radiate, fan out, splay
11 explode, burst, fly apart, fly in all directions, come apart, come unstuck, break up, disintegrate, fragment, decompose, evaporate, dissipate, disappear, vanish
► *375 Disintegration; 526 Disappearance*
12 disperse, scatter, diffract, diffuse, dispel, separate, part, divide, sunder, hive off, detach
► *372 Separation*

13 dismiss, send away, send off, disband, dissolve, demobilize, deactivate, discharge, send home, muster out (US), rout, put to flight, demob (Inf)

14 dilute, water down, dissolve, thin, thin out, attenuate, liquefy, evaporate, boil away, vaporize, volatilize, dissipate

15 decentralize, deconcentrate, regionalize, localize, depopulate

16 distribute, disseminate, circulate, put into circulation, publish, broadcast, spread, deploy, propagate, issue, dispense, deal, deal out, dole out

▶ *740 Publication; 770 Allocation*

17 sow, seed, strew, scatter around, scatter to the winds, throw around, cast, fling, litter

18 sprinkle, spray, splash, shower, spatter, splatter, smatter, dust, powder, flour, dredge, pepper, stud, spot, dot, speckle, speck, freckle

ADJECTIVES

19 dispersed, scattered, diffuse, widespread, sparse, infrequent, sporadic, dotted about, few and far between

▶ *206 Few*

20 separated, separate, discrete, disintegrated, fragmented, decomposed, broken up, split-up

▶ *372 Separation; 375 Disintegration*

21 disbanded, dissolved, unassembled, dismissed, demobilized, deactivated, demobbed (Inf)

22 distributed, disseminated, diffused, broadcast, spread, deployed, strewn, sown, propagated, circulated, published, issued, given out, dispensed

▶ *740 Publication; 770 Allocation*

23 sprinkled, sprayed, spattered, splattered, smattered, dusted, powdered, peppered, studded, spotted, dotted, speckled, freckled

24 divergent, forking, radiating, branching, ramiform, dendriform, dendritic, centrifugal

25 sprawled, sprawling, straggling, straggly, drifting, adrift, astray, wandering, stray, loose, all over the lot (Inf)

26 decentralized, deconcentrated, regionalized, localized, federalized

27 dilute, diluted, watered-down, liquefied, evaporated, boiled away, vaporized, dissipated

28 dispersive, scattering, spreading, diffractive, diffusive, distributive, disseminative, dissipative

ADVERBS

29 dispersively, diffractively, diffusively, distributively, disseminatively, dissipatively

30 diffusely, sparsely, infrequently, sporadically, here and there, in places

31 everywhere, in all quarters, wherever you look (*or* turn), in all directions, to the four winds, to the four corners of the earth

378 Obstruction

There was only one catch and that was Catch-22, which specified that a concern for one's own safety in the face of dangers that were real and immediate was the process of a rational mind.
Joseph Heller.

NOUNS

1 hindrance, hindering, impediment, encumbrance, let or hindrance (Lit), obstruction, obstructiveness, restriction, circumscription, restraint, retardation, control, curb, detention, detainment, limitation, friction, interruption, interference, interception, interposition, intervention, meddling, opposition, contrariness, unwillingness, refusal, interdiction, injunction, resistance, counteraction, countermeasure, obviation, determent, dissuasion, discouragement, frustration, foiling, prevention, repression, preclusion, prohibition, stopping, forestalling, hampering

▶ *113 Opposition; 166 Limit; 226 Stopping; 347 Counteraction; 365 Friction; 383 Resistance; 384 Defence; 481 Dissuasion; 637 Unwillingness; 709 Refusal*

2 obstacle, block, stumbling block, blockage, blockade, roadblock, lockout, log jam (US), stoppage, tollgate, strike, barrier, bar, picket line, embargo, intervention, impediment, turnstile, bottleneck, jam, traffic jam, contraflow, difficulty, deterrent, drawback, joker (US), inconvenience, bureaucracy, red tape, regulations, not plain sailing, hazard, hurdle, hitch, snag, drag, rub, catch, catch-22, vicious circle (*or* cycle), check, stay, arrest, sabotage, filibuster, delay, trouble, mishap, contretemps, accident, breakdown, flat tyre, puncture, technical hitch, technical problems, malfunction, computer malfunction, glitch, engine trouble, teething troubles, flaw, impasse, stalemate, deadlock, botch, mix-up, foul-up (US), hang-up (Inf), hiccup (Inf), bug (US inf), fly in the ointment (Inf), spanner in the works(Inf), spot of bother (Inf), cat among the pigeons (Inf), fox in the henhouse (Inf), nigger in the woodpile (Offensive), sabbing (Inf), cockup (Inf), screw-up (US inf), fuck-up (Inf)

▶ *12 Government and Politics; 40 Computers; 240 Inconvenience; 264 Difficulty; 319 Transport; 333 Slowness; 563 Infertility*

3 barrier, wall, brick wall, stone wall, fence, barbed wire, portcullis, sea wall, jetty, mole, breakwater, levee, dam, dike, bulwark, rampart, bunker, buffer, parapet, breastwork, earthwork, work, embankment, moat, ditch, weir, Iron Curtain, Bamboo Curtain, Berlin Wall, Hadrian's Wall, Great Wall of China, barrier method contraception, prophylaxis, condom, diaphragm, Dutch cap

▶ *165 Enclosure; 309 Closure; 384 Defence*

4 restraint, curb, check, shackles, chains, ball and chain, tether, fetter, bond, tie, apron strings, knot, rein, leash, lead, brake, governor (of speed), wheel clamp, boot, Denver boot, doorstop, anchor

▶ *387 Subjection; 815 Prison*

5 inhibition, introversion, conservativeness, embarrassment, shyness, negativism, hanging back, foot-dragging (Inf)

▶ *172 Inside; 634 Avoidance; 637 Unwillingness; 655 Unsociability*

6 burden, inconvenience, handicap, encumbrance, debts, mortgage, dependents, family responsibilities, white elephant, overload, last straw, weight on one's shoulders, millstone round one's neck, albatross, dead weight, cross to bear, monkey on one's back (US inf)

▶ *414 Heaviness; 784 Debt*

7 hinderer, hindrance, interrupter, obstructer, obstructionist, negativist, introvert, impeder, marplot, filibuster (*or* filibusterer), staller, frustrator, killjoy, spoilsport, heckler, interferer, meddler, intruder, gate-crasher, damper, troublemaker, mischief-maker, gremlin, poltergeist, saboteur, snake in the grass, dog in the manger, interfering so-and-so (Inf), wet blanket (Inf), party-pooper (Inf)

VERBS

8 **hinder**, impede, encumber, obstruct, get in the way of, restrict, circumscribe, choke, stifle, restrain, disable, incapacitate, undermine, impair, control, curb, detain, hold back, hold one back, limit, retard, stall, cause friction, interrupt, interfere, intercept, upset, interpose, intervene, come between, meddle, bother, heckle, barrack, oppose, refuse, resist, counteract, devise countermeasures, obviate, deter, dissuade, discourage, frustrate, thwart, spike, foil, foul up, mix up, prevent, repress, preclude, prohibit, forbid, stop, stop one in the act, bring to a standstill, scotch, forestall, hamper, damper, stymie, cripple, hobble, drag one's feet, cut the ground from under one's feet, nip in the bud, throw cold water on, clip one's wings, take the wind out of one's sails, steal someone's thunder, upset one's applecart, pull the rug from under one's feet, cramp someone's style (Inf), crimp (US inf), put a crimp in (US inf), spike someone's guns (Inf), snooker (Inf), hassle (Inf), crab one's act (*or* deal) (US inf), queer (Inf), louse up (Inf), snafu (US inf)

9 **block**, block up, blockade, throw up a roadblock, create an obstacle, create a barrier, wall, wall up, fence, dam, cut off, create a logjam (US), strike, picket, form a picket line, bar, lock out, embargo, intervene, impede, trip, trip up, cramp one's style, stand in the way of, get under one's feet, get in the way, bottleneck, cause a traffic jam, deter, use a condom, find a joker in the pack (US), inconvenience, snag, hit a snag, find oneself in a catch-22 situation, sabotage, filibuster, delay, stall, protract, play for time, cause trouble, have a mishap, have an accident, have a breakdown, have a flat, develop technical problems, malfunction, develop engine trouble, have teething troubles, reach an impasse, reach a stalemate, deadlock, have a hiccup (Inf), have a fly in the ointment (Inf), gum up (Inf), gum up the works (Inf), throw a spanner in the works (Inf), find a nigger in the woodpile (Offensive), have a cockup (Inf), sab (Inf)

10 **restrain**, curb, check, shackle, chain, tether, fetter, bind, tie one's hands, tie, rein, leash, brake, act as a brake, clamp a wheel, anchor

11 **be inhibited**, be introverted, have a conservative outlook, embarrass, shy, hang back, drag, drag one's feet (Inf)

12 **burden**, inconvenience, handicap, encumber, saddle with, have debts, mortgage one's house, have dependents to support, have family responsibilities, overload, have a weight on one's shoulders, have a millstone round one's neck, have an albatross round one's neck, have a cross to bear, have a monkey on one's back (US inf)

ADJECTIVES

13 **hindering**, hindered, impeding, impeded, held back, held up, unhelpful, uncooperative, unwilling, contrary, encumbering, encumbered, obstructive, restrictive, cramping, circumscriptive, limited, interfering, intrusive, interventional, intervening, meddling, deterrent, dissuasive, discouraging, off-putting, preventive, defensive, prophylactic, counteractive, repressive, preclusive, prohibitive, prohibiting, thwarting, more of a hindrance than a help

14 **blocked**, barred, in the way, walled-in, fenced-in, up against a brick wall, with one's back to the wall, in a corner, restraining, restrained, anchored, curbed, shackled, chained, tethered, leashed, deterrent, interventional, inconvenient, bureaucratic, regulatory, hazardous, fraught with difficulties, not easy, accidental, malfunctioning, deadlocked, at a standstill, at an impasse, burdened, overburdened, heavy-laden, handicapped, saddled with, in debt, indebted, overloaded, backbreaking, lumbered with (Inf), in a fix (Inf), in a pickle (Inf), hairy (Inf)

15 **inhibitive**, introversive, conservative, embarrassing, embarrassed, shy, negative, foot-dragging (Inf)

ADVERBS

16 **with delay**, with much ado, without help, unhelpfully, without assistance, uncooperatively, unwillingly, contrarily, obstructively, restrictively, intrusively, in an intrusive manner, dissuasively, discouragingly, preventively, defensively, counteractively, repressively, preclusively, prohibitively

17 **in the way**, interventionally, inconveniently, bureaucratically, hazardously, with difficulty, the hard way, up against a brick wall, with one's back to the wall, in a corner, accidentally

18 **inhibitively**, with inhibitions, in an inhibited way, conservatively, embarrassingly, with embarrassment, shyly, negatively, in a negative manner

379 Trap

In baiting a mouse-trap with cheese, always leave room for the mouse. Saki.

NOUNS

1 **trap**, pitfall, pit, snare, gin, springe, trap door, trap for the unwary, danger, hazard, catch, snag, catch-22, pons asinorum, obstacle, stumbling block, booby trap, deathtrap, firetrap, mine, minefield, tank trap, dragon's teeth, trick, deception, con (Inf), ruse, subterfuge, artifice, stratagem, surprise, unexpected event, lying in wait, unexpected attack, ambush, sleeping dog, wolf in sheep's clothing, thin ice, quagmire, quicksand, marsh, sand bar, sandbank, shoal, shoal water, breakers, shallows, shallow water, reef, sunken reef, coral reef, rock, ironbound coast, lee shore, steep, chasm, abyss, crevasse, precipice, rapids, white-water, current, crosscurrent, undertow, vortex, maelstrom, whirlpool, eddy, rising water, incoming tide, tidal wave, flash flood, storm, squall, gale, hurricane, tornado, cyclone, twister (US), volcano, furnace, earthquake, dynamite, powder keg, time bomb, terrorist bomb, trouble spot, area of contamination, hotbed, source of trouble, Pandora's box, hornet's nest, bane

► *157 Shallowness; 254 Danger; 378 Obstruction; 587 Weapon; 630 Surprise; 700 Deception; 736 Concealment*

VERBS

2 **trap**, entrap, snare, ensnare, net, catch, catch out, catch unawares, surprise, take by surprise, lie in wait, ambush, trick, deceive, dupe, inveigle, cause trouble, make mischief

▶ *630 Surprise; 700 Deception*

380 Violence

So soon as the man overtook me, he was but a word and a blow.
John Bunyan.

NOUNS

1 **violence**, ferocity, vehemence, excess, force, severity, virulence, intensity, power, strength, vigour, bluster, roughness, rough handling, harshness, fierceness, aggression, wildness, fury, frenzy, passion, ferment, effervescence, agitation, turbulence, storminess, impetuosity, forcefulness, might, energy, boisterousness, destructiveness, murderousness

▶ *327 Agitation; 334 Power; 336 Strength; 338 Vigour; 357 Destruction; 647 Severity*

2 **physical violence**, physical cruelty, physical abuse, child abuse, torture, hammer blows, strong-arm tactics, thuggery, hooliganism, vandalism, terrorism, brute force, brutality, bestiality, savagery, barbarity, bloodlust, bloodthirstiness, blood-letting, slaughter, homicide, murder, rape, sexual assault, indecent assault, violation, gang rape, male rape

▶ *382 Killing; 491 Physical Pain; 651 Malevolence*

3 **instance of violence**, onrush, assault, charge, sortie, attack, outburst, outbreak, rush, commotion, disturbance, tumult, brouhaha, riot, row, uproar, roughhouse, fisticuffs, fracas, clash, crash, twist, sprain, fracture, wrench, dislocation, shock, outrage, atrocity, murder, bloodbath, throe, paroxysm, fit, convulsion, spasm, tremor, earthquake, quake, tidal wave, flood, cataclysm, eruption, explosion, detonation, blow-up, flare-up, blast, burst, bursting open, dissilience, rumpus (Inf), ruckus (US inf), punch-up (Inf)

▶ *234 Distortion; 381 Attack; 507 Loudness*

4 **violent creature**, savage, beast, savage beast, wild beast, brute, monster, dragon, demon, devil, hellhound, hound of Hell, Hound of the Baskervilles, mad dog, wolf, she-wolf, tiger, tigress, hellcat, he-man, hulk, caveman, Neanderthal, barbarian, vandal, rough, tough, tough guy, ruffian, mugger, thug, hooligan, bully, bullyboy, bovver boy, terror, holy terror, terrorist, revolutionary, militant, anarchist, agitator, assassin, murderer, mass murderer, sex murderer, serial killer, rapist, hangman, executioner, butcher, slaughterer, man of blood, Herod, Boadicea, psychopath, homicidal maniac, madman, thunderer, fire raiser, arsonist, pyromaniac, firebrand, fire-eater, hotspur (Lit), madcap, hell-raiser, bravo, desperado, termagant, fury, spitfire, shrew, virago, Amazon

▶ *382 Killing; 461 Insanity; 588 Anarchy*

5 **violent weather**, storm, tempest, cloudburst, downpour, rainstorm, hailstorm, snowstorm, blizzard, flood, flash flood, gully washer (US), thunder, thunder and lightning, fulguration, squall, tornado, cyclone, hurricane, typhoon, gale, strong wind, war of the elements, weather, bad weather, inclement weather, rough weather, dirty weather, foul weather, magnetic storm, dust storm, sandstorm, sirocco

ADJECTIVES

6 **violent**, ferocious, vehement, excessive, outrageous, severe, virulent, intense, extreme, acute, unmitigated, sharp, blustering, blustery, brisk, abrupt, brusque, rude, bluff, rough, harsh, fierce, aggressive, tyrannical, heavy-handed, forceful, forcible, strong, powerful, mighty, vigorous, energetic, wild, furious, infuriated, angry, on the rampage, on the warpath, fuming, frenzied, frantic, frenetic, in hysterics, hysterical, kicking, struggling, thrashing, mad, insane, maddened, crazed, enraged, berserk, intemperate, immoderate, unbridled, unrestrained, out of control, uncontrollable, ungovernable, unruly, untamed, raging, rabid, like a mad dog, like a mad bull, like a raging bull, inextinguishable, irrepressible, ebullient, heated, inflamed, hot, red-hot, flaming, scorching, fiery, impassioned, passionate, ardent, fervent, eruptive, bursting, convulsive, spasmodic, destructive, ruinous, catastrophic, cataclysmic, overwhelming, devastating, explosive, volcanic, seismic, boiling, effervescent, agitated, disturbed, turbulent, tumultuous, tempestuous, stormy, impetuous, riotous, uproarious, boisterous, rampant, charging, roaring, desperate, gnashing, howling, murderous, barbarous, savage, brutal, bestial, cruel, vicious, bloody, bloodthirsty, ravening, hot-blooded, hotheaded, headstrong, bellicose, warlike, threatening, tigerish, waspish

▶ *327 Agitation; 334 Power; 336 Strength; 338 Vigour; 357 Destruction; 382 Killing; 461 Insanity; 507 Loudness; 647 Severity; 651 Malevolence*

VERBS

7 **be violent**, rush about, run riot, run wild, run amok, dash, rush headlong, hurtle, hurl oneself, crash in, burst in, break out, burst out, surge forward, charge, stampede, break the peace, raise a storm, riot, roughhouse, kick up a row, kick up a shindig, rampage, go on the rampage, go on the warpath, rage, storm, bluster, roar, come in like a lion, see red, go berserk, lose control, resort to violence, resort to fisticuffs, take up arms, take to arms, rebel

▶ *262 Haste; 507 Loudness*

8 **use violence**, force, use force, strike, hit, mug, beat up, do violence to, assault, abuse, violate, rape, ravish, torture, ill-treat, break, smash, destroy, strain, pull, wrench, twist, sprain, dislocate, fracture, force open, blow open, break open, break in, burst in, shock, shake, clobber (Inf)

▶ *234 Distortion; 327 Agitation; 351 Misuse; 357 Destruction; 381 Attack; 491 Physical Pain; 651 Malevolence*

9 **make violent**, stir up, jolt, goad, whip, whip up, lash, incite, fire, fire up, inflame, blow on the embers, add fuel to the flames, foment, exacerbate, aggravate, whet, sharpen, irritate, exasperate, anger, infuriate, lash (*or* whip up) into a fury, enrage, madden, make mad, wave a red flag before a bull

▶ *607 Annoyance and Aggravation*

ADVERBS

10 **violently**, ferociously, vehemently, severely, intensely, abruptly, rudely, harshly, fiercely, forcefully, forcibly, powerfully, vigorously, by storm, by force, hammer

and tongs, tooth and nail, like mad, headlong, precipitately, head first, head foremost, like Gadarene swine, like a bull at a gate, like a battering ram, at the point of a sword (*or* gun *or* knife), at gunpoint, at knifepoint, tyrannously, tyrannically, high-handedly, neck and crop, bodily, at one fell swoop, with a vengeance, beyond all reason

381 Attack

Kill the other guy before he kills you. Jack Dempsey.

VERBS

1 **attack**, launch an attack, break the peace, start a fight, take the offensive, assume the offensive, go (over) onto the offensive, go on the attack, engage, strike first, strike the first blow, fire the first shot, sound the charge, advance, advance against, march against, ride against, drive against, sail against, fly against, go over the top, bear down on, charge, charge against, rush, rush at, run at, dash at, gallop at, go full belt at, tilt at, ride full tilt at, go for, make a dead set at, drive, thrust, push, raid, foray, strike, pound, assault, blitz, bombard, assail, harry, hunt, ram, collide with, ambush, surprise

2 **fire**, fire on, open fire (on), fire at, level, draw a bead on, aim, find (*or* get) in the cross hairs, pull (*or* squeeze) the trigger, take a pot shot, pop at, snipe at, pick off, shoot, shoot at, let fly, volley, volley and thunder, rattle, blast, pour a broadside into, shoot down, bring down, torpedo, strafe, cannonade, shell, fusillade, pepper, rake, straddle, enfilade

3 **bomb**, throw bombs, drop bombs, carpet-bomb, drop the payload, hit the target, make the rubble bounce, blitz, nuke (Inf), lay eggs (Inf), plaster (Inf), prang (Inf)

4 **besiege**, lay siege to, starve out, surround, enclose, encircle, encroach, infringe, blockade, hem in, beset, beleaguer, invest

5 **strike**, hit, go for, set on, have a fling at, have a go at, pounce upon, fall upon, pitch into, sail into, launch out at, let fly at, lash out at, let someone have it, lay into, tear into, lace into, round on, strike at, raise one's hand against, grapple with, close with, fetch a blow, lay about one, swipe (at), flail, hammer, punch, butt, push, poke (at), kick, knock down, bring down, lay low, beat up, mug, attack tooth and nail, go berserk, run amok, savage, maul, jump (Inf), kick ass (US inf)

6 **stab**, make a pass at, have a cut at, lunge, thrust, thrust at, pierce, cut, slash, knife, spear, lance, bayonet, impale, run through, cut down

7 **stone**, throw a stone, heave a brick, lapidate, sling, pelt, shy, throw at, hurl at, chuck (Inf)

8 **counterattack**, fight back, retaliate, resist, oppose, rebel (against), confront, defy, challenge, take on, stand against, take a stand against, withstand, strike back at, return blow for blow, break out, sally, make a sortie

► *383 Resistance; 385 Retaliation; 661 Defiance*

9 **attack successfully**, break through, breach, take over, board, lay aboard, grapple, capture, storm, take by storm, carry, escalade, burst in, invade, incur upon, overrun, overcome, overmaster, overwhelm, overpower, ride down, run down, trample, beat, corner, bring to bay, go on the rampage, slaughter, kill, ravage, rape, terrorize, torture, wreak havoc, scorch, burn, lay waste

► *387 Subjection*

10 **criticize**, censure, cast aspersions on, inveigh against, disparage, denigrate, malign, decry, denounce, condemn, slander, defame, libel, berate, vituperate, abuse, vilify, revile, slur, smear

► *670 Disapproval; 678 Scornfulness*

NOUNS

11 **attack**, assault, aggression, aggressiveness, pugnacity, hostility, intimidation, harassment, belligerence, combativeness, bellicosity

12 **military attack**, hostile attack, offensive, offensive operations, offensive campaign, strike, pre-emptive strike, onslaught, onset, charge, drive, push, thrust, rush, run, dead set, shock, surprise attack, raid, forray, find-and-destroy mission, surprise offensive, surprise blow, shock tactics, blitzkrieg, *coup de main* (Fr), land attack, armoured attack, ground-force attack, infantry assault, tank assault, pincer movement, flanking attack, enfilade, air attack, sea attack, boarding, combined attack, blind attack, night attack, camisado, concentrated attack, blitz, massed attack, relentless attack, day-and-night attack, bombardment, heavy bombardment, artillery bombardment, barrage, mortar attack, cannonade

► *585 War*

13 **air attack**, air strike, air raid, air campaign, aerial bombardment, bomb-dropping, bomb run, bombing, conventional bombing, strategic bombing, tactical bombing, precision bombing, dive-bombing, surgical air strike, saturation bombing, carpet bombing, indiscriminate bombing, kamikaze bombing, suicide bombing, high-level bombing, low-level bombing, missile strike, laser targeting, anti-aircraft fire, anti-aircraft artillery, triple-A, ack-ack, tracer flare, strafe

14 **siege**, blockade, encirclement, encroachment, infringement, inroad, investment, counterattack, counteroffensive, retaliation, rebellion, sally, sortie, breakout, breakthrough, taking by storm, storm, escalade, irruption, overstepping, overrunning, ingress, invasion, incursion, occupation, subjection, dragonnade, bloodbath, slaughter, devastation, laying waste, pillage, rape, havoc

15 **firing**, fire, shooting, musketry, gunnery, gunfire, broadside, shot across the bows, volley, salvo, burst, spray, machine-gun fire, strafe, rifle fire, fusillade, burst of fire, rapid-fire, crossfire, plunging fire, raking fire, sharpshooting, sniping

► *587 Weapon*

16 **terrorist attack**, terror tactics, hostage taking, kidnapping, assassination, bombing, letter bombing, mail-bombing, car bombing, guerrilla attack, sniping, war of attrition,

17 **personal attack**, physical attack, physical violence, mugging, armed robbery, assault and battery, grievous bodily harm (GBH), rape, date rape, indecent (*or* sexual) assault, foul play, stab in the back, injustice, verbal attack, criticism, censure, aspersion, disparagement, denigration, decrial, denunciation, slander, defamation, libel, calumny, abuse, vilification, revilement, slur, smear

▶ *380 Violence; 607 Annoyance and Aggravation; 670 Disapproval; 678 Scornfulness*

18 hit, blow, punch, knock, swipe, kick, stab, jab, cut, cut and thrust, thrust, swordthrust, home-thrust, lunge, foin, pass, passado, quarte and tierce, stabbing, knifing, bayonetting, impalement, goring, stoning, lapidation

19 attacker, assailant, aggressor, warrior, crusader, holy warrior, hawk, militant, attacking force, spearhead, strike force, storm trooper, fighter pilot, air ace, top gun, bomber, dive bomber, bombardier, sharpshooter, sniper, terrorist, guerrilla, besieger, blockader, raider, invader, stormer, escalader, mugger, rapist, murderer, assassin, killer

▶ *586 Combatant*

20 bout, spell, spasm, fit, seizure, paroxysm, match, contest, fight, round

▶ *260 Ill Health*

ADJECTIVES

21 aggressive, antagonistic, unfriendly, hostile, inimical, pugnacious, truculent, threatening, provocative, quarrelsome, contentious, disputatious, litigious

22 militant, militaristic, martial, belligerent, bellicose, combative, hawkish, warlike, warring, warmongering, sabre-rattling, offensive, on the offensive, spoiling for a fight, on the warpath, up in arms

▶ *585 War*

23 attacking, assaulting, invading, storming, charging, boarding, fighting, striking, harrying, kicking, punching, flailing, cutting, slashing, destructive, violent, bloodthirsty, savage, brutal, brutish, cruel, barbarous, bloody, uncontrollable, overpowering, overwhelming, frenzied, raging, berserk

▶ *380 Violence*

24 counterattacking, resisting, opposing, retaliatory, challenging, defiant, rebellious

▶ *113 Opposition; 383 Resistance*

25 critical, censorious, disparaging, denigrating, maligning, decrying, denunciatory, defamatory, slanderous, libellous, vituperative, abusive

▶ *678 Scornfulness; 712 Curse*

ADVERBS

26 aggresively, forcefully, assertively, offensively, with hostility, on the offensive, on the attack, on the warpath, in combat

382 Killing

There's no difference between one's killing and making decisions that will send others to kill. It's exactly the same thing, or even worse. Golda Meir.

Yet each man kills the thing he loves,
By each let this be heard,
Some do it with a bitter look,
Some with a flattering word.
The coward does it with a kiss,
The brave man with a sword! Oscar Wilde.

NOUNS

1 killing, slaying, murder, manslaughter, revenge killing, senseless killing, destruction, destruction of life, taking life, causing death, dealing death, execution, blood-shedding, blood-letting, ritual killing, accidental killing, mercy killing, euthanasia

▶ *357 Destruction; 582 Death*

2 murder, first-degree murder, second-degree murder, premeditated murder, capital murder, assassination, contract murder, mass murder, gang murder, St Valentine's Day murder, terrorist killing, brutal murder, murder most foul, classic murder, crime of passion, manslaughter, unlawful killing, thuggery, shooting, knifing, poisoning, drowning, suffocation, asphyxiation, strangulation, garrotting, hanging, murder weapon, gun, knife, blunt instrument, rope, (terrorist) bomb, bumping off (Inf), rubbing out (Inf), blowing away (Inf), wasting (Inf)

3 homicide, regicide, tyrannicide, parricide, patricide, matricide, uxoricide, fratricide, sororicide, infanticide, exposure of infants, genocide, ethnic cleansing

4 slaughter, massacre, bloodbath, carnage, butchery, wholesale murder, high casualties, great bloodshed, noyade, battue, holocaust, pogrom, purge, ethnic cleansing, annihilation, liquidation, decimation, extermination, destruction, genocide, ethnocide, the Holocaust, Final Solution, war, battle, Custer's Last Stand, Roman holiday, gladiatorial combat, duel, Massacre of the Innocents, Sicilian Vespers, St Bartholomew's Day Massacre, Night of the Long Knives

▶ *357 Destruction; 585 War*

5 execution, capital punishment, death penalty, legalized killing, judicial murder, auto-da-fé, hanging, rope, scaffold, gallows, gibbet, electrocution, electric chair, shooting, firing squad, lethal injection, gas chamber, beheading, guillotine, axe, burning alive, the stake, stoning, extrajudicial execution, lynching, dispatch, death-blow, *coup de grâce* (Fr), final stroke, quietus

▶ *814 Punishment*

6 ritual killing, sacrifice, religious sacrifice, martyrdom, martyrization, immolation, crucifixion, field of blood, Aceldama

▶ *7 Religion*

7 suicide, self-destruction, self-slaughter, killing oneself, doing away with oneself, dying by one's own hand, felo de se, slashing one's wrists, jumping from a high place, hanging oneself, shooting oneself, taking an overdose, overdose of sleeping pills, drug overdose, gas, gassing oneself, self-immolation, suttee, seppuku, hara-kiri, kamikaze, attempted suicide, mass suicide, parasuicide, fake suicide, suicide pact

8 accidental killing, death by misadventure, manslaughter, violent death, fatal accident, traffic death, death on the roads, fatal car crash, fatal train crash, fatal plane crash

▶ *582 Death*

9 animal killing, blood sports, bullfighting, hunting, fox-hunting, deer hunting, rabbit hunting, duck hunting, wildfowling, chase, shooting, grouse shooting, pheasant shooting, trapping, selective killing, cull, extermination, slaughtering, knackery, vivisection, animal suicide, lemmings, Gadarene swine, whale (*or* dolphin) beaching

► *59 Horse Riding and Racing*

10 killer, slayer, murderer, man of blood, mercy killer, soldier, combatant, guerrilla, urban guerrilla, terrorist, slaughterer, butcher, executioner, hangman, punisher, tribal killer, head-hunter, cannibal, killer dog, poisonous snake, rabid animal, shark, man-eater

► *586 Combatant*

11 murderer, murderess, cold-blooded murderer, killer, assassin, hired killer, hired assassin, contract killer, professional killer, professional murderer, mass murderer, serial killer, psychopathic killer, psychopath, pathological killer, homicidal maniac, Cain, terrorist, bomber, poisoner, strangler, garrotter, axe murderer, hatchet man, gangster, gang member, gunman, hired gun, bravo, desperado, cutthroat, thug, ruffian, homicide, regicide, tyrannicide, parricide, patricide, matricide, uxoricide, fratricide, sororicide, infanticide, hit man (Inf), Mafia hit man (Inf), psycho (Inf)

12 executioner, hangman, firing squad member, axeman, headsman (Lit), Jack Ketch (Lit)

13 animal killer, hunter, huntsman, fox-hunter, beagler, deer hunter, rabbit hunter, duck hunter, wildfowler, grouse shooter, pheasant shooter, trapper, slaughterman, knacker, bullfighter, matador, toreador, picador, pest exterminator, rat-catcher, mole-catcher, knacker, vivisectionist, predator, bird of prey, beast of prey, poison, pesticide, insecticide, ratsbane, rodenticide, vermicide, germicide

14 plant killer, weedkiller, herbicide, fungicide, algicide

► *43 Agriculture*

15 slaughterhouse, abattoir, knacker's yard, shambles, bullring, arena, battleground, field of battle, battlefield, killing fields, the Alamo, Little Bighorn, Wounded Knee, the Somme, Pearl Harbor, Stalingrad, Mylai, civilian targets, Dresden, Hiroshima, Nagasaki, gas chamber, gas oven, Auschwitz, Dachau, Belsen

VERBS

16 kill, slay, murder, shed blood, take life, deprive of life, rob of life, shorten someone's life, hasten someone's end, end someone's life, dispatch, destroy, do away with, make away with, get rid of, cut off, nip in the bud, put down, put to sleep, bring down to the grave, drive to death, work to death, send out of the world, send to one's account, send to one's Maker, launch into eternity, snuff (Inf), put out of one's misery (Inf)

► *582 Death*

17 murder, commit murder, assassinate, poison, stab, stab to death, knife, sabre, spear, put to the sword, lance, bayonet, run through, shoot, shoot down, gun down, pick off, pistol, blow out the brains of, bomb, strangle, wring the neck of, garrotte, choke, smother, burke, suffocate, asphyxiate, stifle, drown, wall up, bury alive, strike, smite, brain, spill the brains of, poleaxe, sandbag, beat to death, burn, burn alive, roast alive, gas, electrocute, starve to death, arrange a fatal accident, eliminate (Inf), waste (US inf), do in (Inf), do for (Inf), bump off (Inf), rub out (Inf), take for a ride (Inf), make to walk the plank (Inf)

18 slaughter, butcher, poleaxe, cut the throat of, drain the lifeblood of, massacre, slay en masse, smite hip and thigh, put to the sword, cut to pieces, cut to ribbons, cut down, decimate, mow down, shoot down, gun down, steep one's hands in blood, wade in blood, give no quarter, spare none, take no prisoners, destroy, wipe out, wipe off the face of the earth, annihilate, exterminate, liquidate, purge, send to the gas chamber, commit genocide

► *357 Destruction*

19 execute, condemn to death, condemn, sign the death warrant, put to death, hang, send to the scaffold, electrocute, gas, give a lethal injection, shoot, behead, guillotine, send to the stake, burn alive, stone to death, lynch, garrotte, deal a deathblow, give one's quietus, string up (Inf)

► *814 Punishment*

20 kill ritually, sacrifice, offer up, martyr, martyrize, crucify, immolate, burn

► *7 Religion*

21 commit suicide, kill oneself, take one's own life, put an end to one's life, do away with oneself, die by one's own hand, make away with oneself, commit hara-kiri, commit suttee, hang oneself, shoot oneself, blow out one's brains, cut one's throat, slash one's wrists, fall on one's sword, die Roman fashion, put one's head in the oven, gas oneself, take poison, take an overdose, jump from a high place, jump overboard, drown oneself, get oneself killed, request euthanasia, do oneself in (Inf), top oneself (Inf)

22 kill animals, hunt, shoot, trap, fish, angle, poison, cull, exterminate, put to sleep, put down, experiment on, perform vivisection on

ADJECTIVES

23 deadly, lethal, killing, mortal, fatal, deathly, fell (Lit), life-threatening, capital, death-bringing, malignant, poisonous, toxic, asphyxiant, suffocating, stifling, unhealthy, miasmic, pathological, insalubrious, inoperable, incurable, terminal

► *260 Ill Health; 582 Death*

24 murderous, homicidal, psychopathic, genocidal, internecine, slaughterous, destructive, death-dealing, trigger-happy, cold-blooded, sanguinary, ensanguined, bloody, gory, blood-stained, red-handed, bloodthirsty, thirsting for blood, cruel, savage, brutal, head-hunting, man-eating, cannibalistic, self-destructive, suicidal

► *357 Destruction; 651 Malevolence*

ADVERBS

25 lethally, mortally, fatally, malignantly, terminally, murderously, homicidally, bloodthirstily, suicidally, in at the death, in at the kill

INTERJECTIONS

26 no quarter!, take no prisoners!, cry havoc!, shoot to kill!, string him up!, hang 'em high!, nuke 'em! (Inf)

383 Resistance

I shall earnestly and persistently continue to urge all women to the practical recognition of the old Revolutionary maxim, 'Resistance to tyranny is obedience to God.' Doris Stephens.

NOUNS

1 **resistance**, refusal, unwillingness, noncooperation, uncooperativeness, opposition, objection, challenge, stand, brave front, refusal to work, strike, walkout, deprecation, protest, dissent, defiance, repulse, repulsion, repellence, rebuff, reluctance, renitency, negativeness

► *113 Opposition; 364 Repulsion; 637 Unwillingness; 661 Defiance; 709 Refusal; 753 Protest*

2 **obstinacy**, intractability, refractoriness, recalcitrance, stubbornness, obduracy, firmness, hardness, toughness, callousness, stiffness, starchiness, rigidity, inflexibility, inelasticity, not bending, not yielding

► *418 Hardness; 641 Obstinacy*

3 **resistance movement**, self-defence, withstanding, nonviolent resistance, passive resistance, civil disobedience, mutiny, uprising, insurgence, insurrection, revolution, revolt, guerrilla warfare, terrorism

► *384 Defence; 585 War; 661 Defiance*

4 **desisting**, desistance, denial, self-denial, self-restraint, denying oneself, refusal, refusing oneself, refraining, abstaining, forbearance, forbearing, doing without, not touching

► *684 Self-Restraint*

5 **resister**, defender, repeller, opponent, opposer, revolutionary, freedom fighter, reactionary, terrorist, anarchist, die-hard, traditionalist, reactionary, conservative, hardliner, stick-in-the-mud, hard-head (US), refuser, conscientious objector, pacifist, refusenik, refrainer, abstainer, forbearer

► *12 Government and Politics*

VERBS

6 **resist**, offer resistance, withstand, endure, make a stand, stand against, put up a brave front, not give way, show reluctance, refuse, strike, walk out, come out, not cooperate, not be tempted by, oppose, object to, confront, contend with, obstruct, hinder, challenge, deprecate, protest, dissent, defy, refuse to bow down, repulse, repel, rebuff, hold off, keep at arm's length, keep at bay

7 **be obstinate**, stand firm, stand rigid, show no flexibility, not bend, not yield, stick to one's guns, dig in one's heels, refuse to budge

8 **revolt**, mutiny, rise up, not take it lying down, fight off, defend oneself

9 **desist**, deny oneself, refuse oneself, restrain from, refrain from, abstain from, forbear, do without, not touch

ADJECTIVES

10 **resistant**, resisting, renitent, withstanding, reluctant, negative, refusing, striking, unwilling, noncooperative, uncooperative, opposing, opposed, objecting, challenging, challenged, deprecative, deprecating, protesting, dissenting, defiant, rebuffing, repulsing, repellent, repelling, obstructive, hard-headed (US), hard-shell (US), hardcore, hard-nosed (Inf)

11 **obstinate**, intractable, refractory, recalcitrant, callous, hard, rigid, firm, standing firm, tough, stiff, starchy, stubborn, obdurate, inflexible, unbending, unyielding, unmalleable, die-hard, hardline, traditional, conservative

12 **resisting**, unsubmissive, up in arms, undefeated, unsubdued, unbowed, unquelled, unbeatable, invincible, bulletproof, self-defensive, revolutionary, rebellious, mutinous, insurgent, reactionary, terrorist, anarchist

13 **desisting**, denying, self-denying, refraining, abstaining, abstemious, forbearing

ADVERBS

14 **resistingly**, resistantly, reluctantly, negatively, unwillingly, noncooperatively, challengingly, deprecatingly, protestingly, under protest, dissentingly, repellently, obstinately, hard-headedly (US), intractably, traditionally, conservatively, callously, firmly, rigidly, toughly, stiffly, inflexibly, unbendingly, invincibly, defiantly, unsubmissively, mutinously, rebelliously

15 **abstemiously**, abstinently, forbearingly, with forbearance, through self-denial

INTERJECTIONS

16 **fight on!**, no surrender!, rise up!, resist!, we shall overcome!

384 Defence

NOUNS

1 **defence**, defensive move, defensive tactic, the defensive, resistance, passive resistance, active resistance, parry, warding off, safeguarding, safekeeping, preserving, preservation

2 **safeguard**, protection, buffer, screen, rampart, bulwark, buffer, fender, bumper

3 **counter**, counterforce, counteraction, counterstroke

► *385 Retaliation*

4 **defensiveness**, defence mechanism camouflage, protective colouring, elusiveness, shyness, nervousness

5 **self-defence**, boxing, martial arts, judo, karate, security, surveillance, burglar alarm, car alarm, personal alarm, rape alarm, whistle, Mace™, guard dog

6 **protective clothing**, helmet, crash helmet, head guard, goggles, visor, body padding, shoulder pad, shin pad, gloves, gauntlets, protective belt, body belt, box, fireproof clothing, bulletproof vest, flak jacket, gas mask, breathing apparatus

7 **armour**, jousting armour, body armour, harness, full armour, panoply, mail, chain mail, chain armour, scale armour, fluted armour, splint armour, steel-plate armour, armour plate, breastplate, backplate, cuirass, lance rest, lorica, plastron, hauberk, habergeon, brigandine, coat of mail, corslet, helmet, helm, coif, gorget, casque, basinet, sallet, morion, siege cap, steel helmet, tin hat, bowl, skull, visor, beaver, shako, bearskin, busby, vambrace, brassard, cubitiere, elbow-cop, gauntlet, cuisse, greave, shield, buckler, scutum, target, pavis, mantelet, testudo

8 **military defences**, defensive line, fortified line, entrenchment, fixed position, fieldwork, redoubt, redan, lunette, breastwork, parados, contravallation, outwork, circumvallation, earthwork, embankment, mound, sandbag, moat, ditch, fosse, trench, dugout, foxhole, tripwire, trap, mine

9 barrier, barricade, blockade, boom, fence, wall, roadblock, stakes, pales, paling, abatis, palisade, stockade, zareba, defensive circle, circle of wagons, laager, entanglements, razor wire, electric fence, spike, caltrop, chevaux-de-frise, Maginot Line, Siegfried Line, Hadrian's Wall, Antonine Wall, Great Wall of China

10 shelter, air-raid shelter, fallout shelter, concrete shelter, underground shelter, bunker, blockhouse, blackout, smokescreen

11 fortification, box fortification, triangle fortification, circumvallation, bulwark, rampart, wall, town wall, parapet, battlement, bailey, machicolation, embrasure, casemate, merlon, loophole, banquette, barbette, emplacement, gun emplacement, vallum, scarp, escarp, counterscarp, glacis, curtain, bastion, demibastion, ravelin, demilune, outwork, buttress, abutment, gabion, gabionade

12 fort, fortress, fortalice, rampart, stockade, earthwork, castle, keep, ward, barbican, tower, turret, battlements, curtain, bartizan, donjon, portcullis, drawbridge, moat, gate, gatehouse, postern, sally port, citadel, capitol, acropolis, refuge, Martello tower, pillbox, blockhouse, strong point, stronghold, fastness, laager, zareba

13 defender, champion, patron, aider, supporter, henchman, angel (Inf), knight, knight errant, white knight, paladin

14 guard, bodyguard, lifeguard, watch, sentry, sentinel, vigilante, patrol, patrolman, patrolwoman, security guard, watchman, night watchman, night watch, doorman, bouncer (Inf), garrison, picket, armed guard, vanguard, rearguard, escort

15 protector, guardian, warden, warder, custodian, keeper, park keeper, gamekeeper, goalkeeper, wicketkeeper,

16 rescuer, deliverer, saviour

VERBS

17 defend, guard, protect, secure, keep, watch, safeguard, lock up, ward

18 fence, wall, hedge, moat, booby trap, mine, circumscribe, enclose, barricade, palisade, block, obstruct

19 buffer, cushion, pad, shield, camouflage, curtain, cover, screen, cloak, conceal

20 reinforce, armour, fortify, strengthen, beef up (Inf)

21 entrench, dig in, make a stand, stand firm, stand in front, stand by, stand ready, garrison, man the fort, man the guns, man the defences, man the breach, man, plug the gap, stop the gap

22 plead for, hold a brief for, argue for, take up the cause of, protect the interests of, support, champion, vindicate, fight for, take up arms for, break a lance for, take up the cudgels for

23 rescue, come to the rescue, save, deliver

24 parry, counter, riposte, fence, fend off, throw back, ward off, hold off, keep off, fight off, stave off, repulse, hold (*or* keep) at bay, keep at arm's length, avoid, turn, avert, deflect

25 stall, beat about the bush, quibble, vacillate, blow hot and cold, stonewall, block, obstruct, delay

26 act on the defensive, fight a defensive battle, take evasive action, play for a draw, stalemate,

27 retaliate, fight back, come back, show fight, show one's mettle, give a warm reception to, resist, repulse, repel, butt away

28 survive, withstand, escape, bear the brunt, hold one's own, fall back on, beat a strategic retreat, get out while the going is good, retire, turn back, scrape through, live to fight another day

ADJECTIVES

29 defending, defensive, on the defensive, on guard, resisting, extenuating, excusing, vindicating, challenged, protective, tutelary, responsible

30 defended, protected, secured, armoured, armour-plated, heavy-armed, mailed, mail-clad, armour-clad, ironclad, panoplied, accoutred, prepared, harnessed (Lit), moated, palisaded, barricaded, walled, fortified, machicolated, castellated, battlemented, loopholed

31 entrenched, dug in, bombproof, bulletproof, invulnerable, unconquerable

ADVERBS

32 defensively, protectively, on the defensive, on guard, at bay, in defence, self-defensively, in self-defence

385 Retaliation

This animal is very bad; when attacked it defends itself.
Anonymous.

NOUNS

1 retaliation, reprisal, revenge, just revenge, vengeance, redress, desert, deserts, just deserts, dueness, justice, retribution, reparation, repayment, Nemesis, comeuppance (Inf), punishment, negative reaction, negative feedback, backlash, boomerang, counter, counterpunch, counterstroke, counteraction, counterblast, counterplot, countermine, counter suit, answering back, comeback, riposte, retort, rejoinder, returning good for evil, heaping coals of fire, reciprocation, talion, like for like, tit for tat, quid pro quo, measure for measure, blow for blow, an eye for an eye and a tooth for a tooth, a taste of one's own medicine, a Roland for an Oliver, a game at which two can play

2 revenger, avenger, vigilante, guerrilla, saboteur, member of the resistance, member of the underground

VERBS

3 retaliate, take reprisals, get satisfaction, exact compensation, recoup, repay, redress, redress the balance, inflict punishment, punish, revenge, make good, counter, riposte, parry, make a requital, pay one out, pay one back, shoot back, pay off old scores, wipe out a score, square the account, be quits, get even with, get one's own back, reciprocate, give and take, avenge, live by the golden rule, do unto others as you would be done by, return good for evil, heap coals of fire on one's head, fight fire with fire, return like for like, return the compliment, give as good as one got, pay one in his own coin, give a quid pro quo, return, retort, cap, answer back, answer, countercharge, react, boomerang, recoil, round on, kick back, hit back, not take it lying down, resist, requite

4 serve one right, be rightly served, be one's own fault, make one's bed and lie in it, be taught a lesson, have had one's lesson, restitute, pay off, find one's match, meet

one's match, get what one deserves, get one's deserts, get what was due, get what was coming, get a dose of one's own medicine, be hoisted with one's own petard, be chastised, be punished

ADJECTIVES

5 **retaliatory**, in retaliation, in reprisal, in self-defence, retaliative, retributive, punitive, recriminatory, like for like, reciprocal, revengeful, vindictive, vengeful, rightly served

ADVERBS

6 **with vengeance**, by way of return, in requital, tit for tat

INTERJECTIONS

7 **revenge!**, it serves you right!, take that!, see how it feels!, put that in your pipe and smoke it!, the laugh's on you!

386 Compulsion

The use of force alone is but temporary. It may subdue for a moment; but it does not remove the necessity of subduing again: and a nation is not governed, which is perpetually to be conquered. Edmund Burke.

NOUNS

1 **compulsion**, compulsiveness, irresistibility, irresistible force, obsessiveness, obsessive need, obsession, preoccupation, need, urge, drive, essential, necessity, obligation, requirement, prerequisite, zero options, no choice, Hobson's choice, a must (Inf)

▶ *810 Duty*

2 **coercion**, pressure, order, command, mandate, forcing, force, legal force, enforcement, force majeure (Lit), main force, physical force, duress, restraint, constraint, intimidation, bullying, browbeating, threat, violence, brute force

▶ *251 Restraint; 334 Power; 380 Violence; 387 Subjection; 397 Command*

3 **coercive methods**, blackmail, extortion, bribery, carrot and stick, big stick, bludgeon, strong-arm tactics, arm-twisting, force-feeding, kidnapping, forced labour, labour camp, slavery, impressment, pressgang, sanctions, conscription, call-up, draft (US), penalty clause, fine, jail, torture

▶ *585 War; 647 Severity; 814 Punishment*

4 **coercive person**, forceful person, steamroller, bulldozer (Inf), bully, blackmailer, extortionist, briber, robber, kidnapper, hijacker, gunman, terrorist, torturer, mugger (Inf)

5 **compulsive person**, addict, monomaniac, compulsive eater, compulsive gambler, compulsive talker, compulsive liar, compulsive shopper, shoplifter, kleptomaniac, obsessive dieter, anorexic, alcoholic, smoker, workaholic, chocaholic (Inf), megalomaniac, completist

VERBS

6 **compel**, coerce, urge, oblige, make, insist on, insist, make a point of, emphasize, not take no for an answer, pressure, bring pressure to bear upon, put pressure on, apply pressure, bear down on, press, put under duress, squeeze, impel, drive, force someone's hand, twist one's arm, leave no choice, leave no option, leave no escape, pin down, tie down, bind, constrain, restrain, hold back, oppress, necessitate, require, command, demand, dictate, mandate, order, regiment, discipline, impose, impose a duty, enforce, lean on (Inf)

7 **force**, intimidate, threaten, force upon, force to accept, force-feed, foist on, fob off on, take, take by force, requisition, commandeer, constrain, extort, blackmail, kidnap, hold to ransom, exact, wring from, drag from, use force against, bring legal force to bear, conscript, call up, draft (US), impress, dragoon, use physical force, inflict, bully, bully into, browbeat, steamroller, bludgeon, press-gang, use violence, ram down one's throat, stampede, take the gloves off (Inf), turn the heat on (Inf), strong-arm (Inf), bulldoze (Inf), railroad (Inf), put the screws on (Inf)

8 **be compelled**, be coerced, yield to pressure, have no choice, have no option, must, should, have to, cannot help but, cannot do otherwise, have got to, cannot be helped

ADJECTIVES

9 **compelling**, compulsive, coercive, irresistible, hypnotic, mesmeric, cogent, convincing, inspiring, influential, persuasive, involuntary, unavoidable, inevitable, necessary, of necessity, commanding, imperative, urgent, overriding, pressing, driving, high-pressure, oppressive, dictatorial, enforcing, binding, restraining, constraining, steamroller, steamrolling, forceful, forcible, violent, bludgeoning, strong-arm (Inf), bulldozing (Inf)

10 **compulsory**, mandatory, necessary, unavoidable, ineluctable, obligatory, required, requisite, prerequisite

ADVERBS

11 **compellingly**, compulsively, on compulsion, coercively, irresistibly, hypnotically, cogently, convincingly, influentially, persuasively, involuntarily, unavoidably, inevitably, willy-nilly, necessarily, of necessity, perforce, obligatorily, imperatively, urgently, oppressively, under pressure to, under pressure, under duress, commandingly, violently, forcefully, forcibly, by force, by force majeure (Lit), by main force, by force of arms, *vi et armis* (L), at the sword's point, at the point of a gun, at gunpoint, at knifepoint

387 Subjection

If you want a picture of the future, imagine a boot stamping on a human face – for ever. George Orwell.

NOUNS

1 **subjection**, subjugation, inferiority, inferior status, lower status, inferior rank, satellite status, subordination, subordinate position, subordinate role, subordinacy, junior rank, juniority, dependence, dependency, mutual dependence, symbiosis, wardship, tutelage, apprenticeship, obedience, subservience, servitude, servility, service, employment, employ, allegiance, loss of rights, disenfranchisement, disfranchisement, loss of battle, defeat, loss of freedom, captivity, compulsory servitude, involuntary servitude, constraint, indentureship, bondage, enslavement, slavery, white slavery, peonage, feudalism, vassalage, thraldom, serfdom, villeinage

► *122 Inferiority; 247 Failure; 585 War; 663 Obedience; 664 Servility; 747 Cooperation; 796 Immorality; 810 Duty; 815 Prison*

2 **domination**, mastery, overpowering, overcoming, discipline, restraint, control, conquest, conquoring, suppression, oppression, repression, intimidation, colonialism, tyranny

► *12 Government and Politics; 395 Influence; 396 Authority; 647 Severity*

3 **subordinate**, inferior, assistant, helper, apprentice, student, learner, servant, right-hand man, secretary, employee, staff member, conscript, substitute, underling, minion, tool, lackey, flunkey, sycophant, fag, low man on the totem pole (Inf), sidekick (Inf), gofer (US inf), grunt (US inf), stooge (Inf)

► *401 Servant*

4 **dependent**, child, foster child, orphan, junior, protégé, charge, ward, hanger-on, follower, satellite, parasite

► *555 Youth*

5 **subjected person**, loser, surrenderer, captive, hostage, prisoner, POW (prisoner of war), inmate, slave, white slave, liege, chattel, indentured servant, bondsman, bondwoman, bondslave, thrall, concubine, galley salve, serf, villein, peon, puppet

VERBS

6 **subject**, subjugate, subdue, make inferior, lower, humble, subordinate, hold down, keep down, give a subordinate role to, have at one's mercy, do what one likes with, humiliate, walk (all) over, walk on, sit on, regiment, tame, bring into line, bring to one's knees, bring to heel, bring low, keep under one's thumb, twist around one's little finger, keep at one's beck and call, lead by the nose, kick around, browbeat, henpeck, treat like dirt (under one's feet), exploit, treat like shit (Inf), trample on, tread on, make dependent, tutor, apprentice, employ, disenfranchise, disfranchise, reduce to servitude, take away one's freedom, rob of freedom, indenture, colonize, railroad (Inf), use as a doormat (Inf)

7 **defeat**, vanquish, capture, take prisoner, lead in triumph, lead captive, make a hostage of, constrain, dominate, overpower, overcome, master, prevail over, discipline, restrain, control, conquer, suppress, oppress, repress, intimidate, tyrannize

8 **be subject to**, be subjected to, have inferior rank, hold a subordinate position, depend on, have a mutual dependence, pay tribute to, pay homage to, grovel, eat out of one's hands, obey, bear allegiance to, owe loyalty to, serve, wait on, serve involuntarily, lose a battle, lose one's freedom, become a slave, become a hostage, fall into the clutches of, lose one's rights, serve as a doormat for (Inf)

ADJECTIVES

9 **subject**, subjecting, subjected, in subjection, in one's power, in one's control, in one's pocket, under one's thumb, like putty in one's hands, eating out of one's hands, subjugated, brought to one's knees, brought low, made to grovel, brought to heel, treated like dirt (under one's feet), treated like shit (Inf), led by the nose, kicked around, browbeaten, henpecked, inferior, lower, substitute, subordinate, under one's command, under the sway of, in the hands of, in the clutches of, like a puppet on a string, at one's feet, at one's beck and call, junior, dependent, tied to one's apron strings, at one's mercy, symbiotic(al), tutorial, apprenticed, subservient, obedient, servile, serving, employed, in the pay of, answering to, employable, captive, in captivity, taken prisoner, in bondage, in bonds, in chains, in harness, unfree, not independent, compulsory, involuntary, indentured, enslaving, enslaved, in slavery, reduced to slavery, sold into slavery, feudal

10 **dominating**, overpowering, overcoming, controlling, controllable, conquering, suppressive, suppressing, oppressive, oppressing, repressive, repressing, intimidating, colonial, tyrannical

ADVERBS

11 **under subjection**, while in one's power, under orders, at the beck and call of, dependently, subserviently, servilely, like a servant, in the pay of, in captivity, in slavery, involuntarily, against one's will

388 Submission

To great evils we submit; we resent little provocations. William Hazlitt.

NOUNS

1 **submission**, submissiveness, appeasement, deference, obedience, tameness, submitting, succumbing, subservience, slavishness, servitude, collaboration, sell-out (Inf), consent, acquiescence, compliance, concession, assent, agreeing, nonresistance, passivity, passiveness, peace at any price, line of least resistance, resignation, fatalism, supineness, lethargy, apathy, cop-out (Inf), inactivity, surrender, yielding, giving way, giving in, giving up the fort, caving in (Inf), the white flag, capitulation, surrender, unconditional surrender, cession, abandonment, relinquishment, abdication, resignation, deference, abject loyalty, homage, bow, curtsy, humble submission, humility, kneeling, genuflection, kowtow, prostration, grovelling, obeisance, sexual submission, passive sex, masochism

2 **appeaser**, defeatist, quitter, pushover (Inf), mouse, doormat, wet (Inf), wimp (Inf), coward, sycophant, groveller, toady, brown-noser (US inf), brown-nose (US inf), Uriah Heep, Uncle Tom (Offensive), servant, menial, grunt (US inf), gofer (Inf), slave, masochist

VERBS

3 **submit**, yield, obey, give in, not resist, not insist, make no waves, keep quiet, pussyfoot (around) (Inf), defer to, bow to, accept, face reality, face the facts, resign oneself, be resigned, make a virtue of necessity, appease, collaborate with, sell out (Inf), yield with a good grace, admit defeat, yield the palm, play it low-key, take things easy, take the heat off (Inf), cool it (Inf), acquiesce, condone, buy (Inf), comply, consent, assent, relent, abide, overlook, ignore, disregard, allow, go along with, play along with, grant, concede, shrug one's shoulders, be indifferent, turn a blind eye toward, show apathy for, avoid responsibility for, cop out (Inf), withdraw, retreat, retire, hang it up (Inf), fade into the background, leave, step aside, make way for, turn back, not contest, let judgment

go by default, pass up, pull out, be inactive, capitulate, surrender, be defeated, cease resistance, stop fighting, sue for peace, subdue oneself, call it a day, have no fight left, have all the fight knocked out of one, give up, give way, cry quits, cry uncle (US inf), have had enough, abandon one's cause, relinquish, throw in the towel, hold up one's hands, show the white flag, ask for terms, haul down the flag, strike colours, ask for mercy, give oneself up, yield oneself, lay down one's arms, hand over one's sword, abdicate, renounce authority, resign, stand down

4 **succumb**, knuckle under, break under pressure, yield to the pressure, be out for the count, cave in (Inf), collapse, sag, wilt, tire, faint, drop, show no fight, take the line of least resistance, bow before the inevitable, bow before the storm, be swept aside, be submissive, submit, learn obedience, keep in one's place, know one's place, do homage, bow, curtsy, take it on the chin, swallow the pill, bite the bullet, apologize, eat humble pie, eat dirt, eat crow (US inf), be humble, take it, take it from one, take it lying down, pocket the insult, grin and bear it, bear, lump it (Inf), take one's lumps (Inf), suffer in patience, endure, digest, stomach, put up with, take the heat (Inf), suffer, bend, kneel, kowtow, toady, crouch, cringe, crawl, bow and scrape, stoop, grovel, lick the dust, lick the boots of, kiss the rod, brown-nose (Inf)

ADJECTIVES

5 **submitting**, surrendering, quiet, meek, humble, tame, docile, unresisting, nonresisting, law-abiding, peaceful, submissive, subservient, servile, menial, lowly, low, abject, obedient, slavish, unconcerned, fatalistic, resigned, subdued, acquiescent, concessionary, assenting, pliant, accommodating, malleable, biddable, tractable, soft, amenable, agreeable, weak-kneed, bending, crouching, crawling, cringing, lying down, supine, prostrate, bootlicking, bowing and scraping, kneeling, on bended knee, sycophantic, toadying, humble, masochistic

ADVERBS

6 **with humility**, humbly, meekly, obediently, without resistance

INTERJECTIONS

7 **I/we surrender!**, enough!, mercy!, uncle! (US inf)

389 Escape

NOUNS

1 **escape**, breakout, getaway, get-out, jailbreak, freedom, decampment, flight, departure, withdrawal, retreat, hasty retreat, disappearance, disappearing trick, vanishing, vanishing into thin air, French leave, truancy, elopement, runaway wedding, elusion, evasion, avoidance, nonpayment, financial escape, tax avoidance, tax evasion, tax-dodging, tax shelter, tax haven, creative economy, black economy, moonlighting, narrow escape, hairbreadth escape, near miss, near thing, reprieve, overturned conviction, acquittal, release, setting free, liberation, immunity, impunity, exemption, escapology, escapism, rescue, deliverance, riddance, relief, hooky (US inf), flit (Inf), moonlight flit (Inf), close shave (Inf), close call (US inf), narrow squeak (Inf)

▶ *250 Freedom; 254 Danger; 303 Backward Motion; 313 Departure; 391 Liberation; 526 Disappearance; 634 Avoidance; 758 Exemption; 786 Nonpayment*

2 **means of escape**, exit, emergency exit, way out, egress, back door, trap door, escape hatch, hidden panel, secret passage, backstairs, ladder, fire escape, drawbridge, vent, safety valve, camouflage, disguise, dodge, device, trick, contrivance, loophole, escape clause, technicality, let-out

▶ *136 Qualification; 252 Safety; 315 Exit; 484 Plan*

3 **escaper**, escapee, fugitive, runaway, fleer, retreater, eloper, truant, evader, tax evader, tax dodger, reprieved prisoner, released prisoner, escaped prisoner, jail-breaker, refugee, survivor, escapist, escapologist, Houdini

4 **leak**, leakage, air leakage, gas leakage, water loss, loss, emission, issue, seepage, discharge, outflow

▶ *315 Exit*

VERBS

5 **escape**, break out, get out, escape from jail, break out of prison, break loose, break one's chains, go over the wall, break away, get away, make a getaway, decamp, flee, fly, take flight, bolt, run away, abscond, depart, duck and run, make good one's escape, effect one's escape, get free, win freedom, find freedom, slip one's collar, slip one's lead (*or* leash), take to one's heels, retreat, beat a hasty retreat, disappear, vanish, vanish into thin air, make oneself scarce, sneak off, sneak out, steal away, go absent without leave (AWOL), take French leave, play truant, jump bail, elope, deliver oneself, save oneself, save one's skin, have a narrow escape, have a hairbreadth escape, escape by the skin of one's teeth, slip through someone's fingers, wiggle (*or* wriggle) out of, bluff one's way out, scrape through, slip through, break through, get a reprieve, have one's conviction overturned, secure an acquittal, receive immunity, secure exemption, go unpunished, go scot-free, get away with it, get off, get off on a technicality, get off lightly, survive, weather the storm, find relief, skip (US inf), vamoose (US inf), take it on the lam (US inf), do a bunk (*or* runner) (Inf), do a moonlight flit (Inf), play hooky (Inf), skive off (Inf), have a close shave (Inf), have a close call (US inf), have a narrow squeak (Inf), save one's bacon (Inf)

▶ *250 Freedom; 313 Departure; 390 Deliverance; 391 Liberation; 526 Disappearance; 608 Relief; 634 Avoidance; 758 Exemption*

6 **elude**, evade, avoid, dodge, miss, get rid of, rid oneself of, hide, lie low, stay underground, escape detection, give one the slip, shake off, throw off the trail, throw off the scent, give one a run for one's money, escape notice, avoid taxes, evade taxes, moonlight

▶ *634 Avoidance; 736 Concealment; 786 Nonpayment*

7 **leak**, leak away, leak air, leak gas, lose water, flow out, emerge, issue, seep out, gush, spurt

▶ *315 Exit*

ADJECTIVES

8 **escaping**, evasive, elusive, fugitive, runaway, truant, escaped, loose, free, scot-free, reprieved, acquitted, immune, exempt, relieved, emancipated, liberated, untied, unbound, unchained

▶ *250 Freedom; 391 Liberation*

ADVERBS

9 **fugitively**, in flight, in hiding, out of range (*or* sight), away, over the hills and far away, freely

390 Deliverance

Lord, deliver me from myself. Thomas Browne.

VERBS

1 **deliver**, save, rescue, come to the rescue, throw a lifeline to, snatch from the jaws of death, save at the last second (*or* minute), rescue at the eleventh hour, save by the bell, extricate, unravel, untangle, extract, get out, unfasten, unloose, untie, unbind, unfetter, unchain, unburden, disburden, disencumber, rid of, save from, relieve, release, emancipate, liberate, free, declare free, set free, set at large, unlock, unbar, let out, let go, let off, get off, reprieve, acquit, exempt, excuse, dispense with, spare, redeem, ransom, bail out, buy off, purchase, salvage, retrieve, recover, bring back, restore

► *250 Freedom; 252 Safety; 319 Transport; 369 Extraction; 372 Separation; 389 Escape; 391 Liberation; 409 Arrangement; 608 Relief; 758 Exemption; 768 Giving*

NOUNS

2 **deliverance**, delivery, saving, life-saving, rescue, air-sea rescue, extrication, unravelling, untangling, extraction, disencumberment, riddance, good riddance, relief, release, emancipation, freedom, liberation, let-off, amnesty, discharge, reprieve, reprieval, acquittal, dispensation, excuse, exemption, escape, let-out, way out, salvation, redemption, ransom, bail, buying off, purchase, salvage, retrieval, recovery, restoration, day of grace, respite, delay, truce, standstill, cessation

► *226 Stopping; 250 Freedom; 369 Extraction; 389 Escape; 391 Liberation; 608 Relief*

3 **deliverer**, saviour, life-saver, rescuer, rescue team, air-sea rescue helicopter, lifeboat, lifeboatman, liberator, emancipator, redeemer, salvage company

► *252 Safety; 391 Liberation*

ADJECTIVES

4 **deliverable**, saveable, salvable, rescuable, extricable, redeemable, salvageable, fit for release, delivered, saved, rescued, liberated, free, saving, life-saving, saved by the bell

INTERJECTIONS

5 **to the rescue!**, man overboard!, all hands on deck!, all hands to the pump!, help!

ADVERBS

6 **extricably**, redeemably, free, salvably

391 Liberation

I cannot and will not give any undertaking at a time when I, and you, the people, are not free. Your freedom and mine cannot be separated. Nelson Mandela.

Liberty does not consist in mere declarations of the rights of man. It consists in the translation of those declarations into definite action. Woodrow Wilson.

NOUNS

1 **liberation**, freedom, freeing, setting free, deliverance, delivery, release, disencumberment, emancipation, Emancipation Proclamation (US), manumission, unhanding, unbinding, unchaining, unshackling, unfettering, unknotting, unleashing, unbridling, unburdening, mental freedom, independent mind, liberated spirit, liberal thinking, loosing, unloosing, disengagement, decontrol, deregulation, liberalization, relaxation, discharge, dismissal, extrication, parole, bail, demobilization, disbanding, escape, rescue, redemption, pardoning, absolving, salvation, relief, reprieve, exemption, exemptibility, absolution, forgiveness of sins, forgiveness, acquittal, acquittance, quittance, quitclaim

► *250 Freedom; 372 Separation; 390 Deliverance; 458 Wisdom; 608 Relief; 649 Forgiveness; 758 Exemption*

2 **equal opportunity**, equal status, equal rights, ERA (Equal Rights Amendment) (US), civil rights, women's liberation, feminism, minority rights, animal liberation, animal-rights activism, gay liberation, women's lib (Inf)

► *466 Discrimination*

3 **liberator**, emancipator, manumitter, deliverer, rescuer, absolver, redeemer, The Redeemer, saviour, The Saviour, escapee, parolee, animal-rights activist, ERA supporter (US), women's libber (Inf)

► *7 Religion*

VERBS

4 **liberate**, free, set free, set at liberty, set at large, deliver, release, emancipate, manumit, disencumber, unhand, untie one's hands, unbind, unchain, unbolt, unlock, uncage, unshackle, unfetter, unknot, unleash, unbridle, unburden, give free rein, free mentally, have an independent mind, loose, loosen, unloose, unloosen, cast loose, let (*or* turn) loose, let out, let go of, let go free, disengage, decontrol, deregulate, liberalize, relax restrictions, lift controls, life a curfew, discharge, dismiss, extricate, parole, put on parole, bail, let out on bail, grant bail to, discharge, demobilize, disband, send home, release, escape, rescue, redeem, save, deliver, relieve, exempt, reprieve, acquit, pardon, absolve, pay off a debt, pay off a mortgage, go over the hill (Inf), go over the wall (Inf), go bail for (Inf), demob (Inf), let off the hook (Inf)

5 **be liberated**, achieve liberty, free oneself, gain one's freedom, go free, go scot-free, go at liberty, go AWOL (absent without leave), extricate oneself, break loose, eluctate, break out, break away, get away, get free, get off, get off scot-free, get out of, tear loose, get out, break (*or* burst) one's bonds, throw off the yoke, throw off, shake off, slip the collar, assert oneself, get the bit between one's teeth, stand on one's own two feet, fight for freedom, jump the wall, tunnel out, shake (US inf), shake free (US inf), go on the lam (US inf)

6 **treat equally**, grant equal rights to, grant equality to, enforce civil rights, enfranchise, abolish discrimination, end racial discrimination, end sexual discrimination, support women's liberation, end age discrimination, adopt affirmative action

ADJECTIVES

7 **liberated**, liberating, free, freed, emancipated, unshackled, unfettered, independent-minded, deregulated, liberalized, released, paroled, on parole, bailed, out on bail, redemptive, absolving, absolved, saved, rescued, exemptible, exempted, acquitted, scot-free

ADVERBS

8 **free**, scot-free, freely, with a free spirit, in a liberating atmosphere, carefree, without a care, without regulations, unshackled, unrestricted, unconfined, without chains, without discrimination, fairly, with equal chance

392 Help

Many hands make light work. Proverb.

NOUNS

1 **help**, aid, assistance, helping hand, hand, assist (US), springboard, instrument, means to an end, avail, use, benefit, advantage, improvement, following wind, fair wind, tailwind, leg-up (Inf)

► *244 Improvement; 349 Use; 352 Means*

2 **support**, moral support, backing, succour, relief, comfort, ease, remedy, ministration, ministry, offices, good offices, kind offices, service, benefit, advice, counsel, guidance, constructive criticism, intercession, prayer, benediction, lift, boost, good turn, good deed, favour, kindness, rescue, deliverance

► *263 Ease; 390 Deliverance; 394 Remedy; 608 Relief; 713 Advice; 797 Good*

3 **sustenance**, support, subsistence, sustainment, sustention, sustentation, maintenance, upkeep, livelihood, living, keep, daily bread, manna, provision, nourishment, nurture, mothering, care, tender loving care (TLC), sympathy

► *413 Support; 436 Provisions*

4 **social assistance**, income support, public assistance (US), private insurance, national insurance, state insurance, health insurance, unemployment insurance, life assurance, benefit, relief, welfare, welfare (*or* relief) payment, jobseeker's allowance, unemployment benefit, unemployment compensation (US), housing benefit, sickness benefit, disablement benefit, maternity benefit, maternity allowance, maternity grant, child benefit, family allowance, child allowance, family benefit, family credit, pension, retirement pension, state pension, old age pension, widow's pension, company pension, personal pension, noncontributory benefit, maintenance, alimony, aliment (Scot), guaranteed annual income (US), social security, public provision, state provision, social services, welfare services, National Health Service (NHS), welfare state, protection, dole (Inf), the welfare (Inf)

► *2 Sociology; 252 Safety*

5 **medical assistance**, therapy, treatment, surgery, remedy, cure, medicine, first aid,

► *35 Medicine; 393 Repair; 394 Remedy*

6 **financial assistance**, subsidy, subvention, grant, allowance, stipend, donation, contribution, endowment, settlement, bestowal, dowry, scholarship, bursary, fellowship, sponsorship, financial backing, funding, loan, advance, credit, monetary aid, economic aid, hand-out, charity

► *14 Finance; 768 Giving; 771 Lending; 783 Credit; 785 Payment*

7 **convenience**, facility, amenity, accommodation, appliance, aid, tool, labour-saving device, time-saving device, safeguard

► *239 Convenience; 252 Safety; 265 Easiness; 438 Tool*

8 **furtherance**, advancement, facilitation, expediting, forwarding, promotion, preferment, special (*or* preferential) treatment

9 **patronage**, fosterage, tutelage, auspices, aegis, championship, sponsorship, subsidization, seconding, advocacy, encouragement, backing, support, abetment, countenance

► *413 Support; 652 Philanthropy*

10 **helpfulness**, cooperation, collaboration, willingness, usefulness, utility, benevolence, kindness, goodwill, advantageousness, profitability

► *237 Usefulness; 636 Willingness; 650 Benevolence; 747 Cooperation; 765 Profit*

11 **helper**, assistant, assister, aid, aider, enabler, aide, mate, abettor, collaborator, colleague, partner, ally, attendant, adjutant, coadjutant, adjuvant, helping hand, facilitator, auxiliary, second, subordinate, deputy, lieutenant, backup, standby, henchman, right-hand man (*or* woman), man Friday, girl Friday, support, backing, backing group, back-room boys (*or* girls), second line, reinforcements, reserves, staff, workers, employees, hands, sidekick (Inf), gofer (Inf)

► *578 Worker*

12 **recipient**, beneficiary, heir

► *769 Receiving*

13 **supporter**, mainstay, comfort, prop, succourer, tower of strength, friend in need, good neighbour, good Samaritan, ministering angel, carer, helpmate, helpmeet, friendly critic

► *569 Friendship; 797 Good*

14 **adviser**, mentor, guide, counsellor, minister, pastor, consultant, arbitrator, advocate, troubleshooter

► *7 Religion; 713 Advice; 748 Mediation*

15 **benefactor**, benefactress, well-wisher, philanthropist, patron, sponsor, promoter, backer, guardian angel, patron saint, tutelary, fairy godmother, genie, angel (Inf)

► *652 Philanthropy*

16 **home help**, housekeeper, help, daily help, daily, domestic help, domestic, cleaner, cleaning lady, charwoman, charlady, hired help, servant, Mrs Mop (Inf), char (Inf)

► *401 Servant*

VERBS

17 **help**, aid, assist, abet, aid and abet, help out, make oneself useful, be of assistance, be of help, do something, give a hand, lend (*or* bear) a hand, give (*or* render) assistance, give an assist (US), proffer aid, come to the aid (*or* assistance) of, rush (*or* fly) to the assistance of, go (*or* come) to the relief of, rescue, deliver, save, go for help

► *237 Usefulness; 390 Deliverance*

18 **receive help**, accept aid, collect unemployment, receive welfare payments, take charity

19 **support**, succour, comfort, hearten, give relief to, min-

ister to, care for, tend, look after, nurse, alleviate, relieve, ease, remedy, treat, doctor, bolster, strengthen, reinforce, buttress, shore, shore up, prop, prop up, undergird, crutch, boost, lift, rally, revive, restore, give new life to
▶ *263 Ease; 393 Repair; 394 Remedy; 413 Support; 608 Relief*
20 sustain, support, maintain, keep, provide for, nourish, nurture, mother, hold someone's hand, pamper, coddle, cosset, protect, sympathize
▶ *252 Safety; 436 Provisions*
21 be helpful, benefit, advantage, do one good, do one a world of good, serve, avail, profit, gain
▶ *237 Usefulness; 765 Profit; 797 Good*
22 improve, better, ameliorate, enhance, do something for (*or* to), do a good turn, do a favour, give a leg-up, help a lame dog over a stile, help a lame duck, accommodate, oblige, indulge, favour, collaborate, cooperate, pitch in
▶ *244 Improvement; 747 Cooperation; 810 Duty*
23 advise, counsel, guide, countenance, encourage, uphold, support, subscribe to, cultivate, give (*or* lend *or* furnish) support, lend oneself, endorse, sanction, advocate, champion, argue for, hold a brief for, intercede, take by the hand, hold out a hand to, take under one's wing, patronize, sponsor, take up, propose, second, back, foster, take in hand, take in tow, plump for (Inf)
▶ *413 Support; 713 Advice; 748 Mediation*
24 back, back up, stand behind, stand back of (US), get in back of (US), get behind, stand by, stick by, take the part of, go to bat for (US), take up the cudgels for, stick up for, run interference for (US), side with, align with, associate oneself with, come down (*or* range oneself) on the side of, ally with
25 serve, attend, wait on, tend, look after, work for, labour on behalf of, cater for (*or* to), pander to, do for (Inf)
▶ *401 Servant; 578 Worker*
26 be useful, come in useful, not come (*or* go) amiss, fill a need, lend itself, augment, supplement, produce results
27 find useful, need, could (*or* can) do with, avail oneself of
▶ *211 Addition; 237 Usefulness; 349 Use*
28 further, advance, forward, promote, prefer, favour, advantage, facilitate, expedite, subserve, subvene, contribute to, make for, have a hand in, help along, boost, conduce to, ease (*or* smooth) the way, clear the track, grease the wheels, quicken, hasten, speed, lend wings to
▶ *262 Haste; 265 Easiness; 268 Slipperiness; 302 Forward Motion*
29 finance, fund, sponsor, back, support, subsidize, subventionize, guarantee, endow, settle, bestow, donate, contribute to (*or* towards), pitch in, lend, loan, advance, set up, set (*or* put) on one's feet, provide the means, be the making of, help out, tide over, see through, bale (*or* bail) out, chip in (Inf)
▶ *14 Finance; 768 Giving; 771 Lending; 780 Money; 783 Credit; 785 Payment*

ADJECTIVES

30 helping, aiding, assisting, adjuvant, serving, supporting, supplementing, of assistance, of service, of help, facilitative, facilitating, instrumental, promoting, favouring
▶ *265 Easiness; 302 Forward Motion; 413 Support*
31 supplementary, auxiliary, subsidiary, ancillary, accessory, subservient, on call, at one's service (*or* command), at one's beck and call
32 supportive, comforting, reassuring, succouring, morale-boosting, caring, tending, attending, ministering, ministrant, ministrative, encouraging, heartening, sustaining, fostering, nurturing
▶ *608 Relief*
33 helpful, assistant (Lit), useful, utilitarian, serviceable, convenient, handy, informative, practical, constructive, positive, furthering, promoting, contributory, conducive
▶ *237 Usefulness; 239 Convenience*
34 beneficial, good, salutary, advantageous, favourable, propitious, expedient, profitable, gainful, valuable, remedial, therapeutic
▶ *235 Worth; 394 Remedy; 765 Profit; 797 Good*
35 benevolent, kind, kindly, considerate, benign, sympathetic, friendly, neighbourly, cooperative, willing, accommodating, obliging, generous, charitable, beneficent, philanthropic, indulgent, well-disposed, favourably disposed, well-affected, well-meaning, well-meant, well-intentioned
▶ *636 Willingness; 650 Benevolence; 652 Philanthropy; 747 Cooperation*

ADVERBS

36 helpfully, supportively, usefully, serviceably, conveniently, practically, constructively, positively, beneficially, to the good, advantageously, favourably, profitably, to advantage
37 in aid of, for the sake of, on behalf of, by the aid of, thanks to, under the auspices (*or* aegis) of, in the name of, in the service of
38 benevolently, kindly, considerately, sympathetically, cooperatively, willingly, obligingly, charitably

393 Repair

VERBS

1 repair, do repairs, mend, patch up, fix, right, put right, set to rights, rectify, correct, straighten out, put in order, put into working order, get working, put back into operation, reactivate, remedy, amend, edit, emend, adjust, tune (up), overhaul, service, maintain, cobble, sole, resole, heel, retread, reface, cover, recover, resurface, thatch, line, reline, make good, splice, bind, bind up, tie, tie up, darn, patch, reupholster, stop, fill, fill in, plug, plug up, plug a hole, stop a gap, fill in the cracks, plaster, seal, paper over, caulk, pick up the pieces, piece together, glue together, reassemble, put back together, cannibalize, join
▶ *244 Improvement; 309 Closure; 394 Remedy; 550 Covering; 801 Right*
2 refurbish, renovate, redecorate, repaint, repaper, recondition, revamp, refit, restore, renew, remodel, refashion, reform, retouch, touch up, freshen up, make over, change, smarten up, give a face-lift, improve, upgrade, modernize, do wonders with, gentrify, do up (Inf), fix up (US inf), yuppify (Inf), trendify (Inf)
▶ *256 Cleanness; 295 Newness*
3 restore, return, replace, retrocede, repatriate, give back, hand back, put back, bring back, yield up, restitute, make amends, pay back, atone, recall, reappoint, rein-

stall, re-establish, reinstitute, reintroduce, relaunch, refound, rehabilitate, reconstitute, reformulate, reprogramme, reinforce, reconstruct, reform, reorganize, reorient, rebuild, re-erect, remake, redo, make like new, return to mint condition, make as good as new, service, overhaul, valet, clean, make whole, reintegrate, redintegrate (Lit), replant, reclaim, reforest, reafforest, recycle, reprocess, revalidate, revive, rally, strengthen, replenish, fill up again, restock, reassemble, reconvene, bring together, redeem, ransom, rescue, save, salvage, deliver, release, free, liberate, cough up (Inf)

► *259 Health; 336 Strength; 376 Gathering; 390 Deliverance; 391 Liberation; 436 Provisions; 775 Giving Back; 807 Atonement*

4 **be restored**, recover, come round, come to, revive, pick up, rally, respond to treatment, pull through, get over, get well, get better, bounce back, convalesce, recuperate, regain one's strength, turn the corner, find one's feet again, pick oneself up, get up, weather the storm, survive, live through, sleep through, reawaken, live again, be reborn, be born again, come back to life, come to life again, cheat death, rise from the dead, rise like a phoenix from the ashes, return from the grave, return to the land of the living, reappear, take on a new lease of life, return to normal, get back to normal, go on as before, resume, start again, go back to square one, look like new, look in mint condition, look as good as new, undergo repairs, make a comeback (Inf), sleep off (Inf), snap out of it (Inf)

► *130 Beginning; 244 Improvement; 259 Health; 581 Refreshment*

5 **revive**, revivify, revitalize, resuscitate, regenerate, recall to life, awaken, reawaken, resurrect, reanimate, rekindle, enliven, invigorate, reinvigorate, breathe fresh life into, give a new lease of life, restore vitality, rejuvenate, refresh, freshen, renew, recruit (Lit)

► *581 Refreshment*

6 **cure**, heal, make well, cure of, break of, nurse, nurse through, treat, physic (Lit), medicate, prescribe medication, detoxify, use therapy, doctor, operate, bandage, put a plaster on, bind up one's wounds, work a cure, perform a miracle, snatch from the grave, restore to health, set up, set on one's feet again, set, knit together, cicatrize, heal over, form a scab, scab over, close, right itself, put itself right, heal itself, cure itself, work its own cure

► *244 Improvement; 259 Health; 394 Remedy*

7 **resort**, go, head for, leave for, betake oneself, have recourse

NOUNS

8 **repair**, repairs, reparation, mending, patching up, fixing, putting right, rectification, correction, reactivation, remedy, amendment, editing, emendation, maintenance, running repairs, service, servicing, correcting faults, overhauling, overhaul, tuning, tune-up, adjustment, renovation, restoration, renewal, reconditioning, reintegration, redintegration (Lit), reassembling, do-it-yourself (DIY), making like new, putting in mint condition, making as good as new, mend, invisible mending, darn, darning, patch, patching, clout (Dial), cobbling, soling, resoling, heeling, resurfacing, splicing, binding, insertion, reinforcement, refit, new look, face-lift, beautification

► *244 Improvement; 394 Remedy; 547 Beautification*

9 **restoration**, returning, giving back, replacement, putting back, retrocession, repatriation, restitution, redress, amends, reparation, reparations, atonement, finding again, getting back, retrieval, recovery, recall, reinvestment, reinstitution, reinstallation, reinstalment, rehabilitation, replanting, reafforestation, reforestation, reclamation, recycling, reprocessing, salvage, redemption, ransom, rescue, salvation, deliverance, re-establishment, reconstitution, reintroduction, relaunching, reformulation, re-erection, rebuilding, reformation, reprogramming, reconstruction, reorganization, readjustment, reorientation, remodelling, refashioning, reconversion, reaction, counter-reformation, counteraction, resumption, return to normal, derestriction, recruitment, reinforcement, strengthening, replenishment, provision

► *336 Strength; 390 Deliverance; 436 Provisions; 775 Giving Back; 807 Atonement*

10 **revival**, recovery, renewal, revivification, revitalization, revivescence, reawakening, resurgence, recurrence, comeback, return to fashion, turnabout, turnround, rally, fresh spurt, new energy, refreshment, new supply, recruitment, financial upturn, economic recovery, economic miracle, boom, prosperity, reactivation, reanimation, resuscitation, artificial respiration, rejuvenation, rejuvenescence, second childhood, second youth, second honeymoon, second spring, Indian summer, rebirth, renaissance (*or* renascence), new birth, second birth, palingenesis, regeneration, regeneracy, new life, new hope, second chance, resurrection, rising from the dead, recall from the grave, return to the land of the living, reappearance, resurrection day, the Resurrection, revivalism, evangelism

► *248 Prosperity; 581 Refreshment*

11 **recuperation**, convalescence, recovery, healing, mending, cure, being cured, response to treatment, response to therapy, return to normal, rally, rallying, perking up, upturn, turn for the better, cicatrization, closing, scab formation, scabbing over, healing over, restoration to health, return to health, remedy, moderation, easing, relief, psychological cure, psychotherapy, catharsis, abreaction, curability, curableness

► *244 Improvement; 259 Health; 394 Remedy; 608 Relief*

12 **repairer**, repairman, mender, fixer, handyman, renovator, painter, decorator, interior decorator, do-it-yourselfer (DIYer), mechanic, engineer, amender, emendator, editor, copy editor, subeditor, proofreader, rectifier, rebuilder, restorer, art restorer, refurbisher, darner, tailor, seamstress, patcher, cobbler, shoe-repairer, knife-grinder, tinker, plumber, electrician, salvager, salvor, doctor, surgeon, curer, healer, bonesetter, osteopath, chiropractor, plastic surgeon, psychiatrist, psychotherapist, psychoanalyst, hypnotist, reformist, reformer, faith healer

► *244 Improvement; 394 Remedy*

ADJECTIVES

13 **repaired**, mended, patched up, fixed, right, correct, restored, reconditioned, renovated, redecorated, remade, rebuilt, reconstructed, reconstituted, refurbished, reequipped, refitted, redone, rectified, put right, reinforced, strengthened, improved, like new, in mint condition, as

good as new, renewed, reborn, born again, redeemed, saved, resuscitated, revived, redivivus, renascent, resurgent, phoenix-like, like a phoenix from the ashes, reclaimed, recovered, salvaged, found

► *244 Improvement; 394 Remedy*

14 repairable, reparable, restorable, mendable, amendable, rectifiable, recoverable, retrievable, redeemable (*or* redemptible), curable, operable, treatable, medicable

15 cured, healed, returned to health, healthy, better, like new, as good as new, none the worse, convalescent, on the mend, back on one's feet, back to normal, oneself again, alive and kicking, in one's right mind

► *259 Health; 394 Remedy*

16 restorative, reparative, analeptic, reviving, recuperative, curative, sanative, healing, medicated, medicinal, remedial, redemptive (*or* redemptory)

► *394 Remedy; 581 Refreshment*

ADVERBS

17 repairably, reparably, recoverably, redeemably, remedially

394 Remedy

Well, now, there's a remedy for everything except death. Miguel de Cervantes.

Extreme remedies are most appropriate for extreme diseases. Hippocrates.

NOUNS

1 remedy, cure, antidote, help, aid, succour, relief, oil on troubled waters, moderator, remedial measure, corrective, correction, amendment, redress, amends, restitution, expiation, atonement, certain cure, recuperation, recovery, medicinal value, healing quality (*or* property), healing gift, sovereign remedy, specific remedy, specific, answer, solution, prescribed remedy, prescription, recipe, formula, quack remedy, nostrum, patent medicine, panacea, heal-all, cure-all, catholicon, elixir, *elixir vitae* (L), philosopher's stone

► *244 Improvement; 392 Help; 393 Repair; 608 Relief; 685 Moderation; 706 Answer; 775 Giving Back; 807 Atonement*

2 medicine, remedy, pharmaceutical, drug, prescription (drug), physic, materia medica, pharmacopoeia, pharmacognosy, herbal remedy, vegetable remedy, galenical, herb, medicinal herb, simple, balm, balsam, medication, medicament, over-the-counter medication, patent medicine, proprietary drug, generic drug, ethical drug, placebo, pill, bolus, tablet, tabloid, capsule, lozenge, pastille, draught, dose, drench, drip, injection, shot, jab (Inf), infusion, potion, elixir, decoction, preparation, mixture, powder, electuary, linctus, plaster, medicine chest, medicine cabinet, medicine bottle

► *32 Chemistry; 37 Pharmacology; 691 Drug-Taking*

3 prophylactic, preventive, preventative, contraception, sanitation, sanitary precaution, quarantine, isolation, *cordon sanitaire* (Fr), hygiene, prophylaxis, immunization, inoculation, vaccination, vaccine, triple vaccine, BCG, MMR (measles, mumps, rubella) vaccine, antimalarial pill, quinine, antisepsis, disinfection, sterilization, antiseptic, disinfectant, iodine, carbolic, boric acid, boracic acid, bactericide, germicide, insecticide, poison, fumigant, dentifrice, toothpaste, tooth powder, cleanser, mouthwash, gargle, fluoride, hydrogen peroxide, Mercurochrome™

► *256 Cleanness; 257 Hygiene; 259 Health; 563 Infertility; 634 Avoidance*

4 antidote, countermeasure, antitoxin, counterpoison, counterirritant, antihistamine, antibody, monoclonal antibody, antiserum, mithridate, theriac, antipyretic, febrifuge, quinine, vermifuge, anthelmintic, antigen, interferon, antibiosis, antibiotic, immunosuppressant, antispasmodic, anticonvulsant, anticoagulant, sedative, muscle relaxant

► *347 Counteraction*

5 analgesic, painkiller, pain-reliever, anodyne, nepenthe, palliative, balm, salve, demulcent, arnica, aspirin, paracetamol, codeine, ibuprofen, meperidine, pethidine, nitrous oxide, laughing gas, morphine, morphia, laudanum (Lit), anaesthetic, local anaesthetic, general anaesthetic, analgesia, pain relief, anaesthesia, local anaesthesia, general anaesthesia, acupuncture, hypnosis, mind over matter

► *491 Physical Pain*

6 purgative, purge, cathartic, laxative, aperient, castor oil, Epsom salts, health salts, senna pods, cascara, milk of magnesia, diuretic, expectorant, emetic, nauseant, antacid, ipecacuanha, carminative, digestive, liquorice, dill water, douche, enema

7 tonic, restorative, roborant, cordial, tonic water, reviver, refresher, stimulant, amphetamine, Benzedrine™, caffeine, nicotine, alcohol, smelling salts, sal volatile, hartshorn, infusion, tisane, herb tea, ginseng, royal jelly, vitamin, iron, bracer (Inf), pick-me-up (Inf), pep pill (Inf)

► *338 Vigour; 581 Refreshment*

8 drug, wonder drug, miracle drug, synthetic drug, designer drug, antibiotic, sulpha drug, sulphonamide, penicillin, aureomycin, streptomycin, insulin, cortisone, hormone, steroid, progesterone, oestrogen, tamoxifen, contraceptive pill, analgesic, aspirin, codeine, paracetamol, anaesthetic, tranquillizer, temazepam, diazepam, Valium™, antidepressant, Prozac™, sedative, barbiturate, sleeping pill, soporific, narcotic, dope, heroin, opium, cocaine, morphine, intoxicant, stimulant, drug-taking

► *37 Pharmacology; 343 Inactivity; 489 Insensibility; 563 Infertility; 691 Drug-Taking*

9 balm, balsam, oil, soothing syrup, emollient, moderator, salve, cerate, ointment, cream, face cream, moisturizer, cosmetic, petrolatum, petroleum jelly, Vaseline™, lanolin, liniment, embrocation, lotion, wash, eyewash, collyrium

► *547 Beautification; 685 Moderation*

10 surgical dressing, dressing, lint, gauze, swab, bandage, fingerstall, sling, splint, cast, plaster of Paris, tourniquet, patch, application, external application, plaster, sticking plaster, Elastoplast™, corn plaster, court plaster, mustard plaster, cataplasm, fomentation, poultice, compress, tampon, tent, roll, pledget, pessary, suppository, traumatic

11 medical art, therapeutics, healing, art of healing, gift of healing, healing touch, recuperation, medicine, clinical medicine, preventive medicine, medical advice, practice, medical practice, leechcraft (Lit), allopathy, homoeopathy, naturopathy, nature cure, acupuncture, alternative medicine, complementary medicine, ayurveda, holistic medicine, folk medicine, faith healing, laying on of hands, Christian Science

► *35 Medicine; 260 Ill Health; 393 Repair*

12 surgery, general surgery, brain surgery, heart surgery, cardiac surgery, open-heart surgery, bypass surgery, transplant surgery, grafting, plastic surgery, cosmetic surgery, rhinoplasty, prosthesis, prosthetics, surgical operation, operation, op (Inf), phlebotomy, venesection, bleeding, blood-letting, cupping, transfusion, perfusion, dialysis, transplant, graft, skin graft, renal (*or* kidney) graft, corneal graft, coronary bypass graft, cauterization, amputation, trephination, lobotomy, tonsillectomy, appendicectomy, colostomy, laparotomy, mastectomy, radical mastectomy, hysterectomy, vasectomy, dental surgery, bridging, drawing, extracting, stopping, filling, crowning, chiropody, podiatry, electrolysis

► *35 Medicine*

13 therapy, therapeutics, medical care, healing art, treatment, medical treatment, clinical treatment, nursing, bedside manner, first aid, aftercare, course, cure, faith cure, nature cure, cold-water cure, hydrotherapy, thalassotherapy, regimen, diet, dietary, chiropractic, bonesetting, manipulation, massage, orthopaedics, osteopathy, osteotherapy, hypnotherapy, hormone therapy, hormone replacement therapy (HRT), immunotherapy, chemotherapy, physiotherapy, occupational therapy, radiotherapy, phototherapy, heat treatment, electrotherapy, shock treatment, electroconvulsive therapy (ECT), mental treatment, clinical psychology, child psychology, psychotherapy, psychiatry, psychoanalysis, psychology, group therapy, behavioural therapy, aversion therapy, Gestalt therapy, primal (scream) therapy, rebirthing, acupuncture, acupressure, catheterization, intravenous injection, drip, drip-feed, fomentation, poulticing

► *442 Intellect*

14 hospital, infirmary, sanatorium, dispensary, clinic, nursing home, convalescent home, rest home, home for the dying, hospice, asylum, mental asylum, mental hospital, lazaretto (*or* lazaret *or* lazarette), lazar-house (*or* pest-house), leper asylum, leper colony, hospital ship, HOPE, hospital train, MASH (mobile army surgical hospital) (US), stretcher, ambulance, ward, hospital ward, isolation ward, sick bay, sickroom, sickbed, hospital bed, ripple bed, tent, oxygen tent, iron lung, respirator, life-support system, heart-lung machine, kidney machine, scanner, body scanner, brain scanner, head scanner, CT (*or* CAT) scanner, MR scanner, dressing station, first-aid station, casualty station, operating room, operating theatre, operating table, consulting room, surgery, spa, hydro, watering place, pump room, baths, hot springs, thermae, solarium, sun lamp, sun bed

► *35 Medicine; 461 Insanity*

15 healer, therapeutist, doctor, physician, leech (Lit), surgeon, dental surgeon, dentist, veterinary surgeon, veterinarian, vet, herbalist, herb doctor, faith healer, layer-on of hands, Christian Scientist, allopath, homeopath, naturopath, acupuncturist, hypnotist, hakim (*or* hakeem), flying doctor, witch doctor, medicine man, sorcerer, therapist, psychotherapist, psychiatrist, alienist (US), psychoanalyst, osteopath, bonesetter, chiropractor, masseur, masseuse, pedicurist, podiatrist, chiropodist, optician, oculist, orthoptist, nutritionist, dietician, nurse, Aesculapius, Hippocrates, the father of medicine, Galen, doc (Inf), quack (Inf), horse doctor (Inf), medic (Inf), medico (Inf), sawbones (Inf), headshrinker (Inf), shrink (Inf)

► *35 Medicine; 36 Psychology and Psychiatry*

16 druggist, pharmacist, apothecary, chemist, dispenser, posologist, pharmacologist, pharmacy

► *32 Chemistry; 37 Pharmacology*

ADJECTIVES

17 remedial, corrective, therapeutic, medicinal, analeptic, curative, first aid, restorative, helpful, beneficial, healing, curing, hygienic, sanitary, salubrious, salutiferous, health-giving, specific, sovereign, panacean, all-healing, soothing, paregoric, balsamic, demulcent, emollient, palliative, lenitive, anodyne, analgesic, narcotic, hypnotic, anaesthetic, insensible, peptic, digestive, purging, cleansing, cathartic, emetic, vomitory, laxative, antidotal, counteracting, theriacal, prophylactic, preventive, preventative, disinfectant, antiseptic, antipyretic, febrifugal, tonic, stimulative, dietetic, alimentary, nutritive, nutritional

► *37 Pharmacology; 235 Worth; 256 Cleanness; 257 Hygiene; 347 Counteraction; 393 Repair; 489 Insensibility; 685 Moderation*

18 medical, pathological, Aesculapian, Hippocratic, Galenic, allopathic, homoeopathic, herbal, surgical, anaplastic, rhinoplastic, orthopaedic, orthotic, vulnerary, traumatic, obstetric, obstetrical, gynaecological, paediatric, geriatric, clinical, medicable, operable, curable

► *35 Medicine*

VERBS

19 remedy, correct, restore, fix, mend, put right, help, aid, succour, apply a remedy, treat, heal, cure, work a cure, palliate, alleviate, soothe, demulce, neutralize, relieve, ease

► *244 Improvement; 392 Help; 393 Repair; 608 Relief*

20 doctor, be a doctor, practise, have a practice, practise medicine, treat, prescribe, advise, attend, minister to, tend, nurse, give first aid, give the kiss of life, revive, hospitalize, put on the sick list, put to bed, physic, medicate, drench, dose, purge, inject, give a shot, dress, bind, swathe, bandage, put a plaster on, plaster, stop the bleeding, apply a tourniquet, staunch, poultice, foment, set, put in splints, drug, dope, anaesthetize, operate, use the knife, cut open, amputate, trepan, trephine, curette, cauterize, bleed, phlebotomize, transfuse, perfuse, massage, rub, manipulate, draw, extract, pull, stop, fill, crown, immunize, vaccinate, inoculate, sterilize, pasteurize, antisepticize, disinfect, sanitate

► *35 Medicine; 257 Hygiene*

ADVERBS

21 remedially, therapeutically, medicinally, medically, pathologically, surgically, clinically

395 Influence

How to Win Friends and Influence People. Dale Carnegie.

The hand that rocks the cradle
Is the hand that rules the world. William Ross Wallace.

NOUNS

1 **influence**, power, powerful influence, potency, potentiality, ability, capability, superior power, strength, might, mightiness, force, force to be reckoned with, predominance, prevalence, greatness, magnitude, importance, significance, advantage, authority, whip hand, upper hand, final say, casting vote, vital role, leading part, leverage, grip, hold, footing, play, weight, impact, pressure, pull, drag, magnetism, gravity, attraction, fascination, repulsion, drive, push, thrust, impulse, motive, motivation, interest, vested interest, emotion, impression, inspiration, persuasion, encouragement, cause, contagion, infection, climate, atmosphere, circumstances, fate, destiny, clout (Inf)

▶ *121 Superiority; 123 Importance; 331 Impulsion; 334 Power; 363 Attraction; 364 Repulsion; 386 Compulsion; 396 Authority; 471 Attention; 480 Persuasion; 811 Reputation*

2 **occult influence**, magic, magic spell, witchcraft, sorcery, charm, mesmerism, hypnotism, planetary influence, heaven, stars, astrology, horoscope, malevolence, malign influence, curse, voodoo (*or* hoodoo)

▶ *11 Occultism*

3 **personal influence**, personality, magnetic personality, charisma, repute, reputation, credit, prestige, leadership, ascendancy, hegemony, domination, dominance, dominion, tyranny, authority, sway, control, reign

4 **indirect influence**, favour, friend at court, amicus curiae (Lit), patronage, wires, wirepulling (US), strings, lever, hold, hidden influence, secret influence, hidden hand, power broker, kingmaker, *éminence grise* (Fr), grey eminence, power behind the throne, woman behind the (great) man, hand that rocks the cradle, pull (Inf)

5 **influential person**, president, prime minister, premier, chair, chairman, chairwoman, director, parent, best friend, priest, preacher, doctor, lawyer, lobbyist, manager, manipulator, uncrowned king (*or* queen), big noise (Inf), big shot (Inf), bigwig (Inf), big wheel (Inf), big cheese (Inf), queen bee (Inf), brass hat (Inf), top brass (Inf), wheeler-dealer (Inf), influence pedlar (Inf)

▶ *392 Help*

6 **group influence**, pressure group, self-help group, lobby, public opinion, the powers that be, the Establishment, Big Brother, multinational company, superpower

7 **sphere of influence**, area (*or* field) of influence, territory, orbit, ambit, bailiwick, turf (US inf)

VERBS

8 **influence**, have influence, exercise influence, exert influence, command influence, have charisma, impress, motivate, actuate, activate, encourage, suggest, persuade, carry weight, have importance, be recognized, be listened to, have a voice, make one's voice heard, have a say in, play a role (*or* part) in, have a part to play, gain a footing (*or* foothold), take root, strike root in, gain a hearing, make oneself felt, affect, bear upon, tell upon, work upon, have the right connections, know the right people, have friends in high places, have the ear of, pressurize, put pressure on, lobby, pull (the) strings, pull (the) wires (US), guide, direct, lead, establish the trend, set the trend, set the fashion, serve as a model, promote, prejudice, bias, brainwash, predispose, dispose, colour, lure, tempt, appeal, have pull (Inf), have pulling power (Inf), have clout (Inf), carry clout (Inf), wheel and deal (Inf), weigh in (Inf)

9 **change**, change for better or for worse, make or mar, counterbalance, tip (*or* turn) the scales, influence positively, make better, improve, leaven, influence negatively, discourage, repulse, disgust, repel, put off, militate against, infect, dilute, contaminate, adulterate, mar, spoil, impair, ruin

10 **be a prevailing influence**, be prevalent, prevail, predominate, fascinate, mesmerize, hypnotize, practise witchcraft, outweigh, override, overbear, gain (*or* have) the upper hand, have the final say, have the casting vote, have sway, force, compel, pull, drag, tyrannize, dominate, have power over, tower over, have a hold over (*or* on), have in one's power, bestride, subdue, subjugate, overawe, overcome, gain full play, master, gain mastery, overmaster, reign supreme, rule, run, control, monopolize, take over, take a firm grip, take (a) hold, rage, be all the rage, be rife, spread, spread like wildfire, run through, pervade, permeate, hold all the cards, hold all the aces, hold the whip hand, be in the driving seat, lead by the nose, have under one's thumb, wind (*or* twist) around one's little finger, wear the trousers (Inf), wear the pants (US inf), throw one's weight around (Inf), catch on (Inf)

ADJECTIVES

11 **influential**, causal, effectual, effective, persuasive, important, vital, significant, contributing, contributory, decisive, momentous, world-shattering, earth-shaking, telling, prestigious, impressive, potent, powerful, strong, active, busy, meddling, interfering, mighty, forceful, great, superior, ruling, leading, guiding, directing, instructive, educative, reigning, regnant, in the ascendant, rising, in authority, of authority, commanding, authoritative, tyrannical

12 **appealing**, emotional, moving, affecting, charming, attractive, gripping, fascinating, irresistible, charismatic, magnetic, mesmeric, hypnotic, compelling, inspirational, encouraging, inspiring, motivating, suggestive, seductive, tempting, addictive, habit-forming, infectious, contagious, catching

13 **dominant**, predominant, wide-ranging, international, multinational, monopolistic, prevailing, prevalent, ubiquitous, pervasive, all-pervading, in the driving seat, on the up and up (Inf)

ADVERBS

14 **influentially**, causally, effectually, to good effect, with great (*or* telling) effect, persuasively, importantly, vitally, significantly, prestigiously, impressively, potently, powerfully, strongly, forcefully, predominantly, commandingly, authoritatively, with (*or* by) authority, under someone's influence, within someone's orbit, tyrannically,

internationally, encouragingly, decisively, momentously, emotionally, charmingly, irresistibly, charismatically, hypnotically, inspirationally, suggestively, seductively, infectiously, contagiously, ubiquitously, pervasively

396 Authority

NOUNS

1 **authority**, power, control, command, leadership, direction, governance, domination, predominance, overbearance, dominance, ascendancy, hegemony, mastery, magistrality, superiority, supremacy, seniority, might, strength, potency, potence, absolute power, absolutism, legitimacy, legality, legal power, law, lawful authority, right, rightful authority, eminent domain, divine right, prerogative, royal prerogative, regality, royalty, nobility, constituted authority, derived authority, delegated authority, the upper hand, the whip hand, financial control, purse strings, indirect authority, hidden power, power behind the throne, string pulling, wirepulling (US), manipulation, influence, pressure, patronage, puissance (Lit), clout (Inf)

► *121 Superiority; 334 Power; 780 Money*

2 **authoritativeness**, powerfulness, greatness, mightiness, masterfulness, lordliness, peremptoriness, imperativeness, imperiousness, majesty, self-assertion, confidence, knowledge

► *452 Certainty; 455 Knowledge*

3 **acquisition of power**, empowerment, election, selection, delegation, deputation, appointment, authorization, grant, succession, legitimate succession, accession, coronation, anointment, consecration, seizure of power, usurpation, coup d'état, coup, revolution, overthrowing, taking over

► *12 Government and Politics; 129 Precedence*

4 **governance**, reins of government, government, politics, administration, management, bureaucracy, red tape, civil service, officialism, beadledom, jurisdiction, direction, command, rule, sway, hold, grip, reign, sovereignty, suzerainty, dominion, officialdom, the government, the administration, the authorities, the Establishment, the ruling class (*or* classes), the system, the power structure, the powers that be, Big Brother, the top, the high command, the inner circle, the board, the directorship, higher-ups (Inf)

5 **position of authority**, office of power, high office, government post, federal post (US), seat of government, cabinet seat, governorship, mayoralty, consulate, proconsulate, prefecture, magistracy, headship, presidency, premiership, chairmanship, directorship, secretariat, superintendency, inspectorship, judgeship, police rank, military rank

► *16 Law; 586 Combatant*

6 **place of authority**, capital, palace, corridors of power, Whitehall, Downing Street, Number Ten, Parliament, Westminster, Washington (US), the White House (US), Congress (US), the Hill (US), the Capitol (US), Capitol Hill (US), classroom, courtroom, police station, prison, military base, military unit

7 **type of rule**, monarchy, constitutional monarchy, regnancy, regency, dynasty, aristocracy, plutocracy, meritocracy, oligarchy, tribalism, heteronomy, imperialism, colonialism, puppet government, caretaker government, representative government, majority rule, democracy, proportional representation, pluralism, republicanism, federalism, parliamentary government, constitutional government, egalitarianism, government of the people, by the people, for the people, self-government, rule of law, autonomy, home rule, theocracy, papal rule, ecclesiasticism, state control, collectivism, socialism, communism, Leninism, Marxism, Bolshevism, dictatorship of the proletariat, demagogy, demagoguery, despotism, benevolent despotism, authoritarianism, autocracy, autarchy, tyranny, dictatorship, totalitarianism, Fascism, Nazism, National Socialism, military government, martial law, police state, rule of terror, ochlocracy, mobocracy, mob rule, mob law, anarchy, syndicalism, anarcho-syndicalism, White supremacy, Black power

► *190 Expansion; 250 Freedom; 251 Restraint; 469 Selection; 588 Anarchy; 647 Severity*

8 **governmental organization**, body politic, regime, city, city state, state, county, district, province, canton, territory, nation, country, realm, kingdom, duchy, dukedom, principality, palatinate, republic, empire, colony, dependency, protectorate, mandate, dominion, commonwealth, federation, confederation

► *86 Regions*

9 **permission**, authorization, sanction, justification, testimonial, testimony, declaration, evidence, permit, warrant, licence, visa, credential, reference, avowal, say-so (Inf)

► *716 Evidence; 757 Permission*

10 **person of authority**, authority, leader, director, executive, manager, superior, head, chief, top man, patrician, ruler, autocrat, tyrant, dictator, despot, sovereign, monarch, king, queen, emperor, empress, pope, cardinal, primate, archbishop, bishop, dean, archdeacon, rabbi, president, prime minister, premier, minister of state, MP (Member of Parliament), MEP (Member of the European Parliament), Senator (US), Congressman (US), Congresswoman (US), representative (US), cabinet member, governor, high commissioner, commissioner, military governor, seneschal, proconsul, consul general, consul, mayor, mayoress, judge, associate justice (US), chief justice of the United States (US), magistrate, sheriff, constable, marshal, justice of the peace, official, party official, chief whip, whip, party whip, Democratic whip (US), Republican whip (US), stringpuller, wirepuller (US), policeman, policewoman, military officer, commander-in-chief, commanding officer, commander, executive officer, educator, principal, headmaster, headmistress, chancellor, vice chancellor, provost, teacher, mentor, sage, wise man, guru, swami, exec (US inf), the Old Man (Inf), bobby (Inf), bluebottle (Inf), bigwig (Inf), big shot (Inf), big wheel (Inf), big cheese (Inf), top dog (Inf), boss (Inf), beak (Inf), head honcho (Inf), copper (Inf), cop (Inf), Smokey (US inf)

► *7 Religion; 400 Master; 573 Aristocrat; 579 Management*

11 **expert**, genius, intellectual, researcher, professor, don, scholar, scientist, historian, musical genius, maestro, virtuoso, master of the violin, specialist, connoisseur, past master, adept, practitioner, physician, consultant, guide,

professional, old master, old hand, walking encyclopedia, lexicographer, pro (Inf), ace (Inf), dab hand (*or* dab) (Inf), highbrow (Inf), egghead (Inf), boffin (Inf)

▶ *18 Music; 19 Painting and Sculpture; 25 Cookery; 442 Intellect; 455 Knowledge; 458 Wisdom; 485 Skill*

ADJECTIVES

12 **authoritative**, official, definitive, ex officio, powerful, empowered, regal, royal, noble, controlling, commanding, holding the reins of government, leading, governing, ruling, reigning, on the throne, authoritarian, dominant, predominant, high-handed, overbearing, masterful, domineering, condescending, patronizing, imperative, imperious, arrogant, coercive, lordly, superior, supreme, senior, mighty, strong, potent, absolute, legitimate, legal, lawful, rightful, influential, pre-eminent, peremptory, overruling, self-assertive, confident, knowledgeable, puissant (Lit), bossy (Inf)

13 **elected**, selected, chosen, delegated, deputized, appointed, authorized, granted, successional, accessional

14 **governmental**, political, administrative, ministerial, managerial, bureaucratic, official, jurisdictional, sovereign, royal, regal, majestic, monarchal (*or* monarchial), kinglike, kingly, queenly, princely, aristocratic, imperial, oligarchic, plutocratic, suzerain, presidential, congressional, parliamentary, colonial, territorial, national, gubernatorial (US), democratic, popular, classless, republican, federal, constitutional, self-governing, autonomous, autarchic, independent, socialistic, communistic, Marxist, authoritarian, autocratic, tyrannical, dictatorial, totalitarian, Fascist, Nazi, patriarchal, matriarchal, anarchic

15 **true**, authentic, authenticated, official, legitimate, genuine, reliable, conclusive, certain, positive, sure

16 **authorized**, sanctioned, accredited, approved, allowed, permitted, licenced, warranted, chartered, made legal, legalized

17 **expert**, masterly, skilled, accomplished, professional, knowledgeable, intellectual

VERBS

18 **have authority**, have power, possess power, control, command, lead, direct, rule, govern, hold the reins of government, hold office, hold power, exercise power, wield authority, preside over, legislate, administer, manage, rule absolutely, hold sway, reign, reign supreme, sit on the throne, wear the crown, wield the sceptre, predominate, have the upper hand, have the whip hand, rule the roost, keep order, police, control the purse strings, pull strings, pull wires (US), manipulate, have under one's thumb, bend to one's will, influence, pressure, hold in the palm of one's hand (Inf), have over a barrel (Inf), have clout (Inf), have the say-so (Inf)

19 **be authoritarian**, dominate, domineer, discipline, drill, subjugate, dictate to, tyrannize, oppress, lord it over, play god, lay down the law, rule with an iron rod, hold all the aces, rule the roost, condescend, wear the trousers, wear the pants (US), crack the whip, call the shots, call the tune, ride roughshod over, lead by the nose, twist round one's little finger, boss (Inf), throw one's weight around (Inf)

20 **take authority**, assume authority, acquire authority, succeed, accede, mount the throne, take office, take command, assume command, take the helm, take over the reins (of government), gain the upper hand, get the whip hand, seize power, usurp power, lead a coup d'état), overthrow, take over

21 **grant authority**, delegate authority, give authority, empower, power, elect, select, delegate, deputize, appoint, authorize, legitimatize, coronate, anoint, consecrate, give permission, patronize, allow, permit, approve, grant, sanction, declare, accredit, license, charter, make legal, legalize

22 **be an authority on**, be an expert on, specialize in, have expertise, know, know all about, know the ropes, be well up on, know inside out, know back to front, know one's stuff (Inf), have the know-how (Inf)

ADVERBS

23 **authoritatively**, with (*or* by) authority, with (*or* by) power, ex cathedra, in the name of, by warrant of, in (*or* by) virtue of one's authority, in authority, in charge, in control, officially, powerfully, in power, royally, on the throne, nobly, commandingly, in command, in the driving seat, at the wheel, at the helm, at the reins, in the saddle, high-handedly, dominantly, arrogantly, supremely, strongly, potently, absolutely, legitimately, legally, lawfully, rightfully, knowledgeably, confidently

24 **ministerially**, presidentially, congressionally, administratively, colonially, nationally, politically, in a political context, democratically, constitutionally, independently, socialistically, communistically

25 **authentically**, truly, offically, with official approval, legitimately, genuinely, reliably, conclusively, certainly, positively, surely

26 **expertly**, in an expert manner, masterly, skilfully, with skill, professionally, knowledgeably, intellectually

397 Command

I don't mind how much my ministers talk – as long as they do what I say. Margaret Thatcher.

NOUNS

1 **command**, commandment, order, legal order, direct order, instruction, direction, ruling, rule, regulation, directive, word, sign, signal, law, act, enactment, legislation, manifesto, prescription, precept, charge, behest, dictate, ordinance, edict, fiat, canon, bull, encyclical, papal decree, decree, ukase, decree nisi, decree absolute, prescript, order of the day, marching orders, statement, pronouncement, proclamation, declaration, dictum, invitation, royal command, negative command, prohibition, proscription, counterorder, countermand, interdict, veto, ban, embargo

▶ *12 Government and Politics; 386 Compulsion; 399 Veto; 693 Information; 707 Affirmation*

2 **demand**, claim, requisition, warning notice, final warning, red demand, final demand, ultimatum, legal order, tax demand, levy, warrant, bench warrant, warrant of arrest, search warrant, mittimus, writ, process, summons, writ of summons, subpoena, citation, habeas corpus, injunction, interdict, bidding, beck, call, beck and call, threat, extortion, blackmail

▶ *710 Request*

3 authority, rule, control, government, power, sway, mastery, sovereignty, suzerainty, dominion, domination

4 authorization, commission, charge, written authority, permit, letters patent, patronage, appointment, mandate, electoral mandate, the go-ahead (Inf)

▶ *396 Authority; 469 Selection; 757 Permission*

5 self-assurance, self-confidence, presence, authority, look of power

6 person in command, head of state, chief executive, chief executive officer (CEO), president, prime minister, premier, chancellor, judge, policeman, jailer, process-server, summoner, commander, commander-in-chief, commanding officer (CO), commandant, general, lieutenant general, major general, brigadier, brigadier general (US), field marshal, air marshal, admiral, fleet admiral, admiral of the fleet

▶ *16 Law; 586 Combatant*

7 overview, survey, ballpark view, bird's-eye view, summary

8 vantage point, observation post, watchtower, crow's nest, bridge, cockpit

VERBS

9 command, issue a command, order, give an order, direct, instruct, rule, regulate, signal, enact, legislate, make law, lay down the law, issue a manifesto, promulgate, prescribe, give a direction, give a mandate, charge, call upon, dictate, decree, sign a decree, pass a decree, issue an edict, issue a statement, pronounce, pontificate, proclaim, declare, say so, invite, prohibit, proscribe, countermand, counterorder, interdict, veto, ban, impose a ban, embargo, impose an embargo

10 demand, make demands, ask for, call for, insist on, lay upon, require, impose, make obligatory, claim, make claims upon, requisition, order up, indent, issue a warning notice, give final notice, present with an ultimatum, take a strong line, demand tax payment, levy, exact, warrant, issue a warrant, subpoena, issue an injunction, interdict, threaten, extort, blackmail, put one's foot down (Inf)

11 have authority over, have power over, have sway over, rule over, rule, control, compel, impose, govern, dominate, dictate to, judge, pass judgment, give a ruling, show authority, have the look of power, call the shots (Inf), call the signals (US inf)

12 be available to one, have at one's command, have at one's disposal, have at one's beck and call

13 authorize, commission, charge, permit, appoint, mandate

ADJECTIVES

14 commanding, ordering, imperative, directive, compelling, ruling, regulatory, enacted, legislative, prescriptive, encyclical, papal, pontifical, authoritative, governmental, mandatory, obligatory, compulsory, dictatorial, prohibitive, proscriptive, injunctive, countermanded, interdicted, vetoed, banned, embargoed

15 self-assured, self-confident, controlling, domineering, superior, lordly, powerful, autocratic, imperious, high-handed, authorized, commissioned, appointed, mandated, bossy (Inf)

ADVERBS

16 commandingly, by command, at the word of command, by order, as ordered, as required, imperatively, compellingly, prescriptively, to order, authoritatively, governmentally, obligatorily, dictatorially, prohibitively, proscriptively, self-assuredly, self-confidently, with confidence, domineeringly, superiorly, powerfully, autocratically, imperiously, high-handedly

398 Delegate

Not all the water in the rough rude sea.
Can wash the balm from an anointed king;
The breath of worldly men cannot depose
The deputy elected by the Lord. William Shakespeare.

NOUNS

1 delegate, elected person, nominee, appointed person, appointee, envoy, emissary, representative, elected representative, official representative, political representative, member of parliament (MP), Parliamentarian, Congressman (US), Congresswoman (US), Representative (US), Senator (US), minister, cabinet member, diplomat (*or* diplomatist), diplomatic officer, ambassador, legate, high commissioner, commissioner, chargé d'affaires, consul, negotiator, messenger, agent, middleman, intermediary, clerk, councillor, deputy, depute (Scot), convention delegate, conference delegate, workshop delegate

▶ *12 Government and Politics*

2 representative body, delegation, legation, diplomatic staff, diplomatic corps, corps diplomatique (CD), diplomatic service, foreign service, consulate service, embassy, consulate, mission, trade delegation, Parliament, Congress (US), Senate (US), council, town council, county council, parish council, town meeting (US), city council (US), board of aldermen, aldermanic board, official body, negotiating body, committee, forum, quorum, working party, round table, panel, workshop, convention, conference, conclave

3 delegation, authorization, appointment, nomination, assignment, election, delegation of work, delegation of power, shared responsibility, decentralization, devolution, devolvement, job sharing, deputation, deputizing, deputing, assignment of work, consignation

▶ *316 Transfer*

4 deputy, assistant, right-hand man, second-in-command, number two, aide, lieutenant, deputy prime minister, deputy chairman, deputy sheriff (US), vice-regent, nuncio, vice president, vice chairman, vice chancellor, vice admiral, viceroy, vice consul, proconsul, propraetor (*or* propretor), vicar, vicar-general, executive assistant, helper, secretary, girl Friday, auxiliary, relief worker, temporary worker, spokesperson, spokesman, spokeswoman, public relations man (*or* woman), messenger, power behind the throne, temp (Inf), *éminence grise* (Fr)

▶ *392 Help; 480 Persuasion; 579 Management; 741 News*

5 alternative, alternate (US), surrogate, proxy, substitute, sub, scrub (US), replacement, locum (tenens), reserve, understudy, double, stand-in, backup, stunt man (*or* woman), twelfth man, twentieth man (Aus), ghostwriter, whipping boy, pinch hitter (US), redshirt (US inf)

► *46 American Football; 48 Baseball; 53 Cricket; 66 Soccer; 762 Substitution*

6 **agent**, go-between, representative, delegate, intermediary, middleman, trustee, broker, literary agent, contact, negotiator, arbitrator, mediator, lawyer, solicitor, attorney, barrister, diplomat, diplomatic agent, emissary, envoy, minister, ambassador, minister plenipotentiary, commissioner, legate, attaché, consul, consular agent, vice consul, consul-general, brief (Inf), matchmaker, pander (*or* panderer), pimp

► *12 Government and Politics; 16 Law; 398 Delegate; 747 Cooperation*

VERBS

7 **delegate**, depute, deputize, assign, consign, appoint, nominate, elect, authorize, commission, empower, entrust, charge, designate, spread the load, job-share, share the work, devolve, decentralize, transfer, turn over to

8 **represent**, act for, stand for, speak for, substitute for, understudy, stand in, represent the interests of, serve as a representative, act as proxy for, attend a council meeting, attend a convention, attend a conference, serve on a working party

ADJECTIVES

9 **delegated**, delegable, elected, nominated, appointed, representative, Parliamentary, Congressional (US), Senatorial (US), ministerial, diplomatic, ambassadorial, legatine, legationary, consular, intermediary, deputy

10 **decentralized**, devolved, shared, deputized, deputed, assigned, consigned

ADVERBS

11 **representatively**, as a representative, in Parliament, in Congress (US), Congressionally (US), in the Senate (US), Senatorially (US), ministerially, diplomatically, with diplomacy, like an ambassador

12 **by proxy**, indirectly, in (*or* on) behalf of, *pro persona* (p.p.) (L), for, diplomatically, like a diplomat, ministerially, imitatively, in imitation of

399 Veto

NOUNS

1 **veto**, ban, embargo, injunction, interdiction, interdict, counterorder, countermand, check, curfew, thumbs down, turndown (US), red light, no, suspension, cancellation, denial, rejection, refusal, pocket veto (US), rebuff, abrogation, annulment, repealing, restriction, circumscription, exclusion, ostracism, debarment, forbidding, prohibition, taboo, repressive regime, repression, suppression, prevention, restraint, zoning law (US), obstruction, impediment, obstacle, interference, disallowance, abolition, prohibition of alcohol, temperance, Eighteenth Amendment (US), Volstead Act (US), unpermissibility, illicitness, illegality, illegitimacy, crackdown, excommunication

► *128 Exclusion; 371 Expulsion; 378 Obstruction; 470 Rejection; 670 Disapproval; 709 Refusal*

2 **censorship**, proscription, deletion, blue pencil, classified document, secret document, top-secret document, restricted information, Official Secrets Act, news blackout, D-notice, banned book, the Index, *Index Librorum Prohibitorum* (L), film classification, R18 certificate, motion-picture rating (US), X-rated movie (US)

► *12 Government and Politics; 17 Literature; 525 Appearance; 736 Concealment; 737 Secrecy*

VERBS

3 **veto**, ban, impose a ban, embargo, interdict, counterorder, contermand, check, decide against, turn down, turn the thumbs down, give the thumbs down, withhold permission, refuse permission, deny, say no to, give the red light to, suspend, cancel, not tolerate, reject, refuse, rebuff, abrogate, annul, repeal, revoke, restrict, circumscribe, put out of bounds, make off-limits (US), exclude, shut the door on, ostracize, send to Coventry, blackball, debar, forbid, prohibit, disallow, prevent, obstruct, impede, inhibit, place an obstacle in someone's path, interfere, abolish, make illegal, outlaw, criminalize, put outside the law, crack down on, excommunicate

4 **censor**, proscribe, delete, blue-pencil, classify secret, make taboo, restrict, stop, repress, suppress, restrain, stifle, cancel, prohibit, ban a book, put on the Index, invoke the Official Secrets Act, issue a D-notice, black out, bleep out (US), classify a film, rate a movie (US), kill (Inf)

ADJECTIVES

5 **vetoed**, banned, embargoed, contraband, injunctive, interdictive, suspended, cancelled, null and void, denied, rejected, refused, blackballed, restrictive, forbidden, *verboten* (Ger), impermissible, unauthorized, not allowed, circumscriptive, exclusive, prohibitive, prohibited, prohibiting, prohibitory, barred, out of bounds, off-limits (US), taboo, repressive, suppressive, preventive, preventative, obstructive, inhibiting, illicit, illegal, unlawful, illegitimate, excommunicated

6 **censored**, proscriptive, proscribed, deleted, blue-pencilled, blacked out, unprintable, bleeped out (US), unmentionable, unsayable, classified, secretive, secret, top-secret, restrictive, restricted, banned

ADVERBS

7 **by veto**, injunctively, under an injunction, interdictively, impermissibly, without permission, without authorization, circumscriptively, exclusively, prohibitively, repressively, in a repressive way, suppressively, preventively, in order to prevent, obstructively, illicitly, illegally, unlawfully, illegitimately

8 **under censorship**, proscriptively, with deletions, secretively, in a secret manner, restrictively, with restrictions

400 Master

I shall be an autocrat: that's my trade. And the good Lord will forgive me: that's his. Catherine the Great.

So long as men worship the Caesars and Napoleons, Caesars and Napoleons will arise to make them miserable. Aldous Huxley.

NOUNS

1 **master**, mistress, lord, lord and master, lord paramount,

overlord, liege lord, liege, nobleman, aristocrat, lady, dame, lord of the manor, lady of the manor, master of the house, mistress of the house, man of the house, husband, lady of the house, wife, sir, madam, matron, mother superior, housemother, patriarch, matriarch, dowager, elder, owner, property owner, landowner, squire, laird (Scot), landlord, landlady, proprietor, governor, sahib, bwana, seigneur, guvnor (*or* guv) (Inf)

▶ *567 Male; 568 Female; 573 Aristocrat; 575 Title; 763 Possession*

2 **sovereign**, crowned head, monarch, absolute monarch, king, Rex, divine king, queen, Regina, Your Majesty, His (*or* Her) Highness, Your Royal Highness, His (*or* Her) Royal Highness, queen mother, queen regent, prince, crown prince, Prince of Wales, prince regent, princess, crown princess, emperor, Caesar, empress, rajah, rani (*or* ranee), Kaiser, Kaiserin, tsar (*or* czar), tsarina (*or* czarina), Pharaoh, shah, khan, mikado, Mogul, Great Mogul, maharajah, nabob, sultan, caliph, Dalai Lama

▶ *121 Superiority; 123 Importance; 396 Authority*

3 **leader**, head of state, chief of state, chief executive, president, prime minister, premier, chancellor, minister, minister of state, secretary, secretary of state, MP (Member of Parliament), MEP (Member of the European Parliament), Senator (US), Congressman (*or* -woman) (US), representative (US), cabinet member, governor, governor general, lieutenant governor, high commissioner, commissioner, military governor, pasha, suzerain, viceroy, proconsul, consul general, consul, mayor, Lord Mayor, Lady Mayor, mayoress, Supreme Court judge (US), judge, associate justice (US), chief justice of the United States (US), chief magistrate, magistrate, bailie (Scot), bailiff, sheriff, constable, marshal, justice of the peace, justice, official, party official, chief whip, whip, Democratic whip (US), Republican whip (US), officer, functionary, dignitary, person in office, person in authority, ruler, potentate, protector, chief, chieftain, headman, sheik, rajah, mandarin, Your Excellency (*or* Excellence), His (*or* Her) Excellency (*or* Excellence)

▶ *12 Government and Politics*

4 **absolute ruler**, autocrat, *Führer* (Ger), *der Führer* (Ger), Hitler, *Duce* (It), tyrant, dictator, despot, satrap, warlord, shogun, oppressor, captor, martinet, Big Brother, tin god, petty tyrant, jack-in-office, little Hitler (Inf), gauleiter (Inf)

5 **company leader**, company official, superior, senior, executive, director, chairman of the board, board member, chair, chairman, chairwoman, chairperson, manager, controller, capitalist, plutocrat, oligarch, tycoon, captain of industry, head, chief, employer, VIP (very important person), doyen, doyenne, cock of the walk, kingpin, bigwig (Inf), big gun (Inf), big shot (Inf), big wheel (Inf), big cheese (Inf), head honcho (Inf), top dog (Inf), kingfish (US inf), boss (Inf)

▶ *579 Management*

6 **religious leader**, pope, pontiff, cardinal, dean, rabbi, guru, archbishop, bishop, provost, high priest, priest, ayatollah, imam, ecclesiastical governor

▶ *7 Religion*

7 **military leader**, military officer, commissioned officer, commander-in-chief, commanding officer, commander, commandant, general, generalissimo, field marshal, air marshal, admiral, fleet admiral, admiral of the fleet, executive officer, exec (US inf), the Old Man (Inf), brass hat (Inf)

▶ *586 Combatant*

8 **the power structure**, the ruling class (*or* classes), ruling party, the Establishment, the authorities, officialdom, principalities and powers, the powers that be, Big Brother, the Government, Whitehall, Downing Street, Westminster, Washington (US), the White House (US), the Hill (US), Capitol Hill (US), the Capitol (US), the Pentagon (US), the Kremlin, the high command, the board, the directorship, the top, the corridors of power, the inner circle, the in-group, the top brass (Inf), higher-ups (Inf)

9 **educational leader**, scholar, pedagogue, intellectual, thinker, philosopher, sage, wise man, mentor, guru, swami, trustee, regent (US), instructor, college president (US), university president (US), chancellor, vice chancellor, provost, principal, dean, professor, don, fellow, reader, lecturer, governor, head, master, headmaster, headmistress, head teacher, head of department, head of sixth-form, schoolmaster, schoolmistress, teacher, tutor, housemaster, housemistress, schoolmarm (Inf), highbrow (Inf), egghead (Inf), beak (Inf)

▶ *442 Intellect*

10 **expert**, grand master, master, champion, genius, musical genius, maestro, virtuoso, master of the violin, specialist, past master, adept, sailing master, master thief, practitioner, graduate, consultant, guide, professional, master carpenter, skilled worker, the right man for the job, old master, old hand, walking encyclopedia, champ (Inf), pro (Inf), ace (Inf), dab hand (*or* dab) (Inf)

11 **masterpiece**, masterwork, *chef-d'oeuvre* (Fr), *tour de force* (Fr), magnum opus, classic, treasure, work of art, thing of beauty and a joy forever, feat of creation, epic, perfection, *crème de la crème* (Fr)

▶ *19 Painting and Sculpture*

ADJECTIVES

12 **masterful**, magistral, lordly, noble, aristocratic, magisterial, majestic, matronly, patriarchal, matriarchal, elder, sovereign, crowned, absolute, divine, royal, head, chief, principal, main, major, great, leading, controlling, parliamentary, senatorial (US), congressional (US), autocratic, authoritarian, dominating, domineering, coercive, imperious, dictatorial, despotic, oppressive, executive, managerial, capitalistic, plutocratic, oligarchic, papal, pontifical, cardinal, rabbic, rabbinical, commissioned, commanding, able

13 **excellent**, expert, master, champion, specialist, professional, scholarly, intellectual, philosophical, masterly, skilled, skilful, adept, proficient, first-rate, supreme, consummate, polished, finished, competent, good at, experienced, qualified, ace (Inf), highbrow (Inf), bossy (Inf)

VERBS

14 **master**, rule, lead, govern, dictate, oppress, lord it over, conquer, vanquish, defeat, beat, overpower, overcome, crush, quell, subdue, subjugate, dominate, control, command, direct, manage, head, operate in the corridors of power, sit on the board, hold a directorship, reach the

top, head an institution, head a school, teach, instruct, tutor, specialize, win, paint a masterpiece, create a treasure, boss (Inf)

15 learn, understand, comprehend, apprehend, grasp, acquire, become proficient, retain, remember, know how to, assimilate, learn a trade, work an apprenticeship, practise at, learn by heart, memorize, research into, specialize in, know all the answers, get the hang of (Inf), ace (US inf), bone up on (Inf)

ADVERBS

16 masterfully, nobly, in a noble manner, aristocratically, absolutely, royally, autocratically, dominatingly, domineeringly, imperiously, dictatorially, oppressively, in order to oppress, executively, managerially, excellently, expertly, with expertise, professionally, intellectually, philosophically, skilfully, adeptly, proficiently, supremely, consummately, competently

401 Servant

All English shop assistants are Miltonists. All Miltonists firmly believe that 'they serve who only stand and wait.' George Mikes.

NOUNS

1 servant, paid helper, help, retainer, household servant, domestic, worker, hired hand, farmhand, labourer, handyman, odd-job man, employee, assistant, subordinate, subaltern, attendant, servitor (Lit), orderly, factotum, general servant, humble servant, follower, henchman, liegeman, daily help (*or* daily), cleaning lady, occasional help, hired help, menial, underling, hireling, inferior, minion, flunky, lackey, drudge, mister fix-it (US inf)

► *122 Inferiority; 237 Usefulness; 392 Help; 578 Worker; 663 Obedience*

2 public servant, public official, civil servant, politician, public office holder

3 attendant, usher, server, maître d'hôtel, maître d' (US), maid, valet, butler, batman, hostess, airline hostess, airline attendant, flight attendant, cabin crew, head waiter, waiter, waitress, steward, wine steward, sommelier, stewardess, bus boy (US), carhop (US), barperson, barman, barmaid, bartender (US), barkeeper (US), barkeep (US), potboy, page, bellboy (US), bellhop (US), porter, redcap (US), skycap (US), caddie, cloakroom attendant, hatcheck girl (US), counterman (US), shop assistant, salesclerk (*or* clerk) (US), shoeblack, bootblack (US), shoeshine boy (US), caretaker, concierge, janitor, soda jerk (US inf)

► *342 Activity; 778 Sale*

4 personal attendant, personal servant, companion, confidante, nurse, nursemaid, au pair, governess, nanny, chaperon, driver, chauffeur, batman, bodyguard, henchman, tutor, barber, hairdresser, masseur, masseuse

5 office assistant, assistant, personal assistant (PA), executive assistant, secretary, clerk, right-hand man, man (*or* girl) Friday, office boy (*or* girl), errand boy (*or* girl), tea lady, copy aide (US), messenger, runner, courier, employee, office worker, staff member, peon, dogsbody (Inf), gofer (US inf)

► *579 Management*

6 domestic servant, domestic, steward, house steward, bailiff, housekeeper, chamberlain, butler, major-domo, cook, maid, maidservant, housemaid, parlourmaid, chambermaid, *femme de chambre* (Fr), upstairs maid, nursemaid, nurse, nanny, ayah (India), amah (China), girl, servant girl, wench (Lit), au pair, boy, house boy, live-in maid, handmaid, handmaiden, lady's maid, maid-in-waiting, lady-in-waiting, lord-in-waiting, lady of the bedchamber, lord of the bedchamber, gentleman's gentleman, gentleman, man, manservant, serving man, serving maid, serving girl, kitchen maid, dishwasher, kitchen boy, laundry maid, cleaning woman, daily help (*or* daily), charwoman (*or* charlady), char (Inf), Mrs Mop (Inf), chauffeur, driver, gardener, footman, stableman, stableboy, groom, domestic drudge, skivvy, slavey (Inf)

► *256 Cleanness*

7 slave, serf, slave-girl, bondservant, bondsman, bondmaid, thrall, vassal, galley slave, captive

VERBS

8 serve, be in service, do service, work for, care for, take care of, help, tend, look after, wait upon, attend upon, live in, make oneself useful, minister to, administer to, assist, do housework, do chores, clean for, accompany, follow, oblige, obey, pander to, wait on hand and foot, dance attendance upon, char (Inf), do for (Inf)

ADJECTIVES

9 serving, attending, attendant, in (domestic) service, working, in employment, in one's employ, on the staff, on the payroll, in one's pay, helping, ministering, aiding, waiting on, menial, obedient, subject, servile, at one's beck and call, unfree, in servitude, in slavery, in captivity, in bonds

ADVERBS

10 obediently, menially, servilely, in servitude, in slavery, in captivity

Substance and Structure

402 Material World

And even the most solid of things and the most real, the best-loved and the well-known, are only hand-shadows on the wall. Empty space and points of light. Jeanette Winterson.

NOUNS

1 **material world**, physical world, empirical world, real world, world of experience, world of nature, nature, laws of nature, material existence, materiality, materialness, existence, corporeity, corporeality, corporality, bodiliness, substantiality, physical being, physical existence, physical condition, concreteness, tangibility, palpability, solidity, density, weight, gravity, personality, individuality

▶ *93 Existence; 95 Reality; 171 Outside; 403 Structure; 414 Heaviness; 416 Density*

2 **materialization**, embodiment, incarnation, corporation, epiphany, manifestation, reincarnation, metempsychosis, realization, positivism, materialism, dialectical materialism, empiricism, scientism, unspirituality, worldliness, sensuality, sensualism

▶ *8 Divinity*

3 **materialist**, dialectical materialist, Marxist, realist, humanist, positivist, chemist, physicist, geophysicist, atomist, scientist, collector, consumer, capitalist

▶ *4 Philosophy; 28 Physics; 30 Earth Science; 32 Chemistry*

4 **matter**, prime matter, brute matter, material, raw material, basic materials, materials, materiality, stuff, mass, fabric, body, frame, structure, substance, solid substance, corpus, organic matter, flesh, flesh and blood, plasma, protoplasm, cells, organism, element, elementary unit, fundamental particle, building block, principle, first principle, unit of being, origin, the four elements, earth, air, fire, and water, ingredient, factor, component, constituent, mineral, monad, chemical element, basic substance, isotope, physical element, atom, molecule, elementary particle, electron, neutron, meson, proton, quark, nucleus, nucleon, photon, quantum, ion, minuteness, nuts and bolts (Inf), the nitty-gritty (Inf)

▶ *28 Physics; 32 Chemistry; 34 Life Science; 99 Essence; 405 Component*

5 **object**, inanimate object, tangible object, still-life, physical presence, body, human object, person, real person, flesh and blood, thing, something, commodity, article, item, artefact, gadget, thingumabob (Inf), thingumajig (Inf), thingummy (Inf), what's-its-name (Inf)

▶ *93 Existence; 95 Reality; 554 Life; 566 Humankind*

6 **natural science**, physical science, science of matter, science of physical properties, science, biology, chemistry, organic chemistry, inorganic chemistry, physical chemistry, geophysics, physics, mechanics, Newtonian mechanics, quantum mechanics, theory of relativity, thermodynamics, electromagnetism, applied physics, technology, atomic physics, nuclear physics, nucleonics

ADJECTIVES

7 **material**, tangible, substantial, sensible, real, natural, massy, solid, massive, concrete, palpable, ponderable, weighty, physical, empirical, spatiotemporal, objective, impersonal, clinical, neuter, incarnate, embodied, somatic, corporal, corporeal, bodily, fleshly, of flesh and blood, in the flesh, carnal, reincarnated, realized, materialized, materialistic, worldly, earthly, unspiritual, nonspiritual, sensual

▶ *95 Reality*

VERBS

8 **be material**, exist, materialize, substantialize, substantiate, make concrete, reify, objectify, externalize, realize, make real, corporealize, embody, incarnate, personify, reincarnate

▶ *93 Existence*

ADVERBS

9 **materially**, of material, with material, tangibly, substantially, sensibly, naturally, in a natural way, solidly, concretely, palpably, physically, objectively, with objectivity, impersonally, clinically, corporally, sensually

403 Structure

Who could have foretold, from the structure of the brain, that wine could derange its functions? Hippocrates.

NOUNS

1 **structure**, arrangement, organization, organic structure, plan, pattern, tectonics, architecture, architectonics

▶ *409 Arrangement; 484 Plan*

2 **fabric**, build, texture, contexture, tissue, warp, weft, weave, content, substance, materials, work, brickwork

▶ *404 Texture; 435 Materials*
3 **form**, formation, morphology, shape, mould, architecture, physique, build, setup, make-up, fashion, fabrication, conformation, configuration, format, composition, constitution, creation, body, anatomy, get-up (Inf)
▶ *160 Form*
4 **framework**, frame, framing, bodywork, skeleton, lattice, latticework, scaffold, rack, shell, chassis, cadre, doorframe, window case (*or* frame), casement, picture frame, cantilever, space frame
5 **structuring**, formation, making, shaping, creation, building, production, forging, patterning, moulding
▶ *130 Beginning; 356 Creation*
6 **construction**, building, edifice, construct, erection, elevation, establishment, house, skyscraper, tower, pyramid, pile, prefab, prefabrication, superstructure, complex, works, workings, substructure, infrastructure, understructure, foundations, underbuilding
▶ *20 Architecture; 38 Engineering*
7 **skeleton**, exoskeleton, carapace, endoskeleton, axial skeleton, appendicular skeleton, bone, horn, cartilage, keratin, ossicle, ossification, osteoblast, osteoclast, osteocyte, chondroblast, tendon, ligament
8 **science of structure**, adenography, adenology, anatomy, angiography, angiology, anthropotomy, histology, morphology, myology, neurology, organology, osteography, osteology, promorphology, splanchnography, splanchnology, zootomy, geomorphology, plate tectonics, tectology
▶ *30 Earth Science; 34 Life Science; 35 Medicine*
9 **artistic structure**, musical structure, structuralism, post-structuralism, constructionism, deconstructionism, composition, choreography, design, balance, unity, rhythm, theme, subject
▶ *17 Literature; 18 Music; 19 Painting and Sculpture; 21 Drama; 22 Dancing*
10 **anatomist**, histologist, morphologist, geomorphologist

ADJECTIVES

11 **structural**, constructional, organizational, superstructural, substructural, infrastructural, textural, architectural, tectonic, architectonic
12 **organic**, organismal, organological, morphological, anatomical, formal
13 **skeletal**, bony, osteal, osseous, ossiferous, ossicular, ossified

VERBS

14 **structure**, organize, plan, pattern, arrange, prepare, design, draw up, invent
15 **shape**, form, formulate, evolve, raise, make, manufacture, fashion, fabricate, elaborate, mould, frame, compose, create, unify
16 **construct**, build, erect, devise, concoct, put up, set up, get up
17 **assemble**, put together, piece together, patch together

ADVERBS

18 **structurally**, architecturally, constructionally, superstructurally, substructurally, tectonically, architectonically, organically, skeletally, morphologically, anatomically
19 **in production**, under construction, in hand

404 Texture

NOUNS

1 **texture**, surface texture, surface, finish, feel, touch, sensation, intertexture, contexture, structure, constitution, consistency
▶ *403 Structure; 488 Sensation; 492 Touch*
2 **grain**, denier, fineness (*or* coarseness) of grain, smoothness, fineness, refinement, softness, delicacy, daintiness, filminess, gossameriness, fluffiness, fluff, downiness, down, fuzziness, peachiness, satin, satininess, silk, silkiness, roughness, graininess, granular texture, granulation, grittiness, grit, hardness
▶ *418 Hardness; 419 Softness; 421 Smoothness; 549 Refinement*
3 **nap**, pile, shag, nub, knub, protuberance, indentation, pit, pock
4 **weave**, weaving, web, network, weftage, warp and woof (*or* weft)
5 **textile**, fabric, cloth, stuff, staple, material, tissue
▶ *435 Materials*
6 **fibre**, yarn, thread, string, tow, filament

ADJECTIVES

7 **textural**, textured, woven
8 **rough**, coarse, coarse-woven, coarse-grained, grained, grainy, granular, granulated, gritty, ribbed, twilled, tweedy, woolly, hairy, fibrous, homespun, hodden, linsey-woolsey
9 **smooth**, fine, fine-grained, close-woven, fine-woven, refined, satin, satiny, silky, cottony
10 **delicate**, dainty, filmy, gossamer, gossamery, finespun, thin-spun, subtle, fine-drawn, wire-drawn
11 **fluffy**, downy, fuzzy, velvety, velutinous

VERBS

12 **coarsen**, roughen, rough up, granulate, grain, gnarl, knob
13 **smooth**, smooth out, flatten, iron out, press
14 **go against the grain**, rub the wrong way, rumple, wrinkle

ADVERBS

15 **texturally**, structurally, roughly, fuzzily, coarsely, fibrously, smoothly, finely, silkily, delicately, daintily, subtly, on the surface, to the touch

405 Component

NOUNS

1 **component**, content, constituent, part, integral part, integrant, ingredient, element, aspect, feature, facet, detail, particular, factor, item, link, part and parcel
▶ *205 Part*
2 **piece**, bit, portion, part, fragment, fraction, segment, section, sector, division, subdivision, category, faction, class, branch, department, unit
▶ *205 Part*
3 **unit**, module, building block, building brick, cell, particle, molecule, atom, jigsaw piece, Meccano™, Lego™, spare part, basic materials
4 **components**, works, workings, mechanism, machinery, engine, innards, guts, insides (Inf)

▶ *172 Inside; 406 Contents*
5 **member**, team member, member of staff, one of, one of us, co-worker, colleague, associate, fellow, cog in the wheel
▶ *578 Worker*
ADJECTIVES
6 **component**, constituent, integral, integrant, ingredient, elemental, elementary, formative, fractional, segmental, departmental, categorical
▶ *205 Part*
7 **modular**, cellular, molecular, atomic, integral, joined, linked, fitted, built-in
8 **belonging**, appurtenant, part of, one of, essential, fundamental, intrinsic, inherent, integral, particular
▶ *99 Essence*
9 **composing**, constituting, comprising, including, inclusive of, containing, embodying, incorporating
▶ *127 Inclusion; 204 Whole*
VERBS
10 **compose**, constitute, comprise, make up, form part of, combine in, merge in, amalgamate, participate in, join, contribute
▶ *374 Combination*
11 **consist of**, comprise, contain, include, embrace, encompass, subsume, embody, incorporate, be made up of, be composed of, involve, cover
▶ *127 Inclusion; 204 Whole*
12 **be one of**, belong to, be part of, inhere, reside in, consist in
▶ *205 Part*
13 **make**, make up, construct, build, build up, erect, structure, assemble, put together, piece together, connect together, fit together, set up, compound, fabricate, fashion, form, compile, compose, knock together (Inf)
▶ *356 Creation*
ADVERBS
14 **constituently**, elementally, atomically, inclusively, integrally, inherently, essentially, fundamentally, constructively, departmentally, fractionally

406 Contents

Don't you know each cloud contains
Pennies from Heaven? Johnny Burke.

NOUNS
1 **contents**, content, what is contained, things contained, ingredients, components, constituents, constitution, composition, make-up, structure, embodiment, parts, elements, factors, features, substance, stuff, material, matter, spirit, essence, quintessence, gist, meat, nub
▶ *99 Essence; 403 Structure; 405 Component; 409 Arrangement; 694 Meaning*
2 **load**, lading, cargo, payload, freight, burden, charge, containerload, carload, truckload, busload, trainload, boatload, shipment, stowage, tonnage
▶ *141 Space; 158 Size; 203 Quantity; 319 Transport; 360 Retention; 410 Container*
3 **insides**, inside, inner workings, guts, pith, marrow, heart, core, kernel, entrails, bowels, offal, innards (Inf)
▶ *172 Inside*
4 **stuffing**, filling, filler, wadding, padding, packing, lining, interlining
▶ *435 Materials*
5 **divisions**, subdivisions, sections, chapters, subject matter, themes, topics, items, index, inventory, code, table, list, checklist, tally, chart, catalogue, glossary, register, schedule, scheme, agenda
▶ *137 Class; 220 List; 740 Publication; 770 Allocation*
VERBS
6 **contain**, hold, enclose, conceal, package, parcel, box up, containerize, load, lade, freight, take on board
▶ *360 Retention; 410 Container*
7 **stuff**, fill, pad, pack, pack in (*or* into), cram, jam, squeeze in, insert, pour in, make full, fill up, top up
8 **embody**, subsume, include, compose, constitute, make up, structure, build, assemble, put together
▶ *127 Inclusion*
9 **itemize**, index, list, enumerate, tabulate, catalogue, classify, divide, subdivide, section, register, file, tally, schedule, schematize, programme
ADJECTIVES
10 **containing**, component, constituent, constituted, composed, made-up, embodying, subsuming, including, inclusive, structured, featuring, elemental, substantial, material, essential, quintessential
11 **loaded**, laden, holding, containing, charged, burdened, burdensome, stuffed, full, lined, padded, packed, crammed, squeezed, topped up
12 **itemized**, indexed, listed, coded, tabled, tabular, tabulated, charted, catalogued, registered, scheduled, programmed, sectioned, divided, subdivided, thematic, topical, schematic
ADVERBS
13 **structurally**, elementally, substantially, materially, in essence, essentially, quintessentially
14 **internally**, inside, within, to the core, inclusively, fully, to the brim, to the top
15 **thematically**, indexically, topically, schematically, sectionally, divisionally

407 Order

Order is heaven's first law. Alexander Pope.

A place for everything, and everything in its place. Samuel Smiles.

NOUNS
1 **order**, organization, formalization, formalism, arrangement, array, disposition, layout, pattern, composition, formation, structure, setup, distribution, line-up, putting in order, prioritization, system, scheme, schedule
▶ *160 Form; 403 Structure; 409 Arrangement*
2 **grouping**, categorization, classification, codification, specification, pigeonholing, cataloguing, indexing, listing, taxonomy
▶ *137 Class*
3 **hierarchy**, pecking order, series, sequence, gradation, progression, alphabetical order, numerical order, serial

order, ascending (*or* descending) order, reverse order, logical order
► *132 Consecutiveness*
4 position, place, class, grade, category, degree, rank, ranking, status, subordination
► *137 Class*
5 orderliness, state of order, tidiness, neatness, cleanness, smoothness, straightness, correctness, good condition, good trim, fine fettle, a place for everything and everything in its place, apple-pie order (Inf), good nick (Inf), (all ship-shape and) Bristol fashion (Inf)
► *256 Cleanness; 801 Right*
6 methodicalness, methodology, meticulousness, punctiliousness, accuracy, straightness, systematization, systematism, systematics, systematology
► *273 Accuracy*
7 method, system, discipline, organization, routine, custom, habit, rule, pattern, plan, scheme, structure, coherence, coordination, uniformity, regularity, symmetry, proportion
► *162 Symmetry; 352 Means; 484 Plan; 632 Habit*
8 harmony, concord, stability, quiet, quietude, peace, peace and quiet, calm, tranquillity, stillness, quietness, detachment
► *4 Philosophy; 301 Motionlessness; 506 Silence; 750 Agreement*
9 discipline, law, law and order, rule of law, control, stability
► *16 Law*

ADJECTIVES

10 ordered, organized, formalized, formal, formalistic, arranged, arrayed, disposed, composed, structured, schematic, systematic, symmetrical, balanced, ordained
► *162 Symmetry; 403 Structure; 409 Arrangement; 484 Plan*
11 grouped, categorized, categorical, classified, classificatory, codified, specified, pigeonholed, indexed, indexical, catalogued, listed
► *137 Class*
12 hierarchical, serial, sequential, gradational, taxonomic(al), progressive, alphabetical, numerical, in order, graded, ranked
► *132 Consecutiveness*
13 orderly, tidy, neat, neat and tidy, spick-and-span, clean, smooth, straight, correct, trim, spruce, dapper, smart, sleek, slick, groomed, well-groomed, not a hair out of place, kempt, well-kept, well-cared for, in good order, in perfect order, in good trim, in good condition, in the pink, in fine fettle, shipshape, all shipshape and Bristol fashion, neat as a button (*or* pin), dinky (Inf), in apple-pie order (Inf), in good nick (Inf)
► *256 Cleanness; 801 Right*
14 well-ordered, well-organized, methodical, meticulous, punctilious, systematic, scientific, businesslike, formal, accurate, straight, regular, uniform, coherent, intelligible
► *273 Accuracy; 695 Intelligibility*
15 habitual, routine, usual, regular, customary
► *632 Habit*
16 harmonious, concordant, stable, steady, quiet, peaceful, calm, tranquil
► *301 Motionlessness; 506 Silence; 750 Agreement*
17 disciplined, controlled, under control, restrained, lawful, law-abiding, peaceable, docile, obedient, well-behaved, well-drilled, well-regulated, according to rule, decorous, mannerly
► *16 Law; 388 Submission; 631 Behaviour; 663 Obedience*

VERBS

18 order, put in order, set in order, arrange, array, dispose, lay out, organize, marshal, manage, compose, form, structure, set up, line up, align, ordain
► *403 Structure; 409 Arrangement; 579 Management*
19 systematize, methodize, rationalize, standardize, sort, sort out, sift, group, categorize, class, classify, catalogue, codify, index, pigeonhole, rank, grade, place, position, tabulate, prioritize
► *137 Class*
20 harmonize, stabilize, regularize, regulate, synchronize, accord
► *750 Agreement*
21 tidy, tidy up, neaten, clean, straighten, smooth, straighten up, correct, put (*or* set) to rights, smarten up, spruce up, groom, lick (*or* knock *or* whip) into shape
22 pacify, calm, cool down, cool off, pour oil on troubled water, restore order, keep order, discipline, take in hand, control, govern, police, clean up, tighten up on, clamp down on
► *396 Authority; 749 Pacification*
23 be in order, be in working order, work, function, operate, go like clockwork, go
► *346 Operation*
24 line up, fall in, take one's place, queue up, place oneself, draw up, fall into place, find one's level

ADVERBS

25 in order, in turn, hierarchically, taxonomically, formalistically, in series, step by step, by stages, progressively, sequentially, alphabetically, numerically, according to plan
26 orderly, in orderly fashion, in order, neatly, tidily, just so
27 methodically, systematically, symmetrically, uniformly, regularly, routinely, by the book

408 Disorder

A sweet disorder in the dress
Kindles in clothes a wantonness. Robert Herrick.

NOUNS

1 disorder, disorderliness, disorganization, disarrangement, disarray, derangement, disjunction, disharmony, discord, disruption, disturbance, upset, discomposure, discomfiture, disconcertedness, disintegration, incoherence, unintelligibility, confusion
► *328 Disturbance; 375 Disintegration; 696 Unintelligibility; 751 Disagreement*
2 irregular order, irregularity, randomness, haphazardness, nonuniformity, unsymmetry, nonsymmetry, disproportion, misshapenness, shapelessness, no pattern, no rhyme or reason

▶ *114 Diversity; 161 Shapelessness*

3 **untidiness**, dirtiness, uncleanness, grubbiness, messiness, unkemptness, dishevelment, scruffiness, shabbiness, neglect, negligence, carelessness, slipshodness, shoddiness, sloppiness, sluttishness, slovenliness, slatternliness, sordidness, squalidness, slobbishness (Inf)

▶ *258 Dirtiness; 666 Negligence*

4 **litter**, rubbish, garbage, trash, mess, clutter, muddle, jumble, lumber, hodgepodge (*or* hotchpotch), hash, mishmash, pickle, topsy-turvy, topsy-turviness, shambles, rat's nest, pigsty, midden, dump, tip, slum, (junk) heap, higgledy-piggledy (Inf), unholy (*or* god-awful) mess (Inf)

▶ *238 Uselessness; 412 Mixture; 441 Waste; 767 Disposal*

5 **confusion**, chaos, muddle, mess, jumble, welter, bedlam, pandemonium, hell, all hell let loose, inferno, madhouse, bear garden, tumult, turmoil, turbulence, upheaval, ferment, hullabaloo (*or* hullaballoo), hubbub, racket, cacophony, uproar

▶ *507 Loudness; 517 Dissonance*

6 **mix-up**, snarl-up, foul-up, mess, hash (Inf), pig's ear (Inf), cockup (Inf), balls-up (Inf), screw-up (Inf), fuck-up (Inf), snafu (situation normal: all fucked up) (Inf)

▶ *486 Unskilfulness*

7 **tangle**, snarl, labyrinth, maze, web, jungle

▶ *264 Difficulty*

8 **lawlessness**, anarchy, chaos, disorder, disobedience, disorderly behaviour, unruliness, boisterousness, rowdiness, laddishness, disruptiveness, no discipline, nihilism, amorality, lack of discipline, rebelliousness, revolution, uprising, upheaval, vandalism, hooliganism

▶ *588 Anarchy; 662 Disobedience*

9 **disorder**, disturbance, disruption, commotion, pother, stir, fuss, bother, spot of bother, trouble, ado, to-do, hurly-burly, all hell let loose, fight, argument, brawl, row, fistfight, fisticuffs, rumpus, ruckus, ruction, mêlée, rough and tumble, free-for-all, donnybrook, affray, fray, breach of the peace, riot, rampage, anarchy, mob rule, set-to (Inf), shindig (*or* shindy) (Inf), argy-bargy (Inf), punch-up (Inf), roughhouse (Inf), aggro (Inf), dust-up (Inf)

▶ *588 Anarchy*

10 **slattern**, sloven, slut, slob (Inf), slag (Inf), litterbug (Inf), litter lout (Inf)

11 **troublemaker**, rioter, lord of misrule, nihilist, amorality, anarchist, pest, nuisance, irritant, agitator, loot, hooligan, vandal, pain in the neck (Inf), stirrer (Inf)

ADJECTIVES

12 **disordered**, orderless, in disorder, in disarray, disarranged, deranged, disrupted, disorganized, muddled, jumbled, shuffled, out of order, displaced, misplaced, out of place, out of joint, disjointed, dislocated

▶ *144 Displacement*

13 **unordered**, unorganized, unarranged, ungraded, unsorted, unsifted, unclassified

14 **irregular**, random, haphazard, erratic, hit-or-miss, sporadic, spasmodic, desultory, nonuniform, unsymmetrical, nonsymmetrical, misshapen, disproportionate, shapeless, formless

▶ *161 Shapelessness*

15 **untidy**, dirty, filthy, unclean, grubby, messy, in a mess, scruffy, shabby, ragged, in rags, down-at-heel, unsightly, unkempt, dishevelled, bedraggled, tousled, uncombed, windblown, pulled through a hedge backwards, like something the cat brought in, ruffled, crumpled, frumpish, sluttish, slovenly, slatternly, neglectful, negligent, careless, slipshod, shoddy, slack, sordid, squalid, shambolic (Inf), slobbish (Inf)

▶ *245 Deterioration; 258 Dirtiness; 666 Negligence*

16 **confused**, incoherent, convoluted, disorganized, muddleheaded, scatterbrained, featherbrained, unsystematic, unmethodical

▶ *696 Unintelligibility*

17 **discomposed**, discomfited, disconcerted, unsettled, disturbed, perturbed, upset, deranged, convulsed

18 **muddled**, jumbled, scrambled, confused, chaotic, tangled, labyrinthine, awry, askew, amiss, topsy-turvy, upside-down, at sixes and sevens, head over heels, higgledy-piggledy (Inf), arsy-versy (Inf), cockeyed (Inf), haywire (Inf)

▶ *264 Difficulty*

19 **mixed-up**, snarled-up, fouled-up, messed-up, mucked-up (Inf), ballsed-up (Inf), screwed-up (Inf), fucked-up (Inf), snafu (Inf)

▶ *486 Unskilfulness*

20 **disorderly**, chaotic, lawless, unruly, undisciplined, uncontrolled, out of control, unmanageable, boisterous, disruptive, stroppy (Inf), laddish (Inf), rowdy, hell-raising, harum-scarum, wild, turbulent, rampageous, riotous, rebellious, insubordinate, contumacious, mutinous, obstreperous, disobedient, anarchic, nihilistic

▶ *588 Anarchy; 641 Obstinacy; 662 Disobedience*

VERBS

21 **disorder**, disorganize, disarrange, derange, throw into disarray, muddle, jumble, shuffle, mix up, scramble, disperse, scatter, break up, disrupt, disturb

▶ *144 Displacement; 328 Disturbance; 377 Dispersal*

22 **discompose**, disconcert, disturb, perturb, upset, hassle (Inf), pester, unsettle, disorient, addle, befuddle, confuse, tie in knots, knock galley-west (US inf)

23 **confuse**, muddle (up), mess (up), hash (up), botch, bungle, mix up, snarl up, foul up, make a hash (*or* mess) of (Inf), make a pig's ear of (Inf), cock up (Inf), screw up (Inf), balls up (Inf), fuck up (Inf), bollix up (Inf)

▶ *486 Unskilfulness*

24 **make disordered**, untidy, mess up, dishevel, bedraggle, tousle, ruffle, rumple, crumple, crease, turn upside down, tangle, snarl

25 **be disordered**, lapse into disorder, fall into confusion, fall into disarray, degenerate, disintegrate, come apart, come unstuck, dissolve into chaos

▶ *245 Deterioration; 375 Disintegration*

26 **be disorderly**, get out of hand, get out of control, disobey, throw off discipline, make trouble, raise a rumpus, run wild, run amok (*or* amuck), riot, run riot, rampage, go on the rampage, roister, storm, mob, kick up a row (Inf), raise hell (Inf), raise the devil (Inf), horse around (Inf), cut up rough (Inf)

▶ *507 Loudness; 588 Anarchy; 662 Disobedience*

ADVERBS

27 **in disorder**, in disarray, in confusion, in a muddle, in a mess, in a jumble, by chance, unmethodically, unsys-

tematically, irregularly, haphazardly, erratically, indiscriminately, randomly, at random, sporadically, spasmodically, by fits and starts, without rhyme or reason, chaotically, confusedly

28 anyhow, all anyhow, all over, all over the place, upside-down, topsy-turvy, pell-mell, helter-skelter, harum-scarum, off the rails, at sixes and sevens, at cross purposes, all over the shop (Inf), arsy-versy (Inf), higgledy-piggledy (Inf), every which way (Inf)

29 riotously, on the rampage, anarchically, rebelliously, boisterously, disruptively

409 Arrangement

I wish our clever young poets would remember my homely definitions of prose and poetry; that is, prose = words in their best order; – poetry = the best words in the best order. Samuel Taylor Coleridge.

NOUNS

1 arrangement, order, ordering, putting in order, arranging, arraying, marshalling, disposition, disposal, placing, placement, location, structuring, composition, grouping, alignment, line-up

► *142 Location; 403 Structure; 407 Order*

2 array, assemblage, arrangement, display, pattern, design, decoration, style, layout, structure, composition, flower arrangement

► *738 Display*

3 organization, method, methodization, system, systematization, structuring, planning, charting, routinization, rationalization, standardization, centralization, coordination

► *352 Means; 484 Plan; 579 Management*

4 rearrangement, reordering, reorganization, restructuring, realignment, regrouping, simplification, streamlining, shake-up (Inf)

► *137 Class; 224 Change; 403 Structure*

5 categorization, classification, codification, taxonomy, grouping, placing, placement, pigeonholing, compartmentalization, grading, gradation, ranking, rating, seeding (sport), hierarchy, stratification, graduation, sorting, sorting out, sifting, screening, selection, analysis, tabulation, alphabetization, alpha-sorting, cataloguing, listing, indexing, filing

► *137 Class; 220 List; 407 Order; 469 Selection*

6 category, subcategory, class, subclass, group, subgroup, order, suborder, division, subdivision, family, set, bracket, head, heading, department, section, grade, rank, level, position, place, status, slot, niche, pigeonhole, compartment

► *137 Class*

7 catalogue, directory, gazetteer, register, digest, compendium, index, list, inventory, record, file, computer file, computer listing

► *40 Computers; 220 List; 744 Record*

8 chart, diagram, table, graph, flow chart, pie chart, bar chart, scatter diagram, flow sheet, spreadsheet, Venn diagram, plan, scheme, schema, schedule, programme

► *484 Plan*

9 musical arrangement, adaptation, interpretation, version, orchestration, score, instrumentation, choreography

► *18 Music*

10 agreement, understanding, arrangement, settlement, deal, compact, contract, covenant, terms

► *754 Compromise; 755 Contract*

11 arrangements, plans, preparations, making arrangements, planning, preparing, groundwork

► *243 Preparation; 484 Plan*

VERBS

12 arrange, order, put (*or* set) in order, reduce to order, structure, range, array, marshal, dispose, place, position, locate, set, set out, lay out, display, align, line up, put into shape, compose, group, space, space out, distribute, allocate, settle

► *142 Location; 403 Structure; 407 Order; 738 Display; 770 Allocation*

13 organize, methodize, systematize, rationalize, standardize, normalize, centralize, coordinate, plan, schematize

► *484 Plan; 579 Management*

14 rearrange, reorder, reorganize, restructure, shake up, realign, adjust, simplify, streamline

► *224 Change*

15 categorize, classify, class, codify, digest, program, group, pigeonhole, compartmentalize, place, place in order, put in order, grade, rank, rate, seed, sort, sort out, assort, sift, sift out, sieve, screen, select, analyse, process, process data, tabulate, alphabetize, catalogue, index, list, inventory, record, register, file

► *137 Class; 220 List; 469 Selection; 744 Record*

16 adapt, arrange, interpret, compose, orchestrate, score, instrument, choreograph

► *18 Music*

17 come to an arrangement, come to an agreement, compromise, agree, settle, make a deal, come to terms, fix up (Inf)

► *754 Compromise*

18 make arrangements, arrange for, prearrange, prepare, plan, schedule, organize, manage, contrive, devise

► *243 Preparation; 484 Plan; 579 Management*

19 tidy, tidy up, neaten, rearrange, straighten, straighten up, clean up, put to rights, put in trim, clear up, clear the decks, untangle, disentangle, unravel, unsnarl, iron out, smooth, debug

► *407 Order; 421 Smoothness*

ADJECTIVES

20 arranged, ordered, in order, orderly, structured, ranged, arrayed, marshalled, disposed, placed, aligned, grouped

► *142 Location; 403 Structure; 407 Order; 738 Display*

21 organized, methodized, systematized, rationalized, planned, prearranged

► *484 Plan*

22 organizational, methodical, systematic, schematic, rational, formational

► *579 Management*

23 rearranged, reordered, reorganized, restructured, realigned, adjusted, simplified, streamlined

► *224 Change*

24 categorized, classified, codified, grouped, pigeonholed, compartmentalized, placed, graded, ranked, rated, seeded, stratified, sorted, sorted out, assorted, sifted, screened, selected, analysed, processed, tabulated, alphabetized, catalogued, indexed, listed, filed, on file, on record

► *137 Class; 220 List; 744 Record*

25 categorical, classificatory, hierarchical, taxonomic(al)

► *407 Order*

26 diagrammatic, graphic, tabular, schematic, analytic

27 tidied, tidy, neatened, neat, straightened, straightened out, cleared up, untangled, disentangled, unravelled, unsnarled

ADVERBS

28 in place, in order, rationally, tidily, neatly, methodically, systematically, schematically, taxonomically, diagrammatically, indexically, analytically

410 Container

NOUNS

1 container, receptacle, holder, frame, vessel, repository, depository, reservoir, store

► *141 Space; 158 Size; 165 Enclosure; 166 Limit; 203 Quantity; 406 Contents; 736 Concealment*

2 compartment, cell, cage, cubicle, booth, stall, box, pew, niche, recess, nook, inglenook, cranny, bay, alcove, cubby, cubbyhole, snuggery, hole in the wall (Inf)

3 cabinet, cupboard, built-in cupboard, fitted unit, highboy (US), lowboy (US), tallboy, whatnot, chest, commode, chest of drawers, drawer, shelf, bookshelf, bookcase, unit, wall unit, hi-fi unit, dresser, Welsh dresser, drinks cabinet, sideboard, bureau, davenport, escritoire, secretaire, desk, writing desk, filing cabinet, kitchen unit (*or* cabinet), freezer, fridge-freezer, fridge, refrigerator, dishwasher

► *23 Furniture and Woodwork; 439 Store*

4 rack, shelf, shelving, layer, level, storey, floor, deck

5 packet, pack, packaging, cover, wrapper, sheath, envelope, jacket, document, wallet, file, folder, parcel, bundle

► *576 Work; 577 Workshop*

6 box, chest, coffer, casket, caddy, case, locker, canister, tin can, tin, can, carton, punnet, cardboard box, shoe box, cool box, Esky (Aus), moneybox, safe, jewellery box, cigarette case, snuffbox, matchbox, tinderbox, ammunition box, powder box, file, boxfile, dispatch box, packing box (*or* case), crate, (freight) container, tea chest, coffin, sarcophagus

► *439 Store*

7 basket, shopping basket, hamper, picnic hamper (*or* basket), rush basket, reed basket, wicker basket, wire basket, flower basket, fruit basket, bread basket, laundry basket, clothes basket, wastepaper basket, wastebasket, log basket, pannier, punnet, Moses basket, bassinet, creel, skep, trug

8 bag, sack, string bag, carrier bag, plastic bag, polythene bag, freezer bag, paper bag, shopping bag, carryall, holdall, grip, poke (Dial), pouch, diplomatic pouch, purse, handbag, shoulder bag, duffel bag, clutch bag, tote bag, bum bag, evening bag, sponge bag, carpetbag, overnight bag, school bag, satchel, sports bag, kitbag, golf bag, game bag, cool bag, tucker bag (Aus), swag (Aus), bundle, saddlebag, nosebag

9 baggage, luggage, suitcase, travel bag, grip, holdall, carryall, Gladstone bag, Boston bag, portmanteau, valise, trunk, overnight bag, flight bag, carry on bag, backpack, knapsack, rucksack, haversack, daysack, briefcase, attaché case, portfolio, wallet, money belt

10 cart, pushcart, handcart, trolley, shopping trolley, barrow, wheelbarrow, wagon, truck, lorry, van, transit van, removal van, freight train, boot, luggage rack, overhead locker

► *319 Transport*

11 vessel, urn, jar, tea caddy, coffee jar, kilner jar, vase, ewer, pitcher, jug, amphora, cask, vat, barrel, keg, drum, wine cask, pipe, beer barrel, puncheon, hogshead, firkin, tun, mash tun, tank, cistern, bucket, pail, watering can, dustbin, bin, litter bin, rubbish bin, trash can (US inf), wheelie bin, scuttle, coal scuttle, silo, hopper

12 bath, bathtub, hip bath, footbath, eyebath, sitzbath, Jacuzzi™, tin bath, bidet, tub, washtub, sink, kitchen sink, basin, washbasin, bowl, vat, trough

13 drinking vessel, cup, teacup, coffee cup, eggcup, mug, stoup (Dial), beaker, drinking cup, glass, tumbler, highball glass, beer glass, *Stein* (Ger), pint glass, half-pint glass, straight glass, lager glass, tankard, toby jug, horn, drinking horn, cannikin, pannikin, noggin, chalice, goblet, wineglass, champagne flute, schooner, rummer, brandy balloon, brandy snifter, jigger, liqueur glass, pony, sherry glass, loving cup

14 bottle, flask, flagon, vial, phial, decanter, carafe, wine bottle, demijohn, magnum, jeroboam, rehoboam, methuselah, balthazar, gourd, calabash, wineskin, beer bottle, milk bottle, hip flask, hot-water bottle, thermos (flask)

15 pot, pan, pots and pans, cooking pot, cauldron, saucepan, wok, frying pan, skillet, steamer, fish kettle, roasting tin, double boiler, bain marie, casserole, roaster, cake tin, bread tin, boiler, brazier, kettle, jug kettle, coffeepot, coffee urn, percolator, coffee maker, cafetière, teapot, tea urn, jamjar, honeypot, storage jar, plastic container, warming pan, chamber pot, potty

16 crockery, china, chinaware, dishware, pottery, teaset, dinner service, glassware, Tupperware™, utensils, bowl, finger bowl, mixing bowl, cereal bowl, soup bowl, porringer, sugar bowl, salad bowl, punch bowl, tureen, ramekin, terrine, jelly mould, gravy (*or* sauce) boat, rose bowl, plate, dinner plate, platter, dish, saucer, charger, salver, tray

17 ladle, ice-cream scoop, scoop, dipper, spatula, spoon, wooden spoon, tablespoon, dessertspoon, soup spoon, teaspoon, eggspoon, sugar spoon, shovel, spade, trowel

► *25 Cookery*

18 stomach, belly, gut, abdomen, paunch, midriff, tummy (tum) (Inf), bread basket (Inf), potbelly (Inf), beergut (Inf), spare tyre (Inf), bay window (Inf)

► *557 Eating*

19 inflatable, balloon, inner tube, football, gasbag, bubble, blister, sac

ADJECTIVES

20 containing, contained, holding, held, enclosing, enclosed, covering, covered, enveloping, enveloped, wrapping, wrapped, sheathed, surrounded, cocooning, cocooned, stabling, stabled, sheltering, sheltered, storing, storage, stored, reserved, packing, packed, bundled, boxed, caged, canning, canned, tinning, tinned, potting, potted, bottling, bottled, ladled, scooped, spooned, shovelled, binned, shelved, garaged, bagged, in the bag, locked up, entombed

VERBS

21 put (*or* **place**) **in a container**, store, reserve, containerize, crate up, bundle, can, tin, pot, box up, pour in, bottle, cover, wrap, pack, package, sheath, cocoon, envelope, enclose, cage, surround, shelter, stable, garage, entomb

411 Layer

NOUNS

1 **layer**, stratum, seam, zone, vein, lode, bed, belt, strip, band, course, table, thickness, ply, interlining, fold, pleat, lap, flap, superstratum, overlayer, topcoat, topsoil, overlap, substratum, underlayer, underlay, lining, undercoat, bedding

► *152 Thickness; 187 Horizontality; 550 Covering*

2 **level**, tier, row, storey, floor, landing, deck, terrace, ledge, shelf, step, stage

► *175 Base; 413 Support*

3 **coat**, coating, covering, sheet, blanket, foil, leaf, lamina, lamella, plate, plating, veneer, facing, fascia, overlay, sheathe, bark, membrane, skin, peel, pellicle, film, patina, bloom, scum, dross

► *153 Thinness; 435 Materials*

4 **slice**, sliver, wafer, disc, chip, rasher, collop (Dial), cut, slab, tablet, plaque, plank, slat, lath, panel, pane, tile, slate, shaving, paring, scale, squama, flake, dandruff, scurf, flock, floccus

5 **layered thing**, laminate, Formica™, laminated wood, plywood, laminated glass, safety glass, sandwich, club sandwich (US), double-decker, layer cake, onion, nest of tables, Russian doll, coalmine, shingled roof, clapboard house (US), atmosphere

6 **layering**, stratification, lamination, lamellation, foliation, scaliness, flakiness, squamation, delamination, exfoliation, desquamation

ADJECTIVES

7 **layered**, in layers, stratified, stratiform, straticulate, foliated, laminate, laminated, two-ply, three-ply, two-tiered, three-tiered, two-storeyed, three-storeyed, double-decker, terraced, multistage

8 **coated**, undercoated, plated, veneered, faced, lined, overlaid, overlaying, overlapped, overlapping, sheathed, laminated

9 **platelike**, leaflike, foliate, lamellar, lamellate, lamellated, lamelliform, placoid, membranous, pellicular, filmy, scummy, drossy, scaly, furfuraceous, squamous, squamose, squamulose, flaky, scurfy, flocculent, floccose

VERBS

10 layer, lay, lay down, arrange in layers, stratify, laminate, tier, deck, shingle, sandwich, coat, spread, cover, plate, veneer, face, line, overlay, overlap

11 scale, peel off, peel, flake off, flake, strip, shave, delaminate, exfoliate, desquamate

ADVERBS

12 in layers, in strips, on several levels, membraneously, furfuraceously, squamously, squamosely, flocculently

412 Mixture

NOUNS

1 **mixture**, admixture, commixture, intermixture, mixing, mingling, intermingling, stirring, shaking, blending, harmonization, association, combination, integration, syncretism, eclecticism, fusion, merger, union, amalgamation, conglomeration, composition, miscibility, solubility, infusion, interfusion, suffusion, transfusion, instillation, infiltration, pervasion, permeation, saturation, penetration, impregnation, contamination, pollution, contagion, infection, adulteration, dilution, watering down, qualification, sophistication, involvement, complexity, complication, entanglement, confusion, disorder, jumble, muddle, scramble, chaos, entropy, randomness, nonuniformity, patchiness, heterogeneity, hybridization, mongrelism, cross-breeding, interbreeding, miscegenation, intermarriage, syngamy, allogamy

2 **mixed thing**, mix, mixture, blend, mélange, composition, harmony, association, synthesis, marriage, interracial marriage, interfaith marriage, combination, compound, alloy, bronze, brass, pewter, billon, electrum, steel, magma, amalgam, fusion, infusion, solution, colloid, suspension, cocktail, punch, brew, witch's brew, medicinal compound, linctus, cough linctus, cough mixture, patent medicine, potion, concoction, confection, potpourri, pastiche, pasticcio, paste, stew, Irish stew, gumbo (US), soup, broth, goulash, Hungarian goulash, hash, ragout, salmagundi, olla podrida, bubble and squeak, fry-up (Inf), combo (Inf), Mickey Finn (Inf)

3 **miscellany**, miscellaneous collection, medley, miscellanea, anthology, collection, thesaurus, chrestomathy (Lit), variety, patchwork, mosaic, variegation, dappling, speckling, speckled effect, mottled effect, motley, job lot, hotchpotch, hash, mess, farrago, gallimaufry, potpourri, mishmash, linsey-woolsey, ragbag, jumble, lucky dip, grab bag (US), tombola, conglomeration, muddle, tangle, entanglement, imbroglio, confusion, complexity, kaleidoscope, phantasmagoria, babel, Tower of Babel, topsy-turvydom (US), bear garden, clatter, clamour, pandemonium, omnium-gatherum, motley crew, menagerie, zoo, circus, variety show, assortment, all sorts, bits and pieces, bits and bobs, oddments, snippets, paraphernalia, odds and ends, odds and sods (Inf), dog's dinner (*or* breakfast) (Inf)

4 **admixture**, ingredient, element, vein, streak, strain, dash, tincture, tinge, infusion, sprinkling, *soupçon* (Fr), touch, pinch, smack, modicum, suspicion, flavour, seasoning, condiment, herb, spice, *bouquet garni* (Fr), colouring, colour, dye, hue, stain, blot, smidgen (US inf)

5 **hybrid**, cross, hybrid flower, hybrid rose, cross-breed, half-breed (Offensive), half-blood (Offensive), half-caste (Offensive), mestizo, métis, quadroon, octaroon, mu-

latto, high yellow (Inf), Creole, Cape Coloured (*or* Coloured) (S Afr), Eurasian, mongrel, cur, alley cat (US), mule, hinny, tigon (*or* tiglon), loganberry, boysenberry, tayberry, clementine

6 **mixer**, electric mixer, beater, shaker, cocktail shaker, stirrer, spoon, wooden spoon, blender, liquidizer, food processor, whisk, churn, cream-maker, creamer, scrambler, mixing bowl, crucible, melting pot

► *25 Cookery*

7 **person who mixes**, chef, cook, baker, bartender, chemist, alchemist, witch, socialite, stirrer, mixer (Inf), mixologist (US inf)

VERBS

8 **mix**, admix, commix, immix, mix up, mix and match, stir, shake, knead, pound, pulverize, mash, brew, infuse, instil, imbue, impregnate, tinge, dye, colour, speckle, bespeckle, dapple, variegate, suffuse, combine, integrate, fuse, compound, alloy, amalgamate, merge, blend, harmonize, mingle, commingle, intermingle, intersperse, intermix, interlard, interleave, interlay, intertwine, intertwist, interweave, interlace, plait, braid, sprinkle, besprinkle, dash, dilute, water, water down, qualify, weaken, adulterate, sophisticate, temper, spice, season, fortify, lace, spike, pep up, doctor, meddle with, interfere with, tamper with, spoil, mar, debase, contaminate, cross, cross-fertilize, cross-breed, interbreed, hybridize, mongrelize

9 **mix up**, muddle, scramble, jumble, shuffle, confuse, bewilder, puzzle, confound, mistake, entangle, do wrong, mess up (Inf)

10 **become mixed**, blend, mix together, integrate, run through, penetrate, permeate, pervade, stain, infiltrate, infect, pollute, contaminate, become tainted with, become inextricably linked with, become entangled with, become involved with, intermarry, interbreed

11 **be mixed up**, misunderstand, not understand, puzzle over, get wrong, forget

ADJECTIVES

12 **mixed**, mixed-up, intermixed, mingled, intermingled, interracial, interfaith, interspersed, interlaced, interwoven, intertwisted, intertwined, plaited, braided, miscible, soluble, colloidal, dissolved, stirred, shaken, blended, harmonized, combined, integrated, syncretic, eclectic, fused, mashed, alloyed, merged, amalgamated, conglomerated, composite, half-and-half, tempered, sophisticated, adulterated, dilute, diluted, watered-down, weakened, qualified, involved, involved in, complex, complicated, in the melting pot, tangled, entangled, unclassified, unsorted, unordered, disordered, jumbled, confused, out of order, orderless, shuffled, scrambled, chaotic, topsy-turvy, miscellaneous, random, nonuniform, patchy, patched, heterogeneous, hybrid, mongrel, half-breed (*or* half-bred) (Offensive), cross-bred, crossed, half-caste (Offensive), half-blooded (Offensive), of mixed blood, miscegenetic, interbred, intermarried, multiracial, multicultural, kaleidoscopic, phantasmagorical, variegated, dappled, speckled, mottled, motley, shot, shot through with, tinged, dyed, coloured, pervasive, all-pervading, fifty-fifty (Inf), higgledy-piggledy (Inf)

13 **mixed-up**, muddled, jumbled, scrambled, confused, bewildered, puzzled, confounded, mistaken, forgetful

ADVERBS

14 **in the midst**, among many, among others, *inter alios* (L), among other things, *inter alia* (L), among (*or* amongst), amidst, in the midst of, in the middle of, interracially, between races, complexly, complicatedly, with complications, out of order, chaotically, miscellaneously, randomly, at random, patchily, heterogeneously, with different parts, kaleidoscopically, phantasmagorically, pervasively, contagiously, infectiously, higgledy-piggledy (Inf)

413 Support

While I cannot be regarded as a pillar, I must be regarded as a buttress of the church, because I support it from the outside. Lord Melbourne.

NOUNS

1 **support**, buttress, abutment, reinforcement, underpinning, strengthening, holding up, propping up, backing up

► *403 Structure*

2 **supporting part**, support, mainstay, prop, fulcrum, brace, buttress, flying buttress, abutment, bulwark, rampart, wall, retaining wall, embankment, mounting, scaffolding, frame, framework, skeleton, backbone, spine, ribs, A-frame, transom, chassis, underframe, undercarriage, underpinning, underlay, bracket, strut, pier, girder, rafter, beam, crossbeam, crossbar, lintel, king post, balustrade, pilaster, column, post, pillar, caryatid, shaft, stem, pile, foundation, foundation stone, cornerstone, keystone, bedrock, basement, groundwork, substructure, pedestal, base, stand, music stand, tripod, table, worktable, mantelpiece, shelf

► *38 Engineering; 175 Base; 186 Verticality; 187 Horizontality; 373 Connection*

3 **body support**, sling, bandage, splint, crutch, cane, stick, walking stick, walking frame, walker, Zimmer™, staff, alpenstock

4 **rest**, headrest, footrest, footstool, back rest, chair, easy chair, dentist's chair, shooting stick, saddle, sofa, couch, ottoman, davenport, bed, cradle, crib, mattress, springs, box springs, pillow, bolster

5 **supporting garment**, girdle, corset, brassiere, bra, athletic belt, athletic support, jockstrap

► *553 Fashion*

6 **moral support**, encouragement, furtherance, backing, advocacy, championship, protection, friendship, sympathy, empathy, aid, abetment, help, succour, assistance, cooperation, corroboration, collaboration, approval, endorsement, preferential treatment, intercession, favour, security blanket (US)

► *384 Defence; 747 Cooperation*

7 **financial support**, financial aid, pecuniary assistance, provision, sponsorship, backing, patronage, sustenance, sustainment, maintenance, subsistence, contribution, grant, allowance, stipend, pension, subsidy, upkeep, child support, alimony

► *392 Help; 780 Money; 785 Payment*

8 **supporter**, helper, aide, auxiliary, assistant, sidekick, spear-carrier, helpmate, helping hand, fund-raiser, char-

ity worker, tower of strength, substitute, backup (US), well-wisher, disciple, adherent, follower, fan, admirer, attendant, acolyte, collaborator, colleague, ally, corroborator, cooperator, sympathizer, fellow traveller, advocate, upholder, defender, protector, champion, proposer, seconder, benefactor, backer, underwriter, patron, sponsor, angel, sustainer, maintainer, friend, guardian, guardian angel, fairy godmother, Social Security, Social Services, Child Support Agency

► *608 Relief; 679 Generosity*

ADJECTIVES

9 **supportive**, supporting, retaining, foundational, ground, basal, upholding, sustaining, maintaining, helpful, encouraging, kindly, sympathetic, empathetic, understanding, reassuring, cooperative, corroborative, collaborative, benevolent, patronal, well-disposed, favourable, contributory, stipendiary, advocatory, preferential, intercessional, auxiliary, subsidiary, ancillary, substitute, discipular, attending, guardian

10 **supportable**, bearable, tolerable, endurable, sufferable, acceptable, manageable, passable, average, not (so) bad, so-so (Inf)

VERBS

11 **support**, bear, carry, hold up, prop up, prop, back up, shore up, strengthen, buttress, reinforce, bolster, brace, abut, bulwark, rampart, wall, embank, scaffold, frame, underframe, underpin, bracket, post, dig (*or* sink) a foundation, lay a foundation stone, lay a cornerstone

12 **bear**, tolerate, endure, stomach, brook, abide, countenance, suffer, submit to, undergo, stand (for), put up with (Inf), stick (Inf)

13 **support financially**, finance, pay for, fund, provide for, back, subsidize, sponsor, patronize, underwrite, maintain, keep, pension, contribute, grant, bankroll (US inf)

14 **give moral support**, stand by, back up, encourage, wish well, strengthen, buoy up, carry, back, champion, stand up for, stand behind, uphold, defend, assist, substitute for, lend a helping hand, aid, further, forward, abet, help, succour, sustain, foster, cooperate, corroborate, collaborate, intercede (on behalf of), propose, second, favour, praise, honour, approve of, endorse, advocate, recommend, give the seal of approval to, give one's blessing to, stick up for (Inf)

414 Heaviness

That blessed mood,
In which the burthen of the mystery,
In which the heavy and the weary weight
Of all this unintelligible world,
Is lightened. William Wordsworth.

ADJECTIVES

1 **heavy**, weighty, having weight, weighted, with a weight of, weighing, weigh-in, weigh-out, weighed, heavyweight, middleweight, lightweight, featherweight, leaden, solid, dense, massive, massy (Lit), considerable, great, stout, large, lumpish, lumpy, bulky, fat, overweight, obese, corpulent, heavy as a horse, heavy as lead, hefty (Inf), beefy (Inf), chunky (Inf)

2 **loaded**, laden, charged, overloaded, overladen, overweighed, overweighted

► *152 Thickness; 158 Size; 416 Density*

3 **ponderous**, onerous, heavy-handed, cumbersome, cumbrous, weighed (*or* weighted) down, burdensome, burdened, taxed, saddled, overburdened, overloaded, overladen, oppressive, oppressed, taxing, overtaxing, overtaxed, overbalanced, top-heavy, unwieldy, pressing, incumbent on, pressurized, handicapped

► *249 Adversity*

NOUNS

4 **heaviness**, weightiness, weight, poundage, tonnage, body weight, birthweight, solid body, massiveness, mass, lumpiness, lump, bulkiness, bulk, extra weight, fatness, obesity, corpulence, brawn, beefiness (Inf), beef (Inf), heftiness (Inf), heft (Inf)

► *152 Thickness; 158 Size; 416 Density*

5 **gravity**, specific gravity, gravitation, force of gravity, gravitational pull, G, G-force

6 **displacement**, draught, sinkage, load, loading, freight, cargo, bale, ballast, lading, charging, charge, overload, overloading, overweighting, surcharge

► *319 Transport; 406 Contents*

7 **weighing**, weighing-in, weigh-in, weighing-out, weigh-out, dead weight, dead load, live load, gross weight, net weight, neat weight, overweight, underweight, boxing weight, heavyweight, light-heavyweight, middleweight, welterweight, lightweight, featherweight, cruiserweight, bantamweight, flyweight, hefting (US inf)

► *52 Combat Sports and Martial Arts; 59 Horse Riding and Racing*

8 **weighing down**, weighting down, saddling, burdensomeness, burdening, burden, overburdening, ponderousness, ponderosity, incubus, onerousness, oppressiveness, oppression, taxing, tax, overtaxing, overbalance, unwieldiness, pressure, cumbersomeness, cumbrance, encumbrance, handicap, drag, stone, millstone

► *120 Inequality; 264 Difficulty; 305 Descent; 367 Lowering; 378 Obstruction*

9 **avoirdupois weight**, troy weight, apothecaries' weight, atomic weight, molecular weight, ounce, pound, stone, ton, pennyweight, hundredweight, milligram, gram, kilogram, kilo, dram, drachm, carat, scruple, axle load, laden weight

► *26 Measurement*

10 **scales**, pair of scales, scale, calibrator, weighing machine, weighbridge, bathroom scales, kitchen scales, counter scale, platform scale, spring scale, torsion scale, barrel scale, drum scale, fan scale, steelyard, balance, spring balance, spiral balance, Roman balance, counterbalance, counterpoise, makeweight, ballast, ballasting

► *438 Tool*

11 **weight**, sinker, lead, plumb, plumb bob, plummet, lead balloon, ton of bricks (Inf)

VERBS

12 **be heavy**, have weight, gain weight, put on weight, exert weight, carry weight, weigh the same, balance, counterweigh, counterpoise, outweigh, overweigh, outbalance, overbalance, tip the scales, turn the scales, tip the balance, wallow, sink, gravitate, settle, founder, descend, weigh a ton (Inf)

13 weigh on, weigh (*or* lie) heavy upon, press upon, weigh one down, oppress, hang like a millstone

▶ *119 Equality*

14 make heavy, load, lade, weigh down, weigh one down, hang weights on, ballast, burden, make overweight, overburden, overload, encumber, cumber, charge, tax, hinder, handicap, hamper, saddle, oppress, lie heavy upon, bear (*or* rest) hard upon, overweigh, overtax

15 weigh, take (*or* find) the weight of, put (*or* stand) on the scales, lay on the scale, measure, weigh oneself, weigh in, weigh out, weigh in the balance, strike a balance, heft (US inf)

ADVERBS

16 heavily, heavy, weightily, with great weight, massively, greatly, stoutly, largely, densely, leadenly, like a ton of bricks, like a lead balloon, like lead, like a horse

17 burdensomely, under a burden, oppressively, with oppression, ponderously, onerously, cumbersomely, cumbrously

415 Lightness

Angels can fly because they take themselves lightly. G. K. Chesterton.

ADJECTIVES

1 light, unheavy, weighing little, portable, handy, lowweight, lightweight, featherweight, bantamweight, underweight, light-footed, light on one's feet, light-handed, light-fingered, having a light touch, light as air, lighter-than-air, light as a feather, light as thistledown, light as a fairy, weightless, without weight, unweighable, imponderable, imponderous

▶ *153 Thinness*

2 insubstantial, ethereal, rare, sublime, airy, gaseous, volatile, frothy, foamy, foaming, whipped, whisked, bubbly, bubbling, effervescent, *pétillant* (Fr), sparkling, downy, feathery, cobwebby, gossamery, fluffy, uncompressed, soft, gentle, delicate, dainty, tender, flimsy, floaty, floating, floatable, buoyant, buoyed up, unsinkable, levitative, levitational, levitating

▶ *153 Thinness*

3 lightening, unloading, unloaded, off-loaded, aerating, aerated, easing, relieving, alleviating, alleviative, disburdening, unburdening, disencumbering

4 leavening, fermenting, fermentative, raising, self-raising, yeasty, enzymic, diastasic, zymotic

NOUNS

5 lightness, rarity, thinness, unheaviness, portability, airiness, ethereality, gaseousness, volatileness, volatility, vaporization, foaminess, frothiness, bubbliness, effervescence, sparkling, yeastiness, downiness, fluffiness, softness, gentleness, tenderness, flimsiness, delicacy, daintiness, unweighableness, imponderableness, imponderability, lack of weight, weightlessness, defiance of gravity, levitation, levitating, floating, floatability, ascent, buoyancy, levity (Lit)

▶ *96 Unreality; 159 Smallness; 304 Ascent; 417 Sparseness; 419 Softness; 432 Gas; 434 Air*

6 lightening, easing, easement, aeration, alleviation, relief, unburdening, unloading, unlading, unsaddling, untaxing

▶ *265 Easiness; 371 Expulsion*

7 light thing, air, hot air, helium, ether, bubble, balloon, snowflake, feather, down, thistledown, fluff, fuzz, oose (Scot), gossamer, cobweb, straw, dust, mote, cork, froth, foam, spume, soufflé, mousse, sponge, floating thing, float, life buoy, life belt, life jacket, life preserver (US), mae west (Inf)

8 leavening, leaven, fermentation, ferment, raising agent, yeast, enzyme, barm (Lit), baking powder, self-raising flour

▶ *25 Cookery; 366 Raising*

VERBS

9 be light, weigh little, have little weight, lack weight, defy gravity, levitate, ascend, rise, elevate, surface, float to the surface, float, swim, drift, waft, glide, soar, hover

10 lighten, make light, make lighter, gasify, vaporize, aerate, volatilize, buoy, buoy up, hold up, uplift, fluff, upraise, leaven, ferment, work, raise, empty, unload, offload, unlade, lighten ship, unballast, throw overboard, jettison, disencumber, disburden, unburden, unsaddle, untax, relieve, alleviate, ease, reduce weight, lose weight

ADVERBS

11 lightly, with a light touch, insubstantially, without substance, ethereally, sublimely, effervescently, softly, gently, with gentleness, delicately, daintily, tenderly, with tenderness, flimsily, fluffily, imponderably, zymotically

416 Density

NOUNS

1 density, denseness, solidity, solidness, bulk, mass, thickness, thickening, compactness, concreteness, toughness, hardness, hardening, closeness, cohesion, coalescence, consistency, impenetrability, impermeability, imperviousness, indissolubility, indivisibility, inseparability, coherence, incompressibility

▶ *152 Thickness; 267 Stickiness; 336 Strength; 402 Material World; 414 Heaviness; 418 Hardness; 423 Toughness*

2 concentration, consolidation, condensation, coagulation, constriction, haemostasis, thrombosis, concretion, concretization, solidification, congealment, constipation, nucleation, gelatinization, glaciation, ossification, petrifaction, fossilization, crystallization, sedimentation, precipitation

3 relative density, specific gravity, densimeter, hydrometer, aerometer

▶ *438 Tool*

4 solid body, solid mass, solid, mass, aggregate, conglomerate, hardcore, nucleus, precipitate, deposit, sediment, coagulum, curd, clot, blood clot, thrombosis, thrombus, embolus, concretion, concrete, cement, earth, clay, hardpan, block, rock, crystal, stone, lump, chunk, clod, clump, cluster, cake, nugget, knot, node, nodule, burl, bone, gristle, cartilage, ossicle, obstacle, wall, forest, thicket

▶ *260 Ill Health; 378 Obstruction*
5 **condenser**, compressor, thickener, thickening, gelatine, rennet, pepsin

ADJECTIVES

6 **dense**, thick, compact, cohesive, close-knit, close-packed, close-textured, close-woven, incompressible, close, firm-packed, firm, full, densely arrayed, assembled, serried, massed, thick on the ground, massive, massy, heavy, weighty, monolithic, solid, concrete, rigid, inelastic, constrictive, styptic, astringent, haemostatic, strong, unbreakable, infrangible, indivisible, inseparable, consistent, impenetrable, thickset, thick-growing, bushy, luxuriant, plenteous, impermeable, impervious, without holes

7 **condensed**, consolidated, concentrated, solidified, solidifying, binding, congealed, congealing, coagulated, coagulating, constipated, constipating, costive, curdled, clotted, clotting, jelled (*or* gelled), jelling (*or* gelling), set, setting, freezing, frozen, deep-frozen, unthawed, unmelted, undissolved, insoluble, indissoluble, infusible, crystalline, crystallized, caked, matted, knotted, knotty, ropy, tangled, gnarled, lumpy, close, stuffy, foggy, murky, smoky, thick enough to be cut with a knife

VERBS

8 **be dense**, densify, become thick, thicken, cohere, solidify, become solid, harden, cement, set, gelatinize, jellify, jell (*or* gell), congeal, coagulate, clot, curdle, cake, crust, consolidate, constipate, conglomerate, contract, form a core, form a kernel, nucleate, crystallize, fossilize, petrify, ossify, freeze, glaciate, deposit, condense, evaporate, precipitate, inspissate (Lit)

9 **make dense**, bring together, bind, crowd, mass, squeeze (*or* pack) together, pack, squeeze in, squeeze, load tightly, cram, tamp, ram down, make smaller, compact, compress, concentrate, firm up (*or* down)

ADVERBS

10 **densely**, thickly, compactly, cohesively, firmly, with firmness, fully, massively, heavily, solidly, concretely, rigidly, constrictively, strongly, plenteously, imperviously, costively, insolubly

417 Sparseness

As for the grass, it grew as scant as hair
In leprosy. Robert Browning.

ADJECTIVES

1 **sparse**, thin, empty, vacuous, vacuum, void, scarce, rare, tenuous, delicate, fine, wispy, light, low-pressure, windy, airy, gaseous, vaporous, volatilizable, volatilized, ethereal, buoyant, insubstantial (*or* unsubstantial), immaterial, slight, flimsy, incorporeal, uncompressed, uncompact, spongy, compressible, soft, airy-fairy (Inf)
▶ *94 Nonexistence; 96 Unreality; 98 Absence; 101 Unworldliness; 415 Lightness; 419 Softness*

2 **rarefied**, rarefactional (*or* rarefactive), expansive, expanding, expanded, extensive, extending, extended, attenuated, attenuate, dilative, dilatational, dilatable, dilatant, dilating, etherealized, thinning, thinned, thinned-out, diluted, dilute, weak, adulterated, watered, watered-down, cut
▶ *190 Expansion; 191 Contraction; 337 Weakness; 377 Dispersal*

NOUNS

3 **sparseness**, thinness, emptiness, vacuity, vacuousness, voidness, scarcity, scarceness, rarity, rareness, tenuity, tenuousness, delicacy, fineness, wispiness, lightness, low pressure, windiness, airiness, gaseousness, volatility, volatileness, ethereality, buoyancy, lack of substance, insubstantiality (*or* unsubstantiality), immateriality, lack of solidity, slightness, flimsiness, incorporeality, reduced pressure, compressibility, sponginess, softness

4 **rarefaction**, expansion, extension, attenuation, dilation, dilatation, etherealization, thinning, dilution, weakness, adulteration

5 **gas**, air, atmosphere, oxygen, hydrogen, ether, wind, vacuum, near vacuum
▶ *432 Gas; 434 Air*

VERBS

6 **make sparse**, thin, thin out, rarefy, gasify, vaporize, volatilize, reduce pressure, create a vacuum, hermetically seal, pump out, empty, exhaust, expand, extend, attenuate, dilate, etherealize, dilute, water, water down, cut, weaken, adulterate

ADVERBS

7 **sparsely**, thinly, emptily, with emptiness, vacuously, in a vacuum, tenuously, delicately, finely, lightly, airily, ethereally, insubstantially (*or* unsubstantially), expansively, by expanding, extensively

418 Hardness

A Hard Rain's A-Gonna Fall. Bob Dylan.

In the bleak mid-winter
Frosty wind made moan,
Earth stood hard as iron,
Water like a stone. Christina Rossetti.

ADJECTIVES

1 **hard**, hard as steel, hard as nails, steely, steel, diamond-like, iron, hard as iron, stone, stony, hard as stone, lithic, granite, granitic, marble, rock, rocky, rock-hard, hard as a rock, rocklike, lapideous, lithoid (*or* lithoidal), lithic, flinty, pebbly, gravelly, gritty, lumpy, horny, corneous, callous, leathery, bony, osseous, ossific, cartilaginous, gristly, sclerotic, crusty, incrusted, glassy, crystalline, vitreous, petrifactive, petrifying
▶ *336 Strength; 416 Density; 492 Touch*

2 **tough**, strong, firm, solid, rock-solid, unbreakable, adamant, indestructible, shatterproof, resistant, starchy, starched, boned, whaleboned, stark, stiff, rigid, inflexible, inelastic, unsprung, unrelaxed, tight, taut, tense, pokerlike, muscle-bound, muscular, stiff as a board, stiff as a poker, stiff as a ramrod, stiff as buckram
▶ *423 Toughness*

3 **hardened**, toughened, fortified, strengthened, stiffened, reinforced, backed, braced, buttressed, proofed, tempered, heat-treated, annealed, oil-tempered, indurate,

indurated, case-hardened, hard-boiled, steeled, armoured, armour-plated, callous, calloused, ossified, hornified, calcified, crusted, crystallized, granulated, vitrified, petrified, fossilized, sunbaked, solidified, set, frozen, frozen solid, frozen over, icy

4 **mentally hard**, inflexible, stubborn, obdurate, obstinate, firm, tough, intransigent, unadaptable, unpliable, unpliant, unmalleable, intractable, intractile, unbending, unyielding, ungiving, unalterable, immutable, difficult, callous, case-hardened, hardhearted, stony-hearted, heartless, insensitive, thick-skinned, hard-boiled, tough as old boots (Inf)

NOUNS

5 **hardness**, strength, firmness, solidity, impenetrability, resistance, density, hardcore, hard centre, toughness, toughening, steeliness, stoniness, rockiness, cragginess, grittiness, lumpiness, nodularity, nodosity, rigidity, rigidness, rigour, temper, stiffness, stiffening, starchiness, starching, tautness, tightness, inflexibility, inelasticity, inextensibility, tension, tenseness, tensity, backing

6 **solidification**, hardening, setting, crystallization, granulation, petrifaction (*or* petrification), fossilization, lapidification, ossification, vitrification, glaciation, steeling, tempering, vulcanization, calcification, sclerosis, atherosclerosis, multiple sclerosis, arteriosclerosis, hardening of the arteries

▶ *30 Earth Science; 260 Ill Health*

7 **hard substance**, diamond, steel, hard steel, hammer, iron, wrought iron, cast iron, metal, aluminium, Duralumin™, nail, hardware, stoneware, rock, stone, stone wall, adamant, pebble, grit, boulder, silica, flint, granite, quartz, marble, brick, cement, concrete, concrete block, reinforced concrete, ferroconcrete, baked brick, brick wall, brick house, bulletproof glass, armour, wood, hardwood, heartwood, duramen, oak, heart of oak, teak, board, bone, gristle, cartilage, spine, backbone, fingernail, toenail, horn, ivory, shell, wart, corn, callus, node, nodule, lump, crust, jawbreaker (*or* jawcrusher)

▶ *30 Earth Science*

8 **mental hardness**, toughness, hardness of heart, hardheartedness, callousness, obduracy, obstinacy, intransigence, intractability, inflexibility, unpliability, unmalleability, unbendingness, unyieldingness, immovability, stubbornness, asperity

▶ *641 Obstinacy*

VERBS

9 **harden**, make hard, render hard, toughen, case-harden, strengthen, steel, temper, reinforce, brace, buttress, shore, shore up, back, tighten, stiffen, tauten, starch, wax, tense, vulcanize, crisp, bake, heat, heat-treat, hardboil, anneal, freeze, refrigerate

10 **solidify**, petrify, fossilize, ossify, calcify, vitrify, crystallize, glaciate, granulate, candy, set, firm, stiffen, condense, thicken, jell (*or* gel)

11 **be stubborn**, remain intransigent, not yield, not bend, not give, not alter

ADVERBS

12 **toughly**, strongly, resistantly, by offering resistance, starkly, stiffly, with stiffness, rigidly, tightly, tautly, tensely, in a tense manner, stonily, grittily, crustily, icily

13 **inflexibly**, without flexibility, stubbornly, in a stubborn manner, firmly, with firmness, intransigently, intractably, unalterably, immutably, callously, hardheartedly

419 Softness

ADJECTIVES

1 **soft**, softening, softened, unstarched, unstiffened, nonrigid, flaccid, limp, rubbery, flabby, floppy, flimsy, unstrung, relaxed, slack, lax, loose, sprung, fluid

▶ *431 Fluid*

2 **pliant**, pliable, giving, yielding, melting, flexible, flexile, bendable, stretchable, elastic, lithe, lithesome, willowy, supple, lissom, limber, loose-limbed, double-jointed, springy, acrobatic, athletic, plastic, extensile, extensible, extendible, ductile, tractile, tractable, adaptable, malleable, mouldable, shapable, impressible, waxy, doughy, pasty, putty-like

▶ *422 Elasticity*

3 **smooth**, satiny, satinlike, silky, silken, velvety, velvet, velvetlike, plushy, plush, downy, feathery, fluffy, flossy, woolly, fleecy, flocculent, furry

▶ *421 Smoothness*

4 **compressible**, squeezable, padded, foam-filled, cushiony, pneumatic, pillowed, podgy, pudgy, spongy, mashy, soggy, squashy, squishy, squelchy, juicy, overripe, pulpy, pithy, medullary, muddy, boggy, marshy, mossy, grassy, turfy, loamy, clayey, argillaceous

5 **soft as butter**, soft as wax, soft as soap, soft as down, soft as velvet, soft as silk, soft as putty, soft as dough, soft (*or* smooth) as a baby's bottom, soft as a kiss, soft as a whisper, soft as a sigh, tender as a spring chicken

6 **soft-hearted**, tender-hearted, kind-hearted, warm-hearted, sympathetic, compassionate, gentle, tender, kind, delicate, mild, easy, easy-going, relaxed, lenient, lax, complaisant, mellow, laid-back (Inf)

7 **impressionable**, susceptible, formable, sensitive, formative, nonresistive, easing, mollifying, mollified, showing leniency, appeasing, complying, adapting, adaptable

NOUNS

8 **softness**, softening, softening-up, pliability, pliableness, pliancy, flexibility, bendability, give, suppleness, willowiness, limberness, litheness, nonrigidity, springiness, springing, elasticity, plasticity, ductility, tensileness, tractability, malleability, impressibility, rubberiness, extendibility, extensibility, looseness, slackness, flaccidity, flaccidness, flabbiness, floppiness, limpness

9 **smoothness**, downiness, fluffiness, furriness, woolliness, flocculence, flossiness, featheriness, silkiness, velvetiness, satininess, plushiness

10 **compressibility**, sponginess, pulpiness, doughiness, semiliquidity, sogginess, marshiness, bogginess, squashiness, squelchiness

11 **soft thing**, feather, feather bed, eiderdown, swan's-down, duvet, continental quilt, pillow, cushion, armchair, easy chair, sofa, pad, padding, upholstery, wadding, foam-filling, foam, fluff, puff, fur, cotton wool, wool, fleece, silk, satin, velvet, velveteen, plush, down, thistledown, kapok, hair, paste, modelling clay, Plasticine™, play dough, dough, putty, wax, soap, butter, pulp, mousse, mud, marsh, bog, snowflake, snow, breeze, zephyr

▶ *31 Meteorology and Climatology; 72 Birds; 490 Physical Pleasure*

12 gentleness, tenderness, delicacy, mellowness, mildness, kindness, sensitiveness, easiness, easing up, leniency, laxity, laxness, laxation, mollification, mollifying, appeasement, compliance, complying, obedience, adaptability

▶ *388 Submission; 588 Anarchy; 648 Leniency*

VERBS

13 soften, soften up, unstiffen, sag, flop, unstring, relax, slacken, loosen, bend, unbend, spring, mould, shape, make an impression in, impress, wax, smooth out, pad, cushion, plump up, plump, fluff up, fluff, shake up, featherbed, render soft, tenderize, mellow, mature, ripen, overripen, oil, grease, lubricate, knead, massage, mash, whip, pulp, squash, pulverize, chew, masticate, macerate, marinate, steep, drench, melt, thaw, liquefy

14 ease, relax, unwind, mellow, temper, lessen, mitigate, demulce, assuage, soothe, subdue, soften the tone, tone down, turn down, simmer down, mollify, limber up, massage, loosen, loosen up, hang loose (Inf), cool it (Inf), cool (*or* chill) out (Inf)

15 be kind, show gentleness, show tenderness, show leniency, have compassion, ease up

16 yield, give way, give in, give, relent, appease, comply, obey, adapt, submit

ADVERBS

17 softly, with softness, limply, flaccidly, flimsily, slackly, loosely, laxly, fluidly, pliantly, flexibly, elastically, lithely, lissomly, limberly, acrobatically, like an acrobat, athletically, like an athlete, waxily, smoothly, pneumatically, silkily, fluffily, soggily

18 soft-heartedly, gently, tenderly, with tenderness, sensitively, delicately, easily, leniently, laxly, compassionately, with compassion, mildly, complaisantly, impressionably, susceptibly, compliantly, submissively

420 Roughness

The rough male kiss of blankets. Rupert Brooke.

ADJECTIVES

1 rough, roughened, rough-hewn, roughcast, unsmooth, textured, rippled, rippling, ripply, undulatory, wrinkled, wrinkly, crinkled, crinkly, crumpled, crumply, rugose (*or* rugous), uneven, corrugated, nonuniform, irregular, ruffled, muricate (*or* muricated), inequal, rugged, ragged, unsifted

▶ *365 Friction; 404 Texture*

2 coarse, coarse-grained, rough-grained, cross-grained, grainy, granulated, gravelly, stony, rocky, rockbound, ironbound, craggy, cragged, scraggly, scraggy, snaggy, snagged, snaggled, nodose (*or* nodous), nodular, lumpy, slubbed, hispid, villous, spiny, nubby, studded, knobby, knobbly, knotted, knotty, gnarled, gnarly, knurled, bouclé, shattered, broken, jagged, jaggy, sharp, serrated, ridged, rough-edged, deckle-edged, corrugated, grated, tweed, tweedy, potholed, furrowed, rutty, rutted, pitted, pockmarked, pocked, pocky, pimply, scabby, scabrous, encrusted, scaly, warty, blistered, cracked, chapped

3 barbed, prickly, scratchy, notched, hacked, hairy, unshorn, hirsute, shockheaded, pigtailed, ponytailed, bushy, woolly, flocculent, lanate, furry, matted, curly, frizzy, fuzzy, shaggy, shagged, bristly, bristling, bristled, barbellate, setiform, setose, strigose, hispid, unkempt, unshaven, stubbled, stubbly, bearded, bewhiskered, moustached

▶ *425 Sharpness*

4 bumpy, jolting, agitated, turbulent, choppy, tempestuous, storm-tossed

5 unfinished, incomplete, unpolished, unrefined, shapeless, rudimentary, preliminary, cursory, crude, raw, rough and ready, sketchy, vague, approximate

NOUNS

6 roughness, unsmoothness, wrinkliness, rugosity, unevenness, corrugation, nonuniformity, irregularity, inequality, rough going, joltiness, bumpiness, rough surface, rough ground, ruggedness, raggedness, granulation, coarseness, coarse grain, coarse cloth, cragginess, scraggliness, nodosity, lumpiness, rough air, strong wind, turbulence, rough water, choppiness, hispidity, bristliness, horripilation, villosity, spininess, nubbiness, nubbliness, rough skin, scaliness, scabrousness, hairiness, rough hair, shagginess, knobbliness, scratchiness, rough texture, rough fibre, shattered surface, brokenness, jaggedness, sharp edge, serration, saw-edge, rough edge, deckle edge, scalloped edge

▶ *164 Edge; 365 Friction; 404 Texture; 433 Water; 434 Air; 550 Covering*

7 rough thing, roughcast, sandpaper, glasspaper, emery paper, emery board, emery wheel, file, corrugated iron, washboard, grater, steel wool, scrubbing brush, nailbrush, sackcloth, homespun, tweed, linsey-woolsey, corduroy, knot, kink, bouclé, chapped hands, bumpy face, acne, creeping flesh, goose flesh, goose pimples, goose bumps, barbed wire, broken glass, notched wood, splinter, burr, bristle, awn, thistle, prickle, barb, thorn, scale, scab, matted hair, shag, stubble, five-o'clock shadow, plaid, braid, pigtail, ponytail, dreadlocks, beard, goatee, whiskers, muttonchops, moustache, handlebars, horsehair, designer stubble (Inf)

▶ *180 Convolution; 548 Blemish; 551 Dress*

8 rough ground, broken ground, canyon, mountain, sierra, rough road, potholed road (*or* street), dirt road, dirt track, sheeptrack, furrow, rut, crack, undergrowth, overgrowth

▶ *319 Transport*

9 broken water, ripple, big wave, tidal wave, tsunami, choppy sea, air pocket, hurricane, tornado, cyclone, twister (US inf)

▶ *30 Earth Science*

10 rough idea, rough working, rough copy, rough approximation, rough, mock-up, draft, preliminary sketch, unfinished piece, crudeness, incompleteness, shapelessness, rudiment, cursoriness, sketchiness, vagueness, approximateness

▶ *125 Imitation; 270 Vagueness; 446 Idea*

VERBS

11 be rough, lack uniformity, lack regularity, lack equality, have a rough surface (*or* texture), ripple, crack, chap, have a bumpy face, have acne, creep (of flesh), horripilate, bristle, bristle up, prickle, scale, bump, jolt, jerk

12 **make rough**, rough, rough up, roughen, roughen up, roughcast, rough-hew, ruffle, wrinkle, crease, fold, crinkle, crumple, rumple, corrugate, granulate, coarsen, stud, emboss, boss, break, crack, hack, serrate, crenate, notch, engrail, indent, mill, sandpaper, grate, go against the grain, rub up the wrong way, set on edge, knot, kink, tousle, tangle, gnarl, pothole, furrow, plaid, braid

13 **be unfinished**, leave unfinished (*or* incomplete), give a rough idea, make a rough copy, approximate, sketch, make a preliminary sketch, draft, rough out, mock up

ADVERBS

14 **roughly**, rough, in the rough, unsmoothly, against the grain, against the nap, the wrong way, choppily, unevenly, rugosely, irregularly, without regularity, inequally, without equality, ruggedly, coarsely, stonily, lumpily, turbulently, bumpily, villously, sharply, brokenly, jaggedly

15 **incompletely**, in unfinished form, shapelessly, without shape, preliminarily, crudely, sketchily, vaguely, approximately

421 Smoothness

He gave the impression that very many cities had rubbed him smooth. Graham Greene.

ADJECTIVES

1 **smooth**, smoothing, smoothed, smooth-surfaced, smooth-textured, streamlined, nonfrictional, frictionless, even, unrough, flush, sleek, slick (US), bald, clean-shaven, hairless, glabrous (*or* glabrate), smooth-haired, well-brushed, combed, brushed, groomed, carded, silken, silky, satiny, velvety, smooth-skinned, peachlike, fleecy, woolly, soft, downy

2 **uniform**, even, regular, horizontal, plane, level, harrowed, rolled, steamrolled, flattened, unsharpened, blunt, edgeless, rounded, curved, waterworn, flat, ironed, unwrinkled, uncrumpled, unruffled, unbroken

▶ *177 Curve; 181 Roundness; 426 Bluntness*

3 **soothing**, peaceful, still, quiet, calm, dead, quiescent

4 **polished**, varnished, burnished, waxed, enamelled, lacquered, glazed, glacé, gleaming, shiny, glossy, glassy, mirror-like, reflective, slippery, slick (US), skiddy, slithery, buttery, lubricated, lubricious, oily, oiled, greasy, greased, soapy

5 **smooth as a peach**, smooth as a baby's bottom, smooth as glass, smooth as velvet, smooth as satin, satin-smooth, smooth as marble, slippery as an eel, slippery as a greased pig, calm as a mill pond

6 **smooth-mannered**, well-mannered, suave, smooth-spoken, sophisticated, urbane, glib, slick, sleek, sycophantic, unctuous, ingratiating, creepy (Inf), smarmy (Inf)

NOUNS

7 **smoothness**, evenness, flushness, smooth texture, smooth surface, uniformity, regularity, horizontality, levelness, flatness, peacefulness, stillness, calmness, serenity, calm, dead calm, unruffled surface, quiescence, making smooth, levigation, sleekness, silkiness, satininess, velvetiness, fleeciness, softness, shininess, shine, lustre, finish, glossiness, glassiness, slickness (US), slipperiness, slitheriness, unctuousness, lubrication, lubricity, oiliness, greasiness

▶ *187 Horizontality; 301 Motionlessness; 522 Light*

8 **smooth thing**, silk, satin, velvet, velveteen, velour, down, swan's-down, hair, baby's bottom, bald head, mahogany, marble, alabaster, ivory, glass, mirror, ice, dance floor, ice rink, lawn, plumb wicket, bowling alley, bowling green, artificial turf, Astroturf™, desert, plain, billiard table, billiard ball, tennis court, paving, asphalt, Tarmac™, flagstone, slide, chute, slipway, millpond, smooth water, dead water, calm water

9 **smoother**, roller, garden roller, steamroller, bulldozer, rolling pin, flattener, trowel, iron, electric iron, smoothing iron, flatiron, tailor's goose, mangle, wringer, press, hot press, trouser press, plane, spokeshave, drawknife, rake, harrow, card, comb, brush, hairbrush, sandpaper, glasspaper, emery paper, emery board, file, nailfile, buffer, floor polisher, sander, burnisher, chamois, waxer

▶ *256 Cleanness; 365 Friction; 553 Fashion*

10 **polish**, shoe polish, car polish, floor polish, furniture polish, silver polish, French polish, varnish, burnish, enamel, gloss, glaze, patina, wax, facing, lubricant, grease, oil, lubricator, grease gun, oilcan

▶ *268 Slipperiness*

VERBS

11 **smooth**, smoothen, smooth out (*or* away), remove friction, streamline, plane, planish, even, level, harrow, mow, rake, flatten, flatten down, plaster down, comb, rub down, rub, roll, calender, press, hot-press, uncrease, iron, iron out, unravel, mangle, shave, cut, shorten, smooth down, file down, sand, sandpaper, emery, levigate, slick down (US), slick (US), starch, launder, clean, shine, burnish, make bright, buff, polish, glaze, glacé, butter, gloss, wax, varnish, paint, coat, finish, pave, Tarmac™, overlay, Astroturf™, lubricate, oil, grease

12 **go smoothly**, feel no friction, glide, skate, ice-skate, roller-skate, roll, ski, float, bowl along, run on rails, slip, slide, skid, coast, freewheel

▶ *300 Motion*

13 **smooth over**, soothe, calm, appease, pacify, allay, ameliorate, assuage, mitigate, alleviate, charm, ingratiate, toady, creep up to (Inf), suck up to (Inf)

ADVERBS

14 **smoothly**, evenly, unroughly, without roughness, flushly, sleekly, slickly (US), uniformly, on an even keel, regularly, horizontally, levelly, flatly, bluntly

15 **soothingly**, peacefully, without trouble, stilly, quietly, calmly, softly, quiescently

16 **suavely**, sophisticatedly, glibly, urbanely, sleekly, sycophantically, unctuously, creepily (Inf), smarmily (Inf)

422 Elasticity

All my clothes have stretch marks, darling. Jennifer Saunders.

NOUNS

1 **elasticity**, stretch, stretchability, stretchiness, stretching,

suppleness, plasticity, rubberiness, extensibility, extension, distension, flexibility, pliancy, pliability, tensibility, tension, strain, ductility, tonicity, tonus, tone, springiness, spring, resilience (*or* resiliency), give, snap, snapback, recoil, rebound, bounciness, bounce, flex (Inf)

▶ *144 Displacement; 224 Change; 419 Softness*

2 adaptability, resilience (*or* resiliency), buoyance (*or* buoyancy), flexibility, adjustability, responsiveness, liveliness, compliance, accommodation, yielding

▶ *227 Changeableness; 265 Easiness; 471 Attention; 747 Cooperation; 750 Agreement*

3 elastic thing, elastic tissue, whalebone, baleen, elastic band, rubber band, rubber ball, tennis ball, handball, basketball, stretch fabric, Lycra™, spandex, stretch jeans, gum, chewing gum, bubble gum, spring, springboard, diving board, trampoline, pogo stick, bungee rope, racket, jumping jack, catapult, slingshot (US), bouncy castle, condom

▶ *19 Painting and Sculpture; 553 Fashion*

4 rubber, gum elastic, elastomer, crude rubber, natural rubber, latex, caoutchouc, guttapercha, plantation rubber, india rubber, foam rubber, sponge rubber, hard rubber, vulcanized rubber, vulcanite, ebonite, synthetic rubber, Thiokol™, cold rubber, Buna™, nitrile, neoprene, silicone rubber, crepe rubber, Butyl (rubber)™, polyurethane rubber, reclaimed rubber, rubber plantation, rubber plant, rubber tree

5 spring, mainspring, hairspring, coil spring, spiral spring, volute spring, leaf spring, bedspring (US), box spring, suspension system, shock absorber

▶ *180 Convolution*

ADJECTIVES

6 elastic, rubber, rubbery, rubberlike, rubberized, stretchable, stretchy, stretching, stretch, stretched, supple, plastic, extensible (*or* extensile), extending, extended, distensible, distending, distended, flexible, flexing, flexed, pliant, pliable, tensile, tensible, ductile, tonic, springy, springing, sprung, well-sprung, coiling, coiled, resilient, giving, yielding, snapping, recoiling, rebounding, bouncy, bouncing

7 adaptive, adaptable, adapting, adapted, resilient, buoyant, flexible, adjustable, adjusting, adjusted, responsive, responding, lively, compliant, complying, yielding, accommodating

VERBS

8 be elastic, stretch, extend, expand, distend, flex, have flexibility, have tone, show resilience, give, spring, snap, snap back, recoil, rebound, bounce

9 make elastic, elasticize, elasticate, rubberize, rubber, vulcanize, plasticize

10 be adaptable, adapt, have resilience, have buoyancy, stay flexible, comply, adjust, respond quickly, accommodate, yield, bounce back

ADVERBS

11 elastically, supplely, with suppleness, plastically, flexibly, pliantly, springily, bouncily

12 adaptably, resiliently, flexibly, responsively, compliantly, accommodatingly

423 Toughness

Horny-handed sons of toil. Denis Kearney.

ADJECTIVES

1 tough, strong, rugged, solid, sturdy, resistant, resisting, durable, hard-wearing, lasting, long-lasting, infrangible, untearable, unbreakable, nonbreakable, unshatterable, shatterproof, shockproof, chip-proof, fractureproof, bulletproof, bombproof, fireproof, indestructible

2 toughened, case-hardened, tanned, hardened, tempered, annealed, vulcanized, strengthened

3 hard, rock-hard, rigid, stiff, nonelastic, inelastic, unsprung, leathery, leatherlike, coriaceous, firm, clinging, stuck, cohesive, coherent, viscid, chewy, fibrous, woody, ligneous, gristly, cartilaginous, rubbery, overdone, hard-boiled, inedible, indigestible, tough as nails, tough as old boots, tough as (shoe) leather

▶ *418 Hardness*

4 powerful, athletic, muscular, brawny, burly, sinewy, strapping, weather-beaten, lean, wiry, stringy, full of vitality, blessed with stamina, robust, enduring, untiring, unflagging, indefatigable, tenacious, resilient, hardy, stalwart, rough, brutal, vicious, bullying

▶ *336 Strength*

5 mentally tough, mentally strong, resolved, single-minded, unyielding, stubborn, obstinate, obdurate, inflexible, hardhearted, stern, unfeeling, callous, cynical, case-hardened, thick-skinned, hard-boiled (Inf), hard-nosed (Inf)

▶ *451 Disbelief; 635 Will; 640 Perseverance*

NOUNS

6 toughness, strength, ruggedness, solidness, sturdiness, resistance, durability, survivability, lastingness, infrangibility, unbreakableness, unbreakability, hardness, rigidness, stiffness, firmness, clinging, cohesiveness, cohesion, coherence, viscidity, leatheriness, stringiness, rubberiness, chewiness, inedibility, indigestibility

▶ *267 Stickiness; 277 Duration; 416 Density; 418 Hardness*

7 tough thing, leather, gristle, cartilage, bulletproof glass, bulletproof vest, air-raid shelter, nut, coconut

8 physical strength, physical power, powerful build, athletic build, muscularity, muscles, sinews, brawn, leanness, wiriness, stringiness, vitality, vigorousness, vigour, stamina, robustness, stalwartness, tenacity, endurance, resilience, hardiness, lasting power, physical roughness, brutality, brute force, viciousness, bullying

▶ *338 Vigour; 380 Violence*

9 mental toughness, mental strength, resolve, single-mindedness, unyieldingness, stubbornness, obstinacy, obdurateness, inflexibility, hardheartedness, sternness, unfeelingness, callousness, cynicalness

▶ *451 Disbelief; 635 Will; 640 Perseverance*

VERBS

10 be tough, show strength, resist, last, outlast, survive, have survivability, endure, stay the course, resist breaking, toughen, harden, stiffen, cling, stick fast, have physical strength, have an athletic build, flex one's muscles, show stamina, have tenacity, refuse to yield, have no feelings, act roughly, brutalize, use brute force, bully, hang tough (Inf), tough something out (Inf)

► *277 Duration; 607 Annoyance and Aggravation*

11 **make tough**, strengthen, harden, tan, mercerize, vulcanize, temper, anneal, case-harden, make unbreakable, shatterproof, bulletproof, bombproof, fireproof

ADVERBS

12 **toughly**, strongly, using strength, ruggedly, solidly, sturdily, resistantly, resistingly, durably, lastingly, infrangibly, indestructibly, rigidly, stiffly, firmly, cohesively, coherently, viscidly, indigestibly

13 **powerfully**, athletically, muscularly, leanly, robustly, enduringly, untiringly, tenaciously, resiliently, hardily, stalwartly, roughly, brutally, with brute force

14 **single-mindedly**, stubbornly, obstinately, obdurately, inflexibly, hardheartedly, sternly, unfeelingly, callously, cynically

424 Brittleness

ADJECTIVES

1 **brittle**, brittle as glass, fragile, fragile as an eggshell, frangible, delicate, papery, wafer-thin, flimsy, frail, unsturdy, unsteady, insubstantial, shoddy, gimcrack, jerry-built, dilapidated, tumbledown, weak, vulnerable, breakable, ready to break, breaking, broken, ready to burst, bursting, burst, explosive, crackable, ready to crack, cracking, cracked, crackled, chipping, chipped, shatterable, shattering, shattered, ready to split, splitting, split, splintery, splintering, scissile, tearable, tearing, torn, crushable, crushing, crushed, crumbly, crumbling, crumbled, short, friable, fissile, flaky, flaking, powdery, crispy, crisp, inelastic, rigid, like parchment, crazy (Lit)

► *245 Deterioration; 337 Weakness; 372 Separation; 418 Hardness; 425 Sharpness*

NOUNS

2 **brittleness**, fragility, fragileness, frangibility, frangibleness, delicacy, flimsiness, frailty, unsturdiness, weakness, vulnerability, breakableness, breakability, breaking, breakup, cracking, splitting, split, splintering, scission, crushability, crumbliness, crumbling, deterioration, friability, friableness, fissility, flakiness, crispness, crispiness, inelasticity, rigidness

3 **brittle thing**, eggshell, icicle, thin ice, ice sculpture, old paper, parchment, rice paper, old bone, lamina, dead leaf, piecrust, pastry, matchwood, balsa (*or* balsawood), shale, slate, glass, windowpane, glasshouse, greenhouse, crystal, porcelain, pottery, weak thing, jerry-built house, house of cards, sand castle, snowman, bubble

VERBS

4 **be brittle**, be fragile, deteriorate, wear thin, crash, give way, fall in, tumble, fall to pieces, break, break down, break apart (*or* up), craze (Dial), disintegrate, burst, explode, crack, crack off, fracture, shatter, break off, snap off, snap, split, splinter, chip, chip off, crush, crumble, flake, fragment, shiver, live in a glass house

ADVERBS

5 **fragilely**, delicately, flimsily, frailly, unsteadily, insubstantially, shoddily, weakly, vulnerably, explosively, crispily, rigidly, without flexibility

425 Sharpness

ADJECTIVES

1 **sharp**, sharpened, pointed, pointy, sharp-pointed, needle-pointed, needle-like, acicular, aciculate (*or* aciculated), mucronate, acuminate, needle-sharp, sharp as a needle, spearlike, lanceolate, lance-shaped, hastate, arrow-like, sagittal, sagittate (*or* sagittiform), unblunted, tapered, tapering, fastigiate, conical, pyramidal, convergent, spindle-shaped, fusiform, wedge-shaped, wedgy

2 **spiked**, spiky, star-pointed, star-shaped, starlike, stellate, stellular, barbed, spiny, spinose, spinous, acanthoid, acanthous, prickly, pricky, pricking, bristly, bristling, hispid, awned, stinging, stingy, thorny, brambly, briery, thistly, sharp as broken glass

► *424 Brittleness*

3 **sharp-edged**, sharp-set, honed, razor-edged, razor-sharp, sharp as a razor, knife-edged, knifelike, cultrate, keen, keen as a razor, keen-edged, double-edged, cutting, swordlike, ensiform, saw-edged

4 **toothed**, toothy, fanged, fanglike, tusked, tusklike, horned, hornlike, corniculate, cornute (*or* cornuted), toothlike, odontoid, dentiform, denticulate, cusped, cuspidate (*or* cuspate), muricate (*or* muricated), serrated, notched, emarginate (*or* emarginated), comblike, pectinate (*or* pectinated), snagged, snaggy, snaggle-toothed, craggy, rough, jagged

5 **mentally sharp**, sharp-witted, quick-witted, keen-minded, acute, astute, alert, bright, shrewd, clever, smart, intelligent, perspicacious, discerning, observant, perceptive, sharp-eyed, keen, acuminous, sharp as a tack, razor-sharp, sharp-tongued, acerbic

► *442 Intellect*

NOUNS

6 **sharpness**, pointedness, acumination, mucronation, spininess, spinosity, thorniness, bristliness, prickliness, denticulation, dentition, serration

► *310 Convergence*

7 **sharp point**, point, knife point, pencil point, sword point, cusp, vertex, prong, tine, sting, dent, notch, sharp edge, saw-edge, cutting edge, knife edge, razor edge, jagged edge

► *587 Weapon*

8 **sharp-pointed thing**, pyramid, summit, peak, crag, arête, projection, spire, steeple, flèche, nail, tack, stylus, pin, hatpin, drawing pin, thumbtack (US), pushpin (US), burin, rowel, staple, nib, needle, knitting needle, bodkin, hypodermic needle, pick, pickaxe, icepick, toothpick, fork, pitchfork, harrow, rake, comb, cog, sprocket, ratchet, awl, auger, drill, borer, gimlet, broach, perforator, spear, spearhead, bayonet, lance, lancet, fleam, marlinespike (*or* marlinspike), caltrop, cheval-de-frise, bodkin, barb, barbed wire, barbwire (US), harpoon, fluke, hook, fish-hook, gaff, nippers, sword, dagger, dirk, stiletto, rapier, pike, skewer, spit, arrowhead, arrow, quarrel, goad, ankus, prod, sticker (US inf), horn, antler, claw, talon, cockspur (*or* spur), porcupine, hedgehog, quill, spine, prick, sting, spicule (*or* spiculum), pine needle, prickle, thorn, brier, burr, bramble, thistle, nettle,

awn, cactus, yucca, Adam's-needle, Spanish bayonet, bristle, hair, beard, moustache
▶ *174 Top; 438 Tool; 550 Covering; 551 Dress; 587 Weapon*
9 **sharp-edged thing**, broken glass, razor, razor blade, blade, wedge, fingernail, edge tool, chisel, plane, scraper, drawknife, spokeshave, cutter, saw, scissors, shears, pinking shears, pruning shears, pruner, clippers, secateurs, billhook, grass cutter, lawn mower, scythe, sickle, shovel, spade, trowel, adze, adz (US), mattock, ploughshare, share, coulter, colter (US), hatchet, axe
▶ *43 Agriculture*
10 **knife**, surgical knife, scalpel, bistoury, cook's knife, cleaver, chopper, carving knife, carver, whittle (Dial), slicer, kitchen knife, bread knife, fish knife, paring knife, skiver, penknife, pocketknife, craft knife, clasp knife, flick knife, switchblade (US), sheath knife, jackknife, hunting knife, bowie knife, bush knife, machete, kris, parang, panga, sword, broadsword, cutlass, scimitar
▶ *25 Cookery; 35 Medicine*
11 **tooth**, first tooth, milk tooth, baby tooth, deciduous tooth, permanent tooth, front tooth, incisor, cutter, canine (tooth), eyetooth, carnassial, bicuspid, premolar, back tooth, grinder, molar, wisdom tooth, bucktooth, snaggletooth, gold tooth, crown, false tooth, fang, tusk, denticle, set of teeth, uppers and lowers (Inf), fangs (Inf), ivories (Inf), pearls (Inf)
12 **sharpener**, knife sharpener, steel, pencil sharpener, whetstone, grindstone, oilstone, hone, file, emery, emery board, emery paper, sandpaper, glasspaper, Carborundum™, strap, strop
13 **mental sharpness**, sharp-wittedness, quick-wittedness, acuteness, acuity, astuteness, alertness, brightness, shrewdness, cleverness, intelligence, smartness, perspicacity, perspicaciousness, keenness, discernment, acumen
▶ *442 Intellect*

VERBS

14 **be sharp**, be pointed, have a point, end in a point, taper (*or* come) to a point, peak, converge, acuminate, spiculate, bristle, bristle with, prickle, prick, stick, pierce, sting, have prongs, have an edge, have a jagged edge, cut, needle, have horns, gore, bite, chew, cut a tooth
15 **make sharp**, sharpen, hone, file, sandpaper, grind, oilstone, strop, strap, whet, taper, edge, put an edge on, point, make pointed, put a point on, notch, serrate, barb, spur, break glass
16 **use a sharp tool** (*or* **weapon**), scrape, chisel, plane, cut, scissor, saw, shear, clip, prune, cut (*or* mow) the lawn (*or* grass), fork, harrow, rake, comb, scythe, sickle, shovel, spade, trowel, plough, axe, knife, razor, cleave, chop, carve, whittle, slice, skive, drill, bore, perforate, spear, bayonet, lance, spike, harpoon, hook, gaff, nip, stick, skewer, shoot an arrow, shoot with an arrow, goad, prod, claw, scratch
▶ *381 Attack*
17 **be mentally sharp**, have sharp wits, have quick wits, show acuteness, stay alert, show intelligence, discern
▶ *442 Intellect*

ADVERBS

18 **sharply**, pointedly, acutely, smartly, astutely, alertly, brightly, shrewdly, cleverly, intelligently, perspicaciously, discerningly, keenly
19 **suddenly**, sharply, cleanly, without warning
▶ *630 Surprise*

426 Bluntness

So sicken waning moons too near the sun,
And blunt their crescents on the edge of day. John Dryden.

ADJECTIVES

1 **blunt**, bluntish, blunted, dull, unsharp, unsharpened, unwhetted, worn, smooth, smoothed, faired, stub, stubby, snub, blunt-nosed, rounded, square, curving, flat, flattened, unedged, edgeless, unpointed, pointless, blunt-edged, blunt-ended, blunt-pointed, dull-edged, dull-pointed, bated
▶ *177 Curve; 181 Roundness; 421 Smoothness*
2 **outspoken**, straightforward, frank, direct, plain-spoken, candid, curt, bluff, abrupt
▶ *269 Brevity; 660 Insolence; 799 Honour*
3 **dull**, obtuse, insensitive, unperceptive, hebetudinous, dense, slow, numb, unfeeling
▶ *489 Insensibility; 592 Insensitivity*
4 **toothless**, edentate, edental, edentulous, teethless, biteless

NOUNS

5 **bluntness**, unsharpness, dullness, smoothness, flatness, stubbiness, roundness
6 **outspokenness**, straightforwardness, frankness, directness, plain-spokenness, candidness, curtness, bluffness, abruptness
7 **dullness**, obtuseness, obtundity, insensitivity, insensitiveness, hebetude, impercipience, numbness
8 **toothlessness**, lack of bite, lack of incisiveness, toothless tiger
9 **blunt instrument**, blunt edge, foil, spatula, palette knife

VERBS

10 **blunt**, dull, obtund, take the edge off, disedge, flatten, round, smooth, turn, turn the edge, bate (a foil), draw the teeth (*or* fangs) of

ADVERBS

11 **smoothly**, dully, stubbily, flatly, roundly, pointlessly, toothlessly
12 **bluntly**, frankly, to the point, candidly, curtly, plainly, straightforwardly, directly, abruptly
13 **obtusely**, insensitively, imperceptively, numbly

427 Powderiness

NOUNS

1 **powderiness**, pulverulence, dustiness, chalkiness, flouriness, efflorescence, bloom
2 **crumbliness**, flakiness, friability, friableness, pulverableness, brittleness, looseness
▶ *424 Brittleness*
3 **graininess**, granularity, granulation, mealiness, branniness, grittiness, sandiness, sabulosity, gravelliness
▶ *404 Texture*
4 **pulverization**, powdering, milling, multure, reducing to dust, dusting, frosting, grinding, trituration, crushing,

mashing, smashing, beating, pounding, contusion, grating, shredding, crumbling, flaking, levigation, granulation, granulization, comminution, erosion, abrasion, attrition, detrition, brecciation, fragmentation, sharding, atomization, micronization, disintegration, attenuation, decomposition, limation

► *375 Disintegration; 377 Dispersal*

5 powder, dust, dirt, chalk, efflorescence, flowers, flowers of sulphur, pounce, talc (talcum powder), face powder, cosmetics, attritus, dustball, fluff, pussies, kittens, slut's wool, lint, soot, smuts, ash, sawdust, coal dust, airborne particles, fallout, air pollution, smog, cosmic dust, dust cloud, dust storm, dust devil

6 crumb, flake, crumble, dandruff, scurf, filings, raspings, snowflake, fragment, smithereens

7 grain, granule, granulet, speck, mote, particle

8 meal, groats, bran, flour, atta, farina, grist

9 grit, sand, gravel, shingle, detritus, debris, breccia, collapse breccia

► *30 Earth Science*

10 spore, pollen, pollen grain, microspore, sporule

► *78 Flowers; 561 Reproduction*

11 pulverizer, comminutor, kominuter, triturator, levigator, crusher, rock crusher, food processor, mill, grinder, coffee grinder (*or* mill), pepper mill, atomizer, grindstone, bulldozer, masher, pounder, millstone, pestle, pestle and mortar, muller, quern, quernstone, roller, steamroller

12 abrasive, file, sandpaper, glasspaper, emery paper, emery board, nailfile

13 grater, cheese grater, nutmeg grater, shredder

► *438 Tool*

14 koniology, konimeter

ADJECTIVES

15 powdery, dusty, dust-covered, pulverulent, pulverous, scobiform, scobicula, dirty, sooty, chalky, chalklike, calcareous, flocculent

16 mealy, branny, floury, farinaceous, furfuraceous

17 grainy, gritty, granular, sandy, sabulous, arenose, arenaceous, arenarious, gravelly, shingly, shingled, pebbly, pebbled, breccial, brecciated, detrited, detrital

18 pulverized, powdered, ground, granulated, disintegrated, ground to dust, crushed, grated, shredded, sifted, pestled, comminuted, triturated, levigated, sharded

19 crumbly, friable, crumbled, crumbling, crisp, flaky, scaly, scurfy

20 pulverizable, pulverable, pulverulent, triturable

VERBS

21 powder, dust, flour, sand, sprinkle, scatter, dredge

22 pulverize, powder, comminute, reduce (*or* grind) to powder (*or* dust), triturate, contriturate, levigate, bray, pestle, disintegrate, fragment, shard, brecciate, atomize, micronize

23 crumble, crumb, chip, flake

24 grind, granulate, granulize, grain, mill, flour, mince

25 grate, shred, abrade, rub down, scrape, rasp, file

26 beat, pound, bray, smash, mash, hammer, bruise, knead, crush, squash, crunch, kibble, kevel, scrunch (Inf)

27 come (*or* **fall**) **to dust**, crumble into dust, disintegrate, fall to bits (*or* pieces), break up, granulate, decompose, effloresce

28 weather, erode, wear down, rust

ADVERBS

29 flakily, granularly, grittily, dustily, abrasively, dirtily

428 Dryness

I must get out of these wet clothes and into a dry Martini.
Alexander Woollcott.

ADJECTIVES

1 dry, arid, waterless, moistureless, unwatered, unirrigated, unmoistened, needing water, undamped, anhydrous, droughty, high and dry

2 thirsty, thirsting, athirst, dry, dry as a bone, parched, drouthy (Scot)

3 dried-up, dried, dehydrated, desiccated, exsiccated, withered, shrivelled, sere (*or* sear) (Lit), faded, wizened, weazened, parchment-like, mummified, corky, juiceless, sapless, dry as a bone, bone-dry, dry as dust, dry as parchment, dry as a stick, dry as a biscuit, dry as a mummy

4 dried-out, drained, evaporated, squeezed dry, mangled

5 rainless, fair, set fair, hot, sunny, fine, cloudless, pleasant

► *31 Meteorology and Climatology*

6 desert, arid, Saharan, dusty, powdery, sandy, barren, bare, brown, grassless

► *427 Powderiness*

7 adapted to drought, xerophilous, xerophytic, xeromorphic

8 baked, parched, sun-dried, sunbaked, burnt, scorched, bleached, sunned, insolated, aired, wind-dried, air-dried

► *493 Heat*

9 drying, desiccative, desiccant, dehydrating, exsiccative, exsiccant, siccative, siccant, evaporative

10 waterproof, protected from wet, waterproofed, proof, moistureproof, rainproof, stormproof, flood proof, showerproof, dampproof, leakproof, watertight, snug, dryshod

NOUNS

11 dryness, aridness, aridity, siccity, parchedness, waterlessness, drought

12 thirst, thirstiness, drought (Scot), dryness, dehydration, xerostomia

13 drying, drying up, desiccation, exsiccation, dehydration, airing, anhydration, air-drying, dehumidification, withering, fading, bleaching, searing, mummification, insolation, sunning, blotting, mopping-up

14 desert, sand dune, barren land, badlands, dust bowl, salt flat, wasteland, Death Valley, Sahara, Kalahari, Gobi, Sinai, karoo (Africa), dry (*or* arid) climate, sun, heat, sunniness, sunny South

15 dryer (or drier), absorbent, blotting paper, blotter, mop, sponge, swab, swabber, brush, towel, towelling, desiccator, desiccative, siccative, exsiccative, exsiccator, dehydrator, dehydrant, dehumidifier, evaporator, hairdryer, wringer, mangle, spin-dryer, tumble-dryer, clothes-dryer, clotheshorse

16 dry skin, xeroderma (*or* xerodermia), ichthyosis, fishskin disease, xerophthalmia

VERBS

17 dry, become dry, dry up, dry off, dry out, dehydrate, anhydrate, drain, evaporate, vaporize, desiccate, exsiccate, freeze-dry, dehumidify, air-dry, wind-dry, smoke, smoke-dry, kipper, cure

18 thirst, be thirsty, thirst for, parch

19 bake, sun, expose to sunlight, insolate, sun-dry, toast, roast, scorch, bleach, apricate, burn, fire, kiln, torrefy

20 absorb, drink up, soak up, blot, blot up, mop, mop up, swab, wipe, wipe up, wipe dry, sponge, towel, rub, brush

21 dry up, parch, wither, shrivel, wilt, wizen, weazen, mummify, preserve

22 keep dry, keep watertight, wear a macintosh, hold off the wet, waterproof

23 drip-dry, spin-dry, tumble-dry, wring, mangle, hang out to dry, hang out, peg out, air, evaporate

ADVERBS

24 drily, aridly, anhydrously, thirstily, dustily, xerically, xerophytically

429 Moisture

I am sick o' wastin' leather on these gritty pavin'-stones,
An' the blasted English drizzle wakes the fever in my bones.
Rudyard Kipling.

NOUNS

1 moisture, moistness, moistiness, dampness, wetness, wettishness, wateriness, humour (Lit), humectation (Lit), sogginess, soddenness, soppiness

► *431 Fluid; 433 Water*

2 mistiness, fogginess, fog, fog band, cloud, rain, raininess, rainfall, pluviosity, showeriness, Scotch mist, drizzle, mizzle, wet weather

► *31 Meteorology and Climatology*

3 humidity, humidness, dankness, dankishness, mugginess, stickiness, clamminess, closeness, humidification, absolute humidity, relative humidity, dew point, saturation, saturation point

4 seepage, percolation, permeation, rising damp, wet rot

5 sprinkle, sprinkling, spraying, sparge, asperge, aspersion, hosing, splash, spatter, splatter, affusion

► *377 Dispersal*

6 dew, dewdrops, night dew, dawn dew, rain dew, evening damp, fog drip, false dew, tear dew, guttation

7 bogginess, swampiness, marshiness, muddiness, dewiness

8 marsh, swamp, fen, bog, quagmire, wetlands, salt marsh, flood plain, quicksand, mud, slime, ooze, mire, wet, sludge, squelch

ADJECTIVES

9 moist, damp, wet, moisty, dampish, wettish, soggy, sodden, humid, clammy, sticky, muggy, close, dank, tacky, humectant

10 misty, foggy, cloudy, watery, rainy, showery, drizzling, drizzly, mizzly, dewy, bedewed, roric

11 marshy, swampy, boggy, fenny, soggy, oozy, squashy, squelchy, splashy, sludgy, slushy, muddy, sodden, waterlogged, flooded

12 seeping, dripping, drip-dropping, percolating, splashed, spattered, weeping, tear-stained, tearful, dribbling, drivelling, drooling, sweating, perspiring

► *433 Water*

VERBS

13 moisten, dampen, wet, add water, humidify, humectate (Lit), humect (Lit)

14 sprinkle, spatter, spray, hose, splash, dabble, slosh (Inf)

15 be moist, be damp, be soggy, squelch, not have a dry thread (*or* stitch), drizzle, mizzle

16 seep, drip, percolate, leak, ooze, trickle, shed tears, weep, sweat, perspire, exude, bleed, salivate, dribble, drool, slobber

► *433 Water*

ADVERBS

17 moistly, wetly, succulently, damply, clammily, humidly, stickily, dankly, soggily, oozily

430 Viscosity

NOUNS

1 viscosity, viscidity, viscousness, thickening, spissitude, inspissation, incrassation, stickiness, tackiness, glueyness, gluelikeness, adhesiveness, glutinousness, glutinosity, gumminess, gummosity, gauminess (Dial), gumlikeness, syrupiness, treacliness, mucilaginousness, gelatinousness, jelly-likeness, jellification, gelatinity, clabbering (Dial), loppering (Dial), colloidality, doughiness, pastiness, clamminess, slabbinness (Lit), lentor (Lit), ropiness, stringiness, toughness, tenacity, tenaciousness, gooeyness (Inf)

► *152 Thickness; 267 Stickiness; 423 Toughness*

2 adhesive, glue, gluten, mastic, wax, beeswax, gum, chewing gum, bubble gum, chicle, chicle gum, guar gum, resin, paste, size, birdlime, tar

► *267 Stickiness*

3 paste, size, glair, glaze

4 emulsion, collodion (*or* collodium), colloid

5 mucus, phlegm, albumen, pus, matter, snot (Inf)

► *431 Fluid*

6 gelatin, gel, jelly, syrup, honey, treacle, jam

► *25 Cookery*

7 slime, goo (Inf), gunge (Inf), gunk (Inf), gook (Inf), glop (Inf), guck (Inf)

ADJECTIVES

8 viscous, viscose, viscid, inspissate, incrassate, sticky, tacky, adhesive, gluey, gluelike, waxy, glutinous, glutinose, glutenous, colloidal, emulsive, gumbo, gumbolike, gummy, gaumy (Dial), gummous, gumlike, slabby (Lit), thick, stodgy, heavy, mucilaginous, clammy, ropy, stringy, tough

9 gelatinous, jelly-like, jellied, jelled, syrupy, treacly, jammy, tremelloid (*or* tremellose)

VERBS

10 stick, glue, gum, gum up, paste, adhere

► *267 Stickiness*

11 thicken, jellify, jelly, gelatinize, emulsify, clabber (Dial), lopper (Dial), incrassate (Lit), inspissate (Lit)

► *152 Thickness*

ADVERBS

12 viscously, viscidly, thickly, stickily, tackily, adhesively, tenaciously

431 Fluid

NOUNS

1 fluid, liquid, liquid state, liquor, water, drink, beverage, liquid extract, fluid extract, condensation, elastic fluid, nonelastic fluid

▶ *429 Moisture; 433 Water; 558 Drinking*

2 juice, sap, extract, latex, milk, whey, buttermilk, ghee, water, running water, gravy, stock, meat juice, sauce, gippo, soup

▶ *25 Cookery; 79 Trees*

3 body fluid, lymph, plasma, blood, humour, chyle, rheum, serous fluid, serum, pus, matter, purulence, suppuration, ichor, sanies, discharge, gleet, leucorrhoea, the whites (Inf), mucus, mucor, phlegm, snot (Inf), saliva, spittle, urine, piss (Inf), pee (Inf), wee (Inf), excrement, shit (Inf), semen, menstrual flow, sweat, perspiration, tear, tears, teardrop, milk, mother's milk, colostrum, lactation, dropsy, oedema, hydrocele

▶ *560 Excretion*

4 blood, lifeblood, arterial blood, venous blood, gore, claret, blood serum, blood substitute, blood plasma, plasma substitute, synthetic plasma, dextran, clinical dextran, blood cell (*or* corpuscle), red blood cell (*or* corpuscle), erythrocyte, white blood cell (*or* corpuscle), leucocyte, lymphocyte, neutrophil, phagocyte, blood platelet, haemoglobin, clot, blood clot, thrombosis, blood pressure, blood group (*or* type), O (*or* A *or* B *or* AB) blood groups, Rhesus factor, Rh factor, Rh-positive, Rh-negative, antigen, antibody, isoantibody, globulin, opsonin, blood count, blood picture, circulation, bloodstream, blood bank, bloodmobile (US), blood transfusion

▶ *35 Medicine; 394 Remedy*

5 fluidity, fluidness, liquidity, liquidness, fluxure, fluxility, liquefaction, colliquation, juiciness, sappiness, pulpiness, wateriness, runniness, rheuminess, nonviscosity, noncoagulation, haemophilia, solubleness, liquidescence, bloodiness, goriness, semiliquidity

6 flow, fluency, flux, fluxion, fluxility (Lit), haemorrhage, suppuration, secretion

7 juiciness, sappiness, milkiness, succulence, lactescence, lactation, chylifaction, chylification, serosity, moisture

8 fluidification, liquefaction, liquidization, liquescence, colliquefaction, solubility, deliquation, liquescency, deliquescence, fluxibility, dissolution, solution, dissolving, decoagulation, unclotting, melting, thaw, thawing, unfreezing, running, fusing, fusion, solubilization, lixiviation, percolation, leaching

9 solvent, liquifier, liquefacient, dissolvent, dissolver, dissolving agent, menstruum, anticoagulant, hydragogue, resolvent, resolutive, thinner, diluent (*or* dilutant), flux, universal solvent, alkahest (*or* alcahest)

10 solution, infusion, decoction, suspension, emulsion, apozem, flux, lixivium, lye

▶ *412 Mixture*

11 liquidizer, blender, food processor, juice extractor

▶ *25 Cookery*

12 flowmeter, fluidmeter, hydrometer

13 fluid mechanics, hydraulics, hydrogeology, hydrology, hydrometry, hydrostatics, hydrodynamics, hydrokinetics

▶ *28 Physics*

ADJECTIVES

14 fluid, liquid, fluidal, fluidic, liquiform, uncongealed, unclotted

15 flowing, fluent, fluxive, fluxible (Lit), fluxile (Lit), fluxional, fluxionary (Lit), watery, runny, juicy, sappy, moist, succulent, squashy

16 rheumy, weeping, pussy, purulent, suppurating, suppurative, suppurated, sanious, ichorous, phlegmy, humoral, serous, chylific, chylifactive, chylifactory, tearlike, lachrymal, lachrymatory

17 milky, lacteal, lacteous, lactic, lactescent, lactiferous

18 bloody, gory, bleeding, sanguineous, haemic, haemal, haemogenic, haemophilic

19 liquefied, dissolved, deliquescent, melted, molten, thawed, decoagulated, in solution, in suspension, liquescent, liquefacient, solvent

20 liquefying, liquefactive, colliquative, thawing, melting, fusing, dissolving, dissolutional, anticoagulant

21 liquefiable, soluble, meltable, fusible, thawable, dissolvable, dissoluble

VERBS

22 make fluid, liquefy, liquate, liquidize, fluidize, fluidify, liquesce, blend, emulsify

23 dissolve, solve, thin, solubilize, decoagulate, unclot, hold in solution, leach, lixiviate, percolate, decoct, infuse, resolve

24 melt, run, thaw, melt down, smelt, defrost, unfreeze, render, clarify, deliquesce, fuse, flux

25 flow, run, stream, pour, well up, gush, spout, vomit forth, spew out, bleed, flood, weep, seep, sweat, ooze

ADVERBS

26 fluidly, liquidly, fluently, runnily, juicily, moistly, succulently, purulently, weepily, tearfully, lacteally, sanguinely, sanguinarily, sweatily, oozily

432 Gas

If silicon had been a gas I should have been a major-general.
James Abbott McNeill.

NOUNS

1 gas, rare (*or* inert *or* noble) gas, air, atmosphere, atmospheric air, vapour, elastic fluid, ether, volatile

▶ *32 Chemistry; 434 Air*

2 exhalation, breath, exspiration, effluvium

3 miasma, mephitis, malaria (Lit), foetid air, rank air fume(s), reek, smoke, wisp (*or* puff *or* plume) of smoke, smog, poisonous gas, damp, firedamp, blackdamp, afterdamp, chokedamp, biogas

▶ *500 Smell*

4 water vapour, steam, cloud, mist, fog

▶ *31 Meteorology and Climatology; 433 Water*

5 belch, ructation, eructation, hiccup, flatulence, flatulency, flatuosity, flatus, wind, windiness, gas, burp (Inf), fart (Inf)

6 aerogastria, aerogenesis, aerodontalgia, aeroneurosis, aerophagia, gas gangrene

► *260 Ill Health*

7 gaseousness, gassiness, gaseity, gaseous state, fizziness, effervescence, fermentation, vaporousness, vaporosity, vapouriness, vapour, pressure (*or* tension)

8 volatility, vapourability, vapourizability, evaporability

► *415 Lightness*

9 aeriness, etherealism, etheriability

10 vaporization, evaporation, volatilization, gasification, aeration, etherification, aerification, sublimation, distillation, fractionation, atomization, exhalation, etherealization, steaming, smoking, fumigation

11 vaporizer, spray, aerosol, aerosol spray, CFC (chlorofluorocarbon), Freon™, propellant, atomizer, condenser, retort, still

12 aerostatics, aerodynamics, pneumatostatics, pneumatics, pneumodynamics

► *28 Physics*

13 gas balloon, air balloon, helium balloon, hydrogen balloon, aerostat, airship, bladder, air bladder, bicycle tube, inner tube

14 gasworks, gas plant, gasholder, gasometer, gasolier, gaslight, gaslamp

15 vaporimeter, manometer, pressure gauge, gasometer, gas meter, airometer, aerometer, spirometer, eudiometer, pneumatometer

ADJECTIVES

16 gaseous, gaslike, gasiform, gassy, gasified, in the gaseous state, vaporous, vapour-like, vapoury, vapourish

17 airy, aery, aerial, ethereal, atmospheric

18 miasmic, miasmal, miasmatic, mephitic, foetid, reeking, fumy, fuming, effluvial

19 smoky, smoking, smoggy, steamy, steaming, vaporing, cloudy, misty, foggy

20 flatulent, windy, gassy

21 gassy, fizzy, effervescent, bubbly, sparkling, carbonated, aerated

22 aerostatic, aerodynamic, pneumatic

23 volatile, volatilizable, vapourable, vaporific, vaporizable, vaporescent, evaporable, evaporative

24 oxygenous, oxygenic, ozonous, ozonic, ozone-friendly

VERBS

25 gasify, evaporate, vaporize, volatilize, atomize, sublimate, sublime, distil, fractionate, etherify

26 aerate, fumigate, aerify, etherize, carbonate, oxygenate, hydrogenate, atomize, spray, perfume, fluidize

27 give off, emit, exhale, reek, fume, send out, smoke, steam, let off (*or* blow off) steam, turn on the gas, combine with gas

ADVERBS

28 aerily, ethereally, atmospherically, vaporously

29 aerostatically, aerodynamically, pneumatically, pneumodynamically

30 smokily, steamily, mistily, effervescently, effervescingly

433 Water

Water, water, every where,
And all the boards did shrink;
Water, water, every where,
Nor any drop to drink. Samuel Taylor Coleridge.

Human beings were invented by water as a device for transporting itself from one place to another. Tom Robbins.

NOUNS

1 water, H_2O, *aqua* (L), *eau* (Fr), Adam's ale, Adam's wine, hydrol, fluid, liquid, moisture, heavy water (D_2O), distilled water, hard water, soft water, mineral water(s), limewater, rain(s), rainwater, running water, spring, fountain, spring water, well water, hydrothermal water, fresh water, sea water, salt water, brine, the briny (Inf), meltwater, ice, standing water

► *31 Meteorology and Climatology; 88 Lakes; 90 Rivers; 91 Seas; 429 Moisture; 431 Fluid*

2 drinking water, tap water, bottled water, spa water, mineral water, soda water, carbonated water, fizzy water

► *558 Drinking*

3 wateriness, wet, wetness, wettishness, damp, dampness, runniness, moistness, raininess, rainfall, dewiness, vapour, water vapour, steam, condensation, haze, mist, fog, cloud

► *432 Gas*

4 exudate, exudation, tears, weeping, sweat, perspiration, saliva, spittle, urine, urination, piss (Inf), pee (Inf), wee (Inf)

► *560 Excretion; 602 Sorrow; 603 Lamentation*

5 dilution, solution, adulteration, saturation, watering down

6 hydrate, hydration, hydrolysis, wetting agent, wetting-out agent

7 hydrotherapeutics, hydropathy, hydrotherapy, irrigation, water cure, taking the waters

► *394 Remedy*

8 watering, irrigation, wetting, hosing, hosing down, sprinkling, spraying, squirting, sparging, spargefaction, aspersion, aspergation, splashing, spattering, swashing, affusion

► *377 Dispersal*

9 soaking, soakage, soak, drenching, drench, sousing, souse, drowning, flooding, inundation, immersion, submersion, imbruement, ducking, saturation, permeation, percolation, leaching, lixiviation, dunking (Inf)

10 steeping, infusion, brewing, maceration, seething, impregnation, infiltration, injection, pulping

11 wash, washing, rinse, rinsing, laving, bath, bathing, dip, soap and water, splash, ablution, cleansing, balneation, bidet, shower, showering, shower bath, shower head, needle bath, Jacuzzi™, whirlpool bath, douche, syringe, fountain syringe, enema, clyster

► *256 Cleanness*

12 sprinkler, watering can, spray can, rose, nozzle, sparger, sparge, sprayer, speed sprayer, mist, concentrate sprayer, spray, aspergillum (*or* aspergill), sprinkling system, sprinkler head, aerosol, atomizer, vaporizer, water pistol (*or*

gun), squirt gun
▶ *438 Tool*
13 **irrigator**, well, oasis, conduit, hydrant, water hydrant, garden hose, hosepipe, tap, standpipe, water pipe, pump, fire engine, shadoof (*or* shaduf), Persian wheel, Archimedes' screw
▶ *43 Agriculture; 44 Horticulture*
14 **lavender water**, rose water, scent, perfume, eau de Cologne
▶ *502 Fragrance*
15 **holy water**, baptism, immersion, christening, hydromancy, religious rite
▶ *10 Ritual*
16 **water carrier**, water cart, watering cart, water jug, ewer, pitcher, jug, reservoir, dam, cistern, water tank
▶ *410 Container*
17 **water cycle**, hydrologic cycle, hydrosphere, hydrometeor, head, hydrostatic head, head of pressure
▶ *90 Rivers; 91 Seas*
18 **hydrography**, hydrology, hydrometry, hygrometry, hydraulics, hydrodynamics, hydromechanics, hydrokinetics, hydrostatics, hydroponics, aquiculture
▶ *28 Physics; 44 Horticulture*
19 **measuring instrument**, hygrometer, hair hygrometer, hygrograph, hydrograph, hygrodeik, hygroscope, hygrothermagraph, psychrometer, wet-and-dry bulb thermometer, sling psychrometer, humidor, hydrostat, rain gauge, udometer, pluviometer, Nilometer, weather house
20 **hydrologist**, hydrographer, water diviner
▶ *11 Occultism*

ADJECTIVES

21 **watery**, waterish, fluid, liquid, aqueous, aquatic, moist, hydrous, hydrated, hydraulic, hydrodynamic, hydrometric, hydrostatic
22 **diluted**, saturated, watered-down, thinned, adulterated, weak, wishy-washy (Inf)
▶ *153 Thinness*
23 **wet**, soaked, drenched, soaking wet, soaked to the skin, like a drowned rat, sodden, wringing, wringing wet, sopping, sopping wet, saturated, soused, waterlogged, watersoaked, streaming, dripping, dripping wet, awash, soggy, bathed, steeped
24 **flooded**, overflowed, awash, whelmed, inundated, swamped, engulfed, deluged, drowned, submerged, submersed, immersed, dipped, ducked, dunked, weltering
25 **seeping**, weeping, oozing, dribbling, dripping
26 **wetting**, watering, moistening, damping, humectant, irrigational, irriguous (Lit)
27 **cleansing**, hydrotherapeutic
28 **hygric**, hygrometric, hygroscopic, hygrophilous, hygrothermal

VERBS

29 **water**, moisten, sprinkle, irrigate, hydrate, wet, soak, drench, douse, souse, drown, drouk (Scot), immerse, submerse, imbrue, permeate, percolate, leach, lixiviate, flood, inundate, saturate, waterlog, deluge, swamp, submerge, pour on, flow on, duck, dunk, sluice, come down cats and dogs
30 **dilute**, water down, add water, thin, adulterate, cut, dissolve
31 **steep**, infuse, imbue, macerate, pickle, brine, impregnate, infiltrate, seethe, inject
32 **seep**, weep, bleed, ooze, percolate, dribble, drip, exude, perspire, sweat, salivate, spit, dribble, cry, weep, urinate, pass water, piss (Inf), pee (Inf), wee (Inf)
33 **sprinkle**, spray, sparge, asperge, mist, atomize, shower, scatter, splash, splatter, spatter, bespatter, clash, paddle, slop, slobber
34 **hose**, hose down, syringe, squirt, inject, douche, sponge, wash, rinse, lave (Lit), (take a) bath, bathe, (take a) shower, perform one's ablutions

ADVERBS

35 **wetly**, moistly, damply, fluidly (*or* fluidally), liquidly, weepily, runnily, oozily
36 **hydraulically**, hydrodynamically, hydrometrically, hydrostatically, hydroscopically

434 Air

Gentlemen know that fresh air should be kept in its proper place – out of doors – and that, God having given us indoors and out-of-doors, we should not attempt to do away with this distinction.
Rose Macaulay.

NOUNS

1 **air**, ether, atmosphere, oxygen, gas, thin air, rarity, airspace, gaseous medium (*or* environment *or* envelope), the sky, blue sky, the heavens, welkin (Lit), lift (Dial), ozone (Inf)
▶ *432 Gas*
2 **aerosphere**, ecosphere, biosphere, noosphere
3 **atmospheric layers**, troposphere, substratosphere, tropopause, stratosphere, strato-isothermal region, isothermal layer, ozone layer (*or* ozonosphere), ionosphere, exosphere, D region, Heaviside (*or* Heaviside-Kennelly *or* Kennelly-Heaviside) layer (*or* region), E region, Appleton layer, F region, Van Allen belt (*or* radiation belt), photosphere, chemosphere, lower atmosphere, upper atmosphere, outer atmosphere, stratum, layer, belt
▶ *30 Earth Science*
4 **air flow**, wind, breeze, blast, gust, air current, current of air, updraught, downdraught, crosscurrent, monsoon, headwind, tailwind, following wind, jetstream
▶ *31 Meteorology and Climatology; 304 Ascent; 305 Descent*
5 **open air**, fresh air, out-of-doors, exposure, the great outdoors, sea air, ozone (Inf)
6 **ventilation**, airing, fanning, aeration, aerage, cross-ventilation, refreshment, perflation, air conditioning, air cooling, refrigeration, oxygenation, oxygenization
▶ *494 Cold*
7 **ventilator**, aerator, fan, blower, air conditioner, AC (Aus inf), air filter, air cooler, ventilating system, air passage
8 **respiration**, breathing, inhalation, inspiration, exhalation, expiration, air flow, windpipe, trachea, bronchus, bronchiole, exchange of gases, respiratory organ, lung, alveoli, gills
9 **airiness**, lightness, weightlessness, buoyancy, ethereality
▶ *415 Lightness*

10 **air bubble**, froth, foam, fluff, sponge, lather, suds, spray, spume, spindrift, cushion of air, air pocket, soufflé, mousse, meringue, balloon, air balloon, air bladder
11 **aeration**, fermentation, leavening, raising agent, yeast, leaven, ferment

ADJECTIVES

12 **airy**, aery, aerial, aeriform, aeriferous, airlike, ethereal, insubstantial, light, lighter-than-air, weightless, exposed, roomy, rare, rarified, thin
13 **atmospheric**, stratospheric, tropospheric
14 **aerial**, buoyant, inflated, blown-up, flatulent, pneumatic
15 **breezy**, windy, blowy, fresh, gusty
16 **open-air**, outdoor, out-of-doors, alfresco
17 **ventilated**, well-ventilated, fresh, air-conditioned, fanned, cooled, air-cooled
18 **bubbly**, foamy, frothy, fizzy, effervescent, aerated, yeasty
19 **respiratory**, breathing, respiring, inhaling, exhaling, bronchial, pulmonary, pneumonic

VERBS

20 **aerate**, aerify, oxygenate, air, ventilate, air-condition, air-cool, expose, freshen, deodorize, clean, take an airing
21 **respire**, breathe, breathe in, inhale, inspire, breathe out, exhale, expire
22 **blow**, blast, gust, huff, puff, make a draught, fan
23 **whisk**, aerate, whip, beat
24 **bubble**, froth, foam, fizz, effervesce, sparkle, gurgle, ferment, simmer

ADVERBS

25 **airily**, lightly, frothily, effervescently, effervescingly, atmospherically, pneumatically
26 **out-of-doors**, outside, in the open, in the open air, alfresco, under the open sky, in the sun, abroad, *en plein air* (Fr)

435 Materials

The materials of city planning are: sky, space, trees, steel and cement; in that order and that hierarchy. Le Corbusier.

NOUNS

1 **materials**, raw materials, basic materials, resources, the essentials, the basics, means, elements, components, constituents, material, stuff, substance, matter, staple, stock, grain, grist, food, fodder, meat, fuel, oil, crude oil, petroleum, petrochemical, coal, anthracite, hard coal, bituminous coal, soft coal, gas, natural gas, ore, mineral, uranium, yellow cake, metal ore, metal, pig iron, ingot, clay, adobe, china clay, potter's clay, gypsum, soil, sand, glass, plastic, synthetic resin, polymers, thermoplastic, celluloid, melamine formaldehyde, Formica™, polyethylene, polythene, polypropylene, polystyrene, ABS, PVS (polyvinyl chloride), PTFE (polytetrafluoroethylene), fluorocarbon, Teflon™, acrylic, nylon, polyamide, thermoset, urea-formaldehyde, phenon formaldehyde, polyester, epoxy, polyurethane, latex, cellulose, fibreglass, carbon fibre, rope, yarn, filament, fibre, wool, cotton, silk, rayon, fabric, cloth, felt, textile, leather, hide, skin, rawhide, parchment, vellum, chamois, cowhide, sheephide, sheepskin, horsehide, goathide, goatskin, pighide, pigskin, doeskin, wood, timber, log, faggot, stick, rafter, board, beam, plank, planking, plywood, lath, stave
► *25 Cookery; 42 Fabrics and Dyeing; 95 Reality; 352 Means; 437 Fuel; 527 Transparency*
2 **building material**, building block, breeze block, brick, stone, marble, granite, ashlar, masonry, combined structure, bricks and mortar, lath and plaster, wattle and daub, roofing material, shingle, tile, slate, thatch, paving material, paving, paving stone, flag, flagstone, cobble, compo, composition, mortar, plaster, cement, Portland cement, concrete, reinforced concrete, ferroconcrete, prestressed concrete, hardcore, gravel, Tarmac™, asphalt, macadam, blacktop (US)
► *24 Ceramics; 319 Transport; 550 Covering*
3 **paper**, stationery, sheet, quire, ream, foolscap, imperial paper, A4 paper, writing paper, notepaper, typing paper, computer paper, wrapping paper, toilet paper, fibre paper, cotton paper, rag paper, rice paper, greaseproof paper, newsprint, cardboard, card, pasteboard, Bristol board, calendered paper, art paper, glossy paper, laminated paper, cartridge paper, India paper, Bible paper, tissue paper, tracing paper, carbon paper, crepe paper, wax paper, waterproof paper, Cellophane™, papier-mâché, pulp, imperial wood pulp, cellulose fibre
4 **board**, millboard, strawboard, fibreboard, plasterboard, chipboard, hardboard
► *17 Literature*

436 Provisions

The Chinese do not draw any distinction between food and medicine. Lin Yutang.

NOUNS

1 **provision**, supplying, providing, furnishing, equipping, logistics, fitting out, outfitting, purveying, purveyance, catering, catered affair, service, delivery, distribution, self-service, takeaway, procuring, pandering, feeding, entertainment, clothing, accommodation, bed and breakfast, bed and board, board and lodging, boarding house, boarding school, maintenance, support, assistance, lending, subsidy, subvention, equipment, stock, supply, food supply, water supply, constant supply, feed, pipeline, supply line, source, commissariat, provisioning, victualling, supplies, stores, reserves, rations, iron rations, K rations, food rations, food stamps (US), starvation rations, emergency rations, ration, helping, portion, share, reinforcement, replenishment, refill, topping-up, plenitude, grist to the mill, fuel to the flame, yield, produce, product, return, increase, gain, conservation, resource management, economy, budgeting, budget, cash flow, possible need, preparation, precaution, measure, step
► *25 Cookery; 136 Qualification; 232 Completeness; 243 Preparation; 316 Transfer; 356 Creation; 392 Help; 397 Command; 439 Store; 484 Plan; 680 Thrift; 764 Sharing; 765 Profit; 768 Giving*
2 **provisions**, food, provender, sustenance, foodstuffs, victuals, comestibles, eatables, drinkables, groceries, grub (Inf), nosh (Inf)
► *25 Cookery*

3 **provider**, supplier, donor, giver, creditor, lender, moneylender, bursar, purser, treasurer, waiter, waitress, steward, butler, commissary (US), quartermaster, storekeeper, victualler, sutler, provision merchant, ship chandler, drysalter, grocer, greengrocer, baker, poulterer, fishmonger, butcher, vintner, wine merchant, milkman, wholesaler, retailer, middleman, shopkeeper, wet nurse, feeder, procurer, panderer, pander, pimp, bawd

▶ *768 Giving; 771 Lending; 776 Trade; 780 Money; 796 Immorality*

4 **caterer**, private caterer, wedding caterer, purveyor, hotelier, hotelkeeper, hotel manager, restaurateur, head waiter, maître d'hôtel, innkeeper, host, publican, licensee, alewife, landlord, landlady, housekeeper, housewife, cook, chef, pastrycook, confectioner, mine host (Inf)

▶ *25 Cookery*

VERBS

5 **provision**, supply, provide, furnish, equip, purvey, cater, afford, offer, lend, contributes, give, endow, present, find, arm, man, staff, fit out, outfit, kit out (*or* up), fix up, prepare, make ready, get ready, maintain supply, keep supplied, yield, produce, bring in, bring in a supply, truck in (US), fly in, pump in, procure, pander, pimp, service, service an order, meet an order, meet a demand, sell, distribute, deliver, make deliveries, deliver the goods, hand-out, hand round, serve, serve up, dish up, victual, feed, cook for, clothe, accommodate, board, put up, maintain, keep, support, provide for, stock, keep a stock, budget, make provision, make due provision, provide for oneself, provision oneself, take on supplies, take in supplies, stock up, lay in a stock, store, stockpile, hoard, bunker, gather food, forage, fuel, coal, water, take on water, tap, draw, draw on, milk, extract, export, import, trade, dish out (Inf), do for (Inf), do for oneself (Inf)

▶ *243 Preparation; 356 Creation; 369 Extraction; 439 Store; 665 Carefulness; 768 Giving; 771 Lending; 776 Trade; 778 Sale*

6 **replenish**, resupply, reinforce, fill, refill, fill up, top up, restock, revictual, refuel, reload, make up, make good, refresh, revitalize

▶ *232 Completeness*

ADJECTIVES

7 **provisioning**, supplying, providing, furnishing, equipping, catering, commissarial, self-service, takeaway, sufficing, all-sufficing, sufficient, available, available on request, in stock, on tap, on the menu

▶ *217 Sufficiency; 768 Giving*

8 **provisional**, supplied, provided, furnished, equipped, all found, all-in, well-appointed, catered, offered, given, staffed, prepared, ready, stocked, victualled

▶ *243 Preparation ; 768 Giving*

437 Fuel

Her own mother lived the latter years of her life in the horrible suspicion that electricity was dripping invisibly all over the house. James Thurber.

NOUNS

1 **fuel**, fossil fuel, gas, oil, solid fuel, coal, wood, charcoal, peat, peat bog, peat moss, electricity, nuclear power, renewable energy source, nonrenewable energy source

2 **lighter**, firelighter, tinder, tinderbox, kindling, wood, firewood, log, Yule log, faggot, charcoal, turf, dung, brushwood, spunk, punk, touchpaper, taper, match, spill, vesta, lucifer, safety match, matchbox, wick, spark, scintilla, flint, burning glass, torch, firebrand, brand (Lit), cigarette lighter, cap, percussion cap, ignition system, sparking plug, detonator, fuse, time-fuse, explosive, high explosive, firebomb *or* incendiary bomb, fire ship

▶ *493 Heat*

3 **gas**, coal, gas, natural gas, town gas, producer gas, North Sea gas, Calor gas, propane, butane, methane, lighter fuel, gasfield, gasworks, gasholder, gasometer, gas tank, gas main, gas pipe, gas meter, gas poker, gas burner, gas turbine, rocket fuel, liquid oxygen, lox

▶ *319 Transport; 330 Propulsion; 431 Fluid; 432 Gas*

4 **electricity**, hydroelectricity, generating station, power station, generator, turbine, power pack, magneto, dynamo, electricity supply, electric current, national grid, pylon, underground cable, power cable, electric lead, flex, power point, socket, electric switch, light switch, electricity meter, fuel cell, electric battery, battery, electrification, electrocution, electric chair, electric motor, power cut, blackout, brownout (US)

5 **coal**, bituminous coal, brown coal, cannel coal, lignite, coke, anthracite, briquette (*or* briquet), coal dust, slack, coalbed, Coal Measures, coalfield, coalmine, pit, coalface, coal cellar, coal bunker, coal hole (Inf), coal box, coal bin, coal scuttle, black diamonds

▶ *30 Earth Science*

6 **oil**, petroleum, mineral oil, crude oil, crude, petrol, gasoline (*or* gas) (US), unleaded petrol, diesel oil (*or* fuel), derv, paraffin, coal oil (US), aviation fuel, methylated spirits (*or* spirit), naphtha, gas oil, oil reserves, oilfield, Alaskan oil, oil well, oil rig, offshore rig, oil platform, North Sea oil, oil refinery, refining, fractionation, cracking, oil pipeline, oil tanker, oil drum, oilcan, petrol can, octane number (*or* rating), petrol station, filling station, petrol pump, oil shale, oil slick, fuel injection, petrodollar diesel (Inf), meths (Inf), nodding donkey (Inf)

▶ *268 Slipperiness; 412 Mixture*

7 **nuclear power**, nuclear energy, nuclear generating station, Windscale, Sellafield, nuclear reactor, thermal reactor, gas-cooled reactor, magnox reactor, advanced gas-cooled reactor (AGR), water-cooled reactor, pressurized-water reactor (PWR), boiling-water reactor (BWR), fast-breeder reactor, nuclear fuel, core, fuel rod, uranium, enriched uranium, plutonium, nuclear fission, nuclear fusion, nuclear waste, nuclear accident, Chernobyl, Three Mile Island

8 **renewable energy**, solar power, solar energy, solar battery, photovoltaic cell, wind power, windmill, wind pump, wind generator, wind turbine, geothermal energy, water mill, water turbine, wave power, tidal power, tidal energy, biomass

9 **power-worker**, stoker, charcoal-burner, coal merchant, coal miner, gas-fitter, gasman, boilermaker, meter-reader, electrician, oil-worker, oilman, lumberjack, woodcutter, peat cutter, firebomber

► 576 Work

ADJECTIVES

10 **powered**, charged, combustible, inflammable, flammable, explosive, incendiary, raw, refined, carbonaceous, carboniferous, coaly, bituminous, lignitic, coal-fired, gaseous, gas-fired, fuel-efficient, electric, hydroelectric, electrical, electrifying, woody, ligneous, wood-burning, oil-fired, petrol-driven, high-octane, unleaded, thermal, nuclear, thermonuclear, nuclear-powered, wind-driven, wind-powered, geothermal, water-driven, steam-operated, solar, solar-powered, renewable, gas-guzzling (US inf)

VERBS

11 **fuel**, stoke, fill up, refuel, light, light the touchpaper, strike, put a match to, kindle, fire up, fire, burn gas, detonate, set off, touch off, trigger (off), explode, power, charge, recharge, electrify, plug in, switch on, dig coal, mine coal, burn coal, strike oil, pump oil, refine oil, pump petrol, have a meltdown, heat with solar power, step on the gas (Inf)

ADVERBS

12 **powerfully**, combustibly, explosively, electrically, hydroelectrically, thermally, at full power, at full steam

438 Tool

Give us the tools, and we will finish the job. Winston Churchill.

NOUNS

1 **tool**, implement, instrument, utensil, precision tool, machine tool, hand tool, garden tool, apparatus, appliance, machine, device, mechanical device, mechanical aid, contraption, gadget, contrivance, screwdriver, hammer, ram, drill, electric drill, perforator, punch, wrench, torque wrench, spanner, adjustable spanner, pipe wrench, Stillson™, pliers, pincers, tweezers, nippers, chisel, sander, plane, wedge, edged tool, axe, knife, Stanley knife™, saw, jigsaw, fretsaw, chain saw, rope, cable, peg, nail, tack, screw, nut, bolt, nuts and bolts, hanger, hook, support, prop, leverage, lever, jemmy, crowbar, handspike, jack, pivot, grip, lug, handle, helve, haft, shaft, tiller, helm, rudder, pulley, sheave, wheel, switch, stopcock, cock gunlock, trigger, pedal, pole, weapon, arm, arms, gizmo (US inf), doodah (Inf), thingumabob (Inf), thingummy (Inf), doohickey (US inf), whatsit (Inf), whatnot (Inf)

► *372 Separation; 373 Connection; 413 Support; 484 Plan; 587 Weapon*

2 **toolroom**, tool shed, toolhouse (US), tool-kit, bag of tricks

3 **garden tool**, spade, shovel, trowel, fork, pitchfork, pickaxe, sickle, scythe, billhook, rake, hoe, cultivator, mattock, clough, dibber, riddle, roller, edging iron (*or* knife), pruning saw, hedge clipper (*or* trimmer), lopper, secateurs, shears, Rotavator™, lawn mower, motor mower, Strimmer™

4 **prehistoric tool**, pebble hand-axe, flint chisel, bronze axe, iron sickle

5 **machine**, mechanical device, machinery, mechanism, works, clockwork, wheelwork, wheels within wheels, nuts and bolts, part, component, spring, mainspring, hairspring, cam, gear, gears, gearing, spur gear, spur wheel, bevel gear, clutch, synchromesh, automatic transmission, motor, engine, internal-combustion engine, lean-burn engine, rotary engine, Wankel engine, diesel engine, steam engine, turbine, generator, dynamo, dynamotor, servomechanism, servomotor, robot, automaton, computer

► *40 Computers; 61 Motor Racing; 334 Power; 405 Component*

6 **mechanics**, engineering, mechanical engineering, civil engineering, chemical engineering, electrical engineering, electronics, hydrodynamics, hydromechanics, hydraulics, cybernetics, automatic control, automation, computerization, robotics, artificial intelligence (AI), mechanical power, mechanical advantage, technics, technology, advanced technology, high technology, high tech, low technology, low tech, terotechnology

► *38 Engineering; 39 Electronics; 40 Computers*

7 **equipment**, tools, utensils, furniture, appointments, fittings, fixtures, fixture, adjunct, upholstery, furnishing, trappings, accoutrement, dress, outfit, kit, gear, tackle, harness, paraphernalia, chattels, impedimenta, property, wares, stock-in-trade, merchandise

► *440 Possessions; 551 Dress*

8 **machinist**, operator, operative, driver, minder, machine-minder, engineer, technician, mechanician, mechanist, mechanic, fitter, tool-user, craftsman, artisan, manual worker, skilled worker

ADJECTIVES

9 **mechanical**, mechanized, mechanistic, motorized, technological, hydraulic, electronic, powered, power-driven, labour-saving, automatic, robotic, automated, computerized, computer-literate, machine-minded, tool-using, instrumental

VERBS

10 **use tools**, hammer, screw, ram, drill, punch, wrench, chisel, chop, saw, nail, tack, hook, lever, crowbar, shovel, rake, hoe, riddle, mow, mechanize

ADVERBS

11 **instrumentally**, mechanically, automatically, hydraulically, electronically, cybernetically, technologically

439 Store

Old Mother Hubbard
Went to the cupboard,
To fetch her poor dog a bone;
But when she got there
The cupboard was bare
And so the poor dog had none. Nursery Rhyme.

NOUNS

1 **store**, accumulation, hoard, mass, heap, load, stack, pile, stockpile, build-up, backlog, food mountain, butter mountain, wine lake, reservoir, bundle, bag(ful), packet, bucket(ful), amount, quantity, crop, harvest, vintage, mow, haystack, haycock, hayrick, stock, stock-in-trade, merchandise, property, assets, capital, holding, invest-

ment, fund, reserve fund, reserves, emergency reserves, something in reserve, something in hand, unexpended balance, savings, savings account, nest egg, deposit, treasure, buried treasure, cache, hiding place, bottom drawer, trousseau, provision, pool, kitty, common fund, appeal fund, charity, community chest

▶ *203 Quantity; 376 Gathering; 436 Provisions; 736 Concealment; 765 Profit; 779 Market*

2 **resource**, deposits, natural resource, natural deposit, quarry, mine, gold mine, coalmine, coalfield, coalbed, colliery, working, shaft, coalface, coal deposit, seam, stringer, lode, pipe, pipe vein, rich vein, vein, mineral deposit, gasfield, oilfield, well, oil well, gusher, fountain, fount, spring, source, bonanza (US), strike, discovery

▶ *344 Cause; 449 Discovery*

3 **supply**, constant supply, stream, tap, pipeline, artesian well, milch cow, the goose that lays the golden eggs, cornucopia, abundance, plenty, repertoire, range, collection, depleted supply, broken pipeline, scarcity

▶ *217 Sufficiency; 218 Insufficiency*

4 **storage**, stowage, gathering, garnering, accumulation, conservation, preservation, silage, ensilage, bottling, safe-deposit, protection, stabling, warehousing, space, room, accommodation, storage space, shelf space, shelf room, cupboard space, cupboard room, box room, loft, attic, hold, bunker, basement, cellar, wine cellar, storeship, supply base, storehouse, storeroom, stockroom, warehouse, shed, stable, garage, depository, depot, entrepot, dock, wharf, magazine, arsenal, armoury, gunroom, treasure house, treasury, exchequer, strongroom, vault, gold vault, silver vault, coffer, moneybox, moneybag, till, money drawer, strongbox, safe, night safe, bank, blood bank, sperm bank, data bank, memory, store of memories, hive, honeycomb, granary, garner, barn, silo, water tower, reservoir, cistern, tank, petrol tank, gasholder, gasometer, battery, storage battery, dry battery, wet battery, petrol station, filling station, petrol pump, dump, tip, rubbish dump, refuse dump, trash dump (US), landfill, sump, drain, cesspool, septic tank, sewage works (*or* farm), pantry, larder, buttery, still room, chamber, cupboard, cabinet, shelf, chest of drawers, drawer, refrigerator, icebox (US), deepfreeze, freezer, portmanteau, suitcase, holdall, chest, trunk, packing case, box, container, receptacle, holder, quiver, fridge (Inf), fridge-freezer (Inf)

▶ *40 Computers; 141 Space; 252 Safety; 258 Dirtiness; 359 Preservation; 376 Gathering; 410 Container; 462 Memory; 565 Habitat*

5 **collection**, accumulation, set, complete set, archives, inventory, record, file, folder, bundle, portfolio, stamp collection, coin collection, record collection, tape collection, video collection, book collection, archive, repository, museum, art museum, gallery, art gallery, library, yearbook, diary, almanac, farmer's almanac, encyclopedia, dictionary, thesaurus, zoo, menagerie, aquarium, waxworks, Madame Tussaud's™, exhibition, exhibit, repertory, repertoire, bag of tricks (Inf)

▶ *17 Literature; 284 Past Time; 376 Gathering; 738 Display; 744 Record*

VERBS

6 **store**, amass, accumulate, heap, stack, pile up, load, stow, pack, bundle, stow away, pack away, put away, put in mothballs, mothball, lay up, fold up, roll up, store in the garage, store in the barn, stable, warehouse, garner, gather, bring together, harvest, reap, mow, pick, glean, stock, stock up, stock up one's cupboards, stock up one's larder, stock up one's freezer, lay in, bulk-buy, panic buy, board, stockpile, build up, build up one's stocks, increase, augment, store fuel, store coal, bunker, provision, provide, supply, take on, take in, fill, fill up, fuel, fuel up, top up, refill, refuel, replenish, save, keep, retain, hang on to, hold, put by, keep by, file, bottle, pickle, conserve, preserve, leave, set aside, put aside, lay away, lay by, keep back, keep in hand, reserve, fund, bank, deposit, invest, treasure, hive, bury, hide, conceal, secrete, cache, squirrel away, stash away, salt away, husband, economize, save up, make a nest egg, prepare for a rainy day, equip oneself, prepare oneself, put in the the bottom drawer, pool, put in the kitty, share, go together, communalize, sock away (US inf)

▶ *43 Agriculture; 213 Increase; 243 Preparation; 359 Preservation; 360 Retention; 376 Gathering; 406 Contents; 436 Provisions; 680 Thrift; 736 Concealment*

ADJECTIVES

7 **stored**, amassed, accumulated, heaped, abundant, plentiful, stacked, piled up, loaded, stowed (away), packed (away), in store, in storage, in mothballs, laid up, hoarded, in deposit, in hand, held, saved, put aside, set aside, put by, kept by, in reserve, unused, unspent, unexpended, banked, funded, invested, available, in stock, spare, supernumerary, preserved, conserved, bottled, pickled

▶ *350 Nonuse; 359 Preservation ; 376 Gathering*

440 Possessions

In a consumer society there are inevitably two kinds of slaves: the prisoners of addiction and the prisoners of envy. Ivan Illich.

The spread of personal ownership is in harmony with the deepest instincts of the British people. Few changes have done more to create one nation. Nigel Lawson.

NOUNS

1 **property**, possession, realty, real property, real estate (US), freehold, leasehold, estate, legal estate, *praedium* (L), title, right, copyright, patent, receipt, claim, rent-roll, domain, building, public property, common property, church property, benefice, living, holding, smallholding, homestead, farm, cottage, bungalow, house, ranch, hacienda, chalet, villa, manor, mansion, flat, apartment, tenement, penthouse, plantation, castle, land, lands, acres, broad acres, acreage, tract, grounds, lot, plot, parcel, allotment, landed estate, landed property, common land, common, crown lands, political possession, territory, dependency, dominion

▶ *7 Religion; 12 Government and Politics; 396 Authority; 763 Possession; 764 Sharing*

2 **legal terms**, personalty, domain, demesne, chose, chose in possession, chose in action, messuage, tenement, tenure, hereditament, fee simple, fee tail, mortmain,

dead hand, immovables, movables, jointure, entail, remainder, reversion, limitation

3 **historic property terms**, toft, allodium, feu, frankalmoign, fee, fief, feud, fiefdom, feudality, villeinage, villeinhold, socage, free socage, burgage, copyhold, seigneury, appanage

4 **possessions**, personal property, effects, personal effects, estate and effects, belongings, gear, stuff, things, material things, what one can call one's own, what one has to one's name, one's all, chattels (Lit), goods and chattels, worldly goods, trappings, temporalities, paraphernalia, accoutrements, appurtenances, duffel (*or* duffle) (US), accessories, appendages, impedimenta, luggage, baggage, bag and baggage, furniture, fixtures and fittings, bits and pieces

► *406 Contents*

5 **personal estate**, one's worth, what one is worth, net worth, circumstances, state, assessed valuation, assets, resources, collateral, valuables, one's money, one's fortune, wealth, inheritance, legacy, heirloom, funds, income, capital, revenue, means, substance, securities, stocks and shares, stocks and bonds, portfolio, tangible assets, tangibles, intangible assets, intangibles, fixed assets, frozen assets, liquid assets, net assets, current assets, stock, stock-in-trade, merchandise, wares, goods, contents, plant

► *352 Means; 768 Giving; 781 Wealth*

6 **marriage settlement**, dowry, dower, bride price, dot, portion, marriage portion, allotment, allowance, pin money, maintenance, alimony, aliment (Scot), palimony (US)

► *570 Marriage*

7 **property man** (*or* **woman**), dealer in real property, estate agent, real-estate agent (US), realtor (US), speculator, investor, stockholder, shareholder, developer, property owner, man (*or* woman) of property, man (*or* lady) of the house, lord (*or* lady) of the manor, freeholder, owner, landowner, holder, householder, leaseholder, lessee, tenant, sitting tenant

ADJECTIVES

8 **propertied**, proprietary, possessing, possessed, freehold, leasehold, copyhold, movable, immovable, real, allotted, territorial, landed, praedial, manorial, seignorial, feudal, feudatory, feodal, allodial, patrimonial, hereditary, heritable, testamentary, limited, assessed, collateral, secured, tangible, intangible, fixed, frozen, liquid, net, endowed, dowered, established, copyrighted, patented

VERBS

9 **own property**, possess, buy property, have an estate, occupy a freehold, rule a territory, own personal effects, have belongings, have to one's name, own assets, have resources, put up collateral, inherit, have substance, own stocks and shares (*or* bonds), have a portfolio, put in possession, endow, dower, possess with, bless with, give, devise, bequeath, grant, allot, assign

ADVERBS

10 **proprietarily**, hereditarily, heritably, with a dowry, patrimonially, collaterally, territorially

441 Waste

VERBS

1 **waste**, squander, fritter (away), spend, spend money like water, overspend, run through, lavish, splurge, throw away, pour down the drain, dissipate, scatter, disperse, throw to the four winds, slop, spill, overwork, overcrop, overfish, overgraze, impoverish, milk dry, misuse, abuse, put to the wrong use, misapply, misspend, cast pearls before swine, not use, make no use of, waste effort, labour in vain, consume, eat, devour, gobble up, swallow, make a dent in, make inroads on, wade into, expend, lay out, take, use up, exhaust, deplete, drain, suck dry, empty, wear, wear away, wear out, erode, gnaw, damage, impair, pollute, be wasted, go to waste, suffer loss, waste away, emaciate, wither, wilt, shrivel, decay, decline, decrease, diminish, leak, ebb away, flow out, run low, dry up, melt, melt away, liquefy, evaporate, vaporize, run out, give out, burn, burn down, burn out, burn away, gut, deteriorate, run to seed, run to waste, go to ruin, go down the drain, go to pot, weaken, fade, wane, blow (Inf), blue (Inf), piss away (Inf)

► *214 Decrease; 218 Insufficiency; 238 Uselessness; 245 Deterioration; 315 Exit; 337 Weakness; 349 Use; 350 Nonuse; 351 Misuse; 431 Fluid; 432 Gas; 681 Extravagance; 787 Expenditure*

2 **lay waste**, devastate, ravage, ruin, destroy, demolish, sabotage, vandalize, loot, plunder, sack, raze, despoil, pillage, kill, murder, wipe out, obliterate, nuke (Inf), trash (Inf)

► *357 Destruction; 382 Killing; 774 Stealing*

NOUNS

3 **waste**, wastage, wastefulness, squandering, frittering (away), extravagance, overspending, economy, thriftlessness, improvidence, useless expenditure, unnecessary expenditure, prodigality, lavishness, splurge, spree, spending, outlay, expense, expenditure, dissipation, dispersion, spillage, overwork, misuse, abuse, misapplication, consumption, inroads, using up, exhaustion, depletion, wear and tear, erosion, damage, wasting away, emaciation, atrophy, decay, decline, decrease, drainage, leakage, ebb, outflow, loss, melting, liquefaction, evaporation, vaporization, deterioration, (built-in) obsolescence, overproduction, superfluity

► *214 Decrease; 219 Excess; 245 Deterioration; 315 Exit; 337 Weakness; 351 Misuse; 431 Fluid; 432 Gas; 681 Extravagance; 787 Expenditure*

4 **destruction**, destructiveness, wilful destruction, vandalism, arson, sabotage, disaster area, scene of destruction, havoc, devastation, wreck, ruin, looting, pillage

► *357 Destruction; 774 Stealing*

5 **waste product**, litter, refuse, rubbish, trash (US), garbage, leftovers, scraps

► *215 Remainder; 236 Worthlessness; 238 Uselessness; 258 Dirtiness*

6 **waster**, big spender, last of the big spenders, squanderer, wastrel, spendthrift, prodigal

► *681 Extravagance; 787 Expenditure*

7 **destroyer**, scourge, bane, polluter, vandal, arsonist, killer, murderer, Angel of Death

► *357 Destruction; 382 Killing*

ADJECTIVES

8 **wasteful**, extravagant, unnecessary, uneconomic, uneconomical, improvident, thriftless, prodigal, lavish, spendthrift, penny wise and pound foolish, time-consuming, energy-consuming

► *681 Extravagance; 787 Expenditure*

9 **waste**, superfluous, unwanted, unused, leftover, useless, worthless, throwaway

► *219 Excess; 236 Worthlessness; 238 Uselessness*

ADVERBS

10 **wastefully**, extravagantly, unnecessarily, uneconomically, improvidently, ruinously, thriftlessly, immoderately, prodigally, profligately, lavishly, superfluously, uselessly

11 **destructively**, damagingly, devastatingly, abusively

The Mind

442 Intellect

We should take care not to make the intellect our god; it has, of course, powerful muscles, but no personality. Albert Einstein.

The highest intellects, like the tops of mountains, are the first to catch and to reflect the dawn. Lord Macaulay.

NOUNS

1 **mind**, mentality, rationality, ratiocination, conception, intellectualism, intellectuality, consciousness, awareness, cognition, perception, perceptiveness, apperception, percipience
▶ *36 Psychology and Psychiatry; 443 Thought; 460 Sanity; 462 Memory*

2 **ways of thinking**, logic, formal reasoning, deduction, induction, reasoning, insight, acumen, inspiration, instinct, rationale, ratiocination, intuition, sixth sense, extrasensory perception (ESP), quantum leap (Inf)
▶ *4 Philosophy; 11 Occultism; 444 Reason; 445 Intuition*

3 **intelligence**, intellect, understanding, comprehension, sense, judgment, mentality, mind, brain, brains, wit, wits, reason, nous, IQ (intelligence quotient)

4 **cleverness**, genius, flair, brains, wit, wisdom, sagacity, sapience, erudition, knowledgeableness, brightness, incisiveness, shrewdness, astuteness, aptitude, brilliance, alertness, sharpness, acuity, acuteness, quickness, quickwittedness, keen-wittedness, canniness, subtlety, braininess (Inf)
▶ *455 Knowledge; 458 Wisdom*

5 **common sense**, sense, sensibleness, sound judgment, discernment, clear thinking, horse sense, native wit, mother wit, savvy, nous (Inf), street smarts (US inf)

6 **thoughtfulness**, judiciousness, consideration, reflection, reflectiveness, circumspection, profundity, profoundness, depth

7 **brain**, head, cerebrum, grey matter, seat of thought, upper storey (Inf), noddle (Inf), noodle (US inf), noggin (Inf)

8 **intellectual person**, intellectual, scholar, academic, academician, thinker, genius, wise man, sage, savant, master, guru, elder statesman, oracle, pundit, polymath, littérateur, illuminati, bookman, bookworm, bibliophile, bluestocking, highbrow, egghead (Inf), intellect (Inf), boffin (Inf), brainbox (Inf), know-all (Inf), know-it-all (US inf), clever clogs (Inf), swot (Inf), smart aleck (Inf), smarty pants (Inf), smartarse (Inf)

ADJECTIVES

9 **mental**, intellectual, rational, reasoning, thinking, conceptual, conceptive, cerebral, cephalic, noetic, phrenic, psychological, logical, deductive, instinctive, intuitive

10 **intelligent**, understanding, clever, learned, erudite, knowledgeable, wise, sage, sagacious, bright, smart, shrewd, astute, brilliant, alert, sharp, acute, quick-witted, keen-witted, gifted, brainy (Inf)

11 **thoughtful**, judicious, reflective, circumspect, sapient, profound, sensible, reasonable, sound, deep

VERBS

12 **think**, reason, rationalize, ratiocinate, conceptualize, cognize, perceive, apperceive, ideate, deduce, induce, intuit

13 **be intelligent**, use one's head (Inf), have one's head screwed on (Inf), have one's wits about one (Inf), have a head on one's shoulders (Inf), know what's what (Inf)

ADVERBS

14 **mentally**, intellectually, cerebrally, conceptually, instinctively, intuitively

15 **intelligently**, sensibly, reasonably, rationally, logically, knowledgeably, wisely, cleverly, sagaciously, profoundly, reflectively, judiciously, thoughtfully, shrewdly, astutely, alertly, acutely, smartly

443 Thought

It is a good morning exercise for a research scientist to discard a pet hypothesis every day before breakfast. It keeps him young. Konrad Lorenz.

NOUNS

1 **thought**, thinking, cognition, reasoning, reason, cogitation, mental process, thought process, mental activity, cerebration, deduction, ratiocination, rumination, workings of the mind

2 **intellectual exercise**, deep thinking, hard thinking, profound thought, headwork, brainwork, ideation
▶ *446 Idea*

3 **thoughtfulness**, concentration, contemplation, reflection, consideration, speculation, retrospection, pensiveness, reverie, brown study, introspection, musing, day-

dreaming, innermost thought, meditation, meditativeness

▶ *4 Philosophy*

4 **deliberation**, pondering, abstract thought, abstractedness, profundity

5 **creative thought**, lateral thinking, inventiveness, originality, inventive power, flow of ideas, inspiration, train of thoughts, stream of consciousness, thinking cap (Inf)

▶ *442 Intellect; 458 Wisdom; 462 Memory; 471 Attention; 477 Imagination*

6 **idea**, thought, notion, concept, conception, belief, premise, theory, hypothesis, conjecture, fancy, supposition, surmise, intuition, inkling, conclusion, principle, precept, point of view, attitude, novel idea, crazy idea, good idea, quantum leap, flash of inspiration, brainwave (Inf), brainstorm (US inf), good wheeze (Inf)

▶ *446 Idea; 447 Topic; 450 Belief; 476 Supposition; 701 Argument; 705 Question*

7 **thinker**, logical thinker, rational person, wise man, philosopher, professor, academic, intellectual, highbrow, genius, scholar, student, ideologist, dreamer, egghead (Inf), walking encyclopedia (Inf), brainbox (Inf)

▶ *455 Knowledge*

ADJECTIVES

8 **thoughtful**, thinking, reasoning, mental, intellectual, cognitive, cerebral, ruminative, philosophical, considerate

9 **concentrating**, contemplative, pensive, reflective, absorbed, lost in thought

10 **speculative**, introspective, meditative, profound, deliberative, pondered, pondering, musing, inventive, dreamy, notional, conceptual, fanciful, theoretical, conjectural, suppositional, in a brown study, in a world of one's own, miles away (Inf)

11 **reasoning**, intelligent, rational, logical, intellectual, philosophical, professorial, scholarly, ideological, highbrow

VERBS

12 **think**, reason, cogitate, ruminate, ponder, consider, meditate, exercise one's intellect, cerebrate, ratiocinate, think deeply, think hard, think profoundly, use one's head, use one's brain, rack one's brains, ideate, speculate, imagine

13 **concentrate**, contemplate, mull over, reflect, reflect upon, study, apply one's mind

14 **have second thoughts**, think over, rethink, reconsider, think again, sleep on it

15 **think about**, work out, weigh up, take stock of, deliberate, ponder, use lateral thinking, get one's brain into gear (Inf)

16 **have an idea**, conceive of, premise, theorize, conjecture, hypothesize, deduce, infer, speculate, suppose, surmise, conclude, hold a point of view, defend one's attitude, originate, invent, have a good idea, have a brainwave (Inf)

17 **philosophize**, intellectualize, internalize, introspect, show genius

ADVERBS

18 **thoughtfully**, reflectively, philosophically, contemplatively, on reconsideration, on second thoughts, rationally, logically, intuitively, introspectively, creatively, inventively

444 Reason

Reason is itself a matter of faith. It is an act of faith to assert that our thoughts have any relation to reality at all. G. K. Chesterton.

NOUNS

1 **reason**, mind, intellect, power of reason, rationality, intelligence, understanding, perception, judgment, wisdom, sense, sanity, saneness, power of conception

▶ *442 Intellect; 443 Thought; 455 Knowledge; 460 Sanity; 466 Discrimination*

2 **reasoning**, rationalizing, rationalism, rationality, rationalization, logical process, logical thought, logic, ratiocination, plain reason, generalization, inference, deductive reasoning, deduction, inductive reasoning, induction, a priori reasoning, a posteriori reasoning, syllogism, analysis, discursive reasoning

▶ *27 Mathematics; 445 Intuition*

3 **debate**, polemics, dialectics, dialecticism, apologetics, argumentation, argument, formal argument, legal argument, dissent, dispute, disputation, litigation

▶ *751 Disagreement*

4 **explanation**, cause, motive, grounds, premise, pretext, theory, basis, assumption, justification, defence, speculation, hypothesis, valid point, excuse

▶ *344 Cause; 453 Uncertainty; 476 Supposition; 745 Maxim*

5 **reasoner**, thinker, intellectual, academic, philosopher, logician, rationalist, apologist, dialectician, syllogist

6 **arguer**, debater, litigator, disputant, plaintiff, defendant, jurist, polemicist (*or* polemist), casuist, proponent, wrangler, barrack-room lawyer, jailhouse lawyer (US), Philadelphia lawyer (US), ambulance chaser (US)

▶ *701 Argument*

ADJECTIVES

7 **reasoning**, reasonable, rational, thinking, intellectual, intelligent, understanding, perceptive, knowledgeable, judgmental, wise, sensible, sane

8 **rational**, rationalistic, logical, ratiocinative, analytic(al), inferential, deductive, inductive, a priori, a posteriori

9 **argumentative**, dissenting, disputing, litigious, polemic (*or* polemical), dialectical

10 **causal**, theoretical, assumptive, valid, explanatory, justified, defended, defensive, excused

VERBS

11 **reason**, rationalize, analyse, think, think logically, logicalize, understand, perceive, judge, ratiocinate, generalize, synthesize, infer, deduce, induce

12 **be reasonable**, show wisdom, make sense, hold water (Inf)

13 **debate**, argue, dissent, dispute, litigate, enter into argument, exchange opinions

14 **premise**, theorize, postulate, philosophize, assume, explain, justify, defend, excuse

ADVERBS

15 **reasonably**, rationally, logically, sensibly, sanely, within bounds, as far as possible

445 Intuition

A moment's insight is sometimes worth a life's experience. Oliver Wendell Holmes.

NOUNS

1 intuition, intuitiveness, intuitive reasoning, feminine intuition, feeling, insight, perception, inspiration

2 precognition, a priori knowledge, sixth sense, second sight, clairvoyance, divination, telepathy, extrasensory perception (ESP), presentiment

▶ *442 Intellect; 478 Improvisation; 590 Feelings; 475 Prediction; 11 Occultism*

3 insight, foreboding, impression, feeling, impulse, hunch, flash

4 instinct, innate reaction, proclivity, subconscious, unconscious, automatic reaction, Pavlovian response, knee-jerk (Inf), gut reaction (Inf)

5 intuitive person, feeling person, medium, clairvoyant, seer, prophet, diviner, sibyl, carer

ADJECTIVES

6 intuitive, insightful, perceptive, sensitive, sensing, inspired

7 precognitive, a priori, unmediated, second-sighted, clairvoyant, divinatory, telepathic, extrasensory, presentient

8 instinctive, instinctual, automatic, spontaneous, reflex, innate, Pavlovian, knee-jerk (Inf)

VERBS

9 be intuitive, intuit, feel, have a feeling about, go on one's feelings, perceive, divine, work on a hunch, follow one's hunch, feel it in one's bones (*or* water), have a funny feeling about, just know

10 be instinctive, react automatically, give a knee-jerk reaction

ADVERBS

11 intuitively, by intuition, instinctively, by (*or* on) instinct, automatically, spontaneously

446 Idea

When the torrent sweeps a man against a boulder, you must expect him to scream, and you need not be surprised if the scream is sometimes a theory. Robert Louis Stevenson.

NOUNS

1 idea, notion, abstraction, thought, thinking, concept, conception, observation, perception, understanding, awareness, apprehension, comprehension, reflection, assumption, presumption, reaction, estimation, feeling, sentiment, memory, construct, mental picture, mental image, mental object, imago, ideatum, noumenon, essence, Platonic Idea, the Absolute Idea

▶ *4 Philosophy; 7 Religion; 8 Divinity; 99 Essence; 101 Unworldliness; 442 Intellect; 443 Thought; 445 Intuition; 462 Memory; 476 Supposition; 591 Sensitivity*

2 theory, idea, hypothesis, suggestion, conjecture, speculation, supposition, suspicion, indication, fancy, clue, hint, guess, feeling, intuition, hunch (Inf)

▶ *4 Philosophy; 476 Supposition*

3 plan, intention, scheme, project, proposal, invention, idea, brainwave, bright idea, brainstorm, brainchild, cunning plan, wizard wheeze (Inf)

▶ *126 Originality; 482 Intention; 484 Plan*

4 purpose, aim, design, function, goal, object, objective, target, end, point, reason, significance, meaning

▶ *131 End; 444 Reason; 482 Intention; 483 Motive; 484 Plan; 635 Will; 694 Meaning*

5 ideology, opinion, view, viewpoint, stand, stance, position, philosophy, ideas, beliefs, principles, creed, credo, teachings, tenets, ideals, morals, standards, prejudices

▶ *4 Philosophy; 7 Religion; 450 Belief*

6 ideal, model, example, exemplar, paragon, paradigm, standard, pattern, quintessence, epitome, prototype, archetype, vision, dream, Utopia, fantasy, fancy, wishful thinking, castle in the air (*or* in Spain)

▶ *230 Perfection; 477 Imagination; 610 Hope*

7 idealism, idealization, optimism, visionariness, Utopianism, romanticism, daydreaming, wishful thinking, impracticality, ideality, idealness

▶ *4 Philosophy; 230 Perfection; 610 Hope*

8 imagination, imaginativeness, inventiveness, originality, creativity, ingenuity, inspiration, perception, visualization, conceptualization

▶ *126 Originality; 477 Imagination; 591 Sensitivity; 619 Wonder*

9 person of ideas, thinker, philosopher, theorizer, theoretician, idealist, ideologue, ideologist, dreamer, optimist, Utopian, visionary, creator, mentor, romantic, creative artist, inventor, boffin (Inf), egghead (Inf), back-room boy (Inf), ideas person (Inf)

▶ *4 Philosophy; 6 Education; 11 Occultism; 17 Literature; 18 Music; 19 Painting and Sculpture; 21 Drama; 442 Intellect; 458 Wisdom; 518 Vision*

ADJECTIVES

10 theoretical, notional, abstract, putative, conceptual, perceptual, philosophical, hypothetical, conjectural, speculative, suppositional, propositional, suggestive, indicative, suspected, assumed, presumed, estimated, guesstimated (*or* guestimated) (Inf)

11 ideational, mental, cerebral, intellectual, in the mind, in the mind's eye, in one's head, imagined, visualized, conceived, conceptualized, inspired, aware, reflective, imaginative, inventive, creative, original, ingenious, fanciful

12 purposive, functional, goal-directed, teleological, aiming, functioning, targeting, intentional, proposed, aimed, targeted, schematic, designed, planned, reasoned, well-reasoned, reasonable, significant, meaningful

▶ *344 Cause*

13 ideal, model, exemplary, paradigmatic, epitomical, quintessential, prototypical, archetypical, visionary, fantastic, idealistic, idealized, optimistic, Utopian, romantic, sentimental, dreamy, impractical, ideological

▶ *4 Philosophy; 230 Perfection; 610 Hope*

VERBS

14 have an idea, come to mind, enter one's head, cross one's mind, suggest itself, dawn upon, realize, perceive, remember, come to one, occur to one, hit one, strike one, be struck by, deduce, understand, apprehend, intuit,

see, grasp, grab one (Inf), get (Inf), suss (out) (Inf), pop into one's head (Inf)
▶ *706 Answer*

15 imagine, ideate, think, reflect, deliberate, feel, conceive, visualize, conceptualize, picture, envision, envisage, formulate, create, invent, originate, think up, conjure up, dream up, dream, fancy, fantasize, idealize, romanticize, daydream, pipe dream, see through rose-coloured (*or* tinted) glasses, build castles in the air
▶ *442 Intellect; 443 Thought; 477 Imagination*

16 inspire, inspirit, fire one's imagination, animate, exhilarate, enliven

17 theorize, hypothesize, conjecture, suggest, suspect, guess, reckon, estimate, suppose, opine, believe, assume, presume, have a hunch (Inf), guesstimate (*or* guestimate) (Inf)
▶ *4 Philosophy; 443 Thought*

18 aim, plan, plot, scheme, design, propose, intend, target, point to, head for, get ideas, set one's sights on, aspire, aim high, overreach, overstep oneself, have thoughts above one's station, go all out for (Inf)
▶ *329 Overstepping; 482 Intention; 483 Motive; 484 Plan; 633 Pursuit; 635 Will*

19 epitomize, exemplify, set an example, model, pattern, indicate, represent, signify, mean

ADVERBS

20 theoretically, notionally, in theory, abstractly, abstractedly, putatively, philosophically, thoughtfully, conceptually, hypothetically, conjecturally, reflectively, mentally, in the mind, in the mind's eye, in one's head, upstairs (Inf)

21 purposively, intentionally, schematically, indicatively, functionally, significantly, meaningfully, reasonably, to the point, with an aim in mind, with a view to, on purpose, deliberately

22 imaginatively, originally, inventively, creatively, ingeniously, perceptively, inspirationally, optimistically, romantically, sentimentally, impractically, dreamily, fantastically, idealistically, through rose-coloured (*or* -tinted) glasses

23 ideally, perfectly, under the best circumstances, in a perfect world, at best, all things being equal

24 ideologically, standardly, archetypally, paradigmatically, so it seems, as one sees it, to one's way of thinking, in one's opinion

INTERJECTIONS

25 got it!, eureka!, I see!, that's it!, aha!, that's the idea!

447 Topic

NOUNS

1 topic, subject, contents, text, subject matter, matter, theme, plot, angle, interest, concern, point, motif, leitmotiv, programme, statement, message, argument, thesis, theorem, proposition, supposition, heart of the matter, main point, keynote, essence, idea, gist, drift, pith, meat, basis, foundation, rubric
▶ *99 Essence; 176 Angle; 406 Contents; 446 Idea; 476 Supposition; 694 Meaning; 722 Essay; 723 Summary*

2 issue, point at issue, concern, focus, question, topic, problem, bone of contention, moot point, living issue, matter for discussion, case, point, item, motion, agenda, business on hand, any other business
▶ *701 Argument; 705 Question; 746 Negotiation; 751 Disagreement*

3 matter of interest, topic for discussion, events, news, happenings, rumour, gossip, story, affair, business, proceedings, goings-on (Inf)
▶ *693 Information; 731 Talkativeness; 741 News*

4 sphere, domain, business, concern, area, branch, course, discipline, topic, field, field of inquiry, subject of investigation
▶ *143 Situation; 705 Question*

5 educational topic, subject, field of study, course, project, class project, individual project, art project, special topic, nature topic, science topic, local-history topic, tract, treatise, lecture course
▶ *6 Education; 722 Essay*

ADJECTIVES

6 topical, in the news, current, present, immediate, contemporary, up-to-date, up-to-the-minute, hot off the press, straight from the horse's mouth, timely, happening (Inf)
▶ *741 News*

7 focused, subjective, angled, pointed, founded, based, concerned with, dealing with, supposed, proposed, programmed, thematic, central, basic
▶ *99 Essence*

8 problematic, moot, mooted, undecided, questioned, challenged, challenging, curious, interesting, thought-provoking, debatable, worthy of discussion, on the agenda

9 local, familiar, domestic, nearby, local-interest, gossipy, telltale
▶ *147 Closeness*

VERBS

10 focus on, concentrate on, centre on, point to, be concerned with, contain, include, state, argue, propose, suppose
▶ *99 Essence; 127 Inclusion*

11 raise the point, raise the issue, point out, make a point, put on the agenda, put forward (a suggestion), deal with, discuss, debate, contend, question, inquire, study, get to the heart of the matter, do a project on (Inf)
▶ *4 Philosophy; 701 Argument; 746 Negotiation; 751 Disagreement*

ADVERBS

12 topically, locally, domestically, currently, in the news, as it happens, up to date, up to the minute, in the mind, on the brain, in one's thoughts
▶ *142 Location; 170 Surroundings; 275 Time*

13 problematically, curiously, interestingly, challengingly, questionably, debatably, in question, under consideration, under discussion, afoot, on the agenda, on the table, before the house, before the committee
▶ *746 Negotiation*

14 thematically, essentially, basically, centrally, supposedly, pointedly, to the point, in essence, in short
▶ *99 Essence; 723 Summary*

448 Experiment

I'm really an experimentalist. I used to say 'I think with my hands.' Dorothy Hodgkin.

NOUNS

1 experiment, investigation, probe, analysis, diagnosis, assay, essay, test, acid test, blood test, trial, inquiry (*or* enquiry), probation, sounding out, sounder, sound, feeler, check, tentation, venture, bid, endeavour, effort, gambit, risk, try, trial and error, hit and miss, cut and try (Inf), shot (Inf), go (Inf), fling (Inf), crack (Inf), whack (Inf), stab (Inf)

▶ *35 Medicine; 346 Operation; 353 Attempt; 449 Discovery; 464 Judgment; 640 Perseverance; 716 Evidence*

2 rehearsal, practice, audition, hearing, model, mock-up, rough draft, sketch, trial, trial run, single-blind trial, double-blind trial, tryout, dummy run, practice run, pilot run, dry run, road test, flight test, test flight, trial balloon, sample, control

▶ *125 Imitation*

3 experimentation, experimentalism, empiricism, pragmatism, instrumentalism, testing, trying, research, research and development (R and D), vivisection, investigation, examination, exploration, verification, determination, ascertainment, speculation, conjecture, guesswork, estimation, rule of thumb

▶ *4 Philosophy; 26 Measurement; 345 Effect; 454 Verification; 475 Prediction; 619 Wonder; 703 Demonstration; 705 Question; 716 Evidence; 743 Identification*

4 originality, experimentation, inventiveness, creativity, innovation, novelty, newness, unfamiliarity, strangeness, avant-garde, modernism, daring, recklessness, risk, nothing ventured, nothing gained

▶ *17 Literature; 18 Music; 19 Painting and Sculpture; 21 Drama; 126 Originality; 295 Newness; 446 Idea; 477 Imagination*

5 experimenter, experimentalist, empiricist, investigator, scientist, researcher, research scientist, research worker, vivisectionist, R and D worker, analyst, assayer, quester, striver, inquirer (*or* enquirer), trier, tester, test-driver, test pilot, speculator, inventor, innovator, creator, creative artist

▶ *19 Painting and Sculpture; 28 Physics; 29 Astronomy; 32 Chemistry; 37 Pharmacology*

6 place of experimentation, laboratory, lab (Inf), research establishment, field station, proving ground, think tank, workshop, studio

▶ *6 Education; 28 Physics; 32 Chemistry*

7 experimentee, testee, patient, subject, guinea pig, laboratory animal, lab rat (Inf)

▶ *37 Pharmacology; 70 Animals*

ADJECTIVES

8 experimental, empirical, pragmatic, scientific, analytic, instrumental, probational, probationary, exploratory, investigative, trying, experimenting, inquiring, testing, researching, verifying, verifiable, determining, determinable, speculative, conjectural, tentative, provisional, mock, rough, trial, test, dummy, practice, model, simulated

LABORATORY APPARATUS

alembic	dropper	pipette
aludel	Erlenmeyer flask	platinum wire
aspirator	evaporating dish	pneumatic trough
balance	filter funnel	reagent bottle
beaker	filter paper	receiver
Beckmann thermometer	filter pump	reflux condenser
beehive shelf	flask	round–bottomed flask
blowpipe	fluted funnel	separating funnel
boiling tube	fume cupboard	sintered–glass crucible
Bückner funnel	gas jar	spatula
Bunsen burner	graduated flask	stand
burette	hotplate	still
capillary tube	Kipp's apparatus	stirrer
centrifuge	Leibig condenser	thermometer
clamp	measuring cylinder	trough
condenser	melting–point apparatus	U–tube
conical flask	mortar	vacuum still
crucible	muttle furnace	volumetric flask
deflagrating spoon	oven	watch glass
dessicator	pestle	

▶ *125 Imitation*

9 original, experimental, inventive, creative, innovative, novel, modern, new, unfamiliar, strange, avant-garde, modernist, venturesome, daring, enterprising, reckless, risky, chancy

▶ *295 Newness; 477 Imagination*

10 tested, experimented upon, tried, researched, determined, verified, checked, essayed, ventured, estimated, risked, chanced

VERBS

11 experiment, experimentalize, conduct an experiment, test, try, essay, assay, try out, put on trial, put to the test (*or* proof), research, sound out, test the water, explore, analyse, feel the pulse, test the depth, investigate, probe, sample, examine, inquire (*or* enquire), verify, substantiate, confirm, check, check out, determine, prove, ascertain, speculate, prospect, conjecture, guess, estimate

▶ *26 Measurement; 705 Question*

12 rehearse, practise, audition, mock up, sketch, try out, road-test, flight-test, simulate, model

▶ *125 Imitation*

13 invent, create, innovate, dare, risk, chance, take chances, gamble, try one's luck, try one's hand, try one's strength, venture, attempt, endeavour, try, undertake, take the bull by the horns, have a go (Inf), have a fling (Inf), give it a go (Inf), have a stab at (Inf), take a crack at (Inf)

▶ *107 Chance; 126 Originality; 353 Attempt; 477 Imagination*

ADVERBS

14 experimentally, empirically, scientifically, analytically, investigatively, provisionally, conjecturally, speculatively, on spec, by rule of thumb, by trial and error, by hit and miss, by guess and God, on trial, on probation, under examination, on the slab (Inf)

15 inventively, experimentally, creatively, innovatively, daringly, recklessly, riskily, strangely, for the first time, as never before

449 Discovery

Eureka! (I have found it!) Archimedes.

VERBS

1 discover, find, locate, place, come across, come upon, happen upon, stumble on, hit upon, encounter, meet with, meet, see, spy, espy, spot, descry, perceive, sight, glimpse, catch a glimpse of, set eyes on, notice, observe, watch, recognize, identify

▶ *142 Location; 518 Vision; 743 Identification*

2 detect, ferret out, worm out, track down, run down, run to earth, hunt, seek, smell out, sniff out, get wind of, get warm, find a clue, set a trap for, ensnare, catch, catch red-handed, catch in the act, acquire, unearth, disinter, dig up, uncover, bring to light, expose, lay bare, unveil, lift the veil on, unmask, disclose, reveal, divulge, betray, show up, show in one's true colours, spill the beans (Inf)

▶ *633 Pursuit; 705 Question; 739 Disclosure; 765 Profit*

3 find out, find out about, learn, ascertain, determine, realize, understand, see the light, catch on (Inf), get it (Inf)

▶ *455 Knowledge; 693 Information; 695 Intelligibility*

4 invent, design, devise, contrive, hit upon an idea, originate, create, pioneer, herald, be in the vanguard, lead the way to, explore, rediscover

▶ *130 Beginning; 356 Creation; 448 Experiment*

5 be discovered, be unmasked, come to light, appear, show up, turn up

▶ *525 Appearance*

NOUNS

6 discovery, finding, location, accidental discovery, serendipity, encounter, meeting, spotting, perception, sight, sighting, glimpse, observation, recognition, identification

▶ *142 Location; 518 Vision; 743 Identification*

7 detection, ferreting out, tracking down, search, hunt, hunting, pursuit, catching, catch, acquisition, excavation, archaeology (*or* archeology), uncovering, exposure, unveiling, unmasking, disclosure, leak, manifestation, revelation, divulgence, betrayal, eye-opener (Inf), showdown (Inf)

▶ *633 Pursuit; 705 Question; 739 Disclosure*

8 finding out, learning, ascertaining, realization, understanding, enlightenment, illumination

▶ *455 Knowledge; 693 Information; 695 Intelligibility*

9 invention, designing, design, device, idea, contrivance, inspiration, origination, creation, pioneering, exploration, experiment, rediscovery

▶ *130 Beginning; 356 Creation; 448 Experiment*

10 find, discovery, lucky find, *trouvaille* (Fr), treasure-trove, strike

11 detector, metal detector, divining rod, lie detector, sonar, radar, probe, sensor, scanner

12 discoverer, finder, spotter, scout, spy, observer, dowser, water diviner, prospector, archaeologist (*or* archeologist), detective, private detective, sniffer dog, inventor, designer, author, founder, parent, producer, agent, motivator, originator, forerunner, herald, pioneer, pathfinder, explorer, traveller, mole (Inf), private eye (Inf), gumshoe (US inf)

▶ *130 Beginning; 356 Creation; 518 Vision*

ADJECTIVES

13 discovering, finding, on the trail of, on the right track, warm, revelatory, revealing, inventive, pioneering, exploratory, experimental

▶ *448 Experiment; 739 Disclosure*

14 discovered, found, located, seen, spotted, unearthed, uncovered, exposed, unmasked, revealed

▶ *142 Location; 518 Vision*

15 discoverable, findable, recognizable, identifiable, perceptible, detectable, heuristic

ADVERBS

16 originally, experimentally, inventively, at first sight, at a glance, apparently, identifiably, recognizably, obviously, manifestly, revealingly

450 Belief

Push on, and faith will catch up with you. Jean D'Alembert.

NOUNS

1 belief, opinion, view, point of view, angle, viewpoint, stand, standpoint, position, attitude, stance, impression, feeling, sentiment, intuition, thought, idea, notion, premise (*or* premiss), principle, proposition, theory, hypothesis, judgment, conjecture, supposition, surmise, speculation, popular belief, climate of opinion, persuasion, conviction, certainty, truth

▶ *443 Thought; 445 Intuition; 446 Idea; 452 Certainty; 464 Judgment; 476 Supposition; 590 Feelings; 698 Truth*

2 religious belief, religion, faith, religious feeling, persuasion, creed, credo, dogma, canon, principle, tenet, *aberglaube* (Ger), articles of faith, declaration of faith, statement of belief, catechism, manifesto, doctrine, school, cult, philosophy, ideology, traditional belief, superstition, old wives' tale, folklore, obi, obeah, pishogue, voodoo, myalisma, ism (Inf)

▶ *4 Philosophy; 7 Religion; 745 Maxim*

3 believing, faith, trust, confidence, assurance, reliance, dependence, credence, credit, credulity, credulousness, gullibility, blind faith, suspension of disbelief, expectation, hope, acceptance, pledge, word of honour

▶ *610 Hope; 799 Honour*

4 believability, credibility, plausibility, trustworthiness, reliability

5 believer, true believer, conformer, conformist, traditionalist, theist, deist, pilgrim, sanyasin, devotee, hajji, communicant, worshipper, church member, churchgoer, practising Christian, man (*or* woman) of prayer, nun, monk, contemplative, mystic, convert, born-again Christian, Jesus freak (Inf)

▶ *7 Religion*

6 trusting person, innocent, ingenue, lamb to the slaughter (Inf), sucker (Inf)

VERBS

7 believe, have faith in, put one's faith in, have no doubts about, credit, accept, be led to believe, take someone's word for, accept on faith, take on trust, trust, confide in, rely on, depend on, count on, bank on, swear by, take for granted, rest assured, know, maintain, hold, declare, affirm, profess, confess, fall for (Inf), buy (Inf), swallow (Inf), swallow (*or* fall for) hook, line, and sinker (Inf)

▶ *455 Knowledge; 707 Affirmation*

8 **be of the opinion**, opine, presume, assume, surmise, guess, suppose, think, suspect, understand, be under the impression, get it into one's head, have in mind, imagine, fancy, regard, consider, deem, esteem

▶ *443 Thought; 476 Supposition*

9 **make someone believe**, assure, convince, persuade, influence, convert, win over, evangelize, proselytize, propagandize, spread the word, indoctrinate, brainwash, deceive, dupe, take in (Inf)

▶ *395 Influence; 700 Deception*

10 **be believed**, gain acceptance, go down well, find credence

ADJECTIVES

11 **believing**, assured, confident, convinced, sure, certain, positive, opinionated, dogmatic, trusting, trustful, unhesitating, unquestioning, undoubting, unsuspecting, credulous, gullible, faithful, conformist, orthodox, converted, born-again

▶ *7 Religion; 452 Certainty; 646 Naivety*

12 **gullible**, credulous, innocent, naive, green, wet behind the ears (Inf)

13 **believable**, credible, creditable, tenable, plausible, reasonable, realistic, possible, probable, likely, convincing, persuasive, impressive, commanding, reliable, trustworthy

▶ *102 Possibility; 104 Probability*

14 **believed**, undisputed, unquestioned, authoritative, accredited, doctrinal, creedal, received, accepted, maintained, putative, supposed, alleged, hypothetical

ADVERBS

15 **believingly**, confidently, positively, dogmatically, trustfully, unhesitatingly, unsuspectingly, faithfully, credulously, gullibly, like a lamb to the slaughter (Inf)

16 **believably**, credibly, plausibly, reasonably, convincingly, persuasively, supposedly, allegedly, hypothetically

451 Disbelief

NOUNS

1 **disbelief**, doubt, doubtfulness, dubiousness, dubiety, uncertainty, hesitancy, hesitation, distrust, mistrust, misgiving, qualm, scruple, reservation, scepticism, scorn, suspiciousness, suspicion, disagreement, dissent, demur

▶ *453 Uncertainty; 621 Derision; 751 Disagreement*

2 **unbelievability**, incredibility, impossibility, improbability, implausibility, untenability

▶ *103 Impossibility; 105 Improbability*

3 **incredulity**, amazement, bewilderment, bafflement, perplexity, nonbelief, discredit, rejection, denial

▶ *630 Surprise; 708 Negation*

4 **unbelief**, infidelity, paganism, heathenism, misbelief, heresy, agnosticism, atheism, irreligion, loss of faith

▶ *7 Religion*

5 **disbeliever**, unbeliever, nonbeliever, heretic, pagan, heathen, infidel, agnostic, atheist, doubter, doubting Thomas, apostate, dissenter, dissident, nonconformist, sceptic, mocker, detractor, irreligionist, secularist, rationalist, free-thinker, materialist, Marxist, conscientious objector

▶ *7 Religion*

ADJECTIVES

6 **disbelieving**, unbelieving, incredulous, sceptical, scornful, doubtful, doubting, dubious, uncertain, hesitant, distrustful, mistrustful, suspicious, dissenting, heretical, atheistic, agnostic, pagan, heathen, faithless, unfaithful

▶ *7 Religion; 453 Uncertainty; 621 Derision*

7 **disbelieved**, unbelieved, discredited, exploded, unbelievable, incredible, beyond belief, impossible, improbable, implausible, untenable, hard to believe, far-fetched, unreliable, suspect, suspected, suspicious, so-called, self-styled, questionable, disputable

▶ *103 Impossibility; 105 Improbability; 272 Ridiculousness*

VERBS

8 **disbelieve**, discredit, refuse to believe, dissent, disagree, scorn, ridicule, mock, scoff at, deny, negate, challenge, dispute, question, doubt, have doubts about, hesitate, waver, half-believe, have reservations, distrust, mistrust, suspect, smell a rat, take with a pinch (*or* grain) of salt, apostatize, lapse

▶ *621 Derision; 705 Question; 708 Negation*

9 **cause disbelief**, cast doubt, call into question, discredit, raise suspicions, amaze, stagger

▶ *630 Surprise; 705 Question*

ADVERBS

10 **disbelievingly**, unbelievingly, incredulously, sceptically, doubtfully, dubiously, uncertainly, hesitantly, distrustfully, mistrustfully, suspiciously

11 **unbelievably**, incredibly, implausibly, unreliably, questionably, disputably

452 Certainty

The trouble with the world is that the stupid are cocksure and the intelligent full of doubt. Bertrand Russell.

ADJECTIVES

1 **certain**, known, factual, actual, historical, real, true, veracious, definite, sure, secure, absolute, given, verifiable, demonstrable, well-grounded, well-founded, proved, documented, certified, ascertained, demonstrated, established, tried and tested, safe, self-evident, unmistakable, unmistaken, ostensible, obvious, necessary, realistic, accurate, authoritative

▶ *95 Reality; 273 Accuracy; 396 Authority; 448 Experiment; 454 Verification; 455 Knowledge; 520 Visibility; 703 Demonstration; 725 Clarity; 745 Maxim; 801 Right*

2 **convinced**, certain, sure, positive, believing, accepting, trusting, unquestioning, undoubting, unswerving, unhesitating, undeviating, assured, satisfied, persuaded, confident, self-assured, self-confident, opinionated, cocksure, assertive, overconfident, doctrinaire, dogmatic, orthodox, narrow-minded, obstinate, stubborn, bigoted, biased, partisan, fanatical

▶ *7 Religion; 450 Belief; 466 Discrimination; 641 Obstinacy*

3 **decided**, settled, fixed, established, open-and-shut, undisputed, unrefuted, irrefutable, undeniable, uncon-

testable, unchallengeable, incontrovertible, indubitable, unimpeachable, unambiguous, unequivocal
▶ *716 Evidence*
4 **guaranteed**, assured, insured, warranted, pledged, promised
▶ *756 Promise*
5 **inevitable**, destined, predestined, determined, predetermined, fixed, set, fated, fateful, unstoppable, ineluctable, necessary, inescapable, unavoidable, inevasible, unpreventable, relentless, inflexible, inexorable, unyielding, directed, headed for
▶ *106 Predetermination*
6 **infallible**, reliable, dependable, trustworthy, predictable, regular, stable, solid, secure, unshakable, unwavering, unchanging, undeviating, steady, steadfast, firm, sound, staunch, faithful, loyal, stoical
▶ *225 Permanence; 228 Stability; 253 Security; 298 Regularity*
7 **particular**, specific, specified, definite, determined, stipulated, indicated, named, fixed, pinned down, distinct, singular, single, individual
▶ *197 One; 685 Moderation; 743 Identification*
8 **unspecified**, indeterminate, undetermined, indefinite, unnamed, unmentioned, several, few, many
▶ *203 Quantity; 206 Few; 207 Plurality; 453 Uncertainty*

NOUNS

9 **certainty**, surety, knowledge, factuality, reality, actuality, historicity, truth, trueness, verity, veracity, absoluteness, authoritativeness, indubitability, indisputability, definiteness, validity, accuracy, evidence, proof, obviousness, necessity
▶ *3 History; 93 Existence; 95 Reality; 185 Bulge; 273 Accuracy; 396 Authority; 448 Experiment; 455 Knowledge; 520 Visibility; 698 Truth; 716 Evidence*
10 **conviction**, certainty, certainness, certitude, belief, acceptance, credence, trust, faith, assurance, assuredness, sureness, surety, positiveness, confidence, self-assurance, cocksureness, self-confidence, assertiveness, overconfidence, dogmatism, positivism, orthodoxy, narrow-mindedness, obstinacy, stubbornness, bigotry, bias, partisanship, fanaticism, fideism
▶ *7 Religion; 450 Belief; 466 Discrimination; 641 Obstinacy*
11 **opinionist**, convinced person, believer, overconfident person, show-off, exhibitionist, positivist, doctrinaire, dogmatist, bigot, zealot, fanatic, partisan, stick-in-the-mud (Inf), old fogy (Inf)
▶ *7 Religion; 450 Belief; 641 Obstinacy*
12 **something certain**, fact, foregone conclusion, open-and-shut case, winner, safe bet, dead certainty, dead cert (Inf), cinch (Inf), sure thing (Inf)
▶ *95 Reality; 104 Probability; 698 Truth*
13 **confirmation**, assurance, verification, affirmation, affirmativeness, demonstration, proof, ascertainment, establishment, evidence, grounds, facts, signs
▶ *454 Verification; 703 Demonstration; 707 Affirmation; 716 Evidence; 742 Sign*
14 **guarantee**, assurance, insurance, warrant, warranty, pledge, promise
▶ *669 Approval; 756 Promise*
15 **guarantor**, insurer, warrantor, pledger, promiser
16 **inevitability**, inevitableness, certainty, fate, destiny, fatefulness, predestination, determination, predetermination, ineluctability, necessity, unavoidability, inescapableness, inevasibleness, unpreventability, irrevocability, relentlessness, inexorability, force majeure, *vis major* (L), act of God
▶ *106 Predetermination; 131 End; 334 Power*
17 **infallibility**, reliability, dependability, trustworthiness, predictability, regularity, stability, solidity, security, steadiness, steadfastness, firmness, soundness, staunchness, fidelity, loyalty, stoicism
▶ *4 Philosophy; 228 Stability; 253 Security; 298 Regularity; 475 Prediction*
18 **particularity**, particularization, specification, specificness, definiteness, determination, stipulation, indication, fixing, pinning down, distinctness, singularity, the specific, the particular, the case in point, quantity, amount, number, measure
▶ *166 Limit; 197 One; 436 Provisions*
19 **indeterminacy**, inexactness, imprecision, generality, vagueness
▶ *453 Uncertainty*

VERBS

20 **be certain**, know, know for sure, feel sure, have no doubt, believe, be convinced, accept, credit, rely on, depend on, have faith in, assert oneself, lay down the law, pontificate, stick to one's guns, dogmatize, dig in one's heels
21 **make certain**, make sure, ensure, confirm, verify, affirm, demonstrate, prove, ascertain, establish, determine, find out, settle, fix, pin down, clear up, check, decide, convince, evince, ground, guarantee, warrant, pledge, promise, authenticate, certify, endorse, substantiate, secure, stabilize, steady, solidify
22 **specify**, particularize, define, determine, stipulate, indicate, measure, quantify

ADVERBS

23 **certainly**, surely, really, truly, actually, absolutely, positively, firmly, definitely, undoubtedly, indubitably, unquestionably, without question, without a shadow of doubt
24 **with certainty**, confidently, assuredly, assertively, dogmatically, obstinately, stubbornly
25 **inevitably**, certainly, ineluctably, unavoidably, inescapably, irrevocably, relentlessly, inexorably, surely, fatefully, in the end

INTERJECTIONS

26 **certainly**!, naturally!, definitely!, of course!, by all means!, be my guest!, go ahead!, help yourself!

453 Uncertainty

ADJECTIVES

1 **uncertain**, unsure, unknown, doubtful, dubious, speculative, conjectural, hypothetical, provisional, disputable, contestable, controversial, controvertible, moot, questionable, suspicious, distrustful, mistrustful, unbelieving, sceptical, agnostic, open-minded
▶ *7 Religion; 451 Disbelief; 456 Ignorance; 701 Argument; 705 Question*
2 **irresolute**, indecisive, vacillating, wavering, hesitant,

hesitating, hanging (*or* holding) back, faltering, undecided, unsettled, ambivalent, unresolved, unanswered
▶ *326 Oscillation; 479 Equivocation; 639 Vacillation*
3 **confused**, bewildered, disconcerted, worried, perplexed, nonplussed, confounded, baffled, puzzled, discomposed, in a quandary, at a loss for words, embarrassed, shy, timid, bewildering, disconcerting, worrying, perplexing, baffling, puzzling, difficult, enigmatic, problematic, cryptic
▶ *264 Difficulty; 328 Disturbance; 378 Obstruction; 696 Unintelligibility; 705 Question*
4 **indemonstrable**, unverifiable, unprovable, unconfirmable, unlikely, improbable, unpredictable
▶ *105 Improbability; 802 Wrong*
5 **uncertified**, undocumented, unchecked, uncorroborated, unverified, unauthenticated, unsigned, unratified, unascertained, unofficial, unproved, untried, untested, speculative, experimental, apocryphal
▶ *448 Experiment*
6 **indeterminate**, indefinite, vague, unclear, undefined, borderline, ambiguous, equivocal, indistinct, faint, hazy, foggy, misty, fuzzy, obscure, inaccurate, inexact, imprecise, loose, lax, broad, general, amorphous, incoherent
▶ *138 Generality; 161 Shapelessness; 266 Obscurity; 270 Vagueness; 408 Disorder; 479 Equivocation; 524 Dimness; 528 Opaqueness; 702 Sophistry*
7 **unreliable**, fallible, undependable, untrustworthy, treacherous, dishonest, perfidious, insecure, transient, infirm, insubstantial, unsound, unstable, unsteady, inconsistent, shifty, shaky, precarious, slippery, risky, hazardous, dangerous, perilous, eccentric, erratic, irregular, unpredictable
▶ *247 Failure; 254 Danger; 278 Transience; 299 Irregularity; 337 Weakness; 700 Deception*
8 **capricious**, whimsical, fickle, irresponsible, skittish, volatile, mercurial, fitful, changeable, mutable, fluid, fluctuating, wavering, flexible, mobile, aleatoric, inconstant, variable, random, chancy, haphazard
▶ *107 Chance; 133 Discontinuity; 224 Change; 227 Changeableness; 300 Motion; 325 Deviation; 422 Elasticity; 541 Variegation; 642 Frivolity*

NOUNS

9 **uncertainty**, incertitude, unsureness, uncertainness, contestability, controvertibility, doubtfulness, dubiousness, disputability, questionableness, open mind, open verdict, question mark, guesswork, guess, anyone's guess, wild guess, enigma
▶ *451 Disbelief; 701 Argument; 705 Question*
10 **suspicion**, suspiciousness, conjecture, doubt, distrust, mistrust, caution, disbelief, incredulity, denial, rejection, scepticism, agnosticism, atheism
▶ *4 Philosophy; 7 Religion; 470 Rejection; 704 Refutation*
11 **irresoluteness**, irresolution, indecision, indecisiveness, unsettledness, vacillation, wavering, hesitation, ambivalence, faltering, cleft stick, horns of a dilemma, borderline case
▶ *639 Vacillation*
12 **confusion**, bewilderment, disconcertion, disconcertedness, confoundment, perplexity, bafflement, puzzlement, predicament, quandary, embarrassment, discomposure, shyness, timidity
▶ *264 Difficulty; 705 Question*
13 **indemonstrability**, unverifiability, unprovability, unconfirmability, unlikelihood, unlikeliness, improbability
▶ *103 Impossibility; 105 Improbability; 708 Negation*
14 **indeterminacy**, indefiniteness, vagueness, unclearness, ambiguity, equivocalness, indistinctness, neither one thing nor the other, faintness, haziness, fogginess, mistiness, fuzziness, obscurity, inaccuracy, inexactness, imprecision, looseness, laxity, broadness, generality, amorphousness, incoherence
▶ *138 Generality; 161 Shapelessness*
15 **unreliability**, fallibility, untrustworthiness, treacherousness, insecurity, transience, infirmity, insubstantiality, unsoundness, instability, unstableness, unsteadiness, inconsistency, shiftiness, shakiness, precariousness, eccentricity, irregularity, unpredictability, risk, hazard, adventure, gamble
▶ *105 Improbability; 247 Failure; 254 Danger; 299 Irregularity; 337 Weakness*
16 **capriciousness**, whimsicality, fickleness, volatility, volatileness, fitfulness, changeableness, mutability, fluidity, fluctuation, wavering, inconstancy, flexibility, mobility, variability, randomness, chance
▶ *107 Chance; 227 Changeableness; 300 Motion; 326 Oscillation; 642 Frivolity*
17 **uncertain person**, agnostic, doubting Thomas, doubter, worrier, questioner, sceptic, erratic
▶ *705 Question*

VERBS

18 **be uncertain**, have one's doubts, doubt, question, moot, distrust, mistrust, disbelieve, have a suspicion about, suspect, wait and see, wonder about, speculate, conjecture, dispute, contest, controvert
▶ *701 Argument; 705 Question*
19 **hesitate**, vacillate, dither, waver, hang (*or* hold) back, falter, be irresolute, be in two minds about, equivocate, prevaricate, sit on the fence, keep an open mind
▶ *639 Vacillation; 702 Sophistry*
20 **make uncertain**, obscure, mystify, baffle, faze, confound, confuse, perplex, daze, haze, fog, disturb, disconcert, embarrass, worry, bewilder, flummox, nonplus, puzzle, stump, keep someone guessing
▶ *266 Obscurity; 457 Stupidity*
21 **change**, mutate, fluctuate, vary, move, shift, shake, slip, fail, betray
▶ *247 Failure; 300 Motion*
22 **risk**, chance, gamble, hazard, venture, dare, speculate
▶ *107 Chance*

ADVERBS

23 **uncertainly**, doubtfully, dubiously, suspiciously, sceptically, irresolutely, hesitantly, indecisively, speculatively, conjecturally, disputably, controversially, questionably, in question
▶ *451 Disbelief; 701 Argument; 705 Question*
24 **confusingly**, bewilderingly, worryingly, puzzlingly, problematically, enigmatically, embarrassingly, in a quandary, on the horns of a dilemma
▶ *264 Difficulty; 328 Disturbance; 630 Surprise; 705 Question; 730 Voicelessness*
25 **indeterminately**, indefinitely, vaguely, ambiguously,

equivocally, indistinctly, faintly, hazily, foggily, mistily, fuzzily, obscurely, inaccurately, imprecisely, loosely, broadly, generally, amorphously, incoherently

▶ *161 Shapelessness; 266 Obscurity*

26 **unreliably**, fallibly, treacherously, dishonestly, insecurely, transiently, insubstantially, unsteadily, inconsistently, shiftily, shakily, precariously, dangerously, perilously, riskily, hazardously, eccentrically, erratically, irregularly, unpredictably, improbably

▶ *105 Improbability; 107 Chance; 254 Danger; 299 Irregularity*

27 **capriciously**, on a whim, whimsically, irresponsibly, fitfully, intermittently, changeably, fluidly, flexibly, inconstantly, variably, randomly

▶ *227 Changeableness ; 642 Frivolity*

454 Verification

And ye shall know the truth, and the truth shall make you free. Bible: John.

VERBS

1 **verify**, validate, confirm, ratify, authenticate, certify, record, document, assure, guarantee, warrant, second, support, sign, countersign, endorse, vindicate, make certain, remove doubt, make good, ensure, check, double-check, crosscheck, recheck, collate

▶ *253 Security; 714 Vindication*

2 **prove**, demonstrate, illustrate, clarify, clear up, show, evince, corroborate, sustain, bear out, support, substantiate, circumstantiate, determine, ascertain, establish, witness

▶ *703 Demonstration*

3 **testify**, attest, affirm, state, assert, avow, aver, give evidence, turn queen's evidence, witness, inform, grass (Inf), rat (US inf), squeal (Inf), sing (Inf), lag (Aus inf), dob (Aus inf)

▶ *715 Accusation; 716 Evidence*

NOUNS

4 **verification**, validation, confirmation, ratification, authentication, certification, documentation, attestation, affirmation, avouchment, avowal, averment, assurance, surety, check, double-check, crosscheck, collation

▶ *136 Qualification; 253 Security; 273 Accuracy; 452 Certainty; 698 Truth; 707 Affirmation; 714 Vindication; 743 Identification*

5 **proof**, proving, demonstration, illustration, clarification, corroboration, support, substantiation, circumstantiation, determination, ascertainment, establishment

▶ *448 Experiment; 449 Discovery; 701 Argument; 703 Demonstration*

6 **evidence**, counterevidence, confirmation, statement, credential, testimonial, reference, character reference, recommendation, seal, signature, documentation, documents, ticket, passport, visa, permit

▶ *136 Qualification; 693 Information; 716 Evidence; 742 Sign*

7 **verifier**, testifier, voucher, swearer, attestant, signatory, witness, eyewitness, spectator, bystander, passer-by, informant, informer, snout (Inf), grass (Inf), rat (US inf), squealer (Inf), nark (Inf), dobber (Aus inf), lagger (Aus inf)

▶ *693 Information*

ADJECTIVES

8 **verifiable**, certifiable, documented, authentic, recorded, seconded, proved, witnessed

▶ *3 History; 698 Truth; 721 Description*

9 **verificatory**, verificative, demonstrative, illustrative, evidential, determining, validating, assuring, establishing, confirming, testificatory, ratificatory, prima facie, corroborative, supportive, substantial, circumstantial, probative, collative, checking, crosschecking, double-checking

10 **verified**, validated, confirmed, ratified, authenticated, certified, documented, attested, affirmed, avouched, avowed, averred, assured, sure, certain, checked, double-checked, crosschecked, collated

ADVERBS

11 **verifiably**, corroboratively, demonstratively, illustratively, supportively, circumstantially, authentically, genuinely, certifiably, with appropriate papers, with all documents

▶ *95 Reality*

12 **assuredly**, certainly, surely, indisputably, really, for certain, for sure, in truth, most certainly, indeed, to be sure, sure enough, beyond question, no two ways about it

▶ *452 Certainty; 455 Knowledge; 698 Truth*

INTERJECTIONS

13 **really!**, honestly!, honest!, that's the one!, I swear!, marry! (Lit)

455 Knowledge

Nam et ipsa scientia potestas est. (Knowledge itself is power.) Francis Bacon.

For in much wisdom is much grief: and he that increaseth knowledge increaseth sorrow. Bible: Ecclesiastes.

His had been an intellectual decision founded on his conviction that if a little knowledge was a dangerous thing, a lot was lethal. Tom Sharpe.

NOUNS

1 **knowledge**, knowing, ken, cognition, cognizance, gnosis, realization, perception, understanding, comprehension, apprehension, grasp, mastery, awareness, consciousness, acquaintance, familiarity, illumination, enlightenment, foresight, foreknowledge, intuition, savoir-faire, *Aufklärung* (Ger), savvy (Inf)

▶ *445 Intuition; 695 Intelligibility*

2 **information**, data, common knowledge, general knowledge, facts, know-how, expertise, skill, aptitude, forte, métier, touch, technique, accomplishment, partial knowledge, half-knowledge, smattering, inkling, intimation, suspicion

▶ *456 Ignorance; 485 Skill; 693 Information*

3 **learning**, lore, erudition, sagacity, wisdom, scholarship, letters, omniscience, polymathy, proficiency, mastery,

craftsmanship, literacy, numeracy, cleverness, intelligence, acquired knowledge, booklearning, bookishness, education, schooling, instruction, teaching, culture, cultivation, civilization, self-education, self-instruction, autodidactism, accomplishments, acquirements, attainments, attainment targets, experience, practical experience, practice
▶ *458 Wisdom*
4 **intellect**, mind, brain, intelligence, wit, faculty, brains (Inf), smarts (US inf), street smarts (US inf), suss (Inf)
▶ *442 Intellect*
5 **science**, natural science, applied science, technology, the arts, the humanities, letters, literature, ology (Inf)
6 **knowledgeable person**, mastermind, genius, sage, wise man, savant(e), mine of information, walking encyclopedia, expert, authority, scholar, don, academic, pedant, scientist, teacher, intellectual, highbrow, egghead (Inf), bluestocking (Inf), know-all (Inf), clever dick (Inf), clever clogs (Inf), smartarse (Inf), smarty pants (Inf), smart alec (Inf), wise guy (Inf), brainbox (Inf), bright spark (Inf), boffin (Inf)
▶ *442 Intellect; 458 Wisdom*
7 **academia**, groves of academe, intelligentsia, literati, illuminati

ADJECTIVES

8 **knowledgeable**, knowing, well-informed, all-knowing, omniscient, polymathic, encyclopedic, clever, intelligent, sagacious, wise, enlightened, informed, instructed, trained, cognizant, qualified, experienced, practised, versed, competent, skilled, proficient, efficient, expert, well-versed, gifted, talented, good at, aware, conscious, mindful, attentive, acquainted with, no stranger to, familiar with, conversant with, briefed, primed, *au fait* (Fr), *au courant* (Fr), in the picture, streetwise, shrewd, astute, perceptive, smart, brainy (Inf), wise to (Inf), in the know (Inf), sussed (Inf)
▶ *442 Intellect; 458 Wisdom; 485 Skill; 693 Information*
9 **literate**, numerate, schooled, educated, well-educated, erudite, scholarly, donnish, academic, intellectual, highbrow, cultured, cultivated, sophisticated, worldly, pedantic, well-qualified, highly qualified, overqualified
▶ *442 Intellect*
10 **known**, verified, proved, true, certain, discovered, explored, recognized, perceived, seen, knowable, heard of, well-known, famous, infamous, notorious, celebrated, renowned, common, public, no secret
▶ *452 Certainty; 698 Truth; 716 Evidence*

VERBS

11 **know**, understand, comprehend, apprehend, realize, conceive, appreciate, recognize, identify, distinguish, discern, perceive, see, ken (Dial), master, retain, savvy (Inf), twig (Inf), catch on (Inf)
▶ *442 Intellect; 695 Intelligibility; 743 Identification*
12 **know by heart**, know inside out, know backwards, know forward and backward (US), learn by rote, memorize, know all the answers, know one's stuff, know the ropes, know from A to Z, know like the back of one's hand, know full well
▶ *462 Memory*
13 **get to know**, acquaint oneself with, familiarize oneself with, experience, study, con, learn, discover, find out, take in, grasp, get wise to (Inf), suss (out) (Inf)
▶ *449 Discovery*
14 **cause to know**, tell, inform, brief, prime, teach, instruct, train, school, educate, coach
▶ *693 Information*

ADVERBS

15 **knowledgeably**, knowingly, intelligently, wisely, proficiently, consciously, intellectually, academically, pedantically, cognitively, as far as one knows, as every schoolboy (*or* schoolgirl) knows

456 Ignorance

Yet ah! why should they know their fate?
Since sorrow never comes too late,
And happiness too swiftly flies.
Thought would destroy their paradise.
No more; where ignorance is bliss,
'Tis folly to be wise. Thomas Gray.

I count religion but a childish toy,
And hold there is no sin but ignorance. Christopher Marlowe.

NOUNS

1 **ignorance**, lack of knowledge, nescience, incognizance, incomprehension, unawareness, insensibility, unconsciousness, blankness, nonrecognition, unfamiliarity, awkwardness, gaucherie, uncertainty, illiteracy, backwardness, unenlightenment, unskilfulness, artlessness, naivety, innocence, unintelligence, empty-headedness, folly, stupidity
▶ *457 Stupidity; 459 Folly; 486 Unskilfulness; 489 Insensibility; 646 Naivety*
2 **half-knowledge**, inexperience, inexpertness, amateurism, amateurishness, semi-literacy, smattering of knowledge, dabbling, superficiality, sciolism, dilettantism, quackery, charlatanism, bluff
3 **unknown thing**, unknown quantity, mystery, enigma, secret, anonymity, the unknown, unknown territory, *terra incognita* (L), guesswork, anybody's guess, complete blank, closed (*or* sealed) book, all Greek, pig in a poke, mystery tour, UFO (unidentified flying object)
▶ *696 Unintelligibility; 737 Secrecy*
4 **unknown person**, anonymous person, person(s) unknown, John (*or* Jane) Doe, dark horse, anon., Mr X, A. N. Other, any Tom, Dick, or Harry, Mr Nobody, blind date
5 **ignorant person**, ignoramus, simpleton, fool, bungler, charlatan, quack, amateur, dilettante, cowboy (Inf), dabbler, layman, Philistine, humbug, bluffer, illiterate, dunce, blockhead, novice, greenhorn, boofhead (Aus), thimblewit, divvy (Inf), goof (Inf), bozo (Inf), duffer (Inf), berk (Inf), thicko (Inf), dickhead (Inf), fuckwit (Inf), shagwit (Inf), smeghead (Inf), dumbo (Inf), plonker (Inf), dim bulb (Inf), dimbo (Inf), bimbo (Inf), himbo (Inf), dummy (Inf), dumdum (Inf), dumbbell (Inf), dumb cluck (Inf), nerd (*or* nurd) (Inf)

ADJECTIVES

6 **ignorant**, unknowing, nescient, incognizant, unwitting, unaware, oblivious, unconscious, blank, unin-

formed, in the dark, misinformed, misled, unskilled, uninitiated, green, naive, simple, innocent, gauche, awkward, unenlightened, backward, illiterate, unlettered, unschooled, untutored, uneducated, untaught, uninstructed, unscholarly, low-brow, Philistine, stupid, dull, dim, dim-witted, slow, slow-witted, thick, thickheaded, thick as two short planks, empty-headed, clueless (Inf), dumb (Inf), nerdy (Inf), pig ignorant (Inf), dead from the neck up (Inf), fuckwitted (Inf)

▶ *457 Stupidity; 459 Folly; 486 Unskilfulness; 646 Naivety*

7 semiskilled, semi-literate, semi-schooled, lay, amateur, amateurish, inexperienced, inexpert, unqualified, quack, shallow, superficial, dilettante, half-baked (Inf)

8 unknown, mysterious, strange, unfamiliar, unrecognized, unnamed, anonymous, unidentified, secret, obscure, unbeknown, unseen, unheard of, unspoken, ineffable, untold, unrealized, unperceived, unexplored, uncharted, unknowable, beyond the frontiers of knowledge

▶ *696 Unintelligibility; 737 Secrecy*

VERBS

9 be ignorant, not know, know nothing, wallow in ignorance, be in the dark, lack information, have nothing to go on, have a lot to learn, be stumped, give up, not have a clue, not have the foggiest idea, shrug one's shoulders

10 know little, have a smattering of knowledge, dabble in, have a go at

11 make ignorant, keep in the dark, mystify, mislead, misinform

ADVERBS

12 ignorantly, unknowingly, unwittingly, unconsciously, stupidly, in ignorance, for all one knows

INTERJECTIONS

13 who knows?, God knows!, search me!, I give up!

457 Stupidity

NOUNS

1 lack of intellect, absence of intellect, poverty of intellect, intellectual weakness, mental weakness, lack of brains, low IQ, low mental age, low reading age, feeble-mindedness, simple-mindedness, backwardness, slowness, imbecility, idiocy, mindlessness, senselessness, brainlessness, vacancy, vacuity, mental deficiency, mental retardation, mental handicap, brain damage, senility, dementia, lack of reason, unreason, irrationality, insanity

▶ *461 Insanity*

2 unintelligence, ignorance, stupidity, denseness, lack of knowledge, lack of wisdom, foolishness, folly, thoughtlessness, illogicality, empty-headedness, inanity, fatuity, puerility, childishness, immaturity, lack of understanding, incomprehension, unperceptiveness (*or* imperceptiveness), obtuseness, stolidity, thickheadedness, hebetude, oafishness, boorishness, lack of wit, witlessness, dim-wittedness, dimness, unoriginality, uninventiveness, unimaginativeness, imitativeness, imitation

▶ *125 Imitation; 271 Simplicity; 456 Ignorance; 459 Folly; 472 Inattention; 486 Unskilfulness; 555 Youth; 646 Naivety*

3 unintelligent person, ignoramus, fool, dunce, simpleton, Simple Simon, idiot, complete idiot, imbecile, moron, cretin, dolt, dullard, blockhead, clod, oaf, boor, numbskull (*or* numskull), halfwit, dunderhead, bumpkin, ninny, nincompoop, silly idiot (Inf), scatterbrain (Inf), dummy (Inf), dumbo (Inf), thickie (*or* thicky) (Inf), twit (Inf), nitwit (Inf), dimwit (Inf), wally (Inf), dope (Inf), lamebrain (Inf), pinhead (Inf), peabrain (Inf), birdbrain (Inf), vegetable (Inf), dumbbell (US inf), klutz (US inf), plonker (Inf), prat (Inf)

4 nonhuman existence, irrationality, unreason, animality, instinct, brute instinct, brute creation, vegetation, vegetable life, inanimate nature, inanimate objects, sticks and stones

▶ *30 Earth Science; 70 Animals; 77 Plants; 93 Existence*

ADJECTIVES

5 lacking intellect, intellectually weak, mentally weak, feeble-minded, simple, simple-minded, slow, backward, educationally subnormal (ESN), dull, vacuous, vacant, mindless, senseless, brainless, imbecilic, idiotic, cretinous, moronic, mentally deficient, mentally retarded, mentally handicapped, brain-damaged, senile, in one's second childhood, demented, insane, irrational

6 unintelligent, ignorant, stupid, dense, foolish, thoughtless, unthinking, illogical, inane, fatuous, empty-headed, puerile, childish, childlike, infantile, immature, unwise, unperceptive (*or* imperceptive), obtuse, stolid, thickheaded, blockheaded, oafish, boorish, doltish, witless, unoriginal, uninventive, unimaginative, imitative, dimwitted (Inf), dim (Inf), thick (Inf), thick as two short planks (Inf), dumb (Inf), dopey (Inf), silly (Inf), daft (Inf), loony (*or* looney) (Inf), nutty (Inf), klutzy (US inf), soft (Inf), soft in the head (Inf), not all there (Inf), not sixteen ounces to the pound (Inf), not playing with a full deck (Inf), not sixteen annas to the rupee (Inf), a brick short of a load (Inf), two sandwiches short of a picnic (Inf), not the full pound note (Inf), two bangers short of a barbie (Aus inf), out to lunch (Inf)

▶ *272 Ridiculousness; 456 Ignorance; 461 Insanity*

7 intellectually subnormal, mentally subnormal, educationally subnormal (ESN), subnormal, mentally deficient, mentally handicapped, retarded, backward, simple, simple-minded, feeble-minded, imbecilic, idiotic, moronic, cretinous, autistic, brain-damaged, senile, confused, incoherent, witless, gaga (Inf)

8 nonhuman, irrational, without reason, dumb, brute, animal, instinctive, instinctual, vegetable, vegetative, inanimate, inorganic, mineral

▶ *339 Inertness; 341 Inaction; 343 Inactivity*

VERBS

9 lack intellect, have a low IQ, lack reason, be of unsound mind, be out of one's mind, show ignorance, be stupid, not have enough sense to come in out of the rain, not see an inch beyond one's nose, not find one's way to first base (US), fail to see, play the fool, be not all there (Inf)

10 bemuse, confound, confuse, muddle, befuddle, fuddle, bewilder, mystify, perplex, flummox, baffle, bedazzle, addle, stump, stun, knock out, paralyse, make one's head spin, drive to one's wits end, blunt, dull, obscure, drug, anaesthetize

▶ *327 Agitation; 328 Disturbance; 408 Disorder; 489 Insensibility; 691 Drug-Taking; 696 Unintelligibility; 730 Voicelessness*

ADVERBS

11 unintelligently, without intelligence, unthinkingly, without thinking, empty-headedly, absently, vacantly, vacuously, inanely, fatuously, ignorantly, stupidly, mindlessly, senselessly, brainlessly, feeble-mindedly, simple-mindedly, idiotically, moronically, insanely, senilely, irrationally, illogically, unwisely, foolishly, imperceptively, obtusely, stolidly, childishly, puerilely, immaturely, imitatively, uninventively, unimaginatively

12 nonhumanly, irrationally, unreasoningly, without rationality, without reason, instinctively, instinctually, from instinct, inanimately

458 Wisdom

For in much wisdom is much grief: and he that increaseth knowledge increaseth sorrow. Bible: Ecclesiastes.

Wisdom is the principal thing; therefore get wisdom: and with all thy getting get understanding. Bible: Proverbs.

It is the province of knowledge to speak and it is the privilege of wisdom to listen. Oliver Wendell Holmes.

NOUNS

1 wisdom, sagacity, sagaciousness, sapience, reason, judgment, discretion, discernment, discrimination, perspicacity, penetration, perception, insight, intuition, understanding, comprehension, breadth of vision, profundity, knowledge, erudition, learning, experience, enlightenment, objectivity, soundness of mind, shrewdness, acumen, astuteness, tact, level-headedness, prudence, judiciousness, far-sightedness, foresight, forethought, cunning, craftiness

▶ *455 Knowledge; 464 Judgment; 466 Discrimination; 616 Caution; 645 Cunning*

2 intelligence, intellectualism, intellect, mind, understanding, quick-wittedness, cleverness, smartness, brightness, brilliance, aptitude, talent, genius, high IQ (intelligence quotient), inspiration, bright idea, brainwave, wit, wits, mother wit, sense, common sense, horse sense, good sense, brain (Inf), brains (Inf), little grey cells (Inf), grey matter (Inf), gumption (Inf), nous (Inf)

▶ *442 Intellect*

3 wise man, wise woman, sage, guru, witch, shaman, sibyl, oracle, seer, prophet, thinker, philosopher, Solomon

▶ *4 Philosophy; 475 Prediction*

4 intellectual, scholar, academic, genius, Mensa member, bright spark (Inf), brainbox (Inf), clever dick (Inf), smartarse (Inf), smart alec (Inf), wise guy (Inf)

▶ *442 Intellect; 455 Knowledge*

ADJECTIVES

5 wise, sagacious, sapient, thoughtful, thinking, reflecting, reasoning, rational, sensible, profound, deep, intellectual, highbrow, knowledgeable, knowing, erudite, learned, perspicacious, perceptive, oracular, level-headed, prudent, judicious, balanced, objective, impartial, just, fair-minded, broad-minded, circumspect, unprejudiced, statesmanlike, diplomatic, discreet, tactful, politic, well-advised

▶ *460 Sanity; 464 Judgment; 473 Disinterestedness; 616 Caution*

6 intelligent, clever, smart, bright, brilliant, talented, gifted, highly capable, able, skilful, skilled, quick, quick-witted, sharp, sharp-witted, alert, astute, shrewd, street-wise, canny, far-sighted, clear-headed, calculating, crafty, cunning, brainy (Inf), all there (Inf), on the ball (Inf), too clever by half (Inf), clever-clever (Inf), smartarse (Inf)

▶ *442 Intellect; 485 Skill; 645 Cunning*

VERBS

7 be wise, understand, grasp, fathom, discern, see through, distinguish, discriminate, judge, intuit, use one's head, use one's intelligence, have one's wits about one, know the score, know what's what

▶ *464 Judgment; 466 Discrimination; 695 Intelligibility*

8 be intelligent, have brains, know, shine, scintillate, know how many beans make five, have one's head screwed on the right way (Inf)

▶ *442 Intellect; 455 Knowledge*

ADVERBS

9 wisely, sagaciously, thoughtfully, rationally, sensibly, perspicaciously, prudently, judiciously, objectively, diplomatically, discreetly

10 intelligently, cleverly, brilliantly, astutely, shrewdly

459 Folly

Mix a little foolishness with your serious plans: it's lovely to be silly at the right moment. Horace.

Fools are in a terrible, overwhelming majority, all the wide world over. Henrik Ibsen.

NOUNS

1 folly, foolishness, stupidity, ineptitude, inanity, rashness, recklessness, madness, senselessness, silliness, absurdity, ridiculousness, ludicrousness, asininity, childishness, puerility, fatuousness, pointlessness, extravagance, frivolity, flippancy, giddiness, thoughtlessness, irresponsibility, imprudence, indiscretion, conceit, heedlessness, ignorance, unintelligence, low IQ (intelligence quotient), eccentricity, insanity, lunacy, idiocy, imbecility, feeble-mindedness, empty-headedness, senility, dotage, craziness (Inf), daftness (Inf)

▶ *272 Ridiculousness; 456 Ignorance; 457 Stupidity; 461 Insanity; 615 Rashness*

2 act of folly, foolery, tomfoolery, mistake, error, misjudgment, gaffe, blunder, bloomer (Inf), blooper (US inf)

▶ *274 Error; 465 Misjudgment; 697 Nonsense*

3 foolish person, fool, simpleton, imbecile, idiot, moron, cretin, halfwit, ass, jackass, dolt, blockhead, dunce, dotard, dimwit (Inf), dumbo (Inf), dimbo (Inf), birdbrain (Inf), dope (Inf), nincompoop (Inf), ninny (Inf), nitwit (Inf), twit (Inf), dingbat (US inf), noodle (Inf), pinhead (Inf), pillock (Inf), right Charlie (Inf), wally (Inf), meathead (Inf), jerk (Inf), asshole (US inf), sucker (Inf), prat (Inf), fuckwit (Inf)

▶ *456 Ignorance; 461 Insanity*

4 **rash person**, hothead, daredevil, adventurer, madcap, eccentric

ADJECTIVES

5 **foolish**, stupid, inept, inane, mad, unwise, ill-advised, ill-considered, imprudent, injudicious, uncircumspect, incautious, rash, reckless, foolhardy, harebrained, heedless, inattentive, hotheaded, hellbent, headstrong, wild, prodigal, devil-may-care, couldn't-care-less, frivolous, flippant, silly, asinine, idiotic, imbecilic, moronic, anserine, lunatic, insane, senseless, brainless, ignorant, unintelligent, dim-witted, feeble-minded, empty-headed, simple, slow, doltish, dull, gormless, fatuous, pointless, absurd, ludicrous, ridiculous, nonsensical, preposterous, childish, puerile, senile, eccentric, bird-brained (Inf), nutty (Inf), daft (Inf), crazy (Inf), barmy (Inf), spaced-out (Inf), potty (Inf), gaga (Inf)

▶ *272 Ridiculousness; 456 Ignorance; 457 Stupidity; 461 Insanity; 615 Rashness*

VERBS

6 **be foolish**, take leave of one's senses, go mad, lose one's head, throw caution to the wind, stick one's neck out, take a leap in the dark, play with fire, have no thought for the consequences, ask for trouble, tempt fate, buy a pig in a poke, never learn, not have the sense one was born with

▶ *456 Ignorance; 461 Insanity; 615 Rashness*

7 **play the fool**, act the goat, make a fool of oneself, clown around, play silly buggers (Inf)

▶ *697 Nonsense*

ADVERBS

8 **foolishly**, stupidly, unwisely, imprudently, rashly, recklessly, idiotically, insanely, senselessly, brainlessly, unintelligently, absurdly, ludicrously, ridiculously, nonsensically

460 Sanity

There is less harm to be suffered in being mad among madmen than in being sane all by oneself. Denis Diderot.

NOUNS

1 **sanity**, saneness, sound mind, soundness of mind, *mens sana* (L), stability, balanced mind, mental equilibrium, mental health, normality, sobriety

▶ *689 Sobriety*

2 **rationality**, reasonableness, reason, intelligibility, lucidity, coherence, good sense, common sense, wits, intelligence

▶ *458 Wisdom; 695 Intelligibility*

3 **sane person**, Mr (*or* Mrs) Normal, reasonable person, voice of reason, rock (of Gibraltar)

ADJECTIVES

4 **sane**, not mad, *compos mentis* (L), in one's right mind, in full possession of one's faculties, of sound mind, mentally sound, normal, sober, all there (Inf), together (Inf), with both oars in the water (Inf), right in the head (Inf)

▶ *689 Sobriety*

5 **rational**, reasonable, coherent, intelligible, lucid, clear-headed, balanced, well-balanced, level-headed, stable, steady, sound, sensible, common-sensical, intelligent

▶ *458 Wisdom; 695 Intelligibility*

VERBS

6 **be sane**, have one's wits about one, become sane, ratiocinate, come to one's senses, sober down, sober up, make sane, restore to sanity

ADVERBS

7 **sanely**, soberly, rationally, reasonably, coherently, lucidly

461 Insanity

The madman is not the man who has lost his reason. The madman is the man who has lost everything except his reason. G. K. Chesterton.

NOUNS

1 **insanity**, madness, lunacy, idiocy, irrationality, unsound mind, sick mind, mental illness (*or* disorder), (mental) derangement, mental instability, unbalanced mind, balance of mind disturbed, criminal insanity, McNaghten Rules, diminished responsibility, abnormality, aberration, incoherence, eccentricity, oddness, freakishness, crankiness, craziness, kinkiness (Inf), nuttiness (Inf), battiness (Inf), bats in the belfry (Inf), screw loose (Inf), slate loose (Inf)

▶ *16 Law; 36 Psychology and Psychiatry; 118 Nonconformity; 459 Folly*

2 **subnormality**, mental subnormality, intellectual subnormality, (mental) retardation, mental deficiency, amentia, aphrenia, mental handicap, oligophrenia, mental impairment, backwardness, learning difficulties, Down's syndrome, autism, cretinism, feeble-mindedness, imbecility, idiocy

▶ *36 Psychology and Psychiatry; 260 Ill Health; 457 Stupidity*

3 **mental deterioration**, dementia, confusion, softening of the brain, senile dementia, presenile dementia, Alzheimer's disease, Pick's disease, brain damage, brain disease, brain disorder, encephalopathy, spongiform encephalopathy, mad-cow disease, Creutzfeld-Jakob disease, kuru, general paralysis of the insane (GPI), fit, convulsion, paroxysm, seizure, stroke, rabies, hydrophobia, epilepsy, epileptic fit, grand mal, tonic-clonic fit, petit mal

▶ *260 Ill Health*

4 **delusion**, illusion, hallucination, paraphrenia, shared delusions, communicated insanity, folie à deux, personality disorder, paranoia, monomania, obsessive behaviour, hypochondria, obsession, complex (Inf), phobia, persecution mania, fixation, compulsion, urge, craving, craze, passion, elation, ecstasy, hypomania, mania, frenzy, hysteria, ravings, delirium, delirium tremens, DT's (Inf), dipsomania, megalomania, delusions of grandeur, kleptomania, pyromania, agromania, ono-

matomania, theomania, religious mania, nymphomania, satyriasis, erotomania, necromania, fetishism, homicidal mania

▶ *36 Psychology and Psychiatry; 96 Unreality; 477 Imagination; 612 Fear; 796 Immorality*

5 psychosis, psychopathy, schizophrenia, dementia praecox, split personality, schizoid personality, hebephrenia, catatonia, manic-depressive psychosis, cyclothymia, alcoholic psychosis, Korsakoff's psychosis (*or* syndrome)

▶ *36 Psychology and Psychiatry*

6 mental breakdown, nervous breakdown, neurosis, psychoneurosis, neuroticism, neurasthenia, anxiety, (personal) crisis, depression, clinical depression, melancholia, involutional melancholia, hysteria, shell shock, nervous tic, nerves (Inf), attack of nerves (Inf), brainstorm (Inf), crack-up (Inf)

▶ *36 Psychology and Psychiatry; 327 Agitation; 602 Sorrow; 612 Fear*

7 insane person, madman, madwoman, lunatic, mental case, maniac, manic-depressive, homicidal maniac, megalomaniac, monomaniac, hypomaniac, kleptomaniac, nymphomaniac, sex maniac, psychopath, psychotic, paranoiac, obsessive, hysteric, neurotic, hypochondriac, schizoid, schizophrenic, melancholic, depressive, idiot, idiot savant, cretin, moron, imbecile, eccentric, crank (Inf), crackpot (Inf), kook (US inf), headcase (Inf), nut (Inf), nutcase (Inf), nutter (Inf), screwball (Inf), oddball (Inf), fruitcake (Inf), booby (Inf), dummy (Inf), loony (Inf), loony tune (US inf), loon (Inf), psycho (Inf), sicko (Inf), space-case (US inf), space cadet (US inf)

8 mental hospital, mental institution, mental home, lunatic asylum, insane asylum, madhouse, Bedlam, psychiatric hospital, special hospital, psychiatric unit, psychiatric ward, padded cell, special school, loony bin (Inf), bin (Inf), nuthouse (Inf), funny farm (Inf), funny place (Inf), funny house (Inf), nut college (Inf), nut farm (Inf), nut hatch (Inf), screw factory (Inf), squirrel tank (Inf), acorn academy (Inf), bughouse (US inf), booby hutch (Inf), loony school (Inf)

▶ *36 Psychology and Psychiatry*

9 treatment, psychiatric care, psychoanalysis, analysis, psychotherapy, counselling, electroconvulsive therapy (ECT), shock therapy (*or* treatment)

10 psychiatrist, psychoanalyst, psychotherapist, mad doctor (Inf), head doctor (Inf), headshrinker (Inf), shrink (Inf), trick cyclist (Inf), barred-window boys (Inf), men in white coats (Inf)

▶ *35 Medicine; 394 Remedy*

ADJECTIVES

11 insane, mad, of unsound mind, *non compos mentis* (L), deranged, demented, abnormal, disturbed, unbalanced, unhinged, alienated, weird, peculiar, odd, anile, doited, out of one's mind (*or* senses), raving mad, stark raving mad, stark staring mad, mad as a march hare, mad as a hatter, mental (Inf), certifiable (Inf), funny (in the head) (Inf), wacky (Inf), screwy (Inf), kinky (Inf), cranky (Inf), crazy (Inf), daft (Inf), queer in the head (Inf), touched (Inf), daft as a brush (Inf), cracked (Inf), crackers (Inf), crack-brained (Inf), cuckoo (Inf), dolally (*or* dolally-tap) (Dial), bonkers (Inf), nutty (Inf), nutty as a fruitcake (Inf), nuts (Inf), barmy (*or* balmy) (Inf), bananas (Inf), bats (Inf), batty (Inf), dotty (Inf), barking mad (Inf), (clean) round the bend (*or* twist) (Inf), dippy (Inf), loco (US inf), loopy (Inf), loose in the attic (Inf), loose in the head (Inf), in left field (US inf), off one's head (Inf), off one's chump (Inf), off one's trolley (Inf), off one's rocker (Inf), off one's nuts (Inf), off one's block (Inf), off one's crust (Inf), off one's onion (Inf), off the side (US inf), off the wall (US inf), up the pole (Inf), out of one's head (Inf), out of one's skull (Inf), out of one's tree (Inf), ape (US inf)

12 manic, ranting, raving, frenzied, frenetic, frantic, hysterical, demented, rabid, foaming at the mouth, wild, berserk, delirious, deluded, hallucinating

13 mentally ill, disturbed, sick, abnormal, neurotic, depressed, depressive, melancholic, paranoid (*or* paranoiac), fixated, psychotic, schizophrenic, schizoid, catatonic, psychopathic, certified, schizo (Inf)

▶ *36 Psychology and Psychiatry; 260 Ill Health*

VERBS

14 become insane, go mad, lose one's wits, be insane, rave, ramble, run amok, have a screw loose (Inf), have bats in the belfry (Inf), lose one's marbles (Inf), go off one's head (Inf), go round the bend (Inf), start climbing the wall (Inf), go ape (Inf)

15 make insane, madden, drive mad, derange, dement, unbalance, unhinge, confuse, drive crazy, drive up the wall (Inf), drive round the bend (Inf), send over the edge (Inf)

16 certify, commit, section, put away

ADVERBS

17 insanely, madly, dementedly, psychotically, abnormally, neurotically, crazily (Inf)

462 Memory

Memories are hunting horns whose sound dies on the wind. Guillaume Apollinaire.

Thanks For the Memory. Leo Robin.

Better by far you should forget and smile
Than that you should remember and be sad. Christina Rossetti.

NOUNS

1 memory, recollection, remembrance, remembering, recall, total recall, good memory, photographic memory, retention, retentiveness, memorization, learning by heart (*or* rote), reminiscence, anamnesis, retrospection, reflection, hindsight, evocation, mind's eye, nostalgia, recognition, identification, collective memory, race memory, Mother of the Muses, Mnemosyne

▶ *455 Knowledge; 743 Identification*

2 retrospect, retrospective, review, flashback, *déjà vu* (Fr), history, memoirs, autobiography, anecdote

▶ *3 History; 744 Record*

3 memento, souvenir, token, keepsake, memorabilia, trophy, relic, commemoration, memorial, monument, statue, plaque, tribute

4 reminder, memorandum, memo, note, diary, engagement diary, album, photograph album, scrapbook, record, mnemonic, *aide-mémoire* (Fr), cue, prompt, prompter

▶ *693 Information; 744 Record*

5 day to remember, memory, centenary, bicentenary, tercentenary, quatercentenary, quincentenary, sexcentenary, anniversary, place in history, fame, notoriety

▶ *601 Celebration; 811 Reputation*

6 artificial memory, computer memory, RAM (random access memory), ROM (read only memory), data bank, database

▶ *40 Computers; 439 Store*

ADJECTIVES

7 memorable, unforgettable, notable, noteworthy, remembered, unforgotten, indelible, stamped on one's memory, forever in one's memory, haunting, evocative, reminiscent, nostalgic, reminding, mnemonic

▶ *123 Importance*

8 remembering, unable to forget, retrospective, mindful, bearing (*or* keeping) in mind

9 memorized, learnt by heart (*or* rote), committed to memory

10 memorial, commemorative, celebratory

VERBS

11 memorize, fix in one's mind, commit to memory, learn by heart, learn by rote, learn, remember, retain, hold in one's mind, bear (*or* keep) in mind, store in one's heart

▶ *455 Knowledge*

12 remember, recall, call to mind, recollect, think of, call up, summon up, conjure up, recognize, identify, know again, review, retrace, recapture, hark back, look back, think back, reminisce, reflect, rake up the past, write one's memoirs

▶ *743 Identification*

13 remind, bring to mind, bring back, take back, prompt, jog one's memory, ring a bell, refresh one's memory, brush up, recapitulate, review, haunt, not allow to forget, remind oneself, tie a knot in one's handkerchief, make a note

▶ *112 Repetition; 744 Record*

14 commemorate, memorialize, remember, honour, pay tribute to, toast, observe, celebrate, mark the occasion

▶ *601 Celebration*

15 be remembered, make history, live on, make an impression, stick in the mind, be engraved on one's memory, recur, come back, be unforgotten

ADVERBS

16 memorably, unforgettably, reminiscently, mnemonically, retrospectively, commemoratively, in memory of, in memoriam, by heart, by rote

463 Forgetfulness

Many brave men lived before Agamemnon's time; but they are all, unmourned and unknown, covered by the long night, because they lack their sacred poet. Horace.

NOUNS

1 oblivion, obliviousness, abstractedness, detachment, ataraxia, withdrawal, absorption, self-absorption, introspection, self-loss, depersonalization, catatonia, senselessness, insensibility, unconsciousness, coma, stupor, narcosis, trance, meditative trance, yoga trance, rapture, ecstasy, ecstasis, hypnosis

▶ *266 Obscurity; 472 Inattention; 489 Insensibility*

2 blankness, vacancy, vacuity, emptiness of mind, emptyheadedness, absent-mindedness, forgetfulness, loss of memory, amnesia, total blank, mental block, blackout

▶ *472 Inattention*

3 poor memory, dim memory, hazy recollection, lapse of memory, mind (*or* brain) like a sieve

4 unthinkingness, thoughtlessness, unmindfulness, heedlessness, inattention, disregard, neglect, carelessness, selfishness, ingratitude, indifference

▶ *672 Ingratitude; 683 Selfishness*

5 death, annihilation, obliteration, nirvana

▶ *8 Divinity; 582 Death*

6 amnesty, pardon, forgiveness, absolution

▶ *649 Forgiveness*

7 forgetful person, absent-minded professor, scatterbrain, amnesiac

ADJECTIVES

8 oblivious, abstracted, detached, withdrawn, introspective, (self-)absorbed, head in the clouds, wandering, distracted, preoccupied, otherwise engaged, blind, deaf, unaware, in a world of one's own, depersonalized, catatonic, senseless, insensible, unconscious, rapturous, ecstatic, hypnotic, trance-like, spaced-out (Inf), out to lunch (Inf), miles away (Inf)

▶ *472 Inattention; 666 Negligence*

9 blank, vacant, vacuous, empty-headed, absent-minded, forgetful, forgetting, amnesic, Lethean, nirvanic

10 unthinking, thoughtless, unmindful, heedless, inattentive, disregarding, neglectful, negligent, careless, selfish, ungrateful, indifferent

11 forgotten, not remembered, out of sight, out of mind, not missed, forgettable, unmemorable, best forgotten, dead and buried, lost to oblivion, past, gone, lost, beyond recall, half-remembered, on the tip of one's tongue

VERBS

12 be forgotten, slip one's mind, fade from one's memory, sink into oblivion, sink without trace, drop from view, go in one ear and out of the other

13 forget, have no recollection of, not remember, miss, overlook, neglect, omit, think no more of, not give another thought to, erase (*or* efface) from one's memory, unlearn, leave behind, break with the past, consign to oblivion, clean forget (Inf)

▶ *358 Obliteration; 472 Inattention*

14 be forgetful, have a mind (*or* brain) like a sieve, have a short memory, misremember, remember wrongly, forget one's lines, fluff one's lines, dry

15 forgive, forgive and forget, let bygones be bygones, bury the hatchet

▶ *649 Forgiveness*

ADVERBS

16 obliviously, unconsciously, senselessly, blankly, vacantly, vacuously, forgetfully, absent-mindedly, abstractedly, distractedly, negligently, inattentively, unthinkingly, thoughtlessly, heedlessly, carelessly, indifferently, hypnotically, ecstatically, in a dream, in a trance

464 Judgment

No man can justly censure or condemn another, because indeed no man truly knows another. Thomas Browne.

NOUNS

1 **judgment**, discrimination, discernment, distinction, differentiation, selection, choice, discretion, taste, wisdom, sense, judging, adjudication, arbitration, umpirage, faculty of judgment, reasoning, deduction, inference, dissertation, corollary, consideration, view, belief, opinion, assessment, evaluation, speculation, conjecture, surmise, sensibility, guesswork, guess, estimate, estimation, calculation, rating, valuation, appraisal, appreciation, survey, inspection, report, review, notice, remark, comment, critique, criticism, constructive criticism, censure, value judgment, second opinion, public opinion, vox populi, vote, referendum, plebiscite

▶ *26 Measurement; 210 Calculation; 444 Reason; 450 Belief; 458 Wisdom; 466 Discrimination; 469 Selection; 669 Approval; 670 Disapproval*

2 **verdict**, judgment, adjudication, summing up, recapitulation, decision, conclusion, ruling, finding, award, sentence, pronouncement, order, edict, decree, decree nisi, decree absolute, acquittal, condemnation, execution of judgment, law, canon, act, legislation

▶ *16 Law; 397 Command; 723 Summary*

3 **place of judgment**, judgment seat, seat of justice, tribunal, the Woolsack, law court, court of law, criminal court, civil court, Court of Appeal, Star Chamber, High Court, Queen's Bench, circuit court, assizes, assize sessions, quarter sessions, crown court, petty sessions, magistrates' court, police court, coroner's court, court martial, kangaroo court, courtroom, the bench, jury box, dock, witness box, chair

▶ *16 Law*

4 **judgment day**, day of judgment, Last Judgment, the Last Day, Doomsday, millennium, resurrection day, afterlife, hereafter

▶ *7 Religion*

5 **judge**, adjudicator, arbitrator, jurist, arbiter, umpire, referee, mediator, assessor, valuer, appraiser, surveyor, inspector, examiner, tester, reporter, commentator, censor, editor, critic, reviewer, expert, connoisseur, adviser, counsellor, panel of judges, panel, jury

▶ *466 Discrimination; 713 Advice; 748 Mediation*

6 **justice**, judge, judge advocate general, his Lordship, his Worship, judge advocate, chief justice, crown court judge, public prosecutor, procurator fiscal, district attorney, county court judge, trial judge, sessions judge, assize judge, recorder, magistrate, coroner, stipendiary magistrate, justice of the peace (JP), associate justice, the bench, the judiciary, the magistracy, the beak (Inf)

▶ *16 Law*

7 **jury**, jury, juryman, jurywoman, juror, foreman of the jury, grand jury, special jury, coroner's jury, jury list, trial jury, twelve good men and true (Inf)

▶ *16 Law*

ADJECTIVES

8 **judging**, discriminating, discerning, selecting, selective, criticizing, critical, judgmental, inquisitional, moralistic, sententious, approving, appreciative, disapproving, condemnatory, censorious

▶ *466 Discrimination; 469 Selection; 669 Approval; 670 Disapproval*

9 **judicious**, discerning, discriminating, sensitive, accurate, right, just, fair, unbiased, dispassionate, wise, shrewd, judicial, judicatory, juridical

▶ *458 Wisdom; 466 Discrimination; 473 Disinterestedness; 801 Right*

10 **judged**, submitted for judgment, under consideration, on trial, up for trial, sub judice, before the bar, up before the beak (Inf)

VERBS

11 **judge**, umpire, referee, sit in judgment, arbitrate, hear, hear the case, commit for trial, try, sum up, award, decree, adjudge, adjudicate, decide, conclude, find, find for, find against, determine, settle, settle the matter, rule, pronounce sentence, pass judgment, charge the jury, bring a verdict, acquit, condemn, censure, censor, criticize, disapprove of, approve of

▶ *16 Law; 669 Approval; 670 Disapproval*

12 **estimate**, judge, gauge, calculate, reckon, size up, evaluate, assess, value, appraise, rate, regard, deem, esteem, think, believe, guess, surmise, conjecture, judge by eye, weigh up, ponder over, consider, reason, deduce, infer, examine, investigate, inspect, survey, vet, make a report on, review, criticize, comment on, scan, check, check out (Inf)

▶ *210 Calculation; 444 Reason*

ADVERBS

13 **judicially**, judiciously, selectively, critically, approvingly, disapprovingly

14 **considering**, taking into account, all things considered, everything being equal

465 Misjudgment

I too well know its truth, from experience, that whenever any poor Gipsies are encamped anywhere and crimes and robberies &c. occur, it is invariably laid to their account, which is shocking; and if they are always looked upon as vagabonds, how can they become good people? Queen Victoria.

NOUNS

1 **misjudgment**, poor judgment, miscalculation, misconception, misconstruction, misinterpretation, misunderstanding, wrong impression, cross purposes, inexactness, underestimation, overestimation, undervaluation, overvaluation, false reading, distortion, fallacy, deception, fallibility, gullibility, self-deception, fool's paradise, wrong end of the stick (Inf)

▶ *467 Overestimation; 468 Underestimation; 700 Deception*

2 **mistake**, error, blunder, bungling, clanger (Inf), howler (Inf), blooper (Inf), boob (Inf), boo-boo (Inf), bloomer (Inf), dog's breakfast (Inf)

▶ *274 Error*

3 injustice, miscarriage of justice, mistrial, packed jury, partiality, partisanship, one-sidedness, predilection, predisposition, preferential treatment, favouritism, nepotism, intolerance, discrimination, unfairness, inequality, unlawfulness, bias, prejudice, prejudicial treatment, chauvinism, sectarianism, provincialism, parochialism, insularity, xenophobia, racism, racialism, racial prejudice, racial intolerance, Aryanism, apartheid, anti-Semitism, sexism, ageism, homophobia, bigotry, fanaticism, narrow-mindedness, tunnel vision, overspecialization, narrow mind, closed mind, jaundiced eye, foul play (Inf), not cricket (Inf), one-track mind (Inf)

▶ *120 Inequality; 466 Discrimination; 594 Hate*

4 prejudgment, preconception, preconceived idea, *parti pris* (Fr), mind made up, *idée fixe* (Fr), fixed idea, fixation, obsession, predetermination, foregone conclusion, presupposition

▶ *106 Predetermination*

5 misjudging person, bigot, zealot, fanatic, partisan, chauvinist, xenophobe, racist, racialist, Nazi, sexist, homophobe, pervert, fool, bungler

6 misjudged person, victim, scapegoat, prey, guy, butt

ADJECTIVES

7 misjudging, in error, mistaken, wrong, wrong-headed, muddled, fallible, gullible, misguided, misled, deluded, deceived

▶ *274 Error; 700 Deception*

8 unjust, unfair, discriminatory, prejudicial, partial, partisan, subjective, one-sided, predisposed, preferential, intolerant, prejudiced, biased, jaundiced, warped, twisted, chauvinistic, sectarian, provincial, parochial, insular, xenophobic, racist, colour-prejudiced, anti-Semitic, sexist, ageist, class-prejudiced, homophobic, snobbish, bigoted, fanatical, narrow-minded, narrow, hidebound, pedantic, unimaginative, prejudged, preconceived, fixed

▶ *106 Predetermination; 234 Distortion; 466 Discrimination*

9 misjudged, misunderstood, wrongly accused, unfairly treated, misconstrued, misinterpreted, underestimated, overestimated, undervalued, overvalued, underrated, overrated, out, wrong, mistaken, ill-timed, untimely, inconvenient, ill-advised, foolish

▶ *240 Inconvenience; 274 Error; 459 Folly; 467 Overestimation; 468 Underestimation*

VERBS

10 misjudge, miscalculate, misreckon, misinterpret, misconstrue, misunderstand, misconceive, misread, get wrong, mistake, twist, distort, let slip, waste an opportunity, miss, trip, slip, stumble, blunder, bungle, time badly, mistime, overestimate, underestimate, overvalue, undervalue, overrate, underrate, be unable to see the wood for the trees, get hold of the wrong end of the stick (Inf)

▶ *234 Distortion; 274 Error; 467 Overestimation; 468 Underestimation*

11 be unjust, treat unfairly, discriminate, take sides, prejudge, preconceive

▶ *466 Discrimination*

12 bias, prejudice, jaundice, warp, twist, predispose

▶ *234 Distortion*

ADVERBS

13 misguidedly, mistakenly, in error, wrongly, fallibly, gullibly, foolishly

14 unjustly, unfairly, partially, subjectively, preferentially, intolerantly, chauvinistically, parochially, fanatically, narrow-mindedly

466 Discrimination

Everyone complains of his memory, but no one complains of his judgment. Duc de la Rochefoucauld.

NOUNS

1 discrimination, selection, selectivity, selectiveness, distinction, differentiation, appraisal, sorting, graduation, separation, demarcation, division, segregation, diagnosis, interpretation

▶ *26 Measurement; 209 Grading; 372 Separation; 409 Arrangement; 469 Selection; 719 Interpretation*

2 judiciousness, judgment, discrimination, discretion, taste, good taste, sensitivity, sensibility, discernment, criticism, appreciation, feel, perception, insight, connoisseurship, acumen, flair, dilettantism, palate, refined palate, refinement, delicacy, finesse, fastidiousness, meticulousness, perfectionism, quibbling, hair-splitting (Inf)

▶ *230 Perfection; 464 Judgment; 495 Taste; 591 Sensitivity; 702 Sophistry*

3 prejudice, discrimination, bias, bigotry, narrowness, narrow-mindedness, pettiness, small-mindedness, intolerance, insularism, parochialism, one-sidedness, partisanship, jaundice, prejudgment, inequity, unfairness, foul play (Inf), not cricket (Inf)

▶ *120 Inequality; 395 Influence; 641 Obstinacy*

4 social discrimination, sexual discrimination, sexism, heterosexism, male chauvinism, misogyny, misandry, homophobia, racial discrimination, racism, racialism, race hatred, anti-Semitism, apartheid, segregation (US), ghettoization, xenophobia, ethnocentricity, ethnic cleansing, ethnocide, pogrom, political persecution, McCarthyism, elitism, glass ceiling, class prejudice, class discrimination, classism, class war, fascism, Nazism, Aryanism, jingoism, chauvinism, ultranationalism, superpatriotism, religious persecution, fundamentalism, fanaticism, witch-hunting, heresy-hunting, ableism, fattism, ageism, granny-bashing (Inf), queer-bashing (Inf), Paki-bashing (Inf), redbaiting (US inf)

▶ *7 Religion; 137 Class; 351 Misuse; 380 Violence; 381 Attack; 594 Hate*

5 favouritism, nepotism, cronyism, partisanship, positive discrimination, preferential treatment

6 discriminating person, critic, selector, judge, connoisseur, dilettante, gourmet, epicure, idealist, purist, pedant, perfectionist, quibbler, hair-splitter (Inf), fusspot (Inf)

▶ *557 Eating*

7 bigot, dogmatist, partisan, elitist, fanatic, persecutor, ageist, sexist, male chauvinist, misogynist, misandrist, homophobe, racist, racialist, anti-Semite, xenophobe, fascist, Nazi, jingo, jingoist, ultranationalist, chauvinist, superpatriot, fundamentalist, witch-hunter, male chauvinist pig (Inf), pig (Inf), redneck (Inf), granny-basher (Inf), queer-basher (Inf), Paki-basher (Inf), red-baiter (US inf)

► *641 Obstinacy*

8 victim of discrimination, victim of oppression, sufferer, prey, martyr, unlucky person, unfortunate, scapegoat, the persecuted, the exploited, the oppressed, slave, underdog (Inf)

► *249 Adversity*

ADJECTIVES

9 discriminating, judicious, selective, tasteful, sensitive, differential, separating, discerning, divisional, critical, diagnostic, interpretational, appreciative, epicurean, perceptive, insightful, refined, delicate, fastidious, meticulous, perfectionist, pedantic, quibbling, hair-splitting (Inf), choosy (Inf), picky (Inf)

► *372 Separation; 469 Selection; 665 Carefulness; 702 Sophistry*

10 discriminatory, prejudicial, one-sided, partisan, jaundiced, inequitable, unfair, partial, preferential, nepotistic, prejudiced, biased, bigoted, narrow-minded, blinkered, small-minded, petty, intolerant, dogmatic, insular, parochial, elitist, classist, ageist, disablist, ableist, sexist, misogynist, misogynous, misandrist, misandrous, homophobic, heterosexist, racist, racialist, anti-Semitic, xenophobic, jingoistic, ethnocentric, fascist, Nazi, ultranationalistic, superpatriotic, chauvinist, chauvinistic, fundamentalist, fanatical

11 judged, selected, distinct, discrete, diagnosed, interpreted, differentiated, sorted, graded, graduated, separate, demarcated, divided, segregated, discriminated against, persecuted, exploited, oppressed

VERBS

12 discriminate, select, choose, favour, prefer, judge, distinguish, differentiate, discern, pick, pick out, pick and choose, compare and contrast, sort, analyse, grade, graduate, separate, demarcate, divide, segregate, diagnose, interpret, quibble, split hairs (Inf), sort the sheep from the goats (Inf), sort the grain (*or* wheat) from the chaff (Inf)

► *464 Judgment; 469 Selection*

13 prejudge, forejudge, precondemn, bias, prejudice, warp, not see beyond one's nose, put on blinkers, blind oneself, close one's mind, listen with deaf ears

► *234 Distortion; 395 Influence; 456 Ignorance; 505 Deafness*

14 discriminate against, criticize, persecute, harass, be hard on, treat unfairly, oppress, exploit, witch-hunt, pick on (Inf), granny-bash (Inf), queer-bash (Inf), redbait (US inf), Paki-bash (Inf)

ADVERBS

15 discriminatingly, selectively, distinctly, separately, differentially, divisively, diagnostically

16 judiciously, judgmentally, with discretion, tastefully, sensitively, discerningly, critically, analytically, appreciatively, perceptively, insightfully, delicately, fastidiously, meticulously, pedantically

17 prejudicially, preferentially, dogmatically, inequitably, unfairly, narrow-mindedly, small-mindedly, intolerantly, parochially, fanatically, homophobically, xenophobically, ethnocentrically, racially, chauvinistically, ultranationalistically, superpatriotically, jingoistically

467 Overestimation

NOUNS

1 overestimation, overvaluation, overrating, misjudgment, miscalculation, overconfidence, rashness, overoptimism, idealism, overweening pride, conceit, hubris, arrogance, egomania, exaggeration, overstatement, hype, hyperbole, megalomania, vanity, showing off, blowing one's own trumpet (Inf)

► *465 Misjudgment; 615 Rashness; 673 Vanity; 727 Exaggeration*

2 overestimate, much ado about nothing, storm in a teacup, pipe dream, castles in Spain, castles in the air, fool's paradise, Utopia, panegyric, fuss, hue and cry, hot air (Inf), big deal (Inf)

► *610 Hope*

3 optimist, young hopeful, idealist, megalomaniac, panjandrum, exaggerator, promoter

VERBS

4 overestimate, overvalue, overrate, overprize, overprice, price oneself out of the market, overcharge, misjudge, miscalculate, exaggerate, overstate, make a mountain out of a molehill, make a fuss about, hype, overpraise, panegyrize, maximize, make the most of, be too good to be true

► *465 Misjudgment; 727 Exaggeration; 792 Dearness*

ADJECTIVES

5 overestimating, overconfident, rash, overoptimistic, overenthusiastic, hubristic, arrogant

► *610 Hope; 615 Rashness*

6 overestimated, overvalued, overrated, overpriced, dear, expensive, misjudged, exaggerated, overpraised, not all it's cracked up to be (Inf)

► *727 Exaggeration; 792 Dearness*

ADVERBS

7 overoptimistically, idealistically, overenthusiastically, hyperbolically, arrogantly, overconfidently, rashly, vainly

468 Underestimation

No one ever went broke underestimating the intelligence of the American people. H. L. Mencken.

NOUNS

1 underestimation, undervaluation, underrating, misjudgment, miscalculation, underestimate, conservative estimate, minimization, deprecation, self-deprecation, depreciation, self-depreciation, detraction, understatement, litotes, self-effacement, humility, modesty, false modesty, affectation, pessimism, defeatism, negative outlook, cynicism

► *465 Misjudgment; 611 Despair; 623 Humility; 674 Modesty; 676 Affectation; 678 Scornfulness; 728 Understatement*

2 pessimist, defeatist, minimizer, detractor, cynic

VERBS

3 underestimate, undervalue, underrate, misprize, misjudge, miscalculate, minimize, play down, understate, make little of, make light of, shrug off, pooh-pooh, belittle, disparage, underpraise, underprice, discount, mark down, hold cheap, scorn, set no store by, not do justice to, soft-pedal (Inf)

▶ *465 Misjudgment; 621 Derision; 678 Scornfulness; 728 Understatement; 793 Cheapness*

ADJECTIVES

4 **underestimating**, deprecating, depreciatory, detracting, disparaging, scornful, minimizing, conservative, moderate, pessimistic, defeatist, modest, humble

▶ *611 Despair; 623 Humility; 674 Modesty; 678 Scornfulness*

5 **underestimated**, undervalued, underrated, misjudged, miscalculated, underpriced, cheap

▶ *465 Misjudgment; 793 Cheapness*

ADVERBS

6 **pessimistically**, cynically, scornfully, disparagingly, affectedly, conservatively, moderately, modestly, humbly

469 Selection

VERBS

1 **select**, choose, make a choice, eliminate the alternatives, decide, determine, make up one's mind, decide on, settle on, plump for, opt, opt for, take up an option, take up, accept, adopt, coopt, have a choice, have a voice, have free will, judge, exercise one's discretion

▶ *464 Judgment; 635 Will*

2 **prefer**, have a preference, like better, like best, would like, would rather, favour, fancy, incline, lean, have a bias, tend, might as well, might do worse, see fit, think fit, think it best to

▶ *595 Liking; 669 Approval*

3 **side with**, back, support, endorse, embrace, espouse, cast (*or* throw) in one's lot with, come out (*or* down) for, come out (*or* down) on one side, take sides, commit oneself, take the plunge, leap into, cross the Rubicon, burn one's bridges, burn one's boats, take for better or for worse, take for richer or for poorer, take in sickness and in health

▶ *392 Help; 570 Marriage; 638 Resolution*

4 **pick**, pick out, hand-pick, single out, pass, approve, recommend, put up, propose, nominate, second, appoint, commission, designate, delegate, detail, highlight, mark out, mark down, preselect, earmark, reserve, set aside, set apart, distinguish, identify, separate, isolate, abstract, excerpt, cull, anthologize, glean, winnow, sift, skim, skim off, cream, skim off the cream, pick the best, take one's pick, indulge one's fancy, discriminate, pick and choose

▶ *372 Separation; 466 Discrimination; 743 Identification*

5 **vote**, choose by ballot, go to the polls, have a vote, have a voice, have a say, have the vote, be enfranchised, be on the electoral roll, cast a vote, register one's vote, cast one's ballot, be counted, raise one's hand, divide, vote for, vote in, elect, re-elect, return, vote out, vote down, deselect, reject, vote with one's feet, electioneer, canvass, accept a nomination, accept a candidacy (*or* candidature), run (US), stand, put to the vote, hold a referendum, poll, take a poll, take an opinion poll, measure public opinion, count votes, count ballots, count hands, count heads, count noses, count straws, hold an election, go to the country, appeal to the electorate, ask for a vote of confidence

▶ *12 Government and Politics; 470 Rejection*

NOUNS

6 **selection**, choice, choosing, decision, determination, making up one's mind, judgment, discretion, discrimination, picking and choosing, eclecticism, finickiness, fastidiousness, picking out, adoption, cooption, cooptation, nomination, appointment, commission, designation, right of choice, free will, freedom of choice, pick, variety, range, range of choice, list, shortlist, *embarras de richesses* (Fr), *embarras de choix* (Fr)

▶ *464 Judgment; 466 Discrimination; 635 Will; 752 Offer*

7 **preference**, predilection, partiality, inclination, leaning, tendency, prejudice, bias, favouritism, taste, liking, favour, fancy, preferability, desirability

▶ *595 Liking*

8 **choice**, possible choice, option, alternative, difficult choice, tough decision, dilemma, limited choice, limited options, only choice, Hobson's choice, no real alternative, no choice, zero option, nothing for it but, blind choice, blind date, unlucky choice, bad bargain, best option, better choice, greater good, lesser evil, lesser of two evils

9 **chosen thing**, pick, first choice, selection, assortment, pickings, gleanings, excerpts, anthology, the best, the cream, *crème de la crème* (Fr), the chosen, chosen people, elite

▶ *121 Superiority; 235 Worth*

10 **vote**, voice, cast vote, cumulative vote, transferable vote, majority vote, deciding vote, voice vote, positive vote, aye, yea, vote of confidence, negative vote, no, nay, vote of no confidence, blackball vote, blackballing, absentee vote, absentee ballot, mail-in vote (US), postal vote, card vote, ballot, secret ballot, open vote, show of hands, poll, opinion poll, public opinion poll, Gallup poll™, MORI (Market and Opinion Research Institute) poll™, straw poll, jury poll (US), direct vote, plebiscite, referendum, amendment referendum (US), vox populi

11 **franchise**, right of representation, suffrage, universal suffrage, adult suffrage, manhood suffrage, women's suffrage, votes for women, suffragettism, democracy, democratic system, parliamentary system, congressional system (US), electoral system, electoral college (US), proportional representation, first-past-the-post system, counting hands, counting heads, counting noses

12 **election**, general election, national election, federal election (US), state election (US), by-election, local election, local-government election, indirect election, primary election (US), primary (US), direct primary (US), open primary (US), closed primary (US), polls, polling, voting, political campaign, ticket, manifesto, electioneering, whistle-stop tour, whistle-stopping, canvassing, stumping (US), doorstepping, hustings, candidacy (*or* candidature), polling day, polling place, polling station, polling booth, voting paper, ballot paper, ballot box, returns, vote counting, tabulation of ballots, evaluation of returns, voting machine, psephology, electoral roll, voting list, constituency, marginal constituency, electoral district, polling district, precinct (US), borough, pocket

borough (Lit), rotten borough (Lit)

13 **electorate**, voters, voter, registered voter, absentee voter, constituent, elector (US), balloter, candidate, nominee, victorious candidate, president-elect (US), minister designate, losing candidate, also-ran, psephologist, suffragette, suffragist, poll watcher

ADJECTIVES

14 **selecting**, choosing, deciding, decisive, eclectic, optional, discretional, volitional, exercising choice, selective, particular, discriminating, discerning, showing preference, preferential, favouring, choosy (Inf), picky (Inf)

▶ *466 Discrimination; 595 Liking; 635 Will; 669 Approval*

15 **chosen**, selected, picked, sorted, assorted, seeded, well-chosen, worth choosing, to be jumped at, not to be sniffed at, select, choice, A1, recherché, hand-picked, elite, elect, designate, elected, returned, adopted, deselected, on approval, preferable, better, desirable, advisable, preferred, special, favourite, fancy, pet, God's own, by appointment, not to be sneezed at (Inf)

▶ *235 Worth; 595 Liking*

16 **elective**, electoral, voting, enfranchised, vote-catching, electioneering, canvassing, psephological

ADVERBS

17 **selectively**, eclectically, optionally, by choice, by ballot, by referendum, alternatively, either…or, preferentially, preferably, rather, sooner, à la carte

470 Rejection

Go, and never darken my towels again! Groucho Marx.

VERBS

1 **reject**, decline, turn down, not accept, say no to, refuse, draw the line at, rebuff, repulse, repel, spurn, dismiss out of hand, disallow, not approve, not pass, return, send back, look a gift horse in the mouth, not consider, pass over, ignore, disregard, not select, vote against, cast a negative vote, not vote for, deselect

▶ *666 Negligence; 670 Disapproval; 709 Refusal*

2 **discard**, throw away, scrap, ditch, throw aside, lay aside, set aside, renounce, give up, abandon, eliminate, get rid of, throw out, cast out, eject, jettison, expel, dismiss, oust, depose, supersede, junk (Inf), sling out (Inf), chuck out (Inf), kick out (Inf), boot out (Inf), kick downstairs (Inf)

▶ *350 Nonuse; 371 Expulsion*

3 **exclude**, except, count out, not count, exempt, blackball, cold-shoulder, turn one's back on, slight, snub, brush off, freeze out, scout (Lit), give a cold reception to, give a cool welcome to, make unwelcome, not cater for, not want, turn up one's nose at, sniff at, scorn, disdain, mock, deride, laugh at, ridicule, sneeze at (Inf)

▶ *128 Exclusion; 621 Derision; 655 Unsociability; 659 Discourtesy*

4 **revoke**, cancel, abrogate, negate, abnegate, repudiate, apostatize, recant, deny, disclaim, disavow

▶ *479 Equivocation; 708 Negation*

NOUNS

5 **rejection**, declining, nonacceptance, refusal, nonapproval, disapproval, slight, snub, rebuff, repulse, spurn, kick, brush-off, cold shoulder, cold reception, cool welcome, more kicks than ha'pence , more bricks than bouquets, exclusion, exception, exemption, blackballing

▶ *128 Exclusion; 655 Unsociability; 670 Disapproval; 709 Refusal*

6 **discarding**, disuse, nonuse, abandonment, elimination, ejection, expulsion, dismissal, unemployment, disemployment (US), redundancy, defeat, electoral defeat, nonelection, deselection, lost election, forfeiture of deposit

▶ *247 Failure; 350 Nonuse; 371 Expulsion*

7 **abrogation**, cancellation, negation, abnegation, repudiation, apostasy, recantation, denial, disavowal

▶ *479 Equivocation; 708 Negation*

8 **rejected thing**, reject, discard, unpopular cause, lost cause, failure, flop (Inf)

▶ *247 Failure*

9 **rejected person**, loser, born loser, defeated candidate, unsuccessful applicant, redundant worker, 4-F recruit (US), fired employee, spurned lover, ineligible athlete, no-hoper (Inf), wallflower (Inf)

ADJECTIVES

10 **rejected**, declined, turned down, not accepted, unchosen, unselected, ineligible, unqualified, unsuitable, unacceptable, unaccepted, unrequited, returned, sent back, unusable, unfit for human consumption, unfit for consideration, not be thought of, out of the question, unwanted, discarded, disused, thrown away, cast out, dismissed, redundant, excluded, snubbed

471 Attention

The idea that He would take his attention away from the universe in order to give me a bicycle with three speeds is just so unlikely I can't go along with it. Quentin Crisp.

NOUNS

1 **attention**, attentiveness, notice, regard, concern, consideration, mindfulness

2 **close attention**, undivided attention, attention to detail, close observance, examination, watchfulness, alertness, finickiness, nit-picking (Inf)

3 **carefulness**, meticulousness, fastidiousness, sedulousness, circumspection, scrutiny, surveillance, vigilance, wariness, heed, concentration, application, assiduousness

4 **diligence**, studiousness, single-mindedness, fixation, pedantry, purism, obsession, preoccupation, tunnel vision, hang-up (Inf)

▶ *443 Thought; 616 Caution; 644 Curiosity; 665 Carefulness*

5 **solicitude**, care, consideration, protection, indulgence, attendance, courtesy, gallantry, spoiling, fussing over (Inf)

6 **attentive person**, doctor, lawyer, examiner, scholar, lover, suitor, chaperon

ADJECTIVES

7 **watchful**, alert, attentive, observant, sharp-eyed, vigilant, on guard, careful, wary, circumspect, scrutinizing, surveying, heedful, curious

8 **diligent**, studious, painstaking, meticulous, fastidious, sedulous, assiduous, undistracted, single-minded, rapt,

engrossed, obsessed, fixated, pedantic, preoccupied, purist, hung-up (Inf), all eyes (Inf), all ears (Inf)
9 **solicitous**, caring, concerned, protective, considerate, mindful, indulgent, attentive, courteous, gallant

VERBS

10 **be attentive**, regard, consider, notice, note, pay attention to, hover over, dance attendance on, attend, care for
11 **take note of**, register, mark, keep an eye on, give undivided attention to, watch, observe, examine, miss nothing, stay alert, guard against, prick up one's ears (Inf)
12 **scrutinize**, survey, heed, study, fix upon, nit-pick (Inf)
13 **attract attention**, draw attention, excite the attention of, be the centre of attention, catch the eye of, act as a magnet
14 **be solicitous**, indulge, pay attention to, show consideration for, shower attention on, court, spoil, flirt, grovel, toady, fawn over, crawl, fuss over (Inf), suck up to (Inf), brown-nose (Inf), arse-lick (Inf)

ADVERBS

15 **attentively**, mindfully, observantly, watchfully, alertly, carefully, meticulously, fastidiously, sedulously, circumspectly, vigilantly, warily, assiduously, diligently, studiously, pedantically

472 Inattention

There is a wicked inclination in most people to suppose an old man decayed in his intellects. If a young or middle-aged man, when leaving a company, does not recollect where he laid his hat, it is nothing; but if the same inattention is discovered in an old man, people will shrug up their shoulders, and say, 'His memory is going.' Samuel Johnson.

NOUNS

1 **inattention**, inattentiveness, incuriosity, thoughtlessness, unmindfulness, forgetfulness, aberration, heedlessness, unconcern, detachment, obliviousness, apathy, disregard, distraction, nonobservance, carelessness, rashness, desultoriness, superficiality, indifference, cold shoulder
2 **impetuosity**, precipitance, impulsiveness, rashness, recklessness, foolhardiness, flightiness
3 **absent-mindedness**, daydreaming, dizziness, frivolity, woolgathering, stargazing, head in the clouds, castles in the air, Walter Mitty
► *157 Shallowness; 618 Indifference*
4 **thoughtlessness**, inconsideration, disregard, indifference, ignoring, insensitivity, selfishness
► *683 Selfishness*
5 **inattentive act**, oversight, lapse, slip, error, mistake, blunder, mishap, forgotten name, forgotten anniversary, forgotten birthday, slip-up (Inf)
► *274 Error*
6 **inattentive person**, daydreamer, dreamer, scatterbrain, woolgatherer, absent-minded professor

ADJECTIVES

7 **inattentive**, thoughtless, unthinking, not concentrating, incurious, unmindful, forgetful, heedless, unheeding, unconcerned, detached, oblivious, apathetic, listless, disregarding, distracted, unobservant
8 **absent-minded**, lost in thought, daydreaming, woolgathering, stargazing, in a brown study, in a world of one's own (Inf), out to lunch (Inf), not with it (Inf)
9 **thoughtless**, inconsiderate, uncaring, selfish, insensitive, unthinking
10 **careless**, negligent, neglectful, slack, remiss, sloppy, slapdash, slipshod, hit-or-miss, dizzy, flighty, rash, precipitous
11 **perfunctory**, casual, lackadaisical, desultory, superficial

VERBS

12 **be inattentive**, show unconcern, disregard, ignore, not notice, not listen, pay no attention, take no notice (*or* note) of, pay no heed to, overlook, put out of mind, allow one's mind to wander, daydream, stargaze, woolgather, be elsewhere (Inf), build castles in the air (Inf)
13 **be thoughtless**, be inattentive, show inconsideration for, disregard, ignore, slight, turn one's back on, make unwelcome, cold-shoulder, give someone the cold shoulder

ADVERBS

14 **inattentively**, incuriously, thoughtlessly, unmindfully, forgetfully, heedlessly, selfishly, inconsiderately, indifferently, obliviously, apathetically, carelessly, rashly, impetuously, recklessly, impulsively

473 Disinterestedness

There is no such thing on earth as an uninteresting subject; the only thing that can exist is an uninterested person. G. K. Chesterton.

NOUNS

1 **disinterestedness**, disinterest, indifference, detachment, ataraxia, impartiality, lack of bias, lack of prejudice, objectivity, equitableness, fair-mindedness, fairness, open-mindedness, justice, neutrality, nonalignment, noninvolvement, lack of emotion, self-control, self-restraint, dispassion, stoicism, keeping a stiff upper lip, keeping cool (Inf)
► *684 Self-Restraint; 799 Honour; 801 Right*
2 **unselfishness**, selflessness, altruism, considerateness, consideration, thought for others, kindness, compassion, sympathy, pity, humility, modesty, self-denial, self-effacement, self-abnegation, self-sacrifice, martyrdom, idealism, high-mindedness, honesty, honourableness, sublimity, loftiness, magnanimity, nobleness, munificence, benevolence, charity, generosity, open-handedness, big-heartedness
3 **impartial person**, judge, jury member, arbitrator, moderator, referee, umpire
► *623 Humility; 627 Pity; 650 Benevolence; 652 Philanthropy; 658 Courtesy; 768 Giving*

ADJECTIVES

4 **disinterested**, indifferent, detached, impersonal, impartial, unbiased, unprejudiced, objective, equitable, nonpartisan, fair, fair-minded, open-minded, open, just, neutral, nonaligned, uninvolved, not bothered, self-controlled, dispassionate, stoical (*or* stoic), cool (Inf)

5 **unselfish**, selfless, altruistic, considerate, kind, compassionate, sympathetic, humble, modest, self-abnegating, self-sacrificing, self-denying, self-effacing, ready to die for, martyred, idealistic, high-minded, honest, honourable, sublime, lofty, magnanimous, noble, munificent, benevolent, charitable, generous, open-handed, big-hearted

VERBS

6 **be disinterested**, show (*or* take) no interest in, show indifference towards, lack bias, lack prejudice, keep an open mind, open one's mind to, do the fair thing, lack emotion, demonstrate self-control, keep a stiff upper lip, mind one's own business, live and let live, keep cool (Inf)

7 **be unselfish**, think of others first, put oneself last, sacrifice oneself, make a sacrifice, sacrifice, rise above oneself, do the right thing by, show compassion for, sympathize with, pity, give generously, have a big heart, take a back seat (Inf), bend (*or* lean) over backwards (Inf)

ADVERBS

8 **disinterestedly**, indifferently, impersonally, impartially, objectively, without bias, without prejudice, equitably, fairly, open-mindedly, with an open mind, openly, justly, neutrally, dispassionately, stoically, with a stiff upper lip, coolly (Inf)

9 **unselfishly**, selflessly, altruistically, with others in mind, for the sake of others, considerately, kindly, compassionately, sympathetically, humbly, in a humble manner, modestly, with modesty, idealistically, high-mindedly, honestly, honourably, sublimely, loftily, magnanimously, nobly, with noble intentions, munificently, benevolently, charitably, generously, open-handedly, big-heartedly

474 Expectation

Unhappiness is best defined as the difference between our talents and our expectations. Edward de Bono.

NOUNS

1 **expectation**, expectancy, expectance, anticipation, contemplation, prospect, hope, hopefulness, optimism, presumption, assumption, confidence, assurance, reliance, trust, belief, waiting, suspense, apprehension, apprehensiveness, pessimism, dread, fear, foreboding, anxiety, uncertainty, possibility, probability, likelihood, certainty

► *102 Possibility; 104 Probability; 293 Earliness; 294 Lateness; 450 Belief; 452 Certainty; 453 Uncertainty; 610 Hope; 611 Despair; 612 Fear*

2 **expectations**, demands, desires, hopes, prospects, outlook, forecast, prognosis, prediction, accountability, responsibility, contingency, possibility, dream, aspiration, ambition, castles in Spain, castles in the air

► *283 Future Time; 475 Prediction; 610 Hope*

3 **the expected thing**, the done thing, the usual, the normal, normal behaviour, custom, tradition, habit, just what one would have expected

► *632 Habit*

4 **expectant person**, expectant, anticipant, omen, portent, augury, heir, heiress, beneficiary, recipient, inheritor, successor, next of kin, expectant mother, mother-to-be, prospective parents

► *561 Reproduction; 769 Receiving*

ADJECTIVES

5 **expecting**, expectant, in expectation, in high hopes, full of hope, hopeful, confident, sanguine, optimistic, desiring, wanting, on the waiting list, sure, certain, anticipating, anticipant, anticipative, anticipatory, prepared, ready, waiting, on stand-by, forewarned, forearmed, unsurprised, on the lookout, vigilant, watchful, on tenterhooks, in suspense, excited, eager, prognostic, apprehensive, dreading, pessimistic, anxious

► *243 Preparation; 452 Certainty; 610 Hope; 611 Despair; 612 Fear; 617 Desire*

6 **expectant**, expecting, pregnant, gravid, with child, in the family way

7 **expected**, predicted, foreseen, unsurprising, designated, chosen, promised, due, anticipated, probable, likely, apparent, predictable, foreseeable, sure, certain, long-awaited, future, prospective, contemplated, impending, imminent, on the cards, hoped for, desired, feared, dreaded

► *283 Future Time; 469 Selection; 475 Prediction; 612 Fear; 617 Desire*

VERBS

8 **expect**, anticipate, look forward to, look for, see coming, look at, contemplate, face, have in prospect, intend, plan, envisage, hope, hope for, apprehend, dread, fear, expect the worst

► *482 Intention; 484 Plan; 610 Hope; 612 Fear*

9 **predict**, foresee, forecast, think, believe, estimate, reckon, calculate, bargain for, count on, bank on, take for granted, assume, presume, count one's chickens before they are hatched

► *450 Belief; 464 Judgment; 475 Prediction; 610 Hope*

10 **wait**, bide one's time, wait for, await, be on the waiting list for, queue up for, stand by, be on stand-by, be on call, look out for, watch out for

11 **demand**, insist on, call for, require, need, want, wish

► *135 Requirement; 617 Desire*

ADVERBS

12 **expectantly**, hopefully, confidently, optimistically, anticipatively, anticipatorily, apprehensively, pessimistically, anxiously, in suspense, on tenterhooks, with bated breath

13 **expectedly**, unsurprisingly, predictably, foreseeably

475 Prediction

NOUNS

1 **prediction**, forecast, forecasting, foretelling, forewarning, prophecy, apocalypse, revelation, prognosis, prognostication, presentiment, premonition, hunch, feeling, foreboding, foresight, presage, prefiguration, prefigurement, prior consideration, expectation, prospect, weather forecast, horoscope, fortune

► *283 Future Time; 474 Expectation*

2 **divination**, clairvoyance, augury, taking the auspices, soothsaying, astrology, horoscopy, haruspicy, vaticination, casting nativities, fortune-telling, palmistry, chiromancy, crystal-gazing, reading cards, cartomancy, I Ching, casting lots, sortilege, bibliomancy, interpreting dreams, oneiromancy, hydromancy, pyromancy, geomancy, necromancy, occultism, dowsing, discovery, guesswork, speculation

▶ *11 Occultism*

3 plan, planning, forward planning, long-range plan, emergency plan, contingency plan, programme, prospectus, schedule, itinerary, appointments calendar, calendar of events, almanac, preview, announcement, notice, advance notice, publication, prepublication, warning, preliminary warning, warning sign, warning shot, danger signal, hint, suggestion, intimation

▶ *484 Plan; 711 Warning; 740 Publication*

4 model, working model, test model, test design, prototype, shape of things to come

5 omen, good omen, bad omen, sign, indication, portent, presage, augury, auspice, writing on the wall, prognostic, prognostication, syndrome, symptom, caution, warning, forewarning, harbinger, precursor, forerunner, herald, messenger, prefigurement, foretoken, type, ominousness, portentousness, signs of the times

▶ *129 Precedence; 254 Danger; 711 Warning; 741 News; 743 Identification*

6 good-luck sign, good-luck charm, talisman, mascot, horseshoe, four-leaf (*or* four-leaved) clover, rabbit's foot, Saint Christopher's medal, shooting star, amber, bloodstone, lodestone, black cat, finding a penny, touching a sailor, seeing a bride, seeing a chimney sweep, knocking on wood

▶ *107 Chance*

7 bad-luck sign, broken mirror, clock that stops, spilt salt, gathering clouds, peacock feather, bird of ill omen, owl, raven, walking under a ladder, opening an umbrella indoors, stepping on a crack, telling one's dream before breakfast

▶ *107 Chance*

8 oracle, sage, prophet, prophetess, prophet of doom, doom merchant, doomster, doomwatcher, Cassandra, warner, seer, visionary, vaticinator, soothsayer, clairvoyant, telepathist, medium, occultist, pythoness, sorcerer, witch, warlock, Delphic oracle, Pythian oracle, Pythia, sibyl, Sibylline books, Nostradamus, Witch of Endor

▶ *464 Judgment; 711 Warning*

9 forecaster, consultant, weather forecaster, meteorologist, weatherman (*or* weatherwoman), financial forecaster, sports forecaster, racing forecaster, odds-maker, tipster, gambler, speculator, prognosticator, futurologist, diviner, water diviner, dowser, astrologer, caster of nativities, fortune teller, palmreader, palmist, crystal gazer, interpreter of dreams, augur, auspex, haruspex

10 cards, Tarot cards, Ouija board™, runes, dice, lot, tripod, crystal ball, mirror, tea leaves, palm, head, entrails, texts, Bible, *sortes Biblicae* (L), *sortes Virgilianae* (L), *sortes Homericae* (L)

VERBS

11 predict, foresee, forecast, foretell, prophesy, reveal, make a prediction, make an educated guess, guess, guesstimate, speculate, prognosticate, make a prognosis, vaticinate, forebode, bode, augur, foretoken, presage,

SIGNS OF THE ZODIAC

Aries	♈	(Ram; 21 Mar – 19 Apr)
Taurus	♉	(Bull; 20 Apr – 20 May)
Gemini	♊	(Twins; 21 May – 21 June)
Cancer *or* Moon Child	♋	(Crab; 22 June – 22 July)
Leo	♌	(Lion; 23 July – 22 Aug)
Virgo	♍	(Virgin *or* Maiden; 23 Aug – 22 Sept)
Libra	♎	(Balance *or* Scales; 24 Sept – 23 Oct)
Scorpio	♏	(Scorpion; 24 Oct – 21 Nov)
Sagittarius	♐	(Archer; 22 Nov – 21 Dec)
Capricornus *or* Capricorn	♑	(Goat *or* Sea Goat; 22 Dec – 19 Jan)
Aquarius	♒	(Water Carrier; 20 Jan – 18 Feb)
Pisces	♓	(Fishes; 19 Feb – 20 Mar)

portend, foreshow, foreshadow, prefigure, shadow forth, forerun, herald, harbinger, usher in, go before, come before, point to, indicate, signify, betoken, represent, typify, hint, suggest, announce, give notice, notify, advertise, forewarn, warn, give warning, look black, look ominous, lower (*or* lour), menace, threaten, depress, promise, augur well, bid fair, give hope, hold out hopes, build up hopes, raise expectations, excite expectations, cheer up

▶ *129 Precedence; 610 Hope; 711 Warning; 740 Publication; 743 Identification*

12 divine, soothsay, take (*or* read) the auspices, take (*or* read) the omens, interpret dreams, vaticinate, cast a horoscope, cast a nativity, cast lots, gamble, tell fortunes, gaze into a crystal ball, read the future, read the signs, read the stars, read the cards, read the runes, read the entrails, read one's hand, read one's palm

ADJECTIVES

13 predicting, predictive, foretelling, forewarning, presentient, prescient, foreseeing, clairvoyant, fortune-telling, weather-wise, prophetic, oracular, mantic, vatic (*or* vaticinal), fatidic (*or* fatidical), apocalyptic, sibylline, sibyllic (*or* sibylic), monitory, premonitory, foreboding, cautionary, heralding, prefiguring, precursory, signifying, indicative, symptomatic

14 predicted, foretold, forecast, predictable, foreseeable

15 presageful, portentous, significant, fateful, augural, auspicial, haruspical, of good omen, auspicious, propitious, promising, fortunate, favourable, prosperous, of ill omen, ominous, big with fate, pregnant with doom, inauspicious, sinister, adverse, unfavourable

▶ *107 Chance; 248 Prosperity; 249 Adversity*

ADVERBS

16 predictively, prophetically, predictably, foreseeably, portentously, significantly, fatefully, auspiciously, promisingly, inauspiciously, ominously

476 Supposition

My own suspicion is that the universe is not only queerer than we suppose, but queerer than we can suppose. J. B. S. Haldane.

NOUNS

1 supposition, assumption, presumption, notion, idea,

the idea of, fancy, conceit, ideality, pretence, pretending, affectation, presupposition, condition, stipulation, *sine qua non* (L), conditions, proposal, proposition, offer, submission, argument, hypothetical argument, postulation, postulate, premise, theory, hypothesis, working hypothesis, explanation, tentative explanation, model, theorem, mathematical theorem, topic, thesis, position, stand, attitude, orientation, point of view, standpoint, opinion, suggestion, casual suggestion, suggestiveness
▶ *446 Idea; 447 Topic; 450 Belief; 477 Imagination; 676 Affectation; 693 Information; 701 Argument; 746 Negotiation; 752 Offer*
2 **basis of supposition**, hint, clue, evidence, data, research data, datum, deduction, induction, inference, suspicion, sneaking suspicion, hunch, inkling, intimation, intuition, instinct, association of ideas, causal relationship, thought, thinking, lateral thinking, supposability, conjecturability, probability, possibility
▶ *102 Possibility; 104 Probability; 443 Thought; 445 Intuition; 716 Evidence*
3 **conjecture**, unverified supposition, bare supposition, speculation, pure speculation, vague suspicion, suspicion, guess, surmise, mere notion, gamble, try, shot, shot in the dark, gambling, guessing, guesswork, rough guess, crude estimate, shrewd idea, intuition, construction, reconstruction, guesstimate (Inf)
▶ *445 Intuition; 464 Judgment*
4 **theorist**, theorizer, theoretician, hypothesist, thinker, philosopher, academic, researcher, research worker, academic researcher, scientific researcher, experimenter, experimental scientist, scientist, theory builder, model builder, supposer, surmiser, guesser, critic, armchair critic, armchair strategist, armchair detective, armchair quarterback (US), doctrinarian, doctrinaire, speculator, gambler, planner, boffin (Inf)
▶ *443 Thought; 452 Certainty; 484 Plan*

VERBS

5 **suppose**, assume, presume, have a notion, have an idea, imagine, pretend, fancy, dream, think, conceive, draw a mental picture, take into one's head, get into one's head, opine, divine, suspect, have a hunch, have an inkling, intuit, infer, deduce, conclude, surmise, conjecture, guess, make a guess, hazard a guess, guesstimate, suppose so, dare say, convince oneself, persuade oneself, believe, understand, gather, presuppose, presurmise, premise, posit, postulate, lay down, assert, affirm, predicate, take for granted, take, take it, reason, speculate, form a hypothesis, hypothesize, have a theory, theorize, let, sketch, draft, outline, plan, rely on supposition, gamble
▶ *443 Thought; 444 Reason; 445 Intuition; 450 Belief; 477 Imagination; 484 Plan; 701 Argument; 707 Affirmation*
6 **propound**, propose, suggest, make a suggestion, mean seriously, offer, put on the agenda, moot, move, propose a motion, bring up for debate, request, plead (*or* argue) a case, put a case, submit, make one's submission, argue, put forth, put forward, advance, venture to say, make a point, put forward a notion, throw out an idea, throw into the melting pot, advise, outline, adumbrate, allude, hint, put an idea into one's head, persuade, urge, motivate, influence
▶ *444 Reason; 480 Persuasion; 693 Information; 710 Request; 713 Advice; 752 Offer*

ADJECTIVES

7 **suppositional**, suppositive, supposing, assumptive, presumptive, notional, conjectural, guessing, intuitive, propositional, hypothetical, theoretical, postulatory, putative, suppositious (*or* supposititious), unverified, moot, armchair, speculative, wildly speculative, blue-sky (US), gratuitous, suggestive, hinting, allusive, hard to pin down, stimulating, thought-provoking, of academic interest, academic, guesstimating (Inf)
▶ *445 Intuition; 450 Belief*
8 **supposed**, assumed, presumed, premised, a priori, postulated, surmised, conjectured, guessed, hypothesized, understood, taken, taken as read, taken for granted, proposed, suggested, mooted, topical, given, granted, granted for the sake of argument, assented, suppositive, putative, inferred, deduced, pretended, alleged, reputed, so-called, titular, quasi, not real, unreal, abstract, fanciful, fancied, imagined, imaginary, fabled, untrue, supposable, assumable, presumable, surmisable, imaginable
▶ *94 Nonexistence; 447 Topic; 477 Imagination*
9 **meant**, intended, designed, expected, obliged, required
▶ *135 Requirement; 482 Intention*

ADVERBS

10 **supposedly**, allegedly, reputedly, as rumour has it, seemingly, possibly, conjecturally, hypothetically, theoretically, speculatively, in a speculative way, for the sake of argument, as an academic exercise, ex hypothesi, in theory, as it were, at a guess

CONJUNCTIONS

11 **supposing**, if, in the event that, assuming that, on the assumption that, even if, though, although, as if, as though
▶ *136 Qualification; 222 Circumstances*

477 Imagination

Imagination and fiction make up more than three quarters of our real life. Simone Weil.

NOUNS

1 **imagination**, imaginativeness, perception, vision, creativity, creativeness, invention, inventiveness, originality, ingenuity, resourcefulness, enterprise, skill, fancy, fancifulness, fantasy, fantasticality (*or* fantasticalness), stretch of the imagination, power of imagination, visual imagination, vivid imagination, highly-coloured imagination, bold imagination, fertile imagination, lively imagination, poetic imagination, the mind's eye, visualization, objectification, conceptualization, imagery, image-building, word-painting, artistry, creative thought, creative work, creative force
▶ *126 Originality; 485 Skill*
2 **inspiration**, muse, inspiration from the muse, afflatus, divine afflatus, frenzy, poetic frenzy, ecstasy, genius
3 **insight**, understanding, empathy, sympathy, moral sensibility, sensitivity
▶ *591 Sensitivity*
4 **ideality**, mental image, mental picture, impression, con-

cept, conception, thought, idealization, ideal, ego ideal, appearance, image, picture, projection, fancy, conceit (Lit), coinage of the brain, brain-creation, brainchild, notion, idea, whim, maggot, vagary, caprice, whimsy (*or* whimsey), whimsical notion, whim-wham (Lit), crinkum-crankum, absurdity, unreality, figment, figment of the imagination, fiction, work of fiction, creative writing, story, novel, romance, science fiction, fantasy, fairy tale, imaginary world, imaginative exercise, creative exercise, flight of fancy, play of fancy, daydream, uncontrolled imagination, extravaganza, rhapsody, exaggeration, falsehood, poetic licence, poetry, quixotry, knight errantry, tilting at windmills, shadow boxing, sciamachy

▶ *17 Literature; 96 Unreality; 443 Thought; 446 Idea; 525 Appearance; 642 Frivolity; 697 Nonsense; 699 Falsehood; 721 Description; 727 Exaggeration*

5 **fantasy**, fabrication, improvisation, make-believe, vision, wildest dreams, dream, bad dream, nightmare, bogey (*or* bogy), phantom, ghost, apparition, spectre, shadow, vapour (Lit), dimness, mirage, Fata Morgana, visual fallacy, fancy, illusion, optical illusion, trompe l'oeil, delusion, hallucination, chimera, error

▶ *118 Nonconformity; 274 Error; 518 Vision; 524 Dimness*

6 **reverie**, daydream, brown study, abstractedness, abstraction, head in the clouds, sleepwalking, somnambulism, trance, insensibility, delirium, frenzy, subjectivism, autosuggestion, wishful thinking, sophistry, window-shopping, golden dream, pipe dream, fantasia, wish, desire, romance, stardust, romanticism, escapism

▶ *461 Insanity; 472 Inattention; 489 Insensibility; 617 Desire; 702 Sophistry*

7 **idealism**, Utopianism, castles in the air, castles in Spain, castles in the sand, pie in the sky, end of the rainbow, good times coming, millennium, idle fancy, myth, fable, jam tomorrow (Inf)

▶ *283 Future Time; 617 Desire*

8 **dreamland**, dream world, Utopia, Erewhon, promised land, land of milk and honey, Garden of Eden, El Dorado, Happy Valley, Fortunate Isles, Isles of the Blest, Cockaigne, Ruritania, Arcadia, Shangri-la, Atlantis, Lyonnesse, Middle-earth, Narnia, Oz, never-never land, wonderland, fairyland, cloud-cuckoo-land, the end of the rainbow

▶ *283 Future Time*

9 **visionary**, seer, diviner, dreamer, daydreamer, somnambulist, fantast, fantasist, idealist, Utopian, philanthropist, escapist, ostrich, avoider, lotus-eater, wishful thinker, romantic, romancer, romanticist, myth-maker, rhapsodist, enthusiast, knight errant, Don Quixote, eccentric, crank, creative worker, artist, poet

▶ *461 Insanity; 472 Inattention; 475 Prediction; 634 Avoidance*

ADJECTIVES

10 **imaginative**, creative, inventive, innovative, original, ingenious, resourceful, clever, enterprising, skilful, eidetic, visualizing, perceptive, fertile, fecund, productive, inspired, fancy-led, romancing, romantic, high-flown, rhapsodic (*or* rhapsodical), enthusiastic, carried away, exaggerated, lively, vivid, poetic, fictional, Utopian, idealistic, dreamy, dreaming, daydreaming, in a brown study, in a trance

▶ *472 Inattention; 485 Skill; 562 Fertility; 727 Exaggeration*

11 **fantastical**, fantastic, unreal, bizarre, grotesque, extravagant, whimsical, fanciful, airy-fairy (Inf), preposterous, absurd, outlandish, impractical, Heath Robinson, Rube Goldberg (US), visionary, otherworldly, starry-eyed, quixotic, Laputan

▶ *96 Unreality; 697 Nonsense*

12 **imaginary**, imagined, unreal, abstract, illusory, illusive, fanciful, fancied, chimerical, ethereal, unsubstantial, insubstantial, lacking substance, subjective, hypothetical, suppositional, conceptual, notional, ideal, dreamy, dreamlike, visionary, not of this world, of another world, cloudy, vaporous, shadowy, fictitious, fictional, fictive, storybook, make-believe, thought-up, dreamed-up, created, invented, fabricated, contrived, devised, pretend, not real, simulated, imitated, nonexistent, untrue, unhistorical, mythical (*or* mythic), mythological, legendary, fabulous, fabled

▶ *96 Unreality; 274 Error; 476 Supposition; 524 Dimness*

13 **imaginable**, conceivable, thinkable, fanciable

VERBS

14 **imagine**, perceive, conceive, create, invent, think, suppose, think of, think up, conjure up, fancy, dream up, make up, devise, concoct, coin, hatch, produce, fabricate, originate, excogitate, have an inspiration, improvise, visualize, envisage, envision, see in the mind's eye, see, picture, conceptualize, conjure up a vision, form an image of, get a mental picture of, picture to oneself, represent to oneself, represent, paint, write, compose, paint in words, write a portrait of, realize, objectify, capture, recapture, call to mind, call up, summon up, use one's imagination, give rein to one's imagination, let one's imagination run riot, exaggerate, play with one's thoughts, pretend, make believe, hallucinate

▶ *356 Creation; 443 Thought; 476 Supposition; 478 Improvisation; 518 Vision; 717 Representation*

15 **fantasize**, live in a dream world, build Utopias, build castles in the air, build castles in Spain, build castles in the sand, see visions, dream of other worlds, dream dreams, daydream, muse, go into a brown study, idealize, see through rose-coloured glasses (*or* spectacles), romanticize, poeticize, fictionalize, rhapsodize, exaggerate

▶ *472 Inattention; 727 Exaggeration*

16 **have insight**, have understanding, understand, empathize, sympathize

▶ *591 Sensitivity; 695 Intelligibility*

ADVERBS

17 **imaginatively**, creatively, inventively, ingeniously, resourcefully, with imagination, with a flight of fancy, in the mind's eye, with one's head in the clouds, fancifully, romantically, idealistically

478 Improvisation

A master of improvised speech and improvised policies. A. J. P. Taylor.

ADJECTIVES

1 **improvised**, makeshift, provisional, jury-rigged, inventive, ad hoc, impromptu, ad-lib, extemporaneous, extemporary, extempore, unrehearsed, unprepared, unpremeditated, unmeditated, uncalculated, catch-as-catch-can (US), offhand, offhanded, off the cuff (Inf)

2 **spontaneous**, sudden, snap, spur-of-the-moment, unprompted, unmotivated, unprovoked, unforced, voluntary, willing, unguarded, incautious, rash, impetuous, impulsive, natural, instinctive, involuntary, automatic, knee-jerk, intuitive, untaught, emotional

▶ *445 Intuition; 590 Feelings; 615 Rashness; 636 Willingness; 646 Naivety*

VERBS

3 **improvise**, make do, throw together, invent, devise, contrive, come up with, think up, dream up, ad-lib, extemporize, vamp, think on one's feet, act on impulse, act on the spur of the moment, come out with, blurt, say whatever comes into one's mind, say whatever pops into one's head, flash out with, rise to the occasion, have a sudden brainwave (Inf), jam (Inf)

NOUNS

4 **improvisation**, invention, ad hoc measures, extemporization, jam session, cadenza, ad-libbing, ad-lib, impromptu talk, unpremeditation, thinking on one's feet, offhandedness

5 **spontaneity**, involuntariness, reflex, automatic reflex, knee-jerk reaction, impulsiveness, impulse, blind impulse, instinct, intuition, hunch, sudden thought, idea, flash, inspiration, snap decision, spurt of activity, burst of confidence

▶ *445 Intuition; 446 Idea*

6 **improviser**, innovator, inventor, extemporizer, adlibber, improvisatore, improvisatrice, creature of impulse, spontaneous person

ADVERBS

7 **extempore**, extemporaneously, impromptu, ad hoc, ad lib, spontaneously, suddenly, on the spur of the moment, involuntarily, instinctively, in an offhand manner, offhand, on the run, off the top of one's head, out of thin air, off the cuff (Inf)

479 Equivocation

We ought to see far enough into a hypocrite to see even his sincerity. G. K. Chesterton.

VERBS

1 **be equivocal**, be ambiguous, cut both ways, play on words, pun, have two meanings, have a double meaning, have a second meaning, speak oracles, speak with two voices, double talk, dissemble, deceive, mislead, fudge, hedge, beat about the bush, fence, sit on the fence, quibble, equivocate, avoid, evade, dodge, sidestep, trim, prevaricate, change the subject, waffle (Inf), speak with forked tongue (US inf), weasel (out) (Inf), change the channel (US inf), pussyfoot (Inf), shillyshally (Inf)

▶ *634 Avoidance; 694 Meaning; 699 Falsehood; 700 Deception; 702 Sophistry*

2 **equivocate**, tergiversate, change one's mind, think again, think better of it, change one's tune, shift one's ground, shift gears, move the goalposts, vacillate, shuffle, face both ways, be two-faced, run with the hare and hunt with the hounds, change round, swerve, tack, do a U-turn, wheel about, change front, turn one's back on, turn against, back out, withdraw, get cold feet, resign, forsake, wash one's hands of, turn over a new leaf, become a new man (*or* woman)

▶ *224 Change; 244 Improvement; 245 Deterioration; 355 Relinquishment; 605 Resignation; 639 Vacillation; 808 Remorse*

3 **apostatize**, change sides, change one's colours, change one's allegiance, turn one's coat, let the side down, turn renegade, turn traitor, switch, switch over, cross over, cross the floor, join the opposition, go over, desert, defect, blackleg, collaborate, betray, jump ship, jump (*or* climb) on the bandwagon, follow the rising star, stool (on) (US inf), rat (on) (Inf)

4 **recant**, unsay, take back (one's words), recall one's words, withdraw, retract, apologize, eat one's words, crawl, cringe, back down, back-pedal, go back on, renege, disavow, disclaim, repudiate, refute, deny, negate, renounce, abjure, forswear, swear off, recall, revoke, rescind, abrogate, eat one's hat (Inf), eat humble pie (Inf), eat crow (US inf)

▶ *623 Humility; 664 Servility; 708 Negation*

NOUNS

5 **equivocalness**, equivocation, ambiguity, ambivalence, indefiniteness, vagueness, uncertainty, mental reservation, concealment, prevarication, evasion, balancing act, white lie, untruth, quibble, quibbling, sophistry, two voices, contrariety, double meaning, amphibology, enigma, wordplay, play upon words, double entendre, pun, paronomasia, calembour, equivoque, newspeak, Pentagonese (US), double talk, gobbledegook, circumlocution, conundrum, riddle, oracle, oracular utterance, parable, polysemy, weasel word (Inf)

▶ *5 Language and Linguistics; 453 Uncertainty; 599 Humour; 634 Avoidance; 694 Meaning; 696 Unintelligibility; 702 Sophistry; 736 Concealment*

6 **equivocation**, tergiversation, change of mind, irresolution, vacillation, inconsistency, better thoughts, afterthought, second thoughts, change of purpose, alteration of plan, change of direction, deviation, shifting one's ground, versatility, back-pedalling, reversal, about-turn, U-turn, volte-face, withdrawal, change of mood, temperament, whim, caprice

▶ *224 Change; 325 Deviation; 355 Relinquishment; 639 Vacillation; 642 Frivolity; 808 Remorse*

7 **apostasy**, change of allegiance, conversion, turning renegade, turning traitor, going over, recreancy, desertion, defection, collaboration, betrayal, treachery, perfidy, unreliableness, untrustworthiness, improbity, ratting (Inf)

▶ *800 Dishonour*

8 **recantation**, taking back one's words, withdrawal, retraction, retractation, apology, eating one's words, disavowal, disclaimer, repudiation, denial, negation, renunciation, abjuration, forswearing, revocation, revoking, recall, abrogation, humble pie (Inf), eating crow (US inf)

► *708 Negation*

9 equivocator, tergiversator, opportunist, timeserver, toady, Vicar of Bray, double-dealer, weasel, two-faced person, trimmer, Janus, jilt, flirt, coquette, weathercock, recanter, forswearer, recreant, apostate, renegade, turncoat, reneger, traitor, Judas, betrayer, disloyal (*or* fair-weather) friend, quisling, fifth columnist, collaborationist, collaborator, lost leader, deserter, defector, quitter, runaway, informer, telltale, tattler, strike-breaker, blackleg, deviationist, secessionist, seceder, recidivist, backslider, proselyte, slippery customer (Inf), rat (Inf), ratter (Inf), grass (Inf), squealer (Inf), stool pigeon (Inf), scab (Inf)

► *227 Changeableness; 634 Avoidance; 693 Information; 700 Deception; 747 Cooperation*

ADJECTIVES

10 equivocal, ambiguous, ambivalent, epicene, not univocal, double, double-tongued, two-edged, facing both ways, left-handed, backhanded, equivocating, prevaricating, vague, evasive, misleading, roundabout, circumlocutory, oracular, amphibolous, homonymous, anagrammatic

► *179 Circularity*

11 equivocating, tergiversating, shuffling, slippery, supple, versatile, perfidious, double-dealing, hypocritical, two-faced, false, unfaithful, disloyal, traitorous, treacherous, apostate, recanting, renegade, recidivist, relapsed, going back, back-pedalling, vacillating, irresolute, fickle, whimsical, capricious, timeserving, flattering

► *639 Vacillation; 642 Frivolity; 677 Flattery; 699 Falsehood*

ADVERBS

12 equivocally, ambiguously, ambivalently, evasively, amphibolously

13 perfidiously, traitorously, treacherously, unfaithfully, disloyally

480 Persuasion

They will conquer, but they will not convince. Miguel de Unamuno y Jugo.

NOUNS

1 persuasion, persuasiveness, influence, clout (Inf), inducement, pressure, insistence, prompting, lobbying, salesmanship, sales pitch, sales talk, patter

2 flattery, cajolery, coaxing, teasing, wheedling, blandishment, honeyed words, side pressure, urging, incitement, encouragement, lecture, pleading, advocacy, solicitation, invitation, temptation, enticement, turn-on (Inf), soft soap (Inf)

3 incentive, lure, allure, allurement, seduction, seductiveness, tantalization, attractiveness, attraction, witchery, bewitchment, carrot, siren song, voice of the tempter, winning ways, fascination, charm, sex appeal, charisma, magnetism, it (Inf)

4 exhortation, pep talk (Inf), pep rally (US), rallying cry, clarion call, trumpet call

5 propaganda, promotion, self-promotion, publicity, advertising, pamphleteering, agitprop, consciousness raising, indoctrination, hard selling, brainwashing

6 advertising, advertisement, sales promotion, promotional literature, direct mail, soft sell, hard sell, public relations (PR), publicity, Madison Avenue, flackery (US inf), ballyhoo (Inf), hype (Inf)

► *740 Publication*

7 persuadability, docility, tractability, teachableness, willingness, pliancy, pliability, softness, susceptibility, susceptivity, credulity, suggestibility, credulousness, impressibility, sensitivity, putty in one's hands (Inf)

8 incentive, inducement, stimulus, fillip, nudge, threat, prod, slap, spur, goad, whip, rod, crack of the whip, big stick, carrot, carrot and stick, sop, jam tomorrow (Inf)

9 enticement, lure, trap, decoy, decoy duck, bait, baited trap, greased palm, special offer, sale of the century, loss leader, come-on (Inf)

10 bribe, kickback, backhander, slush fund, offer of a lifetime, offer one cannot refuse, pork barrel (US inf)

11 motive, reason, cause, cause of action, rationale, reasoning, justification, grounds, motivation, driving force, impetus, mainspring, causation, intention, objective, aim, goal, aspiration, ambition, ideal, guiding principle, words to live by, guiding light, direction, calling, call, vocation, conscience, dictate of conscience, honour, duty, personal reasons, ulterior motive, impulse, spur-of-the-moment

► *344 Cause; 478 Improvisation; 483 Motive; 610 Hope; 683 Selfishness; 810 Duty*

12 persuader, orator, rhetorician, advocate, pleader, coaxer, wheedler, salesman (*or* saleswoman), advertiser, ad man (*or* woman), promoter, propagandist, publicizer, publicist, publicity agent, public relations officer, PR man (*or* woman), vote-catcher (Inf), vote-snatcher (Inf), flak-catcher (Inf), spin doctor (Inf)

► *677 Flattery; 729 Speech; 740 Publication*

13 tempter, tantalizer, seducer, Romeo, rake, Casanova, temptress, seductress, Eve, vamp, *femme fatale* (Fr), Mata Hari, siren, Circe, Lorelei, Satan

14 motivator, mover, prime mover, manipulator, manager, agent, manoeuvrer, tactician, strategist, planner, instigator, prompter, suggester, hinter, inspirer, influence, counsellor, adviser, abettor, aider and abettor, *agent provocateur* (Fr), ringleader, firebrand, rabble-rouser, demagogue, seditionist, agitator, activist, lobbyist, lobbyer, lobby, pressure group, special-interest group, watchdog group, political association, ginger group, movers and shakers (Inf), wirepuller (US inf)

► *392 Help; 395 Influence; 484 Plan; 579 Management; 713 Advice*

VERBS

15 persuade, influence, advise, counsel, induce, pressure, lobby, insist, move, motivate, incline, dispose, prompt, instigate, bring about, cause, convince, win over, carry with one, carry one's point, prevail upon, talk into, urge, impel, push into, drive into, nag into, bully into, wear down, intimidate, browbeat, coerce, twist one's arm, compel, force, bring round, talk round, convert, indoctrinate, brainwash, bring to one's side, get in one's corner, bring over, make one of us, procure, enlist, engage, coax, wheedle, cajole, sweet-talk, blandish, turn someone's head, lay it on thick, conciliate, appease, pacify, take by storm (Inf), put the screws on (Inf)

▶ *395 Influence; 450 Belief; 677 Flattery; 749 Pacification; 760 Conversion*

16 **tempt**, lead into temptation, allure, lure, entice, seduce, hold out a carrot to, dangle before one's eyes, make one's mouth water, tantalize, tease, inveigle, ensnare, coax, wheedle, pander to, facilitate, make things easy for, clear the path for, grease the wheels, gild the pill, sugar the pill, sweeten the pot (Inf)

▶ *265 Easiness; 379 Trap*

17 **bribe**, offer a bribe, offer an inducement, hold out a carrot, give a sop to Cerberus, tip, reward, suborn, corrupt, buy off, square (Inf), pay under the table (Inf), offer a sweetener (Inf), grease the palm (Inf), oil (Inf), oil the hand (Inf)

▶ *752 Offer; 813 Reward*

18 **be persuaded**, yield, succumb, submit, give up, concede, agree, consent, believe, fall for, obey one's conscience, act on principle, come (*or* fall) under the influence, hear the call, feel the urge, buy (Inf), get it bad (Inf), catch the bug (Inf)

ADJECTIVES

19 **persuasive**, influential, impressive, convincing, cogent, hortatory, didactic, protreptic, directive, compelling, forceful, effective, telling, winning, inducing, incentive, motivating, encouraging, exciting, energizing, stimulating, tonic, challenging, rousing, inflaming, provocative, teasing, tantalizing, tempting, alluring, attractive, inviting, magnetic, fascinating, bewitching, hypnotic, mesmeric, charismatic, charming, sexy, irresistible, habit-forming, addictive

▶ *363 Attraction; 395 Influence; 450 Belief; 632 Habit*

20 **persuadable**, persuasible, credulous, receptive, open to suggestion, tractable, docile, inspired, motivated, goal-oriented, spurred on, incited, encouraged, egged on, spellbound, bewitched, induced, pressured

ADVERBS

21 **persuasively**, impressively, convincingly, cogently, forcefully, encouragingly, provocatively, temptingly, invitingly, irresistibly

481 Dissuasion

VERBS

1 **dissuade**, discourage, caution, warn, advise against, persuade against, convince to the contrary, talk out of, put off, argue against, confute, castigate, reprove, expostulate, remonstrate, cry out against, protest against

▶ *670 Disapproval; 704 Refutation; 711 Warning; 753 Protest*

2 **deter**, frighten off, frighten away, unnerve, rattle, shake, stagger, make one stop in one's tracks, give one pause, daunt, cow, intimidate, threaten, terrorize

▶ *612 Fear*

3 **deflect**, head off, steer one away from, turn one aside, wean away from, disaccustom, halt one's progress, ruin one's plans, hold back, keep back, restrain, crush, nip in the bud, stop, prevent

▶ *251 Restraint; 325 Deviation; 487 Unaccustomedness*

4 **put off**, disincline, disaffect, indispose, set against, turn against, repel, disgust, fill with distaste, render averse

▶ *596 Dislike*

5 **discourage**, dishearten, dispirit, depress, disillusion, disenchant, throw cold water on, dampen, extinguish, quench, squelch, cool, chill, damp the ardour, be a wet blanket, take the edge off, blunt, calm, quiet

▶ *602 Sorrow; 685 Moderation*

NOUNS

6 **dissuasion**, discouragement, no encouragement, contrary advice, caution, warning, reproof, admonition, expostulation, remonstrance, objection, protest, resistance, opposition, hindrance, setback, closed door, roadblock, red light, contraindication

▶ *113 Opposition; 378 Obstruction; 383 Resistance; 711 Warning*

7 **deterrence**, deterrent, disincentive, intimidation, terrorism, deflection, restraint, disinclination, disaffection, disheartenment, disenchantment, cold water, damper

▶ *251 Restraint; 325 Deviation; 596 Dislike; 612 Fear*

8 **cautionary person**, wet blanket, killjoy, spoilsport, party-pooper (Inf)

ADJECTIVES

9 **dissuasive**, discouraging, contrary, contradictory, cautionary, warning, monitory, expostulatory, chilling, damping, disheartening, deterrent

10 **dissuaded**, discouraged, disenchanted, disillusioned, disheartened, dampened, reluctant, unwilling

▶ *637 Unwillingness*

ADVERBS

11 **dissuasively**, discouragingly, dishearteningly, as a deterrent

482 Intention

NOUNS

1 **intention**, intent, meaning, purpose, set purpose, settled purpose, motive, *mens rea* (L), criminal intent, good intention, benevolence, ulterior motive, axe to grind

▶ *483 Motive; 650 Benevolence; 651 Malevolence; 694 Meaning*

2 **intentionality**, deliberateness, calculation, calculated risk, determination, resolve, resolution, predetermination, premeditation

▶ *106 Predetermination; 210 Calculation; 638 Resolution*

3 **future intention**, prospect, view, purview, plan, proposal, design, project, enterprise, undertaking, pursuit, study, occupation, preoccupation, ambition, aspiration, hope, desire

▶ *283 Future Time; 354 Undertaking; 617 Desire*

4 **formulated intention**, decision, judgment, final decision, final word, ultimatum, threat, promise, engagement, bid, bid for, attempt

▶ *353 Attempt; 464 Judgment; 711 Warning; 756 Promise*

5 **final intention**, overall design, ultimate purpose, ultimate aim, teleology, final cause, God's purpose, eschatology, the four last things, the grand scheme, the big picture, *raison d'être* (Fr), trend, tendency, intentional bias, tendentiousness, be-all and end-all (Inf)

▶ *131 End; 344 Cause*

6 **objective**, final objective, end, end in view, destination, aim, object, goal, mark, target, stationary target, butt, quintain (Lit), moving target, target area, bull's-eye, finishing line, finishing tape, winning post, place of pilgrimage, Mecca, Lourdes, Canterbury, prey, quarry, game, prize, cup, trophy, silver cup, silver plate, crown, wreath, laurels, dream, lifelong dream, vision, heart's desire, Promised Land, land of milk and honey, El Dorado, Fountain of Youth, Shangri-la, Holy Grail, philosopher's stone, pot (*or* crock) of gold at the end of the rainbow

▶ *131 End; 312 Arrival; 617 Desire; 633 Pursuit; 794 Prize*

VERBS

7 **intend**, mean, purpose, propose, have in mind, have in view, have an eye to, contemplate, think of, ponder, meditate, calculate, reckon on, plan, plan for, prepare for, look for, expect, foresee

▶ *474 Expectation; 484 Plan*

8 **resolve**, determine, determine to, mean to, have a mind to, really mean, have every intention, premeditate, predetermine, project, design, harbour a design, have a purpose, have a motive, undertake, engage, take on oneself, shoulder, promise, threaten

▶ *354 Undertaking; 638 Resolution; 711 Warning; 756 Promise*

9 **intend for**, destine for, predestine, mark down for, earmark, put aside for, hold for, keep for, reserve for, put on layaway (US)

10 **aim**, aim at, go for, try for, bid for, aspire to, dream of, strive after, work for, have designs on, set one's sights on, take aim, focus on, point at

▶ *324 Direction; 353 Attempt*

ADJECTIVES

11 **intending**, intent on, determined to, resolute, serious, serious-minded, seeking, out to, out for, with designs on, having in view, purposive, teleological, inclined, disposed, so minded, so inclined, prospective, would-be, hopeful, aspiring, ambitious, hellbent (Inf)

▶ *617 Desire; 638 Resolution*

12 **intended**, meant, for a purpose, for a reason, deliberate, intentional, voluntary, volitional, wilful, calculated, studied, planned, designed, purposed, purposeful, premeditated, aforethought, predetermined, determined, eschatological

▶ *106 Predetermination; 484 Plan; 635 Will*

ADVERBS

13 **intentionally**, deliberately, purposely, purposefully, on purpose, by design, wittingly, knowingly, with full knowledge, with one's eyes open, pointedly, designedly, advisedly, voluntarily, wilfully, with meditation, with forethought, with malice aforethought, ruthlessly, in cold blood

14 **for**, for a purpose, in order to, with the intention of, with a view to, with an eye to, with the object of, in pursuance of, pursuant to

15 **according to plan**, as planned, as arranged, to design, to one's own design, to one's own specifications

483 Motive

Never ascribe to an opponent motives meaner than your own. J. M. Barrie.

Nobody ever did anything very foolish except from some strong principle. Lord Melbourne.

NOUNS

1 **motive**, cause, reason, rationale, grounds, excuse, pretext, motivation, driving force, guiding principle, guiding light, guiding star, lodestar, ideal, intention, objective, object, design, purpose, aim, goal, hope, desire, ambition, driving ambition, impetus, stimulation, impulse, compulsion, inspiration, bright idea, call, calling, vocation, aspiration, selfish motive, ulterior motive, what makes one tick (Inf), brainwave (Inf)

▶ *344 Cause; 482 Intention; 610 Hope; 683 Selfishness; 810 Duty*

2 **inducement**, influence, encouragement, invitation, incentive, provocation, enticement, lure, allurement, attraction, attractiveness, charm, fascination, bewitchment, magnetism, magnetic personality, seductiveness, seduction, blandishment, cajolery, coaxing, flattering, teasing, wheedling, pleading, advocacy, advice, persuasion, persuasiveness, propaganda, agitprop, pressure, lobbying, solicitation, advertising, hard sell (Inf), soft sell (Inf), sales talk, patter, promises

▶ *363 Attraction; 677 Flattery; 710 Request; 713 Advice*

3 **stimulus**, stimulant, fillip, tonic, sop, prod, goad, spur, carrot and stick (Inf)

4 **negative stimulus**, threat, castigation, big stick, whip, lash, crack of the whip, threat of dismissal

5 **positive stimulus**, flattery, carrot, charm, spell, lure, bait, loss leader, special offer, limited offer, added attraction, profit, money, cash, pay, payment, salary, wages, benefits, pay increase, rise, raise (US), bonus, hand-out, gift, donation, gratuity, tip, bribe, kickback, baksheesh, slush fund, political favours, spoils system (US), tempting offer, offer one cannot refuse, golden apple, perk (Inf), sweet-talk (Inf), come-on (Inf), turn-on (Inf), freebie (US inf), pork barrel (US inf), hush money (Inf)

▶ *392 Help; 612 Fear*

6 **suggestibility**, susceptibility, receptivity, impressibility, tractability, malleability, adaptability, docility, compliance, willingness, putty in one's hands

▶ *636 Willingness*

7 **motivator**, prime mover, moving spirit, orator, rhetorician, preacher, lawyer, politician, instigator, rabble-rouser, demagogue, agitator, troublemaker, firebrand, ringleader, manipulator, manoeuvrer, strategist, tactician, manager, prompter, adviser, counsellor, aider and abettor, *agent provocateur* (Fr), tempter, temptress, seducer, seductress, *femme fatale* (Fr), siren, flatterer, coaxer, Svengali, Rasputin, hypnotizer, hypnotist, persuader, advertiser, salesman (*or* saleswoman), propagandist, public relations person, publicist, press agent, lobbyist, lobby, pressure group, special-interest group, ginger group, vamp (Inf), sexpot (Inf), flack (US inf)

VERBS

8 be motivated, be induced, succumb, submit, concede, give in, come (*or* fall) under the influence of, fall for, heed the call, feel the urge, follow (*or* obey) one's conscience, follow (*or* obey) one's instincts, catch the bug (Inf), be bitten by the bug (Inf), get it bad (Inf)

9 motivate, start, initiate, begin, set in motion, instigate, bring about, induce, prompt, actuate, move, cause, bring on, influence, persuade, convince, suggest, recommend, advocate, advise, counsel, talk into, bring (*or* talk) someone round, bring over, win over, enlist, recruit, bring to one's side, procure, carry with one, make one's point, carry one's point, have an impact with, interest, intrigue, prevail upon, act upon, appeal to, attract, captivate, fascinate, charm, coax, cajole, blandish, flatter, tantalize, make things easy for, energize, galvanize, electrify, encourage, cheer on, sound the trumpet, rally, inspire, inspirit, animate, rouse, arouse, exhort, stimulate, excite, evoke, call forth, challenge, provoke, impel, impress, jolt, jog, prick, spur, spur on, drive on, hurry, hustle, bend, incline, dispose, pull, draw, direct, lead, give a lead, set the pace, set a trend, set the fashion, be a trendsetter, hold out a carrot, make someone's mouth water, sugar the pill, sweet-talk (Inf), root for (Inf), turn on (Inf)

10 manipulate, play on (*or* upon), operate on (*or* upon), call the tune, put up to, abet, aid and abet, lobby, prejudice, bias, predetermine, predispose, lead astray, misdirect, mislead, insinuate, hint, lead into temptation, tempt, entice, seduce, lure, hypnotize, mesmerize, bewitch, infect, exert pressure, bring pressure to bear, force, compel, nag, drive, push, bully, browbeat, override, prevail upon, press, prod, goad, whip, lash, inveigle, incite, egg on, ensnare, entrap, get round someone, twist someone's arm (Inf), needle (Inf)

ADJECTIVES

11 motivational, influential, directional, directive, incentive, attractive, magnetic, persuasive, hortatory, hortative, provocative, incitive, instigative, inflammatory, hypnotic, mesmeric, irresistible, suggestive, motivating, influencing, convincing, compelling, encouraging, challenging, provoking, stimulating, electrifying, inciting, instigating, energizing, kinetic, galvanizing, inflaming, rousing, insinuating, teasing, tantalizing, alluring, tempting, inviting, charming, fascinating, bewitching, spellbinding

12 motivated, persuaded, moved, influenced, induced, prompted, impelled, caused, directed, encouraged, exhorted, challenged, urged, egged on, spurred on, pressured, lobbied, prodded, goaded, whipped, provoked, stimulated, electrified, energized, animated, inspired, inflamed, incited, roused, galvanized, charmed, enticed, lured, attracted, seduced, bewitched, coaxed, flattered, spellbound, hypnotized, mesmerized, self-motivated, goal-oriented

13 suggestible, susceptible, receptive, impressible, tractable, malleable, adaptable, docile, compliant, willing, easily led

► *636 Willingness*

ADVERBS

14 influentially, in order to influence, persuasively, provocatively, hypnotically, irresistibly, suggestively, convincingly, to convince, compellingly, rousingly, hortatorily, hortatively, insinuatingly, teasingly, tantalizingly, alluringly, temptingly, as a temptation, invitingly, charmingly, fascinatingly, bewitchingly, stimulatingly, inspirationally, encouragingly, seductively, susceptibly, receptively, tractably, docilely, compliantly, willingly

484 Plan

The best laid schemes o' mice an' men
Gang aft a-gley,
An' lea'e us nought but grief an' pain
For promis'd joy. Robert Burns.

Life is what happens to you while you're busy making other plans. John Lennon.

NOUNS

1 plan, scheme, design, programme, project, proposal, proposition, suggestion, motion, amendment, resolution, intention, proposed action, proposed line of action, master plan, overall plan, corporate plan, management by objectives, financial plan, budget, national planning, five-year plan, schedule, schedule of events, timetable, agenda, order of the day, plan of the day, new business, old business, any other business (AOB)

► *482 Intention*

2 policy, procedure, system, strategy, plan of action, contingency plan, emergency plan, emergency procedure, course of action, working plan, company policy, tactics, preventive action, forethought, foresight, statesmanship, diplomacy, operational research, management review, way, approach, address, attack, steps, measures, countermeasures, actions, reactions, counteractions, stroke of policy, coup, coup d'état, *coup de main* (Fr), scenario, forecast, prediction, brochure, prospectus, manifesto, political party platform, platform, political plank, political party ticket, ticket, slate (US), political line, party line, mandate, formula, rule

► *12 Government and Politics; 140 Rule; 317 Way; 340 Action; 352 Means; 475 Prediction*

3 expedient plan, expedient, contrivance, resource, resort, last resort, *pis aller* (Fr), last-minute rescue, eleventh-hour rescue, winning card, trump card, card up one's sleeve, ace in the hole, recipe, nostrum, antidote, remedy, answer, loophole, way out, technicality, income-tax haven, flag of convenience, device, gimmick, trick, stratagem, artifice, ruse, dodge, evasion, ploy, shift, fiddle, swindle, knack, stunt, feat, *tour de force* (Fr), masterstroke, bold move, inspiration, brainwave, brainstorm (US), ingenious plan, happy thought, bright idea, right idea, idea, notion, invention, contraption, gadget, ad hoc measure, improvisation, makeshift, stopgap, wangle (Inf), sting (Inf), wheeze (Inf), gizmo (Inf)

► *352 Means; 389 Escape; 394 Remedy; 446 Idea; 478 Improvisation; 485 Skill; 645 Cunning*

4 plot, secret plan, scheme, intrigue, web of intrigue, web, cabal, conspiracy, inside job, insider trading, insider dealing, racket, game, manipulation, machination, wire-pulling (US), string pulling, put-up, put-up job, secret influence, secrecy, latency, counterplot, countermine, frame-up (Inf), fit-up (Inf)

▶ *384 Defence; 737 Secrecy*

5 **map**, plan, ground plan, floor plan, town plan, street map, road map, A to Z, atlas, scale drawing, blueprint, layout, diagram, chart, flow chart

▶ *717 Representation*

6 **outline**, summary, skeleton, rough, roughcast, sketch, model, pattern, pilot scheme, prototype, draft, first draft, proof, proof copy, revision, revise, revised copy

▶ *723 Summary*

7 **planning**, scheming, contrivance, organization, order, systematization, rationalization, centralization, headquarters, base, planning office, board room, committee room, back-room, operations room, drawing board

▶ *407 Order; 579 Management*

8 **planner**, organizer, manager, deviser, contriver, framer, inventor, originator, hatcher, proposer, promoter, projector, founder, designer, architect, town-planner, backroom boy (*or* girl), mastermind, systematizer, systems analyst, strategist, tactician, manoeuvrer, diplomat, statesman, politician, Machiavelli, schemer, plotter, intriguer, intrigant (Lit), plot-spinner, cabal, conspirator, boffin (Inf), brains (Inf), wheeler-dealer (Inf), axe-grinder (Inf), go-getter (Inf)

VERBS

9 **plan**, scheme, design, contrive, organize, systematize, methodize, rationalize, centralize, order, programme, propose, suggest, resolve, intend, project, aim, approach, approach a problem, confront a problem, attack a problem, make (*or* draw up) a plan, conceive (*or* form) a plan

▶ *407 Order; 482 Intention*

10 **plan out**, draw up, draft, frame, shape, form, work out, map out, lay out, sketch, sketch out, chalk out, design, design a prototype, programme, draw up a programme, lay the foundation, lay the cornerstone, map out a course, mark out a course, shape a course, schedule, draw up a schedule, timetable, phase (US), adjust, revise, redo, recast, improve

▶ *160 Form; 244 Improvement; 717 Representation*

11 **invent**, create, concoct, hatch, formulate, think up, hit upon, fall on, discover, find a way, contrive, devise, engineer

▶ *449 Discovery; 477 Imagination*

12 **plan ahead**, prepare, arrange, prearrange, predetermine, think ahead, look ahead, calculate, budget, forecast, predict, foresee, envisage, expect, follow a plan, have a policy, work to a schedule

▶ *106 Predetermination; 243 Preparation; 409 Arrangement; 474 Expectation; 475 Prediction*

13 **plot**, scheme, have designs, be up to something, conspire, intrigue, machinate, cabal, concoct, brew a plot, brew, hatch a plot, hatch, undermine, countermine, set a trap for, dig a pit for, trap, ensnare, work against, manoeuvre, manipulate, wheel and deal (Inf), pull strings (Inf), pull wires (US inf), cook up (Inf), frame (Inf), fit up (Inf)

▶ *379 Trap; 395 Influence; 645 Cunning; 699 Falsehood*

ADJECTIVES

14 **planned**, intended, intentional, rational, meant, premeditated, contrived, designed, organized, schematic, systematic, orderly, methodical, worked out, prepared, strategic, tactical, under discussion, under consideration, at the planning stage, on the drawing board, in draft, in proof, on the stocks, drawn up

15 **planning**, scheming, cunning, contriving, resourceful, ingenious, purposeful, up to something, involved, in deep, intriguing, plotting, conspiratorial, Machiavellian, wheeler-dealing (Inf)

ADVERBS

16 **as planned**, intentionally, purposefully, according to schedule, schematically, methodically, systematically, strategically, tactically

17 **conspiratorially**, cunningly, intriguingly, resourcefully, ingeniously

485 Skill

There must be love
Without love you will be merely skilful. Frédérick Leboyer.

NOUNS

1 **skill**, skilfulness, mental skill, manual skill, professional skill, technical skill, social skill, ability, proficiency, competence, efficiency, faculty, special faculty, capability, capacity, adroitness, dexterity, dexterousness, handiness, deftness, adeptness, address, ease, facility, grace, style, elegance, neatness, many-sidedness, all-round capacity, versatility, adaptability, amphibiousness, ambidexterity, ambidextrousness, flexibility, suppleness, touch, grip, control, mastery, mastership, wizardry, virtuosity, excellence, prowess, expertise, expertness, professionalism, goodness, forte, strength, strong point, strong card, major suit, speciality, specialty (US), specialism, major subject (US), major (US), métier, accomplishment, attainment, acquirement, experience, knowledge, technical knowledge, practical knowledge, everyday knowledge, practical ability, technique, clever hands, deft fingers, craftsmanship, art, artistry, delicacy, fine workmanship, art that conceals art, execution, finish, perfection, ingenuity, resourcefulness, craft, craftiness, cunning, cleverness, sharpness, common sense, worldly wisdom, sophistication, sagacity, savoir-faire, finesse, tact, discretion, discrimination, gimmick, dodge, contrivance, trick, stratagem, tactics, skilful use, exploitation, use, nous (Inf)

▶ *230 Perfection; 235 Worth; 265 Easiness; 334 Power; 349 Use; 455 Knowledge; 458 Wisdom; 466 Discrimination; 484 Plan; 543 Elegance; 631 Behaviour; 645 Cunning; 700 Deception*

2 **aptitude**, talent, natural talent, inborn aptitude, innate ability, inherent ability, feeling for, eye for, ear for, propensity, inclination, tendency, bent, natural bent, faculty, endowment, gift, flair, knack, turn, green fingers, genius, genius for, aptness, fitness, qualification, good head for (Inf), know-how (Inf)

▶ *229 Tendency*

3 **masterpiece**, work of art, great work of literature, creation of genius, creation, beauty, jewel, *chef-d'oeuvre* (Fr), *pièce de résistance* (Fr), masterwork, magnum opus, work-

manlike job, stroke of genius, masterstroke, *coup-de-maître* (Fr), coup, exploit, feat, feat of skill, stunt, sporting feat, hat trick, act, deed, *tour de force* (Fr), brilliance, bravura, fireworks, ace, trump, clincher, exceller, *objet d'art* (Fr), curio, collectable, collector's piece (*or* item), classic, best-seller, hit (Inf), smash hit (Inf)

▶ *235 Worth; 340 Action*

4 skilled person, skilful person, proficient person, expert, adept, craftsman, craftswoman, do-it-yourselfer (US), DIY type, all-rounder, jack of all trades, handyman, admirable Crichton, paragon, Renaissance man, person of many parts, master, past master, graduate, intellectual, mastermind, sage, genius, wizard, gifted child, prodigy, maestro, virtuoso, bravura player, musician, first fiddle, prima donna, diva, prima ballerina, prizewinner, star, champion, world champion, Olympic champion, gold medallist, silver medallist, bronze medallist, *cordon bleu* (Fr), blue-ribbon winner, titleholder, belt-holder, black belt, brown belt, dan, cup-holder, ace, exceller, top selection, picked man, capped player, lettered player (US), varsity player (US), first-string, first-string player, All-Pro (US), All-American (US), star player, seeded player, seed, top seed, crack shot, dead shot, acrobat, gymnast, athlete, dab hand (Inf), dabster (Inf), white hope (Inf)

▶ *230 Perfection; 235 Worth; 336 Strength; 458 Wisdom; 619 Wonder*

5 expert, no novice, professional, practitioner, specialist, authority, doyen, learned person, intellectual, professor, teacher, scholar, pundit, guru, savant, polymath, scientist, veteran, old hand, old stager, old soldier, old dog, sea dog, practised hand, practised eye, knowing person, cunning fellow, slyboots, smart guy (US), fraud, trickster, sophisticate, member of the smart set, cosmopolitan, citizen of the world, man (*or* woman) of the world, man (*or* woman) about town, businessman, businesswoman, salesman (*or* saleswoman) of the month (*or* year), career woman, careerist, tactician, strategist, diplomatist, artist, artisan, craftsman, craftswoman, technician, skilled worker, experienced hand, right person for the job, key man, consultant, adviser, back-room boy, planner, connoisseur, cognoscente, fancier, pro (Inf), boffin (Inf), walking encyclopedia (Inf), brain (Inf), egghead (Inf), highbrow (Inf), wise guy (Inf), whiz kid (Inf), shellback (Inf), warhorse (Inf), smart customer (Inf), smart cookie (US inf), clever clogs (Inf), sharp (Inf)

▶ *455 Knowledge; 484 Plan; 578 Worker; 645 Cunning; 713 Advice*

ADJECTIVES

6 skilful, skilled, able, proficient, competent, efficient, talented, gifted, good, good at, excellent, superb, top-notch, top-flight, top-level, apt, handy, adroit, dexterous, ambidextrous, deft, adept, slick, neat, agile, sure-footed, nimble, nimble-fingered, green-fingered, clever, quick, quick-witted, shrewd, cunning, crafty, smart, intelligent, politic, diplomatic, statesmanlike, wise, sagacious, many-sided, versatile, adaptable, flexible, ingenious, resourceful, ready, ready for anything, panurgic, sound, competitive, masterful, masterly, magisterial, expert, highly qualified, accomplished, finished, perfect, first-rate (Inf), A1 (Inf), ace (Inf), crack (Inf), wizard (Inf)

▶ *230 Perfection; 235 Worth; 458 Wisdom*

7 gifted, naturally gifted, talented, blessed with talent, of many parts, endowed, well-endowed, born for, suited for, cut out for

8 expert, skilled, experienced, tried, seasoned, veteran, versed in, *au fait* (Fr), instructed, practised, well-practised, well-prepared, trained, finished, passed, qualified, highly qualified, specialized, matured, proficient, competent, efficient, professional, businesslike, up on (Inf), well up on (Inf)

▶ *243 Preparation; 455 Knowledge*

9 well-made, expertly made, well-crafted, professional, workmanlike, shipshape, finished, stylish, elegant, sophisticated, happy, felicitous, artistic, artificial, Daedalian, cunning, clever, craftily contrived, deep-laid

▶ *543 Elegance*

VERBS

10 be skilful, excel, do well, shine, have a flair for, have a knack for, have the knack, have a gift for, show a talent for, show aptitude, have the trick of, have (just) the right touch, have an eye for, have an ear for, have one's hand in, play one's cards well, not put a foot wrong, know what one is about, know just when to stop, use skilfully, exploit, take advantage of, squeeze the last ounce out of, make hay while the sun shines, profit by, live by one's wits, get around, know all the answers, have one's wits about one, be wise, exercise discretion, discriminate, know what's what (Inf), have a good head for (Inf)

▶ *121 Superiority; 235 Worth; 287 Timeliness; 349 Use; 458 Wisdom; 466 Discrimination*

11 be expert, turn professional, know, know backwards, know forward and backward, know one's stuff, know the ropes, know all the ins and outs, have the knowledge, have experience, take in one's stride, display one's skill, demonstrate, play with, stunt, show off, have the know-how (Inf), know one's onions (Inf)

▶ *6 Education; 455 Knowledge*

ADVERBS

12 skilfully, ably, adroitly, dexterously, proficiently, competently, efficiently, well, with skill, with aplomb, like an expert, like a master, handily, deftly, adeptly, neatly, stylishly, artistically, ingeniously, resourcefully, cleverly, shrewdly, intelligently, knowledgeably, expertly, professionally, scientifically, without fault, like a machine, naturally, swimmingly, in one's stride, as to the manner born

486 Unskilfulness

In a hierarchy every employee tends to rise to his level of incompetence. Laurence J. Peter.

ADJECTIVES

1 unskilful, ungifted, untalented, talentless, unendowed, unaccomplished, unremarkable, unimpressive, unpromising, unversatile, disqualified, unfit, inept, unapt, unable, incapable, impotent, undependable, untrained, uninstructed, unenlightened, unequipped, incompetent, inefficient, ineffectual, unpractical, unadapted, unadaptable, like a fish out of water, unadventurous, unbusinesslike, unprofessional, unstatesmanlike, undiplomatic, impolitic, ill-considered, uninformed, stupid, silly, foolish, unwise, thoughtless, inattentive, undiscerning, wild, giddy, impulsive, scatterbrained, carefree, easygoing, happy-go-lucky, light-minded, feckless, futile, failed, unsuccessful, unacclaimed, inadequate, insufficient, dumb (Inf), dim-witted (Inf), not up to scratch (Inf)

▶ *218 Insufficiency; 247 Failure; 335 Powerlessness; 343 Inactivity; 459 Folly; 472 Inattention; 751 Disagreement*

2 unskilled, raw, green, unripe, undeveloped, young, callow, immature, inexperienced, uninitiated, wet behind the ears, in (*or* under) training, apprenticed, half-skilled, semiskilled, unseasoned, unprepared, unqualified, inexpert, scratch, ignorant, unversed, unconversant, untrained, uninstructed, uneducated, untaught, untutored, uneducable, unteachable, unfinished, nonprofessional, nonspecialist, lay, amateurish, amateur, self-taught, self-made, autodidactic, unscientific, unsound, charlatan, quack, quackish, specious, pretentious, affected, pickup (US inf), ham (Inf)

▶ *456 Ignorance; 676 Affectation*

3 clumsy, awkward, gauche, gawky, gawkish, ungainly, uneasy, uncertain, boorish, churlish, discourteous, uncouth, unrefined, ill-mannered, rude, surly, stuttering, stammering, tactless, indiscreet, indiscriminating, bumbling, bungling, lubberly, maladroit, unhandy, all thumbs, left-handed, one-handed, heavy-handed, heavy-footed, unsteady, unbalanced, lumbering, hulking, gangling, stumbling, shambling, wobbly-legged, stiff, rusty, unused, on the shelf, unaccustomed, unhabituated, unpractised, out of practice, out of training, out of kilter, off one's timing, off one's stride, off form, out-of-touch, losing one's touch, losing one's feel, losing it, slipping, careless, hasty, haphazard, slapdash, negligent, slovenly, slatternly, fumbling, groping, tentative, experimental, ungraceful, graceless, inelegant, clownish, top-heavy, lopsided, unequal, cumbersome, ponderous, clumsily built, unmanageable, unsteerable, unwieldy, inexact, unadjusted, dribbling (US inf), babbling (US inf), out of sync (Inf), ham-handed (*or* ham-fisted) (Inf), cack-handed (Inf), butterfingered (Inf), rubber-legged (Inf)

▶ *120 Inequality; 158 Size; 274 Error; 350 Nonuse; 448 Experiment; 487 Unaccustomedness; 544 Inelegance; 659 Discourtesy; 666 Negligence; 729 Speech*

4 bungled, badly done, botched, messed-up, fouled-up, foozled, mismanaged, mishandled, maladministered, misapplied, botchy, messy, faulty, imperfect, misguided, ill-advised, ill-judged, ill-timed, unhappy, infelicitous, unplanned, unprepared, ill-contrived, ill-defined, ill-considered, ill-devised, ill-prepared, thrown together, cobbled together, crude, unpolished, rough and ready, inartistic, amateurish, amateur, jerry-built, home-made, do-it-yourself, DIY, artless, slapdash, superficial, perfunctory, neglected, uncompleted, bodged (Inf), screwed-up (Inf), fucked-up (Inf), half-baked (Inf), half-assed (US inf)

▶ *231 Imperfection; 646 Naivety; 666 Negligence*

VERBS

5 be unskilful, lack skill, lack talent, not have the skills, not know how, not know, show one's ignorance, not have a clue, go the wrong way about it, start at the wrong end, do things backwards, do things halfway, do things by halves, not complete, not finish the job, tinker, paper over the cracks, burn one's fingers, put one's foot in it, catch a Tartar, reckon without one's host, not expect, mishandle, mismanage, maladminister, misconduct, misrule, misgovern, misapply, misuse, misdirect, blunder, err, make a mistake, miss one's cue, forget one's words, overact, underact, lose one's touch, lose one's feel, lose one's cunning, lose one's skill, lose it, go rusty, get out of practice, disaccustom, fail, face disaster, come unstuck, fluff one's lines (Inf), ham it up (Inf), come a cropper (Inf), lose out (Inf), lose one's nerve (Inf), lose one's head (Inf)

▶ *247 Failure; 274 Error; 456 Ignorance; 463 Forgetfulness; 487 Unaccustomedness; 612 Fear; 630 Surprise*

6 act foolishly, make a fool of oneself, make an ass of oneself, lose face, not know what one is about, not know one's own business, be one's own worst enemy, act in one's own worst interests, stand in one's own light, cut one's own throat, cut off one's nose to spite one's face, paint oneself into a corner, throw the baby out with the bath water, have egg on one's face, become an object lesson, quarrel with one's bread and butter, bite the hand that feeds one, kill the goose that lays the golden eggs, spoil the ship for a ha'p'orth of tar, bring one's house about one's ears, saw off the limb one sits on, shoot oneself in the foot, fall in one's own trap, knock one's head against a brick wall, put the cart before the horse, be penny-wise and pound-foolish, put all one's eggs in one basket, bite off more than one can chew, have too many irons in the fire, try to put a square peg in a round hole, put new wine into old bottles, blunder, labour in vain, attempt the impossible, go on a fool's errand, go on a wild goose chase, waste effort, lean on a broken reed, strain at a gnat and swallow a camel

▶ *103 Impossibility; 238 Uselessness; 697 Nonsense*

7 be clumsy, blunder, fumble, bumble, flounder, stumble, trip, trip over, not look where one is going, grope, lumber, hulk, get in the way, stand in the light, stutter, stammer, muff, fluff, foozle, pull, slice, mishit, misthrow, overthrow, overshoot, overstep, play into the hands of, spill, slop, drop, drop a catch, drop a sitter, drop a pop-up, let fall, catch a crab, score an own goal, let the cat out of the bag, make a faux pas, put one's foot in one's mouth, put one's foot in it, get egg on one's face, do a bad job, do badly, bungle, botch, foul up, mess up, make a mess of, spoil, mar, blot, impair, meddle, miscarry, fail, bobble (US inf), boob, galumph, bodge (Inf), dribble (US inf), drop a brick (Inf), screw up (Inf), fuck up (Inf), cock up (Inf), balls up (Inf), blow (Inf), make a hash of (Inf), fool with (Inf)

▶ *245 Deterioration; 247 Failure; 274 Error; 329 Overstepping; 342 Activity; 367 Lowering; 448 Experiment; 472 Inattention*

NOUNS

8 unskilfulness, lack of skill, want of skill, lack of ability, lack of proficiency, lack of professionalism, amateurism, lack of talent, no gift for, ineptitude, ineptness, unaptness, inability, impotence, incompetence, inexpertness, inefficiency, ineffectuality, lack of practice, rustiness, nonuse, ignorance, inexperience, immaturity, rawness, greenness, unripeness, underdevelopment, incapacity, disqualification, unfitness, pretension, quackery, charlatanism, clumsiness, awkwardness, gaucherie, lubberliness, unhandiness, left-handedness, heavy-handedness, backwardness, slowness, unintelligence, booby prize, wooden spoon, cack-handedness (Inf), ham-handedness (*or* ham-fistedness) (Inf)

▶ *335 Powerlessness; 350 Nonuse; 456 Ignorance; 459 Folly; 676 Affectation*

9 **bungling**, botching, bumbling, tinkering, half measures, pale imitation, travesty, noncompletion, bungle, botch, mess, shambles, foul-up, bad day, off day, one of those days, poor performance, poor show, bad job, unsatisfactory work, failure, flop, missed chance, untimeliness, dropped catch, fumble, foozle, muff, fluff, flub, miss, misfire, mishit, slice, misthrow, overthrow, own goal, mistake, error, thoughtlessness, inattention, tactlessness, indiscretion, infelicity, gaffe, faux pas, mishandling, mismanagement, misapplication, misuse, too many cooks, too many chiefs and not enough Indians, misrule, misgovernment, maladministration, misjudgment, misperception, misconduct, antics, much ado about nothing, wild-goose chase, wasted effort, lost labour, bobbling (US inf), dog's dinner (*or* breakfast) (Inf), pig's breakfast (Inf), pig's ear (Inf), cockup (Inf), balls-up (Inf), butterfingers (Inf)

▶ *238 Uselessness; 247 Failure; 274 Error; 351 Misuse; 465 Misjudgment; 472 Inattention*

10 **unskilled person**, learner, apprentice, trainee, student, probationer, beginner, novice, greenhorn, raw recruit, colt, rookie (Inf), dude (US), amateur, dabbler, tinker, bungler, failure, loser, bad learner, one's despair, incompetent, botcher, bumbler, blunderer, bungling idiot, marplot, mismanager, fumbler, muffer, muff, lump, hulk, lubber, lout, clumsy lout, oaf, clumsy oaf, bull in a china shop, dolt, ass, fool, booby, looby, clown, buffoon, joke, butt, bumpkin, country bumpkin, clod, scribbler, hack, dauber, bad hand, poor hand, bad shot, poor shot, no marksman, jack of all trades and master of none, landlubber, fair-weather sailor, freshwater sailor, horse marine (US), ass in a lion's skin, jackdaw in peacock's feathers, imposter, quack, charlatan, mountebank, cowboy (Inf), nerd (Inf), wally (Inf), dipstick (Inf), ham (Inf), blunderbuss (Inf), boob (Inf), butterfingers (Inf), clumsy clot (Inf), swab (Inf), duffer (Inf), nitwit (Inf), nit (Inf), stooge (Inf), (big) galoot (US inf), bozo (US inf), jerk (Inf), stick (Inf), hick (US inf), rube (US inf), slob (Inf)

▶ *247 Failure; 408 Disorder; 459 Folly*

ADVERBS

11 **unskilfully**, ineptly, incompetently, inefficiently, unprofessionally, undiplomatically, foolishly, unsuccessfully, inexpertly, amateurishly, clumsily, awkwardly, carelessly, negligently, badly, imperfectly

487 Unaccustomedness

ADJECTIVES

1 **unaccustomed**, not used to, uncomfortable with, not in the habit of, nonobservant, unfamiliar, unwonted, unhabituated, untaught, untrained, uneducated, inexperienced, ignorant of, innocent, naive, new to, new, fresh, raw, callow, green, uninstructed, out of the habit, disaccustomed, rusty, unskilful, unseasoned, unripe, immature, undomesticated, untamed, unbroken, not broken, wild, still wet behind the ears (Inf)

▶ *456 Ignorance; 486 Unskilfulness; 555 Youth; 646 Naivety*

2 **not customary**, not done, out of the ordinary, not current, nonprevalent, unwonted, unpractised, not observed, unnecessary, not de rigueur, not in vogue, unfashionable, bad form, tactless, without manners, gauche, vulgar, out of step, out of fashion, antiquated, old-fashioned, old hat, stale, defunct, past, outgrown, discarded, disused, unconventional, nonconformist, unsanctified by custom, untraditional, unprecedented, unhackneyed, avant-garde, original, experimental, odd, strange, unusual, uncommon, way out (Inf), far out (Inf), non-U (Inf), out of time (Inf)

▶ *114 Diversity; 118 Nonconformity; 497 Blandness; 659 Discourtesy*

NOUNS

3 **unaccustomedness**, disusage, disuse, discontinuance, inexperience, unfamiliarity, unskilfulness, deterioration, staleness, lack of practice, rustiness, unconventionality, nonconformity

VERBS

4 **be unaccustomed**, slip, lapse, fall into disuse, grow rusty, deteriorate

5 **disaccustom**, wean from, cure, reform, break (*or* drop) a habit, give up, throw off, slough off, shed, kick (Inf)

ADVERBS

6 **unaccustomedly**, uncomfortably, ignorantly, innocently, naively, immaturely

7 **unskilfully**, inexpertly, incapably, inadequately, incompetently

8 **unusually**, uncommonly, oddly, strangely, unconventionally, eccentrically, originally, experimentally

Sensations

488 Sensation

O for a life of sensations rather than of thoughts! John Keats.

NOUNS

1 **sensation**, feeling, awareness, sentience, perception, experience, sense perception, impression, sense datum, sensum, response, reaction, receptivity, receptiveness, consciousness, emotion, sentiment, the senses, sight, hearing, touch, taste, smell, sixth sense, second sight, extrasensory perception, ESP, telepathy, clairvoyance, agitation, excitement, thrill

2 **ability to sense**, sensitivity, feelings, susceptibility, threshold of pain, irritability, tenderness, thin skin, vulnerability, soft underbelly, prickliness, ticklishness, touchiness, delicacy, sensuousness, sensuality, warm-bloodedness, oversensitivity, hyperaesthesia, allergy

3 **stimulus**, goad, prick, stimulant, heightener, thrill, throb, prickle, tingle, *frisson* (Fr), fluttering, buzz, kick, tickle, itch, horripilation, goose pimples, goose flesh, the shivers, formication, pins and needles, sore spot, titillation, stimulation, the creeps (Inf), heebie-jeebies (Inf)

4 **someone or something that feels**, aesthete, epicure, epicurean, shrinking violet, sensitive plant, cry-baby, sense organ, sensorium, nervous system, nerve, nerve fibre, raw nerve, nerve-ending, nerve cell, neurone, whisker, tentacle, proboscis, finger, fingertip, antenna, nerve centre

ADJECTIVES

5 **sensible**, sensitive, aware, aware of, alive to, sentient, feeling, percipient, switched on (Inf), clued up (*or* in) (Inf), in the picture (Inf)

6 **conscious**, awake, wide awake, sleepless, insomniac

7 **susceptible**, impressionable, perceptive, responsive, oversensitive, thin-skinned, allergic, delicate, tender, touchy, irritable, tetchy, jumpy, excited, temperamental, agitated, irritated, thrilled, stirred, overexcited, hyperactive, hyped up (Inf), hot-blooded, carnal, epicurean, sensuous, aesthetic

8 **sensate**, perceptible, tactile, palpable, tangible, audible, visible, noticeable

9 **exciting**, sensational, titillating, thrilling, stimulating, keen, breathtaking, impressive, stirring, emotive, poignant, striking, electric, electrifying, hair-raising, itchy, prickly, tingly, tickly

10 **sensory**, sensorial, nerval, nervous, neurological

VERBS

11 **sense**, be sensitive, be alive to, respond, react, tingle, prickle, tickle, itch, be itchy, be irritated, be irritable, have gooseflesh, have goose-pimples, horripilate, be aware, be aware of, detect, feel, have one's senses, perceive, see, hear, touch, taste, smell, realize, experience

12 **awake**, wake up, regain consciousness, come to one's senses, be on a high, have one's wits about one, be on the ball, have one's nerves stretched, be on tenterhooks

13 **arouse sensation**, wake, wake up, enliven, activate, stir, disturb, agitate, impress, invigorate, quicken, animate, stimulate, titillate, whet, galvanize, cause a sensation, thrill, excite, arouse, touch a raw nerve, heighten awareness, raise one's consciousness

ADVERBS

14 **sensationally**, feelingly, emotionally, excitingly, melodramatically

489 Insensibility

NOUNS

1 **lack of feeling**, lack of awareness, ignorance, lack of sensation, analgesia, paralysis, anaesthesia, clumsiness, heavy-handedness, dullness, insensitiveness, apathy

2 **unconsciousness**, coma, faint, swoon, sleep, doze, snooze, torpor, daydream, nap, catnap, stupor, trance, suspended animation, etherism, sleepiness, somnolence, numbness

3 **heedlessness**, impassivity, hardness, callousness, hard-heartedness, heartlessness, thick skin

4 **anaesthetic**, painkiller, analgesic, narcotic, opium, laudanum, dope, drug, ether, novocaine, cocaine, pethidine, barbiturate, halothane, lignocaine, acupuncture, hypnosis, Mickey Finn, sleeping pill, somnifer, sleeping draught, knockout drops, tranquillizer

5 **unfeeling person**, sleepwalker, somnambulist, robot, android, zombie, hearty, pachyderm, Sleeping Beauty

ADJECTIVES

6 **unfeeling**, blind, deaf, insentient, nerveless, senseless, insensitive, clumsy, heavy-handed, unresponsive, impassive, cold-blooded, apathetic, heedless, oblivious, unmindful, forgetful, unwary, impervious, unemotional, hardened, stolid, blockish

7 **anaesthetized**, etherized, frozen, hypnotized, insensible, numb, knocked out (Inf), deadened, inured

8 **unconscious**, stunned, concussed, in a coma, comatose, asleep, out cold, catatonic, away with the fairies, out for the count, dead to the world, wigged out (Inf), zonked out (Inf), knocked out (Inf)

► *690 Drunkenness*

9 **anaesthetic**, analgesic, deadening, numbing, hypnotic, narcotic, soporific, somnific, somniferous

10 **sleepy**, somnolent, dopey, drowsy, fuzzy, woozy (Inf)

VERBS

11 **be unfeeling**, be impassive, be apathetic, drowse, doze, sleep, sleepwalk, somnambulate, fall asleep, go to sleep, nod off, drop off, faint, pass out, black out, shut off, shut oneself off, switch off, ignore, be oblivious

12 **anaesthetize**, render insensible, etherize, put to sleep, put under, desensitize, deaden, blunt, benumb, freeze, hypnotize, mesmerize, narcotize, stun, stupefy, knock out, brain, render unconscious, concuss

ADVERBS

13 **insensibly**, unfeelingly, bluntly, insensitively, sleepily, somnolently, unconsciously, obliviously, imperceptibly, in one's sleep

490 Physical Pleasure

Great lords have their pleasures, but the people have fun. Baron de Montesquieu.

All the things I really like to do are either immoral, illegal, or fattening. Alexander Woollcott.

NOUNS

1 **physical pleasure**, pleasant sensation, feeling good, well-being, ease, contentment, comfort, pleasantness, cosiness, enjoyment, conviviality, fun, zest, *joie de vivre* (Fr), happiness, felicity, delight, bliss, euphoria, indulgence, the good life, luxury, opulence, sensuousness, loveliness, softness, smoothness, tastiness, sweetness, fragrance, self-indulgence, self-gratification, profligacy, gourmandising, epicureanism, *la dolce vita* (It), sensual pleasure, sensualism, hedonism, pleasure principle, dissipation, carnality, voluptuousness, sexual pleasure, eroticism, titillation, arousal, satisfaction, gratification, orgasm, climax, masturbation, sexual intercourse

► *241 Pleasantness; 263 Ease; 419 Softness; 581 Refreshment*

2 **good time**, happy hour, fun time, whale of a time, wine, women and song, bread and circuses, just what the doctor ordered, just the ticket (Inf), the life of Riley (Inf)

► *241 Pleasantness; 248 Prosperity; 263 Ease; 419 Softness; 581 Refreshment; 593 Love; 617 Desire; 781 Wealth*

3 **pleasure-seeker**, jet-setter, connoisseur, *bon viveur* (Fr), epicure, epicurean, gourmet, gourmand, lotus-eater, sybarite, playboy, sensualist, hedonist, voluptuary, roué, libertine, philanderer, rake, seducer, seductress, *fille de joie* (Fr), mistress, nymphomaniac, courtesan, good-time girl, sexpot (Inf), swinger (Inf)

► *617 Desire*

4 **pleasurable things**, comforter, amenity, cushion, comfort blanket, feather bed, snuggery, entertainment, feast, treat, banquet, beanfeast (Inf), spread, jamboree, splurge, sweetmeats, ambrosia, nectar, creature comforts, wall-to-wall carpeting, free lunch, luxury goods, revelry, carnival, spree, orgy, a good time, love-in, aphrodisiac, love potion, philtre, fleshpots

5 **idealized pleasure**, easy street, bed of roses, land of milk and honey, Elysium, Elysian fields, heaven, heaven on earth, earthly paradise

ADJECTIVES

6 **pleasant**, comfortable, easeful, restful, relaxing, soothing, comforting, warm, congenial, agreeable, likable, nice, pleasing, pleasurable, pleasure-giving, satisfying, gratifying, attractive, refreshing, enjoyable, convivial, delectable, charming, delightful, idyllic, Elysian, paradisiacal (*or* paradisiac), generous, luscious, opulent, luxuriant, luxurious, exquisite, sumptuous, de luxe, lush, lovely, silken, smooth, fun, welcome, inviting, snug, cosy, soft, cuddly, cuddlesome, heart-warming, lovable, blissful, palatable, delicious, mouthwatering, ambrosial, sweet, succulent, juicy, sweet-smelling, perfumed, fragrant, euphonious, dulcet, mellifluous, titillating, seductive, sensual, sexy, erotic, carnal, voluptuous, to one's taste, to one's liking, scrumptious (Inf), cushy (Inf)

7 **pleased**, relaxed, comfortable, warm, snug, cosy, content, contented, happy, delighted, at ease, sensual, self-indulgent, profligate, voluptuous, pleasure-seeking, licentious, hedonistic, fun-loving, wanton, sybaritic, nymphomaniac, aroused, excited, titillated, gratified, satisfied, coddled, mollycoddled, cosseted, pampered, spoiled, merry, euphoric, chuffed (Inf), gruntled, tickled pink (Inf), tickled to death (Inf), snug as a bug in a rug (Inf), in clover (Inf), in the pink (Inf), high (Inf), turned on (Inf), on a high (Inf), high as a kite (Inf)

VERBS

8 **feel pleasure**, feel good, enjoy, relish, revel in, take pleasure in, delight in, enjoy oneself, please oneself, have fun, make merry, bask, bask in, indulge oneself, gormandize, splurge, luxuriate, wallow, purr, nestle, snuggle, enjoy sex, have an orgasm, climax, kill the fatted calf, feather one's nest, have a ball (Inf), get a kick out of (Inf), paint the town red (Inf)

9 **give pleasure**, please, cheer, gladden, delight, charm, gratify, indulge, entertain, amuse, treat, regale, wine and dine, cuddle, hug, fondle, pet, stimulate, arouse, tickle, titillate, thrill, excite, satisfy, sate, satiate, make love to, warm the cockles of one's heart, take one's fancy, sugar the pill, gild the pill, tickle pink (Inf)

10 **comfort**, ease, relieve, slake, alleviate, appease, salve, soothe, soften, sympathize with, offer sympathy to, refresh, content, hug, cuddle, warm, mother, pet, make comfortable, coddle, mollycoddle, cosset, pamper, spoil, featherbed

ADVERBS

11 **pleasingly**, satisfyingly, luxuriously, indulgently, enjoyably, comfortably, happily, painlessly, warmly, cosily, blissfully, with pleasure, for kicks

491 Physical Pain

Whipping and abuse are like laudanum: You have to double the dose as the sensibilities decline. Harriet Beecher Stowe.

He that lives long suffers much. Proverb.

NOUNS

1 **pain**, hurt, painfulness, hurtfulness, soreness, suffering, dolour (Lit), malaise, affliction, misery, discomfort, distress, irritation, tenderness, sore spot, inflammation, pinprick, pins and needles, twinge, pang, pangs, smarting, prick, throes, cramp, spasm, stitch, ache, aching, aches and pains, throb, throbbing, agony, convulsion, anguish, ordeal, hell, martyrdom, passion, purgatory, lancination, stab, torment, hell on earth, punishment, physical punishment, flogging, torture

▶ *242 Unpleasantness; 814 Punishment*

2 **painful condition**, headache, splitting headache (*or* head), migraine, megrim (Lit), sick headache, toothache, earache, sore throat, laryngitis, ulcer, hunger pains, indigestion, heartburn, pyrosis, upset stomach, dyspepsia, stomachache, colic, grips, hernia, rupture, backache, lumbago, sciatica, rheumatism, arthritis, myalgia, neuralgia, heart pain, angina pectoris, angina, dysmenorrhoea, period pains, labour pains, afterpains, crick in the neck (Inf), tummyache (Inf), bellyache (Inf), gutache (Inf)

▶ *260 Ill Health; 591 Sensitivity*

3 **injury**, wound, lesion, trauma, scratch, scrape, graze, abrasion, bruise, contusion, bump, hit, sprain, burn, scald, cut, stab, puncture, jab, tear, slash, gash, laceration, bite, fracture, broken bone, broken jaw, mauling, savaging, bloody nose, black eye, shiner (Inf)

4 **pain relief**, analgesia

▶ *37 Pharmacology; 394 Remedy*

ADJECTIVES

5 **painful**, sore, hurting, uncomfortable, distressing, miserable, chronic, acute, stinging, tingling, smarting, cramping, lancinating, aching, tender, raw, throbbing, biting, gnawing, gripping, stabbing, shooting, grinding, splitting, pounding, agonizing, purgatorial, excruciating, exquisite, racking, harrowing, burning, searing, scalding, traumatic, extreme, unbearable, intolerable

6 **injured**, wounded, bruised, grazed, cut, punctured, scraped, sprained, lacerated, torn, fractured, broken, blackened

7 **feeling pain**, pained, suffering, hurting, distressed, sore, hurt, aching, anguished, in agony, agonized, convulsed, wincing, writhing, aching all over, tormented, tortured, afflicted, martyred, raw, black-and-blue, bleeding, blistered, traumatized

8 **inflicting pain**, painful, hurtful, hurting, torturing, tormenting, brutal, cruel, sadistic

VERBS

9 **feel pain**, suffer, hurt, ache, agonize, be afflicted, smart, wince, flinch, twitch, chafe, writhe, squirm, go through hell, be a martyr, show fortitude, bite the bullet

10 **be painful**, hurt, sting, tingle, smart, cramp, ache, throb, bite, gnaw, grip, stab, shoot, grind, pound, burn, sear

11 **inflict pain**, pain, hurt, injure, wound, hit, scratch, scrape, graze, prick, pinch, nip, tweak, sting, bruise, contuse, bump, sprain, burn, scald, jab, cut, tear, slash, gash, draw blood, bloody, puncture, run through, impale, fracture, punish, shoot, maul, mangle, savage, bite, claw, knife, stab, beat, beat up, beat black and blue, batter, smash, flog, thrash, convulse, traumatize, excruciate, wring, harrow, torment, torture, rack, martyr, crucify, touch a raw nerve, cut to the quick, give someone a bad time, carve up (Inf)

12 **express pain**, cry sob, wail, moan, gasp, whimper, groan, squeal, squawk, yelp, scream, shriek, screech, howl, yowl, yell

ADVERBS

13 **painfully**, throbbingly, achingly, excruciatingly, hurtfully, to the quick

492 Touch

And the stately ships go on
To their haven under the hill;
But O for the touch of a vanish'd hand,
And the sound of a voice that is still! Alfred, Lord Tennyson.

NOUNS

1 **touch**, sense of touch, feeling, tactile, sensation, impression, sense perception, aesthesia, aesthesis, sensitivity, tactility, tangibility, solidity, concreteness, reality, palpability, texture, consistency, feel, vibration

▶ *404 Texture; 421 Smoothness; 488 Sensation*

2 **touching**, physical contact, handling, fingering, palpating, manipulating, applying pressure, massaging, stroking, rubbing, fondling, holding, grasping, gripping, clutching, laying on of hands, osteopathy, chiropractic, fondling, caressing, petting (Inf), groping (Inf), goosing (Inf)

3 **press**, brush, graze, skim, flick, tickle, pinch, nip, tweak, twitch, pull, tug, yang, top, pot, dab, nudge, push, poke, prod, blow, hit, knock, strike, jab, bump, slap, punch, bot, smash, kick

4 **kiss**, caress, fondle, rub, stroke, nuzzle, maul, paw, pet (Inf), grope (Inf), goose (Inf)

5 **toucher**, massager, massagist, masseur, masseuse, osteopath, chiropractor, bonesetter, right-handed, left-handed

▶ *35 Medicine*

6 **contiguity**, convergence, confluence, conjunction, meeting, joining, node, connection, nexus, meeting place, meeting point, joint, junction, intersection, overlap, seam, interface

▶ *267 Stickiness*

7 **sense organ**, nerve, nerve-ending, feeler, toucher, whisker, antenna, proboscis, tentacle, palpus, palp, paw, claw, flipper, hand, right-handedness, dextrality, left-handedness, sinistrality, thumb, finger, first finger, forefinger, index finger, second finger, middle finger, third finger, ring finger, fourth finger, little finger, fingernail, fingertip, fist, toe, big toe, hallux, little toe, pinkie (Inf), dukes (Inf), knuckle sandwich (Inf)

ADJECTIVES

8 touchable, palpable, tangible, solid, concrete, material, real, substantial, perceptible, sensuous, attainable, at hand, handy, reachable, gettable, sensory, tactual, tactile, touch-sensitive, sensitive to touch, sensitive, tender, get-at-able (Inf)

9 touching, adjacent, adjoining, meeting, contiguous, bordering, abutting, intersecting, glancing, colliding, crashing, overlapping, interfacing, connecting, hand-in-hand, hand-in-glove

10 handed, right-handed, dextral, left-handed, sinistral, ambidextrous, light-handed, neat, delicate, heavy-handed, clumsy, manual, hand-operated, touch-operated, hands-on, able, artistic, skilful

VERBS

11 touch, contact, feel, finger, handle, palpate, manipulate, manoeuvre, massage, rub, rub noses, nuzzle, knead, caress, kiss, stroke, fumble, fondle, maul, paw, grope, graze, skim, shave, brush, flick, tickle, nip, pinch, stick, tweak, twitch, pull, pluck, tug, yank, hit, strike, pat, tap, dab, knock, slap, bat, punch, smash, kick, press, jab, poke, prod, nudge, elbow, play with, tamper with, tinker, tinker with, toy with, fiddle, fiddle with, buttonhole, pick up, seize, catch, hold, hold fast, hold on, lay hands on, grab, snatch, clutch, grasp, grip, pet (Inf), touch up (Inf), feel up (Inf), grope (Inf), goose (Inf), collar (Inf), nab (Inf), cop (Inf)

12 abut, adjoin, border, verge on, contact, come into contact, make contact, meet, touch, reach, converge, interface, come together, join, connect, overlap, attach, couple, splice, conjoin, impinge, brush, skim, graze, glance, kiss, collide, impact, bump into, bump, clash, crash, crunch, run into, intersect, link up, amalgamate, keep in touch, come to hand, shake hands, touch a sore point, make someone's hackles rise

13 be touched by, feel, be sensitive, tingle, itch, have gooseflesh (*or* goosebumps *or* goosepimples), bruise, become black-and-blue

ADVERBS

14 palpably, tangibly, solidly, substantially

15 insensitively, clumsily, heavy-handedly, with a heavy hand

16 sensitively, perceptibly, caressingly, light-handedly, with a light touch

17 manually, by hand, hand to hand

493 Heat

If you can't stand the heat, get out of the kitchen. Harry S. Truman.

NOUNS

1 heat, hotness, warmness, warmth, lukewarmness, tepidity, tepidness, temperature, room temperature, radiant heat, body heat, blood heat, warm-bloodedness, raised temperature, calescence, high temperature, fever, pyrexia, feverishness, inflammation, flush, hot flush, blush, fug, stuffiness, steam, steaminess, overheating, sweatiness, sweat, perspiration, white heat, incandescence, flash point, melting point, boiling point, first-degree burn, second-degree burn, third-degree burn, burn

► *35 Medicine; 437 Fuel*

2 heat measurement, temperature, calorific value, joule, calorie, kilocalorie, heat unit, BTU (British thermal unit), therm, calorimeter, thermometer, clinical thermometer, thermograph, Fahrenheit scale, Celsius scale, centigrade scale, Réaumur scale, specific heat, latent heat

► *26 Measurement*

3 heater, warmer, heating element, space heater, space heating, fan heater, convection heater, gas heater, central heating, radiator, hot-water tank, hot-water pipes, boiler, copper, immersion heater, geyser, thermostat, underfloor heating, hypocaust, hot-air vent (*or* duct), solar heating, solar panel, antifreeze, ethylene glycol, de-icer, double glazing, lagging, insulation, polystyrene, Thermos™, winter clothes, thermal wear, winter woollies, overcoat, British warm, fur coat, fur hat, parka, foot-warmer, poultice, fomentation, warming pan, hot-water bottle, electric blanket, blanket, duvet, quilt, iron, electric iron, steam iron, branding iron, soldering iron, crucible, long johns (Inf), hottie (Aus and NZ inf)

► *551 Dress*

4 burner, cooker, stove, hob, hotplate, grill, griddle, kitchen range, oven, kettle, toaster, waffle iron (US), sandwich-maker, barbecue pit, spit, microwave oven, haybox, Dutch oven, gas ring

► *25 Cookery*

5 hot weather, summer, summertime, high summer, flaming June, midsummer, dog days, warm spell, hot spell, long hot summer, heat haze, midday sun, sunbathing, sunbath, sun bed, sun lamp, solarium, suntan, tan, tanning, browning, bronzing, sunburn, peeling, redness, blister, heat rash, sunstroke, heat exhaustion, heatstroke, sunbather, sun worshipper, nudist, warm front, summer drought, heat wave, tropical heat, sultriness, Indian summer, St Luke's summer, St Martin's summer, thaw, melting, global warming, greenhouse effect, greenhouse gases, warming of the earth's atmosphere, sizzler (Inf), scorcher (Inf)

► *522 Light*

6 fire, combustion, fireplace, hearth, chimney corner, inglenook, grate, hearthstone, flue, chimney, brazier, firebrand, flame, flames, blaze, glow, conflagration, holocaust, fireball, smoke, embers, ash, cinders, clinker, coke, charcoal, bonfire, beacon fire, kiln, furnace, smelter, forge, oast house (*or* oast), incinerator, torch, blowtorch, flamethrower, oxyacetylene burner, pyre, funeral pyre, coal fire, open fire, wood fire, campfire, wood stove, firebox, gas fire, gas jet, pilot light, gas oven, paraffin stove, Bunsen burner, electric fire, heat lamp, forest fire, house fire, arson, pyromania, firebomb, incendiary bomb, Greek fire, wildfire, firestorm, sheet of fire, sea of flames, towering inferno, flammability, inflammability, combustibility, spontaneous combustion, ignition, the stake, crematorium

► *308 Opening; 582 Death; 814 Punishment*

7 fireman, fire fighter, arsonist, pyromaniac, incendiary, firebomber, fire raiser, firebug (Inf)

8 hot place, hot spot, sun deck, sun lounge, *thermae* (L), *calidarium* (L), sauna, Jacuzzi™, Turkish bath, boiler room, greenhouse, hothouse, hotbed, conservatory, equator, tropics, Tropic of Cancer, Tropic of Capricorn, Africa, South Pacific, rainforest, equatorial rainforest, jungle, Amazon Basin, desert, Sahara, Kalahari, Gobi, Death Valley, Sunbelt, Deep South Torrid Zone, subtropics, Mediterranean, hot spring, geyser, Old Faithful, warm current, Gulf Stream, hot-air current, thermal, south wind, Zephyr, sirocco, volcano, magma, lava, Vesuvius, Etna, Hell, inferno, hellfire

ADJECTIVES

9 **hot**, thermal, thermic, feeling hot, warm, mild, tepid, lukewarm room-temperature, chambré, snug, fuggy, stuffy, heating, warming, calefacient, calorific, overheated, suffocating, piping hot, baking hot, fiery, fierce, scalding, searing, scorching, cauterizing, roasting, boiling, on the boil, simmering, steaming, sizzling, smoking, smouldering, red-hot, white-hot, incandescent, candent (Lit), molten, glowing

10 **on fire**, alight, flaming, in flames, burning, ablaze, flaring, burnt to a crisp, burnt to a cinder, inflammable, flammable, combustible, incendiary, igneous, caustic, thermonuclear, volcanic, pyrogenic, warm as toast, hot as hell, hot enough to fry an egg on, frazzled (Inf)

11 **warm**, balmy, temperate, springlike, mild, fair, clement, summery, sunny, sunbaked, blistering, scorching, humid, muggy, close, steamy, sticky, sizzling, sweltering, stifling, sultry subtropical, tropical, equatorial

12 **warm-hearted**, cordial, heart-warming, hot-blooded, ebullient, warm-blooded, homoiothermic, blushing, pyrexial (*or* pyrexic), fevered, feverish, flushed, hot and bothered, passionate, ardent, vehement, hot-tempered, fire-breathing, burning, torrid, seething, inflaming

13 **heated**, insulated, lined, padded, fur-lined, double-glazed, lagged, centrally heated, coal-fired, coal-burning, wood-burning, gas-fired, oil-fired, warmed up, warmed through, defrosted, heated up, preheated, baked, roasted, boiled, toasted, reheated, burnt, fired, burnt out, burnt down, singed, scorched, molten

VERBS

14 **be hot**, heat, heat up, glow, heat through, defrost, thaw, melt, de-ice, warm, warm up, reheat, cook, roast, toast, simmer, boil, scald, parboil, steam, bake, stew, braise, grill, fry, parch, wither, shrivel (up), melt down, smelt, solder, weld, fuse, lag, insulate, line, pad, double glaze, rub, chafe, take the chill off, stamp one's feet

15 **burn**, set fire to, set on fire, fire, set alight, torch, kindle, ignite, put a match to, catch fire, be on fire, flame, flare, blaze, crackle, smoke, fume, smoulder, burn up, burn down, burn out, singe, scorch, sear, calcine, char, carbonize, cremate, incinerate, vaporize, cauterize, brand, reduce to ashes, burn to a cinder, burn at the stake, burn to the ground, burst into flames, go up in flames

16 **feel hot**, keep warm, dress warmly, get overheated, blush, flush, sweat, perspire, run a temperature, be feverish, swelter, bask, sunbathe, sun oneself, suntan, tan, get a tan, brown, burn, peel, blister

ADVERBS

17 **warmly**, hotly, ardently, fierily, feverishly, to the boiling point, to a cinder

494 Cold

Cold hands, warm heart. Proverb.

NOUNS

1 **coldness**, lack of heat, chill, chilliness, coolness, cooling, low temperature, freshness, nippiness

2 **freezing**, frost, freezing cold, icing, iciness, frigidity, gelidity, algidity, sub-zero temperature, absolute zero

► *28 Physics*

3 **chill**, common cold, pneumonia, coryza, hypothermia, exposure, chilblain, frostbite

4 **cooler**, chiller, fan, air conditioning, air conditioner, ventilator, punkah, cooling tower, refrigerator, fridge, icebox (US), cool box, cool bag, Esky (Aus), ice bag, ice bucket, ice pack, chilled counter, chill cupboard, ice house, ice machine, freezer, deep freezer, deep freeze, fridge-freezer, refrigerant, coolant, liquid oxygen, lox, cryogenics, cryogen, cryonics, cryostat, cryosurgery

► *25 Cookery*

5 **ice**, ice cube, cracked ice, frosting, glaze, dry ice, glacier, ice sheet, pack ice, icecap, ice field, ice floe, frost, frostiness, hoar frost, white frost, frost hollow, rime, freeze-up, Jack Frost, black frost, hard frost, black ice, icicle, wintry shower, frozen rain, sleet, snow, snow flurry, flurry, snowfall, snowstorm, blizzard, white-out, snowflake, snow crystal, wet snow, slush, powder snow, granular snow, dry snow, snowball, driven snow, snowdrift, avalanche, hail, hailstorm, hailstone, snowman, Snow Queen

6 **Arctic**, North Pole, Antarctic, South Pole, Siberia, Arctic Circle, Land of the Midnight Sun, permafrost, snowline, snow house, igloo, Eskimo, iceberg, frigidarium, hibernacle, hibernaculum, winter quarters, frigid zone

7 **cold weather**, cold spell, cold snap, nippiness, severe weather, nip in the air, cold season, inclemency, cold front, chill factor, wind-chill factor, North Wind, Boreas, ice age, winter, December, January, February, wintriness, arctic conditions, dead of winter, depths of winter, brass monkey weather (Inf)

ADJECTIVES

8 **cold**, fresh, bracing, nippy, sharp, inclement, parky, breezy, invigorating, raw, chill, chilly, cool, coolish, unheated, chilled, shivery, pinched, biting, bitter, bleak, wintry, severe, snowy, sleety, frosty, icy, snowbound, snowed in, iced up, ice-bound, blue with cold, stiff with cold, perishing, ice-cold, algid, glacial, frigid, freezing, frozen, gelid, polar, Arctic, Siberian, frost-bitten, frozen solid (*or* stiff), frosted, hoar, frappé, iced, glazed, on ice, on the rocks, chilled to the bone, chilled to the marrow, cold as the grave, cold as marble, cold as charity, cold enough to freeze the balls off a brass monkey (Inf)

9 **heat-resistant**, heat-proof, insulated, air-conditioned, air-cooled, water-cooled, cooling, chilling, refrigerant, frigorific, freezable, freezing, refrigerated, unmelted, quick-frozen, freeze-dried, cryogenic, cryonic

VERBS

10 **be cold**, shiver, tremble, shudder, perish, quiver, have gooseflesh (*or* goose-pimples), freeze, catch cold, take a

chill, have the shivers, stamp one's feet, one's teeth chatter

11 become cold, cool down, lose heat, cool off, freeze, freeze over, congeal, ice over, ice up, be snowed in, be snowed under, freeze to death, get frostbite, be so cold one's toes (*or* fingers) drop off

12 make cold, chill, freshen, sharpen, ventilate, air-condition, fan, benumb, freeze, refrigerate, glaciate, freeze-dry

ADVERBS

13 coldly, coolly, wintrily, frigidly, icily, bitterly, frostily

495 Taste

Good taste is better than bad taste, but bad taste is better than no taste. Arnold Bennett.

NOUNS

1 taste, sense of taste, palate, tastiness, pleasant taste, sapidity, deliciousness, palatability, unpleasant taste, unpalatability, sharp taste, acid taste, tart taste, salty taste, spicy taste, sweet taste, sour taste, bitter taste, pungent taste, aftertaste

2 taste of life, experience, liking, preference, inclination, predilection, good taste, refinement, discrimination, elegance, cultivation, bad taste, vulgarity, lack of style, sweet taste, enjoyment, success, sour taste, bitter taste, disappointment, failure

▶ *25 Cookery; 241 Pleasantness; 464 Judgment; 466 Discrimination; 496 Flavour; 498 Sweetness; 499 Sourness; 549 Refinement; 595 Liking; 596 Dislike*

3 appetizer, starter, hors d'oeuvre, *bonne bouche* (Fr), apéritif, delicacy, dainty, titbit, sample, sampler, drop, morsel, mouthful, nibble, nip, *soupçon* (Fr), tasting, sampling, gustation, degustation

4 flavour, gusto, relish, savour, richness, sweetness, saltiness, sourness, bitterness, strong flavour, delicate flavour, flavouring, seasoning, flavour enhancer, monosodium glutamate (MSG)

5 taster, sampler, nibbler, eater, drinker, wine taster, diner, connoisseur, gourmet, epicure, gourmand, *bon vivant* (Fr), foodie (Inf),

▶ *557 Eating*

6 taste bud, appetite, taste test, taste treat, tasting cup, tester

ADJECTIVES

7 tasty, palatable, delicious, having flavour, tastable, edible (*or* eatable), esculent, comestible, sapid, tasteful, savorous, savoury, appetizing, inviting, relishable, delectable, dainty, epicurean, flavourful (*or* flavoursome), ambrosial, potable, drinkable, toothsome, mouthwatering, succulent, sharp, unpleasant, unpalatable, acid, spicy, sweet, sour, tart, bitter, pungent, salty, scrumptious (Inf), yummy (Inf), finger-lickin' good (Inf), done to a turn (Inf), moreish (*or* morish) (Inf)

8 tasteful, having good taste, cultivated, refined, discriminating, elegant, having bad taste, vulgar, lacking style, experiencing the sweet taste of success, experiencing the sour (*or* bitter) taste of failure

▶ *549 Refinement*

VERBS

9 taste, try, sample, eat, nibble, drink, test, experience, savour, degust, smack, enjoy, appreciate, relish, tickle one's palate, tickle one's fancy

10 make taste, add taste to, enhance, flavour, dress, garnish, spice, sauce

ADVERBS

11 tastily, deliciously, full of flavour, palatably, succulently, sweetly, bitterly, pungently, scrumptiously (Inf), mouthwateringly, tastefully, elegantly, tastelessly, vulgarly

496 Flavour

Then to the spicy nut-brown ale. John Milton.

NOUNS

1 piquancy, pungency, strong flavour, spiciness, sting, tang, tanginess, smokiness, tartness, bite, kick, sourness, bitterness, gaminess, raciness, poignancy, aroma

▶ *25 Cookery; 495 Taste*

2 seasoning, flavouring, condiment, salt, sea salt, pepper, black pepper, white pepper, peppercorn, garnish, dressing, salad dressing, mayonnaise, French dressing, vinaigrette, marinade, relish, sauce, soy (*or* soya) sauce, Worcestershire sauce, ketchup, barbecue sauce, horseradish sauce, mint sauce, cranberry sauce, chutney, pickle, dill pickle, gherkin, piccalilli, Tabasco™, onion, pickled onion, garlic, garlic salt, curry, Madras, curry powder

3 curing, smoking

4 stimulation, titillation, liveliness, spirit, zest, archness, harshness, roughness, poignancy

5 herbs, spices, allspice, angelica, aniseed, balm, basil, bay leaf, borage, camomile, caper, caraway seeds, cassia, cayenne, chervil, chilli, chives, cinnamon, clove, co-

HERBS AND SPICES

allspice	cloves	mustard
amandine	comfrey	nutmeg
angelica	coriander	oregano
anise	cumin	paprika
basil	curry	parakelia
bay leaf	dill	parsley
bergamot	dillseed	peppermint
black pepper	fennel	pimento
borage	fenugreek	rosemary
camomile (*or*	five spices	rue
chamomile)	garam masala	saffron
campion	garlic	sage
caper	garlic salt	savory
capsicum	ginger	sesame
caraway seeds	ginseng	sorrel
cardamom	hyssop	spearmint
cayenne pepper	juniper berries	stacte (Lit)
celery salt	lavender	sweet cicely
chervil	lemon mint	tarragon
chicory	lovage	thyme
chilli	mace	turmeric
chives	marjoram	vanilla
cinnamon	mint	white pepper

riander, cumin, dill, fennel, fenugreek, gentian, ginger, horseradish, hyssop, juniper, lemon thyme, lemon verbena, liquorice, lovage, mace, marjoram, mint, mustard, French mustard, English mustard, myrrh, nutmeg, oregano, paprika, parsley, peppermint, rosemary, rue, saffron, sage, savory, sesame seeds, sorrel, tarragon, thyme, vanilla, verbena, wormwood, *bouquet garni* (Fr), mixed herbs, *fines herbes* (Fr)

6 **cordial**, stimulant, reviver, restorative, tonic, medicinal drink, nip, toddy, smelling salts, sal volatile, pick-me-up (Inf)

7 **tobacco**, Virginia tobacco, Turkish tobacco, nicotine, tar, cigar, Havana, corona, panatella, cheroot, cigarillo, humidor, cigarette, filter-tip, cork-tip, king-size, high tar, low tar, menthol, cigarette case, cigarette lighter, packet, carton, box, cigarette end, stub, butt, cigarette paper, roll-your-own, rolling tobacco, cigarette machine, ashtry, snuff, snuffbox, pinch of snuff, oral tobacco, chewing tobacoo, plug, quid, tobacco sachet, pipe tobacco, shag, flake, clay pipe, meerschaum, churchwarden, water pipe, hubble-bubble, narghile, hookah, pipe of peace, culumet, tobacco pouch, stem, pbow, the weed (Inf), baccy, cig (Inf), ciggie (Inf), fag (Inf), cancer stick (Inf), coffin nail (Inf), fag end (Inf), dog-end (Inf)

8 **smoking**, draw, puff, drag, chain-smoking, passive smoking, smoking area, smoking compartment, smoker, nonsmoker, smoke-free area, smoker's requisites, tobacconist, smoker's cough, bronchitis, lung cancer

ADJECTIVES

9 **piquant**, pungent, aromatic, flavourful, appetizing, stinging, biting, hot, peppery, seasoned, spiced, herby, savoury, tangy, tart, sharp, sour, bitter, minty, highly flavoured, highly seasoned, spicy, salty, strong, smoky, smoked, cured, kippered, pickled, soused, gamy, racy

10 **stimulating**, interesting, intriguing, titillating, exciting, lively, restorative, medicinal, provocative, spirited, thought-provoking, poignant, arch

11 **tobacco**, smoking, smoke-free, smokingrelated, filter-tip, cork-tip, king-size, high-tar, low-tar, roll-your-own

VERBS

12 **season**, flavour, salt, pepper, marinate, souse, smoke, kipper, cure, dry, pickle, curry

13 **be piquant**, sting, bite, pique, goad, interest, stimulate, revive, restore, titillate, intrigue, excite, provoke, stir

14 **smoke**, smoke cigarettes, smoke cigars, smoke a pipe, draw, puff, drag, inhale, chain-smoke

ADVERBS

15 **piquantly**, pungently, aromatically, tartly, sharply, bitterly, medicinally

16 **stimulatingly**, interestingly, intriguingly, provocatively, spiritedly, poignantly

497 Blandness

NOUNS

1 **tastelessness**, blandness, mildness, insipidity, insipidness, plainness, unsavouriness, tameness, dullness, vapidness, vapidity, weakness, weakening, thinness, feebleness, adulteration, dilution, wateriness,

2 **dilution**, watering, watering down, staleness, flatness, banality, triteness, lifelessness, dryness, aridity, monotony, boredom, wishy-washiness (Inf), jejuneness, dissatisfaction, indifference

▶ *25 Cookery; 296 Oldness; 337 Weakness; 606 Dissatisfaction; 618 Indifference; 620 Boredom*

3 **tasteless items**, pap, mash, pulp, gruel, skilly, bread and milk, bread and water, weak coffee, dishwater, slop (Inf)

4 **bad taste**, tastelessness, lack of (good) taste, lack of refinement, inelegance, insensitivity, raciness, coarseness, crudeness, crassness, tackiness, tawdriness, gaucheness, vulgarity, indecency, obscenity

▶ *544 Inelegance; 675 Vulgarity*

ADJECTIVES

5 **tasteless**, bland, mild, insipid, plain, tame, dull, rapid, weak, thin, feeble, flat, stale, dry, arid, humdrum, monotonous, nondescript, unexciting, uninviting, lifeless, flavourless, unflavoured, unsalted, unseasoned, watered, watered-down, diluted, adulterated, dilute, milk-and-water, unappetizing, banal, trite, uninspired, boring, jejune, unsatisfying, indifferent, characterless, as dull as ditchwater, dry as dust, wishy-washy (Inf)

6 **coarse**, lacking refinement, having bad taste, tasteless, lacking (good) taste, inelegant, insensitive, undiscriminating, racy, tacky, tawdry, gauche, gaudy, vulgar, crude, crass, indecent, obscene, sick (Inf), gross (Inf)

VERBS

7 **be tasteless**, have no taste, taste stale, taste flat, lose taste, lose interest, show indifference, bore, pall

8 **dilute**, water down, thin, weaken, adulterate

9 **have bad taste**, lack (good) taste, lack refinement, act vulgarly

ADVERBS

10 **without taste**, blandly, insipidly, mildly, dully, weakly, flatly, drily, aridly, monotonously

11 **tastelessly**, coarsely, inelegantly, insensitively, racily, tackily, gauchely, vulgarly, crudely, crassly, indecently, obscenely

498 Sweetness

Things sweet to taste prove in digestion sour. William Shakespeare.

NOUNS

1 **sweetness**, sugariness, syrupiness, cloying, sweetness, sickliness, saccharinity, sweet tooth, fragrance, pleasantness, melodiousness, freshness, smoothness

▶ *25 Cookery; 241 Pleasantness; 421 Smoothness; 502 Fragrance; 516 Tunefulness; 595 Liking*

2 **sweetener**, sweetening, sugar, sucrose, glucose, fructose, dextrose, lactose, cane sugar, beet sugar, sugar lump, sugar loaf, caster sugar, granulated sugar, powdered sugar, icing sugar, refined sugar, unrefined sugar, brown sugar, demerara sugar, syrup, maple syrup, treacle, molasses, glycerine, artificial sweetener, saccharine, aspartame, Nutrasweet™, cyclamate, honey, honeycomb, Hymettus honey, clover honey, honeydew, jam, jelly, preserve, conserve, marmalade, nectar, delicacies, sweetmeats, fruit, candied fruit, glacé fruit, ambrosia, a spoonful of sugar, sugar and spice and all things nice

COMMON SUGARS

arabinose	mannose
fructose (*or* laevulose *or* fruit sugar)	raffinose
	rhamnose
fucose	ribose
galactose	sorbose
glucose (*or* dextrose *or* grape sugar)	sucrose (*or* cane sugar *or* beet sugar *or* saccharose)
lactose (*or* milk sugar)	xylose
maltose (*or* malt sugar)	

3 **dessert**, pudding, sweet, ice cream, chocolate mousse, custard, whipped cream, cake, chocolate cake, fruitcake, cheesecake, sponge cake, gateau, brownie, pie, apple pie, pastry, Danish pastry, patisserie, icing, frosting (US), marzipan, afters (Inf)

4 **confectionery**, sweets, sweeties (Inf), comfit, candy (US), bonbon, dragée, chocolate, milk chocolate, white chocolate, toffee, fudge, boiled sweet, jawbreaker (US), lollipop, liquorice, dolly mixture, peppermint, gumdrop, fruit gum, fondant, candyfloss, confectioner's shop, sweet shop

5 **sweet drink**, cocoa, hot chocolate, cordial, fruit juice, fruit squash, fruit crush, lemonade, orangeade, soft drink, Coca-Cola™, cream soda, ice-cream soda (US), sherbet, mead, sweet wine, dessert wine, muscatel, Sauternes, mulled wine, spiced wine, gluhwein, hot toddy, fruit cup, punch, liqueur

ADJECTIVES

6 **sweet**, sweetish, sweetened, saccharine, cloying, sickly, sickly-sweet, honeyed, sugared, sugary, sugar-coated, treacly, syrupy, ambrosial, nectared, nectareous, candied, crystallized, glazed, iced, frosted (US), bittersweet, sweet-and-sour, sweet as a nut

7 **pleasant**, fresh, smooth, fragrant, melodious

VERBS

8 **sweeten**, sugar, sugar-coat, honey, ice, frost (US), glaze, candy, mull, make pleasant, make fragrant, sugar the pill

ADVERBS

9 **sweetly**, pleasantly, freshly, smoothly, fragrantly, melodiously

499 Sourness

I am sure the grapes are sour. Aesop.

NOUNS

1 **sourness**, sour taste, tartness, bitterness, sharp flavouring, sharpness, dryness, acerbity, acidity, astringency, acidulousness, subacidity, vinegariness, unripeness, greenness

2 **unpalatability**, bitterness, gall, acridity, bile, nasty taste, foul taste, staleness, rancidness, mould, rottenness, unwholesomeness, rankness, brackishness, dankness

3 **sour thing**, crab apple, green apple, lemon, lime, aloes, sloe, vinegar, vinaigrette, bitters, Angostura bitters, wormwood, sour milk, sour cream, soured cream, sloe gin, whisky sour, dry wine, sour wine, acid rain, tartaric acid, acetic acid, gall and wormwood

4 **spleen**, rancour, bile, biliousness, crabbedness, moroseness, sullenness, bitterness, sour grapes, crosspatch (Inf), sourpuss (Inf)

ADJECTIVES

5 **acid**, acidic, sharp, sour, tangy, tart, pungent, acerbic, acidulous, lemony, vinegary, acidulated, subacid, unripe, green, immature, hard, unsweetened, dry, acrid, biting, bitter

6 **unpalatable**, unappetizing, uninviting, unsavoury, unpleasant, disagreeable, nasty, disgusting, foul-tasting, nauseating, uneatable, inedible, dank, brackish, undrinkable, corked, harsh, stale, rough, rancid, overripe, mouldy, rotten, high, bad, off, curdled, fermented, on the turn, turned, unwholesome, contaminated, poisonous, toxic

7 **splenetic**, rancorous, bilious, sarcastic, harsh, crabbed, crabby, bitter, morose, sullen, grumpy

VERBS

8 **sour**, be sour, go sour, turn sour, acidify, sharpen, taste bad, taste foul, curdle, spoil, turn, ferment, go off, go bad, go mouldy, moulder, set one's teeth on edge

9 **disgust**, nauseate, sicken, embitter, turn one's stomach, get up one's nose (Inf)

ADVERBS

10 **sourly**, bitterly, tartly, sharply, drily, pungently, harshly, unpleasantly, inedibly, nauseatingly

11 **splenetically**, rancorously, harshly, sarcastically, morosely, sullenly, grumpily

500 Smell

Music, when soft voices die,
Vibrates in the memory –
Odours, when sweet violets sicken,
Live within the sense they quicken. Percy Bysshe Shelley.

NOUNS

1 **odour**, smell, smelliness, odorousness, scent, sweet smell, fragrance, perfume, unpleasant smell, stench, stink, slight smell, faint smell, aroma, aromaticity, bouquet, nose, savour, breath, air, suggestion, whiff, waft, smoke, vapour, exhalation, emanation, heady scent, redolence, strong smell, fruitiness, pungency, fresh smell, olfactology, olfactologist, olfactronics, odorimetry, olfactometry

▶ *99 Essence; 432 Gas; 502 Fragrance; 503 Stench*

2 **sense of smell**, smelling, act of smelling, olfaction, inhalation, sniff, sniffing, sniffle, nosing, nose, nostril, naris, nasal cavity, olfactory nerve, smelling bottle, smelling salts, herbs, spices, sniffer dog, bloodhound, keen nose, good nose, snuffler, snout (Inf), hooter (Inf), schnozzle (Inf), snoot (Inf), smeller (Inf), conk (Inf), proboscis (Inf), beak (Inf)

▶ *185 Bulge; 434 Air; 466 Discrimination*

3 **scent**, trail, scent gland, pheromone

▶ *633 Pursuit; 744 Record*

4 **reputation**, repute, regard, aura, tone, character, savour, emanation, good odour, bad odour, odour of sanctity, smell of success

ADJECTIVES

5 **odorous**, odoriferous, smelling, olent, redolent, pungent, heady, fragrant, perfumed, scented, smelly, stinking, noisome, noxious, whiffy (Inf), aromatic, savorous, herby, spicy, downwind of, emanative, olfactible, pheromonal, keen-scented, sharp-nosed

▶ *466 Discrimination; 502 Fragrance; 503 Stench*

6 **olfactory**, olfactive, nasal, rhinological

VERBS

7 **smell**, breathe, breathe in, inhale, sniff, nose, sniff at, smell at, snuff, snuffle, sniffle, sniff out, smell out, nose out, catch a whiff of, get wind of, follow the scent, follow one's nose

▶ *434 Air; 633 Pursuit*

8 **have odour**, smell, smell of, emanate, exhale, stink, reek, pong (Inf), whiff (Inf)

▶ *503 Stench*

9 **impart odour to**, perfume, scent, aromatize

▶ *502 Fragrance*

ADVERBS

10 **odorously**, odoriferously, olfactorily, nasally, aromatically, headily

501 Odourlessness

NOUNS

1 **odourlessness**, inodorousness, lack of smell, scentlessness, deodorization, fumigation, freshness, cleanness, fresh air, ventilation, lack of sense of smell, anosmia, bad nose, nasal congestion, blocked nose, cold in the nose (*or* head), head cold, a breath of fresh air, smoke-free zone (*or* area), smokeless zone, no-smoking area

▶ *94 Nonexistence; 98 Absence; 256 Cleanness; 434 Air; 489 Insensibility*

2 **deodorant**, anti-perspirant, spray deodorant, roll-on, stick, mouthwash, breath-freshener, breath-sweetener, cachou, deodorizer, fumigator, ventilator, extractor fan, exhaust fan (US), air filter, air purifier, air freshener, cooker hood, disinfectant, drain cleaner, smell trap, stench trap, stink trap

▶ *255 Purity; 257 Hygiene; 497 Blandness; 502 Fragrance*

ADJECTIVES

3 **odourless**, inodorous, scentless, unperfumed, unscented, fragrance-free, odour-free, smoke-free, smokeless, smell-less, noseless, deodorized, disinfected, fumigated, clean, fresh, ventilated, upwind of, in the fresh air

▶ *255 Purity; 256 Cleanness; 257 Hygiene; 434 Air*

4 **deodorizing**, deodorant, cleansing, freshening, disinfectant

VERBS

5 **deodorize**, disinfect, fumigate, ventilate, freshen, clean, cleanse, clear the air, open a window, put off the scent

6 **have no smell**, lose one's sense of smell, have a cold in the nose, hold one's nose, be upwind of, lose the scent

ADVERBS

7 **odourlessly**, cleanly, freshly, upwind, in the fresh air

502 Fragrance

Here's the smell of the blood still. All the perfumes of Arabia will not sweeten this little hand. William Shakespeare.

NOUNS

1 **fragrance**, fragrancy, sweet smell, bouquet, aroma, scent, perfume, *parfum* (Fr), musk, muskiness, spice, spiciness, balm, balminess, perfume dynamics, aromatherapy, aromatherapist

▶ *256 Cleanness; 498 Sweetness; 500 Smell*

2 **fragrant thing**, new-baked bread, fresh coffee, wax polish, sea air, new-mown hay, flower garden, herb garden, herbs, spices, flower, bunch of flowers, bouquet, posy, nosegay, buttonhole, corsage, orange blossom, honeysuckle, lily, sweet pea, gardenia, lavender, jasmine, rose, bed of roses, rose garden, stephanotis, violet, carnation, tuberose, cloves, vanilla, sweet cicely, essence, essential oil, fixative, toiletries, body lotion, talcum powder, bath oil, shower gel, scented soap, rose water, lavender water, eau de Cologne, cologne, toilet water, eau de toilette, scent, perfume, French perfume, Chanel No. 5™, after-shave, pomade, scent bottle, perfume bottle, flacon, atomizer, perfume spray, lavender bag, lavender sachet, perfumer, *parfumier* (Fr), perfumery, all the perfumes of Arabia, pomander, potpourri, pastille, cachou

▶ *78 Flowers; 99 Essence; 241 Pleasantness; 490 Physical Pleasure; 545 Beauty; 547 Beautification*

3 **incense**, frangipani, resin, olibanum, frankincense, myrrh, camphor, eucalyptus, spikenard, musk, civet, otto (*or* attar), ambergris, patchouli, sandalwood, vetiver, chypre, censer, thurible, thurifer, joss stick

▶ *7 Religion; 10 Ritual*

ADJECTIVES

4 **fragrant**, sweet-smelling, scented, sweet-scented, perfumed, aromatic, flowery, floral, spicy, musky, fruity, pungent, heady, camphorated, balmy, ambrosial, aromatherapeutic

▶ *241 Pleasantness; 496 Flavour; 498 Sweetness; 500 Smell*

VERBS

5 **be fragrant**, smell sweet, smell like a flower garden

▶ *498 Sweetness; 500 Smell*

6 **perfume**, scent, aromatize, spray, burn incense, cense, thurify, embalm, lay up in lavender

▶ *7 Religion*

ADVERBS

7 **fragrantly**, aromatically, florally, spicily, muskily, pungently

503 Stench

O! my offence is rank, it smells to heaven. William Shakespeare.

NOUNS

1 **stench**, stink, unpleasant smell, bad odour, malodour, malodorousness, smelliness, fetor (*or* foetor), fetidness (*or* foetidness), mephitis, miasma, gas, effluvium, reek, exhalation, osmidrosis, sweatiness, fug, staleness, musti-

ness, frowstiness, frowziness, fustiness, fust, lack of ventilation, whiff (Inf), hum (Inf), pong (Inf), niff (Inf)

▶ *242 Unpleasantness; 500 Smell*

2 **something that makes an unpleasant smell**, bad drains, smell of drains, sewer, sewer gas, cesspit, cesspool, latrine, exhaust fumes, air pollution, cigarette smoke, cooking smells, boiled cabbage, rotting vegetables, sour milk, strong cheese, stinker, stink-bomb, hydrogen sulphide, sulphur dioxide, bad egg, rotten egg, body odour (BO), sweat, armpits, smelly feet, sweaty socks, halitosis, bad breath, dogbreath, ammonia, urine, excrement, sewage, dung, farmyard smells, breaking wind, flatus, fart (Inf), skunk, polecat, billy goat, stinkard, stinkhorn, garlic, asafoetida (*or* asafetida), putrefaction, putrescence, decomposition, decay, rancidity, gaminess, corruption, the great unwashed

▶ *32 Chemistry; 43 Agriculture; 245 Deterioration; 258 Dirtiness; 296 Oldness; 432 Gas; 499 Sourness; 560 Excretion*

ADJECTIVES

3 **stinking**, smelly, reeking, noisome, offensive, malodorous, foul-smelling, evil-smelling, mephitic, miasmic, miasmal, overpowering, unwholesome, sweaty, unwashed, fetid (*or* foetid), frowsty, frowzy, musty, unventilated, fusty, fuggy, stale, rank, olid, graveolent, gassy, asphyxiating, sulphurous, ammoniacal, whiffy (Inf), niffy (Inf), pongy (Inf)

▶ *258 Dirtiness; 296 Oldness; 500 Smell*

4 **putrid**, putrescent, decaying, rotting, rotten, decomposed, high, off, gamy, rancid, sour, tainted

▶ *245 Deterioration; 499 Sourness*

VERBS

5 **stink**, smell, smell bad, smell foul, reek, stink out, have bad breath, have halitosis, have BO, stink to high heaven, smell like a drain, smell like a midden, smell of rotten eggs, whiff (Inf), pong (Inf), hum (Inf), niff (Inf), break wind, fart (Inf), let off (Inf), let fly (Inf), drop one (Inf)

▶ *258 Dirtiness; 500 Smell; 560 Excretion*

ADVERBS

6 **stinkingly**, smellily, malodorously, sourly, mustily, fustily, rankly

504 Hearing

The song that we hear with our ears is only the song that is sung in our hearts. Ouida.

NOUNS

1 **hearing**, sense of hearing, audition, sharp ear, keen sense of hearing, good ear, musical ear, musicality, perfect pitch, absolute pitch, bad ear, poor ear, earshot, hearing distance, auditory range, range, audibility, listening, listening in, eavesdropping, attention, heed, heeding, mind, auscultation, sounding, acoustics, radiophonics

▶ *18 Music; 28 Physics; 505 Deafness; 507 Loudness; 695 Intelligibility*

2 **hearer**, listener, auditor, hearkener, ear witness, audience, congregation, house, audiophile, hi-fi enthusiast, eavesdropper, listener in, telephone tapper, monitor

3 **auditorium**, hall, concert hall, opera house, music room, listening post

4 **ear**, outer ear, earlobe, earhole, cauliflower ear, jug ears, bat ears, pierced ears, lug (Inf), lughole (Inf), shell-like (Inf)

5 **internal ear**, middle ear, tympanic cavity, eardrum, tympanum, tympanic membrane, auditory ossicle, incus, anvil, malleus, hammer, stapes, stirrup bone, Eustachian tube, inner ear, labyrinth, cochlea, cochlear nerve, semicircular canals

6 **otology**, otolaryngology, otorhinolaryngology, ENT (ear, nose, and throat), audiology, ear wax, ear drops, earache, otalgia, otitis, labyrinthitis, otologist, otolaryngologist, otorhinolaryngologist, ENT specialist, audiologist, aurist, hearing specialist, auriscope, audiometer

7 **ear attachments**, earmuffs, ear flaps, earring, ear clip, ear stud, ear plug, grommet, hearing aid, ear trumpet, earphone

8 **something heard**, noise, sound, speech, conversation, talk, hearsay, hearsay evidence, report, rumour, gossip, *on dit* (Fr), grapevine, jungle telegraph, word of mouth, word (*or* whisper) in one's ear, Chinese whisper, tattle, tittle-tattle, ringing in the ears, tinnitus, reflected sound, echo, reverberation, alarm clock, clock radio, doorbell, Entryphone™, earful (Inf)

▶ *28 Physics; 510 Resonance; 729 Speech; 734 Conversation*

9 **audio device**, sound receiver, hearing aid, deaf aid, ear trumpet, earphones, headphones, headset, telephone tap, wiretap, auscultator, stethoscope, audio, amplification, amplifier, volume control, broadcasting device, pickup, microphone, megaphone, loud-hailer, bullhorn (US), loudspeaker, speaker, loudspeaker van, public-address system (PA), Tannoy™, ultrasound scanner, echolocation, radar, sonar, asdic, sonic depth finder, sonobuoy, radio, radio receiver, wireless, transistor radio, car radio, spoken radio, talk radio, Citizens' Band radio (CB), telephone, phone, handset, earpiece, mobile telephone, mobile phone, car phone, Cellnet™, cellphone, cellular telephone, cellular radio, connection, call, radiotelephone, radiotelephony, radiophone, transceiver, intercom, telephone answering machine, answering machine, answerphone, Ansafone™, answering service, bleeper, pager, radiopager, radiopaging, tape recorder, cassette recorder, personal stereo, personal CD player, Walkman™, cassette, tape, record, disc, vinyl disc, compact disc (CD), bug (Inf), cans (Inf), mike (Inf), amp (Inf), steam radio (Inf), walkie-talkie (Inf), ghetto blaster (Inf), boom box (US inf)

▶ *18 Music; 692 Communications*

10 **sound quality**, monophonic sound, stereophonic sound, quadraphonic sound, listenability, reception, tone control, graphic equalizer, equalization, bias, phase, bass, treble, range, level, echo, reverb (Inf)

ADJECTIVES

11 **aural**, auricular, auditory, audile, auditive, acoustic, audio, radio, wireless, broadcast, transmitted, telephone, telephonic, radiophonic, audiovisual, hearing, audient, listening, attentive, musical, all ears (Inf), bugged (Inf)

► 18 Music; 28 Physics; 466 Discrimination; 471 Attention

12 **eared**, having ears, auricular, auriculate, ear-shaped, earlike, auriform, big-eared, long-eared, jug-eared, cauliflower-eared, lop-eared, crop-eared

13 **otological**, audiological, otolaryngological, otorhinolaryngological, ENT (ear, nose, and throat), otalgic, otoscopic

► 35 Medicine

14 **hearable**, audible, reachable, within range, within earshot, loud, soft, resonant, sonorous, echoing, echoic, carrying, listenable, easy-listening, easy on the ear, harsh, ear-splitting, loud enough to wake the dead

► 507 Loudness; 510 Resonance; 511 Faintness; 513 Harsh Sound

VERBS

15 **hear**, hear things, hear voices, perceive, catch, have an ear for, have a good ear, have perfect (*or* absolute) pitch, have a poor ear, have no ear, hear of, hear tell, hear tell of, hear on the grapevine, hear from, be in touch with, listen, give ear, lend an ear, hearken, hark, listen to, give a hearing, hear out, attend, pay attention, concentrate, heed, mind, learn, gather, auscultate, sound, listen in, tune in, pick up, overhear, eavesdrop, tape, tap, wiretap, intercept, monitor, pin back one's ears, prick up one's ears, be all ears, keep one's ear to the ground, keep one's ears open, have long ears, make someone's ears burn, have someone's ear, hang on someone's words (*or* lips), bug (Inf), get an earful (Inf)

► 471 Attention; 692 Communications

16 **be heard**, fall on the ear, reach, carry, come within earshot, sound, resound, reverberate, echo, transmit, broadcast, go on the air

► 510 Resonance

ADVERBS

17 **aurally**, auricularly, within earshot, within range, within hearing, within call, hearably, audibly, aloud, out loud, telephonically, by telephone, on the air, on the radio, audiovisually, attentively, auscultatorily, by ear, at first hearing

INTERJECTIONS

18 **hear hear!**, listen!, hark!, oyez!, hist!

505 Deafness

There are two kinds of deafness. One is due to wax and is curable; the other is not due to wax and is not curable. William Wilde.

NOUNS

1 **deafness**, hearing loss, hearing impairment, partial deafness, total deafness, deaf-mutism, poor hearing, defective hearing, failure to hear, tone deafness, unmusicalness, inattention, lack of attention, daydreaming, indifference, heedlessness, oblivion, insensitivity, deaf ears, lip-reading, lip-reader, sign language, American Sign Language (AMSLAN), signing, dactylology, finger alphabet, smoke signals, semaphore, hearing aid, deaf aid, ear trumpet

► 35 Medicine; 463 Forgetfulness; 489 Insensibility; 504 Hearing; 506 Silence; 556 Age; 592 Insensitivity; 618 Indifference; 692 Communications

2 **deaf people**, the deaf, the hard of hearing, deaf-mute

3 **inaudibility**, faintness, faint sound, ear plug, silencer, damper, mute, sordino, sourdine, soft pedal, soundproofing, sound insulation, baffle, threshold of hearing, ultrasound, poor reception, interference, jamming, mute button

► 39 Electronics; 511 Faintness

ADJECTIVES

4 **deaf**, unhearing, without hearing, hard of hearing, hearing-impaired, partially deaf, totally deaf, stone deaf, deaf as a post, deaf-mute, deaf and dumb, tone-deaf, unmusical, earless, deafened, stunned, wearing earplugs

► 35 Medicine; 504 Hearing

5 **unhearing**, unaware, oblivious, deaf to, heedless, unheeding, unconcerned, indifferent, insensitive, inattentive, dead to the world

► 463 Forgetfulness; 472 Inattention; 592 Insensitivity; 618 Indifference

6 **deafening**, ear-splitting, piercing, earshattering

► 507 Loudness

7 **unheard**, inaudible, toneless, faint, difficult to hear, muted, soundproof, ultrasonic, out of range, out of earshot, off-air, off the air, turned off, switched off, unheard of, deaf to all pleas, none so deaf as those who will not hear

► 506 Silence; 511 Faintness; 618 Indifference

VERBS

8 **be deaf**, go deaf, lose one's hearing, fail to hear, miss, ignore, turn a deaf ear, close one's ears, not listen, tune out, lip-read, use sign language, sign, have no ear for

► 463 Forgetfulness; 472 Inattention; 504 Hearing; 692 Communications

9 **deafen**, make deaf, burst the eardrums, stun

► 507 Loudness

10 **muffle**, mute, baffle, deaden, silence, soundproof, insulate, jam, drown out, use earplugs, put one's fingers in one's ears, turn the sound down (*or* off)

► 506 Silence; 511 Faintness

11 **be unheard**, fall on deaf ears, go in (at) one ear and out (of) the other, go off the air

ADVERBS

12 **deafly**, deafeningly, inaudibly, tonelessly, out of earshot, out of range

506 Silence

When you have nothing to say, say nothing. Charles Caleb Colton.

Silence is as full of potential wisdom and wit as the unhewn marble of great sculpture. Aldous Huxley.

Whereof one cannot speak, thereon one must remain silent. Ludwig Wittgenstein.

VERBS

1 **be silent**, be quiet, keep silent, keep quiet, keep mum,

not speak, not say a word, not open one's mouth, hold one's tongue, clench one's teeth, hold one's breath, make no noise, not make a sound, not make a peep, not utter a squeak, become silent, fall silent, stop talking, relapse into silence, lose one's voice, be struck dumb, get laryngitis, clam up (Inf), pipe down (Inf), knock it off (Inf)

▶ *511 Faintness; 730 Voicelessness; 732 Shyness*

2 **silence**, make silent, quiet, make quiet, quieten, hush, still, lull, quell, subdue, mute, stifle, smother, muffle, muzzle, gag, stop, put to silence, soft-pedal, play down, drown the noise, drown (out), can it (US inf), put the lid on (Inf), stop someone's mouth (Inf)

▶ *301 Motionlessness; 507 Loudness; 511 Faintness; 730 Voicelessness*

ADJECTIVES

3 **silent**, quiet, inaudible, noiseless, soundless, taciturn, mute, mum, tight-lipped, dumb, voiceless, aphonic, aphasic, tongueless, speechless, dumbfounded, wordless, hushed, still, stilly (Lit), calm, peaceful, quiescent, soft, faint, muted, soundproof, unsounded, unuttered, unspoken, tacit, solemn, awful, deathlike, quiet as a mouse, quiet as a lamb, silent as the grave, silent as the tomb, so silent one could hear a pin drop, clammed up (Inf)

▶ *301 Motionlessness; 511 Faintness; 589 Peace; 730 Voicelessness; 732 Shyness*

NOUNS

4 **silence**, quiet, quietness, noiselessness, inaudibility, soundlessness, taciturnity, muteness, dumbness, voicelessness, aphonia, laryngitis, speechlessness, wordlessness, hush, stillness, lull, rest, calm, peace, quietude, quiescence, softness, faintness, mutedness, solemnity, solemnness, solemn silence, awful silence, dead silence, deathlike silence, deathly hush, uncanny silence, perfect silence, total silence, not a sound, not a squeak

▶ *301 Motionlessness; 511 Faintness; 589 Peace; 730 Voicelessness; 732 Shyness*

ADVERBS

5 **silently**, in silence, quietly, inaudibly, noiselessly, soundlessly, calmly, peacefully, softly, faintly

INTERJECTIONS

6 **hush!**, sh!, silence!, quiet!, shut up!, that's enough!, peace!, soft!, mum's the word!, whist! (Dial), hold your tongue!, keep your mouth shut!, keep your trap shut! (Inf), dry up! (Inf), pipe down! (Inf), cut the cackle! (Inf), stow it! (Inf), can it! (US inf), knock it off! (Inf)

507 Loudness

Like German opera, too long and too loud. Evelyn Waugh.

NOUNS

1 **loudness**, high volume, noise, loud noise, ear-splitting noise, shattered silence, burst of sound, report, loud report, explosion, bang, blast, boom, sonic boom, burst, shell burst, slam, clap, thunderclap, alarm, siren, honk, toot, prolonged noise, reverberation, loud laughter, cachinnation, laughter, loud breathing, stertorousness, snoring, rumble, roll, rattle, thunder, storm, thundering storm, rumbling thunder, rattling thunder, thunderbolts of Thor, war in heaven, dashing, surging, hissing, sibilation, retort, fire, gunfire, artillery, bombardment, blitz, dissonance, cacophony, stridency, stridor, brassiness, shrillness, blare, bray, fanfare, flourish, trumpet blast, clarion call, call, view halloo, sonority, sonorousness, organ notes, clang, clangour, stentorian tones, plangency, resonance, ringing tones, bells, peal, chimes, campanology, diapason, swell, surge, crescendo, forte, fortissimo, tutti, full blast, full chorus

▶ *18 Music; 508 Sudden Sound; 509 Repeated Sound; 510 Resonance; 512 Hissing Sound; 513 Harsh Sound; 517 Dissonance; 711 Warning*

2 **outcry**, vociferation, clamour, shouting, screaming, roaring, bawling, yelling, hooting, chanting, shout, scream, shriek, cry, roar, whoop, howl, ululation, hubbub, hullabaloo, song and dance, slamming, banging, stamping, crash, clash, clatter, din, row, uproar, tumult, deafening row, noisiness, racket, bedlam, pandemonium, turmoil, rumpus, all hell let loose, enough noise to wake the dead, stramash (Scot), ballyhoo (Inf), shemozzle (Inf)

▶ *380 Violence; 408 Disorder; 514 Human Cry; 515 Animal Cry; 600 Rejoicing*

3 **audibility**, distinctness, sound, noise, broken silence

▶ *504 Hearing*

4 **sound maker**, voice, larynx, voice box, vocal chords, loud pedal, amplifier, public-address system, PA (system), loudspeaker, speaker, megaphone, loud-hailer, microphone, ear trumpet, hearing aid, loud instrument, gong, whistle, siren, horn, hooter, klaxon, rattle, bullroarer, buzzer, bell, alarm, door knocker, brass horn, trumpet, bugle, portable stereo player, stentorian voice, lungs, good lungs, good pair of lungs, lungs of brass, iron throat, mike (Inf), amp (Inf), ghetto blaster (Inf)

5 **loud person**, opera singer, Shakespearean actor, hog caller, drill sergeant, tobacco auctioneer, Stentor, Hermes, town crier

ADJECTIVES

6 **loud**, noisy, full of noise, on full volume, at full pitch, full, booming, ringing, carrying, deafening, ear-splitting, ear-rending, thundering, thunderous, rattling, crashing, pealing, clangorous, dinning, rackety, shrill, piercing, high-sounding, strident, braying, blaring, brassy, echoing, resounding, resonant, sonorous, plangent, deep, discordant, cacophonous, shouting, yelling, whooping, screaming, bellowing, crying, big-mouthed, loud-mouthed, lusty, powerful, full-throated, at the top of one's voice (*or* lungs), stentorian, brazen-mouthed, trumpet-tongued, uproarious, rowdy, rumbustious, rambunctious, boisterous, disorderly, multisonous, many-tongued, vociferous, clamorous, clamant, swelling, crescendo, forte, fortissimo, enough to wake the dead

▶ *408 Disorder; 510 Resonance; 513 Harsh Sound; 514 Human Cry; 515 Animal Cry; 517 Dissonance*

7 **heard**, hearable, audible, distinct

▶ *504 Hearing*

VERBS

8 **be loud**, sound, break the silence, speak, give tongue, speak up, raise one's voice, strain one's voice, crack one's voice, vociferate, shout, yell, roar, bellow, call, catcall, caterwaul, yowl, howl, ululate, shriek, cry, scream, squawk, skirl (Scot), trumpet, bugle, blare, whistle, shrill, bray, cachinnate, laugh, snore, clap, stamp, reverberate, resound, ring, peal, clang, rattle, thunder, fulminate, storm, clash, crash, clatter, slam, bang, blast, burst, boom, explode, detonate, go off, knock, knock hard, hammer, drill, din, shatter the peace, stun, deafen, split the ears, rend the eardrums, shatter the eardrums, ring in the ear, swell, fill the air, rend the skies, make the welkin ring (Lit), rattle the windows, bring the house down, raise the roof, blow the roof off, raise the rafters, raise all hell, awake the echoes, wake the dead, raise Cain, make a devil of a row, rampage, go on a rampage, kick up a shindy (Inf)

▶ *408 Disorder; 508 Sudden Sound; 510 Resonance; 513 Harsh Sound; 514 Human Cry; 515 Animal Cry; 600 Rejoicing*

ADVERBS

9 **loudly**, noisily, stridently, sonorously, uproariously, vociferously, lustily, at the top of one's voice, in full cry, full blast, full chorus, tutti, with a deafening roar, like all hell let loose, forte, fortissimo, crescendo

10 **aloud**, audibly, distinctly

508 Sudden Sound

Though I speak with the tongues of men and of angels, and have not charity, I am become as sounding brass, or a tinkling cymbal. Bible: I Corinthians.

NOUNS

1 **bang**, slam, wham, whack, thump, thud, blast, report, discharge, explosion, burst, volley, round, salvo, shot, pistol-shot, detonation, blowout, backfire, boom, sonic boom, peal, thunderclap, clap of thunder, crash, clash, kaboom (Inf), kapow (Inf), zap (Inf), Kazam (Inf)

▶ *507 Loudness*

2 **crack**, crackle, crackling, crepitation, sizzling, spitting, click, snap, slap, smack, clap, tap, rap, rat-tat-tat, knock, pop, plop, plunk

▶ *509 Repeated Sound*

3 **banger**, cracker, firecracker, squib, explosive, bomb, grenade, firearm, gun, shotgun, pop gun, rifle, air rifle, air gun

4 **belch**, hiccup, eructation, flatulence, burp (Inf), fart (Inf)

▶ *371 Expulsion*

VERBS

5 **bang**, slam, wham, blast, discharge, burst, burst on the ear, explode, blow up, detonate, backfire, boom, thunder, resound, echo, rumble, peal, crash, clash

6 **crack**, crackle, crepitate, sizzle, fizzle, spit, effervesce, click, clunk, clatter, rattle, snap, clap, rap, tap, slap, smack, pop, plop, plonk, plunk

7 **belch**, hiccup, eruct, break wind, burp (Inf), fart (Inf)

ADJECTIVES

8 **banging**, crashing, slamming, bursting, exploding, explosive, booming, thundering, thundrous, ear-splitting, deafening

9 **crackling**, crepitant, sizzling, spitting, clicking, rattling, popping, staccato

ADVERBS

10 **explosively**, like a bolt from the blue, bang, abruptly, suddenly, staccato

▶ *630 Surprise*

509 Repeated Sound

The most persistent sound which reverberates through men's history is the beating of war drums. Arthur Koestler.

NOUNS

1 **drumming**, thrumming, roll, rumble, rumbling, grumbling, booming, reverberation, echo, vibration, pulsation, palpitation, throbbing, pounding, beat, pulse, beating, drum, drumbeat, drum roll, tattoo, devil's tattoo, tom-tom

▶ *112 Repetition; 507 Loudness; 510 Resonance*

2 **humming**, whirring, buzzing, hum, whirr, buzz, purr, drone, bombination (*or* bombilation) (Lit), mutter, murmur, background murmur, blah-blah

3 **rattle**, clatter, clitter-clatter, chatter, babble, clack, racket

▶ *508 Sudden Sound*

4 **knocking**, knock-knock, rat-a-tat, rat-tat-tat, rub-a-dub, pitter-patter, pitapat, tick, ticktock, drip-drop

5 **ringing**, pinging, ping, pip, ring-ring, chiming, pealing, carillon, ding-dong

6 **musical repetition**, rhythm, trill, tremolo, vibrato, refrain, burden, chorus, canon, round

▶ *18 Music; 516 Tunefulness*

7 **repeated word**, reiteration, restatement, anaphora, epistrophe, catchword, buzz word, cliché, truism, catchphrase, slogan, rhyme, assonance

▶ *5 Language and Linguistics; 17 Literature; 553 Fashion*

VERBS

8 **drum**, thrum, roll, rumble, grumble, boom, reverberate, resound, resonate, echo, re-echo, vibrate, pulse, pulsate, throb, pound, beat, beat (*or* sound) a tattoo, tattoo

9 **hum**, whirr, buzz, purr, drone, bombinate (*or* bombilate) (Lit), mutter, murmur, witter

10 **rattle**, clatter, clack, chatter, babble, sputter, chug, rev up (Inf)

11 **knock**, tap, tick, ticktock, patter, drip

12 **ring**, ping, clang, chime, peal, toll, carillon

13 **trill**, quaver, warble, chorus, sing in a round

14 **repeat**, reiterate, restate, say it again, trot out clichés, talk in clichés

ADJECTIVES

15 **drumming**, rolling, thrumming, reverberant, reverberative, resonant, throbbing, pounding, beating, loud, insistent, persistent, incessant, repeated

16 **humming**, whirring, buzzing, droning, monotonous, repetitive, unvaried

17 **rattling**, clattering, chattering, sputtering, clicking, ticking, knocking

18 **pealing**, chiming, repeating

ADVERBS

19 **repeatedly**, resonantly, over and over again, rhythmically, insistently, persistently, repetitively, monotonously, incessantly

510 Resonance

NOUNS

1 **resonance**, resonation, reverberation, resounding, rebounding, hollowness, echo, re-echo, lingering note, reflection, recurrence, vibration, whirring, humming, buzzing, oscillation, sympathetic resonance, morphogenetic resonance

▶ *326 Oscillation; 509 Repeated Sound*

2 **ringing**, bell-ringing, tintinnabulation, campanology, peal, toll, knell, chime, tinkle, jingle, chink, clink, ping, ting-a-ling, clang, clangour, sounding brass, brass, blare, flourish, fanfare, tucket

▶ *507 Loudness*

3 **deepness**, lowness, profundity, booming, thundering, fillness, richness, sonorousness, sonority, plangency, deep note, low note, bass note, grave note, pedal note, low voice, bass, basso, basso profondo, baritone, bass baritone, contralto

4 **sources of resonance**, tube, tunnel, bell, handbell, church bell, doorbell, chimes, telephone bell, fire bell, cowbell, clapper, gong, triangle, trumpet, horn, stringed instrument

5 **resonator**, sounding board, sound box, resonating chamber (*or* cavity), sustaining pedal

ADJECTIVES

6 **resonant**, resonating, reverberating, reverberative, reboant, stentorian, resounding, rebounding, hollow, echoing, re-echoing, vibrating, pulsating, carrying, echoic, lingering, persisting, persistent, humming, whirring, buzzing

7 **ringing**, tintinnabular (*or* tintinnabulary), pealing, tolling, sounding, chiming, tinkling, jingling, pinging, clanging, loud

8 **deep**, low, deep-toned, deep-pitched, deep-sounding, deep-voiced, sepulchral, sonorous, vibrant, booming, thundering, full, rich, plangent, mellow, melodious, rounded, orotund, full-throated

▶ *516 Tunefulness*

VERBS

9 **resonate**, reverberate, resound, rebound, boom, echo, re-echo, be repeated, be reflected, recur, vibrate, whir, hum, buzz, oscillate

10 **ring**, ring in the ear, tintinnabulate, peal, toll, sound, knell, chime, tinkle, jingle, jangle, chink, clink, ping, twang, clang, blare, trumpet, tootle, toot

ADVERBS

11 **resonantly**, reverberantly, resoundingly, reflectively, recurrently, deeply, profoundly, richly, vibrantly, sonorously, plangently

511 Faintness

The harp that once through Tara's halls
The soul of music shed,
Now hangs as mute on Tara's walls
As if that soul were fled. Thomas Moore.

ADJECTIVES

1 **faint-sounding**, faint, subdued, hushed, muted, low, quiet, soft, gentle, piano, pianissimo, indistinct, unclear, distant, weak, muffled, stifled, whispered, murmured, muttered, mumbled, half-heard, inaudible, imperceptible

▶ *506 Silence; 730 Voicelessness*

2 **nonresonant**, deadened, dulled, damped, dampened, muted, muffled, stifled, smothered, silenced, soundproof(ed), dull, heavy, flat, dead

NOUNS

3 **mutedness**, faintness, lowness, softness, indistinctness, lack of clarity, nonresonance

4 **faint sound**, soft sound, undertone, bated breath, murmuring, murmuration, muttering, mumble, mumbling, whispering, susurration, rustle, rustling, crackle, sighing, moaning, whine, whining, humming, drone, droning, purring

▶ *512 Hissing Sound*

5 **dull sound**, heavy sound, thud, clunk, thump, bump, plump, plunk, plonk, plop

6 **silencer**, mute, damper, soft pedal, sordino

VERBS

7 **mute**, lower, subdue, dampen, damp down, soft-pedal, deaden, dull, muffle, stifle, hush, quieten, quiet, soften, still, silence

8 **sound faint**, drop (*or* lower) one's voice, murmur, mutter, mumble, whisper, breathe, susurrate, rustle, crackle, sigh, moan, whine, hum, croon, drone, purr

9 **be nonresonant**, sound dead, fall dead on the ear, arouse no echoes, thud, clunk, thump, plump, plunk, plonk, plop

ADVERBS

10 **faintly**, softly, quietly, piano, pianissimo, in an undertone, with bated breath, *sotto voce* (It), aside, in an aside, out of earshot

512 Hissing Sound

Sighs are the natural language of the heart. Thomas Shadwell.

NOUNS

1 **hiss**, hissing, sibilation, sibilance, assibilation, lisping, whispering, stage whisper, susurration, shushing, hushing, rustle, rustling, swish, swoosh, froufrou, sputter, splutter, splash, plash, wheezing, whistling, white noise, rhonchus, rale (*or* râle), sneeze, sneezing, wheeze, fizzing, effervescence, sizzle, sizzling, whizzing, squish, squash, squelch

2 **catcall**, jeer, boo, hoot, raspberry, derision, Bronx cheer (US inf)

▶ *670 Disapproval; 712 Curse*

3 **hisser**, snake, serpent, cat, goose, leaking tyre, sibilant, letter *s*, sigma

VERBS

4 **hiss**, sibilate, assibilate, lisp, whisper, shush, hush, rustle, susurrate, swish, swoosh, sputter, splutter, splash, plash, wheeze, rasp, whistle, snuffle, sneeze, fizz, effervesce, fizzle, sizzle, whiz, squish, squash, squelch

5 **catcall**, jeer, boo, hoot, blow a raspberry, deride, disparage

ADJECTIVES

6 **hissing**, sibilant, rustling, whispering, sneezing, wheezy, asthmatic, fizzy, effervescent, sizzling, fizzling

7 **catcalling**, jeering, booing, hooting, disapproving, derisive, scornful

ADVERBS

8 **sibilantly**, swishingly, squashily, effervescently, asthmatically, wheezily

INTERJECTIONS

9 **sh!**, hist!, whist!, whisht!, wheesh!, tsk!, tush!

513 Harsh Sound

NOUNS

1 **stridency** (*or* stridence), harshness, discord, discordance, clamour, harsh sound, stridor, cacophony, raucousness, dissonance, squawk, yawp, yelp, yell, howl, wail, ululation, bray, brassiness, brass, blare, skirl, blast, tantara

▶ *507 Loudness; 517 Dissonance*

2 **hoarseness**, roughness, huskiness, gruffness, lowness, gutteralness, throatiness, gutteral sound, rasping sound, caw, croak, grunt, snort, snore, stertor, cough, belch, cracked voice, frog in the throat, rustiness, friction, scrape, scratch, nasality, nasal tone, twang, drone

3 **shrillness**, high pitch, shriek, scream, squeal, screech, squeak, piping, whistling, whistle, catcall, wolf whistle, penny whistle, tin whistle, bleep, bleeper, high note, falsetto, acute note, sharp note, squeakiness, creakiness, creak, creaking door, rusty hinge

VERBS

4 **be strident**, jar, clash, discord, jangle, rasp, grind, grate, grate on one's ears, set one's teeth on edge, go right through one, squawk, yawp, yelp, yawl, yell, howl, wail, ululate, bray, blare, skirl, blast, split one's ears, lift the roof (Inf)

5 **sound hoarse**, rasp, grate, grind, crunch, scrunch, gutteralize, caw, croak, grunt, snort, snore, cough, hawk, clear one's throat, hem, belch, choke, gasp, crack one's voice, have a frog in one's throat, scrape, saw, scratch, twang, drone, clank, clink

6 **be shrill**, shriek, scream, screech, squeal, squeak, creak, pipe, whistle, wolf whistle, catcall

ADJECTIVES

7 **strident**, stridulous (*or* stridulant), harsh, raucous, discordant, grating, jarring, flat, inharmonious, unmelodious, unmusical, metallic, twangy, penetrating, loud, clamorous, cacophonous, dissonant, ear-splitting, squawky, squawking, howling, ululant, brassy, brazen, braying, blaring

8 **hoarse**, husky, rough, gruff, low, gutteral, throaty, gravelly, rasping, cawing, croaky, croaking, grunting, snorting, snoring, stertorous, cracked, nonresonant, dry, rusty, unoiled, scraping, scratchy, droning, clanking, clinking

9 **shrill**, high, high-pitched, sharp, acute, piercing, earpiercing, squeaky, squeaking, creaky, creaking, tinny, reedy, piping, whistling, bleeping

ADVERBS

10 **stridently**, loudly, harshly, discordantly, raspingly, gutterally, shrilly

514 Human Cry

Swans sing before they die – 'twere no bad thing,
Did certain persons die before they sing. Samuel Taylor Coleridge.

NOUNS

1 **cry**, call, loud cry, outcry, outburst, battle cry, war cry, rallying cry, vociferation, clamour, uproar, hullabaloo, hubbub, shout, scream, screech, shriek, yell, roar, bellow, bawl, yawl, caterwaul, holler (Inf)

▶ *507 Loudness*

2 **cry of joy**, laugh, laughter, cachinnation, horse laugh, guffaw, hoot, whoop, yippee, chortle, chuckle, giggle, titter, snigger

▶ *597 Joy; 599 Humour; 600 Rejoicing*

3 **cry of praise**, acclamation, paean, hallelujah, alleluia, hosanna, glossolalia, applause, cheer, whoop, bravo, hurrah, hooray, hip-hip hurrah (*or* hooray), huzzah (Lit)

▶ *669 Approval*

4 **cry of greeting**, hello (*or* hullo), hail, greetings, salutation

▶ *654 Sociability; 658 Courtesy*

5 **hunting cry**, cry of the chase, hue and cry, halloo (or halloa), whoa, view halloo, tally-ho, yoicks (Lit)

6 **cry of pain**, scream, shriek, squeal, gasp, whine, whimper, groan, moan, crying, weeping, weeping and wailing, keening, ululation, lamentation, wail, howl, bawl, sob, sigh, boohoo, ouch, ow

▶ *602 Sorrow; 603 Lamentation*

7 **cry of disapproval**, exclamation, ejaculation, interjection, expletive, hoot, jeer, boo, hiss, catcall, curse, raspberry, bird (US inf), Bronx cheer (US inf)

▶ *670 Disapproval; 712 Curse*

8 **musical cry**, song, yodel, chant, chorus, solo

▶ *18 Music; 516 Tunefulness*

9 **crier**, town crier, barker, street trader, hawker, huntsman, master of hounds, yodeller, shouter, yeller, bawler, cheerer, cheerleader, rooter (Inf)

VERBS

10 **cry out**, call, call out, vociferate, raise a cry, raise one's voice, strain one's lungs (*or* voice, vocal cords), crack one's throat, shout, shout out, shout oneself hoarse, shout at the top of one's voice (*or* lungs), blast out, thunder out, explode, scream, shriek, yell, roar, bellow, bawl, yawl, yowl, squall, caterwaul, holler (Inf), yawp (US inf)

11 **laugh**, cachinnate, guffaw, hoot, whoop, chortle, chuckle, giggle, titter, snigger, split one's sides, blow a gut (US inf)

▶ *599 Humour*

12 **cheer**, cheer for, give three cheers, hurrah, hurray, sing the praises of, shout for, root for (Inf), pull for (US inf)

13 **cry**, sob, sigh, groan, moan, whine, whimper, yammer, mewl, pule, gasp, fret, lament, weep, wail, keen, ululate, howl, bawl, blubber, blub (Inf)

14 **hiss**, hoot, boo, jeer, catcall, exclaim, ejaculate, curse, tell off, shout down, bawl out

15 **sing out**, give voice, yodel, chant, chorus, belt out (Inf)

ADJECTIVES

16 **vociferous**, noisy, loud, vocal, stentorian, full-throated, thundering, thunderous, booming, deafening, shouting, screaming, yelling, bellowing, roaring, uproarious, clamorous, obstreperous, loudmouthed (Inf)

17 **cheering**, rousing, shooping, laughing, chuckling, giggling

18 **crying**, sobbing, sighing, groaning, moaning, whimpering, weeping, wailing, howling, ululant, blubbering, blubbing (Inf)

19 **hissing**, booing, jeering, cursing, exclamatory, ejaculatory

ADVERBS

20 **vociferously**, noisily, loudly, vocally, thunderously, deafeningly, uproariously, clamorously, obstreperously, at the top of one's voice

515 Animal Cry

We think caged birds sing, when indeed they cry. John Webster.

NOUNS

1 **animal cry**, warning cry, mating call, animal call, barking, baying, howling, belling, wailing, yowling, yawling, bleating, bellowing, roaring, ululation, bark, yelp, yap, snap, snarl, growl, woof, hiss, meow (*or* miaow, miaou), mew, purr, baa, moo, neigh, whinny, hee-haw, yawp (US inf)

2 **bird song**, bird call, note, woodnote, chirping, chirruping, chattering, twittering, warble, squeak, cheep, twitter, tweet-tweet, cuckoo, hoot, tu-whit tu-whoo, cock-a-doodle-doo, croak, caw, coo, whoop, hiss, quack, cluck, squawk, screech

3 **insect noise**, buzzing, humming, droning, whining, stridulation, bombination (*or* bombilation) (Lit)

VERBS

4 **cry**, call, ululate, give tongue, bay, bay at the moon, howl, bell, troat, wail, yowl, yawl, caterwaul, bark, yelp, yap, whine, snap, snarl, growl, meow (*or* miaow, miaou), purr, mew, mewl, hiss, bleat, baa, moo, low, bellow, roar, trumpet, neigh, bray, whinny, whicker, nicker, grunt, snort, croak, squeal, squeak, gibber, yawp (US inf)

5 **sing**, sing like a bird, warble, trill, carol, whistle, chirp, chirr, chirrup, cheep, peep, pule, pipe, tweet, twitter, chatter, whirr, coo, caw, hoot, screech, honk, oink, quack, cluck, clack, crow, cackle, chuckle, gaggle, gobble, squawk

6 **buzz**, hum, drone, whine, stridulate, grate, rasp, bombinate (*or* bombilate) (Lit)

ADJECTIVES

7 **ululant**, howling, yowling, wailing, wailful, bellowing, full-throated, deep-throated

8 **singing**, warbling, carolling, tweeting, twittering, twittery, chattering

9 **humming**, buzzing, droning, stridulous (*or* stridulant)

ADVERBS

10 **howlingly**, wailfully, stridulously, stridulantly, chattily, croakily

516 Tunefulness

The heart of the melody can never be put down on paper. Pablo Casals.

NOUNS

1 **melody**, tune, air, song, aria, strain, measure, theme, subject, motif, leitmotiv, line, melodic line, cantus, cantus firmus, canto, refrain, reprise, descant, chorus, solo, theme song, signature tune, Broadway melody, simple melody, popular melody, lost melody

2 **song**, lied, chanson, aubade, serenade, lullaby, cradle song, berceuse, barcarolle, part song, round, madrigal, folksong, glee, lay, roundelay, lilt, shanty, yodel, popular song, lyric, calypso, spiritual, love song, torch song, chant, plainchant, cantide, chorale, carol, Christmas carol, hymn, psalm, anthem, national anthem, cavatina

3 **melodiousness**, musicality, musicalness, musical quality, musical texture, euphony, euphoniousness, harmoniousness, harmony, chime, concord, consonance, attunement

4 **harmonics**, harmonization, harmonic progression, unison, homophony, monophony, monody, counterpoint, polyphony, heterophony, cantus firmus, tonality, resolution, cadence, perfect cadence, fauxbourdon, faburden, thorough bass, basso continuo, continuo, figured bass, ground bass, walking bass, syncopation, timing, rhythm, tempo, beat, phrasing, phrase, passage, figure, sequence, tonal sequence, orchestration, instrumentation, arrangement, passacaglia, chaconne, musica ficta

▶ *18 Music*

5 **melodist**, harmonist, songwriter, lyricist, psalmist, singer, balladeer, minstrel, lieder singer, Meistersinger, minnesinger, troubadour, trouvère, serenader, chanteuse, crooner, soprano, contralto, alto, tenor, bass, soloist, chorister, songster, warbler, songbird, nightingale, canary

ADJECTIVES

6 **melodious**, melodic, musical, tuneful, lyrical, canorous, lilting, singable, catchy, tripping, soft, sweet, dulcet, velvety, mellow, smooth, sweet-sounding, honeyed, mellifluous, mellifluent, Orphean, silvery, silver-toned, golden-toned, fine-toned, true, well-pitched, clear, clear as a bell, chiming, full-toned, resonant, full, rich, euphonious, euphonic, harmonious

7 **harmonious**, harmonizing, harmonic, in harmony, concordant, consonant, agreeing, in concord, in consent, *en rapport* (Fr), unanimous, attuned, in tune, in unison, in chorus, homophonic, monophonic, monodic, polyphonic, synchronous, synchronized, syncopated, corresponding, assonant, rhyming, matching

▶ *18 Music; 750 Agreement*

VERBS

8 **harmonize**, accord, chime in, be in harmony, synchronize, attune, tune, tune up, be together, be in unison, agree, be at one, conform, correspond, rhyme, match

9 **set to music**, melodize, harmonize, symphonize, orchestrate, syncopate, score, accompany

10 **sing**, vocalize, lilt, warble, trill, carol, croon

▶ *515 Animal Cry*

ADVERBS

11 **melodiously**, melodically, tunefully, lyrically, sweetly, melifluously, euphoniously, resonantly

12 **harmoniously**, in harmony, in accord, in concord, in consent, *en rapport*, unanimously, in tune, in unison, in chorus, synchronously, in sync (Inf)

517 Dissonance

NOUNS

1 **dissonance**, discord, discordance, disharmony, harshness, jarring, jangling, clashing, stridency, hoarseness

2 **dissonant noise**, cacophony, Babel, cat's concert, caterwauling, yowling, row, din, noise, clamour, uproar, racket, hullabaloo, hubbub, pandemonium, bedlam, tumult, turmoil

▶ *507 Loudness; 513 Harsh Sound*

3 **musical dissonance**, tunelessness, unmelodiousness, flatness, sharpness, dissonant chord, wrong note, clinker (US inf)

4 **atonality**, twelve-note (*or* twelve-tone) composition, twelve-note (*or* twelve-tone) scale, note (*or* tone) row, series, serialism, dodecaphony, total serialism, preparation (of dissonance), imperfect cadence, emancipation of the dissonance

▶ *18 Music*

5 **atmospheric dissonance**, static, wow, flutter, hiss, white noise, interference

6 **disagreement**, disaccord, discord, dissension, dissent, difference, conflict, clash, argument, quarrel

▶ *751 Disagreement*

ADJECTIVES

7 **dissonant**, discordant, inharmonious, jangling, jarring, clashing, grating, scraping, rasping, harsh, raucous, cacophonous, strident, shrill

8 **disagreeing**, conflicting, at variance, contrary, unresolved

9 **unmelodious**, unmusical, unharmonized, untuneful, tuneless, droning, singsong, untuned, cracked, off-pitch, off-key, off, out of tune, sharp, flat, flat-toned, toneless, atonal, serial

VERBS

10 **lack harmony**, jangle, jar, grate, clash, crash, saw, scrape, rasp, drone, whine, thrum, play sharp, play flat, hurt the ears, fluff (Inf), hit a clinker (US inf)

11 **disagree**, differ, conflict, be in conflict, be at odds, clash, argue, quarrel, cross swords

ADVERBS

12 **dissonantly**, discordantly, disharmoniously, cacophonously, tunelessly, unmelodiously, raucously, atonally, harshly, stridently, hoarsely, hissingly, raspingly

518 Vision

Our sight is the most perfect and most delightful of all our senses. It fills the mind with the largest variety of ideas, converses with its objects at the greatest distance, and continues the longest in action without being tired or satiated with its proper enjoyments.
Joseph Addison.

NOUNS

1 **vision**, seeing, sight, eyesight, visual sense, visual acuity, sense of sight, faculty of sight, power of seeing, normal sight, normal vision, perfect vision, 20/20 vision, night vision, scotopia, good eyesight, long sight, far sight (US), short sight, near sight (US)

2 **eye**, orb, eyeball, eyesocket, orbit, white of the eye, sclera, cornea, iris, pupil, lens, aqueous humour, vitreous humour, light-sensitive cell, retina, cone, rod, blind spot, optic nerve, eye muscle, eyebrow, eyelid, conjunctiva, eyelash, sharp eye, keen eye, penetrating eye, gimlet eye, X-ray eye, eagle eye, eagle, hawk, cat, lynx, Argus, basilisk, Gorgon, gazehound, optic (Inf), peepers (Inf), sparklers (Inf)

3 **observation**, examination, scanning, inspection, supervision, perusal, scrutiny, scan, study, survey, watching, watchfulness, surveillance, espionage, spying, peering, prying, voyeurism, I-spy, reconnaissance, recce (Inf), look-see (Inf), once-over (Inf)

4 **visualization**, consideration, contemplation, imagination, mind's eye, insight, prevision, anticipation, foresight, far-sightedness, planning, perception, discernment, awareness, understanding, perspicacity, perspicuity

▶ *725 Clarity*

5 **imagination**, dreaming, daydreaming, stargazing, dream, daydream, pipe dream, second sight, the sight, clairvoyance, crystal-gazing, scrying, illusion, *déjà vu* (Fr), optical illusion, mirage, hallucination, will-o'-the-wisp, ignis fatuus, Fata Morgana, pink elephant, chimera, figment, apparition, semblance, phantom, phantasm, spectre, phantasmagoria, wraith, ghost, vision, fantasy

▶ *96 Unreality; 274 Error; 477 Imagination*

6 **look**, glance, glimpse, *coup d'oeil* (Fr), peep, peek, squint, sideways look, sidelong look, gaze, stare, gape, grimace, black look, glare, glower, scowl, evil eye, dirty look, leer, ogle, old-fashioned look, glad eye, roving eye, come-hither look, sheep's eyes, melting look, gander (Inf), dekko (Inf), butcher's (Inf), shufty (Inf)

7 **view**, sight, aspect, vista, panorama, prospect, outlook, scene, scenery, landscape, townscape, cityscape, seascape, show, peepshow, spectacle, pageant, display, tableau, exhibition, spectator sport, performance, showing, picture, painting, drawing, photograph, film, overview, eyesore, blemish, blot (on the landscape), eyeful (Inf), eye-opener (Inf), sight for sore eyes (Inf), sight (Inf), fright (Inf)

8 **reflection**, image, mirror image, likeness, representation, mirror, glass, looking glass, hand mirror, magnifying mirror, shaving mirror, dressing-table mirror, full-length mirror, cheval glass, pier glass, reflector, wing mirror, rear-view mirror, Catseye™, speculum, distorting mirror, image recorder, camera, cine camera, video camera, telephoto lens, zoom lens, wide-angle lens, fish-eye lens, slide, projector, magic lantern

▶ *41 Photography*

9 **viewpoint**, perspective, scope, range, eyeshot, field of vision, bird's-eye view, worm's-eye view, point of view, peephole, sight hole, spyhole, window, windscreen, picture window, shop window, judas-window, squint, belvedere, mirador, gazebo, watchtower, observation

point, conning tower, bridge, crow's nest, observatory, planetarium, observation car, theatre, stalls, pit, dress circle, circle, gallery, gods (Inf), cinema, stadium, amphitheatre, arena, ringside seat, terrace, stand, grandstand, bleachers (Inf)

10 visual aid, eyeglass, reading glass, spectacles, pair of spectacles, specs (Inf), glasses, frames, lenses, contact lenses, hard (*or* soft *or* gas permeable) lenses, disposable lenses, contacts (Inf), gold-rimmed glasses, steel-rimmed glasses, horn-rimmed glasses, reading glasses, pebble glasses, granny glasses, bifocals, half-moon glasses, contact lenses, monocle, lorgnette, pince-nez, quizzing glass, eyeshade, sight screen, sunglasses, dark glasses, night glasses, tinted glasses, polaroid glasses, shades (Inf), protective glasses, goggles, magnifier, magnifying glass, loupe, microfilm reader, microreader, opera glasses, binoculars, field glasses, optical instrument, spyglass, telescope, telescopic sight, gunsight, foresight, backsight, cross hairs, peep sight, microscope, optics, magnification, microscopy, telescopy, stereoscopy, spectroscopy

▶ *28 Physics; 519 Blindness*

11 observer, spectator, audience, sightseer, tourist, beholder, viewer, looker, onlooker, looker-on, witness, eyewitness, bystander, watcher, birdwatcher, spotter, train spotter, lookout, sentry, sentinel, scout, watchman, night watchman, caretaker, janitor, guard, watchdog, vigilante, patrolman, security man, inspector, supervisor, overseer, monitor, scanner, invigilator, scrutinizer, scrutineer, scrutator, gazer, stargazer, crystal gazer, clairvoyant, seer, seeress, visionary, starer, gaper, peerer, nosy parker, prier, peeping Tom, voyeur, gawper (Inf), rubbernecker (US inf)

VERBS

12 see, use one's eyes, behold (Lit), sight, catch sight of, glimpse, catch a glimpse of, espy, spy, notice, witness, spot, perceive, see with the naked eye, see with half an eye, have x-ray eyes, have eyes in the back of one's head, see through a brick wall, see round corners, discern, distinguish, descry, make out, recognize, pick out, discover, sightsee, spectate, see the sights, rubberneck (US inf), keep one's eye in (Inf), lay eyes on (Inf), clap eyes on (Inf)

13 look, look at, regard, focus (on), eye, look straight at, look someone in the face (*or* eye), feast one's eyes on, devour with one's eyes, gaze (at), stare (at), gape (at), goggle (at), look sideways (at), glance (at), steal a glance (at), peep (at), peek (at), squint (at), grimace, give someone a black (*or* dirty) look, glare (at), glower (at), scowl (at), look down one's nose (at), look askance (at), look daggers (at), leer (at), ogle, eye up, flutter one's eyelashes (at), make (sheep's) eyes at (Inf), give someone the glad eye (Inf), be all eyes (Inf), gawk (Inf), gawp (Inf)

14 inspect, examine, view, reconnoitre, scout, look closely at, scrutinize, study, pore over, look over, survey, scan, peruse, read, cast (*or* run) one's eye(s) over, have (*or* take) a look at, give someone (*or* something) the once-over (Inf), have a look-see (Inf), take (*or* have) a gander (at) (Inf), have a dekko (Inf), have a butcher's (Inf), take a shufty (at) (Inf), eyeball (Inf)

15 watch, observe, keep under observation, keep one's eyes (*or* an eye) on, monitor, watch over, oversee, invigilate, supervise, watch out for, keep a look out for, keep an eye out for (*or* open for), spy on, watch like a hawk, keep one's eyes skinned (*or* peeled)

16 visualize, picture, imagine, see in the mind's eye, consider, contemplate, take stock of, anticipate, foresee, plan, perceive, discern, be aware of, understand

17 imagine, fancy, dream, dream up, conjure up, daydream, stargaze, crystal-gaze, scry, foresee, have second sight, hallucinate, see things (Inf)

18 make visible, reveal, reflect, mirror, show, display, exhibit, bring to light, demonstrate, point out, uncover, unmask, expose

▶ *739 Disclosure*

19 be visible, appear, come into view, come to light, emerge, catch the eye, loom up, loom large, show, show through, stand out

▶ *520 Visibility*

ADJECTIVES

20 visual, optical, optic, ophthalmic, eyelike, ocular, binocular, mirror-like, reflecting, two-dimensional, telescopic, microscopic, stereoscopic, three-dimensional, panoramic, scenic, visional, illusionary, illusory, imaginary

21 seeing, sighted, eyed, sharp-eyed, lynx-eyed, eagle-eyed, hawk-eyed, gimlet-eyed, Argus-eyed, staring, glaring, goggle-eyed, popeyed, noticing, watching, looking, on the lookout, observant, watchful, vigilant, aware, perceptive, clear-sighted, clear-eyed, far-seeing, far-sighted, perspicacious, discerning, imaginative, visionary

22 bespectacled, long-sighted, far-sighted (US), short-sighted, near-sighted (US), four-eyed (Inf)

23 visible, perceivable, in view, before one's eyes, perceptible, discernible, detectable, recognizable, apparent, observable, distinct, clear, clear-cut, evident, manifest, plain, obvious, patent, conspicuous, noticeable, watchable, viewable, worth watching, easy on the eye, eye-catching, eye-opening, spectacular

ADVERBS

24 visually, optically, by eye, by sight, in sight, within sight, at sight, at first sight, prima facie, eye to eye, eyeball to eyeball (Inf)

25 visibly, perceptibly, recognizably, apparently, observably, distinctly, clearly, at a glance, evidently, manifestly, plainly, obviously, patently, conspicuously, noticeably

26 watchfully, observantly, vigilantly, sideways, sidelong, glancingly, out of the corner of one's eye

519 Blindness

My darkness has been filled with the light of intelligence, and behold, the outer day-light world was stumbling and groping in social blindness. Helen Keller.

Ask for this great deliverer now, and find him
Eyeless in Gaza at the mill with slaves. John Milton.

NOUNS

1 blindness, sightlessness, eyelessness, lack of sight, stone-blindness, loss of vision, amaurosis, ablepsia, glaucoma, river blindness, onchocerciasis, trachoma, cataract, going blind, darkness, white-out, snow blindness, blackout

2 **poor sight**, failing sight, visual handicap, faulty vision, defective sight, impaired vision, day blindness, hemeralopia, night blindness, nyctalopia, colour-blindness, daltonism, red-blindness, protanopia, deuteranopia, tritanopia, poor vision, amblyopia, dim sight, sand-blindness, purblindness, long sight, long-sightedness, far sight (US), far-sightedness (US), hypermetropia, presbyopia, short sight, near sight (US), near-sightedness (US), shortsightedness, myopia, astigmatism, tunnel vision, detached retina, squint, strabismus, heterotropia, wandering eye, cast, cockeye (Inf), walleye, divergent strabismus, exotropia, cross-eye, convergent strabismus, esotropia, nystagmus, winking, blinking, nictitation, (eye)tic, eyestrain, double vision, diplopia, seeing double, blurred vision, bleariness, bloodshot eyes, red eyes, eye disease, ophthalmia, ophthalmitis, retinopathy, diabetic retinopathy, conjunctivitis, pink eye

3 **aid for poor sight**, eye hospital, eye clinic, ophthalmology, ophthalmologist, eyewash, eye drops, optometry, optometrist, optician, large-print book, spectacles, glasses, Braille, talking book, guide dog, white stick (*or* cane), glass eye, artificial eye, blind register, partially sighted register

▶ *518 Vision*

4 **blind people**, the blind, the sightless, mole, bat, the visually handicapped, the visually impaired, the partially sighted

5 **visual distortion**, prism, refraction, reflection, optical illusion, distorting mirror, hall of mirrors

▶ *234 Distortion*

6 **blinder**, blindfold, blinkers, eyepatch, patch, cover, covering, cloak, screen, smoke, smokescreen, curtain, blind, eclipse, camouflage, façade

▶ *550 Covering*

7 **figurative blindness**, lack of perception, inability to see, blind side, blind flying, fly-by-wire, unawareness, unconcern, disregard, obliviousness, unconsciousness, blind eye, thoughtlessness, lack of consideration, ignorance, invincible ignorance, prejudice, unenlightenment, lack of enlightenment, blind spot, lack of discernment, benightedness

▶ *456 Ignorance; 472 Inattention*

ADJECTIVES

8 **blind**, lacking sight, sightless, unsighted, deprived of vision, unseeing, eyeless, amaurotic, glaucomatous, registered blind, visionless, stone-blind, snow-blind, blind as a bat, blind as a mole

9 **weak-sighted**, having poor sight (*or* vision), visually handicapped, visually impaired, partially sighted, one-eyed, day-blind, hemeralopic, night-blind, nyctalopic, colour-blind, red-blind, protanopic, deuteranopic, tritanopic, amblyopic, dim-sighted, purblind, sand-blind, long-sighted, far-sighted (US), hypermetropic, presbyopic, short-sighted, near-sighted (US), myopic, astigmatic, squinting, stabismic, walleyed, cross-eyed, cockeyed (Inf), boss-eyed (Inf), blinking, winking, nystagmatic, bleary, bleary-eyed, bloodshot, blurry, watery-eyed, red-eyed, seeing double

10 **blinded**, snow-blind, snow-blinded, dazzled, blindfold(ed), blinkered

11 **blinding**, dazzling, bedazzling, stunning, darkening, obscuring, hiding, masking, deceptive, misleading

▶ *700 Deception*

12 **blind to**, imperceptive, unaware (of), unconcerned, oblivious (of), unconscious (of), thoughtless, inconsiderate, unobservant, unmindful, ignorant, in the dark, unenlightened, blinkered, undiscerning, benighted

13 **hidden**, dark, obscure, indistinct, camouflaged, invisible, unseen

▶ *736 Concealment*

VERBS

14 **be blind**, not see, go blind, lose one's sight, black out, see badly, feel one's way, grope, have defective sight, squint, blink, wink, screw up one's eyes, see double, have something in one's eye, have spots in front of one's eyes, be unable to see straight, be unable to see something under one's nose (*or* in front of one's eyes), be unable to see the wood for the trees, have a blind spot

15 **blind**, deprive of sight, make blind, strike blind, put (*or* gouge) someone's eyes out, darken, obscure, blur, eclipse, dazzle, bedazzle, blindfold, blinker, camouflage, mask, screen, deceive, hoodwink

16 **be blind to**, ignore, disregard, overlook, look away, look the other way, drop one's eyes, avert one's gaze (*or* eyes), shut one's eyes to, turn a blind eye (to), take no notice of, wink at, blink at

ADVERBS

17 **blindly**, blindfold, without looking, by touch, by feel, by ear

18 **blindingly**, dazzlingly

520 Visibility

The visible universe was an illusion or, more precisely, a sophism. Mirrors and fatherhood are abominable because they multiply it and extend it. Jorge Luis Borges.

ADJECTIVES

1 **visible**, seeable, in sight, viewable, in view, in full view, observable, distinguishable, discernible, perceptible, perceivable, discoverable, detectable, above the horizon, noticeable, conspicuous, clear, open, overt, plain, evident, manifest, obvious, patent, unhidden, unconcealed, undisguised, exposed, showing, apparent, distinct, easily distinguished, identifiable, recognizable, unmistakable, public, available, present, concrete, material, tangible, palpable, external, outward, superficial, surface, in focus, visible to the naked eye

▶ *97 Presence; 171 Outside; 402 Material World; 518 Vision; 525 Appearance; 725 Clarity; 739 Disclosure; 743 Identification*

2 **clear**, plain, easy to see, bright, light, signed, signposted, clear-cut, distinct, defined, in focus, sharp, high-definition, open, exposed, exposed to view, uncovered, naked, showy, garish, gaudy, lurid, vivid, brilliant, spectacular, glitzy, glaring, unmissable, eye-catching, remarkable, outstanding, striking, blatant, salient, prominent, stark, crystal-clear, lucid, visual, lit (up), well-lit, highlighted, spotlighted, illuminated, picked out, in high relief, in bold relief, on show, on display, high-profile, as clear as

day, in front of one's face (*or* eyes), staring one in the face, under one's nose, plain to see, open to view, open to the public, in the public eye, for all to see, plain as a pikestaff, plain as the nose on one's face

▶ *522 Light; 725 Clarity; 726 Emphasis; 738 Display; 739 Disclosure*

NOUNS

3 **visibility**, visibleness, eyesight, eyeshot, naked eye, range, horizon, visible horizon, skyline, sightline, line of sight, observability, discernibility, perceptibility, perceivability, detectability, identifiability, recognizability, distinctness, conspicuousness, overtness, evidence, availability, presence, tangibility, lack of concealment, revelation

▶ *97 Presence; 518 Vision; 525 Appearance; 739 Disclosure; 743 Identification*

4 **clarity**, clearness, plainness, brightness, brilliance, definition, focus, sharpness, ease of viewing, publicity, exposure, high profile, prominence, starkness, obviousness, blatancy, showiness, vividness, gaudiness, glitz

▶ *725 Clarity*

5 **manifestation**, display, demonstration, exposition, exhibition, show, performance, exposure, pointing out

▶ *21 Drama; 738 Display*

6 **visible thing**, sight, field of vision, field of view, light, visible radiation, outside, exterior, surface, skin, façade, feature, badge, insignia, packaging, sign, signpost, signboard, signal, landmark, outcrop, illustration, high relief, bold relief, exhibit, attraction, cynosure

▶ *171 Outside; 525 Appearance; 743 Identification*

7 **that which makes visible**, visual aid, light, illumination, spotlight, highlighter, underlining, pointer, sign, signpost, high relief, bold relief, fluorescent paint, fluorescent clothing, reflector, shop window, showcase, rangefinder, optical instrument, spectacles, telescope, microscope, X-rays

▶ *35 Medicine; 190 Expansion; 518 Vision; 522 Light; 726 Emphasis*

VERBS

8 **be visible**, be seen, show, stand out, stick out, be obvious, have a high profile, hit one in the eye, stare one in the face, strike one in the face (*or* eye), stick out like a sore thumb (Inf)

▶ *518 Vision*

9 **appear**, materialize, become visible, manifest (itself), come to light, crop up, open (out), meet the eye, show up, turn up, show through, shine through, come to the surface, loom, heave in sight, come over the horizon, come into focus, come out from the woodwork, make an entrance, put in an appearance, pop up (Inf), pop out (Inf)

▶ *312 Arrival; 314 Entry; 525 Appearance; 739 Disclosure*

10 **make visible**, focus, focus on, show, reveal, disclose, demonstrate, manifest, put on view, display, put on display, exhibit, signal, indicate, sign, signpost, point out, open (up), bring to light, uncover, unwrap, expose, illuminate, light (up), unmask, lay bare, raise the curtain on, take the lid off, spotlight, highlight, underline, clarify, elucidate, illustrate, keep sight of, keep in sight, keep in view, not let out of one's sight

▶ *522 Light; 725 Clarity; 739 Disclosure; 743 Identification*

ADVERBS

11 **visibly**, in sight, in view, into sight, into view, out of hiding, outward, outwardly, externally, superficially, on the surface, apparently, ostensibly, to all appearances, evidently, seemingly, in public, openly, in plain view, clearly, plainly, distinctly, obviously, patently, blatantly, manifestly, conspicuously, noticeably, perceptibly, discernibly

521 Invisibility

ADJECTIVES

1 **invisible**, unable to be seen, unseeable, out of sight, unperceivable, imperceptible, indistinguishable, indiscernible, unnoticeable, undetectable, unrecognizable, unidentifiable, unrecognized, unidentified, unmarked, not signposted, not apparent, unapparent, inappreciable, immaterial, insubstantial, unsubstantial, transparent, unseen, unsighted, unobserved, unwitnessed, unnoticed, unperceived, eclipsed, latent, buried, submerged, lurking, in ambush, over the horizon, below the horizon, out of range, out of sight, out of mind

▶ *101 Unworldliness; 145 Distance; 527 Transparency*

2 **difficult to see**, partly visible, half-seen, inconspicuous, low-profile, very small, infinitesimal, microscopic, subliminal, distant, remote, lost in the distance, dark, darkened, faint, pale, indefinite, unclear, indistinct, unfocused, undefined, blurred, blurry, bleared, bleary, hazy, misty, foggy, filmy, shadowy, obscured, dim, fuzzy, low-definition, out of focus, ill-defined, clear as mud (Inf)

▶ *266 Obscurity; 523 Darkness; 524 Dimness; 528 Opaqueness*

3 **private**, internal, inward, hidden, concealed, covert, secret, clandestine, disguised, camouflaged, screened, masked, covered, veiled, recondite, under wraps, dark, blacked out, obscure, obscured, obstructed, behind the scenes, backstage, in camera

▶ *266 Obscurity; 523 Darkness; 550 Covering; 736 Concealment; 737 Secrecy*

NOUNS

4 **invisibility**, disappearance, vanishing, nonappearance, nonpresence, absence, transparency, insubstantiality, darkness, blackness, obscurity, poor visibility, bad visibility, haze, haziness, mist, mistiness, fog, fogginess, fuzziness, indistinctness, faintness, paleness, low definition, poor definition, imperceptibility, indistinguishability, indiscernibility, undetectability, zero visibility, low profile, latency, concealment, hiding, secrecy, privacy

▶ *98 Absence; 524 Dimness; 526 Disappearance; 528 Opaqueness; 736 Concealment; 737 Secrecy*

5 **invisible thing**, the unseen, vanisher, dark corner, blind corner, blind spot, black hole, hidden camera, secret surveillance system, vanishing cream, black ice, invisible ink, the invisible man, back-room boys (*or* girls), spirit world, the fourth dimension, invisible imports (*or* exports), more than meets the eye, hide-and-seek, blind man's buff

▶ *101 Unworldliness*

6 **that which makes invisible**, darkness, night, mist, fog, peasouper, haze, smoke, smokescreen, film, membrane, muddy waters, black light, eraser, rubber, cor-

rection fluid, Tippex™, masking tape, eclipse, distance, remoteness, horizon, edge of sight, vanishing point, veil, yashmak, chador, purdah, mask, domino, disguise, front, camouflage, protective colouring, shroud, curtain, blind, shade, shutter, screen, partition, brick wall, blank wall, plain wrapper, hide, hiding place, hidy-hole, interference, jamming, snow (Inf)

▶ *358 Obliteration; 523 Darkness; 524 Dimness; 528 Opaqueness; 550 Covering; 736 Concealment*

VERBS

7 **become invisible**, disappear, vanish, fade, fade away, blur, dim, darken, escape notice, hide, retreat, go into purdah, go into hiding, play hide-and-seek, lurk, lie low, keep one's head down, keep a low profile, blend into the background, sink without trace, lose sight of, cease to see, see through a glass darkly, now you see it now you don't

▶ *524 Dimness; 526 Disappearance; 736 Concealment*

8 **make invisible**, put out of sight, hide, hide away, bury, conceal, mask, screen, cloak, veil, eclipse, cover (up), put under wraps, obscure, disguise, erase, delete, rub out, white out, Tippex™, black out, blank out, blur, dim, darken, put a lid on, hide under a bushel, sweep under the carpet

▶ *266 Obscurity; 358 Obliteration; 523 Darkness; 550 Covering; 736 Concealment*

ADVERBS

9 **invisibly**, out of view, out of sight, out of range, imperceptibly, indistinguishably, indiscernibly, unnoticeably, unrecognizably, unidentifiably, sight unseen, under plain cover, in hiding, behind the scenes, backstage, in camera, in private, secretly, under cover, internally, inwardly, inwards, underneath, indistinctly, dimly, indefinitely, hazily, on the blind side

522 Light

Music is the arithmetic of sounds as optics is the geometry of light.
Claude Debussy.

NOUNS

1 **light**, luminosity, luminousness, lucency, phosphorescence, fluorescence, luminescence, illumination, candescence, incandescence, lustre, radiance, radiation, refulgence, splendour, resplendence, brightness, brilliance, vividness, visible radiation, light ray, light wave, ray, beam, rays of the sun, sunlight, sunbeam, electromagnetic radiation, ultraviolet light, infrared radiation, photon, monochromatic light, coherent light, visible spectrum

▶ *28 Physics; 518 Vision; 520 Visibility*

2 **quality of light**, soft light, glow, shimmer, shimmering, gleam, glint, glister, sheen, gloss, patina, polish, lustre, iridescence, opalescence, shine, shininess, glassiness, glistening, shining, beam, bright light, brightness, effulgence, glare, dazzle, flare, brilliance, sparkle, twinkle, twinkling, scintillation, glitter, spangle, tinsel, sequin, diamanté, Lurex™, cloth of gold, spark, flash, coruscation, flashing, flicker, flickering

3 **lightening**, illumination, making light, giving light, shedding light, brightening, bleaching, peroxide, overexposure

▶ *290 Daytime*

4 **natural light**, daylight, sun, sunlight, sunshine, rays of the sun, sunbeam, moon, moonlight, moonshine, moonbeam, moonrise, full moon, harvest moon, star, starlight, starshine, nova, supernova, Pole Star, North Star, Polaris, Star of Bethlehem, Milky Way, meteor, falling star, shooting star, comet, Halley's Comet, northern lights, aurora borealis, southern lights, aurora australis, merry dancers, streamers, gegenschein, counterglow, zodiacal light, earthshine, lightning, sheet (*or* forked *or* ball) lightning, summer lightning, flash, thunderbolt, streak

▶ *29 Astronomy; 30 Earth Science; 31 Meteorology and Climatology*

5 **incandescent light**, artificial light, light source, lighting, lamp, lamplight, candle, candlelight, tallow candle, wax candle, cake candle, church candle, rush light, dip, wick, candlestick, candleholder, candelabrum, candelabra, oil lamp, paraffin lamp, hurricane lamp, spirit lamp, acetylene lamp, gaslamp, gaslight, gas mantle, gas jet, gasolier

6 **electric light**, light bulb, bulb, mushroom bulb, pearl bulb, clear bulb, light socket, lampholder, ceiling rose, light switch, light fitting, ceiling light, wall light, sconce, standard lamp, table lamp, bedside lamp, reading lamp, desk lamp, Anglepoise™, strip light, fluorescent light, halogen light, quartz–iodine light, sun lamp, sunray lamp, stroboscope, strobe lighting, searchlight, floodlight, spotlight, limelight, klieg light, footlights, house lights, one's name in lights, neon light, neon lighting, illuminated sign, fairy lights, Christmas tree lights, headlight, headlamp, dipped headlights, dimmed headlights, dims (US inf), sidelight, parking light, rear light, tail light, brake light, reversing light, indicator light, indicator, trafficator, fog lamp, interior light, courtesy light, lighting-up time, streetlight, streetlamp, mercury-vapour lamp, sodium lamp, lamppost, lamp-standard, traffic lights, traffic signals, red light, amber light, green light, stop light, pedestrian lights, green (*or* red) man, Belisha beacon, beacon, lighthouse, pharos, flashing light, occulting light, lightship, light buoy, navigation lights, masthead light, stern light, anchor light, riding lights, running lights, aviation beacon, flare path, approach light, runway lights, light signal, warning light, winker (Inf)

▶ *319 Transport; 711 Warning*

7 **lantern**, horn lantern, dark lantern, link, link-boy, lamplighter, torch, torchlight, flambeau, brand, flashlight (US), pocket torch, pumpkin lantern, turnip lantern, Chinese lantern, nightlight, miner's lamp, safety lamp, Davy lamp, flashlamp, flashgun, flashbulb, photoflood, arc lamp

▶ *28 Physics; 41 Photography*

8 **fire**, flame, firelight, embers, glow, red glow, red heat, white heat, blaze, conflagration, wildfire, fireball, bonfire, watch fire, balefire, signal fire, beacon, spill, match, friction match, vesta, lucifer, safety match, taper, firelighter, lighter, spark, scintilla, ignition, pyrophoric alloy, fireworks, pyrotechnics, Bengal light, sparkler, Roman

candle, Catherine wheel, pinwheel, banger, jumping jack, rocket, Very light, flare

▶ *437 Fuel; 493 Heat*

9 firefly, glow-worm, corposant, St Elmo's fire, will-o'-the-wisp, jack-o'-lantern, marshlight, corpse candle, ignis fatuus

10 window, windowpane, skylight, fanlight, rose window, stained glass, clear glass, frosted glass, bad light, poor light, good light, north light

▶ *308 Opening; 527 Transparency; 528 Opaqueness*

11 photoelectricity, photoemission, photoconduction, photosensor, photometer, photoelectric cell, photosensitivity, exposure meter, LED (light-emitting diode), LCD (liquid-crystal display), light pen, solar energy

12 highlight, downlight, uplighting, uplighter, reflection, *chiaroscuro* (It), black-and-white, half-tone, light show, *son et lumière* (Fr), laser, laser show, holography, hologram, halo, aureole, gloriole, nimbus, corona, rainbow, spectrum

▶ *19 Painting and Sculpture; 529 Colour*

13 enlightenment, elucidation, illumination, clarification, clarity, knowledge, understanding, comprehension, insight, clue, guiding star, leading light, star, shining light, illuminati

▶ *442 Intellect; 455 Knowledge; 725 Clarity*

14 light colour, pale colour, lightness, colourlessness, paleness, pallor, pastiness, blondness, fairness, pastel colour, cream, ivory, off-white

▶ *530 Colourlessness; 531 Whiteness*

ADJECTIVES

15 lucent, luminous, radiant, refulgent, glowing, glimmering, burning, candescent, incandescent, aglow, phosphorescent, fluorescent, shining, lambent, flickering, flickery, blinking, winking, flashing, occulting, stroboscopic, lighting, lightening, illuminating, shedding light on, brightening, beaming

▶ *518 Vision; 520 Visibility*

16 bright, vivid, brilliant, flamboyant, garish, lurid, flashy, effulgent, splendid, resplendent, kaleidoscopic, shining, dazzling, fluorescent, Day-Glo™, blinding, glaring, flashing, sparking, coruscating, glinting, sparkling, scintillating, twinkling, glittering, glittery, tinselly, spangly, sequined, diamanté, Lurex™, fiery, flaming, aflame, alight, blazing, ablaze, flaring

▶ *493 Heat; 520 Visibility*

17 lustrous, glossy, gleaming, shiny, polished, burnished, glacé, glassy, glistening, shimmering, shimmery, opalescent, iridescent, pearly, pearlized, haloed

18 lit, illuminated, lightened, brightened, lit up, well-lit, light, bright, lamplit, candlelit, torchlit, firelit, spotlit, floodlit, flashlit, highlighted, sunlit, starlit, moonlit

19 sunny, daylight, light as day, sunshiny, cloudless, unclouded, clear, daylight saving

20 starry, starbright, star-spangled, star-studded

21 light, lightish, pale, light-coloured, pastel, cream-coloured, ivory, pallid, pasty, colourless, white, whitish, albino, blond(e), fair, flaxen, tow-headed, faded, bleached, peroxided, lightened, overexposed

▶ *530 Colourlessness; 531 Whiteness*

22 enlightened, elucidated, clarified, (crystal) clear, lucid, illuminated, bright, brilliant, intelligent, sparky (Inf)

▶ *442 Intellect; 725 Clarity*

23 photoelectric, photoconductive, photoemissive, photometric, photosensitive, light-sensitive, phototropic, photophobic, spectral, photic, optic

▶ *28 Physics; 41 Photography*

VERBS

24 light, give light, illuminate, illumine, light up, lighten, brighten, switch (*or* turn *or* put) on a light, switch on, turn on, put on, strike a light, strike, ignite, set alight, kindle, fire, set fire to, floodlight, spotlight, highlight, irradiate, dazzle, bedazzle, blind

▶ *493 Heat*

25 light up, gleam, glint, glance, glisten, glimmer, blink, wink, flicker, twinkle, sparkle, spark, flash, coruscate, scintillate, glitter, spangle, shine, glow, glare, flare, flare up, flame, blaze, burn, incandesce, radiate, radiate light, beam, fluoresce, phosphoresce, iridesce

26 grow light, get light, dawn, break, lighten, brighten

27 glaze, polish, burnish, rub up, take a shine, shine like a new pin, reflect, refract

28 bleach, lighten, whiten, dye, peroxide, overexpose, fade, pale, grow pale, lose colour, blench, blanch

▶ *530 Colourlessness; 531 Whiteness*

29 clarify, elucidate, throw light on, shed light on, draw back the curtains, open the shutters, roll up the blind

ADVERBS

30 lightly, brightly, palely, radiantly, incandescently, gleamingly, twinklingly, scintillatingly, glowingly, luminously, illuminatingly, dazzlingly, brilliantly, vividly, flamboyantly, at first light, by day, by daylight, by artificial light

523 Darkness

O dark, dark, dark, amid the blaze of noon,
Irrecoverably dark, total eclipse,
Without all hope of day! John Milton.

She would rather light candles than curse the darkness, and her glow has warmed the world. Adlai Stevenson.

NOUNS

1 darkness, dark, lack of light, sunlessness, dimness, shadow, shadows, shade, gloom, gloominess, murk, murkiness, lividness, leadenness, sombreness, drabness, obscurity, bad light, poor light, twilight, blindness, blackout, eclipse, total eclipse, eclipse of the sun, solar eclipse, eclipse of the moon, lunar eclipse, blackness, pitch-darkness, Stygian gloom, night blindness, darkest hour

▶ *266 Obscurity; 291 Night-Time; 416 Density; 519 Blindness; 521 Invisibility; 522 Light; 524 Dimness; 532 Blackness; 550 Covering; 551 Dress; 736 Concealment*

2 darkening, dimming, turning the lights down (*or* off *or* out), extinguishment, obscuration, obfuscation, occultation, underexposure, blackening, blackout, eclipse, fade-out, lights out, power cut, dimmer switch, dip switch, dipper, cut-out, shading, shading-in, hatching, cross-hatching, benday

▶ *19 Painting and Sculpture; 522 Light*

3 dark colour, deep colour, dark hair, brunette, dark skin, swarthiness, dark brown, slate-grey, aubergine, navy blue, midnight blue, black, blackness, dirt, grime, stain, drabness

► *258 Dirtiness; 529 Colour; 532 Blackness; 533 Greyness; 534 Brownness; 539 Blueness; 540 Purpleness*

4 **dark thing**, dark glasses, dark lantern, cloud, thundercloud, soot, smut, ink, jet, obsidian, pitch, raven, ebony, darkroom, dungeon, cellar, dark clothes, business suit, man's evening dress, little black dress, mourning clothes, black, silhouette, shadow, the man in black, dark star, dark matter

► *41 Photography; 532 Blackness; 551 Dress*

5 **figurative dark thing**, Dark Ages, Darkest Africa, Dark Continent, dark horse

6 **shade**, parasol, beach umbrella, sunshade, awning, smoked glass, eyeshade, sun visor, dark glasses, sunglasses, sun hat, shutters, curtain, blind, roller blind, Venetian blind, festoon blind, blackout, blindfold, hood, shroud, cover, lid, shades (Inf)

► *252 Safety; 528 Opaqueness; 550 Covering*

7 **spiritual darkness**, dark powers, black magic, malignity, evil, ignorance, blindness, oblivion, dejection, depression, despair, gloom, murk, obscurity, shadow, sombreness, grimness, deadness

► *266 Obscurity; 456 Ignorance; 463 Forgetfulness; 519 Blindness; 602 Sorrow; 737 Secrecy; 798 Evil*

ADJECTIVES

8 **dark**, unlit, unlighted, unilluminated, darkish, dim, badly lit, ill-lit, underexposed, light-tight, lightproof, lightless, sunless, moonless, starless, pitch-dark, shady, shaded, umbrageous, overcast, cloudy, stormy, thundery, louring (*or* lowering), dusky, gloomy, dingy, murky, tenebrous, black, Stygian, Cimmerian, nocturnal

► *522 Light; 524 Dimness; 528 Opaqueness*

9 **darkening**, extinguishing, shading, shadowing, screening, obscuring, dimming, dipping, dyeing, casting a shadow

► *42 Fabrics and Dyeing; 550 Covering; 736 Concealment*

10 **dark-coloured**, dark, deep-coloured, deep, subfusc, dark-haired, brunette, dark-skinned, swarthy, black-skinned, dusky, darkling, black, pitch-black, pitchy, jet-black, inky, black as ink, black as night, ebony, melanic, melanous, sable, livid, leaden, grimy, dirty, stained, drab, funereal

► *258 Dirtiness; 532 Blackness*

11 **benighted**, dismal, gloomy, cheerless, depressed, dejected, mournful, clouded, murky, wicked, evil, ominous, menacing, threatening, sinister, shadowy, shady, sombre, grim, forbidding, unenlightened, ignorant, blind, oblivious, obfuscated, obscure, cryptic, mysterious, enigmatic, mystic, inscrutable, secret, arcane, hidden, occult, esoteric

► *11 Occultism; 266 Obscurity; 456 Ignorance; 602 Sorrow; 736 Concealment; 737 Secrecy; 798 Evil*

VERBS

12 **be dark**, lack light, wear mourning, lurk in the shadows

13 **become dark**, darken, deepen, blacken, grow dark, cloud over, look like rain, lour (*or* lower), dim, be extinguished, go out, night falls, the sun sets (*or* goes down), the light fails

► *524 Dimness; 532 Blackness*

14 **make dark**, darken, obscure, obfuscate, turn (*or* switch) the lights out (*or* off), extinguish, douse, quench, snuff, snuff out, blow out (the candle), dim, dip, shade, shadow, adumbrate, overshadow, cast a shadow over, put in the shade, occult, eclipse, shutter, close the shutters, draw the curtains, pull down the blind, black out, block out light, blot out light, underexpose, blindfold, hood, cover (over), veil, shroud, silhouette, shade in, hatch, cross-hatch, deject, depress, keep dark, keep in the dark

► *19 Painting and Sculpture; 266 Obscurity; 524 Dimness; 532 Blackness; 550 Covering; 602 Sorrow; 736 Concealment; 737 Secrecy*

ADVERBS

15 **darkly**, dimly, obscurely, blackly, at nightfall, by night, in the night, at midnight, nocturnally, in the dark, in the shade, shadily, gloomily, mournfully, sombrely, grimly, ominously, mysteriously, inscrutably

524 Dimness

NOUNS

1 **dimness**, faintness, paleness, half-light, semidarkness, twilight, gloaming, evening light, late evening, dusk, duskiness, first light, early morning, thick cloud, waning of the moon, partial eclipse, penumbra, oblique light, bad light, poor light, shadiness, shade, shadow, dim lighting, romantic lighting, dimmed lights, dipped lights, sidelights, lampshade, light filter, dimmer switch

► *290 Daytime; 291 Night-Time; 522 Light; 523 Darkness*

2 **murk**, murkiness, fog, fogginess, dense fog, peasouper, smog, mist, mistiness, sea mist, haar, fret vapour, condensation, steam, miasma, exhalation, smoke, cloudiness, haze, haziness, dusty air, sandstorm, low visibility, poor visibility, impaired visibility, obscurity, distance, remoteness, vagueness, indistinctness, low definition, soft focus, blur, blurriness, fuzziness, bleariness, poor sight, cataract, dullness, matt finish, tarnish, greyness, dinginess, drabness, opaqueness, semitransparency, smoked glass, frosted glass, film, filminess, veil, muslin, sheer fabric

► *266 Obscurity; 518 Vision; 519 Blindness; 520 Visibility; 521 Invisibility; 528 Opaqueness; 533 Greyness*

3 **dimming**, making dim, becoming dim, clouding over, shading, shadowing, overshadowing, blackening

4 **stupidity**, dimness, dim-wittedness, thickness, denseness, lack of intelligence, obtuseness

► *457 Stupidity; 459 Folly*

ADJECTIVES

5 **dim**, half-lit, half-dark, semidark, twilit, crepuscular, waning, dimly lit, ill-lit, dark, darkish, sombre, livid, leaden, dusky, grey, dull, overcast, cloudy, louring (*or* lowering), stormy, sunless, shady, shadowy, tenebrous

► *523 Darkness; 533 Greyness*

6 **murky**, foggy, smoggy, smog-laden, thick, dusty, smoky, smoke-laden, smoke-filled, misty, steamy, steamed up, miasmal, miasmic, cloudy, nebulous, hazy, distant, remote, vague, indistinct, unclear, low-definition, soft-focus, blurred, blurry, fuzzy, blear, bleary, bleared, muzzy, opaque, smoked, frosted, milky, veiled, filmy, obscured, obscure, shadowy, ill-defined, indistinguishable, faint,

feeble, weak, muted, diffused, pale, white, clear as mud (Inf)

▶ *266 Obscurity; 528 Opaqueness; 531 Whiteness*

7 dimmed, clouded, dull, dulled, faded, drab, dingy, gloomy, lacklustre, lustreless, matt, unpolished, tarnished, rusty, dusty, dirty

▶ *258 Dirtiness*

8 stupid, dim, dull, dense, thick, unintelligent, obtuse, doltish, dim-witted

▶ *457 Stupidity; 459 Folly*

VERBS

9 be dim, become dim, grow dim, darken, cloud over, film over, glaze over, mist over, steam up, lour (*or* lower), become grey, pale, grow pale (*or* faint), wane, fade, fade out, gutter

▶ *523 Darkness; 528 Opaqueness; 533 Greyness*

10 make dim, bedim, fade, cloud, becloud, fog, befog, blur, blear, mist, film, smear, glaze, darken, lower (the lights), turn (the lights) down, dip, shade, shadow, cast a shadow, obscure, obfuscate, veil, shroud

▶ *266 Obscurity; 528 Opaqueness; 736 Concealment*

11 tarnish, rust, dull, lose (its) shine, deaden, tone down, dirty, sully, muddy

▶ *258 Dirtiness*

ADVERBS

12 dimly, cloudily, hazily, foggily, mistily, blearily, muzzily, obscurely, darkly, vaguely, indistinctly, faintly, dingily, drably, in the twilight, in the gloaming, through a glass darkly

525 Appearance

Alas, after a certain age every man is responsible for his face. Albert Camus.

The Lord prefers common-looking people. That is why he makes so many of them. Abraham Lincoln.

Gentlemen always seem to remember blondes. Anita Loos.

NOUNS

1 **appearance**, appearing, coming into view, coming into being, materialization, manifestation, embodiment, incarnation, realization, birth, formation, dawning, dawn, beginning, emergence, onset, arising, rise, coming, advent, arrival, debut, entrance, introduction, presentation, first appearance, publication, issue, issuing forth, launch, release, preview, opening, opening night, first night, premiere, first screening, opening up, unfolding, blooming, waxing, disclosure, revelation, exposure

▶ *95 Reality; 130 Beginning; 308 Opening; 312 Arrival; 402 Material World; 738 Display; 739 Disclosure; 740 Publication*

2 **being in view**, visibility, presence, attendance, court appearance, existence, being, being there, occurrence, happening, phenomenon, performance, stage appearance, showing, show, parade, display, exhibition

▶ *21 Drama; 93 Existence; 97 Presence; 520 Visibility; 738 Display*

3 **external appearance**, look, outward form, superficies, surface, form, shape, format, dimensions, outline, contour, silhouette, relief, elevation, section, aspect, side, facet, angle, point of view, facies, outside, exterior, externals, front, façade, fascia, facing, covering, veneer, dress, clothes, clothing, garb, fashion, dressing up, cut, style, demeanour, manner, mien, bearing, posture, carriage, deportment, air, feature, characteristic, marking, trait, figure, body, body type, physical type, face, physiognomy, visage, countenance, lineaments, features, forehead, brow, eye, nose, mouth, lips, cheek, cheekbone, jaw, chin, ear, full-face, half-face, profile, backview, expression, facial expression, body language, skin, skin colour, complexion, looks, good looks, beauty, ugliness, homeliness

▶ *160 Form; 167 Front; 171 Outside; 545 Beauty; 546 Ugliness; 550 Covering; 551 Dress; 553 Fashion*

4 **something that appears**, spectacle, sight, revelation, apocalypse, theophany, epiphany, miracle, marvel, prodigy, apparition, ghost, spectre, phantom, emanation, ectoplasm, illusion, hallucination, vision, dream, chimera, image, after-image, mirage, hologram, seeming, semblance, pretence, pose, guise, disguise

5 **impression**, effect, first impression, impact, visual appeal, face value, public persona, public image, reflection, mirror image, likeness, similarity, match, lookalike, double, copy, clone, imitation, ringer, representation, picture, photograph, model, replica

▶ *19 Painting and Sculpture; 41 Photography; 96 Unreality; 101 Unworldliness; 115 Similarity; 125 Imitation; 518 Vision; 526 Disappearance; 550 Covering; 700 Deception; 736 Concealment*

6 **reappearance**, return, reissue, republication, second showing, repeat, recurrence, second coming, *déjà vu* (Fr)

▶ *112 Repetition*

ADJECTIVES

7 **appearing**, apparent, material, embodied, incarnate, realized, there, present, all there, obvious, evident, patent, manifest, showing, visible, in sight, on show, on view, exposed, displayed, revealed, epiphanic, theophanic, salient, prominent, conspicuous, jutting, impressive, effective, spectacular, phenomenal, apocalyptic, coming into sight, coming into view, coming into being, beginning, coming, arriving, entering, coming on the scene, emergent, arising, developing, unfolding, waxing, recurring, repeated

▶ *97 Presence; 130 Beginning; 312 Arrival; 520 Visibility*

8 **outer**, outward, superficial, surface, external, exterior, visual, reflected, mirrored, reflecting, mirroring, visible

9 **ostensible**, seeming, deceptive, specious, illusory, visionary, dreamlike, chimerical, imaginary, hallucinatory

▶ *96 Unreality; 101 Unworldliness; 171 Outside; 700 Deception*

10 **aspectual**, beautiful, attractive, sightly, decorated, decorative, well-dressed, fashionable, ugly, unattractive, homely, unsightly, plain, ill-dressed, unfashionable, easy on the eye (Inf)

▶ *545 Beauty; 546 Ugliness; 553 Fashion*

VERBS

11 **appear**, show, show up, be present, attend, be at, be there, be, look, seem, appear like, look like, seem like,

seem to be, look to be, appear to be, have a look of, have the appearance of, take the shape of, take the guise of, disguise oneself as, dress up as, imitate, copy, reflect, mirror, match, resemble

▶ *97 Presence; 115 Similarity; 125 Imitation; 520 Visibility*

12 become visible, materialize, appear, come to light, see the light, begin, dawn, come forth, come forward, come out, emerge, issue, rise, arise, surface, come to the surface, come up, crop up, show, show up, show oneself, turn up, come, arrive, enter, present itself (*or* oneself), make (*or* put in) an appearance, come into the picture, come on the scene, reveal itself (*or* oneself), peep, peep out, crawl out of the woodwork, come over the horizon, loom, wax, fade in, heave in sight, come in sight, rear its (ugly) head, pop up (Inf)

▶ *130 Beginning; 312 Arrival; 402 Material World; 520 Visibility*

13 occur, happen, perform, play, act, appear in, act in, star in, appear on stage, come on the stage, appear on film (*or* screen), be published, come out, become available, appear in the shops, appear in court, recur, reappear, come round again

▶ *21 Drama; 740 Publication*

14 present, put forward, make apparent, realize, show, show up, reveal, disclose, expose, display, exhibit, expose oneself, publish, issue, launch, release, screen, point out, point up, highlight, silhouette, outline, wrap, giftwrap, wrap up in clean linen, disguise, flash (Inf), prettify (Inf), tart up (Inf)

▶ *547 Beautification; 738 Display; 739 Disclosure; 740 Publication*

ADVERBS

15 apparently, evidently, obviously, plainly, clearly, manifestly, to all appearances, seemingly, ostensibly, on the face of it, on the surface, superficially, outwardly, externally, facially, for the sake of appearances, at face value, at sight, at first sight, at first blush, on sight, into sight, in outline

526 Disappearance

This time it vanished quite slowly, beginning with the end of the tail, and ending with the grin, which remained some time after the rest of it had gone. Lewis Carroll.

VERBS

1 disappear, cease, end, cease to be, cease to exist, become extinct, die out, die, expire, perish, pass away, pass, wane, ebb, recede, vanish, dematerialize, become invisible, evanesce, evaporate, dissolve, melt, fade, fade away, fade out, dwindle, dwindle away, peter out, disguise oneself, hide, lie low, go to ground, lurk, disappear into thin air, blend into the background, sink below the horizon, sink without trace, go out of use, become obsolete, cease publication, go out of print, go off the air, close, close down

▶ *94 Nonexistence; 131 End; 214 Decrease; 226 Stopping; 521 Invisibility; 582 Death; 736 Concealment*

2 depart, decamp, go, go away, escape, run, run away, flee, fly, withdraw, retire, go into retirement, retreat, go into retreat, melt away, absent oneself, play (Dial), go AWOL, take French leave, play truant, not appear, fail to appear, stay away, play hooky (Inf), do a runner (Inf), scarper (Inf), vamoose (Inf)

▶ *98 Absence; 313 Departure; 315 Exit*

3 cause to disappear, vaporize, liquidate, disembody, destroy, annihilate, waste, disperse, dissipate, dispel, scatter, dismiss, send away, expel, hide, conceal, obscure, bury, disguise, camouflage, erase, blot out, obliterate, rub, rub out, wipe, wipe out, scrub, cancel, get rid of, eliminate, remove, take away, spirit away, steal, rip off (Inf)

▶ *357 Destruction; 358 Obliteration; 371 Expulsion; 583 Burial; 736 Concealment*

NOUNS

4 disappearance, disappearing, cessation, end, extinction, dying out, death, dying, passing away, passing, wane, ebb, vanishing, dematerialization, disembodiment, vaporization, evaporation, evanescence, dissolution, melting, fading, fading away, fading out, dwindling, erosion, wearing away, dispersal, dispersion, dissipation, scattering, departure, exit, going, going away, escape, running away, flight, withdrawal, retreat, desertion, truancy, nonappearance, staying away, absence, nonexistence, invisibility, vanishing trick, escapology, escapee, missing person, runaway, truant, fade-out, blackout, vanishing point, horizon, disappearing act (Inf)

▶ *94 Nonexistence; 98 Absence; 131 End; 226 Stopping; 313 Departure; 315 Exit; 582 Death*

5 disguise, protective coloration, camouflage, blacking up, blacking out, occultation, eclipse, obscuring, obscuration, hiding, concealment, burial, erasure, obliteration, cancellation, elimination, annihilation, destruction, loss

▶ *358 Obliteration; 523 Darkness; 525 Appearance; 583 Burial; 736 Concealment*

ADJECTIVES

6 disappearing, vanishing, evanescent, fugitive, going, departing, escaping, transient, fleeting, passing, fading, waning, dying, dissolving, evaporating, hiding, obsolescent, here today gone tomorrow, now you see it now you don't

▶ *278 Transience*

7 disappeared, vanished, absent, not present, gone, gone away, away, missing, lost, dead, extinct, obsolete, past, past and gone, nonexistent, invisible, eclipsed, occulted, hidden, gone to ground, concealed, buried, disguised, camouflaged, obscured, dispersed, dissipated, worn away, eroded, out of the picture, out of sight, lost to sight, out of range

▶ *94 Nonexistence; 98 Absence; 313 Departure; 521 Invisibility; 736 Concealment*

ADVERBS

8 fleetingly, transiently, evanescently, meltingly, fugitively, away, absently, invisibly, inwardly, below the surface, below the horizon, in hiding, in disguise, underground, obsolescently

527 Transparency

ADJECTIVES

1 **transparent**, clear, limpid, pellucid, colourless, crystal, crystalline, crystal-clear, glassy, vitreous, glass-like, hyaline, transpicuous, dioptric, refractive, nonreflective, watery, liquid, clarified, pure, cloudless, unclouded, unobstructed, as clear as crystal, clear as air

▶ *255 Purity; 256 Cleanness; 433 Water; 434 Air; 521 Invisibility; 522 Light; 530 Colourlessness*

2 **translucent**, see-through, revealing, diaphanous, lucent, gauzy, open-textured, sheer, thin, flimsy, filmy, fine, insubstantial, vaporous

▶ *94 Nonexistence; 153 Thinness*

3 **semitransparent**, translucent, milky, misty, smoky, smoked, tinted, stained, frosted, pearly, opalescent, opaline, semiopaque

▶ *528 Opaqueness*

4 **easily seen through**, open, guileless, ingenuous, direct, forthright, straightforward, frank, candid, open-hearted, undisguised, evident, obvious, patent, easily detected, manifest, plain, unambiguous, lucid

▶ *520 Visibility; 695 Intelligibility; 725 Clarity; 739 Disclosure*

NOUNS

5 **transparency**, clarity, clearness, limpidity, limpidness, pellucidity, pellucidness, colourlessness, glassiness, vitreousness, vitreosity, crystallinity, wateriness, purity, cleanness, unobstructed view, cloudlessness

▶ *255 Purity; 256 Cleanness; 433 Water; 521 Invisibility*

6 **translucency**, translucence, diaphanousness, gauziness, open texture, sheerness, thinness, flimsiness, filminess, fineness, insubstantiality, vaporousness

▶ *94 Nonexistence; 153 Thinness*

7 **semitransparency**, translucency, milkiness, pearliness, mistiness, smokiness, opalescence

▶ *528 Opaqueness*

8 **transparent thing**, water, ice, vapour, air, glass, window, shop window, showcase, glass case, display case, goldfish bowl, glasshouse, greenhouse, conservatory, watch glass, lens, eyeglass, spectacles, glasses, crystal ball, hyalite, hyalin, clear varnish, Perspex™, Plexiglass™ (US), Cellophane™, plastic wrap, clingfilm, bubble pack, blister pack, window envelope, slide, transparency, negative, film, gossamer, sheer fabric, muslin, scrim, gauze, chiffon, organdie, organza, tiffany, voile, net, lace, smoke, mist, haze

▶ *308 Opening; 518 Vision; 528 Opaqueness*

9 **glass**, clear glass, crystal, crystal glass, rock crystal, lead glass, lead crystal, bottle glass, crown glass, flint glass, plate glass, sheet glass, window glass, bulletproof glass, laminated glass, safety glass, toughened glass, reinforced glass, opal glass, frosted glass, ground glass, stained glass, fibreglass, quartz glass, glassware, window, windowpane, pane, window light, light, windshield, windscreen, two-way mirror

▶ *308 Opening; 522 Light*

10 **openness**, apparentness, obviousness, plainness, lucidity, guilelessness, ingenuousness, straightforwardness, forthrightness, frankness, open-heartedness

▶ *520 Visibility; 695 Intelligibility; 725 Clarity; 739 Disclosure*

VERBS

11 **be transparent**, reveal, show through, shine through, transmit light, become transparent, crystallize, liquefy, vaporize

12 **make transparent**, crystallize, purify, clarify, refine, brighten, wipe, clean, cleanse, open, open out, demist, uncloud, see through, see through a brick wall, see round corners, have x-ray eyes (Inf)

▶ *255 Purity; 256 Cleanness*

ADVERBS

13 **transparently**, clearly, limpidly, pellucidly, translucently, diaphanously, flimsily, insubstantially, mistily, smokily, openly, directly, obviously, plainly

528 Opaqueness

ADJECTIVES

1 **opaque**, nontransparent, nontranslucent, dense, thick, solid, impenetrable, impermeable, impervious, light-tight, lightproof, dark, black, windowless, blank, covered, coated

▶ *152 Thickness; 416 Density; 523 Darkness; 532 Blackness; 550 Covering*

2 **shady**, obscure, dark, murky, dirty, grimy, dusty, dull, lustreless, matt, muddy, muddied, turbid, cloudy, milky, fuzzy, blurred, vague, dim, hazy, smoky, foggy, misty, misted, steamed up, clouded, obfuscated, opaline, frosted, smoked, filmy, semiopaque

▶ *258 Dirtiness; 266 Obscurity; 523 Darkness; 524 Dimness; 527 Transparency*

3 **mirror-like**, mirrored, reflecting, reflective, mirroring, shiny, glassy

▶ *28 Physics*

4 **inscrutable**, baffling, mystifying, cryptic, enigmatic, arcane, recondite, unclear, ambiguous, indefinite, unknowable, unfathomable, unintelligible, clear as mud (Inf)

▶ *696 Unintelligibility; 736 Concealment; 737 Secrecy*

5 **unintelligent**, dim, dim-witted, stupid, dense, thick, thickheaded, dull, dull-witted, obtuse, doltish, stolid, having a closed mind, not open to new ideas, thick as a plank (*or* two short planks) (Inf)

NOUNS

6 **opaqueness**, opacity, filminess, density, thickness, solidity, impenetrability, impermeability, imperviousness, darkness, blackness, murkiness, dirtiness, dullness, muddiness, turbidity, cloudiness, milkiness, fuzziness, dimness, haziness, fogginess, obfuscation, reflection, mirroring

▶ *28 Physics; 152 Thickness; 258 Dirtiness; 416 Density; 523 Darkness; 524 Dimness; 527 Transparency; 532 Blackness*

7 **opaque thing**, brick wall, muddy water, haze, mist, film, steam, smoke, cloud, fog, peasouper, blizzard, dust storm, sandstorm, smokescreen, frosted glass, ground glass, screen, curtain, drapes (US), blind, shutter

▶ *524 Dimness; 736 Concealment*

8 **obscurity**, inscrutability, abstruseness, ambiguity, unclearness, unintelligibility, opacity

► *266 Obscurity; 696 Unintelligibility*

9 **stupidity**, thickheadedness, stolidity, dull-wittedness, hebetude

► *457 Stupidity*

VERBS

10 **be opaque**, become opaque, cloud over, steam up, mist, fog, thicken

11 **make opaque**, thicken, muddy, stir up, cloud, darken, dim, frost, smoke, devitrify, screen, cover, coat, obfuscate, obscure

► *152 Thickness; 523 Darkness; 524 Dimness; 550 Covering*

12 **obscure**, mystify, puzzle, baffle, perplex

► *266 Obscurity; 696 Unintelligibility*

ADVERBS

13 **opaquely**, densely, solidly, impenetrably, impermeably, imperviously, obscurely, cloudily, foggily, mistily, inscrutably, cryptically, ambiguously, unintelligibly, stupidly, stolidly

529 Colour

All colours will agree in the dark. Francis Bacon.

NOUNS

1 **colour**, colouring, coloration, biological coloration, pigmentation, monochrome, spectral colour, primary colour, primary triads, secondary colour, secondary triads, natural colour, complementary colour, neutral colour, heraldic colour, chromatic colour, chromaticism, chromatism, chromatic aberration, colour vision, colour perception, colour-blindness

► *531 Whiteness; 532 Blackness; 533 Greyness; 534 Brownness; 535 Redness; 536 Orangeness; 537 Yellowness; 538 Greenness; 539 Blueness; 540 Purpleness*

2 **colourfulness**, spectrum, rainbow, prism, refracted colour, range of colour, variegation, multicolour, polychrome, polychromatism, riot of colour, splash of colour, colour disk, colour wheel, colour circle, colour scheme, colour harmony, colour coordination, colour chart, pigment chart, colour code, colourcast

► *541 Variegation*

3 **hue**, colour temperature, warm hue, cool hue, chroma, chromaticity, saturation, purity, colour quality, tone, value, tint, tincture, tinge, shade, cast, darkness, loudness, intensity, brilliance, luminosity, softness, warmth, dullness, deadness, paleness, faded hue, discoloration, patina, half-tone, half-light, mezzotint

► *522 Light*

4 **pigment**, colorant, staining pigment, organic pigment, inorganic pigment, opaque pigment, semitransparent pigment, transparent pigment, metallic pigment, colouring, colouring matter, additive colour, subtractive colour, artificial colouring, dye, dyestuff, stain, fast dye, natural dye, vegetable dye, artificial dye, synthetic dye, aniline, red dye, cochineal, grain, purple dye, indigo, madder, blue dye, woad, tint, paint, varnish, lacquer, enamel, glaze, luminous glaze, wash, colourwash, whitewash, distemper, fixative, mordant, colourfastness

5 **paint**, medium, emulsion paint, gloss paint, undercoat, primer, oil paints, acrylic paints, gouache, poster paint, watercolours, watercolour pigments, artist colours, basic palette, standard palette, expanded palette, coloured pencil, coloured crayon, coloured chalk, coloured paper, art equipment, art supplies

► *19 Painting and Sculpture*

6 **painter**, colourist, watercolourist, chromatist, chromatic painter, colour-field painter, colour photographer, chromolithographer, colour coordinator

7 **colour painting**, chromatic painting, colour-field painting, colour photography, colour film, colour slides, colour transparencies, colour negative, colour prints, colour printing, colour reproduction, colour filter, colourization, chromolithography, Technicolor™

► *19 Painting and Sculpture; 41 Photography*

8 **chromatics**, chromatology, science of colour, colour theory, colorimetry, spectrum analysis, spectrography, spectrophotometry, spectroscope, chromascope, colorimeter, spectrometer, tintometer, spectrophotometer, spectrograph, chromaticity chart, chromaticity diagram

9 **complexion**, natural colour, healthy hue, flush, blush, glow, rosy cheeks, ruddiness, sickly hue, paleness, pallor, cosmetics, make-up, rouge, blusher, lipstick, eyeshadow, war paint (Inf)

► *259 Health; 260 Ill Health; 547 Beautification*

ADJECTIVES

10 **coloured**, in colour, in Technicolor™, painted, pigmented, stained, dyed, tinted, tinct, tinged, toned, shaded, technicoloured, colourized, multicoloured, many-coloured, polychrome, polychromatic, variegated, kaleidoscopic, prismatic, spectroscopic, chromatic, monochromatic, colourable, colorific, tinctorial, colourfast, fast, unfading, constant

11 **colourful**, full-coloured, uniform, matching, agreeing, harmonious, toning, intense, strong, emphatic, florid, high-coloured, deep, deep-coloured, rich, warm, glowing, bright, brilliant, vivid, gay

► *522 Light; 750 Agreement*

12 **gaudy**, garish, overstated, showy, flashy, lurid, loud, glaring, flaring, flaunting, spectacular, clashing, disagreeing, discordant, screaming, shrieking, harsh, stark, raw, crude

► *517 Dissonance*

13 **soft-hued**, soft, quiet, understated, mellow, delicate, refined, discreet, whitish, pearly, creamy, light, pale, pastel, muted, dull, flat, matt, dead, simple, plain, sober, sombre, dark, drab, dingy, black, faded, discoloured, patinated, weathered

► *523 Darkness; 531 Whiteness*

14 **chromolithographic**, colorimetric, spectrophotometric, spectrographic, chromatological, photochromic, calorochromic

VERBS

15 **colour**, colour in, paint, watercolour, crayon, colour print, colourize, variegate, pigment, stain, dye, tie-dye, imbue, imbrue, tint, tincture, tinge, tone, shade, wash, colourwash, distemper, lacquer, enamel, coat, discolour, fade, weather, mellow, tone down, whiten, whitewash, silver, yellow, gild, redden, rouge, tan, darken, blacken, brighten, illuminate, emblazon

16 **make up**, powder, rouge, flush, blush, redden, glow, pale

► *547 Beautification*
17 colourcast, transmit colour

ADVERBS

18 colourfully, colouristically, brightly, brilliantly, gaudily, garishly, polychromatically, in Technicolour™

530 Colourlessness

NOUNS

1 **colourlessness**, achromatism, achromaticity, neutral hue, decoloration, decolorization, etiolation, bleaching, blanching, fading, weathering, whitening, whiteness, neutral tint

2 **paleness**, pallor, pallidity, lightness, faintness, anaemia, bloodlessness, albinism, albinoism, pigment deficiency

3 **pen-and-ink sketch**, black-and-white drawing, overexposed photograph, overexposed negative, overexposure, underexposed photograph, underexposed negative, underexposure, black-and-white photograph, black-and-white print

4 **colour remover,** bleacher, bleach, bleaching powder, blancher, whitener, decolorant, hydrogen peroxide, peroxide, lime, chloride of lime, chlorinated lime

VERBS

5 **lose colour**, pale, fade, run, bleach, blanch, whiten, come out in the wash, turn pale, peak, change countenance, go as white as a sheet, go white around the gills

6 **decolour**, achromatize, fade, etiolate, bleach, blanch, peroxide, whiten, drain of colour, wash out, tone down, deaden, weaken, pale, dim, bedim, dull, tarnish, discolour

ADJECTIVES

7 **colourless**, hueless, toneless, neutral, uncoloured, achromatic, decoloured, discoloured, bleached, etiolated, overexposed, underexposed, weathered, faint, faded, fading, washed out, washy, wishy-washy, unpigmented, whitish, yellowish, lustreless, mousy, dingy, milky, dull, leaden, grey, lacklustre, without gloss, dim

8 **drained of colour**, white-skinned, light-skinned, white, faint-coloured, bloodless, anaemic, albino, albinotic, emaciated, peaky, peakish, peaked (US), pale, pallid, mousy, ashy, ashen, ashen-hued, livid, tallow-faced, pasty, doughy, mealy, sallow, sickly, unhealthy, blank, glassy, lacklustre, insipid, lurid, ghastly, wan, deathly, deathlike, deathly pale, pale as death, dead, pale as ashes, white as a sheet, white (*or* green) around the gills, cadaverous, ghostlike, ghostly

ADVERBS

9 **colourlessly**, tonelessly, achromatically, neutrally, faintly, dimly, dully, dingily, blankly

531 Whiteness

There can be no whitewash at the White House. Richard Milhous Nixon.

ADJECTIVES

1 **white**, pure-white, snow-white, snowy, lily-white, milk-white, milky, lactescent, whitish, albescent, off-white, half-white, oyster-white, pearly, ivory, alabaster, marble, chalky, creamy, magnolia, ecru, unbleached, undyed, greige, mushroom, beige, silver, silvery, silvered, argent, argentine, argental, white as the driven snow, white as a lily, white as milk, white as marble, white like ivory, fair-skinned, light- (*or* pale-) complexioned, albinotic, albinistic, Caucasian

► *1 Anthropology; 2 Sociology; 525 Appearance; 534 Brownness*

2 **whitened**, bleached, blanched, decolorized, faded, colourless, achromatic, semitransparent, whitewashed, snow-capped, snow-covered, ice-covered, hoary, frosty, frosted, foam-flecked, foaming, spumy, soapy, lathery, white with dust, dusty, white-hot

► *493 Heat; 530 Colourlessness*

3 **white-haired**, fair-haired, fair, blond(e), ash-blond(e), platinum-blond(e), golden-haired, flaxen-haired, tow-headed, Nordic, grey-haired, grey, canescent, hoary, grizzled, pepper-and-salt, mottled

► *533 Greyness*

4 **pale**, pallid, sallow, waxen, ashen, ashy, livid, ghastly, white as a sheet

► *530 Colourlessness*

5 **pure**, chaste, virginal, clean, spotless, immaculate

► *255 Purity; 256 Cleanness*

6 **light**, luminous, bright, dazzling

► *522 Light*

NOUNS

7 **whiteness**, snowiness, milkiness, lactescence, whitishness, albescence, off-whiteness, pearliness, chalkiness, creaminess, silveriness, fairness, greyness, canescence, hoariness, colourlessness, achromatism, etiolation, semitransparency, paleness, pallor, sallowness, albinism, albinoism, lack of pigment, leucoderma

► *1 Anthropology; 2 Sociology; 119 Equality; 530 Colourlessness*

8 **whitener**, whiting, blanco, white alkali, white arsenic, white lead, pipeclay, whitewash, calcimine, white paint, Chinese white, Luma white, Paris white, flake white, zinc white, titanium white, achromatic hue

9 **white thing**, whites, white goods, white sale, white tie, hoar, frost, snow, driven snow, new-fallen snow, chalk, paper, white paper, teeth, milk, flour, white flag, white wall, white light, white heat, marble, alabaster, ivory, pearl, lily, whitecap, white horse, white dwarf, white blood cell, silver, white metal, white gold, pewter, platinum, white oak, white spruce, white poplar, white rose, whitethorn, white clover, swan, whitefish, white whale, white shark, whitetail, white-tailed deer, whitethroat, white admiral, whitefly, white ant, whitebait, white bread, white sauce, white wine, white coffee, white pepper, white meat, White House, White Friar, White Cliffs of Dover

10 **figurative usage**, white-collar worker, white elephant, white hat, white knight, white feather, white hope, white lie, whited sepulchre, White Nile, White Mountains, White Russia, White Sea, White Volta, white lightning (US inf), white stuff (Inf)

11 **purity**, chastity, cleanness, spotlessness

► *255 Purity; 256 Cleanness*

12 **light**, luminosity, brightness

► *522 Light*

VERBS

13 **whiten**, white, bleach, blanch, blanco, pipeclay, whitewash, calcimine, wash, clean, pale, blench, fade, decolorize, etiolate, frost, silver, grizzle

ADVERBS

14 **whitely**, palely, pallidly, achromatically, lightly, luminously, chalkily, creamily, semitransparently, foamily

532 Blackness

Any colour, so long as it's black. Henry Ford.

ADJECTIVES

1 **black**, sable, raven, ebon, ebony, jet, jet-black, jetty, pitch-black, pitchy, inky, sooty, fuliginous, coal-black, sloe-black, blackish, nigrescent, blue-black, grey-black, brown-black, black as coal, black as soot, black as jet, black as pitch, black as night, black as midnight, black as ink, black as my hat, black as a tinker's pot, black as thunder, black as hell

2 **dark**, deep, of the deepest dye, achromatic, low-toned, low in tone, dim, dingy, murky, smudgy, smoky, dusky, swarthy, swart (Lit), pigmented, melanistic, dark-complexioned, Black, Negro, Negroid

► *1 Anthropology; 2 Sociology; 523 Darkness; 525 Appearance*

3 **blackened**, singed, charred, tanned, suntanned, sunburnt, black-and-blue

► *493 Heat; 534 Brownness*

4 **black-haired**, black-locked, raven-haired, dark-haired, dark-headed, brunette, black-eyed, sloe-eyed

5 **black-hearted**, evil, wicked, nefarious, heinous, villainous, blackguardly

► *798 Evil*

6 **sad**, sombre, gloomy, depressed, depressing, mournful, mourning, funereal

► *583 Burial; 602 Sorrow; 603 Lamentation*

NOUNS

7 **blackness**, inkiness, blackishness, nigrescence, nigritude, darkness, dark, night, dark colour, dark colouring, pigmentation, pigment, colour, depth, deep tone, blackening, darkening, obscuration, Negroism, melanism, melanosis, swarthiness, swartness, duskiness, black-and-white, *chiaroscuro* (It), chequer

► *1 Anthropology; 523 Darkness*

8 **black pigment**, melanin, blacking, lampblack, black lead, ivory black, blue-black, nigrosine, japan, niello, burnt cork, ink, Indian ink, China ink, printer's ink, newsprint ink, indelible ink

9 **black thing**, ink, tar, pitch, coal, charcoal, silhouette, shadow, ebony, jet, obsidian, soot, smut, sable, black belt, black tie, crepe, mourning clothes, black hat, blacktop (US), black flag, blackboard, blackjack, blackout, black light, black hole, black pudding, black coffee, black pepper, crow, raven, blackbird, black swan, black Angus, black snake, black bear, black grouse, black widow, blacktail deer, blackfish, black bass, blackfly, blackberry, blackcurrant, black spruce, black nightshade, blackthorn, sloe, black-eyed Susan, blackface, black eye, bruise, blackhead, Black Friar, Black Rod, Black and Tan, Black Watch, Black Shirt, Black Maria

10 **figurative usage**, blackmail, blackball, blacklist, blackguard, black magic, black art, black market, black economy, black sheep, black ice, black spot, black box, black book, black bottom, Black Mass, Black Death, Black Prince, Black Forest, Black Hills, Black Sea, Black Country, blackleg (Inf), black stuff (Inf), black diamonds (Inf)

VERBS

11 **blacken**, black, blacklead, japan, niello, ink, ink in, dirty, blot, smudge, smirch, sully, darken, deepen, singe, char, burn, tan, suntan, blackball, blacklist, boycott

ADVERBS

12 **blackly**, darkly, deeply, inkily, duskily, swarthily, obscurely, gloomily

533 Greyness

One that is ever kind said yesterday:
'Your well-belovèd's hair has threads of grey,
And little shadows come about her eyes.' W. B. Yeats.

ADJECTIVES

1 **grey**, greyish, canescent, griseous, silver-grey, silver, silvery, silvered, light-grey, pale-grey, powder-grey, dove-grey, pearl-grey, pearly, mouse-coloured, mousy, taupe, dun, brown-grey, donkey-grey, steel-grey, steely, iron-grey, leaden, charcoal-grey, dark-grey, blue-grey, slate-grey, slate-coloured, ash-grey, ashen, ashy, cinereous, smoky, fuliginous, dapple-grey, neutral, unbleached, undyed, greige, ecru

► *531 Whiteness*

2 **grey-haired**, grey-headed, grizzled, grizzly, pepper-and-salt, hoary, hoar, greying, elderly, old, aged

► *531 Whiteness; 556 Age*

3 **dull**, drab, dreary, gloomy, sombre, dark, leaden, overcast, cloudy, murky, misty, foggy

► *524 Dimness*

NOUNS

4 **greyness**, grey colour, greyishness, canescence, grey pigment, Payne's grey, neutral tint, grisaille, oyster, taupe, greige

5 **grey thing**, slate, silver, pewter, iron, steel, lead, gunmetal, ashes, Grey Friar, greyhound, grey wolf, grey whale, greyhen, grey squirrel, greylag, greywacke, grey hair

6 **figurative usage**, grey area, grey matter, grey population, Old Grey Whistle Test, greybeard, grey market, grey knight, Gray Panther (US), grey man (Inf)

7 **dullness**, drabness, dreariness, gloominess, darkness, cloudiness, murk

VERBS

8 **grey**, turn grey, go grey, silver, frost

ADVERBS

9 **greyly**, dully, drably, drearily, gloomily, sombrely, cloudily, mistily, murkily, foggily, smokily

534 Brownness

Oh, good gigantic smile o' the brown old earth. Robert Browning.

ADJECTIVES

1 **brown**, pale brown, oatmeal, beige, buff, fawn, biscuit, mushroom, café-au-lait, ecru, snuff-coloured, yellow-brown, dun, khaki, hazel, walnut, orange-brown, amber, bronze, tawny, fulvous, sorrel, reddish-brown, nut-brown, tan, foxy, bay, roan, chestnut, auburn, mahogany, copper, coppery, copper-coloured, cupreous, russet, rust-coloured, rusty, rubiginous, ferruginous, liver-coloured, maroon, purple-brown, puce, dark brown, peat-brown, mocha, chocolate, coffee, coffee-coloured, fuscous

2 **browned**, bronzed, dark, brunette, tanned, suntanned, brown as a berry, brown as a nut, sunburnt, toasted, grilled, charred, singed

NOUNS

3 **brownness**, brown colour, brown pigmentation, melanin, mole, freckle, suntan, sunburn, brunette, dark skin, dark complexion

▶ *566 Humankind*

4 **brown pigment**, bistre, ochre, sepia, raw sienna, burnt sienna, raw umber, burnt umber, Vandyke brown, brown dye, Bismarck brown

5 **brown thing**, cinnamon, coffee, chocolate, butterscotch, caramel, toffee, burnt almond, brown sugar, demerara, muscovado, brown bread, wholemeal bread, brown rice, brownie, brown betty (US), tobacco leaf, dead leaf, autumn colours, fall colours (US), brown coal, lignite, brownstone (US), brown algae, brown fat, brown rot, brown-lung disease, brown bear, brown trout, brown recluse spider (US), brown-tail moth, Brown Swiss cattle, Burmese cat, seal-point (Siamese cat), chocolate-point (Siamese cat), brown paper bag, brown belt, shit (Inf)

6 **figurative usage**, brownie, brown study, brownout (US), Brown Owl, Brownie Guide, Brownie Girl Scout (US), Brownie point, Brown Shirt, brown stuff (Inf), brown-bagger (US inf), brown-noser (US tab inf), brown-trousers (Inf)

VERBS

7 **brown**, embrown, tan, suntan, bronze, sunburn, burn, singe, char, grill, toast

535 Redness

My mistress' eyes are nothing like the sun;
Coral is far more red than her lips' red. William Shakespeare.

ADJECTIVES

1 **red**, pink, coral, coral-pink, orange-pink, shell-pink, flesh-pink, flesh-coloured, peach-coloured, salmon-pink, shocking pink, rose-pink, damask, carnation, rosy, roseate, rose-coloured, rose-red, cherry, cherry-red, cerise, bright red, blood-red, carmine, crimson, cramoisy (Lit), scarlet, cardinal red, Turkey red, vermilion, vermeil, gules, brick-red, pillarbox red, flame-coloured, deep red, ruby, winecoloured, purple-red, beetroot-red, fuchsia, cyclamen, magenta, maroon, murrey (Lit), brownish-red, oxblood, rust-coloured, rufous, rufescent, russet

▶ *534 Brownness; 540 Purpleness*

2 **red-faced**, red-cheeked, rosy-cheeked, rosy, glowing, blooming, flushing, blushing, rubescent (Lit), ruddy, sanguine, rubicund, florid, blowzy, rouged, reddened, flushed, red as a beetroot, red as a lobster, sunburnt, hectic, fevered, feverish, fiery, red-hot

▶ *260 Ill Health; 493 Heat*

3 **red-haired**, ginger-haired, carroty, sandy, Titian, auburn, chestnut

4 **bloody**, blood-stained, bloodshot, gory, sanguineous, sanguinary, ensanguined, incarnadine (Lit)

NOUNS

5 **redness**, reddening, rubescence, rubefaction, rubefacient, rufescence, red colour, red complexion, blush, flush, hectic flush, red rash, scarlet fever, glow, warmth, rosiness, bloom, ruddiness, floridness, rubicundity

6 **red pigment**, red dye, cadmium red, cadmium scarlet, Windsor red, Grumbacher red, Thalo red, Indian red, murex, cochineal, carmine, kermes, dragon's blood, cinnabar, vermilion, minium, red lead, ruddle, madder, rose madder, brown madder, alizarin, alizarin crimson, crimson lake, Venetian red, rosaniline, solferino, red ochre, light red oxide, red cosmetic, henna, rouge, blusher, lipstick, nail polish

7 **red thing**, ruby, garnet, carnelian, fire, flame, fireglow, sunset, dawn, rust, brick, blood, gore, red blood cell (*or* corpuscle), rose, geranium, carnation, poppy, peony, cherry, strawberry, raspberry, mulberry, redcurrant, plum, peach, tomato, beetroot, red clover, red pepper, redwood, red bird, cardinal, robin redbreast, redwing, red deer, red fox, red squirrel, red salmon, red snapper, red admiral, red bug (US), red grouse, red meat, red wine, claret, port, burgundy, red planet, Mars, red giant, red dwarf, red card, red ink, red light, danger signal, fire engine, pillarbox, red cheeks, rosy cheeks, apple cheeks, cherry lips, high colour, strawberry mark, red hair, redhead, carrot-top (Inf), gingernob (Inf)

8 **figurative usage**, red carpet, red herring, red-letter day, red tape, red alert, red-light district, red-hot mama, Red Cross, Red Crescent, Red Sea, Communist, Red (Inf), better red than dead, reds under the bed, redcoat, redneck (US inf), red-eye flight (US inf)

VERBS

9 **redden**, flush, blush, glow, colour, colour up, crimson, make red, rubefy, ruddle, rouge, raddle, rubricate, mantle, incarnadine (Lit)

ADVERBS

10 **ruddily**, rosily, blushingly, in the pink, floridly, sanguineously, sanguinarily, warmly

536 Orangeness

ADJECTIVES

1 **orange**, reddish-yellow, yellowish-red, ochreous, amber, saffron, apricot, peach, golden, old-gold, or, carroty, Titian, ginger, tan, bronze, brassy, flame-coloured, coppery

▶ *534 Brownness; 535 Redness; 537 Yellowness*

NOUNS

2 **orangeness**, orange colour, orange pigment, ochre, raw sienna, Mars orange, cadmium orange, ginger, henna, carotene

3 **orange thing**, orange, marmalade, orangeade, orange squash, orange juice, tangerine, mandarin, clementine, satsuma, minneola, ortaline, Jaffa orange, blood orange, peach, apricot, nectarine, kumquat, carrot, pumpkin, marigold, sunflower, saffron, orange hawkweed, goldfish, amber, amber light, brass, copper, sand, tequila sunrise, buck's fizz, orange sunshine (Inf)

4 **figurative usage**, orange blossom, orangewood, orangery, orange pekoe, orange stick, orange-flower water, Orangeman, Orangeman's Day, Orange March, Orange Free State

537 Yellowness

There's a one-eyed yellow idol to the north of Khatmandu,
There's a little marble cross below the town;
There's a broken-hearted woman tends the grave of Mad Carew
And the Yellow God forever gazes down. J. Milton Hayes.

ADJECTIVES

1 **yellow**, pale yellow, cream-coloured, creamy, beige, honey-coloured, straw-coloured, fallow, champagne, greenish-yellow, citron, chartreuse, primrose-yellow, lemon-yellow, citrine, bright yellow, canary-yellow, sunshine-yellow, gold, golden, golden-yellow, gilt, gilded, aureate, or, amber, honey-coloured, brownish-yellow, old-gold, mustard-yellow, mustard, buff, tawny

2 **yellowish**, xanthous, luteous, fulvous, flavescent, sulphurous

3 **yellow-haired**, fair-haired, flaxen-haired, golden-haired, tow-haired, blond, ash-blond, platinum-blond, strawberry-blond, honey-blond

4 **yellow-faced**, sallow, jaundiced, bilious

5 **cowardly**, craven, spineless, chicken-hearted, lily-livered, yellow (Inf), chicken (Inf)

▶ *614 Cowardice*

NOUNS

6 **yellowness**, yellow colour, yellow hair, fair hair, blond(e), towhead, yellow skin, jaundice, icterus, yellow fever, biliousness

7 **yellow pigment**, cadmium yellow, cadmium lemon, gamboge, chrome yellow, Windsor yellow, Indian yellow, Naples yellow, lemon yellow, orpiment, yellow ochre, Claude tint, massicot, weld, luteolin, xanthene, xanthophyll

8 **yellow thing**, gold, topaz, amber, old ivory, yellow metal, sulphur, brimstone, lemon, citron, banana, mustard, honey, butter, buttercup, daffodil, crocus, primrose, cowslip, dandelion, winter jasmine, yellowhammer, yellowtail, yellowthroat, yellow underwing, yellow jacket (US), Yellow Pages, yellow line, yellow rain, yellow card, yellow spot, yellow jacket (US inf), yellows (Inf), yellow sunshine (Inf)

9 **figurative usage**, Yellow Sea, Yellow River, Yellowstone National Park, yellow journalism, yellow peril, yellow streak, yellow press, yellow-belly (Inf)

VERBS

10 **make** (*or* **become**) **yellow**, yellow, gild

ADVERBS

11 **yellowly**, goldenly, creamily

538 Greenness

Let us take as our emblem green cockades, green the colour of hope! Camille Desmoulins.

ADJECTIVES

1 **green**, emerald, jade, vert, grass-green, leaf-green, pea-green, leek-green, greenish, virescent, viridescent, yellow-green, lime-green, chartreuse, eau-de-nil, Lincoln green, bice-green, olive-green, grey-green, sage-green, avocado, celadon, reseda, mignonette, blue-green, glaucous, sea-green, Nile green, loden green, aquamarine, dull green, dark green, bottle green, jungle green, forest green

▶ *537 Yellowness; 539 Blueness*

2 **verdant**, grassy, leafy, green, fresh, rural

3 **raw**, unripe, unseasoned, immature, callow, green, inexperienced, unskilled, inexpert, untrained, untried, untested, unsophisticated, naive, ingenuous, artless, innocent, credulous, gullible, gauche, awkward, wet behind the ears (Inf)

▶ *456 Ignorance; 555 Youth*

4 **fresh**, new, young, youthful, evergreen, sappy, springlike, vernal, vigorous, flourishing, blooming

5 **green-eyed**, jealous, envious, green with envy, covetous, resentful

▶ *629 Jealousy*

6 **sick**, nauseated, green, bilious, greensick, green around the gills (Inf)

▶ *260 Ill Health*

7 **environmental**, conservationist, green, environment-friendly, ozone-friendly

NOUNS

8 **greenness**, viridity, viridescence, virescence, verdancy, verdure, greenery, woodland, greenwood, evergreen, foliage, leaves, grass, moss, turf, sward, grassland, farmland, pasture, common, green belt, park, lawn, green, village green, bowling green, greenkeeper, green fingers

9 **greenstuff**, greens, spring greens, cabbage, lettuce, broccoli, green leek, green bean, green pepper, greengage, lime, avocado, greengrocer

10 **green pigment**, chlorophyll, terre verte, celadonite, viridian, verditer, Paris green, Windsor green, Thalo yellow green, Hooker's green

11 **green thing**, greenstone, jade, emerald, malachite, beryl, chrysoprase, olivine, verd antique, green porphyry, aquamarine, greensand, verdigris, patina, green turtle, green snake, greenfinch, greenshank, greenlet, greenfly, greenheart, green card, little green men, green paper, green ice (US inf), green dragon (Inf), green hornet (Inf)

12 **figurative usage**, Greenland, Greenland Sea, Green

Mountains, Green River, Green Bay, Green Berets, greenroom, greenhouse, greenhouse effect, green pound, greenback (US inf), greenmail (US inf), the green stuff (US inf)

13 **young thing**, immature thing, greenhorn, greenstick fracture, green tea

14 **green-eyed monster**, jealousy, envy, covetousness, green envy

15 **green light**, traffic light, go-ahead, all clear, permission, approval, consent

▶ *669 Approval; 757 Permission*

16 **green politics**, Green Party, Greens, environmentalism, ecology, preservationism, conservationism, greening, green labelling, Greenpeace, Friends of the Earth

VERBS

17 **green**, become green, make green

ADVERBS

18 **greenly**, verdantly, freshly, youthfully

539 Blueness

I never saw a man who looked
With such a wistful eye
Upon that little tent of blue
Which prisoners call the sky. Oscar Wilde.

ADJECTIVES

1 **blue**, light blue, sky blue, pale blue, ice blue, powder blue, Cambridge blue, Wedgwood blue, grey-blue, saxe blue, slate blue, smoke blue, steel blue, green-blue, robin's-egg blue (US), duck-egg blue, eggshell blue, aquamarine, turquoise, peacock blue, kingfisher blue, cobalt blue, cyan, cyanic, bright blue, cerulean, sapphire, air force blue, electric blue, ultramarine, deep blue, royal blue, dark blue, Oxford blue, midnight blue, navy blue, navy, French navy, perse, purplish-blue, azure, indigo, hyacinthine

▶ *538 Greenness; 540 Purpleness*

2 **bluish**, black-and-blue, livid, bruised, cyanotic, cyanosed, caesious, blue with cold, freezing, blue around the gills (Inf), blue in the face

3 **depressed**, dejected, downcast, despondent, blue, unhappy, sad, melancholy, gloomy, glum

4 **indecent**, smutty, risqué, bawdy, blue, coarse, obscene, near the knuckle

▶ *796 Immorality*

NOUNS

5 **blueness**, blue colour, blue pigment, blue dye, azure, cyan, indigo, woad, bice, Prussian blue, Saxon blue, French blue, ultramarine, cobalt blue, cerulean blue, Antwerp blue, phthalocyanine blue zaffre, smalt, methylene blue, gentian blue

6 **blue thing**, sky, sea, bluejeans, blueprint, blue pencil, blue ribbon, bluebook, blue peter, bluestone, sapphire, aquamarine, turquoise, lapis lazuli, beryl, bluebonnet, bluegrass, bluebell, cornflower, forget-me-not, iris, hyacinth, blueberry, blue cheese, Stilton, blue mould, bluebird, bluetit, blue jay, bluebill, bluefish, blue whale, bluegill, blue crab, bluepoint oyster (US), blue fox, blue racer, Blue Cross (US), Bluebeard, Blue Ridge Mountains, Blue Mountains, Blue Nile, blue cheer (Inf), blue velvet (Inf)

7 **figurative usage**, blues, blue devils, blue note, blue streak, blue murder, blueblood, bluestocking, blueprint, bluejacket, blue-chip, blue-collar worker, blue-eyed boy, bluegrass (US), blue moon, blue film, blue pencil, blue law (US), blue-sky law (US), blue-plate special (US), blue language, blue funk (Inf), blue balls (Inf), blue flu (US inf)

8 **bluishness**, cyanosis, blue baby, lividness, lividity, bruising

VERBS

9 **blue**, turn blue, dye blue, woad, azure

10 **blue-pencil**, edit

540 Purpleness

I think it pisses God off if you walk by the color purple in a field somewhere and don't notice it. Alice Walker.

NOUNS

1 **purpleness**, purplishness, blue and red, purple colour, imperial purple, bishop's purple, mourning colour, funeral colour

2 **purple pigment**, purple dye, Tyrian purple, gentian violet, Parma violet, cobalt violet, methyl violet, mauveine, amaranth, permanent magenta, Windsor violet, Thalo purple, Thio violet

3 **purple thing**, lavender, lilac, violet, pansy, heather, foxglove, hyancinth, heliotrope, clematis, rhododendron, purple-fringed orchid, plum, damson, aubergine, beetroot, purple gallinule, purple grackle, purple martin, purple emperor, amethyst, Purple Heart (US), purple heart (Inf), purple haze (Inf)

4 **figurative usage**, purple prose, purple patch, purple passage, born to the purple

5 **lividness**, lividity, bruising, bruise

ADJECTIVES

6 **purple**, purplish, purply, purpled, pale purple, lavender, lilac, mauve, purple-red, fuchsia, magenta, maroon, plum, plum-coloured, damson-coloured, puce, amaranthine, hyacinthine, heliotrope, violet, violaceous, amethystine, purpure, deep purple, dark purple, aubergine, mulberry, murrey (Lit); purple-blue, indigo

▶ *535 Redness; 539 Blueness*

7 **livid**, black-and-blue, bruised

8 **furious**, livid, purple with rage

VERBS

9 **empurple**, purple, bruise

541 Variegation

Glory be to God for dappled things –
For skies of couple-colour as a brindled cow;
For rose-moles all in stipple upon trout that swim. Gerard Manley Hopkins.

NOUNS

1 **variegation**, variety, difference, diversification, diversity,

diversity of colours, dichroism (*or* dichromatism), trichroism, trichromatism, polychromatism, polychromy, motley, medley of colour, riot of colour, spectrum, rainbow effect, play of colour, iridescence, opalescence, pearliness, chatoyancy, moiré

2 **check**, chequer, Prince of Wales chequer, hound's tooth check, plaid, tartan, mosaic, patch, patchiness, patchwork, inlay, damascene, marquetry, parquetry, tessellation, tessera

3 **striping**, striation, stripe, stria, band, bar, line, streak, streakiness, marbling, crack, craze, crackle, reticulation

4 **maculation**, mottling, mottle, mottlement, dappling, brindling, stippling, pointillism, freckling, spottiness, patchiness patch, speck, speckle, spot, sunspot, dot, polka dot, macula, foxing, brindle, fleck, freckle, pimple, blotch, splotch, birthmark, strawberry mark, splodge, splash

5 **variegated thing**, stained glass, kaleidoscope, spectrum, prism, rainbow, Joseph's coat, Harlequin, motley, patchwork quilt, tartan, collage, confetti, peacock, peacock's tail, zebra, tiger, leopard, jaguar, tortoiseshell cat, calico cat, tabby cat, Dalmatian, chameleon, tortoiseshell butterfly, dragonfly, mackerel sky, buttermilk sky, dancing light, glancing light, shot silk, watered silk, moiré, opal, mother-of-pearl, nacre, tiger's-eye, agate, jasper, cymophane, tortoiseshell, serpentine, spangle, sequin, marbled paper, parquet floor, enamelwork, chessboard, draughtboard, tricolour, bar code, crazy paving, cracked glass

ADJECTIVES

6 **variegated**, bicolour (*or* bicoloured), dichroic (*or* dichromatic), trichoic, trichomatic, polychrome, polychromatic, multicoloured, parti-coloured, pied, varicoloured, versicolour, many-coloured, many-hued, rainbow-coloured, motley, kaleidoscopic, spectral, prismatic, colourful, florid, ornamental, patterned, embroidered, worked, chameleonic, changeable

7 **iridescent**, opalescent, opaline, nacreous, pearly, semitransparent, shot, shot through with, pavonine, moiré, watered, chatoyant

8 **checked**, chequered, plaid, tartan, tortoiseshell, inlaid, tessellated, patched, patchy, pied, black-and-white, piebald, pinto, skewbald, fasciate, stripy

9 **striped**, stripy, striate (*or* striated), banded, barred, lined, streaked, marbled, marbly, veined, jaspé, reticulate, panelled, paned

10 **mottled**, dappled, brindled, tabby, grizzled, pepper-and-salt, roan, spotted, maculate, macular, dotted, studded, peppered, sprinkled, powdered, dusted, dusty, cloudy, hazy, blemished, fly-spotted, speckled, speckledy, freckled, spotty, pimply, pocked, pockmarked

VERBS

11 **variegate**, diversify, pattern, chequer, check, patch, spangle, damascene, inlay, enamel, tessellate, mottle, dapple, brindle, stipple, grizzle, spot, maculate, dot (with), stud, pepper, sprinkle, powder, dust, speckle, freckle, stripe, striate, band, bar, streak, marble, vein, craze, crack, cloud, stain, blot, discolour, fox

ADVERBS

12 **variedly**, diversely, polychromatically, kaleidoscopically, floridly, ornamentally, iridescently, nacreously, patchily, fasciately, reticulately

542 Decoration

To gild refined gold, to paint the lily,
To throw a perfume on the violet,
To smooth the ice, or add another hue
Unto the rainbow, or with taper-light
To seek the beauteous eye of heaven to garnish,
Is wasteful and ridiculous excess. William Shakespeare.

NOUNS

1 **ornament**, ornamentation, adornment, decoration, garnish, trimming, embellishment, colour, flourish, embroidery, frills, *épergne* (Fr), arrangement, flower arrangement, floral arrangement, table setting, interior decoration, colour decoration, colour design, floridness, floweriness, flowers of speech, arabesques, purple passages, preciosity, preciousness, euphuism, euphemism, rhetoric, figurativeness, figure of speech, metaphor, simile, trope, alliteration, assonance, hyperbaton, antithesis

▶ *17 Literature; 18 Music; 547 Beautification*

2 **affectation**, pomposity, pretension, pretentiousness, ostentation, showiness, false show, false front, putting on airs, magniloquence, grandiloquence, loftiness, high tone, high-sounding words, eloquence, rhetoric, orotundity, vigour, extravagance, overstatement, exaggeration, hyperbole, turgidity, turgescence, flatulence, talking big, boasting, bombast, rant, fustian, rodomontade, empty talk, Johnsonese, long words, diffuseness, circumlocution, convolution, tortuousness

▶ *270 Vagueness; 507 Loudness; 676 Affectation; 726 Emphasis; 727 Exaggeration*

GEMSTONES

adularia	chrysoprase	opal
agate	citrine	Oriental almandine
alexandrite	corundum	Oriental emerald
almandine	diamond	Oriental topaz
amazonite	diopside	plasma (or plasm)
amber	emerald	rhodolite
amethyst	fire opal	rubellite
andalusite	garnet	ruby
andradite	grossularite	ruby spinel
aquamarine	hawk's–eye	sapphire
aventurine *or* aventurin	heliodor	sard
balas (or balas ruby)	hiddenite	sardonyx
bloodstone	hyacinth	Spanish topaz
bone turquoise	jasper	spessartite
cairngorm	kunzite	sphene
carbuncle	lapis lazuli	spodumene
carnelian	Madagascar aquamarine	staurolite
cat's–eye	morganite	topaz
chalcedony	morion	turquoise
chatoyant	moss agate	vesuvianite
chrysoberyl	New Zealand greenstone	water sapphire
chrysolite	onyx	white sapphire
		zircon

3 **pattern**, design, fancywork, detail, flourish, illustration, etching, tattooing, pokerwork, pyrography, filigree, gilding, gilt, gold leaf, scrollwork, illumination, lettering, moulding, beading, breadwork, fluting, ormolu, mosaic, needlework, embroidery, tapestry, cross-stitch, patchwork, appliqué, crochet, lacework, lace, broderie anglaise, smocking, crewel work
4 **honour**, decoration, medal, honours, title, spurs, badge, pips, stripes, star, gold star, garter, order, blue, gong (Inf)
5 **decorating**, painting and decorating, housepainting, wallpapering, interior decorating, interior design
6 **decorative articles**, trinkets, knick-knacks (Inf), gewgaws (Inf), spangles, sparklers, gandery, frippery, flounce, ruffle, frill, furbelow, fringe, ribbon, braid, feathers
7 **jewellery**, costume jewellery, baubles, necklace, bracelet, bangle, ear ring, ring, tiara, torque, badge, pin, brooch, tiepin, hatpin, anklet, medallion, nose-ring, stud, ear-cuff, chain
8 **decorator**, painter, illustrator, illuminator, embroiderer, crewelist, jeweller, gilder, scroll worker, pyrographer, lace maker, smocker
9 **phrasemonger**, stylist, euphuist, flowery writer, flowery speaker, speaker, orator, rhetorician, politician, wordspinner (Inf)
▶ *543 Elegance; 724 Style; 729 Speech*

ADJECTIVES

10 **ornate**, elaborate, fancy, ornamented, ornamental, decorated, richly decorated, decorative, adorned, garnished, trimmed, embellished, beautified, gilded, coloured, rich, luxuriant, florid, flowery, precious, euphuistic, euphemistic, extravagant, overstated, exaggerated, hyperbolic, affected, pompous, pretentious, ostentatious, flashy, flamboyant, showy, meretricious, frothy, fussy, overloaded, stiff, stilted, pedantic, ponderous, long-worded, Latinate, sesquipedalian, Johnsonian, diffuse, circumlocutory, convoluted, tortuous, rhetorical, declamatory, oratorical, eloquent, grandiloquent, magniloquent, lofty, high-flown, high-flying, loud, brassy, resonant, sonorous, ringing, singing, ranting, orotund, high-pitched, high-sounding, grandiose, stately, bombastic, fustian, inflated, tumid, turgid, swollen, antithetical, alliterative, metaphorical, figurative, highfalutin (Inf)
▶ *270 Vagueness; 507 Loudness; 547 Beautification; 676 Affectation; 726 Emphasis; 727 Exaggeration*
11 **decorated**, knighted, honoured

VERBS

12 **ornament**, adorn, decorate, garnish, trim, deck, festoon, embellish, beautify, enhance, grace, embroider, enrich, gild, overlay, load with ornament, overload, gild the lily, euphuize, euphemize, elaborate, overelaborate, overstate, use long words, ring, sing, boast, rant, rave
▶ *507 Loudness; 547 Beautification; 676 Affectation*

ADVERBS

13 **ornately**, elaborately, floridly, preciously, extravagantly, hyperbolically, pompously, pretentiously, ostentatiously, flamboyantly, pedantically, ponderously, grandiloquently, magniloquently, bombastically, turgidly, metaphorically, figuratively

543 Elegance

Somehow importing to the peeling of a banana the elegant nonchalance of a duke drawing a monogrammed cigarette from a platinum case. Alexander Woollcott.

NOUNS

1 **elegance**, elegancy, style, stylishness, perfect style, grace, gracefulness, delicacy, harmony, euphony, taste, tastefulness, good taste, propriety, beauty, politeness, gentility, refinement, sophistication, suavity, suaveness, culture, purity, perspicuity, clarity, plainness, simplicity, restraint, dignity, distinction, grandeur, naturalness, classicism, Atticism, proportion, symmetry, balance, rhythm, ease, readability, flow, fluidity, smoothness, fluency, aptness, fittingness, felicity, the right word in the right place, *mot juste* (Fr), polish, finish, neatness, well-turned phrase, elaboration, ornament, flourish, florid style, artificiality
▶ *162 Symmetry; 230 Perfection; 271 Simplicity; 485 Skill; 542 Decoration; 545 Beauty; 549 Refinement; 551 Dress; 553 Fashion; 724 Style; 725 Clarity*
2 **stylist**, stylish writer, euphuist, classical author, classic, classicist, purist
▶ *17 Literature; 542 Decoration; 724 Style*

ADJECTIVES

3 **elegant**, stylish, smart, graceful, delicate, harmonious, euphonious, tasteful, fine, beautiful, majestic, stately, exquisite, polite, courtly, refined, sophisticated, suave, cultivated, pure, perspicacious, clear, lucid, cogent, plain, simple, restrained, dignified, distinguished, distinctive, natural, idiomatic, good, correct, expressive, sensitive, readable, classic, well-proportioned, proportional, symmetrical, balanced, gracile, rhythmic, tripping, easy, fluid, smooth, flawless, mellifluous, fluent, eloquent, apt, fitting, felicitous, polished, manicured, soigné, well-groomed, finished, unlaboured, well-turned, round, neat, neatly put, neatly wrought, artistic, artistically done, elaborate, ornamented, artificial, classical, Attic, Augustan, Ciceronian
▶ *17 Literature; 162 Symmetry; 230 Perfection; 271 Simplicity; 485 Skill; 542 Decoration; 545 Beauty; 549 Refinement; 551 Dress; 553 Fashion; 724 Style; 725 Clarity*

VERBS

4 **be elegant**, have a good style, show style, be stylish, write well, show taste, have taste, have a light touch, turn a phrase, perfect, polish, refine, edit, rewrite, elaborate, ornament, do artistically
▶ *17 Literature; 230 Perfection; 542 Decoration; 545 Beauty; 549 Refinement; 553 Fashion; 724 Style*

ADVERBS

5 **elegantly**, stylishly, smartly, gracefully, delicately, harmoniously, euphoniously, tastefully, beautifully, suavely, perspicaciously, clearly, plainly, simply, naturally, expressively, readably, symmetrically, rhythmically, easily, smoothly, mellifluously, fluently, aptly, felicitously, neatly, artistically, elaborately, artificially

544 Inelegance

What dreadful hot weather we have! It keeps me in a continual state of inelegance. Jane Austen.

NOUNS

1 **inelegance**, inelegancy, gracelessness, clumsiness, awkwardness, gaucheness, lack of finesse, gaucherie, gawkiness, gawkishness, lack of style, lack of polish, cack-handedness (Inf), klutziness (US inf)

► *231 Imperfection; 486 Unskilfulness*

2 **impropriety**, indelicacy, crudeness, vulgarity, tastelessness, bad taste, rudeness, discourtesy, grossness, coarseness, roughness, boorishness, churlishness, uncouthness, unrefinement

► *659 Discourtesy; 660 Insolence; 675 Vulgarity*

3 **ugliness**, plainness, drabness, shabbiness, bad taste, garishness, gaudiness, loudness, tawdriness, vulgarity, commonness, tackiness (Inf)

► *497 Blandness; 546 Ugliness; 675 Vulgarity*

4 **inelegance of speech**, incorrectness, bad grammar, solecism, vulgarism, vulgarity, dysphemism, clumsy construction, clumsiness, long-windedness, sesquipedalianism, stiffness, stiltedness, cumbrousness, ponderousness, turgidity, bombast, pomposity, grandiloquence, cacology, bad language, cursing, effing and blinding (Inf)

► *5 Language and Linguistics; 479 Equivocation; 702 Sophistry*

5 **mispronunciation**, poor diction, speech defect, speech impediment

6 **blunder**, faux pas, gaffe, gaucherie, bloomer (Inf), clanger (Inf), howler (Inf), cock up (Inf), dog's breakfast (Inf), pig's ear (Inf), balls-up (Inf)

► *274 Error*

ADJECTIVES

7 **graceless**, ungraceful, inelegant, clumsy, awkward, cumbersome, ill-proportioned, ungainly, dumpy, clownish, gauche, gawky, gawkish, undignified, ham-fisted, heavy-handed, heavy-footed, all fingers and thumbs (Inf), cack-handed (Inf), klutzy (US inf)

► *231 Imperfection; 486 Unskilfulness*

8 **indecorous**, unseemly, improper, indelicate, crude, vulgar, tasteless, in bad taste, beyond the pale, rude, discourteous, impolite, gross, coarse, boorish, churlish, uncouth, barbaric, barbarous, unrefined, unpolished, *infra dignitatem* (L), infra dig

► *659 Discourtesy; 675 Vulgarity*

9 **inelegant**, dysphemistic, cacological, turgid, pompous, rhetorical, grandiloquent, formal, stiff, stilted, wooden, unfluent, ill-sounding, cacophonous, uneuphonious, jarring, grating, incorrect, solecistic, doggerel, artless, unnatural, artificial, mannered, affected, laboured, tortuous, ludicrous, grotesque

► *656 Formality; 676 Affectation*

10 **ugly**, unattractive, unaesthetic, plain, drab, dingy, dreary, dull, shabby, seedy, squalid, rough, mousy, lank, dowdy, badly dressed, unfashionable, in bad taste, tasteless, common, vulgar, garish, gaudy, loud, tawdry, meretricious, overdressed, tacky (Inf), tarty (Inf), dressed up like a dog's dinner (Inf), common as muck (Inf)

► *546 Ugliness; 675 Vulgarity*

ADVERBS

11 **inelegantly**, gracelessly, clumsily, awkwardly, indecorously, indelicately, grossly, coarsely, shabbily, unfashionably, tastelessly

545 Beauty

There is no excellent beauty that hath not some strangeness in the proportion. Francis Bacon.

She walks in beauty, like the night
Of cloudless climes and starry skies;
And all that's best of dark and bright
Meet in her aspect and her eyes. Lord Byron.

Beauty is altogether in the eye of the beholder. Margaret Wolfe Hungerford.

A thing of beauty is a joy for ever:
Its loveliness increases; it will never
Pass into nothingness; but still will keep
A bower quiet for us, and a sleep
Full of sweet dreams, and health, and quiet breathing. John Keats.

'Beauty is truth, truth beauty,' – that is all Ye know on earth, and all ye need to know. John Keats.

NOUNS

1 **gorgeousness**, brightness, brilliance, beauteousness, pulchritude, radiance, magnificence, fairness, loveliness, comeliness, prettiness, attractiveness, beauty, pulchritude, agreeableness, good looks, handsomenesss, shapeliness, grace, gracefulness, refinement, elegance, chic, splendour, exquisiteness, nobility, appeal, charm, glamour, delicacy, harmony, symmetry

2 **beautiful thing**, ornament, adornment, decoration, masterpiece, thing of beauty, *chef-d'oeuvre* (Fr), cynosure (*or* cynosura)

3 **attractive female**, beauty, masterpiece, belle, belle of the ball, raving beauty, dream, vision, pearl, pretty, jewel, treasure, dazzler, bobby dazzler, looker (Inf), beauty queen, smasher (Inf), lulu (Inf), pin-up girl, *femme fatale* (Fr), lovely

4 **attractive male**, dreamboat (Inf), hunk (Inf), dish (Inf), dream man, beau, charmer, looker, Adonis

ADJECTIVES

5 **beautiful**, beauteous, of beauty, lovely, lush (Inf), gorgeous, handsome, pretty, fine, good-looking, attractive, fair, bright, comely, shapely, bonny, cute, sweet, winsome, exquisite, glamorous, pulchritudinous, well-made, well-proportioned, gracile, well-built, manly, statuesque, Junoesque, aesthetically pleasing, aesthetic, tasteful, picturesque, scenic, ornamental

6 **personable**, appealing, enchanting, agreeable, charming, becoming presentable, tidy (Inf), trim, attractive, peachy, blooming, rosy, elegant, tasteful

VERBS

7 **be beautiful**, shine, dazzle, glow, sparkle

8 **beautify**, adorn, prettify, decorate, bejewel, transform, transfigure, primp (Inf), glamorize, tart up (Inf), titivate

546 Ugliness

And you, madam, are ugly. But I shall be sober in the morning. Winston Churchill, to a woman who accused him of being drunk.

NOUNS

1 **ugliness**, hideousness, unsightliness, repulsiveness, gracelessness, inelegance, homeliness, plainness, hideosity, deformity, contortedness, mutilation, defacement, disfigurement

2 **ugly person**, no beauty, no oil painting (Inf), no Adonis (Inf), back end of a bus (Inf), something the cat brought in (Inf), something the cat sicked up (Inf), dog's breakfast (Inf), fright (Inf), scarecrow, monster, gargoyle, monster, horror, old witch, not one's type, paper-bag job (Inf), dog (Inf), howler (Inf), pizza face (Inf)

3 **ugly place**, eyesore, blot on the landscape, carbuncle, blemish, slum

ADJECTIVES

4 **ugly**, plug ugly (Inf), hideous, repulsive, graceless, plain, homely, unsightly, unseemly, unshapely, not fit to be seen, deformed, contorted, mutilated, defaced, disfigured, unlovely, gross (Inf), unprepossessing, ill-favoured, monstrous, misshapen, misbegotten, gruesome, wan, grisly, graceless, inelegant, unaesthetic, unbecoming, unattractive, indelicate, uncouth, ungainly, distasteful, grotty (Inf), coarse, awkward

VERBS

5 **make ugly**, disfigure, deface, distort, deform, mutilate, blemish, mask, misshape, impair, spoil, scar

ADVERBS

6 **hideously**, grossly, repulsively, disgustingly, gracelessly, inelegantly

547 Beautification

Ladies and gentlemen, I stand before you tonight in my green chiffon evening gown, my face softly made up, my fair hair gently waved…the Iron Lady of the Western World. Me? A cold war warrior? Well, yes – if that is how they wish to interpret my defence of values, and freedoms fundamental to our way of life. Margaret Thatcher.

NOUNS

1 **transfiguration**, transformation, improvement, refurbishment, restoration, rebuilding

2 **plastic surgery**, cosmetic surgery, face-lift, liposuction, breast reduction, breast enlargement, nose job (Inf), boob job (Inf), nip and tuck (Inf)

3 **beauty treatment**, facial, face pack, toilet, toilette, manicure, pedicure, wash and brush up (Inf)

4 **cosmetics**, make-up, war paint (Inf), paint, greasepaint, slap (Inf), rouge, powder, eye make-up, blusher, lipstick, kohl, mascara, eye-liner, eye-shadow, nail polish, nail varnish

5 **make-up box**, paintbox, toilet bag, wash bag, manicure set

6 **toiletries** , perfume, scent, toilet water, eau de toilette, eau de cologne, perfume oil, essential oil, smellies (Inf)

7 **hairdressing**, trichology, hair cutting, hair styling, hair colour, hair dyeing, barbering

8 **haircut**, coiffure, trim, style, hairstyle, crop, cut and blow dry, hair-do, permanent wave, perm (Inf), hair straightening, curl removal, beehive, Eton crop, bob, ponytail, plait, braids, fringe, chignon, dreadlocks, dreads (Inf), frizz, Afro, wet-look, curls, quiff, mullet, short-back-and-sides, mohican, skinhead, suedehead

9 **hair removal**, depilation, shaving, shave, waxing, sugaring, electrolysis, eyebrow plucking

10 **wig**, false hair, toupé, hair extension, rug (Inf)

11 **hairdressing salon**, hairdressers, barber shop, crimpers (Inf)

12 **beauty parlour**, beauty shop, beauty salon

13 **beautician**, beauty specialist, make-up artist, cosmetician, hairdresser, barber, trichologist, hair-stylist, crimper (Inf), coiffeur, coiffeuse, manicurist, pedicurist, plastic surgeon

ADJECTIVES

14 **beautified**, decorated, adorned, embellished, embroidered, trimmed, tricked out, decked out, improved, touched up, tarted up (Inf)

VERBS

15 **beautify**, prettily, glamorize, smarten up, spruce up, primp, prink, titivate

16 **make up**, doll up (Inf), paint, tart up (Inf), apply the war paint (Inf), stick on some slap (Inf), put a face on (Inf), perfume

17 **crimp**, coif, clop, curl

548 Blemish

Through tatter'd clothes small vices do appear;
Robes and furr'd gowns hide all. William Shakespeare.

NOUNS

1 **spot**, mark, scar, pockmark, welt, weal, flaw, defect, blot, imperfection, crud (Inf), disfigurement, distortion, defect, stigma, smudge, smear, stain, blotch, tarnish, speck

2 **pimple**, spot, pustule, boil, swelling, carbuncle, bubo, blackhead, whitehead, acne, zit (Inf)

3 **blot on the landscape**, eyesore, smur, carbuncle

ADJECTIVES

4 **blemished**, flawed, masked, defective, deformed, defaced, disfigured, imperfect, spoiled, spoilt, soiled, shop-soiled, damaged, polluted, cracked

5 **marked**, scarred, spotted, pitted, pockmarked, scabrous, scabrid

6 **seedy**, shabby, tatty, tacky, down-at-heel, moth-eaten, dog-eared

VERBS

7 **blemish**, flaw, crack, disfigure, deface, distort, deform, spot, smudge, smear, stain, soil, impair, spoil, mutilate, pustulate, misshape, impair, mar

549 Refinement

This Englishwoman is so refined
She has no bosom and no behind. Stevie Smith.

NOUNS

1 **elegance**, style, grace, taste, good taste, tastefulness, distinction, dignity, quality, polish, finish, culture, civility, good breeding, good manners, correctness, delicacy, beauty, courtesy, decency, seemliness, decorum, urbanity, propriety, sophistication, gracious living, connoisseurship

2 **subletly**, distinction, delicacy

3 **etiquette**, custom, protocol, politeness, snobbery, the done thing (Inf), keeping up appearances (Inf)

4 **refined person**, connoisseur, aesthete, dilettante, man of taste, woman of taste, gentleman, gentlewoman

ADJECTIVES

5 **refined**, elegant, graceful, tasteful, dignified, polished, delicate, U(Inf), well-finished, well-bred, urbane, well-mannered, well-spoken, courteous, distingué, ladylike, gentlemanly, genteel, civilized, cosmopolitan, sophisticated, discriminating, fastidious, sensitive, artistic, aesthetic, appreciative, critical, refined

VERBS

6 **refine**, purify, distil

550 Covering

You can say what you like about long dresses, but they cover a multitude of shins. Mae West.

NOUNS

1 **covering**, covering up, covering over, coverage, cover, overarching, spanning, overlaying, laying on, stratification, superimposition, overlapping, imbrication, coating, topping, paving, blanketing, cloaking, enclosement, walling in, walling up, envelopment, enfoldment, enwrapment, wrapping, casing, screening, shielding, overshadowing, eclipsing, blotting out, flooding over, obscuring, hiding

▶ *736 Concealment*

2 **cover**, top, lid, cap, cork, plug, stopper, bung, crust, piecrust, flap, shutter, gravestone, shroud, pall, topsoil, mulch, cloud, smokescreen

3 **coating**, coat, layer, film, plastering, topping, icing, frosting, glaze, varnish, veneer, enamel, lacquer, japan, stain, creosote, paint, wax, furniture polish, plate, silver plate, electroplate, copperplate, gold plate

4 **wrapping**, wrapping paper, giftwrapping, wrapper, tissue paper, packaging, box, envelope, involucre, shroud, sheath, sheathing, book cover, dust jacket, binding, binder, foil, Cellophane™, polythene, wax paper, aluminium foil, plastic wrap, clingfilm

5 **body covering**, clothing, armour, hat, hard hat, coat, jacket, cloak, robe, vestment, sweater, cowl, hood, veil, scarf, comforter, shroud, sunbonnet, afghan, lap robe, rug

▶ *551 Dress*

6 **medical covering**, dressing, bandage, bandaging, elastic bandage, adhesive tape, plaster, Elastoplast™, cast, plaster cast, surgical dressing, surgical mask

▶ *35 Medicine; 394 Remedy*

7 **overhead covering**, roof, pitched roof, gable roof, flat roof, rooftop, housetop, dome, cupola, roofing, slates, tiles, shingles, thatch, ceiling plaster, ceiling, overhead, overhead beam, rafters, canopy, awning, marquee, tent, big top, tepee (*or* teepee *or* tipi), wigwam, ciborium, canvas, tarpaulin, tarp (US inf), mosquito netting

8 **wall covering**, facing, revetment, rendering, cladding, bricks, adobe, mortar, grout, pebble-dash, panelling, plywood, wallboard, planking, boarding, weatherboard, clapboard, wall tiles, ceramic tiles, paint, whitewash, plaster work, plaster, size (*or* sizing), stucco, Artex™, parget (*or* pargeting), wallpaper, curtain, drape, drapery, hanging, tapestry, soft furnishings, mould, encrustation (*or* incrustation)

9 **floor covering**, rug, hooked rug, throw rug (US), area rug, hearth rug, braided rug, drugget, carpet, wall-to-wall carpet, fitted carpet, carpeting, broadloom carpet, pile carpet, Persian carpet (*or* rug), Turkish carpet (*or* rug), stair carpet, runner, mat, doormat, bathmat, matting, dropcloth (US), groundsheet (*or* ground cloth), tiles, tiling, linoleum, lino, vinyl, floorboards, duckboards, parquet, parquet floor, wax

10 **bed covering**, bed cover, mattress cover, dust ruffle (US), bedding, bedclothes, bed linen, blanket, duvet, continental quilt, quilt, patchwork quilt, eiderdown, comforter (US), bedspread, spread, counterpane, coverlet, cover, bedsheet, fitted sheet, sheet, pillowcase (*or* pillowslip), pillow sham (US), bed canopy, valance

11 **paving**, surfacing, road surface, pavement, sidewalk (US), crazy paving, concrete, cement, Portland cement, tar, blacktop (US), Tarmac™, asphalt, macadam, gravel, chippings, cobble, cobblestone, flagstone, stepping stone

12 **protective covering**, shield, sunshade, parasol, sun hat, pith helmet, topee, visor, eyeshade, sunglasses, shades (Inf), suntan lotion, sunscreen, life jacket, life belt, umbrella, brolly (Inf), bumbershoot (US inf), insulation, lagging, fibreglass, awning, blind, Venetian blind, shade, lampshade, placemat, tablecloth, doily, Formica™, upholstery, furniture cover, chair cover, slipcover, antimacassar, cushion cover, bulletproof glass, unbreakable glass, watch glass, screen, fire curtain, car bonnet, car silencer, housing, armour, mail

13 **casing**, case, watchcase, ammunition case, crate, box, capsule, shell, nutshell, artillery shell, pastry shell, eggshell, pod, hull, husk, chaff, cornhusk (US), shuck, skin, jacket, peel, rind, bark, seed coat, testa, integument, tegumen

14 **animal covering**, cortex, skin, outer skin, epidermis, scar, eschar, scab, scalp, cuticle, eyelid, hair, fell, hide, rawhide, horsehide, pigskin, leather, kid, calf, suede, chamois, morocco, buckskin, doeskin, fur, mink, sable, ermine, chinchilla, fleece, pelt, beaver pelt, feathers, plumage, shell, oyster shell, clamshell, snail shell, turtle shell, conch, scallop, scale, scute, carapace, lorica, operculum, cocoon, chrysalis, horse blanket, saddlecloth

15 **shelter**, protection, secrecy, concealment, hiding place, hideout, hideaway, safe house, retreat, refuge, den, lair,

secret drawer, secret passageway, hidden panel, cache, cover, screen, covert, hide

16 **disguise**, mask, domino, veil, camouflage, protective colouring, false beard, masquerade

17 **coverer**, tailor, furrier, painter, whitewasher, plasterer, roofer, thatcher, draper, wallpaperer, bricklayer, carpetlayer, upholsterer, bookbinder, electroplater, giftwrapper, packager, tiler, paver, tanner, quilter, disguiser, camouflager, masker, masquerader, incorporator

18 **fixer**, handler, publicist, journalist, public relations man (*or* woman), spin doctor

19 **inclusion**, embodiment, incorporation, comprehension, comprehensive insurance policy, blanket coverage

20 **fixing**, handling, news coverage, news item, publicity

21 **substitution**, substitute, replacement, alternative, alternate, surrogate, surrogate mother, stepmother, stepfather, foster parent, proxy, fill-in, stand-in, backup, relief, locum, reserve, understudy, double, stunt man (*or* woman), ghostwriter

► *413 Support*

22 **progression**, making progress, traversal, traversing, continuation, continuing, continuing on, passing through, travelling through, traveller, tourist, traverser, wanderer, student, reader

VERBS

23 **cover**, lay on, superimpose, lay over, put a lid on, top, crown, cap, cork, plug, bung, stopper, stop

24 **coat**, spread, spread on, spread over, overlay, carpet, blanket, tile, parquet, upholster, layer, daub, plaster, top, ice, frost, glaze, varnish, veneer, enamel, lacquer, japan, stain, tan, creosote, paint, whitewash, wax, polish, plate, silver, gild, electroplate, copperplate

25 **wrap**, enwrap, wrap up, wrap round, surround, envelop, enfold, shroud, enshroud, giftwrap, package, box, pack, enclose, case, encase, crate, sheathe, bandage, bind, swathe, dress

26 **overlie**, lie over, overlap, lap, imbricate, jut, shingle, span, bridge, overarch, overhang, overshadow

27 **roof**, roof in (*or* over), dome, tile, thatch, plaster, ceil, canopy

28 **face**, front, revet, render, clad, brick, lay bricks, mortar, grout, pebble-dash, panel, plank, board, paint, whitewash, plaster, size, stucco, parget, wallpaper, paper, curtain, drape, mould, encrust (*or* incrust)

29 **surface**, pave, concrete, cement, tar, blacktop (US), Tarmac™, macadamize, gravel, cobble

30 **protect**, shield, screen, shade, insulate, lag, house, guard, defend, armour, watch over, hide out, retreat

31 **hide**, conceal, keep under cover, cover up, mask, veil, cloak, cowl, shroud, hood, disguise, camouflage, masquerade, cloud, obscure, blot out, eclipse, blot, flood, inundate

32 **include**, embody, incorporate, contain, comprise, encompass

33 **fix**, handle, take care of, pay attention to, give news coverage to, report, publicize

34 **cover for**, substitute for, replace, alternate, surrogate, foster, fill in, stand in, back up, relieve, understudy, double for, ghostwrite

35 **progress**, traverse, continue, continue on, pass through, travel through, study, read

ADJECTIVES

36 **covered**, covered up, topped, capped, corked, glazed, varnished, stained, painted, whitewashed, copperplated, roofed, tiled, thatched, tented, faced, bricked, panelled, papered, wallpapered, covered over, roofed in (*or* over)

37 **protected**, shielded, enclosed, wrapped, packaged, boxed, crated, encased, bound, sheathed, swathed, bandaged, hidden, concealed, screened, masked, veiled, shrouded, enshrouded, cloaked, robed, hooded, camouflaged, disguised, secret, obscured, walled-in, walled up

38 **covering**, overlaying, overlying, spanning, superimposed, epidermal, cuticular, integumental

39 **inclusive**, embodied, incorporated (*or* incorporate), comprehensive, encompassing

40 **substitutive**, substitutable, substitute, alternative, surrogate, foster, stand-in, backup, relief, locum, reserve

41 **progressing**, continuous, passing, travelling, studious, well-read

ADVERBS

42 **inclusively**, comprehensively, universally, all around, on all sides, from all directions, over, above, around, under, below, above and below

43 **alternatively**, as substitute, on behalf of, in behalf of, per pro (p.p.)

551 Dress

NOUNS

1 **dress**, clothing, clothes, suit of clothes, wear, apparel, accoutrement, article of clothing, garment, garb, frock, creation, linen, habiliments, attire, kit, rig, outfit, wardrobe, tailor-made clothes, bespoke clothes, ready-to-wear clothes, off-the-peg clothes, wash-and-wear clothes, store-bought clothes (Dial), unisex clothes, men's clothing, menswear, women's clothing, womenswear, trousseau, wedding clothes, bridal outfit, maternity wear, work (*or* working) clothes, formal clothes, best clothes, Sunday best, Sunday go-to-meeting clothes (US), best bib and tucker, finery, regalia, caparison, panoply, array, frippery, ostrich feathers, informal clothes, sportswear, old clothes, worn clothes, castoffs, second-hand clothes, tatters, slops, seconds, (fine) raiment (Lit), vesture (Lit), number (Inf), rag (Inf), rags (Inf), glad rags (Inf), togs (Inf), toggery (Inf), get-up (Inf), rigout (Inf), (full) fig (Inf), duds (Inf), front (US inf), gear (Inf), hand-me-down (Inf), reach-me-down (Inf), threads (Inf), clobber, dry goods (US inf)

► *550 Covering*

2 **dressing**, covering, vestiture, investiture, investment, toilet, toilette (Lit), wardrobe, turnout, dressing up, overdressing, foppishness, underdressing, casualness, fashion, the latest fashion, the latest style, the fashion world, fashion designing, Paris fashion, high fashion, couture, *haute couture* (Fr), Savile Row, Carnaby Street, Garment District (US), Fifth Avenue (US), Rodeo Drive (US), the clothing business, tailoring, dressmaking, garmentmaking, habilimentation, millinery, hosiery, hatmaking, hatting, shoemaking, bootmaking, cobbling, the rag trade (Inf)

► *295 Newness; 543 Elegance; 553 Fashion; 776 Trade*

3 formal dress, formal (US), correct dress, court dress, full dress, dress suit, morning dress, tail coat (*or* swallow-tailed coat), tails (Inf), white tie and tails (Inf), soup and fish (Inf), morning coat, dinner dress, party dress, evening dress, evening gown, dinner jacket, tuxedo (US), tux (US), black tie, bow tie, dicky bow, cummerbund, academic dress, academicals, cap and gown, academic robe, vestment, vesture, subfusc, the tartan, kilt, pearlies, uniform, military uniform, dress uniform, full-dress uniform, blues, dress blues, whites, dress whites, mess kit, uniform slops, battledress, khaki uniform, khakis (US), regimentals, fatigues, school uniform, clerical dress, clerical garb, canonicals, nun's habit, nurse's uniform, policeman's (*or* policewoman's) uniform, servant's uniform, livery, riding habit, national dress, national costume, folk costume, mourning clothes, black, (widow's) weeds

► *7 Religion; 656 Formality; 743 Identification*

4 informal dress, casual clothes, plain clothes, leisure wear, sportswear, tracksuit, shell suit, dishabille, slacks, lounge suit, slack suit (US), blazer, sports jacket, denims, sweat shirt, T-shirt, blouson, smoking jacket, housecoat, lounging pyjamas, bed jacket, wrapper, dressing gown, bathrobe, slippers, mufti, civvies (Inf)

► *45 Sport; 552 Undress; 580 Leisure*

5 fancy dress, costume, guise, masquerade, bedizenment (Lit), motley, silks, colours, character dress, outfit, rig, gear, disguise, camouflage, theatrical costume, ballet costume, dance costume, Hollywood costume, Broadway costume, symbolic costume, animal costume, antique costume, novelty costume, medieval costume, classical costume, baroque costume, neoclassic costume, Wagnerian costume, Kabuki costume, buskin, cothurnus, sock and buskin, cap and bells, mask, wooden mask, papier mâché mask, rubber mask, tunic, plume, gown, armour, make-up, greasepaint, powder, lipstick, wig, beard

► *21 Drama; 22 Dancing; 736 Concealment*

6 skirt, maxiskirt (*or* maxi), midiskirt (*or* midi), miniskirt (*or* mini), microskirt (*or* micro), pleated skirt, full skirt, flared skirt, A-line skirt, gored skirt, dirndl, kilt, filibeg (*or* fillibeg), straight skirt, slit skirt, divided skirt, culottes, sarong, tight skirt, hobble skirt, sports skirt, riding habit, tennis skirt, ballet skirt, tutu, overskirt, hoop skirt, crinoline, grass skirt, kirtle (Lit)

► *22 Dancing*

7 frock, dress, cocktail dress, dinner dress, gown, ball gown, dinner gown, tea gown, evening gown, overdress, shirtdress, mantua, cheongsam, muu-muu, Mother Hubbard, maxidress (*or* maxi), minidress (*or* mini), pinafore dress, jumper (US), tube dress, sheath dress, sack, shirtwaister, shirtwaist (US), gymslip, sundress, backless dress, strapless dress, topless dress, maternity dress, wedding dress, little black dress, little black number (Inf)

8 shirt, long-sleeved shirt, dress shirt, evening shirt, office shirt, body shirt (*or* bodysuit) (US), olive-drab shirt (*or* OD shirt) (US), short-sleeved shirt, sports shirt, pullover shirt, blouse, middy blouse (*or* middy), overblouse, top, tank top, halter, bustier, smock, dashiki, polo shirt, T-shirt, sweat shirt, sark (Scot), dicky, hair shirt, doublet (Lit)

9 trousers, pants (US), trews (Scot), long trousers, long pants (US), cords, flannels, pinstripes, hipsters, hip-huggers (US), Capri pants (*or* Capris), toreador pants, bell-bottoms, slacks, Oxford bags, pegged trousers, pegged pants (US), knickerbockers, knickers (US), plus fours, galligaskins, breeches, breeks (Scot), knee breeches, riding breeches, riding pants (US), buckskins (US), overalls, jodhpurs, pedal pushers, dungarees, denims, jeans, blue-jeans, Levi's™, lederhosen, bloomers, pantaloons, palazzo pants, gym pants (US), ski pants, shorts, short pants (US), Bermuda shorts, hot pants, short shorts, cycling shorts, britches (Inf), drainpipes (Inf), flares (Inf), bags (Inf), striders (*or* strides) (US inf), pistols (US inf), joggers (Inf)

10 suit, outfit, costume, ensemble, coordinates, separates, dress suit, one-piece suit, two-piece suit, three-piece suit, business suit, lounge suit, pinstripe suit, tweed suit, tweeds, trouser suit, pantsuit (US), catsuit, slack suit (US), leisure suit (US), zoot suit, jump suit, leotard, coveralls, boiler suit, tracksuit, shell suit, jog suit, jogging suit (US), wet suit, G-suit, spacesuit

11 jacket, cutaway, morning (*or* tail *or* swallow-tailed) coat, tails (Inf), claw-hammer coat (US), tweed coat, sack coat (US), topper (US), midicoat, sports jacket, sports coat (US), blazer, sporting jacket, Eton jacket, mess jacket, shell jacket, cardigan (jacket), cardie (Inf), Nehru jacket, Mao jacket, loden, dolman jacket, Mackinaw coat (US), lumber-jacket, lumberjack (US), leather jacket, bomber jacket, parka, anorak, cagoule, reefer, windcheater, windbreaker (US), hunting jacket, shooting jacket, Norfolk jacket, donkey jacket, riding jacket, hacking jacket (*or* coat), Eisenhower jacket (US), jerkin, spencer, bolero, tunic, tabard, waistcoat, vest (US), monkey jacket (Inf), bumfreezer (Inf), boolhipper (US inf)

12 coat, overcoat, topcoat, surcoat, fur, mink, greatcoat, frock coat (*or* frock), Prince Albert, chesterfield, redingote, paletot, surtout, raglan, ulster, duffel (*or* duffle) coat, pea jacket (*or* pea coat), fearnought (*or* fearnaught), dreadnought (*or* dreadnaught), light coat, duster, raincoat, waterproof, mackintosh, Burberry™, Barbour™, gaberdine (*or* gabardine) coat, trench coat, oilskins, slicker (US), southwester (*or* sou'wester), mac (Inf), crombie (Inf)

► *550 Covering*

13 sweater, jersey, cardigan, pullover, slipover, woolly, cashmere sweater, knitted sweater, knit, hand-knit (*or* hand-knitted) sweater, jumper, V-neck, polo-neck (*or* polo), ski sweater, turtleneck, crew-neck, Guernsey, Aran sweater, fisherman's jersey, Fair Isle, twinset, sloppy joe (Inf), cardie (Inf)

14 neckwear, scarf, muffler, comforter, fichu, stock, neckpiece, neckerchief, bandanna (*or* bandana), kerchief, shawl, tallith, stole, fur, boa, tippet, jabot, tucker, chemisette, guimpe, cravat, neckcloth, ascot, tie, necktie (US), bow tie, dicky bow, Windsor tie, four-in-hand, string tie, necklace, neckband, band, collar, starched collar, stiff collar, high collar, choker, Vandyke collar, Peter Pan collar, bertha collar, Eton collar, Mandarin collar, stand-up collar, rabato, button-down collar, shawl collar, clerical (*or* Roman) collar, ruff, dog collar (Inf)

► *7 Religion*

15 headgear, headdress, millinery, hat, chapeau, top hat, high hat, silk hat, stovepipe hat, bowler, derby (US), felt hat, homburg, fedora, trilby, pork-pie hat, deerstalker, Tyrolean hat, straw hat, boater, panama, cowboy hat, stetson, ten-gallon hat, sombrero, slouch hat, beaver, beaverskin, coonskin hat (*or* cap), busby, cocked hat, tricorn (*or* tricorne), mortarboard, bonnet, Easter bonnet, poke bonnet, sunbonnet, sun hat, picture hat, pillbox, toque, cloche, rain hat, southwester (*or* sou'wester), clerical hat, biretta, shovel hat, woolly hat, bobble hat, helmet, pith helmet (*or* topee), hard hat, safety hat, crash helmet, work hat, coolie hat, witch's hat, wizard's hat, cap, cloth cap, beanie (*or* beany) (US), baseball cap (US), jockey cap, beret, tam-o'shanter, (*or* tam), glengarry, balmoral, skullcap, coif, mobcap (*or* mob), Juliet cap, Dutch cap, stocking cap, military cap, forage cap, kepi, shako, fez, dunce cap (*or* dunce's cap *or* fool's cap), jester's cap, coxcomb, balaclava helmet, scarf, mantilla, plumes, crown, coronet, tiara, net, snood, headscarf, headband, ribbon, fillet, sweatband, turban, hood, cowl, wimple, veil, yashmak, wig, hairpiece, toupee, false hair, peruke, periwig, barrister's wig, bagwig (Lit), powdered wig, hair transplant, topper (Inf), tin hat (Inf), lid (Inf), tile (Inf), titfer, skid lid (Inf), plug hat (US inf), rug (Inf)

► *16 Law; 48 Baseball; 401 Servant; 578 Worker; 586 Combatant*

16 robe, bathrobe, lounging robe, gown, dressing gown, *robe-de-chambre* (Fr), peignoir, negligée, housecoat, wrapper, bed jacket, boudoir dress, tunic, sari, kimono, caftan (*or* kaftan), jubbah, burka, kanga, chiton, himation, toga, toga virilis, pallium, clerical robe, cassock

► *7 Religion; 10 Ritual*

17 grave clothes, shroud, winding sheet

► *583 Burial*

18 underwear, undergarments, underclothes, underthings, scanties, lingerie, unmentionables, thermal underwear, long underwear, combinations (*or* combs), union suit (US), drawers (*or* underdrawers), pants (*or* underpants), shorts (*or* undershorts) (US), boxer shorts, trunks, briefs, Y-fronts, BVD's (US), jockey shorts (US), jockstrap (*or* athletic support), panties, pantalets (*or* pantalettes), bloomers, knickers, French knickers, camiknickers (*or* camiknicks), vest (*or* undervest), singlet, undershirt (US), T-shirt (US), semmit (Scot), camisole, chemise, shift, step-ins, slip, half-slip, underskirt, petticoat, crinoline, Balmoral, teddy, crop top, body stocking, body, foundation garment, corset, stays, girdle, panty girdle, roll-on, supporter, brassiere, bra, suspender belt, garter belt (US), braces, bustle, hoop, farthingale, pannier, smock (Lit), long johns (Inf), undies (Inf), smalls, skivvy shirt (*or* skivvy) (US inf), skivvies (US inf)

► *413 Support; 493 Heat; 552 Undress*

19 footwear, footgear, shoes, leather shoes, lace-ups, Oxfords, pumps, court shoes, winkle-pickers, buckled shoes, square-toed shoes, pointed shoes, high heels, spike (*or* stiletto) heels, platform heels, Cuban heels, wedge heels, wedgies (US), canvas shoes, plimsolls (*or* plimsoles), trainers, sneakers (US), gym shoes, running shoes, spikes, football boots, rugby boots, tennis shoes, trainers, espadrilles, rubber-soled shoes, crepe-soled shoes, ballet shoes (*or* slippers), casuals, flat shoes, sling (*or* sling-back) shoes, walking shoes, brogues, moccasins, loafers (US), Hush Puppies™, slippers, mules, slip-ons, scuffs, sandals, open-toed sandals, buskins, chappals, flip-flops, thongs (US), zoris, wooden shoes, clogs, sabots, pattens, work shoes, boots, riding boots, fashion boots, high boots, top boots, thigh boots, hip boots, waders, Wellington boots (*or* wellingtons *or* gumboots), hobnail boots, walking boots, fell boots, Doc Martens (DMs)™, stogies (US), cowboy boots, ski boots, paratrooper boots, combat boots, desert boots, jackboots, chukka boots, snowshoes, overshoes, galoshes, gumshoes, rubbers (US), bumpers (Inf), daps (Inf), clodhoppers (Inf), flatties (Inf), wellies (Inf), Jesus boots (Inf), brothel creepers (Inf), beetle-crushers (Inf)

20 legwear, hosiery, hose, stockings, sheer stockings, seamless stockings, seamed stockings, silk stockings, lisle stockings, nylons, tights, fishnet tights, pantyhose (US and Aus), fleshings, half-hose, socks, argyles, crew socks, knee-length (*or* knee) socks, over-the-knee socks, bobby socks, ankle socks, anklets (US), sweat socks, ski socks, galligaskins, leggings, legwarmers, chaps (US), gaiters, spats, suspender, garter (US), puttees, spatterdashes

21 beachwear, swimsuit, swimming (*or* bathing) costume, bathing (*or* swimming) suit, (swimming) trunks, bathers (Aus), bikini, tanga, thong, one-piece swimsuit, monokini, maillot, two-piece swimsuit, wet suit, sundress, beach robe, sunglasses, shades (Inf)

► *67 Swimming; 552 Undress*

22 nightwear, sleepwear, nightclothes, nightdress (*or* nightgown), nightshirt, bedgown, negligée, pyjamas, baby doll pyjamas, dressing gown, bed jacket, nightcap, bedsocks, nightie (Inf), PJs (Inf)

► *343 Inactivity; 552 Undress*

23 children's clothes, infants' wear, baby clothes, layette, rompers, jumpers (US), creepers (US), matinée coat (*or* jacket), coatee, playsuit, sunsuit, bootees, bib, nappy (*or* napkin), diaper (US), swaddling clothes, beanie (US), babygro™, sleepsuit

24 part of garment, neck, yoke, collar, top, bodice, bosom, corsage, bib, stomacher, shirt-front, waistline, peplum, train, gusset, crotch, codpiece, arm, armhole, sleeve, short sleeve, long sleeve, dolmen sleeve, raglan sleeve, puff sleeve, leg-of-mutton sleeve, flap, coat-tail, placket, opening, pocket, patch pocket, gore, pleat, kick pleat, lapel, fold, turn-up, cuff, hemline, edging, garniture, trim, button, fly, zip, hook and eye, Velcro™

► *164 Edge; 373 Connection; 547 Beautification*

25 accessories, accoutrements, paraphernalia, muff, earmuffs, cloak, capote, cape, mantle, shawl, wrap, poncho, afghan, apron, pinafore, pinny (Inf), overall, armlet, armband, shoulder pad, belt, cincture, bandoleer, sash, baldric, codpiece, obi, gloves, kid gloves, suede gloves, driving gloves, long gloves, evening gloves, gauntlets, mittens, mitts, wristband, sunglasses, shades (Inf), handkerchief, loincloth, waistcloth, lungi (*or* lungee), dhoti, fig leaf, G-string, jockstrap, falsies (Inf)

► *205 Part; 405 Component; 552 Undress*

26 fashion designer, couturier (*or* couturiere), costumer, *costumier* (Fr), costume designer, dressmaker, tailor, sartor (Lit), garment-maker, clothier, outfitter, milliner, modiste, hatter, hosier, glover, furrier, haberdasher (US), draper, fabric dealer (US), mercer, dry-goods dealer (US), shoemaker, cobbler, souter (Scot), bootmaker, booter, garmentworker, cutter, needleworker, needlewoman, seamstress, sewer, stitcher, finisher, fitter, busheller, cordwainer (Lit)

▶ *42 Fabrics and Dyeing; 356 Creation; 435 Materials; 776 Trade*

27 model, fashion model, male model, Beau, Beau Brummel, dandy, fop, trendsetter, snappy dresser (Inf), poser (Inf), clotheshorse (Inf), coat hanger (Inf), face (Inf)

28 valet, dresser, batman, lady's maid, wardrobe mistress

▶ *401 Servant*

ADJECTIVES

29 dressed, clothed, clad, attired, garbed, apparelled, bedecked, arrayed, vested, invested, habited, habilimented, wrapped, draped, robed, frocked, mantled, cloaked, gowned, hatted, capped, bonneted, hooded, bewigged, gloved, shod, shoed, booted, decked out, turned out, rigged, kitted out, costumed, uniformed, liveried

▶ *736 Concealment*

30 dressed-up, smart, clothes-conscious, fashionable, stylish, modish, à la mode, chic, dapper, spruced up, spruce, well-dressed, groomed, well turned out, tricked out (*or* up), soigné (*or* soignée), *en grande tenue* (Fr), *en grande toilette* (Fr), in Sunday best, in Sunday go-to-meeting clothes (US), in full dress, in white tie and tails, in tails, bedight (Lit), bedizened (Lit), natty (Inf), dressed to kill (Inf), dressed up to the nines (Inf), in fine feather (Inf), in one's best bib and tucker (Inf), done (*or* got) up like a dog's dinner (Inf), togged (Inf), fancied up (Inf), slicked up (US inf), tarted up (Inf), tarty (Inf), gussied up (US inf), dolled up (Inf), spiffed up (Inf), dap (US inf)

▶ *543 Elegance; 553 Fashion*

31 styled, tailored, sartorial, tailor-made, bespoke, made-to-measure, made-to-order, custom-made, designer, store-bought (Dial), off-the-peg, ready-made, ready-to-wear, single-breasted, double-breasted, one-piece, two-piece, unisex, well-cut, fully fashioned, stylish, dressy, smart, matching, colour-coordinated, classic, princess-line, Empire-line, A-line, step-in, pull-on, button-through, buttoned-up, zip-up, casual, informal, sporty, baggy, sloppy, gathered, rucked, ruched, tucked, darted, hemmed, laced, long-sleeved, short-sleeved, gusseted, pleated, trimmed, folded, bloused, bouffant, skintight, slinky (Inf), natty (Inf), snazzy (Inf)

VERBS

32 dress, clothe, clad, garment, apparel, accoutre, attire, robe, enrobe, gown, drape, cloak, mantle, garb, enfold, envelop, wrap, roll up in, swaddle, swathe, shroud, sheathe, cover, vest, invest, cap, hood, glove, shoe, uniform, costume

33 dress up, deck out, turn out, rig out, spruce up, titivate, bedeck, array, beautify, primp, prink, comparison, dight (Lit), bedizen (Lit), dress to kill (Inf), dress up to the nines (Inf), dress in one's best bib and tucker (Inf), fancy up (Inf), tart up (Inf), gussy up (US inf), doll up (Inf), spiff up (Inf)

34 wear, dress in, have on, don, clothe oneself, attire oneself, get dressed, get one's clothes on, put on, pull on, slip on, slip (*or* get) into, step in, button up, zip up, do up, lace up, tie, get changed, change one's clothes, change, try on

35 make clothing, outfit, tailor, tailor-make, custom-make, make to order, accoutre, costume, powder, bewig, uniform, equip, rig out, fit out, design, style, cobble, measure, adjust, gather, fold, blouse, seam, sew, stitch, pleat, finish, fit, bushel (US)

ADVERBS

36 dressily, fashionably, stylishly, modishly, in vogue, chicly, elegantly, smartly, glamorously, casually, informally, sportily, nattily (Inf), snazzily (Inf)

552 Undress

NOUNS

1 undress, undressing, unclothing, uncovering, disrobing, disrobement, divestment, denuding, denudation, stripping, stripping bare, laying bare, baring, bareness, nudism, naturism, gymnosophy, revealing, exposing, exposure, toplessness, indecent exposure, striptease, dance of the seven veils, exhibitionism, streaking, strip poker, strip-search (*or* skin-search), skinny-dipping (Inf), flashing (Inf), mooning (Inf)

▶ *22 Dancing; 551 Dress; 738 Display; 739 Disclosure*

2 nudity, nakedness, bareness, state of nature, the nude, the buff (Inf), the raw (Inf), the altogether (Inf), birthday suit (Inf), not a stitch on (Inf), not a stitch to one's name (Inf), nudie (US inf), pornographic magazine, erotica, nude painting, strip (*or* striptease) club, strip-o-gram (Inf), strip (*or* striptease) joint (US inf)

▶ *19 Painting and Sculpture; 21 Drama; 41 Photography*

4 dishabille (*or* **deshabille**), informality, informal dress, nightwear, nightdress, nightgown, nightie (Inf), pyjamas, dressing gown, bathrobe, housecoat, kimono, underwear, swimwear, revealing dress, miniskirt, microskirt, shorts, hot pants, G-string, thong, posing pouch, jockstrap, décolletage, plunging neckline, careless dress, negligent dress, poor dress, second-hand clothes, hand-me-downs, rags, tatters

▶ *553 Fashion; 657 Informality; 666 Negligence*

5 baldness, hairlessness, alopecia, calvities, premature baldness, baldheadedness, bare head, baldpatedness, bald top, beardlessness, bald person, bald head, baldpate, skinhead, baldy (Inf), slaphead (Inf)

▶ *421 Smoothness*

6 peeling, shedding, moulting, moult, decortication, excoriation, desquamation, exfoliation, abscission, ecdysis, exuviation

▶ *72 Birds; 76 Insects and Arachnids; 372 Separation*

7 depilation, falling hair, alopecia, hair remover, denuder, depilatory, electrolysis, wax, razor, shaving, shave, plucking, shearing, shear, haircut, tonsure

8 nude person, naked person, naked lady, disrober, nude, nude model, nude figure, nudist, naturist, gymnosophist, stripper, male stripper, stripteaser, striptease dancer, striptease artiste (*or* artist), exotic dancer, topless dancer, topless waitress, ecdysiast, exhibitionist, streaker, exposer, skinny-dipper (Inf), strip-o-gram (Inf), flasher (Inf), peeler (US inf)

► 19 Painting and Sculpture

ADJECTIVES

9 **undressed**, unclothed, clothesless, uncovered, unclad, without a stitch on, bared, bare, nude, in the nude, naked, stark-naked (*or* stark), stripped, stripped naked (*or* bare *or* nude), strip-searched (*or* skin-searched), disrobed, unrobed, unattired, undraped, ungarbed, in a state of nature, au naturel, *in puris naturalibus* (L), in nature's garb, naked as the day one was born, naked as a jaybird (US), nudist, naturistic, gymnosophical, buck naked (US inf), nuddy (Inf), raw (Inf), in the raw (Inf), in the buff (Inf), stripped to the buff (Inf), in the altogether (Inf), starkers (Inf), in one's birthday suit (Inf), bare-ass (*or* bare-assed) (US inf), bare-bollock (Inf)

10 **in dishabille**, *en deshabille* (Fr), underdressed, underclothed, half-dressed, half-clothed, informally dressed, bare-headed, hatless, topless, décolleté, low-necked, low-cut, off-the-shoulder, strapless, miniskirted, microskirted, swimsuited, bikini-clad, casually dressed, negligently dressed, in one's shirtsleeves, poorly dressed, tattered, threadbare, out at elbows, ragged, barefoot, barelegged

11 **exposed**, exposable, divested, unveiled, denuded (*or* denudated), laid bare, barebacked, barebreasted, topless, barechested, barelegged, barefoot (*or* barefooted), discalced (*or* discalceate), barenecked, indecently dressed, pornographic, X-rated, stripped, peeled, skinny-dipping (Inf), debagged (Inf), flashing (Inf), mooning (Inf)

► 675 Vulgarity

12 **peeling**, peeled, shedding, shed, sloughy, exuvial, exfoliatory (*or* exfoliative), leafless, desquamative, ecdysial, moulting, moulted, unfledged, unfeathered, plucked

13 **hairless**, bald, baldheaded, baldpated, thin, thin on top, tonsured, shaved, shaven, clean-shaven, beardless, smooth-shaven, smooth-faced, smooth, glabrous (*or* glabrate), hair removing, depilatory, bald as a coot, bald as an egg, bald as a billiard ball, bare as the back of one's hand

VERBS

14 **undress**, unclothe, uncover, disrobe, unrobe, unveil, uncloak, undrape, divest, doff, take off, strip off, slip off, slip out of, step out of, remove, put off, drop, undo, unbutton, unzip, unhook, unlace, untie, change one's clothes, change, strip, bare, strip bare, lay bare, expose, lay open, disclose, reveal, expose oneself, streak, go topless, practise nudism, peel off (Inf), strip to the buff (Inf), wear a smile (US inf), skinny-dip (Inf), flash (Inf), moon (Inf)

15 **make nude**, denude, denudate, strip, force someone to strip, pull (*or* rip) off someone's clothes, disrobe, strip-search (*or* skin-search), unwrap, fleece, shear, shave, pluck, deplume, tear off, scrape off, peel, pare, flay, abrade, rub off, scalp, debark, debag (Inf)

16 **peel**, shed, slough, lose feathers, moult, throw off, cast off, scale off, scale, flake off, flake, decorticate, excoriate, desquamate, exfoliate, exuviate

ADVERBS

17 **nakedly**, with nothing on, without a stitch on, barely, in the nude, pornographically, explicitly, indecently, in one's shirtsleeves, informally, casually, revealingly, baldly, in the raw (Inf), in the buff (Inf), in the altogether (Inf), in one's birthday suit (Inf)

553 Fashion

One had as good be out of the world, as out of the fashion. Colley Cibber.

One week he's in polka dots, the next week he's in stripes.
Cos he's a dedicated follower of fashion. Ray Davies.

Fashions, after all, are only induced epidemics. George Bernard Shaw.

NOUNS

1 **fashion**, style, mode, vogue, look, new look, craze, trend, set, rage, the latest, *dernier cri* (Fr), *haute couture* (Fr), high fashion, elegance, designer label

2 **fashionableness**, chic, stylishness, à la mode

3 **fashion business**, the rag trade (Inf), schmutter business (Inf)

4 **design**, mode, style, structure, set, mould, aspect, light, appearance, tendency, convention, usage, protocol, form

5 **fashion model**, model, mannequin, supermodel, fashion plate, clotheshorse (Inf), snappy dresser, coathanger (Inf)

6 **fashionable élite**, high society, café society, beau monde, *crème de la crème* (Fr), beautiful people (Inf), jet set (Inf), jet-setter (Inf), Sloane Ranger (Inf)

ADJECTIVES

7 **fashionable**, smart, stylish, à la mode, modish, voguish, snazzy, clothes-conscious, well-dressed, dressy, trend-setting, tasteful, classy, posh, glamorous, well-groomed, chic, trendy (Inf), dressed up to the nines (Inf), cool (Inf), with it (Inf), swish (Inf), all the rage (Inf), crucial (Inf), hip (Inf), groovy (Inf)

VERBS

8 **dress up**, don, get oneself done up, tart up (Inf), doll up (Inf), put on one's glad rags (Inf)

9 **fashion**, shape, produce, figure, turn, round, cut, style, tailor, cut out, create, model, chisel, carve, sculpt, hew, mould, cast, hammer out, forge, build, formulate, construct, knock into shape, shape

ADVERBS

10 **fashionably**, stylishly, tastefully, glamorously, trendily (Inf)

Life and Society

554 Life

Life is a tragedy when seen in close-up, but a comedy in long-shot. Charlie Chaplin.

Life is an incurable disease. Abraham Cowley.

Life is like a sewer. What you get out of it depends on what you put into it. Tom Lehrer.

Life's but a walking shadow, a poor player,
That struts and frets his hour upon the stage,
And then is heard no more; it is a tale
Told by an idiot, full of sound and fury,
Signifying nothing. William Shakespeare.

NOUNS

1 life, living, being alive, being, existing, existence, subsistence, entity, animate existence, animation, living things, animal life, the animal kingdom, human life, humankind, mankind, vegetable life, plant life, life on earth, the living and breathing world, the living, living being, human being, living person, person, individual, survivor, living soul, soul, spirit, animal spirits, life force, vital force, vital spark, vital flame, *élan vital* (Fr), seat of life, essential part, beating heart, strong pulse, liveliness, vivacity, energy, sprightliness, vitality, vitalization, vivification, sensation, sentience, sensibility, moral sensibility, imparting of life, cooperative living, symbiosis, association, ginger (Inf)

▶ *70 Animals; 77 Plants; 93 Existence; 99 Essence; 334 Power; 336 Strength; 338 Vigour; 342 Activity; 566 Humankind; 747 Cooperation*

2 living matter, protoplasm, bioplasm, tissue, living tissue, macromolecule, bioplast, cell, gene, unicellular organism, organism

3 life requirements, vital necessities, subsistence, sustenance, nourishment, food, staff of life, bread, daily bread, manna, water, oxygen, air, vital air, breath of life, breath of one's nostrils, lifeblood, heart's blood, heart, artery

4 biological function, life senses, sight, smell, touch, taste, hearing, breathing, respiration, life activity, biological clock, fertility, parenthood, motherhood, fatherhood, procreation, propagation, reproduction, sexual reproduction, sex, sexual activity, coition, copulation, sexual intercourse, conception, pregnancy, confinement, delivery, birth, gift of life, nativity, viability, viableness, origin

▶ *130 Beginning; 488 Sensation; 561 Reproduction; 562 Fertility*

5 life cycle, seven ages of man, birth, childhood, youth, adolescence, adulthood, middle age, old age, death, lifetime, life span, life expectancy, average life, allotted span, allotted days, one's born days, threescore years and ten, biometry, longevity, survival, survivability, capacity for life, hold on life, will to live, life-support system, cat's nine lives, new birth, renaissance, revivification, revival, reanimation, reincarnation, resurrection, Lazarus, life to come, immortal life, immortality, eternal life, eternity, future state, the hereafter, afterlife, heaven, paradise

▶ *130 Beginning; 275 Time; 277 Duration; 279 Eternity; 393 Repair; 556 Age; 582 Death*

6 things brought to life, Pinocchio, Frankenstein's monster, the portrait of Dorian Gray, nutcracker, witch's broom, magic carpet, scarecrow and tin man in *The Wizard of Oz*, Pygmalion's statue

7 studies of life, life sciences, biology, genetics, botany, zoology, anthropology, humanities, sociology

▶ *1 Anthropology*

8 theories of life, creation, evolution, Bhavachakra, reincarnation, samsara

9 classifications of life, taxonomy, viruses, bacteria, plants, algae, fungi, bryophytes, pteridophytes, spermatophytes, animals, protozoa, parazoa, metazoa, vertebrates, amphibians, mammals

▶ *137 Class*

10 lifestyle, way of life, existence

▶ *317 Way; 631 Behaviour; 632 Habit*

11 life story, history, biography, autobiography, memoirs

▶ *3 History; 17 Literature; 721 Description; 744 Record*

ADJECTIVES

12 alive, live, living, quick (Lit), alive and kicking, animate, conscious, breathing, in life, incarnate, in the flesh, not dead, existent, extant, surviving, ongoing, in the land of the living, (still) with us, still breathing, above ground, on this side of the grave, long-lived, old, aged, ancient, tenacious of life, lasting, lifelong, capable of life, viable, vital, vivifying, life-giving, Promethean, vivified, enlivened, revived, restored, reborn

▶ *93 Existence; 95 Reality; 393 Repair; 556 Age; 582 Death*

13 lively, animated, vivacious, spirited, energetic, vigorous, dynamic, active, sprightly, gingery (Inf)

▶ *334 Power; 336 Strength; 338 Vigour; 342 Activity*

14 biotic, biotical (US), symbiotic, biological, biologic (US), biogenetic, biogenetical, protoplasmatic, protoplasmic, protoplastic, bioplastic

15 born, born alive, newly born, newborn, begotten, out of, by, fathered, sired, mothered, dammed, foaled, dropped, spawned, littered, laid, new-laid, hatched, produced

▶ *108 Relatedness; 130 Beginning; 356 Creation; 561 Reproduction*

VERBS

16 live, be alive, have life, be, have being, exist, draw breath, breathe, respire, subsist, walk the earth, live one's life, live life to the fullest, liven (up), quicken, come to life, come to, come round, regain consciousness, revive, not die, be spared, survive, endure, come through, carry on, continue, last, persist, cheat death, have nine lives, be reborn

▶ *93 Existence; 393 Repair*

17 dwell, live at (*or* in), reside at (*or* in), inhabit, lodge, stay, abide

▶ *565 Habitat*

18 be born, come into the world, have one's nativity, come into existence, first see the light (of day), begin, draw breath, draw first breath, fetch breath

▶ *130 Beginning*

19 give birth to, give life to, create life, impart life, beget, hear the patter of little (*or* tiny) feet, have an extra mouth to feed, breed, spawn, procreate, reproduce, conceive, generate, vitalize, vivify, liven (up), breathe life into, bring (back) to life, raise up, raise from the dead, resuscitate, revive, bring round, restore to consciousness

▶ *393 Repair; 561 Reproduction*

20 support life, provide for, provide a living for, support, maintain, keep alive, save the life of, keep body and soul together, make ends meet, keep the wolf from the door, feed, nourish

21 invigorate, revitalize, put new life into, rejuvenate, give hope, give a shot in the arm, give a new lease of (*or* on) life, put zest into, reanimate, revive the spirit, resurrect, restore

▶ *581 Refreshment*

ADVERBS

22 vitally, viably, lively, animatedly, vivaciously, biologically, biotically

555 Youth

Better is a poor and a wise child than an old and foolish king, who will no more be admonished. Bible: Ecclesiastes.

Les enfants terribles. (The embarrassing young.) Paul Gavarni.

Youth is a malady of which one becomes cured a little every day. Benito Mussolini.

My salad days,
When I was green in judgment, cold in blood,
To say as I said then! William Shakespeare.

NOUNS

1 **youth**, adolescence, pubescence, puberty, age of puberty, teens, preteens, boyhood, girlhood, maidenhood, childhood, babyhood, infancy, young days, younger days, school age, schooldays, college days, student days, pupilage, apprenticeship, wardship, happiest days of one's life, salad days, the prime of life, heyday of the blood, early life, springtime of life, bloom of youth, tender age, awkward age, immaturity, puerility, nonage, minority

▶ *130 Beginning; 295 Newness*

2 **youthfulness**, juvenescence, juvenility, juvenilia, youngness, childishness, boyishness, girlishness, maidenliness, young blood, vigour, freshness, sappiness, juiciness, growing pains

3 **immaturity**, inexperience, undevelopment, greenness, rawness, naivety, ingenuousness, awkwardness, callowness, unreadiness, unpreparedness

4 **young animal**, young, yearling, fawn, kitten, puppy, pup, kid, lamb, lambkin, cub, whelp, piglet, duckling, cygnet, chick, fry, fledgling, nestling, calf, colt, foal, filly, larva, grub, nymph, pupa, chrysalis, cocoon, caterpillar, tadpole, polliwog, brood, clutch, spawn, farrow, litter

5 **young plant**, sprout, seedling, set, shoot, offshoot, sucker, twig, sprig, scion, sapling

6 **young person**, youngster, youth, youngling (Lit), young'un (Inf), minor, adolescent, teenager, young adult, juvenile, junior, young hopeful, kid (Inf), teenybopper (Inf), weenybopper (Inf), groupie (Inf)

7 **young man**, youth, boy, lad, laddie (Scot), stripling, schoolboy, urchin, street urchin, cub, kid (Inf), young shaver (Inf), pup (Inf), young pup (Inf)

8 **young woman**, girl, young lady, miss, lass, lassie (Scot), chit of a girl, slip of a girl, schoolgirl, maid, maiden, virgin, tomboy, hoyden, mademoiselle, minx, hussy, nymph, nymphet, missy (Inf), baggage (Offensive), chick (Inf), bird (Inf), baby (Inf), babe (US inf)

9 **child**, baby, babe, bairn (Scot), bouncing baby, nursling (*or* nurseling), bundle of joy, babe in arms, infant, tiny tot, mite, toddler, little one, darling, little angel, little monkey, little cherub, little imp, youngster, boy, lad, laddie (Scot), girl, lass, lassie (Scot), kid (Inf), kiddie (Inf), peewee (US inf), nipper (Inf), brat (Inf), moppet (Inf), poppet (Inf), whippersnapper (Inf), rugrat (Inf), ankle-biter (Inf)

10 **the young**, young people, youth, young blood, children, schoolchildren, the rising young, the rising generation, the younger generation, the new generation, kids (Inf)

ADJECTIVES

11 **young**, youthful, juvenile, juvenescent, childlike, childish, boylike, boyish, beardless, girllike, girlish, maidenly, virginal, innocent, underage, underaged, undeveloped, minor, pre-school, school-age, junior, teenage, teenaged, in one's teens, sweet sixteen, adolescent, pubescent, sweet and twenty, in the flower of youth, infantile, infant, in one's infancy, baby, babyish, unfledged, fledgling, new-fledged, in the cradle, at the breast, in arms, in nappies, knee-high, knee-high to a grasshopper

12 **immature**, inexperienced, undeveloped, green, raw, naive, naïf, ingenuous, awkward, callow, unready, unprepared
13 **maturing**, growing, budding, pullulating, burgeoning, developing, rounding out, flowering, blooming, in bloom

ADVERBS

14 **youthfully**, juvenilely, childishly, boyishly, girlishly, virginally, innocently, in one's infancy, in one's teens, in the flower of youth, in the cradle, at the breast
15 **immaturely**, greenly, rawly, awkwardly, unreadily, unpreparedly

VERBS

16 **be young**, have the bloom of youth, stay young
17 **make young**, youthen, rejuvenate, reinvigorate
18 **grow**, have growing pains, bud, pullulate, burgeon, develop, round out, flower, bloom, mature

556 Age

I am past thirty, and three parts iced over. Matthew Arnold.

What is an adult? A child blown up by age. Simone de Beauvoir.

Youth is a blunder; manhood a struggle; old age a regret. Benjamin Disraeli.

Life begins at forty. Sophie Tucker.

NOUNS

1 **age**, time span, lifetime, life span, (number of) years, one's age, one's time of life
► *277 Duration*
2 **adulthood**, adultness, maturity, maturation, manhood, womanhood, matronliness, middle age, prime of life, seniority, oldness, old age, ripeness
► *296 Oldness*
3 **maturity**, matureness, experience, professionalism, confidence, readiness, preparedness, leadership
► *129 Precedence; 243 Preparation*
4 **middle age**, middle life, middle years, maturity, mellowness, ripeness, the riper years, years of discretion, one's prime, the prime of life, change of life, menopause, male menopause, climacteric, midlife crisis, dangerous age, wrong side of forty (Inf)
5 **old age**, elderliness, senescence, longevity, seniority, retirement age, pensionable age, ripe old age, green old age, golden years, third age, advanced years, allotted span, threescore years and ten, declining years, decline, hoariness, greyness, frailty, infirmity, anility, senility, second childhood, dotage, anecdotage, evening of one's life, autumn of one's life, winter of one's life
► *337 Weakness; 461 Insanity*
6 **gerontology**, geriatric medicine, gerontologist, geriatrician
► *35 Medicine*
7 **older person**, adult, grown-up, elder, senior, doyen (*or* doyenne), retired person, pensioner, old person, old age pensioner (OAP), retiree (US), senior citizen, veteran, geriatric, greybeard, sexagenarian, septuagenarian, octogenarian, nonagenarian, centenarian, Methuselah, old fogy, dotard, the old folks, Darby and Joan, Gray Panther (US), oldster (Inf), oldie (Inf), golden oldie (Inf), no spring chicken (Inf), crumbly (Inf), wrinkly (Inf), dodderer (Inf)
8 **man**, husband, father, grandfather, patron, widower, old bachelor, man of the world, older man, old man, old boy, veteran, greybeard, old guy (Inf), old codger (Inf), old buffer (Inf), old duffer (Inf), old-timer (US inf), old geezer (Inf), old git (Inf)
9 **woman**, wife, mother, grandmother, matron, widow, old spinster, older woman, old woman, old witch, woman of the world, granny (Inf), old gal (Inf), old bag (Inf), old bat (Inf)
10 **the old**, the elderly, old people, the older generation, the over-the-hill gang (Inf), woopies (well-off older people) (Inf)

ADJECTIVES

11 **adult**, mature, senior, experienced, prepared, grown-up, ripe, developed, full-grown, in full bloom, in one's prime
12 **ageing**, growing old, getting old, senescent, getting on (*or* along), getting on (*or* along) in years, going grey, greying, getting crow's-feet, getting a middle-aged spread, declining, weakening, waning, on the wane, running (*or* going) to seed, sinking, moribund
13 **middle-aged**, mature, of mature years, fatherly, motherly, matronly, menopausal, climacteric, overblown, run (*or* gone) to seed, gone to pot, not as young as one was, long in the tooth, thirtysomething (Inf), fortysomething (Inf), no chicken (Inf), no spring chicken (Inf)
14 **aged**, old, grown old, elderly, venerable, patriarchal, matriarchal, geriatric, advanced in years, at an advanced age, past one's prime, well-preserved, white-haired, grey-haired, old and grey, hoary, wrinkled, wizened, shrivelled, lined, decrepit, failing, senile, anile, burdened with age, stricken in years, moribund, living on borrowed time, not long for this world, with one foot in the grave, ancient, old as the hills, old as Methuselah, still in full possession of one's faculties, doddering, past it (Inf), too old to cut the mustard (US inf), gaga (Inf)
15 **age-related**, geriatric, gerontologic, ageist

ADVERBS

16 **maturely**, with maturity, preparedly, ripely, in full bloom, in one's prime, venerably, patriarchally, matriarchally, past one's prime, at an advanced age, in one's old age, climacterically, hoarily, senilely, burdened with age, stricken in years, moribundly, on borrowed time, with one foot in the grave

VERBS

17 **age**, be (some) years old, see one's (specified) summer, grow up, grow old, get old, mature, ripen, mellow, pass one's prime, get on, get on in years, show one's years, go to seed, go to pot, decline, sink, weaken, deteriorate, get a middle-aged spread, get crow's-feet, wrinkle, wizen, shrivel, wither, grey, go grey, turn white, live to a ripe old age, become long in the tooth, dodder, have a second childhood, have had one's day, have seen better days, have one foot in the grave, become too old to cut the mustard (US inf)
18 **mature**, grow up, grow, develop, ripen, mellow, flower, bloom, come of age, leave the nest, come to maturity, at-

tain majority, reach one's majority, assume responsibility, reach manhood (*or* womanhood), reach the prime of one's life

557 Eating

NOUNS

1 **eating**, consuming, consumption, feeding, taking (in) food, ingesting, ingestion, ingurgitation, chewing, mastication, munching, manducation, biting, gnashing, champing, chomping, swallowing, deglutition, downing, getting down, gulping, slurping, engulfment, digestion, absorption

2 **appetite**, hunger, craving, voracity, voraciousness, wolfishness, gluttony, greed, gormandizing, gourmandism, voracious eating, devouring, devourment, engorgement, gobbling, bolting, guzzling, overeating, overindulgence, feasting, gorging, bingeing, binge, stuffing oneself, excessive consumption, compulsive eating, bulimia, bulimia nervosa, bulimarexia, pigout (US inf)

▶ *617 Desire; 686 Self-Indulgence; 688 Gluttony*

3 **delicate eating**, tasting, relishing, savouring, palate-tickling, refined palate, educated palate, epicurism, gourmandism, dainty palate, nibbling, licking, pecking, lack of appetite, picking at one's food, playing with one's food, toying with one's food, dieting, pathological dieting, anorexia, anorexia nervosa, starving

▶ *25 Cookery; 153 Thinness; 687 Fasting*

4 **eating meals**, dining, lunching, breakfasting, supping, having tea, snacking, grazing, eating on the run, eating in bed, breakfast in bed, eating alone, eating out, dining out, communal eating, eating together, messing, partaking, formal dining, feasting, banqueting, regalement, hospitality, entertainment, table manners

▶ *581 Refreshment; 632 Habit; 654 Sociability*

5 **eating habit**, meat-eating, flesh-eating, carnivorousness, omophagy, creophagy, ichthyophagy, insectivorousness, anthropophagy, man-eating, cannibalism, vegetarianism, veganism, herbivorousness, rumination, chewing the cud, grazing, pasturing, cropping, graminivorousness, frugivorousness, omnivorousness

6 **nutrition**, diet, dietetics, healthy eating, proper eating, balanced diet, recommended diet, special diet, macrobiotic diet, vegetarian diet, protein diet, carbohydrate diet, fruit diet, salt-free diet, low-fat diet, fat-free diet, low-cholesterol diet, diabetic diet, sugar-free diet, calorie-controlled diet, slimming diet, crash diet, liquid diet, Cambridge Diet™, food-combining diet, Hay Diet™, slimming, dieting, weight-watching, losing weight, reducing, regaining one's figure, regulated diet, diet regimen, regimen, regime, course, dietary plan, dietary, diet sheet, calorie counter

7 **food**, sustenance, nourishment, aliment, alimentation, nutriment, nutrition, nurture, fare, baby food, Pablum™, pabulum, pap, food for the body, food for the mind, food for the spirit, manna, food of the gods, ambrosia, amrita, bread, daily bread, staff of life, meat, staple food, foodstuffs, groceries, provisions, stores, supplies, commissariat, comestibles, edibles, eatables, victuals, vittles (Dial), viands, provender, rations, emergency rations, wartime rations, iron rations, emergency food supply, tack, hard tack, biscuit, salt pork, pemmican, rich food, heavy food, bulk, stodge, packaged food, vacuum-packed food, tinned food, frozen food, freezer stock, freeze-dried food, dried food, dehydrated food, long-life food, processed food, convenience food, junk food, fast food, short-order food (US), microwave food, healthy food, health food, wholefood, organic food, hydroponic food, home-grown food, high-fibre food, low-fat food, low-salt food, good food, savoury food, good cheer (Lit), cheer (Lit), fat of the land, creature comforts, cakes and ale, delicacies, dainties, luxuries, titbits, snacks, eats (Inf), grub (Inf), tuck (Inf), tucker (Aus inf), nosh (Inf), scoff (Inf), chow (Inf), chuck (US inf), peckings (US inf), soul food (US inf), goodies (Inf)

▶ *25 Cookery; 80 Fruits; 245 Deterioration; 248 Prosperity; 436 Provisions; 439 Store; 770 Allocation*

8 **animal food**, pet food, dog food, cat food, rabbit food, gerbil food, hamster food, fish food, bird food, birdseed, feed, feedstuff, chickenfeed, provender, fodder, pasture, pasturage, forage, corn, oats, barley, grain, hay, grass, clover, alfalfa, lucerne, silage, nuts, acorns, beech mast, dry feed, winter feed, pigswill, cattle cake, saltlick

▶ *43 Agriculture*

9 **plenty**, oversupply of food, food mountain, cornucopia, milk and honey, fleshpots, good table, loaded table, festal cheer, festive board, groaning board

▶ *217 Sufficiency; 219 Excess*

10 **scarcity**, lack of food, insufficient diet, meagre diet, bread-and-water diet, poor table, bare cupboard, malnutrition, rickets, beriberi, pellagra, scurvy, starvation, famine

▶ *218 Insufficiency; 260 Ill Health; 617 Desire*

11 **food content**, vitamins, calories, roughage, bulk, fibre, water, minerals, salt, calcium, iron, protein, amino acid, carbohydrates, cholesterol, oil, fat, saturated fats, polyunsaturates, starch, sugar, glucose, sucrose, lactose, fructose, (food) additive, E number, preservative, flavour enhancer (*or* intensifier), monosodium glutamate, (artificial) flavouring, (artificial) colouring, artificial sweetener, emulsifier

▶ *211 Addition; 495 Taste*

12 **meal**, refreshment, refection, repast, collation, informal meal, light meal, stand-up meal, buffet, snack, bite to eat, piece to eat, chance meal, potluck, full meal, square meal, three-course meal, formal meal, sit-down meal, family meal, breakfast, English breakfast, continental breakfast, brunch, elevenses, lunch, luncheon, Sunday lunch, light lunch, austerity lunch, bread-and-cheese lunch, ploughman's lunch, packed lunch, pack-lunch, tiffin, tea, afternoon tea, five o'clock, high tea, cream tea, tea for two, evening meal, dinner, TV dinner, supper, fork supper

13 **feast**, banquet, state banquet, regale (Lit), harvest supper, harvest home, reception, wedding reception, wedding breakfast, formal dinner, formal occasion, annual dinner, annual company get-together, employee dinner (*or* party), dinner dance, Christmas dinner, festive gathering, party, tea party, picnic, *fête champêtre* (Fr), tailgate picnic (US), barbecue, cookout (US), wiener roast (US), weenie roast (US inf), clambake (US), spread, junket, orgy, Roman orgy, bacchanalia, Lucullan banquet, bean-

feast (Inf), beano (Inf), do (Inf), bunfight (Inf), nosh-up (Inf), thrash (Inf), blowout (Inf)

► *601 Celebration; 654 Sociability*

14 mouthful, bite, nibble, piece, morsel, bolus, gobbet, slice, sliver, appetizer, hors d'oeuvre, titbit, helping, serving, portion, second helping, seconds (Inf), dish, course, first course, starter, soup, fish course, entrée, remove, main course, side-dish, entremets, dessert, sweet, pudding, afters (Inf)

► *25 Cookery*

15 eating place, dining room, dinette, dining hall, banquet hall, banqueting hall, refectory, refreshment room, lunchroom (US), canteen, company canteen, mess room, military canteen, military mess, Naafi, restaurant, health-food restaurant, wholefood restaurant, fast-food restaurant, hamburger place, McDonald's™, café, cafeteria, self-service restaurant, automat (US), eating house, diner (US), luncheonette (US), beanery (US), kebab house, crêperie, trattoria, spaghetti house, pizzeria, bistro, brasserie, steakhouse, chophouse, grill room, rotisserie, carvery, coffee house, espresso café, coffee bar, milk bar, ice-cream parlour, soda fountain (US), drug-store counter (US), lunch counter, fast-food counter, snack bar, sandwich bar, teahouse, teashop, tearoom, pancake house, waffle house (US), drive-in (US), drive-in window (US), take-away window, fish-and-chip shop, coffee stall, hot-dog stand, motorway restaurant, pull-in, transport café, roadside café (US), buffet, dining car, diner, vending machine, takeaway, eatery (US inf), greasy spoon (Inf), chippy (Inf)

16 eating utensil, knife, carving knife, fish knife, steak knife, butter knife, fork, fish fork, salad fork, fondue fork, spoon, teaspoon, tablespoon, dessertspoon, soup spoon, chopsticks, plate, dish, bowl, feeding organ, teeth, jaws, mandibles, mouth, tongue, throat, gullet, stomach, belly, paunch, crop, maw, intestines, bowels, guts

► *410 Container*

17 food shop, supermarket, hypermarket, grocery (store), grocer's (shop), fish store (US), fishmonger, bakery, baker's (shop), butcher's (shop), butcher, greengrocer('s), fruit stall, delicatessen, deli (Inf), health-food shop, food department, food hall, market, confectionary('s), sweet shop, tuck shop, commissary (US), commissariat

► *778 Sale; 779 Market*

18 eater, feeder, consumer, partaker, diner, luncher, small eater, light eater, dainty eater, taster, nibbler, dieter, slimmer, weight watcher, anorexic, big eater, hearty eater, heavy eater, feaster, banqueter, glutton, gourmand, bulimic, *bon vivant* (Fr), trencherman (*or* trencherwoman), Lucullus, bacchanal, bacchant, diner-in, boarder, messer, messmate, diner-out, frequenter of restaurants, dining-club member, picnicker, gourmet, epicure, connoisseur, meat-eater, flesh-eater, carnivore, man-eater, cannibal, anthropophagite, insectivore, omnivore, vegetarian, vegan, herbivore, fussy eater (Inf), picky eater (Inf), picker (Inf), pecker (Inf), gobbler (Inf), pig (Inf), hog (Inf), wolf (Inf), hyena (Inf), gannet (Inf), locust (Inf), foodie (Inf), veggie (Inf)

► *466 Discrimination; 654 Sociability; 688 Gluttony*

19 dietitian, dietician, dietary expert, nutritionist, nutrition expert

20 food provider, farmer, fisherman, rancher, grocer, greengrocer, fishmonger, butcher, baker, confectioner, milkman, restaurateur, chef, cook, caterer

► *25 Cookery*

VERBS

21 eat, take nourishment, subsist, fare (Lit), consume, feed, ingest, ingurgitate, engulf, take in food, graze, browse, pasture, crop, chew, chew up, munch, crunch, scrunch, masticate, manducate, gnash, champ, chomp, mouth, worry, gnaw, grind, bite, nibble, peck, tear, rend, ruminate, chew the cud, swallow, gulp, gulp down, slurp, suck, devour, take down, get down, digest, absorb

22 eat well, have a good appetite, water at the mouth, drool, salivate, raven, hunger, starve, fall to, pitch in, set to, tuck in to, lay into, get one's teeth into, sink one's teeth into, devour, gobble, snap up, dispatch, bolt, wolf (down), overeat, overindulge, gorge oneself, engorge, stuff oneself, binge, fill one's stomach, feed oneself full (US), sate, guzzle, gormandize, gluttonize, eat like a pig, take every course, eat everything in sight, eat up, clean one's plate, leave a clean plate, lick the platter clean, put away, polish off, make short work of, ask for seconds, ask for more, fatten on, batten on, prey on, nosh (Inf), scoff (Inf), put on the feedbag (Inf), lay it on (Inf), do justice to (Inf), get the hungries (US inf), fork in (Inf), spoon in (Inf), shovel in (Inf), feed one's face (Inf), feed one's tapeworm (Inf), pig out (US inf), scarf up (*or* down) (US inf)

23 taste, relish, savour, nibble (at), lick, sample, peck at, pick at, play with one's food, toy with one's food, have a poor appetite, sniff at, eat less, diet, count the calories, reduce

► *153 Thinness*

24 have a meal, board, mess, partake, have a feed, break bread, break one's fast, breakfast, brunch, lunch, have (*or* take) tea, dine, sup, snack, graze, eat between meals, eat out, dine out, regale, feast, banquet, carouse, revel

25 provide food, feed, give to eat, nourish, nurture, sustain, aliment, take care of, board, victual, provision, cater, purvey, dine, wine and dine, feast, banquet, fête, regale, have to dinner, invite over, cook for, nurse, breast-feed, suckle, give suck, force-feed, drip-feed, graze, pasture, put out to grass, fatten, fatten up

► *25 Cookery; 436 Provisions; 654 Sociability*

ADJECTIVES

26 eating, feeding, dining, grazing, meat-eating, flesh-eating, carnivorous, creophagous, man-eating, cannibalistic, omophagic, omophagous, insectivorous, herbivorous, graminivorous, frugivorous, vegetarian, vegan, omnivorous, greedy, gluttonous, hungry, ravenous, voracious, devouring, guzzling, bulimic, wolfish, gannet-like, well-fed, well-nourished, full, full up, bloated, stuffed, sated

► *617 Desire; 687 Fasting; 688 Gluttony*

27 edible, eatable, consumable, esculent, comestible, digestible, predigested, nourishing, nutritious, nutritive, nutritional, feeding, sustaining, alimental, alimentary, dietary, dietetic, slimming, low-calorie, low-fat, wholesome, good, appetizing, palate-tickling, palatable, mouthwatering, dainty, tasty, savoury, sweet, calorific, high-calorie, fattening, body-building, protein-rich, rich, succulent, delicious, scrumptious, moreish (Inf), finger-licking (US inf)

▶ *259 Health; 495 Taste*

ADVERBS

28 **carnivorously**, creophagously, cannibalistically, omophagically, omophagously, insectivorously, herbivorously, omnivorously, gluttonously, hungrily, ravenously, voraciously, greedily

29 **edibly**, eatably, consumably, digestibly, nutritiously, calorifically, succulently, tastily, deliciously

558 Drinking

Drink no longer water, but use a little wine for thy stomach's sake and thine often infirmities. Bible: I Timothy.

NOUNS

1 **drinking**, imbibing, imbibition, fluid intake, potation, sucking, lapping, sipping, tasting, nipping, supping, gulping, swallowing, swilling, swigging, quaffing, toping, soaking, pulling, wine tasting, wine-bibbing, drinking to excess, drunkenness, alcoholism, dipsomania

▶ *260 Ill Health; 601 Celebration; 654 Sociability; 690 Drunkenness*

2 **drink**, beverage, potation, libation, oblation, toast, health, mixed drink, concoction, cocktail, potion, decoction, infusion, cup of tea, cuppa (Inf), drink of the gods, nectar, thirst-quencher, draught, gulp, swallow, sip, sup (Dial), bottle(ful), can, glass(ful), cup(ful), pint (Dial), long drink, tall drink, bumper, stiff one, two fingers, short drink, short one, short, quick one (US inf), snifter (Inf), sundowner (Inf), pick-me-up (Inf), bevvy (Inf), jar (Inf)

▶ *394 Remedy; 412 Mixture; 581 Refreshment*

3 **tea**, green tea, black tea, iced tea, lemon tea, herbal tea, fruit tea, jasmine tea, camomile tea, peppermint tea, Earl Grey, Indian tea, Darjeeling, Assam, China tea, pekoe, orange pekoe, Keemun, Lapsang Souchong, gunpowder, Ceylon tea, Russian tea, mate, tisane, char (Inf)

4 **coffee**, black coffee, white coffee, instant coffee, filter coffee, freshly ground coffee, mocha, decaffeinated coffee, decaf (Inf), java (US inf)

5 **milk**, fresh milk, pint of milk, pinta (Inf), quart of milk (US), cow's milk, goat's milk, mare's milk, kumiss (*or* koumiss), camel's milk, pasteurized milk, homogenized milk, long-life milk, UHT milk, beestings, mother's milk, breast milk, colostrum, dried milk, powdered milk, skimmed milk, semiskimmed milk, condensed milk, evaporated milk, Pet Milk™ (US), ice milk (US), milk shake, milky drink, malted milk, chocolate milk, hot chocolate, cocoa, Horlicks™, top of the milk, cream, drinking yoghurt, lassi

▶ *25 Cookery; 557 Eating*

6 **soft drink**, nonalcoholic beverage, thirst-quencher, water, drinking water, filtered water, *eau potable* (Fr), spring water, mineral water, Perrier™, sparkling water, carbonated water, fizzy water, soda water, soda, cream soda, soda fountain, tonic water, barley water, squash, cordial, mixer, low-calorie drink, ginger beer, sarasparilla, root beer, near beer, cream soda, ginger ale, cola, Coca-Cola™, Coke™, Pepsi (Cola)™, fizz, fizzy drink, lemonade, bitter lemon, orangeade, fruit juice, apple juice, orange juice, grapefruit juice, pineapple juice, tomato juice, Virgin Mary, vegetable juice, V-8 juice™ (US), coconut milk, julep, sherbet (US), pop (Inf), black cow (US inf)

7 **alcoholic drink**, alcohol, liquor, wood alcohol, fermented drink, wine, corn liquor, corn whisky, corn, malt liquor, John Barleycorn, beer, hops, bottled beer, draught beer, keg beer, bitter, mild, ale, strong ale, pale ale, real ale, stout, porterwhisky, usquebaugh, Scotch whisky, Scotch, rye (US), rye whiskey (US), bourbon (US), bourbon whiskey (US), Irish whiskey, poteen, vodka, aquavit, absinthe, raki, arrack, ouzo, rum, dark rum, light rum, Jamaica rum, demerara rum, white rum, Bacardi™, grog, hot grog, toddy, hot toddy, punch, rum punch, milk punch, eggnog, egg flip, advocaat, cordial, grenadine, spiced wine, mulled wine, negus, posset, hippocras, caudle, cup, claret cup, apéritif, liqueur, frappé, Cointreau™, Tia Maria™, Drambuie™, crème de menthe, cassis, alcopop, booze (Inf), poison (Inf), hooch (US inf), rotgut (Inf), moonshine (US inf), mountain dew (US inf), mother's ruin (Inf)

8 **mixed drink**, gin and tonic, gin and It, pink gin, brandy and soda, whisky and soda, rum and Coke, rum and pep, rum and black, vodka and tonic, cocktail, Bucks fizz, Bloody Mary, brandy Alexander, collins, Tom Collins, Rum Collins, daiquiri, sling, gin sling, Singapore sling, highball, julep, mint julep, kir, kir rose, black velvet, Manhattan, margarita, martini, Old Fashioned, Pimms™, pina colada, red-eye, sangria, screwdriver, snakebite, snowball, spritzer, tequila sunrise, whiskey sour, whisky mac, white lady, mixer, tonic, soda, vermouth, Angostura Bitters, Worcester sauce, Tabasco™

9 **wine**, the grape, juice of the grape, blood of the grape, red wine, white wine, rosé, vin rosé, Rhine wine, sparkling wine, spumante, champagne, still wine, sweet wine, dessert wine, dry wine, light wine, heavy wine, full-bodied wine, vintage wine, vin ordinaire, vin de table, table wine, vin du pays, Bordeaux, claret, white Bordeaux, Sauternes, burgundy, chablis, sparkling burgundy, beaujolais, Muscadet, chardonnay, hock, Moselle, riesling, frascati, Tokay, chianti, Bulls Blood, rioja, retsina, vinho verde, cabernet sauvignon, vermouth, fortified wine, sherry, sweet sherry, cream sherry, dry sherry, sack, port, white port, ruby port, tawny port, vintage port, crusted port, madeira, marsala, vermouth, Martini™, vino (Inf), plonk (Inf), bubbly (Inf), champers (Inf)

10 **drink container**, bottle, flask, hip flask, cafetière, Thermos™ (flask), vacuum flask (*or* bottle *or* jug), canteen, can, decanter, glass, tumbler, rummer, wineglass, sherry glass, tankard, *Stein* (Ger), mug, cup, coffee cup, teacup, Styrofoam™ cup (US), loving cup, stirrup cup, bowl

▶ *410 Container*

11 **drink provider**, drinking place, teashop, coffee bar, licensed premises, public house (US), liquor store (US)

▶ *581 Refreshment; 776 Trade; 779 Market*

12 **drinker**, light drinker, social drinker, sipper, wine taster, heavy drinker, hard drinker, guzzler, bibber, swiller,

quaffer, toper, drunkard, wino (Inf), boozer (Inf), pisshead (Inf), alehead (Inf), lush (Inf), alkie (Inf)

VERBS

13 **drink**, imbibe, potate, suck, lap, sip, taste, nip, have a drink, wet one's lips, wet one's whistle (Inf), draw the cork, crack a bottle, drink up, quaff, sup, swallow, gulp, gulp down, down, drain, knock back, put away, lap up, soak up, sponge up, wash down, swill, swig, slake one's thirst, drink one's fill, toss off one's glass, empty the glass (*or* bottle), drain one's glass, have a refill, sweeten (US), have another, have one for the road, tipple, tope, get drunk, drink like a fish, indulge (Inf), booze (Inf), chug (Inf), get pissed (Inf), go out on the ale (Inf)

▶ *601 Celebration; 690 Drunkenness*

14 **drink to**, drink the health of, raise one's glass, pledge, toast, salute

15 **provide drink**, water, wine, suckle, give suck, nurse, lay in drink, lay down a cellar, give someone a refill, sweeten (US)

ADJECTIVES

16 **drinking**, nursed, suckled, breast-fed, imbibing, swilling, tippling, drunken, bibulous, vinous, dipsomaniacal, off the wagon (Inf), boozing (Inf)

▶ *689 Sobriety; 690 Drunkenness*

17 **drinkable**, potable, milky, lactic, white, diluted, weak, strong, undiluted, black, nonalcoholic, soft, fizzy, alcoholic, fermented, distilled, spiritous, hard, vinous, sparkling, still, sweet, dry, light, full-bodied, vintage

INTERJECTIONS

18 **cheers!**, here's health!, to us!, here's to you!, here's looking at you!, here's mud in your eye!, bottoms up!, down the hatch!, slàinte!, *prosit!*, (Ger), skol!, chug-a-lug! (Inf)

559 Secretion

Falstaff sweats to death.
And lards the lean earth as he walks along. William Shakespeare.

NOUNS

1 **secretion**, exudation, emission, transudation, excretion, discharge, release, voidance, ejection, emanation, secernment, lactation, lacrimation, crying, weeping, guttation, salivation, sweating, perspiration, secretory mechanism, merocrine secretion, eccrine secretion, apocrine secretion, holocrine secretion

▶ *560 Excretion*

2 **secreted substance**, secretion, internal secretion, hormone, chalone, digestive juice, gastric juice, succus entericus, pancreatic juice, bile, gall, mucus, external secretion, phlegm, sputum, saliva, tears, rheum, seminal fluid, semen, milk, colostrum, sweat, sebum, musk, pheromone, ectohormone, honeydew, plant secretion, nectar, latex, resin, tannin, gum

▶ *33 Biochemistry; 79 Trees; 431 Fluid; 560 Excretion*

3 **gland**, endocrine gland, ductless gland, exocrine gland, eccrine gland, intestinal gland, sweat gland, mammary gland, lacrimal (*or* lachrymal) gland, scent gland, plant gland, oil gland, salt gland, nectary, laticifer, hydathode

ENDOCRINE GLANDS

adrenal gland, suprarenal gland	pineal gland
corpora allata	pituitary gland
corpora cardiaca	placenta
corpus luteum	suprarenal gland, adrenal gland
islets of Langerhans	testis
ovary	thyroid gland
parathyroid gland	

EXOCRINE GLANDS

Bartholin's gland	liver	sebaceous gland
breast	mammary gland	sublingual gland
Brunner's gland	meibomian gland, tarsal gland	submandibular gland, submaxillary gland
buccal gland	nabothian gland	
Cowper's gland, bulbourethral gland	pancreas	
	parotid gland	sweat gland
gastric gland	preputial gland	tarsal gland, meibomian gland
lacrimal gland	prostate gland	
Lieberkühn's gland	salivary gland	vestibular gland

ADJECTIVES

4 **secretory**, secretionary, secretive, exudative, transudatory, emissive, excretory, emanative, emanatory, emanational, glandular, merocrine, eccrine, apocrine, holocrine, secreting, lactating, lactational, lactescent, lactiferous, laticiferous, lacrimatory, crying, weeping, sebaceous, sebiferous, sweating, sweaty, sudatory, salivating

5 **of a secretion**, glandular, glandulous, hormonal, endocrine, adrenal, ovarian, testicular, seminal, pineal, pituitary, placental, luteal, thyroidal, exocrine, eccrine, lacrimal (*or* lachrymal), lacrimatory, mammary, lacteal (*or* lacteous), mucous (*or* mucose), mucoid, sudoral, sebaceous, salivary, parotid, sialoid, gastric, pyloric, pancreatic, prostatic

6 **inducing secretion**, lactogenic, sialogogic, lacrimatory, sudatory, sudorific, cholagogic

▶ *37 Pharmacology*

VERBS

7 **secrete**, exude, transude, produce, emit, excrete, discharge, release, liberate, void, eject, give up, give off, emanate, secern, produce, produce secretion, lactate, lacrimate, cry, weep, salivate, sweat, perspire

▶ *371 Expulsion; 560 Excretion*

ADVERBS

8 **glandularly**, glandulously, lactationally, lacteally, weepily, tearfully, sweatily

560 Excretion

What is man, when you come to think upon him, but a minutely set, ingenious machine for turning, with infinite artfulness, the red wine of Shiraz into urine? Karen Blixen.

NOUNS

1 **excretion**, egestion, elimination, expulsion, discharge, ejection, extrusion, emission, emanation, secretion, tran-

sudation, exudation, extravasation, flux, flow, expectoration, ejaculation, ecchymosis, effusion

▶ *371 Expulsion*

2 **defecation**, evacuation, voidance, dejection, purge, purgation, catharsis, clearance, bowel movement (BM), movement, motion, regular motion, diarrhoea, loose bowels, flux, bloody flux, dysentery, lientery, copremesis, constipation, the runs (Inf), the trots (Inf), the shits (Inf), Delhi belly (Inf), GI's (*or* GI shits) (US inf), turistas (US inf), Montezuma's revenge (Inf), Aztec two-step (Inf)

▶ *35 Medicine; 260 Ill Health; 394 Remedy*

3 **urination**, micturation, call of nature, incontinence, weak bladder, enuresis, bed-wetting, nocturnal enuresis, urinalysis, urinometer, wee (Inf), pee (Inf), piss (Inf), slash (Inf), Jimmy Riddle (Inf), leak (Inf)

4 **excrement**, excreta, egesta, ejecta, ejectamenta, waste, waste matter, dejection, dejecture, dejecta, exudation, exudate, transudation, transudate, extravasation, extravasate, effluent, sewage, sewerage

▶ *441 Waste*

5 **faeces**, stool, motion, turd (Inf), feculence, ordure, night soil, jakes (Dial), dung, muck, manure, cow pats, cow flops, cow chips, buffalo chips, guano, dirt, droppings, sheep's currants, coprolite, coprolith, shit (Inf), crap (Inf), poo (Inf), poo-poo (Inf), poop (Inf), ca-ca (Inf), number twos (Inf), big jobs (Inf), dingleberry (Inf), clinker (Inf)

▶ *258 Dirtiness*

6 **urine**, water, urea, uric acid, number ones (Inf), little jobs (Inf), pee (Inf), pee-pee (Inf), wee (Inf), wee-wee (Inf), piss (Inf), piddle (Inf), widdle (Inf)

▶ *433 Water*

7 **pus**, discharge, matter, pustule, mucopus, seropus, ichor, sanies, purulence, pussiness, suppuration, festering, mattering, running, weeping, rankling, gleet, leucorrhoea

8 **sweat**, perspiration, sudor, sweating, perspiring, sudation, sudoresis, diaphoresis, exudation, exudate, induced sweat, honest sweat, cold sweat, sweat of one's brows, beads of sweat, streams of sweat, BO (body odour)

9 **saliva**, spit, spittle, salivation, salivary gland, ptyalism, sialorrhoea, dribble, drivel, slaver, slobber, slabber, froth, foam, cough, coughing, expectoration, spitting, phlegm, catarrh, mucus, rheum, snot

10 **bleeding**, extravasation of blood, nosebleed, ecchymosis, petechia, bruising, bruise, haemorrhage, haemorrhoea, haematemesis, haemoptysis, haematuria, haemophilia

11 **menstruation**, menses, menstrual flow (*or* flux *or* discharge), monthly discharge, catamenia, catamenial discharge, period(s), monthlies, courses, the curse, the Curse of Eve, time of the month, menopause, menarche, amenorrhoea, dysmenorrhoea, epimenorrhoea, hypomenorrhoea, menorrhagia, oligomenorrhoea

12 **dead tissue**, slough, cast, exuviae, ecdysis, moulting, desquamation

13 **lavatory**, toilet, convenience, public convenience, WC (water closet), latrine, head, bathroom, washroom, basement, rest room, comfort station (US), ladies, ladies' (*or* women's) room, little girls' room, powder room, gents, little boys' room, urinal, privy, outhouse, backhouse, earth closet, chemical toilet, loo (Inf), bog (Inf), john (US inf), can (US inf), crapper (Inf), khazi (Inf), shithouse (Inf)

14 **toilet**, stool, throne, commode, closestool, chamber pot, chamber, potty, bedpan, po (*or* poe) (Inf), jerry (Inf), thunderbox (Inf), gazunder (Inf), pisspot (Inf)

VERBS

15 **excrete**, egest, eliminate, pass, expel, discharge, eject, extrude, emit, give off, secrete, transude, exude, extravasate, weep, expectorate, ejaculate, relieve (*or* ease) oneself, go to the toilet, go, answer the call of nature, pay a call (Inf)

▶ *371 Expulsion*

16 **defecate**, have a bowel movement (BM), move one's bowels, move, pass, evacuate, void, purge, shit, have (*or* take) a shit, shit oneself, be caught short, foul, soil, crap (Inf), poo (Inf), do a poo (Inf), ca-ca (Inf), do number twos (Inf), have the runs (*or* trots *or* shits) (Inf)

17 **urinate**, micturate, pass (*or* make) water, wet, wet oneself, wet the bed, stale, piss (Inf), pee (Inf), pee-pee (Inf), wee (Inf), wee-wee (Inf), piddle (Inf), widdle (Inf), do number ones (Inf), spend a penny (Inf), have a slash (Inf), take a leak (Inf), have a Jimmy Riddle (Inf), pump bilge (Inf), siphon the python (Inf), point Percy at the porcelain (Inf), pee oneself (Inf)

18 **fester**, suppurate, run, weep, rankle, matter, come to a head

19 **sweat**, perspire, exude, break out in a sweat, sweat like a trooper (*or* horse *or* pig), swelter, wilt, steam, glow

▶ *493 Heat*

20 **salivate**, water at the mouth, spit, splutter, slobber, slabber, slaver, dribble, drivel, drool, froth (*or* foam) at the mouth, cough, cough up, expectorate, hawk, clear one's throat, blow one's nose

21 **bleed**, spill (*or* lose) blood, bloody, ecchymose, extravasate, haemorrhage

22 **menstruate**, bleed, be on, come on, have one's period, have the curse, have visitors, have one's friends and relations

23 **cast**, slough, shed one's skin, ecdyse, moult, desquamate

ADJECTIVES

24 **excretory**, excretive, excretionary, egestive, eliminative, eliminant, ejective, exudative, transudative, secretory

25 **faecal**, feculent, excremental, excrementary, scatologic, scatological, stercoral, stercorous, stercoraceous, shitty, dungy, cathartic, purgative, laxative, aperient

26 **urinary**, urinative, diuretic, enuretic, incontinent, continent, potty-trained, toilet-trained, house-trained

27 **purulent**, suppurative, festering, pussy, mattering, running

28 **sweaty**, sudatory, sudoric, sudorific, diaphoretic, sweating, perspiring, bathed in sweat, drenched with sweat, wet with sweat, clammy, sticky, wilting, glowing

29 **salivating**, spitting, coughing, spluttering, slobbering, slavering, dribbling, drooling, frothing, foaming, rheumy, watery, mucous, expectorant

30 **bleeding**, haemorrhaging, blood-soaked, bloody, ecchymosed

31 menstrual, catamenial, monthly, menopausal, menstruating, on, on the rag (Inf)

32 cast-off, shed, exuvial, moulting, ecdysial, desquamated

ADVERBS

33 scatologically, shittily, crappily, diuretically, bloodily, sweatily, clammily, stickily

561 Reproduction

Population growth is the primary source of environmental damage. Jacques Cousteau.

NOUNS

1 reproduction, multiplication, proliferation, repetition, replication, duplication, reduplication, copying, photocopying, photocopy, Xerox™, photoreproduction, PMT (photomechanical transfer), printing, letterpress printing, hot-metal printing, offset lithography, publishing, mass production, reconstruction, renovation, renewal, restoration, revival, resuscitation, reanimation, regeneration, resurrection, resurgence, reincarnation, rebirth, palingenesis

► *111 Sameness; 112 Repetition; 125 Imitation; 207 Plurality; 393 Repair; 740 Publication*

2 print, reprint, offprint, photocopy, copy, duplicate, facsimile, edition, new edition, revised edition, clone, replica

► *19 Painting and Sculpture; 41 Photography*

3 propagation, generation, procreation, sex, facts of life, the birds and the bees, sexual intercourse, copulation, coition, breeding, spawning, genetic engineering, gene manipulation, eugenics, genesis, biogenesis, abiogenesis, autogenesis, spontaneous generation, parthenogenesis, virgin birth, fertilization, impregnation, pollination, fecundation, insemination, artificial insemination (AI), AID (artificial insemination by donor), DI (donor insemination), AIH (artificial insemination by husband), IVF (in vitro fertilization), GIFT (gamete intra-Fallopian transfer), test-tube baby, conception, germination, pregnancy, gestation, incubation, hatching, birth, parturition, nativity, happy event, the patter of tiny feet, childbirth, birth rate, natality, fructification, fruition, florescence, efflorescence, flowering

4 development, growth, adolescence, sexual awakening, puberty, adulthood, parenthood, parentage, paternity, maternity, fatherhood, motherhood, loins, womb

► *130 Beginning; 555 Youth; 562 Fertility; 796 Immorality*

5 propagator, pollinator, fertilizer, cultivator, procreator, begetter, parent, father, mother, sire, dam

6 progeny, offspring, child, baby, young, fruit of someone's loins, kid (Inf), nipper (Inf), sprog (Inf)

► *108 Relatedness; 356 Creation*

7 obstetrics, midwifery, childbirth, natural childbirth, childbed, lying-in, confinement, labour, accouchement, travail (Lit), contractions, labour pains, epidural, amniotic fluid, waters, breaking of the waters, birth pangs, breech presentation, delivery, forceps delivery, Caesarian section, Caesarian, embryo, fetus, amniotic sac, bag of waters, caul, umbilical cord, placenta, afterbirth, amniocentesis, alpha-fetoprotein test, afp test, obstetrician, gynaecologist, midwife, pregnant woman, mother-to-be, primigravida, unigravida, multigravida, gooseberry bush, stork

► *35 Medicine; 560 Excretion*

8 organs of reproduction, reproductive organs, genitalia, genitals, pudenda, private parts, privates, female sex organs, vulva, clitoris, labia majora, labia minora, vagina, uterus, womb, cervix, neck of the womb, ovary, Fallopian tubes, ovipositor, ovum, egg, male sex organs, penis, phallus, intromittent organ, male member, privvy member, glans penis, foreskin, testicles, testes, scrotum, prostate, prostate gland, vas deferens, semen, seminal fluid, sperm, spermatozoa, seed, pollen, stigma, style, gynoecium, stamen, anther, cunt (Inf), quim (Inf), pussy (Inf), fanny (Inf), twat (Inf), slit (Inf), cock (Inf), knob (Inf), prick (Inf), dick (Inf), weapon (Inf), tool (Inf), pecker (US inf), willy (*or* willie) (Inf), chopper (Inf), John Thomas (Inf), balls (Inf), nuts (Inf), goolies (Inf), bollocks (Inf), rocks (Inf)

VERBS

9 reproduce, repeat, echo, duplicate, replicate, clone, copy, make a copy of, photocopy, Xerox™, mass-produce, print, reprint, print off, bash off, bash out, turn out, churn out

10 reproduce oneself, conceive, get (*or* become) pregnant, fall, carry, give birth, bring to birth, bring forth, bear, be brought to bed of (Lit), have a baby, have children, drop sprogs (Inf)

11 have young, have progeny, have offspring, lay (eggs), spawn, hatch, drop, foal, lamb, farrow, pup, whelp, calve, cub, kitten, litter, have one's birth, be born, seed oneself, germinate, sprout, bloom, flower, fruit, bear fruit, fructify

12 multiply, burgeon, proliferate, spring up like mushrooms, crop up all over the place, recreate

► *108 Relatedness; 111 Sameness; 125 Imitation; 207 Plurality; 562 Fertility; 740 Publication*

13 propagate, generate, produce, produce offspring, procreate, breed, bring into existence, bring (*or* call) into being, bring into the world, give life to, beget, spawn, engender, father, sire, carry on the line, make pregnant, impregnate, fertilize, fecundate, inseminate, pollinate, hatch, incubate, raise, rear, bring up, raise from seed, bud, graft, take cuttings, layer, air-layer, knock up (Inf)

► *108 Relatedness; 356 Creation; 562 Fertility*

14 have sex, have sexual intercourse, make love, copulate, do it, fuck (Inf), shag (Inf), screw (Inf), shaft (Inf), roger (Inf), lay (Inf), knock (Inf), knock off (Inf), bonk (Inf), have it off (Inf), have it away (Inf)

► *796 Immorality*

ADJECTIVES

15 reproduced, printed, duplicated, copied, repeated, renewed, renewing, re-created, re-creating, reborn, renascent, resurgent, resurrectional, resurrectionary, reappearing, hydra-headed, Phoenix-like

16 reproductive, generative, procreative, procreant, life-giving, originative, seminal, spermatic, germinal, genetic, sexual, unisexual, bisexual, genital, vulvar, clitoral, vaginal, cervical, ovarian, penile, phallic, scrotal, in season, on (*or* in) heat, pregnant, impregnated, fertilized, fecundated, breeding, broody, enceinte, with child, big with, heavy with, gravid, expecting, expecting a baby, expecting a happy event, expectant, in the family way, in an interesting condition, in a delicate condition, eating for two, about to give birth, parturient, in labour, antenatal, perinatal, postnatal, puerperal, obstetric, live-bearing, viviparous, oviparous, parthenogenetic, up the spout (Inf), up the stick (Inf), up the pole (Inf), in the club (Inf), in the pudding club (Inf), with a bun in the oven (Inf), preggers (Inf)

► *35 Medicine; 560 Excretion*

ADVERBS

17 **repeatedly**, in duplicate, in triplicate

18 **reproductively**, genetically, sexually, genitally

562 Fertility

We have been God-like in our planned breeding of our domesticated plants and animals, but we have been rabbit-like in our unplanned breeding of ourselves. Arnold Toynbee.

NOUNS

1 **fertility**, fecundity, fruitfulness, exuberance, luxuriance, lushness, richness, embarrassment of riches, *embarras de richesses* (Fr), abundance, plenty, plenitude, wealth, riot, profusion, rich harvest, bounty, nature's bounty, rich soil, rich earth, Mother earth, hotbed, seedbed, nursery, propagator, cornucopia, horn of plenty, land flowing with milk and honey, milch cow, second crop, aftermath, aftergrowth, Green Revolution

► *43 Agriculture; 217 Sufficiency; 219 Excess*

2 **productiveness**, mass production, productivity, high productivity, boom, economic boom, economic upturn, booming economy, prosperity, overproductiveness, superabundance, superfluity, glut, butter mountain, wine lake, high birth rate, population explosion, baby boom, biotic potential, productive capacity, menarche, menstruation, procreation, reproduction, propagation, fructification, fecundation, fertilization, pollination, resourcefulness, inventiveness, imaginativeness, fertile imagination

► *13 Economics; 219 Excess; 248 Prosperity; 356 Creation; 477 Imagination; 560 Excretion; 561 Reproduction*

3 **fertilizer**, organic fertilizer, manure, farmyard manure, dung, cow dung, guano, compost, bonemeal, hoof and horn, fishmeal, slurry, artificial fertilizer, chemical fertilizer, phosphates, nitrates, potash, ammonium salts, sulphates, lime, marl, dressing, top dressing, mulch, seed, semen, sperm, fertility drug, gonadotrophin

► *43 Agriculture; 258 Dirtiness; 560 Excretion; 561 Reproduction*

4 **fertility cult**, fertility rite, fertility symbol, phallic symbol, phallus, lingam, yoni, Earth Goddess, Earth Mother, Demeter, Ceres

ADJECTIVES

5 **fertile**, fecund, fruitful, fructiferous, fruit-bearing, productive, highly productive, profitable, paying, lucrative, remunerative, high-yielding, generative, prolific, philoprogenitive (Lit), multiparous, teeming, streaming, pouring, copious, abundant, plentiful, plenteous, profuse, bountiful, bounteous, fat, lush, verdant, luxuriant, rich, rife, exuberant, thriving, flourishing, prosperous, booming, pregnant, parturient, heavy with, big with, procreant, procreative, propagatory, regenerative, creative, inventive, resourceful

► *217 Sufficiency; 219 Excess; 248 Prosperity; 356 Creation; 477 Imagination; 561 Reproduction*

VERBS

6 **be fertile**, thrive, flourish, burgeon, bloom, blossom, fructify, produce seeds, seed itself, germinate, conceive, give birth, bear, teem, swarm, pullulate, proliferate, mushroom, spring up like mushrooms, multiply, boom, populate, overpopulate, prosper

► *208 Multitude; 248 Prosperity; 561 Reproduction*

7 **make fertile**, fecundate, fructify, green the desert, make the desert bloom, plant, fertilize, manure, compost, dress, top-dress, mulch, marl, enrich, feed, water, irrigate, impregnate, inseminate, pollinate, propagate, produce, procreate, generate

► *43 Agriculture; 561 Reproduction*

ADVERBS

8 **fruitfully**, productively, profitably, prolifically, abundantly, through nature's bounty, thanks to Mother Nature, creatively, inventively, resourcefully

563 Infertility

Why should human females become sterile in the forties, while female crocodiles continue to lay eggs into their third century? Aldous Huxley.

NOUNS

1 **infertility**, infecundity, fruitlessness, unproductiveness, unproductivity, barrenness, sterility, impotence, celibacy, childlessness, fallowness, aridity, aridness, dryness, drought-stricken land, desert, desert sands, sand dunes, dust bowl, desert island, waste, wasteland, lunar landscape, Arctic waste, Antarctic waste, barren waste, wild, wilderness, desolation, desertification, soil erosion, deforestation, defoliation, scorched earth policy, waste of waters, dying race, menopause, change of life, abortion, spontaneous abortion, miscarriage, falling birth rate, low birth rate, zero population growth, economic decline, recession, stagnation, economic stagnation, slump, depression, unprofitableness, unprofitability, poor return, low yield, dearth, famine, waste of time, waste of effort

► *214 Decrease; 218 Insufficiency; 238 Uselessness; 357 Destruction; 428 Dryness; 441 Waste; 766 Loss*

2 **making infertile**, sterilization, tying the tubes (Inf), hysterectomy, vasectomy, castration, neutering, spaying, gelding

3 **birth control**, contraception, prophylactic, planned parenthood, family planning, contraceptive, IUD (intrauterine device), IUCD (intrauterine contraceptive device), coil, loop, barrier contraceptive, diaphragm, Dutch cap, condom, sheath, French letter (Inf), rubber (Inf), johnny (Inf), female condom, femidom, contraceptive sponge, spermicide, contraceptive pill, the pill, minipill, morning-after pill, abortion pill, male pill, contraceptive injection, rhythm method, coitus interruptus,

ADJECTIVES

4 **infertile**, infecund, fruitless, unfruitful, unproductive, unprolific, barren, sterile, impotent, celibate, childless, fallow, arid, dry, drought-stricken, desert, poor, empty, treeless, gaunt, bleak, stark, bare, sparse, uncultivated, stony, shallow, eroded, withered, shrivelled, dead, blasted, waste, wild, desolate, wasted, stagnating, stagnant, recessionary, unprofitable, depressed, low-yield

▶ *218 Insufficiency; 428 Dryness*

5 **rendered infertile**, unfertilized, on the pill, sterilized, vasectomized, castrated, gelded, neutered, spayed

6 **having no effect**, ineffective, unsuccessful, failed, null and void, addled, abortive

▶ *236 Worthlessness; 238 Uselessness; 247 Failure; 335 Powerlessness*

VERBS

7 **be infertile**, lie fallow, stagnate, rust, rot, run to seed, hide one's abilities, bury one's talents, hide one's light under a bushel, hang fire, prove infertile, fail, come to nothing, come to naught, abort, miscarry, lose the baby, have no issue, have no offspring, die without issue (*or* offspring), be childless

▶ *238 Uselessness; 245 Deterioration; 247 Failure*

8 **make infertile**, sterilize, vasectomize, unman, emasculate, castrate, geld, spay, neuter

9 **practise birth control**, plan one's family, take precautions, use a condom, go on the pill

10 **waste**, lay waste, desolate, deforest, overgraze, overfish

▶ *257 Hygiene; 357 Destruction*

ADVERBS

11 **unproductively**, fruitlessly, impotently, unprofitably

12 **without issue**, without offspring, o.s.p. (obit sine prole)

564 Inhabitant

I am not an Athenian or a Greek, but a citizen of the world.
Socrates.

NOUNS

1 **inhabitant**, inhabiter, native, aborigine, autochthon, indigene, Indian, earliest inhabitant, first comer, local, occupant, occupier, dweller, resident, resider, residentiary, denizen, indweller, inmate, incumbent

▶ *565 Habitat; 566 Humankind; 815 Prison*

2 **inhabitants**, population, native population, populace, people, people at large, public, general public, citizenry, colony, commune, community, neighbourhood, dwellers, residents, household, family, ménage, tribe, clan

▶ *1 Anthropology; 566 Humankind; 574 Commoner*

3 **householder**, head of the household, owner-occupier, freeholder, tenant, sitting tenant, renter, lessee, leaseholder, lodger, roomer, paying guest, boarder, roommate, flatmate, addressee, guest, visitor

▶ *440 Possessions; 733 Address; 763 Possession*

4 **townsman**, townswoman, townsfolk, townspeople, townsperson, towndweller, burgess, burgher, oppidan, citizen, city dweller, city person, metropolitan, urbanite, suburbanite, commuter, townee (Inf), city slicker (Inf), slicker (Inf)

▶ *87 Cities, Towns, and Villages*

5 **countryman**, countrywoman, country gentleman, country-dweller, country cousin, country bumpkin, ruralist, provincial, rustic, peasant, yokel, villager, parishioner, cottager, farmer, smallholder, crofter, Highlander, lowlander, backsettler, bushman (Aus), frontiersman, backwoodsman, apple-knocker (Inf), clod (Inf), hick (US inf), redneck (Inf), cracker (US inf), hayseed (US inf), hillbilly (US inf)

6 **illegal occupant**, squatter, trespasser, illegal immigrant, uninvited guest, invader, gate-crasher, cuckoo (Inf)

7 **settler**, pioneer, precursor, incomer, immigrant, colonist, colonizer, colonial, planter

▶ *126 Originality*

8 **national**, subject, citizen, naturalized citizen, citizen by adoption, holder of dual nationality, citizen of the world, compatriot, fellow countryman (*or* countrywoman), fellow citizen, home towner (US inf)

OFFENSIVE NAMES

Abo (Aus; Aborigine)
Anglo (Aus; person of British descent)
Argie (Argentinian)
Aussie (Australian)
Balt (Aus; person of Baltic descent)
binghi (Aus; Aborigine)
bogtrotter (Irish)
bohunk (US; person from E *or* central Europe)
Canuck (Can; French Canadian)
Chink (*or* Chinky) (Chinese)
crunchie (South African; Afrikaner)
dago (person of Latin descent)
ding (Aus; Italian *or* Greek)
Eyetie (Brit; Italian)
Frog (French person)
gook (US; person from Far East)
goy (gentile)
greaseball (US; Italian)
greaser (US; Mexican)
gringo (person from English–speaking country)
guinea (US; Italian)
gyppo (Brit; Egyptian)
honky (US; White person)
hori (NZ; Maori)
Hun (German)
Hunk (*or* Hunkie) (US; person from E *or* central Europe)
Jackie (*or* Jacky) (Aus; Aborigine)
Jap (Japanese)
Jerry (German)
jim crow (US; Black person)
Jock (Brit; Scots person)
kike (Jew)
kipper (Aus; English person)
Kraut (German)
limey (US; British person)
Mick (Irish person)
munt (Zimbabwe; Black African)
Nip (Japanese)
ofay (US; White person)
Paddy (Irish person)
Paki (Brit; Pakistani)
Pepsi (Can; French Canadian)
polak (Pole)
pom (*or* pommie) (Aus; English person)
redleg (Carib; poor White)
Ruskie (Russian)
Sawney (Scots person)
sheeny (Jew)
shiksa (non–Jewish girl)
Siwash (US; North American Indian)
spade (Black person)
spic (*or* spick *or* spik) (US; Latin American)
spook (White person)
Taffy (Brit; Welsh person)
Uncle Tom (servile *or* obsequious Black person)
Wasp (US; White Anglo–Saxon Protestant)
wetback (US; Mexican)
whitey (*or* whity) (US; White person)
wog (Brit; non–White)
wop (Italian, Spanish, *or* Portuguese)
Yank (*or* Yankee) (American)
yid (Jew)

9 **British inhabitant**, Brit, Briton, John Bull, Englishman (*or* Englishwoman), Pom (Aus inf), Limey (US inf), Scot, Jock (Inf), Jimmy (Inf), Welshman (*or* Welshwoman), Taffy (Inf), Celt, Gael, Northerner, Southerner, Westcountryman (*or* Westcountrywoman), Londoner, cockney, Bristolian, Brummie (Inf), Mancunian, Geordie, Liverpudlian, Scouse (Inf), Glaswegian, Aberdonian

▶ *85 Countries; 86 Regions; 87 Cities, Towns, and Villages; 142 Location; 143 Situation*

10 **US inhabitant**, American, Uncle Sam, Easterner, Eastlander, Westerner, Westlander, Northerner, New Englander, New Yorker, Yankee (Inf), Yank (Inf), GI Joe (Inf)

ADJECTIVES

11 **inhabited**, occupied, occupied by, populated, lived in, indwelt, residential, tenanted, rented, leased, let, freehold, squatted, communal

12 **native**, indigenous, aboriginal, autochthonous (*or* autochthonic *or* autochthonal), ethnic, tribal, local, metropolitan, urban, suburban, rustic, provincial

13 **resident**, residing, living in, dwelling, settled, domiciled, colonial, colonized, naturalized, immigrant

VERBS

14 **inhabit**, dwell, reside, live in, abide in, occupy, lease, rent, lodge, board, take rooms, stay, sojourn, visit

▶ *565 Habitat*

15 **settle**, move in, set up house, domicile, pioneer, immigrate, colonize, people, populate, squat, trespass, gatecrash, crash down (Inf)

565 Habitat

The emergence of intelligence, I am convinced, tends to unbalance the ecology. In other words, intelligence is the great polluter. It is not until a creature begins to manage its environment that nature is thrown into disorder. Clifford D. Simak.

NOUNS

1 **habitat**, habitation, abode, dwelling, dwelling place, domicile, place, place where one lives (*or* resides), residence, place of residence, house, home, roof over one's head, accommodation, quarters, living quarters, lodgings, lodging, billet, rooms, sleeping place, squat, crash pad (Inf), digs (diggings) (Inf), pad (Inf), crib (Inf)

▶ *564 Inhabitant*

2 **environment**, surroundings, habitat, microhabitat, ecosystem, niche, abode, locality, locale, haunt, domain, range, territory, terrain, element, home ground, base, bailiwick, own back yard, neighbourhood, hangout (Inf), stamping ground (Inf)

▶ *30 Earth Science; 142 Location; 143 Situation; 170 Surroundings; 222 Circumstances*

3 **home**, homestead, home-sweet-home, hearth and home, hearth, fireside, inglenook, base, nest, place where one hangs one's hat, home town, birthplace, cradle, homeland, native land, motherland, fatherland

▶ *175 Base*

4 **official residence**, presidential palace, governor's mansion, White House, 10 Downing Street, Chequers, Mansion House, Buckingham Palace, Windsor Castle, Balmoral, embassy, consulate, vicarage, rectory, parsonage, deanery, manse, mansion, palace, castle, château, villa, manor house, grange, hall, lodge, stately home, ancestral hall (*or* seat), estate, pile (Inf)

▶ *7 Religion; 20 Architecture; 573 Aristocrat*

5 **house**, town house, semidetached house, semi, duplex (US), detached house, terraced house, row house, back-to-back, two-up-two-down , split-level house, ranch house, farmhouse, villa, bungalow, dormer bungalow, chalet, cottage, cabin, log cabin, flat, apartment, maisonette, penthouse, duplex apartment, bedsit (*or* bedsitter), studio, granny flat, *pied-à-terre* (Fr), snuggery, love nest

6 **apartment block**, tower block, high-rise flats (*or* apartments), tenement, condominium (US), housing estate

▶ *141 Space; 403 Structure; 410 Container*

7 **room**, chamber, hall, entrance hall, lobby, vestibule, anteroom, gallery, porch, portico, foyer, corridor, passage, landing, mezzanine, living room, sitting room, lounge, reception room, drawing room, front room, best room, parlour, salon, dining room, breakfast room, dinette, dining hall, dining kitchen, canteen, mess, mess room, restaurant, cafeteria, kitchen, kitchenette, back kitchen, galley, utility room, laundry room, larder, pantry, scullery, still room, study, library, studio, workroom, office, den, snuggery, snug, games room, family room, rumpus room (US), playroom, recreation room, bedroom, bedchamber, boudoir, sleeping room, nursery, dormitory, dressing room, bathroom, shower room, washroom, cloakroom, toilet, lavatory, WC, water closet, comfort station (US), smallest room, loo (Inf), lav (Inf), bog (Inf), storeroom, junk room, box room, lumber room, glory hole, cellar, bunker, basement, subbasement, coal hole, attic, garret, loft, garden room, conservatory, sun lounge, solarium, sun porch, greenhouse, glasshouse, orangery, lean-to, outhouse, summer house, gazebo, belvedere, garage, carport, boathouse, hangar, veranda, balcony, patio, piazza

▶ *20 Architecture; 557 Eating*

8 **shelter**, shed, shack, hut, lean-to, outhouse, hutch, booth, bothy (Scot), shanty, hovel, tumbledown shack, squat, derelict house, slum, deri (Inf), hole (Inf), dump (Inf), pigsty (Inf), pigpen (Inf), dive (Inf), joint (Inf), dosshouse (doss) (Inf), flophouse (US inf), kiphouse (Inf), fleabag (US inf)

▶ *782 Poverty*

9 **mobile home**, caravan, trailer, camper, campervan, houseboat, tent, tepee (*or* tipi), wigwam, pavilion

10 **hotel**, motel, motor inn, inn, hostelry, guest house, boarding house, *pension* (Fr), bed and breakfast (B & B), bed and board, board and lodging, hostel, youth hostel, pub (public house), tavern, local (Inf), boozer (Inf)

11 **retreat**, haven, refuge, sanctuary, hideaway, halfway house, sheltered housing, hospice

12 **stall**, fold, barn, stable, byre, sty, pigsty, cowshed, cowhouse, kennel, pound, cattery, coop, henhouse, chicken coop, run, battery, cage, zoo, zoological garden, menagerie, aquarium, fishtank, marine park, sea zoo, aviary, birdhouse, birdcage, dovecote, pigeon loft

► *71 Mammals; 72 Birds; 74 Fishes; 76 Insects and Arachnids; 165 Enclosure*

13 lair, den, cave, hole, covert, sett, holt, burrow, warren, tunnel, earth, drey, nest, eyrie, perch, roost, beehive, anthill

ADJECTIVES

14 inhabiting, abiding, residing, residential, fit for habitation, residentiary, resident, in residence, at home, dwelling, living, staying, domiciled, housed, roofed, lodged, billeted, sheltered

15 environmental, surrounding, neighbourhood, territorial, local, urban, suburban, built-up, metropolitan, towny, inner-city

► *30 Earth Science; 87 Cities, Towns, and Villages*

16 manorial, palatial, presidential, grand, detached, semidetached, terraced, back-to-back, duplex, split-level, single-storey, multistorey, high-rise

VERBS

17 inhabit, abide in, dwell, dwell in, reside in, live in, occupy, squat, stay, sojourn, settle, colonize, populate, people

18 take up residence, hang up one's hat, move in, make one's nest, nest, nestle, perch, roost, burrow, stable, pitch one's tent, camp, encamp, bivouac, quarter, room, board, lodge, put up at (Inf), doss down (Inf), crash (Inf), park one's carcass (Inf), drop anchor (Inf)

19 frequent, haunt, visit, hang out at (Inf)

ADVERBS

20 environmentally, territorially, locally, around, in the vicinity, in the neighbourhood

566 Humankind

The human race will be the cancer of the planet. Julian Huxley.

I love mankind – it's people I can't stand. Charles M. Schultz.

How beauteous mankind is! O brave new world
That has such people in't! William Shakespeare.

NOUNS

1 humankind, people, mankind, womankind, humanity, human race, human species, human beings, Homo sapiens, hominid, man, men, generations of man, peoples of the earth, earthlings, the world, the world population, everyone, everybody, folk, every living soul, the living, the quick (Lit), us, ourselves, grains of sand, blades of grass, fish in the sea

2 human nature, human fallibility, human failing, human frailty, human weakness, mortality, flesh

► *337 Weakness*

3 early human, primitive human, primitive humanity, barbarians, pagans, savages, bushmen, aborigines, ancient man, early humanity, primeval man, primeval humanity, Homo erectus, Stone-Age man, Cro-Magnon man, Homo neanderthalensis, Neanderthal man, anthropoid ape, apeman (*or* apewoman), caveman (*or* cavewoman), cave dweller, troglodytes, Ramapithecus, Pithecanthropus, Peking man, Java man

► *3 History*

4 modern human, civilized humanity, modern man, modern woman, well-bred person, gentleman, lady, educated person, scientific man (*or* woman), political animal, the civilized world, culture, civilization, early civilizations, the ancients, Sumerian, Egyptian, Ethiopian, Babylonian, Assyrian, Persian, Hittite, Hebrew, Aegean, Phoenician, Greek, Roman, Mogul, Chinese, Aztec, Inca

► *244 Improvement; 549 Refinement*

5 study of mankind, anthropology, anthropography, anthropometry, craniometry, craniology, anthropogenesis, somatology, social anthropology, demography, social science, sociology, humanitarianism, humanism, anthroposophy, anthropomorphism, ethnology, ethnography, folklore, mythology

► *1 Anthropology; 2 Sociology*

6 studier of mankind, anthropologist, craniologist, social anthropologist, demographer, sociologist, humanist, ethnographer, folklorist, mythologist

7 person, individual, human being, human, being, man, woman, adult, girl, boy, teenager, adolescent, child, baby, Adamite, mortal, creature, fellow creature, body, soul, living soul, flesh and blood, average person, ordinary person, common man, everyman, everywoman, man (*or* woman) in the street, man on the Clapham omnibus, John Doe, the noble animal, the naked ape, earthling, tellurian, Lord of Creation, God's image, God's creation, I, one, somebody, someone, so and so, such a one, party, customer, character, type, element, important figure, important person, personage, person of note, VIP, man (*or* woman) at the top, celebrity, star, favourite, all (those) concerned, personnel, cast, list of characters, dramatis personae, counted person, head, hand, nose, unit, bod (Inf), guy (US inf), chap (Inf), bugger (Inf), sod (Inf), joe (US inf), Joe Bloggs (Inf), Joe Soap (Inf), the average punter (Inf), top dog (Inf), suit (US inf), the man (US inf), cele (Inf)

► *123 Importance; 555 Youth; 556 Age; 567 Male; 568 Female*

8 humanlike machine, robot, automaton, android, humanoid, cyborg, bionic man, bionic woman

9 group, kinship group, family, clan, brotherhood, fraternity, sorority, clique, set, social group, society, organized society, stratified society, class, social classes, nobility, aristocracy, gentility, upper class, bourgeoisie, middle classes, upper middle class, lower middle class, working class, lower class, public, general public, general population, generality, populace, citizenry, inhabitants, the masses, commonalty, plebs, hoi polloi, common people, common persons, people, folk, you and me, community at large, community, neighbourhood, ghetto, ethnic minority, ethnic group, racial group (*or* type), race, primitive society, tribe, tribalism, the human family, socio-political group, international society, community of nations, European Community (EC), European Economic Community (EEC), comity of nations, United Nations (UN), international cooperation, Joe Public (Inf)

► *2 Sociology; 108 Relatedness; 376 Gathering; 564 Inhabitant; 573 Aristocrat; 574 Commoner; 747 Cooperation*

10 member of society, citizen, nobleman, noblewoman,

aristocrat, patrician, gentleman, lady, bourgeois, white-collar worker, commoner, blue-collar worker, worker, co-worker, colleague, comrade

▶ *573 Aristocrat; 574 Commoner; 578 Worker*

11 **nation**, people, state, country, realm, kingdom, national entity, nationality, statehood, civil society, body politic, political entity, demos, city state, welfare state, civil state, nation state, multiracial state, melting pot, isolationism, noninvolvement, neutrality, Swiss neutrality, Austrian neutrality, alliance of states, commonwealth, Commonwealth of Nations, the Commonwealth, polity, democratic state, democracy, republican state, republic, socialist state, socialism, communistic state, communism, totalitarian state, totalitarianism, dictatorship, nationalism, national consciousness, race consciousness, Pan-Africanism, ultranationalism, chauvinism, jingoism, expansionism, imperialism, colonialism, Lebensraum

▶ *12 Government and Politics; 85 Countries*

ADJECTIVES

12 **human**, mortal, creaturely, fleshly, earthborn, tellurian, anthropoid, humanoid, hominoid, humanlike, subhuman, civilized, anthropological, ethnographical, racial, ethnic, anthropocentric, anthropomorphic, personal, individual, humanistic, bionic

13 **national**, state, civic, civil, governmental, democratic, republican, socialistic, communistic, totalitarian, public, general, communal, tribal, social, societal, cosmopolitan, international, interracial

VERBS

14 **make human**, humanize, anthropomorphize, civilize

ADVERBS

15 **humanly**, mortally, anthropologically, ethnographically, racially, ethnically, personally, individually, personally, humanistically, socially, nationally, internationally

567 Male

How beastly the bourgeois is
especially the male of the species. D. H. Lawrence.

NOUNS

1 **male sex**, masculine gender, man, mankind, manhood, masculinity, manliness, mannishness, virility, virilism, machismo, male chauvinism, misogyny, male exclusiveness, male-dominated society, patriarchy, laddishness (Inf)

2 **male**, male person, man, gentleman, old man, young man, youth, boy, little boy, lad, fellow, he, him, himself, Adam, blade (Lit), swain (Lit), bloke (Inf), guy (US inf), chap (Inf), chappie (Inf), dude (US inf), bozo (US inf), prick (Inf), joker (Inf), card (Inf), cove (Inf), gay dog (Inf), gent (Inf), (old) geezer (Inf), (old) gaffer (Inf), (old) codger (Inf), (old) buffer (Inf), blue-eyed boy (Inf), yob (Inf), young buck (Inf), young Turk (Inf)

▶ *555 Youth; 556 Age*

3 **male title of address**, Mr, mister, Sir (*or* sir), esquire, Esq., Father, master, Lord (*or* lord), my lord (*or* m'lud), his lordship, my good man, my dear man (*or* sir), gentleman, goodman (Lit), monsieur, Herr, Don, dom, señor, senhor, signor, sahib, Sri, babu, tovarisch, comrade, boy, son, sonny, lad, boyo (Inf), man (US inf), fellow (US inf), Mac (Inf), mate (Inf), pal (Inf), chum (Inf), buddy (US inf), bud (US inf), buster (US inf), sport (Aus inf), cock (Inf), squire (Inf), governor (Inf), guvnor (Inf), guv (Inf), Jock (Inf), Jimmy (Inf), Johnny (Inf), pop (Inf), old man (Inf), Mister Charlie (US inf)

▶ *569 Friendship; 575 Title*

4 **boyfriend**, boy, sweetheart, engaged man, fiancé, bridegroom, groom, beau, escort, date, partner, lover, Adonis, lover boy, toy boy (Inf), sugar daddy (Inf), beefcake (Inf), dish (Inf), hunk (Inf), prime beef (Inf), choice meat (Inf)

▶ *593 Love*

5 **single man**, unmarried man, bachelor, available man, unattached male, divorcé, exhusband, widower

6 **macho man**, muscleman, he-man, cocksman (Inf), caveman (Inf), male chauvinist pig (MCP) (Inf)

7 **libertine**, rake, cad, bounder, philanderer, heartbreaker, Casanova, Don Juan, buck, stallion, man of the world, worldly man, gigolo, ladies' man, male prostitute, rent boy, stud (Inf), slag (Inf)

▶ *118 Nonconformity; 796 Immorality*

8 **homosexual**, gay

9 **offensive terms for homosexual**, sissy, pretty boy (Inf), mummy's boy (Inf), nancy (boy) (Inf), homo (Inf), queer (Inf), queen (Inf), faggot (US inf), fag (US inf), pansy (Inf)

10 **bisexual**, AC/DC guy, bi-guy (Inf)

11 **transsexual**, transvestite, cross-dresser

12 **eunuch**, castrate, castrato, capon (US inf)

▶ *337 Weakness*

13 **man in the family**, family man, married man, husband, spouse, live-in lover, widower, househusband, man about the house, father, patriarch, paterfamilias, paternity, fatherhood, son, boy, brother, uncle, nephew, godfather, godson, grandfather, grandson, old man (Inf), daddy (Inf), dad (Inf), pop (Inf), pater (Inf)

▶ *108 Relatedness; 570 Marriage*

14 **liberated man**, new man, male feminist, sensitive man, caring father

15 **menfolk**, men, the boys, the boys in the back room, spear side, stag party (Inf), the lads (Inf)

16 **male animal**, lion, tiger, bull, bullock, bull-calf, ox, steer, stallion, studhorse, stud, entire horse, colt, gelding, stag, buck, hart, boar, hog, ram, tup, he-goat, billy goat, dog, dog fox, tom cat, jack, cock, cockerel, rooster, capon, drake, gander

ADJECTIVES

17 **male**, masculine, manly, macho, virile, muscular, gentlemanly, chivalrous, mannish, manlike, unmanly, effeminate, gay, homosexual, laddish (Inf), butch (Inf), homo (Inf), queer (Inf)

568 Female

One is not born a woman, one becomes one. Simone de Beauvoir.

NOUNS

1 **female sex**, feminine gender, second sex, weaker sex,

gentle sex, fair sex, woman, womankind, womanhood, femininity, feminineness, feminality, muliebrity, womanliness, womanishness, the eternal feminine, girlishness, feminism, women's rights, equal rights, Women's Movement, Women's Liberation, women's lib, gynography, matriarchy, gynarchy, gynocracy, effeminacy, androgyny, gynaecology, gyniatrics, gyniatry, obstetrics

▶ *35 Medicine; 119 Equality; 561 Reproduction*

2 female, female person, woman, lady, old woman, matron, dowager, young woman, girl, little girl, she, her, herself, Eve, maiden (Lit), damsel (Lit), colleen, grisette, midinette, virago, Amazon, sheila (Aus inf), gal (Inf), lassie (Inf)

▶ *555 Youth; 556 Age*

3 female title of address, Miss (*or* miss), Mrs, Ms, Madam (*or* madam), ma'am, marm, mistress, missus, goody (Lit), goodwife (Lit), Dame, Lady, lady, milady, her ladyship, my good lady, my dear woman (*or* lady), mademoiselle, madame, Frau, Fraulein, Donna, signora, signorina, señora, señorita, memsahib, hinny (Dial), lass, lassie (Inf), sister (US inf)

4 girlfriend, girl, sweetheart, bride, escort, date, lover, engaged woman, fiancée, mistress, kept woman

5 single girl, single woman, unmarried woman, virgin, maiden, unmarried mother, bachelor girl, spinster, old maid, unattached female, divorcée, widow

6 loose woman, nymph, nymphet, hussy, *femme fatale* (Fr), nymphomaniac, goer (Inf), slag (Inf), nympho (Inf)

7 prostitute, whore, sex-worker, lady of the night, call girl, harlot, strumpet, tart (Inf), tom (Inf)

▶ *796 Immorality*

8 nasty woman, jade, shrew, minx, nag, witch, bitch (Inf), (old) cow (Inf), (old) bag (Inf)

9 woman considered as a sex object, skirt (Inf), bit of skirt (Inf), doll (Inf), dolly bird (Inf), bird (Inf), chick (Inf), fine fryer (US inf), honey (US inf), a real honey (US inf), cupcake (US inf), baby (Inf), babe (US inf), little mama (US inf), moll (Inf), bint (Inf), crumpet (Inf), cheesecake (Inf), bit of fluff (Inf), piece of fluff (US inf), broad (US inf), dame (US inf), baggage (Inf), tart (Inf), ball-breaker (Inf), cunt (Inf)

10 homosexual, gay, lesbian, Sapphic, tribade, les (Inf), lez (Inf), dyke (Inf), butch (Inf), bulldyke (US inf), bisexual, transsexual, female transvestite, drag king (Inf)

▶ *118 Nonconformity; 593 Love*

11 liberated woman, modern woman, new woman, feminist, sister, women's libber, bra burner, suffragette, career woman, working woman, working wife (*or* mother), superwoman

▶ *391 Liberation; 576 Work*

12 woman in the family, married woman, wife, spouse, live-in lover, ex-wife, widow, housewife, mother, matriarch, materfamilias, maternity, motherhood, daughter, girl, sister, aunt, auntie, niece, godmother, goddaughter, grandmother, granddaughter, old lady (Inf), old woman (Inf), trouble and strife (Inf), ball and chain (Inf), squaw (Inf), mummy (Inf), mum (Inf), mom (Inf), mater (Inf), sis (Inf)

▶ *108 Relatedness; 570 Marriage*

13 womenfolk, women, the girls, the sisterhood, matronage, distaff side, women's quarters, harem, seraglio, zenana, purdah, hen party (Inf), the second (*or* weaker *or* lesser *or* subordinate) sex (Offensive)

14 female animal, lioness, tigress, cow, heifer, mare, filly, hind, doe, vixen, sow, gilt, ewe, ewe-lamb, she-goat, nanny goat, bitch, hen, pen

ADJECTIVES

15 female, feminine, womanly, womanish, effeminate, ladylike, girlish, maidenly, matronly, child-bearing, feminist, feministic, virago-like, Amazonian, lesbian, butch (Inf), dykey (Inf)

569 Friendship

Two are better than one; because they have a good reward for their labour. For if they fall, the one will lift up his fellow: but woe to him that is alone when he falleth; for he hath not another to help him up. Bible: Ecclesiastes.

It is not so much our friends' help that helps us as the confident knowledge that they will help us. Epicurus.

NOUNS

1 friendship, fellowship, companionship, amicableness, amicability, amiableness, amity, acquaintanceship, camaraderie, fraternization, comradeship, colleagueship, togetherness, solidarity, cooperation, concord, harmony, friendliness, making friends, sociability, neighbourliness, goodwill, benevolence, philanthropy, kindness, kindliness, hospitality, warmth, warm-heartedness, warmness, ardency, love, cordiality, courtesy, regard, heartiness, bonhomie, geniality, brotherhood, fraternalism, fraternity, sodality, confraternity, brotherly interest, freemasonry, sorority, sisterhood, sisterly interest, partiality, prejudice, favouritism, partisanship, support, loyal support, mateyness (Inf), palliness (Inf), chuminess (Inf)

▶ *567 Male; 568 Female; 593 Love; 650 Benevolence; 652 Philanthropy; 654 Sociability; 658 Courtesy; 747 Cooperation; 749 Pacification*

2 friendly relations, compatibility, harmony, rapport, sympathy, understanding, good understanding, fellow feeling, community of interest, *esprit de corps* (Fr), mutual support, mutual respect, mutual regard, mutual good will, entente, entente cordiale, good terms, two minds with but a single thought, hands across the sea

3 familiarity, intimacy, fast friendship, close friendship, warm friendship, passionate friendship, closeness, nearness, inseparability, affinity, special affinity, devotion, devotedness, dedication, steadfastness, commitment, firmness, staunchness, constancy, trueness, triedness

▶ *7 Religion; 663 Obedience*

4 act of friendship, vow of loyalty, toast, handshake, handclasp (US), embrace, hug, kiss, peck on the cheek, rubbing noses, open arms, holding hands, dining together

5 friend, mutual friend, acquaintance, companion, fellow, fellow creature, colleague, comrade, shipmate, messmate, playmate, roommate, classmate, schoolmate, schoolfellow, amigo, friend in need (is a friend indeed), circle of friends, butty (Dial), crony (Inf), chum (Inf), pal

(Inf), mate (Inf), compadre (Inf), my man (US inf), buddy (US inf), sidekick (Inf)

6 **close friend**, best friend, dear friend, intimate friend, childhood friend, lifelong friend, friend of the family, girlfriend, boyfriend, boon companion, intimate, confidant (*or* confidante), familiar, brother, sister, best man, bridesmaid, maid (*or* matron) of honour, alter ego, other self, shadow, stable companion, mutual friends, inseparables, birds of a feather, two peas in a pod, bosom pal (Inf), bosom buddy (US inf)

► *555 Youth; 570 Marriage*

7 **famous friendships**, Achilles and Patroclus, Castor and Pollux, Damon and Pythias, David and Jonathan, Nisus and Euryalus, Lewis Carroll and Alice, Wordsworth and Coleridge, Robinson Crusoe and Friday, John Smith and Pocahontas, Tom Sawyer and Huckleberry Finn, Don Quixote and Sancho Panza, the Three Musketeers, the Lone Ranger and Tonto

ADJECTIVES

8 **friendly**, friendlike, cordial, courteous, amicable, amiable, kindly, kind, peaceable, unhostile, sociable, affectionate, gracious, harmonious, pleasant, congenial, compatible, cooperative, agreeable, favourable, hospitable, demonstrative, effusive, back-slapping, ardent, warm, warm-hearted, well-meaning, genial, well-disposed, well-intended, generous, benevolent, philanthropic, companionable, fraternal, confraternal, brotherly, sisterly, neighbourly, welcoming, receptive, hearty, sympathetic, understanding, comradely, simpatico (Inf), matey (Inf), chummy (Inf), pally (Inf), palsy-walsy (Inf), buddy-buddy (Inf)

9 **friends with**, friendly with, acquainted, at home with, in favour, on good terms with, on a good footing, on the right side of, in the good graces of, in the good books of, regarded highly by, in (good) with (Inf)

10 **familiar**, on familiar terms, intimate, on intimate terms, close, near, inseparable, arm-in-arm, hand-in-hand, hand-in-glove, free-and-easy, on visiting terms, on a first-name basis, favourite, hail-fellow-well-met, thick (Inf), thick as thieves (Inf)

11 **devoted**, dedicated, supportive, loyal, true, tried-and-true, tested, faithful, steadfast, constant, committed, firm, fast, staunch, trustful, trustworthy

12 **favourable**, beneficial, helpful, promising, auspicious, propitious, advantageous, useful, profitable

VERBS

13 **befriend**, be friendly with, make friends, make friends with, win friends, cultivate friends, strike up a friendship, strike up an acquaintance, gain the friendship of, have friends, enjoy friendship with, fraternize with, hobnob with, have a wide acquaintance with, get to know, get acquainted, break the ice, make overtures, win friends, win friends and influence people, warm to, show benevolence, have dealings with, keep company with, go around with, become inseparable, stay on good terms, take up with (Inf), knock about with (Inf), get chummy with (Inf), get pally with (Inf), buddy up with (Inf), hit it off with (Inf), become as thick as thieves (Inf)

14 **seek the friendship of**, make friendly overtures to, extend the hand of friendship, seek the company of, make advances, court, pay court to, pay addresses to, woo, run after, date, take out, go out with, make up to (Inf), play up to (Inf), frat (Inf), cotton up (*or* on) to (US inf), shine up to (US inf), suck up to (Inf)

15 **be hospitable**, entertain friends, serve as host (*or* hostess), act as host (*or* hostess), entertain, greet, shake hands, clasp hands (US), welcome, welcome with open arms, embrace, introduce, acquaint, present, make a toast, carve, serve, do the honours

16 **be favourable**, provide a benefit, help, promise, seem propitious, serve a use, profit

ADVERBS

17 **in friendship**, in a friendly way, in a friendly spirit, as friends, cordially, courteously, with a courteous manner, amicably, amiably, peaceably, sociably, affectionately, with affection, graciously, harmoniously, pleasantly, under pleasant circumstances, compatibly, cooperatively, agreeably, favourably, kindly, with kindness, hospitably, effusively, ardently, warmly, with warmth, warm-heartedly, with a warm heart, heartily, genially, generously, benevolently, fraternally, receptively, with open arms, sympathetically

18 **intimately**, in an intimate fashion, familiarly, closely, inseparably, arm in arm, hand in hand, hand in glove

19 **devotedly**, with devotion, supportively, in support, loyally, from loyalty, with loyalty, truly, faithfully, steadfastly, constantly, committedly, firmly, fastly, staunchly, trustfully, in (*or* with) good trust, trustworthily

20 **favourably**, beneficially, helpfully, with a helping hand, promisingly, with promise, auspiciously, propitiously, advantageously, usefully, profitably, in a profitable way

570 Marriage

Happiness in marriage is entirely a matter of chance. Jane Austen.

Wives are young men's mistresses, companions for middle age, and old men's nurses. Francis Bacon.

But if they cannot contain, let them marry: for it is better to marry than to burn. Bible: I Corinthians.

One fool at least in every married couple. Henry Fielding.

Marriage is a great instititition, but I'm not ready for an institution, yet. Mae West.

NOUNS

1 **marriage**, matrimony, holy matrimony, wedlock, holy wedlock, conjugality, union, sacrament of marriage, match, one flesh, alliance, married status, married state, wedded state, state of matrimony, conjugal bliss, nuptial bond, marriage tie, wedded bliss, weddedness, wifehood, husbandhood, spousehood, coverture (Lit), bridal bed, marriage bed, bridebed, cohabitation, living as man and wife, tying the knot (Inf), taking the plunge (Inf), getting hitched (Inf), shacking up (Inf)

► *7 Religion; 593 Love; 597 Joy*

2 **alliance**, merger, union, link, connection, consolida-

tion, association, amalgamation, partnership, tie-up, hook-up

3 types of marriage, monogamy, monogyny, monandry, polygamy, Mormonism, polygyny, polyandry, bigamy, digamy, deuterogamy, trigamy, second marriage, remarriage, morganatic marriage, marriage of convenience, *mariage de convenance* (Fr), love match, levirate, leviration, left-handed marriage, companionate marriage, trial marriage, common-law marriage, picture marriage, interfaith marriage, mixed marriage, intermarriage, interracial marriage, intercaste marriage, miscegenation, exogamy, endogamy, misalliance, mésalliance, spiritual marriage, free union, free love, compulsory marriage, arranged marriage, concubinage, homosexual marriage, lesbian marriage, marriage by proxy

4 marriageability, marriageableness, nubility, marriageable age, age of consent, ripeness, fitness for marriage, good match, proper match, suitable match, suitable party, eligible party, eligible bachelor

5 wedding, wedding ceremony, wedding service, white wedding, church wedding, nuptial Mass, nuptial benediction, marriage vows, nuptial vows, nuptials, hymeneal rites, betrothal, spousal, civil wedding, civil ceremony, registry (*or* register) office wedding, court house wedding (US), marriage by the justice of the peace (US), solemn wedding, quiet wedding, elopement, Gretna Green wedding, Las Vegas wedding (US), forcible wedlock, espousal (Lit), tying the knot (Inf), shotgun wedding (Inf)

6 general terms, marriage licence, wedding announcement, wedding shower (US and Aus), wedding invitation, wedding rehearsal, wedding day, wedding morning, wedding bells, ring, wedding ring, wedding banns, wedding canopy, wedding march, wedding music, wedding song, marriage song, nuptial song, nuptial ode, hymeneal, prothalamium, epithalamium, marriage procession, wedding dress, wedding veil, saffron veil, saffron robe, wedding reception, wedding present (*or* gift), bridal bouquet, wedding cake, wedding breakfast, marriage feast, marriage toast, wedding photographs, honeymoon, bridal chamber, honeymoon suite, bridal suite, marriage lines (Inf)

► *601 Celebration*

7 bridal party, bride, bridal attendant, bridesmaid, maid (*or* matron) of honour, young matron, attendant, flower girl, bridegroom, groom, best man, usher, page, pageboy, train-bearer

8 spouse, espouser, espoused, bride, blushing bride, war bride, bridegroom, groom, one's promised, one's betrothed, soul mate, helpmate, helpmeet, affinity, marriage partner, partner, faithful spouse, better half (Inf), GI bride (US inf)

9 married couple, the happy couple, bridal pair, newlyweds, honeymooners, man and wife, *vir et uxor* (L), one flesh, Mr and Mrs, Darby and Joan, Philemon and Baucis

10 married man, husband, househusband, consort, benedick, monogamist, monogynist, old man, lord and master, henpecked husband, injured husband, cuckold, second husband, much-married man, bigamist, polygamist, polygynist, Solomon, Mormon, Bluebeard, hubby (Inf), goodman (Lit)

11 married woman, wife, housewife, lady, good lady, old lady, matron, feme covert (Lit), second wife, wife in all but name, common-law wife, concubine, goodwife (Lit), goody (Lit), better half, missis (*or* missus) (Inf), trouble and strife (Inf), squaw (Inf), old dutch

12 partner, cohabitant, live-in lover, common-law wife (*or* husband)

13 matchmaker, marriage broker, *shadchan* (Yiddish), matrimonial agent, go-between, marriage adviser, marriage guidance counsellor, mediator, marriage bureau, dating agency, lonely hearts club, lonely hearts column, dating service, computer dating

► *748 Mediation*

14 gods and goddesses of marriage, Hymen, Hera, Juno, Teleia, Pronuba, Frigg

VERBS

15 marry, get married, wed, say "I do", couple, become one, affiance, publish the banns, contract matrimony, take a wife, ask for one's hand, take a husband, bestow one's hand upon, accept a proposal, take for better or for worse, quit the single state, elope, run away, cohabit, live together, live as man and wife, share one's bed and board, set up house together, honeymoon, go on honeymoon, consummate one's marriage, marry well, marry into money, make a good match, mismarry, make a bad match, marry in haste, repent at leisure, remarry, rewed, commit bigamy, intermarry, miscegenate, betroth (Lit), plight one's troth (Lit), espouse (Lit), wive (Lit), receive one's marriage lines (Inf), get spliced (Inf), tie the knot (Inf), take the plunge (Inf), make an honest woman of (Inf), lead to the altar (Inf), get hitched (Inf), hook up with (Inf)

16 join in marriage, join in holy wedlock, join, unite in holy wedlock, unite, celebrate a marriage, conduct the ceremony, conduct the wedding, read the wedding vows, read the wedding service, tie the wedding knot, tie the nuptial knot, make one, pronounce man and wife, give in marriage, give away, marry off, bestow in marriage

17 matchmake, make a match, match, mate, find a mate for, find a husband for, find a wife for, arrange a marriage

18 live together, cohabit, shack up with (Inf)

19 merge, unite, ally, link, connect, consolidate, associate, amalgamate, form a partnership, tie up with, hook up with

ADJECTIVES

20 matrimonial, marital, conjugal, connubial, nuptial, hymeneal, spousal, premarital, concubinal, concubinary, matronly, wifely, bridal, husbandly

21 married, wedded, united, espoused, partnered, joined, paired, coupled, mated, newlywed, matched, ill-matched, made man and wife, one, made one, one bone and one flesh, in double harness, remarried, hitched (Inf), spliced (Inf), hooked (Inf)

22 marriageable, nubile, eligible, suitable, fit for marriage, ripe for marriage, of (marriageable) age, betrothed, engaged, promised, affianced, plighted, spoken for

23 monogamous, bigamous, digamous, polygamous, polygynous, polyandrous, morganatic, miscegenetic

ADVERBS

24 matrimonially, in the way of marriage, in holy wedlock, like man and wife, maritally, conjugally, connubially, nuptially, in double harness, as one, monogamously, bigamously, with two wives, polygamously, morganatically

571 Divorce and Widowhood

Divorce? Never. But murder often! Sybil Thorndike, when asked if she had considered divorcing her husband.

NOUNS

1 divorce, divorcement, dissolution of marriage, divorce decree, decree nisi, decree absolute, annulment, decree of nullity, no marriage, breakdown of marriage, nonconsummation of marriage, broken marriage, broken home, marriage on the rocks, breakup, split-up, split, grass widowhood, grass widowerhood

► *372 Separation*

2 separation, legal separation, judicial separation, estrangement, living apart, desertion, impediment (Lit)

► *355 Relinquishment*

3 divorce court, divorce case, matrimonial cause, co-respondent, grounds for divorce, incompatibility, cruelty, mental cruelty, adultery, divorce settlement, maintenance, alimony, custody of children, visiting rights

► *651 Malevolence; 780 Money; 796 Immorality*

4 divorced person, divorcer, divorced woman, divorcée, divorced man, divorcé, grass widow (*or* widower)

5 widowhood, widowerhood, weeds, widow's weeds, grass widowhood, grass widowerhood

► *551 Dress; 582 Death*

6 surviving spouse, survivor, widow, dowager, dowager queen, queen mother, war widow, grass widow, widow woman (Dial), merry widow, widower, grass widower, widowman (Dial), relic (Lit), golf widow (Inf), baseball widow (US inf)

VERBS

7 divorce, obtain a divorce, get divorced, dissolve one's marriage, separate, live separately, live apart, part, break up, split up, split, sever, come to a parting of the ways, unmarry, untie the knot, sue for divorce, file (suit) for divorce, grant a final decree, grant an annulment, grant a decree of nullity (Lit), annul a marriage, put asunder, put away, revert to the single state, revert to bachelorhood, regain one's freedom

8 desert, abandon, leave, walk out, come to a parting (of the ways)

9 widow, bereave, die before one's spouse, make a widow, make a widower, leave one's wife a widow, leave one's husband a widower

10 be widowed, outlive one's spouse, survive one's spouse, lose one's husband (*or* wife), mourn one's husband (*or* wife), put on widow's weeds

ADJECTIVES

11 divorced, dissolved, separated, legally separated, split, estranged, living apart, deserted, abandoned, on the rocks (Inf)

12 widowed, husbandless, widowered, wifeless, widowish, widowlike

ADVERBS

13 without one's spouse, without one's husband, without one's wife, by decree nisi (Lit), by decree absolute (Lit), by decree of nullity (Lit), by annulment, in estrangement, apart

572 Celibacy

Marriage may often be a stormy lake, but celibacy is almost always a muddy horse-pond. Thomas Love Peacock.

NOUNS

1 celibacy, unmarried condition, unwed condition, singleness, single state, single blessedness, bachelorhood, spinsterhood, independence, misogamy, misogyny, misandry

► *250 Freedom; 653 Misanthropy*

2 virginity, chastity, continence, abstinence, life of abstinence, self-denial, lack of sex, maidenhood, maidenhead, purity

► *795 Morality*

3 monasticism, monastic order, celibate order, holy orders, reclusive life, solitary state, Encratism, spiritual marriage, the veil

► *7 Religion*

4 celibate person, celibate, eunuch, religious celibate, Encratite, monk, monastic, priest, nun, bride of Christ, agamist, recluse, hermit, virgin, virgo intacta, vestal, vestal virgin, Virgin Mary, the Virgin, virtuous man, Galahad, virtuous woman, Lucretia, celibate goddess, Diana, Artemis

5 single person, single man (*or* woman), unmarried man (*or* woman), unwed man (*or* woman), unattached man (*or* woman), single, bachelor, confirmed bachelor, spinster (*or* spinstress), *femme sole* (Lit), debutant (*or* debutante), maiden, maiden lady, maid, single girl, bachelor girl, lone woman, maiden aunt, old maid, enemy of marriage, misogamist, misogynist, misandrist, (old) bach (Inf)

ADJECTIVES

6 celibate, celibatarian, unmarried, unwedded, unwed, single, sole (Lit), spouseless, wifeless, husbandless, unpartnered, unmated, mateless, spinsterly, spinsterish, spinsterlike, old-maidish, maiden, maidenly, bachelorly, bachelorlike, unwooed, unasked, unconsummated, independent, unattached, free, fancy-free, on the shelf, misogamic, misogynous, misandrous

► *247 Failure*

7 virginal, virgin, continent, abstinent, chaste, pure, innocent, maidenly, intact

8 monastic, monachal, monkish, nunnish, priestly, Encratite

VERBS

9 be celibate, practise celibacy, impose celibacy on oneself, remain unmarried, stay single, live alone, have a bachelor's flat, have a bachelor's apartment (US), keep bachelor's hall, live in single blessedness, have no offers, receive no proposals, sit on the shelf, bach (it) (Inf)

10 be continent, be chaste, remain a virgin, abstain, stay pure, have no sex, forgo sex

11 be monastic, live like a monk, live like a nun, take the veil, take oneself to a nunnery, become a bride of Christ, take holy orders, live like a hermit

ADVERBS

12 celibately, singly, solitarily, by oneself, independently, freely, without obligations, virginally, continently, abstinently, chastely, purely, monastically, like a monk, like a nun

573 Aristocrat

Democracy means government by the uneducated, while aristocracy means government by the badly educated. G. K. Chesterton.

The Stately Homes of England
How beautiful they stand,
To prove the upper classes
Have still the upper hand. Noël Coward.

NOUNS

1 nobleman, noblewoman, noble, lord, lady, duke, duchess, marquis, marquess, marquise, marchioness, margrave, margravine, count, countess, earl, viscount, viscountess, baron, baronet, knight, gentleman, gentlewoman, grand duke, peer, life peer, titled person, blueblood, optimate, patrician, toff (Inf), upper-class twit (Inf), Lord Muck (Inf), Lady Muck (Inf), Sloane Ranger (Inf), nob (Inf), gent (Inf)

2 aristocracy, nobility, lordship, *ancien régime* (Fr), peerage, dukedom, earldom, viscounty, viscountcy, baronetcy, gentry, landed gentry, ruling class, upper classe, gentlefolk, elite, high society, beau monde, nobs (Inf), top set (Inf), jet set (Inf)

3 nobleness, nobility, kingliness, quality, virtue, distinction, lineage, pedigree, gentility, noble family, dynasty, good breeding, line, ancestory

ADJECTIVES

4 aristocratic, noble, blue blooded, thoroughbred, ennobled, titled, high-class, upper-class, U (Inf), gentlemanly, ladylike, well-bred, ducal, lordly, princely, wellborn, high-born, patrician, baronial, high-caste, classy (Inf), first-class, top-drawer (Inf), of good family

VERBS

5 make noble, ennoble, raise to the peerage, knight, kick upstairs (Inf)

574 Commoner

I have no concern for the common man except that he should not be so common. Angus Wilson.

NOUNS

1 plebeian, pleb (Inf), man-in-the-street, normal person, ordinary bloke, regular guy, prole, proletarian, everyman, underling, Mr Nobody, John Bull, common man, little man, bourgeois, yokel, peasant, rustic, bumpkin, country bumpkin, country cousin, hillbilly, hick (Inf), serf, villein, husbandman, churl, Essex man (*or* girl) (Inf), Joe Public (Inf)

2 the common people, the commons, commonalty, the people, the masses, proletariat, hoi polloi, rank and file, grass roots, lower orders, middle classes, suburbanites, working classes, bourgeoisie, vulgar herd, great unwashed, have nots, the world and his wife (Inf), Tom, Dick, and Harry (Inf), normals (Inf), Sharons (Inf)

ADJECTIVES

3 common, usual, normal, average, plebeian, provincial, of the people, titleless, low-down, second-class, lowborn, low-caste, proletarian, plebby (Inf), of humble birth

4 ordinary, plebeian, simple, rustic, unsophisticated, plain, common, parvenu, vulgar, uncultured, primitive, infra dig, non-U (Inf)

575 Title

Do you want a dukedom or anything like that? Queen Elizabeth II, to Winston Churchill on his retirement.

NOUNS

1 right, birthright, honour, knighthood, glorification, celebrity, renown, name, note, fame, glory, station, order, lionization, handle, dedication, commeration, conservation, sanctification, enthronement, knighting, ennoblement, exalting, canonization, beatification

2 entitlement, due, expectation, obligation, duty

3 honours, battle honours, accolade, favour, award, medal, ribbon, prize, gong (Inf)

4 titleholder, possessor, holder, owner, landowner, landlord, honoured, guest, knight, lord, lady

ADJECTIVES

5 entitled, worthy, deserving, meritorious, renowned, celebrated, sung, famous, fabled, illustrious

6 worshipful, honoured, right honourable, reverent, princely, lordly, majestic

VERBS

7 be entitled to, earn, deserve, be worthy of, claim, expect

576 Work

When work is a pleasure, life is a joy! When work is a duty, life is slavery. Maxim Gorky.

Work expands so as to fill the time available for its completion. Cyril Northcote Parkinson.

The only place where success comes before work is a dictionary. Vidal Sassoon.

NOUNS

1 work, labour, toil, industry, assigned work, assignment, easy work, labour of love, hard work, heavy work, uphill work, a long haul, warm work, exhausting work, punishing work, backbreaking work, spadework, donkey-work, legwork, manual work, manual labour, getting one's hands dirty, sweat of one's brow, sweat, everyday work, daily grind, housework, kitchen work, garden work, fieldwork, farmwork, school work, chores, travail, thankless task, drudgery, work without pay, slavery, grind, strain, swink (Lit), dreary routine, treadmill, grindstone, hack work, penal work, hard labour, breaking stones, penalty, forced labour, corvee, compulsion, fatigue, fatigue duty, spell of duty, duty, piecework, taskwork, take-home work, homework, outwork, journeywork, fag (Inf), shitwork (Inf)

2 **task**, chore, job, unpleasant job, operation, exercise, assignment, project, commission, deed, feat, trick, shift, stint, stretch, bout, spell of work, period of work, extra work, overtime, job of work, stroke of work, hand's turn, working life, working week, working day, man-hours

▶ *276 Time Span; 340 Action; 354 Undertaking; 356 Creation; 810 Duty*

3 **job**, occupation, employment, profession, trade, métier, business, line of work, line of business, career, vocation, calling, mission, craft, racket (Inf), game (Inf)

4 **exertion**, effort, attempt, endeavour, struggle, straining, strain, stress, might and main, tug, squeeze, pull, push, stretch, rub, scrub, heave, lift, throw, drive, force, pressure, full pressure, maximum pressure, unbearable pressure, energy, applied energy, directed energy, power, manpower, horsepower, ergonomics, mighty effort, impressive effort, the hard way, muscle, muscle power, elbow grease, sweat of one's brow, pains, taking pains, operoseness, assiduity, elaboration, overwork, overexertion, overactivity, overdoing it, working oneself to death, battle, campaign, fray, ado, hassle, trouble, toil and trouble, busman's holiday (Inf)

▶ *334 Power; 342 Activity; 353 Attempt*

5 **exercise**, practice, regular practice, drill, training, the bar, preparation, warm-up, PE (physical education), PT (physical training), keep fit, keeping fit, running, jogging, cycling, walking, swimming, rowing, gymnastics, weightlifting, yoga, isometrics, eurhythmics, callisthenics, work-out, aerobics, athletics, games, sports, races, sport, pumping iron (Inf)

▶ *243 Preparation; 336 Strength; 342 Activity*

VERBS

6 **work**, labour, be busy, do easy work, do hard work, work at home, freelance, work in the field, toil, drudge, fag, grind, slog, peg away, moil (Dial), sweat, work up a sweat, work up a lather, clean, scrub, rub, lift, heave, pull, haul, tug, push, shove, dig, spade, do the work, soil one's hands, get one's hands dirty, spit on one's palms, clock in (*or* on), punch in (US), begin, get down to it, set about, set to, take one's coat off, roll up one's sleeves, finish the job, quit work, clock out (*or* off), punch out (US), earn a wage, be a breadwinner, get on the gravy train (Inf), make short work of, make up for lost time, go slow, continue working, keep at it, plod, persevere, work hard, work all day, work all week, work a forty-hour week, do a nine-to-five (Inf), work overtime, work double time, do two jobs, work double, work shifts, work day shifts, work night shifts, shift, work all hours, work night and day, burn the midnight oil, burn the candle at both ends, slave, slave away, beaver away, work one's fingers to the bone, work like a galley slave, work like a horse, work like a Trojan, work oneself to death, work oneself into the grave, overdo it, overwork, make work, sweat blood (Inf), hump (Inf), ply the oar (Inf), moonlight (Inf)

▶ *130 Beginning; 340 Action; 342 Activity; 346 Operation; 640 Perseverance*

7 **work for**, serve, minister to, put to work, employ, task, tax, fatigue

▶ *261 Tiredness; 392 Help*

8 **exert oneself**, strive, strain, struggle, apply oneself, put one's best foot forward, make an effort, try, attempt, endeavour, travail, bestir oneself, spare no effort, do one's utmost, try one's best, put oneself out, trouble oneself, leave no stone unturned, turn every stone, use one's best endeavours, do all one can, go to any lengths, move heaven and earth, pull out all the stops, put one's heart and soul into it, put one's back into it, strain to the utmost, strain every nerve, use every muscle, give one's all, love one's job, have one's heart in one's work, force one's way, elbow one's way, drive through, wade through, persevere, hammer at, slog at, battle, campaign, take action, go all out (Inf), bend over backwards (Inf), sweat blood (Inf)

▶ *340 Action; 342 Activity; 353 Attempt; 636 Willingness*

9 **exercise**, practise, drill, train, prepare, warm up, limber up, keep fit, run, jog, cycle, walk, swim, work out

ADJECTIVES

10 **working**, labouring, busy, industrious, employed, born to toil, horny-handed, drudging, sweating, grinding, slogging, hard-working, plodding, persevering, tireless, energetic, active, painstaking, thorough, attentive, diligent, assiduous, exercising, practising, gymnastic, athletic, on the go (Inf), hard at it (Inf)

▶ *342 Activity; 471 Attention; 640 Perseverance*

11 **laborious**, strenuous, full of labour, involving effort, requiring great effort, gruelling, punishing, unremitting, tiring, very tiring, exhausting, backbreaking, crushing, killing, toilsome, troublesome, weary, wearisome, painful, burdensome, heroic, Herculean, arduous, hard, heavy, uphill, difficult, hard-fought, hard-won, thorough, painstaking, laboured, elaborate, detailed, fiddling, fussy, nit-picking (Inf)

▶ *264 Difficulty*

ADVERBS

12 **laboriously**, arduously, strenuously, energetically, lustily, heartily, the hard way, manually, by hand, by the sweat of one's brow, on the treadmill, with heart and soul, with might and main, with all one's might, on all cylinders, tooth and nail, hammer and tongs, for all one is worth, to one's utmost, on overtime, on double time

577 Workshop

The Continent will not suffer England to be the workshop of the world. Benjamin Disraeli.

An art can only be learned in the workshop of those who are winning their bread by it. Samuel Butler.

NOUNS

1 **workshop**, workroom, workplace, place of work, work-

ing area, working space, laboratory, research laboratory, lab, studio, atelier, study, den, library, plant, installation, industrial estate, science park, works, factory, manufacturing plant, yard, sweatshop, mill, cotton mill, loom, sawmill, paper mill, foundry, metalworks, steelyard, steelworks, smelter, furnace, blast furnace, forge, smithy, stithy (Dial), power station, power plant, powerhouse (US), gasworks, waterworks, brickworks, quarry, mine, colliery, coalmine, pit, coalface, stannary, tin mine, mint, store, arsenal, armoury, dockyard, shipyard, slips, wharf, dock, barn, stable, construction site, building site, brownfield site, excavation site, refinery, distillery, brewery, malt house, malting, shop floor, bench, assembly line, production line, farm, dairy, creamery, stock farm, nursery, tree farm, sewing room, kitchen, laundry room, laundry, shop, office, main office, head office, branch office, subsidiary office, large office, executive office, small office, cubbyhole, bureau, business house, company headquarters, company, firm, offices, government offices, congressional offices (US), parliamentary offices, secretariat, industrial area, polluted area, industrial town, manufacturing town, hive of industry, activity, Rust Belt (US inf)

▶ *43 Agriculture; 334 Power; 342 Activity ; 356 Creation; 439 Store; 565 Habitat*

578 Worker

Workers of the world, unite. Karl Marx.

NOUNS

1 **worker**, employee, hand, operative, working man (*or* woman), voluntary worker, charity worker, volunteer, participator, social worker, philanthropist, independent worker, freelance, freelancer, self-employed person, housewife, hausfrau, chief cook and bottle-washer, toiler, moiler (Dial), drudge, hack, flunky (*or* flunkey), menial, factotum, handyman, wallah (*or* walla), servant, domestic, servant, domestic, butler, maid, cook, chauffeur, gardener, cleaner, charwoman, help, home help, hewer of wood and drawer of water, beast of burden, busy person, Stakhanovite, jack of all trades, maid of all work, professional person, businessman, businesswoman, career woman, executive, breadwinner, earner, salary earner, wage earner, trade unionist, intellectual, professor, teacher, brain worker, scientist, artist, artistic worker, writer, performer, player, actor, actress, dancer, ballet dancer, singer, opera singer, musician, orchestra conductor, orchestra director (US), executant, journalist, newsman (*or* woman), newscaster, anchorperson, anchorman, anchorwoman, presenter, clerical worker, office worker, desk worker, white-collar worker, blackcoat worker, secretary, executive assistant, personal assistant (PA), girl Friday, shop assistant, seller, artisan, workman, labourer, unskilled labourer, casual labourer, day labourer, agricultural labourer, farm worker, farmhand, farmer, pieceworker, manual worker, blue-collar worker, factory worker, factory hand, construction worker, excavator, road worker, roadman, ganger, platelayer, docker, stevedore, packer, meatpacker, porter, coolie (*or* cooly), dustman, gofer (US inf), dogsbody (Inf), fag (Inf), slave (Inf), galley slave (Inf), beaver (Inf), bee (Inf), busy bee (Inf), ant (Inf), wage slave (Inf), boffin (Inf), navvy (Inf)

▶ *43 Agriculture; 117 Conformity; 137 Class; 256 Cleanness; 342 Activity; 401 Servant; 636 Willingness; 652 Philanthropy; 764 Sharing; 778 Sale*

2 **artisan**, artificer, skilled worker, master, proficient person, technician, semiskilled worker, tradesman, journeyman, apprentice, learner, craftsman, craftswoman, handicraftsman, handicraftswoman, potter, carpenter, joiner, carver, woodworker, cabinet-maker, turner, sawyer, cooper, wright, wheelwright, wainwright, coachbuilder, shipwright, shipbuilder, boat-builder, builder, architect, master mason, mason, housebuilder, bricklayer, plasterer, tiler, thatcher, painter, decorator, metalworker, forger, smith, blacksmith, tinsmith, goldsmith, silversmith, gunsmith, locksmith, tinker, repairman, knife-grinder, miner, coal miner, collier, steelworker, foundryman, mechanic, automobile mechanic, car mechanic, aircraft mechanic, machinist, fitter, engineer, civil engineer, mining engineer, mechanical engineer, electrical engineer, radio engineer, television engineer, computer engineer, power-plant worker, gasman, plumber, welder, electrician, weaver, spinner, tailor, cutter, needlewoman, clothier, watchmaker, clockmaker, jeweller, glass-blower, chippie (Inf), mister fix-it (US inf), grease monkey (Inf)

3 **agent**, operator, doer, practitioner, perpetrator, minister, officer, functionary, instrument, tool, representative, rep, delegate, convention delegate, official, spokesman, spokeswoman, spokesperson, mediator, go-between, deputy, proxy, substitute, executor, executrix, executive, operative, administrator, manager, industrialist, manufacturer, producer, maker, wholesaler, middleman, merchant, dealer, broker, store owner, shop owner, employer

▶ *340 Action; 348 Instrumentality; 356 Creation; 398 Delegate; 400 Master; 762 Substitution; 776 Trade; 778 Sale*

4 **personnel**, employees, workers, workpeople, staff, workforce, labour force, company, organization, team, gang, squad, crew, complement, cadre, nucleus, band, cast, dramatis personae, hands, men, women, payroll, labour, casual labour, labour pool, manpower, working classes, proletariat

▶ *21 Drama; 137 Class; 376 Gathering*

5 **partner**, associate, co-worker, fellow worker, colleague, workmate, mate

▶ *392 Help; 747 Cooperation*

579 Management

By working faithfully eight hours a day you may eventually get to be a boss and work twelve hours a day. Robert Frost.

VERBS

1 **manage**, administer, organize, orchestrate, mastermind, carry out goals, govern, rule, regulate, control, control results, supervise, supervise staff, watch over, superintend, motivate, direct, lead, oversee, have charge of, have in one's charge, manipulate, manoeuvre, pull the

strings, influence, have the measure of, know, handle, conduct, run, carry on, minister, prescribe, caretake, invigilate, proctor (US), nurse, look after, take care of, hold the portfolio, hold the purse strings, hold the reins, keep order, police, legislate, pass laws, make legal, sway, have a way with, be the boss, have taped (Inf), call the shots (Inf)

► *246 Success; 395 Influence; 396 Authority; 436 Provisions; 455 Knowledge; 480 Persuasion; 665 Carefulness*

2 **direct**, command, lead, be in charge, head, head up (Inf), boss, lead the way, pioneer, precede, come before, dictate, wear the trousers, hold power, hold office, hold (*or* have) a responsible position, have responsibility, have overall responsibility, assume command, assume responsibility, incur a duty, preside, take the chair, be in the chair, chair, captain, skipper, pilot, stroke, cox, steer, navigate, take the helm, hold the tiller, hold the reins, crack the whip, point, point to, show, show the way, indicate, advise, counsel, shepherd, guide, conduct, lead on, escort, accompany, channel, canalize, funnel, route, train, lead over, lead through, introduce, compere, host, act as a master of ceremonies, honcho (US inf), call the shots (Inf), emcee (Inf)

► *129 Precedence; 223 Accompaniment; 324 Direction; 397 Command; 713 Advice; 743 Identification; 810 Duty*

NOUNS

3 **management**, managing, administration, organization, orchestration, control, conduct, conduct of affairs, motivation, manipulation, running, handling, managership, stewardship, proctorship, agency, commission, power, authority, supervision, superintendence, overview, surveillance, care, charge, patronage, protection, art of management, tact, man-management, human relations, public relations, way with, judgment, skill, business management, decision-making, work study, management study, time and motion study, operational research, cost-benefit analysis, policy, home economics, household management, housekeeping, housewifery, husbandry, economics, political economy, statesmanship, statecraft, government, governance, regimen, regime, regulation, legislation, lawmaking, reins of government, reins, department, ministry, cabinet, inner cabinet, staff work, bureaucracy, civil service, secretariat, government office, workshop

► *252 Safety; 396 Authority; 484 Plan; 485 Skill; 577 Workshop; 665 Carefulness*

4 **directorship**, direction, directing, responsibility, command, control, administrative control, managerial control, supreme control, dictatorship, leadership, premiership, chairmanship, captaincy (*or* captainship), superiority, guidance, steering, steerage, pilotage, steersmanship, helmsmanship

► *121 Superiority; 397 Command*

5 **guide**, controls, reins, helm, rudder, wheel, tiller, joystick, pole star, lodestar, needle, magnetic needle, compass, binnacle, gyrocompass (*or* gyro), automatic pilot (*or* autopilot *or* gyropilot), navigational aid, direction-finding, beam, radar, lighthouse, lightship, light vessel, foghorn, buoy, direction, remote control

6 **governing body**, controlling body, supervisory body, administration, quango, committee, steering committee, standing committee, select committee, cabinet, inner cabinet, council, board, board of directors, directorate, directors, management, managers, executive, employers, bosses, staff, brass (Inf), top brass (Inf)

7 **council**, council board, round table, council chamber, board room, court, tribunal, Privy Council, Star Chamber, Curia Regis, Sanhedrin, presidium, ecclesiastical council, Curia, consistory, vestry, cabinet, kitchen cabinet (US), panel, board, advisory board, consultative body, commission, Royal Commission, assembly, conference, conventicle, congregation, ecclesia, conclave, convocation, synod, convention, congress, meeting, top-level meeting, summit, durbar, diet, moot, folkmoot, comitia, zemstvo, soviet, council of elders, elder statesmen, genro, federal council, League of Nations, United Nations (UNO), Security Council, hearing, audience, sitting, session, think tank (Inf)

► *7 Religion; 376 Gathering; 713 Advice; 734 Conversation*

8 **British administrative council**, town council, parish council, community council, municipal council, county council, regional council, district council

9 **US administrative council**, town council, city council, mayor-council system, city commission, council-manager system, county commission, county board, board of aldermen, aldermanic board

10 **legislative body**, legislative branch, legislative assembly, legislature, government, deliberative assembly, deliberative body, consultative assembly, division, quorum, senatus, senate, parliament, European Parliament, Dáil Éireann (*or* Dáil), Seanad Éireann (*or* Seanad), National Assembly, Chambre des Députés, Bundesrat, Bundestag, States General, Storting, Folketing, Cortes, Majlis, Supreme Soviet

► *12 Government and Politics*

11 **British government**, Parliament, Mother of Parliaments, Westminster, House of Commons, Lower House, Lower Chamber, House of Lords, Upper House, Upper Chamber, House of Peers, another place

12 **US government**, Congress, Capitol Hill, Senate, Upper House, Upper Chamber, House of Representatives, House, Lower House, Lower Chamber

13 **director**, manager, governor, controller, legislator, lawgiver, lawmaker, president, vice president, prime minister, premier, governor general, capitalist, VIP, employer, boss, master, head, headman, chief, overseer, head of the household, head of state, superior, principal (US), headmaster (*or* mistress), superintendent (US), moderator, dean, rector, chancellor, vice chancellor, chair, chairperson, chairman (*or* chairwoman), speaker, captain, skipper, stroke, cox, mariner, steersman, helmsman, navigator, pilot, guide, conductor, forerunner, precursor, drill sergeant, trainer, academic adviser, director of studies, professor, teacher, tutor, instructor, mentor, adviser, political economist, kingmaker, wirepuller (US), animator, motivator, hidden hand, influence, back-seat driver (Inf)

► *12 Government and Politics; 121 Superiority; 395 Influence; 400 Master; 480 Persuasion; 713 Advice; 719 Interpretation*

14 **leader**, charismatic leader, governor, Messiah, Mahdi, ayatollah, guru, maharajah, Senate majority leader (US),

House majority leader (US), leader of the House of Commons, leader of the House of Lords, Senate minority leader (US), House minority leader (US), leader of the Opposition, floor leader, spearhead, team captain, quarterback, centre forward, shepherd, teamster, cowboy (*or* cowhand), ranch foreman (US), drover, herdsman, bellwether, fugleman, pacemaker, pacesetter, toastmaster, symposiarch, master of ceremonies (MC), compere, ringmaster, high priest, mystagogue, chorus leader, choragus, coryphaeus, conductor, director (US), leader of the orchestra, first violin, precentor, drum major, drum majorette, cheerleader (US), ringleader, demagogue, rabble-rouser, agitator, captain, condottiere, autocrat, dictator, *Führer* (Ger), *Duce* (It)

▶ *12 Government and Politics; 400 Master; 662 Disobedience*

15 manager, manageress, person in responsibility, responsible person, person in charge, key person, VIP, kingpin, administrator, executive, chief executive officer (CEO), company director, managing director, store manager (*or* manageress), shop manager (*or* manageress), office manager, banker, bank official, bank manager, executor, doer, statesman (*or* stateswoman), politician, procurator, housekeeper, housewife, househusband, chatelaine, steward, farm manager, bailiff, reeve, agent, factor, consignee, superintendent, supervisor, inspector, overseer, foreman (*or* -woman), ganger, gaffer, charge hand, warden, matron, sister, charge nurse, nurse, senior nursing officer, protector, proctor, disciplinarian, party chairman, party manager, whip, party whip, majority whip (US), minority whip (US), chief whip, custodian, caretaker, curator, librarian, keeper, master of hounds, whipper-in, huntsman, circus manager, bigwig (Inf), big shot (Inf), big cheese (Inf), pol (US inf)

▶ *123 Importance; 252 Safety; 340 Action; 398 Delegate*

16 official, officer, office-holder, office bearer, Jack-in-office, tin god, marshal, steward, shop steward, representative, deputy, delegate, senator, Areopagite, Sanhedrist, member of parliament (MP), Parliamentarian, backbencher, peer, life peer, Lords Spiritual, Lords Temporal, member of Congress (US), Senator (US), Congressman (*or* Congresswoman) (US), Representative (US), government servant, public servant, civil servant, apparatchik, servant, officer of state, high official, vizier, grand vizier, cabinet minister, cabinet member (US), secretary, minister, undersecretary, junior minister, secretary-general, United Nations secretary-general, permanent secretary, bureaucrat, Eurocrat, European commissioner, European Parliament member, Euro-MP, MEP, mandarin, judicial officer, district officer, regional official, magistrate, justice of the peace (JP), commissioner, prefect, intendant, consul, proconsul, first secretary, counsellor, praetor, quaestor, aedile, ambassador, envoy, envoy extraordinary, special envoy, alderman, mayor, city manager (US), councillor, councilman (*or* councilwoman) (US), functionary, party official, petty official, administrative officer, clerk, school prefect, monitor, jobsworth (Inf)

▶ *12 Government and Politics; 396 Authority; 398 Delegate; 400 Master; 401 Servant; 713 Advice*

ADJECTIVES

17 managerial, administrative, executive, organizational, directorial, directing, leading, heading up, hegemonic, directional, guiding, steering, navigational, governing, controlling, political, official, bureaucratic, governmental, presidential, gubernatorial, legislative, judicial, economic, in charge, at the helm, holding the reins, in the driving seat, in the chair, authoritative, authoritarian, officious, dictatorial, despotic, tyrannical, supervisory, managing, nomothetic (*or* nomothetical), high-level, top-level, important

▶ *123 Importance; 396 Authority*

18 parliamentary, congressional, senatorial, legislative, deliberative, unicameral, bicameral, conciliar, convocational, ecclesiastical, synodal, canonical, decretal

ADVERBS

19 managerially, administratively, officially, politically, economically, authoritatively, in control, in charge, in command, at the helm, at the wheel, on the bridge, in the driving seat, in the saddle, in the chair, at the head, ex officio, on the cutting edge (US), with diplomacy, with statesmanship, in the hot seat (Inf)

580 Leisure

The wisdom of a learned man cometh by opportunity of leisure: and he that hath little business shall become wise. How can he get wisdom that holdeth the plough, and that glorieth in the goad, that driveth oxen, and is occupied in their labours, and whose talk is of bullocks? Bible: Ecclesiasticus.

If all the year were playing holidays, To sport would be as tedious as to work. William Shakespeare.

NOUNS

1 leisure, free time, spare time, spare hours, free moments, vacant moments, idle moments, odd moments, time to oneself, time for oneself, time one can call one's own, breathing space (*or* room), freedom, liberty, convenience, opportunity, time on one's hands, time to kill, no work, not enough work, sinecure, idleness, *dolce far niente* (It), inactivity, rest, repose, ease, relaxation, no hurry, time to spare, ample time, all the time in the world

▶ *263 Ease; 343 Inactivity*

2 time off, holiday, vacation, leave, day off, half-holiday, sabbatical, furlough, off duty, break, recess, time-out (US), respite, relief, peace, quiet, recreation, breather (Inf)

▶ *146 Interval*

3 unemployment, joblessness, redundancy, lay-off, no more work, dismissal, discharge, retirement, resignation, calling it quits, the sack (Inf), being fired (Inf)

▶ *605 Resignation*

VERBS

4 have leisure, have free time, have spare time, find time for, have plenty of time, have all the time in the world, have time on one's hand, be master of one's time, take one's ease, see no cause for haste, be in no hurry, take one's (own good) time, take time to smell the flowers

(US), move slowly, spend, pass, while away, want something to do, find time hangs heavy on one's hands, take a holiday, take a vacation (US), take a break, take time out (US), take leave, take a sabbatical, go on a furlough, rest, repose, resign, give up work, retire, go into retirement, take early retirement, get laid off, get the sack (Inf), get fired (Inf)

5 **dismiss**, discharge, lay off, make redundant, fire (Inf), sack (Inf)

ADJECTIVES

6 **leisure**, free, spare, unoccupied, recreational

7 **leisurely**, unhurried, slow, deliberate, relaxed, easy, labour-saving, idle, inactive, resting, reposeful, leisured, at leisure, unoccupied, free, available, disengaged, at a loose end, at ease, off duty, on holiday, on vacation, on leave, on furlough, on sabbatical, retired, in retirement, redundant, dismissed, discharged, laid off, unemployed, jobless, out of work, non-working, fired (Inf), sacked (Inf)

▶ *263 Ease; 333 Slowness; 343 Inactivity; 605 Resignation*

ADVERBS

8 **leisurely**, unhurriedly, conveniently, at one's convenience, at one's leisure, in one's own time, at any odd moment, in one's spare time

581 Refreshment

VERBS

1 **refresh**, freshen, freshen up, tidy, tidy up, spruce up, clean, clean up, air, ventilate, aerate, air-condition, provide more oxygen, open windows, fan, shade, cool, cool off, cool down, chill, refrigerate, brace, stimulate, exhilarate, invigorate, enliven, vitalize, animate, strengthen, fortify, give a second wind to, give renewed strength to, restore, renew, recruit, recreate, resuscitate, breathe new life into, revive, reanimate, reinvigorate, revitalize, rejuvenate, renovate, repair, ease, relieve, dispel, allow rest, give a break, feed, give food and drink, cheer, give a breather (Inf)

▶ *25 Cookery; 256 Cleanness; 338 Vigour; 393 Repair; 434 Air; 494 Cold; 608 Relief*

2 **be refreshed**, feel refreshed, refresh oneself, breathe deeply, draw breath, get one's breath back, regain (*or* recover) one's breath, get one's second wind, take a deep breath, take in oxygen, fill one's lungs, respire, clear one's head, come to, perk up, feel like a giant refreshed, feel like a new man (*or* woman), feel twice the man (*or* woman) one was, feel like a kid again, feel oneself again, be restored, recover, recuperate, revive, renew oneself, cool off, mop one's brow, stretch one's legs, take a break, take a recess, rest, have a rest, repose, sleep it off, have a change, have a change of pace, go on leave, clear the cobwebs out (Inf), snap out of it (Inf), come around (Inf), take a breather (Inf), take five (*or* ten) (Inf), sack out (Inf)

▶ *263 Ease; 393 Repair; 494 Cold*

ADJECTIVES

3 **refreshing**, bracing, stimulating, exhilarating, invigorating, fortifying, revitalizing, fresh, cool, cooling, cold, comforting, relieving, recreative, recreational, reviving, restorative, tonic

4 **refreshed**, freshened up, cool, cooled off, braced, stimulated, exhilarated, invigorated, enlivened, fortified, revitalized, recovered, revived, restored, like a giant refreshed, like a new man (*or* woman), twice the man (*or* woman) one was, like a kid again, oneself again, rested, perked up, ready for more, ready for another round

NOUNS

5 **refreshment**, freshness, freshening up, tidiness, tidying up, cleanness, cleanliness, ventilation, aeration, respiration, shade, coolness, cooling off, cooling down, refrigeration, stimulation, exhilaration, invigoration, vitalization, animation, perking up, restoration, renewal, recruitment, recreation, R and R (rest and recreation), recovery, recuperation, resuscitation, new life, revival, reanimation, reinvigoration, revitalization, rejuvenation, renovation, repair, ease, relief, rest, repose

▶ *256 Cleanness; 338 Vigour; 393 Repair; 434 Air; 494 Cold; 608 Relief*

6 **refresher**, reviver, restorative, stimulant, tonic, air, breath of air, breath of fresh air, breeze, cool breeze, oxygen, breath of oxygen, shower, cold shower, wash, wash and brush up, rest, repose, break, vacation, holiday, change of scene, recess, leave, lull

7 **refreshments**, refection, food, drink, sustenance, snack, pick-me-up (Inf), breather (Inf), quick one (Inf), one for the road (Inf), nineteenth hole (Inf)

ADVERBS

8 **refreshingly**, exhilaratingly, invigoratingly, freshly, coolly, restfully

582 Death

God grants an easy death only to the just. Svetlana Alliluyeva.

O Death, where is thy sting-a-ling-a-ling,
O Grave, thy victoree?
The bells of hell go ting-a-ling-a-ling
For you but not for me. Anonymous.

Men fear death, as children fear to go in the dark; and as that natural fear in children is increased with tales, so is the other. Francis Bacon.

To die will be an awfully big adventure. J. M. Barrie.

Darkling I listen; and, for many a time I have been half in love with easeful Death. John Keats.

Whom the gods love dies young. Menander.

NOUNS

1 **death**, biological death, clinical death, brain death, cerebral death, dying, act of dying, expiration, expiry, decease, demise, mortality, extinction, end of life, end, no life, stillbirth, loss of life, exit, departure, passing, passing away (*or* over), process of death, perishability, putrefaction, mortification, necrosis, decay, deathliness, cadaverousness, ephemerality, transience, transiency, hand

of death, cold fingers of death, jaws of death, dance of death, shadow of death, shades of death, the beyond, the other side, the great divide, rest, eternal rest, quietude, the great adventure (Inf), the last debt (Inf), the final thrill (US inf), curtains (Inf), crossing the bar (Inf), crossing the Styx (*or* Lethe *or* River Jordan) (Inf), the long sleep (Inf), the big sleep (Inf)

► *94 Nonexistence; 245 Deterioration; 278 Transience; 530 Colourlessness*

2 death personified, Death, the Grim Reaper, the Great Leveller, the Thief in the Night, the Last Summoner, Angel of Death, Azrael, King of Death, King of Terrors, Mors, Thanatos

3 symbol of death, death's-head, skull, skull and crossbones, memento mori

4 death sentence, doom, crack of doom, knell, death knell, martyrdom, quietus, execution, capital punishment, legalized killing, hanging, electric chair, electrocution, gas chamber, lethal injection, guillotine, firing squad, crucifixion, death row (US), death chamber, death house (US inf)

► *382 Killing; 814 Punishment*

5 ways of dying, natural death, old-age death, easy death, quiet end, euthanasia, release, happy release, welcome end, suicide, violent death, sudden death, unexpected loss of life, untimely end, accidental death, death by misadventure, fatality, fatal accident, drowning, watery grave, road fatality, traffic accident, starvation, fatal disease, mortal illness, terminal illness (*or* disease)

6 killing, murder, poisoning, stabbing, shooting

► *382 Killing*

7 dying day, last hour, valley of the shadow of death, deathbed, deathwatch, deathbed repentance, deathbed confession, final words, last words, death scene, last breath, last gasp, dying breath, death rattle, death throes, last agony, finality, extreme unction, passing bell, last rites, funeral rites, obsequies, swan song (Inf)

► *131 End; 583 Burial*

8 after death, rigor mortis, postmortem, postmortem examination, autopsy, necropsy, inquest, mortuary, morgue, charnel house, embalming, mourning, lamentation, wake, Irish wake, viewing the body, funeral, funeral parlour, crematorium, cemetery, graveyard, graveside services, eulogy, coffin, grave, tomb, dead-house (Inf), cold meat party (US inf), pine drape (US inf), deep six (US inf), six (US inf)

► *583 Burial*

9 person dealing with the dead, doctor, coroner, police, undertaker, mortician (US), funeral director, embalmer

► *583 Burial*

10 dying person, dying patient, terminal patient, hopeless case, condemned man (*or* woman), the condemned, dead duck (Inf), dead pigeon (Inf), goner (Inf)

► *260 Ill Health*

11 dead person, fatality, casualty, victim, stillbirth, the deceased, the defunct, the late lamented, dead body, body, corpse, cadaver, carcass, mummy, embalmed body, skeleton, fossil, remains, mortal remains, relics, ashes, carrion, stiff (Inf), food for worms (Inf)

12 death count, mortality rate, mortality table, bill of mortality, mortality, death rate, death register, death roll, death toll, fatality list, casualty list, martyrology, necrology, deaths column, obituary (obit), death notice, death record, death certificate, fatalities, casualties, the dead, the dead and dying, the fallen (Inf), the lost (Inf)

13 the dead, ancestors, forefathers, precursors, those who have gone before, loved ones, dear (*or* dearly) departed

14 the spiritual world, world of spirits, unseen world, next world, future state, afterlife, hereafter, the shades, saints, souls, spirits, ghosts, phantoms, underworld, the lower regions, nether world, nether regions, Sheol, Styx, Stygian shore, Stygian darkness, Hades, hell, mythic hell, Elysian fields, meads of asphodel, happy hunting grounds, Abraham's bosom, Davy Jones's locker, heaven, paradise, mythic heaven, halls of death (Inf)

► *7 Religion; 8 Divinity; 283 Future Time*

VERBS

15 die, be dead, lose one's life, succumb, expire, perish, decease, pass away (*or* over), pass, depart this life, depart, be taken, meet one's death, meet one's end, meet one's fate, be no more, cease to be, cease to live, be gone, stop breathing, breathe one's last, give up the ghost, curl up and die, drop off, close one's eyes, fall asleep, predecease, become extinct, come (*or* turn) to dust, decompose, lie in the grave, sleep one's last sleep (Inf), turn up one's toes (Inf), push up daisies (Inf), be six feet under (Inf), ring down the curtain (Inf), shuffle off this mortal coil (Inf), pay the debt of nature (Inf), go the way of all flesh (Inf), go to one's reward (Inf), go to one's last home (Inf), go west (Inf), go to the last roundup (US inf), go to one's long account (Inf), cash in one's chips (Inf), have had one's chips (Inf), quit the scene (US inf), quit it (US inf), cross the bar (Inf), cross the Styx (*or* Lethe *or* River Jordan) (Inf), go up Salt River (US inf), join the majority (Inf), join the choir invisible (Inf), join the angels (Inf), meet one's Maker (Inf), meet Saint Peter (Inf), enter the Golden Gate (Inf), go to glory (Inf), reach a better world (Inf), awake to life immortal (Inf), kick the bucket (Inf), kick it (Inf), bite the dust (Inf), croak (Inf), peg it (Inf), peg out (Inf), snuff it (Inf), cop it (Inf), buy it (Inf), buy the farm (US inf), conk out (Inf), go for a burton (Inf), pop off (Inf), pop one's clogs (Inf), hop the twig (US inf), go belly up (US inf)

► *94 Nonexistence; 131 End; 214 Decrease; 226 Stopping; 245 Deterioration*

16 meet one's fate, die peacefully, die in one's sleep, die in bed, drop (down) dead, die a natural death, die in poverty, die well, die with honour, die young, die before one's time, die prematurely, come to an untimely end, die of old age, catch one's death, die of neglect, starve to death, die hard, die fighting (for one's country), die in combat, die in action, fall, get cut down, get killed, surrender one's life, lay down one's life, relinquish one's life, give (up) one's life for another, make the supreme sacrifice, die (*or* meet) a violent death, break one's neck, bleed to death, drown, go to Davy Jones's locker, founder, receive one's death warrant, receive a death sentence, be put to death, suffer execution, die the death, hang, walk the plank, commit euthanasia, commit suicide, end one's life, kill oneself, die by one's own hand, snuff out like a candle (Inf), die in harness (Inf), die with one's boots on (Inf), meet a sticky end (Inf)

▶ *382 Killing*

17 bury, entomb, embalm, view the body, mourn, grieve, lament, bemoan, regret, eulogize, plant (Inf), deep six (US inf)

▶ *583 Burial; 602 Sorrow*

ADJECTIVES

18 dying, expiring, deathly, deathlike, deathly pale, white as a sheet, cadaverous, skeletal, on the danger list, in intensive care, in a critical condition, terminally ill, sick unto death, hopeless, doomed (to die), fated (to die), fey (Scot), condemned to die, condemned to death, sentenced to death, under sentence of death, on one's deathbed, at the point of death, moribund, *in extremis* (L), half-dead, slipping away, slipping, sinking, sinking fast, fading, fading fast, hanging by a thread, struggling for breath, at one's last gasp, not long for this world, not long to go, going, about gone, far gone, done for (Inf), having had it (Inf), on one's last legs (Inf), with one foot in the grave (Inf), at death's door (Inf), death knocking at the door (Inf), sands of time running out (Inf), one's hour having come (Inf), one's time being up (Inf), one's number being up (Inf)

▶ *131 End; 260 Ill Health; 814 Punishment*

19 dead, deceased, defunct, demised, lifeless, breathless, still, inanimate, exanimate, bereft of life, no more, passed away, passed over, passed, released, out of one's misery, departed this life, departed, gone, dead on arrival (DOA), born dead, stillborn, extinct, finished, out of this world, numbered with the dead, taken by God, called by God, called to one's eternal rest, gathered to one's fathers, in Abraham's bosom, asleep in Jesus, in Paradise, at the Pearly Gates, gone before, gone to join one's ancestors, long gone, gone but not forgotten, late, lamented, late lamented, regretted, dead and gone, dead and buried, buried, in the grave, killed, murdered, slaughtered, massacred, sacrificed, martyred, sainted, (as) dead as a doornail, (as) dead as mutton, (as) dead as a dodo, done for (Inf), kaput (Inf), six feet under (Inf), under hatches (Inf), beyond the grave (Inf), launched into eternity (Inf), on the other side (Inf), behind the veil (Inf), beyond mortal ken (Inf), gone to Elysium (Inf), gone to the Elysian fields (Inf), gone to the happy hunting grounds (US inf), gone for a burton (Inf), cold (Inf), stiff (Inf), stone dead (Inf)

▶ *94 Nonexistence; 131 End; 489 Insensibility; 583 Burial*

20 deadly, mortal, fatal, terminal, lethal, murderous, perishable, ephemeral, transient

▶ *278 Transience; 382 Killing*

21 deathly, deathlike, corpse-like, cadaverous, ghastly, livid, pale, pallid, wan, ghostly, ashen, haggard, skeletal

▶ *153 Thinness; 530 Colourlessness*

22 postmortem, post-obit, posthumous, funereal, embalmed, mummified, fossilized

ADVERBS

23 fatally, terminally, moribundly, lifelessly, inanimately, postmortem, after death, posthumously, in the event of death

INTERJECTIONS

24 I'm dying!, I'm done for!, I've had it!, it's curtains!, this is it!, it's all over!, it is all up with me!

583 Burial

John Brown's body lies a-mouldering in the grave,
His soul is marching on! Charles Sprague Hall.

NOUNS

1 burial, burying, disposal of the dead, burial customs, interment, inhumation, entombment, sepulture, urn burial, cremation, incineration, scattering of the ashes, mass burial, burial at sea, military burial, full military rites, embalmment, embalming, mummification, myrrh, spices, natron, mummy-case, sarcophagus, pyre, funeral pile, crematorium, mortuary, morgue, charnel house, deadhouse (Inf)

▶ *582 Death*

2 funeral, funeral rites, funeral ceremony, funeral service, burial service, graveside service, memorial service, requiem, obsequies, exequies, obituary, funeral parlour, crematorium, mourning, weeping and wailing, keen, lamentation, wake, Irish wake, lying-in-state, viewing the body, receiving family friends, funeral procession, cortege, dead march, knell, passing bell, muffled drum, last post, taps, funeral hymn, *Dies Irae* (L), funeral oration, funeral sermon, eulogy, elegy, dirge, lament, lowering the body, closing the grave, cold meat party (US inf), obit (Inf)

▶ *582 Death; 603 Lamentation*

3 funeral director, undertaker, mortician (US), pallbearer, grave digger, sexton, priest, minister, mourner, weeper, keener, hired mourner, mute, embalmer, monument mason, eulogist, eulogizer, elegist, epitaphist, obituary writer, obituarist, necrologist

▶ *7 Religion; 603 Lamentation*

4 funeral objects, hearse, coffin, casket, shell, cist, bier, pall, catafalque, urn, cinerary urn, funeral urn, bone urn, ossuary, canopic urn (*or* jar *or* vase), inscription, Rest in Peace (RIP), here lies, *hic jacet* (L), epitaph, lapidary phrases, monument, sepulchral monument, tombstone, gravestone, headstone, footstone, brass, hatchment, cross, memorial, war memorial, cenotaph, burial clothes, grave clothes, cerements, cerecloth, shroud, winding sheet, mummy wrapping, flowers, wreath, pine drape (US inf)

▶ *462 Memory*

5 cemetery, graveyard, churchyard, burial place, burial ground, plot, family plot, final resting place, God's acre, catacomb, columbarium, cinerarium, necropolis, city of the dead, golgotha, chapel of remembrance, garden of remembrance, garden of rest, military cemetery, pet cemetery, boneyard (Inf)

6 grave, grave pit, plague pit, common grave, mass grave, open grave, tomb, mausoleum, vault, crypt, burial chamber, sepulchre, mummy chamber, King Tutankhamen's (*or* Tut's) tomb, pyramid, mastaba, pantheon, dakhma, fogou, Tower of Silence, narrow house, long home, beehive tomb, shaft tomb, barrow, mound, tumulus, earthwork, cromlech, dolmen, menhir, cairn, shrine, memorial, cenotaph, deep six (US inf), six (US inf)

▶ *182 Convexity*

7 inquest, autopsy, necropsy, post-mortem examination,

postmortem, exhumation, disinterment, disentombment, removal of the body, digging up the body

► 705 *Question*

VERBS

8 **bury**, inter, inhume, lay to rest, lay in the grave, consign to earth, lower the body, put to bed with a shovel, lay out, prepare for burial, close the eyes, embalm, mummify, coffin, encoffin, entomb, ensepulchre, urn, cremate, incinerate, burn on the pyre, pay one's last respects, go to a funeral, toll the knell, sing a requiem, sound the last post, mourn, keen, lament, hold a wake, plant (Inf), deep six (US inf)

► *582 Death; 603 Lamentation*

9 **exhume**, disinter, dig up, unearth, unbury, disentomb

ADJECTIVES

10 **buried**, dead and buried, interred, inhumed, laid to rest, entombed, coffined, urned, cremated, embalmed, mummified, in the grave, below ground, six feet under, pushing up daisies (Inf)

► *582 Death*

11 **funeral**, burial, funerary, funebrial, funereal, sombre, black, dark, sad, mournful, mourning, lamenting, dirgelike, dirgeful, mortuary, cinerary, crematory, crematorial (US), sepulchral, memorial, obsequial, eulogistic, eulogistical (US), elegiac, elegiacal (US), obituary, necrological, lapidary, epitaphic

► *523 Darkness; 532 Blackness; 602 Sorrow; 603 Lamentation*

ADVERBS

12 **funereally**, sombrely, sepulchrally, eulogistically, elegiacally, necrologically, in memoriam, post-obitum, postmortem, beneath the sod, six feet deep

584 Military Affairs

I'd like to see the government get out of war altogether and leave the whole feud to private industry. Joseph Heller.

I am tired and sick of war. Its glory is all moonshine… War is hell. General William Sherman.

NOUNS

1 **military affairs**, military science, military strategy, grand strategy, general policy, war, war plans, warcraft, arms, art of war, siegecraft, military tactics, logistics, campaign, theatre of operations, strategic objectives, command of the sea, command of the air, mobilization, military service, recruiting, compulsory service, conscription, conscripting, the draft (US), impressment, operations, rank, military installations, headquarters (HQ), base, camp, barracks, billet, military equipment

► *243 Preparation; 484 Plan; 585 War*

2 **the military**, national defence, military forces, the services, army, land forces, ground forces, navy, air force, marines, special forces, standing army, professional army, regular forces, mercenary forces, nonprofessional army, volunteer army, irregular forces, irregulars, reserve forces, reserves, Territorial Army, Home Guard, US National Guard (US), Senior Service, Special Boat Service (SBS), Special Air Service (SAS), militia, citizen's army, military arm, arm of the service, military branch, branch of the service, military–industrial complex

3 **military training**, national military college, Imperial Defence College, US National War College (US), military academy, United States Military Academy (*or* West Point), United States Naval Academy (*or* Annapolis), Air Force Academy, British military academies: Royal Military Academy (*or* Sandhurst), Royal Naval College (*or* Dartmouth), Royal Air Force Academy (*or* Cranwell), Royal Military College of Canada, Royal Military College (*or* Duntroon) (Aus), *École Spéciale Militaire* (Fr), staff college

► *6 Education*

4 **military organization**, national defence headquarters, Ministry of Defence, Government Communications Headquarters (GCHQ), Department of Defense (US), operational command, military unit, tactical unit, support unit, administrative unit, commando unit, medical service, Mobile Army Surgical Hospital (MASH), communication service, maintenance service, supply service, evacuation service, group, battle group, column, rank, file, detail, kitchen police (KP), detachment, combat team, task force, squad, section, platoon, company, troop, battery, battalion, infantry battalion, mechanized battalion, missile battalion, signal battalion, engineer battalion, reconnaissance battalion, regiment, infantry regiment, brigade, artillery brigade, division, infantry division, armoured division, motorized division, mechanized division (US), air division, airborne division, parachute division, aircraft division, destroyer division, cruiser division, submarine division, army corps, armoured corps, medical corps, dental corps, nurse corps, army service corps, drum corps, bugle corps, quartermaster corps, transportation corps, military police corps, field army, flight, squadron, wing, fleet, operational fleet, task group, amphibious force squadron, flotilla, destroyer flotilla, support fleet, auxiliary fleet, reserve fleet, outfit (Inf)

5 **military staff**, general staff, Defence Council, Joint

BRITISH MILITARY RANKS

Army
Field Marshal
General
Lieutenant-General
Major-General
Brigadier
Colonel
Lieutenant-Colonel
Major
Captain
Lieutenant
Second Lieutenant
Cadet

Royal Navy
Admiral of the Fleet
Admiral
Vice-Admiral
Rear-Admiral
Commodore
Captain
Commander
Lieutenant Commander
Lieutenant
Sub-Lieutenant
Acting Sub-Lieutenant
Cadet

Royal Air Force
Marshal of the Royal Air Force
Air Chief Marshal
Air Marshal
Air Vice–Marshal
Air Commodore
Group Captain
Wing Commander
Squadron Leader
Flight Lieutenant
Flying Officer
Pilot Officer
Cadet

BRITISH MILITARY MEDALS AND DECORATIONS	
Victoria Cross	Distinguished Service Medal (Navy)
Distinguished Service Cross	Distinguished Conduct Medal
Military Cross	Military Medal (Army)
Distinguished Flying Cross	Distinguished Flying Medal
Air Force Cross	Air Force Medal
Conspicuous Gallantry Medal	

Chiefs of Staff (US), SHAPE (Supreme Headquarters, Allied Powers in Europe), army staff, air force staff, navy staff, military headquarters staff, commander, chief of staff, deputy chief of staff, staff officers, plans and operations staff, training staff, supply staff, personnel staff, intelligence staff, commanding officer, company grade officer, junior officer, noncommissioned officer (NCO), platoon commander, company commander, field grade officer, senior officer, battalion commander, regimental commander, brigade commander, cavalry commander, artillery commander, general officer, flag officer, senior commander, divisional commander, corps commander, field army commander, task force commander

▶ *586 Combatant*

6 **military law**, Uniform Code of Military Justice (US), court martial, general court martial, district court martial, field general court martial, special court martial (US), summary court martial (US), military police, military police corps, Royal Military Police (RMP), Military Police (MP) (US)

▶ *16 Law*

7 **miscellaneous terms**, militarism, military government, military tradition, military bearing, military salute, military band, military music, military honours, military spirit, morale, gung-ho attitude (Inf)

ADJECTIVES

8 **military**, martial, militant, naval, service, fighting, soldierly, gladiatorial, strategic, tactical, offensive, defensive, pre-emptive, aggressive, pugnacious, combative, bellicose, warlike, belligerent, gung-ho (Inf)

9 **enlisted**, conscripted, drafted, volunteer, commissioned, noncommissioned, regular, irregular, reserve, combatant, noncombatant

VERBS

10 **enlist**, join up, join the colours, take the Queen's shilling, recruit, conscript, draft, impress, mobilize, demobilize, demob (Inf)

ADVERBS

11 **militarily**, martially, strategically, tactically, offensively, defensively, pre-emptively

585 War

Then said Jesus unto him, Put up again thy sword into his place: for all they that take the sword shall perish with the sword. Bible: Matthew.

C'est magnifique, mais ce n'est pas la guerre. (It is magnificent, but it is not war.) Pierre Bosquet.

The first casualty when war comes is truth. Hiram Warren Johnson.

NOUNS

1 **war**, warfare, modern warfare, conflict, armed conflict, military conflict, military operation, intervention, armed intervention, arms, the sword, grim-visaged war, *horrida bella* (L), *ultima ratio regum* (L), fortunes of war, wager of battle, arbitrament of war, armed neutrality, defensive weapons, Fortress America, paper war, war of words, polemic, quarrel, war of nerves, sabre-rattling, gunboat diplomacy, superpower diplomacy, psychological warfare, intimidation, undeclared war, uneasy peace, cold war, half-war, doubtful war, phoney war, disguised war, economic war, trade war, Cod war, real war, hot war, civil war, brother war, internecine war, revolt, revolution, war of independence, ideological war, class war, war on want, war of liberation, holy war, religious war, crusade, jihad, aggressive war, war of conquest, war of expansion, imperialist war, ethnic cleansing, limited war, war of containment, localized war, desert war, triphibious war, war on all fronts, all-out war, major war, general war, world war, First World War, Second World War, global war, total war, mother of all battles, war to end all wars, The Great War, Armageddon, blitzkrieg, blitz, atomic war, nuclear war, total destruction, push-button war, high-tech war, computer war, war of attrition, chemical warfare, truceless war, war to the knife, war to the end (*or* death), no prisoners taken, no holds barred

▶ *381 Attack; 382 Killing; 384 Defence; 587 Weapon; 612 Fear; 661 Defiance*

2 **glory of war**, pomp and circumstance of war, panoply of war, triumphal procession, chivalry, shining armour, red coats, rows of nodding plumes, martial music, military band, drums, bugle, trumpet, bugle call, battle call, battle cry, battle yell, rallying cry, rebel yell (US), war cry, war whoop, war song, war dance

3 **gods and goddesses of war**, Mars, Ares, Odin, Wotan, Bellona, Athena, Eris, Fea, Indra, Kartikeya, Tyr

▶ *8 Divinity*

4 **belligerency**, militancy, hostilities, state of war, state of siege, resort to arms, declaration of war, outbreak of war, wartime, wartime conditions, time of war, the war years

5 **bellicosity**, war fever, love of war, warlike habits, military spirit, fighting spirit, pugnacity, pugnaciousness, combativeness, aggressiveness, aggression, hawkishness, Ramboism, sabre-rattling, militancy, militarism, military tradition, expansionism, war policy, patriotism, fervent patriotism, jingoism, chauvinism, my country right or wrong, might is right

▶ *465 Misjudgment; 701 Argument; 751 Disagreement*

6 **art of war**, tactics of war, war strategy, war skills, grand strategy, warcraft, siegecraft, castrametation, fortification, military leadership, generalship, soldiership, seamanship, airmanship, military academy, Royal Military Academy, Sandhurst, Britannia Royal Naval College, war college, staff college, training drill, march, obstacle course, ballistics, gunnery, rifle practice, musketry practice, staff work, logistics, planning, plan, plan of battle,

battle plan, campaign plan, military evolutions, manoeuvres, tactics, strategy, war games, military experience, battlefield knowledge, knowledge of the enemy

► *455 Knowledge; 484 Plan; 485 Skill*

7 war measures, war policy, war footing, war readiness, war preparations, war effort, war work, arming, appeal to arms, call to arms, clarion call, call, rally, fiery cross, call-up, mobilization, recruitment, conscription, the draft (US), national service, military duty, enlisting, volunteering, joining up, doing one's duty for king (*or* queen) and country, rationing, blackout, civilian evacuation, victory gardens, censorship, propaganda, internment

► *243 Preparation; 742 Sign*

8 warfare, war, warring, waging war, making war, declaring war, open war, warpath, battles, skirmishes, sieges, bloodshed, deeds of blood, violence, fighting, campaigning, soldiering, active service, military service, infantry service, naval service, air force service, serving one's country, bombing, bombardment, saturation bombing, strategic bombing, tactical bombing, carpet bombing, sea battles, sea bombardment, sea raiding, fleet blockade, blockading, besieging, investment, enclosure, artillery warfare, aerial warfare, naval warfare, submarine warfare, undersea warfare, amphibious warfare, chemical warfare, gas warfare, biological warfare, bacteriological warfare, germ warfare, atomic warfare, nuclear warfare, limited nuclear warfare, theatre nuclear warfare, tactical nuclear warfare, economic warfare, sanctions, economic sanctions, military sanctions, arms sanctions, blockade, attrition, scorched earth policy, ethnic cleansing, psychological warfare, wartime propaganda, wartime censorship, offensive warfare, attack, defensive warfare, defence, Star Wars, Strategic Defense Initiative (SDI), mobile warfare, blitzkrieg, blitz, static warfare, trench warfare, desert warfare, mountain warfare, jungle warfare, bush-fighting, guerrilla warfare, sniping, campaign, expedition, mission, operation, operations, land operations, sea operations, naval operations, air operations, amphibious operations, combined operation, allied operation, joint operation, invasion, incursion, raid, word of command, order, military orders, battle orders, command, password, watchword

► *381 Attack; 384 Defence; 586 Combatant; 587 Weapon*

9 battle, pitched battle, battle royal, armed conflict, action, fight, scrap, skirmish, brush, collision, clash, shoot-out, offensive, blitz, attack, defence, defensive battle, stand, engagement, infantry engagement, naval engagement, sea fight, air fight, dogfight, line of battle, order of battle

10 battleground, battlefield, field of battle, field of conflict, killing field, battle zone, war zone, theatre of war, combat zone, area of hostilities, front line, front, firing line, beachhead, bridgehead, sector, salient, bulge, pocket, field of blood, Aceldama (New Testament)

► *381 Attack; 384 Defence*

11 recruit, conscript, draftee (US), volunteer, soldier, infantryman, navy man, seaman, marine, air force pilot, mercenary, veteran, legionnaire, old soldier, Chelsea Pensioner, GI (US inf), Tommy (Inf), tar (Inf), swabby (US inf), jarhead (US inf), fly-boy (US inf)

► *586 Combatant*

VERBS

12 go to war, declare war, resort to war (*or* arms), choose the military solution, open hostilities, call to arms, appeal to arms, take to arms, fly to arms, unleash the war dogs, unsheathe the sword, throw away the scabbard, whet the sword, take up the cause, take up the cudgels, fight, rise, rebel, revolt, overthrow, display the flag, fly one's flag, raise one's banner, show the flag, show one's colours, set up one's standard, arm, militarize, mobilize, prepare for war, put on a war footing, rally, call up, call to the colours, rally round the flag, recruit, conscript, draft (US), commission, give a commission, join the army, join up, enlist, enrol, volunteer, take a commission, serve one's country, serve one's king (*or* queen), answer the call, get one's call-up papers, receive a letter from Uncle Sam (US), put on a uniform

13 be at war, make war, wage war (against), engage in war (*or* hostilities), march to war, go on the warpath, war, war against, war upon, go on active service, ship out, shoulder a musket, smell powder, taste battle, flesh one's sword, open a campaign, campaign, soldier, take the field, take the offensive, invade, attack, raid, ambush, cut down, keep the field, hold one's ground, resist incursions, stand firm, defend, act on the defensive, counterattack, counter, manoeuvre, march, countermarch, blockade, cut off, beleaguer, besiege, starve out, invest, surround, shed blood, bloody, put to the sword, slaughter, mow down, slay, kill, ravage, rape, burn, scorch, lay waste, destroy, demolish, press the button, drop the bomb, nuke (Inf), kick ass (US inf)

► *357 Destruction; 381 Attack; 382 Killing; 384 Defence*

14 battle, do battle, give battle, offer battle, accept battle, cross swords with, take issue with, contest, dispute, re-

WARS

- Peloponnesian Wars (431–404 BC)
- Samnite Wars (350–200 BC)
- Punic War (264–146 BC)
- Hundred Years' War (1337–1453)
- Wars of the Roses (1455–85)
- Thirty Years' War (1618–48)
- (English) Civil War (1642–46)
- War of the Spanish Succession (1701–13)
- War of the Austrian Succession (1740–48)
- Seven Years' War (1756–63)
- French and Indian War (1754)
- War of American Independence (1775–83)
- Napoleonic Wars (1805–15)
- War of 1812
- Opium Wars (1839–42, 1856–60)
- Mexican War (1846–48)
- Crimean War (1853–56)
- (American) Civil War (*or* War Between the States) (1861–65)
- Franco–Prussian War (1870–71)
- Sino–Japanese War (1894–95)
- Spanish–American War (1898)
- Boer War (1880–81, 1899–1902)
- Russo–Japanese War (1904–05)
- World War I (1914–18)
- Spanish Civil War (1936–39)
- World War II (1939–45)
- Korean War (1950–53)
- Vietnam War (1959–75)
- Six Day War (1967)
- Iran–Iraq War (1980–88)
- Falklands War (1982)
- Gulf War (1991)
- Bosnian Civil War (1992–95)

sist, make (*or* take) a stand, stand, take a position, choose one's ground, dig in, sound the charge, beat the drum, go over the top, charge, engage, provoke an engagement, confront, open fire, fire (at), shoot (at), stage a shoot-out, call for a show-down, join battle, meet on the battlefield, skirmish, brush with, contend, combat, fight it out, fight to the finish, fight to the last man, fight the good fight, fight, close the ranks, rally

▶ *383 Resistance; 661 Defiance*

ADJECTIVES

15 warring, fighting, battling, campaigning, at war, waging war, engaged in war, on the warpath, in a state of war, belligerent, aggressive, bellicose, militant, mobilized, called, called up, drafted (US), conscripted, armed, uniformed, in the army (*or* military), arrayed, embattled, up in arms, sword in hand, at the front, on active duty, in battle, on the offensive, attacking, on the defensive, defending, engaged, at grips, at loggerheads

▶ *243 Preparation; 381 Attack; 384 Defence; 751 Disagreement*

16 warlike, militaristic, bellicose, hawkish, unpacific, Ramboesque, militant, aggressive, belligerent, pugnacious, pugilistic, combative, gung-ho, war-loving, warmongering, bloodthirsty, battle-hungry, war-fevered, fierce, tough, cruel, ass-kicking (US inf)

▶ *380 Violence*

17 military, paramilitary, mercenary, martial, exercised in arms, bearing arms, veteran, battle-scarred, shell-shocked, knightly, chivalrous, soldierly, soldierlike, naval, operational, strategical, tactical

ADVERBS

18 to war, at arms, at the front, at sword's point, at the point of a bayonet, at the cannon's mouth, in the face of death, belligerently, militantly, militarily, militaristically

586 Combatant

Older men declare war. But it is youth that must fight and die. Herbert Clark Hoover.

If I were fierce and bald and short of breath,
I'd live with scarlet Majors at the Base,
And speed glum heroes up the line to death. Siegfried Sassoon.

NOUNS

1 combatant, fighter, battler, struggler, contender, adversary, opponent, agonist, aggressor, assailant, assaulter, attacker, besieger, stormer, escalader, soldier, fighting man, belligerent, militarist, man-at-arms, storm trooper, shock trooper, warrior, brave, dueller, duellist, swordsman, sabreur, sword, good sword, blade (Lit), knight, knight errant, paladin, gunman, strong-arm man, assassin, killer, bully, hoodlum, rowdy, ruffian, neo-Nazi, National Front (NF) member, skinhead, Hell's Angel, thug, rough, tough, bravo, phansigar, fire-eater, swashbuckler, swaggerer, *miles gloriosus* (L), hit man (Inf), hooligan (Inf), bovver (*or* bully) boy (Inf)

▶ *380 Violence; 381 Attack; 382 Killing*

2 defender, protector, policeman, bodyguard, Secret Service member (US), Home Guard, Guardian Angel (US), vigilante, minder (Inf), bouncer (Inf)

▶ *384 Defence*

3 athlete, sportsman, sportswoman, bullfighter, toreador, matador, picador, jouster, tilter, fencer, foilsman, gladiator, retiarius, fighter, prizefighter, boxer, pugilist, champion, bruiser, slogger, puncher, sparring partner, flyweight, bantamweight, featherweight, lightweight, welterweight, middleweight, cruiserweight, heavyweight, wrestler, Graeco-Roman wrestler, freestyle wrestler, sumo wrestler, grappler, jujitsuist, judoist, karate expert, champ (Inf), pug (Inf), grunt-and-groaner (US inf)

4 fighting animal, fighting dog, pit bull terrier, fighting bird, fighting cock, gamecock, fighting fish, bear and dog, badger and dog, snake and mongoose

5 arguer, reasoner, advocate, barrister, lawyer, litigant, quarreller, disputer, debater, wrangler, controversialist, troublemaker, firebrand, rabble-rouser

▶ *16 Law; 701 Argument; 751 Disagreement*

6 militarist, warmonger, hawk, militant, hardliner, Dr. Strangelove, jingoist, chauvinist, imperialist, expansionist, crusader, militant Christian, warrior for God, conqueror, conquistador, Rajput, Ghazi, Kshatriya, Mameluke, samurai, professional soldier, Gurkha, sepoy, sowar, centurion, vexillary, mercenary, auxiliary, myrmidon, freelance, freelancer, soldier of fortune, adventurer, Hessian, condottiere, privateer, pirate, buccaneer, freebooter, marauder, raider, plunderer, robber

▶ *585 War; 774 Stealing*

7 militarist nation, nation in arms, martial race, Spartan race, warlike people

▶ *585 War*

8 soldier, serviceman, servicewoman, military man, fighting man, professional soldier, army man, warrior, hero, officer, standard-bearer, colours-bearer, ensign, redcoat, private soldier, private, common soldier, recruit, volunteer, conscript, enlisted man (US), draftee (US), pressed man, effective, Anzac, poilu, heavy-armed soldier, man-at-arms, hoplite, light-armed soldier, kern, bashi-bazouk, velites, tribal warrior, brave, skirmisher, sharpshooter, sniper, *franc-tireur* (Fr), shooter, long-term soldier, trooper, regular, campaigner, reservist, Guardsman (US), Territorial, Home Guardsman, militiaman, irregular, fencible, GI (US inf), rookie (Inf), tommy (Inf), Tommy Atkins (Inf), doughboy (US inf), weekend warrior (US inf)

9 guerrilla, freedom fighter, resistance fighter, underground fighter, partisan, terrorist, mosstrooper, raider, cateran, rapparee, fedayeen, Maquis, IRA member, PLO member

▶ *383 Resistance; 585 War*

10 woman soldier, servicewoman, WRAC, WRAF, Wren (Inf), female warrior, heroine, battlemaid, Amazon, Boadicea, Joan of Arc, Valkyrie

11 former soldier, old soldier, old trooper, old campaigner, ex-serviceman, ex-servicewoman, veteran, vet (Inf), Chelsea pensioner, legionnaire, legionary, British Legion member

12 ceremonial troops, Guardsman, Grenadier Guard, Coldstream Guard, Scots Guard, Irish Guard, Welsh

Guard, Life Guard, Horse Guard, Foot Guard, Swiss Guard, Praetorian Guard, colour guard, housecarl, janissary, protector

► *252 Safety*

13 historical soldiery, archer, bowman, crossbowman, arbalester, spearman, pikeman, halberdier, lancer, arquebusier, matchlockman, musketeer, fusilier, rifleman, pistoleer, carabineer, grenadier, cannoneer, miner

14 armed forces, military forces, services, fighting forces, combat troops, troops, combat-ready forces, allied forces, army, navy, air force, marines, coastguard, men, personnel, effectives, contingents, armament, armada, army of occupation, occupying force, occupation troops, garrison, *corps d'élite* (Fr), picked troops, crack troops, SAS (Special Air Service), Special Forces (US), shock troops, storm troops, Nazi SA (Sturmabteilung), Iraqi Republican Guards, spearhead, advance party, reconnaissance party, expeditionary force, striking force, flying column, assault troops, parachute troops, paratroops, commandoes, task force, raiding party, field army, line, front line, front-line troops, thin red line, first echelon, wing, van, vanguard, centre, main body, rear, rearguard, detachment, party, detail, patrol, night patrol, night watch, picket, sentry, sentinel, vedette, second echelon, base troops, base, staff, reserves, recruits, reinforcements, replacements, levy, general levy, draft (US), *arrière-ban* (Fr), mercenaries, auxiliaries, ceremonial troops, protector, Guards, household troops, Household Cavalry, guerrilla force, underground, resistance, Maquis, IRA (Irish Republican Army), PLO (Palestine Liberation Organization)

► *252 Safety; 383 Resistance; 384 Defence; 612 Fear*

15 army, professional army, standing army, regular army, volunteer army, conscript army, US Army, British Army, mercenary army, militia, Home Guard, Territorial Army (TA), Women's Royal Army Corps (WRAC), Queen Alexandra's Royal Army Nursing Corps (QARANC), Queen Alexandra's Royal Naval Nursing Service (QARNNS), British Army Reserve

16 army unit, corps, army corps, medical corps, division, armoured division, panzer division, brigade, heavy brigade, artillery brigade, light brigade, rifle brigade, battery, regiment, cavalry regiment, foot regiment, infantry, line infantry, light infantry, mountain infantry, squadron, troop, battalion, company, platoon, section, squad, detail, party, band, unit, group, detachment, army formation, array, line, column, file, rank, square, phalanx, legion, cohort, century, decury, maniple

17 army person, army officer field-marshal, general, lieutenant-general, major general, brigadier, colonel, lieutenant-colonel, major, captain, lieutenant, second lieutenant, cadet, warrant officer, noncommissioned officer, sergeant, corporal, lance-corporal, bombardier, enlisted person, private, common soldier, the ranks, rank and file, man-at-arms, cannon fodder, food for powder, gallant company, merry men, infantryman, foot soldier, foot, footslogger, peon, *chasseur* (Fr), Zouave, artillery man, gunner, machine-gunner, bazookaman, sapper, pioneer

18 army of people, multitude, mass, host, horde, legion, mob

► *208 Multitude*

19 cavalry, yeomanry, heavy cavalry, light cavalry, sabres, horse, light horse, cavalry regiment, mounted troops, mounted rifles, mounted police, mounted infantry, horse artillery, warhorse, charger, destrier (Lit)

20 cavalryman, mounted soldier, mounted infantryman, horse soldier, horseman, rider, cavalier, trooper, man-at-arms, yeoman, knight, lancer, chivalry, sowar (India), uhlan (Poland), hussar, cuirassier, dragoon, light dragoon, heavy dragoon, Ironsides, Cossack, spahi (Turkey), rough-rider, cameleer

21 armoured cavalry, armoured division, armoured car, armoured personnel carrier, tank, Challenger, M1A1 (US), Leopard (Ger), Panzer (Ger), tank transporter

22 navy, fleet, fleet arm, admiralty, naval service, senior service, silent service, naval armament, sea power, gunboat diplomacy, sail, wooden walls, mothball fleet, Royal Navy (RN), Women's Royal Naval Service (WRNS), Royal Naval Reserve, Royal Naval Volunteer Reserve, merchant navy, merchant marine

23 naval unit, fleet, flotilla, squadron, little ships, convoy, armada, argosy, Fleet Air Arm

24 warship, war vessel, man-of-war, ship of the line, flagship, command ship, flotilla leader, capital ship, aircraft carrier, battleship, dreadnought, cruiser, light cruiser, anti-submarine cruiser, armoured cruiser, battle cruiser, destroyer, guided-missile destroyer, destroyer escort, frigate, corvette, sloop, fast patrol boat, patrol boat, PT boat, gunboat, motor torpedo boat, torpedo boat, E-boat, submarine, nuclear submarine, U-boat, anti-submarine submarine, hunter-killer, submarine chaser, minelayer, minesweeper, fire ship, blockship, Q-ship, landing craft, amphibious ship, amphibian, duck, fleet auxiliary vessels, attack transport ship, attack cargo ship, fast transport ship, transport ship, troopship, tender, submarine tender, repair ship, storeship, depot ship, ammunition ship, supply ship, fuel ship, oil tanker, guard ship, hospital ship, icebreaker, ocean radar station ship, flattop (US inf)

► *323 Water Transport*

25 historical naval ships, war galley, bireme, trireme, quinquereme, galleon, galleass, three-decker, *Sovereign of the Seas, Victory*, turret ship, *Devastation*, ironclad, *Warrior*, *Monitor, Merrimack*, battleship, *Dreadnought*, raider, privateer, pirate ship

26 naval mine, torpedo, depth charge

27 naval man, navy man, naval officer, admiral of the fleet, admiral, vice admiral, rear-admiral, commodore, captain, commander, lieutenant-commander, lieutenant, sub-lieutenant, midshipman, fleet chief petty officer, chief petty officer, petty officer, rating, able rating, ordinary rating, seaman, able seaman, ordinary seaman, sailor, bluejacket, mariner, buccaneer, pressed man, coastguardsman, submariner, naval airman, Seabee (US), woman sailor, Wren, Wave (US), Wran (Aus), powder monkey, powder boy, cabin boy, naval reservist, Royal Naval Reservist, Royal Naval Volunteer Reservist gob (US inf), swab (US inf), swabbie (US inf), limey (Inf), wavy navy (Inf)

28 marines, Royal Marines, Royal Marine Commandos, marine, leatherneck (US), jarhead (US), jolly (Inf)

29 air force, air arm, air corps, flying corps, air service, Fleet Air Arm, Royal Air Force (RAF), US Air Force (USAF), Women's Royal Air Force (WRAF), Royal Air Force Volunteer Reserve

30 air force unit, airborne division, air group, wing, squadron, flight

31 military aircraft, aircraft, plane, aeroplane, warplane, battle plane, bomber, fighter-bomber, heavy bomber, light bomber, jump jet, fighter, night fighter, interceptor, anti-submarine plane, ground-attack aircraft, interdictor, spy plane, AWACS (airborne warning and control system), patrol plane, scout, transport plane, troop carrier, flying boat, trainer, helicopter, helicopter gunship, zeppelin, captive balloon, observation balloon, barrage balloon, airship, tank-buster (Inf)

▶ *319 Transport; 434 Air*

32 airman, air force officer, marshal of the Royal Air Force, air chief marshal, air marshal, air vice-marshal, air commodore, group captain, wing commander, squadron leader, flight-lieutenant, flying officer, pilot officer, master aircrew, flight sergeant, flight sergeant aircrew, chief technician, sergeant aircrew, junior technician, senior aircraftman (*or* -woman), leading aircraftman (*or* -woman), air troops, parachute troops, paratrooper, ground staff, fighter pilot, bomber pilot, co-pilot, navigator, gunner, bombardier, observer, aircrew, para (Inf), Wingco (Inf)

ADJECTIVES

33 combative, aggressive, hostile, adversarial, opposing, inimical, agonistic, antagonistic, bellicose, belligerent, pugnacious, militant, militaristic, warlike, expansionistic, imperialistic, jingoistic, chauvinistic, hardline, crusading, buccaneering, piratical, bloodthirsty, rowdy, rough, tough, thuggish, trigger-happy (Inf), gung-ho (Inf)

▶ *381 Attack; 584 Military Affairs; 585 War*

34 argumentative, quarrelsome, litigious, controversial, troublemaking, rabble-rousing

▶ *701 Argument; 751 Disagreement*

35 martial, naval, gladiatorial, pugilistic, mercenary, auxiliary, soldierly, soldierlike, brave, heroic, armed, armoured, enlisted, drafted, conscripted, recruited, signed up (Inf)

VERBS

36 combat, make trouble, rabble-rouse, warmonger, crusade, break ceasefire, shatter the peace, declare war, wage a campaign, send (in) the marines, attack, assault, assail, storm, besiege, lay siege to

▶ *381 Attack; 585 War*

37 fight, shoot, fire, pull the trigger, gun down, bomb, blast, plant mines, enter the lists, charge, strike, spear, lance, joust, tilt, fence, spar, put on one's boxing globes, box, punch, hit, wrestle, grapple

▶ *584 Military Affairs; 585 War*

38 conquer, win, subdue, quell, overcome, storm, take over, invade, maraud, raid, plunder, rob, kill, assassinate, massacre, terrorize

▶ *382 Killing; 773 Taking*

39 defend, protect, police, guard, resist, oppose, picket, protest

▶ *113 Opposition; 383 Resistance; 384 Defence; 753 Protest*

40 argue, contend, dispute, debate, disagree, quarrel, wrangle

▶ *701 Argument; 751 Disagreement*

ADVERBS

41 aggressively, inimically, agonistically, antagonistically, belligerently, pugnaciously, militantly, militaristically, imperialistically, jingoistically, chauvinistically, bloodthirstily, rowdily, argumentatively, litigiously, controversially

42 martially, pugilistically, bravely, heroically, at war, up in arms, under fire, under siege, on the front line, in the cannon's mouth, in the thick of the fray

587 Weapon

NOUNS

1 weapon, arm, deterrent, deadly weapon, defensive weapon, armour, plate, steel-plate armour, mail, chain mail, defence, offensive weapon, attack, air attack (*or* assault), air raid, artillery barrage, conventional weapon, nuclear weapon, theatre nuclear weapon, tactical nuclear weapon, nuclear deterrent, (nuclear) fallout, radioactivity, radioactive cloud, mushroom cloud, radiation, secret weapon, death ray, laser, natural weapon, teeth, fist, claws, nails

▶ *381 Attack; 384 Defence; 425 Sharpness; 585 War*

2 arms, weapons, weaponry, side arms, small arms, armament, munitions, armaments, rocketry, missilery, gunnery, musketry, archery, bowmanship

3 arms race, defence, arms traffic, (nuclear) proliferation, arms trade, gun-running

▶ *384 Defence; 436 Provisions*

4 arsenal, armoury, arms depot, ammunition ship, ammunition room, ammunition dump, ammunition chest, gunroom, gun rack, magazine, powder magazine, powder barrel, powder keg, powder flask, powder horn, caisson, ammunition box, bullet-pouch, cartridge belt, bandoleer, arrow-case, quiver, scabbard, sheath, holster, ammo dump (Inf)

▶ *410 Container; 439 Store*

5 missile weapon, missile, ballistic missile, intercontinental ballistic missile (ICBM), multiple independently targeted re-entry vehicle (MIRV), guided missile, surface-to-air missile (SAM), Cruise missile, Exocet™, Scud (Inf), defensive missile, antimissile missile, antiballistic missile (ABM), Patriot, submarine, torpedo boat, torpedo, nuclear submarine, Polaris, Trident, Strategic Defense Initiative (SDI), Star Wars, antitank weapon, bazooka, rocket-launcher, rocket, shell, star shell, flare, gas shell, shrapnel, whiz-bang, V-1, V-2, bullet, pellet, rocket site, launching pad, silo

6 historical missile weapon, javelin, harpoon, dart, bola, lasso, boomerang, catapult, woomera (Aus), throwstick, arrow, barbed arrow, poisoned arrow, shaft, bolt, quarrel, arrowhead, barb, stone, brick, brickbat, fléchette, bow, longbow, crossbow, arbalest, ballista, mangonel, trebuchet, sling, blowpipe, ball, shot

▶ *330 Propulsion*

7 blunt weapon, blunt instrument, club, bludgeon, truncheon, cudgel, cosh, life preserver, blackjack (US), shillelagh (*or* shillala), lathi, mace, knobkerrie, knobstick, battering ram, ram, warhammer, hammer, staff, stave, stick, switch, quarterstaff, sandbag, knuckle-duster, brass knuckles (US), bicycle chain, bottle, baseball bat

► *331 Impulsion*

8 sharp weapon, lance, javelin, jerid, harpoon, gaff, pike, assegai, partisan, bill, halberd, axe, battle-axe, poleaxe, tomahawk, hatchet, chopper, gisarme, sword, cold steel, naked steel, broadsword, two-edged sword, two-handed sword, cutlass, glaive (Lit), claymore, hanger, short sword, swordstick, cavalry sword, sabre, scimitar (*or* simitar), yataghan, falchion, blade, fine blade, trusty blade, bilbo, Toledo, rapier, tuck (Lit), fencing sword, foil, épée, bayonet, dagger, poniard, snickersnee (Lit), dirk, skean, sgian-dhu (*or* skean-dhu), dudgeon (Lit), misericord (*or* misericorde) (Lit), stylet, stiletto, machete, matchet, kukri, kris, parang, panga, knife, bowie knife, flick knife, pigsticker (US inf)

► *425 Sharpness*

9 firearm, gun, handgun (US), revolver, pistol, piece, automatic, semiautomatic, Colt™, repeater, rifle, magazine rifle, repeating rifle, Winchester, fowling piece, sporting gun, shotgun, sawn-off shotgun, single-barrelled gun, double-barrelled gun, smoothbore, rifled bore, bore, calibre, carbine, breechloader, elephant gun, muzzle, trigger, lock, magazine, breech, butt, gunstock, sight, backsight, ramrod, six-shooter (US inf), rod (US inf), zipgun (US inf), Saturday night special (US inf), gat (US inf), shooting iron (US inf)

► *584 Military Affairs*

10 historical gun, arquebus, hackbut, hagbut, matchlock, wheel lock, flintlock, fusil, musket, Brown Bess, blunderbuss, muzzleloader, chassepot, needlegun, Enfield rifle, duelling pistol, horse pistol, petronel, pistolet, cannon, brass cannon, horse artillery

11 guns, ordnance, cannonry, artillery, light artillery, heavy artillery, mountain artillery, galloping guns, battery, broadside, artillery park, gun park, piece, field piece, field gun, rifle, M-1 rifle (US), Garand rifle (US), siege gun, great gun, heavy gun, heavy metal, howitzer, trench-mortar, mine-thrower, *minenwerfer* (Ger), Minnie, trench gun, anti-aircraft gun, Bofers gun, anti-aircraft artillery, bazooka, assault gun, quick-firing gun, machine gun, pom-pom, M-60 machine gun, light machine gun, Bren gun, Sten gun, submachine gun, subgun, Thompson submachine gun™, Tommy gun™, uzi, kalashnikov, AK-47, gat, flamethrower, guncarriage, limber, caisson, gun emplacement

12 historical guns, bombard, falconet, swivel, basilisk, petard, carronade, culverin, mortar, cannon royal, seventy-four, Big Bertha, Whistling Dick (US), Gatling gun, mitrailleuse, pom-pom, Maxim gun, Lewis gun, Winchester

13 ammunition, live ammunition, live shot, round of ammunition, round, powder and shot, shot, small shot, buckshot, ball, bullet, expanding bullet, soft-nosed bullet, dumdum (bullet), rubber bullet, plastic bullet, baton round, projectile, missile, slug, pellet, shell, shrapnel, flak, ack-ack, wad, cartouche, cartridge, live cartridge, spent cartridge, dud, blank cartridge, blank, cartridge belt, cartridge clip, cartridge case, ammo (Inf)

14 historical ammunition, round shot, canister (shot), case shot, grapeshot, chain shot, mitraille, buckshot, ball, cannonball

► *330 Propulsion*

15 explosive, powder, gunpowder, propellant, saltpetre, high explosive, dynamite, gelignite, TNT (trinitrotoluene), nitroglycerine, lyddite, melinite, cordite, guncotton, plastic explosive, Semtex™, cap, detonator, fuse, priming, charge, warhead, atomic warhead, fissionable material, fireworks

16 bomb, explosive device, shell, bombshell, grenade, hand grenade, Molotov cocktail, megaton bomb, atom (*or* atomic) bomb, A-bomb, nuclear bomb, hydrogen bomb, H-bomb, neutron bomb, enhanced radiation bomb, radioactivity, radiation, (nuclear) fallout, radioactive cloud, mushroom cloud, cluster bomb, fragmentation bomb, nailbomb, firebomb, incendiary bomb, napalm bomb, carcass, mine, landmine, magnetic mine, acoustic mine, limpet mine, letter bomb, mailbomb, car bomb, booby trap, infernal machine (Lit), depth charge, torpedo, tin fish, flying bomb, V-1, doodlebug, V-2, rocket bomb, time bomb, Greek fire, pineapple (Inf), blockbuster (Inf)

► *379 Trap*

588 Anarchy

They that are discontented under monarchy, *call it* tyranny; *and they that are displeased with* aristocracy, *call it* oligarchy: *so also, they which find themselves grieved under a* democracy, *call it* anarchy, *which signifies the want of government; and yet I think no man believes, that want of government, is any new kind of government.* Thomas Hobbes.

NOUNS

1 anarchy, lawlessness, disorder, breakdown of law and order, no authority, interregnum, power vacuum, powerlessness, impotence, disorganization, misgovernment, misrule, unrestraint, unruliness, disruption, irresponsibility, indiscipline, disobedience, insubordination, defiance of authority, arrogation, breakdown of government, chaos, turmoil, mob rule, mob law, lynch law, sedition, subversion, fifth column, revolution, rebellion, guerrilla tactics, the underground, usurpation, abdication, forced resignation, overthrow, coup d'état, coup, dethronement, mutiny, reign of terror, law of the jungle, every man for himself, dog-eat-dog

► *335 Powerlessness; 408 Disorder; 660 Insolence; 662 Disobedience*

2 anarchism, nihilism, antinomianism, syndicalism, anarcho-syndicalism, ochlocracy, mobocracy

3 anarchist, anarch (Lit), revolutionary, subversive, seditionary, rebel, mutineer, fifth columnist, terrorist, guerrilla, assassin, arrogator, antinomian, nihilist, syndicalist, ochlocrat, mobocrat

VERBS

4 be anarchic, be anarchistic, cause anarchy, cause disorder, defy authority, resist authority, reject authority, usurp authority, usurp, undermine, subvert, arrogate, resist control, disobey, not obey, act without authority, answer to no man, be a law unto oneself, take the law into one's own hands, please oneself, do as one pleases, indulge oneself, let oneself go, practise subversion, go underground, disrupt, revolt, rebel, mutiny, overthrow, depose, lead a coup d'état, lead a coup, topple a government, assassinate (a leader), unseat, dethrone, unthrone, uncrown, seize the crown, cause to abdicate, force to resign

5 **misgovern**, misrule, mismanage, exert no authority, become disorganized, reduce to chaos

ADJECTIVES

6 **anarchic**, anarchical, disorganized, ungoverned, lawless, unofficial, wildcat, disobedient, insubordinate, seditious, self-willed, wilful, headstrong, heady, rash, disorderly, confused, uncontrolled, undisciplined, unrestrained, unbridled, unreined, unaccountable, irresponsible, rampant, unruly, wild, riotous, chaotic, rebellious, revolutionary, mutinous, dog-eat-dog

7 **anarchistic**, nihilistic, antinomian, syndicalistic, ochlocratic, mobocratic

ADVERBS

8 **anarchically**, lawlessly, unofficially, disobediently, insubordinately, seditiously, without authority, wilfully, to please oneself, rashly, irresponsibly, wildly, chaotically, rebelliously, mutinously

589 Peace

Give peace in our time, O Lord. The Book of Common Prayer.

Don't tell me peace has broken out. Bertolt Brecht.

Nation shall speak peace unto nation. Montague John Rendall.

NOUNS

1 **peace**, freedom from war, peacetime, state of peace, peaceable kingdom, peace that passeth all understanding, quiet life, the line of least resistance, no hassle, peacefulness, peace and quiet, quiescence, rest, stillness, peace of mind, harmony, concord, piping times of peace, palmy days, golden times, bed of roses, lasting peace, universal peace, Pax Romana, Pax Britannica, Pax Americana, imposed peace, law and order, order, truce, temporary truce, uneasy truce, lull in hostilities, cessation, end of war, end of hostilities, armistice, cease-fire, surrender, demobilization, military discharge (US), coexistence, armed neutrality, neutrality, nonalignment, nonaligned nations, noninvolvment, indifference, nonintervention, avoidance, peaceableness, nonaggression, cordial relations, amity, friendship, pacifism, pacification, peace at any price, mutually assured destruction, peace in our time, nonviolence, ahimsa, disarmament, nuclear disarmament, Campaign for Nuclear Disarmament (CND), ban-the-bomb movement, anti-war movement, anti-Vietnam War movement, peace movement, peace party, peace camp, peacemaking, irenics, irenic theology, peace offering, peace pipe, calumet, peace proposal, peace talks, peace treaty, peace agreement, nonaggression pact, disarmament treaty, arms limitation treaty, Strategic Arms Limitation Talks (SALT), Strategic Arms Reduction Talks (START), burying the hatchet, amnesty, pardon, forgiveness, no aggro (Inf), demob (Inf), civvy street (Inf)

▶ *226 Stopping; 263 Ease; 301 Motionlessness; 506 Silence; 569 Friendship; 585 War; 618 Indifference; 634 Avoidance; 649 Forgiveness; 685 Moderation; 748 Mediation; 749 Pacification; 750 Agreement*

2 **symbol of peace**, dove, lamb, olive branch, flag of truce, white flag, peace sign, V-sign, peace pipe, Christ, angel, broken arrow (*or* lance), United Nations (UN), International Red Cross, Peace Corps

▶ *749 Pacification*

3 **pacifist**, pacifier, man (*or* woman) of peace, peacemaker, peacemonger, peace-lover, CND member, draft dodger (US), draft evader (US), draft protester (US), draft exile (US), draft-card burner (US), peacenik, dove, neutral, civilian, noncombatant, nonbelligerent, passive resister, conscientious objector, Quaker, peace negotiator, mediator, intermediary, peacekeeper, United Nations peacekeeping force, conchie (Inf)

▶ *748 Mediation; 749 Pacification*

4 **Nobel Peace Prize**, Willy Brandt, Mikhail Gorbachev, Dag Hammarskjöld, Martin Luther King, Henry Kissinger, Anwar Sadat and Menachem Begin, Andre Sakharov, Albert Schweitzer, Mother Teresa, Bishop Desmond Tutu, Lech Wałesa, Woodrow Wilson, Rigoberta Menchu, Aung San Suu Kyi, Dalai Lama, Nelson Mandela and F. W. de Klerk, Yasser Arafat with Shimon Peres and Yitzhak Rabin, Joseph Rotblat, Bishop Carlos Filipe Ximenes Belo and José Ramos-Horta

VERBS

5 **be at peace**, enjoy peace, stay at peace, observe neutrality, keep the peace, keep out of war, make love – not war, jaw, jaw – not war, war, avoid bloodshed, keep out of trouble, mean no harm, end hostilities, call a truce, forget one's differences, bury the hatchet, smoke the peace pipe, beat swords into ploughshares, play it cool (Inf)

▶ *749 Pacification*

6 **make peace**, work for peace, ban the bomb, pacify, mediate, settle one's differences, halt the arms race, disarm, make the world a safer place, make the lion lie down with the lamb, surrender, sue for peace

▶ *748 Mediation*

ADJECTIVES

7 **peaceful**, quiet, quiet as a lamb, quiescent, tranquil, serene, still, calm, halcyon, piping, palmy, golden, bloodless, harmonious, peacelike, dovelike, harmless, inoffensive, innocent, mild, mild-mannered, easy-going, good-natured, agreeable, amiable, friendly, liberal, tolerant, uncompetitive, uncontentious, peaceable, law-abiding, peace-loving, pacific, unmilitary, unwarlike, unmilitant, nonaggressive, unaggressive, war-weary, pacifist, nonviolent, unresisting, passive, submissive, submitting, unarmed, noncombatant, civilian, neutral, nonaligned, peacemaking, conciliatory, placatory, irenic, without enemies, at peace (with the world), not at war, prewar, antebellum, postwar, postbellum, peacetime, in civvies (Inf), on civvy street (Inf)

► *263 Ease; 301 Motionlessness; 388 Submission; 506 Silence; 569 Friendship; 585 War; 748 Mediation; 749 Pacification; 750 Agreement*

ADVERBS

8 **peacefully**, peaceably, pacifically, without violence, without fear, bloodlessly, safely, quietly, softly, tranquilly, serenely, in peace, in a peaceful way, at peace

INTERJECTIONS

9 **peace**!, keep the peace!, God's peace!, peace be with you!

Emotions

590 Feelings

One may not regard the world as a sort of metaphysical brothel for emotions. Arthur Koestler.

NOUNS

1 **feeling**, perception, sensation, sense, experience, aesthesia, awareness, consciousness, realization, understanding, knowledge, reaction
▶ *455 Knowledge; 488 Sensation*

2 **impression**, fancy, belief, idea, notion, shade of feeling, inkling, intimation, suggestion, hint, nuance, undercurrent, instinctive feeling, intuition, sixth sense, insight, extrasensory perception (ESP), clairvoyance, presentiment, divination, instinct, impulse, reflex, hunch, gut reaction (Inf), vibes (Inf)
▶ *11 Occultism; 445 Intuition*

3 **feelings**, sentiments, sensibilities, susceptibilities, affections, sympathies, finer feelings, attitudes, beliefs, opinion, view, viewpoint
▶ *591 Sensitivity*

4 **emotion**, mood, attitude, frame of mind, state of mind, strong feeling, passion, ardour, fervour, fire, heat, verve, ecstasy, rapture, zeal, intensity, vehemence, obsession, fanaticism, mania
▶ *219 Excess; 594 Hate; 597 Joy*

5 **good feeling**, fellow feeling, tender feeling, fondness, sympathy, empathy, identification, cordiality, warmth, friendliness, amicability, responsiveness, involvement, liking, love, devotion
▶ *591 Sensitivity; 593 Love*

6 **bad feeling**, hard feelings, animosity, resentment, bitterness, ill will, offence, dislike, intolerance, spite, jealousy, grudge, envy, hatred, fury, rage, bad atmosphere, bad vibes (Inf)
▶ *596 Dislike; 629 Jealousy*

7 **emotionalism**, emotionality, emotiveness, nostalgia, romanticism, sentimentality, overemotionalism, mawkishness, bathos, excitability, emotional instability
▶ *591 Sensitivity*

8 **seat of feelings**, deepest feelings, core of one's being, secret places, heart, bosom, soul, spirit, bottom of one's heart, cockles of one's heart, pit of one's stomach, bones, guts (Inf)

9 **feeling person**, sympathizer, friend, carer, sensitive person, emotional person, hothead, wild boy, wild man, virago, shrew, spitfire
▶ *219 Excess; 591 Sensitivity; 593 Love*

ADJECTIVES

10 **feeling**, sensing, sentient, sensible, perceptive, aware, conscious, knowing, realizing, understanding, responsive, sensitive, impressionable, susceptible
▶ *488 Sensation; 591 Sensitivity*

11 **intuitive**, instinctive, impulsive, inspirational, clairvoyant, fey
▶ *11 Occultism*

12 **sensitive**, sympathetic, empathetic, feeling, caring, involved with, fond, cordial, friendly, amicable, warm, warm-hearted, soft-hearted, tender, romantic, nostalgic, sentimental, bathetic, maudlin, mawkish, sloppy (Inf), emotional, overemotional, tearful, overcome, overwhelmed, overwrought, hypersensitive, highly strung
▶ *591 Sensitivity; 593 Love*

13 **passionate**, impassioned, intense, effusive, ardent, fervent, zealous, vehement, rapturous, ecstatic, fiery, heated, inflamed, excitable, impetuous, hotheaded, temperamental, touchy, volatile, mercurial, unstable, melodramatic, hysterical, obsessed, jealous, envious, fanatical, manic, raving, raging, over-the-top (OTT) (Inf)
▶ *219 Excess; 594 Hate; 597 Joy; 629 Jealousy*

14 **emotive**, affecting, touching, moving, deeply felt, heartfelt, overwhelming

VERBS

15 **feel**, experience, sense, perceive, be aware of, realize, understand, go through, live through, undergo

16 **feel in one's bones**, sense, intuit, feel instinctively, know by instinct, guess at, have a hunch about (Inf)

17 **feel deeply**, take to heart, show signs of emotion, get agitated about, go into ecstasies over, have hysterics, throw a tantrum, go mad, see red, run amok, explode, throw a wobbly (Inf), be a prima donna (Inf), be a little madam (Inf), have a nervous breakdown (Inf), throw a fit (Inf), hit the roof (Inf), freak out (Inf), go bananas (Inf)
▶ *445 Intuition*

18 **feel for**, empathize, relate to, enter into the spirit of, sympathize, commiserate, pity, be sorry for, grieve for, bleed for
▶ *591 Sensitivity; 627 Pity*

19 **believe**, think, opine, maintain, hold

▶ *450 Belief*

ADVERBS

20 **with feeling**, feelingly, affectingly, touchingly, warmly, with all one's heart, from the bottom of one's heart, passionately, ardently, fervently, intensely, zealously, vehemently, rapturously, ecstatically, hysterically

21 **emotionally**, sentimentally, mawkishly

591 Sensitivity

True kindness presupposes the faculty of imagining as one's own the suffering and joy of others. André Gide.

ADJECTIVES

1 **sensitive**, impressionable, suggestible, impressible, susceptible, affectible, receptive, responsive, perceptive, sentient, feeling, delicate, aware, empathetic, sympathetic, compassionate, caring, tender, tender-hearted, soft-hearted, emotional, sentimental

▶ *590 Feelings*

2 **oversensitive**, touchy, irritable, irascible, thin-skinned, highly strung, temperamental, nervy, jumpy, like a cat on a hot tin roof

▶ *590 Feelings*

3 **sore**, painful, raw, tender, allergic, sensitized, ticklish, itchy, tingling

4 **accurate**, precise

▶ *273 Accuracy*

NOUNS

5 **sensitivity,** sensitiveness, sensibility, impressionability, suggestibility, impressibility, susceptibility, affectibility, receptivity, responsiveness, awareness, delicacy, finer feelings, tenderness, empathy, sympathy, commiseration, compassion, pity, sentimentality

▶ *488 Sensation; 590 Feelings*

6 **oversensitivity**, touchiness, irritability, irascibility, raw feelings, sore point

▶ *590 Feelings*

7 **soreness**, rawness, tenderness, ticklishness, allergy, itchiness, tingling

▶ *491 Physical Pain*

8 **sensitive person**, sympathizer, carer, counsellor, good listener, good Samaritan, new man

9 **oversensitive person**, bundle of nerves, neurotic, jitterbug, sensitive plant (*or* flower) (Inf), shrinking violet (Inf), mouse (Inf)

10 **accuracy**, pinpoint accuracy, precision, high fidelity, hi-fi, fine tuning

▶ *273 Accuracy*

VERBS

11 **be sensitive**, feel for, pity, sympathize, empathize, commiserate, show feelings, feel deeply, take to heart, be all heart, need kid-glove treatment (Inf)

ADVERBS

12 **sensitively**, feelingly, with feeling, perceptively, delicately, sympathetically, tenderly, caringly

13 **oversensitively**, emotionally, irritably, temperamentally

592 Insensitivity

Just as the meanest and most vicious deeds require spirit and talent, so even the greatest deeds require a certain insensitiveness which on other occasions is called stupidity. Georg Christoph Lichtenberg.

ADJECTIVES

1 **insensitive**, insensible, unsusceptible, immune, unresponsive, unimpressionable, unimpressible, unaffected, indifferent, apathetic, impassive, unfeeling, insensate, unemotional, frigid, cold, cold-hearted, cold-blooded, heartless, thick-skinned, impervious, proof against, rhino-hided, obtuse, blunt, tactless, unimaginative, callous, uncaring, tough, hard, hardened, blind, deaf, unaware, unconscious, imperceptive, impercipient, dull, thick (Inf)

▶ *618 Indifference*

2 **desensitized**, numb, frozen, paralysed, anaesthetized, dopey, groggy, torpid, sluggish, drugged, stupefied, comatose, unfeeling, unconscious, quiescent, inert, dead

▶ *339 Inertness; 343 Inactivity; 489 Insensibility*

NOUNS

3 **insensitiveness**, insensibility, unsusceptibility, unresponsiveness, indifference, apathy, impassivity, lack of feeling, coldness, cold-heartedness, heartlessness, callousness, tactlessness, bluntness, hardness, unawareness, dullness, Philistinism

▶ *628 Cruelty*

4 **desensitization**, narcotization, stupefaction, hypnosis, numbness, paralysis, stupor, torpor, sluggishness, grogginess, trance, coma, catalepsy, catatonia, narcosis, analgesia, anaesthesia, unconsciousness, stagnation, quiescence

▶ *339 Inertness; 343 Inactivity; 489 Insensibility*

5 **insensitive person**, ascetic, stoic, Philistine, bigot, hardnut (Inf), redneck (Inf), meathead (Inf), cold fish (Inf), iceberg (Inf), icicle (Inf), ice queen (Inf)

▶ *4 Philosophy; 466 Discrimination*

6 **desensitizing substance**, narcotic, anaesthetic, drug, soporific, painkiller, analgesic, sleeping draught, sleeping pill, nepenthes, tranquillizer, barbiturate, knockout drops (Inf), Mickey Finn (Inf), downers (Inf), barbs (Inf), reds (Inf), red devils (Inf), dope (Inf), black bombers (Inf), green and blacks (Inf)

▶ *37 Pharmacology*

VERBS

7 **render insensitive**, desensitize, numb, benumb, paralyse, freeze, stupefy, anaesthetize, narcotize, drug, dope, hypnotize, deaden, blunt, concuss, knock out, knock senseless, brain (Inf)

▶ *489 Insensibility*

ADVERBS

8 **unfeelingly**, insensitively, in cold blood, indifferently, apathetically, unemotionally, coldly, heartlessly, bluntly, tactlessly, callously

593 Love

All the world loves a lover. Proverb.

NOUNS

1 **love**, affection, natural affection, sentiment, fondness, liking, like, attachment, devotion, parental love, filial love, maternal love, paternal love, adoration, worship, hero worship, admiration, fascination, idolization, idolatry, firm attachment, regard, popular regard, popularity, respect, brotherly love, Christian love, Christian charity, charity, Agape, spiritual love, Platonic love, friendship, loyalty, compatibility, fellow feeling, understanding, mutual understanding, mutual affection, mutual attraction, mutual love, love for one's country, patriotism, self-love, narcissism, egotism

► *569 Friendship; 590 Feelings; 591 Sensitivity; 595 Liking; 650 Benevolence; 652 Philanthropy; 667 Respect*

2 **romantic love**, ardour, ardency, fervour, ecstasy, transport, transport of love, light of love, infatuation, dawn of love, first love, young love, calf love, puppy love, fancy, passing fancy, love-hate relationship, fascination, enchantment, bewitchment, possessive love, possessiveness, jealousy, free love, true love, the real thing, faithful love, sexual love, lust, married love, conjugal love, uxoriousness, Cupid's string, Oedipus complex, Electra complex, crush (Inf), mush (Inf), shine (Inf), pash (Inf)

► *663 Obedience*

3 **lovingness**, amorousness, amativeness, affectionateness, tenderness, kindness, sentiment, sentimentality, sentimental attachment, demonstrativeness, feeling, tender feeling, susceptibility, emotion, romanticism, lovesickness, lovelornness

4 **lovability**, lovableness, loveliness, likability, amiability, agreeability, attractiveness, beauty, appeal, sweetness, charm, charms, endearment, adorability, desirability, sex appeal, sexiness, flirtatiousness, coquetry, enchantment, allurement, winsomeness, winning ways, gift of pleasing, pleasing qualities, endearing qualities

► *545 Beauty*

5 **desire**, lust, passion, yearning, longing, abnormal affection, itching, amorousness, aphrodisia, flames of love, flame, fire of love, lasciviousness, licentiousness, caprice, ecstasy, intimacy, bodily love, desires of the flesh, lovemaking, making love, sex, libido, sexual urge, sexual love, act of love, sex act, sexual intercourse, sexual relations, sexual union, pairing, connection, copula (Lit), coupling, copulation, coition, coitus, cohabitation, fornication, carnal knowledge, sleeping together, sleeping with, marital relations, marriage act, mating, consummation, sexiness, eroticism, erotomania, wantonness, libertinage, prurience, venery (Lit), fucking (Inf), sleeping around (Inf), diddling (Inf), randiness (Inf), horniness (Inf), making someone (Inf), making it with (Inf), nooky (Inf), screwing (Inf), bonking (Inf), rogering (Inf), balling (US inf), humping (Inf), rumpy-pumpy (Inf), having it off (Inf), getting one's leg over (Inf)

► *796 Immorality*

6 **courtship**, pursuit of love, pursuit of a loved one, courting, wooing, dating, suit, going together, going with, going out, taking out, walking out (Dial), flirtation, flirtatiousness, flirting, coquetry, coyness, dalliance, dallying, toying, sheep's eyes, coquettish glances, sly looks, ogle, side-glance, flattering, honeying, pressing one's suit, laying siege, gallantry, hoping for conquest, advances, addresses, billing and cooing, sighing, proposing, proposal, bestowal of love, favours, suing (Lit), going steady (Inf), getting pinned (US inf), come-hither look (Inf), necking (Inf), lollygagging (US inf), fooling around (Inf), making out (US inf), making whoopee (Inf), petting (Inf), smooching (Inf), smoodging (*or* smooging) (Aus and NZ inf), spooning (Inf), goo-goo eyes (Inf), poodle-faking (Inf)

7 **choice**, preference, sympathy, predilection, inclination, tendency

► *469 Selection*

8 **love affair**, romance, relationship, amour, liaison, intrigue, flirtation, seduction, illicit love, eternal triangle, *ménage à trois* (Fr), forbidden love, affair, affair of the heart, adultery, infidelity, unfaithfulness, cuckoldry, romantic tie, entanglement, amourette, flirtation, falling in love, course of love, something between them, the old, old story, betrothal, engagement, wedding bells, espousal (Lit), hanky-panky (Inf)

► *570 Marriage*

9 **lover**, wooer, suitor, pursuer, paramour, amorist, sweetheart, conquest, captive, admirer, adorer, follower, aficionado, fan, pop fan, hero-worshipper, date, girlfriend, lass, goddess, temptress, dangerous woman, *femme fatale* (Fr), flirt, coquette, fiancée, bride-to-be, old girl, old lady, mistress, the other woman, lady in amorata, jo (Scot), Amaryllis, Dulcinea, boyfriend, young man, beau, fiancé, escort, squire, cavalier, gallant, old man, gigolo, seducer, lecher, libertine, ladies' man, woman-chaser, skirt-chaser, heartbreaker, philanderer, womanizer, Casanova, Don Juan, Lothario, Romeo, swain (Lit), strumpet (Lit), gill (Lit), blind date (Inf), steady (Inf), girl (Inf), dream girl (Inf), dream man (Inf), heart-throb (Inf), catch (Inf), (old) flame (Inf), gold-digger (Inf), vamp (Inf), lady-killer (Inf), wolf (Inf), sheik (*or* sheikh) (Inf), dreamboat (Inf), bird (Inf), sweet potato (pie) (US inf), fella (US inf), man (*or* woman) on the make (Inf), make-out artist (US inf), masher (Inf), sugar daddy (Inf), teenybopper (Inf), groupie (Inf)

10 **lovers**, soul mates, mutual lovers, loving couple, engaged couple, turtledoves, star-crossed lovers, tragic loves, Romeo and Juliet, Daphnis and Chloe, David and Bathsheba, Antony and Cleopatra, Harlequin and Columbine, Benedick and Beatrice, Pyramus and Thisbe, Hero and Leander, Tristan and Isolde, Lancelot and Guinevere, Paris and Helen, Troilus and Cressida, Heloise and Abelard, Dante and Beatrice, Heathcliff and Cathy, Napoleon and Josephine, Lord Nelson and Lady Hamilton, King Edward and Wallis Simpson, Scarlett and Rhett, lovebirds (Inf)

11 **loved one**, love, true love, beloved, dearly beloved, beloved object, object of one's affections, light of one's life, dear love, well-beloved, valentine, soul mate, favoured suitor, favourite, preference, apple of one's eye, lucky man, man after one's own heart, kept woman, mistress, jewel in the crown, future, betrothed, bride-to-be, idol, matinée idol, pop star, hero, heroine, spoiled

child, teacher's pet, family pet, cosset, blue-eyed boy (Inf), intended (Inf), bit on the side (Inf)

12 nicknames for lovers, love names, terms of endearment, love, lover, darling, dear, dear heart, precious, precious heart, cherub, angel, chickabiddy, lamb, honey (US), pet, poppet, sweetheart, sweetie (Inf), sweets (Inf), sweetkins (Inf), cookie (US inf), deary (*or* dearie) (Inf), honeybunch (US inf), lovey (Inf), sugar (US inf), petkins (Inf), snookums (Inf), honey child (US inf), lambkins (Inf), duck (*or* ducks) (Inf), ducky (Inf), hon (US inf), baby (Inf), baby doll (Inf), babe (US inf), chick (Inf), doll (Inf)

13 abode of love, love nest, bower, bower of bliss, boudoir, honeymoon suite, honeymoon cottage, bridal suite, nuptial chamber, bridal bed, woman's quarters, gynaeceum, zenana, harem, seraglio

14 communication of love, loving words, soft words, honeyed words, sweet nothings, flattery, blandishments, pet names, pretty names, billing and cooing, loving looks, fond look, amorous glance, side-glance, ogle, languishing look, sheep's eyes, wink, coquettish smile, loving touch, cuddling, tickling, snuggling, hugging, embracing, nuzzling, squeezing, caressing, fondling, bundling, kissing, kiss, osculation, French kiss, smack, smack on the lips, lovebite, bear hug, poke, pat, love slap, pinch, nip, tickle, stroke, hug, embrace, squeeze, clasp, enfoldment, caress, cuddle, nuzzle, fondle, buss (Dial), sweet-talk (Inf), petting (Inf), necking (Inf), smooching (Inf), smoodging (*or* smooging) (Aus and NZ inf), peck (Inf), peck on the cheek (Inf), nibble (Inf), (a bit of) slap and tickle (Inf), footsie (Inf), smacker (Inf), spooning (Inf), groping (Inf), grope (Inf), goose (Inf)

15 love item, love token, ribbon, pin, love letter, billet-doux, love poem, love sonnet, love song, serenade, love lyric, amorous ditty, caterwauling, valentine, aubade

16 gods and goddesses of love, Venus, Aphrodite, Astarte, Freya (*or* Freyja), Cupid, Eros, Amor, Kama

ADJECTIVES

17 loving, amorous, amative, affectionate, demonstrative, fond, attached, devoted, kind, friendly, amicable, sympathetic, charitable, agapistic, sentimental, faithful, loyal, uxorious, motherly, paternal, fraternal, platonic, charitable, Christian, brotherly, patriotic

18 in love, falling in love, head over heels in love, happily in love, blissfully in love, in love with, infatuated with, smitten (with), bitten, taken with, enamoured of, fond of, sweet on, keen on (*or* about), mad about, set on, attached to, engaged to, wedded to, caught, have a thing about (Inf), wild about (Inf), crazy about (Inf), nuts about (Inf), stuck on (Inf), sold on (Inf), (far) gone on (Inf), hipped on (US inf), hooked (Inf)

19 enamoured, attracted, charmed, becharmed, fervent, doting, devoted, gallant, enslaved, ensnared, enraptured, rapturous, infatuated, enchanted, captivated, fascinated, bewitched, besotted, mad, insane, crazed, lovesick, lovelorn, languishing, smitten, heartsmitten

20 amorous, amatory, romantic, sentimental, emotional, tender, soft, adoring, melting, flirtatious, flirty, coquettish, seductive, coy, passionate, lustful, ardent, yearning, longing, moping, mooning, desirous, lascivious, capricious, ecstatic, excited, erotic, sexy, sexual, alluring, erogenous, sexually enslaving, ensnaring, possessive, jealous, randy (Inf), horny (Inf)

21 beloved, loved, well-beloved, dearly loved, cherished, adored, esteemed, revered, preferred, fancied, favourite, chosen, pet, darling, dear, prized, treasured, dear to one's heart, after one's heart, admired, regarded, respected, well-liked, liked

22 lovable, loveworthy, lovesome, charming, endearing, adorable, appealing, interesting, intriguing, enchanting, captivating, beguiling, desirable, tempting, alluring, seductive, beautiful, lovely, winsome, sweet, winning, pleasing, engaging, graceful, angelic, seraphic, divine, kissable, cuddly, cuddlesome, caressable, huggable, popular, likable, congenial, compatible, to one's taste, to one's fancy, to one's mind

VERBS

23 love, dearly love, have love (only) for, love to distraction, adore, be sweet on, cherish, relish, treasure, hold dear, prize, value, esteem, have a high regard for, appreciate, like, desire, fancy, have a fancy for, have eyes for, go for, care for, have a soft spot for, have a weakness for, have a fondness for, hold in affection, make much of, revere, admire, idolize, worship, take pleasure in, delight in, take an interest in, feel for, think the world of, have a kind heart, have a kindness for, sympathize with

24 be in love, be sweet on, dote on, lose one's heart, have an infatuation, cling to, embrace, become enamoured with, fall for, yearn for, long for, become attached to, fall head over heels in love, burn (with love), sweat, faint, die of (*or* for) love, burn with love, burn with passion, flame with passion, warm to, take to, take a fancy to, take a liking to, have a mash on (Lit), be crazy about (Inf), have a crush on (Inf), take a shine to (Inf), cotton to (US inf), have it bad (Inf)

25 be loved, be courted, have many dates, become a favourite, steal every heart, break hearts, arouse, rouse, stir, excite, warm, heat up, inflame, draw interest, turn heads, turn on (Inf)

26 court, go courting, pay court to, woo, squire, escort, pursue, chase, press one's suit, bestow one's affections, lay siege to, set one's cap at (*or* for), lose one's heart, date, go out with, walk out with, have a date, make a date, make addresses, make advances, make passes, philander, tempt, tantalize, bait, lure, flirt, tease, trifle, dally, toy, draw on, lead on, coquet, vamp, make eyes, wink, ogle, whisper sweet nothings, sigh, serenade, run around, play around, declare one's love, offer one's heart to, sue (Lit), sweet-talk (Inf), give a come-hither look (Inf), go steady with (Inf), get pinned (US inf), pin (US inf), spoon (Inf), turn on (Inf)

27 kiss, blow a kiss, give a French kiss, smack, buss (Dial), osculate, bill and coo, pat the head, pat the cheek, pat the bottom, chuck under the chin, caress, cuddle, bundle, squeeze, fold, enfold, embrace, embosom, press (*or* clasp) to one's bosom, throw one's arms around, take into one's arms, fold to one's heart, stroke, snuggle (up), nestle (up), nuzzle (up), fondle, drool over, slobber over, dandle, coddle, cosset, pet (Inf), neck (Inf), smooch (Inf), smoodge (*or* smooge) (Aus and NZ inf), fool around (Inf), play footsie (Inf), make out (US inf), make whoopee (Inf), lollygag (US inf), have a bit of slap and tickle (Inf), spoon (Inf)

28 win the love of, enamour, enchant, becharm, charm, beguile, captivate, fascinate, enrapture, enthral, hold in thrall, bewitch, allure, attract, make oneself attractive, appeal, endear oneself, ingratiate oneself, flatter, curry favour, worm oneself into the affections, carry away, sweep off one's feet, turn one's head, flutter someone's heart, dazzle, bedazzle, ensnare, win the affection of, win the love of, win the heart of, take the fancy of, make a conquest, catch, propose (marriage), become engaged, ask for one's hand, announce one's engagement, publish the banns, marry, honeymoon, plight one's troth (Lit), make (*or* score) a hit (Inf), bowl over (Inf), pop the question (Inf), lead to the altar (Inf)

29 make love, have sex, have intercourse, sleep with, sleep together, bestow one's favours, mate, couple, copulate, cohabit, fornicate, fuck (Inf), sleep around (Inf), diddle (Inf), have one's way with, make someone (Inf), make it with (Inf), have it off (with) (Inf), screw (Inf), ball (US inf)

ADVERBS

30 lovingly, with love, with all one's love, fondly, with fondness, affectionately, with affection, tenderly, dearly, amorously, adoringly, in an affectionate way, devotedly, charitably, with charity, faithfully, fervently, romantically, with romance, sentimentally, dotingly, emotionally, under an emotional strain, with great emotion, attractively, flirtatiously, coquettishly, seductively, jealously, passionately, ardently, madly, lustfully, with lust, in heat, lasciviously, sexily, lovably, charmingly, with great charm, endearingly, adorably, appealingly, excitedly, enchantingly, captivatingly, dazzlingly, desirably, temptingly, alluringly, tantalizingly, seductively, kindly, sympathetically, with a come-hither look (Inf)

594 Hate

We can scarcely hate any one that we know. William Hazlitt.

Few people can be happy unless they hate some other person, nation or creed. Bertrand Russell.

NOUNS

1 hate, hatred, dislike, aversion, loathing, detestation, spleen, disfavour, displeasure, disaffection, disapproval, disapprobation, repugnance, revulsion, repulsion, disgust, abhorrence, abomination, antipathy, antagonism, animosity, enmity, hostility, odium, execration, spite, spitefulness, malice, malice aforethought, malevolence, malediction, malignity, bitterness, gall, rancour, acrimony, ill nature, ill feeling, ill will, ill wishes, bad wishes, sullenness, resentment, grudge, hard feelings, jealousy, envy, the green-eyed monster, venom, virulence, bad blood, bone to pick, baring one's fangs, despitefulness (Lit)

▶ *596 Dislike; 624 Anger and Resentment; 626 Sullenness; 651 Malevolence; 670 Disapproval; 751 Disagreement*

2 curse, voodoo curse, spell, evil spell, evil eye, hex, pishogue, whammy (Inf), double whammy (Inf)

▶ *712 Curse*

3 race (*or* racial) hatred, racism (*or* racialism), colour prejudice, segregation, apartheid, prejudice, bigotry, anti-Semitism, racial phobia, xenophobia, Anglophobia, Francophobia

▶ *465 Misjudgment*

4 hatefulness, loathsomeness, obnoxiousness, despicability, contemptibility, unpopularity, alienation, estrangement, discredit, disrepute, black books, bad books, bad odour, beastliness (Inf), shitlist (Inf)

▶ *470 Rejection; 668 Disrespect; 812 Notoriety*

5 anger, burst of anger, wrath, rage, tears of rage, ire, fury, raging fury, temper, fit of temper, crossness, choler

6 swearing, cursing, profanity, shouting, foul mouth

7 hated thing, pet hate, pet aversion, abomination, anathema, bugbear, bitter pill, unwelcome necessity, embarrassing situation, phobia, fear, *bête noire* (Fr), filth, illness, injury, death, pet peeve (Inf)

▶ *612 Fear*

8 hated person, not one's type, menace, pest, devil, foe, enemy, sworn enemy, archenemy, tyrant, Hitler, Stalin, nobody's darling, shrew, virago, bane, heretic, blackleg, scab, public nuisance, public enemy, criminal, murderer, Dr Fell, dastard (Lit), cad (Inf), bastard (Inf), bad news (Inf), git (Inf), bitch (Offensive)

▶ *113 Opposition; 586 Combatant*

9 hater, misanthrope, misanthropist, misogamist, misogynist, woman-hater, misandrist, man-hater, homophobe, bigot, racist (*or* racialist), anti-Semite, phobic, xenophobe, Anglophobe, Francophobe

▶ *653 Misanthropy*

ADJECTIVES

10 hating, hateful, full of hate, loathing, detesting, abhorring, antipathetic, antagonistic, hostile, execrative, averse, spiteful, spleenful, vindictive, vicious, contemptuous, malicious, full of malice, malevolent, maledictive, malignant, rancorous, acrimonious, poisonous, bitter, sharp, ill-natured, set against, resentful, grudging, sour, sullen, jealous, envious, green-eyed, venomous, virulent

11 racist, racialist, prejudiced, bigoted, anti-American, anti-Semitic, phobic, xenophobic, Anglophobic, Francophobic

12 hated, loathed, hateful, loathsome, not nice, detestable, disgusting, abhorrent, odious, obnoxious, despicable, contemptible, execrable, accursed, unlovable, invidious, unpopular, out of favour, discredited, disliked, unwelcome, unwanted, baneful, nasty, horrid, repugnant, revolting, repelling, abominable, disgusting, vile, repulsive, nauseous, nauseating, alien, strange, foreign, unloved, loveless, scorned, jilted, lovelorn, crossed in love, unvalued, unmissed, unlamented, unmourned, unchosen, spurned, condemned, in someone's bad books, in someone's black books, beastly (Inf), on someone's shitlist (Inf)

13 angry, wrathful, irate, furious, bad-tempered, in a bad temper, cross, choleric, implacable, profane, evil-speaking, cursing, swearing, foul-mouthed

VERBS

14 hate, dislike, have no love for, detest, utterly detest, loathe, find loathsome, abhor, execrate, hold in disgust, hold in contempt, despise, abominate, bear malice towards, take an aversion to, show displeasure, have hard feelings towards, disapprove, shudder at, turn away from, recoil at, shrink from, reject, spurn, refuse, not choose, object to, resent, bear a grudge, envy, disrelish, condemn, denounce, avoid, curse, have a bone to pick, bare one's fangs, have a down on (Inf), spit upon (Inf), have it in for (Inf), hate one's guts (Inf)

15 curse, cast a spell upon, give someone the evil eye, throw (*or* put) the whammy on (Inf), throw (*or* put) the double whammy on (Inf)

16 cause hate, excite hate, cause loathing, antagonize, aggravate, exacerbate, alienate, estrange, sour, envenom, embitter, poison, incense, enrage, disgust, repel, nauseate, make enemies, sow dissension, create bad blood, destroy good will, set by the ears, grate, jar, end up in someone's black books, mix it (Inf)

17 anger, have a burst of anger, rage, show ire, have a fit of temper, utter profanities, curse, swear, have a foul mouth, spit tacks (Aus inf)

ADVERBS

18 hatefully, in a hateful manner, loathingly, antipathetically, antagonistically, in an antagonistic way, hostilely, with hostility, execratively, aversely, spitefully, with spite, spleenfully, vindictively, viciously, contemptuously, with contempt, maliciously, with malice, malevolently, maledictively, malignantly, rancorously, acrimoniously, poisonously, bitterly, sharply, ill-naturedly, with an ill nature, resentfully, grudgingly, sourly, sullenly, jealously, enviously, venomously, virulently, obnoxiously, despicably, contemptibly, disreputably

595 Liking

NOUNS

1 liking, attachment, sentimental attachment, tender feeling, tenderness, fond feeling, fondness, affection, attraction, affinity, mutual affinity, friendship, friendliness, intimacy, empathy, sympathy, approval, favourable attitude, admiration, infatuation, titillation, fascination, temptation, allurement, devotion, loyal devotion, patriotism, adoration, love, mutual love, desire, passion, appetite, weakness, zest, wishing, longing, yearning, hankering

► *569 Friendship; 593 Love; 654 Sociability*

2 inclination, tendency, penchant, propensity, proclivity, preference, favour, predilection, predisposition, disposition, intention, partiality, prejudice, bias, leaning, selection, choice, readiness, willingness, eagerness, mind, cast of mind, turn, bent, aptitude

► *106 Predetermination; 469 Selection; 480 Persuasion; 482 Intention*

3 likes, hobby, fancy, caprice, whim, whimsy, phase, trend, craze, pleasure, relish, taste, mania, wish, craving, infatuation, soft spot, selection, choice, fad (Inf), crush (Inf), shine (Inf)

4 likable person, good person, kind person, helpful person, good Samaritan, rescuer, saviour, good acquaintance, close associate, friend, close friend, best friend, intimate friend, bosom friend, good neighbour, companion, confidant, confidante, dear one, dear, treasure, beloved one, darling, love, lover, childhood playmate, schoolmate, mate (Inf), pal (Inf), chum (Inf), buddy (US inf), bosom buddy (US inf), sidekick (Inf)

ADJECTIVES

5 likable, liked, favoured, admired, appreciated, popular, wished for, good, amicable, congenial, friendly, affectionate, appealing, fascinating, adorable, lovely, attractive, pleasing, endearing, captivating, infatuating, titillating, tempting, alluring, lovable, intimate

6 liking, admiring, fascinated, devoted, inclined towards, empathetic, sympathetic, tending, intending, turning, bending, leaning, predisposed, disposed, prejudiced, biased, favouring, favourable towards, preferrring, approving, partial to, wishing, hankering, longing, yearning, loving, infatuated, titillated, desirous, passionate, ready, willing, eager

VERBS

7 like, care for, have an affinity for, act in a friendly manner, show empathy, sympathize with, hold dear, cherish, appreciate, esteem, treasure, prize, think the world of, have high regard for, enjoy, delight in, adore, admire, relish, savour, have an attachment for, take a fancy to, take to, stay devoted to, feel fondness for, love, desire, have passion for, show a weakness for, wish, wish for oneself, set one's heart on, have designs, on, long, yearn, hanker after, be sweet on, be infatuated with, fancy (Inf), have a crush on (Inf)

8 prefer, want, have a preference for, have a propensity for, be inclined towards, approve, show approval for, favour, predispose oneself, lean towards, intend, select, choose, have a cast of mind, turn, bend, show aptitude for

9 like to, want to, wish to, love to, dearly love to, long to, choose to

ADVERBS

10 with great liking, with a likeable manner, popularly, amicably, congenially, affectionately, with affection, appealingly, fascinatingly, adorably, attractively, pleasingly, in a pleasing way, endearingly, captivatingly, infatuatingly, titillatingly, temptingly, lovably, intimately

11 admiringly, with great admiration, empathetically, sympathetically, in a sympathetic manner, favourably, approvingly, longingly, yearningly, lovingly, with love, desirously, passionately, in a passionate moment, readily, willingly, eagerly

596 Dislike

NOUNS

1 dislike, instinctive dislike, instant dislike, disapproval, disfavour, disaffection, aversion, prejudice, bias, ill feeling, distaste, disrelish, dissatisfaction, discontent, displeasure, avoidance, rejection, disinclination, no inclination for, no stomach for, reluctance, unwillingness, ill will, resentment, disagreement, dissent, antipathy, antagonism, enmity, animosity, bad blood, abhorrence, detestation, abomination, hatred, mutual hatred, common hatred, hate, loathing, hostility, repugnance, repulsion, disgust, horror, mortal horror, fear, phobia, xenophobia, claustrophobia, bitterness, sourness, gall and wormwood, allergy (Inf)

▶ *242 Unpleasantness; 364 Repulsion; 470 Rejection; 594 Hate; 606 Dissatisfaction; 612 Fear; 624 Anger and Resentment; 634 Avoidance; 637 Unwillingness; 670 Disapproval*

2 disliked thing, object of dislike, pet aversion, pet hate, pet peeve, embarrassing situation, failure, defeat, dangerous encounter, danger

▶ *247 Failure; 254 Danger; 264 Difficulty*

3 disliked person, not one's type, rude person, mannerless brat, fault-finder, unfair opponent, ill-wisher, bad neighbour, antagonist, enemy, sworn enemy, *persona non grata* (L), *bête noire* (Fr), loudmouth (Inf)

▶ *113 Opposition; 249 Adversity; 655 Unsociability*

4 sign of dislike, shyness, drawing back, frown, scowl, shuddering, nausea, queasiness, heaving stomach, vomiting, cold sweat, creeping flesh

▶ *260 Ill Health*

VERBS

5 dislike, have no liking for, take a dislike to, not care for, have no inclination for, have no desire for, have no use for, have no stomach for, have no heart for, have no time for, not endure, prefer not to, disapprove, reject, object to, feel an aversion for, disfavour, disrelish, find not to one's taste, not like the look of, take a dim view of, have it in for, can't stand, can't bear, not be able to bear, take offence at, mind, demonstrate ill will, show resentment, resent, have a grudge against, disagree, dissent, antagonize, loathe, abhor, detest, despise, abominate, hate, share a common hatred, fear, feel fear, feel disgust, sicken at, feel sick at, want to vomit, mislike (Lit)

6 react against, vote against, not choose, avoid, recoil, shun, turn away, shrink from, look askance, make a face, sniff at, sneer at, yell at, grimace, shudder, vomit, fight, hit, attack, have one's knife in, turn up the nose (Inf)

7 cause dislike, repel, disgust, disincline, deter, frighten, go against the grain, rub the wrong way, annoy, antagonize, put one's back up, enrage, set against, set at odds, turn one against, make bad blood, excite hate, pall, pall on, jade, sate, disagree with, disagree, upset, put off, revolt, repel, offend, grate, jar, displease, torment, disgust, nauseate, sicken, make one sick, shock, scandalize, create a scandal, incur blame, get on one's nerves (Inf), stick in one's throat (Inf), get up one's nose (Inf), get one's goat (Inf), gross out (US inf)

ADJECTIVES

8 disliking, not liking, displeased, discontented, dissatisfied, disenchanted, disillusioned, without love, loveless, undesirous, unsympathetic, out of sympathy, disinclined, loath, unwilling, reluctant, averse, not charmed, put off, disaffected, shy, avoiding, squeamish, queasy, disagreeing, dissenting, averse, resentful, fearful, unfriendly, hostile, antipathetic, antagonistic, bitter, inimical, repelled, not tolerating, prejudiced against, biased against, disapproving, disgusted, despising, abhorring, loathing, detesting, hating, hateful, fearing, fearful, sickened, sated, nauseous, nauseated, vomiting, sick of (Inf), sick and tired of (Inf), allergic (Inf)

9 disliked, dislikable, unlikable, unpopular, unappreciated, out of favour, disapproved, disfavoured, not one's sort, not to one's taste, uncared for, unwanted, avoided, undesired, undesirable, unprepossessing, unloved, unlovable, rejected, jilted, spurned, thrown over, unchosen, unwelcome, unrelished, distasteful, uncomforting, unconsoling, disagreeing, disagreeable, insufferable, not tolerated, intolerable, despised, loathsome, feared, fearsome, abhorred, abhorrent, disgusting, repulsive, repugnant, rebarbative, abominable, revolting, foul, stinking, unsavoury, nauseating, sickening, in one's bad book, not one's cup of tea (Inf), yucky (Inf)

ADVERBS

10 discontentedly, unsympathetically, unwillingly, under duress, reluctantly, with misgivings, shyly, aversely, resentfully

11 disgustingly, repulsively, repugnantly, rebarbatively

597 Joy

There are those who believe Black people possess the secret of joy and that it is this that will sustain them through any spiritual or moral or physical devastation. Alice Walker.

NOUNS

1 happiness, contentment, euphoria, gladness, lightheartedness, cheerfulness, merriment, delight, pleasure, enjoyment, delectation, joy, joyfulness, joyousness, felicity, gaiety, glee, gleefulness, high spirits, *joie de vivre* (Fr), gusto, zest, exuberance, ebullience, transport, exaltation, exhilaration, rapture, ecstasy, bliss, enchantment, intoxication, delirium

▶ *598 Happiness; 600 Rejoicing; 609 Satisfaction*

2 fun, entertainment, party, treat, holiday, celebration, merrymaking, revelry, honeymoon period, halcyon days, heaven, paradise, joy, thrill, kick (Inf), buzz (Inf), lark (Inf), whizz (Inf), high (Inf)

▶ *601 Celebration*

3 joyful person, merrymaker, reveller, party-goer, groover (Inf), raver (Inf)

ADJECTIVES

4 happy, contented, euphoric, pleased, glad, gladsome, cheerful, joyful, joyous, full of joy, felicitous, gay, blithe, merry, delighted, exuberant, ebullient, blissful, starry-eyed, elated, overjoyed, thrilled, transported, ecstatic, celebratory, jubilant, captivated, enchanted, enraptured, delirious, intoxicated, beside oneself, beside oneself with joy, like a child with a new toy, pleased as Punch (Inf), happy as a sandboy (Inf), over the moon (Inf), on cloud nine (Inf), in seventh heaven (Inf), tickled pink (Inf), tickled to death (Inf), high as a kite (Inf), blissed out (Inf)

5 delightful, lovely, wonderful, marvellous, heavenly, enchanting, gorgeous, entrancing, charming, enthralling, captivating, Elysian (Lit), out of this world (Inf)

▶ *241 Pleasantness*

VERBS

6 enjoy, have fun, celebrate, relish, delight in, take pleasure in, have a good time, eat, drink, and be merry, kick up one's heels (Inf)

7 show joy, smile, grin, beam, laugh, chuckle, giggle, chortle, guffaw, crow, sing, purr, rejoice

8 cause joy, gladden, please, cheer, thrill, delight, charm, enchant, enrapture, enthral, captivate, intoxicate, send (Inf)

ADVERBS

9 joyfully, happily, gladly, cheerfully, with pleasure, merrily, gaily, gleefully

598 Happiness

ADJECTIVES

1 cheerful, cheery, happy, glad, joyful, in good spirits, radiant, sunny, smiling, grinning, beaming, laughing, genial, good-natured, good-humoured, optimistic, sociable, light-hearted, exhilarated, merry, jolly, jovial, convivial, genial, gay, funny, buoyant, carefree, jaunty, perky, vivacious, lively, animated, sparkling, high-spirited, in high spirits, bouncing, bouncy, chirpy, bonhomous, high (Inf), up (Inf)

▶ *597 Joy*

2 cheering, encouraging, heart-warming, reviving, uplifting, amusing, diverting, entertaining, wacky (Inf)

NOUNS

3 cheerfulness, cheer, cheeriness, happiness, joy, good spirits, sunniness, geniality, good humour, sociability, light-heartedness, exhilaration, optimism, good cheer, jollity, joviality, conviviality, geniality, gaiety, levity, mirth, vivacity, jauntiness, liveliness, animation, high spirits, laughter, merriment, merrymaking, fun

▶ *599 Humour*

4 cheerful person, optimist, life and soul of the party (Inf), ray of sunshine (Inf), smiler (Inf)

5 cheer, whoop, shout, yell, applause, clap, clapping

VERBS

6 bring cheer, cheer, gladden, cheer up, revive (the spirits of), brighten, lighten, hearten, enliven, uplift, animate, exhilarate, perk up (Inf), buck up (Inf), jolly along (Inf)

7 be cheerful, have fun, enjoy, smile, grin, beam, laugh, sparkle, grin and bear it, put on a brave face, look on the bright side

8 cheer, whoop, shout, yell, applaud, clap, hurrah, give three cheers, encourage, spur, spur on

▶ *601 Celebration*

ADVERBS

9 cheerfully, cheerily, with good cheer, with a cheerful heart, happily, gladly, joyfully, radiantly, light-heartedly, merrily, gaily, jauntily, perkily, buoyantly, with high spirits

599 Humour

No mind is thoroughly well organized that is deficient in a sense of humour. Samuel Taylor Coleridge.

It's hard to be funny when you have to be clean. Mae West.

NOUNS

1 humorousness, humour, funniness, wit, wittiness, jokiness, drollery, dryness, facetiousness, flippancy, pawkiness

2 amusement, entertainment, diversion, fun, merriment, mirth, laughter, enjoyment, hilarity

3 wit, ready wit, joking, jesting, joshing, teasing, kidding, clowning, buffoonery, quipping, wordplay, banter, badinage, repartee, dry wit, sarcasm, irony, gallows humour, black humour, sick humour, blue humour

4 entertainment, comedy, satire, parody, caricature, send-up, takeoff, farce, lampoon, burlesque, slapstick, stand-up comedy, comedy routine, comedy skit, comedy hour, sitcom (situation comedy), musical comedy, cartoon, comic strip

▶ *21 Drama*

5 joke, jest, jape, caper, practical joke, prank, trick, witticism, gag, pun, one-liner, wisecrack, quip, pleasantry, funny story, yarn, old chestnut, shaggy dog story, tall story, blue joke, double entendre, dirty story, belly laugh, a laugh (Inf), lark (Inf), leg-pull (Inf)

▶ *700 Deception*

6 humorist, wit, wag, joker, jester, tease, teaser, gagster, wisecracker, jokesmith, nimblewit (US), comic, comedian, stand-up comic (*or* comedian), alternative comedian, straight man, clown, buffoon, gag writer, ironist, satirist, lampooner, caricaturist, cartoonist, top banana (US inf), second banana (US inf)

▶ *21 Drama*

7 person who humours, sycophant, toady, flatterer, bootlicker (Inf), brown-nose (US inf), creep (Inf)

▶ *664 Servility; 677 Flattery*

8 temperament, disposition, humour

▶ *99 Essence*

ADJECTIVES

9 funny, amusing, diverting, entertaining, laughable, risible, hilarious, uproarious, side-splitting, hysterical (Inf)

10 humorous, witty, funny, jocular, jocose, joking, slapstick, waggish, nimble-witted, quick-witted, smart, comic, droll, amusing, whimsical, quirky, zany, Pythonesque, merry, pawky, dry, facetious, farcical, sarcastic, ironic, satirical, flippant, teasing, jokey (Inf), corny (Inf)

11 humouring, pleasing, placating, indulging, pampering, cossetting, spoiling, cajoling, flattering, sycophantic, servile, ingratiating, toadying, unctuous, oily, slimy (Inf), smarmy (Inf), bootlicking (Inf), brown-nosing (US inf)

12 four humours, phlegmatic, sanguine, choleric, melancholic

VERBS

13 be humorous, entertain, amuse, regale, divert, joke, crack a joke, josh, jest, banter, pun, quip, wisecrack, clown, play the fool, make fun of, poke fun at, play a joke on, pull someone's leg, tease, rag, twit, kid, rib, scoff, mock, satirize, parody, send up, take off, lampoon, caricature

14 laugh, giggle, snigger, snicker, titter, chuckle, chortle, guffaw, howl, roar, slap one's thighs, split one's sides, roll in the aisles, laugh like a drain, laugh till one cries, laugh one's head off, hoot (Inf)

▶ *597 Joy; 598 Happiness; 600 Rejoicing*

15 humour, gratify, please, placate, indulge, pamper, cosset, spoil, cajole, flatter, patronize, condescend, smarm, cultivate, toady to, suck up to (Inf), butter up (Inf), bootlick (Inf), soft-soap (Inf), brown-nose (US inf)

ADVERBS

16 **humorously**, wittily, amusingly, funnily, laughably, hilariously, comically, drolly, whimsically, drily, facetiously, farcically, sarcastically, ironically, satirically

17 **jokingly**, as a joke, for fun, in fun, in sport, for sport, with tongue in cheek

600 Rejoicing

All my life through, the new sights of Nature made me rejoice like a child. Marie Curie.

NOUNS

1 **rejoicing**, celebrating, jubilation, exultation, triumph, happiness, joyfulness, joy, delight, jolliness, merriment, jollification, roistering, merrymaking, festivity, festivities, celebration, special day, holiday, festival, high days and holidays, anniversary, jubilee, party, revel, great day, feast, feast day, street party, banquet, field day, rave (Inf), beano (Inf)

▶ *25 Cookery; 597 Joy; 601 Celebration*

2 **fanfare**, salute, applause, ovation, cry, shout, yell, cheer, three cheers, hurrah, huzzah, hosanna, hallelujah, hallelujah chorus, hymn, praise, glory, thanksgiving, congratulation, congratulations

▶ *7 Religion; 507 Loudness; 669 Approval*

3 **laughter**, giggling, tittering, hilarity, laugh, giggle, titter, chortle, snigger, the giggles

▶ *597 Joy; 599 Humour*

4 **rejoicer**, celebrator, laugher, giggler, titterer, cackler, reveller, merrymaker, roisterer, raver (Inf)

VERBS

5 **rejoice**, celebrate, jubilate, exult, triumph, glory, leap for joy, make merry, have a party, roister, revel, carouse, feast, banquet, have a ball (Inf), make whoopee (Inf), paint the town red (Inf), go on a binge (Inf), rave (Inf), whoop it up (Inf), throw a party (Inf), have a knees-up (Inf)

▶ *597 Joy; 601 Celebration*

6 **fête**, lionize, sing the praises of, praise, honour, pay respects to, salute, kill the fatted calf for, give a hero's welcome to

▶ *669 Approval*

7 **dance**, skip, frolic, rollick, clap, applaud, cry, shout, yell, cheer, give thanks, congratulate

▶ *22 Dancing; 507 Loudness; 669 Approval*

8 **laugh**, titter, giggle, chortle, get the giggles (Inf), split one's sides (Inf), fall about (Inf), roll in the aisles (Inf)

▶ *599 Humour*

ADJECTIVES

9 **rejoicing**, celebratory, jubilant, exultant, triumphant, glorious, ecstatic, euphoric, happy, joyful, cheery, merry, jolly, revelling, applauding, cheering, high (Inf)

▶ *597 Joy; 601 Celebration; 669 Approval*

10 **laughing**, giggling, tittering, laughable, comic, humorous, funny, hilarious, side-splitting (Inf)

▶ *599 Humour*

ADVERBS

11 **rejoicingly**, jubilantly, triumphantly, ecstatically, euphorically, joyfully, merrily

INTERJECTIONS

12 **hurrah!**, hip, hip, hurrah!, hooray!, hip, hip, hooray!, hosanna!, hallelujah!, yippee!

601 Celebration

On with the dance! let joy be unconfined;
No sleep till morn, when Youth and Pleasure meet
To chase the glowing Hours with flying feet. Lord Byron.

NOUNS

1 **celebration**, celebrating, observance, festivity, festivities, festive occasion, fête, fiesta, festa, function, picnic, party, feast, banquet, beanfeast, rejoicing, revel, revelry, revels, carousal, orgy, debauch, drinking bout, dithyramb, *Oktoberfest* (Ger), Mardi Gras, saturnalia, performance, occasion, jubilation, jubilee, merrymaking, merriment, gaiety, jollity, jollification, conviviality, Whoopee, skylarking, holiday(-making), gala (affair), jamboree, high jinks, fair, carnival, binge (Inf), bender (Inf), blowout (Inf), do (Inf), bit of a do (Inf)

2 **commemoration,** memorialization, honouring, remembrance, memory, observance, ceremonial, solemnization, marking the occasion, jubilee, holiday, memorial service, remembrance service, anniversary

3 **ceremony**, ceremonial function, function, ritual, service, office, solemn observance, ritual observance, rite, liturgy, ovation, coronation, enthronement, triumph, rite of passage, bar mitzvah, convocation, graduation, inauguration, initiation, mummery

4 **reception**, hero's welcome, ticker-tape welcome, red-carpet treatment, reception committee, triumphal arch

5 **anniversary**, special day, day to remember, great day, gala day, flag day, feast day, fast day, field day, holy day, saint's day, high day, Armistice Day, Remembrance Sunday, poppy day, D-day, Fourth of July, Thanksgiving, Independence Day, Republic Day, Bastille Day, V-E Day, birthday, name day, wedding anniversary, silver wedding, ruby wedding, golden wedding, diamond wedding, centenary, bicentenary, sesquicentenary, jubilee, silver jubilee, golden jubilee, diamond jubilee

6 **tribute**, testimonial, testimonial banquet (*or* dinner), toast, health, congratulation

7 **thanksgiving**, harvest home, Te Deum, thanks, hosanna, hallelujah

8 **salute**, salvo, fanfare, triumph, fanfare, fanfaronade, dressing ship, flypast, march past, drum roll, tattoo, flags, banners, waving, bunting, streamers, ticker tape, decorations, Chinese lanterns, illuminations, fireworks, bonfire

9 **rejoicing**, cheering, applause, ovation, standing ovation, flag waving, mafficking

ADJECTIVES

10 **celebrative**, celebratory, festive, merry, gay, convivial, dithyrambic

11 **commemorative**, ceremonial, solemn, memorial, honourable

12 ceremonial, ritual, solemn, triumphal, crowning
13 congratulatory, welcoming, complimentary, auspicious
14 centennial, bicentennial, tricentennial, sesquicentennial

VERBS

15 celebrate, rejoice, revel, merrymake, fête, party, junket, felicitate, maffick
16 commemorate, honour, keep, mark, remember, memorialize, solemnize, observe, jubilate, jubilize, signalize, hallow, keep holy, perform, sanctify, mark the occasion, pay one's respects
17 congratulate, toast, drink the health of, drink to, raise (*or* fill) one's glass, praise, pay tribute to, sing the praises of, reward, drain a bumper, sing Happy Birthday
18 salute, welcome, cheer, applaud, roll out the red carpet, kill the fatted calf, fête, chair, lionize, hang out the flags (*or* bunting), garland, throw a party, make much of, do one proud, carry shoulder high, mob, deck (*or* wreathe) with flowers, fling wide the gates, beat a tattoo, blow the trumpets, fire a salvo
19 install, enthrone, crown, inaugurate, launch, induct, initiate, instate, present, auspicate
20 come out, pass out, graduate

ADVERBS

21 in honour of, in memory of, in commemoration of, on the occasion of, in remembrance of

602 Sorrow

Do you hear the children weeping, O my brothers,
Ere the sorrow comes with years? Elizabeth Barrett Browning.

A moment of time may make us unhappy for ever. John Gay.

Down, thou climbing sorrow,
Thy element's below. William Shakespeare.

NOUNS

1 sorrow, sadness, regret, unhappiness, sorrowfulness, heartache, sadheartedness, downheartedness, heavyheartedness, wretchedness, misery, desolation, heartbreak, suffering, distress, anguish, languishment, agony, pain, torment, woe, grief, dolour, mourning, weeping and wailing and gnashing of teeth (Inf)
► *249 Adversity; 603 Lamentation*
2 depression, melancholy, malaise, droopiness, dreariness, joylessness, cheerlessness, low spirits, lowness, dejection, dejectedness, despondency, Slough of Despond, gloom, gloominess, the doldrums, dispiritedness, glumness, despair, black despair, death wish, the dumps (Inf), the blues (Inf)
► *611 Despair*
3 sad person, sufferer, languisher, wretch, poor wretch, downer (Inf)
4 depressing person, depressive, melancholic, moper, whiner, whinger (Inf), complainer, Job's comforter, Jonah, killjoy, spoilsport (Inf), sourpuss (Inf), wet blanket (Inf), Eeyore (Inf), misery (Inf), miseryguts (Inf), bring-down (Inf)

ADJECTIVES

5 sad, unhappy, sorrowful, crestfallen, saddened, sadhearted, downhearted, heavyhearted, disheartened, distressed, miserable, wretched, forlorn, languishing, tormented, woebegone, tearful, doleful, dolorous, mournful, pining, heartbroken, broken-hearted, disconsolate, inconsolable, desolate, grief-stricken, ululant, cut up (Inf)
6 depressed, melancholic, downcast, low, droopy, dreary, joyless, dejected, dispirited, despondent, in the doldrums, atrabilious, lugubrious, grey, lacklustre, listless, gloomy, morose, glum, dismal, long-faced, moody, moping, suicidal, out of sorts (Inf), down (Inf), down in the dumps (Inf), Eeyorish (Inf), bad (Inf), face like a tombstone (Inf), face like a wet weekend (Inf), blue (Inf), sunk (Inf), in the depths (Inf), in a black hole (Inf)
7 distressing, depressing, dispiriting, sorry, lamentable, heartbreaking, harrowing, painful, tragic, grievous

VERBS

8 grieve, sorrow, sadden, languish, mourn, pine, sigh, lament, cry, weep, sob, moan, howl, wail, ululate, eat one's heart out (Inf), be cut up (Inf)
9 despair, despond, lose heart, lose hope, give way, droop, mope, wilt, flag, brood, sulk, hit bottom (Inf), hit rock bottom (Inf), be a wet blanket (Inf)
10 depress, bring down, dishearten, dispirit, dampen, dampen the spirits of, put a wet blanket on (Inf), pour cold water on (Inf)

ADVERBS

11 sadly, sorrowfully, unhappily, miserably, mournfully, dolefully, with a sad heart, with tears in one's eyes
12 joylessly, gloomily, glumly, drearily, listlessly, dismally, lugubriously, with a long face

603 Lamentation

I weep for Adonais – he is dead!
O, weep for Adonais! though our tears
Thaw not the frost which binds so dear a head! Percy Bysshe Shelley.

NOUNS

1 lamentation, lamenting, grieving, crying, weeping, wailing, weeping and wailing and gnashing of teeth, keening, mourning, wake, last rites, widow's weeds, sackcloth and ashes, dolefulness, tearfulness, sobbing, sadness, sorrow, sorrowfulness, mournfulness, plangency, wretchedness, woe
► *583 Burial; 602 Sorrow*
2 lament, lamentation, requiem, obsequies, dirge, elegy, swan song, threnody, coronach, knell, funeral oration, thanatopsis, last post, keen, howl, ululation, cry, moan, groan, sigh, complaint, sob story, tale of woe
► *18 Music; 602 Sorrow; 606 Dissatisfaction*
3 lamenter, griever, weeper, wailer, keener, mourner, elegist, threnodist, blubberer, cry-baby, sniveller

ADJECTIVES

4 lamenting, grieving, crying, weeping, lachrymose, tearful, wailing, keening, mourning, mournful, miserable, doleful, wretched, woebegone, disconsolate, unhappy, sad, sorrowful, wet-eyed, red-eyed, plaintive, plangent, dirgelike, elegiac, threnodic, depressed, down (Inf)

5 **lamentable**, pitiful, tear-jerking, distressing, depressing, deplorable, regrettable

VERBS

6 **lament**, grieve, sorrow, mourn, mourn for, go into mourning for, elegize, threnodize, weep for, wail, keen, beat one's breast, bemoan, bewail, complain, deplore, regret, rue

▶ *583 Burial; 602 Sorrow; 606 Dissatisfaction*

7 **weep**, cry, sob, wail, shed tears over, weep over, cry one's eyes out, howl, ululate, sigh, snivel, blubber, blub (Inf)

ADVERBS

8 **mournfully**, tearfully, dolefully, sadly, plaintively, plangently, in mourning, in black, in sackcloth and ashes, at half-mast

604 Disappointment

Mountains will heave in childbirth, and a silly little mouse will be born. Horace.

Look in my face; my name is Might-have-been.
I am also called No-more, Too-late, Farewell. Dante Gabriel Rossetti.

NOUNS

1 **disappointment**, bitter disappointment, discouragement, mortification, chagrin, regret, regrets, frustration, feeling of frustration, frustrated expectations, partial success, near failure, noncompletion, nonfulfilment, unfulfilled expectations, tantalization, tease, raised expectations, false hopes, blighted hopes, unsatisfied hopes, hopes unrealized, betrayed hopes, hopelessness, despair, bafflement, false expectation, vain expectation, forlorn hope, overestimation, miscalculation, misjudgment

▶ *465 Misjudgment; 467 Overestimation; 602 Sorrow; 611 Despair*

2 **bad outcome**, bad result, bad news, not what one had hoped for, not what one had expected, disenchantment, disillusionment, disillusion, discontent, dissatisfaction, shock, blow, setback, balk, hitch, impediment, obstacle, bad luck, misfortune, trick of fortune, slip 'twixt the cup and the lip, anticlimax, damp squib, comedown, letdown, bringing down to earth, humiliation, humbling, failure, defeat, disaster, fiasco, one in the eye for (Inf), bummer (Inf)

▶ *247 Failure; 249 Adversity; 378 Obstruction; 606 Dissatisfaction; 623 Humility; 630 Surprise; 741 News; 794 Prize*

3 **mirage**, trick of the light, false dawn, fool's paradise, fool's gold

VERBS

4 **be disappointed**, try in vain, fail, come up short, fall short, not realize one's expectations, miscalculate, misjudge, expect more, expect better, have hoped for better, have hoped for something better, have hoped better of, expect otherwise, have one's plans ruined, have a bad outcome, have a bad result, find to one's cost, regret, follow bad advice, listen to a false prophet, be duped, be led astray

▶ *247 Failure; 700 Deception*

5 **be crestfallen**, look blue, look blank, laugh on the other side of one's face, be sick with disappointment, be sick at heart, despair

▶ *602 Sorrow; 611 Despair; 623 Humility*

6 **disappoint**, fall short, fail to deliver, not come up to expectations, belie one's expectations, ruin one's plans, go wrong, turn sour, defeat one's hopes, dash one's hopes, crush one's hopes, blight one's hopes, deceive one's hopes, betray one's hopes, burst the bubble, bring down to earth, disenchant, disillusion, serve badly, fail, let down, leave in the lurch, not come up to scratch, dash the cup from one's lips, tantalize, tease, raise one's expectations, leave unsatisfied, dissatisfy, dishearten, sadden, upset, spoil one's pleasure, dumbfound, boggle one's mind, surprise, amaze

▶ *378 Obstruction; 602 Sorrow; 623 Humility; 630 Surprise*

7 **thwart**, frustrate, balk, bilk, foil, baffle, confound, hinder, hamper, refuse, deny, stonewall, turn away, reject, jilt, befool, humble, humiliate, put one's nose out of joint, disconcert, discontent, sour, embitter with disappointment, cause discontent, stand up (Inf)

▶ *470 Rejection; 499 Sourness; 606 Dissatisfaction; 623 Humility*

8 **be dishonest**, betray, cheat, deceive, mislead, delude, dupe, trick, swindle, play false, betray one's trust, play a trick, con (Inf), flimflam (Inf), sting (Inf), take to the cleaners (Inf)

▶ *700 Deception; 800 Dishonour*

ADJECTIVES

9 **disappointed**, disenchanted, disillusioned, expecting more, expecting better, expecting otherwise, badly served, let down, frustrated, thwarted, balked, bilked, foiled, baffled, confounded, confused, hindered, hampered, denied, refused, stonewalled, rejected, turned away, jilted, defeated, disconcerted, crestfallen, dejected, depressed, disheartened, discouraged, mortified, chagrined, humiliated, humbled, disgruntled, soured, dissatisfied, sad, discontented, upset, sick with disappointment, hopeless, heartbroken, crushed, devastated

▶ *247 Failure; 378 Obstruction; 470 Rejection; 602 Sorrow; 606 Dissatisfaction; 611 Despair; 623 Humility; 630 Surprise*

10 **deceived**, misled, deluded, duped, betrayed, tricked, cheated, swindled, conned (Inf), taken to the cleaners (Inf)

▶ *700 Deception*

11 **disappointing**, frustrating, unfulfilling, unsatisfying, unsatisfactory, insufficient, inadequate, falling short, not up to expectations, less than one's hopes, second-best, second-rate, poor, inferior, discontenting, miscarried, abortive, unsuccessful

▶ *218 Insufficiency; 247 Failure; 606 Dissatisfaction*

12 **deceptive**, misleading, deceiving, dishonest, untrustworthy, cheating

ADVERBS

13 **disappointingly**, with a disappointing result, without meeting expectations, frustratingly, tantalizingly, so near and yet so far, deceptively, misleadingly

605 Resignation

NOUNS

1 **resignation**, relinquishment, departure, withdrawal, renouncement, renunciation, surrender, quitting, quitting work, giving notice, handing in one's notice, calling it quits, notice of resignation, forced resignation, voluntary resignation, retirement, retiral (Scot), abdication, abandonment, throwing in the towel (*or* sponge) (Inf)

▶ *12 Government and Politics; 313 Departure; 355 Relinquishment; 813 Reward*

2 **stoicism**, sanguinity, phlegm, indifference, coldness

3 **resigner**, retiree, pensioner, abdicator, quitter, relinquisher, renouncer

4 **resignedness**, acceptance, reconciliation, acquiescence, coming to terms, resigned to one's fate

VERBS

5 **resign**, offer (*or* tender) one's resignation, hand in one's resignation, send in one's papers, give notice, quit work, quit, call it quits (US), hand in one's notice, retire (from), go into retirement, take early retirement, draw one's social security benefits, draw one's pension, stand down, stand (*or* step) aside, abdicate, renounce the throne, give up the crown, abandon, desert, leave one's post, leave, depart, withdraw, vacate, tear oneself away from, drop, let go of, give up, resign under pressure, forgo, renunciate, surrender, relinquish, throw in the towel (*or* sponge) (Inf), chuck (in *or* up) (Inf), jack (*or* pack) it in (Inf), take someone's job and shove it (US inf)

6 **resign oneself**, accept, acquiesce, come to terms with

ADJECTIVES

7 **resigning**, resigned, abdicating, abdicated, retiring, retired, in retirement, past, former, one-time, sometime, late, emeritus, on social security benefits, on a pension, pensioned, pensioned-off, forced out, outgoing, renunciatory

8 **resigned**, accepting, acquiescent, stoical, sanguine, phlegmatic, indifferent

ADVERBS

9 **stoically**, sanguinely, phlegmatically, indifferently

10 **by resigning**, by retiring, in retirement, formerly, lately

606 Dissatisfaction

Oh, I wish that God had not given me what I prayed for! It was not so good as I thought. Johanna Spyri.

NOUNS

1 **dissatisfaction**, displeasure, disgruntlement, discontent, discontentment, disappointment, disillusionment, consternation, disapprobation, disapproval, rejection, reprobation, censure, dislike, derision, deprecation, disgust, contempt, contemptuousness, scorn

2 **expression of dissatisfaction**, complaint, criticism, boo, hiss, whistle, snub, reprimand, remonstration, rebuke, reproof, black mark (Inf), gripe (Inf), rocket (Inf), telling off (Inf)

3 **dissatisfied person**, dissatisfied customer, reprover, complainer, grumbler, grouser, carper, moaner, whiner, bleater, spoilsport, malcontent, moper, sulker, brooder, angry young man, bellyacher (Inf), griper (Inf), whinger (Inf), kvetch (US inf)

ADJECTIVES

4 **dissatisfied**, displeased, disgruntled, discontented, discontent, malcontent, malcontented, sulking, sulky, brooding, disaffected, complaining, whingeing, disappointed, disillusioned, disapproving, unapproving, unimpressed, critical of, perjorative, disgusted, contemptuous, scornful, derisive, derisory

5 **unsatisfactory**, dissatisfactory, disappointing, disapproved of, unapproved, unpopular, rejected, substandard, not up to scratch (Inf)

VERBS

6 **dissatisfy**, displease, disappoint, disillusion, disgust, revolt, sicken

7 **be dissatisfied**, disapprove, not hold with, not think much of, dislike, resent, disfavour, criticize, find fault with, pick holes in, look askance at, tut-tut at, object to, cavil, grumble, grouse, carp, complain, whine, moan, sulk, brood, run down, belittle, deride, deprecate, deplore, reprove, rebuke, condemn, perjorate, reject, abhor, scorn, defame, revile, vilify, boo, hiss, whistle at, slate (Inf), bellyache (Inf), whinge (Inf), gripe (Inf), kvetch (US inf), slag off (Inf)

ADVERBS

8 **discontentedly**, disapprovingly, disgustedly, contemptuously, scornfully

607 Annoyance and Aggravation

NOUNS

1 **aggravation**, exacerbation, worsening, deterioration, intensification, heightening, deepening, magnification, augmentation, enhancement, exaggeration

▶ *213 Increase; 245 Deterioration*

2 **annoyance**, exasperation, irritation, vexation, provocation, anger

3 **nuisance**, bother, trouble, victimization, bullying, harassment, hassle (Inf), spot of bother (Inf), aggro (Inf), seeing to (Inf)

▶ *242 Unpleasantness; 381 Attack*

ADJECTIVES

4 **aggravated**, worsened, not improved, exacerbated, intensified, heightened, deepened, increased, magnified, enhanced, enlarged

5 **aggravating**, annoying, irritating, exasperating, provoking, vexing, vexatious

VERBS

6 **aggravate**, make worse, worsen, exacerbate, inflame, intensify, heighten, deepen, increase, augment, magnify, enhance, exaggerate, bring to a head, rub it in (Inf), rub salt in the wound (Inf), rub one's nose in it (Inf)

7 **become aggravated**, get worse, worsen, build up, go from bad to worse, deteriorate, degenerate, decline

8 **annoy**, irritate, exasperate, goad, provoke, antagonize, anger, vex, tease, peeve, hassle (Inf)

ADVERBS

9 **from bad to worse**, out of the frying pan into the fire

10 **annoyingly**, irritatingly, vexatiously

608 Relief

And thou wilt give thyself relief, if thou doest every act of thy life as if it were the last. Marcus Aurelius.

NOUNS

1 **ease**, solace, comfort, consolation, alleviation, reassurance, relaxation, mollification, appeasement, mitigation, assuagement, abatement, remission, respite, lull, palliation, anaesthetization, tranquillization, sedation, a load off one's mind (*or* one's shoulders) (Inf)

2 **aid**, assistance, help, succour, support, helping hand, rescue, deliverance, liberation, release, emancipation, salvation, salvage

3 **reliever**, comforter, consoler, mollifier, remedy, cure, balm, palliative, anodyne, analgesic, painkiller, anaesthetic, tranquillizer, sedative, opiate, soporific, hypnotic, sleeping pill, sleeping draught, ray of sunshine (Inf), oil on troubled waters (Inf)

► *394 Remedy*

4 **charity**, alms, alms-giving, poor relief, benefaction, gift, donation; relief, aid, emergency aid, disaster relief, famine relief

5 **helper**, auxiliary, deputy, assistant, helpmate, helpmeet, aide, aide-de-camp, medic, paramedic, doctor, nurse, girl (*or* man) Friday, right-hand man (*or* woman), understudy, substitute, replacement, stand-in, locum, locum tenens, reserve, stopgap, backup, supporter, twelfth man, good right arm (Inf)

6 **profile**, silhouette, delineation, lineament, outline, form, contour, elevation, embossment, projection, rilievo (*or* relievo), bas-relief, low relief, *basso rilievo* (It), high relief, *alto-rilievo* (It), *mezzo rilievo* (It)

ADJECTIVES

7 **relieved**, calmed, restored, refreshed, eased, comforted, soothed, consoled, reassured, mollified, appeased, relaxed, sedated, assuaged, cured

8 **relieving**, helping, helpful, refreshing, restorative, comforting, consoling, reassuring, relaxing, easing, calming, soothing, balsamic, curative, remedial, assuaging, palliative, sedative, hypnotic

VERBS

9 **relieve**, ease, solace, comfort, pacify, soothe, calm, quiet, console, alleviate, reassure, allay, mollify, appease, mitigate, moderate, temper, assuage, abate, diminish, lessen, soften, relax, palliate, tranquillize, sedate, anaesthetize, take the sting out of (Inf)

10 **save**, rescue, throw a lifeline to, come to the rescue of, reprieve, deliver, free, set free, liberate, emancipate, release, rid

11 **assist**, help, aid, deputize for, stand in for, do duty for, substitute for, understudy for, step into the shoes of, take over from, replace, succeed

12 **relieve from duty**, dismiss, fire, let go, lay off, sack (Inf), axe (Inf), can (Inf)

13 **relieve oneself**, urinate, pee (Inf), take a pee (Inf), piddle (Inf), tinkle (Inf), go to the rest room (US inf), go to the men's (*or* women's) room (US inf), go to the little boys' (*or* little girls') room (US inf), use the bathroom (US inf), piss (Inf), go to the john (US inf), go to the bog (Inf), aim Archie at the Armitage (Inf), point Percy at the porcelain (Inf)

► *560 Excretion*

14 **take away**, confiscate, disencumber, sequestrate, commandeer, dispossess, snatch, steal, rob, mug, run away with (Inf), do out of (Inf)

ADVERBS

15 **comfortingly**, reassuringly, refreshingly, soothingly, helpfully

609 Satisfaction

Youth will be served, every dog has his day, and mine has been a fine one. George Henry Borrow.

The reward of a thing well done is to have done it. Ralph Waldo Emerson.

NOUNS

1 **satisfaction**, fulfilment, gratification, thankfulness, contentedness, contentment, content, peace of mind, serenity, equanimity, happiness, pleasure, enjoyment, comfort, ease, satiation, satiety, self-satisfaction, smugness, complacency

► *241 Pleasantness; 490 Physical Pleasure; 597 Joy; 608 Relief*

2 **reparation**, recompense, compensation, atonement, amends, apology, indemnity, expiation, reconciliation, appeasement, propitiation

► *807 Atonement*

3 **satisfactoriness**, sufficiency, adequacy, tolerability

ADJECTIVES

4 **satisfied**, fulfilled, gratified, thankful, content, contented, serene, uncomplaining, without complaints, undemanding, secure, safe, happy, pleased, satiated, full, full up, comfortable, self-satisfied, smug, complacent

5 **satisfying**, fulfilling, gratifying, pleasing, pacifying, comforting, satiating, filling, ample

6 **satisfactory**, sufficient, sufficing, enough, adequate, acceptable, passable, tolerable, all right, not bad, good enough, fair, so-so (Inf), OK (Inf)

VERBS

7 **be satisfied**, have nothing to complain about, have nothing to grumble about, be at ease, delight in, have one's heart's desire, have all one could ask for, purr (Inf), be like the cat that stole the cream (Inf), look like the cat that swallowed the canary (US inf)

8 **satisfy**, gratify, fulfil, content, please, indulge, satiate, sate, fill, quench, slake

9 **comfort**, pacify, placate, lull, appease, reassure, assure, convince, persuade, put someone's mind at rest, set at ease

10 **suffice**, serve, do, answer, settle, meet, meet the needs of

11 **recompense**, compensate, atone, make amends, apologize, indemnify, expiate, reconcile, appease, propitiate

ADVERBS

12 **satisfactorily**, adequately, enough

13 **with satisfaction**, thankfully, contentedly, serenely, happily

610 Hope

After all, tomorrow is another day. Margaret Mitchell.

Hope springs eternal in the human breast;
Man never is, but always to be blest. Alexander Pope.

NOUNS

1 **hope**, hoping, hopefulness, optimism, cheerfulness, buoyancy, positive thinking, bright side, silver lining, rose-coloured glasses (*or* spectacles), rose-tinted view, wishful thinking, false hope, hope and a prayer, faint hope, ray of hope, last hope
► *598 Happiness*

2 **expectation**, expectations, anticipation, assumption, presumption, trust, confidence, faith, belief, conviction
► *450 Belief; 474 Expectation*

3 **aspiration**, ambition, dream, vision, high hopes, great expectations, aim, intention, wish, desire, longing, yearning, castles in the air, castles in Spain, pipe dream, fool's paradise, Utopia, Erewhon, promised land, cloud-cuckoo-land, dream world, fantasy
► *96 Unreality; 617 Desire*

4 **comfort**, cheer, reassurance, encouragement, support, security, promise, auspiciousness, propitiousness, prospects
► *756 Promise*

5 **hoper**, aspirant, hopeful, young hopeful, wannabe (Inf), dreamer, optimist, idealist, Pollyanna, utopian

VERBS

6 **hope**, live in hope, hope against hope, hope and pray, hope to God, pin one's hopes on, count on, rely on, bank on, put one's trust in, trust, believe, feel confident, rest assured, assume, presume
► *450 Belief*

7 **aspire**, aim, dream, have high hopes, wish, desire, long, yearn, expect, look forward to, await, anticipate
► *474 Expectation; 617 Desire*

8 **be optimistic**, hope for the best, think positively, have faith, make the best of it, look on the bright side, look (*or* see) through rosecoloured glasses (*or* spectacles), not cross one's bridges before one comes to them, count one's chickens before they are hatched

9 **be hopeful**, cross one's fingers, keep one's fingers crossed, touch (*or* knock on) wood, take heart, cheer up, buck up, keep smiling, never say die, keep one's hopes (*or* spirits) up, see light at the end of the tunnel

10 **inspire hope**, comfort, cheer, cheer up, reassure, encourage, raise one's hopes, promise, augur well, bid fair
► *102 Possibility; 475 Prediction; 598 Happiness; 756 Promise*

ADJECTIVES

11 **hopeful**, hoping, full of hope, optimistic, sanguine, cheerful, buoyant, positive, starry-eyed, bullish (Inf), upbeat (Inf), up (Inf)
► *598 Happiness*

12 **expectant**, expecting, anticipating, confident, poised, assured
► *450 Belief; 474 Expectation*

13 **aspirant**, aspiring, ambitious, go-getting, dreaming, wishful, desirous, longing, yearning
► *617 Desire*

14 **cheering**, heartening, reassuring, encouraging, promising, auspicious, propitious, favourable, bright, sunny, golden, rosy, rose-coloured, rose-tinted
► *756 Promise*

ADVERBS

15 **hopefully**, with hope, optimistically, cheerfully, buoyantly, positively, confidently, expectantly, ambitiously, encouragingly, promisingly, auspiciously, propitiously

INTERJECTIONS

16 **never say die!**, nil desperandum!, where there's life, there's hope!

611 Despair

The mass of men lead lives of quiet desperation. Henry David Thoreau.

NOUNS

1 **hopelessness**, lack of hope, no hope, loss of hope, despondency, alarm and despondency, discouragement, defeatism, scepticism, negativism, pessimism, cynicism, dejection, despair, black despair, desperation, melancholy, depression, doubt, self-doubt, gloom, gloominess, gloom and doom
► *602 Sorrow*

2 **hopeless situation**, lost cause, quandary, predicament, catch-22 (situation), bleak outlook, dashed hopes, disappointment, downer (Inf), write-off (Inf), letdown (Inf)
► *264 Difficulty; 604 Disappointment*

3 **hopeless person**, loser, born loser, failure, defeatist, negativist, pessimist, cynic, melancholic, moper, Cassandra, prophet of doom, Job's comforter, no-hoper (Inf), drag (Inf), hopeless case (Inf), goner (Inf), dead duck (Inf), Eeyore (Inf), drongo (Aus inf)
► *247 Failure*

ADJECTIVES

4 **hopeless**, without hope, forlorn, despondent, comfortless, cheerless, discouraged, defeated, defeatist, negative, sceptical, negativistic, pessimistic, cynical, dejected, downcast, despairing, desperate, suicidal, desolate, disconsolate, melancholic, depressed, gloomy, down in the dumps (Inf), down at the mouth (Inf), in the doldrums (*or* depths) (Inf), down (Inf)
► *602 Sorrow*

5 **past hope**, terminal, incurable, inoperable, irremediable, irreparable, irrevocable, irreversible, incorrigible, irredeemable, irretrievable, beyond recall, lost, gone
► *582 Death*

6 **inauspicious**, unpropitious, ill-omened, ill-starred, doomed, ominous, black

7 **futile**, useless, worthless, pointless, vain, impossible
► *103 Impossibility; 236 Worthlessness; 238 Uselessness*

8 **bad**, poor, inferior, no good, without skill, incompetent, lamentable, awful, terrible, clumsy, inept, hopeless (Inf), pathetic (Inf), ham-fisted (Inf), cack-handed (Inf)

▶ *486 Unskilfulness*

VERBS

9 **be hopeless**, lack hope, lose hope, give up hope, give up, despair, doubt, lose heart, look on the black (*or* dark) side, think negatively, think the worst of, write off (Inf)

▶ *602 Sorrow*

10 **disappoint**, crush, shatter one's hopes, dash the cup from one's lips, drive to despair

▶ *515 Disappointment*

ADVERBS

11 **hopelessly**, despondently, negatively, pessimistically, cynically, dejectedly, despairingly, desperately, gloomily, incurably, irredeemably

612 Fear

Fear has many eyes and can see things underground. Miguel de Cervantes.

Let me assert my firm belief that the only thing we have to fear is fear itself. Franklin D. Roosevelt.

Fear lent wings to his feet. Virgil.

NOUNS

1 **fear**, fright, terror, horror, horrification, affright (Lit), dread, awe, panic, phobia, aversion, mortal fear, fear and trembling, unholy terror, fit of terror, blind panic, icy fingers, cold sweat, blood running cold, hair standing on end, chattering teeth, knocking knees, funk (Inf), blue funk (Inf)

2 **fearfulness**, nervousness, timorousness, apprehension, apprehensiveness, anxiety, uneasiness, tension, trepidation, consternation, perturbation, alarm, unease, disquiet, dismay, foreboding, misgivings, qualms, agitation, nerves, palpitations, shivers, quaking, shaking, trembling, goose flesh, goose bumps, butterflies in the stomach, sinking stomach, stage fright, shivers up and down the spine, the jitters (Inf), the jumps (Inf), the willies (Inf), the jimjams (Inf), the collywobbles (Inf), the heebie-jeebies (Inf), a flat spin (Inf)

▶ *614 Cowardice*

3 **worry**, anxiety, uneasiness, angst, fretting, concern, care, solicitude

▶ *650 Benevolence; 652 Philanthropy*

4 **intimidation**, frightening, terrorism, terrorization, threatening, cowing, bullying, hectoring, demoralization, reign of terror, war of nerves, psychological warfare, Sword of Damocles

▶ *381 Attack; 607 Annoyance and Aggravation*

5 **frightener**, scarer, terrorist, bully, alarmist, scaremonger, doom merchant, spreader of alarm and despondency, bogeyman, bogey, spectre, ghost, bugbear, nightmare, bane, pet hate, *bête noire* (Fr)

▶ *381 Attack*

6 **frightened person**, chicken, mouse, rabbit, bag (*or* bundle) of nerves, nervous wreck, scarebaby (Inf), scaredy-cat (Inf)

▶ *614 Cowardice*

ADJECTIVES

7 **frightened**, afraid, scared, fearing, fear-stricken, terrified, terror-struck, horrified, horror-struck, aghast, petrified, panic-stricken, terrorized, intimidated, cowed, demoralized, affright (Lit), in fear and trembling, paralysed with fear, rigid with fear, rooted to the spot, frightened (*or* terrified *or* scared) out of one's wits, frightened (*or* scared) to death, white as a sheet, pale as a ghost, deadly pale, blanched, ashen-faced, in a cold sweat, frit (Inf), reduced to a jelly (Inf), in a funk (Inf), in a blue funk (Inf), scared stiff (Inf), scared shitless (Inf), shit scared (Inf)

▶ *614 Cowardice*

8 **fearful**, nervous, timorous, apprehensive, anxious, uneasy, alarmed, disquieted, agitated, jittery, jumpy, timid, tremulous, trembling, shaky, shaking, quaking, twitchy, tense, strained, highly strung, nervy, edge, panicky, distressed, on edge, on tenterhooks, on pins and needles, on a cliff edge, waiting for the bomb to drop, waiting for the other shoe to fall, with one's heart in one's mouth, afraid of one's shadow, shaking like a leaf (*or* jelly), uptight (Inf)

9 **worried**, troubled, concerned, solicitous, caring, anxious, fretting, harassed, plagued, haunted, tormented

10 **frightening**, fearsome, awesome, daunting, dismaying, formidable, menacing, intimidating, alarming, unnerving, startling, scaring, enervating, shocking, horrifying, terrifying, petrifying, terrible, frightful, fearful, dreadful, dire, grim, horrible, horrific, horrendous, ghastly, hideous, awful, appalling, hair-raising, scary (Inf), spooky (Inf)

VERBS

11 **be afraid**, be afraid of, be frightened (of), fear, dread, be in mortal dread (of), stand aghast, take fright, panic, show fear, tremble, shake, shiver, shudder, quiver, flinch, shrink, draw back, recoil, quail, blench, quake in one's boots (*or* shoes), shake like a leaf (*or* jelly), turn pale (*or* white *or* ashen), look as if one had seen a ghost, be paralysed with fear, jump out of one's skin, be petrified, freeze with horror, be rooted to the spot, feel one's blood (*or* bowels) turn to water, feel one's hair stand on end, shit oneself (*or* one's pants) (Inf)

12 **be fearful**, be nervous, shrink, start, flutter, palpitate, twitch, be on edge, have qualms, think twice, get cold feet, be all of a doodah (Inf), have kittens (Inf), funk (Inf)

13 **frighten**, scare, daunt, dismay, distress, alarm, fright (Lit), affright (Lit), menace, intimidate, cow, bully, terrorize, browbeat, bulldoze, unnerve, give someone a fright, enervate, make someone jump, shake, shock, stagger, startle, panic, horrify, appal, terrify, petrify, make someone's blood run cold, put the fear of God into, put the wind up (Inf), put the frighteners on (Inf), scare someone half to death (Inf), frighten (*or* scare) someone out of their wits (*or* to death) (Inf), scare the living daylights out of (Inf), scare the pants off (Inf), scare shitless (Inf)

14 **worry**, concern, trouble, harass, fret, plague, haunt, torment, be worried (about), fear for, be fearful for, be anxious for (*or* about), agonize over, bite (*or* chew) one's nails, sweat blood (Inf)

ADVERBS

15 **fearfully**, in fear of, nervously, timorously, timidly,

tremulously, apprehensively, anxiously, uneasily, with fear and trembling, in mortal fear (*or* dread)

16 **frighteningly**, alarmingly, menacingly, horrifingly, frightfully, dreadfully, horribly, horrifically, hideously

613 Courage

NOUNS

1 **courage**, bravery, valour, valiance, courageousness, braveness, mettle, pluck, nerve, daring, audacity, audaciousness, boldness, hardiness, hardihood, fearlessness, dauntlessness, undauntedness, spirit, vim, nerves of steel, stout-heartedness, lion-heartedness, doughtiness, fighting spirit, backbone, grit, toughness, stamina, derring-do (Inf), bottle (Inf), guts (Inf), spunk (Inf), balls (Inf)

▶ *336 Strength*

2 **heroism**, chivalry, knightliness, gallantry, prowess, manliness, virility, stiff upper lip, aggressiveness, bellicosity

▶ *585 War; 658 Courtesy; 799 Honour*

3 **steadfastness**, confidence, self-reliance, fortitude, perseverance, endurance, tenacity, determination, resoluteness, intrepidity

▶ *638 Resolution; 640 Perseverance*

4 **adventurousness**, gameness, foolhardiness, rashness

▶ *615 Rashness*

5 **bold front**, bold façade, brave face, bravado, Dutch courage

▶ *525 Appearance*

6 **encouragement**, heartening, assurance, reassurance, incitement, exhortation, animation, bucking up (Inf)

▶ *483 Motive*

7 **courageous person**, brave person, brave (Lit), hero, heroine, knight, knight in shining armour, he-man, superman, superwoman, warrior, heart of oak, daredevil, stunt man (*or* woman), lion, tiger, bulldog, fighting cock

▶ *586 Combatant*

8 **courageous act**, act of courage, feat, feat of endurance, exploit, heroic exploit, deed, knightly deed, chivalry, prowess, derring-do, adventure, gallantry, heroics, *coup de grâce* (Fr)

▶ *340 Action*

ADJECTIVES

9 **courageous**, brave, heroic, gallant, valorous, valiant, mettlesome, mettled, plucky, daring, audacious, bold, hardy, fearless, dauntless, undaunted, spirited, stout-hearted, lion-hearted, unflinching, unshrinking, unshakable, unbowed, undismayed, indomitable, doughty, tough, bold as a lion, spunky (Inf), gutsy (Inf), ballsy (Inf)

▶ *336 Strength*

10 **chivalrous**, knightly, heroic, gallant, manly, soldierly

▶ *658 Courtesy; 799 Honour*

11 **militant**, aggressive, bellicose, martial, warlike

▶ *585 War*

12 **self-reliant**, confident, unafraid, unfearing, steadfast, persevering, tenacious, dogged, determined, resolute, intrepid

▶ *638 Resolution; 640 Perseverance*

13 **adventurous**, venturesome, game, foolhardy, rash, danger-loving

▶ *615 Rashness*

14 **encouraging**, heartening, assuring, reassuring

VERBS

15 **be courageous**, dare, venture, brave, face, confront, face (the) danger, face the odds, beard, defy, outface, look in the face (*or* eyes), stand up to, bell the cat, keep a stiff upper lip, brazen out, screw one's courage to the sticking place, take the plunge, take the bull by the horns, face the music, have the courage of one's convictions, court disaster, laugh at danger, show one's mettle, fight, win one's spurs, have a lot of bottle (Inf), have guts (Inf)

▶ *354 Undertaking; 615 Rashness; 661 Defiance*

16 **take courage**, take heart, pluck up courage, dare, steel oneself, screw up one's courage, put on a brave face, grin and bear it, endure, persevere, keep one's chin up

▶ *640 Perseverance*

17 **give courage**, encourage, hearten, assure, reassure, embolden, inspirit, inspire, incite, exhort, animate

▶ *483 Motive*

ADVERBS

18 **courageously**, bravely, heroically, valiantly, audaciously, boldly, fearlessly, dauntlessly, steadfastly, tenaciously, defiantly, intrepidly, adventurously, rashly

614 Cowardice

None but a coward dares to boast that he has never known fear.
Marshal Foch.

NOUNS

1 **cowardice**, cowardliness, lack of courage, timidity, pusillanimity, chicken-heartedness, faint-heartedness, faint heart, dastardliness, cravenness, poltroonery, timorousness, fearfulness, abject fear, lack of spirit, lack of moral fibre, defeatism, desertion, cowering, overcaution, weakness, funk (Inf), blue funk (Inf), cold feet (Inf), yellow streak (Inf), white feather (Inf)

▶ *611 Despair; 612 Fear; 616 Caution*

2 **coward**, dastard, craven, poltroon, deserter, milksop, milquetoast (US), rat (Inf), yellow-belly (Inf), chicken (Inf), rabbit (Inf), jellyfish (Inf), mouse (Inf), sissy (Inf), weed (Inf), wimp (Inf), baby (Inf), funk (Inf), scaredy-cat (Inf)

▶ *337 Weakness*

ADJECTIVES

3 **cowardly**, dastardly, craven, recreant (Lit), pusillanimous, timid, shy, spineless, soft, namby-pamby, chicken-hearted, chicken-livered, lily-livered, faint-hearted, weak-kneed, timorous, wet, fearful, afraid, scared, frightened, rattled, daunted, cowed, unstaunch, unsteadfast, panicky, unheroic, defeatist, cowering, unable to say boo to a goose, chicken (Inf), gutless (Inf), sissy (Inf), windy (Inf), yellow (Inf), yellow-bellied (Inf)

▶ *337 Weakness; 612 Fear; 674 Modesty*

VERBS

4 **be a coward**, lack courage, lose one's nerve, back out, cower, quail, cringe, shrink, recoil, skulk, sneak, have no stomach for, show the white feather, retreat, desert, run away, turn tail, flee, beat a hasty retreat, scuttle, cut and

run, live to fight another day, lose one's bottle (Inf), get cold feet (Inf), chicken out (Inf), funk (Inf), wet oneself (Inf), have no guts (Inf), do a bunk (Inf), throw a wobbly (*or* wobbler) (Inf)

► *303 Backward Motion; 337 Weakness; 612 Fear*

ADVERBS

5 **cravenly**, pusillanimously, timidly, spinelessly, chicken-heartedly, faint-heartedly, timorously, fearfully

615 Rashness

NOUNS

1 **rashness**, recklessness, hastiness, haste, impetuousness, impetuosity, overhaste, precipitancy, precipitateness, precipitance, imprudence, improvidence, indiscretion, inattention, negligence, carelessness, heedlessness, regardlessness, incautiousness, inconsideration, unwariness, irresponsibility, wildness, impulsiveness, capriciousness, frivolity, levity, flippancy, foolhardiness, folly, daring, audacity, audaciousness, temerity, presumption, overconfidence, overenthusiasm, impatience, hotheadedness, excitability, desperation, desperateness, adventurousness, brinkmanship, playing with fire, daredevilry

► *262 Haste; 459 Folly; 472 Inattention; 613 Courage; 666 Negligence*

2 **rash move**, risk, needless risk, dangerous game, leap in the dark, gamble

► *107 Chance; 254 Danger*

3 **rash person**, daredevil, hothead, madcap, brinkman, wild boy, desperado, hooligan, adventurer, gambler

ADJECTIVES

4 **rash**, reckless, hasty, impetuous, overhasty, precipitate, precipitant, headlong, breakneck, imprudent, improvident, injudicious, indiscreet, inconsiderate, ill-considered, ill-advised, thoughtless, inattentive, negligent, slapdash, hit-and-miss, careless, heedless, regardless, incautious, uncircumspect, unwary, irresponsible, wild, impulsive, capricious, frivolous, flippant, couldn't-care-less, devil-may-care, free-and-easy, happy-go-lucky, foolhardy, foolish, harebrained, hotheaded, madcap, daredevil, death-defying, danger-loving, risk-taking, adventurous, daring, bold, audacious, overconfident, overambitious, overenthusiastic, overzealous, impatient, desperate, do-or-die, trigger-happy (Inf), asking for trouble (Inf), asking for it (Inf), over-the-top (OTT) (Inf)

► *254 Danger; 262 Haste; 459 Folly; 472 Inattention; 613 Courage; 666 Negligence*

VERBS

5 **be rash**, rush into, rush one's fences, rush in where angels fear to tread, carry on regardless, ignore the consequences, gamble, take risks, play with fire, ride the tiger, bell the cat, throw caution to the wind, chance one's arm, stick one's neck out, drop one's guard, court danger (*or* disaster), tempt providence (*or* fate), count one's chickens before they are hatched, buy a pig in a poke, take a leap in the dark, ask for trouble (Inf), ask for it (Inf)

► *107 Chance; 254 Danger; 262 Haste*

ADVERBS

6 **rashly**, recklessly, hastily, impetuously, headlong, head first, carelessly, heedlessly, irresponsibly, wildly, impulsively, foolishly, overconfidently, impatiently

616 Caution

The only way to be absolutely safe is never to try anything for the first time. Magnus Pyke.

NOUNS

1 **caution**, cautiousness, carefulness, care, wariness, chariness, watchfulness, vigilance, alertness, heedfulness, heed, wisdom, prudence, circumspection, judiciousness, guardedness, scepticism, discretion, reticence, tentativeness, reluctance, slowness, hesitance, hesitancy, hesitation, deliberation, careful consideration, second thoughts, doubt, suspicion, self-preservation, self-protection, protection, providence, foresight, forethought, wait-and-see policy, waiting game, overcaution, overcautiousness

► *252 Safety; 253 Security; 333 Slowness; 436 Provisions; 443 Thought; 458 Wisdom; 471 Attention; 665 Carefulness*

2 **insurance**, insurance policy, rainy day policy, nest egg, savings, warning, safeguard, safety first, precaution

► *252 Safety; 333 Slowness; 680 Thrift; 711 Warning*

3 **cautious person**, slow starter, hesitator, doubter

ADJECTIVES

4 **cautious**, careful, wary, chary, watchful, vigilant, alert, on one's guard, heedful, mindful, prudent, circumspect, sceptic, once bitten twice shy, suspicious, doubtful, tentative, reluctant, slow, hesitant, nervous, experimental, gingerly, anticipatory, provident, thrifty, economical, frugal, canny, guarded, secretive, conservative, discreet, reticent, politic, judicious, on the safe side, overcautious, unadventurous, cagey (Inf)

► *252 Safety; 333 Slowness; 436 Provisions; 443 Thought; 458 Wisdom; 471 Attention; 665 Carefulness; 680 Thrift*

VERBS

5 **be cautious**, take care, hold back, hang back, count to ten, take one's time, take one step at a time, take it easy, take it slowly, tread warily, take tentative steps, feel one's way, proceed with caution, hedge, beat about the bush, take no risks, play safe, hedge one's bets, take pains, make sure, make certain, look twice, look before one leaps, watch one's step, safeguard oneself, beware, look out, keep a look out, keep tabs on, keep an eye on, see how the land lies, see how the wind blows, put a toe in the water, play it by ear, anticipate, take precautions, leave nothing to chance, cover oneself, take out insurance, count the cost, economize, save, hesitate, think twice, have second thoughts, doubt, suspect, pussyfoot (Inf)

► *252 Safety; 333 Slowness; 436 Provisions; 665 Carefulness; 680 Thrift*

6 **caution**, warn, forewarn, advise

► *711 Warning; 713 Advice*

ADVERBS

7 **cautiously**, carefully, warily, watchfully, heedfully, prudently, circumspectly, tentatively, reluctantly, hesitantly,

gingerly, providently, judiciously, sceptically, overcautiously

617 Desire

Sooner murder an infant in its cradle than nurse unacted desires. William Blake.

O, she is the antidote to desire. William Congreve.

There are two tragedies in life. One is to lose your heart's desire. The other is to gain it. George Bernard Shaw.

Desire is the very essence of man. Benedict Spinoza.

NOUNS

1 desire, wish, want, longing, craving, need, requirement, demand, will, urge, impulse, itch, eagerness, avidity, willingness, zeal, passion, ardour, aspiration, ambition, hope, covetousness, cupidity, greed, voracity, fascination, curiosity, inclination, leaning, penchant, predilection, preference, taste, appetancy, weakness, partiality, liking, fancy, fondness, love, lust, appetite, hunger, thirst, yearning, yen (Inf), pining, hankering, wistfulness, nostalgia, homesickness

► *135 Requirement; 229 Tendency; 595 Liking; 610 Hope; 635 Will; 636 Willingness; 644 Curiosity; 688 Gluttony*

2 desirability, expedience, suitability, advisability, meritoriousness, acceptability

► *239 Convenience*

3 appetite, keen appetite, hunger, hungriness, starvation, famine, empty stomach, thirst, thirstiness, dryness, dry throat

► *25 Cookery; 557 Eating; 687 Fasting; 690 Drunkenness*

4 sexual desire, carnal desire, concupiscence, lust, lechery, lecherousness, sexual appetite, sexual urge, libido, libidinousness, passion, ardour, sexuality, carnality, nymphomania, satyriasis, randiness (Inf), the hots (Inf), hot pants (Inf)

► *593 Love; 796 Immorality*

5 object of desire, desired object, one's heart's desire, desideratum, requirement, request, appeal, aim, objective, goal, catch, prize, trophy, lure, draw, attraction, ideal, the unattainable, forbidden fruit, the brass ring

► *363 Attraction; 482 Intention; 710 Request; 794 Prize*

6 desirer, wisher, wanter, fancier, worshipper, devotee, aspirant, wannabe (Inf), hoper, coveter, envier, lecher, lech (*or* letch), libertine, glutton, greedy pig (Inf)

► *688 Gluttony*

ADJECTIVES

7 desired, wished for, wanted, needed, necessary, required, desirable, requested, longed for, yearned for, coveted, envied, enviable, in demand, popular, sought-after

► *135 Requirement; 710 Request*

8 desirable, acceptable, welcome, pleasurable, pleasant, attractive, likable, appealing, inviting, tempting, appetizing, mouthwatering, admirable, creditable, laudable, praiseworthy, worthy, meritorious, deserving, worthwhile, good, beneficial, advantageous, profitable, expedient, convenient, suitable, fitting, apt, proper

► *235 Worth; 239 Convenience; 241 Pleasantness; 765 Profit; 797 Good*

9 desirous, desiring, wishful, wishing for, wanting, needing, demanding, longing for, coveting, craving, itching for, dying for, ardent, passionate, avid, eager, keen, partial to, fond, covetous, envious, gluttonous, voracious, greedy, acquisitive, possessive, insatiable, hoping, hopeful, aspiring, would-be, yearning, pining, wistful, nostalgic, homesick

► *610 Hope; 688 Gluttony*

10 hungry, starving, starved, famished, ravenous, empty, half-starved, peckish, thirsty, dry, parched, dehydrated

11 lustful, libidinous, lecherous, lascivious, concupiscent, randy, hot for, sexually desirable, sexy, seductive, provocative, titillating, fanciable (Inf)

► *796 Immorality*

VERBS

12 desire, wish for, want, need, require, demand, cry out for, ask for, request, call, summon, welcome, long for, pray for, covet, envy, have one's eye on, set one's heart on, dream of, hope for, aspire to, aim for, set one's sights on, crave, itch for, hanker after, yearn for, pine for, miss, hunger for, thirst for, be dying for, pant for, lust after, prefer, favour, like, fancy

► *135 Requirement; 397 Command; 595 Liking; 710 Request*

13 like, love, want, desire, woo, court, chase, run after, pursue, lust after, fancy (Inf), be turned on by (Inf), have the hots for (Inf)

► *593 Love; 633 Pursuit; 796 Immorality*

14 be hungry, hunger, starve, raven, be thirsty, thirst, lick one's lips, salivate

15 cause desire, awaken desire, fill with longing, tempt, tantalize, attract, allure, lure, draw, fill with desire, excite, titillate, stimulate, motivate, whet one's appetite, make one's mouth water, turn on (Inf)

► *363 Attraction*

16 be desirable, suit, befit, answer the problem, fit the bill, serve

► *237 Usefulness*

ADVERBS

17 desirably, acceptably, pleasantly, attractively, temptingly, appetizingly, meritoriously, beneficially, expediently, suitably

18 desirously, wishfully, avidly, eagerly, covetously, enviously, wistfully

19 hungrily, ravenously, thirstily

20 lustfully, libidinously, lecherously, lasciviously, sexily, seductively, provocatively

618 Indifference

But what is past my help is past my care. Francis Beaumont.

At length the morn and cold indifference came. Nicholas Rowe.

NOUNS

1 indifference, unconcern, lack of interest, apathy, disinterestedness, incuriosity, incuriousness, aloofness, detachment, dispassion, noninvolvement, inertia, inactivity, passiveness, passivity, ataraxia (*or* ataraxy), phlegmaticalness (*or* phlegmaticness), phlegm, lethargy, listlessness, dispiritedness, spiritlessness, sluggishness, oscitation, inappetence, inappetency, lethargy, half-heartedness, perfunctoriness, inexcitability, calmness, lukewarmness, coldness, cold-heartedness, cold-bloodedness, coolness, want of zeal, want of excitement, nonchalance, insouciance, indifferentism, no desire for, lack of appetite, lackadaisicalness, insensibility, insensitivity, dullness, numbness, the blahs (US inf)

► *343 Inactivity; 472 Inattention; 592 Insensitivity; 637 Unwillingness*

2 **carelessness**, disregard, inattention, laxity, heedlessness, negligence, neglect, recklessness, rashness, promiscuousness, amorality

► *615 Rashness; 666 Negligence*

3 **impartiality**, indiscrimination, disinterest, objectivity, no prejudice, unbiased attitude, open mind, no preference, don't-care attitude, neutrality, middle way, moderation, justice, fairness

► *685 Moderation; 801 Right*

4 **mediocrity**, averageness, ordinariness, tolerability, passableness

► *117 Conformity*

5 **insignificance**, unimportance, triviality, irrelevance, inconsequence, immateriality

► *124 Unimportance*

6 **indifferent person**, neutral, neutralist, moderate, middle-of-the-roader, fence-sitter, slacker, pococurante, laodicean, indifferentist, third party, impartial observer, cold fish, wet blanket (Inf)

► *341 Inaction*

ADJECTIVES

7 **indifferent**, disinterested, incurious, uninquisitive, uninterested, apathetic, detached, dispassionate, uninvolved, not involved, withdrawn, aloof, carefree, fancy-free, noncommittal, impersonal, matter-of-fact, unconcerned, uncaring, unresponsive, in one's shell, unaware, oblivious, insensible to, blind to, deaf to, dead to, lost to, unconscious, comatose, inert, inactive, ataractic, listless, dispirited, spiritless, sluggish, inappetent, phlegmatic(al), lethargic, half-hearted, perfunctory, impassive, pococurante, blasé, easy-going, unsurprised, inexcitable, unimpressed, unaffected, unfeeling, untouched, unemotional, unmoved, unruffled, calm, lukewarm, cool, cold, cold-hearted, cold-blooded, frigid, frosty, unmoved, nonchalant, insouciant, unaffectionate, undesirous, passionless, lackadaisical, insensible, insensitive, thick-skinned, dull, deadpan, numb, benumbed, laid-back (Inf)

8 **careless**, disregarding, negligent, inattentive, lax, heedless, reckless, rash, devil-may-care, promiscuous, amoral

9 **impartial**, indiscriminate, disinterested, happy either way, don't-care, objective, unbiased, unprejudiced, open-minded, neutral, moderate, just, fair

10 **mediocre**, average, middling, ordinary, fair, unexceptional, unaspiring, tolerable, passable, all right, so-so (Inf), no great shakes (Inf)

► *216 Average*

11 **insignificant**, unimportant, trivial, irrelevant, inconsequential, immaterial, boring, blah (Inf)

VERBS

12 **be indifferent**, be incurious, mind one's own business, close one's eyes to, look the other way, disregard, dismiss, let go, not mind, care nothing for, not care, not think twice about, not lose any sleep over, not have one's heart in it, have no taste for, not give a fig for, not care a straw about, not give a hoot, shrug off, detach oneself, withdraw, become aloof, show no concern for, take no interest, yawn, oscitate, fail to move, fail to act, not respond, not be affected by, remain unmoved, have a thick skin, have a heart of stone, harden, harden one's heart, not turn a hair, stay in one's shell, lose interest, cool off, be left cold (Inf), not give a damn (Inf)

13 **make indifferent**, make insensitive, dull, blunt, desensitize, numb, benumb, deaden, bore, turn off (Inf)

14 **be careless**, disregard, act negligently, show poor attention, fail to heed, act recklessly, have no morals

15 **be impartial**, be objective, be unbiased, have no prejudice, be non-partisan, remain neutral about, not take sides, take neither side, sit on the fence

16 **be mediocre**, have no aspirations, get by, pass, not set the world on fire, sit and watch the world go by, lose someone's attention, fail to move, fail to inspire, make no impact upon

ADVERBS

17 **indifferently**, disinterestedly, with no interest, incuriously, apathetically, aloofly, impersonally, matter-of-factly, uncaringly, unresponsively, obliviously, in oblivion, unconsciously, inertly, inactively, listlessly, dispiritedly, spiritlessly, sluggishly, phlegmatically, half-heartedly, unfeelingly, impassively, unemotionally, with dry eyes, with a straight face, deadpan, calmly, coolly, coldly, cold-heartedly, cold-bloodedly, in cold blood, nonchalantly, insouciantly, dispassionately, insensibly, insensitively, numbly

18 **carelessly**, without a worry, inattentively, negligently, heedlessly, recklessly, rashly, promiscuously, amorally, without morals

19 **impartially**, indiscriminately, objectively, open-mindedly, with an open mind, justly, fairly

20 **unexceptionally**, tolerably, middlingly, passably, fairly, insignificantly, without significance, unimportantly, trivially, irrelevantly, boringly, so-so (Inf)

INTERJECTIONS

21 **never mind!**, forget it!, what does it matter!, who cares?, so what?

619 Wonder

Two things fill the mind with ever new and increasing wonder and awe, the more often and the more seriously reflection concentrates upon them: the starry heaven above me and the moral law within me. Immanuel Kant.

Philosophy is the product of wonder. A. N. Whitehead.

NOUNS

1 wonder, sense of wonder, state of wonder, breathless wonder, wonderment, awe, fascination, admiration, raptness, hero worship, love, lack of expectation, surprise, astonishment, astoundment, dumbfoundment, amazement, bafflement, bewilderment, puzzlement, sense of mystery, stupor, stupefaction, uncertainty, consternation, shock, fear

► *453 Uncertainty; 593 Love; 630 Surprise; 696 Unintelligibility*

2 sign of wonderment, exclamation, exclamation mark, shocked silence, silence, open mouth, popping eyes, eyes on stalks, cry of wonder, gasp of admiration, whistle

► *612 Fear*

3 wonder-working, miracle-working, magic, sorcery, spellbinding, wonderful works, thaumatology, teratology, thaumaturgy, stroke of genius, feat, exploit, deed, transformation, *coup de théâtre* (Fr), dramaturgy

► *7 Religion; 11 Occultism; 485 Skill*

4 wonder, object of wonder, object of admiration, something incredible, eye-opener, quite something, one for the book, one in a thousand, phenomenon, best-seller, miracle, portent, omen, sign, marvel, masterpiece, masterstroke, *chef-d'oeuvre* (Fr), drama, sensation, cause célèbre, *annus mirabilis* (L), fantasy, cloud-cuckoo-land, Utopia, wonderland, fairyland, fantasy, theme park, Disneyland, spectacle, sight, Seven Wonders of the World, UFO (unidentified flying object)

► *477 Imagination*

5 person of wonder, amazing person, wonder, prodigy, child prodigy, infant prodigy, wonder boy (*or* girl), whiz kid, *wunderkind* (Ger), genius, man (*or* woman) of genius, nine-days wonder, miracle-worker, wizard, witch, fairy godmother, thaumaturge, sorcerer, hero, heroine, superman, superwoman, bionic man, wonder woman, paragon, curiosity, puzzle, enigma, idiot savant, oddity, freak, monster, monstrosity, *rara avis* (L), exceptional person, proficient person, millionaire, best-selling author, world champion, Olympic champion, star, idol, hit (Inf), knockout (Inf), stunner (Inf), wow (Inf)

► *630 Surprise*

ADJECTIVES

6 wondering, in wonderment, lost in wonder, astonished, astounded, amazed, lost in amazement, awed, awestruck, fascinated, admiring, impressed, surprised, inexpectant, marvelling, spellbound, rapt, unable to believe one's eyes (*or* senses), dazzled, blinded, dumbfounded, flabbergasted, shocked, scandalized, bowled over, thunderstruck, dazed, stupefied, bewildered, puzzled, aghast, fazed (US inf), gobsmacked (Inf)

7 wide-eyed, round-eyed, popeyed, with one's eyes starting out of one's head, with eyes on stalks, agog, all agog, open-mouthed, agape, gaping, dumb, struck dumb, dumbstruck, inarticulate, speechless, breathless, wordless, left without words, silenced, silent, transfixed, rooted to the spot

8 wonderful, to wonder at, wondrous, marvellous, miraculous, astounding, aweful, amazing, beguiling, fantastic, too good to be true, too bad to be true, imaginary, impossible, hardly possible, surprising, unexpected, improbable, unbelievable, incredible, inconceivable, unimaginable, indescribable, unutterable, unspeakable, ineffable, inexpressible, mind-boggling, mind-blowing, striking, overwhelming, awesome, awe-inspiring, breathtaking, impressive, admirable, exquisite, excellent, record-breaking, best, rare, exceptional, extraordinary, unprecedented, unusual, remarkable, noteworthy, dramatic, sensational, shocking, scandalizing, exotic, outlandish, unheard of, strange, odd, very odd, outré, weird, weird and wonderful, bizarre, peculiar, unaccountable, mysterious, enigmatic, puzzling, shattering, bewildering, wonder-working, thaumaturgic, magical, like magic, monstrous, prodigous, phenomenal, stupendous, fearful, frightening, grotesque

VERBS

9 wonder, marvel, admire, whistle, hold one's breath, gasp, gasp with admiration, idolize, hero-worship, stare, gaze and gaze, goggle at, gawk, open one's eyes wide, rub one's eyes, not believe one's eyes (*or* ears), look aghast, gape, open one's mouth, have no words to express, not know what to say, stand in amazement, not expect, fear, become fazed by (US inf), gawp (Inf)

10 be wonderful, be marvellous, inspire awe, impress, surpass belief, stagger belief, boggle the mind, cause doubt, beggar all description, baffle description, spellbind, enchant, bewitch, dazzle, strike with admiration, turn one's head, excite love, strike dumb, stun, daze, stupefy, awe, electrify, impress, petrify, dumbfound, confound, astound, astonish, amaze, flabbergast, surprise, baffle, bewilder, boggle (the mind), puzzle, startle, shock, make one's eyes open, make one's head swim, make one sit up and take notice, take one's breath away, stagger, frighten, scandalize, faze (US inf), bowl over (Inf), blow one's mind (Inf)

11 do wonders, work wonders, work miracles, do magic, achieve marvels

12 wonder whether, speculate, conjecture, ponder, meditate, muse, think, question, query, suspect, have a suspicion, take a guess at, hazard a guess, ask oneself

► *453 Uncertainty; 705 Question*

ADVERBS

13 wonderfully, wondrously, in wonder, marvellously, miraculously, fantastically, fabulously, stupendously, awesomely, mysteriously, weirdly, bizarrely, astonishingly, in astonishment, amazingly, in amazement, in awe, astoundingly, surprisingly, to one's surprise, to one's amazement, with gaping mouth, indescribably, ineffably, unspeakably, remarkably, splendidly, fearfully, strange to say, wonderful to relate, *mirabile dictu* (L), to the wonder of all

INTERJECTIONS

14 wonderful!, amazing!, incredible!, awesome!, smashing!, I don't believe it!, can you beat that!, really!, what!, go on!, well I never!, blow me down!, did you ever!, gosh!, wow!, how about that!, bless my soul!, wonders will never cease!, goodness gracious!, whatever next!, never!, fab! (Inf), ace! (Inf), brill! (Inf), magic! (Inf), cool! (Inf), wicked! (Inf), holy cow! (Inf), holy mackerel! (Inf), holy Moses! (Inf), holy smoke! (Inf), holy shit! (Inf)

620 Boredom

I wanted to be bored to death, as good a way to go as any. Peter De Vries.

Is not life a hundred times too short for us to bore ourselves? Friedrich Wilhelm Nietzsche.

NOUNS

1 **boredom**, boringness, tedium, tediousness, tiresomeness, ennui, dullness, dreariness, weariness, fatigue, irksomeness, slowness, inactivity, languor, longueur, thumb-twiddling, devil's tattoo, dissatisfaction, dislike, lack of enjoyment, flatness, tastelessness, insipidity, monotony, dull monotony, sameness, plainness, uniformity, lack of variation, humdrum, humdrumness, staleness, dryness, aridity, repetition, repetitiousness, repetitiveness, long-windedness, drawing out, prolixity, stodginess, stuffiness, heaviness, ponderousness, satiety, banality, triteness, prosaicness, prosiness, commonplaceness, indifference, sullenness, lack of interest, melancholy, boring life, *taedium vitae* (L), world-weariness, *Weltschmerz* (Ger)

▶ *117 Conformity; 261 Tiredness; 270 Vagueness; 271 Simplicity; 343 Inactivity; 497 Blandness; 596 Dislike; 606 Dissatisfaction; 618 Indifference*

2 **boring thing**, same old thing, broken record, time to kill, time on one's hands, leaden hours, real bore, utter bore, no fun, too much of a good thing, twice-told tale, dull speech, unfunny joke, beaten track (*or* path), rut, monotony, assembly line, conveyor belt, production line, chore, treadmill, grindstone, bromide, drag (Inf), bind (Inf), same old story (Inf), old chestnut (Inf), same damn thing (Inf), downer (Inf), bummer (US inf), snore (Inf), yawnsville (Inf)

▶ *112 Repetition*

3 **boring person**, bore, utter bore, egoist, egotist, long-winded speaker, humourless comedian, pest, buttonholer, killjoy, moper, bromide, Mrs Grundy, crashing bore, crasher (Inf), crusher (Inf), drag (Inf), drip (Inf), pain (Inf), pain in the neck (Inf), pain in the arse (Inf), misery (Inf), stick-in-the-mud (Inf), drag-ass (US inf), wet blanket (Inf), anorak (Inf), trainspotter (Inf), dweeb (Inf), nerd (Inf), bummer (US inf), wanker (Inf), boring old fart (Inf)

▶ *683 Selfishness*

ADJECTIVES

4 **boring**, boresome (US), tedious, tiresome, tiring, uninteresting, dull, dreary, dreich (*or* dreigh) (Scot), drab, weary, wearisome, wearying, wearing, irksome, slow, inactive, languorous, time-killing, thumb-twiddling, disliked, unenjoyable, repeated, repetitious, repetitive, plain, flat, tasteless, insipid, cloying, satiating, too much, monotonous, uniform, unvarying, invariable, humdrum, pedestrian, suburban, prosaic, prosy, commonplace, stale, unfunny, humourless, soporific, sleep-inducing, unreadable, arid, dry, dry as dust, long-winded, overlong, drawn out, prolix, dragging, stodgy, stuffy, heavy, ponderous, leaden, banal, trite, indifferent, melancholy, world-weary, deadly (Inf), draggy (Inf), heavy (Inf), blah (Inf)

5 **bored**, afflicted with boredom, bored to death, bored to tears, tired, good and tired, tired to death, fatigued, drowsy, dreary, weary, wearied, world-weary, tired of living, jaded, sated, satiated, sick of, tired of, sick and tired of, dissatisfied, disinterested, sullen, twiddling one's thumbs, bored stiff (Inf), fed-up (Inf), cheesed off (Inf)

VERBS

6 **be boring**, be tedious, bore, bore to death, bore to tears, pall, tire, make one tired, send (*or* put) one to sleep, make one yawn, dull, weary, fatigue, irk, dissatisfy, provide no enjoyment, repeat, lack variation, lack variety, draw out, go on forever, go on and on, drone on, never end, harp on, dwell upon, repeat oneself, sound like a broken record, play the same old tune, drag, move slowly, sate, satiate, jade, cloy, glut, cause dislike, lack interest, fail to interest, tell the same old story, buttonhole, talk too long, stay too long, outstay one's welcome, bore the pants off (Inf), bore stiff (Inf), pain (Inf), leave one cold (Inf), make one fed-up (Inf), cheese one off (Inf), give one a bellyful (Inf)

7 **suffer boredom**, lead a boring life, have a monotonous job, do boring work, do dull work, have (*or* keep) one's nose to the grindstone, do the same old thing, stay in a rut, have time to kill, have time on one's hands, twiddle one's thumbs, dislike, have no enjoyment from, grow weary of the world

ADVERBS

8 **boringly**, tediously, tiringly, uninterestingly, dully, drearily, drably, without excitement, without variety, on the beaten track, wearily, without a change of scenery, slowly, inactively, languorously, repeatedly, repetitiously, repetitively, to death, ad nauseam, flatly, tastelessly, insipidly, plainly, with no frills, monotonously, uniformly, without a change of pace, invariably, in the expected way, prosaically, stalely, soporifically, aridly, drily, long-windedly, stodgily, stuffily, heavily, ponderously, banally, tritely, indifferently, depressingly

621 Derision

Damn with faint praise, assent with civil leer,
And, without sneering, teach the rest to sneer. Alexander Pope.

How strange, when I saw you acting in The Glorious Adventure *I laughed all the time.* Noël Coward.

NOUNS

1 **mockery**, derisiveness, jeering, banter, badinage, scorn, sarcasm, scoffing, aping (Inf)

2 **act of derision**, satire, parody, spoof, pasquinade, pasquil, caricature, cartoon, burlesque, farce, travesty, lampoon, joke, denunciation, mockery, putdown, take off (Inf), send-up (Inf), wind-up (Inf), piss-take (Inf)

3 **derider**, satirist, lampooner, lampoonist, joker, mimic, caricaturist, cartoonist

4 **laughing stock**, butt, foil, figure of fun, dupe, patsy, fall guy, straight man, Aunt Sally, stooge (Inf)

ADJECTIVES

5 **derisive**, ridiculing, scornful, farcical, satirical, sarcastic, sardonic, quizzical

VERBS

6 **deride**, laugh at, snigger about, poke fun at, send up, mock, scoff at, jeer at, put down, dis (Inf), make a mockery of, mock, pillary, pasquinade, satirize, lampoon, caricature, guy, denounce, debunk, deflate, take the mick (Inf), take the mickey (Inf), take the piss (Inf)

ADVERBS

7 **mockingly**, laughingly, sneeringly, scornfully, satirically, jovially

622 Pride

Pride goeth before destruction, and an haughty spirit before a fall. Bible: Proverbs.

We are not ashamed of what we have done, because, when you have a great cause to fight for, the moment of greatest humiliation is the moment when the spirit is proudest. Christabel Pankhurst.

NOUNS

1 **pride**, proudness, pridefulness, self-esteem, self-confidence, self-importance, self-regard, self-respect, *amour propre* (Fr), honour, courage, spirit

2 **unapproachability**, disdain, obstinacy, stiff-necked pride, stiff-neckedness, touchiness, self-sufficiency, independence

► *655 Unsociability*

3 **conceit**, vanity, arrogance, insolence, haughtiness, self-admiration, overconfidence, overproudness, overweening pride, pretension, egotism, egoism, affectation, uppitiness, self-praise, snobbery, inverted snobbery, false pride, vainglory, purse-pride, overambitiousness, hubris

► *673 Vanity; 676 Affectation*

4 **prestige**, honour, merit, desert, dignity, reputation, augustness, style, high-flier

5 **stateliness**, loftiness, proud bearing, nobility, condescension, hauteur

6 **majesty**, grandeur, grandiosity, venerability, sedateness, lordliness, princeliness, pomp, pomposity, pomp and circumstance, solemnity, gravity

► *643 Solemnity*

7 **satisfaction,** job well done, good work, fulfilment, success, achievement

► *246 Success; 609 Satisfaction*

8 **worthiness**, merit, credit, excellence, quality, value

► *235 Worth; 803 Virtue*

9 **ostentation**, display, show

► *673 Vanity*

10 **boastfulness**, swank, side, big-headedness, puffed-out chest, self-glorification, bumptiousness

11 **prejudice**, contempt, class consciousness, class distinction, snobbery, superiority complex, racial prejudice, social discrimination, (male) chauvinism, heterosexism, white (*or* black) supremacy

12 **object of pride**, favourite, jewel in the crown, pick, pick of the bunch, source of pride, pride of place, pride and joy, boast

13 **proud person**, vain person, egoist, paragon, boaster, snob, parvenu, swank, swankpot, prima donna, Lord of Creation, swelled head, swollen head, true gentleman, grande dame, peacock, cock of the walk, swaggerer, bragger, braggart, blusterer, aristocrat, Lord (*or* Lady) Muck (Inf), his nibs (Inf), bighead (Inf), bigwig (Inf), toffeenose (Inf), *crach* (Welsh)

ADJECTIVES

14 **proud**, prideful, self-important, self-confident, self-esteeming, self-regarding, spirited, high-spirited, courageous, proudspirited, proud-looking, pleased as Punch, as proud as Lucifer, house-proud, proud as a peacock, holier-than-thou, hoity-toity, supercilious, high-hatted, pleased as a dog with two tails, honourable

15 **unapproachable**, disdainful, obstinate, starchy, erect, stiff, stiff-necked (*or* -backed), prickly, touchy, independent, self-sufficient, hardened, unbending, distant, aloof, standoffish

16 **oppressive**, overweening, overbearing, hubristic

17 **conceited**, vain, arrogant, pompous, insolent, brazen, unblushing, unabashed, condescending, haughty, self-admiring, affected, uppity, self-praising, snobbish, vainglorious, purse-proud, strutting, conceited, nose-in-the-air, snooty, on one's dignity, on one's high horse, inches taller, smug, pleased with oneself, like a cat that got the cream, stuck-up (Inf), toffee-nosed (Inf)

18 **prestigious**, dignified, august, high-flying, stylish, commanding, patronizing, impressive, mighty, highfalutin(g) (Inf)

19 **stately**, lofty, condescending, aristocratic, noble, majestic, majesterial, imposing, grand, venerable, sedate, solemn, grave, sombre, worthy, august, pompous, high-and-mighty, high-minded, high-nosed, regal, lordly, princely, royal, kingly, queenly, statuesque, elevated, imperious, authoritative, high-handed

20 **fulfilled**, satisfied

21 **ostentatious**, showy, plumed, crested, fine, grand, fashionable, flaunting

22 **boastful**, puffed up, inflated, swollen, swollen-headed, big-headed, ungracious, strutting, swaggering, swanky, cocky, bumptious, self-glorifying, bursting (*or* bloated) with pride, elated, flushed with pride

23 **prejudiced**, contemptuous, class conscious, despising, undemocratic, xenophobic, racially prejudiced, anti-Semitic, sexist, ageist, feminist, (male) chauvinist

VERBS

24 **be proud**, have one's pride, hold one's head (high), stand erect, stand up straight, hold oneself erect, refuse to stoop, look one in the face (*or* eye), have one's self-respect, stand on one's dignity

25 **be proud of**, take pride in, glory in, exult in

26 **be too proud**, give oneself airs, be vain, be on one's high horse, hold one's nose in the air, be too grand to, be stuck up, be snooty, think too much of oneself, be on an ego trip (Inf)

27 **be ostentatious**, show off, swank, swagger, strut

28 **disdain**, despise, condescend, patronize, think it beneath one, look down on, display hauteur, pull rank,

overween, lord it over, queen it over, come it over, throw one's weight around
29 feel pride, swell with pride, take pride in, preen oneself, congratulate oneself, boast, hug oneself, pat oneself on the back, flatter oneself, think a lot of oneself
30 make proud, do (someone) proud, gratify, elate, flush, turn (someone's) head
31 save face, save one's face, preserve one's dignity, preserve one's honour, preserve one's reputation, guard one's pride, be jealous of one's good name

ADVERBS

32 proudly, pridefully, self-confidently, self-reliantly, erectly, with head held high, with one's nose in the air, stiff-neckedly, egoistically, egotistically
33 with dignity, nobly, worthily, sedately, solemnly, soberly, gravely
34 imposingly, loftily, grandly, magisterially
35 ostentatiously, swankily, swaggeringly, showily
36 majestically, regally, royally, venerably, nobly, like a lord, *en grand seigneur* (Fr)

623 Humility

Blessed are the meek: for they shall inherit the earth. Bible: Matthew.

Humility is only doubt,
And does the sun and moon blot out. William Blake.

It is difficult to be humble. Even if you aim at humility, there is no guarantee that when you have attained the state you will not be proud of the feat. Bonamy Dobrée.

ADJECTIVES

1 humble, meek, unpretentious, unassuming, modest, mouselike, harmless, inoffensive, not proud, undistinguished, unimportant, without airs, without side
2 lowly, low, poor, mean, small, low-born, plebeian, working-class
3 humbled, humiliated, embarrassed, mortified, deflated, wounded, shamed, scorned, abject, chagrined, crushed, hangdog, let down, set down, taken down a peg or two, cut down to size, put down, squashed, slapped in the face, debunked, slapped down, rebuked, disapproved, discomfited, defeated, reduced, diminished, dejected, degraded, deflated, lowered, brought down, laid low, bowed down, on one's knees, in the dust, ashamed, shamefaced, crestfallen, disconcerted, out of countenance, broken-spirited, dashed, abashed, sheepish, not proud of
4 self-abasing, self-effacing, deferent, self-submitting, diminished, self-abnegating, dispirited, self-doubting, self-deprecating, condescending, submitting
5 submissive, subservient, obedient, resigned, disinterested
6 humiliating, embarrassing, mortifying, wounding, chastening, crushing

NOUNS

7 humility, humbleness, meekness, modesty, unpretentiousness, simplicity, undistinguished, unimportance
▶ *674 Modesty*
8 lowliness, lowlihood, poorness, meanness, smallness
▶ *122 Inferiority*
9 humiliation, embarrassment, mortification, comedown, descent, deflation, wounded (*or* humbled) pride, kenosis, hangdog look (*or* expression), hurt pride, injured pride, tail between the legs, offended dignity
10 abasement, debasement, degradation, letdown, setdown, putdown, climbdown, slap in the face, dump (Inf)
11 self-abasement, self-effacement, deference, self-submission, self-abnegation, diminishment, genuflection (*or* genuflexion)
12 submissiveness, subservience, obedience, resignation, disinterestedness
▶ *663 Obedience; 664 Servility*
13 disrepute, shame, disgrace, mortification, shamefacedness, shamefastness, shamefaced look
14 rebuke, retort, crushing reply, reprimand, chastening thought
15 condescension, condescendence, deigning, lowering oneself, stooping
16 humble person, mouse, shrinking violet, no boaster, Uriah Heep, sycophant, wimp (Inf)

VERBS

17 humiliate, humble, mortify, embarrass, put out, put out of countenance, chasten, disconcert, abash, make one feel small (*or* this high), teach one his place, rub one's nose in it, make one eat dirt, snub, cut, cut down to size, crush, squash, slight, sit on, send away with a flea in the ear
18 condescend, deign, stoop, lower oneself, demean oneself, unbend, patronize
19 be humble, have no sense of pride, play second fiddle, take a back seat, put others first
20 submit, crawl, eat humble pie, knuckle under, eat dirt, swallow one's pride, lick the dust, come on bended knee, grovel, come hat in hand, draw in one's horns, sing small, lower one's tone (*or* note), tuck one's tail, come down a peg or two
21 humble oneself, resign oneself, turn the other cheek, demean oneself, genuflect, bow, scrape, crawl, climb down, get down from one's high horse, put one's pride in one's pocket, deprecate oneself, set one's dignity aside, eat dirt (Inf)
22 shame, put to shame, disgrace, mortify, be rude, put a person's nose out of joint, make a fool of, put in the shade
23 abase, debase, crush, degrade, abash, reduce, diminish, demean, lower, bring low (*or* down), trip up, take down, set down, put down, dump (on), knock off one's perch, take down a peg (or two)
24 be humiliated, be put out of countenance, feel small, feel cheap, look foolish (*or* silly), sink through the floor, take shame, be ashamed, have a (very) red face, hang one's head (in shame), hide one's face, not dare to show one's face, not have a good word to say for oneself, drink the cup of humiliation, be cold-shouldered, get a slap in the face, be put in one's place
25 deflate, take the wind out of someone's sails, take the

shine out of, take it out of, take the starch out of, put a person's nose out of joint, put a tuck in one's tail
26 **outdo**, outstare, frown down, daunt, get the better of, gain the upper (*or* whip) hand, triumph over, crow, gain ascendancy over

ADVERBS

27 **humbly**, meekly, modestly
28 **subserviently**, deferentially, with due deference, with bated breath, submissively, abjectly, on bended knee, on one's knees, on all fours, with one's tail between one's legs, with hat in hand

624 Anger and Resentment

Anger supplies the arms. Virgil.

NOUNS

1 **resentment**, bitterness, bitter resentment, burning resentment, resentfulness, rancour, rankling, acrimony, spleen, gall, acid, acidity, acidulousness, heartburning, soreness, slow burn, grudge, malice, jealousy, envy, displeasure, dissatisfaction, disapproval, disapprobation, ill humour, animosity, hard feelings, ill feelings, irritation, vexation, discontent, annoyance, aggravation, exasperation, pique, peevishness, asperity, bone to pick
► *242 Unpleasantness; 327 Agitation; 606 Dissatisfaction*
2 **offence**, umbrage, hurt, indignity, insult, affront, wrong, huff, dudgeon (Lit), high dudgeon (Lit), miff (Inf)
3 **cause of offence**, provocation, last straw, red rag to a bull, sore point, tender spot, dangerous subject, pinprick, raw nerve
4 **anger**, wrath, wrathfulness, rage, blind rage, furious rage, fury, blind fury, passion, ire, choler, aggression, belligerence, bellicosity, crossness, snappishness, sullenness, heat, vehemence, violence, fit of anger, fit of temper, tearing rage, outburst, tantrum, temper tantrum, paroxysm (of rage), convulsion, storm, scene, ferment, fret, tears of rage, explosion, going on the rampage, gnashing the teeth, stamping the foot, shouting, roaring, raging, tizzy (Inf), duck-fit (Inf), cat-fit (Inf), blow-up (Inf), flare-up (Inf), paddy (*or* paddywhack) (Inf), stew (Inf), wax (Inf), dander (US inf), conniption (fit) (US inf)
► *380 Violence; 507 Loudness; 625 Grumpiness; 651 Malevolence*
5 **quarrel**, argument, tiff, fight, box on the ear, rap on the knuckles, slap in the face, coming to blows, fisticuffs
► *751 Disagreement*
6 **sign of anger**, angry look, black look, frown, scowl, glower, glare, growl, snarl, bark, bite, snap
7 **gods and goddesses of anger**, the Furies, Allecto, Megaera, Tisiphone, the Eumenides, the Erinys, Ira, Nemesis

VERBS

8 **resent**, feel resentment, nurse resentment, feel offended, feel insulted, feel piqued, feel sore, feel discontented, bear malice, bear a grudge, have a bone to pick, find intolerable, not be able to bear, not be able to stomach, suffer, feel, smart under, take amiss, take exception to
9 **offend**, provoke, vex, annoy, aggravate, goad, sting, exasperate, irritate, antagonize, incense, arouse, inflame, nettle, fret, insult, affront, outrage, give umbrage, grieve, aggrieve, wound, hurt (the feelings), chafe, pique, huff, rile, rankle, ruffle, work up, get on one's nerves, get to one, bother, harass, pester, tease, bait, pinprick, torment, goad, sting, taunt, get one's back up, put one's fur up, put one's bristles up, ruffle the dignity, ruffle one's feathers, raise someone's hackles, step (*or* tread) on someone's toes, put someone's nose out of joint (Inf), stir the blood (Inf), stick in one's craw (*or* throat) (Inf), needle (Inf), miff (Inf), stir up (Inf), rub up the wrong way (Inf)
10 **be offended**, take offence, feel hurt, feel pique, take amiss, take ill, take in bad part, take to heart, mind, not take a joke, take umbrage, get huffy, get miffed (Inf), have one's nose out of joint (Inf)
11 **be angry**, rage, rave, rant, rant and rave, bluster, fulminate, burn, fume, seethe, simmer, smoke, smoulder, boil, glower, glare, frown, scowl, lour (*or* lower), look black, look like thunder, look daggers, snarl, growl, snap, create a scene, make a scene, weep with rage, quiver with rage, fret, chafe, storm, breathe fire, quarrel, have a tiff, fight, bite someone's head off, raise Cain, raise hell, raise the devil, raise the roof, throw a fit, have a (temper) tantrum, go berserk, rampage, foam at the mouth, shake with passion, stamp one's foot, paw the ground (Inf), champ (*or* chafe) at the bit (Inf), take on (Inf), carry on (Inf), kick up a row (Inf), kick up dirt (Inf), make a shindy (Inf), cut up rough (Inf), stew (Inf), sizzle (Inf), throw a cat-fit (Inf), throw a conniption fit (US inf), be pissed (off) (Inf), throw a wobbler (Inf)
12 **become angry**, get angry, anger, lose one's temper, lose patience, get cross, get sore, fly into a rage, fly into a passion, explode, throw a tantrum, colour, redden, flush with anger, do a slow burn, ignite, kindle, take fire, forget oneself, lose control, get sore, bridle, bristle, raise one's hackles, get one's back up, get one's gorge up, get one's blood up, get mad (Inf), get one's Irish up (Inf), see red (Inf), get steamed up (Inf), get hot under the collar (Inf), flare up (Inf), reach boiling point (Inf), boil over (Inf), work up into a lather (Inf), work up into a sweat (Inf), work up into a stew (Inf), let fly (Inf), fly off the handle (Inf), hit the roof (*or* ceiling) (Inf), blow one's top (Inf), blow one's lid (*or* stack) (US inf), become red (Inf), lose one's rag (Inf), have a haemorrhage (Inf), go off the deep end (Inf), out-Lear Lear (Inf), blow one's cool (Inf), blow a fuse (Inf), blow a gasket (Inf), go up the wall (Inf), go spare (Inf), go ballistic (Inf), go postal (Inf), flip one's lid (*or* wig) (Inf), wig out (Inf), freak out (Inf), get one's dander up (US inf), get one's monkey up (Inf), kick up shit (Inf)
13 **vent one's anger**, vent one's rancour, vent one's spleen, pour wrath onto, snap at, bite (*or* snap) someone's head off, express one's feelings, take it out on (Inf), jump down someone's throat (Inf)
14 **make angry**, make sore, aggravate, huff, put out, enrage, infuriate, madden, drive into a frenzy, work up into a passion, make someone's blood boil, make all hell break loose, disturb someone's equanimity, ruffle someone's temper, push too far, ulcerate, envenom, poison, set at loggerheads, set by the ears, make mad (Inf), brown off (Inf), drive up the wall (Inf), piss off (Inf)

ADJECTIVES

15 **resentful**, offended, insulted, affronted, hurt, pained, put-out, indignant, reproachful, bitter, embittered, virulent, acrimonious, sharp, acid, acidulous, splenetic, acerbic, caustic, irritated, vexed, wrought-up, discontented, disapproving, displeased, not amused, up in arms, provoked, riled, worked up, annoyed, aggravated, exasperated, piqued, peeved, in a pet, nettled, stung, smarting, hurt, sore, grudging, moody, malicious, jealous, envious, green with envy, full of hate, bileful, bilious, spiteful, ill-humoured, impatient, shirty (Inf), stroppy (Inf)

16 **angry**, angered, irate, ireful, cross, aggressive, belligerent, bellicose, wrathful, furious, infuriated, choleric, indignant, livid, pale with anger, red with rage, red with anger, enraged, raging, incensed, fuming, flushed with rage, warm, boiling with rage, boiling, burning, smouldering, sulphurous, in a rage, in a huff, huffed, in a temper, beside oneself, crying with rage, frenzied, foaming at the mouth, foaming, rabid, berserk, fighting mad, hopping mad, hopping, mad as a hornet, mad as a wet hen, good and mad, speechless with rage, stuttering, gnashing, growling, snapping, dangerous, violent, fierce, savage, rampaging, roaring, in high dudgeon, rubbed (up) the wrong way, mad (Inf), apoplectic (Inf), sizzling (Inf), in a stew (Inf), in a strop (Inf), in a paddy (Inf), seeing red (Inf), hot under the collar (Inf), ratty (Inf), waxy (Inf), browned off (Inf), het up (Inf), pissed off (Inf), PO'd (US inf)

ADVERBS

17 **resentfully**, with resentment, hurtfully, in a hurtful manner, indignantly, reproachfully, with reproach, virulently, acrimoniously, bitterly, with bitterness, sharply, acidly, caustically, irritatingly, discontentedly, annoyingly, aggravatingly, exasperatingly, maddeningly, grudgingly, maliciously, with malice, jealously, with a jealous heart, enviously, biliously, spitefully, disapprovingly, with one's nose out of joint (Inf)

18 **angrily**, in anger, irately, infuriatingly, crossly, wrathfully, furiously, with (*or* in) fury, indignantly, lividly, warmly, heatedly, sulphurously, in the heat of passion, in the height of passion, in the heat of the moment, in hot blood, rabidly, apoplectically (Inf), in a paddy (Inf), while seeing red (Inf), with one's dander up (US inf), with one's monkey up (Inf)

625 Grumpiness

He could enrage his antagonists by making them feel their own impotence to enrage him. Anonymous.

NOUNS

1 **irascibility**, irritability, impatience, temperamentalness, sharp temper, quick temper, fiery temper, short temper, bad temper, dangerous temper, thin skin, touchiness, tetchiness, prickliness, grumpiness, gruffness, readiness to take offence, quick passions, peevishness, pepperiness, testiness, petulance, querulousness, fretfulness, resentfulness, sullenness, shrewishness, vixenishness, fractiousness, crankiness, crossness, crabbedness, huffiness, cussedness, cantankerousness, churlishness, sharpness, tartness, acerbity, asperity, gall, bile, vinegar, sourness, acidity, acidness, shrewishness, waspishness, meanness, contentiousness, quarrelsomeness, disputatiousness, argumentativeness, belligerence, orneriness (US inf), grouchiness (Inf), crabbiness (Inf), bitchiness (Inf), short fuse

► *591 Sensitivity; 606 Dissatisfaction; 615 Rashness; 624 Anger and Resentment; 626 Sullenness; 655 Unsociability; 751 Disagreement*

2 **sign of irascibility**, bad temper, black look, frown, scowl, glare, grimace, glower, lour (*or* lower), growl, snarl, snap

3 **irascible person**, hothead, tartar, bear, bear with a sore head, crank (US), ugly customer, shrew, virago, vixen, termagant, fury, witch, tigress, spitfire, fishwife, nag, harridan, scold, grouch (Inf), grump (Inf), crosspatch (Inf), sorehead (US inf), cat (Inf), dragon (Inf), battle-axe (Inf), she-devil (Inf), bitch (Inf)

ADJECTIVES

4 **irascible**, irritable, impatient, nervous, jumpy, strained, fretful, oversensitive, touchy, tetchy, thin-skinned, petulant, peevish, querulous, testy, temperamental, highly strung, short-tempered, short, huffy, annoyed, resentful, sullen, sore, riled, nettled, ill-humoured, snappish, snappy, bellicose, waspish, sharp-tongued, sharp, tart, acerbic, sour, acid, shrewish, vixenish, crusty, ornery, prickly, peppery, hot-blooded, hot-tempered, quick-tempered, short-tempered, easily roused, grumpy, gruff, cross, cantankerous, churlish, fractious, bilious, dyspeptic, contentious, quarrelsome, disputatious, argumentative, belligerent, angry, mean, bearish, like a bear with a sore head, grouchy (Inf), crotchety (Inf), cranky (US inf), crabby (Inf), uptight (Inf)

5 **showing irascibility**, frowning, scowling, glowering, louring (*or* lowering), pouting, grimacing, growling, snarling

VERBS

6 **be irascible**, strain, fret, rouse easily, have a short temper, have a temper, have a bad temper, have an uncontrollable temper, have a short fuse, have a bad liver, show impatience, become annoyed, resent, have a sharp tongue, turn sour, act like a vixen, quarrel, dispute, argue, get angry, turn against (*or* on), fly at, snap at, snap (*or* bite) one's head off, act like a bear, jump down someone's throat (Inf), act like a bitch (Inf)

7 **frown**, scowl, glower lour (*or* lower), pout, grimace, growl, snarl

8 **make irascible**, irritate, make impatient, vex, annoy, bother, rile, nettle, rouse, test someone's patience, cause resentment, make angry, make uptight (Inf), peeve (Inf)

ADVERBS

9 **irascibly**, irritably, in an irritable mood, impatiently, without patience, petulantly, peevishly, querulously, temperamentally, resentfully, sullenly, ill-humouredly, waspishly, sharply, in a sharp tone, sourly, in a sour disposition, acidly, like a shrew, like a vixen, nervously, in a nervous state, fretfully, touchily, tetchily, grumpily, hot-bloodedly, gruffly, in a gruff manner, crossly, cantankerously, churlishly, biliously, contentiously, argumentatively, belligerently, angrily, with anger, meanly,

with a frown, with a scowl, with a grimace, grouchily (Inf), crankily (Inf), like a bitch (Inf)

626 Sullenness

NOUNS

1 **sullenness**, sulkiness, surliness, glumness, moroseness, moodiness, mopiness, melancholy, atrabiliousness, dejection, grumpishness, whininess, ill humour, ill nature, unsociability, lack of communication, lack of talk, sourness, grimness, sternness, mumpishness (Lit)

▶ *499 Sourness; 624 Anger and Resentment; 655 Unsociability*

2 **sign of sullenness**, sullen look, hangdog look, long face, pout, *moue* (Fr), sigh, moan, the blues, blue devils, the sulks, fit of the sulks, the sullens, the pouts, the mopes, the mumps (Lit), the dumps (Inf), the grumps (Inf), the mulligrubs (Inf)

3 **irritableness**, irritability, irascibility, discontent, dissatisfaction, petulance, temperament, ill temper, bad temper, shocking temper, touchiness, peevishness, grumpiness, gruffness, crossness, crankiness, cussedness, spitefulness, spleen, liver, bile, grouchiness (Inf), biliousness (Inf), bitchiness (Inf)

▶ *606 Dissatisfaction; 625 Grumpiness; 659 Discourtesy*

4 **sign of irritableness**, bad temper, scowl, frown, grimace, lour (*or* lower), glower, glare, wry face, black look, growl, snarl, snort, snap, mow (Lit), short fuse (Inf)

5 **sullen person**, sulker, grumbler, grouser, whiner, whinger, bear, bear with a sore head, hothead, witch, grouch (Inf), grump (Inf), crosspatch (Inf), sorehead (US inf), bellyacher (Inf), bitch (Inf)

ADJECTIVES

6 **sullen**, sulky, surly, serious, pouting, melancholy, melancholic, atrabilious, moody, morose, glum, grim, stern, dour, sour, gloomy, sombre, dismal, dark, black, dejected, depressed, cheerless, ill-humoured, ill-natured, blue, saturnine

7 **irritable**, irascible, disagreeable, discontented, dissatisfied, smouldering, temperamental, bad-tempered, ill-tempered, surly, resentful, churlish, touchy, tetchy, testy, acid, tart, vinegary, grumpy, quarrelsome, cantankerous, curmudgeonly, out of humour, in a bad humour, out of temper, dyspeptic, bitter, peevish, petulant, shrewish, vixenish, cross, abrupt, brusque, gruff, frowning, unsmiling, louring (or lowering), glowering, scowling, grumbling, grousing, snarling, snapping, snappish, put-out, mumpish (Lit), (down) in the dumps (Inf), bilious (Inf), grouchy (Inf), bitchy (Inf), cranky (US inf), bellyaching (Inf), beefing (Inf), shirty (Inf)

8 **overcast**, cloudy, louring (*or* lowering), glowering, dismal

▶ *31 Meteorology and Climatology*

VERBS

9 **be sullen**, sulk, get oneself into a sulk, mope, brood, fret, pout, whine, whinge, have the blues, have a long face, make a lip, hang one's lip, moan, have the pip (Inf)

10 **make sullen**, deject, depress, sour, give someone the blues, put someone in a melancholy mood, pip (Inf), give someone the pip (Inf)

11 **be irritable**, glare, lour (*or* lower), glower, smoulder, look black, make a wry face, knit one's brows, frown, scowl, grimace, bare one's teeth, show one's fangs, growl, grouch, snarl, snap, spit, grumble, mutter, complain, grouse, carp, get out of bed on the wrong side (Inf), grouch (Inf), crab (Inf), bitch (Inf), bellyache (Inf), beef (Inf)

12 **make irritable**, irritate, annoy, acerbate, exacerbate, embitter, bitter, make bitter, envenom, put in a bad temper, put in a bad humour, discontent, dissatisfy, rub the wrong way

ADVERBS

13 **sullenly**, sulkily, seriously, in a serious mood, moodily, morosely, glumly, ill-humouredly, in an ill humour, grimly, sternly, dourly, sourly, gloomily, sombrely, dismally, darkly, blackly, under a black cloud, dejectedly, depressingly, in a fit of depression, cheerlessly, without cheer, saturninely

14 **irritably**, with irritation, irascibly, disagreeably, discontentedly, with bad grace, temperamentally, ill-naturedly, with an ill nature, resentfully, with resentment, churlishly, touchily, testily, acidly, with an acid tongue, tartly, grumpily, cantankerously, bitterly, crossly, peevishly, petulantly, abruptly, brusquely, gruffly, grouchily (Inf), crankily (Inf)

627 Pity

To show pity is felt as a sign of contempt because one has clearly ceased to be an object of fear *as soon as one is pitied.* Friedrich Wilhelm Nietzsche.

NOUNS

1 **pity**, sympathy, commiseration, condolence, feeling, fellow feeling, empathy, understanding, compassion, compassionateness, mercifulness, charity, humanity, kindness, benevolence, tenderness, gentleness, caring, soft-heartedness, warm-heartedness, tender-heartedness, soft heart, warm heart, tender heart, self-pity, tears of self-pity, tears for oneself, self-commiseration, self-compassion

▶ *602 Sorrow; 648 Leniency; 650 Benevolence*

2 **condolence**, condolences, sympathy, tears of sympathy, sympathy in grief, shared grief, mourning, sorrow, shared sorrow, shared suffering, comfort, balm, consolation, commiseration, remorse, compunction, regret, ruth (Lit), lament, wake, keen

3 **mercy**, compassion, grace, favour, quarter, forgiveness, mercifulness, forbearance, long-suffering, second chance, letting off, clemency, leniency, reprieve, relief, mitigation, pardon, acquittal

▶ *649 Forgiveness; 814 Punishment*

4 **pitying person**, sympathizer, commiserator, mourner, social reformer, bleeding heart (Inf)

5 **misfortune**, bad luck, disappointment, regret, a pity, a shame, a crying shame, a sin

ADJECTIVES

6 **pitying**, sympathetic, sympathizing, sorry for, comforting, consoling, commiserative, commiserating, condolent, understanding, compassionate, caring, tender, tender-hearted, gentle, kind, kind-hearted, soft, soft-

hearted, warm-hearted, benevolent, gracious, generous, clement, yielding, lenient, forbearant, charitable, humane, human, merciful, full of mercy, forgiving, full of forgiveness

7 **pitiful**, pitiable, piteous, arousing pity, demanding pity, heart-rending, heartbreaking, pathetic, sad, distressing, grievous, touching, moving, tear-jerking, affecting, arousing compassion, ruthful (Lit), self-pitying, sorry for oneself

VERBS

8 **pity**, show pity, feel pity, have pity for, feel sorry for, feel sorrow for, feel for, take pity on, sympathize, sympathize with, empathize, empathize with, understand, show understanding, support

9 **sorrow**, grieve, grieve for, share grief, lament, condole with, commiserate, comfort, offer comfort, console, offer consolation, soothe, wipe away one's tears, weep with, weep for, bleed, bleed for, share one's sorrow, express sympathy for, express one's condolences, send one's condolences, pay one's respects

10 **show mercy**, have mercy on, have pity, take pity on, forgive, pardon, grant a pardon, absolve, reprieve, spare, forbear, give a second chance, give a last chance, relent, unbend, relax, give quarter, go easy on, give respite, be lenient, not be too hard on, put out of one's misery, give a break (Inf)

11 **excite pity**, move to compassion, melt, melt the heart, thaw, soften, move, touch, affect, reach, grieve, move to tears, disarm, appeal to one's better feelings

12 **ask for mercy**, plead for mercy, beg for mercy, ask for pity, plead with, cry for quarter, plead (*or* beg) for one's life, fall on one's knees, throw oneself upon another's mercy, plead (*or* beg) for forgiveness

ADVERBS

13 **pitifully**, pitiably, piteously, sympathetically, in sympathy, compassionately, with compassion, mercifully, with mercy, humanely, for humane reasons, tenderly, tender-heartedly, gently, kindly, kind-heartedly, in a kind-hearted way, warm-heartedly, in a warmhearted manner, benevolently, graciously, generously, charitably

INTERJECTIONS

14 **have pity!**, have mercy!, have a heart!, take pity!, for pity's sake!, for mercy's sake!, for the love of God!

628 Cruelty

Man's inhumanity to man
Makes countless thousands mourn! Robert Burns.

NOUNS

1 **pitilessness**, lack of pity, without pity, unsympatheticness, uncompassionateness, intolerance, unfeelingness, mercilessness, unmercifulness, inclemency, ruthlessness, hardheartedness, heartlessness, hardness of heart, heart of stone, heart of flint, hardness, flintiness, callousness, inhumanity, cruelty, severity, remorselessness, unremorsefulness, unforgivingness, revengefulness, pound of flesh, short shrift

► *418 Hardness; 592 Insensitivity; 647 Severity; 651 Malevolence*

2 **inflexibility**, implacability, unyieldingness, intractability, inexorableness, relentlessness

3 **pitiless person**, callous person, cold-blooded killer, sadistic tyrant, hard case (Inf), loan shark (Inf)

ADJECTIVES

4 **pitiless**, unpitying, unpitiful, unfeeling, without feelings, unmoved, unresponsive, impassive, uncaring, obdurate, unsympathetic, unsympathizing, without compassion, heartless, hardhearted, cold, cold-hearted, stony-hearted, hard, hardened, harsh, severe, flinty, tough, callous, ruthless, cruel, soulless, brutal, cold-blooded, sadistic, barbarous, barbaric, remorseless, unremorseful, vengeful, revengeful, vindictive, unforgiving

5 **inflexible**, unbending, unrelenting, relentless, inexorable, implacable, unyielding, intractable

VERBS

6 **be pitiless**, have no pity, show no pity, have no mercy, show no mercy, show no sympathy, lack compassion, have no feelings, have no heart, show no leniency, give no quarter, insist on (*or* claim) one's pound of flesh, stand by (*or* on) the letter of the law, go by the rule book, show no flexibility, be unmoved, not be moved, turn a deaf ear, harden one's heart, not forgive, stop at nothing, let nothing stand in one's way, make short shrift of

ADVERBS

7 **pitilessly**, without pity, unsympathetically, mercilessly, unmercifully, unforgivingly, unyieldingly, heartlessly, unfeelingly, without feelings, without batting an eye (*or* eyelid), unresponsively, impassively, obdurately, coldly, cold-heartedly, without a twinge of conscience, harshly, severely, toughly, callously, cruelly, brutally, cold-bloodedly, in cold blood, sadistically, barbarously, remorselessly, vengefully, vindictively, unrelentingly, relentlessly

629 Jealousy

For the ear of jealousy heareth all things: and the noise of murmurings is not hid. Bible: Wisdom.

O, beware, my lord, of jealousy;
It is the green-ey'd monster which doth mock
The meat it feeds on. William Shakespeare.

NOUNS

1 **jealousy**, jealousness, pangs of jealousy, enviousness, envy, covetousness, sexual jealousy, heartburning, heartburn, jaundice, jaundiced eye, jaundiced view, jaundiced look, green-eyed jealousy, sour grapes, resentment, hostility, possessiveness, rivalry, competition, competitiveness, competitive spirit, eternal triangle, crime of passion, green-eyed monster (Inf)

► *593 Love; 594 Hate; 624 Anger and Resentment*

2 **distrust**, distrustfulness, mistrust, mistrustfulness, suspicion, suspiciousness, doubt, misdoubt, watchfulness, vigilance, possessiveness, solicitousness, anxiousness, apprehensiveness

► *451 Disbelief*

3 **rival**, rival in love, competitor, the other man, the other woman

ADJECTIVES

4 **jealous**, envious, covetous, devoured with jealousy, consumed with jealousy, eaten up with jealousy, obsessed with jealousy, jaundiced, jaundice-eyed, green, green-eyed, yellow, yellow-eyed, lynx-eyed, sour, resentful, possessive, overpossessive, hostile, invidious, rival, competitive, competing, emulative, emulous

5 **distrustful**, mistrustful, suspicious, doubtful, misdoubtful, watchful, vigilant, Argus-eyed, solicitous, anxious, apprehensive

VERBS

6 **be jealous**, envy, covet, view with jealousy, view with a jaundiced eye, suffer pangs of jealousy, have heartburn, eat one's heart out, resent, resent competition, brook no rival

7 **arouse jealousy**, make jealous, create resentment, give someone an inferiority complex, put someone's nose out of joint (Inf)

8 **distrust**, mistrust, be suspicious, be wary, doubt, misdoubt, be possessive, be overpossessive, strive to keep for oneself, not allow out of one's sight

ADVERBS

9 **jealously**, with a jealous heart, enviously, with envy, covetously, resentfully, possessively, in a possessive manner, hostilely, invidiously, competitively, emulously, distrustfully, mistrustfully, suspiciously, doubtfully, watchfully, vigilantly, solicitously, anxiously, apprehensively

630 Surprise

No, my dear, it is I *who am surprised; you are merely astonished.*
Noah Webster, replying to his wife who said she was surprised to see him embracing their maid.

NOUNS

1 **surprise**, lack of warning, lack of expectation, unexpectedness, unpredictability, unpreparedness, unreadiness, miscalculation, misjudgment, improbability

2 **amazement**, wonder, astonishment, astoundment, stupefaction, incredulity, disconcertment, disappointment, anticlimax

▶ *451 Disbelief; 604 Disappointment; 619 Wonder*

3 **shock**, horror, surprisal, start, jump, fright, turn, jolt, blow, bolt from the blue, thunderbolt, bombshell, facer

▶ *612 Fear*

4 **surprising thing**, wonder, the unexpected, the unforeseen, serendipity, the unpredictable, unexpected gift, treat, special treat, windfall, unexpected occurrence, unforeseen result, twist, reversal, revelation, eye-opener

▶ *224 Change; 765 Profit*

5 **surpriser**, wonderman, wonder woman, superman, superwoman, miracle-worker, thaumaturge, magician

ADJECTIVES

6 **surprised**, off guard, unprepared, unsuspecting, unaware, caught unawares, caught napping, taken aback, startled, ambushed, trapped

▶ *612 Fear*

7 **amazed**, awed, awestruck, marvelling, admiring, impressed, astonished, astounded, stupefied, stunned, stunned into silence, struck dumb, speechless, dumbfounded, thunderstruck, staggered, shocked, disconcerted, disappointed, flabbergasted (Inf), bowled over (Inf), gobsmacked (Inf)

▶ *604 Disappointment; 619 Wonder*

8 **surprising**, sudden, unexpected, unforeseen, unpredictable, unanticipated, unannounced, amazing, astounding, astonishing, staggering, shocking, out of the ordinary, full of surprises, serendipitous, unusual, unprecedented, odd, abnormal, freakish, weird and wonderful, peculiar, freaky (Inf)

▶ *118 Nonconformity; 619 Wonder*

VERBS

9 **surprise**, discover, take unawares, take by surprise, catch out, catch off-guard, catch unawares, catch napping, catch red-handed, startle, jolt, frighten, give one a fright, make one jump, give one (quite) a turn, take aback, spring on, catch with one's pants (*or* trousers) down (Inf)

▶ *449 Discovery; 612 Fear*

10 **ambush**, capture, ensnare, trap, creep up on, pounce on, spring upon

▶ *379 Trap*

11 **amaze**, astonish, astound, dumbfound, strike dumb, leave speechless, stupefy, stagger, boggle, stun, shock, disconcert, disappoint, electrify, impress, come out of the blue, be a surprise, be one in the eye for, flabbergast (Inf), bowl over (Inf), floor (Inf), gobsmack (Inf), knock for six (Inf), knock for a loop (US inf)

▶ *604 Disappointment; 619 Wonder*

12 **be surprised**, not expect, start, jump, jump out of one's skin, shy, be taken aback, fall into a trap

▶ *612 Fear*

ADVERBS

13 **surprisingly**, amazingly, astoundingly, unexpectedly, suddenly, without warning, out of the blue, like a bolt from the blue, unawares, off (one's) guard

▶ *280 Immediacy*

INTERJECTIONS

14 **good heavens!**, well I never!, you don't say!, I don't believe it!, you could have knocked me down with a feather!, marry! (Lit)

▶ *619 Wonder*

Character and Behaviour

631 Behaviour

Men are rewarded and punished not for what they do, but rather for how their acts are defined. This is why men are more interested in better justifying themselves than in better behaving themselves. Thomas Szasz.

NOUNS

1 **conduct**, behaviour, deportment, bearing, personal bearing, comportment, carriage, posture, port, demeanour, mien, attitude, mental attitude, aspect, outlook, mood, opinion, feeling, look, look in one's eyes, appearance, tone, tone of voice, voice, delivery, motion, action, actions, gesticulation, gesture, mode of behaviour, manners, manner, style, fashion, guise, air, pose, affectation, role-playing, role model, example, democratic behaviour, gesture of equality, common touch, past behaviour, known attitudes, record, track record, history, study of conduct, psychology, behaviourism, reward of conduct, reciprocal manners, deserts, dueness, proposed conduct, intentions, good intentions, line of action, policy, course, race, walk, walk of life, vocation, career, observance, rule, rules, rules of life, the golden rule, rules of business, rules of the road (Inf)

▶ *450 Belief; 484 Plan; 525 Appearance; 590 Feelings; 676 Affectation; 729 Speech; 743 Identification*

2 **good conduct**, good behaviour, goodness, virtue, breeding, poise, dignity, presence, savoir-faire, etiquette, protocol, good manners, gracious manners, graciousness, courtesy, politeness, gentlemanly behaviour, ladylike behaviour

▶ *235 Worth; 581 Refreshment; 658 Courtesy; 797 Good; 803 Virtue*

3 **well-behaved person**, well-mannered person, gentleman, lady, gracious host (*or* hostess), polite listener, good child, law-abiding citizen, saint, moralist

▶ *235 Worth; 658 Courtesy; 663 Obedience; 797 Good; 803 Virtue*

4 **bad conduct**, misconduct, bad behaviour, misbehaviour, mischief, naughtiness, badness, vice, wickedness, ill-breeding, bad manners, ungraciousness, boorishness, rudeness, discourtesy, selfishness, vileness

▶ *659 Discourtesy; 662 Disobedience; 798 Evil; 804 Wickedness*

5 **badly behaved person**, ill-mannered person, rude person, obnoxious person, boor, lout, cad, bounder, naughty child, criminal, egomaniac, immoralist, amoralist, inconsiderate driver, loud drunk, git (Inf), asshole (Inf)

▶ *236 Worthlessness; 659 Discourtesy; 662 Disobedience; 798 Evil; 804 Wickedness*

6 **way of life**, lifestyle, ethos, morals, principles, ideals, customs, traditions, conventions, mores, praxis, modus vivendi, manners, habits

▶ *4 Philosophy; 7 Religion; 632 Habit*

7 **way**, proven way, new way, method, method of operating, modus operandi, tried-and-true method, experimental method, practice, routine, procedure, routine procedure, process

▶ *317 Way*

8 **treatment**, handling, manipulation, control, discipline, regulation, direction, management, administration, operation, organization, orchestration, masterminding, leadership, command, guidance, supervision, dealings, actions, transactions, affairs, deeds, gentle handling, tact, diplomacy, leniency, kid gloves, velvet glove, iron hand in a velvet glove, rough handling, severity, iron hand, boot, jackboot, kick in the pants (US), putting the boot in (Inf), kick in the ass (Inf)

▶ *324 Direction; 579 Management; 647 Severity; 648 Leniency; 813 Reward; 814 Punishment*

9 **tactics**, strategy, campaign, plan, plan of campaign, plan of attack, game plan, logistics, programme, policy, line, party line, rules of the game, game rules, political science, politics, art of the possible, opportunism, realpolitik, diplomacy, statesmanship, governance, lifemanship, gamesmanship, cunning, brinkmanship, generalship, seamanship, skill, manoeuvres, manoeuvring, marching and countermarching, outflanking, jockeying, jockeying for position, wheeling and dealing, advantage, tactical advantage, built-in advantage, vantage ground, starting ahead of the game, stalling for time, playing for time, delay, manoeuvre, move, gambit, deed, game, little game, tactic, stratagem, trick, shift, contrivance, one-upmanship (Inf)

▶ *121 Superiority; 294 Lateness; 340 Action; 396 Authority; 484 Plan; 485 Skill; 645 Cunning*

10 **conductor**, guide, leader, director, escort, usher, carrier, driver, pilot

VERBS

11 **conduct oneself**, behave, carry oneself, bear oneself, deport oneself, comport oneself, acquit oneself, act, do,

set an example, provide a role model, gesture, gesticulate, posture, pose, affect, indulge in, play one's part, participate, pursue, follow a course, follow one's career, shape one's career, steer one's career, steer for, conduct one's affairs, busy oneself, paddle one's own canoe, be master of one's own ship, shift for oneself, employ tactics, manoeuvre, manipulate, mastermind, jockey, twist, turn, take advantage of, use

▶ *250 Freedom; 324 Direction; 340 Action; 342 Activity; 676 Affectation; 743 Identification; 764 Sharing*

12 behave well, behave oneself, behave, be good, keep out of mischief, conduct oneself properly, comport oneself well, lead a good life, set a good example, mind one's p's and q's, abide by the rules, play the game

▶ *235 Worth; 797 Good; 803 Virtue*

13 behave badly, misbehave, demean oneself, lead a bad life, set a bad example, break (all) the rules, deserve ill of, carry on (Inf), try it on (Inf), play up (Inf), have one's mind in the mud (US inf)

▶ *236 Worthlessness; 798 Evil; 804 Wickedness*

14 behave towards, treat, deal with, handle, do, see to, put on one's calendar, have in one's book, have on one's plate, have to do with, conduct, operate, carry on, run, direct, manage, cope with, manipulate, control, organize, orchestrate, mastermind, lead, do the necessary thing, do the needful (Inf), act, transact, enact, execute, dispatch, carry out, carry through, put into practice, put into effect, initiate, plan, work out, programme, work at, think through, work through, wade through, go through, read, study, research

▶ *340 Action; 484 Plan; 576 Work; 579 Management*

15 conduct, guide, lead, direct, navigate, steer, pilot, escort, usher, carry, transmit, convey

ADJECTIVES

16 behaving, behavioural, behaviouristic, ethological, tactical, strategical, political, statesmanlike, governmental, businesslike

17 well-behaved, on one's best behaviour, well-bred, gentlemanly, ladylike, dignified, well-mannered, gracious, courteous, polite, good, ethical, virtuous, law-abiding

▶ *235 Worth; 658 Courtesy; 797 Good; 803 Virtue*

18 badly behaved, bad, ill-bred, mischievous, naughty, wicked, ill-mannered, ungracious, boorish, rude, discourteous, impolite, selfish, inconsiderate, obnoxious, playing up (Inf), bad news (Inf)

▶ *236 Worthlessness; 659 Discourtesy; 798 Evil; 804 Wickedness*

ADVERBS

19 well, in a gentlemanly (*or* ladylike) manner, properly, with propriety, politely, graciously, courteously, virtuously, ethically

20 badly, in an ungentlemanly (*or* unladylike) manner, wickedly, naughtily, ungraciously, rudely, discourteously, impolitely, selfishly, inconsiderately, obnoxiously

632 Habit

Curious things, habits. People themselves never knew they had them. Agatha Christie.

Men's natures are alike; it is their habits that carry them far apart. Confucius.

NOUNS

1 habit, habitual action, force of habit, second nature, matter of course, custom, use, usage, wont, pattern, praxis, regularity, familiarity, inveteracy, confirmed habit, long habit, addiction, compulsion, bad habit, cacoethes, mania, obsession, fixation, complex

▶ *298 Regularity*

2 tendency, habitude, leaning, bent, propensity, proclivity, instinct, knack, trick, trait, idiosyncrasy, mannerism

▶ *229 Tendency*

3 way, ways, established ways, fixed ways, lifestyle, way of life, daily habit, constitutional, routine, run, round, daily round, routine work, repetitive job, groove, rut, tramlines, beaten track, treadmill, grind (Inf), daily grind (Inf), the nine-to-five (Inf)

4 custom, usage, standard usage, established custom, standing custom, native custom, old custom, the old way, tradition, lore, folklore, social custom, social usage, mores, manners and customs, behaviour patterns, institution, ritual, rite, ceremony, observance, religious observance, religion, cult, cultus, trend, fashion, craze, the in thing (Inf)

▶ *7 Religion; 134 Continuity; 277 Duration; 553 Fashion*

5 tradition, consuetude, law, prescription, legal precedent, rules, rules and regulations, house rules, rules of business, convention, protocol, unwritten law, order of the day, formality, form, etiquette, manners, social manners, table manners, eating habits, conduct, behaviour, military conduct, military discipline, the done thing (Inf), spit and polish (Inf)

▶ *16 Law; 140 Rule; 631 Behaviour; 656 Formality*

6 procedure, official procedure, standard procedure, recognized procedure, policy, usual policy, practice, standard practice, common practice, routine, system, drill, bureaucracy, red tape, beadledom, petty officialdom, conventionalism, conventionality, traditionalism, conservatism, old school, conformism, conformity

▶ *117 Conformity; 407 Order*

7 habituation, training, drilling, memorization, rote, indoctrination, brainwashing, inurement, institutionalization, hardening, seasoning, maturing, maturation, naturalization, acclimatization, adaptation, orientation, conditioning, association, reflex, conditioned reflex

▶ *243 Preparation; 462 Memory*

8 creature of habit, habitué, old fogy, conservative, old guard, traditionalist, conventionalist, hardliner, regular, regular customer, frequent patron, frequenter, long-standing client, addict, drug addict, alcoholic, workaholic, devotee, fan, enthusiast, camp follower, stick-in-the-mud (Inf), dodo (Inf), groupie (Inf)

▶ *117 Conformity; 690 Drunkenness; 691 Drug-Taking; 777 Purchase*

ADJECTIVES

9 habitual, customary, accustomed, wonted, predictable, invariable, usual, regular, routine, everyday, daily, quotidian, weekly, monthly, annual, professional, occupational

► 228 Stability; 275 Time; 297 Frequency; 298 Regularity
10 **familiar**, known, well-known, everyday, household, ordinary, common, commonplace, unexceptional, unoriginal, stock, trite, banal, hackneyed, clichéd, well-worn, trodden, beaten, current, prevalent, widespread, obtaining, universal, common or garden (Inf)
► *138 Generality*
11 **normal**, natural, in character, typical, stereotyped, conventional, orthodox, traditional, traditionary (US), traditive, ritual, time-honoured, old, old-fashioned, old-world, old-line (US), permanent, lasting
► *117 Conformity; 225 Permanence*
12 **established**, official, *de rigueur* (Fr), done, practised, approved, accepted, socially accepted, received, admitted, acknowledged, recognized, understood, accredited, instituted, institutionalized, hallowed by custom, in, fashionable, in fashion, in vogue, modish, in the mode, with it (Inf)
► *386 Compulsion; 553 Fashion; 669 Approval*
13 **fixed**, set, set in one's ways, staunch, true-blue, dyed-in-the-wool, ingrained, implanted, rooted, deep-rooted, deep-seated, imbued, permeated, soaked, dyed
► *99 Essence*
14 **habituated**, in the habit, used, accustomed, familiar, at home, conversant, *au fait* (Fr), practised, trained, tamed, broken in, acclimatized, naturalized, conditioned, inured, seasoned, hardened, confirmed, chronic, inveterate, addicted, given, dedicated, devoted, wedded, habitual, frequent, recurrent, constant, perpetual
► *112 Repetition; 134 Continuity; 243 Preparation; 297 Frequency; 455 Knowledge*
15 **habit-forming**, addictive, obsessive, haunting, besetting, clinging
► *480 Persuasion*

VERBS

16 **have a habit**, have the habit of, do regularly, be known to, have a tendency, go regularly, haunt, frequent, habituate (US), make a habit of, take up, go in for, never vary, observe routine, be in a rut, be stuck in a groove, tread the beaten path (*or* track), cling to custom, observe tradition
17 **become a habit**, become acceptable, catch on, grow on one, take hold of one, become part of one, stick, cling, adhere, settle, take root, be the rule, obtain, prevail, come into use, acquire the force of habit (*or* custom)
18 **habituate**, accustom, inure, season, harden, case-harden, teach, train, domesticate, tame, break in, naturalize, acclimatize, adapt, orient, orientate, implant, ingraft, imbue, indoctrinate, brainwash, condition, accustom oneself, get used to, get the feel of, get the knack of, warm up, get into one's stride, take to, take to like a duck to water, get into the way of, acquire the habit, learn a habit, develop a habit, cultivate a habit, fall into a habit, get into a habit, be slave to a habit, become addicted, catch oneself doing, keep one's hand in, practise, get the hang of (Inf)
► *395 Influence*

ADVERBS

19 **habitually**, by force of habit, by tradition, by custom, customarily, wontedly, invariably, usually, regularly, with regularity, professionally, occupationally, as usual, as always, as is one's wont, systematically, mechanically, automatically, without thinking, in one's stride, traditionally, conventionally

633 Pursuit

The English country gentleman galloping after a fox – the unspeakable in full pursuit of the uneatable. Oscar Wilde.

NOUNS

1 **pursuit**, pursuing, pursuance, going after, seeking, looking for, search, quest, hunting, tracking, trailing, stalking, spooring, chasing, following, dogging, shadowing, manhunt, dragnet, APB (all points bulletin) (US), persecution, witch-hunt, McCarthyism (US), kangaroo court, hounding, persistence, perseverance, prosecution, execution, effectuation, tailing (Inf)
► *640 Perseverance; 705 Question*
2 **chase**, pursuit, hot pursuit, run, paper chase, steeplechase, race, racing, hunt, hunting, hounding, casting, hue and cry, tally-ho, beat, drive, battue, beating, shooting, gunning, hunting, shooting, and fishing, blood sport, fox hunt, stag hunt, elk hunt, pheasant shoot, grouse shoot, duck shoot, turkey shoot, big-game hunt, safari hunt, lion hunt, tiger hunt, elephant hunt, bear hunt, boar hunt, pigsticking, stalking, deerstalking, hawking, falconry, fowling, wildfowling, fishing, angling, fly-fishing, coarse fishing, inshore fishing, offshore fishing, freshwater fishing, trout fishing, salmon fishing, sea fishing, deep-sea fishing, game fishing, marlin fishing, whaling, ice fishing, beagling, coursing, ratting, trapping, badger hunting, woodchuck hunting (US), groundhog hunting (US), ferreting, rabbiting, lamping, mole-catching, possuming (US), catch
► *382 Killing; 765 Profit*
3 **hunting and fishing equipment**, fishing pole, fishing rod, fishing line, casting rod, rod and line, rod and reel, rod and tackle, bait, fly, fishing net, fishnet, keepnet, dragnet, hunting rifle, gun, rifle, shotgun, fowling piece, trap
► *379 Trap; 587 Weapon*
4 **activity**, work, business, occupation, career, leisure pursuit, hobby, pastime, interest, recreation
► *576 Work*
5 **pursuer**, seeker, searcher, researcher, quester, search party member, vigilante committee member, chaser, follower, dogger, shadow, sleuth, tail (Inf)
6 **hunter**, tracker, trailer, stalker, huntsman, huntress, Nimrod, Diana, whip, whipper-in, beater, hounds, pack, field, hound, foxhound, otterhound, bloodhound, gundog, athlete, sportsman, sportswoman, marksman, markswoman, shot, good shot, gun, big-game hunter, safari hunter, lion hunter, tiger hunter, buffalo hunter, fox-hunter, deerstalker, poacher, guddler, trapper, ratcatcher, mole-catcher, bird-catcher, fowler, wildfowler, falconer, hawker, fisherman, piscator, angler, compleat angler, shrimper, oysterman, trawler, trawlerman, whaler, head-hunter, cannibal, man-eater, beast of prey, mouser, bird of prey, hawk, falcon
7 **the hunted**, prey, quarry, game, victim, fugitive, es-

capee, deserter, missing person, lost child, criminal, suspect on the lam(US inf)

▶ *389 Escape*

VERBS

8 **pursue**, go after, seek, look for, search for, hunt for, quest after, cast about for, fish for, dig for, organize a search party, organize a vigilante committee, organize a dragnet, be gunning for, send after, send for, send out a search party, be in hot pursuit, conduct a witch-hunt, set up a kangaroo court, persecute, oppress, harass, harry, chivy, chevy

▶ *705 Question*

9 **follow**, track, trail, stalk, spoor, prowl after, sneak after, walk as quiet as an Indian (US), dog, shadow, sleuth, dog one's footsteps, dog one's every step, stick like glue, follow the scent, follow the trail, scent out, sniff out, run to ground, discover, tail (Inf), sit on one's tail (Inf)

▶ *449 Discovery*

10 **chase**, give chase, run after, whoop, halloo, hark, cry on, raise the hunt, raise the hue and cry, run down, ride down, rush at, charge at, tilt at, ride full tilt at, leap at, jump at, grab away, snatch at

▶ *381 Attack; 773 Taking*

11 **hunt**, go hunting, go big-game hunting, go shooting, shoot, bag, follow the chase, ride to hounds, go fishing, fish, fly-fish, angle, cast one's net, trawl, whale, shrimp, ice fish, catch, net, hook, reel in, guddle, trap, ensnare, mouse, play cat and mouse, stalk, deer-stalk, fowl, hawk, course, start game, start up, beat, flush, lay traps, set snares, poach

▶ *379 Trap; 382 Killing*

12 **aim at**, be after, mark as one's prey, make one's quarry, set one's course, steer for, woo, court, throw oneself at, mob, swarm over, strive for (*or* after), make it one's business to, pursue one's goals, pursue one's ends, pursue one's interest, set one's cap for (*or* at) (Inf), look out for number one (Inf)

▶ *324 Direction; 482 Intention*

13 **follow up**, contact again, persist, persevere, press on, progress, push one's way, elbow one's way, force one's way, fight one's way

▶ *302 Forward Motion; 640 Perseverance*

14 **carry on**, continue, practise, conduct, prosecute, execute, perform, undertake

▶ *340 Action; 354 Undertaking*

ADJECTIVES

15 **pursuing**, pursuant, seeking, searching, questing, in quest of, sent after, following, chasing, in pursuit, in hot pursuit, in full cry, on the trail, on one's scent, on one's tail (Inf)

16 **hunting**, shooting, fishing, piscatorial

17 **pursued**, sought, followed, chased, hounded, hunted

ADVERBS

18 **pursuant to**, in pursuance of, in search of, in quest of, on the lookout for, with a search party, on the trail, on the track, on the scent, after, in pursuit, in hot pursuit, hot on the trail, in full cry

INTERJECTIONS

19 **after him!**, stop thief!, follow that car!, shoot!, fire!, halloo!, view halloo!, yoicks!, tally-ho!, there she blows!, Geronimo!

634 Avoidance

One of the best ways of avoiding necessary and even urgent tasks is to seem to be busily employed on things that are already done.
John Kenneth Galbraith.

VERBS

1 **avoid**, keep away from, keep from, stay away from, not go near, bypass, circumvent, steer clear, keep clear, stand clear, get out of the way, make way for, stand back, hold off, keep one's distance, keep at arm's length, give a wide berth to, shun, eschew, leave, let alone, have nothing to do with, keep out of, not touch with a bargepole, stand aloof, stand apart, keep oneself to oneself, have no hand in, play no part in, keep one's hands clean, turn away, turn aside, look the other way, turn a blind eye, ignore, cold-shoulder, snub, give the go-by, not give the time of day, cut (Inf)

▶ *145 Distance; 325 Deviation; 470 Rejection; 655 Unsociability*

2 **avert**, prevent, foil, obstruct, hinder

▶ *378 Obstruction*

3 **abstain**, forswear, deny oneself, do (*or* go) without, pass up, not indulge, not touch, refrain, forbear, spare, hold back, temper, moderate, pull one's punches, soften the blow, kick the habit (Inf), go on the wagon (Inf)

▶ *684 Self-Restraint; 685 Moderation; 689 Sobriety*

4 **shy**, shrink, flinch, blink, blench, fight shy, balk at, start aside, jib, refuse, give a miss, not try, not attempt, back away, back off, draw back, retreat, hang back, demur, drag one's feet, not push oneself forward, funk (Inf), turn tail (Inf)

▶ *612 Fear; 637 Unwillingness; 709 Refusal*

5 **shirk**, get out of, make excuses, malinger, pass the buck (Inf), cop out (Inf), skive (Inf), gold brick (US inf), scrimshank (Inf)

▶ *343 Inactivity; 666 Negligence*

6 **evade**, take evasive action, dodge, duck, deflect, ward off, parry, escape, elude, give one the slip, skulk, cower, hide, play hide-and-seek, send on a wild goose chase, lead one a dance, throw dust in one's eyes, throw off the scent, go on the lam (US inf)

▶ *384 Defence; 389 Escape; 736 Concealment*

7 **be evasive**, avoid the issue, duck the issue, sidestep, skirt round, talk round, equivocate, hedge, fence, fudge, prevaricate, procrastinate, delay, postpone, shelve, table, deny, disown, bury one's head in the sand, repress, suppress, ban, censor, beat about the bush (Inf), waffle (Inf), pussyfoot (Inf)

▶ *294 Lateness; 399 Veto; 479 Equivocation; 708 Negation*

8 **run away**, run off, escape, desert, play truant, jump bail, take French leave, go absent without leave (AWOL), abscond, elope, absent oneself, decamp, depart, leave, go, quit, shoot through (Aus), withdraw, retire, retreat, beat a retreat, turn one's back, make tracks, flee, fly, take flight, be off, make off, bolt, run, run for it, run for one's life, take to one's heels, show a clean pair of heels, make oneself scarce, scoot, part company, break away, slip the cable, shake the dust from one's feet, steal away, sneak off, slink off, shuffle off, creep off

9 **play truant**, truant, play hooky (*or* hookey) (US inf), do a bunk (Inf), flit (Inf), bug off (*or* out) (US inf), quit the scene (US inf), dust (US inf), bottle up and go (US inf), turn tail (Inf), slope off (*or* away), skive (Inf), mitch (Inf), cut (Inf), cut and run (Inf), scram (Inf), scat (Inf), skedaddle (Inf), beat it (Inf)

▶ *98 Absence; 262 Haste; 303 Backward Motion; 313 Departure; 389 Escape*

NOUNS

10 **avoidance**, bypassing, circumvention, averting, prevention, obstruction, hindrance, distance, safe distance, wide berth, shunning, aloofness, cold shoulder, snub

▶ *145 Distance; 325 Deviation; 378 Obstruction; 470 Rejection; 655 Unsociability*

11 **abstinence**, abstention, forswearing, self-denial, refraining, forbearance, temperance, moderation

▶ *684 Self-Restraint; 685 Moderation; 689 Sobriety*

12 **shyness**, shrinking, unwillingness, reluctance, flinching, blinking, blenching, jibbing, refusal, revulsion, recoil, retreat, withdrawal, retirement, neutrality, noninvolvement, nonintervention, isolationism, escapism

▶ *612 Fear; 618 Indifference; 637 Unwillingness; 709 Refusal*

13 **shirking**, inaction, apathy, inactivity, passivity, passing the buck (Inf), cop-out (Inf), skiving (Inf)

▶ *343 Inactivity; 666 Negligence*

14 **evasion**, evasive action, dodge, duck, deflection, parry, defence mechanism, defensive reaction, escape, elusiveness, skulking, cowering, hide-and-seek, wild-goose chase, red herring

▶ *384 Defence; 389 Escape; 736 Concealment*

15 **evasiveness**, avoiding the issue, sidestep, equivocation, prevarication, procrastination, delaying action, noncooperation, denial, repression, suppression, waffle (Inf), pussyfooting (Inf)

▶ *294 Lateness; 399 Veto; 479 Equivocation; 708 Negation*

16 **desertion**, truancy, French leave, elopement, absence, departure, flight, hookey (*or* hooky) (US inf), flit (Inf)

▶ *98 Absence; 313 Departure; 389 Escape*

17 **avoider**, abstainer, nondrinker, teetotaller, dodger, sidestepper, evader, tax evader, coward, shrinker, quitter, shirker, slacker, idler, skulker, draft dodger, truant, deserter, apostate, renegade, absentee, runaway, teenage runaway, deserting husband, refugee, displaced person, escapee, escaper, fugitive, nonrealist, escapist, dreamer, visionary, ostrich, possum, welsher (Inf), couch potato (Inf), gold brick (US inf), gold bricker (US inf), scrimshanker (Inf), skiver (Inf), suspect on the lam (US inf)

▶ *343 Inactivity; 389 Escape; 477 Imagination; 614 Cowardice; 684 Self-Restraint; 689 Sobriety*

ADJECTIVES

18 **avoiding**, evasive, equivocal, elusive, slippery, hard to catch, untamed, wild, shy, flinching, blinking, blenching, shrinking, backward, reluctant, unwilling, noncooperative, noncommittal, unforthcoming, taciturn, passive, inert, inactive, not involved, apathetic, noncommitted, uncommitted, neutral, centrifugal, fugitive, escaped, runaway, hunted, hiding, skulking, cowering, hidden, latent, repressive, suppressive, preventive, censorial, defensive, on the defensive, fly-by-night (Inf), on the lam (US inf)

▶ *479 Equivocation; 612 Fear; 637 Unwillingness; 732 Shyness*

19 **abstaining**, abstinent, ascetic, dry, on the wagon, shunning, going (*or* doing) without, temperate, moderate

20 **avoidable**, avertable, preventable, escapable, unsought, unattempted

ADVERBS

21 **away**, clear, aloof, apart, distantly, abstinently, temperately, moderately

22 **evasively**, equivocally, elusively, avoidably, avertably, preventably, preventively, obstructively

23 **shyly**, reluctantly, unwillingly, hesitantly, apathetically, passively

INTERJECTIONS

24 **hands off!**, keep off!, keep your distance!, run for it!, run for your life!, beware!, forbear!, beat it! (Inf), scram! (Inf)

635 Will

Where there's a will there's a way. Proverb.

NOUNS

1 **will**, volition, conation, willing, intention, intent, purpose, wish, desire, pleasure, fancy, choice, option, preference, inclination, disposition, mind

▶ *617 Desire*

2 **willpower**, strength of will, strength of purpose, firmness of purpose, iron will, determination, steadfastness, resoluteness, resolution, resolve, tenacity, single-mindedness, mind over matter, self-control

3 **wilfulness**, self-will, one's own sweet will, will of one's own, waywardness, obstinacy, obduracy, doggedness, intransigence, stubbornness, pig-headedness, mulishness, bloody-mindedness (Inf)

▶ *683 Selfishness*

4 **free will**, independence, self-determination, autonomy, freedom of choice, personal freedom, discretion, free hand, free spirit

5 **will**, testament, last will and testament, codicil, privileged will, inheritance, estate, legacy, bequest

▶ *16 Law*

ADJECTIVES

6 **willed**, volitional, volitive, intentional, deliberate, willing, disposed, conative

▶ *636 Willingness*

7 **iron-willed**, determined, purposeful, steadfast, resolute, adamant, unyielding, tenacious, single-minded, self-controlled

8 **wilful**, self-willed, headstrong, wayward, stubborn, dogged, obstinate, obdurate, intransigent, pig-headed, bull-headed, mulish, bloody-minded (Inf)

9 **autocratic**, authoritarian, arbitrary, dictatorial

10 **free**, independent, self-determined, autonomous, discretionary, optional

VERBS

11 **wish**, will, want, desire

12 **choose**, decide, select, opt for, plump for, favour, think best, see fit

13 intend, determine, purpose, plan, cause, bring about, effect, be (hell) bent on (Inf)

14 follow one's own will, do as one likes (chooses *or* pleases), do what one likes (chooses *or* pleases), please oneself, go one's own way, know one's own mind, have a mind of one's own, be one's own man (*or* woman)

15 impose one's will, assert oneself, dominate, command, demand, order, ordain, decree, have one's own way, have it all one's own way, trample over, bulldoze, bully, force

16 bequeath, will, leave, pass on, hand down, transfer, give, confer

ADVERBS

17 at will, as one pleases (*or* wishes), when and how one pleases, at one's pleasure, as one thinks fit (*or* best), ad libitum, ad lib

636 Willingness

ADJECTIVES

1 willing, agreeable, content, disposed, inclined, prone, ready, game, receptive, assenting, consenting, in favour, prepared

2 eager, enthusiastic, keen, prompt, ready and willing, willing and able, alacritous, zealous, overzealous, overenthusiastic, overeager, overkeen, fanatical, no holding back, keen as mustard (Inf), raring to go (Inf), spoiling for, gung-ho (Inf), champing at the bit (Inf)

3 amenable, compliant, acquiescent, biddable, persuadable, pliable, pliant, tractable, manageable, obedient, docile

4 helpful, cooperative, collaborative, cordial, gracious, benevolent, philanthropic

► *650 Benevolence; 652 Philanthropy*

5 voluntary, unprompted, spontaneous, offered, unbidden, unforced, volunteering, offering, self-appointed

NOUNS

6 willingness, readiness, cheerful compliance, gameness, consent, receptiveness

7 eagerness, enthusiasm, keenness, promptness, alacrity, ardour, fervour, zeal, zealousness, overeagerness, overenthusiasm, overzealousness, excessive zeal, zealotry, ardour of the chase, fanaticism

8 acquiescence, amenability, compliance, pliancy, pliability, tractability, persuasability, docility, obedience

9 goodwill, benevolence, graciousness, cordiality, helpfulness, cooperation, collaboration, right mood

10 voluntary work, voluntary service, voluntary aid, unpaid work, self-appointed task, labour of love, charitable work, community work, voluntaryism (*or* voluntarism)

► *608 Relief*

11 willing worker, willing hands, helping hand, volunteer, unpaid worker, aid worker, charity worker, eager beaver (Inf)

12 philanthropist, helper, volunteer, donor, benefactor, do-gooder (Inf)

► *679 Generosity*

VERBS

13 be willing, agree, assent, comply, acquiesce, consent, abide by, accept, go along with, have a mind to, have a good mind to, be ready, show willing, go off like a shot, go off at the drop of a hat, jump at, leap at, catch at, go out of one's way to, bend over backwards, lean over backwards

14 cooperate, collaborate, help, aid, assist, lend a hand

15 volunteer, offer, put forward, put oneself in the firing line, sacrifice oneself

ADVERBS

16 willingly, with a will, without demur, cheerfully, readily, agreeably, gladly, with (great) gusto, with good grace, with all one's heart, with open arms

17 spontaneously, at the drop of a hat, without hesitation, like a shot

18 voluntarily, of one's own free will, off one's own bat, without prompting, of one's own accord, on one's own initiative, on one's own volition

637 Unwillingness

He that complies against his will,
Is of his own opinion still. Samuel Butler.

ADJECTIVES

1 unwilling, disinclined, indisposed, loath, reluctant, demurring, averse, not prepared, not so minded, not in the mood, not feeling like, not ready

2 refusing, unconsenting, unreconciled, unconvinced, dissenting, dissident, adverse, opposed, opting out, disagreeing, antipathetic, digging in one's toes (*or* heels) (Inf)

3 cautious, wary, chary, hesitant, shy, bashful, modest, shrinking, shirking, unzealous, unenthusiastic, unsympathetic, half-hearted, lukewarm, backward, unhelpful, uncooperative, apathetic

4 procrastinating, postponing, delaying, sluggish, lazy, neglectful, negligent, remiss

5 reluctant, resistant, protesting, sulky, dissenting, sceptical, atheistic

VERBS

6 be unwilling, resist, reject, disagree, dissent, protest, not have the heart to, have no stomach for, stickle, stick, have scruples, boggle at (Inf), give the thumbs down to (Inf), give the red light to (Inf)

► *470 Rejection; 751 Disagreement; 753 Protest*

7 refuse, recoil, turn away, back away, edge away, not face, blench, flinch, fight, shy away, shrink from, duck, jib, shirk, elude, neglect

► *709 Refusal*

8 hold back, postpone, delay, demur, procrastinate, shelve, hang back, drag one's feet, look over one's shoulder, sit back, sit tight, hesitate, balk, tread warily, look before one leaps, put off (till tomorrow), put on the back burner, hang fire (Inf)

9 not cooperate, dissent, obstruct, not do one's part, not pull one's weight, not play, not play ball, dissociate oneself, have no truck with, turn one's back, drop out, abstain, opt out, stonewall

10 grudge, begrudge, turn up one's nose, show one's distaste, force oneself, make oneself, do with a heavy heart, sulk

NOUNS

11 unwillingness, loathness, reluctance, disinclination, indisposition, dislike, disagreement, demur, objection, protest

▶ *751 Disagreement; 753 Protest*

12 opposition, resistance, renitency, recalcitrance, filibuster, balking, refusal, rejection, opt-out, rebuff, turndown (US), unhelpfulness, noncooperation, hindrance

▶ *113 Opposition; 378 Obstruction; 709 Refusal*

13 dissociation, nonassociation, abstention, unenthusiasm, lack of zeal, half-heartedness, apathy, indifference, lifelessness, faint-heartedness, want of alacrity, backwardness, slowness, hesitation, wariness, scruple, qualm, doubt, repugnance, abhorrence, recoil, aversion, averseness, no stomach for, shrinking, shyness, bashfulness, modesty

▶ *333 Slowness; 618 Indifference; 634 Avoidance; 674 Modesty*

14 disobedience, nonobservance, noncompliance, indocility, refractoriness, fractiousness, the sulks, sulkiness, sullenness, grudging service, perfunctoriness, undependability, unreliability, dereliction

▶ *626 Sullenness; 662 Disobedience*

15 delay, shelving, postponement, putting on the back burner, putting off (till tomorrow), procrastination, mañana attitude, sluggishness, laziness, neglect, negligence, remissness

▶ *343 Inactivity; 666 Negligence*

16 reluctant person, objector, resister, protester, abstainer, dropout, shirker, sulker, nonactivist, procrastinator, dissenter, dissident, sceptic, nonbeliever, atheist

ADVERBS

17 unwillingly, reluctantly, under protest, under duress, under pressure, with a bad grace, in spite of oneself, against one's will, against the grain, regretfully, with regret, without enthusiasm, unenthusiastically, half-heartedly, with dragging feet, with a heavy heart, with a long face, hesitantly, warily

638 Resolution

Like all weak men he laid an exaggerated stress on not changing one's mind. W. Somerset Maugham.

ADJECTIVES

1 resolute, resolved, determined, decided, decisive, deliberate, single-minded, concentrated, purposive, purposeful, intent, (dead) set, intent upon, set upon, bent upon, obsessed, hellbent (Inf)

▶ *482 Intention*

2 tenacious, persevering, persistent, dogged, zealous, thorough, all-consuming, earnest, serious, insistent, pressing, urgent, driving, forceful, energetic, vigorous, hard-hitting, desperate, stopping at nothing, all out, wholehearted, committed, devoted, dedicated, tireless, indefatigable, whole hog (Inf), gung-ho (Inf), bodacious (US inf)

▶ *338 Vigour; 471 Attention; 640 Perseverance*

3 strong-willed, iron-willed, strong-minded, uncompromising, unbending, inflexible, unyielding, intransigent, adamant, obstinate, stubborn, relentless, ruthless, merciless, pitiless, inexorable, implacable, stern, grim, unfeeling, stony, icy, hard, rock-hard, hard as iron, iron, cast-iron, steely, tough as steel

▶ *418 Hardness; 423 Toughness; 628 Cruelty; 641 Obstinacy*

4 undaunted, nothing daunted, heroic, game, unfearing, unshaken, unshakable, unshrinking, unflinching, unwavering, unhesitant, steadfast, indomitable, unconquered, unbeaten, steeled, armoured

▶ *246 Success; 613 Courage*

5 steady, constant, firm, solid, like the Rock of Gibraltar, immovable, unchangeable, reliable, staunch, dependable, self-controlled, self-restrained, self-mastered, self-possessed

▶ *228 Stability; 684 Self-Restraint*

VERBS

6 be resolute, know one's own mind, mean business, stop at nothing, stick at nothing, not stop at trifles, go through fire and water, go to all lengths, go to any length, push to extremes, see through, carry through, go the whole hog (Inf)

7 resolve, make up one's mind, decide, determine, purpose, intend, will, make a resolution, take a resolution, fix, settle, seal, conclude, terminate

▶ *131 End; 482 Intention; 635 Will*

8 brace oneself, steel oneself, clench one's teeth, grit one's teeth, face, face the issue, face the odds, rise to the occasion, dare, defy, take on all comers, bell the cat, outface, stare down, take the bull by the horns, take the bit between one's teeth, bite the bullet, take the plunge, throw down the gauntlet, cross the Rubicon, burn one's boats, burn one's bridges, show one's colours, nail one's colours to the mast, set one's face (Inf), go for it (Inf), go for broke (Inf)

▶ *254 Danger; 661 Defiance*

9 undertake, take on, take up, go in for, get down to, set to, buckle to, roll one's sleeves up, put one's shoulder to the wheel, tackle, grapple with, commit oneself, devote oneself, dedicate oneself, give oneself to, put one's heart into, grasp the nettle, give up everything for, set one's heart on, pursue, go after, bear down on, get a move on (Inf), get weaving (Inf), stir the possum (Aus inf), get on the stick (Inf), get one's ass moving (Inf), get one's ass in gear (Inf), go to it (Inf), get after (Inf), go get it (Inf), get going (Inf)

▶ *342 Activity*

10 insist, urge, press, make something happen, not take no for an answer, put one's foot down, stand no nonsense, stand firm, dig in, dig one's toes (*or* heels) in, hold (*or* stand) one's ground, stay put, not budge, not yield, not compromise, not give an inch, stand up for one's principles, stand fast, hold fast, stick fast, adhere

11 persist, persevere, soldier on, stick it out, endure, grin and bear it, hold out, hold out one's own, never despair, never say die, never surrender, fight to the finish, fight to the death, die fighting, die with one's boots on, go down with (colours) flying, go down with one's ship, die hard, hang in (Inf)

▶ *640 Perseverance*

NOUNS

12 resolution, resolve, fixed resolve, resoluteness, determination, grim determination, doggedness, decidedness, mind made up, decisiveness, decision, purposefulness, purpose, intention

▶ *482 Intention*

13 concentration, seriousness, fixity of purpose, single-mindedness, commitment, total commitment, devotion, utter devotion, self-devotion, devotedness, dedication, earnestness, zeal, ardour, eagerness, drive, vigour, energy, desperation

▶ *338 Vigour; 342 Activity*

14 tenacity, persistence, perseverance, stubbornness, obstinacy, relentlessness, ruthlessness, inexorability, implacability, sternness, pitilessness, hardness, steeliness, inflexibility, insistence, pressure, compulsion

▶ *386 Compulsion; 628 Cruelty; 640 Perseverance; 641 Obstinacy*

15 will, iron will, willpower, intent, strength of character, self-control, self-restraint, self-mastery, self-command, self-possession, steadiness, constancy, firmness, stability, staunchness, reliability, steadfastness

▶ *228 Stability; 635 Will; 684 Self-Restraint*

16 fortitude, spirit, grit, backbone, mettle, daring, dauntlessness, courage, pluck, dash, aplomb, élan, moral fibre, stiff upper lip, gritted teeth, clenched teeth, clenched jaw, rock, iron, cast iron, steel, backbone of steel, hearts of oak, bulldog breed, spunk (Inf), guts (Inf), moxie (US inf), bottle (Inf)

▶ *613 Courage*

ADVERBS

17 resolutely, decisively, purposefully, deliberately, single-mindedly, intently, seriously, earnestly, in earnest, with body and soul, with tooth and nail, with might and main, at all costs, at any price, come what may, come rain or shine, come hell or high water, persistently, doggedly, manfully, like a man, live or die, neck or nothing, once and for all

INTERJECTIONS

18 here goes!, go for it!, once more unto the breach!, damn the consequences!, full speed ahead!

639 Vacillation

One day the don't-knows will get in, and then where will we be?
Spike Milligan.

ADJECTIVES

1 vacillating, wavering, irresolute, unresolved, undecided, uncommitted, equivocal, tergiversating, noncommittal, undetermined, of (*or* in) two minds, unable to make up one's mind, indecisive, unsure, uncertain, hesitating, hesitant, dithering, wobbling, boggling, stalling, evasive, shifty, wobbly

▶ *453 Uncertainty; 479 Equivocation; 637 Unwillingness*

2 changeable, variable, unstable, inconstant, temperamental, mercurial, fickle, whimsical, capricious, not to be pinned down, without ballast, restless, fidgety, irresponsible, giddy, flighty, featherbrained, light-minded, superficial, unpersevering, unfaithful, adulterous, as changeable as a weathercock (*or* the weather *or* the moon)

▶ *227 Changeableness; 642 Frivolity*

3 timid, tremulous, nervy, jumpy, jittery, panicky, shaken, rattled, faint-hearted, cowardly, unheroic, nerveless, squeamish, weak, weak-willed, pusillanimous, weak-minded, weak-kneed, spineless, insipid, ineffectual, wimpish (Inf), wet (Inf), wishy-washy (Inf)

▶ *337 Weakness; 612 Fear; 614 Cowardice*

4 unsteady, unreliable, unstaunch, unsteadfast, teetering, tottering, apathetic, indifferent, characterless, featureless, suggestible, impressionable, flexible, pliant, putty-like, easy-going, good-natured

VERBS

5 vacillate, waver, fluctuate, vary, oscillate, seesaw, wobble, teeter, sway, go back and forth, go to and fro, boggle, dither, stall, equivocate, tergiversate, quibble, palter, shuffle, shillyshally (Inf)

▶ *227 Changeableness; 326 Oscillation; 479 Equivocation*

6 hesitate, have second thoughts, change one's mind, blow hot and cold, back away, balk, shy, jib, shirk, evade, avoid

▶ *634 Avoidance*

7 be irresolute, be of (*or* in) two minds, not know one's own mind, not know what to do, sit on the fence, go where the wind blows, go round in circles, put off a decision, delay, put off (till tomorrow), procrastinate, dally, dilly-dally, leave undecided, leave in suspense

▶ *294 Lateness; 453 Uncertainty*

8 balance, weigh up the pros and cons, discuss, debate, argue, hum (*or* hem) and haw, will and will not

▶ *701 Argument*

9 change sides, go over, apostatize, cross the floor, shift one's ground, be unfaithful, commit adultery, play around, go catting (Inf), jump ship (Inf), sell out (Inf)

10 compromise, yield, give way, take half measures, meet halfway, give up, not persevere

▶ *388 Submission; 754 Compromise*

NOUNS

11 vacillation, irresolution, indecision, uncertainty, equivocation, tergiversation, doubt, hesitation, hesitancy, infirmity of purpose, lack of resolution, lack of commitment, nonperseverance, broken resolve, broken promise, uncommitted vote, floating vote

▶ *453 Uncertainty; 479 Equivocation*

12 inconstancy, fluctuation, changeableness, variability, blowing hot and cold, fickleness, whimsicality, capriciousness, irresponsibility, levity, lack of willpower, lack of drive

▶ *227 Changeableness; 642 Frivolity*

13 timidity, tremulousness, nervousness, nerviness, jumpiness, jitteriness, faint-heartedness, cowardice, loss of nerve, squeamishness, weakness, pusillanimity, weak will, spinelessness, no backbone, no grit, wishy-washiness (Inf)

▶ *337 Weakness; 612 Fear; 614 Cowardice*

14 apathy, indifference, no strong feelings, lukewarmness, half-heartedness, listlessness, no will of one's own, impressibility, impressionability, suggestibility, pliancy, easy-going nature, putty in one's hands, passivity, inertness, submission, submissiveness, servitude

▶ *388 Submission; 618 Indifference*

15 indecisive person, uncommitted voter, floating voter, independent (US), dabbler, dilettante, weakling, compromiser, waverer, wobbler, ditherer, staller, tergiversator, turncoat, adulterer, butterfly, feather, weathercock, chameleon, don't-know (Inf), man of straw (Inf), funker (Inf), wimp (Inf), wet (Inf), piss-ant (US inf)

ADVERBS

16 **irresolutely**, indecisively, equivocally, noncommittally, uncertainly, hesitantly, nervously, pusillanimously, from pillar to post, between the devil and the deep blue sea, between Scylla and Charybdis, between a rock and a hard place, in a catch-22 situation

640 Perseverance

Constant dripping hollows out a stone. Lucretius.

NOUNS

1 **perseverance**, persistence, doggedness, determination, resolution, tenacity, pertinacity, pertinaciousness, stubbornness, obstinacy, insistence, patience, plodding

► *638 Resolution; 641 Obstinacy*

2 **commitment**, total commitment, single-mindedness, singleness of purpose, concentration, attention, application, sedulity, sedulousness, assiduity, assiduousness, industriousness, tirelessness, indefatigability, effort, exertion, hard work, repeated efforts, unflagging efforts

► *342 Activity; 471 Attention; 576 Work*

3 **constancy**, steadfastness, fidelity, staunchness, maintenance, continuance, ceaselessness, diligence, permanence, iteration, reiteration, repetition

► *112 Repetition; 134 Continuity; 225 Permanence*

4 **stamina**, endurance, staying power, fortitude, strength, courage, bulldog courage, grit, true grit, backbone, gameness, pluck, guts (Inf), gutsiness (Inf), moxie (US inf), bottle (Inf)

► *336 Strength; 613 Courage*

5 **tenacious person**, loyal supporter, hard-core supporter, die-hard, old guard, trier, willing worker, workaholic, workhorse (Inf), stayer (Inf)

VERBS

6 **persevere**, persist, keep at it, keep on trying, try and try again, repeat, iterate, reiterate, renew one's efforts, double one's efforts, plod, slog, slog away, peg away, hammer away at, work at, work round the clock, work one's fingers to the bone, work till one drops, die in harness, die with one's boots on, move heaven and earth, work miracles, keep on keeping on (US inf), plug away (Inf), work one's ass (*or* butt *or* tail) off (Inf)

► *353 Attempt; 576 Work*

7 **maintain**, sustain, keep up, follow through, continue, carry on, go on, keep on, keep going, keep the pot boiling (Inf), keep the ball rolling (Inf)

► *134 Continuity*

8 **hold out**, hold out for, not take no for an answer, stand firm, maintain one's ground, not budge, dig in one's toes (*or* heels), hold out to the last, die at one's post, go down with one's ship, not despair, never despair, never say die, never give up hope, hope on, grit one's teeth, hang on, not let go, hold fast, maintain one's grip, cling, stick like glue, hang on by one's teeth, hang on for dear life, hang on like grim death, sink or swim, stick to one's guns (Inf)

► *360 Retention; 610 Hope; 638 Resolution*

9 **endure**, have what it takes, come up (*or* back) for more, survive, remain, stick it out, see it through, stay till the bitter end, carry through, complete, take a licking and keep on ticking (US inf)

ADJECTIVES

10 **persevering**, persistent, tenacious, sedulous, assiduous, dogged, determined, resolute, stubborn, obstinate, enduring, staunch, faithful, diligent, surviving, patient, trying hard, plodding, slogging away, industrious, strenuous, hanging in there (Inf)

► *342 Activity; 353 Attempt; 576 Work; 638 Resolution; 641 Obstinacy*

11 **steady**, unfaltering, unwavering, unflagging, undrooping, unwearied, untiring, indefatigable, unsleeping, sleepless, vigilant, unfailing, unremitting, constant, continual, unceasing, renewed, iterated, reiterated, repeated

► *112 Repetition; 134 Continuity*

12 **indomitable**, undefeated, unconquerable, unconquered, unbeaten, undaunted, undiscouraged, undeterred, game, plucky, game to the last (*or* end), going down fighting, going down with guns blazing, true to the bitter end, gutsy (Inf)

► *246 Success; 613 Courage*

ADVERBS

13 **persistently**, perseveringly, doggedly, tenaciously, resolutely, patiently, for better or for worse, through thick and thin, through fire and water, to the last man, to the bitter end

14 **continually**, repeatedly, unendingly, ceaselessly, till the cows come home (Inf)

641 Obstinacy

U-turn if you want to. The lady's not for turning. Margaret Thatcher.

ADJECTIVES

1 **obstinate**, stubborn, obdurate, headstrong, bull-headed, pig-headed, mulish, stubborn as a mule, pertinacious, wilful, self-willed, froward (Lit), *entêté* (Fr), awkward, bloody-minded (Inf)

2 **refractory**, recalcitrant, wayward, arbitrary, perverse, contrary, contumacious, disobedient, unruly, restive, unmanageable, intractable, uncontrollable, ungovernable, unpersuadable, incorrigible, irrepressible, indocile, stiff-necked, hard-mouthed, cross-grained, crotchety, irascible

► *383 Resistance; 625 Grumpiness; 626 Sullenness; 661 Defiance; 662 Disobedience; 809 Shamelessness*

3 **unyielding**, firm, determined, resolute, dogged, bulldog-like, tenacious, persevering, stiff, wooden, rigid, adamant, inelastic, inflexible, unbending, obdurate, hardened, hard (*or* tough) as nails, case-hardened, hardheaded, uncompromising, hardcore, intransigent, unmoved, uninfluenced, unrelenting, with heels dug in, immovable, irremovable, irreversible, persistent, incurable, chronic, dour, grim, inexorable, unappeasable, im-

placable, merciless, pitiless, hard-nosed (Inf), hard-boiled (Inf)

► *225 Permanence; 418 Hardness; 628 Cruelty; 638 Resolution; 640 Perseverance*

4 **set**, set in one's ways, habituated, hidebound, conservative, ultraconservative, obscurantist, reactionary, blimpish, unteachable, impervious, blind, blinded, deaf, opinionated, dogmatic, hardline, hard-shelled (US), pedantic, obsessed, bigoted, fanatical, dry (Inf), blinkered (Inf)

► *465 Misjudgment; 632 Habit*

NOUNS

5 **obstinacy**, stubbornness, obduracy, obdurateness, adamantine, bull-headedness, pig-headedness, mulishness, pertinaciousness, pertinacity, self-will, mind of one's own, perversity, contumacy, disobedience, resistance, intractability, incorrigibility, stiff neck, wrongheadedness, cussedness, dourness, indocility, bloody-mindedness (Inf)

► *383 Resistance; 626 Sullenness; 635 Will; 662 Disobedience*

6 **determination**, will, single-mindedness, resolution, grimness, doggedness, tenacity, bulldog tenacity, perseverance, stubborn persistence, inelasticity, inflexibility, woodenness, toughness, hardness, intransigence, immovability, hard line, no compromise, irreversibility, fixity

► *418 Hardness; 638 Resolution; 640 Perseverance*

7 **opinionatedness**, opiniativeness, self-opinion, dogmatism, rigorism, intolerance, prejudice, bias, bigotry, zealotry, fanaticism, ruling passion, obsession, *idée fixe* (Fr), blind side, blindness, closed mind, narrow-mindedness, illiberality, obscurantism, ignorance, old school, *ancien régime* (Fr)

► *452 Certainty; 456 Ignorance; 465 Misjudgment; 519 Blindness*

8 **obstinate person**, hardliner, hard-head, rigorist, stickler, pedant, dogmatist, fanatic, zealot, bigot, persecutor, stayer, die-hard, old fogy, conservative, dog in the manger, obscurantist, reactionary, Colonel Blimp, blimp, mule (Inf), stick-in-the-mud (Inf), hard-nose (Inf), hard-ass (US inf), dry (Inf), last-ditcher (Inf), bitter-ender (US inf)

► *383 Resistance; 638 Resolution; 753 Protest*

VERBS

9 **be obstinate**, persist, persevere, brazen it out, stick to one's guns, dig in one's toes (*or* heels), not budge, sit tight, stay put, stand firm, insist, brook no denial, not take no for an answer, not change one's mind, go one's own way, want one's own way, dogmatize, have a closed mind, stay in a rut, cling to custom, ignore, not listen, turn a deaf ear, take no advice,

► *383 Resistance; 452 Certainty; 615 Rashness; 632 Habit; 638 Resolution; 640 Perseverance; 683 Selfishness; 809 Shamelessness*

ADVERBS

10 **obstinately**, stubbornly, obdurately, pig-headedly, mulishly, like a mule, wilfully, doggedly, tenaciously, for oneself, in an uncompromising way, intransigently, inexorably

642 Frivolity

Ever let the fancy roam,
Pleasure never is at home. John Keats.

ADJECTIVES

1 **capricious**, arbitrary, erratic, fitful, uncertain, unpredictable, idiosyncratic, unexpected, volatile, mercurial, inconsistent, inconstant, variable, changeable, unstable, unreliable, fickle, feckless, irresponsible, flighty, flirtatious, coquettish, frivolous, skittish, giddy, featherbrained, light-minded, whimsical, fanciful, fantastic, eccentric, offbeat, freakish, quirky, humoursome, temperamental, moody, crotchety, irascible, fretful, hysterical, mad, weird, crazy, playful, mischievous, prankish, wanton, motiveless, purposeless, wayward, perverse, contrary, undisciplined, refractory, wilful, particular, faddy, faddish, captious, unreasonable

► *227 Changeableness; 453 Uncertainty; 461 Insanity; 472 Inattention; 630 Surprise*

NOUNS

2 **caprice**, capriciousness, arbitrariness, fitfulness, flightiness, uncertainty, unpredictability, inconsistency, inconstancy, changeableness, changeability, variability, instability, unreliability, fickleness, fecklessness, irresponsibility, coquettishness, flirtatiousness, frivolousness, frivolity, giddiness, levity, light-mindedness, whimsicality, eccentricity, crankiness, freakishness, quirkiness, fretfulness, pettishness, irascibility, playfulness, mischief, waywardness, motivelessness, purposelessness, faddishness, faddism

3 **whim**, whimsy, caprice, megrim (Lit), idea, notion, fancy, passing fancy, impulse, change of mind, flip-flop, vagary, outlandish notion, crotchet, maggot, bee in the bonnet, humour, mood, temperament, fit, peculiarity, idiosyncrasy, quirk, kink, fad, craze, freak, escapade, prank, boutade, wild-goose chase, coquetry, flirtation, the whim-whams (US inf), brainstorm (Inf)

► *459 Folly; 461 Insanity; 477 Imagination; 478 Improvisation*

4 **capricious person**, man (*or* woman) of impulse, eccentric, freak, oddball (Inf), crank, flirt, coquette, tease, trifler, featherbrain, butterfly, fair-weather friend, prankster, imp (Inf), monkey (Inf)

VERBS

5 **be capricious**, submit to a whim, take it into one's head, have a sudden flight of fancy, pick and choose, chop and change, blow hot and cold, flip-flop, vary, change, vacillate, fluctuate, have a bee in one's bonnet, show fickleness, trifle with, take up a thing and drop it, do by fits and starts, tease, flirt, coquet

► *227 Changeableness; 459 Folly; 639 Vacillation*

ADVERBS

6 **capriciously**, arbitrarily, erratically, fitfully, by fits and starts, by dribs and drabs, now this, now that, from one extreme to the other, frivolously, fancifully, on impulse, as the mood takes one, as the fancy takes one, at the drop of a hat, at one's own sweet will

643 Solemnity

You must not think me necessarily foolish because I am facetious, nor will I consider you necessarily wise because you are grave.
Sydney Smith.

ADJECTIVES

1 **solemn**, grave, serious, thoughtful, pensive, sedate, staid, sober, sober as a judge, stern, severe, unsmiling, straight-faced, grim, poker-faced, stony-faced, deadpan, humourless, sombre, dour, sullen, glum, long-faced, frowning

▶ *622 Pride; 626 Sullenness*

2 **earnest**, sincere, genuine, resolute, determined, purposeful, intent, dedicated, committed, eager, enthusiastic

▶ *636 Willingness*

3 **important**, significant, of consequence, serious, weighty, momentous, crucial, vital, life-and-death, critical, dangerous, ominous, perilous

▶ *123 Importance*

NOUNS

4 **solemnity**, gravity, gravitas, no laughing matter, no joke, straight face, thoughtfulness, staidness, sternness, severity, humourlessness, grimness, dourness, sullenness, gloom, long face

5 **earnestness**, sincerity, resolution, determination, dedication, commitment, eagerness, enthusiasm

▶ *636 Willingness*

6 **importance**, import, significance, consequence, weightiness, momentousness, moment, gravity, severity

7 **serious person**, heavyweight, intellectual, highbrow, egghead (Inf), sobersides (Inf)

▶ *442 Intellect*

VERBS

8 **be serious**, look serious, keep a straight face, compose one's features, keep from laughing, repress a smile, wipe the smile off one's face, pull (*or* make) a long face, frown, glare, glower

9 **take seriously**, be in earnest

ADVERBS

10 **solemnly**, gravely, seriously, soberly, with a straight face, thoughtfully, sternly, severely, sullenly, glumly

11 **earnestly**, sincerely, genuinely, really, actually, truly, honestly, in all seriousness

12 **indeed**, really, certainly, seriously, in all conscience, absolutely, definitely, unquestionably, undeniably

644 Curiosity

NOUNS

1 **curiosity**, curiousness, inquisitiveness, questioning, interest, inquisition, inquiry (*or* enquiry), desire (*or* thirst) for knowledge, inquiring mind

2 **prying**, nosiness, snooping, meddling, officiousness, gossip, tittle-tattle, morbid curiosity, prurience, voyeurism, rubbernecking (Inf)

▶ *342 Activity; 471 Attention; 705 Question; 741 News*

3 **curious person**, inquirer (*or* enquirer), inquisitor, investigator, examiner, questioner, detective, lawyer, teacher, explorer, adventurer, sightseer, tourist, spectator, traveller, journalist

4 **meddler**, gossip, gossipmonger, scandalmonger, stirrer, prier, pry, spy, tittle-tattler, eavesdropper, voyeur, Peeping Tom, quidnunc, kibitzer (US), Paul Pry, busybody (Inf), snoop (Inf), nosy parker (Inf), mole (Inf), big-ears (Inf), rubbernecker (Inf)

ADJECTIVES

5 **curious**, inquisitive, inquiring, inquisitorial, questioning, interested, with ears burning, wanting to know, keen to learn, keen, adventurous, sightseeing

6 **prying**, officious, meddlesome, meddling, prurient, gossipy, snooping (Inf), snoopy (Inf), nosy (Inf)

VERBS

7 **be curious**, inquire (*or* enquire), inquire (*or* enquire) after, question, quiz, interrogate, search for, show interest, desire knowledge, thirst for knowledge, want to know, seek out, feel concern for, show interest in, gossip, tittle-tattle, sightsee, eavesdrop, pry, meddle, poke one's nose in, prick up one's ears, sniff out (Inf), nose around (Inf), snoop (Inf), rubberneck (Inf)

ADVERBS

8 **curiously**, inquisitively, inquisitorially, questioningly, keenly, adventurously

9 **officiously**, pruriently, nosily (Inf)

645 Cunning

NOUNS

1 **cunning**, cunningness, slyness, wiliness, foxiness, artfulness, craftiness, craft, art, skill, lore, knowledge, resourcefulness, inventiveness, ingenuity, imagination, knack, guile, cleverness, smartness, sharpness, acuity, shrewdness, sophistication, intelligence, stealth, stealthiness, subtlety, latency, concealment, caution, wariness, suppleness, slipperiness, shiftiness, knavery, chicanery, chicane, trickery, imposture, foul play, finesse, jugglery, sleight, cheating, circumvention, deception, deceit, duplicity, sophistry, double-dealing, double-crossing, false political promises, chicken in every pot (US), forty acres and a mule (US), peace with honour, smoothness, flattery, beguilement, disguise, insincerity, hypocrisy, manoeuvring, evasion, temporizing, tactics, policy, diplomacy, Machiavellianism (*or* Machiavellism), realpolitik, jobbery, gerrymandering, improbity, sharp practice, underhanded (*or* underhand) deal, under-the-table deal, under-the-counter purchase, secret influence, backstage dealings, back-room influence, old boy network, gentleman's club, politics in a smoke-filled room (US), backdoor influence, intrigue, plot, conspiracy, know-how (Inf), gamesmanship (Inf), cageyness (Inf), monkey business (Inf), wheeling and dealing (Inf)

▶ *395 Influence; 455 Knowledge; 477 Imagination; 479 Equivocation; 484 Plan; 485 Skill; 631 Behaviour; 677 Flattery; 699 Falsehood; 700 Deception; 702 Sophistry; 737 Secrecy; 800 Dishonour*

2 **stratagem**, ruse, wile, art, artifice, device, resource, resort, ploy, shift, dodge, contrivance, expedient, machination, game, (dirty) little game, plot, subterfuge, evasion, excuse, pretext, white lie, lie, cheat, deception,

sham, swindle, fraud, confidence trick, trick, old trick, bag of tricks, box of tricks, tricks of the trade, feint, catch, net, web, ambush, Greek gift, Trojan horse, political trick, stalking-horse, trial balloon, *ballon d'essai* (Fr), trap, ditch, pit, pitfall, Parthian shot, web of cunning, web of deceit, blind, smokescreen, dust thrown in the eyes, red herring, flag of convenience, thin end of the wedge, manoeuvre, move, tactic, tactics, wrinkle (Inf), scam (Inf), con (Inf), flimflam (Inf)

► *379 Trap; 484 Plan; 631 Behaviour; 700 Deception*

3 **cunning person**, wily person, crafty fellow, slyboots, artful dodger, fast talker, sophist, casuist, logic-chopper, fox, Reynard, lurker, hider, serpent, snake, snake in the grass, troublemaker, fraud, dissembler, shammer, wolf in sheep's clothing, hypocrite, double-crosser, deceiver, forked tongue, liar, cheat, trickster, sharper, swindler, confidence trickster, knave (Lit), juggler, conjuror, flatterer, glib tongue, smooth talker, diplomat, diplomatist, self-serving politician, timeserver, Machiavelli, intriguer, conspirator, plotter, schemer, strategist, tactician, manoeuvrer, wirepuller (US), con man (Inf), flimflam man (Inf), sharp (Inf), fly-by-night(er) (Inf), smoothie (*or* smoothy) (Inf), wheeler-dealer (Inf)

► *379 Trap; 480 Persuasion; 484 Plan; 677 Flattery; 736 Concealment*

ADJECTIVES

4 **cunning**, sly, wily, foxy, artful, crafty, clever, skilful, knowledgeable, resourceful, inventive, ingenious, guileful, imaginative, disingenuous, subtle, serpentine, vulpine, feline, full of ruses, tricky, tricksy, devious, secret, stealthy, clandestine, underhand (*or* underhanded), under-the-table, under-the-counter, scheming, contriving, practising, plotting, planning, intriguing, conspiring, calculating, Machiavellian, arch, knowing, intelligent, smart, sharp, astute, shrewd, wise, acute, sophisticated, urbane, canny, pawky (Dial), too clever for, too clever by half, too smart for one's own good, up to everything, not to be caught napping, not born yesterday, experienced, reticent, reserved, not to be drawn, cautious, wary, tactical, strategical, well-laid, well-planned, full of snares, insidious, perfidious, shifty, slippery, timeserving, temporizing, equivocal, sophistical, flattering, beguiling, hypocritical, insincere, deceitful, deceiving, rascally, crooked, dishonest, knavish (Lit), slick (Inf), fly (Inf), no flies on (Inf), cagey (Inf)

► *458 Wisdom; 479 Equivocation; 484 Plan; 485 Skill; 700 Deception; 737 Secrecy; 800 Dishonour*

VERBS

5 **be cunning**, finesse, play the fox, shift, dodge, manoeuvre, jockey, twist, turn, wriggle, hide, lie low, skulk, lurk, scheme, intrigue, conspire, plot, plan, devise, contrive, wangle, know a trick or two, fix the game, play a dangerous game, spin a web, weave a plot, confuse, muddy the waters, have method in one's madness, have an ulterior motive, have an axe to grind, play tricks with, monkey about with, tinker, circumvent, gerrymander, overreach, outsmart, outwit, outdo, be too quick for, be too clever for, trick, cheat, swindle, defraud, double-cross, deceive, betray, steal a march on, snatch from under one's nose, coax, flatter, beguile, cajole, wheedle, blarney, have the blarney, temporize, play for time, juggle, ambush, waylay, dig a pit for, undermine, bait the trap, get one's foot in the door, create a catch-22 situation, match in cunning, expose the trick, avoid the trap, see the catch, have a card up one's sleeve, have a shot in one's locker, know all the answers, live by one's wits, fly by the seat of one's pants, con (Inf), flimflam (Inf), sweet-talk (Inf), pull a fast one (Inf), put one over (Inf), be one up on (Inf), go one better (Inf), pip at the post (Inf)

► *180 Convolution; 329 Overstepping; 480 Persuasion; 484 Plan; 677 Flattery; 700 Deception; 736 Concealment*

ADVERBS

6 **cunningly**, artfully, craftily, slyly, on the sly, secretly, stealthily, shrewdly, astutely, tactically, strategically, deceitfully, guilefully, dishonestly, with a glib tongue

646 Naivety

Credulity is the man's weakness, but the child's strength.
Charles Lamb.

I'd the upbringing a nun would envy and that's the truth. Until I was fifteen I was more familiar with Africa than my own body.
Joe Orton.

ADJECTIVES

1 **naive**, naïf, artless, without art, simple, simple-minded, ingenuous, guileless, free from guile, without artifice, without tricks, childlike, uncontrived, unstudied, uncomplicated, unadorned, unvarnished, plain, homespun, home-made, do-it-yourself, DIY, unskilled, uncivilized, uncultured, unrefined, unpolished, native, natural, unartificial, in a state of nature, primitive, wild, savage, untaught, self-taught, uneducated, untutored, self-made, unguided, unlearned, unscientific, unprogressive, backward, ignorant, Arcadian, young, innocent, unversed, uninitiated, born yesterday, green, immature, inexperienced, unworldly, unsophisticated, callow, wet behind the ears, not dry behind the ears, not on guard, unsuspecting, unsuspicious, trusting, confiding, credulous, gullible, unconstrained, uninhibited, unreserved, unaffected, undissembling, spontaneous, candid, frank, open, straightforward, undesigning, truthful, veracious, single-hearted, honest, sincere, out in the open, on the up and up, blunt, outspoken, free-spoken, transparent, undisguised, unpoetical, prosaic, no-nonsense, matter-of-fact, down-to-earth, literal, literal-minded, accurate, modest, shy, inarticulate, unassuming, unpretentious, unpretending, inartistic, Philistine, unmusical, tone-deaf, uncouth, vulgar, hoydenish, ill-bred, on the level (Inf)

► *255 Purity; 271 Simplicity; 273 Accuracy; 456 Ignorance; 459 Folly; 478 Improvisation; 486 Unskilfulness; 674 Modesty; 675 Vulgarity; 698 Truth; 738 Display; 799 Honour; 805 Innocence*

NOUNS

2 **naivety**, artlessness, guilelessness, simplicity, simple-mindedness, ingenuousness, freedom from artifice, youth, innocence, greenness, immaturity, inexperience, unworldliness, unsophistication, callowness, credulity, gullibility, plainness, unaffectedness, naturalness, igno-

rance, backwardness, uncivilized state, primitiveness, savagery, darkness, barbarism, nescience, indifference to art, candour, frankness, openness, straightforwardness, bluntness, matter-of-factness, outspokenness, veracity, truth, honesty, probity, sincerity, modesty, unpretentiousness, Philistinism, imperfection, uncouthness, vulgarity, crudity, bad taste

▶ *231 Imperfection; 271 Simplicity; 456 Ignorance; 675 Vulgarity; 698 Truth; 799 Honour; 805 Innocence*

3 **naive person**, unsophisticated person, ingenuous person, ingenue, Candide, child of nature, savage, noble savage, *enfant terrible* (Fr), lamb, babe in arms, child, youth, innocent, beginner, novice, greenhorn, rough diamond, simpleton, dolt, fool, ninny, dupe, plain man, simple soul, pure heart, candid speaker, Philistine, provincial, country-dweller, country cousin, rustic, yokel, clod, bumpkin, country bumpkin, hillbilly (US), stick (Inf), hick (US inf), rube (US inf), hayseed (US inf), sucker (Inf)

▶ *459 Folly; 574 Commoner; 805 Innocence*

VERBS

4 **be naive**, live a simple life, live in a state of nature, live in ignorance, know no better, be wet behind the ears, eschew artifice, have no guile, have no tricks, have no affectations, trust, confide, look one in the face, look one straight in the eyes, speak plainly, call a spade a spade, wear one's heart upon one's sleeve, say what is in one's mind, speak one's mind, not mince one's words, have no hang-ups (Inf)

▶ *271 Simplicity; 698 Truth; 805 Innocence*

ADVERBS

5 **naively**, artlessly, ingenuously, without guile, without artifice, innocently, credulously, gullibly, without pretensions, without affectation, frankly, candidly, openly, sincerely, straightforwardly, bluntly, matter-of-factly, with an open heart

647 Severity

NOUNS

1 **severity**, strictness, fastidiousness, pedantry, meticulousness, stringency, sternness, ruggedness, toughness, harshness, hardness, intolerance, no compromise, uncharitableness, rigorousness, rigour, fundamentalism, Draconian measures, rigidity, formality, orthodoxy, firmness, firm hand, strong hand, hard hand, firm control, tight rein, restraint, inflexibility, stubbornness, obstinacy, bigotry, regimentation, discipline, strict discipline, clampdown, martial law, letter of the law, authority, power, arbitrary power, no appeal, inclemency, lack of mercy, harsh treatment, asperity, callousness, pitilessness, inhumanity, cruelty, bullying, outrage, pound of flesh, tight ship (Inf)

▶ *334 Power; 396 Authority; 418 Hardness; 628 Cruelty; 641 Obstinacy*

2 **suppression**, oppression, repression, subjugation, subjection, persecution, coercion, harassment, victimization, extortion, exploitation, Rachmanism, inquisition, censorship, expurgation, blue laws (US), Official Secrets Act, absolutism, authoritarianism, autocracy, totalitarianism, militarism, dictatorship, despotism, tyranny, Fascism, Nazism, Stalinism, brute force, naked force, show of force, iron rule, iron hand, mailed fist, jackboot, atrocity, torture, execution

▶ *251 Restraint; 380 Violence; 387 Subjection; 796 Immorality; 802 Wrong; 804 Wickedness; 814 Punishment*

3 **unadornment**, plainness, simplicity, austerity, asceticism, ascesis, restraint, self-restraint, self-denial, self-mortification, Spartanism, prudery, puritanism

▶ *417 Sparseness*

4 **strict person**, Spartan, puritan, purist, pedant, stickler, bureaucrat, disciplinarian, martinet, petty tyrant, militarist, sergeant major, hanging judge, oppressive person, oppressor, Big Brother, authoritarian, despot, dictator, autocrat, inquisitor, persecutor, bully, hard master, taskmaster, taskmistress, slave-driver, bloodsucker, hardliner, hawk, dry (Inf), Dutch uncle (Inf)

▶ *400 Master*

VERBS

5 **be severe**, restrain, regiment, discipline, chastise, punish, wield power, exert authority, maintain firm control, keep a tight rein, take Draconian measures, get tough, deal harshly with, come down on, intimidate, frighten, take the heart out of, clamp down on, put a stop to, not tolerate, squeeze, crush, impose martial law, allow no appeal, give no quarter, offer no compromise, lack mercy, show no mercy, show no pity, shove around, boss around, wave the big stick, bully, bait, hassle, stick to the letter of the law, have one's pound of flesh, put one's foot down (Inf), run a tight ship (Inf)

6 **suppress**, oppress, repress, subjugate, subject, persecute, hunt down, coerce, harass, abuse, abuse one's authority, misgovern, misrule, mishandle, victimize, extort, exploit, enslave, censor, expurgate, tyrannize, use brute force, have a show of force, treat rough, ride roughshod over, stamp on, tread on, tread under foot, walk over, pull no punches, torment, terrorize, rule with an iron hand, torture, commit an atrocity, execute, shed blood, put to the sword, get tough with (Inf), take off the gloves (Inf), put the screws on (Inf), put the frighteners on (Inf)

7 **be unadorned**, have simplicity, restrain oneself, show self-restraint, live a spartan life, be austere

ADJECTIVES

8 **severe**, strict, rigorous, harsh, hard, hard as nails, uncompromising, unbending, stubborn, obstinate, hardheaded (US), stern, rigid, firm, inflexible, uncharitable, Draconian, exacting, exact, pedantic, formal, orthodox, fundamental, fastidious, meticulous, stringent, censorious, censorial, regimented, disciplined, rugged, tough, hardhearted, intolerant, inquisitorial, bigoted, inclement, callous, pitiless, merciless, unsparing, unforgiving, inhumane, cruel, brutal, coercive, oppressive, repressive, exploitative, undemocratic, militaristic, authoritarian, totalitarian, despotic, dictatorial, autocratic, Fascist, tyrannical, domineering, dominating, high-handed, overbearing, heavy-handed, bossy (Inf)

9 **suppressed**, oppressed, repressed, subjugated, subjected, persecuted, coerced, harassed, censored, expurgated, exploited, victimized, tyrannized, tortured, executed

10 **unadorned**, plain, simple, purist, restrained, self-

restrained, austere, ascetic, Spartan, prudish, puritanical, strait-laced

ADVERBS

11 **severely**, strictly, under strict regulations, rigorously, harshly, stubbornly, obstinately, sternly, rigidly, firmly, inflexibly, stringently, uncharitably, exactingly, pedantically, formally, fundamentally, fastidiously, meticulously, uncompromisingly, without compromise, unsparingly, relentlessly, unrelentingly, intolerantly, callously, hard-heartedly, inhumanely, cruelly, toughly, unyieldingly, mercilessly, brutally, high-handedly, in a high-handed manner, arbitrarily, heavy-handedly, with a heavy hand, with an iron hand, oppressively, repressively, dictatorially, autocratically, tyrannically

12 **plainly**, simply, without adornment, austerely, ascetically, prudishly, puritanically

648 Leniency

NOUNS

1 **leniency**, lenience, lenity, laxity, easiness, mildness, moderation, gentleness, softness, tenderness, patience, tolerance, toleration, forbearance, compassion, pity, mercifulness, mercy, quarter, forgiveness, pardon, amnesty, clemency, reasonableness, humanity, humaneness, benevolence, kindness, kindliness, graciousness, charitableness, charity, magnanimity, generousness, favour, concession, sop, humouring, consideration, leave, allowance, permission, permissiveness, indulgence, *laissez faire* (Fr), spoiling, gratification, light rein, light hand, velvet glove, cotton-wool treatment (Inf), kid-glove treatment, kid gloves

▶ *627 Pity; 649 Forgiveness; 650 Benevolence; 685 Moderation; 757 Permission*

2 **lenient person**, permissive parent, philanthropist, latitudinarian, liberal, bleeding-heart liberal (Inf), wet (Inf), old softy (Inf)

VERBS

3 **be lenient**, show leniency, go easy on, moderate, treat kindly, treat lightly, make no demands, make few demands, deal gently, handle tenderly, tolerate, forbear, not press, bear with, stretch a point, bend a rule, give quarter, have compassion, have pity, pity, show mercy, forgive, forget, pardon, spare, grant amnesty, favour, concede, humour, show consideration, allow, permit, indulge, oblige, gratify, spare the rod, handle with kid (*or* velvet) gloves, keep (*or* use) a light rein, use a light hand, pull one's punches (Inf), let off the hook (Inf)

ADJECTIVES

4 **lenient**, lax, easy, easy-going, mild, moderate, clement, gentle, soft, tender, patient, tolerant, forbearing, long-suffering, compassionate, pitying, merciful, forgiving, reasonable, considerate, humane, benevolent, kind, kindly, gracious, charitable, accepting, magnanimous, accommodating, generous, permissive, indulgent, spoiling, kid-glove, live-and-let-live

5 **given consideration**, given permission, allowed, permitted, granted amnesty, pardoned, forgiven, indulged, gratified, pitied, spoiled, spoiled rotten (Inf)

ADVERBS

6 **leniently**, easily, mildly, moderately, gently, softly, tenderly, patiently, with kid gloves, with a light rein, with a light hand, tolerantly, compassionately, mercifully, reasonably, considerately, humanely, benevolently, kindly, with kindness, graciously, in a gracious manner, charitably, magnanimously, accommodatingly, generously, permissively, indulgently, gratifyingly

649 Forgiveness

Then said Jesus, Father, forgive them; for they know not what they do. And they parted his raiment, and cast lots. Bible: Luke.

To err is human, to forgive, divine. Alexander Pope.

NOUNS

1 **forgiveness**, pardon, full pardon, free pardon, amnesty, excuse, reprieve, sparing, indemnity, exemption, immunity, grace, dispensation, forgiveness of sin, absolution, remission, remission of sin, indulgence, shrift (Lit)

▶ *7 Religion; 627 Pity; 648 Leniency*

2 **forgivingness**, forgiving nature, mercifulness, clemency, compassion, kindness, benevolence, magnanimity, unresentfulness, unrevengefulness, placability, placableness, lenity, long-suffering, forbearance, patience, tolerance, indulgence, stoicism, overlooking, disregard

▶ *650 Benevolence*

3 **absolution**, acquittal, cancellation, discharge, release, deliverance, freeing, exoneration, condonation, exculpation, vindication, justification, reconciliation, conciliation, redemption, pacification, rehabilitation, atonement

▶ *714 Vindication; 749 Pacification*

ADJECTIVES

4 **forgiving**, pardoning, excusing, reprieving, sparing, absolving, shriving, exonerating, condoning, vindicating, justifying, reconciling, conciliatory, redeeming, pacifying, rehabilitating

5 **merciful**, compassionate, kind, clement, benevolent, magnanimous, unresentful, unrevengeful, unreproachful, placable, lenient, long-suffering, forbearing, patient, tolerant, indulgent, stoic

6 **forgiven**, pardoned, excused, granted amnesty, reprieved, spared, absolved, shriven, indulged, remitted, acquitted, cancelled, discharged, released, delivered, freed, let off, exonerated, condoned, exculpated, vindicated, justified, reconciled, redeemed, pacified, rehabilitated, atoned, restored, reinstated, taken back, let off the hook (Inf)

7 **forgivable**, pardonable, venial, excusable, easily excused

8 **overlooked**, disregarded, not held against one, blotted (out), wiped away, swept clean, removed from the record, erased from the record

VERBS

9 **forgive**, give (*or* grant) forgiveness, pardon, grant amnesty to, excuse, reprieve, spare, indemnify, exempt, grant immunity, forgive one's sins, absolve, grant absolution, shrive, forgive and forget, forget, reconcile, be rec-

onciled, conciliate, redeem, make peace, shake hands, kiss and make up, bury the hatchet, smoke the peace pipe, let bygones be bygones, dismiss from one's thoughts, think no more of, not give it another (*or* a second) thought, let it go, let it pass, charge to experience, come to an understanding, shake on it (Inf), make it up (Inf)

10 **absolve**, acquit, vindicate, cancel, discharge, release, deliver, free, set free, let off, let one off this time, exonerate, exculpate, remit, dismiss, clear one's name, clear, wipe the slate clean, sweep clean, blot out one's sins, start afresh, assoil (Lit), let one off the hook (Inf)

11 **condone**, overlook, disregard, connive, justify, give one the benefit of the doubt, wink at, close (*or* shut) one's eyes to, turn a blind eye to, ignore, let pass, pass over, let it go

12 **show mercy**, be merciful, show compassion, leave unavenged, turn the other cheek, return good for evil, pocket the affront, bear no malice, take no offence, take in good part, be lenient, be patient with, tolerate, show tolerance, endure, bear with, make allowances for, unbend, soften, relent, accept an apology, forbear (Lit), put up with (Inf)

13 **ask forgiveness**, plead (*or* beg) for forgiveness, beg pardon, offer apologies, ask (*or* beg) for mercy, ask for absolution

ADVERBS

14 **forgivingly**, with a forgiving heart, mercifully, compassionately, kindly, benevolently, magnanimously, patiently, with patience, tolerantly, indulgently, conciliatorily, venially, without bearing a grudge

650 Benevolence

I have always depended on the kindness of strangers. Tennessee Williams.

NOUNS

1 **benevolence**, benevolentness, benevolent disposition, kindness, kindliness, kind-heartedness, loving kindness, milk of human kindness, goodness, niceness, goodwill, benignity, cordiality, geniality, affability, helpfulness, kindly disposition, open-heartedness, heart of gold, amiability, sociability, bonhomie, friendship, good-naturedness, love, grace, grace of God, pity, mercy, goodness and mercy, forgiveness, compassion, tolerance, toleration, soft-heartedness, consideration, thoughtfulness, courteousness, attentiveness, mindfulness, decent feeling, fellow feeling, humaneness, humanity, humanitarianism, love of mankind, goodwill towards man, brotherly love, brotherliness, brotherhood of man

► *392 Help; 569 Friendship; 590 Feelings; 593 Love; 627 Pity; 648 Leniency; 649 Forgiveness; 654 Sociability; 658 Courtesy; 747 Cooperation; 797 Good*

2 **charity**, charitableness, hospitality, philanthropy, good works, Christian charity, generosity, generousness, bountifulness, liberality, patronage, magnanimity, altruism, unselfishness, selflessness, big-heartedness, open-handedness, Red Cross, OXFAM, Salvation Army, Amnesty International

► *652 Philanthropy; 679 Generosity; 768 Giving*

3 **welfare**, welfarism, welfare state, welfare work, social services, social security, social welfare, social work, public welfare, child welfare, community service, health care, unemployment benefits, retirement benefits, pension, socialism, liberalism, the dole (Inf)

4 **benevolent act**, kind act, helpful act, act of grace, kindness, kind deed, good deed, good turn, good work, mitzvah (Judaism), favour, courtesy, service, benefit, charitable act (*or* deed), rescue, relief, loan, alms, alms-giving, labour of love, offices, good offices

5 **benevolent person**, kind person, Good Samaritan, Christian, good neighbour, sympathizer, well-wisher, philanthropist, altruist, welfarist, humanitarian, man (*or* woman) of goodwill, welfare worker, social worker, patron, reformer, alms-giver, almoner, Mother Teresa, do-gooder (Inf), goody-goody (Inf), bleeding heart (Inf)

ADJECTIVES

6 **benevolent**, kind, kind-hearted, warm-hearted, good, nice, benign, helpful, amiable, sociable, friendly, affectionate, loving, considerate, decent, thoughtful, attentive, solicitous, courteous, mindful, condolent, sympathetic, empathetic, good-hearted, good-natured, good-humoured, cordial, genial, affable, well-meant, well-meaning, well-intentioned, tolerant, compassionate, open-hearted, humane, forgiving, indulgent, soft-hearted, lax, lenient, obliging, accommodating, neighbourly, fatherly, paternal, motherly, maternal, brotherly, fraternal, sisterly, cousinly, full of the milk of human kindness

7 **charitable**, beneficent, hospitable, philanthropic, Christian, generous, bountiful, magnanimous, altruistic, unselfish, big-hearted, open-handed, liberal, giving, alms-giving

VERBS

8 **be benevolent**, be kind, do a kindness, do a favour, do the offices, do right by, treat well, mean well, have the best intentions, love, make love – not war, show consideration, show concern, have regard for, remember, understand, sympathize, empathize, comfort, relieve, mother, nurse, accommodate, indulge, tolerate, show mercy, forgive, return good for evil, do as one would be done by, practise the golden rule, have a heart of gold, have a generous heart, have a big heart, have one's heart in the right place, reform, oblige, respect, wish well, wish the best for, give one's blessing, support, encourage, look with a favourable eye

9 **be charitable**, give financial support, give freely, aid, provide aid, provide needed funds, raise money for, practise philanthropy, benefit, act like a Christian, patronize

ADVERBS

10 **benevolently**, kindly, kind-heartedly, with kindness, in kindness, out of kindness, tenderly, lovingly, with tender loving care, with love, while in love, benignly, helpfully, in a helpful manner, amiably, sociably, affectionately, considerately, decently, thoughtfully, attentively, solicitously, courteously, mindfully, condolently, compassionately, with compassion, by the grace of God, humanely, forgivingly, soft-heartedly, sympathetically, good-heartedly, with a good heart, good-naturedly, with

a good nature, tolerantly, indulgently, obligingly, accommodatingly, paternally, like a father, maternally, like a mother, fraternally, like a brother

11 **charitably**, through charity, beneficently, hospitably, philanthropically, generously, bountifully, magnanimously, altruistically, unselfishly, big-heartedly, with a big heart, open-handedly, with open hands, liberally

651 Malevolence

A cruel story runs on wheels, and every hand oils the wheels as they run. Ouida.

NOUNS

1 **malevolence**, evilness, badness, ill will, bad will, ill nature, ill disposition, evil disposition, malignity, malignance, hate, hatred, hatefulness, loathing, blind fury, misanthropy, misandry, misogyny, lack of humanity, malice, maliciousness, malice aforethought, maleficence, evil intent, wickedness, devilry, devilishment, bad intention, worst intention, enmity, truculence, truculency, hostility, animosity, antagonism, meanness, nastiness, bad blood, cussedness (Inf), bloody-mindedness (Inf)

► *594 Hate; 628 Cruelty; 798 Evil; 804 Wickedness*

2 **cruelness**, cruelty, cruel conduct, inhumanity, inhumaneness, barbarism, barbarity, brutality, brutalness, brutishness, savagery, savageness, atrocity, bestiality, animality, viciousness, ferocity, ferociousness, violence, vandalism, sadism, sadistic cruelty, monstrousness, terrorism, heinousness, fiendishness, bloodthirstiness, bloodthirst, bloodlust, cannibalism

► *254 Danger; 382 Killing*

3 **callousness**, callosity, unfeelingness, unnaturalness, hardness, hardheartedness, heartlessness, obduracy, obdurateness, heart of stone, stony-heartedness, heart of marble, heart of flint, coldness, cold-heartedness, cold-bloodedness, gloating, gloating pleasure, unholy joy, *Schadenfreude* (Ger), harshness, roughness, severity, ruthlessness, sternness, grimness

4 **bitterness**, tartness, acrimony, asperity, resentment, acerbity, sourness, sharpness, sharp tongue, ill feeling, vengefulness, mordacity, mordancy, acidity, causticity, causticness, caustic reply, biting comment, spite, spitefulness, rancour, gall, spleen, bile, virulence, venom, venomousness, vitriol, vindictiveness, grudge, beastliness, waspishness, snideness, bitchiness (Inf), cattiness (Inf)

5 **intolerance**, persecution, intimidation, victimization, tyrannization, bullying, harassment, sexual harassment, racial harassment, racial hatred, racism, racialism

6 **inconsiderateness**, inconsideration, insensitivity, lack of care, lack of concern, thoughtlessness, heedlessness, unmindfulness, unhelpfulness, unobligingness, unkindness, unkindliness, unfriendliness, ungraciousness, uncharitableness, ungenerousness

7 **act of malevolence**, bad deed, bad turn, harm, disservice, ill service, ill turn, mischief, misfortune, crime, threat, menace, intimidation, blackmail, foul play, atrocity, brutal act, outrage, evil act, act of inhumanity, crime against humanity, cruel act, act of cruelty, reign of terror, bloodshed, torture, slaughter, murder, killing, mass murder, massacre, serial killing, homicide, genocide, fratricide, patricide, matricide, infanticide, abuse, physical abuse, verbal abuse, sexual abuse, child abuse, harm, hurt, grievous bodily harm (GBH), assault, sexual assault, rape, personal violence, ill-treatment, misuse, maltreatment

8 **malefactor**, bad person, evildoer, wrongdoer, malfeasant, miscreant, sinner, racist, vandal, larrikin (Aus), destroyer, nihilist, wrecker, spoiler, traitor, back-stabber, betrayer, double-crosser, Judas, villain, rogue, ruffian, scoundrel, caitiff, blackguard, bully, bullyboy, thug, phansigar, lout, punk, bruiser, criminal, offender, lawbreaker, felon, outlaw, desperado, gangster, hoodlum (US), sadist, torturer, molester, abuser, rapist, tyrant, Attila, vulture, hyena, predator, snake, viper, terrorist, anarchist, murderer, mass murderer, serial killer, homicidal maniac, killer, butcher, cutthroat, gunman, contract killer, assassin, hired assassin, baddie (Inf), bad egg (Inf), bad lot (Inf), terror (Inf), unholy terror (Inf), tough (Inf), rough (Inf), crook (Inf), mugger (Inf), con man (Inf), snake in the grass (Inf), Hun (Inf), hatchet man (Inf), hit man (Inf), crim (Inf), mobster (US inf), roughneck (Inf), yob (Inf), yobbo (Inf), skinhead (Inf), hood (US inf), hooligan (Inf), ugly customer (Inf), nasty piece of work (Inf)

9 **vixen**, hellcat, wildcat, tigress, shrew, virago, fury, siren, witch, hag, hell-hag (Inf), she-devil (Inf), bitch (Inf)

ADJECTIVES

10 **malevolent**, ill-willed, ill-intentioned, ill-wishing, ill-natured, ill-disposed, evil, evil-disposed, evil-minded, malignant, malign, meaning harm, pernicious, wicked, hating, full of hate, hateful, full of loathing, malicious, malefic, baleful, intolerant, persecuting, oppressive, tyrannical, intimidatory, menacing, harassing, racist

11 **cruel**, cruel-hearted, inhuman, inhumane, subhuman, dehumanized, atrocious, outrageous, barbaric, barbarous, brutal, brutish, savage, bestial, beastly, animal, vicious, ferocious, violent, sadistic, monstrous, terrorful, terroristic, heinous, bloodthirsty, bloody, cannibalistic, torturous, murderous, homicidal, fiendish, fiendlike, devilish, satanic, demoniac, demoniacal, diabolical, hellish, infernal, ghoulish

12 **callous**, calloused, unfeeling, unnatural, obdurate, hard, hardhearted, hardened, hard of heart, heartless, cold, cold-hearted, cold of heart, cold-eyed, cold-blooded, steely, steely-eyed, stony, stony-hearted, flinty, flint-hearted, marble-hearted, harsh, rough, ungentle, severe, stern, grim, dour, gruff, rugged, tough, austere

13 **merciless**, pitiless, ruthless, revengeful, full of revenge, vengeful

14 **hostile**, truculent, antagonistic, mean, nasty, spiteful, despiteful, rancorous, splenetic, virulent, venomous, envenomed, poisonous, baneful, vitriolic, vindictive, beastly, snide, waspish, viperish, bitter, bitter and twisted, tart, acrimonious, resentful, acerbic, sour, astringent, mordant, mordacious, sarcastic, acidic, acid, acrid, caustic, sharp, cutting, whipping, piercing, penetrating, biting, stinging, stabbing, cussed (Inf), bloody-minded (Inf), cattish (Inf), catty (Inf), bitchy (Inf)

15 **inconsiderate**, unthoughtful, thoughtless, insensitive,

uncaring, unconcerned, unfeeling, unresponsive, unheedful, heedless, unmindful, unhelpful, unobliging, disobliging, unaccommodating, unsympathetic, unkind, unkindly, unfriendly, unamiable, sullen, ungenial, ungracious, uncordial, inhospitable, unchristian, unbenevolent, uncharitable, unphilanthropic, ungenerous

VERBS

16 **be malevolent**, bear malice, hate, show ill will, bear ill will, bear a grudge, cherish a grudge, loathe, spite, wreak one's spite, do one a bad turn, do one's worst, disoblige

17 **kill**, murder, slaughter, massacre, savage, thirst for blood, kill in cold blood

18 **torment**, attack, harm, hurt, injure, abuse, sexually abuse, rape, molest, maltreat, ill-treat, beat, tyrannize, oppress, persecute, intimidate, bully, harass, victimize, terrorize, torture, menace, hound, harry, threaten, frighten, scare, demand, blackmail, hold to ransom, use bully-boy tactics, beat up (Inf), bash (Inf), bullyrag (Inf), do over (Inf), bash up (Inf), cut up nasty (*or* ugly) (Inf), put the wind up (Inf), put the frighteners on (Inf), have it in for (Inf)

19 **be pitiless**, be merciless, have no mercy, exact revenge, take one's revenge

ADVERBS

20 **malevolently**, with evil intent, with the worst intentions, maliciously, with malice aforethought, spitefully, out of spite, in spite, unkindly, perniciously, with hate, wickedly, hatefully, with malice, cruelly, brutally, savagely, sadistically, callously, meanly, heartlessly, coldheartedly, without mercy, without pity, truculently, acrimoniously, caustically, intolerantly, tyrannically, harshly, severely, inconsiderately, ungraciously

652 Philanthropy

The spacious philanthropy which he exhaled upon Europe stopped quite sharply at the coasts of his own country. Winston Churchill.

NOUNS

1 **philanthropy**, philanthropism, humanitarianism, humaneness, humanity, welfarism, benevolence, charitableness, charity, welfare, altruism, dedication, helpfulness, kind-heartedness, kindness, compassion, brotherly love, goodwill, grace, beneficence, unselfishness, generosity, open-handedness, munificence, munificentness, bounty, liberality, do-gooding (Inf)

▶ *392 Help; 627 Pity; 636 Willingness; 650 Benevolence; 803 Virtue*

2 **public spiritedness**, public spirit, social conscience, social consciousness, citizenship, good citizenship, civism, utilitarianism, Benthamism, humanitarianism, universal benevolence, socialism, communism, reformism, urge to set the world to rights, greatest good of the greatest number

▶ *244 Improvement*

3 **philanthropist**, benefactor, benefactress, humanitarian, idealist, ideologist, altruist, visionary, utopian, utilitarian, Benthamite, internationalist, friend of the human race, welfare worker, social worker, community service worker, almoner, charity worker, voluntary worker, volunteer, aid worker, missionary, mission worker, helper, helping hand, aider, assister, befriender, succourer, Samaritan, Good Samaritan, kind person, good neighbour, do-gooder (Inf)

4 **welfare state**, social welfare, child welfare, social services, social security, poor relief, assistance, food stamps (US), benefit, unemployment benefit, the dole (Inf), income support, child support, nanny state (Inf)

5 **charity**, aid, good works, worthy cause, relief, disaster relief, gift, hand-out, donation, fund, flag day, charity event, fund-raiser, telethon, charitable foundation, Red Cross, community chest (*or* fund) (US), United Way (US), OXFAM, Save the Children

ADJECTIVES

6 **philanthropic**, philanthropical, humanitarian, benevolent, beneficent, humane, charitable, altruistic, aidgiving, aiding, alms-giving, generous, munificent, eleemosynary, kind, kind-hearted, kindly, compassionate, gracious, big-hearted, large-hearted, public spirited, civic, idealistic, enlightened, reforming, visionary, liberal, utilitarian, socialistic, communistic

VERBS

7 **be charitable**, philanthropize, show benevolence, have a social conscience, do good, do a good turn, do a good deed, help, benefit, render assistance, have one's heart in the right place

ADVERBS

8 **philanthropically**, benevolently, beneficently, humanely, from the heart, charitably, altruistically, for the public good, generously, munificently, kind-heartedly, compassionately, with compassion, with good will, idealistically, socialistically, communistically, *pro bono publico* (L)

653 Misanthropy

What though the spicy breezes
Blow soft o'er Ceylon's isle;
Though every prospect pleases,
And only man is vile... Reginald Heber.

NOUNS

1 **misanthropy**, misanthropism, hatred of mankind, distrust of mankind, misandry, misogyny, cynicism, unsociability, antisociability, unsociableness, antisocial attitude, antisocial behaviour, selfishness, egotism, egoism, inhumanity, malevolence

▶ *606 Dissatisfaction; 655 Unsociability; 683 Selfishness*

2 **misanthrope**, misanthropist, hater of mankind, mankind-hater, world-hater, hater of man, man-hater, misandrist, hater of women, woman-hater, misogynist, male chauvinist, antifeminist, sexist loner, solitary, unsocial person, cynic, egotist, egoist, Diogenes, Alceste, male chauvinist pig (Inf)

ADJECTIVES

3 **misanthropic**, antisocial, unsociable, inhuman, cynical, egoistic, egotistical, selfish, misandrous, man-hating, woman-hating, misogynous, sexist

VERBS

4 **become a misanthrope** (*or* **misanthropist**), lose faith in human nature, hate the world, hate mankind, hate men (*or* women), distrust people

ADVERBS

5 **misanthropically**, cynically, antisocially, inhumanly, with inhumanity, egotistically, in an egotistical manner, egoistically, selfishly, from a selfish standpoint

654 Sociability

Society is no comfort
To one not sociable. William Shakespeare.

NOUNS

1 **sociability**, sociableness, socialness, sociality, social-mindedness, affability, amicability, amiability, friendliness, neighbourliness, gregariousness, kindness, warmth, fondness for company, fondness for society, geniality, congeniality, cordiality, conviviality, enjoyment, joviality, jollity, revelry, festivity, merriment, merrymaking, gaiety, cheer, good cheer, hospitality, companionability, compatibility, clubbishness, fraternization, participation, membership, cooperation, sharing, partaking, hobnobbing, conversation, intercourse, communicativeness, communication, intercommunication, communion, intercommunion, social skills, social ability, social relations, social intercourse, social activity, group activity, association, consociation, affiliation, familiarity, intimacy, consorting, fratting (Inf)

▶ *376 Gathering; 597 Joy; 598 Happiness; 658 Courtesy; 679 Generosity; 692 Communications; 734 Conversation; 747 Cooperation*

2 **social ambition**, ambition, social climbing, status-seeking, social success, popularity, social graces, good manners, savoir-vivre, refinement, breeding, courtesy, easy manner, savoir-faire, ability to mix, affability, conversableness, social demand, upward mobility, keeping up with the Joneses (Inf)

▶ *246 Success; 631 Behaviour; 658 Courtesy*

3 **meeting**, appointment, engagement, rendezvous, assignation, date, double date, social gathering, social, social affair, gathering, at home, meeting one's friends, tête-à-tête, *conversazione* (It), soirée, coffee, coffee morning, tea, afternoon tea, high tea, reception, wedding reception, entertainment, seeing one's family, family reunion, class reunion, visiting, visit, formal visit, official visit, visitation, interview, calling, call, social call, courtesy call, frequenting, frequentation, stay, social round, round of visits, social whirl, mad round, calling card, tryst (Lit), get-together (Inf), dropping in (Inf), blind date (Inf), elevenses (Inf), dirty weekend (Inf)

4 **meeting place**, stadium, public hall, restaurant, salon, drawing room, love nest, pub

5 **party**, entertainment, festivity, feast, banquet, dinner, dinner party, supper party, tea party, house party, weekend party, at home, open day, open house (US), house-warming, house-raising, barn-raising, surprise party, garden party, lawn party, *fête champêtre* (Fr), costume party, fancy-dress party, ball, hunt ball, masked ball, masquerade, masque (*or* mask), cocktail party, sherry party, beer party, drinks party, bottle party, drug party, smoker, mixed party, birthday party, coming-out party, coming out, debut, presentation, wedding party, dance, barn dance, square dance (US), hoedown (dance) (US), disco, discotheque, barbecue, barbie (Inf), BBQ, wienie roast (US), gala, (bit of a) do (Inf), knees-up (Inf), shindig (Inf), shindy (Inf), stag party (Inf), hen party (Inf), potluck dinner (Inf), hop (Inf), bop (Inf), rave (*or* rave-up) (Inf), blowout (Inf)

▶ *22 Dancing; 691 Drug-Taking*

6 **social person**, convivial person, social butterfly, good host (*or* hostess), socialite, debutante, good neighbour, good fellow, charming fellow, conversationalist, friend, visitor, guest, welcome guest, one of the family, good company, good companion, *bon vivant* (Fr), playboy, man about town, social lion, habitué, clubman (*or* club-woman), active member, back-slapper, unwelcome guest, gate-crasher, parasite, mine host (Lit), pal (Inf), chum (Inf), mate (Inf), mixer (Inf), good mixer (Inf), joiner (Inf), life (and soul) of the party (Inf), raver (Inf)

7 **human society**, humanity, mankind, humankind, community, commune, public, social group, social circle, social set, one's set, social class, upper class, elite, high society, beau monde, gentry, nobility, aristocracy, middle class, working class, caste, peer group, one's group, one's gang, one's club, the crowd, family, one-parent family, family circle, home circle, friends and relations, friends and acquaintances

▶ *117 Conformity; 549 Refinement; 553 Fashion*

8 **good company**, company, comradeship, friendship, fellowship, good fellowship, fraternity, camaraderie, togetherness, bonhomie, cordiality, hospitality

9 **welcome**, welcoming, hearty welcome, cordial welcome, warm welcome, warmth, warm reception, smiling reception, greeting, handshake, handclasp (US), embrace, welcoming embrace, kiss, hug, peck on the cheek, back-slapping

10 **social animal**, ape, lion, bird, marmot, ant, bee, termite, wasp, dolphin, rook

▶ *71 Mammals; 72 Birds; 76 Insects and Arachnids*

VERBS

11 **be sociable**, be social, enjoy company, love company, entertain, invite, host, be hospitable, throw a party, act as host, act the host, act as hostess, act the hostess, have an open day, hold open house (US), welcome, bid welcome, make welcome, welcome with open arms, put out the welcome mat (US), hug, embrace, do the honours, preside, participate, mix with, mingle with, get together, join in, be a good mixer, know how to mix, get about (*or* around), go out, dine out, go to parties, fish for invitations, accept invitations, share, eat off the same platter, crack a bottle with, toast, drink to, pledge, love a party, go partying, gate-crash, go clubbing, go nightclubbing, go pubbing, go out on the town, go on a spree, kill the fatted calf, associate with, consort with, rub shoulders (*or* elbows) with (Inf), go Dutch (Inf), go shares (Inf), take potluck (Inf), go pub-crawling (Inf), paint the town red (Inf), keep up with the Joneses (Inf), freeload (Inf)

12 **visit**, call on, pay a visit, look up, see, stop off, stop over, make oneself welcome, make oneself at home, make oneself one of the family, unbend, relax, leave one's calling card, sojourn, stay, weekend, keep up with, be on visiting terms, winter, summer, drop in on (Inf), drop by (Inf)

13 fraternize, have friends, make friends (easily), hobnob, glad-hand, back-slap, have fun, introduce oneself, get along with, get on well with, keep company with, hang around with, walk hand in hand with, club together with, date, make a date, seek acquaintance, make acquaintance, live it up (Inf), hang out with (Inf), pal up with (Inf), gang up with (Inf), hook up with (Inf)

14 welcome, greet, shake hands with, embrace, kiss

ADJECTIVES

15 sociable, social, affable, social-minded, socially disposed, communal, collective, common, public, civic, companionable, amicable, amiable, affable, clubbish, clubby, communicative, friendly, fond of company, courteous, civil, urbane, easy, easy-going, free-and-easy, party-minded, cordial, genial, witty, amusing, charming, charismatic, extrovert, gregarious, outgoing, hearty, lively, hail-fellow-well-met, convivial, jolly, jovial, merry, cheerful, smiling, welcoming, warm, affectionate, hospitable, neighbourly, inviting, matey (Inf), pally (Inf)

16 popular, beloved, liked, sought-after, welcome, ever-welcome, welcomed with open arms, socially accepted, accepted as one of the family, made to feel at home, socially successful, entertained, fêted, dined, wined and dined

17 festive, carnival-like, entertaining, fun, joyous, Christmassy

ADVERBS

18 sociably, socially, affably, amicably, amiably, convivially, family-oriented, *en famille* (Fr), genially, in friendship, in a friendly fashion, like friends, companionably, arm in arm, hand in hand, affectionately, with love, as lovers, communicatively, courteously, civilly, easily, cordially, hospitably, wittily, amusingly, in an amusing way, charmingly, with great charm, gregariously, heartily, with open arms, warmly, merrily, cheerfully, with good cheer, joyously, festively, entertainingly

655 Unsociability

I never said, 'I want to be alone.' I only said, 'I want to be left *alone.' There is all the difference.* Greta Garbo.

NOUNS

1 unsociability, unsociableness, dissociability, dissociableness, unsocial habits, antisocial habits, ungregariousness, unclubability, uncongeniality, incompatibility, unfriendliness, unhappiness, sullenness, mopishness, moroseness, taciturnity, reticence, uncommunicativeness, standoffishness, haughtiness, lonely pride, reserve, aloofness, remoteness, detachment, indifference, apartness, distance, maintaining one's distance, reclusiveness, coolness, coldness, frigidity, chill, chilliness, iciness, frostiness, inhospitality, unreceptiveness, ungraciousness, discourtesy, avoidance, withdrawal, refusal to mix, cutting someone off, privacy, keeping one's own company, keeping (oneself) to oneself, domesticity, homelife, seclusiveness, self-containment, retirement, singleness, celibacy, unapproachability, inaccessibility, exclusivity, privacy, private world, sending to Coventry, cutting someone dead (Inf)

► *128 Exclusion; 622 Pride; 626 Sullenness; 634 Avoidance; 659 Discourtesy; 732 Shyness*

2 shyness, bashfulness, timidity, diffidence, modesty, introversion, anthropophobia, agoraphobia

► *674 Modesty*

3 separation, seclusion, isolation, splendid isolation, solitariness, solitude, loneliness, exclusion, retreat, rejection, exile, banishment, deportation, expulsion, segregation, apartheid, blacklist, blackball, ostracism, sending to Coventry, boycott, quarantine, concealment, purdah, Balkanization

► *371 Expulsion; 372 Separation; 470 Rejection; 736 Concealment*

4 place of confinement, reserve, enclave, haven, reservation, American Indian reservation, homeland, Bantustan, ghetto, native quarter, prison, concentration camp, Dachau, prison camp, POW (prisoner of war) camp, jail (*or* gaol), penitentiary, penal institution, maximum-security prison, borstal, reformatory (*or* reform school), penal settlement, penal colony, Devil's Island, Siberia, pen (US inf)

► *565 Habitat; 815 Prison*

5 solitary place, retreat, sanctuary, sanctum, den, study, cloister, cell, sequestered nook, ivory tower, private quarters, secret garden, backwater, back of beyond, back o'Bourke (Aus), desert island, hiding place, hideout, godforsaken hole (Inf), hick town (US inf), Podunk (US inf), jerkwater town (US inf)

6 unsocial person, solitary person, stay-at-home, recluse, hermit, anchorite, ascetic, Hieronymite, guellemin, cave dweller, coenobite (*or* cenobite), santon, marabout, sannyasi, eremite, monk, outsider, not one of us, odd man out, oddity, eccentric, misfit, fish out of water, *persona non grata* (L), marooned person, castaway, Robinson Crusoe, loner (Inf), lone wolf (Inf), homebody (Inf), troglodyte (Inf), square peg (in a round hole) (Inf), iceberg (US inf)

► *100 Otherness*

7 outsider, foreigner, expatriate, exile, evacuee, refugee, outcast, outcaste, untouchable, pariah, leper, reject, deported person, deportee, displaced person (DP), stateless person, flotsam, flotsam and jetsam, homeless person, trash (US), poor white trash (US), outlaw, bandit, prisoner, POW (prisoner of war), vagabond, orphan, waif, stray, foundling, expat (Inf)

► *2 Sociology*

ADJECTIVES

8 unsociable, dissociable, dissocial, antisocial, ungregarious, uncompanionable, uncongenial, uncommunicative, reclusive, reticent, silent, sullen, mopy, morose, private, close, autistic, unforthcoming, unapproachable, withdrawn, in one's shell, domestic, seclusive, retiring, standoffish, aloof, haughty, remote, removed, distant, apart, detached, indifferent, Olympian, exclusive, self-sufficient, self-contained, inaccessible, forbidding, discourteous, impolite, uncivil, unmannerly, ungracious, rude, disrespectful, unfriendly, cool, cold, chilly, icy, frigid, frosty, unneighbourly, unwelcoming

9 **shy**, bashful, timid, taciturn, silent, introverted, afraid of the opposite sex, afraid of company

10 **lonely**, lonesome, alone, on one's own, solitary, isolated, secluded, stay-at-home, unpopular, friendless, boycotted, shunned, banned, frozen-out, prohibited, outlawed, desolate, lorn (Lit), forlorn, godforsaken, uninvited, deserted, avoided, rejected, ostracized, sent to Coventry, exiled, banished, deported, expelled, displaced, disbarred, confined, concealed, behind the veil, in purdah, single, celibate, unmarried, unwedded, separated, divorced, incompatible, not fit to live with, out of place, like a fish out of water, blanked (Inf), cold-shouldered (Inf), on one's tod (Inf)

11 **secluded**, private, isolated, quiet, off the beaten track, out-of-the-way, remote, deserted, desolate, hidden, screened, cloistered, sequestered, unvisited, unexplored, uninhabited, unknown

VERBS

12 **be unsocial**, keep (oneself) to oneself, keep one's distance, shun company, stand aloof, seclude oneself, go into seclusion, retire, go into retirement, retire from the world, give up one's friends, give up one's social life, stay at home, shut oneself up, withdraw, see no one, bury oneself, creep into a corner, stay in one's shell, stew in one's own juice, abandon the world, take the veil, lead a cloistered life

13 **ignore**, not acknowledge, avoid, have nothing to do with, exclude, shun, ban, shut (*or* close) the door on, segregate, blacklist, blackball, treat as a leper, treat as an outsider, keep at arm's length, repel, act rudely, snub, rebuff, frown on, turn one's back on, isolate, ostracize, freeze out, cut off, send to Coventry, shut out, reject, ban, boycott, prohibit, outlaw, turn out, displace, exile, banish, deport, expel, cast out, disbar, conceal, keep (in) private, keep in purdah, confine, shut up, quarantine, seclude, sequester, imprison, jail (*or* gaol), cold-shoulder (Inf), cut someone dead (Inf), blank someone (out) (Inf)

ADVERBS

14 **unsocially**, antisocially, inhospitably, incompatibly, taciturnly, reticently, quietly, silently, without a word, sullenly, morosely, privately, in private, at home, domestically, aloofly, haughtily, with disdain, remotely, distantly, indifferently, inaccessibly, behind closed doors, exclusively, self-sufficiently, without assistance, forbiddingly, discourteously, impolitely, uncivilly, ungraciously, rudely, with rudeness, disrespectfully, coolly, coldly, icily, frigidly, shyly, in a shy manner, bashfully, timidly

656 Formality

I think she must have been very strictly brought up, she's so desperately anxious to do the wrong thing correctly. Saki.

NOUNS

1 **formality**, form, formalness, state, stateliness, state occasion, dignity, ceremoniousness, stiffness, sedateness, staidness, starchiness, solemnity, solemness, royal we, etiquette, correct behaviour, protocol, the thing to do, doing the right thing, smartness, spit and polish, correctness, correctitude, fastidiousness, decorum, decorousness, stuffiness, stiff-neckedness, strait-lacedness, hideboundness, preciseness, red carpet, conventionality, propriety, best behaviour, stylization, primness, rigidness, pomp, circumstance, pride, gravity, weightiness

2 **formalism**, ritualism, ceremonialism, pedantry, preciseness, precisionism, preciousness, preciosity, purism, punctiliousness, scrupulousness, conventionalism, conventionality, over-refinement, over-preciseness, goody-goodyism

3 **formal occasion**, ceremony, ceremonial, procedure, ritual, drill, practice, routine, drill attention, celebration, *son et lumière* (Fr), spectacle, set piece, tableau, scene, show, Lord Mayor's show, changing the guard, trooping the Colour, turnout, review, (grand) parade, march past, flypast, pageant, fête, gala, gala performance, tournament, tattoo, field day, red-letter day, rite, liturgy, religious ceremony, service, Christening, wedding, funeral, confirmation, baptism, coronation, rite of passage, convocation, graduation, inauguration, initiation, bar mitzvah

► *601 Celebration*

4 **formal dress**, full dress, court dress, grand toilette, robes, regalia, finery, tails, black tie, white tie, white tie and tails, correct dress, uniform, formal attire, morning dress, evening dress, evening gown, ball gown, dinner jacket, dress suit, tuxedo, tux, lounge suit, long dress, cocktail dress, best bib and tucker, Sunday best, academic dress, cap and gown, subfusc, mourning black, widow's weeds, uniform, regimentals, livery, dress uniform, mess kit, battledress, fatigues, khaki, school uniform, vestments, clerical dress

5 **etiquette**, rules of conduct, social code, formalities, prescribed form, set form, social procedures, social graces, social conduct, social convention, social image, custom, good manners, politeness, *politesse* (Fr), natural politeness, civilities, comity, decencies, elegancies, mores, proprieties, decorum, good form, right form, protocol, diplomatic code, punctilio, point of etiquette, convention

ADJECTIVES

6 **formal**, formulary, formalistic, legalistic, pedantic, stately, dignified, ceremonious, ceremonial, stiff, refined, starchy, sedate, staid, stilted, rigid, solemn, royal, correct, smart, precise, conventional, ritual, procedural, standing on ceremony, official, stylized, prim, punctilious, precise, scrupulous, fastidious, precious, puristic, exact, meticulous, orderly, methodical, elegant, decorous, proud, grave, pompous, weighty

7 **dressed-up**, formally dressed, uniformed, in full dress, black tie, white tie, in white tie and tails, in tails, dressed to kill, dressed fit to kill, in Sunday best, in one's best bib and tucker, in fine feather, *en grande toilette* (Fr), chic, soignée, stylish, modish, fashionable, well turned out, dolled up, dressed (*or* dolled) up to the nines (Inf), spiffed (*or* fancied *or* slicked) up, glitzy (Inf), ritzy (Inf), right-on (Inf)

8 **ceremonious**, ceremonial, ritual, ritualistic, solemn, pompous, liturgic, stately

VERBS

9 **formalize**, ritualize, solemnize, conventionalize, stylize

10 **celebrate**, dignify, honour, fête, observe

11 be formal, observe the formalities, stand on ceremony, do things by the book, follow protocol

ADVERBS

12 formally, in due form, in set form, pro forma, as a matter of form, precisely, smartly, officially, starchily, stiffly, stiltedly, rigidly, primly, solemnly, procedurally, conventionally, ritually, royally, correctly, ceremoniously

657 Informality

Not least among the qualities in a great King is a capacity to permit his ministers to serve him. Cardinal Richelieu.

NOUNS

1 informality, informalness, lack of formality, lack of ceremony, unceremoniousness, lack of convention, unconventional, unofficial, indifference, nonconformity, casualness, offhandedness

2 sociability, affability, graciousness, cordiality, relaxedness, Bohemianism

3 familiarity, naturalness, simplicity, plainness, homeliness, homeyness, folksiness, the common touch, unaffectedness

4 freedom, licence, indulgence, tolerance, toleration, free speech, free will, free thought, free-and-easiness, a free hand, leeway, margin, unconstraint, latitude, independence, freedom of action, laxity, permissiveness, relaxation, forbearance, ease, easiness, leave, looseness, irregularity, permissive society

5 nonobservance, nonadherence, breach of etiquette, bad form, gaffe, bad taste, bad manners, incorrectness, gaucherie

6 informal dress, casual dress, undress, mufti, casual clothes, leisure wear, slacks, jeans, tracksuits, shell suits, *déshabillé* (Fr), dishabille, dressing gown, loungewear, day dress, peignoir, bathrobe, robe, wrapper, housecoat, smoking jacket, slippers, shirtsleeves, civvies (Inf)

ADJECTIVES

7 informal, unceremonious, unconventional, unofficial, indifferent, nonconformist, casual, offhand, unstuffy, unaffected, unassuming

8 sociable, affable, gracious, cordial, relaxed, Bohemian

9 familiar, natural, simple, plain, homely, folksy, common, unaffected, *haymish* (Yiddish)

10 free, indulgent, tolerant, unconstrained, independent, lax, permissive, easy-going, free-and-easy, loose, irregular

VERBS

11 not stand on ceremony, let one's hair down, be oneself, be natural, relax, feel at home, make oneself at home, not insist, waive the rules, come as you are, be footloose and fancy free, go native, show no respect for

ADVERBS

12 informally, unceremoniously, without ceremony

13 casually, offhand, offhandedly, relaxedly, familiarly

14 naturally, simply, plainly

15 unaffectedly, unassumingly, unconstrainedly, unofficially, *en famille* (Fr)

658 Courtesy

If a man be gracious and courteous to strangers, it shews he is a citizen of the world. Francis Bacon.

NOUNS

1 courtesy, courteousness, common courtesy, politeness, civility, kindness, kindliness, amiability, sweetness, niceness, amenity, agreeableness, affability, comity, graciousness, humility, consideration, thoughtfulness, solicitousness, solicitude, decency, tact, tactfulness, discretion, charity, generosity, benevolence, help, friendliness, sociability, gallantry, chivalry, chivalrousness, courtliness, comity, noblesse oblige, graciousness, gracefulness, suavity, suaveness, blandness, social tact, smoothness, flattery, sweet tongue, soft tongue, honeyed tongue, fair words, soft words, easy temper, even temper, good humour, gentleness, mildness, mild manner, obligingness, the common touch, mansuetude (Lit), soft soap (Inf), sweet-talking (Inf)

▶ *392 Help; 569 Friendship; 623 Humility; 650 Benevolence; 654 Sociability; 677 Flattery*

2 good manners, exquisite manners, mannerliness, etiquette, good behaviour, breeding, good breeding, good deportment, refinement, polish, culture, gentility, genteelness, sophistication, elegance, urbanity, savoir-vivre, savoir-faire, gentlemanliness, ladylikeness, formality, correctness, convention, protocol, custom, diplomacy

▶ *549 Refinement; 553 Fashion*

3 courtesies, social courtesies, civilities, urbanities, amenities, graces, gentilities, pleasantries, compliments (of the season), regards, best regards, best wishes, best respects, love, kind remembrances, elegances, dignities, respect, respectfulness, formalities, rites, rituals, ceremonies, invitation, presentation, welcome, introduction, reception, acknowledgment, compliment, toast, recognition, mark of recognition, valediction, fond farewell

▶ *313 Departure; 471 Attention; 593 Love; 667 Respect*

4 deference, obeisance, compliance, complaisance, condescension, oiliness, unctuousness, glibness, fulsomeness, sycophancy, ingratiation, doffing one's cap, touching one's cap, kissing someone's hand, bowing, nodding, kowtowing, salaaming, laying it on (Inf)

▶ *367 Lowering; 663 Obedience*

5 sign of courtesy, sign of politeness, act of kindness, salutation, salute, greeting, handshake, handclasp (US), hug, kiss, embrace, smile, wave, graceful gesture, bow, curtsy

6 courteous person, willing servant, sycophant, helpful neighbour, gallant, knight, chevalier, lady, gentleman, proper gentleman (*or* lady)

▶ *401 Servant; 573 Aristocrat*

ADJECTIVES

7 courteous, polite, civil, urbane, agreeable, affable, genial, amiable, gracious, humble, fair, considerate, thoughtful, solicitous, decent, tactful, discreet, generous, benevolent, charitable, accommodating, lenient, even-tempered, gentle, mild, mild-mannered, good-humoured, obliging, amenable, sociable, friendly, kind, kindly, sweet, nice, welcoming, gallant, chivalrous, courtly, graceful, old-fashioned, old-world

8 good-mannered, well-behaved, well-bred, well-spoken, refined, cultured, cultivated, genteel, gentlemanly, ladylike, correct, urbane, polished, elegant, conventional, suave, bland, smooth, flattering, sweet-talking, soft-tongued, sweet-tongued, honey-tongued, formal, *de rigueur* (Fr), ceremonious, diplomatic, respectful

9 deferential, obeisant, compliant, condescending, complaisant, glib, fulsome, sycophantic, ingratiating, bowing, nodding, kowtowing, smug, oily, unctuous, buttery (Inf), soapy (Inf), slimy (Inf)

VERBS

10 be courteous, show courtesies, show kindness, give consideration, care, use tact, oblige, invite, receive, welcome, introduce, acknowledge, compliment, recognize, toast, drink to, give one's best regards, give one's best wishes, send one's respects, give respect, send one's regrets, express regrets, show love, love, flatter, have a sweet tongue, use soft words, possess an even temper, have a mild manner, not take offence, take in good part, remain good-humoured, have the common touch, soft-soap (Inf)

11 have good manners, mind one's manners, behave well, behave properly, remain on one's best behaviour, treat with politeness, observe etiquette, mind one's p's and q's, have good breeding, show refinement, act like a gentleman, act like a lady, observe protocol, follow custom, use diplomacy, not give offence

12 greet, welcome, welcome home, welcome with open arms, advance to meet, salute, hail, wave, smile, hug, squeeze, embrace, kiss, blow a kiss, say hello, bid good day, raise one's hat (*or* cap), shake hands, clasp hands (US), squeeze one's hand, pump one's hand, honour, fire a salute, parade, present arms, turn out, give a hero's welcome, crown, wreathe, garland, fête, celebrate

13 defer to, treat with deference, pay respects, pay homage, make obeisance, comply, condescend, ingratiate oneself, act sycophantically, bow, curtsy, bob, nod, duck, touch one's forelock, doff one's hat, touch one's cap, kiss someone's hand, kneel, kowtow, salaam, prostrate oneself, toady to, fawn on, lay it on (Inf)

ADVERBS

14 courteously, with courtesy, politely, in a polite manner, civilly, agreeably, affably, amiably, graciously, humbly, considerately, thoughtfully, solicitously, decently, tactfully, discreetly, generously, benevolently, charitably, accommodatingly, leniently, gently, mildly, good-humouredly, obligingly, amenably, sociably, kindly, with kindness, sweetly, nicely, gallantly, chivalrously, courtly, knightly, like a knight in shining armour, gracefully, with good grace, old-worldly

15 genteelly, correctly, urbanely, elegantly, conventionally, suavely, blandly, smoothly, politely, respectfully, considerately, thoughtfully, as a thoughtful gesture, generously, benevolently, solicitously, decently, tactfully, discretely, charitably, accommodatingly, formally, ceremoniously, diplomatically

16 deferentially, with deference, obeisantly, compliantly, condescendingly, complaisantly, glibly, fulsomely, sycophantically, ingratiatingly, unctuously

659 Discourtesy

JUDGE WILLIS: *You are extremely offensive, young man.*
F. E. SMITH: *As a matter of fact, we both are, and the only difference between us is that I am trying to be, and you can't help it.* F. E. Smith.

NOUNS

1 discourtesy, discourteousness, impoliteness, unpoliteness, incivility, inurbanity, disagreeableness, ungraciousness, ungallantness, uncourtliness, ungentlemanliness, thoughtlessness, shortness, inconsiderateness, lack of consideration, unsolicitousness, tactlessness, insensitivity, inattention, sullenness, excessive frankness, bluntness, acerbity, sharpness, tartness, asperity, gruffness, bluffness, roughness, harshness, severity, brusqueness, ungentleness, unfriendliness, unpleasantness, surliness, crustiness, nastiness, anger, ridicule, derision, mockery, raillery, scoffing, jeering, beastliness (Inf)

▶ *269 Brevity; 472 Inattention; 621 Derision; 624 Anger and Resentment; 626 Sullenness; 647 Severity; 668 Disrespect*

2 bad manners, shocking manners, no manners, lack of manners, unmannerliness, want of chivalry, lack of politeness, scant courtesy, rudeness, insolence, impudence, truculence, churlishness, impatience, interruption, vulgarity, offensiveness, coarseness, boorishness, caddishness, grossness, gross behaviour, crudeness, loutishness, ill-breeding, misconduct, bad behaviour, conduct unbecoming, cheek (Inf), sauce (Inf), lip (Inf)

▶ *606 Dissatisfaction; 625 Grumpiness; 660 Insolence; 675 Vulgarity*

3 act of discourtesy, short answer, angry reply, rebuff, insult, jeer, snub, abuse, rude gesture, V-sign, sticking out one's tongue, black look, sour look, scowl, frown, bad language, bad words, rude words, dirty joke, cold shoulder (Inf)

4 discourteous person, rude person, insolent person, fault-finder, boor, lout, brute, yahoo, savage, barbarian, no shining knight, no gentleman, mannerless imp, curmudgeon, bear, grouser, sulker, grouch (Inf), crosspatch (Inf), loudmouth (Inf), pig (Inf), bellyacher (Inf), yob (*or* yobbo) (Inf), nerd (US inf), shithouse (Inf)

ADJECTIVES

5 discourteous, impolite, uncivil, disagreeable, inurbane, ungracious, ungallant, uncourtly, ungentlemanly, ungentlemanlike, unladylike, unfeminine, unpleasant, surly, sullen, crusty, nasty, unkind, thoughtless, offhanded, inconsiderate, unsolicitous, tactless, insensitive, inattentive, cavalier, abusive, vituperative, not anxious to please, unsmiling, grim, unneighbourly, unsociable, unfriendly, uncomplimentary, unflattering, disrespectful, familiar, gruff, blunt, over-blunt, over-frank, harsh, severe, ungentle, rough, rugged, brutal, brusque, curt, short, abrupt, impatient, discontented, peevish, testy, acerbic, sharp, sharp-tongued, tart, snappy, biting, growling, bearish, acrimonious, aggressive, beastly (Inf), cold-shoulder (Inf)

6 **bad-mannered**, ill-mannered, unmannerly, unchivalrous, badly behaved, rude, insolent, impudent, impertinent, saucy, churlish, truculent, abusive, cursing, obstreperous, forward, irascible, difficult, vulgar, offensive, injurious, coarse, boorish, caddish, gross, crude, loutish, ill-bred, unrefined, uncouth, uncultured, barbarian, savage, foul-mouthed, growling, grumbling, swearing, cheeky (Inf), sassy (US inf), lippy (US inf)

VERBS

7 **be discourteous**, not respect, ruffle feelings, show no regard for someone's feelings, abuse, affront, outrage, take liberties, make free with, make bold, treat rudely, have no manners, display bad manners, flout etiquette, cause offence, insult, know no better, refuse to say thank you, refuse to say sorry, stare, ogle, gaze, ignore, interrupt, cut, snub, look right through, have no time for, turn one's back on, make unwelcome, show the door, behave badly, behave cheekily (Inf), cut dead (Inf), cold-shoulder (Inf), give someone lip (Inf)

► *371 Expulsion*

8 **get angry**, be sullen, pout, glower, lour (*or* lower), frown, scowl, growl, curse, swear, shout down, lose one's temper, rant, hit the roof, blow one's top (Inf), blow one's lid (*or* stack) (US inf)

ADVERBS

9 **discourteously**, without courteousness, impolitely, uncivilly, uncourtly, ungallantly, ungraciously, ungentlemanly, unlike a gentleman, charmlessly, without charm, disagreeably, unchivalrously, unpleasantly, in an unpleasant manner, sullenly, sulkily, nastily, unkindly, thoughtlessly, offhandedly, inconsiderately, tactlessly, insensitively, inattentively, abusively, vituperatively, grimly, unsociably, without warmth, impatiently, discontentedly, peevishly, gruffly, bluntly, harshly, severely, ungently, roughly, brutally, brusquely, curtly, abruptly, tartly, sharply, in a sharp tone, angrily, with (*or* in) anger, crossly, acrimoniously, aggressively

10 **rudely**, disrespectfully, without respect, insolently, impudently, impertinently, saucily, churlishly, abusively, with a volley of abuse, obstreperously, irascibly, vulgarly, offensively, in an offensive way, injuriously, coarsely, boorishly, like a boor, caddishly, loutishly, grossly, crudely, uncouthly, savagely, derisively, mockingly, scoffingly, jeeringly, cheekily (Inf), yobbishly (Inf), like a yob (Inf), like a nerd (US inf)

660 Insolence

A man should not insult his wife publicly, at parties. He should insult her in the privacy of the home. James Thurber.

NOUNS

1 **insolence**, procacity, effrontery, impudence, impertinence, rudeness, bumptiousness, contumely, incivility

2 **cheek**, face, mouth, sass, brass, brass neck, nerve, gall, crust, lip, chutzpah, brazenness

3 **audacity**, boldness, assurance, hubris, brazen face, hardened face, blatancy, flagrancy, presumptiousness, overweening

4 **arrogance**, loftiness, uppishness, uppitiness, pushiness, haughtiness, pride, tyranny, shamelessness

5 **bravado**, defiance, bluster, presumption

6 **contempt**, disdain, sneer, sneering, disparagement

7 **insult**, gesture, taunt, affront, snook, V-sign, throwaway manner

8 **rudeness**, disrespectfulness, contempt, derision, ridicule

9 **discourtesy**, petulance, defiance, answering back, backchat, back talk, rejoinder, raillery, banter, disrespectfulness

10 **impudence**, impertinence, flippancy, cockiness, cheek, cheekiness, freshness, brazen-facedness, brassiness

11 **sauciness**, disrespect, impertinence, pertness, impudence, freshness, sassiness

12 **impudent person**, upstart, young pup, whippersnapper, smart aleck, cheeky devil, brazen face, *chutzpadik* (Yiddish), swaggerer, smartarse (Inf), minx, hussy, baggage, madame, beggar-on-horseback, Jack-in-office, tin god, braggart, blusterer, boaster, cockalorum, cock of the walk, smarty pants (Inf), wise guy (Inf), saucebox (Inf)

ADJECTIVES

13 **insolent**, impudent, malapert, impertinent, bumptious, contumelious, flip (Inf)

14 **cheeky**, brazen, mouthy, brassy, saucy, sassy, crusty, gally, nervy, smart-alecky (Inf), smart-arsed (Inf), wise-arsed (Inf)

15 **audacious**, bold, assured, brazen-faced, blatant, flagrant, precocious, obtrusive, familiar, unabashed

16 **arrogant**, lofty, haughty, uppish, uppity, pushy, proud, tyrannical, shameless, presumptuous, overweening

17 **contemptuous**, disdainful, sneering, cool, cold, disparaging, aweless

18 **insulting**, taunting, uncalled-for, gratuitous

19 **rude**, disrespectful, contemptuous, derisive, bluff, brash, barefaced

20 **discourteous**, petulant, defiant, backchatting, bantering, disrespectful

21 **impudent**, impertinent, pert, flippant, cocky, cheeky, fresh, brazen, brazen-faced, brassy, bold as brass, bold, unblushing, shameless

VERBS

22 **be rude**, have the cheek, have the audacity, make bold, make free with, have the gall, have the nerve, have the brass neck, dare, presume, take liberties, hold in contempt, forget one's place (*or* manners), get personal, get fresh (*or* smart) (Inf)

23 **be proud**, presume, put on airs, put one's nose in the air

24 **be vain**, brag, swagger, swank, swell, talk big, boast, brook no restraint

25 **answer back**, cheek, talk back, sass, backchat, provoke, retort, shout down, lip (Inf), give lip (Inf)

26 **oppress**, hector, bully, throw one's weight around, browbeat, grind down, trample on, ride roughshod over, treat with a high hand

27 **dare**, presume, take liberties, outface, brazen it out, brave it out, take a high tone, lord it, queen it, outlook, outface, lay down the law

28 get above oneself, presume, step out of line, lord it, come the high and mighty, forget one's place, confute, rise above one's station, throw one's weight around, be a law unto oneself, teach one's grandmother to suck eggs (Inf)

29 ridicule, express contempt, snort, sneer, jeer, cock a snook, snap one's fingers at, make a V sign, blow a raspberry, put one's tongue out, not give a fig, send to blazes, taunt, deride, despise, scorn, scoff, laugh in the face of, laugh out of court, guy

ADVERBS

30 insolently, impertinently, impudently, flippantly, bumptiously, pertly, precociously

31 cheekily, brazenly, cockily, saucily, sassily

32 audaciously, boldly, blatantly, flagrantly, precociously, obtrusively, brashly

33 arrogantly, presumptuously, loftily, haughtily, proudly, shamelessly, pushily

34 contemptuously, disdainfully, sneeringly, coolly, disparagingly

35 rudely, brashly, disrespectfully, derisively

36 discourteously, petulantly, disrespectfully

661 Defiance

NOUNS

1 defiance, defying, audacity, nerve, impertinence, pertness, impudence, insolence, belligerence, courage, boldness, bold front, brave face, bravura, bravado, daringness, daring, presumption, temerity, self-assertion, assurance, self-assurance, arrogance, bluster, bumptiousness, shamelessness, contrariness, cockiness, brashness, brassiness, brazenness, rashness, effrontery, barefaced effrontery, provocativeness, sauce, sauciness, cheekiness, nerviness (US inf), (brass) neck (Inf), (barefaced) cheek (Inf), cussedness (Inf), chutzpah (US inf), lip (Inf), bottle (Inf)

► *613 Courage; 615 Rashness; 622 Pride; 660 Insolence*

2 disobedience, insubordination, resistance, opposition, dissent, disagreement, confrontation, challenge, rebelliousness, rebellion, refusal, contumacy, contemptuousness, contempt, derision, disdain, disregard

► *113 Opposition; 662 Disobedience; 751 Disagreement*

3 act of defiance, challenge, dare, threat, taunt, insult, rude remark, contumely, answering back, impudent talk, opposition rally, demonstration, sit-in, march, treason, insurrection, revolution, declaration of war, battle cry, rebel yell (US), backchat (Inf), back talk (US inf), sass (US inf)

► *585 War; 668 Disrespect*

4 defiant person, challenger, opponent, usurper, militant, protestor, rebel, leader of the opposition, demonstrator, marcher, activist, martyr, nonconformist, conscientious objector, devil's advocate, cheeky monkey (Inf), bigmouth (Inf)

VERBS

5 defy, challenge, oppose, protest, bid defiance to, hurl defiance at, flout, show insolence, show courage, face danger, dare, brave, bare one's teeth, fly in the face of, stand up to, withstand, refuse to bow to, call one's bluff, run the gauntlet, take one up on, present a bold front, present a brave face, outstare, brazen it out, presume, bluster, crow over, provoke, affront, have temerity, have (a) nerve, have barefaced cheek (Inf), have a cheek (Inf), cheek (Inf), cock a snook (Inf), have chutzpah (US inf), get on one's high horse (Inf), give someone lip (Inf), sass (US inf)

6 be insubordinate, show contempt, scorn, spurn, slight, disregard, ignore, resist, refuse, confront, disobey, disagree, threaten, challenge, oppose, dissent, throw down the gauntlet, throw one's hat in the ring, dare, taunt, act insolent, snap one's fingers at, laugh in someone's face, insult, make a rude remark, answer back, play the devil's advocate, demonstrate, hold a demonstration, stage (*or* hold) a sit-in, march, rebel, usurp, declare war, give the battle cry, give a rebel yell (US)

ADJECTIVES

7 defiant, outspoken, assertive, emphatic, assured, self-assured, unabashed, audacious, bold, arrogant, presumptuous, stubborn, obstinate, stiff-necked, bumptious, offensive, impudent, impertinent, pert, insolent, insulting, contemptuous, disdainful, derisive, shameless, brash, bold as brass, brassy, brazen, courageous, daring, reckless, saucy, cocky, cheeky, nervy (US inf), sassy (US inf)

8 defying, challenging, disagreeing, disobedient, recalcitrant, refractory, obstinate, antagonistic, belligerent, bellicose, provocative, aggressive, rebellious, militant, warlike

ADVERBS

9 defiantly, assertively, emphatically, with emphasis, courageously, in a courageous way, in the face of, in the teeth of, assuredly, self-assuredly, unabashedly, audaciously, boldly, to one's face, daringly, as a dare, arrogantly, presumptuously, stubbornly, obstinately, bumptiously, offensively, impudently, impertinently, pertly, insolently, insultingly, contemptuously, disdainfully, derisively, shamelessly, without shame, without embarrassment, brashly, with a lot of nerve, brazenly, under the very nose of, courageously, recklessly, saucily, cockily, cheekily, nervily (US inf)

10 in defiance, challengingly, as a challenge, disobediently, obstinately, antagonistically, with antagonism, belligerently, in a belligerent way, bellicosely, provocatively, aggressively, rebelliously, in open rebellion, militantly, like a war

INTERJECTIONS

11 how dare you!, what cheek!

662 Disobedience

Of Man's first disobedience, and the fruit
Of that forbidden tree, whose mortal taste
Brought death into the World, and all our woe... John Milton.

NOUNS

1 disobedience, noncompliance, noncooperation, uncooperativeness, nonconformity, nonobservance, undutifulness, unwillingness, opposition, recalcitrance, refractoriness, obstinacy, stubbornness, intractability, hindrance, obstruction, obstructionism, obstreperousness, indiscipline, restlessness, restiveness, wildness, delinquency, unruliness, dissension, defiance, defiance of orders, refusal to obey orders, violation of orders, disloyalty, perfidiousness, perfidy, unfaithfulness, faithlessness, defection, desertion, AWOL (absent without leave), tergiversation, insubordination, strike, mutinousness, mutineering, mutiny, civil disobedience, passive resistance, resistance, conscientious objection, religious disobedience, immorality, wickedness, sin, sinfulness, orneriness (US inf), misbehaviour, mischief-making, naughtiness, stroppiness (Inf), monkey tricks (Inf), monkey shines (US inf)

▶ *113 Opposition; 118 Nonconformity; 327 Agitation; 357 Destruction; 378 Obstruction; 380 Violence; 408 Disorder; 637 Unwillingness; 661 Defiance; 804 Wickedness*

2 violation of the law, infraction, infringement, transgression, felony, trespass, extortion, breach of the peace, civil disturbance, disorder, riot, street riot, rioting, street fight, gang warfare, tumult, turmoil, lawlessness, lawbreaking, criminality, crime, vandalism, robbery, murder, regicide, tyrannicide, homicide

▶ *382 Killing; 774 Stealing; 800 Dishonour*

3 subversion, subversiveness, underground activities, sedition, seditiousness, conspiracy, intrigue, plot, cabal, faction, secret society, agitprop, infiltration, spying, espionage, fifth columnism, fifth column, agitation, sabotage, terrorism, anarchy, treasonable activities, treason, high treason, lese-majesty

▶ *383 Resistance; 484 Plan*

4 revolution, rebellion, rebelliousness, revolt, sansculottism, uprising, mutiny, mutinousness, coup d'état, coup, putsch, breakaway, schism, secession, sedition, insurrection, insurgence, insurgency, resistance movement, resistance, terrorism, guerrilla warfare, civil war, war

▶ *585 War*

5 troublemaker, mischief-maker, naughty child, scamp, pest, nuisance, rascal, scallywag, imp, handful, little monkey (Inf), pain in the neck (Inf), pain in the arse (Inf)

6 nonconformist, protestant, deviationist, radical, Jacobin, maverick, opponent, malcontent, Frondeur

7 protester, civil rights activist, suffragist, suffragette, women's libber, environmental activist, campaigner, demonstrator, marcher, dissident, recusant, recalcitrant, striker, picketer

8 agitator, *agent provocateur* (Fr), ringleader, rabble-rouser, soapbox orator, demagogue, firebrand

9 criminal, lawbreaker, robber, bandit, thief, burglar, housebreaker, murderer, assassin, extortionist, killer, rapist, sexual abuser, wife-batterer, gang member, gangster, Mafia member, Mafioso, petty criminal, mugger (Inf), hood (US inf), mobster (US inf), brawler, rowdy, ruffian, hoodlum (US), handful (Inf), bolshie (Inf), hooligan (Inf), bovver boy (Inf)

10 seditionist, seditionary, subversive, conspirator, Guy Fawkes, John Brown (US), traitor, collaborator, quisling, tergiversator, extremist, Black Panther (US), National Front member, insurrectionist, insurgent, infiltrator, fifth columnist, anarchist, rioter, terrorist, Weatherman (US), IRA (Irish Republican Army) member, Provisional, Provo, guerrilla, urban guerrilla, partisan, saboteur, Luddite

11 rebel, secessionist, seceder, revolutionary, revolutionist, sans-culotte, revolter, mutineer, Contra, Bolshevist, Trotskyist, Red (Inf), commie (Inf), pinko (Inf), leftie (Inf)

12 reactionary, counter-revolutionary, conservative, monarchist, White Russian, counterterrorist, nonstriker, strike-breaker, scab, blackleg

ADJECTIVES

13 disobedient, noncompliant, uncomplying, noncooperative, uncooperative, nonobservant, undutiful, unwilling, opposing, recalcitrant, obstinate, stubborn, intractable, obstructive, insubordinate, obstreperous, undisciplined, poorly disciplined, transgressing, restless, restive, wild, out of control, unmanageable, disobeying, misbehaved, mischief-making, naughty, delinquent, disorderly, riotous, tumultuous, unruly, dissenting, defiant, recusant, disloyal, perfidious, deserting, tergiversatory, mutinous, lawless, lawbreaking, criminal, immoral, wicked, sinning, ornery (US inf), bloody-minded (Inf)

14 subversive, seditious, conspiratorial, factional, anarchic, anarchical, treasonable, revolutionary, rebellious, in rebellion, mutinous, breakaway, schismatic, insurgent, insurrectional, insurrectionary

VERBS

15 be disobedient, disobey, not obey, not listen to, not heed, pay no attention to, ignore instructions, not do as one is told, refuse to cooperate, not cooperate, not comply with, not conform, oppose, hinder, obstruct, misbehave, make mischief, get into mischief, dissent, flout authority, show insubordination, defy, defy orders, refuse to obey orders, violate orders, defect, desert, go AWOL (absent without leave), tergiversate, strike, take industrial action, break the law, violate the law, commit a crime, infringe, transgress, breach the peace, trespass, riot, vandalize, rob, murder, sin, snap one's fingers at

16 be subversive, subvert, conspire, plot, betray, infiltrate, spy, agitate, sabotage, terrorize, create anarchy, lead a rebellion, uprise, rise in arms, mount the barricades, mutiny, secede, revolt, stage a revolt, rebel, fight, overthrow, lead a coup, kick over the traces

ADVERBS

17 disobediently, contrary to orders, unwillingly, obstinately, stubbornly, intractably, insubordinately, obstreperously, restlessly, restively, wildly, naughtily, delinquently, riotously, tumultuously, dissentingly, defiantly, as a protest, disloyally, perfidiously, mutinously, lawlessly, criminally, immorally, without regard to morality, wickedly, in a wicked way

18 subversively, seditiously, conspiratorially, rebelliously, mutinously, schismatically

663 Obedience

It is much safer to obey than to rule. Thomas à Kempis.

NOUNS

1 obedience, compliance, complaisance, acquiescence, deference, obsequiousness, dutifulness, duty, abiding by the law, goodness, observance, conformity, willingness, readiness, nonresistance, meekness, submissiveness, submission, passivity, passiveness, yielding, docility, subservience, servility, slavishness, tractability, pliance, malleability, softness, tameness, inactivity

▶ *117 Conformity; 343 Inactivity; 388 Submission; 419 Softness; 589 Peace; 636 Willingness; 664 Servility; 749 Pacification; 799 Honour; 810 Duty*

2 **loyalty**, fidelity, fealty, allegiance, service, faithfulness, good faith, good behaviour, devotion, constancy, comity, steadfastness, staunchness

3 **obeisance**, homage, worship, reverence, kneeling, humility, respect, courtesy, bow, curtsy, genuflection (*or* genuflexion), obsequy, salaam, prostration, grovelling, kowtow

4 **obedient person**, conformist, traditionalist, loyalist, loyal party member, law-abiding citizen, pillar of the community, soldier, wellbehaved child, teacher's pet, henpecked husband, servant, slave, gofer (US inf)

▶ *122 Inferiority; 392 Help; 401 Servant*

VERBS

5 **obey**, comply, comply with, acquiesce, consent, assent, defer, defer to, yield to, do one's duty, show good faith, behave well, show devotion to, abide by the law, keep the law, observe the rules, follow the book, conform, not resist, obey orders, take orders, follow orders, follow like sheep, wait for the command, do as one is told, do the will of, carry out orders, discharge, perform, heed, mind, come to heel, toe the line, stay in line, submit, yield, bear allegiance, give allegiance to, go along with, follow the party line, serve, do service, put oneself at one's service, do one's bidding, come at one's call, wait upon, minister to, follow to the ends of the earth

6 **show obeisance to**, pay homage, offer homage, keep the faith, worship, kneel, show humility, show respect, pay tribute, show courtesy, bow, curtsy, bend, stoop, genuflect, salaam, prostrate oneself, grovel, scrape, kowtow

ADJECTIVES

7 **obedient**, compliant, complying, complaisant, acquiescent, deferential, obsequious, dutiful, duteous (Lit), conforming, law-abiding, observant, good, willing, ready, nonresisting, unresisting, meek, sheep-like, submitting, submissive, passive, yielding, docile, resigned, disciplined, well-behaved, well-trained, biddable, under control, at one's beck and call, at one's command, at one's pleasure, at one's disposal, subservient, servile, slavish, tractable, amenable, pliant, inactive, manageable, malleable, soft, tame, trained, regimented, under one's thumb, like putty in one's hands, like a puppet on a string, on a leash (*or* lead)

8 **loyal**, faithful, devoted, devoted to, dedicated to, sworn to, constant, steadfast, staunch, true, sycophantic, trueblue, leal (Scot)

9 **obeisant**, offering homage, worshipping, reverential, kneeling, humble, respectful, courteous

ADVERBS

10 **obediently**, in obedience to, compliantly, in compliance with, under orders, to order, as ordered, complaisantly, acquiescently, deferentially, obsequiously, dutifully, in conformity with, conformingly, observantly, willingly, readily, unresistingly, meekly, submissively, passively, docilely, subserviently, servilely, slavishly, tractably, pliantly, inactively, softly, tamely, loyally, faithfully, devotedly, steadfastly, staunchly, constantly, reverentially, respectfully, courteously

11 **yours to command**, at your command, at your orders, at your service, as you please, as you will

664 Servility

I am well aware that I am the 'umblest person going....My mother is likewise a very 'umble person. We live in a numble abode. Charles Dickens.

Wit that can creep, and pride that licks the dust. Alexander Pope.

Whenever he met a great man he grovelled before him, and mylorded him as only a free-born Briton can do. William Makepeace Thackeray.

NOUNS

1 **servility**, slavishness, deference, compliance, pliancy, subservience, menialness, abjectness, submission, submissiveness, slavery, serfdom, helotism, peonage, lack of self-respect

2 **sycophancy**, obsequiousness, fawning, grovelling, toadying, sponging, parasitism, cringing, footlicking, bootlicking, backscratching, apple-polishing, handshaking, timeserving, obeisance, prostration, crawling, mealymouthing, bowing and scraping, ingratiation, truckling, bent back, ducking, bobbing, soft-soaping, arse-licking (*or* kissing) (Inf), brown-nosing (Inf)

3 **sycophant**, toady, toad, toadeater, timeserver, creep, Uriah Heep, crawler, bootlicker, groveller, lickspittle, suck, mealy-mouth, assentor, yes-man, smoothie, lapdog, spaniel, poodle, jackal, creature, cat's-paw, dupe, stooge, footstool, doormat, instrument, tool, puppet, minion, lackie, courtier, faithful servant, man, slave, helot, serf, peon, kowtower, creeping Jesus (Inf), arselicker (*or* -kisser) (Inf), brownie (Inf), brown-noser (Inf),

4 **sponger**, parasite, leech, sponge, barnacle, freeloader, deadbeat, gigolo, toy boy

5 **adherent**, hanger-on, follower, appendage, satellite, dangler, dependent, shadow, collaborator, retainer, servant, man

ADJECTIVES

6 **servile**, slavish, deferential, compliant, pliant, puttylike, supple, subservient, menial, abject, submissive, not free, dependent, under the thumb (Inf)

7 **sycophantic**, obsequious, flattering, fawning, grovelling, toadying, sponging, parasitic, cringing, footlicking, bootlicking, backscratching, apple-polishing, handshaking, timeserving, obeisant, prostrate, mealy-mouthed, crawling, ingratiating, truckling, soft-soaping, smarmy, whining, freeloading, cringing, cowering, snivelling, leechlike, beggarly, hangdog, on one's knees, on bended knee, bowed, stooping, kowtowing, bowing, scraping, crawling, sneaking, creepy, unctuous, soapy, oily, slimy,

overattentive, arse-licking (*or* -kissing) (Inf), brown-nosing (Inf)

VERBS

8 **be servile**, lose (*or* forfeit) one's self-respect, let oneself be walked all over, act as a footstool, swallow insults, stoop, fall (all) over

9 **fawn**, toady, ingratiate oneself, insinuate oneself, flatter, truckle, crawl, grovel, curry favour, bootlick, lickspittle, lick the feet of, lick the shoes (*or* boots) of, suck up to, creep to, make up to, spaniel, soft-soap, pay court to, worm oneself into, lick the hem of one's garment, pay court to, play (*or* act) up to, handshake, polish the apple, get into the good graces of, get on the right side of, rub up the right way, lick the arse of (Inf), brown-nose (Inf)

10 **knuckle under**, demean oneself, cower, cringe, crouch, kneel, make obeisance, stoop, bend the knee, fall on one's knees, prostrate oneself, throw oneself at the feet of, defer to, tug one's forelock, bow, kowtow, bow and scrape, fetch and carry, bend, bob, duck, be the tool of, lick the dust, agree to anything

11 **pander to**, wait on (*or* upon), wait on hand and foot, cater for, fetch and carry, do service, serve, jump at the bidding of, do the dirty work of, stooge for, squire, dance attendance on, comply, fall at a person's feet, do the bidding of, run after

12 **beg**, beg for favours, wheedle, whine, beg for crumbs

13 **conform**, comply, serve the times, fall into line

14 **follow**, batten on, hang on, adhere to, jump on the bandwagon, run with the hare and hunt with the hounds, follow at heel, follow the crowd, go with the stream, swim with the tide, pin on to, latch on to, hang on the skirts (*or* sleeve) of

15 **sponge**, sponge on, feed on, live off, parasitize, fatten on, use, make use of, use as a meal ticket

ADVERBS

16 **with servility**, slavishly, subserviently, abjectly, menially, submissively, with cap in hand

17 **sycophantically**, obsequiously, ingratiatingly, fawningly, grovellingly, on one's knees, creepily

18 **parasitically**, like a leech

665 Carefulness

Any girl who was a lady would not even think of having such a good time that she did not remember to hang on to her jewelry. Anita Loos.

NOUNS

1 **carefulness**, care, caution, attentiveness, attention, mindfulness, diligence, heed, assiduity, thoroughness, exactness, precision, meticulousness

2 **consideration**, solicitude, compassion, mindfulness, care, loving care, tender loving care (TLC)

3 **circumspection**, watchfulness, alertness, vigilance, readiness, preparation, prudence, scruples, scrupulousness

4 **fastidiousness**, particularity, exactitude, perfectionism, orderliness, tidiness, neatness, perfection, attention to detail, niceness, pedantry, pernicketiness, faddiness

▶ *243 Preparation; 273 Accuracy; 342 Activity; 407 Order; 471 Attention; 616 Caution*

5 **watchfulness**, surveillance, vigilance, wariness, guarding, guardedness, watching, watch, lookout, inspection, invigilation, vigil, guard-duty, baby-sitting, baby-minding, neighbourhood watch, stake-out

▶ *252 Safety*

6 **careful person**, perfectionist, pedant, miser, hoarder, Scrooge, bomb-disposal expert, shrewd businessman (*or* businesswoman)

7 **caring person**, carer, nurse, doctor, social worker

8 **watchful person**, baby-sitter, baby-minder, guard, caretaker, guardian, chaperon, bodyguard, sentry, sentinel, vigilante, neighbourhood watchman, Guardian Angel (US)

ADJECTIVES

9 **careful**, attentive, mindful, diligent, heedful, assiduous, thorough, meticulous, circumspect, watchful, wide awake, alert, vigilant, observant, guarding, watching, on guard, ready, prepared, prudent, scrupulous, precise, painstaking, pedantic, perfect, perfectionist, fastidious, nice, pernickety, faddy, particular, exact, orderly, tidy, neat

VERBS

10 **be careful**, mind, heed, watch, prepare, be vigilant, be cautious, tread carefully, pay attention to, tread warily, walk on eggshells (Inf)

11 **care for**, take charge of, safeguard, guard, stand guard, look out for, survey, check, inspect, invigilate, watch over, keep an eye on, attend to, take care of, chaperon, baby-sit, baby-mind, nurse, keep tabs on (Inf)

ADVERBS

12 **carefully**, with care, cautiously, gingerly, diligently, with precision, in detail, with exactitude, thoroughly, precisely, perfectly, alertly, warily

13 **caringly**, tenderly, attentively, gently

666 Negligence

Celerity is never more admir'd
Than by the negligent. William Shakespeare.

NOUNS

1 **negligence**, carelessness, inattention, thoughtlessness, unmindfulness, nonchalance, unconcern, oblivion, insouciance, disregard, neglectfulness, dereliction, forgetfulness, heedlessness, remissness

2 **indifference**, informality, casualness, *laissez faire* (Fr), inexactitude, unscrupulousness, superficiality, shallowness, offhandedness, slackness, shoddiness, laziness, untidiness, messiness, slovenliness, sloppiness, sluttishness, procrastination, avoidance, delay

3 **negligent person**, procrastinator, idler, shirker, sloven, slut, slob (Inf)

ADJECTIVES

4 **negligent**, neglectful, careless, inattentive, thoughtless, unmindful, nonchalant, unconcerned, uncaring, oblivious, insouciant, disregardful, forgetful, heedless, remiss

5 **indifferent**, informal, casual, lackadaisical, inexact, unscrupulous, superficial, shallow, offhanded, procrasti-

nating, avoiding, delaying, slack, lax, half-done, slipshod, slapdash, incomplete, shoddy, lazy, untidy, dirty, messy, slovenly, sluttish, sloppy (Inf), grotty (Inf)

VERBS

6 **be neglectful**, neglect, disregard, take no notice of, not care for, ignore, turn a blind eye to, forget, not heed, procrastinate, take things slowly, put off until tomorrow, take it easy, put one's feet up, avoid, delay, leave undone, leave half-done, not complete, give a lick and a promise (Inf)

ADVERBS

7 **negligently**, neglectfully, carelessly, cursorily, any old way (Inf), sloppily (Inf)

667 Respect

We owe respect to the living; to the dead we owe only truth.
Voltaire.

NOUNS

1 **respect**, regard, esteem, consideration, attention, honour, favour, approbation, approval, appreciation, repute, recognition, good opinion, high opinion, high standing, prestige, authority
▶ *396 Authority; 669 Approval*

2 **admiration**, adoration, breathless adoration, adulation, worship, hero worship, idolization, veneration, awe, reverence, homage, fealty, obeisance, great respect, high regard
▶ *619 Wonder*

3 **respectfulness**, due respect, deference, humbleness, humility, devotion, loyalty, courtesy, comity, polite regard, attentions
▶ *623 Humility; 658 Courtesy; 663 Obedience*

4 **mark of respect**, show of respect, salute, nod, inclination, bend, bending, bow, bowing and scraping, scrape, stooping, curtsy, bob, bending the knee, genuflection (*or* genuflexion), kneeling, prostration, kissing the hem, salaam, kowtow, obeisance

5 **presenting arms**, standing at (*or* to) attention, dipping the colours, guard of honour, parade of honour, flypast, red carpet, ticker-tape parade (*or* reception)

6 **greeting**, welcome, salutation, salute, obeisance, obsequy

7 **respects**, regards, kind regards, kindest regards, greetings, salutations, compliments, devoirs, good wishes, best wishes

ADJECTIVES

8 **respectful**, regardful, considerate, attentive, honorific, ceremonious, appreciative

9 **showing respect**, deferential, courteous, polite, gracious, dutiful, obeisant, humble, knowing one's place, conscious of one's place, submissive, submitting, compliant, obsequious, servile, ingratiating, fawning, kowtowing, bootlicking (Inf)
▶ *623 Humility; 658 Courtesy; 664 Servility; 810 Duty*

10 **reverent**, reverential, venerative, venerational, admiring, adoring, worshipping, worshipful, adulatory, deifying, hero-worshipping, idolizing, in awe, awestruck, awestricken, wondering

11 **in a respectful stance**, standing, on one's feet, upstanding, rising, kneeling, on bended knee, on one's knees, prostrate, saluting, cap in hand, bare-headed, forelock-tugging, nodding, bending, bowing, curtsying, bobbing, bowing and scraping, stooping

12 **respected**, held in respect, well respected, highly regarded, esteemed, honoured, revered, reverenced, admired, well thought of, highly thought of, highly considered, appreciated, valued, prized, time-honoured, prestigious
▶ *669 Approval*

13 **respectable**, reputable, upright, worthy, venerable, estimable, praiseworthy, laudable
▶ *235 Worth*

14 **awe-inspiring**, imposing, impressive, important, authoritative, august, sage, wise
▶ *123 Importance; 396 Authority; 458 Wisdom*

VERBS

15 **respect**, regard, esteem, entertain respect for, think well of, think highly of, regard highly, hold in high regard, hold in high esteem, have (*or* hold) a high opinion of, look up to, rank high (*or* highly), hold dear, value, admire, prize, treasure, favour, appreciate, set store by (Inf)
▶ *235 Worth; 669 Approval*

16 **revere**, reverence, hold in reverence, venerate, honour, admire, adore, cherish, think the world of, look up to, worship, lionize, hero-worship, put on a pedestal, worship the ground one walks on, idolize, idolatrize, deify, apotheosize

17 **praise**, exalt, extol, acclaim, glorify, laud, sing the praises of

18 **show respect**, pay respect, accord respect to, defer to, heed, obey, consider, do (*or* pay) homage, pay one's respects, pay tribute to, acknowledge, do the honours, carry shoulder high
▶ *663 Obedience*

19 **take off one's hat to**, uncover one's head, doff one's cap to, tug one's forelock, rise, stand, rise to one's feet, be upstanding, nod, incline the head, bow one's head, bow, bow and scrape, bow down, bend, stoop, salaam, curtsy, bob, bob down, genuflect, bend the knee, kneel, get down on one's knees, fall on one's knees, fall down before, fall at the feet of, prostrate oneself, kiss the hem of one's garment, kiss the ring of, make obeisance, grovel, kowtow
▶ *623 Humility; 664 Servility*

20 **salute**, present arms, fire a salute, turn out the guard, roll out the red carpet, put out the bunting, raise the flag, greet, welcome, address

21 **command respect**, compel respect, inspire respect, impose, impress, rank high, stand high, awe, overawe, overwhelm
▶ *123 Importance*

ADVERBS

22 **respectfully**, with due respect, with all respect, with all due respect, deferentially, courteously, politely, graciously, reverentially, reverently, worshipfully, humbly, obsequiously

23 **saving your grace**, saving your reverence, excusing the liberty

668 Disrespect

Never speak disrespectfully of Society, Algernon. Only people who can't get into it do that. Oscar Wilde.

NOUNS

1 **disrespect**, disrespectfulness, lack of respect, want of respect, rudeness, discourtesy, impoliteness, unmannerliness, incivility, impertinence, impudence, insolence, irreverence, lack of veneration, blasphemy, scurrility, defamation, obloquy, opprobrium

▶ *659 Discourtesy; 660 Insolence; 678 Scornfulness*

2 **disesteem**, undervaluation, underestimation, disregard, neglect, dishonour, disrepute, disfavour, disapprobation, disapproval

▶ *468 Underestimation; 666 Negligence; 670 Disapproval*

3 **contempt**, contemptuousness, scorn, scornfulness, disdain, disdainfulness, superciliousness, superiority, loftiness, contumely, despite, low opinion, low esteem

4 **ridicule**, mockery, derision, sarcasm, irony, satire, imitation, impersonation, burlesque, caricature, lampoon, parody, takeoff (Inf), send-up (Inf)

▶ *125 Imitation; 621 Derision*

5 **insult**, aspersion, affront, snub, slight, rebuff, repulse, spurn, spurning, cold shoulder, slap in the face, backhanded compliment, left-handed compliment, cut, cutting remark, unkindest cut of all, putdown, the go-by (Inf)

6 **taunt**, jeer, mock, scoff, jibe (*or* gibe), dig, barb, sneer, snort, sniff, hiss, boo, catcall, hoot, raspberry, brickbat, banter, chaff, teasing, barracking (Inf), the bird (Inf), Bronx cheer (US inf)

▶ *670 Disapproval*

7 **sign of disrespect**, rude gesture, snook, V-sign, two-fingered salute, Harvey Smith salute, mooning

8 **indignity**, humiliation, degradation, mortification, chagrin, embarrassment, loss of face, egg on one's face (Inf)

▶ *623 Humility; 674 Modesty*

9 **butt**, dupe, target, victim, game, fair game, easy mark, Aunt Sally, fall guy, fool, everybody's fool, jest, joke, figure of fun, laughing stock, monkey, stooge (Inf), mug (Inf)

ADJECTIVES

10 **disrespectful**, wanting in respect, irreverent, irreverential, blasphemous, scurrilous, rude, discourteous, impolite, unmannered, uncivil, impertinent, cheeky, saucy, pert, impudent, insolent, insubordinate, brazen, brazen-faced, bold, audacious, forward, familiar, sassy (US inf), fresh (Inf)

▶ *659 Discourtesy; 660 Insolence*

11 **insulting**, abusive, offensive, pejorative, defamatory, opprobrious, contumacious, outrageous, snubbing, slighting, rebuffing, repulsing, spurning, backhanded, left-handed, cutting

▶ *678 Scornfulness*

12 **disregardful**, neglectful, negligent, dishonourable, disreputable, contemptible, despicable, worthless, shameful, base, low

▶ *236 Worthlessness; 666 Negligence; 812 Notoriety*

13 **contemptuous**, scornful, disdainful, pejorative, supercilious, lofty, haughty, arrogant, snobbish, snooty, contumelious, snotty (Inf)

14 **ridiculing**, mocking, derisive, derisory, sarcastic, ironic, satirical, imitating, burlesque, caricatural, parodic

▶ *125 Imitation; 621 Derision*

15 **taunting**, jeering, mocking, flouting, scoffing, scorning, jibing (*or* gibing), sneering, hissing, booing, catcalling, hooting, bantering, chaffing, teasing, barracking (Inf)

16 **humiliating**, degrading, mortifying, embarrassing

▶ *623 Humility; 674 Modesty*

17 **unrespected**, disrespected, unrevered, unreverenced, unvenerated, held in low esteem, trivialized, of no value, of no account

▶ *236 Worthlessness*

18 **undervalued**, underestimated, underrated, disparaged, belittled, denigrated, ignored, disregarded, unregarded, neglected

▶ *468 Underestimation; 666 Negligence*

VERBS

19 **disrespect**, have no respect for, have no regard for, have a low opinion of, hold in low esteem, hold in contempt, have no time for, rank low, hold cheap, underrate, underestimate, undervalue, perjorate, misprize

▶ *468 Underestimation*

20 **scorn**, disdain, despise, asperse, look down on, hold in contempt, disparage, belittle, trivialize, denigrate, depreciate, run down, defame, look down one's nose at (Inf)

▶ *678 Scornfulness*

21 **disregard**, ignore, neglect, dishonour, disgrace, shame, put to shame, drag in the mud

▶ *666 Negligence*

22 **show disrespect**, show no respect, be rude, lack courtesy, turn one's back on, tread on someone's toes, ride roughshod over, brush aside, shove aside, elbow aside, crowd, jostle, remain seated, keep one's hat on

▶ *659 Discourtesy; 660 Insolence*

23 **insult**, offend, affront, snub, slight, rebuff, repulse, spurn, give the cold shoulder, cold shoulder, cut dead, put down, slap in the face, add insult to injury, give the go-by (Inf), dump on (Inf)

24 **ridicule**, mock, deride, make fun of, satirize, imitate, caricature, make a laughing stock of, poke fun at, tease, send up (Inf), take off (Inf), pan (Inf), roast (Inf), rag (Inf), pull one's leg (Inf)

▶ *621 Derision*

25 **taunt**, jeer, mock, scoff, jibe (*or* gibe) at, dig at, sneer, snort, sniff, hiss, boo, catcall, hoot, blow a raspberry, heckle, rail at, laugh at, call names, twit, guy, give one the bird (Inf), barrack (Inf)

▶ *670 Disapproval*

26 **cock a snook**, thumb one's nose at, stick out one's tongue at, make faces at, spit at, moon

27 **desecrate**, despoil, defile, profane, commit sacrilege, cheapen, lower, degrade, humiliate, treat like dirt, treat like shit (Inf)

ADVERBS

28 **disrespectfully**, irreverently, rudely, discourteously, impertinently, impudently, insolently, sassily (US inf)

29 **mockingly**, derisively, sarcastically, satirically

30 contemptuously, scornfully, disdainfully, superciliously

669 Approval

NOUNS

1 approval, approbation, satisfaction, acceptance, adoption, sanction, countenance, blessing, agreement, formal agreement, permission, authorization, assent, consent, acquiescence, vote, imprimatur, endorsement, mandate, support, backing, advocacy, championship, patronage, recommendation, licence, rubber stamp, stamp of approval, seal of approval, nod of approval, nod, wink, OK (*or* okay) (Inf), go-ahead (Inf), thumbs up (Inf), green light (Inf)

▶ *392 Help; 609 Satisfaction; 747 Cooperation; 757 Permission*

2 admiration, respect, regard, esteem, credit, acknowledgment, recognition, appreciation, gratitude, honour, favour, good opinion, good books, good graces, popularity, prestige, liking, affection, love

▶ *593 Love; 595 Liking; 667 Respect*

3 praise, honour, laud, laudation, glory, glorification, extolment, exaltation, overpraise, overestimation, flattery, compliments, adulation, idolatry, deification, apotheosis, lionization, hero worship

▶ *467 Overestimation; 677 Flattery*

4 compliment, complimentary remark, praise, word of praise, congratulation, felicitation, pat on the back, good word, commendation, citation, honourable mention, accolade, kudos, glowing terms, eulogy, encomium, panegyric, tribute, favourable review, rave review, good notice, good press, bouquet, paean

5 acclaim, acclamation, plaudit, applause, round of applause, thunderous applause, clap, handclap, clapping, handclapping, hand, big hand, ovation, standing ovation, cheers, three cheers, cheering, huzzah (US), whistling, stamping, curtain call, encore

6 recommendation, testimonial, reference, character reference, credential, letter of introduction

7 advocate, champion, supporter, backer, patron, sponsor, recommender, favourable critic

8 admirer, supporter, follower, fan, supporters' club, fan club, hero-worshipper, rooter (Inf), groupie (Inf)

9 praiser, commender, laudator, eulogist, eulogizer, panegyrist, extoller

10 applauder, clapper, *claqueur* (Fr), *claque* (Fr), cheerer, cheerleader

VERBS

11 approve, approve of, hold with, like, think well of, think highly of, think the best of, have no fault to find, find no fault, admire, respect, regard highly, hold in high regard, esteem, value, prize

▶ *235 Worth; 595 Liking; 667 Respect*

12 accept, pass, adopt, sanction, countenance, give one's blessing, agree, grant permission, authorize, ratify, assent, give one's assent, consent, give one's consent, acquiesce, condone, endorse, license, give the stamp (*or* seal *or* nod) of approval, rubber stamp, nod, wink, tip the wink (Inf), OK (*or* okay) (Inf), give the OK (*or* okay) (Inf), give the go-ahead (Inf), give the thumbs up (Inf), give the green light (Inf)

▶ *757 Permission*

13 support, back, lend one's backing to, uphold, advocate, champion, recommend, favour, commend, speak well of, speak highly of, speak up for, put in a good word for, give a reference for, act as referee for

14 praise, laud, glorify, honour, exalt, extol, magnify, overpraise, overestimate, flatter, compliment, adulate, idolize, deify, apotheosize, lionize, hero-worship

▶ *467 Overestimation; 677 Flattery*

15 compliment, pay a compliment, praise, congratulate, pat on the back, give a bouquet (*or* posy), take one's hat off to, doff one's hat to, hand it to, commend, eulogize, panegyrize, pay tribute to, sing the praises of, sound the praises of, wax lyrical, trumpet, praise to the skies, cry up, boost, puff, puff up, hype, hype up, rave about (Inf)

16 acclaim, hail, applaud, clap, clap one's hands, give a big hand, give a standing ovation, cheer, give three cheers, huzzah (US), whistle, stamp, shout for more, encore, shout bravo, roar one's approval, bring the house down, raise the roof, throw flowers, root for (Inf)

17 meet with approval, meet with approbation, win praise, find favour, gain credit, satisfy, pass, pass muster, pass the test, come up to scratch, gain one's spurs

▶ *246 Success; 609 Satisfaction*

ADJECTIVES

18 approving, satisfied, content, appreciatory, appreciative, grateful, approbatory, respectful, well-inclined, favourable, complimentary, commendatory, laudatory, admiring, eulogistic, encomiastic, panegyric, acclamatory, fulsome, overpraising, overappreciative, uncritical, undiscriminating, flattering, adulatory, idolatrous, lionizing, hero-worshipping

▶ *595 Liking; 609 Satisfaction; 671 Gratitude; 677 Flattery*

19 supporting, supportive, backing, advocating, championing, recommending, in favour, for, pro

▶ *392 Help*

20 acclamatory, applauding, clapping, cheering

21 praiseworthy, laudable, commendable, worthy, estimable, creditable, admirable, unimpeachable, meritorious, deserving, welldeserving

▶ *235 Worth*

22 approvable, satisfactory, acceptable, passable, permissible, worthwhile

23 approved, passed, tested, accepted, supported, backed, endorsed, favoured, recommended

24 admired, respected, well thought of, popular, in demand, in good odour, in high esteem

▶ *667 Respect*

ADVERBS

25 approvingly, admiringly, with compliments, with praise

26 approvably, satisfactorily, acceptably, passably, to approval, to satisfaction

INTERJECTIONS

27 bravo!, encore!, more!, *bis*! (Fr), well done!, congratulations!, hear hear!, hurrah!

670 Disapproval

NOUNS

1 disapproval, disapprobation, dissatisfaction, discontent, discontentment, discontentedness, unhappiness, displeasure, disfavour, disgruntlement, indignation, distaste, dislike, unpopularity

▶ *596 Dislike; 602 Sorrow; 606 Dissatisfaction*

2 disrespect, disesteem, disrepute, contempt, despite, low opinion, poor opinion, low esteem (*or* estimation), dim view

▶ *668 Disrespect; 812 Notoriety*

3 nonacceptance, rejection, refusal, ostracism, cold shoulder, sending to Coventry, blackballing, ban, bar, boycott, veto, negative veto, thumbs down (Inf), red light (Inf)

▶ *128 Exclusion; 399 Veto; 470 Rejection; 708 Negation; 709 Refusal*

4 disagreement, dissension, opposition, hostility, objection, complaint, exception, contradiction, cavil

▶ *113 Opposition; 701 Argument; 751 Disagreement*

5 criticism, hostile criticism, critical remarks, critical review, unfavourable review, bad press, bad notice, dispraise, brickbat, rap, flak (Inf), slating (Inf), panning (Inf), knock (Inf), slam (Inf)

▶ *678 Scornfulness*

6 fault-finding, carping, cavilling, pettifoggery, captiousness, hair-splitting, niggling, quibbling, fastidiousness, fussing, pestering, nagging, henpecking, overcriticalness, hypercriticism, hypercriticalness, censoriousness, crabbing (Inf), nit-picking (Inf)

7 blame, censure, reprobation, recrimination, complaint, charge, accusation, condemnation, denunciation, denouncement, impeachment, castigation, chastisement, reproof, reprehension, reprimand, rebuke, reproach, stricture, upbraiding, scolding, chiding, admonishment, admonition, warning, lesson, lecture, sermon, set-down, taking to task, hauling (*or* raking) over the coals, home truths, piece of one's mind, rap over the knuckles, black mark, telling off (Inf), ticking-off (Inf), talking-to (Inf), flea in one's ear (Inf), earful (Inf), wigging (Inf), carpeting (Inf), dressing-down (Inf), rocket (Inf)

▶ *711 Warning; 715 Accusation; 814 Punishment*

8 berating, railing, abuse, tirade, diatribe, onslaught, attack, verbal attack, harsh words, rough edge of one's tongue, tongue-lashing, laying into, pitching into, lambasting, vituperation, execration, revilement, vilification, skinning alive (Inf), roasting (Inf)

▶ *381 Attack; 594 Hate*

9 show of disapproval, display of disapproval, slow handclap, hiss, hissing, boo, catcall, raspberry, taunt, jeer, sneer, derision, ridicule, protest, clamour, outcry

▶ *621 Derision; 668 Disrespect; 753 Protest*

10 disapproving look, dirty look, black look, reproving look (*or* glance), raised eyebrow, glare, silent reproach, frown, scowl

11 disapprover, objector, opposer, opponent, attacker, prude, puritan, censor, censurer, castigator

12 critic, criticizer, fault-finder, pettifogger, quibbler, knocker (Inf), nit-picker (Inf)

13 pessimist, misery, killjoy, moaner, grouser, wet blanket (Inf), spoilsport (Inf), grouch (Inf), sourpuss (Inf)

▶ *602 Sorrow; 611 Despair*

VERBS

14 disapprove, disapprove of, not approve, express disapproval, express disapprobation, disfavour, view with disfavour, take a dim view of, dislike, not admire, have a low (*or* poor) opinion of, think little of, hold in low esteem (*or* estimation), hold in contempt, have no respect for, have no regard for, think ill of, discountenance, look down on, frown on, look down one's nose at, turn up one's nose at

▶ *596 Dislike; 668 Disrespect*

15 withhold approval, say no to, not hear of, turn down, reject, refuse, exclude, ostracize, cold shoulder, give the cold shoulder, send to Coventry, black, blacklist, blackball, ban, bar, boycott, veto, disallow, prohibit, give the thumbs down (Inf), turn thumbs down on (Inf), give the red light (Inf)

▶ *128 Exclusion; 399 Veto; 470 Rejection; 709 Refusal*

16 disagree, oppose, object to, remonstrate, complain, show hostility, set oneself against, set one's face against

▶ *113 Opposition; 751 Disagreement*

17 criticize, fault, deplore, deprecate, depreciate, decry, denigrate, disparage, dispraise, belittle, cry down, run down, tear apart, hand out brickbats, snipe at, rap, knock (Inf), slate (Inf), pan (Inf), slam (Inf)

▶ *678 Scornfulness*

18 find fault, carp, carp at, cavil, derogate, split hairs, niggle, quibble, pick holes, pick to pieces, pester, nag, henpeck, crab (Inf), bug (Inf), hassle (Inf), nit-pick (Inf)

19 blame, hold responsible, accuse, charge, reprobate, recriminate, condemn, denunciate, denounce, impeach, incriminate

▶ *715 Accusation*

20 censure, castigate, chastise, reprove, reprehend, reprimand, rebuke, reproach, upbraid, scold, chide, admonish, warn, lecture, deliver a sermon (*or* lesson), set down, take to task, haul (*or* rake) over the coals, give a piece of one's mind, rap over the knuckles, give a black mark, call to account, dress down (Inf), give a dressing-down (Inf), tell off (Inf), tick off (Inf), give an earful (Inf), give a wigging (Inf), carpet (Inf), come down on like a ton of bricks (Inf)

▶ *711 Warning; 814 Punishment*

21 berate, rail, rail (*or* rage) against, assail, attack, abuse, give the rough edge of one's tongue, lash, tongue-lash, lay into, pitch into, lambast (*or* lambaste), read the riot act, throw the book at, give one what for (Inf), bawl out (Inf), skin alive (Inf), give a roasting (Inf)

22 vituperate, execrate, revile, pour vitriol, curse, vilify, blacken, defame

▶ *594 Hate; 678 Scornfulness*

23 show disapproval, tut-tut, frown, scowl, raise one's eyebrows, hiss, boo, catcall, jeer, heckle, shout down, throw mud, throw stones, pelt with rotten eggs, deride, ridicule, mob, lynch

▶ *621 Derision; 668 Disrespect*

24 be open to criticism, get a bad press, meet with disapproval, get a bad name, take the blame, take the rap (Inf), carry the can (Inf)

ADJECTIVES

25 disapproving, unapproving, disapprobatory, dissatisfied, discontented, unhappy, disappointed, displeased, disgruntled, indignant, disrespectful

▶ *596 Dislike; 602 Sorrow; 606 Dissatisfaction; 668 Disrespect*

26 disagreeing, dissenting, opposing, hostile, contradicting, contradictory, against, agin, objecting, protesting

▶ *751 Disagreement*

27 critical, dispraising, abusive, execratory, vituperative, disparaging, deprecatory, damaging, defamatory, unfavourable, poor, uncomplimentary

▶ *678 Scornfulness*

28 fault-finding, captious, carping, cavilling, pettifogging, hair-splitting, nagging, niggling, quibbling, fastidious, overcritical, hypercritical, ultracritical, censorious, crabbing (Inf), nit-picking (Inf)

29 blaming, blameful, accusatory, accusing, judgmental, damning, condemning, condemnatory, denunciatory, recriminative

▶ *715 Accusation*

30 censuring, castigatory, chastising, reprimanding, rebuking, reproaching, reproachful, upbraiding, chiding, scolding, admonitory, stern

31 disapproved, unapproved, rejected, refused, unaccepted, opposed, excluded, ostracized, blacked, blacklisted, blackballed, banned, barred, boycotted, vetoed

▶ *128 Exclusion; 399 Veto; 470 Rejection; 709 Refusal*

32 unsatisfactory, unacceptable, unpraiseworthy, uncommendable, not to be recommended, found wanting, not good enough, inadequate, insufficient

▶ *218 Insufficiency; 606 Dissatisfaction*

33 criticized, dispraised, uncommended, run down, given a bad press, panned (Inf), slated (Inf)

34 censured, castigated, chastised, reprimanded, rebuked, reproached, upbraided, scolded, admonished, lambasted, berated, assailed, attacked, abused, given the rough edge of one's tongue, laid into, skinned alive (Inf)

▶ *381 Attack*

35 hissed, booed, taunted, jeered, sneered at, derided, ridiculed

36 blameworthy, blamable, to blame, responsible, culpable, criminal, guilty, open to criticism, reprehensible, objectionable, impeachable

ADVERBS

37 disapprovingly, critically, censoriously, reproachfully

671 Gratitude

Thank me no thankings, nor proud me no prouds. William Shakespeare.

NOUNS

1 gratitude, gratefulness, thankfulness, appreciation, appreciativeness, obligation, sense (*or* feeling) of obligation, sense (*or* feeling) of indebtedness, awareness, mindfulness, cognizance

▶ *483 Motive; 601 Celebration; 669 Approval*

2 thanks, thank you, grateful thanks, hearty thanks, sincere thanks, thanksgiving, Eucharist, blessing, benediction, Magnificat, Te Deum, prayer, prayer of thanks, paean, praise, hymn, grace, grace before meals

3 recognition, acknowledgment, credit, credit line, credits, by-line, thank-you letter, thank-you card (*or* note), bread-and-butter letter, thank offering, thank-you gift (*or* present), reward, tip, bonus, gratuity, token of one's gratitude, recognition of one's services, leaving present, retirement gift, parting gift, gold watch, vote of thanks, tribute, praise, testimonial, applause, round of applause, golden handshake (Inf)

▶ *813 Reward*

ADJECTIVES

4 grateful, thankful, appreciative, pleased, gratified, pleased as punch, indebted, beholden, obliged, much obliged, under obligation, obligated, mindful of obligations, in one's debt, owing a favour

5 thanking, blessing, praising, crediting, giving credit, cognizant of, acknowledging

VERBS

6 be grateful, be thankful, feel (*or* have) an obligation, appreciate, express gratitude, thank, give thanks, express thanks, render thanks, return thanks, say thank you, receive with grateful thanks, receive with open arms, return a favour, show gratitude, show appreciation, reward, tip, give a bonus, acknowledge, express acknowledgments, pay tribute, praise, recognize, applaud, give a (big) hand, give three cheers, give credit, attribute

7 give thanks, say grace, bless, say a prayer of thanks, thank (*or* bless) one's lucky stars, count one's blessings, thank God, praise heaven, be thankful for small mercies

ADVERBS

8 gratefully, with gratitude, thankfully, with (special) thanks, appreciatively, to express appreciation(s), with a grateful heart, from a sense of obligation, in recognition of one's service(s), as a token of one's gratitude

INTERJECTIONS

9 thank you!, thank you very much!, bless you!, much obliged!, thank heaven!, thank God!, thank goodness!, heaven be praised!, Allah be praised!, gramercy! (Lit), thanks! (Inf), many thanks! (Inf), thanks a lot! (Inf), ta! (Inf), cheers! (Inf)

672 Ingratitude

And having looked to government for bread, on the very first scarcity they will turn and bite the hand that fed them. Edmund Burke.

Blow, blow, thou winter wind,
Thou art not so unkind
As man's ingratitude. William Shakespeare.

NOUNS

1 ingratitude, lack of gratitude, ungratefulness, thanklessness, unthankfulness, lack of appreciation, unappreciation, unappreciativeness, ungraciousness, thoughtlessness, discourteousness, forgetfulness, inconsiderateness, rudeness, selfishness, nonrecognition, nonacknowledgment, taking for granted, no thanks, no reward, lack of (due) credit, grudging thanks, half-hearted thanks, thankless task

▶ *592 Insensitivity; 659 Discourtesy*

2 thankless person, unappreciative person, ingrate (Lit), ungrateful wretch, ungrateful yob (Inf)

ADJECTIVES

3 **ungrateful**, unthankful, unappreciative, ungracious, discourteous, ill-mannered, bad-mannered, forgetful, thoughtless, inconsiderate, unmindful, heedless, rude, selfish

4 **unthanked**, unrewarded, unacknowledged, unrecognized, uncredited, unrequited, forgotten, neglected, ignored

5 **thankless**, unrewarding, useless, fruitless, unprofitable, without thanks, without appreciation, without acknowledgment, without (due) credit

VERBS

6 **be ungrateful**, be unappreciative, fail to appreciate, see no reason to thank, give no credit, feel no obligation, be forgetful, forget, unrequite, be thoughtless, take for granted, be rude, begrudge, ignore, neglect, look a gift horse in the mouth, bite the hand that feeds one

ADVERBS

7 **ungratefully**, unappreciatively, without appreciation, ungraciously, discourteously, forgetfully, thoughtlessly, inconsiderately, heedlessly, rudely, selfishly, thanklessly, without thanks, without acknowledgment, without (due) credit, uselessly, fruitlessly, unprofitably

673 Vanity

We are so vain that we even care for the opinion of those we don't care for. Marie Ebner von Eschenbach.

NOUNS

1 **vanity**, vainness, immodesty, overproudness, insubstantiality, vain pride, empty pride, conceit, conceitedness, self-importance, swollen headedness, big-headedness, megalomania, pomposity, grandiloquence

▶ *622 Pride*

2 **self-satisfaction**, self-congratulation, self-assurance, smugness, self-approbation, self-content, complacency, self-sufficiency, solipsism

3 **cockiness**, perkiness, bumptiousness, pertness, brazenness, shamelessness, flagrancy, aggressiveness, obtrusiveness, brashness, flashiness, bombast, flamboyance, self-confidence, self-assertiveness, swank, airs and graces, pompousness, loftiness, high-and-mightiness, delusions of grandeur, high-falutin ways (Inf)

4 **self-admiration**, self-esteem, self-praise, self-applause, self-flattery, self-worship, self-love, self-endearment, *amour propre* (Fr), self-infatuation, narcissism, narcism, vaingloriousness

5 **self-interest**, selfishness, egotism, egoism, egoisticalness, egotisticalness, self-centredness, me-ism, Thatcher's children

6 **boastfulness**, pride, conceit, arrogance, bravado, machismo, heroics, sensationalism, side, showing off, exhibitionism, demonstrativeness, self-conceit, self-display, ostentation, showiness, dramatics, histrionics, theatricality

7 **vain person**, egotist, show-off, swank, self-admirer, exhibitionist, peacock, turkey cock, Narcissus, braggart, know-all, know-it-all, bighead, toffeenose, swollen head, God's gift to women, Mr Clever, smarty pants (Inf), Miss Clever, pompous twit, stuffed shirt, empty head, fop, smart aleck (Inf), clever clogs (Inf), clever dick (Inf), wiseacre (Inf), wise guy (Inf), smartarse (Inf), drama queen (Inf)

ADJECTIVES

8 **vain**, immodest, overproud, insubstantial, conceited, self-important, arrogant, stuck-up, snooty, big-headed, swollen-headed, megalomaniac

9 **self-satisfied**, self-congratulatory, self-assured, self-contented, complacent, contented, smug, self-sufficient

10 **self-admiring**, self-worshipping, self-loving, self-endearing, self-infatuated, narcissistic, self-glorifying, supercilious, self-respecting, vainglorious, smug, self-approving, stuck on oneself, impressed (*or* pleased) with oneself, all wrapped up in oneself

11 **cocky**, perky, pert, bumptious, pompous, aggressive, self-confident, self-assertive, swanky, pretentious, affected, foppish, obtrusive, full of oneself, overclever, too clever by half, too smart for one's own good

12 **self-interested**, selfish, egotistic, egotistical, egoistic, egoistical, egocentric, solipsistic, self-centred, self-styled

13 **boastful**, proud, prideful, arrogant, exhibitionistic, self-conceited, ostentatious, self-opinionated, stuck-up, too big for one's boots, peacockish, know-it-all, overwise, wise in one's own conceit, dogmatic, opinionated, puffed up, blatant, swaggering, pompous, pretentious, putting on airs, affected, smart-alecky (Inf), smart-arsed (Inf)

14 **opinionated**, dogmatic, too big for one's boots

VERBS

15 **be vain**, have a high opinion of oneself, be stuck on oneself, be impressed with oneself, think a lot of oneself, flatter oneself, be puffed up, think one knows it all, fish for compliments, be pleased with oneself, be full of oneself, be wrapped up in oneself, set a high value on oneself, think oneself the cat's pyjamas (*or* whiskers), think oneself God Almighty, think oneself God's gift to mankind, think well of oneself, think one is it, have no self-doubt, love the sound of one's own voice, give oneself airs, get above oneself, give oneself a pat on the back

16 **show off**, feel pride, blow one's own trumpet, boast, hug oneself, swank, strut, put on airs, talk big, talk for effect, put on side, show one's paces, preen oneself, push oneself forward, go to one's head

17 **be affected**, dress up, doll up, play the fop, dandify, toot one's own horn

18 **make conceited**, fill with conceit, inflate, puff up with pride, turn one's head

ADVERBS

19 **vainly**, immodestly, conceitedly, vaingloriously, self-importantly

20 **smugly**, complacently, self-assuredly, self-congratulatory, self-sufficiently, self-contentedly

21 **cockily**, perkily, pertly, bumptiously, aggressively, self-confidently, self-assertively, obtrusively, blatantly, flamboyantly, swankily, pretentiously, affectedly, foppishly, superciliously

22 **selfishly**, egotistically, egocentrically, solipsistically

23 **boastfully**, proudly, arrogantly, conceitedly, ostentatiously

24 **pompously**, dogmatically, grandiloquently, bombastically, theatrically

674 Modesty

She just wore
Enough for modesty – no more. Robert Williams Buchanan.

Be modest! It is the kind of pride least likely to offend. Jules Renard.

NOUNS

1 modesty, meekness, humility, unpretentiousness, unassumingness, unassuming nature, unostentatious, unobtrusiveness, unboastfulness

► *623 Humility*

2 blushing, blush, flushing, flush, colouring, reddening, crimsoning, red face

3 bashfulness, coyness, prudishness, demureness, demurity, shamefacedness, shamefastness, skittishness, chastity, virtue

4 shyness, timidity, timidness, diffidence, self-consciousness, retiring, disposition, timorousness, embarrassment, stage fright

5 self-deprecation, self-effacement, distrust, undervaluing the self, self-doubt, lack of self-confidence, weak ego

6 reserve, restraint, reticence, constraint, backwardness, retiring disposition, reluctance

7 modest person, mouse, shrinking violet, doormat, stammerer, stutterer, blusher

ADJECTIVES

8 modest, meek, humble, unpretentious, unpretending, unassuming, unostentatious, unobtrusive, unboastful, unimposing, unimpressive, unaspiring

9 blushing, flushed, red, ruddy, reddening, crimsoning, nervous, awkward, shamefaced, sheepish

10 bashful, coy, prudish, shockable, demure, demuring, chaste, pure, shamefaced, confused, chaste, virtuous

11 shy, overshy, timid, diffident, self-conscious, retiring, timorous, embarrassed, frightened, mouselike, shrinking, unimportant, unsure of oneself, inarticulate, stammering

12 self-deprecating, self-effacing, self-doubting, unambitious, deprecating, self-distrustful

13 reserved, restrained, reticent, constrained, backward, retiring, reluctant, unseen, unheard, quiet

VERBS

14 be modest, deprecate oneself, show moderation, ration oneself, be temperate, not blow one's own trumpet, not push oneself forward, yield to others, play second fiddle, know one's place, not look for praise

15 escape notice, avoid, hide one's light under a bushel, take a back seat, keep a low profile, keep in (*or* merge into) the background, shun the limelight, hang back, shrink back, hesitate, crawl (*or* creep) into one's shell, be a back-room boy (*or* girl), blush unseen, shrink from public gaze, retire

16 be self-conscious, blush, flush, crimson, colour up, squirm, turn red, stammer, die of embarrassment, feel shame, die of shame

ADVERBS

17 modestly, quietly, demurely, meekly, humbly, unpretentiously, unobtrusively, without ceremony, without fuss (*or* frills), privately

18 shyly, timidly, bashfully, diffidently, timorously, chastely, virtuously, coyly, shamefacedly, shamefastly, sheepishly, blushingly, with downcast eyes

675 Vulgarity

The aristocratic pleasure of displeasing is not the only delight that bad taste can yield. One can love a certain kind of vulgarity for its own sake. Aldous Huxley.

NOUNS

1 tastelessness, no taste, bad taste, coarseness, gaudiness, showiness, glitz (Inf)

2 tawdriness, shoddiness, tackiness, cheapness

3 grossness, impropriety, unseemliness, ill-breeding, commonness, incivility, bad form, incorrectness, bad manners, boorishness, discourtesy, coarseness, crudeness, loutishness (Inf)

4 inelegance, uncouthness, solecism, putting one's foot in it

5 vulgar person, cad, bounder, slob, Philistine, barbarian, boor, parvenu, nouveau riche, vulgarian, prole, pleb, savage, yokel, yob (Inf), lout (Inf), show-off (Inf)

6 vulgar herd, the people, hoi polloi, the great unwashed (Inf), the proles, rank and file, rabble, riff-raff, scum, Tom, Dick, and Harry (Inf)

ADJECTIVES

7 vulgar, coarse, gross, cheap, ill-bred, infra dig, *infra dignitatem* (L), inelegant, ungentlemanly, unladylike, unfeminine, non-U (Inf), plebeian, plebby (Inf), loud, showy, meretricious, ostentatious, garish, Day-Glo™, gaudy, tawdry, glitzy

8 discourteous, boorish, uncouth, unseemly, unrefined, gauche, awkward, disorderly, unpolished, tasteless, unfashionable, uncultured, barbarian, parvenu, nouveau riche

9 ribald, bawdy, Rabelaisian, provocative, immoral, blue, unmentionable, unquotable, unprintable, filthy, obscene, smutty, barbarius, lewd, indecent, scatological, in the worst possible taste, in bad taste

VERBS

10 vulgarize, coarsen, cheapen, lower, lower the tone, commercialize

676 Affectation

Don't you sit there and sigh gal like you was Lady Nevershit. Arnold Wesker.

NOUNS

1 affectedness, pretentiousness, artifice, histrionics, theatricality, euphuism, showmanship, euphemism, sanctimoniousness, sanctimony, irony, speciosity, speciarness, deceptiveness, puffery (Inf), exhibition, artifice, pretension, pretence, falsity, false display, posture, pose, delusions of grandeur, airs and graces (Inf)

2 pretender, humbug (Inf), actor, bluffer, deceiver,

poseur, poser (Inf), charlatan, attitudinizer, ironist, hypocrite, swank (Inf), exhibitionist, show-off (Inf), Tartuffe, drama queen (Inf)

ADJECTIVES

3 **affected**, precious, pretentious, mannered, chichi (Inf), self-conscious, conceited, artificial, unnatural, stilted, sanctimonious, stagey, euphemistic, showy, meretricious, theatrical, histrionic, puffed up, ironic, ironical, boastful, swanky, mouthy (Inf), puffy (Inf), specious, tongue-in-cheek (Inf), all wind and water (Inf), all piss and wind (Inf), all mouth and trousers (Inf)

VERBS

4 **be affected**, affect, attitudinize, pose, put on airs, pretend, assume, posture, bluff, show off, play-act, play to the gallery, put on airs and graces, swank

ADVERBS

5 **affectedly**, pretentiously, self-consciously, theatrically, histrionically

677 Flattery

It is happy for you that you possess the talent of flattering with delicacy. May I ask whether these pleasing attentions proceed from the impulse of the moment, or are the result of previous study? Jane Austen.

NOUNS

1 **flattery**, adulation, compliments, praise, overpraise, excessive praise, overlaudation, overcommendation, hagiography, panegyric, hype, insincere praise, insincerity, hypocrisy, eyewash (Inf)

► *669 Approval; 700 Deception; 727 Exaggeration*

2 **blarney**, honeyed words, honeyed phrases, salve, sweet-talk (Inf), soft soap (Inf), flannel (Inf), bunkum (Inf)

3 **cajolery**, wheedling, inveiglement, blandishments, ingratiation, getting round (Inf)

► *480 Persuasion*

4 **unctuousness**, unctuosity, oiliness, smarm, smarminess, sliminess

5 **sycophancy**, servility, toadyism, fawning, bootlicking, backscratching, arse-licking (Inf)

6 **flatterer**, adulator, charmer, smooth talker, cajoler, wheedler, inveigler

7 **sycophant**, obligor, toady, fawner, yes-man, bootlicker, backscratcher, Uriah Heep, crawler (Inf), creep (Inf), hanger-on (Inf), arse-licker (Inf), brown-nose (Inf)

VERBS

8 **flatter**, adulate, compliment, praise, overpraise, overlaud, overcommend, overesteem, overestimate, hype, puff, overdo it (Inf), lay it on (Inf), lay it on thick (Inf), lay it on with a trowel (Inf)

► *467 Overestimation; 547 Beautification; 669 Approval; 727 Exaggeration*

9 **blarney**, sugar, charm, smarm, oil, oil the tongue, flatter to deceive, sweet-talk, soft-soap (Inf), butter (Inf), butter up (Inf), soften up (Inf), flannel (Inf)

10 **cajole**, wheedle, inveigle, blandish, coax, court, ingratiate oneself, curry favour, suck up to (Inf), make up to (Inf), get round (Inf)

11 **be sycophantic**, insinuate oneself, toady, fawn, fawn on, creep, crawl, bootlick, backscratch, arse-lick (Inf), brown-nose (Inf)

► *664 Servility*

ADJECTIVES

12 **flattering**, adulatory, complimentary, laudatory, praising, insincere, hypocritical, tongue-in-cheek

► *547 Beautification; 669 Approval; 700 Deception*

13 **honeyed**, sugary, saccharine, saccharine sweet, blarneying, honey-tongued, smooth-tongued, smooth-spoken, buttery (Inf), sweet-talking (Inf), soft-soaping (Inf)

14 **cajoling**, wheedling, inveigling, blandishing, coaxing, ingratiating

15 **unctuous**, oily, smarmy, slimy, greasy

16 **sycophantic**, servile, obsequious, toadyish, fawning, creeping, crawling, bootlicking, backscratching, arse-licking (Inf)

► *664 Servility*

ADVERBS

17 **flatteringly**, with honeyed words, unctuously, smarmily, sycophantically, obsequiously

678 Scornfulness

The pleasure of criticizing robs us of the pleasure of being moved by some very fine things. Jean de La Bruyère.

NOUNS

1 **disparagement**, deprecation, depreciation, decrial, detraction, derogation, denigration, belittlement, slighting, crying down, underestimation, understatement, faint praise, lukewarm support, fault-finding, nit-picking (Inf), running down (Inf), putting down (Inf)

► *468 Underestimation*

2 **criticism**, hostile criticism, critical remarks, bad review, bad press, brickbat (Inf), flak (Inf), knocking (Inf), panning (Inf), slating (Inf), slam (Inf), hatchet job (Inf)

► *670 Disapproval*

3 **defamation**, obloquy, defamation of character, character assassination, slander, libel, traducement, calumny, obloquy, smear campaign, muckraking, mudslinging, scandal, gossip, malicious gossip, backbiting

► *381 Attack; 718 Misrepresentation*

4 **aspersion**, insinuation, innuendo, slur, smear, disparaging remark, defamatory remark, slighting remark, poison-pen letter

► *715 Accusation; 812 Notoriety*

5 **scorn**, contempt, disdain, derision, revilement, vilification, abuse, insult, degradation, debasement, scurrility, defilement, blackening, tarnishing

► *621 Derision*

6 **ridicule**, lampoon, satire, pasquinade, burlesque, skit, squib, caricature, send-up (Inf), takeoff (Inf)

► *668 Disrespect*

7 **disparager**, depreciator, decrier, detractor, derogator, belittler, critic, hostile critic, hatchet man (Inf), knocker (Inf)

8 **defamer**, slanderer, libeller, muckraker, mudslinger, backbiter, smircher, smearer, gossiper, gossip, scandalmonger, gossip columnist

9 **ridiculer**, lampooner, lampoonist, satirist, caricaturist, mocker

VERBS

10 **disparage**, deprecate, depreciate, decry, detract, derogate, denigrate, belittle, slight, cry down, minimize, play down, underestimate, underrate, undervalue, understate, run down (Inf), put down (Inf), dis (Inf), do down (Inf), sell short (Inf)

▶ *367 Lowering; 468 Underestimation*

11 **criticize**, find fault, dispraise, put down, knock (Inf), pan (Inf), slate (Inf), slam (Inf), pull to pieces (Inf), tear to shreds (Inf), nit-pick (Inf), slag off (Inf)

▶ *670 Disapproval*

12 **defame**, slander, libel, traduce, calumniate, malign, damage, compromise, discredit, dishonour, bring into disrepute, blacken, tarnish, sully, soil, smear, besmear, smirch, besmirch, bespatter, drag through the gutter, drag through the mud, throw mud, sling mud, muckrake, backbite, stab in the back, bad-mouth (US inf)

▶ *812 Notoriety*

13 **vilify**, revile, abuse, degrade, debase, defile, asperse, cast aspersions on, insinuate, slur, cast a slur on, whisper, gossip, talk about, talk about behind one's back, speak ill of

14 **ridicule**, lampoon, satirize, caricature, make fun of, poke fun at, mock, guy, scoff, sneer, deride, scorn, send up (Inf), take off (Inf)

▶ *621 Derision; 668 Disrespect*

ADJECTIVES

15 **disparaging**, deprecatory, depreciatory, decrying, detractory, derogatory, pejorative, denigratory, belittling, slighting, minimizing, critical, knocking (Inf), nit- picking (Inf)

▶ *670 Disapproval*

16 **defamatory**, slanderous, libellous, calumnious, calumniatory, scandalous, scurrilous, abusive, insulting, aspersive, insinuating, gossiping, whispering, mudslinging, smearing, besmirching, blackening, tarnishing, damaging, injurious, destructive, venomous, caustic, bitter, backbiting, snide, catty (Inf), bitchy (Inf)

▶ *812 Notoriety*

17 **scornful**, contemptuous, contumelious, sarcastic, ridiculing, mocking, scoffing, sneering, derisive

▶ *621 Derision; 668 Disrespect*

ADVERBS

18 **disparagingly**, derogatorily, pejoratively, slightingly, critically, slanderously, libellously, scornfully, contemptuously, derisively

679 Generosity

A bit of fragrance always clings to the hand that gives you roses.
Chinese Proverb.

ADJECTIVES

1 **generous**, liberal, open-handed, hospitable, giving, unstinting, ungrudging, beneficent, munificent, bountiful, bounteous, lavish, princely, handsome

2 **magnanimous**, charitable, benevolent, humanitarian, philanthropic

3 **abundant**, plentiful, ample, lavish, more than enough, copious, overflowing, profuse, superabundant

▶ *219 Excess*

4 **big**, roomy, large, capacious, spacious, commodious

NOUNS

5 **generosity**, liberality, open-handedness, beneficence, charity, bounty, bounteousness, munificence, hospitality

6 **magnanimity**, charitableness, benevolence, philanthropy

7 **gift**, contribution, subscription, donation, covenant, bonus, tip, hand-out, alms, baksheesh

▶ *608 Relief; 780 Money; 785 Payment*

8 **abundance**, plenty, plenteousness, profusion, superabundance

9 **generous person**, benefactor, backer, donor, donator, contributor, subscriber, philanthropist, humanitarian, good Samaritan, willing giver, Lady Bountiful, Father Christmas, Santa Claus, fairy godmother, angel (Inf)

VERBS

10 **be generous**, give generously, give freely, give away, keep open house, spare no expense, pay towards, give with both hands, tip well, splash out (Inf), cough up (Inf)

11 **give**, contribute, subscribe, donate, covenant, bequeath, endow, finance, fund, aid, support

▶ *413 Support*

ADVERBS

12 **generously**, liberally, freely, lavishly, copiously, amply, abundantly, plentifully, ungrudgingly, with open hands, with no expense spared

680 Thrift

I knew once a very covetous, sordid fellow, who used to say, 'Take care of the pence, for the pounds will take care of themselves.'
Earl of Chesterfield.

NOUNS

1 **thrift**, thriftiness, economy, good husbandry, good management, good housekeeping, carefulness, prudence, frugality, austerity, cheeseparing

▶ *682 Meanness*

2 **act of thrift**, economy drive, retrenchment, cutting back, cutback, budget, spending plan

3 **saver**, economizer, scrimper

ADJECTIVES

4 **thrifty**, economical, unlavish, unwasteful, conserving, saving, labour-saving, time-saving, money-saving, good with money, canny, careful, prudent, economizing, sparing, frugal, Spartan, austere, meagre, scrimpy, cheeseparing

VERBS

5 **be thrifty**, make do, budget, live on a budget, live (*or* keep) within one's means, make both ends meet, conserve, husband, husband one's resources

6 **save**, economize, keep costs down, retrench, cut down, cut costs, cut back, cut corners, scrimp, scrape, cut one's coat according to one's cloth (Inf), tighten one's belt (Inf), batten down the hatches (Inf)

ADVERBS

7 **economically**, thriftily, prudently, frugally, with a sparing hand

681 Extravagance

I expect I shall have to die beyond my means. Oscar Wilde.

...we owe something to extravagance, for thrift and adventure seldom go hand in hand. Jennie Jerome Churchill.

ADJECTIVES

1 **extravagant**, wasteful, lavish, uneconomic, spendthrift, prodigal, profligate, thriftless, unthrifty, improvident, easy come easy go (Inf)

▶ *679 Generosity*

2 **unrestrained**, excessive, inordinate, immoderate, extreme, wild, exaggerated, hyperbolic, magnified, profuse, showy, ostentatious, preposterous, outrageous, fantastical

▶ *213 Increase; 219 Excess*

3 **costly**, high-priced, expensive, dear, overpriced, exorbitant, inflationary, sky-high, unaffordable, prohibitive, extortionate, steep (Inf), pricey (Inf), going through the roof (Inf)

NOUNS

4 **extravagance**, prodigality, lavishness, wastefulness, profligacy, conspicuous consumption, unthriftiness, squandering, improvidence, spending spree

5 **unrestrainedness**, immoderation, exaggeration, hyperbole, profusion, superfluity, dissipation, extremes

6 **spendthrift**, prodigal, prodigal son, profligate, wastrel, squanderer, waster, big spender (Inf), spender (Inf), Mrs (*or* Mr) Spend Spend Spend (Inf)

VERBS

7 **waste**, squander, fritter, fritter away, misspend, dissipate, lavish, go through, use up, exhaust, pour down the drain (Inf), blow (Inf)

8 **overspend**, overdraw, live beyond one's means, throw money away, throw good money after bad, go on a spending spree, spend money like water, spend, spend, spend (Inf), splash out on (Inf), spend (money) like it's going out of style (*or* fashion) (Inf)

ADVERBS

9 **extravagantly**, wastefully, lavishly, uneconomically, excessively, inordinately, immoderately, inexhaustibly, to the full, no end (Inf)

682 Meanness

He who meanly admires mean things is a Snob. William Makepeace Thackeray.

ADJECTIVES

1 **mean**, miserly, parsimonious, ungenerous, grudging, tight, tightfisted, close, close-fisted, money-grubbing, near, niggardly, penurious, penny-pinching, penny-wise, scrimping, cheeseparing, mingy, stingy, tight-arsed (Inf)

▶ *680 Thrift*

2 **unpleasant**, nasty, unkind, hurtful, spiteful, petty, small, small-minded, despicable, base, shabby, sordid, squalid, lowly, beastly (Inf)

▶ *122 Inferiority; 242 Unpleasantness*

NOUNS

3 **parsimony**, parsimoniousness, niggardliness, miserliness, ungenerousness, ungenerosity, tightness, tightfistedness, close-fistedness, cheeseparing, stinginess, minginess

4 **unpleasantness**, nastiness, hurtfulness, pettiness, spite, baseness, beastliness, shabbiness, lowliness, squalor

5 **miser**, niggard, skinflint, hoarder, money-grubber, Scrooge, penny-pincher, misanthrope, mean old stick (Inf), meanie (Inf), tight-wad (US inf), tight-arse (Inf)

6 **nasty person**, meanie (Inf), git (Inf)

▶ *242 Unpleasantness*

VERBS

7 **hoard**, save up, save, stint, scrimp, skimp, starve

8 **grudge**, begrudge, resent

ADVERBS

9 **meanly**, parsimoniously, ungenerously, niggardly, grudgingly, on a shoestring

683 Selfishness

It's 'Damn you, Jack – I'm all right!' with you chaps. David Bone.

NOUNS

1 **selfishness**, self-interest, self-concern, self-pity, self-preservation, self-consideration, self-indulgence, self-pleasing, self-serving, self-seeking, personal desires, personal aims, possessiveness, keeping for oneself, covetousness, jealousy, envy, avarice, acquisitiveness, mundaneness, worldliness, materialism, greed, ambition, careerism, opportunism, individualism, stinginess, miserliness, niggardliness, littleness, meanness, mean-mindedness, mean-spiritedness, parsimony, charity that begins at home, every man for himself (Inf), looking after number one (Inf)

▶ *360 Retention; 617 Desire; 629 Jealousy; 682 Meanness; 686 Self-Indulgence; 763 Possession*

2 **egoism**, egotism, ego, conceit, vanity, self-love, self-devotion, self-absorption, narcissism, self-centredness, no thought for others, egocentrism, egocentricity, egocentredness, self-praise, ego trip (Inf)

▶ *673 Vanity*

3 **selfish person**, egoist, egotist, egomaniac, narcissist, self-seeker, self-pleaser, self-server, opportunist, monopolist, dog in the manger, money-grubber (Inf), hog (Inf), road hog (Inf)

ADJECTIVES

4 **selfish**, self-concerned, self-indulgent, self-interested, self-seeking, possessive, covetous, jealous, envious, avaricious, acquisitive, materialistic, worldly, ambitious, greedy, monopolistic, opportunistic, individualistic, ungenerous, uncharitable, stingy, miserly, niggardly, mean, mean-minded, mean-spirited, parsimonious, cold-hearted, on the make (Inf), money-grubbing (Inf)

5 **egoistic**, egoistical, egotistic, egotistical, conceited, vain, narcissistic, self-loving, self-absorbed, self-centred, egocentric, ego-centred, wrapped up in oneself (Inf), concerned with number one (Inf), stuck on oneself (Inf)

VERBS

6 **be selfish**, indulge oneself, spoil oneself, please oneself, put oneself first, think only of oneself, pursue one's interests, advance one's own interests, sacrifice the interests of others, have personal motives, have ambition, covet, envy, acquire, monopolize, possess, keep for oneself, hang on to, feather one's nest, have an axe to grind, hog (Inf)

7 **be egoistic**, be egotistic, love oneself, have no thought for others, praise oneself, brag, take an ego trip (Inf), take care of (*or* look after) number one (Inf)

ADVERBS

8 **selfishly**, only for oneself, for one's own sake, self-indulgently, possessively, covetously, jealously, enviously, avariciously, acquisitively, materialistically, ambitiously, for profit, from personal motives, for private ends, greedily, individualistically, ungenerously, uncharitably, stingily, meanly, parsimoniously, cold-heartedly, on the make (Inf)

9 **egoistically**, egotistically, conceitedly, self-lovingly, vainly, with self-love, egocentrically, with no thought for others, as an ego trip (Inf)

684 Self-Restraint

You know, she speaks eighteen languages. And she can't say 'No' in any of them. Dorothy Parker.

NOUNS

1 **self-restraint**, self-control, self-discipline, self-denial, self-abnegation, self-mastery, restraint, constraint, restriction, repression, avoidance, eschewal, forbearance, renunciation, relinquishment, refrainment, abstaining, abstinence, abstention, abstemiousness, sexual abstinence, ascesis, celibacy, chastity, purity, puritanism, continence, temperance, temperateness, soberness, sobriety, total abstinence, teetotalism, prohibition, Rechabitism, Volstead Act (US), Eighteenth Amendment (US), Woman's Christian Temperance Union (WCTU), Church of England Temperance Society, diet, dieting, Weightwatchers, vegetarianism, veganism, fast, fasting, Lenten fare, fish day, asceticism, Spartanism, frugality, parsimony, economy, simple life, plain living, plainness, self-sufficiency, passing up (Inf)

▶ *25 Cookery; 151 Narrowness; 355 Relinquishment; 473 Disinterestedness; 634 Avoidance; 680 Thrift; 682 Meanness; 687 Fasting; 795 Morality*

2 **moderation**, moderateness, prudence, reasonableness, nothing in excess, middle way, happy medium, golden mean

▶ *685 Moderation*

3 **calmness**, composure, lack of emotion, stoicism, keeping a stiff upper lip, sang-froid

▶ *378 Obstruction; 489 Insensibility*

4 **self-restrained person**, sober person, (total) abstainer, teetotaller, Rechabite, prohibitionist, nonsmoker, vegetarian, vegan, ascetic, dieter, faster, puritan, Spartan, sobersides, dry (US inf), tight-arse (*or* tight-ass) (Inf)

VERBS

5 **be self-restrained**, restrain oneself, control oneself, exercise self-control, discipline oneself, restrict oneself, limit oneself, deny oneself, do without, never touch, constrain oneself, ration oneself, refrain, abstain, repress, retard, hold back, rein in, avoid excess, avoid, eschew, forbear, renounce, relinquish, put a stop to, swear off, give up, forgo, ban, curb, brake, veto, know when to stop, know when one has had enough, temper, drink in moderation, shun alcohol, prohibit drinking, renounce drinking, take (*or* sign) the pledge, diet, go on a diet, lose weight, control one's appetite, eat sparingly, eat in moderation, eat to live, not live to eat, half starve, starve, fast, control one's lusts, repress one's desires, mortify the flesh, economize, live plainly, live simply, live frugally, tighten one's belt, pass up (Inf), go dry (US inf), go on the wagon (Inf)

6 **moderate**, do nothing in excess, keep within bounds, circumscribe, confine, observe a limit, keep to the middle way, keep a happy medium, keep the golden mean

7 **be calm**, have composure, lack emotion, keep a stiff upper lip

ADJECTIVES

8 **self-restrained**, self-controlled, self-disciplined, self-denying, restrictive, restricted, strict, repressive, repressed, prohibited, renunciative, relinquished, restrained, anal-retentive, refraining, forbearing, abstaining, abstemious, abstinent, sexually abstinent, celibate, continent, chaste, pure, puritanical, temperate, tempered, not excessive, not overdoing it, sober, teetotal, sworn off, dieting, vegetarian, vegan, fasting, Lenten, ascetic, plain, Spartan, frugal, economical, parsimonious, stinting, sparing, costive, self-sufficient, on the wagon (Inf), dry (US inf), strait-laced (Inf), uptight (Inf), tight-arsed (*or* tight-assed) (Inf)

9 **moderate**, prudent, reasonable, measured, within bounds, circumscribed, confined, within reasonable limits, limiting, limited, under control

10 **calm**, composed, lacking emotion, stoic, keeping a stiff upper lip

ADVERBS

11 **with self-restraint**, with self-control, restrictively, strictly, repressively, forbearingly, abstemiously, chastely, purely, puritanically, temperately, teetotally, without excess, without overdoing it, ascetically, plainly, frugally, economically, parsimoniously, stintingly, sparingly, self-sufficiently

12 **moderately**, with moderation, prudently, with prudence, reasonably, within reason, within bounds, within reasonable limits, under control

13 **calmly**, without emotion, stoically, with a stiff upper lip

685 Moderation

By God, Mr Chairman, at this moment I stand astonished at my own moderation! Clive of India.

Moderation is a fatal thing, Lady Hunstanton. Nothing succeeds like excess. Oscar Wilde.

NOUNS

1 **moderation**, moderateness, reasonableness, restraint, check, control, self-control, equanimity, composure, sang-froid, sedateness, self-possession, sobriety, coolness, calmness, quietness, mildness, gentleness, nonviolence, temperance, steadiness, impartiality, neutrality, fairness, justness, judiciousness, justice, due measure, golden mean, average, happy medium, middle way, halfway house, correction, adjustment, modulation, regulation, mutual concession, trade-off, give and take, compromise, mitigation, relaxation, relief, let-up, remission, alleviation, easing, assuagement, mollification, calming, quietening, sedation, tranquillization, abatement, lessening, reduction, diminution, decrease

▶ *214 Decrease; 216 Average; 263 Ease; 301 Motionlessness; 393 Repair; 394 Remedy; 506 Silence; 689 Sobriety; 754 Compromise*

2 **moderator**, controller, calming influence, restraining hand, mollifier, peacemaker, pacifier, mediator, arbitrator, arbiter, judge, referee, umpire, chairperson, cushion, buffer, shock absorber, damper, restraint, brake, clamp, killjoy, wet blanket, stopper, downer, dummy, sedative, tranquillizer, soporific, sleeping pill, barbiturate, bromide, nightcap, lullaby, soothing influence, palliative, lenitive, demulcent, alleviative, rose water, painkiller, analgesic, anodyne, anaesthetic, opiate, opium, laudanum, oil on troubled waters, balm, balm of Gilead

▶ *251 Restraint; 394 Remedy; 748 Mediation*

VERBS

3 **be moderate**, take the middle way, follow the golden mean, stay on an even keel, stay within bounds, sober up, calm down, settle, settle down, keep the peace, give up arms, disarm, go quietly, go out like a lamb, remit, relent, relax, ease off, go easy, compromise

▶ *263 Ease; 689 Sobriety; 754 Compromise*

4 **moderate**, correct, adjust, modulate, regulate, mediate, judge, arbitrate, chair, take the chair, preside, referee, umpire, curb, tame, check, keep within bounds, restrict, constrict, constrain, limit, keep within limits, repress, restrain, chasten, govern, control, clamp, clamp down on, calm, pour oil on troubled waters, temper, mollify, soften, cushion, break the fall of, put a damper on, damp, dampen, deaden, cool, subdue, sedate, tranquillize, anaesthetize, still, quiet, quieten, hush, lull, rock, rock to sleep, sweeten, keep sweet, dulcify, mitigate, palliate, extenuate, qualify, weaken, obtund, blunt, dull, take the edge off, assuage, ease, soothe, relieve, alleviate, lighten, neutralize, take the sting out of, deactivate, smooth over, bring round, talk round, disarm, appease, pacify, allay, abate, lessen, reduce, diminish, decrease, play down, moderate one's language, censor, blue-pencil, tone down, euphemize, sober, sober down, throw cold water on, reduce the temperature, bank down the fires, slacken, relax, comfort, soft-pedal (Inf)

▶ *214 Decrease; 251 Restraint; 263 Ease; 347 Counteraction; 393 Repair; 394 Remedy; 579 Management; 748 Mediation; 749 Pacification*

5 **moderate one's hunger**, assuage one's hunger, satisfy one's appetite, assuage one's thirst, quench one's thirst, slake one's thirst

ADJECTIVES

6 **moderate**, medium, equable, balanced, steady, not extreme, not excessive, modest, judicious, just, fair, nonviolent, harmless, gentle, gentle as a lamb, mild, mild as milk, milk-and-water, weak, poor, middling, fair to middling, mediocre, indifferent, average, ordinary, passable, unexceptional, unremarkable, limited, restricted, measured, sensible, rational, reasonable, within reason, within limits (*or* bounds), restrained, controlled, chastened, subdued, quiet, peaceable, pacific, still, untroubled, peaceful, tranquil, self-controlled, low-key, temperate, tempered, sober, calm, cool, composed, cool, calm, and collected, so-so (Inf)

▶ *216 Average; 301 Motionlessness; 506 Silence; 689 Sobriety*

7 **politically moderate**, neutral, liberal, tolerant, middle-of-the-road, centre, left of centre, nonextreme, nonradical, non-reactionary, mugwumpish, noncommittal, wishy-washy

8 **moderating**, lenitive, soothing, nonirritant, alleviative, assuaging, easing, painkilling, analgesic, anodyne, calming, calmative, sedative, tranquillizing, narcotic, hypnotic, mesmeric, soporific, smooth, soft, bland, emollient, demulcent, lubricating, comforting, disarming, pacificatory

▶ *394 Remedy; 749 Pacification*

ADVERBS

9 **moderately**, in moderation, with moderation, within limits, within bounds, within reason, reasonably, within range, to a degree, to some extent, fairly, pretty, quite, rather, somewhat, slightly, at half speed, equably, judiciously, gently, weakly, temperately, calmly, half-heartedly, nervously

686 Self-Indulgence

The key to his behaviour was self-indulgence, which he made almost a rule of life. Stephen Spender.

NOUNS

1 **self-indulgence**, self-gratification, pleasure-seeking, hedonism, sybaritism, epicureanism, luxury, sensuality, voluptuousness, carnality

▶ *490 Physical Pleasure*

2 **dissipation**, riotous living, fast living, high living, free living, dissoluteness, licentiousness, debauchery, profligacy, carousal, orgy, saturnalia

3 **overindulgence**, immoderation, uncontrol, unrestraint, abandon, indiscipline, inordinateness, inordinancy, overdoing, excess, excessiveness, incontinence, concupiscence, intemperance, drunkenness, crapulence, addiction, overeating, greed, gluttony, gourmandising, extravagance, wastefulness, prodigality

▶ *219 Excess; 681 Extravagance; 688 Gluttony; 690 Drunkenness*

4 **self-absorption**, self-obsession, self-devotion, self-worship, self-love, narcissism, vanity, self-centredness, egoism, selfishness, I'm all right Jack (Inf)

▶ *683 Selfishness*

5 self-indulgent person, pleasure-seeker, free-liver, high-liver, fast-liver, hedonist, sybarite, epicure, *bon vivant* (Fr), gourmet, gourmand, glutton, toper, voluptuary, sensualist, debauchee, narcissist, egoist

ADJECTIVES

6 self-indulgent, self-gratifying, pleasure-seeking, pleasure-bound, hedonistic, sybaritic, epicurean, sensual, voluptuous, carnal

7 dissipated, dissipating, dissolute, riotous, fast-living, high-living, free-living, licentious, debauched, debauching, profligate

8 overindulgent, immoderate, uncontrolled, unrestrained, undisciplined, ill-disciplined, abandoned, inordinate, excessive, incontinent, concupiscent, intemperate, drunk, crapulent, addicted, greedy, gluttonous, gourmandising, extravagant, wasteful, prodigal

9 self-absorbed, self-obsessed, self-devoted, self-worshipping, self-loving, narcissistic, vain, self-centred, egotistic, selfish

VERBS

10 indulge oneself, indulge in, luxuriate in, wallow in, deny oneself nothing, put oneself first, look after number one

11 overindulge, overdo, waste, squander, dissipate, gorge, debauch, carouse, not know when to stop, burn the candle at both ends, sow one's wild oats, have a fling (Inf), go on a bender (Inf), binge (Inf)

ADVERBS

12 self-indulgently, intemperately, incontinently, immoderately, excessively, in (*or* to) excess, beyond all bounds

687 Fasting

The month of Ramadan shall ye fast, in which the Koran was sent down from heaven, a direction unto men, and declarations of direction, and the distinction between good and evil. Koran.

NOUNS

1 fasting, fast, abstinence from food, abstinence, abstemiousness, austerity, atrophy, religious fasting, Lenten fare, Quadragesimal fare, dieting, diet, prescribed diet, health diet, crash diet, starvation diet, slimming diet, liquid diet, weight loss, lean cuisine, slimming, reducing, weight-watching, Weightwatchers, losing weight, counting calories, anorexia (nervosa)

2 short rations, military rations, K rations (US), iron rations, short commons, asceticism, Spartan fare, prison fare, diet of bread and water, hunger striking, bare subsistence, bare cupboard, insufficient diet, hunger, famishment, starvation

▶ *218 Insufficiency; 226 Stopping; 260 Ill Health; 684 Self-Restraint*

3 fast day, fast, *jour maigre* (Fr), day of abstinence, meatless day, fish day, Lent, Friday, Good Friday, Yom Kippur, Tishah b'Av, Ramadan

▶ *7 Religion*

4 fasting person, faster, dieter, hunger striker, anorexic, ascetic, weight watcher, calorie counter

VERBS

5 fast, abstain from eating, abstain, eat nothing, having nothing to eat, live on air, go hungry, hunger, clem (*or* clam) (Dial), go without food, go without, avoid food, have an empty stomach, suffer from anorexia (nervosa), give up eating, refuse food, go on a hunger strike, eat sparingly, eat no meat, keep Lent, keep a Spartan regimen, live on bread and water, live on rations, eat less, control one's appetite, lose weight, take off weight, join Weightwatchers, diet, go on a diet, go on a crash diet, go on a starvation diet, go on a liquid diet, slim, reduce, count calories, half starve, starve, famish, die for food, tighten one's belt, make a little go a long way

ADJECTIVES

6 fasting, abstinent, abstemious, not eating, anorexic, without food, off food, unfed, going without, with an empty stomach, empty, keeping one's fast, keeping Lent, Lenten, Quadragesimal, keeping a Spartan regimen, Spartan, on a diet, slimming, reducing, on a crash diet, austere, ascetic, on a starvation diet, on a liquid diet, on meagre rations, on (a) hunger strike, on bread and water, underfed, poorly fed, half-starved, starving, starved, famishing, famished, ravenous, clemmed (*or* clammed) (Dial), hungry, dying for food, wasting away, thin, anorexic, hungry enough to eat a horse

ADVERBS

7 abstemiously, in a Spartan manner, on bread and water, without food, ravenously, hungrily, to near starvation

688 Gluttony

The eye is bigger than the belly. Proverb.

NOUNS

1 gluttony, greediness, greed, overeating, self-indulgence, overindulgence, overindulging, intemperance, insatiability, voraciousness, voracity, ravenousness, rapacity, edaciousness, edacity, polyphagia, hedonism, concupiscence, big appetite, wolfishness, piggishness (Inf), hoggishness (Inf), bingeing (Inf)

▶ *557 Eating; 617 Desire; 686 Self-Indulgence*

2 epicurism, epicureanism, gourmandise, gourmandism, gastronomy

3 act of gluttony, banquet, feast, bacchanalia, Lucullan banquet, clambake (US), feeding frenzy (Inf), spread (Inf), food orgy (Inf), beano (Inf), beanfeast (Inf), blowout (Inf), pigout (US inf), nosh-up (Inf)

4 glutton, greedy person, good eater, big eater, hearty eater, heavy eater, guzzler, gorger, trencherman, trencherwoman, omnivore, bacchanal, Lucullus, gourmet, gourmand, gormandizer, gastronome, epicure, epicurean, *bon vivant* (Fr), cormorant, wolf, binger (Inf), foodie (Inf), gobbler (Inf), pig (Inf), greedy pig (Inf), porker (Inf), hog (Inf), hyena (Inf), locust (Inf), bottomless pit (Inf), human garbage can (US inf), gannet (Inf), greedy guts (Inf)

VERBS

5 be greedy, gluttonize, gormandize, hedonize, overeat, self-indulge, overindulge, indulge one's appetite, indulge oneself, have a big appetite, love food, love to eat, live to eat, eat up, set to, wipe the plate clean, devour, bolt, guzzle, gobble, gulp, snap up, wolf, make a pig (*or* hog) of oneself, fill oneself, stuff oneself, stuff, cram, glut oneself, glut, gorge, engorge, have eyes bigger than one's stomach, eat like a horse, eat one's head off, eat out of house and home, tuck in to (Inf), binge (Inf), go on a binge (Inf), graze (Inf), pig out (US inf)

ADJECTIVES

6 **gluttonous**, greedy, insatiable, never full, intemperate, hedonistic, self-indulgent, overeating, overindulgent, voracious, ravenous, rapacious, well-nourished, edacious, polyphagous, epicurean, gastronomic, omnivorous, devouring, all-devouring, stuffing, stuffed, cramming, bolting, gobbling, gulping, glutting, gluttonizing, gorging, gorged, overgorging, overgorged, engorged, guzzling, wolfing, wolfish, esurient, piggish (Inf), hoggish (Inf), bingeing (Inf)

ADVERBS

7 **gluttonously**, greedily, with pure greed, self-indulgently, hungrily, with one bite, at a gulp, voraciously, ravenously, out of house and home, gastronomically, edaciously, like a horse, wolfishly, like a wolf, piggishly (Inf), like a pig (Inf), hoggishly (Inf), like a hog (Inf)

689 Sobriety

If someone asks for a soft drink at a party, we no longer think he is a wimp. Edwina Currie.

ADJECTIVES

1 **sober**, not drunk, unintoxicated, clear-headed, with a clear head, without a hangover, sobered up, abstinent, abstemious, temperate, teetotal (TT), strictly teetotal, prohibitionist, nondrinking, off drink, off the hard stuff, on soft drinks, water-drinking, tea-drinking, sober as a judge, stone-cold sober (Inf), unfuddled (Inf), on the (water) wagon (Inf), not indulging (Inf), dry (Inf), off the bottle (Inf), drying out (Inf)

▶ *634 Avoidance; 684 Self-Restraint; 685 Moderation*

2 **nonalcoholic**, alcohol-free, unfermented, soft

VERBS

3 **be sober**, stay sober, keep (*or* have) a clear head, not drink, abstain, avoid alcohol, keep off liquor, stay away from the hard stuff, never touch a drop, never let liquor pass one's lips, drink water, prefer soft drinks, drink moderately, drink sociably, hold one's liquor, carry one's liquor, not imbibe (Inf), not indulge (Inf)

4 **give up alcohol**, give up drinking, become teetotal, become a teetotaller, come off (drink), kick the habit, turn prohibitionist, sign the pledge, join the Band of Hope, go dry (Inf), go on the (water) wagon (Inf)

5 **sober up**, clear one's head, sleep it off, get rid of a hangover, detoxify, get the fumes out of one's brain (Inf), dry out (Inf)

NOUNS

6 **sobriety**, soberness, abstinence, abstemiousness, temperance, teetotalism, water-drinking, tea-drinking, state of sobriety, unintoxicated state, clear head, no hangover, unfuddled brain (Inf)

▶ *634 Avoidance; 684 Self-Restraint; 685 Moderation*

7 **prohibition**, Prohibition (US), the Volstead Prohibition Act (US), the 18th Amendment (US), the noble experiment (US), dry county (US), dry state (US)

8 **sober person**, nondrinker, nonalcoholic, nonaddict, moderate drinker, social drinker, water-drinker, tea-drinker, abstainer, teetotaller, strict teetotaller, prohibitionist, Rechabite, temperance society, Woman's Christian Temperance 135 Union, Alcoholics Anonymous (AA), the Betty Ford Clinic, the Band of Hope

ADVERBS

9 **soberly**, with sobriety, abstemiously, temperately, with a clear head

690 Drunkenness

For when the wine is in, the wit is out. Thomas Becon.

Wine is a mocker, strong drink is raging: and whosoever is deceived thereby is not wise. Bible: Proverbs.

ADJECTIVES

1 **drunk**, inebriated, intoxicated, ebriate, ebriated, ebriose, under the influence (of alcohol), having had (a drop) too much, having had one too many, in liquor, the worse for liquor, comfortably drunk, gloriously drunk, roaring drunk, fighting drunk, pot-valiant, drunk and disorderly, drunken, drunk as a lord, drunk as a fiddler, drunk as a fiddler's bitch, drunk as a skunk (US), drunk as an owl, drunk as David's sow, fou as a coot (Scot), fou as a wulk (Scot), tight (Inf), in one's cups (Inf), half-seas over (Inf), three (*or* four) sheets in (*or* to) the wind (Inf), one over the eight (Inf), boozed up (Inf), ginned up (Inf), liquored up (Inf), lit up (Inf), flushed (Inf), merry (Inf), happy (Inf), high (Inf), elevated (Inf), exhilarated (Inf), tanked up (Inf), bevvied up (Dial), pissed (Inf), Brahms (and Liszt) (Inf), pissed as a newt (Inf), well-oiled (Inf), well-lubricated (Inf), pickled (Inf), potted (Inf), canned (Inf), bottled (Inf), stewed (Inf), fried (Inf), pixilated (Inf), ratted (Inf), rat-faced (Inf), rat-arsed (Inf)

2 **slightly drunk**, tipsy, maudlin, tearful, tired and emotional, muzzy, glazed, glassy-eyed, pie-eyed, seeing double, woozy, dizzy, giddy, reeling, staggering, hiccupping, tiddly (Inf), squiffy (Inf), half-cut (Inf), half-bagged (Inf), half-shot (Inf), fuddled (Inf), muddled (Inf), flustered (Inf), boozy (Inf)

3 **dead drunk**, in a drunken stupor, stupefied, stinking drunk (Inf), stinko (Inf), blind drunk (Inf), blind (Inf), blotto (Inf), stoned (Inf), smashed (Inf), sloshed (Inf), sozzled (Inf), soused (Inf), soaked (Inf), juiced (Inf), lushed (US inf), loaded (US inf), plastered (Inf), bagged (Inf), blasted (Inf), plowed under (US inf), plotzed (US inf), legless (Inf), arseholed (Inf), shitfaced (US inf), paralytic (Inf), gone (Inf), shot (Inf), blitzed (Inf), bombed (out of one's mind) (Inf), zonked (out) (Inf), zonkers (Inf), zonko (Inf), wiped out (Inf), teed (Inf), twisted (US inf), stiff (Inf), out (of it) (Inf), out cold (Inf), under the table (Inf), dead to the world (Inf)

4 **crapulous**, crapulent, hung over, with a hangover, with

a sick headache, with a thick head, with a fuzzy tongue, dizzy, giddy, sick

5 **drunken**, inebriate, intemperate, habitually drunk, never sober, alcoholic, dipsomaniac, dipsomaniacal, with a drink problem, addicted to alcohol, a slave to drink, given to drink, on the bottle, sottish, sodden, gin-sodden, beery, vinous, smelling of drink, stinking of liquor, fond of a drink, thirsty, bibulous, bibbing, wine-bibbing, tippling, toping, swilling, swigging, guzzling, hard drinking, carousing, wassailing, red-nosed, bloodshot, gouty, liverish, boozy (Inf), boozing (Inf), pub-crawling (Inf)

6 **intoxicating**, intoxicant, inebriating, inebriative, inebriant, temulent, stimulant, exhilarating, exciting, going to the head, heady, winy, vinous, beery, spiritous, alcoholic, hard, potent, strong, double-strength, proof, overproof, straight, neat, unmixed, undiluted, addictive, habit-forming

VERBS

7 **be drunk**, have had (a drop) too much, have had one too many, not hold one's liquor, hiccup, slur one's words, stutter, stammer, see double, see pink elephants, not walk straight, lurch, stagger, reel, succumb, pass out

8 **get drunk**, have (a drop) too much, have one too many, drink, drink deep, drink hard, drink like a fish, tipple, tope, guzzle, swig, swill, quaff, crack a bottle, hit the bottle, go on a spree, carouse, wassail, sacrifice to Bacchus, booze (Inf), souse (Inf), soak (Inf), lush (US inf), bib (Lit), fuddle (Inf), liquor up (Inf), tank up (Inf), bend one's elbow (Inf), knock back a few (Inf), chug-a-lug (US inf), have one over the eight (Inf), go on a blind (Inf), go on a bender (Inf), go on the fuddle (Inf), go on a pub-crawl (Inf), pub-crawl (Inf), drown one's sorrows (Inf), commune with the spirits (Inf)

9 **be intoxicating**, inebriate, make drunk, stupefy, stimulate, exhilarate, elevate, excite, go to one's head, make one's head swim, fuddle (Inf), befuddle (Inf), put one under the table (Inf)

NOUNS

10 **drunkenness**, inebriation, intoxication, inebriety, insobriety, ebriety, ebriosity, tipsiness, drunken (*or* alcoholic) stupor, influence of alcohol, stimulation, exhilaration, elevation, excitation, Dutch courage, hiccup, hiccupping, slurred speech, thick speech, stuttering, stammering, seeing double, wooziness, dizziness, staggering, reeling, blackout, befuddlement (Inf), blind staggers (Inf)

11 **drinking**, excessive drinking, hard drinking, getting drunk, intemperance, bibulousness, wine-bibbing, tippling, swilling, weakness for liquor, fondness for the bottle, sottishness, beeriness, vinousness, soaking (Inf)

12 **alcohol**, drink, alcoholic drink, liquor, alcoholic liquor, intoxicating liquor, hard drink, strong drink, Dutch courage, potations, libations, grog, wine, beer, spirits, water of life, John Barleycorn, cocktail, tall (*or* long) drink, bootleg liquor, home brew, booze (Inf), juice (Inf), vino (Inf), plonk (Inf), hooch (Inf), moonshine (Inf), rotgut (Inf), gnat's piss (Inf)

13 **drink**, beverage, potation, compotation, libation, libation to Bacchus, flowing bowl, cup that cheers, tipple, bevvy (Dial), nip, dram, drop, finger, snort, round, round of drinks, snifter (Inf), one for the road (Inf), hair of the dog (that bit one) (Inf), one over the eight (Inf)

► *558 Drinking*

14 **drinking bout**, binge, spree, orgy of drinking, bacchanalia, revel, jag (Inf), lush (Inf), blind (Inf), bender (Inf), pub-crawl (Inf)

15 **crapulence**, crapulousness, hangover, morning after (the night before), (sick) headache, thick head, fuzzy tongue, dizziness, giddiness, sickness

16 **alcoholism**, alcoholic addiction, alcohol abuse, dipsomania, drink problem, tremors, delirium tremens, cirrhosis of the liver, red nose, DT's (Inf), jimjams (Inf), the horrors (Inf), heebie-jeebies (Inf), pink elephants (Inf), grog-blossom (Inf)

17 **drunkard**, drunk, inebriate, intoxicated person, habitual drunkard, sot, alcoholic, dipsomaniac, slave to drink, pathological drunk, drinker, hard drinker, problem drinker, secret drinker, social drinker, bibber, winebibber, tippler, swiller, toper, tosspot, thirsty soul, devotee of Bacchus, bacchanal, bacchant, maenad, Silenus, carouser, reveller, boozer (Inf), soaker (Inf), (old) soak (Inf), souse (Inf), sponge (Inf), juice head (Inf), wineskin (Inf), froth-blower (Inf), pub-crawler (Inf), alehead (Inf), pisshead (Inf), piss-artist (Inf)

ADVERBS

18 **drunkenly**, under the influence, tipsily, in a drunken stupor, crapulously, crapulently

691 Drug-Taking

Americans use drugs as if consumption bestowed a 'special license' to be an asshole. Frank Zappa.

NOUNS

1 **drug-taking**, drug addiction, drug abuse, drug dependence, habit, smoking, sniffing, glue-sniffing, injecting, snorting (Inf), freebasing (Inf), hitting up (Inf), shooting up (Inf), skin-popping (Inf), mainlining (Inf), pill-popping (Inf), chasing the dragon (Inf), belly habit (US inf), banging (Inf), blowing (Inf), cocktailing (US inf), buzz (Inf), trip (Inf), acid trip (Inf), bad trip (Inf), tracks (Inf), trackmarks (Inf), whore scars (US inf), quill (US inf), shooting gallery (Inf)

2 **drug pushing**, drug peddling, drug trafficking, possessing narcotics, carrying (Inf), holding (Inf)

3 **withdrawal**, withdrawal symptoms, withdrawal sickness, cold turkey (Inf), bogue (US inf)

4 **drug taker**, drug user, drug addict, druggie (Inf), junkie (Inf), dope fiend (Inf), drug scorer (Inf), greasy junkie (US inf), DA (Inf), freak (Inf), head (Inf), acid-head (Inf), hophead (Inf), chippy (US inf), coke-head (Inf), mainliner (Inf), hype (Inf), jones (US inf), scag jones (US inf)

5 **drug pusher**, pusher, drug peddler, drug dealer, connection, candy man (US inf), reefer man (Inf), viper (US inf)

6 **drug**, drugs, dope, narcotic, narcotics, fix, hard drug, soft drug, designer drug, ecstasy, cannabis, marijuana, hashish, cocaine, heroin, methadone, barbiturate, morphine, opium, amphetamine, stimulant, excitant, hallu-

cinogen, LSD (lysergic acid diethylamide), PCP (phencyclidine), STP, mescaline, peyote, joint (Inf), the joint (Inf), reefer (Inf), stick (Inf), hit (Inf), bang (Inf), spliff (Inf), roach (Inf), shot (Inf), snort (Inf), blockbuster (US inf), dime's worth (US inf), hash (Inf), Mary Ann (Inf), Mary Jane (Inf), Mary Warner (Inf), OZ (Inf), mooter (Inf), muggles (US inf), birdwood (US inf), tea (Inf), grass (Inf), weed (Inf), rope (Inf), panatella (Inf), black gunion (US inf), ganja (Inf), hemp (Inf), kef (Inf), pot (Inf), Acapulco gold (Inf), gage (*or* gauge) (US inf), gangster (US inf), gungeon (US inf), Jamaican ganja (US inf), coke (Inf), snow (Inf), crack (Inf), crack cocaine (Inf), C (Inf), C and H (Inf), C and M (Inf), white stuff (Inf), speedball (Inf), Peruvian marching powder (US inf), rock (Inf), dynamite (US inf), dyno (Inf), girl (Inf), horse (Inf), junk (Inf), smack (Inf), H (Inf), scag (*or* skag) (Inf), boy (Inf), brown sugar (Inf), hot shot (US inf), black tar (Inf), candy (Inf), needle candy (Inf), nose candy (Inf), gumball (Inf), Mexican mud (US inf), tootsie roll (US inf), peanut butter (Inf), dog food (Inf), downer (Inf), barb (Inf), yellow jacket (Inf), morph (Inf), M (Inf), black stuff (US inf), brown stuff (Inf), blue velvet (US inf), pep pill (Inf), dex (Inf), dexie (Inf), dexo (Inf), upper (Inf), speed (Inf), green dragon (Inf), green hornet (Inf), purple heart (Inf), black beauty (US inf), acid (Inf), blue cheer (Inf), purple haze (US inf), yellow (Inf), yellow sunshine (Inf), orange (US inf), orange sunshine (US inf), angel dust (Inf), magic mushroom (Inf)

ADJECTIVES

7 **drugged**, doped, incapacitated, insensible, high (Inf), stoned (Inf), zonked (out) (Inf), zonkers (Inf), zonko (Inf), spaced-out (Inf), freaked out (Inf), floating (Inf), loaded (US inf), turned on (Inf), bogue (Inf)

8 **addicted**, drug-dependent, hooked (Inf)

9 **addictive**, narcotic, psychedelic, hallucinogenic, mind-blowing (Inf)

VERBS

10 **drug oneself**, take drugs, smoke, inject oneself, possess narcotics, traffic in drugs, have withdrawal symptoms, snort (Inf), chase the dragon (Inf), drop (Inf), drop acid (Inf), freebase (Inf), shoot up (Inf), shoot gravy (US inf), mainline (Inf), hot-shot (US inf), cook up (Inf), turn on (Inf), trip out (Inf), take a trip (Inf), blow one's mind (Inf), freak out (Inf), bang (Inf), blow (Inf), blow smoke (Inf), blow gage (*or* gauge) (US inf), carry (Inf), hold (Inf), dry out (Inf), go cold turkey (Inf)

ADVERBS

11 **in a trance**, insensibly, dopily (Inf), narcotically, psychedelically, habitually, dependently

Communication

692 Communications

The medium is the message. This is merely to say that the personal and social consequences of any medium…result from the new scale that is introduced into our affairs by each extension of ourselves or by any new technology. Marshall McLuhan.

NOUNS

1 **communications**, means of communication, speech, talking, writing, correspondence, long-distance communication, electronic communication, telecommunications, signalling, radio communication, broadcasting, mass communication, communications medium, mass media, radio, television, the press

▶ *693 Information; 729 Speech; 740 Publication; 741 News*

2 **postal communication**, postal service, Post Office, US Postal Service, GPO (General Post Office), Postal Union, post office, sorting office, dead-letter office, returned-letter office, Royal Mail, letter post, domestic mail (US), inland post, international mail, overseas mail, airmail, Swiftair, surface mail, express mail (US), priority mail (US), special handling (US), special delivery, Data Post, first-class mail, second-class mail, third-class mail (US), sea mail, parcel post, Parcel Force™, fourth-class mail (US), COD, collect on delivery (US), cash on delivery, Freepost™, registered mail, recorded delivery, return receipt (US), express delivery, Red Star delivery, insured mail (US), metered mail, forwarded mail, general delivery (US), poste restante, Pony Express

3 **correspondence**, mail, post, letter, airmail letter, air letter, aerogram, registered letter, dead letter, postcard, postal card (US), money order (US), postal order, packet, parcel, envelope, name and address, address, zip code (US), postcode, stamp, postage stamp, airmail stamp, first-class stamp, second-class stamp, mailbox (US), pillarbox, postbox, letterbox, post-office box, private box, pigeonhole, pigeon box, mailbag, mailsack, mail pouch (US), postbag, diplomatic bag, dispatch box, postage (*or* postal) meter (US), franking machine, postmark

4 **postal worker**, postmaster general, postmaster, postmistress, mailman (US), mailwoman (US), mail carrier (US), letter carrier, postman, postwoman, sorter, special-delivery messenger, messenger, courier, Queen's Messenger

5 **correspondent**, letter writer, pen friend, pen pal (Inf)

6 **telecommunication**, transmission, propagation, two-way communication, one-way communication, telephony, radiotelephony, computer networking, telegraphy, radiotelegraphy, teleinformatics, communications technology, communications engineering, radio engineering, telephone engineering, communications system, network, communications network, communications channel, communications link, telecottage, communications line, transmission line, cable, coaxial cable (*or* coax), multiwire cable, fibre cable, fibre-optic cable

7 **satellite communication**, communications satellite, geostationary satellite, Comsat™, Telstar™, Astra™, Marcopole™, Intelsat™, Eutelsat™

8 **data transmission**, text transmission, telegraph, radiotelegraph, Morse code, dot, dash, dit, dah, heliograph, telegram, overseas telegram, cablegram, cable, wire, Telemessage™, telex, telex machine, teleprinter, teletypewriter (US), Teletex™, facsimile transmission, fax, fax machine, fax number, electronic mail, email (*or* e-mail), electronic office

9 **telephone**, phone, telephone set, handset, receiver, earpiece, mouthpiece, microphone, headset, headphones, extension, intercom, answering machine, push-button telephone, dial telephone, cordless telephone, mobile telephone, car telephone, radiotelephone, radiophone, ship-to-shore telephone, videophone, cellular phone, cellphone, Cellnet™, Vodaphone™, public telephone, pay station (US), payphone, cardphone, phonecard, Mercurycard™, telephone box, telephone booth, call box, telephone kiosk, blower (Inf), dog and bone (Inf)

10 **telephone call**, phone call, call, local call, long-distance call, toll call, overseas call, reverse-charge call, collect call (US), personal call, person-to-person call (US), nuisance call, diverted call, hunging, waiting, conference call, Freefone™ call, buzz (Inf), tinkle (Inf), bell (Inf)

11 **dialling**, direct distance dialing (DDD) (US), direct dialling, international direct dialling (IDD), subscriber trunk dialling (STD), telephone number, phone number, dialling code, area code (US), local code, national code, international code, dial tone (US), dialling tone, tone, ring tone, busy signal (US), engaged tone, telephone book, phone book, telephone directory, Yellow Pages

12 **public telephone system**, public telephone (*or* network), telephoneline, subscriber line, party line, trunk

line, hot line, chat line, telephone wire, telephone pole, telegraph pole, telephone exchange, exchange, local exchange, tandem exchange, trunk exchange, automatic exchange, crossbar exchange, private exchange (PX), private branch exchange (PBX), private automatic branch exchange (PABX), private manual branch exchange (PMBX), switchboard

13 **telephoner**, subscriber, caller, phoner, telephone operator, switchboard operator, operator, telephonist, telephone mechanic (US), telephone engineer, linesman

14 **radio transmission**, radio wave, long wave (LW), short wave (SW), medium wave (MW), radio spectrum, microwaves, radio frequency (RF), frequency band, waveband, band, bandwidth, frequency allocation, radio beam, radio signal, pulsed signal, radio link, microwave link, radio channel, modulation, carrier, modulated carrier, demodulation, modulator, demodulator, carrier transmission, frequency modulation (FM), amplitude modulation (AM), phase modulation (PM), sideband, single sideband transmission, pulse code modulation (PCM), multiplex transmission, frequency-division multiplex (FDM), timedivision multiplex (TDM)

15 **transmitted wave**, line-of-sight transmission, direct wave, ground wave, groundreflected wave, ionosphere, F-layer (*or* Fregion), E-layer (*or* E-region), D-layer (*or* Dregion), ionospheric reflection, ionospheric wave, indirect wave, sky wave, space wave, ionospheric disturbance, ionospheric storm

16 **transmitter**, radio transmitter, FM (frequency-modulated) transmitter, LW (long-wave) transmitter, AM (amplitude-modulated) transmitter, MW (medium-wave) transmitter, UHF (ultrahigh-frequency) transmitter, SHF (superhighfrequency) transmitter, VHF (very highfrequency) transmitter, radio microphone, radiophone, mobile phone, car phone, cellular phone, short-wave radio, Citizens' Band (CB)

17 **antenna**, aerial, transmitting antenna, receiving antenna, directional antenna, dipole antenna, dipole, folded dipole, Yagi antenna, loop (*or* frame) antenna, whip antenna, long-wire antenna, dish antenna, dish, horn antenna, omnidirectional antenna, radiator, director, reflector

18 **radio**, radio receiver, receiver, tuned radio-frequency (TRF) receiver, superhet receiver, amplifier, booster, intermediate-frequency (IF) amplifier, audiofrequency (AF) amplifier, loudspeaker, speaker, tuner, tuning, preset tuning, volume control, tone control, wireless, radio set, crystal set, cat's whisker, clock radio, car radio, VHF radio, mobile radio, walkie-talkie, radiopager, pager, bleep (*or* bleeper), portable radio, battery radio, transistor radio, trannie (Inf), Walkman™, personal stereo, ghetto blaster (Inf), boom box (US inf)

19 **radio reception**, reception, fading (*or* fade), drift, creeping, crawling, distortion, interference, noise, atmospherics, static, white noise, cross talk, hum, hiss

20 **radio broadcasting**, broadcasting authority, broadcasting station, BBC (British Broadcasting Corporation), Beeb (Inf), Auntie (Inf), BBC Radio, Radio 1, Radio 2, Radio 3, Radio 4, Radio 5, BBC World Service, National Public Radio (NPR) (US), local radio, college radio, commercial radio, satellite radio (US), pirate radio, Citizens' Band radio, CB radio, amateur radio, radio station, relay station, booster station, radio mast, radio tower, mobile radio station, mobile unit, radio car, radiomobile, station identification, call sign, call letters (US)

21 **television** (TV), black-and-white television, monochrome television, colour television, small screen, high-definition television (HDTV), broadcast television, closed-circuit television (CCTV), cable television, pay (*or* subscription) television, satellite television, television camera, telecamera, mobile camera, television tube (*or* picture tube), cathode-ray tube, tube, video signal, audio signal, sequential scanning, interlaced scanning, line, field, frame, lines per frame, frame frequency, field frequency

22 **television set**, receiver, screen, controls, volume, brightness, colour, contrast, preset tuning, remote control, zapper (Inf), colour television, black-and-white television, portable television, TV, small screen, telly (Inf), the box (Inf), idiot box (Inf), goggle box (Inf), boob tube (US inf)

23 **television reception**, reception, picture quality (*or* picture), video, sound quality (*or* sound), test card, grainy picture, snowy picture, snow, vertical roll, fipples, interference, noise, distortion, picture clarity, definition, high definition

24 **television broadcasting**, broadcasting authority, BBC Television, independent television, commercial television, Independent Broadcasting Authority (IBA), Independent Television Authority (ITA), Independent Television Commission (ITC), FOX (US), broadcasting station, television channel, BBC1, BBC2, ITV (Independent Television), Channel 4 (C4), Channel 5 (C5), Federal Communications Commission (FCC) (US), network television (US), ABC (American Broadcasting), CBS (Columbia Broadcasting System), NBC (National Broadcasting Corporation), public broadcasting (US), PBS (Public Broadcasting Service) (US), local television, cable television, satellite television, Sky, CNN (Cable News Network) (US), television station, relay station, booster station, television mast, television tower, mobile station, TV mobile

25 **broadcast material**, transmission, telecast, simulcast, on-site broadcast (US), outside broadcast (OB), relay, live relay, recording, repeat, rerun, transcription, programme, prime-time programme, syndicated programme (US), audience participation, phone-in, telethon, quiz show, game show, chat show, talk show, variety show, series, miniseries, serial, costume drama, saga, docudrama, faction, soap opera, soap, situation comedy, sitcom (Inf), news, news summary, news roundup, news documentary, news report, live coverage, commercial break, commercial, station break (US), public service announcement (PSA) (US), Teletext™, viewdata, Ceefax™, Oracle™, Prestel™, Skytext™, Viewtron™, CableText™, Antiope™, educational broadcasting, Open University, religious broadcasting, Christian Broadcasting Network (US)

26 **recording**, tape recording, tape recorder, tapedeck cassette, audio cassette, tape, DAT recording, video recording, video, video cassette, video cassette recorder (VCR),

video tape, video game, TV game, video nasty, videodisc, video camera, camcorder

27 signalling, signal, semaphore, flag signals, Morse code, railway signals, smoke signals, radio signalling, radio control, radio navigation, radiobeacon, navigational beacon, radio marker, radio direction-finding (RDF), radio compass, radiogoniometer, radio bearing, radio astronomy

28 radar, pulse (*or* pulsed) radar, continuous-wave (CW) radar, primary radar, secondary radar, MTI (moving-target indication, phrased-array radar, radar station, radar beacon, radar transponder beacon, racon, radar antenna, radar dish, transmit-receive (TR) switch, anti-transmit-receive (ATR) switch, fixed array, radar beam, target, return signal, echo, radar screen, radar indicator, planposition indicator (PPI), radarscope, display, scan, military radar, weather radar, radar navigation, radar guidance, radar tracking, radar surveillance, radar astronomy

29 broadcaster, telegrapher, telegraphist, radio operator, amateur radio operator, radio ham (Inf), radio broadcaster, television broadcaster, announcer, commentator, talking head, newscaster, anchorman, anchorperson, anchorwoman, newsreader, presenter, newsman, newswoman, informant, master of ceremonies (MC), emcee (US), host, compere, question master, disc jockey (DJ), deejay, televangelist (US), media personality

VERBS

30 communicate, communicate with, be in touch, get in touch, make contact, speak (to), talk (to), write (to), signal, transmit, link up, relay, propagate, amplify, modulate, demodulate, radio, page, bleep, broadcast, announce, inform, televise, telecast, repeat, rerun, advertise, receive, tune in, listen in, watch, record, tape-record, tape, video

► *693 Information; 729 Speech; 740 Publication; 741 News*

31 correspond, correspond with, exchange letters, write (to), send a letter to, drop a line to, reply (to), answer, acknowledge, address, stamp, frank, mail, post, airmail, send, send on, forward, dispatch, sort, deliver, send a telegram (to), telegraph, cable, wire, telex, fax

► *316 Transfer*

32 telephone, phone, call (up), ring (up), make a (phone) call, give someone a call (*or* ring), give someone a buzz (Inf), give someone a tinkle (Inf), give someone a bell (Inf), hang up, ring off

ADJECTIVES

33 communicational, communicating, transmissional, oral, verbal, epistolary (*or* epistolatory), postal, relecommunicational, telephonic, telegraphic

► *17 Literature; 729 Speech*

34 communicated, spoken, written, signalled, posted, post-paid, registered, sent, transmitted, relayed, propagated, amplified, modulated, demodulated, broadcast, announced, advertised, radioed, televised, repeated, received, read, seen, heard, transcribed, recorded, taped, videoed

► *740 Publication*

35 communicable, transmittable, transmissible

► *316 Transfer*

693 Information

Facts speak louder than statistics. Geoffrey Streatfield.

NOUNS

1 information, facts, facts and figures, data, knowledge, intelligence, acquaintance, news, tidings, word, info (Inf), the know (Inf), gen (Inf), low-down (Inf), dope (Inf), dirt (Inf)

2 communication, transmission, dissemination, diffusion, notification, announcement, broadcast, publication, narration, account, eyewitness account, statement, review, report, dispatch, communiqué, bulletin, message, wire, fax, telegram, Telemessage™, telex, cable, cablegram, notice, order, briefing, instruction

3 document, paper, certificate, record, report, medical report, police report, review, *compte rendu* (Fr), annual report, progress report, term report, statement, estimate, specification, statement of account, financial statement, return, annual return, tax return, government documents, white paper, green paper, classified information, file, dossier, official documents, bumph (Inf)

4 mass communication, mass media, the media, broadcasting, radio, television, journalism, the press, serious press, tabloid press, yellow press, news, news coverage, blanket coverage, news item, newscast, feature story, scoop, publicity, press release, news release, hand-out, news conference, press conference, mention, obituary, regular feature, letters to the editor, advertisement, advert, ad, classified ad, small ad, births, marriages, and deaths, hatches, matches, and dispatches (Inf), magazines, journals, mailing list, subscription list, correspondence, circular, mailshot, junk mail

► *692 Communications; 740 Publication; 741 News*

5 reference book, encyclopedia, almanac, yearbook, dictionary, thesaurus, directory, index, guidebook, Baedeker, Fodor, Michelin, travelogue, handbook, manual, vade mecum, ABC, A–Z, timetable, Bradshaw, map, atlas, roadbook, road map, route map, itinerary, chart, plan, gazetteer, nautical almanac, astronomical almanac, ephemeris, catalogue, telephone directory, phone book, Yellow Pages

6 information technology, IT, computerized information, data communications, information retrieval, database, viewdata, data processing, information processing, word processing, information theory, statistics

► *40 Computers*

7 advice, tip, word, passing word, word in the ear, word to the wise, subtle word, hint, whisper, aside, suggestion, inference, intimation, insinuation, indication, inside information, pointer, tip-off, word of mouth, rumour, leak, gossip, gesture, prompt, reminder, signal, nod, wink, look, nudge, pinch, kick, kick under the table, caution, warning, scuttlebutt (US inf)

► *713 Advice; 737 Secrecy; 739 Disclosure*

8 source of information, source, authority, grapevine, channel, quarters, information centre, information office, press office, news agency, news syndicate, press service, wire service (US), Reuters, Press Association, Associated Press, United Press International, Agence France Presse

9 **informant**, informer, messenger, herald, teller, witness, eyewitness, testifier, narrator, communicator, announcer, broadcaster, newsreader, newscaster, anchorman (*or* anchor woman), spokesman (*or* spokeswoman), spokesperson, mouthpiece, news commentator, weather forecaster, notifier, advertiser, adviser, promoter, publicizer, publicist, public relations officer, publicity agent, press agent, flack (US), publisher, journalist, correspondent, special correspondent, foreign correspondent, reporter, freelance reporter, freelancer, stringer, feature writer, columnist, gossip columnist, gossip writer, chequebook journalist, newshound (Inf), hack (Inf)

10 **informer**, contact, source, adviser, tipster, tipper, talebearer, telltale, blabber, tattler, gossip, newsmonger, inside agent, betrayer, fifth columnist, accuser, stool pigeon, mole (Inf), nark (Inf), copper's nark (Inf), squealer (Inf), squeaker (Inf), whistle-blower (Inf), rat (Inf), snitch (Inf), fink (US inf), nose (US inf), grass (Inf), supergrass (Inf), delator (Lit)

VERBS

11 **inform**, tell, apprise, acquaint, advise, confide, notify, certify, testify, brief, instruct, teach, enlighten, educate, point out, correct, put right, disabuse, undeceive, disillusion, let know, have know, keep posted, give to understand, put in the picture (Inf), fill in (Inf), put wise (Inf), clue up (Inf), wise up (US inf)

12 **communicate**, make known, impart, transmit, disseminate, convey, recount, narrate, describe, publicize, break the news, broadcast, announce, televise, publish, report, document, post, wire, telegraph, fax, telex, telephone, phone, call, call up

▶ *692 Communications; 740 Publication*

13 **inform on** (*or* **against**), betray, denounce, accuse, turn queen's (*or* king's) evidence, tergiversate, tell, tell on, blab, spill the beans (Inf), let the cat out of the bag (Inf), stool (US inf), sell down the river (Inf), spill one's guts (Inf), sing (Inf), split (Inf), grass (Inf), shop (Inf), snitch (Inf), peach (Inf), squeal (Inf), blow (Inf), blow the lid off (Inf), blow the gaff (Inf), blow the whistle on (Inf), rat (Inf), delate (Lit)

▶ *739 Disclosure*

14 **tip**, tip off, hint, breathe, whisper, indicate, signal, suggest, imply, intimate, insinuate

15 **be informed**, come to know, realize, understand, know, learn, discover, be in the know, infer, get wind of, scent, hear, overhear, be a fly on the wall, get to hear of, become alive to, have it from, have it on good authority, have it from the horse's mouth, be told by a little bird

ADJECTIVES

16 **informative**, informatory, informational, revealing, illuminating, enlightening, explicit, clear, definite, expressive, expository, instructive, instructional, educational, advisory, cautionary, monitory, indicating, insinuating, suggesting, candid, plain-spoken, communicative, overcommunicative, indiscreet, loquacious, talkative, chatty, gossipy, big-mouthed (Inf)

▶ *731 Talkativeness; 739 Disclosure*

17 **newsworthy**, front-page, headline, newsy

▶ *741 News*

18 **informed**, enlightened, alert (to), aware (of), advised (of), briefed, posted, in touch, *au fait* (Fr), *au courant* (Fr), up-to-date, in the know (Inf), in on (Inf), in the picture (Inf), clued up (Inf), wised up (US inf), genned up (Inf)

ADVERBS

19 **reportedly**, as stated, on information received, as it is said, from the grapevine, by word of mouth, straight from the horse's mouth, as the story goes, apparently, from what one can gather, if one can trust one's ears

694 Meaning

The least of things with a meaning is worth more in life than the greatest of things without it. Carl Gustav Jung.

NOUNS

1 **meaning**, signification, sense, message, idea, message conveyed, idea conveyed, denotation, substance, essence, spirit, sum, sum and substance, gist, pith, core, contents, text, matter, subject matter, topic, semantic content, deep structure, value, drift, tenor, purport, import, implication, connotation, colouring, effect, force, relevance, bearing, scope, context, meaningfulness, semantic flow, expression, mode of expression, diction, style, semantics, general semantics, semasiology, sematology, semiotics, semiology, linguistics, nuts and bolts (Inf), nitty-gritty (Inf)

▶ *5 Language and Linguistics; 447 Topic; 724 Style; 742 Sign*

2 **significance**, seriousness, importance, import, substance, pith

▶ *123 Importance*

3 **comprehension**, clarity, plainness, explicitness, clear message, single meaning, univocal, monosemy, unambiguity, unambiguousness, unambiguous passage, lack of clarity, confused message, double meaning, extended meaning, multivocal, polysemy, ambiguity, ambiguousness, ambiguous passage, equivocal passage, equivocalness

▶ *271 Simplicity; 479 Equivocation; 695 Intelligibility*

4 **type of meaning**, level of meaning, denotation, literal meaning, plainness, literality, connotation, interpretation, explanation, definition, reference, application, construction, context, intention, intelligibility, meaningfulness, semantic field, original meaning, main meaning, derivation, etymology, chief meaning, leading sense, received meaning, accepted meaning, allegorical meaning, usage, practice, lexical meaning, grammatical meaning, technical meaning, specialized meaning, special meaning, jargon, idiom, same meaning, equivalent meaning, equivalence, synonym, synonymousness, synonymity, synonymy, identity, opposite meaning, contradictory meaning, opposite, antonym, changed meaning, semantic shift, figurative meaning, metaphorical meaning, metaphor, trope, hidden meaning, latent meaning, tropical meaning, latency, esoteric sense, implied sense, no sense, nonsense, absurdity

▶ *139 Speciality; 271 Simplicity; 344 Cause; 632 Habit; 695 Intelligibility; 697 Nonsense; 719 Interpretation*

5 **point**, purpose, aim, object, end, idea, plan, design, intention, intent, value, worth, use

► *235 Worth; 237 Usefulness; 482 Intention; 484 Plan*

ADJECTIVES

6 **meaningful**, full of meaning, replete with meaning, packed with meaning, pregnant with meaning, having meaning, having sense, etymological, denotative, comprehensible, intelligible, unambiguous, univocal, monosemous, clear, plain, lucid, perspicuous, literal, express, explicit, pointed, declaratory, affirmative, indicative, repeated, tautological (*or* tautologous), identical, similar, synonymous, equivalent, paraphrastic, tantamount, connotative, implied, implicit, inferred, tacit, suggestive, unclear, obscure, confused, technical, professional, special, specialized, contrary, opposite, antonymous, homonymous, extended, transferred, ambiguous, multivocal, polysemous, equivocal, symbolic, figurative, metaphorical, allegorical, idiomatic, significative, importing, purporting, indicating, telltale, evocative, expressive, interpretative, interpretive, telling, eloquent, allusive, without meaning, meaningless, nonsensical, absurd

► *112 Repetition; 115 Similarity; 266 Obscurity; 271 Simplicity; 479 Equivocation; 695 Intelligibility; 696 Unintelligibility; 697 Nonsense; 707 Affirmation; 719 Interpretation; 725 Clarity; 742 Sign; 743 Identification*

7 **significant**, consequential, serious, important, weighty, substantial, pithy, meaty, of moment

► *123 Importance*

8 **semantic**, semasiological, semiotic, semiological, linguistic, philological, verbal, lexical

► *5 Language and Linguistics*

9 **meant**, implied, intended, deliberate, designed, planned, destined, predestined

► *106 Predetermination; 482 Intention*

VERBS

10 **mean**, signify, have a meaning, have a sense, mean something, convey a meaning, convey a message, convey an idea, get across, communicate, denote, say clearly, say plainly, use plain words, say directly, spell out, declare, assert, affirm, express, inform, tell, connote, imply, indicate, symbolize, stand for, represent, betoken, designate, import, purport, intend, point to, add up to, boil down to, spell, convey, bespeak, tell of, speak of, breathe of, savour of, speak volumes, evidence, mean to say, try to say, be getting at, be driving at, really mean, have in mind, contemplate, allude to, refer to, hint at, suggest, intimate, say in other words, put another way, rephrase, paraphrase, repeat, tautologize, have the same meaning, agree in meaning, mean the same thing, coincide, accord, conflict in meaning, mean something else, mean the opposite, mean the reverse, contradict, disagree, talk turkey (US inf)

► *112 Repetition; 693 Information; 695 Intelligibility; 707 Affirmation; 716 Evidence; 717 Representation; 743 Identification; 750 Agreement*

11 **infer**, draw a meaning, deduce, understand, understand by

► *476 Supposition*

12 **intend**, aim, purpose, plan, design, destine, predestine, cause, result in, bring about, entail, involve, portend, presage, augur

► *106 Predetermination; 344 Cause; 475 Prediction; 482 Intention; 484 Plan*

ADVERBS

13 **meaningfully**, meaningly, with meaning, significantly, intelligibly, clearly, directly, explicitly, plainly, unambiguously, in plain words, to the effect that, in the sense that (*or* of), in a sense, in some sense, as meant, as intended, as understood, according to the book, from the context, literally, verbatim, word for word, in other words, so to speak, ambiguously, figuratively, metaphorically, symbolically

► *719 Interpretation*

695 Intelligibility

Unless one is a genius, it is best to aim at being intelligible.
Anthony Hope.

ADJECTIVES

1 **intelligible**, comprehensible, understandable, knowable, apprehensible, fathomable, penetrable, scrutable, interpretable, realizable, coherent, making sense, sane, audible, coming through loud and clear, visible, luminous, unambiguous, unambivalent, unequivocal, univocal, meaningful, explicable, teachable, unblurred, focused, clear-cut, precise, definite, certain, positive, telling, striking, vivid, graphic, highly coloured, descriptive, illustrative, explanatory, explicatory, interpretative, interpretive, informative

► *455 Knowledge; 460 Sanity; 520 Visibility; 694 Meaning; 721 Description*

2 **simple**, clear, crystal-clear, plain, plainly stated, explicit, articulate, well-spoken, distinct, direct, straightforward, unevasive, unadorned, downright, forthright, uninvolved, uncomplicated, obvious, self-explanatory, self-evident, easy, easily understood, easy to comprehend, easy to follow, easy to grasp, made easy, made simple, clear to anyone, easy to read, readable, legible, *lisible* (Fr), decipherable, beautifully handwritten, clearly printed, uncoded, decoded, explained, interpreted, simplified, popularized, popular, exoteric, for everyone, for the layman, for the general public, reaching a mass audience, aiming for the lowest common denominator, available to all, apodeictic, using short words, using simple language, limpid, transparent, lucid, pellucid, perspicuous, as simple as pie, as clear as day, as plain as the nose on one's face

► *265 Easiness; 271 Simplicity; 527 Transparency; 719 Interpretation; 725 Clarity*

3 **recognizable**, distinguishable, identifiable, distinct, defined, well-defined, standing out, definite, unmistakable, knowable

► *139 Speciality; 452 Certainty*

VERBS

4 **be intelligible**, make sense, come through loud and clear, come alive, take on depth, offer readability, read easily, add up, speak to one's understanding, tell its own tale, speak for itself, speak volumes, have no secrets, become apparent, sink in, penetrate, dawn on, register, open one's eyes, come over (Inf), get across (Inf)

▶ *520 Visibility; 701 Argument; 716 Evidence*

5 **simplify**, make clear, make crystal-clear, make plain, state plainly, speak clearly, articulate, repeat, recapitulate, make easy, predigest, make easily understood, popularize, write for the layman, address the general public, reach a mass audience, aim for the lowest common denominator, make available to all, spell out, put in plain words, state in plain English, use short words, use simple language, avoid gobbledegook, offer an easy read, facilitate, explain, explicate, interpret, elucidate, clarify, clear up, labour the obvious, emphasize, put over (Inf)

▶ *112 Repetition; 265 Easiness; 271 Simplicity; 719 Interpretation; 725 Clarity*

6 **understand**, comprehend, know, realize, apprehend, fathom, penetrate, master, learn, have, hold, retain, remember, have understanding, get to the bottom of, grasp, grasp the meaning, get the gist of, get the idea, get hold of, seize, be on to, take in, follow, get, begin to understand, come to understand, have insight, have one's eyes opened, see the light, see through, see it all, be undeceived, get to know, be told, be informed, be with it (Inf), be with one (Inf), twig (Inf), latch on to (Inf), catch on (Inf), get wise to (Inf), get the picture (Inf), see the lay of the land (Inf), catch the drift of (Inf), get the hang of (Inf), tumble to (Inf), rumble (Inf), dig (Inf), savvy (Inf), colly (US inf)

▶ *449 Discovery; 455 Knowledge; 458 Wisdom; 462 Memory; 518 Vision; 693 Information*

7 **recognize**, detect, identify, spot, descry, distinguish, discern, make out, perceive, ken (Scot), conceive, see at a glance, see with half an eye, see, make no mistake

▶ *452 Certainty; 518 Vision; 707 Affirmation; 743 Identification*

8 **be recognizable**, have a distinctive appearance, stand out, leap out

NOUNS

9 **intelligibility**, comprehensibility, understandability, knowability, apprehensibility, fathomableness, penetrability, scrutability, interpretability, explicability, teachability, coherence, unambiguity, unambivalence, precision, preciseness, definiteness, positiveness, certainty, sense, meaningfulness, informativeness, vividness, graphicness, descriptiveness

▶ *455 Knowledge; 694 Meaning*

10 **simplicity**, clarity, clearness, plainness, plain speaking, plain speech, explicitness, articulateness, articulacy, distinctness, directness, straightforwardness, downrightness, forthrightness, uninvolvement, unadornment, unadorned style, simple eloquence, readability, legibility, beautiful handwriting, decipherability, clear printing, decoding, easiness, facility, obviousness, self-evidence, explanation, amplification, interpretation, simplification, popularization, lowest common denominator (LCD), short words, words of one syllable, plain words, simple language, plain English, mother tongue, limpidity, transparency, lucidity, pellucidity, perspicuity

▶ *265 Easiness; 271 Simplicity; 527 Transparency; 719 Interpretation; 725 Clarity*

11 **recognizability**, cognizability, distinction, distinguishability, distinctiveness, definiteness, definition

▶ *452 Certainty*

12 **understanding**, comprehension, mastery, realization, apprehension, grasp, learning, knowledge, perception, recognition

▶ *455 Knowledge; 743 Identification*

ADVERBS

13 **intelligibly**, comprehensibly, understandably, coherently, articulately, expressively, simply, clearly, lucidly, plainly, distinctly, unmistakably, explicitly, concisely, in words of one syllable, with clarity, in a clear style, in plain terms, in no uncertain terms, in plain English, unambiguously, for the layman, for the general public

696 Unintelligibility

ADJECTIVES

1 **unintelligible**, incomprehensible, unclear, meaningless, obscure, esoteric, inconceivable, not understandable, impossible to explain, inexplicable, unexplainable, unaccountable, so much nonsense, gibbering, incoherent, rambling, inarticulate, unknown, undiscoverable, unfathomable, inapprehensible, unbridgeable, impenetrable, unsearchable, inscrutable, blank, expressionless, deadpan, impassive, inaudible, muted, scrambled, garbled, scrawly, scribbled, cramped, crabbed, encoded, hard to decode, undecipherable, unreadable, illegible, undiscernible, unseen, invisible, hidden, unknowable, private, arcane, cryptic, mysterious, shrouded in mystery, enigmatic, esoteric, gnostic, sphinxlike, oracular, profound, deep, occult, mystic, mystical, transcendental, inexpressible, unspeakable, unpronounceable, unutterable, ineffable, incommunicable, untranslatable, indefinable, like double Dutch (Inf), poker-faced (Inf)

▶ *7 Religion; 156 Depth; 266 Obscurity; 732 Shyness; 736 Concealment*

2 **unexplained**, never solved, without a solution, without a clue, unsolvable, insoluble, unsolved, unresolved, uncertain, shrouded in mystery

3 **unrecognizable**, incognizable, indistinguishable, unidentifiable, indistinct, poorly defined, undefined, hidden, indefinite, easily mistaken, unknowable

▶ *456 Ignorance; 592 Insensitivity*

4 **difficult**, confusing, puzzling, baffling, perplexing, hard to understand, complex, complicated, beyond one's comprehension, defying comprehension, beyond one, over one's head, recondite, abstruse, elusive, amorphous, shadowy, obscure, sphinxlike, enigmatic, inscrutable, mysterious, occult, nebulous, vague, murky, muddy, misty, foggy, hazy, fuzzy, dim, clear as mud, unclear, ambiguous, equivocal, paradoxical, of doubtful meaning, oracular

▶ *264 Difficulty; 266 Obscurity; 479 Equivocation; 524 Dimness*

5 **strange**, odd, weird, abnormal, unexpected, bizarre, quaint, eccentric, oddball (Inf)

▶ *118 Nonconformity; 453 Uncertainty; 630 Surprise*

6 **confused**, puzzled, baffled, perplexed, mystified, unable to understand, wondering, bewildered, flummoxed, stumped, confounded, nonplussed, out of one's depth, out of it (Inf), not getting it (Inf)

VERBS

7 **be unintelligible**, defy comprehension, not make sense, elude one, escape one, lose one, make one's head swim (*or* ache), need an interpreter, present a puzzle, keep one guessing, talk in riddles, speak in tongues, talk nonsense, gibber, ramble, mean nothing, speak badly, speak gobbledegook, talk like an idiot, babble, look blank, look expressionless, look deadpan, scribble, doodle, scrawl, cause doubt, puzzle, baffle, perplex, mystify, bewilder, flummox, confound, stump, confuse, bedevil, entangle, go over one's head, be beyond one's reach, talk double Dutch (Inf)

► *328 Disturbance; 451 Disbelief; 453 Uncertainty*

8 **make unintelligible**, scribble, scrawl, scramble, garble, encode, encipher, shroud in mystery, obscure, complicate, confuse

9 **find unintelligible**, not understand, find hard to understand, find too difficult, misjudge, misunderstand, get wrong, get the wrong idea, not know, not register, have a blind spot, have no grasp of, not have the first idea, not make out, not know what to make of, make neither head nor tail of, make nothing of, puzzle, wonder, rack one's brains, be out of one's depth, not know what one is about, be lost, be at sea, not get it (Inf), not grasp it (Inf), throw up one's hands (Inf), be on a different wavelength (Inf)

► *274 Error; 465 Misjudgment; 472 Inattention; 486 Unskilfulness; 519 Blindness; 716 Evidence*

10 **be unexplained**, require explanation, remain unsolved, have no answer, have no solution, give no clue

NOUNS

11 **unintelligibility**, incomprehensibility, inapprehensibility, meaninglessness, lack of meaning, lack of sense, nonsense, unclearness, lack of clarity, obscurity, uncertainty, ambiguity, equivocalness, esotericism, difficulty, perplexity, bafflement, confusion, mystification, impenetrability, inscrutability, the unknown, inconceivability, lack of understanding, inexplicability, unaccountability, impossibility of discovery, secrecy, babbling, mumbling, stuttering, stammering, blankness, lack of expression, impassivity, inaudibility, faintness, muteness, illegibility, unreadability, invisibility, privacy, arcaneness, mystery, profoundness, deepness, occultism, mysticism, transcendentalism, inexpressibility, unspeakableness, ineffability, incommunicability, indefinableness, poker face (Inf)

► *453 Uncertainty; 461 Insanity; 697 Nonsense; 729 Speech; 737 Secrecy*

12 **unintelligible thing**, obscure point, perplexing question, puzzle, puzzler, problem, conundrum, knotty problem, hard (*or* tough) nut to crack, baffling attitude, mysterious message, secret, secret book, code, cipher (*or* cypher), secret language, idiolect, gibberish, scrawl, scribble, mystery, enigma, enigmatic question, riddle, paradox, double Dutch (Inf)

► *266 Obscurity; 453 Uncertainty; 737 Secrecy*

ADVERBS

13 **unintelligibly**, incomprehensibly, meaninglessly, inconceivably, inexplicably, unaccountably, incoherently, inarticulately, unfathomably, impenetrably, expressionlessly, inscrutably, blankly, impassively, inaudibly, unreadably, illegibly, cryptically, esoterically, mysteriously, enigmatically

697 Nonsense

This particularly rapid, unintelligible patter
Isn't generally heard, and if it is it doesn't matter. W. S. Gilbert.

NOUNS

1 **nonsense**, rubbish, trash, stuff and nonsense, balderdash, rot, twaddle, drivel, gibberish, gobbledegook, absurdity, senselessness, bombast, empty talk, bunkum, amphigory (*or* amphigouri), nonsense verse, doggerel, blah (Inf), hooey (Inf), bilge (Inf), claptrap (Inf), piffle (Inf), bosh (Inf), tosh (Inf), tripe (Inf), poppycock (Inf), crap (Inf), shit (Inf), bullshit (Inf), bull (Inf), cobblers (Inf), balls (Inf), bollocks (Inf)

► *272 Ridiculousness; 459 Folly; 699 Falsehood*

2 **solecism**, malapropism, Freudian slip, spoonerism, wellerism, howler, witticism, *bon mot* (Fr), epigram, riddle, pun, play on words, joke, quip, crack (Inf), gag (Inf), wisecrack (Inf), scream (Inf), laugh (Inf)

► *274 Error; 599 Humour*

3 **tomfoolery**, horseplay, antics, capers, high jinks, silliness, silly season, vagary, whimsicality, banter, buffoonery, drollery, clowning, burlesque, farce, scrape, prank, trick, practical joke, mucking about (Inf), shenanigans (Inf), skylarking (Inf)

► *459 Folly; 621 Derision*

4 **buffoon**, fool, jester, clown, joker, practical joker, prankster, japer, humorist, wit, wag, comedian, tease, teaser, *farceur* (Fr), wisecracker (Inf)

► *599 Humour*

ADJECTIVES

5 **nonsensical**, foolish, silly, absurd, meaningless, senseless, idiotic, mad, crazy, ridiculous, ludicrous, asinine, anserine, preposterous, fanciful, imaginative, fatuous, funny, jocular, humorous, droll, waggish, comic, merry, farcical, laughable, piffling (Inf)

► *272 Ridiculousness; 459 Folly; 461 Insanity; 599 Humour*

VERBS

6 **talk nonsense**, rave, rant, gabble, garble, blarney, talk through one's hat, rhapsodize, romance, joke, pun, play on words, quip, crack jokes, gag (Inf), blah (Inf), bullshit (Inf)

► *599 Humour; 699 Falsehood*

7 **be nonsense**, mean nothing, have no meaning

8 **fool**, fool around, play the fool, act the fool, clown, lark about, skylark, monkey around, horse about, act the goat

► *459 Folly*

ADVERBS

9 **nonsensically**, foolishly, absurdly, meaninglessly, ridiculously, preposterously, humorously

698 Truth

The truth that makes men free is for the most part the truth which men prefer not to hear. Herbert Sebastian Agar.

And ye shall know the truth, and the truth shall make you free. Bible: John.

'Tis strange – but true; for truth is always strange;
Stranger than fiction: if it could be told,
How much would novels gain by the exchange! Lord Byron.

It is hard to believe that a man is telling the truth when you know that you would lie if you were in his place. Henry Louis Mencken.

NOUNS

1 truth, trueness, fact, verity, eternal verities, rightness, unerroneousness, unmistakenness, unfalseness, unfallaciousness, unspeciousness, unspuriousness, unfictitiousness, (good) sooth (Lit), dinkum oil (Aus and NZ inf)

2 reality, actuality, existence, substance, substantiality, tangibility, the real world, things as they are

▶ *93 Existence; 95 Reality*

3 the truth, the facts, facts of the matter, facts of life, facts, the case, the plain truth, the simple truth, the honest truth, the actual truth, the very truth, the absolute truth, the objective truth, the ultimate truth, home truths, the unalloyed truth, the unvarnished truth, the naked truth, the unqualified truth, the sober truth, the exact truth, the straight truth, the honest-to-goodness truth, the honest-to-God truth, God's truth, gospel, the gospel truth, Holy Writ, Biblical truth, the revealed truth, revelation, the heart of the matter, the whole truth and nothing but the truth, how it is (Inf), the lowdown (Inf)

4 truism, basic truth, intrinsic truth, primary premise, axiom, maxim, aphorism, platitude, proverb, precept, principle, dictum

▶ *745 Maxim*

5 truthfulness, frankness, veracity, honesty, lack of disguise, lack of exaggeration, objectivity, lack of bias, probity, candour, sincerity, openness, open-heartedness, forthrightness, straightforwardness, directness, bluntness, lack of flattery, warts and all, plainness, baldness, outspokenness, ingenuousness, naivety, artlessness, guilelessness, simpleness, lack of pretension, lack of pretence, lack of assumption, unaffectedness, downrightness

▶ *799 Honour*

6 authenticity, realness, no illusion, genuineness, officialness, originality, inimitability, uniqueness, purity, unadulteration, sterling silver, hallmarked silver, twenty-four-carat gold, validity, bona fideness, legitimacy, rightfulness, the real thing, the genuine article, the very thing, not a fake, no imitation, soundness, solidity, unquestionability, unquestionableness, unqualifiedness, unrefutability, unconfutability, undeniableness, it (Inf), all wool and a yard wide (US inf), the (real) McCoy (Inf), the real Simon Pure (Inf)

▶ *126 Originality; 716 Evidence*

7 confirmation, determination, ascertainment, authentication, verification, validation, certification, demonstration, establishment, attestation, substantiality, substantiation, corroboration, proof, facts, logic, evidence, statistics

▶ *703 Demonstration*

8 accuracy, perfection, preciseness, precision, exactness, exactitude, meticulousness, pinpoint accuracy, detail, microscopic detail, definition, fastidiousness, correctness, rightness, aptness, rigour, rigorousness, faultlessness, absoluteness, flawlessness, care for the truth, attention to details (*or* facts), particularization, punctiliousness, mathematical exactness, mechanical precision, micrometry, scientific exactness, documentation, fine adjustment, squaring, setting, truing, trimming, delicateness, delicacy, refinement, fineness, niceness, nicety, subtleness, subtlety, faithfulness, fidelity, high fidelity, true report, true representation, hitting the nail on the head, scoring a bull's-eye

▶ *471 Attention*

9 uniformity, regularity, constancy, straightness, lack of deviation, unchangeableness, unerringness

10 literalness, literality, literalism, literal meaning, denotation, following the letter, true to the letter, the very words, verbatim account, textualism, chapter and verse, word-for-word translation

▶ *17 Literature*

11 pedantry, strictness, rigidity, severity, rigour, rigorousness, literal-mindedness, closeness, authority, authoritativeness, cogency, weight, force, legality, lawfulness, legitimacy, acting according to the book, going by the letter of the law

▶ *16 Law; 396 Authority*

12 realism, true look, true sound, ring of truth, look of reality, verisimilitude, veraciousness, appearance of truth, absolute likeness, absolute realism, photographic realism, realistic representation, representationalism, naturalism, naturalness, faithful rendering

▶ *19 Painting and Sculpture*

13 faithfulness, loyalty, fidelity, faith, trueness

▶ *663 Obedience*

14 truthful person, honest John, George Washington

ADJECTIVES

15 true, veritable, veracious, factual, right, unmistaken, not in error, unfictitious, honest-to-goodness, honest-to-God, gospel, Biblical, revealed, holding true, holding good, holding water, holding up, standing up, standing the test, standing the test of time, holding up in the wash (Inf)

16 existing, real, actual, substantial, tangible

17 truistic, intrinsic, primary, axiomatic, aphoristic, platitudinous, proverbial, preceptive, principled

18 truthful, frank, veracious, honest, veridical, undisguised, unexaggerated, objective, unbiased, candid, sincere, open, open-hearted, above board, forthright, straightforward, direct, blunt, unflattering, warts and all, plain, bald, outspoken, ingenuous, naive, artless, guileless, simple, unpretending, unpretentious, unassuming, unaffected, downright, straight from the shoulder

19 authentic, real, without illusion, genuine, official, original, unimitated, inimitable, unique, pure, unadulterated, sterling, hallmarked, twenty-four carat, valid, bona fide, legitimate, rightful, by birth, sound, solid, substantial, undoubted, unquestionable, unquestioned, unqualified, unrefuted, unconfuted, undenied, honest-to-goodness, honest-to-God, pukka (*or* pucka) (Inf), sure enough (Inf), dinkum (Aus and NZ inf)

20 proved, proven, factually proven, logically proven, statistically proven, authenticated, ascertained, verified, validated, certified, demonstrated, logically demonstrated, confirmed, determined, established, attested, substantiated, corroborated

21 accurate, precise, exact, perfect, word-perfect, definitive, meticulous, pinpoint, pinpointed, detailed, particularized, defined, microscopic, correct, right, apt, rigorous, faultless, absolute, flawless, punctilious, mathematical, mathematically exact, mechanically precise, scientific, documented, documentary, documental, fine, finely adjusted, squared, trued, set, trimmed, delicate, refined, nice, subtle, faithful, straight, well-aimed, dead right, true to the facts, OK (*or* okay) (Inf), dead-on (Inf), on the button (Inf), A-OK (*or* A-okay) (US inf), bang-on (Inf), spot on (Inf), on the nose (US inf), straight up (Inf)

22 uniform, regular, constant, straight, undeviating, unchanging, unerring

23 literal, denotative, verbatim, textual, word-for-word, chapter-and-verse, following the letter, true-to-the-letter

24 pedantic, strict, rigid, severe, literal-minded, rigorous, close, authoritative, cogent, weighty, forceful, legal, lawful, legitimate

25 lifelike, true-to-life, ringing true, looking true, sounding true, appearing true, seeming real, verisimilar, realistic, veracious, unmistaken, naturalistic, representative, true-to-nature, faithfully rendered, just right, true to the spirit, coming alive, true to scale

26 faithful, loyal, dependable, trustworthy, honourable, true, true-blue

VERBS

27 be true, be the case, conform to facts, square with facts, square with the evidence, hold true, hold good, hold water, hold up, stand up, stand the test, stand the test of time, hold up in the wash (Inf), wash (Inf)

28 bring into existence, actualize, make tangible, know the real world, see things as they are

29 be truthful, tell the truth, speak the truth, confess the truth, give the true story, stick to the facts, square with the facts (*or* evidence), lack disguise, lack bias, show sincerity, be open, open up, open one's heart, make a clean breast of it, make no bones about it, call a spade a spade

30 prove (to be) true, prove real, confirm, determine, ascertain, authenticate, verify, validate, certify, demonstrate, establish, attest, substantiate, corroborate, offer factual evidence, present the facts

31 be accurate, perfect, pinpoint, detail, define, correct, care for the truth, give attention to details (*or* facts), particularize, document, make fine adjustments, adjust, square, true, set, trim, refine, make fine, make uniform, regularize, straighten, not allow to deviate, aim well, give a true report, make a true representation, get at the truth, hit the nail on the head, score a bull's-eye, dot one's i's and cross one's t's, hit it on the nose (US inf)

32 be literal, give a verbatim account, follow the letter, be a pedant, act according to the book, go by the letter of the law

33 seem lifelike, seem true to life, ring true, hold the ring of truth, look true, sound true, carry conviction, give the appearance of truth, seem real, seem true to nature, come alive

34 render, render faithfully, copy nature, represent, bring alive

ADVERBS

35 truly, really, actually, factually, in point of fact, verily, veritably, in truth, indeed, with truth, to tell the truth, in reality, in fact, as a matter of fact, really-truly (Inf), no buts (about it) (Inf), forsooth (Lit)

36 truthfully, frankly, honestly, veridically, objectively, candidly, sincerely, openly, directly, bluntly, warts and all, simply, not to mince words (*or* matters)

37 authentically, genuinely, really, truly, officially, uniquely, purely, indubitably, undoubtedly, undeniably, certainly, indeed, nothing else but, rightfully, logically, naturally, legitimately

38 literally, strictly speaking, verbatim, word for word, letter for letter, *verbatim et litteratim* (L), by the book, in the same words, to the letter, pedantically, rigorously, legitimately, as it reads, *sic* (L)

39 accurately, correctly, rightly, properly, precisely, exactly, perfectly, straight, expressly, dead right, even, square, plumb, directly, squarely, point-blank, unerringly, undeviatingly, right to an inch, right to a hair, right to a turn, right to a T, in every detail, in all respects, neither more nor less, *tout à fait* (Fr), to be exact, spot on (Inf)

INTERJECTIONS

40 right!, fine!, right you are!, that's it!, you've got it!, that's for sure!, ain't it the truth! (Inf), righto! (Inf), fair dinkum! (Aus and NZ inf)

699 Falsehood

O what a tangled web we weave,
When first we practise to deceive! Sir Walter Scott.

NOUNS

1 falsehood, falseness, falsity, error, mendaciousness, mendacity, inveracity, untruth, untruthfulness, truthlessness, untrueness, unverity, fallaciousness, fallacy, erroneousness, ungenuineness, spuriousness, false conduct, improbity, dissemblance, dishonesty, sleaze, bad faith, lack of integrity, deception, delusion, Machiavellianism, unreality, nonexistence

► *234 Distortion; 700 Deception; 800 Dishonour*

2 duplicity, doubleness, two-facedness, double life, double-mindedness, double facade, double-tongue, forked tongue, double-dealing, ambidexterity

3 hypocrisy, hypocriticalness, insincerity, deception, delusion, disguise, camouflage, concealment, sanctimony, sanctimoniousness, religiosity, false piety, ostentatiousness, uncandidness, uncandour, unfrankness, tokenism, flattery, unctuousness, oiliness, cant, lip service, mummery, mouthing, mealy-mouthedness, empty gesture, emptiness, disingenuousness, mockery, unseriousness, meretriciousness, crossed fingers, tongue-in-cheek, cupboard love, crocodile tears, Tartuffery, Pecksniffery, Pharisaism, blandishments, blarney, sweet-talk (Inf), soft soap (Inf)

4 spuriousness, bogusness, falseness, ungenuineness, unauthenticity, unrealness, forgery, counterfeiting, artificiality, factitiousness, hollowness, humbug, humbuggery, speciousness, sophistry, casuistry, Jesuitism, charlatanism, charlatanry, quackery, quackishness, quackism, mountebankery, imposture, illegitimacy, phoniness (Inf)

▶ *702 Sophistry*

5 deceitfulness, duplicity, fraudulence, falseheartedness, cunning, low cunning, sneakiness, artfulness, artifice, guile, wile, fake conduct, malingering, improbity, lying, treason, treachery, Judas kiss

6 lying, fibbing, fibbery, fabrication, pseudology, pathological lying, habitual lying, shameless lying, barefaced lying, mythomania, perjury, false witness, false swearing, forswearing, perfidy, defamation, libel, slander

7 pretence, pretending, pretension, dissimulation, impersonation, imitation, acting, play-acting, dramatization, fiction, fictionalization, romanticization, poetic licence, representation, feigning, feint, pretext, posture, pose, posing, affectation, apparentness, ostensibility, attitudinizing, exaggeration, overstatement, hyperbole, overestimation

8 fraud, fraudulence, swindle, dishonesty, cheating, trickery, fakery, faking, falsity, imposture, sharp practice, illicit practice, confidence trick, underhanded deal, insider dealing, adulteration, packed jury, stacked deck, loaded dice, salted mine, juggled figures, counterfeiting, forgery, put-up job, hoax, canard, con (Inf), crookedness (Inf), whitewash job (Inf), frame-up (Inf), put-on (US inf), sting (Inf), rip-off (Inf)

9 falsification, falsifying, faking, misrepresentation, misstatement, overstatement, understatement, misquote, misinterpretation, misreporting, misciting, perversion, distortion, straining, warping, slanting, slant, twisting, twist, garbling, garble, sharp practice, nod and a wink, collusion, manipulation, tampering with, doctoring, rigging, juggling, retouching, counterfeiting, forgery, fabrication, trumping up, confabulation, invention, imagination, concoction, canard, fiction, figment, myth, legend, fable, wangle (Inf), fiddle (Inf), fix (Inf), plant (Inf), frame (Inf), frame-up (Inf)

▶ *477 Imagination; 720 Misinterpretation*

10 lie, fib, fable, story, tall story, t tale, tall tale, fairy tale, fantasy, the big lie, downright lie, shameless lie, monstrous lie, barefaced lie, taradiddle (*or* tarradiddle), breach of promise, broken promise, broken word, terminological inexactitude, traveller's tale, flam (Dial), flimflam (Inf), cock-and-bull story (Inf), yarn (Inf), fisherman's yarn (Inf), fish story (US inf), shaggy dog story (Inf), whopper (Inf), all my eye (and Betty Martin) (Inf), dirty lie (Inf)

11 half-truth, half-lie, partial truth, near-truth, equivocation, (little) white lie, economy with the truth, false rumour, empty gossip (*or* talk), canard, old wives' tale, diplomatic excuse, misinterpretation, distorted truth, propaganda, propaganda machine, factory of lies (Inf), gate of ivory (Inf)

▶ *477 Imagination; 720 Misinterpretation; 736 Concealment; 741 News*

12 fake, sham, mock, imitation, copy, counterfeit, bootleg, dummy, tinsel, paste, rubbish, junk, phoney (Inf), pseud (Inf), pseudo (Inf)

13 evasion, equivocation, ambivalence, double talk, shiftiness, dodging, shuffling, fencing, fudging the issue

14 façade, front, mask, show, masquerade, disguise, ostentation, false front, outward show, false show, dressing up, false air, false light, face, appearance, fanfaronade, semblance, seeming, sham, fake, act, bluff, bluffing, simulation, dissimulation, dissemblance, window-dressing, whitewash, gloss, varnish, gild, embellishment, embroidery, touch up, touching up, deodorization, colour, colouring, false colour, falsely colouring, simulacrum (Lit)

15 nonsense, humbug, humbuggery, moonshine, hogwash, eyewash (Inf), bosh (Inf), baloney (Inf), flimflam (Inf), claptrap (Inf), gammon (Inf), bunkum (*or* buncombe) (Inf), bunk (Inf), hooey (Inf), hoke (US inf), hokum (US inf), bull (Inf), bullshit (Inf), crap (Inf), balls (Inf)

16 false thing, forged passport, counterfeit note, Hitler diaries, plagiarized book, simulated wood, paste gem, fool's gold, nine-bob note, Trojan horse, mirage

17 false person, humbug, hoaxer, hypocrite, whited sepulchre, pretender, imposter, charlatan, liar, perjurer, fraud, cheat, swindler, confidence man, counterfeiter, plotter, schemer, saboteur, informer, traitor, betrayer, double-crosser, double agent, Pharisee, Judas Iscariot, Benedict Arnold, seducer, Don Juan, Casanova, goody-goody (Inf), con man (Inf), pseud (Inf)

18 liar, fibber, fibster, fabricator, fabulist, phoney, perjurer, false witness, falsifier, propagandist, prevaricator, pseudologist, pathological liar, confirmed liar, habitual liar, consummate liar, palterer, equivocator, storyteller, romancer, Ananias, Satan, Father of Lies, Baron Münchhausen, Sir John Mandeville, yarn-spinner (Inf), dirty liar (Inf), bullshitter (Inf)

19 cheat, fraud, defrauder, cozener, counterfeiter, forger, swindler, imposter, impersonator, ringer (US), pretender, humbug, fake, faker, shark, phoney, sham, shammer, quack, quackster, mountebank, *saltimbanco* (It), bluff, bluffer, charlatan, poser, poseur, hypocrite, Pharisee, whited sepulchre, Tartuffe, Pecksniff, Joseph Surface, false friend, fair-weather friend, summer soldier, wolf in sheep's clothing, ass in a lion's skin, four-flusher (US inf), mealy-mouth (Inf)

VERBS

20 be false, ring false, not ring true, falsify, lie, not speak the truth, dissemble, show bad faith, lack integrity, deceive, delude, make an error

21 double-deal, play a double role, have it both ways, play both ends against the middle, have one's cake and eat it too, have a foot in both camps, run with the hare and hunt with the hounds, two-time (Inf)

22 be hypocritical, be insincere, deceive, delude, act sanctimoniously, have false piety, be holier than thou, be holier than the Pope, disguise, camouflage, conceal, lack candour, cant, render (*or* pay) lip service, mouth, make an empty gesture, flatter, mock, say one thing and mean another, cross one's fingers, put one's tongue in one's cheek, shed crocodile tears, blandish, be full of blarney, sweet-talk (Inf), soft-soap (Inf)

23 be deceitful, malinger, sneak, show treachery, give a Judas kiss

24 pretend, make a pretense of, make a show of, make like, make as if, dissimulate, impersonate, imitate, act, play-act, play, play a part, dissemble, represent, feign, feint, posture, pose, pose as, assume the guise of, pass oneself off as, affect, attitudinize, assume, put on, put on a (false) front, sail under false colours, play possum, roll over and play dead

25 be fraudulent, swindle, cheat, trick, fake, copy, falsify, deal underhandedly, deal on inside information, pack (a jury), stack, juggle, load, salt, salt a mine, adulterate, counterfeit, forge, hoax, whitewash, con (Inf), put on (Inf), sting (Inf), rip off (Inf), nobble (Inf)

26 falsify, fake, misrepresent, misstate, overstate, understate, misquote, misinterpret, put a false construction on, misreport, miscite, pervert, distort, strain, warp, slant, twist, garble, collude, give a nod and a wink, manipulate, tamper with, retouch, counterfeit, forge, fabricate, trump up, confabulate, invent, imagine, cry wolf, concoct, mythologize, fable, doctor, rig, wangle (Inf), fiddle (Inf), cook the books (Inf), fix (Inf), plant (Inf), frame (Inf)

27 evade, equivocate, be ambivalent, double talk, shuffle, fence, fudge the issue

28 mask, show, masquerade, disguise, impersonate, show a false front, make an outward show, put up a (false) front, give a false show, present a false air, put in a false light, face, appear, seem, fake, act, bluff, simulate, dissimulate, dissemble, window-dress, embellish, embroider, touch up, dress up, overdo, deodorize, make smell like roses, gloss, gloss over, whitewash, varnish, gilt, colour, colour falsely

ADJECTIVES

29 false, fallacious, erroneous, mendaceous, inveracious, untrue, untruthful, truthless, not true, ungenuine, spurious, dissembling, dishonest, deceptive, delusive, Machiavellian

30 duplicitous, two-faced, Janus-faced, double-minded, double-dealing, double-tongued, ambidextrous

31 hypocritical, insincere, disingenuous, meretricious, deceptive, delusive, sanctimonious, religiose, falsely pious, empty, Pharisaic, ostentatious, uncandid, unfrank, unctuous, oily, mealy-mouthed, flattering, Pecksniffian, mocking, unserious, tongue-in-cheek, nonsensical, goody-goody (Inf), sweet-talking (Inf), soft-soaping (Inf)

32 spurious, bogus, ungenuine, unauthentic, unreal, apocryphal, forged, counterfeited, artificial, factitious, hollow, humbug, specious, sophistic, casuistic, charlatan, charlatanistic, quackish, impostrous, illegitimate, phoney (Inf)

33 deceitful, duplicitous, fraudulent, fake, artificial, false-hearted, cunning, sneaky, artful, guileful, wily, crafty, manipulative, malingering, lying, fibbing, fabricating, prevaricating, slandering, libelling, perjuring, falsely swearing, forswearing, perfidious, collusive, treasonous, treacherous, flimflam (Inf)

34 pretending, pretentious, dissembling, dissimulating, acting, play-acting, masquerading, feigning, bluffing, affecting, attitudinizing, posturing, posing, hyperbolic, romantic, romanticized, exaggerated, seeming, apparent, so-called, ostensible, put-on (US inf)

35 fraudulent, swindling, dishonest, cheating, tricky, false, fake, impostrous, illicit, underhanded, counterfeit, forged, copied, put-up, whitewashed, crooked (Inf), put-on (US inf), rip-off (Inf)

36 falsified, faked, fake, misrepresented, exaggerated, distorted, twisted, stretched, half-true, counterfeit, forged, fabricated, made-up, confabulated, invented, slanderous, libellous, perjurious, manipulated, concocted, fictional, fictionalized, imaginative, mythologized, fabled, legendary, cock-and-bull, trumped-up, contrary-to-fact

37 fake, sham, mock, artificial, imitative, bogus, counterfeit, tinselled, rubbishy, junky, phoney (Inf), not all it's cracked up to be (Inf)

38 evasive, equivocal, ambivalent, doubletalking, shifty, shuffling, dodging, fencing

39 disguised, false, seeming, sham, imitative, fake, imitation, simulated, dissembled, dissimulated, glossed, varnished, gilded, embellished, embroidered, overdone, dressed up, touched up, coloured, falsely coloured

ADVERBS

40 falsely, mendaciously, untruthfully, truthlessly, unveraciously, deceitfully, deceptively, fallaciously, under false pretences, erroneously, hypocritically, ungenuinely, bogusly, dishonestly

41 spuriously, artificially, synthetically, unnaturally, ungenuinely, factitiously, speciously, hyperbolically, seemingly, apparently, plausibly, ostensibly, nominally, in name only

42 hypocritically, insincerely, uncandidly, emptily, unseriously, unctuously, mealy-mouthedly

700 Deception

The smyler with the knyf under the cloke. Geoffrey Chaucer.

You can fool some of the people all the time and all the people some of the time; but you can't fool all the people all the time. Abraham Lincoln.

NOUNS

1 deception, calculated deception, deceptiveness, deceit, deceiving, lying, falsehood, falseness, dishonesty, duplicity, double-dealing, circumvention, fraudulence, fraudulency, craftiness, artfulness, guile, cunning, craft, insidiousness, underhandedness, sleaze, sneakiness, deviousness, shiftiness, furtiveness, surreptitiousness, indirection, subterfuge, tongue-in-cheek

► *645 Cunning; 699 Falsehood*

2 self-deception, wishful thinking, fond illusion, delusion, delusiveness, make-believe, living in one's own little world, living in an ivory tower, living in cloud-cuckoo land, living in a fool's paradise

► *274 Error; 459 Folly*

3 hypocrisy, falseness, hypocriticalness, insincerity, mealy-mouthedness, lip service, empty gesture, veneer, hollowness, bubble, sham, pretence, Tartuffery, Tartuffism, Pecksniffery, Pharisaism, artificiality, false face, false front, show, false show, outward show, tokenism, soft soap (Inf), sweet-talk (Inf)

▶ *736 Concealment*

4 **falseheartedness**, duplicity, hypocrisy, treachery, treacherousness, treason, betrayal, perfidy, machination

▶ *800 Dishonour; 804 Wickedness*

5 **falseness**, deceit, trickiness, imposture, fallaciousness, fallacy, misleading, misguidance, misdirection, misinformation, misconception, mockery, false reputation, feet of clay, insubstantiality, hallucination, illusion, phantasm, mirage, will-o'-the-wisp, bum steer (US inf)

6 **imitation**, rubbish, tinsel, paste, ormolu, fool's gold, mosaic gold, nickel silver, German silver, Britannia metal, cultured pearl, synthetic rubber, simulated wood, plastic spoon, man-made lake

▶ *125 Imitation*

7 **tricking**, trickery, fooling, befooling, outsmarting, outmanoeuvring, taking advantage of, bluffing, shamming, circumvention, outwitting, ensnarement, entrapment, entanglement, enmeshment, whitewashing, dupery, hoodwinking, victimization (*or* victimisation), manipulation, quackery, chicanery, chicane, sleight (of hand), wheeling and dealing, sharp practice, dodgery, artifice, machination, sorcery, witchcraft, bag of tricks, connivance, collusion, conspiracy, covin (Lit), tricks of the trade, kidding (Inf), conning (Inf), burning (Inf), putting on (US inf), snow job (US inf), flimflam (Inf), flimflammery (Inf), blag (Inf), blagging (Inf), bamboozlement (Inf), diddling (Inf), fishy transaction (Inf), skulduggery (Inf), shenanigan (Inf), hanky-panky (Inf), monkey business (Inf), jiggery-pokery (Inf), hornswoggling (Inf), boiler room (Inf)

8 **trick**, dirty trick, ploy, gambit, ruse, stratagem, contrivance, catch, artifice, device, scheme, design, *ficelle* (Fr), blind, wile, shift, dodge, artful dodge, sleight, fetch, feint, pass, bluff, gimmick, diversion, joker (US), bag of tricks, confidence trick, gold brick, wrinkle (Inf), put-on (US inf), diddle (Inf), con (Inf), bunco (game) (US inf), rip-off (Inf), (good) wheeze (Inf), sting (Inf)

9 **sleight of hand**, legerdemain, juggling, jugglery, illusion, trickery, subterfuge, conjuring, conjuration, prestidigitation, ventriloquism, magic, mumbo jumbo, hocus-pocus, curve (US), curveball (US), thimblerig, three-card trick, googly (Inf), bosey (Inf), wrong'un (Inf)

10 **fraud**, fraudulence, pious fraud, racket, dodge, swindle, cheat, cheating, dishonesty, foul play, imposture, (piece of) sharp practice, illicit practice, underhanded deal, legal chicanery, insider dealing, counterfeiting, forgery, ballot-box stuffing, ballot rigging, gerrymandering, cardsharping, forcing a card, wangle (Inf), sell (Inf), con (Inf), fix (Inf), flimflam (Inf), diddle (Inf), fiddle (Inf), swizzle (Inf), swiz (Inf), ramp (Inf), scam (Inf), gyp (*or* gip) (Inf), rip-off (Inf)

11 **hoax**, deception, sham, spoof, game, bluff, sport, joke, practical joke, April fool hoax, rag, humbug, Piltdown Man, Loch Ness monster, pulling one's leg, leg-pull (Inf)

▶ *599 Humour*

12 **disguise**, concealment, camouflage, protective coloration, false colours, borrowed plumes, false front, incognito, mask, domino, visor (*or* vizor) (Lit), veil, cloak, masquerade, masque, mummery, diversion, smokescreen, red herring, tub to a whale, trap door, sliding panel, fake bottom, secret passage, secret drawer (*or* compartment), varnish, paint, whitewash, gloss

▶ *736 Concealment*

13 **snare**, trap, gin, deathtrap, ambush, pitfall, deadfall, pit, trap door, mousetrap, mole trap, rat trap, flytrap, flypaper, Venus flytrap, pitcher plant, Dionaea, spring gun, set gun, baited trap, Longworth trap, booby trap, mine, tripwire, decoy, diversion, sprat to catch a mackerel, kidnapping, hijacking (*or* highjacking), car bomb, letter bomb, parcel bomb, net, mesh, trawl, dragnet, seine, purse seine, pound net, gill net, web, cobweb, hook, fish-hook, bait, sniggle, ground bait, lure, fly, jig, squid, plug, wobbler, spinner, lime twig, birdlime, shanghaiing (Inf)

14 **fatal gift**, poisoned apple, Trojan horse, Greek gift

15 **deceiver**, hypocrite, liar, deluder, duper, misleader, beguiler, kidder, ragger, leg-puller, practical joker, Puck, Loki, trickster, swindler, hoaxer, spoofer, cheat, imposter, fake, faker, charlatan, impersonator, pretender, sham, shammer, fraud, ringer (US), humbug, bluff, bluffer, mountebank, *saltimbanco* (It), poser, poseur, malingerer, hypochondriac, masquerader, mummer, guiser, guisard (Scot), incognito (*or* incognita), phoney, quack, quackster, rogue, seducer, Don Juan, Casanova, wolf in sheep's clothing, ass in a lion's skin, jackdaw in peacock's feathers, quacksalver (Lit), pseud (Inf), bamboozler (Inf), four-flusher (US inf)

16 **liar**, fibber, fibster, consumate liar, pathological liar, confirmed liar, habitual liar, perjurer, false witness, mythomaniac, pseudologue, prevaricator, fabricator, equivocator, fabulist, falsifier, storyteller, yarner, yarn-spinner, Ananias, Satan, Father of Lies, Baron Münchhausen, Sir John Mandeville, dirty liar (Inf), bullshitter (Inf)

17 **cheat**, cheater, swindler, defrauder, confidence man, trickster, cozener, gyp, gypper, bilker, crook, short-changer, counterfeiter, horse-trader, horse coper, cardsharp, cardsharper, pettifogger, land pirate, land shark, shark, land-grabber, mortgage shark, crimp, thimblerigger, con man (Inf), con artist (Inf), bunco artist (US inf), bunco steerer (US inf), shyster (US inf), diddler (Inf), wide boy (Inf), cowboy (Inf), two-timer (Inf), flimflammer (Inf), flimflam man (Inf), blackleg (Inf), magsman (Inf), chiseller (Inf), spiv (Inf)

18 **decoy**, *agent provocateur* (Fr), stool pigeon (US inf), stoolie (US inf), shill (Inf), come-on man (Inf), plant (Inf)

19 **hypocrite**, phoney, sham, sanctimonious fraud, false friend, fair-weather friend, summer soldier, pharisee, whited sepulchre, canter, snuffler, mealy-mouth, Tartuffe, Pecksniff, Joseph Surface

20 **plotter**, schemer, intriguer, intrigant (Lit), conspirer, conspirator, Guy Fawkes, machinator, subversive, saboteur, fifth columnist, fellow traveller, security risk, collaborator, collaborationist, fraternizer

21 **traitor**, treasonist, quisling, betrayer, serpent, snake, snake in the grass, double-crosser, double-dealer, double agent, trimmer, timeserver, turncoat, informer, arch-

traitor, Judas, Judas Iscariot, Benedict Arnold, Brutus, rat (Inf)

22 dupe, victim, fool, April fool, laughing stock, fair game, greenhorn, innocent, beginner, trusting soul, puppet, cat's-paw, toy, plaything, pawn, instrument, tool, gull (Lit), soft touch (Inf), easy pickings (Inf), easy mark (US inf), pushover (Inf), babe (Inf), babe in arms (Inf), babe in the woods (Inf), dude (US inf), sitting duck (Inf), pigeon (Inf), mug (Inf), patsy (Inf), cinch (Inf), stooge (Inf), sucker (US inf), fall guy (US inf), schmuck (US inf), schnook (US inf), schlemiel (US inf), sap (Inf), monkey (Inf)

VERBS

23 deceive, be dishonest, give a false impression, sneak, double-cross, double-deal, circumvent, pull a fast one (Inf), two-time (Inf), sell someone a bill of goods (Inf), pull the wool over someone's eyes (Inf)

24 be deceived, fall victim to, fall for, be had (Inf), get taken for a ride (Inf), buy a pig in a poke (Inf)

25 deceive oneself, indulge in wishful thinking, have fond illusions, delude oneself, hallucinate, make believe, live in one's own little world, live in cloud-cuckoo-land (*or* an ivory tower *or* a fool's paradise)

26 be a hypocrite, pay lip service, make an empty gesture, pretend, show a false face, show a false front, show, belie, talk sweetly, soft-soap (Inf)

27 be false, betray, trick, deceive, delude, beguile, mock, misinform, mislead, misguide, misdirect, throw off the scent, lay a false scent, have feet of clay, send on a wild goose chase (Inf), lead up the garden path (Inf), string along (Inf), give someone a bum steer (US inf)

28 trick, play a trick on, fool, befool, make a fool of, make an ass of, make one look silly, mock, make fun of, take advantage of, ridicule, outsmart, outmanoeuvre, spoof, bluff, sham, circumvent, contrive, catch, devise, scheme, design, shift, dodge, fetch, feint, pass, fudge, divert, outwit, ensnare, entrap, entangle, enmesh, whitewash, dupe, swindle, hoodwink, victimize, manipulate, chicane, wheel and deal, machinate, sell a gold brick, practise sorcery, practise witchcraft, have a bag of tricks, connive, collude, conspire, use tricks of the trade, play a confidence trick, fake someone out (US inf), take for a ride (Inf), diddle (Inf), kid (Inf), con (Inf), have (*or* put) someone on (Inf), flimflam (Inf), bamboozle (Inf), snow (US inf), hornswoggle (Inf), make a wally of (Inf), rip off (Inf)

29 juggle, trick, conjure, ventriloquize, practise magic, throw someone a curve (US), throw someone a curveball (US), thimblerig, bowl a googly (Inf), bowl a bosey (Inf), bowl a wrong'un (Inf)

30 be fraudulent, defraud, dodge, swindle, fleece, bilk, cheat, do out of, cheat on, deal on inside information, counterfeit, forge, force a card, mark the cards, stack the deck, deal off the bottom of the deck, load the dice, throw a fight, obtain under false pretenses, leave in the lurch, leave holding the baby, wangle (Inf), sell (Inf), gull (Inf), con (Inf), burn (Inf), fix (Inf), flimflam (Inf), fiddle (Inf), swizzle (*or* swiz) (Inf), short-change (Inf), cook the books (Inf), scam (Inf), gyp (*or* gip) (Inf), rip off (Inf), nick someone for (US inf), screw (Inf), take a dive (Inf)

31 hoax, deceive, spoof, bluff, play a joke on, play a practical joke on, play an April fool joke on, rag, pull one's leg

32 disguise, conceal, camouflage, show false colours, have a false front, mask, veil, cloak, masquerade, divert, throw up a smoke screen, introduce a red herring, varnish, paint, whitewash, gloss

33 snare, ensnare, trap, entrap, lay a trap for, gin, catch, ambush, waylay, kidnap, hijack (*or* highjack), set a gun, bait a trap, set a booby trap, mine, tripwire, trip up, trip, lime, birdlime, decoy, lure, divert, plant a car bomb, post a letter bomb, post a parcel bomb, net, trawl, seine, entangle, ensnarl, tangle, hook, hook in, bait, bait a hook, dangle the bait, sniggle, nab (Inf), nick (Inf), shanghai (Inf)

ADJECTIVES

34 deceiving, misleading, double-dealing, conniving, contriving, covering up, whitewashing, colluding, dodging, feinting, designing, scheming, cheating, calculating, cunning, sharp, artful, guileful, wily, crafty, tricky, shifty, devious, dishonest, sneaky, furtive, surreptitious, indirect, smooth, slippery, slick (US inf), conning (Inf), wangling (Inf), dodgy (Inf)

35 deceptive, deceitful, false, fallacious, duplicitous, dishonest, conspiratorial, fraudulent, sorcerous, insidious, illicit, underhand, ballot-rigged, gerrymandered, contrived, gimmicky, misleading, tongue-in-cheek, fixed (Inf)

36 deceived, duped, tricked, hoaxed, fooled, befooled, outsmarted, hookwinked, victimized, outmanoeuvred, bluffed, cheated, outwitted, ensnared, entrapped, entangled, enmeshed, manipulated, misled, misguided, misdirected, misinformed, self-deceived, mocked, ridiculed, made sport of, made a joke of, ragged, flimflammed (Inf), spoofed (Inf), diddled (Inf), done (Inf), swizzled (Inf), taken in (Inf), taken for a ride (Inf), sold a pig in a poke (Inf), sold a pup (Inf), had (Inf)

37 hypocritical, false, insincere, phoney, sanctimonious, Pharisaic, Tartuffian, Pecksniffian, mealy-mouthed, hollow, pretending, artificial, false-faced, false-fronted, tokenistic

38 treacherous, false-hearted, duplicitous, faithless, unfaithful, inconstant, double-dealing, betraying, treasonous, perfidious, dangerous

39 imitative, imitation, artificial, phoney, synthetic, simulated, substituted, cultured, unnatural, unoriginal, copied, plastic, man-made, fake, bogus, sham, mock, quack, counterfeit, forged, shoddy, rubbishy

40 illusory, illusive, unreal, insubstantial, tricky, conjured, juggled, magic, magical, sleight-of-hand, mumbo-jumbo, hocus-pocus, delusive, delusory, make-believe, imagined, dreamed-up, chimerical, hallucinatory, phantasmic

41 disguised, concealed, hidden, camouflaged, incognito (*or* incognita), masquerading, masked, veiled, cloaked, varnished, painted, whitewashed, glossed, visored (*or* vizored) (Lit)

42 trapped, snared, ginned, ambushed, mined, kidnapped, hijacked (*or* highjacked), baited, trawled, hooked, netted, meshed, webbed, cobwebbed

701 Argument

There is only one way under high heaven to get the best of an argument – and that is to avoid it. Dale Carnegie.

NOUNS

1 **argument**, disagreement, dispute, quarrel, controversy, discord, misunderstanding, incompatibility, diversity, difference, altercation, wrangle, squabble, bickering, tiff, spat, row, scuffle, clash, brawl, conflict, feud, fight, fray, affray, fracas, scrimmage, donnybrook, strife, argy-bargy (Inf), set-to (Inf), scrap (Inf), fisticuffs (Inf), barney (Inf), falling-out (Inf), to-do (Inf), slanging match (Inf), name calling (Inf)

▶ *328 Disturbance; 365 Friction; 381 Attack; 585 War; 751 Disagreement; 759 Exchange*

2 **logical argument**, debate, discussion, disputation, dialogue, dialectic, eristic, polemic, maieutic, hermeneutic, heuristic, elenchus, logic, sophistry, argumentation, discourse, reasoning, ratiocination, deliberation, deduction, induction, consideration, reflection, thought, challenge, reductio ad absurdum, questioning, inquiry, doubt

▶ *4 Philosophy; 27 Mathematics; 443 Thought; 444 Reason; 702 Sophistry; 705 Question; 734 Conversation; 746 Negotiation*

3 **line of argument**, line of reasoning, reasoning, rationale, contention, topic, issue, thesis, hypothesis, postulate, proposition, premise, pretext, point, case, claim, assertion, statement, affirmation, attestation, testimony, position, opinion, stance, grounds, evidence

▶ *446 Idea; 447 Topic; 452 Certainty; 476 Supposition; 716 Evidence*

4 **gist**, outline, summary, essence, theme, subject, topic, idea, point, nub, argument, issue, plot, subplot, scenario, setting, story, moral, allegory, parable

▶ *99 Essence; 447 Topic; 694 Meaning*

5 **plea**, pleading, argument, request, entreaty, cry, suit, consideration, excuse, answer, apology, defence, claim, justification, explanation, rationalization, vindication, cause

▶ *344 Cause; 706 Answer; 710 Request; 714 Vindication*

6 **arguer**, argumentative type, debater, disputant, pleader, lawyer, barrister, disputer, quarreller, troublemaker, wrangler, polemicist, polemist, controversialist, logician, eristic, sophist

▶ *4 Philosophy; 16 Law; 586 Combatant*

ADJECTIVES

7 **arguing**, quibbling, quarrelling, wrangling, squabbling, bickering, at odds, at cross purposes, different, diverse, discordant, incompatible, dissenting, dissentient, rowing, scuffling, clashing, at loggerheads, scrapping (Inf)

▶ *114 Diversity; 328 Disturbance*

8 **argumentative**, quarrelsome, disagreeable, disputatious, litigious, dissentious, factious, querulous, peevish, irritable, contrary, testy, petulant, fractious, choleric, cross, irascible, cantankerous, grouchy (Inf)

▶ *607 Annoyance and Aggravation; 625 Grumpiness; 641 Obstinacy*

9 **hostile**, antagonistic, provocative, polemical, eristic, inimical, pugnacious, belligerent, bellicose, warlike, brawling, conflicting, feuding, fighting, at war, at each other's throats, in battle

▶ *113 Opposition; 380 Violence; 381 Attack; 383 Resistance*

10 **arguable**, debatable, disputable, contentious, topical, controversial, questionable, doubtful, dubious, challenging, problematic, refutable, open to question, in question, moot, unsettled, undecided, misunderstood

11 **logical**, elenctic, sophistic (*or* sophistical), heuristic, hypothetical, propositional, proposed, postulated, claimed, asserted, stated, affirmed, attested

12 **apologetic**, in defence, defensive, pleading, justifiable, explicable, vindicated, justified, rational, explained, causal, caused

VERBS

13 **argue**, disagree, bicker, wrangle, quarrel, quibble, squabble, fall out (Inf), remonstrate, altercate, have words (Inf), gainsay, contradict, polemicize, oppose, dissent, differ, dispute, contest, spar, scuffle, have a set-to (Inf), clash, conflict, brawl, feud, fight, go to war

▶ *708 Negation*

14 **discuss**, debate, exchange opinions, reason, ratiocinate, logicize, logomachize, deliberate, consider, weigh up, reflect, doubt, question, inquire, challenge, moot, deduce, induce, chop logic, cavil, argue the toss

▶ *702 Sophistry; 746 Negotiation; 759 Exchange*

15 **state**, argue, maintain, say, affirm, attest, hold, claim, hypothesize, propose, postulate, suggest, imply, indicate, signify, betoken, denote, show, demonstrate, establish, evince, prove

▶ *452 Certainty; 476 Supposition*

16 **plead**, argue, request, entreat, prevail upon, persuade, canvass, put one's case, apologize, defend, claim, answer, justify, explain, rationalize, vindicate

▶ *710 Request; 714 Vindication*

ADVERBS

17 **argumentatively**, disagreeably, irritably, petulantly, crossly, discordantly, incompatibly, diversely, differently, at odds, at cross purposes, at loggerheads, polemically, antagonistically, provocatively, inimically, belligerently, in conflict, at each other's throats, at war

18 **arguably**, disputedly, topically, controversially, contrarily, on the contrary, on the other hand, at issue, under investigation, in question, doubtfully, hypothetically, plausibly

19 **logically**, dialectically, deductively, inductively, reflectively, thoughtfully, deliberately

20 **apologetically**, in defence, as a defence, in answer, in response, justifiably, explicably, rationally, reasonably, causally

702 Sophistry

Universities incline wits to sophistry and affectation. Francis Bacon.

NOUNS

1 **sophistry**, casuistry, philosophism, jesuitry, false reasoning, specious reasoning, logic-chopping, faulty logic, illogicality, illogicalness, fallaciousness, fallacy, speciousness, invalidity, untenableness, unsoundness, irra-

tionality, inconsistency, circularity, equivocation, subterfuge, sleight, distortion, misapplication, solecism, mere rhetoric, empty words, moonshine

▶ *4 Philosophy; 179 Circularity; 189 Slantedness; 234 Distortion; 274 Error; 479 Equivocation; 697 Nonsense; 701 Argument; 718 Misrepresentation; 802 Wrong*

2 **sophism**, paralogism, pseudosyllogism, solecism, flawed argument, circular argument, non sequitur, paradox, contradiction in terms, antilogy, fallacy, dodge, trick, ruse, shuffle, quibble, quip, quirk, cavil, contrivance, stratagem, subterfuge, red herring, scheme, misinformation, disinformation, propaganda, hogwash, baloney, bosh (Inf), bunkum (Inf), hooey (Inf), hokum (Inf), scam (Inf), blag (Inf), bullshit (Inf)

▶ *266 Obscurity; 484 Plan; 699 Falsehood; 700 Deception; 736 Concealment*

3 **cunning**, sophistication, craftiness, artfulness, art, artifice, slyness, foxiness, slipperiness, shiftiness, trickiness, sneakiness, insidiousness, machination, manipulation, demagoguery, pulling the wool over someone's eyes, mystification, obfuscation

▶ *11 Occultism; 266 Obscurity; 395 Influence; 480 Persuasion; 485 Skill; 528 Opaqueness; 550 Covering; 645 Cunning; 700 Deception*

4 **quibbling**, captiousness, hair-splitting, nit-picking, cavilling, subtlety, oversubtlety, paltering, prevarication, hedging, shuffling, beating about the bush, pettifoggery, pussyfooting (Inf), jiggery-pokery (Inf)

▶ *479 Equivocation*

5 **hypocrisy**, deceit, deception, duplicity, pretence, humbug, double-dealing, insincerity, disingenuousness, guile, evasion, mendacity, fakery, chicanery, quackery, charlatanism, mountebankery, Pharisaism, Tartuffery

▶ *11 Occultism; 157 Shallowness; 699 Falsehood; 700 Deception*

6 **sophist**, sophister, sophisticator, paralogist, philosophist, casuist, Jesuit, solecist, logic-chopper, equivocator, prevaricator, caviller, quibbler, nit-picker, hair-splitter, pussyfooter, pettifogger, waffler, charmer, demagogue, propagandist, sweet-talker, trickster, schemer, hypocrite, faker, liar, quack, charlatan, mountebank, con man (Inf), shyster (Inf)

▶ *4 Philosophy; 700 Deception*

ADJECTIVES

7 **sophistic**, sophistical, casuistic(al), jesuitic(al), solecistic(al), rhetorical, logic-chopping, paralogistic, pseudosyllogistic, specious, fallacious, spurious, faulty, flawed, inconsistent, circular, equivocal, erroneous, illogical, paradoxical, contradictory, unreasonable, irrational, unfounded, baseless, groundless, invalid, untenable, unsound, distorted, misapplied, contrived, tortuous, misleading, spurious, inconsequential, dubious, fictitious, illusory, superficial, empty, misinformed, economical with the truth

▶ *118 Nonconformity; 697 Nonsense; 718 Misrepresentation; 802 Wrong*

8 **cunning**, sophisticated, crafty, artful, sly, foxy, sneaky, shifty, dodgy, tricky, insidious, underhand, perfidious, evasive, elusive, manipulating, demagogic, mystifying, obfuscated

▶ *266 Obscurity; 395 Influence; 480 Persuasion; 485 Skill; 645 Cunning; 700 Deception*

9 **quibbling**, cavilling, captious, hair-splitting, nit-picking, shuffling, hedging, equivocal, equivocating, prevaricating, pettifogging, pussyfooting (Inf)

10 **hypocritical**, deceptive, deceitful, pretended, in pretence, feigning, dissembling, dissimulating, double-dealing, unreliable, insincere, disingenuous, tongue-in-cheek, fraudulent, dishonest, lying, mendacious, false, bogus, sham, counterfeit, fake, faking, sweet-talking, Pharisaic, pseudo (Inf), so-called (Inf), two-timing (Inf), phoney (*or* phony) (Inf)

▶ *699 Falsehood*

VERBS

11 **practise sophistry**, chop logic, misapply, misconstrue, misrepresent, misquote, contradict oneself, falsify, distort, strain, warp, slant, twist, gild, gloss, whitewash, dress up, embroider, disguise, camouflage, mask, juggle, rig, contrive, scheme, manipulate, machinate, propagandize, sway the crowd, misinform, mislead, pull the wool over someone's eyes, mystify, obfuscate, fudge (Inf)

▶ *542 Decoration; 718 Misrepresentation; 731 Talkativeness*

12 **deceive**, dissimulate, dissemble, pretend, feign, bluff, masquerade, put on an act, put up a front, lie, fake, dodge, trick, elude, evade, charm, sweet-talk, have it both ways, double-deal, cheat, work both sides of the street (Inf), con (Inf), two-time (Inf), blag (Inf), talk with one's fingers crossed (Inf), talk shit (Inf), bullshit (Inf)

▶ *125 Imitation; 700 Deception; 736 Concealment; 737 Secrecy*

13 **quibble**, cavil, split hairs, nit-pick, palter, bandy words, hedge, shuffle, pettifog, equivocate, beg the question, prevaricate, beat about the bush, avoid the issue, filibuster, pussyfoot (Inf), argue all round the houses (Inf), argue the hind legs off a donkey (Inf)

▶ *180 Convolution; 479 Equivocation; 701 Argument; 729 Speech; 731 Talkativeness*

ADVERBS

14 **sophistically**, casuistically, jesuitically, solecistically, speciously, falsely, fallaciously, illogically, irrationally, unsoundly, inconsistently, paradoxically, erroneously, groundlessly, circularly, equivocally, captiously, subtly, dubiously, spuriously, rhetorically

15 **hypocritically**, deceitfully, deceptively, dishonestly, insincerely, disingenuously, with tongue in cheek, unreliably, dodgily, sneakily, craftily, artfully, slyly, on the sly, cunningly, insidiously, perfidiously, evasively, elusively, as a gloss, strategically, demagogically, as a con (Inf), behind someone's back (Inf), with fingers crossed (Inf)

703 Demonstration

NOUNS

1 **demonstration**, display, manifestation, showing, show, exhibition, exposition, presentation, disclosure, revelation, presentment, publication, performance, expo

▶ *525 Appearance; 738 Display; 739 Disclosure; 740 Publication*

2 **demonstrativeness**, openness, frankness, candour, emotionality, affection, effusiveness, expansiveness, os-

tentation, showiness, flashiness, flamboyance, exhibitionism, showing off, dramatics, theatrics, staginess, emotionalism, overemotionalism, histrionics

▶ *21 Drama; 36 Psychology and Psychiatry; 738 Display*

3 **explanation**, demonstration, clarification, elucidation, exposition, indication, illustration, description, depiction, delineation, illumination, exemplification, expounding, exegesis, briefing, instructions, lecture, talk, discourse, example, model, sample, specimen

▶ *6 Education; 693 Information; 721 Description; 722 Essay*

4 **proof**, demonstration, evidence, *quod erat demonstrandum* (L) (QED), substantiation, confirmation, verification, determination, ascertainment, settlement, ratification, bearing out, corroboration, justification, affirmation, attestation, testimonial, testimony

▶ *454 Verification; 707 Affirmation; 716 Evidence; 742 Sign*

5 **demonstrability**, demonstrableness, provability, verifiability, confirmability, accountability, certainty, likelihood, probability

▶ *104 Probability; 452 Certainty; 454 Verification*

6 **mass demonstration**, parade, pageant, spectacle, march, protest march, rally, protest, picket, strike, industrial action, boycott, occupation, takeover, sit-in (Inf), sleep-in (Inf), work-in (Inf), demo (Inf)

▶ *15 Industrial Relations; 328 Disturbance; 376 Gathering; 753 Protest*

7 **demonstrator**, explainer, explicator, clarifier, exponent, expositor, expounder, exegetist, illustrator, instructor, lecturer, experimenter, producer, presenter, performer, showman, show-off, exhibitionist, emotionalist, poser (Inf)

▶ *6 Education; 21 Drama; 448 Experiment*

8 **protester**, dissenter, dissident, objector, demonstrator, political activist, agitator, minority voice, voice of opposition, picket, striker

▶ *113 Opposition; 327 Agitation; 383 Resistance; 661 Defiance; 753 Protest*

ADJECTIVES

9 **demonstrated**, on show, on display, obvious, manifest, plain, clear, express, explicit, displayed, exhibited, disclosed, exposed, revealed, made public, published, publicized, expository, expositional, exhibitional, revelatory, apodeictic

▶ *520 Visibility; 738 Display; 739 Disclosure; 740 Publication*

10 **demonstrative**, open, unrestrained, frank, candid, warm, affectionate, effusive, expansive, ostentatious, showy, flashy, flamboyant, dramatic, stagy, theatrical, exhibitionist, emotional, exhibitionistic, emotionalistic, histrionic

▶ *21 Drama; 590 Feelings; 593 Love*

11 **explanatory**, explicatory, illustrative, indicative, descriptive, representative, exemplificatory, exemplifying, illuminating, exegetic, explained, demonstrated, clarified, cleared up, elucidated, illustrated, described, depicted, delineated, illuminated, exemplified, expounded

▶ *721 Description*

12 **demonstrable**, provable, confirmable, attestable, verifiable, evident, self-evident, obvious, undeniable, apparent, perspicuous, distinct, indisputable, unquestionable, positive, certain, conclusive, clear-cut

▶ *452 Certainty; 520 Visibility; 716 Evidence*

13 **proven**, demonstrated, shown, substantiated, confirmed, verified, determined, ascertained, settled, ratified, corroborated, borne out, justified, affirmed, attested, evidential, probative, probatory, corroborative, relevant

▶ *454 Verification; 707 Affirmation*

14 **demonstrating**, protesting, objecting, opposing, dissenting, agitating, rallying, marching, parading, on parade, striking, picketing, boycotting

▶ *113 Opposition; 376 Gathering*

VERBS

15 **demonstrate**, show, display, exhibit, manifest, disclose, expose, point out, bring out, roll out, reveal, produce, air, put forward, publish, perform, flaunt, brandish, flourish

▶ *21 Drama; 738 Display; 739 Disclosure; 740 Publication*

16 **explain**, expound, show how, elucidate, express, indicate, unfold, make clear, clarify, illuminate, exemplify, illustrate, quote, cite, itemize, particularize, give instances, delineate, depict, describe, brief, instruct, lecture

▶ *6 Education; 721 Description*

17 **prove**, evince, substantiate, establish, evidence, validate, ratify, verify, corroborate, support, bear out, circumstantiate, justify, determine, ascertain, fix, settle, confirm, affirm, attest, prove one's point, remove all doubt, clinch (Inf)

▶ *454 Verification; 707 Affirmation; 716 Evidence*

18 **appear**, materialize, come forth, take a stand, stand up and be counted, speak out, raise one's voice, speak one's mind, assert oneself, draw attention to oneself, play to the gallery, perform, show off, dramatize, emotionalize

▶ *21 Drama; 185 Bulge; 525 Appearance*

19 **protest**, dissent, object, complain about, oppose, agitate, demonstrate, rally, march, march for, parade, strike, picket, boycott, occupy, take over, stage a demo (Inf), stage a sit-in (Inf), sit in (Inf)

▶ *113 Opposition*

ADVERBS

20 **manifestly**, obviously, plainly, clearly, publicly, in public, for all to see, in broad daylight, under one's nose, to one's face, as plain as the nose on one's face

21 **demonstratively**, openly, frankly, candidly, emotionally, expressively, affectionately, warmly, effusively, expansively, ostentatiously, flamboyantly, dramatically, theatrically, histrionically

22 **demonstrably**, verifiably, justifiably, accountably, certainly, likely, probably, in all likelihood, illuminatingly, illustratively, indicatively, descriptively, exegetically, as an example, in proof, as proof, as evidence, in evidence, in other words, that is, *id est* (L), that is to say

23 **in protest**, in opposition, on parade, on a demo (Inf)

704 Refutation

I refute it thus. Samuel Johnson.

NOUNS

1 **refutation**, disproof, disproval, invalidation, negation, negativity, naysaying, nullification, annulment, disaffirmation, disconfirmation, confounding, discrediting, abrogation, disallowal, dismissal, reversal, undermining,

subversion, overthrow, destruction, demolition, reductio ad absurdum, conclusive argument, knockdown argument, floorer (Inf), clincher (Inf)

► *357 Destruction; 399 Veto; 481 Dissuasion; 621 Derision; 701 Argument; 708 Negation; 715 Accusation; 751 Disagreement*

2 **denial**, refutation, rebuttal, contradiction, confutation, contravention, contention, negation, disaffirmation, rejection, repudiation, renunciation, abnegation, recantation, recusance, withdrawal, reversal, disclaimer, disavowal, disownment, apostasy

► *381 Attack; 470 Rejection; 708 Negation; 761 Reversion*

3 **countercharge**, refutation, counterclaim, counteraccusation, counterstatement, counterblast, counteraction, comeback, reply, counterargument, rebuttal, rejoinder, answer, response, retort, riposte, retaliation, objection, defence, statement of defence, demurrer, demurral

► *16 Law; 113 Opposition; 347 Counteraction; 384 Defence; 385 Retaliation; 706 Answer; 709 Refusal*

4 **refutability**, confutability, disprovability, defeasibility, weakness, unsoundness, groundlessness

► *247 Failure; 337 Weakness; 453 Uncertainty; 699 Falsehood; 802 Wrong*

5 **refuter**, confuter, negator, nullifier, naysayer, abrogator, denier, repudiator, abnegator, recanter, recusant, responder, defendant, destroyer

► *113 Opposition; 586 Combatant; 714 Vindication; 753 Protest*

ADJECTIVES

6 **refutable**, confutable, disprovable, defeasible, weak, faulty, flawed, unfounded, groundless, unsound, objectionable, inconclusive, without a leg to stand on

► *274 Error; 337 Weakness; 453 Uncertainty; 699 Falsehood; 802 Wrong*

7 **refuting**, confuting, confounding, confutative, refutative, refutatory, contradictory, contrary, counteractive, retaliatory, answering, responding, contravening, rebutting, repudiating, renouncing, abnegating, disclaiming, disowning, discrediting, exploding, disproving, negating, invalidating, overturning, destroying

► *113 Opposition; 357 Destruction; 708 Negation; 709 Refusal; 812 Notoriety*

VERBS

8 **refute**, confute, confound, disprove, prove the contrary, invalidate, nullify, annul, negate, disallow, forbid, dismiss, abrogate, dispose of, disconfirm, discredit, expose, show up, belie, deflate, undermine, overturn, overthrow, defeat, outsmart, outwit, demolish, destroy, explode, crush, squash, quash, floor, silence, have the last word, argue into a corner, argue down, knock down, shout down, not leave a leg to stand on, score points against, force to step down, show them what's what (Inf)

► *357 Destruction; 358 Obliteration; 388 Submission; 506 Silence; 621 Derision; 812 Notoriety*

9 **deny**, refute, contradict, gainsay, naysay, argue against, argue with, raise doubts about, question, dispute, oppose, controvert, contravene, disaffirm, reject, repudiate, renounce, abnegate, recant, reverse, withdraw, disclaim, disavow, disown, repugn

► *453 Uncertainty; 701 Argument; 705 Question*

10 **countercharge**, counter, counterclaim, counterblast, rebut, parry, retaliate, retort, answer, answer back, reply, rejoin, respond, object, offer in defence, demur

► *16 Law; 347 Counteraction*

ADVERBS

11 **in reply**, in response, in answer, as an answer, as a defence, in defence, defensively, dismissively, negatively, destructively, conclusively

12 **refutably**, confutably, disprovably, defeasibly, weakly, unsoundly, groundlessly, without grounds, without a leg to stand on, inconclusively, disputedly

INTERJECTIONS

13 **no!**, nay!, wrong!, I disagree!, I object!, nonsense!, not at all!, no way!

► *274 Error; 697 Nonsense; 699 Falsehood ; 802 Wrong*

705 Question

To be, or not to be – that is the question… William Shakespeare.

NOUNS

1 **question**, query, doubt, uncertainty, reservation, problem, difficulty, confusion, puzzle, challenge, objection, issue, point, proposition, request, entreaty, plea

► *135 Requirement; 264 Difficulty; 446 Idea; 447 Topic; 451 Disbelief; 453 Uncertainty; 456 Ignorance; 710 Request*

2 **questioning**, inquiry (*or* enquiry), querying, interrogation, interpellation, inquisition, cross-questioning, cross-examination, challenge, Socratic elenchus, philosophical inquiry, argument, investigation, analysis, inspection, scrutiny, survey, review, study, probe, inquest, criminal investigation, scientific investigation, research, poll, market research, search, quest, pumping (Inf), grilling (Inf), the third degree (Inf)

► *4 Philosophy; 16 Law; 448 Experiment; 701 Argument*

3 **questionnaire**, question paper, quiz, examination, test, poll, census, checklist, trial, catechism, oral examination, viva voce examination, hearing, audition, question-time, question and answer session, interview, viva (Inf)

► *2 Sociology; 6 Education; 7 Religion; 21 Drama; 136 Qualification; 464 Judgment; 706 Answer*

4 **difficult question**, awkward question, personal question, burning question, sixty-four (thousand) dollar question, leading question, bone of contention, controversy, moot point, catch, trick question, knotty problem, poser, stumper, mystery, tough nut to crack, mind boggler, brain-teaser, conundrum, riddle, enigma, dilemma, moral dilemma, crux, crisis, Hobson's choice, catch-22, sticky moment (Inf)

► *264 Difficulty; 266 Obscurity; 379 Trap; 696 Unintelligibility; 701 Argument; 751 Disagreement; 795 Morality*

5 **easy question**, silly question, stupid question, rhetorical question, formality, trivia quiz, child's play, doddle (Inf), cinch (Inf), breeze (Inf), pushover (Inf), piece of cake (Inf)

► *124 Unimportance; 263 Ease; 265 Easiness; 656 Formality*

6 **uncertainty**, questioning, doubt, doubtfulness, scepticism, Pyrrhonism, agnosticism, misgiving, mistrust, dis-

trust, hesitation, conjecture, guesswork, anybody's guess (Inf)

▶ *4 Philosophy; 451 Disbelief; 453 Uncertainty; 456 Ignorance; 476 Supposition; 639 Vacillation*

7 **questionableness**, dubiousness, doubtfulness, implausibility, unlikelihood, improbability, uncertainty, wild chance, faint hope, risk, riskiness, unreliability, untrustworthiness, deceptiveness, deceitfulness, ambiguity

▶ *105 Improbability; 266 Obscurity; 453 Uncertainty; 479 Equivocation; 700 Deception; 702 Sophistry*

8 **curiosity**, inquisitiveness, inquiring (*or* enquiring) mind, insatiable curiosity, desire (*or* thirst) for knowledge, wonder, puzzlement, soul-searching, probing, prying

▶ *6 Education; 619 Wonder; 644 Curiosity*

9 **questioner**, asker, interrogator, interpellator, investigator, journalist, interviewer, chat show host (*or* hostess), quiz master, game show presenter, prober, examiner, inquisitor, cross-examiner, interlocutor, lawyer, barrister, coroner, detective, inspector, scrutineer, student, researcher, tester, experimenter, scientist, surveyor, reviewer, analyst, pollster, canvasser, market researcher, seeker, doubter, philosopher, sceptic, doubting Thomas, agnostic, dissenter, detractor

▶ *2 Sociology; 4 Philosophy; 6 Education; 7 Religion; 16 Law; 21 Drama; 113 Opposition; 443 Thought; 446 Idea; 448 Experiment; 619 Wonder; 740 Publication; 753 Protest*

10 **person questioned**, interviewee, chat (*or* game) show guest, examinee, candidate, defendant, suspect, witness, plaintiff

▶ *16 Law; 136 Qualification; 715 Accusation*

11 **question mark**, query, interrogation mark, interrogation point, note of interrogation, interrogative pronoun, interrogative clause, future interrogative, indirect question

▶ *5 Language and Linguistics*

ADJECTIVES

12 **questioning**, requesting, pleading, inquiring, interrogative, curious, inquisitive, elenctic, investigative, examining, fact-finding, knowledge-seeking, exploratory, analytic, interpellant, probing, searching, researching, questing, prying, introspective, wondering, doubting

▶ *448 Experiment; 644 Curiosity; 693 Information*

13 **problematic**, difficult, confusing, confused, puzzling, challenging, quizzical, tricky, sticky, knotty, tough, mysterious, riddling, enigmatic, in a dilemma, on the horns of a dilemma, crucial, examinational, catechismic

▶ *11 Occultism; 264 Difficulty; 266 Obscurity; 795 Morality*

14 **questionable**, doubtful, uncertain, moot, at issue, open to question, in question, in doubt, open to debate, debatable, under discussion, controversial, borderline, arguable, disputable, equivocal, suspicious, dubious, implausible, unlikely, improbable, chancy, risky, unreliable, unverifiable, untrustworthy, deceptive, deceitful, ambiguous, shady, spurious

▶ *105 Improbability; 107 Chance; 479 Equivocation; 700 Deception; 701 Argument; 702 Sophistry*

15 **sceptical**, doubting, Pyrrhonist, agnostic, distrustful, journalistic, scientific, criminal, philosophical, legal, experimental, conjectural, guessing, hesitating

▶ *4 Philosophy; 16 Law; 448 Experiment; 451 Disbelief*

16 **questioned**, asked, interrogated, examined, cross-examined, cross-questioned, quizzed, analysed, researched, challenged, investigated, inspected, scrutinized, reviewed, surveyed, studied, probed, polled, canvassed, sought, grilled (Inf), pumped (Inf), given the third degree (Inf)

▶ *2 Sociology; 16 Law; 710 Request*

VERBS

17 **question**, inquire (*or* enquire), ask, quiz, query, plead, entreat, request, appeal, interpellate, examine, test, try, check, catechize, hear, give a viva voce examination, give an audition, interview, sound out, pick the brains of, investigate, analyse, conduct an inquiry into, inspect, scrutinize, survey, scan, review, study, fact-find, hunt the facts, probe, research, poll, canvass, search, wonder, introspect, soul-search, pry, hunt, pursue, search out, seek, quest

▶ *2 Sociology; 4 Philosophy; 7 Religion; 448 Experiment; 693 Information; 710 Request*

18 **interrogate**, question, examine, hold for questioning, cross-question, cross-examine, pump (Inf), grill (Inf), give someone the third degree (Inf), put through the hoop (Inf), torture, witch-hunt

▶ *7 Religion; 16 Law*

19 **be questioned**, help the police with their inquiries, appear on a chat show, sit an examination, take part in a survey

▶ *2 Sociology; 6 Education; 16 Law; 21 Drama; 706 Answer*

20 **doubt**, question, have one's doubts, have misgivings, mistrust, distrust, suspect, disbelieve, cast doubt upon, call into question, moot, raise the issue, make the point, propose, debate, discuss, dispute, contest, impugn, refute, confute, disagree, dissent, object, hesitate, conjecture, guess, risk, chance

▶ *107 Chance; 113 Opposition; 453 Uncertainty; 701 Argument; 751 Disagreement; 753 Protest*

21 **confuse**, challenge, puzzle, pose, set a riddle, boggle, mystify, stump, trick, deceive

▶ *264 Difficulty; 457 Stupidity; 696 Unintelligibility; 700 Deception*

22 **pop the question**, ask for someone's hand in marriage, ask to marry, propose, get engaged, plight one's troth

▶ *570 Marriage; 710 Request*

ADVERBS

23 **questioningly**, curiously, quizzically, inquisitively, probingly, searchingly, on a quest, on a mission, on a fact-finding mission, analytically, investigatively, scientifically, experimentally, agnostically, sceptically, philosophically, introspectively

24 **questionably**, hesitatingly, doubtfully, in doubt, dubiously, challengingly, puzzlingly, arguably, debatably, disputably, in question, under discussion, on the horns of a dilemma, on the borderline, controversially, conjecturally, riskily, suspiciously, equivocally, unreliably, problematically, trickily, enigmatically, deceptively, deceitfully, ambiguously, implausibly, improbably

25 **what?**, how much?, when?, at what time?, where?, at what place?, in what position?, whence?, from what place?, why?, for what reason?, how?, in what way?

706 Answer

The answer, my friend, is blowin' in the wind. Bob Dylan.

NOUNS

1 answer, reply, response, rejoinder, responsion, respondence, replication, retort, riposte, comeback, repartee, witty repartee, short answer, back talk, backchat, insolence, smart alec answer (Inf)

▶ *442 Intellect; 659 Discourtesy; 660 Insolence; 729 Speech; 734 Conversation; 775 Giving Back*

2 acknowledgment, answer, return correspondence, written reply, official reply, rescript, receipt, confirmation, RSVP

▶ *692 Communications; 707 Affirmation; 769 Receiving; 775 Giving Back; 788 Receipt*

3 question and answer, dialogue, interchange, interlocution, interview, exchange, interaction

▶ *4 Philosophy; 110 Reciprocity; 705 Question; 734 Conversation; 759 Exchange*

4 reaction, answer, retroaction, recoil, reflex, return, reflux, rebuff, backlash, kickback, recalcitration, bounceback, repercussion, reverberation, echo, response, responsory, antiphon, antiphonal chant, antistrophe, antithesis

▶ *10 Ritual; 17 Literature; 18 Music; 112 Repetition; 347 Counteraction; 509 Repeated Sound; 510 Resonance*

5 counterstatement, answer, countercharge, counterblast, retaliation, defence, plea, argument, refutation, rebuttal, contradiction, objection, vindication, last word, parting shot, interjection

▶ *131 End; 385 Retaliation; 701 Argument; 704 Refutation; 714 Vindication*

6 solution, answer, result, issue, outcome, upshot, denouement, resolution, conclusion, discovery, resolving, working out, unscrambling, clearing up, sorting out, decoding, interpretation, explanation, reason, resource, contrivance, measure, plan, remedy, antidote

▶ *131 End; 317 Way; 345 Effect; 394 Remedy; 444 Reason; 449 Discovery; 484 Plan; 638 Resolution; 719 Interpretation*

7 numerical result, answer, solution, product, sum, total, difference, equation, remainder, score, tally

▶ *27 Mathematics; 194 Number; 210 Calculation*

8 correspondence, answerableness, correlation, parallelism, symmetry, equivalence, congruence, conformity, twin, match, tally, agreement, aptness, fitness, suitability, relevance, usefulness

▶ *111 Sameness; 117 Conformity; 188 Parallelism; 217 Sufficiency; 237 Usefulness; 750 Agreement*

9 answerability, responsibility, liability, accountability, obligation, duty, requirement

▶ *135 Requirement; 810 Duty*

10 answerer, respondent, replier, correspondent, interlocutor, dialectician, talker, chatterer, conversationalist, addressee, interviewee, inquirer, objector, defendant, solver, planner, decoder, mathematician

▶ *4 Philosophy; 16 Law; 654 Sociability; 705 Question; 731 Talkativeness*

ADJECTIVES

11 answering, replying, responsive, responding, respondent, acknowledged, confirmed, returned, retorted, backchatting, insolent

▶ *660 Insolence*

12 reactive, interlocutory, interactive, retroactive, recoiling, reflexive, returning, refluent, rebuffed, recalcitrant, repercussive, reverberatory, echoing, antiphonal, antithetical

13 retaliatory, counterstated, countercharged, counterblasted, defensive, pleading, argumentative, refutative, refutatory, rebutted, objectionable, objecting, vindicating, vindicated, interjecting, interjected

▶ *385 Retaliation; 701 Argument; 704 Refutation; 714 Vindication*

14 solved, soluble, resultant, issuing, resolved, concluded, discovered, worked out, unscrambled, cleared up, sorted out, decoded, interpreted, interpretational, explanatory, explained, reasoned, contrived, measured, planned, remedial, antidotal

▶ *394 Remedy; 449 Discovery; 484 Plan; 638 Resolution*

15 correspondent, corresponding, correlative, parallel, reciprocal, symmetrical, equivalent, congruent, conforming, twin, matching, tallying, agreeing, apt, fitting, suitable, relevant, useful

▶ *110 Reciprocity; 111 Sameness; 188 Parallelism; 237 Usefulness*

16 answerable, responsible, liable, accountable, required, obliged, obligatory, under obligation, duty-bound, beholden, dutiful

▶ *135 Requirement; 810 Duty*

VERBS

17 answer, reply, respond, rejoin, riposte, retort, return, acknowledge, confirm, come back (Inf), get back (Inf)

18 answer back, talk back, contradict, confute, counterstate, countercharge, counterblast, refute, rebut, defend, vindicate, plead, argue, object, backchat, butt in, interject, insult, taunt, provoke, have the last word, fire the parting shot, have the final say, forget one's manners, be lippy (Inf), give some lip (Inf), lip off (US inf), mouth off (Inf)

▶ *607 Annoyance and Aggravation; 659 Discourtesy; 660 Insolence; 704 Refutation*

19 react, exchange, interact, converse, interview, interlocute, interchange, retroact, recoil, return, rebuff, kick back, recalcitrate, bounce back, reverberate, echo

▶ *510 Resonance*

20 solve, sum, score, equate, total, resolve, conclude, discover, work out, unscramble, clear up, sort out, decode, interpret, explain, reason, contrive, measure, plan, remedy

▶ *210 Calculation; 394 Remedy; 444 Reason; 446 Idea; 449 Discovery; 719 Interpretation; 743 Identification*

21 answer to, correspond, correlate, parallel, reciprocate, conform, twin, match, tally, agree, oblige, require

▶ *110 Reciprocity; 111 Sameness; 117 Conformity; 188 Parallelism; 750 Agreement*

22 be the answer, pertain, fit, suit, fulfil expectations, rise to the occasion, turn up trumps (Inf), be just the job (*or* thing) (Inf), do the trick (Inf)

▶ *217 Sufficiency; 609 Satisfaction; 610 Hope*

23 answer for, be responsible, act on behalf of, represent, speak for, appear for, replace, stand in for, deputize, understudy

▶ *135 Requirement; 354 Undertaking; 398 Delegate; 717 Representation; 810 Duty*

ADVERBS

24 **in answer**, in reply, in response, responsively, reflexively, reactively, retroactively, interactively, interchangeably, reciprocally, exchangeably, conversationally, dialectically, in conversation, argumentatively, insolently, defensively, in defence, recalcitrantly, antithetically, reverberantly, echoingly, on the rebound, on the bounce

25 **conclusively**, in conclusion, in the end, as it turns out, solubly

26 **correspondingly**, answerably, correlatively, in parallel, symmetrically, equivalently, congruently, conformingly, agreeably, aptly, fittingly, suitably, relevantly, usefully, reasonably, remedially

27 **answerably**, responsibly, representatively, accountably, dutifully, instead, in lieu, in place, as a replacement

707 Affirmation

NOUNS

1 **affirmation**, affirmance, assertion, attestation, declaration, averment, asseveration, allegation, swearing, vouching, certification, vouch (Lit)

▶ *452 Certainty; 739 Disclosure*

2 **statement**, pronouncement, profession, utterance, word, say, saying, dictum, *ipse dixit* (L), proposition, maxim, positive declaration, proclamation, enunciation, annunciation, announcement, press announcement, public relations release, position, position paper, stand, stance, manifesto, creed, submission, prepared text, thesis, supposition, predication, conclusion, say-so (Inf)

▶ *464 Judgment; 476 Supposition; 745 Maxim*

3 **vow**, oath, word, pledge, promise, guarantee, solemn word, solemn oath, sworn statement, statement under (*or* on) oath, deposition, affidavit, sworn testimony, solemn affirmation, declaration of truth, assurance, commitment, word of honour, word of a gentleman, swearing in, charging, adjuration, swearing on the Bible, Bible oath, judicial oath, oath of office, official oath, oath of allegiance, loyalty oath, test (Lit)

▶ *716 Evidence; 756 Promise*

4 **confirmation**, corroboration, substantiation, ratification, authentication, proof, establishment, assurance, endorsement, second, support, supportive statement, written statement, backing, backing up, attestation, validation, verification, certification, fortification, reinforcement, lack of retraction, buttressing

5 **admission**, avowal, avouchment, disclosure, deposition, confession

6 **assertiveness**, forcefulness, self-assertion, assurance, decisiveness, incisiveness, pointedness, explicitness, expressness, outspokenness, bluntness, plainness, strong words, thrust, drive, push, pushiness, insistence, peremptoriness, vehemence, vigorousness, vigour, positiveness, chutzpah (US), zip (Inf), go (Inf), get-up-and-go (Inf), oomph (Inf)

▶ *338 Vigour*

7 **emphasis**, stress, stressed point, overstatement

▶ *726 Emphasis*

8 **definiteness**, absoluteness, categoricalness, unequivocalness, certainty, unquestionability, unquestionableness, undisputedness, indubitability, indubitableness

▶ *661 Defiance; 715 Accusation; 753 Protest*

9 **affirmer**, affirmant, asserter (*or* assertor), witness, eyewitness, testifier, attestant, declarer, professor, proclaimer, enunciator, announcer, public relations man (*or* woman), submitter, voucher, vower, discloser, confessor, pledger, swearer, oath-taker, oath administrator, guarantor, authenticator, backer, corroborator, certifier, verifier, ratifier, advocate, assurer, supporter, sponsor, endorser, seconder, promoter, patron, ally, helpmate, tower of strength, champion, fortifier, pusher, insister

ADJECTIVES

10 **affirmative**, affirming, affirmatory, assertive, assertory, supportive, declarative, declaratory, proclamatory, annunciative, annunciatory, enunciative, enunciatory, validatory, creedal, suppositional, predicative, predicational, propositional, conclusive

11 **stated**, declared, asserted, pronounced, professed, uttered, proclaimed, affirmed, attested, alleged, averred, asseverated, enunciated, annunciated, announced, released, read, submitted, admitted, confessed, avowed, avouched, disclosed

12 **vowed**, pledged, promised, assured, guaranteed, committed, vouched, vouched for, sworn, sworn to, on oath, depositional, true, veridical

13 **supported**, confirmed, corroborated, substantiated, ratified, authenticated, attested, validated, verified, certified, established, assured, unretracted, unretractable, endorsed, supported, backed, reinforced, fortified, buttressed

14 **assertive**, self-assertive, assertory, assured, confident, forceful, decisive, decided, incisive, pointed, explicit, express, outspoken, blunt, plain, strongly worded, thrustful, driven, insistent, dogmatic, peremptory, pontifical, ex cathedra, vehement, emphatic, vigorous, positive, not negative, brooking no denial, straight from the shoulder, pushy (Inf)

15 **emphasized**, stressed, strongly worded, pointed, underlined, underscored, overstated, exaggerated

16 **definite**, absolute, categorical, unequivocal, unquestionable, undisputed, indisputable, indubitable

VERBS

17 **affirm**, assert, attest, declare, state, make a statement, pronounce, aver, asseverate, profess, utter, give the word, propose, declare positively, proclaim, enunciate, annunciate, announce, make a press announcement, issue a public relations release, say, speak, give voice to, have one's say, release a paper, issue a manifesto, issue a press release, live by a creed, submit, put forward, write a thesis, set down, predicate, conclude, certify, allege, swear, vouch

18 **vow**, swear (to), swear an oath, swear on oath, state under (*or* on) oath, give one's (solemn) word, give one's (solemn) oath, pledge, promise, guarantee, commit oneself, vouch for, administer an oath, place (*or* put) under oath, swear in, charge, adjure, give a sworn statement,

make a deposition, sign an affidavit, give sworn testimony, testify, bear witness, declare as true, assure, commit, give one's word of honour, give one's word as a gentleman, take the oath of office, swear an oath of allegiance, swear on the Bible, kiss the book, swear to God, swear by all that is holy, cross one's heart (and hope to die)

19 confirm, corroborate, substantiate, ratify, authenticate, prove, establish, assure, endorse, second, support, issue a supportive statement, back, back up, attest, validate, verify, certify, fortify, reinforce, fail to retract, buttress, stick to one's guns (Inf)

20 admit, avow, avouch, disclose, depose, confess, own up

21 be assertive, assert, assure, act forcefully, act decisively, speak ex cathedra, speak out (*or* up), have one's say, say so, have the last word, use strong words, put it bluntly, thrust, drive, push, insist, brook no denial, get on one's soapbox, hold the floor, lay down the law, make no bones about

22 emphasize, stress, stress a point, overstate, mean what one says, be definite, not equivocate, not question, not dispute

ADVERBS

23 affirmatively, positively, absolutely, definitely, categorically, assertively, allegedly, avowedly, undoubtedly, unequivocally, unquestionably, indisputably, indubitably, conclusively, authentically, assuredly, emphatically, with emphasis, without fear of contradiction

24 truthfully, truly, assuredly, decidedly, seriously, in all seriousness, in earnest, in all conscience, upon one's word, upon one's honour, in sworn testimony, on the Bible, under (*or* on) oath

25 explicitly, bluntly, insistently, plainly, dogmatically, ex cathedra, vehemently, pointedly, vigorously, provocatively, defiantly, critically

INTERJECTIONS

26 as God is my witness!, honest to God!, on my word of honour!, as I stand here!, cross my heart and hope to die!, scout's honour!, on my mother's life!

708 Negation

NOUNS

1 negation, abnegation, negative, negativism, negativeness, negativity, negative attitude, pessimism, defeatism, despondence, despondency, noncorroboration, no, nay, naysaying (Lit), nix (US inf)

► *611 Despair*

2 rejection, refusal, denial, disavowal, disallowance, prohibition, invalidation, disclaimer, nonacceptance, declining, refusal of consent, veto, refusal of belief, nonbelief, disbelief, atheism, unbelief, agnosticism, apostasy, nonobservance, disobedience, recusance, recusancy, disownment, repudiation, renunciation, disclamation, dissociation, disassociation, nonassociation

► *451 Disbelief; 470 Rejection; 662 Disobedience; 709 Refusal*

3 rebuttal, refutation, rejoinder, retortion, retort, challenge, objection, demurral, demur, defiance, obstruction, deprecation, dissent, doubtfulness, questioning, protest, denial, flat denial, emphatic denial, contradiction, flat contradiction, contravention, contrary assertion, disagreement, impugnation, disaffirmation, antithesis, reverse, opposite, contrary, contrariness, countering, contesting, taking issue with, disproving, crossing, disproof, appeal, cross-appeal, gainsaying (Lit)

► *661 Defiance; 753 Protest*

4 renunciation, abrogation, recantation, repudiation, abjuration, forswearing, swearing off, relinquishment, revocation, repeal, rescindment, retraction, retractation, cancellation, nullification, annulment, countermand, invalidation

► *355 Relinquishment; 479 Equivocation*

5 cancellation, cancelling, nullification, annulment, repealing, repeal, reversion, discontinuation, discontinuance, waiver, suspension, setting aside, invalidation, disallowance, rescinding, rescindment, abjuration, abrogation, negation, revocation, reversal, recall, rejection, repudiation, amnesty, reprieve, abolition, abolition of sins, salvation, abolishment, elimination, write-off, censorship, deletion, removal, reneging, recantation, retraction, retractation, obliteration, defacement

► *7 Religion; 350 Nonuse; 358 Obliteration; 708 Negation; 761 Reversion*

6 termination, cessation, stoppage, discontinuance, nolle prosequi (Lit), resignation, honourable discharge, dismissal, discharge, expulsion, firing, redundancy, suspension, lay-off, furlough (US), services no longer required, cancellation of contract, recall, removal, ejection, dishonourable discharge, one's cards (Inf), the axe (Inf), the push (Inf), the bowler hat (Inf), golden handshake (Inf), the sack (Inf), the boot (Inf), the shove (Inf), the bounce (US inf), the bullet (Inf), the kiss off (US inf), the chop (Inf), walking papers (US inf), marching orders (Inf), the old heave-ho (Inf), the elbow (Inf), the big E (Inf)

► *226 Stopping; 371 Expulsion*

7 cancelling out, neutralizing, neutralization, making equal, equalizing, balance, equal weight, counterbalance, counterweight, sash weight, counterpoise, counterorder, countermand, counteraction, contradiction, refutation

8 nonexistence, nothingness, nothing, nullity, nonentity, void, vacuity, vacuum, emptiness

► *94 Nonexistence*

9 negativist, pessimist, refuser, vetoer, atheist, agnostic, apostate, rebutter, challenger, protestant, objector, dissenter, protester, recanter, repealer, retractor, nonentity, gainsayer (Lit)

VERBS

10 be negative, be pessimistic, negate, abnegate, not corroborate, shake one's head, say no, reject, refuse, refuse to accept, not accept, deny, not admit, disavow, disallow, prohibit, make impossible, invalidate, decline, refuse consent, veto, not believe, disbelieve, practise atheism, be agnostic, not observe, disobey, disown, repudiate, renunciate, disclaim, dissociate oneself, disassociate oneself, not associate, naysay (Lit)

11 rebut, refute, rejoin, retort, challenge, object, demur, defy, obstruct, deprecate, stand up to, dissent, doubt, express doubts, question, call into question, refuse credence, protest, deny, deny the possibility, issue a flat denial, emphatically deny, contradict, issue a flat contradiction, controvert, contravene, disagree, impugn, disaffirm, reverse, be opposite, affirm the contrary, counter, contest, take issue with, disprove, cross, appeal, cross-appeal, belie, give the lie to, gainsay (Lit)

12 renounce, abrogate, recant, repudiate, abjure, forswear, swear off, relinquish, revoke, repeal, rescind, retract, cancel, nullify, annul, countermand, invalidate, apostasize, tergiversate, take back, go back on one's word, change one's mind, do a U-turn, make a 180-degree turn, do a turn-around, eat one's words (Inf), eat one's hat (Inf)

13 be nothing, have no existence, not exist, not be, be null and void

14 cancel, nullify, make null and void, void, disallow, reject, negate, abolish, eliminate, suspend, call off, abandon, invalidate, withdraw, set aside, waiver, retract, renounce, abjure, quash, overrule, rescind, abrogate, repeal, reverse, recall, revoke, reprieve, offer amnesty to, renege, recant, repudiate, annul, annihilate, obliterate, destroy, delete, cut, erase, efface, write off, do away with, strike out, black out, blot out, cross out, censor, remove all signs of, remove, expunge, scribble out, scrub out, wipe out, deface, kill (Inf)

15 terminate, stop, dismiss, discontinue, cancel one's contract, resign, remove, bench (US), suspend, lay off, eject, discharge, give a dishonourable discharge to, cashier, dethrone, depose, divest, unfrock, strike off the register, oust, demote, fire (Inf), axe (Inf), give someone the axe (Inf), give someone the golden handshake (Inf), give someone the (old) heave-ho (Inf), sack (Inf), bump (Inf), kiss off (Inf), give someone the chop (Inf), get (*or* cop) the bullet (Inf), give someone their marching orders (Inf)

16 cancel out, cancel, eliminate each other, make neutral, neutralize, make equal, equalize, countervail, offset, weigh equally, weigh up against, counterbalance, counterweigh, balance, counterpoise, work both ways, cut both ways, work against, issue a counterorder, countermand, counteract, turn the tables on, contradict, refute

ADJECTIVES

17 negative, pessimistic, defeatist, despondent, abnegative, atheistic, agnostic, recusant, doubtful, protestant, defiant, contrary, obstructive, contradictive, contradictory, repudiative, renunciative, renunciatory, abrogative, revocatory, abjuratory, deprecative, dissociative, disassociative, nonassociative

18 rejected, refused, denied, refuted, rebutted, disobeyed, disavowed, disallowed, prohibited, obstructed, contravened, invalidated, nonaccepted, declined, vetoed, disbelieved, nonobserved, disowned, disclaimed, relinquished, renounced, negated, deprecated, repudiated, repealed, rescinded, retracted, reversed, recanted, cancelled, nullified, annulled, countermanded, challenged, questioned, contested, disproved, crossed, appealed, crossappealed, nixed (US inf)

19 rebutting, refuting, rejecting, prohibiting, refusing, denying, forswearing, rejoining, retorting, objecting, opposing, obstructing, deprecating, dissenting, doubting, questioning, challenging, contradicting, countering, disagreeing, impugning, disaffirming, gainsaying (Lit)

20 cancelled, abrogated, stopped, annulled, nullified, null and void, voided, invalid, invalidated, killed, dead, repealed, revoked, rescinded, rescindable, set aside, recalled, negated, reprieved, terminated, abolished, laid off, suspended, discharged, fired, reborn, reformative, reformed, censored, deleted, struck out, struck off, wiped out, defaced, neutralized, equalized, balanced, counteracting, counteractive, contrary, bowler-hatted (Inf), fired (Inf), axed (Inf), sacked (Inf)

21 nonexistent, unexisting, null and void, vacant, vacuous, empty

ADVERBS

22 negatively, in the negative, not at all, (in) no way, pessimistically, despondently, atheistically, doubtfully, deniably, in denial, defiantly, contrarily, in contradiction, contradictorily, prohibitively, obstructively, invalidly, in opposition, opposingly, deprecatively, dissentingly, questionably, challengingly

INTERJECTIONS

23 no!, nay!, *non!* (Fr), *nein!* (Ger), *nyet!* (Russian), certainly not!, absolutely not!, I think not!, not so!, not really!, not likely!, not if I can help it!, not for the world!, not for the love of money!, not for the life of me!, not at all!, no way!, in no case!, a thousand times no!, to the contrary!, *au contraire!* (Fr), quite the contrary!, far from it!, nothing of the kind!, nothing of the sort!, nothing doing! (Inf), nope! (Inf), nix! (US inf)

24 never!, anything but!, out of the question!, you must be joking!, God forbid!, forget it!, not by a long shot! (Inf), not by a long chalk! (Inf), no sirree! (US inf), fat chance! (Inf), over my dead body! (Inf)

709 Refusal

What is a rebel? A man who says no. Albert Camus.

NOUNS

1 refusal, refusal of consent, lack of consent, turning down, thumbs down, rejection, denial, repulsion, repulse, negative answer, negation, flat refusal, point-blank refusal, red light, noncompliance, resistance, retention, recalcitrance, unwillingness, nonwillingness, noncooperation, nonacceptance, denigration, refusal to work, strike, industrial action, lockout, sit-down strike (*or* sit-in), refusal to pay, nonpayment, default, tax evasion, creative accounting

► *360 Retention; 364 Repulsion; 371 Expulsion; 383 Resistance; 470 Rejection; 634 Avoidance; 637 Unwillingness; 708 Negation*

2 dissent, dissidence, lack of consent, contrary vote, a vote against, veto, disagreement, opposition, objection, discordance, refutation, repudiation, rebuttal, rebuff, contradiction, confutation, renunciation, confrontation, demonstration, civil disobedience, controversy, prohibition, counterorder, interdiction, interdict, ban, embargo, gainsaying (Lit), kick in the teeth (Inf)

► *113 Opposition; 661 Defiance; 753 Protest*

3 abnegation, relinquishment, self-restraint, self-sacrifice, self-renunciation, self-denial, denying oneself, refusing oneself

► *355 Relinquishment; 684 Self-Restraint*

4 **refuser**, refusenik, teetotaller, abstainer, tax evader, draft dodger (US), conscientious objector, deserter, truant, dissident, striker, scab, blackleg, gainsayer (Lit)

VERBS

5 **refuse**, reject, deny, say no, shake one's head, give the thumbs down to, show the red light to, repulse, repel, negate, not comply, resist, refuse permission, refuse flatly, refuse point-blank, retain, not cooperate, denigrate, not be willing to, not accept, decline, turn down, pass up, make one's excuses, send one's apologies, avoid, turn away, shy away from, shrink from, flinch at, balk at, jib at, keep away, not want anything to do with, refuse to work, strike, go on strike, call a strike, lock out, have a sit-down strike, refuse to pay, default, evade taxes, turn one's back on, turn a deaf ear to, harden one's heart to, not buy (Inf), not wear (Inf)

6 **dissent**, withhold consent, withhold assent, express doubts, disagree, oppose, not allow, disallow, not stand for, reject, repudiate, rebuff, spurn, snub, object, refute, rebut, contradict, confute, nullify, renunciate, confront, withstand, not comply with, demonstrate against, cast a contrary vote, vote against, veto, prohibit, forbid, interdict, embargo, ban, gainsay (Lit), tell someone where to go (Inf), tell someone where to get off (Inf), kick someone in the teeth (Inf)

7 **refuse oneself**, deny oneself, deprive oneself of, renounce, forebear, demur, abstain, abstain from, go without, do without, live simply

ADJECTIVES

8 **refused**, refusing, noncooperative, uncooperative, unconsenting, uncompliant, noncompliant, noncomplying, resistant, resisting, negative, negating, recalcitrant, unwilling, nonwilling, nonaccepting, turned down, turned away, thrown out, ejected, excluded, withholding, withheld, kept back, not offered, retained, striking, strike-bound, sit-down, sit-in, given the thumbs down, given the red light, deaf to, not willing to hear of

9 **dissenting**, dissident, disagreeing, repudiating, demurring, opposing, opposite, adversarial, protesting, objecting to, discordant, refuting, denying, denied, disallowed, not allowed, not permitted, not granted, contradictory, contrary, contravening, confutative, renunciative, renunciatory, rejecting, rejected, rebuffed, revoking, revocatory, confrontational, controversial, prohibitionary, prohibited, prohibiting, interdictive, banned, embargoed

10 **abnegating**, abnegated, relinquishing, relinquished, self-sacrificing, self-renunciatory, self-denying

ADVERBS

11 **uncooperatively**, without a cooperative spirit, on no account, not at all, negatively, resistantly, resistingly, with resistance, unwillingly, dissentingly, dissidently, oppositely, discordantly, contradictorily, in contradiction, contrarily, controversially, in a controversial way, interdictively, no fear, not on your life (Inf), no chance (Inf), no way (Inf), not over one's dead body (Inf), not for all the tea in China (Inf), not on your nelly (Inf)

INTERJECTIONS

12 **no!**, no way!, a thousand times no!, never!, not likely!, impossible!, nothing doing!, far from it!, count me out!, over my dead body! (Inf), like hell! (Inf), nix (US inf)

710 Request

When two or three are gathered together in thy Name thou wilt grant their requests. The Book of Common Prayer.

NOUNS

1 **request**, asking, entreaty, solemn entreaty, importunity, pressure, persuasion, insistence, urgency, urging, imploring, soliciting, accosting, invitation, application, appeal, bid, cry, desire, expressed desire, special request, favour, wish, want, petition, round-robin, invocation, incantation, prayer, supplication, adjuration, *cri du coeur* (Fr), begging, beseeching, pestering, solicitation, living will, viatical settlement, suggestion, proposition, proposal, motion, approach, offer, requirement, claim, counterclaim, suit, courting, wooing

► *135 Requirement; 480 Persuasion; 617 Desire; 752 Offer*

2 **demand**, requisition, order, indent, summons, call, notice, claim, demand for payment, final demand, final notice, last time of asking, injunction, dunning, dun, command, ultimatum, forcible demand, demand backed by threats, threat, blackmail, exaction, extortion

► *386 Compulsion; 397 Command; 701 Argument; 740 Publication*

3 **solicitation**, soliciting money, chain letter, mendicancy, begging, cadging, busking, fund-raising, appealing, appeal, charity appeal, canvass, canvassing, charity events, charity show, charity ball, charity match, benefit game (US), (church) bazaar, benefit concert, Band-Aid, telethon, Children in Need Appeal, charity organization, OXFAM, United Way (US), charity funds, benefit gig (Inf), scrounging (Inf), sponging (Inf), bumming (US inf), panhandling (US inf), freeloading (Inf), mooching (Inf), the touch (Inf)

► *650 Benevolence; 772 Borrowing; 773 Taking*

4 **requester**, petitioner, appealer, lobbyist, supplicant, suppliant, appellant, solicitor, canvasser, charity worker, fund-raiser, claimant, counterclaimant, asker, blackmailer, extortionist, hustler, seeker, inquirer, questioner, borrower, customer, applicant, candidate, suitor, lover

5 **beggar**, cadger, busker, mendicant, mendicant friar, hanger-on, vagrant, freebooter, tramp, hobo (US), bum (US inf), scrounger (Inf), sponger (Inf), panhandler (US inf), freeloader (Inf), moocher (Inf), ligger (Inf)

VERBS

6 **request**, make a request, have a request to make, have a need for, lack, want, want to know, demand an answer, ask, ask for, ask for support, ask for one's blessing, ask if it is possible, ask a favour, ask leave, beg leave, ask permission, beg permission, ask to be excused, make a special request, go cap in hand, entreat, pressure, insist, urge, implore, solicit, accost, hustle, invite, request the pleasure of one's company, apply for, appeal, bid, cry, desire, wish, petition, sign a petition, sign a round robin, invoke, incant, pray, pray for, address one's prayers to, kneel to, go down on one's knees to, supplicate, adjure, beg, beseech, cajole, coax, pester, tout, hawk, suggest,

persuade, proposition, propose, move, approach, make overtures to, offer, apply, require, claim, counterclaim, issue a suit, court, woo, request one's hand in marriage, pop the question (Inf), go down on bended knee, bug (Inf)

7 **demand**, requisition, order, indent, summon, call, claim, press a claim, put in a claim, invoice, charge, bill, levy, tax, demand payment, make a final demand, receive a final notice, receive an injunction, dun, command, issue an ultimatum, threaten, demand with threats, blackmail, exact, extort, bleed someone (Inf), put the squeeze on someone (Inf), put the bite on someone (US and Aus inf)

8 **solicit money**, beg, cadge, hold out one's hand, go from door to door, pass around the hat, busk, raise funds, appeal, make a charity appeal, launch an appeal, canvass, hold a charity event, put the squeeze on, scrounge (Inf), sponge (Inf), bum (US inf), panhandle (US inf), freeload (Inf), mooch (Inf), put the touch on (Inf), tap (Inf)

ADJECTIVES

9 **requesting**, requested, asking, insistent, urgent, invitational, inviting, desired, petitioned, round-robin, invocational, incantational, adjuratory, entreating, beseeching, propositional, proposable, proposed, offered, required, courting, wooing

10 **demanding**, demanded, requisitionary, claiming, injunctive, forcible, threatening, threatened, blackmailing, blackmailed, extortive, extorting, extorted

11 **begging**, cadging, mendicant, fund-raising, scrounging (Inf), sponging (Inf), freeloading (Inf), mooching (Inf)

ADVERBS

12 **by request**, insistently, urgently, with urgency, entreatingly, by one's leave, with permission, beseechingly, forcibly, using force, with force

711 Warning

Beware the ides of March. William Shakespeare.

NOUNS

1 **warning**, caution, caveat, example, warning example, advice, counsel, lesson, object lesson, notice, advance notice, notification, information, intelligence, news, word, word of warning, word in the ear, word to the wise, tip, tip-off, kick under the table, wink, pinch, nudge, hint, announcement, publication, public warning, storm warning, hurricane warning, final warning, final notice, final invoice, final demand, ultimatum, monition, admonition, admonishment, reprimand, deterrent, dissuasion, protest, expostulation, forewarning, foreboding, premonition, premonition of disaster, omen, bad omen, evil omen, portent, evil portent, prediction, augury, Mother Carey's chickens, storm(y) petrel, bird of ill omen, gathering clouds, gathering storm, rising river, cloud on the horizon, war cloud, conscience, voice of conscience, warning voice, note of warning, murmur of discontent, muttering, sign, symptom, indication, indicator, signal, signs of the times, knell, death knell, menace, danger, threat

► *254 Danger; 397 Command; 475 Prediction; 481 Dissuasion; 606 Dissatisfaction; 616 Caution; 670 Disapproval; 693 Information; 713 Advice; 740 Publication; 741 News; 742 Sign; 743 Identification; 810 Duty*

2 **danger signal**, alarm, warning alarm, warning sign, writing on the wall, beacon, light, shout, bell, whistle, horn, siren, blast, honk, toot, ring, gale warning, hurricane warning, storm signal, storm cone, alarum (Lit), hue and cry, alarm clock, alarm bell, security alarm, emergency buzzer, panic button, burglar alarm, fire alarm, fire bell, foghorn, fog signal, bell buoy, klaxon, car horn, bicycle bell, police whistle, church bell, curfew bell, tocsin, alert, red alert, beat of drum, tattoo, trumpet call, war cry, war whoop, war dance, battle cry, rallying cry, starter's gun, warning shot, shot across the bows, fiery cross (US), warning light, flashing light, red light, amber light, flare, warning flare, Very signal (*or* light), red flag, yellow flag, distress signal, SOS, mayday, distress flare, sign of alarm, wide eyes, open mouth, start, tremor, paleness, sweat, hair on end

► *254 Danger; 612 Fear; 742 Sign; 743 Identification*

3 **false alarm**, false alert, false warning, alarm test, cry of wolf, scare, hoax, bugbear, bugaboo, bogey (*or* bogy), *bête noire* (Fr), nightmare, bad dream, false pregnancy, blank cartridge, fool's gold, flash in the pan, canard, false report, false rumour, untruth

► *96 Unreality; 242 Unpleasantness; 700 Deception*

4 **warner**, cautioner, caveator, adviser, counsellor, admonisher, prophet, Ezekiel, Nostradamus, Cassandra, medicine man, witch doctor, shaman, diviner, scaremonger, alarmist, flagman, signaller, lighthouse-keeper, watchman, lookout, security guard, security man (*or* woman), watch, guard, picket, sentinel, sentry, scout, advanced guard, vanguard, rear sentry, rearguard, watchdog, protector, spy, informant, mole, rat (Inf), squealer (Inf)

► *252 Safety; 475 Prediction; 616 Caution; 693 Information; 713 Advice*

VERBS

5 **warn**, give fair warning, caution, issue a caveat, advise, counsel, give a word of warning, give a word in the ear, give a word to the wise, tip, tip off, kick under the table, wink, pinch, nudge, hint, drop a hint, give notice, notify, inform, apprise, issue a public warning, put on one's guard, alert, forewarn, forearm, prepare, spell danger, spell disaster, predict, augur, remind, put one in mind, admonish, reprove, lour, menace, threaten, advise against, dissuade, remonstrate, protest, provoke action, cause panic

► *243 Preparation; 462 Memory; 616 Caution; 670 Disapproval; 693 Information; 713 Advice*

6 **be warned**, receive notice, beware, take heed, watch one's step, learn one's lesson, take someone's words to heart, profit by (the) example, profit by one's mistakes

7 **raise the alarm**, give the alarm, sound a warning, sound the alarm, sound the fire alarm, sound a siren, sound one's horn, honk, toot, blow the whistle, ring the bell, pull the emergency handle, press the emergency button, fire a warning flare, toll, knell, alert, arouse, scare, startle, frighten, alarm, cry, scream, raise a hue and cry, call out the troops, turn out the guard, call the po-

lice, dial 999, call a doctor, call an ambulance, call the fire brigade, call the emergency service, call the rescue service, call the AA (Automobile Association), call the RAC (Royal Automobile Club), give a false alarm, cry wolf, cry too soon, test the alarm system, cry blue murder (Inf)

► *612 Fear; 630 Surprise*

ADJECTIVES

8 **warning**, cautionary, exemplary, advisable, counsellable, instructive, informative, notifying, hinting, monitory, admonitory, protesting, symptomatic, prognostic, predicting, premonitory, boding, foreboding, ill-omened, ominous, presageful, menacing, minatory, threatening, deterrent, dissuasive, frightening

► *475 Prediction; 612 Fear; 616 Caution; 693 Information; 713 Advice*

9 **warned**, cautioned, advised, counselled, taught a lesson, cautious, wary, forewarned, forearmed, prepared, once bitten (Inf)

► *243 Preparation; 616 Caution*

INTERJECTIONS

10 **look out!**, beware!, careful!, watch out!, watch it!, take care!, mind your step!, mind the gap!, look where you're going!, cave!, (Inf), fore! (golf)

712 Curse

NOUNS

1 **curse**, curse word, oath, profanity, profanation, obscenity, vulgarity, scurrility, imprecation, dysphemism, naughty word, bad word, swearword, dirty word, four-letter word, expletive, invective, string of invectives, unrepeatable expression, ribaldry, bawdy verse, dirty joke, blue joke, dirty talk, filth, cursing, swearing, foul mouth, foul-mouthing, dirty mouth, billingsgate, scatology, blasphemy, sacrilege, talking dirty, cuss (Inf), cuss word (Inf), no-no (Inf), tinker's damn (*or* cuss) (Inf), effing and blinding (Inf)

► *675 Vulgarity*

2 **offensive language**, bad language, indelicate language, unparliamentary language, colourful language, blue language, foul language, obscene language, profane language, strong language, vile language, dirty language, filthy language, Anglo-Saxon

3 **vilification**, vituperation, denunciation, fulmination, execration, revilement, scurrility, verbal abuse, volley of abuse, thundering, reproach, opprobrium, slander, libel, defamation, calumny, obloquy, threat, evil speaking, onslaught, attack, slanging match

► *668 Disrespect; 670 Disapproval; 678 Scornfulness; 715 Accusation*

4 **malediction**, ill wishes, spell, voodoo spell, the evil eye, *maloccio* (It), curse, charm, jinx, imprecation, damnation, ban, excommunication, anathema, proscription, commination, malison (Lit), hex (US inf), whammy (Inf), double whammy (Inf)

► *7 Religion; 11 Occultism; 651 Malevolence*

VERBS

5 **curse**, use profanity, swear, curse and swear, talk filthy, talk dirty, tell dirty jokes, write bawdy poems, use bad language, use obscene language, use expletives, use billingsgate, scatologize, dysphemize, blaspheme, commit a sacrilege, take the Lord's name in vain, swear like a trooper, swear till one is blue in the face, make the air blue, cuss (Inf), eff and blind (Inf)

6 **vilify**, revile, denunciate, execrate, condemn, fulminate, rebuke, scold, chide, tongue-lash, abuse, heap abuse upon, pour vitriol upon, hurl a volley of abuse at, blackguard, accuse, reproach, vituperate, rail against, inveigh against, thunder, blast, damn and blast, slang, reproach, slander, libel, defame, call names, disgrace, threaten, attack, round upon, send to the devil, have a slanging match, give the rough edge of one's tongue to, send to blazes (Inf)

7 **wish ill**, put a spell on, put a curse on, call a curse down on, give the evil eye to, charm, put a jinx on, damn, curse up hill and down dale, imprecate, anathematize, ban, excommunicate, proscribe, curse with bell, book and candle, curse like hell (Inf), hex (US inf), put a hex on (US inf), throw (*or* put) a whammy on (Inf), throw (*or* put) a double whammy on (Inf)

ADJECTIVES

8 **cursing**, swearing, profane, obscene, vulgar, scurrilous, naughty, offensive, indelicate, blue, four-letter, Anglo-Saxon, invective, dirty, filthy, vile, indecent, ribald, bawdy, Rabelaisian, risqué, raw (US), foul, foul-mouthed, foul-tongued, scatological, dysphemistic, blasphemous, sacrilegious

9 **vituperative**, abusive, vitriolic, vilifying, reviling, denunciatory, denouncing, blasting, reproachful, ignominious, opprobrious, slanderous, libellous, defamatory, calumnious, attacking, threatening

10 **maledictive**, maledictory, imprecatory, damning, cursed, accursed, damned, wished on one, hexed, jinxed, under a spell, bewitched, unblest, execrative, under a ban, banned, excommunicated, proscribed, comminatory, hexed (US inf)

11 **miscellaneous euphemisms**, blessed, blamed (US), blankety-blank (Inf), confounded (Inf), dad-blamed (Inf), dad-blasted (Inf), dad-burned (Inf), doggone (US inf), deuced (Inf), darn (Inf), darned (Inf), goshdarn (Inf), goshdarned (Inf), dang (Inf), danged (Inf), durn (US), durned (US), ruddy (Inf), blasted (Inf), bloody (Inf), goldarn (US inf), crikey (Inf), blazes (Inf), jeepers (creepers) (US inf)

ADVERBS

12 **swearingly**, profanely, obscenely, vulgarly, scurrilously, naughtily, offensively, with offence, indelicately, dirtily, vilely, indecently, in an indecent manner, ribaldly, bawdily, blasphemously, sacrilegiously

13 **vituperatively**, abusively, in an abusive manner, reproachfully, with reproach, slanderously, libellously, defamatorily, ignominiously, opprobriously

14 **damningly**, cursedly, as a curse, bewitchingly, by means of enchantment, while under a spell, execratively

INTERJECTIONS

15 **miscellaneous swearwords**, damn!, blast!, Christ!, Jesus Christ!, Christ Almighty!, Jesus wept!, bloody hell!, bugger it! (Inf), bugger off! (Inf), shit! (Inf), balls! (Inf), bollocks! (Inf), piss off! (Inf), fuck! (Inf), fuck it! (Inf), fuck me! (Inf), fuck off! (Inf), fuck you! (Inf), fucking hell! (Inf)

16 euphemisms, darn!, dang it!, gosh!, dad-blast!, gosh-darn!, the devil take it!, jeepers-creepers!, gee whiz!, gee whillikers! (US)

713 Advice

Advice is seldom welcome; and those who want it the most always like it the least. Earl of Chesterfield.

One gives nothing so freely as advice. Duc de la Rochefoucauld.

NOUNS

1 advice, word of advice, piece of advice, counsel, rede (Lit), tip, hint, word in the ear, word to the wise, words of wisdom, pearls of wisdom, wisdom, counselling, guidance, advising, therapy, didacticism, moralizing, moral injunction, prescription, precept, caution, warning, admonition, suggestion, recommendation, proposition, proposal, motion, supposition, submission, opinion, view, estimate, criticism, constructive criticism, briefing, instruction, information, notification, communication, intelligence, news, word, charge, charge to the jury, advice for, encouragement, advice against, deprecation

▶ *394 Remedy; 458 Wisdom; 464 Judgment; 476 Supposition; 480 Persuasion; 481 Dissuasion; 693 Information; 711 Warning*

2 consultation, taking counsel, seeking advice, deliberation, discussion, mutual consultation, heads together, tête-à-tête, parley, negotiation session, negotiations, conference, round table, meeting of minds, exchange of views, open exchange, reference, referment, council, huddle (Inf), powwow (Inf)

▶ *579 Management; 734 Conversation; 753 Protest*

3 precept, maxim, principle, moral, rule, moral rule, golden rule, guideline, moral guideline, guide, commandment, the Ten Commandments, the Twelve Tables, laws of Medes and the Persians, law, canon law, common law, unwritten law, custom, rule of custom, convention, practice, norm, habit and repute, advice, firm advice, admonition, warning, direction, instruction, general instruction, technicality, nice point, precedent, leading case, example, text, injunction, charge, command, commission, mission, mandate, order, written order, writ, warrant, rescript, decree, decretal, canon, judgment, prescript, prescription, remedy, ordinance, regulation, form, formula, formulary, rubric, recipe, receipt (US), statute, enactment, act, code, penal code, corpus juris, body of law, legislation, tenet, article, set of rules, constitution, party line, party ticket (US)

▶ *16 Law; 117 Conformity; 140 Rule; 394 Remedy; 397 Command; 464 Judgment; 632 Habit; 737 Secrecy; 745 Maxim*

4 adviser, counsellor, guidance counsellor, consultant, professional consultant, management consultant, financial consultant, troubleshooter, expert, referee, independent referee, ombudsman, arbiter, arbitrator, judge, umpire, critic, estimator, prescriber, recommender, commender, advocate, mover, prompter, motivator, medical adviser, doctor, diagnostician, therapist, psychotherapist, psychiatrist, psychoanalyst, analyst, legal adviser, counsel, legal counsel, lawyer, attorney, solicitor, barrister, marriage adviser, marriage guidance counsellor, social worker, guide, cicerone, teacher, tutor, professor, priest, philosopher, mentor, confidante, friend, best friend, aide, helper, monitor, watchdog, admonisher, reminder, remembrancer (Lit), Nestor, Egeria, oracle, prophet, wise man, sage, committee of inquiry, public inquiry, governmental committee, congressional committee (US), parliamentary committee, select committee, consultative body, council, student council, emergency council, intrusive person, meddler, busybody, last word (Inf), Dutch uncle (Inf), back-seat driver (Inf)

▶ *342 Activity; 394 Remedy; 458 Wisdom; 464 Judgment; 480 Persuasion; 485 Skill*

VERBS

5 advise, give advice, offer advice, counsel, give counsel, offer counsel, guide, criticize, moralize, command, dictate, enjoin, prescribe, advocate, recommend, commend, think best, suggest, propose, move, put to, submit, propound, press, urge, encourage, exhort, incite, advise against, dissuade, admonish, warn, caution, prompt, hint, teach, brief, instruct, tell, inform, notify, apprise, charge (a jury)

▶ *239 Convenience; 397 Command; 476 Supposition; 480 Persuasion; 481 Dissuasion; 693 Information; 711 Warning*

6 consult, seek advice, ask for advice, seek opinion, refer to, refer to arbitration, call in, call on, ask for a second opinion, hold a public inquiry, submit one's judgment to another's, confide in, have at one's elbow, accept advice, take advice, follow advice, listen to, learn from, take one's cue from, sit in council, sit in conclave, hold a consultation, deliberate, discuss, confer, huddle, hold a confidential discussion, meet with, swap ideas, iron out problems, negotiate, have a tête-à-tête with, put heads together, have a powwow with, hold a council of war, parley, sit round a table, compare notes

▶ *734 Conversation*

ADJECTIVES

7 advising, advisory, counselling, consultative, deliberative, hortatory, hortative, monitory, recommendatory, therapeutic, prescriptive, didactic, instructive, informative, moral, moralizing, persuasive, encouraging, dissuasive, admonitory, warning, cautionary

▶ *480 Persuasion; 481 Dissuasion; 711 Warning*

8 advisable, recommendable, recommended, prudent, wise, judicious, politic, sensible, practical, expedient

▶ *239 Convenience; 458 Wisdom*

ADVERBS

9 advisably, prudently, wisely, judiciously, hortatorily, hortatively, didactically, instructively, informatively, morally

714 Vindication

NOUNS

1 vindication, exoneration, exculpation, compurgation (Lit), absolution, remission, remittal, acquittal, verdict of acquittal, verdict of innocence, verdict of not guilty, quashing of the charge, discharge, dismissal, release, pardon, clearance, clearing from guilt, clearing of one's name, purging, purgation, reinstatement, restitution, restoration, rehabilitation, triumph of justice, assertion of truth, the OK (Inf), the green light (Inf)

▶ *16 Law; 464 Judgment; 805 Innocence*

2 **defence**, legal defence, successful defence, reply for the defence, rebuttal, refutation, rejoinder, retort, recrimination, *tu quoque* (L), counterargument, argument, plea, justification, explanation, grounds, good grounds, truth, reason, good reason, excuse, good excuse, alibi, cause, just cause, supportive evidence, corroboration, partial excuse, extenuation, extenuating circumstances, mitigation, mitigating circumstances, palliation, qualification, allowance, out (US)

▶ *136 Qualification; 273 Accuracy; 384 Defence; 698 Truth; 706 Answer*

3 **cover-up**, whitewash, whitewashing, cop-out (Inf)

4 **revenge**, vengeance, reprisal, requital, retribution, fitting retribution, punishment, just punishment, poetic justice

▶ *385 Retaliation; 814 Punishment*

5 **vindicator**, justifier, defender, pleader, advocate, proponent, apologist, excuser, champion, palliator, whitewasher

6 **avenger**, vindicator, retaliator, punisher, Nemesis

VERBS

7 **vindicate**, exonerate, exculpate, absolve, remit, grant remission, allow for, make allowances for, excuse, pardon, clear, put in the clear, clear one's name, free from blame, withdraw the charge, acquit, discharge, dismiss, release, liberate, free, set free, purge, reinstate, restore, rehabilitate, make good, assert the truth, do justice to, set right, give the OK to (Inf), give the green light to (Inf)

8 **justify**, defend, make a legal defence, rebut the charge, rebut, refute, rejoin, retort, recriminate, argue, argue for, plead, plead one's own cause, attest to, warrant, explain, show good grounds, prove the truth of, prove, demonstrate, corroborate, substantiate, give supportive evidence, give a good reason, furnish a good excuse, make excuses for, alibi, speak up for, champion, uphold, stand up for, extenuate, mitigate, palliate, soften, ease, qualify, find an out (US), stick up for (Inf)

9 **cover up**, whitewash, cop out

10 **avenge**, revenge, requite, give fitting retribution, punish

ADJECTIVES

11 **vindicatory**, vindicating, exculpatory, exculpating, exonerative, exonerating, justifying, defensive, defending, argumentative, refuting, rejoining, retorting, rebutting, explanatory, excusatory, excusing, supportive, corroborative, apologetic, extenuating, extenuatory, mitigative, mitigating, qualifying, palliative, remissive, justifying

12 **innocent**, not guilty, acquitted, dismissed, discharged, released, pardoned, cleared, restored, rehabilitated

13 **vindicable**, justifiable, defensible, arguable, refutable, rebuttable, warrantable, admissible, allowable, reasonable, explainable, excusable, having an excuse, pardonable, remissible, forgivable, condonable, venial, exemptible, dispensable

14 **vindictive**, vengeful, revengeful, avenging, requiting, retributive, unforgiving, spiteful, venomous, malicious, malevolent, punitive, punishing

ADVERBS

15 **in vindication**, justifyingly, defensively, argumentatively, in explanation, as an excuse, supportively, in support, apologetically, extenuatingly, with qualifications, palliatively, remissively, justifyingly, with justification, forgivably, venially

16 **vindictively**, vengefully, revengefully, retributively, unforgivably, spitefully, in a spiteful manner, venomously, maliciously, with malice, malevolently, punitively, punishingly, as punishment

715 Accusation

I do not know the method of drawing up an indictment against an whole people. Edmund Burke.

J'accuse. (I accuse.) Émile Zola.

NOUNS

1 **accusation**, complaint, accusing, bringing of charges, charge, countercharge, blame, insinuation, implication, reproach, denunciation, denouncement, allegation, imputation, suit, lawsuit, plaint, action, litigation, citation, summons, arrest, booking, prosecution, impeachment, indictment, true bill (US), gravamen, incrimination, recrimination, count, case, court case, case for the prosecution, evidence

▶ *661 Defiance; 670 Disapproval; 678 Scornfulness; 701 Argument; 716 Evidence*

2 **false accusation**, false charge, false evidence, fake confession, perjured testimony, perjury, libel, slander, calumny, scandal, defamation, trumped-up charge, misrepresentation, plant (Inf), cooked-up charge (Inf), put-up job (Inf), put-up (Inf), frame-up (Inf), frame (Inf)

3 **accuser**, denouncer, incriminator, charger, petitioner, plaintiff, complainant, claimant, litigant, appellant, petitioner, party to a suit, witness for the prosecution, hostile witness, indicter, prosecutor, public prosecutor, district attorney (US), impeacher, false witness, perjurer, libeller, libellant, informer, whistle-blower (Inf), stool pigeon (Inf), stoolie (Inf), grass (Inf), supergrass (Inf), nark (Inf), squealer (Inf), fink (US inf), snitcher (Inf), snitch (Inf), canary (Inf)

4 **accused person**, the accused, defendant, respondent, correspondent, culprit, suspect, prisoner, guilty party, marked man

VERBS

5 **accuse**, complain, bring charges, charge with, charge, countercharge, blame, lay the blame on, insinuate, implicate, impute, reproach, denunciate, denounce, allegate, sue, bring a charge, file charges, bring a lawsuit, bring (an) action, bring a case, bring litigation, litigate, serve a citation, serve a summons, summon, serve with a writ, cite, prosecute, impeach, indict, swear (*or* bring) an indictment, inculpate, incriminate, recriminate, arrest, arraign, book, hold a court case, put on trial, hold a trial, try, send before the judge, send before the beak (Inf), put in the dock, bring evidence against, witness,

bear witness, lodge a complaint, inform against (*or* on), point the finger at, throw the book at (Inf), haul up (Inf), blow the whistle (Inf), stool (US inf), put the finger on (US inf), blow the gaff (Inf), grass (Inf), nark (Inf), squeal (Inf), fink (US inf), snitch (Inf), sing (US inf)

6 **accuse falsely**, give false evidence, bear false witness, fake the evidence, fake a confession, commit perjury, perjure oneself, libel, slander, defame, misrepresent, calumniate, trump up a charge, plant evidence, frame (Inf), cook up a charge (Inf), cook the evidence (Inf)

7 **be accused**, stand accused, help (*or* assist) the police with their inquiries, receive a summons, have charges brought against one, await trial, go on trial, stand before the judge, stand in the dock, defend oneself, offer a defence

ADJECTIVES

8 **accusatory**, accusing, accused, imputative, charged, up on a charge, countercharged, blamed, implicated, pointing to, denunciatory, denunciated, denounced, alleging, alleged, under suspicion, litigious, cited, summoned, arrested, booked, awaiting trial, liable to prosecution, prosecuted, impeachable, impeached, indictable, indicted, incriminatory, incriminated, recriminatory, recriminated, hauled up (Inf)

9 **perjurious**, perjured, libellous, libelled, slanderous, slandered, defamatory, defamed, misrepresented, calumnious, trumped-up, planted (Inf), cooked-up (Inf), put-up (Inf), framed (Inf)

ADVERBS

10 **accusingly**, in accusation, allegedly, before the judge, litigiously, perjuriously, libellously, slanderously, defamatorily, in a frame-up (Inf)

716 Evidence

NOUNS

1 **evidence**, grounds, reasons, premises, basis for belief, data, information, facts, relevant facts, record, reference, report, intelligence, gen (Inf), the low-down (Inf)

▶ *3 History; 444 Reason; 450 Belief; 455 Knowledge; 693 Information; 721 Description; 744 Record*

2 **proof**, verification, demonstration, corroboration, substantiation, confirmation, certainty

▶ *452 Certainty; 454 Verification; 701 Argument; 703 Demonstration*

3 **evidentness**, manifestation, obviousness, appearance, self-evidence, visibility, prominence

▶ *185 Bulge; 520 Visibility; 525 Appearance*

4 **indication**, indicator, pointer, telltale sign, token, symptom, clue, remains, mark, track, trail, footprint, wake, vapour trail, spoor, scent

▶ *449 Discovery; 633 Pursuit*

5 **legal evidence**, evidence in chief (US), prima-facie evidence, external (*or* extrinsic) evidence, internal (*or* intrinsic) evidence, primary evidence, secondary evidence, direct evidence, indirect evidence, testimonial evidence, testimony, statement, declaration, admission, deposition, documentary evidence, exhibit, confession, affidavit, collateral evidence, cumulative evidence, circumstantial evidence, hearsay evidence, word-of-mouth evidence, incriminating evidence, counterevidence, inadmissible evidence

▶ *16 Law; 707 Affirmation; 739 Disclosure; 740 Publication*

6 **documentation**, document, authority, papers, case history, record, testimonial, recommendation, character reference, reference, credential, curriculum vitae, CV, résumé (US), warrant, warranty, ticket, chit, receipt, voucher, passport, identity card, i.d., visa, permit, security pass

▶ *3 History; 136 Qualification; 396 Authority; 743 Identification; 744 Record*

7 **person who gives evidence**, witness, eyewitness, bystander, passer-by, attestant, defendant, plaintiff, spectator, spy, informant, telltale, stool pigeon (Inf), rat (US inf), squealer (Inf), snout (Inf), mole (Inf), nark (Inf), grass (Inf), supergrass (Inf), lagger (Aus inf), dobber (Aus inf)

▶ *454 Verification; 693 Information*

ADJECTIVES

8 **evidential**, prima facie, significant, factual, relevant, informed, witnessed, attested, circumstantial, direct, documented, recorded, documentary, reported, corroborative, probative, constructive, indicative, pointing, demonstrative, telltale, authentic, empirical, verified, confirmed, proved, certain

9 **evident**, apparent, manifest, obvious, self-evident, visible, prominent, ostensible

▶ *525 Appearance*

VERBS

10 **make evident**, show, show signs of, represent, speak for itself, suggest, indicate, imply

11 **give evidence**, witness, testify, swear, take the oath, attest, affirm, assert, declare, state, bear witness to, swear to, allege

12 **prove**, verify, validate, corroborate, support, sustain, back up, circumstantiate, authenticate, confirm, certify, countersign, endorse

13 **turn queen's evidence**, inform, betray, save one's own skin, tell tales, nark (Inf), squeal (Inf), sing (Inf), rat (US inf), grass on (Inf), grass (someone) up (Inf), lag (Aus inf), dob (Aus inf)

ADVERBS

14 **as evidence**, in evidence, in proof, certainly, factually, authentically, relevantly, significantly, circumstantially, indicatively, demonstratively, reportedly, with reason, on good grounds

15 **evidently**, manifestly, obviously, apparently, self-evidently, visibly, ostensibly, prominently, on display, for all to see, in broad daylight

717 Representation

Taxation without representation is tyranny. James Otis.

No annihilation without representation. Arnold Toynbee.

NOUNS

1 **representation**, depiction, delineation, portrayal, rendering, embodiment, personification, incarnation, realization, typification, epitome, quintessence, type, figu-

ration, symbolization, indication, conventional representation, manifestation, evocation, presentation, presentment, imitation, impersonation, impression, exemplar, similarity, semblance, likeness, realism, photographic likeness, striking likeness, speaking likeness, lookalike, exact likeness, true picture, spitting image, double, doppelgänger, copy, duplicate, facsimile, fax (Inf), replica, reflection, mirror image, outline, description, writing, picture writing, pictogram, hieroglyphics, runes, notation, mathematical notation, musical notation, bad likeness, poor representation, misrepresentation, dead ringer (Inf)

► *17 Literature; 115 Similarity; 125 Imitation; 163 Outline; 700 Deception; 718 Misrepresentation; 721 Description; 738 Display; 743 Identification*

2 **reproduction**, photograph, carbon copy, photocopy, Xerox™, Identikit™, Photofit™, print, graphics, etching, engraving, lithograph, collotype, blueprint, diagram, chart, graph, plan, draft, rough draft, sketch, cartoon, caricature, picture, illustration, book illustration, tracing, drawing, isometric drawing, isometric projection, axiometric drawing, technical drawing, mechanical drawing, artwork, painting, oil painting, oil, watercolour, portraiture, portrait, fine art, illumination, calligraphy, film, video

► *19 Painting and Sculpture; 41 Photography; 160 Form; 484 Plan*

3 **acting**, portraying, portrayal, playing, playing a character, playing the part of, impersonating, impersonation, posing, characterizing, characterization, performing, performance, enactment, role-playing, mimicry, charade, mime, dumbshow, masquerade

► *21 Drama; 125 Imitation; 356 Creation*

4 **person who makes a representation**, artist, painter, watercolourist, copyist, illustrator, graphic artist, cartoonist, sketcher, caricaturist, etcher, engraver, printmaker, mapmaker, cartographer, photographer, sculptor, sculptress, modeller, model maker, forger, counterfeiter

5 **performer**, player, actor, actress, mime artist, mime, mimic, impersonator, female impersonator, drag artist

6 **image**, symbol, likeness, very image, clear image, exact image, very picture, exact picture, spitting image, visual, visual aid, photograph, duplicate, eidetic image, mental image, idea, thought, afterthought, after-image, reflected image, reflection, mirror image, projection, hologram, shadow figure, silhouette, painted image, icon, idol, graven image, effigy, gargoyle, sculpture, statue, statuette, bust, torso, head, figure, figurine, wax figure, waxwork, model, working model, replica, manikin, dummy, tailor's dummy, doll, china doll, rag doll, golliwog, soft toy, teddy bear, puppet, marionette, *fantoccini* (It), finger puppet, glove puppet, snowman, gingerbread man, scarecrow, guy, Guy Fawkes, robot, automaton

► *7 Religion; 446 Idea; 522 Light; 525 Appearance; 742 Sign*

7 **map**, world map, county map, city map, town plan, A to Z, road map, relief map, survey map, Ordnance Survey map, sketch map, elevation, projection, Mercator's projection, orthographic projection, conic projection, gnomonic projection, chart, cartogram, statistics, atlas, world atlas, globe, map of the heavens, star map, map-making, cartography

► *210 Calculation; 484 Plan*

8 **representative**, example, sample, specimen, cross section, agent, agency, proxy, substitute, replacement, stand-in, deputy, delegate, ambassador, envoy, spokesman (*or* spokeswoman), spokesperson

► *762 Substitution; 778 Sale*

VERBS

9 **represent**, depict, delineate, portray, render, embody, personify, incarnate, realize, typify, symbolize, epitomize, manifest, evoke, present, imitate, impersonate, personate, pretend to be, resemble, look like, copy, duplicate, reproduce, reflect, mirror, image, catch, capture, catch exactly, catch a likeness, register, record, photograph, film, snap, shoot, take a picture, take a photo, shoot a picture, scan, X-ray, process, print, enlarge, blow up, project

► *41 Photography; 115 Similarity; 125 Imitation; 700 Deception; 743 Identification; 744 Record*

10 **act**, portray, present, dramatize, play, play a character, play the part of, act the part of, assume the role of, role-play, characterize, perform, enact, impersonate, take off, pose as, go as, mimic, mime, masquerade, improvise

► *21 Drama; 125 Imitation; 478 Improvisation*

11 **paint**, draw, sketch, caricature, picture, illustrate, draft, sketch out, rough out, block out, plan, diagram, make a diagram, draw a blueprint, design, outline, describe, trace, shape, form, mould, carve, sculpt, cast, cut, engrave, etch, print, plot, map, chart, survey

► *19 Painting and Sculpture; 160 Form; 163 Outline; 484 Plan; 721 Description*

12 **stand for**, mean, denote, exemplify, show, pass for, pass as, replace, substitute for, stand in for, act for

► *694 Meaning; 738 Display; 762 Substitution*

ADJECTIVES

13 **representational**, representing, representative, depictive, delineatory, portraying, symbolic, emblematic, figurative, typical, quintessential, archetypal, characteristic, exemplary, evocative, descriptive, illustrative, graphic, pictorial, hieroglyphic, reflecting, similar, like, imitative, iconic, diagrammatic, vivid, realistic, naturalistic, true-to-life, impressionistic, abstract, nonrepresentational, surrealistic, surreal, artistic, painterly, paintable, photogenic, photographic

► *19 Painting and Sculpture; 41 Photography; 115 Similarity; 125 Imitation; 484 Plan; 721 Description; 742 Sign*

ADVERBS

14 **representationally**, representatively, symbolically, emblematically, figuratively, typically, characteristically, descriptively, illustratively, graphically, pictorially, vividly, realistically

718 Misrepresentation

One to mislead the public, another to mislead the Cabinet, and

the third to mislead itself. Herbert Henry Asquith, explaining why the War Office kept three sets of figures.

NOUNS

1 **misrepresentation**, distortion, deformation, twist, dissimilarity, perversion, falsification, lie, fib, not a true picture, false light, falsehood, unfair representation, bad likeness, poor likeness, exaggeration, grotesquerie, colouring, overemphasis, overdramatization, caricature, travesty, parody, burlesque, guy, flattering, flattery, nonrealism, bad art, daubing, daub, botch, anamorphosis, false image, distorted image, distorting mirror

▶ *19 Painting and Sculpture; 116 Dissimilarity; 234 Distortion; 621 Derision; 677 Flattery; 699 Falsehood; 727 Exaggeration; 802 Wrong*

2 **misinformation**, false information, disinformation, misteaching, misevaluation, misinterpretation, garbling, misstatement, misquotation

▶ *693 Information; 720 Misinterpretation*

3 **deceiver**, liar, dissembler, dissimulator, fraud, cheat, swindler, hoaxer, trickster, adulterer, cardsharp, confidence trickster, Tartuffe, con man (Inf)

VERBS

4 **misrepresent**, distort, deform, twist, make dissimilar, pervert, falsify, slant, put in a false light, lie, belie, represent unfairly, make a poor likeness, make a false image, exaggerate, colour, overemphasize, overdramatize, caricature, parody, travesty, burlesque, guy, flatter, overembellish, gild the lily, create nonrepresentational art, overdraw, daub, botch

▶ *19 Painting and Sculpture; 116 Dissimilarity; 234 Distortion; 621 Derision; 677 Flattery; 699 Falsehood; 727 Exaggeration; 802 Wrong*

5 **misinform**, give false information, disinform, misteach, misevaluate, misinterpret, garble, misstate, misquote

▶ *693 Information; 720 Misinterpretation*

ADJECTIVES

6 **misrepresented**, misrepresenting, biased, slanted, not representative, unrepresentative, distorted, deformed, twisted, perverted, false, untrue, wrong, incorrect, inaccurate, dissimilar, unlike, unfair, unjust, exaggerated, caricatured, parodied, grotesque, flattering, nonrepresentational, cardboard

▶ *116 Dissimilarity; 234 Distortion; 621 Derision; 677 Flattery; 699 Falsehood; 727 Exaggeration; 802 Wrong*

7 **misinformed**, mistaught, misinterpreted, garbled, misstated, misquoted

▶ *693 Information; 720 Misinterpretation*

ADVERBS

8 **unrepresentatively**, falsely, wrongly, incorrectly, inaccurately, unfairly, unjustly, in a false light

719 Interpretation

The soul fortunately, has an interpreter – often an unconscious, but still a truthful interpreter – in the eye. Charlotte Brontë.

NOUNS

1 **interpretation**, construction, rendering, way of putting something, explanation, definition, description, explication, emendation, amendment, editing, simplification, exposition, exegesis, epexegesis, eisegesis, isogesis, judgment, estimate, personal feeling, understanding, enlightenment, light, clarification, insight, elucidation, illumination, illustration, exemplification, demonstration, example, resolution, solution, answer, key, clue, the secret, decipherment, decoding, code cracking, analysis, conflation, application, particular interpretation, twist, turn, reading, lection, meaning, subaudition, connotation, euhemerism, demythologization, allegorization, metaphor, accepted reading, usual text, vulgate, edited text, alternative reading, variant reading, rendition, deconstruction, version, edition, critical edition

▶ *5 Language and Linguistics; 17 Literature; 244 Improvement; 271 Simplicity; 449 Discovery; 464 Judgment; 591 Sensitivity; 694 Meaning; 695 Intelligibility; 706 Answer; 725 Clarity*

2 **annotation**, gloss, footnote, textual note, marginalia, variorum, scholium, apparatus criticus, note, note of explanation, exegesis, legend, appendix, explanatory remark, word of explanation, inscription, comment, editorial comment, additional comment, commentary

▶ *211 Addition*

3 **criticism**, literary criticism, critique, review, notice, theatre review, art review, music review, book review, film review, television review, rave review, puff, favourable review, good review, negative review, bad review, panning, textual criticism, form criticism, higher criticism, New Criticism, lower criticism, practical criticism, personal criticism, critical power, critic's gift

▶ *713 Advice; 722 Essay*

4 **translation**, transcription, rendering, literal translation, faithful translation, word-for-word translation, loose translation, free translation, bilingual text, version, rewording, paraphrase, adaptation, simplification, amplification, transliteration, decoding, unscrambling, decipherment, sign-language reading, lip-reading, key, crib (Inf), pony (Inf), trot (US inf)

▶ *273 Accuracy; 695 Intelligibility; 717 Representation; 723 Summary*

5 **science of interpretation**, exegetics, hermeneutics, tropology, epigraphy, cryptology, cryptography, cryptanalysis, palaeography, semiology (*or* semeiology), lexicography, linguistics, diagnostics, symptomatology, physiognomy, phrenology, graphology, prophecy, divination, criticism

▶ *5 Language and Linguistics; 475 Prediction*

6 **interpreter**, translator, linguist, explainer, clarifier, paraphraser, paraphrast, simplifier, popularizer, lexicographer, definer, teacher, religious teacher, expounder, exponent, reviewer, critic, textual critic, literary critic, Leavisite, editor, copy editor, emender, emendator, annotator, glossator, glossarist, scholiast, commentator, exegete, exegetist (*or* exegesist), isogete, euhemerist, demythologizer, cryptographer, cryptologist, cryptanalyst, decoder, code-breaker, cipher clerk, sign-language reader, lip-reader, oneirocritic, medium, spiritualist, diviner, epigraphist, palaeographer

▶ *5 Language and Linguistics; 7 Religion; 17 Literature; 284 Past Time; 455 Knowledge; 475 Prediction*

7 **news interpreter**, journalist, reporter, commentator,

editorial writer, leader writer, columnist, news source, specialist source, public relations (PR) man (*or* woman), PR representative (*or* officer), press officer, press agent, public information officer, publicizer, spokesman (*or* spokeswoman), company spokesman (*or* spokeswoman), mouthpiece, flack (US inf), spin doctor (Inf)

► *692 Communications; 693 Information; 740 Publication; 741 News*

VERBS

8 **interpret**, construe, put a construction on, render, put, explain, explicate, inform, expound, comment on, give a sense to, ascribe a meaning to, make sense of, understand, take to mean, read, read into, read between the lines, deduce, infer, reason, define, describe, emend, amend, twist, turn, conflate, edit, copy-edit, simplify, spell out, popularize, facilitate, judge, estimate, give insight, give enlightenment, clarify, make clear, elucidate, disambiguate, analyse, illuminate, throw (*or* shed) light on, illustrate, exemplify, give an example, demonstrate, show, act as guide

► *244 Improvement; 271 Simplicity; 449 Discovery; 464 Judgment; 694 Meaning; 695 Intelligibility; 725 Clarity*

9 **decipher**, crack, crack a code, unlock a code, crack the cipher, decode, unscramble, find the meaning, read hieroglyphics, read, spell out, puzzle out, make out, work out, sort out, piece together, find the sense of, find the key to, solve, resolve, find a solution, find a resolution, enucleate, unravel, unriddle, demystify, disentangle

► *695 Intelligibility; 706 Answer*

10 **annotate**, gloss, footnote, add commentary, add explanation, write notes for, inscribe, comment on

► *211 Addition*

11 **criticize**, review, critique, evaluate, give criticism, offer criticism, pan, slate, give (*or* offer) constructive criticism, puff

► *17 Literature; 713 Advice*

12 **translate**, transcribe, transliterate, render, paraphrase, rephrase, reword, restate, rehash, make a new version, put into, turn into, give a literal translation of, adapt, simplify, amplify, encode, decode, put into code, cipher, decipher, use sign language, sign, read sign language, read lips, lip-read, interpret, act as interpreter, offer an interpretation, use a crib (Inf), use a pony (Inf), use a trot (US inf)

► *717 Representation; 723 Summary*

13 **interpret news**, report, cover, slant, comment on, write an editorial, write a leader, write a column, do public relations, serve as press officer for, act as spokesman (*or* woman) for, spin, give a spin (to)

► *692 Communications; 693 Information; 740 Publication; 741 News*

ADJECTIVES

14 **interpretive**, interpretative, interpretational, constructive, explanatory, explicatory, explicative, explaining, descriptive, expositive, expository, insightful, illustrative, demonstrative, definitional, definitive, defining, exemplary, exegetic, exegetical, hermeneutic, clarifying, elucidative, elucidatory, illuminating, semiological (*or* semeiological), euhemeristic, demythologizing

► *271 Simplicity; 694 Meaning; 725 Clarity*

15 **interpreted**, glossed, explained, defined, illustrated, elucidated, clarified, simplified, annotated, commented on, edited, emended, amended, conflated, translated, rendered, deciphered, decoded, unscrambled, cracked, unlocked, coded, encoded, scrambled

► *695 Intelligibility*

16 **annotative**, glossarial, scholiastic, explanatory, critical, editorial, commentarial

► *211 Addition*

17 **translational**, paraphrastic, metaphrastic, polyglot, multilingual, bilingual, synonymous, equivalent, literal, word-for-word, verbatim, faithful, free, loose

► *5 Language and Linguistics*

ADVERBS

18 **in other words**, in words to that effect, that is to say, that is, i.e., *id est* (L), namely, viz, *videlicet* (L), to wit, to put it another way, plainly, in plain words, in plain English, to be clear, to explain, in explanation, interpretively, interpretatively, illustratively, exegetically

720 Misinterpretation

To be great is to be misunderstood. Ralph Waldo Emerson.

VERBS

1 **misinterpret**, misunderstand, misapprehend, mistranslate, render incorrectly, misread, misconstrue, put a wrong construction on, get wrong, get one wrong, take wrong, misconceive, misjudge, miscomputate, misdiagnose, mistake, get hold of the wrong end of the stick, err, blunder, misspell, put in a false light, misteach, miseducate, explain wrongly, misrepresent, stretch the meaning, strain the sense, put a false sense on, put a false construction on, give a false idea, give a false impression, pervert, distort, change the meaning, do violence to the meaning, wrench, twist, give a twist (*or* turn) to, twist the words, manipulate the truth, misquote, equivocate, play upon words, read into, write into, take out of context, add a meaning, add, omit, leave out, suppress, subtract, repeat wrongly, falsify, garble, exaggerate, inflate, overpraise, overrate, overestimate, underpraise, underrate, underestimate, depict falsely, traduce, travesty, parody, caricature, burlesque, ridicule, defame, libel, slander, guy (Inf)

► *211 Addition; 212 Subtraction; 234 Distortion; 274 Error; 456 Ignorance; 465 Misjudgment; 467 Overestimation; 468 Underestimation; 479 Equivocation; 621 Derision; 678 Scornfulness; 718 Misrepresentation; 727 Exaggeration*

NOUNS

2 **misinterpretation**, wrong interpretation, misunderstanding, misapprehension, mistranslation, translator's error, misreading, false reading, wrong words, misconstruction, false construction, misapplication, misdiagnosis, misconception, misjudgment, miscomputation, mistake, wrong end of the stick, error, blunder, solecism, misspelling, false light, misteaching, wrong instruction, wrong explanation, misrepresentation, stretching the meaning, straining the sense, overdoing it, strained sense, false sense, false idea, false impression, colouring the truth, lying, perversion, distortion, wrenching, twist-

ing, twist, turn, manipulation, misquotation, equivocalness, circumlocution, wordplay, misuse of words, catachresis, abuse of language, addition, omission, suppression, subtraction, falsification, garbling, garble, overestimation, underestimation, exaggeration, inflation, different wavelength, false depiction, traducement, travesty, parody, caricature, burlesque, ridiculing, defamation, libel, slander

▶ *211 Addition; 212 Subtraction; 234 Distortion; 274 Error; 456 Ignorance; 465 Misjudgment; 467 Overestimation; 468 Underestimation; 479 Equivocation; 621 Derision; 678 Scornfulness; 718 Misrepresentation; 727 Exaggeration*

ADJECTIVES

3 **misinterpreted**, misunderstood, mistranslated, misread, misconstrued, misconceived, mistaken, wrong, misspelt, solecistic, catachrestic, misquoted, garbled, falsified, distorted, exaggerated, inflated, misrepresented, libellous, slanderous

ADVERBS

4 **mistakenly**, erroneously, in error, wrongly, falsely

5 **misrepresentedly**, distortedly, exaggeratedly, libellously, slanderously

721 Description

NOUNS

1 **description**, account, detailed description, detailed account, statement, statement of facts, details, particulars, specification, report, record, delineation, depiction, picture, portrait, portrayal, characterization, profile, character sketch, case history, version, explanation

▶ *693 Information; 744 Record*

2 **brief description**, caption, legend, indication, heading, subtitle, word portrait, thumbnail sketch, summary, outline, cameo, vignette, exposé

▶ *723 Summary*

3 **narration**, narrative, narrative writing, account, essay, story, storyline, plot, subplot, scenario, tale, *conte* (Fr), yarn, fairy tale, folk tale, myth, legend, saga, epic, narrative poem, serial, soap opera, kitchen-sink drama, fable, cautionary tale, parable, allegory, metaphor, simile, stream of consciousness, ballad, anecdote, reminiscence, chronicle, annals, history, record, journal, diary, drama, documentary, documentary drama, docudrama, faction, reportage, travelogue, fiction, fantasy, tall story (Inf), soap (Inf)

▶ *3 History; 17 Literature*

4 **factual account**, nonfiction, documentary, documentary account, report, journalism, biography, autobiography, life story, curriculum vitae (CV), résumé (US), hagiography, obituary, real-life story, personal account, confessions, memoirs, diary, journal, letter, personal correspondence

▶ *722 Essay; 744 Record*

5 **fiction**, descriptive writing, creative writing, creative composition, novel, short story, novella, historical novel, picaresque novel, *roman à clef* (Fr), fictional biography, *Bildungsroman* (Ger), crime fiction, detective novel, thriller, spy story, science fiction, sci-fi, adventure story, western, romance, love story, Gothic novel, ghost story, pulp fiction, best-seller, blockbuster (Inf), whodunit (Inf), potboiler (Inf)

▶ *17 Literature*

6 **sort**, kind, type, genre, variety, breed, species, ilk, kidney

▶ *137 Class*

7 **nomenclature**, naming, addressing, calling, roll call, appellation, denomination, terminology, taxonomy, classification, designation, description, identification, indication, antonomasia, naming ceremony, christening, baptising, baptism, nicknaming, study of names, eponymy, onomastics, onomatology, orismology, study of place names, toponymy, misnaming, pseudonymity

▶ *743 Identification*

8 **name**, nomen, noun, proper noun, appellation, appellative, full name, forename, first name, praenomen, Christian name, baptismal name, given name, Confirmation name, middle name, second name, agnomen, last name, married name, surname, family name, patronymic, matronymic, cognomen, maiden name, pet name, diminutive, sweetheart name, familiar name, pen name, nom de plume, false name, alias, assumed name, pseudonym, allonym, stage name, sobriquet, nickname, tautonym, namesake, epithet, title, autograph, signature, label, tag, term, technical term, password, place name, eponym, toponym, trademark, tradename, hallmark, markings, moniker (*or* monicker) (Inf), handle (Inf)

▶ *10 Ritual; 575 Title; 593 Love; 733 Address; 743 Identification*

9 **representation**, imitation, likeness, striking likeness, impression, picture, true picture, portrait, sketch, drawing, mechanical drawing, freehand drawing, technical drawing, duplicate, double, spitting image, facsimile, tracing, photocopy, Xerox™, lithograph

▶ *19 Painting and Sculpture; 111 Sameness; 717 Representation*

10 **descriptive writer**, creative writer, wordsmith, literary person, man (*or* woman) of letters, writer, author, novelist, fiction writer, fictionist, crime writer, essayist, poet, playwright, dramatist, librettist, script writer, fabulist, teller of tales, storyteller, raconteur, anecdotist, biographer, hagiographer, diarist, historian, chronicler, annalist, recorder, historiographer, journalist, reporter, correspondent, special correspondent, war correspondent, sports correspondent, columnist, gossip columnist, agony aunt, scribbler, pen pusher, ghostwriter, hack (Inf)

▶ *17 Literature; 740 Publication; 741 News*

ADJECTIVES

11 **descriptive**, representational, graphic, vivid, detailed, full, informative, illustrative, explicatory, explanatory, elucidatory, illuminating, expository, expositive, interpretive, amplifying, well-drawn, true-to-life, real-life, realistic, naturalistic, photographic, eidetic, convincing, picturesque, expressive, impressionistic, suggestive, evocative, moving, poignant, thrilling, exciting, striking, highly coloured, forceful

▶ *693 Information*

12 **narrative**, fictional, imaginative, kitchen-sink, factual, documentary, biographical, autobiographical, factional, mythological, epic, heroic, romantic, picaresque

▶ *17 Literature*

13 representing, representative, iconic, pictorial, emblematic, symbolic, figurative, diagrammatic, representational, realistic, true-to-life, photographic, artistic, primitive, naive, impressionistic, surrealistic, surreal, abstract

▶ *19 Painting and Sculpture; 41 Photography*

VERBS

14 describe, delineate, draw, sketch, picture, depict, portray, limn, paint, represent, illustrate, characterize, form, shape, fashion, design, draft, sketch out, adumbrate, rough out, outline, make a diagram of, do a portrait, catch a likeness, capture an expression, doodle, scribble

15 recount, relate, tell, retell, narrate, tell a story, tell a tale, spin a yarn, reminisce, evoke, bring to life, characterize, detail, recapitulate, review, record, chronicle, repeat, recite, rehearse, pass on the information, communicate, report, cover, submit a report, make a statement, testify, keep posted, correspond, write an account of, write a story about, fictionalize, dramatize, romanticize, mythologize, imagine

▶ *477 Imagination; 693 Information*

16 define, specify, name, mention, detail, particularize, itemize, inventorize, explain, interpret

17 describe a circle, draw a circle, circumscribe, mark out, trace

ADVERBS

18 descriptively, graphically, vividly, realistically, illustratively, imaginatively

722 Essay

They will review a book by a writer much older than themselves as if it were an over-ambitious essay by a second-year student…It is the little dons I complain about, like so many corgis trotting up, hoping to nip your ankles. J. B. Priestley.

NOUNS

1 dissertation, discourse, disquisition, treatise, tract, tractate, exposition, summary, theme, argument, descant, thesis, essay, composition, study, lucubration, examination, survey, inquiry, discussion, symposium, paper, monograph, memoir, screed, harangue, homily, sermon, oration, peroration, tirade, lecture, lesson, prolegomenon, exegesis, interpretation, explanation, gloss, annotation, comment, commentary

▶ *701 Argument; 723 Summary; 729 Speech*

2 article, leading article, leader, editorial comment, editorial, column, news item, review, notice, critique, criticism, write-up, puff (Inf)

▶ *740 Publication; 741 News*

3 dissertator, essayist, pamphleteer, propagandist, preacher, orator, speaker, lecturer, teacher, publicizer, publicist, writer, author, editor, leader writer, journalist, contributor, reviewer, critic, commentator, exponent, expounder, expositor, proselytizer, proselyte, interpreter, Leavisite, exegete, glossarist, annotator

VERBS

4 dissertate, discourse, descant, speak about, write about, put forward an argument about, argue, develop a thesis, go into, deal with in depth, do a paper on, write a treatise on, hold a symposium, inquire into, survey, discuss, comment on, criticize, commentate, gloss, annotate, interpret, explain, elucidate, define, expound, proselytize, harangue, orate, perorate, sermonize, preach, pontificate

▶ *701 Argument; 719 Interpretation; 729 Speech*

ADJECTIVES

5 expository, discursive, disquisitional, critical, interpretive, interpretative, exegetical, illuminating, editorial, glossarial, annotative

723 Summary

I take the view, and always have done, that if you cannot say what you have to say in twenty minutes, you should go away and write a book about it. Lord Brabazon of Tara.

NOUNS

1 summary, synopsis, precis, résumé, *aperçu* (Fr), digest, epitome, abstract, review, recapitulation, gist, drift, conspectus, survey, bird's-eye view, overview, run-down, sketch, thumbnail sketch, CV (curriculum vitae), recap (Inf)

2 outline, skeleton, plan, blueprint, syllabus, prospectus, brochure, abridgment (*or* abridgement), concise version, potted version, abbreviation, shortening, diminution, contraction, truncation, pruning, compression, apheresis, apocope, syncope, elision

▶ *191 Contraction; 220 List; 269 Brevity; 484 Plan*

3 compendium, anthology, treasury, collection, compilation, corpus, chrestomathy, miscellany, miscellanea, album, scrapbook, ephemera, cuttings, extracts, excerpts, selection

▶ *376 Gathering; 469 Selection*

4 summariness, briefness, brevity, shortness, terseness, brusqueness, conciseness, pithiness, succinctness, compactness, pointedness, compendiousness, laconism, laconicism

▶ *149 Shortness; 269 Brevity*

5 summarizer, precis writer, abridger, epitomizer, abbreviator, shortener, cutter, editor

ADJECTIVES

6 summary, brief, short, short and sweet, curt, brusque, terse, concise, pithy, compendious, succinct, compact, pointed, short and to the point, epigrammatic, epigrammatical, laconic, irreducible

▶ *149 Shortness; 262 Haste; 269 Brevity*

7 shortened, abbreviated, abridged, summarized, synopsized, clipped, pruned, docked, truncated, cut short, cut, contracted, compacted, potted, collected

▶ *149 Shortness; 191 Contraction*

VERBS

8 summarize, precis, make a résumé, synopsize, make a synopsis of, condense, digest, epitomize, encapsulate, reduce, shorten, abbreviate, abridge, contract, pot, truncate, cut short, give an outline of, outline, sketch, sketch out, boil down, sum up, resume, recapitulate, abstract, express pithily, epigrammatize, recap (Inf)

▶ *149 Shortness; 191 Contraction; 269 Brevity*

9 **compile**, consolidate, collect together, anthologize, excerpt, select

▶ *376 Gathering; 469 Selection*

10 **be brief**, come to the point, cut a long story short

ADVERBS

11 **summarily**, briefly, shortly, brusquely, tersely, crisply, laconically, concisely, pithily, succintly, pointedly

12 **in brief**, in short, without wasting words, in a word, in a nutshell, in a few words, epigrammatically

724 Style

Style is the man himself. Comte de Buffon.

All styles are good except the tiresome sort. Voltaire.

In matters of grave importance, style, not sincerity, is the vital thing. Oscar Wilde.

NOUNS

1 **style**, fashion, mode, manner, way, technique, approach, tone, tenor, idiom, vein, strain, quality, character, personal style, mannerism, speciality, peculiarity, affectation, idiosyncrasy

▶ *139 Speciality; 352 Means; 553 Fashion; 726 Emphasis*

2 **stylishness**, elegance, grace, charm, flair, panache, élan, chic, perfect touch

▶ *271 Simplicity; 542 Decoration; 543 Elegance; 549 Refinement; 553 Fashion*

3 **inelegance**, plainness, lack of refinement, affectation, overelaboration, heaviness, heavy-handedness, lumpishness, commonness

▶ *544 Inelegance*

4 **literary style**, mode of expression, manner of speaking, form of speech, diction, phrasing, wording, sentence structure, phraseology, phrase, choice of words, idiolect, vocabulary, language, expression of ideas, command of language, oratory, rhetoric, word power, command of idiom, feeling for language, sense of language, word magic

5 **stylist**, stylish writer, fine writer, classical author, rhetorician, orator, phrasemonger, wordsmith, word-spinner (Inf)

▶ *542 Decoration; 543 Elegance*

ADJECTIVES

6 **styled**, phrased, worded, expressed, put

7 **stylish**, elegant, graceful, chic, sophisticated, fashionable

8 **inelegant**, common, vernacular, heavy, heavy-handed, clumsy, plain, dowdy, dumpy, frumpy, overelaborate

▶ *5 Language and Linguistics; 17 Literature; 271 Simplicity; 542 Decoration; 543 Elegance; 544 Inelegance; 549 Refinement; 553 Fashion; 725 Clarity; 729 Speech*

VERBS

9 **style**, show style, demonstrate style, develop a literary style, state, put, express, express in words, find words to express, choose one's words carefully, phrase, word, formulate, frame, couch, set out, present, use the vernacular, overwrite, spin words (Inf)

ADVERBS

10 **stylistically**, linguistically, rhetorically, idiomatically, idiosyncratically, ornately, elaborately, gracefully, elegantly, stylishly, with style, with flair, fluently, plainly

725 Clarity

NOUNS

1 **clarity**, clearness, lucidity, pellucidity, perspicuity, perspicuousness, transparency, purity, limpidity, coherence, intelligibility, comprehensibility, plainness, simplicity, austerity, starkness, straightforwardness, directness, unambiguousness, explicitness, definition, definiteness, distinctness, obviousness, exactness, accuracy

▶ *271 Simplicity; 273 Accuracy; 520 Visibility; 522 Light; 527 Transparency; 695 Intelligibility*

VERBS

2 **clarify**, make clear, disambiguate, define, demonstrate, explicate, interpret, decipher, elucidate, illuminate, enlighten, fill in

ADJECTIVES

3 **clear**, lucid, pellucid, perspicuous, limpid, transparent, pure, coherent, intelligible, comprehensible, apodeictic, plain, unadorned, simple, austere, stark, straightforward, direct, unambiguous, explicit, clear-cut, definite, distinct, obvious, exact, accurate, uninvolved

▶ *271 Simplicity; 273 Accuracy; 520 Visibility; 522 Light; 527 Transparency; 695 Intelligibility*

ADVERBS

4 **clearly**, lucidly, pellucidly, perspicuously, limpidly, transparently, purely, coherently, intelligibly, comprehensibly, plainly, simply, straightforwardly, directly, unambiguously, explicitly, distinctly, obviously, exactly, accurately

726 Emphasis

NOUNS

1 **emphasis**, stress, accent, accentuation, underlining, underscoring, italics, vehemence, insistence, urgency, priority, iteration, reiteration, repetition, enthusiasm, fervour, passion, feeling, ardour, fire, warmth, glow, spirit, inspiration, vigour, vigorousness, vim, gusto, zest, verve, boldness, dash, raciness, sparkle, panache, liveliness, vitality, vivaciousness, vivacity, vividness, positive outlook, affirmation, piquancy, poignancy, bite, sharpness, mordancy, pungency, penetration, asperity, acuity, intensity, incisiveness, keenness, trenchancy, strength, strong language, power, force, forcefulness, energy, drive, punch, oomph (Inf)

▶ *112 Repetition; 334 Power; 336 Strength; 338 Vigour; 386 Compulsion; 425 Sharpness; 496 Flavour; 542 Decoration; 707 Affirmation; 717 Representation; 727 Exaggeration; 729 Speech*

2 **seriousness**, solemnity, gravity, weight, importance, significance, attention, prominence, impressiveness, loftiness, elevation, sublimity, eloquence, grandeur, grandiloquence, magniloquence

▶ *123 Importance; 471 Attention*

ADJECTIVES

3 **emphatic**, vehement, earnest, insistent, urgent, firm,

uncompromising, dogmatic, iterative, reiterative, repetitive, enthusiastic, fervent, passionate, impassioned, ardent, fiery, glowing, warm, spirited, inspired, vigorous, zestful, bold, dashing, racy, sparkling, lively, vivacious, positive, affirmative, categorical, unequivocal, definite, sure, certain, incisive, cutting, slashing, pulling no punches, penetrating, keen, trenchant, pointed, sententious, pithy, meaty, thought-provoking, pungent, sharp, mordant, piquant, poignant, vivid, graphic, strong, strongly worded, eloquent, compelling, convincing, effective, cogent, forceful, powerful, strenuous, energetic, brisk, peppy (Inf), punchy (Inf), zingy (Inf)

▶ *112 Repetition; 334 Power; 336 Strength; 338 Vigour; 386 Compulsion; 425 Sharpness; 452 Certainty; 496 Flavour; 542 Decoration; 591 Sensitivity; 717 Representation; 729 Speech*

4 **emphasized**, stressed, accentuated, highlighted, enhanced, underlined, in italics, pointed out, pointed up, marked, pronounced, *accusé* (Fr)

▶ *707 Affirmation*

5 **serious**, solemn, grave, weighty, important, significant, heavy, intense, solid, impressive, lofty, elevated, sublime, grand, grandiloquent, majestic, magniloquent

▶ *123 Importance*

VERBS

6 **emphasize**, stress, accent, accentuate, highlight, enhance, spotlight, feature, underline, underscore, italicize, put in italics, point out, call (*or* draw) attention to, point up, insist, urge, reaffirm, reassert, reiterate, repeat, dwell on, plug, raise one's voice, shout, roar, thunder, bellow, glow, dash, sparkle, pull no punches, penetrate, provoke thought, convince, impress on, press home, drive home, din in, rub in, hammer home

▶ *112 Repetition; 123 Importance; 471 Attention; 707 Affirmation; 727 Exaggeration; 729 Speech*

ADVERBS

7 **emphatically**, vehemently, earnestly, insistently, urgently, dogmatically, enthusiastically, fervently, passionately, ardently, positively, incisively, strongly, forcefully, vigorously, energetically, strenuously, solemnly, gravely, with conviction, in no uncertain terms, with eloquence, in glowing terms, grandiloquently, magniloquently, majestically

727 Exaggeration

Reports of my death are greatly exaggerated. Mark Twain.

NOUNS

1 **exaggeration**, exaggerating, overemphasis, overstatement, excessiveness, intensification, overenthusiasm, overstress, overexposure, extremism, extremes, exacerbation, exorbitance, inordinacy, overkill, aggravation, hyperbolism, hyperbole, superlative, sensationalism, sensation, overdoing, excitement, hype (Inf), overselling, embellishment, embroidery, touching up, varnish, overcolouring, prodigality, overreaction, fuss, pother, commotion, to-do, leaning (*or* bending) over backwards, stretching, straining, labouring, overestimation, overvaluation, exaggerated lengths, overcompensation, enhancement, gilding the lily, overacting, histrionics, hamming, overdrawing, overwriting, purple patch, melodrama, burlesque, travesty, caricature, making a mountain out of a molehill, storm in a teacup, ballyhoo (Inf), puffery (Inf)

▶ *234 Distortion; 327 Agitation; 465 Misjudgment; 467 Overestimation; 477 Imagination; 542 Decoration; 607 Annoyance and Aggravation; 621 Derision*

2 **enlargement**, magnification, amplification, dilation, dilatation, maximization, inflation, expansion, aggrandizement, heightening, blowing up, puffing up

▶ *190 Expansion; 211 Addition*

3 **extravagance**, excessiveness, flamboyance, ostentation, outrageousness, profuseness, profusion, lavishness, overindulgence, overspending, pound-foolishness, intemperance, inordinacy, exorbitance, going to extremes, running riot, overdoing it, carrying too far, going too far, overshooting, overstepping the mark, piling Ossa upon Pelion, piling it on (Inf)

▶ *686 Self-Indulgence*

4 **bombast**, pomposity, inflatedness, magniloquence, grandiloquence, boasting, boast, bragging, self-glorification, ranting, raving, huckstering, talking in superlatives, hype, overpraise, flattery, overrating, depiction in glowing terms, purple prose, making much of, excessive loyalty, chauvinism, hot air (Inf)

▶ *677 Flattery; 740 Publication*

5 **tall story**, traveller's tale, fisherman's (*or* angler's) tale, flight of fancy, stretch of the imagination, drawing on the imagination, dealing in the marvellous, teratology, yarn (Inf), fish story (US inf), fisherman's tale (Inf), shaggy dog story (Inf)

6 **exaggerator**, extremist, miracle-monger, teratologist, panjandrum, liar, Baron Münchhausen, sensationalist, radical, fanatic, boaster, braggart, braggadocio, brag, blusterer, hector, fanfaron, windbag (Inf), bullshitter (Inf)

VERBS

7 **exaggerate**, overemphasize, intensify, overstate, overenthuse, overstress, hyperbolize, sensationalize, overdo, hype, embellish, embroider, touch up, varnish, colour highly, overcolour, overexpose, exacerbate, overkill, aggravate, overreact, fuss, pother, make a commotion, make a to-do, lean (*or* bend) over backwards, stretch, strain, labour, go to exaggerated lengths, overestimate, overvalue, overcompensate, enhance, gild the lily, overact, have histrionics, ham, ham it up, chew the scenery (Inf), overdraw, overwrite, write a purple patch, burlesque, travesty, caricature, make a mountain out of a molehill, be a storm in a teacup, ballyhoo (Inf)

8 **enlarge**, magnify, amplify, dilate, maximize, inflate, expand, distend, heighten, aggrandize, blow up, puff up

9 **be extravagant**, overdo, overdo it, lavish, overindulge, overspend, run riot, go to extremes, carry too far, go too far, overshoot, overstep the mark, not know when to stop, pile Ossa upon Pelion, pile it on (Inf)

10 **boast**, brag, bombast, rant, rave, huckster, hype, talk in superlatives, blow up (out of all proportion), oversell, overrate, overpraise, flatter, inflate, depict in glowing terms, make much of, self-glorify, out-Herod Herod, pile it on (Inf), lay it on (Inf), lay it on thick (Inf), lay it on with a trowel (Inf)

11 tell a tall story, have a flight of fancy, stretch the imagination, draw on the imagination, deal in the marvellous, spin a yarn (Inf)

ADJECTIVES

12 exaggerated, overemphasized, overstated, sensationalized, overdone, inflated, hyped, puffed, overrated, overpraised, oversold, flattered, embellished, embroidered, touched up, blown-up, varnished, highly coloured, overcoloured, overdrawn, far-fetched, excessive, intensified, overstressed, overenthusiastic, overemphatic, hyperbolic, overexposed, exacerbated, exorbitant, extreme, inordinate, aggravated, superlative, prodigious, stretched, strained, laboured, overestimated, overvalued, overcompensated, enhanced, overwritten, purple patch, overacted, histrionic, histrionical, melodramatic, teratologic, teratological, ballyhooed (Inf)

13 enlarged, magnified, amplified, dilated, maximized, inflated, expanded, aggrandized, heightened, blown-up, puffed up

14 extravagant, excessive, flamboyant, ostentatious, outrageous, profuse, lavish, grandiose, overindulgent, overspending, pound-foolish, intemperate, inordinate, exorbitant, overdone, overshot, overstepped, meretricious, piled-on (Inf)

15 bombastic, boasting, bragging, raving, inflating, self-glorifying, hyping, magniloquent, grandiloquent, pompous, fustian

ADVERBS

16 exaggeratedly, hyperbolically, superlatively, overenthusiastically, overemphatically, excitedly, sensationally, histrionically, melodramatically, magniloquently, grandiloquently, bombastically, pompously

17 excessively, extremely, outrageously, extravagantly, exorbitantly, inordinately, prodigiously, flamboyantly, ostentatiously, lavishly, profusely, intemperately, too much, *in extremis* (L)

728 Understatement

NOUNS

1 understatement, underemphasis, conservativeness, minimization, underestimation, unobtrusiveness, unsubstantiality, undervaluation, conservative estimate, underreckoning

► *468 Underestimation*

2 detraction, belittlement, faint praise, two cheers

3 subtlety, delicacy, restraint, restrainedness, elegance, refinement, good taste, finesse, discrimination, fastidiousness

► *466 Discrimination; 549 Refinement*

4 simplicity, simpleness, plainness, clinicalness, modesty, Spartan simplicity, bareness, austerity, austereness, starkness, unelaborateness, unfanciness, unfussiness, minimalism, beauty unadorned, unpretentiousness, unostentatiousness, unaffectedness

► *271 Simplicity*

5 reserve, reticence, restraint, constraint, diffidence, modesty, quietness, subduedness, retiring disposition

► *251 Restraint; 674 Modesty*

6 suggestion, trace, touch, dash, smattering, sprinkling, tinge, taste, jot, iota, suspicion, *soupçon* (Fr), inkling, intimation, smack, taint, thought, shade, tempering, smidgen (*or* smidgin) (US inf)

7 imperceptibility, imperceptibleness, inconspicuousness, unimpressiveness, faintness, shadowiness, vagueness

8 insipidness, insipidity, pallidness, blandness, tastelessness, flavourlessness, vapidity, wateriness, half-heartedness, wishy-washiness (Inf)

9 downplaying, de-emphasis, dilution, watering down, diminishment, curtailment, moderation, restraint, constraint, disregard, playing down, deprecation, underplaying, making light of, shrugging off, paring down, cutting down to size

10 deflation, puncturing, depreciation, cutting down, cutting back

11 modest person, quiet person, shy person, introvert, mouse, shrinking violet (Inf)

ADJECTIVES

12 understated, underemphasized, conservative, minimized, underestimated, unobtrusive, unsubstantial, undervalued, underreckoned, underrated

13 subtle, delicate, restrained, elegant, refined, tasteful, discriminating, fastidious, pastel

14 simple, plain, modest, bare, austere, stark, clinical, unelaborate, unfancy, unfussy, unpretentious, unostentatious, unadorned, unaffected, minimal

15 reserved, reticent, restrained, constrained, diffident, modest, quiet, subdued, retiring, unassuming, low-profile

16 imperceptible, inconspicuous, unimpressive, faint, shadowy, vague, indistinct, impalpable, slight, underwhelming (Inf)

17 insipid, pallid, bland, diluted, watered-down, tasteless, flavourless, half-hearted, vapid, watery, wersh (Scot), wishy-washy (Inf)

18 deflated, punctured, depreciated, cut down, cut back

19 downplayed, played-down, underplayed, toned-down, moderated, de-emphasized, diluted, watered-down, reduced, diminished, curtailed, restrained, constrained, disregarded, made light of, shrugged-off, pared, pared-down

VERBS

20 understate, underemphasize, underreckon, minimize, underplay, underestimate, undervalue, underrate, sell short (Inf)

21 detract from, underpraise, belittle, damn with faint praise, give two cheers, deflate, puncture, depreciate, cut down, cut back, bring down to earth, cut down to size, let the air out of, take the wind out of one's sails

22 play down, downplay, underplay, tone down, moderate, de-emphasize, deprecate, dilute, water down, reduce, diminish, curtail, restrain, constrain, disregard, make light of, set no store by, shrug off, pare, pare down, spare one's blushes

ADVERBS

23 unobtrusively, conservatively, unnoticeably

24 simply, plainly, austerely, starkly, unelaborately, unfussily, unpretentiously, unostentatiously, minimally

25 reservedly, reticently, diffidently, modestly, quietly, unassumingly

26 insipidly, pallidly, vapidly, blandly, tastelessly, half-heartedly

27 imperceptibly, inconspicuously, unimpressively, faintly, vaguely, indistinctly

28 moderately, with restraint, in a constrained manner

729 Speech

Most men make little use of their speech than to give evidence against their own understanding. Lord Halifax.

But words once spoke can never be recall'd. Earl of Roscommon.

NOUNS

1 faculty of speech, oral communication, language, talk, talking, speaking, verbal intercourse, dialogue, conversation, colloquy, discourse, voice, speaking voice, tongue, *langue* (Fr), parole, vocabulary, spoken language, living language, mother tongue, native tongue, Queen's English, English as she is spoken, vernacular, vulgar tongue, colloquial speech, idiomatic speech, idiom, dialect, patois, parlance, private language, code, idiolect, slang, cant, jargon, gobbledegook, computerspeak, technobabble, newspeak, patter, chat, natter, chatter, psychobabble (Inf), lingo (Inf), yakking (Inf), yakkety-yak (Inf), chinwag (Inf), rabbit (Inf), spiel (Inf), rap (Inf)

▶ *5 Language and Linguistics; 692 Communications; 733 Address; 734 Conversation*

2 power of speech, articulateness, articulacy, eloquence, fluency, command of language, way with words, word power, style, rich vocabulary, grandiloquence, magniloquence, orotundity, purple passage, flowery speech, talkativeness, volubility, loquacity, glossolalia, speaking in tongues, prolixity, logorrhoea, verbosity, verbiage, wordiness, verbal diarrhoea, long-windedness, repetitiveness, blah (Inf), blarney (Inf), gift of the gab (Inf)

▶ *112 Repetition; 270 Vagueness; 724 Style; 731 Talkativeness*

3 mode of speech, tone of voice, voice, tone, voice quality, timbre, intonation, pitch, modulation, inflection, stress, emphasis, pronunciation, accent, regional accent, native accent, foreign accent, broad accent, brogue, twang, burr, trill, drawl, suburban whine, nasality, stridor, lisping, stammer, stutter, speech impediment, speech defect, mispronunciation, cacoepy

4 articulation, diction, elocution, voicing, enunciation, phonation, vocalization, utterance, delivery, attack, ventriloquism, sign language, meaningful looks, gesticulation, gesture

▶ *730 Voicelessness; 742 Sign*

5 organ of speech, articulator, voice, mouth, tongue, teeth, lips, vocal organs, vocal chords, vocal folds, voice box, larynx, Adam's apple, glottis, epiglottis, hard palate, alveolar palate, soft palate, uvula, nasal cavity, oral cavity, pharynx, throat

6 phonetics, phonology, articulatory phonetics, acoustic phonetics, orthoepy, pronunciation, accentuation, rhythmic pattern, cadence, prosody, prosodics, metrics, linguistics, agogics

▶ *5 Language and Linguistics*

7 utterance, vocalization, spoken word, word of mouth, word, phrase, sentence, expression, locution, articulate sound, speech sound, phoneme, vowel, diphthong, voiced consonant, syllable, remark, observation, comment, dictum, statement, affirmation, assertion, averment, declaration, pronouncement, allegation, thought, reflection, interjection, exclamation, ejaculation, gasp, mutter, murmur, whisper, aside, question, answer, reply, response, address, greeting, opinion, contribution, say, crack (Dial), one's two cents' worth (US inf), one's twopennyworth (Inf), one's bit (Inf), one's piece (Inf)

▶ *707 Affirmation*

8 speech, oration, address, welcoming address, panegyric, eulogy, encomium, farewell oration, farewell address, valedictory, obsequies, after-dinner speech, vote of thanks, reading, recital, declaration, broadcast, sermon, exhortation, homily, harangue, mouthful, earful, tirade, diatribe, invective, obloquy, flea in one's ear, lecture, dissertation, peroration, preamble, proem, prologue, foreword, monologue, soliloquy

▶ *130 Beginning; 722 Essay; 733 Address; 735 Soliloquy*

9 art of public speaking, oratory, rhetoric, stump oratory, speech-making, speechifying, tub-thumping, declamation, ranting, rant, blarney, vituperation, address, soapbox oratory

10 speaker, utterer, talker, sayer, chatterer, prattler, gossip, gossiper, communicator, conversationalist, interlocutor, monologist, soliloquizer, soliloquist, public speaker, after-dinner speaker, speech-maker, speechifier, orator, oratrix, rhetorician, ranter, soapbox orator, tub-thumper, haranguer, demagogue, sermonizer, preacher, lecturer, presenter, announcer, broadcaster, narrator, chorus, spokesperson, spokesman, spokeswoman, delegate, advocate, mediator, intermediary, salesperson, salesman, saleswoman, representative, rep, smooth talker (Inf), blabbermouth (Inf), bigmouth (Inf)

▶ *734 Conversation; 735 Soliloquy; 748 Mediation*

VERBS

11 speak, talk, say, utter, declare, proclaim, state, aver, assert, affirm, allege, tell, relate, recite, quote, cite, give utterance to, enunciate, voice, express, verbalize, put into words, find words for, find words to express, formulate, convey, impart, communicate, disclose, blurt out, interject, exclaim, ejaculate, interrupt, have one's say, answer, reply, respond, call attention to, refer to, allude to, mention

▶ *707 Affirmation; 739 Disclosure*

12 speak loudly, speak up, shout, yell, cry, bawl, roar, boom, thunder, trumpet, blare, scream, shriek, screech, exclaim

▶ *507 Loudness; 513 Harsh Sound*

13 speak in a particular way, breathe, whisper, murmur, mutter, mumble, sigh, gasp, pant, pipe, flute, warble, coo, sing out, chant, cackle, crow, bark, yelp, growl, snap, snarl, squeak, whine, sob, wail, drawl, sibilate

▶ *512 Hissing Sound; 514 Human Cry*

14 speak to, address, talk to, apostrophize, discourse, lecture, sermonize, preach to, hold forth, orate, deliver a speech, make speeches, speechify, take the floor, perorate, rant, tub-thump, rail, harangue, invoke, appeal to

▶ *478 Improvisation; 677 Flattery; 731 Talkativeness; 733 Address; 734 Conversation*

15 **talk to oneself**, soliloquize, monologize

▶ *735 Soliloquy*

ADJECTIVES

16 **speech**, lingual, linguistic, vocal, spoken, uttered, said, articulated, voiced, vocalized, pronounced, enunciated

17 **oral**, verbal, unwritten, *viva voce* (L), nuncupative, parol

18 **phonetic**, phonic, tonic, tonal, pitched, accented, stressed, unstressed, unaccented, nasal, twangy, throaty, guttural, aspirated, aspirate, voiced, voiceless

▶ *5 Language and Linguistics*

19 **speaking**, talking, able to speak, with a tongue in one's head, articulate, fluent, talkative, loquacious, voluble, free-speaking, true-speaking, plain-speaking, plain-spoken, outspoken, out-speaking, loud-spoken, loud-speaking, soft-spoken, soft-speaking, quietly spoken, well-spoken, Anglophone, English-speaking, monolingual, unilingual, bilingual, trilingual, multilingual, polyglot, monoglot

▶ *731 Talkativeness*

20 **eloquent**, silver-tongued, smooth-talking, rhetorical, grandiloquent, magniloquent, tub-thumping, ranting, declamatory, bombastic, dithyrambic

ADVERBS

21 **orally**, vocally, verbally, *viva voce* (L), by word of mouth, phonetically, linguistically, eloquently, articulately, rhetorically, grandiloquently, magniloquently

730 Voicelessness

No voice; but oh! the silence sank
Like music on my heart. Samuel Taylor Coleridge.

NOUNS

1 **voicelessness**, loss of voice, no voice, aphonia, dysphonia

2 **inarticulation**, inarticulateness, difficulty in speaking, hoarseness, huskiness, croakiness, changing voice, breaking voice, thickness of voice, raucousness, harsh voice, unmusicality, tuneless voice

▶ *513 Harsh Sound*

3 **speech defect**, speech impediment, aphasia, dysphasia, dysphemia, stammer, stammering, stutter, stuttering, unintelligible speech, paraphasia, lallation, babbling, lisping, sibilation

▶ *512 Hissing Sound; 696 Unintelligibility; 697 Nonsense*

4 **whispering**, whisper, stage whisper, murmur, mumble, muffled voice, low voice, undertone, aside, mutter, voiceless consonant, surd, sigh, hiss

▶ *511 Faintness*

5 **mutism**, deaf-mutism, muteness, dumbness, speechlessness, taciturnity, reticence, silence

▶ *505 Deafness; 506 Silence; 732 Shyness*

6 **silent speech**, sign language, signing, Ameslan (US), deaf-and-dumb language, body language, gesture, gesticulation, meaningful look, signalling, semaphore

▶ *742 Sign*

7 **voiceless person**, mute, deaf-mute, deaf-and-dumb person, infant, fracastorius

8 **mute**, damper, silencer, soft pedal

ADJECTIVES

9 **voiceless**, unvoiced, aphonic, dysphonic, surd, silent, infant

▶ *506 Silence*

10 **low-voiced**, whispering, whispered, inaudible, muted, muttering, murmuring, mumbling, muffled, faint, low, breaking, cracked, hoarse, husky, croaking, with a frog in one's throat

▶ *511 Faintness*

11 **speechless**, inarticulate, mute, dumb, deaf and dumb, tongue-tied, taciturn, reticent, silent, silenced, gagged, choked, dumbfounded, struck dumb, mum (Inf), shtoom (Inf), gobsmacked (Inf)

▶ *505 Deafness; 506 Silence; 630 Surprise; 732 Shyness*

12 **inarticulate**, unintelligible, aphasic, dysphasic, dysphemic, stammering, stuttering, paraphasic, babbling, lisping, sibilant, hissing, sighing

▶ *696 Unintelligibility*

VERBS

13 **be voiceless**, not speak, be silent, keep quiet, hold one's tongue, not breathe a word, button one's lip (Inf), keep mum (Inf), keep shtoom (Inf)

14 **have difficulty speaking**, stammer, stutter, babble, lisp, hiss, lose one's voice, be struck dumb, lose one's powers of speech, lose one's tongue, let the cat get one's tongue, use sign language, sign, exchange meaningful looks, gesture, gesticulate

▶ *742 Sign*

15 **strike dumb**, make mute, dumbfound, take one's breath away, muffle, mute, deaden, silence, hush, gag, suppress, reduce to silence, cut short, hang up on, shout down, gobsmack (Inf)

▶ *506 Silence*

16 **speak in a low voice**, speak softly, whisper, stage whisper, whisper in one's ear, mutter, mumble, murmur, speak *sotto voce*, drop one's voice, speak under one's breath, speak in muted tones, sound faint, sigh

▶ *511 Faintness*

ADVERBS

17 **voicelessly**, silently, hoarsely, huskily, low, in an undertone, *sotto voce* (It), under one's breath, in a whisper, with bated breath

731 Talkativeness

It is with narrow-souled people as with narrow-necked bottles: the less they have in them, the more noise they make in pouring it out. Alexander Pope.

NOUNS

1 **talkativeness**, loquacity, loquaciousness, volubility, garrulousness, garrulity, verbosity, wordiness, prolixity, logorrhoea, logomania, verbal diarrhoea, runaway tongue, long-windedness, windiness, fluency, glibness, fluent tongue, multiloquence, multiloquy, eloquence, flow of words, chattiness, gabbiness (Inf), gassiness (Inf), bigmouth (Inf), gift of the gab (Inf), spiel (Inf)

► *270 Vagueness; 729 Speech*

2 **effusiveness**, effusion, gushiness, gush, candour, openness, frankness, communicativeness, sociability

► *654 Sociability*

3 **talk**, chat, chatter, chattering, babble, gabble, jabber, jabbering, rap, prattle, prating, palaver, gab, blab, blabber, small talk, gossip, idle gossip, tittle-tattle, waffle, gas, hot air, empty talk, chinwag (Inf), yak (Inf), yakkety-yak (Inf), witter (Inf), jaw (Inf), jaw-jaw (Inf), guff (Inf), blah (Inf), blah-blah (Inf)

► *697 Nonsense; 729 Speech; 734 Conversation*

4 **talker**, speaker, nonstop talker, chatterer, chatterbox, babbler, jabberer, gossip, tattler, tittle-tattler, driveller, waffler, ranter, quacker, gasser, magpie, jay, gabber, blabber, informer, blabbermouth (Inf), grass (Inf), bigmouth (Inf), windbag (Inf), gasbag (Inf), motor-mouth (Inf)

► *693 Information*

ADJECTIVES

5 **talkative**, loquacious, voluble, garrulous, verbose, wordy, prolix, long-winded, windy, chattering, babbling, gabbling, jabbering, jibbering, running on, fluent, glib, multiloquent, eloquent, gassy (Inf), gabby (Inf)

► *270 Vagueness; 729 Speech*

6 **effusive**, gushing, expansive, candid, frank, communicative, sociable, chatty, conversational, gossipy, tattling, prattling, prating, blabbing, yakking (Inf), bigmouthed (Inf), all mouth (Inf), mouthy (Inf), lippy (Inf), flip (Inf)

► *654 Sociability; 734 Conversation*

VERBS

7 **be talkative**, talk at length, talk, chat, chatter, babble, gabble, jabber, gibber, prate, gab, natter, gas, prattle on, rattle on, ramble on, blab, blabber, waffle, blah (Inf), rabbit on (Inf), witter (Inf), jaw (Inf), go on and on (Inf), run off at the mouth (Inf)

8 **talk too much**, talk nineteen to the dozen, talk the hind leg(s) off a donkey, talk one's head off, oil one's tongue, have a big mouth, spin out, expatiate, gush, spout, hold forth, drone on, bore, buttonhole, monopolize the conversation, not let anyone get a word in edgeways, like the sound of one's own voice, talk until one is blue in the face, shoot one's mouth off (Inf)

9 **out-talk**, shout down, bamboozle, filibuster, stonewall

► *702 Sophistry*

ADVERBS

10 **talkatively**, loquaciously, volubly, garrulously, fluently, glibly, eloquently

11 **effusively**, gushingly, expansively, candidly, frankly, sociably, communicatively, chattily

INTERJECTIONS

12 **rhubarb! rhubarb!** , blah! blah!, yak! yak!, yakkety-yak!

732 Shyness

Shyness is just egotism out of its depth. Penelope Keith.

ADJECTIVES

1 **shy**, timid, nervous, bashful, coy, mousy, shrinking, apprehensive, pusillanimous, timorous, self-conscious, quiet, modest, blushing, self-effacing, humble, unassertive, passive, reticent, withdrawn, incommunicative, uncommunicative, unforthcoming, diffident, taciturn, reserved, not to be drawn, tight-lipped, antisocial, unsociable, sullen, self-contained, mum (Inf), shtoom (Inf)

► *623 Humility; 655 Unsociability*

2 **sparing with words**, saying little, laconic, monosyllabic, silent, mute, dumb, voiceless, speechless, inarticulate, guarded, cautious, playing one's cards close to one's chest, secretive, with sealed lips, uninformative, vague, evasive, cagey (Inf), brusque, short, curt, terse, concise

► *506 Silence; 616 Caution; 730 Voicelessness; 737 Secrecy*

NOUNS

3 **shyness**, quietness, bashfulness, nervousness, timidness, timidity, coyness, self-consciousness, humility, modesty, reticence, reserve, diffidence, incommunicativeness, uncommunicativeness, taciturnity, shortness, brevity, brusqueness, curtness, gruffness, sullenness, evasiveness, secrecy

► *737 Secrecy*

4 **guarded speech**, laconism, laconicism, laconicness, conciseness, succinctness, terseness, silence, muteness, dumbness, voicelessness, speechlessness, inarticulacy, stuttering, stammering

► *269 Brevity*

5 **shy person**, mouse, coquette, doormat, wallflower, person of few words, no orator, strong silent type, clam, Trappist

VERBS

6 **be shy**, shrink, withdraw, hide, blend into the background, flinch, hide one's light under a bushel, keep out of the limelight, blush

7 **keep quiet**, spare one's words, use few words, keep one's counsel, refuse to comment, hold one's tongue, keep one's mouth shut, keep oneself to oneself, keep one's trap shut (Inf), keep shtoom (Inf), stammer, stutter, falter

ADVERBS

8 **shyly**, coyly, timidly, diffidently, reservedly, pusillanimously, self-consciously, nervously, nervily, modestly, humbly, quietly, reticently, apprehensively, incommunicatively, uncommunicatively, silently, voicelessly, without a word

733 Address

I dreamt that I was making a speech in the House. I woke up, and by Jove I was! Duke of Devonshire.

NOUNS

1 **address**, allocution, apostrophe, lecture, discourse, recitation, recital, reading, talk, presentation, speech, oration, public speech, formal speech, set speech, prepared speech, disquisition, declamation, tirade, diatribe, jeremiad, invective, harangue, screed, rodomontade, philippic, sermon, homily, rant (Inf), earful (Inf), mouthful (Inf)

► *729 Speech*

2 salutation, greeting, salaam, hail, salutatory address, address of welcome, valedictory address, valedictory, valediction, inaugural address, pep talk, exhortation, peroration, appeal, invocation, interpellation, interjection, advances, suit, court

▶ *658 Courtesy; 710 Request*

3 skill, address, adroitness, dexterity, deftness, neatness, expertness, expertise, ability, cleverness, ingenuity, art, tact

▶ *485 Skill*

4 approach, method, way, mode, line, attack

▶ *317 Way; 352 Means*

5 place of residence, residence, domicile, habitation, abode, home, house, habitat, location, whereabouts, house number, number, road name, street name, district, postcode, zip code (US), no fixed abode (NFA)

▶ *142 Location; 565 Habitat*

6 public speaker, speech-maker, spokesperson, spokesman, spokeswoman, lecturer, discourser, reader, orator, declaimer, ranter, tub-thumper, rhetorician, silver-tongued orator, soapbox orator, stump orator, rabble-rouser, demagogue, pulpiteer, preacher, sermonizer, sermoner, sermonist, pontificator, expositor, expounder

VERBS

7 address, speak to, talk to, lecture, apostrophize, take the floor, give a talk, make a speech (*or* presentation), deliver an address, discourse, speechify, hold forth, declaim, orate, harangue, perorate, pontificate, rant, tub-thump, rabble-rouse, sermonize, preach at

8 appeal to, invoke, entreat, pray to, apply to, petition, go cap in hand to

9 approach, accost, buttonhole, call to, salute, hail, greet, say good morning to, pass the time of day with, parley with, converse with

▶ *658 Courtesy; 734 Conversation*

10 send, direct, address, consign, transmit, dispatch, post, mail, seal, stamp, frank, send on, forward, redirect, readdress

11 title, entitle, style, term, call sir, call madam

▶ *575 Title; 658 Courtesy*

12 address oneself to, go in for, take up, undertake, engage in, apply oneself to, devote oneself to

▶ *354 Undertaking*

ADJECTIVES

13 oratorical, rhetorical, declamatory, demagogic, demagogical

14 vocative, invocatory, salutatory, valedictory

INTERJECTIONS

15 hail!, greetings!, hello!, hi!

734 Conversation

I wish you would read a little poetry sometimes. Your ignorance cramps my conversation. Anthony Hope.

He has occasional flashes of silence, that make his conversation perfectly delightful. Sydney Smith.

NOUNS

1 conversation, talk, chat, dialogue, duologue, two-hander, interlocution, colloquy, converse, discourse, intercourse, verbal intercourse, social intercourse, communication, intercommunication, communion

2 chat, natter, crack (Dial), small talk, table talk, friendly talk, heart-to-heart, tête-à-tête, fireside chat, cosy chat, causerie, idle talk, prattle, tattle, tittle-tattle, gossip, idle gossip, chit-chat, backchat, repartee, banter, confabulation, confab (Inf), conflab (Inf), chinwag (Inf)

▶ *731 Talkativeness*

3 social gathering, social, party, soirée, *conversazione* (It)

▶ *654 Sociability*

4 conference, parley, powwow, congress, conclave, meeting, gathering, assembly, convention, forum, open forum, symposium, talk-in, teach-in, seminar, polemics, dialectic, exchange of views, discussion, debate, debating, colloquium, *convivio* (It), consultation, council, council of war, round-table conference, huddle, putting one's heads together

▶ *376 Gathering*

5 talks, high-level talks, summit meeting, summit talks, summit, negotiations, bargaining, treaty-making

▶ *746 Negotiation*

6 interview, audience, audition, interrogation, interlocution, examination, investigation, analysis, review, consideration, question and answer session

▶ *705 Question*

7 conversationalist, converser, talker, discourser, confabulator, colloquist, collocutor, interlocutor, interviewer, examiner, cross-examiner, interrogator, interpellator, inquirer, respondent

8 chatterer, natterer, gossip, tittle-tattler, gasser (Inf), gasbag (Inf), windbag (Inf)

VERBS

9 converse, discourse, talk together, talk, speak, parley, communicate, commune, confabulate, have a talk, hold a conversation, engage in conversation, carry on a conversation, have a word with, have a quick word with, exchange words, exchange pleasantries, pass the time of day, chew the fat (Inf)

10 chat, natter, chatter, prattle, prate, gossip, have a cosy chat, have a little chat, have a heart-to-heart, talk tête-à-tête, go in a huddle, talk privately, whisper together, have a chinwag (Inf)

11 confer, hold a conference, parley, powwow, sit down together, meet around a conference table, get round the table, talk over, thrash out, debate, discuss, exchange views, sit in council, sit in committee, consider the pros and cons, deliberate over, analyse, canvass, consult, refer to, negotiate, bargain, hold talks, hold a summit, hold a council of war

ADJECTIVES

12 conversing, talking, chatting, interlocutory, confabulatory, talkative, loquacious, communicative, unreserved

▶ *731 Talkativeness*

13 discussing, conferring, conferential, in conference, in committee, consultatory, consultative, advisory

14 conversational, chatty, colloquial, informal, gossipy, newsy, informative

ADVERBS

15 conversationally, colloquially, informally, tête-à-tête, loquaciously, communicatively, unreservedly, off the record

735 Soliloquy

NOUNS

1 **soliloquy**, monologue, monology, monody, monodrama, interior monologue, stream of consciousness, apostrophe, aside, lecture, rant, harangue, oration, sermon, speech, one-man show, one-woman show, ravings (Inf)

▶ *197 One*

2 **soliloquist**, soliloquizer, monologist, monodist, sole performer, soloist, lecturer, orator, preacher

VERBS

3 **soliloquize**, monologize, talk to oneself, talk to the wall, have an audience of one, say to oneself, tell oneself, think aloud, apostrophize

4 **monopolize the conversation**, do all the talking, hold forth without interruption, rabbit on (Inf), rave on (Inf), run off at the mouth (Inf)

▶ *731 Talkativeness*

ADJECTIVES

5 **soliloquizing**, monologic, monological, apostrophic, monodramatic, soloistic, thinking aloud, talking to oneself, raving (Inf)

736 Concealment

NOUNS

1 **concealment**, invisibility, disappearance, eclipse, occultation, hiding, secretion, reconditeness

2 **hiding place**, mother's skirt, foxhole, dugout, bolt hole, bomb shelter, refuge, shelter, sanctuary, asylum, safe house, hidden cave, nook, cranny, niche, hideout, hideaway, cubbyhole, hidy-hole, cache, stash, closet, attic, cellar, doormat, mattress, secret compartment, secret panel, secret passage, fake book, hollow tree, safe, safe-deposit, bank vault

3 **covering up**, purdah, masking, screening, veiling, anonymity, disguise, mask, masked ball, *bal masqué* (Fr), costume party, camouflage, screen, smokescreen, ambush, trap

4 **silence**, reticence, taciturnity, reserve, closeness, discretion, confidentiality, privacy, suppression, censorship, clampdown, national security, classified information, D-notice, Official Secrets Act, Privy Councillor's oath

▶ *737 Secrecy*

5 **evasion**, evasiveness, equivocation, equivocality, equivocalness, prevarication, vagueness, obscurity, mystification, obfuscation, deception, misinformation, disinformation, lie, untruth, cover-up, Watergate, Irangate, Chernobyl, dishonesty, false evidence, perjury, deceitfulness, dissimulation, duplicity, trickery, subterfuge

▶ *699 Falsehood; 700 Deception*

6 **privacy**, seclusion, retreat, sanctum, monastery, convent, nunnery, closed order, private garden, private club, lair, den, study, library, boudoir, bedroom, bath, toilet, desert island, lighthouse, mountaintop, ivory tower

7 **concealer**, hider, hermit, recluse, lone wolf, power behind the throne, *éminence grise* (Fr), undercover agent, face in the crowd, no name, X, code name, alias, stage name, pen name, pseudonym, nom de plume, masquerader, evader, Freemason, Klansman, mafioso, dissembler, deceiver, conspirator, boogerboo (US inf)

▶ *737 Secrecy*

VERBS

8 **conceal**, hide, hide away, secrete, bury, inter, confine, seclude, ensconce, stow away, lock up, seal up, wall up, bottle up, store, stash (away), sweep under the carpet (mat *or* rug), cover up, cover, wrap up, paper over, whitewash, varnish, gloss over, overlay, paint over, smother, stifle, suppress, censor, screen, cloak, shroud, curtain, blanket, veil, draw a veil over, keep under wraps, muffle, mask

9 **disguise**, camouflage, encode, obscure, eclipse, darken, fog, befog, cloud, becloud, muddle, obfuscate, dim, bedim, muddy the waters,

10 **deceive**, dissemble, masquerade, blindfold, mislead, confuse, pull the wool over someone's eyes, bamboozle (Inf)

11 **conceal oneself**, evade, shun, hide from, retreat into one's shell, keep (fade *or* stay) in the background, keep a low profile, stay out of the limelight, stay in the shadows, dodge, avoid, play hide-and-seek, steal away, slip by, slink, glide, creep, tiptoe, leave no address, cover one's tracks, lay a false scent (*or* trail), take cover, go to earth, go underground, lie low, hide out, be on the run, take to the hills, vanish, vanish into thin air, disappear, exit, skip town (US inf), hit the road (US inf), lie doggo (Inf), go on the lam (US inf)

12 **be silent**, keep one's mouth shut, hold one's tongue, look blank, look natural, keep a straight face, keep mum, shut up, act dumb (Inf), shut one's trap (*or* face) (Inf), zip (*or* button) one's lips (*or* mouth) (Inf), zip it (Inf)

▶ *506 Silence; 737 Secrecy*

13 **equivocate**, prevaricate, evade, hedge, fence, stonewall, beat about the bush (Inf)

ADJECTIVES

14 **concealed**, hidden, unseen, secluded, sequestered, reclusive, incommunicado, out-of-touch, private, screened, hooded, masked, recondite, veiled, covered, overprinted, eclipsed, obscured, blotted out, under wraps, smothered, stifled, suppressed, censored

15 **disguised**, distorted, camouflaged, unrecognized, unrecognizable, incognito, anonymous, cryptic, secret, covert, occult, latent, coded, codified, cryptographic, unintelligible

16 **silent**, taciturn, reticent, reserved, aloof, unsociable, withdrawn

17 **noncommittal**, uncommunicative, uninformative, clamlike, tight-lipped, poker-faced, vague, evasive, close, discreet, secretive, cagey (Inf), buttoned-up (Inf)

ADVERBS

18 **privately**, in private, secretly, in secret, behind closed doors

▶ *737 Secrecy*

737 Secrecy

Stolen waters are sweet, and bread eaten in secret is pleasant. Bible: Proverbs.

Mum's the word. George Colman, the Younger.

Three may keep a secret, if two of them are dead. Benjamin Franklin.

NOUNS

1 **secrecy**, silence, privacy, confidentiality, confidence, secret, confidant (*or* confidante), seal of the confessional, family secret, skeleton in the cupboard, secret meeting, private meeting, closed session, meeting in camera, confidential information, sealed orders, state secret, classified information, Official Secrets Act, top-secret file, censorship, suppression

► *736 Concealment*

2 **secretiveness**, stealth, stealthiness, furtiveness, clandestineness, covertness, Secret Service, intelligence service, MI5, MI6, CIA, KGB, espionage, counterintelligence, undercover agent, secret agent, spy, double agent, mole, industrial espionage, underhand dealing, intrigue, plot, conspiracy, cabal, *omertà* (It)

3 **mystification**, mystery, enigma, puzzle, problem, poser, intricacy, complexity, difficulty

4 **brain-teaser**, teaser, brain-twister, charade, Chinese puzzle, tangram, Rubik Cube™, maze, labyrinth, word-puzzle, crossword, anagram, acrostic, riddle, riddle-me-ree, conundrum, rebus, cipher, code, cryptogram, cryptography, cryptographer, coder, public-key cryptography, decoder, hieroglyphics

5 **difficult problem**, knotty problem, hard nut to crack, Gordian knot, Hyrcanian wood, squaring the circle, duplicating the cube, riddle of the sphinx

6 **natural mystery**, ghosts, Bermuda Triangle, Atlantis, Stonehenge, Lourdes, Easter Island, flying saucers, UFOs (unidentified flying objects), crop circles, Fortean animals, Loch Ness Monster, Yeti, Abominable Snowman, Bigfoot

7 **esotericism**, mystery, obscurity, secrecy, secret society, Freemasonry, Freemason, lodge, Ku Klux Klan, Klansman, initiate, Mafia, mafioso, Know-Nothings (US), occultism, gnosis, cabbalism, cabbala, arcanum, esoterica, secret lore, secret art, secret formula, alchemy, alchemist

8 **anonymity**, unknown quantity, unknown person, mysterious stranger, no name, Unknown Warrior, invisible man, code name, X, Anon., assumed name, stage name, pen name, pseudonym, nom de plume, alias, unknown country, *terra incognita* (L), Dark Continent

ADJECTIVES

9 **secret**, private, privy, intimate, confidential, closed, secluded, sealed, isolated, unrevealed, undisclosed, undivulged, unspoken, untold, top-secret, classified, restricted, censored, suppressed, off-the-record, hush-hush (Inf)

10 **secretive**, silent, close, reticent, surreptitious, stealthy, furtive, sly, clandestine, covert, undercover, underhand, conspirational, cabalistic, cloak-and-dagger (Inf)

11 **mysterious**, enigmatic, inscrutable, unknowable, esoteric, cabbalistic, arcane, occult, abstruse, mystifying, confusing, bewildering, puzzling, perplexing, unresolved, unintelligible, problematic, complex, intricate, labyrinthine, difficult, knotty, cryptic, hidden, concealed, camouflaged, disguised, incognito, unknown, anonymous

VERBS

12 **keep secret**, conceal, hide, withhold, keep back, suppress, censor, seal, ban, restrict, classify, put a D-notice on, keep under wraps, keep close, keep (it) to oneself, keep under one's hat, play (it) close to one's chest, keep (it) dark, give nothing away, keep one's mouth shut, hold one's tongue, not breathe a word, keep mum, keep one's counsel, make no sign, neither confirm nor deny, make no comment, let (it) go no further, hush up, cover up, clam up (Inf), put (*or* keep) the lid on (Inf), black out (Inf)

► *736 Concealment*

13 **mystify**, puzzle, baffle, perplex, bewilder, confuse, deceive, keep (someone) in the dark, stump (Inf)

14 **make mysterious**, obscure, obfuscate, code, encode, cipher, encipher

ADVERBS

15 **in secret**, secretly, privately, behind closed doors, in camera, sub rosa, confidentially, in confidence, (just *or* strictly) between ourselves, *entre nous* (Fr), off the record, between you, me, and the gatepost, for your ears only, *sotto voce* (It), in a whisper, in an undertone, anonymously, incognito, with nobody (any) the wiser

16 **stealthily**, furtively, conspiratorially, in secrecy, like a thief in the night, under cloak of darkness, invisibly, behind one's back, by the back door, under the counter, huggermugger (Lit), in a hole-and-corner way (Inf), on the sly, on the quiet, on the q.t. (Inf)

738 Display

That's it, baby, if you've got it, flaunt it. Mel Brooks.

VERBS

1 **display**, show, put on display, put on view, put on show, exhibit, manifest, present, bring forward, reveal to the public, expose, expose to view, disclose, offer for approval, set out, set before someone's eyes, give a guided tour, show round, bring to notice, draw attention to, feature, spotlight, illuminate, put in bold (*or* high) relief, headline, emphasize, point out, indicate, teach, instruct, explain, make a show of, flourish, brandish, wave, dangle, flaunt, vaunt, show off, parade, air, sport, model, demonstrate, perform, act, enact, dramatize, put on, stage, release, publish, flash (Inf)

► *21 Drama; 125 Imitation; 326 Oscillation; 455 Knowledge; 471 Attention; 551 Dress; 676 Affectation; 703 Demonstration; 717 Representation; 726 Emphasis; 739 Disclosure; 743 Identification*

2 **display something**, screen, televise, put on television, broadcast, put on radio, stage a play, hold an exhibition, exhibit, hang a picture, show photographs, place in a shop window, advertise

► *19 Painting and Sculpture; 21 Drama*

3 **reveal**, manifest, divulge, disclose, discover, uncover, unearth, bring to light, illuminate, throw light on, make plain, make obvious, bring to notice, bring up, point up, point out, indicate, accentuate, enhance, make important, throw into relief, emphasize, highlight, spotlight, place in the spotlight, place in the foreground, proclaim, publicize, promote, advertise, publish, cite, mention, make reference to, adduce, quote, extract, invent, develop, formulate, produce, bring out, bring forth, expose, open up, lay bare, lay open, throw open, unmask, unveil, drag out, draw out, draw forth, express, trot out, come out with, show off, evidence, show, evince, give away, betray, draw attention to, unfurl, unroll, unfold, spread out, solve, decipher, decode, explain, interpret

► *123 Importance; 171 Outside; 213 Increase; 308 Opening; 356 Creation; 369 Extraction; 449 Discovery; 522 Light; 707 Affirmation; 716 Evidence; 719 Interpretation; 739 Disclosure; 740 Publication*

4 **show oneself**, show one's face, reveal oneself, appear, materialize, rear one's head, show up, be seen, show the flag, come out into the open, come forth, unmask oneself, unveil oneself, tear off the mask, show (oneself in) one's true colours, stand in the open, stand in full view, confront, force a confrontation, come face to face, come eyeball to eyeball, assert onself, speak up, speak out, raise one's voice, stand up, stand up and be counted, take a stand, speak plainly, put one's cards on the table, have no secrets, make no mystery, make no secret of, not try to hide, have no shame, wash one's dirty linen in public, wear one's heart on one's sleeve, reveal one's mind, reveal one's thoughts, reveal one's opinions, tell to one's face, give straight from the shoulder, make no bones about

► *525 Appearance; 698 Truth*

5 **be visible**, attract attention, attract notice, stand out, stand out a mile, have the spotlight on one, be in the limelight, hold centre stage, show up, show up well, require no explanation, go without saying, stand to reason, tell its own story, speak for itself, make an impression, loom large, stare one in the face, openly happen, come to light, transpire, emanate

► *147 Closeness; 271 Simplicity; 471 Attention; 520 Visibility; 695 Intelligibility; 703 Demonstration*

NOUNS

6 **display**, show, exhibition, exposition, expo, demonstration, presentation, spectacle, showing, viewing, collection, retrospective, fair, market, fashion show, motor show, boat show, dog show, cat show, art show, craft show, crafts fair, antique show, antiques fair, parade, array

► *19 Painting and Sculpture; 117 Conformity; 439 Store; 551 Dress; 703 Demonstration; 779 Market*

7 **showpiece**, exhibit, collector's piece, pride, jewel in the crown, collectable (*or* collectible), curio, antique, museum piece, model, sample, specimen, example, mock-up, dummy, piece of evidence

8 **showplace**, showroom, exhibition hall, exhibition centre, gallery, museum, hall, auditorium, scene, showcase, display case, display cabinet, dumpbin, store window, shop window, notice board, bulletin board, pegboard, hoarding, sign, advertisement, poster, placard, sandwich boards, label, bill, citation

9 **production**, performance, presentation, enactment, show, spectacle, musical, concert, play, ballet, film, motion picture, cinema, television programme, TV programme, radio programme, preview

► *21 Drama; 717 Representation*

10 **manifestation**, manifestness, revelation, disclosure, exposure, laying open, unfolding, unrolling, discovery, uncovering, bringing to light, shedding of daylight on, visibility, publicity, promotion, advertising, flagrancy, blatancy, conspicuousness, ostentation, showing off, accentuation, emphasis, highlight, spotlight, ceremony, pageant, pageantry, pomp, expression, formulation, affirmation, proof, evidence, confrontation, comparison, projection, representation, symbolization, typification, personification, indication, sign, token, signal, symptom, syndrome, omen, press conference, proclamation, publication, apparition, appearance, materialization, epiphany, incarnation, theophany, avatar, seance, occultism, splash (Inf)

► *7 Religion; 471 Attention; 475 Prediction; 518 Vision; 726 Emphasis; 739 Disclosure; 743 Identification*

11 **openness**, obviousness, plainness, candour, glasnost, plain speech, unadulterated truth, simple truth, home truth, open-and-shut case

► *698 Truth*

12 **displayer**, exhibitor, demonstrator, presenter, publicist, publicizer, advertiser, press agent, flack (US inf), public relations (PR) man (*or* woman), promotional manager, barker, showman, master of ceremonies (MC), impresario, stage manager, exhibitionist, flaunter, striptease artiste, stripteaser, stripper, model, male model, mannequin, vain person, peacock

► *21 Drama; 551 Dress; 673 Vanity*

ADJECTIVES

13 **displayed**, on display, exhibited, presented, shown, on show, on view, on, made public, brought to public notice, brought to one's notice, brought to attention, manifested, apodeictic, featured, visible, apparent, brought forth, produced, mentioned, adduced, cited, quoted, confronted, brought face to face, worn, sported, paraded, shown off, flaunted, waved, unfurled, brandished, flourished, advertised, publicized, promoted, published, expressible, producible, showable

► *139 Speciality; 326 Oscillation; 525 Appearance*

14 **manifest**, revealed, disclosed, divulged, exposed, uncovered, discovered, declared, overt, palpable, open, in the open, public, on the surface, staring one in the face, unconcealed, uncamouflaged, undisguised, noticeable, conspicuous, notable, apparent, visible, obvious, ostensible, open-and-shut, appearing, token, indicative, typical, symbolic, personified, representative, definite, defined, identifiable, recognizable, certain, unmistakable, incontestable, pronounced, prominent, clear as daylight, intelligible, signal, marked, striking, in relief, bold, in bold (*or* high) relief, salient, highlighted, accentuated, emphasized, in the foreground, in the limelight, patent, evident, self-evident, written all over one for all to see, obtrusive, flagrant, blatant, arrant, glaring, stark-staring, ostentatious, catching the eye, eye-catching, well-

known, notorious, famous, infamous, gaudy, showy, loud, shouting from the rooftops

▶ *452 Certainty; 716 Evidence; 726 Emphasis; 743 Identification*

15 open, candid, frank, explicit, plain, plain-speaking, plain-spoken, plain as the nose on one's face, clear, crystal-clear, truthful, honest, veracious, free, unreserved, honest-to-goodness, honest-to-God, downright, forthright, straightforward, blunt, heart-to-heart, off-the-record, outspoken, emphatic, no-nonsense, bold, daring, brazen, immodest, shameless, impudent, defiant, barefaced, bare, uncovered, naked, flaunting

▶ *661 Defiance; 698 Truth; 796 Immorality; 799 Honour*

ADVERBS

16 manifestly, obviously, evidently, plainly, apparently, openly, overtly, publicly, in public, for public notice, for all to see, conspicuously, flagrantly, undisguisedly, palpably, notoriously, at first blush, externally, on the face of it, on the surface, superficially, open and above-board, with one's cards on the table, before one, before all, before God, under the eye of heaven, on exhibition, in full view, in broad daylight, out in the open, in open court, on the stage

17 frankly, candidly, honestly, forthrightly, to one's face, face to face, off the record, boldly, defiantly

739 Disclosure

NOUNS

1 disclosure, exposure, uncovering, unveiling, revelation, manifestation, epiphany, anagnorisis, discovery, diagnosis, denouement, resolution, explanation, showdown, catastrophe, apocalypse

▶ *449 Discovery*

2 divulgence (*or* **divulgement**), communication, broadcast, announcement, declaration, publication, full report, investigative journalism, exposé, betrayal, leak, hint, telltale sign, giveaway, state's evidence (US), queen's (*or* king's) evidence, tergiversation, admission, acknowledgment, avowal, affirmation, confession

3 openness, full details, no holds barred, plain speaking, downrightness, candour, frankness, truth, honesty, unreservedness, outspokenness, indiscretion

▶ *698 Truth; 731 Talkativeness*

4 discloser, revealer, discoverer, researcher, exposer, investigator, investigative journalist, reporter, communicator, publicizer, broadcaster, announcer, source, informant, confessor, informer, betrayer, maieusis, telltale (Inf), blabberer (Inf), blabbermouth (Inf), whistle-blower (Inf), squealer (Inf), peacher (Inf), grass (Inf), supergrass (Inf)

▶ *693 Information*

VERBS

5 disclose, reveal, expose, show, make known, bring to light, bring into the open, open the windows, discover, diagnose, take the lid off, let out, unleash, unkennel, hold up to view, take the wraps off, bare, lay bare, strip bare, denude, unfold, unroll, unfurl, unpack, unwrap, uncover, unshroud, unscreen, uncurtain, unveil, lift (*or* draw) the veil, raise the curtain, shine some light on, let in daylight, let some light in, unclose, unseal, break the seal, break the wax, open, lay open, open up, dig up, disinter, show up, manifest, uncloak, unmask, tear off the mask, go public, let slip, show for what it is, show oneself in one's true colours

6 divulge, declare, broadcast, announce, communicate, inform, educate, publicize, publish, break the news, break it to, give out, vent, give vent to, ventilate, air, speak out, come out with, tell all, let on, tell, talk, speak, utter, breathe, hint, confide, leak, let one in on, let drop, let fall, let out, open the books, set straight (*or* right), set the record straight, straighten the record, show one's hand, show one's cards, put one's cards on the table, talk straight, talk turkey (US inf), blow the lid off (Inf), blow the gaff (Inf), let it all hang out (US inf)

7 betray, give away, tell on, inform on, accuse, name names, turn state's evidence (US), turn queen's (*or* king's) evidence, tergiversate, blurt out, talk out of turn, blab, tell tales out of school (Inf), let the cat out of the bag (Inf), spill the beans (Inf), give the game away (Inf), blow the whistle on (Inf), shoot off one's mouth (Inf), blow someone's cover (Inf), split (Inf), sing (US inf), sing like a canary (US inf), peach (Inf), squeal (Inf), grass (Inf), rat (on) (Inf)

8 admit, allow, acknowledge, concede, grant, assent, affirm, avow, own, confess, own up, plead guilty, come clean, make a clean breast of it, get it off one's chest, open one's heart to, unbosom oneself, unburden oneself, bare one's breast to

9 be disclosed, appear, stand revealed, emerge, transpire, come to light, become known, come out, break, blow up, get out, leak out, become public knowledge, break forth, break through the clouds, show through, show its face, show its true colours, come as a revelation, come with a blinding flash, flash on the mind, dawn upon

ADJECTIVES

10 disclosed, revealed, shown, showing, visible, clear, obvious, transparent, open, laid bare, exposed, leaked, confessed, admitted, avowed, acknowledged, uncovered, unearthed, unmasked

11 disclosing, revealing, divulging, maieutic, open, candid, frank, downright, unreserved, outspoken, forthcoming, informative, communicative, talkative, garrulous, loquacious, indiscreet, imprudent, chatty, leaky

12 revelatory, expository, explicatory, explanatory, interpretive, apocalyptic, manifesting, epiphanic

ADVERBS

13 openly, unreservedly, in the open, with no holds barred, outright, freely, frankly, plainly, candidly, forthrightly, indiscreetly

740 Publication

NOUNS

1 publication, publishing, dissemination, circulation, ventilation, divulgence (*or* divulgency), divulgation, disclosure, promulgation, broadcasting, public-address system, loudspeaker, Tannoy™, loud-hailer, bullhorn (US), spreading the word, spreading abroad, broadcast, announcement, declaration, proclamation, pronouncement, public notice, speech, statement, sermon, notification, official notice, report, communiqué, bulletin, manifesto, pronunciamento, edict, decree, encyclical, ukase, ban, unconfirmed report, rumour, hearsay, gossip, trial balloon

► *729 Speech; 739 Disclosure*

2 **mass media**, the media, communication, mass communication, telecommunication, television, radio, broadcasting, telecasting, cable television, narrowcasting, cablecasting, cable-vision (US), readership, audience, viewership, viewing figures, ratings, television ratings, A.C. Nielsen ratings (US), BARB (Broadcasters' Audience Research Board) ratings, radio audience measurement, BBC's BRD (Broadcasting Research Department) Daily Survey of Listening, audience survey

► *692 Communications*

3 **journalism**, the press, fourth estate, newspaper world, Fleet Street, Street of Shame (Inf), serious press, tabloid press, popular press, gutter press, yellow press, underground press, reporting, rapportage, newspapering (US), coverage, report, notice, write-up, broadsheet, scoop, editorial comment, editorial, leader, leading article, gossip column, advice column, agony column (Inf), personal column, personals (Inf), public comment, correspondence column, open letter, letters to the editor, headline, banner headline, streamer, screamer (US inf)

► *741 News*

4 **newspaper**, paper, international paper, national paper, provincial paper, local paper, freesheet, giveaway, morning paper, evening paper, weekly paper, Sunday paper, daily paper, daily, quality daily, broadsheet, the heavies (Inf), tabloid, sheet, rag (Inf), edition, early edition, late edition, stop-press edition, extra edition, extra, late extra, special edition, sports edition, magazine section, supplement, colour supplement, feuilleton, trade supplement

5 **journal**, periodical, review, gazette, magazine, glossy magazine, picture magazine, newsmagazine, women's magazine, men's magazine, business magazine, comic magazine, comic, comic strip, in-flight magazine, literary magazine, pulp magazine, serial, series, part work, daily, weekly, biweekly, fortnightly, semimonthly, monthly, quarterly, seasonal, annual, specialist publication, organ, academic journal, professional journal, technical journal, trade journal, trade paper, trade organ, house magazine, in-house magazine, house organ, newsletter, newssheet, pamphlet

6 **book publishing**, publishing, book trade, bookselling, bookshop, library, Public Lending Right (PLR), book club, book, hardback, paperback, coffee-table book, textbook, trade book, reference book, dictionary, thesaurus, guidebook, cookbook, cookery book, sports book, children's book, novel, best-seller, romantic novel, Mills & Boon, bodice ripper, thriller, general fiction, adult fiction, juvenile fiction, pulp fiction, book serialization, book review, book fair, Frankfurt Book Fair, promotion tour, Pulitzer Prize (US), Booker Prize

► *693 Information*

7 **publicity**, limelight, spotlight, coverage, public recognition, public eye, fame, famousness, renown, blaze of publicity, the talk of the town, the flavour of the month, the cover of *Time*, notoriety, infamy, common knowledge, public knowledge, openness, manifestation, publicness, currency, wide currency, wide circulation, nationwide circulation, country-wide circulation, public discussion, conference, public forum, town-hall meeting, pulpit, platform, soapbox, rostrum, hustings, ballyhoo (Inf)

8 **public relations** (PR), press office, press conference, news conference, press release, press announcement, propaganda, media event, staged event, exhibition, media blitz, photocall, photo-opportunity, display, name in (bright) lights, letters a foot high, letters of fire (*or* gold), top billing, showmanship, P. T. Barnum, medicine show (US), window-dressing, ostentation, sensationalism, exaggeration, puff, three-ring circus, The Greatest Show on Earth, promo (Inf), flackery (US inf), hype (Inf), media hype (Inf)

9 **advertisement**, notice, announcement, commercial, trailer, poster, flier (US), *affiche* (Fr), insertion, insert, leaflet, pamphlet, flyer, blad, brochure, blurb, circular, hand-out, handbill, bill, billboard, hoarding, placard, banner, sandwich board, display board, notice board, classified advertisement, commercial listing, Yellow Pages, advertorial, advert (Inf), ad (Inf), small ad (Inf), classified ad (Inf), want ad (Inf), plug (Inf), teaser (Inf), puff job (Inf), puff piece (Inf)

10 **publicizer**, publicist, promoter, propagandist, publicity agent, press agent, image-maker, advertiser, advertising agent, advertising account executive, hidden persuader, copywriter, blurb writer, public relations officer (PRO), PR man, PR woman, PR person, notifier, announcer, messenger, proclaimer, crier, herald, barker, spieler, tout, pamphleteer, bill poster, bill sticker, sandwichman, spin doctor (Inf), flack (US inf), shill (US inf)

11 **newspaperman**, newsman, newspaperwoman, newswoman, newspaper proprietor, press baron, journalist, reporter, news reporter, correspondent, special correspondent, foreign correspondent, war correspondent, investigative journalist, chequebook journalist, editorial writer, leader writer, columnist, gossip columnist, agony aunt, freelancer, stringer, press photographer, critic, editor, news editor, city editor, features editor, sports editor, copy editor, subeditor, hack (Inf)

12 **publisher**, book publisher, university press, bookperson, author, writer, novelist, ghostwriter, literary agent, agent, editor, managing editor, editor-in-chief, copy editor, manuscript editor, desk editor, fiction editor, reference editor, proofreader, printer, typesetter, compositor, comp (Inf), bookbinder, bookseller, librarian

VERBS

13 **make public**, bring to public notice, bring into the open, tell the world, inform, go public, let it be known, make known, divulge, reveal, disclose, expose, ventilate, air, communicate, broadcast, transmit, relay, telecast, televise, radio, narrowcast, cablecast (US), disseminate, diffuse, propagate, get out, put out, give out, promulgate, release, circulate, spread, spread the word, spread abroad, put about, rumour, spread a rumour, fly a kite, launch a trial balloon, bruit (about), bruit abroad, noise abroad, bring up, mention, talk about, gossip, retail, pass round, bandy about, hawk about, buzz about

14 **proclaim**, publish, announce, notify, pronounce, declare, declaim, herald, trumpet, blast, blazon, blaze, blaze abroad, cry, shout, scream, thunder, shout from the rooftops, beat the big drum, announce with a flourish of trumpets, raise a hue and cry, raise the roof, raise hell, come on like gangbusters (US), pitch a bitch (US inf)

15 publish, prepare for publication, report, cover, write, write up, serialize, syndicate, edit, copy-edit, subedit, sub(Inf), typeset, set, print, put to bed, go to press, issue a publication, issue, bring out, break a story, scoop, put out, distribute, circularize

16 publicize, advertise, advertise for, request, place (*or* insert) an advertisement, bill, post bills, placard, pamphleteer, propagandize, promote, build up, boost, sell, push, feature, highlight, spotlight, pinpoint, emphasize, headline, put in headlines, splash, blitz the media, make famous, put on the map, make one's name (known), make someone, make a cynosure of, make much of, extol, glorify, rave about, overrate, puff, tout, plug (Inf), ballyhoo (Inf), hype (up) (Inf), shill (US inf)

17 be published, become public knowledge, come out, see oneself in print, get in print, circulate, spread, pass round, go the rounds, get around (*or* about), spread abroad, spread like wildfire, fly about, buzz about

18 become famous, be in the news, get into the papers, hit the headlines, make the front page, make it to the top, become known from coast to coast (US) be sold, have a circulation, sell well, sell like hot cakes (Inf)

ADJECTIVES

19 published, in print, printed, in circulation, circulating, in the air, current, in the news, in the open, open, public, made public, revealed, disclosed, exposed, announced, declared, proclaimed, ventilated, aired, communicated, disseminated, distributed, circularized, spread around (*or* about), broadcast, on the air, televised

20 well-known, widely known, on everyone's lips, in the headlines, in the public eye, celebrated, renowned, famed, famous, popular, infamous, notorious, crying, flagrant, blatant, glaring, sensational, manifest

21 publishing, declaratory, notificatory

ADVERBS

22 publicly, openly, blatantly, (out) in the open, out front, in open court, with open doors, in full view, on stage, in the public eye, for all to see, in the limelight

741 News

NOUNS

1 news, breaking news, hard news, straight news, facts, information, intelligence, current affairs, journalism, print journalism, electronic journalism, Fourth Estate, public relations (PR)

▶ *692 Communications; 740 Publication*

2 news event, news happening, news account, eyewitness account, press conference, news conference

3 reporting, news reporting, reportage, news gathering, coverage, live coverage, newscasting, sportscasting, newspapering, investigative reporting, in-depth reporting, political reporting, parliamentary reporting, interpretive reporting, analytical journalism, objective reporting, scoop, exclusive, spoiler, legwork (Inf), muckraking (Inf), doorstopping (Inf), knee-jerk journalism (Inf)

4 journalist, broadcast journalist, news reporter, reporter, cub reporter, newspaperman (*or* -woman), newsman (*or* -woman), newshound, journo (Inf), newscaster, news staff, news crew, news pool, news photographer, news cameraman (*or* -woman), news camera crew, sports reporter, sportscaster, fashion reporter, freelance reporter, freelance writer, correspondent, foreign correspondent, lobby correspondent, columnist, gossip columnist, critic, chequebook journalism, hack, hackette, scandalmonger, muckraker, leader writer, editor, gatekeeper (US), managing editor, subeditor, foreign editor, sports editor, anchorman (*or* -woman), anchorperson, newsreader, news commentator, news bureau chief, press secretary, press officer, press agent, public relations practitioner, spokesman (*or* -woman)

5 mass communication, mass media, news organization, news outlet, news media, print media, electronic media, press, quality press, tabloid press, popular press, yellow press, gutter press, newspaper, broadsheet, heavy, scandal sheet, popular newspaper, national newspaper, provincial newspaper, local newspaper, Sunday newspaper, weekly newspaper, special edition, special issue, extra, newsmagazine, colour supplement

6 radio news, television news, newscast, sportscast, evening news, 6 o'clock news, 10 o'clock news, documentary, newsreel

7 press agency, news agency, news service, wire service, syndicate, Reuters, Press Association, Associated Press, United Press International, Agence France Presse

8 newsroom, press room, news desk, sports desk, press office, copy desk

9 news story, news article, news item, news report, news review, running story, feature story, feature article, editorial, leader, column, opinion column, gossip column, humour column, news programme, latest news, news update, news brief, news flash, news bulletin, scoop, exclusive, extra, news dispatch, news release, press release, press notice, hand out, hard news, straight news, fresh news, breaking news, hot news (Inf), feature news, news analysis, news style, media hype, journalese (Inf), Timese (US inf)

10 copy, feature copy, time copy (US), evergreen copy (US), subbed copy, take

11 news source, newsstand, newsdealer (US), news stall, newsagent, news vendor, newsboy (*or* -girl), newsie (US), newsletter, newssheet, newsprint, news beat

12 headline, head, by-line, banner head, masthead, flag

VERBS

13 report, broadcast, transmit, document, cover, disclose, break, issue, dispatch, scoop, publish, publicize, circulate, interview, write, freelance, edit, subedit, sub (Inf), syndicate

ADJECTIVES

14 journalistic, reportorial, reportable, editorial, newsworthy, newsy, full of news, informative, reported, going the rounds, hot off the press

ADVERBS

15 journalistically, reportorially, reportedly, editorially, informatively, as reported, as stated

742 Sign

I have known many an instance of a man writing a letter and forgetting to sign his name, but this is the only instance I have ever known of a man signing his name and forgetting to write the letter. Henry Ward Beecher, congregational minister, said on receiving a note containing only the word 'Fool'.

NOUNS

1 **sign**, symbol, signification, meaning, connotation, representation, signal, indicator, indication, pointing out, identification sign, signature, autograph, mark, 'X', fingerprint, name tag, directional sign, signpost, roadsign, motorway sign, highway sign (US), banner, poster, placard, protest sign, 'for sale' sign, warning sign, 'no parking' sign, 'no trespassing' sign, danger sign, rallying symbol, fiery cross, political symbol, emblem, eagle, hammer and sickle, sun, swastika, religious symbol, sacred symbol, cross, crescent, mandala, magic symbol, talisman, mojo (US), conventional symbol, image, token, letter, sure sign, evidence, telltale sign, omen, sign of the times, identifying sign, brand, trademark, hallmark, imprint, track, trail, piste, condensation trail, signs, traces, scent, clue, cue, key, lead, marker, weather sign, dark clouds, falling leaves, thunder and lightning, sign of illness, symptom, syndrome, fever, pain, dizziness, nausea, secret symbol, secret sign, shibboleth, high sign, countersign, password, cipher, code, picture writing, hieroglyphics, hieroglyph, rune, gypsy signs, scout signs, musical notation, mathematical notation, plus sign, minus sign, multiplication sign, division sign, equal (*or* equals) sign, decimal point, symbol list, sigla

▶ *18 Music; 27 Mathematics; 220 List; 319 Transport; 693 Information; 694 Meaning; 717 Representation; 719 Interpretation; 737 Secrecy; 738 Display; 743 Identification*

2 **symbolism**, symbology, symbolization, semiotics, semiology, symptomatology, iconology, iconography

3 **gesture**, gesticulation, body language, sign language, signing, dactylology, deaf-and-dumb language, ticktack, baseball sign (US), kinesics, demeanour, look, beckoning look, come-hither look, twinkle, glance, smile, blush, ogle, leer, wink, fluttering eyelashes, raised eyebrows, tic, twitch, frown, scowl, pout, *moue* (Fr), pursed lips, grimace, clenched jaw, clenched teeth, arms akimbo, stuck-out tongue, nod of the head, shake of the head, laugh, cheer, hiss, sigh, moan, hoot, boo, whistle, catcall, hand signal, fist, clenched fist, wringing hands, hands on hips, hands in pockets, praying gesture, tearing one's hair, pointing, point, wave, hat waving, flag waving, V-sign, two-finger gesture, middle-finger gesture, wagging forefinger, drumming fingers, clapping, applause, touch, handshake, grip, shoulder clasping, head patting, bottom patting, bottom pinching, poking someone in the ribs, hug, nudge, push, shove, slap, tapping foot, stamping foot, kick, kick under the table, crossed legs, folded arms, wolf whistle (Inf), raspberry (Inf), Bronx cheer (US inf), Harvey Smith salute (Inf), footsie (Inf), goose (Inf)

▶ *48 Baseball; 300 Motion; 331 Impulsion; 597 Joy; 598 Happiness; 600 Rejoicing; 601 Celebration; 602 Sorrow; 606 Dissatisfaction; 625 Grumpiness; 626 Sullenness*

4 **signal**, message, time signal, pips, telegraph signal, Morse code, heliograph, semaphore, wigwag flag, signal lamp, fire, watch fire, smoke signal, danger signal, warning signal, warning flag, red flag, signal lamp (*or* light), traffic light (*or* signal), green light, go light, red light, stop light, amber light, caution light, warning light, beacon, beacon fire, balefire, flashing light, lighthouse beacon, railway signal, Belisha beacon, distress signal, SOS, rocket, signal rocket, flare, Very light, Very pistol, minute gun, warning sound, horn, hooter, foghorn, starter's gun, whistle, referee's whistle, police whistle, alarm, fire alarm, burglar alarm, car alarm, alarm clock, siren, police siren, ambulance siren, fire-engine siren, air-raid siren, all-clear siren, alarm bell, Lutine bell, summoning sound, telephone ring, bleep, bleeper, door buzzer, door knocker, doorbell, bell, church bell, Angelus bell, sacring bell, dinner bell, dinner gong, passing knell, knell, muffled drum, manifestation, signalling, alarum (Lit)

▶ *359 Preservation; 437 Fuel; 493 Heat; 692 Communications*

5 **indicator**, guide, index, gauge, thermometer, barometer, speedometer, mileometer, odometer (US), cynosure, pointer, finger, index finger, forefinger, arm, needle, arrow, cursor, time indicator, timekeeper, clock, watch, stopwatch, hour hand, minute hand, second hand, direction indicator, turn indicator, blinker, winker, compass, compass needle, magnetic needle, radar, weather vane, weathercock, windsock, wind sleeve, white line, Catseye™, signpost, roadsign, motorway sign, highway sign (US), guidepost, crossroad sign, finger post, milepost, milestone, landmark, benchmark, earthwork, cairn, monument, sea mark, lighthouse, lightship, buoy, star, guiding star, lodestar, North Star, Pole Star, Polaris, Southern Cross, depth indicator, water line, watermark, tidemark, load line, Plimsoll line, triangulation point

▶ *26 Measurement; 281 Timekeeping*

6 **word**, catchword, slogan, watchword, shibboleth, call, cry, hue and cry, shout, hail, proclamation, publication, announcement, marriage banns, invitation, summons, call to prayer, church bell, muezzin's call, command, word of command, rallying cry, war cry, battle cry, rebel yell (US), call to arms, bugle call, trumpet call, fanfare, sennet, flourish, reveille, assemble, charge, advance, rally, tattoo, retreat, lights out, last post, taps (US), drumbeat, cry for help, distress call, SOS, Mayday, Hey rube! (US inf)

▶ *392 Help; 507 Loudness; 585 War; 740 Publication; 741 News*

7 **punctuation**, punctuation mark, point, stop, full stop, period, comma, colon, semicolon, quotation mark, inverted comma, turned comma, quotes (Inf), single quotes, double quotes, exclamation mark, question mark, query, interrobang, apostrophe, parentheses, brackets, square brackets, braces, hyphen, dash, en rule, em rule, blank, ellipsis, swung dash, reference mark, asterisk, star, asterism, cross-reference mark, dagger, obelus, solidus, stroke, virgule, omission mark, caret, accent, grave accent, acute accent, circumflex, breve, umlaut, tilde, cedilla, háček, hamse, dieresis, diacritical

mark, diacritic, macron, vowel point, indention, paragraph, printing mark, hand, fist, index, underlining

► *269 Brevity; 725 Clarity*

8 **signer**, autographer, signatory, orthologist, symbolist, symbologist, symbolizer, iconographer, semiologist, semiotician, iconologist, letterer, sign-maker, imprinter, marker, communicator, gesturer, gesticulator, telegraph operator, telegrapher, telegraphist, telegraph messenger, heliographer, telecommunicator, signaller, timekeeper, lighthouse operator, shouter, hailer, proclaimer, messenger, publisher, announcer, inviter, summoner, bell-ringer, muezzin, commander, bugler, trumpeter, alarmist, referee, policeman (*or* policewoman), fireman, air-raid warden

► *692 Communications; 739 Disclosure; 740 Publication*

VERBS

9 **use signs**, sign, sign one's name, put one's signature to, sign on the dotted line, autograph, initial, countersign, use symbols, signal, gesture, indicate, point to, point out, signpost, mark, mark the way, point the way, show the way, direct, guide, blaze, demarcate, mark out, chalk out, lay out, delineate, fingerprint, carry a protest sign, burn a cross, give someone a secret sign, give a password, code, put the finger on (US inf), finger (US inf)

10 **signify**, represent, symbolize, stand for, mean, denote, connote, imply, indicate, suggest, intimate, hint at, give evidence of, show signs of, symptomize, characterize, bear the marks of, bear the stamp of, smack of, smell of, witness to, bear witness to, typify, betoken, disclose, reveal, signalize, emphasize, highlight, blazon

11 **gesture**, use body language, gesture, motion, gesticulate, attract notice, pantomime, mime, mimic, imitate, use sign language, sign, suit the action to the word, give a look, shrug, nod one's head, shake one's head, beckon, gaze, glance, look (*or* speak) volumes, ogle, leer, look daggers (at), wink, flutter (*or* bat) one's eyelashes, raise one's eyebrows, frown, scowl, pout, *moue* (Fr), purse one's lips, grimace, show anger, curl one's lip, snap, bite, clench one's jaw, clench one's teeth, grit one's teeth, gnash one's teeth, stick out one's tongue, pull faces, twinkle, smile, laugh, hiss, sigh, moan, hoot, boo, whistle, give a catcall, give a hand-signal, clench one's fist, wring one's hands, raise one's hand, wave, chop the air, flag down, wave to, wave on, wave by, wave through, wave one's hat, tear one's hair, point, point one's finger, point at (*or* to), give the V-sign, drum one's fingers, clap, applaud, hold out one's hand, salute, greet, squeeze someone's hand, clasp someone's shoulder, clap someone on the back, pat someone's head, pat someone's bottom, pinch someone's bottom, poke someone in the ribs, hug, nudge, pat, stroke, caress, jog, push, shove, poke, prod, slap, tap one's foot, stamp, stomp, kick, shuffle, scrape one's feet, paw the ground, cross one's legs, fold one's arms, give a wolf whistle (Inf), play footsie (Inf), blow a raspberry (Inf), cock a snook (Inf), goose someone (Inf)

12 **signal**, make a signal, hang out a signal, send a signal, semaphore, wigwag, send smoke signals, exchange signals, communicate, publish, inform, announce, declare, herald, hail, proclaim, call, cry, shout, summon, command, call to prayer, send a message, tap out a message, use Morse code, call for help, send out a distress call, send an SOS, warn, fire a warning shot, alert, honk, whistle, set off an alarm, raise the alarm, ring the church bells, sound the trumpets, beat the drum, beat a retreat

► *692 Communications; 740 Publication*

13 **punctuate**, abbreviate, accent, indent, parenthesize, underline, italicize, underscore, stress, emphasize, dot, dash, hyphenate, cross, cross out, obelize, asterisk, dot one's i's and cross one's t's, put in quotes (Inf)

ADJECTIVES

14 **signifying**, indicative, indicatory, significative, identifying, directional, pointing, connotative, denotative, signalizing, disclosing, revealing, explanatory, betraying, giving away, telltale, signalling, symbolic, symbolical, symbolistic, symbological, semiotic, semiological, symptomatic, symptomatological, diagnostic, expressive, implicative, demonstrative, meaningful, suggestive, suggesting, representative, representing, evidential, nominal, diagrammatic, typical, characteristic, individual, special, interpretive, prophetic, presageful, ominous

15 **gestural**, gesticulative, dactylographic, pantomimic, signing, thumbing, looking, glancing, smiling, winking, grimacing, laughing, sighing, moaning, whistling, clapping, patting, pushing, slapping, stamping

16 **signalling**, telegraphic, heliographic(al), semaphoric(al), flashing, warning, summoning, ringing, bell-ringing, bleeping, shouting, hailing, proclaiming, publishing, announcing, inviting, calling, commanding

17 **punctuated**, quoted, hyphenated, referenced, cross-referenced, accented, abbreviated, apostrophized, indented, paragraphed, underlined, italicized

ADVERBS

18 **indicatively**, revealingly, symptomatically, diagnostically, expressively, with expression, demonstratively, meaningfully, signficantly, with meaning, suggestively, in a suggestive manner, evidentially, by this token, in token of, representatively, symbolically, as a symbol, symbolistically, semiologically, in pantomime, in sign language, diagrammatically, typically, characteristically, individually, specially, interpretively, prophetically, as a sign, ominously, telegraphically, semaphorically

743 Identification

I would venture to guess that Anon, who wrote so many poems without signing them, was often a woman. Virginia Woolf.

NOUNS

1 **identification**, recognition, detection, distinguishing, differentiation, diagnosis, indicating, indication, pointing out, pinpointing, designation, naming, labelling, characterization, characteristic, form, shape, outline, size, colour, colouring, mannerism, trait, denomination, classifying, classification, analysis, categorization, cataloguing, establishing, establishment, authentication, verification, substantiation, corroboration

► *35 Medicine; 160 Form; 163 Outline; 194 Number; 707 Affirmation; 717 Representation; 721 Description*

2 **identity**, particularity, individuality, distinctiveness, uniqueness, personality, self, name

► *99 Essence*

3 means of identification, ID, name, title, letters after one's name, name and address, signature, autograph, paraph, initials, mark, 'X', monogram, identification papers, identity (*or* ID) card, passport, visa, letter of introduction, permit, credentials, endorsement, fingerprint, thumbprint, footprint, dental record, genetic fingerprinting, DNA fingerprinting, photograph, passport photograph, Identikit™, identity number, National Insurance number, Social Security number (US), student number, military service number, driving licence number, bank-account number, telephone number, credit-card number, numberplate registration number, license plate number (US), personalized numberplate, ISBN (International Standard Book Number), call sign, call letters (US), secret word, password, 'open sesame,' watchword, token, countersign, shibboleth, secret signal, dactylography (US), trademark, brand, brand name, tradename, copyright, logo, logotype, hallmark, cachet, official stamp, seal, great seal, privy seal, signet, sigil, superscription, impress (*or* impression), imprint, watermark, letterhead, masthead, colophon, bookplate, ex-libris, marque, model, earmark, caste mark, tattoo, birthmark, strawberry mark, blemish, scar, stigma, label, luggage label, tie-on label, clothes marking, prisoner's broad arrow, clothes label, tag, tally, tessera, counter, chip, adhesive label, sticker, badge, emblem, name badge, nametape, plate, nameplate, brass plate, card, visiting card, business card, place card, sign, signboard, trade sign, fascia, inn sign, pub sign, tavern's bush, barber's striped pole, pawnshop's three balls, certificate, birth certificate, marriage certificate, death certificate, ticket, airline ticket, train ticket, bus ticket, theatre ticket, cinema ticket, raffle ticket, cloakroom ticket, ticket counterfoil, ticket stub (US), chit, chitty, docket, invoice, bill, bill of lading, waybill, copy, duplicate, dog tag (US inf)

► *575 Title; 737 Secrecy; 742 Sign*

4 insignia, badge, markings, military markings, badge of sovereignty, throne, sceptre, orb, crown, regalia, robes of office, badge of office, chain of office, mark of authority, sword of state, gavel, mace, staff, pastoral staff, wand, baton, keys, military insignia, badge of rank, spread eagle (US), star, bar, stripe, chevron, wings, epaulette, brassard (*or* brassart), aiguillette, cockade, hackle, sash, medal, Congressional Medal of Honor (US), ribbon, decoration, cross, Victoria Cross (VC), George Cross, Iron Cross, *Croix de Guerre* (Fr), badge of merit, victory laurels, garland, wreath, bays, chaplet, trophy, gold medal, silver medal, bronze medal, silver cup, silver plate, rosette, blue ribbon, school letter (US), pip (Inf), gong (Inf), chicken (US inf), hash mark (US inf), Hershey bar (US inf)

► *575 Title; 794 Prize*

5 uniform, military uniform, army uniform, navy uniform, air force uniform, marine's uniform, regimentals, school uniform, sports outfit, sports uniform (US), baseball uniform (US), nurse's uniform, Boy Scout uniform, chauffeur's uniform, livery, stable colours, jockey's colours, national dress, tartan, kilt, stetson, lederhosen, prison clothes, mourning clothes, widow's weeds, crepe, black dress, black armband, cardinal's cap, dunce's cap, cap and gown, mortarboard, tie, club tie, old school tie, school ring (US), class ring (US), signet ring, lapel pin, sphragistics

► *551 Dress; 553 Fashion*

6 national emblem, national device, American spread eagle, British lion and unicorn, English rose, Scottish thistle, Welsh leek, Welsh daffodil, Irish shamrock, Canadian maple leaf, French fleur-de-lis, Russian bear, Soviet hammer and sickle, Japanese rising sun, Turkish crescent and star, Swiss cross, Nazi swastika, fylfot, Roman eagle

► *85 Countries*

7 flag, standard, banner, ensign, bunting, colours, national colours, national flag, Stars and Stripes, Star-Spangled Banner, Old Glory, the red, white, and blue, jack, Union Jack, Union flag, St Andrew's cross, St George's cross, St Patrick's cross, Tricolour, *drapeau tricolore* (Fr), Confederate flag, Stars and Bars, red flag, regimental colours, ship's colours, King's (*or* Queen's) Colour, Red Ensign, White Ensign, Blue Ensign, pilot jack, merchant jack, blue peter, flag of convenience, pirate flag, skull and crossbones, black flag, Jolly Roger, military flag, vexillum, labarum, gonfalon, guidon, oriflamme, bannerette (*or* banneret), streamer, pennon, banderole, bannerol, pennant, swallowtail, burgee, quarantine flag, yellow flag, flag of truce, flag of surrender, white flag, flagpole, flagstaff, canton, hoist, fly, grommet, halyard, heading, sleeve, truck, clip, red duster (Inf)

8 heraldic device, armory, blazonry, blazon, armorial bearings, coat of arms, arms, achievement, hatchment, shield, escutcheon (*or* scutcheon), crest, torse, wreath, helmet, crown, coronet, mantling, garland, chaplet, bandeau, lambrequin, supporters, motto, field, quarter, rustre, tresure, dexter, bar, bar sinister, chief, base, charge, device, bearing, ordinary, label, pale, bend, bend sinister, chevron, pile, saltire, cross, canton, bordure, lozenge, fusil, gyron, flanch, fret, marshalling, quartering, impaling, impalement, dimidiation, differencing, difference, fesse point, honour point, nombril point, animal charge, lion, lion rampant, lion couchant, antelope, bear and ragged staff, unicorn, griffin, cockatrice, eagle, spread eagle, falcon, martlet, crescent, mullet, annulet, floral charge, fleur-de-lis, Tudor rose, cinquefoil, trefoil, planta genista, badge, rebus, baton, portcullis, heraldic tincture, gules, azure, vert, sable, purpore, tenne, murrey, metal, or, argent, fur, ermine, ermines, erminites, erminois, pean, vair, potent

9 herald, heraldist, heraldic official, herald extraordinary, Earl Marshal, king of arms, Clarenceux, Lyon King of Arms, Lord Lyon, pursuivant, Rouge Croix, Rouge Dragon, heraldic register, Roll of Arms, College of Arms, College of Heralds

VERBS

10 identify, recognize, detect, distinguish, differentiate, diagnose, analyse, indicate, show, exhibit, point out, pinpoint, establish, authenticate, verify, substantiate, corroborate, designate, name, give a name to, specify, characterize, hallmark, earmark, label, docket, tag, tab, keep tabs on, classify, categorize, catalogue, reference, number, letter, page, paginate, record, photograph, picture, fingerprint, register, ticket, delimit, limit, note, annotate, mark, put a mark on, underline, underscore, tick, check (US), tick off, check off (US), mark off, etch, engrave, imprint, tattoo, pierce, notch, chalk, chalk up, scar, disfigure, blaze, brand, burn in, stamp, seal, punch, impress, emboss, overprint, emblazon, blazon, impale, dimidiate, quarter, difference, marshal, charge

11 **identify oneself**, sign, ratify, countersign, endorse, autograph, write one's signature, write one's name, inscribe, put one's hand to, subscribe, undersign, initial, paraph, put one's mark on, put one's cross on, be identified, leave fingerprints, leave footprints, have a birthmark, be conspicuous, stand out, stick out

ADJECTIVES

12 **identified**, recognized, established, authenticated, verified, substantiated, corroborated, identifiable, recognizable, shown, shown up, known, known by, known as, designated, denoted, named, labelled, tagged, marked, hallmarked, trademarked, earmarked, characterized, classified, categorized, referenced, catalogued, indexed, lettered, numbered, patterned, signed, signatory, symbolical, sigillary, titled, imprinted, fingerprinted, photographed, pictured, stigmatized, scarred, branded, tattooed

13 **heraldic**, emblematic, crested, armorial, blazoned, emblazoned, paly, barry, dexter, sinister, gules, azure, vert, purpure, sable, tenne, murrey, or, argent, ermine, fleury, seme, pomme, rampant, gardant, regardant, couchant, statant, sejant, passant

ADVERBS

14 **identifiably**, indicatively, symbolically, as a symbol, emblematically, heraldically

744 Record

What is a diary as a rule? A document useful to the person who keeps it, dull to the contemporary who reads it, invaluable to the student, centuries afterwards, who treasures it! Ellen Terry.

NOUNS

1 **record**, recording, documentation, document, form, documents, papers, chronicle, history, historical record, historical documents, annals, archives, account, narrative, memoir, autobiography, biography, biographical record, case history, obituary, personal history, curriculum vitae (CV), vita (US), résumé, correspondence, memorabilia, cutting, press cutting, visual record, photograph, picture, snapshot, portrait, sketch, representation, list, inventory, waiting list, jury list, file, dossier, portfolio, personal file, public record, public file, police record, criminal record, official record, official publication, Congressional Record (US), Hansard, government papers, recorded material, recorded proceedings, transactions, minutes, report, official report, company report, annual report, school report, report card, office memorandum, memo, reminder, note, entry, item, return, income-tax return, invoice, bill, check (US), statement, receipt, voucher, docket, counterfoil, stub, cheque stub, tally, scoresheet, scoreboard

► *3 History; 220 List; 253 Security; 462 Memory; 693 Information; 716 Evidence; 717 Representation; 721 Description; 743 Identification*

2 **certificate**, credential, charter, authorization, birth certificate, marriage certificate, death certificate, passport, ID (identification), diploma, muniments, deed, title, title deed, ownership papers, car papers, registration document, insurance papers, insurance certificate, ticket, warranty, testimonial, sworn statement, affidavit, notarized statement, deposition, daybook

3 **notes**, school notes, annotations, margin notes, marginalia, adversaria, jottings, writing

► *719 Interpretation*

4 **inscription**, personal note, signature, autograph, initials, legend, wall writing, graffiti

5 **copy**, photocopy, Xerox™, Xerox™ copy, laser copy, carbon copy, spare copy, duplicate copy, duplicate

6 **record book**, notebook, scrapbook, album, commonplace book, minute book, registry, register, roll, rollbook, directory, address book, logbook, log, diary, journal, calendar, cartulary, tablet, table, notepad, memo pad, scratchpad, jotter, ledger, cashbook, account book, chequebook, catalogue, index, card, index card, microfilm, microfiche, microcard, tape, magnetic tape, computer tape, disk, database, data processing

► *40 Computers; 159 Smallness; 210 Calculation; 789 Accounting*

7 **recording**, phonograph record, gramophone record, record, LP (long-playing record), single, EP (extended-play record), disc, minidisc, CD (compact disc), digital compact cassette, pressing, cassette tape, cassette, tape, magnetic tape, DAT tape, film, motion-picture film, video tape, vid (Inf)

8 **registration**, registry, record-keeping, recording, writing, printing, inscribing, engraving, epigraphy, enrolment, enlistment, empanelment, booking, reservation, entry, double entry, book-keeping, accountancy, accounts, filing, indexing, cataloguing, listing

► *789 Accounting*

9 **recorder**, record-keeper, registrar, chronicler, annalist, archivist, historian, archaeologist, antiquarian, diarist, columnist, journalist, reporter, newsman (*or* newswoman), press photographer, writer, biographer, autobiographer, amanuensis, notary, stenographer, typist, computer operator, keyboarder, scribe, secretary, receptionist, clerk, filing clerk, book-keeper, accountant, petitioner, artist, engraver, draughtsman, photographer, cameraman, scorekeeper, timekeeper

► *3 History; 41 Photography; 741 News*

10 **recording instrument**, photocopier, camera, video camera, camcorder, recorder, tape recorder, tape machine, cassette recorder, electronic listening device, wiretap, bug (Inf), answering machine, video tape recorder, video cassette recorder (VCR), dictaphone, cash register, seismograph, speedometer, gauge, flight recorder, black box, stopwatch

► *26 Measurement; 41 Photography; 281 Timekeeping; 692 Communications*

11 **monument**, memorial, war memorial, memorial arch, victory arch, column, pillar, national monument, tomb of an unknown soldier, tomb, mausoleum, pyramid, shrine, statue, bust, plaque, tablet, slab, memorial inscription, gravestone, tombstone, ancient monument, monolith, obelisk, megalith, dolmen, menhir, cromlech,

cairn, barrow, earthwork, mound, testimonial, cup, trophy, prize, ribbon, medal, decoration, memento, souvenir

▶ *284 Past Time; 462 Memory; 583 Burial; 794 Prize*

12 vestige, trace, track, trail, piste, scent, spoor, mark, print, footprint, footstep, fingermark, tyremark, tidemark, stain, relic, remains

▶ *441 Waste; 548 Blemish; 716 Evidence; 742 Sign*

VERBS

13 record, document, chronicle, log, put (*or* place) on record, put in the minutes, inscribe, register, enrol, file, index, catalogue, tabulate, list, empanel, copy, photocopy, print, store in a database, input, tape, tape-record, video-tape, film, photograph, take a picture, capture on film, preserve for posterity, store in the archives, paint, represent, relate, narrate, recount, recite

▶ *3 History; 693 Information; 717 Representation; 721 Description*

14 inscribe, transcribe, write, write down, commit to writing, put on paper, put (*or* set) down, set down in black and white, enter in a book, take minutes, make notes, note, note down, take down, mark down, jot, jot down, engrave, cut, incise, etch, carve

▶ *17 Literature*

15 register, enter, docket, enter names, tick off names, put on the list, put on the waiting list, enrol, enlist, empanel, book, reserve, list, itemize, tabulate, score, tally, notch up (Inf)

▶ *220 List*

ADJECTIVES

16 recorded, on record, in the minutes, documented, chronicled, logged, noted, inscribed, written down, on paper, in black and white, printed, entered, registered, enrolled, on the books, in the book, filed, in the file, indexed, in the index, listed, on the list, on the waiting list, copied, photographed, photocopied, input, in the database, taped, on tape, video-taped, filmed, on film, official, documentary

▶ *220 List; 693 Information*

ADVERBS

17 on the record, in black and white, on paper, officially

745 Maxim

NOUNS

1 maxim, saying, proverb, adage, aphorism, apophthegm (*or* apothegm), words of wisdom, saw, gnome, gnomic formula, oracle, mot, witticism, epigram, epigraph, motto, slogan, catchphrase, catchword, watchword, byword, epithet, tag, moral, axiom, truth, truism, banality, cliché, platitude, commonplace, bromide, hackneyed phrase, stock phrase, precept, order, dictum, formula, mantra, theorem, rule, law, observation, principle, old chestnut (Inf)

▶ *269 Brevity; 458 Wisdom; 599 Humour; 713 Advice*

ADJECTIVES

2 proverbial, aphoristic, gnomic, epigrammatic, axiomatic, banal, clichéd, platitudinous, commonplace, trite, hackneyed, stock, stereotyped, sententious, moralistic, moralizing, preceptive, witty, pithy, enigmatic, oracular

VERBS

3 aphorize, epigrammatize, coin a phrase, proverb, moralize, pronounce, utter, theorize, formulate, observe, propose, remark

ADVERBS

4 proverbially, aphoristically, epigrammatically, axiomatically, platitudinously, as they say, as the saying goes, to coin a phrase, in a nutshell

Negotiations and Transactions

746 Negotiation

Let us never negotiate out of fear, but let us never fear to negotiate. John Fitzgerald Kennedy.

NOUNS

1 **negotiation**, negotiations, mediation, arbitration, conciliation, compromising, compromise, exchange, discussions, bargaining, collective bargaining, hard bargaining, barter, bartering, horse-trading, trade-off, haggling, wrangling, making terms, treaty-making, diplomacy, communication, intercommunication, dealing (Inf), an offer one can't refuse (Inf)

▶ *692 Communications; 754 Compromise; 776 Trade*

2 **basis for negotiations**, frame of reference, contract, terms, written terms, set of terms, conditions, part of the bargain, offer, provision, article, articles of agreement, requirement, qualification, clause, essential clause, *sine qua non* (L), escape clause, let-out clause, proviso, stipulation, concession, reservation, strings, small print

▶ *135 Requirement; 136 Qualification; 752 Offer; 755 Contract*

3 **discussion**, round-table discussion, conference, teleconference, videoconference, bargaining session, debate, high-level talks, summit meeting, summit conference, summit, cabinet meeting, moot, exchange of views, powwow (Inf), argy-bargy (Inf)

▶ *734 Conversation*

4 **negotiator**, mediator, intermediary, intercessor, go-between, diplomat (*or* diplomatist), ambassador, chargé d'affaires, matchmaker, link, broker, arbitrator, lawyer, solicitor, middleman, stockbroker, ACAS (Advisory Conciliation and Arbitration Service

▶ *12 Government and Politics; 16 Law*

VERBS

5 **negotiate**, mediate, arbitrate, seek agreement, seek accord, settle, conciliate, cooperate, compromise, exchange, exchange views, discuss, communicate, intercommunicate, bargain, do collective bargaining, do hard bargaining, barter, horse trade, trade off, trade, haggle, wrangle, come to terms, make terms, make conditions, stipulate, make concessions, add strings, read the small print, use diplomacy, treat (Lit), make a treaty, hold a conference, attend a conference, have a summit meeting, hold a summit, confer, hold talks, get round the table, deliberate, have a discussion, put heads together, transact business, do business, do transactions, work at reaching an agreement, make overtures, test the ground, offer a solution, work out a formula, work something out, get something through, deal (Inf), make (*or* do) a deal (Inf), powwow (Inf), argy-bargy (Inf)

6 **make conditions**, impose conditions, make proposals, make a bid, make demands, stipulate, put in clauses, leave a loophole, add an escape clause, write in a let-out clause, leave the options open, hedge one's bets

7 **act as a go-between**, broker, matchmake, act as a middleman, act as a link, stand in for, replace, proxy

ADJECTIVES

8 **negotiated**, mediated, arbitrated, negotiable, practicable, practical, feasible, workable, pragmatic, transferable, conveyable, exchangeable, trade-off, subject to terms, conditional, provisional, provisory, stipulatory, concessionary, conciliatory, compromising, collective, haggling, wrangling, treaty-making, diplomatic, communicative, intercommunicative

ADVERBS

9 **feasibly**, pragmatically, conditionally, under certain conditions, provisionally, with provisions, conciliatorily, compromisingly, as a compromise, as a trade-off, collectively, diplomatically, in diplomatic language, like a diplomat, communicatively

747 Cooperation

NOUNS

1 **cooperation**, collaboration, coaction, concurrence, synergy, synergism, cooperativeness, assistance, support, backup, helpfulness, help

▶ *392 Help; 413 Support*

2 **fellowship**, comradeship, friendship, sodality, solidarity, togetherness, sympathy, fellow feeling, fraternalism, fraternity, sorority, clanship, freemasonry, community spirit, team spirit, morale, *esprit de corps* (Fr), concord, concordance, harmony, accord, consensus, concurrence, agreement, bipartisanship

▶ *569 Friendship; 750 Agreement*

3 **mutual relationship**, correlation, interaction, symbiosis, synergy, sharing, participation, mutualism, mutualness, mutuality, reciprocity, interplay, mutual assistance, coadjuvancy, networking, aiding and abetting,

logrolling (US), compromise, concession, give-and-take, exchanging favours, backscratching (Inf)

▶ *110 Reciprocity; 654 Sociability; 754 Compromise*

4 joint operation, combined operation, common endeavour, joint effort (*or* venture), combined effort, concerted effort, communal effort, pulling together, joining of forces, pooling of resources, teamwork, working together, joint action, concerted action, collective action, united action, mass action, united front, cooperative enterprise, cooperative, collective, community, commune

▶ *13 Economics; 340 Action; 576 Work; 764 Sharing*

5 joint control, coagency, coadministration, comanagement, cochairmanship, co-directorship, partnership, copartnership, copartnery, codetermination, co-ownership, collegialism, federalism, federation, confederation, confederacy, cahoots (US inf)

▶ *579 Management*

6 movement, communalism, collectivism, socialism, communism, ecumenicalism (*or* ecumenicism)

▶ *7 Religion; 12 Government and Politics*

7 association, alliance, alignment, affiliation, combination, combine, cartel, consortium, union, unification, coalition, fusion, merging, merger, coalescence, coadunation, amalgamation, consolidation, incorporation, integration, hook-up (Inf), tie-up (Inf), tie-in (Inf)

8 conferring, conference, teleconferencing, consultation, connivance, collusion, complicity, conspiracy

▶ *484 Plan*

9 team, team mates, partners, co-workers, colleagues, associates, fellows, collaborators, coauthors, community, congregation, brotherhood, fraternity, confraternity, sisterhood, sorority, duet, duumvirate, trio, triumvirate, troika, quartet, quintet, sextet, septet, octet, nonet, league, federation, confederation

▶ *18 Music*

10 cooperator, helper, assistant, partner, co-worker, ally, fellow, coadjutor, conspirator, collaborator, quisling

VERBS

11 cooperate, collaborate, concur, coact, help, assist, support, play ball (Inf)

▶ *392 Help; 413 Support*

12 reciprocate, respond, interrelate, interact, interplay, mesh, lend oneself, requite, repay, give and take, return the compliment, aid and abet, compromise

▶ *110 Reciprocity; 754 Compromise*

13 work together, act in concert, work as a team, pitch in, rally round, show willing, pull together, hang together, keep together, hold together, stand together, put heads together, make common cause, unite efforts, sail (*or* row) in the same boat (US), stand shoulder to shoulder, stand or fall together, sink or swim together, contribute, join in, participate, share, throw in together (US inf)

▶ *576 Work; 636 Willingness; 654 Sociability*

14 join with, join up with, join hands with, go in with, do business with, get together with, team up with, ally (oneself) with, align (oneself) with, range (oneself) with, line up with, cast in one's lot with, join one's fortunes to, get together, band together, club together, gang together, join forces, pool resources, pool interests, merge with, go into partnership, go partners (Inf), gang up with (Inf), swing in with (US inf), stand in with (US inf), throw in with (US inf), string along with (Inf)

15 concur, go along with, harmonize, concert, collude, connive, conspire, be in cahoots (Inf)

▶ *750 Agreement*

16 join, associate, ally, affiliate, combine, amalgamate, unite, fuse, merge, coalesce, consolidate, federate, confederate, hook up (Inf), tie up (Inf), tie in (Inf)

ADJECTIVES

17 cooperative, cooperating, cooperant, collaborative, coactive, coacting, concurrent, synergetic(al), synergistic(al), synergic(al), coadjutant, coadjuvant, symbiotic(al), helpful, obliging, willing, accommodating, supportive, contributory, participatory

▶ *388 Submission; 392 Help; 413 Support; 636 Willingness*

18 joint, shared, combined, collective, concerted, united, common, communal, pooled, mutual, reciprocal, correlational, interrelating, interactive, communalist(ic), collectivist(ic), communist, socialist, ecumenical

▶ *110 Reciprocity; 764 Sharing*

19 associating, allied, affiliated, comradely, fraternal, friendly, concordant, harmonious, *en rapport* (Fr), concurring, commensal, uncompetitive, noncompetitive, conniving, collusive, conspiratorial, hand-in-glove, in cahoots (Inf)

▶ *750 Agreement*

ADVERBS

20 cooperatively, cooperatingly, collaboratively, coactively, concurrently, synergistically, synergetically, jointly, together, collectively, combinedly, conjointly, concertedly, communally, harmoniously, concordantly, as one, with one accord, with one voice, unanimously, hand in glove, shoulder to shoulder, hand in hand, back to back, all for one, one for all

21 in cooperation, in collaboration, in conjunction, in concert, in tandem, in collusion, in league, in cahoots (Inf)

PREPOSITIONS

22 with, together with, jointly with, in cooperation with, in collaboration with, in conjunction with, in concert with, in association with

748 Mediation

Your 'If' is the only peace-maker; much virtue in 'If'. William Shakespeare.

VERBS

1 mediate, intermediate, negotiate, arbitrate, referee, umpire, judge, officiate, find agreement, settle differences, reconcile, conciliate, negotiate peace, pacify, propitiate, moderate, intercede, be a go-between, put oneself between, jump in the middle of, intervene, interpose, step in, bring together, bring to the table, act as a pander for, act as agent for, run messages for, offer one's intercession, proffer one's good offices, meddle, intermeddle, interfere, stick one's nose in (Inf)

▶ *342 Activity; 464 Judgment; 685 Moderation; 713 Advice; 749 Pacification*

NOUNS

2 **mediation**, intermediation, negotiation, arbitration, give-and-take, coming together, conciliation, reconciliation, diplomacy, gunboat diplomacy, statesmanship, judgment, umpirage, pacification, propitiation, moderation, intervention, interposition, intercession, stepping-in, troubleshooting, good offices, meddling, intermeddling

▶ *342 Activity; 464 Judgment; 685 Moderation; 713 Advice; 749 Pacification*

3 **mediator**, intermediary, intermediator, intercessor, interceder, negotiator, arbiter, arbitrator, referee, umpire, judge, diplomat, diplomatist, statesman, pacifier, propitiator, peacemaker, dove, appeaser, conciliator, moderator, moderating influence, troubleshooter, common friend, middleman, go-between, liaison, third party, matchmaker, marriage broker, pander, panderer, Pandarus, adviser, counsellor, marriage adviser, marriage counsellor, marriage guidance counsellor, Advisory Conciliation and Arbitration Service (ACAS), meddler

▶ *342 Activity; 464 Judgment; 685 Moderation*

4 **representative**, rep, delegate, spokesman, spokeswoman, spokesperson, mouthpiece, agent, publicist, public relations officer, press agent, ombudsman, attorney, accountant, consultant, adviser, counsellor, pleader, propitiator, peacemaker

▶ *713 Advice*

5 **conference**, peace conference, parley, talks

▶ *734 Conversation*

ADJECTIVES

6 **mediatory**, mediatorial, arbitral, arbitrational, diplomatic, intercessory, intercessional, pacificatory, propitiatory, conciliatory, advisory

▶ *464 Judgment; 713 Advice; 749 Pacification*

ADVERBS

7 **mediatorially**, mediately, intermediately, conciliatorily, diplomatically, judgmentally

749 Pacification

Since wars begin in the minds of men, it is in the minds of men that the defences of peace must be constructed. Anonymous.

NOUNS

1 **pacification**, pacifying, peacemaking, irenics, nonviolence, ahimsa, satyagraha, conciliation, propitiation, appeasement, peace at any price, peace in our time, mollification, moderation, reconciliation, reconcilement, improved relations, détente, rapprochement, accommodation, adjustment, agreement, compromise, composition of differences, mediation, arbitration, good offices, convention, entente, understanding, treaty, peace treaty, nonaggression pact, Strategic Arms Limitation Talks (SALT), SALT I Treaty, Strategic Arms Control Treaty (START), START 2, suspension of hostilities, truce, temporary truce, lull, cessation, armistice, cease-fire, burying the hatchet, imposed peace, forced reconciliation, compulsive cease-fire, moratorium, moratorium on nuclear testing, ban on testing, test ban, comprehensive test ban, disarmament, unilateral disarmament, defence cuts, arms cuts, arms reduction, arms control, reduction of nuclear stockpiles, destruction of weapons, de-escalation of the arms race, freedom from war, Campaign for Nuclear Disarmament (CND), ban-the-bomb movement, peace movement, anti-war movement, anti-Vietnam War movement, the peace process, demobilization, demob, disbanding, nuclear-free zone, peace camp

▶ *226 Stopping; 386 Compulsion; 589 Peace; 685 Moderation; 748 Mediation; 754 Compromise; 755 Contract*

2 **peace offering**, irenicon, dove of peace, olive branch, peace overture, peaceful approach, friendly approach, hand of friendship, outstretched hand, friendliness, flag of truce, white flag, peace pipe, calumet, wergild, blood money, compensation, reparation, atonement, restitution, fair offer, easy terms, plea for peace, amnesty, pardon, full pardon, mercy, forgiveness, leniency, clemency

▶ *463 Forgetfulness; 589 Peace; 649 Forgiveness; 685 Moderation; 807 Atonement*

3 **pacifist**, pacifier, conscientious objector, peace protester, passive resister, CND member, peacemaker, peace negotiator, negotiator, mediator, Sabine women

▶ *589 Peace; 748 Mediation*

VERBS

4 **pacify**, make peace, live in peace, enjoy peace, keep the peace, stay at peace, avoid war, avoid strife, impose peace, give peace to, halt the arms race, hold out the olive branch, hold out the peace pipe, hold out one's hand, return a soft answer, turn the other cheek, coo like a dove, conciliate, propitiate, disarm, reconcile, placate, appease, satisfy, content, make happy, make content, pour oil on troubled waters, put out the fire, douse the flames, allay, ease, alleviate, soothe, take the sting out of, tranquillize, mollify, assuage, calm down, cool one's temper, quell, subdue, smooth over, smooth one's ruffled feathers, compose, pour balm into (*or* on) one's wounds, restore, make well, heal, cure, restore peace, restore harmony, harmonize, win over, bring to terms, resolve problems, settle differences, accommodate, adjust, bridge over, bring together, mediate, show (tender) mercy, grant clemency, grant a truce, grant an armistice, grant peace, give terms

▶ *301 Motionlessness; 393 Repair; 589 Peace; 609 Satisfaction; 649 Forgiveness; 685 Moderation; 748 Mediation*

5 **make peace**, sue for peace, stop fighting, halt hostilities, call it quits, cry quits, break it up, bury the hatchet, let bygones be bygones, forgive and forget, forget grievances, pretend it never happened, make friends, shake hands, shake on it, make it up, kiss and make up, patch up a quarrel, come to an understanding, make a deal, get together, learn to live together, compose differences, compromise, meet halfway, agree, agree to differ, agree to disagree, disarm, lay down one's arms, put down one's gun, sheathe the sword, put up one's sword, beat swords into ploughshares, sign (*or* make *or* call) a truce, suspend hostilities, demilitarize, demobilize, smoke the peace pipe, leash the dogs of war, close the gates of Janus (Lit), cool it (Inf)

▶ *226 Stopping; 463 Forgetfulness; 649 Forgiveness; 754 Compromise; 755 Contract*

ADJECTIVES

6 **pacificatory**, pacifying, conciliatory, placatory, propitiatory, appeasing, irenic, irenical, peacemaking, peace-loving, dovelike, disarming, friendly, satisfying, calming, soothing, emollient, lenitive, mediatory, negotiated, pacifiable, pacified, satisfied, happy, content

▶ *589 Peace; 685 Moderation; 748 Mediation*

ADVERBS

7 **pacifically**, peacefully, irenically, moderately, mediatorially, accommodatingly, leniently, mercifully, forgivingly, clemently, soothingly, balmily, agreeably, in agreement, together

▶ *748 Mediation; 750 Agreement*

750 Agreement

NOUNS

1 **accord**, accordance, unanimity, unanimousness, harmony, unity, agreement, consensus, concert, consentaneity, concurrence, confluence, concourse, concord, concordance, one voice, vox populi, meeting of minds, like-mindedness, one (*or* same) mind, mutual understanding, sympathy, acceptance, acquiescence, accedence, accommodation, concession, reconciliation, capitulation, compromise, compliance, solidarity, kinship, compatibility, affinity, rapport, empathy, identity, similarity, mutuality, closeness, communion, peace, happy family, team spirit, *esprit de corps* (Fr)

▶ *569 Friendship; 589 Peace; 747 Cooperation; 754 Compromise*

2 **alliance**, league, union, federation, entente (cordiale), affiliation, guild, coalition, collusion, conspiracy, collaboration, synergy, partnership, fellowship, society, community, association, cartel, consortium, team, crew, group, band, bunch, gang, posse, mob, combo (Inf)

▶ *12 Government and Politics; 376 Gathering*

3 **arrangement**, settlement, compact, pact, treaty, covenant, contract, convention, bargain, deal, bond, transaction, pledge, promise

▶ *746 Negotiation; 747 Cooperation; 754 Compromise; 755 Contract*

4 **harmony**, harmonization, coordination, synchronization, synchronism, coincidence, concomitance, conjunction, symmetry, balance, equilibrium, regularity, consonance, consonancy, assonance, resonance, echo, rhyme, alliteration, melody, counterpoint, chime, chiming, homophony, euphony, euphoniousness, symphony, unison, chorus, choir, resolution (of a discord), blend, modulation, attunement, adjustment, orchestration

▶ *18 Music; 162 Symmetry; 510 Resonance; 516 Tunefulness*

5 **conformity**, conformance, conformation, uniformity, uniformness, constancy, continuity, consistency, coherence, homogeneity, homology, sameness, oneness, equipollence, parity, isotropy, synonymity, synonymy, indistinguishability, equivalence, interchangeability, congruence, congruity, correspondence, correlation, reciprocation, parallelism, likeness, similarity, analogousness, analogy, match, twin, brother, sister, complement, counterpart, alter ego, doppelgänger, clone, lookalike, spitting image, birds of a feather

▶ *110 Reciprocity; 111 Sameness; 115 Similarity; 117 Conformity; 125 Imitation; 188 Parallelism*

6 **convention**, orthodoxy, tradition, institution, custom, habit, praxis, pattern, order, system, method, routine, stereotype, type, norm, standard

▶ *117 Conformity; 298 Regularity; 632 Habit*

7 **consent**, assent, hearty assent, affirmation, blessing, approval, agreement, authorization, authority, ratification, certification, vouchsafement, endorsement, recognition, support, leave, liberty, attestation, tick, check (US), okay (OK) (Inf), go-ahead (Inf), green light (Inf)

▶ *669 Approval; 707 Affirmation*

8 **permit**, permission, sanction, allowance, clearance, licence, charter, warrant, warranty, certificate, patent, exemption, entitlement, dispensation

▶ *136 Qualification; 669 Approval; 758 Exemption*

9 **grant**, gift, present, donation, bestowal, presentment, conferment, conferral, provision, privilege, investiture, endowment, perquisite, perk

▶ *768 Giving*

ADJECTIVES

10 **in accord**, accordant, unanimous, harmonious, united, agreeing, agreed, *en rapport* (Fr), in rapport, consenting, consentient, consentaneous, in concert, concerted, concurrent, confluent, concordant, at one, with one voice, sympathetic, like-minded, understanding, empathizing, identifying with, amicable, frictionless, congenial, compatible, conciliatory, reconciling, reconcilable, complying, compliant, conceding, concessive, compromising, accepting, accepted, accommodating, acquiescing, acquiescent

▶ *111 Sameness; 569 Friendship; 754 Compromise*

11 **allied**, corporate, affiliated, filiated, associated, bonded, joint, conjoint, combined, combining, connected, linked, merged, in communion, communal, contributing, coactive, synergic, colluding, conspiring, conspiratorial, collaborating, collaborative, fraternal, fraternizing, coexisting, ganging up (Inf)

▶ *12 Government and Politics; 376 Gathering; 747 Cooperation*

12 **arranged**, settled, negotiated, negotiating, covenanted, covenantal, contractual, bargaining, pledged, promised

▶ *409 Arrangement; 746 Negotiation; 755 Contract*

13 **harmonious**, coordinated, synchronized, synchronous, coincident, coinciding, conjoint, concomitant, symmetrical, balanced, in equilibrium, regular, regulated, shaped, adjusted, attuned, homophonic, euphonious, euphonic, symphonious, symphonic, unisonous, blended, merged, orchestrated, modulated, modulating, in concert, choral, melodic, melodious, contrapuntal, harmonic, enharmonic, sounding, chiming, echoing, resounding, resonant, resonating, assonant, consonant, rhyming, alliterative, in tune (Inf), in sync (Inf)

▶ *18 Music; 162 Symmetry; 510 Resonance; 516 Tunefulness*

14 **conforming**, conformable, uniform, homogenous, homogenetic, homologous, level, equal, isotropic, identical, indistinguishable, same, constant, steady, unbroken, consistent, coherent, continuous, undeviating, orderly, straight, even, monotonous, unvarying, invariable, undifferentiated, equipollent, equivalent, interchangeable, synonymous, reciprocal, parallel, correspondent, corre-

sponding, congruous, congruent, correlated, correlative, interrelated, commensurate, complementary, reflecting, resembling, like, similar, analogous, analogical, matching, paired, twinned, twin, held together, hanging together (Inf), all of a piece (Inf)
▶ *110 Reciprocity; 111 Sameness; 117 Conformity; 125 Imitation; 188 Parallelism*

15 **conventional**, orthodox, strict, conservative, typical, typifying, traditional, customary, stock, usual, habitual, mundane, normal, ordinary, commonplace, stereotypical, quintessential, regular, regulated, standard, standardized, institutional, institutionalized, *comme il faut (Fr)*
▶ *117 Conformity; 298 Regularity; 632 Habit*

16 **fitting**, befitting, relevant, belonging, pertaining, appertaining, germane, pertinent, apposite, expedient, suitable, serving the purpose, qualified for, cut out for (Inf)
▶ *136 Qualification*

17 **consenting**, consentient, consentaneous, assenting, assentient, assentatious, affirming, affirmative, confirming, confirmed, approving, approved, recognized, agreeing, agreed, ratifying, ratified, ratificatory, authorizing, authorized, accredited, supported, seconded, backed, underwritten, endorsed, signed, sealed, stamped, rubber-stamped, ticked, checked (US)
▶ *669 Approval; 707 Affirmation*

18 **permitting**, permitted, entitled, cleared, validated, valid, passed, certificated, licensed, chartered, vouchsafed, sanctioned, warranted, allowing, allowed, legalized, legal, licit, decriminalized, exempt, exempted
▶ *136 Qualification; 669 Approval; 758 Exemption, Legality*

19 **granted**, donated, bestowed, presented, conferred, afforded, privileged, vested, rendered, enabled
▶ *768 Giving*

20 **agreeable**, uncontested, acceptable, uncontradicted, incontrovertible, unopposed, unobjectionable, viable, bipartisan, apolitical

VERBS

21 **be in accord**, be in accordance, accord, concord, concur, agree, have no objection, be at one, be in harmony, see eye to eye (with), empathize, identify with, go along with, comply, accede, concede, acquiesce, be reconciled, hit it off with (Inf)
▶ *569 Friendship*

22 **form an alliance**, ally, affiliate, unite, collude, conspire, collaborate, pull together, associate with, side with, team up (with), partner, fraternize, combine with, join with, conjoin, coact, cowork, synergize, gang up (with) (Inf), be in cahoots (with) (Inf)
▶ *376 Gathering*

23 **arrange**, settle, make terms, bargain, deal, negotiate, compromise, contract, transact, covenant, pledge, promise, shake hands on
▶ *409 Arrangement; 746 Negotiation; 755 Contract*

24 **harmonize**, coordinate, synchronize, coincide, conjoin, symmetrize, balance, shape, regulate, equalize, equilibrate, blend, merge, concert, orchestrate, symphonize, melodize, modulate, counterpoise, attune, tune in, adjust, resolve, rhyme, alliterate, assonate, resonate, chime, sound, resound, echo
▶ *18 Music; 162 Symmetry; 510 Resonance; 516 Tunefulness*

25 **conform**, be uniform, match, mirror, tally, square with, be like, resemble, look like, sound like, reflect, interrelate, correlate, correspond, complement, parallel, reciprocate, be consistent, cohere, hold together, hang together, tie in with, be conventional, follow, take one's place, line up, fall in, know one's place, go with the flow (Inf), follow the crowd (Inf), jump on the bandwagon (Inf), toe the line (Inf)
▶ *110 Reciprocity; 111 Sameness; 115 Similarity; 117 Conformity; 188 Parallelism*

26 **make uniform**, standardize, normalize, regularize, systematize, order, equalize, level, even out (*or* up), homogenize, assimilate, habituate, conventionalize, institutionalize, align, liken, stereotype
▶ *117 Conformity; 298 Regularity; 632 Habit*

27 **fit**, serve, suit, belong, appertain, pertain, qualify for, be just the thing (Inf), fill the bill (Inf), check (Inf), jibe (Inf), be just the job (Inf)
▶ *136 Qualification*

28 **consent**, assent, affirm, agree, approve, give one's blessing, authorize, ratify, confirm, certify, vouchsafe, endorse, accredit, validate, authenticate, recognize, tick, check (US), attest, sign, seal, stamp, rubber stamp, underwrite, second, back, back up, support, bless, nod, give the nod, say aye, say hear hear, say the word, OK (Inf), give the OK (Inf), give the thumbs up (Inf), tip the wink (Inf), give the all clear (*or* green light) (Inf), give the go-ahead (Inf)
▶ *669 Approval; 707 Affirmation*

29 **permit**, sanction, allow, warrant, license, pass, charter, patent, clear, give (*or* grant) leave, entitle, exempt, legalize, decriminalize
▶ *136 Qualification; 669 Approval; 758 Exemption*

30 **grant**, donate, give, bestow, present, confer, rend, render, afford, provide, privilege, vest, invest with, endow, patronize, enable, give someone a chance
▶ *768 Giving*

ADVERBS

31 **in accord**, with one accord, unanimously, harmoniously, *en rapport* (Fr), in concert, concertedly, unitedly, with one voice, of one mind, *nem. con.* (*nemine contradicente*) (L), together, all together, as one, solidly, by consensus, sympathetically, understandingly, compatibly, closely, communally, *en masse* (Fr), *en bloc* (Fr), like sheep
▶ *111 Sameness; 569 Friendship; 754 Compromise*

32 **in alliance**, corporately, in league, federally, in partnership, conspiratorially, hand in hand, shoulder to shoulder, cheek by jowl, in cahoots (Inf)
▶ *12 Government and Politics; 376 Gathering; 747 Cooperation*

33 **harmoniously**, agreeably, synchronously, resonantly, homophonically, euphonically, euphoniously, symphonically, melodically, soundingly, resoundingly, chorally, in chorus, in unison, in concert
▶ *18 Music; 510 Resonance; 516 Tunefulness*

34 **uniformly**, identically, equally, indistinguishably, similarly, like, likewise, thus, in the same way, in like manner, by the same token

35 **consistently**, regularly, evenly, steadily, constantly, invariably, continually, continuously, always, without exception

36 **accordingly**, consequently, therefore, ergo, so, it follows

that, hence, whence, wherefore, wherefrom, that (*or* such) being the case, in that case, at that rate, that being so, as it happens, in that way, thus, like that, for that (*or* which) reason, on that ground, under the circumstances, as the matter stands

▶ *132 Consecutiveness*

37 conventionally, traditionally, customarily, ordinarily, usually, routinely, habitually, typically, normally, as a rule

38 fittingly, befittingly, relevantly, pertinently, expediently, suitably, in keeping, appropriately, aptly, appositely

39 with consent, consentingly, assentingly, affirmingly, affirmatively, in the affirmative, approvingly, as agreed upon, as promised, as contracted for, as arranged, with permission, by (*or* with) someone's leave

▶ *707 Affirmation*

751 Disagreement

Quarrels would not last so long if the fault were on only one side.
Duc de la Rochefoucauld.

NOUNS

1 disagreement, difference of opinion, difference, argument, altercation, contention, contentiousness, dissension, dissent, dissidence, criticism, disaccord, discordance, disharmony, unharmoniousness, friction, noncooperation, hatred, unpleasantness, controversy, confrontation, difficulty, misunderstanding, disunity, breach of friendship, parting of the ways, estrangement, division, divisiveness, polarization, severance of cordial relations, incompatibility, irreconcilability, enmity, irascibility, provocativeness, cantankerousness, prickliness, quarrelsomeness, bickering, wrangling, hostility, bellicosity, combativeness, aggressiveness, belligerence, strife, fighting, infighting, clashing, area of disagreement, disputed area, theatre of war, sore point, ticklish issue, bone to pick, bone of contention, *casus belli* (L), house divided against itself, recall of ambassadors, uptightness (Inf)

▶ *113 Opposition; 114 Diversity; 343 Inactivity; 372 Separation; 517 Dissonance*

2 argument, debate, polemic, quarrel, row, dispute, spat, tiff, fuss, slanging match, discord, split, rift, breach, cleft, rupture, schism, struggle, scrimmage, squabble, wrangle, rumpus, tussle, scrap, brawl, fisticuffs, donnybrook, fracas, clash, conflict, open conflict, feud, blood feud, fight, battle, war, all-out war, storm in a teacup, tempest in a teapot (US), falling-out (Inf), hassle (Inf), flap (Inf), shindy (Inf), set-to (Inf), run-in (Inf), dust-up (Inf), ruckus (Inf), ruction (Inf), barney (Inf), argy-bargy (Inf), bobsy-die (NZ inf), knock-down-drag-out fight (Inf), rhubarb (US inf), rumble (US inf)

▶ *585 War; 661 Defiance*

3 difference, dissimilarity, nonconformity, deviation, divergence, variance, disparity, discord, discrepancy, incompatibility, incongruity, inequality, ambiguity, ambivalence, inconsistency, credibility gap, bad match, bad fit, misfitting, mismatching, misaligning, mistiming

▶ *118 Nonconformity; 120 Inequality; 234 Distortion*

4 dissenter, dissident, dissentient, protester, objector, disputer, critic, quarreller, troublemaker, intruder, gatecrasher, noncooperator, outsider, misfit, eccentric, crank, freak, laughing stock, wolf in sheep's clothing, ass in a lion's skin, odd man out, fish out of water, square peg in a round hole, scab, blackleg

▶ *459 Folly; 621 Derision; 700 Deception*

VERBS

5 disagree, differ, differ with, agree to differ, have differences with, hold opposite views, argue, altercate, not get along, contend, dissent, object to, not cooperate, have nothing to do with, hate, confront, quarrel, criticize, bicker, wrangle, misunderstand, divide, polarize, sever relations, part company with, come to a parting of the ways, split up with, break away from, provoke, show hostility, fight, clash, have an area of disagreement, have a bone to pick, fall out with (Inf), have a falling-out (Inf), not play ball (Inf), fight like cats and dogs

6 argue, debate, quarrel, row, dispute, spat (US), tiff, fuss, have a slanging match, split (up), rupture, struggle, squabble, wrangle, tussle, lock horns, go to court, scrap, brawl, engage in fisticuffs, have a donnybrook, clash, conflict, feud, fight, carry on a vendetta, battle, declare war, go to war, make all-out war, hassle (Inf), have a set-to (Inf), have a run-in (Inf), have a dust-up (Inf), kick up a row (*or* fuss) (Inf), kick up a shindy (Inf), kick up bobsy-die (NZ inf), have a knock-down-drag-out fight (Inf)

7 pick a fight, pick a quarrel, sow dissension, divide, provoke, set at odds, stir up trouble, make trouble, look for trouble, go looking for trouble, look for a disagreement, spoil for a fight, challenge, intrude, gate-crash, pick a bone with, have a bone to pick, rub (up) the wrong way, have a chip on one's shoulder (Inf), go on the warpath (Inf)

8 be different, be at variance, vary, deviate, diverge, have a credibility gap, match poorly, fit badly, not fit in with, misfit, mismatch, misalign, mistime, go against the grain, march to a different drummer (Inf)

ADJECTIVES

9 disagreeing, differing, argumentative, polemical, contentious, dissenting, dissident, dissentient, discordant, disharmonious, unharmonious, noncooperative, hating, hateful, unpleasant, controversial, confrontational, disputing, quarrelsome, quarrelling, at odds with, at variance with, at loggerheads with, criticizing, bickering, wrangling, divisive, polarizing, schismatic, incompatible, irreconcilable, irascible, provocative, cantankerous, prickly, hostile, inimical, bellicose, combative, aggressive, militant, antagonistic, belligerent, fighting, squabbling, brawling, warring, at war, at strife, up in arms, like cats and dogs, at cross purposes, knock-down-drag-out (Inf)

10 different, differing, dissimilar, deviating, divergent, variant, odd, alien, unsuitable, discordant, discrepant, incompatible, incongruous, unequal, ambiguous, ambivalent, inconsistent, misfit, mismatched, misaligned, mistimed, like a fish out of water, like a square peg in a round hole

ADVERBS

11 **in disagreement**, argumentatively, contentiously, dissentingly, discordantly, in defiance of, in contempt of, disharmoniously, without harmony, noncooperatively, without cooperation, despite, in spite of, hatefully, in a hateful manner, unpleasantly, controversially, in a controversial way, divisively, schismatically, incompatibly, at odds, irreconcilably, irascibly, provocatively, in order to provoke, cantankerously, hostilely, with hostility, inimically, bellicosely, combatively, aggressively, in an aggressive way, antagonistically, belligerently, like cats and dogs

12 **differently**, in a different way, dissimilarly, without similarity, divergently, unsuitably, discordantly, discrepantly, incompatibly, incongruously, unequally, ambiguously, ambivalently, in more than one way, inconsistently, without consistency, like a fish out of water, like a square peg in a round hole

752 Offer

He's a businessman. I'll make him an offer he can't refuse.
Mario Puzo.

NOUNS

1 **offer**, proffer, proposal, invitation, proposition, bid, approach, offer one cannot refuse, come-on (Inf), freebie (US inf)

2 **tentative offer**, suggestion, presentation, submission, feeler, toe in the water, advance, overture, motion, chance, opening, opportunity, golden opportunity

3 **business offer**, merger, bid, takeover bid, buy-out, final offer, last word, ultimatum, firm price, asking price, fair offer, special offer, sale, special sale, bargain of the month

4 **illegal offer**, bribe, slush fund, blood money, pass (Inf), kickback (Inf), rake-off (Inf)

▶ *363 Attraction; 480 Persuasion; 483 Motive; 756 Promise; 778 Sale*

5 **offer of public service**, (political) candidature, solicitation of votes, bid for votes, request for support, offer to stand for Parliament, offer to run for Congress (US)

▶ *12 Government and Politics*

6 **offering**, sacrifice, martyrdom, gift, present, dedication, consecration, oblation, offertory, collection, votive offering, incense, peace offering, contribution, donation, subscription, propitiation, conciliation, appeasement, expiation, self-immolation, burnt offering, sacrificial offering, sacrificial lamb, hecatomb

▶ *7 Religion; 582 Death*

7 **martyr**, Christian martyr, Stephen, Sebastian, Catherine, willing sacrifice, human sacrifice, sacrificial lamb, suttee, proto-martyr

8 **volunteer**, voluntary worker, VSO (Voluntary Service Overseas), Peace Corps (US), charity worker, unpaid worker, Good Samaritan, philanthropist, humanitarian, benefactor, contributor, altruist, social worker, community service worker, candy striper (US), public servant, candidate, missionary, do-gooder (Inf)

▶ *392 Help; 650 Benevolence; 652 Philanthropy*

VERBS

9 **offer**, proffer, propose, bid, approach, submit, suggest, put out a feeler, advance, make an overture, provide an opportunity, lay before, make an offer, make a fair offer, hold out, keep one's offer open, leave the door open, hold a special sale, offer for sale, put up for sale, invite offers, advertise, hand out a sample, auction, open bidding, hold out an incentive, lure, bait, spur, goad, persuade, induce, bribe, take a kickback (Inf), rake off (Inf)

10 **offer to buy**, attempt to buy, offer a fair price for, make an offer for, make a bid for, bid, negotiate, haggle

11 **volunteer**, do volunteer work, do charity work, do missionary work, work without pay, come forward, take on, lend a helping hand, act on one's own initiative, act without prompting, not wait to be asked, offer help, offer assistance, offer financial assistance, offer hospitality, provide, present, give, furnish, lend, loan, put into one's hands, lay at one's feet

12 **offer one's life**, sacrifice one's life, sacrifice oneself, become a martyr, die for a cause

13 **be a candidate**, offer oneself (for public office), stand as a candidate, run as a candidate (US), stand for office, run for office (US), enter the race, contest an office, solicit votes, bid for votes, request support

14 **offer reparation**, atone, make amends, apologize, offer one's apologies, beg one's pardon, propitiate, conciliate, appease, pacify, expiate, offer satisfaction, give satisfaction, make up for one's error

15 **offer worship**, celebrate mass, celebrate communion, administer the sacraments, minister, officiate, lead the worship, say the prayers, propitiate, appease, pacify

16 **make an offering**, offer a sacrifice, offer a gift, dedicate, consecrate, burn incense, make a peace offering, contribute, donate, subscribe, make a burnt offering, make a sacrificial offering, offer a sacrificial lamb

ADJECTIVES

17 **offered**, offering, inviting, propositional, bid, sale-price, persuasive, advertised, illegal, bribed, bribable, open to offers, on offer, on special offer, up for sale, for sale, cheap, reduced, up for auction, on auction, open for bid, requested, available, on the market, on hire, to let, for rent (US)

18 **voluntary**, unprompted, unforced, of one's own free will, on one's own accord, off one's own bat, charity, unpaid, philanthropic, humanitarian, altruistic

19 **sacrificial**, sacrificed, martyred, consecrated, oblatory, oblational, contributory, donated, propitiatory, conciliatory, expiatory

ADVERBS

20 **persuasively**, in a persuasive manner, for sale, cheaply, with no strings attached, at no extra cost, illegally, voluntarily, for free, philanthropically, altruistically, like a Good Samaritan, sacrificially, as a sacrifice, conciliatorily

753 Protest

The defiance of established authority, religious and secular, social and political, as a world-wide phenomenon may well one day be

accounted the outstanding event of the last decade. Hannah Arendt.

NOUNS

1 **protest**, opposition, objection, dissent, dissatisfaction, disagreement, disapproval, disapprobation, negation, negativity, contravention, hostility, discontent, recalcitrance, refractoriness, challenge, refusal to obey orders, refutation, noncooperation, noncompliance, disobedience, anger, defiance, recusance, mutiny, refusal to pay, nonpayment, protestation, expostulation, deprecation, intercession, counteraction, warning, complaint, clamour, outcry, no, nay, denial, contradiction, repudiation, disclaimer, renunciation, disavowal, kicking against the pricks, gainsaying (Lit), kick (US inf), bitch (Inf), beef (Inf)

▶ *637 Unwillingness; 662 Disobedience; 670 Disapproval; 708 Negation; 709 Refusal; 751 Disagreement*

2 **disorder**, agitation, breach of the peace, lawlessness, anarchism, anarchy, insurgency, sedition, treason, high treason, riot, rioting, rebellion, revolt, mutiny, insurrection, uprising, coup d'état, putsch, terrorism, war, guerrilla war, civil war, assassination, regicide, tyrannicide

▶ *661 Defiance*

3 **gesture of protest**, peaceful protest, strike, sit-down strike (*or* protest), go-slow, work to rule, hunger strike, boycott, picketing, demonstration, protest march, protest meeting, sit-in, work-in, raised fist, raised eyebrows, slow handclap, protest song, boo, hiss, groan, whistle, catcall, jeer, howl, raspberry, V-sign, squawk (Inf), the bird (Inf), the finger (US inf), Bronx cheer (US inf)

▶ *703 Demonstration*

4 **protester**, objector, conscientious objector, ecowarrior, antiroad protester, complainer, dissatisfied customer, grumbler, grouser, whiner, bellyacher, moaner, difficult character, mischief-maker, troublemaker, agitator, malcontent, ranter, rabble-rouser, dissident, dissentient, dissenter, critic, detractor, protestant, separatist, sectarian, dropout, nonconformist, hippie, rebel, demonstrator, striker, picketer, nonstriker, scab, blackleg, marcher, tubthumper, counter-demonstrator, suffragette, suffragist, whinger (Inf), moaning Minnie (Inf)

5 **seditionist**, anarchist, nihilist, spy, counterspy, industrial spy, revolter, revolutionary, urban guerrilla, partisan, resistance fighter, freedom fighter, terrorist, IRA (Irish Republican Army) member

▶ *12 Government and Politics*

VERBS

6 **protest**, oppose, object, raise an objection, dissent, resist, show dissatisfaction, disagree with, disapprove of, show disapproval, deprecate, detract, contravene, show discontent, become agitated about, challenge, refuse to obey orders, not cooperate, not comply, disobey, become angry, raise one's fist, defy, mutiny, expostulate, intercede, counteract, warn, complain, clamour, say no, deny, contradict, repudiate, disclaim, renounce, disavow, speak out against, raise one's voice against, raise the roof over, kick against the pricks, gainsay (Lit), kick (US inf), bitch (Inf), beef (Inf)

7 **complain**, groan, grumble, grouse, whine, gripe, bellyache, moan, rant, boo, hiss, tut-tut, whistle, give a catcall, jeer, howl, give a raspberry, give the V-sign, squawk (Inf), whinge (Inf), cry (*or* scream) blue murder (Inf), cry (*or* scream) bloody murder (US inf), give someone the bird (Inf), give someone the finger (US inf), kick up a fuss about (Inf), give someone the Bronx cheer (US inf)

8 **cause mischief**, cause trouble, strike, come out on strike, go on strike (US), go slow, work to rule, stage a sit-down, take industrial action, go on hunger strike, boycott, picket, cause disorder, breach the peace, agitate against, demonstrate against, go on a protest march, hold a protest meeting, sit in, act lawlessly, cause anarchy, riot, rebel, revolt, mutiny, begin an insurrection, lead an uprising, pull off a coup d'état, lead a putsch, terrorize, belong to a terrorist organization, belong to the IRA (Irish Republican Army), use terrorist tactics, wage war, fight a guerrilla war, assassinate

ADJECTIVES

9 **protesting**, protestant, opposing, dissenting, dissatisfied, disapproving, negative, negating, hostile, critical, discontent, malcontent, discontented, unconsenting, deprecatory, recalcitrant, refractory, challenging, noncooperative, noncompliant, nonconformist, disobedient, angry, contrary, defiant, recusant, counteractive, denying, denied, contradictive, repudiated, clamorous, hissing, booing, jeering, bolshie (Inf), bloody-minded (Inf)

10 **lawbreaking**, lawless, anarchical, anarchic, insubordinate, insurgent, mutinous, seditious, treasonous, riotous, rebellious, revolutionary, anarchist, nihilist, terrorist, guerrilla, counter-revolutionary, insurrectionary, assassinated, regicidal

ADVERBS

11 **disapprovingly**, without approval, in opposition, negatively, hostilely, with hostility, critically, in a critical way, deprecatorily, disobediently, angrily, with anger, contrarily, defiantly, in defiance of, in the face of, contradictively, in conflict with, lawlessly, insubordinately, mutinously, seditiously, rebelliously, in rebellion against

754 Compromise

Compromise used to mean that half a loaf was better than no bread. Among modern statesmen it really seems to mean that half a loaf is better than a whole loaf. G. K. Chesterton.

NOUNS

1 **compromise**, adaptation, adaptability, accommodation, sharing, cooperation, agreement, arrangement, working arrangement, practical compromise, modus vivendi, understanding, concession, mutual concession, give-and-take, adjustment, settlement, negotiation, negotiability, arbitration, middle way, middle course, middle ground, halfway, happy medium, balance, balancing act, central position, meeting halfway, splitting the difference, equal swap, trade-off, bargain, deal (Inf)

▶ *216 Average; 747 Cooperation; 748 Mediation; 750 Agreement; 755 Contract; 776 Trade*

2 **half-measure**, stopgap measure, temporary substitute, second best

▶ *762 Substitution*

3 **irresolution**, hesitation, lack of resolution, lack of con-

viction, lack of committal, lukewarmness, neutrality, desertion of principles, evasion of responsibility, dishonour, shame, cop-out (Inf)

▶ *639 Vacillation; 812 Notoriety*

VERBS

4 **compromise**, reach (*or* make) a compromise, meet halfway, adapt, accommodate, cooperate, make adjustments, adjust, readjust, negotiate, go to arbitration, arbitrate, make mutual concessions, concede, cede, give and take, average out, split the difference, agree to some of it, agree to half of it, strike a balance, stretch a point, play politics, go so far but no further, steer a middle course, strike an average, go half and half, have a foot in both camps, sit on the fence, take what's on offer, take the good with the bad, make the best of a bad job, make a virtue of necessity, make a deal (Inf), go fifty-fifty (Inf), go Dutch (Inf)

5 **be irresolute**, lack resolution, lack conviction, desert one's principles, evade one's responsibilities, duck responsibility (Inf), cop out (Inf)

ADJECTIVES

6 **compromising**, accommodating, adjusted, negotiable, adaptable, averaging out, averaged out, agreeing, agreed, arranged, conceding, give-and-take, settled, halfway, balancing, balanced, neither one thing nor the other, half-measure, stopgap, temporary, second-best

7 **irresolute**, noncommittal, lukewarm, neutral, evasive, discredited, dishonourable, dishonoured, damaging, cop-out (Inf)

ADVERBS

8 **compromisingly**, in equal measures, in equal parts, accommodatingly, in an accommodating manner, by negotiating, agreeably, under an agreement, under an arrangement, halfway, as a half-measure, in a temporary manner

9 **irresolutely**, without resolution, noncommittally, without commitment, lukewarmly, neutrally, evasively, in an evasive manner, dishonourably, without honour, as a cop-out (Inf)

755 Contract

A verbal contract isn't worth the paper it's written on. Samuel Goldwyn.

NOUNS

1 **contract**, undertaking, assignment, engagement, obligation, commitment, promise, formal contract, mise (Lit), compact, arrangement, understanding, cooperation, accord, agreement, deal, mutual agreement, legal agreement, binding agreement, formal agreement, informal agreement, gentleman's agreement, pledge, exchanged vow, marriage contract, betrothal, matrimony, holy matrimony, nuptial bond, conjugal trust, wedlock, bond, union, alliance, partnership, covenant, pact, suicide pact, negotiation, bargain, bargaining, bartering, give and take, mediation, settlement, ratification, completion, confirmation, consent, assent, seal, signet, signature, cosignature, countersignature, security, deed

▶ *253 Security; 354 Undertaking; 570 Marriage; 716 Evidence; 746 Negotiation; 747 Cooperation; 748 Mediation; 750 Agreement; 756 Promise*

2 **purchase contract**, building contract, service contract, rental contract, leasing contract, lease, employment contract, teaching contract, publishing contract, insurance policy, promissory note, IOU, debenture, debenture bond, mortgage deed, deed of trust

▶ *780 Money; 783 Credit; 784 Debt*

3 **alliance**, league, cartel, consortium, trust, entente cordiale, entente, Triple Entente, international agreement, arms-control agreement, SALT (Strategic Arms Limitation Talks), international pact, trade agreement, Treaty of Rome, convention, treaty, peace treaty, Treaty of Paris, Treaty of Versailles, nonaggression pact, concordat, mutual-defence treaty, NATO (North Atlantic Treaty Organization), SEATO (Southeast Asia Treaty Organization), GATT (General Agreement on Tariffs and Trade), Warsaw Pact

▶ *12 Government and Politics; 749 Pacification; 776 Trade*

4 **contractor**, contracting party, signatory, signer, cosigner, countersigner, the undersigned, endorser, ratifier, covenanter, consenting party, assenter, treaty-maker, peacemaker, mediator, negotiator, diplomat, arbitrator, jobber, entrepreneur, doer, operator, dealer, wheeler-dealer (Inf), fast operator (Inf)

VERBS

5 **contract**, enter into a contract, execute a contract, indent, make a compact, sign a pact, commit oneself, bind oneself, contract a marriage, marry, wed, sign (on the dotted line), cosign, countersign, seal, subscribe to, underwrite, endorse, ratify, attest, confirm, covenant, negotiate a treaty, sign a treaty, enter into an alliance, ally, join a consortium, league with, go into league with, form a cartel, bargain, strike a bargain, settle, negotiate, make terms, cooperate, give and take, barter, come to an agreement, come to terms, transfer, convey, deed (US), go into a partnership, form a partnership, work out a deal, conclude (*or* clinch) a deal (Inf), shake on a deal (Inf), close the deal (Inf), tie the knot (Inf), put out a contract on (Inf)

6 **catch**, get, come down with, become infected, break out with

ADJECTIVES

7 **contractual**, contracted, covenantal, covenanted, agreeable, agreed to, agreed, promised, sworn, consensual, assenting, negotiable, negotiated, negotiating, treaty-making, bilateral, multilateral, signed (on the dotted line), cosigned, countersigned, signed sealed and delivered, under one's hand and seal, ratified, assigned, arranged, matrimonial, nuptial, conjugal, allied, united, conspiratorial

ADVERBS

8 **contractually**, as contracted for, according to the contract, covenantally, agreeably, as agreed upon (*or* to), as promised, according to the agreement, consensually, with consent, bilaterally, multilaterally, matrimonially, nuptially, conjugally, conspiratorially

756 Promise

I thought he was a young man of promise; but it appears he was a young man of promises. Arthur Balfour.

NOUNS

1 **promise**, solemn promise, commitment, voluntary commitment, pledge, vow, oath, one's word, testimony, swearing on the Bible, swearing, deposition, adjuration, statement under oath, affidavit, affirmation, firm date, delivery date, assurance, profession, promise-making, gentleman's agreement, unwritten agreement, covenant, bond, handshake, compact, contract, mutual pledge, debt of honour, intention, declaration of intent, post (*or* put up) the banns, read (*or* publish) the banns, engagement, exchange of vows, betrothal, marriage contract

► *482 Intention; 570 Marriage; 698 Truth; 707 Affirmation; 755 Contract; 772 Borrowing; 784 Debt*

2 **guarantee**, security, written guarantee, warrant, warranty, promissory note, contract, insurance premium, IOU, voucher, pawn ticket, chit

► *253 Security*

3 **potential**, possibilities, capacity, capability, ability, good things to come, hope, good omen, favourable auspices, good prospects, bright prospects

► *450 Belief; 716 Evidence*

4 **promised land**, land of promise, land flowing with milk and honey, Canaan, Israel, El Dorado, end of the rainbow, pot of gold (at the end of the rainbow), Utopia, Erewhon, Shangri-la, Holy Grail, Sangreal, Goshen, Elysia, Elysian Fields, Fountain of Youth, eternal youth, eternal life, the millennium, Heaven, Valhalla (*or* Walhalla), the happy hunting ground

5 **promise-maker**, promiser, guarantor, party, surety, signatory, signer, cosignatory, co-signer, bondsman, obligor, swearer, attestor

6 **someone promised**, betrothed, fiancé, fiancée, affianced, engaged person, lucky man, bride-to-be, the intended (Inf)

VERBS

7 **promise**, make a promise, solemnly promise, pledge, confirm, assure, say yes to, say one will, proffer, affirm, give one's word (of honour), vow, commit oneself, swear, swear on (*or* under) oath, swear on the Holy Bible, swear on one's mother's life (*or* head), cross one's heart (and hope to die), testify, take responsibility for, pledge one's word, pledge oneself, pledge one's honour, enter into an agreement, give a firm date, undertake to, make a gentleman's agreement, shake on it, sign on the dotted line, covenant, contract, get engaged to, become engaged, become betrothed to, plight one's troth, exchange vows, espouse, ask for the hand of, accept a proposal, put up the banns, say "I do"

8 **guarantee**, warrant, certify, assure, answer for, vouch for, commit oneself, make it one's duty, take on, accept responsibility, accept obligation, accept liability, secure, insure, underwrite, stand bail for, go bond for, give a written guarantee, sign a promissory note, cosign a note, attest to, make a contract, promise to pay, give one's IOU, receive a voucher, receive a pawn ticket

9 **be auspicious**, be likely, promise well, augur well, hold out hopes for, build up hope, bid fair

10 **show potential**, show promise, have possibilities, hope, receive a good omen, have good prospects, have a bright future, get better, improve, develop, evolve, prove fruitful

11 **promise oneself**, have in mind, look forward to, have one's eye on, contemplate, think of, desire, want, set one's heart on, covet, have designs on

ADJECTIVES

12 **promised**, pledged, bound, committed, testimonial, sworn, on (*or* under) oath, on one's word, under hand and seal, adjuratory, votive, affirmative, assured, professed, engaged, betrothed, spoken for

13 **guaranteeing**, guaranteed, authenticating, authenticated, certified, assured, attested, certain, warranted, underwritten, signed, cosigned, securing, secured, pledging, pledged, committed, bound, obligated, promissory, contracted

14 **auspicious**, propitious, promising, full of promise, encouraging, hopeful, full of hope, potential, full of potential, possible, likely, fortunate, favourable, optimistic, good, bright, fair, golden, rosy, cloudless, clear

15 **future**, eventual, destined, fated, potential, prospective, to come, probable, possible, anticipated, looked for, hoped for, predicted, predictable, foreseeable, sure, certain

ADVERBS

16 **as promised**, as agreed, duly, upon one's word (of honour), on (*or* under) oath, under hand and seal, votively, assuredly, with assurance, certainly

17 **auspiciously**, propitiously, promisingly, full of promise, with promise, encouragingly, hopefully, full of hope, with hope, potentially, possibly, fortunately, favourably, optimistically, in an optimistic way, brightly, rosily, clearly

18 **potentially**, eventually, prospectively, probably, possibly, predictably, surely, certainly

757 Permission

NOUNS

1 **permission**, authorization, leave, approval, nod of approval, consent, implied consent, approbation, blessing, benevolence, clearance, security clearance, top-secret clearance, authority, legality, law, mandate, sanction, endorsement, confirmation, ratification, verification, corroboration, validation, tolerance, toleration, dispensation, exemption, nonliability, connivance, acquiescence, concession, licence, free hand, carte blanche, blank cheque, freedom, easiness, indulgence, leniency, permissiveness, laissez-faire attitude, unconstraint, promiscuity, free love, permissive society, the sixties, the green light, the thumbs-up, the go-ahead (Inf), the OK (Inf), the magic word (Inf), the Open Sesame (Inf), the nod (Inf), the all clear (Inf)

► *250 Freedom; 265 Easiness; 648 Leniency; 650 Benevolence; 669 Approval; 758 Exemption*

2 **permit**, written permission, grant, warrant, warranty,

charter, patent, letters patent, certificate, credentials, diploma, testimonial, recommendation, reference, character reference, seal, signature (on the dotted line), endorsement, voucher, ticket, admission ticket, docket, chit, licence, fishing licence, driving licence, MOT (Ministry of Transport) certificate, release, waiver, nihil obstat (Lit), imprimatur, clearance papers, work permit, green card, pass, passport, visa, password, safe-conduct pass, *laissez passer* (Fr), leave, sick leave, leave of absence, furlough, holiday, vacation, sabbatical, parole, stamp, rubber stamp, mark, cross

▶ *12 Government and Politics; 55 Fishing; 319 Transport; 570 Marriage; 580 Leisure; 716 Evidence*

VERBS

3 **permit**, give permission, allow, let, make possible, authorize, approve, clear, sanction, endorse, confirm, ratify, verify, corroborate, validate, tolerate, exempt, connive, acquiesce, countenance, license, legitimize, legalize, make legal, decriminalize, lift the ban on, not stand in the way of, enable, empower, remove all obstacles, facilitate, say yes to, give the green light, give thumbs up, sign (on the dotted line), consent, bless, give one's blessing, give dispensation, make concessions, grant immunity, compromise, give the OK (Inf), give the all clear (Inf), give the go-ahead (Inf), give the nod (Inf), say the magic word (Inf)

4 **be permissive**, be lax, indulge, spoil, favour, pamper, adopt a laissez-faire attitude, give someone his (*or* her) head, give someone a free hand, bend the rules, stretch the point, not cramp someone's style, not stand in the way of, allow to have the run of, make it easy for, give someone a chance, allow someone to take liberties, let someone get away with it, relinquish authority, resign oneself to, give carte blanche to, give a blank cheque to, open the floodgates, let someone get away with murder (Inf)

5 **be permitted**, have permission, receive permission, have authorization, have clearance, have someone's blessing, have a free hand, take liberties, get away with it, have a blank cheque, get away with murder (Inf)

6 **ask permission**, beg permission, ask leave, beg leave, ask if one may, ask to be excused, request, petition, seek a favour, seek help, ask for someone's blessing

▶ *392 Help; 710 Request*

ADJECTIVES

7 **permitted**, allowed, authorized, warranted, sanctioned, licensed, legal, legalized, lawful, licit, decriminalized, chartered, patent, above board, legitimate, acceptable, worthwhile, approved, passed, unconditional, without strings, legit (Inf)

8 **permitting**, permissive, permissible, admissive, admissible, allowing, allowable, printable, sayable, unprohibitive, easy-going, tolerant, lenient, indulgent, *laissez faire* (Fr), loose, lax, easy come easy go, overindulgent, irresolute, unassertive, conniving

ADVERBS

9 **with permission**, under authorization, under licence, under warrant, under a charter, under a patent, legally, with legal protection, lawfully, legitimately, acceptably, unconditionally, without conditions, without strings, permissively, in a permissive fashion, permissibly, tolerantly, leniently, indulgently, loosely, laxly, with no questions asked, on the nod, irresolutely, unassertively, connivingly

758 Exemption

NOUNS

1 **exemption**, immunity, impunity, nonliability, nonresponsibility, dispensation, special treatment, privilege, exception, exclusion, diplomatic immunity

▶ *128 Exclusion*

2 **acquittal**, absolution, pardon, exoneration, excuse, discharge, release, liberation, freedom, liberty, independence

▶ *250 Freedom; 391 Liberation; 649 Forgiveness*

3 **self-exemption**, self-certification, escapism, evasion of responsibility, dereliction of duty, washing one's hands (Inf), passing the buck (Inf)

4 **licence**, permission, permit, certificate of exemption, charter, franchise, patent, privilege, leave, compassionate leave, leave of absence, aegrotat

▶ *757 Permission*

ADJECTIVES

5 **exempt**, exempted, immune, not subject to, nonliable, not liable, not responsible, unaccountable, not accountable, not answerable, unanswerable, privileged, excepted, excluded, shielded, protected, unpunishable

▶ *128 Exclusion; 252 Safety*

6 **acquitted**, absolved, pardoned, exonerated, excused, let off, spared, clear, free, freed from blame, discharged, released, liberated, off the hook (Inf)

▶ *649 Forgiveness*

7 **independent**, free, unrestricted, unbound, unconstrained, uncontrolled

8 **tax-free**, duty-free, post-free, zero-rated

VERBS

9 **exempt**, exclude, except, leave out, set apart, privilege, grant immunity, grant impunity

▶ *128 Exclusion*

10 **acquit**, exonerate, exculpate, absolve, grant absolution, pardon, excuse, let off, let off scot-free, spare, show mercy, forgive, grant amnesty to, dismiss, discharge, release, liberate, free, set free, set at liberty, let go, drop all charges against

▶ *391 Liberation; 649 Forgiveness*

11 **be exempt**, have no liability, have no responsibility, enjoy immunity, enjoy diplomatic immunity

12 **exempt oneself**, excuse oneself, go on leave, take compassionate leave, escape, evade one's responsibilities, fail in one's duty, admit no responsibility, evade liability, shift (*or* transfer) the responsibility, shift the blame, pass the buck (Inf), shrug off (Inf), wash one's hands of (Inf), get off scot-free (Inf), get away with it (Inf), get away with murder (Inf)

ADVERBS

13 **with impunity**, freely, tax-free, duty-free, unaccountably, unanswerably, unrestrainedly, without fear of reprisal

759 Exchange

Who will change old lamps for new ones?…new lamps for old ones? Anonymous.

NOUNS

1 **exchange**, interchange, change, trade, barter, conversion, commutation, permutation, substitution, transposition, shuffle, shuffling, switch, switching, swap, swapping, pawning, castling (chess), mutuality, reciprocity, reciprocation, give-and-take, tit for tat, quid pro quo, retaliation, blow for blow, eye for an eye, tooth for a tooth, measure for measure, cooperation, logrolling (US), interplay, two-way traffic, repartee, equivalent, correlation, compensation, recompense, consideration, small consideration, redemption, ransom, trade-off, dealing, financial dealing, transaction, truck

► *385 Retaliation; 706 Answer; 747 Cooperation; 754 Compromise; 776 Trade*

2 **place of exchange**, place of trade, market, marketplace, stock exchange, Bourse, rialto, bank, bureau de change, *cambio* (It), *Weschel* (Ger), pawnshop

3 **something in exchange**, new lamps for old, pawn ticket, change, small change, money, cash, bill of exchange, banker's draft, cheque, business cards, valentines, telephone numbers

4 **person who exchanges**, banker, moneychanger, stockbroker, pawnbroker, exchange student, au pair, substitute, wife swapper

VERBS

5 **exchange**, give in exchange, give an equivalent, interchange, shuffle, switch, swap, castle (chess), reciprocate, cooperate, logroll (US), correlate, requite, give as good as one gets, answer back, retort, bandy words with, return the compliment, pay in kind, compensate, recompense, exchange for, change places, transpose, shuttle, commute, substitute, convert, pawn, convert into, change money, barter, trade, trade off, traffic, truck, transact, deal, give in return, give and take, give tit for tat, give blow for blow, take an eye for an eye, rob Peter to pay Paul, take in one another's washing, scratch each other's back

ADJECTIVES

6 **in exchange**, equivalent, complementary, reciprocal, reciprocative, mutual, two-way, tit-for-tat, retaliatory, compensatory, exchangeable, changeable, interchangeable, convertible, commutative, substitutive, substitutable

7 **exchanged**, changed, interchanged, substituted, transposed, traded, bartered, converted, switched, swapped, pawned, reciprocated, requited, compensated, ransomed

ADVERBS

8 **in exchange**, mutually, reciprocally, equivalently, correlatively, changeably, interchangeably, commutatively, au pair, vice versa, back and forth, backwards and forwards, to and fro, by turns, turn and turn about, turn about (US), each in his (*or* her) turn, in kind, in return, in return for, in exchange for

760 Conversion

Provided that the City of London remains as at present, the Clearing-house of the World. Joseph Chamberlain.

NOUNS

1 **conversion**, converting, changeableness, convertibility, change, transition, transposition, movement, shift, transfer, transference, translation, interpretation, misinterpretation, alteration, modification, reorganization, rationalization, transformation, metamorphosis, mutation, processing, chemical change, chemistry, reduction, resolution, fermentation, ferment, leaven, dehydration, crystallization, melting, physical change, transmutation, transfiguration, magic, enchantment, bewitchment, alchemy

► *224 Change; 345 Effect; 356 Creation*

2 **evolution**, evolving, growth, life cycle, development, progress, revolution, reformation, re-education, rebirth, regeneration, rehabilitation, improvement, naturalization, assimilation, degeneration, deterioration, perversion, denaturalization, alienation

► *213 Increase; 244 Improvement; 245 Deterioration; 302 Forward Motion; 393 Repair*

3 **persuasion**, indoctrination, brainwashing, religious conversion, proselytizing, proselytization, evangelism, evangelization, revivalism, revival, spiritual rebirth

► *7 Religion; 395 Influence; 480 Persuasion*

4 **medium of conversion**, Bible, church, school, laboratory, melting pot, crucible, cauldron, test tube, retort, alembic, fermentation vat, workshop, lathe, potter's wheel, sculptor's tools, foundry, anvil

5 **converter**, indoctrinator, teacher, preacher, minister, priest, vicar, evangelist, television evangelist (US), proselyter, proselytizer, missionary, apostle, televangelist (US inf)

6 **convert**, changed person, proselyte, catechumen, neophyte, new man (*or* woman), apostate, tergiversator, backslider, renegade, turncoat, traitor

VERBS

7 **convert into**, metamorphose, mutate, transpose, move, shift, transfer, translate, alter, transform, process, reduce, resolve, ferment, leaven, dehydrate, crystallize, melt, transmute, transfigure, become, be turned into (*or* to), change into, turn into (*or* to), get, come to, develop into, evolve into, pass into, shift into, slide into, mellow into, mature into, ripen into, ferment into, melt into, merge into, dissolve into, sink into

8 **be transformed**, be changed, evolve, develop, wax, grow, ripen, mature, mellow, age, progress, improve, naturalize, assimilate, regenerate, be rejuvenated, denaturalize, deteriorate, degenerate, take the shape of, assume the shape of, assume the character of, assume the nature of, undergo a personality change, not know oneself, suffer a sea change, reform, revolt, enter a new phase, enter a different phase, reach a stage, turn over a new leaf

9 **transform**, transfigure, change the face of, make into, ferment, leaven, process, reduce, reduce to, turn into, convert into, resolve into, conjure into, metamorphose,

transmute, alchemize, mould, shape, lick into shape, knock into shape, rehabilitate, paper over, paper over the cracks, paint over, render, translate, interpret, misinterpret, reinterpret, modify, decorate, redecorate, reshape, remodel, reform, reorganize, restructure, re-educate, rationalize, deform, distort, twist, pervert

10 **be converted**, be saved, be born again, turn to God, change one's ways, turn against, renege, apostatize, desert, turn traitor, turn to sin

11 **persuade**, influence, indoctrinate, brainwash, win over, proselytize, preach, evangelize, convert, save, revive

12 **naturalize**, internationalize, assimilate, orientalize, Indianize, Russify, westernize, Americanize, Anglicize, Frenchify, Germanize, Europeanize, Africanize, denaturalize

ADJECTIVES

13 **converted**, changed, transformed, turned into, transposed, transfigured, transmuted, metamorphosed, mutated, translated, enchanted, bewitched, changed beyond recognition, unrecognizable, brainwashed, proselytized, assimilated, naturalized, improved, regenerated, degenerated

14 **converting**, changing, becoming, growing, developing, maturing, transferring, altering, transforming, mutating, processing, fermenting, leavening, crystallizing, melting, transmuting, transfiguring, evolving, progressing, regenerating, improving, degenerating, deteriorating

15 **convertible**, changeable, transformable, impressionable, influenceable, persuadable, transmutable, transposable, transferable, translatable, alterable, improvable, reducible, resolvable

16 **influenced**, persuaded, brainwashed, converted, saved, revived, born again, reborn, proselytized, evangelized

17 **naturalized**, internationalized, assimilated, orientalized, westernized, Americanized, Anglicized, Frenchified, Germanized, Europeanized, Africanized, denaturalized

ADVERBS

18 **convertibly**, in transition, in transit, en route, on the way to

761 Reversion

NOUNS

1 **reversion**, reversal, turning back, turning backwards, going back, return, regression, recession, retrogression, retrograde state, withdrawal, apostasy, retraction, recantation, repentance, backing down, retreat, retirement, retroversion, retroflexion, looking back, retrospection, reaction, retroaction, retrospective action, counteraction, backfire, ricochet, recoil, boomerang effect, backlash, counter-revolution, counter-reformation, about-turn, right about-turn, U-turn, volte-face, atavism, recidivism, backsliding, relapse

▶ *112 Repetition; 296 Oldness; 303 Backward Motion; 344 Cause; 462 Memory*

2 **restoration**, reconversion, changing back, giving back, reinstatement, transfer, restitution, compensation, revival, new beginning, resumption, recommencement, recovery, retrieval, recycling, taking back, retaliation, reprisal, getting back

▶ *130 Beginning; 765 Profit; 773 Taking; 775 Giving Back*

3 **turning point**, pivotal point, crucial point, crucial moment, crisis point, crisis, watershed, turn of the tide

4 **return**, swing, swing of the pendulum, give and take, comings and goings, shuttling, shuttle, commuting, returning home, round trip, return ticket, commute (US inf)

▶ *177 Curve*

5 **reply**, retort, retortion, answer, response, feedback, confutation, refutation

▶ *704 Refutation; 706 Answer*

VERBS

6 **reverse**, turn back, turn about, turn, go back, return, revert, regress, recede, retrogress, recidivate, withdraw, retract, back down, retreat, retire, recant, renege, backslide, slide back, slip back, relapse, turn backwards, look back, hark back, archaize, turn back the clock, react, counteract, backfire, ricochet, recoil, boomerang, do (*or* make) an about-turn, do (*or* make) a U-turn

7 **restore**, restore the status quo, reconvert, revive, resume, change back, give back, make restitution, compensate, reinstate, restart, recommence, start again, begin again, go back to the beginning, undo, do again, unmake, remake, start afresh, start anew, recover, retrieve, recycle, take back, retaliate, get back at, get one's own back (Inf), take it from the top (Inf)

8 **return**, swing back, swing around, swing, trace back, rebound, recoil, kick back, give and take, come and go, shuttle, commute, return home, make a round trip, buy a return-trip ticket

9 **reply**, retort, answer, respond, give feedback, confute, refute, recant, repent

ADJECTIVES

10 **regressive**, recessive, reversionary, reversional, retroverse, retrograde, restitutive, restitutory, compensatory, retrospective, reflexive, reactive, reactionary, retroactive, atavistic, recidivist, recidivistic, recidivous

11 **reversed**, regressed, retracted, recanted, retreated, retired, reverted, reacted, recoiled, backfired, returned, restored, reinstated, revived, resumed, recovered, retrieved, recycled, replied, retorted, answered, responded, refuted

12 **reversible**, returnable, restorable, recoverable, retrievable, recyclable, refutable

ADVERBS

13 **reversibly**, regressively, retrospectively, reflexively, reactively, retroactively, atavistically, retrievably, refutably, invertedly, inside out, wrong side out, back to front, back to the beginning, as you were, from the top (Inf)

762 Substitution

An old Dutch farmer, who remarked to a companion once that it was not best to swap horses in mid-stream. Abraham Lincoln.

NOUNS

1 **substitution**, change, exchange, quid pro quo, commutation, alternation, switch, swap, shuffle, represen-

tation, replacement, deputing, deputizing, power of attorney, vicariousness, supplanting, supersession, surrogation, surrogacy, alternative choice, equivalence, equivalent, alternative, worse alternative, the lesser of two evils, second best, *pis aller* (Fr), expedient, compromise, modus vivendi, temporary measure, stopgap, compensation, expiation

► *119 Equality; 717 Representation; 754 Compromise; 759 Exchange*

2 **substitute person**, sub, alternate, proxy, agent, representative, deputy, depute (Scot), surrogate, surrogate mother, locum, locum tenens, fill-in, stand-in, understudy, stunt man (*or* stunt woman), body double, double, ringer, lookalike, soundalike, impostor, changeling, Doppelgänger, ghostwriter, reserve, reservist, pinch hitter (US), twelfth man, supply, supply teacher, relief, replacement, successor, supplanter, step father, step dad, step mother, step mum, step family, foster parent, father figure, father substitute, mother figure, mother substitute, scapegoat, whipping boy, fall guy (US inf), patsy (Inf)

► *747 Cooperation*

3 **substitute thing**, symbol, representation, synonym, doublet, metaphor, analogy, transplant, artificial limb, prosthesis, pacemaker, succedaneum, bandage, sticking plaster, Elastoplast, Band-Aid (US), remount, guilt-offering, sacrifice, lamb to the slaughter

► *5 Language and Linguistics; 394 Remedy*

VERBS

4 **be a substitute**, relieve, succeed, supplant, supersede, oust, displace, replace, take the place of, ghostwrite, pinch hit (US), serve as proxy, act as deputy for, represent, act for, do duty for, double for, imitate, fill in, stand in, understudy, deputize, cover, cover for, hold the fort, take over, foster, take responsibility, take on responsibility, shoulder responsibility, take the blame, take the rap, step into the shoes of (Inf)

5 **take a substitute**, exchange for, exchange, commute, choose an alternative, compromise, take in exchange, take second best, make do with, put up with, count as, treat as, regard as, take a rain check (US inf)

6 **give a substitute**, give in exchange, exchange, switch, swap, shuffle, change for, change, interchange, put in place of, compensate for, symbolize, fob off, palm off

ADJECTIVES

7 **substitute**, substitutive, substitutional, alternate, alternative, acting, deputy, proxy, reserve, replacement, equivalent, lookalike, soundalike, surrogate, second, additional, stopgap, makeshift, temporary, provisional

8 **substituted**, changed, exchanged, switched, swapped, replaced, deputized, supplanted, superseded, compensated

ADVERBS

9 **instead**, instead of, in place of, in lieu of, on behalf of, in one's behalf, in one's place, in favour of, at the expense of, as an alternative, alternatively, equivalently, additionally, temporarily, provisionally, for want of anything better, *faux de mieux* (Fr), in default of, by default, by proxy, per pro (p.p.), *in loco parentis* (L), by (*or* through) the agency of, in one's shoes (Inf)

763 Possession

NOUNS

1 **possession**, right of possession, possessorship, possessing, owning, ownership, proprietorship, lawful possession, legal possession, rightful possession, enjoyment, property rights, proprietary rights, mineral rights, lordship, dominion, sovereignty, holding, hold, grasp, grip, retention, making one's own, claiming, laying claim to, taking, taking possession, appropriating, appropriation, control, marking one's territory, occupying, occupancy, occupation, hoisting one's flag over, landownership, landowning, landholding, land tenure, custody, title, original title, lease, leasehold, freehold, tenure, tenancy, tenantry, exclusive possession, sole possession, monopoly, monopolization, cornering of the market, a corner on, engrossment, forestalment, sublease, squatting, squatterism, squatters' rights, claim, legal claim, heirship, heirdom, inheritance, heritage, patrimony, nine tenths of the law, nine points of the law, bird in the hand

► *13 Economics; 14 Finance; 349 Use; 773 Taking*

2 **legal terms**, pre-emption, prescription, fee simple, seisin, de facto possession, de jure possession, uti possidetis, chose in possession, dominium

► *16 Law*

3 **medieval ownership**, villeinage, villeinhold, socage, free socage, burgage, frankalmoign, fee, fief, feud, feudality

4 **possession**, property, owned property, freehold, estate, landed estate, plantation, colony, dependency, protectorate, dominion, personal effects, belongings, accoutrements, appurtenances, chattel, bag and baggage, stuff, gear, things, all one's worldly goods and chattels, clothes off one's back

► *3 History; 440 Possessions*

5 **possessor**, owner, monopolizer, buyer, purchaser, holder, landowner, property owner, leaseholder, lessee, householder, occupant, occupier, owner-occupier, mortgagee, proprietor (*or* proprietress), landlord (*or* landlady), resident, tenant, sitting tenant, rent-payer, lodger, boarder, paying guest, guest, visitor, squatter, taker

► *312 Arrival; 564 Inhabitant*

6 **lord**, lord and master, overlord, master, mistress, lord (*or* lady) of the manor, squire, laird (Scot), thane, earldorman (Lit), man (*or* woman) of property, man (*or* woman) of substance

► *387 Subjection*

VERBS

7 **possess**, own, have in one's possession, have in hand, have in one's grip, have in one's grasp, command, have at one's command, have at one's disposal, buy, take up residence in, move into, take out a tenancy, take out a mortgage, become the proud owner of, have title to, have the deed for, have tenure of, have in one's name, have, have and hold, hold, number among one's possessions, call one's own, enjoy, occupy, dwell in, monopolize, have all to oneself, keep for oneself, have exclusive possession of, have exclusive rights to, forestall, engross, tie up, corner, get a corner on, corner the market, rent, let, claim, squat, squat on, claim squatter's rights, hog (Inf)

ADJECTIVES

8 **possessing**, possessed of, in possession, having possessions, possessory, owning, landowning, landed, property-owning, propertied, having, having and holding, holding, enjoying, proprietorial, occupying, squatting, exclusive, unshared, monopolistic

9 **possessed**, owned, owned by, in (*or* under) the ownership of, one's (very) own, in the possession of, in the hands of, in one's hands, in one's grasp, held, belonging to, in one's name, at one's disposal, at one's command, on hand, in store, in the bank, exclusive, unshared, monopolized by

ADVERBS

10 **possessively**, in the possession of, in one's name, at one's disposal, at one's command, monopolistically, exclusively

764 Sharing

NOUNS

1 **joint possession**, possession in common, having a part, having a share, joint tenancy, tenancy in common, joint ownership, common ownership, shared ownership, time sharing, time-share apartment, condominium (US), part ownership, partnership, copartnership, union, association, alliance, public corporation, public company, joint stock, common stock, common money, profit-sharing, dividend, share, joint bank account, pool, kitty, tontine, common supplies, store, common property, common land, common, public land, (public) park, cooperative system, public domain, nationalization, public ownership, state ownership, socialism, socialization, communism, communization, collectivism, collectivization, collective farm, collective, sharecropping (US), communal living, commune, community, communalization, kolkhoz, kibbutz, joint government, coalition, federation, confederation, commonwealth, commonweal, the Commonwealth of Nations, international organization, United Nations (UN), United Nations Organization (UNO), European Union (EU), European Community (EC), Common Market, global village, cooperative, dependency, dominion, democracy, participatory democracy, town meeting

▶ *12 Government and Politics; 43 Agriculture; 127 Inclusion; 439 Store; 440 Possessions; 747 Cooperation; 763 Possession; 780 Money; 785 Payment*

2 **participation**, group participation, membership, affiliation, association, collaboration, cooperation, joint action, sympathy strike, companionship, fellowship, mutualism, inclusion, involvement, engagement, contribution, partaking, complicity, sharing, co-sharing, shared feelings, fellow feeling, sympathy, empathy

▶ *590 Feelings*

3 **participant**, participator, partaker, sharer, co-tenant, fellow tenant, joint owner, time-share owner, condominium owner (US), roommate, flatmate, apartment sharer (US), partner, copartner, shareholder, ally, confederate, associate, colleague, collaborator, accomplice, accessory, party, a party to, member, community member, commune member, communard, kibbutznik, socialist, communist, party member, union member, sympathizer, empathizer, sharecropper (US), share farmer (Aus)

VERBS

4 **have joint possession**, hold in common, share (in), take a share, share expenses, split the difference, go Dutch, have a stake in, cooperate, contribute, participate (in), become a member, join, associate oneself with (*or* to), take part in, enter into, partake of, involve oneself, have to do with, have a hand in, have a finger in (the pie), have a voice (*or* say) in, join in, be in on, communalize, socialize, communize, nationalize, internationalize, share and share alike, go shares (Inf), go halves (Inf), go fifty-fifty (Inf), go even-Stephen (Inf), have a piece of (Inf), get in on the act (Inf)

ADJECTIVES

5 **jointly possessing**, jointly possessed, joint, united, concerted, associate, corporate, profit-sharing, time sharing, house-sharing, flat-sharing, apartment-sharing (US), cooperative, common, in common, communal, general, public, mutual, collective, socialistic, communistic, the people's, global, international, participating, participatory, participative, accessory, partaking, part of, involved (in), sympathetic, empathetic, in on, in the middle of, in the same boat, share and share alike

ADVERBS

6 **in common**, commonly, together, jointly, unitedly, cooperatively, in cooperation with, collectively, communally, socialistically, communistically, globally, throughout the world, internationally, on the international scene, sympathetically, empathetically

765 Profit

If possible honestly, if not, somehow, make money. Horace.

NOUNS

1 **gain**, gaining, getting, receiving, taking, winning, acquisition, acquirement, obtainment, attainment, attainability, advantage, unfair advantage, benefit, personal benefit, coming by, gathering in, bringing in, securement, procurement, procural, procurance, procuration, earnings, makings, moneymaking, breadwinning, profitableness, profitmaking, profit-taking, profitability, profitable transaction, lucrative deal, successful speculation, realization, gainfulness, remunerativeness, fund-raising, profiteering, usury, greed, grist to the mill, getting hold of (Inf), pulling down (Inf), money-grubbing (Inf), raking (*or* coining) it in (Inf)

▶ *683 Selfishness; 769 Receiving; 773 Taking; 780 Money*

2 **augmentation**, increase, gain in value, appreciation, price increase, pay increase, rise, raise (US), increment, development, crescendo, growth, expansion, gaining weight, gaining height, broadening, widening, spreading, spread, escalation, inflation, dilation, advance, approach, headway, gaining ground, ground gained, improvement, improved mileage, performance gain, betterment, higher jump, faster race, further throw, longer endurance, gaining on, gaining time, overtaking, leaving behind

▶ *47 Athletics; 213 Increase; 293 Earliness; 778 Sale*

3 **acquisition**, collection, gathering, gleaning, bringing

together, assembling, assemblage, accumulation, cumulation, amassment, accretion, catch, hoard, store, heap, stack, pile, stock, stockpile, mountain, pool, bunch (Inf), haul (Inf)

► *376 Gathering; 439 Store*

4 earnings, income, private income, corporate income, earned income, unearned income, advance earnings, advance, royalty, national income, GNP (gross national product), privy purse, revenue, wages, salary, pay, pay packet, pay cheque, money coming in, takings, makings, receipts, box-office receipts, gross receipts, net receipts, gross revenue, turnover, net revenue, return, gross return, net return, returns, proceeds, gate money, gate, winnings, pickings, gleanings, retirement pay, social security payments, pension, stipend, annuity, tontine, maintenance, alimony, palimony (US), fee, remuneration, take (US inf), take-in (US inf)

► *12 Government and Politics; 570 Marriage; 785 Payment; 788 Receipt*

5 profit, gain, gains, capital gains, clear profit, profits, gross profits, gross, net profits, net, emolument, interest, compound interest, simple interest, percentage, dividends, inheritance, bequest, legacy, endowment, dowry, grant, subsidy, compensation, honorarium, fellowship, scholarship, bursary (Scot), benefit, fringe benefit, extra, bonus, perquisite, perk, commission, expense account, allowance, pocket money, pin money, extra money, prosperity, wealth, pelf, lucre, filthy lucre, savings, spending money, money for a rainy day, reward, gratuity, tip, lagniappe (US), baksheesh, award, trophy, prize, jackpot, something for nothing, gift, free gift, giveaway (US), find, finding, discovery, trove, treasure-trove, buried treasure, piece of luck, windfall money, windfall profit, windfall, easy money, illegal gain, ill-gotten gains, theft, stealing, bribe, plunder, booty, spoils, spoils of war, plum (Inf), golden handshake (Inf), golden parachute (US inf), gettings (Inf), killing (Inf), clean up (US inf), rake-off (Inf), gravy (Inf), boodle (Inf), swag (Inf), freebie (US inf), exes (Inf)

► *107 Chance; 248 Prosperity; 265 Easiness; 449 Discovery; 768 Giving; 774 Stealing; 781 Wealth; 794 Prize; 813 Reward*

6 yield, output, production, proceeds, produce, product, crop, vintage crop, bumper crop, cash crop, second crop, gleanings, harvest, fruit, vintage, vintage wine

► *43 Agriculture; 356 Creation*

7 gainer, winner, moneymaker, breadwinner, wealthy person, rich person, billionaire, millionaire (*or* millionairess), parvenu (*or* parvenue), capitalist, tycoon, magnate, heir, heiress, beneficiary, procurer, earner, fundraiser, profiteer, usurer, collector, gatherer, gleaner, hoarder, wage earner, wage worker (US), saver, thief, robber, briber, plunderer, money-spinner (Inf), money-grubber (Inf), gold-digger (Inf), fat cat (US inf)

8 wealthy people, the rich and famous, the well-to-do, the nouveaux riches, the jet set, the upper class, the upper crust (Inf), the well-heeled (Inf), glitterati (Inf), the haves (Inf), Sloanes (Inf)

VERBS

9 gain, get, win, have success, acquire, obtain, make one's own, appropriate, annex, attain, have an advantage, have an unfair advantage, benefit, receive a benefit, come by, gather in, bring in, secure, procure, earn, make, make money, profit, make a profit, realize, raise funds, collect funds, launch an appeal, beg, borrow, or steal, profiteer, lay hands on, get one's fingers on, get hold of (Inf), pull down (Inf), glom on to (US inf)

10 augment, increase, escalate, gain in value, appreciate, rise in price, receive a pay increase, receive a rise, receive a raise (US), reach a crescendo, grow, experience growth, gain height, develop, proliferate, mushroom, flower, expand, snowball, broaden, widen, spread, become larger, put on weight, gain weight, get fatter, inflate, dilate, advance, advance on, approach, get nearer, reach, get to, make headway, make rapid strides, cover the ground, gain ground, improve, perform better, jump higher, run faster, throw further, endure longer, gain on, gain time, recover lost ground, overtake, leave behind

11 acquire, collect, gather together, gather in, have a bumper crop, glean, harvest, assemble, accumulate, cumulate, accrete, amass, save up, save, bring together, get together, scrape together (*or* up), round up, dig up, catch, hoard, store away, heap, stack, pile up, pile, stockpile, stock up, pool together, pool, bunch together (Inf), bunch (Inf), scare up (US inf)

12 earn, earn income, have a private income, earn a living, balance the books, have gainful employment, make money by, turn into money, get in advance, receive an advance, receive royalties, have regular wages, get paid, draw a salary, draw a pay cheque, credit to one's account, have money coming in, have wealth, draw retirement pay, receive social security payments, receive a pension, receive a stipend, receive maintenance, receive alimony (*or* aliment), receive palimony (US), keep the wolf from the door, turn an honest penny (Inf), bring home the bacon (Inf), earn a crust (Inf)

13 be profitable, be financially worthwhile, offer a good living, show a profit, pay, pay well, yield, produce, gross, bring in a return, pay interest, pay a dividend, accrue, roll in

14 profit, make a profit, make a net profit, take a profit, reap a profit, turn to profit, sell at a profit, capitalize on, make capital out of, have capital gains, cash in on, clear, make a good living, make a fortune, have the Midas touch, prosper, draw interest, take a percentage, earn a dividend, pay dividends, inherit, receive a bequest, receive a legacy, succeed to, come into money, fall heir to, compensate, study on a scholarship, receive a fringe benefit, receive a bonus, have an expense account, draw an allowance, have extra money, save, receive a tip, win an award, get a medal, win a trophy, win a prize, break the bank, win the pools, win the lottery, find the pot of gold, get something for nothing, receive a free gift, discover a treasure trove, come across, light upon, have a piece of luck, receive a windfall profit, steal, bribe, plunder, receive a golden handshake (Inf), make a killing (Inf), clean up (US inf), line one's pockets (Inf), make one's pile (Inf), laugh all the way to the bank (Inf), hit the jackpot (Inf), rake it in (Inf), rake off (Inf)

ADJECTIVES

15 gainful, beneficial, acquiring, acquired, obtainable, attainable, available, procurable, inheriting, inherited, beneficiary, compensatory, fund-raising, moneymaking, capitalistic, profitable, profitmaking, profit-taking, gross, net, on the credit side, gratuitous, giveaway (US), windfall, financially worthwhile, useful, paid, paying, well-paying, lucrative, remunerative, rewarding, money-spinning (Inf)

16 **greedy**, avaricious, acquisitive, grasping, plundering, grabby (US inf), money-grubbing (Inf), on the make (Inf), gold-digging (Inf)

17 **well-off**, well-to-do, in the black, comfortably off, doing fine, doing very nicely, solvent, well provided for, doing great, affluent, prosperous, rich, filthy rich, wealthy, worth millions, rich as Croesus, rich as King Midas, well-heeled (Inf), flush (Inf), rolling in it (Inf), loaded (Inf)

18 **acquisitional**, acquisitive, collective, accumulative, cumulative, mountainous, augmentative, augmented, expansive, gaining, ahead of time, widening, inflationary, improvable, improved

19 **yielding**, productive, fruitful, fertile, prolific, bumper, harvested

ADVERBS

20 **gainfully**, beneficially, for money (*or* profit *or* gain), advantageously, acquisitively, profitably, at a profit, gratuitously, lucratively, remuneratively, greedily, avariciously, affluently, prosperously, richly, wealthily, collectively, accumulatively, cumulatively, expansively, productively, fruitfully, fertilely, prolifically, in the black

766 Loss

'Tis better to have loved and lost than never to have lost at all. Samuel Butler.

What's lost upon the roundabouts we pulls up on the swings! Patrick Reginald Chalmers.

To lose one parent, Mr Worthing, may be regarded as a misfortune; to lose both looks like carelessness. Oscar Wilde.

NOUNS

1 **loss**, losing, misplacing, mislaying, taking away, decrease, decrement, subtraction, deprivation, privation, hopeless loss, dead loss, total loss, utter loss, irreparable loss, irretrievable loss, dispossession, eviction, expropriation, divestment, robbery, stripping, asset-stripping, detriment, disadvantage, setback, check, reverse, reversal, failure, defeat, penalty, forfeiture, forfeit, loss of freedom, loss of rights, disentitlement, disenfranchisement (*or* disfranchisement), disqualification, loss of consciousness, coma, death, bereavement, spiritual loss, perdition, sacrifice, denial, loss of weight, weight loss, dieting, slimming, fasting, weight-watching, figure-watching, anorexia, riddance, good riddance, nonrestoration, nonrecovery

▶ *7 Religion; 16 Law; 25 Cookery; 35 Medicine; 98 Absence; 212 Subtraction; 214 Decrease; 526 Disappearance; 773 Taking; 814 Punishment*

2 **financial loss**, loss of profit, lack of profit, loss of earnings, poor return, cut price, cut rate (US), loss leader, diminishing returns, losses, losings, operating at a loss, running at a loss, cost, expense, expenditure, not making ends meet, deficit, deficiency, insufficiency, shortfall, overspending, overdraft, debit, insolvency, bankruptcy, going to the wall, going belly up (US inf)

▶ *780 Money; 782 Poverty; 783 Credit; 784 Debt; 787 Expenditure; 791 Discount*

3 **waste**, wastefulness, wastage, squandering, dissipation, misuse, losing battle, wasted effort, loss of interest, unproductiveness, fruitlessness, spilt milk, waste of breath, waste of time, vain labour, labour of Sisyphus, fool's errand, wild-goose chase

▶ *238 Uselessness; 441 Waste*

4 **lessening**, dwindling, falling off, waning, wasting away, fading out, dimming, wearing, wearing away, erosion, wear and tear, blood, sweat, and tears, exhaustion, depletion, shrinkage, depreciation, diminution, outflow, draining, drain, dribbling away, seeping away, leakage, haemorrhage, evaporation, impoverishment, deterioration

▶ *245 Deterioration*

5 **destruction**, denudation, spoiling, despoilment, spoliation, wilful destruction, sabotage, harm, injury, impairment, damage, ruin, ablation

▶ *357 Destruction*

6 **loser**, born loser, failure, reject, disqualified athlete, unsuccessful candidate, flounderer, black sheep, lost sheep, lost soul, damned soul, fallen angel, sinner, dissipated person, good-for-nothing, ne'er-do-well, scapegoat, victim, dupe, prey, bungler, incompetent, star-crossed lover, lame dog, lame duck, underdog, social outcast, down-and-out, wasteful person, waster, squanderer, polluter, overspender, defaulter, bankrupt, wallflower (Inf), no-hoper (Inf), no-good (US inf), flop (Inf), fall guy (US inf)

7 **dieter**, slimmer, weight watcher, Weightwatchers™, anorexic, faster

8 **lost thing**, lost game, lost chance, lost opportunity, lost cause, lost election, lost labour, lost love, lost art, lost memory, lost time, lost hope, Lost Generation, lost tribes, lost ground, lost battle, lost war, lost life, lost youth, misspent youth

▶ *12 Government and Politics; 585 War*

VERBS

9 **lose**, suffer loss, incur loss, meet with a loss, have no more, not find, lose sight of, not be able to find, look in vain for, misplace, mislay, miss, lose track of, lose contact with, lose one's memory, forget, take away, decrease, subtract, consume, deprive, dispossess, evict, expropriate, divest, rob, strip, asset-strip, have a setback, have a reversal, fail, lose a chance, miss an opportunity, face defeat, lose out, lose the battle, lose the election, lose the day, lose the match, almost win, just lose, lose by a whisker, incur a penalty, forfeit, sacrifice, relinquish, lose one's freedom, become a prisoner, lose one's rights, become disenfranchised (*or* disfranchised), face disqualification, face a total loss, die, lose weight, diet, slim, fast, starve oneself, refuse food, go on a hunger strike, become anorexic, lose consciousness, faint, collapse, say goodbye to, kiss goodbye (Inf), be pipped at the post (Inf)

10 **have a financial loss**, incur losses, sell at a loss, lose money, lose profits, lose earnings, have a poor return, cut prices, have diminishing returns, suffer a setback, have losses, operate at a loss, run at a loss, throw good money after bad, make no profit, not make ends meet, run a deficit, fall short, have nothing to show for, overspend, pour money down the drain, overdraw, run up an overdraft, become insolvent, face bankruptcy, go to the wall, go into the red (Inf), come to a sticky end (Inf), go broke (Inf), go bust (Inf), go belly up (US inf)

11 be wasteful, waste, squander, dissipate, throw away, fritter away, pour down the drain, let slip through one's fingers, waste one's efforts, waste one's breath, waste one's time, labour in vain, draw a blank, go on a fool's errand, go on a wild goose chase

12 lessen, dwindle, wane, fade out, dim, deplete, depreciate, diminish, deteriorate, waste away, wear, wear away, erode, drain, dribble away, leak, haemorrhage, seep away, evaporate, shrink, impoverish, become impoverished, undergo privation, lose the battle, lose interest in

13 destroy, misuse, despoil, spoliate, spoil, denude, destroy, wilfully destroy, sabotage, harm, injure, impair, damage, ruin, ablate

14 go to waste, come to nothing, come to naught, go (*or* run) to seed, go to pot, dissipate, scatter to the winds, throw out of the window, go to the dogs, go (*or* end) up in smoke, go down the drain (*or* tube *or* pan), go up the spout (Inf)

15 lose someone, give someone the slip, avoid, evade, elude, dodge, escape, outrun, outstrip, leave behind, shake off

ADJECTIVES

16 losing, lost, missing, gone missing, misplaced, mislaid, astray, without, lacking, out of sight, out of view, lost from view, fallen by the wayside, nowhere to be found, long-lost, gone forever, gone for good, gone by the board, forgotten, out of mind, dead and buried, lost at sea, sunk, irrecoverable, irretrievable, incorrigible, irredeemable, hopeless, depriving, deprived, failing, failed, out of the window (Inf), squandered, depleted, stripped of, shorn of, bereft, spent, destroyed, ruined, irreclaimable, unsalvageable, the worse for wear, nonrecyclable, gone down the drain

17 unprofitable, profitless, non-profit-making, loss-leading, loss-making, cut-price, cut-rate (US), out-of-pocket, out, unsuccessful, deficient, insufficient, prodigal, wasteful, squandering, overspent, overextended, overdrawn, nonpaying, insolvent, impoverished, ruined, ruinous, bankrupt, poor, cash-poor, in the red (Inf), broke (Inf), bust (Inf), belly up (US inf)

18 at a loss, out of place, off course, off familiar territory, lost in thought, disoriented, confused, bewildered, lost in amazement, astonished, dumbstruck, astray, floundering, out of one's element, out of one's depth, all at sea, like a fish out of water, like a square peg in a round hole, gobsmacked (Inf)

ADVERBS

19 irrecoverably, irretrievably, irredeemably, irreclaimably, hopelessly

20 at a loss, at a cut price, at a cut rate (US), unsuccessfully, deficiently, insufficiently, prodigally, wastefully, in the red (Inf)

21 out of place, incongruously, anomalously, off course, off familiar territory, out of one's element, out of one's depth, out of sight, out of view, like a fish out of water, like a square peg in a round hole

767 Disposal

NOUNS

1 disposal, giving up, getting rid of, discarding, parting with, alienation, transfer, substitution, nonretention, letting go, releasing, release, dismissal, firing, sacking, freeing, liberation, liberating, unfreezing, decontrol, dispensation, exemption, nonliability, dissolution, divorce, cession, abandonment, removal, clearance, ejection, riddance, dumping, scrapping, renunciation, relinquishment, forgoing, forswearing, swearing off, cancellation, abrogation, disuse, desuetude, availability, disposability, outflow, incontinence, excretion, marching orders (Inf), the boot (Inf), the chop (Inf)

▶ *355 Relinquishment; 371 Expulsion; 372 Separation; 391 Liberation; 762 Substitution*

2 disposal of property, sale, selling, selling off, putting on the market, clearance sale, closing-down sale, jumble sale, boot sale, car-boot sale, rummage sale (US), garage sale (US), bazaar, church bazaar, fair, auction, Dutch auction, saleableness, saleability, sale and lease back, disposability

▶ *778 Sale*

3 disposable things, junk, jumble, white elephant, castoffs, flotsam, jetsam, flotsam and jetsam, rubbish, garbage (US), trash (US)

▶ *238 Uselessness*

4 wastebin, wastepaper basket, wastebasket, dustbin, garbage (*or* trash) can (US), rubbish bin, litter bin, bin, rubbish truck, dustcart (US), rubbish scow, skip, dredger, incinerator, waste disposer, waste disposal unit, drain, waste pipe, sewer

▶ *410 Container*

5 wasteyard, junkyard, dump, town (*or* city) dump, landfill site, scrapyard, scrap metal yard, dustheap (US), junk (*or* trash) pile, rubbish heap (*or* pile), refuse heap, compost heap, (kitchen) midden (Dial), cesspit, cesspool, septic tank, sewage farm (*or* works), nuclear reprocessing plant

6 rubbish collector, dustbin man (*or* woman), garbage man (*or* woman) (US), binman, dustman, litter picker, street sweeper, rag-and-bone man, junkman (US)

7 toilet, lavatory, water closet, WC, earth closet, outhouse (US), privy, latrine, head(s) (Naut), portable toilet, chemical toilet, commode, jakes (Dial), toilet bowl, pan, lavatory bowl (*or* pan), stool, chamber pot, bedpan, potty, urinal, Ladies, Gentlemen (*or* Gents), Men (US), Women (US), Men's (Rest) Room (US), Women's (Rest) Room (US), little boys' room, little girls' room, smallest room (in the house), public convenience, cloakroom, bathroom, rest room (US), washroom (US), comfort station (US), powder room, lounge, loo (Inf), bog (Inf), john (US inf), crapper (Inf), khazi (*or* kharzie) (Inf), thunderbox (Inf), thunderbowl (Inf), jerry (Inf), gazunder (Inf)

▶ *560 Excretion*

8 sink, kitchen sink, draining board, cistern, cesspit, cesspool, septic tank, septic (system) (Aus), sump, slough, soakaway, gutter, drain, sewer, cloaca, main, dunghill, midden (Lit), tip, dump, refuse dump, rubbish dump, rubbish pile, trash dump (US), rubbish heap, landfill, compost heap, compose, dustbin, coal cellar, Augean stables, pigsty, pigpen (US), den, slum, tenement building, tenement, shambles, abattoir, slaughterhouse, quarantine, quarantined house, quarantine flag, spittoon, cuspidor (US), coal hole (Inf)

▶ *410 Container; 441 Waste*

VERBS

9 dispose of, get rid of, not retain, dispense with, stop using, do without, get along without, spare, give up, let go, let loose of, release, waive, abandon, cede, yield, surrender, relinquish, part with, marry off, discard, throw away, cast off, eject, jettison, let out, leak, emit, cast away, cast overboard, scrap, dump, destroy, free, liberate, lift, lift restrictions, derestrict, raise an embargo, decontrol, deregulate, deration, substitute, replace, supersede, unhand, relax one's grip, release one's hold, unlock, unclinch, unclench, open, unbind, untie, disentangle, disunite, negate, dissolve, divorce, disinherit, turn one's back on, impoverish, cut off without a penny, cut off with a shilling, disown, maroon, cast out, renounce, abjure, forswear, swear off, disclaim, recant, cancel, revoke, abrogate, forgo, abandon one's stance, wash one's hands of, ditch (Inf)

▶ *371 Expulsion*

10 dismiss, discharge, lay off, give notice (to quit), make redundant, fire, sack, give the sack to, ease out, edge out, elbow out, pension off, put out to grass, put out to pasture (US), kick out (Inf), boot out (Inf), give someone the (old) heave-ho (Inf), give someone their marching orders (Inf), drop (US inf), give someone the boot (Inf), give someone the chop (Inf)

11 dispose of property, sell property, sell, sell off, have a sale, put up for sale, put on the market, vend, peddle, hawk, push, auction, have an auction, put under the hammer, put on the block (US), sell to the highest bidder, sell over the counter, sell under the counter, sell on the black market, flog (Inf)

ADJECTIVES

12 disposed (of), dispensed with, relinquished, released, not retained, not kept, got rid of, discarded, freed, liberated, abandoned, divorced, disowned, disinherited, forgone, forsworn

13 dismissed, discharged, fired, sacked, made redundant, under notice to quit, given notice to quit, laid off, given the sack, given one's marching orders (Inf), given the (old) heave-ho (Inf), given the chop (Inf), given the boot (Inf)

14 for sale, available, saleable, to be disposed of, transferable, inheritable, sold off

15 unclaimed, remaining, left behind, unappropriated, unowned, unpossessed, derelict

ADVERBS

16 disposably, distributively, by letting go, by giving up, by auction, under the hammer, on the block (US), by sale, over the counter, under the counter, without an inheritance, without a penny

768 Giving

When they will not give a doit to relieve a lame beggar, they will lay out ten to see a dead Indian. William Shakespeare.

He gives twice who gives promptly. Publilius Syrus.

NOUNS

1 giving, donation, bestowal, charity, alms-giving, benevolence, benefaction, philanthropy, subvention, subsidization, generosity, generous giving, generous nature, liberality, largess, bounty, contributing, contribution, offering, tithing, subscription, prize-giving, presentation, presentment, awarding, service, commitment, labour of love, voluntary work, charity work, consignment, conveyance, imparting, impartation, delivery, supplying, transfer, provision, concession, surrender, surrendering, endowing, endowment, settlement, dowry, grant, granting, conferral, conferment, investment, investiture, enfeoffment (Lit), infeudation (Lit), bequeathal, leaving, will-making, will, testament, last will and testament, gifting, bribing

▶ *16 Law; 440 Possessions; 570 Marriage; 650 Benevolence; 652 Philanthropy; 679 Generosity; 780 Money*

2 gift, present, birthday present, anniversary present, Christmas present, Christmas box, box, souvenir, memento, keepsake, a little something, token, token of esteem, gift token, gift voucher, tip, fee, honorarium, incentive pay, subsidy, subvention, support, price support, tax benefit, tax write-off, grant, grant-in-aid, allowance, pocket money, stipend, allotment, aid, financial assistance, help, scholarship, fellowship, welfare, public welfare, relief, welfare payment, alimony, palimony (US), social security benefit, retirement benefit, annuity, pension, old-age insurance, bequest, legacy, inheritance, gratuity, baksheesh, cumshaw, *pourboire* (Fr), *Trinkgeld* (Ger), consideration, bribe, kickback, douceur, sensitive payment, slush fund, inducement, prize, reward, award, presentation, trophy, bonus, bonanza, something extra, lagniappe (US), perquisite, expense account, benefit, blessing, boon, grace, favour, free gift, giveaway (US), outright gift, ex gratia payment, piece of luck, windfall, (unsolicited) repayment, conscience money, payment, required giving, tribute, tax, income tax, transfer, handsel (Lit), fairing (Lit), golden handshake (Inf), perk (Inf), whip-round (Inf), palm oil (US inf), grease (Inf), gravy (Inf), freebie (US inf), backhander (Inf), hush money (Inf), cough syrup (Inf), rake-off (Inf), sweetener (Inf), schmear (US inf), eckies (*or* exes) (Inf)

▶ *392 Help; 785 Payment; 794 Prize*

3 offering, dedication, consecration, votive offering, peace offering, thank offering, offertory, collection, sacrifice, self-sacrifice, oblation, Easter offering, Peter's pence (*or* Peter pence), tithe, widow's mite, mite box, contribution, subscription, flag day, tag day (US), appeal, Red Cross, OXFAM, United Way (US), benefit, benefit match, charity game (US), benefit performance, Live Aid, alms, Maundy money, dole, food aid, food parcel, food stamp (US), meal ticket, free meal, bounty, manna, largess, donation, donative, hand-out, giveaway (US)

▶ *679 Generosity*

4 giver, good giver, cheerful giver, generous giver, philanthropist, provider, benefactor, donator, donor, blood donor, organ donor, kidney donor, bestower, rewarder, tipper, briber, grantor, conferrer, awarder, imparter, presenter, prize-giver, settlor (Lit), testator (*or* testatrix) (Lit), legator (Lit), devisor (Lit), bequeather, subscriber, contributor, sacrificer, worshipper, tributary, tribute-payer, subject, almoner, alms-giver, saint, good Samaritan, kind person, helper, saviour, The Saviour, supporter, backer, financer, funder, patron (*or* patroness), distributor of largess, rich uncle, fairy godmother, Lady Bountiful, Santa Claus, Father Christmas, angel (Inf), sugar daddy (Inf)

▶ *636 Willingness; 679 Generosity*

VERBS

5 give, make a gift, make a present of, give a birthday present, give an anniversary gift, give a Christmas present, gift, give away, give free, not charge, treat, entertain, have a generous nature, pour out, lavish upon, shower upon, enrich, spare no expense, subscribe to, present, make a presentation, transmit, impart, convey, deliver, supply, consign, lend, render, provide, honour with, favour with, show favour, make time for, have time for, grant, vouchsafe, bestow upon, confer upon, award, accord, will, give by will, will to, make a will, draw up a will, execute a will, make a bequest, bequeath, leave, provide for, endow, dower, give a prize, tender, put into the hands of, lay at the feet of, transfer, turn over, hand over, give over, make over, give out, deal out, measure out, mete out, dole out, share out, share, share with, dispense, part with, come across with, accommodate with, delegate, allot, commission, dispatch, send, give up, cede, yield, entrust, vest, invest with, subsidize, pay, pay towards, finance, pay taxes, pay tribute, reward, offer a reward, dedicate, devote, consecrate, vow, give praise to, offer, offer up, sacrifice, give a gratuity, tip, cross one's palm (with silver), bribe, slip money to, stand (Inf), sweeten the kitty (Inf), put something in the pot (US inf), chip in (Inf), pay one's whack (Inf), dish out (Inf), shell out (Inf), fork out (*or* over *or* up) (Inf), kick in (US and Aus inf), grease the palm (Inf)

6 give to charity, philanthropize, donate, tithe, contribute to, commit money, commit time, volunteer, give alms, bestow alms, give freely, give generously, open one's purse, put one's hand in one's pocket, pass round the hat, give the shirt off one's back, launch an appeal, help, help fund, help with money, do one's duty, pay one's share, commit oneself, participate, have a whip-round (Inf)

▶ *652 Philanthropy; 679 Generosity*

ADJECTIVES

7 given, giveable, bestowable, impartable, available, saleable, for sale, subventionary, bequeathed, willed, bequeathable, transferable, granted, accorded, bestowed, bonus, giveaway (US), given away, gratis, free (of charge), uncharged, for nothing, costing nothing, for the asking, voluntary, complimentary, courtesy, sacrificial, votive, oblatory, gratuitous, God-given, donative, contributory, tributary, testate (Lit), testamentary (Lit), testamental (Lit), endowed, subsidized, dowered, stipendiary, pensionary, insurable, taxable

8 giving, bestowing, imparting, granting, transferring, alms-giving, charitable, benevolent, philanthropic, generous, open-handed, bountiful, liberal

▶ *636 Willingness; 652 Philanthropy; 679 Generosity*

ADVERBS

9 as a gift, gratuitously, gratis, free (of charge), for free, without payment, on the house, on one, charitably, with charity, benevolently, generously, bountifully, liberally, sacrificially, votively, oblatorily

769 Receiving

Experience was to be taken as showing that one might get a five-pound note as one got a light for a cigarette; but one had to check the friendly impulse to ask for it in the same way. Henry James.

NOUNS

1 receiving, recipience, reception, getting, taking, accepting, acceptance, acquisition, collection, collecting, collectorship, receivership, inheritance, heritage, patrimony, legacy, bequest, bequeathal, birthright, heirship, succession, line of succession, primogeniture, hereditament, heirloom

▶ *763 Possession; 773 Taking*

2 something received, gift, token, tribute, prize, trophy, money received, earnings, profits, income, salary, pay, take-home pay, revenue, net receipts, gross receipts, proceeds, receipts, returns, box-office returns, gate money, the gate, takings, credits, dividend, bursary, stipend, scholarship, fellowship, maintenance, annuity, tontine, fringe benefit, winnings, ill-gotten gains, allowance, pin money, pocket money, alimony, palimony (US), pension, compensation, bonus, commission, perquisite, perk (Inf)

▶ *768 Giving; 780 Money; 794 Prize*

3 acknowledgment of payment, receipt of custom, bill, voucher, ticket, counterfoil, stub (US), docket

4 reception, admitting, admission, admittance, greeting, welcoming, entertaining, welcoming ceremony, baptism, christening, confirmation, initiation, debut, reception room, reception, lobby, living area, living room, drawing room, sitting room

▶ *370 Admittance; 654 Sociability*

5 recipient, receiver, getter, taker, accepter, acceptor, receiver of stolen property, fence (Inf), buyer, purchaser, customer, acquirer, obtainer, procurer, holder, payee, endorsee, consignee, donee (Lit), grantee (Lit), trustee, allottee, lessee, licensee, earner, wage earner, pensioner, old age pensioner (OAP), annuitant, dependent, receiver of honours, scholarship winner, scholar, exhibitioner, fellowship winner, fellow, valedictorian (US), winner, prizewinner, message-receiver, addressee, reader, listener, hearer, viewer, spectator, beholder, audience, one at the receiving end, object of charity, charity case, beggar, sufferer, scapegoat, victim, butt, panhandler (US inf)

▶ *608 Relief; 813 Reward; 814 Punishment*

6 beneficiary, heir, heiress, legal heir, heritor (Lit), heir apparent (Lit), heir presumptive (Lit), heir-at-law (Lit), fiduciary heir (Lit), inheritor, inheritress (*or* inheritrix), successor, legatee (Lit), assignee (Lit), assign (Lit), devisee (Lit), coheir, joint heir, next in line

7 **collector**, tax collector, customs officer, excise officer, exciseman, bill collector, debt collector, rent collector, *rentier* (Fr), bailiff, confiscator, sequestrator, receiver, official receiver, liquidator, administrative receiver

▶ *784 Debt*

8 **receiver**, radio receiver, radar receiver, telephone receiver, headset, headphones, earphones

▶ *692 Communications*

VERBS

9 **receive**, be given, have from, get, take, take in, take up, accept, acquire, gain, collect, obtain, secure, come by, come to hand, earn, have an income, gross, net, clear, bring in, take home, pocket, draw a pension, receive social security, inherit, become an heir (*or* heiress), receive a bequest, succeed to, come to one, come into, come in for, pass into one's hand, fall into one's hands, fall to one's lot, fall to one's share, step into the shoes of, take over, take off someone's hands, stick to one's fingers, acknowledge, receipt, give a receipt, credit, accept stolen property, fence (Inf)

10 **receive someone**, admit, greet, welcome, make welcome, shake hands with, hold out one's hand to, advance to meet, receive guests, usher in, entertain, host, act as host (*or* hostess), be at home to, open one's doors to, keep open house, receive into the church, baptize, christen, confirm

▶ *654 Sociability*

ADJECTIVES

11 **receiving**, recipient, receptive, taking, accepting, acceptant, wage-earning, salaried, paid, compensated, pensioned, pensioned-off, awarded, rewarded, given, allotted, on the receiving end

12 **receptive**, welcoming, open, open-minded, generous-hearted

13 **received**, accepted, taken, taken over, acquired, gained, collected, secured, inherited, admitted, taken in, heard, read, seen, acknowledged, well-received, welcomed, entertained, received into the church, baptized, christened, confirmed

14 **receivable**, takable, gettable, collectable, compensatory, compensative, pensionary, hereditary, primogenitary

ADVERBS

15 **receptively**, in a receptive way, as a wage-earner, hereditarily, with a warm welcome, as a new member, as a convert, with openness, with an open mind, in an open-minded way, with a generous heart, in a generous-hearted manner

770 Allocation

The white man knows how to make everything, but he does not know how to distribute it. Sitting Bull.

NOUNS

1 **allocation**, allotting, allotment, assignment, appointment, job allocation, job sharing, apportionment, apportioning, appropriation, earmarking, tagging, setting aside, division, subdivision, partition, sharing, sharing out, distribution, parcelling out, doling out, dealing out, dispensing, dispensation, delimitation, demarcation, divvying up (US inf)

▶ *205 Part; 764 Sharing*

2 **portion**, share, fair share, dividend, allocation, allotment, lot, plot, strip of land, proportion, ratio, quota, dole, pittance, allowance, ration, dose, dosage, measure, dollop, helping, slice, slice of the cake, piece of the pie (US), piece of the action (Inf)

▶ *166 Limit; 209 Grading*

3 **allotted task**, assigned task, assigned job, chore, stint, shift, stretch, bout, period, spell of work

▶ *768 Giving*

VERBS

4 **allot**, allocate, apportion, appropriate, earmark, tag, demarcate, delimit, limit, divide, divide proportionately, split down the middle, prorate, divide up, subdivide, carve up, bisect, split, cut, share, share out, distribute, spread around, dispense, deal out, deal, portion out, dole out, parcel out, mete out, measure, ration, dose, divvy up (US inf), dish out (Inf)

5 **get one's allotment**, get one's (fair) share, get a share, take a share, take one's cut, be cut in, go shares (Inf), go halves (Inf), get a piece of the action (Inf)

6 **assign**, assign a task, assign a job, assign a part, assign a place, allot a billet, detail

ADJECTIVES

7 **allocated**, allotted, assigned, apportioned, divided, shared out, distributed, dividable, divisible

ADVERBS

8 **proportionately**, respectively, pro rata, per head, per capita, each according to his share

771 Lending

Lend only that which you can afford to lose. Proverb.

NOUNS

1 **lending**, loaning, giving temporarily, giving, lending money, moneylending, advancing, advance on salary, advance on royalties, advance, advancement, accommodation, grant, giving credit, lending at interest, lending on security, lending on collateral, usury, extortion, pawnbroking, loan-sharking (Inf), hocking (US inf), popping (Inf)

▶ *17 Literature; 783 Credit*

2 **loan**, unsecured loan, secured loan, collateral loan, long-term loan, short-term loan, student loan, instalment loan, bank loan, personal loan, business loan, international loan, foreign loan, lend-lease

3 **lender**, loaner, creditor, moneylender, moneybroker, banker, bank manager, loan officer (US), financier, usurer, loan shark, pawnbroker, mortgagee, mortgage holder, hire-purchase dealer, Shylock (Inf), uncle (Inf)

4 **lending institution**, financial institution, building society, friendly society, savings and loan association (US), credit company, credit-card company, American Express™, VISA, finance company (*or* house), loan office

(US), mortgage company, bank, credit union, *mont-de-piété* (Fr), IMP (International Monetary Fund), World Bank, European Bank, hock shop (US inf), pop shop (Inf), uncle's (Inf)

VERBS

5 **lend**, loan, give temporarily, give one a loan, negotiate a loan, float a loan (US), lend money, make an unsecured loan, make a secured loan, lend on security (*or* on collateral), give a long-term loan, give a short-term loan, advance, accommodate, grant, allow credit, give credit, lend at interest, practise usury, extort

ADJECTIVES

6 **loaned**, on loan, lent, lending, accommodative, secured, on collateral, unsecured, usurious, extortionate, on credit

ADVERBS

7 **on loan**, on security, on collateral, on (*or* in) advance, on credit

772 Borrowing

Be not made a beggar by banqueting upon borrowing, when thou hast nothing in thy purse: for thou shalt lie in wait for thine own life, and be talked on. Bible: Ecclesiasticus.

The human species, according to the best theory I can form of it, is composed of two distinct races, the men who borrow, and the men who lend. Charles Lamb.

Neither a borrower nor a lender be;
For loan oft loses both itself and friend,
And borrowing dulls the edge of husbandry. William Shakespeare.

NOUNS

1 **borrowing**, request for money, money-raising, fund-raising, advance on salary, advance on royalties, advance, request for credit, loan application, loan transaction, loan agreement, buying on credit, repayment plan, taking out a loan, financing, mortgaging, pledging, draw-down, pawning, begging, hocking (US inf), popping (Inf), touching (up) (Inf), hitting up (US inf)

▶ *710 Request; 769 Receiving; 771 Lending; 773 Taking*

2 **adoption**, adoptability, appropriation, assumption, using as one's own

▶ *349 Use*

3 **illegal borrowing**, unauthorized borrowing, infringement of copyright, plagiarism, bootlegging, parodying, copying, piracy, pirating, imitating, imitation, fake, pastiche (*or* pasticcio), stealing, autotheft, joyriding (Inf)

▶ *17 Literature; 18 Music; 125 Imitation; 700 Deception; 774 Stealing*

4 **credit**, credit account, credit facility, credit card, charge card, American Express™, VISA™, MasterCard™, phonecard, instalment, buying, instalment plan (US), hire purchase (HP), plastic (Inf), tick (Inf), the never-never (Inf)

▶ *777 Purchase; 783 Credit*

5 **loan**, bank loan, personal loan, business loan, secured loan, mortgage, overdraft, debt, repayable amount, outstanding balance, IOU

▶ *784 Debt*

6 **borrower**, debtor, ower, fund-raiser, mortgagor (*or* mortgager), credit user, credit-card holder, pawner, pledger, sponger, cadger, plagiarist, pirate, imitator

VERBS

7 **borrow**, request money, raise money, take a salary advance, take an advance on royalties, request credit, make a loan application, sign a loan agreement, take out a loan, negotiate a loan, float a loan (US), secure a loan, secure a personal loan, take out a business loan, provide collateral, finance a purchase, give one's IOU, mortgage one's house, take out a (second) mortgage, have an overdraft, pledge, pawn, beg, scrounge, cadge, sponge, touch someone (up) (Inf), hit someone up (US inf), bum (US inf), hock (US inf), pop (Inf)

8 **adopt**, appropriate, take on, avail oneself of, assume, use as one's own

9 **borrow illegally**, borrow without permission, borrow without authorization, infringe a copyright, plagiarize, bootleg, parody, sample, copy, pirate a record, pirate a video, imitate, fake, steal, steal one's stuff (Inf), joy-ride (Inf)

10 **buy on credit**, open a credit account, have a credit facility, use a credit card, get on credit, run up an account, run up a debt, incur liabilities, buy in instalments, buy on the instalment plan (US), buy on HP, buy on the never-never (Inf), get on tick (Inf), get on the cuff (Inf)

ADJECTIVES

11 **borrowed**, loaned, mortgaged, secured, securing, money-raising, repayable, outstanding, credit-card, instalment, pawned, adopted, appropriated, infringed, plagiarized, copied, pirated, imitated, fake, ersatz, stolen, plastic (Inf)

12 **adoptive**, adopting, adopted, adoptable, appropriating, appropriated, appropriable, capable of being used

ADVERBS

13 **on loan**, as an advance, by credit, with a credit card, on one's credit account, in instalments

773 Taking

The good old rule
Sufficeth them, the simple plan,
That they should take, who have the power,
And they should keep who can. William Wordsworth.

NOUNS

1 **taking**, capture, seizure, obtaining, snatching, grabbing, clutching, grasping, grasping nature, avarice, greed, rapacity, taking in, consumption, taking on, employment, engagement, taking in hand, taking hold, possession, taking possession, assuming ownership, inheritance, sexual possession, sexual assault, rape, ravishment, violation, deflowerment, taking over, takeover, takeover bid, buy-out, merger, appropriation, infringement of copyright, plagiarism, arrogation, annexation, colonization, subjection, subjugation, subduing, conquering, confiscation, nationalization, assumption, requisition, in-

dention, indent, acquisition, usurpation, seizure of power, coup, coup d'état, getting, profit-taking, winning, cadging, bumming, scrounging (Inf), touching (up) (Inf), hitting up (US inf), mooching (Inf)

▶ *17 Literature; 125 Imitation; 381 Attack; 617 Desire; 651 Malevolence*

2 **taking back**, recovery, retrieval, recoupment, regaining, recapturing, recapture, reclaiming, taxing, tax-raising, levying, foreclosing, foreclosure, eviction, seizure, confiscation, dispossession, distraint, repossession, expropriation, disinheritance, deprivation, divestment, annexation, impounding, sequestration, withdrawing, withdrawing a statement, retracting, recanting, backtracking, U-turn, nabbing (Inf), nicking (Inf)

3 **taking away**, removal, eradication, deletion, erasure, blotting out, rubbing out, subtraction, extraction, deduction, cut, asset-stripping, taking out, borrowing, plagiarism, imitation, purloining, stealing, thieving, theft, raiding, raid, plundering, pillaging, marauding, sacking, sack, looting, despoiling, spoliation, grabbing, capturing, arresting, apprehending, making a prisoner, abduction, slavery, kidnapping, hijacking, skyjacking, carjacking, piracy, taking money away, extorting, extortion, swindle, embezzlement, blackmail, deception, manipulation, pinch (Inf), protection racket (Inf), rip-off (Inf), shakedown (US inf), cop (Inf), nick (Inf), heist (US inf)

▶ *16 Law; 358 Obliteration; 585 War; 699 Falsehood; 796 Immorality*

4 **taking in**, hospitality, access, shelter, sanctuary, asylum, opening one's doors, granting a visa

▶ *650 Benevolence; 654 Sociability*

5 **takings**, take, catch, capture, tax, levy, ill-gotten gains, pickings, rich pickings, gleanings, revenue, receipts, proceeds, turnover, earnings, winnings, savings, spoils, spoils of war, booty, plunder, prize, haul (Inf), plum (Inf), swag (Inf), boodle (Inf), hot goods (Inf), hot property (Inf)

▶ *780 Money*

6 **taker**, usurper, seizer, remover, snatcher, bag-snatcher, grabber, cadger, appropriator, confiscator, sequestrator, receiver, expropriator, asset-stripper, infringer, plagiarist, bootlegger, taking by storm, spoiler, raider, pillager, marauder, sacker, ransacker, looter, despoiler, abductor, embezzler, robber, mugger, rapist, captor, kidnapper, hijacker, skyjacker, extortionist, extortioner, blackmailer, racketeer, greedy person, leech, parasite, vampire, locust, predator, vulture, wolf, shark, crook (Inf), shakedown artist (US inf)

VERBS

7 **take**, capture, seize, obtain, snatch, grab, clutch at, grasp, have a grasping nature, show greed, take in, accept, consume, take on, employ, engage, take in hand, inherit, take hold of, get hold of, lay one's hands on, stake one's claim to, possess, take possession of, squat, assume ownership of, take sexual possession of, assault sexually, rape, ravish, violate, deflower, take over, buy out, merge, take for oneself, appropriate, infringe a copyright, plagiarize, annex, colonize, conquor, subject, subjugate, subdue, overrun, swarm over, earmark, confiscate, nationalize, communalize, assume, assume ownership, requisition, indent, acquire, usurp, seize power, lead a coup, get, take profits, win, bum, scrounge (Inf), touch up (Inf), hit up (US inf), mooch (Inf)

8 **take back**, recover, retrieve, recoup, recover one's costs, recover one's losses, recapture, regain, reclaim, tax, raise taxes, overtax, levy, foreclose, evict, seize, confiscate, dispossess, cut someone out of one's will, cut off without a penny, repossess, distrain, expropriate, disinherit, deprive, divest, annex, impound, sequester

9 **withdraw a statement**, retract, recant, backtrack, do a U-turn, eat one's words (Inf), eat humble pie (Inf)

10 **take away**, remove, eradicate, delete, erase, blot out, rub out, subtract, extract, deduct, take off, cut, mine, tap, milk, strip the assets of, take out, borrow, plagiarize, imitate, purloin, steal, thieve, pilfer, shoplift, help, oneself to, run away with, carry off, run off with, elope with, raid, plunder, pillage, sack, loot, despoil, grab, take into custody, take captive, capture, make a prisoner, trap, ensnare, hold, arrest, apprehend, run in, abduct, kidnap, take a hostage, enslave, shanghai, hijack, skyjack, take money away, extort, extort protection money, swindle, embezzle, fleece, blackmail, dupe, outwit, outsmart, deceive, manipulate, twist round one's little finger, fool, befool, make a fool of, take to the cleaners (Inf), take for a ride (Inf), run a protection racket (Inf), nab (Inf), pinch (Inf), nick (Inf), cop (Inf), rip off (Inf), shake down (US inf), heist (US inf)

11 **be hospitable**, take in, take on board, allow in, give access to, ask in, have round, give shelter to, shelter, give sanctuary to, give asylum to, grant a visa to, open one's doors to

ADJECTIVES

12 **taking**, avaricious, greedy, grasping, rapacious, predatory, possessive, acquisitive, acquiring, merged, takeover, inheriting, assaulted, raped, appropriated, requisitionary, acquisitional, retrievable, taxable, tax-raising, expropriatory, confiscatory, commandeering, annexed, deductive, asset-stripped, plundering, plundered, extortionate, deceptive, manipulative, thieving, rip-off (Inf)

ADVERBS

13 **avariciously**, with avarice, greedily, in a greedy fashion, graspingly, rapaciously, predatorily, like a predator, possessively, acquisitively, retrievably, deductively, extortionately, deceptively, with deception, manipulatively, in a manipulative way

774 Stealing

The fault is great in man or woman
Who steals a goose from off a common;
But what can plead that man's excuse
Who steals a common from a goose? Anonymous.

NOUNS

1 **stealing**, thieving, thievery, thievishness, theft, petty theft, grand theft, larceny, taking, pilfering, pilferage, filching, filch, petit (*or* petty) larceny, grand larceny, purloining, robbing, robbing the till, putting one's fingers in the till, robbery, bank robbery, train robbery, highway robbery, armed robbery, robbery with violence, daylight robbery, assault and robbery, ram-raiding, mugging,

purse-snatching, pickpocketing, burglarizing, burglary, aggrevated burglary, housebreaking, breaking and entering, unlawful entry, safe-breaking, safe-cracking, safe-blowing, hijacking, skyjacking, carjacking, piracy, cattle raiding, cattle rustling, stock rustling, shoplifting, kleptomania, light-fingeredness, light fingers, poaching, borrowing, snatching, bag-snatching, scrumping (Dial), scrounging (Inf), lifting (Inf), pinching (Inf), sticky fingers (Inf), snitching (Inf), swiping (Inf), nicking (Inf), boosting (Inf), hustling (Inf), fiddling (Inf)

▶ *381 Attack; 651 Malevolence; 773 Taking*

2 kidnapping, abduction, false imprisonment, shanghaiing, impressment, crimping, dognapping (Inf)

3 theft, car theft, autotheft, joyriding (Inf), taking without owner's consent, taking and driving away, hotting (Inf), hot-wiring (Inf), robbery, train robbery, The Great Train Robbery, bank robbery, burglary, break-in, holdup, grab, smash and grab raid, ram-raid, job (Inf), steal (Inf), lift (Inf), snatch (Inf), heist (US inf), caper (US inf), stick-up (US inf), stick-up job (US inf), bag job (US inf), pinch (Inf)

4 stolen goods, ill-gotten gains, spoils, spoils of war, contraband, pillage, booty, loot, plunder, prize, pickings, rich pickings, stealings, gleanings, spoils of office, take (US inf), haul (Inf), steal (US inf), graft (Inf), swag (Inf), boodle (Inf), rip-off (Inf), hot goods (Inf), hot property (Inf)

5 plundering, plunder, pillaging, pillage, raiding, raid, foraging, foray, looting, looting and pillaging, sacking, sack, ransacking, privateering, buccaneering, brigandism, brigandage, banditry, outlawry, freebooting, despoliation, despoiling, despoilment, spoliation, depredation, grave-robbing, ravaging, raping, rape, gang rape, ravishment, date rape (US inf), body-snatching (Inf)

▶ *585 War; 796 Immorality*

6 illegal borrowing, unauthorized borrowing, misappropriation, infringement of copyright, plagiarism, plagiarizing, plagiary, literary theft, cheating, piracy, pirating, record piracy, video piracy, bootleg record, bootlegging, copying, imitating, imitation, fake, cribbing (Inf), lifting (Inf), joyriding (Inf), joyride (Inf)

▶ *17 Literature; 18 Music; 125 Imitation; 699 Falsehood*

7 dishonesty, cheating, deception, graft, embezzlement, misappropriation of funds, fraud, forgery, counterfeiting, extortion, blackmail, tax evasion, computer crime, swindle, confidence trick, confidence game (US), tricky business, shady business (Inf), protection racket (Inf), fiddle (Inf), flimflam (Inf), graft (Inf), con trick (Inf), con game (US inf), skin game (Inf), scam (Inf), blag (Inf), sting (Inf), rip-off (Inf)

▶ *40 Computers; 780 Money*

8 thief, stealer, robber, Robin Hood, bank robber, Bonnie Parker and Clyde Barrow, train robber, Jesse James, highway robber, highwayman, Dick Turpin, bushranger (Aus), mugger, purloiner, taker, pickpocket, Artful Dodger, kleptomaniac, shoplifter, pilferer, filcher, petty thief, sneak thief, prowler, larcenist, bag-snatcher, burglar, cat burglar, housebreaker, safe-breaker, safe-cracker, cracksman, safe-blower, picklock, hijacker, skyjacker, terrorist, kidnapper, abductor, shanghaier, crimp, chicken thief, cattle thief, cattle rustler (US), rustler (US), poacher, cutpurse (Lit), dognapper (Inf), lifter (Inf), scrounger (Inf), dip (Inf), cracksman (Inf), yegg (*or* yeggman) (US inf), peterman (Inf), booster (Inf)

9 plunderer, pillager, sacker, ransacker, brigand, bandit, raider, mosstrooper, marauder, slave-raider, buccaneer, Jean Lafitte, Blackbeard, privateer, corsair, freebooter, ravager, ravisher, rapist, spoiler, despoiler, depredator, wrecker, grave-robber, body-snatcher (Inf)

10 infringer, plagiarist, cheat, pirate, record pirate, video pirate, bootlegger, copier, imitator, cribber (Inf), joyrider (Inf)

11 dishonest person, criminal, confidence man, trickster, receiver of stolen property, cheat, liar, hypocrite, forger, counterfeiter, white-collar criminal, computer criminal, tax evader, creative accountant, defrauder, embezzler, swindler, sharper, shark, peculator, outlaw, thug, gangster, gang member, hoodlum (US), racketeer, gunman, hold-up man, flimflam man (Inf), diddler (Inf), crook (Inf), fiddler (Inf), con man (Inf), blagger (Inf), mob member (Inf), mobster (US inf), stick-up man (US inf), fence (Inf), ganef (US inf)

VERBS

12 steal, thieve, pilfer, filch, appropriate, purloin, rob, commit robbery, rob the till, put one's fingers in the till, borrow, let stick to one's fingers, make off with, sneak off with, walk off with, steal a car, joy-ride, hot-wire (Inf), rob a bank, rob a train, pull off a robbery in broad daylight, ram-raid, mug, hold someone up, snatch a purse, pick one's pockets, pickpocket, relieve one of, burglarize, burgle, commit burglary, break into a house, housebreak, make an unlawful entry, crack a safe, hijack, skyjack, carjack, rustle cattle, shoplift, poach, snatch, snatch a bag, scrounge (Inf), lift (Inf), pinch (Inf), snaffle (Inf), have sticky fingers (Inf), do a job (Inf), snitch (Inf), swipe (Inf), nick (Inf), stick someone up (US inf), knock off (Inf), boost (Inf), hustle (Inf), nobble (Inf), fiddle (Inf), heist (US inf)

13 kidnap, abduct, hold for ransom, shanghai, spirit away, carry off (*or* away), impress, crimp, dognap (Inf)

14 plunder, pillage, raid, prey upon, forage, foray, loot, loot and pillage, sack, ransack, freeboot, despoil, spoliate, depredate, rob a grave, ravage, rape, ravish

15 infringe, plagiarize, cheat, pirate, pirate a record, pirate a video, bootleg, copy, imitate, crib (Inf), lift (Inf), joyride (Inf)

16 act dishonestly, evade taxes, defraud, deceive, bilk, dupe, embezzle, swindle, fleece, extort protection money, chisel (Inf), cook the books (Inf)

ADJECTIVES

17 stolen, purloined, pilfered, thieving, thievish, light-fingered, burglarious, brigandish, kleptomaniac, larcenous, ill-gotten, kidnapped, kidnapping, hijacked, hijacking, skyjacking, poaching, predatory, predacious, buccaneering, privateering, piratelike, raiding, plunderous, plundering, looting, pillaging, spolitory, marauding, foraging, ravaging, grave-robbing, body-snatching (Inf), sticky-fingered (Inf), hot (Inf), rip-off (Inf)

18 fraudulent, dishonest, cheating, cheated, deceptive, infringed, pirated, piratical, plagiarized, misappropriated, unauthorized, blackmailed, blackmailing, swindled, crooked (Inf), scrounging (Inf), joyriding (Inf), fiddling (Inf), on the fiddle (Inf)

ADVERBS

19 **thievishly**, with light fingers, larcenously, with larceny in one's heart, predatorily, like a predator, fraudulently, dishonestly, in a dishonest way, deceptively, with deception, piratically, like a pirate, with sticky fingers (Inf)

775 Giving Back

NOUNS

1 **giving back**, returning, return, handing back, sending back, extradition, restitution, reversion, bringing back, repatriation, reinstatement, reappointment, re-enthronement, re-establishment, restoration, restoring, recycling, recycled paper, retrocession, reinvestment, rehabilitation, replacement, redemption, atonement, deliverance, requital, ransom, rescue

► *390 Deliverance; 393 Repair*

2 **compensation**, repayment, recoupment, refund, reimbursement, indemnification, indemnity, double indemnity (US), damages, penalty, amends, making amends, making good, reparation, recompense, paying back, squaring, conscience money

► *767 Disposal; 785 Payment; 814 Punishment*

3 **returner**, compensator, restorer, reinstator, atoner, redeemer, The Redeemer, refunder, recycler

► *7 Religion*

VERBS

4 **give back**, return, hand back, send back, extradite, make restitution, bring back, repatriate, reinstate, reappoint, re-enthrone, restore one to favour, give back one's position, re-establish, restore, recycle, retrocede, reinvest, rehabilitate, replace, redeem, atone, deliver, requite, ransom, rescue

5 **compensate**, repay, refund, reimburse, give one's money back, indemnify, pay double indemnity (US), pay damages, make redress, make amends for, make good, render good, make reparations, recompense, square, pay back, pay back taxes, pay off a loan, pay conscious money

ADJECTIVES

6 **restoring**, restored, restitutive, restitutory, restorable, redemptive, redemptional, redeeming, redeemed, atoning, refunding, refunded, compensatory, indemnificatory, indemnifying, reparative, reparatory

ADVERBS

7 **redemptively**, in redemption, in recompense, in restitution, in compensation, in amends, in requital, in atonement, to atone for

776 Trade

Nothing links man to man like the frequent passage from hand to hand of cash. Walter Richard Sickert.

VERBS

1 **trade**, exchange, make a fair exchange, barter, truck, swap, do a swap, transact, deal, trade off, do business, merchandise, market, buy and sell, export and import, open a trade, drive a trade, sell, peddle, push, promote, traffic, buy cheap and sell dear, trade in, deal in, handle, traffic in, smuggle, operate on the black market, deal in the black market, racketeer, profiteer, turn over, turn over one's stock, nationalize, privatize, commercialize, put on a business footing, intervene, raise trade barriers, float, incorporate, trade with, do business with, deal with, have dealings with, open an account with, sell to, buy from, solicit business, go out for trade, profit, gain, make a profit, make a killing (Inf), turn ideas into profits, have an eye for (*or* to) business, look to one's profits, know the price of everything and the value of nothing, fence (Inf)

► *759 Exchange; 777 Purchase; 778 Sale*

2 **speculate**, venture, risk, gamble, invest, sink one's capital in, put one's money to work, make one's money work for one, go on the stock exchange, play the stock market, play the futures market, deal in futures, dabble in shares, operate, bull, bear, stag, rig the market, manipulate market prices, do insider trading, make a killing (Inf), go bust (Inf)

3 **bargain**, negotiate, deal, haggle, chaffer, huckster, higgle, dicker, push up, beat down, offer, make an offer, tender, bid, make a bid, outbid, overbid, underbid, gazump, gazunder, make a takeover bid, propose a merger, initiate a (leveraged) buyout, resort to greenmail, act as white knight, pre-empt (a takeover), stickle, drive a (hard) bargain, state one's terms, ask for, charge, settle for, take, agree to, make (*or* do) a deal, shake hands on, shake on, sign on the dotted line, contract, stick out for (Inf), hold out for (Inf)

► *755 Contract*

NOUNS

4 **trade**, commerce, business, exchange, fair exchange, trade-off, barter, truck, swap, exchange of goods, payment in kind, transaction, commercial transaction, deal, business deal, trading, dealing, doing business, merchandising, buying and selling, trafficking, factorage, factorship, brokerage, agiotage, arbitrage, brokering, jobbing, stock-jobbing, share-pushing, profitmaking, traffic, drug traffic, prostitution, white slave traffic, slave trade, smuggling, black market, black economy, racketeering, profiteering

5 **commercial trade**, commercial intercourse, export and import, exporting and importing, visible trade, visible goods, visible earnings, visibles, commodification, invisible trade, invisible goods, invisible earnings, invisibles, foreign trade, international trade, home trade, domestic trade, protection, protectionism, protective tariff, protective duty, protective quota, customs barrier, tariff barrier, trade barrier, trade restriction, intervention, interventionism, free trade, open market, economic zone, free-trade area, European Free Trade Association (EFTA), economic integration, European Union (EU), European Community (EC), European Economic Community (EEC), Common Market, Euromarket, Organization of Petroleum-Exporting Countries (OPEC), General Agreement on Tariffs and Trade (GATT), World Trade Organization (WTO), capitalism, free enterprise, free economy, *laissez faire* (Fr), free-market economy, boom and bust, fluctuation, private sector, private enterprise, privatiza-

tion, public sector, state enterprise, nationalization, chamber of commerce, junior chamber of commerce (US), labor union (US), trade(s) union

► *779 Market*

6 **business**, venture, undertaking, enterprise, industry, profession, vocation, calling, craft, métier, job, occupation, (line of) work

► *354 Undertaking; 576 Work*

7 **company**, firm, concern, corporation, private company, public company, incorporated company (Inc.) (US), limited company (Ltd), public limited company (plc)

8 **speculation**, gambling, investment, playing the stock market, insider trading, insider dealing

9 **bargaining**, negotiation, haggling, higgling, hard bargaining, horse-trading, tender, offer, bid, takeover, (leveraged) buyout, merger, greenmail, bargain, deal, agreement, contract, trade agreement, GATT (General Agreement on Tariffs and Trade), World Trade Organization (WTO)

10 **trader**, businessman, businesswoman, merchant, white knight, dealer, wholesaler, retailer, vendor, seller, marketer, buyer, purchaser, exporter, importer, merchandiser, distributor, broker, stockbroker, market maker, stock-jobber, jobber, speculator, negotiator, barterer, haggler, horse-trader, profiteer, racketeer, smuggler, fence (Inf)

► *777 Purchase; 778 Sale*

11 **chamber of commerce member**, junior chamber of commerce member (US), Jaycee (US), liveryman, guildsman, labor union member (US), trade(s) unionist, shop steward

12 **custom**, customer(s), clientele, client(s), patronage, patron(s)

ADJECTIVES

13 **mercantile**, merchant-like, trading, exchanging, swapping, commercialistic, capitalist, wholesale, retail, exchangeable, marketable, merchantable, saleable

14 **commercial**, economic, monetary, financial, fiscal

15 **profitable**, profitmaking, for profit, risky, speculative

16 **unprofitable**, non-profit-making, charitable, loss-making, unremunerative, break-even

17 **professional**, vocational, occupational, industrial

18 **contractual**, tendered, negotiated, leveraged

19 **corporate**, incorporated, limited, public, nationalized, private, privatized, merged

ADVERBS

20 **in trade**, in commerce, in business, in the marketplace, across the counter, under the counter

777 Purchase

Today you're unhappy? Can't figure it out? What is the salvation? Go shopping. Arthur Miller.

VERBS

1 **purchase**, buy, get, obtain, come by, procure, acquire, acquire by purchase, make a purchase, complete a purchase, purchase by mail order, order, order through a catalogue, order by telephone, teleshop, buy on approval, buy on appro, buy cheaply, buy for a song, buy at a cut price, make a find, make a good buy, get one's money's worth, make a bad buy, afford, pay for, buy outright, buy over the counter, buy on the spot, snap up, pay cash for, pay on the spot, buy on credit, buy on the instalment plan, buy on hire purchase, buy on HP, buy on the never-never, buy on tick, buy on account, pay by credit (*or* charge) card, pay by cheque, buy in, hoard, buy up, buy up the shop, pre-empt, corner, make a corner in, corner the market, monopolize, engross (Lit), buy out, make a (leveraged) buyout, bargain, barter, bid, bid for, bid up, offer, make an offer, buy (oneself) in, buy a piece of, invest in, sink one's money in, buy shares, bull, stag, speculate, make a buy (Inf), be ripped-off (Inf)

► *752 Offer; 769 Receiving; 772 Borrowing; 783 Credit; 785 Payment*

2 **shop**, market, go shopping, shop till one drops, spend, expend, spend lavishly, be out of pocket, shop for, require, have a shopping list, hit the shops (Inf)

► *681 Extravagance; 787 Expenditure*

3 **buy back**, repurchase, redeem, ransom

4 **buy off**, bribe, square, suborn, corrupt, pay off

5 **defray**, pay for, bear the cost of, finance, bankroll (US inf)

NOUNS

6 **purchase**, buy, acquisition, purchases, shopping, good buy, bargain, good bargain, real bargain, find, one's money's worth, bad buy, rip-off (Inf)

7 **purchasing**, buying, outright purchase, on-the-spot purchase, cash purchase, deferred payment, credit (*or* charge) card purchase, Switch™, purchase on account, purchase on credit, the instalment plan, hire purchase, the HP, the never-never, tick, buying up, takeover, (leveraged) buyout, management buyout, greenmail, pre-emption, cornering, forestalling, bid, takeover bid, offer, buy-back (US), first refusal, right of purchase

► *752 Offer; 785 Payment*

8 **shopping**, shopping spree, shopping by mail order, catalogue buying, teleshopping, spending, expenditure, requirement(s), shopping list

► *787 Expenditure*

9 **repurchase**, redemption, ransom

10 **bribery**, subornment, corruption

11 **custom**, patronage, demand, consumer demand

12 **purchaser**, buyer, customer, regular customer, loyal customer, patron, client, clientele, consumer, shopper, emptor, teleshopper, spender, credit-card holder, charge-card holder, bargain hunter, bargainer, haggler, investor, speculator, share-buyer, bull, stag, vendee, transferee, consignee, offerer, bidder, highest bidder, taker, acceptor, hoarder, pre-emptor, redeemer, ransomer, briber

ADJECTIVES

13 **bought**, purchased, paid for, charged, purchasable, emptional, worth buying, ransomed, redeemed, bribed, bribable

14 **buying**, purchasing, shopping, marketing, teleshopping, cash and carry, cash on delivery (COD), cut-price, for a song, bidding, bargaining, haggling, investing, speculative, bullish, pre-emptive, redemptive, acquisitive

► *791 Discount; 792 Dearness; 793 Cheapness*

ADVERBS

15 **cheaply**, inexpensively

16 dearly, expensively
17 acquisitively, pre-emptively, redemptively, profitably

INTERJECTIONS

18 buyer beware!, *caveat emptor!* (L)

778 Sale

Sell a country! Why not sell the air, the great sea, as well as the earth? Did not the Great Spirit make them all for the use of his children? Tecumseh.

VERBS

1 sell, vend, dispose of, transfer, convey, market, merchandise, put on sale, put up for sale, offer for sale, have for sale, have on offer, make a sale, deal, trade, barter, exchange, bring to market, unload on the market, unload, dump, get rid of, hawk, peddle, traffic in, push, promote, canvass, solicit, tout, cater to (*or* for), auction, auction off, put to auction, sell by auction, bring under the hammer, put to (*or* on) the block, sell to the highest bidder, knock down to, wholesale, retail, handle, carry, stock, deal in, sell over the counter, sell under the counter, sell on the black market, sell on the black economy, turn over one's stock, realize, encash, sell at a profit, make a profit, make a killing, gain, sell at a loss, sell at a sacrifice, lose money on, lose, undercut, have a price war, reduce, sell off, remainder, clear stock, hold (*or* have) a sale, hold a clearance sale, hold a going-out-of-business sale, hold a fire sale (US), sell up, sell out, wind up, sell again, resell, sell forward, sell short, flog (Inf)

► *765 Profit; 766 Loss; 776 Trade*

2 be sold, change hands, be on sale, come under the hammer, go to (*or* on) the block, fetch a good price, go for a good price, sell, have a buyer, have a market, meet a demand, be in demand, sell well, sell like hot cakes, sell out, boom, be a best-seller, sell badly, stay on the shelf, gather dust, flop (Inf)

NOUNS

3 selling, sale, vending, vendition, disposal, transfer, conveyance, transaction, deal, marketing, merchandising, distribution, sales coverage, promotion, advertisement, traffic, trade, trading, dealing, barter, exchange, trafficking, peddling, canvassing, soliciting, auction, wholesale, retail, sale of office, simony, private sale, exclusive sale, monopoly, oligopoly

► *776 Trade*

4 sale, sell-out, bargain sale, grand opening sale, sale of the century, spring sale, summer sale, autumn sale, winter sale, stock-taking sale, clearance sale, clearance, closing-down sale, going-out-of-business sale, fire sale (US), white sale, rummage sale, jumble sale, garage sale, car-boot sale, sale of work, charity sale, bazaar, church bazaar, charity bazaar, second-hand sale, junk sale, public sale, auction, art auction, sale by auction, roup (Dial), Dutch auction, vendue (US)

► *779 Market*

5 sales, good sales, boom, bad sales, recession, depression

► *248 Prosperity; 249 Adversity*

6 salesmanship, service, sales talk, pitch, sales patter, spiel, hard sell, soft sell, sales conference, sales forecasting

7 market, market research, consumer questionnaire, product testing, marketability, saleability, vendibility

8 merchandise, product, article, article for sale, vendible, article of commerce, line, range, repertoire, store, selling line, best-seller, loss leader, staple, commodity, salable commodity, stock, stock-in-trade, supplies, wares, goods, goods on approval, goods on assignment, capital goods, shop goods, consumer goods, consumer durables, durables, perishable goods, perishables, canned goods, dry goods, white goods, sundries, freight, load, cargo

► *406 Contents; 439 Store*

9 seller, vendor, consignor, transferor, share-seller, bear, auctioneer

10 salesman, saleswoman, salesperson, salesgirl, shop assistant, shop girl, shopwalker, sales representative, representative, rep, agent, door-to-door salesman, sales force, traveller, commercial traveller, travelling salesman (*or* saleswoman), knight of the road (Inf)

11 pedlar, peddler (US), seller, rag-and-bone man (*or* ragman), junkman (*or* junk dealer) (US), street seller, street vendor, hawker, tinker, Gypsy, traveller, huckster, colporteur, bagman (Inf), chapman (Lit), cheap-jack (Inf), costermonger (*or* coster), barrow boy, market trader, stall-keeper, sutler (Lit)

12 wholesaler, marketer, merchandiser, merchant, wholesale merchant, business person, businessman, businesswoman, entrepreneur, merchant prince, merchant venturer, speculator, operator, monopolist, oligopolist, importer, exporter, dealer, middleman, broker, stockbroker, market maker, stock-jobber, jobber, share-pusher, financier, company promoter, banker, lender, moneylender, moneychanger, foreign exchange dealer, cambist, procurer, trafficker, canvasser, tout, agent, estate agent, house agent, ticket agent, booking clerk, roundsman, milkman, fence (Inf)

13 retailer, middleman, regrater, shopkeeper, storekeeper, shop owner, store owner, dealer, merchant, trader, tradesman, monger, florist, milliner, tailor, shoe seller, fishmonger, ironmonger, mercer, haberdasher, grocer, groceryman (US), greengrocer, provision merchant, provisioner, butcher, baker, tobacconist, newsagent

14 street trader, street vendor, street seller, market trader, stall-keeper, stall-holder, barrow boy, costermonger, coster, sutler, vivandiere

ADJECTIVES

15 saleable, vendible, marketable, merchantable, available, obtainable, on tap

16 sold, sold out, in demand, popular, sought-after, called for

ADVERBS

17 marketably, saleably, commercially, profitably, speculatively, unprofitably

18 on sale, for sale, on the shelves, in the shops (*or* stores), in stock, on the market, up for sale, up for grabs, under the hammer, on the block (US)

779 Market

Send a fool to the market and a fool he will return again. Proverb.

NOUNS

1 **market**, daily market, weekly market, weekend market, farmers' market, mart, open market, street market, bazaar, flea market, Petticoat Lane, Portobello Road, Orchard Street (US), produce market, vegetable market, flower market, Covent Garden, livestock market, meat market, Smithfield, fish market, Billingsgate, Fulton Street (US), auction room, Christie's, Sotheby's, saleroom, exchange, corn exchange, corn market, wheat pit, custom house, horse fair, goose fair

2 **fair**, world fair, international fair, trade fair, industries fair, show, trade show, motor show, boat show, exhibition, exposition, shop window

3 **sellers' market**, buyers' market, bear market, bull market, over-the-counter market, kerb market, black market, black economy, underground economy, grey market

▶ *13 Economics; 14 Finance; 776 Trade*

4 **free market**, free-trade area, open market, European Free Trade Association (EFTA), Common Market, Euromarket, European Economic Community (EEC), European Community (EC), European Union (EU), European Economic Area (EEA), single market, single European market, Latin American Integration Association (LAIA), MERCOSUR, CARICOM, Organization of Petroleum-Exporting Countries (OPEC), General Agreement on Tariffs and Trade (GATT), World Trade Organization (WTO), economic zone, economic integration, open-door policy

▶ *776 Trade*

5 **stock market**, Stock Exchange, securities market, unlisted securities market, commodity market, commodity exchange, change (Lit), bourse, Wall Street (US), the City, Third Market, Rialto, bucket shop, share shop

6 **marketplace**, market town, market cross, forum, agora

7 **emporium**, general market, covered market, arcade, Burlington Arcade, Trump Tower (US), shopping mall, mall, pedestrian precinct, shopping centre, trading centre, trading post, free port, entrepot, depot, warehouse, wharf, quay

▶ *439 Store*

8 **store**, shop, retail outlet, retailer's, department store, chain store, multiple store (*or* shop), boutique, bargain basement, corner shop, convenience store (US), 7-11 (US), mom and pop store (US), supermarket, superstore, hypermarket, megastore, cash and carry, business concern, family concern, concern, firm, establishment, trading company, trading house, house

▶ *577 Workshop*

9 **stall**, booth, stand, newsstand, kiosk, barrow, vending machine, counter, store window, shop window, window display

10 **bazaar**, sale of work, bring-and-buy sale, rummage sale, jumble sale, car-boot sale

780 Money

Money is like muck, not good except it be spread. Francis Bacon.

For the love of money is the root of all evil: which while some coveted after, they have erred from the faith, and pierced themselves through with many sorrows. Bible: I Timothy.

For I don't care too much for money,
For money can't buy me love. John Lennon.

Lack of money is the root of all evil. George Bernard Shaw.

NOUNS

1 **money**, legal tender, medium of exchange, specie, coinage, circulating medium, monetary unit, monetary denomination, currency, decimal currency, managed currency, fluctuating currency, hard currency, soft currency, sound currency, honest money, money of account, sterling, pound sterling, precious metal, gold, ringing gold, clinking gold, silver, siller (Dial), bullion, coin, paper money, shell money, cowrie, wampum

2 **cash**, hard cash, spot cash, petty cash, ready money, pelf, mammon, lucre, filthy lucre, root of all evil, the ready (Inf), readies (Inf), shekels (Inf), dough (Inf), bread (Inf), dosh (Inf), lolly (Inf), jack (US inf), dib(s) (Inf), moolah (Inf), spondulix (*or* spondulicks) (Inf), coin (Inf), brass (Dial), loot (Inf), swag (Inf), boodle (Inf), rhino (Inf), poppy (Inf), wampum (US inf), gelt (Inf), greenstuff (US inf), green (US inf), folding money (Inf), folding cabbage (*or* lettuce) (Inf), folding green (US inf), sugar (Inf), gravy (Inf), palm oil (US inf), palm grease (US inf)

3 **fortune**, wealth, riches, pile of money, heaps of money, stacks of money, mountain of money, mint of money, wads of money, bundle of money, millions, billions, crores, lakhs, scads of money (Inf), packet of money (Inf), big bucks (US inf), megabucks (Inf), cool million (Inf), zillions (Inf), century (Inf), ton (Inf), grand (Inf)

▶ *781 Wealth*

4 **change**, small change, coins, silver, pin money, allowance, pocket money, spending money, paltry sum, centime, sou, paisa, piastre, kopeck, chickenfeed (Inf), peanuts (Inf), coppers (Inf), nickles and dimes (US inf)

5 **sum**, sum of money, round sum, lump sum, figure, ballpark figure (Inf)

6 **funds**, cash supplies, monies, treasure, purse, store, provision, liquidity, hot money, liquid assets, money in the bank, account, bank account, current account, deposit account, savings account, higher interest rate account, bank annuities, trust fund, wherewithal, means, ready money, capital, funds in hand, funds for investment, reserves, capital reserves, dollar reserves, gold reserves, reserve liability, balances, sterling balances, finances, exchequer, financial provision, cash flow, remittance, payment, cash bank

7 **finance**, high finance, world of finance, financial world, financial circles, International Monetary Fund (IMF), World Bank, European Bank, International Finance Cor-

poration (IFC), financial control, money power, dollar diplomacy, purse strings, power of the purse, almighty dollar, money dealings, cash transaction, money market, Euromarket, Eurodollar market, Eurocurrency market, Eurobond market, Eurodollar, ECU (European Currency Unit), hard ECU, green pound, foreign exchange market, stock market, exchange, stock exchange, Big Bang, exchange rate, floating exchange rate, free exchange rate, European Monetary System (EMS), ERM (exchange rate mechanism), exchange rate parity, parity, valuta, par, EC snake, exchange control, managed currency, bank rate, prime lending rate (US), minimum lending rate, agio, agiotage, devaluation, depreciation, falling exchange rate, rising exchange rate, bimetallism, gold and silver standard, monometallism, gold standard, equalization fund, sinking fund, revolving fund, deficit finance, bail out, inflation, inflationary spiral, stagflation, stagnation, reflation, disinflation, deflation

▶ *14 Finance; 779 Market*

8 **American money**, American paper money, American coinage, penny, cent, one cent, nickel, five cents, 5¢, dime, ten cents, 10¢, quarter, twenty-five cents, 25¢, half-dollar, fifty cents, 50¢, dollar, silver dollar, Susan B. Anthony dollar, one-dollar bill, greenback, $1, two-dollar piece, American eagle bullion coin, eagle, five-dollar bill, $5, ten-dollar bill, $10, twenty-dollar bill, $20, fifty-dollar bill, $50, 100-dollar bill, $100, two bits (Inf), four bits (Inf), buck (Inf), smacker (Inf), fiver (Inf), tenner (Inf), sawbuck (Inf), C-note (Inf), one bill (Inf)

9 **British money**, British paper money, British coinage, decimal coinage, penny, new penny, 1p, twopence, 2p, five pence, 5p, ten pence, 10p, twenty pence, 20p, fifty pence, 50p, pound coin, pound note, £1, five-pound note, £5, ten-pound note, £10, twenty-pound note, £20, quid (Inf), nicker (Inf), smacker (Inf), oncer (Inf), sov (Inf), fiver (Inf), tenner (Inf), pony (Inf), monkey (Inf), archer (Inf)

10 **former British money**, former British coinage, predecimal coinage, farthing, halfpenny, ha'penny, 1/2d, penny, old penny, threepenny bit, thrupenny bit, 3d, sixpence, 6d, shilling, 1s, two-shilling piece, florin, 2s, half-crown, half-a-crown, two and six, two shillings and six pence, 2s 6d, 2/6, five shillings, crown, 5s, guinea, 21s, sovereign, gold sovereign, half sovereign, noble, groat, bawbee (Inf), tanner (Inf), bob (Inf), ship halfpenny, cartwheel penny (Inf), bun penny (Inf)

11 **national coins**, foreign coins, franc, new franc, mark, Deutschmark, pfennig, schilling, guilder, krona, krone, markka, drachma, lira, peseta, escudo, peso, cruzado, rupee, rouble, yuan, yen, won, kip, dinar, zloty, lek, riyal, dirham, rand, inti, naira

12 **ancient coins**, shekel, talent, denarius, obolus, soldo, ducat, sou, bezant, pistole, piece of eight

13 **coinage**, coins, minting, issue, specie, metallic currency, fractional currency, stamped coinage, minted coinage, gold coinage, silver coinage, electrum coinage, copper coinage, nickel coinage, billon coinage, bronze coinage, coin, piece, coin of the realm, coin collecting, numismatics, numismatology

14 **paper money**, note, bill (US), fiat money, fiduciary currency, assignat (Lit), banknote, treasury note, bill of exchange, negotiable instrument, draft, order, money order, postal order, cheque, cashier's cheque, certified cheque, giro cheque, traveller's cheque, Eurocheque, letter of credit, certificate, debenture, promissory note, IOU, note of hand, commercial paper, coupon, warrant, scrip, scrip certificate, bond, bearer bond, corporate bond, convertible bond, zero coupon bond, US Savings Bond (US), Premium Savings Bond, premium bond, shinplaster (US inf)

15 **false money**, bad money, counterfeit money, base coin, forgery, forged note, flash note, kite, snide, rap (Lit), clipped coinage, demonetized coinage, withdrawn coinage, obsolete coinage, depreciated currency, devalued currency, bad cheque, bad check (US), rubber cheque, funny money (Inf), dud cheque (Inf)

▶ *786 Nonpayment*

16 **bullion**, bar, gold bar, ingot, nugget, gold, solid gold, silver, solid silver, precious metal, yellow metal, platinum, electrum, billon, white gold, false gold, fool's gold

17 **financier**, money man, moneyer, minter, mint master, coiner, forger, money-dealer, moneychanger, cambist, moneylender, usurer, capitalist, tycoon, magnate, banker, treasurer, cashier, paymaster, bursar, purser, quaestor (Lit), coin collector, numismatist

18 **treasurer**, honorary treasurer, keeper of the purse, cashier, teller, payer, paymaster, bursar, almoner, purser, depositary, stakeholder, trustee, steward, consignee, book-keeper, accountant, banker, financier, controller (*or* comptroller), Chancellor of the Exchequer, Secretary of the Treasury (US), Governor of the Bank of England, Chairman of the Federal Reserve System (US), mint master, minter, quaestor (in Ancient Rome)

19 **treasury**, treasure house, governmental funds, public money, public purse, exchequer, reserves, fund, store, counting house, custom house (*or* customs house), bursary, almonry (Lit), bank, Bank of England, Federal Reserve System (US), Old Lady of Threadneedle Street, commercial bank, financial company, financial house, savings bank, clearing bank, merchant bank, building society, savings and loan association (US), building and loan association (US), Post Office savings bank

20 **money store**, coffer, chest, box, treasure chest, depository, federal depository (US), Fort Knox (US), strongroom, safe, wall safe, safe-deposit (*or* safety-deposit), safe-deposit box, strongbox, cash box, moneybox, moneybag, piggy bank, money belt, pocket, wallet, billfold (US), change purse, handbag, purse (US), pocketbook (US), stocking, mattress

21 **till**, cash register, cash desk, slot machine, cash dispenser, automated teller machine (ATM), personal identification number (PIN)

▶ *410 Container; 439 Store*

ADJECTIVES

22 **monetary**, pecuniary, financial, fiscal, numismatic, chrysological, budgetary, sumptuary, coined, stamped, minted, issued, nummular, nummary, fiduciary, gold-based, sterling-based, inflationary, deflationary, floating, clipped, devalued, depreciated, withdrawn, demonetized, decimal

23 **solvent**, sound, rich, wealthy, loaded (Inf)

▶ *781 Wealth*

VERBS

24 monetize, mint, coin, print, stamp, issue, circulate, counterfeit, forge, pass, utter, pass a bad check (US), kite a check (US inf), bounce a cheque (Inf)

25 demonetize, withdraw, withdraw from circulation, call in, debase, clip, devalue, depreciate, inflate

26 bank, deposit, draw, withdraw, cash, encash, realize, liquidate, cash a cheque, endorse a cheque, write a cheque, pay, change, exchange, get some kick (US inf)

27 invest, save, buy bonds, play the market

ADVERBS

28 financially, fiscally, numismatically, pecuniously, solvently, wealthily, in the money (Inf)

781 Wealth

Wealth covers sin – the poor are naked as a pin. Kassia.

ADJECTIVES

1 wealthy, rich, affluent, well-off, well-paid, prosperous, well-to-do, in the money, moneyed, propertied, worth a lot, worth a mint, worth millions, rolling in money, dripping with wealth, made of money, well-situated, well provided for, well-endowed, well-housed, comfortably off, comfortable, in easy circumstances, doing nicely thank you, rich as Croesus, rich as Rockefeller, rich as Solomon, born with a silver spoon in one's mouth, born in (*or* to) the purple, blessed with this world's goods, stinking rich (Inf), filthy rich (Inf), disgustingly rich (Inf), rolling in it (Inf), rolling (Inf), dripping (Inf), loaded (Inf), flush (Inf), well-heeled (Inf), worth a bundle (Inf), worth a packet (Inf), lousy with money (Inf), in clover (Inf), in the chips (Inf), in the gravy (Inf), in the dough (US inf), in high (*or* tall) cotton (US inf), on Easy Street (Inf), quids in (Inf), raking it in (Inf)

▶ *248 Prosperity*

2 solvent, financially stable, financially sound, sound, solid, taken care of, in the black, in funds, in cash, out of debt, creditworthy, a good credit risk, able to pay, good for it, all straight (Inf)

▶ *783 Credit; 785 Payment*

3 opulent, luxurious, lavish, sumptuous, palatial, splendid, first-class, de luxe, expensive, dear, costly, richly furnished, elegantly upholstered, diamond-studded, gilded, glittering, plush (Inf), plushy (Inf), ritzy (Inf), glitzy (Inf), slap-up (Inf)

4 lush, fat, fertile, fecund, productive, prolific, abundant, plentiful, plenteous, bountiful, flowing with milk and honey

▶ *356 Creation; 562 Fertility*

NOUNS

5 wealth, richness, affluence, prosperity, financial power, fortune, handsome fortune, resources, substantial resources, limitless resources, capital, substantial capital, assets, liquid assets, means, income, high income, high tax bracket, surtax bracket, gain, gains, profit, profits, moneymaking, savings, investments, nest egg, savings account, investment account, large inheritance, generous endowment, estate, money, property, possessions, well-lined purse, bottomless purse, bonanza, mine, gold mine, cash cow, El Dorado, Golconda, pot of gold, end of the rainbow, purse of Fortunatus, philosopher's stone, golden goose, golden touch, Midas touch, nice little earner (Inf)

▶ *14 Finance; 248 Prosperity; 680 Thrift; 765 Profit; 769 Receiving*

6 money, riches, lucre, filthy lucre, mammon, pelf, brass (Dial), cash, old money, new money, mint of money, pots of money, heaps of money, pile of money, mountain of money, wad of notes, riches of Solomon, tidy sum (Inf), king's ransom (Inf), bundle (Inf), packet (Inf), cool million (Inf), zillions (Inf), scads of money (Inf), megabucks (Inf), big bucks (US inf), tall money (US inf), long bread (US inf), long green (US inf)

▶ *780 Money*

7 opulence, luxury, lavishness, sumptuousness, comfort, comfortable circumstances, ease, easy circumstances, the good life, good times, plenty, abundance, profusion, superfluity, bounty, cornucopia, fat of the land, fleshpots, plushness (Inf), easy street (Inf), life of Riley (Inf)

8 solvency, financial stability, financial soundness, soundness, solidity, substance, credit, creditworthiness, fiscal competence, independence, self-sufficiency

▶ *783 Credit*

9 plutocracy, timocracy, capitalism

10 wealthy person, rich person, millionaire, millionairess, multimillionaire, billionaire, moneymaker, big earner, tycoon, magnate, baron, self-made man (*or* woman), man (*or* woman) of means, Croesus, Midas, Dives, Plutus, Rockefeller, capitalist, plutocrat, yuppie, parvenu, heir, beneficiary, heir to a fortune, heiress, moneybags (Inf), money-spinner (Inf), fat cat (Inf), nabob (Inf)

11 the rich, the well-off, the well-to-do, the haves, the privileged, privileged class, moneyed class, propertied class, leisured class, the upper classes, the cream of society, the county set, the country club set (US), the well-heeled (Inf), the jet set, the glitterati, beau monde, beautiful people, *jeunesse dorée* (Fr), the new (*or* newly) rich, nouveaux riches, the upper crust (Inf)

VERBS

12 be rich, have wealth, have money, have money to burn, draw a large income, command capital, have the golden touch, turn all to gold, roll in money, drip with wealth, wallow in riches, have money coming out of one's ears (Inf), stink of money (Inf), rake (*or* coin) it in (Inf), sit on a goldmine (Inf), live on Easy Street (Inf), live the life of Riley (Inf)

13 get rich, prosper, make it, enrich oneself, make money, mint money, coin money, spin money, attract money, come into money, inherit, gain, make a profit, make one's fortune, make a fortune, make a mint, rake in the cash, feather one's nest, line one's pocket, strike it rich, hit the jackpot, win the pools, win the lottery (*or* sweepstake), have one's ship come in (*or* home), find the philosopher's stone, find one's El Dorado, find the pot of gold at the end of the rainbow, rake it in (Inf), make a killing (Inf), make a bundle (Inf), make a packet (Inf), make a pile (Inf), make a bomb (Inf), clean up (Inf)

▶ *248 Prosperity; 765 Profit; 769 Receiving*

14 seek riches, chase fame and fortune, worship the almighty dollar (US), worship the golden calf, pay tribute to mammon

15 make rich, enrich, provide money, bequeath, endow, enhance, improve

ADVERBS

16 wealthily, richly, affluently, prosperously, well, comfortably, opulently, luxuriously, lavishly, in clover (Inf), on the gravy train (Inf), high on the hog (US inf)

782 Poverty

It is only the poor who are forbidden to beg. Anatole France.

I want there to be no peasant in my kingdom so poor that he is unable to have a chicken in his pot every Sunday. Henri IV.

Hard to train to accept being poor. Horace.

ADJECTIVES

1 poor, impecunious, penniless, moneyless, penurious, poverty-stricken, badly off, poorly off, unprovided for, lowpaid, underpaid, underprivileged, deprived, needy, in need, indigent, wanting, in want, in distress, in reduced circumstances, straitened, hand-to-mouth, destitute, necessitous, on the breadline, below the poverty line, in the poverty trap, on the dole, on welfare (US), without prospects, with nothing to hope for, poor as dirt, poor as a church mouse, poor as Lazarus, poor as Job, poor as Mother Hubbard, unable to make both ends meet, unable to get by, unable to pay one's way, unable to keep the wolf from the door, not blessed with this world's goods, hard up (Inf)

▶ *264 Difficulty; 786 Nonpayment*

2 insolvent, indebted, in debt, owing, bankrupt, ruined, financially ruined, financially embarrassed, short, short of cash, short of funds, down to one's last penny, without a sou, without a cent (US), in the red, impoverished, pauperized, reduced to poverty (*or* beggary), broken, dispossessed, stripped, fleeced, robbed, disinherited, dowerless, portionless, in difficulties, not knowing which way to turn, up against it, out-of-pocket, broke (Inf), stone-broke (Inf), stony-broke (Inf), flat broke (Inf), flat (Inf), dead broke (Inf), skint (Inf), hard up (Inf), strapped (Inf), hurting (Inf), pinched (for money) (Inf), pushed (for money) (Inf), pressed (for money) (Inf), hard-pressed (Inf), hard put to it (Inf), put to one's shifts (Inf), on one's uppers (Inf), on one's beam-ends (Inf), on the rocks (Inf), in hock (US inf), in queer street (Inf), cleaned out (Inf), wiped out (US inf), bust (Inf), busted (US inf), without a bean (Inf), belly up (US inf)

3 beggarly, mendicant, down-and-out, on the street, homeless, shelterless, hungry, underfed, starving, barefoot, in rags, ragged, tattered, tatty, patched, threadbare, shabby, scruffy, down-at-heel (*or* the heels), out at (the) elbows, mean, seedy, squalid, dirty, slummy, dilapidated, gone to ruin, gone to pot, melted out (US inf)

4 inadequate, insufficient, deficient, lacking, scarce, meagre, scant, scanty, skimpy

NOUNS

5 poverty, poorness, impecuniousness, impecuniosity, pennilessness, penury, impoverishment, pauperism, deprivation, privation, hardship, need, neediness, necessitousness, necessity, dire necessity, indigence, want, lack, distress, difficulties, dire straits, reduced circumstances, straitened circumstance, hand-to-mouth existence, mere existence, destitution, low pay, low income, insufficient income, slender means, narrow means, meagre resources, subsistence level, breadline, poverty line, poverty trap, wolf at the door, Lady Poverty (Inf)

▶ *264 Difficulty; 786 Nonpayment*

6 insolvency, debt, indebtedness, dependence, unsoundness, financial unsoundness, fiscal incompetence, bankruptcy, ruin, financial ruin, financial collapse, financial embarrassment, loss of fortune, dispossession, disinheritance, hard times, bad times, depression, recession, slump, belt-tightening, shortage of cash, shortage of funds, insufficient funds, light pocket, empty purse, bare cupboard, empty larder, pinch (Inf), queer street (Inf), low water (Inf)

7 beggary, beggardom, beggarliness, mendicancy, homelessness, hunger, fasting, famine, raggedness, rags, tatters, shabbiness, scruffiness, meanness, seediness, squalor, dilapidation, slum, substandard housing, workhouse, poorhouse, rat trap (US inf)

▶ *258 Dirtiness; 682 Meanness*

8 renunciation of wealth, voluntary poverty, vow of poverty, the Franciscan order, asceticism

9 inadequacy, insufficiency, deficiency, lack, shortage, dearth, scarcity, paucity, meagreness, scantness, scantiness, skimpiness

10 poor person, needy person, pauper, indigent, down-and-out, bankrupt, insolvent, broken man (*or* woman), beggar, mendicant, mendicant friar, lazar, Franciscan, Grey Friar, Poor Clare, Job, Lazarus, Cinderella, poor relation, vagrant, bag lady, tramp, hobo (US), homeless person, squatter, slum-dweller, ghetto resident, rag-picker, bum (Inf), freeloader (Inf)

11 the poor, the needy, the have-nots, the underprivileged, the underprivileged class, the disadvantaged, the deprived, Third World, the lower classes, the dregs of society, poor white, white trash, new (*or* newly) poor

VERBS

12 be poor, live poorly, live in poverty, need, want, lack, not have a penny, not have two halfpennies to rub together, earn little or nothing, live on a pittance, eke out a livelihood, scratch (out) a living, live from hand to mouth, watch the pennies, tighten one's belt, fall below the poverty line, be caught in the poverty trap, go on relief, go on welfare (US), go on the dole, claim supplementary benefit, sign on (Inf), go on the parish, beg for one's bread, sing for one's supper, starve, have no prospects, feel the pinch (Inf), pinch pennies (Inf), pinch (Inf), have no more shots in one's locker (Inf)

13 lose one's money, lose everything, go to pot, go to ruin, go bankrupt, fall on hard times, decline in fortune, come down in the world, sell the family silver, go into debt, be deeply in debt, declare Chapter 11 (US), go broke (Inf), go bust (Inf), go busted (US inf), go to the wall (Inf), go belly up (US inf)

14 impoverish, make poor, reduce to poverty, beggar, pauperize, leave destitute, ruin, bankrupt, dispossess, disinherit, disendow, cut off with a shilling (Inf), deprive, strip, fleece, rob, take to the cleaners (Inf)

ADVERBS

15 poorly, impecuniously, penuriously, in need, in reduced circumstances, on the breadline, on the poverty line, in the poverty trap, on welfare (US), on the dole, on one's uppers, on the streets

16 meanly, shabbily, scruffily, seedily

17 inadequately, insufficiently, meagrely, scantly, scantily, skimpily

783 Credit

It is only the poor who pay cash, and that not from virtue, but because they are refused credit. Anatole France.

NOUNS

1 credit, customer credit, banker's credit, creditworthiness, sound proposition, good credit risk, credit rating, borrowing capacity, credit limit, line of credit, credit control, liquidity ratio, overdraft, the red, loan, mortgage, second mortgage, remortgage, debt, account, charge account, credit account, department store account, customer account, budget account, deferred payment, instalment plan, instalment buying, paying off (US), hire purchase (HP), score, tally, bill, accounts payable, unpaid bill, overdue account, outstanding balance, tick (Inf), the never-never (Inf)

► *771 Lending; 772 Borrowing; 784 Debt; 789 Accounting*

2 credit card, bank card, charge card, American Express™, VISA™, MasterCard™, Access™, Diners' Club™, plastic money, plastic, phonecard, credit note, letter of credit

3 deposit, bank (*or* building society) deposit, current account deposit, savings account deposit, credit account, deposit account, the black, credits, balances, credit balance, right-hand entry, receipts

► *788 Receipt*

4 bank, commercial bank, finance company, finance house, savings bank, building society, friendly society, credit union, credit bureau (US), pawnshop, pawnbroker's

► *14 Finance*

5 lender, loan-maker, mortgagee, pledgee, pawnbroker, usurer, extortionist, lender of last resort, debt collector, (debt) collection agency, dun, loan shark (Inf)

6 depositor, investor, saver

7 repute, reputation, standing, prestige, trust, confidence, reliability, probity

► *450 Belief; 667 Respect; 799 Honour*

VERBS

8 credit, give (*or* furnish) credit, extend credit, lend, loan, grant a loan, grant, arrange a mortgage, sell on credit, await payment, seek payment, dun

► *771 Lending; 784 Debt*

9 acquire credit, take out credit, open a charge (*or* credit) account, have an account with, charge, charge to one's account, run up an account, run up a bill, defer payment, forgo repayment, buy on hire purchase (HP), buy on the instalment plan, buy on time (US), put on layaway (US), borrow, take out a loan, mortgage, overdraw, go into the red

► *772 Borrowing*

10 deposit, make a deposit, credit to one's account, place in one's account, place to one's credit, stay in the black

11 recognize, give recognition, ascribe, attribute, give credit where it's due

ADJECTIVES

12 charged, deferred, overdrawn, in the red

13 in credit, in the black, creditworthy

ADVERBS

14 on credit, on account, by deferred payment, by instalments, by hire purchase, on the cuff (Inf), on tick (Inf), on the never-never (Inf), on the slate (Inf)

15 into the black, out of the red, into the red, out of the black

784 Debt

He that dies pays all debts. William Shakespeare.

NOUNS

1 debt, indebtedness, state of indebtedness, owing, liability, obligation, commitment, encumbrance, accountability, responsibility, secured debt, unsecured debt, debt of honour, good debt, bad debt, short-term debt, floating debt, promise to pay, something owing, what one owes, debts, bills, debit, charge, overdraft, the red, charge account, credit account, charge card, credit card, bank card

► *783 Credit*

2 national debt, national credit, government debt, federal debt (US), funded debt, trading deficit, trade gap, negative balance of payments, public sector borrowing, public sector borrowing requirement (PSBR)

3 loan, bank loan, business loan, capital gearage, leverage, personal loan, secured loan, guaranteed loan, mortgage, second mortgage, remortgage, guaranty, collateral security, unsecured loan, sum entrusted, loan capital, debt capital, loan repayment, mortgage repayment, lending, borrowing, prime (lending) rate (US), minimum lending rate, bill discounting rate

► *771 Lending; 772 Borrowing*

4 interest, premium, rate of interest, APR (annualized percentage rate), bank rate, simple interest, compound interest, high interest, excessive interest, usury, pound of flesh (Inf)

5 amount owing, unpaid amount, deficit, bill, account, tally, score, overdraft, balance to pay, accounts receivable, receivables, overdue amount, overdue payment, arrears, accumulated arrears, back pay, back rent, foreclosure, repossession, inability to pay, insufficient funds, defaulting, write-off, bad debt, bounced cheque, payment refused, frozen balance, blocked account, frozen assets

► *766 Loss; 786 Nonpayment*

6 debtor, credit buyer, cardholder, borrower, personal borrower, business borrower, loanee, loan applicant, guarantor, co-signer, obligor, drawee, mortgagor, pledgor, bad debtor, defaulter, nonpayer, bilker, insolvent, bankrupt

VERBS

7 **be in debt**, owe, owe money, borrow money, have to repay, have bills to pay, run up a bill, run up an account, run (*or* get) into debt, overspend, overdraw, go into the red, pay interest, accept a charge, get credit, have an account with, live on credit, buy on credit, buy on the instalment plan, buy on hire purchase, collateralize, charge, charge to one's account, back another's credit, co-sign a loan, make oneself responsible, go bail for

▶ *772 Borrowing; 783 Credit*

8 **not pay**, default, reschedule one's debts, leave one's bills unpaid, cheat one's creditors, bilk, outrun the constable, welsh, levant, do a moonlight flit (Inf)

▶ *786 Nonpayment*

ADJECTIVES

9 **in debt**, indebted, pledged, bound, obliged, committed, encumbered, mortgaged, liable, responsible, accountable, answerable, beholden, borrowing, owing, unpaid, due, overdrawn, in the red, minus, in difficulties, in dire straits, deep in debt, burdened with debt, up to one's ears in debt, over one's head in debt, mortgaged to the hilt, in hock (US inf)

10 **unable to pay**, insolvent, nonpaying, defaulting, at the mercy of one's creditors, in the hands of the receiver, foreclosed, repossessed

ADVERBS

11 **insolvently**, in debt, in over one's head, in the red, in arrears, on loan, on credit, on the slate (Inf), on tick (Inf), on the never-never (Inf), on the tab (Inf), in hock (Inf)

785 Payment

We're overpaying him but he's worth it. Samuel Goldwyn.

NOUNS

1 **payment**, paying, paying out, payout, disbursement, remittance, expenditure, outlay, paying for, meeting the cost, bearing the cost, defrayment, defrayal, defraying, paying off, payoff, discharge, written discharge, quittance, acquittance, release, satisfaction, full satisfaction, liquidation, clearance, settlement, full settlement, settlement on account, accounts receivable, receivables, receipt, receipted payment, receipt for payment, receipt in full, due payment, overdue payment, cash payment, ready cash, money, EFTPOS, plastic (Inf), Switch card™, credit card, payment in kind, advance payment, first payment, partial payment, down payment, deposit, earnest money, earnest, handsel, instalment, premium, standing order, direct debit, deferred payment, charge-account payment, instalment-plan payment, hire-purchase payment, cash on delivery (COD), subscription, tribute, voluntary payment, donation, contribution, offering, appeal, collection, whip-round (Inf)

▶ *787 Expenditure; 788 Receipt*

2 **repayment**, reimbursement, refund, compensation, recompense, indemnity, restitution, payment-in-lieu, substitution, composition

3 **pay**, remuneration, salary, wages, stipend, emolument, honorarium, fee, commission, royalty, advance, payroll, payout, pay packet, pay slip, pay cheque, take-home pay, income, earnings, reward, tip, gratuity, pension, annuity, retirement pension, back pay, retroactive pay, redundancy pay, severance pay, payoff, ex gratia payment, payment-in-lieu, overtime pay, golden handshake (Inf), golden parachute (Inf), golden handcuffs (Inf), golden hello (Inf)

▶ *813 Reward*

4 **grant**, grant-in-aid, subsidy, subvention, donation, contribution, subscription, tribute, damages, indemnity, penalty, tax, ransom, payoff, bribe, payola (US inf), sweetener (Inf)

5 **payer**, paymaster, bursar, purser, cashier, treasurer

VERBS

6 **pay**, pay out, disburse, remit, expend, spend, subscribe, make a payment, get a receipt, pay for, pay cash, pay by cheque, pay by cashier's check (US), pay by standing order (*or* direct debit), pay in kind, trade, negotiate a trade-off, barter, make a down payment, put down, pay in advance, put money up front, pay on sight, pay on call, pay on delivery, pay on demand, pay on the dot, pay dearly, pay an exorbitant price, unloose the purse strings, open one's wallet (*or* purse), empty one's pocket, lay out (Inf), shell out (Inf), fork out (*or* over *or* up) (Inf), ante up (Inf), stump up (Inf), cough up (Inf), come across (Inf), do the needful (Inf), pay on the nail (Inf), pay through the nose (Inf)

▶ *787 Expenditure*

7 **pay off**, discharge, satisfy, redeem, meet, liquidate, clear, settle, settle an account, honour, honour a bill, clear (*or* square) accounts with, pay up, pay in full

8 **defray**, defray the cost, pay for, meet the cost, bear the cost, stand the cost, stand, treat, give, donate, contribute, fund, finance, put up money, pick up the bill (*or* tab), pay the piper, foot the bill (Inf), pay the freight (US inf)

9 **pay one's way**, pay one's share, share expenses, go Dutch, buy a round, stand a round

10 **pay back**, repay, reimburse, refund, compensate, recompense, indemnify, restitute

11 **remunerate**, pay wages, pay a salary, pay commission, distribute, reward, tip, bribe, dole out (Inf), dish out (Inf), tickle (*or* grease) one's palm (Inf), cross one's palm with silver (Inf), pay off (Inf), sweeten the pot (Inf), provide a sweetener (Inf)

▶ *813 Reward*

12 **be profitable**, yield a return, make money, benefit, avail, be worth the effort

▶ *765 Profit*

13 **retaliate**, avenge oneself, revenge oneself, reciprocate, requite, pay back, pay off, pay off old scores, take an eye for an eye, give tit for tat (Inf), settle a score (Inf), get even (Inf), get one's own back (Inf)

▶ *385 Retaliation*

14 **atone**, make amends, suffer, answer

ADJECTIVES

15 **paying**, disbursing, expending, spending

16 **paid**, paid in full, out of debt, liquidated, in the black, out of the red, owing nothing, debt-free, cleared, settled, discharged

17 **payable**, payable on demand, due, owed, owing, remittable, refundable, redeemable
18 **profitable**, worthwhile, advantageous, lucrative, remunerative, rewarding, moneymaking
19 **receiving pay**, earning, salaried, waged, wage- earning, hired, prepaid, paid in advance, post-paid
20 **paying in return**, compensatory, retributive, redemptive

ADVERBS

21 **cash down**, in advance, cash on delivery (COD), in instalments, by cheque, on demand, on the dot, on the nail (Inf)

786 Nonpayment

NOUNS

1 **nonpayment**, default, refusal to pay, avoiding financial obligations, tax avoidance, tax evasion, tax shelter, tax haven, creative accounting, black economy, embezzlement, defalcation, swindling, defrauding, improbity, protest (by creditor), repudiation of debts, forgiveness of debts, cancellation of debts, scam (Inf), fiddle (Inf)
► *634 Avoidance; 800 Dishonour*
2 **stoppage**, deduction, moratorium, embargo, freeze, reduced payment, deferred payment, instalment plan, hire purchase
3 **bad payment**, bad cheque, dishonoured cheque, bogus cheque, dud cheque, bouncing cheque, protested bill, rubber cheque (Inf)
4 **depreciation**, devaluation, devalued currency, counterfeit money
► *13 Economics; 14 Finance; 780 Money*
5 **insolvency**, inability to pay, debt, insurmountable debt, unpayable debt, failure to meet one's obligations, nothing in the kitty, overdrawn account, overdraft, cashflow crisis, financial crisis, crash, collapse, failure, bank failure, failure of credit, bankruptcy, ruin, financial ruin, bankruptcy court, bankruptcy proceedings, Chapter 11 (US)
► *784 Debt*
6 **nonpayer**, miser, Shylock, skinflint, defaulter, bankrupt, discharged bankrupt, undischarged bankrupt, debtor, insolvent debtor, embezzler, defalcator, defrauder, tax dodger, tax evader, tax exile, bilker, absconder, lame duck, welsher (Inf)

VERBS

7 **not pay**, default, refuse to pay, avoid financial obligations, practise tax evasion, evade taxes, divert, sequester, embezzle, defalcate, swindle, defraud, evade one's creditors, outrun the constable, bilk, welsh, levant, abscond, decamp, do a moonlight flit (Inf), fiddle one's income tax (Inf)
8 **stop payment**, withhold payment, freeze, block, refuse payment, disallow payment, bounce a cheque, dishonour a cheque, protest a bill, repudiate
9 **be unable to pay**, have no ready cash, get into debt, fall into arrears, get behindhand, become insolvent, have a cash-flow crisis, go bankrupt, go through the bankruptcy court, go to the wall, sink, fail, break, go bust, crash, collapse, wind up, go into liquidation, go belly up (US inf)
► *784 Debt*
10 **forgive a debt**, cancel a debt, wipe the slate clean, discharge a bankrupt, write off
11 **be parsimonious**, keep one's wallet (*or* purse) shut, economize, scrimp, scrape and save, make ends meet
► *680 Thrift; 682 Meanness*
12 **devalue the currency**, depreciate the currency, lower the official rate of exchange, go off the gold standard, demonetize
► *780 Money*

ADJECTIVES

13 **nonpaying**, miserly, mean, measly, skinflint, defaulting, behindhand, in arrears, unable to pay, insolvent, bankrupt, indebted, up to one's ears in debt, over one's head in debt, poor, beggared, ruined
► *782 Poverty; 784 Debt*
14 **unpaid**, unrewarded, unremunerated, uncompensated, unrecompensed, unpayable, irredeemable

ADVERBS

15 **without paying**, in arrears, in the red, in debt, insolvently, without a penny to one's name

INTERJECTIONS

16 **can't pay!**, won't pay!

787 Expenditure

A budget is a method of worrying before you spend instead of afterwards. Anonymous.

Too caustic? To hell with cost; we'll make the picture anyway. Samuel Goldwyn.

VERBS

1 **expend**, spend, disburse, pay, pay out, shop, buy, purchase, incur costs, incur expenses, invest, sink money, afford, meet the cost, run down one's account, use up one's credit, live on (*or* off) capital, dip into capital, draw on one's savings, dissave, disinvest, untie the pursestrings, empty one's pocket, open one's pocket, spare no expense, spend lavishly, splurge, overspend, be out of pocket, squander, fritter away, throw away, dissipate, go on a spending spree, shop till one drops, fling money around, throw money at, spend money like water, spend money as if it grows on trees, lay out (Inf), fork out (Inf), shell out (Inf), splash out (Inf), open the floodgates (Inf), do proud (Inf), blow (Inf), blow one's cash (Inf), blow a fortune (Inf), blow it (Inf), blue (Inf)
► *681 Extravagance; 777 Purchase; 785 Payment*
2 **consume**, use, use up, exhaust, deplete, go through, run through, get through, waste
► *349 Use; 441 Waste*
3 **donate**, give, give money, give to charity, contribute, support, back, finance, pay for, defray, bear the costs, treat, stand (Inf), bankroll (US inf)
► *679 Generosity; 768 Giving*

NOUNS

4 **expenditure**, spending, disbursement, payment, shopping, buying, buy, good buy, bad buy, purchase
► *777 Purchase; 785 Payment*
5 **expense**, expenses, expense account, miscellaneous ex-

penses, out-of-pocket expenses, extras, outlay, investment, costs, cost of living, monthly bills, outgoings, overheads, fee, charge, price, rate, tax

▶ *790 Price*

6 **extravagance**, prodigality, spending (*or* shopping) spree, spree, splurge, dissaving, disinvestment, run on savings, living off (*or* on) one's capital

▶ *681 Extravagance*

7 **donation**, giving, contribution, support, backing, finance, generosity, liberality

▶ *679 Generosity; 768 Giving*

8 **spender**, shopper, buyer, purchaser, investor

9 **spendthrift**, squanderer, wastrel, shopaholic (Inf)

ADJECTIVES

10 **expending**, spending, sumptuary, out-of-pocket, lighter in one's purse, generous, liberal

11 **spendthrift**, extravagant, profligate, prodigal, spending money like water, spending money as if it grows on trees, living on (*or* off) capital

12 **expended**, spent, disbursed, paid, paid out, invested, contributed, at one's expense, laid out (Inf), blown (Inf)

13 **used**, used up, exhausted, depleted

ADVERBS

14 **generously**, liberally, extravagantly, profligately, prodigally

788 Receipt

How were the receipts today in Madison Square Garden? Phineas Taylor Barnum.

NOUNS

1 **receipt**, voucher, counterfoil, stub, proof of purchase, written acknowledgment of payment

2 **money received**, receipts, gross receipts, net receipts, box-office receipts, gate money, gate, revenue, sales revenue, proceeds, returns, royalty, royalties, money coming in, incomings, credits, profits, gross profits, net profits, mesne profits, turnover, sales volume, interest, gain, capital gain, bonus, premium, tax, taxes, direct tax, indirect tax, sales tax (US), value-added tax (VAT), property tax, rates, dues, duty, customs, tariff, import levy, rent, rent-roll, takings (Inf), take (Inf)

▶ *765 Profit; 769 Receiving*

3 **income**, national income, business income, private income, privy purse, emolument, regular income, earnings, remuneration, salary, wages, pay, half pay, freelance pay, fees, pension, pension fund, retirement benefit (US), annuity, tontine, grant, allowance, personal allowance, spending money, pin money, pocket money, money for a rainy day, financial support, bursary, bursarship, scholarship, fellowship, work-study grant (US), maintenance, aliment, alimony, child support (US), palimony (Inf)

▶ *785 Payment; 813 Reward*

4 **legacy**, inheritance, dower, bequest, heritage, birthright, patrimony

5 **winnings**, prize, draw, lucky draw, raffle, lottery, lucky dip, cut, rake-off (Inf)

▶ *794 Prize*

ADJECTIVES

6 **received**, paid, credited, gained, gotten, accepted, taken, receipted, acknowledged, acknowledged with thanks, inherited, bequeathed, hereditary, patrimonial, bursarial, granted, salaried, waged, profitable, gainful

VERBS

7 **receive**, get, gain, take, acquire, accept, admit, receipt, acknowledge, mark paid, earn, gross, net, come into, inherit, fall to one, accrue, pay, yield, credit, pay off (Inf)

▶ *769 Receiving*

ADVERBS

8 **profitably**, gainfully, in profit, in receipt, at a premium, remuneratively, with interest, patrimonially, supportively, financially

789 Accounting

The only man who has ever run away from the circus to become an accountant. Anonymous, referring to John Major.

NOUNS

1 **accounts**, accountancy, accounting, financial accounting, cost accounting, management accounting, financial records, book-keeping, commercial arithmetic, creative accounting, item, entry, double entry, single entry, credit, debit, account, profit-and-loss account, balance sheet, debit and credit, receipts and expenditures, payments and receipts, running account, current account, cash account, deposit account, savings account, suspense account, expense account

2 **budgeting**, budget, capital budget, materials budget, production budget, production cost budget, creditors budget, debtors budget, cash budget, zero-based budgeting, budget estimates, fund-holding

▶ *436 Provisions*

3 **accounting**, reckoning, calculation, computation, enumeration, score, tally, audit, inspection of accounts, inspection of books

4 **statement**, statement of account, bank statement, bank reconciliation statement, account rendered, *compte rendu* (Fr), invoice, bill, waybill, manifest, account paid, account settled

5 **account book**, bankbook, passbook, chequebook, cashbook, petty-cash book, daybook, journal, ledger, register, books, records, accounts code

▶ *744 Record*

6 **accountant**, chartered accountant (CA), cost accountant, book-keeper, storekeeper, cashier, paymaster, bursar, purser, treasurer, auditor, inspector of accounts, examiner of accounts, actuary, statistician, bean counter (Inf)

VERBS

7 **account**, keep accounts, keep the books, balance accounts, prepare a balance sheet, make up an account, cast an account, write up, write down, book, enter, journalize, post, carry over, carry forward, debit, credit, record, register, cost, value, estimate, prepare a cash-flow forecast, budget, prepare a budget, practise creative accounting, massage the accounts, falsify the accounts,

defraud, garble, fudge, doctor, cook the accounts (*or* books) (Inf), fiddle (Inf)

8 **audit**, inspect accounts, examine the accounts, go through the books, take stock, check stock, inventory, catalogue, list

► *220 List*

9 **settle accounts**, square accounts, pay up, cough up (Inf), finalize accounts, wind up accounts, write off accounts, prepare a statement, present an account, invoice, bill, charge, surcharge, overcharge, undercharge

► *790 Price*

ADJECTIVES

10 **accounting**, book-keeping, reckoning, computing, calculating, accountable, fiscal, financial, economic, commercial, arithmetical, mathematical, statistical, actuarial, bursarial, budgetary, inventorial, itemized, creative

11 **accounted**, audited, balanced, tallied, registered, recorded, credited, debited, deposited, saved, received, spent, invoiced, billed, costed, settled, carried forward

ADVERBS

12 **on account**, on credit, on the bill, on the slate (Inf), on the tab (Inf)

13 **financially**, fiscally, economically, commercially, arithmetically, statistically, creatively, in debt, in credit, at a loss, at cost

790 Price

A man who knows the price of everything and the value of nothing. Oscar Wilde.

NOUNS

1 **price**, cost, charge, price charged, selling price, retail price, wholesale price, factory price, factory-gate price, market price, world price, quoted price, quotation, estimate, amount, figure, sum asked for, standard price, list price, current price, offer price, sale price, cut price, discount price, factory discount price, reduced price rate, price cut, price war, price control, fixed price, *prix fixe* (Fr), price range, price list, tariff, cheapness, dearness

► *778 Sale; 791 Discount; 792 Dearness; 793 Cheapness*

2 **value**, monetary value, face value, par value, fair value, scarcity value, exchange value, worth, money's worth, what it will fetch, valuation, assessment, premium, prize, bounty, reward

► *235 Worth*

3 **fee**, rate, going rate, rate for the job, service fee, piece rate, flat rate, high rate, ceiling, low rate, floor, basement price, commission, cut, refresher, charge, demand, dues, subscription, surcharge, supplement, extra, entrance fee, admission fee, cover charge (US), service charge, corkage, fare, flat fare, hire, rental, rent, ground rent, house rent, quitrent (Lit), overcharge, excessive charge, price-fixing, extortion, rip-off (Inf), rake-off (Inf)

4 **bill**, invoice, reckoning, statement

5 **cost**, buying price, purchase price, outlay, costs, expenses, expenditure, cost of living, cost-of-living index, inflation, damage (Inf)

► *787 Expenditure*

6 **business costs**, start-up costs, running costs, overheads, purchase (*or* rental) of premises, office supplies, postage, utilities, wages, wage bill, salary bill, legal costs, damages, transport charges, freight charges, freightage, wharfage, lighterage, salvage

7 **tax**, taxes, dues, taxation, direct tax, indirect tax, progressive tax, proportional tax, capitation tax, regressive tax, punitive tax, collective tax, income tax, corporate (*or* corporation) tax, company tax, excess profits tax, windfall profits tax, capital gains tax, capital levy, inheritance tax, death duty, estate duty, property tax, rates, community charge, poll tax, council tax, municipal tax (US), state tax (US), city (*or* town) tax (US), local tax, capital transfer tax, gift tax, ecclesiastical tax, Peter's pence, tithe, tenths, purchase tax, sales tax (US), VAT (value added tax), octroi, surtax, supertax, cess, tax system, tax office (*or* bureau), Inland Revenue, pay as you earn (PAYE), National Insurance, tax return, tax form, tax declaration, tax rate, tax table, tax computation, deduction, personal allowance, taxable income, tax demand, tax owed, tax payment, tax refund, rating, assessment, appraisement, valorization, rateable value, estimate

8 **levy**, duty, impost, toll, excise, customs, Customs and Excise, tariff, tonnage and poundage, charge, fine, penalty, imposition, exaction, aid, benevolence, tribute, blackmail, protection money, hush money, ransom, forced saving, involuntary saving

► *785 Payment*

9 **historical taxes**, Danegeld, stamp tax, salt tax, gabelle, window tax, scot and lot, feudal tax, scutage

10 **taxpayer**, ratepayer, tax assessor, tax collector, tax consultant

VERBS

11 **price**, fix the price of, set a price, quote a price, value, valuate, evaluate, appraise, rate, assess

12 **charge**, ask, demand, exact, levy, tax, put a tax on, tithe

13 **cost**, amount to, come to, sell for, fetch, bring (in), set one back (Inf)

ADJECTIVES

14 **priced**, valued, rated, assessed, worth, valued at

15 **chargeable**, rateable, taxable, dutiable, nontaxable, nondutiable, tax-free, tax-exempt, deductible, tax-deductible

ADVERBS

16 **at a price**, for the price of, to the amount of, to the tune of (Inf)

791 Discount

NOUNS

1 **discount**, reduction, price reduction, cut, decrease, decrement, something off, concession, allowance, margin, rebate, refund, drawback, cashback, reward card, loyalty card, tare, tare and tret (Lit), deduction, deferment, contango, backwardation, commission, percentage, poundage, agio, brokerage, one's cut, rake-off (Inf)

► *212 Subtraction; 214 Decrease*

2 **bargain**, special offer, loss leader, incentive, bargain price, special price, cut price, cut rate, basement price, bottom price, dumping, sale, bargain sale, grand opening sale, sale of the century, clearance sale, going-out-of-

business sale, fire sale, rummage sale, garage sale, jumble sale, bring-and-buy sale, car-boot sale, knockdown price (Inf)

▶ *778 Sale; 793 Cheapness*

VERBS

3 **discount**, reduce, lower, reduce the price of, mark down, cut, slash, take something off, give a concession, allow a margin, rebate, refund, tare, deduct, subtract, take off, knock off, depreciate, cheapen, offer a bargain, offer a discount, allow a discount, dump, knock down (Inf)

4 **take a discount**, take one's commission (*or* cut), take one's percentage, let stick to one's finger, rake off (Inf)

5 **buy at a discount**, pick up cheap, get for a song, make a killing, buy wholesale, buy in bulk, buy in the sales, find a bargain, defer payment, make a deposit

ADJECTIVES

6 **discounted**, marked down, cut-price, cut-rate, bargain, cheap, rebated, shopworn (US), shopsoiled

ADVERBS

7 **at a discount**, at cut price, at half price, at bargain prices, on special offer, below par, less than the going rate, less than the market rate, in the sale, in the bargain bin

792 Dearness

The most expensive habit in the world is celluloid not heroin and I need a fix every two years. Steven Spielberg.

NOUNS

1 **high price**, dearness, expensiveness, costliness, big price tag, fancy price, luxury price, up-market price, steep price (Inf), stiff price (Inf), pretty penny (Inf), ritzy price (Inf)

▶ *13 Economics; 14 Finance; 777 Purchase; 780 Money; 785 Payment; 787 Expenditure; 790 Price*

2 **unfair price**, overcharging, overpricing, excessive charge, surcharge, overcharge, exorbitance, exorbitant price, extortionate price, an arm and a leg (Inf), highway robbery (Inf), daylight robbery (Inf)

3 **inflationary price**, rising prices (*or* costs), climbing prices, soaring prices (*or* costs), spiralling prices, skyrocketing price, mounting costs, inflation, inflationary pressure, inflationary spiral, bullish tendency, bull market, sellers' market, prices going through the ceiling (*or* roof)

4 **extortion**, usury, profiteering, rack-rent, loan-sharking (Inf), gouging (US inf), rip-off (Inf)

▶ *219 Excess; 700 Deception; 773 Taking; 774 Stealing; 776 Trade; 779 Market*

5 **overcharger**, usurer, extortionist, shark, Shylock, rack-renter, loan shark (Inf), rip-off artist (Inf), con man (Inf)

▶ *772 Borrowing; 774 Stealing; 784 Debt*

6 **value**, worth, high value, great worth, valuableness, invaluableness, pricelessness, preciousness, scarcity value, rarity, rareness, dearth, scarcity

▶ *235 Worth*

ADJECTIVES

7 **dear**, expensive, costly, high-priced, high-price, dear at the price, dear at any price, extravagant, fancy, luxury, up-market, exorbitant, excessive, overpriced, overcharging, overcharged, unreasonable, prohibitive, beyond one's means, not affordable, more than one can afford, more than one's pocket can stand, extortionate, inflationary, rising, climbing, soaring, spiralling, mounting, rocketing, high-cost, sky-high, bullish, bull, usurious, profiteering, pricey (*or* pricy) (Inf), ritzy (Inf), gouging (US inf), stiff (Inf), steep (Inf), skyrocketing (Inf), going through the roof (Inf), out of sight (US inf)

▶ *218 Insufficiency; 219 Excess; 329 Overstepping*

8 **valuable**, invaluable, high-value, priceless, beyond price, above price, inestimable, precious, too precious for words, at a premium, worth a pretty penny (Inf), worth a fortune, worth a king's ransom, worth its weight in gold, exclusive, rare, scarce, infrequent, like gold dust, not to be had for love or money

VERBS

9 **be dear**, cost a lot, cost one dear, cost a fortune, hurt one's pocket, make a hole in one's pocket, rise in price, appreciate, escalate, soar, mount, rocket, climb, go through the ceiling (*or* roof), run into money, harden, get too dear, price itself out of the market, cost (Inf), cost a pretty penny (Inf), cost the earth (Inf), cost an arm and a leg (Inf), cost a packet (Inf), cost a bundle (Inf)

▶ *13 Economics; 14 Finance; 213 Increase; 235 Worth; 785 Payment; 790 Price*

10 **overcharge**, overprice, surcharge, sell dear, oversell, ask too much, rack-rent, profiteer, raise the price, put up prices, mark up, set the price tag too high, inflate, extort, fleece, swindle, do (Inf), commit highway robbery (Inf), commit daylight robbery (Inf), hold up (US inf), bleed (white) (Inf), gouge (US inf), con (Inf), rip off (Inf), burn (Inf), sting (Inf), soak (US inf), skin (Inf), clip (Inf), screw (Inf)

▶ *219 Excess; 329 Overstepping; 700 Deception; 773 Taking; 774 Stealing*

11 **overpay**, overspend, pay too much, pay more than it's worth, pay dearly, ruin oneself, be overdrawn, go into the red, raise the bid, bid up, pay a pretty penny (Inf), pay through the nose (Inf), be had (Inf), get ripped off (Inf)

▶ *219 Excess; 681 Extravagance; 787 Expenditure*

ADVERBS

12 **dearly**, dear, at great cost, at heavy cost, at great expense, at huge expense, expensively, grossly, extravagantly, outrageously, exorbitantly, excessively, extortionately, prohibitively, beyond one's means, more than one can afford, usuriously, stiffly (Inf), steeply (Inf), out of sight (US inf)

13 **valuably**, at great value, invaluably, inestimably, pricelessly, beyond worth, exclusively, rarely, scarcely, infrequently, preciously, at a premium

793 Cheapness

Pile it high, sell it cheap. Jack Cohen.

NOUNS

1 **cheapness**, inexpensiveness, reasonableness, reason-

able charge, affordability, good value, value for money, money's worth, easy terms, popular price, sensible price, competitive price, sale price, reduced price, discount, budget price, economy price, bargain price, cut price, cut rate (US), price cut, markdown, knockdown price, slashed price, rock-bottom price, giveaway price, nominal price, peppercorn rent, low (*or* small) price tag, cheap rate, reduced rate, concessional rate

2 **declining prices**, fall, price fall, bear market, bearishness, buyers' market, sluggish market, deflation, slump, plunge, recession, depression, cooling off of the economy, devaluation, depreciation, Dutch auction, superfluity, redundance, oversupply, plenty, glut, drug on the market

▶ *13 Economics; 14 Finance; 752 Offer; 777 Purchase; 778 Sale; 780 Money; 787 Expenditure; 790 Price; 791 Discount*

3 **shoddiness**, cheapness, gaudiness, second-ratedness, inferiority, baseness, lowness, poorness, shabbiness, scruffiness, pettiness, paltriness, pokiness, meanness, commonness, vulgarity, kitsch, crumminess (Inf)

▶ *122 Inferiority; 216 Average; 675 Vulgarity; 682 Meanness*

4 **bargain**, good buy, good deal, special offer, two for the price of one, loss leader, sale goods, sale merchandise, *bon marché* (Fr), seconds, rejects, excursion fare, tourist fare, second-class fare, economy fare, off-season fare, off-peak fare, APEX (Advance Purchase Excursion), bucket-shop fare, cheap ticket, discount ticket, season ticket, bus pass, railcard, coachcard, travelcard, Interrail Card™, half fare, stand-by fare, steal (US inf), snip (Inf), twofer (US inf)

▶ *319 Transport; 746 Negotiation; 779 Market*

5 **cheap item**, trifle, gewgaw, gimcrack, frippery, bauble, trinket, gaud, curio, knick-knack, kickshaw, bagatelle, brummagem, toy, plaything, novelty, bric-a-brac, tat, junk, jumble, white elephant

▶ *542 Decoration*

6 **absence of charge**, gift, free gift, giveaway (US), freesheet, complimentary gift, something for nothing, gratuitousness, gratuity, *gratuit* (Fr), free board, free lodging, free quarters, grace-and-favour flat, free drink, free lunch, free postage, Freepost™, 0800 telephone number, Freefone™, free admission, free entry, free seat, free ticket, guest ticket, complimentary ticket, pass, free pass, guest pass, complimentary pass, free port, free trade, free service, free delivery, volunteer work, voluntary work, charity, labour of love, perquisite, perk (Inf), free ride (Inf), freebie (US inf), Annie Oakley (US inf), paper (Inf)

▶ *679 Generosity; 752 Offer; 768 Giving; 786 Nonpayment*

7 **discounter**, street trader, wholesaler, cash and carry, warehouse, bucket shop, bargain basement, bargain bin, discount store, second-hand shop, junk shop, thrift shop, charity shop, flea market, jumble sale, rummage sale (US), car-boot sale, yard sale (US), garage sale, coupons, classified ads (Inf), small ads (Inf)

▶ *776 Trade; 779 Market*

8 **bargain hunter**, off-season traveller, pass holder, gate-crasher, miser, penny-pincher, coupon-clipper (US), skinflint, Scrooge, cheap-jack (Inf), sponger (Inf), free-loader (Inf)

▶ *343 Inactivity; 680 Thrift; 682 Meanness; 773 Taking*

ADJECTIVES

9 **cheap**, inexpensive, unexpensive, uncostly, reasonable, sensible, manageable, affordable, within one's means, easy on the pocket, modest, moderate, bargain-basement, down-market, five-and-ten (US), dime-store (US), twopenny-halfpenny, good-value, low-budget, low-priced, low, underpriced, catchpenny, brummagem, going cheap (*or* cheaply), going for a song, cheap at the price, cheap at half the price, (well) worth the money, sale, sale-priced, off-season, off-peak, excursion, economy-class, tourist-class, second-class, third-class, bucket-shop, concessional, nominal, budget, economical, economy, economy size, bargain, discount, half-price, cut-price, cut-rate (US), markdown, knockdown, marked down, reduced, reduced to clear, slashed, sacrificial, rock-bottom, giveaway, declining, falling, slumping, bearish, bear, devalued, depreciated, superfluous, redundant, oversupplied, a dime a dozen (US), dirt-cheap (Inf), cheap as dirt (Inf), cheapo (Inf), for peanuts (Inf)

10 **shoddy**, shabby, scruffy, base, low, mean, poor, paltry, poky, mangy, scummy, tacky, gaudy, tawdry, tatty, trashy, twopenny (*or* tuppenny), second-rate, inferior, low-grade, low-quality, useless, unsaleable, unsalable (US), unmarketable, valueless, worthless, shopsoiled, shopworn (US), unbought, unwanted, out of fashion, past its sell-by date, crummy (Inf), tinpot (Inf), two-bit (US inf), lousy (Inf), chintzy (US inf)

▶ *236 Worthlessness; 238 Uselessness*

11 **free of charge**, free, scot-free, free for the asking, for free, for nothing, without charge, not charged for, uncharged, unchargeable, gratis, given free, given away, given, giveaway, complimentary, on the house, courtesy, gratuitous, honorary, grace-and-favour, voluntary, unsalaried, unpaid, charity, eleemosynary, untaxed, tax-free, zero-rated, rent-free, post-paid, post-free, f.o.b. (free on board), buckshee (Inf)

▶ *786 Nonpayment*

VERBS

12 **be cheap**, cost next to nothing, go for a song, go dirt-cheap, fall in price, depreciate, decline, sag, fall, drift, slump, plunge, plummet

▶ *367 Lowering*

13 **make cheap**, cheapen, devalue, offer value for money, give someone his money's worth, lower the price, reduce the price, lower charges, trim, cut, mark down, slash, discount, offer easy terms, sacrifice, undercharge, undercut, undersell, let go for a song, flood the market, glut the market, dump, unload, depress the market, give away, knock the bottom out of the market (Inf), knock down (Inf)

▶ *217 Sufficiency; 367 Lowering*

14 **buy cheaply**, economize, shop around, find bargains, buy wholesale, buy in bulk, buy at factory prices, buy at cost, pick up for nothing, travel second-class, travel tourist-class, travel off season, live within one's means, buy for nickles and dimes (US), haggle, beat down, buy dirt-cheap (Inf), sponge (off) (Inf), freeload (Inf)

▶ *680 Thrift; 746 Negotiation; 776 Trade; 779 Market*

ADVERBS

15 **cheaply**, cheap, inexpensively, unexpensively, reasonably, modestly, moderately, economically, nominally, at cost, wholesale, at a discount, *à bon marché* (Fr), for pennies, for nickels and dimes (US), for a (mere) song, for nothing, on the house, as a gift, on the cheap (Inf)

794 Prize

NOUNS

1 **trophy**, award, reward, prize, first prize, consolation prize, sports trophy, medal, gold medal, silver medal, bronze medal, military medal, war medal, *Croix de Guerre* (Fr), George Cross, Victoria Cross, campaign medal, medallion, plate, cup, loving cup, gold cup, silver cup, ribbon, blue ribbon, *cordon bleu* (Fr), military ribbon, figurine, statuette, wreath, chaplet, garland, palm, laurels, laurel wreath, crown, spurs, garter, decoration, military decoration, citation, military citation, honour, honours list, order of merit, order of chivalry, *Légion d'Honneur* (Fr), feather in one's cap, pot (Inf), gong (Inf), *victor ludorum* (L)

▶ *575 Title; 813 Reward*

2 **spoils**, spoils of war, booty, loot, plunder, pillage, winnings, scalp, head, shrunken head, swag (Inf)

3 **memento**, souvenir, keepsake, relic, token, token of remembrance, love token

▶ *462 Memory*

795 Morality

No morality can be founded on authority, even if the authority were divine. A. J. Ayer.

Morality's not practical. Morality's a gesture. A complicated gesture learnt from books. Robert Bolt.

What is moral is what you feel good after, and what is immoral is what you feel bad after. Ernest Hemingway.

We know no spectacle so ridiculous as the British public in one of its periodical fits of morality. Lord Macaulay.

NOUNS

1 morality, moralness, moral climate, moral standards, morals, ethics, ethicalness, principles, standards, ideals, beliefs, scruples, behaviour, conduct, ethos, attitudes, customs, mores, habits, manners

► *4 Philosophy; 7 Religion; 632 Habit*

2 good morals, integrity, propriety, probity, decency, goodness, virtue, honour, honesty, nobility, rectitude, uprightness, righteousness, right, sense of right and wrong, conscience, voice of conscience, justice, fairness, fair play, good taste, spirituality, piousness, saintliness, Moral Rearmament

► *7 Religion; 549 Refinement; 799 Honour; 801 Right; 803 Virtue*

3 moral purity, purity, faultlessness, perfection, sinlessness, sainthood, immaculacy, immaculateness, Immaculate Conception, innocence, modesty, bashfulness, coyness, pudency, shame, chastity, abstinence, continence, celibacy, Encratism, temperance, coldness, frigidity, virginity, maidenhood, maidenhead, cherry (Inf)

► *230 Perfection; 572 Celibacy; 674 Modesty; 805 Innocence*

4 self-righteousness, narrow-mindedness, mealy-mouthedness, prudery, prudishness, Grundyism, priggishness, primness, smugness, sanctimony, sanctimoniousness, pietism, puritanism, gravity, graveness, seriousness, sternness, Sunday-opening laws, blue laws (US), Prohibition (US), censorship, expurgation, bowdlerization, euphemism, genteelism, affectation, shockability, squeamishness, overmodesty, false modesty, false shame, *mauvaise honte* (Fr)

► *647 Severity; 676 Affectation*

5 pure person, virtuous person, virgin, maiden, vestal, vestal virgin, virgo intacta, Sir Galahad, the Virgin Mary, celibate, Encratite, religious celibate, monk, nun, saint

► *7 Religion; 572 Celibacy*

6 moralist, puritan, Victorian, prig, prude, prohibitionist, teetotaller, guardian of morality, censor, watchdog, Watch Committee, Moral Majority, Mrs Grundy, Mrs Mary Whitehouse, Carry Nation (US), wowser (Aus and NZ inf)

7 moral, lesson, teaching, message, point, precept, homily, maxim, apophthegm, adage, proverb, saying, saw, epigram, motto

ADJECTIVES

8 moral, ethical, principled, high-minded, good, decent, honourable, honest, noble, upright, righteous, virtuous, right-minded, right, proper, just, fair, scrupulous, saintly

9 pure, faultless, perfect, sinless, immaculate, spotless, purified, refined, snowy, white, pure as the driven snow, innocent, modest, bashful, blushing, coy, shy, chaste, undefiled, unfallen, virgin, virginal, vestal, maidenly, untouched, unwedded, celibate, continent, temperate, Platonic, sublimated, sexless, cold, frigid

10 moralistic, moralizing, self-righteous, narrow-minded, mealy-mouthed, prudish, priggish, prim, old-maidish, smug, sanctimonious, holier-than-thou, pietistic, pious, puritan, Victorian, strait-laced, grave, serious, severe, stern, censorious, censored, edifying, clean, printable, publishable, quotable, repeatable, mentionable, expurgated, bowdlerized, euphemistic, genteel, affected, overmodest, overdelicate, squeamish, shockable

VERBS

11 be moral, do no wrong, fight the good fight, follow (*or* keep on) the straight and narrow, abstain, wait, forgo sex, practise abstinence, remain celibate, remain a virgin, remain pure

12 moralize, sermonize, preach, pontificate, lecture, harangue, hold forth, go on about, point a moral, have the right moral attitude

ADVERBS

13 morally, ethically, ideally, purely, sanctimoniously, piously, moralistically

796 Immorality

It is worse than immoral, it's a mistake. Dean Acheson.

NOUNS

1 **immorality**, moral badness, bad morals, lack of morals, amorality, lack of principles, unscrupulousness, unethicalness, moral delinquency, moral turpitude, badness, wickedness, vice, viciousness, evil nature, evil, wrong, wrongdoing, criminality, dishonesty

▶ *274 Error; 588 Anarchy; 668 Disrespect; 699 Falsehood; 700 Deception; 774 Stealing; 798 Evil; 800 Dishonour; 802 Wrong; 804 Wickedness; 806 Guilt; 809 Shamelessness*

2 **indecency**, salaciousness, prurience, impure thoughts, lewdness, filthiness, defilement, uncleanness, indelicacy, bad taste, coarseness, vulgarity, grossness, nastiness, ribaldry, bawdiness, bawdry (Lit), loose talk, filthy talk, blue joke, dirty joke, dirty story, naughty story, smoking-room story, double entendre, filth, dirt, smut, obscenity, corruption, depravity, sexually explicit literature, obscene literature, adult literature, dirty books, erotic literature, erotica, facetiae, pornography, porn (Inf), soft-core pornography, soft porn (Inf), page 3 girl, girlie magazine, men's magazine, *Playboy, Lady Chatterley's Lover*, X-rated movie (*or* film) (US), blue movie (*or* film), voyeurism, sexploitation, hard-core pornography, hard porn (Inf), child pornography, video nasty, skin flick (Inf), snuff movie (*or* film) (Inf)

3 **sexual immorality**, unchastity, promiscuity, wantonness, incontinence, easy virtue, lightness, shamelessness, immodesty, laxity, loose morals, no morals, morals of an alley cat, amorality, permissive society, free love, wife swapping, sexual delinquency, roving eye, libido, lust, lecherousness, lickerishness (Lit), concupiscence, carnality, sexuality, eroticism (*or* erotism), fleshliness, the flesh, sexual indulgence, sexiness, lasciviousness, salaciousness, lubricity, dissoluteness, decadence, degeneracy, profligacy, dissipation, debauchery, depravity, licentiousness, sexual licence, libertinism (*or* libertinage), seduction, defloration, venery, lechery, satyriasis, priapism, nymphomania, fornication, whorishness, harlotry, womanizing, whoring, running around, bed hopping (Inf), fooling around (Inf), sleeping around (Inf), screwing around (Inf), wenching (Lit)

▶ *490 Physical Pleasure; 673 Vanity; 686 Self-Indulgence*

4 **illicit love**, forbidden love, guilty love, unlawful desires, forbidden fruit, unlawful carnal knowledge, adultery, criminal conversation, unfaithfulness, infidelity, marital infidelity, extramarital relations, eternal triangle, liaison, intrigue, amour, irregular union, *ménage à trois* (Fr), concubinage, cuckolding, cuckoldry, cheating (Inf), a bit on the side (Inf)

▶ *570 Marriage; 593 Love; 662 Disobedience*

5 **prostitution**, vice, vice squad, soliciting, importuning, kerb crawling, streetwalking, harlot's trade, harlotry, whoredom, oldest profession, Mrs Warren's profession, pimping, pandering, procuring, living on immoral earnings, brothel-keeping, white slave trade (*or* traffic)

6 **brothel**, bordello, bagnio, whorehouse, bawdyhouse (Lit), disorderly house, house of ill repute (*or* ill-fame), massage parlour, red-light district, cathouse (US inf), knocking shop (Inf), juke house (US inf)

7 **sexual assault**, sexual offence, sexual perversion, sexual deviancy, incest, buggery, sodomy, bestiality, sadism, sado-masochism, s and m (Inf), sexual abuse, child abuse, pederasty, indecent assault, rape, ravishment, violation, gang rape, date rape, gangbang (Inf), the train (*or* the choochoo) (US inf), gross indecency, indecent exposure, exposing oneself, flashing (Inf), mooning (US inf)

▶ *381 Attack; 585 War; 594 Hate*

8 **immoral man**, adulterer, rake, rakehell (Lit), Casanova, Don Juan, libertine, lecher, degenerate, debauchee, roué, satyr, dirty old man, womanizer, philanderer, playboy, gigolo, pimp, pander, procurer, hustler (US), male prostitute, catamite, rent boy

9 **immoral woman**, fallen woman, adulteress, loose woman, scarlet woman, nymphomaniac, nympho (Inf), strumpet, trollop, slut, whore, harlot, courtesan, concubine, kept woman, prostitute, streetwalker, call girl, brothel keeper, madam, tart (Inf), hooker (US inf), Cyprian (Lit)

10 **sex offender**, sex fiend, sex criminal, rapist, sadist, child abuser (*or* molester), pederast, pervert, pornographer, flasher (Inf)

ADJECTIVES

11 **immoral**, amoral, unethical, unprincipled, unscrupulous, bad, wicked, wrong, morally wrong, evil, criminal, illegal, dishonest

12 **indecent**, salacious, prurient, lewd, lubricious, indelicate, improper, suggestive, provocative, risqué, titillating, arousing, erotic, naughty, blue, coarse, crude, vulgar, ribald, strong, racy, louche, bawdy, Rabelaisian, unwholesome, insalubrious, defiling, corrupting, depraving, impure, unclean, dirty, smutty, filthy, scrofulous, scabrous, scatological, stinking, rank, offensive, shocking, obscene, pornographic, uncensored, unexpurgated, unmentionable, unquotable, unprintable, fruity (Inf), near the knuckle (Inf), near the bone (Inf)

13 **unchaste**, unvirtuous, of easy virtue, wanton, light, loose, frail, fallen, seduced, prostituted, fast, naughty, immodest, unblushing, shameless, flaunting, brazen, amoral, promiscuous, sex-mad, man-mad, man-crazy, nymphomaniac, scarlet, whorish, tarty, meretricious (Lit), on the game (Inf)

14 **lecherous**, carnal, fleshly, voluptuous, libidinous, lustful, lickerish (Lit), concupiscent, incontinent, Paphian, sexy, hot, rampant, rutting, ruttish, oversexed, sex-mad, sex-crazy, woman-mad, woman-crazy, priapic, lewd, lascivious, licentious, libertine, wild, rakish, amoral, adulterous, unfaithful, dissolute, dissipated, profligate, whoremongering, debauched, depraved, vicious, turned on (Inf), horny (US inf), randy (Inf), goatish (Lit)

15 **unlawful**, abnormal, incestuous, sadistic, sado-masochistic, perverted, bestial, animalistic

VERBS

16 **do wrong**, err, sin, go wrong, stray, go astray, fall, lapse, sink, degenerate, go to the bad, go to rack and ruin, go to the dogs (Inf), go to pot (Inf)

17 **be sexually immoral**, have no morals, have the morals of an alley cat, break the marriage vow, commit adultery,

keep a mistress, see another woman (*or* man), cuckold, fornicate, womanize, philander, whore (around), sleep around (Inf), screw around (Inf), lech (around) (Inf), have the hots for (Inf), cheat (Inf), put the horns on (Inf), have a bit on the side (Inf)

18 prostitute, solicit, importune, streetwalk, pimp, pander, procure, live on immoral earnings, be on the game (Inf), hook (US inf), hustle (US inf)

19 corrupt, debase, demoralize, lead astray, ruin, wreck, disgrace, shame, dishonour, defile, smirch, sully, soil, debauch, deprave, vitiate, pervert

20 seduce, take advantage of, have one's way with, take one's pleasure with, deflower, ravish, rape, force, violate, sexually assault, indecently assault, abuse, sexually abuse, interfere with

ADVERBS

21 immorally, indecently, suggestively, salaciously, immodestly, without shame

797 Good

Do good by stealth, and blush to find it fame. Alexander Pope.

Nothing can harm a good man, either in life or after death. Socrates.

You shouldn't say it is not good. You should say you do not like it; and then, you know, you're perfectly safe. James Whistler.

ADJECTIVES

1 good, excellent, first-rate, first-class, superior, better, superb, splendid, great, famous, fine, superfine, exquisite, high-class, wonderful, magnificent, terrific, impressive, meritorious, praiseworthy, admirable, worthy, valuable, profitable, sound, healthy, salubrious, salutary, favourable, propitious, heaven-sent, auspicious, lucky, suitable, appropriate, apt, right, fabulous (Inf), fine and dandy (Inf), super (Inf), crackerjack (Inf), topnotch (Inf), A-OK (*or* A-okay) (US inf), dandy (Inf), jim-dandy (US inf), smashing (Inf), cool (US inf), hunky-dory (US inf), wizard (Inf), top-hole (Inf), brill (Inf), fab (Inf), radical (Inf), rad (Inf), swell (Inf), spiffy (Inf), corking (Inf), crack (Inf), copacetic (*or* kopasetic) (US inf), bad (Inf), wicked (Inf), deadly (Inf)

► *121 Superiority; 235 Worth; 248 Prosperity; 259 Health; 781 Wealth*

2 best, very best, best ever, top, essential, quintessential, choice, elite, unequalled, nonpareil, peerless, matchless, record-breaking, class A, perfect, flawless, supreme, superlative

► *230 Perfection*

3 kind, goodly, nice, gracious, fair, virtuous, righteous, moral, honest, honourable, benevolent, beneficent, helpful, good-natured, friendly, well-wishing, thoughtful, generous

► *650 Benevolence; 747 Cooperation; 768 Giving; 799 Honour; 803 Virtue*

4 well-behaved, well-mannered, obedient, compliant, docile, willing, biddable, dutiful

► *388 Submission*

5 proficient, efficient, competent, accomplished, expert, handy, skilled, skilful, deft, versatile, dexterous, adroit, talented, gifted, masterful, masterly, wicked (Inf)

► *485 Skill*

6 beneficial, useful, advantageous, worthwhile, profitable, improving, bettering, edifying, beatific

► *237 Usefulness; 244 Improvement; 765 Profit*

7 large, goodly, ample, substantial, large-size(d), ample-size(d), adequate-size(d), sufficient-size(d)

► *158 Size*

NOUNS

8 good, goodness, excellence, first-class, quality, good quality, superiority, superbness, splendidness, greatness, fame, wonderfulness, magnificence, merit, worth, worthiness, praiseworthiness, value, soundness, healthiness, favourableness, propitiousness, auspiciousness, suitableness, appropriateness, aptness, rightness

9 the best, the very best, the best ever, tops, essence, quintessence, choice, pick, elite, cream, cream of the crop, flower, paragon, nonpareil, gem of the first water, jewel in the crown, top marks, class A, superlative, perfection, flawlessness, supremacy

10 kindness, kindliness, goodliness, niceness, graciousness, fairness, virtue, virtuousness, righteousness, rectitude, morality, honesty, honourableness, benevolence, beneficence, thoughtfulness, helpfulness, grace, goodnaturedness, friendliness, well-wishing, generosity, kind act, good turn

11 good behaviour, good manners, obedience, compliance, docility, willingness, biddability, dutifulness

12 proficiency, efficiency, competence, accomplishment, expertise, skilfulness, deftness, versatility, dexterousness, adroitness, handiness, ability, talent, gift, masterfulness, masterliness

13 benefit, well-being, welfare, public weal, common good, interest, behalf, happiness, blessing, benediction, betterment, improvement, advantage, worthwhileness, profitability, prosperity, boon, gift, profit, gain, usefulness, use, advantage, edification

14 largeness, goodliness, ampleness, substantiality, large size, ample size, adequate size, sufficient size

15 good person, saint, priest, nun, monk, Good Samaritan, altruist, philanthropist, friend, good neighbour, well-wisher, helper, rescuer, white knight

16 superior person, star, superstar, champion, superman, superwoman, prodigy, genius, wonder, virtuoso, paragon, high achiever, ace, high flyer, *crème de la crème* (Fr), pick of the bunch, nonesuch (*or* nonsuch), *übermensch* (Ger), first-rater, number one, numero uno (Inf), topnotcher (Inf), whiz kid (Inf), whiz (Inf), the cat's pyjamas (*or* whiskers) (Inf)

17 good thing, the very thing, just the thing, good luck, (good) fortune, favour, blessing, halcyon days, happy ending, treasure, gem, jewel, dream, pride and joy, pride, prize, find, winner, godsend, windfall, masterstroke, *tour de force* (Fr), *chef-d'oeuvre* (Fr), work of art, masterpiece, collector's item, record-breaker, best-seller, hit (Inf), smash (Inf), smash hit (Inf), dandy (Inf), jim-dandy (US inf), crackerjack (Inf), peach (Inf), plum (Inf), knockout (Inf), humdinger (Inf), corker (Inf), doozy (US inf), killer

(Inf), killer-diller (US inf), dilly (US inf), beaut (US and Aus inf), lollapalooza (US inf)

VERBS

18 be good, behave well, obey, comply, conform, show respect, bear allegiance to, pay homage to

19 be good at, do well at, master, excel, qualify for, pass, transcend, have the knack, have a gift for, show skill for, perform skilfully, exploit, play one's cards right

20 do good, help, serve, benefit, avail, make better, do a world of good, do someone a favour, bless, better, improve, advance, profit, bring prosperity

21 do well, thrive, flourish, prosper, succeed, improve, get better, make a profit, gain, turn to good account, make money, get rich, be on top of the world, be on the crest of a wave

ADVERBS

22 well, impressively, admirably, excellently, superbly, splendidly, famously, fabulously, exquisitely, wonderfully, magnificently, perfectly, peerlessly

23 nicely, friendlily, helpfully, benevolently, beneficently, generously, good-naturedly, honestly, morally

24 obediently, willingly, compliantly, dutifully, docilely

25 skilfully, expertly, dexterously, adroitly, giftedly, masterfully, competently

26 usefully, beneficially, advantageously, profitably

INTERJECTIONS

27 great!, super! (Inf), rad! (Inf), brill! (Inf), fab! (Inf), bad! (Inf)

798 Evil

Honi soit qui mal y pense. (Evil be to him who evil thinks.) Anonymous.

The fearsome word-and-thought-defying banality of evil. Hannah Arendt.

NOUNS

1 evil, evilness, badness, wickedness, meanness, wrongness, wrong, sin, improbity, malevolence, maleficence, malignity, malice, viciousness, hatefulness, injustice, untruthfulness, unkindness, ill will, vindictiveness, revengefulness, mischievousness, mischief, devilry, obnoxiousness, offensiveness, iniquity, vice, immorality, corruption, defilement, depravity, foulness, vileness, nastiness, noxiousness, wretchedness, rottenness, worthlessness, terribleness, dreadfulness, horribleness, awfulness, atrociousness, deadliness, beastliness (Inf)

► *651 Malevolence; 800 Dishonour; 802 Wrong*

2 affliction, trouble, troubles, adversity, plague, blight, ruin, destruction, mental affliction, unease, annoyance, angst, depression, mental illness, suffering, distress, misery, grief, sorrow, woe, bodily harm, harmfulness, harm, abuse, hurtfulness, hurt, discomfort, malaise, painfulness, pain, sickness, illness, unhealthiness, sore, running sore, malignancy (*or* malignance), malignity, casualty, accident, damage, injury, wound, tragedy, calamity, disaster, catastrophe, fiasco, sad ending, fatality, mortal blow, deathblow, death, vale of tears

► *249 Adversity; 264 Difficulty; 357 Destruction; 491 Physical Pain; 582 Death; 602 Sorrow*

3 bad luck, misfortune, ill fortune, adversity, inauspiciousness, ominousness, unfavourableness, slings and arrows (of misfortune), ill wind, evil star

► *475 Prediction*

4 evil power, bad influence, malign influence, bad spell, evil spell, the evil eye, malediction, curse, jinx, voodoo, bad karma, whammy (Inf), double whammy (Inf), hex (US inf), hoodoo (Inf)

5 evil thing, evil plight, evil wish, bane, pornography, poison, pollution, pollutant, crime, murder, foul play, skeleton in the cupboard, Pandora's box

► *16 Law; 382 Killing*

6 evil person, bad influence, bane, evil genius, evildoer, wrongdoer, malefactor, troublemaker, mischief-maker, villain, blackguard, scoundrel, bully, holy terror, terrorist, traitor, criminal, robber, kidnapper, pervert, child abuser, pornographer, rapist, killer, serial killer, murderer, mass murderer, homicidal maniac, assassin, cutthroat, poisoner, gang member, mafioso, evil ruler, Hitler, Stalin, devil, Satan, the Evil One, snake in the grass, Old Nick (Inf), baddie (*or* baddy) (Inf), crook (Inf), mobster (US inf)

► *7 Religion*

ADJECTIVES

7 evil, bad, wicked, mean, wrong, sinful, sinister, nefarious, malevolent, maleficent, malignant, malicious, vicious, diabolical, demonic, ungodly, hateful, unkind, untruthful, prejudicial, vindictive, revengeful, mischievous, obnoxious, offensive, odious, iniquitous, immoral, corrupt, defiled, blighted, depraved, foul, vile, nasty, wretched, deplorable, rotten, worthless, terrible, dreadful, horrible, awful, atrocious, despicable, detestable, contemptible, reprehensible, deadly, beastly (Inf), lousy (Inf)

8 afflicted, troubled, plagued, depressed, distressed, miserable, grievous, grief-stricken, sorrowful, woeful, sad, hurt, in pain, sick, ill, unhealthy, sore, damaged, injured, wounded, tragic

9 detrimental, damaging, destructive, deleterious, harmful, injurious, hurtful, distressing, troublous, baleful, baneful, pernicious, noxious, toxic, corruptive, corrosive, malignant, catastrophic, dire, mortal, deadly

10 inauspicious, unfavourable, unfortunate, unlucky, adverse, ominous, accursed, jinxed, voodooed, hoodooed (Inf), hexed (US inf)

VERBS

11 be evil, do evil, work evil, do wrong, do wrong by, wrong, do mischief to, do ill, not tell the truth, trouble, get into trouble, distress, aggrieve, afflict, plague, harass, persecute, threaten, menace, mistreat, maltreat, abuse, molest, defile, violate, despoil, lay a hand on, befoul, torment, condemn, hurt, harm, corrupt, pervert, damage, impair, blight, pollute, wreak havoc on, poison, injure, wound, destroy, doom, kill, curse, jinx, hex (US inf), put the (*or* a) whammy on (Inf), put the (*or* a) double whammy on (Inf)

ADVERBS

12 evilly, badly, ill, wickedly, wrongly, wrong, all wrong, sinfully, sinisterly, nefariously, malevolently, maliciously, with malice, viciously, diabolically, hatefully, with hate, unkindly, prejudicially, with prejudice, untruthfully, vindictively, in a vindictive way, revengefully, for revenge, mischievously, obnoxiously, offensively, odiously, immorally, corruptly, deplorably, terribly, dreadfully, horribly, awfully, atrociously, detestably, reprehensibly

13 **destructively**, in a destructive manner, depressingly, distressingly, miserably, grievously, sorrowfully, to one's sorrow, woefully, sadly, balefully, harmfully, hurtfully, perniciously, with malice, deleteriously, painfully, accidentally, tragically, disastrously, fatally, with fatal results, mortally

14 **inauspiciously**, ominously, as a bad omen, unfavourably, unfortunately, without good fortune, unluckily, adversely

INTERJECTIONS

15 **bad luck!**, terrible!, horrible!, that's awful!, woe is me!, jinxed again!, a plague on you!

799 Honour

NOUNS

1 **probity**, honourableness, honour, goodness, integrity, respectability, decency, incorruptibility, principles, high principles, ethics, morality, morals, moral fibre, high ideals, high-mindedness, uprightness, nobleness, good character, repute, trustworthiness, trustiness, reliability, dependability, honesty, truthfulness, truth, candidness, candour, frankness, openness, veracity, plainness, straightforwardness, sincerity, scrupulousness, scruples, fastidiousness, carefulness, conscientiousness, meticulousness, soundness, sense of duty, sense of responsibility, impartiality, fairness, equity, justice, clean hands, clear conscience, conscience, good faith, bona fides (Lit), faithfulness, fidelity, constancy, steadfastness, trueness, loyalty, devotion, chivalry

► *271 Simplicity; 273 Accuracy; 663 Obedience; 665 Carefulness; 698 Truth; 795 Morality; 797 Good*

2 **purity**, sanctity, faith, virtue, virginity, innocence, righteousness, godliness, holiness, rectitude, pure heart

► *7 Religion; 256 Cleanness; 803 Virtue; 805 Innocence*

3 **honourable person**, honest person, man (*or* woman) of honour, man of his word, woman of her word, good person, perfect gentleman, Galahad, true lady, fair fighter, good loser, sportsman, sportswoman, knight in shining armour, champion of lost causes, salt of the earth, good sort (Inf), brick (Inf), square (*or* straight) shooter (US inf), good sport (Inf)

ADJECTIVES

4 **honourable**, respectable, decent, good, reputable, incorruptible, high-minded, principled, fastidious, high-principled, ethical, moral, upright, upstanding, noble, trustworthy, trusty, sure, reliable, dependable, as good as one's word, responsible, dutiful, honest, true, truthful, candid, frank, open, above board, on the up and up, law-abiding, veracious, plain, plain-spoken, straightforward, sincere, undeceitful, undeceptive, scrupulous, careful, meticulous, conscientious, sound, impartial, fair, fair-dealing, straight, equitable, bona fide, just, faithful, constant, steadfast, loyal, true-blue, true to the core, devoted, chivalrous, gentlemanly, sportsmanlike, sporting, on the level (Inf), fair and square (Inf), square (Inf), straight up (Inf)

5 **pure**, undefiled, sanctified, saintly, pious, religious, godly, virtuous, virginal, innocent, righteous, pure as the driven snow

VERBS

6 **be honourable**, act honourably, preserve one's honour, behave well, behave like a gentleman, act like a lady, live like a Christian, fear God, keep (the) faith, have virtue, have decency, act morally, deal fairly, play by the rules, stick to the rules, go by the book, shoot straight, guard one's reputation, keep one's promise, keep one's word, speak truthfully, speak (*or* tell) the truth, stick to the truth, tell the whole truth and nothing but the truth, tell the truth and shame the devil, speak plainly, tell it like it is, call a spade a spade, put (*or* lay) one's cards on the table, show respect, show a sense of duty, keep steadfast, level with (Inf), give it straight (Inf), keep to the straight and narrow (Inf)

ADVERBS

7 **honourably**, respectably, decently, well, reputably, high-mindedly, ethically, morally, nobly, reliably, dependably, responsibly, dutifully, honestly, truly, truthfully, to tell the truth, in truth, with truth, candidly, frankly, openly, veraciously, plainly, in plain words, in plain English, straight from the shoulder, not to mince words, without equivocation, unequivocally, sincerely, scrupulously, sedulously, carefully, meticulously, conscientiously, in all conscience, impartially, fairly, squarely, in (*or* with) good faith, justly, faithfully, constantly, steadfastly, loyally, devotedly, chivalrously, sportingly, straight up (Inf)

8 **purely**, with pure intentions, piously, religiously, virtuously, innocently, in all innocence, righteously

800 Dishonour

NOUNS

1 **improbity**, dishonour, dishonesty, disrepute, shame, worthlessness, good-for-nothingness, evilness, wickedness, badness, villainy, villainousness, corruption, depravity, venality, turpitude, moral turpitude, knavery, lack of integrity, disrespect, disgrace, debasement, baseness, indecency, immorality, lack of morals, lack of principles, lack of conscience, unscrupulousness, deviousness, opportunism, unfairness, partiality, bias, prejudice, injustice, insincerity, hypocrisy, disingenuousness, untruthfulness, falsehood, lie, foul play, contrivance, chicanery, trickery, trick, dirty trick, not playing the game, crookedness (Inf), hitting below the belt (Inf)

► *479 Equivocation; 645 Cunning; 662 Disobedience; 699 Falsehood; 700 Deception; 802 Wrong; 804 Wickedness*

2 **faithlessness**, unfaithfulness, bad faith, infidelity, perfidy, perfidiousness, deceit, falseness, falsity, breach of faith, broken word, broken promise, breach of promise, unreliability, untrustworthiness, undependability, wavering loyalty, sitting on the fence, disloyalty, disobedience, duplicity, double-dealing, double-crossing, U-turn, volte-face, tergiversation, defection, desertion, betrayal, treachery, Judas kiss, stab in the back, treason, high

treason, sedition, rebellion, running with the hare and hunting with the hounds, sell-out (Inf)

3 **criminality**, crime, lawbreaking, felony, racketeering, fraudulency, fraudulence, fraud, thieving, thievishness, light fingers, embezzlement, bribery, tax evasion, graft, sharp practice, swindle, confidence trick, confidence game (US), underhand dealings, dirty dealings, sleaze, racket, skulduggery (Inf), shadiness (Inf), crookedness (Inf), fishy transaction (Inf), fiddle (Inf), con trick (Inf), con game (US inf), scam (Inf)

▶ *774 Stealing; 796 Immorality; 802 Wrong*

4 **dishonourable person**, dishonest person, man (*or* woman) of dishonour, scoundrel, good-for-nothing, bad influence, rascal, rogue, knave, villain, fraud, double-dealer, double-crosser, traitor, Judas, criminal, gangster, racketeer, lawbreaker, embezzler, felon, snake in the grass, slippery customer (Inf), shady character (Inf), two-timer (Inf), con man (Inf), shyster (US inf), crook (Inf), spiv (Inf), mobster (US inf)

ADJECTIVES

5 **dishonourable**, dishonest, disreputable, shameful, worthless, good-for-nothing, evil, wicked, bad, villainous, nefarious, corrupt, corruptible, unprincipled, unethical, bribable, depraved, venal, disrespectful, disgraceful, ignoble, contemptible, sleazy, debased, base, indecent, immoral, unscrupulous, ungentlemanly, unsportsmanlike, rotten, devious, up to something, up to no good, opportunistic, scheming, unfair, biased, prejudiced, unjust, insincere, hypocritical, disingenuous, uncandid, untruthful, lying, tricky, foxy, vulpine, slippery, wrangling (Inf), shady (Inf), crooked (Inf), low-down (Inf), not cricket (Inf), on the fiddle (Inf)

6 **faithless**, unfaithful, perfidious, deceitful, false, two-faced, untrustworthy, not to be trusted, unreliable, undependable, questionable, shaky, disloyal, disobedient, double-dealing, double-crossing, duplicitous, deserting, betraying, treacherous, treasonous, seditious, rebellious

7 **criminal**, lawbreaking, felonious, fraudulent, underhanded, thieving, light-fingered, embezzling, swindling, bribing, not straight, shady (Inf), crooked (Inf), fishy (Inf), bent (Inf)

VERBS

8 **be dishonourable**, be dishonest, lack honesty, have no morals, forget one's principles, yield to temptation, live by one's wits, evade, shift the blame, falsify, perjure oneself, tell lies, lie, prevaricate, pull the wool over someone's eyes, shed crocodile tears, bend the rules (Inf), pass the buck (Inf), wangle (Inf), finagle (Inf), smell fishy (Inf), do the dirty on (Inf), play dirty pool (US inf)

9 **prove false**, dissemble, deceive, double-cross, break one's word, break faith, go back on one's promises, let down one's side, let down, turn against, forsake, betray, stab in the back, go over to the enemy, collaborate, run with the hare and hunt with the hounds, bite the hand that feeds one, sell out (Inf), two-time (Inf), sell down the river (Inf)

10 **be criminal**, lead a life of crime, smuggle, defraud, cheat, rob, embezzle, racketeer, fence, swindle, steal, thieve, pilfer, shoplift, fiddle (Inf), do someone out of (Inf), cook the books (Inf), scam (Inf)

ADVERBS

11 **dishonourably**, without honour, dishonestly, without regard for honesty, shamefully, like a thief in the night, worthlessly, wickedly, badly, corruptly, unethically, by fair means or foul, disrespectfully, disgracefully, ignobly, indecently, immorally, unscrupulously, deviously, mala fide, unfairly, naughtily, insincerely, hypocritically, uncandidly, untruthfully, faithlessly, unfaithfully, deceitfully, falsely, unreliably, shakily, disloyally, disobediently, treacherously, seditiously, rebelliously, criminally, fraudulently, underhandedly, shadily (Inf)

801 Right

Right is more precious than peace. Woodrow Wilson.

NOUNS

1 **fairness**, rightness, justice, equity, equitableness, impartiality, equality, equalness, fair-mindedness, fair play (*or* treatment), even handedness, square deal, even deal, lack of bias, even break (Inf), fair crack of the whip (Inf)

▶ *16 Law; 324 Direction*

2 **correctness**, accurateness, accuracy, authenticity, validity, legitimacy, truth, trueness, genuineness, veracity, precision, preciseness

▶ *273 Accuracy; 698 Truth*

3 **properness**, correctness, honesty, decency, propriety, seemliness, probity, integrity, honour, etiquette

▶ *795 Morality; 797 Good*

4 **righteousness**, virtue, virtuousness, uprightness, integrity, rectitude, uprightness, probity, godliness

▶ *7 Religion; 8 Divinity; 797 Good; 799 Honour; 803 Virtue*

5 **righting wrong**, reform, reformation, rectification, correction

▶ *12 Government and Politics; 224 Change*

6 **right**, entitlement, due, desert, claim, prerogative

ADJECTIVES

7 **right**, fair, just, equitable, equal, impartial, fair-minded, open-minded, square, unbiased, disinterested, even-handed, objective, neutral, unprejudiced

8 **correct**, accurate, true, authentic, genuine, valid, legitimate, veracious, unerring, precise, exact, dead right (Inf), spot on (Inf), bang-on (Inf), on the button (Inf)

9 **in the right**, justified, justifiable, excusable, forgivable, unimpeachable, unchallengeable, rightful, deserved, due, entitled

10 **moral**, moralistic, ethical, high-principled, righteous, virtuous, godly, clean, pure, honest, honourable, truthful, upright, upstanding, straight, straightforward, blameless

11 **right-minded**, decent, law-abiding, sporting, sportsmanlike, on the side of the angels, squeaky clean (Inf)

12 **all right**, fine, fit, well, healthy, in good health, balanced, all there (Inf), in the pink (Inf), up to par (Inf), OK (Inf)

VERBS

13 **be right**, be in the right, have right on one's side, be within one's rights, have grounds for, be justified, deserve, merit, have a claim to, be entitled to

14 **be fair**, see justice done, see fair play, do the right thing,

play the game, hear both sides, arbitrate, give the Devil his due

15 put right, set right, set to rights, right a wrong, rectify, redress, reform, mend, fix, repair, compensate for, make reparation for, sort out

ADVERBS

16 right, rightly, rightfully, deservedly

17 by rights, by right, properly, justly, in fairness

18 properly, correctly, as is fitting, as is befitting, aptly, befittingly, fittingly, satisfactorily, suitably

19 equally, fairly, justly, impartially, without bias, without distinction, without fear or favour

20 correctly, aright, accurately, truly, precisely, genuinely, bang, squarely

21 in the right, within one's rights

802 Wrong

Wrongdoing can only be avoided if those who are not wronged feel the same indignation at it as those who are. Solon.

NOUNS

1 unfairness, wrongness, injustice, inequity, discrimination, bias, one-sidedness, unevenness, favouritism, partiality, prejudice, partisanship

▶ *465 Misjudgment; 466 Discrimination*

2 incorrectness, falseness, error, mistake, untruthfulness, inaccuracy, fallaciousness, erroneousness, unsoundness, invalidity, mistakenness

▶ *274 Error*

3 impropriety, unseemliness, indecorousness, vulgarity, vulgarness, bad taste

▶ *497 Blandness; 675 Vulgarity; 796 Immorality; 798 Evil; 800 Dishonour*

4 abnormality, irregularity, oddity, oddness, queerness, aberrance, aberration, perversion

▶ *118 Nonconformity; 299 Irregularity*

5 unrighteousness, sinfulness, wickedness, badness, evilness

▶ *796 Immorality; 798 Evil; 804 Wickedness*

6 unlawfulness, lawlessness, illegality, illegitimacy, illicitness, infraction, violation, delinquency, criminality, foul play

7 sense of wrong, complaint, grouse, grievance, injury, wrong, injustice, tort, foul, foul play, raw deal (Inf), gripe (Inf)

8 wrongdoing, wrong, sin, vice, guilty act, bad deed, evil deed, misdeed, abomination, crime, felony, misdemeanour, offence, misdoing, transgression, trespass, infraction, infringement, injury, harm, hurt, abuse, error, mistake, mischief

▶ *274 Error; 631 Behaviour*

9 dishonour, disgrace, scandal, shame, crying shame, slur, stain, stigma, blot, blot on one's copybook (Inf)

10 wrongdoer, sinner, offender, culprit, criminal, felon, lawbreaker, delinquent, juvenile delinquent, trespasser, transgressor, infractor, miscreant, villain, malefactor, crook (Inf), crim (Inf)

ADJECTIVES

11 wrong, wrongful, unjust, unfair, inequitable, biased, prejudiced, racially prejudiced, discriminatory, favouring, partial, partisan, uneven, unbalanced, weighted, one-sided, leaning to one side, unsportsmanlike, not playing the game, not cricket (Inf), below the belt (Inf), out of line (Inf)

▶ *465 Misjudgment*

12 incorrect, not right, inaccurate, imprecise, false, untrue, untruthful, fallacious, unsound, invalid, erroneous, mistaken, misinformed, at fault, off course, off beam, off-target, off base (US), wide of the mark

▶ *274 Error*

13 improper, incorrect, unsuitable, unfit, unfitting, unbefitting, inappropriate, inapt, incongruous, indecorous, unseemly, unbecoming, undesirable, vulgar, tasteless, not done (Inf), not the done thing (Inf), not the thing (Inf)

▶ *497 Blandness; 675 Vulgarity*

14 abnormal, irregular, odd, queer, aberrant, perverted, deviant, unsound, unhinged, wrong in the head (Inf)

▶ *118 Nonconformity; 299 Irregularity; 461 Insanity*

15 immoral, amoral, corrupt, unprincipled, unethical, dishonest, dishonourable, disgraceful, shameful, shamefaced, shameless, scandalous, infamous, sacrilegious

▶ *796 Immorality; 800 Dishonour*

16 in the wrong, guilty, at fault, blameworthy, to be blamed, culpable, sinful, unrighteous, bad, wicked, evil, vicious, abominable, unlawful, lawless, illegal, illegitimate, illicit, criminal, felonious, delinquent, transgressive, infringing, violative, offensive, abusive, injurious, hurtful, harmful, mischievous, crooked (Inf)

▶ *806 Guilt*

17 unforgivable, unpardonable, unjustifiable, inexcusable, reprehensible, objectionable

18 gone wrong, not working, broken down, out of commission, out of order, in need of repair, awry, askew, defective, malfunctioning, on the blink (Inf), conked out (Inf), kaput (Inf), buggered up (Inf)

VERBS

19 be wrong, make a mistake, give the wrong answer, blunder, slip up (Inf), make a bloomer (Inf)

▶ *274 Error*

20 wrong, hurt, harm, injure, offend, abuse, maltreat, ill-treat, ill-use, oppress, malign, defame

▶ *678 Scornfulness*

21 do wrong, break the law, break (*or* not play by) the rules, commit a crime, commit an offence, offend, trespass, transgress, infringe, violate, cheat, not play the game, commit a foul, hit below the belt (Inf)

22 discriminate, discriminate against, be biased, show partiality, show favouritism, favour, lean towards, lean to one side

▶ *465 Misjudgment*

23 sin, fall from grace, err, go astray, stray from the straight and narrow, go to the bad, go to the dogs (Inf)

▶ *798 Evil; 804 Wickedness*

24 go wrong, break down, go out of commission, be out of order, fail, malfunction, conk out (Inf), go on the blink (Inf), go phut (Inf), go kaput (Inf)

ADVERBS

25 wrongly, wrongfully, unjustly, unfairly

26 **wrong**, incorrectly, inaccurately, imprecisely, falsely, untruthfully, erroneously, mistakenly
27 **improperly**, unsuitably, inappropriately, indecorously
28 **immorally**, dishonestly, sinfully, wickedly, unlawfully, illicitly

803 Virtue

To be able to practise five things everywhere under heaven constitutes perfect virtue…gravity, generosity of soul, sincerity, earnestness, and kindness. Confucius.

The greatest offence against virtue is to speak ill of it. William Hazlitt.

Most men admire
Virtue, who follow not her lore. John Milton.

NOUNS

1 **virtue**, virtuousness, righteousness, probity, goodness, good behaviour, virtuous conduct, Christian conduct, moral goodness, moral rectitude, rectitude, morality, moral strength, moral tone, spirituality, saintliness, sanctity, godliness, holiness, perfection, nobleness, magnanimity, philanthropy, benevolence, generosity, altruism, unselfishness, disinterestedness, idealism, uprightness, irreproachability, guiltlessness, blamelessness, stainlessness, uncorruptness, sinlessness, innocence, honour, personal honour, integrity, decency, chivalry, properness, good conscience, clear conscience, the straight and narrow (path)
▶ *7 Religion; 230 Perfection; 650 Benevolence; 795 Morality; 799 Honour; 801 Right; 805 Innocence*
2 **virtues**, morals, mores, ethics, principles, high principles, ideals, cardinal virtues, moral virtues, theological virtues, moral laws, faith, hope, charity, love, natural virtues, prudence, justice, temperance, soberness, self-control, character, chastity, purity, virginity, fortitude, honesty, duty, obedience, grace, saving grace, qualities, fine qualities, saving qualities, heroic qualities
▶ *684 Self-Restraint; 810 Duty*
3 **worth**, worthiness, excellence, credit, merit, desert
▶ *235 Worth; 669 Approval*
4 **virtuous person**, good person, honest person, saint, angel, priest, nun, monk, paragon, paragon of virtue, altruist, virgin, martyr, white knight, knight in shining armour, Good Samaritan, good example, goody-goody (Inf)

ADJECTIVES

5 **virtuous**, righteous, good, good as gold, Christian, moral, spiritual, saintly, saintlike, seraphic, angelic, sanctified, godly, holy, perfect, unerring, noble, magnanimous, philanthropic, benevolent, generous, altruistic, unselfish, disinterested, idealistic, upright, irreproachable, above reproach, impeccable, above temptation, guiltless, blameless, stainless, spotless, without blemish, immaculate, uncorrupt, uncorrupted, sinless, innocent, honourable, decent, chivalrous, proper, on the side of the angels, pure as driven snow
6 **ethical**, principled, high-principled, faithful, charitable, loving, prudent, just, honest, dutiful, obedient, temperate, self-controlled, sober, chaste, pure, virginal
7 **worthy**, praiseworthy, commendable, excellent, meritorious, exemplary

VERBS

8 **be virtuous**, be good, do good, love good, do no evil, hate evil, hear no evil, see no evil, speak no evil, behave, stay on one's good (*or* best) behaviour, practise virtue, have all the virtues, resist temptation, rise above temptation, control one's passions, control oneself, fight the good fight, keep straight, go straight, follow one's conscience, keep to (*or* on) the straight and narrow path, follow the straight and narrow, walk humbly with one's God, shame the devil, discharge one's obligations, do one's duty, set a good example, be a shining light, have saving grace

ADVERBS

9 **virtuously**, righteously, innocently, in all innocence, goodly, with good intentions, morally, spiritually, angelically, perfectly, nobly, for noble reasons, magnanimously, benevolently, generously, altruistically, for the benefit of others, unselfishly, idealistically, uprightly, irreproachably, impeccably, guiltlessly, without guilt, blamelessly, without blame, stainlessly, immaculately, sinlessly, without sin, honourably, decently, chivalrously, properly
10 **ethically**, faithfully, charitably, lovingly, with a loving heart, prudently, justly, honestly, with honesty, dutifully, obediently, temperately, soberly, chastely, purely, virginally
11 **worthily**, commendably, excellently, in an excellent manner, meritoriously

804 Wickedness

The wickedness of the world is so great you have to run your legs off to avoid having them stolen from under you. Bertolt Brecht.

NOUNS

1 **wickedness**, badness, sinfulness, sin, evil, cruelty, brutality, wrong, improbity, iniquity, flagitiousness, unrighteousness, wrongdoing, evildoing, bad behaviour, misbehaviour, wicked ways, bad ways, bad conduct, bad character, disrepute, fallen nature, recidivism, backsliding, deterioration, naughtiness, disobedience, dishonesty, wicked deed, peccability, transgression, trespass, delinquency, criminality, corruption, vitiation, loss of innocence, shamelessness, vileness, baseness, heinousness, viciousness, cruelness, hellishness, malevolence, hardness of heart, villainy, knavery, roguery, enormity, inhumanity, infamy, flagrancy, outrage, abomination, atrocity
▶ *236 Worthlessness; 245 Deterioration; 651 Malevolence; 662 Disobedience; 798 Evil; 800 Dishonour; 802 Wrong; 812 Notoriety*
2 **vice**, immorality, amorality, amoralism, no morals, loose morals, unvirtuousness, impurity, indecency, lust, vulgarity, carnality, debauchery, degeneration, degeneracy, profligacy, depravity, turpitude, moral turpitude, degradation, perversion

► *796 Immorality*

3 **venial sin**, small fault, flaw, fatal flaw, imperfection, shortcoming, failing, frailty, human frailty, foible, weakness, human weakness, moral weakness, weakness of the flesh, weak point, laxity, lack of principle, infirmity, fault, defect, demerit, deficiency, limitation, indecorum, impropriety, indiscretion, unseemliness, bad taste, peccadillo, slight transgression, minor offence

► *337 Weakness*

4 **sin**, original sin, capital sin, mortal sin, deadly sin

5 **seven deadly sins**, pride, covetousness, lust, anger, gluttony, envy, sloth

6 **religious sin**, impiety, ungodliness, blasphemy, sacrilege, desecration, profaneness, idolatry, devilry, devil worship, Satanism, diabolism, witchcraft, sorcery, the Old Adam, devil, Satan, Mephistopheles

► *7 Religion; 622 Pride*

7 **criminality**, criminal act, criminal offence, guilty act, guilt, foul play, illegality, unlawful act, lawbreaking, crime, misdemeanour, white-collar crime, shoplifting, delinquency, juvenile delinquency, felony, drug peddling, robbery, rape, assault, assault and battery, murder, capital crime, deadly crime, hanging offence, career of crime, criminal world, underworld, gangland, organized crime, the syndicate (US), the Mafia, Cosa Nostra, Black Hand, the rackets (Inf), the mob (Inf)

► *381 Attack; 382 Killing; 691 Drug-Taking; 806 Guilt*

8 **wicked place**, den of iniquity, den of vice, brothel, house of prostitution, opium den, gambling den, road to hell, hell, Hades (Inf), robbers' lair (Inf), cathouse (US inf)

9 **wicked person**, wrongdoer, evildoer, transgressor, sinner, lost soul, lost sheep, prodigal son, black sheep, outcast, undesirable, troublemaker, good-for-nothing, ne'er-do-well, scamp, rake, knave, rogue, rascal, scoundrel, rapscallion, reprobate, wastrel, profligate, degenerate, lecher, pervert, child abuser, paedophile, fallen woman, fallen angel, demimonde, hussy, whore, streetwalker, call girl, pimp, nasty type, thug, bully, tyrant, fiend, brute, savage, sadist, ogre, monster, demon, ghoul, Satanist, devil worshipper, devil, devil incarnate, miscreant, renegade, recreant, blasphemer, idolater, profaner, traitor, betrayer, quisling, Judas, snake, snake in the grass, swine, swindler, villain, blackguard, criminal, lawbreaker, malefactor, outlaw, desperado, culprit, offender, felon, cheat, thief, robber, rapist, drug peddler, hoodlum (US), gangster, racketeer, hired killer, killer, murderer, assassin, terrorist, the wicked, the bad, scum of the earth, dregs of society

► *796 Immorality; 798 Evil*

10 **bad person**, ugly customer (Inf), bad egg (Inf), baddie (Inf), bad lot (Inf), rotten apple (Inf), crook (Inf), bastard (Inf), rat (Inf), skunk (Inf), polecat (US inf), bitch (Inf), stinker (Inf), rotter (Inf), wrong'un (Inf), lowlife (Inf), son of a bitch (s.o.b.) (US inf), hooker (US inf), hood (Inf), hooligan (Inf), hit man (Inf), tea leaf (Inf), mobster (US inf), bounder (Inf), gross-out (US inf), bad news (Inf), louse (Inf)

ADJECTIVES

11 **wicked**, bad, sinful, full of sin, sinning, evil, evildoing, wrong, wrongdoing, erring, iniquitous, nefarious, flagitious, unrighteous, badly behaved, misbehaved, misbehaving, improper, disreputable, disgraceful, fallen, knavish, roguish, rascally, slipping, sliding, backsliding, recidivous, deteriorating, naughty, disobedient, dishonest, transgressing, trespassing, delinquent, criminal, corrupt, rotten, rotten to the core, shameless, unprincipled, worthless, unscrupulous, conscienceless, despicable, reprehensible, vile, base, foul, beastly, heinous, vicious, cruel, brutal, brutalized, hellish, maleficent, malevolent, hardhearted, hardened, callous, villainous, miscreant, inhuman, infamous, flagrant, outrageous, abominable, atrocious, hopeless, incorrigible, irreclaimable, unredeemed, irredeemable, unforgivable, unexcusable, inexcusable, unpardonable, irremissible, inexpiable, unatonable

► *798 Evil*

12 **immoral**, steeped in vice, vicious, unvirtuous, virtueless, ruined, scarlet, without morals, unchaste, impure, indecent, obscene, gross, shocking, outrageous, lustful, vulgar, carnal, debauched, degenerate, profligate, depraved, degraded, perverse, perverted, amoral

► *796 Immorality*

13 **venial**, vulnerable, not above temptation, easily tempted, not perfect, imperfect, failing, frail, infirm, feeble, weak, morally weak, lax, having a weaker side, having one's foibles, having a touch of human frailty, human, only human, too human, defective, deficient, indecorous, indiscreet, unseemly, flagrant, scandalous, scandalizing

14 **impious**, irreligious, ungodly, godless, godforsaken, blasphemous, sacrilegious, profane, accursed, damned, reprobate, not in a state of grace, infernal, devilish, diabolical, satanic, fiendish, Mephistophelian

15 **criminal**, offensive, culpable, accusable, blameworthy, guilty, foul, illegal, unlawful, lawbreaking, delinquent, felonious

► *802 Wrong*

VERBS

16 **be wicked**, do wrong, err, make a mistake, slip, trip, stumble, fall, fall from grace, stray, have one's foibles, have one's weak side, misbehave, sin, commit sin, transgress, trespass, offend, shock, scoff at virtue, become corrupt, go to the bad, fall into evil ways, shame oneself, disgrace oneself, ruin one's name, sow one's (wild) oats, kick over the traces, have an affair, lapse, relapse, backslide, deviate from the path of virtue, stray from (*or* leave) the straight and narrow, blot one's copybook (Inf), go to the dogs (Inf), carry on (Inf), gross someone out (US inf)

17 **make wicked**, set a bad example, mislead, lead astray, teach wickedness, tempt, pervert, corrupt, distort, demoralize, brutalize, seduce, shame, dehumanize, diabolize

ADVERBS

18 **wickedly**, badly, sinfully, evilly, with evil intentions, wrongly, iniquitously, disreputably, to one's discredit, disgracefully, disobediently, dishonestly, corruptly, unscrupulously, vilely, viciously, cruelly, without regard to feelings, brutally, malevolently, flagrantly, scandalously, hardheartedly, callously, inhumanly, incorrigibly, irredeemably, inexcusably, unpardonably

19 vulnerably, imperfectly, indecorously, indiscreetly
20 immorally, without morals, amorally, indecently, obscenely, in an obscene manner, lustfully, vulgarly, carnally, degenerately, mortally, impiously, irreligiously, blasphemously, sacrilegiously, profanely, devilishly, diabolically, satanically, fiendishly
21 criminally, offensively, with offence, culpably, guiltily, illegally, unlawfully, delinquently, feloniously

805 Innocence

NOUNS

1 innocence, innocentness, virtue, goodness, morality, uprightness, probity, purity, virginity, chastity, purity of heart, saintliness, state of grace, perfection, immaculacy, cleanness, cleanliness, spotlessness, stainlessness, whiteness, incorruption, incorruptibility, incorruptedness, sinlessness, freedom from sin, guiltlessness, inculpability, clear conscience, clean hands, faultlessness, impeccability, blamelessness, freedom from blame, unblameworthiness, irreproachability, nothing to confess, nothing to declare, innocent intentions, pure motives, inoffensiveness, harmlessness, playfulness
► *7 Religion; 256 Cleanness; 795 Morality; 799 Honour; 803 Virtue*
2 legal innocence, verdict of innocence, finding of innocence, acquittal, exoneration, exculpation, absolution
► *16 Law*
3 naivety, ingenuousness, guilelessness, artlessness, unsophistication, inexperience, immaturity, callowness, greenness, unworldliness, naturalness, simplicity, credulousness, childhood, days of innocence, golden age, prelapsarian innocence, salad days
► *456 Ignorance; 555 Youth; 646 Naivety*
4 innocent person, innocent party, innocent, beginner, ingenue, virgin, newcomer, greenhorn, tenderfoot, infant, child, good person, saint, lamb, dove, angel (Inf), goody-goody (Inf), babe (Inf), newborn babe (Inf), babe in arms (Inf)

ADJECTIVES

5 innocent, virtuous, good, upright, pure, virginal, chaste, pure of heart, saintly, perfect, angelic, immaculate, unblemished, untainted, stainless, spotless, unspotted, unsullied, undefiled, unsoiled, clean, pristine, white, sinless, free from sin, prelapsarian, untouched by evil, faultless, impeccable, unerring, blameless, unblamable, unblameworthy, irreprehensible, inculpable, reproachless, irreproachable, above suspicion, not guilty, guiltless, cleared, in the clear, with clean hands, clean-handed, uncorrupt, uncorruptible, uncorrupted, incorrupt, incorruptible, innocent as a lamb, lamblike, innocent as a dove, dovelike, gentle, inoffensive, harmless, innocuous, safe, playful, holier-than-thou, goody-goody (Inf), clean (Inf)
6 declared innocent, found innocent, found not guilty, cleared, acquitted, exonerated, exculpated, absolved
7 naive, ingenuous, guileless, artless, unsophisticated, credulous, inexperienced, immature, callow, green, unworldly, natural, simple, knowing no wrong, knowing no better, prelapsarian, childlike, innocent as a child, innocent as a newborn babe (Inf)

VERBS

8 be innocent, have no guilt, stand above suspicion, wrong no-one, have clean hands, have a clear conscience, have nothing to be ashamed of, have nothing to hide, have nothing to declare, have nothing to confess, live in a state of grace, not fall from grace, mean no harm, have the best intentions, salve one's conscience, look as if butter would not melt in one's mouth
9 declare innocent, find innocent, find not guilty, clear, acquit, exonerate, exculpate, absolve
10 be naive, have no guile, lack sophistication, lack experience, lack maturity, know no wrong, know no better, have the innocence of a child, have the innocence of a newborn babe (Inf)

ADVERBS

11 innocently, in all innocence, with clean hands, with a clear conscience, with an easy conscience, virtuously, uprightly, purely, with pure intentions, virginally, chastely, perfectly, to perfection, in a perfect way, angelically, immaculately, spotlessly, faultlessly, impeccably, unerringly, guiltlessly, with no guilt, blamelessly, irreproachably, inoffensively, harmlessly, in a harmless way, innocuously, with the best (of) intentions, unknowingly, unconsciously, unawares, playfully
12 naively, ingenuously, guilelessly, artlessly, without affectation, credulously, immaturely, naturally, simply, like an innocent child, with the innocence of a newborn babe (Inf)

806 Guilt

NOUNS

1 guilt, guiltiness, culpability, liability, one's fault, blood guilt, red-handedness, delinquency, illegality, criminality, implication, complicity, aiding and abetting, responsibility, reproach, reproachfulness, censure, blame, peccancy, inculpation, reprehensibility, blameworthiness, impeachability, indictability, accusation of guilt, accusation, conviction of guilt, conviction
► *16 Law; 715 Accusation; 739 Disclosure; 804 Wickedness*
2 signs of guilt, burden of guilt, onus of guilt, guilt complex, guilty feelings, guilty conscience, bad conscience, twinge of conscience, qualms, remorse, shame, contrition, regret, self-reproach, self-accusation, penitence, guilty behaviour, blush, stammer, embarrassment, dirty hands, bloody hands, red hands
► *808 Remorse*
3 sin, sinfulness, sinning, deadly sin, venial sin, original sin, vice, iniquity, wickedness, guilty act, wrongdoing, misconduct, misdoing, misdeed, misbehaviour, lapse, slip, faux pas, blunder, mistake, fault, failure, dereliction of duty, injury, wrong, sin of omission, negligence, culpable omission, unprofessional conduct, indiscretion, impropriety, peccadillo, naughtiness, wicked deed, transgression, trespass, injustice, illegality, tort (Lit), delict (Lit), crime, criminal offence, offence, misdemeanour, white-collar crime, malpractice, felony, atrocity, outrage, enormity
► *274 Error; 651 Malevolence; 666 Negligence; 802 Wrong*
4 guilty person, guilty party, offender, culprit, wrongdoer, reprobate, recidivist, malefactor, delinquent, accomplice,

criminal, confessed criminal, convicted criminal, felon, convict, prisoner, prison inmate, jailbird (*or* gaolbird), old lag (Inf)

ADJECTIVES

5 **guilty**, blood-guilty, responsible, reprehensible, reprehensive, censurable, inexcusable, without excuse, unjustifiable, unpardonable, unforgivable, reproachable, reproachful, reprovable, in the wrong, at fault, to blame, on one's head, culpable, inculpated, caught in the act, caught red-handed, caught with one's trousers down, caught with one's pants down (US), caught with one's hand in the till, impeachable, chargeable, accusable, blameworthy, blameful, blamed, implicated, censured, peccant, condemned, convicted, found guilty, proved guilty

6 **appearing guilty**, looking guilty, shamefaced, shameful, ashamed, sheepish, blushing, stammering, hangdog, red-handed, feeling guilty, contrite, conscience-stricken, remorseful, regretful, sorry

7 **sinful**, wicked, illegal, criminal, trespassing, transgressing, heinous, mortal, deadly, murderous

VERBS

8 **be guilty**, be at fault, have no excuse, have no alibi, have nothing to say for oneself, get caught in the act, get caught red-handed, get caught with one's trousers down, get caught with one's pants down (US), get caught with one's hand in the till, have crimes to answer for, have blood on one's hands, acknowledge one's guilt, acknowledge one's sins, bear the blame, plead guilty, confess, stand condemned

9 **appear guilty**, look guilty, seem guilty, look ashamed, look embarrassed, look sheepish, blush, stammer, feel guilty, have a bad conscience, accuse oneself, torture oneself, punish oneself, wear a hair shirt, look like the cat that swallowed the canary (*or* that got the cream)

10 **sin**, trespass, transgress, commit a crime, commit a white-collar crime, commit a misdemeanour, commit a felony, rob, steal, kidnap, murder, assassinate

ADVERBS

11 **guiltily**, reprehensibly, reprehensively, inexcusably, without excuse, unjustifiably, unpardonably, unforgivably, reproachfully, with reproach, blamefully, criminally, red-handed, red-handedly, in the (very) act, in flagrante delicto (Lit), shamefacedly, shamefully, ashamedly, sheepishly, blushingly, contritely, remorsefully, regretfully, sorrily, with sorrow, with a guilty conscience

807 Atonement

Undeservedly you will atone for the sins of your fathers. Horace.

NOUNS

1 **atonement**, amends, making amends, satisfaction, expiation, reparation, rectification, redress, compensation, payment, repayment, indemnity, indemnification, reimbursement, restitution, requital, recompense, redemption, making right, making good, making up for, quittance, squaring, measure for measure, blood money, wergild, eye for an eye, propitiation, appeasement, conciliation, reconciliation, pacification, pouring oil on troubled waters, quits (Inf)

▶ *749 Pacification; 754 Compromise; 775 Giving Back*

2 **apology**, abject apology, regrets, expression of regret, excuse, acknowledgment, acknowledgment of guilt, *mea culpa* (L), repentance, remorse, confession, penitence, penance, contrition, breast-beating, expiatory offering, offering, oblation, sacrifice, piaculum, burnt offering, peace offering, votive offering, penitential act, penitential exercise, mortification, flagellation, lustration, fasting, cleansing, purification, maceration, austerities, asceticism, purgation, purgatory, sackcloth and ashes, hair shirt, bed of nails, shrift (Lit), Day of Atonement, Yom Kippur

▶ *7 Religion; 256 Cleanness; 808 Remorse; 814 Punishment*

3 **atoner**, penitent, expiator, confessor, repenter, born-again Christian, faster, flagellant, scapegoat, whipping boy

▶ *7 Religion; 10 Ritual*

ADJECTIVES

4 **atoning**, making amends, expiatory, reparatory, reparative, rectifying, redressing, compensatory, compensational, repaying, indemnificatory, restitutive, restitutory, restitutional, recompensing, righting, squaring, propitiatory, appeasing, satisfying, conciliatory, reconciliatory, pacifying, apologetic, apologetical, sorry, regretting, penitent, repentant, contrite, penitential, penitentiary, doing penance, lustral, lustrative, lustrational, purgative, purgatorial, cleansing, purifying, piacular, offering, oblatory, sacrificial

VERBS

5 **atone**, atone for, make amends for, satisfy, give satisfaction, expiate, propitiate, appease, conciliate, reconcile, pacify, repair, rectify, redress, compensate, pay back, pay the penalty, pay the forfeit, repay, indemnify, reimburse, requite, redeem, make right, make good, make up for, make matters up, square it, square things, clear the air, pour oil on troubled waters, pay one's dues (Inf), call it quits (Inf)

6 **apologize**, apologize to, make one's apologies, offer one's apologies, say one is sorry, express regret, express one's regrets, beg pardon, beg (*or* ask) forgiveness, come cap in hand, get down on one's knees, confess, go to confession, repent, express one's remorse, pray, offer, offer an oblation, offer sacrifice, sacrifice to, pay the price, pay the penalty, do penance, mortify oneself, mortify one's flesh, flagellate oneself, purify oneself, cleanse oneself of sin, cleanse oneself of guilt, fast, suffer purgatory, put on (*or* wear) sackcloth and ashes, don (*or* wear) a hair shirt, lie on a bed of nails, shrive oneself (Lit), put oneself through hell (Inf)

7 **be punished**, take one's punishment, swallow one's medicine, receive absolution, receive forgiveness, be saved, become a born-again Christian

ADVERBS

8 **penitently**, repentantly, in repentance, as penance, as atonement, to make amends, conciliatorily, apologetically, contritely, purgatively, purgatorially, sacrificially

808 Remorse

From that time Jesus began to preach, and to say, Repent: for the kingdom of heaven is at hand. Bible: Matthew.

NOUNS

1 **penitence**, repentance, contrition, remorsefulness, remorse, self-remorse, self-reproach, regretfulness, regret, regrets, regretting, sorriness, shamefulness, shame, scruples, qualms, soul-searching, compunction, guilt, guilt feelings, self-accusation, self-condemnation, hair shirt, guilty conscience, bad conscience, uneasy conscience, twinge of conscience, pangs of conscience, pangs, pricking of conscience, voice of one's conscience, weight on one's mind, confession, humble confession, recantation, apology, apologies, heartfelt apology, humble apology, abject apology, grudging apology, deathbed repentance, deathbed confession, reformation, conversion, change of heart

▶ *7 Religion; 244 Improvement; 603 Lamentation; 739 Disclosure; 760 Conversion; 806 Guilt*

2 **type of penance**, atonement, reparation, mortification, mortification of the flesh, breast-beating, sackcloth and ashes, wearing a sackcloth, wearing a hair shirt, flagellation, self-flagellation, self-scourging, prostration, self-punishment, self-humiliation, purification, purgation

▶ *388 Submission; 623 Humility; 807 Atonement*

3 **penitent person**, penitent, confessor, flagellant, ascetic, prodigal son, prodigal returned, contrite sinner, born-again Christian, reformed character, reformed prostitute, magdalen (Lit), sadder but wiser man (*or* woman)

VERBS

4 **be penitent**, do penance, repent, feel contrite, feel remorse, blame oneself, reprove oneself, accuse oneself, reproach oneself, search one's soul, rue the day, wish undone, regret, have regrets, express regrets, feel sorry, say one is sorry, apologize, feel shame, hang one's head in shame, show compunction, feel guilty, have guilt feelings, blame oneself, accuse oneself, condemn oneself, bewail one's sins, confess one's sins, confess, go to confession, acknowledge one's sins, acknowledge one's faults, recant one's errors, recant, think again, have second thoughts, think better of, learn one's lesson, learn from (bitter) experience, see the error of one's ways, see the light, reform, make a fresh start, turn from sin, return to the straight and narrow, become a born-again Christian, turn over a new leaf, wipe the slate clean

5 **do penance**, atone, atone for, make amends, salve one's conscience, mortify one's flesh, beat one's breast, repent in sackcloth and ashes, wear a sackcloth, wear a hair shirt, flagellate oneself, scourge oneself, prostrate oneself, punish oneself, humiliate oneself

ADJECTIVES

6 **penitent**, repentant, repenting, contrite, remorseful, full of remorse, remorsing, regretful, full of regrets, regretting, lamenting, sorry, apologetic, sorrowful, ashamed, shameful, shamefaced, rueful, self-reproachful, self-reproaching, self-accusing, self-condemning, compunctious, guilty, full of guilt, conscience-stricken, conscience-smitten, pricked by conscience, plagued by conscience, confessing, confessed, reformed, regenerate, reclaimed, converted, born-again

7 **penitential**, penitentiary, doing penance, atoning, atoned, self-punishing, humiliating, humiliated

ADVERBS

8 **penitently**, repentantly, with repentance, contritely, remorsefully, regretfully, with regret, apologetically, to apologize, sorrowfully, ruefully, shamefully, shamefacedly, in self-reproach, self-accusingly, compunctiously, guiltily, with a guilty conscience, penitentially, like a penitent, in sackcloth and ashes, humiliatingly, to make a fresh start

INTERJECTIONS

9 **sorry**!, I confess!, I'm guilty!, *mea culpa*! (L), I repent!

809 Shamelessness

NOUNS

1 **impenitence**, impenitentness, nonrepentance, lack of contrition, refusal to recant, lack of confession, incorrigibility, obstinacy, stubbornness, obduracy, hardness, hardness of heart, cold-heartedness, hardheartedness, heart of stone, callousness, induration, remorselessness, pitilessness, shamelessness, seared conscience, no apologies, no regrets, no remorse, no going back

▶ *418 Hardness; 628 Cruelty; 640 Perseverance; 641 Obstinacy*

2 **impenitent person**, cold-hearted person, hardhearted person, hardened sinner, inveterate sinner, dyed-in-the-wool sinner, shameless hussy, brazen hussy, callous murderer, lost cause, hopeless case, hard case (Inf)

▶ *651 Malevolence; 804 Wickedness*

ADJECTIVES

3 **impenitent**, unrepentant, unrepenting, incorrigible, inveterate, obdurate, obstinate, brazen, shameless, unreformed, unregretting, not sorry, unsorry, unapologetic, uncontrite, unmoved, unashamed, unblushing, unremorseful, without remorse, remorseless, having no remorse, unsorrowful, having no sorrow, unregretful, without regrets, having no regrets, regretless, unregretting, without a pang of regret, without compunction, without a conscience, conscienceless, cold-hearted, heartless, hardhearted, hardened, hard, callous, indurative, untouched, hopeless, lost, irreclaimable, irredeemable, not redeemable, not redeemed, unredeemed, unreconciled, unreformed, unregenerated, unchastened, unrecanting, unshriven, not confessing, rotten to the core, dyed-in-the-wool

4 **unatoned**, unrepented, unregretted, unapologized for

VERBS

5 **be impenitent**, remain unrepentant, not reform, have no regrets, have no remorse, have no conscience, feel nothing, remain obstinate, refuse to recant, make no confession, not confess, offer no apologies, want no forgiveness, feel no remorse, harden one's heart, steel oneself, indurate, refuse to see the error of one's ways

ADVERBS

6 **impenitently**, unregretfully, with no regrets, without regret, unremorsefully, remorselessly, with no remorse,

without remorse, without compunction, unashamedly, shamelessly, unblushingly, cold-heartedly, hardheartedly, without any qualms, without any scruples, without looking back, without seeing the error of one's ways

810 Duty

Do your duty and leave the rest to the Gods. Pierre Corneille.

England expects every man will do his duty. Lord Nelson.

When a stupid man is doing something he is ashamed of, he always declares that it is his duty. George Bernard Shaw.

NOUNS

1 **duty**, one's duty, the right thing, the proper thing, bounden duty, obligation, imposition, onus, burden, charge, assignment, responsibility, responsibleness, liability, accountability, accountableness, answerability

2 **task**, function, work, service, line of duty, office, station, profession, business, place, calling, engagement, commission, mission, assignment, fatigue, shift, watch

▶ *576 Work*

3 **allegiance**, loyalty, fealty, homage, devotion, dedication, deference, respect, reverence, obedience, compliance, comity, submission, docility

▶ *388 Submission; 663 Obedience; 667 Respect*

4 **sense of duty**, dutifulness, duteousness, devotion (*or* dedication) to duty, moral obligation, moral imperative, call of duty, moral sense, claims of conscience, conscience, inner voice, still small voice, stern daughter of the voice of God, willingness

▶ *636 Willingness; 795 Morality*

5 **discharge of duty**, performance, acquittal, observance

6 **ethics**, rules, regulations, maxim, precept, morals, rule of conduct, code of conduct, code of duty, code of honour, unwritten code, professional code, Hippocratic oath, Ten Commandments, Decalogue

▶ *140 Rule; 745 Maxim*

7 **commitment**, promise, pledge, vow, oath, word, word of honour, contract, engagement, obligation, tie, bond, covenant, assurance, understanding, gentleman's agreement

▶ *755 Contract; 756 Promise*

ADJECTIVES

8 **dutiful**, duteous, conscientious, scrupulous, punctilious, ethical, moral, principled, virtuous, honourable, decent, upright

▶ *795 Morality; 797 Good; 799 Honour; 803 Virtue*

9 **loyal**, devoted, dedicated, deferential, respectful, reverential, obedient, compliant, submissive, docile, tractable, amenable, willing

▶ *388 Submission; 636 Willingness; 663 Obedience; 667 Respect*

10 **liable**, accountable, answerable, responsible

11 **duty-bound**, bound, bound by duty, obligated, obliged, beholden, tied, committed, engaged, pledged, sworn, saddled

12 **obligatory**, mandatory, compulsory, *de rigueur* (Fr), binding, incumbent on, inescapable, unavoidable, unconditional, categorical, peremptory, imperative

▶ *386 Compulsion*

13 **on duty**, on call, at work

VERBS

14 **be the duty of**, fall to, fall to the lot of, rest with, rest on the shoulders of, devolve upon, belong to, pertain to, lie at the door of, be up to, behove, become, befit, must, should, ought to, had better, had best

▶ *386 Compulsion*

15 **be liable**, answer for, account for, stand responsible for, incur a duty, incur a responsibility, make it one's duty, take on the responsibility, accept the responsibility, take upon one's shoulders, make oneself liable, commit oneself, engage oneself, pledge oneself

16 **do one's duty**, discharge one's duty, carry out (*or* perform) one's duty, fulfil one's duty, do what one has to do, shoulder one's responsibilities, obey, acquit, do the needful, do what is necessary, do what is expected, do one's bit, act (*or* play) one's part, stay at one's post, go down with one's ship, (lie back and) think of England (Inf)

▶ *663 Obedience*

17 **impose a duty**, oblige, put under an obligation, obligate, bind, saddle with, make incumbent, tie, commit, engage, pledge, require, order, command, decree, call upon, enjoin, expect, expect it of, look to

▶ *135 Requirement; 397 Command*

ADVERBS

18 **on duty**, in the line of duty, dutifully, duteously, ethically, morally, loyally, respectfully, accountably, responsibly

811 Reputation

Reputation, reputation, reputation! O, I have lost my reputation! I have lost the immortal part of myself, and what remains is bestial. William Shakespeare.

NOUNS

1 **estimation**, reputation, report, good report, good reference, reference, regard, esteem, favour, good colour, cachet, approval, approbation, distinction, eminence, mark, prestige, credit, credibility, claim to fame (Inf), street credibility (Inf), street cred (Inf)

2 **person of repute**, man (*or* woman) of honour, pillar of the community, man (*or* woman) of high standing, optimate, emeritus, authority, somebody, VIP, celebrity, star, megastar, notable, favourite, big shot (Inf)

ADJECTIVES

3 **reputable**, of repute, creditworthy, creditable, respected, respectable, well thought of, highly thought of, honoured, honourable, emeritus, popular, in good odour with, favoured by, in favour with, distinguished, eminent, approved, renowned, famous, fabled, above board

4 **reputed**, alleged, supposed

VERBS

5 **have repute**, have a good reputation, be famous, be well thought of, be highly thought of, make a name for oneself, win renown, be acclaimed

ADVERBS

6 **reputedly**, allegedly, supposedly, so they say, as the story goes

7 **eminently**, prestigiously, honourably, distinctively, to one's credit

812 Notoriety

Caesar's wife must be above suspicion. Julius Caesar.

NOUNS

1 **disrespect**, bad name, shady past, notoriety, bad odour, bad light, infamy, ill-repute, disreputability, hatefulness, obnoxiousness, loathsomeness, unseemliness, disfavour, discredit, dishonour, slur, ignominy, degradation, disgrace, shame, scandal, skeleton in the cupboard (Inf)

2 **disreputable character**, rogue, rascal, scallywag, blackguard, undesirable, ugly customer, scoundrel, bad lot, bad egg, bad influence, black sheep, ne'er-do-well, cad, bounder, talk of the town, bad scene (Inf), shit (Inf), lowlife (Inf)

3 **disreputable action**, foul play, dirty trick, skullduggery, fraud, sharp practice, con trick, con (Inf), hanky-panky (Inf), scam (Inf)

ADJECTIVES

4 **disreputable**, ignominious, degrading, notorious, infamous, nefarious, shady, questionable, scandalous, dishonourable, shameless, immoral, underhand, fraudulent, devious, suspicious, iffy (Inf), dodgy (Inf), not on the level (Inf),

VERBS

5 **bring into disrepute**, lose repute, shame, fall from grace, fall from favour, disgrace oneself, lower oneself, demean oneself, degrade oneself, put to shame, bring shame upon, show oneself up, humiliate oneself, forfeit one's reputation, desecrate, defile, dishonour, discredit, cast a slur

813 Reward

NOUNS

1 **reward**, financial reward, remuneration, recompense, deserved reward, deserts, just deserts, justice, guerdon, meed (Lit), satisfaction, job satisfaction, personal reward, recognition, public recognition, due recognition, credit, due credit, acknowledgment, thanks, gratitude, favour, tribute, deserved tribute, proof of regard, acclaim, acclamation, bouquet, praise, honour, honours, decoration, title, honorary degree, honorary title, letters after one's name, peerage, Birthday Honours, New Year Honours

▶ *575 Title; 609 Satisfaction; 669 Approval; 671 Gratitude; 814 Punishment*

2 **prize**, award, crown, trophy, cup, pot, shield, certificate, medal, kewpie doll (US), consolation prize, second prize, runner-up prize, booby prize, wooden spoon, cash prize, prize money, jackpot, kitty, Nobel Prize, Pulitzer Prize (US), Booker Prize, Academy Award (US), Oscar (US), Emmy (US), BAFTA Award, Man/Woman of the Year, Olympic Gold (*or* Silver *or* Bronze) Medal, America's Cup, Blue Riband, blue ribbon

▶ *794 Prize*

3 **grant**, aid, assistance, subsidy, subvention, fellowship, scholarship, stipend, exhibition, bursary, bursarship, allowance

4 **reward for service**, remuneration, fee, retainer, honorarium, emolument, payment, payment in kind, payoff, pension, retirement pension, pay, wage, wages, salary, basic salary, take-home pay, compensation (US), severance pay, redundancy money, income, earnings, wage (*or* salary) scale, (pay) rise, raise (US), increment, overtime pay, commission, bonus, incentive, inducement, enticement, offer, tempting offer, bait, lure, perquisite, fringe benefits, hidden income, expense account, perk (Inf), golden hello (Inf), golden handcuffs (Inf), golden handshake (Inf), golden parachute (Inf)

▶ *752 Offer; 785 Payment*

5 **turnover**, return, profitable return, gain, profit, gross profit, net profit, pre-tax profit, profit after tax, profit margin, margin of profit, bottom line

▶ *765 Profit*

6 **compensation**, indemnification, indemnity, satisfaction, consideration, solatium, damages, quid pro quo, requital, retaliation, reparation, amends, restitution, comeuppance (Inf)

▶ *385 Retaliation; 775 Giving Back*

7 **bounty**, premium, gift, gratuity, baksheesh, tip, *douceur* (Fr), *pourboire* (Fr), *trinkgeld* (Ger)

▶ *768 Giving*

8 **secret money**, laundered money, slush fund, smart money, protection money, blackmail, kickback, bribe, rake-off (Inf), payoff (Inf), sweetener (Inf), hush money (Inf)

VERBS

9 **reward**, offer (*or* give) a reward, remunerate, recompense, give financial reward, give a deserved reward, guerdon, satisfy, give job satisfaction, give personal reward, recognize, credit, acknowledge, thank, show one's gratitude, pay tribute, pat on the back, acclaim, praise, hand out bouquets, award, present, offer (*or* give) a prize, honour, decorate, bestow a medal, bestow an honorary degree, honour with a title

▶ *575 Title; 669 Approval; 671 Gratitude; 811 Reputation*

10 **grant**, aid, assist, subsidize, award a fellowship, give a scholarship

11 **pay**, remunerate, give, tip, tip well, bribe, offer a bribe, pay off, repay, pay back, give what is due, pay back in his (*or* her) own coin, retaliate, settle up, compensate, indemnify, requite, make reparation, make amends, restitute, pay under the table (Inf), offer a sweetener (Inf), grease the palm (Inf), make it worth one's while (Inf)

▶ *385 Retaliation; 768 Giving; 775 Giving Back; 785 Payment*

12 **be rewarded**, get a reward, gain a reward, have one's reward, get one's deserts, receive one's due, get what is coming to one, get job satisfaction, win a prize, get a medal, receive an honorary degree, receive a title, get one's comeuppance (Inf)

13 **get paid**, draw a salary, earn an income, have a gainful occupation, accept payment, accept a gratification, take

a bribe, have one's palm greased (Inf), receive a sweetener (Inf)

► *769 Receiving*

14 gain, reap, reap a profit, reap the fruits, win, accept, harvest, get results

► *765 Profit*

ADJECTIVES

15 rewarding, financially rewarding, satisfying, paying, profitable, moneymaking, lucrative, remunerative, gainful

► *765 Profit; 785 Payment*

16 rewarded, recognized, credited, acknowledged, acclaimed, praised

17 compensatory, indemnificatory, reparatory, retributive, retaliatory

18 giving, generous, open-handed, liberal, offering

► *679 Generosity; 752 Offer; 768 Giving*

ADVERBS

19 rewardingly, satisfyingly, as a reward, as a prize, for one's service, in compensation

20 profitably, lucratively, remuneratively, gainfully, fruitfully, productively

814 Punishment

Love is a boy, by poets styl'd,
Then spare the rod, and spoil the child. Samuel Butler.

Punishment is not for revenge, but to lessen crime and reform the criminal. Elizabeth Fry.

My object all sublime
I shall achieve in time –
To let the punishment fit the crime –
The punishment fit the crime. W. S. Gilbert.

VERBS

1 punish, inflict punishment (upon), discipline, take disciplinary action, give (*or* teach) a lesson, chastise, chasten, correct, administer correction, castigate, admonish, reprimand, reprove, rebuke, chide, scold, tell off, dust down, take to task, rap across the knuckles, smack on the wrist, have one's head for, hurt, inflict pain (upon), afflict, inflict, visit, impose, persecute, victimize, make an example of, shame, pillory, put in the stocks, tar and feather, toss in a blanket, duck, masthead, keelhaul, picket, spread-eagle, imprison, jail, incarcerate, intern, lock up, transport, condemn to the galleys, demote, degrade, downgrade, unfrock, reduce to the ranks, suspend, expel, send down, cashier, drum out, ban, proscribe, banish, exile, deport, ostracize, blackball, outlaw, put in the corner, send out of the room, put in detention, keep in, give lines, confiscate, take away, sequestrate, deprive, forfeit, fine, amerce, mulct, bind over, strafe (Inf), have (*or* call) on the carpet (Inf), dress down (Inf), give a dressing-down (Inf), put away (Inf), send down (*or* up) (Inf), send to Coventry (Inf), gate (Inf), ground (US inf)

► *647 Severity; 815 Prison*

2 penalize, come down on, come down hard on, come down on like a ton of bricks, impose a penalty, exact a penalty, condemn, sentence, execute (*or* carry out) a sentence, execute justice, exact retribution, settle, fix, bring to book, give what was coming to him (*or* her), retaliate, settle with, get even with, pay back, avenge, revenge oneself, throw the book at (Inf), give what for (Inf), give his (*or* her) comeuppance (Inf)

► *385 Retaliation*

3 hit, strike, smack, slap, slap on the wrist, lambaste, paddle, slipper, put across one's knee, cuff, clout, box someone's ears, clip on (*or* round) the ear, rap over the knuckles, drub, trounce, beat, beat black and blue, beat the living daylights out of, belt, strap, leather, larrup (Dial), wallop, welt, tan, tan one's hide, cane, birch, switch, whack, thwack, thrash, flog, whip, horsewhip, lash, lay on the lash, scourge, give stripes, give strokes, give the cat, flay, flay one's back, lay one's back open, flail, flagellate, bastinado, cudgel, belabour, fustigate (Lit), give a hiding (Inf), hide (Inf), lather (Inf), dust (off) (Inf)

4 torture, put to torture, torment, inflict pain, give the third degree, thumbscrew, rack, put on the rack, break on the wheel, press, apply *peine forte et dure* (Fr), mutilate, kneecap, persecute, martyr, martyrize, work over, give the works (Inf)

► *491 Physical Pain*

5 execute, put to death, punish with death, condemn, condemn to death, sentence to death, kill, lynch, electrocute, send to the chair, hang, hang by the neck, string up, send to the gallows, send to the scaffold, gibbet, hang, draw, and quarter, gas, put in the gas chamber, give a lethal injection, shoot, put in front of a firing squad, stand against a wall, guillotine, behead, cut off one's head, decapitate, decollate, send to the block, strangle, garrotte, bow-string, burn, burn alive, burn at the stake, send to the stake, flay, flay alive, stone, stone to death, lapidate, dismember, tear limb from limb, impale, crucify, hold mass executions, commit genocide, purge, massacre, decimate, slaughter, murder, butcher (Inf), send to the hot seat (US inf), stretch one's neck (Inf), necklace (S Afr inf), give one a necklace (S Afr inf)

► *382 Killing*

6 be punished, suffer punishment, take the consequences, have it coming to one, get what one was asking for, get one's deserts, regret it, smart for it, hold one's hand out, pay the ultimate price, pay for it with one's head, die the death, come to execution, lay one's head on the block, come to the gallows, get one's comeuppance (Inf), be for the high jump (Inf), catch it (Inf), catch (*or* get) it in the neck (Inf), take the rap (Inf), stand the racket (Inf), face the music (Inf), take one's medicine (Inf), take one's gruel (Inf), take a ride to Tyburn (Lit), kick the air (Inf), dance upon nothing (Inf), swing (Inf)

NOUNS

7 punishment, penalization, discipline, disciplinary action, chastisement, chastening, chiding, correction, lesson, castigation, admonition, reprimand, reproof, rebuke, scolding, telling off, dusting down, rap across the knuckles, smack on the wrist, persecution, victimization, example, shame, tarring and feathering, tossing in a blanket, ducking, keelhauling, walking the plank, detention, house arrest, imprisonment, incarceration, confinement, internment, prison (*or* jail) sentence, debt to society, penal servitude, hard labour, chain gang, labour camp, penal colony, Gulag, transportation, galleys, demotion, degrading, downgrading, unfrocking, suspension, expulsion, banishment, exile, deportation, ostracism, blackballing, outlawing, proscription, banning, keeping in, lines, confiscation, sequestration, escheat, deprivation, expropriation, forfeit, forfeiture, fine, fining, court fine, amercement, mulct, deodand, binding over, dressing-down (Inf), high jump (Inf), chewing out (Inf), kicking ass (US inf), sending to Coventry (Inf), gating (Inf), grounding (US inf)

▶ *647 Severity; 815 Prison*

8 penalty, official punishment, legal punishment, prescribed punishment, pains and penalties, condemnation, sentence, sentencing, execution of sentence, execution of justice, exaction of penalty, liability, legal liability, legal obligation, legal debt, dueness, court award, damages, costs, compensation, restoration, restitution, payment, court payment, compulsory payment, compensatory payment, ransom

9 retribution, just retribution, fitting retribution, Nemesis, deserts, just deserts, meet reward (Lit), justice, poetic justice, divine justice, retributive justice, doom, doomsday, judgment, day of judgment, day of reckoning, reckoning, what is coming to one, retaliation, reprisal, requital, repayment, revenge, getting even, what for (Inf), comeuppance (Inf), hell (*or* the devil) to pay (Inf)

▶ *385 Retaliation*

10 affliction, infliction, visitation, imposition, trial, task, punishing experience, dose, hard dose, pill, bitter pill, hard (*or* tough) row (to hoe), hard lines, adversity, suffering, damage, loss, injury

▶ *249 Adversity*

11 penance, self-punishment, atonement, self-mortification, self-discipline, asceticism, hara-kiri, seppuku, felo de se, suicide

12 corporal punishment, chastisement of the flesh, bodily chastisement, hitting, striking, spanking, smacking, slapping, paddling, drubbing, trouncing, beating, caning, birching, thrashing, thrashing of a lifetime, flogging, whipping, horsewhipping, scourging, flagellation, running the gauntlet, hit, spank, smack, slap, slap on the wrist, rap, rap over the knuckles, box on the ear, clip on (*or* round) the ear, blow, buffet, cuff, clout, stroke, stripe, torture, third degree, racking, breaking on the wheel, hanging by the wrists, strappado, bastinado, death by a thousand cuts, hiding (Inf), dusting (Inf)

▶ *491 Physical Pain*

13 capital punishment, execution, legalized killing, judicial murder, extreme penalty, death sentence, death penalty, death warrant, traitor's death, electrocution, hanging, hanging, drawing, and quartering, gas, poison, injection, shooting, guillotining, beheading, decapitation, decollation, strangulation, garrotte, stoning, lapidation, impalement, crucifixion, flaying alive, burning, burning at the stake, auto-da-fé, drowning, noyade, massacre, mass murder, mass execution, purge, genocide, the Holocaust, Final Solution, slaughter, martyrdom, martyrization, persecution to the death, illegal execution, lynching, lynch law

▶ *382 Killing*

14 instrument of punishment, pillory, stocks, ducking stool, cucking stool, stool of repentance, cutty stool (Scot), corner, dunce's cap, open hand, hairbrush, belt, strap, tawse (Scot), thong, quirt, lash, whip, horsewhip, cowhide, sjambok (S Afr), knout, scourge, cat-o'-nine-tails, cat, rope's end, whipping post, ruler, ferule, stick, birch, birch-rod, switch, big stick, rattan, cane, rod, cudgel, cosh, club, rubber hose, bicycle chain, sandbag, chain, irons, bilboes, fetters, cell, jail, prison, prison house

▶ *251 Restraint; 815 Prison*

15 instrument of torture, rack, thumbscrew, iron boot, pilliwinks, triangle, wheel, treadmill, tightened headband, weights, *peine forte et dure* (Fr), spiked device, Iron Maiden, *Fass* (Ger), crushing device, Scavenger's Daughter, torture chamber, the Inquisition, the Star Chamber

16 instrument of execution, electric chair, the chair, hanging rope, rope, noose, halter, hempen collar, drop, scaffold, gallows, gibbet, gas, gas chamber, hemlock, poison, lethal injection, bullet, firing squad, wall, axe, headsman's axe, block, guillotine, maiden (Scot), garrotte, bow-string, cross, stake, condemned cell, death chamber, lethal chamber, death house (US), death row (US), the hot seat (Inf), Tyburn tree (Inf), necklace (S Afr inf)

17 punisher, discipliner, chastiser, chastener, corrector, castigator, persecutor, tyrant, vindicator, revenger, avenger, retaliator, sentencer, justiciary, magistrate, judge, caner, whipper, flogger, flagellator, scourger, torturer, inquisitor, witch-hunter, executioner, high executioner, hangman, Jack Ketch (Lit), hanging judge (US), headsman, garrotter, bowstringer, lyncher, hit man, assassin, murderer, hatchet man (Inf)

18 penology, poenology, criminal psychology, prison management, penal code, penologist

ADJECTIVES

19 punitive, punitory, punishing, penalizing, penal, penological, capital, corporal, disciplinary, corrective, correctional, instructive, castigatory, admonitory, vindictive, retributive, revengeful, retaliatory

20 punished, disciplined, castigated, imprisoned, in confinement, under house arrest, fined, beaten, tortured, executed, gated (Inf), grounded (US inf)

21 punishing, hard, arduous, strenuous, exhausting, gruelling, laborious, backbreaking, demanding, taxing, torturous, painful

22 punishable, liable, amerceable, mulctable, deserving punishment, condemned, awaiting execution

ADVERBS

23 punitively, penally, penologically, vindictively, retributively, punishingly, punishably

INTERJECTIONS

24 string him up!, lynch him!, hang 'em high!, off with his head!, throw the book at him! (Inf), heads will roll! (Inf)

815 Prison

Oh they're taking him to prison for the colour of his hair. A. E. Housman.

Stone walls do not a prison make,
Nor iron bars a cage. Richard Lovelace.

NOUNS

1 **prison**, jail (*or* gaol), county jail (US), city jail (US), jailhouse (US), (state) penitentiary (US), Sing Sing (US), women's penitentiary (US), federal prison (US), state prison (US), lockup, compound, pound, dungeon, oubliette, prison camp, concentration camp, Auschwitz, Buchenwald, labour camp, Gulag, prison colony, Devil's Island, prison farm (US), debtor's prison, maximum-security prison, Wormwood Scrubs, Dartmoor, Broadmoor, Alcatraz (US), minimum-security prison, house of detention, house of correction, correction facility (US), halfway house, reformatory, reform school, detention centre, borstal, young offender institution, youth custody centre, detention home (US), community home, approved school, military prison, guardhouse, bring (US), stockade (US)

2 **the inside (Inf)**, borstal (Inf), pen (US inf), glasshouse (Inf), little school (US inf), nick (Inf), quod (Inf), clink (Inf), cooler (Inf), stir (Inf), slammer (Inf), sneezer (US inf), jug (Inf), can (Inf), bucket (Inf), tank (US inf), hoosegow (*or* hoosgow) (US inf), chokey (*or* choky) (Inf), poky (*or* pokey) (US inf), the big house (US inf), big school (US inf)

▶ *378 Obstruction*

3 **prison cell**, jail cell, solitary confinement, death cell, death row (US), solitary (Inf), bullpen (US inf), flowery (dell) (Inf), birdcage (Inf), icebox (US inf), the hole (Inf)

4 **prison sentence**, period of detention, life, time (Inf), BOT (balance of time) (US inf), stretch (Inf), fistful (Inf), handful (Inf), five fingers (Inf), both hands (Inf), the book (Inf), porridge (Inf), vacation (US inf), lag (Inf), bird (Inf)

5 **prisoner**, prisoner behind bars, POW (prisoner of war), prisoner of conscience, political prisoner, condemned prisoner, hostage, captive, convict, inmate, detainee, chain-gang member (US), government man (Aus), lifer (Inf), jailbird (*or* gaolbird), guest of His (or Her) Majesty (Inf), con (Inf), yardbird (US inf), rock crusher (US inf), zebra (US inf), old lag (Inf)

6 **prison officer**, prison governor, warder, warden (US), prison guard, keeper, correctional officer (US), custodian, jailer (*or* gaoler), turnkey, screw (Inf), the Man (US inf), horse (US inf)

7 **imprisonment**, confinement, solitary confinement, detention, detainment at His (*or* Her) Majesty's pleasure, detention in a young offender institution, internment, captivity, corrective training, durance (Lit), forced labour, immurement (Lit), solitary (Inf), porridge (Inf)

ADJECTIVES

8 **imprisoned**, in prison, under arrest, serving a sentence, captive, in captivity, on remand, in detention, detained, detained at His (*or* Her) Majesty's pleasure, confined, interned, incarcerated, restricted, locked up, under lock and key, behind bars, in solitary confinement, in solitary (Inf), doing time (Inf), in (Inf), inside (Inf), in the nick (Inf), in stir (Inf), in the cooler (Inf), on ice (Inf), buried (US inf), doing porridge (Inf), up the river (US inf), in the big house (US inf)

VERBS

9 **imprison**, take prisoner, jail, confine, intern, incarcerate, impound, lock up, put away, detain, detain at His (*or* Her) Majesty's pleasure, lock up and throw away the key, put in solitary confinement, immure (Lit), put in solitary (Inf), throw in the tank (US inf), throw in the cooler (Inf), jug (Inf), send up the river (US inf), send up (US inf), send down (Inf), put in the big house (US inf)

10 **be in prison**, serve a sentence, join the chain gang (US), do time (Inf), enjoy His (*or* Her) Majesty's hospitality (Inf), land in the cooler (Inf), serve a stretch (Inf), do porridge (Inf), do bird (Inf), lag (Inf)

ADVERBS

11 **captively**, while in prison, under lock and key, on the inside (Inf)

Index

A 2.7 *social stratification*
A1 121.14, 235.2 *best*; 469.15 *chosen*; 56.5 *golf ball*; 123.6 *notable*; 230.1 *perfect*; 485.6 *skilful*; 235.1 *worthy*
A4 paper 435.3 *paper*
aa 30.25 *eruption*
aardvark 71.6 *insect-eating mammal*
abacist 210.6 *calculator*
aback 50.20 *offshore*
abacus 174.3 *architectural summit*; 27.67 *calculator*; 40.3, 210.5 *computer*; 20.9 *miscellaneous architectural features*
Abaddon 8.7 *devil*; 8.12 *hell*
abaft 50.20 *offshore*
abandon 708.14 *cancel*; 571.8 *desert*; 470.2 *discard*; 767.9 *dispose of*; 372.13 *diverge*; 342.4 *energy*; 128.7 *exclude*; 215.8 *leave*; 98.19 *leave empty*; 250.6 *liberality*; 686.3 *overindulgence*; 605.5 *resign*; 313.2, 355.2 *withdraw*
abandon discussion 355.2 *withdraw*
abandoned 197.16 *alone*; 767.12 *disposed*; 350.4 *disused*; 571.11 *divorced*; 686.8 *overindulgent*; 355.5 *relinquished*; 215.9 *remaining*; 250.12 *unconditional*; 372.17 *unjoined*; 98.14 *unoccupied*; 254.3 *vulnerable*
abandon hope 341.4 *not act*
abandonment 226.1 *cessation*; 313.7 *departure*; 470.6 *discarding*; 767.1 *disposal*; 350.10 *disuse*; 250.6 *liberality*; 355.3 *relinquishment*; 605.1 *resignation*; 388.1 *submission*
abandon one's cause 388.3 *submit*
abandon one's stance 767.9 *dispose of*
abandon the world 655.12 *be unsocial*
abase **623.23**; 367.4 *debase*; 245.6 *pervert*
abasement **623.10**; 122.1 *inferiority*; 245.8 *perversion*
abash 623.23 *abase*; 623.17 *humiliate*
abashed 623.3 *humbled*
abate 209.6 *change gradually*; 214.4 *decrease*; 305.9 *descend*; 685.4 *moderate*; 608.9 *relieve*
abatement 214.1 *decrease*; 608.1 *ease*; 685.1 *moderation*
abating 214.6 *decreasing*
abatis 384.9 *barrier*
abattoir 767.8 *sink*; 382.15 *slaughterhouse*
abbacomes 7.7 *monk*
abbacy 7.9 *priesthood*
abbess 7.7 *monk*
abbey 10.11 *place of worship*
abbot 7.7 *monk*
abbreviate 269.4 *be concise*; 191.5, 214.5 *make smaller*; 163.5 *outline*; 742.13 *punctuate*; 149.10 *shorten*; 212.3 *subtract*; 723.8 *summarize*
abbreviated 269.3 *concise*; 233.4 *incomplete*; 163.6 *outlined*; 742.17 *punctuated*; 212.7 *reduced*; 149.8, 723.7 *shortened*; 191.7 *smaller*
abbreviation 269.1 *conciseness*; 191.1 *contraction*; 214.1 *decrease*; 163.1, 723.2 *outline*; 149.3 *shortened version*; 149.2 *shortening*; 212.1 *subtraction*
abbreviator 723.5 *summarizer*
ABC 5.14 *alphabet*; 40.3 *computer*; 693.5 *reference book*; 692.24 *television broadcasting*
abdicate 355.1 *relinquish*; 605.5 *resign*; 388.3 *submit*; 355.2 *withdraw*
abdicated 605.7 *resigning*
abdicating 605.7 *resigning*
abdicating monarch 355.4 *deserter*
abdication 588.1 *anarchy*; 355.3 *relinquishment*; 605.1 *resignation*; 388.1 *submission*
abdicator 355.4 *deserter*; 605.3 *resigner*
Abdiel 8.6 *angel*
abdomen 172.4 *insides*; 410.18 *stomach*
abdominable 236.3 *bad*
abdominal 172.10 *visceral*
abdominal protector 58.1 *hockey*
abdominous 158.16 *fat*
abducent **364.9**
abduct 774.13 *kidnap*; 773.10 *take away*
abduction 774.2 *kidnapping*; 773.3 *taking away*
abductive 364.9 *abducent*
abductor 773.6 *taker*; 774.8 *thief*
abeam 50.20 *offshore*; 50.10 *sailing*
abecedarian 6.7 *learner*
abecedarium 6.14 *school book*
Aberdeen 87.4 *British cities*
Aberdonian 564.9 *British inhabitant*
aberglaube 450.2 *religious belief*
aberrance 802.4 *abnormality*; 299.2 *unusualness*
aberrancy 325.13 *deviation*; 274.7 *errancy*
aberrant 118.17, 802.14 *abnormal*; 325.20 *deviant*; 311.6 *divergent*; 274.16 *errant*; 299.5 *unusual*
aberrantly 311.16 *divergently*
aberrate 311.10 *diverge*
aberration 802.4 *abnormality*; 118.6, 325.13 *deviation*; 144.1 *displacement*; 311.1 *divergence*; 472.1 *inattention*; 461.1 *insanity*; 28.31 *lens element*; 299.2 *unusualness*
aberrational 325.20 *deviant*
abet 344.12 *determine*; 413.14 *give moral support*; 392.17 *help*; 483.10 *manipulate*
abetment 413.6 *moral support*; 392.9 *patronage*
abettor 344.8 *contributor*; 392.11 *helper*; 480.14 *motivator*
abeyance 341.1 *inaction*; 361.6 *interruption*; 301.1 *motionlessness*; 350.8 *nonuse*
abeyant 361.9 *interrupted*; 301.5 *sedentary*
Abfahrt 68.1 *skiing*
Abhayagiri 10.13 *shrine*
abhiseka 10.7 *non-Christian ritual*
abhor 606.7 *be dissatisfied*; 596.5 *dislike*; 594.14 *hate*
abhorred 596.9 *disliked*
abhorrence 596.1 *dislike*; 637.13 *dissociation*; 594.1 *hate*
abhorrent 596.9 *disliked*; 594.12 *hated*; 364.8 *repulsive*
abhorrently 364.11 *repulsively*
abhorring 596.8 *disliking*; 594.10 *hating*
abidance 117.2 *compliance*; 225.1 *permanence*
abide 413.12 *bear*; 301.8 *be motionless*; 225.5 *be permanent*; 554.17 *dwell*; 277.6 *last*; 134.4 *protract*; 388.3 *submit*
abide by 636.13 *be willing*; 117.8 *comply*
abide by the law 16.67 *follow the law*; 663.5 *obey*
abide by the rules 631.12 *behave well*
abide in 564.14, 565.17 *inhabit*
abiding 565.14 *inhabiting*; 93.12, 277.8 *lasting*; 225.7 *permanent*
abiding by the law 663.1 *obedience*
abidingly 225.9 *permanently*
ability **136.2**; **334.2**; 229.3 *aptitude*; 265.1 *easiness*; 395.1 *influence*; 237.7 *instrumentality*; 352.1 *means*; 102.2 *possibleness*; 756.3 *potential*; 797.12 *proficiency*; 136.1 *qualification*; 485.1, 733.3 *skill*
ability to mix 654.2 *social ambition*
ability to sense **488.2**
ab initio 130.39 *from the beginning*
abiogenesis 561.3 *propagation*
abirritant 37.7 *ointment*
a bit 275.3 *duration*; 205.12 *partly*; 209.11 *to a degree*
abject 623.3 *humbled*; 236.4 *poor*; 664.6 *servile*; 388.5 *submitting*
abject apology 807.2 *apology*; 808.1 *penitence*
abject fear 614.1 *cowardice*
abject loyalty 388.1 *submission*
abjectly 623.28 *subserviently*; 664.16 *with servility*; 236.15 *worthlessly*
abjectness 236.10 *poverty*; 664.1 *servility*
abjuration 708.5 *cancellation*; 479.8 *recantation*; 708.4 *renunciation*
abjuratory 708.17 *negative*
abjure 708.14 *cancel*; 767.9 *dispose of*; 479.4 *recant*; 708.12 *renounce*
ablate 766.13 *destroy*
ablation 766.5 *destruction*; 365.2 *wearing away*
ablative 5.31 *case*; 365.10 *frictional*
ablative absolute 5.35 *part of speech*
ablaut 5.36 *accent*
ablaze 522.16 *bright*; 493.10 *on fire*
able 342.18 *active*; 119.9 *adequate*; 492.10 *handed*; 237.3 *instrumental*; 458.6 *intelligent*; 400.12 *masterful*; 323.11 *nautical*; 160.12 *on form*; 102.5 *possible*; 334.13 *powerful*; 136.9 *qualified*; 485.6 *skilful*
able-bodied 342.18 *active*; 323.11 *nautical*; 336.9 *physically strong*; 204.8 *sound*
able-bodied seaman 323.7 *nautical person*
abled 336.9 *physically strong*
ableism 466.4 *social discrimination*
ableist 466.10 *discriminatory*
ableness 136.1 *qualification*
ablepsia 519.1 *blindness*
able rating 586.27 *naval man*
able seaman 323.7 *nautical person*; 586.27 *naval man*
able to pay 781.2 *solvent*
able to speak 729.19 *speaking*
ablution 10.5 *Christian rite*; 433.11 *wash*
ablutionary 256.18 *cleansing*; 255.15 *purifying*
ablutions **256.5**
ably 136.17 *capably*; 485.12 *skilfully*
abnegate 708.10 *be negative*; 704.9 *deny*; 355.1 *relinquish*; 470.4 *revoke*
abnegated 709.10 *abnegating*
abnegating **709.10**; 704.7 *refuting*
abnegation **709.3**; 470.7 *abrogation*; 704.2 *denial*; 708.1 *negation*; 355.3 *relinquishment*
abnegative 708.17 *negative*
abnegator 355.4 *deserter*; 704.5 *refuter*
abnormal **118.17**; **802.14**; 114.5 *diverse*; 461.11 *insane*; 461.13 *mentally ill*; 696.5 *strange*; 630.8 *surprising*; 796.15 *unlawful*; 299.5 *unusual*
abnormal affection 593.5 *desire*
abnormality **802.4**; 118.6 *deviation*; 114.1 *diversity*; 461.1 *insanity*; 299.2 *unusualness*
abnormally 114.10 *diversely*; 461.17 *insanely*; 118.21 *unconformably*; 299.9 *unusually*
abnormal psychology 36.1 *psychology*
abodah 10.4 *public worship*
abode 565.2 *environment*; 565.1 *habitat*; 733.5 *place of residence*
abode of love **593.13**
abode of mammals **71.20**
Abode of the Gods 8.11 *heaven*
abolish 708.14 *cancel*; 357.8 *destroy*; 399.3 *veto*; 355.2 *withdraw*
abolish discrimination 391.6 *treat equally*
abolished 708.20 *cancelled*; 355.5 *relinquished*
abolishment 708.5 *cancellation*; 357.1 *destruction*
abolition 708.5 *cancellation*; 357.1 *destruction*; 355.3 *relinquishment*; 399.1 *veto*
abolitionist 355.4 *deserter*
abolition of sins 708.5 *cancellation*
A-bomb 587.16 *bomb*
abominable 596.9 *disliked*; 594.12 *hated*; 802.16 *in the wrong*; 258.8 *unclean*; 804.11 *wicked*
Abominable Snowman 70.7 *legendary beast*; 89.3 *mountaineer*; 737.6 *natural mystery*
abominably 236.15 *worthlessly*
abominate 596.5 *dislike*; 594.14 *hate*
abomination 236.9 *badness*; 596.1 *dislike*; 594.1 *hate*; 594.7 *hated thing*; 258.2 *uncleanness*; 804.1 *wickedness*; 802.8 *wrongdoing*
à bon marché 793.15 *cheaply*
abonnement 68.1 *skiing*
aboriginal 344.13 *causal*; 3.15 *historic*; 564.12 *native*; 293.15 *precursory*; 130.31 *prime*; 1.13 *racial*
aboriginally 3.24 *historically*; 293.19 *primevally*
Aborigine 293.4 *early comer*
aborigine 293.4 *early comer*; 564.1 *inhabitant*; 1.6 *race*
ab origine 130.39 *from the beginning*
Aborigines 284.6 *people of the past*
aborigines 566.3 *early human*
abort **40.20**; 563.7 *be infertile*; 94.13 *cause not to exist*; 131.16 *cease*; 247.8 *miscarry*; 357.11 *ruin*
aborted 247.10 *failed*
abortifacient 37.4 *drug type*; 37.17 *stimulating*
abortion 563.1 *infertility*; 247.4 *unsuccessful thing*
abortion pill 563.3 *birth control*
abortive 604.11 *disappointing*; 247.10 *failed*; 238.2 *futile*; 563.6 *having no effect*
abortively 247.12 *unsuccessfully*
abound 219.4 *be excessive*
about **217.5**; 27.87 *mathematically*; 147.12 *near*; 50.20 *offshore*; 216.11 *on average*; 203.6 *quantitative*; 203.7 *quantitatively*; 170.8 *round*

about-face 303.13 *about-turn*; 303.9 *turn round*
about gone 582.18 *dying*
about this big 158.13 *this size*
about this size 158.13 *this size*
about to 229.5 *tending to*
about to give birth 561.16 *reproductive*
about to go 245.13 *dilapidated*
about-turn 303.13; 479.6 *equivocation*; 761.1 *reversion*; 303.9, 325.11 *turn round*
above 154.19 *high*; 550.42 *inclusively*; 89.11 *on the mountain*; 129.11 *prior*; 21.17 *stage*; 121.12 *superior*
above all 123.9 *importantly*; 121.17 *supremely*
above and below 550.42 *inclusively*
above average 121.12 *superior*; 121.16 *superiorly*
above board 799.4 *honourable*; 757.7 *permitted*; 811.3 *reputable*; 698.18 *truthful*
above expectations 219.8 *excessively*
above ground 554.12 *alive*
above-mentioned 129.11 *prior*
above one's head 154.19 *high*; 335.14 *powerlessly*
above par 121.16 *superiorly*; 235.1 *worthy*
above price 235.3, 792.8 *valuable*
above reproach 803.5 *virtuous*
above stairs 154.19 *high*
above suspicion 805.5 *innocent*
above temptation 803.5 *virtuous*
above the horizon 520.1 *visible*
above the law 16.62
above water 252.6 *safe*
ab ovo 130.39 *from the beginning*
abracadabra 11.5 *spell*
abrade 365.13; 427.25 *grate*; 552.15 *make nude*
abraded 30.59 *weathered*
Abraham's bosom 582.14 *the spiritual world*
abrase 365.13 *abrade*
abrasion 28.10 *force*; 491.3 *injury*; 427.4 *pulverization*; 157.4 *shallow thing*; 365.2 *wearing away*; 30.35 *weathering*
abrasive 427.12; 256.9 *cleaning agent*; 358.4 *eraser*; 365.10 *frictional*
abrasively 365.17; 427.29 *flakily*
abraxas 11.5 *spell*
abreaction 36.3 *psychiatric treatment*; 393.11 *recuperation*
abreast 119.12 *equally*; 188.7 *in parallel*; 119.8 *on equal terms*
abreast of the times 302.17 *forward*
abridge 269.4 *be concise*; 191.5, 214.5 *make smaller*; 163.5 *outline*; 149.10 *shorten*; 212.3 *subtract*; 723.8 *summarize*; 5.46 *translate*
abridged 269.3 *concise*; 233.4 *incomplete*; 163.6 *outlined*; 212.7 *reduced*; 149.8, 723.7 *shortened*; 191.7 *smaller*; 5.40 *translated*
abridger 723.5 *summarizer*
abridgment 269.1 *conciseness*; 191.1 *contraction*; 214.1 *decrease*; 163.1, 723.2 *outline*; 149.3 *shortened version*; 149.2 *shortening*; 212.1 *subtraction*; 5.12 *translation*
abroad 145.10 *distantly*; 100.18 *extraneously*; 434.26 *out-of-doors*
abrogate 16.78 *acquit*; 16.77 *annul*; 708.14 *cancel*; 131.16 *cease*; 347.3 *counteract*; 357.8 *destroy*; 767.9 *dispose of*; 238.8 *make useless*; 358.1 *obliterate*; 479.4 *recant*; 704.8 *refute*; 335.7 *remove power from*; 708.12 *renounce*; 470.4 *revoke*; 350.6 *stop using*; 399.3 *veto*; 355.2 *withdraw*
abrogated 708.20 *cancelled*; 16.57 *null*; 339.6 *suspended*; 238.1 *useless*
abrogation 470.7; 708.5 *cancellation*; 131.2 *cessation*; 347.1 *counteraction*; 767.1 *disposal*; 358.3 *obliteration*; 479.8 *recantation*; 704.1 *refutation*; 355.3 *relinquishment*; 708.4 *renunciation*; 399.1 *veto*
abrogative 708.17 *negative*
abrogator 704.5 *refuter*
abrupt 149.9; 659.5 *discourteous*; 626.7 *irritable*; 426.2 *outspoken*; 380.6 *violent*
abruptly 426.12 *bluntly*; 659.9 *discourteously*; 508.10 *explosively*; 626.14 *irritably*; 149.12 *short*; 380.10 *violently*
abruptness 149.6; 426.6 *outspokenness*
ABS 435.1 *materials*
abscess 260.15 *ulcer*
abscise 77.22 *be dormant*
abscisic acid 33.17 *plant hormone*
abscissa 27.33 *coordinates*; 26.4 *size*
abscission 77.6 *leaf*; 552.6 *peeling*; 372.3 *separateness*
abscond 98.18; 389.5 *escape*; 786.7 *not pay*; 313.3 *quit*; 634.8 *run away*
absconded 98.9 *away*
absconder 786.6 *nonpayer*
abseil 62.3 *climbing technique*; 305.9 *descend*; 62.9 *mountaineer*
abseiling down 62.3 *climbing technique*
Absence 98
absence 94.6; **98.1**; 634.16 *desertion*; 526.4 *disappearance*; 521.4 *invisibility*; 355.3 *relinquishment*
absence of charge 793.6
absence of dirt 256.1 *cleanness*
absence of intellect 457.1 *lack of intellect*
absence of power 335.1 *powerlessness*
absent 98.8; 355.6 *apathetic*; 526.7 *disappeared*; 128.11 *excluded*; 94.9 *nonexistent*; 135.4 *required*; 218.2 *unprovided*; 350.1 *unused*
absentation 98.4 *absenteeism*
absentee 98.6; 634.17 *avoider*; 98.11 *truant*
absentee ballot 469.10 *vote*
absenteeism 98.4; 343.7 *idleness*
absentee landlord 343.8 *nonworker*
absentee vote 469.10 *vote*
absentee voter 469.13 *electorate*
absently 98.20; **195.12**; 355.8 *apathetically*; 526.8 *fleetingly*; 457.11 *unintelligently*
absent-minded 472.8; 463.9 *blank*; 372.17 *unjoined*
absent-mindedly 372.22 *in isolation*; 463.16 *obliviously*
absent-mindedness 472.3; 463.2 *blankness*; 358.5 *forgetfulness*
absent-minded professor 463.7 *forgetful person*; 472.6 *inattentive person*
absent oneself 98.16; 526.2 *depart*; 313.3 *quit*; 634.8 *run away*
absinthe 558.7 *alcoholic drink*
absolute 698.21 *accurate*; 396.12 *authoritative*; 452.1 *certain*; 232.7 *complete*; 707.16 *definite*; 8.13 *divine*; 400.12 *masterful*; 230.1 *perfect*; 250.12 *unconditional*
absolute age 30.41 *geological time*
absolute ceiling 322.5 *flight*
absolute command 12.3 *governance*
absolute frequency 27.58 *frequency distribution*
absolute humidity 429.3 *humidity*; 31.6 *weather data*
absolute idealism 101.5 *idealism*
absolute likeness 698.12 *realism*
absolutely 707.23 *affirmatively*; 396.23 *authoritatively*; 452.23 *certainly*; 256.20 *clean*; 230.8, 232.9 *completely*; 8.19 *divinely*; 643.12 *indeed*; 400.16 *masterfully*; 204.11 *wholly*
absolutely it 126.2 *original*
absolutely not 708.23 *no!*; 94.14 *not at all*
absolute magnitude 29.13 *luminosity*
absolute monarch 400.2 *sovereign*
absoluteness 698.8 *accuracy*; 452.9 *certainty*; 707.8 *definiteness*; 255.8 *simplicity*
absolute pitch 504.1 *hearing*; 18.21 *tone*
absolute power 396.1 *authority*
absolute rate theory 32.14 *chemical reaction*
absolute realism 698.12 *realism*
absolute ruler 400.4
absolute value 27.6 *complex number*; 27.50 *scalar quantity*
absolute zero 494.2 *freezing*; 28.38 *thermodynamics*; 195.1 *zero*
absolution 649.3; 16.42, 758.2 *acquittal*; 463.6 *amnesty*; 649.1 *forgiveness*; 805.2 *legal innocence*; 391.1 *liberation*; 714.1 *vindication*
absolutism 396.1 *authority*; 647.2 *suppression*
absolve 649.10; 16.78, 758.10 *acquit*; 805.9 *declare innocent*; 649.9 *forgive*; 391.4 *liberate*; 10.18 *perform rites*; 627.10 *show mercy*; 714.7 *vindicate*
absolved 16.63, 758.6 *acquitted*; 805.6 *declared innocent*; 649.6 *forgiven*; 391.7 *liberated*
absolver 391.3 *liberator*
absolving 649.4 *forgiving*; 391.7 *liberated*; 391.1 *liberation*
absorb 32.29; **370.13**; **428.20**; 211.6 *add*; 374.5 *combine*; 557.21 *eat*; 172.15 *keep inside*; 29.37 *observe*; 349.1 *use*
absorbed 32.43; 374.7 *combined*; 443.9 *concentrating*; 6.18 *educated*; 463.8 *oblivious*; 111.12 *same*; 4.17 *thoughtful*
absorbed dose 28.70 *radioactivity*
absorbency 370.5 *absorption*
absorbent 370.17; 428.15 *dryer*; 370.6 *sponge*
absorption 370.5; 31.9 *atmospheric process*; 374.1 *combination*; 42.6 *dye*; 557.1 *eating*; 28.68 *emission*; 6.8 *learning*; 463.1 *oblivion*; 34.5 *physiology*; 32.20 *surface chemistry*; 28.15 *wave property*
absorption indicator 32.18 *gravimetric analysis*
absorption nebula 29.8 *interstellar medium*
absorption spectrum 28.68 *emission*
absorptive 370.17 *absorbent*
absquatulate 313.4 *hurry off*
abstain 634.3; 572.10 *be continent*; 795.11 *be moral*; 684.5 *be self-restrained*; 689.3 *be sober*; 687.5 *fast*; 341.4 *not act*; 637.9 *not cooperate*; 350.5 *not use*; 709.7 *refuse oneself*; 355.1 *relinquish*; 251.10 *restrain oneself*
abstainer 634.17 *avoider*; 355.4 *deserter*; 341.2 *nonacting person*; 709.4 *refuser*; 637.16 *reluctant person*; 383.5 *resister*; 689.8 *sober person*
abstain from 383.9 *desist*; 709.7 *refuse oneself*
abstain from eating 687.5 *fast*
abstaining 634.19; 383.4, 383.13 *desisting*; 341.3 *inactive*; 684.8 *self-restrained*; 684.1 *self-restraint*
abstemious 383.13 *desisting*; 687.6 *fasting*; 251.14, 684.8 *self-restrained*; 689.6 *sober*
abstemiously 383.15; **687.7**; 689.9 *soberly*; 251.17, 684.11 *with self-restraint*
abstemiousness 687.1 *fasting*; 251.3, 684.1 *self-restraint*; 689.6 *sobriety*
abstention 634.11 *abstinence*; 637.13 *dissociation*; 341.1 *inaction*; 684.1 *self-restraint*
abstentious 341.3 *inactive*
abstergent 256.18 *cleansing*
abstinence 634.11; 687.1 *fasting*; 795.3 *moral purity*; 350.8 *nonuse*; 355.3 *relinquishment*; 251.3, 684.1 *self-restraint*; 689.6 *sobriety*; 572.2 *virginity*
abstinence from action 341.1 *inaction*
abstinence from food 687.1 *fasting*
abstinent 634.19 *abstaining*; 687.6 *fasting*; 251.14, 684.8 *self-restrained*; 689.1 *sober*; 572.7 *virginal*
abstinently 383.15 *abstemiously*; 634.21 *away*; 572.12 *celibately*
abstract 269.4 *be concise*; 138.8 *generalization*; 138.20 *generalized*; 477.12 *imaginary*; 101.11 *internal*; 266.2 *obscure*; 4.13 *of philosophy*; 163.1, 163.5 *outline*; 469.4 *pick*; 41.4 *portrait*; 19.29 *realist*; 717.13 *representational*; 721.13 *representing*; 149.10 *shorten*; 149.3 *shortened version*; 212.3 *subtract*; 212.6 *subtractive*; 723.8 *summarize*; 723.1 *summary*; 476.8 *supposed*; 27.69, 96.10, 446.10 *theoretical*
abstract algebra 27.23 *algebra*
abstracted 463.8 *oblivious*; 149.8 *shortened*; 212.5 *subtracted*; 372.17 *unjoined*; 325.25 *wandering*
abstractedly 463.16 *obliviously*; 446.20 *theoretically*
abstractedness 443.4 *deliberation*; 463.1 *oblivion*; 477.6 *reverie*; 325.16 *wandering*
abstraction 36.13 *depression*; 138.8 *generalization*; 446.1 *idea*; 266.1 *obscurity*; 477.6 *reverie*; 212.1 *subtraction*; 27.65 *theory*
abstractly 372.22 *in isolation*; 19.30 *pictorially*; 101.14 *subjectively*; 4.25, 446.20 *theoretically*
abstract sculptor 19.17 *sculptor*
abstract sculpture 19.12 *sculpture*
abstract thought 443.4 *deliberation*; 4.4 *philosophical investigation*
abstruse 696.4 *difficult*; 737.11 *mysterious*; 266.2 *obscure*; 264.12 *problematic*
abstrusely 266.4 *obscurely*
abstruseness 264.1 *difficulty*; 266.1, 528.8 *obscurity*
absurd 477.11 *fantastical*; 459.5 *foolish*; 103.1 *impossible*; 694.6 *meaningful*; 697.5 *nonsensical*; 272.5 *ridiculous*
absurdity 459.1 *folly*; 477.4 *ideality*; 103.5 *impossibility*; 272.1 *ludicrousness*; 697.1 *nonsense*; 694.4 *type of meaning*
absurdly 459.8 *foolishly*; 103.11 *impossibly*; 697.9 *nonsensically*; 272.8 *ridiculously*
a bunch of fives 201.1 *five*
abundance 679.8; 152.6 *denseness*; 270.1 *diffuseness*; 219.1 *excess*; 562.1 *fertility*; 781.7 *opulence*; 217.8 *plenty*; 208.3 *profuseness*; 439.3 *supply*; 215.4 *surplus*
abundant 679.3; 208.9 *ample*; 152.2 *dense*; 270.3 *diffuse*; 219.6 *excessive*; 562.5 *fertile*; 781.4 *lush*; 217.2 *plentiful*; 439.7 *stored*
abundantly 270.7 *diffusely*; 217.9 *enough*; 219.8 *excessively*; 562.8 *fruitfully*; 679.12 *generously*; 215.11 *residually*
abuse 659.3 *act of discourtesy*; 651.7 *act of malevolence*; 798.2 *affliction*; 659.7 *be discourteous*; 798.11 *be evil*; 670.21 *berate*; 670.8 *berating*; 381.10 *criticize*; 349.3 *exploit*; 236.11 *harmfulness*; 236.14 *ill-treat*; 351.1, 351.2 *misuse*; 381.16 *personal attack*; 245.8 *perversion*; 245.6 *pervert*; 678.5 *scorn*; 796.20 *seduce*; 647.6 *suppress*; 651.18 *torment*; 349.6 *use*; 380.8 *use violence*; 678.13, 712.6 *vilify*; 441.1, 441.3 *waste*; 802.20 *wrong*; 802.8 *wrongdoing*
abused 670.34 *censured*; 351.4 *misused*
abuse of language 274.11 *grammatical error*; 720.2 *misinterpretation*
abuse of terms 274.11 *grammatical error*
abuse one's authority 647.6 *suppress*
abuse power 351.1 *misuse*
abuser 351.3; 651.8 *malefactor*; 349.8 *user*
abuse the environment 351.1 *misuse*
abusive 351.5; 659.6 *bad-mannered*; 381.25, 670.27 *critical*; 678.16 *defamatory*; 659.5 *discourteous*; 668.11 *insulting*; 802.16 *in the wrong*; 712.9 *vituperative*
abusive language 58.3 *ice hockey*
abusively 351.6; 441.11 *destructively*; 659.9 *discourteously*; 659.10 *rudely*; 712.13 *vituperatively*
abut 492.12; 20.19 *decorate*; 147.18 *juxtapose*; 413.11 *support*
abutment 38.21 *bridge*; 20.8 *column*; 384.11 *fortification*; 147.3 *juxtaposition*; 38.27 *superstructure*; 413.1 *support*; 413.2 *supporting part*; 360.4 *wall*
abuttal 147.3 *juxtaposition*
abutting 147.10 *juxtaposed*; 20.17 *structured*; 492.9 *touching*
Abydos 10.13 *shrine*
a bygone age 284.1 *past time*
abysmal 156.8 *deep*; 8.16 *devilish*
abyss 183.2 *concave land*; 156.4 *deep thing*; 146.3 *gulf*; 8.12 *hell*; 379.1 *trap*
abyssal 156.8 *deep*; 30.51, 91.7 *oceanic*
abyssal hill 30.16 *ocean floor*
abyssal plain 30.16 *ocean floor*
AC 275.29 *one day*; 434.7 *ventilator*
academia 455.7
academic 6.18 *educated*; 6.16 *educational*; 6.4 *educator*; 458.4 *intellectual*; 442.8 *intellectual person*; 455.6 *knowledgeable person*; 4.19 *learned*; 455.9 *literate*; 4.13 *of philosophy*; 4.10 *philosopher*; 444.5 *reasoner*; 4.12 *sage*; 476.7 *suppositional*; 476.4 *theorist*; 443.7 *thinker*
academic adviser 579.13 *director*
academically 455.15 *knowledgeably*; 6.26 *studiously*; 4.25 *theoretically*
academicals 551.3 *formal dress*
academic dress 551.3, 656.4 *formal dress*
academic freedom 250.2 *free speech*
academician 19.16 *artist*; 442.8 *intellectual person*
academic journal 740.5 *journal*; 276.7 *periodical*
academic psychology 36.1 *psychology*
academic researcher 476.4 *theorist*
academic robe 551.3 *formal dress*
academic year 276.4 *period of activity*
academy 6.12 *educational institution*
Academy Award 813.2 *prize*
Academy Awards 21.6 *cinema*
Acanthocephala 75.6 *worm*
acanthocephalan 75.6 *worm*
acanthoid 425.2 *spiked*
acanthous 425.2 *spiked*
Acapulco gold 691.6 *drug*
acarid 76.2 *arachnid*; 76.11 *arachnidan*
acaroid 76.11 *arachnidan*
acarological 76.15 *arachnological*
acarologist 76.9 *arachnologist*
acarology 76.7 *study*
ACAS 746.5 *negotiate*

accede 750.21 *be in accord;* 117.8 *comply;* 396.20 *take authority*
accedence 750.1 *accord*
accede to 289.11 *follow in office*
accede to the throne 12.12 *take authority*
accelerando 332.14 *swiftly*
accelerate **332.6**; 302.8 *further;* 262.1 *hasten;* 331.1 *impel;* 213.5 *make bigger;* 265.16 *make easy;* 262.2 *make haste;* 47.7 *race*
accelerated 332.3 *accelerating;* 213.7 *increased*
accelerating 332.3
acceleration **332.9**; 262.4 *haste;* 213.1 *increase;* 28.8 *time;* 47.1 *track events*
acceleration due to gravity 28.8 *time*
acceleration path 47.2 *field events*
accelerator 32.15 *catalysis;* 28.94 *particle accelerator*
accelerometer 26.8 *meter;* 332.8 *speed*
accent **5.36**; 5.26 *dialect;* 726.1 *emphasis;* 726.6 *emphasize;* 17.9 *metre;* 729.3 *mode of speech;* 334.1 *power;* 742.13 *punctuate;* 742.7 *punctuation*
accented 729.18 *phonetic;* 742.17 *punctuated*
accentual 17.20 *metrical*
accentual metre 17.9 *metre*
accentual-syllabic metre 17.9 *metre*
accentuate 726.6 *emphasize;* 738.3 *reveal*
accentuated 726.4 *emphasized;* 738.14 *manifest*
accentuation 726.1 *emphasis;* 738.10 *manifestation;* 17.9 *metre;* 729.6 *phonetics;* 5.30 *syntax*
accept **669.12**; 452.20 *be certain;* 450.7 *believe;* 636.13 *be willing;* 769.9, 788.7 *receive;* 605.6 *resign oneself;* 469.1 *select;* 388.3 *submit;* 773.7 *take;* 370.9 *welcome*
acceptability 617.2 *desirability;* 370.3 *introduction;* 136.1 *qualification;* 217.7 *sufficiency*
acceptable 370.14 *admissive;* 750.20 *agreeable;* 669.22 *approvable;* 239.1 *convenient;* 617.8 *desirable;* 757.7 *permitted;* 241.1 *pleasant;* 136.9 *qualified;* 609.6 *satisfactory;* 217.1 *sufficient;* 413.10 *supportable*
acceptably 669.26 *approvably;* 136.17 *capably;* 617.17 *desirably;* 217.9 *enough;* 757.9 *with permission*
accept a candidacy 469.5 *vote*
accept a charge 784.7 *be in debt*
accept advice 713.6 *consult*
accept a gratification 813.13 *get paid*
accept aid 392.18 *receive help*
accept an apology 649.12 *show mercy*
acceptance 750.1 *accord;* 370.1 *admittance;* 669.1 *approval;* 450.3 *believing;* 452.10 *conviction;* 769.1 *receiving;* 605.4 *resignedness*
accept a nomination 469.5 *vote*
acceptant 769.11 *receiving*
accept a proposal 570.15 *marry;* 756.7 *promise*
accept battle 585.14 *battle*
accepted 669.23 *approved;* 216.1 *average;* 450.14 *believed;* 632.12 *established;* 750.10 *in accord;* 138.19 *prevailing;* 769.13, 788.6 *received*
accepted meaning 694.4 *type of meaning*
accepted reading 719.1 *interpretation*
accepter 769.5 *recipient*
accepting 452.2 *convinced;* 750.10 *in accord;* 648.4 *lenient;* 769.1, 769.11 *receiving;* 605.8 *resigned*
accept invitations 654.11 *be sociable*
accept liability 756.8 *guarantee*
accept obligation 756.8 *guarantee*
accept on faith 450.7 *believe*
acceptor 32.11 *chemical bond;* 777.12 *purchaser;* 769.5 *recipient*
acceptor impurity 28.44, 39.4 *semiconductor*
accept payment 813.13 *get paid*
accept responsibility 756.8 *guarantee*
accept stolen property 769.9 *receive*
accept the Lord 7.19 *be religious*
accept the responsibility 810.15 *be liable*
Access™ 783.2 *credit card*
access **318.4**; 40.20 *abort;* 40.19 *computing terms;* 314.5 *entrance;* 314.1 *entry;* 308.19 *open up;* 370.2 *receptivity;* 314.4 *right of entry;* 317.2 *route;* 327.8 *spasm;* 773.4 *taking in*
accessibility 97.4 *availability;* 147.1, 239.4 *nearness;* 102.2 *possibleness*
accessible **317.15**; 312.20 *attainable;* 97.10 *available;* 265.11 *made easy;* 147.9 *near;* 239.2 *nearby;* 308.13 *opened up;* 102.5 *possible;* 370.15 *receptive*
accessibly 239.7 *conveniently;* 308.25 *obviously*
accession **289.4**; 312.17 *achievement;* 396.3 *acquisition of power;* 211.1 *addition*
accessional 396.13 *elected*
accessories **551.25**; 440.4 *possessions;* 372.7 *separates*
accessory 223.17 *accompanying;* 211.1 *addition;* 223.4 *concomitant;* 344.8 *contributor;* 764.5 *jointly possessing;* 764.3 *participant;* 219.3 *superfluity;* 392.31 *supplementary;* 124.8 *trifle*
accessory cord 62.4 *climbing equipment*
access road 373.5 *road*
acciaccatura 18.16 *musical note*
accident 249.1 *adversity;* 798.2 *affliction;* 107.1 *chance;* 288.4 *mishap;* 378.2 *obstacle*
accidental **288.17**; 378.14 *blocked;* 107.8 *chance;* 18.16 *musical note;* 105.3 *unexpected*
accidental death 582.5 *ways of dying*
accidental discovery 449.6 *discovery*
accidental killing **382.8**; 382.1 *killing*
accidentally 107.13 *by chance;* 798.13 *destructively;* 249.12 *in adversity;* 378.17 *in the way;* 288.21 *mistakenly*
accident neurosis 36.10 *neurosis*
accident prevention 15.2 *industrial negotiations*
accident-prone 249.8 *unlucky*
acclaim **669.5**; **669.16**; 667.17 *praise;* 813.1, 813.9 *reward;* 9.7 *worship*
acclaimed 813.16 *rewarded*
acclamation 669.5 *acclaim;* 514.3 *cry of praise;* 813.1 *reward*
acclamatory **669.20**; 669.18 *approving*
acclimate 292.7 *season*
acclimatization 243.13 *development;* 632.7 *habituation;* 117.3 *pliancy*
acclimatize 117.10 *assimilate;* 243.7 *develop;* 632.18 *habituate;* 292.7 *season*
acclimatized 632.14 *habituated*
acclivity 154.2 *heights;* 305.6 *slide*
accolade 669.4 *compliment;* 575.3 *honours*
accommodate 422.10 *be adaptable;* 650.8 *be benevolent;* 754.4 *compromise;* 119.11 *equalize;* 392.22 *improve;* 127.4 *include;* 771.5 *lend;* 117.9 *make conform;* 324.8 *orient;* 749.4 *pacify;* 436.5 *provision;* 370.9 *welcome*
accommodate oneself 117.8 *comply*
accommodate with 768.5 *give*
accommodating 422.7 *adaptive;* 392.35, 650.6 *benevolent;* 117.13 *compliant;* 754.6 *compromising;* 747.17 *cooperative;* 658.7 *courteous;* 750.10 *in accord;* 127.7 *including;* 648.4 *lenient;* 388.5 *submitting*
accommodatingly 422.12 *adaptably;* 650.10 *benevolently;* 754.8 *compromisingly;* 658.14 *courteously;* 658.15 *genteelly;* 648.6 *leniently;* 749.7 *pacifically*
accommodation 750.1 *accord;* 422.2 *adaptability;* 754.1 *compromise;* 392.7 *convenience;* 565.1 *habitat;* 127.1 *inclusion;* 771.1 *lending;* 324.3 *orientation;* 749.1 *pacification;* 117.3 *pliancy;* 436.1 *provision;* 141.5 *reserved space;* 158.1 *size;* 439.4 *storage*
accommodation ladder 304.9 *ladder*
accommodative 771.6 *loaned*
accompanied **223.20**; 108.4 *related*
accompanier 223.6
Accompaniment 223
accompaniment **223.1**; 18.15 *composition;* 97.2 *omnipresence;* 108.1 *relatedness;* 285.1 *same time*
accompanist 223.6 *accompanier*
accompany **223.13**; 285.6 *be simultaneous;* 579.2 *direct;* 401.8 *serve;* 516.9 *set to music*
accompanying **223.17**; 97.8 *attendant;* 285.9 *simultaneous*
accomplice 806.4 *guilty person;* 764.3 *participant*
accomplish 312.9 *achieve;* 340.4 *act;* 246.6 *be successful;* 204.10, 232.4 *complete;* 230.5 *perfect;* 356.10 *produce;* 253.13 *secure one's objective;* 345.5 *show an effect*
accomplished **253.8**; 232.7 *complete;* 396.17 *expert;* 6.19 *knowledgeable;* 4.19 *learned;* 797.5 *proficient;* 485.6 *skilful*
accomplishment 312.17 *achievement;* 340.1 *action;* 232.3 *completion;* 340.2 *deed;* 455.2 *information;* 356.1 *production;* 797.12 *proficiency;* 485.1 *skill;* 246.1 *success*
accomplishments 455.3 *learning*
accomplish nothing 238.9 *waste effort*
accord **750.1**; 239.6 *be convenient;* 750.21 *be in accord;* 108.8 *be proportionate to;* 115.10 *be similar;* 117.7 *conform;* 117.1 *conformity;* 755.1 *contract;* 747.2 *fellowship;* 768.5 *give;* 407.20, 516.8 *harmonize;* 694.10 *mean*
accordance 750.1 *accord;* 117.1 *conformity;* 111.2 *equivalence;* 115.1 *similarity*
accordant 117.12 *conforming;* 111.13 *equivalent;* 750.10 *in accord*
accorded 768.7 *given*
accordingly **750.36**; 222.15 *under the circumstances;* 345.12 *with the effect of*
according to chance 107.14 *perchance*
according to circumstances 222.15 *under the circumstances*
according to law 16.44 *legal;* 16.81 *legally;* 298.17 *orderly*
according to order 298.17 *orderly*
according to plan **482.15**; 407.25 *in order*
according to rule **117.19**; 407.17 *disciplined;* 298.17 *orderly*
according to schedule 484.16 *as planned*
according to the agreement 755.8 *contractually*
according to the book 694.13 *meaningfully*
according to the contract 755.8 *contractually*
according to the rules 140.19 *to rule*
according to tradition 298.17 *orderly*
accordion pleat 184.3 *pleat*
accord respect to 667.18 *show respect*
accord with 119.10 *be equal*
accost 733.9 *approach;* 710.6 *request*
accosting 710.1 *request*
accouchement 561.7 *obstetrics*
account **789.7**; 789.1 *accounts;* 784.5 *amount owing;* 220.4 *bill;* 210.12 *check;* 3.5 *chronicle;* 693.2 *communication;* 783.1 *credit;* 721.1 *description;* 780.6 *funds;* 123.1 *importance;* 721.3 *narration;* 744.1 *record*
accountability 706.9 *answerability;* 784.1 *debt;* 703.5 *demonstrability;* 810.1 *duty;* 474.2 *expectations*
accountable 789.10 *accounting;* 706.16 *answerable;* 784.9 *in debt;* 810.10 *liable*
accountableness 810.1 *duty*
accountably 706.27 *answerably;* 703.22 *demonstrably;* 810.18 *on duty*
accountancy 789.1 *accounts;* 744.8 *registration*
accountant **789.6**; 210.7 *mathematician;* 744.9 *recorder;* 748.4 *representative;* 780.18 *treasurer*
account book **789.5**; 744.6 *record book*
account books 220.4 *bill*
accounted 789.11
accounted for 282.8 *available*
account for 810.15 *be liable;* 4.21 *rationalize*
Accounting 789
accounting **789.3**; **789.10**; 789.1 *accounts;* 210.3 *count;* 14.1 *finance*
account paid 789.4 *statement*
account rendered 789.4 *statement*
accounts **789.1**; 744.8 *registration*
accounts code 789.5 *account book*
account settled 789.4 *statement*
accounts payable 783.1 *credit*
accounts receivable 784.5 *amount owing;* 785.1 *payment*
accoutre 551.32 *dress;* 551.35 *make clothing*
accoutred 384.30 *defended;* 243.18 *prepared*
accoutrement 551.1 *dress;* 438.7 *equipment*
accoutrements 551.25 *accessories;* 211.3 *additional item;* 763.4 *possession;* 440.4 *possessions*
accredit 750.28 *consent;* 396.21 *grant authority*
accredited 396.16 *authorized;* 450.14 *believed;* 750.17 *consenting;* 632.12 *established*
accrete 765.11 *acquire;* 211.6 *add*
accretion 765.3 *acquisition;* 211.1 *addition;* 213.1 *increase*
accretionary 211.8 *additional*
accretive 211.8 *additional*
accrual 211.1 *addition;* 213.1 *increase*
accrue 211.6 *add;* 765.13 *be profitable;* 345.8 *grow;* 788.7 *receive*
accrue to 213.5 *make bigger*
acculturation 6.1 *education*
accumbency 187.1 *horizontality*
accumbent 187.10 *lying*
accumulate 765.11 *acquire;* 376.37 *assemble;* 213.4 *increase;* 439.6 *store*
accumulated 376.47 *collected;* 439.7 *stored*
accumulated arrears 784.5 *amount owing*
accumulation 765.3 *acquisition;* 376.25 *assemblage;* 439.5 *collection;* 213.1 *increase;* 439.4 *storage;* 439.1 *store*
accumulative 765.18 *acquisitional*
accumulatively 765.20 *gainfully*
accumulator 376.35 *collector;* 334.7 *electrical power;* 39.29 *power source*
Accuracy 273
accuracy **273.1**; **591.10**; **698.8**; 452.9 *certainty;* 725.1 *clarity;* 801.2 *correctness;* 407.6 *methodicalness;* 27.8 *number system;* 230.3 *perfection;* 28.83 *sensitivity*
accuracy event 55.1 *angling*
accurate **273.5**; **591.4**; **698.21**; 452.1 *certain;* 725.3 *clear;* 801.8 *correct;* 464.9 *judicious;* 646.1 *naive;* 230.1 *perfect;* 407.14 *well-ordered*
accurately **273.8**; **698.39**; 725.4 *clearly;* 801.20 *correctly*
accurateness 801.2 *correctness*
accurate person 273.4
accurate thing 273.3
accursed 236.3 *bad;* 236.6 *damnable;* 236.5 *harmful;* 594.12 *hated;* 804.14 *impious;* 798.10 *inauspicious;* 712.10 *maledictive;* 249.8 *unlucky*
accusable 804.15 *criminal;* 806.5 *guilty;* 16.47 *liable to law;* 16.54 *litigated;* 16.58 *unjust*
Accusation 715
accusation **715.1**; 670.7 *blame;* 806.1 *guilt;* 16.5 *litigation*
accusation of guilt 806.1 *guilt*
accusative 5.31 *case*
accusatory **715.8**; 670.29 *blaming*
accuse **715.5**; 739.7 *betray;* 670.19 *blame;* 693.13 *inform on;* 16.70 *litigate;* 712.6 *vilify*
accusé 726.4 *emphasized*
accused 715.8 *accusatory;* 16.8 *litigant*
accused person **715.4**; 16.8 *litigant*
accuse falsely 715.6
accuse oneself 806.9 *appear guilty;* 808.4 *be penitent*
accuser **715.3**; 693.10 *informer;* 16.8 *litigant*
accusing 715.1 *accusation;* 715.8 *accusatory;* 670.29 *blaming;* 16.53 *litigating*
accusingly 715.10
accustom 632.18 *habituate;* 292.7 *season*
accustomed 216.1 *average;* 138.21 *common;* 140.10 *customary;* 632.9 *habitual;* 632.14 *habituated;* 292.15 *seasoned*
accustom oneself 632.18 *habituate*
AC/DC 198.10 *two-sided*
AC/DC guy 567.10 *bisexual*
ACE 40.3 *computer*
ace 235.2 *best;* 69.3 *card game terms;* 400.13 *excellent;* 396.11, 400.10 *expert;* 56.7 *golf;* 56.3 *golf shots;* 400.15 *learn;* 485.3 *masterpiece;* 352.1 *means;* 197.1 *one;* 121.6 *paragon;* 136.8 *qualified person;* 147.2 *short distance;* 485.6 *skilful;* 485.4 *skilled person;* 246.3 *successful thing;* 797.16 *superior person;* 63.2 *tennis strokes;* 619.14 *wonderful!;* 235.1 *worthy*
ace in the hole 121.3, 164.4 *advantage;* 123.3 *chief thing;* 484.3 *expedient plan*
Aceldama 585.10 *battleground;* 382.6 *ritual killing*
acellular 34.23 *cellular*
acerbate 626.12 *make irritable*
acerbic 499.5 *acid;* 659.5 *discourteous;* 651.14 *hostile;* 625.4 *irascible;* 425.5 *mentally sharp;* 624.15 *resentful*
acerbity 651.4 *bitterness;* 659.1 *discourtesy;* 625.1 *irascibility;* 499.1 *sourness*
acetic acid 499.3 *sour thing*

acetylate 32.26 *react*
acetylene lamp 522.5 *incandescent light*
a.c. generator 39.30 *generator*
ache 242.12, 491.10 *be painful*; 491.9 *feel pain*; 236.11 *harmfulness*; 491.1 *pain*
ache in every muscle 261.5 *be fatigued*
achene 80.2 *botanical fruit*
aches and pains 491.1 *pain*
achievable 312.20 *attainable*; 102.5 *possible*; 95.9 *realizable*
achieve **312.9**; 340.4 *act*; 348.4 *be an instrument*; 246.6 *be successful*; 204.10, 232.4 *complete*; 131.15 *end*; 230.5 *perfect*; 356.10 *produce*; 345.5 *show an effect*
achieved 232.7 *complete*
achieve liberty 391.5 *be liberated*
achieve marvels 619.11 *do wonders*
achievement **312.17**; 340.1 *action*; 302.12 *advance*; 232.3 *completion*; 340.2 *deed*; 345.1 *effect*; 743.8 *heraldic device*; 348.1 *instrumentality*; 356.1 *production*; 622.7 *satisfaction*; 246.1 *success*
achieve nothing 238.7 *be useless*
achiever 340.3 *doer*; 246.4 *successful person*
achieve victory 246.9 *be victorious*
Achilles and Patroclus 569.7 *famous friendships*
Achilles' heel 231.7 *defect*; 254.7 *vulnerability*; 337.1 *weakness*
aching 261.1 *fatigued*; 491.7 *feeling pain*; 491.1 *pain*; 242.4, 491.5 *painful*
aching all over 491.7 *feeling pain*
achingly 491.13 *painfully*
aching muscles 261.7 *fatigue*
achondrite 29.20 *meteor*
achromatic 530.7 *colourless*; 532.2 *dark*; 531.2 *whitened*
achromatically 530.9 *colourlessly*; 531.14 *whitely*
achromatic hue 531.8 *whitener*
achromaticity 530.1 *colourlessness*
achromatic lens 28.29 *optical element*
achromatism 530.1 *colourlessness*; 531.7 *whiteness*
achromatize 530.6 *decolour*
Achtung! 68.18 *danger!*
acicular 425.1 *sharp*
aciculate 425.1 *sharp*
acid **32.8**; **32.36**; **499.5**; 357.7 *agent of destruction*; 691.6 *drug*; 236.5 *harmful*; 651.14 *hostile*; 625.4 *irascible*; 626.7 *irritable*; 624.15 *resentful*; 624.1 *resentment*; 495.7 *tasty*; 242.3 *unpalatable*
acid–base catalysis 32.15 *catalysis*
acid dye 42.6 *dye*
acid-head 691.4 *drug taker*
acid house 18.9 *popular music*
acid-house party 376.10 *dance*
acidic 32.36, 499.5 *acid*; 651.14 *hostile*
acidify 32.26 *react*; 499.8 *sour*
acidimeter 26.8 *meter*
acidimetric 26.16 *micrometric*
acidimetry 26.2 *micrometry*
acidity 651.4 *bitterness*; 260.8 *indigestion*; 625.1 *irascibility*; 624.1 *resentment*; 499.1 *sourness*
acid jazz 18.8 *jazz*
acid kiln 24.6 *ceramic workshop*
acidly 625.9 *irascibly*; 626.14 *irritably*; 624.17 *resentfully*
acidness 625.1 *irascibility*
acidosis 260.8 *indigestion*
acid rain 245.10 *impairment*; 31.26 *raininess*; 499.3 *sour thing*
acid rock 30.30 *igneous rock*; 18.9 *popular music*
acid salt 32.10 *salt*
acid stop 41.12 *development*
acid taste 495.1 *taste*
acid test 448.1 *experiment*
acid trip 691.1 *drug-taking*
acidulated 499.5 *acid*
acidulous 499.5 *acid*; 624.15 *resentful*
acidulousness 624.1 *resentment*; 499.1 *sourness*
ACK 40.14 *data transfer*
ack-ack 381.13 *air attack*; 587.13 *ammunition*
acknowledge 739.8 *admit*; 706.17 *answer*; 658.10 *be courteous*; 671.6 *be grateful*; 692.31 *correspond*; 769.9, 788.7 *receive*; 813.9 *reward*; 667.18 *show respect*
acknowledged 706.11 *answering*; 739.10 *disclosed*; 632.12 *established*; 769.13, 788.6 *received*; 813.16 *rewarded*
acknowledged with thanks 788.6 *received*
acknowledge one's faults 808.4 *be penitent*
acknowledge one's guilt 806.8 *be guilty*
acknowledge one's sins 806.8 *be guilty*; 808.4 *be penitent*
acknowledging 671.5 *thanking*
acknowledgment **706.2**; 669.2 *admiration*; 807.2 *apology*; 658.3 *courtesies*; 40.14 *data transfer*; 739.2 *divulgence*; 671.3 *recognition*; 813.1 *reward*
acknowledgment of guilt 807.2 *apology*
acknowledgment of payment **769.3**
aclinic line 30.45 *magnetic pole*
acme 154.2 *heights*; 230.3 *perfection*; 121.4, 174.1 *summit*
acme of perfection 230.3 *perfection*
acne 548.2 *pimple*; 420.7 *rough thing*; 260.13 *skin disease*
A.C. Nielsen ratings 740.2 *mass media*
acoelomate 75.16 *invertebrate*
acolyte 7.8 *priest*; 7.3 *religious person*; 413.8 *supporter*
Aconcagua 89.6 *other major mountains and ranges*
aconite 33.19 *alkaloid*
acorn academy 461.8 *mental hospital*
acorn barnacle 75.4 *arthropod*
a corner on 763.1 *possession*
acorns 557.8 *animal food*
acorn worm 75.2 *protochordate*; 75.6 *worm*
a couple 207.1 *plurality*
acoustic 504.11 *aural*; 28.98 *physical*
acoustically 28.100 *physically*
acoustic coupler 40.14 *data transfer*; 40.7 *peripheral*
acoustic mine 587.16 *bomb*
acoustic phonetics 729.6 *phonetics*
acoustics 28.2 *classical physics*; 504.1 *hearing*
acoustic wave 28.14 *sound wave*; 326.5 *wave*
acquaint 569.15 *be hospitable*; 6.22 *educate*; 693.11 *inform*
acquaintance 569.5 *friend*; 693.1 *information*; 455.1 *knowledge*
acquaintanceship 569.1 *friendship*
acquainted 569.9 *friends with*
acquainted with 455.8 *knowledgeable*
acquaint oneself with 455.13 *get to know*
acquest 215.5 *estate*
acquiesce 669.12 *accept*; 750.21 *be in accord*; 636.13 *be willing*; 117.8 *comply*; 663.5 *obey*; 757.3 *permit*; 605.6 *resign oneself*; 388.3 *submit*
acquiescence **636.8**; 750.1 *accord*; 669.1 *approval*; 117.2 *compliance*; 663.1 *obedience*; 757.1 *permission*; 605.4 *resignedness*; 388.1 *submission*
acquiescent 636.3 *amenable*; 117.13 *compliant*; 265.13 *easy-going*; 750.10 *in accord*; 663.7 *obedient*; 605.8 *resigned*; 388.5 *submitting*
acquiescently 663.10 *obediently*
acquiescing 750.10 *in accord*
acquire **765.11**; 683.6 *be selfish*; 449.2 *detect*; 352.6 *find means*; 765.9 *gain*; 400.15 *learn*; 777.1 *purchase*; 769.9, 788.7 *receive*; 773.7 *take*
acquire a reputation 340.4 *act*
acquire authority 396.20 *take authority*
acquire by purchase 777.1 *purchase*
acquire credit **783.9**
acquired 765.15 *gainful*; 769.13 *received*
acquired knowledge 455.3 *learning*
acquire knowledge 6.23 *learn*
acquirement 765.1 *gain*; 485.1 *skill*
acquirements 455.3 *learning*
acquirer 769.5 *recipient*
acquire the habit 632.18 *habituate*
acquiring 765.15 *gainful*; 773.12 *taking*
acquisition **765.3**; 449.7 *detection*; 765.1 *gain*; 777.6 *purchase*; 769.1 *receiving*; 773.1 *taking*
acquisitional **765.18**; 773.12 *taking*
acquisition of knowledge 6.8 *learning*
acquisition of power **396.3**
acquisitive 765.18 *acquisitional*; 777.14 *buying*; 617.9 *desirous*; 765.16 *greedy*; 683.4 *selfish*; 773.12 *taking*
acquisitively **777.17**; 773.13 *avariciously*; 765.20 *gainfully*; 683.8 *selfishly*
acquisitiveness 683.1 *selfishness*
acquit **16.78**; **758.10**; 649.10 *absolve*; 805.9 *declare innocent*; 390.1 *deliver*; 810.16 *do one's duty*; 464.11 *judge*; 391.4 *liberate*; 714.7 *vindicate*
acquit oneself 631.11 *conduct oneself*
acquittal **16.42**; **758.2**; 649.3 *absolution*; 390.2 *deliverance*; 810.5 *discharge of duty*; 389.1 *escape*; 805.2 *legal innocence*; 16.7 *legal trial*; 391.1 *liberation*; 627.3 *mercy*; 464.2 *verdict*; 714.1 *vindication*
acquittance 391.1 *liberation*; 785.1 *payment*; 253.2 *promise*
acquitted **16.63**; **758.6**; 805.6 *declared innocent*; 389.8 *escaping*; 649.6 *forgiven*; 250.9 *free*; 714.12 *innocent*; 391.7 *liberated*
acraniate 75.16 *invertebrate*
acreage 43.11 *farmland*; 86.12 *plot*; 440.1 *property*
acres 440.1 *property*
acrid 499.5 *acid*; 651.14 *hostile*
acridine dye 42.6 *dye*
acridity 499.2 *unpalatability*
acrimonious 659.5 *discourteous*; 594.10 *hating*; 651.14 *hostile*; 624.15 *resentful*
acrimoniously 659.9 *discourteously*; 594.18 *hatefully*; 651.20 *malevolently*; 624.17 *resentfully*
acrimony 651.4 *bitterness*; 594.1 *hate*; 624.1 *resentment*
acrobat 336.5 *athlete*; 21.31 *circus performer*; 485.4 *skilled person*
acrobatic 419.2 *pliant*; 68.12 *ski*; 45.5 *sporting*
acrobatically 68.17 *on a ski run*; 419.17 *softly*; 45.7 *sportingly*
acrobatic jump 68.1 *skiing*
acrobatic skiing 68.1 *skiing*
acromegaly 158.4 *gigantism*
acronym 5.13 *letter*
acronymic 5.41 *lettered*
acronymous 5.41 *lettered*
acropolis 356.8 *construction*; 384.12 *fort*; 252.5 *refuge*
acrospire 77.9 *seed*
across 150.8 *breadthwise*; 318.14 *by the way*; 189.8 *obliquely*
across-the-board 216.1 *average*; 138.15 *general*; 127.7 *including*; 204.6 *whole*
across the counter 776.20 *in trade*
across the line 329.17 *ahead*
across the sea 91.11 *nautically*
acrostic 737.4 *brain-teaser*; 5.13 *letter*; 5.41 *lettered*
a crying shame 627.5 *misfortune*
acrylic 435.1 *materials*; 19.8 *painting*
acrylic paints 529.5 *paint*
act **21.34**; **340.4**; **717.10**; 342.12 *be active*; 348.4 *be an instrument*; 631.14 *behave towards*; 346.7 *be operational*; 397.1 *command*; 631.11 *conduct oneself*; 340.2 *deed*; 738.1 *display*; 21.29 *entertainer*; 699.14 *façade*; 3.14 *historicalness*; 699.28 *mask*; 485.3 *masterpiece*; 525.13 *occur*; 713.3 *precept*; 699.24 *pretend*; 140.1 *rule*; 21.8 *scene*; 345.5 *show an effect*; 464.2 *verdict*
act against 113.21 *counteract*; 113.14 *oppose*
act as a brake 251.8, 378.10 *restrain*
act as a footstool 664.8 *be servile*
act as agent for 748.1 *mediate*
act as a go-between **746.7**
act as a link 746.7 *act as a go-between*
act as a magnet 471.13 *attract attention*
act as a middleman 746.7 *act as a go-between*
act as deputy for 762.4 *be a substitute*
act as guarantor 253.11 *promise*
act as guide 719.8 *interpret*
act as host 569.15 *be hospitable*; 654.11 *be sociable*; 769.10 *receive someone*
act as hostess 654.11 *be sociable*
act as interpreter 719.12 *translate*
act as proxy for 398.8 *represent*
act as referee for 669.13 *support*
act as security 253.11 *promise*
act as spokesman for 719.13 *interpret news*
act as white knight 776.3 *bargain*
act curtain 21.19 *stage set*
act decisively 707.21 *be assertive*
act dishonestly **774.16**
act drop 21.19 *stage set*
act dumb 736.12 *be silent*
act eccentrically 250.16 *be independent*
act erratically 299.7 *be unusual*
act foolishly **486.6**
act for 762.4 *be a substitute*; 398.8 *represent*; 717.12 *stand for*
act forcefully 707.21 *be assertive*
act honourably 799.6 *be honourable*
act in 525.13 *occur*
act in concert 747.13 *work together*
acting **21.22**; **340.5**; **717.3**; 12.10 *governing*; 699.7 *pretence*; 699.34 *pretending*; 762.7 *substitute*
acting area 21.17 *stage*
actinoid 32.6 *chemical element*
actinometer 26.8 *meter*
actinometric 26.16 *micrometric*
actinometry 26.2 *micrometry*
actinomycin 83.6 *fungal antibiotic*
act insolent 661.6 *be insubordinate*
Action 340
action **340.1**; 715.1 *accusation*; 342.1 *activity*; 17.3 *aspect of fiction*; 585.9 *battle*; 631.1 *conduct*; 340.2 *deed*; 21.9 *dramaturgy*; 345.1 *effect*; 15.4 *industrial dispute*; 16.5 *litigation*; 300.2 *momentum*; 346.1 *operation*; 344.6 *undertaking*
actionable 16.47 *liable to law*; 16.54 *litigated*; 16.58 *unjust*
action painter 19.16 *artist*
action painting 19.2, 19.8 *painting*
actions 631.1 *conduct*; 340.2 *deed*; 484.2 *policy*; 631.8 *treatment*
action sequence 41.4 *portrait*
action shot 41.4 *portrait*
activate **130.20**; **346.8**; 488.13 *arouse sensation*; 224.8 *cause change*; 395.8 *influence*; 338.3 *invigorate*; 32.26 *react*
activated 342.18 *active*; 32.39 *catalytic*
activated complex 32.14 *chemical reaction*
activation 224.1 *change*; 342.4 *energy*
activation energy 32.14 *chemical reaction*
activator 224.5 *changer*
active **342.18**; 340.5 *acting*; 342.19 *busy*; 395.11 *influential*; 554.13 *lively*; 300.16 *moving*; 346.10 *operational*; 338.4 *vigorous*; 5.32 *voice*; 576.10 *working*
active galaxy 29.7 *galaxy*
active interest 342.2 *social activity*
active list 220.6 *list of names*
actively **340.7**; **342.22**; 300.18 *in motion*; 346.13 *operationally*
actively involved 342.18 *active*
active member 654.6 *social person*
activeness 340.1 *action*; 342.1 *activity*
active participation 342.2 *social activity*
active person 342.10 *busy person*
active power 39.26 *electrical energy*
active principle 37.5 *prescription*
active resistance 384.1 *defence*
active-ride 61.10 *racing*
active service 585.8 *warfare*
active site 33.11 *enzyme*
active sun 29.15 *sun*
active supporter 340.3 *doer*
active suspension system 61.6 *motor-racing terms*
active treatment 35.8 *treatment*
active volcano 30.24 *volcanic activity*
activism **342.5**; 340.1 *action*; **21.10** *theatre movements*
activist **21.42**; 353.7 *attempter*; **342.10** *busy person*; 661.4 *defiant person*; **340.3** *doer*; 480.14 *motivator*
Activity 342
activity **342.1**; **633.4**; 340.1 *action*; 262.4 *haste*; 300.2 *momentum*; 69.8 *pastime*; 28.70 *radioactivity*; 338.1 *vigour*; 577.1 *workshop*
act lawlessly 753.8 *cause mischief*
act like a bear 625.6 *be irascible*
act like a bitch 625.6 *be irascible*
act like a charm 246.8 *be effective*
act like a Christian 650.9 *be charitable*
act like a gentleman 658.11 *have good manners*
act like a lady 799.6 *be honourable*; 658.11 *have good manners*
act like a tonic 338.3 *invigorate*
act like a vixen 625.6 *be irascible*
act morally 799.6 *be honourable*
act negligently 618.14 *be careless*
act oddly 299.7 *be unusual*
act of courage 613.8 *courageous act*
act of cruelty 651.7 *act of malevolence*
act of defiance **661.3**
act of derision **621.2**
act of discourtesy **659.3**
act of dying 582.1 *death*
act of folly **459.2**
act of friendship **569.4**
act of gluttony **688.3**

act of God 452.16 *inevitability*; 357.4 *ruin*
act of grace 650.4 *benevolent act*
act of inhumanity 651.7 *act of malevolence*
act of kindness 658.5 *sign of courtesy*
act of love 593.5 *desire*
act of malevolence **651.7**
act of smelling 500.2 *sense of smell*
act of thrift **680.2**
act on behalf of 706.23 *answer for*
act one's part 810.16 *do one's duty*
act on impulse 478.3 *improvise*
act on principle 480.18 *be persuaded*
act on the defensive **384.26**; 585.13 *be at war*
actor **21.24**; 340.3 *doer*; 717.5 *performer*; 227.8 *person who changes costume*; 676.2 *pretender*; 578.1 *worker*
actor-manager 21.24 *actor*; 21.27 *producer*
a.c. transmission 39.33 *power distribution*
act recklessly 618.14 *be careless*
actress 21.24 *actor*; 340.3 *doer*; 717.5 *performer*; 227.8 *person who changes costume*; 578.1 *worker*
act roughly 423.10 *be tough*
act rudely 655.13 *ignore*
act sanctimoniously 699.22 *be hypocritical*
act sycophantically 658.13 *defer to*
act the fool 697.8 *fool*
act the goat 697.8 *fool*; 459.7 *play the fool*
act the host 654.11 *be sociable*
act the hostess 654.11 *be sociable*
act the part of 717.10 *act*
act together 374.6 *come together*
actual 452.1 *certain*; 3.19 *chronicled*; 698.16 *existing*; 97.7, 282.6 *present*; 93.13, 95.6 *real*
actuality **282.3**; 452.9 *certainty*; 93.4 *demonstrable existence*; 3.14 *historicalness*; 97.1 *presence*; 95.1, 698.2 *reality*
actualization 93.8 *creation*
actualize 93.20 *bring into being*; 698.28 *bring into existence*; 95.11 *make real*
actualized 93.15 *created*
actually 452.23 *certainly*; 643.11 *earnestly*; 97.14 *in person*; 93.22, 95.13 *really*; 3.25 *reportedly*; 698.35 *truly*
actual thing 111.1 *sameness*
actuarial 789.10 *accounting*; 210.13 *calculative*
actuarial calculation 107.7 *calculation of chance*
actuary 789.6 *accountant*; 210.7 *mathematician*; 26.9 *measurer*
actuate 346.8 *activate*; 331.1 *impel*; 395.8 *influence*; 483.9 *motivate*; 300.14 *set in motion*
actuation 300.2 *momentum*; 300.1 *motion*
act upon 340.4 *act*; 483.9 *motivate*; 346.9 *take action*
act vulgarly 497.9 *have bad taste*
act without authority 588.4 *be anarchic*
act without ceremony 262.2 *make haste*
act without prompting 752.11 *volunteer*
ACU 40.12 *electronic office*
acuity 273.1 *accuracy*; 442.4 *cleverness*; 645.1 *cunning*; 726.1 *emphasis*; 336.2 *healthiness*; 425.13 *mental sharpness*; 156.3 *profundity*
acumen 466.2 *judiciousness*; 425.13 *mental sharpness*; 6.11 *refinement*; 442.2 *ways of thinking*; 458.1 *wisdom*
acuminate 425.14 *be sharp*; 425.1 *sharp*
acumination 425.6 *sharpness*
acuminous 425.5 *mentally sharp*
acupressure 35.2 *natural medicine*; 394.13 *therapy*
acupuncture 489.4 *anaesthetic*; 394.5 *analgesic*; 394.11 *medical art*; 35.2 *natural medicine*; 35.9 *surgery*; 394.13 *therapy*
acupuncturist 35.12, 394.15 *healer*
a cut above 235.2 *best*
acutance 41.8 *composition*
acute 5.36 *accent*; 164.10 *advantaged*; 645.4 *cunning*; 442.10 *intelligent*; 425.5 *mentally sharp*; 491.5 *painful*; 513.9 *shrill*; 336.11 *strong in spirit*; 380.6 *violent*; 156.11 *wise*
acute accent 742.7 *punctuation*
acute angle 27.39, 176.1 *angle*
acute-angled 176.9 *angled*
acute-angled triangle 27.43 *triangle*
acute attack 260.2 *illness*
acute dilemma 254.5 *danger*
acutely **336.15**; 164.12 *at an advantage*; 442.15 *intelligently*; 425.18 *sharply*
acuteness 442.4 *cleverness*; 425.13 *mental sharpness*
acute note 513.3 *shrillness*
acyclic 32.35 *combined*
acyclic compound 32.7 *chemical compound*
acylate 32.26 *react*
acylglycerol 33.7 *fat*
AD 275.29 *one day*
ad 740.9 *advertisement*; 693.4 *mass communication*
adage 5.21 *catchword*; 745.1 *maxim*; 795.7 *moral*
adagio 333.16 *slowly*; 18.19 *tempo*
Adam 567.2 *male*
adamant 418.7 *hard substance*; 635.7 *iron-willed*; 638.3 *strong-willed*; 418.2 *tough*; 641.3 *unyielding*
adamantine 641.5 *obstinacy*
Adam Hepplewhite 23.7 *furniture style*
adamic 296.12 *olden*
Adamite 566.7 *person*
Adam's ale 433.1 *water*
Adam's apple 80.5 *figurative usage*; 729.5 *organ of speech*
Adam's-needle 425.8 *sharp-pointed thing*
Adam's Peak 10.13 *shrine*
Adam's wine 433.1 *water*
adapt **409.16**; 422.10 *be adaptable*; 224.7 *be changed*; 224.8 *cause change*; 117.8 *comply*; 18.35 *compose*; 754.4 *compromise*; 632.18 *habituate*; 136.15 *modify*; 324.8 *orient*; 719.12 *translate*; 419.16 *yield*
adaptability **422.2**; 754.1 *compromise*; 419.12 *gentleness*; 117.3 *pliancy*; 485.1 *skill*; 483.6 *suggestibility*; 237.5 *usefulness*; 265.3 *wieldiness*
adaptable 422.7 *adaptive*; 754.6 *compromising*; 117.11 *conformable*; 419.7 *impressionable*; 419.2 *pliant*; 485.6 *skilful*; 483.13 *suggestible*; 237.1 *useful*; 265.12 *wieldy*
adaptably **117.16**; **422.12**
adaptation 224.1 *change*; 18.15 *composition*; 754.1 *compromise*; 239.3 *convenience*; 632.7 *habituation*; 136.5 *modification*; 409.9 *musical arrangement*; 324.3 *orientation*; 117.3 *pliancy*; 719.4 *translation*
adapted 422.7 *adaptive*; 136.11 *modified*
adapted for speed 332.1 *swift*
adapted to 239.1 *convenient*
adapted to drought **428.7**
adapter 224.5 *changer*
adapt for the stage 21.38 *dramatize*
adapting 422.7 *adaptive*; 419.7 *impressionable*
adaption 117.3 *pliancy*
adaptive **422.7**; 117.11 *conformable*
adapt oneself 117.8 *comply*
add **27.91**; **210.9**; **211.6**; 134.3 *continue*; 368.1 *insert*; 720.1 *misinterpret*; 194.10 *number*; 203.8 *quantify*; 32.26 *react*
add a meaning 720.1 *misinterpret*
add an escape clause 746.6 *make conditions*
add commentary 719.10 *annotate*
added 211.8 *additional*; 127.8 *included*; 368.12 *inserted*; 203.6 *quantitative*; 108.4 *related*; 295.14 *renewed*
added attraction 483.5 *positive stimulus*
added contribution 213.1 *increase*
added extra 211.4 *extra*
addend 27.15 *addition*
addendum 211.1 *addition*; 211.3 *additional item*
add explanation 719.10 *annotate*
add frills 244.1 *improve*
add fuel to 213.5 *make bigger*
addict 386.5 *compulsive person*; 632.8 *creature of habit*; 260.19 *sick person*
addicted **691.8**; 632.14 *habituated*; 686.8 *overindulgent*
addicted to alcohol 690.5 *drunken*
addiction 36.15 *compulsion*; 632.1 *habit*; 686.3 *overindulgence*; 245.8 *perversion*
addictive **691.9**; 395.12 *appealing*; 632.15 *habit-forming*; 690.6 *intoxicating*; 480.19 *persuasive*
adding 211.1 *addition*; 210.3 *count*
adding machine 27.67 *calculator*; 40.3, 210.5 *computer*
adding-up 211.2 *mathematical addition*
add insult to injury 668.23 *insult*
additament 211.3 *additional item*
Addition 211
addition **27.15**; **211.1**; 211.3 *additional item*; 210.1 *calculation*; 203.2 *certain amount*; 32.14 *chemical reaction*; 295.5 *fresh start*; 190.1 *growth*; 213.1 *increase*; 120.1 *inequality*; 368.8 *insertion*; 720.2 *misinterpretation*; 205.7 *piece*; 134.2 *protraction*; 108.1 *relatedness*
additional **211.8**; 134.5 *continual*; 213.6 *increasing*; 295.14 *renewed*; 762.7 *substitute*
additional comment 719.2 *annotation*
additional item **211.3**
additionally **211.10**; 134.7 *continually*; 213.8 *increasingly*; 762.9 *instead*; 190.10 *largely*
additional part 211.3 *additional item*
additional power 334.1 *power*
addition polymer 32.21 *polymer*
additive 211.8 *additional*; 211.3 *additional item*; 32.38 *reactive*; 127.2 *thing included*
additive colour 529.4 *pigment*
additive process 28.28 *colour*
addle 258.10 *be dirty*; 457.10 *bemuse*; 408.22 *discompose*
addled 563.6 *having no effect*
add nothing 119.11 *equalize*
add on 295.20 *make new*
add-on 211.3 *additional item*
add one's share 211.6 *add*
add one's support 211.7 *support*
add one's two penn'orth 211.6 *add*
add-ons 372.7 *separates*
Address 733
address **733.1**; **733.7**; 40.20 *abort*; 729.9 *art of public speaking*; 40.19 *computing terms*; 692.31 *correspond*; 692.3 *correspondence*; 142.2 *exact location*; 484.2 *policy*; 316.13 *post*; 667.20 *salute*; 733.10 *send*; 485.1, 733.3 *skill*; 729.14 *speak to*; 729.8 *speech*; 729.7 *utterance*
address book 220.3 *dictionary*; 744.6 *record book*
addressee 706.10 *answerer*; 564.3 *householder*; 769.5 *recipient*
addresses 593.6 *courtship*
addressing 721.7 *nomenclature*
addressing the ball 56.3 *golf shots*
address of welcome 733.2 *salutation*
address oneself to **733.12**; 243.2 *do the groundwork*; 354.1 *undertake*
address one's prayers to 710.6 *request*
address the general public 695.5 *simplify*
address the question 108.7 *relate to*
add taste to 495.10 *make taste*
add to 211.6 *add*; 190.5, 213.5 *make bigger*; 127.6 *subsume*
adduce 222.11 *circumstantiate*; 738.3 *reveal*
adduced 738.13 *displayed*
adducent 363.8 *attracting*
adduct 363.11 *attract*
adduction 363.2 *pulling power*
adductive 363.8 *attracting*
add up 27.91, 210.9, 211.6 *add*; 695.4 *be intelligible*
add up to 204.9 *be whole*; 694.10 *mean*; 210.10 *total*
add value 211.6 *add*
add water 374.5 *combine*; 433.30 *dilute*; 429.13 *moisten*
adenography 403.8 *science of structure*
adenology 403.8 *science of structure*
adenosine 34.12 *molecular biology*
adept 400.13 *excellent*; 396.11, 400.10 *expert*; 11.12 *occultist*; 485.6 *skilful*; 485.4 *skilled person*
adeptly 400.16 *masterfully*; 485.12 *skilfully*
adeptness 485.1 *skill*
adequacy 237.7 *instrumentality*; 216.6 *mediocrity*; 136.1 *qualification*; 609.3 *satisfactoriness*; 217.7 *sufficiency*
adequate **119.9**; 232.7 *complete*; 237.3 *instrumental*; 216.3 *mediocre*; 235.5 *not bad*; 334.13 *powerful*; 609.6 *satisfactory*; 217.1 *sufficient*
adequate amount 217.7 *sufficiency*
adequate income 217.7 *sufficiency*
adequately 217.9 *enough*; 334.18 *powerfully*; 609.12 *satisfactorily*
adequate size 797.14 *largeness*
adequate-size 797.7 *large*
adesnine 33.10 *nucleoside*
ad eundem 119.12 *equally*
à deux 198.9 *two*
adhere **267.6**; 632.17 *become a habit*; 228.6 *be stable*; 267.8 *be tenacious*; 638.10 *insist*; 373.13 *intercommunicate*; 360.6 *retain*; 430.10 *stick*
adherence 267.2 *tenacity*
adherence to the law 16.28 *legality*
adherent **267.4**; **664.5**; 267.9 *adhesive*; 267.5 *follower*; 413.8 *supporter*; 9.5 *worshipper*
adhere to 664.14 *follow*; 4.22 *propound a philosophy*; 211.7 *support*
adhesion **267.1**; 373.1 *connection*; 362.4 *friction*; 363.2 *pulling power*; 360.1 *retention*
adhesive **267.3**; **267.9**; **430.2**; 373.14 *connective*; 360.9 *retentive*; 360.3 *tools for gripping*; 430.8 *viscous*
adhesive label 743.3 *means of identification*
adhesively 363.13 *attractionally*; 373.17 *in connection with*; 362.16 *magnetically*; 360.11 *tenaciously*; 430.12 *viscously*
adhesiveness 267.1 *adhesion*; 430.1 *viscosity*
adhesive tape 267.3 *adhesive*; 373.6 *line*; 550.6 *medical covering*
ad hoc 478.7 *extempore*; 478.1 *improvised*
ad hoc measure 484.3 *expedient plan*; 352.1 *means*
ad hoc measures 478.4 *improvisation*
adiabatic 31.43 *atmospheric*
adiabatic change 28.39 *expansion*
adiabatic cooling 31.9 *atmospheric process*
adiabatic lapse rate 31.9 *atmospheric process*
adiabatic process 31.9 *atmospheric process*
adieu 313.14 *goodbye!*; 313.9 *parting*
a dime a dozen 793.9 *cheap*
ad infinitum 202.10 *infinitely*; 148.11 *lengthily*
adios! 313.14 *goodbye!*
adipocere 375.1 *disintegration*
adipose 158.16 *fat*; 268.13 *slippery*
adiposity 158.5 *fatness*
Adirondack Mountains 89.4 *US mountains*
adit 314.5 *entrance*; 317.2 *route*
adjacency 147.3 *juxtaposition*; 239.4 *nearness*
adjacent 147.10 *juxtaposed*; 239.2 *nearby*; 492.9 *touching*; 27.43 *triangle*
adjacently 147.14 *beside*
adjectival 5.44 *grammatical*
adjectival phrase 5.23 *phrase*
adjective 211.3 *additional item*; 5.35 *part of speech*
adjoin 492.12 *abut*; 147.18 *juxtapose*
adjoined 211.8 *additional*
adjoining 147.10 *juxtaposed*; 147.9 *near*; 492.9 *touching*
adjoining section 147.7 *interface*
adjourn 294.8 *delay*; 361.12 *interrupt*; 226.9 *pause*
adjourned 226.10 *finished*; 294.10 *held up*; 361.9 *interrupted*
adjournment 294.3 *delayed action*; 361.6 *interruption*
adjudge 16.76, 464.11 *judge*
adjudicate 16.76, 464.11 *judge*; 140.13 *rule*; 16.71 *try a case*
adjudication 464.1 *judgment*; 464.2 *verdict*
adjudicator 464.5 *judge*
adjunct 211.8 *additional*; 211.3 *additional item*; 223.4 *concomitant*; 438.7 *equipment*; 108.1 *relatedness*
adjunctive 211.8 *additional*
adjunctly 211.10 *additionally*
adjuration 756.1 *promise*; 710.1 *request*; 707.3 *vow*
adjuratory 756.12 *promised*; 710.9 *requesting*
adjure 710.6 *request*; 707.18 *vow*
adjust 698.31 *be accurate*; 422.10 *be adaptable*; 224.7 *be changed*; 224.8 *cause change*; 117.8 *comply*; 754.4 *compromise*; 119.11 *equalize*; 750.24 *harmonize*; 551.35 *make clothing*; 117.9 *make conform*; 298.10 *make regular*; 158.18 *measure*; 685.4 *moderate*; 136.15 *modify*; 324.8 *orient*; 749.4 *pacify*; 484.10 *plan out*; 243.4

prepare for action; 409.14 *rearrange*; 244.3 *rectify*; 393.1 *repair*
adjustability 422.2 *adaptability*
adjustable 422.7 *adaptive*; 117.11 *conformable*
adjustable spanner 438.1 *tool*
adjusted 422.7 *adaptive*; 754.6 *compromising*; 750.13 *harmonious*; 136.11 *modified*; 409.23 *rearranged*
adjusting 422.7 *adaptive*
adjustment 224.1 *change*; 754.1 *compromise*; 119.3 *equalization*; 750.4 *harmony*; 685.1 *moderation*; 136.5 *modification*; 324.3 *orientation*; 749.1 *pacification*; 117.3 *pliancy*; 244.6 *rectification*; 393.8 *repair*
adjust the clock 275.18
adjutant 392.11 *helper*
adjuvant 392.11 *helper*; 392.30 *helping*
Adler 36.29 *psychologist*
Adlerian 36.33 *Freudian*
Adlerian psychology 36.1 *psychology*
ad lib 635.17 *at will*; 217.9 *enough*; 478.7 *extempore*
ad-lib 478.4 *improvisation*; 478.3 *improvise*; 478.1 *improvised*; 21.35 *overact*
ad-libber 478.6 *improviser*
ad-libbing 478.4 *improvisation*
ad libitum 635.17 *at will*; 217.9 *enough*
ad man 480.12 *persuader*
admeasure 26.10 *measure*
admeasured 26.13 *measured*
admeasurement 26.1 *measurement*
administer 37.19; 340.4 *act*; 140.16 *direct*; 396.18 *have authority*; 579.1 *manage*; 35.19 *practise medicine*; 349.1 *use*
administer an oath 707.18 *vow*
administer correction 814.1 *punish*
administer justice 16.69 *have jurisdiction over*; 16.76 *judge*
administer the sacraments 752.15 *offer worship*
administer to 401.8 *serve*
administrate 340.4 *act*
administration 37.13; 340.1 *action*; 140.8 *authority*; 396.4 *governance*; 579.6 *governing body*; 12.1 *government*; 579.3 *management*; 631.8 *treatment*
administrational 16.48 *jurisdictional*
administration of justice 16.2 *jurisdiction*
administrative 340.6 *effective*; 12.9, 396.14 *governmental*; 16.48 *jurisdictional*; 140.9 *legal*; 579.17 *managerial*
administrative area 86.5 *state*
administrative control 579.4 *directorship*
administratively 16.86 *jurisdictionally*; 579.19 *managerially*; 396.24 *ministerially*; 12.14 *politically*
administrative officer 579.16 *official*
administrative receiver 769.7 *collector*
administrative unit 584.4 *military organization*
administrator 578.3 *agent*; 340.3 *doer*; 579.15 *manager*; 346.5 *operator*
admirable 617.8 *desirable*; 797.1 *good*; 669.21 *praiseworthy*; 619.8 *wonderful*; 235.1 *worthy*
Admirable Crichton 235.8 *exceller*; 485.4 *skilled person*
admirably 797.22 *well*; 235.11 *worthily*
admiral 400.7 *military leader*; 323.7 *nautical person*; 586.27 *naval man*; 397.6 *person in command*
Admiral of the Fleet 323.7 *nautical person*; 400.7 *military leader*; 586.27 *naval man*; 397.6 *person in command*
Admiral's Cup series 50.1 *sailing*
admiralty 586.22 *navy*
Admiralty chart 323.5 *navigation*; 91.5 *oceanography*
Admiralty Division 16.20 *British court*
admiration 667.2; **669.2**; 595.1 *liking*; 593.1 *love*; 619.1 *wonder*; 235.6 *worth*
admire 669.11 *approve*; 9.8 *idolatrize*; 595.7 *like*; 593.23 *love*; 667.15 *respect*; 667.16 *revere*; 619.9 *wonder*
admired 669.24; 593.21 *beloved*; 595.5 *likable*; 667.12 *respected*; 9.11 *worshipped*; 235.1 *worthy*
admirer 669.8; 593.9 *lover*; 413.8 *supporter*; 9.5 *worshipper*
admiring 630.7 *amazed*; 669.18 *approving*; 595.6 *liking*; 667.10 *reverent*; 619.6 *wondering*
admiringly 595.11; 669.25 *approvingly*
admissibility 127.1 *inclusion*; 370.3 *introduction*; 102.2 *possibleness*
admissible 370.14 *admissive*; 127.8 *included*; 757.8 *permitting*; 102.5 *possible*; 714.13 *vindicable*
admission 707.5; 370.1 *admittance*; 739.2 *divulgence*; 314.1 *entry*; 127.1 *inclusion*; 716.5 *legal evidence*; 769.4 *reception*; 314.4 *right of entry*
admission fee 790.3 *fee*
admission ticket 757.2 *permit*
admissive 370.14; 757.8 *permitting*
admissory 370.14 *admissive*
admit 370.7; **707.20**; **739.8**; 314.14 *enrol*; 127.4 *include*; 368.7 *install*; 788.7 *receive*; 769.10 *receive someone*
admit defeat 226.6 *cease*; 388.3 *submit*
admit no responsibility 758.12 *exempt oneself*
admit of 127.4 *include*
Admittance 370
admittance 370.1; 127.1 *inclusion*; 769.4 *reception*; 314.4 *right of entry*
admitted 739.10 *disclosed*; 632.12 *established*; 127.8 *included*; 769.13 *received*; 707.11 *stated*
admitting 769.4 *reception*
admix 412.8 *mix*
admixture 412.4; 211.1 *addition*; 412.1 *mixture*
admonish 713.5 *advise*; 670.20 *censure*; 814.1 *punish*; 711.5 *warn*
admonished 670.34 *censured*
admonisher 713.4 *adviser*; 711.4 *warner*
admonishment 670.7 *blame*; 711.1 *warning*
admonition 713.1 *advice*; 670.7 *blame*; 481.6 *dissuasion*; 713.3 *precept*; 814.7 *punishment*; 711.1 *warning*
admonitory 713.7 *advising*; 670.30 *censuring*; 814.19 *punitive*; 711.8 *warning*
adnate 83.10 *of fungi*
ad nauseam 620.8 *boringly*; 270.7 *diffusely*; 112.23 *repeatedly*
adnexed 83.10 *of fungi*
ado 342.1 *activity*; 328.5 *commotion*; 408.9 *disorder*; 576.4 *exertion*
adobe 24.9 *industrial ceramics*; 435.1 *materials*; 24.2 *raw material*; 550.8 *wall covering*
adolescence 561.4 *development*; 554.5 *life cycle*; 555.1 *youth*
adolescent 566.7 *person*; 555.11 *young*; 555.6 *young person*
Adonai 8.3 *God*
Adonis 545.4 *attractive male*; 567.4 *boyfriend*; 363.6 *charmer*
adopt 772.8; 669.12 *accept*; 469.1 *select*; 349.1 *use*; 370.9 *welcome*
adoptability 772.2 *adoption*
adoptable 772.12 *adoptive*
adopt affirmative action 391.6 *treat equally*
adopt a laissez-faire attitude 757.4 *be permissive*
adopted 772.12 *adoptive*; 772.11 *borrowed*; 469.15 *chosen*
adopting 772.12 *adoptive*
adoption 772.2; 669.1 *approval*; 469.6 *selection*
adoptive 772.12
adorability 593.4 *lovability*
adorable 595.5 *likable*; 593.22 *lovable*
adorably 593.30 *lovingly*; 595.10 *with great liking*
adoration 667.2 *admiration*; 595.1 *liking*; 593.1 *love*; 7.2 *religiousness*; 10.3 *rite of worship*; 9.1 *worship*
adorational 9.9 *worshipful*
adore 7.19 *be religious*; 595.7 *like*; 593.23 *love*; 10.19 *offer worship*; 667.16 *revere*; 9.7 *worship*
adored 593.21 *beloved*; 9.11 *worshipped*
adorer 593.9 *lover*; 9.5 *worshipper*
adoring 593.20 *amorous*; 667.10 *reverent*; 9.9 *worshipful*
adoringly 593.30 *lovingly*; 9.12 *worshipfully*
adorn 545.8 *beautify*; 244.1 *improve*; 542.12 *ornament*
adorned 547.14 *beautified*; 542.10 *ornate*
adornment 545.2 *beautiful thing*; 244.5 *improvement*; 542.1 *ornament*
adown 305.19 *down*
ADP 33.22 *bioenergetics*
adrenal 559.5 *of a secretion*
adrift 325.27 *astray*; 92.13 *continentally*; 372.22 *in isolation*; 50.20 *offshore*; 50.10 *sailing*; 377.25 *sprawled*; 372.17 *unjoined*
adroit 797.5 *proficient*; 485.6 *skilful*
adroitly 485.12, 797.25 *skilfully*
adroitness 797.12 *proficiency*; 485.1, 733.3 *skill*
adscititious 211.8 *additional*
adsorb 32.29, 370.13 *absorb*
adsorbed 32.43 *absorbed*
adsorbent 370.17 *absorbent*; 370.6 *sponge*
adsorption 370.5 *absorption*; 32.5 *process*; 32.20 *surface chemistry*
adulate 8.17 *deify*; 677.8 *flatter*; 669.14 *praise*; 9.7 *worship*
adulated 8.15 *deified*
adulation 667.2 *admiration*; 8.9 *deification*; 677.1 *flattery*; 669.3 *praise*; 9.1 *worship*
adulator 677.6 *flatterer*
adulatory 669.18 *approving*; 677.12 *flattering*; 667.10 *reverent*
adult 556.11; 243.20 *developed*; 258.9 *obscene*; 556.7 *older person*; 566.7 *person*
adult education 6.2 *educational system*
adult-education centre 6.12 *educational institution*
adulterate 699.25 *be fraudulent*; 224.8 *cause change*; 395.9 *change*; 367.4 *debase*; 433.30, 497.8 *dilute*; 417.6 *make sparse*; 245.3 *make worse*; 412.8 *mix*; 337.7 *weaken*
adulterated 433.22 *diluted*; 412.12 *mixed*; 417.2 *rarefied*; 497.5 *tasteless*
adulteration 224.1 *change*; 433.5 *dilution*; 699.8 *fraud*; 245.10 *impairment*; 231.5 *imperfection*; 412.1 *mixture*; 417.4 *rarefaction*; 497.1 *tastelessness*; 337.1 *weakness*
adulterer 718.3 *deceiver*; 227.6 *fickle person*; 796.8 *immoral man*; 639.15 *indecisive person*
adulteress 796.9 *immoral woman*
adulterous 639.2 *changeable*; 796.14 *lecherous*
adultery 571.3 *divorce court*; 796.4 *illicit love*; 593.8 *love affair*
adult fiction 740.6 *book publishing*
adulthood 556.2; 561.4 *development*; 554.5 *life cycle*
adult literature 796.2 *indecency*
adultness 556.2 *adulthood*
adult suffrage 469.11 *franchise*
adumbrate 721.14 *describe*; 523.14 *make dark*; 476.6 *propound*
advance 302.12; 310.2 *approach*; 312.10 *arrival*; 381.1 *attack*; 765.10 *augment*; 765.2 *augmentation*; 295.16 *avant-garde*; 348.4 *be an instrument*; 239.6 *be convenient*; 300.13 *be in motion*; 248.5 *be prosperous*; 246.6 *be successful*; 237.9 *be useful*; 772.1 *borrowing*; 134.3 *continue*; 344.12 *determine*; 300.17 *directional*; 797.20 *do good*; 765.4 *earnings*; 6.22 *educate*; 392.29 *finance*; 392.6 *financial assistance*; 302.10 *forward motion*; 302.8, 392.28 *further*; 244.2 *get better*; 300.19 *go!*; 302.1 *go forward*; 244.1 *improve*; 244.5 *improvement*; 213.1, 213.4 *increase*; 771.5 *lend*; 771.1 *lending*; 265.16 *make easy*; 300.3 *motion towards*; 330.21 *move forward*; 752.9 *offer*; 205.2 *particular*; 785.3 *pay*; 476.6 *propound*; 752.2 *tentative offer*; 742.6 *word*
advance against 381.1 *attack*
advance agent 21.27 *producer*
advance camp 62.1 *mountaineering*
advanced 295.16 *avant-garde*; 293.12 *early*; 302.17 *forward*; 295.10 *new*; 6.20 *refined*
advanced gas-cooled reactor 334.8, 437.7 *nuclear power*; 28.73 *nuclear reactor*
advanced guard 711.4 *warner*
advanced hour 294.2 *late hour*
advanced in years 556.14 *aged*; 296.11 *old*
advanced stage 293.3 *early stage*
advanced technology 438.6 *mechanics*
advanced thinker 295.9 *modern person*
advanced years 556.5 *old age*
advance earnings 765.4 *earnings*
advance guard 295.6 *avant-garde*; 167.1 *front*
advance man 293.4 *early comer*; 21.27 *producer*
advancement 302.12 *advance*; 6.1 *education*; 392.8 *furtherance*; 244.5 *improvement*; 213.1 *increase*; 348.1 *instrumentality*; 771.1 *lending*; 35.9 *surgery*
advance notice 475.3 *plan*; 711.1 *warning*
advance on 765.10 *augment*
advance one's own interests 683.6 *be selfish*
advance on royalties 772.1 *borrowing*; 771.1 *lending*
advance on salary 772.1 *borrowing*; 771.1 *lending*
advance party 586.14 *armed forces*
advance payment 785.1 *payment*
advances 593.6 *courtship*; 733.2 *salutation*
advance to meet 658.12 *greet*; 769.10 *receive someone*
advance to the rear 303.2, 303.11 *retreat*
advancing 310.8; 312.19 *approaching*; 300.17 *directional*; 302.17 *forward*; 244.16 *improving*; 348.6 *instrumental*; 771.1 *lending*
advantage 121.3; **164.4**; 239.6 *be convenient*; 392.21 *be helpful*; 237.8, 237.10, 797.13 *benefit*; 239.3 *convenience*; 66.2 *football play*; 392.28 *further*; 765.1 *gain*; 392.1 *help*; 395.1 *influence*; 631.9 *tactics*; 63.4 *tennis terms*; 349.6 *use*
advantaged 164.10
advantageous 392.34, 797.6 *beneficial*; 239.1 *convenient*; 617.8 *desirable*; 569.12 *favourable*; 237.4, 785.18 *profitable*; 246.14 *rewarding*; 349.10 *usable*; 235.4 *worthwhile*
advantageously 569.20 *favourably*; 765.20 *gainfully*; 392.36 *helpfully*; 246.16 *successfully*; 121.16 *superiorly*; 237.12, 349.11, 797.26 *usefully*
advantageousness 392.10 *helpfulness*
advection 31.9 *atmospheric process*
advection fog 31.33 *fog*
advection frost 31.36 *frost*
advective 31.43 *atmospheric*
Advent 10.16 *religious festival*
advent 525.1 *appearance*; 312.10 *arrival*; 283.6 *future event*
Adventist 7.5 *Christian*
adventitious 211.8 *additional*; 107.8 *chance*; 222.7 *circumstantial*; 100.8 *extraneous*
adventitious bud 77.8 *bud*
adventitiously 100.18 *extraneously*; 222.16 *relatively*
adventitious root 77.7 *root*
Advent season 292.1 *season*
adventure 613.8 *courageous act*; 354.1 *undertake*; 354.2 *undertaking*; 453.15 *unreliability*; 353.6 *venture*
adventurer 353.7 *attempter*; 644.3 *curious person*; 586.6 *militarist*; 227.7 *person who moves around*; 459.4, 615.3 *rash person*; 354.4 *volunteer*
adventure story 17.2, 721.5 *fiction*
adventurous 613.13; 644.5 *curious*; 354.6 *enterprising*; 615.4 *rash*
adventurously 353.10 *ambitiously*; 613.18 *courageously*; 644.8 *curiously*; 354.9 *enterprisingly*
adventurousness 613.4; 615.1 *rashness*
adventurous person 353.7 *attempter*
adverb 211.3 *additional item*; 5.35 *part of speech*
adverbial 5.44 *grammatical*
adverbially 5.52 *grammatically*
adverbial phrase 5.23 *phrase*
adversaria 744.3 *notes*
adversarial 586.33 *combative*; 113.24 *discordant*; 709.9 *dissenting*
adversary 586.1 *combatant*; 113.13 *opponent*
adversative 113.25 *contrary*
adverse 249.6; 357.14 *destructive*; 372.18 *disagreeable*; 236.5 *harmful*; 798.10 *inauspicious*; 240.1 *inconvenient*; 113.22 *oppositional*; 475.15 *presageful*; 637.2 *refusing*
adverse circumstances 249.1 *adversity*
adversely 372.23 *disagreeably*; 249.12 *in adversity*; 798.14 *inauspiciously*; 113.27 *opposingly*
Adversity 249
adversity 249.1; 798.2, 814.10 *affliction*; 798.3 *bad luck*; 264.6 *critical situation*; 236.11 *harmfulness*
advert 740.9 *advertisement*; 693.4 *mass communication*
advertise 692.30 *communicate*; 738.2 *display something*; 123.8 *make important*;

752.9 *offer*; 475.11 *predict*; 740.16 *publicize*; 738.3 *reveal*
advertised 692.34 *communicated*; 738.13 *displayed*; 752.17 *offered*
advertise for 740.16 *publicize*
advertisement **740.9**; 480.6 *advertising*; 693.4 *mass communication*; 778.3 *selling*; 738.8 *showplace*
advertisement curtain 21.19 *stage set*
advertiser 738.12 *displayer*; 693.9 *informant*; 483.7 *motivator*; 480.12 *persuader*; 740.10 *publicizer*
advertising **480.6**; 483.2 *inducement*; 738.10 *manifestation*; 480.5 *propaganda*
advertising account executive 740.10 *publicizer*
advertising agent 740.10 *publicizer*
advertorial 740.9 *advertisement*
Advice 713
advice **693.7**; **713.1**; 6.1 *education*; 483.2 *inducement*; 713.3 *precept*; 392.2 *support*; 711.1 *warning*
advice against 713.1 *advice*
advice column 740.3 *journalism*
advice for 713.1 *advice*
advisability 239.3 *convenience*; 617.2 *desirability*
advisable **713.8**; 469.15 *chosen*; 239.1 *convenient*; 237.1 *useful*; 711.8 *warning*
advisably **713.9**; 4.29 *wisely*
advise **392.23**; **713.5**; 616.6 *caution*; 579.2 *direct*; 394.20 *doctor*; 6.22 *educate*; 693.11 *inform*; 483.9 *motivate*; 480.15 *persuade*; 35.19 *practise medicine*; 476.6 *propound*; 711.5 *warn*
advise against 713.5 *advise*; 481.1 *dissuade*; 711.5 *warn*
advised 106.4 *deliberate*; 693.18 *informed*; 711.9 *warned*
advisedly 6.25 *educationally*; 482.13 *intentionally*; 4.29 *wisely*
adviser **392.14**; **713.4**; 579.13 *director*; 6.4 *educator*; 485.5 *expert*; 693.9 *informant*; 693.10 *informer*; 464.5 *judge*; 342.11 *meddler*; 748.3 *mediator*; 480.14, 483.7 *motivator*; 136.8 *qualified person*; 748.4 *representative*; 4.12 *sage*; 711.4 *warner*
advising **713.7**; 713.1 *advice*
advisory 713.7 *advising*; 734.13 *discussing*; 6.16 *educational*; 693.16 *informative*; 748.6 *mediatory*
advisory board 579.7 *council*
advocaat 558.7 *alcoholic drink*
advocacy 669.1 *approval*; 480.2 *flattery*; 483.2 *inducement*; 413.6 *moral support*; 392.9 *patronage*
advocate **669.7**; 392.23, 713.5 *advise*; 392.14, 713.4 *adviser*; 707.9 *affirmer*; 586.5 *arguer*; 413.14 *give moral support*; 16.13 *lawyer*; 16.70 *litigate*; 483.9 *motivate*; 480.12 *persuader*; 729.10 *speaker*; 669.13 *support*; 413.8 *supporter*; 714.5 *vindicator*
advocating 669.19 *supporting*
advocatory 413.9 *supportive*
adz 425.9 *sharp-edged thing*
adze 62.4 *climbing equipment*; 425.9 *sharp-edged thing*; 23.11 *woodworking tool*
aedile 579.16 *official*
a-effect 21.9 *dramaturgy*
Aegean 566.4 *modern human*
aegis 392.9 *patronage*; 252.2 *protection*
aegrotat 758.4 *licence*
aeolian 31.47 *windy*
Aeolian mode 18.20 *key*
aeon 279.2 *a long time*; 275.5 *indefinite period*; 275.4 *term*; 276.2 *time period*
aeonian 279.9 *agelong*
aeons 277.5 *long duration*
Aepyornis 72.8 *extinct bird*
aerage 434.6 *ventilation*
aerate **432.26**; **434.20**; 415.10 *lighten*; 257.6 *make hygienic*; 581.1 *refresh*; 434.23 *whisk*
aerated 434.18 *bubbly*; 432.21 *gassy*; 415.3 *lightening*
aerating 415.3 *lightening*
aeration **434.11**; 415.6 *lightening*; 581.5 *refreshment*; 432.10 *vaporization*; 434.6 *ventilation*
aerator 434.7 *ventilator*
aerial **434.14**; 432.17, 434.12 *airy*; 692.17 *antenna*; 154.9 *high*; 19.24 *pictorial*; 68.12 *ski*; 68.1 *skiing*
aerial bombardment 381.13 *air attack*
aerial perspective 19.4 *treatment*
aerial photography 41.1 *photography*
aerial reconnaissance 322.1 *aviation*
aerial root 77.7 *root*
aerial warfare 585.8 *warfare*
aerie 72.14 *nest*
aeriferous 434.12 *airy*
aerification 432.10 *vaporization*
aeriform 434.12 *airy*
aerify 432.26, 434.20 *aerate*
aerily **432.28**
aeriness **432.9**
aeriolate 83.10 *of fungi*
aeroballistics 322.2 *aeronautics*
aerobatic 322.9 *aeronautical*
aerobatically 322.11 *aeronautically*
aerobatics 322.1 *aviation*
aerobe 34.3 *organism*
aerobic 34.22 *physiological*
aerobic respiration 34.6 *cell biology*; 33.24 *respiration*
aerobics 300.11 *bodily movement*; 22.1 *dancing*; 576.5 *exercise*; 244.9 *physical improvement*
aerodontalgia 432.6 *aerogastria*
aerodrome 322.4 *airport*; 312.15 *destination*
aerodynamic 322.9 *aeronautical*; 432.22 *aerostatic*; 28.98 *physical*
aerodynamically 322.11 *aeronautically*; 432.29 *aerostatically*; 28.100 *physically*
aerodynamics 432.12 *aerostatics*; 28.2 *classical physics*
aero engine 38.11 *engine*
aerofoil 228.3 *stabilizer*
aerogastria **432.6**
aerogenesis 432.6 *aerogastria*
aerogram 692.3 *correspondence*
aerolite 29.20 *meteor*
aerology 31.1 *meteorology*
aerometer 26.8 *meter*; 416.3 *relative density*; 432.15 *vaporimeter*
aerometric 26.16 *micrometric*
aerometry 26.2 *micrometry*
aeronaut 305.8 *descender*
aeronautical **322.9**
aeronautical engineering 322.2 *aeronautics*; 38.1 *engineering*; 38.3 *mechanical engineering*
aeronautically **322.11**
aeronautics **322.2**
aeroneurosis 432.6 *aerogastria*
aero-optics 322.2 *aeronautics*
aeropause 322.5 *flight*
aerophagia 432.6 *aerogastria*
aerophone 18.25 *musical instrument*
aeroplane 322.8 *aircraft*; 586.31 *military aircraft*; 319.5 *transportable*
aerosol 37.10 *inhalant*; 32.3 *phase*; 433.12 *sprinkler*; 432.11 *vaporizer*
aerospace 141.2 *empty space*
aerosphere **434.2**
aerostat 322.8 *aircraft*; 432.13 *gas balloon*
aerostatic **432.22**
aerostatically **432.29**
aerostatics **432.12**
aerothermodynamics 322.2 *aeronautics*
aerotowing 322.7 *miscellaneous aviation terms*
aery 432.17, 434.12 *airy*
Aeschylean tragedy 21.11 *tragedy*
Aesculapian 394.18 *medical*
Aesculapius 394.15 *healer*
Aeshma 8.7 *devil*
Aesma 8.6 *angel*
aesthesia 590.1 *feeling*; 492.1 *touch*
aesthesis 492.1 *touch*
aesthete 549.4 *refined person*; 488.4 *someone or something that feels*
aesthetic 19.26 *artistic*; 545.5 *beautiful*; 4.11 *follower of a doctrine*; 4.14 *of a philosophy*; 549.5 *refined*; 488.7 *susceptible*
aesthetically 19.31 *artistically*
aesthetically pleasing 545.5 *beautiful*
aestheticism 4.7 *school of thought*
aesthetics 4.6 *branch of philosophy*
aestival 292.11 *summer*
aestivate 343.13 *sleep*
aestivating 343.4 *not awake*
aestivation 343.9 *sleep*; 292.3 *summer*
aetiology 35.3 *medical specialty*
AEW 322.6 *flight control*
afar 145.10 *distantly*
a far cry from 116.4 *dissimilar*
AFC 46.1 *football*
a few 206.1, 206.5 *few*; 207.1 *plurality*
affability 241.8 *amiability*; 650.1 *benevolence*; 658.1 *courtesy*; 654.1, 657.2 *sociability*; 654.2 *social ambition*
affable 650.6 *benevolent*; 658.7 *courteous*; 241.2 *likable*; 654.15, 657.8 *sociable*
affably 658.14 *courteously*; 654.18 *sociably*
affair 346.3 *business*; 593.8 *love affair*; 447.3 *matter of interest*; 354.2 *undertaking*
affair of the heart 593.8 *love affair*
affairs 340.2 *deed*; 631.8 *treatment*
affect 676.4 *be affected*; 123.7 *be important*; 224.8 *cause change*; 631.11 *conduct oneself*; 627.11 *excite pity*; 395.8 *influence*; 699.24 *pretend*; 108.7 *relate to*; 345.5 *show an effect*; 229.4 *tend*
Affectation 676
affectation **542.2**; 622.3 *conceit*; 631.1 *conduct*; 340.2 *deed*; 724.3 *inelegance*; 699.7 *pretence*; 795.4 *self-righteousness*; 724.1 *style*; 476.1 *supposition*; 468.1 *underestimation*
affected **676.3**; 673.13 *boastful*; 673.11 *cocky*; 622.17 *conceited*; 260.23 *diseased*; 329.13 *exaggerated*; 544.9 *inelegant*; 795.10 *moralistic*; 542.10 *ornate*; 236.4 *poor*; 486.2 *unskilled*
affectedly **676.5**; 673.21 *cockily*; 468.6 *pessimistically*
affectedness **676.1**
affectibility 591.5 *sensitivity*
affectible 591.1 *sensitive*
affecting 395.12 *appealing*; 590.14 *emotive*; 627.7 *pitiful*; 699.34 *pretending*
affectingly 590.20 *with feeling*
affection 669.2 *admiration*; 703.2 *demonstrativeness*; 595.1 *liking*; 593.1 *love*
affectionate 650.6 *benevolent*; 703.10 *demonstrative*; 569.8 *friendly*; 595.5 *likable*; 593.17 *loving*; 654.15 *sociable*
affectionately 650.10 *benevolently*; 703.21 *demonstratively*; 569.17 *in friendship*; 593.30 *lovingly*; 654.18 *sociably*; 595.10 *with great liking*
affectionateness 593.3 *lovingness*
affections 590.3 *feelings*
affective psychosis 36.11 *psychosis*
affiance 570.15 *marry*
affianced 570.22 *marriageable*; 756.6 *someone promised*
affiche 740.9 *advertisement*
affidavit 744.2 *certificate*; 716.5 *legal evidence*; 16.5 *litigation*; 756.1 *promise*; 707.3 *vow*
affiliate 750.22 *form an alliance*; 747.16 *join*
affiliated 750.11 *allied*; 747.19 *associating*; 108.4 *related*
affiliation 750.2 *alliance*; 747.7 *association*; 764.2 *participation*; 108.1 *relatedness*; 654.1 *sociability*
affine transformation 27.48 *transformation*
affinity 750.1 *accord*; 229.2 *attitude*; 363.1 *attraction*; 569.3 *familiarity*; 595.1 *liking*; 108.1 *relatedness*; 115.1 *similarity*; 570.8 *spouse*
affirm **707.17**; 739.8 *admit*; 450.7 *believe*; 750.28 *consent*; 716.11 *give evidence*; 16.68 *legislate*; 452.21 *make certain*; 694.10 *mean*; 756.7 *promise*; 703.17 *prove*; 729.11 *speak*; 701.15 *state*; 476.5 *suppose*; 454.3 *testify*
affirmance 707.1 *affirmation*
affirmant 707.9 *affirmer*
Affirmation 707
affirmation **707.1**; 452.13 *confirmation*; 750.7 *consent*; 739.2 *divulgence*; 726.1 *emphasis*; 123.1 *importance*; 16.31 *legislation*; 701.3 *line of argument*; 16.5 *litigation*; 738.10 *manifestation*; 27.63 *mathematical logic*; 756.1 *promise*; 703.4 *proof*; 729.7 *utterance*; 454.4 *verification*
affirmative **707.10**; 750.17 *consenting*; 726.3 *emphatic*; 694.6 *meaningful*; 756.12 *promised*
affirmative action 119.3 *equalization*
affirmatively **707.23**; 750.39 *with consent*
affirmativeness 452.13 *confirmation*
affirmatory 707.10 *affirmative*
affirmed 701.11 *logical*; 703.13 *proven*; 707.11 *stated*; 454.10 *verified*
affirmer **707.9**
affirming 707.10 *affirmative*; 750.17 *consenting*
affirmingly 750.39 *with consent*
affirm the contrary 708.11 *rebut*
affix 211.6 *add*; 211.3 *additional item*; 5.35 *part of speech*
affixing 5.39 *of language*
affixing language 5.10 *language type*
affix to 267.7 *cause to adhere*
affixture 211.1 *addition*
afflatus 477.2 *inspiration*; 17.13 *poetic genius*
afflict 798.11 *be evil*; 814.1 *punish*
afflicted **798.8**; 491.7 *feeling pain*
afflicted with boredom 620.5 *bored*
affliction **798.2**; **814.10**; 249.1 *adversity*; 260.2 *illness*; 491.1 *pain*
affluence 314.2 *influx*; 217.8 *plenty*; 248.1 *prosperity*; 90.6 *river flow*; 246.1 *success*; 781.5 *wealth*
affluent 90.10 *fluvial*; 217.2 *plentiful*; 248.8 *prosperous*; 90.1 *river*; 781.1 *wealthy*; 765.17 *well-off*
affluently 90.13 *fluently*; 765.20 *gainfully*; 248.9 *prosperously*; 781.16 *wealthily*
affluent society 248.1 *prosperity*
afflux 314.2 *influx*; 90.6 *river flow*
affluxion 314.2 *influx*
afford 787.1 *expend*; 750.30 *grant*; 217.6 *have enough*; 436.5 *provision*; 777.1 *purchase*
affordability 793.1 *cheapness*
affordable 793.9 *cheap*
afforded 750.19 *granted*
afford sanctuary 252.10 *protect*
afforestation 79.5 *forestry*
afforested 79.16 *wooded*
affray 701.1 *argument*; 408.9 *disorder*
affriction 365.1 *friction*
affright 612.1 *fear*; 612.13 *frighten*; 612.7 *frightened*
affront 659.7 *be discourteous*; 661.5 *defy*; 660.7, 668.5, 668.23 *insult*; 624.2 *offence*; 624.9 *offend*; 242.5 *unpleasantness*
affronted 624.15 *resentful*
affusion 10.5 *Christian rite*; 429.5 *sprinkle*; 433.8 *watering*
afghan 551.25 *accessories*; 550.5 *body covering*
aficionado 593.9 *lover*; 9.5 *worshipper*
afield 145.10 *distantly*
aflame 522.16 *bright*
a flat spin 612.2 *fearfulness*
AFL-CIO 15.3 *organized labour*
afloat 90.11 *flooded*; 323.11 *nautical*; 91.11, 323.12 *nautically*
afoot 342.19 *busy*; 243.17 *developing*; 447.13 *problematically*
aforementioned 129.11 *prior*
aforenamed 129.11 *prior*
aforesaid 129.11 *prior*
aforethought 106.4 *deliberate*; 482.12 *intended*
aforetime 3.24 *historically*; 284.22 *in the past*
a fortiori 4.16 *dialectical*
afp test 561.7 *obstetrics*
afraid 614.3 *cowardly*; 612.7 *frightened*
afraid of company 655.9 *shy*
afraid of one's shadow 612.8 *fearful*
A-frame 176.1 *angle*; 413.2 *supporting part*
A-framed 176.7 *angular*
a free hand 657.4 *freedom*
afreet 8.7 *devil*
afresh 112.24, 295.22 *again*
Africa 92.1 *continent*; 493.8 *hot place*
African 5.11 *family of languages*
African-American 1.6 *race*; 1.13 *racial*
African dish **25.53**
Africanism 5.26 *dialect*
Africanize 760.12 *naturalize*
Africanized 760.17 *naturalized*
Afro 547.8 *haircut*
Afro-American 1.6 *race*; 1.13 *racial*
Afro-Asiatic 5.11 *family of languages*
Afro-Caribbean 1.6 *race*; 1.13 *racial*
Afro-Cuban 18.8 *jazz*
aft 168.9 *in the rear*; 50.10 *sailing*
after **283.15**; 290.4 *afternoon*; 168.9 *in the rear*; 633.18 *pursuant to*
after a fashion 317.16 *how*
after ages 283.1 *future time*
after a while 294.17 *later*
after back rest 50.8 *punting*
afterbirth 561.7 *obstetrics*
aftercare 394.13 *therapy*; 35.8 *treatment*
afterdamp 432.3 *miasma*
after dark 291.7 *evening*
after death **582.8**; 582.23 *fatally*; 301.10 *motionlessly*

after-dinner 263.4 *at ease*; 25.56 *culinary*
after-dinner speaker 729.10 *speaker*
after-dinner speech 729.8 *speech*
aftereffect 211.3 *additional item*; 345.1 *effect*; 215.1 *remainder*
afterglow 215.1 *remainder*
aftergrowth 562.1 *fertility*
after him! 633.19
after-image 717.6 *image*; 525.4 *something that appears*
afterlife 464.4 *judgment day*; 554.5 *life cycle*; 101.1 *nonmaterial world*; 582.14 *the spiritual world*
after life's fitful fever 301.10 *motionlessly*
aftermath 345.1 *effect*; 562.1 *fertility*; 132.4 *repercussion*; 289.9 *sequel*
aftermost 168.9 *in the rear*
afternoon 290.4; **290.7**; 291.6, 291.7 *evening*
afternoons 111.20 *regularly*
afternoon tea 290.4 *afternoon*; 291.4 *evening thing*; 557.12 *meal*; 654.3 *meeting*
after one's heart 593.21 *beloved*
afterpains 491.2 *painful condition*
afterpart 50.3 *parts of a sailing boat*; 168.1 *rear*
afterpiece 168.1 *rear*; 21.8 *scene*
afterquarters 168.1 *rear*
afters 498.3 *dessert*; 25.9 *dish*; 557.14 *mouthful*
aftershaft 72.17 *plumage*
after-shave 502.2 *fragrant thing*
aftershock 30.22 *seismic activity*
after-shove 50.8 *punting*
aftertaste 495.1 *taste*
after this fashion 317.16 *how*
afterthought 294.3 *delayed action*; 479.6 *equivocation*; 717.6 *image*; 168.1 *rear*
afterwards 283.15 *after*
afterword 168.1 *rear*; 289.9 *sequel*
aft mast 50.3 *parts of a sailing boat*
a full plate 342.6 *business*
Aga™ 25.5 *cooker*
again 112.24; **295.22**; 111.18 *identically*; 198.19 *twice*
again and again 297.1 *frequently*; 112.23 *repeatedly*
against 347.5 *counter*; 364.12 *defensively*; 670.26 *disagreeing*; 113.31 *opposed to*
against one's will 387.11 *under subjection*; 637.17 *unwillingly*
against the clock 262.6 *hastily*
against-the-clock competition 59.9 *jumping*
against the grain 303.29 *in reverse*; 420.14 *roughly*; 637.17 *unwillingly*
against the law 16.89 *guiltily*; 16.55 *illegal*; 16.82 *illegally*
against the nap 420.14 *roughly*
against the rules 118.15 *irregular*
against the stream 264.25 *difficultly*
against the tide 113.30 *contrariwise*
against the wind 264.25 *difficultly*; 324.11 *in all directions*
Agama 7.12 *religious text*
agamist 572.4 *celibate person*
Agape 593.1 *love*; 10.16 *religious festival*
agape 308.12 *open*; 619.7 *wide-eyed*
agapistic 593.17 *loving*
agar 84.5 *algal product*; 33.4 *polysaccharide*
agarics 83.3 *fungi*
agate 541.5 *variegated thing*
agateware 24.1 *ceramics*
Age 556
age 556.1; **556.17**; 279.2 *a long time*; 760.8 *be transformed*; 245.1 *deteriorate*; 243.7 *develop*; 296.17 *grow old*; 275.5 *indefinite period*; 296.1 *oldness*; 276.2 *time period*
aged 556.14; 554.12 *alive*; 533.2 *grey-haired*; 296.11 *old*
age group 285.5 *contemporary*; 376.18 *generation*; 2.6 *social group*
ageing 556.12; 245.12 *deteriorated*
ageism 465.3 *injustice*; 466.4 *social discrimination*
ageist 556.15 *age-related*; 466.7 *bigot*; 466.10 *discriminatory*; 622.23 *prejudiced*; 465.8 *unjust*
agelong 279.9
Agence France Presse 741.7 *press agency*; 693.8 *source of information*
agency 340.1 *action*; 348.2 *instrument*; 348.1 *instrumentality*; 579.3 *management*; 352.1 *means*; 717.8 *representative*
agenda 406.5 *divisions*; 447.2 *issue*; 220.5 *list of appointments*; 484.1 *plan*; 106.6 *premeditation*
ageneric 139.17 *exceptional*
agent 398.6; **578.3**; 348.3 *assistant*; 224.5 *changer*; 344.4 *contributing factor*; 344.8 *contributor*; 398.1 *delegate*; 449.12 *discoverer*; 340.3 *doer*; 122.6 *inferior*; 579.15 *manager*; 480.14 *motivator*; 346.5 *operator*; 21.27 *producer*; 740.12 *publisher*; 717.8, 748.4 *representative*; 778.10 *salesman*; 762.2 *substitute person*; 778.12 *wholesaler*
agential 348.7 *causal*
agent of destruction 357.7
Agent Orange 357.7 *agent of destruction*
agent provocateur 662.8 *agitator*; 700.18 *decoy*; 480.14, 483.7 *motivator*
age of Aquarius 248.3 *time of plenty*
age of consent 570.4 *marriageability*
Age of Enlightenment 284.5 *historical period*
age of puberty 555.1 *youth*
Age of Reason 284.5 *historical period*; 3.10 *past age*
age-old 296.12 *olden*
age-related 556.15
ages 275.5 *indefinite period*; 277.5 *long duration*
ages ago 296.19 *anciently*; 284.22 *in the past*
age set 1.5 *anthropological concept*
agglomerate 267.6 *adhere*; 376.37 *assemble*; 376.48 *cumulate*
agglomeration 267.1 *adhesion*; 376.25 *assemblage*; 374.3 *assembly*
agglutinate 211.6 *add*; 267.7 *cause to adhere*; 360.6 *retain*
agglutination 211.1 *addition*; 267.1 *adhesion*
agglutinative 211.8 *additional*; 5.39 *of language*
agglutinative language 5.10 *language type*
aggrandize 727.8 *enlarge*; 190.5, 213.5 *make bigger*
aggrandized 727.13 *enlarged*
aggrandizement 727.2 *enlargement*; 190.1 *growth*; 213.1 *increase*
aggravate 607.6; 594.16 *cause hate*; 264.22 *cause trouble*; 727.7 *exaggerate*; 624.14 *make angry*; 213.5 *make bigger*; 380.9 *make violent*; 245.3 *make worse*; 624.9 *offend*
aggravated 607.4; 245.12 *deteriorated*; 727.12 *exaggerated*; 624.15 *resentful*
aggravating 607.5; 264.13 *inconvenient*
aggravatingly 624.17 *resentfully*
aggravation 607.1; 242.7 *dissension*; 727.1 *exaggeration*; 245.10 *impairment*; 213.1 *increase*; 624.1 *resentment*; 264.8 *snag*
aggregate 27.91 *add*; 27.15 *addition*; 376.37 *assemble*; 374.9 *assembled*; 374.3 *assembly*; 374.5 *combine*; 376.48 *cumulate*; 194.4 *mathematical result*; 416.4 *solid body*; 203.4, 210.10 *total*; 204.2 *whole thing*
aggregated 374.9 *assembled*
aggregate fruit 80.2 *botanical fruit*
aggregation 376.25 *assemblage*; 374.3 *assembly*
aggresively 381.26
aggression 624.4 *anger*; 381.11 *attack*; 585.5 *bellicosity*; 336.1 *strength*; 380.1 *violence*
aggressive 381.21; 342.18 *active*; 624.16 *angry*; 673.11 *cocky*; 586.33 *combative*; 661.8 *defying*; 751.9 *disagreeing*; 659.5 *discourteous*; 613.11 *militant*; 584.8 *military*; 242.2 *objectionable*; 336.11 *strong in spirit*; 338.4 *vigorous*; 380.6 *violent*; 585.16 *warlike*; 585.15 *warring*
aggressively 586.41; 673.21 *cockily*; 659.9 *discourteously*; 661.10 *in defiance*; 751.11 *in disagreement*; 336.14 *strongly*; 242.13 *unpleasantly*
aggressiveness 381.11 *attack*; 585.5 *bellicosity*; 673.3 *cockiness*; 751.1 *disagreement*; 342.4 *energy*; 613.2 *heroism*; 242.6 *objectionability*; 336.1 *strength*
aggressive war 585.1 *war*
aggressor 381.19 *attacker*; 586.1 *combatant*; 242.9 *unpleasant person*
aggrevated burglary 774.1 *stealing*
aggrieve 798.11 *be evil*; 236.14 *ill-treat*; 624.9 *offend*
aggro 408.9 *disorder*; 607.3 *nuisance*; 242.8 *quarrel*
aghast 612.7 *frightened*; 619.6 *wondering*
agile 342.18 *active*; 485.6 *skilful*; 332.1 *swift*
agilely 332.14 *swiftly*
agility 332.8 *speed*
agin 670.26 *disagreeing*; 113.31 *opposed to*
agio 791.1 *discount*; 14.1, 780.7 *finance*
agiotage 14.1, 780.7 *finance*; 776.4 *trade*
agitate 327.22; 488.13 *arouse sensation*; 342.12 *be active*; 662.16 *be subversive*; 328.7 *disturb*; 703.19 *protest*; 326.9 *vibrate*
agitate against 753.8 *cause mischief*; 347.3 *counteract*
agitated 327.15; 342.18 *active*; 420.4 *bumpy*; 328.12 *disturbed*; 612.8 *fearful*; 300.16 *moving*; 488.7 *susceptible*; 380.6 *violent*
agitated depression 36.13 *depression*
agitated for 243.17 *developing*
agitatedly 327.27
agitating 703.14 *demonstrating*; 300.17 *directional*; 326.14 *vibrating*
Agitation 327
agitation 327.1; 342.1 *activity*; 300.5 *circuition*; 753.2 *disorder*; 328.1 *disturbance*; 612.2 *fearfulness*; 262.4 *haste*; 227.2 *irresolution*; 300.2 *momentum*; 342.7 *restlessness*; 488.1 *sensation*; 662.3 *subversion*; 326.2 *vibration*; 380.1 *violence*
agitator 327.14; **662.8**; 579.14 *leader*; 480.14, 483.7 *motivator*; 113.11 *opposer*; 703.8, 753.4 *protester*; 244.12 *reformer*; 408.11 *troublemaker*; 380.4 *violent creature*
agitprop 483.2 *inducement*; 480.5 *propaganda*; 662.3 *subversion*
aglow 522.15 *lucent*
agnate 108.4 *related*
agnomen 721.8 *name*
agnostic 451.5 *disbeliever*; 451.6 *disbelieving*; 4.11 *follower of a doctrine*; 708.17 *negative*; 708.9 *negativist*; 4.14 *of a philosophy*; 705.9 *questioner*; 705.15 *sceptical*; 453.1 *uncertain*; 453.17 *uncertain person*
agnostically 705.23 *questioningly*
agnosticism 708.2 *rejection*; 4.7 *school of thought*; 453.10 *suspicion*; 451.4 *unbelief*; 705.6 *uncertainty*
Agnus Dei 10.9 *prayer*
ago 3.24 *historically*; 284.22 *in the past*
agog 619.7 *wide-eyed*
agogic 18.30 *harmonic*
agogics 729.6 *phonetics*
agon 21.9 *dramaturgy*
agonic line 30.45 *magnetic pole*
agonist 586.1 *combatant*
agonistic 586.33 *combative*; 45.5 *sporting*
agonistically 586.41 *aggressively*
agonize 491.9 *feel pain*; 236.14 *ill-treat*
agonized 491.7 *feeling pain*
agonize over 612.14 *worry*
agonizing 491.5 *painful*
agony 236.11 *harmfulness*; 491.1 *pain*; 602.1 *sorrow*
agony aunt 721.10 *descriptive writer*; 740.11 *newspaperman*
agony column 740.3 *journalism*
a good credit risk 781.2 *solvent*
a good few 208.6 *many*
a good hand 107.2 *luck*
a good many 208.6 *many*
a good time 490.4 *pleasurable things*
agora 779.6 *marketplace*
agoraphobia 655.2 *shyness*
agrarian 43.19 *agricultural*
agrarianism 43.1 *agriculture*
a greater number 207.1 *plurality*
agree 669.12 *accept*; 706.21 *answer to*; 750.21 *be in accord*; 480.18 *be persuaded*; 115.10 *be similar*; 111.7 *be the same*; 636.13 *be willing*; 409.17 *come to an arrangement*; 374.6 *come together*; 117.8 *comply*; 117.7 *conform*; 750.28 *consent*; 516.8 *harmonize*; 749.5 *make peace*; 354.1 *undertake*
agreeability 593.4 *lovability*
agreeable 750.20; 117.13 *compliant*; 755.7 *contractual*; 658.7 *courteous*; 111.13 *equivalent*; 569.8 *friendly*; 589.7 *peaceful*; 545.6 *personable*; 241.1, 490.6 *pleasant*; 388.5 *submitting*; 636.1 *willing*
agreeableness 658.1 *courtesy*; 545.1 *gorgeousness*; 241.6 *pleasantness*
agreeably 754.8 *compromisingly*; 755.8 *contractually*; 706.26 *correspondingly*; 658.14 *courteously*; 750.33 *harmoniously*; 111.18 *identically*; 569.17 *in friendship*; 749.7 *pacifically*; 241.15 *pleasantly*; 636.16 *willingly*
agree beforehand 106.2 *premeditate*
agreed 754.6 *compromising*; 750.17 *consenting*; 755.7 *contractual*; 750.10 *in accord*; 108.5 *interrelated*; 111.12 *same*
agreed result 106.6 *premeditation*
agreed to 755.7 *contractual*
agreeing 529.11 *colourful*; 754.6 *compromising*; 117.12 *conforming*; 750.17 *consenting*; 706.15 *correspondent*; 111.13 *equivalent*; 516.7 *harmonious*; 750.10 *in accord*; 388.1 *submission*
agree in meaning 694.10 *mean*
Agreement 750
agreement 409.10; 750.1 *accord*; 669.1 *approval*; 776.9 *bargaining*; 754.1 *compromise*; 117.1 *conformity*; 750.7 *consent*; 354.3, 755.1 *contract*; 374.2 *cooperation*; 706.8 *correspondence*; 111.2 *equivalence*; 747.2 *fellowship*; 749.1 *pacification*; 108.1 *relatedness*; 111.1 *sameness*; 115.1 *similarity*; 5.30 *syntax*
agree on a verdict 16.76 *judge*
agree to 776.3 *bargain*
agree to anything 664.10 *knuckle under*
agree to differ 751.5 *disagree*; 749.5 *make peace*
agree to disagree 749.5 *make peace*
agree with 119.10 *be equal*; 241.13 *give pleasure*
agree with one 257.5 *by hygienic*
agrestic 43.19 *agricultural*
agribusiness 43.1 *agriculture*
agricultural 43.19; 356.11 *productive*
agricultural dance 22.4 *historic dancing*
agricultural engineering 38.1 *engineering*
agriculturalist 43.15 *agriculturist*; 243.15 *preparer*
agricultural labourer 578.1 *worker*
agriculturally 43.22
agricultural meteorology 31.1 *meteorology*
agricultural sale 43.1 *agriculture*
agricultural science 43.1 *agriculture*
Agriculture 43
agriculture 43.1; 356.2 *manufacture*
agriculturist 43.15
Agrionia 10.16 *religious festival*
Agrippa 56.5 *golf ball*
agrobiological 43.19 *agricultural*
agrobiologist 43.15 *agriculturist*; 77.12 *plant scientist*
agrobiology 43.1 *agriculture*; 77.10 *plant science*
agrochemicals 43.14 *pest control*
agroecological 43.19 *agricultural*
agroecologist 43.15 *agriculturist*
agroecology 43.1 *agriculture*
agroecosystem 43.1 *agriculture*
agroforestry 43.1 *agriculture*; 79.5 *forestry*
agrogeologist 43.15 *agriculturist*
agrogeology 43.1 *agriculture*
agrological 43.19 *agricultural*
agrologist 43.15 *agriculturist*
agrology 43.1 *agriculture*
agromania 461.4 *delusion*
agronomic 43.19 *agricultural*
agronomics 43.1 *agriculture*
agronomist 43.15 *agriculturist*
agronomy 43.1 *agriculture*
agroscience 43.1 *agriculture*
aground 312.22 *on arrival*; 228.9 *stable*
ague 327.7 *shake*; 260.3 *symptom*; 260.7 *tropical disease*
aguey 327.18 *shaky*
aguish 260.23 *diseased*
AH 275.29 *one day*
aha 446.25 *got it!*
a handful 207.1 *plurality*
ahead 329.17; 164.10 *advantaged*; 145.10 *distantly*; 129.21 *first*; 302.19 *forward*; 283.11 *future*; 167.11 *in front*; 121.12 *superior*
ahead of its time 293.17 *early*
ahead of oneself 293.17 *early*
ahead of one's time 288.18 *out of chronological order*; 293.16 *premature*; 293.20 *prematurely*; 288.11 *too early*
ahead of schedule 293.12, 293.17 *early*
ahead of the times 286.2 *occurring at a different time*
ahead of time 765.18 *acquisitional*; 293.12, 293.17 *early*; 288.18 *out of chronological order*; 288.11 *too early*

ahimsa 749.1 *pacification;* 589.1 *peace;* 4.7 *school of thought*
A horizon 30.36 *soil*
Ahriman 8.7 *devil*
a-hull 50.20 *offshore*
a hundred and one 208.7 *myriad*
Ahura Mazda 8.3 *God*
AID 561.3 *propagation*
aid **608.2**; 340.4 *act;* 608.11 *assist;* 348.4 *be an instrument;* 650.9 *be charitable;* 239.6 *be convenient;* 237.9 *be useful;* 608.4, 652.5 *charity;* 392.7 *convenience;* 636.14 *cooperate;* 344.12 *determine;* 302.8 *further;* 768.2 *gift;* 679.11 *give;* 413.14 *give moral support;* 813.3, 813.10 *grant;* 392.1, 392.17 *help;* 392.11 *helper;* 348.1 *instrumentality;* 790.8 *levy;* 366.7 *lift;* 265.16 *make easy;* 413.6 *moral support;* 62.8 *mountaineering;* 366.3 *promote;* 252.2 *protection;* 394.1, 394.19 *remedy;* 237.5 *usefulness*
aid and abet 392.17 *help;* 483.10 *manipulate;* 747.12 *reciprocate*
aid climbing 62.1 *mountaineering*
aide 713.4 *adviser;* 348.3 *assistant;* 398.4 *deputy;* 392.11, 608.5 *helper;* 413.8 *supporter*
aide-de-camp 608.5 *helper*
aide-mémoire 462.4 *reminder*
aider 344.8 *contributor;* 384.13 *defender;* 392.11 *helper;* 652.3 *philanthropist*
aider and abettor 480.14, 483.7 *motivator*
aid for poor sight **519.3**
aid-giving 652.6 *philanthropic*
aiding 392.30 *helping;* 348.6 *instrumental;* 652.6 *philanthropic;* 401.9 *serving*
aiding and abetting 806.1 *guilt;* 747.3 *mutual relationship*
AIDS 357.7 *agent of destruction;* 260.4 *disease;* 260.14 *venereal disease*
AIDS-related complex 260.14 *venereal disease*
aid worker 652.3 *philanthropist;* 636.11 *willing worker*
aiguillette 743.4 *insignia*
AIH 561.3 *propagation*
aikido **52.10**; 52.1 *combat sports*
aikido grade 52.10 *aikido*
aikido technique 52.10 *aikido*
aikido throws 52.10 *aikido*
ail 260.24 *be unhealthy;* 247.6 *fail*
aileron 119.4 *equilizer;* 228.3 *stabilizer*
ailing 247.10 *failed;* 247.1 *failure;* 260.22 *sick*
ailment 260.2 *illness*
aim **131.14**; **446.18**; **482.10**; 610.3 *aspiration;* 610.7 *aspire;* 353.1 *attempt;* 324.6 *direct;* 324.1 *direction;* 381.2 *fire;* 694.12 *intend;* 480.11, 483.1 *motive;* 482.6 *objective;* 617.5 *object of desire;* 484.9 *plan;* 694.5 *point;* 446.4 *purpose;* 344.5 *reason;* 324.7 *take a direction;* 353.6 *venture*
aim a blow 331.3 *hit*
aim at **633.12**; 482.10 *aim;* 60.7 *shoot;* 324.7 *take a direction*
aimed 324.14 *directed;* 446.12 *purposive*
aim for 617.12 *desire*
aim high 446.18 *aim*
aiming 51.9 *bowls;* 446.12 *purposive;* 353.6 *venture*
aiming at 229.5 *tending to*
aiming point 51.2 *grip*
aimless 270.4 *circumlocutory*
aimless activity 342.7 *restlessness*
aimlessness 270.2 *circumlocution;* 342.7 *restlessness*
aim to 353.1 *attempt*
aim too high 329.1 *overstep*
aim well 698.31 *be accurate*
ain't it the truth 698.40 *right!*
aïoli 25.15 *sauce*
Air 434
air **434.1**; 434.20 *aerate;* 31.8 *atmosphere;* 631.1 *conduct;* 703.15 *demonstrate;* 738.1 *display;* 739.6 *divulge;* 428.23 *drip-dry;* 525.3 *external appearance;* 417.5, 432.1 *gas;* 554.3 *life requirements;* 415.7 *light thing;* 740.13 *make public;* 18.13, 516.1 *melody;* 500.1 *odour;* 256.15 *purify;* 581.1 *refresh;* 581.6 *refresher;* 527.8 *transparent thing;* 319.1 *transport;* 319.5 *transportable*
air ace 381.19 *attacker*
air arm 586.29 *air force*
air attack **381.13**; 381.12 *military attack;* 587.1 *weapon*
air bag 359.2 *preserver;* 252.4 *safety device*
air ball 49.4 *playing terms*
air balloon 434.10 *air bubble;* 432.13 *gas balloon*
airbase 322.4 *airport*
air bladder 434.10 *air bubble;* 74.5 *fish anatomy;* 432.13 *gas balloon;* 84.3 *plant body*
airborne 304.23 *rising*
airborne division 586.30 *air force unit;* 584.4 *military organization*
airborne particles 427.5 *powder*
airbrush 19.11 *artist's materials*
airbrush painting 19.8 *painting*
air bubble **434.10**
air campaign 381.13 *air attack*
air cargo 322.1 *aviation*
air-cargo 319.5 *transportable*
air chief marshal 586.32 *airman*
air commodore 586.32 *airman*
air-condition 434.20 *aerate;* 494.12 *make cold;* 581.1 *refresh*
air-conditioned 494.9 *heat-resistant;* 434.17 *ventilated*
air conditioner 494.4 *cooler;* 434.7 *ventilator*
air conditioning 494.4 *cooler;* 434.6 *ventilation*
air-cool 434.20 *aerate*
air-cooled 494.9 *heat-resistant;* 434.17 *ventilated*
air cooler 434.7 *ventilator*
air cooling 434.6 *ventilation*
air corps 586.29 *air force*
air corridor 322.1 *aviation;* 317.13 *flight path*
aircraft **322.8**; 586.31 *military aircraft*
aircraft carrier 586.24 *warship*
aircraft design 322.2 *aeronautics*
aircraft division 584.4 *military organization*
aircraft mechanic 578.2 *artisan*
aircraft personnel **322.3**
aircraftsman 322.3 *aircraft personnel*
aircrew 322.3 *aircraft personnel;* 586.32 *airman*
air current 434.4 *air flow;* 31.10 *air movement*
air density 31.6 *weather data*
air division 584.4 *military organization*
air-dried 428.8 *baked*
airdrop 322.1 *aviation*
air-dry 428.17 *dry*
air-drying 428.13 *drying*
aired 428.8 *baked;* 740.19 *published*
air express 316.2 *transportation*
air-express 316.13 *post*
airfield 322.4 *airport*
air fight 585.9 *battle*
air filter 256.10 *cleaning object;* 501.2 *deodorant;* 434.7 *ventilator*
air flow **434.4**; 31.10 *air movement;* 322.7 *miscellaneous aviation terms;* 434.8 *respiration*
air force **586.29**; 586.14 *armed forces;* 376.14 *force;* 253.4 *security forces;* 584.2 *the military*
Air Force Academy 584.3 *military training*
air force blue 539.1 *blue*
air force officer 586.32 *airman*
air force pilot 585.11 *recruit*
air force service 585.8 *warfare*
air force staff 584.5 *military staff*
air force uniform 743.5 *uniform*
air force unit **586.30**
air freight 322.1 *aviation;* 316.2 *transportation*
air freshener 256.9 *cleaning agent;* 501.2 *deodorant;* 255.3 *purifier*
air frost 31.36 *frost*
air group 586.30 *air force unit*
air gun 508.3 *banger*
airhole 308.5 *hole*
air hostess 322.3 *aircraft personnel*
airily **434.25**; 101.13 *metaphysically;* 417.7 *sparsely*
airiness **434.9**; 415.5 *lightness;* 417.3 *sparseness*
airing 256.2 *cleaning;* 428.13 *drying;* 255.2 *purification;* 434.6 *ventilation*
airlane 317.13 *flight path;* 318.2 *passing along*
air-layer 561.13 *propagate*
air leakage 389.4 *leak*
airless 301.4 *motionless*
airlessness 301.2 *repose*
air letter 692.3 *correspondence*
airlift 322.1 *aviation;* 316.12 *transport;* 316.2 *transportation*
airlike 434.12 *airy*
airline attendant 401.3 *attendant*
airline hostess 401.3 *attendant*
airline pilot 322.3 *aircraft personnel*
airliner 322.8 *aircraft*
airline ticket 743.3 *means of identification*
airmail 322.1 *aviation;* 692.31 *correspond;* 316.13 *post;* 692.2 *postal communication*
airmail letter 692.3 *correspondence*
airmail stamp 692.3 *correspondence*
airman **586.32**
airmanship 585.6 *art of war*
air marshal 586.32 *airman;* 400.7 *military leader;* 397.6 *person in command*
air mass 31.10 *air movement*
air miss 322.7 *miscellaneous aviation terms*
air movement **31.10**; 31.6 *weather data*
airometer 432.15 *vaporimeter*
air operations 585.8 *warfare*
air passage 434.7 *ventilator*
air-pistol shooting 60.1 *target shooting*
airplane 322.8 *aircraft*
air plant 77.2 *plant*
air pocket 434.10 *air bubble;* 420.9 *broken water;* 322.7 *miscellaneous aviation terms*
air point 62.5 *rock face*
air pollution 427.5 *powder;* 503.2 *something that makes an unpleasant smell*
airport **322.4**; 173.4 *centre of activity;* 312.15 *destination;* 313.10 *place of departure;* 226.4 *stopping place*
airport engineering 38.17 *civil engineering*
airport police 16.14 *police*
air pressure 31.6 *weather data*
air purifier 501.2 *deodorant*
air raid 381.13 *air attack;* 587.1 *weapon*
air-raid shelter 252.5 *refuge;* 384.10 *shelter;* 423.7 *tough thing*
air-raid siren 742.4 *signal*
air-raid warden 742.8 *signer*
air rifle 508.3 *banger*
air-rifle shooting 60.1 *target shooting*
air route 322.1 *aviation;* 317.13 *flight path;* 62.1 *mountaineering*
airs and graces 676.1 *affectedness;* 673.3 *cockiness*
airscrew 307.6 *rotator*
air-sea rescue 390.2 *deliverance*
air-sea rescue helicopter 390.3 *deliverer*
air service 586.29 *air force*
airship 432.13 *gas balloon;* 586.31 *military aircraft*
airsick 371.30 *vomiting*
airsickness 322.7 *miscellaneous aviation terms*
airside 322.4 *airport*
airspace 434.1 *air;* 141.6 *available space;* 141.2 *empty space;* 86.3 *regional boundary*
airspeed 322.5 *flight;* 332.8 *speed*
air squadron 374.3 *assembly*
air station 322.4 *airport*
air stream 31.10 *air movement*
air strike 381.13 *air attack*
airstrip 322.4 *airport;* 317.13 *flight path*
air temperature 31.6 *weather data*
air terminal 312.15 *destination;* 226.4 *stopping place*
airtight 309.12 *closed;* 230.1 *perfect*
air-traffic control 322.6 *flight control*
air-traffic controller 322.3 *aircraft personnel;* 318.7 *traffic controller*
air transport 322.1 *aviation;* 316.5 *means of transport*
air travel 322.1 *aviation;* 300.2 *momentum*
air troops 586.32 *airman*
air vice-marshal 586.32 *airman*
airworthy 252.7 *invulnerable;* 316.17 *transferable;* 319.5 *transportable*
airy **432.17**; **434.12**; 154.9 *high;* 415.2 *insubstantial;* 101.8 *nonmaterial;* 141.13 *spacious;* 417.1 *sparse;* 11.18 *spiritual;* 124.4 *trivial;* 96.8 *unreal*
airy-fairy 477.11 *fantastical;* 417.1 *sparse*
aisle 317.7 *arcade;* 317.11 *channel;* 10.12 *church;* 308.7 *passageway;* 317.2 *route*
ait 92.2 *island*
aitiou 25.53 *African dish*
ajar 308.12 *open*
AK-47 587.11 *guns*
akin 127.8 *included;* 115.7 *similar*
akin to 108.4 *related*
akrasia 4.9 *philosophical problem*
Akshobhya 8.3 *God*
Aktie Tomaat 21.10 *theatre movements*
Alabama 90.3 *US rivers*
alabaster 421.8 *smooth thing;* 531.1 *white;* 531.9 *white thing*
à la carte 25.56 *culinary;* 469.17 *selectively*
alacritous 636.2 *eager;* 293.12 *early;* 332.1 *swift*
alacrity 636.7 *eagerness;* 293.1 *earliness;* 262.4 *haste;* 342.3 *nimbleness;* 332.10 *quickness of mind*
à la mode 295.16 *avant-garde;* 25.56 *culinary;* 551.30 *dressed-up;* 553.7 *fashionable;* 553.2 *fashionableness*
alarm 711.2 *danger signal;* 328.7 *disturb;* 612.2 *fearfulness;* 612.13 *frighten;* 507.1 *loudness;* 711.7 *raise the alarm;* 252.4 *safety device;* 742.4 *signal;* 507.4 *sound maker;* 337.7 *weaken*
alarm and despondency 611.1 *hopelessness*
alarm bell 711.2 *danger signal;* 742.4 *signal*
alarm clock 281.6 *clock;* 711.2 *danger signal;* 742.4 *signal;* 504.8 *something heard*
alarmed 328.12 *disturbed;* 612.8 *fearful*
alarming 254.1 *dangerous;* 328.17 *disturbing;* 612.10 *frightening*
alarmingly 328.18 *disturbingly;* 612.16 *frighteningly*
alarmist 612.5 *frightener;* 742.8 *signer;* 711.4 *warner*
alarm system 252.2, 253.1 *protection*
alarm test 711.3 *false alarm*
alarum 711.2 *danger signal;* 742.4 *signal*
alarums and excursions 21.8 *scene*
alas 249.13 *too bad!*
Alaska–Hawaii Daylight Time 275.9 *time zone*
Alaska–Hawaii Standard Time 275.9 *time zone*
Alaskan oil 437.6 *oil*
a laugh 599.5 *joke*
alb 7.11 *vestment*
alba 17.7 *poem*
albatross 378.6 *burden;* 56.2 *golfing terms;* 72.3 *water bird*
albedo 29.16 *planet*
Alberich 159.4 *little person*
Albert 88.5 *other major lakes*
Albert Schweitzer 589.4 *Nobel Peace Prize*
albescence 531.7 *whiteness*
albescent 531.1 *white*
albinic 1.13 *racial*
albiniotic 1.13 *racial*
albinism 530.2 *paleness;* 260.13 *skin disease;* 531.7 *whiteness*
albinistic 1.13 *racial;* 531.1 *white*
albino 530.8 *drained of colour;* 522.21 *light*
albinoism 530.2 *paleness;* 531.7 *whiteness*
albinotic 530.8 *drained of colour;* 531.1 *white*
Al Borak 59.1 *horse*
album 723.3 *compendium;* 744.6 *record book;* 462.4 *reminder*
albumen 430.5 *mucus;* 33.9 *protein*
albumin 33.9 *protein*
alburum 79.3 *timber*
Alcaics 17.10 *verse form*
Alcatraz 815.1 *prison*
Alceste 653.2 *misanthrope*
alchemic 32.31 *chemical;* 11.15 *witchlike*
alchemist 32.2 *chemist;* 224.6, 227.4 *editor;* 737.7 *esotericism;* 11.12 *occultist;* 412.7 *person who mixes*
alchemistic 11.15 *witchlike*
alchemize 760.9 *transform*
alchemy 32.1 *chemistry;* 760.1 *conversion;* 737.7 *esotericism;* 11.1 *occultism;* 11.3 *witchcraft*
alcohol **690.12**; 558.7 *alcoholic drink;* 359.2 *preserver;* 394.7 *tonic*
alcohol abuse 690.16 *alcoholism;* 260.4 *disease*
alcohol-free 689.2 *nonalcoholic*
alcoholic 386.5 *compulsive person;* 632.8 *creature of habit;* 558.17 *drinkable;* 690.17 *drunkard;* 690.5 *drunken;* 690.6 *intoxicating;* 260.19 *sick person*
alcoholic addiction 690.16 *alcoholism*
alcoholic drink **558.7**; 690.12 *alcohol*
alcoholic liquor 690.12 *alcohol*
alcoholic psychosis 36.11, 461.5 *psychosis*

Alcoholics Anonymous 689.8 *sober person*
alcoholism 690.16; 260.4 *disease*; 558.1 *drinking*
alcoholometer 26.8 *meter*
alcohol thermometer 28.89 *thermometer*
alcopop 558.7 *alcoholic drink*
alcove 183.3 *cavity*; 410.2 *compartment*
aldaric acid 33.3 *carbohydrate*
al dente 25.56 *culinary*
alderman 579.16 *official*
aldermanic board 16.2 *jurisdiction*; 398.2 *representative body*; 579.9 *US administrative council*
aldoheptose 33.3 *carbohydrate*
aldohexose 33.3 *carbohydrate*
aldonic acid 33.3 *carbohydrate*
aldooctose 33.3 *carbohydrate*
aldopentose 33.3 *carbohydrate*
aldose 33.3 *carbohydrate*
aldotetrose 33.3 *carbohydrate*
aldotriose 33.3 *carbohydrate*
aldrin 43.14 *pest control*
ale 558.7 *alcoholic drink*
aleatoric 453.8 *capricious*; 107.8 *chance*; 109.7 *illogical*
aleatorics 107.7 *calculation of chance*
aleatory 107.8 *chance*
alehead 558.12 *drinker*; 690.17 *drunkard*
alembic 760.4 *medium of conversion*
alenu 10.9 *prayer*
alert 342.18 *active*; 665.9 *careful*; 616.4 *cautious*; 711.2 *danger signal*; 693.18 *informed*; 442.10, 458.6 *intelligent*; 425.5 *mentally sharp*; 243.18 *prepared*; 711.7 *raise the alarm*; 742.12 *signal*; 711.5 *warn*; 471.7 *watchful*
alertly 471.15 *attentively*; 665.12 *carefully*; 442.15 *intelligently*; 425.18 *sharply*
alertness 616.1 *caution*; 665.3 *circumspection*; 442.4 *cleverness*; 471.2 *close attention*; 425.13 *mental sharpness*
alevin 74.3 *young fish*
alewife 436.4 *caterer*
Alexandrine 17.9 *metre*
alfalfa 557.8 *animal food*; 43.12 *crop*
alfar 11.11 *ghost*
Alfardaws 8.11 *heaven*
alfresco 171.15 *externally*; 434.16 *open-air*; 434.26 *out-of-doors*; 171.7 *outside*
alga 84.1; 77.4 *lower plant*; 82.3 *moss*
algae 84.2; 554.9 *classifications of life*
Algae and Lichens 84
algal 84.7
algal bloom 84.1 *alga*
algal constituent 84.6 *lichen*
algal pigment 84.3 *plant body*
algal product 84.5
algebra 27.23; 210.1 *calculation*; 27.1 *mathematics*
algebraic 27.68, 210.15 *mathematical*
algebraically 210.16 *mathematically*
algebraic expression 27.25
algebraic geometry 27.34 *geometry*
algebraic number 27.6 *complex number*; 194.2 *kind of number*
algebraic operation 27.14 *operation*
algebraic topology 27.47 *topology*
algebraist 27.2, 210.7 *mathematician*
algebra of propositions 27.23 *algebra*
algicide 382.14 *plant killer*
algid 494.8 *cold*
algidity 494.2 *freezing*
algin 84.5 *algal product*
alginate 84.5 *algal product*
algoid 84.7 *algal*
algological 84.7 *algal*
algologically 84.9; 77.25 *botanically*
algologist 84.2 *algae*; 77.12 *plant scientist*
algology 84.2 *algae*; 34.1 *life science*; 77.10 *plant science*
Algol variable 29.12 *variable star*
algometer 26.8 *meter*
algometry 26.2 *micrometry*
algorithm 27.28; 210.1 *calculation*; 40.19 *computing terms*; 317.1 *way*
algorithmic 210.15 *mathematical*; 194.8 *odd*
alias 737.8 *anonymity*; 736.7 *concealer*; 721.8 *name*
alibi 714.2 *defence*; 714.8 *justify*
Alicia Markova 22.14 *famous ballet dancers*
alicyclic 32.7 *chemical compound*; 32.35 *combined*
alidade 38.17 *civil engineering*; 26.8 *meter*
alien 751.10 *different*; 128.5 *excluded person*; 171.10 *extraneous*; 100.10 *foreign*; 11.11 *ghost*; 594.12 *hated*; 295.8 *new arrival*; 113.22 *oppositional*; 100.6 *outsider*; 29.34 *SETI*; 11.18 *spiritual*; 109.3 *unconnected person*; 372.17 *unjoined*; 109.6 *unrelated*; 77.15 *wild*
alienage 100.2 *foreignness*
alienate 594.16 *cause hate*; 372.11 *divide*
alienated 461.11 *insane*
alienation 36.19 *defence mechanism*; 36.13 *depression*; 767.1 *disposal*; 760.2 *evolution*; 594.4 *hatefulness*
alienation effect 21.9 *dramaturgy*
alien encounter 11.10 *psychic phenomenon*
alienism 100.2 *foreignness*
alienist 394.15 *healer*; 36.30 *psychiatrist*
alif 5.36 *accent*
a life sentence 277.5 *long duration*
a lifetime 277.5 *long duration*
alight 301.8 *be motionless*; 522.16 *bright*; 305.9 *descend*; 312.4 *land*; 493.10 *on fire*; 367.8 *sit*
alight upon 305.12 *drop*
align 27.97; 409.12 *arrange*; 132.16 *arrange consecutively*; 188.6 *correlate*; 117.9 *make conform*; 750.26 *make uniform*; 407.18 *order*
aligned 409.20 *arranged*; 188.4 *correlated*; 324.14 *directed*
aligned wheels 188.2 *parallel thing*
alignment 409.1 *arrangement*; 747.7 *association*; 324.3 *orientation*; 188.1 *parallelism*
align one's march 324.7 *take a direction*
align with 392.24 *back*; 747.14 *join with*
alike 111.18 *identically*; 111.14 *lookalike*; 115.7 *similar*
alikeness 115.1 *similarity*
aliment 557.7 *food*; 788.3 *income*; 440.6 *marriage settlement*; 557.25 *provide food*; 392.4 *social assistance*
alimental 557.27 *edible*
alimentary 557.27 *edible*; 34.22 *physiological*; 308.15 *providing passage*; 394.17 *remedial*
alimentary canal 308.7 *passageway*
alimentation 557.7 *food*
alimony 571.3 *divorce court*; 765.4 *earnings*; 413.7 *financial support*; 768.2 *gift*; 788.3 *income*; 440.6 *marriage settlement*; 392.4 *social assistance*; 769.2 *something received*
A-line 551.31 *styled*
A-line skirt 551.6 *skirt*
aliphatic 32.7 *chemical compound*; 32.35 *combined*
aliquant 205.1 *part*
aliquot 194.9 *fractional*; 205.1 *part*; 205.11 *partial*
aliquot part 27.18 *division*
a little 206.1, 206.5 *few*; 205.12 *partly*; 209.11 *to a degree*
a little something 768.2 *gift*
alive 554.12; 342.18 *active*; 34.21 *living*; 359.7 *preserved*
alive and kicking 342.18 *active*; 554.12 *alive*; 393.15 *cured*
alive to 488.5 *sensible*
alive to opportunity 354.6 *enterprising*
alive with 232.8 *full*
alizarin 535.6 *red pigment*
alizarin crimson 535.6 *red pigment*
alizarin dye 42.6 *dye*
alkahest 431.9 *solvent*
alkali 32.9 *base*
alkali feldspar 30.34 *mineral*
alkali metal 32.6 *chemical element*
alkalimeter 26.8 *meter*
alkalimetric 26.16 *micrometric*
alkalimetry 26.2 *micrometry*
alkaline 32.36 *acid*
alkaline battery 39.29 *power source*
alkaline-earth element 32.6 *chemical element*
alkaloid 33.19; 37.4 *drug type*
alkie 558.12 *drinker*
alkylating agent 37.4 *drug type*
all 204.4; 138.10 *everyone*; 203.6 *quantitative*; 203.4 *total*; 204.6 *whole*
all agog 619.7 *wide-eyed*
Allah 8.3 *God*
Allah be praised 671.9 *thank you!*
all along 275.26 *all the time*
All-American 48.2 *baseball player*; 49.2 *basketball player*; 46.2 *football player*; 485.4 *skilled person*
all-American 336.5 *athlete*; 235.1 *worthy*
all and sundry 114.6 *assorted*; 138.10 *everyone*
all and then some 376.20 *crowd*; 138.10 *everyone*
allantoic 34.26 *developmental*
allantois 34.15 *developmental biology*
all anyhow 408.28 *anyhow*
allargando 333.17 *in slow motion*
all around 232.9 *completely*; 141.16 *extensively*; 550.42 *inclusively*
all-around 114.5 *diverse*; 57.11 *gymnastic*
All-Around Champion 59.12 *rodeo*
All-Around Cow Horse 59.12 *rodeo*
all around the houses 180.8 *circularly*
all at sea 766.18 *at a loss*; 120.7 *unequally*
allay 685.4 *moderate*; 749.4 *pacify*; 608.9 *relieve*; 421.13 *smooth over*
all but 231.11 *imperfectly*; 205.5 *largest part*; 147.13 *nearly*; 204.13 *on the whole*
all by oneself 197.21 *alone*
all clear 538.15 *green light*; 252.1 *safety*
all-clear siren 742.4 *signal*
all-comers 113.10 *the opposition*
all-comprehending 138.15 *general*
all concerned 566.7 *person*
all-consuming 357.14 *destructive*; 638.2 *tenacious*
all-covering 138.15 *general*
all-devouring 688.6 *gluttonous*
all ears 504.11 *aural*; 471.8 *diligent*
Allecto 624.7 *gods and goddesses of anger*
allegate 715.5 *accuse*
allegation 715.1 *accusation*; 707.1 *affirmation*; 729.7 *utterance*
allege 707.17 *affirm*; 716.11 *give evidence*; 729.11 *speak*
alleged 715.8 *accusatory*; 450.14 *believed*; 811.4 *reputed*; 707.11 *stated*; 476.8 *supposed*
allegedly 715.10 *accusingly*; 707.23 *affirmatively*; 96.19 *apparently*; 450.16 *believably*; 811.6 *reputedly*; 476.10 *supposedly*
Allegheny Mountains 89.4 *US mountains*
allegiance 810.3; 663.2 *loyalty*; 387.1 *subjection*
alleging 715.8 *accusatory*
allegorical 110.6 *correlative*; 17.17 *fictional*; 694.6 *meaningful*
allegorically 110.11 *correlatively*
allegorical meaning 694.4 *type of meaning*
allegorist 17.14 *author*
allegorization 719.1 *interpretation*
allegory 110.3 *correlation*; 701.4 *gist*; 721.3 *narration*; 115.1 *similarity*
allegro 262.3 *hasty*; 332.14 *swiftly*
allele 34.13 *genetic material*
Alleluia 10.8 *hymn*
alleluia 514.3 *cry of praise*
allemande 22.4 *historic dancing*
all-embracing 232.7 *complete*; 138.15 *general*; 127.7 *including*; 204.6 *whole*
all-encompassing 138.15 *general*
All-England Championships 63.1 *tennis*
allergic 260.23 *diseased*; 596.8 *disliking*; 591.3 *sore*; 488.7 *susceptible*
allergy 488.2 *ability to sense*; 596.1 *dislike*; 260.1 *ill health*; 591.7 *soreness*
allerome 34.14 *chromosome*
alleviate 490.10 *comfort*; 265.18 *disentangle*; 263.3 *ease*; 244.1 *improve*; 415.10 *lighten*; 214.5 *make smaller*; 685.4 *moderate*; 749.4 *pacify*; 608.9 *relieve*; 394.19 *remedy*; 421.13 *smooth over*; 212.3 *subtract*; 392.19 *support*
alleviating 415.3 *lightening*
alleviation 608.1 *ease*; 244.5 *improvement*; 415.6 *lightening*; 685.1 *moderation*; 212.1 *subtraction*
alleviative 415.3 *lightening*; 685.8 *moderating*; 685.2 *moderator*
alley 317.11 *channel*; 317.3 *road*; 45.2 *sportsground*
alley cat 412.5 *hybrid*
all eyes 471.8 *diligent*
alley-oop! 304.27
alleyway 317.3 *road*
all fingers and thumbs 544.7 *graceless*
all found 436.8 *provisional*
all gone 195.6 *zero*
all Greek 456.3 *unknown thing*
All Hallows' Day 10.15 *holy day*
all hands 138.10 *everyone*
all hands on deck 390.5 *to the rescue!*
all-healing 394.17 *remedial*
all hell let loose 408.5 *confusion*; 408.9 *disorder*; 507.2 *outcry*
alliance 570.2; **750.2**; **755.3**; 376.15, 747.7 *association*; 755.1 *contract*; 374.2 *cooperation*; 764.1 *joint possession*; 570.1 *marriage*; 108.1 *relatedness*
alliance of states 566.11 *nation*
allied 750.11; 747.19 *associating*; 755.7 *contractual*; 374.8 *cooperative*; 108.4 *related*; 115.7 *similar*
allied forces 586.14 *armed forces*
allied operation 585.8 *warfare*
alligator 73.5 *crocodilian*
all impatience 262.3 *hasty*
all in 261.1 *fatigued*; 335.12 *impotent*
all-in 232.7 *complete*; 127.7 *including*; 436.8 *provisional*; 52.15 *wrestling*
all in all 232.9 *completely*; 216.11 *on average*; 204.13 *on the whole*; 138.31 *overall*
all-inclusive 232.7 *complete*; 138.15 *general*; 127.7 *including*; 204.6 *whole*
all-in wrestling 52.5 *wrestling*
alliterate 750.24 *harmonize*; 115.12 *imitate*; 112.22 *resound*
alliterating 112.15 *reverberatory*
alliteration 750.4 *harmony*; 542.1 *ornament*; 17.12 *poetic language*; 112.6 *reverberation*
alliterative 750.13 *harmonious*; 17.20 *metrical*; 542.10 *ornate*; 112.15 *reverberatory*; 115.7 *similar*
alliteratively 115.14 *comparably*
alliterative verse 17.10 *verse form*
all-knowing 8.13 *divine*; 455.8 *knowledgeable*
all mouth 731.6 *effusive*
all mouth and trousers 676.3 *affected*
all my eye 699.10 *lie*
all my own work 126.1 *originality*
allocate 770.4 *allot*; 409.12 *arrange*; 349.5 *dispose of*; 216.10 *make average*; 203.8 *quantify*
allocated 770.7
Allocation 770
allocation 770.1; 770.2 *portion*
allocation of work 15.2 *industrial negotiations*
allocution 733.1 *address*; 10.9 *prayer*
allodial 440.8 *propertied*
allodium 440.3 *historic property terms*
all of 203.7 *quantitatively*
all of a flutter 327.16 *restless*
all of a piece 750.14 *conforming*; 255.16 *simple*; 204.6 *whole*
all of a sudden 149.12 *short*
all of a tizz 327.16 *restless*
all of a twitter 327.28 *shakily*
all off 131.22 *cancelled*
allogamy 412.1 *mixture*
all one 119.8 *on equal terms*; 111.12 *same*
all one can manage 264.9 *difficult person*
all on one's lonesome 250.20 *freely*
allonym 721.8 *name*
allopath 394.15 *healer*
allopathic 35.22, 394.18 *medical*
allopathic medicine 35.1 *medicine*
allopathy 394.11 *medical art*; 35.8 *treatment*
allopolyploidy 34.14 *chromosome*
allot 770.4; 349.5 *dispose of*; 768.5 *give*; 166.7 *limit*; 26.11 *measure out*; 440.9 *own property*; 203.8 *quantify*; 251.8 *restrain*; 349.1 *use*
allot a billet 770.6 *assign*
allotheism 9.2 *idolatry*
allotheist 9.6 *idolater*
allotheistic 9.10 *idolatrous*
allotment 770.1 *allocation*; 44.2 *garden*; 768.2 *gift*; 166.2 *limiting factor*; 440.6 *marriage settlement*; 205.7 *piece*; 86.12 *plot*; 770.2 *portion*; 440.1 *property*; 251.1 *restraint*
allotropic 114.6 *assorted*
allotropy 114.2 *assortment*
allotted 770.7 *allocated*; 440.8 *propertied*; 769.11 *receiving*
allotted days 554.5 *life cycle*
allotted span 275.3 *duration*; 554.5 *life cycle*; 556.5 *old age*
allotted task 770.3
allottee 769.5 *recipient*
allotting 770.1 *allocation*
all out 355.9 *forget it!*; 332.14 *swiftly*; 638.2 *tenacious*; 338.6 *with vigour*

all-out 232.7 *complete;* 332.1 *swift*
all-out war 751.2 *argument;* 585.1 *war*
all over 408.28 *anyhow;* 131.21 *ended;* 141.16 *extensively;* 94.11 *no more*
all-over 97.7 *present*
all over again 295.22 *again*
all over hell 141.16 *extensively*
all over the lot 377.25 *sprawled*
all over the map 141.16 *extensively*
all over the place 408.28 *anyhow;* 114.11 *irregularly*
all over the shop 408.28 *anyhow;* 141.16 *extensively*
allow 739.8 *admit;* 648.3 *be lenient;* 396.21 *grant authority;* 127.4 *include;* 265.16 *make easy;* 16.65 *make legal;* 102.7 *make possible;* 136.15 *modify;* 750.29, 757.3 *permit;* 388.3 *submit;* 212.3 *subtract*
allowable 16.44 *legal;* 757.8 *permitting;* 714.13 *vindicable*
allow access 370.7 *admit*
allow a discount 791.3 *discount*
allow a dismissal 16.78 *acquit*
allow a margin 791.3 *discount*
allow an appeal 16.78 *acquit*
allowance 780.4 *change;* 714.2 *defence;* 791.1 *discount;* 392.6 *financial assistance;* 413.7 *financial support;* 768.2 *gift;* 813.3 *grant;* 127.1 *inclusion;* 788.3 *income;* 648.1 *leniency;* 440.6 *marriage settlement;* 136.5 *modification;* 750.8 *permit;* 770.2 *portion;* 765.5 *profit;* 769.2 *something received;* 212.2 *subtracted item*
allow credit 771.5 *lend*
allowed 136.10, 396.16 *authorized;* 648.5 *given consideration;* 127.8 *included;* 757.7 *permitted;* 750.18 *permitting*
allowed in 314.15 *entering*
allow enough rope 250.15 *set free*
allow for 127.4 *include;* 714.7 *vindicate*
allow full play 250.15 *set free*
allow in 370.7 *admit;* 773.11 *be hospitable*
allowing 127.7 *including;* 750.18, 757.8 *permitting;* 222.15 *under the circumstances*
allowing no delay 280.6
allowing no time 262.3 *hasty*
allow initiative 250.15 *set free*
allow no appeal 647.5 *be severe*
allow no rest 261.6 *fatigue*
allow no time 262.1 *hasten*
allow rest 581.1 *refresh*
alloy 32.7 *chemical compound;* 374.4 *compound;* 32.30 *extract;* 245.3 *make worse;* 412.8 *mix;* 412.2 *mixed thing*
alloyed 32.45 *metallurgical;* 412.12 *mixed*
alloy extractive metallurgy 32.23 *metallurgy*
all-pervading 395.13 *dominant;* 138.15 *general;* 412.12 *mixed*
all-pervasive 97.7 *present*
all piss and wind 676.3 *affected*
Allport-Vernon draw-a-person test 36.5 *psychological test*
Allport-Vernon study of values 36.5 *psychological test*
all-powerful 8.13 *divine*
all-presence 97.2 *omnipresence*
all-present 97.7 *present*
All-Pro 49.2 *basketball player;* 46.2 *football player;* 485.4 *skilled person*
all-purpose 237.1 *useful*
all-red 52.15 *wrestling*
all right 801.12; 235.12 *fantastic!;* 618.10 *mediocre;* 235.5 *not bad;* 609.6 *satisfactory;* 235.11 *worthily*
all round 232.9 *completely;* 324.11 *in all directions;* 170.8 *round*
all-round 114.5 *diverse*
all-round capacity 485.1 *skill*
all-rounder 336.5 *athlete;* 207.5 *pluralist;* 485.4 *skilled person;* 53.4 *team*
all-round gymnast 57.9 *gymnasts*
all-round player 336.5 *athlete*
all round the globe 141.16 *extensively*
All Saints' Day 10.15 *holy day*
all seats taken 232.8 *full*
all-seeing 8.13 *divine*
all set 243.18 *prepared*
all shapes and sizes 114.2 *assortment*
all sorts 412.3 *miscellany*
all sorts and conditions 114.2 *assortment*
All Souls' Day 10.15 *holy day*
allspice 496.5 *herbs*
all square match 56.2 *golfing terms*
All-Star 48.2 *baseball player*
all-star 21.41 *stagestruck;* 235.1 *worthy*
All-Star Game 48.1 *baseball*
all steamed up 259.1 *healthy*
all straight 781.2 *solvent*
all-sufficing 436.7 *provisioning;* 217.1 *sufficient*
all-terrain vehicle 43.10 *farm tool*
all that is left 215.1 *remainder*
all that is possible 217.7 *sufficiency*
all the best 248.10 *good luck!*
all the better for 244.14 *improved*
all the more 213.8 *increasingly;* 121.17 *supremely*
all the rage 295.16 *avant-garde;* 553.7 *fashionable*
all there 801.12 *all right;* 525.7 *appearing;* 232.7 *complete;* 458.6 *intelligent;* 460.4 *sane*
all the same 119.8 *on equal terms;* 111.12 *same*
all the time 275.26; 134.7 *continually;* 297.1 *frequently*
all the trimmings 211.3 *additional item*
all the way 232.9 *completely*
all the way across 150.8 *breadthwise*
all the world 204.4 *all*
all things being equal 446.23 *ideally;* 216.11 *on average*
all things considered 464.14 *considering;* 216.11 *on average;* 204.13 *on the whole;* 138.31 *overall;* 104.11 *probably*
all through 275.26 *all the time;* 317.17 *via*
all through the night 291.7 *evening*
all thumbs 486.3 *clumsy*
all-time 235.2 *best*
all-time low 122.5 *inferior state*
all together 750.31 *in accord;* 204.12 *one and all;* 285.12 *simultaneously;* 223.21, 376.51 *together*
all told 232.9 *completely*
allude 476.6 *propound*
allude to 694.10 *mean;* 729.11 *speak*
all up 131.21 *ended*
allure 363.4 *allurement;* 617.15 *cause desire;* 480.3 *incentive;* 363.12 *lure;* 480.16 *tempt;* 593.28 *win the love of*
allurement 363.4; 480.3 *incentive;* 483.2 *inducement;* 595.1 *liking;* 593.4 *lovability*
alluring 593.20 *amorous;* 363.9 *attractive;* 595.5 *likable;* 593.22 *lovable;* 483.11 *motivational;* 480.19 *persuasive*
alluringly 483.14 *influentially;* 593.30 *lovingly*
allusion 266.1 *obscurity*
allusive 694.6 *meaningful;* 266.2 *obscure;* 476.7 *suppositional*
allusively 266.4 *obscurely*
alluvial 30.52 *coastal;* 92.11 *continental*
alluvial deposit 30.27 *sediment*
alluvial plain 92.6 *lowland*
alluvion 316.10 *transferred thing*
alluvium 215.2 *residue;* 90.6 *river flow;* 30.36 *soil;* 316.10 *transferred thing*
all wind and water 676.3 *affected*
all wrong 798.12 *evilly;* 274.17 *mistaken*
ally 707.9 *affirmer;* 373.3 *associate;* 374.6 *come together;* 755.5 *contract;* 747.10 *cooperator;* 85.3 *dominion;* 750.22 *form an alliance;* 392.11 *helper;* 747.16 *join;* 570.19 *merge;* 764.3 *participant;* 413.8 *supporter*
ally with 392.24 *back;* 747.14 *join with*
almanac 439.5 *collection;* 220.3 *dictionary;* 475.3 *plan;* 693.5 *reference book*
almightily 8.19 *divinely*
almightiness 8.2 *divine attribute*
almighty 158.15 *big;* 8.13 *divine;* 334.13 *powerful*
almighty dollar 780.7 *finance*
Almighty God 8.3 *God*
almoner 650.5 *benevolent person;* 768.4 *giver;* 652.3 *philanthropist;* 7.8 *priest;* 780.18 *treasurer*
almonry 780.19 *treasury*
almost 231.11 *imperfectly;* 27.87 *mathematically;* 147.13 *nearly;* 204.13 *on the whole*
almost all 205.5 *largest part*
almost always 138.30 *usually*
almost entirely 99.13 *in essence*
almost none 206.1 *few*
almost the same way 115.14 *comparably*
almost win 766.9 *lose*
alms 650.4 *benevolent act;* 608.4 *charity;* 679.7 *gift;* 768.3 *offering*
alms-giver 650.5 *benevolent person;* 768.4 *giver*
alms-giving 650.4 *benevolent act;* 650.7 *charitable;* 608.4 *charity;* 768.1, 768.8 *giving;* 652.6 *philanthropic;* 10.3 *rite of worship*
aloes 499.3 *sour thing*
aloft 154.19 *high;* 366.13 *highly;* 50.20 *offshore;* 89.11 *on the mountain;* 50.10 *sailing*
aloha 312.12 *reception*
alone 197.16; 197.21; 250.20 *freely;* 655.10 *lonely;* 197.15 *solo;* 372.17 *unjoined*
aloneness 197.5
along 302.19 *forward;* 148.12 *longitudinally*
a long haul 576.1 *work*
alongside 147.14 *beside;* 188.7 *in parallel;* 169.10 *laterally*
a long stretch 277.5 *long duration*
along these lines 317.16 *how*
a long time 279.2; 277.5 *long duration*
a long time ago 3.24 *historically*
a long way away 145.10 *distantly*
a long way off 145.10 *distantly*
along with 211.10 *additionally;* 223.24 *with*
aloof 197.16 *alone;* 355.6 *apathetic;* 634.21 *away;* 145.10 *distantly;* 618.7 *indifferent;* 372.22 *in isolation;* 145.9 *reserved;* 736.16 *silent;* 118.16 *solitary;* 622.15 *unapproachable;* 655.8 *unsociable*
aloofly 618.17 *indifferently;* 145.11 *reservedly;* 655.14 *unsocially*
aloofness 197.5 *aloneness;* 634.10 *avoidance;* 145.1 *distance;* 618.1 *indifference;* 145.4 *reserve;* 655.1 *unsociability*
alopecia 552.5 *baldness;* 552.7 *depilation*
a lot 208.2 *multitude*
a lot to ask 354.2 *undertaking*
aloud 507.10; 504.17 *aurally*
alp 89.1, 154.3 *mountain*
alpaca 193.4 *textile*
alpenstock 413.3 *body support*
alpestrine 89.7, 154.13 *mountainous*
Alpha and Omega 204.4 *all;* 8.3 *God*
alphabet 5.14
alphabetical 407.12 *hierarchical;* 5.41 *lettered*
alphabetically 407.25 *in order;* 220.13 *inventorially;* 5.48 *linguistically*
alphabetical order 407.3 *hierarchy*
alphabetization 409.5 *categorization*
alphabetize 409.15 *categorize;* 5.47 *word*
alphabetized 409.24 *categorized*
alpha decay 28.70 *radioactivity*
alpha emitter 28.70 *radioactivity*
alpha-fetoprotein test 561.7 *obstetrics*
alpha-helix 33.9 *protein*
alpha-naphthol test 33.5 *sugar test*
alphanumeric character 40.10 *character*
alpha particle 28.70 *radioactivity*
alpha plus 235.1 *worthy*
alpha rays 28.70 *radioactivity*
alpha rhythm 298.2 *cycle*
alpha-sorting 409.5 *categorization*
alpha test 36.6 *intelligence test*
alpha to omega 127.9 *inclusively*
alpha wave 298.2 *cycle*
alpigene 89.7 *mountainous*
Alpine 1.13 *racial*
alpine 44.9 *garden plant;* 89.7, 154.13 *mountainous;* 44.19 *ornamental;* 68.12 *ski*
alpine chain 30.21 *mountain building*
Alpine Club 62.6 *mountaineering association*
Alpine Club of Canada 62.6 *mountaineering association*
alpine garden 44.2 *garden*
alpine glacier 30.38 *glacier*
alpine race 68.3 *ski racing*
alpine racing 68.3 *ski racing*
alpine ski 68.14 *ski;* 68.5 *ski equipment*
alpine skiing 68.1 *skiing*
Alpine type 1.6 *race*
alpinism 62.1 *mountaineering;* 304.6 *mounting*
alpinist 304.11 *ascender;* 62.7, 89.3 *mountaineer*
Alps 154.4 *mountain range;* 89.6 *other major mountains and ranges*
already 284.23 *before now*
alright 216.3 *mediocre;* 312.23 *hello!*
also 211.10 *additionally*
also-ran 469.13 *electorate;* 247.5 *failing person;* 289.8 *follower;* 59.7 *horseracing;* 122.6 *inferior*
altar 10.12 *church*
altarpiece 19.8 *painting*
altazimuth mounting 29.25 *mounting*
alter 224.7 *be changed;* 224.8 *cause change;* 760.7 *convert into;* 295.20 *make new;* 136.15 *modify;* 244.3 *rectify;* 212.4 *take off*
alterability 114.1 *diversity*
alterable 224.11, 227.13 *changeable;* 760.15 *convertible;* 295.15 *renewable*
alterably 224.15, 227.15 *changeably*
alteration 224.1 *change;* 760.1 *conversion;* 295.5 *fresh start;* 136.5 *modification;* 244.6 *rectification*
alteration of plan 479.6 *equivocation*
altercate 701.13 *argue;* 751.5 *disagree*
altercation 701.1 *argument;* 751.1 *disagreement;* 242.8 *quarrel*
altered 224.12 *changed;* 136.11 *modified;* 295.14 *renewed*
alter ego 569.6 *close friend;* 750.5 *conformity;* 115.5 *counterpart;* 139.11 *identity;* 110.2 *interconnection;* 111.3 *lookalike*
alterer 224.6 *editor*
alter from one's course 325.1 *deviate*
altering 760.14 *converting;* 212.1 *subtraction*
alternate 398.5 *alternative;* 227.11 *be changeable;* 298.7 *be regular;* 550.34 *cover for;* 133.8 *discontinuous;* 224.10 *exchange;* 326.8 *oscillate;* 326.13 *oscillating;* 110.4 *reciprocal;* 110.7 *reciprocate;* 298.11 *regular;* 762.7 *substitute;* 762.2 *substitute person;* 550.21 *substitution;* 289.12 *succeeding*
alternate angles 27.39 *angle*
alternate breathing 67.2 *swimming technique*
alternately 298.15 *regularly*
alternating 227.13 *changeable;* 133.8 *discontinuous;* 326.13 *oscillating;* 110.4 *reciprocal;* 298.11 *regular*
alternating current 334.7 *electrical power;* 28.51, 39.9 *electric current;* 298.5 *regular thing*
alternating personality 36.8 *disordered personality;* 36.16 *dissociation*
alternating voltage 39.10 *electric potential*
alternation 227.1 *changeableness;* 224.4 *exchange;* 110.1 *interchange;* 108.2 *interrelatedness;* 27.63 *mathematical logic;* 326.1 *oscillation;* 298.1 *regularity;* 762.1 *substitution*
alternative 398.5; 469.8 *choice;* 352.1 *means;* 326.13 *oscillating;* 110.4 *reciprocal;* 298.11 *regular;* 762.7 *substitute;* 550.21, 762.1 *substitution;* 550.40 *substitutive*
alternative choice 762.1 *substitution*
alternative comedian 599.6 *humorist*
alternative comedy 21.12 *comedy*
alternative hypothesis 27.54 *hypothesis testing*
alternatively 550.43; 227.15 *changeably;* 762.9 *instead;* 110.10 *reciprocally;* 298.15 *regularly;* 469.17 *selectively*
alternative medicine 394.11 *medical art;* 35.2 *natural medicine*
alternative practitioner 35.12 *healer*
Alternative Prayer Book 10.10 *religious manual*
alternative reading 719.1 *interpretation*
alternative route 318.2 *passing along*
alternative theatre 21.1 *drama*
alternator 39.30 *generator;* 334.6 *source of energy*
although 347.5 *counter;* 476.11 *supposing*
altimeter 28.84; 154.5 *height measure;* 26.8 *meter*
altimetric 154.14; 26.16 *micrometric*
altimetry 154.5 *height measure;* 26.2 *micrometry*
altitude 29.5 *celestial sphere;* 209.1 *degree;* 154.1 *height;* 27.37 *line;* 203.1 *quantity;* 143.1 *situation;* 26.4 *size;* 28.7 *space;* 121.1 *superiority;* 27.43 *triangle*
altitude sickness 62.2 *climbing dangers*
altitudinal 154.9 *high*
altitudinous 154.9 *high;* 89.7 *mountainous*
alto 18.32 *instrumental;* 516.5 *melodist*
alto clef 18.17 *notation*
altocumuliform 31.49 *cloudy*
altocumulous 31.49 *cloudy*
altocumulus 31.18 *cloud*
altogether 256.20 *clean;* 232.9 *completely;* 216.11 *on average;* 204.12 *one and all;* 204.13 *on the whole*

alto relievo 19.13 *relief-carving;* 608.6 *profile*
altostratous 31.49 *cloudy*
altostratus 31.18 *cloud*
altricial 72.22 *newly hatched*
altruism 650.2 *charity;* 652.1 *philanthropy;* 4.7 *school of thought;* 473.2 *unselfishness;* 803.1 *virtue*
altruist 650.5 *benevolent person;* 4.11 *follower of a doctrine;* 797.15 *good person;* 652.3 *philanthropist;* 803.4 *virtuous person;* 752.8 *volunteer*
altruistic 650.7 *charitable;* 4.14 *of a philosophy;* 652.6 *philanthropic;* 473.5 *unselfish;* 803.5 *virtuous;* 752.18 *voluntary*
altruistically 650.11 *charitably;* 752.20 *persuasively;* 652.8 *philanthropically;* 473.9 *unselfishly;* 803.9 *virtuously*
ALU 40.5 *processor*
alula 72.17 *plumage*
alum 32.10 *salt*
aluminiferous 32.34 *elemental*
aluminium 20.4 *building material;* 39.3 *electricity;* 418.7 *hard substance*
aluminium alloy 38.25 *construction material;* 323.4 *shipbuilding*
aluminium coating 28.29 *optical element*
aluminium foil 25.6 *kitchen equipment;* 550.4 *wrapping*
aluminous 32.34 *elemental*
alumna 6.7 *learner*
alumnus 6.7 *learner*
alveolar palate 729.5 *organ of speech*
alveolate 83.10 *of fungi*
alveoli 434.8 *respiration*
always 275.26 *all the time;* 750.35 *consistently;* 134.7 *continually;* 225.9 *permanently;* 111.20 *regularly*
always ill 260.21 *unhealthy*
always the same 111.17 *regular*
always victorious 246.15 *victorious*
Alzheimer's disease 335.4 *disability;* 461.3 *mental deterioration*
a.m. 281.18 *horologically;* 290.1 *morning*
amah 401.6 *domestic servant*
amain 332.14 *swiftly*
amalgam 32.7 *chemical compound;* 374.4 *compound;* 412.2 *mixed thing*
amalgamate 492.12 *abut;* 374.5 *combine;* 405.10 *compose;* 747.16 *join;* 570.19 *merge;* 412.8 *mix*
amalgamated 374.9 *assembled;* 412.12 *mixed*
amalgamation 570.2 *alliance;* 747.7 *association;* 374.1 *combination;* 412.1 *mixture*
amanuensis 348.3 *assistant;* 744.9 *recorder*
amaranth 540.2 *purple pigment*
amaranthine 540.6 *purple*
Amaravati 8.11 *heaven*
Amaryllis 593.9 *lover*
amass 765.11 *acquire;* 376.37 *assemble;* 439.6 *store*
amassed 376.47 *collected;* 439.7 *stored*
amassment 765.3 *acquisition*
a match for 217.1 *sufficient*
amateur 486.4 *bungled;* 52.14 *combat;* 456.5 *ignorant person;* 295.12 *immature;* 295.8 *new arrival;* 456.7 *semiskilled;* 486.2 *unskilled;* 486.10 *unskilled person*
amateur athlete 47.3, 336.5 *athlete*
amateur boxer 52.4 *boxer*
amateur dramatics 21.1 *drama*
amateurish 486.4 *bungled;* 295.12 *immature;* 456.7 *semiskilled;* 486.2 *unskilled*
amateurishly 295.24 *immaturely;* 486.11 *unskilfully*
amateurishness 456.2 *half-knowledge*
amateurism 456.2 *half-knowledge;* 486.8 *unskilfulness*
amateur radio 692.20 *radio broadcasting*
amateur radio operator 692.29 *broadcaster*
amateur rowing 50.4 *rowing*
Amateur Swimming Association 67.5 *swimming association*
amateur wrestler 52.6 *wrestler*
amateur wrestling 52.5 *wrestling*
amative 593.17 *loving*
amativeness 593.3 *lovingness*
amatory 593.20 *amorous*
amaurosis 519.1 *blindness*
amaurotic 519.8 *blind*
amaze **630.11**; 619.10 *be wonderful;* 451.9 *cause disbelief;* 604.6 *disappoint*
amazed **630.7**; 619.6 *wondering*
amazement **630.2**; 451.3 *incredulity;* 619.1 *wonder*
amazing 630.8 *surprising;* 619.8 *wonderful;* 619.14 *wonderful!;* 235.1 *worthy*
amazingly 630.13 *surprisingly;* 619.13 *wonderfully*
amazing person 619.5 *person of wonder*
Amazon 158.10 *big person;* 568.2 *female;* 336.6 *muscleman;* 90.5 *other major rivers;* 154.7 *tall person;* 380.4 *violent creature;* 586.10 *woman soldier*
Amazon Basin 493.8 *hot place*
Amazonian 568.15 *female;* 336.9 *physically strong;* 154.12 *tall*
ambage 270.2 *circumlocution*
ambages 306.2 *circuitousness*
ambagious 270.4 *circumlocutory;* 306.9 *orbital*
ambarvalia 10.7 *non-Christian ritual*
ambassador 398.6 *agent;* 398.1 *delegate;* 746.4 *negotiator;* 579.16 *official;* 717.8 *representative*
ambassadorial 398.9 *delegated*
amber 534.1 *brown;* 284.10 *fossilization;* 475.6 *good-luck sign;* 536.1 *orange;* 536.3 *orange thing;* 359.2 *preserver;* 537.1 *yellow;* 537.8 *yellow thing*
ambergris 502.3 *incense*
amber light 711.2 *danger signal;* 522.6 *electric light;* 536.3 *orange thing;* 742.4 *signal*
ambidexterity 198.3 *duality;* 699.2 *duplicity;* 485.1 *skill*
ambidextrous 699.30 *duplicitous;* 492.10 *handed;* 485.6 *skilful;* 198.10 *two-sided*
ambidextrousness 485.1 *skill*
ambience 170.3 *atmosphere;* 19.4 *treatment*
ambient 170.6 *atmospheric;* 18.9 *popular music*
ambient light 41.15 *lighting*
ambiguity 694.3 *comprehension;* 751.3 *difference;* 198.3 *duality;* 479.5 *equivocalness;* 274.11 *grammatical error;* 453.14 *indeterminacy;* 266.1, 528.8 *obscurity;* 705.7 *questionableness;* 696.11 *unintelligibility*
ambiguous **180.5**; 751.10 *different;* 696.4 *difficult;* 198.11 *double-edged;* 479.10 *equivocal;* 453.6 *indeterminate;* 528.4 *inscrutable;* 694.6 *meaningful;* 266.2 *obscure;* 705.14 *questionable*
ambiguously 180.8 *circularly;* 751.12 *differently;* 479.12 *equivocally;* 453.25 *indeterminately;* 694.13 *meaningfully;* 266.4 *obscurely;* 528.13 *opaquely;* 705.24 *questionably*
ambiguousness 694.3 *comprehension*
ambiguous passage 694.3 *comprehension*
ambit 179.2 *circle;* 306.3 *orbit;* 181.6 *round;* 86.14 *sphere;* 395.7 *sphere of influence*
ambition 610.3 *aspiration;* 617.1 *desire;* 342.4 *energy;* 474.2 *expectations;* 482.3 *future intention;* 480.11, 483.1 *motive;* 683.1 *selfishness;* 654.2 *social ambition*
ambitious 610.13 *aspirant;* 353.8 *attempting;* 354.6 *enterprising;* 482.11 *intending;* 683.4 *selfish*
ambitiously **353.10**; 354.9 *enterprisingly;* 610.15 *hopefully;* 683.8 *selfishly*
ambivalence 751.3 *difference;* 198.3 *duality;* 479.5 *equivocalness;* 699.13 *evasion;* 453.11 *irresoluteness;* 36.12 *stress*
ambivalent 751.10 *different;* 198.11 *double-edged;* 479.10 *equivocal;* 699.38 *evasive;* 453.2 *irresolute*
ambivalently 751.12 *differently;* 479.12 *equivocally*
ambiversion 36.7 *personality type*
ambivert 36.7 *personality type*
amble 300.12 *gait;* 333.1 *move slowly;* 333.10 *slow motion;* 300.15 *walk*
ambler 59.4 *saddle horse*
ambling 333.4 *slow*
amblyopia 519.2 *poor sight*
amblyopic 519.9 *weak-sighted*
ambrosia 557.7 *food;* 490.4 *pleasurable things;* 498.2 *sweetener*
ambrosial 502.4 *fragrant;* 490.6 *pleasant;* 498.6 *sweet;* 495.7 *tasty*
Ambrosian chant 10.8 *hymn*
ambulance 394.14 *hospital*
ambulance chaser 444.6 *arguer*
ambulanceman 35.17 *paramedic*
ambulance siren 742.4 *signal*
ambulant 300.16 *moving*
ambulatory 317.7 *arcade;* 20.10 *church architecture;* 20.9 *miscellaneous architectural features*
ambush **630.10**; 381.1 *attack;* 585.13 *be at war;* 645.5 *be cunning;* 736.3 *covering up;* 254.5 *danger;* 700.13, 700.33 *snare;* 645.2 *stratagem;* 379.1, 379.2 *trap*
ambushed 630.6 *surprised;* 700.42 *trapped*
ameliorable 244.15 *improvable*
ameliorate 224.8 *cause change;* 244.1, 392.22 *improve;* 230.5 *perfect;* 421.13 *smooth over*
amelioration 224.1 *change;* 6.1 *education;* 244.5 *improvement*
ameliorative 224.11 *changeable;* 244.16 *improving*
amenability 636.8 *acquiescence*
amenable **636.3**; 658.7 *courteous;* 810.9 *loyal;* 663.7 *obedient;* 388.5 *submitting*
amenable to law 16.47 *liable to law*
amenably 658.14 *courteously*
amend 224.8 *cause change;* 719.8 *interpret;* 244.3 *rectify;* 393.1 *repair*
amendable 393.14 *repairable*
amended 224.12 *changed;* 719.15 *interpreted*
amender 227.4 *editor;* 393.12 *repairer;* 244.13 *reviser*
amendment 224.1 *change;* 719.1 *interpretation;* 484.1 *plan;* 244.6 *rectification;* 394.1 *remedy;* 393.8 *repair*
amendment referendum 469.10 *vote*
amends 807.1 *atonement;* 775.2, 813.6 *compensation;* 394.1 *remedy;* 609.2 *reparation;* 393.9 *restoration*
amenities 658.3 *courtesies*
amenity 392.7 *convenience;* 658.1 *courtesy;* 490.4 *pleasurable things*
amenity tree 79.1 *tree*
amenorrhoea 560.11 *menstruation*
ament 78.4 *flower head*
Amenti 8.12 *hell*
amentia 461.2 *subnormality*
Amerasian 1.6 *race*
amerce 814.1 *punish*
amerceable 814.22 *punishable*
amercement 814.7 *punishment*
America 92.1 *continent;* 85.7 *United States*
American 564.10 *US inhabitant*
Americana 85.7 *United States*
American accent 5.26 *dialect*
American Alpine Club 62.6 *mountaineering association*
American art glass 24.1 *ceramics*
American Ballet 22.12 *ballet companies*
American Birkebeiner 68.2 *cross-country skiing*
American Canoe Association 50.6 *canoeing*
American Casting Association 55.1 *angling*
American cities **87.2**
American coinage 780.8 *American money*
American eagle 85.7 *United States*
American eagle bullion coin 780.8 *American money*
American elk 60.5 *game*
American Express™ 772.4 *credit;* 783.2 *credit card;* 771.4 *lending institution*
American Football **46**
American game fish **55.4**
American household china 24.1 *ceramics*
American Indian 293.4 *early comer*
American Indian reservation 655.4 *place of confinement*
American Indians 284.6 *people of the past*
Americanism 5.26 *dialect;* 85.7 *United States*
Americanization 85.7 *United States*
Americanize 85.18 *exert sovereignty;* 760.12 *naturalize*
Americanized 760.17 *naturalized*
American League 48.1 *baseball*
American money **780.8**
American Motorcycle Association 61.7 *racing governing body*
American paper money 780.8 *American money*
American pocket billiards 65.6 *pool*
American Rowing Association 50.4 *rowing*
American saddle 59.14 *horse-riding terms*
American Sign Language 505.1 *deafness*
American spread eagle 743.6 *national emblem*
American stroke 50.4 *rowing*
American Triple Crown 59.7 *horseracing*
American twist service 63.2 *tennis strokes*
American water spaniel 60.6 *sporting dog*
America's Cup 813.2 *prize*
America's national sport 48.1 *baseball*
Amerindian 1.6 *race;* 1.13 *racial*
Amesha Spentas 8.6 *angel*
Ameslan 730.6 *silent speech*
amethyst 540.3 *purple thing*
amethystine 540.6 *purple*
amiability **241.8**; 650.1 *benevolence;* 658.1 *courtesy;* 593.4 *lovability;* 654.1 *sociability*
amiable 650.6 *benevolent;* 658.7 *courteous;* 569.8 *friendly;* 241.2 *likable;* 589.7 *peaceful;* 654.15 *sociable*
amiableness 569.1 *friendship*
amiably 650.10 *benevolently;* 658.14 *courteously;* 569.17 *in friendship;* 654.18 *sociably*
amicability 569.1 *friendship;* 590.5 *good feeling;* 654.1 *sociability*
amicable 569.8 *friendly;* 750.10 *in accord;* 595.5 *likable;* 593.17 *loving;* 590.12 *sensitive;* 654.15 *sociable*
amicableness 569.1 *friendship*
amicably 569.17 *in friendship;* 654.18 *sociably;* 595.10 *with great liking*
amice 7.11 *vestment*
amicus curiae 395.4 *indirect influence*
Amida 8.3 *God*
amidships 50.3 *parts of a sailing boat*
amidst 412.14 *in the midst*
amigo 569.5 *friend*
a mile long 148.1 *long*
a mile off 116.4 *dissimilar*
amimation 19.9 *drawing*
amino acid **33.8**; 557.11 *food content*
amino-acid residue 33.8 *amino acid*
amino-acid sequence 34.12 *molecular biology*
a minute or two 278.3 *short duration*
amiss 408.18 *muddled;* 236.15 *worthlessly;* 274.22 *wrongly*
amitosis 34.10 *cell division*
amity 569.1 *friendship;* 589.1 *peace*
ammeter **28.90**; 39.23 *electrical instrument;* 26.8 *meter*
ammine 32.7 *chemical compound*
ammo 587.13 *ammunition*
ammo dump 587.4 *arsenal*
ammonia 503.2 *something that makes an unpleasant smell*
ammoniacal 503.3 *stinking*
ammonite 180.3 *convoluted thing;* 30.43 *fossil;* 284.10 *fossilization;* 296.8 *prehistoric animal*
ammonium salts 562.3 *fertilizer*
ammunition **587.13**; 60.3 *hunting equipment;* 352.2 *supplies*
ammunition box 587.4 *arsenal;* 410.6 *box*
ammunition case 550.13 *casing*
ammunition chest 587.4 *arsenal*
ammunition dump 587.4 *arsenal*
ammunition room 587.4 *arsenal*
ammunition round 60.3 *hunting equipment*
ammunition ship 587.4 *arsenal;* 586.24 *warship*
amnesia 463.2 *blankness;* 358.5 *forgetfulness;* 36.14 *trance*
amnesiac 463.7 *forgetful person*
amnesic 463.9 *blank*
amnesty **463.6**; 708.5 *cancellation;* 390.2 *deliverance;* 649.1 *forgiveness;* 648.1 *leniency;* 358.3 *obliteration;* 589.1 *peace;* 479.2 *peace offering*
Amnesty International 650.2 *charity*
amniocentesis 35.7 *diagnosis;* 561.7 *obstetrics*
amnion 34.15 *developmental biology*
amniotic 34.26 *developmental*
amniotic fluid 561.7 *obstetrics*
amniotic sac 561.7 *obstetrics*
amoeba 159.2 *little thing;* 161.2 *shapeless thing*
amoebiasis 75.12 *protozoal disease*
amoebic 159.7 *little;* 75.23 *protozoan*

amoebic dysentery 75.12 *protozoal disease*
amoeboid 159.7 *little;* 75.23 *protozoan*
amoeboid protozoan 75.9 *protozoan*
among 412.14 *in the midst*
among many 412.14 *in the midst*
among others 412.14 *in the midst*
among other things 412.14 *in the midst*
among the also-rans 247.11 *defeated*
among those remaining 215.12 *with a remainder*
a month of Sundays 277.5 *long duration*
Amor 593.16 *gods and goddesses of love*
amoral 618.8 *careless;* 796.11, 802.15, 804.12 *immoral;* 796.14 *lecherous;* 796.13 *unchaste*
amoralism 804.2 *vice*
amoralist 631.5 *badly behaved person*
amorality 618.2 *carelessness;* 796.1 *immorality;* 408.8 *lawlessness;* 796.3 *sexual immorality;* 408.11 *troublemaker;* 804.2 *vice*
amorally 618.18 *carelessly;* 804.20 *immorally*
amorist 593.9 *lover*
amorous **593.20**; 593.17 *loving*
amorous ditty 593.15 *love item*
amorous glance 593.14 *communication of love*
amorously 593.30 *lovingly*
amorousness 593.5 *desire;* 593.3 *lovingness*
amorphism 161.1 *shapelessness*
amorphous 32.33 *crystalline;* 696.4 *difficult;* 453.6 *indeterminate;* 266.2 *obscure;* 161.5 *shapeless*
amorphously 32.46 *chemically;* 453.25 *indeterminately;* 161.6 *shapelessly*
amorphous mineral 30.34 *mineral*
amorphousness 453.14 *indeterminacy;* 266.1 *obscurity;* 161.1 *shapelessness*
amorphous substance 32.4 *crystal*
amount 209.1 *degree;* 194.4 *mathematical result;* 452.18 *particularity;* 790.1 *price;* 203.1 *quantity;* 26.4 *size;* 439.1 *store*
amount of substance 28.9 *mass*
amount outstanding 215.3 *difference*
amount owing **784.5**
amount to 204.9 *be whole;* 790.13 *cost;* 194.11, 210.10 *total*
amour 796.4 *illicit love;* 593.8 *love affair*
amourette 593.8 *love affair*
amour propre 622.1 *pride;* 673.4 *self-admiration*
AMP 33.22 *bioenergetics*
amp 504.9 *audio device;* 507.4 *sound maker;* 334.5 *unit of work*
amperage 334.5 *unit of work*
ampere 334.5 *unit of work*
amphetamine 691.6 *drug;* 394.7 *tonic*
Amphibia 73.7 *amphibian*
amphibian **73.7**; **73.13**; 323.11 *nautical;* 70.4 *type of animal;* 586.24 *warship*
amphibians 554.9 *classifications of life*
amphibious 323.11 *nautical*
amphibious force squadron 584.4 *military organization*
amphibiously 323.12 *nautically*
amphibiousness 485.1 *skill*
amphibious operations 585.8 *warfare*
amphibious ship 586.24 *warship*
amphibious warfare 585.8 *warfare*
amphibole 30.34 *mineral*
amphibology 479.5 *equivocalness*
amphibolous 479.10 *equivocal*
amphibolously 479.12 *equivocally*
amphibrach 17.9 *metre*
amphigory 697.1 *nonsense*
amphimacer 17.9 *metre*
Amphineura 75.5 *mollusc*
amphineuran 75.5 *mollusc*
amphioxus 75.2 *protochordate*
amphipod 75.4 *arthropod*
amphitheatre 62.5 *rock face;* 21.16 *theatre;* 518.9 *viewpoint*
Amphitrite 91.4 *sea god*
amphora 24.8 *ceramic object;* 410.11 *vessel*
amphoteric 32.36 *acid*
amphoteric compound 32.9 *base*
ample **208.9**; 679.3 *abundant;* 158.15 *big;* 150.1 *broad;* 797.7 *large;* 217.2 *plentiful;* 203.6 *quantitative;* 609.5 *satisfying;* 141.13 *spacious;* 152.1 *thick*
ampleness 158.2 *bigness;* 150.4 *breadth;* 797.14 *largeness*
ample size 797.14 *largeness*
ample-size 797.7 *large*
ample time 580.1 *leisure*
amplifiable 190.9 *enlargeable*
amplification 504.9 *audio device;* 39.15 *circuit function;* 270.1 *diffuseness;* 727.2 *enlargement;* 190.1 *growth;* 213.1 *increase;* 695.10 *simplicity;* 719.4 *translation*
amplified 190.7 *bigger;* 692.34 *communicated;* 270.3 *diffuse;* 727.13 *enlarged*
amplifier 504.9 *audio device;* 28.55 *circuit;* 692.18 *radio;* 39.21 *rectifier;* 507.4 *sound maker;* 28.18 *source of sound*
amplify 190.6 *become bigger;* 270.5 *be diffuse;* 692.30 *communicate;* 39.35 *conduct;* 727.8 *enlarge;* 334.12 *generate power;* 190.5, 213.5 *make bigger;* 719.12 *translate*
amplifying 721.11 *descriptive*
amplitude 141.6 *available space;* 150.4 *breadth;* 209.1 *degree;* 270.1 *diffuseness;* 217.8 *plenty;* 203.1 *quantity;* 158.1 *size;* 326.5 *wave;* 28.16 *waveform*
amplitude modulation 297.6 *radio frequency;* 692.14 *radio transmission*
amplitudinous 141.13 *spacious*
amply 217.9 *enough;* 679.12 *generously;* 158.20 *largely;* 203.7 *quantitatively;* 141.15 *spaciously*
ampulla 24.8 *ceramic object*
amputate 394.20 *doctor;* 35.20 *practise surgery;* 372.10 *set apart;* 212.4 *take off*
amputation 372.3 *separateness;* 212.1 *subtraction;* 35.9, 394.12 *surgery*
amrita 557.7 *food*
Amtrak 321.10 *miscellaneous*
AM transmitter 692.16 *transmitter*
amulet 359.2 *preserver;* 10.14 *sacred object;* 11.6 *talisman*
amuse 599.13 *be humorous;* 490.9 *give pleasure*
amusement **599.2**; 69.8 *pastime;* 241.7 *pleasure;* 124.8 *trifle*
amusing 598.2 *cheering;* 599.9 *funny;* 599.10 *humorous;* 241.2 *likable;* 69.9 *recreational;* 654.15 *sociable*
amusingly 599.16 *humorously;* 654.18 *sociably*
a must 386.1 *compulsion;* 135.1 *requirement*
amygdalectomy 36.3 *psychiatric treatment*
amylase 33.11 *enzyme*
amyloid 83.10 *of fungi*
amylopectin 33.4 *polysaccharide*
amylose 33.4 *polysaccharide*
anabasis 304.6 *mounting*
anabatic 304.23 *rising;* 50.10 *sailing*
anabatic wind 50.1 *sailing;* 31.12 *wind*
anabolic 33.26 *biochemical;* 34.22 *physiological;* 37.17 *stimulating*
anabolically 33.27 *biochemically*
anabolic steroid 47.5 *competition;* 37.4 *drug type;* 33.16 *hormone*
anabolism 33.21 *metabolism;* 34.5 *physiology*
anabranch 90.1 *river*
anachronic 286.2 *occurring at a different time*
anachronically 286.4 *mistime*
anachronism 286.1 *different time;* 288.1 *wrong time*
anachronistic **288.14**; 284.19 *antiquarian;* 288.10 *mistimed;* 286.2 *occurring at a different time*
anachronistically **288.20**; 286.4 *mistime;* 288.18 *out of chronological order*
anacoluthia 274.11 *grammatical error*
anaconda 73.3 *snake*
Anacreontics 17.10 *verse form*
anacrusis 17.9 *metre*
anaemia 260.11 *blood disease;* 260.4 *disease;* 218.8 *insufficiency;* 530.2 *paleness;* 337.3 *poor health*
anaemic 260.23 *diseased;* 530.8 *drained of colour;* 337.10 *ill;* 260.21 *unhealthy*
anaerobe 34.3 *organism*
anaerobic 34.22 *physiological*
anaerobic respiration 34.6 *cell biology;* 33.24 *respiration*
anaesthesia 394.5 *analgesic;* 592.4 *desensitization;* 489.1 *lack of feeling;* 35.9 *surgery*
anaesthesiologist 35.13 *medical specialist*
anaesthesiology 35.3 *medical specialty*
anaesthetic **489.4**; **489.9**; 394.5 *analgesic;* 37.14 *counteracting;* 592.6 *desensitizing substance;* 394.8 *drug;* 37.4 *drug type;* 685.2 *moderator;* 608.3 *reliever;* 394.17 *remedial;* 343.10 *soporific*
anaesthetics 35.3 *medical specialty*
anaesthetist 35.13 *medical specialist;* 35.17 *paramedic*
anaesthetization 608.1 *ease*
anaesthetize **489.12**; 457.10 *bemuse;* 394.20 *doctor;* 685.4 *moderate;* 35.20 *practise surgery;* 592.7 *render insensitive;* 608.9 *relieve*
anaesthetized **489.7**; 592.2 *desensitized;* 343.4 *not awake*
anaesthetize hypnotize 343.14 *make inactive*
anagalactic nebula 29.7 *galaxy*
an age 277.5 *long duration*
anaglyph 19.13 *relief-carving*
anaglyptic 19.25 *sculptural*
anaglyptics 19.13 *relief-carving*
anaglyptography 19.13 *relief-carving*
anagnorisis 17.3 *aspect of fiction;* 739.1 *disclosure*
anagogic 11.14 *occult*
anagogics 11.1 *occultism*
anagram 737.4 *brain-teaser;* 5.13 *letter*
anagrammatic 479.10 *equivocal;* 5.41 *lettered*
anagrammatically 5.48 *linguistically*
anagrammatism 5.13 *letter*
anagrammatize 5.45 *use language*
Anahita 8.5 *deity*
anal 308.15 *providing passage;* 168.4 *rear*
anal canal 308.7 *passageway*
analeptic 37.4 *drug type;* 394.17 *remedial;* 393.16 *restorative;* 37.17 *stimulating*
anal fin 74.5 *fish anatomy*
analgesia 394.5 *analgesic;* 592.4 *desensitization;* 489.1 *lack of feeling;* 491.4 *pain relief*
analgesic **394.5**, 489.4, 489.9 *anaesthetic;* 37.14 *counteracting;* 592.6 *desensitizing substance;* 394.8 *drug;* 37.4 *drug type;* 685.8 *moderating;* 685.2 *moderator;* 608.3 *reliever;* 394.17 *remedial*
anally 308.27 *cavernously*
analog 111.2 *equivalence*
analog dial 281.8 *face*
analogical 750.14 *conforming*
analogous 750.14 *conforming;* 110.6 *correlative;* 111.13 *equivalent;* 108.5 *interrelated;* 115.7 *similar*
analogously 115.14 *comparably;* 110.11 *correlatively;* 111.18 *identically;* 108.10 *relevantly*
analogousness 750.5 *conformity*
analogue 110.3 *correlation;* 111.2 *equivalence*
analogue clock 28.87 *clock*
analogue watch 281.7 *watch*
analogy 750.5 *conformity;* 110.3 *correlation;* 111.2 *equivalence;* 4.8 *philosophical term;* 108.1 *relatedness;* 115.1 *similarity;* 762.3 *substitute thing*
anal-retentive 684.8 *self-restrained*
analyse 409.15 *categorize;* 734.11 *confer;* 375.4 *deconstruct;* 466.12 *discriminate;* 4.23 *discuss philosophically;* 372.11 *divide;* 448.11 *experiment;* 743.10 *identify;* 719.8 *interpret;* 4.20 *philosophize;* 36.38 *psychologize;* 705.17 *question;* 444.11 *reason;* 137.14 *sort;* 32.27 *synthesize;* 27.89 *theorize*
analysed 409.24 *categorized;* 705.16 *questioned*
analyser 40.8 *software*
analysis **32.17**; 210.1 *calculation;* 27.30 *calculus;* 409.5 *categorization;* 32.1 *chemistry;* 375.2 *deconstruction;* 448.1 *experiment;* 743.1 *identification;* 719.1 *interpretation;* 734.6 *interview;* 27.1 *mathematics;* 4.4 *philosophical investigation;* 36.3 *psychiatric treatment;* 705.2 *questioning;* 444.2 *reasoning;* 372.1 *separation;* 461.9 *treatment*
analysis of variance 27.55 *statistical methods*
analysis situs 27.47 *topology*
analyst 713.4 *adviser;* 32.2 *chemist;* 448.5 *experimenter;* 4.10 *philosopher;* 36.30 *psychiatrist;* 36.29 *psychologist;* 705.9 *questioner*
analytic **32.41**; 32.31 *chemical;* 409.26 *diagrammatic;* 4.16 *dialectical;* 448.8 *experimental;* 5.38 *linguistic;* 27.68, 210.15 *mathematical;* 5.39 *of language;* 705.12 *questioning;* 444.8 *rational;* 19.29 *realist;* 27.69 *theoretical*
analytical chemist 32.2 *chemist*
analytical chemistry 32.1 *chemistry*
Analytical Engine 40.3 *computer*
analytical journalism 741.3 *reporting*
analytically 32.46 *chemically;* 448.14 *experimentally;* 409.28 *in place;* 466.16 *judiciously;* 5.48 *linguistically;* 27.87 *mathematically;* 4.24 *philosophically;* 705.23 *questioningly;* 375.7 *to pieces*
analytical philosophy 4.6 *branch of philosophy*
analytic geometry 27.34 *geometry*
analytic language 5.10 *language type*
analytic psychology 36.1 *psychology*
anamnesis 462.1 *memory;* 10.9 *prayer*
anamorphosis 718.1 *misrepresentation*
Ananias 699.18, 700.16 *liar*
anapaest 17.9 *metre*
anapaestic 17.20 *metrical*
anaphase 34.10 *cell division*
anaphora 17.12 *poetic language;* 509.7 *repeated word;* 112.1 *repetition*
anaplastic 394.18 *medical*
anarch 588.3 *anarchist*
anarchic **588.6**; 408.20 *disorderly;* 12.9, 396.14 *governmental;* 250.10 *independent;* 753.10 *lawbreaking;* 16.61 *lawless;* 118.12 *nonconformist;* 4.14 *of a philosophy;* 100.11 *separate;* 662.14 *subversive*
anarchical 588.6 *anarchic;* 753.10 *lawbreaking;* 662.14 *subversive*
anarchically **588.8**; 16.84 *lawlessly;* 408.29 *riotously*
anarchism **588.2**; 753.2 *disorder;* 4.7 *school of thought*
anarchist **588.3**; 357.6 *destroyer;* 118.8 *dissenter;* 4.11 *follower of a doctrine;* 753.10 *lawbreaking;* 651.8 *malefactor;* 100.5 *nonconformist;* 12.6 *political party;* 383.5 *resister;* 383.12 *resisting;* 662.10, 753.5 *seditionist;* 408.11 *troublemaker;* 380.4 *violent creature*
anarchistic **588.7**; 357.14 *destructive;* 100.11 *separate*
anarcho-syndicalism 588.2 *anarchism;* 4.7 *school of thought;* 396.7 *type of rule*
anarcho-syndicalist 4.11 *follower of a doctrine;* 4.14 *of a philosophy;* 12.6 *political party*
Anarchy 588
anarchy **588.1**; 408.9, 753.2 *disorder;* 12.1 *government;* 16.41, 408.8 *lawlessness;* 662.3 *subversion;* 396.7 *type of rule*
anathema 594.7 *hated thing;* 712.4 *malediction*
anathematize 712.7 *wish ill*
Anatolian 5.11 *family of languages*
Anatolic 5.11 *family of languages*
anatomical 1.11 *anthropological;* 34.20 *biological;* 403.12 *organic*
anatomically 34.29 *biologically;* 403.18 *structurally*
anatomist **403.10**; 34.19 *life scientist*
anatomization 375.2 *deconstruction*
anatomize 222.11 *circumstantiate;* 372.11 *divide*
anatomy **34.4**; 403.3 *form;* 34.1 *life science;* 160.6 *nature;* 17.4 *nonfiction;* 403.8 *science of structure*
anatriptic 365.10 *frictional*
ancestor 293.4 *early comer;* 129.9 *predecessor;* 344.7 *Prime Mover*
ancestors 296.2 *old people;* 582.13 *the dead*
ancestor worship 9.2 *idolatry*
ancestor worshipper 9.6 *idolater*
ancestor-worshipping 9.10 *idolatrous*
ancestory 573.3 *nobleness*
ancestral 284.19 *antiquarian;* 3.15 *historic;* 296.12 *olden;* 293.15 *precursory*
ancestral hall 565.4 *official residence*
ancestrally 296.21 *archaically;* 3.24 *historically;* 293.19 *primevally*
ancestry 137.8 *genealogy*
anchor 175.4 *base;* 373.12 *bind;* 62.4 *climbing equipment;* 252.2, 253.1 *protection;* 378.10 *restrain;* 378.4 *restraint;* 252.4 *safety device;* 253.10 *secure;* 360.3 *tools for gripping;* 373.9 *yoke*
anchor bait 55.7 *angle*
anchor chain 373.7 *tackle*
anchored 378.14 *blocked;* 228.10 *stabilized*
anchoretic 7.15 *religious*
anchorite 118.9 *hermit;* 197.8 *loner;* 7.7 *monk;* 655.6 *unsocial person*
anchor light 522.6 *electric light*
anchorman 692.29 *broadcaster;* 693.9 *informant;* 741.4 *journalist;* 578.1 *worker*

anchorperson 692.29 *broadcaster;* 741.4 *journalist;* 578.1 *worker*
anchor ring 27.45 *curved surface*
anchor space 65.4 *carom*
anchorwoman 692.29 *broadcaster;* 578.1 *worker*
ancien régime 296.3 *antiquity;* 573.2 *aristocracy;* 284.5 *historical period;* 641.7 *opinionatedness;* 3.8 *past time*
ancient 556.14 *aged;* 554.12 *alive;* 3.15 *historic;* 5.39 *of language;* 296.12 *olden;* 284.17 *past;* 293.14 *primeval*
ancient and modern 113.3 *opposites*
ancient coins 780.12
Ancient Egyptian text 7.12 *religious text*
ancient flint 284.7 *thing of the past*
ancient Greeks 284.6 *people of the past*
ancient history 293.3 *early stage;* 3.8 *past time*
ancient language 5.9
ancient lineage 284.12 *genealogy*
anciently 296.19; 293.19 *primevally*
ancient man 566.3 *early human*
ancient manuscript 296.5 *old thing*
Ancient Mariner 323.7 *nautical person*
ancient monument 356.8 *construction;* 744.11 *monument;* 296.5 *old thing;* 3.11 *relic;* 284.7 *thing of the past*
ancientness 296.3 *antiquity*
ancient people 296.7
ancient Romans 284.6 *people of the past*
ancient ruin 284.7 *thing of the past*
ancient ruins 357.4 *ruin*
ancient tale 296.6 *tradition*
ancient times 296.3 *antiquity;* 3.9 *distant past;* 3.10 *past age;* 284.1 *past time*
ancient wisdom 1.8, 296.6 *tradition*
ancient woodland 79.4 *trees*
ancillary 122.15 *subordinate;* 392.31 *supplementary;* 413.9 *supportive*
ancon 20.9 *miscellaneous architectural features*
ancylostomiasis 260.7 *tropical disease*
and 211.10 *additionally*
andante 333.16 *slowly;* 18.19 *tempo*
Andean 154.13 *mountainous*
Anderson shelter 252.5 *refuge*
Andes 154.4 *mountain range*
Andes Mountains 89.6 *other major mountains and ranges*
and others 207.12 *et cetera*
Andre Agassi 63.7 *famous tennis players*
Andre Sakharov 589.4 *Nobel Peace Prize*
androecium 78.3 *flower part*
androgen 37.4 *drug type;* 33.16 *hormone*
androgyny 568.1 *female sex*
android 566.8 *humanlike machine;* 489.5 *unfeeling person*
and so 222.15 *under the circumstances;* 345.12 *with the effect of*
and so forth 211.10 *additionally;* 127.9 *inclusively*
and so on 211.10 *additionally;* 207.12 *et cetera;* 127.9 *inclusively*
and then some 232.10 *fully*
and there 345.12 *with the effect of*
and the rest 207.12 *et cetera*
anecdotage 556.5 *old age*
anecdote 721.3 *narration;* 462.2 *retrospect*
anecdotist 721.10 *descriptive writer*
anechoic chamber 28.21 *architectural acoustics*
anemogram 31.6 *weather data*
anemograph 31.7 *weather instruments*
anemographic 31.42 *barometric*
anemological 31.47 *windy*
anemology 31.1 *meteorology*
anemometer 26.8 *meter;* 332.8 *speed;* 31.7 *weather instruments*
anemometric 31.42 *barometric;* 26.16 *micrometric*
anemometry 26.2 *micrometry*
aneroid 62.8 *mountaineering*
aneroid barometer 28.88 *barometer;* 62.4 *climbing equipment;* 31.7 *weather instruments*
an eternity 277.5 *long duration*
aneurysm 260.10 *cardiovascular disease*
anew 112.24, 295.22 *again*
anfractuosity 180.1 *convolution*
angel 8.6; 392.15 *benefactor;* 384.13 *defender;* 679.9 *generous person;* 768.4 *giver;* 805.4 *innocent person;* 593.12 *nicknames for lovers;* 21.27 *producer;* 255.5 *pure person;* 413.8 *supporter;* 589.2 *symbol of peace;* 803.4 *virtuous person*
angel cake 25.36 *cake*
angel dust 691.6 *drug*
angelhood 8.6 *angel*
angelic 8.14 *heavenly;* 805.5 *innocent;* 593.22 *lovable;* 255.12 *morally pure;* 803.5 *virtuous*
angelica 496.5 *herbs*
angelical 8.14 *heavenly*
angelically 8.19 *divinely;* 805.11 *innocently;* 255.18, 803.9 *virtuously*
angelic host 8.6 *angel*
angelization 8.9 *deification*
angelize 8.17 *deify*
angelized 8.15 *deified*
Angel of Death 582.2 *death personified;* 441.7 *destroyer*
angel of death 8.6 *angel*
angel of light 8.6 *angel*
angel of love 8.6 *angel*
angel of mercy 35.16 *nurse*
angelology 7.13 *theology*
angelophany 8.8 *divine manifestation*
Angelus 10.9 *prayer*
Angelus bell 742.4 *signal*
anger 594.5; 594.17; 624.4; 607.8 *annoy;* 607.2 *annoyance;* 624.12 *become angry;* 659.1 *discourtesy;* 380.9 *make violent;* 753.1 *protest;* 804.5 *seven deadly sins*
Anger and Resentment 624
angered 624.16 *angry*
angina 260.10 *cardiovascular disease;* 491.2 *painful condition*
angina pectoris 260.10 *cardiovascular disease;* 491.2 *painful condition*
angiogram 35.7 *diagnosis*
angiography 35.7 *diagnosis;* 403.8 *science of structure*
angiology 403.8 *science of structure*
angiosperm 78.2 *flowering plant;* 77.3 *seed plant*
Angiospermae 77.3 *seed plant*
Angkor Wat 10.13 *shrine*
Anglais 59.13 *breeding*
Angle 176
angle 27.39; 55.7; 176.1; 176.11; 450.1 *belief;* 525.3 *external appearance;* 74.15 *fish;* 633.11 *hunt;* 382.22 *kill animals;* 176.6 *motive;* 28.7 *space;* 447.1 *topic*
angle bracket 373.4 *means of connection*
angle brackets 27.25 *algebraic expression*
angled 176.9; 447.7 *focused;* 27.80 *linear*
angled figure 176.3
angled toward 176.10 *biased*
angle iron 176.1 *angle*
angle of bank 322.7 *miscellaneous aviation terms*
angle of depression 27.39 *angle*
angle of elevation 27.39 *angle*
angle off 189.6 *be oblique*
angle of incidence 322.7 *miscellaneous aviation terms*
angle of view 41.17 *lens*
Anglepoise™ 522.6 *electric light*
angler 55.6; 74.10 *fisher;* 633.6 *hunter*
Angles 284.6 *people of the past*
angle subtended 27.39 *angle*
Anglican 7.5 *Christian;* 7.16 *denominational*
Anglicism 5.26 *dialect;* 85.9 *England*
Anglicization 85.9 *England*
Anglicize 85.18 *exert sovereignty;* 760.12 *naturalize*
Anglicized 760.17 *naturalized*
angling 55.1; 55.8; 633.2 *chase;* 74.7 *fishing*
Anglo-African 1.6 *race;* 1.13 *racial*
Anglo-American 1.6 *race*
Anglo-Australian Observatory 29.23 *observatory*
Anglo-Australian Telescope 29.24 *telescope*
Anglo-Catholic 7.5 *Christian*
Anglo-Indian 1.6 *race;* 1.13 *racial*
Anglophile 85.9 *England*
Anglophobe 85.9 *England;* 594.9 *hater*
Anglophobia 594.3 *race hatred*
Anglophobic 594.11 *racist*
Anglophone 729.19 *speaking*
Anglo-Saxon 712.8 *cursing;* 712.2 *offensive language;* 5.19 *swearword*
angora 193.4 *textile*
Angostura bitters 558.8 *mixed drink;* 499.3 *sour thing*
Angra Mainyu 8.7 *devil*
angrily 624.18; 753.11 *disapprovingly;* 659.9 *discourteously;* 625.9 *irascibly*
angry 594.13; 624.16; 625.4 *irascible;* 91.7 *oceanic;* 753.9 *protesting;* 380.6 *violent*
angry look 624.6 *sign of anger*
angry reply 659.3 *act of discourtesy*
angry sea 91.3 *wave*
angry young man 606.3 *dissatisfied person;* 118.8 *dissenter*
Angry Young Men 21.10 *theatre movements*
angst 798.2 *affliction;* 236.11 *harmfulness;* 612.3 *worry*
anguilliform 74.13 *fishlike*
anguine 73.12 *snakelike*
anguish 236.11 *harmfulness;* 491.1 *pain;* 602.1 *sorrow*
anguished 491.7 *feeling pain*
angular 176.7; 300.17 *directional;* 27.80 *linear*
angular acceleration 28.8 *time*
angular deformation 38.16 *deformation*
angular direction 27.39 *angle*
angular distance 27.39 *angle*
angular frequency 28.8 *time*
angular measure 323.5 *navigation*
angular measurement 176.4; 27.39 *angle*
angular momentum 334.4 *energy;* 28.9 *mass*
angular motion 300.5 *circuition;* 307.1 *rotation*
angular resolution 29.28 *resolution*
angular velocity 28.8 *time*
angustifoliate 151.4 *narrow-leaved*
angustirostrate 151.4 *narrow-leaved*
anhedral 322.7 *miscellaneous aviation terms*
anhydrate 428.17 *dry*
anhydration 428.13 *drying*
anhydride 32.10 *salt*
anhydrous 32.36 *acid;* 428.1 *dry*
anhydrously 428.24 *drily*
anhydrous salt 32.10 *salt*
anile 556.14 *aged;* 461.11 *insane*
aniline 529.4 *pigment*
aniline dye 42.6 *dye*
anility 556.5 *old age*
anima 172.5 *inner nature;* 36.21 *psyche;* 11.7 *spirit*
animal 70.2; 70.14 *animalian;* 651.11 *cruel;* 34.21 *living;* 457.8 *nonhuman;* 34.3 *organism*
animal anatomy 70.9 *animal science*
animal behaviour 70.9 *animal science;* 36.1 *psychology*
animal biochemistry 70.9 *animal science*
animal breeding 70.8 *animal welfare;* 43.3 *livestock farming*
animal call 515.1 *animal cry*
animal cell 34.7 *cell*
animal charge 743.8 *heraldic device*
animal conservation 70.8 *animal welfare*
animal costume 551.5 *fancy dress*
animal covering 550.14
Animal Cry 515
animal cry 515.1
animalcular 159.7 *little;* 70.15 *of animals*
animalcule 159.2 *little thing;* 34.3 *organism;* 70.4 *type of animal*
animal dance 22.4 *historic dancing*
animal doctor 35.15 *veterinarian*
animal ecologist 70.11 *zoologist*
animal ecology 70.9 *animal science;* 34.18 *ecology*
animal-fearing 70.18
animal feedstuff 43.9
animal food 557.8
animal health 70.8 *animal welfare;* 43.3 *livestock farming*
animal husbandry 43.3 *livestock farming;* 356.2 *manufacture*
Animalia 70.1 *animals*
animalian 70.14
animalic 70.14 *animalian*
animalism 70.12 *zoophilism*
animalistic 70.14 *animalian;* 796.15 *unlawful*
animality 651.2 *cruelness;* 457.4 *nonhuman existence;* 70.12 *zoophilism*
animal killer 382.13
animal killing 382.9
animal kingdom 70.1 *animals*
animal liberation 70.8 *animal welfare;* 391.2 *equal opportunity*
Animal Liberation Front 70.8 *animal welfare*
animal liberationist 70.10 *animal welfarist*
animal life 70.1 *animals;* 554.1 *life*
animal-like 70.14 *animalian*
animal lover 70.10 *animal welfarist*
animal-loving 70.17
animal magnetism 363.4 *allurement*
animal nutrition 43.3 *livestock farming*
animal painter 19.16 *artist*
animal painting 19.10 *art subject*
animal pathology 70.9 *animal science*
animal physiologist 70.11 *zoologist*
animal physiology 70.9 *animal science*
animal production 43.3 *livestock farming*
animal products 356.7 *produce*
animal protection 70.8 *animal welfare*
animal psychology 70.9 *animal science;* 36.1 *psychology*
animal-rights activism 391.2 *equal opportunity*
animal-rights activist 70.10 *animal welfarist;* 391.3 *liberator*
animal rights movement 70.8 *animal welfare*
Animals 70
animals 70.1; 554.9 *classifications of life*
animal science 70.9
animal spirits 554.1 *life*
animal starch 33.4 *polysaccharide*
animal suicide 382.9 *animal killing*
animal taxonomist 70.11 *zoologist*
animal taxonomy 70.9 *animal science*
animal transport 320.9
animal welfare 70.8; 35.5 *veterinary medicine*
animal welfarist 70.10
animal worship 9.2 *idolatry*
animal worshipper 9.6 *idolater*
animal-worshipping 9.10 *idolatrous*
animate 554.12 *alive;* 488.13 *arouse sensation;* 598.6 *bring cheer;* 613.17 *give courage;* 334.11 *give power;* 331.1 *impel;* 446.16 *inspire;* 34.21 *living;* 483.9 *motivate;* 581.1 *refresh;* 336.8 *strengthen*
animated 342.18 *active;* 598.1 *cheerful;* 334.15 *full of energy;* 554.13 *lively;* 483.12 *motivated;* 338.4 *vigorous*
animated cartoon 19.9 *drawing*
animatedly 554.22 *vitally*
animate existence 554.1 *life*
animation 598.3 *cheerfulness;* 613.6 *encouragement;* 342.4 *energy;* 554.1 *life;* 581.5 *refreshment;* 338.1 *vigour;* 334.3 *vitality*
animatism 9.2 *idolatry;* 101.3 *spiritual world*
animatist 9.6 *idolater*
animatistic 9.10 *idolatrous*
animator 19.16 *artist;* 579.13 *director*
animism 9.2 *idolatry;* 11.1 *occultism;* 4.7 *school of thought;* 101.3 *spiritual world*
animist 101.7 *believer in a nonmaterial world;* 4.11 *follower of a doctrine;* 9.6 *idolater;* 101.9 *parapsychological*
animistic 9.10 *idolatrous;* 4.14 *of a philosophy;* 101.9 *parapsychological*
animistic spirit 8.5 *deity*
animosity 590.6 *bad feeling;* 596.1 *dislike;* 594.1 *hate;* 651.1 *malevolence;* 624.1 *resentment*
animus 172.5 *inner nature;* 36.21 *psyche;* 11.7 *spirit*
anion 39.5 *electrolytic conduction;* 28.66 *ion*
aniseed 496.5 *herbs*
anisogamy 84.4 *reproductive body*
Ankara 87.6 *other cities*
ankh 11.6 *talisman*
ankle-biter 130.15 *baby;* 555.9 *child*
ankle-deep 156.8 *deep;* 157.1 *shallow*
ankle-high 155.5 *low*
ankle-length 148.1 *long*
ankle socks 551.20 *legwear*
anklet 179.3 *circular thing;* 542.7 *jewellery*
anklets 551.20 *legwear*
ankus 425.8 *sharp-pointed thing*
annalist 17.14 *author;* 281.13 *chronicler;* 721.10 *descriptive writer;* 744.9 *recorder;* 275.14 *timekeeper*
annalistic 275.25 *of known date;* 281.17 *timekeeping*
annalistically 281.18 *horologically*
annals 3.5 *chronicle;* 721.3 *narration;* 17.4 *nonfiction;* 744.1 *record*

Anna Pavlova 22.14 *famous ballet dancers*
Annapurna 89.6 *other major mountains and ranges*
anneal 32.30 *extract;* 418.9 *harden;* 423.11 *make tough;* 292.7 *season*
annealed 418.3 *hardened;* 423.2 *toughened*
annelid 75.20 *wormlike*
Annelida 75.6 *worm*
annelidan 75.20 *wormlike*
annelid worm 75.6 *worm*
annex 211.6 *add;* 765.9 *gain;* 773.7 *take;* 773.8 *take back*
annexation 211.1 *addition;* 773.1 *taking;* 773.2 *taking back*
annexe 211.3 *additional item*
annexed 211.8 *additional;* 773.12 *taking*
Annie Oakley 793.6 *absence of charge;* 48.4 *pitching terms*
annihilate 195.9; 708.14 *cancel;* 94.13 *cause not to exist;* 526.3 *cause to disappear;* 357.8 *destroy;* 131.17 *kill;* 358.1 *obliterate;* 382.18 *slaughter*
annihilated 131.23; 94.11 *no more;* 358.6 *obliterated*
annihilating 357.14 *destructive*
annihilation 131.4; 463.5 *death;* 357.1 *destruction;* 526.5 *disguise;* 94.8 *extinction;* 358.3 *obliteration;* 382.4 *slaughter*
annihilationist 357.6 *destroyer*
anniversary 298.3; **298.13**; **601.5**; 601.2 *commemoration;* 275.11 *date;* 462.5 *day to remember;* 600.1 *rejoicing*
anniversary present 768.2 *gift*
annotate 719.10; 722.4 *dissertate;* 743.10 *identify*
annotated 719.15 *interpreted*
annotation 719.2; 211.3 *additional item;* 722.1 *dissertation*
annotations 744.3 *notes*
annotative 719.16; 722.5 *expository*
annotator 722.3 *dissertator;* 719.6 *interpreter*
announce 707.17 *affirm;* 692.30, 693.12 *communicate;* 739.6 *divulge;* 123.8 *make important;* 475.11 *predict;* 740.14 *proclaim;* 742.12 *signal*
announced 692.34 *communicated;* 740.19 *published;* 707.11 *stated*
announcement 740.9 *advertisement;* 693.2 *communication;* 739.2 *divulgence;* 475.3 *plan;* 740.1 *publication;* 707.2 *statement;* 711.1 *warning;* 742.6 *word*
announce one's engagement 593.28 *win the love of*
announcer 707.9 *affirmer;* 692.29 *broadcaster;* 739.4 *discloser;* 693.9 *informant;* 129.8 *precursor;* 740.10 *publicizer;* 742.8 *signer;* 729.10 *speaker*
announcing 742.16 *signalling*
annoy 607.8; 240.5 *be inconvenient;* 596.7 *cause dislike;* 264.22 *cause trouble;* 328.7 *disturb;* 261.6 *fatigue;* 625.8 *make irascible;* 626.12 *make irritable;* 342.17 *meddle;* 624.9 *offend*
annoyance 607.2; 798.2 *affliction;* 236.9 *badness;* 328.1 *disturbance;* 240.3 *inconvenience;* 624.1 *resentment;* 264.8 *snag*
Annoyance and Aggravation 607
annoyed 328.12 *disturbed;* 625.4 *irascible;* 624.15 *resentful;* 264.16 *troubled*
annoying 607.5 *aggravating;* 236.3 *bad;* 328.17 *disturbing;* 261.4 *fatiguing;* 240.1, 264.13 *inconvenient;* 342.21 *meddling;* 242.1 *unpleasant*
annoyingly 607.10; 264.28 *awkwardly;* 328.18 *disturbingly;* 240.6 *inconveniently;* 624.17 *resentfully;* 261.9 *tiringly*
annual 298.13 *anniversary;* 44.17 *botanical;* 298.12 *cyclic;* 78.2 *flowering plant;* 44.9 *garden plant;* 632.9 *habitual;* 740.5 *journal;* 77.14 *of plants;* 275.22 *periodic;* 276.7, 276.8 *periodical;* 77.2 *plant;* 111.17 *regular*
annual company get-together 557.13 *feast*
annual dinner 557.13 *feast*
annually 275.30 *chronologically;* 298.16 *cyclically;* 276.13 *for specified periods;* 77.24 *herbaceously;* 44.20 *horticulturally;* 111.20 *regularly*
annually celebrated day 298.6
annual occurrence 298.3 *anniversary*
annual period 292.1 *season*
annual report 693.3 *document;* 744.1 *record*
annual return 693.3 *document*
annual ring 79.3 *timber*
annual vacation 298.5 *regular thing*
annuitant 769.5 *recipient*
annuity 765.4 *earnings;* 768.2 *gift;* 788.3 *income;* 785.3 *pay;* 769.2 *something received*
annul 16.77; 708.14 *cancel;* 94.13 *cause not to exist;* 131.16 *cease;* 347.3 *counteract;* 357.8 *destroy;* 358.1 *obliterate;* 704.8 *refute;* 708.12 *renounce;* 399.3 *veto;* 355.2 *withdraw*
annul a marriage 571.7 *divorce*
annular 179.5 *circular;* 27.81 *curvilinear*
annularity 179.1 *circularity*
annularly 179.8 *circularly*
annulate 179.5 *circular*
annulation 179.2 *circle*
annulet 743.8 *heraldic device*
annulled 708.20 *cancelled;* 16.57 *null;* 708.18 *rejected*
annulment 708.5 *cancellation;* 131.2 *cessation;* 571.1 *divorce;* 358.3 *obliteration;* 704.1 *refutation;* 355.3 *relinquishment;* 708.4 *renunciation;* 399.1 *veto*
annulus 27.42, 179.2 *circle;* 83.4 *fungal body*
annunciate 707.17 *affirm*
annunciated 707.11 *stated*
annunciation 19.10 *art subject;* 8.8 *divine manifestation;* 707.2 *statement*
annunciative 707.10 *affirmative*
annunciatory 707.10 *affirmative*
annus mirabilis 619.4 *wonder*
Annwn 8.12 *hell*
a nobody 96.5 *insubstantial person*
anode 28.43 *electrical conduction;* 334.7 *electrical power;* 32.19 *electrochemistry;* 39.5 *electrolytic conduction;* 39.20 *electron tube*
anode sludge 32.19 *electrochemistry*
anodic 32.42 *electrochemical*
anodyne 394.5 *analgesic;* 37.4 *drug type;* 685.8 *moderating;* 685.2 *moderator;* 608.3 *reliever;* 394.17 *remedial;* 37.16 *soothing*
anoint 268.19; 37.19 *administer;* 396.21 *grant authority;* 7.21 *ordain;* 10.18 *perform rites*
anointing the sick 10.5 *Christian rite*
anointment 268.4; 396.3 *acquisition of power*
anomalous 118.17 *abnormal;* 299.5 *unusual*
anomalously 766.21 *out of place;* 299.9 *unusually*
anomalousness 118.6 *deviation;* 299.2 *unusualness*
anomaly 118.6 *deviation;* 139.6 *exception*
anomer 32.13 *structure*
anomeric 32.37 *structural*
anomerism 32.13 *structure*
anon 293.17 *early*
Anon. 737.8 *anonymity*
anon. 456.4 *unknown person*
anonymity 737.8; 736.3 *covering up;* 195.5 *nonentity;* 456.3 *unknown thing*
anonymous 736.15 *disguised;* 737.11 *mysterious;* 456.8 *unknown*
anonymously 195.12 *absently;* 737.15 *in secret*
anonymous person 456.4 *unknown person*
anopluran 76.10 *insectan*
anorak 620.3 *boring person;* 551.11 *jacket;* 68.5 *ski equipment*
anorexia 557.3 *delicate eating;* 153.8 *emaciation;* 687.1 *fasting;* 218.8 *insufficiency;* 766.1 *loss;* 337.3 *poor health*
anorexia nervosa 36.15 *compulsion;* 557.3 *delicate eating;* 260.4 *disease;* 153.8 *emaciation;* 218.8 *insufficiency;* 337.3 *poor health*
anorexic 386.5 *compulsive person;* 766.7 *dieter;* 557.18 *eater;* 153.2 *emaciated;* 687.6 *fasting;* 687.4 *fasting person;* 337.10 *ill;* 153.9 *thin person;* 218.3 *underfed;* 260.21 *unhealthy*
anosmia 501.1 *odourlessness*
another 211.8 *additional;* 289.12 *succeeding*
A. N. Other 456.4 *unknown person*
another edition 115.5 *counterpart*
another idea 244.8 *better thing*
another matter 116.2 *unlikeness*
another place 579.11 *British government*
another story 116.2 *unlikeness*
another time 286.3; 286.1 *different time*
another world 101.1 *nonmaterial world*
a nothing 96.5 *insubstantial person*
Ansafone™ 504.9 *audio device*
anse de panier 20.5 *arch*
anseriform 72.21 *avian*
anserine 72.21 *avian;* 459.5 *foolish;* 697.5 *nonsensical*
Answer 706
answer 706.1; **706.17**; 706.2 *acknowledgment;* 785.14 *atone;* 239.6 *be convenient;* 246.8 *be effective;* 111.7 *be the same;* 237.9 *be useful;* 110.9 *correlate;* 692.31 *correspond;* 704.3, 704.10 *countercharge;* 706.5 *counterstatement;* 4.23 *discuss philosophically;* 484.3 *expedient plan;* 719.1 *interpretation;* 706.7 *numerical result;* 701.5 *plea;* 701.16 *plead;* 4.21 *rationalize;* 706.4 *reaction;* 344.5 *reason;* 394.1 *remedy;* 761.5, 761.9 *reply;* 385.3 *retaliate;* 706.6 *solution;* 729.11 *speak;* 217.4, 609.10 *suffice;* 729.7 *utterance*
answerability 706.9; 810.1 *duty*
answerable 706.16; 344.13 *causal;* 784.9 *in debt;* 810.10 *liable*
answerableness 706.8 *correspondence*
answerably 706.27; 344.14 *causally;* 706.26 *correspondingly*
answer back 660.25; **706.18**; 661.6 *be insubordinate;* 704.10 *countercharge;* 759.5 *exchange;* 385.3 *retaliate*
answer book 6.14 *school book*
answered 761.11 *reversed*
answerer 706.10
answer for 706.23; 810.15 *be liable;* 756.8 *guarantee*
answering 706.11; 704.7 *refuting*
answering back 661.3 *act of defiance;* 660.9 *discourtesy;* 385.1 *retaliation*
answering machine 504.9 *audio device;* 744.10 *recording instrument;* 692.9 *telephone*
answering service 504.9 *audio device*
answering to 387.9 *subject*
answerphone 504.9 *audio device*
answer the call 585.12 *go to war*
answer the problem 617.16 *be desirable*
answer the purpose 246.8 *be effective*
answer to 706.21; 108.7 *relate to*
answer to no man 588.4 *be anarchic*
ant 342.10 *busy person;* 76.1 *insect;* 654.10 *social animal;* 76.4 *social insect;* 578.1 *worker*
anta 20.9 *miscellaneous architectural features*
antacid 37.14 *counteracting;* 37.4 *drug type;* 394.6 *purgative*
antagonism 347.1 *counteraction;* 596.1 *dislike;* 242.7 *dissension;* 594.1 *hate;* 651.1 *malevolence;* 113.1 *opposition*
antagonist 596.3 *disliked person;* 113.13 *opponent;* 37.5 *prescription;* 21.23 *role*
antagonistic 249.6 *adverse;* 381.21 *aggressive;* 586.33 *combative;* 347.4 *counteracting;* 661.8 *defying;* 751.9 *disagreeing;* 596.8 *disliking;* 21.39 *dramatic;* 594.10 *hating;* 651.14, 701.9 *hostile;* 113.22 *oppositional*
antagonistically 586.41 *aggressively;* 701.17 *argumentatively;* 347.5 *counter;* 21.44 *dramatically;* 594.18 *hatefully;* 249.12 *in adversity;* 661.10 *in defiance;* 751.11 *in disagreement;* 113.27 *opposingly*
antagonize 607.8 *annoy;* 596.7 *cause dislike;* 594.16 *cause hate;* 113.21, 347.3 *counteract;* 596.5 *dislike;* 624.9 *offend*
Antarctic 494.6 *Arctic*
antarctic 324.13 *directional*
Antarctica 92.1 *continent*
Antarctic waste 563.1 *infertility*
ant bear 71.6 *insect-eating mammal*
ante 167.10 *be in front;* 69.3 *card game terms*
anteater 71.6 *insect-eating mammal*
anteating 71.26 *insectivorous*
antebellum 296.12 *olden;* 589.7 *peaceful*
antecede 129.15 *precede*
antecedence 129.1 *precedence*
antecedency 129.1 *precedence*
antecedent 284.19 *antiquarian;* 4.8 *philosophical term;* 129.4 *precedent;* 129.10 *preceding*
antechamber 167.1 *front*
antedate 288.5 *mistime;* 129.15 *precede*
antedated 288.11 *too early*
antediluvian 3.15 *historic;* 296.12 *olden;* 296.15 *primal*
antelope 60.5 *game;* 743.8 *heraldic device;* 332.12 *swift animal*
antemeridian 290.5 *morning*
ante meridiem 290.8 *in the morning*
antenatal 561.16 *reproductive*
antenatal clinic 35.10 *hospital*
antenna 692.17; 205.4 *component;* 185.3 *protuberance;* 29.26 *radio telescope;* 492.7 *sense organ;* 488.4 *someone or something that feels*
anteposition 129.1 *precedence*
antepost betting 59.7 *horseracing*
anterior 167.6 *front;* 129.10 *preceding*
anteriority 129.1 *precedence*
anteroom 167.1 *front;* 565.7 *room*
ante up 785.6 *pay*
antheap 76.4 *social insect*
anthelion 31.22 *sun*
anthelmintic 394.4 *antidote;* 37.14 *counteracting;* 37.4 *drug type*
anthem 10.8 *hymn;* 18.5 *sacred music;* 516.2 *song*
anthemic 10.21 *ritualistic*
anther 205.6 *branch;* 78.3 *flower part;* 561.8 *organs of reproduction*
antheridium 82.2 *fern plant;* 82.4 *moss plant;* 84.4 *reproductive body*
antherozoid 84.4 *reproductive body*
anthesis 78.5 *flowering*
Anthesteria 10.16 *religious festival*
anthill 565.13 *lair;* 76.4 *social insect*
anthocyanin 33.18 *pigment*
anthologize 723.9 *compile;* 469.4 *pick*
anthology 374.3 *assembly;* 469.9 *chosen thing;* 723.3 *compendium;* 376.30 *compilation;* 412.3 *miscellany*
Anthozoa 75.7 *coelenterate*
anthozoan 75.7 *coelenterate*
anthracite 437.5 *coal;* 435.1 *materials*
anthracosis 260.9 *respiratory disease*
anthrax 260.18 *veterinary disease*
anthrometry 1.10 *measurement*
anthropocentric 566.12 *human*
anthropogenesis 566.5 *study of mankind*
anthropogenic 1.11 *anthropological*
anthropogeny 1.1 *anthropology*
anthropogeographer 1.3 *anthropologist*
anthropogeographic 1.11 *anthropological*
anthropogeographical 1.11 *anthropological*
anthropogeographically 1.16 *anthropologically*
anthropogeography 1.1 *anthropology*
anthropographical 1.11 *anthropological*
anthropographically 1.16 *anthropologically*
anthropography 1.1 *anthropology;* 566.5 *study of mankind*
anthropoid 566.12 *human;* 71.34 *primate*
anthropoid ape 566.3 *early human*
anthropoid apes 71.16 *primate*
anthropoids 71.16 *primate*
anthropolatrous 9.9 *worshipful*
anthropolatry 9.2 *idolatry*
anthropological 1.11; 566.12 *human*
anthropological concept 1.5
anthropological linguistics 5.1 *linguistics*
anthropologically 1.16; 566.15 *humanly*
anthropologist 1.3; 566.6 *studier of mankind*
Anthropology 1
anthropology 1.1; 554.7 *studies of life;* 566.5 *study of mankind*
anthropometric 1.11 *anthropological;* 26.16 *micrometric*
anthropometrical 1.11 *anthropological*
anthropometrically 1.16 *anthropologically*
anthropometrist 1.3 *anthropologist*
anthropometry 1.1 *anthropology;* 26.2 *micrometry;* 566.5 *study of mankind*
anthropomorphic 566.12 *human;* 9.10 *idolatrous*
anthropomorphism 9.2 *idolatry;* 566.5 *study of mankind*
anthropomorphist 9.6 *idolater*
anthropomorphize 9.8 *idolatrize;* 566.14 *make human*
anthropophagite 557.18 *eater*
anthropophagy 557.5 *eating habit*
anthropophobia 655.2 *shyness*
anthroposcopic 1.11 *anthropological*
anthroposophical 11.16 *psychic*
anthroposophist 11.12 *occultist*
anthroposophy 11.1 *occultism;* 566.5 *study of mankind*
anthropotomy 403.8 *science of structure*

anthroscopy 1.10 *measurement*
anthrozoan 75.21 *coelenterate*
anti 113.24 *discordant;* 113.11 *opposer*
anti-aircraft artillery 381.13 *air attack;* 587.11 *guns*
anti-aircraft fire 381.13 *air attack*
anti-aircraft gun 587.11 *guns*
anti-American 594.11 *racist*
antibacterial 37.14 *counteracting*
antiballistic missile 587.5 *missile weapon*
antibiosis 394.4 *antidote*
antibiotic 394.4 *antidote;* 37.14 *counteracting;* 394.8 *drug;* 37.4 *drug type*
antibody 394.4 *antidote;* 431.4 *blood*
antibonding orbital 32.12 *valence*
anticathexis 36.28 *cathexis*
anticholinergic 37.14 *counteracting*
anticholinergic drug 37.4 *drug type*
Antichrist 8.7 *devil*
anticipant 474.4 *expectant person;* 474.5 *expecting*
anticipate 610.7 *aspire;* 616.5 *be cautious;* 293.7 *be early;* 243.3 *be prepared;* 283.10, 474.8 *expect;* 288.5 *mistime;* 293.9 *prepare;* 342.14 *push;* 104.10 *think likely;* 518.16 *visualize*
anticipated 474.7 *expected;* 283.13 *foreseen;* 756.15 *future;* 104.6 *probable*
anticipating 610.12 *expectant;* 474.5 *expecting*
anticipation 474.1, 610.2 *expectation;* 283.4 *looking to the future;* 293.5 *prematurity;* 243.9 *preparation;* 104.1 *probability;* 518.4 *visualization;* 288.1 *wrong time*
anticipative 474.5 *expecting;* 293.16 *premature*
anticipatively 474.12 *expectantly;* 293.20 *prematurely*
anticipatorily 474.12 *expectantly;* 293.20 *prematurely*
anticipatory 616.4 *cautious;* 474.5 *expecting;* 293.16 *premature*
anticlastic surface 27.38 *surface*
anticlimax 630.2 *amazement;* 604.2 *bad outcome*
anticline 30.20 *earth movement;* 184.1 *wrinkle*
anticlockwise 324.10 *clockwise;* 303.29 *in reverse;* 303.25 *reversed;* 307.13 *round*
anticoagulant 394.4 *antidote;* 37.14 *counteracting;* 37.4 *drug type;* 431.20 *liquefying;* 431.9 *solvent*
anticodon 34.13 *genetic material*
anticonvulsant 394.4 *antidote;* 37.4 *drug type*
antics 486.9 *bungling;* 697.3 *tomfoolery*
anticyclone 301.2 *repose;* 31.11 *weather system*
anticyclonic 31.44 *frontal*
antidepressant 37.14 *counteracting;* 394.8 *drug;* 37.4 *drug type*
antidotal 37.14, 347.4 *counteracting;* 394.17 *remedial;* 706.14 *solved*
antidotally 347.5 *counter*
antidote **394.4**; 347.2 *counteracting thing;* 37.4 *drug type;* 484.3 *expedient plan;* 394.1 *remedy;* 706.6 *solution;* 11.6 *talisman*
antielectron 28.77 *elementary particle*
antiemetic 37.14 *counteracting;* 37.4 *drug type*
antifascism 244.11 *reformism*
antifascist 244.12 *reformer*
antifebrile 37.4 *drug type*
antifeminist 653.2 *misanthrope*
antiferromagnetism 28.59 *ferromagnetism*
antifreeze 493.3 *heater*
anti-friction 268.5 *lubricant;* 68.12 *ski*
anti-friction pad 68.5 *ski equipment*
antifungal 37.14 *counteracting*
antifungal agent **83.7**
antifungal drug 37.4 *drug type*
antigen 394.4 *antidote;* 431.4 *blood*
antigravity 366.6 *raising;* 364.5 *repulsion*
antihero 21.23 *role*
antihistamine 394.4 *antidote;* 37.4 *drug type*
antihydrotic 37.14 *counteracting;* 37.4 *drug type*
anti-inflammatory 37.14 *counteracting;* 37.4 *drug type*
antilock braking system 320.21 *miscellaneous motoring terms*
antilog 194.6 *power*
antilogarithm 27.19 *logarithm;* 194.6 *power*
antilogy 702.2 *sophism*
antimacassar 550.12 *protective covering*
antimalarial 37.14 *counteracting*
antimalarial drug 37.4 *drug type*
antimalarial pill 394.3 *prophylactic*
antimasque 21.2 *play*
antimetabolite 37.4 *drug type*
antimissile missile 587.5 *missile weapon*
antimitotic 37.14 *counteracting*
antimonic 32.34 *elemental*
antimonous 32.34 *elemental*
antimycotic 83.7 *antifungal agent;* 37.14 *counteracting;* 37.4 *drug type*
antineutron 28.77 *elementary particle*
antinode 28.12, 326.5 *wave*
antinomian 588.3 *anarchist;* 588.7 *anarchistic;* 16.61 *lawless*
antinomianism 588.2 *anarchism;* 16.41 *lawlessness*
antinomy 16.4 *bad law*
antinovel 17.2 *fiction*
Antiope™ 692.25 *broadcast material*
antiparallel 188.3 *parallel*
antiparticle 28.77 *elementary particle*
antipasto 25.12 *hors d'oeuvre;* 25.47 *Italian dish*
antipathetic 347.4 *counteracting;* 372.18 *disagreeable;* 596.8 *disliking;* 594.10 *hating;* 113.22 *oppositional;* 637.2 *refusing;* 364.8 *repulsive*
antipathetically 347.5 *counter;* 372.23 *disagreeably;* 594.18 *hatefully;* 113.27 *opposingly;* 364.11 *repulsively*
antipathy 347.1 *counteraction;* 596.1 *dislike;* 594.1 *hate;* 113.1 *opposition*
anti-perspirant 501.2 *deodorant*
antiphon 10.8 *hymn;* 706.4 *reaction*
antiphonal 706.12 *reactive*
antiphonal chant 706.4 *reaction*
antipodal 27.81 *curvilinear;* 113.23 *opposite*
antipodal points 113.2 *oppositeness*
antipodean 145.8 *distant;* 86.16 *regional*
Antipodes 86.7 *regions of the world*
antipodes 145.3 *distant place;* 113.2 *oppositeness*
anti-private language argument 4.9 *philosophical problem*
antiproton 28.77 *elementary particle*
antipruritic 37.14 *counteracting;* 37.4 *drug type*
antipsychiatry 36.2 *psychiatry*
antipsychotic 37.14 *counteracting*
antipsychotic drug 37.4 *drug type*
antipyretic 394.4 *antidote;* 37.14 *counteracting;* 37.4 *drug type;* 394.17 *remedial*
antiquarian **284.11**; **284.19**; **296.9**; 296.12 *olden;* 744.9 *recorder*
antiquarianism **284.9**; **296.4**; 3.12 *historicism*
antiquarianize **3.21**; 284.15 *look back*
antiquark 28.77 *elementary particle*
antiquary 284.11, 296.9 *antiquarian*
antiquated 284.19 *antiquarian;* 350.4 *disused;* 3.15 *historic;* 487.2 *not customary;* 296.12 *olden;* 238.1 *useless*
antique 296.12 *olden;* 296.5 *old thing;* 3.11 *relic;* 738.7 *showpiece;* 284.7 *thing of the past*
antique collector 296.9 *antiquarian*
antique costume 551.5 *fancy dress*
antiqued 296.12 *olden*
antique dealer 296.9 *antiquarian*
antiques fair 738.6 *display*
antique show 738.6 *display*
antiquity **296.3**; 3.9 *distant past;* 284.1 *past time;* 3.11 *relic*
antiracism 244.11 *reformism*
antiracist 244.12 *reformer*
anti-realism 4.7 *school of thought*
anti-realist 4.11 *follower of a doctrine;* 4.14 *of a philosophy*
antireflection coating 28.29 *optical element*
antiroad protester 320.21 *miscellaneous motoring terms;* 753.4 *protester*
antiscorbutic 37.14 *counteracting*
anti-Semite 466.7 *bigot;* 594.9 *hater*
anti-Semitic 466.10 *discriminatory;* 622.23 *prejudiced;* 594.11 *racist;* 465.8 *unjust*
anti-Semitism 465.3 *injustice;* 594.3 *race hatred;* 466.4 *social discrimination*
antisepsis 256.2 *cleaning;* 257.1 *hygiene;* 394.3 *prophylactic;* 255.2 *purification*
antiseptic 256.16 *clean;* 256.9 *cleaning agent;* 37.14 *counteracting;* 37.4 *drug type;* 257.4 *hygienic;* 394.3 *prophylactic;* 255.14 *purified;* 394.17 *remedial;* 252.8 *tutelary*
antiseptically 257.7 *hygienically;* 255.19 *purely*
antisepticize 394.20 *doctor;* 257.6 *make hygienic;* 256.15 *purify*
antiserum 394.4 *antidote;* 37.4 *drug type*
antisociability 653.1 *misanthropy*
antisocial 653.3 *misanthropic;* 732.1 *shy;* 118.16 *solitary;* 655.8 *unsociable*
antisocial attitude 653.1 *misanthropy*
antisocial behaviour 653.1 *misanthropy*
antisocial habits 655.1 *unsociability*
antisocially 653.5 *misanthropically;* 655.14 *unsocially*
antisocial personality 36.8 *disordered personality*
antispasmodic 394.4 *antidote;* 37.14 *counteracting;* 37.4 *drug type*
antispastic 37.14 *counteracting;* 37.4 *drug type*
antistrophe 17.8 *part of poem;* 706.4 *reaction*
anti-submarine cruiser 586.24 *warship*
anti-submarine plane 586.31 *military aircraft*
anti-submarine submarine 586.24 *warship*
antisymmetric relation 27.63 *mathematical logic*
antitank weapon 587.5 *missile weapon*
antithesis 113.8 *contrariety;* 192.1 *inversion;* 113.2 *oppositeness;* 542.1 *ornament;* 4.5 *philosophical argument;* 4.8 *philosophical term;* 706.4 *reaction;* 708.3 *rebuttal*
antithetical 113.25 *contrary;* 113.23 *opposite;* 542.10 *ornate;* 706.12 *reactive*
antithetically 706.24 *in answer;* 113.27 *opposingly*
antithrombin 37.4 *drug type*
antitoxin 394.4 *antidote;* 347.2 *counteracting thing*
antitrade winds 31.17 *wind system*
anti-transmit-receive switch 692.28 *radar*
Anti-Trust laws 251.2 *economic restraint*
antitussive 37.14 *counteracting;* 37.4 *drug type*
antivenene 37.4 *drug type*
antivenin 347.2 *counteracting thing*
antivenom 347.2 *counteracting thing*
anti-Vietnam War movement 749.1 *pacification;* 589.1 *peace*
antiviral 37.14 *counteracting*
antiviral drug 37.4 *drug type*
antivivisectionist 70.10 *animal welfarist*
anti-war movement 749.1 *pacification;* 589.1 *peace*
antler 425.8 *sharp-pointed thing*
antlion 76.5 *larva*
Antonine Wall 384.9 *barrier;* 147.7 *interface*
antonomasia 721.7 *nomenclature;* 17.12 *poetic language*
Antony and Cleopatra 593.10 *lovers*
antonym 694.4 *type of meaning;* 5.17 *word*
antonymous 694.6 *meaningful;* 5.42 *worded*
Antwerp blue 539.5 *blueness*
a number 207.1 *plurality*
anuran 73.7, 73.13 *amphibian*
anus 308.4 *body orifice;* 315.7 *outlet;* 168.2 *rear end*
anvil 504.5 *internal ear;* 760.4 *medium of conversion*
anvil cloud 31.18 *cloud*
anxiety 254.5 *danger;* 328.1 *disturbance;* 474.1 *expectation;* 612.2 *fearfulness;* 236.11 *harmfulness;* 461.6 *mental breakdown;* 264.4 *problem;* 36.12 *stress;* 612.3 *worry*
anxiety equivalent 36.12 *stress*
anxiety hysteria 36.12 *stress*
anxiety neurosis 36.10 *neurosis*
anxiety reaction 36.10 *neurosis*
anxiety state 36.12 *stress*
anxious 629.5 *distrustful;* 328.12 *disturbed;* 474.5 *expecting;* 612.8 *fearful;* 264.16 *troubled;* 612.9 *worried*
anxiously 328.19 *distractedly;* 474.12 *expectantly;* 612.15 *fearfully;* 629.9 *jealously*
anxiousness 629.2 *distrust*
any **138.12**; 203.6 *quantitative;* 204.6 *whole*
anybody 138.12 *any*
anybody's guess 705.6 *uncertainty;* 456.3 *unknown thing*
any day 275.27 *at what time*
anyhow **408.28**; 317.16 *how*
any old way 666.7 *negligently*
anyone 138.12 *any*
anyone's guess 453.9 *uncertainty*
any other business 447.2 *issue;* 484.1 *plan*
anything 138.12 *any*
anything but 708.24 *never!*
anything goes 250.12 *unconditional*
any time 286.3 *another time;* 275.27 *at what time*
any time but this 286.1 *different time*
anyway 317.16 *how*
anywhere 97.15 *here*
anywise 317.16 *how*
Anzac 586.8 *soldier*
A-OK 698.21 *accurate;* 797.1 *good;* 230.1 *perfect;* 235.1 *worthy*
AOR 18.9 *popular music*
aorist 5.34 *tense*
apace 262.6 *hastily;* 332.14 *swiftly*
Apadana 7.12 *religious text*
apart **146.8**; **372.16**; **372.21**; 197.16 *alone;* 369.21, 634.21 *away;* 145.8 *distant;* 145.10 *distantly;* 311.16 *divergently;* 100.18 *extraneously;* 315.18 *forth;* 372.22 *in isolation;* 197.22 *one by one;* 100.11 *separate;* 109.6 *unrelated;* 655.8 *unsociable;* 571.13 *without one's spouse*
apart from 211.10 *additionally;* 128.12 *exclusively*
apartheid 128.4 *exclusiveness;* 465.3 *injustice;* 594.3 *race hatred;* 100.3 *separateness;* 655.3 *separation;* 372.2 *setting apart;* 466.4 *social discrimination*
apartment 565.5 *house;* 440.1 *property*
apartment block **565.6**
apartment building 38.20 *building;* 356.8 *construction*
apartment sharer 764.3 *participant*
apartment-sharing 764.5 *jointly possessing*
apartness 197.5 *aloneness;* 655.1 *unsociability*
a party to 764.3 *participant*
apathetic **355.6**; 634.18 *avoiding;* 637.3 *cautious;* 341.3 *inactive;* 472.7 *inattentive;* 618.7 *indifferent;* 339.5 *inert;* 592.1 *insensitive;* 343.3 *not participating;* 301.5 *sedentary;* 489.6 *unfeeling;* 333.5 *unhurried;* 639.4 *unsteady*
apathetically **355.8**; 343.16 *impassively;* 472.14 *inattentively;* 618.17 *indifferently;* 339.7 *inertly;* 301.10 *motionlessly;* 634.23 *shyly;* 592.8 *unfeelingly;* 341.5 *without action*
apathy **639.14**; 36.13 *depression;* 637.13 *dissociation;* 343.7 *idleness;* 341.1 *inaction;* 472.1 *inattention;* 618.1 *indifference;* 339.1 *inertness;* 592.3 *insensitiveness;* 489.1 *lack of feeling;* 301.1 *motionlessness;* 634.13 *shirking;* 388.1 *submission*
Apaturia 10.16 *religious festival*
Apaya 8.12 *hell*
APB 633.1 *pursuit*
ape 111.9 *duplicate;* 115.12, 125.9 *imitate;* 125.7 *imitator;* 461.11 *insane;* 654.10 *social animal*
aped 115.8 *simulated*
apellative 721.8 *name*
apeman 296.7 *ancient people;* 566.3 *early human*
aperçu 723.1 *summary*
aperient 256.2 *cleaning;* 37.4 *drug type;* 560.25 *faecal;* 371.28 *propellant;* 255.4, 394.6 *purgative;* 37.17 *stimulating*
apéritif 558.7 *alcoholic drink;* 495.3 *appetizer;* 129.5 *preface*
aperture 146.2 *crack;* 41.18 *exposure time;* 308.1 *opening;* 29.28 *resolution*
aperture priority 41.18 *exposure time*
aperture setting 41.18 *exposure time*
aperture stop 28.32 *optical instrument*
aperture synthesis 29.26 *radio telescope*
apery 125.3 *mockery*
apes 71.16 *primate*
APEX 793.4 *bargain*
apex 27.39 *angle;* 154.2 *heights;* 61.6 *motor-racing terms;* 174.1 *summit*
Apfelstrudel 25.46 *German dish*
aphaeresis 149.2 *shortening*
aphanitic texture 30.28 *rock*
aphasia 730.3 *speech defect;* 36.14 *trance*
aphasic 730.12 *inarticulate;* 506.3 *silent*
aphelion 29.21 *orbit*

apheresis 723.2 *outline*
aphid 76.3 *pest;* 44.12 *pests and diseases*
aphonia 506.4 *silence;* 36.14 *trance;* 730.1 *voicelessness*
aphonic 506.3 *silent;* 730.9 *voiceless*
aphorism 745.1 *maxim;* 269.2 *outline;* 4.1 *philosophy;* 698.4 *truism*
aphoristic 269.3 *concise;* 745.2 *proverbial;* 698.17 *truistic*
aphoristically 745.4 *proverbially*
aphorize **745.3**; 4.22 *propound a philosophy*
aphrenia 461.2 *subnormality*
aphrodisia 593.5 *desire*
aphrodisiac 490.4 *pleasurable things*
Aphrodite 593.16 *gods and goddesses of love*
apiarian 76.14 *entomological*
apiarist 76.8 *entomologist*
apiary 76.4 *social insect*
apical 174.5 *top*
apical bud 77.8 *bud*
a picture of health 259.1 *healthy*
apiece 139.32 *severally*
aping 125.12 *imitative;* 621.1 *mockery;* 115.1 *similarity*
apish 125.12 *imitative*
apishly 125.14 *imitatively*
a pity 627.5 *misfortune*
a plague on you 798.15 *bad luck!*
aplanospore 84.4 *reproductive body*
aplastic anaemia 260.11 *blood disease*
a pleasure 265.6 *easy thing*
aplenty 208.13 *numerously*
aplomb 4.3 *detachment;* 228.2 *determination;* 638.16 *fortitude*
apoandrous 78.12 *of flowers*
apocalypse 739.1 *disclosure;* 131.5 *fate;* 475.1 *prediction;* 357.4 *ruin;* 525.4 *something that appears*
apocalyptic 525.7 *appearing;* 357.14 *destructive;* 131.20 *ending;* 475.13 *predicting;* 739.12 *revelatory*
apocarpous 80.9 *of a fruit*
apocope 269.1 *conciseness;* 723.2 *outline;* 149.2 *shortening*
apocrine 559.4 *secretory*
apocrine secretion 559.1 *secretion*
Apocrypha 7.12 *religious text*
apocryphal 699.32 *spurious;* 453.5 *uncertified*
Apoda 73.7 *amphibian*
apodal 73.11 *reptilian*
apodan 73.7, 73.13 *amphibian*
apodasis 5.23 *phrase*
apodeictic 725.3 *clear;* 703.9 *demonstrated;* 4.16 *dialectical;* 738.13 *displayed;* 695.2 *simple*
apoenzyme 33.11 *enzyme*
apogee 29.35 *rocketry;* 174.1 *summit*
apolitical 750.20 *agreeable*
Apollo 17.13 *poetic genius;* 29.31 *space travel*
Apollyon 8.7 *devil*
apologetic **701.12**; 807.4 *atoning;* 808.6 *penitent;* 714.11 *vindicatory*
apologetical 807.4 *atoning*
apologetically **701.20**; 714.15 *in vindication;* 807.8, 808.8 *penitently*
apologetics 444.3 *debate;* 7.13 *theology*
apologies 808.1 *penitence*
apologist 444.5 *reasoner;* 714.5 *vindicator*
apologize **807.6**; 808.4 *be penitent;* 752.14 *offer reparation;* 701.16 *plead;* 479.4 *recant;* 609.11 *recompense;* 388.4 *succumb*
apologize to 807.6 *apologize*
apology **807.2**; 17.4 *nonfiction;* 808.1 *penitence;* 701.5 *plea;* 479.8 *recantation;* 609.2 *reparation*
apopetalous 78.12 *of flowers*
apophthegm 745.1 *maxim;* 795.7 *moral*
apoplectic 624.16 *angry;* 1.15 *physical*
apoplectically 624.18 *angrily*
apoplectic build 1.9 *physical type*
apoplexy 335.4 *disability;* 260.2 *illness;* 327.8 *spasm*
apoptosis 34.10 *cell division*
aporetic 4.16 *dialectical*
aposepalous 78.12 *of flowers*
apostasize 708.12 *renounce*
apostasy **479.7**; 470.7 *abrogation;* 704.2 *denial;* 708.2 *rejection;* 761.1 *reversion*
apostate 634.17 *avoider;* 760.6 *convert;* 451.5 *disbeliever;* 118.8 *dissenter;* 479.11 *equivocating;* 479.9 *equivocator;* 708.9 *negativist*
apostatical 355.5 *relinquished*
apostatically 355.8 *apathetically*
apostatize **479.3**; 760.10 *be converted;* 639.9 *change sides;* 451.8 *disbelieve;* 470.4 *revoke;* 355.2 *withdraw*
a posteriori 4.16 *dialectical;* 444.8 *rational*
a posteriori reasoning 444.2 *reasoning*
apostle 760.5 *converter;* 267.5 *follower*
apostrophe 5.36 *accent;* 733.1 *address;* 17.12 *poetic language;* 742.7 *punctuation;* 735.1 *soliloquy*
apostrophic 735.5 *soliloquizing*
apostrophize 733.7 *address;* 735.3 *soliloquize;* 729.14 *speak to*
apostrophized 742.17 *punctuated*
apothecaries' measure 26.5 *measuring system*
apothecaries' weight 414.9 *avoirdupois weight;* 26.5 *measuring system*
apothecary 394.16 *druggist*
apotheosis 8.9 *deification;* 366.7 *lift;* 669.3 *praise*
apotheosize 8.17 *deify;* 9.8 *idolatrize;* 669.14 *praise;* 366.3 *promote;* 667.16 *revere*
apotheosized 366.12 *exalted*
apozem 431.10 *solution*
appal 364.4 *be repulsive;* 242.10 *displease;* 612.13 *frighten*
Appalachian Mountains 89.4 *US mountains*
appalling 612.10 *frightening;* 364.8 *repulsive*
appanage 211.1 *addition;* 440.3 *historic property terms*
apparat 12.3 *governance*
apparatchik 579.16 *official*
apparatus 348.2 *instrument;* 438.1 *tool*
apparatus criticus 719.2 *annotation*
apparel 551.1, 551.32 *dress*
apparelled 551.29 *dressed*
apparent **171.8**; 525.7 *appearing;* 703.12 *demonstrable;* 738.13 *displayed;* 716.9 *evident;* 474.7 *expected;* 738.14 *manifest;* 308.13 *opened up;* 699.34 *pretending;* 104.6 *probable;* 518.23, 520.1 *visible*
apparently **96.19**; **525.15**; 716.15 *evidently;* 171.15 *externally;* 738.16 *manifestly;* 308.25 *obviously;* 449.16 *originally;* 104.11 *probably;* 693.19 *reportedly;* 699.41 *spuriously;* 518.25, 520.11 *visibly*
apparent magnitude 29.13 *luminosity*
apparentness 171.3 *appearance;* 527.10 *openness;* 699.7 *pretence*
apparent power 39.26 *electrical energy*
apparent wind 50.1 *sailing*
apparition 8.8 *divine manifestation;* 477.5 *fantasy;* 11.11 *ghost;* 97.6 *ghostly presence;* 518.5 *imagination;* 738.10 *manifestation;* 525.4 *something that appears*
apparitor 16.10 *law officer*
appeal 363.4 *allurement;* 363.11 *attract;* 53.19 *dismiss;* 545.1 *gorgeousness;* 395.8 *influence;* 16.7 *legal trial;* 593.4 *lovability;* 617.5 *object of desire;* 768.3 *offering;* 785.1 *payment;* 241.6 *pleasantness;* 705.17 *question;* 708.11 *rebut;* 708.3 *rebuttal;* 710.1, 710.6 *request;* 733.2 *salutation;* 710.3 *solicitation;* 710.8 *solicit money;* 593.28 *win the love of*
appealed 708.18 *rejected*
appealer 710.4 *requester*
appeal fund 439.1 *store*
appealing **395.12**; 363.9 *attractive;* 617.8 *desirable;* 595.5 *likable;* 593.22 *lovable;* 545.6 *personable;* 241.1 *pleasant;* 710.3 *solicitation*
appealingly 363.14 *attractively;* 593.30 *lovingly;* 595.10 *with great liking*
appeal to **733.8**; 483.9 *motivate;* 729.14 *speak to*
appeal to arms 585.12 *go to war;* 585.7 *war measures*
appeal to law 16.70 *litigate*
appeal to the electorate 469.5 *vote*
appear **520.9**; **525.11**; **703.18**; 21.34 *act;* 171.13 *appear outwardly;* 312.1 *arrive;* 97.12 *attend;* 525.12 *become visible;* 739.9 *be disclosed;* 449.5 *be discovered;* 97.11 *be present;* 518.19 *be visible;* 130.27, 315.10 *emerge;* 699.28 *mask;* 738.4 *show oneself*
Appearance **525**
appearance **171.3**; **525.1**; 312.10 *arrival;* 631.1 *conduct;* 130.2 *creation;* 553.4 *design;* 8.8 *divine manifestation;* 314.1 *entry;* 716.3 *evidentness;* 699.14 *façade;* 477.4 *ideality;* 96.2 *illusion;* 738.10 *manifestation;* 160.6 *nature;* 97.2 *omnipresence;* 221.1 *state*
appearance of truth 698.12 *realism*
appear for 706.23 *answer for*
appear guilty **806.9**
appear in 525.13 *occur*
appear in court 525.13 *occur*
appearing **525.7**; 525.1 *appearance;* 312.18 *arriving;* 738.14 *manifest*
appearing before the judge 16.53 *litigating*
appearing guilty **806.6**
appearing in court 16.53 *litigating*
appearing true 698.25 *lifelike*
appear in the shops 525.13 *occur*
appear like 525.11 *appear*
appear on film 525.13 *occur*
appear on stage 525.13 *occur*
appear outwardly **171.13**
appear to be 525.11 *appear*
appease 807.5 *atone;* 490.10, 609.9 *comfort;* 685.4 *moderate;* 752.14 *offer reparation;* 752.15 *offer worship;* 749.4 *pacify;* 480.15 *persuade;* 609.11 *recompense;* 608.9 *relieve;* 421.13 *smooth over;* 388.3 *submit;* 9.7 *worship;* 419.16 *yield*
appeased 608.7 *relieved*
appeasement 807.1 *atonement;* 608.1 *ease;* 419.12 *gentleness;* 752.6 *offering;* 749.1 *pacification;* 609.2 *reparation;* 388.1 *submission;* 9.1 *worship*
appeaser **388.2**; 748.3 *mediator*
appeasing 807.4 *atoning;* 419.7 *impressionable;* 749.6 *pacificatory*
appellant 715.3 *accuser;* 16.8 *litigant;* 710.4 *requester*
appellate 16.49 *judicatory*
appellate court 16.19 *law court*
appellation 721.8 *name;* 721.7 *nomenclature*
append 211.6 *add*
appendage 211.1 *addition;* 664.5 *adherent;* 205.4 *component;* 223.4 *concomitant*
appendages 440.4 *possessions*
appendicectomy 394.12 *surgery*
appendicular skeleton 403.7 *skeleton*
appendix 211.3 *additional item;* 719.2 *annotation;* 131.10 *ending;* 168.1 *rear;* 108.1 *relatedness*
apperceive 442.12 *think*
apperception 442.1 *mind*
apperceptionism 36.1 *psychology*
appertain 750.27 *fit;* 108.7 *relate to*
appertaining 750.16 *fitting*
appertain to 127.5 *be included*
appetancy 617.1 *desire*
appetite **557.2**; **617.3**; 617.1 *desire;* 595.1 *liking;* 495.5 *taste bud*
appetizer **495.3**; 25.12 *hors d'oeuvre;* 557.14 *mouthful;* 205.2 *particular;* 129.5 *preface*
appetizing 617.8 *desirable;* 557.27 *edible;* 496.9 *piquant;* 241.4, 495.7 *tasty*
appetizingly 617.17 *desirably*
applaud 669.16 *acclaim;* 671.6 *be grateful;* 598.8 *cheer;* 600.7 *dance;* 742.11 *gesture;* 601.18 *salute;* 9.7 *worship*
applauder **669.10**
applauding 669.20 *acclamatory;* 600.9 *rejoicing*
applause 669.5 *acclaim;* 598.5 *cheer;* 514.3 *cry of praise;* 600.2 *fanfare;* 742.3 *gesture;* 671.3 *recognition;* 601.9 *rejoicing;* 21.8 *scene*
apple 48.3 *baseball equipment;* 49.3 *basketball equipment*
apple aphid 44.12 *pests and diseases*
apple blossom 78.1 *flower*
apple blossom weevil 44.12 *pests and diseases*
apple cheeks 259.3 *health;* 535.7 *red thing*
apple corer 369.9 *extractor*
apple fritter 25.36 *cake*
apple juice 558.6 *soft drink*
apple-knocker 564.5 *countryman*
apple of discord 80.5 *figurative usage*
apple of one's eye 80.5 *figurative usage;* 593.11 *loved one*
apple peel 238.6 *refuse*
apple pie 25.36 *cake;* 498.3 *dessert*
apple-pie order 407.5 *orderliness*
apple polisher 80.5 *figurative usage*
apple-polishing 664.2 *sycophancy;* 664.7 *sycophantic*
apples 80.5 *figurative usage*
apple sauce 80.5 *figurative usage;* 25.15 *sauce*
apple sawfly 44.12 *pests and diseases*
Appleton layer 434.3 *atmospheric layers*
appliance 392.7 *convenience;* 348.2 *instrument;* 438.1 *tool;* 349.6 *use*
appliances 352.1 *means*
applicability 136.1 *qualification;* 349.6 *use;* 237.5 *usefulness*
applicable 239.1 *convenient;* 348.6 *instrumental;* 349.10 *usable;* 237.1 *useful*
applicant 710.4 *requester*
application **40.11**; 342.8 *assiduity;* 471.3 *carefulness;* 640.2 *commitment;* 239.3 *convenience;* 348.1 *instrumentality;* 719.1 *interpretation;* 710.1 *request;* 394.10 *surgical dressing;* 694.4 *type of meaning;* 349.6 *use;* 237.5 *usefulness*
applications program 40.8 *software*
applied 348.8 *practical;* 28.99 *theoretical;* 237.1 *useful*
applied arts 19.1 *art*
applied energy 576.4 *exertion*
applied linguistics 5.1 *linguistics*
applied load 38.14 *load*
applied mathematics **27.3**
applied physics 28.4 *experimental physics;* 402.6 *natural science*
applied psychology 36.1 *psychology*
applied science 455.5 *science*
applied sociology 2.1 *sociology*
appliqué 542.3 *pattern*
apply 37.19 *administer;* 136.14 *be qualified;* 108.7 *relate to;* 710.6 *request*
apply a remedy 394.19 *remedy*
apply a tourniquet 394.20 *doctor*
apply for 135.8 *miss;* 710.6 *request*
applying pressure 492.2 *touching*
apply oneself 576.8 *exert oneself*
apply oneself to 733.12 *address oneself to;* 354.1 *undertake*
apply one's mind 443.13 *concentrate*
apply pressure 386.6 *compel*
apply the match 130.20 *activate*
apply the war paint 547.16 *make up*
apply to 733.8 *appeal to;* 108.7 *relate to*
apply try out 349.1 *use*
appoggiatura 18.16 *musical note*
appoint 397.13 *authorize;* 398.7 *delegate;* 396.21 *grant authority;* 7.21 *ordain;* 469.4 *pick;* 106.1 *predetermine*
appointed 398.9 *delegated;* 396.13 *elected;* 106.3 *predetermined;* 397.15 *self-assured;* 143.6 *situated*
appointed day 275.11 *date*
appointed person 398.1 *delegate*
appointee 398.1 *delegate*
appointment 396.3 *acquisition of power;* 770.1 *allocation;* 397.4 *authorization;* 398.3 *delegation;* 243.11 *fitting out;* 654.3 *meeting;* 7.9 *priesthood;* 376.8 *rendezvous;* 469.6 *selection*
appointments 438.7 *equipment*
appointments calendar 475.3 *plan*
apportion 770.4 *allot;* 349.5 *dispose of;* 372.11 *divide;* 26.11 *measure out;* 205.10 *part;* 203.8 *quantify*
apportioned 770.7 *allocated*
apportioning 770.1 *allocation*
apportionment 770.1 *allocation*
appose 147.18 *juxtapose*
apposite 750.16 *fitting;* 108.4 *related*
appositely 750.38 *fittingly;* 108.10 *relevantly*
appositeness 136.1 *qualification;* 108.1 *relatedness*
apposition 147.3 *juxtaposition;* 5.30 *syntax*
appraisable 26.14 *measurable*
appraisal 466.1 *discrimination;* 464.1 *judgment;* 26.1 *measurement*
appraise 464.12 *estimate;* 26.10 *measure;* 790.11 *price*
appraisement 26.1 *measurement;* 790.7 *tax*
appraiser 464.5 *judge;* 26.9 *measurer*
appreciate 765.10 *augment;* 792.9 *be dear;* 671.6 *be grateful;* 213.4 *increase;* 455.11 *know;* 241.14, 595.7 *like;* 593.23 *love;* 667.15 *respect;* 495.9 *taste*
appreciated 595.5 *likable;* 667.12 *respected*
appreciation 669.2 *admiration;* 765.2 *augmentation;* 671.1 *gratitude;* 213.1 *increase;* 464.1 *judgment;* 466.2 *judiciousness;* 667.1 *respect*
appreciative 669.18 *approving;* 466.9 *discriminating;* 671.4 *grateful;* 464.8 *judging;* 549.5 *refined;* 667.8 *respectful*

appreciatively 671.8 *gratefully*; 466.16 *judiciously*
appreciativeness 671.1 *gratitude*
appreciatory 669.18 *approving*
apprehend 251.11 *detain*; 474.8 *expect*; 446.14 *have an idea*; 455.11 *know*; 400.15 *learn*; 4.21 *rationalize*; 773.10 *take away*; 695.6 *understand*
apprehending 773.3 *taking away*
apprehensibility 695.9 *intelligibility*
apprehensible 695.1 *intelligible*
apprehension 254.5 *danger*; 474.1 *expectation*; 612.2 *fearfulness*; 446.1 *idea*; 455.1 *knowledge*; 16.6 *legal process*; 695.12 *understanding*
apprehensive 629.5 *distrustful*; 474.5 *expecting*; 612.8 *fearful*; 732.1 *shy*
apprehensively 474.12 *expectantly*; 612.15 *fearfully*; 629.9 *jealously*; 732.8 *shyly*
apprehensiveness 629.2 *distrust*; 474.1 *expectation*; 612.2 *fearfulness*
apprentice 578.2 *artisan*; 130.14 *beginner*; 295.12 *immature*; 6.7 *learner*; 387.6 *subject*; 387.3 *subordinate*; 486.10 *unskilled person*
apprentice chef 25.2 *cook*
apprenticed 387.9 *subject*; 486.2 *unskilled*
apprentice oneself 354.1 *undertake*
apprenticeship 243.12 *briefing*; 387.1 *subjection*; 555.1 *youth*
apprise 713.5 *advise*; 6.22 *educate*; 693.11 *inform*; 711.5 *warn*
approach **310.2**; **312.3**; **733.4**; **733.9**; 318.4 *access*; 312.10 *arrival*; 765.10 *augment*; 765.2 *augmentation*; 283.7 *be in the future*; 310.9 *converge*; 314.5 *entrance*; 47.2 *field events*; 317.14 *find one's way*; 322.5 *flight*; 56.1 *golf*; 352.1 *means*; 300.3 *motion towards*; 147.16 *near*; 147.1 *nearness*; 752.1, 752.9 *offer*; 27.94 *order*; 484.9 *plan*; 484.2 *policy*; 710.1, 710.6 *request*; 317.2 *route*; 724.1 *style*; 229.4 *tend*; 317.1 *way*
approachability 102.2 *possibleness*
approachable 312.20 *attainable*; 102.5 *possible*
approach a problem 484.9 *plan*
approaches 147.5 *near place*
approaching **312.19**; 310.8 *advancing*; 283.11 *future*; 147.9 *near*
approaching shot 56.3 *golf shots*
approach light 522.6 *electric light*
approach of time 283.6 *future event*
approbation 669.1 *approval*; 811.1 *estimation*; 757.1 *permission*; 667.1 *respect*
approbatory 669.18 *approving*
appropriable 772.12 *adoptive*
appropriate 119.9 *adequate*; 772.8 *adopt*; 770.4 *allot*; 239.1 *convenient*; 765.9 *gain*; 797.1 *good*; 287.9 *opportunely*; 136.9 *qualified*; 292.14 *seasonable*; 774.12 *steal*; 773.7 *take*; 287.6 *timely*
appropriated 772.12 *adoptive*; 772.11 *borrowed*; 773.12 *taking*
appropriately 136.17 *capably*; 750.38 *fittingly*
appropriateness 797.8 *good*; 136.1 *qualification*; 287.1 *timeliness*
appropriating 772.12 *adoptive*; 763.1 *possession*
appropriation 772.2 *adoption*; 770.1 *allocation*; 763.1 *possession*; 773.1 *taking*
appropriation of land 165.1 *enclosure*
appropriator 773.6 *taker*
approvable **669.22**
approvably **669.26**
Approval 669
approval **669.1**; 750.7 *consent*; 811.1 *estimation*; 538.15 *green light*; 595.1 *liking*; 413.6 *moral support*; 757.1 *permission*; 667.1 *respect*
approve **669.11**; 750.28 *consent*; 396.21 *grant authority*; 757.3 *permit*; 469.4 *pick*; 595.8 *prefer*
approved **669.23**; 396.16 *authorized*; 750.17 *consenting*; 239.1 *convenient*; 632.12 *established*; 757.7 *permitted*; 811.3 *reputable*; 235.1 *worthy*
approved for use 237.2 *usable*
approved school 815.1 *prison*
approved strike 15.4 *industrial dispute*
approve of 669.11 *approve*; 413.14 *give moral support*; 464.11 *judge*
approving **669.18**; 750.17 *consenting*; 464.8 *judging*; 595.6 *liking*
approvingly **669.25**; 595.11 *admiringly*; 464.13 *judicially*; 750.39 *with consent*
approximate 420.13 *be unfinished*; 27.93 *equate*; 138.20 *generalized*; 147.9 *near*; 203.6 *quantitative*; 115.7 *similar*; 420.5 *unfinished*
approximately 115.14 *comparably*; 138.29 *generally*; 420.15 *incompletely*; 27.87 *mathematically*; 147.13 *nearly*; 203.7 *quantitatively*; 274.22 *wrongly*
approximately equal to 27.88 *equal to*
approximateness 420.10 *rough idea*
approximate to 115.11 *make similar*
approximating 147.9 *near*; 115.7 *similar*
approximation 210.1 *calculation*; 274.2 *inaccuracy*; 26.1 *measurement*; 147.1 *nearness*; 27.66 *proof*; 115.1 *similarity*
appulse 147.1 *nearness*
appurtenance 211.1 *addition*; 223.4 *concomitant*; 127.2 *thing included*
appurtenances 763.4 *possession*; 440.4 *possessions*
appurtenant 405.8 *belonging*; 127.8 *included*
APR 784.4 *interest*
apricate 428.19 *bake*
apricot 536.1 *orange*; 536.3 *orange thing*
April fool 700.22 *dupe*
April fool hoax 700.11 *hoax*
April Fools' Day 298.6 *annually celebrated day*
April shower 227.3 *changeable thing*
April showers 31.25 *rain*
a priori 4.16 *dialectical*; 445.7 *precognitive*; 444.8 *rational*; 476.8 *supposed*
a priori knowledge 4.9 *philosophical problem*; 445.2 *precognition*
a priori reasoning 444.2 *reasoning*
apriorism 4.7 *school of thought*
apriorist 4.11 *follower of a doctrine*
apron 551.25 *accessories*; 322.4 *airport*; 256.11 *cleaning cloth*; 21.17 *stage*; 7.11 *vestment*
apron stage 21.17 *stage*
apron strings 378.4 *restraint*
apropos 287.9 *opportunely*; 287.6 *timely*
apse 20.10 *church architecture*
APT 321.10 *miscellaneous*
apt 698.21 *accurate*; 119.9 *adequate*; 706.15 *correspondent*; 617.8 *desirable*; 6.17 *educable*; 543.3 *elegant*; 797.1 *good*; 102.5 *possible*; 104.6 *probable*; 136.9 *qualified*; 485.6 *skilful*; 287.6 *timely*
apterium 72.17 *plumage*
aptitude **229.3**; **485.2**; 334.2 *ability*; 442.4 *cleverness*; 265.1 *easiness*; 6.10 *educability*; 595.2 *inclination*; 455.2 *information*; 458.2 *intelligence*; 102.2 *possibleness*; 136.1 *qualification*; 139.7 *special skill*
aptitude test 36.5 *psychological test*
aptly 136.17 *capably*; 706.26 *correspondingly*; 543.5 *elegantly*; 750.38 *fittingly*; 287.9 *opportunely*; 801.18 *properly*; 6.26 *studiously*
aptness 698.8 *accuracy*; 485.2 *aptitude*; 706.8 *correspondence*; 6.10 *educability*; 543.1 *elegance*; 797.8 *good*; 136.1 *qualification*; 287.1 *timeliness*
apt to 229.5 *tending to*
aqua 433.1 *water*
aquaculture 91.5 *oceanography*
aquamarine 539.1 *blue*; 539.6 *blue thing*; 538.1 *green*; 538.11 *green thing*
aquaplaning 320.21 *miscellaneous motoring terms*
aquarelle 19.8 *painting*
aquarellist 19.16 *artist*
aquarist 74.12 *ichthyologist*
aquarium 439.5 *collection*; 376.31 *exhibition*; 565.12 *stall*; 74.6 *study of fish*
aquarium fish 74.2 *fish*
Aquarius 316.7 *transferor*
aquatic 323.11 *nautical*; 70.15 *of animals*; 77.14 *of plants*; 77.2 *plant*; 433.21 *watery*
aquatic animal **70.5**
aquatint 19.22 *engrave*; 19.15 *engraving*; 19.7 *picture*
aquatinter 19.18 *engraver*
aquavit 558.7 *alcoholic drink*
aqueduct 38.21, 317.9 *bridge*
aqueous 433.21 *watery*
aqueous humour 518.2 *eye*
aquicultural 44.16 *horticultural*
aquiculture 44.5 *gardening*; 433.18 *hydrography*
aquifer 30.9 *groundwater*
aquiline 72.21 *avian*
arabesque 22.9 *ballet steps*; 193.2 *braid*; 68.7 *ice-dancing*
arabesque penchée 22.9 *ballet steps*
arabesques 542.1 *ornament*
Arabic 5.41 *lettered*
Arabic alphabet 5.14 *alphabet*
Arabic numeral 194.1 *number*; 27.9 *numeral*
arabinan 33.4 *polysaccharide*
Arabist 284.11 *antiquarian*
arable 43.20 *farmable*; 43.11 *farmland*
arable farm 43.6 *farm*
arable farmer 43.15 *agriculturist*
arable farming **43.4**; 43.1 *agriculture*
arable land 43.11 *farmland*
arachnid **76.2**; 75.4 *arthropod*
Arachnida 76.2 *arachnid*; 75.4 *arthropod*
arachnidan **76.11**; 75.18 *arthropodous*
arachnoid 76.11 *arachnidan*; 75.18 *arthropodous*
arachnological **76.15**; 75.18 *arthropodous*
arachnologist **76.9**; 75.15 *invertebrate zoologist*
arachnology 75.14 *invertebrate zoology*; 76.7 *study*
Aral Sea 88.5 *other major lakes*
Aralu 8.12 *hell*
Aran sweater 551.13 *sweater*
Aranyaka 7.12 *religious text*
Ararat 89.6 *other major mountains and ranges*
Arat Duzzakh 8.12 *hell*
Arawaks 284.6 *people of the past*
arbalest 587.6 *historical missile weapon*
arbalester 586.13 *historical soldiery*
arbiter 713.4 *adviser*; 16.23, 464.5 *judge*; 748.3 *mediator*; 685.2 *moderator*
arbitrage 776.4 *trade*
arbitral 748.6 *mediatory*
arbitrament of war 585.1 *war*
arbitrarily 642.6 *capriciously*; 250.21 *excessively*; 647.11 *severely*; 16.85 *summarily*
arbitrariness 642.2 *caprice*; 109.1 *unrelatedness*
arbitrary 635.9 *autocratic*; 642.1 *capricious*; 109.7 *illogical*; 641.2 *refractory*; 250.12 *unconditional*
arbitrary power 647.1 *severity*
arbitrate 801.14 *be fair*; 754.4 *compromise*; 15.12 *have an industrial dispute*; 464.11 *judge*; 748.1 *mediate*; 685.4 *moderate*
arbitrated 746.8 *negotiated*; 15.10 *unionized*
arbitrating 15.10 *unionized*
arbitration 754.1 *compromise*; 15.4 *industrial dispute*; 464.1 *judgment*; 748.2 *mediation*; 746.1 *negotiation*; 749.1 *pacification*
arbitrational 748.6 *mediatory*
arbitration award 15.4 *industrial dispute*
arbitration court 15.4 *industrial dispute*
arbitration of interests 15.4 *industrial dispute*
arbitration of rights 15.4 *industrial dispute*
arbitration tribunal 15.4 *industrial dispute*
arbitrator 392.14, 713.4 *adviser*; 398.6 *agent*; 755.4 *contractor*; 15.6 *employer*; 473.3 *impartial person*; 16.23, 464.5 *judge*; 52.8 *karate*; 748.3 *mediator*; 685.2 *moderator*; 746.4 *negotiator*
arboraceous 79.14 *treelike*
arboreal 311.9 *branched*; 44.16 *horticultural*; 70.15 *of animals*; 79.14 *treelike*
arboreous 79.16 *wooded*
arborescence 311.4 *branching*
arborescent 311.9 *branched*; 79.14 *treelike*
arboretum 44.2 *garden*; 79.4 *trees*
arborical 44.16 *horticultural*
arboricultural **79.17**; 44.16 *horticultural*
arboriculturally **79.20**
arboriculture 79.5 *forestry*; 44.1 *horticulture*; 77.10 *plant science*
arboriculturist 79.8 *forester*; 44.13 *horticulturist*
arboriform 311.9 *branched*
arborist 79.8 *forester*
arborization 311.4 *branching*
arbour 44.3 *ornamental garden*; 79.4 *trees*
Arbroath smokey 25.16 *fish dish*
arc 177.2 *bend*; 182.2 *bulge*; 27.42, 179.2 *circle*; 177.6 *curve*; 182.3 *dome*; 28.46, 39.6 *electric discharge*; 27.37 *line*; 205.1 *part*; 179.4 *parts of a circle*; 21.20 *stage lighting*
arcade **317.7**; 779.7 *emporium*; 20.9 *miscellaneous architectural features*
Arcadia 477.8 *dreamland*
Arcadian 646.1 *naive*
arcane 523.11 *benighted*; 528.4 *inscrutable*; 737.11 *mysterious*; 266.2 *obscure*; 11.14 *occult*; 696.1 *unintelligible*
arcanely 11.25 *occultly*
arcaneness 696.11 *unintelligibility*
arcanum 737.7 *esotericism*; 11.2 *the occult*
arc discharge 28.46, 39.6 *electric discharge*
arch **20.5**; 182.5 *be convex*; 177.2 *bend*; 645.4 *cunning*; 177.6 *curve*; 20.19 *decorate*; 182.3 *dome*; 373.4 *means of connection*; 308.7 *passageway*; 496.10 *stimulating*; 121.12 *superior*; 38.27 *superstructure*
archaeological **3.17**
archaeological anthropologist 1.4 *palaeoanthropologist*
archaeological anthropology 1.2 *palaeoanthropology*
archaeological dig 284.8 *excavation*
archaeologist **3.4**; 284.11, 296.9 *antiquarian*; 183.5 *digger*; 449.12 *discoverer*; 744.9 *recorder*
archaeologize 284.16 *excavate*
archaeology **3.2**; 284.9, 296.4 *antiquarianism*; 449.7 *detection*
Archaeopteryx 72.8 *extinct bird*
archaic 350.4 *disused*; 3.15 *historic*; 286.2 *occurring at a different time*; 296.12 *olden*; 5.42 *worded*
archaically **296.21**; 3.24 *historically*; 5.50 *lexically*
archaicism 17.12 *poetic language*
archaic speech 5.9 *ancient language*
archaism 5.9 *ancient language*; 296.4 *antiquarianism*; 286.1 *different time*; 3.12 *historicism*; 296.5 *old thing*; 3.11 *relic*
archaist 296.9 *antiquarian*
archaistic 296.12 *olden*
archaize 3.21 *antiquarianize*; 284.15 *look back*; 761.6 *reverse*
archangel 8.6 *angel*
archangelic 8.14 *heavenly*
archangelship 8.6 *angel*
archbishop 396.10 *person of authority*; 7.8 *priest*; 400.6 *religious leader*; 121.5 *superior*
archbishopric 86.5 *state*
arch bridge 38.21 *bridge*
arch dam 38.23 *dam*
archdeacon 396.10 *person of authority*
archdeaconry 7.10 *priestly dwelling*
archdiocese 7.9 *priesthood*; 86.5 *state*
Arch Druid 7.8 *priest*
Arch Druidess 7.8 *priest*
archduchy 85.3 *dominion*; 12.5 *political organization*
archdukedom 85.3 *dominion*
arched **20.13**; 317.15 *accessible*; 182.4 *convex*; 177.4 *curved*
arched bridge 317.9 *bridge*
archegonium 82.2 *fern plant*; 82.4 *moss plant*
archenemy 594.8 *hated person*
archer **330.16**; 780.9 *British money*; 586.13 *historical soldiery*; 201.10 *thousand*
archer's bow 177.3 *curved things*
archery 587.2 *arms*; 330.6 *shooting*
archetypal 126.4 *original*; 230.1 *perfect*; 717.13 *representational*; 1.14 *societal*
archetypal image 36.24 *symbolism*
archetypally 446.24 *ideologically*; 1.18 *societally*
archetypal myth 1.8 *tradition*
archetype 446.6 *ideal*; 126.2 *original*; 230.3 *perfection*; 99.3 *quintessence*; 36.24 *symbolism*; 1.8 *tradition*
archetypical 446.13 *ideal*; 99.8 *quintessential*
Archfiend 8.7 *devil*
archiform 177.4 *curved*
Archimedes' screw 433.13 *irrigator*; 307.6 *rotator*
Archimedes spiral 27.40 *curve*
arching 177.1 *curvature*
archipelagic 92.11 *continental*
archipelago 92.2 *island*
architect **20.2**; 578.2 *artisan*; 130.16 *originator*; 484.8 *planner*; 356.9 *producer*
architect-designed 356.12 *produced*

architectonic 20.11 architectural; 356.11 productive; 38.32, 403.11 structural
architectonically 20.20 architecturally; 38.33, 403.18 structurally
architectonics 20.1 architecture; 403.1 structure
architectural **20.11**; 38.32, 403.11 structural
architectural acoustics **28.21**
architectural artist 19.16 artist
architectural design 20.1 architecture
architectural engineer 20.2 architect
architectural engineering 20.1 architecture; 38.17 civil engineering
architecturally **20.20**; 38.33, 403.18 structurally
architecturally designed 20.11 architectural
architecturally engineered 20.11 architectural
architectural monstrosity 20.3 building
architectural photography 41.1 photography
architectural sculptor 19.17 sculptor
architectural sculpture 19.12 sculpture
architectural summit **174.3**
architectural tile 24.9 industrial ceramics
Architecture 20
architecture **20.1**; 17.3 aspect of fiction; 40.4 computer; 403.3 form; 356.2 manufacture; 403.1 structure
architrave 174.3 architectural summit
archival 3.19 chronicled
archive 40.20 abort; 3.5 chronicle; 439.5 collection; 40.19 computing terms
archives 439.5 collection; 744.1 record
archivist 3.3 historian; 744.9 recorder
archness 496.4 stimulation
archtraitor 700.21 traitor
archway 314.6 means of entry
arciform 177.4 curved
arc lamp 522.7 lantern
arc light 21.20 stage lighting
Arctic **494.6**; 494.8 cold
arctic 31.55 cool; 324.13 directional
arctic char 55.4 American game fish
Arctic Circle 494.6 Arctic
arctic conditions 494.7 cold weather
Arctic waste 563.1 infertility
arcuate 20.13 arched; 182.5 be convex; 27.81 curvilinear
arcuated 20.13 arched; 182.4 convex; 20.17 structured
arcuation 20.5 arch
ardency 569.1 friendship; 593.2 romantic love
ardent 342.18 active; 593.20 amorous; 617.9 desirous; 726.3 emphatic; 569.8 friendly; 262.3 hasty; 590.13 passionate; 7.15 religious; 380.6 violent; 493.12 warmhearted
ardently 726.7 emphatically; 569.17 in friendship; 593.30 lovingly; 7.23 religiously; 493.17 warmly; 590.20 with feeling
ardour 638.13 concentration; 617.1 desire; 636.7 eagerness; 590.4 emotion; 726.1 emphasis; 342.4 energy; 593.2 romantic love; 617.4 sexual desire
ardour of the chase 636.7 eagerness
arduous 264.10 difficult; 576.11 laborious; 814.21 punishing
arduously **264.26**; 576.12 laboriously
arduousness 264.1 difficulty
area 86.13 locality; 205.1 part; 203.1 quantity; 141.7 range; 86.1 region; 158.1 size; 27.35, 28.7, 141.1 space; 139.8 specialization; 447.4 sphere; 6.3 subject; 27.38 surface; 170.1 surroundings
area code 692.11 dialling
areal 86.16 regional
a real honey 568.9 woman considered as a sex object
areal linguistics 5.1 linguistics
area of contamination 379.1 trap
area of disagreement 751.1 disagreement
area of high pressure 31.11 weather system
area of hostilities 585.10 battleground
area of influence 395.7 sphere of influence
area of low pressure 31.11 weather system
arear 303.28 backwards
area rug 550.9 floor covering
à rebours 303.29 in reverse
arena 382.15 slaughterhouse; 86.14 sphere; 45.2 sportsground; 170.1 surroundings; 21.16 theatre; 518.9 viewpoint
arenaceous 427.17 grainy
arenarious 427.17 grainy
arena theatre 21.16 theatre
arenose 427.17 grainy
Areopagite 579.16 official
Areopagus 16.18 tribunal
Ares 585.3 gods and goddesses of war
arête 154.4 mountain range; 62.5 rock face; 425.8 sharp-pointed thing
argent 743.13 heraldic; 743.8 heraldic device; 531.1 white
argental 531.1 white
argentic 32.34 elemental
argentiferous 32.34 elemental
argentine 531.1 white
Argentine tango 68.7 ice-dancing
argentous 32.34 elemental
argil 24.2 raw material
argillaceous 419.4 compressible
argonaut 323.7 nautical person
argosy 586.23 naval unit
argot 5.26 dialect; 5.20 jargon word; 139.10 specialized language; 5.3 spoken language
argotic 5.42 worded
arguable **701.10**; 16.54 litigated; 705.14 questionable; 714.13 vindicable
arguably **701.18**; 705.24 questionably
argue **586.40**; **701.13**; **751.6**; 706.18 answer back; 639.8 balance; 625.6 be irascible; 444.13 debate; 517.11, 751.5 disagree; 4.23 discuss philosophically; 722.4 dissertate; 447.10 focus on; 714.8 justify; 16.70 litigate; 701.16 plead; 476.6 propound; 242.11 quarrel; 701.15 state
argue against 704.9 deny; 481.1 dissuade
argued 16.54 litigated
argue down 704.8 refute
argue for 392.23 advise; 714.8 justify; 384.22 plead for
argue into a corner 704.8 refute
argue one's case 16.70 litigate
arguer **444.6**; **586.5**; **701.6**
argue the toss 701.14 discuss
argue with 704.9 deny
arguing **701.7**; 16.53 litigating
Argument 701
argument **701.1**; **751.2**; 17.3 aspect of fiction; 27.6 complex number; 706.5 counterstatement; 444.3 debate; 714.2 defence; 517.6, 751.1 disagreement; 408.9 disorder; 722.1 dissertation; 701.4 gist; 27.29 mathematical function; 113.4 objection; 4.5 philosophical argument; 701.5 plea; 242.8, 624.5 quarrel; 705.2 questioning; 27.64 reasoning; 476.1 supposition; 447.1 topic
argument ad hominem 4.8 philosophical term
argument a fortiori 4.8 philosophical term
argument a posteriori 4.8 philosophical term
argument a priori 4.8 philosophical term
argumentation 444.3 debate; 701.2 logical argument
argumentative **444.9**; **586.34**; **701.8**; 751.9 disagreeing; 625.4 irascible; 16.53 litigating; 706.13 retaliatory; 714.11 vindicatory
argumentatively **701.17**; 586.41 aggressively; 706.24 in answer; 751.11 in disagreement; 714.15 in vindication; 625.9 irascibly; 4.24 philosophically
argumentativeness 625.1 irascibility
argumentative type 701.6 arguer
argument from first principles 4.8 philosophical term
arguments 16.7 legal trial
Argus 518.2 eye; 252.3 protector
Argus-eyed 629.5 distrustful; 518.21 seeing
argy-bargy 701.1, 751.2 argument; 746.3 discussion; 408.9 disorder; 746.5 negotiate
argyles 551.20 legwear
aria 18.13, 516.1 melody; 18.4 opera
Ariane 29.35 rocketry
Arica movement 36.3 psychiatric treatment
arid 620.4 boring; 428.6 desert; 428.1 dry; 563.3 infertile; 497.5 tasteless
arid climate 31.38 climate
aridity 620.1 boredom; 497.1 dilution; 428.11 dryness; 563.1 infertility
aridly 620.8 boringly; 428.24 drily; 497.10 without taste
aridness 428.11 dryness; 563.1 infertility
Ariel 332.13 swift person
aright 801.20 correctly
arise **366.5**; 304.13 ascend; 525.12 become visible; 186.5 be vertical; 93.18 come to be; 130.27, 315.10 emerge; 345.9 take effect
arise from 345.7 follow from
arising 525.1 appearance; 525.7 appearing; 315.15 outgoing
arising from 345.10 caused
aristocracy **573.2**; 235.7 elite; 12.1 government; 566.9 group; 654.7 human society; 121.7 the best people; 396.7 type of rule
Aristocrat 573
aristocrat 123.4 bigwig; 235.7 elite; 400.1 master; 566.10 member of society; 622.13 proud person
aristocratic **573.4**; 12.9, 396.14 governmental; 400.12 masterful; 622.19 stately
aristocratically 400.16 masterfully
Aristophanean comedy 21.12 comedy
aristos 121.7 the best people
Aristotelian 4.11 follower of a doctrine; 4.14 of a philosophy
Aristotelianism 4.7 school of thought
Aristotelian philosophy 4.7 school of thought
arithmetic 211.2 mathematical addition; 27.1 mathematics
arithmetical 789.10 accounting; 27.68, 210.15 mathematical; 194.8 odd
arithmetically 789.13 financially; 210.16 mathematically; 194.12 numerically
arithmetician 27.2, 210.7 mathematician
arithmetic mean 27.60 parameter
arithmetic operation 27.14 operation
arithmetic operator 27.13 mathematical symbol
arithmetic progression 302.10 forward motion; 27.20 sequence
arithmetic series 27.20 sequence
arithmomancy 11.9 divination
ark 252.5 refuge; 10.14 sacred object
arm 205.4 component; 243.5 equip; 29.7 galaxy; 334.11 give power; 585.12 go to war; 742.5 indicator; 551.24 part of garment; 252.10 protect; 436.5 provision; 438.1 tool; 587.1 weapon
armada 586.14 armed forces; 586.23 naval unit
Armageddon 585.1 war
armament 586.14 armed forces; 587.2 arms; 243.11 fitting out
armaments 587.2 arms
armature 39.30 generator; 19.14 sculptor's materials
armband 551.25 accessories; 67.3 survival swimming
armchair 23.2 chair; 419.11 soft thing; 476.7 suppositional
armchair critic 4.10 philosopher; 476.4 theorist
armchair detective 476.4 theorist
armchair quarterback 476.4 theorist
armchair strategist 476.4 theorist
Armco™ 61.6 motor-racing terms
armed 586.35 martial; 334.14 operative; 243.18 prepared; 336.13 strengthened; 585.15 warring
armed at all points 243.18 prepared
armed conflict 585.9 battle; 585.1 war
armed force 376.14 force; 252.2 protection
armed forces **586.14**; 253.4 security forces
armed guard 384.14 guard; 252.3 protector
armed intervention 585.1 war
armed neutrality 589.1 peace; 585.1 war
armed robbery 381.16 personal attack; 774.1 stealing
armed to the teeth 243.18 prepared
Armenian 5.11 family of languages
armful 203.3 container
arm-guard 58.3 ice hockey
armhole 551.24 part of garment
arm in arm 223.22 hand in hand; 569.18 intimately; 654.18 sociably
arm-in-arm 569.10 familiar; 147.9 near
arming 585.7 war measures
armistice 749.1 pacification; 226.3 pause; 589.1 peace
Armistice Day 601.5 anniversary
armless 231.3 deformed; 233.4 incomplete; 205.11 partial
armlet 551.25 accessories
armlock 52.5 wrestling
arm of the sea 92.9 inlet
arm of the service 584.2 the military
armorial 743.13 heraldic
armorial bearings 743.8 heraldic device
armory 743.8 heraldic device
armour **384.7**; 550.5 body covering; 551.5 fancy dress; 418.7 hard substance; 252.10, 550.30 protect; 252.2 protection; 550.12 protective covering; 384.20 reinforce; 252.4 safety device; 587.1 weapon
armour-clad 384.30 defended
armoured 384.30 defended; 418.3 hardened; 252.7 invulnerable; 586.35 martial; 638.4 undaunted
armoured attack 381.12 military attack
armoured car 586.21 armoured cavalry
armoured cavalry **586.21**
armoured corps 584.4 military organization
armoured cruiser 586.24 warship
armoured division 586.21 armoured cavalry; 586.16 army unit; 584.4 military organization
armoured personnel carrier 586.21 armoured cavalry
armour plate 384.7 armour; 252.2 protection
armour-plate 252.10 protect
armour-plated 384.30 defended; 418.3 hardened
armoury 587.4 arsenal; 439.4 storage; 577.1 workshop
arm pad 58.5 lacrosse
armpits 503.2 something that makes an unpleasant smell
arms **587.2**; 743.8 heraldic device; 584.1 military affairs; 438.1 tool; 585.1 war
arms akimbo 742.3 gesture
arms control 749.1 pacification
arms-control agreement 755.3 alliance
arms cuts 749.1 pacification
arms depot 587.4 arsenal
arms limitation treaty 589.1 peace
arms race **587.3**
arms reduction 749.1 pacification
arms sanctions 585.8 warfare
arms trade 587.3 arms race
arms traffic 587.3 arms race
arm stroke 67.2 swimming technique
arm-twisting 386.3 coercive methods
army **586.15**; 586.14 armed forces; 374.3 assembly; 376.23 flock; 376.14 force; 253.4 security forces; 76.4 social insect; 584.2 the military; 208.4 throng
Army Alpha test 36.6 intelligence test
army ant 76.4 social insect
Army Beta test 36.6 intelligence test
army corps 586.16 army unit; 584.4 military organization
army formation 586.16 army unit
Army General Classification Test 36.6 intelligence test
army man 586.8 soldier
army officer field-marshal 586.17 army person
army of occupation 586.14 armed forces
army of people **586.18**
army person **586.17**
army rule 12.1 government
army service corps 584.4 military organization
army staff 584.5 military staff
army uniform 743.5 uniform
army unit **586.16**
army worm 76.5 larva
arnica 394.5 analgesic
A road 317.3, 320.2, 373.5 road
aroma 139.3 characteristic; 502.1 fragrance; 500.1 odour; 496.1 piquancy
aromatherapeutic 502.4 fragrant
aromatherapist 502.1 fragrance; 35.12 healer
aromatherapy 502.1 fragrance; 35.2 natural medicine
aromatic 32.7 chemical compound; 32.35 combined; 502.4 fragrant; 500.5 odorous; 496.9 piquant
aromatically 502.7 fragrantly; 500.10 odorously; 496.15 piquantly
aromaticity 500.1 odour
aromatization 32.14 chemical reaction
aromatize 500.9 impart odour to; 502.6 perfume
arondissement 86.5 state

aronha-kodesh 10.14 *sacred object*
around 565.20 *environmentally;* 143.11 *geographically;* 324.11 *in all directions;* 550.42 *inclusively;* 147.12 *near;* 307.13 *round;* 317.17 *via*
around and about 147.12 *near*
arousal 369.5 *drawing out;* 490.1 *physical pleasure*
arouse 488.13 *arouse sensation;* 593.25 *be loved;* 369.15 *draw out;* 490.9 *give pleasure;* 483.9 *motivate;* 624.9 *offend;* 711.7 *raise the alarm*
aroused 490.7 *pleased*
arouse jealousy 629.7
arouse no echoes 511.9 *be nonresonant*
arouse sensation 488.13
arousing 369.18 *extractive;* 796.12 *indecent*
arousing compassion 627.7 *pitiful*
arousing pity 627.7 *pitiful*
Arpanet 40.15 *network*
arpeggio 132.2 *consecution;* 18.16 *musical note*
arquebus 587.10 *historical gun*
arquebusade 37.7 *ointment*
arquebusier 586.13 *historical soldiery*
arrack 558.7 *alcoholic drink*
arraign 715.5 *accuse;* 16.70 *litigate*
arraignment 16.5 *litigation*
arrange 409.12; 750.23; 409.16 *adapt;* 224.8 *cause change;* 18.35 *compose;* 19.23 *design;* 160.7 *form;* 244.1 *improve;* 407.18 *order;* 484.12 *plan ahead;* 106.2 *premeditate;* 243.4 *prepare for action;* 356.10 *produce;* 137.14 *sort;* 403.14 *structure*
arrange a fatal accident 382.17 *murder*
arrange a marriage 570.17 *matchmake*
arrange a mortgage 783.8 *credit*
arrange consecutively 132.16
arranged 409.20; 750.12; 18.31 *composed;* 754.6 *compromising;* 755.7 *contractual;* 407.10 *ordered;* 289.12 *succeeding*
arranged marriage 570.3 *types of marriage*
arrange for 409.18 *make arrangements*
arrange in 127.6 *subsume*
arrange in a circle 179.7 *make circular*
arrange in layers 411.10 *layer*
arrange in succession 132.16 *arrange consecutively*
Arrangement 409
arrangement 409.1; 750.3; 409.10 *agreement;* 409.2 *array;* 18.15 *composition;* 754.1 *compromise;* 755.1 *contract;* 160.1 *form;* 516.4 *harmonics;* 407.1 *order;* 542.1 *ornament;* 243.10 *preparations;* 403.1 *structure;* 289.1 *succession;* 19.4 *treatment*
arrangements 409.11; 243.10 *preparations*
arranger 18.24 *musician*
arranging 409.1 *arrangement*
arrant 738.14 *manifest*
array 409.2; 586.16 *army unit;* 409.12 *arrange;* 132.16 *arrange consecutively;* 738.6 *display;* 551.1 *dress;* 551.33 *dress up;* 243.11 *fitting out;* 407.1, 407.18 *order;* 243.4 *prepare for action;* 29.26 *radio telescope;* 141.7 *range;* 141.21 *space;* 208.4 *throng*
arrayed 409.20 *arranged;* 551.29 *dressed;* 407.10 *ordered;* 585.15 *warring*
arraying 409.1 *arrangement*
arrears 784.5 *amount owing;* 233.1 *incompleteness;* 233.2 *omission*
arrest 715.1 *accusation;* 715.5 *accuse;* 226.8 *cause to cease;* 251.11 *detain;* 251.4 *detention;* 333.12 *hesitation;* 361.12 *interrupt;* 16.6 *legal process;* 378.2 *obstacle;* 333.3 *slow down;* 773.10 *take away*
arrested 715.8 *accusatory;* 333.7 *delayed;* 251.15 *detained*
arrested development 36.17 *fixation*
arresting 773.3 *taking away*
arrête 30.7 *landform*
arrhythmia 260.10 *cardiovascular disease;* 326.2 *vibration*
arridge 68.10 *curling*
arrière-ban 586.14 *armed forces*
Arrival 312
arrival 312.10; 525.1 *appearance;* 130.2 *creation;* 314.7 *entrant;* 314.1 *entry;* 300.3 *motion towards*
arrive 312.1; 525.12 *become visible;* 248.5 *be prosperous;* 246.6 *be successful;* 130.27 *emerge;* 314.9 *enter*
arrive ahead of schedule 293.7 *be early*
arrive ahead of time 293.7 *be early*
arrive at 312.2 *reach*
arrive early 293.7 *be early;* 288.6 *take untimely action*
arrive first 293.7 *be early*
arrive last 294.6 *be late*
arrive late 294.6 *be late;* 288.6 *take untimely action*
arriving 312.18; 525.7 *appearing*
arrogance 660.4; 673.6 *boastfulness;* 167.5 *boldness;* 622.3 *conceit;* 661.1 *defiance;* 467.1 *overestimation*
arrogant 167.9; 660.16; 396.12 *authoritative;* 673.13 *boastful;* 622.17 *conceited;* 668.13 *contemptuous;* 661.7 *defiant;* 467.5 *overestimating;* 673.8 *vain*
arrogantly 660.33; 396.23 *authoritatively;* 673.23 *boastfully;* 661.9 *defiantly;* 467.7 *overoptimistically*
arrogate 588.4 *be anarchic*
arrogation 588.1 *anarchy;* 329.9 *excessiveness;* 16.41 *lawlessness;* 773.1 *taking*
arrogator 588.3 *anarchist*
arrow 330.10 *ball;* 69.6 *darts;* 587.6 *historical missile weapon;* 742.5 *indicator;* 330.8 *missile;* 425.8 *sharp-pointed thing;* 332.11 *swift thing*
arrow-case 587.4 *arsenal*
arrowhead 587.6 *historical missile weapon;* 425.8 *sharp-pointed thing;* 284.7 *thing of the past*
arrow-like 425.1 *sharp*
arrow of time 275.1 *time*
arrow worm 75.6 *worm*
arroyo 90.1 *river*
arse 308.4 *body orifice;* 168.2 *rear end*
arse about 272.6 *be ridiculous*
arsehole 308.4 *body orifice*
arseholed 690.3 *dead drunk*
arse-lick 471.14 *be solicitous;* 677.11 *be sycophantic*
arse-licker 664.3, 677.7 *sycophant*
arse-licking 664.2, 677.5 *sycophancy;* 664.7, 677.16 *sycophantic*
arsenal 587.4; 439.4 *storage;* 577.1 *workshop*
arsenic 32.34 *elemental*
arsenious 32.34 *elemental*
arsenous 32.34 *elemental*
arse over tit 192.4 *inversely*
arson 441.4 *destruction;* 357.3 *destructiveness;* 493.6 *fire*
arsonist 357.6, 441.7 *destroyer;* 493.7 *fireman;* 380.4 *violent creature*
arsy-versy 408.28 *anyhow;* 192.4 *inversely;* 192.2 *inverted;* 408.18 *muddled*
art 19.1; 19.5 *artistry;* 645.1, 702.3 *cunning;* 356.1 *production;* 485.1, 733.3 *skill;* 645.2 *stratagem*
art auction 778.4 *sale*
art college 6.12 *educational institution*
artefact 402.5 *object;* 296.5 *old thing;* 356.3 *product;* 3.11 *relic;* 284.7 *thing of the past*
Artemis 330.16 *archer;* 572.4 *celibate person;* 29.17 *moon*
art equipment 529.5 *paint*
arterial 317.15 *accessible;* 308.15 *providing passage*
arterial blood 431.4 *blood*
arterially 308.27 *cavernously*
arterial road 317.3, 373.5 *road*
arterial street 317.3 *road*
arteriography 35.7 *diagnosis*
arteriosclerosis 260.10 *cardiovascular disease;* 418.6 *solidification*
arteritis 260.10 *cardiovascular disease*
artery 554.3 *life requirements;* 308.7 *passageway;* 317.3 *road*
artesian basin 30.9 *groundwater*
artesian spring 30.9 *groundwater*
artesian well 439.3 *supply*
Artex™ 550.8 *wall covering*
art form 160.3 *kind*
artful 645.4, 702.8 *cunning;* 699.33 *deceitful;* 700.34 *deceiving*
artful dodge 700.8 *trick*
Artful Dodger 645.3 *cunning person;* 774.8 *thief*
artfully 645.6 *cunningly;* 702.15 *hypocritically*
artfulness 645.1, 702.3 *cunning;* 699.5 *deceitfulness;* 700.1 *deception*
art gallery 439.5 *collection*
arthritic 260.23 *diseased;* 260.19 *sick person*
arthritis 491.2 *painful condition;* 260.16 *rheumatism*
arthrodire 74.4 *fossil fish*
arthropod 75.4; 70.4 *type of animal*
Arthropoda 75.4 *arthropod*
arthropodial 75.18 *arthropodous*
arthropod-like invertebrate 75.4 *arthropod*
arthropodous 75.18
Arthur Ashe 63.7 *famous tennis players*
article 722.2; 746.2 *basis for negotiations;* 778.8 *merchandise;* 402.5 *object;* 197.1 *one;* 205.2 *particular;* 5.35 *part of speech;* 713.3 *precept;* 356.3 *product;* 356.5 *work of art*
article for sale 778.8 *merchandise*
article of clothing 551.1 *dress*
article of commerce 778.8 *merchandise*
article of virtu 19.6 *work of art*
articles of agreement 746.2 *basis for negotiations*
articles of faith 450.2 *religious belief*
articulacy 729.2 *power of speech;* 695.10 *simplicity*
articulate 20.19 *decorate;* 695.2 *simple;* 695.5 *simplify;* 729.19 *speaking;* 5.45 *use language*
articulated 729.16 *speech;* 20.17 *structured*
articulated vehicle 320.20 *truck*
articulately 695.13 *intelligibly;* 729.21 *orally*
articulateness 729.2 *power of speech;* 695.10 *simplicity*
articulate sound 729.7 *utterance*
articulation 729.4; 20.9 *miscellaneous architectural features*
articulator 729.5 *organ of speech*
articulatory phonetics 729.6 *phonetics*
artifact 96.7 *artificiality*
artifice 676.1 *affectedness;* 702.3 *cunning;* 699.5 *deceitfulness;* 484.3 *expedient plan;* 645.2 *stratagem;* 379.1 *trap;* 700.8 *trick;* 700.7 *tricking*
artificer 578.2 *artisan;* 356.9 *producer*
artificial 96.12; 676.3 *affected;* 55.8 *angling;* 699.33 *deceitful;* 543.3 *elegant;* 699.37 *fake;* 700.37 *hypocritical;* 125.13 *imitation;* 700.39 *imitative;* 544.9 *inelegant;* 5.39 *of language;* 356.12 *produced;* 115.8 *simulated;* 699.32 *spurious;* 485.9 *well-made*
artificial colouring 529.4 *pigment*
artificial dye 529.4 *pigment*
artificial eye 519.3 *aid for poor sight*
artificial fertilizer 562.3 *fertilizer*
artificial fly 55.2
artificial fly-fishing 55.1 *angling*
artificial grass 46.4 *stadium*
artificial insemination 43.3 *livestock farming;* 561.3 *propagation*
artificial intelligence 40.17; 438.6 *mechanics;* 4.9 *philosophical problem*
artificiality 96.7; 543.1 *elegance;* 700.3 *hypocrisy;* 699.4 *spuriousness*
artificial lake 88.1 *lake*
artificial language 5.8
artificial light 522.5 *incandescent light;* 41.15 *lighting*
artificial limb 762.3 *substitute thing*
artificial lure 55.2 *artificial fly*
artificially 115.14 *comparably;* 543.5 *elegantly;* 125.14 *imitatively;* 68.17 *on a ski run;* 55.9 *on the water;* 699.41 *spuriously*
artificial magnet 363.3 *magnet*
artificial memory 462.6
artificial minnow 55.2 *artificial fly*
artificial reality 96.7 *artificiality;* 40.18 *virtual reality*
artificial respiration 393.10 *revival;* 67.3 *survival swimming*
artificial route 62.1 *mountaineering*
artificial satellite 29.32 *satellite*
artificial slope 68.1 *skiing*
artificial sweetener 557.11 *food content;* 498.2 *sweetener*
artificial turf 421.8 *smooth thing*
artillery 587.11 *guns;* 507.1 *loudness;* 330.6 *shooting*
artillery barrage 587.1 *weapon*
artillery bombardment 381.12 *military attack*
artillery brigade 586.16 *army unit;* 584.4 *military organization*
artillery commander 584.5 *military staff*
artillery man 586.17 *army person;* 330.15 *shooter*
artillery park 587.11 *guns*
artillery shell 550.13 *casing*
artillery warfare 585.8 *warfare*
artiness 19.5 *artistry*
artiodactyl 71.15 *hoofed mammal;* 71.33 *ungulate*
Artiodactyla 71.15 *hoofed mammal*
artiodactylous 71.33 *ungulate*
artisan 578.2; 19.16 *artist;* 340.3 *doer;* 485.5 *expert;* 438.8 *machinist;* 356.9 *producer;* 578.1 *worker*
artisanship 19.5 *artistry*
artist 19.16; 340.3 *doer;* 21.29 *entertainer;* 485.5 *expert;* 717.4 *person who makes a representation;* 356.9 *producer;* 744.9 *recorder;* 477.9 *visionary;* 578.1 *worker*
artist colours 529.5 *paint*
artiste 21.29 *entertainer;* 18.24 *musician*
artistic 19.26; 340.5 *acting;* 543.3 *elegant;* 57.11 *gymnastic;* 492.10 *handed;* 549.5 *refined;* 717.13 *representational;* 721.13 *representing;* 485.9 *well-made*
artistically 19.31; 543.5 *elegantly;* 485.12 *skilfully*
artistically done 543.3 *elegant*
artistic creation 19.6 *work of art*
artistic flair 19.5 *artistry*
artistic gymnastics 57.1 *gymnastics*
artistic invention 19.5 *artistry*
artistic licence 250.1 *freedom*
artistic movement 295.2 *trendiness*
artistic person 340.3 *doer*
artistic production 19.6 *work of art*
artistic quality 19.5 *artistry*
artistic skill 19.5 *artistry*
artistic structure 403.9
artistic taste 19.5 *artistry*
artistic technique 19.5 *artistry*
artistic temperament 19.5 *artistry*
artistic worker 578.1 *worker*
artistry 19.5; 477.1 *imagination;* 485.1 *skill*
artist's materials 19.11
artless 486.4 *bungled;* 544.9 *inelegant;* 646.1, 805.7 *naive;* 271.3 *natural;* 308.16 *open;* 538.3 *raw;* 698.18 *truthful*
artlessly 646.5, 805.12 *naively;* 308.26 *openly*
artlessness 456.1 *ignorance;* 646.2, 805.3 *naivety;* 271.6 *naturalness;* 308.9 *openness;* 698.5 *truthfulness*
art museum 19.11 *artist's materials;* 439.5 *collection*
Art Nouveau 23.7 *furniture style*
art object 19.6 *work of art*
art of healing 394.11 *medical art*
art of management 579.3 *management*
art of public speaking 729.9
art of the possible 631.9 *tactics*
art of war 585.6; 584.1 *military affairs*
art paper 19.11 *artist's materials;* 435.3 *paper*
art pottery 24.1 *ceramics*
art project 447.5 *educational topic*
art restorer 393.12 *repairer*
art review 719.3 *criticism*
art room 6.15 *schoolroom*
arts 6.3 *subject*
arts and crafts 19.1 *art*
art show 738.6 *display*
arts of design 19.1 *art*
art subject 19.10
art supplies 529.5 *paint*
artsy-craftiness 19.5 *artistry*
artsy-fartsiness 19.5 *artistry*
art that conceals art 485.1 *skill*
artwork 717.2 *reproduction;* 19.6 *work of art*
arty 19.26 *artistic*
arty-craftiness 19.5 *artistry*
arty-crafty 19.26 *artistic*
arty-farty 19.26 *artistic*
Aryan 5.11 *family of languages;* 1.6 *race;* 1.13 *racial*
Aryanism 465.3 *injustice;* 466.4 *social discrimination*
as 285.15; 317.16 *how;* 115.13 *similarly*
as a bad omen 798.14 *inauspiciously*
as a challenge 661.10 *in defiance*
as a compromise 746.9 *feasibly*
as a con 702.15 *hypocritically*
as a consequence 345.12 *with the effect of*
as a convert 769.15 *receptively*
as a cop-out 754.9 *irresolutely*
as a curse 712.14 *damningly*
as a dare 661.9 *defiantly*
as a defence 701.20 *apologetically;* 704.11 *in reply*
as a deterrent 481.11 *dissuasively*

asafoetida 503.2 *something that makes an unpleasant smell*
as a formality 251.17 *with self-restraint*
as a general rule 216.11 *on average*
as a gift **768.9**; 793.15 *cheaply*
as a gloss 702.15 *hypocritically*
as agreed 756.16 *as promised*; 354.8 *responsibly*
as agreed upon 755.8 *contractually*; 750.39 *with consent*
as a group 204.12 *one and all*
as a half-measure 754.8 *compromisingly*
as a joke 599.17 *jokingly*
as a lagniappe 211.10 *additionally*
as always 117.18 *as usual*; 632.19 *habitually*
as an academic exercise 476.10 *supposedly*
as an advance 772.13 *on loan*
as an alternative 762.9 *instead*; 144.20 *out of place*
as an answer 704.11 *in reply*
as an approximation 216.11 *on average*
as an ego trip 683.9 *egoistically*
as a new member 769.15 *receptively*
as an example 703.22 *demonstrably*
as an excuse 714.15 *in vindication*
as an individual 109.12 *irrelevantly*
ASA number 41.10 *graininess*
ASAP 262.6 *hastily*; 280.9 *in the shortest possible time*; 332.14 *swiftly*
asapao 25.51 *West Indian dish*
as a preliminary 129.22 *in anticipation*
as a prelude 129.22 *in anticipation*
as a prize 813.19 *rewardingly*
as a protest 662.17 *disobediently*
as a replacement 706.27 *answerably*
as a representative 398.11 *representatively*
as a result 345.12 *with the effect of*
as a reward 813.19 *rewardingly*
as arranged 482.15 *according to plan*; 750.39 *with consent*
as a rule **140.18**; 750.37 *conventionally*; 216.11 *on average*; 204.13 *on the whole*; 138.30 *usually*
as a sacrifice 752.20 *persuasively*
as a sign 742.18 *indicatively*
as ... as possible 232.10 *fully*
as a start 130.40 *first*
as a symbol 743.14 *identifiably*; 742.18 *indicatively*
as a team 204.12 *one and all*
as a temptation 483.14 *influentially*
as a thoughtful gesture 658.15 *genteelly*
as a tip 211.10 *additionally*
as atonement 807.8 *penitently*
as a trade-off 746.9 *feasibly*
as a unit 204.12 *one and all*
as a wage-earner 769.15 *receptively*
as a whole 216.11 *on average*; 204.12 *one and all*; 138.31 *overall*
as before 117.18 *as usual*; 225.9 *permanently*
asbestosis 260.9 *respiratory disease*
as broad as long 119.6 *equal*
as can be 158.20 *largely*
ascariasis 75.11 *helminthic disease*; 260.7 *tropical disease*
ascend **304.13**; 300.13 *be in motion*; 415.9 *be light*; 334.10 *be powerful*; 8.17 *deify*; 244.2 *get better*; 62.9 *mountaineer*; 154.16 *rise*
ascendancy 396.1 *authority*; 12.3 *governance*; 395.3 *personal influence*; 334.1 *power*; 246.1 *success*; 121.1 *superiority*
ascendant 304.23 *rising*; 121.12 *superior*
ascender **304.11**; 62.4 *climbing equipment*; 62.7 *mountaineer*
ascending **304.22**; 300.7 *ascending motion*; 62.3 *climbing technique*; 300.17 *directional*; 154.9 *high*; 89.7 *mountainous*
ascending motion **300.7**
ascending order 132.2 *consecution*; 407.3 *hierarchy*; 178.7 *straight line*
ascend the throne 12.12 *take authority*
ascension 304.1 *ascent*
ascensional 304.23 *rising*
Ascension Day 10.15 *holy day*
Ascent 304
ascent **304.1**; 302.12 *advance*; 300.7 *ascending motion*; 62.3 *climbing technique*; 244.5 *improvement*; 415.5 *lightness*; 366.6 *raising*; 313.8 *start*
ascentive 304.23 *rising*
ascertain 95.12 *establish reality*; 448.11 *experiment*; 449.3 *find out*; 6.23 *learn*; 452.21 *make certain*; 454.2, 703.17 *prove*; 698.30 *prove true*
ascertained 452.1 *certain*; 698.20 *proved*; 703.13 *proven*
ascertaining 449.8 *finding out*
ascertainment 452.13, 698.7 *confirmation*; 448.3 *experimentation*; 454.5, 703.4 *proof*
ascesis 251.3, 684.1 *self-restraint*; 271.4 *simplicity*; 647.3 *unadornment*
ascetic 634.19 *abstaining*; 687.6 *fasting*; 687.4 *fasting person*; 118.9 *hermit*; 592.5 *insensitive person*; 251.6 *lawmaker*; 197.8 *loner*; 7.7 *monk*; 808.3 *penitent person*; 7.15 *religious*; 251.14, 684.8 *self-restrained*; 684.4 *self-restrained person*; 271.1 *simple*; 647.10 *unadorned*; 655.6 *unsocial person*; 9.9 *worshipful*
ascetically 647.12 *plainly*; 684.11 *with self-restraint*; 9.12 *worshipfully*
asceticism 807.2 *apology*; 218.8 *insufficiency*; 814.11 *penance*; 782.8 *renunciation of wealth*; 251.3, 684.1 *self-restraint*; 687.2 *short rations*; 271.4 *simplicity*; 647.3 *unadornment*; 9.1 *worship*
aschelminth 75.6 *worm*
ascidian 75.2 *protochordate*
ASCII 40.10 *character*
as clear as crystal 527.1 *transparent*
as clear as day 520.2 *clear*; 695.2 *simple*
as clear as mud 266.2 *obscure*
ascocarp 83.4 *fungal body*
ascogenous 83.10 *of fungi*
ascomycetes 83.3 *fungi*
Ascomycotina 83.3 *fungi*
as contracted for 755.8 *contractually*; 750.39 *with consent*
ascospore 83.4 *fungal body*
ascot 551.14 *neckwear*
ascribe 783.11 *recognize*
ascribe a meaning to 719.8 *interpret*
ascus 83.4 *fungal body*
ASDE 322.6 *flight control*
as deep as hell 156.8 *deep*
asdic 504.9 *audio device*
as dull as ditchwater 497.5 *tasteless*
a sec 280.3 *instant*
a second or two 278.3 *short duration*
aseity 93.7 *self-existence*
asepsis 256.2 *cleaning*; 257.1 *hygiene*
aseptic 256.16 *clean*; 257.4 *hygienic*; 255.14 *purified*
aseptically 257.7 *hygienically*; 255.19 *purely*
as ever 225.9 *permanently*
as every schoolboy knows 455.15 *knowledgeably*
as evidence **716.14**; 703.22 *demonstrably*
as expected 104.11 *probably*
as far as possible 444.15 *reasonably*
as follows **289.15**
as freight 319.6 *commercially*
as friends 569.17 *in friendship*
Asgard 8.11 *heaven*
as God 8.19 *divinely*
as good as 111.16 *equal*; 119.12 *equally*; 147.13 *nearly*; 204.13 *on the whole*
as good as new 393.15 *cured*; 393.13 *repaired*
ash 258.4 *dirt*; 30.25 *eruption*; 493.6 *fire*; 427.5 *powder*; 238.6 *refuse*
a shame 627.5 *misfortune*
ashamed 806.6 *appearing guilty*; 623.3 *humbled*; 808.6 *penitent*
ashamedly 806.11 *guiltily*
ash-blond 531.3 *white-haired*; 537.3 *yellow-haired*
ashen 582.21 *deathly*; 530.8 *drained of colour*; 533.1 *grey*; 531.4 *pale*; 79.15 *woody*
ashen-faced 612.7 *frightened*
ashen-hued 530.8 *drained of colour*
ashes 582.11 *dead person*; 533.5 *grey thing*; 215.2 *residue*
ash-grey 533.1 *grey*
ashi-waza 52.7 *judo*
ashlar 435.2 *building material*; 20.9 *miscellaneous architectural features*
ashore 92.11 *continental*; 92.13 *continentally*; 312.22 *on arrival*
a short time ago 295.21 *newly*
a short while 275.3 *duration*
ashram 7.10 *priestly dwelling*
ashtry 496.7 *tobacco*
Ash Wednesday 10.15 *holy day*
ashy 530.8 *drained of colour*; 533.1 *grey*; 531.4 *pale*
Asia 92.1 *continent*
Asian 1.6 *race*; 1.13 *racial*
Asiatic cholera 260.7 *tropical disease*
aside 21.22 *acting*; 693.7 *advice*; 325.13 *deviation*; 145.10 *distantly*; 511.10 *faintly*; 350.12 *out of use*; 735.1 *soliloquy*; 729.7 *utterance*; 730.4 *whispering*
as if 115.13 *similarly*; 476.11 *supposing*
a sin 627.5 *misfortune*
as in a mirror 115.13 *similarly*
asinine 459.5 *foolish*; 697.5 *nonsensical*; 272.5 *ridiculous*; 71.33 *ungulate*
asininity 459.1 *folly*
as intended 694.13 *meaningfully*
as is 225.9 *permanently*
as is befitting 801.18 *properly*
as is fitting 801.18 *properly*
as is one's wont 140.13 *as a rule*; 632.19 *habitually*
as I stand here 707.26 *as God is my witness!*
as it happened 222.15 *under the circumstances*
as it happens 750.36 *accordingly*; 93.22 *really*; 447.12 *topically*
as it is 221.9 *conditionally*; 222.15 *under the circumstances*
as it is said 693.19 *reportedly*
as it may be 107.14 *perchance*
as it may chance 107.14 *perchance*
as it may happen 107.14 *perchance*; 222.15 *under the circumstances*
as it reads 698.38 *literally*
as it stands 143.12 *circumstantially*; 221.9 *conditionally*
as it turns out 706.25 *conclusively*; 222.15 *under the circumstances*
as it were 115.13 *similarly*; 476.10 *supposedly*
ask 790.12 *charge*; 4.20 *philosophize*; 705.17 *question*; 710.6 *request*
ask a favour 710.6 *request*
askance 189.8 *obliquely*
asked 705.16 *questioned*
asker 4.10 *philosopher*; 705.9 *questioner*; 710.4 *requester*
askew **176.12**; 234.6 *distorted*; 802.18 *gone wrong*; 408.18 *muddled*; 189.4 *oblique*; 189.8 *obliquely*; 120.3 *unequal*
ask favours of 349.4 *resort to*
ask for 776.3 *bargain*; 397.10 *demand*; 617.12 *desire*; 135.8 *miss*; 710.6 *request*
ask for absolution 649.13 *ask forgiveness*
ask for advice 713.6 *consult*
ask forgiveness **649.13**
ask for it 615.5 *be rash*
ask for mercy **627.12**; 649.13 *ask forgiveness*; 388.3 *submit*
ask for more 218.6 *be unsatisfied*; 557.22 *eat well*
ask for one's blessing 710.6 *request*
ask for one's hand 570.15 *marry*; 593.28 *win the love of*
ask for pity 627.12 *ask for mercy*
ask for seconds 557.22 *eat well*
ask for someone's blessing 757.6 *ask permission*
ask for support 710.6 *request*
ask for terms 388.3 *submit*
ask for trouble 459.6 *be foolish*; 615.5 *be rash*
ask if one may 757.6 *ask permission*
ask in 773.11 *be hospitable*
asking 4.4 *philosophical investigation*; 710.1 *request*; 710.9 *requesting*
asking for it 615.4 *rash*
asking for trouble 615.4 *rash*
asking price 752.3 *business offer*
ask leave 757.6 *ask permission*; 710.6 *request*
ask no favours 250.16 *be independent*
ask oneself 619.12 *wonder whether*
ask permission **757.6**; 710.6 *request*
ask to be excused 757.6 *ask permission*; 710.6 *request*
ask to be tried 16.72 *stand trial*
ask to marry 705.22 *pop the question*
ask too much 218.7 *make insufficient*; 792.10 *overcharge*
aslant 176.12 *askew*
a slave to drink 690.5 *drunken*
asleep 343.4 *not awake*; 489.8 *unconscious*
asleep in Jesus 582.19 *dead*
asleep on one's feet 261.1 *fatigued*
as likely as not 104.11 *probably*
as lovers 654.18 *sociably*
as matters stand 222.15 *under the circumstances*
as meant 694.13 *meaningfully*
Asmodeus 8.7 *devil*
as much again 198.19 *twice*
as much as 203.7 *quantitatively*
as never before 354.9 *enterprisingly*; 448.15 *inventively*
as new 295.21 *newly*
as often as not 297.1 *frequently*
as old as Adam 296.12 *olden*
as old as Methuselah 296.12 *olden*
as old as time 296.12 *olden*
as one 747.20 *cooperatively*; 750.31 *in accord*; 374.10 *in combination*; 570.24 *matrimonially*; 285.13 *synchronously*; 376.51 *together*; 197.23 *wholly*
as one goes 316.18 *in transit*
as one man 285.13 *synchronously*
as one pleases 635.17 *at will*
as one sees it 446.24 *ideologically*
as one thinks fit 635.17 *at will*
as ordered 397.16 *commandingly*; 663.10 *obediently*
asp 73.3 *snake*
asparagus beetle 44.12 *pests and diseases*
asparagus fern 82.1 *fern*
asparagus soup 25.13 *soup*
aspartame 498.2 *sweetener*
aspect **169.4**; **222.6**; 171.3 *appearance*; 405.1 *component*; 631.1 *conduct*; 553.4 *design*; 525.3 *external appearance*; 160.6 *nature*; 143.1 *situation*; 221.1 *state*; 518.7 *view*; 176.5 *viewpoint*
Aspect experiment 28.80 *quantum theory*
aspect of fiction 17.3
aspectual 525.10
aspen 327.15 *agitated*; 327.6 *shaking*
as penance 807.8 *penitently*
aspergation 433.8 *watering*
asperge 429.5, 433.33 *sprinkle*
asperger 10.14 *sacred object*
Asperges 10.5 *Christian rite*; 255.2 *purification*; 256.3 *religious cleansing*
aspergillosis 83.5 *fungal association*
aspergillum 10.14 *sacred object*; 433.12 *sprinkler*
asperity 651.4 *bitterness*; 659.1 *discourtesy*; 726.1 *emphasis*; 625.1 *irascibility*; 418.8 *mental hardness*; 624.1 *resentment*; 647.1 *severity*
asperse 10.18 *perform rites*; 668.20 *scorn*; 678.13 *vilify*
aspersion **678.4**; 10.5 *Christian rite*; 668.5 *insult*; 381.16 *personal attack*; 429.5 *sprinkle*; 433.8 *watering*
aspersive 678.16 *defamatory*
as per usual 216.11 *on average*
asphalt 435.2 *building material*; 38.25 *construction material*; 550.11 *paving*; 317.4 *road surface*; 421.8 *smooth thing*
asphyxiant 382.23 *deadly*
asphyxiate 382.17 *murder*
asphyxiating 503.3 *stinking*
asphyxiation 382.2 *murder*
aspic 25.7 *basic ingredient*; 359.2 *preserver*
aspirant **610.13**; 617.6 *desirer*; 610.5 *hoper*
aspirate 370.12 *draw in*; 729.18 *phonetic*; 5.16 *spoken letter*; 369.14 *suck*
aspirated 729.18 *phonetic*
aspiration **610.3**; 131.14 *aim*; 617.1 *desire*; 474.2 *expectations*; 482.3 *future intention*; 370.4 *intake*; 480.11, 483.1 *motive*; 369.4 *sucking*
aspirator 369.9 *extractor*
aspire **610.7**; 446.18 *aim*; 304.13 *ascend*; 154.15 *be high*
aspire to 482.10 *aim*; 617.12 *desire*
aspirin 394.5 *analgesic*; 394.8 *drug*
aspiring 610.13 *aspirant*; 617.9 *desirous*; 154.9 *high*; 295.12 *immature*; 482.11 *intending*
aspiringly 295.24 *immaturely*
as planned **484.16**; 482.15 *according to plan*
a spoonful of sugar 498.2 *sweetener*
asportation 316.2 *transportation*
as promised **756.16**; 755.8 *contractually*; 750.39 *with consent*
as proof 703.22 *demonstrably*
as proud as Lucifer 622.14 *proud*
as punishment 714.16 *vindictively*
as quick as lightning 280.8 *immediately*
as regards 108.10 *relevantly*
as reported 741.15 *journalistically*

as required 397.16 *commandingly*
as rumour has it 476.10 *supposedly*
ass 316.6 *beast of burden*; 459.3 *foolish person*; 486.10 *unskilled person*
assail 381.1 *attack*; 670.21 *berate*; 331.8 *club*; 586.36 *combat*; 113.18 *object*
assailant 381.19 *attacker*; 586.1 *combatant*
assailed 670.34 *censured*
Assam 558.3 *tea*
Assama 8.11 *heaven*
Assam-Burmese 5.11 *family of languages*
assassin 588.3 *anarchist*; 381.19 *attacker*; 586.1 *combatant*; 662.9 *criminal*; 357.6 *destroyer*; 798.6 *evil person*; 651.8 *malefactor*; 382.11 *murderer*; 814.17 *punisher*; 380.4 *violent creature*; 804.9 *wicked person*
assassinate 588.4 *be anarchic*; 753.8 *cause mischief*; 586.38 *conquer*; 382.17 *murder*; 806.10 *sin*
assassinated 753.10 *lawbreaking*
assassination 753.2 *disorder*; 382.2 *murder*; 381.16 *terrorist attack*
assault 651.7 *act of malevolence*; 381.1, 381.11 *attack*; 331.12 *collision*; 586.36 *combat*; 16.39 *crime*; 804.7 *criminality*; 245.10 *impairment*; 380.3 *instance of violence*; 351.2 *misuse*; 380.8 *use violence*
assault and battery 331.12 *collision*; 804.7 *criminality*; 381.16 *personal attack*
assault and robbery 774.1 *stealing*
assaulted 773.12 *taking*
assaulter 586.1 *combatant*
assault gun 587.11 *guns*
assaulting 381.23 *attacking*
assault sexually 773.7 *take*
assault troops 586.14 *armed forces*
assay 448.1, 448.11 *experiment*; 26.10 *measure*
assayer 448.5 *experimenter*
ass backwards 192.4 *inversely*
assegai 587.8 *sharp weapon*
assemblage **376.25**; 765.3 *acquisition*; 409.2 *array*; 374.3, 376.1 *assembly*; 376.33 *putting together*; 19.12 *sculpture*
assemblage of birds 72.13
assemblage of mammals 71.21
assemble **376.37**; **403.17**; 765.11 *acquire*; 374.5 *combine*; 310.10 *come together*; 406.8 *embody*; 405.13 *make*; 312.8 *meet*; 243.4 *prepare for action*; 356.10 *produce*; 742.6 *word*
assembled **374.9**; **376.46**; 416.6 *dense*
assembler 376.34
assembling 765.3 *acquisition*
assembly **374.3**; **376.1**; 734.4 *conference*; 579.7 *council*; 356.2 *manufacture*; 376.3 *meeting*; 310.4 *meeting place*; 376.33 *putting together*; 10.17 *worshipper*
assembly hall 6.15 *schoolroom*
assembly language 5.8 *artificial language*
assembly line 620.2 *boring thing*; 132.6 *continuum*; 356.2 *manufacture*; 376.33 *putting together*; 111.6 *regularity*; 577.1 *workshop*
assembly of materials 356.1 *production*
assent 669.12 *accept*; 739.8 *admit*; 669.1 *approval*; 636.13 *be willing*; 750.7, 750.28 *consent*; 755.1 *contract*; 663.5 *obey*; 388.1 *submission*; 388.3 *submit*
assentatious 750.17 *consenting*
assented 476.8 *supposed*
assenter 755.4 *contractor*
assentient 750.17 *consenting*
assenting 750.17 *consenting*; 755.7 *contractual*; 388.5 *submitting*; 636.1 *willing*
assentingly 750.39 *with consent*
assentor 664.3 *sycophant*
assert 707.17 *affirm*; 707.21 *be assertive*; 716.11 *give evidence*; 694.10 *mean*; 4.22 *propound a philosophy*; 729.11 *speak*; 476.5 *suppose*; 454.3 *testify*
asserted 701.11 *logical*; 707.11 *stated*
asserter 707.9 *affirmer*
assertion 707.1 *affirmation*; 701.3 *line of argument*; 16.5 *litigation*; 27.63 *mathematical logic*; 4.1 *philosophy*; 729.7 *utterance*
assertion of truth 714.1 *vindication*
assertion sign 4.8 *philosophical term*
assertive **707.14**; 707.10 *affirmative*; 452.2 *convinced*; 661.7 *defiant*; 336.11 *strong in spirit*
assertively 707.23 *affirmatively*; 381.26 *aggresively*; 661.9 *defiantly*; 336.14 *strongly*; 452.24 *with certainty*
assertiveness **707.6**; 452.10 *conviction*; 336.1 *strength*
assertiveness training 36.3 *psychiatric treatment*
assert oneself 703.18 *appear*; 452.20 *be certain*; 391.5 *be liberated*; 635.15 *impose one's will*; 342.14 *push*
assert onself 738.4 *show oneself*
assertory 707.10 *affirmative*; 707.14 *assertive*
assert the truth 714.7 *vindicate*
assess 464.12 *estimate*; 26.10 *measure*; 790.11 *price*
assessable 26.14 *measurable*
assessed 26.13 *measured*; 790.14 *priced*; 440.8 *propertied*
assessed valuation 440.5 *personal estate*
assessment 210.1 *calculation*; 464.1 *judgment*; 26.1 *measurement*; 790.7 *tax*; 790.2 *value*
assessor 16.23, 464.5 *judge*; 26.9 *measurer*
assets 13.7 *corporation*; 352.4 *financial resources*; 440.5 *personal estate*; 439.1 *store*; 217.7 *sufficiency*; 781.5 *wealth*
asset-strip 245.5 *hurt*; 766.9 *lose*
asset-stripped 773.12 *taking*
asset-stripper 773.6 *taker*
asset-stripping 766.1 *loss*; 773.3 *taking away*
asseverate 707.17 *affirm*
asseverated 707.11 *stated*
asseveration 707.1 *affirmation*
asshole 631.5 *badly behaved person*; 459.3 *foolish person*
assibilate 512.4 *hiss*
assibilation 512.1 *hiss*
assidously 297.1 *frequently*
assiduity **342.8**; 665.1 *carefulness*; 640.2 *commitment*; 576.4 *exertion*; 297.4 *frequency*
assiduous 665.9 *careful*; 471.8 *diligent*; 297.3 *frequent*; 342.20 *industrious*; 640.10 *persevering*; 576.10 *working*
assiduously 471.15 *attentively*; 222.19 *meticulously*
assiduousness 471.3 *carefulness*; 640.2 *commitment*; 297.4 *frequency*
assign **770.6**; 769.6 *beneficiary*; 316.14 *bring back*; 137.13 *class*; 398.7 *delegate*; 349.5 *dispose of*; 440.9 *own property*; 355.1 *relinquish*; 139.24 *specify*; 316.11 *transfer*
assign a date to 275.17 *date*
assign a job 770.6 *assign*
assign a part 770.6 *assign*
assign a place 770.6 *assign*
assignat 780.14 *paper money*
assign a task 770.6 *assign*
assignation 654.3 *meeting*; 376.8 *rendezvous*
assigned 770.7 *allocated*; 755.7 *contractual*; 398.10 *decentralized*; 354.5 *undertaken*
assigned job 770.3 *allotted task*
assigned task 770.3 *allotted task*
assigned work 576.1 *work*
assignee 769.6 *beneficiary*
assignment 770.1 *allocation*; 755.1 *contract*; 398.3 *delegation*; 810.1 *duty*; 576.2, 810.2 *task*; 354.2 *undertaking*; 576.1 *work*
assignment of work 398.3 *delegation*
assign to 349.1 *use*
assimilate **117.10**; 370.13 *absorb*; 760.8 *be transformed*; 374.5 *combine*; 99.12 *embody*; 400.15 *learn*; 115.11 *make similar*; 111.8 *make the same*; 750.26 *make uniform*; 760.12 *naturalize*
assimilated 760.13 *converted*; 760.17 *naturalized*; 111.12 *same*
assimilation 370.5 *absorption*; 374.1 *combination*; 760.2 *evolution*; 117.3 *pliancy*; 111.1 *sameness*; 115.1 *similarity*; 5.30 *syntax*
assimilationism 244.11 *reformism*
assimilationist 244.12 *reformer*
assimilative 370.17 *absorbent*
as simple as pie 695.2 *simple*
assist **608.11**; 348.4 *be an instrument*; 636.14, 747.11 *cooperate*; 413.14 *give moral support*; 813.10 *grant*; 392.1, 392.17 *help*; 58.3 *ice hockey*; 265.16 *make easy*; 58.9 *play hockey*; 401.8 *serve*
assistance 608.2 *aid*; 747.1 *cooperation*; 813.3 *grant*; 392.1 *help*; 348.1 *instrumentality*; 413.6 *moral support*; 436.1 *provision*; 265.5 *smoothness*; 652.4 *welfare state*
assistant **348.3**; 747.10 *cooperator*; 398.4 *deputy*; 392.11, 608.5 *helper*; 392.33 *helpful*; 122.6 *inferior*; 401.5 *office assistant*; 401.1 *servant*; 289.7, 387.3 *subordinate*; 413.8 *supporter*
assistant coach 49.2 *basketball player*; 46.2 *football player*
assister 392.11 *helper*; 652.3 *philanthropist*
assisting 392.30 *helping*; 58.8 *hockey*; 58.3 *ice hockey*; 348.6 *instrumental*
assize 16.26 *jury*; 16.7 *legal trial*
assize judge 16.25 *British judge*; 464.6 *justice*
assizes 16.20 *British court*; 16.19 *law court*; 464.3 *place of judgment*
assize sessions 464.3 *place of judgment*
ass-kicking 585.16 *warlike*
associate **373.3**; 374.6 *come together*; 223.11 *companion*; 373.13 *intercommunicate*; 747.16 *join*; 764.5 *jointly possessing*; 405.5 *member*; 570.19 *merge*; 764.3 *participant*; 578.5 *partner*; 108.7 *relate to*
associated **223.19**; 750.11 *allied*; 97.8 *attendant*; 373.14 *connective*; 374.8 *cooperative*; 108.5 *interrelated*; 108.4 *related*
Associated Press 741.7 *press agency*; 693.8 *source of information*
associate justice 464.6 *justice*; 400.3 *leader*; 396.10 *person of authority*
associate oneself with 392.24 *back*; 764.4 *have joint possession*
associates 747.9 *team*
associate with 654.11 *be sociable*; 750.22 *form an alliance*; 223.14 *keep company with*
associating 747.19
association **373.2**; **376.15**; **747.7**; 223.1 *accompaniment*; 570.2, 750.2 *alliance*; 374.3 *assembly*; 36.27 *association of ideas*; 374.2 *cooperation*; 27.61 *correlation*; 632.7 *habituation*; 108.2 *interrelatedness*; 764.1 *joint possession*; 554.1 *life*; 412.2 *mixed thing*; 412.1 *mixture*; 97.2 *omnipresence*; 764.2 *participation*; 108.1 *relatedness*; 654.1 *sociability*
association bargaining 15.1 *industrial relations*
association by contiguity 36.27 *association of ideas*
association by sound 36.27 *association of ideas*
Association Football 66.1 *soccer*
associationism 36.1 *psychology*
association of ideas **36.27**; 476.2 *basis of supposition*
association psychology 36.1 *psychology*
association test 36.5 *psychological test*
associative 374.9 *assembled*; 363.8 *attracting*
associatively 374.10 *in combination*
associative operation 27.14 *operation*
assoil 649.10 *absolve*
assonance 750.4 *harmony*; 542.1 *ornament*; 17.12 *poetic language*; 509.7 *repeated word*; 112.6 *reverberation*
assonant 516.7, 750.13 *harmonious*; 17.20 *metrical*; 112.15 *reverberatory*; 115.7 *similar*
assonate 18.34, 750.24 *harmonize*
as soon as 285.15 *as*
as soon as possible 293.17 *early*
assort 409.15 *categorize*; 137.14 *sort*
assorted **114.6**; 409.24 *categorized*; 469.15 *chosen*
assortment **114.2**; 469.9 *chosen thing*; 376.32, 412.3 *miscellany*
as stated 741.15 *journalistically*; 693.19 *reportedly*
assuage 419.14 *ease*; 301.9 *make motionless*; 685.4 *moderate*; 749.4 *pacify*; 608.9 *relieve*; 421.13 *smooth over*
assuaged 608.7 *relieved*
assuagement 608.1 *ease*; 685.1 *moderation*
assuage one's hunger 685.5 *moderate one's hunger*
assuage one's thirst 685.5 *moderate one's hunger*
assuaging 685.8 *moderating*; 608.8 *relieving*
as substitute 550.43 *alternatively*
assumable 476.8 *supposed*
assume 772.8 *adopt*; 676.4 *be affected*; 450.8 *be of the opinion*; 289.11 *follow in office*; 610.6 *hope*; 474.9 *predict*; 444.14 *premise*; 699.24 *pretend*; 4.22 *propound a philosophy*; 476.5 *suppose*; 773.7 *take*; 27.89, 446.17 *theorize*; 354.1 *undertake*
assume an obligation 354.1 *undertake*
assume authority 12.12, 396.20 *take authority*
assume command 579.2 *direct*; 12.12, 396.20 *take authority*
assumed 27.77 *given*; 167.7 *outward*; 476.8 *supposed*; 96.10, 446.10 *theoretical*; 354.5 *undertaken*
assumed name 737.8 *anonymity*; 721.8 *name*
assume office 289.11 *follow in office*
assume ownership 773.7 *take*
assume responsibility 579.2 *direct*; 556.18 *mature*; 354.1 *undertake*
assume the character of 760.8 *be transformed*
assume the guise of 699.24 *pretend*
assume the mantle 289.11 *follow in office*
assume the nature of 760.8 *be transformed*
assume the offensive 381.1 *attack*
assume the role of 717.10 *act*
assume the shape of 760.8 *be transformed*
assuming 222.15 *under the circumstances*
assuming ownership 773.1 *taking*
assuming that 476.11 *supposing*
Assumption 10.15 *holy day*
assumption 289.4 *accession*; 772.2 *adoption*; 304.1 *ascent*; 8.9 *deification*; 474.1, 610.2 *expectation*; 444.4 *explanation*; 446.1 *idea*; 366.7 *lift*; 4.1 *philosophy*; 476.1 *supposition*; 773.1 *taking*; 96.4 *theorization*
assumption of office 289.4 *accession*
assumptive 444.10 *causal*; 476.7 *suppositional*
assumptively 4.25 *theoretically*
assurance **167.4**; 707.6 *assertiveness*; 660.3 *audacity*; 450.3 *believing*; 107.7 *calculation of chance*; 810.7 *commitment*; 452.13, 707.4 *confirmation*; 354.3 *contract*; 452.10 *conviction*; 661.1 *defiance*; 613.6 *encouragement*; 474.1 *expectation*; 452.14 *guarantee*; 253.2, 756.1 *promise*; 252.1 *safety*; 454.4 *verification*; 707.3 *vow*
assure 707.21 *be assertive*; 609.9 *comfort*; 707.19 *confirm*; 613.17 *give courage*; 756.8 *guarantee*; 450.9 *make someone believe*; 253.11, 756.7 *promise*; 252.10 *protect*; 454.1 *verify*; 707.18 *vow*
assured **167.8**; 707.14 *assertive*; 660.15 *audacious*; 450.11 *believing*; 452.2 *convinced*; 661.7 *defiant*; 610.12 *expectant*; 253.7, 452.4 *guaranteed*; 756.13 *guaranteeing*; 756.12 *promised*; 252.6 *safe*; 707.13 *supported*; 454.10 *verified*; 707.12 *vowed*
assuredly **454.12**; 707.23 *affirmatively*; 756.16 *as promised*; 661.9 *defiantly*; 253.16 *surely*; 707.24 *truthfully*; 452.24 *with certainty*
assuredness 452.10 *conviction*
assurer 707.9 *affirmer*
assuring 613.14 *encouraging*; 454.9 *verificatory*
Assyrian 566.4 *modern human*
Assyriological 3.17 *archaeological*
Assyriologist 284.11 *antiquarian*; 3.4 *archaeologist*; 1.4 *palaeoanthropologist*
Assyriology 3.2 *archaeology*; 1.2 *palaeoanthropology*
A star 29.13 *luminosity*
Astarte 593.16 *gods and goddesses of love*
aster 34.10 *cell division*
asterisk 742.13 *punctuate*; 742.7 *punctuation*; 10.14 *sacred object*
asterism 742.7 *punctuation*
astern 303.28 *backwards*; 50.20 *offshore*
asteroid 75.3 *echinoderm*; 75.17 *echinodermal*; 306.4 *orbiting body*; 29.16 *planet*
asteroidal 29.36 *astronomical*
asteroid belt 29.16 *planet*
as the crow flies 324.9 *directly*; 178.1, 178.12 *straight*
as the matter stands 750.36 *accordingly*; 221.9 *conditionally*
asthenia 337.3 *poor health*
asthenic 337.10 *ill*
asthenosphere 30.5 *earth*; 30.18 *earth's crust*
as the saying goes 745.4 *proverbially*
as the story goes 693.19 *reportedly*; 811.6 *reputedly*

as the winds blow 222.15 *under the circumstances*
as they say 745.4 *proverbially;* 4.25 *theoretically*
as things are 221.9 *conditionally*
as things may fall 222.15 *under the circumstances*
as things stand 222.15 *under the circumstances*
asthma 260.4 *disease;* 260.9 *respiratory disease*
asthmatic 260.23 *diseased;* 512.6 *hissing;* 260.19 *sick person*
asthmatically 512.8 *sibilantly*
as though 476.11 *supposing*
astiamnu 10.3 *rite of worship*
astigmatic 519.9 *weak-sighted*
astigmatism 28.31 *lens element;* 29.25 *mounting;* 519.2 *poor sight*
astir 342.19 *busy;* 300.18 *in motion*
as to 108.10 *relevantly*
a stone's throw away 147.12 *near*
astonish 630.11 *amaze;* 619.10 *be wonderful*
astonished 630.7 *amazed;* 766.18 *at a loss;* 619.6 *wondering*
astonishing 630.8 *surprising*
astonishingly 619.13 *wonderfully*
astonishment 630.2 *amazement;* 619.1 *wonder*
astound 630.11 *amaze;* 619.10 *be wonderful*
astounded 630.7 *amazed;* 619.6 *wondering*
astounding 630.8 *surprising;* 619.8 *wonderful*
astoundingly 630.13 *surprisingly;* 619.13 *wonderfully*
astoundment 630.2 *amazement;* 619.1 *wonder*
Astra™ 692.7 *satellite communication*
astral 29.36 *astronomical;* 101.9 *parapsychological;* 11.18 *spiritual*
astral body 11.7 *spirit;* 101.3 *spiritual world*
astral plane 101.3 *spiritual world;* 11.2 *the occult*
astral-project 11.24 *experience psychic phenomena*
astral projection 11.1 *occultism*
astray **325.27**; 766.18 *at a loss;* 145.10 *distantly;* 325.21 *indirect;* 766.16 *losing;* 377.25 *sprawled*
astringence 191.1 *contraction*
astringency 191.1 *contraction;* 499.1 *sourness*
astringent 191.8 *contracting;* 191.4 *contractor;* 416.6 *dense;* 37.4 *drug type;* 651.14 *hostile;* 37.17 *stimulating*
astrobiology 29.1 *astronomy;* 34.1 *life science*
astrobotany 29.1 *astronomy*
astrochemical 32.31 *chemical*
astrochemist 32.2 *chemist*
astrochemistry 29.1 *astronomy;* 32.1 *chemistry*
astrocompass 323.5 *navigation*
astrodiagnosis 11.9 *divination*
astrodynamics 29.1 *astronomy*
astrogeology 29.1 *astronomy;* 30.1 *earth science*
astrolabe 26.6 *measuring instrument;* 29.23 *observatory*
astrologer 344.8 *contributor;* 11.13 *diviner;* 475.9 *forecaster;* 283.5 *predictor*
astrological 11.17 *divinatory*
astrological angle 176.4 *angular measurement*
astrological influence 344.4 *contributing factor*
astrologically 11.25 *occultly*
astrology 11.9, 475.2 *divination;* 283.4 *looking to the future;* 395.2 *occult influence;* 11.1 *occultism*
astromancer 11.13 *diviner*
astromancy 11.9 *divination*
astrometric 26.16 *micrometric*
astrometry 29.1 *astronomy;* 26.2 *micrometry*
astronaut 141.10 *spaceman;* 29.31 *space travel*
astronautic 29.36 *astronomical*
astronautics **29.29**
astronavigation 323.5 *navigation*
astronavigator 141.10 *spaceman*
astronomer **29.2**
astronomer royal 29.2 *astronomer*
astronomical **29.36**; 158.15 *big;* 202.2 *immeasurable*
astronomical almanac 693.5 *reference book*
astronomical distance 145.1 *distance*
astronomically **29.39**; 202.11 *immeasurably*
astronomical number 194.3 *large number*
astronomical observatory 29.23 *observatory*
astronomical satellite 29.32 *satellite*
astronomical telescope 29.24 *telescope*
astronomical time 281.3 *chronology*
astronomical unit **29.22**
Astronomy 29
astronomy 29.1
astrophotography 29.1 *astronomy;* 41.1 *photography*
astrophysical 29.36 *astronomical*
astrophysically 29.39 *astronomically*
astrophysicist 29.2 *astronomer*
astrophysics 29.1 *astronomy;* 28.4 *experimental physics*
Astroturf™ 421.11 *smooth;* 421.8 *smooth thing;* 46.4 *stadium*
astute 645.4 *cunning;* 442.10, 458.6 *intelligent;* 455.8 *knowledgeable;* 425.5 *mentally sharp;* 6.20 *refined;* 156.11 *wise*
astutely 645.6 *cunningly;* 442.15, 458.10 *intelligently;* 425.18 *sharply*
astuteness 442.4 *cleverness;* 425.13 *mental sharpness;* 156.3 *profundity;* 458.1 *wisdom*
astylar 20.9 *miscellaneous architectural features*
asunder 372.16, 372.21 *apart;* 369.21 *away;* 145.8 *distant;* 145.10 *distantly*
as understood 694.13 *meaningfully*
as usual **117.18**; 632.19 *habitually;* 225.9 *permanently;* 104.11 *probably*
asvamedha 10.3 *rite of worship*
as well 211.10 *additionally*
as well as 127.9 *inclusively*
as yet 284.23 *before now*
asylum 736.2 *hiding place;* 394.14 *hospital;* 252.2, 253.1 *protection;* 370.2 *receptivity;* 252.5 *refuge;* 773.4 *taking in*
asymmetric 234.6 *distorted;* 299.4 *irregular;* 27.79 *spatial;* 32.37 *structural*
asymmetrical 116.4 *dissimilar;* 109.8 *distorted;* 299.4 *irregular;* 27.79 *spatial;* 120.3 *unequal*
asymmetrically **234.13**; 109.13 *disproportionately;* 299.8 *irregularly;* 120.7 *unequally*
asymmetric centre 32.13 *structure*
asymmetric relation 27.63 *mathematical logic*
asymmetry 109.4, 234.1 *distortion;* 120.1 *inequality;* 299.1 *irregularity;* 116.2 *unlikeness*
asymptote 310.5 *focus;* 27.37 *line*
asymptotic 310.7 *convergent;* 27.80 *linear*
asynchronism 286.1 *different time*
asynchronous 286.2 *occurring at a different time*
asynchronously 286.3 *another time*
asynchronous motor 39.31 *electric motor*
asyndeton 5.30 *syntax*
as you please 663.11 *yours to command*
as you were 761.13 *reversibly*
as you will 663.11 *yours to command*
at a crucial point 222.17 *difficultly*
at a crucial time 222.17 *difficultly*
atactic 32.44 *polymeric*
atactic polymer 32.21 *polymer*
at a cut price 766.20 *at a loss*
at a cut rate 766.20 *at a loss*
at a disadvantage 120.3 *unequal;* 120.7 *unequally*
at a discount **791.7**; 212.8 *by subtraction;* 793.15 *cheaply*
at a distance 145.10 *distantly*
at a funeral pace 333.17 *in slow motion*
at a glance 449.16 *originally;* 518.25 *visibly*
at a good pace 47.10 *fast*
at a guess 216.11 *on average;* 476.10 *supposedly*
at a gulp 688.7 *gluttonously*
at a halt 301.10 *motionlessly*
at a late hour **294.16**
at a later time 294.17 *later*
at all 317.16 *how*
at all costs 638.17 *resolutely*
at a loose end 580.7 *leisurely;* 343.2 *not working*
at a loss **766.18**; **766.20**; 789.13 *financially;* 264.16 *troubled*
at a low ebb 367.24 *down;* 122.19 *inferiorly;* 218.10 *insufficiently;* 367.18 *lowering*
at a lower price 214.8 *decreasingly*
at a lower rate 214.8 *decreasingly*
at an advanced age 556.14 *aged;* 556.16 *maturely*
at an advantage **164.12**; 120.3 *unequal;* 120.7 *unequally*
at an angle 176.12 *askew;* 27.80 *linear;* 189.8 *obliquely*
at anchor 301.4 *motionless;* 252.6 *safe;* 228.9 *stable*
at an early time 293.17 *early*
at an end 131.21 *ended;* 226.10 *finished*
at an impasse 378.14 *blocked;* 264.16 *troubled*
at any odd moment 580.8 *leisurely*
at any price 638.17 *resolutely*
at any rate 317.16 *how*
at a pinch 264.25 *difficultly*
at a premium 788.8 *profitably;* 218.4 *scarce;* 792.8 *valuable;* 792.13 *valuably*
at a price **790.16**
at a profit 765.20 *gainfully*
ataractic 618.7 *indifferent*
ataraxia 4.3 *detachment;* 473.1 *disinterestedness;* 618.1 *indifference;* 463.1 *oblivion;* 301.2 *repose*
at arms 585.18 *to war*
at arm's length 145.10 *distantly*
at a slow pace 333.17 *in slow motion*
at a snail's pace 333.17 *in slow motion*
at a stand 301.10 *motionlessly*
at a standstill 378.14 *blocked;* 341.3 *inactive;* 343.15 *inactively;* 343.2 *not working;* 225.9 *permanently;* 264.16 *troubled*
at a stroke 357.16 *destructively*
at a tangent 325.28 *indirectly*
atavism 761.1 *reversion*
atavistic 3.15 *historic;* 761.10 *regressive*
atavistically 761.13 *reversibly*
ataxia 335.4 *disability*
ATB 320.12 *bicycle*
at bargain prices 791.7 *at a discount*
at bay 384.32 *defensively;* 254.4 *endangered*
at best 446.23 *ideally*
at bottom 99.14 *at heart*
at break of day 290.8 *in the morning*
at close quarters 147.12 *near*
at close range 147.12 *near*
at cockcrow 290.8 *in the morning*
at cost 793.15 *cheaply;* 789.13 *financially*
at cross purposes 408.28 *anyhow;* 701.7 *arguing;* 701.17 *argumentatively;* 113.29 *at odds;* 751.9 *disagreeing;* 113.24 *discordant*
at cut price 791.7 *at a discount*
at daggers drawn 113.29 *at odds*
at dawn 290.8 *in the morning*
at daybreak 290.8 *in the morning*
at death's door 582.18 *dying*
at different times 116.7 *dissimilarly*
at each other's throats 701.17 *argumentatively;* 701.9 *hostile*
at ease **263.4**; 250.13 *informal;* 580.7 *leisurely;* 490.7 *pleased;* 248.8 *prosperous*
atelier 19.11 *artist's materials;* 577.1 *workshop*
at express speed 332.14 *swiftly*
at face value 525.15 *apparently*
at fault 806.5 *guilty;* 802.12 *incorrect;* 802.16 *in the wrong;* 274.17 *mistaken*
at first 130.40 *first*
at first blush 525.15 *apparently;* 738.16 *manifestly*
at first hearing 504.17 *aurally*
at first light 290.8 *in the morning;* 522.30 *lightly*
at first sight 525.15 *apparently;* 449.16 *originally;* 518.24 *visually*
at fixed intervals 298.15 *regularly*
at fixed periods 298.15 *regularly*
at full blast 332.14 *swiftly*
at full pitch 507.6 *loud*
at full power 437.12 *powerfully*
at full speed 332.14 *swiftly*
at full steam 437.12 *powerfully*
at full stretch 232.10 *fully*
at full throttle 332.14 *swiftly*
at full tilt 332.14 *swiftly;* 338.6 *with vigour*
at great cost 792.12 *dearly*
at great expense 792.12 *dearly*
at great intervals 206.6 *sparse*
at great length 270.7 *diffusely*
at great value 792.13 *valuably*
at grips 585.15 *warring*
at gunpoint 386.11 *compellingly;* 380.10 *violently*
Athabasca 88.5 *other major lakes*
at half-mast 367.24 *down;* 603.8 *mournfully*
at half price 791.7 *at a discount*
at half speed 333.17 *in slow motion;* 685.9 *moderately*
at hand 97.10, 282.8 *available;* 283.11 *future;* 293.13 *imminent;* 147.9, 147.12 *near;* 239.8 *nearby;* 492.8 *touchable;* 237.1 *useful*
Atharvaveda 7.12 *religious text*
at heart **99.14**
at heavy cost 792.12 *dearly*
atheism 708.2 *rejection;* 453.10 *suspicion;* 451.4 *unbelief*
atheist 451.5 *disbeliever;* 250.8 *freethinker;* 708.9 *negativist;* 637.16 *reluctant person*
atheistic 451.6 *disbelieving;* 250.10 *independent;* 708.17 *negative;* 637.5 *reluctant*
atheistically 250.20 *freely;* 708.22 *negatively*
Athena 585.3 *gods and goddesses of war*
Athens 87.6 *other cities;* 12.5 *political organization*
atheroma 260.10 *cardiovascular disease*
atherosclerosis 418.6 *solidification*
athirst 428.2 *thirsty*
athlete **47.3**; **336.5**; **586.3**; 633.6 *hunter;* 485.4 *skilled person;* 45.3 *sportsman*
athlete's foot 83.5 *fungal association;* 260.13 *skin disease*
athlete's heart 260.10 *cardiovascular disease*
athletic 336.9 *physically strong;* 419.2 *pliant;* 423.4 *powerful;* 45.5 *sporting;* 576.10 *working*
athletically 423.13 *powerfully;* 419.17 *softly;* 45.7 *sportingly*
athletic belt 413.5 *supporting garment*
athletic build 423.8 *physical strength*
athleticism 336.1 *strength*
Athletics 47
athletics 300.11 *bodily movement;* 576.5 *exercise*
athletics track 317.6 *path*
athletic support 47.4 *sports equipment;* 413.5 *supporting garment*
at home **97.17**; 632.14 *habituated;* 250.13 *informal;* 565.14 *inhabiting;* 654.3 *meeting;* 654.5 *party;* 97.9 *resident;* 376.9 *social gathering;* 655.14 *unsocially*
at home with 569.9 *friends with;* 6.19 *knowledgeable*
a thousand and one 208.7 *myriad*
a thousand times no 708.23, 709.12 *no!*
at huge expense 792.12 *dearly*
athwart 150.8 *breadthwise;* 50.20 *offshore*
atilt 189.4 *oblique*
at intervals 146.8 *apart;* 133.17 *discontinuously*
at issue 701.18 *arguably;* 113.29 *at odds;* 113.24 *discordant;* 705.14 *questionable*
at journey's end 312.22 *on arrival*
at knifepoint 386.11 *compellingly;* 380.10 *violently*
Atlanta 87.2 *American cities*
atlantes 19.12 *sculpture*
Atlantic Daylight Time 275.9 *time zone*
Atlantic salmon 55.4 *American game fish;* 25.17 *freshwater fish*
Atlantic Standard Time 275.9 *time zone*
Atlantis 477.8 *dreamland;* 737.6 *natural mystery;* 29.30 *spacecraft*
at large 250.9 *free*
ATLAS 40.3 *computer*
Atlas 158.10 *big person;* 336.6 *muscleman*
atlas 220.3 *dictionary;* 163.4, 484.5, 717.7 *map;* 693.5 *reference book;* 6.14 *school book*
Atlas Mountains 89.6 *other major mountains and ranges*
at last 294.16 *at a late hour;* 131.26, 309.17 *finally*
at law 16.87 *in litigation*
at law with 16.53 *litigating*

at leisure 250.13 *informal*; 580.7 *leisurely*
at length 270.7 *diffusely*; 148.11 *lengthily*
at loggerheads 701.7 *arguing*; 701.17 *argumentatively*; 751.9 *disagreeing*; 585.15 *warring*
at long last 294.16 *at a late hour*; 131.26 *finally*
at low ebb 214.8 *decreasingly*; 245.12 *deteriorated*
ATM 40.12 *electronic office*
Atman 8.3 *God*
atman 11.7 *spirit*
at maximum speed 61.11 *in a race*
at midnight 523.15 *darkly*
atmometer 26.8 *meter*
atmometry 26.2 *micrometry*
atmosphere 31.8; **170.3**; 434.1 *air*; 17.3 *aspect of fiction*; 143.2 *circumstances*; 30.5 *earth*; 417.5, 432.1 *gas*; 395.1 *influence*; 411.5 *layered thing*; 19.24 *pictorial*; 19.4 *treatment*
atmospheric 31.43; **170.6**; **434.13**; 432.17 *airy*; 143.8 *circumstantial*; 30.50 *terrestrial*
atmospheric air 432.1 *gas*
atmospherically 432.28 *aerily*; 434.25 *airily*; 19.31 *artistically*
atmospheric circulation 31.10 *air movement*
atmospheric dissonance 517.5
atmospheric dust 31.8 *atmosphere*
atmospheric electricity 28.42 *electricity*
atmospheric layer 31.8 *atmosphere*
atmospheric layers 434.3
atmospheric model 28.6 *law*
atmospheric physics 31.1 *meteorology*
atmospheric pressure 28.10 *force*
atmospheric process 31.9
atmospherics 692.19 *radio reception*; 327.13 *tempest*
atmospheric water vapour 31.8 *atmosphere*
at night 291.7 *evening*
at nightfall 523.15 *darkly*
at no extra cost 752.20 *persuasively*
at no time 94.15 *not ever*
at odds 113.29; 701.7 *arguing*; 701.17 *argumentatively*; 113.24 *discordant*; 751.11 *in disagreement*
at odds with 751.9 *disagreeing*
at odd times 276.14 *for short periods*
atoll 92.2 *island*; 30.16 *ocean floor*
atom 28.65; 196.3 *fragment*; 159.2 *little thing*; 402.4 *matter*; 197.1 *one*; 405.3 *unit*
atom bomb 587.16 *bomb*
atomic 159.7 *little*; 405.7 *modular*; 197.11 *one*; 205.11 *partial*; 28.98 *physical*; 334.17 *powered*
atomically 405.14 *constituently*; 159.9 *microscopically*
atomic bomb 334.8 *nuclear power*; 587.16 *bomb*
atomic clock 273.3 *accurate thing*; 28.87, 281.6 *clock*
atomic energy 334.4 *energy*; 28.72 *nuclear fission*
atomic-force microscope 28.85 *microscope*
atomic mass 28.69 *isotope*
atomic mass constant 28.69 *isotope*
atomic number 28.69 *isotope*
atomic orbital 28.65 *atom*
atomic physics 28.3 *modern physics*; 402.6 *natural science*
atomic pile 334.8 *nuclear power*; 28.73 *nuclear reactor*
atomic power 334.4 *energy*; 334.8 *nuclear power*
atomic structure 28.65 *atom*
atomic war 585.1 *war*
atomic warfare 585.8 *warfare*
atomic warhead 587.15 *explosive*
atomic weight 414.9 *avoirdupois weight*; 28.69 *isotope*
atomism 4.7 *school of thought*
atomist 4.11 *follower of a doctrine*; 402.3 *materialist*
atomistic 4.14 *of a philosophy*
atomization 375.2 *deconstruction*; 427.4 *pulverization*; 432.10 *vaporization*
atomize 432.26 *aerate*; 222.11 *circumstantiate*; 375.4 *deconstruct*; 357.9 *demolish*; 432.25 *gasify*; 427.22 *pulverize*; 433.33 *sprinkle*
atomizer 502.2 *fragrant thing*; 37.10 *inhalant*; 427.11 *pulverizer*; 433.12 *sprinkler*; 432.11 *vaporizer*
atom smasher 334.8 *nuclear power*
atom-smashing 375.2 *deconstruction*; 28.72 *nuclear fission*
atonal 517.9 *unmelodious*
atonality 517.4
atonally 517.12 *dissonantly*
at once 280.8 *immediately*
atone 785.14; **807.5**; 808.5 *do penance*; 775.4 *give back*; 752.14 *offer reparation*; 609.11 *recompense*; 393.3 *restore*; 9.7 *worship*
at one 750.10 *in accord*
atoned 649.6 *forgiven*; 808.7 *penitential*
at one fell swoop 380.10 *violently*
atone for 807.5 *atone*; 808.5 *do penance*
at one go 132.19 *continuously*
Atonement 807
atonement 807.1; 649.3 *absolution*; 775.1 *giving back*; 749.2 *peace offering*; 814.11 *penance*; 394.1 *remedy*; 609.2 *reparation*; 393.9 *restoration*; 808.2 *type of penance*; 9.1 *worship*
atoner 807.3; 775.3 *returner*
at one remove 325.28 *indirectly*
at one's command 663.7 *obedient*; 763.9 *possessed*; 763.10 *possessively*
at one's convenience 580.8 *leisurely*
at one's desk 342.19 *busy*
at one's disposal 663.7 *obedient*; 763.9 *possessed*; 763.10 *possessively*
at one's elbow 147.12 *near*
at one's expense 787.12 *expended*
at one's feet 147.12 *near*; 387.9 *subject*
at one's fingertips 97.10 *available*; 147.9, 147.12 *near*; 239.8 *nearby*
at one's last gasp 582.18 *dying*
at one's leisure 294.15 *late*; 580.8 *leisurely*
at one's lowest ebb 122.19 *inferiorly*
at one's mercy 387.9 *subject*
at one's own discretion 250.20 *freely*
at one's pleasure 635.17 *at will*; 663.7 *obedient*
at one's service 392.31 *supplementary*; 349.10 *usable*
at one's side 147.12 *near*
at one's top speed 332.14 *swiftly*
at one's wits' end 264.16 *troubled*
at one time 285.13 *synchronously*
atoning 807.4; 808.7 *penitential*; 775.6 *restoring*
atop 89.11 *on the mountain*
A to Z 163.4, 484.5, 717.7 *map*
ATP 33.22 *bioenergetics*
at par 119.8 *on equal terms*
ATP cycle 33.22 *bioenergetics*
at peace 589.7 *peaceful*; 589.8 *peacefully*
at poverty level 135.5 *necessitous*
at present 282.9
atrabilious 602.6 *depressed*; 626.6 *sullen*
atrabiliousness 626.1 *sullenness*
at random 107.13 *by chance*; 408.27 *in disorder*; 412.14 *in the midst*; 299.8 *irregularly*
at regular intervals 298.15 *regularly*
at rest 343.15 *inactively*; 339.7 *inertly*; 301.6 *quiescent*; 228.9 *stable*; 263.6 *with ease*; 341.5 *without action*
at right angles 186.12 *perpendicularly*
at risk 254.4 *endangered*
atrocious 651.11 *cruel*; 798.7 *evil*; 804.11 *wicked*
atrociously 798.12 *evilly*
atrociousness 798.1 *evil*
atrocity 651.7 *act of malevolence*; 651.2 *cruelness*; 380.3 *instance of violence*; 806.3 *sin*; 647.2 *suppression*; 804.1 *wickedness*
at rock bottom 156.16 *deep*; 367.24 *down*
atrophy 191.1 *contraction*; 214.1, 214.4 *decrease*; 245.9 *dilapidation*; 335.4 *disability*; 260.4 *disease*; 153.8 *emaciation*; 687.1 *fasting*; 260.17 *nervous disorder*; 441.3 *waste*
atropine 33.19 *alkaloid*
at sea 323.11 *nautical*; 91.11, 323.12 *nautically*
at sea level 155.7 *lowland*
at short notice 262.6 *hastily*; 293.18 *soon*
at sight 525.15 *apparently*; 518.24 *visually*
at sixes and sevens 408.28 *anyhow*; 114.11 *irregularly*; 408.18 *muddled*
at specified times 298.15 *regularly*
at stake 254.1 *dangerous*
at stated times 298.15 *regularly*
at strife 751.9 *disagreeing*
at sunrise 290.8 *in the morning*
at sunup 290.8 *in the morning*
at sword's point 585.18 *to war*
atta 427.8 *meal*
attach 492.12 *abut*; 211.6 *add*; 373.11 *connect*
attaché 398.6 *agent*
attaché case 410.9 *baggage*
attached 211.8 *additional*; 373.15 *connected*; 593.17 *loving*; 108.4 *related*; 267.10 *tenacious*
attached to 593.18 *in love*
attach importance to 123.8 *make important*
attachment 211.1 *addition*; 211.3 *additional item*; 267.1 *adhesion*; 373.1 *connection*; 595.1 *liking*; 593.1 *love*; 108.1 *relatedness*; 267.2 *tenacity*
attach oneself to 223.16 *attend*; 267.8 *be tenacious*
Attack 381
attack 381.1; **381.11**; 733.4 *approach*; 729.4 *articulation*; 585.9 *battle*; 585.13 *be at war*; 670.21 *berate*; 670.8 *berating*; 331.8 *club*; 331.2 *collide*; 331.12 *collision*; 586.36 *combat*; 113.5 *conflict*; 54.5 *fence*; 54.3 *fencing movements*; 260.2 *illness*; 245.10 *impairment*; 314.3 *inroad*; 380.3 *instance of violence*; 314.10 *invade*; 351.1 *misuse*; 304.6 *mounting*; 113.18 *object*; 64.5 *play rugby*; 484.2 *policy*; 596.6 *react against*; 327.8 *spasm*; 651.18 *torment*; 712.3 *vilification*; 712.6 *vilify*; 585.8 *warfare*; 587.1 *weapon*
attack a problem 484.9 *plan*
attack cargo ship 586.24 *warship*
attacked 670.34 *censured*
attacker 381.19; 586.1 *combatant*; 670.11 *disapprover*; 314.8 *intruder*; 64.4 *rugby player*
attacking 381.23; 54.6 *fencing*; 314.16 *invasive*; 712.9 *vituperative*; 585.15 *warring*
attacking force 381.19 *attacker*
attacking stroke 53.9 *stroke*
attacking zone 58.3 *ice hockey*
attack of nerves 461.6 *mental breakdown*
attack player 58.6 *lacrosse player*
attack successfully 381.9
attack tooth and nail 381.5 *strike*
attack transport ship 586.24 *warship*
attain 312.9 *achieve*; 765.9 *gain*
attainability 765.1 *gain*
attainable 312.20; 765.15 *gainful*; 102.5 *possible*; 95.9 *realizable*; 492.8 *touchable*
attainder 16.43 *conviction*
attain majority 556.18 *mature*
attainment 312.17 *achievement*; 232.3 *completion*; 765.1 *gain*; 485.1 *skill*; 246.1 *success*
attainments 455.3 *learning*
attainment targets 455.3 *learning*
attaint 16.79 *convict*
attar of roses 78.8 *flower product*
Attempt 353
attempt 353.1; **353.5**; 340.4 *act*; 340.1 *action*; 576.4 *exertion*; 576.8 *exert oneself*; 482.4 *formulated intention*; 448.13 *invent*; 356.1 *production*; 342.15 *try*; 354.1 *undertake*; 344.6, 354.2 *undertaking*
attempted suicide 382.7 *suicide*
attempter 353.7
attempting 353.8
attempt the impossible 103.10; 486.6 *act foolishly*; 238.9 *waste effort*
attempt to buy 752.10 *offer to buy*
attempt too much 353.3 *tackle*
attend 97.12; **223.16**; 525.11 *appear*; 471.10 *be attentive*; 394.20 *doctor*; 504.15 *hear*; 35.19 *practise medicine*; 392.25 *serve*
attend a conference 746.5 *negotiate*; 398.8 *represent*
attend a convention 398.8 *represent*
attend a council meeting 398.8 *represent*
attendance 223.10; 525.2 *being in view*; 97.2 *omnipresence*; 471.5 *solicitude*
attendant 97.8; **223.7**; **401.3**; 223.17 *accompanying*; 570.7 *bridal party*; 223.4 *concomitant*; 392.11 *helper*; 401.1 *servant*; 401.9 *serving*; 413.8 *supporter*
attend classes 6.23 *learn*
attended 223.20 *accompanied*
attendee 97.5 *someone present*
attender 97.5 *someone present*
attending 223.17 *accompanying*; 401.9 *serving*; 392.32, 413.9 *supportive*
attending regularly 297.5 *frequenting*
attend regularly 297.8 *frequent*
attend to 665.11 *care for*
attend upon 401.8 *serve*
Attention 471
attention 471.1; 342.8 *assiduity*; 665.1 *carefulness*; 640.2 *commitment*; 504.1 *hearing*; 667.1 *respect*; 726.2 *seriousness*
attentions 667.3 *respectfulness*
attention to detail 273.1 *accuracy*; 342.8 *assiduity*; 471.2 *close attention*; 665.4 *fastidiousness*
attention to details 698.8 *accuracy*
attention to fact 273.2 *correctness*
attentive 504.11 *aural*; 650.6 *benevolent*; 665.9 *careful*; 455.8 *knowledgeable*; 667.8 *respectful*; 471.9 *solicitous*; 4.17 *thoughtful*; 471.7 *watchful*; 576.10 *working*
attentively 471.15; 504.17 *aurally*; 650.10 *benevolently*; 4.28 *thoughtfully*
attentiveness 471.1 *attention*; 650.1 *benevolence*; 665.1 *carefulness*
attentive person 471.6
attenuate 377.14 *dilute*; 417.6 *make sparse*; 153.16 *make thin*; 151.10 *narrow*; 417.2 *rarefied*; 151.3 *tapered*; 153.5 *thinned*
attenuated 417.2 *rarefied*; 151.3 *tapered*; 153.5 *thinned*
attenuation 377.3 *dilution*; 151.9 *narrowing*; 427.4 *pulverization*; 417.4 *rarefaction*; 153.12 *thinning*; 28.15 *wave property*
attest 707.17 *affirm*; 707.19 *confirm*; 750.28 *consent*; 755.5 *contract*; 95.12 *establish reality*; 716.11 *give evidence*; 703.17 *prove*; 698.30 *prove true*; 701.15 *state*; 454.3 *testify*
attestable 703.12 *demonstrable*
attestant 707.9 *affirmer*; 716.7 *person who gives evidence*; 454.7 *verifier*
attestation 707.1 *affirmation*; 698.7, 707.4 *confirmation*; 750.7 *consent*; 701.3 *line of argument*; 703.4 *proof*; 454.4 *verification*
attested 716.8 *evidential*; 756.13 *guaranteeing*; 701.11 *logical*; 698.20 *proved*; 703.13 *proven*; 707.11 *stated*; 707.13 *supported*; 454.10 *verified*
attestor 756.5 *promise-maker*
attest to 756.8 *guarantee*; 714.8 *justify*
at that hour 281.18 *horologically*
at that moment 275.27 *at what time*
at that rate 750.36 *accordingly*; 222.15 *under the circumstances*
at that time 281.18 *horologically*
at the bar 16.86 *jurisdictionally*
at the beginning 130.38 *in the beginning*
at the boiling point 254.1 *dangerous*
at the bottom 155.10 *low*
at the bottom of 344.13 *causal*
at the breast 555.11 *young*; 555.14 *youthfully*
at the cannon's mouth 585.18 *to war*
at the committee stage 243.17 *developing*
at the core 99.14 *at heart*; 173.10 *centrally*
at the door 312.22 *on arrival*
at the double 262.8 *hurry up!*
at the earliest 293.17 *early*
at the eleventh hour 294.16 *at a late hour*; 287.11 *in time*
at the end 226.11 *finally*; 168.9 *in the rear*
at the expense of 762.9 *instead*
at the extreme 164.11 *marginally*
at the finish 226.11 *finally*
at the first 130.38 *in the beginning*
at the first opportunity 293.17 *early*
at the flash point 254.1 *dangerous*
at the foot 155.10 *low*
at the front 585.18 *to war*; 585.15 *warring*
at the hands of 348.9 *instrumentally*
at the head 579.19 *managerially*
at the heart of 173.10 *centrally*
at the helm 396.23 *authoritatively*; 579.17 *managerial*; 579.19 *managerially*; 323.11 *nautical*; 323.12 *nautically*
at the highest level 174.8 *on top*
at the last minute 294.16 *at a late hour*; 287.11 *in time*
at the last stand 254.4 *endangered*
at the limit 164.11 *marginally*
at the lowest point 156.16 *deep*
at the mercy of 254.3 *vulnerable*
at the moment 93.23 *now*
at the moment of 285.15 *as*

at the peak 121.17 *supremely*
at the Pearly Gates 582.19 *dead*
at the planning stage 484.14 *planned*
at the ready 243.18 *prepared*
at the reins 396.23 *authoritatively*
at the right time 283.14 *in the future*
at the same rate 119.12 *equally*
at the same time 211.10 *additionally*; 115.14 *comparably*; 111.18 *identically*; 285.12 *simultaneously*
at the starting grid 61.11 *in a race*
at the summit 174.8 *on top*
at the sword's point 386.11 *compellingly*
at the three-mile limit 166.6 *furthest*
at the time 275.27 *at what time*
at the top 154.19 *high*; 174.8 *on top*
at the very start 130.38 *in the beginning*
at the wheel 396.23 *authoritatively*; 579.19 *managerially*; 323.12 *nautically*
at the whim of 254.3 *vulnerable*
at the wrong time 288.19
at the zenith 121.17 *supremely*
at this hour 281.18 *horologically*
at this moment 282.9 *at present*; 275.27 *at what time*
at this point 142.12 *where*
at this time 282.9 *at present*; 281.18 *horologically*
Attic 543.3 *elegant*
attic 736.2 *hiding place*; 154.8 *high thing*; 20.9 *miscellaneous architectural features*; 565.7 *room*; 439.4 *storage*
Atticism 543.1 *elegance*
Attila 651.8 *malefactor*
attire 551.1, 551.32 *dress*
attired 551.29 *dressed*
attire oneself 551.34 *wear*
attitude 229.2; 22.9 *ballet steps*; 450.1 *belief*; 222.1 *circumstances*; 631.1 *conduct*; 590.4 *emotion*; 443.6 *idea*; 160.6 *nature*; 4.1 *philosophy*; 7.1 *religion*; 221.4 *state of mind*; 476.1 *supposition*
attitudes 590.3 *feelings*; 795.1 *morality*
attitudinize 676.4 *be affected*; 699.24 *pretend*
attitudinizer 676.2 *pretender*
attitudinizing 699.7 *pretence*; 699.34 *pretending*
attollent 366.11 *raised*
attorney 713.4 *adviser*; 398.6 *agent*; 16.13 *lawyer*; 748.4 *representative*
attorney-at-law 16.13 *lawyer*
Attorney General 16.11 *British law officer*; 16.12 *US law officer*
attract 363.11; 617.15 *cause desire*; 483.9 *motivate*; 362.15 *pull towards*; 593.28 *win the love of*
attractance 363.1 *attraction*
attractancy 363.1 *attraction*
attract attention 471.13; 123.7 *be important*; 738.5 *be visible*
attracted 593.19 *enamoured*; 483.12 *motivated*
attracting 363.8; 362.8 *tractional*
Attraction 363
attraction 363.1; 229.2 *attitude*; 334.4 *energy*; 480.3 *incentive*; 483.2 *inducement*; 395.1 *influence*; 595.1 *liking*; 362.5 *magnetism*; 617.5 *object of desire*; 5.30 *syntax*; 520.6 *visible thing*
attractionally 363.13
attractive 363.9; 395.12 *appealing*; **525.10** *aspectual*; 545.5 *beautiful*; 617.8 *desirable*; **334.15** *full of energy*; 241.2, **595.5** *likable*; **362.10** *magnetic*; 483.11 *motivational*; **545.6** *personable*; 480.19 *persuasive*; 490.6 *pleasant*
attractive female 545.3
attractively 363.14; **363.13** *attractionally*; 617.17 *desirably*; **593.30** *lovingly*; 362.16 *magnetically*; 595.10 *with great liking*
attractive male 545.4
attractiveness 241.8 *amiability*; 363.1 *attraction*; 545.1 *gorgeousness*; 480.3 *incentive*; 483.2 *inducement*; 593.4 *lovability*
attractivity 363.1 *attraction*
attract money 781.13 *get rich*
attract notice 738.5 *be visible*; 742.11 *gesture*
attributable to 345.10 *caused*
attribute 136.2, 334.2 *ability*; 671.6 *be grateful*; 139.3 *characteristic*; 223.4 *concomitant*; 99.4 *nature*; 783.11 *recognize*
attributed to 345.10 *caused*
attribution 344.1 *cause*
attributive 5.44 *grammatical*
attributively 5.52 *grammatically*; 345.12 *with the effect of*
attrition 214.1 *decrease*; 427.4 *pulverization*; 585.8 *warfare*; 365.2 *wearing away*
attritive 365.10 *frictional*
attritus 427.5 *powder*
attune 18.34, 516.8, 750.24 *harmonize*; 136.15 *modify*
attuned 18.30 *harmonic*; 516.7, 750.13 *harmonious*; 136.11 *modified*
attunement 750.4 *harmony*; 516.3 *melodiousness*; 18.13 *melody*; 136.5 *modification*
ATU tape 40.7 *peripheral*
at variance 113.29 *at odds*; 517.8 *disagreeing*; 113.24 *discordant*
at variance with 751.9 *disagreeing*; 113.31 *opposed to*
at war 701.17 *argumentatively*; 751.9 *disagreeing*; 701.9 *hostile*; 586.42 *martially*; 585.15 *warring*
at what place? 705.25 *what?*
at what time 275.27
at what time? 705.25 *what?*
at will 635.17
at work 340.5 *acting*; 342.19 *busy*; 810.13 *on duty*
at your command 663.11 *yours to command*
at your orders 663.11 *yours to command*
at your service 663.11 *yours to command*
atypical 116.4 *dissimilar*
aubade 593.15 *love item*; 17.7 *poem*; 516.2 *song*
aubergine 523.3 *dark colour*; 540.6 *purple*; 540.3 *purple thing*
aubergine and tomato pie 25.34 *vegetarian dish*
aubergine roll 25.34 *vegetarian dish*
auburn 534.1 *brown*; 535.3 *red-haired*
AUC 275.29 *one day*
au contraire 113.30 *contrariwise*; 708.23 *no!*
au courant 693.18 *informed*; 6.19, 455.8 *knowledgeable*
auction 767.2 *disposal of property*; 767.11 *dispose of property*; 752.9 *offer*; 778.4 *sale*; 778.1 *sell*; 778.3 *selling*
auctioneer 778.9 *seller*
auction off 778.1 *sell*
auction room 779.1 *market*
audacious 660.15; 613.9 *courageous*; 661.7 *defiant*; 668.10 *disrespectful*; 615.4 *rash*
audaciously 660.32; 613.18 *courageously*; 661.9 *defiantly*
audaciousness 613.1 *courage*; 615.1 *rashness*
audacity 660.3; 167.5 *boldness*; 613.1 *courage*; 661.1 *defiance*; 615.1 *rashness*
audibility 507.3; 504.1 *hearing*; 28.17 *sound*
audible 504.14 *hearable*; 507.7 *heard*; 46.8 *huddle*; 695.1 *intelligible*; 488.8 *sensate*
audibly 507.10 *aloud*; 504.17 *aurally*
audience 374.3 *assembly*; 579.7 *council*; 314.7 *entrant*; 504.2 *hearer*; 734.6 *interview*; 740.2 *mass media*; 518.11 *observer*; 769.5 *recipient*; 97.5 *someone present*; 21.33 *theatregoer*
audience participation 692.25 *broadcast material*
audience survey 740.2 *mass media*
audient 504.11 *aural*
audile 504.11 *aural*
audio 504.9 *audio device*; 504.11 *aural*
audio amplifier 39.21 *rectifier*
audio cassette 692.26 *recording*
audio device 504.9
audiofrequency 28.19 *sound propagation*
audiofrequency amplifier 692.18 *radio*
audiological 504.13 *otological*
audiologist 504.6 *otology*
audiology 504.6 *otology*
audiometer 26.8 *meter*; 504.6 *otology*
audiometric 26.16 *micrometric*
audiometry 26.2 *micrometry*
audiophile 504.2 *hearer*
audio signal 692.21 *television*
audiovisual 504.11 *aural*
audiovisually 504.17 *aurally*
audit 789.8; 789.3 *accounting*; 210.12 *check*
audited 789.11 *accounted*
audition 504.1 *hearing*; 734.6 *interview*; 21.14 *production*; 705.3 *questionnaire*; 448.2 *rehearsal*; 448.12 *rehearse*
auditive 504.11 *aural*
auditor 789.6 *accountant*; 504.2 *hearer*
auditorium 21.18; **504.3**; 28.21 *architectural acoustics*; 38.20 *building*; 6.15 *schoolroom*; 738.8 *showplace*; 21.16 *theatre*
auditory 504.11 *aural*
auditory ossicle 504.5 *internal ear*
auditory range 504.1 *hearing*
au fait 485.8 *expert*; 632.14 *habituated*; 693.18 *informed*; 6.19, 455.8 *knowledgeable*
Aufklärung 455.1 *knowledge*
au fond 99.14 *at heart*
auf Wiedersehn! 313.14 *goodbye!*
Augean stables 767.8 *sink*
augend 27.15 *addition*
auger 38.29 *construction equipment*; 308.2 *opener*; 425.8 *sharp-pointed thing*
aught 195.2 *nothing*
augment 765.10; 211.6 *add*; 211.3 *additional item*; 607.6 *aggravate*; 190.6 *become bigger*; 392.26 *be useful*; 209.6 *change gradually*; 302.8 *further*; 190.5, 213.5 *make bigger*; 439.6 *store*
augmentation 765.2; 211.1 *addition*; 211.3 *additional item*; 607.1 *aggravation*; 190.1 *growth*; 213.1 *increase*
augmentative 765.18 *acquisitional*; 190.9 *enlargeable*; 5.44 *grammatical*; 213.6 *increasing*; 5.35 *part of speech*
augmented 765.18 *acquisitional*; 190.7 *bigger*; 213.7 *increased*
augmenter 190.4 *enlarger*
augmentor 190.4 *enlarger*
au gratin 25.56 *culinary*
augur 11.13 *diviner*; 475.9 *forecaster*; 694.12 *intend*; 283.9 *look ahead*; 475.11 *predict*; 283.5 *predictor*; 7.8 *priest*; 711.5 *warn*
augural 11.17 *divinatory*; 475.15 *presageful*
augur well 248.7, 756.9 *be auspicious*; 610.10 *inspire hope*; 475.11 *predict*
augury 11.9, 475.2 *divination*; 474.4 *expectant person*; 475.5 *omen*; 711.1 *warning*
august 667.14 *awe-inspiring*; 123.6 *notable*; 622.18 *prestigious*; 622.19 *stately*
Augusta 56.1 *golf*
Augustan 543.3 *elegant*; 17.19 *narrative*; 230.1 *perfect*
Augustinian 4.11 *follower of a doctrine*; 4.14 *of a philosophy*
Augustinian philosophy 4.7 *school of thought*
augustness 622.4 *prestige*
auk 72.3 *water bird*
auld lang syne 3.8, 284.1 *past time*
au naturel 25.56 *culinary*; 552.9 *undressed*
Aung San Suu Kyi 589.4 *Nobel Peace Prize*
aunt 568.12 *woman in the family*
Auntie 692.20 *radio broadcasting*
auntie 568.12 *woman in the family*
Aunt Sally 668.9 *butt*; 621.4 *laughing stock*
au pair 401.6 *domestic servant*; 759.8 *in exchange*; 401.4 *personal attendant*; 759.4 *person who exchanges*
aura 170.3 *atmosphere*; 11.10 *psychic phenomenon*; 500.4 *reputation*
aural 504.11; 170.6 *atmospheric*
aural cavity 308.4 *body orifice*
aurally 504.17
aureate 537.1 *yellow*
aureate diction 17.12 *poetic language*
aureole 522.12 *highlight*
aureomycin 394.8 *drug*
au revoir! 313.14 *goodbye!*
auric 32.34 *elemental*
auricle 81.3 *grass plant*
auricular 504.11 *aural*; 504.12 *eared*
auricularly 504.17 *aurally*
auriculate 504.12 *eared*
auriferous 32.34 *elemental*
auriform 504.12 *eared*
auriscope 35.7 *diagnosis*; 504.6 *otology*
aurist 35.13 *medical specialist*; 504.6 *otology*
Aurora 290.1 *morning*
aurora 30.46; 29.16 *planet*
aurora australis 30.46 *aurora*; 522.4 *natural light*
aurora borealis 30.46 *aurora*; 522.4 *natural light*
auroral 290.5 *morning*
auroral display 30.46 *aurora*
aurorally 290.8 *in the morning*
aurous 32.34 *elemental*
Auschwitz 815.1 *prison*; 382.15 *slaughterhouse*
auscultate 504.15 *hear*
auscultation 504.1 *hearing*
auscultator 504.9 *audio device*
auscultatorily 504.17 *aurally*
auspex 11.13 *diviner*; 475.9 *forecaster*
auspicate 130.23 *inaugurate*; 601.19 *install*; 126.7 *originate*
auspication 295.4 *beginning*
auspice 475.5 *omen*
auspices 392.9 *patronage*; 252.2 *protection*
auspicial 475.15 *presageful*
auspicious 756.14; 610.14 *cheering*; 222.9 *comfortable*; 601.13 *congratulatory*; 239.1 *convenient*; 569.12 *favourable*; 797.1 *good*; 475.15 *presageful*; 248.8 *prosperous*; 287.6 *timely*
auspiciously 756.17; 222.18 *comfortably*; 569.20 *favourably*; 610.15 *hopefully*; 287.9 *opportunely*; 475.16 *predictively*; 248.9 *prosperously*
auspicious moment 287.1 *timeliness*
auspiciousness 610.4 *comfort*; 239.3 *convenience*; 797.8 *good*; 248.2 *good fortune*; 287.1 *timeliness*
Auster 31.15 *wind direction*
austere 651.12 *callous*; 725.3 *clear*; 687.6 *fasting*; 271.1, 728.14 *simple*; 680.4 *thrifty*; 647.10 *unadorned*
austerely 647.12 *plainly*; 728.24 *simply*
austereness 728.4 *simplicity*
austerities 807.2 *apology*
austerity 725.1 *clarity*; 687.1 *fasting*; 218.8 *insufficiency*; 271.4, 728.4 *simplicity*; 680.1 *thrift*; 647.3 *unadornment*
austerity lunch 557.12 *meal*
austral 324.13 *directional*
Australasia 92.1 *continent*
Australasian 1.6 *race*; 1.13 *racial*
Australia Day 298.6 *annually celebrated day*
Australian crawl 67.1 *swimming*
Australian GP at Adelaide 61.2 *Formula 1 race*
Australopithecus 296.7 *ancient people*
Austrian neutrality 566.11 *nation*
Austric 5.11 *family of languages*
Austronesian 5.11 *family of languages*
autarchic 12.9, 396.14 *governmental*
autarchy 12.1 *government*; 396.7 *type of rule*
autarkic 250.9 *free*
autarky 250.3 *independence*; 217.7 *sufficiency*
autecology 34.18 *ecology*
auteur 21.27 *producer*
authentic 126.6; **698.19**; 3.19 *chronicled*; 801.8 *correct*; 716.8 *evidential*; 16.51 *legitimate*; 93.13 *real*; 95.7 *realistic*; 396.15 *true*; 454.8 *verifiable*
authentically 396.25; **698.37**; 707.23 *affirmatively*; 716.14 *as evidence*; 454.11 *verifiably*
authenticate 253.12 *certify*; 707.19 *confirm*; 750.28 *consent*; 95.12 *establish reality*; 743.10 *identify*; 452.21 *make certain*; 716.12 *prove*; 698.30 *prove true*; 454.1 *verify*
authenticated 253.7 *guaranteed*; 756.13 *guaranteeing*; 743.12 *identified*; 698.20 *proved*; 707.13 *supported*; 396.15 *true*; 454.10 *verified*
authenticating 756.13 *guaranteeing*
authentication 698.7, 707.4 *confirmation*; 743.1 *identification*; 253.2 *promise*; 454.4 *verification*
authenticator 707.9 *affirmer*
authenticity 698.6; 801.2 *correctness*; 93.4 *demonstrable existence*; 16.30 *legitimacy*; 126.1 *originality*; 95.3 *realism*
author 17.14; 344.9 *be the cause of*; 721.10 *descriptive writer*; 449.12 *discoverer*; 722.3 *dissertator*; 5.2 *linguist*; 344.7 *Prime Mover*; 356.10 *produce*; 356.9 *producer*; 740.12 *publisher*
authoritarian 396.12 *authoritative*; 635.9 *autocratic*; 396.14 *governmental*; 579.17 *managerial*; 400.12 *masterful*; 647.8 *severe*; 647.4 *strict person*
authoritarianism 647.2 *suppression*; 396.7 *type of rule*
authoritative 396.12; 167.8 *assured*;

667.14 *awe-inspiring*; 450.14 *believed*; 452.1 *certain*; 397.14 *commanding*; 121.13 *dominant*; 6.16 *educational*; 395.11 *influential*; 579.17 *managerial*; 698.24 *pedantic*; 334.13 *powerful*; 209.8 *ranked*; 251.13 *restraining*; 140.12 *ruling*; 139.21 *specialized*; 622.19 *stately*
authoritatively 396.23; 397.16 *commandingly*; 209.9 *differentially*; 6.25 *educationally*; 395.14 *influentially*; 579.19 *managerially*; 334.18 *powerfully*; 121.16 *superiorly*; 251.16 *under restraints*; 4.29 *wisely*
authoritativeness 396.2; 452.9 *certainty*; 698.11 *pedantry*
Authority 396
authority 140.8; **396.1**; **397.3**; 167.4 *assurance*; 750.7 *consent*; 716.6 *documentation*; 6.4 *educator*; 485.5 *expert*; 250.3 *independence*; 395.1 *influence*; 16.2 *jurisdiction*; 455.6 *knowledgeable person*; 121.2 *leadership*; 16.29 *legalization*; 579.3 *management*; 698.11 *pedantry*; 757.1 *permission*; 395.3 *personal influence*; 396.10 *person of authority*; 811.2 *person of repute*; 334.1 *power*; 253.2 *promise*; 209.2 *rank*; 667.1 *respect*; 251.1 *restraint*; 4.12 *sage*; 397.5 *self-assurance*; 647.1 *severity*; 693.8 *source of information*; 139.14 *specialist*
authorization 397.4; 396.3 *acquisition of power*; 669.1 *approval*; 744.2 *certificate*; 750.7 *consent*; 398.3 *delegation*; 121.2 *leadership*; 16.29 *legalization*; 136.4, 396.9, 757.1 *permission*; 253.2 *promise*; 136.3 *qualifications*
authorize 397.13; 669.12 *accept*; 750.28 *consent*; 398.7 *delegate*; 334.11 *give power*; 396.21 *grant authority*; 16.65 *make legal*; 757.3 *permit*; 136.13 *qualify*
authorized 136.10; **396.16**; 750.17 *consenting*; 396.13 *elected*; 250.9 *free*; 16.50 *law-abiding*; 16.44 *legal*; 757.7 *permitted*; 397.15 *self-assured*
Authorized Version 7.12 *religious text*
authorizing 750.17 *consenting*
authorship 344.1 *cause*; 356.1 *production*
autism 36.19 *defence mechanism*; 461.2 *subnormality*
autistic 457.7 *intellectually subnormal*; 655.8 *unsociable*
auto 320.16 *car*
Autobahn 317.3, 320.2 *road*
autobiographer 17.14 *author*; 744.9 *recorder*
autobiographical 3.19 *chronicled*; 17.19, 721.12 *narrative*
autobiographically 3.25 *reportedly*
autobiographical novel 17.2 *fiction*
autobiography 3.6 *biography*; 721.4 *factual account*; 554.11 *life story*; 17.4 *nonfiction*; 744.1 *record*; 462.2 *retrospect*
autocade 320.21 *miscellaneous motoring terms*
autocatalysis 32.15 *catalysis*
autocatalytic 32.39 *catalytic*
autochthon 564.1 *inhabitant*
autochthonous 564.12 *native*
autocracy 12.1 *government*; 647.2 *suppression*; 396.7 *type of rule*
autocrat 400.4 *absolute ruler*; 579.14 *leader*; 396.10 *person of authority*; 647.4 *strict person*
autocratic 635.9; 396.14 *governmental*; 400.12 *masterful*; 397.15 *self-assured*; 647.8 *severe*
autocratically 397.16 *commandingly*; 400.16 *masterfully*; 647.11 *severely*
autocross 61.1 *motor racing*
autocycle 320.13 *motorcycle*
Auto-Cycle Union 61.7 *racing governing body*
auto-da-fé 814.13 *capital punishment*; 382.5 *execution*
autodidact 6.7 *learner*
autodidactic 6.17 *educable*; 486.2 *unskilled*
autodidactics 6.2 *educational system*
autodidactism 455.3 *learning*
autoexposure 41.18 *exposure time*
autofocus 41.18 *exposure time*
autogenesis 561.3 *propagation*
autograph 743.11 *identify oneself*; 744.4 *inscription*; 743.3 *means of identification*; 721.8 *name*; 126.2 *original*; 742.1 *sign*; 742.9 *use signs*
autographer 742.8 *signer*
autogyro 307.6 *rotator*
autohypnosis 36.3 *psychiatric treatment*
autohypnotic 11.15 *witchlike*
autohypnotism 11.1 *occultism*
autointoxication 245.10 *impairment*
auto-loading 60.8 *shooting*
auto-loading rifle 60.3 *hunting equipment*
automat 557.15 *eating place*
automate 15.11 *conduct industrial relations*; 111.8 *make the same*; 356.10 *produce*
automated 334.15 *full of energy*; 438.9 *mechanical*; 15.9 *negotiated*; 348.8 *practical*; 356.11 *productive*; 111.17 *regular*
automated teller machine 780.21 *till*
automatic 587.9 *firearm*; 445.8 *instinctive*; 438.9 *mechanical*; 15.9 *negotiated*; 348.8 *practical*; 478.2 *spontaneous*
automatically 632.19 *habitually*; 348.9, 438.11 *instrumentally*; 445.11 *intuitively*
automatic buoy 31.5 *weather station*
automatic camera 41.16 *camera*
automatic control 438.6 *mechanics*
automatic direction finder 323.5 *navigation*
automatic exchange 692.12 *public telephone system*
automatic pilot 579.5 *guide*
automatic pin-setter 51.4 *bowling*
automatic reaction 445.4 *instinct*
automatic reflex 478.5 *spontaneity*
automatic transmission 438.5 *machine*
automatic writing 11.1 *occultism*
automation 13.6 *economic factors*; 334.9 *electronics*; 15.2 *industrial negotiations*; 348.1 *instrumentality*; 356.2 *manufacture*; 438.6 *mechanics*; 111.6 *regularity*
automatism 11.1 *occultism*
automatist 11.12 *occultist*
automative 111.17 *regular*
automaton 112.8 *creature of habit*; 566.8 *humanlike machine*; 717.6 *image*; 438.5 *machine*
autometamorphism 30.32 *metamorphism*
automobile 320.16 *car*; 316.5 *means of transport*
automobile mechanic 578.2 *artisan*
automobile race 61.1 *motor racing*
automobile racer 61.8 *driver*
automobile rally 61.1 *motor racing*
automobile trial 61.1 *motor racing*
automobilia 320.21 *miscellaneous motoring terms*
automotive 300.16 *moving*
automotive engine 38.11 *engine*
automotive engineering 38.1 *engineering*; 38.3 *mechanical engineering*; 320.21 *miscellaneous motoring terms*
automotively 300.18 *in motion*
autonomous 250.9, 635.10 *free*; 12.9, 396.14 *governmental*
autonomously 250.20 *freely*
autonomy 635.4 *free will*; 12.3 *governance*; 12.1 *government*; 250.3 *independence*; 396.7 *type of rule*
autopista 320.2 *road*
autopolyploidy 34.14 *chromosome*
autopsy 582.8 *after death*; 35.7 *diagnosis*; 583.7 *inquest*
auto race 61.9 *race*
auto racing 61.1 *motor racing*
autorickshaw 320.13 *motorcycle*
autoroute 317.3, 320.2 *road*
autosome 34.14 *chromosome*
autospore 84.4 *reproductive body*
autostrada 317.3, 320.2 *road*
autosuggestion 36.3 *psychiatric treatment*; 477.6 *reverie*
autotheft 772.3 *illegal borrowing*; 774.3 *theft*
autotoxaemia 245.10 *impairment*
autumn 292.4; **292.12**; 298.5 *regular thing*
autumnal 292.12 *autumn*; 31.46 *seasonal*
autumnal equinox 292.4 *autumn*; 29.5 *celestial sphere*; 10.15 *holy day*
autumnally 292.18 *seasonally*
autumn colours 534.5 *brown thing*
autumnlike 292.12 *autumn*
autumn of one's life 556.5 *old age*
autumn sale 778.4 *sale*
autumn wood 79.3 *timber*
auxiliaries 586.14 *armed forces*; 211.4 *extra*
auxiliary 211.8 *additional*; 398.4 *deputy*; 211.5 *extra person*; 392.11, 608.5 *helper*; 586.35 *martial*; 586.6 *militarist*; 122.15 *subordinate*; 392.31 *supplementary*; 413.8 *supporter*; 413.9 *supportive*
auxiliary fleet 584.4 *military organization*
auxiliary forces 211.4 *extra*
auxiliary memory 40.6 *memory*
auxin 33.17 *plant hormone*
Avadana 7.12 *religious text*
avail 392.21 *be helpful*; 785.12 *be profitable*; 237.9 *be useful*; 797.20 *do good*; 392.1 *help*; 349.6 *use*; 237.5 *usefulness*
availability 97.4; 767.1 *disposal*; 239.4 *nearness*; 102.2 *possibleness*; 237.5 *usefulness*; 520.3 *visibility*
available 97.10; **282.8**; 767.14 *for sale*; 765.15 *gainful*; 768.7 *given*; 580.7 *leisurely*; 239.2 *nearby*; 343.2 *not working*; 752.17 *offered*; 308.13 *opened up*; 102.5 *possible*; 436.7 *provisioning*; 778.15 *saleable*; 439.7 *stored*; 98.14 *unoccupied*; 349.10 *usable*; 237.1 *useful*; 520.1 *visible*
available man 567.5 *single man*
available on request 436.7 *provisioning*
available post 308.10 *opportunity*
available space 141.6
available to all 695.2 *simple*
availably 308.25 *obviously*
avail nothing 335.6 *be powerless*
avail oneself of 772.8 *adopt*; 392.27 *find useful*; 349.2 *frequent*
avalanche 357.7 *agent of destruction*; 62.2 *climbing dangers*; 305.3 *downflow*; 305.13 *drip*; 219.1 *excess*; 494.5 *ice*; 30.26 *mass movement*; 31.30 *snow*
avalement 68.4 *skiing technique*
Avalon 8.11 *heaven*
avant-garde 295.6; **295.16**; 167.1 *front*; 18.33 *jazz*; 487.2 *not customary*; 126.5 *novel*; 286.2 *occurring at a different time*; 448.9 *original*; 448.4 *originality*; 129.8 *precursor*; 129.14 *preparatory*
avant-garde artist 295.9 *modern person*
avant-garde jazz 18.8 *jazz*
avant-gardism 129.3 *preparation*
avant-gardist 295.9 *modern person*; 129.8 *precursor*
avarice 683.1 *selfishness*; 773.1 *taking*
avaricious 765.16 *greedy*; 683.4 *selfish*; 773.12 *taking*
avariciously 773.13; 765.20 *gainfully*; 683.8 *selfishly*
avast! 50.21
avatar 8.8 *divine manifestation*; 738.10 *manifestation*
Ave 10.9 *prayer*
Avebury 10.13 *shrine*
Ave Maria 10.9 *prayer*
avenge 714.10; 814.2 *penalize*; 385.3 *retaliate*
avenge oneself 785.13 *retaliate*
avenger 714.6; 814.17 *punisher*; 385.2 *revenger*
avenging 714.14 *vindictive*
avenging angel 357.7 *agent of destruction*
avenue 317.3 *road*; 315.6 *way out*
aver 707.17 *affirm*; 729.11 *speak*; 454.3 *testify*
Average 216
average 138.6; **216.1**; **216.4**; 173.6 *central*; 138.21, 574.3 *common*; 117.15 *everyday*; 216.3, 618.10 *mediocre*; 158.14, 216.2, 216.5 *medium*; 685.6 *moderate*; 685.1 *moderation*; 235.5 *not bad*; 203.5 *numbers*; 231.4 *ordinary*; 27.60 *parameter*; 203.6 *quantitative*; 413.10 *supportable*
averaged out 754.6 *compromising*
average life 554.5 *life cycle*
averageness 138.5; 216.4 *average*; 216.6, 618.4 *mediocrity*; 231.8 *ordinariness*
average out 754.4 *compromise*; 216.10 *make average*
average person 216.7; 566.7 *person*
averages 210.2 *statistics*
average-size 158.14 *medium*
average value 27.60 *parameter*
averaging out 754.6 *compromising*
averment 707.1 *affirmation*; 16.5 *litigation*; 729.7 *utterance*; 454.4 *verification*
Avernal 8.16 *devilish*
Avernus 8.12 *hell*
averred 707.11 *stated*; 454.10 *verified*
Averroism 4.7 *school of thought*
Averroist 4.11 *follower of a doctrine*; 4.14 *of a philosophy*
averse 596.8 *disliking*; 594.10 *hating*; 113.22 *oppositional*; 637.1 *unwilling*
aversely 596.10 *discontentedly*; 594.18 *hatefully*
averseness 637.13 *dissociation*
aversion 596.1 *dislike*; 637.13 *dissociation*; 612.1 *fear*; 594.1 *hate*; 113.1 *opposition*
aversion therapy 36.3 *psychiatric treatment*; 394.13 *therapy*
avert 634.2; 325.7 *misdirect*; 384.24 *parry*; 325.8 *sidestep*
avertable 634.20 *avoidable*
avertably 634.22 *evasively*
averting 634.10 *avoidance*
avert one's gaze 519.16 *be blind to*
Aves 72.1 *birds*
Avesta 7.12 *religious text*
avian 72.21
avian anatomy 72.16
aviary 376.31 *exhibition*; 43.7 *farm building*; 72.19 *ornithology*; 565.12 *stall*
Aviation 322
aviation 322.1
aviation beacon 522.6 *electric light*
aviation fuel 437.6 *oil*
aviation meteorology 31.1 *meteorology*
aviator 322.3 *aircraft personnel*
avici 8.12 *hell*
avicultural 72.23 *ornithological*
aviculture 72.19 *ornithology*
aviculturist 72.20 *ornithologist*
avid 617.9 *desirous*
avidity 617.1 *desire*
avidly 617.18 *desirously*
avifauna 72.1 *birds*
avionic 322.9 *aeronautical*
avionically 322.11 *aeronautically*
avionics 322.2 *aeronautics*
avitaminosis 260.4 *disease*
avocado 538.1 *green*; 538.9 *greenstuff*
avocet 72.3 *water bird*
Avogadro constant 28.97 *fundamental constant*
avoid 634.1; 479.1 *be equivocal*; 666.6 *be neglectful*; 252.9 *be safe*; 684.5 *be self-restrained*; 736.11 *conceal oneself*; 389.6 *elude*; 674.15 *escape notice*; 594.14 *hate*; 639.6 *hesitate*; 655.13 *ignore*; 766.15 *lose someone*; 169.8 *move sideways*; 341.4 *not act*; 350.5 *not use*; 384.24 *parry*; 596.6 *react against*; 709.5 *refuse*; 355.1 *relinquish*; 303.6 *shrink back*; 325.8 *sidestep*
avoidable 634.20
avoidably 634.22 *evasively*
avoid alcohol 689.3 *be sober*
Avoidance 634
avoidance 634.10; 36.19 *defence mechanism*; 596.1 *dislike*; 389.1 *escape*; 341.1 *inaction*; 666.2 *indifference*; 350.8 *nonuse*; 589.1 *peace*; 355.3 *relinquishment*; 252.1 *safety*; 684.1 *self-restraint*; 372.2 *setting apart*; 655.1 *unsociability*
avoidance conditioning 36.20 *conditioning*
avoid a parry 54.5 *fence*
avoid bloodshed 589.5 *be at peace*
avoid defeat 246.7 *overcome obstacles*
avoided 596.9 *disliked*; 655.10 *lonely*
avoider 634.17; 477.9 *visionary*
avoid excess 684.5 *be self-restrained*
avoid financial obligations 786.7 *not pay*
avoid food 687.5 *fast*
avoid gobbledegook 695.5 *simplify*
avoiding 634.18; 596.8 *disliking*; 666.5 *indifferent*
avoiding financial obligations 786.1 *nonpayment*
avoiding the issue 634.15 *evasiveness*
avoid responsibility for 388.3 *submit*
avoid strife 749.4 *pacify*
avoid taxes 389.6 *elude*
avoid the issue 634.7 *be evasive*; 109.10 *be unrelated*; 702.13 *quibble*
avoid the trap 645.5 *be cunning*
avoid war 749.4 *pacify*
avoirdupois 26.12 *metrical*
avoirdupois weight 414.9; 26.5 *measuring system*

Avon 90.4 *British rivers*
a vote against 709.2 *dissent*
avouch 707.20 *admit*
avouched 707.11 *stated;* 454.10 *verified*
avouchment 707.5 *admission;* 454.4 *verification*
avow 707.20, 739.8 *admit;* 454.3 *testify*
avowal 707.5 *admission;* 739.2 *divulgence;* 396.9 *permission;* 454.4 *verification*
avowed 739.10 *disclosed;* 707.11 *stated;* 454.10 *verified*
avowedly 707.23 *affirmatively;* 96.19 *apparently*
avulse 369.11 *extract*
avulsion 369.1 *extraction*
AWACS 586.31 *military aircraft*
await 610.7 *aspire;* 283.10 *expect;* 294.7, 474.10 *wait*
awaited 283.13 *foreseen*
awaiting execution 254.4 *endangered;* 814.22 *punishable*
awaiting trial 715.8 *accusatory*
await payment 783.8 *credit*
await trial 715.7 *be accused*
awake 488.12; 342.18 *active;* 488.6 *conscious*
awake late 294.6 *be late*
awaken 344.10; 393.5 *revive*
awaken desire 617.15 *cause desire*
awake the echoes 507.8 *be loud*
awake to life immortal 582.15 *die*
award 768.2 *gift;* 768.5 *give;* 575.3 *honours;* 464.11 *judge;* 813.2 *prize;* 765.5 *profit;* 813.9 *reward;* 794.1 *trophy;* 464.2 *verdict*
award a fellowship 813.10 *grant*
awarded 769.11 *receiving*
awarder 768.4 *giver*
awarding 768.1 *giving*
aware 590.10 *feeling;* 446.11 *ideational;* 693.18 *informed;* 455.8 *knowledgeable;* 518.21 *seeing;* 488.5 *sensible;* 591.1 *sensitive*
awareness 590.1 *feeling;* 671.1 *gratitude;* 446.1 *idea;* 455.1 *knowledge;* 442.1 *mind;* 488.1 *sensation;* 591.5 *sensitivity;* 518.4 *visualization*
aware of 488.5 *sensible*
awash 90.11, 433.24 *flooded;* 433.23 *wet*
away 98.9; **98.21**; **369.21**; **634.21**; 526.7 *disappeared;* 145.8 *distant;* 145.10 *distantly;* 526.8 *fleetingly;* 315.18 *forth;* 389.9 *fugitively;* 371.33 *go away!;* 103.3 *hopeless;* 372.22 *in isolation*
away from 100.18 *extraneously*
away from home 98.10 *nonresident*
away side 169.5 *team*
away with the fairies 489.8 *unconscious*
away with you 371.33 *go away!*
awe 667.2 *admiration;* 619.10 *be wonderful;* 667.21 *command respect;* 612.1 *fear;* 619.1 *wonder;* 9.1 *worship*
awed 630.7 *amazed;* 619.6 *wondering*
aweful 619.8 *wonderful*
aweigh 50.10 *sailing*
awe-inspiring 667.14; 619.8 *wonderful*
aweless 660.17 *contemptuous*
awesome 612.10 *frightening;* 619.8 *wonderful;* 619.14 *wonderful!*
awesomely 619.13 *wonderfully*
awestricken 667.10 *reverent*
awestruck 630.7 *amazed;* 667.10 *reverent;* 619.6 *wondering*
awful 236.3, 611.8 *bad;* 798.7 *evil;* 612.10 *frightening;* 506.3 *silent*
awfully 798.12 *evilly;* 236.15 *worthlessly*
awfulness 236.9 *badness;* 798.1 *evil*
awful silence 506.4 *silence*
a while 275.3 *duration;* 275.5 *indefinite period*
a while ago 284.22 *in the past*
a while back 284.22 *in the past*
awkward 674.9 *blushing;* 264.15, 486.3 *clumsy;* 222.8 *difficult;* 675.8 *discourteous;* 544.7 *graceless;* 456.6 *ignorant;* 555.12 *immature;* 240.1, 264.13 *inconvenient;* 242.2 *objectionable;* 641.1 *obstinate;* 538.3 *raw;* 546.4 *ugly;* 288.13 *untimely*
awkward age 555.1 *youth*
awkwardly 264.28; 288.19 *at the wrong time;* 222.17 *difficultly;* 555.15 *immaturely;* 240.6 *inconveniently;* 544.11 *inelegantly;* 486.11 *unskilfully*
awkwardness 264.2; 456.1 *ignorance;* 555.3 *immaturity;* 240.3 *inconvenience;* 544.1 *inelegance;* 242.6 *objectionability;* 486.8 *unskilfulness;* 288.2 *untimeliness*
awkward occurrence 288.2 *untimeliness*
awkward position 264.7 *awkward situation*
awkward question 705.4 *difficult question*
awkward situation 264.7; 222.4 *difficult circumstances*
awl 308.2 *opener;* 425.8 *sharp-pointed thing*
awn 81.3 *grass plant;* 420.7 *rough thing;* 425.8 *sharp-pointed thing*
awned 425.2 *spiked*
awning 550.7 *overhead covering;* 550.12 *protective covering;* 523.6 *shade*
AWOL 98.4 *absenteeism;* 662.1 *disobedience;* 98.11 *truant*
awry 802.18 *gone wrong;* 408.18 *muddled;* 120.3 *unequal;* 274.22 *wrongly*
axe 62.4 *climbing equipment;* 357.8 *destroy;* 371.2 *dismiss;* 382.5 *execution;* 814.16 *instrument of execution;* 308.2 *opener;* 608.12 *relieve from duty;* 425.9 *sharp-edged thing;* 587.8 *sharp weapon;* 149.10 *shorten;* 708.15 *terminate;* 79.7 *timber production;* 438.1 *tool;* 425.16 *use a sharp tool*
axed 708.20 *cancelled*
axe-grinder 484.8 *planner*
axe kick 52.9 *tae kwon do*
axel jump 68.6 *ice-skating*
axel lift 68.6 *ice-skating*
axeltree 79.12 *figurative usage*
axeman 382.12 *executioner*
axe murderer 382.11 *murderer*
axe to grind 482.1 *intention*
axial 173.6 *central;* 324.14 *directed;* 300.17 *directional;* 77.17 *of stems*
axial motion 300.5 *circuition;* 307.1 *rotation*
axial ray 28.31 *lens element*
axial skeleton 403.7 *skeleton*
axil 77.5 *stem*
axillary 77.17 *of stems*
axillary bud 77.8 *bud*
axing 371.18 *dismissal*
axiological 4.14 *of a philosophy*
axiologically 4.24 *philosophically*
axiologist 4.11 *follower of a doctrine*
axiology 4.6 *branch of philosophy*
axiom 140.4 *guide;* 28.6 *law;* 745.1 *maxim;* 4.8 *philosophical term;* 4.1 *philosophy;* 27.65 *theory;* 698.4 *truism*
axiomatic 745.2 *proverbial;* 27.69 *theoretical;* 698.17 *truistic*
axiomatically 745.4 *proverbially*
axiomatic set theory 4.6 *branch of philosophy*
axiometric drawing 717.2 *reproduction*
axis 307.4 *axle;* 173.1 *centre;* 27.32 *graph;* 77.5 *stem*
axis of symmetry 162.2 *symmetry operation*
axle 307.4; 68.9 *bobsledding;* 38.8 *machine element*
axlebar 307.4 *axle*
axlebox 307.4 *axle*
axle load 414.9 *avoirdupois weight*
axle shaft 307.4 *axle*
axle spindle 307.4 *axle*
axle-true 307.4 *axle*
Axminster 42.3 *fabric*
axolotl 73.8 *young amphibian*
ayah 401.6 *domestic servant*
ayatollah 579.14 *leader;* 7.8 *priest;* 400.6 *religious leader*
aye 469.10 *vote*
Ayers Rock 10.13 *shrine*
Aylesbury duck 25.44 *British dish*
ayn 5.36 *accent*
ayurveda 394.11 *medical art;* 35.2 *natural medicine*
ayurvedic medicine 35.2 *natural medicine*
A–Z 693.5 *reference book*
azan 10.4 *public worship*
Azazil 8.7 *devil*
Azidahaka 8.7 *devil*
azimuth 29.5 *celestial sphere;* 187.2 *horizontal surface;* 324.3 *orientation;* 26.4 *size*
azo dye 42.6 *dye*
Azores high 31.11 *weather system*
Azrael 8.6 *angel;* 582.2 *death personified*
Aztec 566.4 *modern human*
Aztecs 284.6 *people of the past*
Aztec two-step 560.2 *defecation*
azure 539.1, 539.9 *blue;* 539.5 *blueness;* 743.13 *heraldic;* 743.8 *heraldic device*
B 2.7 *social stratification*
ba 111.3 *lookalike*
baa 515.1 *animal cry;* 515.4 *cry*
Baal 9.3 *idol*
Babbitt 117.6 *conformist;* 216.8 *middle classes*
Babbittry 117.4 *conventionalism*
babble 731.7 *be talkative;* 696.7 *be unintelligible;* 90.7 *flow;* 730.14 *have difficulty speaking;* 5.5 *nonstandard language;* 509.3, 509.10 *rattle;* 731.3 *talk*
babbler 731.4 *talker*
babbling 486.3 *clumsy;* 730.12 *inarticulate;* 5.22 *many words;* 730.3 *speech defect;* 731.5 *talkative;* 696.11 *unintelligibility*
babbling brook 90.1 *river*
Babcock-Levy test 36.6 *intelligence test*
babe 555.9 *child;* 700.22 *dupe;* 805.4 *innocent person;* 593.12 *nicknames for lovers;* 568.9 *woman considered as a sex object;* 555.8 *young woman*
babe in arms 130.15 *baby;* 555.9 *child;* 700.22 *dupe;* 805.4 *innocent person;* 646.3 *naive person;* 337.4 *weakling*
babe in the woods 700.22 *dupe*
Babel 517.2 *dissonant noise;* 5.5 *nonstandard language*
babel 412.3 *miscellany*
babesiosis 75.12 *protozoal disease*
babu 567.3 *male title of address*
baby 130.15; 555.9 *child;* 614.2 *coward;* 130.32 *embryonic;* 159.7 *little;* 159.2 *little thing;* 593.12 *nicknames for lovers;* 566.7 *person;* 356.7 *produce;* 561.6 *progeny;* 139.8 *specialization;* 337.4 *weakling;* 568.9 *woman considered as a sex object;* 555.11 *young;* 555.8 *young woman*
baby boom 562.2 *productiveness*
baby buggy 320.8 *baby carriage*
baby carriage 320.8
baby clothes 551.23 *children's clothes*
baby doll 593.12 *nicknames for lovers*
baby doll pyjamas 551.22 *nightwear*
baby food 557.7 *food*
babygro™ 551.23 *children's clothes*
babyhood 130.4 *conception;* 335.3 *helplessness;* 555.1 *youth*
babyish 555.11 *young*
Babylonian 566.4 *modern human*
Babylonians 284.6 *people of the past*
baby-mind 665.11 *care for*
baby-minder 665.8 *watchful person*
baby-minding 665.5 *watchfulness*
baby's bottom 421.8 *smooth thing*
baby-sit 665.11 *care for*
baby-sitter 252.3 *protector;* 665.8 *watchful person*
baby-sitting 665.5 *watchfulness*
baby talk 5.5 *nonstandard language*
baby tooth 425.11 *tooth*
baby walker 320.8 *baby carriage*
Bacardi™ 558.7 *alcoholic drink*
baccalaureate 136.3 *qualifications*
bacchanal 690.17 *drunkard;* 557.18 *eater;* 688.4 *glutton*
bacchanalia 688.3 *act of gluttony;* 690.14 *drinking bout;* 557.13 *feast*
bacchant 690.17 *drunkard;* 557.18 *eater*
baccy 496.7 *tobacco*
bach 572.9 *be celibate*
bachelor 567.5 *single man;* 197.7, 572.5 *single person*
bachelor girl 568.5 *single girl;* 197.7, 572.5 *single person*
bachelorhood 572.1 *celibacy;* 250.3 *independence*
bachelorlike 572.6 *celibate*
bachelorly 572.6 *celibate*
bacillary 151.2 *fine*
bacilliform 151.2 *fine*
bacillus 260.6 *infection;* 159.2 *little thing;* 34.3 *organism*
Back 168
back 392.24; 392.23 *advise;* 227.11 *be changeable;* 300.13 *be in motion;* 31.58 *blow;* 707.19 *confirm;* 750.28 *consent;* 325.1 *deviate;* 300.17 *directional;* 787.3 *donate;* 392.29 *finance;* 413.14 *give moral support;* 418.9 *harden;* 131.25 *hindmost;* 58.2 *hockey player;* 304.15 *mount;* 323.9 *navigate;* 113.2 *oppositeness;* 168.4 *rear;* 168.2 *rear end;* 303.3 *reverse;* 169.9, 469.3 *side with;* 669.13 *support;* 413.13 *support financially;* 169.2 *surface*
backache 491.2 *painful condition*
back and fill 323.9 *navigate;* 326.8 *oscillate*
back and foot 62.3 *climbing technique*
back and forth 224.15, 227.15 *changeably;* 759.8 *in exchange;* 326.18 *to and fro*
back-and-forth 326.13 *oscillating*
back and front 57.5 *horizontal bar*
back and knee 62.3 *climbing technique*
back another's credit 784.7 *be in debt*
back a sail 50.15 *sail*
back away 639.6 *hesitate;* 637.7 *refuse;* 303.3 *reverse;* 634.4 *shy*
back bacon 25.30 *bacon*
back beat 18.19 *tempo*
backbencher 122.6 *inferior;* 579.16 *official;* 12.8 *politician*
backbend 57.8 *floor exercises*
backbite 678.12 *defame*
backbiter 678.8 *defamer*
backbiting 678.3 *defamation;* 678.16 *defamatory*
backboard 49.3 *basketball equipment;* 51.1 *green bowling*
backbone 173.1 *centre;* 613.1 *courage;* 99.2 *essential content;* 638.16 *fortitude;* 418.7 *hard substance;* 640.4 *stamina;* 336.1 *strength;* 413.2 *supporting part*
backbone of steel 638.16 *fortitude*
back boundary line 63.12 *badminton terms*
backbreaker 264.3 *difficult task*
backbreaking 378.14 *blocked;* 264.10 *difficult;* 576.11 *laborious;* 814.21 *punishing*
backbreaking work 576.1 *work*
backchat 661.3 *act of defiance;* 706.1 *answer;* 660.25, 706.18 *answer back;* 734.2 *chat;* 660.9 *discourtesy*
backchatting 706.11 *answering;* 660.20 *discourteous*
backcheck 58.3 *ice hockey;* 58.9 *play hockey*
backchecked 58.8 *hockey*
backchecker 58.4 *ice hockey player*
backchecking 58.8 *hockey;* 58.3 *ice hockey*
backcloth 21.19 *stage set*
back-country 141.3 *geographical space;* 86.18 *local;* 86.6 *regions*
back court 49.1 *basketball*
back crawl 67.1 *swimming*
back door 314.6 *means of entry;* 389.2 *means of escape;* 168.1 *rear;* 317.2 *route;* 252.1 *safety;* 315.6 *way out*
backdoor influence 645.1 *cunning*
back down 479.4 *recant;* 355.1 *relinquish;* 303.2 *retreat;* 761.6 *reverse*
backdrop 21.19 *stage set;* 170.1 *surroundings*
backed 669.23 *approved;* 750.17 *consenting;* 418.3 *hardened;* 707.13 *supported*
back e.m.f. 28.52, 39.10 *electric potential*
back end 292.4 *autumn;* 168.1 *rear*
backer 669.7 *advocate;* 707.9 *affirmer;* 392.15 *benefactor;* 679.9 *generous person;* 768.4 *giver;* 21.27 *producer;* 14.3 *stockbroker;* 413.8 *supporter*
backest 51.9 *bowls*
backest bowl 51.2 *grip*
backfill 38.28 *substructure*
backfire 508.1, 508.5 *bang;* 347.3 *counteract;* 347.1 *counteraction;* 761.6 *reverse;* 761.1 *reversion*
backfired 761.11 *reversed*
back floating 67.1 *swimming*
backflow 90.6 *river flow*
backflowing 300.4 *backward motion;* 300.17 *directional*
back formation 5.17 *word*
back-formed 5.42 *worded*
background 223.17 *accompanying;* 17.3 *aspect of fiction;* 3.5 *chronicle;* 143.2, 222.1 *circumstances;* 222.7 *circumstantial;* 223.4 *concomitant;* 145.3 *distant place;* 136.3 *qualifications;* 168.1 *rear;* 6.11 *refinement;* 170.4 *surrounding;* 170.1 *surroundings*
background murmur 509.2 *humming*
backhand 51.9 *bowls;* 189.5 *devious;* 63.14 *forehand;* 58.8 *hockey;* 331.14 *sporting hit*
backhand drive 63.2 *tennis strokes*
backhanded 189.5 *devious;* 479.10 *equivocal;* 668.11 *insulting*
backhanded compliment 668.5 *insult*
backhandedness 189.3 *deviousness*
backhander 480.10 *bribe;* 768.2 *gift;* 331.14 *sporting hit*
backhand grip 51.2 *grip*
backhand shot 51.2 *grip;* 58.3 *ice hockey*
backhand volley 63.2 *tennis strokes*
backhoe 38.29 *construction equipment*

back home 312.22 *on arrival*
backhouse 560.13 *lavatory*
backing 669.1 *approval;* 300.4 *backward motion;* 707.4 *confirmation;* 787.7 *donation;* 41.11 *emulsion;* 352.4 *financial resources;* 413.7 *financial support;* 418.5 *hardness;* 392.11 *helper;* 413.6 *moral support;* 392.9 *patronage;* 303.12 *reversal;* 392.2 *support;* 669.19 *supporting;* 31.15 *wind direction*
backing band 223.6 *accompanier*
backing down 761.1 *reversion*
backing group 392.11 *helper*
backing store 40.6 *memory;* 40.7 *peripheral*
backing up 707.4 *confirmation;* 303.12 *reversal;* 413.1 *support*
backing vocalist 18.23 *singer*
backing vocalists 223.6 *accompanier*
back into a corner 303.2 *retreat*
back judge 46.2 *football player*
back kick 52.9 *tae kwon do*
back kitchen 565.7 *room*
backlash 347.1 *counteraction;* 706.4 *reaction;* 132.4 *repercussion;* 385.1 *retaliation;* 761.1 *reversion*
back-layout 47.9 *track*
back-layout style 47.2 *field events*
backless dress 551.7 *frock*
backlighting 41.15 *lighting*
back line 68.10 *curling*
backlog 439.1 *store*
back matter 131.10 *ending;* 168.1 *rear*
back o'Bourke 145.3 *distant place;* 655.5 *solitary place*
back of beyond 166.3 *furthest point;* 141.3 *geographical space;* 86.6 *regions;* 655.5 *solitary place*
back off 303.3 *reverse;* 634.4 *shy*
back on one's feet 393.15 *cured*
back out 614.4 *be a coward;* 479.2 *equivocate;* 303.2 *retreat*
back out of 303.2 *retreat*
backpack 410.9 *baggage;* 320.5 *pack;* 316.10 *transferred thing*
back part 168.1 *rear*
back pass 66.2 *football play*
back passage 168.2 *rear end*
back pay 784.5 *amount owing;* 785.3 *pay*
back-pedal 479.4 *recant;* 303.3 *reverse;* 333.3 *slow down*
back-pedalling 479.11 *equivocating;* 479.6 *equivocation*
backplate 384.7 *armour*
back rent 784.5 *amount owing*
back rest 413.4 *rest*
back rib 25.23 *beef*
back-room 484.7 *planning*
back-room boy 485.5 *expert;* 446.9 *person of ideas;* 484.8 *planner*
back-room boys 392.11 *helper;* 521.5 *invisible thing*
back-room influence 645.1 *cunning*
back rope 62.3 *climbing technique*
back row 64.4 *rugby player*
back-saving 263.5 *labour-saving*
backscratch 677.11 *be sycophantic*
backscratcher 677.7 *sycophant*
backscratching 747.3 *mutual relationship;* 664.2, 677.5 *sycophancy;* 664.7, 677.16 *sycophantic*
back seat 122.1 *inferiority*
back-seat driver 713.4 *adviser;* 579.13 *director;* 342.11 *meddler*
backset 303.18 *setback*
backsettler 564.5 *countryman*
back-shove 50.8 *punting*
backside 168.2 *rear end*
backsight 587.9 *firearm;* 518.10 *visual aid*
back slang 5.18 *slang*
back-slap 654.13 *fraternize*
back-slapper 654.6 *social person*
back-slapping 569.8 *friendly;* 654.9 *welcome*
backslide 804.16 *be wicked;* 303.1 *go backwards;* 761.6 *reverse*
backslider **303.21**; 760.6 *convert;* 479.9 *equivocator*
backsliding **303.19**; 245.7 *deterioration;* 303.23 *receding;* 761.1 *reversion;* 804.11 *wicked;* 804.1 *wickedness*
backspin 56.3 *golf shots*
back-stabber 651.8 *malefactor*
backstage 521.9 *invisibly;* 21.43 *on stage;* 521.3 *private;* 168.1 *rear;* 21.17 *stage*
backstage dealings 645.1 *cunning*
backstairs 304.7 *means of ascent;* 389.2 *means of escape*
back stalls 21.18 *auditorium*
backstay 50.3 *parts of a sailing boat*
back stream 90.6 *river flow*
backstreet 245.9 *dilapidation*
backstroke 331.14 *sporting hit;* 67.1 *swimming*
back surfaced 28.29 *optical element*
backswing 56.3 *golf shots*
back talk 661.3 *act of defiance;* 706.1 *answer;* 660.9 *discourtesy*
back the wrong horse 274.18 *be in error;* 247.6 *fail*
back to back 747.20 *cooperatively*
back-to-back 565.5 *house;* 565.16 *manorial*
back to front 761.13 *reversibly*
back-to-front 192.2 *inverted*
back to normal 393.15 *cured*
back tooth 425.11 *tooth*
back to sail 50.20 *offshore*
back to the beginning 761.13 *reversibly*
backtrack 303.13 *about-turn;* 303.3 *reverse;* 773.9 *withdraw a statement*
backtracking 303.13 *about-turn;* 300.17 *directional;* 773.2 *taking back*
back trail 303.13 *about-turn;* 303.3 *reverse*
backup 398.5 *alternative;* 51.10 *bowling;* 51.5 *bowling delivery;* 40.19 *computing terms;* 747.1 *cooperation;* 211.5 *extra person;* 392.11, 608.5 *helper;* 352.5 *reserves;* 303.12 *reversal;* 550.21 *substitution;* 550.40 *substitutive;* 413.8 *supporter*
back up 40.20 *abort;* 392.24 *back;* 300.13 *be in motion;* 707.19 *confirm;* 750.28 *consent;* 550.34 *cover for;* 95.12 *establish reality;* 413.14 *give moral support;* 716.12 *prove;* 303.3 *reverse;* 413.11 *support*
back-view 525.3 *external appearance*
back wall 63.8 *squash*
backward **303.22**; 634.18 *avoiding;* 637.3 *cautious;* 333.7 *delayed;* 245.12 *deteriorated;* 300.17 *directional;* 57.11 *gymnastic;* 456.6 *ignorant;* 457.7 *intellectually subnormal;* 168.9 *in the rear;* 457.5 *lacking intellect;* 646.1 *naive;* 674.13 *reserved;* 67.11 *swimming*
backwardation 791.1 *discount*
backward dislocate circle 57.7 *stationary rings*
backward dive 67.6 *diving*
backward-looking 303.24 *retroactive;* 284.21 *retrospective*
Backward Motion 303
backward motion **300.4**; **303.10**
backwardness 637.13 *dissociation;* 456.1 *ignorance;* 457.1 *lack of intellect;* 646.2 *naivety;* 674.6 *reserve;* 461.2 *subnormality;* 486.8 *unskilfulness*
backwards **303.28**; 57.12 *competitively;* 192.4 *inversely*
backwards and forwards 759.8 *in exchange;* 326.18 *to and fro*
backward somersault 57.8 *floor exercises;* 57.5 *horizontal bar*
backward step 303.10 *backward motion*
backward swing 57.5 *horizontal bar*
backward uprise 57.7 *stationary rings*
backward upstart 57.7 *stationary rings*
backwash 90.6 *river flow;* 345.2 *visible effect*
backwater 90.2 *channel;* 92.9 *inlet;* 86.6 *regions;* 88.2 *small lake;* 655.5 *solitary place*
back water 303.3 *reverse;* 333.3 *slow down*
backwood bowl 51.2 *grip*
back-woods 86.18 *local;* 86.6 *regions*
backwoodsman 564.5 *countryman*
back yard 165.2 *enclosed place;* 86.13 *locality*
bacon **25.30**
baconer 43.8 *livestock*
Baconian 4.11 *follower of a doctrine;* 4.14 *of a philosophy*
bacon joint 25.30 *bacon*
bacteria 554.9 *classifications of life;* 260.6 *infection*
bacterial 159.7 *little;* 34.21 *living*
bacterial cell 34.7 *cell*
bacterial disease 260.4 *disease*
bactericide 37.4 *drug type;* 394.3 *prophylactic*
bacteriocidal 37.14 *counteracting*
bacteriological 34.20 *biological*
bacteriological warfare 585.8 *warfare*
bacteriologist 34.19 *life scientist;* 35.13 *medical specialist*
bacteriology 34.1 *life science;* 35.3 *medical specialty;* 260.20 *pathology*
bacteriophage 34.3 *organism*
bacteriostatic 37.14 *counteracting;* 37.4 *drug type*
bacterium 260.6 *infection;* 159.2 *little thing;* 34.3 *organism*
bad **236.3**; **611.8**; 249.6 *adverse;* 631.18 *badly behaved;* 236.9 *badness;* 602.6 *depressed;* 245.12 *deteriorated;* 800.5 *dishonourable;* 375.5 *disintegrated;* 798.7 *evil;* 797.1 *good;* 797.27 *great!;* 796.11 *immoral;* 231.1 *imperfect;* 236.2 *inferior;* 802.16 *in the wrong;* 16.60 *offending;* 122.14 *poor;* 260.22 *sick;* 124.4 *trivial;* 499.6 *unpalatable;* 804.11 *wicked;* 235.1 *worthy*
bad apple 224.6 *editor*
bad art 718.1 *misrepresentation*
bad atmosphere 590.6 *bad feeling*
bad bargain 469.8 *choice*
bad behaviour 631.4 *bad conduct;* 659.2 *bad manners;* 804.1 *wickedness*
bad blood 113.5 *conflict;* 596.1 *dislike;* 594.1 *hate;* 651.1 *malevolence*
bad books 594.4 *hatefulness*
bad breath 503.2 *something that makes an unpleasant smell*
bad buy 787.4 *expenditure;* 777.6 *purchase*
bad character 236.12 *bad person;* 804.1 *wickedness*
bad cheque 786.3 *bad payment;* 780.15 *false money*
bad condition 221.5 *physical state*
bad conduct **631.4**; 804.1 *wickedness*
bad connection 109.5 *misconnection*
bad conscience 808.1 *penitence;* 806.2 *signs of guilt*
bad day 486.9 *bungling*
bad debt 784.5 *amount owing;* 784.1 *debt*
bad debtor 784.6 *debtor*
bad deed 651.7 *act of malevolence;* 340.2 *deed;* 802.8 *wrongdoing*
baddie 804.10 *bad person;* 798.6 *evil person;* 651.8 *malefactor*
bad drains 503.2 *something that makes an unpleasant smell*
bad dream 711.3 *false alarm;* 477.5 *fantasy*
bad ear 504.1 *hearing*
bad egg 804.10 *bad person;* 812.2 *disreputable character;* 651.8 *malefactor;* 503.2 *something that makes an unpleasant smell*
bad ending 245.7 *deterioration*
bad fairy 236.12 *bad person*
bad faith 800.2 *faithlessness;* 699.1 *falsehood*
bad feeling **590.6**; 242.7 *dissension*
bad fit 751.3 *difference*
bad form 675.3 *grossness;* 657.5 *nonobservance;* 487.2 *not customary*
bad fortune **249.3**
badge 743.8 *heraldic device;* 542.4 *honour;* 743.4 *insignia;* 542.7 *jewellery;* 743.3 *means of identification;* 520.6 *visible thing*
badge of merit 743.4 *insignia*
badge of office 743.4 *insignia*
badge of rank 743.4 *insignia*
badge of sovereignty 743.4 *insignia*
badger and dog 586.4 *fighting animal*
badger hunting 633.2 *chase*
bad grammar 5.29 *grammar;* 274.11 *grammatical error;* 544.4 *inelegance of speech*
bad guy 21.23 *role*
bad habit 632.1 *habit*
bad hair day 247.4 *unsuccessful thing*
bad hand 486.10 *unskilled person*
bad health 260.1 *ill health*
bad heart 260.10 *cardiovascular disease*
bad humour 221.4 *state of mind*
bad-humoured 221.8 *in a state of mind*
bad-humouredly 221.9 *conditionally*
bad idea 247.4 *unsuccessful thing*
badinage 621.1 *mockery;* 599.3 *wit*
bad influence 236.12 *bad person;* 800.4 *dishonourable person;* 812.2 *disreputable character;* 224.6 *editor;* 798.6 *evil person;* 798.4 *evil power*
bad intention 651.1 *malevolence*
bad job 486.9 *bungling*
bad judgment 16.4 *bad law*
bad karma 798.4 *evil power*
badlands 428.14 *desert*
bad language 659.3 *act of discourtesy;* 544.4 *inelegance of speech;* 712.2 *offensive language*
bad law **16.4**
bad learner 486.10 *unskilled person*
bad light 523.1 *darkness;* 524.1 *dimness;* 812.1 *disrespect;* 522.10 *window*
bad likeness 116.3 *disguise;* 718.1 *misrepresentation;* 717.1 *representation*
bad lot 804.10 *bad person;* 812.2 *disreputable character;* 651.8 *malefactor*
bad luck **798.3**; 249.3 *bad fortune;* 604.2 *bad outcome;* 288.3 *lost chance;* 107.2 *luck;* 627.5 *misfortune;* 249.13 *too bad!*
bad luck! **798.15**
bad-luck sign **475.7**
badly **122.21**; **631.20**; 351.6 *abusively;* 800.11 *dishonourably;* 798.12 *evilly;* 486.11 *unskilfully;* 804.18 *wickedly;* 245.14 *worse;* 236.15 *worthlessly;* 274.22 *wrongly*
badly behaved **631.18**; 659.6 *bad-mannered;* 264.14 *troublesome;* 804.11 *wicked*
badly behaved person **631.5**
badly done 486.4 *bungled;* 236.2 *inferior*
badly dressed 544.10 *ugly*
badly lit 523.8 *dark*
badly made 236.2 *inferior*
badly off 782.1 *poor;* 249.7 *unprosperous*
badly served 604.9 *disappointed*
bad-mannered **659.6**; 672.3 *ungrateful*
bad manners **659.2**; 631.4 *bad conduct;* 675.3 *grossness;* 657.5 *nonobservance;* 242.6 *objectionability*
bad match 751.3 *difference*
Badminton 59.11 *eventing*
badminton **63.10**
badminton court 63.11 *badminton equipment*
badminton equipment **63.11**
badminton terms **63.12**
bad money 780.15 *false money*
bad morals 796.1 *immorality*
bad-mouth 678.12 *defame*
bad move 274.1 *mistake*
bad name 812.1 *disrespect*
bad neighbour 596.3 *disliked person*
badness **236.9**; 631.4 *bad conduct;* 798.1 *evil;* 796.1 *immorality;* 800.1 *improbity;* 236.8 *inferiority;* 651.1 *malevolence;* 122.4 *poor quality;* 802.5 *unrighteousness;* 804.1 *wickedness*
bad news 249.1 *adversity;* 631.18 *badly behaved;* 604.2 *bad outcome;* 804.10 *bad person;* 245.7 *deterioration;* 594.8 *hated person*
bad nose 501.1 *odourlessness*
bad notice 670.5 *criticism*
bad odour 812.1 *disrespect;* 594.4 *hatefulness;* 500.4 *reputation;* 503.1 *stench*
bad omen 236.11 *harmfulness;* 475.5 *omen;* 711.1 *warning*
bad outcome **604.2**
bad patch 264.7 *awkward situation;* 249.4 *time of adversity*
bad payment **786.3**
bad person **236.12**; **804.10**; 651.8 *malefactor*
bad policy 240.3 *inconvenience*
bad press 670.5, 678.2 *criticism*
bad result 604.2 *bad outcome*
bad review 678.2, 719.3 *criticism*
Badrinath 10.13 *shrine*
bad sailor 323.7 *nautical person*
bad sales 778.5 *sales*
bad scene 245.7 *deterioration;* 812.2 *disreputable character*
bad shot 486.10 *unskilled person*
bad spell 798.4 *evil power;* 249.4 *time of adversity*
bad spirits 221.4 *state of mind*
bad taste **497.4**; 544.2, 802.3 *impropriety;* 796.2 *indecency;* 646.2 *naivety;* 657.5 *nonobservance;* 122.4 *poor quality;* 675.1 *tastelessness;* 495.2 *taste of life;* 544.3 *ugliness;* 804.3 *venial sin*
bad temper 625.1 *irascibility;* 626.3 *irritableness;* 625.2 *sign of irascibility;* 626.4 *sign of irritableness*
bad-tempered 594.13 *angry;* 626.7 *irritable*
bad time 288.2 *untimeliness*
bad times 782.6 *insolvency;* 249.4 *time of adversity*
bad timing 288.2 *untimeliness*
bad trip 691.1 *drug-taking*
bad turn 651.7 *act of malevolence*
bad use 351.2 *misuse*
bad vibes 590.6 *bad feeling*

bad visibility 521.4 *invisibility*
bad ways 804.1 *wickedness*
bad weather 62.2 *climbing dangers*; 380.5 *violent weather*
bad will 651.1 *malevolence*
bad wishes 594.1 *hate*
bad word 712.1 *curse*; 5.19 *swearword*
bad words 659.3 *act of discourtesy*
Baedeker 693.5 *reference book*
baffle 457.10 *bemuse*; 696.7 *be unintelligible*; 619.10 *be wonderful*; 264.23 *cause difficulties*; 505.3 *inaudibility*; 453.20 *make uncertain*; 505.10 *muffle*; 737.13 *mystify*; 528.12 *obscure*; 604.7 *thwart*
baffled 453.3, 696.6 *confused*; 604.9 *disappointed*; 264.16 *troubled*
baffle description 619.10 *be wonderful*
bafflement 453.12 *confusion*; 604.1 *disappointment*; 451.3 *incredulity*; 696.11 *unintelligibility*; 619.1 *wonder*
baffling 453.3 *confused*; 696.4 *difficult*; 528.4 *inscrutable*; 264.12 *problematic*
baffling attitude 696.12 *unintelligible thing*
baffy 56.4 *golf club*
BAFTA Award 813.2 *prize*
bag 410.8; 203.3 *container*; 633.11 *hunt*; 139.8 *specialization*; 439.1 *store*
bag and baggage 763.4 *possession*; 440.4 *possessions*
bagatelle 124.9 *bauble*; 793.5 *cheap item*; 124.8 *trifle*
bagel 25.39 *loaf*
baggage 410.9; 660.12 *impudent person*; 440.4 *possessions*; 319.2 *thing transported*; 316.10 *transferred thing*; 568.9 *woman considered as a sex object*; 555.8 *young woman*
baggage car 321.6 *rolling stock*
bagged 410.20 *containing*; 690.3 *dead drunk*
baggily 158.20 *largely*
bagginess 158.2 *bigness*; 150.4 *breadth*; 268.2 *runniness*
baggy 158.15 *big*; 150.1 *broad*; 551.31 *styled*
bag job 774.3 *theft*
bag lady 118.7 *nonconformist*; 249.5 *person in adversity*; 782.10 *poor person*
bag limit 60.2 *hunting*
bagman 778.11 *pedlar*
bagmuck 43.13 *fertilizer*
bagnio 796.6 *brothel*
bag of bones 153.9 *thin person*
bag of nerves 612.6 *frightened person*
bag of tricks 439.5 *collection*; 352.1 *means*; 645.2 *stratagem*; 438.2 *toolroom*; 700.8 *trick*; 700.7 *tricking*
bag of waters 561.7 *obstetrics*
bags 208.3 *profuseness*; 551.9 *trousers*
bag-snatcher 773.6 *taker*; 774.8 *thief*
bag-snatching 774.1 *stealing*
bag trolley 320.7 *handcart*
baguette 25.39 *loaf*
baguio 31.16 *wind vortex*
bagwig 551.15 *headgear*
bagworm 76.5 *larva*
Baha'i 7.6 *non-Christian*
Bahir 7.12 *religious text*
bail 390.2 *deliverance*; 16.6 *legal process*; 391.4 *liberate*; 391.1 *liberation*; 316.15 *take away*; 53.5 *wicket*
bailed 391.7 *liberated*
bailey 384.11 *fortification*
Bailey bridge 38.21, 317.9 *bridge*
bailie 400.3 *leader*
bailiff 769.7 *collector*; 401.6 *domestic servant*; 43.16 *farm worker*; 16.10 *law officer*; 400.3 *leader*; 579.15 *manager*
bailiwick 565.2 *environment*; 16.2 *jurisdiction*; 86.14 *sphere*; 395.7 *sphere of influence*; 86.5 *state*
bail out 390.1 *deliver*; 780.7 *finance*
bain marie 25.8 *cooking technique*; 410.15 *pot*
bairn 555.9 *child*
bait 55.1 *angling*; 647.5 *be severe*; 593.26 *court*; 480.9 *enticement*; 633.3 *hunting and fishing equipment*; 363.5, 363.12 *lure*; 624.9 *offend*; 752.9 *offer*; 483.5 *positive stimulus*; 813.4 *reward for service*; 700.13, 700.33 *snare*
bait a hook 700.33 *snare*
bait a trap 700.33 *snare*
bait casting 55.1 *angling*
baited 55.8 *angling*; 700.42 *trapped*
baited trap 480.9 *enticement*; 700.13 *snare*
bait fishing 55.1 *angling*
baiting 55.8 *angling*
bait the hook 55.7 *angle*
bait the trap 645.5 *be cunning*
baize 65.1 *billiards*
bake 428.19; 493.14 *be hot*; 25.55 *cook*; 418.9 *harden*; 24.11 *make ceramics*
baked 428.8; 493.13 *heated*
baked brick 418.7 *hard substance*
bakehouse 25.3 *kitchen*
Bakelite™ 32.21 *polymer*
baker 25.2 *cook*; 557.20 *food provider*; 412.7 *person who mixes*; 436.3 *provider*; 778.13 *retailer*
baker's 557.17 *food shop*
baker's dozen 201.7 *double figures*
bakery 557.17 *food shop*; 25.3 *kitchen*
Bakewell tart 25.36 *cake*
baking 25.1 *cookery*; 25.8 *cooking technique*
baking hot 493.9 *hot*
baking powder 25.7 *basic ingredient*; 415.8 *leavening*
baking sheet 25.6 *kitchen equipment*
baking soda 256.9 *cleaning agent*
baklava 25.52 *Greek dish*
baksheesh 813.7 *bounty*; 679.7, 768.2 *gift*; 483.5 *positive stimulus*; 765.5 *profit*
Bala 88.4 *British lakes*
balaclava helmet 551.15 *headgear*
balance 639.8; 403.9 *artistic structure*; 22.3 *ballroom dance steps*; 111.10 *be equal*; 414.12 *be heavy*; 108.8 *be proportionate to*; 708.7 *cancelling out*; 708.16 *cancel out*; 210.12 *check*; 57.10 *compete in gymnastics*; 232.1 *completeness*; 754.1 *compromise*; 188.6 *correlate*; 19.23 *design*; 4.3 *detachment*; 543.1 *elegance*; 111.5 *equality*; 119.11 *equalize*; 119.2 *equilibrium*; 57.8 *floor exercises*; 750.24 *harmonize*; 750.4 *harmony*; 57.5 *horizontal bar*; 110.1 *interchange*; 216.10 *make average*; 298.10 *make regular*; 228.7 *make stable*; 111.8 *make the same*; 216.5 *medium*; 301.1 *motionlessness*; 298.4 *orderliness*; 188.1 *parallelism*; 205.1 *part*; 110.7 *reciprocate*; 50.16 *row*; 50.4 *rowing*; 414.10 *scales*; 132.7, 228.1 *stability*; 26.7 *standard*; 219.3 *superfluity*; 162.6 *symmetrize*; 162.1 *symmetry*; 19.4 *treatment*; 28.86 *weighing instrument*
balance accounts 789.7 *account*
balance beam 57.6 *pommel horse*
balance carried forward 215.3 *difference*
balance climbing 62.1 *mountaineering*
balanced 789.11 *accounted*; 801.12 *all right*; 708.20 *cancelled*; 754.6 *compromising*; 188.4 *correlated*; 543.3 *elegant*; 111.16, 119.6 *equal*; 750.13 *harmonious*; 216.2 *medium*; 685.6 *moderate*; 301.4 *motionless*; 407.10 *ordered*; 298.14 *orderly*; 460.5 *rational*; 50.11 *rowing*; 228.10 *stabilized*; 162.4 *symmetrical*; 458.5 *wise*
balanced diet 557.6 *nutrition*
balanced line 46.7 *offence*
balanced mind 460.1 *sanity*
balance due 135.2 *need*
balance movement 57.7 *stationary rings*
balance of form 162.1 *symmetry*
balance of mind disturbed 461.1 *insanity*
balance of payments 13.6 *economic factors*; 13.5 *international trade*
balance of power 119.2 *equilibrium*
balance of terror 119.2 *equilibrium*
balance of trade 13.5 *international trade*
balance out 216.10 *make average*
balances 783.3 *deposit*; 780.6 *funds*
balance sheet 789.1 *accounts*; 13.7 *corporation*
balance the books 210.12 *check*; 765.12 *earn*
balance to pay 784.5 *amount owing*
balance wheel 307.6 *rotator*
balancing 754.6 *compromising*; 347.4 *counteracting*; 119.3 *equalization*; 57.11 *gymnastic*; 110.4 *reciprocal*; 50.11 *rowing*
balancing act 754.1 *compromise*; 479.5 *equivocalness*
balancing exercises 57.1 *gymnastics*
balcony 21.18 *auditorium*; 20.9 *miscellaneous architectural features*; 361.5 *projecting object*; 185.2 *projection*; 565.7 *room*; 21.33 *theatregoer*
bal costumé 22.1 *dancing*
bald 552.13 *hairless*; 271.1 *simple*; 421.1 *smooth*; 698.18 *truthful*
bald as a coot 552.13 *hairless*
bald as an egg 552.13 *hairless*
balderdash 697.1 *nonsense*
bald head 552.5 *baldness*; 421.8 *smooth thing*
baldheaded 552.13 *hairless*
baldheadedness 552.5 *baldness*
baldly 552.17 *nakedly*; 271.8 *simply*
baldness 552.5; 271.4 *simplicity*; 698.5 *truthfulness*
baldpate 552.5 *baldness*
baldpated 552.13 *hairless*
baldpatedness 552.5 *baldness*
bald person 552.5 *baldness*
baldric 551.25 *accessories*
bald top 552.5 *baldness*
baldy 552.5 *baldness*
bale 43.9 *animal feedstuff*; 376.27 *bundle*; 414.6 *displacement*; 43.17 *farm*; 376.38 *group*
bale carrier 43.10 *farm tool*
bale-carting 43.5 *cultivation*
baled 376.49 *grouped*
baleen 422.3 *elastic thing*
balefire 522.8 *fire*; 742.4 *signal*
baleful 798.9 *detrimental*; 236.5 *harmful*; 651.10 *malevolent*
balefully 798.13 *destructively*
balefulness 236.11 *harmfulness*
bale out 315.10 *emerge*; 392.29 *finance*
baler 43.10 *farm tool*
bale sledge 43.10 *farm tool*
bale wrapper 43.10 *farm tool*
balk 604.2 *bad outcome*; 639.6 *hesitate*; 637.8 *hold back*; 48.4 *pitching terms*; 48.7 *play baseball*; 604.7 *thwart*
Balkanization 655.3 *separation*
Balkanize 12.11 *govern*
balk at 709.5 *refuse*; 634.4 *shy*
balked 604.9 *disappointed*
Balkhash 88.5 *other major lakes*
balking 637.12 *opposition*
ball 330.10; 587.13 *ammunition*; 53.7 *bat*; 376.10 *dance*; 22.1 *dancing*; 587.14 *historical ammunition*; 587.6 *historical missile weapon*; 593.29 *make love*; 181.11 *make round*; 330.8 *missile*; 654.5 *party*; 48.4 *pitching terms*; 181.3 *round thing*
ballad 721.3 *narration*; 17.7 *poem*
ballade 17.7 *poem*; 17.10 *verse form*
balladeer 17.14 *author*; 516.5 *melodist*; 18.24 *musician*
ballad maker 17.14 *author*
ballad monger 17.14 *author*
ballad opera 21.4 *musical drama*
balladry 17.6 *poetry*
ball and chain 251.5 *means of restraint*; 378.4 *restraint*; 568.12 *woman in the family*
ball-and-claw leg 23.3 *chair leg*
ballast 414.6 *displacement*; 119.4 *equilizer*; 414.14 *make heavy*; 50.3 *parts of a sailing boat*; 321.3 *rail*; 252.4 *safety device*; 414.10 *scales*; 228.3 *stabilizer*
ballasting 414.10 *scales*
ball bearing 307.4 *axle*; 38.8 *machine element*
ball boy 63.6 *tennis player*
ball-breaker 568.9 *woman considered as a sex object*
ballbuster 264.3 *difficult task*
ball-carrier 64.4 *rugby player*
ball clay 24.2 *raw material*
ball-control offence 49.4 *playing terms*
ballerina 22.13 *ballet dancer*; 21.30 *dancer*
ballet 22.8; 21.4 *musical drama*; 738.9 *production*; 68.12 *ski*; 356.5 *work of art*
ballet companies 22.12
ballet costume 551.5 *fancy dress*
ballet dancer 22.13; 21.30 *dancer*; 578.1 *worker*
ballet dancing 22.8 *ballet*; 22.1 *dancing*
balletgoer 21.33 *theatregoer*
balletic 21.39 *dramatic*
ballet music 18.7 *dance music*
balletomane 21.33 *theatregoer*
Ballet Rambert 22.12 *ballet companies*
ballet school 6.12 *educational institution*
ballet shoes 551.19 *footwear*
ballet-skiing 68.1 *skiing*
ballet skirt 551.6 *skirt*
ballet steps 22.9
ball game 143.2 *circumstances*; 69.1 *game*
ball gown 656.4 *formal dress*; 551.7 *frock*
balling 593.5 *desire*
ball in touch 64.3 *rugby play*
ballista 587.6 *historical missile weapon*
ballistic 330.18 *projectile*
ballistically 330.34 *forward*
ballistic missile 330.8 *missile*; 587.5 *missile weapon*
ballistics 585.6 *art of war*; 330.6 *shooting*
ball lightning 31.21 *thunderstorm*
ball milling 24.5 *ceramic process*
ball of fire 302.16 *progressive person*
ballon d'essai 645.2 *stratagem*
ballong 22.9 *ballet steps*
balloon 434.10 *air bubble*; 322.8 *aircraft*; 190.6 *become bigger*; 190.3 *enlarged thing*; 410.19 *inflatable*; 415.7 *light thing*; 181.3 *round thing*
balloon out 182.5 *be convex*; 181.11 *make round*
ballot 469.10 *vote*
ballot box 469.12 *election*
ballot-box stuffing 700.10 *fraud*
balloter 469.13 *electorate*
ballot paper 469.12 *election*
ballot-rigged 700.35 *deceptive*
ballot rigging 700.10 *fraud*
ballpark figure 780.5 *sum*
ballpark view 397.7 *overview*
ball return 51.4 *bowling*
ballroom 22.6 *dance hall*
ballroom dance 22.2 *dance*
ballroom dance steps 22.3
ballroom dancing 22.1 *dancing*
ballroom music 18.7 *dance music*
balls 182.2 *bulge*; 613.1 *courage*; 712.15 *miscellaneous swearwords*; 697.1, 699.15 *nonsense*; 561.8 *organs of reproduction*; 338.1 *vigour*
ballsed-up 408.19 *mixed-up*
balls up 486.7 *be clumsy*; 408.23 *confuse*; 247.6 *fail*; 245.4 *impair*; 274.19 *make a mistake*
balls-up 274.10, 544.6 *blunder*; 486.9 *bungling*; 408.6 *mix-up*
ballsy 613.9 *courageous*
ball the jack 332.5 *run like a shot*
ball up 247.6 *fail*; 181.11 *make round*
ballyhoo 480.6 *advertising*; 727.7 *exaggerate*; 727.1 *exaggeration*; 507.2 *outcry*; 740.7 *publicity*; 740.16 *publicize*
ballyhooed 727.12 *exaggerated*
balm 394.9; 394.5 *analgesic*; 627.2 *condolence*; 502.1 *fragrance*; 496.5 *herbs*; 394.2 *medicine*; 685.2 *moderator*; 37.7, 268.6 *ointment*; 608.3 *reliever*
bal masqué 736.3 *covering up*; 22.1 *dancing*
balmily 749.7 *pacifically*
balminess 502.1 *fragrance*
balm of Gilead 685.2 *moderator*
Balmoral 565.4 *official residence*; 551.18 *underwear*
balmoral 551.15 *headgear*
balmy 502.4 *fragrant*; 248.8 *prosperous*; 31.50, 493.11 *warm*
balneal 256.18 *cleansing*
balneation 433.11 *wash*
baloney 699.15 *nonsense*; 702.2 *sophism*
balsa 424.3 *brittle thing*
balsam 394.9 *balm*; 25.7 *basic ingredient*; 394.2 *medicine*; 37.7, 268.6 *ointment*
balsamic 608.8 *relieving*; 394.17 *remedial*; 37.16 *soothing*
balthazar 410.14 *bottle*
balti 25.54 *other dishes*
Baltic 5.11 *family of languages*
Balto-Slavic 5.11 *family of languages*
balustrade 165.3 *enclosing thing*; 413.2 *supporting part*
bambino 10.14 *sacred object*
Bamboo Curtain 378.3 *barrier*; 128.3 *exclusion zone*; 81.7 *figurative usage*; 147.7 *interface*
bamboo pole 55.3 *fishing tackle*
bamboo shoot 77.9 *seed*
bamboozle 736.9 *deceive*; 731.9 *out-talk*; 700.28 *trick*
bamboozlement 700.7 *tricking*
bamboozler 700.15 *deceiver*
ban 634.7 *be evasive*; 684.5 *be self-restrained*; 397.1, 397.9 *command*; 709.2, 709.6 *dissent*; 128.7 *exclude*; 128.1 *exclusion*; 655.13 *ignore*; 16.35 *illegality*; 737.12 *keep secret*; 166.7 *limit*; 166.2 *limiting factor*; 16.75 *make illegal*; 103.8 *make impossible*; 712.4 *malediction*; 251.5 *means of restraint*; 670.3 *nonacceptance*; 371.4 *ostracize*; 740.1 *publication*; 814.1 *punish*; 251.8 *restrain*; 251.1 *restraint*; 372.10 *set apart*; 350.6 *stop using*; 399.1, 399.3 *veto*; 712.7 *wish ill*; 670.15 *withhold approval*
ban a book 399.4 *censor*
banal 620.4 *boring*; 632.10 *familiar*;

216.3 *mediocre;* 745.2 *proverbial;* 497.5 *tasteless*
banality 620.1 *boredom;* 497.1 *dilution;* 745.1 *maxim*
banally 620.8 *boringly*
banana 537.8 *yellow thing*
Banana bender 80.5 *figurative usage*
banana bond 32.11 *chemical bond*
banana-nut bread 25.38 *bread*
banana republic 80.5 *figurative usage;* 12.5 *political organization*
bananas 461.11 *insane*
banana skin 274.10 *blunder;* 80.5 *figurative usage;* 238.6 *refuse*
banana split 25.35 *dessert*
band **373.10**; 750.2 *alliance;* 586.16 *army unit;* 374.3, 376.1 *assembly;* 179.3 *circular thing;* 376.11 *group;* 411.1 *layer;* 373.6 *line;* 373.4 *means of connection;* 18.26 *musical group;* 151.8 *narrow thing;* 551.14 *neckwear;* 578.4 *personnel;* 148.5 *piece;* 692.14 *radio transmission;* 137.5 *social class;* 541.3 *striping;* 376.12 *team;* 63.3 *tennis equipment;* 541.11 *variegate*
bandage 413.3 *body support;* 373.11 *connect;* 393.6 *cure;* 394.20 *doctor;* 373.6 *line;* 550.6 *medical covering;* 309.8 *stop;* 309.2 *stopper;* 762.3 *substitute thing;* 394.10 *surgical dressing;* 165.6, 550.25 *wrap;* 165.4 *wrapper*
bandaged 550.37 *protected;* 309.13 *stopped*
bandaging 550.6 *medical covering*
Band-Aid 267.3 *adhesive;* 710.3 *solicitation;* 762.3 *substitute thing*
bandanna 551.14 *neckwear*
bandeau 743.8 *heraldic device*
banded 541.9 *striped*
banderole 743.7 *flag*
bandit 662.9 *criminal;* 655.7 *outsider;* 774.9 *plunderer*
banditry 774.5 *plundering*
bandleader 18.24 *musician;* 281.11 *person keeping time*
bandmaster 18.24 *musician*
band of cloud 31.20 *cloud appearance*
bandoleer 551.25 *accessories;* 587.4 *arsenal;* 373.10 *band;* 62.4 *climbing equipment*
band-pass filter 39.22 *transformer*
band printer 40.7 *peripheral*
band rate 40.19 *computing terms*
band saw 38.9 *machine tool;* 79.7 *timber production;* 23.11 *woodworking tool*
band spectrum 28.68 *emission*
bandstand 21.17 *stage*
band-stop filter 39.22 *transformer*
band together **376.41**; 374.6 *come together;* 747.14 *join with*
bandwidth 692.14 *radio transmission*
bandy about 740.13 *make public*
bandy words 702.13 *quibble*
bandy words with 759.5 *exchange*
bane 249.1 *adversity;* 441.7 *destroyer;* 798.6 *evil person;* 798.5 *evil thing;* 612.5 *frightener;* 594.8 *hated person;* 260.5 *plague;* 236.10 *poverty;* 379.1 *trap*
baneful 357.14 *destructive;* 798.9 *detrimental;* 236.5 *harmful;* 594.12 *hated;* 651.14 *hostile*
banefulness 236.11 *harmfulness*
bang **508.1**; **508.5**; 507.8 *be loud;* 331.13 *blow;* 331.2 *collide;* 801.20 *correctly;* 691.6 *drug;* 691.10 *drug oneself;* 508.10 *explosively;* 331.3 *hit;* 507.1 *loudness*
banger **508.3**; 320.16 *car;* 522.8 *fire;* 25.29 *sausage*
banger racing 61.1 *motor racing*
bangers and mash 25.44 *British dish*
banging **508.8**; 691.1 *drug-taking;* 507.2 *outcry*
bangle 542.7 *jewellery*
bang-on 273.5, 698.21 *accurate;* 801.8 *correct;* 235.1 *worthy*
bangtail 59.1 *horse*
bang up 309.10 *enclose*
bang-up 235.1 *worthy*
bang up-to-date 295.10 *new;* 282.6 *present*
banish 128.8 *eject;* 655.13 *ignore;* 371.4 *ostracize;* 814.1 *punish;* 144.16 *replace;* 372.10 *set apart*
banished 655.10 *lonely;* 144.10 *replaced*
banishment 128.2 *ejection;* 371.19 *ostracism;* 814.7 *punishment;* 144.3 *replacement;* 655.3 *separation*
bank **780.26**; **783.4**; 176.11 *angle;* 376.37 *assemble;* 189.6 *be oblique;* 164.1 *edge;* 322.5 *flight;* 322.10 *fly;* 51.1 *green bowling;* 771.4 *lending institution;* 376.26 *mass;* 154.4 *mountain range;* 189.1 *obliqueness;* 759.2 *place of exchange;* 69.10 *play;* 157.4 *shallow thing;* 439.4 *storage;* 439.6 *store;* 780.19 *treasury*
bank account 780.6 *funds;* 14.4 *personal finance*
bank-account number 743.3 *means of identification*
bank annuities 780.6 *funds*
bankbook 789.5 *account book*
bank card 783.2 *credit card;* 784.1 *debt*
bank deposit 783.3 *deposit*
bank down the fires 685.4 *moderate*
banked 61.10 *racing;* 439.7 *stored*
banked circuit 61.6 *motor-racing terms*
banker 69.3 *card game terms;* 780.17 *financier;* 771.3 *lender;* 579.15 *manager;* 759.4 *person who exchanges;* 14.3 *stockbroker;* 780.18 *treasurer;* 778.12 *wholesaler*
banker's credit 783.1 *credit*
banker's draft 759.3 *something in exchange*
bank failure 786.5 *insolvency*
bank holiday 263.1 *ease;* 298.5 *regular thing*
banking 14.1 *finance;* 322.5 *flight*
bank loan 771.2, 772.5, 784.3 *loan*
bank manager 771.3 *lender;* 579.15 *manager*
banknote 780.14 *paper money*
bank of cloud 31.20 *cloud appearance*
Bank of England 780.19 *treasury*
bank official 579.15 *manager*
bank of snow 31.30 *snow*
bank on 450.7 *believe;* 610.6 *hope;* 474.9 *predict*
bank rate 14.1, 780.7 *finance;* 784.4 *interest*
bank reconciliation statement 789.4 *statement*
bank robber 16.40 *lawbreaker;* 774.8 *thief*
bank robbery 774.1 *stealing;* 774.3 *theft*
bankroll 13.11 *deal;* 777.5 *defray;* 787.3 *donate;* 413.13 *support financially*
bankrupt 784.6 *debtor;* 246.10 *defeat heavily;* 357.8 *destroy;* 357.15 *destroyed;* 247.10 *failed;* 247.5 *failing person;* 782.14 *impoverish;* 782.2 *insolvent;* 766.6 *loser;* 135.5 *necessitous;* 786.6 *nonpayer;* 786.13 *nonpaying;* 249.5 *person in adversity;* 782.10 *poor person;* 766.17 *unprofitable;* 249.7 *unprosperous*
bankruptcy 247.1 *failure;* 766.2 *financial loss;* 782.6, 786.5 *insolvency;* 218.8 *insufficiency;* 357.4 *ruin;* 247.4 *unsuccessful thing*
bankruptcy court 786.5 *insolvency*
bankruptcy proceedings 786.5 *insolvency*
bank shot 65.2 *billiards play;* 49.4 *playing terms*
bank statement 789.4 *statement*
bank up 376.37 *assemble*
bank vault 736.2 *hiding place;* 253.5 *safe*
banned 399.6 *censored;* 397.14 *commanding;* 670.31 *disapproved;* 709.9 *dissenting;* 128.11 *excluded;* 103.4 *forbidden;* 16.55 *illegal;* 655.10 *lonely;* 712.10 *maledictive;* 251.13 *restraining;* 399.5 *vetoed*
banned book 399.2 *censorship*
banner 740.9 *advertisement;* 121.15 *excellent;* 743.7 *flag;* 742.1 *sign*
bannerette 743.7 *flag*
banner head 741.12 *headline*
banner headline 740.3 *journalism*
bannerol 743.7 *flag*
banners 601.8 *salute*
banning 371.19 *ostracism;* 814.7 *punishment*
bannock 25.39 *loaf*
ban on testing 749.1 *pacification*
banquet 688.3 *act of gluttony;* 601.1 *celebration;* 557.13 *feast;* 557.24 *have a meal;* 654.5 *party;* 490.4 *pleasurable things;* 217.8 *plenty;* 557.25 *provide food;* 600.5 *rejoice;* 600.1 *rejoicing*
banqueter 557.18 *eater*
banquet hall 557.15 *eating place*
banqueting 557.4 *eating meals*
banqueting hall 557.15 *eating place*
banquette 384.11 *fortification*
banshee 70.7 *legendary beast*
bantam 159.7 *little;* 159.4 *little person;* 149.5 *short person*
bantamweight 586.3 *athlete;* 52.4 *boxer;* 52.3 *boxing weight divisions;* 52.14 *combat;* 415.1 *light;* 414.7 *weighing*
banter 599.13 *be humorous;* 734.2 *chat;* 660.9 *discourtesy;* 621.1 *mockery;* 668.6 *taunt;* 697.3 *tomfoolery;* 599.3 *wit*
bantering 660.20 *discourteous;* 668.15 *taunting*
ban the bomb 589.6 *make peace*
ban-the-bomb movement 749.1 *pacification;* 589.1 *peace*
Bantu 5.11 *family of languages*
Bantustan 655.4 *place of confinement*
banty 149.5 *short person*
Banyan tree 10.14 *sacred object*
bap 25.39 *loaf*
baptising 721.7 *nomenclature*
baptism 10.5 *Christian rite;* 130.8 *enrolment;* 656.3 *formal occasion;* 433.15 *holy water;* 368.10 *immersion;* 370.3 *introduction;* 721.7 *nomenclature;* 769.4 *reception;* 256.3 *religious cleansing*
baptismal 130.36, 370.16 *introductory;* 129.13 *precursory;* 10.21 *ritualistic*
baptismal name 721.8 *name*
baptism of fire 130.8 *enrolment*
Baptist 7.5 *Christian*
baptize 130.25 *enrol;* 368.4 *immerse;* 370.10 *introduce;* 10.18 *perform rites;* 7.20 *preach;* 769.10 *receive someone*
baptized 130.37 *enrolled;* 368.14 *immersed;* 769.13 *received*
baptizer 5.2 *linguist*
bar 378.9 *block;* 780.16 *bullion;* 212.8 *by subtraction;* 309.7 *close;* 309.1 *closure;* 30.11 *coast;* 16.79 *convict;* 16.27 *courtroom;* 128.7 *exclude;* 128.1 *exclusion;* 128.12 *exclusively;* 373.8 *fastening;* 209.3 *gradation;* 743.8 *heraldic device;* 743.4 *insignia;* 103.8 *make impossible;* 670.3 *nonacceptance;* 18.17 *notation;* 378.2 *obstacle;* 148.5, 205.7 *piece;* 251.8 *restrain;* 309.3 *restrainer;* 251.1 *restraint;* 252.4 *safety device;* 372.10 *set apart;* 157.4 *shallow thing;* 309.8 *stop;* 541.3 *striping;* 16.18 *tribunal;* 541.11 *variegate;* 670.15 *withhold approval;* 113.20 *withstand*
Baraim 10.16 *religious festival*
barb 691.6 *drug;* 587.6 *historical missile weapon;* 425.15 *make sharp;* 420.7 *rough thing;* 425.8 *sharp-pointed thing;* 668.6 *taunt*
barbarian 659.6 *bad-mannered;* 357.6 *destroyer;* 675.8 *discourteous;* 659.4 *discourteous person;* 100.10 *foreign;* 380.4 *violent creature;* 675.5 *vulgar person*
barbarians 566.3 *early human*
barbaric 651.11 *cruel;* 100.10 *foreign;* 544.8 *indecorous;* 628.4 *pitiless*
barbarism 651.2 *cruelness;* 274.11 *grammatical error;* 351.2 *misuse;* 646.2 *naivety;* 5.5 *nonstandard language;* 245.8 *perversion*
barbarity 651.2 *cruelness;* 380.2 *physical violence*
barbarius 675.9 *ribald*
barbarize 245.6 *pervert*
barbarous 351.5 *abusive;* 381.23 *attacking;* 651.11 *cruel;* 544.8 *indecorous;* 628.4 *pitiless;* 380.6 *violent;* 5.42 *worded*
barbarously 351.6 *abusively;* 628.7 *pitilessly*
barbecue 25.55 *cook;* 25.5 *cooker;* 557.13 *feast;* 44.3 *ornamental garden;* 654.5 *party*
barbecue cook 25.2 *cook*
barbecued 25.56 *culinary*
barbecued spare ribs 25.43 *US dish*
barbecue pit 493.4 *burner*
barbecue sandwich 25.11 *sandwich*
barbecue sauce 25.15 *sauce;* 496.2 *seasoning*
barbecuing 25.8 *cooking technique*
barbed **420.3**; 425.2 *spiked*
barbed arrow 587.6 *historical missile weapon*
barbed wire 378.3 *barrier;* 43.11 *farmland;* 420.7 *rough thing;* 425.8 *sharp-pointed thing;* 360.4 *wall*
barbel 55.5 *British game fish*
barbellate 420.3 *barbed*
barber 547.13 *beautician;* 256.12 *cleaner;* 401.4 *personal attendant*
barber hauler 50.3 *parts of a sailing boat*
barbering 547.7 *hairdressing*
Barber paradox 4.9 *philosophical problem*
barber shop 547.11 *hairdressing salon*
barber's striped pole 743.3 *means of identification*
barbette 384.11 *fortification*
Barbican 87.5 *London*
barbican 384.12 *fort;* 154.6 *tall thing*
barbicel 72.17 *plumage*
barbie 44.3 *ornamental garden;* 654.5 *party*
barbiturate 489.4 *anaesthetic;* 592.6 *desensitizing substance;* 394.8, 691.6 *drug;* 37.4 *drug type;* 685.2 *moderator;* 343.10 *soporific*
Barbour™ 551.12 *coat*
BARB ratings 740.2 *mass media*
barbs 592.6 *desensitizing substance*
barbule 72.17 *plumage*
barbwire 425.8 *sharp-pointed thing*
barcarolle 516.2 *song*
barchan 30.37 *dune*
bar chart 409.8 *chart;* 27.32 *graph*
bar code 541.5 *variegated thing*
bar-code reader 40.7 *peripheral*
bard 17.14 *author;* 25.55 *cook;* 18.24 *musician*
bare 428.6 *desert;* 255.17 *direct;* 739.5 *disclose;* 563.3 *infertile;* 738.15 *open;* 308.13 *opened up;* 271.1, 728.14 *simple;* 552.14 *undress;* 552.9 *undressed;* 218.2 *unprovided;* 98.13 *vacant;* 254.3 *vulnerable*
bare-ass 552.9 *undressed*
barebacked 552.11 *exposed*
bareback rider 336.5 *athlete;* 21.31 *circus performer;* 59.15 *horse person*
bareback riding 59.6 *horsemanship*
bareback-riding 59.12 *rodeo*
bare-bollock 552.9 *undressed*
bare bones 163.1 *outline*
barebreasted 552.11 *exposed*
barechested 552.11 *exposed*
bare cupboard 782.6 *insolvency;* 557.10 *scarcity;* 687.2 *short rations*
bared 552.9 *undressed*
bare essentials 205.5 *largest part;* 163.1 *outline;* 135.1 *requirement*
barefaced 738.15 *open;* 660.19 *rude*
barefaced effrontery 661.1 *defiance*
barefaced lie 699.10 *lie*
barefaced lying 699.6 *lying*
barefoot 782.3 *beggarly;* 552.11 *exposed;* 552.10 *in dishabille*
bare head 552.5 *baldness*
bare-headed 667.11 *in a respectful stance;* 552.10 *in dishabille*
barelegged 552.11 *exposed;* 552.10 *in dishabille*
barely 231.11 *imperfectly;* 552.17 *nakedly;* 151.11 *narrowly;* 206.11 *sparsely*
barely move 333.2 *hesitate;* 333.1 *move slowly*
barely pass 231.9 *be imperfect*
barely sufficient 217.1 *sufficient*
bare minimum 135.3 *needfulness;* 217.7 *sufficiency*
barenecked 552.11 *exposed*
bareness 98.3 *emptiness;* 552.2 *nudity;* 271.4, 728.4 *simplicity;* 552.1 *undress*
bare one's breast to 739.8 *admit*
bare one's fangs 594.14 *hate*
bare one's teeth 626.11 *be irritable;* 661.5 *defy*
bare subsistence 218.8 *insufficiency;* 687.2 *short rations*
bare supposition 476.3 *conjecture*
barf 371.15 *vomit*
Barfoed's test 33.5 *sugar test*
bargain **776.3**; **791.2**; **793.4**; 750.23 *arrange;* 750.3 *arrangement;* 776.9 *bargaining;* 793.9 *cheap;* 754.1 *compromise;* 734.11 *confer;* 755.1, 755.5 *contract;* 791.6 *discounted;* 777.1, 777.6 *purchase*
bargain basement 793.7 *discounter;* 779.8 *store*
bargain-basement 793.9 *cheap*
bargain bin 793.7 *discounter*
bargainer 777.12 *purchaser*
bargain for 474.9 *predict*
bargain hunter **793.8**; 777.12 *purchaser*
bargaining **776.9**; 750.12 *arranged;* 777.14 *buying;* 755.1 *contract;* 746.1 *negotiation;* 734.5 *talks*
bargaining session 746.3 *discussion*
bargain of the month 752.3 *business offer*
bargain price 791.2 *bargain;* 793.1 *cheapness*
bargain sale 791.2 *bargain;* 778.4 *sale*
barge 316.12 *transport;* 323.3 *vessel*
bargee 323.8 *boatman*
barge in 314.10 *invade;* 329.5 *transgress*
barge in on 133.16 *interrupt*

bargeman 323.8 *boatman*
bar graph 27.32 *graph*; 163.1 *outline*
baring 552.1 *undress*
baring one's fangs 594.1 *hate*
baritone 510.3 *deepness*; 18.32 *instrumental*
barium enema 35.7 *diagnosis*
barium meal 35.7 *diagnosis*
bark 365.13 *abrade*; 515.1 *animal cry*; 550.13 *casing*; 411.3 *coat*; 515.4 *cry*; 624.6 *sign of anger*; 729.13 *speak in a particular way*; 79.3 *timber*
barkeep 401.3 *attendant*
barkeeper 401.3 *attendant*
barker 21.31 *circus performer*; 514.9 *crier*; 738.12 *displayer*; 740.10 *publicizer*
barking 515.1 *animal cry*
barking mad 461.11 *insane*
barley 557.8 *animal food*; 43.12 *crop*
barley baron 43.15 *agriculturist*
barley beef 43.8 *livestock*
barleycorn 81.4 *cereal grass*
barleycorn lead 55.3 *fishing tackle*
barley straw 43.9 *animal feedstuff*
barley sugar 25.41 *sweet*
barley water 558.6 *soft drink*
barm 415.8 *leavening*
bar magnet 28.60, 363.3 *magnet*
barmaid 401.3 *attendant*
barman 401.3 *attendant*
barm cake 25.39 *loaf*
bar mitzvah 601.3 *ceremony*; 656.3 *formal occasion*; 10.7 *non-Christian ritual*
barmy 459.5 *foolish*; 461.11 *insane*
barn 43.7 *farm building*; 565.12 *stall*; 439.4 *storage*; 577.1 *workshop*
barnacle 267.4 *adherent*; 75.4 *arthropod*; 664.3 *sponger*
barn dance 376.10 *dance*; 22.1 *dancing*; 22.4 *historic dancing*; 654.5 *party*
barney 701.1, 751.2 *argument*
barn owl 72.5 *bird of prey*
barn-raising 654.5 *party*
barnstorm 21.35 *overact*
barnstormer 21.24 *actor*
barnstorming 21.22 *acting*
barnyard 43.7 *farm building*
bar of justice 16.18 *tribunal*
barograph 31.7 *weather instruments*
barographic 31.42 *barometric*
barometer **28.88**; 742.5 *indicator*; 26.8 *meter*; 31.7 *weather instruments*
barometric **31.42**; 26.16 *micrometric*
barometry 26.2 *micrometry*
baron 573.1 *nobleman*; 781.10 *wealthy person*
baronet 573.1 *nobleman*
baronetcy 573.2 *aristocracy*
baronial 573.4 *aristocratic*
Baron Münchhausen 727.6 *exaggerator*; 699.18, 700.16 *liar*
barony 86.5 *state*
baroque 19.26 *artistic*; 23.7 *furniture style*; 19.29 *realist*
baroque costume 551.5 *fancy dress*
barperson 401.3 *attendant*
barrack 378.8 *hinder*; 668.25 *taunt*
barracking 668.6 *taunt*; 668.15 *taunting*
barrack-room lawyer 444.6 *arguer*
barracks 584.1 *military affairs*
barracuda 55.4 *American game fish*
barrage 38.23 *dam*; 59.9 *jumping*; 381.12 *military attack*; 38.24 *water system*
barrage balloon 366.10 *elevator*; 586.31 *military aircraft*
barred 378.14 *blocked*; 309.12 *closed*; 670.31 *disapproved*; 128.11 *excluded*; 103.4 *forbidden*; 541.9 *striped*; 399.5 *vetoed*
barred spiral galaxy 29.7 *galaxy*
barred-window boys 36.30, 461.10 *psychiatrist*
barrel 203.3 *container*; 410.11 *vessel*
barrel along 332.4 *be swift*
barrel chair 23.2 *chair*
barrel-chested 152.1 *thick*
barrelling 332.8 *speed*; 332.1 *swift*
barrel printer 40.7 *peripheral*
barrel-racing 59.12 *rodeo*
barrel roll 322.5 *flight*
barrels 208.3 *profuseness*
barrel scale 414.10 *scales*
barrel vault 20.7 *vault*
barren 428.6 *desert*; 238.2 *futile*; 563.3 *infertile*; 335.13 *unsexed*; 98.13 *vacant*
barren cow 43.8 *livestock*
barren land 428.14 *desert*
barrenness 98.3 *emptiness*; 247.1 *failure*; 238.4 *futility*; 563.1 *infertility*; 335.1 *powerlessness*
barren waste 563.1 *infertility*
barrette 373.8 *fastening*
barricade 384.9 *barrier*; 372.6 *boundary*; 128.3 *exclusion zone*; 384.18 *fence*
barricaded 384.30 *defended*
barrier **378.3**; **384.9**; 372.6 *boundary*; 309.1 *closure*; 347.1 *counteraction*; 165.3 *enclosing thing*; 128.3 *exclusion zone*; 103.7, 378.2 *obstacle*; 321.8 *railway station*; 47.1 *track events*
barrier board 58.3 *ice hockey*
barrier contraceptive 563.3 *birth control*
barrier cream 31.22 *sun*
barrier island 30.11 *coast*
barrier method contraception 378.3 *barrier*
barrier reef 30.11 *coast*
barring 212.8 *by subtraction*; 128.12 *exclusively*
barrio 87.7 *city district*
barrister 713.4 *adviser*; 398.6 *agent*; 586.5, 701.6 *arguer*; 16.13 *lawyer*; 705.9 *questioner*
barrister's wig 551.15 *headgear*
barrow 410.10 *cart*; 182.3 *dome*; 583.6 *grave*; 320.7 *handcart*; 43.8 *livestock*; 744.11 *monument*; 154.3 *mountain*; 3.11 *relic*; 779.9 *stall*; 284.7 *thing of the past*
barrow boy 778.11 *pedlar*; 778.14 *street trader*
barry 743.13 *heraldic*
bar sinister 743.8 *heraldic device*
barspoon 55.2 *artificial fly*
bar stool 23.2 *chair*
bartender 401.3 *attendant*; 412.7 *person who mixes*
barter 755.5 *contract*; 13.11 *deal*; 119.3 *equalization*; 224.4, 224.10, 759.1, 759.5 *exchange*; 110.1 *interchange*; 746.1 *negotiation*; 785.6 *pay*; 777.1 *purchase*; 110.7 *reciprocate*; 778.1 *sell*; 778.3 *selling*; 776.1, 776.4 *trade*; 316.1, 316.11 *transfer*
bartered 759.7 *exchanged*; 110.4 *reciprocal*
barterer 13.9 *economist*; 776.10 *trader*
bartering 755.1 *contract*; 110.1 *interchange*; 746.1 *negotiation*
bartizan 384.12 *fort*
barton 43.7 *farm building*
baryon 28.77 *elementary particle*
basal 175.3 *base*; 413.9 *supportive*
basal body 34.8 *cell organ*
basaltic 30.57 *chalky*
basaltware 24.1 *ceramics*
bascule bridge 38.21 *bridge*
Base 175
base **32.9**; **175.1**; **175.3**; **175.4**; 586.14 *armed forces*; 236.3 *bad*; 800.5 *dishonourable*; 668.12 *disregardful*; 565.2 *environment*; 743.8 *heraldic device*; 565.3 *home*; 122.5 *inferior state*; 142.9 *locate*; 142.1 *location*; 27.19 *logarithm*; 155.4 *low thing*; 584.1 *military affairs*; 20.9 *miscellaneous architectural features*; 27.8 *number system*; 122.16 *ordinary*; 313.10 *place of departure*; 484.7 *planning*; 344.3 *rudiment*; 793.10 *shoddy*; 413.2 *supporting part*; 39.19 *transistor*; 27.43 *triangle*; 682.2 *unpleasant*; 804.11 *wicked*
Baseball 48
baseball **48.1**; 48.3 *baseball equipment*
baseball bat 48.3 *baseball equipment*; 587.7 *blunt weapon*; 331.15 *ram*
baseball cap 551.15 *headgear*
baseball equipment 48.3
baseball field 48.1 *baseball*
baseball game 48.1 *baseball*
baseball pass 49.4 *playing terms*
baseball player **48.2**; 336.5 *athlete*
baseball season 292.1 *season*
baseball shoes 48.3 *baseball equipment*
baseball sign 742.3 *gesture*
baseball stadium 48.1 *baseball*
baseball uniform 48.3 *baseball equipment*; 743.5 *uniform*
baseball widow 571.6 *surviving spouse*
baseboard 175.2 *foot*
base camp 62.1 *mountaineering*
base coin 780.15 *false money*
based 143.8 *circumstantial*; 447.7 *focused*
base electrode 39.19 *transistor*
baseless 702.7 *sophistic*
baseline 63.4 *tennis terms*
basely **122.22**
basement 175.2 *foot*; 560.13 *lavatory*; 155.4 *low thing*; 565.7 *room*; 439.4 *storage*; 413.2 *supporting part*
basement price 791.2 *bargain*; 790.3 *fee*
baseness 236.9 *badness*; 800.1 *improbity*; 122.1 *inferiority*; 793.3 *shoddiness*; 682.4 *unpleasantness*; 804.1 *wickedness*
base on balls 48.4 *pitching terms*
baseplate 175.2 *foot*
base runner 48.2 *baseball player*
base troops 586.14 *armed forces*
bash 353.5 *attempt*; 331.13 *blow*; 331.2 *collide*; 331.3 *hit*; 376.9 *social gathering*; 651.18 *torment*
bashful **674.10**; 637.3 *cautious*; 795.9 *pure*; 655.9, 732.1 *shy*
bashfully 674.18 *shyly*; 655.14 *unsocially*
bashfulness **674.3**; 637.13 *dissociation*; 795.3 *moral purity*; 655.2, 732.3 *shyness*
bashi-bazouk 586.8 *soldier*
bashing 331.12 *collision*
bash off 561.9 *reproduce*
bash out 356.10 *produce*; 561.9 *reproduce*
bash up 651.18 *torment*
basic 32.36 *acid*; 175.3 *base*; 344.13 *causal*; 447.7 *focused*; 123.5 *important*; 93.11, 99.6 *intrinsic*; 129.13 *precursory*; 243.16 *preparatory*; 130.35 *rudimentary*; 255.16, 271.1 *simple*; 27.70 *universal*
basically **175.5**; 99.14 *at heart*; 344.14 *causally*; 27.87 *mathematically*; 130.42 *principally*; 93.22 *really*; 271.8 *simply*; 447.14 *thematically*
basic dye 42.6 *dye*
basic English 5.4 *parent language*
basichromatin 34.9 *cell nucleus*
basic ingredient 25.7
basic materials 435.1 *materials*; 402.4 *matter*; 405.3 *unit*
basic palette 529.5 *paint*
basic rock 30.30 *igneous rock*
basics 123.3 *chief thing*; 95.5 *realities*; 344.3 *rudiment*; 130.7 *rudiments*
basic salary 813.4 *reward for service*
basic salt 32.10 *salt*
basic slag 43.13 *fertilizer*
basic substance 402.4 *matter*
basic supplies 352.2 *supplies*
basic swing 68.4 *skiing technique*
basic truth 698.4 *truism*
basidiocarp 83.4 *fungal body*
basidiomycetes 83.3 *fungi*
Basidiomycotina 83.3 *fungi*
basidiospore 83.4 *fungal body*
basidium 83.4 *fungal body*
basil 496.5 *herbs*
basilar 175.3 *base*
basilary 175.3 *base*
basilica 20.10 *church architecture*; 10.11 *place of worship*
basilisk 518.2 *eye*; 587.12 *historical guns*; 70.7 *legendary beast*; 73.2 *lizard*; 73.3 *snake*
basin 256.6, 410.12 *bath*; 183.3 *cavity*; 156.4 *deep thing*; 30.7 *landform*; 29.17 *moon*
basin and ewer 256.6 *bath*
basin and pitcher 256.6 *bath*
basinet 384.7 *armour*
basis 175.1 *base*; 143.2 *circumstances*; 99.2 *essential content*; 444.4 *explanation*; 243.10 *preparations*; 344.5 *reason*; 344.3 *rudiment*; 447.1 *topic*
basis for belief 716.1 *evidence*
basis for negotiations 746.2
basis of supposition 476.2
bask 493.16 *feel hot*; 490.8 *feel pleasure*
basket **410.7**; 49.3 *basketball equipment*; 203.3 *container*; 68.5 *ski equipment*
basket arch 20.5 *arch*
Basketball 49
basketball **49.1**; 49.3 *basketball equipment*; 422.3 *elastic thing*
basketball arena 49.1 *basketball*
basketball equipment 49.3
basketball game 49.1 *basketball*
basketball gym 49.1 *basketball*
basketball gymnasium 49.1 *basketball*
Basketball Hall of Fame 49.1 *basketball*
basketball player **49.2**; 154.7 *tall person*
basketball season 292.1 *season*
basketcase 118.10 *eccentric*
bask in 490.8 *feel pleasure*
bask in the sunshine 248.5 *be prosperous*
bas-relief 608.6 *profile*; 19.13 *relief-carving*
bass 510.3 *deepness*; 25.17 *freshwater fish*; 18.32 *instrumental*; 516.5 *melodist*; 504.10 *sound quality*
bass baritone 510.3 *deepness*
bass clef 18.20 *key*; 18.17 *notation*
Bassenthwaite 88.4 *British lakes*
bassinet 410.7 *basket*
bass note 510.3 *deepness*
basso 510.3 *deepness*
basso continuo 516.4 *harmonics*
basso profondo 510.3 *deepness*
basso rilievo 608.6 *profile*; 19.13 *relief-carving*
bast 373.6 *line*
bastard 804.10 *bad person*; 264.3 *difficult task*; 594.8 *hated person*
bastardize 16.75 *make illegal*
bastard-trench 44.15 *cultivate*
bastard wing 72.17 *plumage*
baste 331.5 *beat*; 25.55 *cook*
Bastille Day 601.5 *anniversary*; 298.6 *annually celebrated day*
bastinado 814.12 *corporal punishment*; 814.3 *hit*
basting 373.8 *fastening*
bastion 384.11 *fortification*; 252.2 *protection*; 252.5 *refuge*
bat **53.7**; **53.17**; **330.26**; **331.10**; 48.3 *baseball equipment*; 519.4 *blind people*; 70.6 *flying animal*; 331.3 *hit*; 331.15 *ram*; 332.8 *speed*; 492.11 *touch*
batch 376.25 *assemblage*; 376.24 *brace*; 376.27 *bundle*; 203.2 *certain amount*; 376.38 *group*
batch processing 40.19 *computing terms*
bate 426.10 *blunt*
bat ears 504.4 *ear*
bated 426.1 *blunt*
bated breath 511.4 *faint sound*
bath **256.6**; **410.12**; 256.6 *bath*; 368.10 *immersion*; 736.6 *privacy*; 433.11 *wash*
Bath bun 25.36 *cake*
Bath chap 25.31 *offal*
bathe **256.14**; 433.34 *hose*
bathed 433.23 *wet*
bathed in sweat 560.28 *sweaty*
bathers 551.21 *beachwear*; 67.8 *swimwear*
bathetic 590.12 *sensitive*
bathing 256.5 *ablutions*; 10.7 *non-Christian ritual*; 67.11 *swimming*; 433.11 *wash*
bathing cap 67.8 *swimwear*
bathing suit 551.21 *beachwear*; 67.8 *swimwear*
bathmat 550.9 *floor covering*
bath oil 502.2 *fragrant thing*
batholith 30.30 *igneous rock*; 30.28 *rock*
bathometer 156.4 *deep thing*; 26.8 *meter*
bathometric 156.13 *bathymetric*; 26.16 *micrometric*
bathometry 156.6 *bathymetry*; 26.2 *micrometry*
bathos 590.7 *emotionalism*; 272.1 *ludicrousness*
bathrobe 552.4 *dishabille*; 551.4, 657.6 *informal dress*; 551.16 *robe*
bathroom 256.6 *bath*; 560.13 *lavatory*; 565.7 *room*; 767.7 *toilet*
bathroom scales 414.10 *scales*
baths 256.6 *bath*; 394.14 *hospital*
bath sponge 75.8 *sponge*
bath towel 256.11 *cleaning cloth*
bathtub 256.6, 410.12 *bath*
bathyal 156.12 *under*
bathymal 30.51 *oceanic*
bathymetric **156.13**; 30.49 *geophysical*; 26.16 *micrometric*; 91.8 *oceanographic*
bathymetrically 30.66 *geographically*; 91.12 *oceanographically*
bathymetry **156.6**; 26.2 *micrometry*; 91.5 *oceanography*; 30.17 *ocean research vessel*
bathypelagic 156.12 *under*
bathyscaph 156.4 *deep thing*; 91.5 *oceanography*; 30.17 *ocean research vessel*
bathysphere 156.4 *deep thing*; 305.8 *descender*; 91.5 *oceanography*; 30.17 *ocean research vessel*
bathythermograph 91.5 *oceanography*
batik 19.1 *art*; 42.7 *dyeing*
bat in a run 48.7 *play baseball*
Bat Kol 8.8 *divine manifestation*
batman 401.3 *attendant*; 401.4 *personal attendant*; 551.28 *valet*
Batman and Robin 336.6 *muscleman*
bat mitzvah 10.7 *non-Christian ritual*

baton 743.8 *heraldic device*; 743.4 *insignia*; 47.9 *track*; 47.1 *track events*
baton change 47.1 *track events*
baton changing 47.1 *track events*
baton round 587.13 *ammunition*
bat out of hell 332.12 *swift animal*
batrachian 73.7, 73.13 *amphibian*
bats 461.11 *insane*
bats in the belfry 461.1 *insanity*
batsman 53.4 *team*
battalion 586.16 *army unit*; 376.14 *force*; 584.4 *military organization*
battalion commander 584.5 *military staff*
battement 22.10 *positions at the barre*
batten 373.12 *bind*; 373.8 *fastening*; 21.19 *stage set*
batten down 309.7 *close*; 228.7 *make stable*
batten down the hatches 309.7 *close*; 243.4 *prepare for action*; 680.6 *save*
battened 373.16 *bound*
battening down the hatches 243.9 *preparation*
batten on 557.22 *eat well*; 664.14 *follow*
battens 50.3 *parts of a sailing boat*; 21.20 *stage lighting*
batter 48.2 *baseball player*; 331.5 *beat*; 121.8 *be superior*; 357.9 *demolish*; 236.14 *ill-treat*; 491.11 *inflict pain*; 351.1 *misuse*; 53.4 *team*
battercake 25.39 *loaf*
battered 245.13 *dilapidated*; 351.4 *misused*
battered women's shelter 252.2 *protection*
batterie 22.9 *ballet steps*
batterie de cuisine 25.6 *kitchen equipment*
battering ram 357.7 *agent of destruction*; 587.7 *blunt weapon*; 331.15 *ram*
batter's box 48.1 *baseball*
batter's helmet 48.3 *baseball equipment*
battery 586.16 *army unit*; 28.43 *electrical conduction*; 334.7 *electrical power*; 437.4 *electricity*; 32.19 *electrochemistry*; 39.5 *electrolytic conduction*; 587.11 *guns*; 584.4 *military organization*; 351.2 *misuse*; 39.29 *power source*; 565.12 *stall*; 439.4 *storage*
battery charger 39.29 *power source*
battery hen 43.8 *livestock*
battery house 43.7 *farm building*
battery of tests 35.7 *diagnosis*
battery radio 692.18 *radio*
battiness 461.1 *insanity*
batting 53.12 *cricketing*
batting average 48.5 *batting terms*
batting champion 48.2 *baseball player*
batting coach 48.2 *baseball player*
batting crease 53.5 *wicket*
batting hit 331.14 *sporting hit*
batting side 53.4 *team*
batting terms 48.5
battle 585.9; **585.14**; 340.1 *action*; 751.6 *argue*; 751.2 *argument*; 113.5 *conflict*; 576.4 *exertion*; 576.8 *exert oneself*; 382.4 *slaughter*
battle-axe 625.3 *irascible person*; 587.8 *sharp weapon*
battle call 585.2 *glory of war*
battle cruiser 586.24 *warship*
battle cry 661.3 *act of defiance*; 514.1 *cry*; 711.2 *danger signal*; 585.2 *glory of war*; 742.6 *word*
battledore 63.10 *badminton*
battledress 551.3, 656.4 *formal dress*
battle fatigue 36.10 *neurosis*
battlefield 585.10 *battleground*; 382.15 *slaughterhouse*
battlefield knowledge 585.6 *art of war*
battlefront 167.1 *front*; 147.7 *interface*
battleground 585.10; 167.1 *front*; 382.15 *slaughterhouse*
battle group 584.4 *military organization*
battle honours 575.3 *honours*
battle-hungry 585.16 *warlike*
battlemaid 586.10 *woman soldier*
battlement 384.11 *fortification*; 252.5 *refuge*
battlemented 384.30 *defended*
battlements 384.12 *fort*
battle orders 585.8 *warfare*
battle painting 19.10 *art subject*
battle plan 585.6 *art of war*
battle plane 586.31 *military aircraft*
battler 586.1 *combatant*
battle royal 585.9 *battle*
battles 585.8 *warfare*
battle-scarred 585.17 *military*
battle scene 21.8 *scene*
battleship 586.25 *historical naval ships*; 586.24 *warship*
battle yell 585.2 *glory of war*
battle zone 585.10 *battleground*
battling 585.15 *warring*
battue 633.2 *chase*; 382.4 *slaughter*
batty 461.11 *insane*
bauble 124.9; 793.5 *cheap item*
baubles 542.7 *jewellery*
baud rate 40.19 *computing terms*
Bauhaus 23.7 *furniture style*
baulk 65.5 *snooker*
baulk cushion 65.3 *English billiards*
baulk line 65.3 *English billiards*; 65.5 *snooker*
baulk-line 65.9 *billiard*; 65.4 *carom*
baulk-line game 65.4 *carom*
baulk-line spot 65.3 *English billiards*
baulk spot 65.5 *snooker*
bawbee 780.10 *former British money*; 124.8 *trifle*
bawd 436.3 *provider*
bawdily 712.12 *swearingly*
bawdiness 796.2 *indecency*
bawdry 796.2 *indecency*
bawdy 712.8 *cursing*; 539.4, 796.12 *indecent*; 675.9 *ribald*
bawdyhouse 796.6 *brothel*
bawdy verse 712.1 *curse*
bawl 514.1, 514.13 *cry*; 514.6 *cry of pain*; 514.10 *cry out*; 729.12 *speak loudly*
bawler 514.9 *crier*
bawling 507.2 *outcry*
bawl out 670.21 *berate*; 514.14 *hiss*
bay 534.1 *brown*; 410.2 *compartment*; 515.4 *cry*; 59.1 *horse*; 92.9 *inlet*; 321.8 *railway station*
Bayard 59.1 *horse*
bay at the moon 515.4 *cry*
Bayerd–Alpert gauge 32.20 *surface chemistry*
baying 515.1 *animal cry*; 59.8 *hunting*
Baykal 88.5 *other major lakes*
bay leaf 496.5 *herbs*
bayo coyote 59.1 *horse*
Bay of Bengal 92.9 *inlet*
Bay of Biscay 92.9 *inlet*
Bayon 10.13 *shrine*
bayonet 308.20 *hole*; 382.17 *murder*; 308.2 *opener*; 425.8 *sharp-pointed thing*; 587.8 *sharp weapon*; 381.6 *stab*; 425.16 *use a sharp tool*
bayoneted 308.14 *holed*
bayonet-fence 54.5 *fence*
bayonet fencing 54.1 *fencing*
bayonetting 381.18 *hit*
bayou 92.9 *inlet*; 92.3 *marsh*; 90.1 *river*; 88.2 *small lake*
bays 743.4 *insignia*
bay window 410.18 *stomach*
bazaar 779.10; 767.2 *disposal of property*; 779.1 *market*; 778.4 *sale*
bazooka 587.11 *guns*; 587.5 *missile weapon*
bazookaman 586.17 *army person*
BBC 692.20 *radio broadcasting*
BBC1 692.24 *television broadcasting*
BBC2 692.24 *television broadcasting*
BBC English 5.6 *official language*
BBC Radio 692.20 *radio broadcasting*
BBC Television 692.24 *television broadcasting*
BBC World Service 692.20 *radio broadcasting*
BBQ 654.5 *party*
BC 275.29 *one day*
BCE 275.29 *one day*
BCG 394.3 *prophylactic*
be 525.11 *appear*; 97.11, 282.5 *be present*; 143.9 *be situated*; 93.17 *exist*; 554.16 *live*
be a back-room boy 674.15 *escape notice*
be a best-seller 778.2 *be sold*
be able 334.10 *be powerful*; 352.6 *find means*
be a botanist 77.23 *study plants*
be about right 216.9 *be average*
be about to 283.8 *intend*
be a breadwinner 576.6 *work*
be absent 98.15; 195.8 *not exist*
be a candidate 752.13
be acclaimed 811.5 *have repute*
be accurate 273.7; **698.31**
be accused 715.7
beach 30.11, 92.4 *coast*; 164.1 *edge*; 164.8 *edging*; 312.4 *land*; 308.8 *open space*; 67.7 *swimming pool*
beach-casting 55.1 *angling*
beachcomber 256.12 *cleaner*; 376.35 *collector*; 258.6 *dirty person*; 124.10 *nonentity*
beachhead 585.10 *battleground*
beach robe 551.21 *beachwear*
beach umbrella 523.6 *shade*
beachwear 551.21
beacon 711.2 *danger signal*; 522.6 *electric light*; 522.8 *fire*; 742.4 *signal*
beacon fire 493.6 *fire*; 742.4 *signal*
be a coward 614.4
be active 342.12
be active in 340.4 *act*
be a customer of 349.2 *frequent*
bead 181.3 *round thing*
be adaptable 422.10
beading 542.3 *pattern*
beadle 16.10 *law officer*; 7.8 *priest*
beadledom 12.3, 396.4 *governance*; 342.9 *overactivity*; 632.6 *procedure*
be admitted 314.9 *enter*
be a doctor 394.20 *doctor*
beadroll 10.14 *sacred object*
beadsman 7.7 *monk*
beads of sweat 560.8 *sweat*
be affected 673.17; **676.4**
be afflicted 491.9 *feel pain*
be a founder member 130.23 *inaugurate*
be afraid 612.11
be afraid of 612.11 *be afraid*
be after 633.12 *aim at*
be against 113.17
be agitated 327.21
beagler 382.13 *animal killer*
beagling 633.2 *chase*; 60.2 *hunting*; 71.23 *mammal hunting*
be agnostic 708.10 *be negative*
be a go-between 748.1 *mediate*
be a good mixer 654.11 *be sociable*
be ahead 121.11 *get ahead*; 164.7 *have an advantage*
be ahead of 167.10 *be in front*
be a hypocrite 700.26
beak 72.16 *avian anatomy*; 400.9 *educational leader*; 20.9 *miscellaneous architectural features*; 396.10 *person of authority*; 185.3 *protuberance*; 500.2 *sense of smell*
beaked 185.5 *protuberant*
beaker 410.13 *drinking vessel*
beaky 185.5 *protuberant*
be alert 342.14 *push*
be a little madam 590.17 *feel deeply*
be alive 554.16 *live*
be alive to 488.11 *sense*
be-all and end-all 204.4 *all*; 482.5 *final intention*; 123.2 *important matter*; 121.1 *superiority*
be all ears 504.15 *hear*
be all eyes 518.13 *look*
be all heart 591.11 *be sensitive*
be all the rage 395.10 *be a prevailing influence*
be alongside 169.7
be always the same 225.5 *be permanent*
beam 598.7 *be cheerful*; 150.4 *breadth*; 579.5 *guide*; 522.1 *light*; 522.25 *light up*; 435.1 *materials*; 373.4 *means of connection*; 50.3 *parts of a sailing boat*; 57.6 *pommel horse*; 522.2 *quality of light*; 597.7 *show joy*; 228.3 *stabilizer*; 38.27 *superstructure*; 413.2 *supporting part*; 23.12 *wood*
be a martyr 491.9 *feel pain*
be ambiguous 180.7; 479.1 *be equivocal*
be ambivalent 699.27 *evade*
beam bridge 38.21 *bridge*
beamed 23.16 *joined*
beamer 53.8 *delivery*
beaming 598.1 *cheerful*; 522.15 *lucent*
beam reaching 50.1 *sailing*
beamy 150.1 *broad*
bean 44.11 *vegetable*
be anarchic 588.4
be anarchistic 588.4 *be anarchic*
be an architect 20.18
be an authority on 396.22
bean counter 789.6 *accountant*
bean curd 25.21 *meat substitute*
beanery 557.15 *eating place*
be an expert on 396.22 *be an authority on*
beanfeast 688.3 *act of gluttony*; 601.1 *celebration*; 557.13 *feast*; 490.4 *pleasurable things*; 376.9 *social gathering*
be angry 624.11; 327.21 *be agitated*
beanie 551.23 *children's clothes*; 551.15 *headgear*
be an instrument 348.4
beano 688.3 *act of gluttony*; 557.13 *feast*; 600.1 *rejoicing*; 376.9 *social gathering*
be a nobody 216.9 *be average*
beanpole 44.6 *garden tool*; 154.7, 158.11 *tall person*; 153.9 *thin person*
beans 43.12 *crop*
be anxious for 612.14 *worry*
be apathetic 489.11 *be unfeeling*
be a pedant 698.32 *be literal*
be a prevailing influence 395.10
be a prima donna 590.17 *feel deeply*
Bear 88.3 *US lakes*
bear 413.12; 562.6 *be fertile*; 793.9 *cheap*; 659.4 *discourteous person*; 14.6 *financial*; 60.5 *game*; 331.1 *impel*; 14.5 *invest*; 625.3 *irascible person*; 130.26, 356.10 *produce*; 561.10 *reproduce oneself*; 253.3 *security officer*; 778.9 *seller*; 776.2 *speculate*; 14.3 *stockbroker*; 388.4 *succumb*; 626.5 *sullen person*; 413.11 *support*; 324.7 *take a direction*; 316.12 *transport*
bearable 231.4 *ordinary*; 413.10 *supportable*
bear a charmed life 252.9 *be safe*
bear a date 281.15 *chronologize*
bear a grudge 651.16 *be malevolent*; 594.14 *hate*; 624.8 *resent*
bear allegiance 663.5 *obey*
bear allegiance to 797.18 *be good*; 387.8 *be subject to*
bear and dog 586.4 *fighting animal*
bear and ragged staff 743.8 *heraldic device*
bear-baiting 71.23 *mammal hunting*
bear comparison 235.9 *be worthy*
beard 613.15 *be courageous*; 551.5 *fancy dress*; 420.7 *rough thing*; 425.8 *sharp-pointed thing*
bearded 420.3 *barbed*
beardless 552.13 *hairless*; 555.11 *young*
beardlessness 552.5 *baldness*
bear down 50.15 *sail*
bear down on 367.5; 381.1 *attack*; 386.6 *compel*; 236.14 *ill-treat*; 638.9 *undertake*
beard worm 75.6 *worm*
bearer 320.5 *pack*; 316.7 *transferor*
bearer bond 780.14 *paper money*
bear false witness 715.6 *accuse falsely*
bear for 324.7 *take a direction*
bear fruit 246.8 *be effective*; 237.10 *benefit*; 80.10 *fruit*; 244.2 *get better*; 345.8 *grow*; 561.11 *have young*
bear garden 408.5 *confusion*; 412.3 *miscellany*
bear hard upon 414.14 *make heavy*
bear hug 593.14 *communication of love*; 360.1 *retention*
bear hunt 633.2 *chase*; 60.2 *hunting*
bear hunting 60.2 *hunting*
bear ill will 651.16 *be malevolent*
bearing 324.2; 27.39 *angle*; 307.4 *axle*; 631.1 *conduct*; 324.1 *direction*; 137.9 *distinction*; 525.3 *external appearance*; 300.12 *gait*; 743.8 *heraldic device*; 38.8 *machine element*; 694.1 *meaning*; 108.1 *relatedness*; 38.27 *superstructure*; 104.2 *tendency*
bearing arms 585.17 *military*
bearing in mind 462.8 *remembering*
bearing off 50.1 *sailing*
bearing out 703.4 *proof*
bearing plate 38.27 *superstructure*
bearings 27.39 *angle*; 324.1 *direction*; 142.2 *exact location*; 323.5 *navigation*; 324.3 *orientation*; 143.1 *situation*
bearing the cost 785.1 *payment*
bear in mind 462.11 *memorize*
bear interest 211.6 *add*
bearish 71.28 *carnivorous*; 793.9 *cheap*; 305.16 *descending*; 659.5 *discourteous*; 625.4 *irascible*
bearish market 218.9 *scarcity*
bearishness 793.2 *declining prices*
bearlike 71.28 *carnivorous*
bear malice 651.16 *be malevolent*; 624.8 *resent*
bear malice towards 594.14 *hate*
bear market 793.2 *declining prices*; 214.3 *decreasing thing*; 249.2 *economic adversity*; 13.6 *economic factors*; 779.3 *sellers' market*; 14.2 *stock exchange*
béarnaise sauce 25.15 *sauce*
bear no malice 649.12 *show mercy*

bear no resemblance 116.5 *be dissimilar*
bear off 189.6 *be oblique*; 325.1 *deviate*; 50.15 *sail*
bear oneself 631.11 *conduct oneself*
be around 170.7 *surround*
bear out 95.12 *establish reality*; 454.2, 703.17 *prove*
bear resemblance 115.10 *be similar*
bearskin 384.7 *armour*
bear the blame 806.8 *be guilty*
bear the brunt 264.20 *be in difficulty*; 249.9 *be in trouble*; 384.28 *survive*
bear the cost 785.8 *defray*
bear the cost of 777.5 *defray*
bear the costs 787.3 *donate*
bear the marks of 742.10 *signify*
bear the palm 121.8 *be superior*
bear the stamp of 345.7 *follow from*; 742.10 *signify*
bear up 336.7 *be strong*
bear upon 331.1 *impel*; 395.8 *influence*; 108.7 *relate to*; 346.9 *take action*
bear up to 324.7 *take a direction*
bear with 648.3 *be lenient*; 649.12 *show mercy*
bear witness 715.5 *accuse*; 707.18 *vow*
bear witness to 716.11 *give evidence*; 742.10 *signify*
be ashamed 623.24 *be humiliated*
be a shining light 803.8 *be virtuous*
be asking for trouble 264.21 *get into trouble*
be assertive 707.21
beast 70.2 *animal*; 258.6 *dirty person*; 122.6 *inferior*; 242.9 *unpleasant person*; 380.4 *violent creature*
beast fable 17.2 *fiction*
beastlike 70.14 *animalian*
beastliness 236.9 *badness*; 651.4 *bitterness*; 659.1 *discourtesy*; 798.1 *evil*; 594.4 *hatefulness*; 242.6 *objectionability*; 258.2 *uncleanness*; 682.4 *unpleasantness*
beastly 70.14 *animalian*; 236.3 *bad*; 651.11 *cruel*; 659.5 *discourteous*; 798.7 *evil*; 594.12 *hated*; 651.14 *hostile*; 242.2 *objectionable*; 258.8 *unclean*; 682.2 *unpleasant*; 804.11 *wicked*
beast of burden 316.6; 70.3 *domesticated animal*; 59.1 *horse*; 578.1 *worker*
beast of prey 382.13 *animal killer*; 60.5 *game*; 633.6 *hunter*
beasts 43.8 *livestock*
beasts of the field 122.6 *inferior*
be a substitute 762.4
be a surprise 630.11 *amaze*
beat 327.10; **331.5**; **427.26**; 327.22 *agitate*; 381.9 *attack successfully*; 121.8 *be superior*; 246.9 *be victorious*; 633.2 *chase*; 256.13 *clean*; 25.55 *cook*; 298.2 *cycle*; 509.8 *drum*; 509.1 *drumming*; 261.1 *fatigued*; 54.3 *fencing movements*; 516.4 *harmonics*; 814.3 *hit*; 633.11 *hunt*; 335.12 *impotent*; 491.11 *inflict pain*; 86.13 *locality*; 142.1 *location*; 400.14 *master*; 17.9 *metre*; 351.1 *misuse*; 275.12 *musical time*; 306.3 *orbit*; 246.11 *overmaster*; 318.1 *passage*; 298.1 *regularity*; 298.5 *regular thing*; 112.22 *resound*; 112.6 *reverberation*; 317.2 *route*; 50.15 *sail*; 327.24 *shake*; 60.7 *shoot*; 18.38 *sound*; 18.19 *tempo*; 651.18 *torment*; 118.13 *unconventional*; 349.1 *use*; 326.9 *vibrate*; 326.2 *vibration*; 326.5 *wave*; 434.23 *whisk*
be at 525.11 *appear*
beat about the bush 616.5 *be cautious*; 270.6 *be circuitous*; 479.1 *be equivocal*; 634.7 *be evasive*; 100.13 *be extraneous*; 306.8 *detour*; 736.13 *equivocate*; 702.13 *quibble*; 384.25 *stall*
beat a hasty retreat 614.4 *be a coward*; 389.5 *escape*
beat all comers 246.9 *be victorious*
be at a loss 264.20 *be in difficulty*
beat a retreat 252.9 *be safe*; 634.8 *run away*; 742.12 *signal*; 313.2 *withdraw*
beat around the bush 100.13 *be extraneous*
beat a strategic retreat 384.28 *survive*
beat a tattoo 509.8 *drum*; 601.18 *salute*
beat black and blue 814.3 *hit*; 491.11 *inflict pain*
beat down 776.3 *bargain*; 793.14 *buy cheaply*; 357.9 *demolish*
be at ease 609.7 *be satisfied*
beaten 317.15 *accessible*; 25.56 *culinary*; 247.11 *defeated*; 632.10 *familiar*; 351.4 *misused*; 122.18 *outclassed*; 814.20 *punished*; 349.9 *used*
beaten flat 187.9 *flattened*
beaten track 620.2 *boring thing*; 317.2 *route*; 632.3 *way*
beater 327.14 *agitator*; 60.4, 633.6 *hunter*; 25.6 *kitchen equipment*; 412.6 *mixer*
be at fault 806.8 *be guilty*
beat flat 187.7 *make horizontal*
beat hollow 329.3 *exceed*
be at home to 769.10 *receive someone*
beatific 797.6 *beneficial*
beatification 8.9 *deification*; 366.7 *lift*; 575.1 *right*
beatified 8.15 *deified*; 366.12 *exalted*
beatified soul 8.10 *deified person*
beatify 8.17 *deify*; 366.3 *promote*
beating 327.10 *beat*; 633.2 *chase*; 331.12 *collision*; 814.12 *corporal punishment*; 247.2 *defeat*; 509.1, 509.15 *drumming*; 60.2 *hunting*; 427.4 *pulverization*; 298.11 *regular*; 112.15 *reverberatory*; 50.1 *sailing*; 326.14 *vibrating*; 326.2 *vibration*; 246.2 *victory*
beating about the bush 270.2 *circumlocution*; 702.4 *quibbling*
beating heart 554.1 *life*
beating up 79.6 *tree management*
beat it 313.15 *go!*; 371.33 *go away!*; 634.24 *hands off!*; 313.4 *hurry off*; 634.9 *play truant*
beatnik 100.5, 118.7 *nonconformist*
be at odds 517.11 *disagree*
beat of drum 711.2 *danger signal*
beat off 364.3 *fend off*
be at one 750.21 *be in accord*; 516.8 *harmonize*
beat one's breast 808.5 *do penance*; 603.6 *lament*
be at peace 589.5
beat poet 17.14 *author*
be a trendsetter 483.9 *motivate*
be at sea 696.9 *find unintelligible*
beat someone hollow 121.8 *be superior*
beat swords into ploughshares 589.5 *be at peace*; 749.5 *make peace*
be attentive 471.10
beat the air 238.9 *waste effort*
beat the big drum 740.14 *proclaim*
be at the brink 164.5 *border*
beat the drum 585.14 *battle*; 742.12 *signal*
beat the record 121.8 *be superior*
be at the station 312.8 *meet*
beat time 298.7 *be regular*; 281.16 *measure time*; 275.16 *time*; 326.9 *vibrate*
beat to a pulp 246.10 *defeat heavily*
beat to death 382.17 *murder*
beat to windward 323.9 *navigate*
beat up 327.22 *agitate*; 331.5 *beat*; 491.11 *inflict pain*; 381.5 *strike*; 651.18 *torment*; 380.8 *use violence*
be at variance 751.8 *be different*
be at war 585.13
Beau 551.27 *model*
beau 545.4 *attractive male*; 567.4 *boyfriend*; 593.9 *lover*
Beau Brummel 551.27 *model*
Beaufort scale 31.13 *wind strength*
beau geste 340.2 *deed*
beaujolais 558.9 *wine*
beau monde 573.2 *aristocracy*; 553.6 *fashionable élite*; 654.7 *human society*; 781.11 *the rich*
be auspicious 248.7; **756.9**
be austere 647.7 *be unadorned*
beaut 797.17 *good thing*
beauteous 545.5 *beautiful*
beauteousness 545.1 *gorgeousness*
be authoritarian 396.19
beautician 547.13; 256.12 *cleaner*; 365.8 *masseur*
Beautification 547
beautification 244.5 *improvement*; 393.8 *repair*
beautified 547.14; 244.14 *improved*; 542.10 *ornate*
beautiful 545.5; 525.10 *aspectual*; 543.3 *elegant*; 162.5 *even*; 593.22 *lovable*
beautiful handwriting 695.10 *simplicity*
beautifully 543.5 *elegantly*
beautifully handwritten 695.2 *simple*
beautiful people 295.6 *avant-garde*; 553.6 *fashionable élite*; 781.11 *the rich*
beautiful thing 545.2
beautify 545.8; **547.15**; 551.33 *dress up*; 244.1 *improve*; 542.12 *ornament*
Beauty 545
beauty 545.3 *attractive female*; 543.1, 549.1 *elegance*; 162.3 *evenness*; 235.8 *exceller*; 525.3 *external appearance*; 545.1 *gorgeousness*; 593.4 *lovability*; 485.3 *masterpiece*; 28.78 *quantum*
beauty and the beast 113.3 *opposites*
beauty parlour 547.12
beauty queen 545.3 *attractive female*
beauty salon 547.12 *beauty parlour*
beauty shop 547.12 *beauty parlour*
beauty specialist 547.13 *beautician*
beauty treatment 547.3
beauty unadorned 728.4 *simplicity*
beaux arts 19.1 *art*
be available to one 397.12
beaver 384.7 *armour*; 342.10 *busy person*; 551.15 *headgear*; 578.1 *worker*
be average 216.9
beaver away 342.15 *try*; 576.6 *work*
beaver pelt 550.14 *animal covering*
beaverskin 551.15 *headgear*
be aware 488.11 *sense*
be aware of 590.15 *feel*; 488.11 *sense*; 518.16 *visualize*
be a wet blanket 602.9 *despair*; 481.5 *discourage*
be beautiful 545.7
be behind 168.6 *be in the rear*
be behindhand 294.6 *be late*
be behind time 262.2 *make haste*
be believed 450.10
be benevolent 650.8
be bent on 635.13 *intend*
be beside 147.18 *juxtapose*
be better than nothing 239.6 *be convenient*
be beyond one's reach 696.7 *be unintelligible*
be biased 120.6 *be unjust*; 802.22 *discriminate*; 229.4 *tend*
be big 158.19
be blind 519.14
be blind to 519.16
bebop 22.2 *dance*; 18.8 *jazz*
bebopper 22.5 *dancer*
be boring 620.6
be born 554.18; 93.18 *come to be*; 130.27 *emerge*; 561.11 *have young*
be born again 760.10 *be converted*; 393.4 *be restored*
be bound to happen 104.8 *be probable*
be brief 723.10
be brittle 424.4
be broad 150.9
be broad-minded 150.12
be broke 135.11 *be needy*
be brought 312.7
be brushed off 48.7 *play baseball*
be busy 288.8; **342.13**; 576.6 *work*
be called out 35.19 *practise medicine*
becalm 301.9 *make motionless*
be calm 684.7
becalmed 341.3 *inactive*; 301.4 *motionless*
be capable of 334.10 *be powerful*
be capricious 642.5
be careful 665.10
be careless 618.14
be cast away 323.10 *sail*
be caught short 560.16 *defecate*
because 344.14 *causally*
because of 345.12 *with the effect of*
be cautious 616.5; 665.10 *be careful*
be celibate 572.9
be central to 99.10 *be essential*
be certain 452.20
béchamel sauce 25.15 *sauce*
be changeable 227.11
be changed 224.7; 760.8 *be transformed*
be charitable 650.9; **652.7**
becharm 593.28 *win the love of*
becharmed 593.19 *enamoured*
be chaste 572.10 *be continent*
be chastised 385.4 *serve one right*
be cheap 793.12
bêche-de-mer 75.3 *echinoderm*
be cheerful 598.7
be childless 563.7 *be infertile*
be circuitous 270.6
beck 397.2 *demand*; 90.1 *river*
beck and call 397.2 *demand*
beckon 742.11 *gesture*
beckoning look 742.3 *gesture*
becloud 736.9 *disguise*; 524.10 *make dim*
be clumsy 486.7
be coerced 386.8 *be compelled*
be cold 494.10
be cold-shouldered 623.24 *be humiliated*
become 810.14 *be the duty of*; 93.18 *come to be*; 760.7 *convert into*
become a born-again Christian 808.4 *be penitent*; 807.7 *be punished*
become acceptable 632.17 *become a habit*
become addicted 632.18 *habituate*
become adult 232.5 *be complete*
become a factor 108.7 *relate to*
become a favourite 593.25 *be loved*
become a free agent 250.16 *be independent*
become aggravated 607.7
become agitated about 753.6 *protest*
become a habit 632.17
become a hostage 387.8 *be subject to*
become airborne 304.19 *take off*
become a karate expert 52.13 *practise judo*
become alive to 693.15 *be informed*
become aloof 618.12 *be indifferent*
become a martyr 752.12 *offer one's life*
become a member 764.4 *have joint possession*
become a misanthrope 653.4
become a nation 85.17
become a new man 479.2 *equivocate*; 259.6 *get healthy*
become angry 624.12; 753.6 *protest*
become an heir 769.9 *receive*
become an in-patient 260.24 *be unhealthy*
become annoyed 625.6 *be irascible*
become an object lesson 486.6 *act foolishly*
become anorexic 766.9 *lose*; 214.5 *make smaller*
become an out-patient 260.24 *be unhealthy*
become a patient 260.24 *be unhealthy*
become apparent 695.4 *be intelligible*
become a prisoner 766.9 *lose*
become a self-made man 246.6 *be successful*
become a slave 387.8 *be subject to*
become a teetotaller 689.4 *give up alcohol*
become attached to 593.24 *be in love*
become autonomous 85.17 *become a nation*
become available 525.13 *occur*
become aware of 6.23 *learn*
become betrothed to 756.7 *promise*
become bigger 190.6
become black-and-blue 492.13 *be touched by*
become celebrated 340.4 *act*
become champion 246.9 *be victorious*
become choppy 91.10 *billow*
become cold 494.11
become complete 232.5 *be complete*
become convalescent 259.6 *get healthy*
become corrupt 804.16 *be wicked*
become dark 523.13
become different 224.7 *be changed*
become dilapidated 245.1 *deteriorate*
become dim 524.9 *be dim*
become disenfranchised 766.9 *lose*
become disorganized 588.5 *misgovern*
become dry 428.17 *dry*
become enamoured with 593.24 *be in love*
become endangered 214.4 *decrease*
become enemies 372.11 *divide*
become engaged 756.7 *promise*; 593.28 *win the love of*
become entangled with 412.10 *become mixed*
become extinct 214.4 *decrease*; 582.15 *die*; 526.1 *disappear*; 131.19 *expire*; 284.14 *pass*
become famous 740.18; 340.4 *act*; 248.5 *be prosperous*
become fazed by 619.9 *wonder*
become green 538.17 *green*
become grey 524.9 *be dim*
become grown-up 232.5 *be complete*
become impoverished 766.12 *lessen*
become independent 85.17 *become a nation*
become inextricably linked with 412.10 *become mixed*
become infected 755.6 *catch*
become inferior 122.11

become insane 461.14
become inseparable 569.13 *befriend*
become insolvent 786.9 *be unable to pay;* 247.6 *fail;* 766.10 *have a financial loss;* 249.10 *need money*
become invisible 521.7; 214.4 *decrease;* 526.1 *disappear*
become involved with 412.10 *become mixed;* 127.5 *be included*
become irrelevant 109.10 *be unrelated*
become known 739.9 *be disclosed*
become larger 765.10 *augment;* 190.6 *become bigger;* 213.4 *increase*
become law 345.9 *take effect*
become mixed 412.10
become new 295.17
become obsolete 245.1 *deteriorate;* 526.1 *disappear;* 296.17 *grow old*
become one 197.19; 570.15 *marry*
become opaque 528.10 *be opaque*
become overweight 190.6 *become bigger*
become part of one 632.17 *become a habit*
become possessed of 289.11 *follow in office*
become proficient 400.15 *learn*
become public knowledge 739.9 *be disclosed;* 740.17 *be published*
become rancid 245.2 *decay*
become red 624.12 *become angry*
become redundant 15.11 *conduct industrial relations*
become runny 268.17 *liquefy*
become sane 460.6 *be sane*
become scarce 214.4 *decrease*
become self-governing 85.17 *become a nation*
become shabby 245.1 *deteriorate*
become silent 506.1 *be silent*
become smaller 191.6
become solid 416.8 *be dense*
become stronger 336.7 *be strong*
become tainted with 412.10 *become mixed*
become teetotal 689.4 *give up alcohol*
become thick 416.8 *be dense*
become thin 153.14
become threadbare 245.1 *deteriorate*
become transparent 527.11 *be transparent*
become turbulent 91.10 *billow*
become unconscious 335.6 *be powerless*
become visible 525.12; 520.9 *appear*
become weary 261.5 *be fatigued*
be comfortable 222.14
becoming 760.14 *converting*
becoming dim 524.3 *dimming*
becoming law 16.31 *legislation*
becoming presentable 545.6 *personable*
be compelled 386.8
be complete 232.5
be composed of 405.11 *consist of*
be concave 183.8
be concerned with 447.10 *focus on*
be concise 269.4
be consecutive 132.13
be consequent upon 289.10 *succeed*
be consistent 750.25 *conform*
be conspicuous 743.11 *identify oneself;* 185.8 *protrude*
be contemporary 285.6 *be simultaneous*
be continent 572.10
be continuous 132.14 *continue*
be contrary 113.16
be convenient 239.6
be conventional 750.25 *conform*
be converted 760.10; 224.7 *be changed;* 7.19 *be religious*
be convex 182.5
be convinced 452.20 *be certain*
be counted 469.5 *vote*
be courageous 613.15
be courted 593.25 *be loved*
be courteous 658.10
be crazy about 593.24 *be in love*
be crestfallen 604.5
be criminal 800.10
be cunning 645.5
be curious 644.7
be cut in 770.5 *get one's allotment*
be cut up 602.8 *grieve*
be cyclic 298.8
bed 23.6; 175.1 *base;* 187.3 *flat thing;* 411.1 *layer;* 44.3 *ornamental garden;* 43.18 *practise livestock farming;* 252.5 *refuge;* 413.4 *rest;* 226.5, 301.3 *resting place;* 30.31 *sedimentary rock*
be damp 429.15 *be moist*
bed and board 565.10 *hotel;* 436.1 *provision*
bed and breakfast 565.10 *hotel;* 436.1 *provision*
be dark 523.12
be dated 281.15 *chronologize;* 275.17 *date*
bedazzle 457.10 *bemuse;* 519.15 *blind;* 522.24 *light;* 593.28 *win the love of*
bedazzling 519.11 *blinding*
bedbug 76.3 *pest*
bed canopy 550.10 *bed covering*
bedchamber 565.7 *room*
bedclothes 550.10 *bed covering*
bed cover 550.10 *bed covering*
bed covering 550.10
bedding 550.10 *bed covering;* 411.1 *layer;* 30.31 *sedimentary rock*
bedding out 44.5 *gardening*
bedding plane 30.18 *earth's crust;* 187.3 *flat thing*
bedding plant 44.9 *garden plant*
bed down 263.2 *take it easy*
be dead 582.15 *die*
be deaf 505.8
be dear 792.9
be deceitful 699.23
be deceived 700.24
bedeck 551.33 *dress up*
bedecked 551.29 *dressed*
be deeply in debt 782.13 *lose one's money*
be defeated 247.7; 388.3 *submit*
be definite 707.22 *emphasize*
be delivered 312.7 *be brought*
be dense 416.8
be dependent upon 122.10 *follow*
be derived from 345.7 *follow from*
be desirable 617.16
be destroyed 357.13
bedevil 696.7 *be unintelligible;* 11.21 *bewitch;* 264.22 *cause trouble;* 8.18 *devilize;* 357.11 *ruin*
bedevilled 11.19 *bewitched*
bedevilment 11.3 *witchcraft*
be devoted to 9.7 *worship*
bedewed 429.10 *misty*
bedgown 551.22 *nightwear*
bed hopping 796.3 *sexual immorality*
be different 751.8; 100.17 *not conform*
be difficult 264.17
be diffuse 270.5
bedight 551.30 *dressed-up*
bedim 530.6 *decolour;* 736.9 *disguise;* 524.10 *make dim*
be dim 524.9
bed in 368.5 *inset*
be dirty 258.10
be disappointed 604.4
be disclosed 739.9
be discourteous 659.7
be discovered 449.5
be dishonest 604.8; 800.8 *be dishonourable;* 700.23 *deceive*
be dishonourable 800.8
be disinterested 473.6
be disjoined 311.12 *separate*
be dismissed 315.14; 350.7 *stop work*
be disobedient 662.15
be disordered 408.25
be disorderly 408.26
be dispersed 377.9
be disposed 229.4 *tend*
be disposed to 4.22 *propound a philosophy*
be dissatisfied 606.7
be dissimilar 116.5
be distant 145.5
be diverse 114.8
bedizen 551.33 *dress up*
bedizened 551.30 *dressed-up*
bedizenment 551.5 *fancy dress*
bed jacket 551.4 *informal dress;* 551.22 *nightwear;* 551.16 *robe*
Bedlam 461.8 *mental hospital*
bedlam 328.5 *commotion;* 408.5 *confusion;* 517.2 *dissonant noise;* 507.2 *outcry*
bed linen 550.10 *bed covering*
bed of nails 807.2 *apology*
bed of roses 78.9 *figurative usage;* 502.2 *fragrant thing;* 490.5 *idealized pleasure;* 589.1 *peace;* 248.1 *prosperity*
be done with 131.15 *end*
be dormant 77.22
bed out 44.15 *cultivate;* 368.6 *plant*
bedpan 560.14, 767.7 *toilet*
bedraggle 258.11 *dirty;* 408.24 *make disordered*
bedraggled 258.7 *dirty;* 408.15 *untidy*
bedridden 301.5 *sedentary;* 260.22 *sick*
be driving at 694.10 *mean*
bedrock 175.1 *base;* 123.3 *chief thing;* 123.5 *important;* 155.4 *low thing;* 344.3 *rudiment;* 30.27 *sediment;* 255.8 *simplicity;* 228.4 *stable thing;* 413.2 *supporting part*
bedroom 736.6 *privacy;* 252.5 *refuge;* 565.7 *room*
bedroom couch 226.5 *resting place*
bedroom farce 21.12 *comedy*
bedroom suburb 87.8 *suburb*
be drunk 690.7
bedsheet 550.10 *bed covering*
bedside lamp 522.6 *electric light*
bedside manner 394.13 *therapy*
bedside table 23.4 *table*
bedsit 565.5 *house*
bedsocks 551.22 *nightwear*
bedspread 550.10 *bed covering*
bedspring 422.5 *spring*
bedstead 23.6 *bed*
bedtime 291.2 *night*
be due to 345.7 *follow from*
be duped 604.4 *be disappointed*
bed-wetting 560.3 *urination*
be dying for 617.12 *desire*
bee 342.10 *busy person;* 76.1 *insect;* 654.10 *social animal;* 76.4 *social insect;* 578.1 *worker*
be early 293.7
be easy 265.15
be easy as pie 265.15 *be easy*
Beeb 692.20 *radio broadcasting*
be eccentric 299.7 *be unusual*
beechen 79.15 *woody*
beech mast 557.8 *animal food;* 79.4 *trees*
beef 25.22; **25.23**; 626.11 *be irritable;* 414.4 *heaviness;* 25.20 *meat;* 753.1, 753.6 *protest*
beefburger 25.20 *meat*
beefcake 567.4 *boyfriend;* 336.6 *muscleman;* 41.4 *portrait*
beef congee 25.48 *Chinese dish*
beef farm 43.6 *farm*
beef farmer 43.15 *agriculturist*
beef farming 43.3 *livestock farming*
be effective 246.8
be efficacious 246.8 *be effective*
beefiness 414.4 *heaviness;* 158.6 *squatness;* 336.1 *strength*
beefing 626.7 *irritable*
beef mountain 43.2 *Common Agricultural Policy*
beef ranch 43.6 *farm*
beef road 320.2 *road*
beef sausage 25.29 *sausage*
beef up 213.5 *make bigger;* 384.20 *reinforce;* 336.8 *strengthen*
beefy 414.1 *heavy;* 336.9 *physically strong;* 158.17 *stocky*
be egoistic 683.7
be egotistic 683.7 *be egoistic*
beehive 342.6 *business;* 182.3 *dome;* 547.8 *haircut;* 565.13 *lair;* 76.4 *social insect*
beehive kiln 24.6 *ceramic workshop*
beehive tomb 583.6 *grave;* 284.7 *thing of the past*
bee in the bonnet 642.3 *whim*
beekeeper 76.8 *entomologist*
beekeeping 76.7 *study*
be elastic 422.8
be elegant 543.4
be eliminated 247.7 *be defeated*
beeline 324.2 *bearing;* 178.7 *straight line*
be elsewhere 472.12 *be inattentive*
Beelzebub 8.7 *devil*
be emaciated 153.15
be enfranchised 469.5 *vote*
be engaged 288.8 *be busy*
be enough 216.9 *be average;* 217.4 *suffice*
be entitled to 575.7; 801.13 *be right*
be equal 111.10; **119.10**
be equal to 119.10 *be equal*
be equivocal 479.1
beer 690.12 *alcohol;* 558.7 *alcoholic drink*
beer barrel 410.11 *vessel*
beer belly 158.8 *fat*
beer bottle 410.14 *bottle*
beer bread 25.38 *bread*
beer garden 44.2 *garden*
beer glass 410.13 *drinking vessel*
beergut 182.2 *bulge;* 410.18 *stomach*
beeriness 690.11 *drinking*
beer party 654.5 *party*
beery 690.5 *drunken;* 690.6 *intoxicating*
bee's knees 235.8 *exceller*
be essential 99.10
beestings 71.2 *mammalian characteristic;* 558.5 *milk*
beeswax 430.2 *adhesive;* 268.18 *lubricate;* 76.4 *social insect*
be eternal 279.5; 202.9 *be infinite*
beet harvester 43.10 *farm tool*
beetle 154.15 *be high;* 76.1 *insect;* 44.12 *pests and diseases;* 361.11 *project*
beetle-browed 361.8 *projecting*
beetle-crushers 551.19 *footwear*
beetle off 313.4 *hurry off*
beetling 154.9 *high;* 361.8 *projecting*
beet planter 43.10 *farm tool*
beetroot 540.3 *purple thing;* 535.7 *red thing*
beetroot-red 535.1 *red*
beet sugar 498.2 *sweetener*
be evasive 634.7
be everywhere 97.11 *be present*
be evil 798.11
be exalted 185.9 *be prominent*
be excessive 219.4
be excluded 128.9
be exclusive 166.7 *limit*
be exempt 758.11
be expert 485.11
be exterior 171.11
be external 100.16
be extinguished 523.13 *become dark*
be extraneous 100.13
be extravagant 727.9
be fair 801.14
befall 107.10 *chance*
be false 699.20; **700.27**; 234.12 *distort the truth*
be famous 811.5 *have repute*
Befana 11.11 *ghost*
be fast 293.7 *be early;* 288.5 *mistime*
be fatigued 261.5
be favourable 569.16
be fearful 612.12
be fearful for 612.14 *worry*
be fed up 217.6 *have enough*
be fertile 562.6
be feverish 493.16 *feel hot*
be fictitious 195.8 *not exist*
be financially worthwhile 765.13 *be profitable*
be finished with 350.6 *stop using*
be fired 226.7 *stop working*
be first 167.10 *be in front*
befit 239.6 *be convenient;* 617.16 *be desirable;* 810.14 *be the duty of*
be fit for 334.10 *be powerful*
befit the occasion 287.4 *be timely*
befit the time 287.4 *be timely*
befitting 239.1 *convenient;* 750.16 *fitting;* 287.6 *timely*
befittingly 750.38 *fittingly;* 287.9 *opportunely;* 801.18 *properly*
be fleeting 278.4 *be transient*
befog 736.9 *disguise;* 31.64 *fog;* 524.10 *make dim*
befool 349.3 *exploit;* 773.10 *take away;* 604.7 *thwart;* 700.28 *trick*
befooled 700.36 *deceived*
befooling 700.7 *tricking*
be foolish 459.6
before 129.20; 296.20 *formerly;* 167.11 *in front;* 97.16 *on the spot*
before all 738.16 *manifestly*
before everything 130.40 *first*
before God 738.16 *manifestly*
beforehand 129.20 *before;* 293.16 *premature;* 293.20 *prematurely*
be foreign 100.14
before long 293.18 *soon*
beforementioned 129.11 *prior*
before now 284.23; 296.20 *formerly;* 3.24 *historically*
before one 738.16 *manifestly*
before one knows it 280.8 *immediately*
before one's eyes 97.10 *available;* 518.23 *visible*
before one's very eyes 97.16 *on the spot*
before the bar 464.10 *judged*
before the bench 16.81 *legally*
before the committee 447.13 *problematically*
before the Flood 3.15 *historic*
before the house 447.13 *problematically*
before the judge 715.10 *accusingly;* 16.87 *in litigation*

before the mast 323.12 *nautically*
before the wind 324.11 *in all directions*
before time 293.17 *early*
be forgetful 463.14; 672.6 *be ungrateful*
be forgotten 463.12
be formal 160.8; **656.11**
be fortunate 248.6
befoul 798.11 *be evil*; 258.11 *dirty*
befouled 258.7 *dirty*
be found 312.1 *arrive*; 93.17 *exist*
be found at 297.8 *frequent*
be fragile 424.4 *be brittle*
be fragrant 502.5
be fraudulent 699.25; **700.30**
be free 250.14
be frequent 297.7
befriend 569.13; 223.14 *keep company with*
befriender 652.3 *philanthropist*
be friendly with 569.13 *befriend*
be frightened 612.11 *be afraid*
be fruitful 80.10 *fruit*
befuddle 690.9 *be intoxicating*; 457.10 *bemuse*; 408.22 *discompose*
befuddlement 690.10 *drunkenness*
be full 232.5 *be complete*
be full of blarney 699.22 *be hypocritical*
be full of oneself 673.15 *be vain*
be full of vigour 338.2
be funny 272.7 *make one laugh*
beg 664.12; 772.7 *borrow*; 710.6 *request*; 710.8 *solicit money*
beg, borrow, or steal 352.6 *find means*; 765.9 *gain*
be generous 679.10
beget 344.9 *be the cause of*; 554.19 *give birth to*; 356.10 *produce*; 561.13 *propagate*
begetter 344.7 *Prime Mover*; 356.9 *producer*; 561.5 *propagator*
be getting at 694.10 *mean*
beg for crumbs 664.12 *beg*
beg for favours 664.12 *beg*
beg forgiveness 807.6 *apologize*
beg for mercy 627.12 *ask for mercy*
beg for more 218.6 *be unsatisfied*
beg for one's bread 782.12 *be poor*
beg for sleep 261.5 *be fatigued*
beggar 710.5; 258.6 *dirty person*; 782.14 *impoverish*; 343.8 *nonworker*; 782.10 *poor person*; 769.5 *recipient*
beggar all description 619.10 *be wonderful*
beggardom 782.7 *beggary*
beggared 786.13 *nonpaying*
beggarliness 782.7 *beggary*; 122.2 *deficiency*
beggarly 782.3; 664.7 *sycophantic*
beggar-on-horseback 660.12 *impudent person*
beggary 782.7
begging 710.11; 772.1 *borrowing*; 710.1 *request*; 710.3 *solicitation*
begin 130.17; **295.19**; **308.24**; 554.18 *be born*; 525.12 *become visible*; 233.5 *be incomplete*; 243.2 *do the groundwork*; 344.11 *inaugurate*; 483.9 *motivate*; 126.7 *originate*; 354.1 *undertake*; 576.6 *work*
begin again 130.28; 295.17 *become new*; 112.20 *renew*; 761.7 *restore*
begin an insurrection 753.8 *cause mischief*
begin from 345.7 *follow from*
beginner 130.14; 700.22 *dupe*; 314.7 *entrant*; 805.4 *innocent person*; 52.8 *karate*; 6.7 *learner*; 646.3 *naive person*; 295.8 *new arrival*; 486.10 *unskilled person*
beginner's luck 246.1 *success*
Beginning 130
beginning 130.1; **130.29**; **295.4**; **308.11**; **308.17**; 525.1 *appearance*; 525.7 *appearing*; 312.10 *arrival*; 293.3 *early stage*; 167.1 *front*; 126.1 *originality*
beginning again 112.4 *return*
beginning of the end 131.9 *close*
beginning of time 4.9 *philosophical problem*
beginnings 344.3 *rudiment*
begin to understand 695.6 *understand*
be given 769.9 *receive*
beg leave 757.6 *ask permission*; 710.6 *request*
begone 313.15 *go!*; 371.33 *go away!*
be gone 582.15 *die*
beg one's pardon 752.14 *offer reparation*
be good 797.18; 631.12 *behave well*; 803.8 *be virtuous*
be good at 797.19
begotten 554.15 *born*; 356.12 *produced*
be governed 12.13
beg pardon 807.6 *apologize*; 649.13 *ask forgiveness*
beg permission 757.6 *ask permission*; 710.6 *request*
be grateful 671.6
be greedy 688.5
begrime 258.11 *dirty*
begrimed 258.7 *dirty*
be grounded in 6.24 *know*
begrudge 672.6 *be ungrateful*; 637.10, 682.8 *grudge*; 218.7 *make insufficient*
beg the question 702.13 *quibble*
beg to differ 113.18 *object*
beguile 645.5 *be cunning*; 700.27 *be false*; 593.28 *win the love of*
beguilement 645.1 *cunning*
beguiler 700.15 *deceiver*
beguiling 645.4 *cunning*; 593.22 *lovable*; 619.8 *wonderful*
be guilty 806.8
beguine 22.2 *dance*
begun 233.4 *incomplete*
be gunning for 633.8 *pursue*
be had 700.24 *be deceived*; 792.11 *overpay*
behalf 797.13 *benefit*
be half-baked 293.10 *hasten*
be hard on 466.14 *discriminate against*
be hard put 264.19 *have difficulty*
behave 340.4 *act*; 631.12 *behave well*; 803.8 *be virtuous*; 631.11 *conduct oneself*
behave badly 631.13; 659.7 *be discourteous*
behave cheekily 659.7 *be discourteous*
behave like a gentleman 799.6 *be honourable*
behave oneself 631.12 *behave well*
behave properly 658.11 *have good manners*
behave towards 631.14
behave well 631.12; 160.8 *be formal*; 797.18 *be good*; 799.6 *be honourable*; 658.11 *have good manners*; 663.5 *obey*
behaving 631.16
Behaviour 631
behaviour 340.1 *action*; 631.1 *conduct*; 160.5 *formality*; 795.1 *morality*; 632.5 *tradition*; 317.1 *way*
behavioural 631.16 *behaving*; 160.11 *formal*; 2.12 *sociological*
behaviourally 2.16 *sociologically*
behavioural pattern 2.3 *social environment*
behavioural psychology 36.1 *psychology*
behavioural science 1.1 *anthropology*; 2.1 *sociology*
behavioural scientist 1.3 *anthropologist*
behavioural therapy 394.13 *therapy*
behaviourism 631.1 *conduct*; 36.1 *psychology*; 4.7 *school of thought*
behaviourist 4.11 *follower of a doctrine*; 4.14 *of a philosophy*
behaviouristic 631.16 *behaving*
behaviourist zoographer 70.11 *zoologist*
behaviour modification 36.3 *psychiatric treatment*
behaviour patterns 632.4 *custom*
behaviour therapist 36.30 *psychiatrist*
behaviour therapy 36.3 *psychiatric treatment*
behead 382.19, 814.5 *execute*; 372.10 *set apart*; 149.10 *shorten*; 212.4 *take off*
beheaded 212.7 *reduced*; 149.8 *shortened*
beheading 814.13 *capital punishment*; 382.5 *execution*; 372.3 *separateness*; 149.2 *shortening*; 212.1 *subtraction*
be healthy 259.5
be heard 504.16
be heavy 414.12
be helpful 392.21
behemoth 158.9 *big thing*; 70.7 *legendary beast*
be here 97.11 *be present*
be here for good 225.5 *be permanent*
be here to stay 225.5 *be permanent*
behest 397.1 *command*
be high 154.15
be highly thought of 811.5 *have repute*
be hilarious 272.7 *make one laugh*
behind 333.7 *delayed*; 145.10 *distantly*; 168.9 *in the rear*; 168.1 *rear*; 168.2 *rear end*
behind bars 815.8 *imprisoned*; 252.6 *safe*
behind closed doors 737.15 *in secret*; 736.18 *privately*; 655.14 *unsocially*
behindhand 294.9, 294.15 *late*; 786.13 *nonpaying*
behind one's back 98.20 *absently*; 737.16 *stealthily*
behind schedule 294.9, 294.15 *late*
behind someone's back 702.15 *hypocritically*
behind-the-back pass 49.4 *playing terms*
behind the eight ball 264.16 *troubled*
behind the scenes 344.13 *causal*; 344.14 *causally*; 168.9 *in the rear*; 521.9 *invisibly*; 21.43 *on stage*; 521.3 *private*
behind the times 284.19 *antiquarian*; 286.2 *occurring at a different time*; 288.18 *out of chronological order*; 288.12 *too late*
behind the veil 582.19 *dead*; 655.10 *lonely*
behind time 294.9, 294.15 *late*; 288.18 *out of chronological order*; 288.12 *too late*
be history 284.13 *be past*
behold 518.12 *see*
beholden 706.16 *answerable*; 810.11 *duty-bound*; 671.4 *grateful*; 784.9 *in debt*
beholder 518.11 *observer*; 769.5 *recipient*; 97.5 *someone present*
be holier than thou 699.22 *be hypocritical*
be honourable 799.6
be hopeful 610.9
be hopeless 611.9
be horizontal 187.6
be hospitable 569.15; **773.11**; 654.11 *be sociable*
be hospitalized 260.24 *be unhealthy*
be hot 493.14
behove 810.14 *be the duty of*
be humble 623.19; 388.4 *succumb*
be humiliated 623.24
be humorous 599.13
be hungry 617.14
be hypocritical 699.22
be identical 111.7 *be the same*
be identified 743.11 *identify oneself*
beige 534.1 *brown*; 531.1 *white*; 537.1 *yellow*
be ignorant 456.9
Beijing 87.6 *other cities*
be ill 249.9 *be in trouble*; 260.24 *be unhealthy*; 337.6 *be weak*
be illegal 16.73
be impartial 618.15
be impassive 489.11 *be unfeeling*
be impenitent 809.5
be imperfect 231.9
be implicated in 127.5 *be included*
be important 123.7
be impossible 103.9
be impotent 335.6 *be powerless*
be impressed with oneself 673.15 *be vain*
be improbable 105.7
be in 138.28 *prevail*
be in accord 750.21
be in accordance 750.21 *be in accord*
be in action 346.7 *be operational*
be inactive 343.12; 341.4 *not act*; 388.3 *submit*
be in a predicament 221.7
be in a rut 632.16 *have a habit*
be inattentive 472.12; 472.13 *be thoughtless*; 325.4 *lose track of*
be in bloom 78.13 *flower*
be in cahoots 747.15 *concur*; 750.22 *form an alliance*
be in charge 340.4 *act*; 579.2 *direct*; 12.11 *govern*
be inclined towards 595.8 *prefer*
be included 127.5
be incomplete 233.5
be in conflict 517.11 *disagree*
be inconvenient 240.5
be incurious 618.12 *be indifferent*
be in danger 254.8
be in debt 784.7
be in demand 778.2 *be sold*
be independent 118.19; **250.16**; 100.17 *not conform*
be indifferent 618.12; 388.3 *submit*
be in difficulty 264.20
be induced 483.8 *be motivated*
be in earnest 643.9 *take seriously*
be in error 274.18
be inert 339.4; 341.4 *not act*
be infatuated with 595.7 *like*
be inferior 122.8
be infertile 563.7
be infinite 202.9
be in flower 78.13 *flower*
be in force 346.7 *be operational*
be informal 250.17
be informed 693.15; 6.24 *know*; 695.6 *understand*
be in front 167.10
being 525.2 *being in view*; 93.1 *existence*; 93.10 *existing*; 554.1 *life*; 34.3 *organism*; 139.13, 566.7 *person*; 97.1 *presence*; 93.2 *thing*
being ahead 121.3 *advantage*
being alive 554.1 *life*
being a regular customer 297.5 *frequenting*
being at large 250.1 *freedom*
being cured 393.11 *recuperation*
being discussed 243.17 *developing*
being fired 580.3 *unemployment*
being in control 250.3 *independence*
being in view 525.2
being there 525.2 *being in view*
be in harmony 750.21 *be in accord*; 516.8 *harmonize*
be inhibited 378.11; 166.7 *limit*
be in hot pursuit 633.8 *pursue*
be in love 593.24
be in mortal dread 612.11 *be afraid*
be in motion 300.13; 302.1 *go forward*
be innocent 805.8
be in no hurry 580.4 *have leisure*
be in on 764.4 *have joint possession*
be in one's element 265.17 *do easily*
be in order 407.23; 298.7 *be regular*
be in play 346.7 *be operational*
be in power 140.16 *direct*; 12.11 *govern*
be in prison 815.10
be in residence 97.13 *reside*
be insane 461.14 *become insane*
be in service 401.8 *serve*
be insincere 699.22 *be hypocritical*
be instinctive 445.10
be instructed 6.23 *learn*
be instrumental 348.4 *be an instrument*
be insubordinate 661.6
be insufficient 218.5
be intelligent 442.13; **458.8**
be intelligible 695.4
be intentionally walked 48.7 *play baseball*
be interior 172.13
be in the chair 579.2 *direct*
be in the dark 456.9 *be ignorant*
be in the future 283.7
be in the know 693.15 *be informed*
be in the limelight 738.5 *be visible*
be in the news 740.18 *become famous*
be in the past 284.13 *be past*
be in the pink 259.5 *be healthy*
be in the rear 168.6
be in the right 801.13 *be right*
be in the running 104.8 *be probable*
be in the shotgun 46.15 *play offence*
be in the vanguard 167.10 *be in front*; 449.4 *invent*
be into 139.27 *specialize*
be in touch 692.30 *communicate*
be in touch with 504.15 *hear*
be intoxicating 690.9
be in trouble 249.9
be introverted 378.11 *be inhibited*
be intuitive 445.9
be in turmoil 327.21 *be agitated*
be in unison 516.8 *harmonize*
be in vain 238.7 *be useless*; 236.13 *be worthless*
be invalided out 260.24 *be unhealthy*
be in working order 407.23 *be in order*
be irascible 625.6
be irregular 299.6
be irrelevant 100.13 *be extraneous*
be irresolute 227.12; **639.7**; **754.5**; 453.19 *hesitate*
be irritable 626.11; 488.11 *sense*
be irritated 488.11 *sense*
be itchy 488.11 *sense*
be jealous 629.6
bejewel 545.8 *beautify*
be justified 801.13 *be right*
be just the job 706.22 *be the answer*; 750.27 *fit*
be just the thing 750.27 *fit*
be kept waiting 294.7 *wait*
be kind 419.15; 650.8 *be benevolent*
be knowledgeable 156.15 *be profound*
be known to 632.16 *have a habit*
belabour 112.18 *harp*; 814.3 *hit*
be lacking 233.5 *be incomplete*
be laid off 226.7 *stop working*

be laid up 260.24 *be unhealthy*
be last 168.6 *be in the rear*
be late 294.6; 262.2 *make haste*; 288.6 *take untimely action*
belated 294.9 *late*
belatedly 294.15 *late*
belatedness 294.1 *lateness*
be lawless 16.74
be lax 757.4 *be permissive*
belay 50.21 *avast!*; 62.9 *mountaineer*; 62.8 *mountaineering*
belay anchor 62.4 *climbing equipment*
belay brake 62.4 *climbing equipment*
belay braking 62.3 *climbing technique*
belayed 62.8 *mountaineering*
belaying 62.3 *climbing technique*; 62.8 *mountaineering*
bel canto 18.4 *opera*
belch 371.16; **371.24**; **432.5**; **508.4**; **508.7**; 513.2 *hoarseness*; 513.5 *sound hoarse*
belching 371.24 *belch*; 371.31 *eructative*
beleaguer 585.13 *be at war*; 381.4 *besiege*
be led astray 604.4 *be disappointed*
be led to believe 450.7 *believe*
be left 215.7; 246.12 *succeed to*
be left cold 618.12 *be indifferent*
be left over 215.7 *be left*
be legal 16.66
be lenient 648.3; 627.10, 649.12 *show mercy*
be level pegging 285.8 *run equally*
Belfast 87.4 *British cities*
belfry 154.6 *tall thing*
Belgrade 87.6 *other cities*
Belgravia 87.5 *London*
be liable 810.15
Belial 8.7 *devil*
be liberated 391.5
belie 700.26 *be a hypocrite*; 96.16 *delude*; 718.4 *misrepresent*; 113.18 *object*; 708.11 *rebut*; 704.8 *refute*
Belief 450
belief 450.1; 452.10 *conviction*; 474.1, 610.2 *expectation*; 443.6 *idea*; 590.2 *impression*; 464.1 *judgment*; 7.1 *religion*
beliefs 590.3 *feelings*; 446.5 *ideology*; 795.1 *morality*
belief system 4.2 *philosophical system*; 7.1 *religion*; 2.4 *social organization*
belie one's expectations 604.6 *disappoint*
believability 450.4
believable 450.13; 104.7 *plausible*; 102.5 *possible*
believably 450.16; 102.11 *potentially*
believe 450.7; **590.19**; 452.20 *be certain*; 480.18 *be persuaded*; 7.19 *be religious*; 464.12 *estimate*; 610.6 *hope*; 474.9 *predict*; 476.5 *suppose*; 446.17 *theorize*
believed 450.14
believe in 4.22 *propound a philosophy*
believer 450.5; 452.11 *opinionist*; 7.3 *religious person*
believing 450.3; **450.11**; 452.2 *convinced*; 7.15 *religious*
believingly 450.15
be lifeless 341.4 *not act*
be light 415.9
be like 115.10 *be similar*; 750.25 *conform*
be likely 756.9 *be auspicious*
be limiting 164.5 *border*
be linked with 223.13 *accompany*
be lippy 706.18 *answer back*
Belisha beacon 320.3 *carriageway*; 318.5 *crossing point*; 522.6 *electric light*; 742.4 *signal*
be listened to 395.8 *influence*
be literal 698.32
belittle 606.7 *be dissatisfied*; 670.17 *criticize*; 728.21 *detract from*; 678.10 *disparage*; 214.5 *make smaller*; 124.13 *make unimportant*; 668.20 *scorn*; 468.3 *underestimate*
be little 159.6
belittled 214.6 *decreasing*; 668.18 *undervalued*
belittlement 214.1 *decrease*; 728.2 *detraction*; 678.1 *disparagement*
belittler 678.7 *disparager*
belittling 678.15 *disparaging*
bell 52.2 *boxing*; 515.4 *cry*; 711.2 *danger signal*; 281.10, 742.4 *signal*; 507.4 *sound maker*; 510.4 *sources of resonance*; 692.10 *telephone call*
bell, book, and candle 11.6 *talisman*
bell-bottomed 150.1 *broad*
bell-bottoms 551.9 *trousers*
bellboy 401.3 *attendant*; 316.7 *transferor*
bell buoy 711.2 *danger signal*
belle 545.3 *attractive female*
belle of the ball 545.3 *attractive female*
belles-lettres 17.1 *literature*
belletrist 17.15 *literary person*
belletristic 17.16 *literary*
bellhop 401.3 *attendant*
bellicose 624.16 *angry*; 586.33 *combative*; 661.8 *defying*; 751.9 *disagreeing*; 701.9 *hostile*; 625.4 *irascible*; 381.22, 613.11 *militant*; 584.8 *military*; 242.2 *objectionable*; 336.11 *strong in spirit*; 380.6 *violent*; 585.16 *warlike*; 585.15 *warring*
bellicosely 661.10 *in defiance*; 751.11 *in disagreement*
bellicosity 585.5; 624.4 *anger*; 381.11 *attack*; 751.1 *disagreement*; 613.2 *heroism*; 336.1 *strength*
belligerence 624.4 *anger*; 381.11 *attack*; 661.1 *defiance*; 751.1 *disagreement*; 625.1 *irascibility*
belligerency 585.4
belligerent 624.16 *angry*; 586.1 *combatant*; 586.33 *combative*; 661.8 *defying*; 751.9 *disagreeing*; 701.9 *hostile*; 625.4 *irascible*; 381.22 *militant*; 584.8 *military*; 585.16 *warlike*; 585.15 *warring*
belligerently 586.41 *aggressively*; 701.17 *argumentatively*; 661.10 *in defiance*; 751.11 *in disagreement*; 625.9 *irascibly*; 585.18 *to war*
belling 515.1 *animal cry*
Bellona 585.3 *gods and goddesses of war*
bellow 507.8 *be loud*; 514.1, 515.4 *cry*; 514.10 *cry out*; 726.6 *emphasize*
bellowing 515.1 *animal cry*; 507.6 *loud*; 515.7 *ululant*; 514.16 *vociferous*
bell-ringer 742.8 *signer*
bell-ringing 18.6 *campanology*; 510.2 *ringing*; 742.16 *signalling*
bell rope 361.3 *suspended object*
bells 507.1 *loudness*
bell shape 181.5 *cone*
bell-shaped 181.9 *round*
Bell's inequality 28.80 *quantum theory*
bell the cat 613.15 *be courageous*; 615.5 *be rash*; 638.8 *brace oneself*
bell tower 154.6 *tall thing*
bellwether 579.14 *leader*
belly 190.6 *become bigger*; 557.16 *eating utensil*; 172.4 *insides*; 25.24 *pork*; 410.18 *stomach*
bellyache 606.7 *be dissatisfied*; 626.11 *be irritable*; 753.7 *complain*; 260.8 *indigestion*; 491.2 *painful condition*
bellyacher 659.4 *discourteous person*; 606.3 *dissatisfied person*; 753.4 *protester*; 626.5 *sullen person*
bellyaching 626.7 *irritable*
bellyband 373.10 *band*
belly button 173.2 *central thing*
belly dance 22.2 *dance*
belly dancer 21.30 *dancer*
belly flop 67.10, 305.5 *dive*; 305.12 *drop*
bellyful 232.2 *fullness*; 219.2 *overdoing it*; 217.7 *sufficiency*
belly habit 691.1 *drug-taking*
belly landing 322.5 *flight*
belly laugh 599.5 *joke*
belly pork 25.30 *bacon*
belly up 335.12 *impotent*; 782.2 *insolvent*; 766.17 *unprofitable*; 249.7 *unprosperous*
Belmont Stakes 59.7 *horseracing*
be located 143.9 *be situated*
belong 127.5 *be included*; 750.27 *fit*
be long 148.9
belonging 405.8; 223.17 *accompanying*; 750.16 *fitting*; 127.8 *included*
belongings 763.4 *possession*; 440.4 *possessions*; 345.2 *visible effect*
belonging to 763.9 *possessed*
belonging to the past 284.19 *antiquarian*
belong to 127.5 *be included*; 405.12 *be one of*; 810.14 *be the duty of*; 108.7 *relate to*
belong to a class 108.9 *have a relative position*
belong to the IRA 753.8 *cause mischief*
belong to the past 296.16 *be old*
belong with 223.13 *accompany*
be lost 696.9 *find unintelligible*
be lost and gone 284.13 *be past*
be loud 507.8
beloved 593.21; 593.11 *loved one*; 654.16 *popular*
be loved 593.25
beloved object 593.11 *loved one*
beloved one 595.4 *likable person*
below 8.20 *devilishly*; 550.42 *inclusively*; 122.19 *inferiorly*; 155.10 *low*; 21.17 *stage*
be low 155.8
below ground 583.10 *buried*
below par 791.7 *at a discount*; 337.10 *ill*; 231.1 *imperfect*; 231.11 *imperfectly*; 337.13 *insufficient*; 260.22 *sick*; 120.3 *unequal*
below sea level 155.7 *lowland*
below standard 122.19 *inferiorly*
below strength 231.2 *incomplete*
below the belt 52.16 *professionally*; 802.11 *wrong*
below the horizon 526.8 *fleetingly*; 521.1 *invisible*
below the mark 122.19 *inferiorly*
below the poverty line 135.5 *necessitous*; 782.1 *poor*
below the salt 122.12 *inferior*
below the surface 526.8 *fleetingly*
below zero 31.55 *cool*
Belsen 382.15 *slaughterhouse*
belt 551.25 *accessories*; 434.3 *atmospheric layers*; 373.10 *band*; 331.13 *blow*; 179.3 *circular thing*; 331.3, 814.3 *hit*; 814.14 *instrument of punishment*; 411.1 *layer*; 38.8 *machine element*; 86.1 *region*
Beltane 10.16 *religious festival*
belter 18.23 *singer*
belt-holder 485.4 *skilled person*
belt loader 38.29 *construction equipment*
belt of cloud 31.20 *cloud appearance*
belt of rain 31.25 *rain*
belt out 18.39 *sing*; 514.15 *sing out*
belt printer 40.7 *peripheral*
belt sander 23.11 *woodworking tool*
belt-tightening 782.6 *insolvency*; 218.8 *insufficiency*
beltway 317.3 *road*
be lucky 248.6 *be fortunate*; 107.12 *take a chance*
Beluga caviar 25.16 *fish dish*
belvedere 44.3 *ornamental garden*; 565.7 *room*; 518.9 *viewpoint*
be made redundant 226.7 *stop working*
be made up of 405.11 *consist of*; 127.4 *include*
be magnetic 363.11 *attract*
be malevolent 651.16
be marooned 92.12
be marvellous 619.10 *be wonderful*
be material 402.8
be mediocre 618.16
be mentally sharp 425.17
be merciful 649.12 *show mercy*
be merciless 651.19 *be pitiless*
bemire 258.11 *dirty*
bemist 31.64 *fog*
be mixed up 412.11
be mixed up in 127.5 *be included*
bemoan 582.17 *bury*; 603.6 *lament*
be moderate 685.3; 216.9 *be average*
be modern 282.5 *be present*
be modest 674.14
be moist 429.15
be monastic 572.11
be moral 795.11
be motionless 301.8
be motivated 483.8
bemuse 457.10
be my guest 452.26 *certainly!*
ben 89.1, 154.3 *mountain*
be naive 646.4; **805.10**
Benares 10.13 *shrine*
be natural 657.11 *not stand on ceremony*
bench 23.2 *chair*; 16.27 *courtroom*; 16.23 *judge*; 154.4 *mountain range*; 44.3 *ornamental garden*; 708.15 *terminate*; 16.18 *tribunal*; 577.1 *workshop*
benchmark 40.19 *computing terms*; 99.2 *essential content*; 142.2 *exact location*; 742.5 *indicator*; 26.7 *standard*
bench of judges 16.18 *tribunal*
bench warrant 397.2 *demand*
bend 177.2; 176.1, 176.11 *angle*; 155.8 *be low*; 189.6 *be oblique*; 367.9 *bow*; 320.3 *carriageway*; 367.16 *courtesy*; 177.6 *curve*; 325.12 *deflect*; 325.14 *deviating course*; 55.3 *fishing tackle*; 184.9 *fold*; 743.8 *heraldic device*; 664.10 *knuckle under*; 38.31 *load*; 161.3 *make shapeless*; 667.4 *mark of respect*; 483.9 *motivate*; 61.6 *motor-racing terms*; 189.1 *obliqueness*; 64.5 *play rugby*; 595.8 *prefer*; 306.7 *ring*; 663.6 *show obeisance to*; 367.8 *sit*; 419.13 *soften*; 388.4 *succumb*; 667.19 *take off one's hat to*; 229.4 *tend*; 325.5 *twist*; 184.1 *wrinkle*
bendability 419.8 *softness*
bendable 419.2 *pliant*
bend a rule 648.3 *be lenient*
benday 523.2 *darkening*
bend backwards 367.7 *lean*
bender 601.1 *celebration*; 690.14 *drinking bout*
bend forks 11.24 *experience psychic phenomena*
bend forwards 367.7 *lean*
bending 177.1 *curvature*; 38.16 *deformation*; 667.11 *in a respectful stance*; 325.21 *indirect*; 595.6 *liking*; 667.4 *mark of respect*; 189.4 *oblique*; 388.5 *submitting*
bending moment 38.15 *strength of materials*
bending the knee 667.4 *mark of respect*
bend in the road 177.3 *curved things*
bend one's elbow 690.8 *get drunk*
bend over 367.7 *lean*
bend over backwards 473.7 *be unselfish*; 636.13 *be willing*; 576.8 *exert oneself*
bend sinister 743.8 *heraldic device*
bend the knee 664.10 *knuckle under*; 667.19 *take off one's hat to*
bend the law 16.73 *be illegal*
bend the rules 800.8 *be dishonourable*; 757.4 *be permissive*
bend the truth 189.7 *deviate*
bend to one's will 396.18 *have authority*
be near 147.15
beneath 122.19 *inferiorly*; 155.10 *low*
beneath contempt 124.2 *obscure*
beneath notice 124.2 *obscure*
beneath the sod 583.12 *funereally*
Benedicite 10.8 *hymn*
benedick 570.10 *married man*
Benedick and Beatrice 593.10 *lovers*
Benedict Arnold 699.17 *false person*; 700.21 *traitor*
benediction 797.13 *benefit*; 10.9 *prayer*; 10.3 *rite of worship*; 392.2 *support*; 671.2 *thanks*
Benedict's test 33.5 *sugar test*
be needy 135.11
benefaction 608.4 *charity*; 768.1 *giving*
benefactor 392.15; 340.3 *doer*; 679.9 *generous person*; 768.4 *giver*; 652.3 *philanthropist*; 252.3 *protector*; 413.8 *supporter*; 752.8 *volunteer*
benefactress 392.15 *benefactor*; 652.3 *philanthropist*; 252.3 *protector*
benefice 440.1 *property*
beneficence 679.5 *generosity*; 797.10 *kindness*; 652.1 *philanthropy*; 235.6 *worth*
beneficent 392.35 *benevolent*; 650.7 *charitable*; 679.1 *generous*; 797.3 *kind*; 652.6 *philanthropic*
beneficently 650.11 *charitably*; 797.23 *nicely*; 652.8 *philanthropically*
beneficial 392.34; **797.6**; 239.1 *convenient*; 617.8 *desirable*; 569.12 *favourable*; 765.15 *gainful*; 259.2 *healthful*; 257.4 *hygienic*; 237.4 *profitable*; 394.17 *remedial*; 235.4 *worthwhile*
beneficially 617.17 *desirably*; 569.20 *favourably*; 765.20 *gainfully*; 392.36 *helpfully*; 349.11, 797.26 *usefully*; 235.11 *worthily*
beneficiary 769.6; 474.4 *expectant person*; 765.7 *gainer*; 765.15 *gainful*; 392.12 *recipient*; 289.5 *successor*; 781.10 *wealthy person*
benefit 237.8; **237.10**; **797.13**; 650.9, 652.7 *be charitable*; 239.6 *be convenient*; 392.21 *be helpful*; 650.4 *benevolent act*; 785.12 *be profitable*; 239.3 *convenience*; 235.10, 797.20 *do good*; 211.4 *extra*; 765.1, 765.9 *gain*; 768.2 *gift*; 392.1 *help*; 768.3 *offering*; 765.5 *profit*; 392.4 *social assistance*; 392.2 *support*; 21.13 *theatrical performance*; 349.6 *use*; 652.4 *welfare state*
benefit concert 710.3 *solicitation*
benefit game 710.3 *solicitation*
benefit gig 710.3 *solicitation*
benefit match 768.3 *offering*
benefit of the doubt 16.42 *acquittal*
benefit performance 768.3 *offering*
benefits 15.2 *industrial negotiations*; 483.5 *positive stimulus*
be negative 708.10
be neglectful 666.6
Benelux 13.5 *international trade*
be nervous 612.12 *be fearful*

Benevolence 650
benevolence 650.1; 658.1 *courtesy*; 649.2 *forgivingness*; 569.1 *friendship*; 768.1 *giving*; 636.9 *goodwill*; 392.10 *helpfulness*; 482.1 *intention*; 797.10 *kindness*; 648.1 *leniency*; 790.8 *levy*; 679.6 *magnanimity*; 757.1 *permission*; 652.1 *philanthropy*; 627.1 *pity*; 473.2 *unselfishness*; 803.1 *virtue*; 235.6 *worth*
benevolent 392.35; **650.6**; 658.7 *courteous*; 569.8 *friendly*; 768.8 *giving*; 636.4 *helpful*; 797.3 *kind*; 648.4 *lenient*; 679.2 *magnanimous*; 649.5 *merciful*; 652.6 *philanthropic*; 627.6 *pitying*; 413.9 *supportive*; 473.5 *unselfish*; 803.5 *virtuous*
benevolent act 650.4
benevolent despotism 12.1 *government*; 396.7 *type of rule*
benevolent disposition 650.1 *benevolence*
benevolently 392.38; **650.10**; 768.9 *as a gift*; 658.14 *courteously*; 649.14 *forgivingly*; 658.15 *genteelly*; 569.17 *in friendship*; 648.6 *leniently*; 797.23 *nicely*; 652.8 *philanthropically*; 627.13 *pitifully*; 473.9 *unselfishly*; 803.9 *virtuously*
benevolentness 650.1 *benevolence*
benevolent person 650.5
be next to 169.7 *be alongside*; 147.18 *juxtapose*
Bengal light 522.8 *fire*
benighted 523.11; 519.12 *blind to*; 291.6 *evening*
benightedness 519.7 *figurative blindness*
benign 392.35, 650.6 *benevolent*; 257.4 *hygienic*; 252.6 *safe*
benignity 650.1 *benevolence*
benignly 650.10 *benevolently*
benign tumour 260.12 *cancer*
benison 10.9 *prayer*
Ben Lomond 89.5 *British mountains*
Ben Nevis 89.5 *British mountains*; 154.3 *mountain*
be no more 131.18 *come to an end*; 582.15 *die*
be non-partisan 618.15 *be impartial*
be nonresonant 511.9
be nonsense 697.7
be not all there 457.9 *lack intellect*
be nothing 708.13
be now 282.5 *be present*
bent 136.2 *ability*; 176.7 *angular*; 485.2 *aptitude*; 229.2 *attitude*; 324.2 *bearing*; 800.7 *criminal*; 177.4 *curved*; 184.7 *folded*; 595.2 *inclination*; 16.60 *offending*; 367.23 *sedentary*; 16.59 *stolen*; 632.2 *tendency*
bent back 664.2 *sycophancy*
bent bond 32.11 *chemical bond*
bent double 367.23 *sedentary*
bent grass 56.1 *golf*
benthal 156.12 *under*
Benthamism 652.2 *public spiritedness*; 4.7 *school of thought*
Benthamite 4.11 *follower of a doctrine*; 4.14 *of a philosophy*; 652.3 *philanthropist*
benthic 30.51, 91.7 *oceanic*; 70.15 *of animals*; 156.12 *under*
benthonic 156.12 *under*
benthos 70.5 *aquatic animal*; 156.4 *deep thing*; 91.1 *sea*
benthoscope 156.4 *deep thing*
bent upon 638.1 *resolute*
bentwood chair 23.2 *chair*
be null and void 708.13 *be nothing*
benumb 489.12 *anaesthetize*; 494.12 *make cold*; 618.13 *make indifferent*; 335.8 *overpower*; 592.7 *render insensitive*
benumbed 341.3 *inactive*; 618.7 *indifferent*
Benzedrine™ 394.7 *tonic*
benzene hexachloride 44.8 *weedkiller*
benzoylate 32.26 *react*
be objective 618.15 *be impartial*
be oblique 189.6; 325.8 *sidestep*; 305.14 *slide*
be oblivious 489.11 *be unfeeling*
be obstinate 383.7; **641.9**
be obvious 520.8 *be visible*
be of assistance 392.17 *help*
be off 371.33 *go away!*; 634.8 *run away*; 313.5 *set out*
be offended 624.10
be officious 342.17 *meddle*
be offside 46.18 *be penalized*
be of help 392.17 *help*
be of no avail 335.6 *be powerless*
be of no help 335.6 *be powerless*
be often seen at 297.8 *frequent*
be of the opinion 450.8; 4.22 *propound a philosophy*
be of two minds 639.7 *be irresolute*
be of unsound mind 457.9 *lack intellect*
be old 296.16
be on 560.22 *menstruate*
be on a high 488.12 *awake*
be on call 243.8 *prepare oneself*; 474.10 *wait*
be one 197.18
be on edge 612.12 *be fearful*
be one of 405.12; 127.5 *be included*
be oneself 657.11 *not stand on ceremony*
be one's own fault 385.4 *serve one right*
be one's own man 635.14 *follow one's own will*
be one up on 645.5 *be cunning*
be on fire 493.15 *burn*
be on guard 54.5 *fence*
be on hand 97.12 *attend*
be on one's toes 342.14 *push*
be on one's way 313.5 *set out*
be on sale 778.2 *be sold*
be on slippery ground 254.8 *be in danger*
be on stand-by 243.8 *prepare oneself*; 474.10 *wait*
be on tenterhooks 488.12 *awake*
be on the ball 488.12 *awake*
be on the beach 164.5 *border*
be on the cards 104.8 *be probable*
be on the game 796.18 *prostitute*
be on the run 736.11 *conceal oneself*
be on the sideline 164.5 *border*
be on the skids 249.9 *be in trouble*
be on the threshold 312.3 *approach*
be on to 695.6 *understand*
be on trial 16.72 *stand trial*
be on visiting terms 654.12 *visit*
be opaque 528.10
be open 308.22; 698.29 *be truthful*
be open to criticism 670.24
be operational 346.7
be opposite 113.15; 708.11 *rebut*
be optimistic 610.8
be ostentatious 622.27
be out of danger 252.9 *be safe*
be out-of-doors 171.12 *be outside*
be out of order 802.24 *go wrong*
be out of pocket 787.1 *expend*; 777.2 *shop*
be outside 171.12
be over 284.13 *be past*; 131.18 *come to an end*
be overdrawn 249.10 *need money*; 792.11 *overpay*
be overpossessive 629.8 *distrust*
be painful 242.12; **491.10**
be paralysed with fear 612.11 *be afraid*
be parsimonious 786.11
be partisan 169.9 *side with*
be part of 127.5 *be included*; 405.12 *be one of*
be past 284.13
be patient with 649.12 *show mercy*
be penalized 46.18
be penitent 808.4
be penny-wise and pound-foolish 486.6 *act foolishly*
be perfect 230.6
be periodical 276.10
be permanent 225.5; 279.5 *be eternal*
be permissive 757.4
be permitted 757.5
be persuaded 480.18
be pessimistic 708.10 *be negative*
be petrified 612.11 *be afraid*
be piquant 496.13
be pissed 624.11 *be angry*
be pitiless 628.6; **651.19**
be pleased with oneself 673.15 *be vain*
be plentiful 217.5 *about*
be pointed 425.14 *be sharp*
be poor 782.12
be possessive 629.8 *distrust*
be possible 102.8
be powerful 334.10
be powerless 335.6
be prejudiced 120.6 *be unjust*
be prepared 243.3; 243.8 *prepare oneself*
be present 97.11; **282.5**; 525.11 *appear*; 312.1 *arrive*
be present at 97.12 *attend*
be pressed for time 262.2 *make haste*
be prevalent 395.10 *be a prevailing influence*
be probable 104.8
be proficient in 6.24 *know*
be profitable 765.13; **785.12**; 213.4 *increase*
be profound 156.15
be prominent 185.9
be proportionate to 108.8
be prosperous 248.5
be proud 622.24; **660.23**
be proud of 622.25
be published 740.17; 525.13 *occur*
be puffed up 673.15 *be vain*
be punished 807.7; **814.6**; 385.4 *serve one right*
be pure 255.9
be put to death 582.16 *meet one's fate*
be qualified 136.14
bequeath 635.16; 316.14 *bring back*; 679.11, 768.5 *give*; 215.8 *leave*; 781.15 *make rich*; 440.9 *own property*
bequeathable 768.7 *given*
bequeathal 768.1 *giving*; 769.1 *receiving*
bequeathed 768.7 *given*; 788.6 *received*
bequeather 768.4 *giver*
bequest 215.5 *estate*; 768.2 *gift*; 788.4 *legacy*; 765.5 *profit*; 769.1 *receiving*; 316.10 *transferred thing*; 635.5 *will*
be questioned 705.19
be quick 262.8 *hurry up!*
be quiet 506.1 *be silent*; 226.6 *cease*
be quite at home 265.17 *do easily*
be quits 385.3 *retaliate*
berakah 10.9 *prayer*
be rash 615.5
berate 670.21; 381.10 *criticize*
berated 670.34 *censured*
berating 670.8
Beratron 28.94 *particle accelerator*
berceuse 516.2 *song*
be ready 636.13 *be willing*
be ready and waiting 293.7 *be early*
be real 95.10
be reasonable 444.12
bereave 571.9 *widow*
bereavement 766.1 *loss*
be reborn 393.4 *be restored*; 554.16 *live*
be received 312.2 *reach*
be recognizable 695.8
be recognized 395.8 *influence*
be reconciled 750.21 *be in accord*; 649.9 *forgive*
be redundant 341.4 *not act*
be reflected 510.9 *resonate*
be refreshed 581.2
bereft 766.16 *losing*; 215.9 *remaining*
bereft of life 582.19 *dead*
be regular 111.11; **298.7**
be rejuvenated 760.8 *be transformed*
be relieved 48.7 *play baseball*
be religious 7.19
be remembered 462.15
be repeated 112.21; 510.9 *resonate*
be repulsive 364.4
be resigned 388.3 *submit*
be resolute 638.6
be responsible 706.23 *answer for*
be responsible for 348.4 *be an instrument*
be restored 393.4; 581.2 *be refreshed*
beret 551.15 *headgear*
be rewarded 813.12
berg 30.39 *iceberg*
Bergmann's rule 1.10 *measurement*
bergschrund 62.5 *rock face*
Bergsonian 4.11 *follower of a doctrine*; 4.14 *of a philosophy*
Bergsonism 4.7 *school of thought*
beriberi 260.4 *disease*; 557.10 *scarcity*; 260.7 *tropical disease*; 33.14 *vitamin deficiency disease*
be rich 781.12
be ridiculous 272.6
be rife 395.10 *be a prevailing influence*
be right 801.13
be rightly served 385.4 *serve one right*
Bering Daylight Time 275.9 *time zone*
Bering Standard Time 275.9 *time zone*
be ripped-off 777.1 *purchase*
berk 456.5 *ignorant person*
Berkelian 4.11 *follower of a doctrine*; 4.14 *of a philosophy*
Berkelianism 4.7 *school of thought*
Berlin 87.6 *other cities*
Berlin Wall 378.3 *barrier*; 372.6 *boundary*; 147.7 *interface*
berm 317.6 *path*
Bermudan rig 50.3 *parts of a sailing boat*
Bermudan-rigged 50.10 *sailing*
Bermuda Race 50.1 *sailing*
Bermuda shorts 551.9 *trousers*
Bermuda Triangle 737.6 *natural mystery*
Bernreuter personality inventory 36.5 *psychological test*
be rolling in it 248.5 *be prosperous*
be rough 420.11
berry 80.2 *botanical fruit*; 356.7 *produce*
berserk 624.16 *angry*; 381.23 *attacking*; 461.12 *manic*; 380.6 *violent*
berserker 357.6 *destroyer*
berth 23.6 *bed*; 143.4 *employment*; 312.4 *land*; 141.5 *reserved space*; 312.16 *stopover*
bertha collar 551.14 *neckwear*
berthage 141.5 *reserved space*
be rude 660.22; 672.6 *be ungrateful*; 623.22 *shame*; 668.22 *show disrespect*
beryl 539.6 *blue thing*; 538.11 *green thing*
be sacked 226.7 *stop working*
be safe 252.9
be sane 460.6
be satisfied 609.7
be saved 760.10 *be converted*; 807.7 *be punished*; 7.19 *be religious*
be seated 367.8 *sit*
beseech 10.20 *pray*; 710.6 *request*
beseeching 710.1 *request*; 710.9 *requesting*
beseechingly 710.12 *by request*
be seen 520.8 *be visible*; 738.4 *show oneself*
be self-conscious 674.16
be selfish 683.6
be self-restrained 684.5
be sensitive 591.11; 492.13 *be touched by*; 488.11 *sense*
be serious 643.8
be servile 664.8
beset 381.4 *besiege*; 329.11 *overrun*; 264.16 *troubled*
besetting 632.15 *habit-forming*
beset with perils 254.1 *dangerous*
be severe 647.5
be sexually immoral 796.17
be shallow 157.6
be sharp 425.14
be shrill 513.6
be shy 732.6
be sick 371.15 *vomit*
be sick at heart 604.5 *be crestfallen*
be sick with disappointment 604.5 *be crestfallen*
beside 147.14; 211.10 *additionally*
be side by side 147.18 *juxtapose*
beside oneself 624.16 *angry*; 597.4 *happy*
beside oneself with joy 597.4 *happy*
besides 211.10 *additionally*
beside the point 100.18 *extraneously*; 109.7 *illogical*; 109.12 *irrelevantly*
besiege 381.4; 585.13 *be at war*; 586.36 *combat*; 251.11 *detain*
besieged 251.15 *detained*
besieger 381.19 *attacker*; 586.1 *combatant*; 128.5 *excluded person*
besieging 585.8 *warfare*
be silent 506.1; **736.12**; 730.13 *be voiceless*; 226.6 *cease*
be similar 115.10
be simple 271.7
be simultaneous 285.6
be situated 143.9
be six feet under 582.15 *die*
be skilful 485.10
beslime 258.11 *dirty*
be slow 294.6 *be late*; 288.5 *mistime*
be small 159.6 *be little*
besmear 678.12 *defame*; 258.11 *dirty*
besmeared 258.7 *dirty*
besmirch 678.12 *defame*; 258.11 *dirty*
besmirched 258.7 *dirty*
besmirching 678.16 *defamatory*
be snooty 622.26 *be too proud*
be snowed in 494.11 *become cold*
be snowed under 494.11 *become cold*
be so 221.6 *be in a state of*
be sober 689.3
be sociable 342.16; **654.11**
be social 654.11 *be sociable*
be soggy 429.15 *be moist*
be sold 778.2
be solicitous 471.14
besom 256.10 *cleaning object*; 68.10 *curling*
be sorry for 590.18 *feel for*
besotted 593.19 *enamoured*
be sour 499.8 *sour*
be spared 554.16 *live*

bespatter 678.12 *defame;* 258.11 *dirty;* 433.33 *sprinkle*
bespeak 694.10 *mean*
bespeak performance 21.13 *theatrical performance*
bespeckle 412.8 *mix*
bespectacled **518.22**
bespoke 139.20 *personalized;* 551.31 *styled*
bespoke clothes 551.1 *dress*
besprinkle 412.8 *mix*
best **121.14; 235.2; 797.2;** 121.8 *be superior;* 230.1 *perfect;* 619.8 *wonderful*
be stable **228.6**
best-ball match 56.1 *golf*
best behaviour 656.1 *formality*
best bet 104.4 *chance*
best bib and tucker 551.1 *dress;* 656.4 *formal dress*
best bit 205.5 *largest part*
best chance 107.5 *good chance;* 287.2 *opportunity;* 102.3 *strong possibility*
best clothes 551.1 *dress*
bestead 237.10 *benefit*
bested 247.11 *defeated;* 122.18 *outclassed*
best effort 353.5 *attempt*
best end of neck 25.26 *lamb*
best ever 121.14, 235.2, 797.2 *best;* 235.8 *exceller;* 246.13 *successful*
best foot 235.6 *worth*
best forgotten 463.11 *forgotten*
best friend 713.4 *adviser;* 569.6 *close friend;* 223.11 *companion;* 395.5 *influential person;* 595.4 *likable person*
bestial 70.14 *animalian;* 651.11 *cruel;* 796.15 *unlawful;* 380.6 *violent*
bestiality 651.2 *cruelness;* 380.2 *physical violence;* 796.7 *sexual assault;* 70.12 *zoophilism*
bestiary 70.7 *legendary beast*
bestir oneself 342.12 *be active;* 576.8 *exert oneself*
best man 570.7 *bridal party;* 569.6 *close friend*
best of its kind 235.8 *exceller*
best one can do 353.5 *attempt*
best option 469.8 *choice*
bestow 392.29 *finance;* 750.30 *grant*
bestowable 768.7 *given*
bestowal 392.6 *financial assistance;* 768.1 *giving;* 750.9 *grant*
bestow alms 768.6 *give to charity*
bestowal of love 593.6 *courtship*
bestow a medal 813.9 *reward*
bestow an honorary degree 813.9 *reward*
bestowed 768.7 *given;* 750.19 *granted*
bestower 768.4 *giver*
bestowing 768.8 *giving*
bestow in marriage 570.16 *join in marriage*
bestow one's affections 593.26 *court*
bestow one's favours 593.29 *make love*
bestow one's hand upon 570.15 *marry*
bestow upon 768.5 *give*
best part 123.3 *chief thing;* 205.5 *largest part*
best people 235.7 *elite*
bestraddle 304.15 *mount*
be straight **178.11**
best regards 658.3 *courtesies*
best respects 658.3 *courtesies*
bestride 395.10 *be a prevailing influence;* 154.15 *be high;* 318.11 *cross;* 304.15 *mount;* 150.10 *span*
be strident **513.4**
be strong **336.7**
best room 565.7 *room*
be struck by 446.14 *have an idea*
be struck dumb 506.1 *be silent;* 730.14 *have difficulty speaking*
best-seller 740.6 *book publishing;* 235.8 *exceller;* 721.5 *fiction;* 797.17 *good thing;* 485.3 *masterpiece;* 778.8 *merchandise;* 246.3 *successful thing;* 619.4 *wonder*
best-selling 235.2 *best;* 246.13 *successful*
best-selling author 619.5 *person of wonder*
best shot 353.5 *attempt*
best side 235.6 *worth*
be stubborn **418.11**
be stuck on oneself 673.15 *be vain*
be stuck up 622.26 *be too proud*
be stumped 456.9 *be ignorant*
be stupid 457.9 *lack intellect*
best wishes 658.3 *courtesies;* 667.7 *respects*
be stylish 543.4 *be elegant*
be subjected to 387.8 *be subject to*
be subject to **387.8**; 345.7 *follow from*
be submissive 388.4 *succumb*
be subsequent to 289.10 *succeed*
be subversive **662.16**
be successful **246.6**; 312.9 *achieve*
be sullen **626.9**; 659.8 *get angry*
be superfluous **219.5**; 341.4 *not act*
be superior **121.8**; 129.16 *take precedence*
be surprised **630.12**
be suspicious 629.8 *distrust*
be sweet on 593.24 *be in love;* 595.7 *like;* 593.23 *love*
be swept aside 388.4 *succumb*
be swift **332.4**
be sycophantic **677.11**
bet 59.7 *horseracing;* 107.12 *take a chance*
beta blocker 37.4 *drug type*
beta decay 28.70 *radioactivity*
beta emitter 28.70 *radioactivity*
beta function 27.29 *mathematical function*
be taken 582.15 *die*
be taken aback 630.12 *be surprised*
betake oneself 393.7 *resort*
be talkative **731.7**
beta minus 216.6 *mediocrity*
beta particle 28.70 *radioactivity*
beta rays 28.70 *radioactivity*
be tasteless **497.7**
beta test 36.6 *intelligence test*
betatron 28.94 *particle accelerator*
be taught 6.23 *learn*
be taught a lesson 385.4 *serve one right*
be tedious 620.6 *be boring*
be temperate 674.14 *be modest*
be tenacious **267.8**
bête noire 264.9 *difficult person;* 596.3 *disliked person;* 711.3 *false alarm;* 612.5 *frightener;* 594.7 *hated thing*
be thankful 671.6 *be grateful*
be the answer **706.22**
be the author of 344.9 *be the cause of*
be the better for 237.11 *find useful*
be the boss 579.1 *manage*
be the case 698.27 *be true*
be the cause of **344.9**
be the duty of **810.14**
be the field general 46.15 *play offence*
be the in thing 138.28 *prevail*
Bethel 10.13 *shrine*
be the making of 235.10 *do good;* 392.29 *finance;* 244.1 *improve*
be the norm 216.9 *be average*
be the rage 138.28 *prevail*
be there 525.11 *appear;* 97.11 *be present;* 93.17 *exist*
be there in person 97.12 *attend*
be the result of 345.7 *follow from*
be the rule **140.15**; 632.17 *become a habit;* 138.28 *prevail*
be the same **111.7**
be the tool of 664.10 *knuckle under*
be thirsty 617.14 *be hungry;* 428.18 *thirst*
Bethlehem 10.13 *shrine*
be thoughtless **472.13**; 672.6 *be ungrateful*
be thrifty **680.5**
betide 107.10 *chance*
be timely **287.4**
betimes 293.17 *early*
be tired 261.5 *be fatigued*
be to come 283.7 *be in the future*
be together 516.8 *harmonize*
betoken 694.10 *mean;* 475.11 *predict;* 742.10 *signify;* 701.15 *state*
be told 695.6 *understand*
bet on 104.10 *think likely*
be too clever for 645.5 *be cunning*
be too grand to 622.26 *be too proud*
be to one's advantage 237.10 *benefit*
be too proud **622.26**
be too quick for 645.5 *be cunning*
be touched by **492.13**
be tough **423.10**
be trained 136.14 *be qualified*
be transformed **760.8**
be transient **278.4**
be transparent **527.11**
betray **739.7**; 479.3 *apostatize;* 645.5 *be cunning;* 604.8 *be dishonest;* 700.27 *be false;* 662.16 *be subversive;* 453.21 *change;* 449.2 *detect;* 693.13 *inform on;* 800.9 *prove false;* 738.3 *reveal;* 716.13 *turn queen's evidence*
betrayal 479.7 *apostasy;* 449.7 *detection;* 739.2 *divulgence;* 800.2 *faithlessness;* 700.4 *falseheartedness*
betrayed 604.10 *deceived*
betrayed hopes 604.1 *disappointment*
betrayer 739.4 *discloser;* 479.9 *equivocator;* 699.17 *false person;* 693.10 *informer;* 651.8 *malefactor;* 700.21 *traitor;* 804.9 *wicked person*
betraying 800.6 *faithless;* 742.14 *signifying;* 700.38 *treacherous*
betray one's hopes 604.6 *disappoint*
betray one's trust 604.8 *be dishonest*
be trendy **295.18**
be triumphant 246.9 *be victorious*
betroth 570.15 *marry*
betrothal 755.1 *contract;* 593.8 *love affair;* 756.1 *promise;* 570.5 *wedding*
betrothed 593.11 *loved one;* 570.22 *marriageable;* 756.12 *promised;* 756.6 *someone promised*
be true **698.27**; 93.17 *exist*
be truthful **698.29**
better **244.17**; 121.8 *be superior;* 224.8 *cause change;* 224.11 *changeable;* 469.15 *chosen;* 393.15 *cured;* 797.20 *do good;* 302.8 *further;* 797.1 *good;* 59.15 *horse person;* 244.1, 392.22 *improve;* 244.14 *improved;* 204.8 *sound;* 121.12 *superior;* 235.1 *worthy*
better advised 244.14 *improved*
better choice 244.8 *better thing;* 469.8 *choice*
better days 283.3 *future condition*
bettered 244.14 *improved*
better element 205.1 *part*
better half 115.5 *counterpart;* 570.11 *married woman;* 223.12 *partner;* 570.8 *spouse*
better idea 244.8 *better thing*
bettering 797.6 *beneficial;* 6.16 *educational*
better luck next time 107.15 *hard luck!*
betterment 765.2 *augmentation;* 797.13 *benefit;* 224.1 *change;* 6.1 *education;* 244.5, 302.15 *improvement*
better off 244.14 *improved*
better oneself 224.7 *be changed;* 244.2 *get better*
better red than dead 535.8 *figurative usage*
better than nothing 231.4 *ordinary*
better thing **244.8**
better thought 244.8 *better thing*
better thoughts 479.6 *equivocation*
better time 286.1 *different time*
betting 59.7 *horseracing*
betty 25.35 *dessert*
be turned into 760.7 *convert into*
be turned on by 617.13 *like*
between jobs 343.2 *not working*
between races 412.14 *in the midst*
between Scylla and Charybdis 254.4 *endangered;* 639.16 *irresolutely;* 264.16 *troubled*
between times **275.24**
between two chairs 254.4 *endangered*
between two fires 254.4 *endangered*
between two stools 264.16 *troubled*
between whiles 275.26 *all the time;* 278.9 *for the time being*
between you 737.15 *in secret*
betwixt and between 216.12 *mediumly*
be two-faced 479.2 *equivocate*
Beulah 8.11 *heaven*
be unable to pay **786.9**
be unaccustomed **487.4**
be unadorned **647.7**
be unappreciative 672.6 *be ungrateful*
be unbiased 150.12 *be broad-minded;* 618.15 *be impartial*
be uncertain **453.18**
be unclear 161.3 *make shapeless*
be unconcerned **109.11**
be undeceived 695.6 *understand*
be undemocratic 120.6 *be unjust*
be under authority 12.13 *be governed*
be under cover 252.9 *be safe*
be under the impression 450.8 *be of the opinion*
be unequal **120.5**
be unexplained **696.10**
be unfaithful 639.9 *change sides*
be unfeeling **489.11**
be unfinished **420.13**
be unforgotten 462.15 *be remembered*
be ungrateful **672.6**
be unhealthy **260.24**
be unheard **505.11**
be uniform 750.25 *conform*
be unimportant **124.11**
be unintelligible **696.7**
be unjust **120.6**; **465.11**
be unlike 116.5 *be dissimilar*
be unlucky 249.9 *be in trouble;* 288.7 *lose one's chance*
be unmasked 449.5 *be discovered*
be unmoved 628.6 *be pitiless*
be unrelated **109.10**
be unsatisfied **218.6**
be unselfish **473.7**
be unskilful **486.5**
be unsocial **655.12**
be unused 350.6 *stop using*
be unusual **299.7**
be unwilling **637.6**
be up against it 254.8 *be in danger*
be up and doing 342.12 *be active;* 338.2 *be full of vigour*
be up in arms 342.14 *push*
be up on 6.24 *know*
be up shit creek 221.7 *be in a predicament*
be upstanding 366.5 *arise;* 186.5 *be vertical;* 667.19 *take off one's hat to*
be up to 810.14 *be the duty of*
be up to something 484.13 *plot*
be upwardly mobile **244.2** *get better*
be upwind of 501.6 *have no smell*
be useful **237.9; 392.26**; 348.4 *be an instrument*
be useless **238.7**; 341.4 *not act*
be vague 161.3 *make shapeless*
be vain **660.24; 673.15**; 622.26 *be too proud*
bevel 176.11 *angle;* 23.10 *carpenter's term;* 176.2 *obliquity*
bevel bearing 307.4 *axle*
bevel gear 38.7 *gear;* 438.5 *machine*
bevelled 176.8, 189.4 *oblique*
bevelled edge 189.2 *oblique line*
bevel square 176.4 *angular measurement*
beverage 558.2, 690.13 *drink;* 431.1 *fluid*
be verballed 16.80 *convict oneself*
be vertical **186.5**; 366.5 *arise*
be victorious **246.9**
be vigilant 665.10 *be careful*
be violent **380.7**
be virtuous **803.8**
be visible **518.19; 520.8; 738.5**
be voiceless **730.13**
bevvied up 690.1 *drunk*
bevvy 558.2, 690.13 *drink*
bevy 71.21 *assemblage of mammals;* 376.11 *group;* 208.4 *throng*
bewail 603.6 *lament*
bewail one's sins 808.4 *be penitent*
be walked 48.7 *play baseball*
be wanting 233.5 *be incomplete*
beware 616.5 *be cautious;* 711.6 *be warned;* 634.24 *hands off!;* 711.10 *look out!*
be warned **711.6**
be wary 629.8 *distrust*
be wasted 441.1 *waste*
be wasteful **766.11**
be weak **337.6**
be well-preserved 259.5 *be healthy*
be well thought of 811.5 *have repute*
be well up on 396.22 *be an authority on*
bewhiskered 420.3 *barbed*
be whole **204.9**
be wicked **804.16**
be widowed **571.10**
bewig 551.35 *make clothing*
bewigged 551.29 *dressed*
bewilder 457.10 *bemuse;* 696.7 *be unintelligible;* 619.10 *be wonderful;* 264.23 *cause difficulties;* 453.20 *make uncertain;* 412.9 *mix up;* 737.13 *mystify*
bewildered 766.18 *at a loss;* 453.3, 696.6 *confused;* 412.13 *mixed-up;* 264.16 *troubled;* 619.6 *wondering*
bewildering 453.3 *confused;* 737.11 *mysterious;* 619.8 *wonderful*
bewilderingly 453.24 *confusingly*
bewilderment 453.12 *confusion;* 451.3 *incredulity;* 619.1 *wonder*
be willing **636.13**; 342.14 *push*
be wise **458.7**; 156.15 *be profound;* 485.10 *be skilful*
bewitch **11.21**; 619.10 *be wonderful;* 483.10 *manipulate;* 593.28 *win the love of*
bewitched **11.19**; 760.13 *converted;* 593.19 *enamoured;* 712.10 *maledictive;* 483.12 *motivated;* 480.20 *persuadable*
bewitcher 11.4 *witch*

bewitchery 11.3 witchcraft
bewitching 483.11 motivational; 480.19 persuasive; 11.15 witchlike
bewitchingly 712.14 damningly; 483.14 influentially
bewitchment 760.1 conversion; 480.3 incentive; 483.2 inducement; 593.2 romantic love
be within one's rights 801.13 be right
be with it 695.6 understand
be with one 695.6 understand
be without 135.7 require
be wonderful 619.10
be worried 612.14 worry
be worthless 236.13
be worth the effort 785.12 be profitable
be worthy 235.9
be worthy of 575.7 be entitled to
be wrong 802.19
be years old 556.17 age
beyond all bounds 686.12 self-indulgently
beyond all expectation 246.16 successfully
beyond all reason 380.10 violently
beyond belief 451.7 disbelieved; 105.2 questionable; 103.2 unbelievable
beyond compare 121.14 best
beyond comprehension 202.2 immeasurable
beyond control 264.14 troublesome
beyond count 208.13 numerously
beyond criticism 121.14 best
beyond expectations 217.2 plentiful
beyond measure 219.8 excessively; 208.8 numberless; 208.13 numerously
beyond mortal ken 582.19 dead
beyond one 696.4 difficult; 335.14 powerlessly
beyond one's comprehension 696.4 difficult
beyond one's fondest dreams 246.16 successfully
beyond one's means 792.7 dear; 792.12 dearly
beyond one's power 335.14 powerlessly
beyond price 235.3, 792.8 valuable
beyond question 454.12 assuredly
beyond reach 145.10 distantly
beyond recall 463.11 forgotten; 611.5 past hope
beyond reckoning 202.2 immeasurable
beyond repair 245.13 dilapidated
beyond seas 91.11 nautically
beyond the grave 582.19 dead
beyond the pale 128.11 excluded; 544.8 indecorous
beyond worth 792.13 valuably
be young 555.16
bezant 780.12 ancient coins
bezel 176.2 obliquity
B-feature 356.5 work of art
Bhagavad-Gita 7.12 religious text
bhaji 25.49 Indian dish
bhakti 9.1 worship
bhangra 18.10 world music
Bhavachakra 554.8 theories of life
bhikku 7.7 monk
bhikkunis 7.7 monk
bhikshu 7.3 religious person
B horizon 30.36 soil
bhuna 25.49 Indian dish
biannual 298.12 cyclic; 275.22 periodic; 276.8 periodical; 198.10 two-sided
biannually 275.30 chronologically; 298.16 cyclically; 276.13 for specified periods
bias 465.12; 229.2 attitude; 452.10 conviction; 325.13 deviation; 596.1 dislike; 234.9, 325.6 distort; 234.1 distortion; 39.10 electric potential; 274.6 fallibility; 51.1 green bowling; 800.1 improbity; 595.2 inclination; 395.8 influence; 120.2, 465.3 injustice; 483.10 manipulate; 189.1 obliqueness; 641.7 opinionatedness; 27.57 population; 469.7 preference; 466.13 prejudge; 466.3 prejudice; 504.10 sound quality; 802.1 unfairness; 176.5 viewpoint
biased 176.10; 452.2 convinced; 466.10 discriminatory; 800.5 dishonourable; 595.6 liking; 718.6 misrepresented; 274.17 mistaken; 325.23 oblique; 229.5 tending to; 120.4, 465.8 unjust; 802.11 wrong
biased against 596.8 disliking
biased sample 27.57 population
bias slope 176.2 obliquity
bias voltage 39.10 electric potential
biathlon 68.2 cross-country skiing; 198.2 double; 68.12 ski; 68.1 skiing
biathlon race 68.2 cross-country skiing
biathlon relay race 68.2 cross-country skiing
bib 551.23 children's clothes; 256.11 cleaning cloth; 690.8 get drunk; 551.24 part of garment
bibber 558.12 drinker; 690.17 drunkard
bibbing 690.5 drunken
bibelot 124.9 bauble
Bible 475.10 cards; 760.4 medium of conversion; 7.12 religious text
Bible bash 7.20 preach
Bible-basher 7.5 Christian
Bible-bashing 7.15 religious; 7.2 religiousness
Bible oath 707.3 vow
Bible paper 435.3 paper
Bible school 6.12 educational institution
Bible-worship 7.2 religiousness
Bible-worshipping 7.15 religious
Biblical 698.15 true
Biblical interpretation 5.12 translation
Biblical proverb 5.21 catchword
Biblical strong men 336.6 muscleman
Biblical truth 698.3 the truth
bibliography 6.14 school book; 220.2 table
bibliolater 9.6 idolater; 7.4 religionist
bibliolatrous 9.10 idolatrous
bibliolatry 9.2 idolatry; 7.2 religiousness
bibliomancy 475.2 divination
bibliophagic 6.18 educated
bibliophile 442.8 intellectual person
bibulous 370.17 absorbent; 558.16 drinking; 690.5 drunken
bibulousness 690.11 drinking
bicameral 579.18 parliamentary; 198.10 two-sided
bicarbonate of soda 25.7 basic ingredient
bicarpellary 80.9 of a fruit
bice 539.5 blueness
bice-green 538.1 green
bicentenary 298.3, 298.13, 601.5 anniversary; 462.5 day to remember; 201.9 treble figures
bicentennial 601.14 centennial; 201.9 treble figures
bicentennially 298.16 cyclically
biceps 182.2 bulge; 336.1 strength
bicker 701.13 argue; 751.5 disagree; 327.26 flicker; 242.11 quarrel
bickering 701.7 arguing; 701.1 argument; 751.9 disagreeing; 751.1 disagreement; 242.7 dissension
bicolour 541.6 variegated
biconditional 4.8 philosophical term
biconvex lens 28.29 optical element
bicuspid 425.11 tooth
bicycle 320.12; 198.2 double; 316.5 means of transport
bicycle bell 711.2 danger signal
bicycle chain 320.11 bicycle part; 587.7 blunt weapon; 814.14 instrument of punishment; 331.16 weapons
bicycle clips 320.11 bicycle part
bicycle courier 320.14 cyclist
bicycle-made-for-two 320.12 bicycle
bicycle part 320.11
bicycle path 317.6 path
bicycle pump 320.11 bicycle part
bicycle rickshaw 320.12 bicycle
bicycle tube 432.13 gas balloon
bicyclist 320.14 cyclist
bid 353.1, 353.5 attempt; 776.3 bargain; 776.9 bargaining; 752.3 business offer; 69.3 card game terms; 448.1 experiment; 482.4 formulated intention; 752.1, 752.9 offer; 752.17 offered; 752.10 offer to buy; 69.10 play; 777.1 purchase; 777.7 purchasing; 710.1, 710.6 request
biddability 797.11 good behaviour
biddable 636.3 amenable; 265.13 easy-going; 663.7 obedient; 388.5 submitting; 797.4 well-behaved
bid defiance to 661.5 defy
bidder 353.7 attempter; 777.12 purchaser; 14.3 stockbroker
bidding 777.14 buying; 397.2 demand
bidding prayer 10.9 prayer
biddings 10.6 Eucharist
bide one's time 294.8 delay; 341.4 not act; 474.10 wait
bidet 256.6, 410.12 bath; 433.11 wash
bid fair 756.9 be auspicious; 610.10 inspire hope; 475.11 predict; 229.4 tend
bid fair to 104.8 be probable
bid farewell 313.6 part
bid for 482.10 aim; 482.4 formulated intention; 14.5 invest; 777.1 purchase
bid for votes 752.13 be a candidate; 752.5 offer of public service
bid goodbye 313.6 part
bid good day 658.12 greet
bid price 14.2 stock exchange
bid up 792.11 overpay; 777.1 purchase
bid welcome 654.11 be sociable
Biedermeier 23.7 furniture style
biennial 44.17 botanical; 298.12 cyclic; 78.2 flowering plant; 44.9 garden plant; 77.14 of plants; 275.22 periodic; 276.8 periodical; 77.2 plant; 198.10 two-sided
biennially 298.16 cyclically; 276.13 for specified periods; 77.24 herbaceously; 44.20 horticulturally
bier 583.4 funeral objects; 320.6 litter
biff 331.13 blow; 331.3 hit
biflagellate 84.7 algal
bifocal 198.10 two-sided
bifocals 28.29 optical element; 518.10 visual aid
bifold 198.9 two
biforked 311.9 branched
biforking 311.4 branching
biform 198.10 two-sided
Bifrost 317.9 bridge
bifurcate 176.7 angular; 311.14 branch; 372.13 diverge; 198.16 halve; 198.10 two-sided
bifurcated 311.9 branched; 198.13 half
bifurcation 311.4 branching; 198.7 halving
big 158.15; **679.4**; 123.5 important
bigamist 570.10 married man
bigamous 570.23 monogamous
bigamously 570.24 matrimonially
bigamy 570.3 types of marriage
big appetite 688.1 gluttony
Big Apple 86.10 urban area
big as a house 152.1 thick
big baby 337.4 weakling
big-bale silage 43.9 animal feedstuff
Big Bang 780.7 finance; 14.2 stock exchange
big bang 29.4 cosmological model; 293.3 early stage
big-bang theory 93.8 creation
big-bellied 158.16 fat
Big Bertha 587.12 historical guns
big-bottomed 158.16 fat
big boys 121.7 the best people
Big Brother 400.4 absolute ruler; 123.4 bigwig; 396.4 governance; 395.6 group influence; 252.2 protection; 647.4 strict person; 400.8 the power structure
big bucks 780.3 fortune; 781.6 money; 208.2 multitude
big bud mite 44.12 pests and diseases
big but 123.4 bigwig
big cat 71.10 cat
big cheese 123.4 bigwig; 400.5 company leader; 395.5 influential person; 579.15 manager; 396.10 person of authority; 121.5 superior
big Chief 123.4 bigwig
big Daddy 123.4 bigwig
big day 123.2 important matter
big deal 123.2 important matter; 467.2 overestimate
big Dick 201.6 ten
big dooley 123.4 bigwig
big-eared 504.12 eared
big earner 781.10 wealthy person
big-ears 644.4 meddler
big eater 557.18 eater; 688.4 glutton
big enchilada 123.4 bigwig; 121.5 superior
big fish 123.4 bigwig
Bigfoot 70.7 legendary beast; 89.3 mountaineer; 737.6 natural mystery
big freeze 31.32 freeze
big game 70.1 animals; 60.5 game
big-game fisherman 55.6 angler
big-game fishing 55.1 angling; 74.7 fishing
big-game hunt 633.2 chase
big-game hunter 60.4, 71.24, 633.6 hunter
big-game hunting 60.2 hunting; 71.23 mammal hunting
bigger 190.7
bigger and better 213.6 increasing; 213.8 increasingly
bigger and bigger 213.8 increasingly
biggie 123.4 bigwig
big gun 123.4 bigwig; 400.5 company leader; 121.5 superior
big guy 123.4 bigwig
big hand 669.5 acclaim
bighead 622.13 proud person; 673.7 vain person
big-headed 622.22 boastful; 673.8 vain
big-headedness 622.10 boastfulness; 673.1 vanity
big-hearted 650.7 charitable; 652.6 philanthropic; 473.5 unselfish
big-heartedly 650.11 charitably; 473.9 unselfishly
big-heartedness 650.2 charity; 473.2 unselfishness
big hit 246.1 success
Bighorn Mountains 89.4 US mountains
bight 92.9 inlet
Bight of Benin 92.9 inlet
big jobs 560.5 faeces
Big John 123.4 bigwig
big letter 5.15 type style
Big Mac™ 25.11 sandwich
big man 123.4 bigwig
big man on campus 123.4 bigwig
bigmouth 661.4 defiant person; 729.10 speaker; 731.1 talkativeness; 731.4 talker
big-mouthed 731.6 effusive; 693.16 informative; 507.6 loud
big name 123.4 bigwig
bigness 158.2
big news 123.2 important matter
big noise 123.4 bigwig; 395.5 influential person; 121.5 superior
bigot 466.7; 594.9 hater; 592.5 insensitive person; 465.5 misjudging person; 641.8 obstinate person; 452.11 opinionist; 7.4 religionist
bigoted 452.2 convinced; 466.10 discriminatory; 594.11 racist; 7.15 religious; 641.4 set; 647.8 severe; 465.8 unjust
bigotry 452.10 conviction; 465.3 injustice; 641.7 opinionatedness; 466.3 prejudice; 594.3 race hatred; 7.2 religiousness; 647.1 severity
big person 158.10
big play 123.3 chief thing
big price tag 792.1 high price
big school 815.2 the inside
big shot 123.4 bigwig; 400.5 company leader; 395.5 influential person; 579.15 manager; 396.10 person of authority; 811.2 person of repute
big smoke 86.10 urban area
big spender 681.6 spendthrift; 441.6 waster
big stick 386.3 coercive methods; 480.8 incentive; 814.14 instrument of punishment; 483.4 negative stimulus
big thing 158.9
big-time operator 123.4 bigwig
big timer 123.4 bigwig
big toe 492.7 sense organ
big top 550.7 overhead covering; 21.16 theatre
big undertaking 264.3 difficult task; 354.2 undertaking
bi-guy 567.10 bisexual
big wave 420.9 broken water
big wheel 123.4 bigwig; 400.5 company leader; 395.5 influential person; 396.10 person of authority
big white Chief 123.4 bigwig
bigwig 123.4; 400.5 company leader; 395.5 influential person; 579.15 manager; 396.10 person of authority; 622.13 proud person; 121.5 superior
big with 562.5 fertile; 561.16 reproductive
big with fate 475.15 presageful
bijou 159.7 little
bike 320.12 bicycle; 320.13 motorcycle
biked 319.5 transportable
biker 320.14 cyclist
bike rider 320.14 cyclist
bikie 320.14 cyclist
biking 319.5 transportable
bikini 551.21 beachwear; 67.8 swimwear
bikini-clad 552.10 in dishabille
bilateral 755.7 contractual; 110.5 interconnected; 169.6 side; 198.10 two-sided
bilaterally 755.8 contractually; 110.10 reciprocally
bilateral paralysis 260.17 nervous disorder
bilateral symmetry 162.1 symmetry; 162.2 symmetry operation
bilbo 587.8 sharp weapon

bilboes 814.14 *instrument of punishment*; 251.5 *means of restraint*
Bildungsroman 17.2, 721.5 *fiction*
bile 651.4 *bitterness*; 625.1 *irascibility*; 626.3 *irritableness*; 559.2 *secreted substance*; 499.4 *spleen*; 499.2 *unpalatability*
bile acid 33.6 *lipid*
bileful 624.15 *resentful*
bile pigment 33.18 *pigment*
bilge 175.2 *foot*; 697.1 *nonsense*; 50.3 *parts of a sailing boat*; 238.6 *refuse*; 215.2 *residue*; 258.5 *swill*
bilge water 258.5 *swill*
bilharziasis 260.7 *tropical disease*
bilingual 5.2 *linguist*; 5.38 *linguistic*; 729.19 *speaking*; 719.17 *translational*; 198.10 *two-sided*
bilingual dictionary 5.28 *dictionary*
bilingualism 198.3 *duality*; 5.1 *linguistics*
bilingually 5.48 *linguistically*
bilingual text 719.4 *translation*
bilious 625.4 *irascible*; 626.7 *irritable*; 624.15 *resentful*; 538.6 *sick*; 499.7 *splenetic*; 260.21 *unhealthy*; 537.4 *yellow-faced*
biliously 625.9 *irascibly*; 624.17 *resentfully*
biliousness 260.8 *indigestion*; 626.3 *irritableness*; 499.4 *spleen*; 537.6 *yellowness*
bilirubin 33.18 *pigment*
biliverdin 33.18 *pigment*
bilk 774.16 *act dishonestly*; 700.30 *be fraudulent*; 784.8, 786.7 *not pay*; 604.7 *thwart*
bilked 604.9 *disappointed*
bilker 700.17 *cheat*; 784.6 *debtor*; 786.6 *nonpayer*
bill 220.4; **790.4**; 769.3 *acknowledgment of payment*; 740.9 *advertisement*; 784.5 *amount owing*; 72.16 *avian anatomy*; 783.1 *credit*; 710.7 *demand*; 21.38 *dramatize*; 220.8 *list*; 194.4 *mathematical result*; 743.3 *means of identification*; 780.14 *paper money*; 92.5 *peninsula*; 740.16 *publicize*; 744.1 *record*; 21.8 *scene*; 789.9 *settle accounts*; 587.8 *sharp weapon*; 738.8 *showplace*; 789.4 *statement*; 21.13 *theatrical performance*
billabong 90.1 *river*
bill and coo 593.27 *kiss*
billboard 740.9 *advertisement*
bill collector 769.7 *collector*
bill discounting rate 784.3 *loan*
billed 789.11 *accounted*
billet 143.4 *employment*; 565.1 *habitat*; 142.9 *locate*; 584.1 *military affairs*; 226.5 *resting place*; 312.16 *stopover*
billet-doux 593.15 *love item*
billeted 565.14 *inhabiting*
billfold 780.20 *money store*
billhook 438.3 *garden tool*; 425.9 *sharp-edged thing*; 79.7 *timber production*
billiard 65.9
billiard ball 421.8 *smooth thing*
billiard cloth 65.1 *billiards*
billiard cue 331.15 *ram*
billiards 65.1
billiards club 65.1 *billiards*
billiards game 69.1 *game*
billiards play 65.2
billiards player 65.7
billiard spot 65.3 *English billiards*; 65.5 *snooker*
billiard table 65.1 *billiards*; 187.3 *flat thing*; 421.8 *smooth thing*
Billie Jean King 63.7 *famous tennis players*
billing and cooing 593.14 *communication of love*; 593.6 *courtship*
Billingsgate 779.1 *market*
billingsgate 712.1 *curse*; 5.19 *swearword*
billion 194.3 *large number*; 201.11 *million*; 208.7 *myriad*
billionaire 765.7 *gainer*; 201.11 *million*; 248.4 *prosperous person*; 781.10 *wealthy person*
billions 780.3 *fortune*; 208.2 *multitude*
billionth 196.4 *less than one*; 201.22 *millionth*
bill of exchange 780.14 *paper money*; 759.3 *something in exchange*
bill of fare 220.4 *bill*
bill of lading 220.4 *bill*; 743.3 *means of identification*
bill of mortality 582.12 *death count*
billon 780.16 *bullion*; 412.2 *mixed thing*
billon coinage 780.13 *coinage*
billow 91.10; 182.5 *be convex*; 91.3 *wave*
billowing 182.4 *convex*; 182.1 *convexity*; 91.7 *oceanic*
billowy cloud 31.20 *cloud appearance*
bill poster 740.10 *publicizer*
bills 784.1 *debt*
bill sticker 740.10 *publicizer*
Bill Tilden 63.7 *famous tennis players*
billy goat 43.8 *livestock*; 567.16 *male animal*; 71.17 *male mammal*; 503.2 *something that makes an unpleasant smell*
bimbo 456.5 *ignorant person*
bimetallism 14.1, 780.7 *finance*
bimodal distribution 27.59 *probability distribution*
bimolecular 32.38 *reactive*
bimolecular reaction 32.14 *chemical reaction*
bimonthly 298.12 *cyclic*; 298.16 *cyclically*
bin 256.10 *cleaning object*; 203.3 *container*; 461.8 *mental hospital*; 371.13 *throw away*; 410.11 *vessel*; 767.4 *wastebin*
binary 32.35 *combined*; 27.71 *numerical*; 198.9 *two*
binary code 40.10 *character*
binary compound 32.7 *chemical compound*
binary digit 27.9 *numeral*
binary notation 27.8 *number system*
binary number 27.8 *number system*
binary star 29.9 *constellation*
binary system 194.1 *number*; 27.8 *number system*
bind 373.12; 164.5 *border*; 620.2 *boring thing*; 386.6 *compel*; 373.11 *connect*; 394.20 *doctor*; 54.3 *fencing movements*; 251.12 *gag*; 376.38 *group*; 810.17 *impose a duty*; 416.9 *make dense*; 228.7 *make stable*; 64.5 *play rugby*; 264.5 *predicament*; 393.1 *repair*; 309.11, 378.10 *restrain*; 136.16 *specify*; 165.6, 550.25 *wrap*
binder 43.10 *farm tool*; 373.6 *line*; 550.4 *wrapping*
binding 386.9 *compelling*; 416.7 *condensed*; 373.6 *line*; 810.12 *obligatory*; 393.8 *repair*; 68.5 *ski equipment*; 550.4 *wrapping*
binding agreement 755.1 *contract*
binding energy 28.65 *atom*; 334.4 *energy*
binding over 814.7 *punishment*
binding twine 373.6 *line*
bind oneself 755.5 *contract*
bind over 814.1 *punish*
bind up 393.1 *repair*
bind up one's wounds 393.6 *cure*
bin end 131.8 *tail*
bin ends 205.8 *bits and pieces*
Binet test 36.6 *intelligence test*
binge 557.2 *appetite*; 688.5 *be greedy*; 601.1 *celebration*; 690.14 *drinking bout*; 557.22 *eat well*; 686.11 *overindulge*
bingeing 557.2 *appetite*; 688.6 *gluttonous*; 688.1 *gluttony*
binger 688.4 *glutton*
bingo 107.3 *equal chance*
binman 767.6 *rubbish collector*
binnacle 579.5 *guide*; 323.5 *navigation*
binned 410.20 *containing*
binocular 198.10 *two-sided*; 518.20 *visual*
binoculars 198.2 *double*; 60.3 *hunting equipment*; 28.32 *optical instrument*; 518.10 *visual aid*
binomial 27.25 *algebraic expression*; 27.76 *functional*
binomial distribution 27.59 *probability distribution*
binomial expression 27.25 *algebraic expression*
binomial nomenclature 34.17 *taxonomy*
binomial series 27.20 *sequence*
bint 568.9 *woman considered as a sex object*
bioaeronautics 322.2 *aeronautics*
bioastronautics 29.29 *astronautics*
biochemical 33.26; 34.20 *biological*; 32.31 *chemical*
biochemical genetics 34.11 *genetics*
biochemically 33.27; 34.29 *biologically*
biochemical taxonomy 33.1 *biochemistry*
biochemist 33.2; 34.19 *life scientist*
Biochemistry 33
biochemistry 33.1; 34.6 *cell biology*; 32.1 *chemistry*; 34.1 *life science*; 35.3 *medical specialty*
biocytin 33.12 *coenzyme*
biodegradable 375.5 *disintegrated*; 278.7 *impermanent*; 372.19 *separable*
biodiversity 34.18 *ecology*
biodynamic farming 43.1 *agriculture*
bioecology 34.1 *life science*
bioelectricity 28.42 *electricity*
bioenergetic 33.26 *biochemical*
bioenergetics 33.22; 33.1 *biochemistry*; 36.3 *psychiatric treatment*
bioengineering 38.1 *engineering*
biofeedback 36.3 *psychiatric treatment*; 11.10 *psychic phenomenon*
biogas 432.3 *miasma*
biogenesis 561.3 *propagation*
biogenetic 554.14 *biotic*
biogenetical 554.14 *biotic*
biogenetics 34.1 *life science*
biographer 17.14 *author*; 721.10 *descriptive writer*; 3.3 *historian*; 744.9 *recorder*
biographical 3.19 *chronicled*; 17.19, 721.12 *narrative*
biographical dictionary 5.28 *dictionary*
biographically 3.25 *reportedly*
biographical record 3.6 *biography*; 744.1 *record*
biographical sketch 17.4 *nonfiction*
biography 3.6; 721.4 *factual account*; 554.11 *life story*; 17.4 *nonfiction*; 744.1 *record*
biohazard 254.5 *danger*; 34.18 *ecology*
biologic 554.14 *biotic*
biological 34.20; 554.14 *biotic*
biological anthropology 1.1 *anthropology*
biological classification 34.17 *taxonomy*
biological clock 554.4 *biological function*; 281.6 *clock*; 276.5 *recurrent period*
biological coloration 529.1 *colour*
biological death 582.1 *death*
biological function 554.4
biologically 34.29; 554.22 *vitally*
biological molecule 34.12 *molecular biology*
biological science 34.1 *life science*
biological shield 28.73 *nuclear reactor*
biological warfare 585.8 *warfare*
biologist 34.19 *life scientist*
biology 34.1 *life science*; 402.6 *natural science*; 554.7 *studies of life*
bioluminescence 28.24 *light emission*
biomass 437.8 *renewable energy*
biomedicine 35.3 *medical specialty*
biometric 34.20 *biological*; 26.16 *micrometric*
biometrics 1.10 *measurement*; 26.2 *micrometry*
biometrist 34.19 *life scientist*
biometry 554.5 *life cycle*; 34.1 *life science*; 26.2 *micrometry*
biomolecular 33.26 *biochemical*
biomolecule 33.1 *biochemistry*
bionic 34.20 *biological*; 566.12 *human*
bionic man 566.8 *humanlike machine*; 619.5 *person of wonder*
bionics 34.1 *life science*
bionic woman 566.8 *humanlike machine*
bionomic 34.20 *biological*
bionomics 34.1 *life science*
biophysical 34.20 *biological*
biophysicist 34.19 *life scientist*
biophysics 28.4 *experimental physics*; 34.1 *life science*
biopic 21.2 *play*
bioplasm 34.7 *cell*; 554.2 *living matter*
bioplasma 11.10 *psychic phenomenon*
bioplast 554.2 *living matter*
bioplastic 554.14 *biotic*
biopsy 35.7 *diagnosis*
biorhythm 298.2 *cycle*; 276.5 *recurrent period*
biorhythmic 298.12 *cyclic*
biosphere 434.2 *aerosphere*; 30.5 *earth*; 34.2 *living world*
biosynthesis 33.1 *biochemistry*; 32.16 *synthesis*
biosynthetic 33.26 *biochemical*
biosynthetically 33.27 *biochemically*
biosystematic 34.28 *taxonomic*
biosystematics 34.17 *taxonomy*
biota 34.2 *living world*
biotechnological 34.20 *biological*
biotechnology 33.1 *biochemistry*; 34.1 *life science*; 34.12 *molecular biology*; 32.16 *synthesis*
biotic 554.14; 34.21 *living*
biotical 554.14 *biotic*
biotically 554.22 *vitally*
biotic potential 562.2 *productiveness*
biotin 33.13 *vitamin*
biotype 34.11 *genetics*
bipartisan 750.20 *agreeable*
bipartisanship 747.2 *fellowship*
bipartite 372.15 *separate*; 198.10 *two-sided*
bipartition 198.7 *halving*
biped 198.2 *double*; 198.10 *two-sided*; 70.4 *type of animal*
bipedal 70.15 *of animals*; 198.10 *two-sided*
bipinnate 77.18 *of leaves*
biplane 198.2 *double*
bipod 198.2 *double*
bipolar transistor 39.19 *transistor*
biquintile 176.4 *angular measurement*
birch 814.3 *hit*; 814.14 *instrument of punishment*
birchbark canoe 50.6 *canoeing*
birching 814.12 *corporal punishment*
birch-rod 814.14 *instrument of punishment*
bird 63.11 *badminton equipment*; 514.7 *cry of disapproval*; 251.4 *detention*; 70.6 *flying animal*; 593.9 *lover*; 815.4 *prison sentence*; 654.10 *social animal*; 70.4 *type of animal*; 568.9 *woman considered as a sex object*; 555.8 *young woman*
birdbanding 72.19 *ornithology*
birdbath 44.3 *ornamental garden*
bird box 72.14 *nest*; 72.19 *ornithology*
birdbrain 459.3 *foolish person*; 457.3 *unintelligent person*
bird-brained 459.5 *foolish*
birdcage 72.19 *ornithology*; 815.3 *prison cell*; 565.12 *stall*
bird call 72.18, 515.2 *bird song*
bird-catcher 633.6 *hunter*
birder 72.20 *ornithologist*
bird food 557.8 *animal food*
bird god 72.9 *fabulous bird*
birdhouse 72.14 *nest*; 72.19 *ornithology*; 565.12 *stall*
birdie 72.1 *birds*; 56.2 *golfing terms*
bird in the hand 763.1 *possession*
birdlife 72.1 *birds*
birdlike 72.21 *avian*
birdlime 267.3, 430.2 *adhesive*; 700.13, 700.33 *snare*
bird of ill omen 475.7 *bad-luck sign*; 711.1 *warning*
bird of passage 72.1 *birds*; 278.2 *transient thing*
bird of peace 72.1 *birds*
bird of prey 72.5; 382.13 *animal killer*; 633.6 *hunter*
bird reserve 72.19 *ornithology*
Birds 72
birds 72.1
bird sanctuary 72.19 *ornithology*
bird scarer 43.14 *pest control*
birdseed 557.8 *animal food*; 77.9 *seed*
bird's-eye 138.15 *general*
bird's-eye view 19.10 *art subject*; 138.7 *global view*; 397.7 *overview*; 723.1 *summary*; 518.9 *viewpoint*; 204.3 *whole situation*
birdsmouth joint 23.10 *carpenter's term*
birdsnest 68.14 *ski*
birdsnesting 68.1 *skiing*
bird's-nest soup 25.13 *soup*
birds of a feather 267.1 *adhesion*; 569.6 *close friend*; 750.5 *conformity*; 115.6 *couple*; 111.1 *sameness*
bird song 72.18; **515.2**
bird strike 322.7 *miscellaneous aviation terms*
bird table 44.3 *ornamental garden*
birdwatcher 518.11 *observer*; 72.20 *ornithologist*
birdwatching 72.19 *ornithology*
birdwood 691.6 *drug*
birdy 72.21 *avian*
birefringence 28.27 *polarized light*
bireme 586.25 *historical naval ships*
biretta 551.15 *headgear*; 7.11 *vestment*
Birmingham 87.4 *British cities*
Birmingham accent 5.26 *dialect*
birth 525.1 *appearance*; 295.4, 308.11 *beginning*; 554.4 *biological function*; 130.4 *conception*; 93.8 *creation*; 137.8 *genealogy*; 554.5 *life cycle*; 561.3 *propagation*
birth certificate 744.2 *certificate*; 743.3 *means of identification*
birth chart 11.9 *divination*
birth control 563.3

birthday 601.5 *anniversary*; 298.6 *annually celebrated day*; 275.11 *date*
birthday cake 25.36 *cake*
Birthday Honours 813.1 *reward*
birthday party 654.5 *party*
birthday present 768.2 *gift*
birthday suit 552.2 *nudity*
birthmark 541.4 *maculation*; 743.3 *means of identification*; 260.13 *skin disease*
birth pangs 561.7 *obstetrics*
birthplace 565.3 *home*; 85.6 *native land*; 344.2 *source*
birth rate 561.3 *propagation*
birthright 788.4 *legacy*; 769.1 *receiving*; 575.1 *right*
births, marriages, and deaths 693.4 *mass communication*
birthweight 414.4 *heaviness*
biryani 25.49 *Indian dish*
bis 112.24 *again*; 669.27 *bravo!*; 198.19 *twice*
biscuit 534.1 *brown*; 557.7 *food*; 25.39 *loaf*
biscuit barrel 25.4 *kitchen container*
biscuit firing 24.5 *ceramic process*
biscuit ware 24.1 *ceramics*
bisect 27.97 *align*; 770.4 *allot*; 372.11 *divide*; 198.16 *halve*; 216.10 *make average*; 205.10 *part*
bisected 198.13 *half*
bisection 198.7 *halving*
bisection search 40.19 *computing terms*
bisector 119.7 *dividing line*; 198.8 *half*; 27.37 *line*
bisexual 567.10; 568.10 *homosexual*; 561.16 *reproductive*; 198.10 *two-sided*
bisexuality 198.3 *duality*
bishop 69.4 *chess terms*; 396.10 *person of authority*; 7.8 *priest*; 400.6 *religious leader*; 121.5 *superior*
Bishop Desmond Tutu 589.4 *Nobel Peace Prize*
bishopdom 7.9 *priesthood*
bishopric 7.9 *priesthood*; 86.5 *state*
bishop's palace 7.10 *priestly dwelling*
bishop's purple 540.1 *purpleness*
Bismarck brown 534.4 *brown pigment*
bismuthic 32.34 *elemental*
bismuthous 32.34 *elemental*
bismuthyl 32.34 *elemental*
bisque 56.3 *golf shots*; 25.13 *soup*
bissextile 298.12 *cyclic*
bistable circuit 39.13 *circuit*
bistoury 425.10 *knife*
bistre 534.4 *brown pigment*
bistro 557.15 *eating place*
bisymmetric 162.4 *symmetrical*
bit 40.19 *computing terms*; 196.3 *fragment*; 59.14 *horse-riding terms*; 197.2 *item*; 159.3 *little piece*; 251.5 *means of restraint*; 27.9 *numeral*; 308.2 *opener*; 205.7, 405.2 *piece*; 21.23 *role*; 127.2 *thing included*
bit by bit 209.10 *by degrees*; 205.12 *partly*; 372.20 *separately*; 139.32 *severally*; 333.16 *slowly*
bitch 804.10 *bad person*; 626.11 *be irritable*; 264.3 *difficult task*; 71.9 *dog*; 568.14 *female animal*; 71.18 *female mammal*; 594.8 *hated person*; 625.3 *irascible person*; 568.8 *nasty woman*; 753.1, 753.6 *protest*; 626.5 *sullen person*; 651.9 *vixen*
bitchiness 651.4 *bitterness*; 625.1 *irascibility*; 626.3 *irritableness*
bitchy 678.16 *defamatory*; 236.5 *harmful*; 651.14 *hostile*; 626.7 *irritable*
bite 55.1 *angling*; 491.10 *be painful*; 496.13 *be piquant*; 425.14 *be sharp*; 557.21 *eat*; 726.1 *emphasis*; 19.22 *engrave*; 742.11 *gesture*; 236.14 *ill-treat*; 76.16 *infest*; 491.11 *inflict pain*; 491.3 *injury*; 557.14 *mouthful*; 205.7 *piece*; 496.1 *piquancy*; 372.9 *separate*; 624.6 *sign of anger*
bite into 314.11 *infiltrate*; 372.9 *separate*
biteless 426.4 *toothless*
bite one's nails 612.14 *worry*
bite someone's head off 624.11 *be angry*; 624.13 *vent one's anger*
bite the bullet 638.8 *brace oneself*; 491.9 *feel pain*; 388.4 *succumb*
bite the dust 357.13 *be destroyed*; 582.15 *die*; 247.6 *fail*; 305.11 *trip*
bite through 372.9 *separate*
bite to eat 557.12 *meal*
biting 499.5 *acid*; 164.10 *advantaged*; 494.8 *cold*; 659.5 *discourteous*; 557.1 *eating*; 651.14 *hostile*; 491.5 *painful*; 496.9 *piquant*; 336.12 *strong to the senses*; 31.47 *windy*
biting comment 651.4 *bitterness*
bit map 40.19 *computing terms*
BITNET 40.15 *network*
bit of a do 601.1 *celebration*
bit of fluff 568.9 *woman considered as a sex object*
bit of luck 107.2 *luck*
bit of skirt 568.9 *woman considered as a sex object*
bit on the side 211.4 *extra*; 593.11 *loved one*
bit part 21.23 *role*
bit player 21.24 *actor*
bits 238.6 *refuse*; 215.1 *remainder*
bits and bobs 205.8 *bits and pieces*; 376.32, 412.3 *miscellany*; 215.2 *residue*
bits and pieces 205.8; 376.32, 412.3 *miscellany*; 440.4 *possessions*; 238.6 *refuse*; 215.2 *residue*
bitsy 159.7 *little*
bitten 593.18 *in love*
bitter 499.5 *acid*; 558.7 *alcoholic drink*; 494.8 *cold*; 678.16 *defamatory*; 596.8 *disliking*; 594.10 *hating*; 651.14 *hostile*; 626.7 *irritable*; 626.12 *make irritable*; 496.9 *piquant*; 624.15 *resentful*; 499.7 *splenetic*; 495.7 *tasty*; 242.3 *unpalatable*; 31.47 *windy*
bitter and twisted 651.14 *hostile*
bitter comedy 21.12 *comedy*
bitter cup 249.1 *adversity*
bitter disappointment 604.1 *disappointment*
bitter end 131.8 *tail*
bitter-ender 641.8 *obstinate person*; 113.11 *opposer*
bitter lemon 558.6 *soft drink*
bitterly 494.13 *coldly*; 594.18 *hatefully*; 626.14 *irritably*; 496.15 *piquantly*; 624.17 *resentfully*; 499.10 *sourly*; 495.11 *tastily*
bitterly cold 31.55 *cool*
bittern 72.3 *water bird*
bitterness 651.4; 590.6 *bad feeling*; 596.1 *dislike*; 495.4 *flavour*; 236.11 *harmfulness*; 594.1 *hate*; 496.1 *piquancy*; 624.1 *resentment*; 499.1 *sourness*; 499.4 *spleen*; 499.2 *unpalatability*
bitter pill 249.1 *adversity*; 814.10 *affliction*; 594.7 *hated thing*
bitter pit 44.12 *pests and diseases*
bitter resentment 624.1 *resentment*
bitters 499.3 *sour thing*
bittersweet 498.6 *sweet*
bitter taste 495.1 *taste*; 495.2 *taste of life*
bittiness 233.1 *incompleteness*
bitts 50.3 *parts of a sailing boat*
bitty 133.8 *discontinuous*; 233.4 *incomplete*; 205.11 *partial*
bitumen 38.25 *construction material*; 317.4 *road surface*
bituminous 437.10 *powered*
bituminous coal 437.5 *coal*; 435.1 *materials*
biuret test 33.9 *protein*
bivalence 4.8 *philosophical term*
bivalent 32.35 *combined*
bivalve 70.5 *aquatic animal*; 198.2 *double*; 75.5 *mollusc*; 75.19 *molluscan*
Bivalvia 75.5 *mollusc*
bivalvular 75.19 *molluscan*
bivouac 62.1 *mountaineering*; 301.3 *resting place*; 565.18 *take up residence*
biweekly 298.12 *cyclic*; 298.16 *cyclically*; 740.5 *journal*
bizarre 118.14 *eccentric*; 477.11 *fantastical*; 272.5 *ridiculous*; 696.5 *strange*; 103.2 *unbelievable*; 619.8 *wonderful*
bizarrely 619.13 *wonderfully*
bizarreness 272.1 *ludicrousness*; 118.4 *unusualness*
bizzy 16.17 *police officer*; 253.3 *security officer*
Björn Borg 63.7 *famous tennis players*
blab 731.7 *be talkative*; 739.7 *betray*; 693.13 *inform on*; 731.3 *talk*
blabber 731.7 *be talkative*; 693.10 *informer*; 731.3 *talk*; 731.4 *talker*
blabberer 739.4 *discloser*
blabbermouth 739.4 *discloser*; 729.10 *speaker*; 731.4 *talker*
blabbing 731.6 *effusive*
Black 532.2 *dark*; 1.13 *racial*
black 532.1; 236.3 *bad*; 532.11 *blacken*; 256.13 *clean*; 523.8 *dark*; 523.3 *dark colour*; 523.10 *dark-coloured*; 523.4 *dark thing*; 258.7 *dirty*; 558.17 *drinkable*; 551.3 *formal dress*; 583.11 *funeral*; 59.1 *horse*; 611.6 *inauspicious*; 528.1 *opaque*; 529.13 *soft-hued*; 626.6 *sullen*; 670.15 *withhold approval*; 52.15 *wrestling*
black-and-blue 532.3 *blackened*; 539.2 *bluish*; 491.7 *feeling pain*; 540.7 *livid*
Black and Tan 532.9 *black thing*
black and white 113.3 *opposites*
black-and-white 532.7 *blackness*; 541.8 *checked*; 19.9 *drawing*; 522.12 *highlight*; 41.3 *photograph*
black-and-white drawing 530.3 *pen-and-ink sketch*
black-and-white film 41.9 *film*
black-and-white photograph 530.3 *pen-and-ink sketch*
black-and-white photography 41.1 *photography*
black-and-white print 530.3 *pen-and-ink sketch*
black-and-white television 692.21 *television*; 692.22 *television set*
black Angus 532.9 *black thing*
black armband 743.5 *uniform*
black art 532.10 *figurative usage*; 11.3 *witchcraft*
black as coal 532.1 *black*
black as hell 532.1 *black*
black as ink 532.1 *black*; 523.10 *dark-coloured*
black as jet 532.1 *black*
black as midnight 532.1 *black*
black as my hat 532.1 *black*
black as night 532.1 *black*; 523.10 *dark-coloured*
black as pitch 532.1 *black*
black as soot 532.1 *black*
black as thunder 532.1 *black*
blackball 532.11 *blacken*; 128.7, 470.3 *exclude*; 128.1 *exclusion*; 532.10 *figurative usage*; 655.13 *ignore*; 371.4 *ostracize*; 814.1 *punish*; 251.8 *restrain*; 251.1 *restraint*; 655.3 *separation*; 372.10 *set apart*; 399.3 *veto*; 670.15 *withhold approval*
black ball 65.5 *snooker*
blackballed 670.31 *disapproved*; 128.11 *excluded*; 399.5 *vetoed*
blackballing 670.3 *nonacceptance*; 371.19 *ostracism*; 814.7 *punishment*; 470.5 *rejection*; 469.10 *vote*
blackball vote 469.10 *vote*
black bass 532.9 *black thing*
black bean aphid 44.12 *pests and diseases*
black beans 43.12 *crop*
black bean soup 25.50 *Central American dish*
black bear 532.9 *black thing*
Blackbeard 774.9 *plunderer*
Black Beauty 59.1 *horse*
black beauty 691.6 *drug*
black belt 532.9 *black thing*; 43.11 *farmland*; 52.7 *judo*; 485.4 *skilled person*
blackberry 532.9 *black thing*
blackberry cobbler 25.36 *cake*
Black Bess 59.1 *horse*
blackbird 532.9 *black thing*
blackboard 532.9 *black thing*; 349.7 *reused product*
black body 28.40 *heating effect*
black-body radiation 28.40 *heating effect*
black bombers 592.6 *desensitizing substance*
black book 532.10 *figurative usage*
black books 594.4 *hatefulness*
black bottom 25.36 *cake*; 22.2 *dance*; 532.10 *figurative usage*
black box 532.10 *figurative usage*; 744.10 *recording instrument*
black bread 25.38 *bread*
black cap 16.43 *conviction*
black cat 475.6 *good-luck sign*; 11.6 *talisman*
black caviar 25.16 *fish dish*
black-coat worker 578.1 *worker*
blackcock 72.10 *male bird*
black coffee 532.9 *black thing*; 558.4 *coffee*
black comedy 21.12 *comedy*
Black Consciousness 244.11 *reformism*
Black Country 532.10 *figurative usage*
black cow 558.6 *soft drink*
blackcurrant 532.9 *black thing*
blackcurrant midge 44.12 *pests and diseases*
blackdamp 432.3 *miasma*
Black Death 532.10 *figurative usage*; 260.5 *plague*
black despair 602.2 *depression*; 611.1 *hopelessness*
black diamonds 437.5 *coal*; 532.10 *figurative usage*
black dress 743.5 *uniform*
black economy 13.2 *economy*; 389.1 *escape*; 532.10 *figurative usage*; 786.1 *nonpayment*; 779.3 *sellers' market*; 776.4 *trade*
blacked 670.31 *disapproved*
blacked out 399.6 *censored*; 521.3 *private*
blacken 532.11; 523.13 *become dark*; 529.15 *colour*; 678.12 *defame*; 258.11 *dirty*; 245.5 *hurt*; 670.22 *vituperate*
blackened 532.3; 491.6 *injured*
blackening 532.7 *blackness*; 523.2 *darkening*; 678.16 *defamatory*; 524.3 *dimming*; 678.5 *scorn*
black eye 532.9 *black thing*; 491.3 *injury*
black-eyed 532.4 *black-haired*
black-eyed Susan 532.9 *black thing*
blackface 532.9 *black thing*; 21.21 *stage requisite*
blackfish 532.9 *black thing*
black flag 532.9 *black thing*; 743.7 *flag*
blackfly 532.9 *black thing*; 76.3 *pest*; 44.12 *pests and diseases*
Black Forest 532.10 *figurative usage*
Black Forest gateau 25.35 *dessert*
Black Friar 532.9 *black thing*
black frost 494.5 *ice*
Black ghetto 87.7 *city district*
black grouse 532.9 *black thing*
blackguard 812.2 *disreputable character*; 798.6 *evil person*; 532.10 *figurative usage*; 651.8 *malefactor*; 712.6 *vilify*; 804.9 *wicked person*
blackguardly 532.5 *black-hearted*
black gunion 691.6 *drug*
black-haired 532.4
Black Hand 804.7 *criminality*
black hat 532.9 *black thing*
blackhead 532.9 *black thing*; 548.2 *pimple*; 260.13 *skin disease*
black-hearted 532.5
Black Hills 532.10 *figurative usage*
black hole 532.9 *black thing*; 521.5 *invisible thing*; 29.11 *stellar birth*
black humour 599.3 *wit*
black ice 532.10 *figurative usage*; 31.32 *freeze*; 494.5 *ice*; 521.5 *invisible thing*
blacking 532.8 *black pigment*; 256.9 *cleaning agent*
blacking out 526.5 *disguise*
blacking up 526.5 *disguise*
blackish 532.1 *black*
blackishness 532.7 *blackness*
blackjack 532.9 *black thing*; 587.7 *blunt weapon*; 331.8 *club*
blacklead 532.11 *blacken*
black lead 532.8 *black pigment*; 256.13 *clean*; 256.9 *cleaning agent*; 268.5 *lubricant*
blackleg 479.3 *apostatize*; 700.17 *cheat*; 325.19 *deviant person*; 751.4 *dissenter*; 15.7 *employee*; 479.9 *equivocator*; 532.10 *figurative usage*; 594.8 *hated person*; 44.12 *pests and diseases*; 753.4 *protester*; 662.12 *reactionary*; 709.4 *refuser*; 260.18 *veterinary disease*
black light 532.9 *black thing*; 521.6 *that which makes invisible*
black-line 23.15 *woodcrafted*
black-line woodcut 23.8 *woodwork*
blacklist 532.11 *blacken*; 16.79 *convict*; 128.7 *exclude*; 128.1 *exclusion*; 532.10 *figurative usage*; 655.13 *ignore*; 220.8 *list*; 220.6 *list of names*; 655.3 *separation*; 372.10 *set apart*; 670.15 *withhold approval*
blacklisted 670.31 *disapproved*; 128.11 *excluded*
blacklisting 16.43 *conviction*; 128.1 *exclusion*
black-locked 532.4 *black-haired*
black look 659.3 *act of discourtesy*; 670.10 *disapproving look*; 518.6 *look*; 624.6 *sign of anger*; 625.2 *sign of irascibility*; 626.4 *sign of irritableness*
black lung 260.9 *respiratory disease*
blackly 532.12; 523.15 *darkly*; 626.13 *sullenly*
black magic 532.10 *figurative usage*; 236.11 *harmfulness*; 523.7 *spiritual darkness*; 11.3 *witchcraft*
blackmail 651.7 *act of malevolence*; 386.3

coercive methods; 397.2, 397.10, 710.2, 710.7 *demand*; 774.7 *dishonesty*; 532.10 *figurative usage*; 386.7 *force*; 790.8 *levy*; 813.8 *secret money*; 773.10 *take away*; 773.3 *taking away*; 651.18 *torment*

blackmailed 710.10 *demanding*; 774.18 *fraudulent*

blackmailer 386.4 *coercive person*; 710.4 *requester*; 773.6 *taker*

blackmailing 710.10 *demanding*; 774.18 *fraudulent*

Black Maria 532.9 *black thing*; 320.17 *police car*

black mark 670.7 *blame*; 606.2 *expression of dissatisfaction*

black market 13.2 *economy*; 532.10 *figurative usage*; 779.3 *sellers' market*; 16.59 *stolen*; 776.4 *trade*

black-market goods 16.36 *stolen property*

Black Mass 532.10 *figurative usage*

Black Muslim 7.6 *non-Christian*

Blackness 532

blackness 532.7; 236.9 *badness*; 523.3 *dark colour*; 523.1 *darkness*; 258.1 *dirtiness*; 521.4 *invisibility*; 291.2 *night*; 528.6 *opaqueness*

black nightshade 532.9 *black thing*

black notes 18.16 *musical note*

blackout 532.9 *black thing*; 463.2 *blankness*; 519.1 *blindness*; 523.2 *darkening*; 523.1 *darkness*; 526.4 *disappearance*; 690.10 *drunkenness*; 437.4 *electricity*; 261.7 *fatigue*; 39.34 *power supply*; 21.8 *scene*; 523.6 *shade*; 384.10 *shelter*; 585.7 *war measures*

black out 519.14 *be blind*; 489.11 *be unfeeling*; 708.14 *cancel*; 399.4 *censor*; 737.12 *keep secret*; 523.14 *make dark*; 521.8 *make invisible*; 358.1 *obliterate*; 251.8 *restrain*

Black Panther 662.10 *seditionist*

black pepper 532.9 *black thing*; 496.2 *seasoning*

black pigment 532.8

blackplate 25.43 *US dish*

Black Power 12.3 *governance*; 244.11 *reformism*; 396.7 *type of rule*

Black Prince 532.10 *figurative usage*

black pudding 532.9 *black thing*; 25.29 *sausage*

Black Rod 532.9 *black thing*

Black run 68.1 *skiing*

black saddler 59.15 *horse person*

Black Sea 532.10 *figurative usage*

black sheep 812.2 *disreputable character*; 532.10 *figurative usage*; 766.6 *loser*; 804.9 *wicked person*

Black Shirt 532.9 *black thing*

Blackshirts 12.6 *political party*

black-skinned 523.10 *dark-coloured*

blacksmith 578.2 *artisan*; 59.15 *horse person*

black snake 532.9 *black thing*

black spot 254.5 *danger*; 532.10 *figurative usage*

black spruce 532.9 *black thing*

black stone 10.14 *sacred object*

black stoneware 24.1 *ceramics*

black stuff 691.6 *drug*; 532.10 *figurative usage*

black swan 532.9 *black thing*; 325.19 *deviant person*

blacktail deer 532.9 *black thing*

black tar 691.6 *drug*

black tea 558.3 *tea*

black thing 532.9

blackthorn 532.9 *black thing*

blackthorn winter 31.3 *weather*

black tie 532.9 *black thing*; 656.7 *dressed-up*; 551.3, 656.4 *formal dress*

blacktop 532.9 *black thing*; 435.2 *building material*; 550.11 *paving*; 317.4 *road surface*; 550.29 *surface*

black velvet 558.8 *mixed drink*

Black Watch 532.9 *black thing*

blackwater fever 260.7 *tropical disease*

black widow 76.2 *arachnid*; 532.9 *black thing*

blad 740.9 *advertisement*

bladder 21.12 *comedy*; 432.13 *gas balloon*

blade 25.22 *beef*; 586.1 *combatant*; 164.3 *cutting edge*; 54.2 *fencing equipment*; 81.3 *grass plant*; 567.2 *male*; 84.3 *plant body*; 25.24 *pork*; 330.11 *propeller*; 50.4 *rowing*; 425.9 *sharp-edged thing*; 587.8 *sharp weapon*

blade of grass 81.3 *grass plant*

blade shoulder 25.25 *pork*

blade slip 50.4 *rowing*

blades of grass 566.1 *humankind*

blag 702.12 *deceive*; 774.7 *dishonesty*; 702.2 *sophism*; 700.7 *tricking*

blagger 774.11 *dishonest person*

blagging 700.7 *tricking*

blah 731.7 *be talkative*; 620.4 *boring*; 270.1 *diffuseness*; 618.11 *insignificant*; 697.1 *nonsense*; 729.2 *power of speech*; 731.3 *talk*; 697.6 *talk nonsense*

blah! blah! 731.12 *rhubarb! rhubarb!*

blah-blah 509.2 *humming*; 731.3 *talk*

blain 260.15 *ulcer*

blamable 670.36 *blameworthy*

blame 670.7; **670.19**; 715.1 *accusation*; 715.5 *accuse*; 806.1 *guilt*

blamed 715.8 *accusatory*; 806.5 *guilty*; 712.11 *miscellaneous euphemisms*

blameful 670.29 *blaming*; 806.5 *guilty*

blamefully 806.11 *guiltily*

blameless 805.5 *innocent*; 801.10 *moral*; 230.1 *perfect*; 803.5 *virtuous*

blamelessly 805.11 *innocently*; 803.9 *virtuously*

blamelessness 805.1 *innocence*; 230.3 *perfection*; 803.1 *virtue*

blame oneself 808.4 *be penitent*

blame-shifting 36.19 *defence mechanism*

blameworthiness 806.1 *guilt*

blameworthy 670.36; 344.13 *causal*; 16.64 *convicted*; 804.15 *criminal*; 806.5 *guilty*; 802.16 *in the wrong*

blaming 670.29

blanch 522.28 *bleach*; 25.55 *cook*; 530.6 *decolour*; 530.5 *lose colour*; 531.13 *whiten*

blanched 612.7 *frightened*; 531.2 *whitened*

blancher 530.4 *colour remover*

blanching 530.1 *colourlessness*

blancmange 25.35 *dessert*

blanco 531.13 *whiten*; 531.8 *whitener*

bland 245.12 *deteriorated*; 658.8 *good-mannered*; 728.17 *insipid*; 685.8 *moderating*; 497.5 *tasteless*

blandish 699.22 *be hypocritical*; 677.10 *cajole*; 483.9 *motivate*; 480.15 *persuade*

blandishing 677.14 *cajoling*

blandishment 480.2 *flattery*; 483.2 *inducement*

blandishments 677.3 *cajolery*; 593.14 *communication of love*; 699.3 *hypocrisy*

blandly 658.15 *genteelly*; 728.26 *insipidly*; 497.10 *without taste*

Blandness 497

blandness 658.1 *courtesy*; 728.8 *insipidness*; 497.1 *tastelessness*

blank 463.9; 587.13 *ammunition*; 256.16 *clean*; 530.8 *drained of colour*; 94.4 *emptiness*; 456.6 *ignorant*; 141.8 *intervening space*; 350.2 *new*; 94.9 *nonexistent*; 528.1 *opaque*; 160.2 *prototype*; 742.7 *punctuation*; 255.13 *pure*; 696.1 *unintelligible*; 98.13 *vacant*

blank an end 68.16 *bobsled*

blank cartridge 587.13 *ammunition*; 711.3 *false alarm*

blank cheque 250.6 *liberality*; 757.1 *permission*

blanked 655.10 *lonely*

blanket 550.10 *bed covering*; 411.3, 550.24 *coat*; 736.8 *conceal*; 357.8 *destroy*; 138.15 *general*; 493.3 *heater*; 127.7 *including*

blanket bath 256.6 *bath*

blanket coverage 127.1, 550.19 *inclusion*; 693.4 *mass communication*; 138.3 *nonspecificness*

blanketing 550.1 *covering*

blanket of snow 31.30 *snow*

blankety-blank 236.6 *damnable*; 712.11 *miscellaneous euphemisms*

blankly 98.20 *absently*; 530.9 *colourlessly*; 350.13 *newly*; 463.16 *obliviously*; 308.26 *openly*; 696.13 *unintelligibly*

blankness 463.2; 98.3 *emptiness*; 456.1 *ignorance*; 350.9 *newness*; 696.11 *unintelligibility*

blank out 521.8 *make invisible*

blank paper 98.3 *emptiness*

blank slate 98.3 *emptiness*

blank someone 655.13 *ignore*

blank verse 17.11 *rhyme*; 17.10 *verse form*

blank wall 264.8 *snag*; 521.6 *that which makes invisible*

blare 507.8 *be loud*; 513.4 *be strident*; 507.1 *loudness*; 510.10 *ring*; 510.2 *ringing*; 729.12 *speak loudly*; 513.1 *stridency*

blaring 507.6 *loud*; 513.7 *strident*

blarney 677.2; **677.9**; 729.9 *art of public speaking*; 645.5 *be cunning*; 699.3 *hypocrisy*; 729.2 *power of speech*; 697.6 *talk nonsense*

blarneying 677.13 *honeyed*

blasé 618.7 *indifferent*

blaspheme 712.5 *curse*; 5.45 *use language*

blasphemer 804.9 *wicked person*

blasphemous 712.8 *cursing*; 668.10 *disrespectful*; 804.14 *impious*; 5.39 *of language*

blasphemously 5.49 *colloquially*; 804.20 *immorally*; 712.12 *swearingly*

blasphemy 712.1 *curse*; 668.1 *disrespect*; 804.6 *religious sin*

blast 434.4 *air flow*; 508.1, 508.5 *bang*; 507.8 *be loud*; 513.4 *be strident*; 434.22 *blow*; 711.2 *danger signal*; 357.9 *demolish*; 38.30 *engineer*; 586.37 *fight*; 381.2 *fire*; 245.5 *hurt*; 380.3 *instance of violence*; 507.1 *loudness*; 712.15 *miscellaneous swearwords*; 740.14 *proclaim*; 330.28 *shoot*; 513.1 *stridency*; 712.6 *vilify*; 31.14 *windiness*

blast away 130.18 *make a beginning*

blasted 236.6 *damnable*; 690.3 *dead drunk*; 563.3 *infertile*; 712.11 *miscellaneous euphemisms*

blast furnace 32.23 *metallurgy*; 577.1 *workshop*

blasting 712.9 *vituperative*

blasting powder 357.7 *agent of destruction*

blast neurosis 36.10 *neurosis*

blastocyst 34.15 *developmental biology*

blastoff 317.13 *flight path*; 313.8 *start*; 130.11 *starting point*

blast off 317.14 *find one's way*; 130.18 *make a beginning*

blastomere 34.15 *developmental biology*

blastomycosis 83.5 *fungal association*

blast out 514.10 *cry out*

blastula 34.15 *developmental biology*

blastulation 34.15 *developmental biology*

blatancy 660.3 *audacity*; 520.4 *clarity*; 738.10 *manifestation*

blatant 660.15 *audacious*; 673.13 *boastful*; 520.2 *clear*; 738.14 *manifest*; 740.20 *well-known*

blatantly 660.32 *audaciously*; 673.21 *cockily*; 740.22 *publicly*; 520.11 *visibly*

blaze 493.15 *burn*; 493.6, 522.8 *fire*; 743.10 *identify*; 522.25 *light up*; 740.14 *proclaim*; 31.61 *shine*; 742.9 *use signs*

blaze abroad 740.14 *proclaim*

blaze a trail 129.18 *forerun*; 130.21 *pioneer*

blaze of publicity 740.7 *publicity*

blazer 551.4 *informal dress*; 551.11 *jacket*

blazes 712.11 *miscellaneous euphemisms*

blazing 522.16 *bright*

blazon 743.8 *heraldic device*; 743.10 *identify*; 740.14 *proclaim*; 742.10 *signify*

blazoned 743.13 *heraldic*

blazonry 743.8 *heraldic device*

bleach 522.28; 428.19 *bake*; 256.13 *clean*; 256.9 *cleaning agent*; 530.4 *colour remover*; 530.6 *decolour*; 42.6 *dye*; 530.5 *lose colour*; 42.15 *treat*; 531.13 *whiten*

bleached 428.8 *baked*; 256.17 *cleaned*; 530.7 *colourless*; 522.21 *light*; 42.11 *treated*; 531.2 *whitened*

bleacher 530.4 *colour remover*

bleachers 48.1 *baseball*; 518.9 *viewpoint*

bleaching 530.1 *colourlessness*; 245.9 *dilapidation*; 428.13 *drying*; 42.8 *fabric treatment*; 522.3 *lightening*

bleaching powder 530.4 *colour remover*

bleak 249.6 *adverse*; 494.8 *cold*; 31.55 *cool*; 563.3 *infertile*

bleakly 249.12 *in adversity*

bleakness 249.1 *adversity*

bleak outlook 611.2 *hopeless situation*

blear 524.10 *make dim*; 524.6 *murky*

bleared 521.2 *difficult to see*; 524.6 *murky*

blearily 524.12 *dimly*

bleariness 524.2 *murk*; 519.2 *poor sight*

bleary 521.2 *difficult to see*; 524.6 *murky*; 519.9 *weak-sighted*

bleary-eyed 519.9 *weak-sighted*

bleat 515.4 *cry*

bleater 606.3 *dissatisfied person*

bleating 515.1 *animal cry*

bleed 560.21; 394.20 *doctor*; 431.25 *flow*; 371.14 *let out*; 560.22 *menstruate*; 792.10 *overcharge*; 429.16, 433.32 *seep*; 627.9 *sorrow*; 369.14 *suck*

bleeder 260.19 *sick person*

bleeder's disease 260.11 *blood disease*

bleed for 590.18 *feel for*; 627.9 *sorrow*

bleeding 560.10; **560.30**; 260.11 *blood disease*; 431.18 *bloody*; 371.22 *disgorgement*; 491.7 *feeling pain*; 369.4 *sucking*; 394.12 *surgery*; 260.3 *symptom*

bleeding heart 650.5 *benevolent person*; 627.4 *pitying person*

bleeding-heart liberal 648.2 *lenient person*

bleed someone 710.7 *demand*

bleed to death 582.16 *meet one's fate*

bleep 692.30 *communicate*; 692.18 *radio*; 513.3 *shrillness*; 742.4 *signal*

bleeped out 399.6 *censored*

bleeper 504.9 *audio device*; 513.3 *shrillness*; 742.4 *signal*

bleeping 236.6 *damnable*; 513.9 *shrill*; 742.16 *signalling*

bleep out 399.4 *censor*

Blemish 548

blemish 548.7; 231.7 *defect*; 122.2 *deficiency*; 234.11 *deform*; 234.3 *deformity*; 245.5 *hurt*; 546.5 *make ugly*; 743.3 *means of identification*; 260.13 *skin disease*; 546.3 *ugly place*; 518.7 *view*

blemished 548.4; 234.7 *deformed*; 231.1 *imperfect*; 233.4 *incomplete*; 541.10 *mottled*

blemish-free 230.1 *perfect*

blench 612.11 *be afraid*; 522.28 *bleach*; 637.7 *refuse*; 634.4 *shy*; 531.13 *whiten*

blenching 634.18 *avoiding*; 634.12 *shyness*

blend 412.10 *become mixed*; 197.19 *become one*; 114.8 *be diverse*; 374.1 *combination*; 374.5 *combine*; 374.4 *compound*; 25.55 *cook*; 750.24 *harmonize*; 750.4 *harmony*; 147.8 *interaction*; 431.22 *make fluid*; 412.8 *mix*; 412.2 *mixed thing*; 356.10 *produce*

blended 374.7 *combined*; 750.13 *harmonious*; 412.12 *mixed*

blender 25.6 *kitchen equipment*; 431.11 *liquidizer*; 412.6 *mixer*

blending 374.1 *combination*; 412.1 *mixture*

blend into the background 521.7 *become invisible*; 732.6 *be shy*; 526.1 *disappear*

blend with the crowd 216.9 *be average*

blepharoplast 84.3 *plant body*

bless 248.7 *be auspicious*; 750.28 *consent*; 8.17 *deify*; 797.20 *do good*; 671.7 *give thanks*; 10.18 *perform rites*; 757.3 *permit*

blessed 8.13 *divine*; 712.11 *miscellaneous euphemisms*; 248.8 *prosperous*; 9.11 *worshipped*

blessedly 248.9 *prosperously*

blessedness 8.1 *divinity*; 248.1 *prosperity*

blessed state 8.1 *divinity*

blessed with stamina 423.4 *powerful*

blessed with talent 485.7 *gifted*

blessing 669.1 *approval*; 797.13 *benefit*; 750.7 *consent*; 10.6 *Eucharist*; 768.2 *gift*; 797.17 *good thing*; 757.1 *permission*; 10.9 *prayer*; 10.3 *rite of worship*; 671.5 *thanking*; 671.2 *thanks*

blessings 248.2 *good fortune*; 248.1 *prosperity*

bless my soul 619.14 *wonderful!*

bless with 440.9 *own property*

bless you 248.10 *good luck!*; 671.9 *thank you!*

blether on 270.5 *be diffuse*

blewit 25.33 *vegetable*

blight 249.1 *adversity*; 798.2 *affliction*; 357.7 *agent of destruction*; 798.11 *be evil*; 245.9 *dilapidation*; 83.1 *fungus*; 245.5 *hurt*; 44.12 *pests and diseases*; 236.10 *poverty*; 79.10 *tree disease*

blighted 44.17 *botanical*; 798.7 *evil*; 83.9 *fungal*; 87.14 *urban*

blighted area 87.7 *city district*

blighted hopes 604.1 *disappointment*

blighted neighbourhood 87.7 *city district*

blight one's hopes 604.6 *disappoint*

blimp 322.8 *aircraft*; 158.12 *fat person*; 641.8 *obstinate person*

blimpish 641.4 *set*

blind 519.8; **519.15**; 523.11 *benighted*; 519.6 *blinder*; 690.3 *dead drunk*; 231.3 *deformed*; 690.14 *drinking bout*; 56.1 *golf*; 341.3 *inactive*; 592.1 *insensitive*; 522.24

light; 62.8 *mountaineering*; 463.8 *oblivious*; 528.7 *opaque thing*; 550.12 *protective covering*; 641.4 *set*; 523.6 *shade*; 645.2 *stratagem*; 521.6 *that which makes invisible*; 700.8 *trick*; 489.6 *unfeeling*
blind alley 309.4 *closed place*; 317.3 *road*; 264.8 *snag*; 238.5 *waste of effort*
blind as a bat 519.8 *blind*
blind as a mole 519.8 *blind*
blind attack 381.12 *military attack*
blind chance 107.1 *chance*
blind choice 469.8 *choice*
blind corner 521.5 *invisible thing*
blind date 469.8 *choice*; 593.9 *lover*; 654.3 *meeting*; 456.4 *unknown person*
blind drunk 690.3 *dead drunk*
blinded 519.10; 641.4 *set*; 619.6 *wondering*
blinder 519.6
blind eye 519.7 *figurative blindness*
blind faith 450.3 *believing*
blind flying 519.7 *figurative blindness*
blindfold 519.15 *blind*; 519.10 *blinded*; 519.6 *blinder*; 519.17 *blindly*; 736.9 *deceive*; 523.14 *make dark*; 523.6 *shade*
blind fury 624.4 *anger*; 651.1 *malevolence*
blind impulse 478.5 *spontaneity*
blinding 519.11; 522.16 *bright*; 31.53 *rainy*
blindingly 519.18
blind luck 107.2 *luck*
blindly 519.17
blind man's buff 521.5 *invisible thing*
blind move 62.3 *climbing technique*
Blindness 519
blindness 519.1; 523.1 *darkness*; 231.5 *imperfection*; 641.7 *opinionatedness*; 337.3 *poor health*; 523.7 *spiritual darkness*
blind oneself 466.13 *prejudge*
blind panic 612.1 *fear*
blind people 519.4
blind rage 624.4 *anger*
blind register 519.3 *aid for poor sight*
blind side 519.7 *figurative blindness*; 641.7 *opinionatedness*
blind spot 231.7 *defect*; 518.2 *eye*; 519.7 *figurative blindness*; 521.5 *invisible thing*
blind staggers 690.10 *drunkenness*
blindstorey 20.10 *church architecture*
blind to 519.12; 618.7 *indifferent*
blini 25.12 *hors d'oeuvre*
blink 519.14 *be blind*; 522.25 *light up*; 634.4 *shy*
blink at 519.16 *be blind to*
blink comparator 29.27 *imaging*
blinker 519.15 *blind*; 742.5 *indicator*
blinkered 519.10 *blinded*; 519.12 *blind to*; 466.10 *discriminatory*; 641.4 *set*
blinkers 519.6 *blinder*; 59.14 *horse-riding terms*
blinking 634.18 *avoiding*; 236.6 *damnable*; 522.15 *lucent*; 519.2 *poor sight*; 634.12 *shyness*; 519.9 *weak-sighted*
blip 236.8 *inferiority*
bliss 597.1 *happiness*; 490.1 *physical pleasure*; 241.6 *pleasantness*
bliss body 11.7 *spirit*
blissed out 597.4 *happy*
blissful 597.4 *happy*; 241.1, 490.6 *pleasant*; 248.8 *prosperous*
blissfully 490.11 *pleasingly*; 248.9 *prosperously*
blissfully in love 593.18 *in love*
blister 182.2 *bulge*; 493.16 *feel hot*; 493.5 *hot weather*; 410.19 *inflatable*; 260.13 *skin disease*; 260.3 *symptom*
blistered 420.2 *coarse*; 491.7 *feeling pain*
blistering 31.51 *hot*; 493.11 *warm*
blister pack 527.8 *transparent thing*
blithe 597.4 *happy*
blitz 381.1 *attack*; 585.9 *battle*; 381.3 *bomb*; 46.11 *defensive huddle*; 357.9 *demolish*; 357.5 *havoc*; 507.1 *loudness*; 381.12 *military attack*; 46.16 *play defence*; 585.1 *war*; 585.8 *warfare*
blitzed 690.3 *dead drunk*
blitzkrieg 381.12 *military attack*; 585.1 *war*; 585.8 *warfare*
blitz the media 740.16 *publicize*
blizzard 494.5 *ice*; 528.7 *opaque thing*; 31.30, 31.63 *snow*; 380.5 *violent weather*
bloat 190.6 *become bigger*; 232.6 *fill*; 190.1 *growth*; 190.5 *make bigger*; 260.18 *veterinary disease*
bloated 190.7 *bigger*; 557.26 *eating*; 219.6 *excessive*; 158.16 *fat*; 217.3 *filled*; 213.7 *increased*
bloatedness 158.5 *fatness*; 190.1 *growth*
bloater 25.16 *fish dish*; 74.8 *food fish*
bloating 190.1 *growth*
blob 161.2 *shapeless thing*; 195.1 *zero*
bloc 374.3 *assembly*; 376.16 *party*; 12.6 *political party*
block 378.9; 53.17 *bat*; 51.9 *bowls*; 52.2 *boxing*; 226.8 *cause to cease*; 87.7 *city district*; 309.1 *closure*; 40.19 *computing terms*; 347.3 *counteract*; 347.1 *counteraction*; 36.19 *defence mechanism*; 294.8 *delay*; 294.3 *delayed action*; 251.11 *detain*; 19.15 *engraving*; 384.18 *fence*; 52.11 *fight*; 814.16 *instrument of execution*; 103.8 *make impossible*; 158.7 *mass*; 103.7, 378.2 *obstacle*; 50.3 *parts of a sailing boat*; 205.7 *piece*; 46.9 *play*; 49.6 *play basketball*; 49.4 *playing terms*; 46.15 *play offence*; 64.5 *play rugby*; 86.12 *plot*; 52.13 *practise judo*; 21.37 *rehearse*; 62.5 *rock face*; 416.4 *solid body*; 384.25 *stall*; 309.8 *stop*; 786.8 *stop payment*; 53.9 *stroke*; 52.9 *tae kwon do*; 113.20 *withstand*
blockade 384.9 *barrier*; 585.13 *be at war*; 381.4 *besiege*; 378.9 *block*; 309.1 *closure*; 251.11 *detain*; 251.4 *detention*; 378.2 *obstacle*; 381.14 *siege*; 309.8 *stop*; 585.8 *warfare*
blockader 381.19 *attacker*
blockading 585.8 *warfare*
blockage 309.1 *closure*; 36.19 *defence mechanism*; 294.3 *delayed action*; 378.2 *obstacle*; 226.2 *stop*
block an attack 54.5 *fence*
block and tackle 366.9 *lifter*; 38.6 *simple machine*
blockboard 23.12 *wood*
blockbuster 357.7 *agent of destruction*; 587.16 *bomb*; 691.6 *drug*; 17.2, 721.5 *fiction*; 246.3 *successful thing*
blocked 378.14; 103.4 *forbidden*; 294.10 *held up*; 309.13 *stopped*; 36.37 *subconscious*
blocked account 784.5 *amount owing*
blocked nose 501.1 *odourlessness*
blocked up 309.13 *stopped*
blocker 49.2 *basketball player*; 46.7 *offence*; 64.4 *rugby player*
block fault 30.20 *earth movement*
blockhead 459.3 *foolish person*; 456.5 *ignorant person*; 457.3 *unintelligent person*
blockheaded 457.6 *unintelligent*
blockhouse 384.12 *fort*; 252.5 *refuge*; 384.10 *shelter*
blocking 52.2 *boxing*; 52.14 *combat*; 36.19 *defence mechanism*; 294.12 *delaying*; 49.4 *playing terms*; 21.14 *production*; 52.15 *wrestling*
blocking high 31.11 *weather system*
blocking kick 52.9 *tae kwon do*
blocking techniques 52.9 *tae kwon do*
blockish 489.6 *unfeeling*
block of flats 38.20 *building*; 356.8 *construction*
block out 243.2 *do the groundwork*; 358.2 *forget*; 160.7 *form*; 163.5 *outline*; 717.11 *paint*
block out light 523.14 *make dark*
block-print 19.7 *picture*
blocks 47.4 *sports equipment*
blockship 586.24 *warship*
block shot 51.2 *grip*
block up 378.9 *block*; 309.8 *stop*
bloke 567.2 *male*
blond 522.21 *light*; 531.3 *white-haired*; 537.3 *yellow-haired*; 537.6 *yellowness*
blondness 522.14 *light colour*
blood 431.4; 431.3 *body fluid*; 130.25 *enrol*; 137.8 *genealogy*; 535.7 *red thing*
blood and thunder 21.9 *dramaturgy*
blood bank 431.4 *blood*; 439.4 *storage*
bloodbath 380.3 *instance of violence*; 381.14 *siege*; 382.4 *slaughter*
blood brother 115.5 *counterpart*
blood cell 431.4 *blood*; 34.7 *cell*
blood clot 431.4 *blood*; 260.10 *cardiovascular disease*; 416.4 *solid body*; 309.2 *stopper*
blood count 431.4 *blood*
blood disease 260.11; 260.4 *disease*
blood donor 768.4 *giver*
blooded horse 59.13 *breeding*
blood feud 751.2 *argument*
blood fluke 75.10 *parasite*; 75.6 *worm*
blood group 431.4 *blood*
blood guilt 806.1 *guilt*
blood-guilty 806.5 *guilty*
blood heat 493.1 *heat*
blood-horse 59.2 *thoroughbred*
bloodhound 633.6 *hunter*; 500.2 *sense of smell*
bloodily 560.33 *scatologically*
bloodiness 431.5 *fluidity*
blood kin 373.3 *associate*
bloodless 260.23 *diseased*; 530.8 *drained of colour*; 337.10 *ill*; 589.7 *peaceful*
bloodlessly 589.8 *peacefully*
bloodlessness 530.2 *paleness*
blood-letting 371.22 *disgorgement*; 382.1 *killing*; 380.2 *physical violence*; 369.4 *sucking*; 394.12 *surgery*
bloodline 59.13 *breeding*; 132.3 *line*
bloodlust 651.2 *cruelness*; 380.2 *physical violence*
bloodmobile 431.4 *blood*
blood money 807.1 *atonement*; 752.4 *illegal offer*; 749.2 *peace offering*
blood of the grape 558.9 *wine*
blood picture 431.4 *blood*
blood plasma 431.4 *blood*
blood platelet 431.4 *blood*
blood poisoning 260.2 *illness*; 260.6 *infection*
blood pressure 431.4 *blood*; 260.10 *cardiovascular disease*
blood pudding 25.29 *sausage*
blood-red 535.1 *red*
blood relationship 108.1 *relatedness*
blood running cold 612.1 *fear*
blood sample 35.7 *diagnosis*
blood sausage 25.29 *sausage*
blood serum 431.4 *blood*
bloodshed 651.7 *act of malevolence*; 585.8 *warfare*
blood-shedding 382.1 *killing*
bloodshot 535.4 *bloody*; 690.5 *drunken*; 519.9 *weak-sighted*
bloodshot eyes 519.2 *poor sight*
blood-soaked 560.30 *bleeding*
blood sport 633.2 *chase*; 45.4 *sporting activity*
blood sports 382.9 *animal killing*
blood-stained 535.4 *bloody*; 382.24 *murderous*
bloodstock 59.2 *thoroughbred*
bloodstone 475.6 *good-luck sign*
bloodstream 431.4 *blood*
blood substitute 431.4 *blood*
bloodsucker 75.10 *parasite*; 76.3 *pest*; 647.4 *strict person*; 70.4 *type of animal*
bloodsucking 70.15 *of animals*
blood, sweat, and tears 766.4 *lessening*
blood test 35.7 *diagnosis*; 448.1 *experiment*
bloodthirst 651.2 *cruelness*
bloodthirstily 586.41 *aggressively*; 382.25 *lethally*
bloodthirstiness 651.2 *cruelness*; 236.11 *harmfulness*; 380.2 *physical violence*
bloodthirsty 381.23 *attacking*; 586.33 *combative*; 651.11 *cruel*; 236.5 *harmful*; 382.24 *murderous*; 380.6 *violent*; 585.16 *warlike*
blood transfusion 431.4 *blood*
bloodworm 76.5 *larva*
bloody 431.18; **535.4**; 381.23 *attacking*; 585.13 *be at war*; 560.21 *bleed*; 560.30 *bleeding*; 651.11 *cruel*; 236.6 *damnable*; 236.5 *harmful*; 491.11 *inflict pain*; 712.11 *miscellaneous euphemisms*; 382.24 *murderous*; 380.6 *violent*
bloody flux 560.2 *defecation*
bloody hands 806.2 *signs of guilt*
bloody hell 712.15 *miscellaneous swearwords*
Bloody Mary 558.8 *mixed drink*
bloody-minded 662.13 *disobedient*; 651.14 *hostile*; 242.2 *objectionable*; 641.1 *obstinate*; 753.9 *protesting*; 264.14 *troublesome*; 113.26 *uncooperative*; 635.8 *wilful*
bloody-mindedness 651.1 *malevolence*; 641.5 *obstinacy*; 113.6 *uncooperativeness*; 635.3 *wilfulness*
bloody nose 491.3 *injury*
bloom 190.6 *become bigger*; 562.6 *be fertile*; 259.5 *be healthy*; 248.5 *be prosperous*; 411.3 *coat*; 78.1, 78.13 *flower*; 79.19, 555.18 *grow*; 561.11 *have young*; 259.3 *health*; 556.18 *mature*; 427.1 *powderiness*; 535.5 *redness*
bloomed lens 28.29 *optical element*
bloomer 459.2 *act of folly*; 274.10, 544.6 *blunder*; 78.2 *flowering plant*; 25.39 *loaf*; 465.2 *mistake*
bloomers 551.9 *trousers*; 551.18 *underwear*
blooming 525.1 *appearance*; 243.20 *developed*; 243.13 *development*; 78.5, 78.11 *flowering*; 538.4 *fresh*; 190.8 *growing*; 190.1 *growth*; 259.1 *healthy*; 555.13 *maturing*; 545.6 *personable*; 535.2 *red-faced*
bloom of youth 555.1 *youth*
Bloomsbury Thesaurus 5.28 *dictionary*
bloomy 78.10 *floral*
blooper 459.2 *act of folly*; 274.10 *blunder*; 465.2 *mistake*
blossom 190.6 *become bigger*; 562.6 *be fertile*; 248.5 *be prosperous*; 246.6 *be successful*; 78.1, 78.13 *flower*; 345.8 *grow*; 345.3 *growth*; 213.4 *increase*; 356.7 *produce*
blossoming 78.5, 78.11 *flowering*; 190.8, 345.11 *growing*; 190.1 *growth*
blossom time 292.2 *spring*
blot 370.13, 428.20 *absorb*; 412.4 *admixture*; 486.7 *be clumsy*; 532.11 *blacken*; 231.7 *defect*; 258.4 *dirt*; 258.11 *dirty*; 802.9 *dishonour*; 550.31 *hide*; 245.5 *hurt*; 358.1 *obliterate*; 548.1 *spot*; 541.11 *variegate*; 518.7 *view*
blotch 541.4 *maculation*; 548.1 *spot*
blot one's copybook 804.16 *be wicked*; 247.6 *fail*
blot on one's copybook 802.9 *dishonour*
blot on the landscape 548.3; 546.3 *ugly place*
blot out 708.14 *cancel*; 526.3 *cause to disappear*; 357.8 *destroy*; 128.8 *eject*; 550.31 *hide*; 358.1 *obliterate*; 773.10 *take away*
blot out light 523.14 *make dark*
blot out one's sins 649.10 *absolve*
blotted 649.8 *overlooked*
blotted out 736.14 *concealed*
blotter 256.10 *cleaning object*; 428.15 *dryer*; 370.6 *sponge*
blotting 370.17 *absorbent*; 370.5 *absorption*; 428.13 *drying*
blotting out 550.1 *covering*; 773.3 *taking away*
blotting paper 428.15 *dryer*; 370.6 *sponge*
blotto 690.3 *dead drunk*
blot up 370.13, 428.20 *absorb*
blouse 551.35 *make clothing*; 551.8 *shirt*
bloused 551.31 *styled*
blouson 551.4 *informal dress*
blow 31.58; **331.13**; **434.22**; 604.2 *bad outcome*; 342.12 *be active*; 486.7 *be clumsy*; 261.5 *be fatigued*; 814.12 *corporal punishment*; 340.2 *deed*; 691.10 *drug oneself*; 787.1 *expend*; 78.1, 78.13 *flower*; 78.5 *flowering*; 160.7 *form*; 371.33 *go away!*; 381.18 *hit*; 693.13 *inform on*; 371.14 *let out*; 492.3 *press*; 630.3 *shock*; 18.38 *sound*; 371.11 *void*; 441.1, 681.7 *waste*; 31.14 *windiness*
blow a fortune 787.1 *expend*
blow a fuse 624.12 *become angry*
blow a gale 31.59 *storm*
blow a gasket 624.12 *become angry*
blow a gut 514.11 *laugh*
blow a hurricane 31.59 *storm*
blow a kiss 658.12 *greet*; 593.27 *kiss*
blow a raspberry 371.16 *belch*; 512.5 *catcall*; 742.11 *gesture*; 660.29 *ridicule*; 668.25 *taunt*
blow away 357.9 *demolish*; 357.8 *destroy*; 330.28 *shoot*
blow-by-blow account 270.1 *diffuseness*
blow down 357.9 *demolish*; 367.6 *throw down*
blower 692.9 *telephone*; 434.7 *ventilator*
blow for blow 759.1 *exchange*; 110.1 *interchange*; 108.2 *interrelatedness*; 385.1 *retaliation*
blow-for-blow 110.4 *reciprocal*
blow gage 691.10 *drug oneself*
blowhole 308.5 *hole*; 315.7 *outlet*
blow hot and cold 642.5 *be capricious*; 224.7 *be changed*; 227.12 *be irresolute*; 639.6 *hesitate*; 384.25 *stall*
blow in 312.1 *arrive*
blowing 691.1 *drug-taking*; 78.5 *flowering*; 261.3 *panting*
blowing away 382.2 *murder*
blowing hot and cold 639.12 *inconstancy*
blowing one's own trumpet 467.1 *overestimation*
blowing up 727.2 *enlargement*; 190.1 *growth*
blow it 787.1 *expend*; 288.7 *lose one's chance*

blow me down 619.14 *wonderful!*
blown 787.12 *expended;* 160.9 *formed*
blown up 366.11 *raised*
blown-up 434.14 *aerial;* 190.7 *bigger;* 727.13 *enlarged;* 727.12 *exaggerated*
blow off 371.16 *belch*
blow one's cash 787.1 *expend*
blow one's chance 288.7 *lose one's chance*
blow one's cool 624.12 *become angry*
blow one's lid 624.12 *become angry;* 659.8 *get angry*
blow one's mind 619.10 *be wonderful;* 691.10 *drug oneself*
blow one's nose 560.20 *salivate*
blow one's own trumpet 673.16 *show off*
blow one's top 624.12 *become angry;* 659.8 *get angry*
blow on the ears 331.13 *blow*
blow on the embers 380.9 *make violent*
blow open 380.8 *use violence*
blowout 688.3 *act of gluttony;* 508.1 *bang;* 601.1 *celebration;* 371.22 *disgorgement;* 557.13 *feast;* 654.5 *party;* 376.9 *social gathering*
blow out 357.8 *destroy;* 371.14 *let out;* 523.14 *make dark;* 315.11 *run out;* 371.11 *void*
blow out one's brains 382.21 *commit suicide*
blow over 226.6 *cease;* 367.6 *throw down*
blowpipe 330.9 *firearm;* 587.6 *historical missile weapon*
blow smoke 691.10 *drug oneself*
blow someone's cover 739.7 *betray*
blow the gaff 715.5 *accuse;* 739.6 *divulge;* 693.13 *inform on*
blow the lid off 739.6 *divulge;* 693.13 *inform on*
blow the roof off 507.8 *be loud*
blow the trumpets 601.18 *salute*
blow the whistle 715.5 *accuse;* 711.7 *raise the alarm*
blow the whistle on 739.7 *betray;* 693.13 *inform on*
blow to bits 357.9 *demolish*
blow to kingdom come 357.9 *demolish*
blow to pieces 372.9 *separate*
blowtorch 493.6 *fire*
blow to smithereens 357.9 *demolish*
blow up **330.30**; 508.5 *bang;* 739.9 *be disclosed;* 31.58 *blow;* 727.10 *boast;* 357.9 *demolish;* 375.3 *disintegrate;* 727.8 *enlarge;* 190.5, 213.5 *make bigger;* 41.21 *photograph;* 717.9 *represent;* 366.2 *send up;* 372.9 *separate;* 304.17 *spring up*
blow-up 624.4 *anger;* 41.12 *development;* 380.3 *instance of violence*
blowy 434.15 *breezy;* 31.47 *windy*
blowzy 535.2 *red-faced*
blub 514.13 *cry;* 603.7 *weep*
blubber 514.13 *cry;* 158.8 *fat;* 152.5 *thickness;* 603.7 *weep*
blubberer 603.3 *lamenter*
blubbering 514.18 *crying*
blubbery 268.13 *slippery*
blubbing 514.18 *crying*
bludgeon 587.7 *blunt weapon;* 386.3 *coercive methods;* 386.7 *force*
bludgeoning 386.9 *compelling*
blue **539.1**; **539.9**; 28.28 *colour;* 712.8 *cursing;* 539.3, 602.6 *depressed;* 787.1 *expend;* 542.4 *honour;* 539.4, 796.12 *indecent;* 18.33 *jazz;* 258.9 *obscene;* 675.9 *ribald;* 626.6 *sullen;* 441.1 *waste*
blue and red 540.1 *purpleness*
blue and white ware 24.1 *ceramics*
blue around the gills 539.2 *bluish*
blue baby 539.8 *bluishness*
blue ball 65.5 *snooker*
blue ball clay 24.2 *raw material*
blue balls 539.7 *figurative usage*
Bluebeard 539.6 *blue thing;* 570.10 *married man*
bluebell 539.6 *blue thing*
blueberry 539.6 *blue thing*
blueberry muffin 25.39 *loaf*
blueberry pancake 25.39 *loaf*
bluebill 539.6 *blue thing*
bluebird 539.6 *blue thing*
blue-black 532.1 *black;* 532.8 *black pigment*
blueblood 539.7 *figurative usage;* 573.1 *nobleman*
blue blooded 573.4 *aristocratic*
bluebonnet 539.6 *blue thing*
bluebook 539.6 *blue thing*
bluebottle 396.10 *person of authority*
blue cheer 539.6 *blue thing;* 691.6 *drug*
blue cheese 539.6 *blue thing*
blue-chip 121.15 *excellent;* 539.7 *figurative usage;* 235.3 *valuable*
blue-collar 15.10 *unionized*
blue-collar union 15.3 *organized labour*
blue-collar worker 15.7 *employee;* 539.7 *figurative usage;* 566.10 *member of society;* 578.1 *worker*
blue colour 539.5 *blueness*
blue crab 539.6 *blue thing*
Blue Cross 539.6 *blue thing;* 35.1 *medicine;* 253.1 *protection*
blue devils 539.7 *figurative usage;* 626.2 *sign of sullenness*
blue dye 539.5 *blueness;* 529.4 *pigment*
Blue Ensign 743.7 *flag*
blue-eyed boy 539.7 *figurative usage;* 593.11 *loved one;* 567.2 *male*
blue film 539.7 *figurative usage*
bluefish 55.4 *American game fish;* 539.6 *blue thing*
blue flu 539.7 *figurative usage*
blue fox 539.6 *blue thing*
blue funk 614.1 *cowardice;* 612.1 *fear;* 539.7 *figurative usage*
bluegill 539.6 *blue thing*
bluegrass 539.6 *blue thing;* 539.7 *figurative usage;* 18.11 *folk music*
blue-green 538.1 *green*
blue-green algae 84.2 *algae*
blue-grey 533.1 *grey*
blue humour 599.3 *wit*
blue in the face 539.2 *bluish*
bluejacket 539.7 *figurative usage;* 586.27 *naval man*
blue jay 539.6 *blue thing*
bluejeans 539.6 *blue thing;* 551.9 *trousers*
blue joke 712.1 *curse;* 796.2 *indecency;* 599.5 *joke*
blue language 539.7 *figurative usage;* 712.2 *offensive language;* 5.19 *swearword*
blue law 539.7 *figurative usage*
blue laws 795.4 *self-righteousness;* 647.2 *suppression*
blue line 58.3 *ice hockey*
blue marlin 55.4 *American game fish*
blue moon 539.7 *figurative usage*
Blue Mosque 10.13 *shrine*
blue mould 539.6 *blue thing*
Blue Mountains 539.6 *blue thing*
blue movie 796.2 *indecency*
blue murder 539.7 *figurative usage*
Blueness 539
blueness 539.5
Blue Nile 539.6 *blue thing*
blue note 539.7 *figurative usage;* 18.8 *jazz*
blue pencil 539.6 *blue thing;* 399.2 *censorship;* 539.7 *figurative usage;* 358.3 *obliteration;* 244.6 *rectification*
blue-pencil **539.10**; 399.4 *censor;* 128.8 *eject;* 685.4 *moderate;* 358.1 *obliterate;* 255.10, 256.15 *purify;* 244.3 *rectify;* 212.3 *subtract*
blue-pencilled 399.6 *censored*
blue-pencilling 256.4 *censorship*
blue peter 539.6 *blue thing;* 743.7 *flag*
blue pigment 539.5 *blueness*
blue-plate special 539.7 *figurative usage*
bluepoint 25.19 *shellfish*
bluepoint oyster 539.6 *blue thing*
blueprint 539.6 *blue thing;* 243.2 *do the groundwork;* 539.7 *figurative usage;* 484.5 *map;* 126.2 *original;* 126.7 *originate;* 163.1, 163.5, 723.2 *outline;* 243.10 *preparations;* 160.2 *prototype;* 717.2 *reproduction*
blue racer 539.6 *blue thing*
Blue Riband 813.2 *prize*
blue ribbon 539.6 *blue thing;* 743.4 *insignia;* 813.2 *prize;* 794.1 *trophy*
blue-ribbon 235.2 *best*
blue-ribbon winner 485.4 *skilled person*
Blue Ridge Mountains 539.6 *blue thing*
blue run 68.1 *skiing*
blues 22.2 *dance;* 539.7 *figurative usage;* 551.3 *formal dress;* 18.8 *jazz*
blue shark 55.5 *British game fish*
Blue Shield 35.1 *medicine*
blueshift 29.21 *orbit*
blue sky 434.1 *air;* 31.22 *sun*
blue-sky 476.7 *suppositional*
blue-sky law 539.7 *figurative usage*
bluesman 18.24 *musician*
bluestocking 539.7 *figurative usage;* 442.8 *intellectual person;* 455.6 *knowledgeable person;* 6.7 *learner*
bluestone 539.6 *blue thing*
blue streak 539.7 *figurative usage;* 332.8 *speed*
blue thing 539.6
bluetit 539.6 *blue thing*
blue velvet 539.6 *blue thing;* 691.6 *drug*
blue water 91.1 *sea*
blue whale 539.6 *blue thing*
blue with cold 539.2 *bluish;* 494.8 *cold*
bluff 676.4 *be affected;* 699.19 *cheat;* 702.12 *deceive;* 700.15 *deceiver;* 699.14 *façade;* 456.2 *half-knowledge;* 700.11, 700.31 *hoax;* 699.28 *mask;* 154.3 *mountain;* 426.2 *outspoken;* 660.19 *rude;* 700.8, 700.28 *trick;* 186.3 *vertical thing;* 380.6 *violent*
bluffed 700.36 *deceived*
bluffer 699.19 *cheat;* 700.15 *deceiver;* 456.5 *ignorant person;* 676.2 *pretender*
bluffing 699.14 *façade;* 699.34 *pretending;* 700.7 *tricking*
bluffness 659.1 *discourtesy;* 426.6 *outspokenness*
bluff one's way out 389.5 *escape*
bluish 539.2
bluishness 539.8
blunder **274.10**; **544.6**; 486.6 *act foolishly;* 459.2 *act of folly;* 486.7 *be clumsy;* 486.5 *be unskilful;* 802.19 *be wrong;* 247.6 *fail;* 247.1 *failure;* 472.5 *inattentive act;* 325.4 *lose track of;* 288.3 *lost chance;* 274.19, 288.9 *make a mistake;* 720.1 *misinterpret;* 720.2 *misinterpretation;* 465.10 *misjudge;* 465.2 *mistake;* 327.25 *pitch;* 806.3 *sin*
blunderbuss 330.9 *firearm;* 587.10 *historical gun;* 486.10 *unskilled person*
blundered 247.10 *failed*
blunderer 486.10 *unskilled person*
blundering 247.10 *failed;* 288.16 *mistaken*
blunderingly 288.21 *mistakenly;* 247.12 *unsuccessfully*
blunder upon 107.11 *chance upon*
blunge 24.11 *make ceramics*
blunged 24.10 *ceramic*
blunger 24.6 *ceramic workshop*
blunging 24.10 *ceramic;* 24.5 *ceramic process*
blunt **426.1**; **426.10**; 489.12 *anaesthetize;* 707.14 *assertive;* 457.10 *bemuse;* 481.5 *discourage;* 659.5 *discourteous;* 592.1 *insensitive;* 618.13 *make indifferent;* 685.4 *moderate;* 646.1 *naive;* 271.3 *natural;* 308.16, 738.15 *open;* 592.7 *render insensitive;* 698.18 *truthful;* 421.2 *uniform*
blunted 426.1 *blunt*
blunt edge 426.9 *blunt instrument*
blunt-edged 426.1 *blunt*
blunt-ended 426.1 *blunt*
blunt instrument **426.9**; 587.7 *blunt weapon;* 382.2 *murder*
bluntish 426.1 *blunt*
bluntly **426.12**; 659.9 *discourteously;* 707.25 *explicitly;* 489.13 *insensibly;* 646.5 *naively;* 308.26 *openly;* 271.8 *simply;* 421.14 *smoothly;* 698.36 *truthfully;* 592.8 *unfeelingly*
Bluntness 426
bluntness **426.5**; 707.6 *assertiveness;* 659.1 *discourtesy;* 592.3 *insensitiveness;* 646.2 *naivety;* 271.6 *naturalness;* 308.9 *openness;* 698.5 *truthfulness*
blunt-nosed 426.1 *blunt*
blunt-pointed 426.1 *blunt*
blunt weapon 587.7
blur 216.9 *be average;* 521.7 *become invisible;* 519.15 *blind;* 258.11 *dirty;* 524.10 *make dim;* 521.8 *make invisible;* 161.3 *make shapeless;* 524.2 *murk*
blurb 740.9 *advertisement*
blurb writer 740.10 *publicizer*
blurred 521.2 *difficult to see;* 524.6 *murky;* 528.2 *shady;* 161.5 *shapeless;* 96.8 *unreal*
blurred vision 519.2 *poor sight*
blurriness 524.2 *murk;* 161.1 *shapelessness*
blurry 521.2 *difficult to see;* 524.6 *murky;* 519.9 *weak-sighted*
blurt 478.3 *improvise*
blurt out 739.7 *betray;* 729.11 *speak*
blush 806.9 *appear guilty;* 674.16 *be self-conscious;* 732.6 *be shy;* 674.2 *blushing;* 529.9 *complexion;* 493.16 *feel hot;* 742.3 *gesture;* 493.1 *heat;* 529.16 *make up;* 535.9 *redden;* 535.5 *redness;* 806.2 *signs of guilt*
blusher 529.9 *complexion;* 547.4 *cosmetics;* 674.7 *modest person;* 535.6 *red pigment*
blushing **674.2**; **674.9**; 806.6 *appearing guilty;* 795.9 *pure;* 535.2 *red-faced;* 732.1 *shy;* 493.12 *warm-hearted*
blushing bride 570.8 *spouse*
blushingly 806.11 *guiltily;* 535.10 *ruddily;* 674.18 *shyly*
blush unseen 674.15 *escape notice*
bluster 342.12 *be active;* 624.11 *be angry;* 380.7 *be violent;* 31.58 *blow;* 660.5 *bravado;* 661.1 *defiance;* 661.5 *defy;* 327.4 *fuss;* 335.2 *futile effort;* 380.1 *violence*
blusterer 727.6 *exaggerator;* 660.12 *impudent person;* 622.13 *proud person*
blustering 380.6 *violent*
blustery 380.6 *violent;* 31.47 *windy*
Blu-tack 267.3 *adhesive*
B-movie 122.7 *inferior thing;* 356.5 *work of art*
BMX 320.12 *bicycle*
BO 560.8 *sweat*
boa 551.14 *neckwear;* 73.3 *snake*
Boadicea 380.4 *violent creature;* 586.10 *woman soldier*
boar 43.8 *livestock;* 567.16 *male animal;* 71.17 *male mammal*
board **435.4**; 381.9 *attack successfully;* 23.17 *carpenter;* 69.4 *chess terms;* 376.7 *committee;* 579.7 *council;* 69.6 *darts;* 314.9 *enter;* 550.28 *face;* 579.6 *governing body;* 418.7 *hard substance;* 557.24 *have a meal;* 564.14 *inhabit;* 435.1 *materials;* 304.15 *mount;* 58.9 *play hockey;* 557.25 *provide food;* 436.5 *provision;* 313.5 *set out;* 63.8 *squash;* 21.17 *stage;* 439.6 *store;* 23.4 *table;* 565.18 *take up residence;* 16.18 *tribunal;* 50.7 *windsurfing;* 23.12 *wood*
board and lodging 565.10 *hotel;* 436.1 *provision*
boarded 58.8 *hockey;* 23.16 *joined*
boarder 557.18 *eater;* 564.3 *householder;* 763.5 *possessor*
board game 69.1 *game*
boarding 381.23 *attacking;* 58.8 *hockey;* 58.3 *ice hockey;* 23.16 *joined;* 381.12 *military attack;* 313.8 *start;* 550.8 *wall covering;* 23.12 *wood*
boarding card 322.7 *miscellaneous aviation terms*
boarding house 565.10 *hotel;* 436.1 *provision*
boarding school 6.12 *educational institution;* 436.1 *provision*
board meeting 376.6 *sitting*
board member 400.5 *company leader*
board of aldermen 16.2 *jurisdiction;* 398.2 *representative body;* 579.9 *US administrative council*
board of directors 579.6 *governing body*
board of governors 6.5 *educationalist*
board room 579.7 *council;* 484.7 *planning*
boardsurf 50.18 *windsurf*
boardsurfer 50.9 *sailor*
boardsurfing 50.7 *windsurfing*
boar hunt 633.2 *chase*
boar hunting 71.23 *mammal hunting*
boast **727.10**; 660.24 *be vain;* 727.4 *bombast;* 622.29 *feel pride;* 127.4 *include;* 622.12 *object of pride;* 542.12 *ornament;* 673.16 *show off*
boaster 727.6 *exaggerator;* 660.12 *impudent person;* 622.13 *proud person*
boastful **622.22**; **673.13**; 676.3 *affected*
boastfully 673.23
boastfulness **622.10**; **673.6**
boasting 542.2 *affectation;* 727.4 *bombast;* 727.15 *bombastic*
boat 316.12 *transport;* 323.3 *vessel*
boat-builder 578.2 *artisan*
boater 551.15 *headgear*
boathouse 565.7 *room*
boating 323.1 *water travel*
Boating Sports 50
boatload 406.2 *load*
boatman **323.8**; 316.7 *transferor*
boat show 738.6 *display;* 779.2 *fair*
boatswain 323.7 *nautical person*
boat trip 323.1 *water travel*
bob 68.9 *bobsledding;* 367.9 *bow;* 52.2 *boxing;* 367.16 *courtesy;* 658.13 *defer to;* 52.11 *fight;* 780.10 *former British money;* 547.8 *haircut;* 362.3 *jerk;* 327.9, 327.23 *jolt;* 664.10 *knuckle under;* 667.4 *mark of respect;* 326.7 *oscillator;* 326.11 *rock;*

149.10 *shorten*; 67.9 *swim*; 667.19 *take off one's hat to*
bob and weave 227.12 *be irresolute*
bob and wheel 17.8 *part of poem*
bobbed 149.8 *shortened*
bobber 55.3 *fishing tackle*
bobbery 327.2 *tumult*
bobbin 55.3 *fishing tackle*; 307.6 *rotator*; 42.4 *weaving*
bobbing 52.2 *boxing*; 52.14 *combat*; 667.11 *in a respectful stance*; 327.9 *jolt*; 67.1 *swimming*; 664.2 *sycophancy*
bobbing and weaving 227.2 *irresolution*
bobble 486.7 *be clumsy*
bobble hat 551.15 *headgear*
bobbling 486.9 *bungling*
bobby 396.10 *person of authority*; 16.17 *police officer*; 252.3 *protector*; 253.3 *security officer*
bobby dazzler 545.3 *attractive female*
bobby pin 373.8 *fastening*
bobby socks 551.20 *legwear*
bob down 667.19 *take off one's hat to*
Bob Major 18.6 *campanology*
bobrun 68.9 *bobsledding*
bobsled 68.16; 68.9 *bobsledding*; 320.10 *sled*
bobsled captain 68.11 *skier*
bobsledder 68.11 *skier*
bobsledding 68.9
bobsledge 68.16 *bobsled*
bobsleigh 68.16 *bobsled*
bobsy-die 751.2 *argument*
bob up 312.1 *arrive*; 304.17 *spring up*
bob up and down 22.15 *dance*; 326.11 *rock*
bocage 79.4 *trees*
bod 566.7 *person*
bodacious 638.2 *tenacious*
bode 475.11 *predict*
bode ill 254.10 *endanger*
bode well 248.7 *be auspicious*; 229.4 *tend*
bodge 486.7 *be clumsy*
bodged 486.4 *bungled*
Bodhisattva 8.3 *God*
bodhisattva 7.3 *religious person*
bodice 551.24 *part of garment*
bodice ripper 740.6 *book publishing*; 17.2 *fiction*
bodiless 101.8 *nonmaterial*
bodiliness 402.1 *material world*
bodily 97.14 *in person*; 402.7 *material*; 204.12 *one and all*; 380.10 *violently*; 172.10 *visceral*
bodily assumption 366.7 *lift*
bodily chastisement 814.12 *corporal punishment*
bodily harm 798.2 *affliction*
bodily love 593.5 *desire*
bodily movement 300.11
bodily organs 172.4 *insides*
bodily presence 97.1 *presence*
boding 711.8 *warning*
bodkin 308.2 *opener*; 425.8 *sharp-pointed thing*
body 376.1 *assembly*; 376.7 *committee*; 582.11 *dead person*; 525.3 *external appearance*; 403.3 *form*; 376.11 *group*; 402.4 *matter*; 160.6 *nature*; 402.5 *object*; 34.3 *organism*; 566.7 *person*; 203.1 *quantity*; 215.1 *remainder*; 152.5 *thickness*; 93.2 *thing*; 551.18 *underwear*
body and soul 232.9 *completely*; 204.11 *wholly*
body armour 384.7 *armour*
body belt 384.6 *protective clothing*
body blow 331.13 *blow*; 331.14 *sporting hit*
body-builder 336.6 *muscleman*
body-building 557.27 *edible*; 257.4 *hygienic*
body-centred 32.33 *crystalline*
body-centred-cubic crystal 32.4 *crystal*
bodycheck 58.9 *play hockey*
bodychecked 58.8 *hockey*
bodychecking 58.8 *hockey*; 58.3 *ice hockey*; 58.5 *lacrosse*
body clock 281.6 *clock*
body cord 54.2 *fencing equipment*
body covering 550.5
body double 21.24 *actor*; 762.2 *substitute person*
body fluid 431.3
bodyguard 223.7 *attendant*; 586.2 *defender*; 384.14 *guard*; 401.4 *personal attendant*; 252.3 *protector*; 253.3 *security officer*; 665.8 *watchful person*
body harness 62.4 *climbing equipment*
body heat 493.1 *heat*
body language 525.3 *external appearance*; 742.3 *gesture*; 5.5 *nonstandard language*; 730.6 *silent speech*
bodyline bowling 53.8 *delivery*
body lotion 256.9 *cleaning agent*; 502.2 *fragrant thing*
body louse 76.3 *pest*
body odour 503.2 *something that makes an unpleasant smell*
body of law 713.3 *precept*; 16.1 *the law*
body orifice 308.4
body padding 384.6 *protective clothing*
body politic 85.1 *country*; 396.8 *governmental organization*; 566.11 *nation*; 12.5 *political organization*
bodypop 22.15 *dance*
bodypopping 22.1 *dancing*
body scan 35.7 *diagnosis*
body scanner 394.14 *hospital*
body shirt 551.8 *shirt*
body shop 320.21 *miscellaneous motoring terms*
body slam 52.5 *wrestling*
body slip 24.3 *glaze*
body-snatcher 774.9 *plunderer*
body-snatching 774.5 *plundering*; 774.17 *stolen*
body stocking 551.18 *underwear*
body support 413.3
body type 525.3 *external appearance*
body wave 30.23 *seismic wave*
body weight 414.4 *heaviness*
bodywork 403.4 *framework*
boeuf bourgignon 25.45 *French dish*
Bofers gun 587.11 *guns*
boffin 396.11, 485.5 *expert*; 442.8 *intellectual person*; 455.6 *knowledgeable person*; 446.9 *person of ideas*; 484.8 *planner*; 136.8 *qualified person*; 4.12 *sage*; 476.4 *theorist*; 578.1 *worker*
boffo 235.1 *worthy*
bog 258.4 *dirt*; 560.13 *lavatory*; 92.3, 429.8 *marsh*; 565.7 *room*; 419.11 *soft thing*; 767.7 *toilet*
bogey 711.3 *false alarm*; 477.5 *fantasy*; 612.5 *frightener*; 56.2 *golfing terms*
bogeyman 612.5 *frightener*
bogged down 294.10 *held up*
bogginess 429.7; 419.10 *compressibility*
bogging down 341.1 *inaction*
boggle 630.11 *amaze*; 619.10 *be wonderful*; 705.21 *confuse*; 639.5 *vacillate*
boggle at 637.6 *be unwilling*
boggle one's mind 604.6 *disappoint*
boggle the mind 619.10 *be wonderful*
boggling 639.1 *vacillating*
boggy 419.4 *compressible*; 92.11 *continental*; 429.11 *marshy*
bogie 321.7 *train*
bog lady 258.6 *dirty person*
bogle 22.2 *dance*
bog moss 82.3 *moss*
bog off 313.15 *go!*
bog roll 256.11 *cleaning cloth*
bogue 691.7 *drugged*; 691.3 *withdrawal*
bogus 96.12 *artificial*; 699.37 *fake*; 702.10 *hypocritical*; 700.39 *imitative*; 699.32 *spurious*
bogus cheque 786.3 *bad payment*
bogusly 699.40 *falsely*
bogusness 699.4 *spuriousness*
Bohemian 325.19 *deviant person*; 250.8 *free-thinker*; 250.10 *independent*; 100.5, 118.7 *nonconformist*; 19.29 *realist*; 657.8 *sociable*; 118.13 *unconventional*
Bohemianism 250.1 *freedom*; 118.3 *nonconformism*; 657.2 *sociability*
Bohr radius 28.97 *fundamental constant*
boil 327.21 *be agitated*; 624.11 *be angry*; 493.14 *be hot*; 182.2 *bulge*; 25.55 *cook*; 257.6 *make hygienic*; 548.2 *pimple*; 327.3 *turbulence*; 260.15 *ulcer*
boil away 377.14 *dilute*
boil down 191.6 *become smaller*; 191.5 *make smaller*; 163.5 *outline*; 149.10 *shorten*; 723.8 *summarize*; 152.7 *thicken*
boil down to 694.10 *mean*
boiled 25.56 *culinary*; 493.13 *heated*
boiled away 377.27 *dilute*
boiled cabbage 503.2 *something that makes an unpleasant smell*
boiled-down 152.2 *dense*; 191.7 *smaller*
boiled fish 25.16 *fish dish*
boiled ham 25.30 *bacon*
boiled sweet 498.4 *confectionery*; 25.41 *sweet*
boiler 493.3 *heater*; 43.8 *livestock*; 321.5 *locomotive part*; 410.15 *pot*; 256.7 *washer*
boilermaker 437.9 *power-worker*
boiler room 493.8 *hot place*; 700.7 *tricking*
boiler suit 551.10 *suit*
boiling 624.16 *angry*; 25.8 *cooking technique*; 31.51, 493.9 *hot*; 32.3 *phase*; 359.1 *preservation*; 28.37 *temperature*; 327.3 *turbulence*; 327.17 *turbulent*; 380.6 *violent*
boiling away 377.3 *dilution*
boiling point 493.1 *heat*; 28.37 *temperature*
boiling-water reactor 437.7 *nuclear power*; 28.73 *nuclear reactor*
boiling with rage 624.16 *angry*
boil over 327.21 *be agitated*; 624.12 *become angry*
boisterous 408.20 *disorderly*; 262.3 *hasty*; 507.6 *loud*; 380.6 *violent*
boisterously 408.29 *riotously*
boisterousness 408.8 *lawlessness*; 380.1 *violence*
boîte 21.16 *theatre*
boîte de nuit 21.16 *theatre*
bola 587.6 *historical missile weapon*
bold 167.9 *arrogant*; 660.15 *audacious*; 613.9 *courageous*; 661.7 *defiant*; 668.10 *disrespectful*; 726.3 *emphatic*; 660.21 *impudent*; 5.41 *lettered*; 738.14 *manifest*; 62.8 *mountaineering*; 738.15 *open*; 615.4 *rash*; 336.12 *strong to the senses*
bold as a lion 613.9 *courageous*
bold as brass 661.7 *defiant*; 660.21 *impudent*
bold climbing 62.1 *mountaineering*
boldering 62.8 *mountaineering*
bold façade 613.5 *bold front*
bold front 613.5; 661.1 *defiance*
bold imagination 477.1 *imagination*
boldly 660.12 *audaciously*; 613.18 *courageously*; 661.9 *defiantly*; 738.17 *frankly*; 336.14 *strongly*
bold move 484.3 *expedient plan*
boldness 167.5; 660.3 *audacity*; 613.1 *courage*; 661.1 *defiance*; 726.1 *emphasis*
bold relief 520.7 *that which makes visible*; 520.6 *visible thing*
bold type 5.15 *type style*
bole 205.6 *branch*; 181.4 *cylinder*; 79.2 *tree part*
bolero 22.4 *historic dancing*; 551.11 *jacket*
boletus 25.33 *vegetable*
bolide 29.20 *meteor*
bollard 373.8 *fastening*; 62.5 *rock face*
bollix up 408.23 *confuse*; 247.6 *fail*
bollocks 182.2 *bulge*; 712.15 *miscellaneous swearwords*; 697.1 *nonsense*; 561.8 *organs of reproduction*
bollocks up 247.6 *fail*; 245.4 *impair*
boll weevil 76.3 *pest*
Bollywood 21.3 *films*
bologna sausage 25.29 *sausage*
bolognese sauce 25.15 *sauce*
bolometer 28.92 *light meter*; 26.8 *meter*
bolometric 26.16 *micrometric*
bolometry 26.2 *micrometry*
boloney 25.29 *sausage*
bolopunch 331.14 *sporting hit*
Bolsheviks 12.6 *political party*
Bolshevism 12.1 *government*; 396.7 *type of rule*
Bolshevist 662.11 *rebel*
bolshie 662.9 *criminal*; 753.9 *protesting*
Bolshoi Ballet 22.12 *ballet companies*
bolster 20.9 *miscellaneous architectural features*; 359.5 *preserve*; 413.4 *rest*; 392.19, 413.11 *support*
bolt 332.6 *accelerate*; 688.5 *be greedy*; 373.12 *bind*; 376.27 *bundle*; 62.4 *climbing equipment*; 309.7 *close*; 373.11 *connect*; 557.22 *eat well*; 389.5 *escape*; 373.8 *fastening*; 587.6 *historical missile weapon*; 313.4 *hurry off*; 262.2 *make haste*; 330.8 *missile*; 62.8 *mountaineering*; 148.5 *piece*; 309.3 *restrainer*; 634.8 *run away*; 252.4 *safety device*; 38.27 *superstructure*; 438.1 *tool*
bolt-action rifle 60.3 *hunting equipment*
bolt down one's meal 262.2 *make haste*
bolted 373.16 *bound*; 309.12 *closed*
bolt from the blue 630.3 *shock*
bolt hole 736.2 *hiding place*; 252.5 *refuge*
bolting 557.2 *appetite*; 688.6 *gluttonous*
bolt of lightning 31.21 *thunderstorm*
bolt rope 50.3 *parts of a sailing boat*
bolt route 62.1 *mountaineering*
bolt upright 186.8 *vertical*; 186.11 *vertically*
Boltzmann constant 28.97 *fundamental constant*
bolus 394.2 *medicine*; 557.14 *mouthful*
bomb 381.3; **587.16**; 357.7 *agent of destruction*; 508.3 *banger*; 320.16 *car*; 357.9 *demolish*; 586.37 *fight*; 382.17 *murder*; 46.9 *play*; 21.13 *theatrical performance*; 247.4 *unsuccessful thing*
bombard 381.1 *attack*; 357.9 *demolish*; 587.12 *historical guns*; 330.28 *shoot*
bombardier 586.32 *airman*; 586.17 *army person*; 381.19 *attacker*; 320.10 *sled*
bombardment 507.1 *loudness*; 381.12 *military attack*; 330.7 *shot*; 585.8 *warfare*
bombast 727.4; 542.2 *affectation*; 727.10 *boast*; 673.3 *cockiness*; 544.4 *inelegance of speech*; 697.1 *nonsense*
bombastic 727.15; 270.3 *diffuse*; 729.20 *eloquent*; 329.13 *exaggerated*; 542.10 *ornate*
bombastically 270.7 *diffusely*; 727.16 *exaggeratedly*; 542.13 *ornately*; 673.24 *pompously*
Bombay duck 25.18 *sea fish*
bombay mix 25.49 *Indian dish*
bomb-disposal expert 665.6 *careful person*
bomb-dropping 381.13 *air attack*
bombed 690.3 *dead drunk*
bomber 381.19 *attacker*; 586.31 *military aircraft*; 382.11 *murderer*
bomber jacket 551.11 *jacket*
bomber pilot 586.32 *airman*
bombinate 515.6 *buzz*; 509.9 *hum*
bombination 509.2 *humming*; 515.3 *insect noise*
bombing 381.13 *air attack*; 381.16 *terrorist attack*; 585.8 *warfare*
bombproof 384.31 *entrenched*; 252.7 *invulnerable*; 423.11 *make tough*; 423.1 *tough*
bomb run 381.13 *air attack*
bombshell 587.16 *bomb*; 630.3 *shock*
bomb shelter 736.2 *hiding place*; 252.5 *refuge*
bona fide 126.6, 698.19 *authentic*; 799.4 *honourable*
bona fideness 698.6 *authenticity*
bona fides 799.1 *probity*
bonanza 219.1 *excess*; 768.2 *gift*; 248.2 *good fortune*; 217.8 *plenty*; 439.2 *resource*; 781.5 *wealth*
bon appetit! 25.58 *grub's on!*
bonbon 498.4 *confectionery*; 25.41 *sweet*
bond 750.3 *arrangement*; 374.6 *come together*; 810.7 *commitment*; 373.11 *connect*; 755.1 *contract*; 38.26 *masonry*; 373.4 *means of connection*; 780.14 *paper money*; 253.2, 756.1 *promise*; 32.26 *react*; 108.1 *relatedness*; 378.4 *restraint*
bondage 251.4 *detention*; 387.1 *subjection*
bond angle 32.11 *chemical bond*
bonded 267.9 *adhesive*; 750.11 *allied*; 373.15 *connected*; 108.4 *related*
bond energy 32.11 *chemical bond*
bonding 267.1 *adhesion*
bonding agent 373.4 *means of connection*
bonding orbital 32.12 *valence*
bondmaid 401.7 *slave*
bonds 251.5 *means of restraint*
bondservant 401.7 *slave*
bondslave 387.5 *subjected person*
bondsman 756.5 *promise-maker*; 401.7 *slave*; 387.5 *subjected person*
bond strength 32.11 *chemical bond*
bondwoman 387.5 *subjected person*
bone 25.55 *cook*; 418.7 *hard substance*; 403.7 *skeleton*; 416.4 *solid body*; 371.11 *void*
bone ash 24.2 *raw material*
bone cancer 260.12 *cancer*
bone-carving 19.12 *sculpture*
bone cell 34.7 *cell*
bone china 24.1 *ceramics*
boned 418.2 *tough*
bone-dry 428.3 *dried-up*
bonefish 55.4 *American game fish*
boneheaded 152.3 *thick-witted*
bone idle 343.3 *not participating*
boneless rump roast 25.23 *beef*
bonemeal 43.13, 562.3 *fertilizer*
bone of contention 705.4 *difficult question*; 751.1 *disagreement*; 447.2 *issue*
boner 274.10 *blunder*

bones 215.1 *remainder;* 590.8 *seat of feelings*
bonesetter 35.12, 394.15 *healer;* 393.12 *repairer;* 492.5 *toucher*
bone-setting 394.13 *therapy*
boneshaker 320.12 *bicycle*
bone to pick 751.1 *disagreement;* 594.1 *hate;* 624.1 *resentment*
bone up 6.23 *learn*
bone up on 400.15 *learn*
bone urn 583.4 *funeral objects*
boneyard 583.5 *cemetery*
bonfire 493.6, 522.8 *fire;* 601.8 *salute*
bong 62.4 *climbing equipment*
bonhomie 650.1 *benevolence;* 569.1 *friendship;* 654.8 *good company*
bonhomous 598.1 *cheerful*
boniness 153.8 *emaciation;* 153.7 *thinness*
bonito 55.4 *American game fish*
bonk 331.13 *blow;* 561.14 *have sex;* 331.3 *hit*
bonkers 461.11 *insane*
bonking 593.5 *desire*
bon marché 793.4 *bargain*
bon mot 697.2 *solecism*
bonne bouche 495.3 *appetizer*
bonnet 551.15 *headgear*
bonneted 551.29 *dressed*
bonny 545.5 *beautiful;* 158.16 *fat;* 259.1 *healthy*
bonsai 44.2 *garden*
bonsai tree 79.1 *tree*
bonspiel 68.10 *curling*
bonus 211.4 *extra;* 679.7, 768.2 *gift;* 768.7 *given;* 788.2 *money received;* 483.5 *positive stimulus;* 765.5 *profit;* 671.3 *recognition;* 813.4 *reward for service;* 769.2 *something received;* 219.3 *superfluity;* 215.4 *surplus*
bonuses 15.2 *industrial negotiations*
bon vivant 557.18 *eater;* 688.4 *glutton;* 686.5 *self-indulgent person;* 654.6 *social person;* 495.5 *taster*
bon viveur 490.3 *pleasure-seeker*
bon voyage 313.14 *goodbye!*
bony 418.1 *hard;* 403.13 *skeletal;* 153.1 *thin*
bony fish 74.2 *fish*
bonze 7.7 *monk*
boo 606.7 *be dissatisfied;* 512.2, 512.5 *catcall;* 753.7 *complain;* 514.7 *cry of disapproval;* 606.2 *expression of dissatisfaction;* 742.3, 742.11 *gesture;* 753.3 *gesture of protest;* 514.14 *hiss;* 670.23 *show disapproval;* 670.9 *show of disapproval;* 668.6, 668.25 *taunt*
boob 486.7 *be clumsy;* 274.10 *blunder;* 272.4 *joke;* 288.3 *lost chance;* 274.19, 288.9 *make a mistake;* 465.2 *mistake;* 486.10 *unskilled person;* 247.4 *unsuccessful thing*
boob job 547.2 *plastic surgery*
boo-boo 274.10 *blunder;* 272.4 *joke;* 288.3 *lost chance;* 465.2 *mistake;* 247.4 *unsuccessful thing*
boobs 182.2 *bulge*
boob tube 692.22 *television set*
booby 461.7 *insane person;* 486.10 *unskilled person*
booby hutch 461.8 *mental hospital*
booby prize 813.2 *prize;* 486.8 *unskilfulness*
booby trap 587.16 *bomb;* 384.8 *fence;* 700.13 *snare;* 379.1 *trap*
boodle 780.2 *cash;* 765.5 *profit;* 774.4 *stolen goods;* 773.5 *takings*
booed 670.35 *hissed*
boofhead 456.5 *ignorant person*
boogerboo 736.7 *concealer*
boogie-woogie 18.8 *jazz*
boohoo 514.6 *cry of pain*
boo-hurrah theory 4.7 *school of thought*
booing 512.7 *catcalling;* 514.19 *hissing;* 753.9 *protesting;* 668.15 *taunting*
book 789.7 *account;* 715.5 *accuse;* 740.6 *book publishing;* 220.8 *list;* 135.10 *necessitate;* 17.8 *part of poem;* 21.2 *play;* 293.9 *prepare;* 744.15 *register;* 253.15 *reserve;* 356.5 *work of art*
book and candle 712.7 *wish ill*
bookbinder 550.17 *coverer;* 740.12 *publisher*
bookcase 23.5, 410.3 *cabinet*
book club 740.6 *book publishing*
book collection 439.5 *collection*
book cover 550.4 *wrapping*
booked 715.8 *accusatory;* 135.4 *required*
Booker Prize 740.6 *book publishing;* 813.2 *prize*
book fair 740.6 *book publishing*
bookie 59.15 *horse person*
book illustration 717.2 *reproduction*
book in advance 293.9 *prepare*
booking 715.1 *accusation;* 21.15 *engagement;* 744.8 *registration*
booking agent 21.27 *producer*
booking clerk 778.12 *wholesaler*
booking office 321.8 *railway station*
bookish 6.18 *educated;* 4.19 *learned*
bookishly 6.26 *studiously*
bookishness 6.9 *learnedness;* 455.3 *learning*
book-keeper 789.6 *accountant;* 210.7 *mathematician;* 744.9 *recorder;* 780.18 *treasurer*
book-keeping 789.10 *accounting;* 789.1 *accounts;* 744.8 *registration*
booklearning 455.3 *learning*
book list 220.2 *table*
bookmaker 59.15 *horse person*
bookmaking 107.7 *calculation of chance*
bookman 442.8 *intellectual person*
bookmark 40.16 *Internet*
Book of Common Prayer 10.10 *religious manual*
book of hours 10.10 *religious manual*
Book of Mormon 7.12 *religious text*
Book of the Dead 7.12 *religious text*
book of words 21.2 *play*
boo koos 217.8 *plenty*
bookperson 740.12 *publisher*
bookplate 743.3 *means of identification*
book publisher 740.12 *publisher*
book publishing 740.6
book review 740.6 *book publishing;* 719.3 *criticism*
book reviewer 17.15 *literary person*
books 789.5 *account book;* 220.4 *bill*
bookseller 740.12 *publisher*
bookselling 740.6 *book publishing*
book serialization 740.6 *book publishing*
bookshelf 23.5, 410.3 *cabinet*
bookshop 740.6 *book publishing*
book trade 740.6 *book publishing*
book-wise 6.18 *educated*
bookworm 442.8 *intellectual person;* 6.7 *learner;* 76.3 *pest;* 75.6 *worm*
Boolean algebra 27.23 *algebra*
boolhipper 551.11 *jacket*
boom 508.1, 508.5 *bang;* 384.9 *barrier;* 562.6 *be fertile;* 507.8 *be loud;* 778.2 *be sold;* 509.8 *drum;* 13.2 *economy;* 213.4 *increase;* 507.1 *loudness;* 50.3 *parts of a sailing boat;* 562.2 *productiveness;* 248.1 *prosperity;* 510.9 *resonate;* 393.10 *revival;* 778.5 *sales;* 729.12 *speak loudly;* 213.2 *spread;* 38.27 *superstructure;* 50.7 *windsurfing*
boom and bust 776.5 *commercial trade;* 326.1 *oscillation*
boom box 504.9 *audio device;* 692.18 *radio*
boom/bust cycle 13.2 *economy*
boomerang 347.3 *counteract;* 587.6 *historical missile weapon;* 385.3 *retaliate;* 385.1 *retaliation;* 761.6 *reverse*
boomerang effect 347.1 *counteraction;* 761.1 *reversion*
booming 508.8 *banging;* 510.8 *deep;* 510.3 *deepness;* 509.1 *drumming;* 562.5 *fertile;* 507.6 *loud;* 248.8 *prosperous;* 514.16 *vociferous*
booming economy 562.2 *productiveness;* 248.1 *prosperity*
boom off 323.9 *navigate*
boom preventer 50.3 *parts of a sailing boat*
boomps-a-daisy 22.2 *dance*
boom town 86.11 *settlement;* 87.9 *town*
boom vang 50.3 *parts of a sailing boat*
boon 797.13 *benefit;* 768.2 *gift*
boon companion 569.6 *close friend*
boondocks 86.6 *regions*
boonies 86.6 *regions*
boor 631.5 *badly behaved person;* 659.4 *discourteous person;* 457.3 *unintelligent person;* 242.9 *unpleasant person;* 675.5 *vulgar person*
boorish 631.18 *badly behaved;* 659.6 *badmannered;* 486.3 *clumsy;* 675.8 *discourteous;* 544.8 *indecorous;* 242.2 *objectionable;* 457.6 *unintelligent*
boorishly 659.10 *rudely*
boorishness 631.4 *bad conduct;* 659.2 *bad manners;* 675.3 *grossness;* 544.2 *impropriety;* 242.6 *objectionability;* 457.2 *unintelligence*
boost 669.15 *compliment;* 392.28 *further;* 338.3 *invigorate;* 366.7 *lift;* 213.5 *make bigger;* 740.16 *publicize;* 366.1 *raise;* 213.2 *spread;* 774.12 *steal;* 336.8 *strengthen;* 392.2, 392.19 *support*
booster 330.11 *propeller;* 692.18 *radio;* 29.35 *rocketry;* 774.8 *thief*
booster station 692.20 *radio broadcasting;* 692.24 *television broadcasting*
boosting 774.1 *stealing*
boot 40.20 *abort;* 130.20 *activate;* 331.13 *blow;* 410.10 *cart;* 331.7 *kick;* 53.6 *pad;* 144.17 *relegate;* 378.4 *restraint;* 68.5 *ski equipment;* 631.8 *treatment*
boot-axe 62.8 *mountaineering*
boot-axe belay 62.3 *climbing technique*
bootblack 401.3 *attendant;* 256.12 *cleaner*
booted 551.29 *dressed*
booted out 144.11 *relegated*
bootees 551.23 *children's clothes*
booter 551.26 *fashion designer*
booth 410.2 *compartment;* 565.8 *shelter;* 779.9 *stall;* 21.16 *theatre*
booting out 371.17 *expulsion*
bootlace 373.6 *line*
bootleg 772.9 *borrow illegally;* 125.2 *copy;* 699.12 *fake;* 774.15 *infringe;* 46.9 *play;* 46.15 *play offence*
bootleg copy 115.2 *copy*
bootlegger 125.8 *copier;* 774.10 *infringer;* 773.6 *taker*
bootlegging 772.3, 774.6 *illegal borrowing*
bootleg liquor 690.12 *alcohol*
bootleg record 774.6 *illegal borrowing*
bootless 247.10 *failed;* 238.2 *futile*
bootlessly 247.12 *unsuccessfully*
bootlessness 238.4 *futility*
bootlick 677.11 *be sycophantic;* 664.9 *fawn;* 599.15 *humour*
bootlicker 599.7 *person who humours;* 664.3, 677.7 *sycophant*
bootlicking 599.11 *humouring;* 667.9 *showing respect;* 388.5 *submitting;* 664.2, 677.5 *sycophancy;* 664.7, 677.16 *sycophantic*
bootmaker 551.26 *fashion designer*
bootmaking 551.2 *dressing*
boot out 470.2 *discard;* 371.2, 767.10 *dismiss;* 364.2 *eject;* 371.1 *expel;* 144.16 *replace*
boot-out 144.4 *relegation*
boot polish 256.9 *cleaning agent*
boots 551.19 *footwear;* 66.1 *soccer*
boot sale 767.2 *disposal of property*
boot-scraper 256.10 *cleaning object*
bootstrap 40.20 *abort;* 40.19 *computing terms*
booty 765.5 *profit;* 794.2 *spoils;* 774.4 *stolen goods;* 773.5 *takings*
booze 690.12 *alcohol;* 558.7 *alcoholic drink;* 558.13 *drink;* 690.8 *get drunk*
boozed up 690.1 *drunk*
boozer 558.12 *drinker;* 690.17 *drunkard;* 565.10 *hotel*
boozing 558.16 *drinking;* 690.5 *drunken*
boozy 690.5 *drunken;* 690.2 *slightly drunk*
bop 22.2, 22.15, 376.10 *dance;* 22.1 *dancing;* 331.3 *hit;* 18.8 *jazz;* 654.5 *party*
boracic acid 394.3 *prophylactic*
borage 496.5 *herbs*
Bordeaux 558.9 *wine*
Bordeaux mixture 44.8 *weedkiller*
bordelaise sauce 25.15 *sauce*
bordello 796.6 *brothel*
border 164.5; 492.12 *abut;* 211.3 *additional item;* 171.11 *be exterior;* 372.6 *boundary;* 163.3, 164.1, 164.6 *edge;* 164.2 *edging;* 171.1 *exterior;* 166.6 *furthest;* 147.18 *juxtapose;* 147.3 *juxtaposition;* 131.7 *limit;* 44.3 *ornamental garden;* 21.19 *stage set;* 170.7 *surround*
border ballad 18.11 *folk music*
bordered 164.8 *edging*
bordering 166.6 *furthest;* 147.10 *juxtaposed;* 147.3 *juxtaposition;* 131.24 *limiting;* 492.9 *touching*
bordering on 239.2 *nearby*
borderland 147.3 *juxtaposition;* 86.6 *regions*
borderline 453.6 *indeterminate;* 705.14 *questionable*
borderline case 453.11 *irresoluteness*
Borders 86.9 *regions of Britain*
borders 86.6 *regions*
bordure 743.8 *heraldic device*
bore 620.6 *be boring;* 270.5 *be diffuse;* 497.7 *be tasteless;* 620.3 *boring person;* 150.4 *breadth;* 23.17 *carpenter;* 90.2 *channel;* 261.6 *fatigue;* 587.9 *firearm;* 308.20 *hole;* 245.5 *hurt;* 183.9 *make concave;* 618.13 *make indifferent;* 308.1 *opening;* 731.8 *talk too much;* 305.15 *tunnel;* 425.16 *use a sharp tool*
boreal 31.55 *cool;* 324.13 *directional;* 31.47 *windy*
Boreas 494.7 *cold weather;* 31.15 *wind direction*
bored 261.2; **620.5**; 261.2 *bored;* 308.14 *holed*
Boredom 620
boredom 620.1; 497.1 *dilution;* 261.7 *fatigue;* 271.4 *simplicity*
bored stiff 620.5 *bored*
bored to death 620.5 *bored*
bored to tears 620.5 *bored*
bored tunnel 38.22 *tunnel*
borehole 183.2 *concave land;* 308.5 *hole*
bore in 314.11 *infiltrate*
bore into 183.9 *make concave*
borer 183.5 *digger;* 76.3 *pest;* 425.8 *sharp-pointed thing;* 23.11 *woodworking tool*
boresome 620.4 *boring*
bore stiff 620.6 *be boring*
bore the pants off 620.6 *be boring*
bore to death 620.6 *be boring*
bore to tears 620.6 *be boring;* 261.6 *fatigue*
boric acid 394.3 *prophylactic*
boring 620.4; 270.3 *diffuse;* 261.4 *fatiguing;* 240.1, 264.13 *inconvenient;* 618.11 *insignificant;* 112.13 *monotonous;* 271.1 *simple;* 497.5 *tasteless;* 305.7 *tunnelling*
boring life 620.1 *boredom*
boringly 620.8; 240.6 *inconveniently;* 618.20 *unexceptionally*
boring machine 38.9 *machine tool;* 23.11 *woodworking tool*
boringness 620.1 *boredom*
boring old fart 620.3 *boring person*
boring person 620.3
boring thing 620.2
Boris Becker 63.7 *famous tennis players*
born 554.15; 356.12 *produced*
born again 760.16 *influenced;* 393.13 *repaired*
born-again 450.11 *believing;* 808.6 *penitent*
born-again Christian 807.3 *atoner;* 450.5 *believer;* 7.5 *Christian;* 808.3 *penitent person*
born alive 554.15 *born*
born dead 582.19 *dead*
borne out 703.13 *proven*
born for 485.7 *gifted*
born in the purple 781.1 *wealthy*
born leader 228.5 *stable person*
born loser 247.5 *failing person;* 611.3 *hopeless person;* 766.6 *loser;* 249.5 *person in adversity;* 470.9 *rejected person*
born of 345.10 *caused*
born to the purple 540.4 *figurative usage*
born to toil 576.10 *working*
born yesterday 646.1 *naive*
borough 469.12 *election;* 86.5 *state;* 87.9 *town*
borrow 772.7; 783.9 *acquire credit;* 27.91 *add;* 125.10 *copy;* 774.12 *steal;* 773.10 *take away*
borrowed 772.11
borrowed plumes 700.12 *disguise*
borrowed word 5.17 *word*
borrower 772.6; 784.6 *debtor;* 710.4 *requester*
borrow from 345.7 *follow from*
borrow illegally 772.9
Borrowing 772
borrowing 772.1; 68.10 *curling;* 784.9 *in debt;* 784.3 *loan;* 774.1 *stealing;* 773.3 *taking away*
borrowing capacity 783.1 *credit;* 352.4 *financial resources*
borrow money 784.7 *be in debt*
borrow without authorization 772.9 *borrow illegally*
borrow without permission 772.9 *borrow illegally*
borscht 25.13 *soup*
borscht belt 21.15 *engagement*

borstal 309.4 *closed place;* 655.4 *place of confinement;* 815.1 *prison;* 244.10 *reformatory;* 815.2 *the inside*
bo-san 7.7 *monk*
bosey 700.9 *sleight of hand*
bosh 697.1, 699.15 *nonsense;* 702.2 *sophism*
bosie 53.8 *delivery*
bosk 79.4 *trees*
bosket 79.4 *trees*
bosky 79.16 *wooded*
bosom 182.2 *bulge;* 551.24 *part of garment;* 590.8 *seat of feelings*
bosom buddy 569.6 *close friend;* 595.4 *likable person*
bosom friend 595.4 *likable person*
bosom pal 569.6 *close friend*
bosomy 158.16 *fat*
boson 28.77 *elementary particle*
boss 396.19 *be authoritarian;* 182.2 *bulge;* 400.5 *company leader;* 20.19 *decorate;* 579.2 *direct;* 579.13 *director;* 15.6 *employer;* 58.7 *hurling;* 420.12 *make rough;* 400.14 *master;* 342.17 *meddle;* 396.10 *person of authority;* 19.13 *relief-carving;* 121.5 *superior*
bossanova 22.2 *dance*
boss around 647.5 *be severe;* 342.17 *meddle*
bossed 20.17 *structured*
bosses 579.6 *governing body*
boss-eyed 519.9 *weak-sighted*
bossy 396.12 *authoritative;* 400.13 *excellent;* 397.15 *self-assured;* 647.8 *severe*
Boston 87.2 *American cities*
Boston accent 5.26 *dialect*
Boston bag 410.9 *baggage*
Boston brown bread 25.38 *bread*
Boston cream pie 25.36 *cake*
Boston rocker 23.2 *chair*
Boston two-step 22.2 *dance*
bosun's chair 50.3 *parts of a sailing boat*
bosun's mate 323.7 *nautical person*
BOT 251.4 *detention;* 815.4 *prison sentence*
bot 492.3 *press*
botanic 77.20 *botanical*
botanical 44.17; 77.20; 34.20 *biological*
botanical fruit 80.2
botanical garden 44.2 *garden*
botanically 77.25; 34.29 *biologically;* 44.20 *horticulturally*
botanic garden 77.11 *herbarium*
botanist 34.19 *life scientist;* 77.12 *plant scientist*
botanize 77.23 *study plants*
botany 34.1 *life science;* 77.10 *plant science;* 554.7 *studies of life*
botch 486.7 *be clumsy;* 236.13 *be worthless;* 486.9 *bungling;* 408.23 *confuse;* 247.1 *failure;* 245.4 *impair;* 231.5 *imperfection;* 236.8 *inferiority;* 718.4 *misrepresent;* 718.1 *misrepresentation;* 378.2 *obstacle*
botched 486.4 *bungled;* 231.1 *imperfect;* 236.2 *inferior*
botcher 486.10 *unskilled person*
botching 486.9 *bungling*
botch up 274.19 *make a mistake*
botch-up 274.10 *blunder*
botchy 486.4 *bungled*
both 198.9 *two*
bother 264.7 *awkward situation;* 342.12 *be active;* 240.5 *be inconvenient;* 264.23 *cause difficulties;* 328.5 *commotion;* 408.9 *disorder;* 328.7 *disturb;* 328.1 *disturbance;* 261.6 *fatigue;* 327.4 *fuss;* 378.8 *hinder;* 240.3 *inconvenience;* 625.8 *make irascible;* 342.17 *meddle;* 342.3 *nimbleness;* 607.3 *nuisance;* 624.9 *offend;* 242.8 *quarrel*
botheration 342.3 *nimbleness*
bothered 328.12 *disturbed;* 264.16 *troubled*
bothersome 236.6 *damnable;* 328.17 *disturbing;* 240.1, 264.13 *inconvenient*
both hands 815.4 *prison sentence*
bothy 565.8 *shelter*
Bo tree 10.14 *sacred object;* 79.13 *tree mythology*
botrytis 44.12 *pests and diseases*
bottle 410.14; 587.7 *blunt weapon;* 167.5 *boldness;* 203.3 *container;* 613.1 *courage;* 661.1 *defiance;* 558.2 *drink;* 558.10 *drink container;* 638.16 *fortitude;* 359.5 *preserve;* 359.2 *preserver;* 410.21 *put in a container;* 640.4 *stamina;* 439.6 *store*
bottled 410.20 *containing;* 690.1 *drunk;* 359.7 *preserved;* 439.7 *stored*
bottled beer 558.7 *alcoholic drink*
bottled fruit 25.42 *preserve;* 359.3 *preserved thing*
bottled water 433.2 *drinking water*
bottle garden 44.2 *garden*
bottle glass 24.1 *ceramics;* 527.9 *glass*
bottle green 538.1 *green*
bottle kiln 24.6 *ceramic workshop*
bottleneck 378.9 *block;* 191.3 *contracted thing;* 310.6 *narrowing;* 151.6 *narrow place;* 378.2 *obstacle*
bottle-opener 308.2 *opener*
bottle party 654.5 *party*
bottler 359.4 *preservationist*
bottle up 736.8 *conceal;* 360.7 *detain;* 172.15 *keep inside;* 166.7 *limit;* 359.5 *preserve;* 251.8 *restrain*
bottle up and go 634.9 *play truant*
bottling 410.20 *containing;* 439.4 *storage*
bottling plant 359.2 *preserver*
bottling up 360.2 *detention*
bottom 55.8 *angling;* 175.1, 175.3 *base;* 156.10 *deeper;* 122.5 *inferior state;* 166.2 *limiting factor;* 155.6 *lower;* 155.4 *low thing;* 168.2 *rear end;* 169.2 *surface*
bottom cushion 65.5 *snooker*
bottom dollar 131.8 *tail*
bottom drawer 23.5 *cabinet;* 243.10 *preparations;* 439.1 *store*
bottom gear 61.6 *motor-racing terms*
bottoming out 191.1 *contraction;* 214.2 *decline*
bottom land 92.6 *lowland*
bottomless 156.8 *deep;* 202.1 *infinite;* 217.2 *plentiful*
bottomlessness 156.1 *depth*
bottomless pit 156.4 *deep thing;* 688.4 *glutton;* 8.12 *hell;* 202.4 *infinity*
bottomless purse 781.5 *wealth*
bottom line 99.2 *essential content;* 95.5 *realities;* 813.5 *turnover*
bottommost 175.3 *base;* 122.12 *inferior;* 155.6 *lower*
bottom of one's heart 590.8 *seat of feelings*
bottom of the barrel 131.8 *tail*
bottom of the bill 21.8 *scene*
bottom of the inning 48.1 *baseball*
bottom of the sea 156.4 *deep thing*
bottom out 191.6 *become smaller;* 155.8 *be low;* 214.4 *decrease*
bottom patting 742.3 *gesture*
bottom pinching 742.3 *gesture*
bottom pocket 65.3 *English billiards;* 65.5 *snooker*
bottom price 791.2 *bargain*
bottoms up 558.18 *cheers!*
bottom turn 50.1 *sailing*
bottom-up 192.2 *inverted*
botulism 260.8 *indigestion;* 260.6 *infection*
bouclé 420.2 *coarse;* 420.7 *rough thing*
boudoir 593.13 *abode of love;* 736.6 *privacy;* 565.7 *room*
boudoir dress 551.16 *robe*
bouffant 551.31 *styled*
bough 205.6 *branch;* 79.2 *tree part*
bought 777.13
bought-in 43.21 *domesticated*
bouillabaisse 25.13 *soup*
bouillon 25.13 *soup*
boulder 418.7 *hard substance;* 30.27 *sediment*
boulder clay 30.38 *glacier*
bouldering 62.1 *mountaineering*
boulevard 317.3 *road*
boulle 23.9 *decorative woodwork;* 23.7 *furniture style*
bounce 327.21 *be agitated;* 422.8 *be elastic;* 53.18 *bowl;* 53.8 *delivery;* 422.1 *elasticity;* 371.1 *expel;* 327.9, 327.23 *jolt;* 304.5, 304.18 *jump;* 326.11 *rock*
bounce a cheque 780.24 *monetize;* 786.8 *stop payment*
bounceback 706.4 *reaction*
bounce back 422.10 *be adaptable;* 393.4 *be restored;* 259.6 *get healthy;* 706.19 *react;* 303.7 *recoil*
bounced cheque 784.5 *amount owing*
bounced light 41.15 *lighting*
bounce pass 49.4 *playing terms*
bouncer 586.2 *defender;* 53.8 *delivery;* 371.26 *ejector;* 384.14 *guard;* 336.6 *muscleman;* 252.3 *protector*
bounce up 302.8 *further*
bouncily 422.11 *elastically*
bounciness 422.1 *elasticity*
bouncing 598.1 *cheerful;* 422.6 *elastic;* 259.1 *healthy;* 338.5 *invigorating;* 304.24 *leaping*
bouncing baby 555.9 *child*
bouncing billy 56.5 *golf ball*
bouncing cheque 786.3 *bad payment*
bouncy 598.1 *cheerful;* 422.6 *elastic;* 338.5 *invigorating;* 327.17 *turbulent*
bouncy castle 422.3 *elastic thing*
bound 373.16; 332.9 *acceleration;* 332.4 *be swift;* 136.12 *conditional;* 373.15 *connected;* 810.11 *duty-bound;* 756.13 *guaranteeing;* 784.9 *in debt;* 47.8, 304.5, 304.18 *jump;* 756.12 *promised;* 550.37 *protected;* 108.4 *related;* 360.10 *retained;* 27.21 *set*
boundary 372.6; 164.1 *edge;* 166.6 *furthest;* 166.3 *furthest point;* 51.1 *green bowling;* 131.7 *limit;* 131.24 *limiting;* 27.37 *line;* 86.3 *regional boundary;* 53.10 *score*
boundary condition 136.7 *condition*
boundary marker 166.4
boundary stone 166.4 *boundary marker*
bound by duty 810.11 *duty-bound*
bounded volume 27.41 *geometric figure*
bounden duty 810.1 *duty*
bounder 631.5 *badly behaved person;* 804.10 *bad person;* 48.5 *batting terms;* 812.2 *disreputable character;* 567.7 *libertine;* 675.5 *vulgar person*
bound for 324.14 *directed*
bound forward 332.6 *accelerate*
bounding 47.2 *field events;* 304.24 *leaping;* 136.6 *specification*
bounding main 91.1 *sea*
boundless 29.36 *astronomical;* 141.12 *extensive;* 202.1 *infinite;* 208.8 *numberless*
boundlessly 29.39 *astronomically;* 202.10 *infinitely*
boundlessness 202.4 *infinity*
bounds 164.1 *edge;* 86.3 *regional boundary;* 136.6 *specification*
bounteous 562.5 *fertile;* 679.1 *generous*
bounteousness 679.5 *generosity*
bountiful 650.7 *charitable;* 562.5 *fertile;* 679.1 *generous;* 768.8 *giving;* 781.4 *lush;* 217.2 *plentiful*
bountifully 768.9 *as a gift;* 650.11 *charitably*
bountifulness 650.2 *charity*
bountiful supply 217.8 *plenty*
bounty 813.7; 562.1 *fertility;* 679.5 *generosity;* 768.1 *giving;* 768.3 *offering;* 781.7 *opulence;* 652.1 *philanthropy;* 790.2 *value*
bouquet 376.29 *bunch;* 669.4 *compliment;* 78.1 *flower;* 502.1 *fragrance;* 502.2 *fragrant thing;* 500.1 *odour;* 813.1 *reward*
bouquet garni 412.4 *admixture;* 496.5 *herbs*
bourbon 558.7 *alcoholic drink*
bourbon whiskey 558.7 *alcoholic drink*
bourgeois 117.6, 117.14 *conformist;* 250.7 *free person;* 566.10 *member of society;* 216.8 *middle classes;* 574.1 *plebeian*
bourgeois ethic 117.4 *conventionalism*
bourgeoisie 566.9 *group;* 216.8 *middle classes;* 574.2 *the common people*
bourguignonne 25.15 *sauce*
bourn 312.15 *destination;* 90.1 *river*
bourrée 22.9 *ballet steps*
Bourse 759.2 *place of exchange*
bourse 779.5 *stock market*
bout 381.20; 770.3 *allotted task;* 69.2 *contest;* 276.4 *period of activity;* 45.1 *sport;* 576.2 *task*
boutade 642.3 *whim*
boutique 779.8 *store*
bout of sickness 260.2 *illness*
boutonniere 78.1 *flower*
Bouyan 8.11 *heaven*
bovid 71.15 *hoofed mammal;* 71.33 *ungulate*
Bovidae 71.15 *hoofed mammal*
bovine 71.15 *hoofed mammal;* 71.33 *ungulate*
bovver boy 586.1 *combatant;* 662.9 *criminal;* 380.4 *violent creature*
bow 367.9; 182.5 *be convex;* 155.8 *be low;* 50.6 *canoeing;* 367.16 *courtesy;* 177.6 *curve;* 658.13 *defer to;* 330.9 *firearm;* 587.6 *historical missile weapon;* 623.21 *humble oneself;* 664.10 *knuckle under;* 667.4 *mark of respect;* 20.9 *miscellaneous architectural features;* 663.3 *obeisance;* 10.19 *offer worship;* 50.3 *parts of a sailing boat;* 50.9 *sailor;* 663.6 *show obeisance to;* 658.5 *sign of courtesy;* 18.38 *sound;* 388.1 *submission;* 388.4 *succumb;* 667.19 *take off one's hat to*
bow and arrow 357.7 *agent of destruction*
bow and scrape 664.10 *knuckle under;* 388.4 *succumb;* 667.19 *take off one's hat to*
bow before the inevitable 388.4 *succumb*
bow before the storm 388.4 *succumb*
bowdlerization 256.4 *censorship;* 128.2 *ejection;* 255.1 *purity;* 795.4 *self-righteousness;* 212.1 *subtraction*
bowdlerize 224.8 *cause change;* 128.8 *eject;* 245.5 *hurt;* 255.10, 256.15 *purify;* 212.3 *subtract*
bowdlerized 795.10 *moralistic*
bowdlerizer 224.6 *editor*
bow down 367.9 *bow;* 305.12 *drop;* 667.19 *take off one's hat to*
bowed 177.4 *curved;* 664.7 *sycophantic*
bowed down 623.3 *humbled*
bowed out 182.4 *convex*
bowel cancer 260.8 *indigestion*
bowel movement 560.2 *defecation*
bowels 557.16 *eating utensil;* 406.3 *insides*
bowels of the earth 156.4 *deep thing*
bower 593.13 *abode of love;* 44.3 *ornamental garden;* 79.4 *trees*
bower of bliss 593.13 *abode of love*
bowie knife 425.10 *knife;* 587.8 *sharp weapon*
bowing 658.4 *deference;* 658.9 *deferential;* 667.11 *in a respectful stance;* 664.7 *sycophantic*
bowing and scraping 367.15 *debasement;* 667.11 *in a respectful stance;* 667.4 *mark of respect;* 388.5 *submitting;* 664.2 *sycophancy*
bowl 51.7; 51.8; 53.18; 384.7 *armour;* 330.10 *ball;* 410.12 *bath;* 183.3 *cavity;* 24.8 *ceramic object;* 203.3 *container;* 410.16 *crockery;* 53.19 *dismiss;* 558.10 *drink container;* 557.16 *eating utensil;* 51.1 *green bowling;* 307.9, 330.22 *roll;* 181.6 *round;* 46.4 *stadium;* 330.5 *throw*
bowl a bosey 700.29 *juggle*
bowl a googly 700.29 *juggle*
bowl a hook ball 51.8 *bowl*
bowl a hoop 330.22 *roll*
bowl along 332.4 *be swift;* 421.12 *go smoothly*
bowl a wrong'un 700.29 *juggle*
bowled over 630.7 *amazed;* 619.6 *wondering*
bowler 51.6; 551.15 *headgear;* 53.4 *team;* 330.14 *thrower*
bowler-hatted 708.20 *cancelled*
bowl game 46.1 *football*
bowline 373.7 *tackle;* 50.7 *windsurfing*
bowling 51.4; 51.10; 53.13; 53.12 *cricketing;* 53.11 *dismissal;* 51.1 *green bowling;* 307.11 *rotating;* 307.2 *turning*
bowling alley 421.8 *smooth thing*
bowling along 332.8 *speed*
bowling bag 51.4 *bowling*
bowling ball 51.4 *bowling*
bowling delivery 51.5
bowling green 187.3 *flat thing;* 51.1 *green bowling;* 538.8 *greenness;* 421.8 *smooth thing*
bowling lane 51.4 *bowling*
bowling pin 51.4 *bowling*
bowling rink 51.1 *green bowling*
bowling shoes 51.4 *bowling*
bowling side 51.1 *green bowling*
bowl over 630.11 *amaze;* 619.10 *be wonderful;* 367.3 *bring down;* 335.8 *overpower;* 593.28 *win the love of*
bow low 367.9 *bow*
Bowls 51
bowls 51.9; 51.1 *green bowling*
bowl-shaped 183.6 *concave*
bowls match 51.1 *green bowling*
bowls player 51.3
bowl wide 325.2 *divert*
bowman 330.16 *archer;* 586.13 *historical soldiery*
bowmanship 587.2 *arms*
bow one's head 667.19 *take off one's hat to*
bow out 98.16 *absent oneself;* 315.9 *exit;* 313.2 *withdraw*
bowsaw 79.7 *timber production*
bowshot 147.2 *short distance;* 330.7 *shot*
bow side 50.4 *rowing*
bowsprit 167.1 *front*
Bow Street runner 16.11 *British law officer*

bow-string 814.5 *execute;* 814.16 *instrument of execution*
bowstringer 814.17 *punisher*
bow stroke 50.6 *canoeing*
bow tie 551.3 *formal dress;* 551.14 *neckwear*
bow to 388.3 *submit;* 122.9 *yield to*
bow wave 28.14 *sound wave*
bow-wow 71.9 *dog*
bow-wow theory 5.37 *linguistic theory*
box 410.6; 21.18 *auditorium;* 331.13 *blow;* 550.13 *casing;* 410.2 *compartment;* 203.3 *container;* 43.7 *farm building;* 52.11, 331.9, 586.37 *fight;* 768.2 *gift;* 331.3 *hit;* 368.5 *inset;* 780.20 *money store;* 53.6 *pad;* 384.6 *protective clothing;* 50.8 *punting;* 372.2 *setting apart;* 439.4 *storage;* 496.7 *tobacco;* 550.25 *wrap;* 550.4 *wrapping*
box a round 52.11 *fight*
box Brownie 41.16 *camera*
box canyon 146.3 *gulf*
boxcar 201.7 *double figures*
box chair 23.2 *chair*
boxed 410.20 *containing;* 550.37 *protected*
boxer 52.4; 336.5, 586.3 *athlete*
boxer shorts 551.18 *underwear*
boxes 21.33 *theatregoer*
boxfile 410.6 *box*
box fortification 384.11 *fortification*
box-girder bridge 38.21 *bridge*
box in 264.23 *cause difficulties;* 251.8 *restrain*
boxing 52.2; 331.12 *collision;* 52.1 *combat sports;* 384.5 *self-defence*
boxing association 52.2 *boxing*
boxing blow 331.14 *sporting hit*
Boxing Day 298.6 *annually celebrated day*
boxing glove 331.16 *weapons*
boxing gloves 52.2 *boxing*
boxing match 52.2 *boxing*
boxing punch 52.2 *boxing*
boxing purse 52.2 *boxing*
boxing ring 52.2 *boxing*
boxing rules 52.2 *boxing*
boxing scorecard 52.2 *boxing*
boxing shorts 52.2 *boxing*
boxing technique 52.2 *boxing*
boxing weight 414.7 *weighing*
boxing weight divisions 52.3
box junction 320.3 *carriageway*
box off 128.7 *exclude*
box office 21.18 *auditorium*
box-office hit 246.3 *successful thing;* 21.13 *theatrical performance*
box-office receipts 765.4 *earnings;* 788.2 *money received*
box-office returns 769.2 *something received*
box-office staff 21.28 *stagehand*
box-office success 246.3 *successful thing*
box of tricks 645.2 *stratagem*
box on the ear 814.12 *corporal punishment;* 624.5 *quarrel*
box pleat 184.3 *pleat*
box room 565.7 *room;* 439.4 *storage*
box seat 21.18 *auditorium*
box set 21.19 *stage set*
box someone's ears 331.3, 814.3 *hit*
box spring 422.5 *spring*
box springs 413.4 *rest*
box the compass 324.8 *orient;* 303.7 *recoil*
box up 406.6 *contain;* 410.21 *put in a container*
boy 567.4 *boyfriend;* 555.9 *child;* 401.6 *domestic servant;* 691.6 *drug;* 567.2 *male;* 567.3 *male title of address;* 567.13 *man in the family;* 566.7 *person;* 555.7 *young man*
boycott 532.11 *blacken;* 753.8 *cause mischief;* 128.7 *exclude;* 128.1 *exclusion;* 753.3 *gesture of protest;* 15.12 *have an industrial dispute;* 655.13 *ignore;* 15.4 *industrial dispute;* 703.6 *mass demonstration;* 670.3 *nonacceptance;* 703.19 *protest;* 655.3 *separation;* 372.10 *set apart;* 372.2 *setting apart;* 670.15 *withhold approval*
boycotted 670.31 *disapproved;* 655.10 *lonely;* 15.10 *unionized*
boycotting 703.14 *demonstrating;* 15.10 *unionized*
boyfriend 567.4; 569.6 *close friend;* 593.9 *lover;* 223.12 *partner*
boyhood 555.1 *youth*
boyish 153.1 *thin;* 555.11 *young*
boyish figure 153.7 *thinness*
boyishly 555.14 *youthfully*
boyishness 555.2 *youthfulness*
boylike 555.11 *young*
boy next door 216.7 *average person*
boyo 567.3 *male title of address*
Boy Scout uniform 743.5 *uniform*
boysenberry 412.5 *hybrid*
boys in the back-room 344.8 *contributor*
bozo 456.5 *ignorant person;* 567.2 *male;* 486.10 *unskilled person*
bra 413.5 *supporting garment;* 551.18 *underwear*
bra burner 568.11 *liberated woman*
brace 376.24; 373.8 *fastening;* 418.9 *harden;* 373.4 *means of connection;* 18.17 *notation;* 581.1 *refresh;* 336.8 *strengthen;* 413.11 *support;* 413.2 *supporting part;* 198.1 *two*
brace and bit 308.2 *opener*
braced 418.3 *hardened;* 581.4 *refreshed;* 336.13 *strengthened*
bracelet 179.3 *circular thing;* 542.7 *jewellery*
bracelets 373.8 *fastening;* 251.5 *means of restraint*
brace oneself 638.8; 243.8 *prepare oneself*
bracer 394.7 *tonic*
braces 27.25 *algebraic expression;* 373.8 *fastening;* 361.4 *hanger;* 742.7 *punctuation;* 551.18 *underwear*
brachiopod 75.5 *mollusc*
Brachiopoda 75.5 *mollusc*
brachycardia 260.10 *cardiovascular disease*
brachylogous 269.3 *concise*
brachylogy 269.1 *conciseness*
bracing 494.8 *cold;* 31.45 *fine;* 259.2 *healthful;* 338.5 *invigorating;* 581.3 *refreshing*
bracken 82.1 *fern*
bracket 409.6 *category;* 137.2 *class;* 373.11 *connect;* 83.4 *fungal body;* 68.6 *ice-skating;* 373.4 *means of connection;* 198.14 *pair;* 108.7 *relate to;* 413.11 *support;* 413.2 *supporting part*
bracket clock 281.6 *clock*
bracketed 373.15 *connected;* 198.9 *two*
bracketed with 115.7 *similar*
bracket fungi 83.3 *fungi*
bracketing 41.13 *framing*
brackets 27.25 *algebraic expression;* 742.7 *punctuation*
bracket together 374.5 *combine;* 108.7 *relate to*
brackish 499.6 *unpalatable*
brackishness 499.2 *unpalatability*
bract 78.3 *flower part;* 77.6 *leaf*
bracteole 77.6 *leaf*
brad 373.8 *fastening*
Bradshaw 693.5 *reference book*
bradykinin 33.8 *amino acid*
brae 89.1, 154.3 *mountain*
brag 683.7 *be egoistic;* 660.24 *be vain;* 727.10 *boast;* 727.6 *exaggerator*
braggadocio 727.6 *exaggerator*
braggart 727.6 *exaggerator;* 660.12 *impudent person;* 622.13 *proud person;* 673.7 *vain person*
bragger 622.13 *proud person*
bragging 727.4 *bombast;* 727.15 *bombastic*
Bragg's law 32.4 *crystal*
Brahmahood 8.1 *divinity*
Brahman 235.7 *elite;* 7.8 *priest*
Brahmanism 7.9 *priesthood*
Brahms 690.1 *drunk*
braid 193.2; 373.11 *connect;* 180.6 *convolute;* 180.3 *convoluted thing;* 542.6 *decorative articles;* 90.7 *flow;* 193.8 *interweave;* 373.6 *line;* 420.12 *make rough;* 412.8 *mix;* 420.7 *rough thing;* 42.13 *spin;* 42.2 *spinning*
braided 373.15 *connected;* 180.4 *convolutional;* 193.6 *interwoven;* 412.12 *mixed;* 42.9 *spun*
braided fibre 42.1 *fibre*
braided line 55.1 *angling*
braided river 90.1 *river*
braided rug 550.9 *floor covering*
braiding 193.1 *interweaving;* 42.2 *spinning*
braids 547.8 *haircut*
Braille 519.3 *aid for poor sight*
brain 442.7; 489.12 *anaesthetize;* 485.5 *expert;* 455.4 *intellect;* 442.3, 458.2 *intelligence;* 382.17 *murder;* 592.7 *render insensitive*
brainbox 458.4 *intellectual;* 442.8 *intellectual person;* 455.6 *knowledgeable person;* 443.7 *thinker*
brain cancer 260.12 *cancer*
brainchild 477.4 *ideality;* 356.4 *mental product;* 446.3 *plan*
brain-creation 477.4 *ideality*
brain damage 457.1 *lack of intellect;* 461.3 *mental deterioration*
brain-damaged 457.7 *intellectually subnormal;* 457.5 *lacking intellect*
brain death 582.1 *death*
brain disease 260.4 *disease;* 461.3 *mental deterioration*
brain disorder 461.3 *mental deterioration*
brainily 6.26 *studiously*
braininess 442.4 *cleverness*
brainless 459.5 *foolish;* 457.5 *lacking intellect*
brainlessly 459.8 *foolishly;* 457.11 *unintelligently*
brainlessness 457.1 *lack of intellect*
brains 442.4 *cleverness;* 455.4 *intellect;* 442.3, 458.2 *intelligence;* 25.31 *offal;* 484.8 *planner*
brain scanner 394.14 *hospital*
brainstorm 484.3 *expedient plan;* 443.6 *idea;* 461.6 *mental breakdown;* 446.3 *plan;* 642.3 *whim*
brain surgeon 35.13 *medical specialist*
brain surgery 35.9, 394.12 *surgery*
brain-teaser 737.4; 705.4 *difficult question;* 264.4 *problem*
brain-twister 737.4 *brain-teaser;* 264.4 *problem*
brainwash 117.10 *assimilate;* 234.12 *distort the truth;* 632.18 *habituate;* 395.8 *influence;* 450.9 *make someone believe;* 480.15, 760.11 *persuade;* 245.6 *pervert*
brainwashed 760.13 *converted;* 760.16 *influenced*
brainwashing 234.4 *distortion of the truth;* 632.7 *habituation;* 760.3 *persuasion;* 480.5 *propaganda*
brainwave 484.3 *expedient plan;* 443.6 *idea;* 458.2 *intelligence;* 356.4 *mental product;* 483.1 *motive;* 446.3 *plan*
brainwork 443.2 *intellectual exercise;* 6.8 *learning;* 4.4 *philosophical investigation*
brain worker 578.1 *worker*
brainy 6.18 *educated;* 442.10, 458.6 *intelligent;* 455.8 *knowledgeable;* 4.19 *learned*
braise 493.14 *be hot;* 25.55 *cook*
braised 25.56 *culinary*
brake 301.8 *be motionless;* 684.5 *be self-restrained;* 320.11 *bicycle part;* 68.9 *bobsledding;* 226.6 *cease;* 333.9 *deceleration;* 82.1 *fern;* 166.7 *limit;* 166.2 *limiting factor;* 685.2 *moderator;* 251.8, 378.10 *restrain;* 378.4 *restraint;* 252.4 *safety device;* 68.5 *ski equipment;* 333.3 *slow down;* 79.4 *trees*
brake block 320.11 *bicycle part*
brake-fade 320.21 *miscellaneous motoring terms*
brake light 522.6 *electric light*
braky 79.16 *wooded*
bramble 267.4 *adherent;* 425.8 *sharp-pointed thing*
brambly 425.2 *spiked*
bran 43.9 *animal feedstuff;* 25.40 *breakfast cereal;* 81.4 *cereal grass;* 427.8 *meal;* 238.6 *refuse;* 215.2 *residue*
branch 205.6; 311.14; 40.20 *abort;* 190.6 *become bigger;* 137.2 *class;* 40.19 *computing terms;* 325.1 *deviate;* 311.5 *fork;* 198.8 *half;* 198.16 *halve;* 137.3 *kingdom;* 27.1 *mathematics;* 373.4 *means of connection;* 405.2 *piece;* 84.3 *plant body;* 7.1 *religion;* 90.1 *river;* 447.4 *sphere;* 77.5 *stem;* 6.3 *subject;* 79.2 *tree part*
branched 311.9; 198.13 *half;* 77.14 *of plants*
branching 311.4; 311.9 *branched;* 377.5 *divergence;* 377.24 *divergent;* 325.24 *diverging;* 190.8 *growing;* 190.1 *growth;* 198.7 *halving;* 373.4 *means of connection;* 79.14 *treelike*
branching off 325.13 *deviation*
branching out 311.4 *branching;* 377.5 *divergence*
branchiopod 75.4 *arthropod*
branchiuran 75.4 *arthropod*
branchlet 84.3 *plant body*
branchlike 311.9 *branched*
branch line 317.10 *railway;* 321.2 *track*
branch off 311.14 *branch*
branch office 577.1 *workshop*
branch of philosophy 4.6
branch of the service 584.2 *the military*
branch out 190.6 *become bigger;* 114.8 *be diverse;* 325.1 *deviate;* 377.10 *diverge;* 79.19 *grow*
branchwood 79.3 *timber*
brand 493.15 *burn;* 139.3 *characteristic;* 139.22 *characterize;* 137.13 *class;* 743.10 *identify;* 522.7 *lantern;* 437.2 *lighter;* 743.3 *means of identification;* 43.18 *practise livestock farming;* 742.1 *sign;* 137.4 *type*
branded 743.12 *identified*
branding iron 493.3 *heater*
brandish 327.22 *agitate;* 703.15 *demonstrate;* 738.1 *display;* 349.1 *use;* 326.12 *wave*
brandished 738.13 *displayed*
brandishing 326.4 *rock*
brand name 37.3 *drug;* 743.3 *means of identification*
brand new 295.10 *new*
brand spanking new 295.10 *new*
brandy Alexander 558.8 *mixed drink*
brandy and soda 558.8 *mixed drink*
brandy balloon 410.13 *drinking vessel*
brandy snifter 410.13 *drinking vessel*
bran flakes 25.40 *breakfast cereal*
branniness 427.3 *graininess*
branny 427.16 *mealy*
brash 661.7 *defiant;* 660.19 *rude*
brashing 79.6 *tree management*
brashly 660.32 *audaciously;* 661.9 *defiantly;* 660.35 *rudely*
brashness 673.3 *cockiness;* 661.1 *defiance*
brashy 205.11 *partial*
brass 780.2 *cash;* 660.2 *cheek;* 583.4 *funeral objects;* 579.6 *governing body;* 412.2 *mixed thing;* 781.6 *money;* 18.25 *musical instrument;* 536.3 *orange thing;* 510.2 *ringing;* 513.1 *stridency*
brassard 384.7 *armour;* 743.4 *insignia*
brass band 374.3 *assembly;* 18.26 *musical group*
brass cannon 587.10 *historical gun*
brasserie 557.15 *eating place*
brass farthing 124.8 *trifle*
brass hat 123.4 *bigwig;* 395.5 *influential person;* 400.7 *military leader;* 121.5 *superior*
brass horn 507.4 *sound maker*
brassica 25.33, 44.11 *vegetable*
brassicaceous 77.16 *taxonomic*
brassick 135.5 *necessitous*
brassie 56.4 *golf club*
brassiere 413.5 *supporting garment;* 551.18 *underwear*
brassiness 167.5 *boldness;* 661.1 *defiance;* 660.10 *impudence;* 507.1 *loudness;* 513.1 *stridency*
brass inlay 23.9 *decorative woodwork*
brass knuckles 587.7 *blunt weapon;* 331.16 *weapons*
brass monkey weather 31.31 *coldness;* 494.7 *cold weather*
brass neck 167.5 *boldness;* 660.2 *cheek*
brass on shell 23.9 *decorative woodwork*
brass plate 743.3 *means of identification*
brass rubbing 19.7 *picture*
brass tacks 93.5 *fact*
brassy 660.14 *cheeky;* 661.7 *defiant;* 660.21 *impudent;* 507.6 *loud;* 536.1 *orange;* 542.10 *ornate;* 513.7 *strident*
brat 555.9 *child*
Bratwurst 25.46 *German dish;* 25.29 *sausage*
bravado 660.5; 673.6 *boastfulness;* 613.5 *bold front;* 661.1 *defiance*
brave 340.5 *acting;* 613.15 *be courageous;* 586.1 *combatant;* 613.9 *courageous;* 613.7 *courageous person;* 661.5 *defy;* 586.35 *martial;* 586.8 *soldier;* 336.11 *strong in spirit*
brave face 613.5 *bold front;* 661.1 *defiance*
brave front 383.1 *resistance*
brave it out 660.27 *dare*
bravely 613.18 *courageously;* 586.42 *martially;* 336.14 *strongly*
braveness 613.1 *courage*
brave person 613.7 *courageous person;* 340.3 *doer*
bravery 613.1 *courage;* 336.1 *strength*
brave try 353.5 *attempt*
bravo 586.1 *combatant;* 514.3 *cry of praise;* 382.11 *murderer;* 380.4 *violent creature*
bravo! 669.27
bravura 661.1 *defiance;* 485.3 *masterpiece*
bravura player 485.4 *skilled person*
braw 235.1 *worthy*

brawl 342.1 *activity*; 701.13, 751.6 *argue*; 701.1, 751.2 *argument*; 408.9 *disorder*; 242.8, 242.11 *quarrel*
brawler 662.9 *criminal*
brawling 751.9 *disagreeing*; 701.9 *hostile*
brawn 414.4 *heaviness*; 25.31 *offal*; 423.8 *physical strength*; 336.1 *strength*
brawniness 158.6 *squatness*
brawny 336.9 *physically strong*; 423.4 *powerful*; 158.17 *stocky*
bray 427.26 *beat*; 507.8 *be loud*; 513.4 *be strident*; 515.4 *cry*; 507.1 *loudness*; 427.22 *pulverize*; 513.1 *stridency*
braying 507.6 *loud*; 513.7 *strident*
braze 267.7 *cause to adhere*
brazen 167.9 *arrogant*; 660.14 *cheeky*; 622.17 *conceited*; 661.7 *defiant*; 668.10 *disrespectful*; 809.3 *impenitent*; 660.21 *impudent*; 738.15 *open*; 513.7 *strident*; 796.13 *unchaste*
brazen face 660.3 *audacity*; 660.12 *impudent person*
brazen-faced 660.15 *audacious*; 668.10 *disrespectful*; 660.21 *impudent*
brazen-facedness 660.10 *impudence*
brazen hussy 809.2 *impenitent person*
brazen it out 641.9 *be obstinate*; 660.27 *dare*; 661.5 *defy*
brazenly 660.31 *cheekily*; 661.9 *defiantly*
brazen-mouthed 507.6 *loud*
brazenness 167.5 *boldness*; 660.2 *cheek*; 673.3 *cockiness*; 661.1 *defiance*
brazen out 613.15 *be courageous*
brazier 493.6 *fire*; 410.15 *pot*
Brazilian GP at Interlagos 61.2 *Formula 1 race*
breach 751.2 *argument*; 381.9 *attack successfully*; 146.2, 146.5 *crack*; 133.4 *interruption*; 16.38 *lawbreaking*; 308.18 *open*; 308.1 *opening*; 372.3 *separateness*; 329.5 *transgress*; 329.8 *transgression*
breached 308.12 *open*
breaching 16.60 *offending*
breach in the wall 254.7 *vulnerability*
breach of etiquette 657.5 *nonobservance*
breach of faith 800.2 *faithlessness*
breach of friendship 751.1 *disagreement*
breach of promise 800.2 *faithlessness*; 699.10 *lie*
breach of the peace 328.5 *commotion*; 408.9, 753.2 *disorder*; 662.2 *violation of the law*
breach the peace 662.15 *be disobedient*; 753.8 *cause mischief*
bread **25.38**; 55.1 *angling*; 780.2 *cash*; 557.7 *food*; 554.3 *life requirements*
bread-and-butter letter 671.3 *recognition*
bread-and-butter pudding 25.35 *dessert*
bread-and-cheese lunch 557.12 *meal*
bread and circuses 490.2 *good time*
bread and milk 497.3 *tasteless items*
bread and water 218.8 *insufficiency*; 497.3 *tasteless items*
bread-and-water diet 557.10 *scarcity*
bread and wine 10.6 *Eucharist*
bread basket 410.7 *basket*; 410.18 *stomach*
bread bin 25.4 *kitchen container*
bread knife 425.10 *knife*
breadline 135.3 *needfulness*; 782.5 *poverty*
bread sauce 25.15 *sauce*
bread stick 25.39 *loaf*
breadth **150.4**; 209.1 *degree*; 27.37 *line*; 203.1 *quantity*; 26.4, 158.1 *size*; 28.7, 141.1 *space*; 152.5 *thickness*
breadth of vision 458.1 *wisdom*
breadthways 150.8 *breadthwise*
breadthwise **150.8**
bread tin 410.15 *pot*
breadwinner 15.7 *employee*; 765.7 *gainer*; 578.1 *worker*
breadwinning 765.1 *gain*
breadwork 542.3 *pattern*
break 424.4 *be brittle*; 739.9 *be disclosed*; 299.6 *be irregular*; 786.9 *be unable to pay*; 337.6 *be weak*; 65.1 *billiards*; 91.10 *billow*; 224.1 *change*; 31.60 *cloud*; 146.2, 146.5 *crack*; 246.10 *defeat heavily*; 357.9 *demolish*; 325.15 *deviating motion*; 133.14 *disconnect*; 263.1 *ease*; 94.4 *emptiness*; 65.3 *English billiards*; 248.2 *good fortune*; 522.26 *grow light*; 133.4 *interruption*; 133.3, 275.6 *interval*; 141.8 *intervening space*; 98.5 *leave of absence*; 420.12 *make rough*; 247.9 *malfunction*; 233.2 *omission*; 308.18 *open*; 308.1 *opening*; 287.2, 308.10 *opportunity*; 205.10 *part*; 226.3, 226.9 *pause*; 276.1 *period*; 65.8 *play billiards*; 581.6 *refresher*; 741.13 *report*; 21.8 *scene*; 372.9 *separate*; 372.3 *separateness*; 141.21 *space*; 580.2 *time off*; 380.8 *use violence*
breakability 424.2 *brittleness*
breakable 424.1 *brittle*; 372.19 *separable*; 68.12 *ski*; 337.8 *weak*
breakable crust 68.1 *skiing*
breakableness 424.2 *brittleness*
breakage 233.2 *omission*; 372.1 *separation*
break a habit 487.5 *disaccustom*
break a lance for 384.22 *plead for*
break a law 118.20 *infringe a law*
break and enter 314.10 *invade*
break an egg 68.16 *bobsled*
break apart 424.4 *be brittle*
break a story 740.15 *publish*
breakaway 250.10 *independent*; 662.4 *revolution*; 662.14 *subversive*
break away 118.19 *be independent*; 391.5 *be liberated*; 372.13 *diverge*; 389.5 *escape*; 634.8 *run away*
break away from 751.5 *disagree*
break ball 65.6 *pool*
breakbone fever 260.7 *tropical disease*
break bounds 118.19 *be independent*; 329.5 *transgress*
break bread 557.24 *have a meal*
break camp 313.3 *quit*
break ceasefire 586.36 *combat*
break cover 315.10 *emerge*
break crop 43.12 *crop*
breakdance 22.15 *dance*
breakdancing 22.1 *dancing*
breakdown 375.2 *deconstruction*; 245.9 *dilapidation*; 335.4 *disability*; 247.1 *failure*; 36.10 *neurosis*; 378.2 *obstacle*; 357.4 *ruin*; 372.1 *separation*; 226.2 *stop*; 260.3 *symptom*
break down 424.4 *be brittle*; 238.7 *be useless*; 226.6 *cease*; 375.4 *deconstruct*; 357.9 *demolish*; 245.1 *deteriorate*; 375.3 *disintegrate*; 802.24 *go wrong*; 238.8 *make useless*; 372.9 *separate*
breakdown in negotiations 15.4 *industrial dispute*
breakdown of government 588.1 *anarchy*
breakdown of marriage 571.1 *divorce*
breakdown voltage 28.48 *insulation*
breaker 43.10 *farm tool*; 59.15 *horse person*; 48.4 *pitching terms*; 30.14, 91.3 *wave*
breakers 379.1 *trap*
breakers ahead 254.6 *danger signal*
break even 111.10, 119.10 *be equal*
break-even 776.16 *unprofitable*
break faith 800.9 *prove false*
breakfast 557.24 *have a meal*; 557.12 *meal*; 290.2 *morning thing*
breakfast cereal **25.40**
breakfast in bed 557.4 *eating meals*
breakfasting 557.4 *eating meals*
breakfast roll 25.39 *loaf*
breakfast room 565.7 *room*
break forth 739.9 *be disclosed*; 315.10 *emerge*
break glass 425.15 *make sharp*
break hearts 593.25 *be loved*
break in 632.18 *habituate*; 314.10 *invade*; 59.16 *ride*; 380.8 *use violence*
break-in 774.3 *theft*
breaking 424.1 *brittle*; 424.2 *brittleness*; 730.10 *low-voiced*; 91.7 *oceanic*
breaking and entering 314.3 *inroad*; 774.1 *stealing*
breaking away 118.2 *dissent*
breaking news 741.1 *news*; 741.9 *news story*
breaking of bread 10.6 *Eucharist*
breaking off 226.2 *stop*
breaking off of negotiations 226.2 *stop*
breaking of the waters 561.7 *obstetrics*
breaking on the wheel 814.12 *corporal punishment*
breaking out 260.13 *skin disease*
breaking stones 576.1 *work*
breaking surface 304.1 *ascent*
breaking the law 16.60 *offending*
breaking up 357.2 *destroying*
breaking violation 65.6 *pool*
breaking voice 730.2 *inarticulation*
breaking wind 371.24 *belch*; 503.2 *something that makes an unpleasant smell*
break in on 328.10 *disrupt*
break into a house 774.12 *steal*
break into song 18.39 *sing*
break in two 372.9 *separate*
break in upon 288.6 *take untimely action*
break it to 739.6 *divulge*
break it up 749.5 *make peace*; 226.12 *stop!*
break loose 391.5 *be liberated*; 389.5 *escape*
breakneck 262.3 *hasty*; 615.4 *rash*; 332.1 *swift*
breakneck speed 332.8 *speed*
break new ground 130.21 *pioneer*
break no bones 235.10 *do good*
break of 393.6 *cure*
break of day 130.2 *creation*; 290.1 *morning*
breakoff 226.1 *cessation*
break off 424.4 *be brittle*; 226.8 *cause to cease*; 226.6 *cease*; 133.12 *discontinue*; 355.2 *withdraw*
break off a relationship 355.2 *withdraw*
break off negotiations 226.6 *cease*
break one's bonds 391.5 *be liberated*
break one's chains 389.5 *escape*
break one's fast 557.24 *have a meal*
break one's journey 312.6 *stop at*
break one's neck 582.16 *meet one's fate*
break one's word 800.9 *prove false*
break on the wheel 814.4 *torture*
break open 380.8 *use violence*
breakout 389.1 *escape*; 315.1 *exit*; 58.8 *hockey*; 381.14 *siege*
break out 391.5 *be liberated*; 380.7 *be violent*; 381.8 *counterattack*; 315.10 *emerge*; 389.5 *escape*
break out in 260.24 *be unhealthy*
break out of prison 389.5 *escape*
breakout play 58.3 *ice hockey*
break out with 755.6 *catch*
break shot 65.4 *carom*
break step 118.19 *be independent*
break the back of 302.2 *start*
break the bank 246.6 *be successful*; 765.14 *profit*
break the connection 133.14 *disconnect*
break the fall of 685.4 *moderate*
break the habit 118.19 *be independent*
break the ice 569.13 *befriend*; 130.21 *pioneer*
break the law 662.15 *be disobedient*; 16.73 *be illegal*; 802.21 *do wrong*
break the link 372.9 *separate*
break the marriage vow 796.17 *be sexually immoral*
break the mould 118.19 *be independent*
break the news 693.12 *communicate*; 739.6 *divulge*
break the peace 381.1 *attack*; 380.7 *be violent*
break the rules 631.13 *behave badly*; 802.21 *do wrong*; 118.20 *infringe a law*
break the seal 739.5 *disclose*
break the silence 507.8 *be loud*
break the skin 308.20 *hole*
break the sound barrier 332.4 *be swift*
break the speed limit 332.4 *be swift*
break the wax 739.5 *disclose*
breakthrough 129.3 *preparation*; 381.14 *siege*; 246.1 *success*
break through 381.9 *attack successfully*; 389.5 *escape*; 314.11 *infiltrate*; 246.11 *overmaster*
break through the clouds 739.9 *be disclosed*
break under pressure 388.4 *succumb*
breakup 424.2 *brittleness*; 375.1 *disintegration*; 377.5 *divergence*; 571.1 *divorce*; 357.4 *ruin*; 372.1 *separation*
break up 357.13 *be destroyed*; 377.9 *be dispersed*; 427.27 *come to dust*; 375.4 *deconstruct*; 357.9 *demolish*; 375.3 *disintegrate*; 408.21 *disorder*; 571.7 *divorce*; 377.11 *explode*; 238.8 *make useless*; 205.10 *part*; 372.9 *separate*; 146.4 *space*
breakwater 378.3 *barrier*; 185.2 *projection*; 252.4 *safety device*; 38.24 *water system*
break water 323.10 *sail*; 304.17 *spring up*
break wind 371.16, 508.7 *belch*; 503.5 *stink*
break with custom 118.19 *be independent*
break with the past 224.7 *be changed*; 224.1 *change*; 463.13 *forget*
bream 55.5 *British game fish*
breast 182.2 *bulge*; 304.14 *climb*; 113.19 *confront*; 25.26, 25.27 *lamb*; 25.28 *poultry*
breast-beating 807.2 *apology*; 808.2 *type of penance*
breast cancer 260.12 *cancer*
breast enlargement 547.2 *plastic surgery*
breast-fed 558.16 *drinking*
breast-feed 71.36 *lactate*; 557.25 *provide food*
breast line 50.3 *parts of a sailing boat*
breast milk 558.5 *milk*
breast-pang 260.10 *cardiovascular disease*
breastplate 384.7 *armour*; 252.2 *protection*
breast reduction 547.2 *plastic surgery*
breaststroke 67.1 *swimming*
breast the storm 113.20 *withstand*
breast the tape 312.2 *reach*
breastwork 378.3 *barrier*; 384.8 *military defences*
breath 432.2 *exhalation*; 500.1 *odour*
breath control 67.2 *swimming technique*
breathe 97.11 *be present*; 739.6 *divulge*; 93.17 *exist*; 371.14 *let out*; 554.16 *live*; 434.21 *respire*; 500.7 *smell*; 511.8 *sound faint*; 729.13 *speak in a particular way*; 693.14 *tip*
breathe deeply 581.2 *be refreshed*
breathe down someone's neck 262.1 *hasten*
breathe fire 624.11 *be angry*
breathe fresh life into 393.5 *revive*
breathe heavily 261.5 *be fatigued*
breathe in 370.12 *draw in*; 434.21 *respire*; 500.7 *smell*
breathe life into 554.19 *give birth to*
breathe new life into 581.1 *refresh*
breathe of 694.10 *mean*
breathe one's last 582.15 *die*
breathe out 315.12 *leak*; 434.21 *respire*
breather 263.1 *ease*; 275.6 *interval*; 226.3 *pause*; 276.1 *period*; 581.7 *refreshments*; 580.2 *time off*
breathe regularly 298.7 *be regular*
breath-freshener 501.2 *deodorant*
breathing 554.12 *alive*; 554.4 *biological function*; 115.9 *lifelike*; 298.5 *regular thing*; 434.8 *respiration*; 434.19 *respiratory*
breathing apparatus 384.6 *protective clothing*
breathing difficulty 260.3 *symptom*
breathing in 370.4 *intake*
breathing space 141.6 *available space*; 263.1 *ease*; 275.6 *interval*; 580.1 *leisure*; 226.3 *pause*
breathless 582.19 *dead*; 262.3 *hasty*; 261.3 *panting*; 327.16 *restless*; 619.7 *wide-eyed*
breathless adoration 667.2 *admiration*
breathless wonder 619.1 *wonder*
breath of air 581.6 *refresher*
breath of fresh air 581.6 *refresher*
breath of life 123.2 *important matter*; 554.3 *life requirements*
breath of one's nostrils 554.3 *life requirements*
breath of oxygen 581.6 *refresher*
breath of wind 31.14 *windiness*
breath-sweetener 501.2 *deodorant*
breathtaking 488.9 *exciting*; 123.6 *notable*; 619.8 *wonderful*
breccia 427.9 *grit*; 30.31 *sedimentary rock*
breccial 427.17 *grainy*
brecciate 427.22 *pulverize*
brecciated 427.17 *grainy*
brecciation 427.4 *pulverization*
Brecon Beacons 89.5 *British mountains*
bred **168.5**; 43.21 *domesticated*; 356.12 *produced*
bred horse 59.13 *breeding*
bred-in-the-bone 374.7 *combined*; 99.6 *intrinsic*
bred into 374.7 *combined*
breech 587.9 *firearm*
breeches 551.9 *trousers*
Breeches Bible 7.12 *religious text*
breeches buoy 252.4 *safety device*
breeches part 21.23 *role*
breechloader 587.9 *firearm*
breech presentation 561.7 *obstetrics*
breed 190.6 *become bigger*; 44.15 *culti-*

vate; 243.7 *develop;* 137.8 *genealogy;* 554.19 *give birth to;* 213.4 *increase;* 213.5 *make bigger;* 99.4 *nature;* 168.8 *nurture;* 43.18 *practise livestock farming;* 130.26, 356.10 *produce;* 561.13 *propagate;* 721.6 *sort*
breeder 43.15 *agriculturist;* 59.15 *horse person*
breeder reactor 28.73 *nuclear reactor*
breeding **59.13**; 137.9 *distinction;* 631.2 *good conduct;* 658.2 *good manners;* 190.1 *growth;* 561.3 *propagation;* 6.11 *refinement;* 561.16 *reproductive;* 654.2 *social ambition*
breeding ground 344.2 *source*
breeks 551.9 *trousers*
breeze 434.4 *air flow;* 705.5 *easy question;* 265.6 *easy thing;* 581.6 *refresher;* 419.11 *soft thing;* 31.12 *wind;* 31.13 *wind strength*
breeze block 20.4, 435.2 *building material;* 38.26 *masonry*
breeze in 265.17 *do easily*
breeziness 31.14 *windiness*
breezy **434.15**; 494.8 *cold;* 31.47 *windy*
Bren gun 587.11 *guns*
breve 5.36 *accent;* 18.17 *notation;* 742.7 *punctuation*
breviary 10.10 *religious manual*
Brevity 269
brevity 269.1 *conciseness;* 149.1 *shortness;* 732.3 *shyness;* 723.4 *summariness;* 278.1 *transience*
brew 190.6 *become bigger;* 243.7 *develop;* 412.8 *mix;* 412.2 *mixed thing;* 484.13 *plot;* 31.59 *storm*
brew a plot 484.13 *plot*
brewer 243.15 *preparer*
brewers' grains 43.9 *animal feedstuff*
brewers' yeast 43.9 *animal feedstuff*
brewery 577.1 *workshop*
brewing 243.17 *developing;* 243.13 *development;* 190.8 *growing;* 356.1 *production;* 433.10 *steeping*
brewis 25.40 *breakfast cereal*
Breydon Water 88.4 *British lakes*
bribable 777.13 *bought;* 800.5 *dishonourable;* 752.17 *offered*
bribe **480.10**; **480.17**; 777.4 *buy off;* 768.2 *gift;* 768.5 *give;* 785.4 *grant;* 752.4 *illegal offer;* 752.9 *offer;* 813.11 *pay;* 483.5 *positive stimulus;* 765.5, 765.14 *profit;* 785.11 *remunerate;* 813.8 *secret money*
bribed 777.13 *bought;* 752.17 *offered*
briber 386.4 *coercive person;* 765.7 *gainer;* 768.4 *giver;* 777.12 *purchaser*
bribery **777.10**; 386.3 *coercive methods;* 800.3 *criminality*
bribing 800.7 *criminal;* 768.1 *giving*
bric-a-brac 124.9 *bauble;* 793.5 *cheap item*
brick 20.18 *be an architect;* 20.4, 435.2 *building material;* 38.25 *construction material;* 550.28 *face;* 418.7 *hard substance;* 587.6 *historical missile weapon;* 799.3 *honourable person;* 24.9 *industrial ceramics;* 24.11 *make ceramics;* 38.26 *masonry;* 535.7 *red thing;* 317.4 *road surface*
brickbat 670.5, 678.2 *criticism;* 587.6 *historical missile weapon;* 330.8 *missile;* 668.6 *taunt*
bricked 550.36 *covered*
brick house 418.7 *hard substance*
bricking 24.10 *ceramic*
brick kiln 24.6 *ceramic workshop*
bricklayer 578.2 *artisan;* 550.17 *coverer*
bricklaying 38.26 *masonry*
brick-red 535.1 *red*
bricks 550.8 *wall covering*
bricks and mortar 435.2 *building material;* 356.8 *construction*
brick wall 378.3 *barrier;* 418.7 *hard substance;* 528.7 *opaque thing;* 521.6 *that which makes invisible;* 360.4 *wall*
brickwork 20.4 *building material;* 356.8 *construction;* 403.2 *fabric;* 38.26 *masonry*
brickworks 577.1 *workshop*
bridal 570.20 *matrimonial*
bridal attendant 570.7 *bridal party*
bridal bed 593.13 *abode of love;* 570.1 *marriage*
bridal bouquet 570.6 *general terms*
bridal chamber 570.6 *general terms*
bridal outfit 551.1 *dress*
bridal pair 570.9 *married couple*
bridal party 570.7
bridal suite 593.13 *abode of love;* 570.6 *general terms*
bride 570.7 *bridal party;* 568.4 *girlfriend;* 570.8 *spouse*
bridebed 570.1 *marriage*
bridegroom 567.4 *boyfriend;* 570.7 *bridal party;* 570.8 *spouse*
bride of Christ 572.4 *celibate person*
bride price 440.6 *marriage settlement*
bridesmaid 570.7 *bridal party;* 569.6 *close friend*
bride-to-be 593.11 *loved one;* 593.9 *lover;* 756.6 *someone promised*
bridge **38.21**; **317.9**; 28.90 *ammeter;* 348.4 *be an instrument;* 90.2 *channel;* 39.13 *circuit;* 373.11 *connect;* 318.11 *cross;* 318.5 *crossing point;* 62.9 *mountaineer;* 151.6 *narrow place;* 40.15 *network;* 550.26 *overlie;* 243.1 *prepare;* 373.5 *road;* 21.17 *stage;* 38.19 *structure;* 316.2 *transportation;* 397.8 *vantage point;* 518.9 *viewpoint*
bridge a river 317.14 *find one's way*
bridgeboard 304.10 *step*
bridge-builder 243.15 *preparer*
bridged 317.15 *accessible;* 373.15 *connected*
bridgehead 585.10 *battleground*
bridge over 749.4 *pacify*
bridge roll 25.39 *loaf*
bridge the gap 265.16 *make easy*
bridging 62.3 *climbing technique;* 394.12 *surgery*
bridle 624.12 *become angry;* 59.14 *horse-riding terms;* 251.5 *means of restraint;* 43.18 *practise livestock farming*
bridle path 318.4 *access;* 317.6 *path*
brief **243.6**; 713.5 *advise;* 398.6 *agent;* 455.14 *cause to know;* 269.3 *concise;* 6.22 *educate;* 703.16 *explain;* 262.3 *hasty;* 693.11 *inform;* 16.13 *lawyer;* 163.6 *outlined;* 149.7 *short;* 723.6 *summary;* 278.6 *transient*
briefcase 410.9 *baggage*
brief counsel 16.70 *litigate*
brief description **721.2**; 163.1 *outline*
briefed 693.18 *informed;* 6.19, 455.8 *knowledgeable;* 243.18 *prepared*
brief encounter 278.2 *transient thing*
brief impression 163.1 *outline*
briefing **243.12**; 713.1 *advice;* 693.2 *communication;* 703.3 *explanation*
briefly 269.5 *concisely;* 149.12 *short;* 723.11 *summarily;* 278.8 *transiently*
briefness 269.1 *conciseness;* 149.1 *shortness;* 723.4 *summariness*
brief oneself 243.8 *prepare oneself*
briefs 551.18 *underwear*
brief sketch 269.2 *outline*
brief span 278.3 *short duration*
brier 267.4 *adherent;* 425.8 *sharp-pointed thing*
briery 425.2 *spiked*
brigade 586.16 *army unit;* 374.3 *assembly;* 374.6 *come together;* 376.14 *force;* 584.4 *military organization*
brigade commander 584.5 *military staff*
brigadier 586.17 *army person;* 397.6 *person in command*
brigadier general 397.6 *person in command*
brigand 774.9 *plunderer*
brigandage 774.5 *plundering*
brigandine 384.7 *armour*
brigandish 774.17 *stolen*
brigandism 774.5 *plundering*
bright **522.16**; 756.14 *auspicious;* 545.5 *beautiful;* 610.14 *cheering;* 256.16 *clean;* 520.2 *clear;* 529.11 *colourful;* 6.17 *educable;* 522.22 *enlightened;* 31.45 *fine;* 442.10, 458.6 *intelligent;* 531.6 *light;* 241.2 *likable;* 522.18 *lit;* 332.2 *mentally quick;* 425.5 *mentally sharp;* 255.14 *purified;* 336.12 *strong to the senses*
bright and early 293.12, 293.17 *early*
bright as silver 256.16 *clean*
bright blue 539.1 *blue*
brighten 598.6 *bring cheer;* 529.15 *colour;* 522.26 *grow light;* 522.24 *light;* 527.12 *make transparent;* 31.61 *shine*
brightened 522.18 *lit*
brightening 522.3 *lightening;* 522.15 *lucent*
brighten one's day 241.13 *give pleasure*
brighter 31.45 *fine*
bright idea 484.3 *expedient plan;* 458.2 *intelligence;* 483.1 *motive;* 446.3 *plan*
bright light 522.2 *quality of light*
brightly 336.15 *acutely;* 756.17 *auspiciously;* 529.18 *colourfully;* 522.30 *lightly;* 425.18 *sharply;* 6.26 *studiously*
bright nebula 29.8 *interstellar medium*
brightness 520.4 *clarity;* 442.4 *cleverness;* 6.10 *educability;* 545.1 *gorgeousness;* 458.2 *intelligence;* 28.23, 522.1, 531.12 *light;* 425.13 *mental sharpness;* 522.2 *quality of light;* 332.10 *quickness of mind;* 692.22 *television set*
Brighton Belle 321.10 *miscellaneous*
bright prospects 756.3 *potential*
bright red 535.1 *red*
bright side 169.4 *aspect;* 610.1 *hope*
bright spark 458.4 *intellectual;* 455.6 *knowledgeable person*
bright yellow 537.1 *yellow*
bright young thing 295.9 *modern person*
brill 797.1 *good;* 797.27 *great!;* 25.18 *sea fish;* 619.14 *wonderful!;* 235.1 *worthy*
brilliance 520.4 *clarity;* 442.4 *cleverness;* 545.1 *gorgeousness;* 529.3 *hue;* 458.2 *intelligence;* 522.1 *light;* 485.3 *masterpiece;* 230.3 *perfection;* 522.2 *quality of light;* 235.6 *worth*
brilliant 522.16 *bright;* 520.2 *clear;* 529.11 *colourful;* 522.22 *enlightened;* 442.10, 458.6 *intelligent;* 230.1 *perfect;* 336.12 *strong to the senses;* 235.1 *worthy*
brilliantine 268.7 *pomade*
brilliantly 336.15 *acutely;* 529.18 *colourfully;* 458.10 *intelligently;* 522.30 *lightly;* 235.11 *worthily*
brim 217.5 *about;* 208.11 *crowd;* 164.1 *edge*
brimful 232.8 *full*
brimmer 232.2 *fullness*
brimming 232.8 *full;* 232.2 *fullness;* 329.11 *overrun*
brimming over 219.6 *excessive*
brim over 219.4 *be excessive;* 329.1 *overstep*
brimstone 537.8 *yellow thing*
brim with 232.5 *be complete*
brim with good health 259.5 *be healthy*
brindle 541.4 *maculation;* 541.11 *variegate*
brindled 541.10 *mottled*
brindling 541.4 *maculation*
brine 359.2 *preserver;* 91.1 *sea;* 433.31 *steep;* 433.1 *water*
brine shrimp 75.4 *arthropod*
bring 316.14 *bring back;* 790.13 *cost;* 815.1 *prison*
bring about 239.6 *be convenient;* 344.9 *be the cause of;* 635.13, 694.12 *intend;* 483.9 *motivate;* 480.15 *persuade;* 356.10 *produce*
bring a case 715.5 *accuse*
bring a charge 715.5 *accuse*
bring action 715.5 *accuse*
bring a lawsuit 715.5 *accuse;* 16.70 *litigate*
bring alive 698.34 *render*
bring-and-buy sale 791.2 *bargain;* 779.10 *bazaar*
bring a suit 16.70 *litigate*
bring a verdict 464.11 *judge*
bring back **316.14**; 390.1 *deliver;* 775.4 *give back;* 462.13 *remind;* 393.3 *restore*
bring bad luck 249.11 *cause adversity*
bring before the court 16.70 *litigate*
bring charges 715.5 *accuse*
bring cheer **598.6**
bring destruction 357.10 *lay waste*
bring down **367.3**; 602.10 *depress;* 381.2 *fire;* 381.5 *strike*
bring-down 602.4 *depressing person*
bring down to earth 728.21 *detract from;* 604.6 *disappoint*
bring evidence against 715.5 *accuse*
bring forth 369.15 *draw out;* 561.10 *reproduce oneself;* 738.3 *reveal*
bring forward 738.1 *display;* 302.8 *further*
bring home the bacon 246.6 *be successful;* 765.12 *earn*
bring home the charge 16.79 *convict*
bring in 370.7 *admit;* 765.9 *gain;* 368.1 *insert;* 370.10 *introduce;* 436.5 *provision;* 769.9 *receive*
bring in a return 765.13 *be profitable*
bring in a supply 436.5 *provision*
bring in a verdict 16.76 *judge;* 16.71 *try a case*
bringing back 775.1 *giving back*
bringing down to earth 604.2 *bad outcome*
bringing forth 369.5 *drawing out*
bringing in 765.1 *gain;* 370.3 *introduction*
bringing legal action against 16.53 *litigating*
bringing of charges 715.1 *accusation*
bringing together 765.3 *acquisition;* 376.1 *assembly;* 374.1 *combination*
bringing to light 738.10 *manifestation*
bring in new blood 224.8 *cause change*
bring into action 346.8 *activate*
bring into being **93.20**; 344.9 *be the cause of;* 160.7 *form;* 130.26, 356.10 *produce;* 561.13 *propagate*
bring into contact 147.18 *juxtapose*
bring into disrepute **812.4**; 678.12 *defame*
bring into effect 346.8 *activate;* 348.4 *be an instrument*
bring into existence **698.28**; 356.10 *produce;* 561.13 *propagate*
bring into focus 173.9 *centre;* 310.11 *focus*
bring into force 346.8 *activate*
bring into line 117.9 *make conform;* 140.14 *regulate;* 387.6 *subject*
bring into operation 346.8 *activate*
bring into play 346.8 *activate*
bring into the open 739.5 *disclose;* 171.14 *externalize;* 740.13 *make public*
bring into the wind 323.9 *navigate*
bring into the world 344.9 *be the cause of;* 130.26, 356.10 *produce;* 561.13 *propagate*
bring in tow 223.15 *escort*
bring it off 246.6 *be successful;* 253.13 *secure one's objective*
bring legal action 16.70 *litigate*
bring litigation 715.5 *accuse*
bring low 623.23 *abase;* 387.6 *subject*
bring near 147.16 *near*
bring off 246.6 *be successful;* 344.9 *be the cause of*
bring on 344.10 *awaken;* 243.7 *develop;* 302.8 *further;* 483.9 *motivate*
bring out 344.10 *awaken;* 703.15 *demonstrate;* 171.14 *externalize;* 356.10 *produce;* 740.15 *publish;* 738.3 *reveal*
bring over 483.9 *motivate;* 480.15 *persuade*
bring pressure to bear 483.10 *manipulate*
bring prosperity 797.20 *do good*
bring results 237.10 *benefit*
bring round 554.19 *give birth to;* 685.4 *moderate;* 480.15 *persuade*
bring shame upon 812.4 *bring into disrepute*
bring someone round 483.9 *motivate*
bring the house down 669.16 *acclaim;* 507.8 *be loud*
bring to 211.6 *add;* 213.5 *make bigger*
bring to a head 607.6 *aggravate;* 204.10 *complete;* 243.7 *develop;* 213.5 *make bigger*
bring to an end 226.8 *cause to cease;* 131.16 *cease;* 278.5 *make transient*
bring to a standstill 226.8 *cause to cease;* 378.8 *hinder;* 301.9 *make motionless*
bring to attention 123.8 *make important*
bring to bay 381.9 *attack successfully*
bring to bear 349.1 *use*
bring to bear upon 108.7 *relate to*
bring to birth 561.10 *reproduce oneself*
bring to book 814.2 *penalize*
bring to fruition 243.7 *develop;* 244.1 *improve*
bring together 765.11 *acquire;* 376.37 *assemble;* 374.5 *combine;* 416.9 *make dense;* 748.1 *mediate;* 749.4 *pacify;* 393.3 *restore;* 300.14 *set in motion;* 439.6 *store*
bring to heel 387.6 *subject*
bring to justice 16.70 *litigate*
bring to life 554.19 *give birth to;* 721.15 *recount*
bring to light 449.2 *detect;* 739.5 *disclose;* 369.15 *draw out;* 518.18, 520.10 *make visible;* 738.3 *reveal*
bring to market 778.1 *sell*
bring to mind 115.10 *be similar;* 462.13 *remind*
bring to notice 738.1 *display;* 123.8 *make important;* 738.3 *reveal*
bring to one's knees 387.6 *subject*
bring to one's side 483.9 *motivate;* 480.15 *persuade*
bring to pass 344.9 *be the cause of*
bring to perfection 230.5 *perfect*

bring to public notice 740.13 *make public*
bring to rest 323.10 *sail*
bring to ruin 357.11 *ruin*
bring to terms 749.4 *pacify*
bring to the bar 16.70 *litigate*
bring to the boil 213.5 *make bigger*
bring to the fore 123.8 *make important*
bring to the table 748.1 *mediate*
bring to trial 16.70 *litigate*
bring under the hammer 778.1 *sell*
bring up 6.22 *educate;* 740.13 *make public;* 356.10 *produce;* 561.13 *propagate;* 738.3 *reveal;* 50.15 *sail;* 371.15 *vomit*
bring up children 168.8 *nurture*
bring up for debate 476.6 *propound*
bring up the rear 168.6 *be in the rear;* 289.10 *succeed*
bring up to date 243.6 *brief;* 244.1 *improve;* 295.20 *make new*
bring up to scratch 243.4 *prepare for action*
bring up to snuff 243.4 *prepare for action*
bring within the law 16.65 *make legal*
brink 164.1 *edge;* 166.3 *furthest point;* 147.2 *short distance*
brinkman 615.3 *rash person*
brinkmanship 615.1 *rashness;* 631.9 *tactics*
Brinks™ 253.4 *security forces*
briny 91.7 *oceanic*
brioche 25.39 *loaf*
briquette 437.5 *coal*
brisé volé 22.9 *ballet steps*
brisk 342.18 *active;* 269.3 *concise;* 726.3 *emphatic;* 31.45 *fine;* 262.3 *hasty;* 332.2 *mentally quick;* 338.4 *vigorous;* 380.6 *violent;* 31.47 *windy*
brisket 25.22, 25.23 *beef*
briskly 269.5 *concisely*
briskness 269.1 *conciseness;* 262.4 *haste;* 342.3 *nimbleness;* 332.8 *speed*
brisk wind 31.14 *windiness*
brisling 74.8 *food fish*
bristle 624.12 *become angry;* 420.11 *be rough;* 425.14 *be sharp;* 208.11 *crowd;* 186.6 *make vertical;* 71.2 *mammalian characteristic;* 420.7 *rough thing;* 425.8 *sharp-pointed thing*
bristled 420.3 *barbed*
bristle up 420.11 *be rough*
bristle with 217.5 *about;* 219.4 *be excessive;* 425.14 *be sharp*
bristle worm 75.6 *worm*
bristliness 420.6 *roughness;* 425.6 *sharpness*
bristling 420.3 *barbed;* 376.50 *crowded;* 219.6 *excessive;* 25.18 *sea fish;* 425.2 *spiked*
bristly 420.3 *barbed;* 425.2 *spiked*
Bristol board 435.3 *paper*
Bristolian 564.9 *British inhabitant*
Brit 564.9 *British inhabitant;* 85.8 *Great Britain*
Britain 85.8 *Great Britain*
Britannia 85.8 *Great Britain*
Britannia Cup 50.5 *Henley trophies*
Britannia metal 700.6 *imitation*
Britannia Royal Naval College 585.6 *art of war*
britches 551.9 *trousers*
Briticism 5.26 *dialect;* 85.8 *Great Britain*
British accent 5.26 *dialect*
British administrative council 579.8
British Amateur Gymnastics Association 57.4 *gymnastic organization*
British Army 586.15 *army*
British Army Reserve 586.15 *army*
British bulldog 85.8 *Great Britain*
British Canoe Union 50.6 *canoeing*
British cities 87.4
British coinage 780.9 *British money*
British Commonwealth 85.2 *union of nations*
British court 16.20
British dish 25.44
British Empire 85.3 *dominion*
British game fish 55.5
British government 579.11; 12.4 *governing body*
British GP at Silverstone 61.2 *Formula 1 race*
British inhabitant 564.9
Britishism 85.8 *Great Britain*
British judge 16.25
British lakes 88.4
British law officer 16.11
British Legion member 586.11 *former soldier*
British lion and unicorn 743.6 *national emblem*
British money 780.9
British Mountaineering Council 62.6 *mountaineering association*
British mountains 89.5
British paper money 780.9 *British money*
British police 16.15
British Racing Drivers' Club 61.7 *racing governing body*
British Rail 321.10 *miscellaneous*
British rivers 90.4
British Schools Canoeing Association 50.6 *canoeing*
British Ski Federation 68.1 *skiing*
British Summer Time 275.9 *time zone*
British warm 493.3 *heater*
British weather 299.3 *irregular thing*
Briton 564.9 *British inhabitant;* 85.8 *Great Britain*
britpop 18.9 *popular music*
Brittany spaniel 60.6 *sporting dog*
brittle 424.1; 278.7 *impermanent;* 337.8 *weak*
brittle as glass 424.1 *brittle*
Brittleness 424
brittleness 424.2; 427.2 *crumbliness*
brittle star 75.3 *echinoderm*
brittle thing 424.3
broach 344.11 *inaugurate;* 130.18 *make a beginning;* 425.8 *sharp-pointed thing;* 369.14 *suck*
broaching 369.4 *sucking*
broaching machine 38.9 *machine tool*
broach to 50.15 *sail*
B road 317.3, 320.2 *road*
broad 150.1; 158.15 *big;* 138.15 *general;* 138.20 *generalized;* 453.6 *indeterminate;* 88.1 *lake;* 141.13 *spacious;* 152.1 *thick;* 568.9 *woman considered as a sex object*
broad accent 729.3 *mode of speech*
broad acres 440.1 *property*
broad-backed 150.2 *broad-shaped*
broad-based 150.2 *broad-shaped;* 138.15 *general;* 127.7 *including*
broad-beamed 150.2 *broad-shaped*
broadbill 150.5 *broad thing*
broad-billed 150.2 *broad-shaped*
broad-bottomed 150.2 *broad-shaped*
broad-breasted 150.2 *broad-shaped*
broad-brimmed 150.2 *broad-shaped*
broad canvas 138.3 *nonspecificness*
broadcast 138.25; 504.11 *aural;* 504.16 *be heard;* 150.1 *broad;* 692.30, 693.12 *communicate;* 692.34 *communicated;* 693.2 *communication;* 377.1 *dispersion;* 738.2 *display something;* 377.16 *distribute;* 377.22 *distributed;* 739.6 *divulge;* 739.2 *divulgence;* 43.17 *farm;* 740.13 *make public;* 740.1 *publication;* 740.19 *published;* 741.13 *report;* 729.8 *speech;* 367.6 *throw down*
broadcast drama 21.2 *play*
broadcaster 692.29; 739.4 *discloser;* 693.9 *informant;* 729.10 *speaker*
broadcasting 692.1 *communications;* 377.1 *dispersion;* 693.4 *mass communication;* 740.2 *mass media;* 740.1 *publication*
broadcasting authority 692.20 *radio broadcasting;* 692.24 *television broadcasting*
broadcasting device 504.9 *audio device*
broadcasting station 692.20 *radio broadcasting;* 692.24 *television broadcasting*
broadcast journalist 741.4 *journalist*
broadcast material 692.25
broadcast television 692.21 *television*
broad-chested 150.2 *broad-shaped*
Broad Church 138.2 *catholicity*
broadcloth 150.5 *broad thing;* 42.3 *fabric;* 193.4 *textile*
broad comedy 21.12 *comedy*
broaden 138.24; **150.11**; 765.10 *augment;* 190.6 *become bigger;* 213.4 *increase;* 190.5, 213.5 *make bigger*
broadened 190.7 *bigger*
broadener 190.4 *enlarger*
broadening 765.2 *augmentation;* 190.8 *growing;* 190.1 *growth;* 213.1 *increase*
broadening the mind 6.8 *learning*
broaden the mind 6.23 *learn*
broad-faced 150.2 *broad-shaped*
broad gauge 150.5 *broad thing;* 321.3 *rail*
broad-gauge 150.1 *broad*
broad-gauged 150.1 *broad*
broad-headed 150.2 *broad-shaped*
broad in the beam 150.2 *broad-shaped;* 158.16 *fat*
broad jump 47.2 *field events*
broad jumper 47.3 *athlete*
broad jumping 47.2 *field events*
broadleaf 150.5 *broad thing;* 79.1 *tree*
broad-leaved 150.2 *broad-shaped*
broadleaved tree 79.1 *tree*
broad-lipped 150.2 *broad-shaped*
broadloom 150.1 *broad;* 42.3 *fabric*
broadloom carpet 550.9 *floor covering*
broadly 150.7; 145.10 *distantly;* 138.29 *generally;* 453.25 *indeterminately;* 190.10 *largely;* 216.11 *on average*
broadly speaking 138.29 *generally;* 216.11 *on average*
broad-minded 150.3; 250.9 *free;* 458.5 *wise*
broad-mindedly 250.20 *freely*
broad-mindedness 150.6; 250.1 *freedom*
Broadmoor 815.1 *prison*
Broadness 150
broadness 158.2 *bigness;* 150.4 *breadth;* 453.14 *indeterminacy;* 138.3 *nonspecificness*
broad-nosed 150.2 *broad-shaped*
broad reaching 50.1 *sailing*
Broads 86.9 *regions of Britain*
broad-shaped 150.2
broadsheet 740.3 *journalism;* 741.5 *mass communication;* 740.4 *newspaper*
broad-shouldered 150.2 *broad-shaped*
broadside 150.8 *breadthwise;* 381.15 *firing;* 587.11 *guns*
broadside-on 50.20 *offshore*
broad spectrum 138.3 *nonspecificness*
broad-spectrum drug 37.3 *drug*
broadsword 150.5 *broad thing;* 425.10 *knife;* 587.8 *sharp weapon*
broad-tailed 150.2 *broad-shaped*
broad thing 150.5
broad-toothed 150.2 *broad-shaped*
Broadway 21.1 *drama;* 21.5 *show business;* 18.12 *Tin Pan Alley*
Broadway costume 551.5 *fancy dress*
Broadway melody 516.1 *melody*
Broadway musical 21.4 *musical drama*
broadways 150.8 *breadthwise*
broad-winged 150.2 *broad-shaped*
broadwise 150.8 *breadthwise*
broagh 5.26 *dialect*
Brobdingnagian 158.15 *big;* 158.10 *big person*
broccoli 538.9 *greenstuff*
brochette 373.8 *fastening*
brochure 740.9 *advertisement;* 723.2 *outline;* 484.2 *policy*
Brocken Spectre 89.3 *mountaineer*
broderie anglaise 542.3 *pattern*
brogue 5.26 *dialect;* 729.3 *mode of speech*
brogues 551.19 *footwear*
broiler 43.8 *livestock*
broiler house 43.7 *farm building*
broiling 25.8 *cooking technique*
broke 782.2 *insolvent;* 135.5 *necessitous;* 766.17 *unprofitable;* 249.7 *unprosperous*
broken 372.16 *apart;* 424.1 *brittle;* 420.2 *coarse;* 146.7 *cracked;* 357.15 *destroyed;* 245.13, 337.9 *dilapidated;* 133.8 *discontinuous;* 103.3 *hopeless;* 231.1 *imperfect;* 233.4 *incomplete;* 491.6 *injured;* 782.2 *insolvent;* 299.4 *irregular;* 308.12 *open;* 205.11 *partial;* 335.10 *powerless*
broken arrow 589.2 *symbol of peace*
broken bone 491.3 *injury*
broken chord 18.16 *musical note*
broken clock 339.3 *inert thing*
broken cloud 31.19 *cloud cover*
broken down 337.9 *dilapidated;* 375.5 *disintegrated;* 43.20 *farmable;* 802.18 *gone wrong;* 343.2 *not working;* 335.10 *powerless;* 238.1 *useless*
broken English 5.26 *dialect*
broken glass 420.7 *rough thing;* 425.9 *sharp-edged thing*
broken ground 420.8 *rough ground*
broken-hearted 602.5 *sad*
broken home 571.1 *divorce*
broken in 43.21 *domesticated;* 632.14 *habituated*
broken jaw 491.3 *injury*
brokenly 372.21 *apart;* 133.18 *disconnectedly;* 420.14 *roughly*
broken man 782.10 *poor person*
broken marriage 571.1 *divorce*
broken mirror 475.7 *bad-luck sign*
brokenness 133.1 *discontinuity;* 299.1 *irregularity;* 420.6 *roughness*
broken off 133.10 *interrupted*
broken pipeline 439.3 *supply*
broken promise 800.2 *faithlessness;* 699.10 *lie;* 639.11 *vacillation*
broken record 620.2 *boring thing*
broken reed 81.7 *figurative usage;* 96.5 *insubstantial person;* 335.5 *powerless person;* 337.4 *weakling*
broken resolve 639.11 *vacillation*
broken rhyme 17.11 *rhyme*
broken set 231.6 *imperfect item*
broken silence 507.3 *audibility*
broken-spirited 623.3 *humbled*
broken state 233.1 *incompleteness*
broken thread 133.7
broken train of thought 133.7 *broken thread*
broken up 357.15 *destroyed;* 372.15 *separate;* 377.20 *separated*
broken water 420.9; 91.3 *wave*
broken-winded 261.3 *panting*
broken word 800.2 *faithlessness;* 699.10 *lie*
broker 746.7 *act as a go-between;* 398.6, 578.3 *agent;* 746.4 *negotiator;* 14.3 *stockbroker;* 776.10 *trader;* 778.12 *wholesaler*
brokerage 791.1 *discount;* 776.4 *trade*
brokering 776.4 *trade*
brolly 550.12 *protective covering*
bromeliaceous 77.16 *taxonomic*
bromic 32.34 *elemental*
bromide 620.3 *boring person;* 620.2 *boring thing;* 37.4 *drug type;* 745.1 *maxim;* 685.2 *moderator*
bromide paper 41.9 *film*
brominate 32.26 *react*
brominated 32.34 *elemental*
bromous 32.34 *elemental*
bronchial 260.23 *diseased;* 434.19 *respiratory*
bronchiole 434.8 *respiration*
bronchitic 260.23 *diseased;* 260.19 *sick person*
bronchitis 260.9 *respiratory disease;* 496.8 *smoking*
bronchoconstrictor 37.4 *drug type*
bronchodilator 37.4 *drug type*
bronchopneumonia 260.9 *respiratory disease*
bronchoscope 35.7 *diagnosis*
bronchoscopy 35.7 *diagnosis*
bronchus 434.8 *respiration*
bronco 59.1 *horse;* 59.4 *saddle horse*
bronco-buster 43.16 *farm worker;* 59.15 *horse person*
brontosaurus 296.8 *prehistoric animal*
Bronx cheer 512.2 *catcall;* 514.7 *cry of disapproval;* 742.3 *gesture;* 753.3 *gesture of protest;* 668.6 *taunt*
bronze 534.1, 534.7 *brown;* 412.2 *mixed thing;* 536.1 *orange;* 19.14 *sculptor's materials;* 19.12 *sculpture;* 47.9 *track*
Bronze Age 3.10 *past age;* 284.4 *prehistoric age*
Bronze-Age 296.15 *primal*
Bronze-Age man 296.7 *ancient people*
bronze axe 438.4 *prehistoric tool*
bronze coinage 780.13 *coinage*
bronzed 534.2 *browned*
bronze medal 47.5 *competition;* 57.1 *gymnastics;* 743.4 *insignia;* 794.1 *trophy*
bronze-medal 123.6 *notable*
bronze medallist 47.3, 336.5 *athlete;* 485.4 *skilled person*
bronzing 493.5 *hot weather*
brooch 373.8 *fastening;* 542.7 *jewellery*
brood 606.7 *be dissatisfied;* 626.9 *be sullen;* 376.24 *brace;* 602.9 *despair;* 72.24 *nest;* 4.20 *philosophize;* 208.4 *throng;* 555.4 *young animal;* 72.12 *young bird*
brooder 606.3 *dissatisfied person*
broodily 4.28 *thoughtfully*
brooding 243.17 *developing;* 606.4 *dissatisfied;* 4.17 *thoughtful*
brood mare 59.1 *horse*
broody 561.16 *reproductive*
brook 413.12 *bear;* 90.1 *river*
brooking no delay 262.3 *hasty*
brooking no denial 707.14 *assertive*
booklet 90.1 *river*
Brooklyn 87.3 *New York*
Brooklyn accent 5.26 *dialect*
brook no delay 262.1 *hasten*
brook no denial 707.21 *be assertive;* 641.9 *be obstinate*
brook no restraint 660.24 *be vain*

brook no rival 629.6 *be jealous*
brook trout 55.4 *American game fish*
broom 256.10 *cleaning object*
broomstick 153.9 *thin person*
brose 25.40 *breakfast cereal*
broth 412.2 *mixed thing*; 25.13 *soup*
brothel 796.6; 804.8 *wicked place*
brothel creepers 551.19 *footwear*
brothel keeper 796.9 *immoral woman*
brothel-keeping 796.5 *prostitution*
brother 569.6 *close friend*; 750.5 *conformity*; 285.5 *contemporary*; 119.5 *equal*; 567.13 *man in the family*; 7.7 *monk*; 127.3 *person included*
brotherhood 376.15 *association*; 569.1 *friendship*; 566.9 *group*; 747.9 *team*
brotherhood of man 650.1 *benevolence*
brotherliness 650.1 *benevolence*
brotherly 650.6 *benevolent*; 569.8 *friendly*; 593.17 *loving*
brotherly interest 569.1 *friendship*
brotherly love 650.1 *benevolence*; 593.1 *love*; 652.1 *philanthropy*
brother under the skin 115.5 *counterpart*
brother war 585.1 *war*
brought before the court 16.54 *litigated*
brought down 623.3 *humbled*
brought face to face 738.13 *displayed*
brought forth 738.13 *displayed*
brought low 387.9 *subject*
brought to attention 738.13 *displayed*
brought to heel 387.9 *subject*
brought to one's knees 387.9 *subject*
brought to one's notice 738.13 *displayed*
brought to perfection 230.1 *perfect*
brought to public notice 738.13 *displayed*
brought up 356.12 *produced*
brought within the law 16.44 *legal*
brouhaha 328.5 *commotion*; 380.3 *instance of violence*; 327.2 *tumult*
brow 525.3 *external appearance*; 185.3 *protuberance*; 174.1 *summit*
browbeat 386.7 *force*; 612.13 *frighten*; 483.10 *manipulate*; 660.26 *oppress*; 480.15 *persuade*; 387.6 *subject*
browbeaten 387.9 *subject*
browbeating 386.2 *coercion*
brown 534.1; **534.7**; 25.55 *cook*; 428.6 *desert*; 493.16 *feel hot*
brown algae 84.2 *algae*; 534.5 *brown thing*
brown as a berry 534.2 *browned*
brown as a nut 534.2 *browned*
brown-bagger 534.6 *figurative usage*
brown ball 65.5 *snooker*
brown bear 534.5 *brown thing*
brown belt 534.5 *brown thing*; 52.7 *judo*; 485.4 *skilled person*
Brown Bess 587.10 *historical gun*
brown betty 534.5 *brown thing*; 25.35 *dessert*
brown-black 532.1 *black*
brown bread 25.38 *bread*; 534.5 *brown thing*
brown coal 534.5 *brown thing*; 437.5 *coal*; 284.10 *fossilization*
brown colour 534.3 *brownness*
brown dye 534.4 *brown pigment*
browned 534.2; 25.56 *culinary*
browned off 624.16 *angry*
brown fat 534.5 *brown thing*
brownfield site 577.1 *workshop*
brown glass 24.1 *ceramics*
brown goods 356.7 *produce*
brown-grey 533.1 *grey*
Brownian 300.17 *directional*
Brownian movement 300.5 *circuition*
brownie 534.5 *brown thing*; 498.3 *dessert*; 534.6 *figurative usage*; 11.11 *ghost*; 159.4 *little person*; 149.5 *short person*; 664.3 *sycophant*
Brownie Girl Scout 534.6 *figurative usage*
Brownie Guide 534.6 *figurative usage*
Brownie point 534.6 *figurative usage*
brownies 25.36 *cake*
browning 493.5 *hot weather*
brownish-red 535.1 *red*
brownish-yellow 537.1 *yellow*
Brown, Jones, and Robinson 216.7 *average person*
brown-lung disease 534.5 *brown thing*
brown madder 535.6 *red pigment*
Brownness 534
brownness 534.3
brown-nose 388.2 *appeaser*; 471.14 *be solicitous*; 677.11 *be sycophantic*; 664.9 *fawn*; 599.15 *humour*; 599.7 *person who humours*; 388.4 *succumb*; 677.7 *sycophant*
brown-noser 388.2 *appeaser*; 534.6 *figurative usage*; 664.3 *sycophant*
brown-nosing 599.11 *humouring*; 664.2 *sycophancy*; 664.7 *sycophantic*
brown off 624.14 *make angry*
brownout 437.4 *electricity*; 534.6 *figurative usage*; 39.34 *power supply*
Brown Owl 534.6 *figurative usage*
brown paper bag 534.5 *brown thing*
Brown personality inventory 36.5 *psychological test*
brown pigment 534.4
brown pigmentation 534.3 *brownness*
brown recluse spider 534.5 *brown thing*
brown rice 534.5 *brown thing*
brown rot 534.5 *brown thing*; 44.12 *pests and diseases*
brown sauce 25.15 *sauce*
Brown Shirt 534.6 *figurative usage*
Brownshirts 12.6 *political party*
brownstone 534.5 *brown thing*; 20.4 *building material*
brown study 534.6 *figurative usage*; 477.6 *reverie*; 443.3 *thoughtfulness*
brown stuff 691.6 *drug*; 534.6 *figurative usage*
brown sugar 25.7 *basic ingredient*; 534.5 *brown thing*; 691.6 *drug*; 498.2 *sweetener*
Brown Swiss cattle 534.5 *brown thing*
brown-tail moth 534.5 *brown thing*
brown thing 534.5
brown-trousers 534.6 *figurative usage*
brown trout 534.5 *brown thing*; 25.17 *freshwater fish*
browse 557.21 *eat*; 81.11 *eat grass*; 71.37 *graze*
browser 81.6 *grass eater*; 40.16 *Internet*; 70.4 *type of animal*
browsing 81.10 *grass-eating*
bruise 427.26 *beat*; 492.13 *be touched by*; 532.9 *black thing*; 560.10 *bleeding*; 540.9 *empurple*; 236.14 *ill-treat*; 491.11 *inflict pain*; 491.3 *injury*; 540.5 *lividness*
bruised 539.2 *bluish*; 491.6 *injured*; 540.7 *livid*
bruiser 586.3 *athlete*; 651.8 *malefactor*; 336.6 *muscleman*
bruising 560.10 *bleeding*; 539.8 *bluishness*; 540.5 *lividness*
bruit 740.13 *make public*
bruit abroad 740.13 *make public*
brumal 292.13 *winter*
brumby 59.1 *horse*
brume 31.34 *mist*
brummagem 793.9 *cheap*; 793.5 *cheap item*
Brummie 564.9 *British inhabitant*
brunch 557.24 *have a meal*; 557.12 *meal*
brunette 532.4 *black-haired*; 534.2 *browned*; 534.3 *brownness*; 523.3 *dark colour*; 523.10 *dark-coloured*
brunt 331.13 *blow*; 331.2 *collide*
brush 428.20 *absorb*; 492.12 *abut*; 585.9 *battle*; 331.13 *blow*; 256.13 *clean*; 256.10 *cleaning object*; 428.15 *dryer*; 147.19 *meet*; 147.4 *meeting*; 19.19 *paint*; 492.3 *press*; 86.6 *regions*; 365.12 *rub*; 421.9 *smoother*; 331.6 *tap*; 492.11 *touch*; 79.4 *trees*; 42.14 *weave*
brush aside 668.22 *show disrespect*
brushed 256.17 *cleaned*; 421.1 *smooth*; 42.10 *woven*
brushing 147.11 *meeting*
brushing off the batter 48.4 *pitching terms*
brush obstacles aside 246.7 *overcome obstacles*
brush off 256.13 *clean*; 470.3 *exclude*; 358.1 *obliterate*; 371.4 *ostracize*; 364.1 *repel*
brush-off 48.4 *pitching terms*; 470.5 *rejection*; 364.6 *repulse*
brush off the batter 48.7 *play baseball*
brush up 256.13 *clean*; 6.23 *learn*; 462.13 *remind*
brush with 585.14 *battle*
brushwood 437.2 *lighter*; 79.3 *timber*
brushwork 19.4 *treatment*
brusque 149.9 *abrupt*; 269.3 *concise*; 659.5 *discourteous*; 626.7 *irritable*; 732.2 *sparing with words*; 723.6 *summary*; 380.6 *violent*
brusquely 269.5 *concisely*; 659.9 *discourteously*; 626.14 *irritably*; 723.11 *summarily*
brusqueness 149.6 *abruptness*; 269.1 *conciseness*; 659.1 *discourtesy*; 732.3 *shyness*; 723.4 *summariness*
brutal 70.14 *animalian*; 381.23 *attacking*; 651.11 *cruel*; 659.5 *discourteous*; 491.8 *inflicting pain*; 382.24 *murderous*; 628.4 *pitiless*; 423.4 *powerful*; 647.8 *severe*; 380.6 *violent*; 804.11 *wicked*
brutal act 651.7 *act of malevolence*
brutality 651.2 *cruelness*; 423.8 *physical strength*; 380.2 *physical violence*; 804.1 *wickedness*
brutalization 245.8 *perversion*
brutalize 423.10 *be tough*; 804.17 *make wicked*; 245.6 *pervert*
brutalized 804.11 *wicked*
brutally 659.9 *discourteously*; 651.20 *malevolently*; 628.7 *pitilessly*; 423.13 *powerfully*; 647.11 *severely*; 804.18 *wickedly*
brutal murder 382.2 *murder*
brutalness 651.2 *cruelness*
brutal task 264.3 *difficult task*
brute 70.2 *animal*; 659.4 *discourteous person*; 457.8 *nonhuman*; 380.4 *violent creature*; 804.9 *wicked person*
brute creation 457.4 *nonhuman existence*
brute force 386.2 *coercion*; 423.8 *physical strength*; 380.2 *physical violence*; 334.1 *power*; 336.1 *strength*; 647.2 *suppression*
brute instinct 457.4 *nonhuman existence*
brute matter 402.4 *matter*
brute strength 334.1 *power*; 336.1 *strength*
brutish 70.14 *animalian*; 381.23 *attacking*; 651.11 *cruel*
brutishness 651.2 *cruelness*
Brutus 700.21 *traitor*
bryological 82.6 *mosslike*
bryologist 82.4 *moss plant*; 77.12 *plant scientist*
bryology 34.1 *life science*; 82.4 *moss plant*; 77.10 *plant science*
Bryophyta 77.4 *lower plant*
bryophyte 77.4 *lower plant*; 82.3 *moss*; 82.6 *mosslike*
bryophytes 554.9 *classifications of life*
bryophytic 82.6 *mosslike*
bryopsid 82.3 *moss*
Bryopsida 82.3 *moss*
Bryozoa 75.7 *coelenterate*
bryozoan 75.7 *coelenterate*
BSE 260.18 *veterinary disease*
B setting 41.18 *exposure time*
B star 29.13 *luminosity*
BTU 493.2 *heat measurement*
bubble 434.24; 327.21 *be agitated*; 424.3 *brittle thing*; 182.2 *bulge*; 190.3 *enlarged thing*; 90.7 *flow*; 700.3 *hypocrisy*; 410.19 *inflatable*; 415.7 *light thing*; 181.3 *round thing*; 68.1 *skiing*
bubble and squeak 25.44 *British dish*; 412.2 *mixed thing*
bubble bath 256.6 *bath*; 256.9 *cleaning agent*
bubble gum 430.2 *adhesive*; 422.3 *elastic thing*
bubble-jet printer 40.7 *peripheral*
bubble memory 40.6 *memory*
bubble pack 527.8 *transparent thing*
bubblewrap 165.4 *wrapper*
bubbliness 415.5 *lightness*
bubbling 415.2 *insubstantial*
bubbly 434.18; 432.21 *gassy*; 415.2 *insubstantial*; 558.9 *wine*
bubby-jock 72.10 *male bird*
bubo 182.2 *bulge*; 548.2 *pimple*
bubonic plague 357.7 *agent of destruction*; 260.5 *plague*
buccaneer 586.6 *militarist*; 323.7 *nautical person*; 586.27 *naval man*; 774.9 *plunderer*
buccaneering 586.33 *combative*; 774.5 *plundering*; 774.17 *stolen*
Bucephalus 59.3 *warhorse*
Buchenwald 815.1 *prison*
buck 780.8 *American money*; 567.7 *libertine*; 567.16 *male animal*; 71.17 *male mammal*
buckaroo 43.16 *farm worker*; 59.15 *horse person*
bucket 203.3 *container*; 68.1 *skiing*; 439.1 *store*; 316.15 *take away*; 815.2 *the inside*; 410.11 *vessel*
bucket down 31.62 *rain*
bucket seat 23.2 *chair*
bucket shop 793.7 *discounter*; 779.5 *stock market*
bucket-shop 793.9 *cheap*
bucket-shop fare 793.4 *bargain*
Buckingham Palace 565.4 *official residence*
bucking up 613.6 *encouragement*
buckle 373.11 *connect*; 373.8 *fastening*; 184.9 *fold*
buckled 373.15 *connected*
buckle down 342.23 *rise and shine!*; 342.15 *try*
buckled shoes 551.19 *footwear*
buckle on one's armour 243.8 *prepare oneself*
buckler 384.7 *armour*
buckle to 354.1, 638.9 *undertake*
buckling 184.1 *wrinkle*
buck naked 552.9 *undressed*
buckrake 43.10 *farm tool*
Bucks fizz 558.8 *mixed drink*
buckshee 793.11 *free of charge*
buckshot 587.13 *ammunition*; 587.14 *historical ammunition*
buckskin 550.14 *animal covering*
buckskins 551.9 *trousers*
buck the trend 118.19 *be independent*
bucktooth 425.11 *tooth*
buck up 610.9 *be hopeful*; 598.6 *bring cheer*
bucolic 43.19 *agricultural*; 17.19 *narrative*; 17.7 *poem*
bucolically 43.22 *agriculturally*
bud 77.8; 190.6 *become bigger*; 182.2 *bulge*; 44.15 *cultivate*; 78.13 *flower*; 345.8, 555.18 *grow*; 345.3 *growth*; 213.4 *increase*; 567.3 *male title of address*; 368.6 *plant*; 130.26 *produce*; 561.13 *propagate*; 344.3 *rudiment*; 130.3 *source*; 77.21 *vegetate*
Budapest 87.6 *other cities*
Buddha 8.3 *God*
Buddhahood 8.1 *divinity*
Buddhic body 11.7 *spirit*
Buddhism 4.7 *school of thought*
Buddhist 7.16 *denominational*; 4.11 *follower of a doctrine*; 7.6 *non-Christian*; 4.14 *of a philosophy*
Buddhist text 7.12 *religious text*
Buddhology 7.13 *theology*
budding 77.8 *bud*; 130.32 *embryonic*; 44.5 *gardening*; 190.8, 345.11 *growing*; 190.1 *growth*; 295.12 *immature*; 555.13 *maturing*
buddy 223.11 *companion*; 569.5 *friend*; 595.4 *likable person*; 567.3 *male title of address*
buddy-buddy 569.8 *friendly*
buddy up with 569.13 *befriend*
budge 300.13 *be in motion*
budgerigar 72.7 *cagebird*
budget 789.7 *account*; 680.2 *act of thrift*; 680.5 *be thrifty*; 789.2 *budgeting*; 793.9 *cheap*; 13.7 *corporation*; 14.1 *finance*; 484.1 *plan*; 484.12 *plan ahead*; 436.1, 436.5 *provision*
budget account 783.1 *credit*
budgetary 789.10 *accounting*; 13.13 *economic*; 780.22 *monetary*
budgetary control 13.7 *corporation*
budget deficit 13.7 *corporation*; 13.3 *economic statistics*
budget estimates 789.2 *budgeting*
budgeting 789.2; 436.1 *provision*
budget price 793.1 *cheapness*
budget surplus 13.7 *corporation*
budgie 72.7 *cagebird*
budstick 44.5 *gardening*
budtime 292.2 *spring*
buff 534.1 *brown*; 342.10 *busy person*; 256.13 *clean*; 365.12 *rub*; 421.11 *smooth*; 21.33 *theatregoer*; 537.1 *yellow*
buffalo chips 560.5 *faeces*
buffalo hunter 633.6 *hunter*
buffer 384.19; 378.3 *barrier*; 40.6 *memory*; 685.2 *moderator*; 85.16 *national*; 252.10 *protect*; 252.2 *protection*; 321.3 *rail*; 384.2 *safeguard*; 421.9 *smoother*
buffer state 85.3 *dominion*; 147.3 *juxtaposition*; 12.5 *political organization*
buffet 31.58, 331.13 *blow*; 814.12 *corporal punishment*; 557.15 *eating place*; 331.3 *hit*; 236.14 *ill-treat*; 557.12 *meal*
buffeting 322.5 *flight*
buffing 365.5 *polishing*
buffing wheel 307.6 *rotator*
buffo 21.32 *clown*
buffoon 697.4; 21.32 *clown*; 599.6 *hu-*

morist; 272.3 *object of ridicule;* 21.23 *role;* 486.10 *unskilled person*
buffoonery 272.1 *ludicrousness;* 697.3 *tomfoolery;* 599.3 *wit*
bug 504.9 *audio device;* 40.19 *computing terms;* 328.7 *disturb;* 670.18 *find fault;* 504.15 *hear;* 260.2 *illness;* 378.2 *obstacle;* 76.3 *pest;* 744.10 *recording instrument;* 710.6 *request;* 274.14 *technical error*
bugaboo 711.3 *false alarm*
bugbear 711.3 *false alarm;* 612.5 *frightener;* 594.7 *hated thing*
bugged 504.11 *aural;* 328.12 *disturbed*
bugger 264.3 *difficult task;* 566.7 *person*
bugger all 195.2 *nothing*
buggered 357.15 *destroyed;* 335.10 *powerless*
buggered up 802.18 *gone wrong*
bugger it 712.15 *miscellaneous swearwords*
bugger off 313.1 *depart;* 313.15 *go!;* 371.33 *go away!;* 712.15 *miscellaneous swearwords*
bugger up 245.4 *impair*
buggery 796.7 *sexual assault*
Buggins's turn 289.1 *succession*
buggy 320.16 *car;* 76.12 *verminous*
bughouse 461.8 *mental hospital*
bug hunter 76.8 *entomologist*
bugia 10.14 *sacred object*
bug-infested 44.17 *botanical*
bugle 507.8 *be loud;* 585.2 *glory of war;* 185.3 *protuberance;* 507.4 *sound maker*
bugle call 585.2 *glory of war;* 18.22 *phrase;* 742.6 *word*
bugle corps 584.4 *military organization*
bugler 742.8 *signer*
bug off 371.33 *go away!;* 634.9 *play truant*
build 175.4 *base;* 20.18 *be an architect;* 190.6 *become bigger;* 403.16 *construct;* 406.8 *embody;* 38.30 *engineer;* 154.18 *erect;* 403.2 *fabric;* 553.9 *fashion;* 160.7, 403.3 *form;* 405.13 *make;* 190.5 *make bigger;* 186.6 *make vertical;* 160.6 *nature;* 1.9 *physical type;* 356.10 *produce;* 366.1 *raise*
build a breakwater 90.9 *stop the flow*
build a bridge 243.1 *prepare*
build a tree house 79.18 *manage trees*
build buildings 20.18 *be an architect*
build castles in Spain 477.15 *fantasize*
builder 20.2 *architect;* 578.2 *artisan;* 356.9 *producer*
build houses 20.18 *be an architect*
build in 165.5 *enclose;* 23.18 *work wood*
building 20.3; **38.20**; 356.8, 403.6 *construction;* 190.1 *growth;* 186.2 *making vertical;* 356.2 *manufacture;* 440.1 *property;* 38.19 *structure;* 403.5 *structuring*
building and loan association 780.19 *treasury*
building block 20.4, 435.2 *building material;* 402.4 *matter;* 405.3 *unit*
building blocks 99.1 *essence;* 344.3 *rudiment*
building brick 405.3 *unit*
building contract 755.2 *purchase contract*
building design 20.1 *architecture*
building material 20.4; **435.2**; 38.25 *construction material*
building site 577.1 *workshop*
building society 783.4 *bank;* 771.4 *lending institution;* 780.19 *treasury*
building society account 14.4 *personal finance*
building stone 20.4 *building material;* 38.26 *masonry*
building style 20.1 *architecture*
build on a rock 228.7 *make stable*
build up 376.37 *assemble;* 607.7 *become aggravated;* 190.6 *become bigger;* 209.6 *change gradually;* 232.4 *complete;* 405.13 *make;* 190.5, 213.5 *make bigger;* 123.8 *make important;* 740.16 *publicize;* 439.6 *store;* 336.8 *strengthen*
build-up 190.1 *growth;* 213.1 *increase;* 439.1 *store*
build up hope 756.9 *be auspicious*
build up hopes 475.11 *predict*
build up one's stocks 439.6 *store*
build Utopias 477.15 *fantasize*
built-in 165.7 *enclosed;* 127.8 *included;* 99.7 *integral;* 405.7 *modular;* 23.14 *wooden*
built-in advantage 631.9 *tactics*
built-in cupboard 410.3 *cabinet;* 23.1 *furniture*
built-in furniture 23.1 *furniture*
built like a fortress 252.7 *invulnerable*
built on sand 227.13 *changeable;* 254.2 *unsafe*
built on weak foundations 227.13 *changeable*
built-up 190.7 *bigger;* 565.15 *environmental*
built-up area 87.8 *suburb;* 86.10 *urban area*
bulb 522.6 *electric light;* 78.2 *flowering plant;* 44.9 *garden plant;* 181.3 *round thing;* 344.3 *rudiment;* 77.5 *stem*
bulbous 182.4 *convex;* 190.8 *growing;* 83.10 *of fungi;* 77.14 *of plants;* 181.9 *round*
bulbously 182.6 *convexly;* 190.10 *largely;* 181.13 *roundly*
bulbousness 182.1 *convexity;* 190.1 *growth*
Bulge 185
bulge 182.2; 121.3 *advantage;* 585.10 *battleground;* 190.6 *become bigger;* 232.5 *be complete;* 182.5 *be convex;* 190.3 *enlarged thing;* 213.4 *increase;* 62.5 *rock face*
bulginess 182.1 *convexity*
bulging 182.4 *convex;* 182.1 *convexity;* 232.8 *full;* 190.8 *growing;* 190.1 *growth;* 213.1 *increase*
bulgingly 182.6 *convexly*
bulgy 182.4 *convex*
bulimarexia 557.2 *appetite*
bulimia 557.2 *appetite*
bulimia nervosa 557.2 *appetite;* 36.15 *compulsion;* 260.4 *disease*
bulimic 557.18 *eater;* 557.26 *eating*
bulk 158.19 *be big;* 416.1 *density;* 557.7 *food;* 557.11 *food content;* 414.4 *heaviness;* 205.5 *largest part;* 207.3 *majority;* 203.1 *quantity;* 158.1 *size;* 152.5 *thickness*
bulk-buy 439.6 *store*
bulkhead 50.3 *parts of a sailing boat;* 38.19 *structure*
bulkiness 158.2 *bigness;* 414.4 *heaviness;* 152.5 *thickness*
bulk large 123.7 *be important*
bulk memory 40.6 *memory*
bulk strain 38.14 *load*
bulk tank 43.10 *farm tool*
bulky 158.15 *big;* 264.15 *clumsy;* 414.1 *heavy;* 152.1 *thick*
bull 173.2 *central thing;* 397.1 *command;* 69.6 *darts;* 792.7 *dear;* 234.4 *distortion of the truth;* 14.6 *financial;* 274.11 *grammatical error;* 14.5 *invest;* 43.8 *livestock;* 567.16 *male animal;* 71.17 *male mammal;* 697.1, 699.15 *nonsense;* 16.17 *police officer;* 777.1 *purchase;* 777.12 *purchaser;* 776.2 *speculate;* 14.3 *stockbroker*
bull beef 43.8 *livestock*
bull-calf 567.16 *male animal*
bulldog 613.7 *courageous person*
bulldog breed 638.16 *fortitude*
bulldog courage 640.4 *stamina*
bull-dogging 59.12 *rodeo*
bulldog-like 641.3 *unyielding*
bulldog tenacity 641.6 *determination*
bulldoze 331.2 *collide;* 357.9 *demolish;* 386.7 *force;* 612.13 *frighten;* 635.15 *impose one's will*
bulldozer 357.7 *agent of destruction;* 386.4 *coercive person;* 38.29 *construction equipment;* 187.4 *flattener;* 427.11 *pulverizer;* 331.15 *ram;* 421.9 *smoother*
bulldozing 331.12 *collision;* 386.9 *compelling*
bulldyke 568.10 *homosexual*
bullet 587.13 *ammunition;* 814.16 *instrument of execution;* 330.8 *missile;* 587.5 *missile weapon;* 332.11 *swift thing*
bulletin 693.2 *communication;* 276.7 *periodical;* 740.1 *publication;* 31.4 *weather forecast*
bulletin board 40.12 *electronic office;* 738.8 *showplace*
bullet-pouch 587.4 *arsenal*
bulletproof 384.31 *entrenched;* 252.7 *invulnerable;* 423.11 *make tough;* 383.12 *resisting;* 423.1 *tough*
bulletproof car 252.4 *safety device*
bulletproof glass 527.9 *glass;* 418.7 *hard substance;* 550.12 *protective covering;* 252.4 *safety device;* 423.7 *tough thing*
bulletproof vest 384.6 *protective clothing;* 252.4 *safety device;* 423.7 *tough thing*
bullets 181.8 *round*
Bullet Train 321.10 *miscellaneous*
bullfighter 382.13 *animal killer;* 586.3 *athlete*
bullfighting 382.9 *animal killing;* 71.23 *mammal hunting*
bull-headed 641.1 *obstinate;* 267.10 *tenacious;* 635.8 *wilful*
bull-headedness 641.5 *obstinacy;* 267.2 *tenacity*
bullhorn 504.9 *audio device;* 740.1 *publication*
bulling 331.12 *collision*
bullion 780.16; 780.1 *money*
bullish 777.14 *buying;* 792.7 *dear;* 610.11 *hopeful;* 248.8 *prosperous;* 304.23 *rising;* 71.33 *ungulate*
bullishly 248.9 *prosperously*
bullish tendency 792.3 *inflationary price*
bull-like 71.33 *ungulate*
bull market 13.6 *economic factors;* 213.3 *increasing thing;* 792.3 *inflationary price;* 248.1 *prosperity;* 779.3 *sellers' market;* 14.2 *stock exchange*
bull-necked 152.1 *thick*
bullock 43.8 *livestock;* 567.16 *male animal*
bullpen 48.1 *baseball;* 815.3 *prison cell*
bull-riding 59.12 *rodeo*
bullring 382.15 *slaughterhouse*
bullroarer 507.4 *sound maker*
Bulls Blood 558.9 *wine*
bull's-eye 273.3 *accurate thing;* 173.2 *central thing;* 482.6 *objective;* 246.3 *successful thing*
bullshit 702.12 *deceive;* 234.4 *distortion of the truth;* 234.12 *distort the truth;* 697.1, 699.15 *nonsense;* 702.2 *sophism;* 697.6 *talk nonsense*
bullshitter 234.5 *defacer;* 727.6 *exaggerator;* 699.18, 700.16 *liar*
bullshitting 234.8 *exaggerated*
bully 647.5 *be severe;* 423.10 *be tough;* 386.4 *coercive person;* 586.1 *combatant;* 798.6 *evil person;* 386.7 *force;* 612.13 *frighten;* 612.5 *frightener;* 635.15 *impose one's will;* 651.8 *malefactor;* 483.10 *manipulate;* 342.17 *meddle;* 336.6 *muscleman;* 660.26 *oppress;* 647.4 *strict person;* 651.18 *torment;* 380.4 *violent creature;* 804.9 *wicked person;* 235.1 *worthy*
bullyboy 651.8 *malefactor;* 336.6 *muscleman;* 380.4 *violent creature*
bullying 386.2 *coercion;* 612.4 *intimidation;* 651.5 *intolerance;* 607.3 *nuisance;* 423.8 *physical strength;* 423.4 *powerful;* 647.1 *severity*
bully into 386.7 *force;* 480.15 *persuade*
bully off 130.18 *make a beginning;* 330.33 *start;* 130.11 *starting point*
bullyrag 651.18 *torment*
bulwark 378.3 *barrier;* 384.11 *fortification;* 252.2 *protection;* 252.5 *refuge;* 384.2 *safeguard;* 413.11 *support;* 413.2 *supporting part;* 360.4 *wall*
bulwarks 50.3 *parts of a sailing boat*
bum 710.5 *beggar;* 772.7 *borrow;* 258.6 *dirty person;* 343.8 *nonworker;* 782.10 *poor person;* 168.2 *rear end;* 710.8 *solicit money;* 773.7 *take*
bum bag 410.8 *bag*
bumbershoot 550.12 *protective covering*
bumble 486.7 *be clumsy*
bumbledom 12.3 *governance;* 16.2 *jurisdiction*
bumbler 486.10 *unskilled person*
bumbling 486.9 *bungling;* 486.3 *clumsy*
bumfreezer 551.11 *jacket*
bummer 604.2 *bad outcome;* 620.3 *boring person;* 620.2 *boring thing*
bumming 710.3 *solicitation;* 773.1 *taking*
bump 492.12 *abut;* 299.6 *be irregular;* 420.11 *be rough;* 182.2 *bulge;* 331.2 *collide;* 331.12 *collision;* 511.5 *dull sound;* 491.11 *inflict pain;* 491.3 *injury;* 299.1 *irregularity;* 327.9, 327.23 *jolt;* 492.3 *press;* 185.3 *protuberance;* 68.1 *skiing;* 708.15 *terminate*
bump and run 46.11 *defensive huddle;* 46.16 *play defence*
bumper 208.9 *ample;* 158.15 *big;* 558.2 *drink;* 232.2 *fullness;* 65.6 *pool;* 384.2 *safeguard;* 50.7 *windsurfing;* 765.19 *yielding*
bumper crop 217.8 *plenty;* 765.6 *yield*
bumper pool 65.6 *pool*
bumpers 551.19 *footwear*
bumper to bumper 147.14 *beside;* 132.20 *in a line*
bumper-to-bumper 317.15 *accessible;* 147.10 *juxtaposed;* 147.9 *near*
bumph 693.3 *document;* 12.3 *governance*
bumpily 114.10 *diversely;* 299.8 *irregularly;* 420.14 *roughly*
bumpiness 133.1 *discontinuity;* 114.1 *diversity;* 420.6 *roughness;* 327.3 *turbulence*
bumping 299.4 *irregular;* 299.1 *irregularity*
bumping off 382.2 *murder*
bumping race 50.4 *rowing*
bump into 492.12 *abut;* 107.11 *chance upon;* 331.2 *collide;* 312.8 *meet*
bumpkin 646.3 *naive person;* 574.1 *plebeian;* 457.3 *unintelligent person;* 486.10 *unskilled person*
bump off 382.17 *murder*
bump start 320.21 *miscellaneous motoring terms*
bumptious 622.22 *boastful;* 673.11 *cocky;* 661.7 *defiant;* 660.13 *insolent*
bumptiously 673.21 *cockily;* 661.9 *defiantly;* 660.30 *insolently*
bumptiousness 622.10 *boastfulness;* 673.3 *cockiness;* 661.1 *defiance;* 660.1 *insolence*
bump up 338.3 *invigorate;* 213.5 *make bigger*
bumpy 420.4; 133.8 *discontinuous;* 114.5 *diverse;* 299.4 *irregular;* 185.5 *protuberant;* 327.17 *turbulent*
bumpy face 420.7 *rough thing*
bum steer 700.5 *falseness*
bun 25.39 *loaf*
Buna™ 422.4 *rubber*
bunch 376.29; 765.11 *acquire;* 765.3 *acquisition;* 267.6 *adhere;* 750.2 *alliance;* 376.1 *assembly;* 376.27 *bundle;* 203.2 *certain amount;* 376.39 *come together;* 376.11, 376.38 *group;* 208.4 *throng*
bunched 376.49 *grouped;* 203.6 *quantitative*
bunch light 21.20 *stage lighting*
bunch of fives 360.3 *tools for gripping*
bunch of flowers 502.2 *fragrant thing*
bunch together 765.11 *acquire;* 267.6 *adhere*
bunch up 267.6 *adhere*
bunco 700.8 *trick*
bunco artist 700.17 *cheat*
bunco steerer 700.17 *cheat*
Bundesrat 579.10 *legislative body*
Bundestag 579.10 *legislative body*
bundle 376.27; 410.8 *bag;* 439.5 *collection;* 376.38 *group;* 593.27 *kiss;* 781.6 *money;* 410.5 *packet;* 410.21 *put in a container;* 330.33 *start;* 439.1, 439.6 *store*
bundle away 371.6 *send away*
bundled 410.20 *containing;* 376.49 *grouped*
bundle off 371.6 *send away;* 330.33 *start*
bundle of joy 555.9 *child*
bundle of money 780.3 *fortune*
bundle of nerves 591.9 *oversensitive person*
bundle out 262.1 *hasten*
bundling 593.14 *communication of love*
bunfight 557.13 *feast;* 376.9 *social gathering*
bung 550.2, 550.23 *cover;* 309.8 *stop;* 309.2 *stopper;* 330.23 *throw*
bungalow 565.5 *house;* 155.4 *low thing;* 440.1 *property*
bunged up 309.13 *stopped*
bungee jump 361.10 *suspend*
bungee rope 422.3 *elastic thing*
bungle 486.7 *be clumsy;* 236.13 *be worthless;* 274.10 *blunder;* 486.9 *bungling;* 408.23 *confuse;* 247.6 *fail;* 247.1 *failure;* 245.4 *impair;* 231.5 *imperfection;* 236.8 *inferiority;* 288.3 *lost chance;* 274.19, 288.9 *make a mistake;* 465.10 *misjudge;* 351.1 *misuse*
bungled 486.4; 247.10 *failed;* 231.1 *imperfect;* 236.2 *inferior;* 351.4 *misused*
bungler 247.5 *failing person;* 456.5 *ignorant person;* 766.6 *loser;* 465.5 *misjudging person;* 486.10 *unskilled person*
bungling 486.9; 486.3 *clumsy;* 247.10 *failed;* 247.1 *failure;* 465.2 *mistake;* 288.16 *mistaken;* 351.2 *misuse*
bungling idiot 486.10 *unskilled person*
bung up 309.8 *stop*
bunion 182.2 *bulge*
bunk 98.4 *absenteeism;* 699.15 *nonsense*
bunk bed 23.6 *bed*
bunker 378.3 *barrier;* 68.10 *curling;* 56.1

golf; 436.5 *provision*; 565.7 *room*; 384.10 *shelter*; 439.4 *storage*; 439.6 *store*
bunker shot 56.3 *golf shots*
bunk off 98.18 *abscond*
bunkum 677.2 *blarney*; 697.1, 699.15 *nonsense*; 702.2 *sophism*
bunny hop 22.2 *dance*
bun penny 780.10 *former British money*
Bunsen burner 493.6 *fire*
Bunsen cell 32.19 *electrochemistry*
bunt 48.5 *batting terms*; 330.21 *move forward*; 48.7 *play baseball*; 330.1 *propulsion*; 331.14 *sporting hit*
bunting 743.7 *flag*; 322.5 *flight*; 601.8 *salute*; 72.6 *songbird*
buoy 579.5 *guide*; 742.5 *indicator*; 415.10 *lighten*; 323.5 *navigation*
buoyance 422.2 *adaptability*
buoyancy 434.9 *airiness*; 334.4 *energy*; 28.10 *force*; 610.1 *hope*; 415.5 *lightness*; 417.3 *sparseness*; 67.1 *swimming*
buoyancy aid 252.4 *safety device*
buoyancy jacket 252.4 *safety device*
buoyant 422.7 *adaptive*; 434.14 *aerial*; 598.1 *cheerful*; 610.11 *hopeful*; 415.2 *insubstantial*; 323.11 *nautical*; 304.23 *rising*; 417.1 *sparse*; 67.11 *swimming*
buoyantly 598.9 *cheerfully*; 610.15 *hopefully*
buoyed up 415.2 *insubstantial*
buoy up 413.14 *give moral support*; 415.10 *lighten*; 366.1 *raise*
BUPA 35.1 *medicine*; 253.1 *protection*
bur 267.4 *adherent*
Burberry™ 551.12 *coat*
burble 90.7 *flow*
bur-chisel 19.15 *engraving*
burden 378.6; **378.12**; 211.6 *add*; 211.1 *addition*; 249.1 *adversity*; 249.11 *cause adversity*; 810.1 *duty*; 236.14 *ill-treat*; 240.3 *inconvenience*; 406.2 *load*; 414.14 *make heavy*; 509.6 *musical repetition*; 219.2 *overdoing it*; 17.8 *part of poem*; 158.1 *size*; 414.8 *weighing down*
burdened 378.14 *blocked*; 406.11 *loaded*; 414.3 *ponderous*
burdened with age 556.14 *aged*; 556.16 *maturely*
burdened with debt 784.9 *in debt*
burdening 414.8 *weighing down*
burden of guilt 806.2 *signs of guilt*
burdensome 236.3 *bad*; 264.10 *difficult*; 240.1 *inconvenient*; 576.11 *laborious*; 406.11 *loaded*; 414.3 *ponderous*
burdensomely 414.17
burdensomeness 414.8 *weighing down*
burden with 211.6 *add*
bureau 410.3 *cabinet*; 16.2 *jurisdiction*; 23.4 *table*; 577.1 *workshop*
bureaucracy 12.3, 396.4 *governance*; 12.1 *government*; 579.3 *management*; 378.2 *obstacle*; 632.6 *procedure*
bureaucrat 294.5 *delayer*; 579.16 *official*; 647.4 *strict person*
bureaucratic 378.14 *blocked*; 12.9, 396.14 *governmental*; 579.17 *managerial*; 2.12 *sociological*
bureaucratically 378.17 *in the way*; 12.14 *politically*; 2.16 *sociologically*
bureau de change 759.2 *place of exchange*
burg 87.9 *town*; 86.10 *urban area*
burgage 440.3 *historic property terms*; 763.3 *medieval ownership*
burgee 743.7 *flag*; 50.3 *parts of a sailing boat*
burgeon 190.6 *become bigger*; 562.6 *be fertile*; 77.8 *bud*; 555.18 *grow*; 213.4 *increase*; 561.12 *multiply*; 83.12 *mushroom*; 77.21 *vegetate*
burgeoning 190.8 *growing*; 190.1 *growth*; 555.13 *maturing*
burgess 250.7 *free person*; 564.4 *townsman*; 87.11 *urbanite*
burgh 87.9 *town*
burgher 117.6 *conformist*; 250.7 *free person*; 216.8 *middle classes*; 564.4 *townsman*; 87.11 *urbanite*
burgherdom 216.8 *middle classes*
Burghley 59.11 *eventing*
burglar 662.9 *criminal*; 128.5 *excluded person*; 314.8 *intruder*; 16.40 *lawbreaker*; 774.8 *thief*
burglar alarm 347.2 *counteracting thing*; 711.2 *danger signal*; 252.2 *protection*; 252.4 *safety device*; 384.5 *self-defence*; 742.4 *signal*
burglarious 774.17 *stolen*
burglarize 774.12 *steal*
burglarizing 774.1 *stealing*
burglar-proof 309.12 *closed*
burglary 16.39 *crime*; 314.3 *inroad*; 774.1 *stealing*; 774.3 *theft*
burgle 314.10 *invade*; 774.12 *steal*
burgundy 535.7 *red thing*; 558.9 *wine*
Burial 583
burial 583.1; 156.1 *depth*; 526.5 *disguise*; 583.11 *funeral*; 368.10 *immersion*; 358.3 *obliteration*
burial at sea 583.1 *burial*; 368.10 *immersion*
burial chamber 583.6 *grave*; 284.7 *thing of the past*
burial clothes 583.4 *funeral objects*
burial customs 583.1 *burial*
burial ground 583.5 *cemetery*; 301.3 *resting place*
burial mound 3.11 *relic*
burial of the dead 10.5 *Christian rite*
burial place 583.5 *cemetery*
burial service 583.2 *funeral*
buried 583.10; 582.19 *dead*; 526.7 *disappeared*; 368.14 *immersed*; 815.8 *imprisoned*; 521.1 *invisible*; 358.6 *obliterated*; 156.12 *under*
buried treasure 765.5 *profit*; 439.1 *store*
burin 19.15 *engraving*; 19.14 *sculptor's materials*; 425.8 *sharp-pointed thing*; 23.11 *woodworking tool*
burka 551.16 *robe*
burke 382.17 *murder*
burl 416.4 *solid body*; 79.2 *tree part*
burla 21.12 *comedy*
burlesque 621.2 *act of derision*; 21.12 *comedy*; 234.4 *distortion of the truth*; 599.4 *entertainment*; 727.7 *exaggerate*; 727.1 *exaggeration*; 125.9 *imitate*; 720.1 *misinterpret*; 720.2 *misinterpretation*; 718.4 *misrepresent*; 718.1 *misrepresentation*; 125.3 *mockery*; 21.2 *play*; 668.4, 678.6 *ridicule*; 668.14 *ridiculing*; 272.5 *ridiculous*; 21.5 *show business*; 272.2 *slapstick comedy*; 697.3 *tomfoolery*; 21.40 *tragic*
burlesqued 234.8 *exaggerated*
burlesque house 21.16 *theatre*
burlesque queen 21.29 *entertainer*
burlesque show 21.7 *show*
burlesque theatre 21.16 *theatre*
burletta 21.12 *comedy*
burliness 158.6 *squatness*; 336.1 *strength*
Burlington Arcade 779.7 *emporium*
burly 336.9 *physically strong*; 423.4 *powerful*; 158.17 *stocky*
Burmese cat 534.5 *brown thing*
burn 493.15; 381.9 *attack successfully*; 428.19 *bake*; 624.11 *be angry*; 585.13 *be at war*; 700.30 *be fraudulent*; 593.24 *be in love*; 491.10 *be painful*; 532.11 *blacken*; 534.7 *brown*; 357.12 *consume*; 814.5 *execute*; 493.16 *feel hot*; 493.1 *heat*; 491.11 *inflict pain*; 491.3 *injury*; 382.20 *kill ritually*; 522.25 *light up*; 382.17 *murder*; 792.10 *overcharge*; 90.1 *river*; 29.35 *rocketry*; 31.61 *shine*; 441.1 *waste*
burn a cross 742.9 *use signs*
burn alive 382.19, 814.5 *execute*; 382.17 *murder*
burn a stone 68.16 *bobsled*
burn at the stake 493.15 *burn*; 814.5 *execute*
burn away 441.1 *waste*
burn coal 437.11 *fuel*
burn down 493.15 *burn*; 441.1 *waste*
burned out 261.1 *fatigued*
burner 493.4
burn gas 437.11 *fuel*
burn in 743.10 *identify*
burn incense 752.16 *make an offering*; 502.6 *perfume*
burning 280.6 *allowing no delay*; 624.16 *angry*; 814.13 *capital punishment*; 28.35 *heat*; 522.15 *lucent*; 493.10 *on fire*; 491.5 *painful*; 700.7 *tricking*; 493.12 *warm-hearted*
burning alive 382.5 *execution*
burning at the stake 814.13 *capital punishment*
burning glass 437.2 *lighter*
burning in hell 16.64 *convicted*
burning question 705.4 *difficult question*
burning resentment 624.1 *resentment*
burning rubber 332.8 *speed*
burning the midnight oil 342.20 *industrious*
burnish 522.27 *glaze*; 421.10 *polish*; 365.12 *rub*; 421.11 *smooth*
burnished 522.17 *lustrous*; 421.4 *polished*
burnisher 421.9 *smoother*
burnishing 365.5 *polishing*
burn one's boats 638.8 *brace oneself*; 469.3 *side with*
burn one's bridges 638.8 *brace oneself*; 469.3 *side with*
burn one's fingers 486.5 *be unskilful*; 264.21 *get into trouble*
burn on the pyre 583.8 *bury*
burnout 337.3 *poor health*
burn out 493.15 *burn*; 261.6 *fatigue*; 296.17 *grow old*; 441.1 *waste*
burn rubber 332.4 *be swift*
Burns stanza 17.10 *verse form*
burnt 428.8 *baked*; 25.56 *culinary*; 493.13 *heated*
burnt almond 534.5 *brown thing*
burnt cork 532.8 *black pigment*
burnt down 493.13 *heated*
burnt end 51.2 *grip*
burn the guy 298.9 *commemorate*
burn the midnight oil 342.13 *be busy*; 294.6 *be late*; 576.6 *work*
burn to a cinder 493.15 *burn*
burnt offering 807.2 *apology*; 752.6 *offering*
burn to the ground 493.15 *burn*; 358.1 *obliterate*
burnt out 493.13 *heated*; 337.11 *weakened*
burnt sienna 534.4 *brown pigment*
burnt to a cinder 493.10 *on fire*
burnt to a crisp 25.56 *culinary*; 493.10 *on fire*
burnt umber 534.4 *brown pigment*
burn up 493.15 *burn*; 357.12 *consume*
burn-up 332.8 *speed*
burn up the miles 332.4 *be swift*
burn up the track 262.2 *make haste*
burn with love 593.24 *be in love*
burn with passion 593.24 *be in love*
burn with zeal 342.14 *push*
burp 371.16, 432.5, 508.4, 508.7 *belch*
burr 5.26 *dialect*; 729.3 *mode of speech*; 420.7 *rough thing*; 425.8 *sharp-pointed thing*; 79.2 *tree part*
burring 5.39 *of language*
burrito 25.50 *Central American dish*
burro 316.6 *beast of burden*
burrow 71.20 *abode of mammals*; 183.2 *concave land*; 308.20 *hole*; 565.13 *lair*; 183.9 *make concave*; 252.5 *refuge*; 565.18 *take up residence*; 305.15 *tunnel*
burrowed 308.14 *holed*
burrower 183.5 *digger*
burrowing 305.7 *tunnelling*
bursar 789.6 *accountant*; 780.17 *financier*; 785.5 *payer*; 436.3 *provider*; 780.18 *treasurer*
bursarial 789.10 *accounting*; 788.6 *received*
bursarship 813.3 *grant*; 788.3 *income*
bursary 392.6 *financial assistance*; 813.3 *grant*; 788.3 *income*; 765.5 *profit*; 769.2 *something received*; 780.19 *treasury*
bursitis 260.16 *rheumatism*
burst 332.9 *acceleration*; 508.1, 508.5 *bang*; 342.12 *be active*; 424.4 *be brittle*; 507.8 *be loud*; 424.1 *brittle*; 208.11 *crowd*; 377.11 *explode*; 381.15 *firing*; 380.3 *instance of violence*; 507.1 *loudness*; 342.3 *nimbleness*
burst ahead 332.6 *accelerate*
burst at the seams 219.4 *be excessive*
burst forth 130.27 *emerge*
burst in 381.9 *attack successfully*; 380.7 *be violent*; 314.10 *invade*; 380.8 *use violence*
bursting 508.8 *banging*; 424.1 *brittle*; 219.6 *excessive*; 380.6 *violent*
bursting at the seams 232.8 *full*
bursting open 380.3 *instance of violence*
bursting with health 259.1 *healthy*
bursting with pride 622.22 *boastful*
burst into flames 493.15 *burn*
burst its banks 219.4 *be excessive*
burst like a balloon 278.4 *be transient*
burst like a bubble 278.4 *be transient*
burst of anger 594.5 *anger*
burst of confidence 478.5 *spontaneity*
burst of energy 332.9 *acceleration*
burst of fire 381.15 *firing*
burst of sound 507.1 *loudness*
burst of speed 332.9 *acceleration*
burst on the ear 508.5 *bang*
burst open 308.18 *open*
burst out 380.7 *be violent*; 315.10 *emerge*
burst someone's bubble 278.5 *make transient*
burst the bubble 604.6 *disappoint*
burst the eardrums 505.9 *deafen*
burst upon 312.5 *get in*
burst with energy 338.2 *be full of vigour*
burst with health 338.2 *be full of vigour*
bury 582.17; **583.8**; 526.3 *cause to disappear*; 736.8 *conceal*; 156.14 *deepen*; 309.10 *enclose*; 368.4 *immerse*; 521.8 *make invisible*; 358.1 *obliterate*; 439.6 *store*
bury alive 382.17 *murder*
bury a stone 68.16 *bobsled*
burying 583.1 *burial*
burying the hatchet 749.1 *pacification*; 589.1 *peace*
bury oneself 655.12 *be unsocial*
bury oneself in 368.4 *immerse*
bury one's talents 563.7 *be infertile*
bury the hatchet 589.5 *be at peace*; 463.15, 649.9 *forgive*; 749.5 *make peace*
bus 320.19; 316.5 *means of transport*; 40.15 *network*; 316.12, 319.4 *transport*; 39.27 *wire*
bus boy 401.3 *attendant*; 316.7 *transferor*
busby 384.7 *armour*; 551.15 *headgear*
bus driver 316.7 *transferor*
bush 38.8 *machine element*; 77.2 *plant*; 86.6 *regions*; 79.1 *tree*
bushed 261.1 *fatigued*
bushel 551.35 *make clothing*
busheller 551.26 *fashion designer*
bush-fighting 585.8 *warfare*
bushing 307.4 *axle*
bush knife 425.10 *knife*
bush lot 79.4 *trees*
Bushman 5.11 *family of languages*
bushman 564.5 *countryman*
bushmen 566.3 *early human*
bushranger 774.8 *thief*
bush track 59.7 *horseracing*
bush tree 44.10 *fruit tree*
bushy 420.3 *barbed*; 44.17 *botanical*; 416.6 *dense*; 79.14 *treelike*
busily 342.22 *actively*
business 342.6; **346.3**; **776.6**; 21.22 *acting*; 340.1 *action*; 633.4 *activity*; 123.1 *importance*; 576.3 *job*; 356.2 *manufacture*; 447.3 *matter of interest*; 447.4 *sphere*; 810.2 *task*; 776.4 *trade*; 354.2 *undertaking*; 87.14 *urban*
business affairs 13.7 *corporation*
business associate 373.3 *associate*
business association 13.7 *corporation*
business borrower 784.6 *debtor*
business card 743.3 *means of identification*
business cards 759.3 *something in exchange*
business concern 779.8 *store*
business costs 790.6
business cycle 13.6 *economic factors*
business deal 776.4 *trade*
business district 87.7 *city district*
business executive 356.9 *producer*
business house 577.1 *workshop*
business income 788.3 *income*
business language 5.7 *international language*
business law 16.1 *the law*
businesslike 342.18 *active*; 631.16 *behaving*; 485.8 *expert*; 342.20 *industrious*; 95.8 *practical*; 136.9 *qualified*; 407.14 *well-ordered*
business loan 771.2, 772.5, 784.3 *loan*
business magazine 740.5 *journal*
businessman 13.9 *economist*; 485.5 *expert*; 356.9 *producer*; 776.10 *trader*; 778.12 *wholesaler*; 578.1 *worker*
business management 579.3 *management*
business manager 21.27 *producer*
business meeting 376.6 *sitting*
business offer 752.3
business on hand 447.2 *issue*
business person 778.12 *wholesaler*
business school 6.12 *educational institution*

business suit 523.4 *dark thing;* 551.10 *suit*
businesswoman 485.5 *expert;* 356.9 *producer;* 776.10 *trader;* 778.12 *wholesaler;* 578.1 *worker*
business zone 87.7 *city district*
busk 710.8 *solicit money*
busker 710.5 *beggar;* 21.29 *entertainer;* 18.24 *musician*
buskin 551.5 *fancy dress;* 21.11 *tragedy*
buskined 21.40 *tragic*
busking 710.3 *solicitation*
buskins 551.19 *footwear*
busload 406.2 *load*
busman's holiday 576.4 *exertion*
bus pass 793.4 *bargain*
buss 593.14 *communication of love;* 593.27 *kiss*
bussed 319.5 *transportable*
bussing 320.15 *motor transport;* 319.5 *transportable*
bus station 313.10 *place of departure;* 226.4 *stopping place*
bus stop 313.10 *place of departure;* 226.4 *stopping place*
bust 182.2 *bulge;* 357.15 *destroyed;* 371.3 *disbar;* 717.6 *image;* 782.2 *insolvent;* 744.11 *monument;* 135.5 *necessitous;* 19.12 *sculpture;* 766.17 *unprofitable*
busted 782.2 *insolvent*
buster 567.3 *male title of address*
bus ticket 743.3 *means of identification*
bustier 551.8 *shirt*
bustiness 158.5 *fatness*
bust in on 288.6 *take untimely action*
bustle 342.12 *be active;* 327.21 *be agitated;* 327.4 *fuss;* 262.4 *haste;* 262.2 *make haste;* 300.2 *momentum;* 342.3 *nimbleness;* 327.2 *tumult;* 551.18 *underwear*
bustler 342.10 *busy person;* 302.16 *progressive person*
bustling 342.19 *busy;* 300.16 *moving*
busty 158.16 *fat*
busy **288.15**; **342.19**; 317.15 *accessible;* 340.5 *acting;* 395.11 *influential;* 576.10 *working*
busy as a beaver 342.19 *busy*
busy as a bee 342.19 *busy*
busy bee 342.10 *busy person;* 578.1 *worker*
busybody 713.4 *adviser;* 342.11, 644.4 *meddler*
busyness 342.6 *business*
busy oneself 340.4 *act;* 342.13 *be busy;* 631.11 *conduct oneself;* 354.1 *undertake*
busy person **342.10**; 340.3 *doer;* 578.1 *worker*
busy signal 692.11 *dialling*
butane 437.3 *gas*
butch 568.15 *female;* 568.10 *homosexual;* 567.17 *male*
butcher 357.9 *demolish;* 814.5 *execute;* 557.20 *food provider;* 557.17 *food shop;* 382.10 *killer;* 651.8 *malefactor;* 436.3 *provider;* 778.13 *retailer;* 382.18 *slaughter;* 380.4 *violent creature*
butcher's 557.17 *food shop;* 518.6 *look*
butchery 382.4 *slaughter*
butler 401.3 *attendant;* 401.6 *domestic servant;* 436.3 *provider;* 578.1 *worker*
Butsuden 10.13 *shrine*
butt **668.9**; 331.13 *blow;* 52.2 *boxing;* 331.2 *collide;* 52.11 *fight;* 587.9 *firearm;* 331.1 *impel;* 147.18 *juxtapose;* 621.4 *laughing stock;* 465.6 *misjudged person;* 330.21 *move forward;* 482.6 *objective;* 330.1 *propulsion;* 168.2 *rear end;* 769.5 *recipient;* 215.1 *remainder;* 381.5 *strike;* 131.8 *tail;* 496.7 *tobacco;* 486.10 *unskilled person*
butt away 384.26 *retaliate*
butte 154.3 *mountain*
butt end 58.9 *play hockey;* 215.1 *remainder;* 131.8 *tail*
butt-ended 58.8 *hockey*
butt-ending 58.8 *hockey;* 58.3 *ice hockey*
butter 25.7 *basic ingredient;* 677.9 *blarney;* 268.18 *lubricate;* 356.7 *produce;* 421.11 *smooth;* 419.11 *soft thing;* 537.8 *yellow thing*
butter chicken 25.49 *Indian dish*
buttercup 537.8 *yellow thing*
buttercup family 77.3 *seed plant*
butterfingered 486.3 *clumsy*
butterfingers 486.9 *bungling;* 486.10 *unskilled person*
butterflies 327.1 *agitation;* 260.8 *indigestion*
butterflies in the stomach 612.2 *fearfulness*
butterfly 642.4 *capricious person;* 70.6 *flying animal;* 639.15 *indecisive person;* 76.1 *insect;* 67.1 *swimming*
butterfly diagram 29.15 *sun*
butter knife 557.16 *eating utensil*
Buttermere 88.4 *British lakes*
buttermilk 431.2 *juice*
buttermilk biscuit 25.39 *loaf*
buttermilk pancake 25.39 *loaf*
buttermilk sky 31.20 *cloud appearance;* 541.5 *variegated thing*
butter mountain 43.2 *Common Agricultural Policy;* 562.2 *productiveness;* 439.1 *store*
butterscotch 534.5 *brown thing;* 25.41 *sweet*
butter up 677.9 *blarney;* 599.15 *humour*
buttery 658.9 *deferential;* 677.13 *honeyed;* 25.3 *kitchen;* 421.4 *polished;* 268.13 *slippery;* 439.4 *storage*
butt guide 55.3 *fishing tackle*
butt in 706.18 *answer back;* 133.16 *interrupt;* 314.10 *invade;* 342.17 *meddle;* 288.6 *take untimely action*
butting 52.2 *boxing;* 331.12 *collision*
butt in on 328.10 *disrupt*
butt into 312.8 *meet*
buttocks 168.2 *rear end*
button 182.2 *bulge;* 309.7 *close;* 373.11 *connect;* 68.10 *curling;* 373.8 *fastening;* 551.24 *part of garment;* 50.4 *rowing;* 68.1 *skiing;* 124.8 *trifle*
button-down collar 551.14 *neckwear*
buttoned 309.12 *closed;* 373.15 *connected*
buttoned-up 309.12 *closed;* 736.17 *noncommittal;* 551.31 *styled*
buttonhole 733.9 *approach;* 620.6 *be boring;* 373.8 *fastening;* 78.1 *flower;* 502.2 *fragrant thing;* 308.5 *hole;* 360.6 *retain;* 731.8 *talk too much;* 492.11 *touch*
buttonholer 620.3 *boring person*
button mushroom 83.2 *mushroom;* 25.33 *vegetable*
button one's lip 730.13 *be voiceless;* 341.4 *not act*
button-through 551.31 *styled*
button up 309.7 *close;* 551.34 *wear*
buttress 20.8 *column;* 707.19 *confirm;* 20.19 *decorate;* 384.11 *fortification;* 418.9 *harden;* 228.7 *make stable;* 361.5 *projecting object;* 252.5 *refuge;* 62.5 *rock face;* 228.3 *stabilizer;* 336.8 *strengthen;* 38.27 *superstructure;* 392.19, 413.1, 413.11 *support;* 413.2 *supporting part;* 360.4 *wall*
buttress dam 38.23 *dam*
buttressed 20.16 *columned;* 418.3 *hardened;* 336.13 *strengthened;* 707.13 *supported*
buttressing 707.4 *confirmation*
buttress root 77.7 *root*
butt rot 79.10 *tree disease*
butty 569.5 *friend;* 25.11 *sandwich*
Butyl ™ 422.4 *rubber*
butyraceous 268.13 *slippery*
buxom 158.16 *fat;* 152.1 *thick*
buxomly 158.20 *largely*
buxomness 158.5 *fatness;* 152.5 *thickness*
buy 450.7 *believe;* 480.18 *be persuaded;* 787.1 *expend;* 787.4 *expenditure;* 763.7 *possess;* 777.1, 777.6 *purchase;* 388.3 *submit*
buy and sell 776.1 *trade*
buy a piece of 777.1 *purchase*
buy a return-trip ticket 761.8 *return*
buy a round 785.9 *pay one's way*
buy at a discount **791.5**
buy at cost 793.14 *buy cheaply*
buy at factory prices 793.14 *buy cheaply*
buy back **777.3**
buy-back 777.7 *purchasing*
buy bonds 780.27 *invest*
buy cheaply **793.14**; 777.1 *purchase*
buy dirt-cheap 793.14 *buy cheaply*
buyer 13.9 *economist;* 763.5 *possessor;* 777.12 *purchaser;* 769.5 *recipient;* 787.8 *spender;* 776.10 *trader*
buyer beware! **777.18**
buyers' market 793.2 *declining prices;* 13.6 *economic factors;* 779.3 *sellers' market*
buy for a song 777.1 *purchase*
buy from 776.1 *trade*
buy in 777.1 *purchase*
buy in bulk 791.5 *buy at a discount;* 793.14 *buy cheaply*
buying **777.14**; 772.4 *credit;* 787.4 *expenditure;* 777.7 *purchasing*
buying and selling 776.4 *trade*
buying off 390.2 *deliverance*
buying on credit 772.1 *borrowing*
buying price 790.5 *cost*
buying up 777.7 *purchasing*
buy in instalments 772.10 *buy on credit*
buy in the sales 791.5 *buy at a discount*
buy it 582.15 *die*
buy off **777.4**; 480.17 *bribe;* 390.1 *deliver*
buy on account 777.1 *purchase*
buy on appro 777.1 *purchase*
buy on approval 777.1 *purchase*
buy on credit **772.10**; 784.7 *be in debt;* 777.1 *purchase*
buy on hire purchase 783.9 *acquire credit;* 784.7 *be in debt;* 777.1 *purchase*
buy on HP 772.10 *buy on credit;* 777.1 *purchase*
buy on the never-never 772.10 *buy on credit;* 777.1 *purchase*
buy on the spot 777.1 *purchase*
buy on tick 777.1 *purchase*
buy on time 783.9 *acquire credit*
buy out 777.1 *purchase;* 773.7 *take*
buy-out 752.3 *business offer;* 13.7 *corporation;* 346.2 *joint operation;* 773.1 *taking*
buy outright 777.1 *purchase*
buy over the counter 777.1 *purchase*
buy property 440.9 *own property*
buy shares 14.5 *invest;* 777.1 *purchase*
buy supplies 352.6 *find means*
buy the farm 582.15 *die*
buy time 294.8 *delay*
buy up 777.1 *purchase*
buy up the shop 777.1 *purchase*
buy wholesale 791.5 *buy at a discount;* 793.14 *buy cheaply*
buzz **515.6**; 342.1 *activity;* 208.11 *crowd;* 691.1 *drug-taking;* 322.10 *fly;* 597.2 *fun;* 509.9 *hum;* 509.2 *humming;* 76.16 *infest;* 510.9 *resonate;* 488.3 *stimulus;* 692.10 *telephone call*
buzz about 740.17 *be published;* 740.13 *make public*
buzzard 72.5 *bird of prey;* 256.12 *cleaner*
buzzer 507.4 *sound maker*
buzzing 509.2, 509.16, 515.9 *humming;* 515.3 *insect noise;* 510.1 *resonance;* 510.6 *resonant*
buzz off 313.1 *depart;* 313.15 *go!;* 371.33 *go away!*
buzz word 5.21 *catchword;* 509.7 *repeated word*
BVD's 551.18 *underwear*
bwana 400.1 *master*
by 554.15 *born;* 352.7 *by means of;* 345.10 *caused;* 348.9 *instrumentally;* 317.17 *via*
by abstaining 251.17 *with self-restraint*
by accident 107.13 *by chance;* 249.12 *in adversity;* 105.11 *luckily;* 105.9 *unexpectedly*
by a classic route 62.10 *on a climb*
by aeroplane 319.6 *commercially*
by a hair's-breadth 151.11 *narrowly;* 147.12 *near*
by air 319.6 *commercially*
by all means 452.26 *certainly!*
by an artificial route 62.10 *on a climb*
by and by 283.14 *in the future;* 293.18 *soon*
by-and-by 283.1 *future time*
by and large 150.7 *broadly;* 99.13 *in essence;* 216.11 *on average;* 204.13 *on the whole*
by annulment 571.13 *without one's spouse*
by any means 317.16 *how;* 102.9 *possibly*
by appointment 469.15 *chosen*
by artificial light 522.30 *lightly*
by a side door 306.12 *circuitously*
by auction 767.16 *disposably*
by authority 12.14 *politically*
by a whisker 151.11 *narrowly;* 147.12 *near*
by ballot 469.17 *selectively*
by birth 698.19 *authentic*
by bus 319.6 *commercially*
by casting 55.9 *on the water*
by catches 133.18 *disconnectedly*
by chance **107.13**; 408.27 *in disorder;* 105.11 *luckily;* 102.9 *possibly*
by cheque 785.21 *cash down*
by choice 469.17 *selectively*
by coincidence 107.13 *by chance*
by command 397.16 *commandingly*
by comparison 209.9 *differentially*
by compulsion 336.15 *acutely*
by consensus 750.31 *in accord*
by counterattacking 54.7 *on guard*
by credit 772.13 *on loan*
by custom 340.7 *actively;* 632.19 *habitually;* 298.17 *orderly*
by day 522.30 *lightly*
by daylight 522.30 *lightly*
by decree absolute 571.13 *without one's spouse*
by decree nisi 571.13 *without one's spouse*
by decree of nullity 571.13 *without one's spouse*
by default 762.9 *instead*
by deferred payment 783.14 *on credit*
by degrees **209.10**; 133.17 *discontinuously;* 205.12 *partly;* 333.16 *slowly*
by design 20.20 *architecturally;* 160.13 *formatively;* 482.13 *intentionally*
by dint of 352.7 *by means of;* 334.18 *powerfully*
by divine right 8.19 *divinely*
by dribs and drabs 642.6 *capriciously*
bye 313.14 *goodbye!;* 53.10 *score*
by ear 504.17 *aurally;* 519.17 *blindly*
by easy stages 333.16 *slowly*
bye-bye 313.14 *goodbye!*
bye-byes 343.9 *sleep*
bye holes 56.2 *golfing terms*
by-election 469.12 *election*
by enactment 340.7 *actively*
by expanding 417.7 *sparsely*
by express 316.18 *in transit*
by eye 518.24 *visually*
by far 121.17 *supremely*
by feel 519.17 *blindly*
by fits 133.17 *discontinuously*
by fits and starts 642.6 *capriciously;* 133.18 *disconnectedly;* 276.14 *for short periods;* 408.27 *in disorder;* 299.8 *irregularly;* 327.29 *jerkily;* 205.12 *partly*
by force 386.11 *compellingly;* 334.18 *powerfully;* 336.14 *strongly;* 380.10 *violently*
by forced march 262.6 *hastily*
by force majeure 386.11 *compellingly*
by force of arms 386.11 *compellingly;* 334.18 *powerfully*
by force of habit 632.19 *habitually*
by giving up 767.16 *disposably*
by God's will 8.19 *divinely*
bygone 3.18 *in the past;* 284.18 *over*
bygone days 3.8, 284.1 *past time*
bygones 3.8 *past time*
by guess and God 448.14 *experimentally*
by halves 233.6 *incompletely*
by hand 316.18 *in transit;* 576.12 *laboriously;* 492.17 *manually;* 24.12 *ornamentally*
by heart 462.16 *memorably*
by hire purchase 783.14 *on credit*
by hit and miss 448.14 *experimentally*
by hook or crook 352.7 *by means of;* 317.16 *how*
by hygienic **257.5**
by inches 209.10 *by degrees*
by instalments 783.14 *on credit*
by instinct 445.11 *intuitively*
by intuition 445.11 *intuitively*
by itself 197.21 *alone*
by jerks 133.18 *disconnectedly*
bylaw 16.3 *law;* 140.1 *rule*
by law 16.81 *legally;* 12.14 *politically*
by leaps and bounds 302.20 *in progress;* 208.13 *numerously;* 332.14 *swiftly*
by letting go 767.16 *disposably*
by-line 741.12 *headline;* 671.3 *recognition*
by lorry 319.6 *commercially*
by main force 386.11 *compellingly*
by means of **352.7**; 348.9 *instrumentally*
by means of enchantment 712.14 *damningly*
by misadventure 249.12 *in adversity*
by mischance 249.12 *in adversity*
by mistake 274.21 *erroneously*
by motorway 319.6 *commercially*
by negotiating 754.8 *compromisingly*
by night 523.15 *darkly;* 291.7 *evening*
by no means 94.14 *not at all*
by offering resistance 418.12 *toughly*
by oneself 197.21 *alone;* 572.12 *celibately;* 250.20 *freely*
by one's leave 710.12 *by request*
by order 397.16 *commandingly;* 16.81 *legally*

by parrying 54.7 *on guard*
bypass 634.1 *avoid;* 179.2, 179.6 *circle;* 306.8 *detour;* 325.14 *deviating course;* 317.14 *find one's way;* 306.5 *ringroad;* 373.5 *road;* 317.2 *route*
bypassing 634.10 *avoidance*
bypass surgery 35.9, 394.12 *surgery*
bypath 325.14 *deviating course;* 317.6 *path*
by pipeline 319.6 *commercially*
byplay 21.22 *acting*
by-product 345.1 *effect;* 211.4 *extra;* 356.3 *product;* 32.16 *synthesis*
by proxy 398.12; 195.12 *absently;* 762.9 *instead*
by rail 319.6 *commercially;* 316.18 *in transit*
byre 43.7 *farm building;* 565.12 *stall*
by reason of 344.14 *causally*
by referendum 469.17 *selectively*
by remittance 316.18 *in transit*
by request 710.12
by resigning 605.10
by resorting to 352.7 *by means of*
by retiring 605.10 *by resigning*
by right 801.17 *by rights;* 16.44 *legal;* 16.81 *legally*
by rights 801.17
by road 319.6 *commercially*
by rote 462.16 *memorably*
by rule of thumb 448.14 *experimentally*
by sale 767.16 *disposably*
by sea 319.6 *commercially;* 91.11 *nautically*
by sheer force 336.14 *strongly*
by ship 319.6 *commercially*
by-side 124.3 *secondary*
by sight 518.24 *visually*
by skips 133.18 *disconnectedly*
by snatches 327.29 *jerkily*
by some means 317.16 *how*
by someone's leave 750.39 *with consent*
by special delivery 316.18 *in transit*
by stages 209.10 *by degrees;* 407.25 *in order*
bystander 147.6 *neighbour;* 518.11 *observer;* 716.7 *person who gives evidence;* 97.5 *someone present;* 454.7 *verifier*
by storm 380.10 *violently*
by subtraction 212.8
by swimming 67.12
by tanker 319.6 *commercially*
byte 40.19 *computing terms*
by telephone 504.17 *aurally*
by the agency of 762.9 *instead*
by the aid of 392.37 *in aid of*
by the back door 737.16 *stealthily*
by the book 117.19 *according to rule;* 273.8 *accurately;* 698.38 *literally;* 407.27 *methodically;* 7.23 *religiously;* 140.19 *to rule*
by-the-by 368.12 *inserted*
by the clock 281.18 *horologically*
by the hand of 348.9 *instrumentally*
by the head 50.20 *offshore*
by the lee 50.20 *offshore*
by the numbers 117.19 *according to rule*
by the same token 119.12 *equally;* 115.13 *similarly;* 222.15 *under the circumstances;* 750.34 *uniformly*
by the stern 50.20 *offshore*
by the way 318.14; 109.12 *irrelevantly*
by this token 742.18 *indicatively*
by touch 519.17 *blindly*
by tradition 632.19 *habitually*
by train 319.6 *commercially*
by transfer 316.18 *in transit*
by trial and error 448.14 *experimentally*
by trolling 55.9 *on the water*
by turns 759.8 *in exchange;* 110.10 *reciprocally;* 298.15 *regularly*
by use of 352.7 *by means of*
by veto 399.7
by virtue of 348.9 *instrumentally;* 334.18 *powerfully*
by warrant of 396.23 *authoritatively;* 12.14 *politically*
by water 319.6 *commercially;* 91.11 *nautically*
byway 317.3 *road*
by way of 318.14 *by the way;* 348.9 *instrumentally;* 317.17 *via*
by way of return 385.6 *with vengeance*
byword 745.1 *maxim*
by word of mouth 729.21 *orally;* 693.19 *reportedly*
Byzantine 296.14 *historic;* 19.29 *realist*
C 691.6 *drug*
C1 216.8 *middle classes;* 2.7 *social stratification*
C2 216.8 *middle classes;* 2.7 *social stratification*
cab 320.18
cabal 374.2 *cooperation;* 376.16 *party;* 484.8 *planner;* 484.4, 484.13 *plot;* 737.2 *secretiveness;* 662.3 *subversion*
cabalistic 376.49 *grouped;* 266.2 *obscure;* 737.10 *secretive*
cabaret 21.4 *musical drama;* 21.7 *show;* 21.16 *theatre*
cabbage 43.12 *crop;* 538.9 *greenstuff;* 339.2 *inert person*
cabbage aphid 44.12 *pests and diseases*
cabbage fly 44.12 *pests and diseases*
cabbage patch 44.2 *garden*
cabbage white 44.12 *pests and diseases*
cabbala 737.7 *esotericism;* 11.1 *occultism;* 11.2 *the occult*
cabbalism 737.7 *esotericism;* 11.1 *occultism*
cabbalist 11.12 *occultist*
cabbalistic 374.8 *cooperative;* 737.11 *mysterious;* 11.14 *occult*
cabbalistically 374.10 *in combination;* 11.25 *occultly*
caber 330.10 *ball*
cabernet sauvignon 558.9 *wine*
cabin 565.5 *house*
cabin boy 323.7 *nautical person;* 586.27 *naval man*
cabin crew 401.3 *attendant*
cabinet 23.5; **410.3**; 376.7 *committee;* 579.7 *council;* 579.6 *governing body;* 579.3 *management;* 439.4 *storage*
cabinet-maker 578.2 *artisan;* 23.13 *carpenter*
cabinet-making 79.5 *forestry;* 23.1 *furniture;* 23.8 *woodwork*
cabinet meeting 746.3 *discussion*
cabinet member 398.1 *delegate;* 400.3 *leader;* 579.16 *official;* 396.10 *person of authority;* 12.8 *politician*
cabinet minister 579.16 *official;* 12.8 *politician*
cabinet painting 19.8 *painting*
cabinet seat 396.5 *position of authority*
cabinet shop 23.1 *furniture*
cabin lift 68.1 *skiing*
cable 68.9 *bobsledding;* 693.2 *communication;* 692.31 *correspond;* 692.8 *data transmission;* 334.7 *electrical power;* 373.6 *line;* 692.6 *telecommunication;* 438.1 *tool*
cable brake 320.11 *bicycle part*
cable car 304.8 *lift;* 321.1 *railway;* 68.1 *skiing*
cablecast 740.13 *make public*
cablecasting 740.2 *mass media*
cablegram 693.2 *communication;* 692.8 *data transmission*
cable railway 317.12 *cableway;* 317.10, 321.1 *railway*
cable release 41.18 *exposure time*
cable-stayed bridge 38.21 *bridge*
cable stitch 42.5 *knitting*
cable television 740.2 *mass media;* 692.21 *television;* 692.24 *television broadcasting*
CableText™ 692.25 *broadcast material*
cable-vision 740.2 *mass media*
cableway 317.12; 38.29 *construction equipment*
caboose 321.6 *rolling stock*
cabriole 22.9 *ballet steps*
cabriole leg 23.3 *chair leg*
ca-ca 560.16 *defecate;* 560.5 *faeces*
cache 736.2 *hiding place;* 40.6 *memory;* 252.5 *refuge;* 550.15 *shelter;* 439.1, 439.6 *store*
cachet 139.3 *characteristic;* 811.1 *estimation;* 743.3 *means of identification;* 37.6 *pill;* 185.1 *prominence*
cachexia 260.1 *ill health*
cachinnate 507.8 *be loud;* 514.11 *laugh*
cachinnation 514.2 *cry of joy;* 507.1 *loudness*
cachou 501.2 *deodorant;* 502.2 *fragrant thing*
cack-handed 611.8 *bad;* 486.3 *clumsy;* 544.7 *graceless*
cack-handedness 544.1 *inelegance;* 486.8 *unskilfulness*
cackle 515.5 *sing;* 729.13 *speak in a particular way*
cackler 600.4 *rejoicer*
cacoepy 729.3 *mode of speech*
cacoethes 632.1 *habit*
cacographic 5.42 *worded*
cacography 5.27 *spelling*
cacological 544.9 *inelegant*
cacology 274.11 *grammatical error;* 544.4 *inelegance of speech*
cacophonous 517.7 *dissonant;* 544.9 *inelegant;* 507.6 *loud;* 513.7 *strident*
cacophonously 517.12 *dissonantly*
cacophony 408.5 *confusion;* 517.2 *dissonant noise;* 507.1 *loudness;* 513.1 *stridency*
cactus 77.2 *plant;* 425.8 *sharp-pointed thing*
CAD 40.1 *computing;* 38.1 *engineering*
cad 631.5 *badly behaved person;* 812.2 *disreputable character;* 594.8 *hated person;* 567.7 *libertine;* 242.9 *unpleasant person;* 675.5 *vulgar person*
cadaster 220.6 *list of names*
cadastral 220.12 *inventorial*
cadaver 582.11 *dead person*
cadaverous 582.21 *deathly;* 530.8 *drained of colour;* 582.18 *dying;* 153.2 *emaciated*
cadaverousness 582.1 *death;* 153.8 *emaciation*
caddie 401.3 *attendant;* 56.6 *golfer*
caddis fly 76.1 *insect*
caddish 659.6 *bad-mannered*
caddishly 659.10 *rudely*
caddishness 659.2 *bad manners*
caddis worm 76.5 *larva*
caddy 410.6 *box;* 316.7 *transferor*
cadence 516.4 *harmonics;* 18.13 *melody;* 729.6 *phonetics;* 305.2 *sinkage*
cadenza 478.4 *improvisation;* 18.16 *musical note*
Cader Idris 89.5 *British mountains*
cadet 586.17 *army person*
cadge 343.12 *be inactive;* 772.7 *borrow;* 710.8 *solicit money*
cadger 710.5 *beggar;* 772.6 *borrower;* 343.8 *nonworker;* 773.6 *taker*
cadging 710.11 *begging;* 710.3 *solicitation;* 773.1 *taking*
cadmium lemon 537.7 *yellow pigment*
cadmium orange 536.2 *orangeness*
cadmium red 535.6 *red pigment*
cadmium scarlet 535.6 *red pigment*
cadmium yellow 537.7 *yellow pigment*
cadre 403.4 *framework;* 376.16 *party;* 578.4 *personnel*
caducity 337.3 *poor health*
CAE 38.1 *engineering*
caecilian 73.7 *amphibian*
caenurus 75.13 *invertebrate larva*
Caesar 400.2 *sovereign*
Caesarian 561.7 *obstetrics*
Caesarian section 561.7 *obstetrics*
Caesar salad 25.14 *salad*
caesious 539.2 *bluish*
caesium clock 281.6 *clock*
caesiumX clock 28.87 *clock*
caesura 133.5; 146.1 *interval;* 17.9 *metre;* 226.3 *pause;* 372.5 *separator*
café 557.15 *eating place*
café-au-lait 534.1 *brown*
café society 553.6 *fashionable élite*
cafeteria 557.15 *eating place;* 565.7 *room*
cafetière 558.10 *drink container;* 410.15 *pot*
caffeine 33.19 *alkaloid;* 394.7 *tonic*
caftan 551.16 *robe*
cage 71.20 *abode of mammals;* 309.4 *closed place;* 410.2 *compartment;* 309.10 *enclose;* 410.21 *put in a container;* 372.2 *setting apart;* 565.12 *stall*
cagebird 72.7
caged 410.20 *containing*
cage rotor 39.31 *electric motor*
cagey 616.4 *cautious;* 645.4 *cunning;* 736.17 *noncommittal;* 732.2 *sparing with words*
cageyness 645.1 *cunning*
cagoule 551.11 *jacket*
cahoots 747.5 *joint control*
CAI 40.1 *computing*
Cain 382.11 *murderer*
cairn 583.6 *grave;* 742.5 *indicator;* 744.11 *monument*
Cairngorm Mountains 89.5 *British mountains*
Cairo 87.6 *other cities*
caisson 587.4 *arsenal;* 587.11 *guns;* 38.28 *substructure*
caitiff 651.8 *malefactor*
cajole 677.10; 645.5 *be cunning;* 599.15 *humour;* 483.9 *motivate;* 480.15 *persuade;* 710.6 *request*
cajoler 677.6 *flatterer*
cajolery 677.3; 480.2 *flattery;* 483.2 *inducement*
cajoling 677.14; 599.11 *humouring*
Cajun cabin 88.7 *lake dwelling*
Cajun dialect 5.26 *dialect*
cake 25.36; 416.8 *be dense;* 25.35, 498.3 *dessert;* 258.11 *dirty;* 158.7 *mass;* 416.4 *solid body*
cake candle 522.5 *incandescent light*
caked 416.7 *condensed;* 258.7 *dirty*
cakes and ale 557.7 *food*
cake tin 25.4 *kitchen container;* 25.6 *kitchen equipment;* 410.15 *pot*
cakewalk 22.2 *dance*
CAL 40.1 *computing*
calabash 410.14 *bottle*
calalou 25.51 *West Indian dish*
calamari 25.52 *Greek dish;* 25.18 *sea fish*
calamite 82.1 *fern*
calamitous 288.17 *accidental;* 236.5 *harmful*
calamitously 288.21 *mistakenly*
calamity 249.1 *adversity;* 798.2 *affliction;* 236.11 *harmfulness;* 288.4 *mishap;* 357.4 *ruin*
calcareous 30.57 *chalky;* 427.15 *powdery;* 75.22 *spongelike*
calcareous clay 24.2 *raw material*
calciferous 32.34 *elemental*
calcification 418.6 *solidification*
calcified 418.3 *hardened*
calcify 32.26 *react;* 418.10 *solidify*
calcimine 531.13 *whiten;* 531.8 *whitener*
calcine 493.15 *burn;* 32.26 *react*
calcium 33.15 *essential element;* 557.11 *food content*
calculable 210.14; 26.14 *measurable;* 27.73 *numerable*
calculably 210.16 *mathematically*
calculate 210.8; 211.6 *add;* 27.90 *enumerate;* 464.12 *estimate;* 482.7 *intend;* 26.10, 209.5 *measure;* 484.12 *plan ahead;* 474.9 *predict;* 4.21 *rationalize*
calculated 26.15, 106.4 *deliberate;* 482.12 *intended;* 229.5 *tending to*
calculated deception 700.1 *deception*
calculated risk 482.2 *intentionality*
calculated to 229.5 *tending to*
calculate one's position 142.11 *find*
calculating 789.10 *accounting;* 210.13 *calculative;* 210.3 *count;* 645.4 *cunning;* 700.34 *deceiving;* 458.6 *intelligent*
calculating machine 40.3 *computer*
Calculation 210
calculation 210.1; 789.3 *accounting;* 482.2 *intentionality;* 464.1 *judgment;* 211.2 *mathematical addition;* 27.1 *mathematics;* 26.1 *measurement;* 27.12 *numeration;* 4.4 *philosophical investigation*
calculation of chance 107.7
calculative 210.13
calculator 27.67; **210.6**; 40.3, 210.5 *computer*
calculus 27.30; 210.1 *calculation;* 27.1 *mathematics*
calculus of variations 27.30 *calculus*
Calcutta 87.6 *other cities*
Calcutta Cup 64.2 *championship*
caldera 30.24 *volcanic activity*
Caledonia 85.11 *Scotland*
Caledonian 85.11 *Scotland*
calefacient 493.9 *hot*
calembour 479.5 *equivocalness*
calendar 281.15 *chronologize;* 281.3 *chronology;* 275.17 *date;* 220.5 *list of appointments;* 744.6 *record book;* 298.5 *regular thing;* 275.13 *timer;* 281.2 *timetable*
calendarist 275.14 *timekeeper*
calendar-maker 281.12 *chronologist;* 275.14 *timekeeper*
calendar-making 281.1 *timekeeping*
calendar month 275.4 *term*
calendar of events 475.3 *plan*
calender 421.11 *smooth*
calendered paper 435.3 *paper*
calendrical 275.25 *of known date;* 281.17 *timekeeping*
calendrist 281.12 *chronologist*
Calends 275.11 *date*
calenture 260.3 *symptom*
calescence 493.1 *heat*
calf 550.14 *animal covering;* 30.39 *iceberg;* 43.8 *livestock;* 555.4 *young animal;* 71.19 *young mammal*

calf horse 59.12 *rodeo*
calf love 593.2 *romantic love*
calf-roping 59.12 *rodeo*
calf's head 25.31 *offal*
calf's liver 25.31 *offal*
calibrate 26.10, 209.5 *measure*
calibrated 209.7 *gradational;* 26.13 *measured*
calibrated scale 26.6 *measuring instrument*
calibration 209.3 *gradation;* 26.1 *measurement;* 28.83 *sensitivity*
calibrator 414.10 *scales*
calibre 150.4 *breadth;* 209.1 *degree;* 587.9 *firearm;* 158.1 *size*
calico cat 541.5 *variegated thing*
calidarium 493.8 *hot place*
caliper brake 320.11 *bicycle part*
caliph 400.2 *sovereign*
call 504.9 *audio device;* 507.8 *be loud;* 693.12 *communicate;* 514.1, 515.4 *cry;* 514.10 *cry out;* 397.2, 710.2, 710.7 *demand;* 617.12 *desire;* 314.9 *enter;* 507.1 *loudness;* 654.3 *meeting;* 480.11, 483.1 *motive;* 135.2 *need;* 7.21 *ordain;* 18.22 *phrase;* 69.10 *play;* 742.12 *signal;* 692.32 *telephone;* 692.10 *telephone call;* 585.7 *war measures;* 742.6 *word*
call a ball 65.8 *play billiards*
call a doctor 711.7 *raise the alarm*
call a draw 46.15 *play offence*
call a halt 226.8 *cause to cease;* 131.16 *cease*
call a meeting 376.42 *call together*
call an ambulance 711.7 *raise the alarm*
call an audible 46.15 *play offence*
call a pocket 65.8 *play billiards*
call a strike 15.12 *have an industrial dispute;* 709.5 *refuse;* 226.7 *stop working*
call a truce 589.5 *be at peace;* 301.9 *make motionless;* 226.9 *pause*
call attention to 726.6 *emphasize;* 729.11 *speak*
call box 692.9 *telephone*
callboy 21.28 *stagehand*
called 65.9 *billiard;* 585.15 *warring*
called ball 65.6 *pool*
called by God 582.19 *dead*
called for 135.4 *required;* 778.16 *sold*
called off 131.22 *cancelled*
called pocket 65.6 *pool*
called strike 15.4 *industrial dispute*
called up 376.46 *assembled;* 585.15 *warring*
caller 314.7 *entrant;* 692.13 *telephoner*
call evidence 16.70 *litigate*
call for 316.14 *bring back;* 397.10, 474.11 *demand;* 135.8 *miss;* 135.2 *need*
call for a show-down 585.14 *battle*
call for help 742.12 *signal*
call forth 483.9 *motivate*
call girl 796.9 *immoral woman;* 568.7 *prostitute;* 804.9 *wicked person*
calligraphic 19.24 *pictorial*
calligraphy 19.1 *art;* 717.2 *reproduction*
call in 713.6 *consult;* 780.25 *demonetize;* 349.5 *dispose of;* 314.9 *enter;* 376.43 *herd;* 370.9 *welcome*
calling 776.6 *business;* 60.2 *hunting;* 576.3 *job;* 654.3 *meeting;* 480.11, 483.1 *motive;* 721.7 *nomenclature;* 742.16 *signalling;* 810.2 *task*
calling card 654.3 *meeting*
calling for 135.6 *demanding*
calling forth 369.5 *drawing out*
calling it quits 605.1 *resignation;* 580.3 *unemployment*
calling the ball 65.6 *pool*
calling the pocket 65.6 *pool*
call in the receiver 226.7 *stop working*
call into being 130.22 *invent*
call into play 349.5 *dispose of*
call into question 451.9 *cause disbelief;* 705.20 *doubt;* 113.18 *object;* 708.11 *rebut*
callipers 28.84 *altimeter;* 26.6 *measuring instrument*
callisthenics 576.5 *exercise;* 57.8 *floor exercises;* 244.9 *physical improvement*
call it a day 226.6 *cease;* 133.12 *discontinue;* 388.3 *submit*
call it quits 807.5 *atone;* 226.6 *cease;* 133.12 *discontinue;* 749.5 *make peace;* 605.5 *resign*
call letters 743.3 *means of identification;* 692.20 *radio broadcasting*
call madam 733.11 *title*
call names 668.25 *taunt;* 712.6 *vilify*
call no man master 250.16 *be independent*
call of duty 810.4 *sense of duty*
call off 708.14 *cancel;* 226.8 *cause to cease*
call of nature 560.3 *urination*
call on 713.6 *consult;* 654.12 *visit*
call one's bluff 661.5 *defy*
call one's own 763.7 *possess*
call on one's time 342.6 *business*
callosity 651.3 *callousness*
callous 651.12; 418.1 *hard;* 418.3 *hardened;* 809.3 *impenitent;* 592.1 *insensitive;* 418.4 *mentally hard;* 423.5 *mentally tough;* 383.11 *obstinate;* 628.4 *pitiless;* 647.8 *severe;* 152.4 *thick-skinned;* 804.11 *wicked*
calloused 651.12 *callous;* 418.3 *hardened*
callously 418.13 *inflexibly;* 651.20 *malevolently;* 628.7 *pitilessly;* 383.14 *resistingly;* 647.11 *severely;* 423.14 *single-mindedly;* 592.8 *unfeelingly;* 804.18 *wickedly*
callous murderer 809.2 *impenitent person*
callousness 651.3; 489.313 *heedlessness;* 809.1 *impenitence;* 592.3 *insensitiveness;* 418.8 *mental hardness;* 423.9 *mental toughness;* 383.2 *obstinacy;* 628.1 *pitilessness;* 647.1 *severity*
callous person 628.3 *pitiless person*
call out 514.10 *cry out;* 15.12 *have an industrial dispute*
call-out 35.6 *health care*
call out the troops 711.7 *raise the alarm*
callow 295.12, 555.12 *immature;* 646.1, 805.7 *naive;* 538.3 *raw;* 487.1 *unaccustomed;* 486.2 *unskilled*
callowness 295.3, 555.3 *immaturity;* 646.2, 805.3 *naivety*
call sign 743.3 *means of identification;* 692.20 *radio broadcasting*
call signals 46.15 *play offence*
call sir 733.11 *title*
call the AA 711.7 *raise the alarm*
call the emergency service 711.7 *raise the alarm*
call the fire brigade 711.7 *raise the alarm*
call the plays 46.15 *play offence*
call the police 711.7 *raise the alarm*
call the RAC 711.7 *raise the alarm*
call the rescue service 711.7 *raise the alarm*
call the roll 210.11 *number*
call the shots 396.19 *be authoritarian;* 579.2 *direct;* 349.5 *dispose of;* 397.11 *have authority over;* 579.1 *manage*
call the signals 397.11 *have authority over*
call the tune 396.19 *be authoritarian;* 349.5 *dispose of;* 483.10 *manipulate*
call time-out 226.9 *pause*
call to 733.9 *approach*
call to account 670.20 *censure*
call to arms 585.12 *go to war;* 585.7 *war measures;* 742.6 *word*
call together 376.42
call to mind 115.10 *be similar;* 477.14 *imagine;* 3.22, 462.12 *remember*
call to prayer 10.4 *public worship;* 742.12 *signal;* 742.6 *word*
call to the colours 585.12 *go to war*
call up 376.42 *call together;* 693.12 *communicate;* 369.15 *draw out;* 386.7 *force;* 585.12 *go to war;* 477.14 *imagine;* 462.12 *remember*
call-up 376.1 *assembly;* 386.3 *coercive methods;* 585.7 *war measures*
call upon 397.9 *command;* 810.17 *impose a duty*
call up spirits 11.22 *conjure*
callus 418.7 *hard substance*
call witnesses 16.71 *try a case*
calm 684.10; 4.18 *detached;* 481.5 *discourage;* 265.13 *easy-going;* 31.45 *fine;* 407.16 *harmonious;* 407.8 *harmony;* 341.1 *inaction;* 341.3 *inactive;* 618.7 *indifferent;* 301.9 *make motionless;* 685.4, 685.6 *moderate;* 407.22 *pacify;* 589.7 *peaceful;* 301.6 *quiescent;* 608.9 *relieve;* 301.2 *repose;* 506.4 *silence;* 506.3 *silent;* 421.7 *smoothness;* 421.13 *smooth over;* 421.3 *soothing;* 228.1 *stability;* 228.9 *stable;* 31.13 *wind strength*
calmative 685.8 *moderating;* 37.15 *sedative*
calm before the storm 301.2 *repose*
calm down 685.3 *be moderate;* 749.4 *pacify*
calmed 608.7 *relieved*
calming 685.8 *moderating;* 685.1 *moderation;* 749.6 *pacificatory;* 608.8 *relieving*
calming influence 685.2 *moderator*
calmly 684.13; 618.17 *indifferently;* 685.9 *moderately;* 301.10 *motionlessly;* 506.5 *silently;* 421.15 *soothingly;* 228.12 *stably;* 4.27 *stoically;* 341.5 *without action*
calmness 684.3; 4.3 *detachment;* 265.4 *ease of manner;* 341.1 *inaction;* 618.1 *indifference;* 685.1 *moderation;* 301.2 *repose;* 421.7 *smoothness*
calm water 421.8 *smooth thing*
Calor gas 437.3 *gas*
calorie 493.2 *heat measurement;* 334.5 *unit of work*
calorie-controlled diet 557.6 *nutrition*
calorie counter 687.4 *fasting person;* 557.6 *nutrition;* 153.9 *thin person*
calorie-counting 153.10 *diet;* 153.3 *slimming*
calories 557.11 *food content*
calorific 557.27 *edible;* 493.9 *hot;* 28.98 *physical*
calorifically 557.29 *edibly;* 28.100 *physically*
calorific value 493.2 *heat measurement*
calorimeter 493.2 *heat measurement;* 26.8 *meter;* 28.89 *thermometer*
calorimetric 26.16 *micrometric*
calorimetry 26.2 *micrometry*
calorochromic 529.14 *chromolithographic*
calotte 7.11 *vestment*
caloyer 7.7 *monk*
calque 5.17 *word*
caltrop 384.9 *barrier;* 425.8 *sharp-pointed thing*
calumet 589.1 *peace;* 749.2 *peace offering*
calumniate 715.6 *accuse falsely;* 678.12 *defame*
calumniatory 678.16 *defamatory*
calumnious 678.16 *defamatory;* 715.9 *perjurious;* 712.9 *vituperative*
calumny 678.3 *defamation;* 715.2 *false accusation;* 381.16 *personal attack;* 712.3 *vilification*
calve 71.35 *give birth;* 561.11 *have young;* 43.18 *practise livestock farming*
Calvin cycle 33.23 *photosynthesis*
Calvinist 7.5 *Christian*
calvities 552.5 *baldness*
Calypso 91.4 *sea god*
calypso 516.2 *song;* 18.10 *world music*
calyptra 82.4 *moss plant;* 77.7 *root*
calyx 205.6 *branch;* 78.3 *flower part*
CAM 40.1 *computing*
Cam 90.4 *British rivers*
cam 438.5 *machine;* 38.8 *machine element*
camán 58.7 *hurling*
camanachd 58.7 *hurling*
camaraderie 569.1 *friendship;* 654.8 *good company*
camber 176.11 *angle;* 182.5 *be convex;* 177.2 *bend;* 189.6 *be oblique;* 320.3 *carriageway;* 182.1 *convexity;* 120.1 *inequality;* 189.1 *obliqueness*
cambered 177.4 *curved*
camber inducer 50.7 *windsurfing*
cambio 759.2 *place of exchange*
cambist 780.17 *financier;* 778.12 *wholesaler*
cambium 77.5 *stem*
Cambria 85.12 *Wales*
Cambrian Mountains 89.5 *British mountains*
Cambrian period 284.3 *geological period*
Cambridge blue 539.1 *blue*
Cambridge Diet™ 557.6 *nutrition*
Cambridge Platonism 4.7 *school of thought*
Cambridge Platonist 4.11 *follower of a doctrine*
Cambridge roll 43.10 *farm tool*
camcorder 41.16 *camera;* 41.14 *cine film;* 115.3 *copier;* 125.6 *photocopier;* 692.26 *recording;* 744.10 *recording instrument*
camel 316.6 *beast of burden*
cameleer 586.20 *cavalryman*
camelid 71.15 *hoofed mammal;* 71.33 *ungulate*
Camelidae 71.15 *hoofed mammal*
camel-like 71.33 *ungulate*
camel litter 320.6 *litter*
camelopard 71.15 *hoofed mammal*
camel's milk 558.5 *milk*
camel spin 68.6 *ice-skating*
cameo 721.2 *brief description;* 19.13 *relief-carving;* 21.23 *role*
cameo glass 24.1 *ceramics*
camera 41.16; 115.3 *copier;* 28.32 *optical instrument;* 125.6 *photocopier;* 744.10 *recording instrument;* 518.8 *reflection*
camera lens 28.30 *lens system*
camera lucida 19.11 *artist's materials*
cameraman 744.9 *recorder*
camera obscura 19.11 *artist's materials;* 41.16 *camera*
camera-shy 41.22 *photographic*
camiknickers 551.18 *underwear*
camisado 381.12 *military attack*
camisole 551.18 *underwear*
camming 62.8 *mountaineering*
camming device 62.4 *climbing equipment*
camomile 496.5 *herbs*
camomile tea 78.8 *flower product;* 558.3 *tea*
camouflage 125.4; 699.22 *be hypocritical;* 519.15 *blind;* 519.6 *blinder;* 384.19 *buffer;* 526.3 *cause to disappear;* 125.2 *copy;* 736.3 *covering up;* 116.6 *differentiate;* 116.3, 526.5, 550.16, 700.12, 700.32, 736.9 *disguise;* 551.5 *fancy dress;* 550.31 *hide;* 699.3 *hypocrisy;* 115.12 *imitate;* 389.2 *means of escape;* 702.11 *practise sophistry;* 521.6 *that which makes invisible*
camouflaged 526.7 *disappeared;* 700.41, 736.15 *disguised;* 519.13 *hidden;* 737.11 *mysterious;* 521.3 *private;* 550.37 *protected*
camouflager 550.17 *coverer*
camp 584.1 *military affairs;* 62.1 *mountaineering;* 565.18 *take up residence;* 169.5 *team*
campagna 81.2 *grassland*
campaign 340.4 *act;* 340.1 *action;* 585.13 *be at war;* 576.4 *exertion;* 576.8 *exert oneself;* 584.1 *military affairs;* 631.9 *tactics;* 354.2 *undertaking;* 585.8 *warfare*
campaigner 340.3 *doer;* 662.7 *protester;* 586.8 *soldier*
Campaign for Nuclear Disarmament 749.1 *pacification;* 589.1 *peace;* 244.11 *reformism*
campaigning 585.8 *warfare;* 585.15 *warring*
campaign medal 794.1 *trophy*
campaign plan 585.6 *art of war*
campanile 154.6 *tall thing*
campanology 18.6; 507.1 *loudness;* 510.2 *ringing*
camp bed 23.6 *bed*
camp chair 23.2 *chair*
camp-drafting 59.12 *rodeo*
camper 565.9 *mobile home*
campervan 565.9 *mobile home*
campestral 92.11 *continental*
campfire 493.6 *fire*
camp follower 632.8 *creature of habit;* 223.9, 289.8 *follower;* 122.6 *inferior*
camphor 502.3 *incense;* 359.2 *preserver;* 33.20 *terpene*
camphorated 502.4 *fragrant*
camping it up 21.22 *acting*
campo 81.2 *grassland*
campos 92.6 *lowland*
campus 6.15 *schoolroom*
campus novel 17.2 *fiction*
can 410.6 *box;* 309.4 *closed place;* 203.3 *container;* 558.2 *drink;* 558.10 *drink container;* 560.13 *lavatory;* 359.5 *preserve;* 359.2 *preserver;* 410.21 *put in a container;* 238.6 *refuse;* 608.12 *relieve from duty;* 815.2 *the inside*
Canaan 756.4 *promised land*
Canada Day 298.6 *annually celebrated day*
Canadian bacon 25.30 *bacon*
Canadian canoe 50.6 *canoeing*
Canadian Curling Association 68.10 *curling*
Canadian GP at Montreal 61.2 *Formula 1 race*
Canadian maple leaf 743.6 *national emblem*
Canadian Pacific 321.10 *miscellaneous*
Canadian Ski Association 68.1 *skiing*
canaille 122.6 *inferior*
canal 317.11 *channel;* 183.2 *concave land;* 184.2 *furrow;* 373.4 *means of connection;* 90.1 *river;* 319.5 *transportable;* 38.24 *water system;* 323.2 *waterway;* 184.8 *wrinkle*
canal boat 323.3 *vessel*
canal bridge 38.21 *bridge*
canalize 579.2 *direct*

canal travel 323.1 *water travel*
canapé 25.12 *hors d'oeuvre*
canard 711.3 *false alarm*; 699.9 *falsification*; 699.8 *fraud*; 699.11 *half-truth*
canari 25.53 *African dish*
canary 715.3 *accuser*; 72.7 *cagebird*; 516.5 *melodist*
canary-yellow 537.1 *yellow*
can a shot 49.6 *play basketball*
canasta pack 69.3 *card game terms*
cancan 22.2 *dance*
cancan dancer 21.30, 22.5 *dancer*
cancel **708.14**; 649.10 *absolve*; 16.77 *annul*; 708.16 *cancel out*; 94.13 *cause not to exist*; 226.8 *cause to cease*; 526.3 *cause to disappear*; 131.16 *cease*; 399.4 *censor*; 347.3 *counteract*; 357.8 *destroy*; 767.9 *dispose of*; 128.8 *eject*; 27.92 *manipulate*; 358.1 *obliterate*; 708.12 *renounce*; 470.4 *revoke*; 350.6 *stop using*; 212.3 *subtract*; 399.3 *veto*; 355.2 *withdraw*
cancel a debt 786.10 *forgive a debt*
cancellation **708.5**; 470.7 *abrogation*; 649.3 *absolution*; 131.2 *cessation*; 347.1 *counteraction*; 526.5 *disguise*; 767.1 *disposal*; 128.2 *ejection*; 27.24 *evaluation*; 358.3 *obliteration*; 355.3 *relinquishment*; 708.4 *renunciation*; 399.1 *veto*
cancellation of contract 708.6 *termination*
cancellation of debts 786.1 *nonpayment*
cancelled **131.22**; **708.20**; 103.4 *forbidden*; 649.6 *forgiven*; 358.6 *obliterated*; 708.18 *rejected*; 355.5 *relinquished*; 399.5 *vetoed*
cancelling 708.5 *cancellation*
cancelling out **708.7**
cancel one's contract 708.15 *terminate*
cancel out **708.16**; 347.3 *counteract*; 119.11 *equalize*
cancer **260.12**; 249.1 *adversity*; 245.9 *dilapidation*; 260.4 *disease*; 345.3 *growth*; 236.10 *poverty*
cancer of the pancreas 260.12 *cancer*
cancerous 260.23 *diseased*
cancerous growth 260.12 *cancer*
cancerous tumour 260.12 *cancer*
cancer stick 496.7 *tobacco*
candelabra 522.5 *incandescent light*
candelabrum 522.5 *incandescent light*
candent 493.9 *hot*
candescence 522.1 *light*
candescent 522.15 *lucent*
C and H 691.6 *drug*
candid 150.3 *broad-minded*; 703.10 *demonstrative*; 739.11 *disclosing*; 527.4 *easily seen through*; 731.6 *effusive*; 178.5, 799.4 *honourable*; 250.13 *informal*; 693.16 *informative*; 646.1 *naive*; 271.3 *natural*; 308.16, 738.15 *open*; 426.2 *outspoken*; 698.18 *truthful*
candidacy 469.12 *election*
candidate 469.13 *electorate*; 705.10 *person questioned*; 710.4 *requester*; 752.8 *volunteer*
Candide 646.3 *naive person*
candidiasis 83.5 *fungal association*
candidly 426.12 *bluntly*; 703.21 *demonstratively*; 731.11 *effusively*; 738.17 *frankly*; 799.7 *honourably*; 250.22 *informally*; 646.5 *naively*; 308.26, 739.13 *openly*; 271.8 *simply*; 698.36 *truthfully*
candidness 250.4 *informality*; 271.6 *naturalness*; 426.6 *outspokenness*; 799.1 *probity*
candid speaker 646.3 *naive person*
candied 498.6 *sweet*
candied fruit 498.2 *sweetener*
candle 522.5 *incandescent light*; 10.14 *sacred object*
candleholder 522.5 *incandescent light*
candlelight 522.5 *incandescent light*; 28.23 *light*
candlelit 522.18 *lit*
Candlemas 10.15 *holy day*
candlepins 51.4 *bowling*
Candle problem 36.5 *psychological test*
candlestick 522.5 *incandescent light*
C and M 691.6 *drug*
can do no more 261.5 *be fatigued*
candour 703.2 *demonstrativeness*; 178.8 *directness*; 731.2 *effusiveness*; 250.4 *informality*; 646.2 *naivety*; 271.6 *naturalness*; 308.9, 738.11, 739.3 *openness*; 799.1 *probity*; 698.5 *truthfulness*
candy 498.4 *confectionery*; 691.6 *drug*; 418.10 *solidify*; 498.8 *sweeten*
candyfloss 498.4 *confectionery*
candy man 691.5 *drug pusher*
candy striper 752.8 *volunteer*
cane 331.5 *beat*; 413.3 *body support*; 54.1 *fencing*; 81.3 *grass plant*; 814.3 *hit*; 814.14 *instrument of punishment*
cane chair 23.2 *chair*
caner 814.17 *punisher*
canescence 533.4 *greyness*; 531.7 *whiteness*
canescent 533.1 *grey*; 531.3 *white-haired*
cane sugar 498.2 *sweetener*
canid 71.8 *flesh-eating mammal*
Canidae 71.8 *flesh-eating mammal*
canine 71.28 *carnivorous*; 71.9 *dog*; 71.8 *flesh-eating mammal*; 425.11 *tooth*
canine distemper 260.18 *veterinary disease*
caning 814.12 *corporal punishment*
canister 410.6 *box*; 587.14 *historical ammunition*
can it 506.6 *hush!*; 506.2 *silence*; 226.12 *stop!*
canker 245.9 *dilapidation*; 83.1 *fungus*; 245.3 *make worse*; 44.12 *pests and diseases*; 236.10 *poverty*; 79.10 *tree disease*
cankered 83.9 *fungal*
cankerous 260.23 *diseased*
cannabis 691.6 *drug*
canned 410.20 *containing*; 690.1 *drunk*; 359.7 *preserved*
canned food 359.3 *preserved thing*
canned goods 778.8 *merchandise*
cannel coal 437.5 *coal*
canner 359.4 *preservationist*
cannery 359.2 *preserver*
cannibal 557.18 *eater*; 633.6 *hunter*; 382.10 *killer*
cannibalism 651.2 *cruelness*; 557.5 *eating habit*; 10.7 *non-Christian ritual*
cannibalistic 651.11 *cruel*; 557.26 *eating*; 382.24 *murderous*; 10.21 *ritualistic*
cannibalistically 557.28 *carnivorously*
cannibalize 393.1 *repair*; 372.9 *separate*
cannikin 410.13 *drinking vessel*
canniness 442.4 *cleverness*
canning 410.20 *containing*; 359.1 *preservation*
canning factory 359.2 *preserver*
cannon 357.7 *agent of destruction*; 65.2 *billiards play*; 331.12 *collision*; 65.3 *English billiards*; 587.10 *historical gun*; 330.8 *missile*; 65.8 *play billiards*
cannonade 381.2 *fire*; 381.12 *military attack*; 330.28 *shoot*; 330.7 *shot*
cannonball 67.10 *dive*; 587.14 *historical ammunition*; 330.8 *missile*; 332.11 *swift thing*
cannoneer 586.13 *historical soldiery*; 330.15 *shooter*
cannon fodder 586.17 *army person*
cannon into 331.2 *collide*
cannon royal 587.12 *historical guns*
cannonry 587.11 *guns*
cannot 335.6 *be powerless*
cannot be helped 386.8 *be compelled*
cannot do otherwise 386.8 *be compelled*
cannot help but 386.8 *be compelled*
canny 616.4 *cautious*; 645.4 *cunning*; 458.6 *intelligent*; 680.4 *thrifty*
canoe **50.17**
canoe association 50.6 *canoeing*
canoeing **50.6**; **50.12**
canoeist 323.8 *boatman*
canoe poling 50.8 *punting*
canoe race 50.6 *canoeing*
canoe racing 50.6 *canoeing*
canoe techniques 50.6 *canoeing*
canoe trophy 50.6 *canoeing*
can of worms 264.4 *problem*
canon **140.2**; 397.1 *command*; 140.4 *guide*; 125.1 *imitation*; 16.3 *law*; 509.6 *musical repetition*; 4.1 *philosophy*; 713.3 *precept*; 7.8 *priest*; 450.2 *religious belief*; 10.10 *religious manual*; 7.12 *religious text*; 26.7 *standard*; 464.2 *verdict*
canoness 7.7 *monk*
canonical 6.21 *curricular*; 579.18 *parliamentary*; 7.17 *priestly*; 7.18 *theological*; 27.70 *universal*
canonical hour 10.4 *public worship*
canonically 6.25 *educationally*; 7.23 *religiously*
canonicals 551.3 *formal dress*; 7.11 *vestment*
canonical writings 7.12 *religious text*
canonist 7.14 *theologian*
canonization 8.9 *deification*; 366.7 *lift*; 575.1 *right*
canonize 8.17 *deify*; 366.3 *promote*
canonized 8.15 *deified*; 366.12 *exalted*
canonized person 8.10 *deified person*
canon law 713.3 *precept*; 16.1 *the law*
can opener 25.6 *kitchen equipment*
canopic urn 583.4 *funeral objects*
canopied 23.14 *wooden*
canopied bed 23.6 *bed*
canopy 550.7 *overhead covering*; 550.27 *roof*
canorous 516.6 *melodious*
cans 504.9 *audio device*
cant 176.11 *angle*; 699.22 *be hypocritical*; 189.6 *be oblique*; 729.1 *faculty of speech*; 51.2 *grip*; 699.3 *hypocrisy*; 5.20 *jargon word*; 189.1 *obliqueness*; 176.2 *obliquity*; 5.45 *use language*; 5.42 *worded*
cantankerous 701.8 *argumentative*; 751.9 *disagreeing*; 625.4 *irascible*; 626.7 *irritable*; 242.2 *objectionable*
cantankerously 751.11 *in disagreement*; 625.9 *irascibly*; 626.14 *irritably*
cantankerousness 751.1 *disagreement*; 625.1 *irascibility*; 242.6 *objectionability*
cantata 10.8 *hymn*; 18.5 *sacred music*
can't bear 596.5 *dislike*
canteen 558.10 *drink container*; 557.15 *eating place*; 565.7 *room*
canter 332.9 *acceleration*; 332.4 *be swift*; 300.12 *gait*; 700.19 *hypocrite*; 59.16 *ride*
Canterbury 87.4 *British cities*; 482.6 *objective*
canterbury 23.5 *cabinet*
Canterbury hoe 44.6 *garden tool*
cantering 332.1 *swift*
canticle 10.8 *hymn*; 18.5 *sacred music*
cantide 516.2 *song*
cantilever 20.19 *decorate*; 403.4 *framework*; 20.9 *miscellaneous architectural features*; 361.5 *projecting object*; 38.27 *superstructure*
cantilever brake 320.11 *bicycle part*
cantilever bridge 38.21, 317.9 *bridge*
canting 7.15 *religious*; 120.3 *unequal*; 5.42 *worded*
canto 516.1 *melody*; 205.2 *particular*; 17.8 *part of poem*
canton 743.7 *flag*; 396.8 *governmental organization*; 743.8 *heraldic device*; 86.5 *state*
cantor 7.8 *priest*
can't pay! **786.16**
can't stand 596.5 *dislike*
cantus 516.1 *melody*
cantus firmus 516.4 *harmonics*; 516.1 *melody*
canvas 57.8 *floor exercises*; 550.7 *overhead covering*; 19.8 *painting*
canvass 340.4 *act*; 734.11 *confer*; 701.16 *plead*; 705.17 *question*; 778.1 *sell*; 710.3 *solicitation*; 710.8 *solicit money*; 469.5 *vote*
canvassed 705.16 *questioned*
canvasser 340.3 *doer*; 12.6 *political party*; 705.9 *questioner*; 710.4 *requester*; 778.12 *wholesaler*
canvas shoes 551.19 *footwear*
canvassing 469.12 *election*; 469.16 *elective*; 778.3 *selling*; 710.3 *solicitation*
canyon 183.2 *concave land*; 146.3 *gulf*; 30.7 *landform*; 420.8 *rough ground*; 92.8 *valley*
can you beat that 619.14 *wonderful!*
caoutchouc 422.4 *rubber*
cap 48.3 *baseball equipment*; 121.8 *be superior*; 20.8 *column*; 232.4 *complete*; 550.2, 550.23 *cover*; 551.32 *dress*; 131.15 *end*; 587.15 *explosive*; 83.4 *fungal body*; 56.4 *golf club*; 174.2 *head*; 551.15 *headgear*; 437.2 *lighter*; 82.4 *moss plant*; 53.6 *pad*; 385.3 *retaliate*; 309.8 *stop*; 309.2 *stopper*; 174.7 *top*
cap. 5.15 *type style*
capability 136.2, 334.2 *ability*; 265.1 *easiness*; 395.1 *influence*; 352.1 *means*; 756.3 *potential*; 136.1 *qualification*; 485.1 *skill*
capable 119.9 *adequate*; 160.12 *on form*; 102.5 *possible*; 334.13 *powerful*; 136.9 *qualified*
capableness 136.1 *qualification*
capable of being used 772.12 *adoptive*
capable of life 554.12 *alive*
capable of perfection 231.1 *imperfect*
capably **136.17**
capacious 158.15, 679.4 *big*; 141.13 *spacious*
capaciously 158.20 *largely*; 141.15 *spaciously*
capaciousness 158.2 *bigness*; 141.4 *spaciousness*
capacitance 334.7 *electrical power*; 28.53, 39.12 *resistance*
capacitive 39.36 *electronic*
capacitor 28.55 *circuit*; 39.17 *resistor*
capacity 136.2, 334.2 *ability*; 232.2 *fullness*; 127.1 *inclusion*; 352.1 *means*; 102.2 *possibleness*; 756.3 *potential*; 203.1 *quantity*; 141.5 *reserved space*; 39.12 *resistance*; 26.4, 158.1 *size*; 485.1 *skill*; 27.35, 141.1 *space*; 237.6 *usability*
capacity for life 554.5 *life cycle*
cap and bells 21.32 *clown*; 21.12 *comedy*; 551.5 *fancy dress*
cap and gown 551.3, 656.4 *formal dress*; 743.5 *uniform*
caparison 551.1 *dress*
cape 551.25 *accessories*; 92.5 *peninsula*; 185.2 *projection*
Cape Coloured 412.5 *hybrid*
Cape Horn 92.5 *peninsula*
Cape of Good Hope 92.5 *peninsula*
caper 22.15 *dance*; 496.5 *herbs*; 599.5 *joke*; 774.3 *theft*
capers 697.3 *tomfoolery*
capillarity 363.2 *pulling power*
capillary attraction 363.2 *pulling power*
cap in hand 667.11 *in a respectful stance*
capital 174.3 *architectural summit*; 121.14, 235.2 *best*; 173.4 *centre of activity*; 87.1 *city*; 20.8 *column*; 382.23 *deadly*; 13.6 *economic factors*; 352.4 *financial resources*; 780.6 *funds*; 123.5 *important*; 5.41 *lettered*; 440.5 *personal estate*; 396.6 *place of authority*; 814.19 *punitive*; 439.1 *store*; 174.5 *top*; 5.15 *type style*; 781.5 *wealth*; 235.1 *worthy*
capital accumulation 13.4 *economic development*
capital budget 789.2 *budgeting*
capital city 173.4 *centre of activity*; 86.10 *urban area*
capital crime 16.39 *crime*; 804.7 *criminality*
capital gain 788.2 *money received*
capital gains 765.5 *profit*
capital gains tax 790.7 *tax*
capital gearage 784.3 *loan*
capital goods 13.2 *economy*; 778.8 *merchandise*
capital investment 13.4 *economic development*
capitalism 776.5 *commercial trade*; 13.6 *economic factors*; 250.1 *freedom*; 781.9 *plutocracy*; 4.7 *school of thought*
capitalist 400.5 *company leader*; 579.13 *director*; 780.17 *financier*; 4.11 *follower of a doctrine*; 250.7 *free person*; 765.7 *gainer*; 402.3 *materialist*; 776.13 *mercantile*; 4.14 *of a philosophy*; 248.4 *prosperous person*; 14.3 *stockbroker*; 781.10 *wealthy person*
capitalist country 85.1 *country*
capitalistic 250.9 *free*; 765.15 *gainful*; 400.12 *masterful*
capitalize on 349.3 *exploit*; 237.11 *find useful*; 765.14 *profit*; 287.5 *take the opportunity*
cap it all 121.8 *be superior*
capital letter 5.15 *type style*
capital levy 790.7 *tax*
capital murder 382.2 *murder*
capital punishment **814.13**; 582.4 *death sentence*; 382.5 *execution*
capital reserves 780.6 *funds*
capital ship 586.24 *warship*
capital sin 804.4 *sin*
capital transfer tax 790.7 *tax*
capitation tax 790.7 *tax*
capitol 384.12 *fort*
Capitol Hill 12.4 *governing body*; 396.6 *place of authority*; 400.8 *the power structure*; 579.12 *US government*
capitulate 388.3 *submit*
capitulation 750.1 *accord*; 388.1 *submission*
capitulum 78.4 *flower head*
capnomancer 11.13 *diviner*
capnomancy 11.9 *divination*
cap of darkness 11.6 *talisman*
capon 567.12 *eunuch*; 43.8 *livestock*; 567.16 *male animal*
caponize 212.4 *take off*
caponized 335.13 *unsexed*
capote 551.25 *accessories*

capped 550.36 *covered*; 551.29 *dressed*; 309.13 *stopped*; 174.6 *topped*
capped player 485.4 *skilled person*
capping 35.4 *dentistry*; 131.20 *ending*; 121.12 *superior*
cap rates 251.9 *economize*
caprice **642.2**; 224.2 *change of mind*; 593.5 *desire*; 479.6 *equivocation*; 477.4 *ideality*; 299.1 *irregularity*; 227.2 *irresolution*; 595.3 *likes*; 642.3 *whim*
capricious **453.8**; **642.1**; 593.20 *amorous*; 224.11, 639.2 *changeable*; 479.11 *equivocating*; 299.4 *irregular*; 227.14 *irresolute*; 615.4 *rash*
capriciously **453.27**; **642.6**; 224.15, 227.15 *changeably*; 299.8 *irregularly*
capriciousness **453.16**; 642.2 *caprice*; 224.2 *change of mind*; 639.12 *inconstancy*; 299.1 *irregularity*; 227.2 *irresolution*; 615.1 *rashness*
capricious person **642.4**
caprine 71.33 *ungulate*
Capri pants 551.9 *trousers*
capsize 120.5 *be unequal*; 192.3 *invert*; 367.7 *lean*; 323.10 *sail*; 305.11 *trip*
capsized 192.2 *inverted*
capsizing 192.1 *inversion*; 192.2 *inverted*
capstan 366.9 *lifter*; 307.6 *rotator*
capstan lathe 38.9 *machine tool*
capstone 174.3 *architectural summit*; 230.3 *perfection*; 62.5 *rock face*
capsule 80.2 *botanical fruit*; 550.13 *casing*; 394.2 *medicine*; 37.6 *pill*; 149.3 *shortened version*
capsulization 149.2 *shortening*
capsulize 149.10 *shorten*
capsulized 149.8 *shortened*
captain 322.3 *aircraft personnel*; 586.17 *army person*; 49.2 *basketball player*; 579.2 *direct*; 579.13 *director*; 46.2, 66.3 *football player*; 121.10 *lead*; 579.14 *leader*; 323.7 *nautical person*; 586.27 *naval man*; 50.15 *sail*; 50.9 *sailor*; 121.5 *superior*
Captain Ahab 323.7 *nautical person*
Captain America 336.6 *muscleman*
captaincy 579.4 *directorship*; 121.2 *leadership*
Captain Hicks 201.2 *six*
captain of industry 123.4 *bigwig*; 400.5 *company leader*
captain's chair 23.2 *chair*
caption 721.2 *brief description*
captious 642.1 *capricious*; 670.28 *fault-finding*; 702.9 *quibbling*
captiously 702.14 *sophistically*
captiousness 670.6 *fault-finding*; 702.4 *quibbling*
captivate 597.8 *cause joy*; 363.12 *lure*; 483.9 *motivate*; 593.28 *win the love of*
captivated 593.19 *enamoured*; 597.4 *happy*
captivating 363.9 *attractive*; 597.5 *delightful*; 595.5 *likable*; 593.22 *lovable*
captivatingly 593.30 *lovingly*; 595.10 *with great liking*
captive 251.15 *detained*; 815.8 *imprisoned*; 593.9 *lover*; 815.5 *prisoner*; 401.7 *slave*; 387.9 *subject*; 387.5 *subjected person*
captive balloon 586.31 *military aircraft*
captively **815.11**
captive nation 85.3 *dominion*
captivity 251.4 *detention*; 815.7 *imprisonment*; 387.1 *subjection*
captor 400.4 *absolute ruler*; 773.6 *taker*
capture 630.10 *ambush*; 381.9 *attack successfully*; 246.9 *be victorious*; 387.7 *defeat*; 477.14 *imagine*; 717.9 *represent*; 773.7 *take*; 773.10 *take away*; 773.1 *taking*; 773.5 *takings*
capture an expression 721.14 *describe*
captured 247.11 *defeated*
capture on film 744.13 *record*
capturing 773.3 *taking away*
capuche 7.11 *vestment*
car **320.16**; 316.5 *means of transport*; 317.6 *rolling stock*
carabineer 586.13 *historical soldiery*; 330.15 *shooter*
caracole 59.10 *dressage*
carafe 410.14 *bottle*
car alarm 384.5 *self-defence*; 742.4 *signal*
caramel 534.5 *brown thing*; 25.41 *sweet*
carapace 550.14 *animal covering*; 403.7 *skeleton*
carat 414.9 *avoirdupois weight*
caravan 565.9 *mobile home*; 132.8 *procession*
caraway seeds 496.5 *herbs*
carbine 587.9 *firearm*
carbocyclic 32.35 *combined*
carbohydrate **33.3**
carbohydrate diet 557.6 *nutrition*
carbohydrates 557.11 *food content*
carbolic 394.3 *prophylactic*
carbolic acid 256.9 *cleaning agent*; 255.3 *purifier*
carbolize 256.13 *clean*
car bomb 587.16 *bomb*; 700.13 *snare*
car bombing 381.16 *terrorist attack*
carbon 33.15 *essential element*
carbon-14 dating 30.42 *dating*
carbonaceous 437.10 *powered*
carbonaceous chondrite 29.20 *meteor*
carbonate 432.26 *aerate*; 32.26 *react*
carbonated 432.21 *gassy*
carbonated water 433.2 *drinking water*; 558.6 *soft drink*
carbon copy 125.2, 744.5 *copy*; 111.4, 125.5 *duplicate*; 112.7 *replica*; 717.2 *reproduction*; 198.5 *twin*
carbon dating 275.8 *dating*
carbon dioxide laser 28.26 *laser*
carbon fibre 38.25 *construction material*; 435.1 *materials*
carbonic 32.34 *elemental*
carboniferous 32.34 *elemental*; 437.10 *powered*
Carboniferous period 284.3 *geological period*
carbonize 493.15 *burn*
car bonnet 550.12 *protective covering*
carbon paper 435.3 *paper*
car-boot sale 791.2 *bargain*; 779.10 *bazaar*; 793.7 *discounter*; 767.2 *disposal of property*; 778.4 *sale*
Carborundum™ 425.12 *sharpener*
carboxylic acid 32.8 *acid*; 33.7 *fat*
carbuncle 548.3 *blot on the landscape*; 20.3 *building*; 182.2 *bulge*; 548.2 *pimple*; 546.3 *ugly place*; 260.15 *ulcer*
carburation 61.6 *motor-racing terms*
carburize 32.26 *react*
carcass 587.16 *bomb*; 582.11 *dead person*
carcerulus 80.2 *botanical fruit*
carcinogenic 260.23 *diseased*
carcinoma 260.12 *cancer*; 345.3 *growth*; 260.3 *symptom*
carcinomatoid 260.23 *diseased*
card 118.10 *eccentric*; 567.2 *male*; 743.3 *means of identification*; 323.5 *navigation*; 435.3 *paper*; 744.6 *record book*; 421.9 *smoother*; 316.10 *transferred thing*
cardboard 718.6 *misrepresented*; 435.3 *paper*
cardboard box 410.6 *box*
carded 421.1 *smooth*
card game 69.3 *card game terms*; 69.1 *game*
card game terms **69.3**
cardholder 784.6 *debtor*; 314.7 *entrant*
cardiac 35.22 *medical*; 172.10 *visceral*
cardiac arrest 260.10 *cardiovascular disease*
cardiac disease 260.10 *cardiovascular disease*; 260.4 *disease*
cardiac glycoside 33.3 *carbohydrate*
cardiac hypertrophy 260.10 *cardiovascular disease*
cardiac surgery 394.12 *surgery*
cardialgia 260.8 *indigestion*
cardie 551.11 *jacket*; 551.13 *sweater*
Cardiff 87.4 *British cities*
cardigan 551.11 *jacket*; 551.13 *sweater*
cardinal 121.14, 235.2 *best*; 27.75 *equal*; 123.5 *important*; 400.12 *masterful*; 27.7 *natural number*; 194.8 *odd*; 396.10 *person of authority*; 7.8 *priest*; 535.7 *red thing*; 400.6 *religious leader*; 121.5 *superior*
cardinal number 194.2 *kind of number*; 27.7 *natural number*
cardinal point 123.3 *chief thing*; 324.4 *compass point*
cardinal red 535.1 *red*
cardinal's cap 743.5 *uniform*
cardinal's hat 7.11 *vestment*
cardinalship 7.9 *priesthood*
cardinal virtues 803.2 *virtues*
card index 220.2 *table*
cardioid 27.40 *curve*
cardiologist 35.13 *medical specialist*
cardiology 35.3 *medical specialty*
cardiopulmonary disease 260.4 *disease*
cardiovascular 172.10 *visceral*
cardiovascular disease **260.10**; 260.4 *disease*
carditis 260.10 *cardiovascular disease*
cardphone 692.9 *telephone*
card punch 40.7 *peripheral*
cards **475.10**; 69.3 *card game terms*
cardsharp 700.17 *cheat*; 718.3 *deceiver*
cardsharper 700.17 *cheat*
cardsharping 700.10 *fraud*
card table 23.4 *table*
card up one's sleeve 121.3 *advantage*; 484.3 *expedient plan*; 352.5 *reserves*
card vote 469.10 *vote*
care 658.10 *be courteous*; 665.1 *carefulness*; 616.1 *caution*; 665.2 *consideration*; 251.4 *detention*; 579.3 *management*; 252.2 *protection*; 471.5 *solicitude*; 392.3 *sustenance*; 612.3 *worry*
care attendant 35.17 *paramedic*
careen 176.11 *angle*; 299.6 *be irregular*; 332.4 *be swift*; 331.2 *collide*; 299.1 *irregularity*; 327.25 *pitch*; 326.4, 326.11 *rock*; 50.15, 323.10 *sail*; 327.11 *stagger*
careening 299.4 *irregular*; 299.1 *irregularity*; 326.16 *rocking*
career 633.4 *activity*; 332.4 *be swift*; 631.1 *conduct*; 302.11 *course*; 576.3 *job*; 300.2 *momentum*; 332.8 *speed*; 305.11 *trip*
careerism 683.1 *selfishness*
careerist 342.10 *busy person*; 485.5 *expert*
career of crime 804.7 *criminality*
career woman 485.5 *expert*; 568.11 *liberated woman*; 578.1 *worker*
care for **665.11**; 471.10 *be attentive*; 595.7 *like*; 593.23 *love*; 35.19 *practise medicine*; 252.10 *protect*; 401.8 *serve*; 392.19 *support*
care for the truth 698.8 *accuracy*; 698.31 *be accurate*
carefree 263.4 *at ease*; 598.1 *cheerful*; 391.8 *free*; 618.7 *indifferent*; 265.14 *relaxed*; 109.6 *unrelated*; 486.1 *unskilful*
careful **665.9**; 342.18 *active*; 616.4 *cautious*; 799.4 *honourable*; 711.10 *look out!*; 680.4 *thrifty*; 471.7 *watchful*
careful consideration 616.1 *caution*
carefully **665.12**; 471.15 *attentively*; 616.7 *cautiously*; 799.7 *honourably*; 4.28 *thoughtfully*
Carefulness 665
carefulness **471.3**; **665.1**; 616.1 *caution*; 799.1 *probity*; 680.1 *thrift*; 349.6 *use*
careful person **665.6**
careless **472.10**; **618.8**; 486.3 *clumsy*; 262.3 *hasty*; 231.2 *incomplete*; 666.4 *negligent*; 615.4 *rash*; 463.10 *unthinking*; 408.15 *untidy*
careless dress 552.4 *dishabille*
carelessly **618.18**; 472.14 *inattentively*; 666.7 *negligently*; 463.16 *obliviously*; 615.6 *rashly*; 486.11 *unskilfully*; 274.22 *wrongly*
carelessness **618.2**; 262.5 *hastiness*; 231.5 *imperfection*; 274.2 *inaccuracy*; 472.1 *inattention*; 666.1 *negligence*; 615.1 *rashness*; 463.4 *unthinkingness*; 408.3 *untidiness*
car engine 38.11 *engine*
care nothing for 618.12 *be indifferent*
carer 665.7 *caring person*; 590.9 *feeling person*; 445.5 *intuitive person*; 35.17 *paramedic*; 591.8 *sensitive person*; 392.13 *supporter*
cares 249.1 *adversity*
caress 593.14 *communication of love*; 742.11 *gesture*; 492.4, 593.27 *kiss*; 365.16 *massage*; 492.11 *touch*
caressable 593.22 *lovable*
caressing 593.14 *communication of love*; 492.2 *touching*
caressingly 492.16 *sensitively*
caret 742.7 *punctuation*
caretake 579.1 *manage*
caretaker 401.3 *attendant*; 579.15 *manager*; 518.11 *observer*; 309.5 *person who closes*; 665.8 *watchful person*
caretaker government 12.1 *government*; 396.7 *type of rule*
cargo 414.6 *displacement*; 406.2 *load*; 778.8 *merchandise*; 319.2 *thing transported*; 316.10 *transferred thing*
cargo cult 9.2 *idolatry*
cargo handler 316.7 *transferor*
cargo load 316.10 *transferred thing*
cargo vessel 316.5 *means of transport*
carhop 401.3 *attendant*
car horn 711.2 *danger signal*
Carib 5.11 *family of languages*
caribou 60.5 *game*
Caribs 284.6 *people of the past*
caricatural 668.14 *ridiculing*
caricature 621.2 *act of derision*; 599.13 *be humorous*; 621.6 *deride*; 116.6 *differentiate*; 116.3 *disguise*; 19.20 *draw*; 19.9 *drawing*; 599.4 *entertainment*; 727.7 *exaggerate*; 727.1 *exaggeration*; 125.9 *imitate*; 274.19 *make a mistake*; 720.1 *misinterpret*; 720.2 *misinterpretation*; 718.4 *misrepresent*; 274.5, 718.1 *misrepresentation*; 125.3 *mockery*; 717.11 *paint*; 717.2 *reproduction*; 668.4, 668.24, 678.6, 678.14 *ridicule*
caricatured 718.6 *misrepresented*
caricaturist 19.16 *artist*; 621.3 *derider*; 599.6 *humorist*; 717.4 *person who makes a representation*; 678.9 *ridiculer*
CARICOM 779.4 *free market*
caries 375.1 *disintegration*
carillon 18.6 *campanology*; 509.12 *ring*; 509.5 *ringing*
carina 72.16 *avian anatomy*
caring 627.1 *pity*; 627.6 *pitying*; 590.12, 591.1 *sensitive*; 471.9 *solicitous*; 392.32 *supportive*; 612.9 *worried*
caring father 567.14 *liberated man*
caringly **665.13**; 591.12 *sensitively*
caring person **665.7**
car insurance 252.2 *protection*
carious 258.8 *unclean*
carjack 774.12 *steal*
carjacking 774.1 *stealing*; 773.3 *taking away*
carload 406.2 *load*
car mechanic 578.2 *artisan*; 258.6 *dirty person*
carminative 37.4 *drug type*; 394.6 *purgative*
carmine 535.1 *red*; 535.6 *red pigment*
Carnaby Street 551.2 *dressing*
carnage 357.5 *havoc*; 382.4 *slaughter*
carnal 804.12 *immoral*; 796.14 *lecherous*; 402.7 *material*; 490.6 *pleasant*; 686.6 *self-indulgent*; 488.7 *susceptible*
carnal desire 617.4 *sexual desire*
carnality 490.1 *physical pleasure*; 686.1 *self-indulgence*; 617.4 *sexual desire*; 796.3 *sexual immorality*; 804.2 *vice*
carnal knowledge 593.5 *desire*
carnally 804.20 *immorally*
carnassial 425.11 *tooth*
carnation 502.2 *fragrant thing*; 535.1 *red*; 535.7 *red thing*
Carneia 10.16 *religious festival*
carnelian 535.7 *red thing*
carnet 320.21 *miscellaneous motoring terms*
carninomatous 260.23 *diseased*
Carnival 10.16 *religious festival*
carnival 601.1 *celebration*; 490.4 *pleasurable things*; 21.7 *show*
carnival-like 654.17 *festive*
Carnivora 71.8 *flesh-eating mammal*
carnivore 557.18 *eater*; 71.8 *flesh-eating mammal*; 70.4 *type of animal*
carnivorous **71.28**; 557.26 *eating*; 70.15 *of animals*; 77.14 *of plants*
carnivorously **557.28**
carnivorousness 557.5 *eating habit*
Carnot cycle 38.13 *engine cycle*; 28.38 *thermodynamics*
carol 10.8 *hymn*; 18.39, 515.5, 516.10 *sing*; 516.2 *song*
carolling 515.8 *singing*
carom **65.4**; 65.2 *billiards play*; 65.4 *carom*; 331.12 *collision*; 65.8 *play billiards*
carom count 65.4 *carom*
carom into 331.2 *collide*
carom score 65.4 *carom*
caron 5.36 *accent*
carotene 536.2 *orangeness*; 33.18 *pigment*; 84.3 *plant body*
carotenoid 33.18 *pigment*; 33.20 *terpene*
carousal 601.1 *celebration*; 686.2 *dissipation*
carouse 690.8 *get drunk*; 557.24 *have a meal*; 686.11 *overindulge*; 600.5 *rejoice*
carouser 690.17 *drunkard*
carousing 690.5 *drunken*
carp 606.7 *be dissatisfied*; 626.11 *be irritable*; 55.5 *British game fish*; 264.23 *cause difficulties*; 264.24 *create difficulties*; 670.18 *find fault*; 25.17 *freshwater fish*
car papers 744.2 *certificate*
car park 318.2 *passing along*
carp at 670.18 *find fault*
carpe diem 282.5 *be present*; 287.5 *take the opportunity*
carpel 78.3 *flower part*

carpenter 23.13; **23.17**; 578.2 *artisan*; 308.3 *person who opens*
carpenter's term 23.10
carpentry 23.8 *woodwork*
carper 606.3 *dissatisfied person*
carpet 175.1 *base*; 670.20 *censure*; 550.24 *coat*; 42.3 *fabric*; 550.9 *floor covering*; 46.4 *stadium*
carpetbag 410.8 *bag*
carpet-beater 331.15 *ram*
carpet-bomb 381.3 *bomb*
carpet bombing 381.13 *air attack*; 585.8 *warfare*
carpeting 670.7 *blame*; 42.3 *fabric*; 550.9 *floor covering*
carpetlayer 550.17 *coverer*
carpet sweeper 256.10 *cleaning object*
car phone 504.9 *audio device*; 692.16 *transmitter*
carping 670.6, 670.28 *fault-finding*
carplike 74.13 *fishlike*
carpogonium 84.4 *reproductive body*
car polish 421.10 *polish*
carpophore 83.4 *fungal body*
carport 565.7 *room*
carpospore 84.4 *reproductive body*
carr 92.3 *marsh*
car radio 504.9 *audio device*; 692.18 *radio*
carriage 320.9 *animal transport*; 631.1 *conduct*; 525.3 *external appearance*; 300.12 *gait*; 316.5 *means of transport*; 321.6 *rolling stock*; 319.1 *transport*; 316.2 *transportation*
carriageable 316.17 *transferable*
carriage clock 281.6 *clock*
carriage horse 59.2 *thoroughbred*
carriage return 40.19 *computing terms*
carriageway 320.3; 317.3 *road*
carried away 477.10 *imaginative*
carried forward 789.11 *accounted*
carried over 215.10 *surplus*
carrier 32.17 *analysis*; 631.10 *conductor*; 260.6 *infection*; 320.5 *pack*; 692.14 *radio transmission*; 316.7 *transferor*; 319.3 *transporter*
carrier bag 410.8 *bag*; 316.10 *transferred thing*
carrier pigeon 316.8 *messenger*
carrier transmission 692.14 *radio transmission*
carrion 582.11 *dead person*; 258.4 *dirt*; 375.1 *disintegration*; 238.6 *refuse*; 258.8 *unclean*
carronade 587.12 *historical guns*
carrot 480.3, 480.8 *incentive*; 536.3 *orange thing*; 483.5 *positive stimulus*
carrot and stick 386.3 *coercive methods*; 480.8 *incentive*; 483.3 *stimulus*
carrot cake 25.36 *cake*
carrot fly 44.12 *pests and diseases*
carrot-top 535.7 *red thing*
carroty 536.1 *orange*; 535.3 *red-haired*
carry 27.91, 211.6 *add*; 381.9 *attack successfully*; 504.16 *be heard*; 123.7 *be important*; 246.9 *be victorious*; 631.15 *conduct*; 691.10 *drug oneself*; 413.14 *give moral support*; 56.3 *golf shots*; 145.7 *reach*; 561.10 *reproduce oneself*; 778.1 *sell*; 413.11 *support*; 316.12, 319.4 *transport*; 316.2 *transportation*
carry across 318.11 *cross*
carry a date 281.15 *chronologize*; 275.17 *date*
carryall 410.8 *bag*; 410.9 *baggage*
carry all before one 246.10 *defeat heavily*; 265.17 *do easily*
carry a point 246.11 *overmaster*
carry a protest sign 742.9 *use signs*
carry away 357.9 *demolish*; 593.28 *win the love of*
carry clout 395.8 *influence*
carry coals to Newcastle 219.5 *be superfluous*; 238.9 *waste effort*
carry conviction 698.33 *seem lifelike*
carrycot 320.8 *baby carriage*
carry forward 789.7 *account*
carrying 691.2 *drug pushing*; 504.14 *hearable*; 507.6 *loud*; 510.6 *resonant*
carrying force 346.12 *operative*
carrying the puck 58.3 *ice hockey*
carrying too far 727.3 *extravagance*
carry into effect 348.4 *be an instrument*
Carry Nation 795.6 *moralist*
carry no weight 124.11 *be unimportant*
carry off 246.6 *be successful*; 774.13 *kidnap*; 316.15, 773.10 *take away*
carry off the laurels 121.8 *be superior*
carry on 633.14; 340.4 *act*; 624.11 *be angry*; 631.13 *behave badly*; 631.14 *behave towards*; 804.16 *be wicked*; 132.14 *continue*; 134.8 *go on!*; 554.16 *live*; 640.7 *maintain*; 579.1 *manage*; 134.4 *protract*
carry on a conversation 734.9 *converse*
carry on a vendetta 751.6 *argue*
carry on bag 410.9 *baggage*
carry one's bat 134.4 *protract*
carry oneself 631.11 *conduct oneself*
carry one's liquor 689.3 *be sober*
carry one's point 483.9 *motivate*; 480.15 *persuade*
carry on regardless 615.5 *be rash*
carry on the line 561.13 *propagate*
carry out 340.4 *act*; 348.4 *be an instrument*; 631.14 *behave towards*; 232.4 *complete*; 230.5 *perfect*; 356.10 *produce*; 217.4 *suffice*; 354.1 *undertake*
carry out goals 579.1 *manage*
carry out one's duty 810.16 *do one's duty*
carry out orders 663.5 *obey*
carry over 789.7 *account*; 211.6 *add*
carry-over 211.3 *additional item*; 215.3 *difference*
carry sail 323.9 *navigate*
carry shoulder high 601.18 *salute*; 667.18 *show respect*
carry the can 670.24 *be open to criticism*
carry the day 121.8 *be superior*; 246.9 *be victorious*
carry the puck 58.9 *play hockey*
carry through 340.4 *act*; 348.4 *be an instrument*; 631.14 *behave towards*; 638.6 *be resolute*; 204.10, 232.4 *complete*; 243.7 *develop*; 640.9 *endure*
carry to 145.7 *reach*
carry too far 727.9 *be extravagant*
carry weight 414.12 *be heavy*; 123.7 *be important*; 395.8 *influence*
carry with one 483.9 *motivate*; 480.15 *persuade*
carsick 371.30 *vomiting*
carsickness 320.21 *miscellaneous motoring terms*
car silencer 550.12 *protective covering*
cart 410.10; 320.7 *handcart*; 316.12, 319.4 *transport*; 320.20 *truck*
cartage 319.1 *transport*; 316.2 *transportation*
cart away 316.15 *take away*
carte 220.4 *bill*
carte blanche 250.6 *liberality*; 757.1 *permission*
cartel 750.2, 755.3 *alliance*; 376.15, 747.7 *association*; 13.6 *economic factors*; 251.2 *economic restraint*; 166.2 *limiting factor*
car telephone 692.9 *telephone*
carter 316.7 *transferor*
Cartesian 4.11 *follower of a doctrine*; 4.14 *of a philosophy*
Cartesian coordinates 27.33 *coordinates*
Cartesianism 4.7 *school of thought*
Cartesian space 27.35 *space*
cart grease 268.5 *lubricant*
car theft 774.3 *theft*
car thief 16.40 *lawbreaker*
carthorse 320.9 *animal transport*; 59.2 *thoroughbred*
cartilage 418.7 *hard substance*; 403.7 *skeleton*; 416.4 *solid body*; 423.7 *tough thing*
cartilaginous 418.1, 423.3 *hard*
cartilaginous fish 74.2 *fish*
carting 319.1 *transport*
cartogram 717.7 *map*
cartographer 26.9 *measurer*; 717.4 *person who makes a representation*
cartographic 26.12 *metrical*
cartographical 142.8 *locational*
cartographically 26.17 *measurably*; 142.13 *topographically*
cartography 163.4, 717.7 *map*; 26.1 *measurement*; 142.5 *topography*
cartomancy 475.2 *divination*
carton 410.6 *box*; 203.3 *container*; 496.7 *tobacco*
cartoon 621.2 *act of derision*; 19.20 *draw*; 19.9 *drawing*; 599.4 *entertainment*; 163.1 *outline*; 717.2 *reproduction*
cartoonist 19.16 *artist*; 621.3 *derider*; 599.6 *humorist*; 717.4 *person who makes a representation*
cartouche 587.13 *ammunition*
cartridge 587.13 *ammunition*; 41.9 *film*; 40.7 *peripheral*
cartridge belt 587.13 *ammunition*; 587.4 *arsenal*
cartridge case 587.13 *ammunition*
cartridge clip 587.13 *ammunition*
cartridge paper 435.3 *paper*
cartulary 744.6 *record book*
cartwheel 57.8 *floor exercises*; 192.1 *inversion*; 192.3 *invert*; 307.6 *rotator*
cartwheel penny 780.10 *former British money*
carve 569.15 *be hospitable*; 553.9 *fashion*; 160.7 *form*; 744.14 *inscribe*; 717.11 *paint*; 356.10 *produce*; 19.21 *sculpt*; 372.9 *separate*; 425.16 *use a sharp tool*; 23.18 *work wood*
carved 160.9 *formed*; 19.28 *sculpted*; 23.15 *woodcrafted*
carved turn 68.4 *skiing technique*
carvel-built 50.10 *sailing*
carvel-built hull 50.3 *parts of a sailing boat*
carve letters 5.47 *word*
carve one's way 302.7 *make one's way*
carver 578.2 *artisan*; 23.13 *carpenter*; 425.10 *knife*; 19.17 *sculptor*
carver chair 23.2 *chair*
carvery 557.15 *eating place*
carve up 770.4 *allot*; 491.11 *inflict pain*; 372.9 *separate*
carving 19.12 *sculpture*; 23.8 *woodwork*
carving knife 557.16 *eating utensil*; 425.10 *knife*
carvone 33.20 *terpene*
car wash 256.7 *washer*
caryatid 19.12 *sculpture*; 413.2 *supporting part*
caryopsis 80.2 *botanical fruit*
Casanova 363.6 *charmer*; 700.15 *deceiver*; 699.17 *false person*; 796.8 *immoral man*; 567.7 *libertine*; 593.9 *lover*; 480.13 *tempter*
cascade 90.2 *channel*; 305.3 *downflow*; 305.13 *drip*; 90.7 *flow*
Cascade Range 89.4 *US mountains*
cascara 394.6 *purgative*
case 5.31; 715.1 *accusation*; 410.6 *box*; 550.13 *casing*; 143.2 *circumstances*; 203.3 *container*; 118.10 *eccentric*; 368.5 *inset*; 447.2 *issue*; 701.3 *line of argument*; 16.5 *litigation*; 20.9 *miscellaneous architectural features*; 222.2 *occurrence*; 35.18 *patient*; 260.19 *sick person*; 5.30 *syntax*; 344.6 *undertaking*; 550.25 *wrap*
case dismissed 16.42 *acquittal*
case for decision 16.5 *litigation*
case for the prosecution 715.1 *accusation*
case grammar 5.29 *grammar*
case-harden 32.30 *extract*; 632.18 *habituate*; 418.9 *harden*; 423.11 *make tough*; 336.8 *strengthen*
case-hardened 418.3 *hardened*; 418.4 *mentally hard*; 423.5 *mentally tough*; 423.2 *toughened*; 641.3 *unyielding*
case history 3.5 *chronicle*; 721.1 *description*; 716.6 *documentation*; 35.6 *health care*; 744.1 *record*
casein 33.9 *protein*
case law 16.7 *legal trial*
casemate 384.11 *fortification*
casement 403.4 *framework*; 20.9 *miscellaneous architectural features*
case notes 3.5 *chronicle*
case of need 135.3 *needfulness*
case record 16.7 *legal trial*
case shot 587.14 *historical ammunition*
cash 780.2; 780.26 *bank*; 352.4 *financial resources*; 781.6 *money*; 483.5 *positive stimulus*; 759.3 *something in exchange*
cash account 789.1 *accounts*
cash a cheque 780.26 *bank*
cash and carry 777.14 *buying*; 793.7 *discounter*; 779.8 *store*
cashback 791.1 *discount*
cash bank 780.6 *funds*
cashbook 789.5 *account book*; 744.6 *record book*
cash box 780.20 *money store*
cash budget 789.2 *budgeting*
cash cow 781.5 *wealth*
cash crop 43.12 *crop*; 765.6 *yield*
cash desk 780.21 *till*
cash dispenser 780.21 *till*
cash down 785.21
cash flow 352.4 *financial resources*; 780.6 *funds*; 436.1 *provision*
cash-flow crisis 786.5 *insolvency*
cash-flow problems 249.2 *economic adversity*
cashier 789.6 *accountant*; 367.4 *debase*; 371.3 *disbar*; 780.17 *financier*; 785.5 *payer*; 814.1 *punish*; 708.15 *terminate*; 780.18 *treasurer*
cashiering 371.18 *dismissal*
cashier's cheque 780.14 *paper money*
cash in on 349.3 *exploit*; 244.2 *get better*; 765.14 *profit*; 287.5 *take the opportunity*
cash in one's chips 582.15 *die*
cashmere 193.4 *textile*
cashmere sweater 551.13 *sweater*
cash on delivery 777.14 *buying*; 785.21 *cash down*; 785.1 *payment*; 692.2 *postal communication*
cash payment 785.1 *payment*
cash-poor 766.17 *unprofitable*
cash prize 813.2 *prize*
cash purchase 777.7 *purchasing*
cash register 27.67 *calculator*; 210.5 *computer*; 744.10 *recording instrument*; 780.21 *till*
cash supplies 780.6 *funds*
cash transaction 14.1, 780.7 *finance*
casing 550.13; 550.1 *covering*
cask 410.11 *vessel*
casket 410.6 *box*; 583.4 *funeral objects*
Caslon type 5.15 *type style*
Caspian Sea 88.5 *other major lakes*
casque 384.7 *armour*
Cassandra 611.3 *hopeless person*; 475.8 *oracle*; 711.4 *warner*
Cassegrain telescope 29.24 *telescope*
casserole 25.55 *cook*; 25.6 *kitchen equipment*; 25.32 *meat dish*; 410.15 *pot*
casseroling 25.8 *cooking technique*
cassette 504.9 *audio device*; 41.9 *film*; 40.7 *peripheral*; 744.7 *recording*
cassette recorder 504.9 *audio device*; 744.10 *recording instrument*
cassette tape 744.7 *recording*
cassia 496.5 *herbs*
cassis 558.7 *alcoholic drink*
cassock 551.16 *robe*; 7.11 *vestment*
cassone 23.5 *cabinet*
cassoulet 25.45 *French dish*
cassowary 72.2 *flightless bird*
cast 21.25; **560.23**; 55.7 *angle*; 55.8 *angling*; 560.12 *dead tissue*; 21.38 *dramatize*; 553.9 *fashion*; 160.7 *form*; 30.43 *fossil*; 529.3 *hue*; 24.11 *make ceramics*; 550.6 *medical covering*; 160.6 *nature*; 717.11 *paint*; 566.7 *person*; 578.4 *personnel*; 519.2 *poor sight*; 356.10 *produce*; 160.2 *prototype*; 19.21 *sculpt*; 19.12 *sculpture*; 377.17 *sow*; 394.10 *surgical dressing*; 376.12 *team*; 229.1 *tendency*; 330.5, 330.23, 331.4 *throw*; 137.4 *type*; 165.4 *wrapper*
cast about for 633.8 *pursue*
cast a contrary vote 709.6 *dissent*
cast adrift 372.13 *diverge*
cast a horoscope 475.12 *divine*
cast a long shadow 123.7 *be important*
cast a lure 55.7 *angle*
cast an account 789.7 *account*
cast a nativity 475.12 *divine*
cast anchor 323.10 *sail*
cast a negative vote 470.1 *reject*
cast a shadow 524.10 *make dim*
cast a shadow before 283.7 *be in the future*
cast a shadow over 523.14 *make dark*
cast a slur 812.4 *bring into disrepute*
cast a slur on 678.13 *vilify*
cast a spell upon 594.15 *curse*
cast aspersions on 381.10 *criticize*; 678.13 *vilify*
cast a vote 469.5 *vote*
castaway 355.4 *deserter*; 355.5 *relinquished*; 655.6 *unsocial person*
cast away 214.4 *decrease*; 767.9 *dispose of*; 215.8 *leave*
cast bait 55.7 *angle*
cast bones 283.9 *look ahead*
cast doubt 451.9 *cause disbelief*
cast doubt upon 705.20 *doubt*
cast down 367.21 *degraded*; 367.22 *overthrown*; 367.6 *throw down*
caste 654.7 *human society*; 209.2 *rank*; 137.5 *social class*; 76.4 *social insect*
castellated 384.30 *defended*
caste mark 743.3 *means of identification*
caster 19.17 *sculptor*
caster of nativities 475.9 *forecaster*
caster sugar 25.7 *basic ingredient*; 498.2 *sweetener*
cast forth 371.14 *let out*
castigate 670.20 *censure*; 481.1 *dissuade*; 814.1 *punish*

castigated 670.34 *censured*; 814.20 *punished*
castigation 670.7 *blame*; 483.4 *negative stimulus*; 814.7 *punishment*
castigator 670.11 *disapprover*; 814.17 *punisher*
castigatory 670.30 *censuring*; 814.19 *punitive*
Castilian Spring 17.13 *poetic genius*
casting 55.1, 55.8 *angling*; 633.2 *chase*; 377.1 *dispersion*; 21.14, 356.1 *production*; 19.12 *sculpture*; 330.3 *throwing*
casting a shadow 523.9 *darkening*
casting lots 475.2 *divination*
casting nativities 475.2 *divination*
casting rod 55.3 *fishing tackle*; 633.3 *hunting and fishing equipment*
casting vote 120.1 *inequality*; 395.1 *influence*
cast iron 38.25 *construction material*; 638.16 *fortitude*; 418.7 *hard substance*
cast-iron 638.3 *strong-willed*
castle 20.3 *building*; 69.4 *chess terms*; 356.8 *construction*; 759.5 *exchange*; 384.12 *fort*; 565.4 *official residence*; 69.10 *play*; 440.1 *property*; 316.11 *transfer*
castle in Spain 337.5 *weak thing*
castle in the air 446.6 *ideal*; 96.2 *illusion*; 105.4 *improbability*; 337.5 *weak thing*
castles in Spain 610.3 *aspiration*; 474.2 *expectations*; 477.7 *idealism*; 467.2 *overestimate*
castles in the air 472.3 *absent-mindedness*; 610.3 *aspiration*; 474.2 *expectations*; 477.7 *idealism*; 467.2 *overestimate*
castles in the sand 477.7 *idealism*
Castle walk 22.2 *dance*
castling 69.4 *chess terms*; 759.1 *exchange*
cast list 220.6 *list of names*
cast loose 391.4 *liberate*
cast lots 475.12 *divine*
cast nativities 11.23 *divine*
cast off 214.4 *decrease*; 767.9 *dispose of*; 371.10 *exterminate*; 215.8 *leave*; 323.9 *navigate*; 552.16 *peel*; 355.1 *relinquish*; 50.15 *sail*; 313.5 *set out*; 350.6 *stop using*; 372.17 *unjoined*
cast-off **560.32**; 258.4 *dirt*; 350.4 *disused*; 238.6 *refuse*; 355.5 *relinquished*; 215.9 *remaining*; 349.9 *used*
castoffs 767.3 *disposable things*; 551.1 *dress*; 215.2 *residue*; 350.11 *unused thing*
cast-off skin 258.4 *dirt*
cast of mind 229.2 *attitude*; 595.2 *inclination*
cast of thousands 21.25 *cast*
cast one's ballot 469.5 *vote*
cast one's eye over 518.14 *inspect*
cast one's eyes backwards 284.15 *look back*
cast one's net 633.11 *hunt*
Castor and Pollux 569.7 *famous friendships*; 198.6 *twins*
castor oil 394.6 *purgative*
cast out 470.2 *discard*; 767.9 *dispose of*; 128.8 *eject*; 371.1 *expel*; 655.13 *ignore*; 371.14 *let out*; 470.10 *rejected*; 144.16 *replace*; 372.17 *unjoined*
cast overboard 767.9 *dispose of*
cast pearls before swine 357.12 *consume*; 441.1 *waste*
castrametation 585.6 *art of war*
castrate 567.12 *eunuch*; 245.5 *hurt*; 335.9 *make impotent*; 563.8 *make infertile*; 238.8 *make useless*; 43.18 *practise livestock farming*; 212.4 *take off*
castrated 563.5 *rendered infertile*; 335.13 *unsexed*
castration 563.2 *making infertile*; 372.3 *separateness*; 212.1 *subtraction*
castration complex 36.18 *complex*
castrato 567.12 *eunuch*; 18.32 *instrumental*
cast spells 11.21 *bewitch*
cast steel 38.25 *construction material*
cast the deciding vote 120.5 *be unequal*
cast the die 107.12 *take a chance*
cast the I Ching 11.23 *divine*
cast vote 469.10 *vote*
casual 263.4 *at ease*; 107.8 *chance*; 666.5 *indifferent*; 250.13, 657.7 *informal*; 472.11 *perfunctory*; 551.31 *styled*
casual clothes 551.4, 657.6 *informal dress*
casual dress 657.6 *informal dress*
casual labour 13.8 *industrial relations*; 578.4 *personnel*
casual labourer 578.1 *worker*
casually **657.13**; 107.13 *by chance*; 551.36 *dressily*; 250.22 *informally*; 552.17 *nakedly*; 263.6 *with ease*
casually dressed 552.10 *in dishabille*
casualness 107.1 *chance*; 551.2 *dressing*; 666.2 *indifference*; 250.4, 657.1 *informality*
casual relationship 108.1 *relatedness*
casuals 551.19 *footwear*
casual suggestion 476.1 *supposition*
casualties 582.12 *death count*
casualty 249.1 *adversity*; 798.2 *affliction*; 582.11 *dead person*
casualty list 582.12 *death count*
casualty station 394.14 *hospital*
casual water 56.1 *golf*
casuist 444.6 *arguer*; 645.3 *cunning person*; 702.6 *sophist*
casuistic 702.7 *sophistic*; 699.32 *spurious*
casuistically 702.14 *sophistically*
casuistry 4.6 *branch of philosophy*; 702.1 *sophistry*; 699.4 *spuriousness*
casus belli 751.1 *disagreement*
CAT 40.1 *computing*
cat **71.10**; 518.2 *eye*; 512.3 *hisser*; 814.14 *instrument of punishment*; 625.3 *irascible person*; 18.24 *musician*; 371.15 *vomit*
catabolic 33.26 *biochemical*; 375.6 *disintegrating*; 34.22 *physiological*
catabolically 33.27 *biochemically*; 375.7 *to pieces*
catabolism 375.2 *deconstruction*; 33.21 *metabolism*; 34.5 *physiology*
catachresis 274.11 *grammatical error*; 720.2 *misinterpretation*
catachrestic 720.3 *misinterpreted*
cataclasis 30.32 *metamorphism*
cataclysm 380.3 *instance of violence*; 90.6 *river flow*; 357.4 *ruin*
cataclysmic 357.14 *destructive*; 380.6 *violent*
cataclysmically 90.13 *fluently*
cataclysmic variable 29.12 *variable star*
catacomb 583.5 *cemetery*; 156.4 *deep thing*
catadioptric lens 41.17 *lens*
catadioptric system 28.30 *lens system*
catafalque 583.4 *funeral objects*
catalectic 17.20 *metrical*
catalepsy 592.4 *desensitization*; 301.1 *motionlessness*; 380.3 *instance of violence*; 343.9 *sleep*; 327.8 *spasm*; 36.14 *trance*
cataleptic 327.19 *convulsive*; 301.5 *sedentary*
catalexis 17.9 *metre*
catalogue **409.7**; 789.8 *audit*; 409.15 *categorize*; 137.13 *class*; 406.5 *divisions*; 743.10 *identify*; 406.9 *itemize*; 220.8 *list*; 744.13 *record*; 744.6 *record book*; 693.5 *reference book*; 407.19 *systematize*; 220.2 *table*
catalogue buying 777.8 *shopping*
catalogued 409.24 *categorized*; 407.11 *grouped*; 743.12 *identified*; 406.12 *itemized*; 220.11 *listed*
cataloguing 409.5 *categorization*; 407.2 *grouping*; 743.1 *identification*; 220.7 *listing*; 744.8 *registration*
catalyse 375.4 *deconstruct*; 33.25 *metabolize*; 32.26 *react*
catalysis **32.15**; 32.1 *chemistry*; 375.2 *deconstruction*
catalyst 32.15 *catalysis*; 224.5 *changer*; 348.2 *instrument*
catalytic **32.39**; 32.31 *chemical*
catalytic agent 224.5 *changer*
catalytically 32.46 *chemically*; 375.7 *to pieces*
catalytic converter 224.5 *changer*
catamaran 50.6 *canoeing*; 198.2 *double*; 50.2 *sailing boat*
catamenia 560.11 *menstruation*
catamenial 560.31 *menstrual*
catamenial discharge 560.11 *menstruation*
catamite 796.8 *immoral man*
cat among the pigeons 378.2 *obstacle*
cat and mouse 113.3 *opposites*
cataplasm 394.10 *surgical dressing*
cataplexy 36.14 *trance*
catapult 357.7 *agent of destruction*; 422.3 *elastic thing*; 330.9 *firearm*; 587.6 *historical missile weapon*; 330.23, 331.4 *throw*
cataract 519.1 *blindness*; 90.2 *channel*; 305.3 *downflow*; 524.2 *murk*
catarrh 260.1 *ill health*; 260.9 *respiratory disease*; 560.9 *saliva*
catarrhine 151.4 *narrow-leaved*
catastrophe 249.1 *adversity*; 798.2 *affliction*; 739.1 *disclosure*; 131.10 *ending*; 357.4 *ruin*; 21.8 *scene*
catastrophic 357.14 *destructive*; 798.9 *detrimental*; 131.20 *ending*; 380.6 *violent*
catastrophically 357.16 *destructively*
catastrophism 34.16 *evolution*
catatonia 592.4 *desensitization*; 335.4 *disability*; 301.1 *motionlessness*; 463.1 *oblivion*; 36.11, 461.5 *psychosis*
catatonic 335.12 *impotent*; 461.13 *mentally ill*; 463.8 *oblivious*; 301.5 *sedentary*; 489.8 *unconscious*
catatonic fit 335.4 *disability*
catatonic stupor 36.13 *depression*
catatonic trance 36.14 *trance*
cat burglar 774.8 *thief*
catcall **512.2**; **512.5**; 507.8 *be loud*; 513.6 *be shrill*; 514.7 *cry of disapproval*; 742.3 *gesture*; 753.3 *gesture of protest*; 514.14 *hiss*; 670.23 *show disapproval*; 670.9 *show of disapproval*; 513.3 *shrillness*; 668.6, 668.25 *taunt*
catcalling **512.7**; 668.15 *taunting*
catch **755.6**; 765.11 *acquire*; 765.3 *acquisition*; 55.1 *angling*; 260.24 *be unhealthy*; 123.4 *bigwig*; 226.8 *cause to cease*; 633.2 *chase*; 231.7 *defect*; 360.7 *detain*; 449.2 *detect*; 449.7 *detection*; 705.4 *difficult question*; 53.19 *dismiss*; 53.11 *dismissal*; 373.8 *fastening*; 74.7 *fishing*; 365.15 *grind*; 504.15 *hear*; 633.11 *hunt*; 593.9 *lover*; 301.9 *make motionless*; 617.5 *object of desire*; 378.2 *obstacle*; 717.9 *represent*; 309.3 *restrainer*; 50.16 *row*; 50.4 *rowing*; 64.3 *rugby play*; 264.8 *snag*; 700.33 *snare*; 46.12 *special team*; 645.2 *stratagem*; 773.5 *takings*; 492.11 *touch*; 379.1, 379.2 *trap*; 700.8, 700.28 *trick*; 593.28 *win the love of*
catch-22 222.4 *difficult circumstances*; 705.4 *difficult question*; 611.2 *hopeless situation*; 378.2 *obstacle*; 264.5 *predicament*; 379.1 *trap*
catch a crab 486.7 *be clumsy*; 50.16 *row*
catch a fly 48.7 *play baseball*
catch a glimpse of 449.1 *discover*; 518.12 *see*
catch a likeness 721.14 *describe*; 717.9 *represent*
catch-all 138.3 *nonspecificness*
catch an infection 260.24 *be unhealthy*
catch a packet 264.21 *get into trouble*
catch-as-catch-can 353.5 *attempt*; 107.8 *chance*; 478.1 *improvised*; 250.12 *unconditional*; 52.15 *wrestling*
catch-as-catch-can wrestling 52.5 *wrestling*
catch at 636.13 *be willing*
catch a Tartar 486.5 *be unskilful*
catch a whiff of 500.7 *smell*
catch cold 494.10 *be cold*
catch crop 43.12 *crop*
catcher 48.2 *baseball player*
catcher's box 48.1 *baseball*
catcher's glove 48.3 *baseball equipment*
catcher's mask 48.3 *baseball equipment*
catcher's mitt 48.3 *baseball equipment*
catcher's sign 48.4 *pitching terms*
catch exactly 717.9 *represent*
catch fire 493.15 *burn*
catch fish 55.7 *angle*
catch in a run-down 48.7 *play baseball*
catching 395.12 *appealing*; 449.7 *detection*
catching a crab 50.4 *rowing*
catching glove 58.3 *ice hockey*
catching the eye 738.14 *manifest*
catch in the act 449.2 *detect*
catch it 814.6 *be punished*; 264.21 *get into trouble*
catchment area 30.8 *drainage*
catch napping 293.9 *prepare*; 630.9 *surprise*
catch off-guard 630.9 *surprise*
catch on 395.10 *be a prevailing influence*; 632.17 *become a habit*; 449.3 *find out*; 455.11 *know*; 695.6 *understand*
catch one's death 582.16 *meet one's fate*
catch oneself doing 632.18 *habituate*
catch one's eye 185.8 *protrude*
catch out 630.9 *surprise*; 379.2 *trap*
catchpenny 793.9 *cheap*; 124.4 *trivial*
catchphrase 5.21 *catchword*; 745.1 *maxim*; 509.7 *repeated word*
catch points 321.3 *rail*
catchpoll 16.11 *British law officer*
catch red-handed 449.2 *detect*; 630.9 *surprise*
catch sight of 518.12 *see*
catch some Zs 263.2 *take it easy*
catch the bug 483.8 *be motivated*; 480.18 *be persuaded*
catch the drift of 695.6 *understand*
catch the eye 518.19 *be visible*
catch the eye of 471.13 *attract attention*
catch the wind 103.10 *attempt the impossible*
catch unawares 630.9 *surprise*; 379.2 *trap*
catch up 332.6 *accelerate*; 262.8 *hurry up!*; 262.2 *make haste*
catch-waist 68.13 *ice-skating*
catch-waist camel spin 68.6 *ice-skating*
catchword **5.21**; 745.1 *maxim*; 509.7 *repeated word*; 742.6 *word*
catchy 18.30 *harmonic*; 516.6 *melodious*
cat-cracking reforming 32.22 *industrial chemistry*
catechism 705.3 *questionnaire*; 450.2 *religious belief*
catechismic 705.13 *problematic*
catechization 6.1 *education*
catechize 705.17 *question*
catecholamine 33.16 *hormone*
catechumen 760.6 *convert*; 7.3 *religious person*
categorical **409.25**; 137.10 *classificatory*; 405.6 *component*; 707.16 *definite*; 726.3 *emphatic*; 407.11 *grouped*; 810.12 *obligatory*
categorical imperative 4.9 *philosophical problem*
categorically 707.23 *affirmatively*; 4.24 *philosophically*; 137.16 *taxonomically*
categoricalness 707.8 *definiteness*
categorical proposition 4.8 *philosophical term*
categorization **409.5**; 137.1 *classification*; 407.2 *grouping*; 743.1 *identification*
categorize **409.15**; 137.13 *class*; 743.10 *identify*; 407.19 *systematize*
categorize as 127.6 *subsume*
categorized **409.24**; 137.12 *classed*; 407.11 *grouped*; 743.12 *identified*
category **409.6**; 216.4 *average*; 137.2 *class*; 205.1 *part*; 405.2 *piece*; 407.4 *position*; 221.1 *state*
category mistake 4.9 *philosophical problem*
catenary 132.9 *consecutive*; 27.40 *curve*; 305.2 *sinkage*
catenary arch 20.5 *arch*
catenate 132.15 *concatenate*
catenation 132.2 *consecution*
cater 557.25 *provide food*; 436.5 *provision*
cateran 586.9 *guerrilla*
cater-cornered 189.4 *oblique*; 189.8 *obliquely*
catered 436.8 *provisional*
catered affair 436.1 *provision*
caterer **436.4**; 25.2 *cook*; 557.20 *food provider*
cater for 664.11 *pander to*; 392.25 *serve*
catering 25.1 *cookery*; 436.1 *provision*; 436.7 *provisioning*
caterpillar 76.5 *larva*; 44.12 *pests and diseases*; 75.6 *worm*; 555.4 *young animal*
cater to 778.1 *sell*
caterwaul 507.8 *be loud*; 514.1, 515.4 *cry*; 514.10 *cry out*
caterwauling 517.2 *dissonant noise*; 593.15 *love item*
catfish 25.17 *freshwater fish*
cat-fit 624.4 *anger*
cat flea 76.3 *pest*
cat food 557.8 *animal food*
catharsis 17.3 *aspect of fiction*; 560.2 *defecation*; 36.3 *psychiatric treatment*; 393.11 *recuperation*; 371.21 *removal*; 21.11 *tragedy*
cathartic 37.4 *drug type*; 371.29 *expulsive*; 560.25 *faecal*; 255.4, 394.6 *purgative*; 394.17 *remedial*; 37.17 *stimulating*; 21.40 *tragic*
cathartically 371.32 *expulsively*
cathectic energy 36.28 *cathexis*
cathection 36.28 *cathexis*
cathedral 356.8 *construction*; 10.11 *place of worship*
cathedral city 87.4 *British cities*; 86.10 *urban area*
Catherine 752.7 *martyr*
Catherine wheel 522.8 *fire*; 307.6 *rotator*

catheterization 394.13 *therapy*
catheterize 255.10, 256.15 *purify*
cathexis 36.28
cathode 28.43 *electrical conduction;* 334.7 *electrical power;* 32.19 *electrochemistry;* 39.5 *electrolytic conduction;* 39.20 *electron tube*
cathode-ray tube 334.7 *electrical power;* 692.21 *television*
cathodic 32.42 *electrochemical*
Catholic 7.5 *Christian*
catholic 138.15 *general*
catholicism 138.2 *catholicity*
catholicity 138.2; 150.4 *breadth*
catholicize 138.23 *generalize*
catholicon 37.3 *drug;* 394.1 *remedy*
Catholic Roman 7.16 *denominational*
cathouse 796.6 *brothel;* 804.8 *wicked place*
cation 39.5 *electrolytic conduction;* 28.66 *ion*
catkin 78.4 *flower head*
catlike 71.28 *carnivorous*
cat lover 70.10 *animal welfarist*
catnap 263.1 *ease;* 343.9, 343.13 *sleep;* 489.2 *unconsciousness*
cat-o'-nine-tails 814.14 *instrument of punishment*
cat's concert 517.2 *dissonant noise*
cat's cradle 193.2 *braid*
Catseye™ 742.5 *indicator;* 518.8 *reflection*
cat show 738.6 *display*
cat's meow 235.8 *exceller*
cat's nine lives 554.5 *life cycle*
cat's-paw 348.3 *assistant;* 700.22 *dupe;* 664.3 *sycophant*
cat's pyjamas 235.8 *exceller*
catsuit 551.10 *suit*
catsup 25.15 *sauce*
cat's whisker 692.18 *radio*
cat's whiskers 235.8 *exceller*
Cattell's Infant Intelligence Scale 36.6 *intelligence test*
cattery 565.12 *stall*
cattiness 651.4 *bitterness*
cattish 71.28 *carnivorous;* 651.14 *hostile*
cattle 43.8 *livestock*
cattle breeder 43.15 *agriculturist*
cattle cake 557.8 *animal food*
cattleman 43.15 *agriculturist*
cattle raiding 774.1 *stealing*
cattle ranch 43.6 *farm*
cattle rustler 774.8 *thief*
cattle rustling 774.1 *stealing*
cattle thief 774.8 *thief*
cat-train 320.10 *sled*
catty 71.28 *carnivorous;* 678.16 *defamatory;* 651.14 *hostile*
catwalk 38.21, 317.9 *bridge*
Caucasian 1.6 *race;* 1.13 *racial;* 531.1 *white*
Caucasoid 1.13 *racial*
Caucasoid race 1.6 *race*
Caucasus 154.4 *mountain range;* 89.6 *other major mountains and ranges*
caucus 376.5 *conference;* 376.16 *party*
caudal 168.4 *rear*
caudal fin 74.5 *fish anatomy*
caudate 73.7, 73.13 *amphibian*
caudex 77.5 *stem*
caudle 558.7 *alcoholic drink*
caught 593.18 *in love*
caught both ways 254.4 *endangered*
caught in the act 806.5 *guilty*
caught napping 630.6 *surprised*
caught red-handed 806.5 *guilty*
caught unawares 630.6 *surprised*
caul 561.7 *obstetrics*
cauldron 760.4 *medium of conversion;* 410.15 *pot*
caulid 77.5 *stem*
cauliflower cheese 25.34 *vegetarian dish*
cauliflower ear 504.4 *ear*
cauliflower-eared 504.12 *eared*
cauline 77.17 *of stems*
caulis 77.5 *stem*
caulk 393.1 *repair*
causal 344.13; **348.7**; **444.10**; 701.12 *apologetic;* 395.11 *influential;* 132.10 *repercussive*
causal body 11.7 *spirit*
causality 28.81; 344.1 *cause;* 132.4 *repercussion*
causal law 28.81 *causality*
causally 344.14; 701.20 *apologetically;* 395.14 *influentially*
causal relationship 476.2 *basis of supposition*
causal theory of perception 4.9 *philosophical problem*
causation 344.1 *cause;* 480.11 *motive*
causative 344.13 *causal*
causatively 344.14 *causally*
Cause 344
cause 344.1; 348.4 *be an instrument;* 344.9 *be the cause of;* 93.20 *bring into being;* 346.3 *business;* 224.8 *cause change;* 714.2 *defence;* 342.4 *energy;* 444.4 *explanation;* 130.23 *inaugurate;* 395.1 *influence;* 348.1 *instrumentality;* 635.13, 694.12 *intend;* 16.5 *litigation;* 483.9 *motivate;* 480.11, 483.1 *motive;* 480.15 *persuade;* 701.5 *plea;* 356.10 *produce;* 346.9 *take action*
cause a death 249.11 *cause adversity*
cause adversity 249.11
cause an accident 249.11 *cause adversity*
cause anarchy 588.4 *be anarchic;* 753.8 *cause mischief*
cause and effect 28.81 *causality;* 132.4 *repercussion*
cause a sensation 488.13 *arouse sensation*
cause a shambles 357.10 *lay waste*
cause a traffic jam 378.9 *block*
cause célèbre 619.4 *wonder*
cause change 224.8
cause chaos 375.4 *deconstruct;* 161.4 *disorder*
caused 345.10; 701.12 *apologetic;* 483.12 *motivated*
caused by 345.10 *caused*
cause desire 617.15
cause difficulties 264.23
cause disbelief 451.9
cause discontent 604.7 *thwart*
cause dislike 596.7; 620.6 *be boring*
cause disorder 588.4 *be anarchic;* 753.8 *cause mischief*
cause doubt 696.7 *be unintelligible;* 619.10 *be wonderful*
cause for alarm 254.6 *danger signal*
cause friction 378.8 *hinder*
cause grief 249.11 *cause adversity*
cause hate 594.16
cause joy 597.8
causeless 107.9
cause list 16.7 *legal trial*
cause loathing 594.16 *cause hate*
cause mischief 753.8
cause no problems 235.10 *do good*
cause not to exist 94.13
cause of action 480.11 *motive*
cause offence 659.7 *be discourteous*
cause of offence 624.3
cause opposition 347.3 *counteract*
cause panic 711.5 *warn*
cause resentment 625.8 *make irascible*
causerie 734.2 *chat*
cause the downfall of 357.9 *demolish*
cause to abdicate 588.4 *be anarchic*
cause to adhere 267.7
cause to cease 226.8
cause to disappear 526.3
cause to flow 90.8
cause to know 455.14
cause trouble 264.22; 378.9 *block;* 249.11 *cause adversity;* 753.8 *cause mischief;* 379.2 *trap*
causeway 38.21 *bridge;* 317.3, 373.5 *road*
causey 317.4 *road surface*
causing death 382.1 *killing*
caustic 678.16 *defamatory;* 37.4 *drug type;* 651.14 *hostile;* 28.31 *lens element;* 493.10 *on fire;* 624.15 *resentful*
caustically 651.20 *malevolently;* 624.17 *resentfully*
causticity 651.4 *bitterness*
causticness 651.4 *bitterness*
caustic reply 651.4 *bitterness*
cauterization 394.12 *surgery*
cauterize 493.15 *burn;* 394.20 *doctor*
cauterizing 493.9 *hot*
Caution 616
caution 616.1; **616.6**; 693.7, 713.1 *advice;* 713.5 *advise;* 665.1 *carefulness;* 645.1 *cunning;* 481.1 *dissuade;* 481.6 *dissuasion;* 333.12 *hesitation;* 475.5 *omen;* 453.10 *suspicion;* 711.5 *warn;* 711.1 *warning*
cautionary 713.7 *advising;* 481.9 *dissuasive;* 693.16 *informative;* 475.13 *predicting;* 711.8 *warning*
cautionary person 481.8
cautionary tale 721.3 *narration*
cautioned 711.9 *warned*
cautioner 711.4 *warner*
caution light 742.4 *signal*
cautious 616.4; **637.3**; 645.4 *cunning;* 333.6 *hesitant;* 732.2 *sparing with words;* 178.4 *traditional;* 711.9 *warned*
cautiously 616.7; 665.12 *carefully;* 333.16 *slowly*
cautiousness 616.1 *caution;* 333.12 *hesitation*
cautious person 616.3
cavalcade 132.8 *procession*
cavalier 223.7 *attendant;* 586.20 *cavalryman;* 659.5 *discourteous;* 59.15 *horse person;* 593.9 *lover*
cavalry 586.19
cavalry commander 584.5 *military staff*
cavalry horse 59.3 *warhorse*
cavalryman 586.20; 59.15 *horse person*
cavalry regiment 586.16 *army unit;* 586.19 *cavalry;* 59.15 *horse person*
cavalry sword 587.8 *sharp weapon*
cavatate 50.18 *windsurf*
cavatation 50.7 *windsurfing*
cavatina 516.2 *song*
cave 183.2 *concave land;* 305.10 *droop;* 308.5 *hole;* 172.1 *interior;* 565.13 *lair;* 711.10 *look out!;* 62.5 *rock face*
caveat 711.1 *warning*
caveat emptor! 777.18 *buyer beware!*
caveator 711.4 *warner*
cave dweller 296.7 *ancient people;* 566.3 *early human;* 284.6 *people of the past;* 655.6 *unsocial person*
cave in 191.6 *become smaller;* 183.8 *be concave;* 305.10 *droop;* 372.9 *separate;* 388.4 *succumb*
cave-in 191.1 *contraction*
caveman 296.7 *ancient people;* 566.3 *early human;* 567.6 *macho man;* 284.6 *people of the past;* 380.4 *violent creature*
cave painting 19.8 *painting;* 3.11 *relic*
cavern 183.2 *concave land;* 308.5 *hole*
cavernous 183.6 *concave;* 156.8 *deep;* 308.14 *holed;* 141.13 *spacious*
cavernously 308.27; 183.11 *concavely*
cavernousness 156.1 *depth*
cavesson 59.14 *horse-riding terms*
caviar 25.16 *fish dish;* 74.9 *fish product*
cavicorn 71.33 *ungulate*
cavil 606.7 *be dissatisfied;* 670.4 *disagreement;* 701.14 *discuss;* 670.18 *find fault;* 702.13 *quibble;* 702.2 *sophism*
caviller 702.6 *sophist*
cavilling 670.6, 670.28 *fault-finding;* 702.4, 702.9 *quibbling*
caving 305.7 *tunnelling*
caving in 388.1 *submission*
cavity 183.3; 146.2 *crack;* 156.4 *deep thing;* 367.14 *depression;* 308.1 *opening*
cavort 22.15 *dance*
caw 515.2 *bird song;* 513.2 *hoarseness;* 515.5 *sing;* 513.5 *sound hoarse*
cawing 513.8 *hoarse*
cay 92.2 *island*
cayenne 496.5 *herbs*
cayman 73.5 *crocodilian*
cayuse 59.1 *horse*
CBL 40.1 *computing*
CB radio 692.20 *radio broadcasting*
CBS 692.24 *television broadcasting*
C clef 18.20 *key*
CD 744.7 *recording*
CD-ROM 40.6 *memory;* 40.7 *peripheral*
CdS meter 41.18 *exposure time*
CE 275.29 *one day*
cease 131.16; **226.6**; 301.8 *be motionless;* 133.2 *cessation;* 309.9 *close down;* 526.1 *disappear;* 133.12 *discontinue;* 341.4 *not act;* 350.6 *stop using;* 355.2 *withdraw*
ceased 133.9 *discontinued*
cease-fire 294.3 *delayed action;* 749.1 *pacification;* 226.3, 226.9 *pause;* 589.1 *peace*
ceaseless 279.10 *continuing forever;* 132.11 *continuous;* 202.3 *eternal;* 112.14 *recurrent*
ceaseless energy 342.4 *energy*
ceaselessly 640.14 *continually;* 132.19 *continuously*
ceaselessness 640.3 *constancy;* 132.5 *continuity*
cease publication 526.1 *disappear*
cease resistance 388.3 *submit*
cease to be 582.15 *die;* 526.1 *disappear*
cease to exist 94.12; 526.1 *disappear*
cease to live 582.15 *die*
cease to see 521.7 *become invisible*
cease trading 226.7 *stop working*
cease work 313.2 *withdraw*
ceasing 131.2, 133.2, 226.1 *cessation*
cede 754.4 *compromise;* 767.9 *dispose of;* 768.5 *give;* 355.1 *relinquish*
cede to 122.9 *yield to*
cedilla 5.36 *accent;* 742.7 *punctuation*
Ceefax™ 692.25 *broadcast material*
ceil 550.27 *roof*
ceilidh 376.10 *dance;* 22.1 *dancing*
ceiling 174.3 *architectural summit;* 203.2 *certain amount;* 790.3 *fee;* 187.3 *flat thing;* 322.5 *flight;* 154.8 *high thing;* 166.2 *limiting factor;* 550.7 *overhead covering*
ceiling light 522.6 *electric light*
ceiling plaster 550.7 *overhead covering*
ceiling rose 522.6 *electric light*
celadon 538.1 *green*
celadonite 538.10 *green pigment*
cele 566.7 *person*
celebrant 9.5, 10.17 *worshipper*
celebrate 601.15; **656.10**; 462.14 *commemorate;* 597.6 *enjoy;* 658.12 *greet;* 123.8 *make important;* 10.19 *offer worship;* 10.18 *perform rites;* 600.5 *rejoice;* 9.7 *worship*
celebrate a birthday 298.9 *commemorate*
celebrate a marriage 570.16 *join in marriage*
celebrate an anniversary 298.9 *commemorate*
celebrate a victory 246.9 *be victorious*
celebrate Christmas 298.9 *commemorate;* 292.6 *spend the season*
celebrate communion 752.15 *offer worship*
celebrated 575.5 *entitled;* 455.10 *known;* 740.20 *well-known*
celebrate mass 752.15 *offer worship*
celebrate the yuletide 292.6 *spend the season*
celebrating 601.1 *celebration;* 600.1 *rejoicing*
Celebration 601
celebration 601.1; 656.3 *formal occasion;* 597.2 *fun;* 600.1 *rejoicing;* 10.16 *religious festival;* 10.3 *rite of worship;* 376.9 *social gathering;* 246.1 *success;* 9.1 *worship*
celebrative 601.10
celebrator 600.4 *rejoicer*
celebratory 601.10 *celebrative;* 597.4 *happy;* 462.10 *memorial;* 600.9 *rejoicing;* 10.21 *ritualistic*
celebrity 235.8 *exceller;* 9.4 *idolized person;* 121.6 *paragon;* 566.7 *person;* 811.2 *person of repute;* 575.1 *right;* 246.1 *success;* 246.4 *successful person*
celerity 262.4 *haste;* 332.8 *speed*
celery fly 44.12 *pests and diseases*
celery soup 25.13 *soup*
celestial 8.6 *angel;* 29.36 *astronomical;* 8.14 *heavenly;* 101.8 *nonmaterial*
celestial body 29.10 *star*
Celestial City 8.11 *heaven*
celestial equator 29.5 *celestial sphere*
celestial kingdom 8.11 *heaven*
celestial latitude 29.5 *celestial sphere*
celestial longitude 29.5 *celestial sphere*
celestially 29.39 *astronomically;* 8.19 *divinely;* 101.13 *metaphysically*
celestial mechanics 29.1 *astronomy*
celestial navigation 323.5 *navigation*
celestial poles 29.5 *celestial sphere*
celestial sphere 29.5
Celibacy 572
celibacy 572.1; 563.1 *infertility;* 795.3 *moral purity;* 684.1 *self-restraint;* 197.6 *singleness;* 655.1 *unsociability*
celibatarian 572.6 *celibate*
celibate 572.6; 572.4 *celibate person;* 563.3 *infertile;* 655.10 *lonely;* 795.9 *pure;* 795.5 *pure person;* 684.8 *self-restrained;* 197.17 *single*
celibate goddess 572.4 *celibate person*
celibately 572.12
celibate order 572.3 *monasticism*
celibate person 572.4
cell 34.7; 34.23 *cellular;* 309.4 *closed place;* 410.2 *compartment;* 334.7 *electrical power;* 32.19 *electrochemistry;* 39.5 *electrolytic conduction;* 172.2 *inside;* 814.14 *instrument of punishment;* 159.2 *little thing;* 554.2 *living matter;* 376.16 *party;* 10.11 *place of wor-*

ship; 39.29 *power source;* 252.5 *refuge;* 655.5 *solitary place;* 405.3 *unit*
cella 20.9 *miscellaneous architectural features;* 10.13 *shrine*
cellar 523.4 *dark thing;* 175.2 *foot;* 736.2 *hiding place;* 25.3 *kitchen;* 155.4 *low thing;* 565.7 *room;* 439.4 *storage*
cellar door 314.6 *means of entry*
cell biologist 34.19 *life scientist*
cell biology 34.6; 34.1 *life science*
cell cycle 34.10 *cell division*
cell division 34.10
cell membrane 34.7 *cell*
Cellnet™ 504.9 *audio device;* 692.9 *telephone*
cell nucleus 34.9
Cellophane™ 435.3 *paper;* 527.8 *transparent thing;* 165.4 *wrapper;* 550.4 *wrapping*
cell organ 34.8
cellphone 504.9 *audio device;* 692.9 *telephone*
cell physiology 34.6 *cell biology*
cell plate 34.7 *cell*
cell respiration 33.24 *respiration*
cells 402.4 *matter*
cell structure 34.6 *cell biology*
cellular 34.23; 405.7 *modular*
cellular phone 692.9 *telephone;* 692.16 *transmitter*
cellular radio 504.9 *audio device*
cellular slime moulds 83.3 *fungi*
cellular telephone 504.9 *audio device*
cellular tissue 34.7 *cell*
cellule 34.7 *cell*
cellulite 158.8 *fat*
celluloid 435.1 *materials*
cellulose 34.7 *cell;* 435.1 *materials;* 33.4 *polysaccharide*
cellulose fibre 435.3 *paper*
cellulus 34.23 *cellular*
cell wall 34.7 *cell*
Celsius scale 493.2 *heat measurement*
Celt 564.9 *British inhabitant*
Celtic 5.11 *family of languages;* 19.29 *realist*
cement 267.3 *adhesive;* 416.8 *be dense;* 435.2 *building material;* 267.7 *cause to adhere;* 38.25 *construction material;* 418.7 *hard substance;* 24.9 *industrial ceramics;* 30.62 *lithify;* 24.11 *make ceramics;* 38.26 *masonry;* 550.11 *paving;* 317.4 *road surface;* 416.4 *solid body;* 550.29 *surface*
cement a relationship 374.6 *come together*
cementation 267.1 *adhesion;* 30.29 *petrogenesis*
cemented 267.9 *adhesive*
cement kiln 24.6 *ceramic workshop*
cemetery 583.5; 582.8 *after death;* 226.5, 301.3 *resting place*
cenotaph 356.8 *construction;* 583.4 *funeral objects;* 583.6 *grave*
Cenozoic 296.15 *primal*
Cenozoic era 284.3 *geological period*
cense 502.6 *perfume*
censer 502.3 *incense;* 10.14 *sacred object*
censor 399.4; 634.7 *be evasive;* 708.14 *cancel;* 224.8 *cause change;* 736.8 *conceal;* 36.19 *defence mechanism;* 670.11 *disapprover;* 224.6 *editor;* 128.8 *eject;* 245.5 *hurt;* 464.5, 464.11 *judge;* 737.12 *keep secret;* 251.6 *lawmaker;* 166.7 *limit;* 685.4 *moderate;* 795.6 *moralist;* 358.1 *obliterate;* 255.6 *prude;* 255.10, 256.15 *purify;* 251.8 *restrain;* 212.3 *subtract;* 647.6 *suppress*
censored 399.6; 708.20 *cancelled;* 736.14 *concealed;* 795.10 *moralistic;* 358.6 *obliterated;* 251.13 *restraining;* 737.9 *secret;* 647.9 *suppressed*
censorial 634.18 *avoiding;* 251.13 *restraining;* 647.8 *severe;* 251.16 *under restraints*
censoring 251.13 *restraining*
censorious 381.25 *critical;* 670.28 *fault-finding;* 464.8 *judging;* 795.10 *moralistic;* 251.13 *restraining;* 647.8 *severe;* 264.14 *troublesome*
censoriously 670.37 *disapprovingly;* 264.29 *perversely;* 251.16 *under restraints*
censoriousness 670.6 *fault-finding*
censorship 256.4; **399.2**; 708.5 *cancellation;* 128.2 *ejection;* 166.2 *limiting factor;* 358.3 *obliteration;* 255.1 *purity;* 251.1 *restraint;* 737.1 *secrecy;* 795.4 *self-righteousness;* 736.4 *silence;* 647.2 *suppression;* 585.7 *war measures*
censurable 806.5 *guilty*
censure 670.20; 670.7 *blame;* 381.10 *criticize;* 606.1 *dissatisfaction;* 806.1 *guilt;* 464.11 *judge;* 464.1 *judgment;* 381.16 *personal attack*
censured 670.34; 806.5 *guilty*
censurer 670.11 *disapprover*
censuring 670.30
census 210.3 *count;* 220.6 *list of names;* 27.12 *numeration;* 705.3 *questionnaire*
census-taker 210.6 *calculator*
cent 780.8 *American money;* 124.8 *trifle*
centaur 70.7 *legendary beast*
centenarian 201.20 *hundredth;* 556.7 *older person;* 201.9 *treble figures*
centenary 298.3, 298.13, 601.5 *anniversary;* 462.5 *day to remember;* 201.20 *hundredth;* 201.9 *treble figures*
centennial 601.14; 201.20 *hundredth;* 201.9 *treble figures*
centennially 298.16 *cyclically;* 201.24 *fivefold*
centennium 201.9 *treble figures*
centering 20.9 *miscellaneous architectural features*
centesimal 201.20 *hundredth*
centigrade 201.9 *treble figures*
centigrade scale 493.2 *heat measurement*
centime 780.4 *change*
centimetre 148.7 *measure of length;* 201.9 *treble figures*
centipede 201.9 *treble figures*
cento 17.7 *poem*
central 173.6; 121.14 *best;* 344.13, 348.7 *causal;* 27.81 *curvilinear;* 447.7 *focused;* 123.5 *important;* 172.9 *inland;* 172.7 *interior;* 216.2 *medium*
Central American dish 25.50
central body 34.8 *cell organ*
central business district 86.10 *urban area*
central casting 21.23 *role*
central city 87.7 *city district*
Central Criminal Court 16.20 *British court*
Central Daylight Time 275.9 *time zone*
Central European Time 275.9 *time zone*
central heating 493.3 *heater*
centralism 173.3 *centrality*
centrality 173.3; 172.1 *interior*
centralization 173.3 *centrality;* 374.1 *combination;* 409.3 *organization;* 484.7 *planning*
centralize 173.9 *centre;* 374.5 *combine;* 310.11 *focus;* 409.13 *organize;* 484.9 *plan*
centralized 173.7; 374.7 *combined;* 12.9 *governmental*
centrally 173.10; 344.14 *causally;* 216.12 *mediumly;* 121.16 *superiorly;* 447.14 *thematically*
centrally heated 493.13 *heated*
centrally planned economy 13.1 *economics*
centralness 173.3 *centrality*
central office 173.4 *centre of activity*
Central Park 87.3 *New York*
central position 754.1 *compromise*
central processor 40.5 *processor*
central reservation 318.5 *crossing point*
Central Standard Time 275.9 *time zone*
central thing 173.2
Centre 173
centre 173.1; **173.9**; 586.14 *armed forces;* 49.2 *basketball player;* 363.7 *centre of attraction;* 123.3 *chief thing;* 99.2 *essential content;* 310.5, 310.11 *focus;* 58.4 *ice hockey player;* 172.2 *inside;* 58.6 *lacrosse player;* 216.5 *medium;* 46.7 *offence;* 179.4 *parts of a circle;* 46.15 *play offence;* 685.7 *politically moderate;* 12.6 *political party*
centre back 66.3 *football player*
centreboard 50.6 *canoeing;* 50.3 *parts of a sailing boat;* 228.3 *stabilizer*
centre circle 66.1 *soccer*
centre court 49.1 *basketball*
centred 65.9 *billiard;* 173.7 *centralized*
centre fielder 48.2 *baseball player*
centre forward 66.3 *football player;* 58.2 *hockey player;* 579.14 *leader*
centre half 66.3 *football player;* 58.2 *hockey player*
centre line 63.12 *badminton terms;* 49.1 *basketball;* 68.10 *curling;* 65.3 *English billiards;* 58.3 *ice hockey;* 58.5 *lacrosse*
centre of activity 173.4
centre of attention 363.7 *centre of attraction;* 173.5 *focus*
centre of attraction 363.7
centre of effort 50.7 *windsurfing*
centre of gravity 173.1 *centre;* 38.14 *load;* 28.9 *mass*
centre of interest 173.5 *focus*
centre of lateral resistance 50.7 *windsurfing*
centre of mass 28.9 *mass*
centre of symmetry 27.41 *geometric figure*
centre on 173.9 *centre;* 447.10 *focus on;* 345.7 *follow from*
centrepiece 173.2 *central thing*
centre-pin 55.8 *angling*
centre-pin reel 55.3 *fishing tackle*
centre pocket 65.3 *English billiards;* 65.5 *snooker*
centre point 173.1 *centre*
centre spot 65.1 *billiards;* 65.4 *carom;* 65.3 *English billiards;* 58.3 *ice hockey;* 65.5 *snooker*
centrestage 21.43 *on stage;* 21.17 *stage*
centre string 65.4 *carom*
centre zone 58.3 *ice hockey*
centric 173.7 *centralized*
centrical 173.7 *centralized*
centricity 173.3 *centrality*
centrifugal 364.9 *abducent;* 634.18 *avoiding;* 300.17 *directional;* 311.6, 377.24 *divergent;* 307.12 *rotary*
centrifugal force 334.4 *energy;* 28.10 *force;* 364.5 *repulsion*
centrifugally 300.18 *in motion*
centrifugation 307.2 *turning*
centrifuge 307.6 *rotator*
centrifugence 311.2 *parting*
centrillion 194.3 *large number;* 201.11 *million*
centring 173.3 *centrality;* 310.7 *convergent;* 310.5 *focus*
centriole 34.8 *cell organ*
centripetal 173.6 *central;* 310.7 *convergent;* 300.17 *directional;* 363.10 *magnetic;* 307.12 *rotary*
centripetal force 28.10 *force;* 363.2 *pulling power*
centripetally 363.13 *attractionally;* 300.18 *in motion*
centrist 12.6 *political party*
centroid 173.1 *centre;* 27.43 *triangle*
centrolineal 310.7 *convergent*
centromere 34.10 *cell division;* 34.14 *chromosome*
centrosome 34.10 *cell division;* 34.8 *cell organ*
centrosphere 34.8 *cell organ;* 173.2 *central thing*
centuple 201.20 *hundredth;* 201.23 *quintuple;* 201.9 *treble figures*
centuplicate 201.20 *hundredth;* 201.23 *quintuple;* 201.9 *treble figures*
centurion 586.6 *militarist;* 201.9 *treble figures*
century 586.16 *army unit;* 780.3 *fortune;* 148.8 *measure of time;* 53.10 *score;* 275.4 *term;* 276.2 *time period;* 201.9 *treble figures*
cep 25.33 *vegetable*
cephalic 442.9 *mental*
cephalin 33.6 *lipid*
Cephalochordata 75.2 *protochordate*
cephalochordate 75.16 *invertebrate;* 75.2 *protochordate*
cephalometer 26.8 *meter*
cephalometric 26.16 *micrometric*
cephalometry 26.2 *micrometry*
cephalopod 70.5 *aquatic animal;* 75.5 *mollusc*
Cephalopoda 75.5 *mollusc*
cephalopodan 75.19 *molluscan*
cephalopodic 75.19 *molluscan*
cephalopodous 75.19 *molluscan*
Cepheid variable 29.12 *variable star*
ceramic 24.10; 32.7 *chemical compound;* 19.25 *sculptural*
ceramic capacitor 39.17 *resistor*
ceramic decoration 24.1 *ceramics*
ceramic object 24.8
ceramic process 24.5
Ceramics 24
ceramics 24.1; 19.1 *art*
ceramic tiles 550.8 *wall covering*
ceramic ware 24.1 *ceramics*
ceramic workshop 24.6
ceramist 24.7 *potter*
cerate 394.9 *balm*
Cerberus 70.7 *legendary beast;* 252.3 *protector*
cercaria 75.13 *invertebrate larva*
cereal 81.4 *cereal grass;* 44.16 *horticultural;* 77.2 *plant*
cereal bowl 410.16 *crockery*
cereal crop 43.12 *crop*
cereal grass 81.4; 81.1 *grass*
cereals 77.3 *seed plant*
cerebral 446.11 *ideational;* 442.9 *mental;* 443.8 *thoughtful*
cerebral death 582.1 *death*
cerebrally 442.14 *mentally*
cerebral palsy 260.17 *nervous disorder*
cerebrate 443.12 *think*
cerebration 443.1 *thought*
cerebroside 33.6 *lipid*
cerebrum 442.7 *brain*
cerecloth 583.4 *funeral objects*
cerements 583.4 *funeral objects*
ceremonial 601.12; 656.8 *ceremonious;* 601.2 *commemoration;* 601.11 *commemorative;* 160.11, 656.6 *formal;* 656.3 *formal occasion;* 10.1 *ritual;* 10.21 *ritualistic*
ceremonial attire 7.11 *vestment*
ceremonial function 601.3 *ceremony*
ceremonialism 656.2 *formalism;* 10.2 *ritualism*
ceremonially 160.14 *conventionally*
ceremonial troops 586.12; 586.14 *armed forces*
ceremonies 658.3 *courtesies*
ceremonious 656.8; 656.6 *formal;* 658.8 *good-mannered;* 667.8 *respectful*
ceremoniously 656.12 *formally;* 658.15 *genteelly*
ceremoniousness 656.1 *formality*
ceremony 601.3; 632.4 *custom;* 160.5 *formality;* 656.3 *formal occasion;* 738.10 *manifestation;* 10.1 *ritual*
Ceres 562.4 *fertility cult*
ceric 32.34 *elemental*
cerise 535.1 *red*
CERN 334.8 *nuclear power*
cerography 19.15 *engraving*
ceroplastic 19.25 *sculptural*
ceroplastics 19.12 *sculpture*
cerous 32.34 *elemental*
certain 452.1; 450.11 *believing;* 452.2 *convinced;* 703.12 *demonstrable;* 228.11 *determined;* 726.3 *emphatic;* 716.8 *evidential;* 474.7 *expected;* 474.5 *expecting;* 756.15 *future;* 253.7 *guaranteed;* 756.13 *guaranteeing;* 695.1 *intelligible;* 455.10 *known;* 738.14 *manifest;* 207.6 *plural;* 283.12 *predictable;* 203.6 *quantitative;* 252.6 *safe;* 246.13 *successful;* 396.15 *true;* 454.10 *verified*
certain amount 203.2
certain cure 394.1 *remedy*
certainly 95.14; **452.23**; 716.14 *as evidence;* 756.16 *as promised;* 454.12 *assuredly;* 396.25, 698.37 *authentically;* 703.22 *demonstrably;* 643.12 *indeed;* 452.25 *inevitably;* 756.18 *potentially*
certainly! 452.26
certainly not 708.23 *no!*
certainness 452.10 *conviction*
certain proportion 205.1 *part*
Certainty 452
certainty 452.9; 450.1 *belief;* 452.10 *conviction;* 707.8 *definiteness;* 703.5 *demonstrability;* 474.1 *expectation;* 107.5 *good chance;* 59.7 *horseracing;* 452.16 *inevitability;* 695.9 *intelligibility;* 27.62 *probability;* 716.2 *proof;* 252.1 *safety*
certifiable 461.11 *insane;* 454.8 *verifiable*
certifiably 454.11 *verifiably*
certificate 744.2; 693.3 *document;* 743.3 *means of identification;* 780.14 *paper money;* 750.8, 757.2 *permit;* 813.2 *prize;* 253.2 *promise;* 136.3 *qualifications*
certificated 750.18 *permitting*
certificate of exemption 758.4 *licence*
certification 707.1 *affirmation;* 698.7, 707.4 *confirmation;* 750.7 *consent;* 136.3 *qualifications;* 454.4 *verification*
certified 136.10 *authorized;* 452.1 *certain;* 253.7 *guaranteed;* 756.13 *guaranteeing;* 461.13 *mentally ill;* 698.20 *proved;* 707.13 *supported;* 454.10 *verified*
certified cheque 780.14 *paper money*
certifier 707.9 *affirmer*
certify 253.12; **461.16**; 707.17 *affirm;* 707.19 *confirm;* 750.28 *consent;* 95.12 *establish reality;* 756.8 *guarantee;* 693.11 *in-*

form; 452.21 make certain; 716.12 prove; 698.30 prove true; 136.13 qualify; 454.1 verify
certiorari 16.6 legal process
certitude 452.10 conviction
Certosina work 23.9 decorative woodwork
cerulean 539.1 blue; 539.5 blueness
cervical 561.16 reproductive
cervical cancer 260.12 cancer
cervical smear 35.7 diagnosis
cervid 71.15 hoofed mammal; 71.33 ungulate
Cervidae 71.15 hoofed mammal
cervine 71.33 ungulate
cervix 561.8 organs of reproduction
cespitose 83.10 of fungi
cess 790.7 tax
cessation **131.2**; **133.2**; **226.1**; 309.1 closure; 390.2 deliverance; 526.4 disappearance; 343.5 inactivity; 301.1 motionlessness; 358.3 obliteration; 749.1 pacification; 589.1 peace; 708.6 termination
cession 767.1 disposal; 355.3 relinquishment; 388.1 submission
cesspit 767.8 sink; 503.2 something that makes an unpleasant smell; 767.5 wasteyard
cesspool 238.6 refuse; 767.8 sink; 503.2 something that makes an unpleasant smell; 439.4 storage; 767.5 wasteyard
Cestoda 75.6 worm
cestode 75.6 worm
cestoid 75.20 wormlike
Cetacea 71.11 marine mammal
cetacean **71.29**; 70.5 aquatic animal; 71.11 marine mammal
cetaceous 71.29 cetacean
ceteris paribus 119.12 equally
Ceylon tea 558.3 tea
CFC 31.8 atmosphere; 432.11 vaporizer
C grade 216.6 mediocrity
chablis 558.9 wine
cha-cha-cha 22.2 dance
chaconne 516.4 harmonics
Chad 88.5 other major lakes
chador 521.6 that which makes invisible
chaetognath 75.6 worm
Chaetognatha 75.6 worm
chafe 624.11 be angry; 493.14 be hot; 491.9 feel pain; 365.15 grind; 365.3 grinding; 624.9 offend
chafer 76.3 pest
chaff 550.13 casing; 81.4 cereal grass; 238.6 refuse; 215.2 residue; 668.6 taunt; 124.8 trifle
chaffer 776.3 bargain
chaffing 668.15 taunting
chafing 365.3 grinding; 365.11 rough
Chagas' disease 260.7 tropical disease
chagrin 604.1 disappointment; 668.8 indignity
chagrined 604.9 disappointed; 623.3 humbled
chain 373.12 bind; 132.15 concatenate; 132.2 consecution; 251.12 gag; 814.14 instrument of punishment; 542.7 jewellery; 373.4 means of connection; 26.6 measuring instrument; 89.1 mountain; 154.4 mountain range; 32.21 polymer; 309.11, 378.10 restrain; 309.3 restrainer; 289.1 succession; 373.7 tackle
chain armour 384.7 armour
chained 378.14 blocked; 373.16 bound; 228.10 stabilized
chain gang 46.2 football player; 814.7 punishment
chain-gang member 815.5 prisoner
chainguard 320.11 bicycle part
chain harrows 43.10 farm tool
chaining 132.2 consecution
chain letter 710.3 solicitation
chain mail 384.7 armour; 252.4 safety device; 587.1 weapon
chain of office 743.4 insignia
chainplates 50.3 parts of a sailing boat
chain printer 40.7 peripheral
chain reaction 32.14 chemical reaction; 28.72 nuclear fission; 334.8 nuclear power; 132.4 repercussion
chains 251.5 means of restraint; 378.4 restraint; 46.4 stadium
chain saw 79.7 timber production; 438.1 tool
chain-saw mortiser 23.11 woodworking tool
chain shot 587.14 historical ammunition
chain-smoke 496.14 smoke
chain-smoking 496.8 smoking
chain store 779.8 store
chain up 251.12 gag
chair **23.2**; 400.5 company leader; 579.2 direct; 579.13 director; 395.5 influential person; 6.6 instructorship; 685.4 moderate; 464.3 place of judgment; 366.3 promote; 413.4 rest; 601.18 salute
chair cover 256.11 cleaning cloth; 550.12 protective covering
chair leg **23.3**
chair lift 317.12 cableway; 366.10 elevator; 304.8 lift; 68.1 skiing
chairman 400.5 company leader; 579.13 director; 395.5 influential person
chairman of the board 400.5 company leader
chairmanship 579.4 directorship; 396.5 position of authority
chair of Saint Peter 10.14 sacred object
chairperson 400.5 company leader; 579.13 director; 685.2 moderator
chair socket 55.1 angling
chairwoman 400.5 company leader; 395.5 influential person
chaise longue 23.6 bed; 23.2 chair
chalaza 72.15 eggs
chalcography 19.15 engraving
Chalcolithic 296.15 primal
Chalcolithic period 284.4 prehistoric age
chalconide 32.6 chemical element
chalet 565.5 house; 440.1 property
chalice 410.13 drinking vessel; 10.14 sacred object
chalk 19.11 artist's materials; 65.1 billiards; 62.4 climbing equipment; 19.20 draw; 743.10 identify; 427.5 powder; 531.9 white thing
chalk and cheese 113.3 opposites
chalk a stick 65.8 play billiards
chalk bag 62.4 climbing equipment
chalkily 531.14 whitely
chalkiness 427.1 powderiness; 531.7 whiteness
chalklike 427.15 powdery
chalk mark 51.2 grip
chalk out 484.10 plan out; 742.9 use signs
chalk up 743.10 identify
chalky **30.57**; 427.15 powdery; 531.1 white
challenge 661.3 act of defiance; 167.10 be in front; 661.6 be insubordinate; 705.21 confuse; 381.8 counterattack; 661.5 defy; 451.8 disbelieve; 701.14 discuss; 661.2 disobedience; 701.2 logical argument; 483.9 motivate; 113.18 object; 113.4 objection; 4.4 philosophical investigation; 4.20 philosophize; 751.7 pick a fight; 753.1, 753.6 protest; 705.1 question; 705.2 questioning; 708.11 rebut; 708.3 rebuttal; 383.6 resist; 383.1 resistance; 354.1 undertake
challenged 384.29 defending; 483.12 motivated; 447.8 problematic; 705.16 questioned; 708.18 rejected; 383.10 resistant
challenge fate 254.9 face danger
Challenger 586.21 armoured cavalry; 29.30 spacecraft
challenger 336.5 athlete; 353.7 attempter; 52.4 boxer; 661.4 defiant person; 708.9 negativist; 45.3 sportsman
challenging 701.10 arguable; 381.24 counterattacking; 661.8 defying; 264.10 difficult; 113.24 discordant; 483.11 motivational; 480.19 persuasive; 264.12, 447.8, 705.13 problematic; 753.9 protesting; 708.19 rebutting; 383.10 resistant
challengingly 661.10 in defiance; 708.22 negatively; 447.13 problematically; 705.24 questionably; 383.14 resistingly
chalone 559.2 secreted substance
chalukah 10.3 rite of worship
chamber 252.5 refuge; 565.7 room; 439.4 storage; 560.14 toilet
chamber group 18.26 musical group
chamberlain 401.6 domestic servant
chambermaid 401.6 domestic servant
chamber music 18.3 classical music
chamber of commerce 776.5 commercial trade; 13.7 corporation
chamber of commerce member **776.11**; 13.9 economist
chamber orchestra 374.3 assembly; 18.26 musical group
chamber pot 410.15 pot; 560.14, 767.7 toilet
chambré 493.9 hot
Chambre des Députés 579.10 legislative body
chameleon 227.3 changeable thing; 639.15 indecisive person; 73.2 lizard; 541.5 variegated thing
chameleonic 541.6 variegated
chamois 550.14 animal covering; 256.11 cleaning cloth; 435.1 materials; 421.9 smoother
champ 586.3 athlete; 52.4 boxer; 557.21 eat; 400.10 expert; 246.5 victorious person
champagne 558.9 wine; 537.1 yellow
champagne flute 410.13 drinking vessel
champaign 81.2 grassland
champ at the bit 624.11 be angry
champers 558.9 wine
champerty 16.39 crime
champignon 83.2 mushroom; 25.33 vegetable
champing 557.1 eating
champing at the bit 636.2 eager
Champion 59.1 horse
champion 392.23 advise; 669.7 advocate; 707.9 affirmer; 47.3, 336.5, 586.3 athlete; 121.14, 235.2 best; 52.4 boxer; 52.14 combat; 384.13 defender; 400.13 excellent; 235.8 exceller; 400.10 expert; 413.14 give moral support; 714.8 justify; 121.6 paragon; 230.1 perfect; 384.22 plead for; 252.10 protect; 252.3 protector; 485.4 skilled person; 797.16 superior person; 669.13 support; 413.8 supporter; 246.5 victorious person; 714.5 vindicator
championing 669.19 supporting
champion of lost causes 799.3 honourable person
championship **64.2**; 669.1 approval; 413.6 moral support; 392.9 patronage; 246.3 successful thing
championship fight 52.2 boxing
Chamuel 8.6 angel
Chance 107
chance **104.4**; **107.1**; **107.8**; **107.10**; 453.16 capriciousness; 227.3 changeable thing; 705.20 doubt; 448.13 invent; 287.2, 308.10 opportunity; 102.1 possibility; 27.62, 104.1 probability; 453.22 risk; 107.12 take a chance; 752.2 tentative offer; 105.3 unexpected; 105.5 unexpectedness
chanced 448.10 tested
chance discovery 107.2 luck
chance encounter 107.2 luck
chance hit 107.2 luck
chance in a million 107.6 poor chance
chance it 107.12 take a chance
chancel 10.12 church; 20.10 church architecture
chancellor 579.13 director; 400.9 educational leader; 6.4 educator; 12.7 governor; 400.3 leader; 397.6 person in command; 396.10 person of authority
Chancellor of the Exchequer 780.18 treasurer
chance meal 557.12 meal
chance meeting 107.2 luck
chance one's arm 615.5 be rash; 353.3 tackle; 107.12 take a chance
Chancery Division 16.20 British court
chance upon **107.11**; 142.11 find
chancing upon 142.3 locating
chancre 260.14 venereal disease
chancy 453.8 capricious; 107.8 chance; 254.1 dangerous; 448.9 original; 705.14 questionable
chandelier 361.3 suspended object
chandelle 322.5 flight
Chanel No. 5™ 502.2 fragrant thing
Change 224
change **224.1**; **395.9**; **453.21**; **780.4**; 780.26 bank; 642.5 be capricious; 227.11 be changeable; 224.7 be changed; 300.13 be in motion; 299.6 be irregular; 120.5 be unequal; 18.6 campanology; 760.1 conversion; 116.6 differentiate; 759.1 exchange; 295.5 fresh start; 762.6 give a substitute; 110.1 interchange; 299.1 irregularity; 295.20 make new; 136.5 modification; 136.15 modify; 110.7 reciprocate; 393.2 refurbish; 759.3 something in exchange; 779.5 stock market; 762.1 substitution; 552.14 undress; 300.15 walk; 551.34 wear
changeability 642.2 caprice; 227.1 changeableness; 114.1 diversity
changeable **224.11**; **227.13**; **639.2**; 453.8, 642.1 capricious; 760.15 convertible; 114.5 diverse; 759.6 in exchange; 299.4 irregular; 31.46 seasonal; 541.6 variegated
Changeableness 227
changeableness **227.1**; 642.2 caprice; 453.16 capriciousness; 760.1 conversion; 639.12 inconstancy; 299.1 irregularity; 327.3 turbulence
changeable person **227.5**
changeable thing **227.3**
changeably **224.15**; **227.15**; 453.27 capriciously; 114.10 diversely; 759.8 in exchange; 299.8 irregularly
change address 142.10 settle
change allegiances 355.2 withdraw
change back 224.8 cause change; 761.7 restore
change bowler 53.4 team
change countenance 530.5 lose colour
change course 224.7 be changed; 325.2 divert; 323.9 navigate
changed **224.12**; 760.13 converted; 759.7 exchanged; 136.11 modified; 110.4 reciprocal; 295.14 renewed; 762.8 substituted
changed beyond recognition 760.13 converted
changed grip 57.5 horizontal bar
change direction **311.15**; 224.7 be changed; 300.13 be in motion; 325.1 deviate
change directions 299.6 be irregular
changed meaning 694.4 type of meaning
change down 61.9 race
changed person 760.6 convert
change for 762.6 give a substitute
change for the better 224.7 be changed; 224.8 cause change; 224.1 change; 244.1 improve; 244.5 improvement
change for the worse 224.7 be changed; 224.8 cause change; 224.1 change
change front 479.2 equivocate
changeful 224.11, 227.13 changeable; 222.7 circumstantial; 299.4 irregular
changefully 222.16 relatively
changefulness 227.1 changeableness
change gradually **209.6**
change hands 778.2 be sold
change into 760.7 convert into
changeless 279.10 continuing forever; 112.13 monotonous; 225.7 permanent; 111.17 regular; 228.9 stable
changelessly 225.9 permanently; 111.20 regularly
changelessness 279.1 eternity; 225.1 permanence; 111.6 regularity; 228.1 stability
changeling 11.11 ghost; 227.10 person who is exchanged; 762.2 substitute person
change loop 68.6 ice-skating
changement 22.9 ballet steps
change money 759.5 exchange
change of allegiance 479.7 apostasy
change of belief 224.2 change of mind
change of clothes 224.4 exchange
change of course 224.1 change
change of direction 224.1 change; 479.6 equivocation
change of heart 224.2 change of mind; 808.1 penitence
change of life 563.1 infertility; 556.4 middle age
change of mind **224.2**; 479.6 equivocation; 642.3 whim
change of mood 479.6 equivocation
change of opinion 224.2 change of mind
change-of-pace 48.4 pitching terms
change of place 224.1 change
change of position 224.1 change; 300.1 motion
change of purpose 479.6 equivocation
change of scene 581.6 refresher
change of scenery 224.1 change
change of stance 224.2 change of mind
change one's address 300.15 walk
change one's allegiance 479.3 apostatize
change one's belief 224.7 be changed
change one's clothes 224.10 exchange; 552.14 undress; 551.34 wear
change one's colours 479.3 apostatize
change one's expression 224.7 be changed
change one's heart 224.7 be changed
change one's mind 224.7 be changed; 227.12 be irresolute; 479.2 equivocate; 639.6 hesitate; 355.1 relinquish; 708.12 renounce
change one's opinion 224.7 be changed
change one's stance 224.7 be changed

change one's tune 224.7 *be changed*; 479.2 *equivocate*
change one's ways 760.10 *be converted*
changeover 289.4 *accession*; 47.1 *track events*
change place 300.13 *be in motion*
change places 224.7 *be changed*; 759.5 *exchange*
change position 224.7 *be changed*; 300.13 *be in motion*
change purse 780.20 *money store*
changer 224.5
change ringing 18.6 *campanology*
change round 224.8 *cause change*; 479.2 *equivocate*; 224.10 *exchange*
change sides 639.9; 479.3 *apostatize*; 355.2 *withdraw*
change speed 299.6 *be irregular*
change the channel 479.1 *be equivocal*
change the face of 760.9 *transform*
change the field 53.16 *field*
change the meaning 720.1 *misinterpret*
change the rules 227.12 *be irresolute*
change the subject 479.1 *be equivocal*
change the tyres 61.9 *race*
change-up 48.4 *pitching terms*
changing 760.14 *converting*
changing back 761.2 *restoration*
changing down 61.6 *motor-racing terms*
changing scene 227.3 *changeable thing*
changing the guard 656.3 *formal occasion*
changing voice 730.2 *inarticulation*
Chang Jiang 90.5 *other major rivers*
channel 90.2; **317.11**; 318.4 *access*; 348.4 *be an instrument*; 40.19 *computing terms*; 579.2 *direct*; 314.5 *entrance*; 90.7 *flow*; 184.2 *furrow*; 92.9 *inlet*; 151.6 *narrow place*; 693.8 *source of information*; 316.11 *transfer*; 39.19 *transistor*; 38.22 *tunnel*; 315.6 *way out*; 184.8 *wrinkle*
Channel 4 692.24 *television broadcasting*
Channel 5 692.24 *television broadcasting*
channel bass 55.4 *American game fish*
Channel Tunnel 317.8 *tunnel*
chanson 17.7 *poem*; 516.2 *song*
chant 10.8 *hymn*; 514.8 *musical cry*; 10.20 *pray*; 18.39 *sing*; 514.15 *sing out*; 516.2 *song*; 729.13 *speak in a particular way*; 11.5 *spell*
chanterelle 25.33 *vegetable*
chanteuse 516.5 *melodist*
chanticleer 72.10 *male bird*
chanting 507.2 *outcry*; 112.15 *reverberatory*
chant royal 17.10 *verse form*
chantry 10.11 *place of worship*
chaos 588.1 *anarchy*; 408.5 *confusion*; 375.1 *disintegration*; 357.5 *havoc*; 16.41, 408.8 *lawlessness*; 412.1 *mixture*; 161.1 *shapelessness*
chaos magic 11.3 *witchcraft*
chaos theory 28.81 *causality*; 4.7 *school of thought*
chaotic 588.6 *anarchic*; 375.5 *disintegrated*; 408.20 *disorderly*; 16.61 *lawless*; 412.12 *mixed*; 408.18 *muddled*
chaotically 588.8 *anarchically*; 375.8 *destructively*; 408.27 *in disorder*; 412.14 *in the midst*; 114.11 *irregularly*
chap 420.11 *be rough*; 567.2 *male*; 566.7 *person*
chap and lie 68.16 *bobsled*
chaparral 77.1 *plants*; 79.4 *trees*
chapatti 25.38 *bread*; 25.49 *Indian dish*
chapeau 551.15 *headgear*
chapel 356.8 *construction*; 15.3 *organized labour*; 10.11 *place of worship*; 10.13 *shrine*
chapelgoer 10.17 *worshipper*
chapel of remembrance 583.5 *cemetery*
chapel of rest 10.11 *place of worship*
chaperon 223.7 *attendant*; 471.6 *attentive person*; 665.11 *care for*; 401.4 *personal attendant*; 252.10 *protect*; 252.3 *protector*; 665.8 *watchful person*
chaperone 223.15 *escort*
chaperoned 223.20 *accompanied*
chapiter 174.3 *architectural summit*; 20.8 *column*
chaplain 7.8 *priest*
chaplaincy 7.9 *priesthood*
chaplainship 7.9 *priesthood*
chaplet 743.8 *heraldic device*; 743.4 *insignia*; 10.14 *sacred object*; 794.1 *trophy*
chapman 778.11 *pedlar*
chappals 551.19 *footwear*
chapped 420.2 *coarse*
chapped hands 420.7 *rough thing*
chappie 567.2 *male*
chaps 551.20 *legwear*
chapter 205.2 *particular*; 7.1 *religion*
Chapter 11 786.5 *insolvency*
chapter-and-verse 698.23 *literal*; 698.10 *literalness*
chapterhouse 7.10 *priestly dwelling*
chapters 406.5 *divisions*
char 532.11 *blacken*; 534.7 *brown*; 493.15 *burn*; 256.12 *cleaner*; 401.6 *domestic servant*; 392.16 *home help*; 401.8 *serve*; 558.3 *tea*
charabanc 320.19 *bus*
character 40.10; 229.2 *attitude*; 325.19 *deviant person*; 118.10 *eccentric*; 160.3 *kind*; 5.13 *letter*; 99.4, 160.6 *nature*; 194.1 *number*; 205.9 *participation*; 139.13, 566.7 *person*; 139.2 *personality*; 500.4 *reputation*; 21.23 *role*; 724.1 *style*; 137.4 *type*; 803.2 *virtues*
character acting 21.22 *acting*
character actor 21.24 *actor*
character actress 21.24 *actor*
character assassination 678.3 *defamation*
character dress 551.5 *fancy dress*
characteristic 99.9; **139.3**; **139.16**; 216.1 *average*; 525.3 *external appearance*; 27.77 *given*; 743.1 *identification*; 27.19 *logarithm*; 27.60 *parameter*; 717.13 *representational*; 742.14 *signifying*; 137.11 *typical*
characteristically 139.30; 742.18 *indicatively*; 717.14 *representationally*; 137.16 *taxonomically*
characteristic curve 41.10 *graininess*
characteristic impedance 39.12 *resistance*
characterization 21.22, 717.3 *acting*; 17.3 *aspect of fiction*; 721.1 *description*; 21.9 *dramaturgy*; 743.1 *identification*
characterize 99.11; **139.22**; 717.10 *act*; 721.14 *describe*; 743.10 *identify*; 721.15 *recount*; 742.10 *signify*; 17.21 *write*
characterized 21.39 *dramatic*; 743.12 *identified*
characterizing 717.3 *acting*
characterless 497.5 *tasteless*; 639.4 *unsteady*; 98.13 *vacant*
character recognition 40.13
character reference 716.6 *documentation*; 454.6 *evidence*; 757.2 *permit*; 669.6 *recommendation*
characters 21.25 *cast*
character set 40.10 *character*
character sketch 721.1 *description*
charade 717.3 *acting*; 737.4 *brain-teaser*; 21.2 *play*
charbroiling 25.8 *cooking technique*
charcoal 19.11 *artist's materials*; 532.9 *black thing*; 19.9 *drawing*; 493.6 *fire*; 437.1 *fuel*; 437.2 *lighter*
charcoal-burner 437.9 *power-worker*
charcoal drawing 19.9 *drawing*
charcoal-grey 533.1 *grey*
charcoal-grill 25.55 *cook*
chardonnay 558.9 *wine*
charge 251.7; **790.12**; 715.1 *accusation*; 715.5 *accuse*; 783.9 *acquire credit*; 713.1 *advice*; 713.5 *advise*; 381.1 *attack*; 397.4 *authorization*; 397.13 *authorize*; 776.3 *bargain*; 585.14 *battle*; 784.7 *be in debt*; 332.4 *be swift*; 380.7 *be violent*; 670.7, 670.19 *blame*; 36.28 *cathexis*; 331.2 *collide*; 331.12 *collision*; 397.1, 397.9 *command*; 39.35 *conduct*; 784.1 *debt*; 398.7 *delegate*; 710.7 *demand*; 387.4 *dependent*; 251.4 *detention*; 414.6 *displacement*; 810.1 *duty*; 28.50, 39.8 *electric charge*; 334.4 *energy*; 787.5 *expense*; 587.15 *explosive*; 790.3 *fee*; 586.37 *fight*; 232.6 *fill*; 437.11 *fuel*; 334.11 *give power*; 743.8 *heraldic device*; 743.10 *identify*; 380.3 *instance of violence*; 790.8 *levy*; 16.70 *litigate*; 16.5 *litigation*; 330.32, 406.2 *load*; 414.14 *make heavy*; 579.3 *management*; 381.12 *military attack*; 58.9 *play hockey*; 713.3 *precept*; 790.1 *price*; 330.12 *propellant*; 252.2 *protection*; 28.78 *quantum*; 789.9 *settle accounts*; 707.18 *vow*; 742.6 *word*
chargeable 790.15; 806.5 *guilty*
charge account 783.1 *credit*; 784.1 *debt*
charge-account payment 785.1 *payment*
charge against 381.1 *attack*
charge at 633.10 *chase*
charge attraction 28.50 *electric charge*
charge card 772.4 *credit*; 783.2 *credit card*; 784.1 *debt*
charge-card holder 777.12 *purchaser*
charge carrier 39.8 *electric charge*; 28.44, 39.4 *semiconductor*
charged 334.16; **783.12**; 715.8 *accusatory*; 777.13 *bought*; 58.8 *hockey*; 406.11, 414.2 *loaded*; 437.10 *powered*
chargé d'affaires 398.1 *delegate*; 746.4 *negotiator*
charged body 28.50 *electric charge*
charge density 28.50, 39.8 *electric charge*
charged particle 28.50 *electric charge*
charged substance 28.50 *electric charge*
charge hand 579.15 *manager*
charge number 28.66 *ion*
charge nurse 579.15 *manager*; 35.16 *nurse*
charger 715.3 *accuser*; 586.19 *cavalry*; 410.16 *crockery*; 59.3 *warhorse*
charge repulsion 28.50 *electric charge*
charge the jury 464.11 *judge*; 16.71 *try a case*
charge to experience 649.9 *forgive*
charge to one's account 783.9 *acquire credit*; 784.7 *be in debt*
charge to the jury 713.1 *advice*; 16.7 *legal trial*
charge up 334.11 *give power*
charge with 715.5 *accuse*
charging 381.23 *attacking*; 414.6 *displacement*; 58.1 *hockey*; 58.3 *ice hockey*; 332.1 *swift*; 380.6 *violent*; 707.3 *vow*
chariness 616.1 *caution*
charisma 363.4 *allurement*; 480.3 *incentive*; 362.5 *magnetism*; 395.3 *personal influence*; 334.1 *power*
charismatic 395.12 *appealing*; 363.9 *attractive*; 362.10 *magnetic*; 480.19 *persuasive*; 334.13 *powerful*; 7.3 *religious person*; 654.15 *sociable*
charismatically 363.14 *attractively*; 395.14 *influentially*; 362.16 *magnetically*
charismatic leader 579.14 *leader*
charitable 650.7; 392.35 *benevolent*; 658.7 *courteous*; 803.6 *ethical*; 768.8 *giving*; 648.4 *lenient*; 593.17 *loving*; 679.2 *magnanimous*; 652.6 *philanthropic*; 627.6 *pitying*; 776.16 *unprofitable*; 473.5 *unselfish*
charitable act 650.4 *benevolent act*
charitable foundation 652.5 *charity*
charitableness 650.2 *charity*; 648.1 *leniency*; 679.6 *magnanimity*; 652.1 *philanthropy*
charitable work 636.10 *voluntary work*
charitably 650.11; 768.9 *as a gift*; 392.38 *benevolently*; 658.14 *courteously*; 803.10 *ethically*; 658.15 *genteelly*; 648.6 *leniently*; 593.30 *lovingly*; 652.8 *philanthropically*; 627.13 *pitifully*; 473.9 *unselfishly*
charity 608.4; **650.2**; **652.5**; 793.6 *absence of charge*; 658.1 *courtesy*; 392.6 *financial assistance*; 793.11 *free of charge*; 679.5 *generosity*; 768.1 *giving*; 648.1 *leniency*; 593.1 *love*; 652.1 *philanthropy*; 627.1 *pity*; 439.1 *store*; 473.2 *unselfishness*; 803.2 *virtues*; 752.18 *voluntary*
charity appeal 710.3 *solicitation*
charity ball 376.10 *dance*; 710.3 *solicitation*
charity bazaar 778.4 *sale*
charity case 769.5 *recipient*
charity event 652.5 *charity*
charity events 710.3 *solicitation*
charity funds 710.3 *solicitation*
charity gala 21.13 *theatrical performance*
charity game 768.3 *offering*
charity match 710.3 *solicitation*
charity organization 710.3 *solicitation*
charity sale 778.4 *sale*
charity shop 793.7 *discounter*
charity show 710.3 *solicitation*
charity work 768.1 *giving*
charity worker 652.3 *philanthropist*; 710.4 *requester*; 413.8 *supporter*; 752.8 *volunteer*; 636.11 *willing worker*; 578.1 *worker*
charka 307.6 *rotator*
charlady 256.12 *cleaner*; 392.16 *home help*
charlatan 699.19 *cheat*; 700.15 *deceiver*; 699.17 *false person*; 456.5 *ignorant person*; 125.7 *imitator*; 676.2 *pretender*; 702.6 *sophist*; 699.32 *spurious*; 486.2 *unskilled*; 486.10 *unskilled person*
charlatanism 456.2 *half-knowledge*; 702.5 *hypocrisy*; 699.4 *spuriousness*; 486.8 *unskilfulness*
charlatanistic 699.32 *spurious*
charlatanry 699.4 *spuriousness*
Charleston 22.2, 22.15 *dance*
Charley 59.8 *hunting*
charlotte 25.35 *dessert*
charlotte russe 25.35 *dessert*
charm 363.4 *allurement*; 72.13 *assemblage of birds*; 363.11 *attract*; 11.21 *bewitch*; 677.9 *blarney*; 597.8 *cause joy*; 702.12 *deceive*; 241.13, 490.9 *give pleasure*; 545.1 *gorgeousness*; 480.3 *incentive*; 483.2 *inducement*; 593.4 *lovability*; 363.5 *lure*; 712.4 *malediction*; 483.9 *motivate*; 395.2 *occult influence*; 241.6 *pleasantness*; 483.5 *positive stimulus*; 359.2 *preserver*; 28.78 *quantum*; 10.14 *sacred object*; 421.13 *smooth over*; 11.5 *spell*; 724.2 *stylishness*; 11.6 *talisman*; 593.28 *win the love of*; 712.7 *wish ill*
charmed 11.19 *bewitched*; 593.19 *enamoured*; 483.12 *motivated*
charmed circle 235.7 *elite*; 251.1 *restraint*
charmed life 252.1 *safety*
charmer 363.6; 545.4 *attractive male*; 235.8 *exceller*; 677.6 *flatterer*; 241.11 *pleasant person*; 702.6 *sophist*; 11.4 *witch*
charming 395.12 *appealing*; 363.9 *attractive*; 597.5 *delightful*; 593.22 *lovable*; 483.11 *motivational*; 545.6 *personable*; 480.19 *persuasive*; 241.1, 490.6 *pleasant*; 654.15 *sociable*; 11.15 *witchlike*
charming fellow 654.6 *social person*
charmingly 363.14 *attractively*; 395.14, 483.14 *influentially*; 593.30 *lovingly*; 654.18 *sociably*
charmlessly 659.9 *discourteously*
charms 593.4 *lovability*
charnel house 582.8 *after death*; 583.1 *burial*
Charon 323.8 *boatman*
charred 532.3 *blackened*; 534.2 *browned*
chart 409.8; 406.5 *divisions*; 142.2 *exact location*; 27.32 *graph*; 220.1, 220.8 *list*; 30.65, 484.5, 717.7 *map*; 323.9 *navigate*; 323.5 *navigation*; 163.1, 163.5 *outline*; 717.11 *paint*; 693.5 *reference book*; 717.2 *reproduction*; 18.18 *written music*
chart-busting 121.14 *best*
charted 406.12 *itemized*; 220.11 *listed*
charter 140.2 *canon*; 744.2 *certificate*; 396.21 *grant authority*; 758.4 *licence*; 750.8, 750.29, 757.2 *permit*; 16.1 *the law*
chartered 396.16 *authorized*; 757.7 *permitted*; 750.18 *permitting*
chartered accountant 789.6 *accountant*
chartered engineer 38.2 *engineer*
charting 220.7 *listing*; 409.3 *organization*
chart recorder 26.8 *meter*
chartreuse 538.1 *green*; 537.1 *yellow*
charts 18.9 *popular music*
chart-topper 235.8 *exceller*; 121.6 *paragon*; 246.3 *successful thing*
chart-topping 121.14, 235.2 *best*; 246.13 *successful*
charwoman 256.12 *cleaner*; 401.6 *domestic servant*; 392.16 *home help*; 578.1 *worker*
chary 616.4, 637.3 *cautious*
Charybdis 90.6 *river flow*; 307.4 *vortex*
chase 633.2; **633.10**; 382.9 *animal killing*; 332.4 *be swift*; 316.14 *bring back*; 593.26 *court*; 19.22 *engrave*; 617.13 *like*; 71.23 *mammal hunting*; 63.5 *real tennis*
chase after 316.14 *bring back*
chased 633.17 *pursued*
chase fame and fortune 781.14 *seek riches*
chase off 364.1 *repel*
chase one's own tail 342.13 *be busy*; 306.6 *orbit*; 307.8 *rotate*
chase out 371.7 *drive out*
chaser 19.18 *engraver*; 633.5 *pursuer*; 21.8 *scene*
chase the dragon 691.10 *drug oneself*
chasing 19.15 *engraving*; 633.15 *pursuing*; 633.1 *pursuit*; 19.13 *relief-carving*
chasing one's own tail 342.9 *overactivity*
chasing the dragon 691.1 *drug-taking*
chasm 156.4 *deep thing*; 146.3 *gulf*; 308.1 *opening*; 372.3 *separateness*; 379.1 *trap*
chassé 22.9 *ballet steps*; 22.3 *ballroom dance steps*
chassepot 587.10 *historical gun*

chasseur 586.17 *army person*
chassis 175.2 *foot*; 403.4 *framework*; 413.2 *supporting part*
chaste 674.10 *bashful*; 803.6 *ethical*; 805.5 *innocent*; 255.12 *morally pure*; 531.5, 795.9 *pure*; 684.8 *self-restrained*; 271.1 *simple*; 197.17 *single*; 572.7 *virginal*
chastely 572.12 *celibately*; 803.10 *ethically*; 805.11 *innocently*; 674.18 *shyly*; 255.18 *virtuously*; 684.11 *with self-restraint*
chasten 623.17 *humiliate*; 685.4 *moderate*; 814.1 *punish*
chastened 685.6 *moderate*
chastener 814.17 *punisher*
chastening 623.6 *humiliating*; 814.7 *punishment*
chastening thought 623.14 *rebuke*
chastise 647.5 *be severe*; 670.20 *censure*; 814.1 *punish*
chastised 670.34 *censured*
chastisement 670.7 *blame*; 814.7 *punishment*; 242.8 *quarrel*
chastisement of the flesh 814.12 *corporal punishment*
chastiser 814.17 *punisher*
chastising 670.30 *censuring*
chastity 674.3 *bashfulness*; 805.1 *innocence*; 795.3 *moral purity*; 255.1, 531.11 *purity*; 684.1 *self-restraint*; 271.4 *simplicity*; 197.6 *singleness*; 572.2 *virginity*; 803.2 *virtues*
chasuble 7.11 *vestment*
chat **734.2**; **734.10**; 731.7 *be talkative*; 734.1 *conversation*; 729.1 *faculty of speech*; 731.3 *talk*
château 565.4 *official residence*
chateaubriand 25.45 *French dish*
chatelaine 579.15 *manager*
chat line 692.12 *public telephone system*
chatoyancy 541.1 *variegation*
chatoyant 541.7 *iridescent*
chat show 692.25 *broadcast material*
chat show guest 705.10 *person questioned*
chat show host 21.29 *entertainer*; 705.9 *questioner*
chattel 763.4 *possession*; 387.5 *subjected person*
chattels 438.7 *equipment*; 440.4 *possessions*
chatter 731.7 *be talkative*; 734.10 *chat*; 729.1 *faculty of speech*; 509.3, 509.10 *rattle*; 515.5 *sing*; 731.3 *talk*
chatterbox 731.4 *talker*
chatterer **734.8**; 706.10 *answerer*; 729.10 *speaker*; 731.4 *talker*
chattering 515.2 *bird song*; 509.17 *rattling*; 515.8 *singing*; 731.3 *talk*; 731.5 *talkative*
chattering teeth 612.1 *fear*
chattily 731.11 *effusively*; 515.10 *howlingly*
chattiness 731.1 *talkativeness*
chatting 734.12 *conversing*
chatty 734.14 *conversational*; 739.11 *disclosing*; 731.6 *effusive*; 693.16 *informative*
Chaucerian stanza 17.10 *verse form*
chaudfroid 25.15 *sauce*
chauffeur 401.6 *domestic servant*; 401.4 *personal attendant*; 316.7 *transferor*; 578.1 *worker*
chauffeur's uniform 743.5 *uniform*
chauvinism 585.5 *bellicosity*; 727.4 *bombast*; 465.3 *injustice*; 566.11 *nation*; 85.4 *nationalism*; 466.4 *social discrimination*
chauvinist 466.7 *bigot*; 466.10 *discriminatory*; 586.6 *militarist*; 465.5 *misjudging person*
chauvinistic 586.33 *combative*; 466.10 *discriminatory*; 85.16 *national*; 465.8 *unjust*
chauvinistically 586.41 *aggressively*; 85.19 *nationally*; 466.17 *prejudicially*; 465.14 *unjustly*
cheap **793.9**; 793.15 *cheaply*; 791.6 *discounted*; 236.2 *inferior*; 752.17 *offered*; 122.14 *poor*; 124.4 *trivial*; 468.5 *underestimated*; 675.7 *vulgar*
cheap as dirt 793.9 *cheap*
cheap at the price 793.9 *cheap*
cheapen 668.27 *desecrate*; 791.3 *discount*; 793.13 *make cheap*; 238.8 *make useless*; 245.6 *pervert*; 675.10 *vulgarize*
cheapening 245.8 *perversion*
cheap item **793.5**
cheap-jack 793.8 *bargain hunter*; 778.11 *pedlar*
cheaply **777.15**; **793.15**; 122.21 *badly*; 752.20 *persuasively*
Cheapness 793
cheapness **793.1**; 236.8 *inferiority*; 122.4 *poor quality*; 790.1 *price*; 793.3 *shoddiness*; 675.2 *tawdriness*; 124.7 *triviality*
cheapo 793.9 *cheap*
cheap rate 793.1 *cheapness*
cheap ticket 793.4 *bargain*
cheat **13.12**; **268.21**; **699.19**; **700.17**; 800.10 *be criminal*; 645.5 *be cunning*; 604.8 *be dishonest*; 699.25, 700.30 *be fraudulent*; 796.17 *be sexually immoral*; 645.3 *cunning person*; 702.12 *deceive*; 700.15, 718.3 *deceiver*; 774.11 *dishonest person*; 802.21 *do wrong*; 699.17 *false person*; 700.10 *fraud*; 774.15 *infringe*; 774.10 *infringer*; 62.9 *mountaineer*; 645.2 *stratagem*; 804.9 *wicked person*
cheat death 393.4 *be restored*; 554.16 *live*
cheated 604.10, 700.36 *deceived*; 774.18 *fraudulent*
cheater 700.17 *cheat*
cheating 62.3 *climbing technique*; 645.1 *cunning*; 700.34 *deceiving*; 604.12 *deceptive*; 774.7 *dishonesty*; 699.8, 700.10 *fraud*; 699.35, 774.18 *fraudulent*; 774.6 *illegal borrowing*; 796.4 *illicit love*
cheat on 700.30 *be fraudulent*
cheat one's creditors 784.8 *not pay*
check **210.12**; **541.2**; 301.8 *be motionless*; 246.9 *be victorious*; 665.11 *care for*; 226.8 *cause to cease*; 69.4 *chess terms*; 750.7, 750.28 *consent*; 347.3 *counteract*; 347.1 *counteraction*; 146.2, 146.5 *crack*; 464.12 *estimate*; 448.1, 448.11 *experiment*; 750.27 *fit*; 333.12 *hesitation*; 58.3 *ice hockey*; 743.10 *identify*; 166.7 *limit*; 166.2 *limiting factor*; 766.1 *loss*; 452.21 *make certain*; 685.4 *moderate*; 685.1 *moderation*; 378.2 *obstacle*; 58.9 *play hockey*; 705.17 *question*; 744.1 *record*; 251.8, 378.10 *restrain*; 251.1, 378.4 *restraint*; 333.3 *slow down*; 136.6 *specification*; 136.16 *specify*; 26.7 *standard*; 226.2 *stop*; 541.11 *variegate*; 454.4 *verification*; 454.1 *verify*; 399.1, 399.3 *veto*; 113.20 *withstand*
checked **541.8**; 136.12 *conditional*; 750.17 *consenting*; 333.7 *delayed*; 58.8 *hockey*; 448.10 *tested*; 454.10 *verified*
check in 312.5 *get in*
checking 58.8 *hockey*; 58.3 *ice hockey*; 454.9 *verificatory*
checklist 406.5 *divisions*; 220.1 *list*; 705.3 *questionnaire*
checkmate 246.9 *be victorious*; 226.8 *cause to cease*; 69.4 *chess terms*; 226.2 *stop*; 246.3 *successful thing*
check off 743.10 *identify*; 372.10 *set apart*
check one's course 324.8 *orient*
check out 464.12 *estimate*; 448.11 *experiment*; 313.2 *withdraw*
checkpoint 166.4 *boundary marker*; 318.5 *crossing point*
check stock 789.8 *audit*
check-up 35.6 *health care*
cheek **660.2**; 660.25 *answer back*; 659.2 *bad manners*; 167.5 *boldness*; 661.5 *defy*; 525.3 *external appearance*; 660.10 *impudence*; 169.1 *side*
cheekbone 525.3 *external appearance*
cheek by jowl 267.9 *adhesive*; 147.14 *beside*; 267.11 *cohesively*; 223.22 *hand in hand*; 750.32 *in alliance*; 147.10 *juxtaposed*; 147.9 *near*
cheekily **660.31**; 661.9 *defiantly*; 659.10 *rudely*
cheekiness 661.1 *defiance*; 660.10 *impudence*
cheeks 168.2 *rear end*
cheek wall 20.9 *miscellaneous architectural features*
cheeky **660.14**; 659.6 *bad-mannered*; 661.7 *defiant*; 668.10 *disrespectful*; 660.21 *impudent*
cheeky devil 660.12 *impudent person*
cheeky monkey 661.4 *defiant person*
cheep 72.18, 515.2 *bird song*; 72.26, 515.5 *sing*
cheer **514.12**; **598.5**; **598.8**; 669.16 *acclaim*; 598.6 *bring cheer*; 597.8 *cause joy*; 598.3 *cheerfulness*; 610.4 *comfort*; 514.3 *cry of praise*; 600.7 *dance*; 600.2 *fanfare*; 557.7 *food*; 742.3 *gesture*; 490.9 *give pleasure*; 610.10 *inspire hope*; 581.1 *refresh*; 601.18 *salute*; 654.1 *sociability*
cheerer 669.10 *applauder*; 514.9 *crier*
cheer for 514.12 *cheer*
cheerful **598.1**; 597.4 *happy*; 610.11 *hopeful*; 654.15 *sociable*
cheerful compliance 636.6 *willingness*
cheerful giver 768.4 *giver*
cheerfully **598.9**; 610.15 *hopefully*; 597.9 *joyfully*; 654.18 *sociably*; 636.16 *willingly*
cheerfulness **598.3**; 597.1 *happiness*; 610.1 *hope*
cheerful person **598.4**
cheerily 598.9 *cheerfully*
cheeriness 598.3 *cheerfulness*
cheering **514.17**; **598.2**; **610.14**; 669.5 *acclaim*; 669.20 *acclamatory*; 600.9, 601.9 *rejoicing*
cheerio 313.14 *goodbye!*
cheerleader 669.10 *applauder*; 514.9 *crier*; 579.14 *leader*; 46.14 *miscellaneous terms*
cheerless 523.11 *benighted*; 611.4 *hopeless*; 626.6 *sullen*
cheerlessly 626.13 *sullenly*
cheerlessness 602.2 *depression*
cheer on 338.3 *invigorate*; 483.9 *motivate*
cheers 669.5 *acclaim*; 313.14 *goodbye!*; 671.9 *thank you!*
cheers! **558.18**
cheer up 610.9 *be hopeful*; 598.6 *bring cheer*; 610.10 *inspire hope*; 475.11 *predict*
cheery 598.1 *cheerful*; 600.9 *rejoicing*
cheese 25.9 *dish*; 356.7 *produce*
cheese and biscuits 25.35 *dessert*
cheese board 25.35 *dessert*
cheeseburger 25.11 *sandwich*
cheesecake 25.36 *cake*; 498.3 *dessert*; 41.4 *portrait*; 568.9 *woman considered as a sex object*
cheesecloth 193.4 *textile*
cheese dip 25.15 *sauce*
cheesed off 261.2, 620.5 *bored*
cheese grater 427.13 *grater*
cheese it 371.33 *go away!*
cheese one off 620.6 *be boring*
cheeseparing 682.1 *mean*; 682.3 *parsimony*; 680.1 *thrift*; 680.4 *thrifty*
cheese pastry 25.37 *pastry*
cheese sandwich 25.11 *sandwich*
cheese sauce 25.15 *sauce*
cheese straws 25.10 *snack*
cheetah 332.12 *swift animal*
chef 436.4 *caterer*; 25.2 *cook*; 557.20 *food provider*; 412.7 *person who mixes*
chef-d'oeuvre 545.2 *beautiful thing*; 340.2 *deed*; 235.8 *exceller*; 797.17 *good thing*; 356.6 *great work*; 400.11, 485.3 *masterpiece*; 230.3 *perfection*; 619.4 *wonder*; 19.6 *work of art*
chef's salad 25.14 *salad*; 25.43 *US dish*
chef's special 139.9 *special*
chela 7.7 *monk*
chelate 32.7 *chemical compound*
chelicerate 75.18 *arthropodous*
chelonian **73.4**; 73.11 *reptilian*
chelonid 73.4 *chelonian*
Chelsea bun 25.36 *cake*
Chelsea Pensioner 586.11 *former soldier*; 585.11 *recruit*
chemiatrist 32.2 *chemist*
chemical **32.31**
chemical bond **32.11**
chemical change 760.1 *conversion*
chemical compound **32.7**
chemical dye 42.6 *dye*
chemical element **32.6**; 402.4 *matter*
chemical energy 28.11, 334.4 *energy*
chemical engineer 32.2 *chemist*
chemical engineering 32.1 *chemistry*; 38.1 *engineering*; 32.22 *industrial chemistry*; 438.6 *mechanics*
chemical fertilizer 562.3 *fertilizer*
chemical formula 32.13 *structure*
chemically **32.46**
chemical messenger 33.16 *hormone*
chemical physics 32.1 *chemistry*; 28.4 *experimental physics*
chemical porcelain 24.9 *industrial ceramics*
chemical reaction **32.14**
chemical toilet 560.13 *lavatory*; 767.7 *toilet*
chemical warfare 585.1 *war*; 585.8 *warfare*
chemical weathering 30.35 *weathering*
chemise 551.18 *underwear*
chemisette 551.14 *neckwear*
chemisorb 32.29, 370.13 *absorb*
chemisorbed 32.43 *absorbed*
chemisorption 370.5 *absorption*; 32.20 *surface chemistry*
chemisorptive 370.17 *absorbent*
chemist **32.2**; 394.16 *druggist*; 224.6, 227.4 *editor*; 402.3 *materialist*; 412.7 *person who mixes*; 372.8 *person who separates*; 37.2 *pharmacologist*
Chemistry 32
chemistry **32.1**; 760.1 *conversion*; 402.6 *natural science*
chemosphere 434.3 *atmospheric layers*
chemotherapy 37.1 *pharmacology*; 394.13 *therapy*; 35.8 *treatment*
chemurgy 32.1 *chemistry*
chenille 193.4 *textile*
chenopodiaceous 77.16 *taxonomic*
cheongsam 551.7 *frock*
cheque 780.14 *paper money*; 759.3 *something in exchange*
chequebook 789.5 *account book*; 744.6 *record book*
chequebook journalism 741.4 *journalist*
chequebook journalist 693.9 *informant*; 740.11 *newspaperman*
chequer 114.8 *be diverse*; 532.7 *blackness*; 541.2 *check*; 541.11 *variegate*
chequered 114.6 *assorted*; 541.8 *checked*; 114.5 *diverse*
chequered career 114.3 *diverse thing*
chequered flag 61.6 *motor-racing terms*
Chequers 565.4 *official residence*
cheque stub 253.2 *promise*; 744.1 *record*
cherish 360.7 *detain*; 595.7 *like*; 593.23 *love*; 359.5 *preserve*; 252.10 *protect*; 667.16 *revere*
cherish a grudge 651.16 *be malevolent*
cherished 593.21 *beloved*; 359.7 *preserved*
cherishing 360.2 *detention*
Chernobyl 736.5 *evasion*; 28.75 *nuclear accident*; 437.7 *nuclear power*
Cherokee alphabet 5.14 *alphabet*
cheroot 496.7 *tobacco*
cherry 80.5 *figurative usage*; 795.3 *moral purity*; 535.1 *red*; 535.7 *red thing*
cherry blossom 78.1 *flower*
cherry lips 535.7 *red thing*
cherry picker 80.5 *figurative usage*
cherry-red 535.1 *red*
cherry stoner 369.9 *extractor*
chersonese 92.5 *peninsula*
cherub 8.6 *angel*; 593.12 *nicknames for lovers*
cherubic 8.14 *heavenly*; 7.15 *religious*
cherubically 8.19 *divinely*
cherubicon 10.8 *hymn*
chervil 496.5 *herbs*
Chesapeake Bay 92.9 *inlet*
Chesapeake Bay retriever 60.6 *sporting dog*
chesil 30.27 *sediment*
chessboard 541.5 *variegated thing*
chessman 69.4 *chess terms*
chess pie 25.36 *cake*
chess piece 69.4 *chess terms*
chess terms **69.4**
chest 410.6 *box*; 23.5, 410.3 *cabinet*; 780.20 *money store*; 439.4 *storage*
chesterfield 23.2 *chair*; 551.12 *coat*
chest-high 154.12 *tall*
chestnut 534.1 *brown*; 59.1 *horse*; 535.3 *red-haired*
chest of drawers 23.5, 410.3 *cabinet*; 439.4 *storage*
chest-pain 260.10 *cardiovascular disease*
chest protector 54.2 *fencing equipment*; 58.3 *ice hockey*
chest protectors 48.3 *baseball equipment*
chest-spasm 260.10 *cardiovascular disease*
chest X-ray 35.7 *diagnosis*
cheval-de-frise 425.8 *sharp-pointed thing*
cheval glass 518.8 *reflection*
chevalier 658.6 *courteous person*
chevaux-de-frise 384.9 *barrier*
chevet 20.10 *church architecture*
Cheviot Hills 89.5 *British mountains*
chevron 176.1 *angle*; 743.8 *heraldic device*; 743.4 *insignia*
chevy 633.8 *pursue*
chew 425.14 *be sharp*; 557.21 *eat*; 419.13 *soften*
chewiness 423.6 *toughness*

chewing 557.1 *eating*
chewing gum 267.4 *adherent;* 430.2 *adhesive;* 422.3 *elastic thing*
chewing out 814.7 *punishment*
chewing the cud 557.5 *eating habit*
chewing tobacoo 496.7 *tobacco*
chew the cud 557.21 *eat;* 81.11 *eat grass;* 71.37 *graze*
chew the fat 734.9 *converse*
chew the scenery 727.7 *exaggerate*
chew up 557.21 *eat*
chew up the scenery 21.35 *overact*
chewy 423.3 *hard*
Cheyenne Frontier Days 59.12 *rodeo*
chianti 558.9 *wine*
chiaroscuro 532.7 *blackness;* 522.12 *highlight;* 19.4 *treatment*
chiasmus 17.12 *poetic language;* 162.1 *symmetry*
chiastic 162.4 *symmetrical*
chic 137.9 *distinction;* 551.30, 656.7 *dressed-up;* 553.7 *fashionable;* 553.2 *fashionableness;* 545.1 *gorgeousness;* 724.7 *stylish;* 724.2 *stylishness*
Chicago 87.2 *American cities*
chicane 320.3 *carriageway;* 645.1 *cunning;* 61.6 *motor-racing terms;* 700.28 *trick;* 700.7 *tricking*
chicanery 645.1 *cunning;* 702.5 *hypocrisy;* 800.1 *improbity;* 700.7 *tricking*
chichi 676.3 *affected*
chick 43.8 *livestock;* 593.12 *nicknames for lovers;* 568.9 *woman considered as a sex object;* 555.4 *young animal;* 72.12 *young bird;* 555.8 *young woman*
chickabiddy 593.12 *nicknames for lovers*
chicken 614.2 *coward;* 537.5, 614.3 *cowardly;* 612.6 *frightened person;* 743.4 *insignia;* 43.8 *livestock;* 25.20 *meat;* 341.2 *nonacting person;* 337.4 *weakling;* 337.12 *weak-willed*
chicken coop 565.12 *stall*
chicken farm 43.6 *farm*
chicken farming 43.3 *livestock farming*
chickenfeed 557.8 *animal food;* 780.4 *change;* 124.8 *trifle*
chicken-hearted 537.5, 614.3 *cowardly;* 337.12 *weak-willed*
chicken-heartedly 614.5 *cravenly*
chicken-heartedness 614.1 *cowardice*
chicken house 43.7 *farm building*
chicken-in-a-basket circuit 21.15 *engagement*
chicken in every pot 645.1 *cunning*
chicken liver 25.31 *offal*
chicken-livered 614.3 *cowardly*
chicken out 614.4 *be a coward*
chickenpox 260.6 *infection;* 260.13 *skin disease*
chicken run 43.7 *farm building*
chicken sandwich 25.11 *sandwich*
chicken soup 25.13 *soup*
chicken thief 774.8 *thief*
chicken tikka masala 25.49 *Indian dish*
chicken wire 360.4 *wall*
chick pea 25.33 *vegetable*
chicle 430.2 *adhesive*
chicle gum 430.2 *adhesive*
chicly 551.36 *dressily*
chide 670.20 *censure;* 814.1 *punish;* 712.6 *vilify*
chiding 670.7 *blame;* 670.30 *censuring;* 814.7 *punishment*
chief 121.14 *best;* 123.4 *bigwig;* 400.5 *company leader;* 579.13 *director;* 173.8 *focal;* 173.5 *focus;* 743.8 *heraldic device;* 123.5 *important;* 400.3 *leader;* 400.12 *masterful;* 396.10 *person of authority;* 129.12 *primary;* 121.5 *superior;* 174.5 *top*
chief constable 16.17 *police officer*
chief cook and bottle-washer 578.1 *worker*
chief executive 340.3 *doer;* 400.3 *leader;* 397.6 *person in command*
chief executive officer 579.15 *manager;* 397.6 *person in command;* 121.5 *superior*
chief hope 123.3 *chief thing*
chief justice 16.23 *judge;* 464.6 *justice*
chiefly 140.18 *as a rule;* 99.13 *in essence;* 216.11 *on average;* 130.42 *principally;* 121.16 *superiorly*
chief magistrate 400.3 *leader*
chief meaning 694.4 *type of meaning*
chief of police 16.17 *police officer*
chief of staff 584.5 *military staff*
chief of state 400.3 *leader*
chief part 205.5 *largest part;* 21.23 *role*
chief petty officer 586.27 *naval man*
chief rabbi 7.8 *priest*
chieftain 400.3 *leader*
chieftaincy 85.3 *dominion*
chief technician 586.32 *airman*
chief thing 123.3
chief whip 400.3 *leader;* 579.15 *manager;* 396.10 *person of authority;* 12.8 *politician*
chiffon 193.4 *textile;* 527.8 *transparent thing*
chigger 76.3 *pest*
chignon 547.8 *haircut*
chigoe 76.3 *pest*
chilblain 494.3 *chill;* 260.15 *ulcer*
child 555.9; 387.4 *dependent;* 805.4 *innocent person;* 646.3 *naive person;* 566.7 *person;* 356.7 *produce;* 561.6 *progeny*
child abuse 651.7 *act of malevolence;* 236.11 *harmfulness;* 380.2 *physical violence;* 796.7 *sexual assault*
child abuser 351.3 *abuser;* 798.6 *evil person;* 796.10 *sex offender;* 804.9 *wicked person*
child allowance 392.4 *social assistance*
child-bearing 568.15 *female*
childbed 561.7 *obstetrics*
child benefit 392.4 *social assistance*
childbirth 561.7 *obstetrics;* 561.3 *propagation*
child-health clinic 35.10 *hospital*
childhood 130.4 *conception;* 554.5 *life cycle;* 805.3 *naivety;* 555.1 *youth*
childhood friend 569.6 *close friend*
childhood playmate 595.4 *likable person*
childish 459.5 *foolish;* 5.39 *of language;* 124.4 *trivial;* 457.6 *unintelligent;* 555.11 *young*
childish language 5.5 *nonstandard language*
childishly 457.11 *unintelligently;* 555.14 *youthfully*
childishness 459.1 *folly;* 457.2 *unintelligence;* 555.2 *youthfulness*
childless 563.3 *infertile*
childlessness 563.1 *infertility*
childlike 646.1, 805.7 *naive;* 457.6 *unintelligent;* 555.11 *young*
child-minder 252.3 *protector*
child molestation 236.11 *harmfulness*
child of fortune 248.4 *prosperous person*
child of God 7.3 *religious person*
child of nature 646.3 *naive person*
child pornography 796.2 *indecency*
child prodigy 619.5 *person of wonder*
childproof 252.7 *invulnerable*
child psychologist 36.29 *psychologist*
child psychology 36.1 *psychology;* 394.13 *therapy*
children 555.10 *the young*
Children in Need Appeal 710.3 *solicitation*
children's book 740.6 *book publishing*
children's clothes 551.23
children's court 16.19 *law court*
children's dentist 35.14 *dentist*
children's dictionary 5.28 *dictionary*
children's game 69.1 *game*
children's hospital 35.10 *hospital*
children's nurse 35.16 *nurse*
children's swimming pool 67.7 *swimming pool*
child's play 705.5 *easy question;* 265.6 *easy thing;* 124.8 *trifle*
child support 413.7 *financial support;* 788.3 *income;* 652.4 *welfare state*
Child Support Agency 413.8 *supporter*
child welfare 650.3 *welfare;* 652.4 *welfare state*
chiliad 201.10 *thousand;* 276.2 *time period*
chiliasm 244.11 *reformism*
chiliast 244.12 *reformer*
chiliastic 244.16 *improving*
chill 494.3; 494.8 *cold;* 31.31, 494.1 *coldness;* 31.55 *cool;* 481.5 *discourage;* 494.12 *make cold;* 581.1 *refresh;* 260.3 *symptom;* 263.2 *take it easy;* 655.1 *unsociability*
chilladas 25.34 *vegetarian dish*
chill cupboard 494.4 *cooler*
chilled 494.8 *cold*
chilled counter 494.4 *cooler*
chilled to the bone 494.8 *cold*
chilled to the marrow 494.8 *cold*
chiller 494.4 *cooler*
chill factor 494.7 *cold weather;* 31.6 *weather data*
chilli 496.5 *herbs*
chilli con carne 25.50 *Central American dish*
chilliness 31.31, 494.1 *coldness;* 655.1 *unsociability*
chilling 481.9 *dissuasive;* 494.9 *heat-resistant*
chill in the air 31.31 *coldness*
chilly 494.8 *cold;* 31.55 *cool;* 655.8 *unsociable*
chilopod 75.4 *arthropod*
Chilopoda 75.4 *arthropod*
chime 750.24 *harmonize;* 750.4 *harmony;* 516.3 *melodiousness;* 18.13 *melody;* 509.12, 510.10 *ring;* 510.2 *ringing*
chime in 516.8 *harmonize;* 133.16 *interrupt*
chimera 477.5 *fantasy;* 96.2 *illusion;* 518.5 *imagination;* 70.7 *legendary beast;* 525.4 *something that appears*
chimerical 96.9, 700.40 *illusory;* 477.12 *imaginary;* 525.9 *ostensible*
chimes 507.1 *loudness;* 510.4 *sources of resonance*
chiming 750.13 *harmonious;* 750.4 *harmony;* 516.6 *melodious;* 509.18 *pealing;* 112.15 *reverberatory;* 509.5, 510.7 *ringing*
chimney 493.6 *fire;* 146.3 *gulf;* 62.9 *mountaineer;* 308.7 *passageway;* 62.5 *rock face;* 154.6 *tall thing;* 92.8 *valley*
chimney corner 493.6 *fire*
chimneying 62.3 *climbing technique*
chimneystack 308.7 *passageway*
chimney sweep 256.12 *cleaner;* 258.6 *dirty person*
chin 525.3 *external appearance*
china 24.1 *ceramics;* 410.16 *crockery;* 356.7 *produce;* 337.5 *weak thing*
china cabinet 23.5 *cabinet*
china clay 435.1 *materials;* 24.2 *raw material*
china decorator 24.7 *potter*
china doll 717.6 *image*
China ink 532.8 *black pigment*
chinaman 53.8 *delivery*
china painter 24.7 *potter*
china plumbing ware 24.9 *industrial ceramics*
china stone 24.2 *raw material*
China syndrome 357.4 *ruin*
China tea 558.3 *tea*
Chinatown 87.3 *New York*
chinaware 24.1 *ceramics;* 410.16 *crockery*
chinchilla 550.14 *animal covering*
chine 154.4 *mountain range;* 92.8 *valley*
Chinese 566.4 *modern human*
Chinese character 5.13 *letter*
Chinese dish 25.48
Chinese lantern 522.7 *lantern*
Chinese lanterns 601.8 *salute*
Chinese mushroom 25.33 *vegetable*
Chinese New Year 10.16 *religious festival*
Chinese puzzle 737.4 *brain-teaser*
Chinese-Siamese 5.11 *family of languages*
Chinese whisper 504.8 *something heard*
Chinese white 531.8 *whitener*
chink 146.2 *crack;* 231.7 *defect;* 184.2 *furrow;* 151.6 *narrow place;* 510.10 *ring;* 510.2 *ringing;* 184.8 *wrinkle*
chink in one's armour 231.7 *defect;* 254.7 *vulnerability*
chinky 184.6 *wrinkly*
chinoiserie 23.1 *furniture;* 23.7 *furniture style*
chinook salmon 55.4 *American game fish*
chintz 193.4 *textile*
chintzy 793.10 *shoddy*
chinwag 734.2 *chat;* 729.1 *faculty of speech;* 731.3 *talk*
chip 424.4 *be brittle;* 39.13 *circuit;* 40.19 *computing terms;* 427.23 *crumble;* 231.7 *defect;* 196.3 *fragment;* 56.7 *golf;* 56.3 *golf shots;* 159.2 *little thing;* 743.3 *means of identification;* 205.7 *piece;* 66.4 *play soccer;* 19.21 *sculpt;* 372.9 *separate;* 411.4 *slice*
chip a stone 68.16 *bobsled*
chipboard 435.4 *board;* 23.12 *wood*
chip in 392.29 *finance;* 768.5 *give;* 133.16 *interrupt*
chip log 332.8 *speed*
chip off 424.4 *be brittle*
chipolata 25.29 *sausage*
chipped 424.1 *brittle;* 231.1 *imperfect*
Chippendale 23.7 *furniture style*
chipper 79.7 *timber production*
chippie 578.2 *artisan;* 23.13 *carpenter*
chipping 424.1 *brittle*
chippings 550.11 *paving*
chip-proof 423.1 *tough*
chippy 691.4 *drug taker;* 557.15 *eating place*
chiquetaille 25.51 *West Indian dish*
chiral 32.37 *structural*
chiral centre 32.13 *structure*
chirality 32.13 *structure*
chirognomy 11.9 *divination*
chiromancer 11.13 *diviner*
chiromancy 11.9, 475.2 *divination*
chiropodist 394.15 *healer;* 35.17 *paramedic*
chiropody 35.6 *health care;* 394.12 *surgery*
chiropractic 35.2 *natural medicine;* 394.13 *therapy;* 492.2 *touching;* 35.8 *treatment*
chiropractor 35.12, 394.15 *healer;* 393.12 *repairer;* 492.5 *toucher*
Chiroptera 71.7 *flying mammal*
chiropteran 71.27; 71.7 *flying mammal*
chirp 72.18 *bird song;* 72.26, 515.5 *sing*
chirping 515.2 *bird song*
chirpy 598.1 *cheerful*
chirr 515.5 *sing*
chirrup 72.18 *bird song;* 72.26, 515.5 *sing*
chirruping 515.2 *bird song*
chisel 774.16 *act dishonestly;* 23.17 *carpenter;* 19.15 *engraving;* 553.9 *fashion;* 160.7 *form;* 356.10 *produce;* 19.21 *sculpt;* 19.14 *sculptor's materials;* 425.9 *sharp-edged thing;* 438.1 *tool;* 425.16 *use a sharp tool;* 438.10 *use tools;* 23.11 *woodworking tool*
chiseller 700.17 *cheat*
chisel plough 43.10 *farm tool*
chi-square distribution 27.59 *probability distribution*
chit 716.6 *documentation;* 756.2 *guarantee;* 159.4 *little person;* 743.3 *means of identification;* 757.2 *permit*
chit-chat 734.2 *chat*
chitin 34.7 *cell;* 33.4 *polysaccharide*
chit of a girl 555.8 *young woman*
chiton 551.16 *robe*
chitterlings 25.31 *offal*
chitty 743.3 *means of identification*
chivalrous 613.10; 658.7 *courteous;* 799.4 *honourable;* 241.2 *likable;* 567.17 *male;* 585.17 *military;* 803.5 *virtuous*
chivalrously 658.14 *courteously;* 799.7 *honourably;* 803.9 *virtuously*
chivalrousness 658.1 *courtesy*
chivalry 241.8 *amiability;* 586.20 *cavalryman;* 613.8 *courageous act;* 658.1 *courtesy;* 585.2 *glory of war;* 613.2 *heroism;* 59.15 *horse person;* 799.1 *probity;* 803.1 *virtue*
chives 496.5 *herbs*
chivy 71.23 *mammal hunting;* 633.8 *pursue*
chivy along 332.7 *hurry someone up*
Chlamydomonas 75.9 *protozoan*
chloramphenical 83.6 *fungal antibiotic*
chloric 32.34 *elemental*
chloride of lime 530.4 *colour remover*
chlorinate 257.6 *make hygienic;* 252.10 *protect;* 255.10, 256.15 *purify;* 32.26 *react*
chlorinated 32.34 *elemental;* 257.4 *hygienic*
chlorinated lime 530.4 *colour remover*
chlorination 256.2 *cleaning;* 257.1 *hygiene*
chlorine 33.15 *essential element*
chlorophyll 538.10 *green pigment;* 33.18 *pigment;* 84.3 *plant body*
chlorophyll a 33.23 *photosynthesis*
chlorophyll b 33.23 *photosynthesis*
Chlorophyta 84.2 *algae*
chlorophyte 84.2 *algae*
chloroplast 34.8 *cell organ*
chloroprene rubber 32.21 *polymer*
chlorosis 44.12 *pests and diseases*
chlorous 32.34 *elemental*
chocaholic 386.5 *compulsive person*
chock 62.4 *climbing equipment;* 309.1 *closure*
chock-a-block 376.50 *crowded;* 152.2 *dense;* 217.3 *filled;* 232.8 *full*
chocker 217.3 *filled*
chock-full 217.3 *filled;* 232.8 *full*
chockstone 62.5 *rock face*
chocolate 534.1 *brown;* 534.5 *brown thing;* 498.4 *confectionery;* 25.41 *sweet*

chocolate bar 25.41 *sweet*
chocolate cake 25.36 *cake*; 498.3 *dessert*
chocolate gateau 25.36 *cake*
chocolate milk 558.5 *milk*
chocolate mousse 498.3 *dessert*
chocolate-point 534.5 *brown thing*
chohan 7.2 *religiousness*
choice 469.8; **593.7**; 797.2 *best*; 123.3 *chief thing*; 469.15 *chosen*; 128.10 *excluding*; 250.1 *freedom*; 595.2 *inclination*; 464.1 *judgment*; 595.3 *likes*; 352.1 *means*; 469.6 *selection*; 372.2 *setting apart*; 797.9 *the best*; 635.1 *will*; 235.1 *worthy*
choice bit 235.7 *elite*
choice meat 567.4 *boyfriend*
choice of expression 5.24 *phrasing*
choice of words 724.4 *literary style*; 5.24 *phrasing*
choir 374.3 *assembly*; 10.12 *church*; 750.4 *harmony*
choir invisible 8.6 *angel*
choir master 18.24 *musician*
choir school 6.12 *educational institution*
choir stall 23.2 *chair*; 10.12 *church*
choke 219.4 *be excessive*; 378.8 *hinder*; 382.17 *murder*; 335.8 *overpower*; 39.17 *resistor*; 513.5 *sound hoarse*; 309.8 *stop*; 309.2 *stopper*; 52.12 *wrestle*; 52.5 *wrestling*
choked 730.11 *speechless*; 309.13 *stopped*
chokedamp 432.3 *miasma*
choked up 309.13 *stopped*
choker 179.3 *circular thing*; 551.14 *neckwear*
chokey 815.2 *the inside*
choking 52.5 *wrestling*
cholagogic 559.6 *inducing secretion*
choler 594.5, 624.4 *anger*
cholera 357.7 *agent of destruction*; 260.8 *indigestion*; 260.6 *infection*; 260.7 *tropical disease*
choleretic 37.4 *drug type*; 37.17 *stimulating*
choleric 594.13, 624.16 *angry*; 701.8 *argumentative*; 599.12 *four humours*; 36.7 *personality type*
cholesterol 557.11 *food content*; 33.6 *lipid*
choline 33.13 *vitamin*
chomp 557.21 *eat*
chomping 557.1 *eating*
Chomskyan 4.11 *follower of a doctrine*; 4.14 *of a philosophy*
Chondrichthyes 74.2 *fish*
chondriosome 34.8 *cell organ*
chondrite 29.20 *meteor*
chondroblast 403.7 *skeleton*
choo choo 321.4 *locomotive*
choose 635.12; 466.12 *discriminate*; 595.8 *prefer*; 469.1 *select*
choose an alternative 762.5 *take a substitute*
choose by ballot 469.5 *vote*
choose one's ground 585.14 *battle*
choose one's words carefully 724.9 *style*
choose the military solution 585.12 *go to war*
choose to 595.9 *like to*
choosing 469.14 *selecting*; 469.6 *selection*
choosy 466.9 *discriminating*; 469.14 *selecting*
chop 25.55 *cook*; 367.2 *flatten*; 205.7 *piece*; 372.9 *separate*; 425.16 *use a sharp tool*; 438.10 *use tools*
chop and change 642.5 *be capricious*; 227.12 *be irresolute*; 224.8 *cause change*
chop down 367.2 *flatten*
chophouse 557.15 *eating place*
choplogic 274.4 *faulty reasoning*
chop logic 701.14 *discuss*; 702.11 *practise sophistry*
chop off 212.4 *take off*
chopped 25.56 *culinary*; 212.7 *reduced*
chopper 322.8 *aircraft*; 320.12 *bicycle*; 425.10 *knife*; 561.8 *organs of reproduction*; 587.8 *sharp weapon*
choppily 420.14 *roughly*
choppiness 133.1 *discontinuity*; 299.1 *irregularity*; 420.6 *roughness*; 327.3 *turbulence*; 91.3 *wave*
chopping 212.1 *subtraction*
chopping and changing 227.2 *irresolution*
chopping board 25.6 *kitchen equipment*
choppy 420.4 *bumpy*; 133.8 *discontinuous*; 299.4 *irregular*; 91.7 *oceanic*; 327.17 *turbulent*
choppy sea 420.9 *broken water*; 91.3 *wave*; 184.4 *wrinkled thing*
chopsticks 557.16 *eating utensil*
chop suey 25.48 *Chinese dish*
chop the air 742.11 *gesture*
choragus 579.14 *leader*; 21.27 *producer*
choral 21.39 *dramatic*; 750.13 *harmonious*; 18.32 *instrumental*
chorale 18.5 *sacred music*; 516.2 *song*
chorally 21.44 *dramatically*; 750.33 *harmoniously*
choral music 18.3 *classical music*
chord 27.42 *circle*; 374.2 *cooperation*; 27.37 *line*; 18.16 *musical note*; 179.4 *parts of a circle*
Chordata 75.2 *protochordate*
chordate 70.15 *of animals*; 75.2 *protochordate*; 70.4 *type of animal*
chordophone 18.25 *musical instrument*
chore 770.3 *allotted task*; 620.2 *boring thing*; 576.2 *task*
chorea 260.17 *nervous disorder*; 327.7 *shake*
choreal 327.19 *convulsive*
choreic 327.19 *convulsive*
choreograph 409.16 *adapt*; 22.15 *dance*
choreographer 22.5 *dancer*; 21.26 *dramatist*; 21.27 *producer*
choreographic 21.39 *dramatic*
choreographically 21.44 *dramatically*
choreography 403.9 *artistic structure*; 22.8 *ballet*; 22.1 *dancing*; 21.9 *dramaturgy*; 409.9 *musical arrangement*
chores 576.1 *work*
choriamb 17.9 *metre*
choric ode 17.7 *poem*
chorion 34.15 *developmental biology*
chorionic 34.26 *developmental*
chorionic villus sampling 35.7 *diagnosis*
chorister 516.5 *melodist*
C horizon 30.36 *soil*
chorography 142.5 *topography*
Chorten 10.13 *shrine*
chortle 514.2 *cry of joy*; 514.11, 599.14, 600.8 *laugh*; 600.3 *laughter*; 597.7 *show joy*
chorus 374.3 *assembly*; 21.25 *cast*; 750.4 *harmony*; 516.1 *melody*; 514.8 *musical cry*; 509.6 *musical repetition*; 17.8 *part of poem*; 21.23 *role*; 21.8 *scene*; 18.39 *sing*; 514.15 *sing out*; 729.10 *speaker*; 285.7 *synchronize*; 509.13 *trill*
chorus boy 21.29 *entertainer*
chorus girl 21.30 *dancer*; 21.29 *entertainer*
chorus leader 579.14 *leader*
chorus master 18.24 *musician*
chose 440.2 *legal terms*
chose in action 440.2 *legal terms*
chose in possession 440.2, 763.2 *legal terms*
chosen 469.15; 593.21 *beloved*; 396.13 *elected*; 121.15 *excellent*; 474.7 *expected*; 235.1 *worthy*
chosen few 235.7 *elite*; 121.7 *the best people*
chosen people 469.9 *chosen thing*; 235.7 *elite*
chosen thing 469.9
choux pastry 25.37 *pastry*
chow 557.7 *food*
chowder 25.13 *soup*
chow down 25.58 *grub's on!*
chow mein 25.48 *Chinese dish*
chrestomathy 723.3 *compendium*; 376.32, 412.3 *miscellany*
Chris Evert 63.7 *famous tennis players*
Chrism 10.5 *Christian rite*
chrism 268.6 *ointment*; 10.18 *perform rites*
chrismal 10.21 *ritualistic*; 10.14 *sacred object*; 268.14 *unguent*
chrismation 268.4 *anointment*
chrismatory 268.14 *unguent*
Christ 8.4 *God the Son*; 712.15 *miscellaneous swearwords*; 589.2 *symbol of peace*
Christ Almighty 712.15 *miscellaneous swearwords*
christen 130.25 *enrol*; 10.18 *perform rites*; 769.10 *receive someone*
christened 130.37 *enrolled*; 769.13 *received*
christener 5.2 *linguist*
christening 10.5 *Christian rite*; 130.8 *enrolment*; 656.3 *formal occasion*; 433.15 *holy water*; 721.7 *nomenclature*; 769.4 *reception*; 323.4 *shipbuilding*
Christian 7.5; 650.5 *benevolent person*; 650.7 *charitable*; 7.16 *denominational*; 593.17 *loving*; 255.12 *morally pure*; 803.5 *virtuous*
Christian Broadcasting Network 692.25 *broadcast material*
Christian charity 650.2 *charity*; 593.1 *love*
Christian conduct 803.1 *virtue*
Christian Democratic Party 12.6 *political party*
Christian Democratic Union 12.6 *political party*
christiania 68.4 *skiing technique*
Christianize 7.20 *preach*
Christian love 593.1 *love*
Christian martyr 752.7 *martyr*
Christian name 721.8 *name*
Christian rite 10.5
Christian Science 394.11 *medical art*
Christian Scientist 7.5 *Christian*; 394.15 *healer*
Christian text 7.12 *religious text*
christie 68.4 *skiing technique*
Christie's 779.1 *market*
Christlike 8.13 *divine*
Christly 8.13 *divine*
Christmas 298.6 *annually celebrated day*; 10.16 *religious festival*; 292.5 *winter*
Christmas box 768.2 *gift*
Christmas cake 25.36 *cake*
Christmas carol 516.2 *song*
Christmas dinner 557.13 *feast*
Christmas present 768.2 *gift*
Christmas pudding 25.35 *dessert*
Christmassy 654.17 *festive*
Christmas time 292.5 *winter*
Christmas tree 79.1 *tree*
Christmas tree lights 522.6 *electric light*
Christological 7.18 *theological*
Christology 7.13 *theology*
Christophany 8.8 *divine manifestation*
chroma 529.3 *hue*
chromascope 529.8 *chromatics*
chromatic 529.10 *coloured*
chromatic aberration 529.1 *colour*; 28.31 *lens element*; 29.25 *mounting*
chromatic colour 529.1 *colour*
chromaticism 529.1 *colour*
chromaticity 529.3 *hue*
chromaticity chart 529.8 *chromatics*
chromaticity diagram 529.8 *chromatics*
chromatic painter 529.6 *painter*
chromatic painting 529.7 *colour painting*
chromatics 529.8
chromatic scale 18.20 *key*
chromatid 34.14 *chromosome*
chromatin 34.9 *cell nucleus*; 34.14 *chromosome*
chromatin strands 34.9 *cell nucleus*
chromatism 529.1 *colour*
chromatist 529.6 *painter*
chromatogram 32.17 *analysis*
chromatographic 32.41 *analytic*
chromatography 32.17 *analysis*; 32.5 *process*
chromatography paper 370.6 *sponge*
chromatological 529.14 *chromolithographic*
chromatology 529.8 *chromatics*
chromatophore 34.8 *cell organ*
chrome yellow 537.7 *yellow pigment*
chromic 32.34 *elemental*
chromite 30.34 *mineral*
chromium 33.15 *essential element*
chromogenic film 41.9 *film*
chromolithographer 529.6 *painter*
chromolithographic 529.14
chromolithography 529.7 *colour painting*
chromomere 34.14 *chromosome*
chromonema 34.14 *chromosome*
chromophore 42.6 *dye*
chromoplast 34.8 *cell organ*
chromosomal 34.25 *genetic*
chromosome 34.14; 34.14 *chromosome*; 34.11 *genetics*
chromosome mutation 34.14 *chromosome*
chromosome number 34.14 *chromosome*
chromosphere 29.15 *sun*
chromotrope 42.6 *dye*
chromous 32.34 *elemental*
chromyl 32.34 *elemental*
chronic 632.14 *habituated*; 275.21 *lasting through time*; 491.5 *painful*; 260.22 *sick*; 641.3 *unyielding*
chronically 260.25 *unhealthily*
chronically ill 260.21 *unhealthy*
chronically sick 260.21 *unhealthy*
chronic complaint 260.1 *ill health*
chronic ill health 260.1 *ill health*
chronic illness 260.1 *ill health*
chronic invalid 260.19 *sick person*
chronicle 3.5; **3.20**; 281.15 *chronologize*; 220.8 *list*; 721.3 *narration*; 17.4 *nonfiction*; 744.1, 744.13 *record*; 721.15 *recount*
chronicled 3.19; 744.16 *recorded*
chronicler 281.13; 17.14 *author*; 721.10 *descriptive writer*; 744.9 *recorder*; 275.14 *timekeeper*
chronogram 281.8 *face*; 275.13 *timer*
chronogrammatic 275.25 *of known date*; 281.17 *timekeeping*
chronograph 281.9 *hourglass*; 275.13 *timer*
chronographer 281.12 *chronologist*; 275.14 *timekeeper*
chronographic 275.25 *of known date*; 281.17 *timekeeping*
chronographically 281.18 *horologically*
chronography 281.3 *chronology*; 275.7 *time measurement*
chronologer 281.12 *chronologist*
chronologic 281.17 *timekeeping*
chronological 132.9 *consecutive*; 275.25 *of known date*; 281.17 *timekeeping*
chronological error 286.1 *different time*; 288.1 *wrong time*
chronologically 275.30; 132.18 *consecutively*; 281.18 *horologically*
chronological order 132.2 *consecution*
chronologist 281.12; 275.14 *timekeeper*
chronologize 281.15; 275.17 *date*
chronology 281.3; 275.7 *time measurement*
chronometer 28.87 *clock*; 26.8 *meter*; 323.5 *navigation*; 281.5 *timekeeper*; 275.13 *timer*
chronometric 26.16 *micrometric*; 275.25 *of known date*; 281.17 *timekeeping*
chronometry 275.10; 26.2 *micrometry*
chronon 275.1 *time*
chronoscope 281.9 *hourglass*
chronoscopy 275.10 *chronometry*
chronostratigraphic unit 30.41 *geological time*
chrysalid 76.13 *immature*
chrysalis 550.14 *animal covering*; 34.15 *developmental biology*; 76.5 *larva*; 344.3 *rudiment*; 555.4 *young animal*
chrysolite 30.34 *mineral*
chrysological 780.22 *monetary*
Chrysophyta 84.2 *algae*
chrysophyte 84.2 *algae*
chrysoprase 538.11 *green thing*
chthonian 8.16 *devilish*
chthonic 8.16 *devilish*
chub 55.5 *British game fish*
chubbiness 158.5 *fatness*; 181.2 *round body*; 152.5 *thickness*
chubby 158.16 *fat*; 152.1 *thick*; 181.10 *well-rounded*
chubby-cheeked 158.16 *fat*
chubby-faced 158.16 *fat*
chuck 25.22, 25.23 *beef*; 46.18 *be penalized*; 331.13 *blow*; 557.7 *food*; 605.5 *resign*; 381.7 *stone*; 331.6 *tap*; 330.5, 330.23 *throw*; 355.2 *withdraw*
chucker 330.14 *thrower*
chucker-out 371.26 *ejector*; 336.6 *muscleman*
chucking 46.13 *penalty*; 330.3 *throwing*
chuck it 226.12 *stop!*
chuckle 514.2 *cry of joy*; 514.11, 599.14 *laugh*; 597.7 *show joy*; 515.5 *sing*
chuckling 514.17 *cheering*
chuck out 357.8 *destroy*; 470.2 *discard*; 371.1 *expel*
chuck under the chin 593.27 *kiss*
chuck up 371.15 *vomit*
chuck-wagon cook 25.2 *cook*
chuff chuff 321.4 *locomotive*
chuffed 490.7 *pleased*
chuffer 321.4 *locomotive*
chug 558.13 *drink*; 509.10 *rattle*; 300.15 *walk*
chug-a-lug 558.18 *cheers!*; 690.8 *get drunk*
chug on 333.1 *move slowly*
chukka boots 551.19 *footwear*
chukker 181.6 *round*
chum 55.1 *angling*; 569.5 *friend*; 595.4

likable person; 567.3 *male title of address*; 654.6 *social person*
chuminess 569.1 *friendship*
chummy 569.8 *friendly*
chump 25.26 *lamb*
chump chops 25.26 *lamb*
chunder 371.15 *vomit*
chunk 203.2 *certain amount*; 158.7 *mass*; 205.7 *piece*; 215.1 *remainder*; 416.4 *solid body*; 330.5 *throw*
chunkiness 158.6 *squatness*; 152.5 *thickness*
chunky 414.1 *heavy*; 158.17 *stocky*; 152.1 *thick*
Chunnel 317.8 *tunnel*
church **10.12**; 38.20 *building*; 356.8 *construction*; 2.8 *human institution*; 760.4 *medium of conversion*; 10.11 *place of worship*; 7.1 *religion*
church architecture **20.10**
church bazaar 767.2 *disposal of property*; 778.4 *sale*
church bell 711.2 *danger signal*; 742.4 *signal*; 510.4 *sources of resonance*; 742.6 *word*
church book 10.10 *religious manual*
church candle 522.5 *incandescent light*
churchgoer 450.5 *believer*; 9.5, 10.17 *worshipper*
churchgoing 7.15 *religious*
church government 12.1 *government*
churchiness 7.2 *religiousness*
churchly 7.17 *priestly*
churchman 7.8 *priest*
church member 450.5 *believer*
church music 18.5 *sacred music*
church parable 18.5 *sacred music*
church property 440.1 *property*
church service 10.4 *public worship*
churchwarden 7.8 *priest*; 496.7 *tobacco*
church wedding 570.5 *wedding*
churchy 7.15 *religious*
churchyard 583.5 *cemetery*
churl 574.1 *plebeian*
churlish 659.6 *bad-mannered*; 486.3 *clumsy*; 544.8 *indecorous*; 625.4 *irascible*; 626.7 *irritable*
churlishly 625.9 *irascibly*; 626.14 *irritably*; 659.10 *rudely*
churlishness 659.2 *bad manners*; 544.2 *impropriety*; 625.1 *irascibility*
churn 327.22 *agitate*; 327.14 *agitator*; 43.10 *farm tool*; 412.6 *mixer*; 327.3 *turbulence*
churn out 112.18 *harp*; 356.10 *produce*; 561.9 *reproduce*
churn up 327.22 *agitate*
chute 90.2 *channel*; 305.5 *dive*; 305.3 *downflow*; 315.7 *outlet*; 421.8 *smooth thing*
chutney 25.42 *preserve*; 496.2 *seasoning*
chutzpadik 660.12 *impudent person*
chutzpah 707.6 *assertiveness*; 167.5 *boldness*; 660.2 *cheek*; 661.1 *defiance*
chyle 431.3 *body fluid*
chylifaction 431.7 *juiciness*
chylifactive 431.16 *rheumy*
chylifactory 431.16 *rheumy*
chylific 431.16 *rheumy*
chylification 431.7 *juiciness*
chypre 502.3 *incense*
CIA 737.2 *secretiveness*
ciao! 313.14 *goodbye!*; 312.23 *hello!*
ciborium 550.7 *overhead covering*; 10.14 *sacred object*
cicatrix 234.3 *deformity*
cicatrization 393.11 *recuperation*
cicatrize 393.6 *cure*; 234.11 *deform*
cicerone 713.4 *adviser*
Ciceronian 543.3 *elegant*
cig 496.7 *tobacco*
cigar 181.4 *cylinder*; 496.7 *tobacco*
cigarette 496.7 *tobacco*
cigarette butt 215.1 *remainder*
cigarette case 410.6 *box*; 496.7 *tobacco*
cigarette end 215.1 *remainder*; 496.7 *tobacco*
cigarette lighter 437.2 *lighter*; 496.7 *tobacco*
cigarette machine 496.7 *tobacco*
cigarette paper 496.7 *tobacco*
cigarette smoke 503.2 *something that makes an unpleasant smell*
cigarillo 496.7 *tobacco*
ciggie 496.7 *tobacco*
Ciliata 75.9 *protozoan*
ciliate 75.9 *protozoan*; 75.23 *protozoan*
ciliate protozoan 75.9 *protozoan*
cilium 34.8 *cell organ*
CIM 40.1 *computing*
Cimmerian 523.8 *dark*; 266.2 *obscure*
cinch 373.10 *band*; 700.22 *dupe*; 705.5 *easy question*; 265.6 *easy thing*; 452.12 *something certain*
cincture 551.25 *accessories*
cinder 258.4 *dirt*; 238.6 *refuse*
Cinderella 124.10 *nonentity*; 782.10 *poor person*
cinders 493.6 *fire*; 215.2 *residue*
cine camera 41.16 *camera*; 41.14 *cine film*; 518.8 *reflection*
cine film **41.14**
cinema **21.6**; 21.1 *drama*; 738.9 *production*; 21.16 *theatre*; 518.9 *viewpoint*
cinemagoer 97.5 *someone present*
Cinemascope™ 150.5 *broad thing*
cinema ticket 743.3 *means of identification*
cinematographically 41.23 *photographically*
cinematography 21.6 *cinema*; 41.1 *photography*
cinema vérité 95.3 *realism*
cine photography 41.1 *photography*
Cinerama™ 150.5 *broad thing*
cinerarium 583.5 *cemetery*
cinerary 583.11 *funeral*
cinerary urn 583.4 *funeral objects*
cinereous 533.1 *grey*
cingulectomy 36.3 *psychiatric treatment*
cingulum 7.11 *vestment*
cinnabar 535.6 *red pigment*
cinnamon 534.5 *brown thing*; 496.5 *herbs*
cinnamon roll 25.36 *cake*
cinnamon toast 25.38 *bread*
cinque 201.1 *five*
cinquefoil 201.1 *five*; 743.8 *heraldic device*
cipher 737.4 *brain-teaser*; 210.8 *calculate*; 737.14 *make mysterious*; 124.10 *nonentity*; 194.1 *number*; 742.1 *sign*; 11.2 *the occult*; 719.12 *translate*; 696.12 *unintelligible thing*; 195.1 *zero*
cipher clerk 719.6 *interpreter*
ciphered 5.40 *translated*
ciphering 210.3 *count*
circadian rhythm 298.2 *cycle*; 276.5 *recurrent period*
Circe 363.6 *charmer*; 480.13 *tempter*; 11.4 *witch*
Circean 11.15 *witchlike*
circle **27.42**; **179.2**; **179.6**; 27.97 *align*; 21.18 *auditorium*; 298.8 *be cyclic*; 177.2 *bend*; 376.19 *clique*; 132.6 *continuum*; 177.6 *curve*; 47.2 *field events*; 376.11 *group*; 181.12 *move round*; 306.3 *orbit*; 251.1 *restraint*; 306.7 *ring*; 307.8 *rotate*; 181.3 *round thing*; 170.7 *surround*; 169.5 *team*; 21.33 *theatregoer*; 518.9 *viewpoint*
circle of friends 569.5 *friend*
circle of least confusion 28.31 *lens element*
circle of wagons 384.9 *barrier*
circle theatre 21.16 *theatre*
circle upon itself 180.6 *convolute*
circlewise 306.12 *circuitously*
circling 298.12 *cyclic*; 306.1 *orbital motion*; 306.11 *orbiting*; 307.12 *rotary*
circling upon itself 180.1 *convolution*
circuit **28.55**; **39.13**; 177.2 *bend*; 179.2 *circle*; 298.2 *cycle*; 334.7 *electrical power*; 21.15 *engagement*; 59.11 *eventing*; 59.9 *jumping*; 86.13 *locality*; 61.6 *motor-racing terms*; 306.3, 306.6 *orbit*; 307.8 *rotate*; 181.6 *round*; 181.3 *round thing*; 317.2 *route*; 204.3 *whole situation*
circuit breaker 39.28 *plug*; 252.4 *safety device*
circuit court 464.3 *place of judgment*; 16.21 *US court*
circuit court of appeals 16.21 *US court*
circuit design 39.13 *circuit*
circuit diagram 39.13 *circuit*
circuit element **39.16**; 28.55 *circuit*
circuit function **39.15**
circuition **300.5**; 306.2 *circuitousness*
circuit judge 16.24 *US judge*
circuitous 270.4 *circumlocutory*; 189.5 *devious*; 300.17 *directional*; 306.9 *orbital*; 219.7 *superfluous*; 325.25 *wandering*
circuitously **270.8**; **306.12**; 179.8, 180.8 *circularly*; 177.7 *curvedly*; 189.9 *deviously*; 300.18 *in motion*
circuitousness **306.2**; 189.3 *deviousness*; 325.16 *wandering*
circuitous route 179.2 *circle*
circuitous writing 270.2 *circumlocution*; 219.3 *superfluity*
circuitry 39.13 *circuit*; 306.2 *circuitousness*
circular **179.5**; **306.10**; 740.9 *advertisement*; 177.4 *curved*; 27.81 *curvilinear*; 298.12 *cyclic*; 693.4 *mass communication*; 138.3 *nonspecificness*; 702.7 *sophistic*
circular argument 274.4 *faulty reasoning*; 303.17 *resilience*; 702.2 *sophism*
circular decimal 27.18 *division*
circular function 27.52 *trigonometric function*
Circularity 179
circularity **179.1**; 177.1 *curvature*; 306.1 *orbital motion*; 702.1 *sophistry*
circularize 179.7 *make circular*; 740.15 *publish*
circularized 740.19 *published*
circularly **179.8**; **180.8**; 177.7 *curvedly*; 298.16 *cyclically*; 702.14 *sophistically*
circularly polarized light 28.27 *polarized light*
circular motion 28.8 *time*
circularness 177.1 *curvature*
circular path 179.2 *circle*
circular polarization 28.15 *wave property*
circular return 298.2 *cycle*
circular road 179.2 *circle*
circular saw 38.9 *machine tool*; 307.6 *rotator*; 79.7 *timber production*; 23.11 *woodworking tool*
circular thing **179.3**
circular triangle 27.43 *triangle*
circulate 740.17 *be published*; 342.16 *be sociable*; 179.6 *circle*; 377.16 *distribute*; 740.13 *make public*; 780.24 *monetize*; 181.12 *move round*; 306.6 *orbit*; 318.9 *proceed*; 741.13 *report*; 307.8 *rotate*
circulated 377.22 *distributed*
circulating 740.19 *published*
circulating medium 780.1 *money*
circulation 431.4 *blood*; 306.2 *circuitousness*; 377.1 *dispersion*; 306.1 *orbital motion*; 318.2 *passing along*; 740.1 *publication*; 307.1 *rotation*
circulation pattern 30.13 *ocean current*
circulatory 179.5 *circular*; 306.9 *orbital*; 307.12 *rotary*
circulatory disease 260.4 *disease*
circumambience 170.2 *encirclement*; 306.1 *orbital motion*
circumambient 306.9 *orbital*; 170.5 *surrounded*
circumambulate 179.6 *circle*; 181.12 *move round*; 306.7 *ring*
circumambulation 10.7 *non-Christian ritual*; 306.1 *orbital motion*; 181.6 *round*
circumbendibus 306.2 *circuitousness*; 317.2 *route*; 325.16 *wandering*
circumcircle 27.42 *circle*
circumcise 212.4 *take off*
circumcision 10.7 *non-Christian ritual*; 372.3 *separateness*; 212.1 *subtraction*
circumference 27.42, 179.2 *circle*; 145.3 *distant place*; 163.3 *edge*; 171.1 *exterior*; 100.4 *externality*; 27.37 *line*; 179.4 *parts of a circle*; 307.1 *rotation*; 317.2 *route*; 158.1 *size*; 141.1 *space*
circumferential 179.5 *circular*
circumferentially 179.8 *circularly*
circumflex 5.36 *accent*; 742.7 *punctuation*
circumflex angle 176.1 *angle*
circumflexion 306.1 *orbital motion*
circumfusion 377.4 *sprinkling*
circumgyratory 307.12 *rotary*
circumlocute 306.8 *detour*; 189.7 *deviate*
circumlocution **270.2**; 542.2 *affectation*; 306.2 *circuitousness*; 189.3 *deviousness*; 479.5 *equivocalness*; 720.2 *misinterpretation*; 5.24 *phrasing*; 317.2 *route*; 325.16 *wandering*
circumlocutory **270.4**; 180.4 *convolutional*; 189.5 *devious*; 479.10 *equivocal*; 306.9 *orbital*; 542.10 *ornate*; 5.43 *phrasal*
circummigrate 306.7 *ring*
circummigration 306.1 *orbital motion*
circumnavigable 306.9 *orbital*
circumnavigate 179.6 *circle*; 181.12 *move round*; 323.9 *navigate*; 306.7 *ring*
circumnavigation 300.5 *circuition*; 306.1 *orbital motion*; 181.6 *round*; 323.1 *water travel*
circumnavigator 323.7 *nautical person*
circumnutate 307.8 *rotate*
circumnutation 307.1 *rotation*
circumpolar star 29.10 *star*
circumrotation 307.1 *rotation*
circumrotatory 307.12 *rotary*
circumscribability 191.2 *contractibility*
circumscribable 191.9 *contractible*
circumscribe 27.97 *align*; 721.17 *describe a circle*; 372.11 *divide*; 128.7 *exclude*; 384.18 *fence*; 378.8 *hinder*; 368.5 *inset*; 166.7 *limit*; 191.5 *make smaller*; 684.6 *moderate*; 151.10 *narrow*; 251.8 *restrain*; 136.16 *specify*; 399.3 *veto*; 165.6 *wrap*
circumscribed 136.12 *conditional*; 684.9 *moderate*; 151.1 *narrow*; 360.10 *retained*; 191.7 *smaller*; 170.5 *surrounded*
circumscribed figure 27.41 *geometric figure*
circumscription 191.1 *contraction*; 163.3 *edge*; 165.1 *enclosure*; 128.1 *exclusion*; 378.1 *hindrance*; 166.1 *limitation*; 251.1 *restraint*; 136.6 *specification*; 399.1 *veto*
circumscriptive 191.8 *contracting*; 378.13 *hindering*; 163.6 *outlined*; 251.13 *restraining*; 399.5 *vetoed*
circumscriptively 399.7 *by veto*; 251.16 *under restraints*
circumspect 665.9 *careful*; 616.4 *cautious*; 442.11 *thoughtful*; 333.5 *unhurried*; 471.7 *watchful*; 458.5 *wise*
circumspection **665.3**; 471.3 *carefulness*; 616.1 *caution*; 151.5 *narrowness*; 333.8 *slowness*; 442.6 *thoughtfulness*
circumspectly 471.15 *attentively*; 616.7 *cautiously*; 333.16 *slowly*
circumstance 656.1 *formality*; 209.2 *rank*
Circumstances 222
circumstances **143.2**; **222.1**; 395.1 *influence*; 440.5 *personal estate*; 221.1 *state*
circumstantial **143.8**; **222.7**; 716.8 *evidential*; 124.1 *unimportant*; 454.9 *verificatory*
circumstantial evidence 716.5 *legal evidence*; 16.7 *legal trial*
circumstantiality 270.1 *diffuseness*
circumstantially **143.12**; 716.14 *as evidence*; 222.15 *under the circumstances*; 124.14 *unimportantly*; 454.11 *verifiably*
circumstantiate **222.11**; 454.2, 703.17, 716.12 *prove*
circumstantiation 454.5 *proof*
circumvallation 165.1 *enclosure*; 384.11 *fortification*; 384.8 *military defences*
circumvent 634.1 *avoid*; 645.5 *be cunning*; 700.23 *deceive*; 306.7 *ring*; 700.28 *trick*
circumvention 634.10 *avoidance*; 645.1 *cunning*; 700.1 *deception*; 700.7 *tricking*
circumvent the law 16.73 *be illegal*
circumvolute 307.8 *rotate*
circumvolution 180.1 *convolution*; 307.1 *rotation*
circumvolve 307.8 *rotate*
circus 412.3 *miscellany*; 317.3 *road*; 21.7 *show*; 21.16 *theatre*
circus animal 70.3 *domesticated animal*
circus artist 21.31 *circus performer*
circus horse 59.1 *horse*
circus manager 579.15 *manager*
circus performer **21.31**; 336.5 *athlete*
circus troupe 21.25 *cast*
cire-perdue 19.12 *sculpture*
cirque 156.4 *deep thing*; 30.7 *landform*; 92.8 *valley*
cirque glacier 30.38 *glacier*
cirrhosis of the liver 690.16 *alcoholism*
cirriform 31.49 *cloudy*
cirripede 75.4 *arthropod*
cirrocumuliform 31.49 *cloudy*
cirrocumulous 31.49 *cloudy*
cirrocumulus 31.18 *cloud*
cirrose 31.49 *cloudy*
cirrostratous 31.49 *cloudy*
cirrostratus 31.18 *cloud*
cirrus 31.18 *cloud*
CIS 85.2 *union of nations*
cissoid 27.40 *curve*
cist 583.4 *funeral objects*
cistern 767.8 *sink*; 439.4 *storage*; 410.11 *vessel*; 433.16 *water carrier*
cisternum 34.8 *cell organ*
cis–trans isomer 32.13 *structure*
citadel 384.12 *fort*; 252.5 *refuge*
citation 715.1 *accusation*; 669.4 *compliment*; 397.2 *demand*; 108.2 *interrelated-*

ness; 16.6 *legal process*; 205.2 *particular*; 738.8 *showplace*; 794.1 *trophy*
cite 715.5 *accuse*; 222.11 *circumstantiate*; 703.16 *explain*; 112.17 *iterate*; 16.70 *litigate*; 738.3 *reveal*; 729.11 *speak*; 139.24 *specify*
cited 715.8 *accusatory*; 738.13 *displayed*; 112.10 *iterated*
Cities, Towns, and Villages 87
citified 87.14 *urban*
citify 87.15 *urbanize*
citizen 250.7 *free person*; 566.10 *member of society*; 564.8 *national*; 85.13 *native*; 127.3 *person included*; 564.4 *townsman*
citizen by adoption 564.8 *national*
citizen of the world 485.5 *expert*; 85.15 *internationalist*; 564.8 *national*
citizenry 566.9 *group*; 564.2 *inhabitants*
citizen's army 584.2 *the military*
Citizens' Band radio 504.9 *audio device*; 692.20 *radio broadcasting*; 297.6 *radio frequency*; 692.16 *transmitter*
citizenship 250.3 *independence*; 652.2 *public spiritedness*
citric 80.7 *fruitlike*
citric acid cycle 33.24 *respiration*
citriculture 44.1 *horticulture*
citrine 80.7 *fruitlike*; 537.1 *yellow*
citron 537.1 *yellow*; 537 8 *yellow thing*
citrous 80.7 *fruitlike*
citrus 80.7 *fruitlike*
citrus belt 43.11 *farmland*
citrus fruit 80.2 *botanical fruit*; 80.1 *fruits*; 44.10 *fruit tree*
city 87.1; 396.8 *governmental organization*; 12.5 *political organization*; 87.14 *urban*; 86.10 *urban area*
city centre 87.7 *city district*; 86.10 *urban area*
city commission 579.9 *US administrative council*
city council 16.2 *jurisdiction*; 398.2 *representative body*; 579.9 *US administrative council*
city district 87.7
city dweller 564.4 *townsman*; 87.11 *urbanite*
city editor 740.11 *newspaperman*
city farm 43.6 *farm*
city father 87.11 *urbanite*
city hall 87.13 *municipal building*
city hospital 35.10 *hospital*
city jail 815.1 *prison*
city magistrate 16.23 *judge*
city manager 16.10 *law officer*; 579.16 *official*; 87.11 *urbanite*
city map 163.4, 717.7 *map*
city of the dead 583.5 *cemetery*
city person 564.4 *townsman*
city police 16.16 *US police*
cityscape 518.7 *view*
city slicker 564.4 *townsman*; 87.11 *urbanite*
city state 396.8 *governmental organization*; 566.11 *nation*; 12.5 *political organization*
city tax 790.7 *tax*
civet 502.3 *incense*
civic 12.9 *governmental*; 566.13 *national*; 652.6 *philanthropic*; 654.15 *sociable*; 87.14 *urban*
civically 87.16 *municipally*
civic architecture 20.1 *architecture*
civic centre 173.4 *centre of activity*
civic garden 44.2 *garden*
civics 6.3 *subject*
civil 658.7 *courteous*; 12.9 *governmental*; 172.8 *internal*; 241.2 *likable*; 566.13 *national*; 654.15 *sociable*; 87.14 *urban*
civil affairs 12.2 *politics*
civil architect 20.2 *architect*
civil architecture 20.1 *architecture*
civil ceremony 570.5 *wedding*
civil code 16.1 *the law*
civil court 16.19 *law court*; 464.3 *place of judgment*
civil disobedience 662.1 *disobedience*; 709.2 *dissent*; 383.3 *resistance movement*
civil disturbance 662.2 *violation of the law*
civil engineer 38.18; 578.2 *artisan*; 38.2 *engineer*
civil engineering 38.17; 38.1 *engineering*; 356.2 *manufacture*; 438.6 *mechanics*
civilian 589.3 *pacifist*; 589.7 *peaceful*
civilian evacuation 585.7 *war measures*
civilian targets 382.15 *slaughterhouse*
civilities 658.3 *courtesies*; 656.5 *etiquette*
civility 241.8 *amiability*; 658.1 *courtesy*; 549.1 *elegance*
civilization 6.1 *education*; 244.5 *improvement*; 455.3 *learning*; 17.1 *literature*; 566.4 *modern human*
civilize 6.22 *educate*; 244.1 *improve*; 566.14 *make human*; 2.15 *socialize*
civilized 566.12 *human*; 241.2 *likable*; 6.20, 549.5 *refined*
civilized humanity 566.4 *modern human*
civilizing 244.16 *improving*
civil law 16.1 *the law*
civil liberties 250.2 *free speech*
civil list 220.6 *list of names*
civilly 20.20 *architecturally*; 658.14 *courteously*; 654.18 *sociably*
civil rights 391.2 *equal opportunity*; 250.2 *free speech*
civil rights activist 662.7 *protester*
civil servant 579.16 *official*; 401.2 *public servant*
civil service 12.3, 396.4 *governance*; 579.3 *management*
civil society 566.11 *nation*
civil state 566.11 *nation*
civil time 281.3 *chronology*
civil war 753.2 *disorder*; 662.4 *revolution*; 585.1 *war*
civil wedding 570.5 *wedding*
civil wrong 16.39 *crime*
civism 652.2 *public spiritedness*
civvies 551.4, 657.6 *informal dress*
civvy street 589.1 *peace*
CJD 260.17 *nervous disorder*
clabber 430.11 *thicken*
clabbering 430.1 *viscosity*
clack 509.3, 509.10 *rattle*; 515.5 *sing*
clad 551.32 *dress*; 551.29 *dressed*; 550.28 *face*
cladding 550.8 *wall covering*
clade 34.17 *taxonomy*
cladism 34.17 *taxonomy*
cladist 34.19 *life scientist*
cladistic 34.28 *taxonomic*
cladistics 34.17 *taxonomy*
cladode 77.6 *leaf*
claim 575.7 *be entitled to*; 397.2, 397.10, 710.2, 710.7 *demand*; 369.6 *extorsion*; 369.16 *extort*; 15.4 *industrial dispute*; 701.3 *line of argument*; 16.70 *litigate*; 16.5 *litigation*; 135.8 *miss*; 135.2 *need*; 701.5 *plea*; 701.16 *plead*; 86.12 *plot*; 763.7 *possess*; 763.1 *possession*; 440.1 *property*; 710.1, 710.6 *request*; 801.6 *right*; 701.15 *state*
claimant 715.3 *accuser*; 710.4 *requester*
claim a victory 246.9 *be victorious*
claimed 16.54 *litigated*; 701.11 *logical*
claiming 710.10 *demanding*; 16.53 *litigating*; 763.1 *possession*
claims of conscience 810.4 *sense of duty*
claim squatter's rights 763.7 *possess*
claim supplementary benefit 782.12 *be poor*
claim to fame 811.1 *estimation*; 139.8 *specialization*; 235.6 *worth*
clairaudience 11.8 *psychic power*
clairaudient 11.17 *divinatory*; 11.13 *diviner*
clairsentience 11.8 *psychic power*
clairsentient 11.17 *divinatory*; 11.13 *diviner*
clairvoyance 11.9, 475.2 *divination*; 8.8 *divine manifestation*; 518.5 *imagination*; 590.2 *impression*; 101.4 *parapsychology*; 445.2 *precognition*; 11.8 *psychic power*; 488.1 *sensation*
clairvoyant 101.7 *believer in a nonmaterial world*; 11.17 *divinatory*; 11.13 *diviner*; 590.11 *intuitive*; 445.5 *intuitive person*; 518.11 *observer*; 475.8 *oracle*; 101.9 *parapsychological*; 445.7 *precognitive*; 475.13 *predicting*
clairvoyantly 101.13 *metaphysically*; 11.25 *occultly*
clam 732.5 *shy person*
clamant 507.6 *loud*
clambake 688.3 *act of gluttony*; 557.13 *feast*
clamber 304.14 *climb*; 304.6 *mounting*
clamber up 304.14 *climb*
clam chowder 25.13 *soup*; 25.43 *US dish*
clamlike 75.19 *molluscan*; 736.17 *noncommittal*
clammed up 506.3 *silent*
clammily 429.17 *moistly*; 560.33 *scatologically*
clamminess 429.3 *humidity*; 430.1 *viscosity*
clammy 429.9 *moist*; 560.28 *sweaty*; 430.8 *viscous*
clamorous 507.6 *loud*; 753.9 *protesting*; 513.7 *strident*; 514.16 *vociferous*
clamorously 514.20 *vociferously*
clamour 328.5 *commotion*; 514.1 *cry*; 517.2 *dissonant noise*; 412.3 *miscellany*; 113.4 *objection*; 507.2 *outcry*; 753.1, 753.6 *protest*; 670.9 *show of disapproval*; 513.1 *stridency*
clamour for 135.8 *miss*
clamp 373.12 *bind*; 191.4 *contractor*; 373.8 *fastening*; 191.5 *make smaller*; 251.5 *means of restraint*; 685.4 *moderate*; 685.2 *moderator*; 251.8 *restrain*; 309.3 *restrainer*; 360.6 *retain*; 360.1 *retention*; 360.3 *tools for gripping*
clamp a wheel 378.10 *restrain*
clampdown 647.1 *severity*; 736.4 *silence*
clamp down on 647.5 *be severe*; 357.8 *destroy*; 685.4 *moderate*; 407.22 *pacify*; 251.8 *restrain*
clamped 373.16 *bound*
clamping 191.1 *contraction*
clamshell 550.14 *animal covering*; 38.29 *construction equipment*
clam up 506.1 *be silent*; 737.12 *keep secret*
Clan 56.5 *golf ball*
clan 373.3 *associate*; 376.17 *family*; 137.8 *genealogy*; 566.9 *group*; 564.2 *inhabitants*; 1.7 *society*
clandestine 645.4 *cunning*; 521.3 *private*; 737.10 *secretive*
clandestineness 737.2 *secretiveness*
clang 507.8 *be loud*; 507.1 *loudness*; 509.12, 510.10 *ring*; 510.2 *ringing*
clang association 36.27 *association of ideas*
clanger 320.11 *bicycle part*; 274.10, 544.6 *blunder*; 465.2 *mistake*
clanging 510.7 *ringing*
clangorous 507.6 *loud*
clangour 507.1 *loudness*; 510.2 *ringing*
clank 513.5 *sound hoarse*
clanking 513.8 *hoarse*
clannish 128.10 *excluding*
clanship 747.2 *fellowship*
clan system 12.1 *government*
clap 669.5, 669.16 *acclaim*; 507.8 *be loud*; 598.5, 598.8 *cheer*; 508.2, 508.6 *crack*; 600.7 *dance*; 742.11 *gesture*; 507.1 *loudness*
clapboard 550.8 *wall covering*; 23.12 *wood*
clapboard house 411.5 *layered thing*
clap eyes on 518.12 *see*
clap of thunder 508.1 *bang*; 31.21 *thunderstorm*
clap one's hands 669.16 *acclaim*
clapped out 261.1 *fatigued*; 335.12 *impotent*
clapper 669.10 *applauder*; 510.4 *sources of resonance*
clapping 669.5 *acclaim*; 669.20 *acclamatory*; 598.5 *cheer*; 742.15 *gestural*; 742.3 *gesture*
claptrap 697.1, 699.15 *nonsense*
claque 669.10 *applauder*; 21.33 *theatregoer*
claqueur 669.10 *applauder*; 21.33 *theatregoer*
Clarenceux 743.9 *herald*
claret 431.4 *blood*; 535.7 *red thing*; 558.9 *wine*
claret cup 558.7 *alcoholic drink*
clarification 256.2 *cleaning*; 265.7 *easing*; 522.13 *enlightenment*; 703.3 *explanation*; 719.1 *interpretation*; 454.5 *proof*
clarified 522.22 *enlightened*; 703.11 *explanatory*; 719.15 *interpreted*; 255.13 *pure*; 527.1 *transparent*
clarifier 703.7 *demonstrator*; 719.6 *interpreter*; 5.2 *linguist*
clarify 522.29; **725.2**; 703.16 *explain*; 719.8 *interpret*; 265.16 *make easy*; 527.12 *make transparent*; 520.10 *make visible*; 431.24 *melt*; 454.2 *prove*; 255.10, 256.15 *purify*; 4.21 *rationalize*; 695.5 *simplify*
clarifying 719.14 *interpretive*
clarion call 480.4 *exhortation*; 507.1 *loudness*; 585.7 *war measures*
Clarity 725
clarity 520.4; **725.1**; 694.3 *comprehension*; 185.4 *conspicuousness*; 178.8 *directness*; 543.1 *elegance*; 522.13 *enlightenment*; 28.23 *light*; 255.1 *purity*; 265.2, 271.4, 695.10 *simplicity*; 527.5 *transparency*
clash 492.12 *abut*; 701.13, 751.6 *argue*; 701.1, 751.2 *argument*; 508.1, 508.5 *bang*; 585.9 *battle*; 507.8 *be loud*; 513.4 *be strident*; 331.2 *collide*; 113.19 *confront*; 347.3 *counteract*; 347.1 *counteraction*; 517.11, 751.5 *disagree*; 517.6 *disagreement*; 380.3 *instance of violence*; 517.10 *lack harmony*; 507.2 *outcry*; 242.8, 242.11 *quarrel*; 18.38 *sound*; 433.33 *sprinkle*
clashing 701.7 *arguing*; 113.5 *conflict*; 347.4 *counteracting*; 751.1 *disagreement*; 113.24 *discordant*; 517.1 *dissonance*; 517.7 *dissonant*; 529.12 *gaudy*
clasp 267.6 *adhere*; 373.12 *bind*; 593.14 *communication of love*; 184.11 *enfold*; 184.5 *enfoldment*; 373.8 *fastening*; 309.3 *restrainer*; 360.6 *retain*; 360.1 *retention*; 360.3 *tools for gripping*
clasped 373.16 *bound*; 360.10 *retained*
clasp hands 569.15 *be hospitable*; 658.12 *greet*
clasping 360.9 *retentive*
clasp knife 425.10 *knife*
clasp someone's shoulder 742.11 *gesture*
Class 137
class 137.2; **137.13**; 216.4 *average*; 409.15 *categorize*; 409.6 *category*; 285.5 *contemporary*; 376.17 *family*; 566.9 *group*; 137.3 *kingdom*; 137.7 *lecture*; 209.5 *measure*; 205.1 *part*; 405.2 *piece*; 407.4 *position*; 209.2 *rank*; 108.3 *relative position*; 27.21 *set*; 221.1 *state*; 137.6 *students*; 407.19 *systematize*; 34.17 *taxonomy*
class A 797.2 *best*; 797.9 *the best*
class boundary 2.7 *social stratification*
class conflict 2.7 *social stratification*
class conscious 622.23 *prejudiced*
class consciousness 622.11 *prejudice*
class discrimination 466.4 *social discrimination*
class distinction 622.11 *prejudice*
classed 137.12; 221.8 *in a state of*; 108.6 *ranked*
classed with 127.8 *included*
classic 216.1 *average*; 543.3 *elegant*; 121.15 *excellent*; 400.11, 485.3 *masterpiece*; 296.12 *olden*; 230.1 *perfect*; 271.1 *simple*; 551.31 *styled*; 543.2 *stylist*; 235.1 *worthy*
classic abseil 62.3 *climbing technique*
Classical 3.15 *historic*
classical 6.21 *curricular*; 543.3 *elegant*; 296.14 *historic*; 17.16 *literary*; 5.39 *of language*; 296.12 *olden*; 230.1 *perfect*; 28.98 *physical*; 19.29 *realist*
Classical Age 284.5 *historical period*; 3.10 *past age*
classical author 543.2, 724.5 *stylist*
classical ballet 22.8 *ballet*
classical ballets 22.11
classical conditioning 36.20 *conditioning*
classical costume 551.5 *fancy dress*
classical dancer 22.5 *dancer*
classical genetics 34.11 *genetics*
classical language 5.9 *ancient language*
classically 296.21 *archaically*; 28.100 *physically*
classical mathematics 27.1 *mathematics*
classical mechanics 28.2 *classical physics*
classical music 18.3
classical physics 28.2
classical riding 59.6 *horsemanship*
classical taxonomy 34.17 *taxonomy*
classical tragedy 21.11 *tragedy*
classicism 284.9, 296.4 *antiquarianism*; 543.1 *elegance*
classicist 284.11, 296.9 *antiquarian*; 5.2 *linguist*; 543.2 *stylist*
classic murder 382.2 *murder*
classic quality 235.6 *worth*
classic route 62.1 *mountaineering*
classification 137.1; 409.5 *categorization*; 209.3 *gradation*; 407.2 *grouping*; 743.1 *identification*; 220.7 *listing*; 721.7 *nomenclature*; 108.3 *relative position*
classificational 137.10 *classificatory*
classifications of life 554.9
classificatory 137.10; 409.25 *categorical*; 407.11 *grouped*; 220.11 *listed*
classified 409.24 *categorized*; 399.6 *censored*; 137.12 *classed*; 209.7 *gradational*;

407.11 *grouped;* 743.12 *identified;* 108.6 *ranked;* 737.9 *secret*
classified ad 740.9 *advertisement;* 693.4 *mass communication*
classified ads 793.7 *discounter*
classified advertisement 740.9 *advertisement*
classified document 399.2 *censorship*
classified information 693.3 *document;* 737.1 *secrecy;* 736.4 *silence*
classified with 127.8 *included*
classify 409.15 *categorize;* 137.13 *class;* 743.10 *identify;* 406.9 *itemize;* 737.12 *keep secret;* 220.8 *list;* 209.5 *measure;* 407.19 *systematize*
classify a film 399.4 *censor*
classify as 127.6 *subsume*
classifying 743.1 *identification*
classify secret 399.4 *censor*
classism 466.4 *social discrimination*
classist 466.10 *discriminatory*
classless 12.9, 396.14 *governmental*
classmate 223.11 *companion;* 285.5 *contemporary;* 569.5 *friend;* 6.7 *learner*
class notes 163.1 *outline*
class of 285.5 *contemporary*
class prejudice 466.4 *social discrimination*
class-prejudiced 465.8 *unjust*
class project 447.5 *educational topic*
class reunion 654.3 *meeting*
class ring 743.5 *uniform*
classroom 396.6 *place of authority;* 6.15 *schoolroom*
class structure 2.7 *social stratification*
class war 244.11 *reformism;* 466.4 *social discrimination;* 585.1 *war*
class with 127.6 *subsume*
classy 573.4 *aristocratic;* 553.7 *fashionable;* 235.1 *worthy*
clastic 30.56 *petrographic*
clastic rock 30.31 *sedimentary rock*
clathrate 32.7 *chemical compound*
clatter 507.8 *be loud;* 508.6 *crack;* 412.3 *miscellany;* 507.2 *outcry;* 509.3, 509.10 *rattle*
clattering 509.17 *rattling*
Claude glass 19.11 *artist's materials*
Claude tint 537.7 *yellow pigment*
clausal 5.43 *phrasal*
clause 746.2 *basis for negotiations;* 205.2 *particular;* 5.23 *phrase*
claustrophobia 596.1 *dislike*
claustrophobic 165.7 *enclosed*
claustrophobically 165.8 *confinedly*
claw 491.11 *inflict pain;* 492.7 *sense organ;* 425.8 *sharp-pointed thing;* 360.3 *tools for gripping;* 425.16 *use a sharp tool;* 373.9 *yoke*
clawback 212.2 *subtracted item*
claw chisel 19.14 *sculptor's materials*
clawed 71.28 *carnivorous*
claw-hammer coat 551.11 *jacket*
claw one's way up 304.14 *climb*
claw ring 50.3 *parts of a sailing boat*
claws 587.1 *weapon*
claw skyward 304.19 *take off*
clay 267.3 *adhesive;* 258.4 *dirt;* 38.26 *masonry;* 435.1 *materials;* 24.2 *raw material;* 30.27 *sediment;* 30.36 *soil;* 416.4 *solid body*
clayey 419.4 *compressible;* 30.58 *earthy*
clay mineral 30.34 *mineral*
claymore 587.8 *sharp weapon*
clay pigeon shooting 60.1 *target shooting*
clay pipe 496.7 *tobacco*
clay sculpture 19.12 *sculpture*
clayware 24.1 *ceramics*
clean 256.13; 256.16; 256.20; 434.20 *aerate;* 232.9 *completely;* 501.5 *deodorize;* 257.4 *hygienic;* 295.12 *immature;* 295.24 *immaturely;* 244.1 *improve;* 805.5 *innocent;* 257.6 *make hygienic;* 527.12 *make transparent;* 801.10 *moral;* 795.10 *moralistic;* 62.9 *mountaineer;* 62.8 *mountaineering;* 350.2 *new;* 501.3 *odourless;* 407.13 *orderly;* 255.13, 531.5 *pure;* 255.14 *purified;* 255.10 *purify;* 581.1 *refresh;* 393.3 *restore;* 271.1 *simple;* 421.11 *smooth;* 407.21 *tidy;* 98.13 *vacant;* 531.13 *whiten;* 576.6 *work*
clean as a whistle 256.16 *clean*
clean bill of health 259.3 *health*
clean climbing 62.1 *mountaineering*
clean dry air 31.8 *atmosphere*
cleaned 256.17; 255.14 *purified*
cleaned out 256.17 *cleaned;* 782.2 *insolvent*
cleaned up 256.17 *cleaned*
cleaner 256.12; 256.9 *cleaning agent;* 392.16 *home help;* 255.3 *purifier;* 578.1 *worker*
clean for 401.8 *serve*
clean forget 463.13 *forget*
clean-handed 805.5 *innocent*
clean hands 805.1 *innocence;* 799.1 *probity*
cleaning 256.2; 256.18 *cleansing;* 62.3 *climbing technique;* 42.8 *fabric treatment;* 244.5 *improvement;* 62.8 *mountaineering;* 255.2 *purification*
cleaning agent 256.9
cleaning cloth 256.11
cleaning lady 392.16 *home help;* 401.1 *servant*
cleaning object 256.10
cleaning out 371.21 *removal*
cleaning up 256.4 *censorship;* 256.2 *cleaning*
cleaning woman 401.6 *domestic servant*
cleanliness 256.1 *cleanness;* 257.1 *hygiene;* 295.3 *immaturity;* 805.1 *innocence;* 255.1 *purity;* 581.5 *refreshment;* 271.4 *simplicity*
cleanly 256.19; 256.16 *clean;* 295.24 *immaturely;* 350.13 *newly;* 501.7 *odourlessly;* 255.13 *pure;* 255.19 *purely;* 425.19 *suddenly*
Cleanness 256
cleanness 256.1; 257.1 *hygiene;* 295.3 *immaturity;* 805.1 *innocence;* 350.9 *newness;* 501.1 *odourlessness;* 407.5 *orderliness;* 255.1, 531.11 *purity;* 581.5 *refreshment;* 271.4 *simplicity;* 527.5 *transparency*
clean one's plate 557.22 *eat well*
clean out 256.13 *clean;* 255.10, 256.15 *purify;* 371.11 *void*
cleanse 501.5 *deodorize;* 257.6 *make hygienic;* 527.12 *make transparent;* 255.10, 256.15 *purify*
cleansed 256.17 *cleaned;* 255.13 *pure;* 255.14 *purified*
cleanse oneself of guilt 807.6 *apologize*
cleanse oneself of sin 807.6 *apologize*
cleanser 256.9 *cleaning agent;* 358.4 *eraser;* 268.7 *pomade;* 394.3 *prophylactic;* 255.3 *purifier*
clean-shaven 552.13 *hairless;* 421.1 *smooth*
clean sheet 98.3 *emptiness*
cleansing 256.18; 433.27; 807.2 *apology;* 807.4 *atoning;* 10.5 *Christian rite;* 256.2 *cleaning;* 501.4 *deodorizing;* 244.5 *improvement;* 10.7 *non-Christian ritual;* 359.1 *preservation;* 255.2 *purification;* 255.15 *purifying;* 394.17 *remedial;* 433.11 *wash*
cleansing agent 256.9 *cleaning agent;* 255.3 *purifier*
cleansing cream 256.9 *cleaning agent;* 255.3 *purifier*
clean slate 98.3 *emptiness;* 358.4 *eraser;* 295.5 *fresh start*
clean up 256.13 *clean;* 781.13 *get rich;* 244.1 *improve;* 407.22 *pacify;* 765.5, 765.14 *profit;* 256.15 *purify;* 581.1 *refresh;* 409.19 *tidy*
clean-up man 48.2 *baseball player*
clear 520.2; 725.3; 649.10 *absolve;* 16.78 *acquit;* 16.63, 758.6 *acquitted;* 756.14 *auspicious;* 634.21 *away;* 154.15 *be high;* 256.13 *clean;* 304.14 *climb;* 805.9 *declare innocent;* 703.9 *demonstrated;* 739.10 *disclosed;* 265.18 *disentangle;* 145.10 *distantly;* 265.9 *easy;* 543.3 *elegant;* 31.45 *fine;* 693.16 *informative;* 88.9 *lakelike;* 265.16 *make easy;* 79.18 *manage trees;* 694.6 *meaningful;* 516.6 *melodious;* 738.15 *open;* 308.13 *opened up;* 308.19 *open up;* 785.7 *pay off;* 750.29, 757.3 *permit;* 336.10 *potent;* 765.14 *profit;* 255.13 *pure;* 255.10 *purify;* 769.9 *receive;* 252.6 *safe;* 31.61 *shine;* 271.1, 695.2 *simple;* 146.4 *space;* 178.2 *straightforward;* 522.19 *sunny;* 527.1 *transparent;* 98.13 *vacant;* 714.7 *vindicate;* 518.23, 520.1 *visible*
clear accounts with 785.7 *pay off*
clear across 150.8 *breadthwise*
clearage 371.21 *removal*
clear-air turbulence 322.7 *miscellaneous aviation terms*
clearance 16.42 *acquittal;* 141.6 *available space;* 560.2 *defecation;* 767.1 *disposal;* 47.2 *field events;* 146.1 *interval;* 318.6 *passport;* 785.1 *payment;* 757.1 *permission;* 750.8 *permit;* 255.2 *purification;* 371.21 *removal;* 778.4 *sale;* 250.5 *scope;* 714.1 *vindication*
clearance kick 64.3 *rugby play*
clearance papers 318.6 *passport;* 757.2 *permit*
clearance sale 791.2 *bargain;* 767.2 *disposal of property;* 778.4 *sale*
clear as a bell 516.6 *melodious*
clear as air 527.1 *transparent*
clear as daylight 738.14 *manifest*
clear as mud 696.4 *difficult;* 521.2 *difficult to see;* 528.4 *inscrutable;* 524.6 *murky*
clear away 371.11 *void*
clear bulb 522.6 *electric light*
clear coast 265.6 *easy thing*
clear conscience 805.1 *innocence;* 799.1 *probity;* 803.1 *virtue*
clear course 265.6 *easy thing*
clear-cut 520.2, 725.3 *clear;* 185.7 *conspicuous;* 703.12 *demonstrable;* 695.1 *intelligible;* 336.10 *potent;* 518.23 *visible*
cleared 16.63 *acquitted;* 805.6 *declared innocent;* 714.12, 805.5 *innocent;* 785.16 *paid;* 750.18 *permitting*
cleared up 703.11 *explanatory;* 706.14 *solved;* 409.27 *tidied*
clear-eyed 518.21 *seeing*
clear field 287.2 *opportunity*
clear glass 527.9 *glass;* 522.10 *window*
clear head 689.6 *sobriety*
clear-headed 458.6 *intelligent;* 4.15, 460.5 *rational;* 689.1 *sober*
clear image 717.6 *image*
clearing 265.8 *disentanglement;* 43.11 *farmland;* 141.3 *geographical space;* 308.8 *open space;* 371.21 *removal;* 79.4 *trees*
clearing bank 780.19 *treasury*
clearing from guilt 714.1 *vindication*
clearing of one's name 714.1 *vindication*
clearing up 256.2 *cleaning;* 706.6 *solution*
clearly 725.4; 525.15 *apparently;* 756.17 *auspiciously;* 543.5 *elegantly;* 695.13 *intelligibly;* 88.10 *limnologically;* 703.20 *manifestly;* 694.13 *meaningfully;* 308.25 *obviously;* 271.8 *simply;* 527.13 *transparently;* 518.25, 520.11 *visibly*
clearly printed 695.2 *simple*
clearly visible 185.7 *conspicuous*
clear message 694.3 *comprehension*
clearness 520.4, 725.1 *clarity;* 185.4 *conspicuousness;* 255.1 *purity;* 695.10 *simplicity;* 527.5 *transparency*
clear off 313.1 *depart;* 313.15 *go!;* 371.33 *go away!;* 371.11 *void*
clear one's head 581.2 *be refreshed;* 689.5 *sober up*
clear one's name 649.10 *absolve;* 714.7 *vindicate*
clear one's throat 560.20 *salivate;* 513.5 *sound hoarse*
clear out 256.13 *clean;* 313.15 *go!;* 371.33 *go away!;* 255.11 *simplify;* 371.11 *void*
clear pool 88.2 *small lake*
clear printing 695.10 *simplicity*
clear profit 765.5 *profit*
clear road 265.6 *easy thing*
clear round 59.9 *jumping*
clear run 287.2 *opportunity*
clear shot 63.12 *badminton terms*
clear-sighted 518.21 *seeing*
clear sky 31.22 *sun*
clear soup 25.13 *soup*
clear space 141.3 *geographical space*
clear stock 778.1 *sell*
clear the air 807.5 *atone;* 501.5 *deodorize*
clear the cobwebs out 581.2 *be refreshed*
clear the crossbar 47.8 *jump*
clear the decks 243.4 *prepare for action;* 409.19 *tidy;* 371.11 *void*
clear the ground 318.10 *enter;* 265.16 *make easy*
clear the path for 480.16 *tempt*
clear the track 392.28 *further*
clear the water 50.16 *row*
clear the way 265.16 *make easy*
clear the way for 102.7 *make possible*
clear thinking 442.5 *common sense*
clear to anyone 695.2 *simple*
clear up 256.13 *clean;* 452.21 *make certain;* 454.2 *prove;* 4.21 *rationalize;* 695.5 *simplify;* 706.20 *solve;* 409.19 *tidy*
clear varnish 527.8 *transparent thing*
clear view 287.2 *opportunity*
clear visibility 185.4 *conspicuousness*
clearway 322.4 *airport;* 318.2 *passing along;* 317.3, 320.2 *road*
cleat 373.8 *fastening;* 50.3 *parts of a sailing boat;* 50.7 *windsurfing*
cleated 62.8 *mountaineering*
cleated boots 62.4 *climbing equipment*
cleavage 34.15 *developmental biology;* 30.20 *earth movement;* 30.28 *rock;* 372.3 *separateness*
cleave 146.5 *crack;* 30.64 *fold;* 198.16 *halve;* 308.18 *open;* 372.9 *separate;* 425.16 *use a sharp tool*
cleaver 425.10 *knife*
cleave to 267.6 *adhere;* 360.6 *retain*
cleave to the line 324.7 *take a direction*
cleek 56.4 *golf club*
clef 18.20 *key;* 18.17 *notation*
cleft 372.16 *apart;* 751.2 *argument;* 146.2 *crack;* 146.7 *cracked;* 198.13 *half;* 183.4 *notch;* 308.12 *open;* 308.1 *opening;* 372.3 *separateness*
cleft palate 234.3 *deformity*
cleft stick 453.11 *irresoluteness;* 264.5 *predicament*
clem 687.5 *fast*
clematis 540.3 *purple thing*
clemency 649.2 *forgivingness;* 648.1 *leniency;* 627.3 *mercy;* 749.2 *peace offering*
clement 648.4 *lenient;* 649.5 *merciful;* 627.6 *pitying;* 493.11 *warm*
clementine 412.5 *hybrid;* 536.3 *orange thing*
clemently 749.7 *pacifically*
clemmed 687.6 *fasting*
clench 191.5 *make smaller;* 360.6 *retain;* 360.1 *retention*
clenched 191.7 *smaller*
clenched fist 742.3 *gesture;* 360.3 *tools for gripping*
clenched jaw 638.16 *fortitude;* 742.3 *gesture*
clenched teeth 638.16 *fortitude;* 742.3 *gesture*
clenching 191.1 *contraction*
clench one's fist 742.11 *gesture*
clench one's jaw 742.11 *gesture*
clench one's teeth 506.1 *be silent;* 638.8 *brace oneself;* 742.11 *gesture*
Cleopatra's Needle 154.6 *tall thing*
clepsydra 281.6 *clock*
clerestory 10.12 *church;* 20.10 *church architecture;* 154.8 *high thing*
clergyman 7.8 *priest*
clergywoman 7.8 *priest*
cleric 7.8 *priest*
clerical 7.17 *priestly*
clerical collar 551.14 *neckwear;* 7.11 *vestment*
clerical dress 551.3, 656.4 *formal dress*
clerical error 274.12 *typing error*
clerical garb 551.3 *formal dress*
clerical hat 551.15 *headgear*
clericalism 12.1 *government;* 7.9 *priesthood*
clerical robe 551.16 *robe*
clericals 7.11 *vestment*
clerical worker 578.1 *worker*
clerihew 269.2 *outline;* 17.7 *poem*
clerk 398.1 *delegate;* 401.5 *office assistant;* 579.16 *official;* 744.9 *recorder*
clerk in holy orders 7.8 *priest*
clerk of the court 16.10 *law officer*
clever 645.4 *cunning;* 6.17 *educable;* 6.18 *educated;* 477.10 *imaginative;* 442.10, 458.6 *intelligent;* 455.8 *knowledgeable;* 425.5 *mentally sharp;* 485.6 *skilful;* 485.9 *well-made*
clever-clever 458.6 *intelligent*
clever clogs 485.5 *expert;* 442.8 *intellectual person;* 455.6 *knowledgeable person;* 673.7 *vain person*
clever dick 458.4 *intellectual;* 455.6 *knowledgeable person;* 673.7 *vain person*
clever hands 485.1 *skill*
cleverly 442.15, 458.10 *intelligently;* 425.18 *sharply;* 485.12 *skilfully;* 6.26 *studiously*
cleverness 442.4; 645.1 *cunning;* 6.10 *educability;* 458.2 *intelligence;* 455.3 *learning;* 425.13 *mental sharpness;* 485.1, 733.3 *skill*
clew 50.3 *parts of a sailing boat;* 50.10 *sailing;* 50.7 *windsurfing*
clew gybe 50.15 *sail;* 50.1 *sailing*
clew line 373.7 *tackle*
clew tack 50.15 *sail;* 50.1 *sailing*

cliché 5.21 *catchword;* 138.8 *generalization;* 745.1 *maxim;* 509.7 *repeated word;* 112.3 *repetitiveness;* 5.42 *worded*
clichéd 632.10 *familiar;* 112.13 *monotonous;* 745.2 *proverbial;* 5.42 *worded*
cliché-ridden 112.13 *monotonous*
click 246.6 *be successful;* 508.2, 508.6 *crack*
clicking 508.9 *crackling;* 509.17 *rattling*
client 776.12 *custom;* 13.9 *economist;* 35.18 *patient;* 777.12 *purchaser;* 349.8 *user*
client-centred therapy 36.3 *psychiatric treatment*
clientele 776.12 *custom;* 13.9 *economist;* 777.12 *purchaser*
cliff 30.11 *coast;* 154.3 *mountain;* 185.2 *projection;* 186.3 *vertical thing*
cliffhanger 119.2 *equilibrium;* 17.2 *fiction*
climacteric 556.4 *middle age;* 556.13 *middle-aged*
climacterically 556.16 *maturely*
climactic 174.5 *top*
climate 31.38; 143.2 *circumstances;* 395.1 *influence;* 229.1 *tendency*
climate modification 31.40 *climatic change*
climate of opinion 450.1 *belief;* 229.1 *tendency*
climatic 143.8 *circumstantial;* 31.41 *meteorologic*
climatically 31.65 *meteorologically*
climatic change 31.40
climatic trend 31.40 *climatic change*
climatic variation 31.40 *climatic change*
climatic zone 31.39
climatological 30.49 *geophysical;* 31.41 *meteorologic*
climatologically 31.65 *meteorologically*
climatologist 30.4 *geophysicist;* 31.2 *meteorologist*
climatology 30.2 *geophysics;* 31.1 *meteorology*
climax 232.5 *be complete;* 121.8 *be superior;* 204.10 *complete;* 34.18 *ecology;* 131.10 *ending;* 490.8 *feel pleasure;* 213.1 *increase;* 213.5 *make bigger;* 490.1 *physical pleasure;* 21.8 *scene;* 327.8 *spasm;* 121.4, 174.1 *summit;* 174.7 *top*
climb 304.14; 304.13 *ascend;* 792.9 *be dear;* 300.13 *be in motion;* 89.10 *climb a mountain;* 322.5 *flight;* 154.2 *heights;* 213.4 *increase;* 302.7 *make one's way;* 89.1 *mountain;* 62.1 *mountaineering;* 304.6 *mounting;* 302.3 *press on;* 154.16 *rise;* 68.14 *ski;* 213.2 *spread*
climbable 304.25 *ladder-like*
climb a mountain 89.10
climbdown 623.10 *abasement*
climb down 305.9 *descend;* 623.21 *humble oneself*
climbed 62.8 *mountaineering*
climber 304.11 *ascender;* 44.9 *garden plant;* 62.7 *mountaineer;* 77.2 *plant*
climb hand over fist 304.14 *climb*
climbing 304.22 *ascending;* 300.7 *ascending motion;* 792.7 *dear;* 300.17 *directional;* 62.1, 62.8 *mountaineering;* 304.6 *mounting;* 77.14 *of plants;* 68.4 *skiing technique*
climbing boots 62.4 *climbing equipment*
climbing club 62.6 *mountaineering association*
climbing dangers 62.2
climbing equipment 62.4
climbing expedition 62.1 *mountaineering*
climbing gear 62.4 *climbing equipment*
climbing mountains 62.1 *mountaineering*
climbing plant 44.9 *garden plant*
climbing prices 792.3 *inflationary price*
climbing technique 62.3
climbing the pole 50.8 *punting*
climb into the saddle 304.15 *mount*
climb on 304.15 *mount*
climb on the bandwagon 125.11 *emulate*
climb over 304.14 *climb*
climb the pole 50.19 *punt*
clinch 267.6 *adhere;* 95.12 *establish reality;* 54.5 *fence;* 54.3 *fencing movements;* 703.17 *prove;* 360.6 *retain;* 360.1 *retention*
clincher 131.13 *ender;* 485.3 *masterpiece;* 704.1 *refutation*
cling 632.17 *become a habit;* 423.10 *be tough;* 640.8 *hold out*
clinger 267.5 *follower*
Clingfilm™ 25.6 *kitchen equipment;* 527.8 *transparent thing;* 165.4 *wrapper;* 550.4 *wrapping*
clinging 267.9 *adhesive;* 632.15 *habit-forming;* 423.3 *hard;* 151.1 *narrow;* 360.9 *retentive;* 423.6 *toughness*
clinging on 360.1 *retention*
clinging vine 267.4 *adherent;* 267.5 *follower*
cling like ivy 267.6 *adhere*
cling on 360.6 *retain*
cling to 267.6 *adhere;* 593.24 *be in love;* 267.8 *be tenacious;* 147.17 *stay near*
cling to custom 641.9 *be obstinate;* 632.16 *have a habit*
clingy 267.10 *tenacious*
clinic 35.10, 394.14 *hospital*
clinical 402.7 *material;* 35.22, 394.18 *medical;* 728.14 *simple*
clinical death 582.1 *death*
clinical depression 36.13 *depression;* 461.6 *mental breakdown*
clinical dextran 431.4 *blood*
clinically 402.9 *materially;* 35.26 *medically;* 394.21 *remedially*
clinical medicine 394.11 *medical art;* 35.3 *medical specialty*
clinicalness 728.4 *simplicity*
clinical psychologist 36.30 *psychiatrist;* 36.29 *psychologist*
clinical psychology 36.1 *psychology;* 394.13 *therapy*
clinical thermometer 493.2 *heat measurement;* 28.89 *thermometer*
clinical treatment 394.13 *therapy;* 35.8 *treatment*
clinician 35.13 *medical specialist;* 36.29 *psychologist*
clink 309.4 *closed place;* 510.10 *ring;* 510.2 *ringing;* 513.5 *sound hoarse;* 815.2 *the inside*
clinker 258.4 *dirt;* 560.5 *faeces;* 493.6 *fire;* 122.7 *inferior thing;* 517.3 *musical dissonance;* 238.6 *refuse*
clinker-built 50.10 *sailing*
clinker-built hull 50.3 *parts of a sailing boat*
clinking 513.8 *hoarse*
clinking gold 780.1 *money*
clinometer 38.17 *civil engineering;* 26.8 *meter*
clinometric 26.16 *micrometric*
clinometry 26.2 *micrometry*
clinopyroxene 30.34 *mineral*
clip 269.4 *be concise;* 46.18 *be penalized;* 373.11 *connect;* 780.25 *demonetize;* 373.8 *fastening;* 743.7 *flag;* 300.12 *gait;* 191.5, 214.5 *make smaller;* 792.10 *overcharge;* 61.9 *race;* 372.10 *set apart;* 149.10 *shorten;* 360.3 *tools for gripping;* 425.16 *use a sharp tool*
clip one's wings 378.8 *hinder;* 238.8 *make useless*
clip on the ear 814.12 *corporal punishment;* 814.3 *hit*
clipped 269.3 *concise;* 780.22 *monetary;* 149.8, 723.7 *shortened;* 191.7 *smaller;* 5.42 *worded*
clipped accent 5.26 *dialect*
clipped coinage 780.15 *false money*
clipped speech 269.1 *conciseness*
clipped word 5.17 *word*
clipper 332.11 *swift thing*
clippers 425.9 *sharp-edged thing*
clipping 191.1 *contraction;* 61.6 *motor-racing terms;* 46.13 *penalty;* 149.2 *shortening*
clippings 205.8 *bits and pieces;* 215.2 *residue*
clip round the ear 331.3 *hit*
clip the apex 61.9 *race*
clip the wings 245.5 *hurt;* 333.3 *slow down*
clip to 211.6 *add*
clip watch 281.7 *watch*
clique 376.19; 128.4 *exclusiveness;* 566.9 *group;* 137.5 *social class*
cliquey 128.10 *excluding*
cliquish 128.10 *excluding*
clitoral 561.16 *reproductive*
clitoridectomy 10.7 *non-Christian ritual*
clitoris 561.8 *organs of reproduction*
clitter-clatter 509.3 *rattle*
cloaca 308.4 *body orifice;* 767.8 *sink;* 38.22 *tunnel*
cloak 551.25 *accessories;* 519.6 *blinder;* 550.5 *body covering;* 384.19 *buffer;* 736.8 *conceal;* 700.12, 700.32 *disguise;* 551.32 *dress;* 550.31 *hide;* 521.8 *make invisible;* 11.20 *occult;* 252.10 *protect;* 7.11 *vestment*
cloak-and-dagger 737.10 *secretive*
cloaked 700.41 *disguised;* 551.29 *dressed;* 550.37 *protected*
cloaking 550.1 *covering*
cloakroom 565.7 *room;* 767.7 *toilet*
cloakroom attendant 401.3 *attendant*
cloakroom ticket 743.3 *means of identification*
clobber 121.8 *be superior;* 551.1 *dress;* 331.3 *hit;* 357.11 *ruin;* 380.8 *use violence*
cloche 551.15 *headgear;* 44.4 *nursery*
clock 28.87; **281.6**; 40.19 *computing terms;* 167.2 *face;* 742.5 *indicator;* 281.14 *keep time;* 275.16 *time;* 275.13 *timer*
clock case 24.8 *ceramic object*
clockface 281.8 *face*
clock in 275.19 *clock on;* 312.5 *get in;* 281.16 *measure time;* 576.6 *work*
clockmaker 578.2 *artisan;* 281.12 *chronologist;* 275.14 *timekeeper*
clockmaking 275.10 *chronometry;* 281.4 *horology*
clock off 275.19 *clock on*
clock on 275.19
clock out 281.16 *measure time;* 313.2 *withdraw;* 576.6 *work*
clock radio 281.6 *clock;* 692.18 *radio;* 504.8 *something heard*
clock rate 40.19 *computing terms*
clock speed 209.5 *measure*
clock that stops 475.7 *bad-luck sign*
clock time 281.3 *chronology;* 275.7 *time measurement*
clockwatch 275.19 *clock on*
clock watcher 343.8 *nonworker;* 275.14 *timekeeper*
clockwise 324.10; 307.13 *round*
clockwork 438.5 *machine;* 111.17, 298.11 *regular*
clockwork precision 273.1 *accuracy*
clockwork regularity 111.6, 298.1 *regularity*
clod 564.5 *countryman;* 158.7 *mass;* 646.3 *naive person;* 205.7 *piece;* 416.4 *solid body;* 457.3 *unintelligent person;* 486.10 *unskilled person*
clodhoppers 551.19 *footwear*
clog 258.10 *be dirty;* 360.7 *detain;* 258.11 *dirty;* 309.8 *stop*
clog dance 22.2 *dance*
clog dancer 22.5 *dancer*
clog dancing 22.1 *dancing*
clogged 258.7 *dirty;* 360.9 *retentive;* 309.13 *stopped*
clogged up 309.13 *stopped*
clogs 551.19 *footwear*
clog up 251.8 *restrain;* 309.8 *stop*
cloister 317.7 *arcade;* 10.12 *church;* 165.5 *enclose;* 165.2 *enclosed place;* 7.10 *priestly dwelling;* 252.5 *refuge;* 655.5 *solitary place*
cloistered 165.7 *enclosed;* 655.11 *secluded*
cloisteredly 165.8 *confinedly*
clone 750.5 *conformity;* 115.2, 125.2, 125.10 *copy;* 115.5 *counterpart;* 198.15 *double;* 115.12 *imitate;* 525.5 *impression;* 111.3 *lookalike;* 111.8 *make the same;* 207.9 *pluralize;* 561.2 *print;* 561.9 *reproduce;* 198.5 *twin*
cloned 198.12 *double;* 111.14 *lookalike*
cloning 198.4 *doubling*
cloning vector 34.12 *molecular biology*
clop 331.13 *blow;* 547.17 *crimp;* 331.7 *kick*
close 131.9; **309.7**; 267.9 *adhesive;* 97.10 *available;* 232.5 *be complete;* 232.4 *complete;* 232.3 *completion;* 416.7 *condensed;* 310.9 *converge;* 376.50 *crowded;* 393.6 *cure;* 416.6 *dense;* 526.1 *disappear;* 165.5 *enclose;* 165.2 *enclosed place;* 131.1, 131.15 *end;* 128.10 *excluding;* 569.10 *familiar;* 31.52 *humid;* 147.10 *juxtaposed;* 682.1 *mean;* 429.9 *moist;* 151.1 *narrow;* 147.9, 147.12 *near;* 239.2 *nearby;* 736.17 *noncommittal;* 698.24 *pedantic;* 317.3 *road;* 737.10 *secretive;* 115.7 *similar;* 226.7 *stop working;* 289.12 *succeeding;* 655.8 *unsociable;* 493.11 *warm*
close associate 595.4 *likable person*
close at hand 283.11 *future;* 147.12 *near*
close attention 471.2
close binary 29.9 *constellation*
close by 282.8 *available;* 147.12 *near;* 239.8 *nearby*
close call 389.1 *escape*
closed 309.12; 232.7 *complete;* 128.10 *excluding;* 247.10 *failed;* 226.10 *finished;* 737.9 *secret;* 68.12 *ski;* 15.10 *unionized*
closed book 106.6 *premeditation;* 456.3 *unknown thing*
closed circuit 39.13 *circuit;* 334.7 *electrical power*
closed-circuit television 692.21 *television*
closed couplet 17.8 *part of poem*
closed door 481.6 *dissuasion;* 128.1 *exclusion*
closed down 309.14
closed-face 55.8 *angling*
closed-face reel 55.3 *fishing tackle*
closed figure 27.41 *geometric figure*
closed gate 68.3 *ski racing*
closed-in 165.7, 309.15 *enclosed*
closed-in person 309.6
closed mind 465.3 *injustice;* 641.7 *opinionatedness;* 106.6 *premeditation*
closed order 736.6 *privacy*
close down 309.9; 226.8 *cause to cease;* 131.16 *cease;* 526.1 *disappear;* 251.8 *restrain;* 226.7 *stop working*
close-down 309.1 *closure;* 226.2 *stop*
closed place 309.4
closed primary 469.12 *election*
closed season 60.2 *hunting*
closed session 737.1 *secrecy*
closed shop 251.2 *economic restraint;* 128.4 *exclusiveness;* 13.8 *industrial relations;* 15.5 *labour law;* 166.2 *limiting factor;* 15.3 *organized labour*
closed surface 27.45 *curved surface;* 27.38 *surface*
closed universe 29.4 *cosmological model*
closed-up 309.14 *closed down;* 191.7 *smaller*
close finish 312.15 *destination*
close-fisted 682.1 *mean*
close-fistedness 682.3 *parsimony*
close-fitting 267.9 *adhesive;* 151.1 *narrow*
close friend 569.6; 595.4 *likable person*
close friendship 569.3 *familiarity*
close-haul 50.15 *sail*
close-hauled 324.11 *in all directions;* 50.10 *sailing*
close hauling 50.1 *sailing*
close imitation 115.2 *copy*
close in 310.9 *converge;* 165.5 *enclose*
close-knit 416.6 *dense;* 128.10 *excluding*
close likeness 115.1 *similarity*
closely 267.11 *cohesively;* 115.14 *comparably;* 750.31 *in accord;* 569.18 *intimately;* 151.11 *narrowly;* 147.12 *near*
Closeness 147
closeness 280.2; 750.1 *accord;* 152.6 *denseness;* 416.1 *density;* 569.3 *familiarity;* 429.3 *humidity;* 147.3 *juxtaposition;* 151.5 *narrowness;* 147.1, 239.4 *nearness;* 698.11 *pedantry;* 736.4 *silence;* 115.1 *similarity*
close observance 471.2 *close attention*
close of day 291.1 *evening*
close of play 131.11 *finality*
close one's ears 505.8 *be deaf*
close one's eyes 582.15 *die*
close one's eyes to 618.12 *be indifferent;* 649.11 *condone*
close one's mind 466.13 *prejudge*
close-packed 267.9 *adhesive;* 32.33 *crystalline;* 416.6 *dense*
close-passing 64.3 *rugby play*
close quarters 147.2 *short distance*
closer 147.9 *near*
close range 147.2 *short distance*
close ranks 267.6 *adhere*
close reaching 50.1 *sailing*
close-run 147.9 *near*
close season 226.3 *pause;* 292.1 *season*
close shave 254.5 *danger;* 389.1 *escape*
closest 97.10 *available;* 147.9 *near*
closestool 560.14 *toilet*
closet 736.2 *hiding place*
closet drama 21.2 *play*
close-textured 416.6 *dense*
close the deal 755.5 *contract*
close the eyes 583.8 *bury*
close the pleadings 16.71 *try a case*
close the proceedings 16.71 *try a case*
close the ranks 585.14 *battle*
close the shutters 523.14 *make dark*
close to the wind 324.11 *in all directions*

close up 191.6 *become smaller*; 309.7 *close*; 309.9 *close down*; 310.9 *converge*; 247.6 *fail*; 191.5 *make smaller*; 147.16 *near*
close-up 41.4 *portrait*
close with 267.6 *adhere*; 310.9 *converge*; 381.5 *strike*
close-woven 416.6 *dense*; 404.9 *smooth*
closing 226.1 *cessation*; 309.1 *closure*; 131.20 *ending*; 393.11 *recuperation*
closing down 309.1 *closure*; 226.2 *stop*
closing-down sale 767.2 *disposal of property*; 778.4 *sale*
closing in 165.1 *enclosure*; 54.3 *fencing movements*
closing stages 131.9 *close*
closing the grave 583.2 *funeral*
closing time 131.11 *finality*
closing up 309.1 *closure*; 191.1 *contraction*
Closure 309
closure 309.1; 226.8 *cause to cease*; 247.1 *failure*; 27.21 *set*; 226.2 *stop*
closure of debate 226.2 *stop*
clot 416.8 *be dense*; 431.4 *blood*; 260.10 *cardiovascular disease*; 258.11 *dirty*; 416.4 *solid body*; 152.7 *thicken*
cloth 42.3 *fabric*; 435.1 *materials*; 356.7 *produce*; 21.19 *stage set*; 193.4, 404.5 *textile*; 7.11 *vestment*; 42.10 *woven*
cloth cap 551.15 *headgear*
clothe 551.32 *dress*; 436.5 *provision*
clothed 551.29 *dressed*
clothe oneself 551.34 *wear*
clothes 551.1 *dress*; 525.3 *external appearance*
clothes basket 410.7 *basket*
clothes brush 256.10 *cleaning object*
clothes-conscious 551.30 *dressed-up*; 553.7 *fashionable*
clothes-dryer 428.15 *dryer*
clotheshorse 428.15 *dryer*; 553.5 *fashion model*; 361.4 *hanger*; 551.27 *model*; 115.4 *person who copies*
clothes label 743.3 *means of identification*
clothesless 552.9 *undressed*
clothesline 361.4 *hanger*
clothes marking 743.3 *means of identification*
clothes off one's back 763.4 *possession*
clothes peg 361.4 *hanger*
clothier 578.2 *artisan*; 551.26 *fashion designer*
clothing 550.5 *body covering*; 551.1 *dress*; 525.3 *external appearance*; 436.1 *provision*
cloth of gold 522.2 *quality of light*
clotted 416.7 *condensed*; 152.2 *dense*; 258.7 *dirty*
clotting 416.7 *condensed*
cloture 226.8 *cause to cease*; 226.2 *stop*
cloud 31.18; **31.60**; 550.2 *cover*; 523.4 *dark thing*; 736.9 *disguise*; 550.31 *hide*; 524.10 *make dim*; 528.11 *make opaque*; 429.2 *mistiness*; 528.7 *opaque thing*; 208.4 *throng*; 541.11 *variegate*; 433.3 *wateriness*; 432.4 *water vapour*
cloud appearance 31.20
cloud base 31.18 *cloud*
cloudburst 31.25 *rain*; 380.5 *violent weather*
cloud-capped 31.49 *cloudy*; 154.9 *high*; 89.7 *mountainous*
cloud-capped peak 89.1 *mountain*
cloud cover 31.19
cloud-covered 31.49 *cloudy*
cloud-crossed 31.49 *cloudy*
cloud-cuckoo-land 610.3 *aspiration*; 477.8 *dreamland*; 619.4 *wonder*
clouded 523.11 *benighted*; 524.7 *dimmed*; 528.2 *shady*
cloud-flecked 31.49 *cloudy*
cloud forest 79.4 *trees*
cloudily 524.12 *dimly*; 533.9 *greyly*; 31.65 *meteorologically*; 528.13 *opaquely*
cloudiness 31.19 *cloud cover*; 258.1 *dirtiness*; 533.7 *dullness*; 524.2 *murk*; 266.1 *obscurity*; 528.6 *opaqueness*
clouding over 524.3 *dimming*
cloud-laden 31.49 *cloudy*
cloudless 756.14 *auspicious*; 31.45 *fine*; 248.8 *prosperous*; 428.5 *rainless*; 522.19 *sunny*; 527.1 *transparent*
cloudlessness 527.5 *transparency*
cloudless sky 31.22 *sun*
cloud nine 174.1 *summit*
cloud of words 270.1 *diffuseness*
cloud on the horizon 254.6 *danger signal*; 711.1 *warning*
cloud over 523.13 *become dark*; 524.9 *be dim*; 528.10 *be opaque*; 31.60 *cloud*
cloudscape 19.10 *art subject*; 41.4 *portrait*
cloud-seeding 31.26 *raininess*
cloud street 31.20 *cloud appearance*
cloud the issue 109.10 *be unrelated*
cloud-topped 31.49 *cloudy*; 154.9 *high*
cloud tower 31.20 *cloud appearance*
cloudy 31.49; 523.8 *dark*; 524.5 *dim*; 258.7 *dirty*; 533.3 *dull*; 477.12 *imaginary*; 429.10 *misty*; 541.10 *mottled*; 524.6 *murky*; 266.2 *obscure*; 626.8 *overcast*; 528.2 *shady*; 432.19 *smoky*
clough 438.3 *garden tool*; 146.3 *gulf*; 92.8 *valley*
clout 396.1 *authority*; 331.13 *blow*; 814.12 *corporal punishment*; 331.3, 814.3 *hit*; 395.1 *influence*; 237.7 *instrumentality*; 480.1 *persuasion*; 185.1 *prominence*; 393.8 *repair*; 121.1 *superiority*
clove 496.5 *herbs*
cloven 372.16 *apart*; 146.7 *cracked*; 198.13 *half*
cloven-hoofed 71.33 *ungulate*
clover 557.8 *animal food*; 43.12 *crop*; 248.1 *prosperity*
clover honey 498.2 *sweetener*
cloverleaf 320.3 *carriageway*; 318.5 *crossing point*; 193.5 *crossroads*; 317.3, 373.5 *road*
cloves 502.2 *fragrant thing*
clown 21.32; 599.13 *be humorous*; 697.4 *buffoon*; 21.31 *circus performer*; 697.8 *fool*; 599.6 *humorist*; 272.3 *object of ridicule*; 486.10 *unskilled person*
clown around 459.7 *play the fool*
clown face 21.21 *stage requisite*
clowning 272.4 *joke*; 272.1 *ludicrousness*; 697.3 *tomfoolery*; 599.3 *wit*
clownish 486.3 *clumsy*; 544.7 *graceless*; 272.5 *ridiculous*
cloy 620.6 *be boring*; 219.4 *be excessive*
cloyed 219.6 *excessive*
cloying 620.4 *boring*; 219.6 *excessive*; 498.6 *sweet*; 498.1 *sweetness*
club 331.8; 374.3 *assembly*; 376.15 *association*; 587.7 *blunt weapon*; 69.3 *card game terms*; 376.19 *clique*; 814.14 *instrument of punishment*; 21.16 *theatre*
clubbish 654.15 *sociable*
clubbishness 654.1 *sociability*
clubby 654.15 *sociable*
club chair 23.2 *chair*
club circuit 21.15 *engagement*
club foot 234.3 *deformity*
clubfooted 234.7 *deformed*
club fungi 83.3 *fungi*
clubhaul 323.10 *sail*
clubman 654.6 *social person*
clubmoss 82.1 *fern*
Club of Paris 13.5 *international trade*
club root 44.12 *pests and diseases*
club sandwich 411.5 *layered thing*; 25.11 *sandwich*
club tie 743.5 *uniform*
club together 747.14 *join with*; 223.14 *keep company with*
club together with 654.13 *fraternize*
cluck 515.2 *bird song*; 515.5 *sing*
clue 476.2 *basis of supposition*; 522.13 *enlightenment*; 716.4 *indication*; 719.1 *interpretation*; 742.1 *sign*; 446.2 *theory*
clued up 693.18 *informed*; 6.19 *knowledgeable*; 488.5 *sensible*
clueless 456.6 *ignorant*
clue up 693.11 *inform*
clump 331.13 *blow*; 376.27 *bundle*; 81.2 *grassland*; 376.38 *group*; 331.7 *kick*; 158.7 *mass*; 416.4 *solid body*
clumped 376.49 *grouped*
clumsily 264.28 *awkwardly*; 240.6 *inconveniently*; 544.11 *inelegantly*; 492.15 *insensitively*; 486.11 *unskilfully*
clumsily built 486.3 *clumsy*
clumsiness 264.2 *awkwardness*; 544.1 *inelegance*; 544.4 *inelegance of speech*; 236.8 *inferiority*; 489.1 *lack of feeling*; 486.8 *unskilfulness*
clumsy 264.15; **486.3**; 611.8 *bad*; 544.7 *graceless*; 492.10 *handed*; 240.1 *inconvenient*; 724.8 *inelegant*; 236.2 *inferior*; 333.4 *slow*; 489.6 *unfeeling*
clumsy clot 486.10 *unskilled person*
clumsy construction 544.4 *inelegance of speech*
clumsy lout 486.10 *unskilled person*
clumsy oaf 486.10 *unskilled person*
clunk 511.9 *be nonresonant*; 508.6 *crack*; 511.5 *dull sound*
clupeoid 74.13 *fishlike*
cluricaune 11.11 *ghost*
cluster 376.28; 376.27 *bundle*; 310.10, 376.39 *come together*; 29.7 *galaxy*; 376.38 *group*; 158.7 *mass*; 416.4 *solid body*
cluster analysis 27.55 *statistical methods*
cluster bomb 587.16 *bomb*
clustered 376.49 *grouped*
clutch 376.24 *brace*; 254.1 *dangerous*; 72.15 *eggs*; 438.5 *machine*; 264.5 *predicament*; 360.6 *retain*; 360.1 *retention*; 492.11 *touch*; 555.4 *young animal*; 72.12 *young bird*
clutch at 773.7 *take*
clutch bag 410.8 *bag*
clutched 360.10 *retained*
clutches 12.3 *governance*
clutching 773.1 *taking*; 492.2 *touching*
clutch-slip 61.6 *motor-racing terms*; 61.9 *race*
clutter 408.4 *litter*; 208.4 *throng*
cluttered 208.10 *crowded*
Clwyd 90.4 *British rivers*
Clyde 90.4 *British rivers*
clyster 368.11 *thing inserted*; 433.11 *wash*
CMI 40.1 *computing*
CND member 589.3, 749.3 *pacifist*; 244.12 *reformer*
Cnidaria 75.7 *coelenterate*
cnidarian 75.7 *coelenterate*
CNN 692.24 *television broadcasting*
C-note 780.8 *American money*
CoA 33.12 *coenzyme*
coach 117.10 *assimilate*; 47.3 *athlete*; 49.2 *basketball player*; 243.6 *brief*; 320.19 *bus*; 455.14 *cause to know*; 6.22 *educate*; 6.4 *educator*; 46.2 *football player*; 243.15 *preparer*
coach-builder 578.2 *artisan*; 23.13 *carpenter*
coach building 320.21 *miscellaneous motoring terms*
coachcard 793.4 *bargain*
coached 6.19 *knowledgeable*
coach horse 316.6 *beast of burden*; 59.2 *thoroughbred*
coaching 6.1 *education*
coact 747.11 *cooperate*; 750.22 *form an alliance*
coacting 747.17 *cooperative*
coaction 747.1 *cooperation*
coactive 750.11 *allied*; 747.17 *cooperative*
coactively 747.20 *cooperatively*
coadjutant 747.17 *cooperative*; 392.11 *helper*
coadjutor 747.10 *cooperator*
coadjuvancy 747.3 *mutual relationship*
coadjuvant 747.17 *cooperative*
coadministration 747.5 *joint control*
coadunation 747.7 *association*
coagency 223.1 *accompaniment*; 374.2 *cooperation*; 747.5 *joint control*
coagent 374.8 *cooperative*
coagulant 37.4 *drug type*
coagulate 267.6 *adhere*; 416.8 *be dense*; 152.7 *thicken*
coagulated 267.9 *adhesive*; 416.7 *condensed*; 152.2 *dense*
coagulating 416.7 *condensed*
coagulation 416.2 *concentration*; 152.6 *denseness*
coagulum 416.4 *solid body*
coal 437.5; 532.9 *black thing*; 30.43 *fossil*; 284.10 *fossilization*; 330.13, 437.1 *fuel*; 437.3 *gas*; 435.1 *materials*; 436.5 *provision*; 334.6 *source of energy*
coalbed 437.5 *coal*; 439.2 *resource*
coal bin 437.5 *coal*
coal-black 532.1 *black*
coal box 437.5 *coal*
coal bunker 437.5 *coal*
coal-burning 493.13 *heated*
coal cellar 437.5 *coal*; 767.8 *sink*
coal deposit 439.2 *resource*
coal dust 437.5 *coal*; 427.5 *powder*
coalesce 111.7 *be the same*; 374.5 *combine*; 747.16 *join*; 111.8 *make the same*
coalesced 111.12 *same*
coalescence 747.7 *association*; 374.1 *combination*; 416.1 *density*; 111.1 *sameness*
coalescent 374.7 *combined*; 111.12 *same*
coalface 437.5 *coal*; 439.2 *resource*; 577.1 *workshop*
coalfield 437.5 *coal*; 439.2 *resource*
coal fire 493.6 *fire*
coal-fired 493.13 *heated*; 437.10 *powered*
coalfish 25.18 *sea fish*
coal hole 437.5 *coal*; 565.7 *room*; 767.8 *sink*
coalition 750.2 *alliance*; 747.7 *association*; 764.1 *joint possession*; 12.6 *political party*
coalman 258.6 *dirty person*
coal measures 437.5 *coal*; 284.10 *fossilization*
coal merchant 437.9 *power-worker*
coalmine 437.5 *coal*; 183.2 *concave land*; 411.5 *layered thing*; 439.2 *resource*; 577.1 *workshop*
coal miner 578.2 *artisan*; 437.9 *power-worker*
coal oil 437.6 *oil*
Coalsack 29.8 *interstellar medium*
coal scuttle 437.5 *coal*; 410.11 *vessel*
coaly 437.10 *powered*
coarctate 191.7 *smaller*
coarctation 191.1 *contraction*
coarse 420.2; **497.6**; 55.8 *angling*; 659.6 *bad-mannered*; 539.4, 796.12 *indecent*; 544.8 *indecorous*; 236.4 *poor*; 404.8 *rough*; 152.4 *thick-skinned*; 546.4 *ugly*; 258.8 *unclean*; 675.7 *vulgar*; 42.10 *woven*
coarse cloth 420.6 *roughness*
coarse fish 25.17 *freshwater fish*
coarse fishing 55.1 *angling*; 633.2 *chase*; 74.7 *fishing*
coarse grain 41.10 *graininess*; 420.6 *roughness*
coarse-grained 420.2 *coarse*; 404.8 *rough*
coarse-grained texture 30.28 *rock*
coarsely 258.12 *dirtily*; 544.11 *inelegantly*; 420.14 *roughly*; 659.10 *rudely*; 497.11 *tastelessly*; 404.15 *texturally*; 152.9 *thick*
coarsen 404.12; 152.8 *fatten*; 420.12 *make rough*; 245.6 *pervert*; 675.10 *vulgarize*
coarseness 659.2 *bad manners*; 497.4 *bad taste*; 675.3 *grossness*; 544.2 *impropriety*; 796.2 *indecency*; 236.10 *poverty*; 420.6 *roughness*; 675.1 *tastelessness*; 258.2 *uncleanness*
coarsening 245.8 *perversion*
coarse pottery 24.1 *ceramics*
coarse-woven 404.8 *rough*
coast 30.11; **92.4**; 301.8 *be motionless*; 265.17 *do easily*; 164.1 *edge*; 265.19 *go easily*; 421.12 *go smoothly*; 341.4 *not act*; 305.6, 305.14 *slide*; 300.15 *walk*
coastal 30.52; 92.11 *continental*; 164.8 *edging*
coastal dune 30.37 *dune*
coastal engineering 38.17 *civil engineering*
coastal fog 31.33 *fog*
coastal plain 92.4 *coast*; 30.7 *landform*
coastal station 31.5 *weather station*
coastal waters 30.12 *ocean*
coast clear 252.1 *safety*
coastguard 586.14 *armed forces*; 252.3 *protector*
coastguardsman 323.7 *nautical person*; 586.27 *naval man*
coast home 265.17 *do easily*
coasting 305.18 *falling*; 323.11 *nautical*
coastland 92.4 *coast*
coastline 30.11, 92.4 *coast*; 163.3 *edge*
coat 411.3; **550.24**; **551.12**; 211.6 *add*; 550.5 *body covering*; 550.3 *coating*; 529.15 *colour*; 411.10 *layer*; 528.11 *make opaque*; 19.19 *paint*; 421.11 *smooth*
coated 411.8; 528.1 *opaque*; 42.11 *treated*
coated lens 28.29 *optical element*
coatee 551.23 *children's clothes*
coathanger 553.5 *fashion model*; 361.4 *hanger*; 551.27 *model*
coating 550.3; 411.3 *coat*; 550.1 *covering*; 171.1 *exterior*
coat of arms 743.8 *heraldic device*
coat of mail 384.7 *armour*
coat of many colours 114.3 *diverse thing*
coat-tail 551.24 *part of garment*; 361.3 *suspended object*
coauthors 747.9 *team*
coax 645.5 *be cunning*; 677.10 *cajole*; 363.12 *lure*; 483.9 *motivate*; 480.15 *persuade*; 710.6 *request*; 480.16 *tempt*
coaxed 483.12 *motivated*
coaxer 483.7 *motivator*; 480.12 *persuader*

coaxial cable 692.6 *telecommunication;* 39.27 *wire*
coaxing 677.14 *cajoling;* 480.2 *flattery;* 483.2 *inducement*
cob 81.4 *cereal grass;* 59.1 *horse;* 25.39 *loaf;* 72.10 *male bird;* 59.5 *pony*
cobalt 33.15 *essential element;* 28.59 *ferromagnetism*
cobalt blue 539.1 *blue;* 539.5 *blueness*
cobaltic 32.34 *elemental*
cobaltous 32.34 *elemental*
cobalt violet 540.2 *purple pigment*
cobble 435.2 *building material;* 551.35 *make clothing;* 550.11 *paving;* 393.1 *repair;* 550.29 *surface*
cobbled 317.15 *accessible*
cobbled together 486.4 *bungled*
cobbler 551.26 *fashion designer;* 393.12 *repairer*
cobblers 697.1 *nonsense*
cobblestone 550.11 *paving;* 317.4 *road surface*
cobble together 356.10 *produce*
cobbling 551.2 *dressing;* 393.8 *repair*
cobra 73.3 *snake*
cobweb 258.4 *dirt;* 415.7 *light thing;* 700.13 *snare;* 76.6 *spinner;* 124.8 *trifle;* 337.5 *weak thing*
cobwebbed 700.42 *trapped*
cobwebby 258.7 *dirty;* 415.2 *insubstantial*
cobwebs of antiquity 296.3 *antiquity*
Coca-Cola™ 558.6 *soft drink;* 498.5 *sweet drink*
cocaine 33.19 *alkaloid;* 489.4 *anaesthetic;* 394.8, 691.6 *drug*
coccidioidomycosis 83.5 *fungal association*
coccus 34.3 *organism*
cochairmanship 747.5 *joint control*
cochineal 529.4 *pigment;* 535.6 *red pigment*
cochlea 180.3 *convoluted thing;* 504.5 *internal ear*
cochlear nerve 504.5 *internal ear*
cochleate 180.4 *convolutional*
cock 43.8 *livestock;* 330.32 *load;* 567.16 *male animal;* 72.10 *male bird;* 567.3 *male title of address;* 561.8 *organs of reproduction;* 243.4 *prepare for action*
cockade 743.4 *insignia*
cock-a-doodle-doo 72.18, 515.2 *bird song*
Cockaigne 477.8 *dreamland*
cock-a-leekie 25.44 *British dish;* 25.13 *soup*
cockalorum 660.12 *impudent person*
cock-and-bull 699.36 *falsified*
cock-and-bull story 234.4 *distortion of the truth;* 699.10 *lie*
cock and hen 201.6 *ten*
cock a snook **668.26**; 661.5 *defy;* 742.11 *gesture;* 660.29 *ridicule*
cockatoo 72.7 *cagebird*
cockatrice 72.9 *fabulous bird;* 743.8 *heraldic device;* 70.7 *legendary beast;* 73.3 *snake*
cockchafer 76.3 *pest*
cockcrow 290.1 *morning*
cocked hat 551.15 *headgear*
cocked up 186.9 *unbowed*
cockee 68.10 *curling*
cockerel 567.16 *male animal;* 72.10 *male bird*
cockeye 519.2 *poor sight*
cockeyed 234.6 *distorted;* 408.18 *muddled;* 519.9 *weak-sighted*
cock gunlock 438.1 *tool*
cockily **673.21**; 660.31 *cheekily;* 661.9 *defiantly*
cockiness **673.3**; 661.1 *defiance;* 660.10 *impudence*
cocking 243.9 *preparation*
cockle 25.19 *shellfish*
cockles of one's heart 590.8 *seat of feelings*
cockloft 154.8 *high thing*
cockney 564.9 *British inhabitant*
cockney accent 5.26 *dialect*
cockney rhyming slang 5.18 *slang*
cock of the walk 400.5 *company leader;* 235.8 *exceller;* 660.12 *impudent person;* 622.13 *proud person;* 121.5 *superior*
cockpit 50.6 *canoeing;* 50.3 *parts of a sailing boat;* 397.8 *vantage point*
cockroach 76.1 *insect;* 76.3 *pest*
cock-robin 72.10 *male bird*
cocksfoot 43.12 *crop*
cockshy 330.5 *throw*
cocksman 567.6 *macho man*
cock-sparrow 72.10 *male bird*
cockspur 425.8 *sharp-pointed thing*
cocksure 452.2 *convinced*
cocksureness 452.10 *conviction*
cocktail 690.12 *alcohol;* 374.4 *compound;* 558.2 *drink;* 558.8 *mixed drink;* 412.2 *mixed thing*
cocktail dress 656.4 *formal dress;* 551.7 *frock*
cocktailing 691.1 *drug-taking*
cocktail party 654.5 *party*
cocktail sausage 25.29 *sausage*
cocktail shaker 412.6 *mixer*
cock the float 55.7 *angle*
cockup 274.10 *blunder;* 486.9 *bungling;* 408.6 *mix-up;* 378.2 *obstacle*
cock up 486.7 *be clumsy;* 544.6 *blunder;* 408.23 *confuse;* 245.4 *impair;* 274.19 *make a mistake;* 186.6 *make vertical*
cocky **673.11**; 622.22 *boastful;* 661.7 *defiant;* 660.21 *impudent*
cocoa 558.5 *milk;* 498.5 *sweet drink*
coconscious 36.21 *psyche;* 36.37 *subconscious*
coconut 423.7 *tough thing*
coconut meal 43.9 *animal feedstuff*
coconut milk 558.6 *soft drink*
coconut pie 25.36 *cake*
cocoon 550.14 *animal covering;* 76.5 *larva;* 252.10 *protect;* 410.21 *put in a container;* 344.3 *rudiment;* 76.6 *spinner;* 555.4 *young animal*
cocooned 410.20 *containing*
cocooning 410.20 *containing*
cocotte 25.6 *kitchen equipment*
co-counselling 36.3 *psychiatric treatment*
COD 692.2 *postal communication*
cod 74.8 *food fish;* 25.18 *sea fish*
coda 211.3 *additional item;* 131.10 *ending;* 18.13 *melody;* 168.1 *rear;* 289.9 *sequel*
coddle 490.10 *comfort;* 25.55 *cook;* 593.27 *kiss;* 392.20 *sustain*
coddled 25.56 *culinary;* 490.7 *pleased*
coddling 25.8 *cooking technique*
code 737.4 *brain-teaser;* 140.2 *canon;* 40.10 *character;* 406.5 *divisions;* 729.1 *faculty of speech;* 737.14 *make mysterious;* 5.5 *nonstandard language;* 4.2 *philosophical system;* 713.3 *precept;* 742.1 *sign;* 139.10 *specialized language;* 11.2 *the occult;* 696.12 *unintelligible thing;* 742.9 *use signs*
code-breaker 719.6 *interpreter*
codec 40.14 *data transfer*
code cracking 719.1 *interpretation*
coded 736.15 *disguised;* 719.15 *interpreted;* 406.12 *itemized*
codeine 394.5 *analgesic;* 394.8 *drug*
code name 737.8 *anonymity;* 736.7 *concealer*
code of conduct 810.6 *ethics;* 4.2 *philosophical system*
code of duty 810.6 *ethics*
code of honour 810.6 *ethics*
code of practice 4.2 *philosophical system*
coder 737.4 *brain-teaser*
codetermination 747.5 *joint control*
codicil 211.3 *additional item;* 635.5 *will*
codification 409.5 *categorization;* 407.2 *grouping;* 16.31 *legislation;* 16.1 *the law*
codified 409.24 *categorized;* 736.15 *disguised;* 407.11 *grouped;* 16.46 *legislated*
codified law 16.1 *the law*
codify 409.15 *categorize;* 16.68 *legislate;* 137.14 *sort;* 407.19 *systematize*
co-directorship 747.5 *joint control*
codlike 74.13 *fishlike*
codling moth 44.12 *pests and diseases*
cod-liver oil 74.9 *fish product*
codomain 27.29 *mathematical function*
codon 34.13 *genetic material*
codpiece 551.25 *accessories;* 551.24 *part of garment*
Cod war 585.1 *war*
coefficient 27.25 *algebraic expression*
coefficient of friction 365.1 *friction*
coelacanth 74.4 *fossil fish*
coelenterate **75.7**; **75.21**; 70.5 *aquatic animal*
coelomate 75.16 *invertebrate*
coenobial 84.7 *algal*
coenobite 7.7 *monk;* 655.6 *unsocial person*
coenobium 84.4 *reproductive body*
coenocyte 34.7 *cell*
coenocytic 34.23 *cellular*
coenzyme **33.12**; 33.11 *enzyme*
coequal 111.16, 119.5, 119.6 *equal*
coequality 111.5, 119.1 *equality*
coequally 111.19, 119.12 *equally*
coerce 386.6 *compel;* 480.15 *persuade;* 251.8 *restrain;* 647.6 *suppress*
coerced 647.9 *suppressed*
coercion **386.2**; 251.1 *restraint;* 647.2 *suppression*
coercive 396.12 *authoritative;* 386.9 *compelling;* 400.12 *masterful;* 251.13 *restraining;* 647.8 *severe*
coercively 386.11 *compellingly;* 251.16 *under restraints*
coercive methods **386.3**
coercive person **386.4**
coeternal 285.9 *simultaneous*
coeternally 285.12 *simultaneously*
coeval 285.5 *contemporary;* 285.9 *simultaneous*
coevality 285.1 *same time*
coevally 285.12 *simultaneously*
coexist 285.6 *be simultaneous;* 93.17 *exist*
coexistence 223.1 *accompaniment;* 93.1 *existence;* 589.1 *peace;* 285.1 *same time*
coexistent 223.18 *concurrent;* 93.10 *existing;* 285.9 *simultaneous*
coexisting 750.11 *allied;* 223.18 *concurrent;* 285.9 *simultaneous*
coextend 188.5 *parallel*
coextension 188.1 *parallelism*
coextensive 119.6 *equal;* 188.3 *parallel*
coextensively 119.13 *equitably;* 188.7 *in parallel*
cofactor 33.11 *enzyme*
co-favourite 59.7 *horseracing*
C of E 7.16 *denominational*
coffee **558.4**; 534.1 *brown;* 534.5 *brown thing;* 654.3 *meeting*
coffee bar 558.11 *drink provider;* 557.15 *eating place*
coffee cake 25.36 *cake*
coffee-coloured 534.1 *brown*
coffee cup 558.10 *drink container;* 410.13 *drinking vessel*
coffee estate 43.6 *farm*
coffee grinder 25.6 *kitchen equipment;* 50.3 *parts of a sailing boat;* 427.11 *pulverizer*
coffee house 557.15 *eating place*
coffee jar 410.11 *vessel*
coffee maker 410.15 *pot*
coffee morning 654.3 *meeting*
coffee plantation 43.6 *farm*
coffee planter 43.15 *agriculturist*
coffeepot 410.15 *pot*
coffee stall 557.15 *eating place*
coffee table 155.4 *low thing;* 23.4 *table*
coffee-table book 740.6 *book publishing*
coffee urn 410.15 *pot*
coffer 410.6 *box;* 20.19 *decorate;* 780.20 *money store;* 439.4 *storage*
cofferdam 128.3 *exclusion zone;* 38.28 *substructure*
coffin 582.8 *after death;* 410.6 *box;* 583.8 *bury;* 583.4 *funeral objects*
coffined 583.10 *buried*
coffin lead 55.3 *fishing tackle*
coffin nail 496.7 *tobacco*
cog 23.17 *carpenter;* 183.10 *notch;* 307.6 *rotator;* 425.8 *sharp-pointed thing*
cogency 336.3 *intensity;* 698.11 *pedantry;* 334.1 *power*
cogent 386.9 *compelling;* 4.16 *dialectical;* 726.3 *emphatic;* 698.24 *pedantic;* 480.19 *persuasive;* 336.10 *potent;* 334.13 *powerful*
cogently 386.11 *compellingly;* 480.21 *persuasively;* 334.18 *powerfully*
cogged 23.16 *joined;* 183.7 *notched*
cogging 23.10 *carpenter's term;* 23.16 *joined*
cog in the wheel 405.5 *member*
cogitate 4.20 *philosophize;* 356.10 *produce;* 443.12 *think*
cogitate upon 356.10 *produce*
cogitatingly 4.28 *thoughtfully*
cogitation 4.4 *philosophical investigation;* 356.1 *production;* 443.1 *thought*
cogitative 4.17 *thoughtful*
cognate 108.4 *related;* 5.17 *word;* 5.42 *worded*
cognate word 5.17 *word*
cognition 455.1 *knowledge;* 442.1 *mind;* 443.1 *thought*
cognitive 443.8 *thoughtful*
cognitively 455.15 *knowledgeably*
cognitive psychology 36.1 *psychology*
cognizability 695.11 *recognizability*
cognizable 16.47 *liable to law;* 16.58 *unjust*
cognizance 671.1 *gratitude;* 16.2 *jurisdiction;* 455.1 *knowledge*
cognizant 6.19, 455.8 *knowledgeable*
cognizant of 671.5 *thanking*
cognize 442.12 *think*
cognomen 721.8 *name*
cognoscente 485.5 *expert*
cog railway 317.10, 321.1 *railway*
cogwheel 307.6 *rotator*
cohabit 223.14 *keep company with;* 570.18 *live together;* 593.29 *make love;* 570.15 *marry*
cohabitant 223.12, 570.12 *partner*
cohabitation 223.1 *accompaniment;* 223.3 *companionship;* 593.5 *desire;* 570.1 *marriage*
cohabitee 223.12 *partner*
cohabiting 223.18 *concurrent*
coheir 769.6 *beneficiary*
cohere 267.6 *adhere;* 197.19 *become one;* 416.8 *be dense;* 750.25 *conform;* 134.3 *continue;* 373.13 *intercommunicate*
coherence 267.1 *adhesion;* 725.1 *clarity;* 750.5 *conformity;* 416.1 *density;* 695.9 *intelligibility;* 407.7 *method;* 197.3 *oneness;* 460.2 *rationality;* 423.6 *toughness*
coherent 267.9 *adhesive;* 725.3 *clear;* 750.14 *conforming;* 373.16 *connective;* 423.3 *hard;* 695.1 *intelligible;* 460.5 *rational;* 407.14 *well-ordered*
coherent light 522.1 *light*
coherently 725.4 *clearly;* 267.11 *cohesively;* 695.13 *intelligibly;* 460.7 *sanely;* 423.12 *toughly*
coherent radiation 28.26 *laser*
cohesion 267.1 *adhesion;* 373.1 *connection;* 134.1 *continuity;* 416.1 *density;* 363.2 *pulling power;* 423.6 *toughness*
cohesive 267.9 *adhesive;* 373.14 *connective;* 134.5 *continual;* 416.6 *dense;* 423.3 *hard;* 360.9 *retentive*
cohesively **267.11**; 363.13 *attractionally;* 416.10 *densely;* 373.17 *in connection with;* 360.11 *tenaciously;* 423.12 *toughly*
cohesiveness 267.1 *adhesion;* 423.6 *toughness*
cohesive strength 38.15 *strength of materials*
cohort 586.16 *army unit;* 376.18 *generation*
coif 384.7 *armour;* 547.17 *crimp;* 551.15 *headgear*
coiffeur 547.13 *beautician*
coiffeuse 547.13 *beautician*
coiffure 547.8 *haircut*
coign of vantage 121.3 *advantage*
coil **180.2**; 177.2 *bend;* 563.3 *birth control;* 180.6 *convolute;* 177.6 *curve;* 184.9 *fold;* 28.60 *magnet;* 306.1 *orbital motion;* 148.5 *piece;* 184.1 *wrinkle*
coiled 306.10 *circular;* 180.4 *convolutional;* 177.4 *curved;* 422.6 *elastic*
coiling 422.6 *elastic*
coil magnet 363.3 *magnet*
coil spring 422.5 *spring*
coil up 181.11 *make round*
coin 780.2 *cash;* 780.13 *coinage;* 160.7 *form;* 477.14 *imagine;* 130.22 *invent;* 20.9 *miscellaneous architectural features;* 780.24 *monetize;* 780.1 *money;* 356.10 *produce*
coinage **780.13**; 130.5 *invention;* 780.1 *money;* 5.17 *word*
coinage metal 32.6 *chemical element*
coinage of the brain 477.4 *ideality*
coin a phrase 745.3 *aphorize*
coin a word 5.45 *use language*
coincide 223.13 *accompany;* 115.10 *be similar;* 285.6 *be simultaneous;* 111.7 *be the same;* 750.24 *harmonize;* 694.10 *mean*
coincidence 17.3 *aspect of fiction;* 107.1 *chance;* 374.1 *combination;* 111.2 *equivalence;* 750.4 *harmony;* 285.1 *same time;* 223.2 *synchronism;* 109.1 *unrelatedness*
coincident 223.18 *concurrent;* 374.8 *cooperative;* 119.6 *equal;* 750.13 *harmonious;* 285.9 *simultaneous*
coincidental 107.8 *chance;* 111.13 *equivalent;* 109.7 *illogical;* 285.9 *simultaneous*
coincidentally 107.13 *by chance;* 119.13 *equitably;* 111.18 *identically;* 374.10 *in combination;* 109.12 *irrelevantly;* 285.12 *simultaneously*
coincide with 119.10 *be equal*
coinciding 223.18 *concurrent;* 750.13 *harmonious*
coin collecting 780.13 *coinage*

coin collection 439.5 *collection*
coin collector 376.35 *collector;* 780.17 *financier*
coined 780.22 *monetary*
coiner 780.17 *financier*
coin money 781.13 *get rich*
coin of the realm 780.13 *coinage*
coins 780.4 *change;* 780.13 *coinage*
coin-toss 46.14 *miscellaneous terms*
Cointreau™ 558.7 *alcoholic drink*
coition 554.4 *biological function;* 593.5 *desire;* 561.3 *propagation*
coitus 593.5 *desire*
coitus interruptus 563.3 *birth control*
Coke™ 558.6 *soft drink*
coke 437.5 *coal;* 691.6 *drug;* 493.6 *fire*
coke-head 691.4 *drug taker*
col 183.2 *concave land;* 146.3 *gulf;* 373.4 *means of connection;* 154.4 *mountain range*
cola 558.6 *soft drink*
colander 25.6 *kitchen equipment;* 308.6 *porous thing*
colchicine 33.19 *alkaloid*
Cold 494
cold 494.8; 249.6 *adverse;* 651.12 *callous;* 31.31 *coldness;* 660.17 *contemptuous;* 31.55 *cool;* 582.19 *dead;* 28.35 *heat;* 341.3 *inactive;* 618.7 *indifferent;* 260.6 *infection;* 592.1 *insensitive;* 628.4 *pitiless;* 795.9 *pure;* 581.3 *refreshing;* 145.9 *reserved;* 260.9 *respiratory disease;* 655.8 *unsociable;* 31.47 *windy*
cold air 31.10 *air movement*
cold as charity 494.8 *cold*
cold as marble 494.8 *cold*
cold as the grave 494.8 *cold*
cold bath 256.6 *bath*
cold-blooded 651.12 *callous;* 74.13 *fishlike;* 618.7 *indifferent;* 592.1 *insensitive;* 382.24 *murderous;* 628.4 *pitiless;* 73.11 *reptilian;* 489.6 *unfeeling*
cold-blooded animal 73.1 *reptile*
cold-blooded killer 628.3 *pitiless person*
cold-bloodedly 618.17 *indifferently;* 628.7 *pitilessly*
cold-blooded murderer 382.11 *murderer*
cold-bloodedness 651.3 *callousness;* 618.1 *indifference*
cold body 28.35 *heat*
cold climate 31.38 *climate*
coldcock 331.3 *hit*
cold cream 256.9 *cleaning agent;* 268.7 *pomade;* 255.3 *purifier*
cold cuts 25.12 *hors d'oeuvre*
cold day 249.4 *time of adversity*
colder 31.55 *cool*
cold-eyed 651.12 *callous*
cold feet 614.1 *cowardice*
cold fingers of death 582.1 *death*
cold fish 618.6 *indifferent person;* 592.5 *insensitive person*
cold frame 44.4 *nursery*
cold front 31.10 *air movement;* 494.7 *cold weather*
cold fusion 28.72 *nuclear fission*
cold-hearted 651.12 *callous;* 809.3 *impenitent;* 618.7 *indifferent;* 592.1 *insensitive;* 628.4 *pitiless;* 683.4 *selfish*
cold-heartedly 809.6 *impenitently;* 618.17 *indifferently;* 651.20 *malevolently;* 628.7 *pitilessly;* 683.8 *selfishly*
cold-heartedness 651.3 *callousness;* 809.1 *impenitence;* 618.1 *indifference;* 592.3 *insensitiveness*
cold-hearted person 809.2 *impenitent person*
cold in the nose 501.1 *odourlessness*
coldish 31.55 *cool*
coldly 494.13; 618.17 *indifferently;* 31.65 *meteorologically;* 301.10 *motionlessly;* 628.7 *pitilessly;* 145.11 *reservedly;* 592.8 *unfeelingly;* 655.14 *unsocially*
cold meat party 582.8 *after death;* 583.2 *funeral*
coldness 31.31; 494.1; 249.1 *adversity;* 651.3 *callousness;* 618.1 *indifference;* 592.3 *insensitiveness;* 795.3 *moral purity;* 145.4 *reserve;* 605.2 *stoicism;* 655.1 *unsociability*
cold occlusion 31.10 *air movement*
cold of heart 651.12 *callous*
cold reception 470.5 *rejection*
cold rubber 422.4 *rubber*
cold season 494.7 *cold weather*
cold shivers 327.7 *shake*
cold shoulder 659.3 *act of discourtesy;* 634.10 *avoidance;* 472.1 *inattention;* 668.5, 668.23 *insult;* 670.3 *nonacceptance;* 470.5 *rejection;* 364.6 *repulse;* 670.15 *withhold approval*
cold-shoulder 634.1 *avoid;* 659.7 *be discourteous;* 472.13 *be thoughtless;* 659.5 *discourteous;* 128.7, 470.3 *exclude;* 655.13 *ignore;* 364.1 *repel*
cold-shouldered 655.10 *lonely*
cold shower 256.6 *bath;* 581.6 *refresher*
cold snap 31.31 *coldness;* 494.7 *cold weather*
cold spell 494.7 *cold weather*
cold steel 587.8 *sharp weapon*
cold storage 359.1 *preservation*
cold store 25.4 *kitchen container*
Coldstream Guard 586.12 *ceremonial troops*
cold substance 28.35 *heat*
cold sweat 612.1 *fear;* 596.4 *sign of dislike;* 560.8 *sweat*
cold turkey 691.3 *withdrawal*
cold war 585.1 *war*
cold water 481.7 *deterrence*
cold-water cure 394.13 *therapy*
cold wave 31.31 *coldness*
cold weather 494.7; 31.31 *coldness*
cold wind 249.1 *adversity*
coleopteran 76.10 *insectan*
coleoptile 77.9 *seed*
coleorhiza 77.9 *seed*
coleslaw 25.14 *salad*
coley 25.18 *sea fish*
colic 260.8 *indigestion;* 491.2 *painful condition*
Coliseum 356.8 *construction*
colitis 260.8 *indigestion*
collaborate 479.3 *apostatize;* 374.6 *come together;* 636.14, 747.11 *cooperate;* 750.22 *form an alliance;* 413.14 *give moral support;* 392.22 *improve;* 800.9 *prove false;* 388.3 *submit*
collaborating 750.11 *allied*
collaboration 750.2 *alliance;* 479.7 *apostasy;* 374.2, 747.1 *cooperation;* 636.9 *goodwill;* 392.10 *helpfulness;* 413.6 *moral support;* 764.2 *participation;* 388.1 *submission*
collaborationist 479.9 *equivocator;* 700.20 *plotter*
collaborative 750.11 *allied;* 747.17 *cooperative;* 636.4 *helpful;* 413.9 *supportive*
collaboratively 747.20 *cooperatively*
collaborator 664.5 *adherent;* 747.10 *cooperator;* 479.9 *equivocator;* 392.11 *helper;* 764.3 *participant;* 700.20 *plotter;* 662.10 *seditionist;* 413.8 *supporter*
collaborators 747.9 *team*
collage 374.2 *cooperation;* 19.7 *picture;* 376.33 *putting together;* 541.5 *variegated thing*
collagen 33.9 *protein*
collapse 191.6 *become smaller;* 183.8 *be concave;* 261.5 *be fatigued;* 335.6 *be powerless;* 786.9 *be unable to pay;* 260.24 *be unhealthy;* 191.1 *contraction;* 214.2 *decline;* 214.4 *decrease;* 247.2 *defeat;* 245.1 *deteriorate;* 245.9 *dilapidation;* 335.4 *disability;* 375.3 *disintegrate;* 375.1 *disintegration;* 305.10 *droop;* 247.6 *fail;* 247.1 *failure;* 305.4 *fall;* 261.7 *fatigue;* 786.5 *insolvency;* 766.9 *lose;* 191.5 *make smaller;* 357.4 *ruin;* 226.7 *stop working;* 388.4 *succumb;* 260.3 *symptom*
collapse breccia 427.9 *grit*
collapsed 260.22 *sick;* 191.7 *smaller*
collapsibility 191.2 *contractibility*
collapsible 191.9 *contractible*
collapsing 191.8 *contracting;* 305.16 *descending;* 64.6 *rugger*
collapsing scrum 64.3 *rugby play*
collar 373.10 *band;* 179.3 *circular thing;* 251.11 *detain;* 251.12 *gag;* 251.5 *means of restraint;* 551.14 *neckwear;* 551.24 *part of garment;* 50.4 *rowing;* 492.11 *touch;* 79.2 *tree part;* 373.9 *yoke*
collaring 24.5 *ceramic process*
collar stud 373.8 *fastening*
collate 454.1 *verify*
collated 454.10 *verified*
collateral 223.17 *accompanying;* 211.8 *additional;* 440.5 *personal estate;* 253.2 *promise;* 440.8 *propertied;* 252.2 *protection;* 169.6 *side*
collateral evidence 716.5 *legal evidence*
collateralize 784.7 *be in debt*
collateral loan 771.2 *loan*
collaterally 211.10 *additionally;* 188.7 *in parallel;* 440.10 *proprietarily*
collateral security 784.3 *loan*
collation 557.12 *meal;* 454.4 *verification*
collative 454.9 *verificatory*
colleague 223.11 *companion;* 569.5 *friend;* 392.11 *helper;* 405.5 *member;* 566.10 *member of society;* 764.3 *participant;* 578.5 *partner;* 413.8 *supporter*
colleagues 747.9 *team*
colleagueship 569.1 *friendship*
collect 765.11 *acquire;* 376.37 *assemble;* 374.5 *combine;* 10.9 *prayer;* 769.9 *receive*
collectable 485.3 *masterpiece;* 769.14 *receivable;* 738.7 *showpiece*
collectanea 376.32 *miscellany*
collect call 692.10 *telephone call*
collect dust 258.10 *be dirty*
collected 376.47; 374.9 *assembled;* 4.18 *detached;* 769.13 *received;* 723.7 *shortened*
collect funds 765.9 *gain*
collecting 376.1 *assembly;* 341.3 *inactive;* 769.1 *receiving*
collecting unemployment 341.3 *inactive*
collecting yard 43.7 *farm building*
collection 439.5; 765.3 *acquisition;* 376.25 *assemblage;* 374.3, 376.1 *assembly;* 723.3 *compendium;* 376.30 *compilation;* 738.6 *display;* 376.31 *exhibition;* 412.3 *miscellany;* 752.6, 768.3 *offering;* 785.1 *payment;* 769.1 *receiving;* 439.3 *supply*
collective 765.18 *acquisitional;* 374.9 *assembled;* 2.13 *communal;* 376.48 *cumulate;* 15.8 *industrial;* 747.18 *joint;* 764.5 *jointly possessing;* 747.4 *joint operation;* 764.1 *joint possession;* 746.8 *negotiated;* 654.15 *sociable*
collective action 747.4 *joint operation*
collective adaptation 2.5 *society*
collective agreement 15.1 *industrial relations*
collective bargaining 746.1 *negotiation*
collective creation 21.2 *play*
collective farm 43.6 *farm;* 764.1 *joint possession*
collectively 747.20 *cooperatively;* 746.9 *feasibly;* 765.20 *gainfully;* 374.10 *in combination;* 764.6 *in common;* 15.13 *industrially;* 204.12 *one and all;* 2.16 *sociologically;* 223.21, 376.51 *together*
collective memory 462.1 *memory*
collective noun 5.35 *part of speech*
collective tax 790.7 *tax*
collective unconscious 36.21 *psyche;* 1.8 *tradition*
collectivism 12.1 *government;* 764.1 *joint possession;* 747.6 *movement;* 4.7 *school of thought;* 396.7 *type of rule*
collectivist 4.11 *follower of a doctrine;* 747.18 *joint;* 4.14 *of a philosophy*
collectivity 2.5 *society*
collectivization 764.1 *joint possession*
collect on delivery 692.2 *postal communication*
collector 376.35; 769.7; 765.7 *gainer;* 402.3 *materialist;* 39.19 *transistor*
collector electrode 39.19 *transistor*
collectorship 769.1 *receiving*
collector's item 235.8 *exceller;* 797.17 *good thing*
collector's piece 235.8 *exceller;* 485.3 *masterpiece;* 738.7 *showpiece*
collect plants 77.23 *study plants*
Collects 10.6 *Eucharist*
collect together 376.39 *come together;* 723.9 *compile*
collect unemployment 392.18 *receive help*
colleen 568.2 *female*
college 356.8 *construction;* 6.12 *educational institution;* 6.13 *university*
college baseball 48.1 *baseball*
college basketball 49.1 *basketball*
college days 555.1 *youth*
college dictionary 5.28 *dictionary*
college football 46.1 *football*
College of Arms 743.9 *herald*
College of Heralds 743.9 *herald*
college president 400.9 *educational leader*
college radio 692.20 *radio broadcasting*
collegialism 747.5 *joint control*
collegiate 6.21 *curricular;* 46.19 *varsity*
collembolan 76.10 *insectan*
collide 331.2; 492.12 *abut;* 323.9 *navigate*
collider 28.94 *particle accelerator*
collide with 381.1 *attack;* 312.8 *meet*
colliding 492.9 *touching*
collier 578.2 *artisan*
colliery 183.2 *concave land;* 439.2 *resource;* 577.1 *workshop*
colligate 376.44 *put together*
colligation 376.1 *assembly*
colligative 32.32 *solid*
colligative property 32.3 *phase*
collimate 188.5 *parallel;* 324.7 *take a direction*
collimation 29.25 *mounting;* 324.3 *orientation;* 188.1 *parallelism*
collinear 27.80 *linear*
collins 558.8 *mixed drink*
colliquation 431.5 *fluidity*
colliquative 431.20 *liquefying*
colliquefaction 431.8 *fluidification*
collision 331.12; 585.9 *battle;* 113.5 *conflict;* 310.1 *convergence;* 28.71 *nuclear reaction;* 365.2 *wearing away*
collision course 310.2 *approach;* 147.1 *nearness*
collision theory 32.14 *chemical reaction*
collocated 5.43 *phrasal*
collocating 5.43 *phrasal*
collocation 376.1 *assembly;* 5.23 *phrase*
collocutor 734.7 *conversationalist*
collodion 430.4 *emulsion*
colloid 430.4 *emulsion;* 412.2 *mixed thing;* 32.3 *phase*
colloidal 267.9 *adhesive;* 412.12 *mixed;* 430.8 *viscous*
colloidality 430.1 *viscosity*
colloidally 32.46 *chemically*
colloidal solution 32.3 *phase*
collop 205.7 *piece;* 411.4 *slice*
colloquial 734.14 *conversational;* 5.39 *of language*
colloquialism 5.3 *spoken language*
colloquialize 5.45 *use language*
colloquially 5.49; 734.15 *conversationally*
colloquial speech 729.1 *faculty of speech*
colloquist 734.7 *conversationalist*
colloquium 734.4 *conference*
colloquize 4.23 *discuss philosophically*
colloquy 734.1 *conversation;* 729.1 *faculty of speech;* 4.5 *philosophical argument*
collotype 717.2 *reproduction*
collude 747.15 *concur;* 699.26 *falsify;* 750.22 *form an alliance;* 700.28 *trick*
colluding 750.11 *allied;* 700.34 *deceiving*
collusion 750.2 *alliance;* 747.8 *conferring;* 699.9 *falsification;* 700.7 *tricking*
collusive 747.19 *associating;* 699.33 *deceitful*
colly 695.6 *understand*
collyrium 394.9 *balm;* 37.4 *drug type;* 268.7 *pomade*
collywobbles 327.1 *agitation;* 260.8 *indigestion*
cologne 502.2 *fragrant thing*
colon 172.4 *insides;* 308.7 *passageway;* 742.7 *punctuation*
colonel 586.17 *army person*
Colonel Blimp 641.8 *obstinate person*
Colonial 296.14 *historic*
colonial 84.7 *algal;* 387.10 *dominating;* 23.7 *furniture style;* 396.14 *governmental;* 85.16, 86.17 *national;* 70.15 *of animals;* 293.15 *precursory;* 564.13 *resident;* 564.7 *settler;* 20.12 *structural*
Colonial bed 23.6 *bed*
colonial home 20.3 *building*
colonialism 387.2 *domination;* 85.3 *dominion;* 12.3 *governance;* 566.11 *nation;* 396.7 *type of rule*
colonialist 85.14 *nationalist*
colonially 84.9 *algologically;* 396.24 *ministerially;* 85.19, 86.20 *nationally;* 293.19 *primevally*
colonic 308.15 *providing passage;* 172.10 *visceral*
colonist 293.4 *early comer;* 314.7 *entrant;* 315.8 *outgoer;* 564.7 *settler*
colonization 773.1 *taking*
colonize 314.14 *enrol;* 85.18 *exert sovereignty;* 565.17 *inhabit;* 293.8 *precede;* 564.15 *settle;* 387.6 *subject;* 773.7 *take*
colonized 564.13 *resident*
colonizer 564.7 *settler*
colonnade 317.7 *arcade;* 20.8 *column;* 132.2 *consecution;* 178.7 *straight line*
colony 85.3 *dominion;* 376.23 *flock;* 396.8 *governmental organization;* 564.2 *inhabitants;* 12.5 *political organization;* 763.4 *possession;* 86.4 *territorial division;* 208.4 *throng*
colophon 743.3 *means of identification;* 168.1 *rear*

Colorado 90.3 *US rivers*
Colorado beetle 44.12 *pests and diseases*
colorant 529.4 *pigment*
coloration 529.1 *colour*
colorific 529.10 *coloured*
colorimeter 529.8 *chromatics*; 28.92 *light meter*; 26.8 *meter*
colorimetric 529.14 *chromolithographic*; 26.16 *micrometric*
colorimetry 529.8 *chromatics*; 26.2 *micrometry*
colossal 158.15 *big*; 154.12 *tall*
Colosseum 356.8 *construction*
colossus 158.10 *big person*; 154.7, 158.11 *tall person*
colostomy 394.12 *surgery*
colostrum 431.3 *body fluid*; 71.2 *mammalian characteristic*; 558.5 *milk*; 559.2 *secreted substance*
Colour 529
colour 28.28; **529.1**; **529.15**; 412.4 *admixture*; 624.12 *become angry*; 532.7 *blackness*; 699.14 *façade*; 743.1 *identification*; 395.8 *influence*; 699.28 *mask*; 718.4 *misrepresent*; 412.8 *mix*; 136.15 *modify*; 542.1 *ornament*; 19.19 *paint*; 1.6 *race*; 535.9 *redden*; 692.22 *television set*; 19.4 *treatment*; 137.4 *type*
colourable 529.10 *coloured*
colourant 42.6 *dye*
colour balance 41.8 *composition*
colour-balancing filter 41.20 *filter*
colour bar 128.4 *exclusiveness*
colour-blind 519.9 *weak-sighted*
colour-blindness 529.1 *colour*; 519.2 *poor sight*
colourcast 529.17; 529.2 *colourfulness*; 41.8 *composition*
colour chart 529.2 *colourfulness*
colour circle 529.2 *colourfulness*
colour code 529.2 *colourfulness*
colour-coordinated 551.31 *styled*
colour coordination 529.2 *colourfulness*
colour coordinator 529.6 *painter*
colour-correcting filter 41.20 *filter*
colour decoration 542.1 *ornament*
colour design 542.1 *ornament*
colour disk 529.2 *colourfulness*
coloured 529.10; 699.39 *disguised*; 412.12 *mixed*; 542.10 *ornate*; 19.27 *painted*; 42.11 *treated*
coloured chalk 529.5 *paint*
coloured crayon 529.5 *paint*
coloured glaze 24.3 *glaze*
coloured paper 529.5 *paint*
coloured pencil 529.5 *paint*
colour falsely 699.28 *mask*
colourfast 529.10 *coloured*
colourfastness 529.4 *pigment*
colour-field painter 529.6 *painter*
colour-field painting 529.7 *colour painting*
colour film 529.7 *colour painting*; 41.9 *film*
colour filter 529.7 *colour painting*; 21.20 *stage lighting*
colourful 529.11; 541.6 *variegated*
colourful language 712.2 *offensive language*
colourfully 529.18
colourfulness 529.2
colour guard 586.12 *ceremonial troops*
colour harmony 529.2 *colourfulness*
colour highly 727.7 *exaggerate*
colour hologram 41.5 *stereoscopic image*
colour in 529.15 *colour*
colouring 412.4 *admixture*; 674.2 *blushing*; 529.1 *colour*; 42.7 *dyeing*; 699.14 *façade*; 743.1 *identification*; 694.1 *meaning*; 718.1 *misrepresentation*; 19.2 *painting*; 529.4 *pigment*
colouring matter 529.4 *pigment*
colouring the truth 720.2 *misinterpretation*
colourist 19.16 *artist*; 529.6 *painter*
colouristically 529.18 *colourfully*
colourization 529.7 *colour painting*
colourize 529.15 *colour*; 19.19 *paint*
colourized 529.10 *coloured*
colourizing 19.2 *painting*
colourless 530.7; 522.21 *light*; 527.1 *transparent*; 260.21 *unhealthy*; 531.2 *whitened*
colourlessly 530.9
Colourlessness 530
colourlessness 530.1; 522.14 *light colour*; 527.5 *transparency*; 531.7 *whiteness*
colour negative 529.7 *colour painting*; 41.12 *development*
colour painting 529.7
colour perception 529.1 *colour*
colour photo 41.3 *photograph*
colour photographer 529.6 *painter*
colour photography 28.28 *colour*; 529.7 *colour painting*; 41.1 *photography*
colour prejudice 594.3 *race hatred*
colour-prejudiced 465.8 *unjust*
colour print 529.15 *colour*; 41.12 *development*; 19.7 *picture*
colour printer 40.7 *peripheral*
colour printing 28.28 *colour*; 529.7 *colour painting*
colour prints 529.7 *colour painting*
colour processing 41.12 *development*
colour quality 529.3 *hue*
colour remover 530.4
colour reproduction 529.7 *colour painting*
colours 551.5 *fancy dress*; 743.7 *flag*; 65.5 *snooker*
colours-bearer 586.8 *soldier*
colour scheme 529.2 *colourfulness*
colour slides 529.7 *colour painting*
colour supplement 741.5 *mass communication*; 740.4 *newspaper*
colour television 28.28 *colour*; 692.21 *television*; 692.22 *television set*
colour temperature 529.3 *hue*; 41.15 *lighting*
colour theory 529.8 *chromatics*
colour transparencies 529.7 *colour painting*
colour up 674.16 *be self-conscious*; 535.9 *redden*
colour vision 529.1 *colour*; 28.23 *light*
colourwash 529.15 *colour*; 529.4 *pigment*
colour wheel 529.2 *colourfulness*; 21.20 *stage lighting*
colporteur 778.11 *pedlar*
colposcope 35.7 *diagnosis*
colposcopy 35.7 *diagnosis*
Colt™ 587.9 *firearm*
colt 59.1 *horse*; 567.16 *male animal*; 71.17 *male mammal*; 486.10 *unskilled person*; 555.4 *young animal*; 71.19 *young mammal*
colter 425.9 *sharp-edged thing*
coltish 342.18 *active*
colubriform 73.12 *snakelike*
colubrine 73.12 *snakelike*
columbarium 583.5 *cemetery*; 72.19 *ornithology*
Columbia 29.30 *spacecraft*; 85.7 *United States*; 90.3 *US rivers*
columbic 32.34 *elemental*
columbiform 72.21 *avian*
Columbine 21.32 *clown*; 21.23 *role*
columbine 72.21 *avian*
columbous 32.34 *elemental*
column 20.8; 586.16 *army unit*; 722.2 *article*; 181.4 *cylinder*; 27.22 *matrix*; 584.4 *military organization*; 744.11 *monument*; 741.9 *news story*; 132.8 *procession*; 38.27 *superstructure*; 413.2 *supporting part*; 154.6 *tall thing*; 186.3 *vertical thing*
columnar 20.16 *columned*
columnated 20.16 *columned*
column chromatography 32.17 *analysis*
columned 20.16
columniation 20.8 *column*
columnist 721.10 *descriptive writer*; 693.9 *informant*; 741.4 *journalist*; 719.7 *news interpreter*; 740.11 *newspaperman*; 744.9 *recorder*
coma 29.19 *comet*; 592.4 *desensitization*; 335.4 *disability*; 260.2 *illness*; 28.31 *lens element*; 766.1 *loss*; 301.1 *motionlessness*; 29.25 *mounting*; 463.1 *oblivion*; 343.9 *sleep*; 489.2 *unconsciousness*
comanagement 747.5 *joint control*
comatose 592.2 *desensitized*; 335.12 *impotent*; 618.7 *indifferent*; 343.4 *not awake*; 260.22 *sick*; 489.8 *unconscious*
comatose patient 339.2 *inert person*
comb 91.10 *billow*; 256.13 *clean*; 256.10 *cleaning object*; 154.4 *mountain range*; 43.18 *practise livestock farming*; 425.8 *sharp-pointed thing*; 421.11 *smooth*; 421.9 *smoother*; 425.16 *use a sharp tool*
combat 52.14; **586.36**; 585.14 *battle*; 113.18 *object*
Combatant 586
combatant 586.1; 584.9 *enlisted*; 382.10 *killer*; 113.13 *opponent*
combat boots 551.19 *footwear*
combative 586.33; 52.14 *combat*; 751.9 *disagreeing*; 381.22 *militant*; 584.8 *military*; 585.16 *warlike*
combatively 751.11 *in disagreement*
combativeness 381.11 *attack*; 585.5 *bellicosity*; 751.1 *disagreement*
combative sport 52.1 *combat sports*
combat neurosis 36.10 *neurosis*
combat-ready forces 586.14 *armed forces*
combat sports 52.1
combat team 584.4 *military organization*
combat troops 586.14 *armed forces*
combat zone 585.10 *battleground*
combe 183.2 *concave land*
combed 421.1 *smooth*
comber 91.3 *wave*
Combination 374
combination 374.1; 223.1 *accompaniment*; 376.1 *assembly*; 747.7 *association*; 412.2 *mixed thing*; 412.1 *mixture*; 320.13 *motorcycle*; 108.1 *relatedness*; 27.21 *set*
combination lock 373.8 *fastening*
combination obstacle 59.9 *jumping*
combinations 551.18 *underwear*
combinative 374.7 *combined*
combinatory 374.7 *combined*
combine 374.5; 374.3 *assembly*; 747.7 *association*; 197.19 *become one*; 43.10 *farm tool*; 747.16 *join*; 412.8 *mix*; 356.10 *produce*; 376.44 *put together*
combined 32.35; **374.7**; 750.11 *allied*; 223.19 *associated*; 376.48 *cumulate*; 57.11 *gymnastic*; 127.8 *included*; 747.18 *joint*; 412.12 *mixed*; 108.4 *related*
combined attack 381.12 *military attack*
combined effort 747.4 *joint operation*
combinedly 747.20 *cooperatively*
combined movement 57.8 *floor exercises*
combined operation 747.4 *joint operation*; 585.8 *warfare*
combined structure 435.2 *building material*
combined tactics 62.3 *climbing technique*
combine harvester 43.10 *farm tool*
combine in 405.10 *compose*
combine with 750.22 *form an alliance*; 211.7 *support*
combine with gas 432.27 *give off*
combings 215.2 *residue*
combining 750.11 *allied*; 374.1 *combination*
comb jelly 75.7 *coelenterate*
comblike 425.4 *toothed*
combo 750.2 *alliance*; 412.2 *mixed thing*
comb out 178.10 *straighten*
combustibility 493.6 *fire*
combustible 493.10 *on fire*; 437.10 *powered*
combustibly 437.12 *powerfully*
combustion 493.6 *fire*; 28.35 *heat*
come 312.1 *arrive*; 525.12 *become visible*
come about 93.18 *come to be*; 345.9 *take effect*; 303.9 *turn round*
come a cropper 486.5 *be unskilful*; 247.6 *fail*
come across 449.1 *discover*; 142.11 *find*; 785.6 *pay*; 765.14 *profit*
come across with 768.5 *give*
come after 132.13 *be consecutive*; 289.10 *succeed*
come again 298.8 *be cyclic*; 218.6 *be unsatisfied*
come again and again 112.21 *be repeated*
come alive 695.4 *be intelligible*; 698.33 *seem lifelike*
come along 302.1 *go forward*
come amiss 240.5 *be inconvenient*
come and get it 25.58 *grub's on!*
come and go 342.12 *be active*; 298.7 *be regular*; 326.8 *oscillate*; 761.8 *return*
come apart 408.25 *be disordered*; 245.1 *deteriorate*; 375.3 *disintegrate*; 377.11 *explode*; 372.9 *separate*
come around 581.2 *be refreshed*
come as a revelation 739.9 *be disclosed*
come as no surprise 104.8 *be probable*
come as you are 657.11 *not stand on ceremony*
come at one's call 663.5 *obey*
comeback 706.1 *answer*; 704.3 *countercharge*; 110.1 *interchange*; 385.1 *retaliation*; 112.4 *return*; 393.10 *revival*
come back 706.17 *answer*; 462.15 *be remembered*; 218.6 *be unsatisfied*; 112.20 *renew*; 384.26 *retaliate*
come back to life 393.4 *be restored*
come before 123.7 *be important*; 579.2 *direct*; 129.15 *precede*; 475.11 *predict*; 370.8 *show in*; 16.72 *stand trial*
come between 372.14; 340.4 *act*; 378.8 *hinder*
come by 765.9 *gain*; 777.1 *purchase*; 769.9 *receive*
come cap in hand 807.6 *apologize*
come clean 739.8 *admit*
comedian 21.24 *actor*; 697.4 *buffoon*; 21.26 *dramatist*; 21.29 *entertainer*; 599.6 *humorist*
comédie-ballet 21.12 *comedy*
comédie larmoyante 21.12 *comedy*
comedienne 21.24 *actor*; 21.29 *entertainer*
comédie rosse 21.12 *comedy*
comedown 249.1 *adversity*; 604.2 *bad outcome*; 305.1 *descent*; 247.1 *failure*; 305.4 *fall*; 623.9 *humiliation*
come down 214.4 *decrease*; 305.9 *descend*; 31.62 *rain*
come down a peg 305.10 *droop*
come down hard on 814.2 *penalize*
come down in buckets 31.62 *rain*
come down on 647.5 *be severe*; 305.12 *drop*; 814.2 *penalize*
come down with 755.6 *catch*
comedy 21.12; 599.4 *entertainment*
comedy actor 21.24 *actor*
comedy actress 21.24 *actor*
comedy hour 599.4 *entertainment*
comedy of character 21.12 *comedy*
comedy of humours 21.12 *comedy*
comedy of ideas 21.12 *comedy*
comedy of intrigue 21.12 *comedy*
comedy of manners 21.12 *comedy*
comedy of morals 21.12 *comedy*
comedy of situation 21.12 *comedy*
comedy routine 599.4 *entertainment*
comedy skit 599.4 *entertainment*
come eyeball to eyeball 738.4 *show oneself*
come face to face 738.4 *show oneself*
come first 123.7 *be important*; 47.6 *compete in track and field*; 121.10 *lead*
come forth 703.18 *appear*; 525.12 *become visible*; 130.27 *emerge*; 738.4 *show oneself*
come forward 525.12 *become visible*; 167.10 *be in front*; 752.11 *volunteer*
come from another country 100.14 *be foreign*
come from without 100.16 *be external*
come full circle 306.6 *orbit*
come hat in hand 623.20 *submit*
come-hither look 593.6 *courtship*; 742.3 *gesture*; 518.6 *look*
come home 312.4 *land*
come in 314.9 *enter*; 312.5 *get in*
come in for 769.9 *receive*
come in force 336.7 *be strong*
come in front 329.3 *exceed*
come in handy 239.6 *be convenient*; 237.9 *be useful*
come in last 247.7 *be defeated*
come in sight 525.12 *become visible*
come into 289.11 *follow in office*; 769.9, 788.7 *receive*; 246.12 *succeed to*
come into an inheritance 248.6 *be fortunate*
come into being 130.27 *emerge*
come into conflict 113.19 *confront*
come into contact 492.12 *abut*; 147.18 *juxtapose*; 312.8 *meet*
come into effect 346.7 *be operational*; 345.9 *take effect*
come into existence 554.18 *be born*; 130.27 *emerge*
come into focus 520.9 *appear*
come into money 248.6 *be fortunate*; 781.13 *get rich*; 765.14 *profit*
come into operation 340.4 *act*; 346.7 *be operational*
come into ownership of 289.11 *follow in office*
come into possession of 289.11 *follow in office*
come into power 334.10 *be powerful*
come into the picture 525.12 *become visible*

come into the world 554.18 *be born;* 130.27 *emerge*
come into use 632.17 *become a habit*
come into view 518.19 *be visible*
come in useful 239.6 *be convenient;* 392.26 *be useful*
come it over 622.28 *disdain*
come last 289.10 *succeed*
comeliness 545.1 *gorgeousness*
comely 545.5 *beautiful*
come near 147.16 *near*
come next 289.10 *succeed*
come of 345.7 *follow from*
come of age 556.18 *mature*
come off 246.8 *be effective;* 689.4 *give up alcohol;* 345.9 *take effect*
come off best 246.11 *overmaster*
come off it 226.12 *stop!*
come off on 267.6 *adhere*
come off second best 247.7 *be defeated*
come off well 246.6 *be successful*
come on 221.6 *be in a state of;* 302.5 *develop;* 560.22 *menstruate*
come-on 363.4 *allurement;* 480.9 *enticement;* 752.1 *offer;* 483.5 *positive stimulus*
come on bended knee 623.20 *submit*
come on like gangbusters 740.14 *proclaim*
come-on man 700.18 *decoy*
come on the scene 525.12 *become visible*
come on the stage 525.13 *occur*
come out 601.20; 525.12 *become visible;* 739.9 *be disclosed;* 221.6 *be in a state of;* 740.17 *be published;* 130.27, 315.10 *emerge;* 525.13 *occur;* 383.6 *resist;* 355.2 *withdraw*
come out easily 265.15 *be easy*
come out for 469.3 *side with*
come out of 345.7 *follow from*
come out on strike 753.8 *cause mischief;* 226.7 *stop working*
come out with 739.6 *divulge;* 478.3 *improvise;* 738.3 *reveal*
come over 695.4 *be intelligible*
come over all queer 260.24 *be unhealthy*
come over the horizon 520.9 *appear;* 525.12 *become visible*
comer 314.7 *entrant;* 246.4 *successful person*
come rain or shine 638.17 *resolutely*
come round 393.4 *be restored;* 554.16 *live*
come round again 298.8 *be cyclic;* 276.10 *be periodical;* 525.13 *occur*
come short 218.5 *be insufficient*
come short of 122.8 *be inferior*
come soon 283.7 *be in the future*
comestible 557.27 *edible;* 495.7 *tasty*
comestibles 557.7 *food;* 436.2 *provisions*
comet 29.19; 522.4 *natural light;* 298.5 *regular thing*
cometary 29.36 *astronomical*
cometary nucleus 29.19 *comet*
come through 221.6 *be in a state of;* 252.9 *be safe;* 554.16 *live*
come to 581.2 *be refreshed;* 393.4 *be restored;* 204.9 *be whole;* 760.7 *convert into;* 790.13 *cost;* 554.16 *live;* 145.7, 312.2 *reach;* 194.11, 210.10 *total*
come to a close 232.5 *be complete*
come to a crossroads 222.12 *come to a juncture;* 317.14 *find one's way*
come to a focus 310.11 *focus*
come to a halt 301.8 *be motionless;* 226.6 *cease;* 247.9 *malfunction*
come to a head 560.18 *fester*
come to a junction 193.9 *cross*
come to a juncture 222.12
come to an agreement 409.17 *come to an arrangement;* 374.6 *come together;* 755.5 *contract*
come to an arrangement 409.17
come to anchor 50.15 *sail*
come to an end 131.18; 232.5 *be complete;* 357.13 *be destroyed;* 226.6 *cease*
come to an understanding 649.9 *forgive;* 749.5 *make peace*
come to a parting 571.8 *desert*
come to a point 173.9 *centre*
come to a standstill 264.20 *be in difficulty;* 301.8 *be motionless;* 226.6 *cease*
come to a stop 226.6 *cease*
come to bat 48.7 *play baseball*
come to be 93.18; 130.27 *emerge*
come to dust 427.27; 278.4 *be transient;* 582.15 *die*
come to execution 814.6 *be punished*
come to financial ruin 249.10 *need money*
come together 310.10; **374.6**; **376.39**; 492.12 *abut*
come to grief 249.9 *be in trouble;* 247.8 *miscarry*
come to grips with 354.1 *undertake*
come to hand 492.12 *abut;* 312.7 *be brought;* 769.9 *receive*
come to heel 663.5 *obey*
come to journey's end 301.8 *be motionless*
come to know 693.15 *be informed*
come to life 554.16 *live*
come to life again 393.4 *be restored*
come to light 520.9 *appear;* 525.12 *become visible;* 739.9 *be disclosed;* 449.5 *be discovered;* 518.19, 738.5 *be visible*
come to maturity 556.18 *mature*
come to mind 446.14 *have an idea*
come to naught 563.7 *be infertile;* 766.14 *go to waste;* 247.8 *miscarry*
come to nothing 563.7 *be infertile;* 247.6 *fail;* 766.14 *go to waste;* 247.8 *miscarry*
come to often 297.8 *frequent*
come to one 446.14 *have an idea;* 769.9 *receive*
come to one's senses 488.12 *awake;* 460.6 *be sane*
come to pass 345.9 *take effect*
come to pieces 375.3 *disintegrate;* 372.9 *separate*
come to rest 301.8 *be motionless;* 312.2 *reach;* 263.2 *take it easy*
come to stay 225.5 *be permanent*
come to terms 409.17 *come to an arrangement;* 755.5 *contract*
come to terms with 605.6 *resign oneself*
come to the front 167.10 *be in front;* 121.8 *be superior*
come to the gallows 814.6 *be punished*
come to the point 723.10 *be brief;* 269.4 *be concise;* 271.7 *be simple;* 310.11 *focus;* 139.23 *particularize;* 108.7 *relate to*
come to the rescue 390.1 *deliver;* 384.23 *rescue*
come to the surface 520.9 *appear;* 525.12 *become visible*
come to understand 695.6 *understand*
come under fire 254.9 *face danger*
come under the hammer 778.2 *be sold*
come under the influence 480.18 *be persuaded*
come undone 372.9 *separate*
come unstuck 408.25 *be disordered;* 486.5 *be unskilful;* 377.11 *explode;* 264.19 *have difficulty;* 372.9 *separate*
come up 525.12 *become visible*
come up for more 640.9 *endure*
come up for trial 16.72 *stand trial*
come upon 107.11 *chance upon;* 449.1 *discover;* 312.8 *meet;* 312.2 *reach*
comeuppance 813.6 *compensation;* 385.1 *retaliation;* 814.9 *retribution*
come up short 604.4 *be disappointed*
come up smiling 246.7 *overcome obstacles*
come up to 119.10 *be equal*
come up to scratch 669.17 *meet with approval*
come up with 478.3 *improvise;* 130.22 *invent*
come what may 638.17 *resolutely*
come with 223.13 *accompany*
come within earshot 504.16 *be heard*
come within the law 16.66 *be legal*
comfit 498.4 *confectionery;* 25.41 *sweet*
comfort 490.10; **609.9**; **610.4**; 650.8 *be benevolent;* 222.5 *comfortable circumstances;* 627.2 *condolence;* 263.1, 263.3, 608.1 *ease;* 265.1 *easiness;* 241.13 *give pleasure;* 610.10 *inspire hope;* 685.4 *moderate;* 781.7 *opulence;* 490.1 *physical pleasure;* 241.7 *pleasure;* 248.1 *prosperity;* 608.9 *relieve;* 609.1 *satisfaction;* 627.9 *sorrow;* 392.2, 392.19 *support;* 392.13 *supporter*
comfortable 222.9; **241.3**; 263.4 *at ease;* 259.1 *healthy;* 490.6 *pleasant;* 490.7 *pleased;* 248.8 *prosperous;* 265.14 *relaxed;* 609.4 *satisfied;* 781.1 *wealthy*
comfortable circumstances 222.5; 781.7 *opulence*
comfortably 222.18; 265.21 *easily;* 490.11 *pleasingly;* 248.9 *prosperously;* 781.16 *wealthily*
comfortably drunk 690.1 *drunk*
comfortably off 248.8 *prosperous;* 781.1 *wealthy;* 765.17 *well-off*
comfortably situated 248.8 *prosperous*
comfort blanket 490.4 *pleasurable things*
comforted 608.7 *relieved*
comforter 550.10 *bed covering;* 550.5 *body covering;* 551.14 *neckwear;* 490.4 *pleasurable things;* 608.3 *reliever*
comforting 685.8 *moderating;* 627.6 *pitying;* 490.6 *pleasant;* 581.3 *refreshing;* 608.8 *relieving;* 609.5 *satisfying;* 392.32 *supportive*
comfortingly 608.15
comfortless 611.4 *hopeless*
comfort station 560.13 *lavatory;* 565.7 *room;* 767.7 *toilet*
comfy 241.3 *comfortable*
comic 19.9 *drawing;* 21.29 *entertainer;* 599.6 *humorist;* 599.10 *humorous;* 740.5 *journal;* 600.10 *laughing;* 17.19 *narrative;* 697.5 *nonsensical;* 272.5 *ridiculous;* 21.40 *tragic*
comical 272.5 *ridiculous*
comicality 272.1 *ludicrousness*
comically 21.44 *dramatically;* 599.16 *humorously;* 272.8 *ridiculously*
comic business 21.12 *comedy*
comic magazine 740.5 *journal*
comic muse 21.12 *comedy*
comic opera 21.4 *musical drama*
comic poet 17.14 *author;* 21.26 *dramatist*
comic poetry 17.6 *poetry*
comic relief 17.3 *aspect of fiction;* 21.12 *comedy;* 21.23 *role*
comic strip 19.9 *drawing;* 599.4 *entertainment;* 740.5 *journal*
comic-strip artist 19.16 *artist*
coming 525.1 *appearance;* 525.7 *appearing;* 312.19 *approaching;* 312.10 *arrival;* 283.11 *future;* 283.6 *future event*
coming across 142.3 *locating*
coming alive 698.25 *lifelike*
coming and going 342.19 *busy;* 326.1 *oscillation*
coming ashore 312.11 *landing*
coming back 312.13 *return*
coming before 129.1 *precedence*
coming by 765.1 *gain*
coming down in buckets 31.53 *rainy*
coming down with 260.22 *sick*
coming events 283.3 *future condition*
coming from 345.10 *caused*
coming from without 100.4 *externality*
coming into being 525.1 *appearance;* 525.7 *appearing;* 93.8 *creation*
coming into sight 525.7 *appearing*
coming into view 525.1 *appearance;* 525.7 *appearing*
coming later 294.12 *delaying*
coming man 302.16 *progressive person*
coming on the scene 525.7 *appearing*
coming out 315.1 *exit;* 315.15 *outgoing;* 654.5 *party;* 130.9 *premiere*
coming-out party 654.5 *party*
comings and goings 761.4 *return*
coming to blows 624.5 *quarrel*
coming together 376.1 *assembly;* 310.1 *convergence;* 748.2 *mediation*
coming to often 297.5 *frequenting*
coming to terms 605.4 *resignedness*
coming to the point 310.5 *focus*
coming up roses 246.1 *success*
comitia 579.7 *council*
comity 810.3 *allegiance;* 367.16, 658.1 *courtesy;* 656.5 *etiquette;* 663.2 *loyalty;* 667.3 *respectfulness*
comity of nations 566.9 *group*
comma 742.7 *punctuation;* 372.5 *separator*
Command 397
command 397.1; **397.9**; 713.5 *advise;* 140.8, 396.1 *authority;* 154.15 *be high;* 386.2 *coercion;* 386.6 *compel;* 40.19 *computing terms;* 710.2, 710.7 *demand;* 140.16, 579.2 *direct;* 579.4 *directorship;* 349.5 *dispose of;* 12.11 *govern;* 12.3, 396.4 *governance;* 396.18 *have authority;* 810.17 *impose a duty;* 635.15 *impose one's will;* 6.24 *know;* 121.2 *leadership;* 400.14 *master;* 763.7 *possess;* 713.3 *precept;* 135.1 *requirement;* 742.12 *signal;* 89.9 *tower;* 631.8 *treatment;* 585.8 *warfare;* 742.6 *word*
commandant 400.7 *military leader;* 397.6 *person in command*
command capital 781.12 *be rich*
commandeer 386.7 *force;* 608.14 *take away*
commandeering 773.12 *taking*
commander 400.7 *military leader;* 584.5 *military staff;* 586.27 *naval man;* 397.6 *person in command;* 396.10 *person of authority;* 742.8 *signer;* 121.5 *superior*
commander-in-chief 400.7 *military leader;* 397.6 *person in command;* 396.10 *person of authority*
command influence 395.8 *influence*
commanding 397.14; 396.12 *authoritative;* 450.13 *believable;* 386.9 *compelling;* 12.10 *governing;* 395.11 *influential;* 400.12 *masterful;* 123.6 *notable;* 622.18 *prestigious;* 140.12 *ruling;* 742.16 *signalling*
commanding lead 121.3 *advantage*
commandingly 397.16; 396.23 *authoritatively;* 386.11 *compellingly;* 395.14 *influentially*
commanding officer 400.7 *military leader;* 584.5 *military staff;* 397.6 *person in command;* 396.10 *person of authority*
commandment 397.1 *command;* 713.3 *precept;* 140.1 *rule*
commandoes 586.14 *armed forces*
command of idiom 724.4 *literary style*
command of language 724.4 *literary style;* 729.2 *power of speech*
command of the air 584.1 *military affairs*
command of the sea 584.1 *military affairs*
commando unit 584.4 *military organization*
command performance 21.13 *theatrical performance*
command respect 667.21; 123.7 *be important*
command ship 586.24 *warship*
comme ci comme ça 216.3 *mediocre*
commedia a soggetto 21.12 *comedy*
commedia dell'arte 21.12 *comedy;* 21.2 *play*
commedia erudita 21.12 *comedy*
comme il faut 750.15 *conventional*
commemorate 298.9; **462.14**; **601.16**
commemoration 601.2; 298.3 *anniversary;* 462.3 *memento*
commemorative 601.11; 298.13 *anniversary;* 462.10 *memorial*
commemoratively 298.16 *cyclically;* 462.16 *memorably*
commence 130.17, 295.19, 308.24 *begin*
commencement 130.1, 295.4, 308.11 *beginning*
commencing 130.29, 308.17 *beginning*
commencing move 130.12 *first move*
commend 713.5 *advise;* 669.15 *compliment;* 669.13 *support*
commendable 239.1 *convenient;* 669.21 *praiseworthy;* 803.7 *worthy*
commendably 803.11 *worthily*
commendation 669.4 *compliment*
commendatory 669.18 *approving*
commender 713.4 *adviser;* 669.9 *praiser*
commensal 747.19 *associating;* 34.18 *ecology;* 70.15 *of animals;* 70.4 *type of animal*
commensalism 34.18 *ecology*
commensurable 27.74 *divisible;* 115.7 *similar*
commensurate 750.14 *conforming;* 119.6 *equal;* 108.5 *interrelated;* 217.1 *sufficient*
commensurately 108.10 *relevantly*
comment 719.2 *annotation;* 722.1 *dissertation;* 464.1 *judgment;* 729.7 *utterance*
commentarial 719.16 *annotative*
commentary 719.2 *annotation;* 722.1 *dissertation;* 17.4 *nonfiction*
commentate 722.4 *dissertate*
commentator 692.29 *broadcaster;* 722.3 *dissertator;* 719.6 *interpreter;* 464.5 *judge;* 719.7 *news interpreter*
commented on 719.15 *interpreted*
comment on 719.10 *annotate;* 4.23 *discuss philosophically;* 722.4 *dissertate;* 464.12 *estimate;* 719.8 *interpret;* 719.13 *interpret news*
commeration 575.1 *right*
commerce 373.2 *association;* 13.5 *international trade;* 776.4 *trade*
commercial 776.14; 789.10 *accounting;* 740.9 *advertisement;* 692.25 *broadcast ma-*

terial; 13.13 *economic;* 15.8 *industrial;* 319.5 *transportable*
commercial arithmetic 789.1 *accounts*
commercial art 19.1 *art*
commercial artist 19.16 *artist*
commercial bank 783.4 *bank;* 780.19 *treasury*
commercial break 692.25 *broadcast material*
commercial building 38.20 *building*
commercial city 87.1 *city*
commercial intercourse 776.5 *commercial trade*
commercialistic 13.13 *economic;* 776.13 *mercantile*
commercialize 776.1 *trade;* 13.10 *trade with;* 675.10 *vulgarize*
commercial law 16.1 *the law*
commercial listing 740.9 *advertisement*
commercially 319.6; 13.14 *economically;* 789.13 *financially;* 15.13 *industrially;* 778.17 *marketably*
commercial paper 780.14 *paper money*
commercial radio 692.20 *radio broadcasting*
commercial television 692.24 *television broadcasting*
commercial trade 776.5
commercial transaction 776.4 *trade*
commercial transport 319.1 *transport*
commercial traveller 778.10 *salesman*
commie 12.6 *political party;* 662.11 *rebel*
commination 712.4 *malediction*
comminatory 712.10 *maledictive;* 10.21 *ritualistic*
commingle 374.5 *combine;* 412.8 *mix*
comminute 427.22 *pulverize*
comminuted 427.18 *pulverized*
comminution 427.4 *pulverization*
comminutor 427.11 *pulverizer*
commis chef 25.2 *cook*
commiserate 591.11 *be sensitive;* 590.18 *feel for;* 627.9 *sorrow*
commiserating 627.6 *pitying*
commiseration 627.2 *condolence;* 627.1 *pity;* 591.5 *sensitivity*
commiserative 627.6 *pitying*
commiserator 627.4 *pitying person*
commissarial 436.7 *provisioning*
commissariat 557.7 *food;* 557.17 *food shop;* 436.1 *provision*
commissary 557.17 *food shop;* 436.3 *provider*
commission 340.4 *act;* 340.1 *action;* 397.4 *authorization;* 397.13 *authorize;* 376.7 *committee;* 579.7 *council;* 398.7 *delegate;* 791.1 *discount;* 790.3 *fee;* 243.11 *fitting out;* 768.5 *give;* 585.12 *go to war;* 130.23 *inaugurate;* 579.3 *management;* 785.3 *pay;* 469.4 *pick;* 713.3 *precept;* 243.4 *prepare for action;* 765.5 *profit;* 813.4 *reward for service;* 469.6 *selection;* 769.2 *something received;* 576.2, 810.2 *task*
commissionaire 309.5 *person who closes*
commissioned 584.9 *enlisted;* 400.12 *masterful;* 397.15 *self-assured*
commissioned officer 400.7 *military leader*
commissioner 398.6 *agent;* 398.1 *delegate;* 400.3 *leader;* 579.16 *official;* 396.10 *person of authority*
commissioner of police 16.17 *police officer*
commission of the peace 16.2 *jurisdiction;* 16.18 *tribunal*
commit 340.4 *act;* 316.14 *bring back;* 461.16 *certify;* 810.17 *impose a duty;* 707.18 *vow*
commit a crime 662.15 *be disobedient;* 16.73 *be illegal;* 802.21 *do wrong;* 806.10 *sin*
commit adultery 796.17 *be sexually immoral;* 639.9 *change sides*
commit a felony 806.10 *sin*
commit a foul 802.21 *do wrong*
commit a malapropism 351.1 *misuse*
commit a misdemeanour 806.10 *sin*
commit an atrocity 647.6 *suppress*
commit an offence 802.21 *do wrong*
commit a sacrilege 712.5 *curse*
commit a white-collar crime 806.10 *sin*
commit bigamy 570.15 *marry*
commit burglary 774.12 *steal*
commit crime 118.20 *infringe a law*
commit daylight robbery 792.10 *overcharge*
commit euthanasia 582.16 *meet one's fate*
commit for trial 464.11 *judge;* 16.71 *try a case*
commit genocide 814.5 *execute;* 382.18 *slaughter*
commit hara-kiri 382.21 *commit suicide*
commit highway robbery 792.10 *overcharge*
commitment 640.2; **810.7**; 638.13 *concentration;* 354.3, 755.1 *contract;* 784.1 *debt;* 643.5 *earnestness;* 569.3 *familiarity;* 768.1 *giving;* 756.1 *promise;* 707.3 *vow*
commit money 768.6 *give to charity*
commit murder 382.17 *murder*
commit oneself 810.15 *be liable;* 755.5 *contract;* 768.6 *give to charity;* 756.8 *guarantee;* 756.7 *promise;* 469.3 *side with;* 354.1, 638.9 *undertake;* 707.18 *vow*
commit perjury 715.6 *accuse falsely*
commit robbery 774.12 *steal*
commit sacrilege 668.27 *desecrate*
commit sin 804.16 *be wicked*
commit suicide 382.21; 131.19 *expire;* 582.16 *meet one's fate*
commit suttee 382.21 *commit suicide*
committal 16.6 *legal process*
committed 569.11 *devoted;* 810.11 *duty-bound;* 643.2 *earnest;* 756.13 *guaranteeing;* 784.9 *in debt;* 756.12 *promised;* 638.2 *tenacious;* 707.12 *vowed*
committedly 569.19 *devotedly*
committed to memory 462.9 *memorized*
committee 376.7; 579.6 *governing body;* 398.2 *representative body*
committee boat 50.2 *sailing boat*
committee of inquiry 713.4 *adviser*
committee room 484.7 *planning*
committee rule 12.1 *government*
committer 340.3 *doer*
commit time 768.6 *give to charity*
committing move 62.3 *climbing technique*
commit to memory 462.11 *memorize*
commit to writing 744.14 *inscribe*
commit unsportsmanlike conduct 46.18 *be penalized*
commix 412.8 *mix*
commixture 412.1 *mixture*
commode 23.5, 410.3 *cabinet;* 560.14, 767.7 *toilet*
commodification 776.5 *commercial trade*
commodious 679.4 *big;* 239.1 *convenient;* 141.13 *spacious;* 237.1 *useful*
commodity 13.6 *economic factors;* 778.8 *merchandise;* 402.5 *object;* 356.7 *produce;* 237.5 *usefulness*
commodity exchange 779.5 *stock market*
commodity market 779.5 *stock market*
commodore 586.27 *naval man*
common 138.21; **574.3**; 216.1 *average;* 216.7 *average person;* 117.15 *everyday;* 632.10, 657.9 *familiar;* 297.3 *frequent;* 81.2 *grassland;* 538.8 *greenness;* 724.8 *inelegant;* 747.18 *joint;* 764.5 *jointly possessing;* 764.1 *joint possession;* 455.10 *known;* 5.39 *of language;* 122.16, 574.4 *ordinary;* 138.19 *prevailing;* 440.1 *property;* 271.1 *simple;* 654.15 *sociable;* 544.10 *ugly*
Common Agricultural Policy 43.2
commonality 216.4 *average;* 138.5 *averageness*
commonalty 566.9 *group;* 124.10 *nonentity;* 574.2 *the common people*
common as muck 544.10 *ugly*
common border 147.7 *interface*
common boundary 147.7 *interface*
common carrier 316.7 *transferor*
common chord 18.16 *musical note*
common cold 494.3 *chill;* 260.6 *infection;* 260.9 *respiratory disease*
common courtesy 658.1 *courtesy*
common denominator 27.18 *division*
common endeavour 747.4 *joint operation*
Commoner 574
commoner 216.7 *average person;* 566.10 *member of society*
common feature 115.1 *similarity*
common folk 216.7 *average person*
common fraction 27.18 *division;* 196.1 *fraction;* 194.5 *ratio*
common friend 748.3 *mediator*
common fund 439.1 *store*
common good 797.13 *benefit*
common grave 583.6 *grave*
common ground 147.8 *interaction*
common hatred 596.1 *dislike*
common informer 16.8 *litigant*
common jury 16.26 *jury*
common knowledge 455.2 *information;* 740.7 *publicity*
common land 764.1 *joint possession;* 440.1 *property*
common law 713.3 *precept;* 16.1 *the law;* 1.8, 296.6 *tradition*
common-law marriage 570.3 *types of marriage*
common-law spouse 223.12 *partner*
common-law wife 570.11 *married woman;* 570.12 *partner*
common logarithm 27.19 *logarithm;* 194.6 *power*
commonly 140.18 *as a rule;* 297.1 *frequently;* 764.6 *in common;* 122.20 *insignificantly;* 216.11 *on average;* 138.32 *universally*
common man 138.9 *everyman;* 566.7 *person;* 574.1 *plebeian*
Common Market 776.5 *commercial trade;* 779.4 *free market;* 764.1 *joint possession*
common money 764.1 *joint possession*
commonness 216.4 *average;* 138.5 *averageness;* 297.4 *frequency;* 675.3 *grossness;* 724.3 *inelegance;* 793.3 *shoddiness;* 271.4 *simplicity;* 544.3 *ugliness*
common noun 5.35 *part of speech*
common occurrence 297.4 *frequency*
common or garden 216.1 *average;* 138.22 *commonplace;* 117.15 *everyday;* 632.10 *familiar;* 271.1 *simple*
common or garden variety 216.4 *average*
common ownership 764.1 *joint possession*
common people 138.11 *general public;* 566.9 *group*
commonplace 138.22; 620.4 *boring;* 750.15 *conventional;* 117.15 *everyday;* 632.10 *familiar;* 745.1 *maxim;* 216.3 *mediocre;* 231.4 *ordinary;* 745.2 *proverbial;* 271.1 *simple;* 124.4 *trivial;* 5.42 *worded*
commonplace book 744.6 *record book*
commonplaceness 620.1 *boredom*
commonplace saying 5.21 *catchword*
common practice 632.6 *procedure*
common property 764.1 *joint possession;* 440.1 *property*
common room 6.15 *schoolroom*
common run 138.6 *average*
common sense 442.5; 4.3 *detachment;* 458.2 *intelligence;* 460.2 *rationality;* 485.1 *skill*
common-sensical 4.15, 460.5 *rational*
common soldier 586.17 *army person;* 586.8 *soldier*
common speech 271.4 *simplicity;* 5.3 *spoken language*
common stock 764.1 *joint possession*
common supplies 764.1 *joint possession*
common touch 631.1 *conduct*
common type 138.9 *everyman*
common-variety 271.1 *simple*
commonweal 237.8 *benefit;* 764.1 *joint possession;* 85.2 *union of nations*
commonwealth 396.8 *governmental organization;* 764.1 *joint possession;* 566.11 *nation;* 12.5 *political organization;* 86.4 *territorial division;* 85.2 *union of nations*
Commonwealth Games 47.5 *competition*
Commonwealth of Nations 566.11 *nation*
commotion 328.5; 342.1 *activity;* 408.9 *disorder;* 727.1 *exaggeration;* 380.3 *instance of violence;* 327.2 *tumult*
communal 2.13; 750.11 *allied;* 564.11 *inhabited;* 747.18 *joint;* 764.5 *jointly possessing;* 566.13 *national;* 138.19 *prevailing;* 654.15 *sociable;* 1.14 *societal;* 2.12 *sociological;* 87.14 *urban*
communal eating 557.4 *eating meals*
communal effort 747.4 *joint operation*
communalism 747.6 *movement*
communalist 747.18 *joint*
communalization 764.1 *joint possession*
communalize 764.4 *have joint possession;* 439.6 *store;* 773.7 *take*
communal living 764.1 *joint possession*
communally 747.20 *cooperatively;* 750.31 *in accord;* 764.6 *in common;* 16.86 *jurisdictionally;* 87.16 *municipally;* 10.23 *ritually;* 1.18 *societally;* 2.16 *sociologically*
communard 764.3 *participant*
communautaire 12.6 *political party*
commune 734.9 *converse;* 654.7 *human society;* 564.2 *inhabitants;* 747.4 *joint operation;* 764.1 *joint possession;* 10.18 *perform rites*
commune member 764.3 *participant*
commune with God 9.7 *worship*
commune with the spirits 690.8 *get drunk*
communicable 692.35; 316.17 *transferable*
communicable disease 260.4 *disease*
communicably 316.18 *in transit*
communicant 450.5 *believer;* 7.5 *Christian;* 9.5, 10.17 *worshipper*
communicate 692.30; **693.12**; 734.9 *converse;* 739.6 *divulge;* 6.22 *educate;* 373.13 *intercommunicate;* 740.13 *make public;* 694.10 *mean;* 721.15 *recount;* 742.12 *signal;* 2.15 *socialize;* 729.11 *speak;* 5.45 *use language*
communicated 692.34; 740.19 *published*
communicated insanity 461.4 *delusion*
communicate with 692.30 *communicate*
communicate with aliens 11.24 *experience psychic phenomena*
communicating 317.15 *accessible;* 692.33 *communicational*
communication 693.2; 713.1 *advice;* 373.2 *association;* 734.1 *conversation;* 739.2 *divulgence;* 740.2 *mass media;* 746.1 *negotiation;* 654.1 *sociability;* 2.14 *socioeconomic;* 316.3 *transmission*
communicational 692.33
communication cord 373.6 *line*
communication network 373.2 *association*
communication of love 593.14
Communications 692
communications 692.1
communications channel 692.6 *telecommunication*
communications engineering 692.6 *telecommunication*
communication service 584.4 *military organization*
communications line 692.6 *telecommunication*
communications link 692.6 *telecommunication*
communications medium 692.1 *communications*
communications network 692.6 *telecommunication*
communications satellite 29.32 *satellite;* 692.7 *satellite communication*
communications system 692.6 *telecommunication*
communications technology 692.6 *telecommunication*
communicative 373.14 *connective;* 734.12 *conversing;* 739.11 *disclosing;* 6.16 *educational;* 731.6 *effusive;* 693.16 *informative;* 746.8 *negotiated;* 654.15 *sociable;* 2.14 *socioeconomic*
communicatively 734.15 *conversationally;* 731.11 *effusively;* 746.9 *feasibly;* 654.18 *sociably;* 2.16 *sociologically*
communicativeness 731.2 *effusiveness;* 654.1 *sociability*
communicator 739.4 *discloser;* 693.9 *informant;* 742.8 *signer;* 729.10 *speaker*
Communion 10.6 *Eucharist*
communion 750.1 *accord;* 734.1 *conversation;* 654.1 *sociability*
communion with God 7.2 *religiousness;* 9.1 *worship*
communiqué 693.2 *communication;* 740.1 *publication*
communism 12.1 *government;* 764.1 *joint possession;* 747.6 *movement;* 566.11 *nation;* 652.2 *public spiritedness;* 244.11 *reformism;* 4.7 *school of thought;* 396.7 *type of rule*
Communist 535.8 *figurative usage;* 12.9 *governmental*
communist 4.11 *follower of a doctrine;* 747.18 *joint;* 85.16 *national;* 4.14 *of a philosophy;* 764.3 *participant;* 244.12 *reformer*
communist bloc 12.5 *political organization*
communist country 85.1 *country*

communistic 12.9, 396.14 governmental; 764.5 jointly possessing; 85.16, 566.13 national; 652.6 philanthropic
communistically 764.6 in common; 396.24 ministerially; 85.19 nationally; 652.8 philanthropically
communistic state 566.11 nation
Communists 12.6 political party
community 750.2 alliance; 87.1 city; 223.3 companionship; 34.18 ecology; 376.17 family; 566.9 group; 654.7 human society; 564.2 inhabitants; 747.4 joint operation; 764.1 joint possession; 205.1 part; 138.19 prevailing; 2.4 social organization; 1.7, 2.5 society; 747.9 team; 87.9 town; 87.14 urban
community at large 566.9 group
community centre 87.13 municipal building
community charge 790.7 tax
community chest 652.5 charity; 439.1 store
community college 6.12 educational institution
community council 579.8 British administrative council; 16.2 jurisdiction
community drama 21.2 play
community home 815.1 prison
community hospital 35.10 hospital
community medicine 35.6 health care; 35.1 medicine
community member 764.3 participant
community of interest 569.2 friendly relations
community of nations 566.9 group
community physician 35.11 doctor
community planning 38.17 civil engineering
community police 16.15 British police
community relations 2.5 society
community service 2.10 social services; 650.3 welfare
community service worker 652.3 philanthropist; 752.8 volunteer
community spirit 747.2 fellowship
community study 2.2 sociological research
community theatre 21.10 theatre movements
community-wide 2.12 sociological
community work 636.10 voluntary work
communization 764.1 joint possession
communize 85.17 become a nation; 764.4 have joint possession
commutability 224.4 exchange
commutable 224.14 exchangeable
commutation 759.1 exchange; 762.1 substitution
commutative 759.6 in exchange
commutatively 759.8 in exchange
commutative operation 27.14 operation
commutator 39.31 electric motor; 334.6 source of energy
commute 298.7 be regular; 224.8 cause change; 224.10, 759.5 exchange; 761.4, 761.8 return; 2.15 socialize; 762.5 take a substitute; 319.4 transport; 87.15 urbanize
commuter 216.8 middle classes; 564.4 townsman; 87.11 urbanite
commuter belt 216.8 middle classes
commuting 761.4 return; 319.1 transport; 319.5 transportable
comp 740.12 publisher
compact 267.9 adhesive; 409.10 agreement; 750.3 arrangement; 269.4 be concise; 269.3 concise; 755.1 contract; 416.6 dense; 159.7 little; 416.9 make dense; 191.5 make smaller; 756.1 promise; 191.7 smaller; 723.6 summary
compactability 191.2 contractibility
compactable 191.9 contractible
compact camera 41.16 camera
compact dictionary 5.28 dictionary
compact disc 504.9 audio device; 307.6 rotator
compacted 723.7 shortened; 191.7 smaller
compactedness 191.1 contraction
compacter 191.4 contractor
compaction 267.1 adhesion; 191.1 contraction
compactly 267.11 cohesively; 269.5 concisely; 416.10 densely
compactness 269.1 conciseness; 416.1 density; 159.1 littleness; 723.4 summariness
compactor 256.10 cleaning object; 38.29 construction equipment
compact ski 68.5 ski equipment
compadre 569.5 friend
companion **223.11**; 115.5 counterpart; 119.5 equal; 569.5 friend; 595.4 likable person; 304.7 means of ascent; 401.4 personal attendant; 252.3 protector
companionability 654.1 sociability
companionable 97.8 attendant; 569.8 friendly; 654.15 sociable
companionably 654.18 sociably
companionate marriage 570.3 types of marriage
companion ladder 304.9 ladder
companionless 197.16 alone
companionship **223.3**; 569.1 friendship; 97.2 omnipresence; 764.2 participation
companionway 304.7 means of ascent; 50.3 parts of a sailing boat
company **776.7**; 586.16 army unit; 374.3, 376.1 assembly; 21.25 cast; 223.3 companionship; 13.7 corporation; 654.8 good company; 376.11 group; 584.4 military organization; 97.2 omnipresence; 127.3 person included; 578.4 personnel; 376.12 team; 577.1 workshop
company canteen 557.15 eating place
company commander 584.5 military staff
company director 579.15 manager
company grade officer 584.5 military staff
company headquarters 577.1 workshop
company leader 400.5
company man 117.6 conformist
company official 400.5 company leader
company pension 392.4 social assistance
company policy 484.2 policy
company promoter 778.12 wholesaler
company report 744.1 record
company spokesman 719.7 news interpreter
company tax 790.7 tax
company-wide bargaining 15.1 industrial relations
comparability 110.3 correlation; 108.2 interrelatedness; 115.1 similarity
comparable 110.6 correlative; 209.7 gradational; 108.5 interrelated; 115.7 similar
comparably **115.14**; 110.11 correlatively; 209.9 differentially; 108.10 relevantly
comparative 209.7 gradational; 5.44 grammatical; 5.38 linguistic
comparative anatomist 70.11 zoologist
comparative anatomy 34.4 anatomy; 70.9 animal science
comparative grammar 5.1 linguistics; 5.30 syntax
comparative historical linguistics 5.1 linguistics
comparative linguistics 5.1 linguistics
comparatively 209.9 differentially; 5.52 grammatically; 5.48 linguistically; 108.10 relevantly; 2.16 sociologically
comparative macrosociology 2.1 sociology
comparative psychology 36.1 psychology
comparative sociology 2.1 sociology
compare 108.8 be proportionate to; 115.10 be similar; 110.9 correlate; 113.21 counteract; 115.11 make similar; 209.5 measure
compare and contrast 466.12 discriminate
compare notes 713.6 consult
compare with 115.11 make similar
comparison 110.3 correlation; 551.33 dress up; 209.3 gradation; 738.10 manifestation; 108.1 relatedness
compartment **410.2**; 409.6 category; 137.2 class; 205.1 part; 372.2 setting apart
compartmental 205.11 partial
compartmentalization 409.5 categorization; 375.2 deconstruction
compartmentalize 409.15 categorize; 375.4 deconstruct; 372.11 divide; 205.10 part
compartmentalized 409.24 categorized; 205.11 partial
compartmentation 375.2 deconstruction
compass 334.2 ability; 28.84 altimeter; 246.6 be successful; 62.4 climbing equipment; 210.5 computer; 209.1 degree; 27.49 geometric construction; 579.5 guide; 742.5 indicator; 323.5 navigation; 324.3 orientation; 141.7 range; 306.7 ring
compass bearing 324.2 bearing
compass card 323.5 navigation; 324.3 orientation
compass direction 324.2 bearing; 142.2 exact location
compasses 27.49 geometric construction
compassion 650.1 benevolence; 665.2 consideration; 649.2 forgivingness; 648.1 leniency; 627.3 mercy; 652.1 philanthropy; 627.1 pity; 591.5 sensitivity; 473.2 unselfishness
compassionate 650.6 benevolent; 648.4 lenient; 649.5 merciful; 652.6 philanthropic; 627.6 pitying; 591.1 sensitive; 419.6 soft-hearted; 473.5 unselfish
compassionate leave 98.5 leave of absence; 758.4 licence
compassionately 650.10 benevolently; 649.14 forgivingly; 648.6 leniently; 652.8 philanthropically; 627.13 pitifully; 419.18 soft-heartedly; 473.9 unselfishly
compassionateness 627.1 pity
compass needle 742.5 indicator
compass point 324.4
compass reading 323.5 navigation
compass rose 324.3 orientation
compatibilist 4.11 follower of a doctrine; 4.14 of a philosophy
compatibility 750.1 accord; 241.8 amiability; 40.19 computing terms; 117.1 conformity; 569.2 friendly relations; 147.8 interaction; 593.1 love; 27.64 reasoning; 654.1 sociability
compatible 117.12 conforming; 569.8 friendly; 750.10 in accord; 241.2 likable; 27.86 logical; 593.22 lovable
compatibly 117.17 conformingly; 750.31 in accord; 569.17 in friendship
compatriot 564.8 national
compeer 285.5 contemporary; 119.5 equal
compeers 376.18 generation
compel **386.6**; 344.10 awaken; 395.10 be a prevailing influence; 334.10 be powerful; 397.11 have authority over; 331.1 impel; 483.10 manipulate; 135.10 necessitate; 480.15 persuade
compelling **386.9**; 395.12 appealing; 344.13 causal; 344.14 causally; 397.14 commanding; 726.3 emphatic; 483.11 motivational; 480.19 persuasive; 336.10 potent; 334.13 powerful
compellingly **386.11**; 336.15 acutely; 397.16 commandingly; 483.14 influentially; 334.18 powerfully
compel respect 667.21 command respect
compendious 269.3 concise; 149.7 short; 723.6 summary
compendiously 269.5 concisely
compendiousness 269.1 conciseness; 149.1 shortness; 723.4 summariness
compendium **723.3**; 374.3 assembly; 409.7 catalogue; 376.30 compilation; 191.3 contracted thing; 220.5 list of appointments; 269.2 outline; 149.3 shortened version
compensate **775.5**; 807.5 atone; 119.11 equalize; 759.5 exchange; 813.11 pay; 785.10 pay back; 765.14 profit; 110.7 reciprocate; 609.11 recompense; 761.7 restore
compensated 759.7 exchanged; 769.11 receiving; 762.8 substituted
compensate for 347.3 counteract; 762.6 give a substitute; 801.15 put right
compensation **775.2**; **813.6**; 807.1 atonement; 347.1 counteraction; 36.19 defence mechanism; 119.3 equalization; 759.1 exchange; 232.2 fullness; 110.1 interchange; 749.2 peace offering; 814.8 penalty; 765.5 profit; 609.2 reparation; 785.2 repayment; 761.2 restoration; 813.4 reward for service; 769.2 something received; 762.1 substitution
compensational 807.4 atoning
compensation neurosis 36.10 neurosis
compensation technique 68.4 skiing technique
compensative 769.14 receivable
compensator 775.3 returner
compensatory **813.17**; 807.4 atoning; 347.4 counteracting; 765.15 gainful; 759.6 in exchange; 785.20 paying in return; 769.14 receivable; 110.4 reciprocal; 761.10 regressive; 775.6 restoring
compensatory payment 814.8 penalty
compere 692.29 broadcaster; 579.2 direct; 579.14 leader
compete 45.6 participate; 69.10 play
compete in gymnastics 57.10
competence 334.2 ability; 265.1 easiness; 237.7 instrumentality; 16.2 jurisdiction; 797.12 proficiency; 136.1 qualification; 485.1 skill; 217.7 sufficiency
competent 119.9 adequate; 400.13 excellent; 485.8 expert; 237.3 instrumental; 455.8 knowledgeable; 16.50 law-abiding; 334.13 powerful; 797.5 proficient; 136.9 qualified; 485.6 skilful; 217.1 sufficient
competently 136.17 capably; 400.16 masterfully; 334.18 powerfully; 485.12, 797.25 skilfully
compete with 113.19 confront
competing 113.24 discordant; 629.4 jealous
competition **47.5**; 113.5 conflict; 69.2 contest; 34.18 ecology; 13.6 economic factors; 629.1 jealousy
competition aikido 52.10 aikido
competition judo 52.7 judo
competitive 113.24 discordant; 57.11 gymnastic; 629.4 jealous; 69.9 recreational; 485.6 skilful; 45.5 sporting; 67.11 swimming; 52.15 wrestling
competitive canoeing 50.6 canoeing
competitive casting 55.1 angling
competitive diving 67.6 diving
competitive diving marks 67.6 diving
competitive fishing 55.1 angling
competitive gymnast 57.9 gymnasts
competitive gymnastics 57.1 gymnastics
competitive ice-dancing 68.7 ice-dancing
competitive ice-skating 68.6 ice-skating
competitive lugeing 68.9 bobsledding
competitively **57.12**; 67.12 by swimming; 629.9 jealously; 55.9 on the water; 113.27 opposingly; 52.16 professionally; 45.7 sportingly
competitiveness 629.1 jealousy
competitive price 793.1 cheapness
competitive punting 50.8 punting
competitive rowing 50.4 rowing
competitive sailing 50.1 sailing
competitive scoring 68.7 ice-dancing
competitive skiing 68.1 skiing
competitive spirit 629.1 jealousy
competitive swimmer 67.4 swimmer
competitive swimming 67.1 swimming
competitive tae kwon do 52.9 tae kwon do
competitor **113.12**; 47.3 athlete; 314.7 entrant; 119.5 equal; 629.3 rival; 45.3 sportsman; 52.9 tae kwon do
compilation **376.30**; 723.3 compendium
compile **723.9**; 40.20 abort; 405.13 make; 376.44 put together
compiled language 40.9 programming language
compiler 40.8 software
complacency 609.1 satisfaction; 673.2 self-satisfaction
complacent 609.4 satisfied; 673.9 self-satisfied
complacently 673.20 smugly
complain **753.7**; 715.5 accuse; 606.7 be dissatisfied; 626.11 be irritable; 670.16 disagree; 15.12 have an industrial dispute; 603.6 lament; 113.18 object; 753.6 protest
complain about 703.19 protest
complainant 715.3 accuser
complainer 602.4 depressing person; 606.3 dissatisfied person; 753.4 protester
complaining 606.4 dissatisfied
complain of 260.24 be unhealthy
complaint 715.1 accusation; 670.7 blame; 670.4 disagreement; 606.2 expression of dissatisfaction; 260.2 illness; 15.4 industrial dispute; 603.2 lament; 113.4 objection; 17.7 poem; 753.1 protest; 802.7 sense of wrong
complaisance 658.4 deference; 663.1 obedience
complaisant 117.13 compliant; 658.9 deferential; 663.7 obedient; 419.6 soft-hearted
complaisantly 117.16 adaptably; 658.16 deferentially; 663.10 obediently; 419.18 soft-heartedly
compleat 232.7 complete
compleat angler 55.6 angler; 633.6 hunter
complement 223.13 accompany; 211.1 addition; 34.14 chromosome; 232.4 com-

plete; 750.25 *conform;* 750.5 *conformity;* 232.2 *fullness;* 127.1 *inclusion;* 110.2 *interconnection;* 110.8 *interrelate;* 5.35 *part of speech;* 127.3 *person included;* 578.4 *personnel;* 27.21 *set;* 376.12 *team*
complemental 110.5 *interconnected*
complementally 110.10 *reciprocally*
complementarity 108.2 *interrelatedness*
complementary 223.17 *accompanying;* 211.8 *additional;* 232.7 *complete;* 750.14 *conforming;* 5.44 *grammatical;* 759.6 *in exchange;* 110.5 *interconnected;* 108.5 *interrelated*
complementary angle 27.39 *angle*
complementary colour 529.1 *colour*
complementary colours 28.28 *colour*
complementary medicine 394.11 *medical art;* 35.2 *natural medicine*
complete **204.10**; **232.4**; **232.7**; 340.4 *act;* 211.6 *add;* 309.9 *close down;* 131.15 *end;* 131.21 *ended;* 640.9 *endure;* 226.10 *finished;* 27.86 *logical;* 230.1, 230.5 *perfect;* 253.13 *secure one's objective;* 345.5 *show an effect;* 217.1 *sufficient;* 197.13, 204.6 *whole*
complete a circuit 181.12 *move round*
complete a purchase 777.1 *purchase*
complete blank 456.3 *unknown thing*
completed 253.8 *accomplished;* 309.14 *closed down;* 243.20 *developed;* 284.18 *over;* 230.1 *perfect*
complete failure 247.1 *failure*
complete idiot 457.3 *unintelligent person*
complete list 204.5 *unit*
completely **230.8**; **232.9**; 256.20 *clean;* 309.17 *finally;* 197.23, 204.11 *wholly*
completely past 284.18 *over*
Completeness 232
completeness **232.1**; 230.3 *perfection;* 27.64 *reasoning;* 204.1 *whole*
complete pass 46.9 *play*
complete set 439.5 *collection;* 127.1 *inclusion;* 204.5 *unit*
complete works 204.2 *whole thing*
completing 232.3 *completion;* 131.20 *ending*
completion **232.3**; 340.1 *action;* 309.1 *closure;* 755.1 *contract;* 345.1 *effect;* 131.1 *end;* 244.5 *improvement;* 230.3 *perfection;* 217.7 *sufficiency*
completist 386.5 *compulsive person*
completive 131.20 *ending*
complex **27.72**; **36.18**; 180.5 *ambiguous;* 32.7 *chemical compound;* 32.35 *combined;* 403.6 *construction;* 461.4 *delusion;* 696.4 *difficult;* 632.1 *habit;* 412.12 *mixed;* 737.11 *mysterious;* 266.2 *obscure;* 264.12 *problematic;* 204.2 *whole thing*
complex analysis 27.30 *calculus*
complex conjugate 27.6 *complex number*
complex fraction 27.18 *division*
complexion **529.9**; 525.3 *external appearance;* 99.4 *nature;* 221.1 *state;* 137.4 *type*
complexity 264.1 *difficulty;* 412.3 *miscellany;* 412.1 *mixture;* 737.3 *mystification;* 266.1 *obscurity*
complex lipid 33.6 *lipid*
complexly 180.8 *circularly;* 412.14 *in the midst*
complex number **27.6**; 194.2 *kind of number*
complex sugar 33.3 *carbohydrate*
compliance **117.2**; 750.1 *accord;* 636.8 *acquiescence;* 422.2 *adaptability;* 810.3 *allegiance;* 658.4 *deference;* 419.12 *gentleness;* 797.11 *good behaviour;* 663.1 *obedience;* 664.1 *servility;* 388.1 *submission;* 483.6 *suggestibility*
compliant **117.13**; 422.7 *adaptive;* 636.3 *amenable;* 658.9 *deferential;* 265.13 *easygoing;* 750.10 *in accord;* 810.9 *loyal;* 663.7 *obedient;* 664.6 *servile;* 667.9 *showing respect;* 483.13 *suggestible;* 797.4 *well-behaved*
compliantly 117.16, 422.12 *adaptably;* 658.16 *deferentially;* 483.14 *influentially;* 663.10, 797.24 *obediently;* 419.18 *softheartedly*
complicate 180.7 *be ambiguous;* 266.3 *make obscure;* 696.8 *make unintelligible*
complicated 180.5 *ambiguous;* 696.4 *difficult;* 412.12 *mixed;* 264.12 *problematic*
complicatedly 412.14 *in the midst*
complicate matters 264.23 *cause difficulties*
complication 17.3 *aspect of fiction;* 264.1 *difficulty;* 260.2 *illness;* 412.1 *mixture;* 264.8 *snag*
complicity 747.8 *conferring;* 806.1 *guilt;* 764.2 *participation*
compliment **669.4**; **669.15**; 658.10 *be courteous;* 658.3 *courtesies;* 677.8 *flatter;* 241.10 *pleasant thing;* 669.14 *praise*
complimentary 669.18 *approving;* 601.13 *congratulatory;* 677.12 *flattering;* 793.11 *free of charge;* 768.7 *given;* 5.43 *phrasal*
complimentary gift 793.6 *absence of charge*
complimentary pass 793.6 *absence of charge*
complimentary phrase 5.24 *phrasing*
complimentary remark 669.4 *compliment*
complimentary ticket 793.6 *absence of charge*
compliments 658.3 *courtesies;* 677.1 *flattery;* 5.24 *phrasing;* 669.3 *praise;* 667.7 *respects*
compline 10.4 *public worship*
comply **117.8**; 422.10 *be adaptable;* 160.8 *be formal;* 797.18 *be good;* 750.21 *be in accord;* 636.13 *be willing;* 664.13 *conform;* 658.13 *defer to;* 663.5 *obey;* 664.11 *pander to;* 388.3 *submit;* 419.16 *yield*
complying 422.7 *adaptive;* 419.12 *gentleness;* 419.7 *impressionable;* 750.10 *in accord;* 663.7 *obedient*
comply with 117.8 *comply;* 663.5 *obey*
compo 435.2 *building material*
Component 405
component **205.4**; **405.1**; **405.6**; 211.3 *additional item;* 39.16 *circuit element;* 406.10 *containing;* 127.8 *included;* 99.7 *integral;* 438.5 *machine;* 402.4 *matter;* 27.50 *scalar quantity;* 127.2 *thing included*
component part 127.2 *thing included*
components **405.4**; 406.1 *contents;* 435.1 *materials*
comportment 631.1 *conduct*
comport oneself 631.11 *conduct oneself*
comport oneself well 631.12 *behave well*
compose **18.35**; **405.10**; 409.16 *adapt;* 409.12 *arrange;* 93.20 *bring into being;* 374.5 *combine;* 232.4 *complete;* 19.23 *design;* 406.8 *embody;* 477.14 *imagine;* 127.4 *include;* 405.13 *make;* 407.18 *order;* 749.4 *pacify;* 356.10 *produce;* 376.44 *put together;* 403.15 *shape;* 767.8 *sink;* 17.21 *write*
compose an epic 17.21 *write*
composed **18.31**; 167.8 *assured;* 684.10 *calm;* 374.7 *combined;* 406.10 *containing;* 4.18 *detached;* 160.9 *formed;* 685.6 *moderate;* 407.10 *ordered;* 301.6 *quiescent*
compose differences 749.5 *make peace*
composedly 4.27 *stoically*
composed of 127.7 *including*
compose oneself 243.8 *prepare oneself*
compose one's features 643.8 *be serious*
composer 18.24 *musician;* 126.3 *originator;* 356.9 *producer*
composing **405.9**; 127.1 *inclusion;* 18.2 *music making*
Composite 20.16 *columned*
composite 374.4 *compound;* 38.25 *construction material;* 27.74 *divisible;* 54.6 *fencing;* 412.12 *mixed;* 77.16 *taxonomic;* 207.7 *various*
composite attack 54.3 *fencing movements*
composite fruit 80.2 *botanical fruit*
composite function 27.29 *mathematical function*
compositeness 207.2 *multiplicity*
composite number 27.5 *number*
Composite order 20.8 *column*
composite parry 54.3 *fencing movements*
composite volcano 30.24 *volcanic activity*
composition **18.15**; **41.8**; 409.1 *arrangement;* 409.2 *array;* 403.9 *artistic structure;* 435.2 *building material;* 374.1 *combination;* 376.30 *compilation;* 406.1 *contents;* 722.1 *dissertation;* 160.1, 403.3 *form;* 160.4 *forming;* 127.1 *inclusion;* 27.29 *mathematical function;* 412.2 *mixed thing;* 412.1 *mixture;* 18.2 *music making;* 99.4 *nature;* 407.1 *order;* 19.2 *painting;* 356.1 *production;* 785.2 *repayment;* 19.4 *treatment;* 19.6, 356.5 *work of art*
compositional 18.31 *composed*
composition of differences 749.1 *pacification*
compositor 740.12 *publisher*
compos mentis 460.4 *sane*
compost 44.15 *cultivate;* 375.1 *disintegration;* 43.13, 44.7, 562.3 *fertilizer;* 562.7 *make fertile;* 238.6 *refuse*
compostable 375.5 *disintegrated*
composted 375.5 *disintegrated*
compost heap 44.4 *nursery;* 238.6 *refuse;* 767.8 *sink;* 767.5 *wasteyard*
composting 44.5 *gardening*
composure 167.4 *assurance;* 684.3 *calmness;* 4.3 *detachment;* 160.1 *form;* 685.1 *moderation;* 301.2 *repose*
compotation 690.13 *drink*
compote 25.35 *dessert*
compound **374.4**; 32.7 *chemical compound;* 374.5 *combine;* 27.74 *divisible;* 165.2 *enclosed place;* 405.13 *make;* 412.8 *mix;* 412.2 *mixed thing;* 77.18 *of leaves;* 815.1 *prison;* 356.3 *product*
compound epithet 17.12 *poetic language*
compound fertilizer 43.13 *fertilizer*
compound fraction 27.18 *division;* 196.1 *fraction;* 194.5 *ratio*
compound interest 213.3 *increasing thing;* 784.4 *interest;* 765.5 *profit*
compound lens 28.30 *lens system*
compound microscope 28.85 *microscope*
comprecation 10.9 *prayer*
comprehend 127.4 *include;* 455.11 *know;* 400.15 *learn;* 4.21 *rationalize;* 695.6 *understand*
comprehensibility 725.1 *clarity;* 695.9 *intelligibility;* 265.2 *simplicity*
comprehensible 725.3 *clear;* 695.1 *intelligible;* 265.11 *made easy;* 694.6 *meaningful;* 255.16 *simple*
comprehensibly 725.4 *clearly;* 695.13 *intelligibly*
comprehension **694.3**; 522.13 *enlightenment;* 446.1 *idea;* 127.1, 550.19 *inclusion;* 442.3 *intelligence;* 455.1 *knowledge;* 695.12 *understanding;* 458.1 *wisdom*
comprehensive 158.15 *big;* 232.7 *complete;* 138.15 *general;* 127.7 *including;* 550.39 *inclusive;* 265.11 *made easy;* 204.6 *whole*
comprehensive insurance policy 550.19 *inclusion*
comprehensively 127.9, 550.42 *inclusively;* 204.12 *one and all;* 156.17 *profoundly*
comprehensiveness 158.2 *bigness;* 232.1 *completeness;* 138.1 *generality;* 127.1 *inclusion;* 204.1 *whole*
comprehensive school 6.12 *educational institution*
comprehensive test ban 749.1 *pacification*
compress 269.4 *be concise;* 416.9 *make dense;* 191.5, 214.5 *make smaller;* 151.10 *narrow;* 360.6 *retain;* 149.10 *shorten;* 394.10 *surgical dressing;* 152.7 *thicken*
compressed 269.3 *concise;* 151.1 *narrow;* 149.8 *shortened;* 191.7 *smaller*
compressibility **419.10**; 191.2 *contractibility;* 28.39 *expansion;* 417.3 *sparseness*
compressible **419.4**; 191.9 *contractible;* 417.1 *sparse*
compression 269.1 *conciseness;* 191.1 *contraction;* 214.1 *decrease;* 38.16 *deformation;* 334.4 *energy;* 28.39 *expansion;* 38.14 *load;* 723.2 *outline;* 360.1 *retention;* 149.2 *shortening;* 68.1 *skiing*
compression turn 68.4 *skiing technique*
compression wood 79.3 *timber*
compressive 191.8 *contracting*
compressive strength 336.1 *strength*
compressor 416.5 *condenser;* 191.4 *contractor*
comprisal 127.1 *inclusion*
comprise 204.9 *be whole;* 405.10 *compose;* 405.11 *consist of;* 99.12 *embody;* 127.4, 550.32 *include*
comprising 405.9 *composing;* 127.7 *including;* 127.1 *inclusion*
Compromise 754
compromise **639.10**; **754.1**; **754.4**; 750.1 *accord;* 750.23 *arrange;* 348.4 *be an instrument;* 685.3 *be moderate;* 409.17 *come to an arrangement;* 678.12 *defame;* 254.10 *endanger;* 348.2 *instrument;* 110.1 *interchange;* 749.5 *make peace;* 685.1 *moderation;* 747.3 *mutual relationship;* 746.1 *negotiation;* 749.1 *pacification;* 757.3 *permit;* 110.7, 747.12 *reciprocate;* 762.1 *substitution;* 762.5 *take a substitute*
compromiser 639.15 *indecisive person*
compromising **754.6**; 750.10 *in accord;* 746.8 *negotiated;* 746.1 *negotiation;* 110.4 *reciprocal*
compromisingly **754.8**; 746.9 *feasibly;* 110.10 *reciprocally*
compte rendu 693.3 *document;* 789.4 *statement*
Comptometer™ 210.5 *computer*
Compulsion 386
compulsion **36.15**; **386.1**; 344.1 *cause;* 461.4 *delusion;* 632.1 *habit;* 336.2 *healthiness;* 331.11 *impulsion;* 483.1 *motive;* 638.14 *tenacity;* 576.1 *work*
compulsion complex 36.18 *complex*
compulsion neurosis 36.10 *neurosis*
compulsive 386.9 *compelling;* 334.13 *powerful*
compulsive cease-fire 749.1 *pacification*
compulsive eater 386.5 *compulsive person*
compulsive eating 557.2 *appetite*
compulsive gambler 386.5 *compulsive person*
compulsive liar 386.5 *compulsive person*
compulsively 336.15 *acutely;* 386.11 *compellingly;* 334.18 *powerfully*
compulsiveness 386.1 *compulsion*
compulsive person 386.5
compulsive shopper 386.5 *compulsive person*
compulsive talker 386.5 *compulsive person*
compulsory **386.10**; 397.14 *commanding;* 99.5 *essential;* 68.13 *ice-skating;* 140.9 *legal;* 810.12 *obligatory;* 135.4 *required;* 387.9 *subject*
compulsory arbitration 15.4 *industrial dispute*
compulsory dancing 68.7 *ice-dancing*
compulsory figure 68.6 *ice-skating*
compulsory marriage 570.3 *types of marriage*
compulsory payment 814.8 *penalty*
compulsory service 584.1 *military affairs*
compulsory servitude 387.1 *subjection*
compunction 627.2 *condolence;* 808.1 *penitence*
compunctious 808.6 *penitent*
compunctiously 808.8 *penitently*
compurgation 16.42 *acquittal;* 714.1 *vindication*
computable 210.14 *calculable;* 26.14 *measurable;* 27.73 *numerable*
computably 210.16 *mathematically*
computation 789.3 *accounting;* 210.1 *calculation;* 210.4 *computing;* 211.2 *mathematical addition;* 27.1 *mathematics;* 26.1 *measurement;* 27.12 *numeration;* 4.4 *philosophical investigation*
computational 210.13 *calculative*
computational linguistics 5.1 *linguistics*
computative 210.13 *calculative*
compute 211.6 *add;* 210.8 *calculate;* 27.90 *enumerate;* 334.12 *generate power;* 26.10 *measure;* 4.21 *rationalize*
computed value 28.83 *sensitivity*
computer **40.3**; **40.4**; **210.5**; 27.67, 210.6 *calculator;* 438.5 *machine*
computer crime 774.7 *dishonesty*
computer criminal 774.11 *dishonest person*
computer dating 570.13 *matchmaker*
computer electronics 39.1 *electronics*
computer engineer 578.2 *artisan*
computer fault 247.4 *unsuccessful thing*
computer file 409.7 *catalogue*
computer game 69.1 *game*
computerization 334.9 *electronics;* 15.2 *industrial negotiations;* 348.1 *instrumentality;* 356.2 *manufacture;* 438.6 *mechanics*
computerize 15.11 *conduct industrial relations;* 356.10 *produce*
computerized 438.9 *mechanical;* 15.9 *negotiated;* 348.8 *practical;* 356.11 *productive*
computerized information 693.6 *information technology*
computer language 5.8 *artificial language*

computer listing 409.7 *catalogue;* 220.2 *table*
computer-literate 438.9 *mechanical*
computer malfunction 378.2 *obstacle*
computer memory 462.6 *artificial memory*
computer networking 692.6 *telecommunication*
computer operator 210.6 *calculator;* 346.5 *operator;* 744.9 *recorder*
computer paper 435.3 *paper*
computer printer 115.3 *copier;* 125.6 *photocopier*
computer programmer 210.6 *calculator*
Computers 40
computer science 40.1 *computing*
computerspeak 729.1 *faculty of speech*
computer tape 744.6 *record book*
computer technology 210.4 *computing*
computer war 585.1 *war*
computing 40.1; **210.4**; 789.10 *accounting;* 210.13 *calculative;* 334.9 *electronics*
computing terms 40.19
comrade 223.11 *companion;* 119.5 *equal;* 569.5 *friend;* 567.3 *male title of address;* 566.10 *member of society;* 12.6 *political party*
comradely 747.19 *associating;* 569.8 *friendly*
comradeship 747.2 *fellowship;* 569.1 *friendship;* 654.8 *good company*
Comsat™ 692.7 *satellite communication*
con 645.5 *be cunning;* 604.8 *be dishonest;* 699.25, 700.30 *be fraudulent;* 251.7 *charge;* 13.12, 268.21 *cheat;* 113.25 *contrary;* 702.12 *deceive;* 812.3 *disreputable action;* 699.8, 700.10 *fraud;* 455.13 *get to know;* 6.23 *learn;* 792.10 *overcharge;* 815.5 *prisoner;* 21.37 *rehearse;* 645.2 *stratagem;* 379.1 *trap;* 700.8, 700.28 *trick*
con artist 700.17 *cheat*
conation 635.1 *will*
conative 635.6 *willed*
con brio 338.6 *with vigour*
concatenate 132.15
concatenation 132.2 *consecution*
concave 183.6; 177.4 *curved;* 27.81 *curvilinear*
concave land 183.2
concave lens 28.29 *optical element*
concavely 183.11; 177.7 *curvedly*
concave mirror 28.29 *optical element*
concave surface 27.38 *surface*
Concavity 183
concavity 183.1; 177.1 *curvature;* 367.14 *depression;* 27.38 *surface*
conceal 736.8; 699.22 *be hypocritical;* 384.19 *buffer;* 526.3 *cause to disappear;* 406.6 *contain;* 116.6 *differentiate;* 700.32 *disguise;* 550.31 *hide;* 655.13 *ignore;* 172.15 *keep inside;* 737.12 *keep secret;* 521.8 *make invisible;* 358.1 *obliterate;* 252.10 *protect;* 439.6 *store*
concealed 736.14; 526.7 *disappeared;* 700.41 *disguised;* 655.10 *lonely;* 737.11 *mysterious;* 358.6 *obliterated;* 521.3 *private;* 550.37 *protected*
concealed crevasse 62.2 *climbing dangers*
concealer 736.7
Concealment 736
concealment 736.1; 645.1 *cunning;* 116.3, 526.5, 700.12 *disguise;* 479.5 *equivocalness;* 699.3 *hypocrisy;* 521.4 *invisibility;* 358.3 *obliteration;* 655.3 *separation;* 550.15 *shelter*
conceal oneself 736.11
concede 739.8 *admit;* 750.21 *be in accord;* 648.3 *be lenient;* 483.8 *be motivated;* 480.18 *be persuaded;* 754.4 *compromise;* 388.3 *submit*
concede a hole 56.7 *golf*
concede defeat 247.7 *be defeated*
conceded hole 56.2 *golfing terms*
concede the victory to 122.9 *yield to*
conceding 754.6 *compromising;* 750.10 *in accord*
conceit 622.3; 673.6 *boastfulness;* 683.2 *egoism;* 459.1 *folly;* 477.4 *ideality;* 467.1 *overestimation;* 17.12 *poetic language;* 476.1 *supposition;* 673.1 *vanity*
conceited 622.17; 676.3 *affected;* 622.17 *conceited;* 683.5 *egoistic;* 673.8 *vain*
conceitedly 673.23 *boastfully;* 683.9 *egoistically;* 673.19 *vainly*
conceitedness 673.1 *vanity*
conceivability 102.2 *possibleness*
conceivable 477.13 *imaginable;* 102.5 *possible*
conceivableness 102.2 *possibleness*
conceivably 102.11 *potentially*
conceive 562.6 *be fertile;* 554.19 *give birth to;* 446.15, 477.14 *imagine;* 130.22 *invent;* 455.11 *know;* 126.7 *originate;* 356.10 *produce;* 695.7 *recognize;* 561.10 *reproduce oneself;* 476.5 *suppose*
conceive a plan 484.9 *plan*
conceived 446.11 *ideational*
conceive of 443.16 *have an idea*
concentralization 310.5 *focus*
concentralize 310.11 *focus*
concentrate 443.13; 191.6 *become smaller;* 173.9 *centre;* 310.10 *come together;* 32.30, 369.8 *extract;* 310.11 *focus;* 504.15 *hear;* 213.5 *make bigger;* 416.9 *make dense;* 191.5 *make smaller;* 369.17 *obtain an extract;* 99.3 *quintessence;* 32.25 *solidify;* 342.15 *try*
concentrated 267.9 *adhesive;* 173.7 *centralized;* 416.7 *condensed;* 638.1 *resolute;* 191.7 *smaller;* 32.32 *solid;* 336.12 *strong to the senses;* 4.17 *thoughtful*
concentrated attack 381.12 *military attack*
concentrated solution 32.3 *phase*
concentrate on 173.9 *centre;* 447.10 *focus on*
concentrate sprayer 433.12 *sprinkler*
concentrating 443.9; 4.17 *thoughtful*
concentration 416.2; **638.13**; 267.1 *adhesion;* 342.8 *assiduity;* 471.3 *carefulness;* 173.3 *centrality;* 640.2 *commitment;* 191.1 *contraction;* 310.1 *convergence;* 213.1 *increase;* 336.3 *intensity;* 369.7 *obtaining an extract;* 4.4 *philosophical investigation;* 139.8 *specialization;* 443.3 *thoughtfulness*
concentration camp 655.4 *place of confinement;* 815.1 *prison*
concentration cell 32.19 *electrochemistry*
concentre 310.11 *focus*
concentric 173.7 *centralized;* 27.81 *curvilinear;* 188.3 *parallel*
concentric circles 27.42 *circle*
concentricity 173.3 *centrality;* 188.1 *parallelism*
concept 443.6, 446.1 *idea;* 477.4 *ideality;* 4.1 *philosophy*
conceptacle 84.4 *reproductive body*
conception 130.4; 554.4 *biological function;* 443.6, 446.1 *idea;* 477.4 *ideality;* 130.5 *invention;* 442.1 *mind;* 356.1 *production;* 561.3 *propagation*
conceptional 130.33 *inventive*
conceptive 130.33 *inventive;* 442.9 *mental;* 4.13 *of philosophy*
conceptual 477.12 *imaginary;* 442.9 *mental;* 4.13 *of philosophy;* 443.10 *speculative;* 446.10 *theoretical*
conceptualism 4.7 *school of thought*
conceptualist 4.11 *follower of a doctrine*
conceptualistic 4.14 *of a philosophy*
conceptualization 446.8, 477.1 *imagination*
conceptualize 446.15, 477.14 *imagine;* 4.20 *philosophize;* 96.14 *theorize;* 442.12 *think*
conceptualized 446.11 *ideational*
conceptually 19.31 *artistically;* 442.14 *mentally;* 126.8 *originally;* 4.25, 446.20 *theoretically*
conceptual thought 4.4 *philosophical investigation*
concern 471.1 *attention;* 123.7 *be important;* 776.7 *company;* 328.7 *disturb;* 123.1 *importance;* 127.1 *inclusion;* 447.2 *issue;* 447.4 *sphere;* 779.8 *store;* 447.1 *topic;* 612.3, 612.14 *worry*
concerned 328.12 *disturbed;* 471.9 *solicitous;* 612.9 *worried*
concerned with 447.7 *focused*
concerned with number one 683.5 *egoistic*
concerning 108.10 *relevantly*
concert 750.1 *accord;* 747.15 *concur;* 243.2 *do the groundwork;* 750.24 *harmonize;* 18.13 *melody;* 18.27 *performance;* 738.9 *production*
concerted 750.10 *in accord;* 747.18 *joint;* 764.5 *jointly possessing*
concerted action 747.4 *joint operation*
concerted effort 747.4 *joint operation*
concertedly 747.20 *cooperatively;* 750.31 *in accord*
concert hall 18.28; 504.3 *auditorium;* 21.16 *theatre*
concerto 356.5 *work of art*
concert pitch 18.21 *tone*
concession 750.1 *accord;* 746.2 *basis for negotiations;* 754.1 *compromise;* 791.1 *discount;* 768.1 *giving;* 648.1 *leniency;* 747.3 *mutual relationship;* 757.1 *permission;* 388.1 *submission*
concessional 793.9 *cheap*
concessional rate 793.1 *cheapness*
concessionary 746.8 *negotiated;* 388.5 *submitting*
concessive 750.10 *in accord*
conch 550.14 *animal covering;* 20.10 *church architecture*
concha 20.9 *miscellaneous architectural features*
conchie 589.3 *pacifist*
conchological 75.19 *molluscan*
conchologist 75.15 *invertebrate zoologist*
conchology 75.14 *invertebrate zoology*
concierge 401.3 *attendant;* 309.5 *person who closes*
conciliar 579.18 *parliamentary*
conciliate 807.5 *atone;* 649.9 *forgive;* 748.1 *mediate;* 752.14 *offer reparation;* 749.4 *pacify;* 480.15 *persuade*
conciliation 649.3 *absolution;* 807.1 *atonement;* 15.4 *industrial dispute;* 748.2 *mediation;* 746.1 *negotiation;* 752.6 *offering;* 749.1 *pacification*
conciliator 15.6 *employer;* 748.3 *mediator*
conciliatorily 746.9 *feasibly;* 649.14 *forgivingly;* 15.13 *industrially;* 748.7 *mediatorially;* 807.8 *penitently;* 752.20 *persuasively*
conciliatory 807.4 *atoning;* 649.4 *forgiving;* 750.10 *in accord;* 748.6 *mediatory;* 746.8 *negotiated;* 749.6 *pacificatory;* 589.7 *peaceful;* 752.19 *sacrificial;* 15.10 *unionized*
concise 269.3; 149.7 *short;* 732.2 *sparing with words;* 723.6 *summary*
concise dictionary 5.28 *dictionary*
concisely 269.5; 695.13 *intelligibly;* 149.12 *short;* 723.11 *summarily*
concisely styled 269.3 *concise*
conciseness 269.1; 732.4 *guarded speech;* 149.1 *shortness;* 723.4 *summariness*
concise style 269.1 *conciseness*
concise version 723.2 *outline*
concision 269.1 *conciseness*
conclave 376.5, 734.4 *conference;* 579.7 *council;* 398.2 *representative body*
conclude 707.17 *affirm;* 226.6 *cease;* 309.9 *close down;* 232.4 *complete;* 131.15 *end;* 443.16 *have an idea;* 464.11 *judge;* 4.22 *propound a philosophy;* 638.7 *resolve;* 345.5 *show an effect;* 706.20 *solve;* 476.5 *suppose;* 27.89 *theorize*
conclude a deal 755.5 *contract*
concluded 232.7 *complete;* 131.21 *ended;* 706.14 *solved*
concluding 131.20 *ending*
conclusion 211.3 *additional item;* 309.1 *closure;* 232.3 *completion;* 345.1 *effect;* 131.1 *end;* 443.6 *idea;* 4.1 *philosophy;* 27.64 *reasoning;* 289.9 *sequel;* 706.6 *solution;* 707.2 *statement;* 226.2 *stop;* 464.2 *verdict*
conclusive 707.10 *affirmative;* 703.12 *demonstrable;* 131.20 *ending;* 396.15 *true*
conclusive argument 704.1 *refutation*
conclusively 131.28; **706.25**; 707.23 *affirmatively;* 396.25 *authentically;* 704.11 *in reply*
concoct 403.16 *construct;* 243.7 *develop;* 234.12 *distort the truth;* 96.17 *fabricate;* 699.26 *falsify;* 477.14 *imagine;* 484.11 *invent;* 484.13 *plot;* 356.10 *produce*
concocted 699.36 *falsified*
concoction 558.2 *drink;* 699.9 *falsification;* 412.2 *mixed thing;* 356.3 *product;* 356.1 *production*
concomitance 223.1 *accompaniment;* 750.4 *harmony;* 285.1 *same time*
concomitant 223.4; 223.17 *accompanying;* 97.8 *attendant;* 750.13 *harmonious;* 285.9 *simultaneous*
concomitantly 285.12 *simultaneously*
concomitant with 285.12 *simultaneously*
concord 750.1 *accord;* 750.21 *be in accord;* 232.1 *completeness;* 374.2 *cooperation;* 747.2 *fellowship;* 569.1 *friendship;* 407.8 *harmony;* 516.3 *melodiousness;* 18.13 *melody;* 589.1 *peace*
concordance 750.1 *accord;* 5.28 *dictionary;* 111.2 *equivalence;* 747.2 *fellowship*
concordant 747.19 *associating;* 117.12 *conforming;* 111.13 *equivalent;* 407.16, 516.7 *harmonious;* 750.10 *in accord*
concordantly 747.20 *cooperatively;* 111.18 *identically*
concordat 755.3 *alliance*
concours d'élégance 320.21 *miscellaneous motoring terms*
concourse 750.1 *accord;* 310.1 *convergence;* 376.3 *meeting;* 90.6 *river flow;* 10.17 *worshipper*
concrete 267.9 *adhesive;* 175.1 *base;* 20.4, 435.2 *building material;* **38.25** *construction material;* 416.6 *dense;* 160.9 *formed;* 418.7 *hard substance;* 24.9 *industrial ceramics;* 18.32 *instrumental;* 93.11 *intrinsic;* 24.11 *make ceramics;* 402.7 *material;* 550.11 *paving;* 19.29 *realist;* 317.4 *road surface;* 416.4 *solid body;* 550.29 *surface;* 492.8 *touchable;* 520.1 *visible*
concrete block 418.7 *hard substance*
concrete bridge 38.21 *bridge*
concrete dam 38.23 *dam*
concretely 267.11 *cohesively;* 416.10 *densely;* 160.13 *formatively;* 402.9 *materially;* 19.30 *pictorially*
concreteness 416.1 *density;* 402.1 *material world;* 492.1 *touch*
concrete poetry 17.6 *poetry*
concrete shelter 252.5 *refuge;* 384.10 *shelter*
concrete slab 38.27 *superstructure*
concretion 416.2 *concentration;* 416.4 *solid body*
concretization 416.2 *concentration*
concubinage 796.4 *illicit love;* 570.3 *types of marriage*
concubinal 570.20 *matrimonial*
concubinary 570.20 *matrimonial*
concubine 796.9 *immoral woman;* 570.11 *married woman;* 387.5 *subjected person*
concupiscence 688.1 *gluttony;* 686.3 *overindulgence;* 617.4 *sexual desire;* 796.3 *sexual immorality*
concupiscent 796.14 *lecherous;* 617.11 *lustful;* 686.8 *overindulgent*
concur 747.15; 223.13 *accompany;* 750.21 *be in accord;* 285.6 *be simultaneous;* 374.6 *come together;* 117.7 *conform;* 747.11 *cooperate*
concurrence 750.1 *accord;* 374.1 *combination;* 117.1 *conformity;* 310.1 *convergence;* 374.2, 747.1 *cooperation;* 747.2 *fellowship;* 285.1 *same time;* 223.2 *synchronism*
concurrent 223.18; 310.7 *convergent;* 374.8, 747.17 *cooperative;* 750.10 *in accord;* 285.9 *simultaneous*
concurrently 223.23; 310.12 *convergently;* 747.20 *cooperatively;* 374.10 *in combination;* 285.12 *simultaneously*
concurrent with 285.12 *simultaneously*
concurring 747.19 *associating;* 223.18 *concurrent*
concuss 489.12 *anaesthetize;* 331.8 *club;* 331.2 *collide;* 592.7 *render insensitive*
concussed 489.8 *unconscious*
concussion 331.12 *collision*
condemn 606.7 *be dissatisfied;* 798.11 *be evil;* 670.19 *blame;* 16.79 *convict;* 381.10 *criticize;* 8.18 *devilize;* 382.19, 814.5 *execute;* 594.14 *hate;* 464.11 *judge;* 814.2 *penalize;* 712.6 *vilify*
condemnation 670.7 *blame;* 16.43 *conviction;* 16.7 *legal trial;* 814.8 *penalty;* 464.2 *verdict*
condemnatory 670.29 *blaming;* 464.8 *judging*
condemned 16.64 *convicted;* 245.13 *dilapidated;* 254.4 *endangered;* 806.5 *guilty;* 594.12 *hated;* 814.22 *punishable;* 254.2 *unsafe*
condemned cell 16.43 *conviction;* 814.16 *instrument of execution*
condemned man 582.10 *dying person*
condemned prisoner 815.5 *prisoner*
condemned to death 582.18 *dying*
condemning 670.29 *blaming*
condemn oneself 808.4 *be penitent*
condemn to death 382.19, 814.5 *execute*
condemn to the galleys 814.1 *punish*
condensation 267.1 *adhesion;* 31.9 *at-*

mospheric process; 32.14 *chemical reaction*; 416.2 *concentration*; 191.1 *contraction*; 152.6 *denseness*; 431.1 *fluid*; 213.1 *increase*; 524.2 *murk*; 369.7 *obtaining an extract*; 163.1, 269.2 *outline*; 32.3 *phase*; 212.1 *subtraction*; 433.3 *wateriness*

condensation nuclei 31.8 *atmosphere*

condensation polymer 32.21 *polymer*

condensation trail 742.1 *sign*

condense 267.6 *adhere*; 191.6 *become smaller*; 269.4 *be concise*; 416.8 *be dense*; 213.5 *make bigger*; 191.5, 214.5 *make smaller*; 369.17 *obtain an extract*; 163.5 *outline*; 32.26 *react*; 149.10 *shorten*; 32.25, 418.10 *solidify*; 212.3 *subtract*; 723.8 *summarize*; 152.7 *thicken*

condensed **416.7**; 267.9 *adhesive*; 31.43 *atmospheric*; 269.3 *concise*; 152.2 *dense*; 212.7 *reduced*; 149.8 *shortened*; 191.7 *smaller*; 32.32 *solid*

condensed milk 558.5 *milk*

condenser **416.5**; 191.4 *contractor*; 28.30 *lens system*; 39.17 *resistor*; 432.11 *vaporizer*

condensibility 191.2 *contractibility*

condensible 191.9 *contractible*

condescend **623.18**; 396.19 *be authoritarian*; 658.13 *defer to*; 622.28 *disdain*; 599.15 *humour*

condescendence 623.15 *condescension*

condescending 396.12 *authoritative*; 622.17 *conceited*; 658.9 *deferential*; 623.4 *self-abasing*; 622.19 *stately*

condescendingly 658.16 *deferentially*

condescension **623.15**; 658.4 *deference*; 622.5 *stateliness*

condiment 412.4 *admixture*; 496.2 *seasoning*

condiments 223.5 *side-dish*

condition **136.7**; 143.2, 222.1 *circumstances*; 140.4 *guide*; 632.18 *habituate*; 259.3 *health*; 260.2 *illness*; 160.6 *nature*; 36.38 *psychologize*; 27.64 *reasoning*; 135.1 *requirement*; 221.1 *state*; 476.1 *supposition*

conditional **136.12**; 222.7 *circumstantial*; 27.26 *equality*; 221.8 *in a state of*; 27.86 *logical*; 27.63 *mathematical logic*; 746.8 *negotiated*; 4.8 *philosophical term*; 251.13 *restraining*; 5.34 *tense*

conditionally **221.9**; 746.9 *feasibly*; 222.16 *relatively*; 251.16 *under restraints*; 136.18 *with qualification*

conditional phrase 5.23 *phrase*

conditional probability 27.62 *probability*

conditioned 632.14 *habituated*; 136.11 *modified*

conditioned reflex 36.20 *conditioning*; 632.7 *habituation*

conditioner 43.10 *farm tool*

conditioning **36.20**; 632.7 *habituation*; 36.3 *psychiatric treatment*

conditions 746.2 *basis for negotiations*; 222.1 *circumstances*; 135.1 *requirement*; 136.6 *specification*; 139.4 *specifications*; 476.1 *supposition*; 31.3 *weather*

conditions of employment 15.2 *industrial negotiations*

condolence **627.2**; 627.1 *pity*

condolences 627.2 *condolence*

condolent 650.6 *benevolent*; 627.6 *pitying*

condolently 650.10 *benevolently*

condole with 627.9 *sorrow*

condom 378.3 *barrier*; 563.3 *birth control*; 347.2 *counteracting thing*; 422.3 *elastic thing*

condominium 565.6 *apartment block*; 12.3 *governance*; 764.1 *joint possession*

condominium owner 764.3 *participant*

condonable 714.13 *vindicable*

condonation 649.3 *absolution*

condone **649.11**; 669.12 *accept*; 388.3 *submit*

condoned 649.6 *forgiven*

condoning 649.4 *forgiving*

condor 72.5 *bird of prey*

condordance 18.13 *melody*

condottiere 579.14 *leader*; 586.6 *militarist*

conduce 302.8 *further*

conduce to 392.28 *further*; 229.4 *tend*

conducive 392.33 *helpful*; 237.3 *instrumental*

conducive to 229.5 *tending to*

conduct **18.40**; **39.35**; **631.1**; **631.15**; 340.1 *action*; 631.14 *behave towards*; 633.14 *carry on*; 324.6, 579.2 *direct*; 223.15 *escort*; 160.5 *formality*; 579.1 *management*; 579.3 *management*; 795.1 *morality*; 632.5 *tradition*; 316.11 *transfer*; 317.1 *way*

conduct a dig 284.16 *excavate*

conductance 28.53, 39.12 *resistance*

conduct an experiment 448.11 *experiment*

conduct an inquiry into 705.17 *question*

conduct a sea survey 91.9 *sail the high seas*

conduct a trial 16.76 *judge*

conduct a witch-hunt 633.8 *pursue*

conducted 223.20 *accompanied*

conduct industrial relations **15.11**

conducting medium 28.43 *electrical conduction*; 39.3 *electricity*

conductiometric titration 32.18 *gravimetric analysis*

conduction 334.7 *electrical power*; 39.3 *electricity*; 28.36 *heat flow*; 316.3 *transmission*

conductional 316.17 *transferable*

conduction band 28.44 *semiconductor*

conduction current 28.51 *electric current*

conduction of electricity 28.43 *electrical conduction*

conductive 316.17 *transferable*

conductively 316.18 *in transit*

conductivity 28.43 *electrical conduction*; 334.7 *electrical power*; 39.3 *electricity*; 28.53, 39.12 *resistance*

conduct of affairs 579.3 *management*

conduct one's affairs 631.11 *conduct oneself*

conduct oneself **631.11**; 340.4 *act*

conduct oneself properly 631.12 *behave well*

conductor **631.10**; 579.13 *director*; 28.43 *electrical conduction*; 334.7 *electrical power*; 39.3 *electricity*; 579.14 *leader*; 18.24 *musician*; 346.5 *operator*; 281.11 *person keeping time*; 321.9 *railway worker*; 223.8 *usher*

conduct the ceremony 570.16 *join in marriage*

conduct the wedding 570.16 *join in marriage*

conduct unbecoming 659.2 *bad manners*

conduit 317.11 *channel*; 314.5 *entrance*; 184.2 *furrow*; 433.13 *irrigator*; 315.7 *outlet*; 308.7 *passageway*

cone **181.5**; 27.45 *curved surface*; 518.2 *eye*; 151.8 *narrow thing*; 79.2 *tree part*

cone-bearing 77.16 *taxonomic*

cone-shaped 27.83 *spherical*; 151.3 *tapered*

confab 734.2 *chat*

confabulate 734.9 *converse*; 699.26 *falsify*

confabulated 699.36 *falsified*

confabulation 734.2 *chat*; 699.9 *falsification*

confabulator 734.7 *conversationalist*

confabulatory 734.12 *conversing*

confection 412.2 *mixed thing*; 37.5 *prescription*; 356.3 *product*

confectionary 557.17 *food shop*; 25.41 *sweet*

confectioner 436.4 *caterer*; 557.20 *food provider*

confectioner's shop 498.4 *confectionery*

confectionery **498.4**

confederacy 374.2 *cooperation*; 747.5 *joint control*

confederate 374.6 *come together*; 374.8 *cooperative*; 747.16 *join*; 764.3 *participant*

Confederate flag 743.7 *flag*

confederation 374.2 *cooperation*; 396.8 *governmental organization*; 747.5 *joint control*; 764.1 *joint possession*; 12.5 *political organization*; 747.9 *team*; 85.2 *union of nations*

Confederation of British Industry 15.1 *industrial relations*

confer **734.11**; 635.16 *bequeath*; 713.6 *consult*; 750.30 *grant*; 746.5 *negotiate*

confer an obligation 235.10 *do good*

conference **376.5**; **734.4**; **748.5**; 747.8 *conferring*; 713.2 *consultation*; 579.7 *council*; 746.3 *discussion*; 740.7 *publicity*; 398.2 *representative body*

conference call 692.10 *telephone call*

conference championship 246.3 *successful thing*

conference delegate 398.1 *delegate*

conferential 734.13 *discussing*

confer holy orders on 7.21 *ordain*

conferment 768.1 *giving*; 750.9 *grant*; 7.9 *priesthood*

conferral 768.1 *giving*; 750.9 *grant*

conferred 750.19 *granted*

conferrer 768.4 *giver*

conferring **747.8**; 734.13 *discussing*

confer upon 768.5 *give*

conferval 84.7 *algal*

confervoid 84.7 *algal*

confess 707.20, 739.8 *admit*; 807.6 *apologize*; 806.8 *be guilty*; 450.7 *believe*; 808.4 *be penitent*; 16.80 *convict oneself*; 10.18 *perform rites*

confessed 739.10 *disclosed*; 808.6 *penitent*; 707.11 *stated*

confessed criminal 806.4 *guilty person*

confessing 16.64 *convicted*; 808.6 *penitent*

confession 707.5 *admission*; 807.2 *apology*; 10.5 *Christian rite*; 739.2 *divulgence*; 716.5 *legal evidence*; 808.1 *penitence*; 10.3 *rite of worship*; 9.1 *worship*

confessional 10.12 *church*; 16.18 *tribunal*

confessional poetry 17.6 *poetry*

confessions 721.4 *factual account*; 17.4 *nonfiction*

confess one's sins 808.4 *be penitent*

confessor 707.9 *affirmer*; 807.3 *atoner*; 739.4 *discloser*; 808.3 *penitent person*; 7.8 *priest*

confess the truth 698.29 *be truthful*

confetti 541.5 *variegated thing*

confidant 569.6 *close friend*; 595.4 *likable person*; 737.1 *secrecy*

confidante 713.4 *adviser*; 595.4 *likable person*; 401.4 *personal attendant*; 21.23 *role*

confide 646.4 *be naive*; 739.6 *divulge*; 693.11 *inform*

confide in 450.7 *believe*; 713.6 *consult*

confidence 167.4 *assurance*; 396.2 *authoritativeness*; 450.3 *believing*; 452.10 *conviction*; 265.4 *ease of manner*; 474.1, 610.2 *expectation*; 556.3 *maturity*; 253.1 *protection*; 783.7 *repute*; 252.1 *safety*; 737.1 *secrecy*; 613.3 *steadfastness*

confidence game 800.3 *criminality*; 774.7 *dishonesty*

confidence level 27.60 *parameter*

confidence limits 27.60 *parameter*

confidence man 700.17 *cheat*; 774.11 *dishonest person*; 699.17 *false person*

confidence trick 800.3 *criminality*; 774.7 *dishonesty*; 699.8 *fraud*; 645.2 *stratagem*; 700.8 *trick*

confidence trickster 645.3 *cunning person*; 718.3 *deceiver*

confident 707.14 *assertive*; 396.12 *authoritative*; 450.11 *believing*; 452.2 *convinced*; 610.12 *expectant*; 474.5 *expecting*; 613.12 *self-reliant*

confidential 123.5 *important*; 737.9 *secret*

confidential information 737.1 *secrecy*

confidentiality 737.1 *secrecy*; 736.4 *silence*

confidentially 737.15 *in secret*

confidently 396.23 *authoritatively*; 450.15 *believingly*; 474.12 *expectantly*; 610.15 *hopefully*; 452.24 *with certainty*

confiding 646.1 *naive*

configuration 139.3 *characteristic*; 160.1, 403.3 *form*; 27.41 *geometric figure*; 36.26 *gestalt*

configurational 160.9 *formed*

configurationally 160.13 *formatively*

configurationism 36.1 *psychology*

configurative 160.9 *formed*

configure 27.96 *represent*

confine 164.5 *border*; 736.8 *conceal*; 251.11 *detain*; 165.5, 309.10 *enclose*; 165.2 *enclosed place*; 655.13 *ignore*; 815.9 *imprison*; 172.15 *keep inside*; 166.7 *limit*; 684.6 *moderate*; 151.10 *narrow*; 136.16 *specify*

confined 136.12 *conditional*; 251.15 *detained*; 165.7, 309.15 *enclosed*; 815.8 *imprisoned*; 166.5 *limited*; 86.18 *local*; 655.10 *lonely*; 684.9 *moderate*; 151.1 *narrow*; 260.22 *sick*

confinedly **165.8**

confined space 151.6 *narrow place*

confined to bed 251.15 *detained*

confinement 554.4 *biological function*; 251.4 *detention*; 815.7 *imprisonment*; 172.2 *inside*; 151.5 *narrowness*; 561.7 *obstetrics*; 814.7 *punishment*; 136.6 *specification*

confines 164.1 *edge*; 147.5 *near place*; 86.3 *regional boundary*; 170.1 *surroundings*

confirm **707.19**; 706.17 *answer*; 750.28 *consent*; 755.5 *contract*; 95.12 *establish reality*; 448.11 *experiment*; 16.68 *legislate*; 452.21 *make certain*; 228.7 *make stable*; 10.18 *perform rites*; 757.3 *permit*; 756.7 *promise*; 703.17, 716.12 *prove*; 698.30 *prove true*; 769.10 *receive someone*; 336.8 *strengthen*; 454.1 *verify*

confirmability 703.5 *demonstrability*

confirmable 703.12 *demonstrable*

confirmation **452.13**; **698.7**; **707.4**; 706.2 *acknowledgment*; 10.5 *Christian rite*; 755.1 *contract*; 454.6 *evidence*; 656.3 *formal occasion*; 16.31 *legislation*; 757.1 *permission*; 703.4, 716.2 *proof*; 769.4 *reception*; 454.4 *verification*

Confirmation name 721.8 *name*

confirmed 706.11 *answering*; 750.17 *consenting*; 716.8 *evidential*; 632.14 *habituated*; 698.20 *proved*; 703.13 *proven*; 769.13 *received*; 707.13 *supported*; 454.10 *verified*

confirmed bachelor 572.5 *single person*

confirmed habit 632.1 *habit*

confirmed liar 699.18, 700.16 *liar*

confirming 750.17 *consenting*; 454.9 *verificatory*

confiscate 814.1 *punish*; 773.7 *take*; 608.14 *take away*; 773.8 *take back*

confiscation 814.7 *punishment*; 773.1 *taking*; 773.2 *taking back*

confiscator 769.7 *collector*; 773.6 *taker*

confiscatory 773.12 *taking*

conflab 734.2 *chat*

conflagration 493.6, 522.8 *fire*

conflate 719.8 *interpret*

conflated 719.15 *interpreted*

conflation 374.1 *combination*; 719.1 *interpretation*

conflict **113.5**; 701.13, 751.6 *argue*; 701.1, 751.2 *argument*; 116.5 *be dissimilar*; 113.19 *confront*; 347.1 *counteraction*; 517.11 *disagree*; 517.6 *disagreement*; 242.8, 242.11 *quarrel*; 36.12 *stress*; 585.1 *war*

conflicting 249.6 *adverse*; 347.4 *counteracting*; 517.8 *disagreeing*; 113.24 *discordant*; 701.9 *hostile*

conflictingly 347.5 *counter*; 249.12 *in adversity*

conflict in meaning 694.10 *mean*

conflict with 113.16 *be contrary*; 347.3 *counteract*

confluence 750.1 *accord*; 376.1 *assembly*; 173.3 *centrality*; 492.6 *contiguity*; 310.1 *convergence*; 90.1 *river*; 90.6 *river flow*

confluent 173.7 *centralized*; 310.7 *convergent*; 376.48 *cumulate*; 90.10 *fluvial*; 750.10 *in accord*; 90.1 *river*

confluently 310.12 *convergently*

confluent stream 90.1 *river*

conflux 310.1 *convergence*; 90.6 *river flow*

confocal 310.7 *convergent*; 27.81 *curvilinear*

conform **117.7**; **664.13**; **750.25**; 706.21 *answer to*; 216.9 *be average*; 160.8 *be formal*; 797.18 *be good*; 111.11 *be regular*; 516.8 *harmonize*; 117.9 *make conform*; 663.5 *obey*

conformable **117.11**; 750.14 *conforming*; 160.9 *formed*

conformably 117.16 *adaptably*; 160.13 *formatively*

conformance 117.1, 750.5 *conformity*; 111.6 *regularity*

conformation 59.13 *breeding*; 117.1, 750.5 *conformity*; 160.1, 403.3 *form*

conformational 32.37 *structural*

conformer 450.5 *believer*; 117.6 *conformist*

conforming **117.12**; **750.14**; 706.15 *correspondent*; 663.7 *obedient*; 111.17 *regular*

conformingly **117.17**; 706.26 *correspondingly*; 663.10 *obediently*

conformism 117.4 *conventionalism*; 632.6 *procedure*

conformist **117.6**; **117.14**; 450.5 *believer*; 450.11 *believing*; 7.5 *Christian*; 663.4 *obedient person*

Conformity 117

conformity **117.1**; **750.5**; 216.4 *average*; 706.8 *correspondence*; 162.3 *evenness*;

125.1 *imitation*; 663.1 *obedience*; 632.6 *procedure*; 111.6 *regularity*; 115.1 *similarity*
conform to 117.7 *conform*
conform to facts 698.27 *be true*
confound 457.10 *bemuse*; 696.7 *be unintelligible*; 619.10 *be wonderful*; 266.3 *make obscure*; 453.20 *make uncertain*; 412.9 *mix up*; 704.8 *refute*; 604.7 *thwart*
confounded 453.3, 696.6 *confused*; 236.6 *damnable*; 604.9 *disappointed*; 712.11 *miscellaneous euphemisms*; 412.13 *mixed-up*
confounding 704.1 *refutation*; 704.7 *refuting*
confoundment 453.12 *confusion*
confraternal 569.8 *friendly*
confraternity 376.15 *association*; 569.1 *friendship*; 747.9 *team*
confrication 365.1 *friction*
confront **113.19**; 585.14 *battle*; 613.15 *be courageous*; 167.10 *be in front*; 661.6 *be insubordinate*; 113.15 *be opposite*; 331.2 *collide*; 381.8 *counterattack*; 751.5 *disagree*; 709.6 *dissent*; 147.19 *meet*; 383.6 *resist*; 738.4 *show oneself*; 354.1 *undertake*
confront a problem 484.9 *plan*
confrontation 310.2 *approach*; 113.5 *conflict*; 751.1 *disagreement*; 661.2 *disobedience*; 709.2 *dissent*; 738.10 *manifestation*; 147.4 *meeting*
confrontational 751.9 *disagreeing*; 709.9 *dissenting*
confrontation therapy 36.3 *psychiatric treatment*
confronted 738.13 *displayed*
confronting 113.24 *discordant*; 113.23 *opposite*
confrontment 113.2 *oppositeness*
Confucian 4.11 *follower of a doctrine*; 4.14 *of a philosophy*
Confucianism 4.7 *school of thought*
Confucian text 7.12 *religious text*
confuse **408.23**; **705.21**; 645.5 *be cunning*; 457.10 *bemuse*; 696.7 *be unintelligible*; 264.23 *cause difficulties*; 736.9 *deceive*; 328.8 *disarrange*; 408.22 *discompose*; 461.15 *make insane*; 266.3 *make obscure*; 453.20 *make uncertain*; 696.8 *make unintelligible*; 412.9 *mix up*; 737.13 *mystify*
confused **408.16**; **453.3**; **696.6**; 327.15 *agitated*; 588.6 *anarchic*; 766.18 *at a loss*; 674.10 *bashful*; 604.9 *disappointed*; 328.13 *disarranged*; 133.8 *discontinuous*; 328.12 *disturbed*; 457.7 *intellectually subnormal*; 694.6 *meaningful*; 412.12 *mixed*; 412.13 *mixed-up*; 408.18 *muddled*; 266.2 *obscure*; 264.12, 705.13 *problematic*; 264.16 *troubled*
confusedly 408.27 *in disorder*
confused message 694.3 *comprehension*
confusing 696.4 *difficult*; 737.11 *mysterious*; 264.12, 705.13 *problematic*
confusingly **453.24**; 328.18 *disturbingly*
confusion **408.5**; **453.12**; 328.2 *disarrangement*; 133.1 *discontinuity*; 408.1 *disorder*; 357.5 *havoc*; 461.3 *mental deterioration*; 412.3 *miscellany*; 412.1 *mixture*; 266.1 *obscurity*; 705.1 *question*; 327.2 *tumult*; 696.11 *unintelligibility*
confusion of tongues 5.5 *nonstandard language*
confutability 704.4 *refutability*
confutable 704.6 *refutable*
confutably 704.12 *refutably*
confutation 704.2 *denial*; 709.2 *dissent*; 16.7 *legal trial*; 761.5 *reply*
confutative 709.9 *dissenting*; 704.7 *refuting*
confute 706.18 *answer back*; 709.6 *dissent*; 481.1 *dissuade*; 705.20 *doubt*; 660.28 *get above oneself*; 704.8 *refute*; 761.9 *reply*
confuter 704.5 *refuter*
confuting 704.7 *refuting*
conga 22.2 *dance*
conga line 22.2 *dance*
con game 800.3 *criminality*; 774.7 *dishonesty*
congé 371.18 *dismissal*; 313.9 *parting*
congeal 494.11 *become cold*; 416.8 *be dense*; 152.7 *thicken*
congealed 267.9 *adhesive*; 416.7 *condensed*; 152.2 *dense*
congealing 416.7 *condensed*
congealment 267.1 *adhesion*; 416.2 *concentration*; 152.6 *denseness*
congeneric 127.8 *included*
congenerous 127.8 *included*
congenial 569.8 *friendly*; 750.10 *in accord*; 241.2, 595.5 *likable*; 593.22 *lovable*; 490.6 *pleasant*
congenial climate 257.2 *salubrity*
congeniality 241.8 *amiability*; 654.1 *sociability*
congenially 595.10 *with great liking*
congenital disease 260.4 *disease*
conger eel 55.5 *British game fish*
congeries 376.25 *assemblage*
congest 219.4 *be excessive*; 309.8 *stop*
congested 208.10, 376.50 *crowded*; 219.6 *excessive*; 232.8 *full*; 309.13 *stopped*
congestion 309.1 *closure*; 219.1 *excess*; 260.3 *symptom*
conglomerate 267.6 *adhere*; 374.9 *assembled*; 374.3 *assembly*; 376.15 *association*; 416.8 *be dense*; 376.48 *cumulate*; 416.4 *solid body*
conglomerated 412.12 *mixed*
conglomeration 267.1 *adhesion*; 376.25 *assemblage*; 374.3 *assembly*; 412.3 *miscellany*; 412.1 *mixture*
conglutinate 267.7 *cause to adhere*
conglutination 267.1 *adhesion*
Congo 90.5 *other major rivers*
congratulate **601.17**; 669.15 *compliment*; 600.7 *dance*
congratulate oneself 622.29 *feel pride*
congratulation 669.4 *compliment*; 600.2 *fanfare*; 601.6 *tribute*
congratulations 669.27 *bravo!*; 600.2 *fanfare*
congratulatory **601.13**
congregate 376.46 *assembled*; 374.5 *combine*; 310.10, 376.39 *come together*; 208.11 *crowd*; 314.12 *flood in*; 312.8 *meet*
congregated 374.9, 376.46 *assembled*
congregation 374.3, 376.1 *assembly*; 376.5 *conference*; 579.7 *council*; 504.2 *hearer*; 376.3 *meeting*; 310.4 *meeting place*; 747.9 *team*; 208.4 *throng*; 10.17 *worshipper*
congregational 374.9 *assembled*; 376.49 *grouped*; 10.22 *worshipping*
Congregationalist 7.5 *Christian*
congregationally 374.10 *in combination*; 10.23 *ritually*
Congress 12.4 *governing body*; 396.6 *place of authority*; 398.2 *representative body*; 579.12 *US government*
congress 376.5, 734.4 *conference*; 579.7 *council*; 310.4 *meeting place*; 10.17 *worshipper*
congressional 398.9 *delegated*; 396.14 *governmental*; 376.49 *grouped*; 400.12 *masterful*; 579.18 *parliamentary*
congressional committee 713.4 *adviser*
Congressional Cup 50.1 *sailing*
congressional district 86.5 *state*
congressionally 396.24 *ministerially*; 398.11 *representatively*
Congressional Medal of Honor 743.4 *insignia*
congressional offices 577.1 *workshop*
Congressional Record 744.1 *record*
congressional system 469.11 *franchise*
Congressman 398.1 *delegate*; 400.3 *leader*; 579.16 *official*; 396.10 *person of authority*; 12.8 *politician*
Congresswoman 398.1 *delegate*; 396.10 *person of authority*
congruence 750.5 *conformity*; 706.8 *correspondence*; 111.2 *equivalence*; 162.1 *symmetry*; 27.48 *transformation*
congruent 117.12, 750.14 *conforming*; 706.15 *correspondent*; 119.6 *equal*; 111.13 *equivalent*; 162.4 *symmetrical*
congruently 310.12 *convergently*; 706.26 *correspondingly*; 119.13 *equitably*; 111.18 *identically*
congruent triangles 27.43 *triangle*
congruity 117.1, 750.5 *conformity*; 162.1 *symmetry*
congruous 117.12, 750.14 *conforming*
congruously 117.17 *conformingly*
conic 181.9 *round*
conical 310.7 *convergent*; 181.9 *round*; 425.1 *sharp*; 27.83 *spherical*; 151.3 *tapered*
conically 181.13 *roundly*
conic projection 717.7 *map*
conic section 27.42 *circle*
conidium 83.4 *fungal body*
conifer 79.1 *tree*
coniferous 77.16 *taxonomic*; 79.14 *treelike*
coniferous forest 79.4 *trees*
coniferous tree 79.1 *tree*
coniine 33.19 *alkaloid*
Coniston Water 88.4 *British lakes*
conjecturability 476.2 *basis of supposition*
conjectural 222.7 *circumstantial*; 448.8 *experimental*; 4.13 *of philosophy*; 705.15 *sceptical*; 443.10 *speculative*; 476.7 *suppositional*; 446.10 *theoretical*; 453.1 *uncertain*
conjecturally 448.14 *experimentally*; 705.24 *questionably*; 222.16 *relatively*; 476.10 *supposedly*; 446.20 *theoretically*; 453.23 *uncertainly*
conjecture **476.3**; 450.1 *belief*; 453.18 *be uncertain*; 705.20 *doubt*; 464.12 *estimate*; 448.11 *experiment*; 448.3 *experimentation*; 443.16 *have an idea*; 443.6 *idea*; 464.1 *judgment*; 4.20 *philosophize*; 4.1 *philosophy*; 476.5 *suppose*; 453.10 *suspicion*; 96.4 *theorization*; 96.14, 446.17 *theorize*; 27.65, 446.2 *theory*; 705.6 *uncertainty*; 619.12 *wonder whether*
conjectured 476.8 *supposed*
conjoin 492.12 *abut*; 211.6 *add*; 374.5 *combine*; 373.11 *connect*; 750.22 *form an alliance*; 750.24 *harmonize*
conjoined 374.7 *combined*
conjoint 750.11 *allied*; 374.7 *combined*; 750.13 *harmonious*
conjointly 211.10 *additionally*; 747.20 *cooperatively*
conjoint therapy 36.3 *psychiatric treatment*
conjugal 755.7 *contractual*; 570.20 *matrimonial*
conjugal bliss 570.1 *marriage*
conjugality 570.1 *marriage*
conjugal love 593.2 *romantic love*
conjugally 755.8 *contractually*; 570.24 *matrimonially*
conjugal trust 755.1 *contract*
conjugate 374.5 *combine*; 374.7 *combined*
conjugate angles 27.39 *angle*
conjugated protein 33.9 *protein*
conjugation 5.30 *syntax*
conjunction 223.1 *accompaniment*; 374.1 *combination*; 373.1 *connection*; 492.6 *contiguity*; 374.2 *cooperation*; 750.4 *harmony*; 27.63 *mathematical logic*; 147.1 *nearness*; 5.35 *part of speech*; 4.8 *philosophical term*; 29.16 *planet*; 223.2 *synchronism*; 5.30 *syntax*
conjunction-reduction 5.30 *syntax*
conjunctiva 518.2 *eye*
conjunctive 211.8 *additional*; 373.14 *connective*; 374.8 *cooperative*; 5.44 *grammatical*
conjunctively 5.52 *grammatically*; 373.17 *in connection with*
conjunctivitis 519.2 *poor sight*
conjuncture 222.2 *occurrence*
conjural 11.15 *witchlike*
conjuration 700.9 *sleight of hand*; 11.5 *spell*
conjure **11.22**; 224.8 *cause change*; 700.29 *juggle*
conjured 700.40 *illusory*
conjure into 760.9 *transform*
conjurement 11.5 *spell*
conjurer 224.6 *editor*
conjure up 11.22 *conjure*; 96.13, 446.15, 477.14, 518.17 *imagine*; 462.12 *remember*
conjure up a vision 477.14 *imagine*
conjuring 96.3 *delusion*; 700.9 *sleight of hand*
conjuror 645.3 *cunning person*; 21.29 *entertainer*
conk 83.4 *fungal body*; 185.3 *protuberance*; 500.2 *sense of smell*
conked out 802.18 *gone wrong*
conk out 582.15 *die*; 802.24 *go wrong*; 247.9 *malfunction*
con man 700.17 *cheat*; 645.3 *cunning person*; 718.3 *deceiver*; 774.11 *dishonest person*; 800.4 *dishonourable person*; 699.17 *false person*; 651.8 *malefactor*; 792.5 *overcharger*; 702.6 *sophist*
connatural 115.7 *similar*
connect **373.11**; 492.12 *abut*; 374.5 *combine*; 132.15 *concatenate*; 39.35 *conduct*; 134.3 *continue*; 147.18 *juxtapose*; 570.19 *merge*; 376.44 *put together*; 108.7 *relate to*
connected **373.15**; 317.15 *accessible*; 750.11 *allied*; 374.7 *combined*; 134.5 *continual*; 376.48 *cumulate*; 108.4 *related*; 115.7 *similar*
connectedness 267.1 *adhesion*; 134.1 *continuity*; 108.1 *relatedness*
connecting 317.15 *accessible*; 147.10 *juxtaposed*; 492.9 *touching*
Connection 373
connection **373.1**; 267.1 *adhesion*; 570.2 *alliance*; 504.9 *audio device*; 492.6 *contiguity*; 134.1 *continuity*; 593.5 *desire*; 691.5 *drug pusher*; 147.3 *juxtaposition*; 376.33 *putting together*; 108.1 *relatedness*
connective **373.14**; 267.9 *adhesive*; 373.4 *means of connection*
connectively 373.17 *in connection with*
connective tissue 373.6 *line*
connect together 405.13 *make*
connect up 132.15 *concatenate*
conned 604.10 *deceived*
conning 700.34 *deceiving*; 6.8 *learning*; 700.7 *tricking*
conning tower 518.9 *viewpoint*
conniption 624.4 *anger*
connivance 747.8 *conferring*; 757.1 *permission*; 700.7 *tricking*
connive 747.15 *concur*; 649.11 *condone*; 757.3 *permit*; 700.28 *trick*
connivent 310.8 *advancing*
conniving 747.19 *associating*; 700.34 *deceiving*; 757.8 *permitting*
connivingly 757.9 *with permission*
connoisseur 466.6 *discriminating person*; 557.18 *eater*; 396.11, 485.5 *expert*; 464.5 *judge*; 490.3 *pleasure-seeker*; 136.8 *qualified person*; 549.4 *refined person*; 139.14 *specialist*; 495.5 *taster*
connoisseurship 19.5 *artistry*; 549.1 *elegance*; 466.2 *judiciousness*; 6.11 *refinement*
connotation 719.1 *interpretation*; 694.1 *meaning*; 742.1 *sign*; 694.4 *type of meaning*
connotative 694.6 *meaningful*; 742.14 *signifying*
connote 694.10 *mean*; 742.10 *signify*
connubial 570.20 *matrimonial*
connubially 570.24 *matrimonially*
conquer **586.38**; 246.9 *be victorious*; 387.7 *defeat*; 400.14 *master*
conquer a mountain 89.10 *climb a mountain*
conquering 387.10 *dominating*; 773.1 *taking*
conqueror 586.6 *militarist*; 246.5 *victorious person*
conquest 387.2 *domination*; 593.9 *lover*; 246.2 *victory*
conquistador 586.6 *militarist*
conquor 773.7 *take*
conquoring 387.2 *domination*
consanguine 108.4 *related*
consanguinely 108.10 *relevantly*
consanguineous 108.4 *related*
consanguineously 108.10 *relevantly*
consanguinity 1.5 *anthropological concept*; 108.1 *relatedness*
conscience 795.2 *good morals*; 480.11 *motive*; 799.1 *probity*; 810.4 *sense of duty*; 711.1 *warning*
conscienceless 809.3 *impenitent*; 804.11 *wicked*
conscience money 775.2 *compensation*; 768.2 *gift*
conscience-smitten 808.6 *penitent*
conscience-stricken 806.6 *appearing guilty*; 808.6 *penitent*
conscientious 810.8 *dutiful*; 799.4 *honourable*
conscientiously 799.7 *honourably*
conscientiousness 799.1 *probity*
conscientious objection 662.1 *disobedience*
conscientious objector 661.4 *defiant person*; 451.5 *disbeliever*; 589.3, 749.3 *pacifist*; 753.4 *protester*; 709.4 *refuser*; 383.5 *resister*
conscious **488.6**; 554.12 *alive*; 590.10 *feeling*; 101.11 *internal*; 455.8 *knowledgeable*
consciously 455.15 *knowledgeably*; 11.25 *occultly*; 101.14 *subjectively*
conscious mind 36.21 *psyche*
consciousness 590.1 *feeling*; 101.6 *internal world*; 455.1 *knowledge*; 442.1 *mind*; 488.1 *sensation*
consciousness raising 480.5 *propaganda*; 36.3 *psychiatric treatment*
conscious of one's place 667.9 *showing respect*
conscious self 36.21 *psyche*

conscript 584.10 *enlist*; 386.7 *force*; 585.12 *go to war*; 585.11 *recruit*; 586.8 *soldier*; 387.3 *subordinate*
conscript army 586.15 *army*
conscripted 584.9 *enlisted*; 586.35 *martial*; 585.15 *warring*
conscripting 584.1 *military affairs*
conscription 386.3 *coercive methods*; 584.1 *military affairs*; 585.7 *war measures*
consecrate 8.17 *deify*; 768.5 *give*; 396.21 *grant authority*; 752.16 *make an offering*; 7.21 *ordain*
consecrated 8.15 *deified*; 10.21 *ritualistic*; 752.19 *sacrificial*
consecrated elements 10.6 *Eucharist*
consecrate to 349.1 *use*
consecration 396.3 *acquisition of power*; 8.9 *deification*; 10.6 *Eucharist*; 752.6, 768.3 *offering*
consecution 132.2
consecutive 132.9; 297.3 *frequent*; 289.12 *succeeding*
consecutively 132.18; 297.1 *frequently*; 289.14 *in succession*
Consecutiveness 132
consecutiveness 132.1; 297.4 *frequency*
consensual 755.7 *contractual*
consensually 755.8 *contractually*
consensus 750.1 *accord*; 747.2 *fellowship*
consent 750.7; **750.28**; 669.12 *accept*; 669.1 *approval*; 480.18 *be persuaded*; 636.13 *be willing*; 117.8 *comply*; 755.1 *contract*; 538.15 *green light*; 663.5 *obey*; 757.1 *permission*; 757.3 *permit*; 388.1 *submission*; 388.3 *submit*; 636.6 *willingness*
consentaneity 750.1 *accord*
consentaneous 750.17 *consenting*; 750.10 *in accord*
consentient 750.17 *consenting*; 750.10 *in accord*
consenting 750.17; 750.10 *in accord*; 636.1 *willing*
consentingly 750.39 *with consent*
consenting party 755.4 *contractor*
consequence 345.1 *effect*; 131.12 *end result*; 123.1, 643.6 *importance*; 356.3 *product*; 132.4 *repercussion*; 289.9 *sequel*
consequent 345.10 *caused*; 289.12 *succeeding*
consequential 345.10 *caused*; 123.5 *important*; 132.10 *repercussive*; 694.7 *significant*
consequentialism 4.7 *school of thought*
consequentialist 4.11 *follower of a doctrine*; 4.14 *of a philosophy*
consequentially 123.9 *importantly*; 345.12 *with the effect of*
consequently 750.36 *accordingly*; 222.15 *under the circumstances*; 345.12 *with the effect of*
consequent upon 345.10 *caused*
conservancy 225.1 *permanence*; 359.1 *preservation*
conservation 34.18 *ecology*; 79.5 *forestry*; 225.1 *permanence*; 359.1 *preservation*; 436.1 *provision*; 575.1 *right*; 372.2 *setting apart*; 439.4 *storage*
conservational 359.6 *preserving*
conservation area 359.1 *preservation*
conservation campaign 359.2 *preserver*
conservationism 538.16 *green politics*
conservationist 225.4; 70.10 *animal welfarist*; 538.7 *environmental*; 359.4 *preservationist*
conservation of charge 28.50 *electric charge*
conservation of energy 28.11 *energy*
conservation of mass 28.9 *mass*
conservatism 225.2; 117.4 *conventionalism*; 632.6 *procedure*
Conservative 225.3 *conservative person*; 7.16 *denominational*; 12.9 *governmental*
conservative 225.8; 616.4 *cautious*; 117.14 *conformist*; 225.3 *conservative person*; 750.15 *conventional*; 632.8 *creature of habit*; 378.15 *inhibitive*; 383.11 *obstinate*; 641.8 *obstinate person*; 113.11 *opposer*; 359.6 *preserving*; 662.12 *reactionary*; 383.5 *resister*; 641.4 *set*; 178.9 *straight person*; 178.4 *traditional*; 113.26 *uncooperative*; 468.4 *underestimating*; 728.12 *understated*
conservative attitude 225.2 *conservatism*
conservative estimate 468.1 *underestimation*; 728.1 *understatement*
conservatively 225.10; 378.18 *inhibitively*; 468.6 *pessimistically*; 359.8 *preservatively*; 383.14 *resistingly*; 728.23 *unobtrusively*
conservativeness 378.5 *inhibition*; 728.1 *understatement*
Conservative Party 12.6 *political party*
conservative person 225.3
conservative politics 225.2 *conservatism*
conservative treatment 35.8 *treatment*
conservator 225.4 *conservationist*; 359.4 *preservationist*; 252.3 *protector*
conservatory 6.12 *educational institution*; 493.8 *hot place*; 44.4 *nursery*; 565.7 *room*; 527.8 *transparent thing*
conserve 680.5 *be thrifty*; 257.6 *make hygienic*; 225.6 *make permanent*; 25.42, 359.5 *preserve*; 359.3 *preserved thing*; 252.10 *protect*; 372.10 *set apart*; 439.6 *store*; 498.2 *sweetener*
conserved 225.7 *permanent*; 359.7 *preserved*; 439.7 *stored*
conserving 359.6 *preserving*; 680.4 *thrifty*
consider 471.10 *be attentive*; 450.8 *be of the opinion*; 701.14 *discuss*; 464.12 *estimate*; 123.8 *make important*; 4.20 *philosophize*; 4.22 *propound a philosophy*; 667.18 *show respect*; 443.12 *think*; 518.16 *visualize*
considerable 158.15 *big*; 414.1 *heavy*; 123.5 *important*; 208.6 *many*
considerably 123.9 *importantly*; 158.20 *largely*
considerate 392.35, 650.6 *benevolent*; 658.7 *courteous*; 648.4 *lenient*; 667.8 *respectful*; 471.9 *solicitous*; 443.8 *thoughtful*; 473.5 *unselfish*
considerately 392.38, 650.10 *benevolently*; 658.14 *courteously*; 658.15 *genteelly*; 648.6 *leniently*; 473.9 *unselfishly*
considerateness 473.2 *unselfishness*
consideration 665.2; 471.1 *attention*; 650.1 *benevolence*; 813.6 *compensation*; 658.1 *courtesy*; 759.1 *exchange*; 768.2 *gift*; 123.1 *importance*; 734.6 *interview*; 464.1 *judgment*; 648.1 *leniency*; 701.2 *logical argument*; 4.4 *philosophical investigation*; 701.5 *plea*; 667.1 *respect*; 471.5 *solicitude*; 442.6, 443.3 *thoughtfulness*; 473.2 *unselfishness*; 518.4 *visualization*
considered 106.4 *deliberate*
considering 464.14; 127.7 *including*
consign 398.7 *delegate*; 768.5 *give*; 733.10 *send*; 316.11 *transfer*; 316.12, 319.4 *transport*
consignable 316.17 *transferable*
consignation 398.3 *delegation*
consigned 398.10 *decentralized*; 319.5 *transportable*
consignee 579.15 *manager*; 777.12 *purchaser*; 769.5 *recipient*; 319.3 *transporter*; 780.18 *treasurer*
consignment 768.1 *giving*; 319.2 *thing transported*; 316.10 *transferred thing*
consignor 778.9 *seller*
consign to earth 583.8 *bury*
consign to oblivion 463.13 *forget*
consistency 117.1, 750.5 *conformity*; 416.1 *density*; 162.3 *evenness*; 298.4 *orderliness*; 27.64 *reasoning*; 111.6 *regularity*; 228.1 *stability*; 404.1 *texture*; 492.1 *touch*; 140.7 *uniformity*
consistent 117.12, 750.14 *conforming*; 416.6 *dense*; 162.5 *even*; 27.86 *logical*; 298.14 *orderly*; 111.17, 298.11 *regular*; 228.9 *stable*; 140.11 *uniform*
consistently 750.35; 117.17 *conformingly*; 298.17 *orderly*; 298.15 *regularly*; 228.12 *stably*
consist in 405.12 *be one of*
consisting of 127.7 *including*
consist of 405.11; 127.4 *include*
consistory 579.7 *council*
consociation 654.1 *sociability*
consolation 627.2 *condolence*; 608.1 *ease*; 231.6 *imperfect item*
consolation prize 813.2 *prize*; 794.1 *trophy*
console 40.7 *peripheral*; 608.9 *relieve*; 627.9 *sorrow*
consoled 608.7 *relieved*
consoler 608.3 *reliever*
console table 23.4 *table*
consolidate 267.6 *adhere*; 416.8 *be dense*; 374.5 *combine*; 723.9 *compile*; 747.16 *join*; 30.62 *lithify*; 570.19 *merge*
consolidated 416.7 *condensed*; 187.9 *flattened*; 30.56 *petrographic*
consolidated snow 31.30 *snow*
consolidation 267.1 *adhesion*; 570.2 *alliance*; 747.7 *association*; 416.2 *concentration*; 30.29 *petrogenesis*
consoling 627.6 *pitying*; 608.8 *relieving*
consol system 323.5 *navigation*
consommé 25.13 *soup*
consonance 750.4 *harmony*; 516.3 *melodiousness*; 17.12 *poetic language*; 17.11 *rhyme*
consonancy 750.4 *harmony*
consonant 117.12 *conforming*; 516.7, 750.13 *harmonious*; 5.16 *spoken letter*
consonantal 5.41 *lettered*
consort 570.10 *married man*; 223.12 *partner*
consorting 654.1 *sociability*
consortium 750.2, 755.3 *alliance*; 374.3 *assembly*; 747.7 *association*; 376.7 *committee*
consortship 223.3 *companionship*
consort with 654.11 *be sociable*; 223.14 *keep company with*
conspectus 149.3 *shortened version*; 723.1 *summary*; 204.3 *whole situation*
conspicuous 185.7; 525.7 *appearing*; 738.14 *manifest*; 123.6 *notable*; 518.23, 520.1 *visible*
conspicuous consumption 681.4 *extravagance*; 349.6 *use*
conspicuously 738.16 *manifestly*; 185.10 *protuberantly*; 518.25, 520.11 *visibly*
conspicuousness 185.4; 738.10 *manifestation*; 520.3 *visibility*
conspiracy 750.2 *alliance*; 747.8 *conferring*; 374.2 *cooperation*; 645.1 *cunning*; 342.9 *overactivity*; 484.4 *plot*; 737.2 *secretiveness*; 662.3 *subversion*; 700.7 *tricking*
conspirational 737.10 *secretive*
conspirator 736.7 *concealer*; 747.10 *cooperator*; 645.3 *cunning person*; 484.8 *planner*; 700.20 *plotter*; 662.10 *seditionist*
conspiratorial 750.11 *allied*; 747.19 *associating*; 755.7 *contractual*; 374.8 *cooperative*; 700.35 *deceptive*; 484.15 *planning*; 662.14 *subversive*
conspiratorially 484.17; 755.8 *contractually*; 750.32 *in alliance*; 374.10 *in combination*; 737.16 *stealthily*; 662.18 *subversively*
conspire 645.5 *be cunning*; 662.16 *be subversive*; 374.6 *come together*; 747.15 *concur*; 750.22 *form an alliance*; 484.13 *plot*; 700.28 *trick*
conspirer 700.20 *plotter*
conspire with 169.9 *side with*
conspiring 750.11 *allied*; 645.4 *cunning*
constable 400.3 *leader*; 396.10 *person of authority*; 16.17 *police officer*
constabulary 16.14 *police*
constance 298.4 *orderliness*
constancy 640.3; 750.5 *conformity*; 132.5, 134.1 *continuity*; 569.3 *familiarity*; 297.4 *frequency*; 277.4 *long-lastingness*; 663.2 *loyalty*; 298.4 *orderliness*; 225.1 *permanence*; 799.1 *probity*; 111.6 *regularity*; 228.1 *stability*; 140.7, 698.9 *uniformity*; 638.15 *will*
constant 27.25 *algebraic expression*; 529.10 *coloured*; 750.14 *conforming*; 134.5 *continual*; 279.10 *continuing forever*; 132.11 *continuous*; 569.11 *devoted*; 202.3 *eternal*; 297.3 *frequent*; 27.77 *given*; 632.14 *habituated*; 799.4 *honourable*; 275.21 *lasting through time*; 663.8 *loyal*; 194.1 *number*; 298.14 *orderly*; 225.7 *permanent*; 112.14 *recurrent*; 111.17, 298.11 *regular*; 228.9 *stable*; 228.4 *stable thing*; 638.5, 640.11 *steady*; 140.11, 698.22 *uniform*
constant companion 223.12 *partner*
constant flow 132.5 *continuity*
constantly 750.35 *consistently*; 134.7 *continually*; 132.19 *continuously*; 569.19 *devotedly*; 202.12 *eternally*; 297.1 *frequently*; 799.7 *honourably*; 663.10 *obediently*; 298.17 *orderly*; 225.9 *permanently*; 111.20, 298.15 *regularly*; 228.12 *stably*
constant supply 436.1 *provision*; 439.3 *supply*
constellation 29.9; 376.28 *cluster*
consternation 606.1 *dissatisfaction*; 612.2 *fearfulness*; 619.1 *wonder*
constipate 416.8 *be dense*; 360.7 *detain*; 309.8 *stop*
constipated 416.7 *condensed*; 360.9 *retentive*; 309.13 *stopped*
constipating 416.7 *condensed*
constipation 309.1 *closure*; 416.2 *concentration*; 560.2 *defecation*; 260.8 *indigestion*; 360.5 *retentiveness*
constituency 469.12 *election*; 86.5 *state*
constituent 205.4, 405.1, 405.6 *component*; 406.10 *containing*; 469.13 *electorate*; 127.8 *included*; 99.7 *integral*; 402.4 *matter*; 127.2 *thing included*
constituently 405.14
constituents 406.1 *contents*; 435.1 *materials*
constitute 405.10 *compose*; 99.12, 406.8 *embody*; 127.4 *include*; 356.10 *produce*
constituted 406.10 *containing*
constituted authority 396.1 *authority*
constituting 405.9 *composing*; 127.1 *inclusion*
constitution 140.2 *canon*; 406.1 *contents*; 403.3 *form*; 259.3 *health*; 127.1 *inclusion*; 99.4 *nature*; 12.5 *political organization*; 713.3 *precept*; 404.1 *texture*; 16.1 *the law*
constitutional 250.9 *free*; 12.9, 396.14 *governmental*; 257.1 *hygiene*; 172.11 *intrinsic*; 16.46 *legislated*; 99.8 *quintessential*; 632.3 *way*
constitutional anthropology 1.10 *measurement*
constitutional government 12.1 *government*; 396.7 *type of rule*
constitutional history 3.1 *history*
constitutionalism 12.1 *government*; 16.31 *legislation*
constitutionality 16.31 *legislation*
constitutional law 16.1 *the law*
constitutionally 396.24 *ministerially*; 12.14 *politically*
constitutional monarchy 12.1 *government*; 396.7 *type of rule*
constitutional psychology 36.1 *psychology*
constitutional rights 250.2 *free speech*
constrain 386.6 *compel*; 387.7 *defeat*; 386.7 *force*; 166.7 *limit*; 685.4 *moderate*; 728.22 *play down*; 251.8 *restrain*
constrained 728.19 *downplayed*; 674.13, 728.15 *reserved*; 251.13 *restraining*
constraining 386.9 *compelling*
constrain oneself 684.5 *be self-restrained*
constraint 386.2 *coercion*; 728.9 *downplaying*; 166.1 *limitation*; 674.6, 728.5 *reserve*; 251.1 *restraint*; 684.1 *self-restraint*; 387.1 *subjection*
constrict 191.5 *make smaller*; 685.4 *moderate*; 151.10 *narrow*; 251.8 *restrain*; 309.8 *stop*
constricted 151.1 *narrow*; 191.7 *smaller*; 309.13 *stopped*
constricting 191.8 *contracting*
constriction 309.1 *closure*; 416.2 *concentration*; 191.1 *contraction*; 151.5 *narrowness*; 251.1 *restraint*
constrictive 191.8 *contracting*; 416.6 *dense*; 251.13 *restraining*
constrictively 416.10 *densely*
constrictor 191.4 *contractor*; 73.3 *snake*
constringe 191.5 *make smaller*
constringency 191.1 *contraction*
constringent 191.8 *contracting*
construct 403.16; 20.18 *be an architect*; 232.4 *complete*; 403.6 *construction*; 38.30 *engineer*; 154.18 *erect*; 553.9 *fashion*; 160.7 *form*; 446.1 *idea*; 405.13 *make*; 356.10 *produce*; 376.44 *put together*; 27.96 *represent*
constructed 160.9 *formed*
construction 356.8; **403.6**; 38.17 *civil engineering*; 476.3 *conjecture*; 160.1 *form*; 160.4 *forming*; 27.49 *geometric construction*; 127.1 *inclusion*; 719.1 *interpretation*; 356.2 *manufacture*; 376.33 *putting together*; 38.19 *structure*; 694.4 *type of meaning*
constructional 38.32, 403.11 *structural*
constructionally 20.20 *architecturally*; 38.33, 403.18 *structurally*
construction engineering 38.17 *civil engineering*
construction equipment 38.29
constructionism 403.9 *artistic structure*
construction material 38.25
construction site 577.1 *workshop*
construction worker 578.1 *worker*
constructive 716.8 *evidential*; 392.33 *helpful*; 719.14 *interpretive*; 356.11 *productive*

constructive criticism 713.1 *advice*; 464.1 *judgment*; 392.2 *support*
constructively 405.14 *constituently*; 160.13 *formatively*; 392.36 *helpfully*
constructivism 21.10 *theatre movements*
constructivist 21.42 *activist*; 19.29 *realist*
constructor 356.9 *producer*
construe 719.8 *interpret*; 4.21 *rationalize*
construing 5.30 *syntax*
consubstantial 111.12 *same*
consubstantiality 111.1 *sameness*
consubstantially 111.18 *identically*
consubstantiate 111.8 *make the same*
consubstantiation 10.6 *Eucharist*; 111.1 *sameness*
consuetude 632.5 *tradition*
consul 398.6 *agent*; 398.1 *delegate*; 400.3 *leader*; 579.16 *official*; 396.10 *person of authority*
consular 398.9 *delegated*
consular agent 398.6 *agent*
consulate 565.4 *official residence*; 396.5 *position of authority*; 398.2 *representative body*
consulate service 398.2 *representative body*
consul general 400.3 *leader*; 396.10 *person of authority*
consul-general 398.6 *agent*
consult **713.6**; 734.11 *confer*; 35.19 *practise medicine*
consultant 392.14, 713.4 *adviser*; 35.11 *doctor*; 396.11, 400.10, 485.5 *expert*; 475.9 *forecaster*; 35.13 *medical specialist*; 136.8 *qualified person*; 748.4 *representative*; 4.12 *sage*; 139.14 *specialist*
consultation **713.2**; 734.4 *conference*; 747.8 *conferring*; 243.9 *preparation*
consultative 713.7 *advising*; 734.13 *discussing*
consultative assembly 579.10 *legislative body*
consultative body 713.4 *adviser*; 579.7 *council*
consultatory 734.13 *discussing*
consulting room 35.10, 394.14 *hospital*
consumable 557.27 *edible*; 349.10 *usable*
consumably 557.29 *edibly*
consumate liar 700.16 *liar*
consume **357.12**; **787.2**; 375.3 *disintegrate*; 349.5 *dispose of*; 557.21 *eat*; 135.9 *find necessary*; 245.5 *hurt*; 766.9 *lose*; 335.7 *remove power from*; 773.7 *take*; 349.1 *use*; 441.1 *waste*
consumed 349.9 *used*
consumed with jealousy 629.4 *jealous*
consumer 557.18 *eater*; 34.18 *ecology*; 13.9 *economist*; 402.3 *materialist*; 777.12 *purchaser*; 349.8 *user*
consumer confidence 13.6 *economic factors*
consumer consumption 135.2 *need*
consumer demand 777.11 *custom*; 135.2 *need*
consumer durables 778.8 *merchandise*
consumer goods 13.2 *economy*; 778.8 *merchandise*
consumer questionnaire 778.7 *market*
consuming 357.14 *destructive*; 557.1 *eating*; 236.5 *harmful*
consummate 232.7 *complete*; 131.15 *end*; 400.13 *excellent*; 230.1, 230.5 *perfect*; 99.8 *quintessential*; 174.5 *top*
consummate liar 699.18 *liar*
consummately 400.16 *masterfully*; 230.7 *perfectly*
consummate one's marriage 570.15 *marry*
consummation 232.1 *completeness*; 232.3 *completion*; 593.5 *desire*; 230.3 *perfection*
consummative 131.20 *ending*
consummatory 131.20 *ending*
consumption 191.1 *contraction*; 214.1 *decrease*; 557.1 *eating*; 236.11 *harmfulness*; 260.6 *infection*; 370.4 *intake*; 135.2 *need*; 260.9 *respiratory disease*; 773.1 *taking*; 349.6 *use*; 441.3 *waste*
consumptive 260.23 *diseased*; 260.19 *sick person*; 191.7 *smaller*
contact 492.12 *abut*; 398.6 *agent*; 373.3 *associate*; 693.10 *informer*; 373.13 *intercommunicate*; 147.3 *juxtaposition*; 2.15 *socialize*; 492.11 *touch*; 316.3 *transmission*
contact again 633.13 *follow up*
contact herbicide 43.14 *pest control*
contact insecticide 43.14 *pest control*
contact lenses 28.29 *optical element*; 518.10 *visual aid*
contact metamorphism 30.32 *metamorphism*
contact print 41.12 *development*; 111.4 *duplicate*
contacts 518.10 *visual aid*
contact sport 45.4 *sporting activity*
contagion 245.10 *impairment*; 260.6 *infection*; 395.1 *influence*; 412.1 *mixture*; 260.5 *plague*; 316.3 *transmission*
contagious 395.12 *appealing*; 260.23 *diseased*; 316.17 *transferable*
contagious disease 260.4 *disease*; 245.10 *impairment*; 316.10 *transferred thing*
contagiously 395.14 *influentially*; 412.14 *in the midst*; 316.18 *in transit*
contagiousness 260.6 *infection*
contain **406.6**; 309.7 *close*; 405.11 *consist of*; 360.7 *detain*; 141.20 *extend*; 447.10 *focus on*; 127.4, 550.32 *include*; 172.15 *keep inside*; 166.7 *limit*; 170.7 *surround*; 165.6 *wrap*
contained 410.20 *containing*; 360.10 *retained*
Container 410
container **203.3**; **410.1**; 439.4 *storage*; 319.2 *thing transported*; 316.10 *transferred thing*; 319.5 *transportable*; 165.4 *wrapper*
containerization 319.1 *transport*
containerize 406.6 *contain*; 410.21 *put in a container*
containerload 406.2 *load*
containing **406.10**; **410.20**; 405.9 *composing*; 127.7 *including*; 406.11 *loaded*
containment 360.2 *detention*; 127.1 *inclusion*; 166.1 *limitation*
contaminant 128.6 *thing excluded*
contaminate 412.10 *become mixed*; 236.13 *be worthless*; 395.9 *change*; 258.11 *dirty*; 76.16 *infest*; 238.8 *make useless*; 245.3 *make worse*; 412.8 *mix*; 316.11 *transfer*
contaminated 260.23 *diseased*; 258.8 *unclean*; 499.6 *unpalatable*
contaminating 236.5 *harmful*
contamination 245.10 *impairment*; 412.1 *mixture*; 236.10 *poverty*; 316.3 *transmission*; 258.2 *uncleanness*
contaminator 316.9 *disease carrier*
contango 791.1 *discount*
conte 17.2 *fiction*; 721.3 *narration*
contemplate 443.13 *concentrate*; 474.8 *expect*; 482.7 *intend*; 6.23 *learn*; 694.10 *mean*; 4.20 *philosophize*; 756.11 *promise oneself*; 518.16 *visualize*; 9.7 *worship*
contemplated 474.7 *expected*
contemplation 474.1 *expectation*; 6.8 *learning*; 4.4 *philosophical investigation*; 301.2 *repose*; 443.3 *thoughtfulness*; 518.4 *visualization*; 9.1 *worship*
contemplative 450.5 *believer*; 443.9 *concentrating*; 6.18 *educated*; 301.6 *quiescent*; 4.17 *thoughtful*; 9.9 *worshipful*
contemplatively 6.26 *studiously*; 4.28, 443.18 *thoughtfully*; 9.12 *worshipfully*
contemporaneity 295.1 *newness*; 285.1 *same time*; 223.2 *synchronism*
contemporaneous 223.18 *concurrent*; 282.6 *present*; 285.9 *simultaneous*
contemporaneously 223.23 *concurrently*; 285.12 *simultaneously*
contemporaneousness 285.1 *same time*
contemporarily 295.21 *newly*; 285.12 *simultaneously*
contemporariness 285.1 *same time*
contemporary **285.5**; 223.18 *concurrent*; 295.10 *new*; 282.6 *present*; 285.9 *simultaneous*; 447.6 *topical*
contemporary life 282.2 *the present day*
contempt **660.6**; **668.3**; 661.2 *disobedience*; 670.2 *disrespect*; 606.1 *dissatisfaction*; 622.11 *prejudice*; 660.8 *rudeness*; 678.5 *scorn*
contemptibility 594.4 *hatefulness*; 124.6 *obscurity*
contemptible 800.5 *dishonourable*; 668.12 *disregardful*; 798.7 *evil*; 594.12 *hated*; 124.2 *obscure*; 236.4 *poor*
contemptibleness 236.10 *poverty*
contemptibly 594.18 *hatefully*; 236.15 *worthlessly*
contemptuous **660.17**; **668.13**; 661.7 *defiant*; 606.4 *dissatisfied*; 594.10 *hating*; 622.23 *prejudiced*; 660.19 *rude*; 678.17 *scornful*
contemptuously **660.34**; **668.30**; 661.9 *defiantly*; 606.8 *discontentedly*; 678.18 *disparagingly*; 594.18 *hatefully*
contemptuousness 668.3 *contempt*; 661.2 *disobedience*; 606.1 *dissatisfaction*
contend 586.40 *argue*; 585.14 *battle*; 235.9 *be worthy*; 47.6 *compete in track and field*; 113.19 *confront*; 751.5 *disagree*; 4.23 *discuss philosophically*; 314.14 *enrol*; 45.6 *participate*; 447.11 *raise the point*
contender 336.5 *athlete*; 353.7 *attempter*; 586.1 *combatant*; 113.12 *competitor*; 314.7 *entrant*; 45.3 *sportsman*
contending 113.24 *discordant*
contend with 383.6 *resist*
content 669.18 *approving*; 263.4 *at ease*; 490.10 *comfort*; 405.1 *component*; 406.1 *contents*; 263.1 *ease*; 403.2 *fabric*; 217.3 *filled*; 749.6 *pacificatory*; 749.4 *pacify*; 490.7 *pleased*; 609.1 *satisfaction*; 609.4 *satisfied*; 609.8 *satisfy*; 158.1 *size*; 217.4 *suffice*; 217.7 *sufficiency*; 636.1 *willing*
contented 217.3 *filled*; 597.4 *happy*; 490.7 *pleased*; 609.4 *satisfied*; 673.9 *self-satisfied*
contentedly 609.13 *with satisfaction*
contentedness 609.1 *satisfaction*
contenting 217.1 *sufficient*
contention 113.5 *conflict*; 704.2 *denial*; 751.1 *disagreement*; 701.3 *line of argument*
contentious 381.21 *aggressive*; 701.10 *arguable*; 751.9 *disagreeing*; 113.24 *discordant*; 625.4 *irascible*; 16.52 *legalistic*
contentiously 751.11 *in disagreement*; 625.9 *irascibly*
contentiousness 751.1 *disagreement*; 625.1 *irascibility*
contentment 263.1 *ease*; 597.1 *happiness*; 490.1 *physical pleasure*; 609.1 *satisfaction*; 217.7 *sufficiency*
Contents 406
contents **406.1**; 172.4 *insides*; 694.1 *meaning*; 440.5 *personal estate*; 220.2 *table*; 127.2 *thing included*; 319.2 *thing transported*; 447.1 *topic*
contermand 399.3 *veto*
conterminous 147.10 *juxtaposed*
contest **69.2**; 701.13 *argue*; 585.14 *battle*; 453.18 *be uncertain*; 381.20 *bout*; 47.6 *compete in track and field*; 4.23 *discuss philosophically*; 705.20 *doubt*; 16.5 *litigation*; 708.11 *rebut*; 45.1 *sport*
contestability 453.9 *uncertainty*
contestable 453.1 *uncertain*
contest an office 752.13 *be a candidate*
contestant 353.7 *attempter*; 113.12 *competitor*
contest at law 16.70 *litigate*
contested 16.54 *litigated*; 708.18 *rejected*
contesting 16.53 *litigating*; 708.3 *rebuttal*
contest with 113.19 *confront*
context 143.2, 222.1 *circumstances*; 223.4 *concomitant*; 694.1 *meaning*; 694.4 *type of meaning*
contextual 223.17 *accompanying*; 143.8, 222.7 *circumstantial*
contextualism 4.7 *school of thought*
contextualist 4.11 *follower of a doctrine*; 4.14 *of a philosophy*
contextually 143.12 *circumstantially*; 222.16 *relatively*
contexture 403.2 *fabric*; 404.1 *texture*
contiguity **492.6**; 280.2 *closeness*; 147.3 *juxtaposition*
contiguous 147.10 *juxtaposed*; 147.9 *near*; 492.9 *touching*
contiguously 147.14 *beside*
contiguousness 147.3 *juxtaposition*
continence 795.3 *moral purity*; 251.3, 684.1 *self-restraint*; 572.2 *virginity*
continent **30.6**; **92.1**; 795.9 *pure*; 86.1 *region*; 251.14, 684.8 *self-restrained*; 560.26 *urinary*; 572.7 *virginal*
continental **92.11**; 100.10 *foreign*; 172.9 *inland*; 86.16 *regional*; 30.50 *terrestrial*
continental breakfast 557.12 *meal*
continental climate 31.38 *climate*
continental crust 30.18 *earth's crust*
Continental Divide 154.4 *mountain range*
continental divide 30.8 *drainage*
continental drift 30.6 *continent*; 30.19 *plate tectonics*
continental glacier 30.38 *glacier*
continental ice sheet 30.38 *glacier*
continental island 92.2 *island*
continentally **92.13**; 30.66, 86.19 *geographically*
continental margin 30.6 *continent*; 30.16 *ocean floor*
continental quilt 550.10 *bed covering*; 419.11 *soft thing*
continental rise 30.16 *ocean floor*
continental shelf 92.4 *coast*; 30.6 *continent*; 30.16 *ocean floor*; 86.3 *regional boundary*
continental slope 30.16 *ocean floor*
continental zone 31.39 *climatic zone*
continently 572.12 *celibately*
contingency 107.1 *chance*; 143.2, 222.1 *circumstances*; 474.2 *expectations*; 102.1 *possibility*; 27.64 *reasoning*
contingency plan 475.3 *plan*; 484.2 *policy*
contingent 345.10 *caused*; 107.8 *chance*; 143.8, 222.7 *circumstantial*; 136.12 *conditional*; 27.86 *logical*
contingently 143.12 *circumstantially*; 221.9 *conditionally*; 222.16 *relatively*; 136.18 *with qualification*; 345.12 *with the effect of*
contingents 586.14 *armed forces*
contingent truth 4.8 *philosophical term*
contingent upon 345.10 *caused*
continual **134.5**; 132.11 *continuous*; 300.17 *directional*; 202.3 *eternal*; 297.3 *frequent*; 93.12, 277.8 *lasting*; 298.14 *orderly*; 112.14 *recurrent*; 640.11 *steady*
continually **134.7**; **640.14**; 750.35 *consistently*; 132.19 *continuously*; 277.12 *everlastingly*; 297.1 *frequently*; 298.17 *orderly*; 112.23 *repeatedly*
continual movement 300.10 *regular movement*
continualness 132.5 *continuity*
continuance 640.3 *constancy*; 93.6 *continuing existence*; 132.5, 134.1 *continuity*; 225.1 *permanence*
continuation 211.1 *addition*; 134.1, 277.3 *continuity*; 275.3 *duration*; 359.1 *preservation*; 550.22 *progression*; 168.1 *rear*; 289.9 *sequel*; 289.1 *succession*
continue **132.14**; **134.3**; 297.7 *be frequent*; 202.9 *be infinite*; 215.7 *be left*; 225.5 *be permanent*; 633.14 *carry on*; 93.19 *continue to be*; 277.7 *go on*; 148.10 *lengthen*; 554.16 *live*; 640.7 *maintain*; 279.7 *make permanent*; 359.5 *preserve*; 550.35 *progress*; 134.4 *protract*
continued 168.4 *rear*
continued fraction 27.18 *division*
continue forever 279.5 *be eternal*
continue on 550.35 *progress*
continue the same 111.11 *be regular*
continue to be **93.19**
continue working 576.6 *work*
continuing 134.5 *continual*; 233.4 *incomplete*; 277.8 *lasting*; 302.18 *ongoing*; 225.7 *permanent*; 550.22 *progression*
continuing existence **93.6**
continuing forever **279.10**
continuing on 550.22 *progression*
Continuity 134
continuity **132.5**; **134.1**; **277.3**; 267.1 *adhesion*; 17.3 *aspect of fiction*; 750.5 *conformity*; 279.1 *eternity*; 297.4 *frequency*; 147.3 *juxtaposition*; 298.4 *orderliness*; 225.1 *permanence*
continuity of germ plasm 34.16 *evolution*
continuo 516.4 *harmonics*
continuous **132.11**; **178.3**; 267.9 *adhesive*; 750.14 *conforming*; 134.5 *continual*; 279.10 *continuing forever*; 300.17 *directional*; 202.3 *eternal*; 147.10 *juxtaposed*; 93.12, 277.8 *lasting*; 225.7 *permanent*; 550.41 *progressing*; 112.14 *recurrent*; 32.32 *solid*; 27.70 *universal*
continuous beam 38.27 *superstructure*
continuous distortion 27.47 *topology*
continuous distribution 27.59 *probability distribution*
continuous function 27.29 *mathematical function*
continuously **132.19**; 147.14 *beside*; 750.35 *consistently*; 134.7 *continually*; 277.12 *everlastingly*; 27.87 *mathematically*; 225.9 *permanently*
continuous motion 132.6 *continuum*
continuousness 132.5, 134.1, 277.3 *continuity*; 298.4 *orderliness*
continuous phase 32.3 *phase*
continuous spectrum 28.68 *emission*

continuous-wave radar 692.28 *radar*
continuum 132.6; 141.9 *fourth dimension*
contort 234.9 *distort;* 234.10 *make faces*
contorted 180.5 *ambiguous;* 546.4 *ugly*
contortedly 234.13 *asymmetrically*
contortedness 546.1 *ugliness*
contortion 234.1 *distortion;* 234.2 *facial distortion*
contortionist 336.5 *athlete;* 21.31 *circus performer*
contour 525.3 *external appearance;* 160.1 *form;* 27.37 *line;* 163.1 *outline;* 608.6 *profile;* 163.2 *shadow*
contour feather 72.17 *plumage*
contour line 163.1 *outline*
Contra 662.11 *rebel*
contraband 16.59 *stolen;* 774.4 *stolen goods;* 16.36 *stolen property;* 399.5 *vetoed*
contraception 563.3 *birth control;* 394.3 *prophylactic;* 252.2 *protection*
contraceptive 563.3 *birth control;* 347.4 *counteracting;* 347.2 *counteracting thing*
contraceptive injection 563.3 *birth control*
contraceptive pill 563.3 *birth control;* 394.8 *drug*
contraceptive sponge 563.3 *birth control*
Contract 755
contract 354.3; **755.1**; **755.5**; 409.10 *agreement;* 750.23 *arrange;* 750.3 *arrangement;* 776.3 *bargain;* 776.9 *bargaining;* 746.2 *basis for negotiations;* 191.6 *become smaller;* 269.4 *be concise;* 416.8 *be dense;* 69.3 *card game terms;* 810.7 *commitment;* 214.4 *decrease;* 245.1 *deteriorate;* 756.2 *guarantee;* 191.5, 214.5 *make smaller;* 151.10 *narrow;* 163.5 *outline;* 756.1, 756.7 *promise;* 309.8 *stop;* 723.8 *summarize;* 354.1 *undertake*
contract a disease 260.24 *be unhealthy*
contract a marriage 755.5 *contract*
contracted 269.3 *concise;* 755.7 *contractual;* 756.13 *guaranteeing;* 15.8 *industrial;* 159.7 *little;* 151.1 *narrow;* 723.7 *shortened;* 191.7 *smaller*
contracted thing 191.3
contractibility 191.2
contractible 191.9
contractile 191.9 *contractible*
contractility 191.2 *contractibility*
contracting 191.8; 15.8 *industrial*
contracting party 755.4 *contractor*
Contraction 191
contraction 191.1; 309.1 *closure;* 269.1 *conciseness;* 214.1 *decrease;* 305.1 *descent;* 151.9 *narrowing;* 163.1, 723.2 *outline*
contractional 191.8 *contracting*
contractions 561.7 *obstetrics*
contractive 191.8 *contracting*
contract killer 651.8 *malefactor;* 382.11 *murderer*
contract matrimony 570.15 *marry*
contract murder 382.2 *murder*
contract of employment 15.1 *industrial relations*
contractor 191.4; **755.4**; 353.7 *attempter;* 38.18 *civil engineer;* 340.3 *doer;* 356.9 *producer*
contract theory of morality 4.9 *philosophical problem*
contractual 755.7; **776.18**; 750.12 *arranged;* 15.8 *industrial;* 354.5 *undertaken*
contractually 755.8; 15.13 *industrially;* 354.8 *responsibly*
contractual obligations 15.2 *industrial negotiations*
contradict 706.18 *answer back;* 701.13 *argue;* 113.15 *be opposite;* 708.16 *cancel out;* 704.9 *deny;* 4.23 *discuss philosophically;* 709.6 *dissent;* 694.10 *mean;* 113.18 *object;* 753.6 *protest;* 708.11 *rebut*
contradicting 670.26 *disagreeing;* 708.19 *rebutting*
contradiction 708.7 *cancelling out;* 706.5 *counterstatement;* 704.2 *denial;* 670.4 *disagreement;* 709.2 *dissent;* 311.1 *divergence;* 113.4 *objection;* 113.2 *oppositeness;* 753.1 *protest;* 27.64 *reasoning;* 708.3 *rebuttal*
contradiction in terms 702.2 *sophism*
contradictive 708.17 *negative;* 753.9 *protesting*
contradictively 753.11 *disapprovingly*
contradict oneself 702.11 *practise sophistry*
contradictorily 708.22 *negatively;* 113.27 *opposingly;* 709.11 *uncooperatively*
contradictory 113.25 *contrary;* 670.26 *disagreeing;* 709.9 *dissenting;* 481.9 *dissuasive;* 311.6 *divergent;* 27.86 *logical;* 708.17 *negative;* 704.7 *refuting;* 702.7 *sophistic*
contradictory law 16.4 *bad law*
contradictory meaning 694.4 *type of meaning*
contradistinction 113.8 *contrariety*
contraflow 378.2 *obstacle*
contraindication 481.6 *dissuasion*
contralto 510.3 *deepness;* 516.5 *melodist*
contrapose 113.15 *be opposite*
contraposition 113.8 *contrariety;* 113.2 *oppositeness*
contrapositive 113.23 *opposite*
contraption 484.3 *expedient plan;* 348.2 *instrument;* 438.1 *tool*
contrapuntal 750.13 *harmonious;* 18.32 *instrumental*
contrapuntal music 18.3 *classical music*
contraries 113.2 *oppositeness*
contrariety 113.8; 118.2 *dissent;* 311.1 *divergence;* 479.5 *equivocalness;* 113.2 *oppositeness*
contrarily 701.18 *arguably;* 347.5 *counter;* 753.11 *disapprovingly;* 249.12 *in adversity;* 708.22 *negatively;* 709.11 *uncooperatively;* 378.16 *with delay*
contrariness 113.7; 661.1 *defiance;* 378.1 *hindrance;* 113.2 *oppositeness;* 708.3 *rebuttal*
contrariwise 113.30; 192.4 *inversely;* 113.23 *opposite;* 110.10 *reciprocally*
contrary 113.25; 249.6 *adverse;* 701.8 *argumentative;* 708.20 *cancelled;* 642.1 *capricious;* 347.4 *counteracting;* 517.8 *disagreeing;* 709.9 *dissenting;* 481.9 *dissuasive;* 378.13 *hindering;* 192.1 *inversion;* 694.6 *meaningful;* 708.17 *negative;* 118.12 *nonconformist;* 113.23 *opposite;* 113.22 *oppositional;* 753.9 *protesting;* 708.3 *rebuttal;* 641.2 *refractory;* 704.7 *refuting;* 264.14 *troublesome;* 113.26 *uncooperative*
contrary advice 481.6 *dissuasion*
contrary assertion 708.3 *rebuttal*
contrary to 347.5 *counter;* 113.31 *opposed to*
contrary to expectation 105.9 *unexpectedly*
contrary-to-fact 699.36 *falsified*
contrary to law 16.55 *illegal;* 16.82 *illegally*
contrary to orders 662.17 *disobediently*
contrary to reason 103.1 *impossible*
contrary vote 709.2 *dissent*
contrast 116.5 *be dissimilar;* 114.8 *be diverse;* 113.15 *be opposite;* 41.8 *composition;* 113.8 *contrariety;* 113.21 *counteract;* 116.1 *dissimilarity;* 114.1 *diversity;* 108.2 *interrelatedness;* 28.23 *light;* 118.1 *nonconformity;* 113.2 *oppositeness;* 108.7 *relate to;* 692.22 *television set;* 116.2 *unlikeness*
contrasted 113.25 *contrary*
contrasting 113.25 *contrary;* 116.4 *dissimilar;* 114.5 *diverse;* 118.11 *nonconforming;* 113.23 *opposite*
contrastingly 116.7 *dissimilarly;* 113.27 *opposingly*
contrastive linguistics 5.1 *linguistics*
contrastively 113.28 *in opposition*
contravallation 384.8 *military defences*
contravene 347.3 *counteract;* 704.9 *deny;* 113.18 *object;* 753.6 *protest;* 708.11 *rebut*
contravened 708.18 *rejected*
contravening 347.4 *counteracting;* 709.9 *dissenting;* 704.7 *refuting*
contravention 347.1 *counteraction;* 704.2 *denial;* 16.38 *lawbreaking;* 113.4 *objection;* 753.1 *protest;* 708.3 *rebuttal*
contredanse 22.4 *historic dancing*
contre partie 23.9 *decorative woodwork*
contretemps 288.4 *mishap;* 378.2 *obstacle*
contribute 405.10 *compose;* 785.8 *defray;* 787.3 *donate;* 679.11 *give;* 764.4 *have joint possession;* 752.16 *make an offering;* 413.13 *support financially;* 229.4 *tend;* 747.13 *work together*
contributed 787.12 *expended*
contributes 436.5 *provision*
contribute to 211.6 *add;* 344.12 *determine;* 392.29 *finance;* 302.8, 392.28 *further;* 768.6 *give to charity;* 213.5 *make bigger*
contributing 750.11 *allied;* 768.1 *giving;* 395.11 *influential*
contributing factor 344.4
contribution 211.3 *additional item;* 344.4 *contributing factor;* 787.7 *donation;* 392.6 *financial assistance;* 413.7 *financial support;* 679.7 *gift;* 768.1 *giving;* 785.4 *grant;* 752.6, 768.3 *offering;* 764.2 *participation;* 785.1 *payment;* 229.1 *tendency;* 729.7 *utterance*
contributor 344.8; 722.3 *dissertator;* 679.9 *generous person;* 768.4 *giver;* 752.8 *volunteer*
contributory 211.8 *additional;* 747.17 *cooperative;* 768.7 *given;* 392.33 *helpful;* 395.11 *influential;* 752.19 *sacrificial;* 413.9 *supportive*
contributory cause 344.4 *contributing factor*
con trick 800.3 *criminality;* 774.7 *dishonesty;* 812.3 *disreputable action*
contrite 806.6 *appearing guilty;* 807.4 *atoning;* 808.6 *penitent*
contritely 806.11 *guiltily;* 807.8, 808.8 *penitently*
contrite sinner 808.3 *penitent person*
contrition 807.2 *apology;* 808.1 *penitence;* 806.2 *signs of guilt*
contriturate 427.22 *pulverize*
contrivance 17.3 *aspect of fiction;* 239.3 *convenience;* 484.3 *expedient plan;* 800.1 *improbity;* 348.2 *instrument;* 449.9 *invention;* 352.1 *means;* 389.2 *means of escape;* 484.7 *planning;* 485.1 *skill;* 706.6 *solution;* 702.2 *sophism;* 645.2 *stratagem;* 631.9 *tactics;* 438.1 *tool;* 700.8 *trick*
contrive 344.10 *awaken;* 645.5 *be cunning;* 243.2 *do the groundwork;* 352.6 *find means;* 478.3 *improvise;* 449.4, 484.11 *invent;* 409.18 *make arrangements;* 484.9 *plan;* 702.11 *practise sophistry;* 106.2 *premeditate;* 706.20 *solve;* 700.28 *trick*
contrive a result 106.2 *premeditate*
contrived 700.35 *deceptive;* 106.4 *deliberate;* 477.12 *imaginary;* 484.14 *planned;* 706.14 *solved;* 702.7 *sophistic*
contriver 484.8 *planner*
contriving 645.4 *cunning;* 700.34 *deceiving;* 484.15 *planning*
control 340.4 *act;* 340.1 *action;* 140.8, 396.1, 397.3 *authority;* 348.4 *be an instrument;* 395.10 *be a prevailing influence;* 631.14 *behave towards;* 334.10 *be powerful;* 387.7 *defeat;* 4.3 *detachment;* 140.16 *direct;* 579.4 *directorship;* 407.9 *discipline;* 349.5 *dispose of;* 387.2 *domination;* 12.11 *govern;* 12.3 *governance;* 396.18 *have authority;* 397.11 *have authority over;* 378.8 *hinder;* 378.1 *hindrance;* 121.2 *leadership;* 166.7 *limit;* 166.1 *limitation;* 579.1 *manage;* 579.3 *management;* 400.14 *master;* 685.4 *moderate;* 685.1 *moderation;* 407.22 *pacify;* 395.3 *personal influence;* 763.1 *possession;* 334.1 *power;* 448.2 *rehearsal;* 251.8 *restrain;* 251.1 *restraint;* 485.1 *skill;* 136.6 *specification;* 136.16 *specify;* 631.8 *treatment;* 349.6 *use*
control character 40.10 *character*
controllable 387.10 *dominating;* 251.13 *restraining*
controllably 251.16 *under restraints*
controlled 51.9 *bowls;* 136.12 *conditional;* 106.4 *deliberate;* 4.18 *detached;* 407.17 *disciplined;* 685.6 *moderate;* 251.13 *restraining;* 36.37 *subconscious*
controlled access highway 317.3 *road*
controlled association 36.27 *association of ideas*
controlled-association test 36.5 *psychological test*
controlled blur 41.13 *framing*
controlled nuclear fusion 28.72 *nuclear fission*
controlled shot 51.2 *grip*
controller 400.5 *company leader;* 40.19 *computing terms;* 579.13 *director;* 340.3 *doer;* 12.7 *governor;* 685.2 *moderator;* 780.18 *treasurer*
controlling 396.12 *authoritative;* 387.10 *dominating;* 12.10 *governing;* 579.17 *managerial;* 400.12 *masterful;* 251.13 *restraining;* 140.12 *ruling;* 397.15 *self-assured*
controlling body 579.6 *governing body*
control one's appetite 684.5 *be self-restrained;* 687.5 *fast*
control oneself 255.9 *be pure;* 684.5 *be self-restrained;* 803.8 *be virtuous;* 251.10 *restrain oneself*
control one's lusts 684.5 *be self-restrained*
control one's passions 803.8 *be virtuous*
control prices 251.9 *economize*
control results 579.1 *manage*
control rods 28.73 *nuclear reactor*
controls 579.5 *guide;* 692.22 *television set*
control the purse strings 396.18 *have authority*
control tower 322.4 *airport*
controversial 701.10 *arguable;* 586.34 *argumentative;* 751.9 *disagreeing;* 114.7, 709.9 *dissenting;* 705.14 *questionable;* 453.1 *uncertain*
controversialist 586.5, 701.6 *arguer*
controversially 586.41 *aggressively;* 701.18 *arguably;* 751.11 *in disagreement;* 705.24 *questionably;* 453.23 *uncertainly;* 709.11 *uncooperatively*
controversion 113.4 *objection*
controversy 701.1 *argument;* 705.4 *difficult question;* 751.1 *disagreement;* 114.4 *dissension;* 709.2 *dissent;* 113.4 *objection*
controvert 453.18 *be uncertain;* 704.9 *deny;* 113.18 *object;* 708.11 *rebut*
controvertibility 453.9 *uncertainty*
controvertible 453.1 *uncertain*
contumacious 408.20 *disorderly;* 668.11 *insulting;* 118.12 *nonconformist;* 641.2 *refractory*
contumacy 661.2 *disobedience;* 641.5 *obstinacy*
contumelious 668.13 *contemptuous;* 660.13 *insolent;* 678.17 *scornful*
contumely 661.3 *act of defiance;* 668.3 *contempt;* 118.2 *dissent;* 660.1 *insolence*
conturbation 327.1 *agitation*
contuse 491.11 *inflict pain*
contusion 491.3 *injury;* 427.4 *pulverization*
conundrum 737.4 *brain-teaser;* 705.4 *difficult question;* 479.5 *equivocalness;* 264.4 *problem;* 696.12 *unintelligible thing*
conurbation 87.1 *city*
convalesce 393.4 *be restored;* 336.7 *be strong;* 244.2 *get better;* 259.6 *get healthy*
convalescence 259.3 *health;* 244.5 *improvement;* 393.11 *recuperation;* 336.4 *strengthening*
convalescent 393.15 *cured;* 259.1 *healthy*
convalescent home 35.10, 394.14 *hospital*
convalescing 336.4 *strengthening*
convect 316.11 *transfer*
convection 31.9 *atmospheric process;* 28.36 *heat flow;* 316.3 *transmission*
convection cell 31.10 *air movement*
convection heater 493.3 *heater*
convective 31.43 *atmospheric*
convene 376.42 *call together*
convened 376.46 *assembled*
convener 376.34 *assembler;* 15.7 *employee*
Convenience 239
convenience 239.3; **239.5**; **392.7**; 97.4 *availability;* 560.13 *lavatory;* 580.1 *leisure;* 147.1 *nearness;* 280.7 *prepared for immediate use;* 243.21 *ready-made;* 287.1 *timeliness;* 237.5 *usefulness;* 265.3 *wieldiness*
convenience food 557.7 *food*
conveniences 352.1 *means*
convenience store 779.8 *store*
convenient 239.1; 97.10 *available;* 617.8 *desirable;* 392.33 *helpful;* 147.9 *near;* 292.14 *seasonable;* 287.6 *timely;* 349.9 *used;* 237.1 *useful;* 265.12 *wieldy*
conveniently 239.7; 392.36 *helpfully;* 580.8 *leisurely;* 287.9 *opportunely;* 237.12, 349.11 *usefully*
convent 165.2 *enclosed place;* 7.10 *priestly dwelling;* 736.6 *privacy*
conventicle 579.7 *council;* 10.11 *place of worship*
convention 117.5; **750.6**; 755.3 *alliance;* 750.3 *arrangement;* 376.5, 734.4 *conference;* 579.7 *council;* 140.6 *custom;* 553.4 *design;* 656.5 *etiquette;* 160.5 *formality;* 658.2 *good manners;* 749.1 *pacification;* 713.3 *precept;* 398.2 *representative body;* 10.1 *ritual;* 632.5 *tradition*
conventional 750.15; 216.1 *average;* 138.21 *common;* 117.14 *conformist;* 140.10 *customary;* 160.11, 656.6 *formal;* 658.8

good-mannered; 632.11 *normal*; 178.4 *traditional*
conventional bombing 381.13 *air attack*
conventionalism 117.4; 656.2 *formalism*; 632.6 *procedure*
conventionalist 117.6 *conformist*; 632.8 *creature of habit*
conventionality 216.4 *average*; 656.2 *formalism*; 656.1 *formality*; 632.6 *procedure*
conventionalize 656.9 *formalize*; 216.10 *make average*; 750.26 *make uniform*
conventionally 160.14; **750.37**; 117.19 *according to rule*; 656.12 *formally*; 658.15 *genteelly*; 632.19 *habitually*
conventional medicine 35.1 *medicine*
conventional representation 717.1 *representation*
conventional symbol 742.1 *sign*
conventional weapon 587.1 *weapon*
convention delegate 578.3 *agent*; 398.1 *delegate*
conventions 631.6 *way of life*
convent school 6.12 *educational institution*
conventual 165.7 *enclosed*; 7.7 *monk*
converge 310.9; 492.12 *abut*; 27.97 *align*; 425.14 *be sharp*; 173.9 *centre*; 331.2 *collide*; 374.5 *combine*; 90.7 *flow*; 151.10 *narrow*; 147.16 *near*
Convergence 310
convergence 310.1; 376.1 *assembly*; 173.3 *centrality*; 331.12 *collision*; 492.6 *contiguity*; 151.9 *narrowing*; 147.1 *nearness*; 90.6 *river flow*
convergence zone 30.19 *plate tectonics*
convergent 310.7; 173.7 *centralized*; 376.48 *cumulate*; 90.10 *fluvial*; 27.80 *linear*; 363.10 *magnetic*; 147.9 *near*; 425.1 *sharp*; 151.3 *tapered*
convergent evolution 34.16 *evolution*
convergently 310.12; 90.13 *fluently*
convergent series 27.20 *sequence*
convergent strabismus 519.2 *poor sight*
convergent view 310.3
converge on 173.9 *centre*
converging 173.7 *centralized*; 310.1 *convergence*; 310.7 *convergent*; 147.9 *near*
converging lens 28.29 *optical element*
converging line 310.5 *focus*
converging lines 27.37 *line*
conversableness 654.2 *social ambition*
conversant 632.14 *habituated*
conversant with 6.19, 455.8 *knowledgeable*
Conversation 734
conversation 734.1; 729.1 *faculty of speech*; 4.5 *philosophical argument*; 654.1 *sociability*; 504.8 *something heard*
conversational 734.14; 731.6 *effusive*; 5.39 *of language*
conversationalism 5.3 *spoken language*
conversationalist 734.7; 706.10 *answerer*; 654.6 *social person*; 729.10 *speaker*
conversationally 734.15; 5.49 *colloquially*; 706.24 *in answer*
conversation piece 19.10 *art subject*
conversation poem 17.7 *poem*
conversazione 654.3 *meeting*; 734.3 *social gathering*
converse 734.9; 734.1 *conversation*; 192.1 *inversion*; 27.86 *logical*; 113.23 *opposite*; 113.2 *oppositeness*; 706.19 *react*; 27.64 *reasoning*
conversely 113.28 *in opposition*; 192.4 *inversely*
converser 734.7 *conversationalist*
converse with 733.9 *approach*
conversing 734.12
Conversion 760
conversion 760.1; 479.7 *apostasy*; 224.2 *change of mind*; 759.1 *exchange*; 244.5 *improvement*; 808.1 *penitence*; 46.6 *scoring*; 224.3 *transformation*; 349.6 *use*
conversion goal 64.3 *rugby play*
conversion hysteria 36.12 *stress*
conversion neurosis 36.10 *neurosis*
conversion to use 349.6 *use*
convert 760.6; 224.7 *be changed*; 450.5 *believer*; 7.19 *be religious*; 224.8 *cause change*; 116.6 *differentiate*; 759.5 *exchange*; 349.3 *exploit*; 244.1 *improve*; 450.9 *make someone believe*; 480.15, 760.11 *persuade*; 46.15 *play offence*; 7.20 *preach*; 7.3 *religious person*
convert a try 64.5 *play rugby*
converted 760.13; 450.11 *believing*; 51.10 *bowling*; 759.7 *exchanged*; 760.16 *influenced*; 808.6 *penitent*; 64.6 *rugger*
converted split 51.5 *bowling delivery*
converter 760.5; 24.6 *ceramic workshop*; 224.5 *changer*; 39.34 *power supply*
convertibility 760.1 *conversion*; 349.6 *use*
convertible 760.15; 320.16 *car*; 119.6 *equal*; 759.6 *in exchange*; 349.10 *usable*; 23.14 *wooden*
convertible bond 780.14 *paper money*
convertible sofa 23.6 *bed*
convertibly 760.18; 349.11 *usefully*
converting 760.14; 760.1 *conversion*
convert into 760.7; 759.5 *exchange*; 760.9 *transform*
convertive 224.13 *transformative*
convert to use 349.3 *exploit*
convex 182.4; 177.4 *curved*; 27.81 *curvilinear*; 181.9 *round*
Convexity 182
convexity 182.1; 177.1 *curvature*; 181.1 *roundness*; 27.38 *surface*
convex lens 28.29 *optical element*
convexly 182.6; 177.7 *curvedly*; 181.13 *roundly*
convex mirror 28.29 *optical element*
convexness 182.1 *convexity*
convex surface 27.38 *surface*
convey 693.12 *communicate*; 631.15 *conduct*; 755.5 *contract*; 318.11 *cross*; 768.5 *give*; 694.10 *mean*; 778.1 *sell*; 300.14 *set in motion*; 729.11 *speak*; 316.12, 319.4 *transport*
conveyable 746.8 *negotiated*; 316.17 *transferable*
convey a meaning 694.10 *mean*
convey a message 694.10 *mean*
conveyance 768.1 *giving*; 316.5 *means of transport*; 778.3 *selling*; 316.2 *transportation*
conveyancer 316.7 *transferor*
convey an idea 694.10 *mean*
conveyor 38.29 *construction equipment*; 366.10 *elevator*; 316.7 *transferor*; 319.3 *transporter*
conveyor belt 620.2 *boring thing*; 132.6 *continuum*; 356.2 *manufacture*; 316.5 *means of transport*
convict 16.79; 251.7 *charge*; 806.4 *guilty person*; 16.40 *lawbreaker*; 815.5 *prisoner*
convicted 16.64; 806.5 *guilty*
convicted criminal 806.4 *guilty person*
conviction 16.43; **452.10**; 450.1 *belief*; 610.2 *expectation*; 806.1 *guilt*; 7.1 *religion*
conviction of guilt 806.1 *guilt*
convict oneself 16.80
convince 609.9 *comfort*; 726.6 *emphasize*; 452.21 *make certain*; 450.9 *make someone believe*; 483.9 *motivate*; 480.15 *persuade*; 7.20 *preach*
convinced 452.2; 450.11 *believing*
convinced person 452.11 *opinionist*
convince oneself 476.5 *suppose*
convince to the contrary 481.1 *dissuade*
convincing 450.13 *believable*; 386.9 *compelling*; 721.11 *descriptive*; 726.3 *emphatic*; 483.11 *motivational*; 480.19 *persuasive*; 336.10 *potent*
convincingly 336.15 *acutely*; 450.16 *believably*; 386.11 *compellingly*; 483.14 *influentially*; 480.21 *persuasively*
convivial 601.10 *celebrative*; 598.1 *cheerful*; 490.6 *pleasant*; 654.15 *sociable*
conviviality 601.1 *celebration*; 598.3 *cheerfulness*; 490.1 *physical pleasure*; 654.1 *sociability*
convivially 654.18 *sociably*
convivial person 654.6 *social person*
convivio 734.4 *conference*
convocation 601.3 *ceremony*; 376.5 *conference*; 579.7 *council*; 656.3 *formal occasion*; 376.3 *meeting*
convocational 579.18 *parliamentary*
convoke 376.42 *call together*
convolute 180.6
convoluted 408.16 *confused*; 180.4 *convolutional*; 189.4 *oblique*; 266.2 *obscure*; 542.10 *ornate*; 264.12 *problematic*
convolutedness 180.1 *convolution*
convoluted thing 180.3
Convolution 180
convolution 180.1; 542.2 *affectation*; 210.1 *calculation*; 27.31 *differentiation*; 264.1 *difficulty*; 189.1 *obliqueness*; 266.1 *obscurity*
convolutional 180.4
convolve 180.6 *convolute*
convoy 223.1 *accompaniment*; 223.15 *escort*; 586.23 *naval unit*; 252.10 *protect*; 252.2 *protection*
convulse 327.21 *be agitated*; 328.7 *disturb*; 491.11 *inflict pain*
convulsed 408.17 *discomposed*; 328.12 *disturbed*; 491.7 *feeling pain*
convulsion 624.4 *anger*; 328.1 *disturbance*; 380.3 *instance of violence*; 461.3 *mental deterioration*; 491.1 *pain*; 327.8 *spasm*
convulsive 327.19; 380.6 *violent*
convulsively 327.29 *jerkily*
convulsive therapy 36.3 *psychiatric treatment*
Conwy 90.4 *British rivers*
coo 515.2 *bird song*; 515.5 *sing*; 729.13 *speak in a particular way*
co-occurrence 223.2 *synchronism*
cook 25.2; **25.55**; 493.14 *be hot*; 436.4 *caterer*; 243.7 *develop*; 401.6 *domestic servant*; 557.20 *food provider*; 412.7 *person who mixes*; 243.15 *preparer*; 578.1 *worker*
cookbook 740.6 *book publishing*; 25.1 *cookery*
cooked 25.56 *culinary*
cooked-up 715.9 *perjurious*
cooked-up charge 715.2 *false accusation*
cooker 25.5; 493.4 *burner*; 28.35 *heat*
cooker hood 501.2 *deodorant*
Cookery 25
cookery 25.1
cookery book 740.6 *book publishing*; 25.1 *cookery*
cook for 557.25 *provide food*; 436.5 *provision*
cookhouse 25.3 *kitchen*
cookie 25.2 *cook*; 40.16 *Internet*; 25.39 *loaf*; 593.12 *nicknames for lovers*
cooking 25.1 *cookery*; 243.17 *developing*
cooking equipment 62.4 *climbing equipment*
cooking pot 25.6 *kitchen equipment*; 410.15 *pot*
cooking salt 25.7 *basic ingredient*
cooking smells 503.2 *something that makes an unpleasant smell*
cooking technique 25.8
cooking utensil 25.6 *kitchen equipment*
cookout 557.13 *feast*
cook's helper 25.2 *cook*
cook's knife 425.10 *knife*
cook somone's goose 246.10 *defeat heavily*
cook the accounts 789.7 *account*
cook the books 774.16 *act dishonestly*; 800.10 *be criminal*; 700.30 *be fraudulent*; 13.12 *cheat*; 699.26 *falsify*
cook the evidence 715.6 *accuse falsely*
cook up 691.10 *drug oneself*; 96.17 *fabricate*; 484.13 *plot*
cook up a charge 715.6 *accuse falsely*
cool 31.55; 494.8 *cold*; 660.17 *contemptuous*; 4.18 *detached*; 4.3 *detachment*; 228.11 *determined*; 481.5 *discourage*; 473.4 *disinterested*; 553.7 *fashionable*; 334.12 *generate power*; 797.1 *good*; 618.7 *indifferent*; 18.33 *jazz*; 685.4, 685.6 *moderate*; 301.6 *quiescent*; 581.1 *refresh*; 581.4 *refreshed*; 581.3 *refreshing*; 145.9 *reserved*; 251.14 *self-restrained*; 655.8 *unsociable*; 619.14 *wonderful!*; 235.1 *worthy*
coolant 494.4 *cooler*; 38.9 *machine tool*; 334.8 *nuclear power*; 28.73 *nuclear reactor*
cool as a cucumber 301.6 *quiescent*
cool bag 410.8 *bag*; 494.4 *cooler*
cool box 410.6 *box*; 494.4 *cooler*
cool breeze 581.6 *refresher*
cool, calm, and collected 685.6 *moderate*
cool climate 31.38 *climate*
cool down 494.11 *become cold*; 407.22 *pacify*; 581.1 *refresh*
cooled 434.17 *ventilated*
cooled off 581.4 *refreshed*
cooler 494.4; 309.4 *closed place*; 31.55 *cool*; 815.2 *the inside*
cool-headed 4.18 *detached*
cool-headedness 4.3 *detachment*
coolhouse 44.4 *nursery*
cool hue 529.3 *hue*
coolie 316.7 *transferor*; 578.1 *worker*
coolie hat 551.15 *headgear*
coo like a dove 749.4 *pacify*
cooling 494.1 *coldness*; 494.9 *heat-resistant*; 581.3 *refreshing*; 31.47 *windy*
cooling down 581.5 *refreshment*
cooling fluid 38.9 *machine tool*
coolingly 31.65 *meteorologically*
cooling off 581.5 *refreshment*
cooling-off period 294.3 *delayed action*; 361.6 *interruption*; 226.3 *pause*
cooling system 28.35 *heat*
cooling tower 494.4 *cooler*
coolish 494.8 *cold*
cool it 301.8 *be motionless*; 419.14 *ease*; 749.5 *make peace*; 226.12, 301.11 *stop!*; 388.3 *submit*; 265.20 *take it easy*
cool jazz 18.8 *jazz*
coolly 494.13 *coldly*; 660.34 *contemptuously*; 228.13 *determinedly*; 473.8 *disinterestedly*; 618.17 *indifferently*; 581.8 *refreshingly*; 145.11 *reservedly*; 4.27 *stoically*; 655.14 *unsocially*
cool million 780.3 *fortune*; 781.6 *money*
coolness 31.31, 494.1 *coldness*; 4.3 *detachment*; 228.2 *determination*; 618.1 *indifference*; 685.1 *moderation*; 581.5 *refreshment*; 145.4 *reserve*; 655.1 *unsociability*
cool off 494.11 *become cold*; 618.12 *be indifferent*; 581.2 *be refreshed*; 407.22 *pacify*; 226.9 *pause*; 581.1 *refresh*
cool one's heels 294.7 *wait*
cool one's temper 749.4 *pacify*
cool out 419.14 *ease*; 251.10 *restrain oneself*
cool welcome 470.5 *rejection*
coomb 92.8 *valley*
coombe 156.4 *deep thing*
coonskin hat 551.15 *headgear*
coop 309.4 *closed place*; 309.10 *enclose*; 43.7 *farm building*; 565.12 *stall*
cooper 578.2 *artisan*; 23.13 *carpenter*
cooperant 747.17 *cooperative*
cooperate 636.14; **747.11**; 348.4 *be an instrument*; 374.6 *come together*; 754.4 *compromise*; 755.5 *contract*; 759.5 *exchange*; 413.14 *give moral support*; 764.4 *have joint possession*; 392.22 *improve*; 110.8 *interrelate*
cooperating 747.17 *cooperative*
cooperatingly 747.20 *cooperatively*
Cooperation 747
cooperation 374.2; **747.1**; 754.1 *compromise*; 755.1 *contract*; 759.1 *exchange*; 569.1 *friendship*; 636.9 *goodwill*; 392.10 *helpfulness*; 348.1 *instrumentality*; 147.8 *interaction*; 110.2 *interconnection*; 346.2 *joint operation*; 413.6 *moral support*; 764.2 *participation*; 654.1 *sociability*
cooperative 374.8; **747.17**; 392.35 *benevolent*; 13.6 *economic factors*; 569.8 *friendly*; 636.4 *helpful*; 348.6 *instrumental*; 110.5 *interconnected*; 764.5 *jointly possessing*; 747.4 *joint operation*; 764.1 *joint possession*; 413.9 *supportive*
cooperative enterprise 747.4 *joint operation*
cooperative hospital 35.10 *hospital*
cooperative living 554.1 *life*
cooperatively 747.20; 392.38 *benevolently*; 374.10 *in combination*; 764.6 *in common*; 569.17 *in friendship*; 348.9 *instrumentally*; 110.10 *reciprocally*
cooperativeness 747.1 *cooperation*
cooperative system 764.1 *joint possession*
cooperator 747.10; 413.8 *supporter*
coopt 469.1 *select*
cooptation 469.6 *selection*
cooption 469.6 *selection*
coordinate 115.5 *counterpart*; 119.7 *dividing line*; 119.6 *equal*; 119.11 *equalize*; 5.44 *grammatical*; 750.24 *harmonize*; 136.15 *modify*; 409.13 *organize*; 32.26 *react*; 162.4 *symmetrical*; 162.6 *symmetrize*
coordinate bond 32.11 *chemical bond*
coordinate clause 205.2 *particular*
coordinate conjunction 5.35 *part of speech*
coordinated 750.13 *harmonious*; 136.11 *modified*
coordinate geometry 27.34 *geometry*
coordinateness 162.1 *symmetry*
coordinates 27.33; 142.2 *exact location*; 27.36 *point*; 372.7 *separates*; 26.4 *size*; 28.7 *space*; 551.10 *suit*
coordinate system 27.33 *coordinates*
coordination 750.4 *harmony*; 346.2

joint operation; 407.7 *method*; 136.5 *modification*; 409.3 *organization*
coordination complex 32.7 *chemical compound*
coordination compound 32.7 *chemical compound*
coot 72.3 *water bird*
cootie 76.3 *pest*
co-ownership 747.5 *joint control*
cop 396.10 *person of authority*; 16.17 *police officer*; 252.3 *protector*; 253.3 *security officer*; 773.10 *take away*; 773.3 *taking away*; 492.11 *touch*
copacetic 797.1 *good*; 235.1 *worthy*
copartner 764.3 *participant*
copartnership 747.5 *joint control*; 764.1 *joint possession*
copartnery 747.5 *joint control*
cope 174.3 *architectural summit*; 7.11 *vestment*
Copenhagen 59.3 *warhorse*
Copenhagen interpretation 28.80 *quantum theory*
copepod 75.4 *arthropod*
Copernican universe 29.4 *cosmological model*
copestone 174.3 *architectural summit*
cope with 119.10 *be equal*; 631.14 *behave towards*
copied 772.11 *borrowed*; 198.12 *double*; 111.15 *duplicate*; 699.35 *fraudulent*; 125.13 *imitation*; 700.39 *imitative*; 19.27 *painted*; 744.16 *recorded*; 561.15 *reproduced*; 115.8 *simulated*
copier **115.3**; **125.8**; 774.10 *infringer*; 125.6 *photocopier*
co-pilot 322.3 *aircraft personnel*; 586.32 *airman*
coping 174.3 *architectural summit*
coping stone 174.3 *architectural summit*
copious 679.3 *abundant*; 208.9 *ample*; 270.3 *diffuse*; 562.5 *fertile*; 217.2 *plentiful*
copiously 270.7 *diffusely*; 217.9 *enough*; 679.12 *generously*
copiousness 270.1 *diffuseness*; 217.8 *plenty*
cop it 582.15 *die*; 264.21 *get into trouble*
coplanar 27.79 *spatial*
copolymer 32.21 *polymer*
copolymeric 32.44 *polymeric*
cop out 754.5 *be irresolute*; 714.9 *cover up*; 634.5 *shirk*; 388.3 *submit*; 355.2 *withdraw*
cop-out 714.3 *cover-up*; 355.4 *deserter*; 754.7 *irresolute*; 754.3 *irresolution*; 355.3 *relinquishment*; 634.13 *shirking*; 388.1 *submission*
Coppelia 22.11 *classical ballets*
copper 534.1 *brown*; 39.3 *electricity*; 33.15 *essential element*; 493.3 *heater*; 536.3 *orange thing*; 396.10 *person of authority*; 16.17 *police officer*; 252.3 *protector*; 253.3 *security officer*; 256.7 *washer*
copper coinage 780.13 *coinage*
copper-coloured 534.1 *brown*
copper engraving 19.15 *engraving*
copperplate 550.24 *coat*; 550.3 *coating*; 19.15 *engraving*
copperplated 550.36 *covered*
coppers 780.4 *change*
copper's nark 693.10 *informer*
coppery 534.1 *brown*; 536.1 *orange*
coppice 79.18 *manage trees*; 79.1 *tree*; 79.4 *trees*
coppicing 79.6 *tree management*
copremesis 560.2 *defecation*
coprolalia 5.19 *swearword*
coprolite 560.5 *faeces*; 30.43 *fossil*
coprolith 560.5 *faeces*
coprophilous 83.10 *of fungi*
cops and robbers 113.3 *opposites*
copse 79.4 *trees*
copsy 79.16 *wooded*
copter 322.8 *aircraft*
copula 593.5 *desire*; 373.4 *means of connection*; 5.35 *part of speech*
copular 5.44 *grammatical*
copulate 374.6 *come together*; 561.14 *have sex*; 593.29 *make love*
copulation 554.4 *biological function*; 593.5 *desire*; 561.3 *propagation*
copy **115.2**; **125.2**; **125.10**; **741.10**; **744.5**; 40.20 *abort*; 525.11 *appear*; 699.25 *be fraudulent*; 772.9 *borrow illegally*; 117.8 *comply*; 115.5 *counterpart*; 116.3 *disguise*; 198.15 *double*; 19.20 *draw*; 111.4, 111.9 *duplicate*; 699.12 *fake*; 115.12 *imitate*; 525.5 *impression*; 774.15 *infringe*; 743.3 *means of identification*; 19.7 *picture*; 561.2 *print*; 744.13 *record*; 112.16 *repeat*; 112.7 *replica*; 717.9 *represent*; 717.1 *representation*; 561.9 *reproduce*; 316.16 *translate*; 198.5 *twin*
copy after 125.9 *imitate*
copy aide 401.5 *office assistant*
copybook 140.10 *customary*; 6.14 *school book*
copycat 117.6 *conformist*; 112.8 *creature of habit*; 125.13 *imitation*; 115.4 *person who copies*
copy desk 741.8 *newsroom*
copy-edit 719.8 *interpret*; 740.15 *publish*; 244.3 *rectify*
copy editing 244.6 *rectification*
copy editor 719.6 *interpreter*; 740.11 *newspaperman*; 740.12 *publisher*; 393.12 *repairer*; 244.13 *reviser*
copyhold 440.3 *historic property terms*; 440.8 *propertied*
copying 19.3 *drawing*; 772.3, 774.6 *illegal borrowing*; 125.1 *imitation*; 112.1 *repetition*; 561.1 *reproduction*; 115.1 *similarity*; 316.4 *translation*
copyist 19.16 *artist*; 125.8 *copier*; 115.4 *person who copies*; 717.4 *person who makes a representation*
copy nature 698.34 *render*
copyright 166.7 *limit*; 166.2 *limiting factor*; 743.3 *means of identification*; 126.7 *originate*; 440.1 *property*; 251.8 *restrain*; 251.1 *restraint*
copyrighted 126.6 *authentic*; 166.5 *limited*; 440.8 *propertied*; 251.13 *restraining*
copyrighted work 126.2 *original*
copywriter 740.10 *publicizer*
CoQ 33.12 *coenzyme*
coq au vin 25.45 *French dish*
coquet 642.5 *be capricious*; 593.26 *court*
coquetry 593.6 *courtship*; 593.4 *lovability*; 642.3 *whim*
coquette 642.4 *capricious person*; 479.9 *equivocator*; 593.9 *lover*; 732.5 *shy person*
coquettish 593.20 *amorous*; 642.1 *capricious*
coquettish glances 593.6 *courtship*
coquettishly 593.30 *lovingly*
coquettishness 642.2 *caprice*
coquettish smile 593.14 *communication of love*
coral 70.5 *aquatic animal*; 535.1 *red*
coral island 92.2 *island*
coralline 75.21 *coelenterate*
coralloid 75.21 *coelenterate*
coral-pink 535.1 *red*
coral reef 92.2 *island*; 157.4 *shallow thing*; 379.1 *trap*
coram judice 16.87 *in litigation*; 16.54 *litigated*
coram populo 16.87 *in litigation*; 16.54 *litigated*
corbel 20.9 *miscellaneous architectural features*
corbel arch 20.5 *arch*
cord 334.7 *electrical power*; 373.6 *line*; 79.3 *timber*; 39.27 *wire*
cordage 373.7 *tackle*; 79.3 *timber*
cordate 77.18 *of leaves*
cordial **496.6**; 558.7 *alcoholic drink*; 650.6 *benevolent*; 569.8 *friendly*; 636.4 *helpful*; 241.2 *likable*; 590.12 *sensitive*; 654.15, 657.8 *sociable*; 558.6 *soft drink*; 498.5 *sweet drink*; 394.7 *tonic*; 493.12 *warm-hearted*
cordiality 241.8 *amiability*; 650.1 *benevolence*; 569.1 *friendship*; 654.8 *good company*; 590.5 *good feeling*; 636.9 *goodwill*; 654.1, 657.2 *sociability*
cordially 569.17 *in friendship*; 241.15 *pleasantly*; 654.18 *sociably*
cordial relations 589.1 *peace*
cordial welcome 654.9 *welcome*
cordillera 89.1 *mountain*; 154.4 *mountain range*
cordite 587.15 *explosive*; 330.13 *fuel*
cordless 39.36 *electronic*
cordless appliance 39.27 *wire*
cordless telephone 692.9 *telephone*
cordon 44.10 *fruit tree*; 20.9 *miscellaneous architectural features*
cordon bleu 485.4 *skilled person*; 794.1 *trophy*
cordon bleu chef 25.2 *cook*
cordon sanitaire 257.1 *hygiene*; 359.1 *preservation*; 394.3 *prophylactic*; 252.2 *protection*
cords 551.9 *trousers*
corduroy 420.7 *rough thing*; 193.4 *textile*
corduroy material 184.4 *wrinkled thing*
corduroy road 317.3 *road*
cordwainer 551.26 *fashion designer*
cordwood 79.3 *timber*; 23.12 *wood*
core 173.1 *centre*; 123.3 *chief thing*; 30.18 *earth's crust*; 99.2 *essential content*; 172.5 *inner nature*; 172.2 *inside*; 406.3 *insides*; 694.1 *meaning*; 437.7 *nuclear power*; 28.73 *nuclear reactor*
core curriculum 6.3 *subject*
core of one's being 590.8 *seat of feelings*
co-respondent 571.3 *divorce court*; 211.5 *extra person*
core store 40.6 *memory*
coriaceous 423.3 *hard*
coriander 496.5 *herbs*
Corinthian 20.16 *columned*
Corinthian order 20.8 *column*
Coriolis force 31.9 *atmospheric process*
cork 550.2, 550.23 *cover*; 360.7 *detain*; 360.2 *detention*; 55.3 *fishing tackle*; 415.7 *light thing*; 309.8 *stop*; 309.2 *stopper*; 79.3 *timber*
corkage 790.3 *fee*
corked 550.36 *covered*; 245.12 *deteriorated*; 231.1 *imperfect*; 309.13 *stopped*; 499.6 *unpalatable*
corker 235.8 *exceller*; 797.17 *good thing*; 246.4 *successful person*
corking 797.1 *good*; 235.1 *worthy*
corkscrew 180.2 *coil*; 180.6 *convolute*; 369.10 *excavator*; 308.2 *opener*
cork-tip 496.7, 496.11 *tobacco*
corky 428.3 *dried-up*
corm 78.2 *flowering plant*; 44.9 *garden plant*; 77.5 *stem*
cormorant 688.4 *glutton*; 72.3 *water bird*
cormous 77.14 *of plants*
corn 558.7 *alcoholic drink*; 557.8 *animal food*; 182.2 *bulge*; 43.12 *crop*; 418.7 *hard substance*; 260.15 *ulcer*
corn belt 43.11 *farmland*
corn borer 76.3 *pest*
corn bread 25.38 *bread*; 25.43 *US dish*
corn chafer 76.3 *pest*
corncob 81.4 *cereal grass*
corn drill 43.10 *farm tool*
cornea 518.2 *eye*
corneal graft 394.12 *surgery*
corned 359.7 *preserved*
corneous 418.1 *hard*
corner 27.39, 176.1 *angle*; 381.9 *attack successfully*; 52.2 *boxing*; 320.3 *carriageway*; 264.23 *cause difficulties*; 325.14 *deviating course*; 222.4 *difficult circumstances*; 58.1 *hockey*; 814.14 *instrument of punishment*; 61.6 *motor-racing terms*; 763.7 *possess*; 777.1 *purchase*; 62.5 *rock face*; 68.14 *ski*; 52.5 *wrestling*
corner area 66.1 *soccer*
cornerback 46.10 *defence*
corner cupboard 23.5 *cabinet*
cornered 176.7 *angular*; 254.4 *endangered*
corner flag 64.1 *rugger*; 66.1 *soccer*
cornering 306.2 *circuitousness*; 320.21 *miscellaneous motoring terms*; 777.7 *purchasing*; 68.4 *skiing technique*
cornering of the market 763.1 *possession*
corner judge 52.7 *judo*
corner kick 66.2 *football play*
cornerman 61.8 *driver*
corner shop 779.8 *store*
cornerstone 123.3 *chief thing*; 99.2 *essential content*; 228.4 *stable thing*; 413.2 *supporting part*
corner the market 763.7 *possess*; 777.1 *purchase*; 13.10 *trade with*
cornet 181.5 *cone*
corn exchange 779.1 *market*
cornfield 43.11 *farmland*
cornflakes 25.40 *breakfast cereal*
cornflour 25.7 *basic ingredient*
cornflower 539.6 *blue thing*
corn god 8.5 *deity*
cornhusk 550.13 *casing*
cornice 174.3 *architectural summit*; 20.19 *decorate*
corniced 20.17 *structured*
corniculate 425.4 *toothed*
Cornish accent 5.26 *dialect*
Cornish stone 24.2 *raw material*
corn liquor 558.7 *alcoholic drink*
corn market 779.1 *market*
cornmeal 25.7 *basic ingredient*
corn plaster 394.10 *surgical dressing*
corn pone 25.38 *bread*
CORN rule 32.13 *structure*
cornucopia 562.1 *fertility*; 781.7 *opulence*; 217.8, 557.9 *plenty*; 439.3 *supply*
cornute 425.4 *toothed*
corn whisky 558.7 *alcoholic drink*
corny 599.10 *humorous*
corolla 78.3 *flower part*
corollary 211.3 *additional item*; 223.4 *concomitant*; 345.1 *effect*; 5.25 *inscription*; 464.1 *judgment*; 27.65 *theory*
corona 179.3 *circular thing*; 522.12 *highlight*; 29.15, 31.22 *sun*; 496.7 *tobacco*
coronach 603.2 *lament*
corona discharge 39.6 *electric discharge*
coronary 260.10 *cardiovascular disease*
coronary bypass graft 394.12 *surgery*
coronary heart disease 260.10 *cardiovascular disease*
coronary thrombosis 260.10 *cardiovascular disease*; 260.4 *disease*
coronate 396.21 *grant authority*
coronation 396.3 *acquisition of power*; 601.3 *ceremony*; 656.3 *formal occasion*
coroner 16.23 *judge*; 464.6 *justice*; 582.9 *person dealing with the dead*; 705.9 *questioner*
coroner's court 16.19 *law court*; 464.3 *place of judgment*
coroner's jury 464.7 *jury*
coronet 179.3 *circular thing*; 551.15 *headgear*; 743.8 *heraldic device*
corporal 586.17 *army person*; 402.7 *material*; 814.19 *punitive*
corporality 402.1 *material world*
corporally 402.9 *materially*
corporal punishment **814.12**; 331.12 *collision*
corporate **776.19**; 750.11 *allied*; 764.5 *jointly possessing*
corporate bond 780.14 *paper money*
corporate income 765.4 *earnings*
corporately 750.32 *in alliance*; 204.12 *one and all*
corporate plan 484.1 *plan*
corporate sector 13.2 *economy*
corporate tax 790.7 *tax*
corporation **13.7**; 374.3 *assembly*; 376.15 *association*; 776.7 *company*; 158.8 *fat*; 16.2 *jurisdiction*; 402.2 *materialization*
corporative state 12.5 *political organization*
corporeal 402.7 *material*; 95.6 *real*
corporeality 402.1 *material world*; 95.1 *reality*
corporealize 402.8 *be material*
corporeity 402.1 *material world*
corposant 522.9 *firefly*
corps 586.16 *army unit*; 376.1 *assembly*; 376.14 *force*; 376.12 *team*
corps à corps 54.3 *fencing movements*
corps commander 584.5 *military staff*
corps de ballet 22.13 *ballet dancer*; 21.25 *cast*
corps d'élite 586.14 *armed forces*; 235.7 *elite*
corps diplomatique 398.2 *representative body*
corpse 582.11 *dead person*; 215.1 *remainder*
corpse candle 522.9 *firefly*
corpse-like 582.21 *deathly*; 153.2 *emaciated*
corpulence 158.5 *fatness*; 414.4 *heaviness*; 181.2 *round body*; 152.5 *thickness*
corpulent 158.16 *fat*; 414.1 *heavy*; 152.1 *thick*; 181.10 *well-rounded*
corpus 723.3 *compendium*; 376.30 *compilation*; 402.4 *matter*; 204.2 *whole thing*
corpuscle 34.7 *cell*; 159.2 *little thing*
corpuscular 159.7 *little*
corpus juris 713.3 *precept*; 16.1 *the law*
Corpus Juris Canonici 16.1 *the law*
Corpus Juris Civilis 16.1 *the law*
corradiate 310.11 *focus*
corral 71.20 *abode of mammals*; 309.4 *closed place*; 165.5, 309.10 *enclose*; 165.2 *enclosed place*; 43.7 *farm building*; 376.43 *herd*; 43.18 *practise livestock farming*
corralling 376.2 *herding*
correct **273.6**; **801.8**; 698.21 *accurate*; 117.10 *assimilate*; 698.31 *be accurate*; 117.14 *conformist*; 543.3 *elegant*; 656.6 *formal*; 658.8 *good-mannered*; 693.11 *inform*; 27.86 *logical*; 685.4 *moderate*; 5.39 *of language*; 407.13 *orderly*; 230.1, 230.5 *perfect*; 814.1 *punish*; 244.3 *rectify*; 394.19

remedy; 393.1 *repair*; 393.13 *repaired*; 407.21 *tidy*
correct behaviour 656.1 *formality*
correct dress 551.3, 656.4 *formal dress*
corrected copy 244.8 *better thing*
corrected proof 244.8 *better thing*
correct English 5.29 *grammar*
correct for 27.93 *equate*
correcting faults 393.8 *repair*
correction 685.1 *moderation*; 814.7 *punishment*; 244.6 *rectification*; 394.1 *remedy*; 393.8 *repair*; 801.5 *righting wrong*
correctional 2.13 *communal*; 814.19 *punitive*
correctional institution 2.8 *human institution*
correctional officer 815.6 *prison officer*
correction facility 815.1 *prison*
correction fluid 358.4 *eraser*; 521.6 *that which makes invisible*
correctitude 656.1 *formality*; 230.3 *perfection*
corrective 347.4 *counteracting*; 814.19 *punitive*; 394.17 *remedial*; 394.1 *remedy*
correctively 347.5 *counter*
corrective training 815.7 *imprisonment*
correctly **801.20**; 273.8, 698.39 *accurately*; 57.12 *competitively*; 656.12 *formally*; 658.15 *genteelly*; 5.52 *grammatically*; 801.18 *properly*
correctness **273.2**; **801.2**; 698.8 *accuracy*; 549.1 *elegance*; 656.1 *formality*; 658.2 *good manners*; 57.1 *gymnastics*; 407.5 *orderliness*; 230.3 *perfection*; 801.3 *properness*; 27.64 *reasoning*
corrector 227.4 *editor*; 814.17 *punisher*; 244.13 *reviser*
correct speech 5.6 *official language*
correct style 5.29 *grammar*
correlate **110.9**; **188.6**; 706.21 *answer to*; 108.8 *be proportionate to*; 750.25 *conform*; 27.93 *equate*; 759.5 *exchange*; 162.6 *symmetrize*
correlated **188.4**; 750.14 *conforming*; 110.6 *correlative*; 108.5 *interrelated*
correlating 110.6 *correlative*
correlation **27.61**; **110.3**; 750.5 *conformity*; 706.8 *correspondence*; 759.1 *exchange*; 108.2 *interrelatedness*; 747.3 *mutual relationship*; 188.1 *parallelism*; 108.1 *relatedness*; 162.1 *symmetry*
correlational 110.6 *correlative*; 747.18 *joint*; 162.4 *symmetrical*
correlation coefficient 27.61 *correlation*
correlative **110.6**; 223.18 *concurrent*; 750.14 *conforming*; 188.4 *correlated*; 706.15 *correspondent*
correlatively **110.11**; 706.26 *correspondingly*; 759.8 *in exchange*
correlativity 110.3 *correlation*
correspond **692.31**; 706.21 *answer to*; 115.10 *be similar*; 111.7 *be the same*; 117.7, 750.25 *conform*; 110.9, 188.6 *correlate*; 516.8 *harmonize*; 721.15 *recount*
correspondence **692.3**; **706.8**; 692.1 *communications*; 117.1, 750.5 *conformity*; 110.3 *correlation*; 119.1 *equality*; 111.2 *equivalence*; 693.4 *mass communication*; 188.1 *parallelism*; 744.1 *record*; 108.1 *relatedness*; 115.1 *similarity*; 162.1 *symmetry*
correspondence column 740.3 *journalism*
correspondence course 6.2 *educational system*
correspondent **692.5**; **706.15**; 715.4 *accused person*; 706.10 *answerer*; 750.14 *conforming*; 188.4 *correlated*; 110.6 *correlative*; 115.5 *counterpart*; 721.10 *descriptive writer*; 119.6 *equal*; 693.9 *informant*; 741.4 *journalist*; 740.11 *newspaperman*; 162.4 *symmetrical*
correspondently 111.18 *identically*
corresponding 117.12, 750.14 *conforming*; 188.4 *correlated*; 110.6 *correlative*; 706.15 *correspondent*; 119.6 *equal*; 111.13 *equivalent*; 516.7 *harmonious*; 108.5 *interrelated*; 115.7 *similar*; 162.4 *symmetrical*
correspondingly **706.26**; 115.14 *comparably*; 110.11 *correlatively*; 119.12 *equally*; 111.18 *identically*; 108.10 *relevantly*; 115.13 *similarly*; 162.7 *symmetrically*
correspond to 119.10 *be equal*; 108.8 *be proportionate to*
correspond with 239.6 *be convenient*; 692.31 *correspond*
corridor 151.6 *narrow place*; 308.7 *passageway*; 86.6 *regions*; 565.7 *room*; 317.2 *route*
corridors of power 396.6 *place of authority*
corrie 156.4 *deep thing*; 92.8 *valley*
corrigendum 274.12 *typing error*
corrigible 244.15 *improvable*
corrival 113.12 *competitor*
corroborate 707.19 *confirm*; 95.12 *establish reality*; 413.14 *give moral support*; 743.10 *identify*; 714.8 *justify*; 757.3 *permit*; 454.2, 703.17, 716.12 *prove*; 698.30 *prove true*
corroborated 743.12 *identified*; 698.20 *proved*; 703.13 *proven*; 707.13 *supported*
corroboration 698.7, 707.4 *confirmation*; 714.2 *defence*; 743.1 *identification*; 413.6 *moral support*; 757.1 *permission*; 454.5, 703.4, 716.2 *proof*
corroborative 716.8 *evidential*; 703.13 *proven*; 413.9 *supportive*; 454.9 *verificatory*; 714.11 *vindicatory*
corroboratively 454.11 *verifiably*
corroborator 707.9 *affirmer*; 413.8 *supporter*
corroboree 22.4 *historic dancing*
corrode 245.2 *decay*; 214.4 *decrease*; 375.3 *disintegrate*; 365.14 *erode*; 245.5 *hurt*; 212.3 *subtract*
corroded 375.5 *disintegrated*; 212.7 *reduced*
corroding 375.6 *disintegrating*
corrosion 357.7 *agent of destruction*; 38.16 *deformation*; 245.9 *dilapidation*; 375.1 *disintegration*; 212.1 *subtraction*; 365.2 *wearing away*
corrosive 357.7 *agent of destruction*; 214.7 *decrescent*; 798.9 *detrimental*; 236.5 *harmful*
corrosively 212.9 *decreasingly*; 375.8 *destructively*
corrugate 180.6 *convolute*; 420.12 *make rough*; 184.10 *pleat*; 184.8 *wrinkle*
corrugated 420.2 *coarse*; 180.4 *convolutional*; 420.1 *rough*; 184.6 *wrinkly*
corrugated iron 420.7 *rough thing*; 184.4 *wrinkled thing*
corrugated paper 184.4 *wrinkled thing*
corrugation 180.2 *coil*; 184.2 *furrow*; 184.3 *pleat*; 420.6 *roughness*
corrupt **796.19**; 798.11 *be evil*; 236.13 *be worthless*; 480.17 *bribe*; 777.4 *buy off*; 245.2 *decay*; 245.12 *deteriorated*; 258.11 *dirty*; 800.5 *dishonourable*; 375.3 *disintegrate*; 798.7 *evil*; 802.15 *immoral*; 804.17 *make wicked*; 245.3 *make worse*; 16.60 *offending*; 245.6 *pervert*; 236.4 *poor*; 258.8 *unclean*; 804.11 *wicked*
corrupted 375.5 *disintegrated*; 5.42 *worded*
corruptible 800.5 *dishonourable*
corrupting 796.12 *indecent*
corruption 777.10 *bribery*; 16.39 *crime*; 245.9 *dilapidation*; 375.1 *disintegration*; 798.1 *evil*; 800.1 *improbity*; 796.2 *indecency*; 5.5 *nonstandard language*; 245.8 *perversion*; 236.10 *poverty*; 503.2 *something that makes an unpleasant smell*; 258.2 *uncleanness*; 804.1 *wickedness*
corruptive 798.9 *detrimental*
corruptly 800.11 *dishonourably*; 798.12 *evilly*; 804.18 *wickedly*
corsage 502.2 *fragrant thing*; 551.24 *part of garment*
corsair 774.9 *plunderer*
corset 191.4 *contractor*; 251.5 *means of restraint*; 413.5 *supporting garment*; 551.18 *underwear*
corslet 384.7 *armour*
cortege 223.10 *attendance*; 583.2 *funeral*; 132.8 *procession*
Cortes 579.10 *legislative body*
cortex 550.14 *animal covering*; 171.1 *exterior*; 77.5 *stem*
corticolous 84.8 *lichenoid*
corticosteroid 37.4 *drug type*; 33.16 *hormone*
cortisone 394.8 *drug*
coruscate 522.25 *light up*
coruscating 522.16 *bright*
coruscation 522.2 *quality of light*
corvee 576.1 *work*
corvette 586.24 *warship*
corvine 72.21 *avian*
corymb 78.4 *flower head*
corymbose 78.12 *of flowers*
coryphaeus 579.14 *leader*
coryphée 21.30 *dancer*
coryza 494.3 *chill*; 260.9 *respiratory disease*
Cosa Nostra 804.7 *criminality*
cosecant 27.52 *trigonometric function*
cosh 587.7 *blunt weapon*; 331.8 *club*; 814.14 *instrument of punishment*; 331.16 *weapons*
co-sharing 119.6 *equal*; 764.2 *participation*
così-così 216.3 *mediocre*
cosidou 25.53 *African dish*
cosign 755.5 *contract*
cosign a loan 784.7 *be in debt*
cosign a note 756.8 *guarantee*
cosignatory 756.5 *promise-maker*
cosignature 755.1 *contract*
cosigned 755.7 *contractual*; 756.13 *guaranteeing*
cosigner 755.4 *contractor*; 784.6 *debtor*; 756.5 *promise-maker*
cosily 490.11 *pleasingly*; 248.9 *prosperously*
cosine 27.52 *trigonometric function*
cosine rule 27.51 *trigonometry*
cosiness 159.1 *littleness*; 490.1 *physical pleasure*
cosmetic 394.9 *balm*
cosmetician 547.13 *beautician*
cosmetics **547.4**; 125.4 *camouflage*; 529.9 *complexion*; 427.5 *powder*
cosmetic surgery 116.3 *disguise*; 547.2 *plastic surgery*; 394.12 *surgery*
cosmic 29.36 *astronomical*; 11.16 *psychic*; 138.16 *universal*; 235.1 *worthy*
cosmically 29.39 *astronomically*; 138.32 *universally*
cosmic background 29.4 *cosmological model*
cosmic being 11.11 *ghost*; 100.6 *outsider*
cosmic consciousness 11.8 *psychic power*
cosmic dust 29.8 *interstellar medium*; 427.5 *powder*
cosmic rays 29.8 *interstellar medium*; 28.70 *radioactivity*
cosmic vibration 11.10 *psychic phenomenon*
cosmochemist 29.2 *astronomer*
cosmochemistry 29.1 *astronomy*
cosmogenist 29.2 *astronomer*
cosmogeny 29.1 *astronomy*
cosmoid scale 74.5 *fish anatomy*
cosmological 29.36 *astronomical*
cosmologically 29.39 *astronomically*
cosmological model **29.4**; 28.6 *law*
cosmologist 29.2 *astronomer*; 4.10 *philosopher*
cosmology 29.1 *astronomy*; 4.6 *branch of philosophy*; 28.4 *experimental physics*
cosmonaut 141.10 *spaceman*; 29.31 *space travel*
cosmonautics 29.29 *astronautics*
cosmopolitan 485.5 *expert*; 138.15 *general*; 85.15 *internationalist*; 566.13 *national*; 549.5 *refined*; 138.16 *universal*
cosmopolitanism 138.1 *generality*; 85.5 *internationalism*
cosmos 95.2 *real world*; 29.3 *universe*; 204.2 *whole thing*
Cossack 586.20 *cavalryman*; 59.15 *horse person*
Cossack dance 22.4 *historic dancing*
cosset 490.10 *comfort*; 599.15 *humour*; 593.27 *kiss*; 593.11 *loved one*; 392.20 *sustain*
cosseted 490.7 *pleased*
cossetting 599.11 *humouring*
cost **790.5**; **790.13**; 789.7 *account*; 792.9 *be dear*; 766.2 *financial loss*; 26.10 *measure*; 790.1 *price*; 235.6 *worth*
Costa Brava 92.4 *coast*
cost a bundle 792.9 *be dear*
cost accountant 789.6 *accountant*
cost accounting 789.1 *accounts*
Costa del Sol 92.4 *coast*
cost a fortune 792.9 *be dear*
cost a lot 792.9 *be dear*
cost a packet 792.9 *be dear*
cost a pretty penny 792.9 *be dear*
co-star 21.34 *act*
cost-benefit analysis 579.3 *management*
costed 789.11 *accounted*
coster 778.14 *street trader*
costermonger 778.11 *pedlar*; 778.14 *street trader*
coster's barrow 320.7 *handcart*
costing nothing 768.7 *given*
costive 416.7 *condensed*; 360.9 *retentive*; 684.8 *self-restrained*; 309.13 *stopped*
costively 416.10 *densely*; 309.16 *impermeably*
costliness 792.1 *high price*; 235.6 *worth*
costly **681.3**; 792.7 *dear*; 781.3 *opulent*; 235.3 *valuable*
cost next to nothing 793.12 *be cheap*
cost of living 790.5 *cost*; 13.3 *economic statistics*; 787.5 *expense*
cost-of-living adjustment 15.2 *industrial negotiations*
cost-of-living index 790.5 *cost*
cost one dear 792.9 *be dear*
costs 13.7 *corporation*; 790.5 *cost*; 787.5 *expense*; 814.8 *penalty*
cost the earth 792.9 *be dear*
costume 551.32 *dress*; 551.5 *fancy dress*; 551.35 *make clothing*; 21.21 *stage requisite*; 551.10 *suit*
costume ball 22.1 *dancing*
costumed 551.29 *dressed*
costume designer 551.26 *fashion designer*; 21.27 *producer*
costume drama 692.25 *broadcast material*
costume jewellery 542.7 *jewellery*
costume party 736.3 *covering up*; 654.5 *party*
costumer 551.26 *fashion designer*
costumier 551.26 *fashion designer*; 21.27 *producer*
costumière 21.27 *producer*
cosy 241.3 *comfortable*; 159.7 *little*; 490.6 *pleasant*; 490.7 *pleased*; 248.8 *prosperous*
cosy chat 734.2 *chat*
cot 23.6 *bed*
cotangent 27.52 *trigonometric function*
co-tenant 764.3 *participant*
coterie 376.19 *clique*; 137.5 *social class*; 169.5 *team*
coterminous 147.10 *juxtaposed*
cothurnus 551.5 *fancy dress*; 21.11 *tragedy*
cotillion 22.1 *dancing*; 22.4 *historic dancing*
Cotswolds 89.5 *British mountains*
Cotswold stone 20.4 *building material*
cottage 20.3 *building*; 565.5 *house*; 440.1 *property*
cottage hospital 35.10 *hospital*
cottage loaf 25.39 *loaf*
cottage pie 25.44 *British dish*
cottager 564.5 *countryman*
cotter pin 373.8 *fastening*
cotton 43.12 *crop*; 435.1 *materials*; 42.12 *natural*; 193.4 *textile*
cotton belt 43.11 *farmland*
Cotton Bowl 46.1 *football*
cotton jersey 193.4 *textile*
cotton mill 577.1 *workshop*
cotton paper 435.3 *paper*
cottonseed 77.9 *seed*
cottonseed cake 43.9 *animal feedstuff*
cotton seeds 238.6 *refuse*
cotton to 593.24 *be in love*
cotton up to 569.14 *seek the friendship of*
cotton wool 419.11 *soft thing*
cotton-wool treatment 648.1 *leniency*
cottony 404.9 *smooth*
cottony cloud 31.20 *cloud appearance*
cotyledon 77.6 *leaf*; 77.9 *seed*
couch 71.20 *abode of mammals*; 155.8 *be low*; 367.3 *bring down*; 23.2 *chair*; 413.4 *rest*; 367.8 *sit*; 724.9 *style*; 263.2 *take it easy*
couchant 743.13 *heraldic*; 155.5 *low*; 187.10 *lying*
couchette 321.6 *rolling stock*
couch potato 634.17 *avoider*; 343.8 *nonworker*; 301.7 *sedentary person*
cough 513.2 *hoarseness*; 260.9 *respiratory disease*; 560.9 *saliva*; 560.20 *salivate*; 513.5 *sound hoarse*; 260.3 *symptom*
coughing 560.9 *saliva*; 560.29 *salivating*
cough linctus 412.2 *mixed thing*
cough mixture 412.2 *mixed thing*
cough syrup 768.2 *gift*
cough up 679.10 *be generous*; 785.6 *pay*; 355.1 *relinquish*; 393.3 *restore*; 560.20 *salivate*; 789.9 *settle accounts*
could be 102.8 *be possible*
could do with 392.27 *find useful*
couldn't-care-less 459.5 *foolish*; 615.4 *rash*
coulee 146.3 *gulf*
couleur de rose 235.1 *worthy*

couloir 146.3 *gulf;* 62.5 *rock face;* 68.1 *skiing;* 92.8 *valley*
coulometer 26.8 *meter*
coulometric 26.16 *micrometric*
coulometry 26.2 *micrometry*
coulter 425.9 *sharp-edged thing*
council **579.7**; 713.4 *adviser;* 376.7 *committee;* 376.5, 734.4 *conference;* 713.2 *consultation;* 579.6 *governing body;* 16.2 *jurisdiction;* 398.2 *representative body;* 16.18 *tribunal*
council area 86.5 *state*
council board 579.7 *council*
council chamber 579.7 *council*
councillor 398.1 *delegate;* 15.7 *employee;* 579.16 *official*
councilman 579.16 *official*
council-manager system 579.9 *US administrative council*
council of elders 579.7 *council*
council of war 734.4 *conference*
council tax 790.7 *tax*
counsel 713.1 *advice;* 392.23, 713.5 *advise;* 713.4 *adviser;* 579.2 *direct;* 16.13 *lawyer;* 483.9 *motivate;* 480.15 *persuade;* 36.38 *psychologize;* 392.2 *support;* 711.5 *warn;* 711.1 *warning*
counsellable 711.8 *warning*
counselled 711.9 *warned*
counselling 713.1 *advice;* 713.7 *advising;* 36.3 *psychiatric treatment;* 461.9 *treatment*
counsellor 392.14, 713.4 *adviser;* 15.6 *employer;* 464.5 *judge;* 748.3 *mediator;* 480.14, 483.7 *motivator;* 579.16 *official;* 36.30 *psychiatrist;* 748.4 *representative;* 4.12 *sage;* 591.8 *sensitive person;* 711.4 *warner*
count **210.3**; 715.1 *accusation;* 211.6 *add;* 123.7 *be important;* 52.2 *boxing;* 210.8 *calculate;* 27.90 *enumerate;* 127.4 *include;* 26.10 *measure;* 573.1 *nobleman;* 194.10, 210.11 *number;* 27.12 *numeration;* 203.8 *quantify;* 275.16 *time;* 203.4 *total*
countable 210.14 *calculable;* 27.73 *numerable*
count as 762.5 *take a substitute*
count ballots 469.5 *vote*
count calories 687.5 *fast*
count down 243.4 *prepare for action*
counted 203.6 *quantitative*
counted person 566.7 *person*
countenance 669.12 *accept;* 392.23 *advise;* 669.1 *approval;* 413.12 *bear;* 525.3 *external appearance;* 167.2 *face;* 392.9 *patronage;* 757.3 *permit*
counter **347.5**; **384.3**; 585.13 *be at war;* 113.16 *be contrary;* 210.6 *calculator;* 40.19 *computing terms;* 113.30 *contrariwise;* 347.3 *counteract;* 347.4 *counteracting;* 347.1 *counteraction;* 704.10 *countercharge;* 68.6 *ice-skating;* 743.3 *means of identification;* 113.18 *object;* 113.22 *oppositional;* 384.24 *parry;* 50.8 *punting;* 708.11 *rebut;* 385.3 *retaliate;* 385.1 *retaliation;* 303.25 *reversed;* 779.9 *stall;* 275.13 *timer*
counteraccusation 704.3 *countercharge*
counteract **113.21**; **347.3**; 113.15 *be opposite;* 708.16 *cancel out;* 357.8 *destroy;* 378.8 *hinder;* 753.6 *protest;* 110.7 *reciprocate;* 761.6 *reverse;* 345.5 *show an effect*
counteracting **37.14**; **347.4**; 708.20 *cancelled;* 113.22 *oppositional;* 110.4 *reciprocal;* 394.17 *remedial*
counteracting thing 347.2
Counteraction 347
counteraction **347.1**; 708.7 *cancelling out;* 384.3 *counter;* 704.3 *countercharge;* 113.9 *countermeasure;* 303.16 *countermotion;* 345.1 *effect;* 119.3 *equalization;* 378.1 *hindrance;* 110.1 *interchange;* 753.1 *protest;* 393.9 *restoration;* 385.1 *retaliation;* 761.1 *reversion*
counteractions 484.2 *policy*
counteractive 708.20 *cancelled;* 347.4 *counteracting;* 378.13 *hindering;* 113.22 *oppositional;* 753.9 *protesting;* 110.4 *reciprocal;* 704.7 *refuting*
counteractively 347.5 *counter;* 378.16 *with delay*
counterargument 704.3 *countercharge;* 113.9 *countermeasure;* 714.2 *defence;* 16.7 *legal trial*
counterattack **381.8**; 585.13 *be at war;* 113.21 *counteract;* 347.1 *counteraction;* 113.9 *countermeasure;* 364.7 *deflection;* 54.5 *fence;* 54.3 *fencing movements;* 381.14 *siege*
counterattacking **381.24**; 54.6 *fencing*
counterbalance 708.7 *cancelling out;* 708.16 *cancel out;* 395.9 *change;* 113.21, 347.3 *counteract;* 347.1 *counteraction;* 119.11 *equalize;* 414.10 *scales;* 228.3 *stabilizer;* 162.6 *symmetrize;* 162.1 *symmetry*
counterbalanced 162.4 *symmetrical*
counterblast 706.18 *answer back;* 347.1 *counteraction;* 704.3, 704.10 *countercharge;* 706.5 *counterstatement;* 385.1 *retaliation*
counterblasted 706.13 *retaliatory*
countercathexis 36.28 *cathexis*
counterchange 110.7 *reciprocate*
countercharge **704.3**; **704.10**; 715.1 *accusation;* 715.5 *accuse;* 706.18 *answer back;* 706.5 *counterstatement;* 385.3 *retaliate*
countercharged 715.8 *accusatory;* 706.13 *retaliatory*
countercharm 347.1 *counteraction*
countercheck 113.21 *counteract;* 113.9 *countermeasure*
counterclaim 704.3, 704.10 *countercharge;* 16.5 *litigation;* 710.1, 710.6 *request*
counterclaimant 710.4 *requester*
counterclockwise 324.10 *clockwise;* 303.29 *in reverse;* 303.25 *reversed;* 307.13 *round*
counterconditioning 36.20 *conditioning*
countercurrent 90.6 *river flow*
counter-demonstrator 753.4 *protester*
countered 54.6 *fencing*
counterevidence 454.6 *evidence;* 716.5 *legal evidence*
counterexample 4.8 *philosophical term*
counterfactual 4.8 *philosophical term*
counterfactual history 3.1 *history*
counterfeit 96.12 *artificial;* 699.25, 700.30 *be fraudulent;* 125.2, 125.10 *copy;* 116.3 *disguise;* 699.12, 699.37 *fake;* 699.36 *falsified;* 699.26 *falsify;* 699.35 *fraudulent;* 702.10 *hypocritical;* 115.12 *imitate;* 125.13 *imitation;* 700.39 *imitative;* 780.24 *monetize;* 115.8 *simulated*
counterfeited 699.32 *spurious*
counterfeiter 699.19, 700.17 *cheat;* 125.8 *copier;* 774.11 *dishonest person;* 699.17 *false person;* 115.4 *person who copies;* 717.4 *person who makes a representation*
counterfeiting 774.7 *dishonesty;* 699.9 *falsification;* 699.8, 700.10 *fraud;* 699.4 *spuriousness*
counterfeit money 786.4 *depreciation;* 780.15 *false money*
counterfeit note 699.16 *false thing*
counterflow 90.6 *river flow*
counterflux 90.6 *river flow*
counterfoil 769.3 *acknowledgment of payment;* 253.2 *promise;* 788.1 *receipt;* 744.1 *record*
counterforce 384.3 *counter*
counterglow 522.4 *natural light*
countering 54.6 *fencing;* 708.3 *rebuttal;* 708.19 *rebutting*
counterintelligence 347.1 *counteraction;* 737.2 *secretiveness*
counterintuitive 103.2 *unbelievable*
counterinvestment 36.28 *cathexis*
counterirritant 394.4 *antidote;* 37.14 *counteracting;* 347.1 *counteraction;* 37.4 *drug type*
counterman 401.3 *attendant*
countermand 708.7 *cancelling out;* 708.16 *cancel out;* 397.1, 397.9 *command;* 708.12 *renounce;* 708.4 *renunciation;* 399.1 *veto*
countermanded 397.14 *commanding;* 708.18 *rejected*
countermarch 585.13 *be at war;* 303.3 *reverse*
countermarching 303.16 *countermotion*
countermeasure **113.9**; 394.4 *antidote;* 347.1 *counteraction;* 378.1 *hindrance*
countermeasures 484.2 *policy*
countermine 113.21 *counteract;* 484.4, 484.13 *plot;* 385.1 *retaliation*
countermotion 303.16
countermove 347.1 *counteraction;* 113.9 *countermeasure*
countermovement 303.16 *countermotion*
counteroffensive 347.1 *counteraction;* 381.14 *siege*
counterorder 708.7 *cancelling out;* 397.1, 397.9 *command;* 709.2 *dissent;* 399.1, 399.3 *veto*
counterpane 550.10 *bed covering*
counter parry 54.3 *fencing movements*
counterpart **115.5**; 750.5 *conformity;* 119.5 *equal;* 110.2 *interconnection;* 198.5 *twin*
counterplot 484.4 *plot;* 385.1 *retaliation*
counterpoint 374.2 *cooperation;* 516.4 *harmonics;* 750.4 *harmony;* 192.1 *inversion;* 17.9 *metre;* 18.19 *tempo*
counterpoint rhythm 18.19 *tempo*
counterpoise 414.12 *be heavy;* 708.7 *cancelling out;* 708.16 *cancel out;* 347.3 *counteract;* 347.1 *counteraction;* 119.11 *equalize;* 119.2 *equilibrium;* 119.4 *equilizer;* 750.24 *harmonize;* 414.10 *scales*
counterpoison 394.4 *antidote*
counterpole 113.2 *oppositeness*
counterpressure 347.1 *counteraction*
counterproposal 113.9 *countermeasure*
counterpunch 347.1 *counteraction;* 385.1 *retaliation*
counter-reformation 393.9 *restoration;* 761.1 *reversion*
counterrevisionist history 3.1 *history*
counter-revolution 761.1 *reversion*
counter-revolutionary 753.10 *lawbreaking;* 113.11 *opposer;* 662.12 *reactionary*
counter-riposte 54.3 *fencing movements*
counter scale 414.10 *scales*
counterscarp 384.11 *fortification*
countersign 755.5 *contract;* 743.11 *identify oneself;* 743.3 *means of identification;* 253.11 *promise;* 716.12 *prove;* 742.1 *sign;* 742.9 *use signs;* 454.1 *verify*
countersignature 755.1 *contract*
countersigned 755.7 *contractual*
countersigner 755.4 *contractor*
counterspell 347.1 *counteraction*
counterspy 227.6 *fickle person;* 753.5 *seditionist*
counterstaining 34.6 *cell biology*
counterstate 706.18 *answer back*
counterstated 706.13 *retaliatory*
counterstatement **706.5**; 704.3 *countercharge*
counterstrike 110.7 *reciprocate*
counterstroke 384.3 *counter;* 364.7 *deflection;* 110.1 *interchange;* 385.1 *retaliation*
counter suit 385.1 *retaliation*
counterterrorist 662.12 *reactionary*
counter to 347.5 *counter;* 113.31 *opposed to*
countervail 708.16 *cancel out;* 113.21, 347.3 *counteract;* 119.11 *equalize*
counterweigh 414.12 *be heavy;* 708.16 *cancel out*
counterweight 708.7 *cancelling out;* 347.1 *counteraction;* 119.4 *equilizer;* 228.3 *stabilizer*
counterword 5.21 *catchword*
counterwork 113.9 *countermeasure*
countess 573.1 *nobleman*
count for nothing 124.11 *be unimportant*
count hands 210.11 *number;* 469.5 *vote*
count heads 210.11 *number;* 469.5 *vote*
counting 210.3 *count;* 127.7 *including;* 27.12 *numeration*
counting calories 687.1 *fasting*
counting hands 469.11 *franchise*
counting heads 469.11 *franchise*
counting house 780.19 *treasury*
counting noses 469.11 *franchise*
counting system 27.8 *number system*
counting-up 211.2 *mathematical addition*
countless 202.2 *immeasurable;* 208.8 *numberless*
countless as the stars 208.8 *numberless*
countlessly 208.13 *numerously*
countlessness 202.5 *immeasurability;* 208.1 *multiplicity*
count me out 709.12 *no!*
count noses 210.11 *number;* 469.5 *vote*
count on 450.7 *believe;* 610.6 *hope;* 474.9 *predict;* 104.10 *think likely*
count one's beads 10.20 *pray*
count one's blessings 671.7 *give thanks*
count out 128.7, 470.3 *exclude*
Countries 85
countrification 87.1 *city*
countrified 87.14 *urban*
countrify 87.15 *urbanize*
country **85.1**; 396.8 *governmental organization;* 59.8 *hunting;* 18.33 *jazz;* 566.11 *nation;* 12.5 *political organization;* 86.6 *regions;* 86.4 *territorial division;* 87.14 *urban*
country and western 18.11 *folk music*
country bumpkin 564.5 *countryman;* 646.3 *naive person;* 574.1 *plebeian;* 87.12 *rural dweller;* 486.10 *unskilled person*
country cottage 20.3 *building*
country cousin 564.5 *countryman;* 646.3 *naive person;* 574.1 *plebeian*
country dance 22.4 *historic dancing*
country dancing 22.1 *dancing*
country-dweller 564.5 *countryman;* 646.3 *naive person*
country gentleman 564.5 *countryman*
countryman **564.5**; 85.13 *native;* 87.12 *rural dweller*
country music 18.11 *folk music*
country of origin 85.6 *native land;* 86.4 *territorial division*
country road 317.3 *road*
country rock 18.9 *popular music*
country route 306.5 *ringroad*
countryside 86.6 *regions*
country town 87.1 *city;* 87.9 *town*
country village 87.10 *village*
countrywide 138.16 *universal*
countrywide circulation 740.7 *publicity*
countrywoman 564.5 *countryman;* 85.13 *native*
count straws 469.5 *vote*
count the calories 153.14 *become thin;* 557.23 *taste*
count the cost 616.5 *be cautious*
count the hours 275.19 *clock on;* 281.16 *measure time*
count the minutes 281.16 *measure time*
count to ten 616.5 *be cautious*
count up 211.6 *add;* 210.11 *number*
count votes 469.5 *vote*
count with 127.6 *subsume*
county 396.8 *governmental organization;* 205.1 *part;* 12.5 *political organization;* 86.5 *state;* 87.14 *urban*
county board 16.2 *jurisdiction;* 579.9 *US administrative council*
county building 87.13 *municipal building*
county commission 16.2 *jurisdiction;* 579.9 *US administrative council*
county council 579.8 *British administrative council;* 16.2 *jurisdiction;* 398.2 *representative body*
county court 16.19 *law court*
county courthouse 87.13 *municipal building*
county court judge 16.23 *judge;* 464.6 *justice*
county cricket 53.1 *cricket match*
county hospital 35.10 *hospital*
county jail 815.1 *prison*
county map 717.7 *map*
county seat 87.2 *American cities;* 87.9 *town*
county sheriff 16.16 *US police*
county town 87.4 *British cities;* 86.11 *settlement;* 87.9 *town*
coup 396.3 *acquisition of power;* 588.1 *anarchy;* 65.2 *billiards play;* 224.1 *change;* 340.2 *deed;* 485.3 *masterpiece;* 484.2 *policy;* 144.3 *replacement;* 662.4 *revolution;* 773.1 *taking*
coup de grâce 613.8 *courageous act;* 340.2 *deed;* 131.13 *ender;* 382.5 *execution;* 357.4 *ruin*
coup de main 340.2 *deed;* 381.12 *military attack;* 484.2 *policy*
coup-de-maître 485.3 *masterpiece*
coup d'état 396.3 *acquisition of power;* 588.1 *anarchy;* 340.2 *deed;* 753.2 *disorder;* 16.41 *lawlessness;* 484.2 *policy;* 662.4 *revolution;* 773.1 *taking*
coup de théâtre 21.9 *dramaturgy;* 619.3 *wonder-working*
coup d'oeil 518.6 *look*
coupé 320.16 *car*
coupé 54.3 *fencing movements;* 321.6 *rolling stock*
couple **115.6**; 492.12 *abut;* 374.6 *come together;* 373.11 *connect;* 206.1 *few;* 28.10 *force;* 223.14 *keep company with;* 593.29 *make love;* 570.15 *marry;* 198.14 *pair;* 108.7 *relate to;* 198.1 *two*
coupled 223.19 *associated;* 373.15 *connected;* 570.21 *married;* 198.9 *two*

coupled column 20.8 *column*
coupled with 211.10 *additionally;* 223.24 *with*
coupler 373.9 *yoke*
couplet 198.2 *double;* 17.8 *part of poem*
couple up 198.14 *pair*
coupling 373.1 *connection;* 593.5 *desire;* 38.8 *machine element;* 321.7 *train;* 373.9 *yoke*
coupling circuit 39.13 *circuit*
coupon 780.14 *paper money;* 253.2 *promise*
coupon-clipper 793.8 *bargain hunter*
coupons 793.7 *discounter*
Courage 613
courage 613.1; 661.1 *defiance;* 638.16 *fortitude;* 622.1 *pride;* 253.1 *protection;* 640.4 *stamina;* 336.1 *strength*
courageous 613.9; 661.7 *defiant;* 354.6 *enterprising;* 622.14 *proud;* 336.11 *strong in spirit*
courageous act 613.8
courageously 613.18; 661.9 *defiantly;* 354.9 *enterprisingly;* 336.14 *strongly*
courageousness 613.1 *courage*
courageous person 613.7
courante 22.4 *historic dancing*
coure 90.6 *river flow*
courier 59.15 *horse person;* 316.8 *messenger;* 401.5 *office assistant;* 692.4 *postal worker;* 332.13 *swift person;* 319.3 *transporter*
course 302.11; 324.2 *bearing;* 631.1 *conduct;* 132.2 *consecution;* 25.9 *dish;* 275.3, 277.1 *duration;* 447.5 *educational topic;* 59.11 *eventing;* 90.7 *flow;* 633.11 *hunt;* 59.9 *jumping;* 411.1 *layer;* 352.1 *means;* 300.2 *momentum;* 557.14 *mouthful;* 557.6 *nutrition;* 346.1 *operation;* 318.2 *passing along;* 37.5 *prescription;* 317.2 *route;* 50.1 *sailing;* 447.4 *sphere;* 45.2 *sportsground;* 6.3 *subject;* 289.1 *succession;* 229.1 *tendency;* 394.13 *therapy;* 281.2 *timetable*
course of action 346.1 *operation;* 484.2 *policy*
course of law 16.6 *legal process*
course of love 593.8 *love affair*
course of time 275.3, 277.1 *duration*
courser 332.12 *swift animal;* 332.13 *swift person;* 59.2 *thoroughbred;* 59.3 *warhorse*
courses 560.11 *menstruation*
coursing 633.2 *chase;* 90.10 *fluvial*
court 593.26; 633.12 *aim at;* 223.10 *attendance;* 471.14 *be solicitous;* 677.10 *cajole;* 579.7 *council;* 16.19 *law court;* 617.13 *like;* 308.8 *open space;* 63.5 *real tennis;* 710.6 *request;* 317.3 *road;* 733.2 *salutation;* 569.14 *seek the friendship of;* 45.2 *sportsground*
court appearance 525.2 *being in view*
court award 814.8 *penalty*
court card 69.3 *card game terms*
court case 715.1 *accusation*
court costs 16.43 *conviction*
court dance 22.4 *historic dancing*
court danger 615.5 *be rash*
court disaster 613.15 *be courageous;* 254.9 *face danger*
court dress 551.3, 656.4 *formal dress*
courteous 658.7; 650.6 *benevolent;* 367.21 *degraded;* 569.8 *friendly;* 241.2 *likable;* 663.9 *obeisant;* 549.5 *refined;* 667.9 *showing respect;* 654.15 *sociable;* 471.9 *solicitous;* 631.17 *well-behaved*
courteous act 367.16 *courtesy*
courteously 367.25; **658.14**; 650.10 *benevolently;* 569.17 *in friendship;* 663.10 *obediently;* 667.22 *respectfully;* 654.18 *sociably;* 631.19 *well*
courteousness 650.1 *benevolence;* 658.1 *courtesy*
courteous person 658.6
courtesan 796.9 *immoral woman;* 490.3 *pleasure-seeker*
courtesies 658.3
Courtesy 658
courtesy 367.16; **658.1**; 241.8 *amiability;* 650.4 *benevolent act;* 549.1 *elegance;* 793.11 *free of charge;* 569.1 *friendship;* 768.7 *given;* 631.2 *good conduct;* 663.3 *obeisance;* 667.3 *respectfulness;* 654.2 *social ambition;* 471.5 *solicitude*
courtesy call 654.3 *meeting*
courtesy light 522.6 *electric light*
court fine 814.7 *punishment*
courthouse 16.27 *courtroom;* 87.13 *municipal building*
courthouse wedding 570.5 *wedding*
courtier 664.3 *sycophant*
courting 593.6 *courtship;* 710.1 *request;* 710.9 *requesting*
courtliness 658.1 *courtesy*
courtly 658.7 *courteous;* 658.14 *courteously;* 543.3 *elegant*
court martial 16.19 *law court;* 584.6 *military law;* 464.3 *place of judgment*
Court of Appeal 16.20 *British court;* 464.3 *place of judgment*
court of appeals 16.21 *US court*
court of arbitration 16.19 *law court*
Court of Arches 16.22 *ecclesiastical court*
court of chancery 16.21 *US court*
court of claims 16.21 *US court*
Court of Common Pleas 16.20 *British court*
court of common pleas 16.21 *US court*
court of conscience 16.18 *tribunal*
court of equity 16.19 *law court*
Court of Exchequer 16.20 *British court*
court officer 16.10 *law officer*
court of justice 16.19 *law court*
court of law 16.19 *law court;* 16.7 *legal trial;* 464.3 *place of judgment*
court of record 16.19 *law court*
Court of Session 16.20 *British court*
court of session 16.19 *law court*
court payment 814.8 *penalty*
court plaster 394.10 *surgical dressing*
courtroom 16.27; 396.6 *place of authority;* 464.3 *place of judgment*
court sessions 16.7 *legal trial*
courtship 593.6
courtship dance 22.4 *historic dancing*
court shoes 551.19 *footwear*
court sitting 16.7 *legal trial*
courtyard 309.4 *closed place;* 165.2 *enclosed place*
couscous 25.54 *other dishes*
cousinly 650.6 *benevolent*
couture 551.2 *dressing*
couturier 551.26 *fashion designer*
couvade 10.7 *non-Christian ritual*
covalent 32.35 *combined*
covalent bond 32.11 *chemical bond*
covalent compound 32.7 *chemical compound*
covalently 32.46 *chemically*
covariance 27.60 *parameter*
covariation 108.2 *interrelatedness*
cove 183.2 *concave land;* 92.9 *inlet;* 567.2 *male*
coven 11.3 *witchcraft*
covenant 409.10 *agreement;* 750.23 *arrange;* 750.3 *arrangement;* 810.7 *commitment;* 755.1, 755.5 *contract;* 679.7 *gift;* 679.11 *give;* 253.2, 756.1, 756.7 *promise;* 140.1 *rule*
covenantal 750.12 *arranged;* 755.7 *contractual*
covenantally 755.8 *contractually*
covenanted 750.12 *arranged;* 755.7 *contractual;* 253.7 *guaranteed*
covenanter 755.4 *contractor*
Covent Garden 779.1 *market*
cover 550.2; **550.23**; 762.4 *be a substitute;* 550.10 *bed covering;* 171.11 *be exterior;* 519.6 *blinder;* 384.19 *buffer;* 253.12 *certify;* 256.11 *cleaning cloth;* 309.7 *close;* 736.8 *conceal;* 405.11 *consist of;* 550.1 *covering;* 551.32 *dress;* 141.20 *extend;* 232.6 *fill;* 127.4 *include;* 368.5 *inset;* 719.13 *interpret news;* 411.10 *layer;* 523.14 *make dark;* 521.8 *make invisible;* 528.11 *make opaque;* 358.1 *obliterate;* 358.3 *obliteration;* 410.5 *packet;* 252.10 *protect;* 252.2, 253.1 *protection;* 740.15 *publish;* 410.21 *put in a container;* 721.15 *recount;* 393.1 *repair;* 741.13 *report;* 64.3 *rugby play;* 523.6 *shade;* 550.15 *shelter;* 309.2 *stopper;* 53.4 *team;* 174.7 *top*
cover a blade 50.16 *row*
coverage 550.1 *covering;* 127.1 *inclusion;* 740.3 *journalism;* 740.7 *publicity;* 141.7 *range;* 741.3 *reporting;* 158.1 *size*
coveralls 551.10 *suit*
cover charge 790.3 *fee*
cover crop 43.12 *crop*
cover defence 64.3 *rugby play*
covered 550.36; 736.14 *concealed;* 410.20 *containing;* 171.6 *exterior;* 253.7 *guaranteed;* 358.6 *obliterated;* 528.1 *opaque;* 521.3 *private;* 252.6 *safe;* 174.6 *topped*
covered market 779.7 *emporium*
covered over 550.36 *covered*
covered up 550.36 *covered*
covered way 317.7 *arcade*
covered yard 43.7 *farm building*
coverer 550.17
cover for 550.34; 762.4 *be a substitute*
cover ground 302.3 *press on*
Covering 550
covering 550.1; **550.38**; 519.6 *blinder;* 411.3 *coat;* 410.20 *containing;* 551.2 *dressing;* 171.1 *exterior;* 525.3 *external appearance;* 127.7 *including;* 309.2 *stopper*
covering over 550.1 *covering*
covering up 736.3; 550.1 *covering;* 700.34 *deceiving;* 358.3 *obliteration*
coverlet 550.10 *bed covering*
cover oneself 616.5 *be cautious*
cover one's tracks 736.11 *conceal oneself*
cover point 58.6 *lacrosse player*
covert 71.20 *abode of mammals;* 72.13 *assemblage of birds;* 736.15 *disguised;* 565.13 *lair;* 72.14 *nest;* 11.14 *occult;* 72.17 *plumage;* 521.3 *private;* 737.10 *secretive;* 550.15 *shelter;* 79.4 *trees*
cover the ground 765.10 *augment*
covertness 737.2 *secretiveness*
coverture 570.1 *marriage*
cover up 714.9; 736.8 *conceal;* 550.31 *hide;* 737.12 *keep secret;* 358.1 *obliterate*
cover-up 714.3; 736.5 *evasion*
cover up for 252.10 *protect*
cover with dust 258.11 *dirty*
covet 629.6 *be jealous;* 683.6 *be selfish;* 617.12 *desire;* 756.11 *promise oneself*
coveted 617.7 *desired*
coveter 617.6 *desirer*
coveting 617.9 *desirous*
covetous 617.9 *desirous;* 538.5 *green-eyed;* 629.4 *jealous;* 683.4 *selfish*
covetously 617.18 *desirously;* 629.9 *jealously;* 683.8 *selfishly*
covetousness 617.1 *desire;* 538.14 *green-eyed monster;* 629.1 *jealousy;* 683.1 *selfishness;* 804.5 *seven deadly sins*
covey 72.13 *assemblage of birds;* 208.4 *throng*
covin 700.7 *tricking*
cow 481.2 *deter;* 568.14 *female animal;* 71.18 *female mammal;* 612.13 *frighten;* 43.8 *livestock*
coward 614.2; 388.2 *appeaser;* 634.17 *avoider;* 341.2 *nonacting person;* 337.4 *weakling*
Cowardice 614
cowardice 614.1; 341.1 *inaction;* 337.2 *indecisiveness;* 639.13 *timidity*
cowardliness 614.1 *cowardice;* 337.2 *indecisiveness*
cowardly 537.5; **614.3**; 341.3 *inactive;* 639.3 *timid;* 337.14 *weakly;* 337.12 *weak-willed*
cowbell 510.4 *sources of resonance*
cowboy 700.17 *cheat;* 43.16 *farm worker;* 59.15 *horse person;* 456.5 *ignorant person;* 250.10 *independent;* 579.14 *leader;* 486.10 *unskilled person*
cowboy boots 551.19 *footwear*
cowboy hat 551.15 *headgear*
cowboys and Indians 113.3 *opposites*
cowcatcher 252.4 *safety device*
cow chips 560.5 *faeces*
cow dung 562.3 *fertilizer*
cowed 614.3 *cowardly;* 612.7 *frightened*
cower 614.4 *be a coward;* 367.9 *bow;* 634.6 *evade;* 664.10 *knuckle under*
cowering 634.18 *avoiding;* 614.1 *cowardice;* 614.3 *cowardly;* 634.14 *evasion;* 664.7 *sycophantic*
Cowes regatta 50.1 *sailing*
cow flops 560.5 *faeces*
cowgirl 43.16 *farm worker;* 59.15 *horse person*
cowhand 43.16 *farm worker*
cowheel 25.31 *offal*
cowherd 43.16 *farm worker*
cowhide 814.14 *instrument of punishment;* 435.1 *materials*
cow horse 59.12 *rodeo*
cowhouse 565.12 *stall*
cowing 612.4 *intimidation*
cowish 71.33 *ungulate*
cowl 550.5 *body covering;* 551.15 *headgear;* 550.31 *hide*
cowlike 71.33 *ungulate*
cowling 68.9 *bobsledding*
cowman 43.16 *farm worker*
cowork 750.22 *form an alliance*
co-worker 223.11 *companion;* 747.10 *cooperator;* 405.5 *member;* 566.10 *member of society;* 346.5 *operator;* 578.5 *partner;* 127.3 *person included*
co-workers 747.9 *team*
cow pats 560.5 *faeces*
cow-pea soup 25.43 *US dish*
cow pony 59.4 *saddle horse*
cowpox 260.13 *skin disease*
cowpuncher 43.16 *farm worker;* 59.15 *horse person*
cowrie 780.1 *money*
cowshed 43.7 *farm building;* 565.12 *stall*
cowslip 537.8 *yellow thing*
cow's milk 558.5 *milk*
cow's tail 62.4 *climbing equipment*
cow's udder 25.31 *offal*
cox 579.2 *direct;* 579.13 *director;* 50.16 *row*
coxcomb 21.12 *comedy;* 551.15 *headgear*
coxed 50.11 *rowing*
coxed fours 50.4 *rowing*
coxed pairs 50.4 *rowing*
coxswain 323.7 *nautical person;* 50.9 *sailor*
coxswainless 50.11 *rowing*
coxswainless fours 50.4 *rowing*
coxswainless pairs 50.4 *rowing*
coy 593.20 *amorous;* 674.10 *bashful;* 255.12 *morally pure;* 795.9 *pure;* 732.1 *shy*
coyly 674.18, 732.8 *shyly;* 255.18 *virtuously*
coyness 674.3 *bashfulness;* 593.6 *courtship;* 795.3 *moral purity;* 255.1 *purity;* 732.3 *shyness*
cozener 699.19, 700.17 *cheat*
CP/M™ 40.8 *software*
CPU 40.5 *processor*
CR 40.10 *character*
crab 75.4 *arthropod;* 626.11 *be irritable;* 670.18 *find fault;* 322.5 *flight;* 366.9 *lifter;* 323.9 *navigate;* 76.3 *pest;* 25.19 *shellfish*
crab apple 499.3 *sour thing*
crabbed 242.2 *objectionable;* 266.2 *obscure;* 264.12 *problematic;* 499.7 *splenetic;* 696.1 *unintelligible*
crabbedness 625.1 *irascibility;* 499.4 *spleen*
crabbiness 625.1 *irascibility*
crabbing 670.6, 670.28 *fault-finding*
crabby 625.4 *irascible;* 242.2 *objectionable;* 499.7 *splenetic*
crablike 75.18 *arthropodous*
crab louse 76.3 *pest*
Crab nebula 29.8 *interstellar medium*
crab one's act 378.8 *hinder*
crabs 260.14 *venereal disease*
crabwalk 325.15 *deviating motion*
crach 622.13 *proud person*
crack 146.2; **146.5**; **508.2**; **508.6**; 353.5 *attempt;* 424.4 *be brittle;* 420.11 *be rough;* 235.2 *best;* 548.7 *blemish;* 734.2 *chat;* 719.9 *decipher;* 231.7 *defect;* 691.6 *drug;* 448.1 *experiment;* 797.1 *good;* 133.4 *interruption;* 420.12 *make rough;* 151.6 *narrow place;* 308.18 *open;* 308.1 *opening;* 62.5 *rock face;* 420.8 *rough ground;* 372.9 *separate;* 372.3 *separateness;* 485.6 *skilful;* 697.2 *solecism;* 541.3 *striping;* 729.7 *utterance;* 541.11 *variegate*
crackable 424.1 *brittle*
crack a bottle 654.11 *be sociable;* 558.13 *drink;* 690.8 *get drunk*
crack a code 719.9 *decipher*
crack a joke 599.13 *be humorous*
crack a safe 774.12 *steal*
crackback block 46.13 *penalty*
crack-brained 461.11 *insane*
crack cocaine 691.6 *drug*
crackdown 251.1 *restraint;* 399.1 *veto*
crack down 251.8 *restrain*
crack down on 399.3 *veto*
cracked 146.7; 548.4 *blemished;* 424.1 *brittle;* 420.2 *coarse;* 245.13 *dilapidated;* 513.8 *hoarse;* 231.1 *imperfect;* 461.11 *insane;* 719.15 *interpreted;* 730.10 *low-voiced;* 308.12 *open;* 517.9 *unmelodious*
cracked glass 541.5 *variegated thing*
cracked ice 494.5 *ice*
cracked voice 513.2 *hoarseness*
cracker 508.3 *banger;* 564.5 *countryman;* 25.39 *loaf*

crackerjack 797.1 *good;* 797.17 *good thing;* 235.1 *worthy*
crackers 461.11 *insane*
cracking 424.1 *brittle;* 424.2 *brittleness;* 32.22 *industrial chemistry;* 437.6 *oil*
crack jokes 697.6 *talk nonsense*
crackle 493.15 *burn;* 24.1 *ceramics;* 508.2, 508.6 *crack;* 511.4 *faint sound;* 24.3 *glaze;* 511.8 *sound faint;* 541.3 *striping*
crackled 424.1 *brittle*
crackling 508.9; 508.2 *crack*
crackling biscuit 25.43 *US dish*
crack of dawn 290.1 *morning*
crack of doom 582.4 *death sentence;* 131.5 *fate;* 357.4 *ruin*
crack off 424.4 *be brittle*
crack of the whip 480.8 *incentive;* 483.4 *negative stimulus*
crack one's throat 514.10 *cry out*
crack one's voice 507.8 *be loud;* 513.5 *sound hoarse*
crackpot 118.10 *eccentric;* 461.7 *insane person*
crack shot 330.15 *shooter;* 485.4 *skilled person*
cracksman 774.8 *thief*
crack the cipher 719.9 *decipher*
crack the whip 396.19 *be authoritarian;* 579.2 *direct*
crack troops 586.14 *armed forces;* 235.7 *elite*
crack up 261.5 *be fatigued*
crack-up 461.6 *mental breakdown;* 357.4 *ruin*
cradle 23.6 *bed;* 130.4 *conception;* 565.3 *home;* 85.6 *native land;* 326.7 *oscillator;* 413.4 *rest;* 130.3, 344.2 *source*
cradle song 516.2 *song*
craft 19.1 *art;* 776.6 *business;* 645.1 *cunning;* 700.1 *deception;* 268.9 *duplicity;* 576.3 *job;* 356.10 *produce;* 485.1 *skill;* 139.8 *specialization;* 323.3 *vessel*
craftily 645.6 *cunningly;* 702.15 *hypocritically*
craftily contrived 485.9 *well-made*
craftiness 645.1, 702.3 *cunning;* 700.1 *deception;* 485.1 *skill;* 458.1 *wisdom*
craft knife 425.10 *knife*
crafts fair 738.6 *display*
craft show 738.6 *display*
craftsman 578.2 *artisan;* 19.16 *artist;* 340.3 *doer;* 485.5 *expert;* 438.8 *machinist;* 356.9 *producer;* 485.4 *skilled person*
craftsman-built 356.12 *produced*
craftsmanship 19.5 *artistry;* 340.2 *deed;* 455.3 *learning;* 356.1 *production;* 485.1 *skill*
craftswoman 578.2 *artisan;* 485.5 *expert;* 356.9 *producer;* 485.4 *skilled person*
craft union 15.3 *organized labour*
craftworker 356.9 *producer*
crafty 268.15; 645.4, 702.8 *cunning;* 699.33 *deceitful;* 700.34 *deceiving;* 458.6 *intelligent;* 485.6 *skilful*
crafty fellow 645.3 *cunning person*
crag 89.1, 154.3 *mountain;* 62.5 *rock face;* 425.8 *sharp-pointed thing;* 186.3 *vertical thing*
cragged 420.2 *coarse*
cragginess 418.5 *hardness;* 420.6 *roughness*
craggy 420.2 *coarse;* 264.11 *rough;* 425.4 *toothed*
cragsman 304.11 *ascender;* 62.7 *mountaineer*
crake 72.3 *water bird*
cram 219.4 *be excessive;* 688.5 *be greedy;* 376.40 *crowd;* 232.6 *fill;* 6.23 *learn;* 416.9 *make dense;* 191.5 *make smaller;* 406.7 *stuff*
cram-full 232.8 *full*
cram in 314.12 *flood in;* 368.3 *impact*
crammed 376.50 *crowded;* 219.6 *excessive;* 232.8 *full;* 406.11 *loaded*
crammer 6.4 *educator*
cramming 688.6 *gluttonous;* 6.8 *learning*
cramoisy 535.1 *red*
cramp 491.10 *be painful;* 373.8 *fastening;* 245.5 *hurt;* 260.8 *indigestion;* 191.5 *make smaller;* 251.5 *means of restraint;* 151.10 *narrow;* 491.1 *pain;* 251.8 *restrain;* 327.8 *spasm*
cramped 218.1 *insufficient;* 166.5 *limited;* 159.7 *little;* 151.1 *narrow;* 264.12 *problematic;* 251.13 *restraining;* 191.7 *smaller;* 696.1 *unintelligible*
cramping 191.8 *contracting;* 191.1 *contraction;* 378.13 *hindering;* 491.5 *painful*
cramping one's style 251.1 *restraint*
crampit 68.10 *curling*
cramp one's style 218.5 *be insufficient;* 378.9 *block;* 245.5 *hurt;* 238.8 *make useless;* 251.8 *restrain*
crampons 62.4 *climbing equipment*
cramp someone's style 378.8 *hinder*
cranberry sauce 25.15 *sauce;* 496.2 *seasoning*
crane 148.9 *be long;* 38.29 *construction equipment;* 361.4 *hanger;* 366.9 *lifter;* 154.6 *tall thing;* 72.3 *water bird*
cranefly 76.1 *insect*
crane one's neck 148.9 *be long;* 303.9 *turn round*
Craniata 75.2 *protochordate*
craniate 75.2 *protochordate*
cranialoger 1.3 *anthropologist*
craniological 1.11 *anthropological*
craniologically 1.16 *anthropologically*
craniologist 566.6 *studier of mankind*
craniology 1.1 *anthropology;* 566.5 *study of mankind*
craniometer 26.8 *meter*
craniometric 1.11 *anthropological;* 26.16 *micrometric*
craniometrical 1.11 *anthropological*
craniometrically 1.16 *anthropologically*
craniometrist 1.3 *anthropologist*
craniometry 1.1 *anthropology;* 1.10 *measurement;* 26.2 *micrometry;* 566.5 *study of mankind*
crank 320.11 *bicycle part;* 642.4 *capricious person;* 325.19 *deviant person;* 118.8, 751.4 *dissenter;* 38.11 *engine;* 461.7 *insane person;* 625.3 *irascible person;* 38.8 *machine element;* 100.5 *nonconformist;* 243.4 *prepare for action;* 307.9 *roll;* 477.9 *visionary*
crankily 625.9 *irascibly;* 626.14 *irritably*
crankiness 642.2 *caprice;* 461.1 *insanity;* 625.1 *irascibility;* 626.3 *irritableness*
cranking over 61.6 *motor-racing terms*
crank over 61.9 *race*
crankshaft 38.11 *engine*
crank up 243.4 *prepare for action*
cranky 461.11 *insane;* 625.4 *irascible;* 626.7 *irritable*
crannog 88.7 *lake dwelling*
cranny 183.3 *cavity;* 410.2 *compartment;* 146.2 *crack;* 736.2 *hiding place*
crap 560.16 *defecate;* 258.4 *dirt;* 560.5 *faeces;* 236.8 *inferiority;* 697.1, 699.15 *nonsense*
crapper 560.13 *lavatory;* 767.7 *toilet*
crappily 560.33 *scatologically*
crappy 236.2 *inferior;* 122.14 *poor;* 238.1 *useless*
craps 69.5 *dice*
crapulence 690.15; 686.3 *overindulgence*
crapulent 690.4 *crapulous;* 686.8 *overindulgent*
crapulently 690.18 *drunkenly*
crapulous 690.4
crapulously 690.18 *drunkenly*
crapulousness 690.15 *crapulence*
crash 40.20 *abort;* 492.12 *abut;* 508.1, 508.5 *bang;* 424.4 *be brittle;* 507.8 *be loud;* 786.9 *be unable to pay;* 91.10 *billow;* 331.2 *collide;* 331.12 *collision;* 40.19 *computing terms;* 214.3 *decreasing thing;* 305.5 *dive;* 305.10 *droop;* 305.12 *drop;* 247.1 *failure;* 305.4 *fall;* 786.5 *insolvency;* 380.3 *instance of violence;* 517.10 *lack harmony;* 247.9 *malfunction;* 507.2 *outcry;* 357.4 *ruin;* 565.18 *take up residence;* 305.11 *trip*
crash barrier 320.21 *miscellaneous motoring terms;* 252.4 *safety device*
crash diet 687.1 *fasting;* 557.6 *nutrition*
crash-dieting 153.10 *diet*
crash-dive 322.5 *flight*
crash down 564.15 *settle*
crasher 620.3 *boring person*
crash helmet 551.15 *headgear;* 384.6 *protective clothing;* 252.4 *safety device*
crash in 380.7 *be violent*
crashing 508.8 *banging;* 305.16 *descending;* 507.6 *loud;* 492.9 *touching*
crashing bore 620.3 *boring person*
crash into 331.2 *collide*
crashland 305.12 *drop*
crash-landing 305.5 *dive;* 322.5 *flight*
crash pad 565.1 *habitat*
crash team 35.17 *paramedic*
crashworthiness 320.21 *miscellaneous motoring terms*
crass 497.6 *coarse*
crassly 497.11 *tastelessly*
crassness 497.4 *bad taste*
crate 410.6 *box;* 320.16 *car;* 550.13 *casing;* 203.3 *container;* 550.25 *wrap*
crated 550.37 *protected*
crater 183.2 *concave land;* 156.4 *deep thing;* 29.17 *moon;* 30.24 *volcanic activity*
crate up 410.21 *put in a container*
cravat 373.6 *line;* 551.14 *neckwear*
crave 617.12 *desire;* 135.8 *miss*
craven 614.2 *coward;* 537.5, 614.3 *cowardly*
cravenly 614.5
cravenness 614.1 *cowardice*
craving 557.2 *appetite;* 36.15 *compulsion;* 461.4 *delusion;* 617.1 *desire;* 617.9 *desirous;* 595.3 *likes;* 135.5 *necessitous*
crawdad 25.19 *shellfish*
crawfish 75.4 *arthropod;* 303.3 *reverse;* 25.19 *shellfish*
crawl 155.8 *be low;* 471.14 *be solicitous;* 677.11 *be sycophantic;* 208.11, 376.40 *crowd;* 664.9 *fawn;* 623.21 *humble oneself;* 73.16 *live as an amphibian;* 73.15 *live as a reptile;* 333.1 *move slowly;* 479.4 *recant;* 333.10 *slow motion;* 623.20 *submit;* 388.4 *succumb;* 67.1 *swimming*
crawler 664.3, 677.7 *sycophant*
crawler lane 320.3 *carriageway*
crawling 376.50 *crowded;* 219.6 *excessive;* 217.3 *filled;* 692.19 *radio reception;* 333.4 *slow;* 388.5 *submitting;* 664.2 *sycophancy;* 664.7, 677.16 *sycophantic;* 258.8 *unclean*
crawlingly 333.17 *in slow motion*
crawling with 232.8 *full*
crawl into one's shell 674.15 *escape notice*
crawl with 217.5 *about;* 219.4 *be excessive;* 76.16 *infest*
Cray 40.3 *computer*
crayfish 75.4 *arthropod;* 25.19 *shellfish*
crayon 19.11 *artist's materials;* 529.15 *colour;* 19.9 *drawing*
craze 424.4 *be brittle;* 36.15 *compulsion;* 632.4 *custom;* 461.4 *delusion;* 553.1 *fashion;* 595.3 *likes;* 541.3 *striping;* 541.11 *variegate;* 642.3 *whim*
crazed 593.19 *enamoured;* 380.6 *violent*
crazily 328.19 *distractedly;* 461.17 *insanely*
craziness 459.1 *folly;* 461.1 *insanity*
crazing 24.3 *glaze*
crazy 424.1 *brittle;* 642.1 *capricious;* 459.5 *foolish;* 461.11 *insane;* 697.5 *nonsensical;* 254.2 *unsafe*
crazy about 593.18 *in love*
crazy idea 443.6 *idea*
crazy paving 114.3 *diverse thing;* 44.3 *ornamental garden;* 550.11 *paving;* 541.5 *variegated thing*
creak 513.6 *be shrill;* 513.3 *shrillness*
creakiness 513.3 *shrillness*
creaking 513.9 *shrill*
creaking door 513.3 *shrillness*
creaky 513.9 *shrill;* 337.8 *weak*
cream 268.19 *anoint;* 394.9 *balm;* 123.3 *chief thing;* 235.7 *elite;* 245.5 *hurt;* 522.14 *light colour;* 558.5 *milk;* 37.7, 268.6 *ointment;* 469.4 *pick;* 356.7 *produce;* 797.9 *the best;* 121.7 *the best people*
cream-coloured 522.21 *light;* 537.1 *yellow*
creamcracker 25.39 *loaf*
creamer 412.6 *mixer*
creamery 577.1 *workshop*
creamily 531.14 *whitely;* 537.11 *yellowly*
creaminess 531.7 *whiteness*
cream-maker 412.6 *mixer*
cream off 369.17 *obtain an extract*
cream of the crop 797.9 *the best;* 121.7 *the best people*
cream sherry 558.9 *wine*
cream soda 558.6 *soft drink;* 498.5 *sweet drink*
cream soup 25.13 *soup*
cream tea 557.12 *meal*
creamware 24.1 *ceramics*
creamy 529.13 *soft-hued;* 531.1 *white;* 537.1 *yellow*
crease 408.24 *make disordered;* 420.12 *make rough;* 184.3, 184.10 *pleat;* 53.5 *wicket;* 184.1, 184.8 *wrinkle*
creased 184.7 *folded;* 184.6 *wrinkly*
crease-resistant 42.11 *treated*
creasy 184.7 *folded*
create 344.9 *be the cause of;* 93.20 *bring into being;* 19.23 *design;* 553.9 *fashion;* 160.7 *form;* 446.15, 477.14 *imagine;* 130.22, 448.13, 449.4, 484.11 *invent;* 126.7 *originate;* 356.10 *produce;* 403.15 *shape*
create a barrier 378.9 *block*
create a catch-22 situation 645.5 *be cunning*
create a controversy 249.11 *cause adversity*
create a logjam 378.9 *block;* 294.8 *delay*
create anarchy 662.16 *be subversive*
create a need 135.10 *necessitate*
create an obstacle 378.9 *block*
create a scandal 596.7 *cause dislike*
create a scene 624.11 *be angry*
create a sensation 123.7 *be important*
create a treasure 400.14 *master*
create a vacuum 417.6 *make sparse*
create bad blood 594.16 *cause hate*
created 93.15; 160.9 *formed;* 477.12 *imaginary;* 356.12 *produced*
create difficulties 264.24
create life 554.19 *give birth to*
create nonrepresentational art 718.4 *misrepresent*
create problems 249.11 *cause adversity*
create resentment 629.7 *arouse jealousy*
creatine phosphate 33.22 *bioenergetics*
creating a part 21.22 *acting*
creating a role 21.22 *acting*
Creation 356
creation 93.8; **130.2**; 344.1 *cause;* 551.1 *dress;* 293.3 *early stage;* 403.3 *form;* 160.4 *forming;* 130.5, 449.9 *invention;* 485.3 *masterpiece;* 126.1 *originality;* 356.3 *product;* 356.1 *production;* 403.5 *structuring;* 554.8 *theories of life*
creation of genius 485.3 *masterpiece*
creative 789.10 *accounting;* 340.5 *acting;* 344.13 *causal;* 234.8 *exaggerated;* 562.5 *fertile;* 160.9 *formed;* 446.11 *ideational;* 477.10 *imaginative;* 130.33 *inventive;* 126.4, 448.9 *original;* 356.11 *productive*
creative accountant 774.11 *dishonest person*
creative accounting 789.1 *accounts;* 786.1 *nonpayment;* 709.1 *refusal*
creative artist 448.5 *experimenter;* 446.9 *person of ideas;* 356.9 *producer*
creative composition 721.5 *fiction*
creative economy 389.1 *escape*
creative exercise 477.4 *ideality*
creative force 477.1 *imagination*
creative imagination 17.13 *poetic genius*
creative impulse 356.1 *production*
creatively 19.31 *artistically;* 344.14 *causally;* 789.13 *financially;* 160.13 *formatively;* 562.8 *fruitfully;* 446.22, 477.17 *imaginatively;* 448.15 *inventively;* 126.8 *originally;* 356.13 *productively;* 443.18 *thoughtfully*
creativeness 477.1 *imagination;* 126.1 *originality*
creative person 340.3 *doer*
creative thought 443.5; 477.1 *imagination*
creative urge 356.1 *production*
creative work 477.1 *imagination*
creative worker 340.3 *doer;* 477.9 *visionary*
creative writer 721.10 *descriptive writer;* 126.3 *originator*
creative writing 721.5 *fiction;* 477.4 *ideality*
creativity 446.8, 477.1 *imagination;* 126.1, 448.4 *originality*
creator 448.5 *experimenter;* 126.3, 130.16 *originator;* 446.9 *person of ideas;* 356.9 *producer*
creature 70.2 *animal;* 348.3 *assistant;* 34.3 *organism;* 566.7 *person;* 356.3 *product;* 664.3 *sycophant*
creature comforts 557.7 *food;* 490.4 *pleasurable things;* 241.7 *pleasure*
creaturely 566.12 *human*
creature of habit 112.8; **632.8**
creature of impulse 478.6 *improviser*
crèche 6.12 *educational institution*
cred 221.8 *in a state of;* 221.1 *state*
credence 450.3 *believing;* 452.10 *conviction*
credential 744.2 *certificate;* 716.6 *documentation;* 454.6 *evidence;* 396.9 *permission;* 669.6 *recommendation*
credentials 743.3 *means of identification;* 757.2 *permit;* 136.3 *qualifications*
credibility 450.4 *believability;* 811.1 *es-*

timation; 104.3 *plausibility*; 102.2 *possibleness*
credibility gap 751.3 *difference*
credible 450.13 *believable*; 104.7 *plausible*; 102.5 *possible*
credibly 450.16 *believably*; 102.11 *potentially*
Credit 783
credit 772.4; **783.1**; **783.8**; 789.7 *account*; 789.1 *accounts*; 669.2 *admiration*; 452.20 *be certain*; 450.7 *believe*; 450.3 *believing*; 215.3 *difference*; 811.1 *estimation*; 392.6 *financial assistance*; 352.4 *financial resources*; 395.3 *personal influence*; 253.2 *promise*; 769.9, 788.7 *receive*; 671.3 *recognition*; 813.1, 813.9 *reward*; 781.8 *solvency*; 235.6, 803.3 *worth*; 622.8 *worthiness*
creditable 450.13 *believable*; 617.8 *desirable*; 669.21 *praiseworthy*; 811.3 *reputable*; 235.1 *worthy*
credit account 772.4, 783.1 *credit*; 784.1 *debt*; 783.3 *deposit*
credit balance 783.3 *deposit*
credit bureau 783.4 *bank*
credit buyer 784.6 *debtor*
credit card 783.2; 772.4 *credit*; 784.1 *debt*; 28.64 *magnetic recording*; 785.1 *payment*
credit-card 772.11 *borrowed*
credit-card company 771.4 *lending institution*
credit-card holder 772.6 *borrower*; 777.12 *purchaser*
credit-card number 743.3 *means of identification*
credit-card purchase 777.7 *purchasing*
credit company 771.4 *lending institution*
credit control 783.1 *credit*
credited 789.11 *accounted*; 788.6 *received*; 813.16 *rewarded*
credit facility 772.4 *credit*
crediting 671.5 *thanking*
credit limit 783.1 *credit*; 352.4 *financial resources*
credit line 671.3 *recognition*
credit note 783.2 *credit card*
creditor 771.3 *lender*; 436.3 *provider*
creditors budget 789.2 *budgeting*
credit rating 783.1 *credit*; 352.4 *financial resources*
credits 783.3 *deposit*; 352.4 *financial resources*; 220.6 *list of names*; 788.2 *money received*; 671.3 *recognition*; 769.2 *something received*
credit squeeze 251.2 *economic restraint*
credit to one's account 783.10 *deposit*; 765.12 *earn*
credit union 783.4 *bank*; 771.4 *lending institution*
credit user 772.6 *borrower*
creditworthiness 783.1 *credit*; 352.4 *financial resources*; 781.8 *solvency*
creditworthy 783.13 *in credit*; 811.3 *reputable*; 781.2 *solvent*
Credo 10.9 *prayer*
credo 10.6 *Eucharist*; 446.5 *ideology*; 4.2 *philosophical system*; 7.1 *religion*; 450.2 *religious belief*
credulity 450.3 *believing*; 646.2 *naivety*; 480.7 *persuadability*
credulous 450.11 *believing*; 450.12 *gullible*; 646.1, 805.7 *naive*; 480.20 *persuadable*; 538.3 *raw*
credulously 450.15 *believingly*; 646.5, 805.12 *naively*
credulousness 450.3 *believing*; 805.3 *naivety*; 480.7 *persuadability*
creed 10.6 *Eucharist*; 446.5 *ideology*; 4.2 *philosophical system*; 7.1 *religion*; 450.2 *religious belief*; 707.2 *statement*
creedal 707.10 *affirmative*; 450.14 *believed*
creek 90.1 *river*
creel 410.7 *basket*
creep 155.8 *be low*; 420.11 *be rough*; 677.11 *be sycophantic*; 736.11 *conceal oneself*; 38.16 *deformation*; 300.12 *gait*; 73.16 *live as an amphibian*; 73.15 *live as a reptile*; 30.26 *mass movement*; 333.1 *move slowly*; 124.10 *nonentity*; 599.7 *person who humours*; 333.10 *slow motion*; 664.3, 677.7 *sycophant*
creeper 44.9 *garden plant*
creepers 551.23 *children's clothes*
creepily 421.16 *suavely*; 664.17 *sycophantically*
creep in 314.11 *infiltrate*
creeping 77.14 *of plants*; 692.19 *radio reception*; 73.11 *reptilian*; 333.4 *slow*; 333.10 *slow motion*; 677.16 *sycophantic*
creeping flesh 420.7 *rough thing*; 596.4 *sign of dislike*
creeping Jesus 7.5 *Christian*; 664.3 *sycophant*
creepingly 333.17 *in slow motion*
creeping thing 70.2 *animal*
creep into a corner 655.12 *be unsocial*
creep off 634.8 *run away*
creep to 664.9 *fawn*
creep up on 630.10 *ambush*
creep up to 421.13 *smooth over*
creepy 421.6 *smooth-mannered*; 11.18 *spiritual*; 664.7 *sycophantic*
creepy-crawly 76.1 *insect*; 333.14 *slow creature*
cremate 493.15 *burn*; 583.8 *bury*
cremated 583.10 *buried*
cremation 583.1 *burial*
crematorial 583.11 *funeral*
crematorium 582.8 *after death*; 583.1 *burial*; 493.6 *fire*; 583.2 *funeral*
crematory 583.11 *funeral*
crème caramel 25.35 *dessert*
crème de la crème 123.3 *chief thing*; 469.9 *chosen thing*; 235.7 *elite*; 553.6 *fashionable élite*; 400.11 *masterpiece*; 246.4 *successful person*; 797.16 *superior person*; 121.7 *the best people*
crème de menthe 558.7 *alcoholic drink*
cremocarp 80.2 *botanical fruit*
crenate 420.12 *make rough*; 183.7 *notched*; 77.18 *of leaves*
crenated 183.7 *notched*
crenately 183.12 *jaggedly*
crenation 183.4 *notch*
crenature 183.4 *notch*
crenel 183.4 *notch*
crenellate 164.6 *edge*; 183.10 *notch*
crenellation 164.2 *edging*
crenulation 183.4 *notch*
Creole 412.5 *hybrid*
creole 5.10 *language type*
creophagous 557.26 *eating*
creophagously 557.28 *carnivorously*
creophagy 557.5 *eating habit*
creosote 550.24 *coat*; 550.3 *coating*; 359.5 *preserve*; 359.2 *preserver*
crepe 532.9 *black thing*; 743.5 *uniform*
crêpe 25.39 *loaf*
crêpe pan 25.6 *kitchen equipment*
crepe paper 435.3 *paper*
crêpe paper 184.4 *wrinkled thing*
crêperie 557.15 *eating place*
crepe rubber 422.4 *rubber*
crepe-soled shoes 551.19 *footwear*
crêpes suzette 25.45 *French dish*
crepitant 508.9 *crackling*
crepitate 508.6 *crack*
crepitation 508.2 *crack*
crepuscular 524.5 *dim*; 291.6 *evening*
crescendo 765.2 *augmentation*; 190.6 *become bigger*; 209.6 *change gradually*; 190.1 *growth*; 213.4 *increase*; 507.6 *loud*; 507.9 *loudly*; 507.1 *loudness*; 213.2 *spread*
crescent 177.2 *bend*; 27.42 *circle*; 190.8 *growing*; 743.8 *heraldic device*; 213.6 *increasing*; 179.4 *parts of a circle*; 317.3 *road*; 742.1 *sign*; 52.15 *wrestling*
crescent dune 30.37 *dune*
crescentic 177.4 *curved*
crescent kick 52.9 *tae kwon do*
crescent moon 29.17 *moon*
crescent-shaped 27.81 *curvilinear*
crest 743.8 *heraldic device*; 89.1 *mountain*; 154.4 *mountain range*; 72.17 *plumage*; 121.4, 174.1 *summit*; 326.5 *wave*
crested 743.13 *heraldic*; 622.21 *ostentatious*; 174.6 *topped*
crestfallen 604.9 *disappointed*; 623.3 *humbled*; 602.5 *sad*
crest of the wave 121.4, 174.1 *summit*
Cretaceous period 284.3 *geological period*
cretic 17.9 *metre*
cretin 459.3 *foolish person*; 461.7 *insane person*; 457.3 *unintelligent person*
cretinism 461.2 *subnormality*
cretinous 457.7 *intellectually subnormal*; 457.5 *lacking intellect*
Creutzfeld-Jakob disease 461.3 *mental deterioration*; 260.17 *nervous disorder*
crevasse 183.2 *concave land*; 156.4 *deep thing*; 30.38 *glacier*; 146.3 *gulf*; 133.4 *interval*; 62.5 *rock face*; 379.1 *trap*; 92.8 *valley*
crevassed 62.8 *mountaineering*
crevice 146.2 *crack*; 308.1 *opening*
creviced 308.12 *open*
crew 322.3 *aircraft personnel*; 750.2 *alliance*; 243.5 *equip*; 43.16 *farm worker*; 323.9 *navigate*; 127.3 *person included*; 578.4 *personnel*; 50.15 *sail*; 346.9 *take action*; 376.12 *team*; 376.13 *workforce*
crew cut 149.4 *short thing*
crewelist 542.8 *decorator*
crewel work 542.3 *pattern*
crewman 50.9 *sailor*
crew member 127.3 *person included*
crew-neck 551.13 *sweater*
crew socks 551.20 *legwear*
crib 23.6 *bed*; 125.2, 125.10 *copy*; 565.1 *habitat*; 774.15 *infringe*; 413.4 *rest*; 6.14 *school book*; 719.4 *translation*
cribber 774.10 *infringer*
cribbing 774.6 *illegal borrowing*
cribriform 308.14 *holed*
crick 90.1 *river*
Cricket 53
cricket ball 330.10 *ball*
cricketer 336.5 *athlete*; 53.4 *team*
cricketing 53.12
cricket match 53.1
cricket season 292.1 *season*
crick in the neck 491.2 *painful condition*
cri du coeur 710.1 *request*
crier 514.9; 129.8 *precursor*; 740.10 *publicizer*
crikey 712.11 *miscellaneous euphemisms*
crim 651.8 *malefactor*; 802.10 *wrongdoer*
crime 16.39; 651.7 *act of malevolence*; 236.9 *badness*; 800.3, 804.7 *criminality*; 340.2 *deed*; 798.5 *evil thing*; 274.8 *moral error*; 806.3 *sin*; 662.2 *violation of the law*; 802.8 *wrongdoing*
crime against humanity 651.7 *act of malevolence*
crime fiction 721.5 *fiction*
crime of passion 629.1 *jealousy*; 382.2 *murder*
crime story 17.2 *fiction*
crime wave 16.41 *lawlessness*
crime writer 17.14 *author*; 721.10 *descriptive writer*
criminal 662.9; **800.7**; **804.15**; 236.3 *bad*; 631.5 *badly behaved person*; 670.36 *blameworthy*; 325.19 *deviant person*; 264.9 *difficult person*; 774.11 *dishonest person*; 800.4 *dishonourable person*; 662.13 *disobedient*; 340.3 *doer*; 798.6 *evil person*; 806.4 *guilty person*; 594.8 *hated person*; 796.11 *immoral*; 802.16 *in the wrong*; 16.40 *lawbreaker*; 651.8 *malefactor*; 16.60 *offending*; 705.15 *sceptical*; 806.7 *sinful*; 122.15 *subordinate*; 633.7 *the hunted*; 804.11 *wicked*; 804.9 *wicked person*; 802.10 *wrongdoer*
criminal act 804.7 *criminality*; 340.2 *deed*
criminal activity 16.39 *crime*
criminal classes 122.6 *inferior*
criminal conversation 796.4 *illicit love*
criminal court 16.19 *law court*; 464.3 *place of judgment*
criminal insanity 461.1 *insanity*
criminal intent 482.1 *intention*
criminal investigation 705.2 *questioning*
criminality 800.3; **804.7**; 16.39 *crime*; 806.1 *guilt*; 796.1 *immorality*; 16.38 *lawbreaking*; 802.6 *unlawfulness*; 662.2 *violation of the law*; 804.1 *wickedness*
criminalize 16.75 *make illegal*; 399.3 *veto*
criminal law 16.1 *the law*
criminally 804.21; 800.11 *dishonourably*; 662.17 *disobediently*; 806.11 *guiltily*; 16.82 *illegally*
criminal offence 16.39 *crime*; 804.7 *criminality*; 806.3 *sin*
criminal psychology 36.1 *psychology*
criminal record 744.1 *record*
criminal statistics 16.37 *criminology*
criminal world 804.7 *criminality*
criminologist 16.37 *criminology*
criminology 16.37
crimp 547.17; 700.17 *cheat*; 378.8 *hinder*; 774.13 *kidnap*; 184.10 *pleat*; 774.8 *thief*; 184.1 *wrinkle*
crimper 547.13 *beautician*
crimpers 547.11 *hairdressing salon*
crimping 774.2 *kidnapping*
crimson 674.16 *be self-conscious*; 535.1 *red*; 535.9 *redden*
crimsoning 674.2, 674.9 *blushing*
crimson lake 535.6 *red pigment*
cringe 614.4 *be a coward*; 367.9 *bow*; 664.10 *knuckle under*; 479.4 *recant*; 388.4 *succumb*
cringing 388.5 *submitting*; 664.2 *sycophancy*; 664.7 *sycophantic*
crinkle 420.12 *make rough*; 44.12 *pests and diseases*; 184.1, 184.8 *wrinkle*
crinkled 420.1 *rough*; 184.6 *wrinkly*
crinkly 420.1 *rough*; 184.6 *wrinkly*
crinkum-crankum 477.4 *ideality*
crinoid 75.3 *echinoderm*
crinoidal 75.17 *echinodermal*
crinoline 551.6 *skirt*; 551.18 *underwear*
cripple 378.8 *hinder*; 245.5 *hurt*; 238.8 *make useless*; 335.8 *overpower*; 260.19 *sick person*; 337.7 *weaken*
crippled 231.3 *deformed*; 337.10 *ill*; 335.12 *impotent*
crippling 245.11 *hurt*
crisis 287.3 *critical time*; 254.5 *danger*; 222.4 *difficult circumstances*; 705.4 *difficult question*; 123.2 *important matter*; 209.4 *interval*; 135.3 *needfulness*; 761.3 *turning point*
crisis point 761.3 *turning point*; 195.4 *zero level*
crisis theology 7.13 *theology*
crisp 424.1 *brittle*; 269.3 *concise*; 427.19 *crumbly*; 31.45 *fine*; 418.9 *harden*
crispbread 25.39 *loaf*
crispily 424.5 *fragilely*
crispiness 424.2 *brittleness*
crisply 269.5 *concisely*; 723.11 *summarily*
crispness 424.2 *brittleness*; 269.1 *conciseness*
crisps 25.10 *snack*
crispy 424.1 *brittle*
crisscross 193.8 *interweave*; 193.1 *interweaving*; 193.6 *interwoven*
criterion 216.4 *average*; 140.4 *guide*; 28.6 *law*; 129.4 *precedent*; 26.7 *standard*; 27.65 *theory*
critic 670.12; 713.4 *adviser*; 466.6 *discriminating person*; 678.7 *disparager*; 751.4 *dissenter*; 722.3 *dissertator*; 719.6 *interpreter*; 741.4 *journalist*; 464.5 *judge*; 740.11 *newspaperman*; 372.8 *person who separates*; 753.4 *protester*; 21.33 *theatregoer*; 476.4 *theorist*
critical 287.7; **381.25**; **670.27**; 719.16 *annotative*; 254.1 *dangerous*; 222.8 *difficult*; 466.9 *discriminating*; 678.15 *disparaging*; 722.5 *expository*; 123.5, 643.3 *important*; 464.8 *judging*; 16.49 *judicatory*; 17.16 *literary*; 346.12 *operative*; 753.9 *protesting*; 6.20, 549.5 *refined*; 260.22 *sick*; 264.14 *troublesome*; 254.2 *unsafe*
critical edition 719.1 *interpretation*
critical juncture 287.3 *critical time*
critically 287.10; 222.17 *difficultly*; 670.37, 753.11 *disapprovingly*; 678.18 *disparagingly*; 707.25 *explicitly*; 123.9 *importantly*; 464.13 *judicially*; 466.16 *judiciously*; 346.13 *operationally*; 264.29 *perversely*
critical mass 28.72 *nuclear fission*
critical moment 222.3; 287.3 *critical time*
critical of 606.4 *dissatisfied*
critical power 719.3 *criticism*
critical remarks 670.5, 678.2 *criticism*
critical review 670.5 *criticism*
critical situation 264.6
critical state 28.38 *thermodynamics*
critical success 21.13 *theatrical performance*
critical temperature 28.38 *thermodynamics*
critical time 287.3
criticism 670.5; **678.2**; **719.3**; 713.1 *advice*; 722.2 *article*; 751.1 *disagreement*; 606.2 *expression of dissatisfaction*; 464.1 *judgment*; 466.2 *judiciousness*; 17.4 *nonfiction*; 381.16 *personal attack*; 719.5 *science of interpretation*
criticize 381.10; **670.17**; **678.11**; **719.11**; 713.5 *advise*; 606.7 *be dissatisfied*; 264.23 *cause difficulties*; 264.24 *create difficulties*; 751.5 *disagree*; 466.14 *discriminate against*; 4.23 *discuss philosophically*; 722.4 *dissertate*; 464.12 *estimate*; 464.11 *judge*; 113.18 *object*
criticized 670.33
criticizer 670.12 *critic*

criticizing 751.9 *disagreeing*; 464.8 *judging*
critic's gift 719.3 *criticism*
critique 722.2 *article*; 719.3 *criticism*; 719.11 *criticize*; 464.1 *judgment*; 17.4 *nonfiction*
critter 70.2 *animal*
croak 515.2 *bird song*; 515.4 *cry*; 582.15 *die*; 513.2 *hoarseness*; 73.16 *live as an amphibian*; 513.5 *sound hoarse*
croakily 515.10 *howlingly*
croakiness 730.2 *inarticulation*
croaking 513.8 *hoarse*; 730.10 *low-voiced*
croaky 513.8 *hoarse*
croc 73.5 *crocodilian*
crocein 42.6 *dye*
crochet 193.2 *braid*; 193.8 *interweave*; 542.3 *pattern*
crock 24.8 *ceramic object*
crockery **410.16**; 24.1 *ceramics*
crock up 261.5 *be fatigued*; 261.6 *fatigue*
crocodile 73.5 *crocodilian*; 148.5 *piece*; 132.8 *procession*
crocodile tears 699.3 *hypocrisy*
Crocodilia 73.1 *reptile*
crocodilian **73.5**; 73.11 *reptilian*
crocus 537.8 *yellow thing*
Croesus 781.10 *wealthy person*
croft 43.6 *farm*
crofter 43.15 *agriculturist*; 564.5 *countryman*
Crohn's disease 260.8 *indigestion*
croissant 25.39 *loaf*
Croix de Guerre 743.4 *insignia*; 794.1 *trophy*
Cro-Magnon man 296.7 *ancient people*; 566.3 *early human*; 284.6 *people of the past*
crombie 551.12 *coat*
cromlech 583.6 *grave*; 744.11 *monument*; 3.11 *relic*; 10.13 *shrine*; 284.7 *thing of the past*
crony 569.5 *friend*
cronyism 466.5 *favouritism*
crook 804.10 *bad person*; 189.6 *be oblique*; 700.17 *cheat*; 774.11 *dishonest person*; 800.4 *dishonourable person*; 798.6 *evil person*; 16.40 *lawbreaker*; 651.8 *malefactor*; 773.6 *taker*; 325.5 *twist*; 7.11 *vestment*; 802.10 *wrongdoer*
crooked 236.3 *bad*; 800.7 *criminal*; 645.4 *cunning*; 800.5 *dishonourable*; 234.6 *distorted*; 699.35, 774.18 *fraudulent*; 325.21 *indirect*; 802.16 *in the wrong*; 189.4 *oblique*; 16.60 *offending*
crookedly 234.13 *asymmetrically*
crookedness 236.9 *badness*; 800.3 *criminality*; 234.1 *distortion*; 699.8 *fraud*; 800.1 *improbity*; 16.38 *lawbreaking*; 189.1 *obliqueness*
crooked teeth 299.3 *irregular thing*
croon 18.39, 516.10 *sing*; 511.8 *sound faint*
crooner 516.5 *melodist*; 18.23 *singer*
crop **43.12**; 72.16 *avian anatomy*; 376.27 *bundle*; 44.15 *cultivate*; 557.21 *eat*; 81.11 *eat grass*; 557.16 *eating utensil*; 43.17 *farm*; 80.1 *fruits*; 345.3 *growth*; 547.8 *haircut*; 356.7 *produce*; 149.10 *shorten*; 439.1 *store*; 765.6 *yield*
crop circle 11.10 *psychic phenomenon*
crop circles 737.6 *natural mystery*
crop dusting 322.1 *aviation*
crop-eared 504.12 *eared*
crop failure 247.4 *unsuccessful thing*
crop-full 232.8 *full*
crop husbandry 43.4 *arable farming*; 77.10 *plant science*
cropped 43.20 *farmable*; 233.4 *incomplete*; 149.8 *shortened*
cropping 557.5 *eating habit*; 41.13 *framing*
crop rotation 43.4 *arable farming*
crop-spraying 43.5 *cultivation*
crop top 551.18 *underwear*
crop up 520.9 *appear*; 525.12 *become visible*; 112.21 *be repeated*; 107.10 *chance*; 130.27 *emerge*; 345.9 *take effect*
crore 201.11 *million*
crores 780.3 *fortune*
crosier 7.11 *vestment*
cross **193.9**; **318.11**; **329.2**; 594.13, 624.16 *angry*; 701.8 *argumentative*; 113.21, 347.3 *counteract*; 583.4 *funeral objects*; 57.11 *gymnastic*; 743.8 *heraldic device*; 412.5 *hybrid*; 743.4 *insignia*; 814.16 *instrument of execution*; 625.4 *irascible*; 626.7 *irritable*; 412.8 *mix*; 113.22 *oppositional*; 757.2 *permit*; 742.13 *punctuate*; 708.11 *rebut*; 10.14 *sacred object*; 742.1 *sign*; 150.10 *span*; 57.7 *stationary rings*
cross a land bridge 92.12 *be marooned*
cross an isthmus 92.12 *be marooned*
cross-appeal 708.11 *rebut*; 708.3 *rebuttal*
crossappealed 708.18 *rejected*
crossbar 320.11 *bicycle part*; 47.2 *field events*; 58.7 *hurling*; 64.1 *rugger*; 66.1 *soccer*; 46.4 *stadium*; 413.2 *supporting part*
crossbar exchange 692.12 *public telephone system*
crossbeam 150.5 *broad thing*; 228.3 *stabilizer*; 413.2 *supporting part*
cross-bench 250.9 *free*
cross-bencher 250.7 *free person*
cross-benches 113.10 *the opposition*
cross block 46.9 *play*; 46.15 *play offence*
crossbow 357.7 *agent of destruction*; 330.9 *firearm*; 587.6 *historical missile weapon*
crossbowman 586.13 *historical soldiery*
cross-bred 43.21 *domesticated*; 412.12 *mixed*
cross-breed 71.9 *dog*; 412.5 *hybrid*; 412.8 *mix*
cross-breeding 412.1 *mixture*
cross-Channel swimming 67.1, 67.11 *swimming*
crosscheck 58.9 *play hockey*; 454.4 *verification*; 454.1 *verify*
crosschecked 58.8 *hockey*; 454.10 *verified*
crosschecking 58.8 *hockey*; 58.3 *ice hockey*; 454.9 *verificatory*
cross-country 324.14 *directed*; 59.17 *equine*; 59.11 *eventing*; 47.9 *track*
cross-country championships 68.2 *cross-country skiing*
cross-country equipment 68.2 *cross-country skiing*
cross-country racing 47.1 *track events*
cross-country runner 47.3 *athlete*
cross-country ski 68.5 *ski equipment*
cross-country skiing **68.2**; 68.1 *skiing*
cross-country technique 68.2 *cross-country skiing*
crosscurrent 434.4 *air flow*; 113.5 *conflict*; 347.2 *counteracting thing*; 90.6 *river flow*; 379.1 *trap*
crosscut 23.17 *carpenter*
crosscut saw 23.11 *woodworking tool*
cross-dresser 567.11 *transsexual*
crosse 58.5 *lacrosse*
crossed 412.12 *mixed*; 708.18 *rejected*
crossed fingers 699.3 *hypocrisy*
crossed in love 594.12 *hated*
crossed legs 742.3 *gesture*
crossed-loop goniometer 323.5 *navigation*
crossed out 358.6 *obliterated*
cross-examination 16.7 *legal trial*; 705.2 *questioning*
cross-examine 705.18 *interrogate*; 16.71 *try a case*
cross-examined 705.16 *questioned*
cross-examiner 734.7 *conversationalist*; 705.9 *questioner*
cross-eye 519.2 *poor sight*
cross-eyed 519.9 *weak-sighted*
cross-fertilize 412.8 *mix*
crossfire 347.2 *counteracting thing*; 381.15 *firing*
crossflow 90.6 *river flow*
cross-foot spin 68.6 *ice-skating*
cross-grained 420.2 *coarse*; 641.2 *refractory*
cross hairs 518.10 *visual aid*
cross handstand 57.7 *stationary rings*
cross hang 57.7 *stationary rings*
cross-hatch 19.20 *draw*; 523.14 *make dark*
cross-hatching 523.2 *darkening*
crossing **193.7**; **317.5**; **329.7**; 311.4 *branching*; 320.3 *carriageway*; 20.10 *church architecture*; 318.5 *crossing point*; 193.5 *crossroads*; 310.4 *meeting place*; 318.1 *passage*; 318.12 *passing*; 708.3 *rebuttal*; 321.2 *track*; 323.1 *water travel*; 323.2 *waterway*
crossing out 358.3 *obliteration*
crossing over 34.10 *cell division*
crossing point **318.5**
crossing the bar 582.1 *death*
crossing the picket lines 15.4 *industrial dispute*
crossing the Styx 582.1 *death*
cross linking 32.21 *polymer*
crossly 624.18 *angrily*; 701.17 *argumentatively*; 659.9 *discourteously*; 625.9 *irascibly*; 626.14 *irritably*
cross-multiplication 27.24 *evaluation*
cross multiply 27.91 *add*
crossness 594.5, 624.4 *anger*; 625.1 *irascibility*; 626.3 *irritableness*
cross one's bows 323.9 *navigate*
cross oneself 10.19 *offer worship*
cross one's fingers 610.9 *be hopeful*; 699.22 *be hypocritical*
cross one's heart 756.7 *promise*; 707.18 *vow*
cross one's legs 742.11 *gesture*
cross one's mind 446.14 *have an idea*
cross one's palm 768.5 *give*
cross one's Rubicon 222.12 *come to a juncture*
crossopterygian 74.2 *fish*; 74.4 *fossil fish*
cross out 708.14 *cancel*; 128.8 *eject*; 358.1 *obliterate*; 742.13 *punctuate*; 212.3 *subtract*
crossover 50.14 *punting*; 321.3 *rail*; 67.11 *swimming*
cross over 479.3 *apostatize*; 318.11, 329.2 *cross*
crossover kick 67.2 *swimming technique*
crossover recovery 50.8 *punting*
crosspatch 659.4 *discourteous person*; 625.3 *irascible person*; 499.4 *spleen*; 626.5 *sullen person*
cross-pollination 78.6 *pollination*
cross product 27.50 *scalar quantity*
cross purposes 465.1 *misjudgment*
cross-question 705.18 *interrogate*
cross-questioned 705.16 *questioned*
cross-questioning 705.2 *questioning*
cross-refer 108.7 *relate to*
cross-reference 108.2 *interrelatedness*; 108.1 *relatedness*
cross-referenced 742.17 *punctuated*
cross-reference mark 742.7 *punctuation*
cross-referred 108.5 *interrelated*
crossroads **193.5**; 311.4 *branching*; 320.3 *carriageway*; 222.3 *critical moment*; 318.5 *crossing point*; 317.3 *road*; 87.10 *village*
crossroad sign 742.5 *indicator*
cross section 27.41 *geometric figure*; 28.71 *nuclear reaction*; 717.8 *representative*
cross-stitch 542.3 *pattern*
cross swords 331.2 *collide*; 517.11 *disagree*
cross swords with 585.14 *battle*; 242.11 *quarrel*
cross talk 40.19 *computing terms*; 692.19 *radio reception*
cross the bar 582.15 *die*
cross the border 329.2 *cross*
cross the floor 479.3 *apostatize*; 639.9 *change sides*
cross the picket lines 15.12 *have an industrial dispute*
cross the Rubicon 638.8 *brace oneself*; 329.2 *cross*; 469.3 *side with*
cross the street 317.14 *find one's way*
cross the Styx 582.15 *die*
cross the threshold 314.9 *enter*
cross through 358.1 *obliterate*
cross to bear 249.1 *adversity*; 378.6 *burden*
cross-tree 79.12 *figurative usage*; 50.3 *parts of a sailing boat*
cross-ventilation 434.6 *ventilation*
crossways 150.8 *breadthwise*
crosswind 31.15 *wind direction*
crosswise 150.8 *breadthwise*; 189.4 *oblique*; 189.8 *obliquely*
crossword 737.4 *brain-teaser*
crotch 551.24 *part of garment*
crotched 65.9 *billiard*
crotchet 18.17 *notation*; 642.3 *whim*
crotchety 642.1 *capricious*; 625.4 *irascible*; 641.2 *refractory*
crouch 155.8 *be low*; 367.16 *courtesy*; 664.10 *knuckle under*; 367.8 *sit*; 388.4 *succumb*
crouched 155.5 *low*
crouching 155.5 *low*; 367.23 *sedentary*; 388.5 *submitting*
crouch ware 24.1 *ceramics*
croup 57.6 *pommel horse*; 260.9 *respiratory disease*
croupy 260.23 *diseased*
crouton 25.38 *bread*
crow 532.9 *black thing*; 256.12 *cleaner*; 623.26 *outdo*; 597.7 *show joy*; 515.5 *sing*; 72.6 *songbird*; 729.13 *speak in a particular way*
crowbar 369.10 *excavator*; 438.1 *tool*; 438.10 *use tools*
crowd **208.11**; **376.20**; **376.40**; 376.1 *assembly*; 219.1 *excess*; 376.11 *group*; 416.9 *make dense*; 668.22 *show disrespect*; 152.7 *thicken*; 208.4 *throng*
crowd control methods 252.4 *safety device*
crowded **208.10**; **376.50**; 317.15 *accessible*; 152.2 *dense*; 297.3 *frequent*; 232.8 *full*
crowdedly 297.1 *frequently*
crowdedness 297.4 *frequency*
crowd in 314.12 *flood in*; 368.3 *impact*
crowd together 191.6 *become smaller*
crowing cock 290.2 *morning thing*
crowlike 72.21 *avian*
crown 211.6 *add*; 179.3 *circular thing*; 331.8 *club*; 232.4 *complete*; 550.23 *cover*; 20.19 *decorate*; 394.20 *doctor*; 131.15 *end*; 130.25 *enrol*; 780.10 *former British money*; 658.12 *greet*; 174.2 *head*; 551.15 *headgear*; 743.8 *heraldic device*; 743.4 *insignia*; 601.19 *install*; 482.6 *objective*; 230.5 *perfect*; 69.10 *play*; 35.21 *practise dentistry*; 813.2 *prize*; 366.3 *promote*; 425.11 *tooth*; 174.7 *top*; 79.2 *tree part*; 794.1 *trophy*
Crown Attorney 16.10 *law officer*
Crown Counsel 16.11 *British law officer*
crown court 16.20 *British court*; 464.3 *place of judgment*
crown court judge 16.25 *British judge*; 464.6 *justice*
crowned 400.12 *masterful*; 20.17 *structured*; 174.6 *topped*
crowned head 400.2 *sovereign*
crowned with success 246.13 *successful*
crown gall 44.12 *pests and diseases*; 79.10 *tree disease*
crown glass 527.9 *glass*
crown-green 51.9 *bowls*
crown-green bowls 51.1 *green bowling*
crowning 121.14, 235.2 *best*; 601.12 *ceremonial*; 232.7 *complete*; 35.4 *dentistry*; 131.20 *ending*; 246.13 *successful*; 394.12 *surgery*; 174.5 *top*
crowning achievement 356.6 *great work*; 230.3 *perfection*
crowning glory 131.10 *ending*
crown lands 440.1 *property*
crown-of-thorns 75.3 *echinoderm*
crownpiece 174.2 *head*
crown prince 400.2 *sovereign*
crown princess 400.2 *sovereign*
Crown Prosecution Service 16.11 *British law officer*
crown rot 44.12 *pests and diseases*
crown wheel 307.6 *rotator*
crow over 661.5 *defy*
crow's foot 184.1 *wrinkle*
crow's nest 154.8 *high thing*; 397.8 *vantage point*; 518.9 *viewpoint*
CRT 39.20 *electron tube*
crucial 344.13 *causal*; 287.7 *critical*; 254.1 *dangerous*; 222.8 *difficult*; 99.5 *essential*; 553.7 *fashionable*; 173.8 *focal*; 123.5, 643.3 *important*; 346.12 *operative*; 705.13 *problematic*
crucially 344.14 *causally*; 287.10 *critically*; 222.17 *difficultly*; 123.9 *importantly*; 346.13 *operationally*
crucial moment 287.3 *critical time*; 123.2 *important matter*; 761.3 *turning point*
crucial point 761.3 *turning point*
crucial time 287.3 *critical time*
crucible 493.3 *heater*; 760.4 *medium of conversion*; 412.6 *mixer*
cruciferous 77.16 *taxonomic*
crucifix 10.14 *sacred object*; 11.6 *talisman*
crucifixion 19.10 *art subject*; 814.13 *capital punishment*; 582.4 *death sentence*; 382.6 *ritual killing*
cruciform 27.40 *curve*
crucify 814.5 *execute*; 236.14 *ill-treat*; 491.11 *inflict pain*; 382.20 *kill ritually*
crud 258.4 *dirt*; 548.1 *spot*
crude 659.6 *bad-mannered*; 486.4 *bungled*; 497.6 *coarse*; 529.12 *gaudy*; 231.2, 233.4 *incomplete*; 796.12 *indecent*; 544.8 *indecorous*; 437.6 *oil*; 420.5 *unfinished*
crude data 27.57 *population*
crude estimate 476.3 *conjecture*
crudely 233.6, 420.15 *incompletely*; 659.10 *rudely*; 497.11 *tastelessly*
crudeness 659.2 *bad manners*; 497.4 *bad*

taste; 675.3 *grossness*; 231.5 *imperfection*; 544.2 *impropriety*; 420.10 *rough idea*
crude oil 435.1 *materials*; 437.6 *oil*
crude rubber 422.4 *rubber*
crudity 646.2 *naivety*
cruel **651.11**; 381.23 *attacking*; 236.5 *harmful*; 491.8 *inflicting pain*; 382.24 *murderous*; 628.4 *pitiless*; 647.8 *severe*; 380.6 *violent*; 585.16 *warlike*; 804.11 *wicked*
cruel act 651.7 *act of malevolence*
cruel conduct 651.2 *cruelness*
cruel-hearted 651.11 *cruel*
cruelly 651.20 *malevolently*; 628.7 *pitilessly*; 647.11 *severely*; 804.18 *wickedly*; 236.15 *worthlessly*
cruelness **651.2**; 804.1 *wickedness*
cruel side 169.4 *aspect*
Cruelty 628
cruelty 651.2 *cruelness*; 571.3 *divorce court*; 236.11 *harmfulness*; 628.1 *pitilessness*; 647.1 *severity*; 804.1 *wickedness*
cruet 10.14 *sacred object*
cruise 322.10 *fly*; 300.15 *walk*
Cruise missile 587.5 *missile weapon*
cruiser 50.2 *sailing boat*; 586.24 *warship*
cruiser division 584.4 *military organization*
cruiser racing 50.1 *sailing*
cruiserweight 586.3 *athlete*; 52.4 *boxer*; 52.3 *boxing weight divisions*; 52.14 *combat*; 414.7 *weighing*
cruising 50.10 *sailing*; 323.1 *water travel*
cruising canoe 50.6 *canoeing*
cruising hook 50.6 *canoeing*
cruising stroke 50.6 *canoeing*
cruising yacht 50.2 *sailing boat*
crumb **427.6**; 25.38 *bread*; 427.23 *crumble*; 196.3 *fragment*; 159.3 *little piece*; 205.7 *piece*
crumble **427.23**; 424.4 *be brittle*; 357.13 *be destroyed*; 337.6 *be weak*; 427.6 *crumb*; 25.35 *dessert*; 245.1 *deteriorate*; 375.3 *disintegrate*; 296.17 *grow old*; 245.4 *impair*; 372.9 *separate*
crumble away 357.13 *be destroyed*; 278.4 *be transient*
crumbled 424.1 *brittle*; 427.19 *crumbly*
crumble into dust 427.27 *come to dust*; 296.17 *grow old*
crumble to dust 357.13 *be destroyed*
crumblies 296.2 *old people*
crumbliness **427.2**; 424.2 *brittleness*
crumbling 424.1 *brittle*; 424.2 *brittleness*; 427.19 *crumbly*; 357.15 *destroyed*; 375.6 *disintegrating*; 296.12 *olden*; 427.4 *pulverization*; 254.2 *unsafe*
crumbly **427.19**; 424.1 *brittle*; 556.7 *older person*; 205.11 *partial*; 268.10 *slippery*
crumbs 122.7 *inferior thing*; 238.6 *refuse*; 215.2 *residue*
crumminess 236.8 *inferiority*; 793.3 *shoddiness*
crummy 236.2 *inferior*; 122.14 *poor*; 793.10 *shoddy*; 260.22 *sick*
crump 331.2 *collide*
crumpet 25.39 *loaf*; 568.9 *woman considered as a sex object*
crumple 408.24 *make disordered*; 420.12 *make rough*; 184.1, 184.8 *wrinkle*
crumpled 420.1 *rough*; 408.15 *untidy*; 184.6 *wrinkly*
crumple up 357.13 *be destroyed*
crumply 420.1 *rough*; 184.6 *wrinkly*
crunch 492.12 *abut*; 427.26 *beat*; 331.2 *collide*; 331.12 *collision*; 557.21 *eat*; 95.5 *realities*; 372.9 *separate*; 513.5 *sound hoarse*
crusade 340.1 *action*; 586.36 *combat*; 7.20 *preach*; 585.1 *war*
crusader 381.19 *attacker*; 340.3 *doer*; 586.6 *militarist*; 7.4 *religionist*
crusading 340.5 *acting*; 586.33 *combative*; 7.15 *religious*; 7.2 *religiousness*
cruse 24.8 *ceramic object*
crush 623.23 *abase*; 427.26 *beat*; 424.4 *be brittle*; 647.5 *be severe*; 246.9 *be victorious*; 342.6 *business*; 191.1 *contraction*; 208.11 *crowd*; 246.10 *defeat heavily*; 481.3 *deflect*; 357.9 *demolish*; 611.10 *disappoint*; 43.10 *farm tool*; 367.2 *flatten*; 623.17 *humiliate*; 236.14 *ill-treat*; 245.4 *impair*; 595.3 *likes*; 191.5 *make smaller*; 400.14 *master*; 704.8 *refute*; 251.8 *restrain*; 593.2 *romantic love*; 376.21 *scrum*; 208.4 *throng*
crushability 424.2 *brittleness*; 191.2 *contractibility*
crushable 424.1 *brittle*; 191.9 *contractible*
crush barrier 252.4 *safety device*
crushed 424.1 *brittle*; 208.10 *crowded*; 357.15 *destroyed*; 604.9 *disappointed*; 623.3 *humbled*; 427.18 *pulverized*; 191.7 *smaller*; 184.6 *wrinkly*
crushed velvet 184.4 *wrinkled thing*
crusher 620.3 *boring person*; 191.4 *contractor*; 131.13 *ender*; 427.11 *pulverizer*
crushing 424.1 *brittle*; 191.8 *contracting*; 191.1 *contraction*; 357.2 *destroying*; 623.6 *humiliating*; 576.11 *laborious*; 427.4 *pulverization*; 251.1 *restraint*; 246.15 *victorious*
crushing blow 357.4 *ruin*
crushing device 814.15 *instrument of torture*
crushing reply 623.14 *rebuke*
crushing victory 246.2 *victory*
crush note 18.16 *musical note*
crush of shoppers 342.6 *business*
crush one's hopes 604.6 *disappoint*
crush to pieces 357.9 *demolish*
crust 416.8 *be dense*; 25.38 *bread*; 660.2 *cheek*; 550.2 *cover*; 30.18 *earth's crust*; 171.1 *exterior*; 418.7 *hard substance*; 205.7 *piece*
Crustacea 75.4 *arthropod*
crustacean 75.4 *arthropod*; 75.18 *arthropodous*
crustaceous 75.18 *arthropodous*
crustal 30.53 *solid-earth*
crustal movement 30.20 *earth movement*
crusted 171.6 *exterior*; 418.3 *hardened*
crusted port 558.9 *wine*
crustily 418.12 *toughly*
crustiness 659.1 *discourtesy*
crustose 84.8 *lichenoid*
crustose lichen 84.6 *lichen*
crusty 660.14 *cheeky*; 659.5 *discourteous*; 171.6 *exterior*; 418.1 *hard*; 625.4 *irascible*
crutch 413.3 *body support*; 392.19 *support*; 79.2 *tree part*
crux 123.3 *chief thing*; 287.3 *critical time*; 705.4 *difficult question*; 99.2 *essential content*; 264.4 *problem*
crux of the matter 123.3 *chief thing*
cruzado 780.11 *national coins*
cry **514.1**; **514.13**; **515.4**; 507.8 *be loud*; 600.7 *dance*; 600.2 *fanfare*; 602.8 *grieve*; 59.8 *hunting*; 603.2 *lament*; 507.2 *outcry*; 701.5 *plea*; 740.14 *proclaim*; 711.7 *raise the alarm*; 710.1, 710.6 *request*; 559.7 *secrete*; 433.32 *seep*; 742.12 *signal*; 729.12 *speak loudly*; 603.7 *weep*; 742.6 *word*
cry-baby 603.3 *lamenter*; 488.4 *someone or something that feels*; 337.4 *weakling*
cry bloody murder 753.7 *complain*
cry blue murder 753.7 *complain*; 711.7 *raise the alarm*
cry down 670.17 *criticize*; 678.10 *disparage*
cry for help 742.6 *word*
cry for quarter 627.12 *ask for mercy*
cry for the moon 103.10 *attempt the impossible*; 238.9 *waste effort*
cry havoc 382.26 *no quarter!*
cry Hughie 371.15 *vomit*
crying **514.18**; 514.6 *cry of pain*; 135.6 *demanding*; 603.1 *lamentation*; 603.4 *lamenting*; 507.6 *loud*; 559.1 *secretion*; 559.4 *secretory*; 740.20 *well-known*
crying cold 260.9 *respiratory disease*
crying down 678.1 *disparagement*
crying out for 135.6 *demanding*
crying shame 802.9 *dishonour*
crying with rage 624.16 *angry*
cryobiological 34.20 *biological*
cryobiologist 34.19 *life scientist*
cryobiology 34.1 *life science*
cry of disapproval **514.7**
cry of greeting **514.4**
cry of joy **514.2**
cry of pain **514.6**
cry of praise **514.3**
cry of the chase 514.5 *hunting cry*
cry of wolf 711.3 *false alarm*
cry of wonder 619.2 *sign of wonderment*
cryogen 494.4 *cooler*
cryogenic 494.9 *heat-resistant*; 28.98 *physical*
cryogenically 28.100 *physically*
cryogenic memory 40.6 *memory*
cryogenic pump 32.20 *surface chemistry*
cryogenics 494.4 *cooler*; 28.3 *modern physics*
cryohydrate 32.7 *chemical compound*
cryometer 26.8 *meter*
cryometry 26.2 *micrometry*
cry on 633.10 *chase*
cry one's eyes out 603.7 *weep*
cryonic 494.9 *heat-resistant*
cryonics 494.4 *cooler*
cryostat 494.4 *cooler*
cryosurgery 494.4 *cooler*
cry out **514.10**
cry out against 481.1 *dissuade*
cry out for 617.12 *desire*; 135.8 *miss*
cry out for rest 261.5 *be fatigued*
crypt 10.12 *church*; 156.4 *deep thing*; 583.6 *grave*
cryptanalysis 719.5 *science of interpretation*
cryptanalyst 719.6 *interpreter*
cryptic 523.11 *benighted*; 453.3 *confused*; 736.15 *disguised*; 528.4 *inscrutable*; 737.11 *mysterious*; 266.2 *obscure*; 11.14 *occult*; 696.1 *unintelligible*
cryptically 266.4 *obscurely*; 528.13 *opaquely*; 696.13 *unintelligibly*
cryptogam 77.4 *lower plant*
cryptogamic 77.16 *taxonomic*
cryptogram 737.4 *brain-teaser*
cryptographer 737.4 *brain-teaser*; 719.6 *interpreter*
cryptographic 736.15 *disguised*
cryptography 737.4 *brain-teaser*; 719.5 *science of interpretation*
cryptologist 719.6 *interpreter*
cryptology 719.5 *science of interpretation*
cry quits 749.5 *make peace*; 388.3 *submit*
cry sob 491.12 *express pain*
crystal **32.4**; 424.3 *brittle thing*; 527.9 *glass*; 416.4 *solid body*; 527.1 *transparent*
crystal ball 475.10 *cards*; 11.9 *divination*; 527.8 *transparent thing*
crystal-ball gazing 283.4 *looking to the future*
crystal boundary 32.4 *crystal*
crystal-clear 520.2 *clear*; 738.15 *open*; 695.2 *simple*; 527.1 *transparent*
crystal-controlled oscillator 39.21 *rectifier*
crystal-gaze 11.23 *divine*; 518.17 *imagine*
crystal gazer 101.7 *believer in a nonmaterial world*; 11.13 *diviner*; 475.9 *forecaster*; 518.11 *observer*; 283.5 *predictor*
crystal-gazing 11.9, 475.2 *divination*; 518.5 *imagination*; 283.4 *looking to the future*
crystal glass 527.9 *glass*
crystalline **32.33**; 416.7 *condensed*; 418.1 *hard*; 527.1 *transparent*
crystalline mineral 30.34 *mineral*
crystalline texture 30.28 *rock*
crystallinity 527.5 *transparency*
crystallite 32.4 *crystal*
crystallization 416.2 *concentration*; 760.1 *conversion*; 32.4 *crystal*; 30.29 *petrogenesis*; 32.5 *process*; 418.6 *solidification*
crystallize 416.8 *be dense*; 527.11 *be transparent*; 760.7 *convert into*; 30.62 *lithify*; 24.11 *make ceramics*; 527.12 *make transparent*; 32.25, 418.10 *solidify*
crystallized 24.10 *ceramic*; 416.7 *condensed*; 32.33 *crystalline*; 418.3 *hardened*; 498.6 *sweet*
crystallized fruit 25.41 *sweet*
crystallized glass 24.9 *industrial ceramics*
crystallized rose petals 78.8 *flower product*
crystallize out 32.25 *solidify*
crystallizing 760.14 *converting*
crystallographer 32.2 *chemist*
crystallographic 32.31 *chemical*; 28.98 *physical*
crystallographically 28.100 *physically*
crystallography 32.1 *chemistry*; 32.4 *crystal*; 28.3 *modern physics*
crystalloid 32.33 *crystalline*
crystal oscillator 39.21 *rectifier*
crystal set 692.18 *radio*
crystal system 32.4 *crystal*
crystal vision 11.8 *psychic power*
cry too soon 711.7 *raise the alarm*
cry uncle 388.3 *submit*
cry up 669.15 *compliment*
cry wolf 699.26 *falsify*; 711.7 *raise the alarm*
C-shape 50.14 *punting*
C-shape shove 50.8 *punting*
Ctenophora 75.7 *coelenterate*
ctenophoran 75.21 *coelenterate*
ctenophore 75.7 *coelenterate*
CT scan 35.7 *diagnosis*
CT scanner 394.14 *hospital*
CU 40.5 *processor*
cub 71.35 *give birth*; 561.11 *have young*; 555.4 *young animal*; 71.19 *young mammal*; 555.7 *young man*
cubage 158.1 *size*
Cuban heels 551.19 *footwear*
cubature 158.1 *size*
cubby 410.2 *compartment*
cubbyhole 410.2 *compartment*; 736.2 *hiding place*; 159.5 *little space*; 577.1 *workshop*
cube 27.91, 210.9 *add*; 213.5 *make bigger*; 27.17 *multiplication*; 27.46 *polyhedron*; 199.1 *three*; 199.10 *triple*
cubed 199.7 *three*
cube root 27.17 *multiplication*; 194.6 *power*
cubic **27.84**; 32.33 *crystalline*; 27.76 *functional*; 26.12 *metrical*; 141.11 *spatial*
cubic close packed 32.33 *crystalline*
cubic close packing 32.4 *crystal*
cubic content 141.1 *space*
cubic crystal 32.4 *crystal*
cubic equation 27.27 *equation*
cubicle 410.2 *compartment*; 43.7 *farm building*
cubiform 27.84 *cubic*
cubist 19.29 *realist*
cubitiere 384.7 *armour*
cuboid 27.84 *cubic*; 27.46 *polyhedron*
cub reporter 741.4 *journalist*
cucking stool 814.14 *instrument of punishment*
cuckold 796.17 *be sexually immoral*; 570.10 *married man*
cuckolding 796.4 *illicit love*
cuckoldry 796.4 *illicit love*; 593.8 *love affair*
cuckoo 515.2 *bird song*; 371.26 *ejector*; 564.6 *illegal occupant*; 461.11 *insane*
cuckoo clock 281.6 *clock*
cuckoo in the nest 371.26 *ejector*; 100.8 *intruder*; 109.2 *unrelated thing*
cuckoo-like 72.21 *avian*
cuculiform 72.21 *avian*
cucumber sandwich 25.11 *sandwich*
cud-chewer 71.15 *hoofed mammal*
cud-chewing 71.33 *ungulate*
cuddle 490.10 *comfort*; 593.14 *communication of love*; 490.9 *give pleasure*; 593.27 *kiss*; 360.6 *retain*; 360.1 *retention*
cuddlesome 593.22 *lovable*; 490.6 *pleasant*
cuddling 593.14 *communication of love*
cuddly 593.22 *lovable*; 490.6 *pleasant*
cuddy 316.6 *beast of burden*
cudgel 587.7 *blunt weapon*; 331.8 *club*; 814.3 *hit*; 814.14 *instrument of punishment*; 331.16 *weapons*
cue 21.22 *acting*; 21.38 *dramatize*; 65.3 *English billiards*; 331.15 *ram*; 462.4 *reminder*; 742.1 *sign*
cue ball 65.3 *English billiards*; 65.5 *snooker*
cue rest 65.1 *billiards*
cue stick 65.1 *billiards*
cuff 331.13 *blow*; 814.12 *corporal punishment*; 814.3 *hit*; 551.24 *part of garment*
cufflink 373.8 *fastening*
cuffs 251.5 *means of restraint*
cui bono? 237.12 *usefully*
cuirass 384.7 *armour*
cuirassier 586.20 *cavalryman*
cuisine 25.1 *cookery*
cuisinier 25.2 *cook*
cuisse 384.7 *armour*
culbute 305.4 *fall*
cul-de-sac 309.4 *closed place*; 317.3 *road*; 264.8 *snag*
culinarily **25.57**
culinary **25.56**
culinary herb 77.2 *plant*; 44.11 *vegetable*
culinary masterpiece 25.9 *dish*
cull 382.9 *animal killing*; 69.3 *card game terms*; 382.22 *kill animals*; 469.4 *pick*; 60.7 *shoot*; 212.3 *subtract*
culled 60.8 *shooting*
culling 60.2 *hunting*
culm 81.3 *grass plant*
culminate 304.13 *ascend*; 232.5 *be complete*; 121.8 *be superior*; 204.10 *complete*; 131.15 *end*; 213.5 *make bigger*; 154.16 *rise*; 345.5 *show an effect*; 174.7 *top*
culminating 232.7 *complete*; 131.20 *ending*; 174.5 *top*
culmination 232.1 *completeness*; 232.3 *completion*; 345.1 *effect*; 131.10 *ending*;

213.1 *increase*; 304.6 *mounting*; 174.1 *summit*
culminative 131.20 *ending*
culottes 551.6 *skirt*
culpability 274.7 *errancy*; 806.1 *guilt*; 16.38 *lawbreaking*
culpable 670.36 *blameworthy*; 804.15 *criminal*; 274.16 *errant*; 806.5 *guilty*; 802.16 *in the wrong*; 16.60 *offending*
culpable omission 806.3 *sin*
culpably 804.21 *criminally*; 16.89 *guiltily*
culprit 715.4 *accused person*; 806.4 *guilty person*; 16.40 *lawbreaker*; 804.9 *wicked person*; 802.10 *wrongdoer*
cult 632.4 *custom*; 9.10 *idolatrous*; 9.2 *idolatry*; 7.1 *religion*; 450.2 *religious belief*; 10.2 *ritualism*
cultish 9.10 *idolatrous*
cultism 9.2 *idolatry*; 10.2 *ritualism*
cultist 9.6 *idolater*; 9.10 *idolatrous*
cultivable 43.20 *farmable*
cultivar 44.5 *gardening*; 34.17 *taxonomy*
cultivate **44.15**; 392.23 *advise*; 344.9 *be the cause of*; 243.7 *develop*; 6.22 *educate*; 43.17 *farm*; 599.15 *humour*; 244.1 *improve*; 44.14 *practise horticulture*; 356.10 *produce*
cultivate a habit 632.18 *habituate*
cultivated 543.3 *elegant*; 658.8 *good-mannered*; 455.9 *literate*; 44.19 *ornamental*; 6.20 *refined*; 495.8 *tasteful*; 77.15 *wild*
cultivated land 43.11 *farmland*
cultivated mushroom 83.2 *mushroom*
cultivated plant 77.2 *plant*
cultivate friends 569.13 *befriend*
cultivation **43.5**; 344.1 *cause*; 243.13 *development*; 6.1 *education*; 455.3 *learning*; 6.11 *refinement*; 495.2 *taste of life*
cultivator 43.15 *agriculturist*; 43.10 *farm tool*; 44.6, 438.3 *garden tool*; 243.15 *preparer*; 356.9 *producer*; 561.5 *propagator*
cultrate 425.3 *sharp-edged*
cultural 244.16 *improving*; 1.14 *societal*
cultural anthropology 1.1 *anthropology*
cultural commentator 17.15 *literary person*
cultural ecology 2.1 *sociology*
culturally 1.18 *societally*; 2.16 *sociologically*
culture 43.5 *cultivation*; 543.1, 549.1 *elegance*; 658.2 *good manners*; 455.3 *learning*; 17.1 *literature*; 566.4 *modern human*; 1.7 *society*
cultured 658.8 *good-mannered*; 125.13 *imitation*; 700.39 *imitative*; 4.19 *learned*; 455.9 *literate*; 44.19 *ornamental*; 6.20 *refined*; 115.8 *simulated*
cultured pearl 700.6 *imitation*
cultus 632.4 *custom*
culumet 496.7 *tobacco*
culverin 587.12 *historical guns*
culvert 317.11 *channel*; 38.22 *tunnel*
cumber 414.14 *make heavy*
Cumberland sausage 25.29 *sausage*
cumbersome 264.15, 486.3 *clumsy*; 544.7 *graceless*; 240.1 *inconvenient*; 414.3 *ponderous*
cumbersomely 414.17 *burdensomely*
cumbersomeness 158.2 *bigness*; 240.3 *inconvenience*; 414.8 *weighing down*
cumbrance 414.8 *weighing down*
Cumbrian Mountains 89.5 *British mountains*
cumbrous 414.3 *ponderous*
cumbrously 414.17 *burdensomely*
cumbrousness 544.4 *inelegance of speech*
cumin 496.5 *herbs*
cummerbund 373.10 *band*; 179.3 *circular thing*; 551.3 *formal dress*
cumshaw 768.2 *gift*
cumulate **376.48**; 765.11 *acquire*
cumulation 765.3 *acquisition*
cumulative 765.18 *acquisitional*; 211.8 *additional*; 213.6 *increasing*
cumulative distribution function 27.59 *probability distribution*
cumulative effect 213.1 *increase*
cumulative evidence 716.5 *legal evidence*
cumulatively 211.10 *additionally*; 765.20 *gainfully*; 213.8 *increasingly*
cumulativeness 213.1 *increase*
cumulative vote 469.10 *vote*
cumuliform 31.49 *cloudy*
cumulonimbiform 31.49 *cloudy*
cumulonimbus 31.18 *cloud*
cumulous 31.49 *cloudy*
cumulus 31.18 *cloud*
cunctative 341.3 *inactive*
cuneal 5.41 *lettered*
cuneate 176.9 *angled*
cuneiform 176.9 *angled*; 5.13 *letter*; 5.41 *lettered*
cuniform 20.17 *structured*
cuniform church 20.10 *church architecture*
Cunning 645
cunning **645.1**; **645.4**; **702.3**; **702.8**; 699.33 *deceitful*; 699.5 *deceitfulness*; 700.34 *deceiving*; 700.1 *deception*; 268.9 *duplicity*; 458.6 *intelligent*; 484.15 *planning*; 485.6 *skilful*; 485.1 *skill*; 631.9 *tactics*; 485.9 *well-made*; 458.1 *wisdom*
cunning fellow 485.5 *expert*
Cunningham 50.10 *sailing*
Cunningham hole 50.3 *parts of a sailing boat*
Cunningham tackle 50.3 *parts of a sailing boat*
cunningly **645.6**; 484.17 *conspiratorially*; 268.24 *duplicitously*; 702.15 *hypocritically*
cunningness 645.1 *cunning*
cunning person **645.3**
cunning plan 446.3 *plan*
cunt 561.8 *organs of reproduction*; 568.9 *woman considered as a sex object*
cup 558.7 *alcoholic drink*; 183.3 *cavity*; 24.8 *ceramic object*; 203.3 *container*; 68.10 *curling*; 558.2 *drink*; 558.10 *drink container*; 410.13 *drinking vessel*; 56.2 *golfing terms*; 744.11 *monument*; 482.6 *objective*; 813.2 *prize*; 369.14 *suck*; 794.1 *trophy*
cup anemometer 31.7 *weather instruments*
cupbearer 316.7 *transferor*
cupboard 23.5, 410.3 *cabinet*; 439.4 *storage*
cupboard love 699.3 *hypocrisy*
cupboard room 439.4 *storage*
cupboard space 439.4 *storage*
cupcake 25.36 *cake*; 568.9 *woman considered as a sex object*
cup fungi 83.3 *fungi*
cup-holder 121.6 *paragon*; 485.4 *skilled person*
Cupid 593.16 *gods and goddesses of love*
cupidity 617.1 *desire*
Cupid's string 593.2 *romantic love*
cup of sorrows 249.1 *adversity*
cup of tea 558.2 *drink*; 139.8 *specialization*
cupola 182.3 *dome*; 154.8 *high thing*; 20.9 *miscellaneous architectural features*; 550.7 *overhead covering*
cuppa 558.2 *drink*
cupping 371.22 *disgorgement*; 369.4 *sucking*; 394.12 *surgery*
cupreous 534.1 *brown*
cupric 32.34 *elemental*
cupriferous 32.34 *elemental*
cuprous 32.34 *elemental*
cup-shaped 183.6 *concave*
cup that cheers 690.13 *drink*
cur 71.9 *dog*; 412.5 *hybrid*
curability 393.11 *recuperation*
curable 244.15 *improvable*; 394.18 *medical*; 393.14 *repairable*
curableness 393.11 *recuperation*
curacy 7.9 *priesthood*
curate 7.8 *priest*
curate's egg 231.5 *imperfection*
curative 608.8 *relieving*; 394.17 *remedial*; 393.16 *restorative*; 35.25 *therapeutic*
curative dance 22.4 *historic dancing*
curator 579.15 *manager*; 252.3 *protector*
curb 684.5 *be self-restrained*; 333.9 *decelerate*; 378.8 *hinder*; 378.1 *hindrance*; 166.7 *limit*; 166.2 *limiting factor*; 685.4 *moderate*; 251.8, 378.10 *restrain*; 251.1, 378.4 *restraint*; 333.3 *slow down*
curbed 378.14 *blocked*; 136.12 *conditional*
curd 416.4 *solid body*
curdle 416.8 *be dense*; 499.8 *sour*
curdled 416.7 *condensed*; 375.5 *disintegrated*; 499.6 *unpalatable*
cure **393.6**; 347.3 *counteract*; 347.2 *counteracting thing*; 243.7 *develop*; 487.5 *disaccustom*; 428.17 *dry*; 244.1 *improve*; 244.5 *improvement*; 259.7 *make healthy*; 352.1 *means*; 392.5 *medical assistance*; 749.4 *pacify*; 35.19 *practise medicine*; 359.5 *preserve*; 393.11 *recuperation*; 608.3 *reliever*; 394.1, 394.19 *remedy*; 496.12 *season*; 394.13 *therapy*
cure-all 37.3 *drug*; 394.1 *remedy*
cured **393.15**; 259.1 *healthy*; 496.9 *piquant*; 359.7 *preserved*; 608.7 *relieved*
cured fish 25.16 *fish dish*
cure itself 393.6 *cure*
cure of 393.6 *cure*
curer 393.12 *repairer*
curette 394.20 *doctor*; 371.11 *void*
curfew 251.4 *detention*; 166.2 *limiting factor*; 399.1 *veto*
curfew bell 711.2 *danger signal*
Curia 579.7 *council*; 16.22 *ecclesiastical court*
curial 16.49 *judicatory*
Curia Regis 579.7 *council*
curing **496.3**; 25.8 *cooking technique*; 359.1 *preservation*; 394.17 *remedial*
curio 793.5 *cheap item*; 485.3 *masterpiece*; 738.7 *showpiece*
Curiosity 644
curiosity **644.1**; **705.8**; 617.1 *desire*; 6.10 *educability*; 619.5 *person of wonder*; 118.4 *unusualness*
curious **644.5**; 139.16 *characteristic*; 118.14 *eccentric*; 6.17 *educable*; 447.8 *problematic*; 705.12 *questioning*; 471.7 *watchful*
curiously **644.8**; 447.13 *problematically*; 705.23 *questioningly*
curiousness 644.1 *curiosity*
curious person **644.3**
curl 177.2 *bend*; 180.2 *coil*; 180.6 *convolute*; 547.17 *crimp*; 68.10 *curling*; 177.6 *curve*; 27.50 *scalar quantity*
curled 177.4 *curved*
curled-up 191.7 *smaller*
curler 330.14 *thrower*
curlers 373.8 *fastening*
curlew 72.3 *water bird*
curlicue 180.2 *coil*
curliness 177.1 *curvature*
curling 68.10
curling association 68.10 *curling*
curling broom 68.10 *curling*
curling championship 68.10 *curling*
curling ice 68.10 *curling*
curling match 68.10 *curling*
curling player 68.11 *skier*
curling rink 68.10 *curling*
curling stone 330.10 *ball*; 68.10 *curling*
curling technique 68.10 *curling*
curling tee 68.10 *curling*
curl one's lip 742.11 *gesture*
curl pass 46.9 *play*
curl removal 547.8 *haircut*
curls 547.8 *haircut*
curl up 191.6 *become smaller*
curl up and die 582.15 *die*
curl upwards 304.13 *ascend*
curly 420.3 *barbed*
curmudgeon 659.4 *discourteous person*
curmudgeonly 626.7 *irritable*
currant 25.42 *preserve*
currant bun 25.39 *loaf*
currency 780.1 *money*; 295.1 *newness*; 740.7 *publicity*; 282.4 *up-to-dateness*
current 216.1 *average*; 302.11 *course*; 28.51, 39.9 *electric current*; 93.10 *existing*; 632.10 *familiar*; 300.2 *momentum*; 295.10 *new*; 282.6 *present*; 740.19 *published*; 90.6 *river flow*; 229.1 *tendency*; 447.6 *topical*; 379.1 *trap*; 237.2 *usable*
current account 789.1 *accounts*; 780.6 *funds*
current account deposit 783.3 *deposit*
current affairs 741.1 *news*
current assets 440.5 *personal estate*
current density 28.51, 39.9 *electric current*
current electricity 28.42, 39.3 *electricity*
currently 295.21 *newly*; 93.23 *now*; 447.12 *topically*
current of air 434.4 *air flow*
current price 790.1 *price*
current transformer 39.22 *transformer*
curricular **6.21**
curriculum 220.5 *list of appointments*; 6.3 *subject*; 281.2 *timetable*
curriculum vitae 716.6 *documentation*; 721.4 *factual account*; 17.4 *nonfiction*; 744.1 *record*
curried 25.56 *culinary*
curry 25.55 *cook*; 25.49 *Indian dish*; 59.16 *ride*; 365.12 *rub*; 496.12 *season*; 496.2 *seasoning*
currycomb 59.14 *horse-riding terms*; 365.12 *rub*
curry favour 677.10 *cajole*; 664.9 *fawn*; 593.28 *win the love of*
curry powder 496.2 *seasoning*
Curse 712
curse **594.2**; **594.15**; **712.1**; **712.5**; 249.1 *adversity*; 594.17 *anger*; 798.11 *be evil*; 11.21 *bewitch*; 16.79 *convict*; 514.7 *cry of disapproval*; 8.18 *devilize*; 798.4 *evil power*; 659.8 *get angry*; 236.11 *harmfulness*; 594.14 *hate*; 514.14 *hiss*; 712.4 *malediction*; 395.2 *occult influence*; 10.18 *perform rites*; 5.45 *use language*; 670.22 *vituperate*
curse and swear 712.5 *curse*
cursed 11.19 *bewitched*; 236.6 *damnable*; 712.10 *maledictive*; 10.21 *ritualistic*
cursedly 712.14 *damningly*
curse like hell 712.7 *wish ill*
curse with bell 712.7 *wish ill*
curse word 712.1 *curse*
cursing **712.8**; 594.13 *angry*; 659.6 *bad-mannered*; 712.1 *curse*; 514.19 *hissing*; 544.4 *inelegance of speech*; 594.6 *swearing*
cursive 5.41 *lettered*
cursive type 5.15 *type style*
cursor 40.19 *computing terms*; 742.5 *indicator*
cursorily 666.7 *negligently*; 157.8 *shallowly*
cursoriness 231.5 *imperfection*; 420.10 *rough idea*; 157.3 *shallowness*
cursory 262.3 *hasty*; 231.2 *incomplete*; 157.2 *superficial*; 420.5 *unfinished*
curt 149.9 *abrupt*; 269.3 *concise*; 659.5 *discourteous*; 426.2 *outspoken*; 149.7 *short*; 732.2 *sparing with words*; 723.6 *summary*
curtail 245.5 *hurt*; 166.7 *limit*; 191.5, 214.5 *make smaller*; 278.5 *make transient*; 728.22 *play down*; 251.8 *restrain*; 372.10 *set apart*; 149.10 *shorten*; 212.4 *take off*
curtailed 728.19 *downplayed*; 233.4 *incomplete*; 166.5 *limited*; 212.7 *reduced*; 149.8 *shortened*; 191.7 *smaller*
curtailment 191.1 *contraction*; 214.1 *decrease*; 728.9 *downplaying*; 166.2 *limiting factor*; 251.1 *restraint*; 372.3 *separateness*; 149.2 *shortening*; 212.1 *subtraction*
curtain 519.6 *blinder*; 372.6 *boundary*; 384.19 *buffer*; 736.8 *conceal*; 128.3 *exclusion zone*; 550.28 *face*; 384.12 *fort*; 384.11 *fortification*; 528.7 *opaque thing*; 21.8 *scene*; 523.6 *shade*; 21.19 *stage set*; 361.3 *suspended object*; 521.6 *that which makes invisible*; 550.8 *wall covering*
curtain call 669.5 *acclaim*; 112.5 *repeat*; 21.8 *scene*
curtain-lifter 21.2 *play*; 21.8 *scene*
curtain-music 21.8 *scene*
curtain off 128.7 *exclude*
curtain-raiser 21.2 *play*; 129.5 *preface*; 130.9 *premiere*; 21.8 *scene*
curtain rise 130.9 *premiere*
curtain rod 361.4 *hanger*
curtains 131.3, 582.1 *death*; 305.4 *fall*
curtain wall 20.9 *miscellaneous architectural features*
curtal 149.8 *shortened*
curtate 149.8 *shortened*
curtly 426.12 *bluntly*; 269.5 *concisely*; 659.9 *discourteously*; 149.12 *short*
curtness 149.6 *abruptness*; 269.1 *conciseness*; 426.6 *outspokenness*; 149.1 *shortness*; 732.3 *shyness*
curtsy 367.9 *bow*; 367.16 *courtesy*; 658.13 *defer to*; 667.4 *mark of respect*; 663.3 *obeisance*; 663.6 *show obeisance to*; 658.5 *sign of courtesy*; 388.1 *submission*; 388.4 *succumb*; 667.19 *take off one's hat to*
curtsying 667.11 *in a respectful stance*
curvaceous 177.5, 181.10 *well-rounded*
curvaceously 177.7 *curvedly*; 181.13 *roundly*
curvaceousness 181.2 *round body*
curvature **177.1**; 325.13 *deviation*; 27.37 *line*; 189.1 *obliqueness*; 27.38 *surface*
Curve 177
curve **27.40**; **177.6**; 27.97 *align*; 182.5 *be convex*; 189.6 *be oblique*; 51.5 *bowling delivery*; 179.2 *circle*; 325.1 *deviate*; 325.14 *deviating course*; 27.32 *graph*; 27.37 *line*; 205.1 *part*; 306.7 *ring*; 700.9 *sleight of hand*; 330.5 *throw*; 325.5 *twist*
curveball 48.4 *pitching terms*; 700.9 *sleight of hand*
curved **177.4**; 51.10 *bowling*; 306.10 *circular*; 27.81 *curvilinear*; 421.2 *uniform*
curved inwards 183.6 *concave*
curved line 27.37 *line*
curvedly **177.7**

curvedness 179.1 *circularity*
curved surface 27.45; 27.38 *surface*
curved things 177.3
curve inwards 183.8 *be concave*
curve putt 56.3 *golf shots*
curve running 47.1 *track events*
curvet 59.10 *dressage*
curviform 177.4 *curved*
curvilinear 27.81; 177.4 *curved*
curvilinearity 177.1 *curvature*
curvilinearly 177.7 *curvedly*
curving 426.1 *blunt*; 177.4 *curved*; 325.21 *indirect*
curving inwards 183.1 *concavity*
curvy 177.5 *well-rounded*
cushion 65.1 *billiards*; 384.19 *buffer*; 685.4 *moderate*; 685.2 *moderator*; 490.4 *pleasurable things*; 252.10 *protect*; 252.2 *protection*; 419.13 *soften*; 419.11 *soft thing*
cushion cover 550.12 *protective covering*
cushioned 263.4 *at ease*
cushion of air 434.10 *air bubble*
cushiony 419.4 *compressible*
cushy 265.9 *easy*; 490.6 *pleasant*
cushy number 265.6 *easy thing*
cusp 27.39 *angle*; 131.7 *limit*; 425.7 *sharp point*; 174.1 *summit*
cusped 425.4 *toothed*
cuspidate 425.4 *toothed*
cuspidor 767.8 *sink*
cuss 712.1, 712.5 *curse*
cussed 651.14 *hostile*
cussedness 661.1 *defiance*; 625.1 *irascibility*; 626.3 *irritableness*; 651.1 *malevolence*; 641.5 *obstinacy*
cuss word 712.1 *curse*
custard 25.35, 498.3 *dessert*
custard pie 272.2 *slapstick comedy*
Custer's Last Stand 382.4 *slaughter*
custodial 251.15 *detained*; 252.8 *tutelary*
custodian 579.15 *manager*; 815.6 *prison officer*; 252.3, 384.15 *protector*
custodianship 251.4 *detention*; 252.2 *protection*
custody 251.4 *detention*; 763.1 *possession*; 252.2 *protection*
custody of children 571.3 *divorce court*
custom 140.6; **632.4**; **776.12**; **777.11**; 340.1 *action*; 117.5, 750.6 *convention*; 549.3, 656.5 *etiquette*; 160.5 *formality*; 658.2 *good manners*; 632.1 *habit*; 407.7 *method*; 298.4 *orderliness*; 713.3 *precept*; 10.1 *ritual*; 474.3 *the expected thing*; 1.8, 296.6 *tradition*
custom and practice 15.1 *industrial relations*
customarily 140.18 *as a rule*; 750.37 *conventionally*; 632.19 *habitually*; 298.17 *orderly*; 1.18 *societally*
customary 140.10; 216.1 *average*; 138.21 *common*; 750.15 *conventional*; 160.11 *formal*; 407.15, 632.9 *habitual*; 298.14 *orderly*; 1.14 *societal*
custom board 50.7 *windsurfing*
custom-build 356.10 *produce*
custom-built 139.20 *personalized*; 356.12 *produced*; 160.10 *prototypical*
customer 776.12 *custom*; 13.9 *economist*; 566.7 *person*; 777.12 *purchaser*; 769.5 *recipient*; 710.4 *requester*; 349.8 *user*
customer account 783.1 *credit*
customer credit 783.1 *credit*
custom house 779.1 *market*; 780.19 *treasury*
customize 356.10 *produce*
custom-made 551.31 *styled*
custom-make 551.35 *make clothing*
customs 790.8 *levy*; 788.2 *money received*; 795.1 *morality*; 631.6 *way of life*; 50.7 *windsurfing*
Customs and Excise 790.8 *levy*
customs barrier 776.5 *commercial trade*; 13.6 *economic factors*; 128.3 *exclusion zone*
customs officer 769.7 *collector*
customs official 252.3 *protector*
cut 98.18 *abscond*; 98.4 *absenteeism*; 770.4 *allot*; 634.1 *avoid*; 53.17, 330.26, 331.10 *bat*; 331.5 *beat*; 269.4 *be concise*; 659.7 *be discourteous*; 425.14 *be sharp*; 331.13 *blow*; 53.18 *bowl*; 708.14 *cancel*; 69.3 *card game terms*; 23.17 *carpenter*; 139.3 *characteristic*; 269.3 *concise*; 25.55 *cook*; 146.2, 146.5 *crack*; 146.7 *cracked*; 44.15 *cultivate*; 433.30 *dilute*; 133.14 *discontinue*; 791.1, 791.3 *discount*; 525.3 *external appearance*; 43.17 *farm*; 553.9 *fashion*; 790.3 *fee*; 160.7 *form*; 184.2 *furrow*; 331.3, 381.18 *hit*; 623.17 *humiliate*; 313.4 *hurry off*; 491.11 *inflict pain*; 491.6 *injured*; 491.3 *injury*; 744.14 *inscribe*; 668.5 *insult*; 133.4 *interruption*; 793.13 *make cheap*; 214.5 *make smaller*; 417.6 *make sparse*; 81.12 *manage grassland*; 160.6 *nature*; 183.4, 183.10 *notch*; 183.7 *notched*; 308.12, 308.18 *open*; 308.1 *opening*; 44.19 *ornamental*; 371.4 *ostracize*; 717.11 *paint*; 205.7 *piece*; 69.10 *play*; 49.6 *play basketball*; 634.9 *play truant*; 417.2 *rarefied*; 364.1 *repel*; 364.6 *repulse*; 251.8 *restrain*; 90.1 *river*; 19.21 *sculpt*; 372.9, 372.15 *separate*; 149.10 *shorten*; 149.8, 723.7 *shortened*; 149.2 *shortening*; 411.4 *slice*; 421.11 *smooth*; 331.14 *sporting hit*; 381.6 *stab*; 53.9 *stroke*; 212.3 *subtract*; 212.2 *subtracted item*; 212.1 *subtraction*; 773.10 *take away*; 773.3 *taking away*; 425.16 *use a sharp tool*; 323.2 *waterway*; 788.5 *winnings*; 23.8 *woodwork*; 42.10 *woven*; 184.8 *wrinkle*
cut above 121.12 *superior*
cut a corner 149.11 *cut short*
cut across 149.11 *cut short*
cut a dash 123.7 *be important*
cut a figure 123.7 *be important*
cut and blow dry 547.8 *haircut*
cut-and-cover tunnel 38.22 *tunnel*
cut-and-dried 106.3 *predetermined*; 243.21 *ready-made*
cut and run 614.4 *be a coward*; 252.9 *be safe*; 332.4 *be swift*; 313.4 *hurry off*; 262.2 *make haste*; 634.9 *play truant*
cut and thrust 331.12 *collision*; 331.9 *fight*; 381.18 *hit*
cut and try 448.1 *experiment*
cutaneous disease 260.13 *skin disease*
cut a tooth 425.14 *be sharp*
cutaway 551.11 *jacket*
cut away 313.4 *hurry off*
cutback 680.2 *act of thrift*; 214.1 *decrease*; 46.9 *play*; 46.15 *play offence*; 149.2 *shortening*; 212.2 *subtracted item*
cut back 209.6 *change gradually*; 728.18 *deflated*; 728.21 *detract from*; 245.5 *hurt*; 214.5 *make smaller*; 206.8 *reduce*; 680.6 *save*; 149.10 *shorten*
cut both ways 479.1 *be equivocal*; 708.16 *cancel out*
cut corners 262.2 *make haste*; 680.6 *save*
cut costs 680.6 *save*
cut dead 659.7 *be discourteous*; 668.23 *insult*
cut down 585.13 *be at war*; 728.18 *deflated*; 357.9 *demolish*; 728.21 *detract from*; 367.2 *flatten*; 214.5 *make smaller*; 680.6 *save*; 149.10 *shorten*; 382.18 *slaughter*; 381.6 *stab*
cut down to size 728.21 *detract from*; 623.3 *humbled*; 623.17 *humiliate*; 117.9 *make conform*
cute 545.5 *beautiful*
cut flowers 78.1 *flower*
cut free 265.18 *disentangle*
cuticle 550.14 *animal covering*; 171.1 *exterior*; 157.4 *shallow thing*
cuticular 550.38 *covering*; 171.6 *exterior*
cut in 133.16 *interrupt*
cut into 314.11 *infiltrate*
cut it out 226.12 *stop!*
cutlass 425.10 *knife*; 587.8 *sharp weapon*
cutlet 205.7 *piece*
cut loose 372.13 *diverge*; 250.19 *liberalize*
cut no ice 335.6 *be powerless*; 124.11 *be unimportant*
cut off 585.13 *be at war*; 269.4 *be concise*; 378.9 *block*; 226.8 *cause to cease*; 133.12 *discontinue*; 655.13 *ignore*; 382.16 *kill*; 278.5 *make transient*; 329.15 *out of reach*; 357.11 *ruin*; 372.10 *set apart*; 149.10 *shorten*; 212.4 *take off*
cut off one's head 814.5 *execute*
cut of one's jib 160.6 *nature*
cut one's own throat 486.6 *act foolishly*
cut one's throat 382.21 *commit suicide*
cut open 394.20 *doctor*; 308.12, 308.18 *open*
cut out 369.13 *dig out*; 243.2 *do the groundwork*; 553.9 *fashion*; 160.7 *form*; 245.5 *hurt*; 355.2 *withdraw*
cut-out 523.2 *darkening*
cut out for 239.1 *convenient*; 750.16 *fitting*; 485.7 *gifted*; 136.9 *qualified*
cutout switch 309.2 *stopper*
cutover 54.6 *fencing*; 54.3 *fencing movements*
cut price 791.2 *bargain*; 793.1 *cheapness*; 766.2 *financial loss*; 790.1 *price*
cut-price 777.14 *buying*; 793.9 *cheap*; 791.6 *discounted*; 212.7 *reduced*; 766.17 *unprofitable*
cut prices 766.10 *have a financial loss*; 212.3 *subtract*
cutpurse 774.8 *thief*
cut rate 791.2 *bargain*; 793.1 *cheapness*; 766.2 *financial loss*
cut-rate 793.9 *cheap*; 791.6 *discounted*; 212.7 *reduced*; 766.17 *unprofitable*
cuts 251.1 *restraint*
cut short 149.11; 269.4 *be concise*; 226.8 *cause to cease*; 133.12 *discontinue*; 357.11 *ruin*; 149.10 *shorten*; 149.8, 723.7 *shortened*; 730.15 *strike dumb*; 723.8 *summarize*
cut short the preliminaries 262.2 *make haste*
cut someone dead 655.13 *ignore*
cutter 578.2 *artisan*; 53.8 *delivery*; 551.26 *fashion designer*; 43.8 *livestock*; 50.2 *sailing boat*; 425.9 *sharp-edged thing*; 723.5 *summarizer*; 425.11 *tooth*
cut the cackle 269.4 *be concise*; 506.6 *hush!*
cut the first turf 130.24 *open*
cut the Gordian knot 246.7 *overcome obstacles*
cut the knot 372.9 *separate*
cut the lawn 425.16 *use a sharp tool*
cut the ribbon 130.24 *open*
cut the throat of 382.18 *slaughter*
cutthroat 357.14 *destructive*; 798.6 *evil person*; 651.8 *malefactor*; 382.11 *murderer*
cut through 149.11 *cut short*; 372.9 *separate*
cut timber 79.18 *manage trees*
cutting 381.23 *attacking*; 183.2 *concave land*; 726.3 *emphatic*; 44.5 *gardening*; 44.9 *garden plant*; 651.14 *hostile*; 668.11 *insulting*; 317.10 *railway*; 744.1 *record*; 372.3 *separateness*; 425.3 *sharp-edged*; 149.2 *shortening*; 212.1 *subtraction*; 321.2 *track*
cutting away 372.3 *separateness*
cutting back 680.2 *act of thrift*; 728.10 *deflation*; 44.5 *gardening*; 212.1 *subtraction*
cutting down 728.10 *deflation*
cutting down to size 728.9 *downplaying*
cutting edge 164.3; 425.7 *sharp point*
cutting fluid 38.9 *machine tool*
cutting horse 59.4 *saddle horse*
cutting off 212.1 *subtraction*
cutting out 369.3 *digging out*
cutting remark 668.5 *insult*
cuttings 723.3 *compendium*
cutting someone dead 655.1 *unsociability*
cutting someone off 655.1 *unsociability*
cutting the ribbon 130.9 *premiere*
cutting torch 19.14 *sculptor's materials*
cuttlefish 70.5 *aquatic animal*
cut to pieces 372.16 *apart*; 357.9 *demolish*; 382.18 *slaughter*
cut to ribbons 382.18 *slaughter*
cut to the quick 491.11 *inflict pain*
cutty stool 814.14 *instrument of punishment*
cut up 372.16 *apart*; 372.11 *divide*; 205.10 *part*; 602.5 *sad*
cut up nasty 651.18 *torment*
cut up rough 624.11 *be angry*; 408.26 *be disorderly*
cutworm 76.5 *larva*; 76.3 *pest*; 44.12 *pests and diseases*
CV 3.6 *biography*; 716.6 *documentation*; 723.1 *summary*
cwm 156.4 *deep thing*; 146.3 *gulf*; 30.7 *landform*; 92.8 *valley*
cyan 539.1 *blue*; 539.5 *blueness*; 28.28 *colour*
cyanic 539.1 *blue*
cyanobacteria 84.2 *algae*
Cyanophyta 84.2 *algae*
cyanosed 539.2 *bluish*
cyanosis 539.8 *bluishness*
cyanotic 539.2 *bluish*
cybernetic 40.21 *on-line*
cybernetically 438.11 *instrumentally*; 40.22 *on-line*
cybernetics 40.17 *artificial intelligence*; 40.1 *computing*; 34.1 *life science*; 438.6 *mechanics*
cyberpunk novel 17.2 *fiction*
cyberspace 40.18 *virtual reality*
cyborg 566.8 *humanlike machine*
cycad 82.1 *fern*
cycad fern 82.1 *fern*
cyclamate 498.2 *sweetener*
cyclamen 535.1 *red*
cycle 298.2; 298.8 *be cyclic*; 320.12 *bicycle*; 179.2 *circle*; 132.6 *continuum*; 576.9 *exercise*; 297.4 *frequency*; 306.3 *orbit*; 276.5 *recurrent period*; 112.4 *return*; 307.1 *rotation*; 289.1 *succession*; 275.4 *term*
cycle round 298.8 *be cyclic*
cycles per second 297.6 *radio frequency*
cyclic 27.85; **298.12**; 179.5 *circular*; 32.35 *combined*; 297.3 *frequent*; 275.22 *periodic*; 276.8 *periodical*; 32.38 *reactive*; 307.12 *rotary*
cyclical 132.12; 306.10 *circular*; 298.12 *cyclic*; 297.3 *frequent*; 112.14 *recurrent*; 307.12 *rotary*
cyclically 298.16; 179.8 *circularly*; 297.1 *frequently*
cyclic compound 32.7 *chemical compound*
cycling 576.5 *exercise*; 318.2 *passing along*; 320.1 *road transport*
cycling shorts 551.9 *trousers*
cyclist 320.14
cyclization 32.14 *chemical reaction*
cyclize 32.26 *react*
cycloid 27.40 *curve*; 36.8 *disordered personality*
cycloid personality 36.8 *disordered personality*
cycloid psychosis 36.11 *psychosis*
cyclometer 26.8 *meter*; 332.8 *speed*
cyclometry 26.2 *micrometry*
cyclone 420.9 *broken water*; 379.1 *trap*; 380.5 *violent weather*; 307.4 *vortex*; 31.11 *weather system*; 31.16 *wind vortex*
cyclonic 31.44 *frontal*; 307.12 *rotary*; 31.48 *stormy*
Cyclopean 158.15 *big*
Cyclops 75.4 *arthropod*; 158.10 *big person*; 70.7 *legendary beast*
cyclorama 21.19 *stage set*
cyclosilicate 30.34 *mineral*
cyclostome 74.2 *fish*
cyclothyme 36.8 *disordered personality*
cyclothymia 36.8 *disordered personality*; 36.11, 461.5 *psychosis*
cyclothymic personality 36.8 *disordered personality*
cyclotron 334.8 *nuclear power*; 28.94 *particle accelerator*
cygnet 555.4 *young animal*; 72.12 *young bird*
cylinder 181.4; 27.45 *curved surface*; 38.11 *engine*
cylinder mower 44.6 *garden tool*
cylindrical 181.9 *round*; 27.83 *spherical*
cylindrical coordinates 27.33 *coordinates*
cylindricality 181.1 *roundness*
cylindrical lens 28.29 *optical element*
cylindrically 181.13 *roundly*
cymatium 174.3 *architectural summit*
cyme 78.4 *flower head*
cymophane 541.5 *variegated thing*
cymose 78.12 *of flowers*
cymose inflorescence 78.4 *flower head*
Cymru 85.12 *Wales*
Cynic 4.11 *follower of a doctrine*; 4.14 *of a philosophy*
cynic 611.3 *hopeless person*; 653.2 *misanthrope*; 468.2 *pessimist*
cynical 611.4 *hopeless*; 423.5 *mentally tough*; 653.3 *misanthropic*
cynically 611.11 *hopelessly*; 653.5 *misanthropically*; 468.6 *pessimistically*; 423.14 *single-mindedly*
cynicalness 423.9 *mental toughness*
cynicism 611.1 *hopelessness*; 653.1 *misanthropy*; 4.7 *school of thought*; 468.1 *underestimation*
cynosural 173.8 *focal*
cynosure 545.2 *beautiful thing*; 363.7 *centre of attraction*; 173.5 *focus*; 742.5 *indicator*; 520.6 *visible thing*
Cynthia 29.17 *moon*
cyperaceous 77.16 *taxonomic*
cypher 27.10 *zero*
Cyprian 796.9 *immoral woman*
cyprinoid 74.13 *fishlike*
cypsela 80.2 *botanical fruit*
Cyrenaic 4.11 *follower of a doctrine*; 4.14 *of a philosophy*
Cyrillic 5.41 *lettered*
Cyrillic alphabet 5.14 *alphabet*

cyst 182.2 *bulge*; 84.4 *reproductive body*; 260.13 *skin disease*; 260.15 *ulcer*
cysticercus 75.13 *invertebrate larva*
cystic fibrosis 260.9 *respiratory disease*
cystine 33.8 *amino acid*
cystoscope 35.7 *diagnosis*
cystoscopy 35.7 *diagnosis*
cytochemistry 34.6 *cell biology*
cytogenetics 34.11 *genetics*
cytokinesis 34.10 *cell division*
cytokinin 33.17 *plant hormone*
cytological 34.20 *biological*
cytologically 34.29 *biologically*
cytological test 34.6 *cell biology*
cytologist 34.19 *life scientist*
cytology 34.6 *cell biology*; 34.1 *life science*
cytoplasm 34.7 *cell*
cytoplasmic 34.23 *cellular*
cytosine 34.12 *molecular biology*; 33.10 *nucleoside*
cytosome 34.7 *cell*
cytotaxonomy 34.17 *taxonomy*
cytotoxic 37.14 *counteracting*
cytoxic drug 37.4 *drug type*
czardas 22.4 *historic dancing*

D 2.7 *social stratification*
DA 691.4 *drug taker*
dab 331.13 *blow*; 492.3 *press*; 25.18 *sea fish*; 331.6 *tap*; 492.11 *touch*; 124.8 *trifle*
dabble 429.14 *sprinkle*
dabble in 456.10 *know little*
dabble in occultism 101.12 *enter a nonmaterial world*
dabble in shares 776.2 *speculate*
dabble in sorcery 224.8 *cause change*
dabbler 456.5 *ignorant person*; 639.15 *indecisive person*; 342.11 *meddler*; 486.10 *unskilled person*
dabbling 456.2 *half-knowledge*; 342.21 *meddling*
dabbling duck 72.3 *water bird*
dab hand 396.11, 400.10 *expert*; 485.4 *skilled person*
dabster 485.4 *skilled person*
da capo 112.24 *again*
Dachau 655.4 *place of confinement*; 382.15 *slaughterhouse*
dachshund 155.4 *low thing*
dactyl 17.9 *metre*
dactylic 17.20 *metrical*
dactylic hexameter 17.9 *metre*
dactylographic 742.15 *gestural*
dactylography 743.3 *means of identification*
dactylology 505.1 *deafness*; 742.3 *gesture*
dad 567.13 *man in the family*
Dadaist 19.29 *realist*
dad-blamed 236.6 *damnable*; 712.11 *miscellaneous euphemisms*
dad-blast 712.16 *euphemisms*
dad-blasted 236.6 *damnable*; 712.11 *miscellaneous euphemisms*
dad-burned 712.11 *miscellaneous euphemisms*
daddy 567.13 *man in the family*
daddy longlegs 76.1 *insect*
dado 175.2 *foot*; 20.9 *miscellaneous architectural features*
Daedalian 485.9 *well-made*
daemon 8.5 *deity*
daffodil 537.8 *yellow thing*
daft 459.5 *foolish*; 461.11 *insane*; 272.5 *ridiculous*; 457.6 *unintelligent*
daft as a brush 461.11 *insane*
daftness 459.1 *folly*; 272.1 *ludicrousness*
dagger 357.7 *agent of destruction*; 742.7 *punctuation*; 425.8 *sharp-pointed thing*; 587.8 *sharp weapon*
daggerboard 50.3 *parts of a sailing boat*; 50.7 *windsurfing*
Dag Hammarskjöld 589.4 *Nobel Peace Prize*
dagoba 10.13 *shrine*
daguerreotype 41.3 *photograph*
Dagwood sandwich 25.11 *sandwich*
dah 692.8 *data transmission*
Dáil Éireann 12.4 *governing body*; 579.10 *legislative body*
daily 256.12 *cleaner*; 298.12 *cyclic*; 298.16 *cyclically*; 276.13 *for specified periods*; 297.1 *frequently*; 632.9 *habitual*; 392.16 *home help*; 740.5 *journal*; 740.4 *newspaper*; 275.22 *periodic*; 276.8 *periodical*; 111.17 *regular*; 111.20 *regularly*
daily bread 557.7 *food*; 554.3 *life requirements*; 392.3 *sustenance*
daily grind 112.3 *repetitiveness*; 632.3 *way*; 576.1 *work*
daily habit 632.3 *way*
daily help 256.12 *cleaner*; 401.6 *domestic servant*; 392.16 *home help*; 401.1 *servant*
daily market 779.1 *market*
daily paper 740.4 *newspaper*
daily round 298.2 *cycle*; 111.6 *regularity*; 181.6 *round*; 632.3 *way*
daily routine 111.6 *regularity*
Dai Nichi 8.3 *God*
dainties 557.7 *food*
daintily 159.8 *in a small way*; 415.11 *lightly*; 404.15 *texturally*
daintiness 256.1 *cleanness*; 404.2 *grain*; 415.5 *lightness*; 159.1 *littleness*
dainty 495.3 *appetizer*; 256.16 *clean*; 404.10 *delicate*; 557.27 *edible*; 415.2 *insubstantial*; 159.7 *little*; 255.14 *purified*; 495.7 *tasty*
dainty eater 557.18 *eater*
dainty palate 557.3 *delicate eating*
daiquiri 558.8 *mixed drink*
dairy 43.7 *farm building*; 577.1 *workshop*
dairy farm 43.6 *farm*
dairy farmer 43.15 *agriculturist*
dairy farming 43.3 *livestock farming*
dairyhand 43.16 *farm worker*
dairy ice cream 25.35 *dessert*
dairying 43.3 *livestock farming*
dairymaid 43.16 *farm worker*
dairy products 356.7 *produce*
dais 21.17 *stage*
daisy chain 78.1 *flower*
daisycutter 53.8 *delivery*; 78.9 *figurative usage*
daisy family 77.3 *seed plant*
daisywheel 78.9 *figurative usage*
daisywheel printer 40.7 *peripheral*
dakhma 583.6 *grave*
Dalai Lama 589.4 *Nobel Peace Prize*; 7.8 *priest*; 400.2 *sovereign*
dale 92.8 *valley*
Dallas 87.2 *American cities*
dalliance 593.6 *courtship*; 333.11 *lingering*
dally 639.7 *be irresolute*; 593.26 *court*; 333.2 *hesitate*; 294.7 *wait*
dallying 593.6 *courtship*; 333.7 *delayed*; 333.11 *lingering*
Dalmatian 541.5 *variegated thing*
daltonism 519.2 *poor sight*
dam **38.23**; 378.3 *barrier*; 378.9 *block*; 59.13 *breeding*; 128.3 *exclusion zone*; 59.1 *horse*; 561.5 *propagator*; 309.8 *stop*; 90.9 *stop the flow*; 38.19 *structure*; 433.16 *water carrier*
damage 798.2, 814.10 *affliction*; 798.11 *be evil*; 236.13 *be worthless*; 790.5 *cost*; 214.1 *decrease*; 678.12 *defame*; 234.11 *deform*; 766.13 *destroy*; 766.5 *destruction*; 236.11 *harmfulness*; 357.5 *havoc*; 245.4 *impair*; 245.10 *impairment*; 231.5 *imperfection*; 357.10 *lay waste*; 218.7 *make insufficient*; 351.1 *misuse*; 441.1, 441.3 *waste*; 337.7 *weaken*; 337.1 *weakness*
damaged 798.8 *afflicted*; 548.4 *blemished*; 245.12 *deteriorated*; 231.1 *imperfect*
damages 790.6 *business costs*; 775.2, 813.6 *compensation*; 785.4 *grant*; 814.8 *penalty*
damaging 351.5 *abusive*; 670.27 *critical*; 678.16 *defamatory*; 798.9 *detrimental*; 236.5 *harmful*; 754.7 *unkind*
damagingly 441.11 *destructively*
damascene 541.2 *check*; 541.11 *variegate*
damask 535.1 *red*
dam-breaking 90.10 *fluvial*
Dame 568.3 *female title of address*
dame 400.1 *master*; 568.9 *woman considered as a sex object*
dammed 554.15 *born*; 309.13 *stopped*
damn 16.79 *convict*; 8.18 *devilize*; 712.15 *miscellaneous swearwords*; 124.8 *trifle*; 712.7 *wish ill*
damnable **236.6**
damn all 195.2 *nothing*
damn and blast 712.6 *vilify*
damnation 283.3 *future condition*; 712.4 *malediction*
damned 16.64 *convicted*; 236.6 *damnable*; 8.16 *devilish*; 804.14 *impious*; 712.10 *maledictive*
damned little difference 115.7 *similar*
damned soul 766.6 *loser*
damnify 245.5 *hurt*
damning 670.29 *blaming*; 712.10 *maledictive*
damningly **712.14**
damn the consequences 638.18 *here goes!*
damn with faint praise 728.21 *detract from*
Damon and Pythias 569.7 *famous friendships*
damp 31.52 *humid*; 432.3 *miasma*; 685.4 *moderate*; 429.9 *moist*; 433.3 *wateriness*; 31.6 *weather data*
dampcourse 175.2 *foot*
damp down 511.7 *mute*
damped 511.2 *nonresonant*
dampen 602.10 *depress*; 481.5 *discourage*; 685.4 *moderate*; 429.13 *moisten*; 511.7 *mute*
dampened 481.10 *dissuaded*; 511.2 *nonresonant*
dampen the spirits of 602.10 *depress*
damper 481.7 *deterrence*; 378.8 *hinder*; 378.7 *hinderer*; 505.3 *inaudibility*; 251.5 *means of restraint*; 685.2 *moderator*; 730.8 *mute*; 251.8 *restrain*; 511.6 *silencer*; 309.2 *stopper*
damping 481.9 *dissuasive*; 433.26 *wetting*
damping-off 83.5 *fungal association*; 44.12 *pests and diseases*
dampish 429.9 *moist*
damply 429.17 *moistly*; 433.35 *wetly*
dampness 429.1 *moisture*; 433.3 *wateriness*; 31.6 *weather data*
dampproof 428.10 *waterproof*
damp squib 604.2 *bad outcome*; 247.4 *unsuccessful thing*
damp the ardour 481.5 *discourage*
damsel 568.2 *female*
damson 540.3 *purple thing*
damson-coloured 540.6 *purple*
dan 485.4 *skilled person*
dance **22.2**; **22.15**; **376.10**; **600.7**; 22.8 *ballet*; 327.21 *be agitated*; 22.1 *dancing*; 327.26 *flicker*; 654.5 *party*; 307.3 *reel*; 326.4, 326.11 *rock*; 304.17 *spring up*; 300.15 *walk*
dance about 52.11 *fight*
dance attendance on 223.16 *attend*; 471.10 *be attentive*; 664.11 *pander to*
dance attendance upon 401.8 *serve*
dance costume 551.5 *fancy dress*
dance floor 22.6 *dance hall*; 421.8 *smooth thing*
dancehall 18.9 *popular music*
dance hall **22.6**
dance lift 68.7 *ice-dancing*
dance music **18.7**
dance of death 582.1 *death*
dance of Siva 10.7 *non-Christian ritual*
dancer **21.30**; **22.5**; 578.1 *worker*
dance step 300.12 *gait*; 68.7 *ice-dancing*
dance upon nothing 814.6 *be punished*
Dancing 22
dancing **22.1**; 342.18 *active*; 22.8 *ballet*; 52.2 *boxing*; 52.14 *combat*; 326.16 *rocking*; 327.6 *shaking*
dancing girl 21.30 *dancer*
dancing light 541.5 *variegated thing*
dancing on ice 68.7 *ice-dancing*
dandelion 537.8 *yellow thing*
dander 624.4 *anger*
dandify 673.17 *be affected*
dandle 593.27 *kiss*
dandruff 427.6 *crumb*; 258.4 *dirt*; 215.2 *residue*; 411.4 *slice*
dandy 797.1 *good*; 797.17 *good thing*; 551.27 *model*; 235.1 *worthy*
Danegeld 790.9 *historical taxes*
dang 712.11 *miscellaneous euphemisms*
danged 712.11 *miscellaneous euphemisms*
Danger 254
danger **254.5**; 264.6 *critical situation*; 596.2 *disliked thing*; 236.11 *harmfulness*; 379.1 *trap*; 711.1 *warning*
danger! **68.18**
danger-loving 613.13 *adventurous*; 615.4 *rash*
dangerous **254.1**; 624.16 *angry*; 236.5 *harmful*; 643.3 *important*; 700.38 *treacherous*; 453.7 *unreliable*
dangerous age 556.4 *middle age*
dangerous course 254.5 *danger*
dangerous encounter 596.2 *disliked thing*
dangerous game 615.2 *rash move*
dangerously **254.11**; 453.26 *unreliably*
dangerousness 254.5 *danger*
dangerous situation 254.5 *danger*
dangerous speed 332.8 *speed*
dangerous subject 624.3 *cause of offence*
dangerous temper 625.1 *irascibility*
dangerous woman 593.9 *lover*
danger past 252.1 *safety*
danger sign 742.1 *sign*
danger signal **254.6**; **711.2**; 475.3 *plan*; 535.7 *red thing*; 742.4 *signal*
dang it 712.16 *euphemisms*
dangle 738.1 *display*; 326.11 *rock*; 361.10 *suspend*; 361.1 *suspension*
dangle before one's eyes 480.16 *tempt*
dangler 664.5 *adherent*
dangle the bait 700.33 *snare*
dangling 361.7 *suspended*; 361.1 *suspension*
dangling participle 274.11 *grammatical error*
Dan grade 52.7 *judo*; 52.8 *karate*
Daniel come to judgment 16.23 *judge*
Daniell cell 32.19 *electrochemistry*
Danish 25.36 *cake*
Danish bacon 25.30 *bacon*
Danish pastry 25.36 *cake*; 498.3 *dessert*
dank 429.9 *moist*; 499.6 *unpalatable*
dankishness 429.3 *humidity*
dankly 429.17 *moistly*
dankness 429.3 *humidity*; 499.2 *unpalatability*
dansak 25.49 *Indian dish*
danse basse 22.4 *historic dancing*
danseur 22.13 *ballet dancer*; 21.30 *dancer*
danseuse 22.13 *ballet dancer*; 21.30 *dancer*
Dante and Beatrice 593.10 *lovers*
Dantesque 17.19 *narrative*
Danube 90.5 *other major rivers*
dap 551.30 *dressed-up*
Daphne 79.13 *tree mythology*
daphnia 75.4 *arthropod*
Daphnis and Chloe 593.10 *lovers*
dapper 256.16 *clean*; 551.30 *dressed-up*; 407.13 *orderly*
dapping 55.1 *angling*
dapple 114.6 *assorted*; 412.8 *mix*; 541.11 *variegate*
dappled 412.12 *mixed*; 541.10 *mottled*
dapple-grey 533.1 *grey*; 59.1 *horse*
dappleness 114.2 *assortment*
dappling 541.4 *maculation*; 412.3 *miscellany*
daps 551.19 *footwear*
Darby and Joan 570.9 *married couple*; 556.7 *older person*; 228.5 *stable person*; 198.1 *two*
Dardanelles 92.9 *inlet*
dare **660.27**; 661.3 *act of defiance*; 613.15 *be courageous*; 661.6 *be insubordinate*; 638.8 *brace oneself*; 661.5 *defy*; 254.9 *face danger*; 448.13 *invent*; 453.22 *risk*; 613.16 *take courage*; 354.1 *undertake*
D area 65.5 *snooker*
daredevil 613.7 *courageous person*; 615.4 *rash*; 459.4, 615.3 *rash person*
daredevilry 615.1 *rashness*
Dar-el-jannah 8.11 *heaven*
dare say 476.5 *suppose*; 104.10 *think likely*
daring 353.8 *attempting*; 613.1 *courage*; 613.9 *courageous*; 254.5 *danger*; 661.1 *defiance*; 661.7 *defiant*; 354.6 *enterprising*; 638.16 *fortitude*; 738.15 *open*; 448.9 *original*; 448.4 *originality*; 615.4 *rash*; 615.1 *rashness*; 336.12 *strong to the senses*
daringly 661.9 *defiantly*; 354.9 *enterprisingly*; 448.15 *inventively*
daringness 661.1 *defiance*
Darjeeling 558.3 *tea*
dark **523.8**; **532.2**; 332.4 *be swift*; 532.7 *blackness*; 534.2 *browned*; 31.49 *cloudy*; 523.10 *dark-coloured*; 523.1 *darkness*; 521.2 *difficult to see*; 524.5 *dim*; 533.3 *dull*; 291.6 *evening*; 583.11 *funeral*; 519.13 *hidden*; 528.1 *opaque*; 521.3 *private*; 528.2 *shady*; 529.13 *soft-hued*; 626.6 *sullen*
Dark Ages 523.5 *figurative dark thing*; 284.5 *historical period*; 3.10 *past age*
dark blue 539.1 *blue*
dark brown 534.1 *brown*; 523.3 *dark colour*
dark clothes 523.4 *dark thing*
dark cloud 31.18 *cloud*
dark clouds 249.1 *adversity*; 742.1 *sign*
dark colour **523.3**; 532.7 *blackness*
dark-coloured **523.10**
dark colouring 532.7 *blackness*
dark comedy 21.12 *comedy*
dark complexion 534.3 *brownness*
dark-complexioned 532.2 *dark*

Dark Continent 737.8 *anonymity*; 523.5 *figurative dark thing*
dark corner 521.5 *invisible thing*
darken 523.13 *become dark*; 521.7 *become invisible*; 524.9 *be dim*; 532.11 *blacken*; 519.15 *blind*; 31.60 *cloud*; 529.15 *colour*; 736.9 *disguise*; 523.14 *make dark*; 524.10 *make dim*; 521.8 *make invisible*; 528.11 *make opaque*
darkened 521.2 *difficult to see*
darkening **523.2**; **523.9**; 532.7 *blackness*; 519.11 *blinding*
Darkest Africa 145.3 *distant place*; 523.5 *figurative dark thing*
darkest hour 523.1 *darkness*
darkfall 291.1 *evening*
dark glasses 523.4 *dark thing*; 28.29 *optical element*; 523.6 *shade*; 518.10 *visual aid*
dark green 538.1 *green*
dark-grey 533.1 *grey*
dark hair 523.3 *dark colour*
dark-haired 532.4 *black-haired*; 523.10 *dark-coloured*
dark-headed 532.4 *black-haired*
dark horse 523.5 *figurative dark thing*; 59.7 *horseracing*; 456.4 *unknown person*
darkish 523.8 *dark*; 524.5 *dim*
dark lantern 523.4 *dark thing*; 522.7 *lantern*
darkling 523.10 *dark-coloured*
darkly **523.15**; 532.12 *blackly*; 524.12 *dimly*; 626.13 *sullenly*
dark matter 29.4 *cosmological model*; 523.4 *dark thing*
dark meat 25.28 *poultry*
dark nebula 29.8 *interstellar medium*
Darkness 523
darkness **523.1**; 249.1 *adversity*; 532.7 *blackness*; 519.1 *blindness*; 533.7 *dullness*; 529.3 *hue*; 521.4 *invisibility*; 646.2 *naivety*; 291.2 *night*; 528.6 *opaqueness*; 521.6 *that which makes invisible*
dark powers 523.7 *spiritual darkness*
dark purple 540.6 *purple*
dark reaction 33.23 *photosynthesis*
darkroom 523.4 *dark thing*; 41.12 *development*
dark rum 558.7 *alcoholic drink*
dark side 169.4 *aspect*
dark skin 534.3 *brownness*; 523.3 *dark colour*
dark-skinned 523.10 *dark-coloured*
dark star 523.4 *dark thing*
dark thing 523.4
darktime 291.2 *night*
darling 21.24 *actor*; 593.21 *beloved*; 555.9 *child*; 9.4 *idolized person*; 595.4 *likable person*; 593.12 *nicknames for lovers*
darn 712.16 *euphemisms*; 712.11 *miscellaneous euphemisms*; 393.1, 393.8 *repair*
darned 236.6 *damnable*; 712.11 *miscellaneous euphemisms*
darner 393.12 *repairer*
darning 393.8 *repair*
darshan 7.8 *priest*
dart 330.10 *ball*; 227.12 *be irresolute*; 587.6 *historical missile weapon*; 330.8 *missile*; 330.23 *throw*; 300.15 *walk*
darted 551.31 *styled*
darting 227.2 *irresolution*; 332.1 *swift*
Dartmoor 815.1 *prison*
dart off 332.6 *accelerate*
darts 69.6
darts game 69.1 *game*
dart to and fro 262.2 *make haste*
Darwinian 34.27 *evolutionary*
Darwinism 34.16 *evolution*
Darwinist 34.19 *life scientist*
Darwin's finches 72.6 *songbird*
Dasehra 10.16 *religious festival*
dash 332.6 *accelerate*; 332.9 *acceleration*; 412.4 *admixture*; 342.12 *be active*; 332.4 *be swift*; 380.7 *be violent*; 91.10 *billow*; 331.13 *blow*; 692.8 *data transmission*; 726.1 *emphasis*; 726.6 *emphasize*; 206.1 *few*; 638.16 *fortitude*; 262.4 *haste*; 331.3 *hit*; 313.4 *hurry off*; 262.2 *make haste*; 373.4 *means of connection*; 412.8 *mix*; 342.3 *nimbleness*; 742.13 *punctuate*; 742.7 *punctuation*; 372.5 *separator*; 728.6 *suggestion*; 338.1 *vigour*; 300.15 *walk*
dash at 381.1 *attack*
dash down 367.2 *flatten*
dashed 623.3 *humbled*
dashed hopes 611.2 *hopeless situation*
dash for 324.7 *take a direction*
dash forward 332.6 *accelerate*
dashiki 551.8 *shirt*
dashing 342.18 *active*; 726.3 *emphatic*; 507.1 *loudness*; 332.1 *swift*
Dashing White Sergeant 22.4 *historic dancing*
dash off 332.6 *accelerate*; 313.4 *hurry off*; 262.2 *make haste*
dash one's hopes 604.6 *disappoint*
dash someone's hopes 247.6 *fail*
dash through 262.2 *make haste*
dastard 614.2 *coward*; 594.8 *hated person*
dastardliness 614.1 *cowardice*
dastardly 614.3 *cowardly*
Dastur 7.8 *priest*
data 476.2 *basis of supposition*; 40.19 *computing terms*; 716.1 *evidence*; 455.2, 693.1 *information*
data bank 462.6 *artificial memory*; 439.4 *storage*
database 40.11 *application*; 462.6 *artificial memory*; 693.6 *information technology*; 744.6 *record book*; 6.14 *school book*; 220.2 *table*
database management system 40.11 *application*
data collection 27.57 *population*
data communications 693.6 *information technology*
data entry 40.1 *computing*
data manipulation language 40.11 *application*
Data Post 692.2 *postal communication*
data processing 210.4 *computing*; 334.9 *electronics*; 693.6 *information technology*; 744.6 *record book*
data processing language 5.8 *artificial language*
data summarization 27.57 *population*
data tablet 40.7 *peripheral*
data transfer 40.14
data transmission **692.8**; 29.32 *satellite*
date **275.11**; **275.17**; 567.4 *boyfriend*; 281.15 *chronologize*; 281.3 *chronology*; 593.26 *court*; 21.15 *engagement*; 654.13 *fraternize*; 568.4 *girlfriend*; 223.14 *keep company with*; 593.9 *lover*; 654.3 *meeting*; 223.12 *partner*; 376.8 *rendezvous*; 569.14 *seek the friendship of*
dated 3.15 *historic*; 275.25 *of known date*
date line 281.3 *chronology*
date rape 381.16 *personal attack*; 774.5 *plundering*; 796.7 *sexual assault*
dating **30.42**; **275.8**; 593.6 *courtship*; 281.1 *timekeeping*
dating agency 570.13 *matchmaker*
dating error 288.1 *wrong time*
dating service 570.13 *matchmaker*
dative 5.31 *case*
dative bond 32.11 *chemical bond*
DAT tape 744.7 *recording*
datum 222.6 *aspect*; 476.2 *basis of supposition*
daub 268.19 *anoint*; 550.24 *coat*; 258.11 *dirty*; 718.4 *misrepresent*; 718.1 *misrepresentation*; 19.19 *paint*; 19.8 *painting*
daubed 19.27 *painted*
dauber 19.16 *artist*; 486.10 *unskilled person*
daubing 718.1 *misrepresentation*; 19.2 *painting*
daughter 568.12 *woman in the family*
daughter nuclide 28.70 *radioactivity*
daughter product 28.70 *radioactivity*
daunt 481.2 *deter*; 612.13 *frighten*; 623.26 *outdo*
daunted 614.3 *cowardly*
daunting 612.10 *frightening*
dauntless 613.9 *courageous*
dauntlessly 613.18 *courageously*
dauntlessness 613.1 *courage*; 638.16 *fortitude*
davenport 23.6 *bed*; 410.3 *cabinet*; 413.4 *rest*; 23.4 *table*
David and Bathsheba 593.10 *lovers*
David and Jonathan 569.7 *famous friendships*
Davis Cup 63.1 *tennis*
Davy Jones's locker 156.4 *deep thing*; 91.1 *sea*; 582.14 *the spiritual world*
Davy lamp 522.7 *lantern*
dawdle 343.12 *be inactive*; 333.2 *hesitate*; 333.10 *slow motion*; 333.15 *slow person*; 294.7 *wait*
dawdler 343.8 *nonworker*; 333.15 *slow person*
dawdling 333.7 *delayed*; 333.6 *hesitant*; 343.7 *idleness*; 333.11 *lingering*; 343.3 *not participating*; 342.7 *restlessness*
dawn 525.1 *appearance*; 525.12 *become visible*; 308.24 *begin*; 308.11 *beginning*; 130.2 *creation*; 293.2 *early hour*; 130.27 *emerge*; 522.26 *grow light*; 290.1, 290.5 *morning*; 535.7 *red thing*; 304.3 *sunrise*
dawn chorus 72.18 *bird song*; 290.1 *morning*
dawn dew 429.6 *dew*
dawning 525.1 *appearance*; 308.17 *beginning*; 130.32 *embryonic*; 290.5 *morning*
dawn of love 593.2 *romantic love*
dawn on 695.4 *be intelligible*
dawn upon 739.9 *be disclosed*; 446.14 *have an idea*
day 275.11 *date*; 148.8 *measure of time*; 275.4 *term*; 276.2 *time period*
day after day 297.1 *frequently*; 112.23 *repeatedly*
day and night 298.5 *regular thing*
day-and-night attack 381.12 *military attack*
day bed 23.6 *bed*
day-blind 519.9 *weak-sighted*
day blindness 519.2 *poor sight*
daybook 789.5 *account book*; 220.4 *bill*; 744.2 *certificate*; 220.5 *list of appointments*; 275.13 *timer*
daybreak 130.2 *creation*; 293.2 *early hour*; 290.1 *morning*
day by day 275.26 *all the time*; 298.16 *cyclically*
day-care centre 6.12 *educational institution*
daydream 472.12 *be inattentive*; 477.15 *fantasize*; 477.4 *ideality*; 96.2 *illusion*; 518.5 *imagination*; 96.13, 446.15, 518.17 *imagine*; 325.4 *lose track of*; 477.6 *reverie*; 489.2 *unconsciousness*
daydreamer 472.6 *inattentive person*; 341.2 *nonacting person*; 477.9 *visionary*
daydreaming 472.8 *absent-minded*; 472.3 *absent-mindedness*; 505.1 *deafness*; 446.7 *idealism*; 518.5 *imagination*; 477.10 *imaginative*; 443.3 *thoughtfulness*; 36.14 *trance*
day dress 657.6 *informal dress*
Day-Glo™ 522.16 *bright*; 675.7 *vulgar*
day hospital 35.10 *hospital*
day in day out 275.26 *all the time*; 132.19 *continuously*; 297.1 *frequently*; 112.23 *repeatedly*
day labourer 578.1 *worker*
daylight 146.1 *interval*; 28.23 *light*; 41.15 *lighting*; 290.1 *morning*; 522.4 *natural light*; 522.19 *sunny*
daylight robbery 774.1 *stealing*; 792.2 *unfair price*
daylight saving 522.19 *sunny*; 275.9 *time zone*
daylight saving time 281.3 *chronology*
day nurse 35.16 *nurse*
day nursery 6.12 *educational institution*
day of abstinence 687.3 *fast day*
Day of Atonement 807.2 *apology*; 10.15 *holy day*
day off 263.1 *ease*; 98.5 *leave of absence*; 226.3 *pause*; 580.2 *time off*
day of grace 390.2 *deliverance*
day of judgment 131.5 *fate*; 283.3 *future condition*; 464.4 *judgment day*; 814.9 *retribution*
day of reckoning 814.9 *retribution*
day of rest 263.1 *ease*
day one 130.1 *beginning*
days 275.5 *indefinite period*; 277.5 *long duration*; 111.20 *regularly*
daysack 410.9 *baggage*
day school 6.12 *educational institution*
day's end 291.1 *evening*; 294.2 *late hour*
days gone by 3.8 *past time*
day's march 145.2 *great distance*
days of grace 294.3 *delayed action*
days of innocence 805.3 *naivety*
days of old 3.8, 284.1 *past time*
days of the week 298.5 *regular thing*
days of yore 3.8, 284.1 *past time*
daystar 29.15 *sun*
Daytime 290
Daytona 200; 61.5 *motorcycle racing*
day to remember **462.5**; 601.5 *anniversary*
daze 619.10 *be wonderful*; 453.20 *make uncertain*; 36.14 *trance*
dazed 619.6 *wondering*
dazzle 545.7 *be beautiful*; 619.10 *be wonderful*; 519.15 *blind*; 522.24 *light*; 522.2 *quality of light*; 593.28 *win the love of*
dazzled 519.10 *blinded*; 619.6 *wondering*
dazzler 545.3 *attractive female*
dazzling 519.11 *blinding*; 522.16 *bright*; 531.6 *light*; 230.1 *perfect*; 336.12 *strong to the senses*; 235.1 *worthy*
dazzlingly 519.18 *blindingly*; 522.30 *lightly*; 593.30 *lovingly*
dBase™ 40.11 *application*
d-block 32.6 *chemical element*
d.c. transmission 39.33 *power distribution*
D-day 601.5 *anniversary*; 298.6 *annually celebrated day*; 275.11 *date*
d drop 50.8 *punting*
DDT 43.14 *pest control*
deacon 7.8 *priest*
deaconess 7.8 *priest*
deaconry 7.9 *priesthood*
deaconship 7.9 *priesthood*
deactivate 347.3 *counteract*; 377.13 *dismiss*; 245.4 *impair*; 238.8 *make useless*; 685.4 *moderate*
deactivated 32.39 *catalytic*; 377.21 *disbanded*; 335.10 *powerless*; 32.38 *reactive*; 339.6 *suspended*
deactivation 32.15 *catalysis*; 347.1 *counteraction*; 377.2 *disbandment*; 337.1 *weakness*
dead **294.14**; **582.19**; 273.8 *accurately*; 51.9 *bowls*; 708.20 *cancelled*; 592.2 *desensitized*; 324.9 *directly*; 526.7 *disappeared*; 530.8 *drained of colour*; 58.8 *hockey*; 341.3 *inactive*; 339.5 *inert*; 563.3 *infertile*; 94.11 *no more*; 511.2 *nonresonant*; 284.18 *over*; 301.5 *sedentary*; 529.13 *soft-hued*; 421.3 *soothing*
dead ahead 324.9 *directly*
dead and buried 583.10 *buried*; 582.19 *dead*; 131.21 *ended*; 463.11 *forgotten*; 3.18 *in the past*; 766.16 *losing*; 284.18 *over*
dead and gone 582.19 *dead*; 3.18 *in the past*; 94.11 *no more*; 284.18 *over*
dead as a dodo 3.18 *in the past*; 94.11 *no more*; 284.18 *over*
dead ball 65.2 *billiards play*; 56.2 *golfing terms*; 49.4 *playing terms*; 64.6 *rugger*
dead-ball foul 46.13 *penalty*
dead-ball line 64.1 *rugger*
deadbeat 664.3 *sponger*
dead beat 261.1 *fatigued*; 335.12 *impotent*
dead body 582.11 *dead person*
dead bolt 252.4 *safety device*
dead bowl 51.2 *grip*
dead broke 782.2 *insolvent*; 135.5 *necessitous*
dead calm 301.2 *repose*; 421.7 *smoothness*
dead centre 273.3 *accurate thing*; 173.1 *centre*
dead cert 265.6 *easy thing*; 107.5 *good chance*; 452.12 *something certain*
dead certainty 452.12 *something certain*
dead drunk 690.3
dead duck 582.10 *dying person*; 611.3 *hopeless person*
dead easy 265.9 *easy*
deaden 489.12 *anaesthetize*; 530.6 *decolour*; 343.14 *make inactive*; 618.13 *make indifferent*; 685.4 *moderate*; 505.10 *muffle*; 511.7 *mute*; 335.8 *overpower*; 592.7 *render insensitive*; 730.15 *strike dumb*; 524.11 *tarnish*
dead end 309.4 *closed place*; 51.2 *grip*; 317.3 *road*; 264.8 *snag*
deadened 489.7 *anaesthetized*; 511.2 *nonresonant*
deadening 489.9 *anaesthetic*
deadeye 330.15 *shooter*
dead faint 335.4 *disability*
deadfall 700.13 *snare*
dead hand 440.2 *legal terms*
deadhead 44.15 *cultivate*; 21.33 *theatregoer*
dead heat 285.11 *equal*; 111.5 *equality*; 285.4 *equal race*; 119.2 *equilibrium*; 59.7 *horseracing*
dead-house 582.8 *after death*; 583.1 *burial*
dead jack 51.2 *grip*
dead language 5.9 *ancient language*
dead leaf 424.3 *brittle thing*; 534.5 *brown thing*
dead letter 692.3 *correspondence*; 335.2 *futile effort*
dead-letter office 692.2 *postal communication*
deadline 131.11 *finality*; 262.4 *haste*

deadliness 798.1 *evil;* 236.11 *harmfulness;* 301.1 *motionlessness*
dead load 38.14 *load;* 414.7 *weighing*
deadlock 111.10 *be equal;* 378.9 *block;* 309.1 *closure;* 111.5 *equality;* 119.2 *equilibrium;* 341.1 *inaction;* 301.1 *motionlessness;* 103.7, 378.2 *obstacle;* 252.4 *safety device;* 264.8 *snag;* 226.2 *stop*
deadlocked 378.14 *blocked;* 111.16 *equal;* 341.3 *inactive;* 264.16 *troubled*
dead loss 766.1 *loss;* 238.5 *waste of effort*
deadly **382.23**; **582.20**; 620.4 *boring;* 254.1 *dangerous;* 357.14 *destructive;* 798.9 *detrimental;* 798.7 *evil;* 797.1 *good;* 236.5 *harmful;* 806.7 *sinful;* 235.1 *worthy*
deadly crime 804.7 *criminality*
deadly pale 612.7 *frightened*
deadly sin 804.4, 806.3 *sin*
deadly weapon 587.1 *weapon*
deadman 62.8 *mountaineering*
deadman belay 62.3 *climbing technique*
dead-man's float 67.1 *swimming*
dead man's hand 69.3 *card game terms*
dead man's handle 321.5 *locomotive part;* 252.4 *safety device*
dead march 583.2 *funeral*
deadness 529.3 *hue;* 523.7 *spiritual darkness*
dead of winter 494.7 *cold weather*
dead-on 698.21 *accurate*
dead on arrival 582.19 *dead*
deadpan 618.7 *indifferent;* 618.17 *indifferently;* 643.1 *solemn;* 696.1 *unintelligible*
dead person 582.11
dead pigeon 582.10 *dying person*
dead puck 58.3 *ice hockey*
dead reckoning 323.5 *navigation*
dead-reckoning position 323.5 *navigation*
dead right 273.5, 698.21 *accurate;* 698.39 *accurately;* 801.8 *correct;* 324.9 *directly*
dead ringer 111.3 *lookalike;* 717.1 *representation;* 198.5 *twin*
dead room 28.21 *architectural acoustics*
Dead Sea Scrolls 296.5 *old thing;* 3.11 *relic*
dead set 353.5 *attempt;* 381.12 *military attack;* 301.1 *motionlessness*
dead shot 330.15 *shooter;* 485.4 *skilled person*
dead silence 506.4 *silence*
dead simple 265.9 *easy*
dead spit 111.3 *lookalike;* 198.5 *twin*
deadstock 43.10 *farm tool*
dead stop 247.1 *failure;* 301.1 *motionlessness;* 226.2 *stop*
dead straight 178.1 *straight*
dead tired 261.1 *fatigued*
dead tissue 560.12
dead to 618.7 *indifferent*
dead to the world 690.3 *dead drunk;* 261.1 *fatigued;* 343.4 *not awake;* 489.8 *unconscious;* 505.5 *unhearing*
dead water 88.2 *small lake;* 421.8 *smooth thing*
dead weight 378.6 *burden;* 414.7 *weighing*
dead wood 238.6 *refuse*
deaf **505.4**; 231.3 *deformed;* 341.3 *inactive;* 592.1 *insensitive;* 463.8 *oblivious;* 641.4 *set;* 489.6 *unfeeling*
deaf aid 504.9 *audio device;* 505.1 *deafness*
deaf and dumb 505.4 *deaf;* 231.3 *deformed;* 730.11 *speechless*
deaf-and-dumb language 742.3 *gesture;* 730.6 *silent speech*
deaf-and-dumb person 730.7 *voiceless person*
deaf as a post 505.4 *deaf*
deaf ears 505.1 *deafness*
deafen **505.9**; 507.8 *be loud*
deafened 505.4 *deaf*
deafening **505.6**; 508.8 *banging;* 507.6 *loud;* 514.16 *vociferous*
deafeningly 505.12 *deafly;* 514.20 *vociferously*
deafening row 507.2 *outcry*
deafly 505.12
deaf-mute 505.4 *deaf;* 505.2 *deaf people;* 231.3 *deformed;* 730.7 *voiceless person*
deaf-mutism 505.1 *deafness;* 730.5 *mutism*
Deafness 505
deafness **505.1**; 231.5 *imperfection;* 337.3 *poor health*
deaf people 505.2
deaf to 618.7 *indifferent;* 709.8 *refused;* 505.5 *unhearing*
deaf to all pleas 505.7 *unheard*
de-air 24.11 *make ceramics*
de-airing 24.5 *ceramic process*
deal **13.11**; 340.4 *act;* 409.10 *agreement;* 770.4 *allot;* 750.23 *arrange;* 750.3 *arrangement;* 776.3 *bargain;* 776.9 *bargaining;* 69.3 *card game terms;* 754.1 *compromise;* 755.1 *contract;* 340.2 *deed;* 377.16 *distribute;* 759.5 *exchange;* 746.5 *negotiate;* 69.10 *play;* 778.1 *sell;* 778.3 *selling;* 776.1, 776.4 *trade;* 23.12 *wood*
deal a blow 331.3 *hit*
deal a deathblow 382.19 *execute*
deal destruction 357.10 *lay waste*
dealer 578.3 *agent;* 755.4 *contractor;* 13.9 *economist;* 227.4 *editor;* 346.5 *operator;* 778.13 *retailer;* 776.10 *trader;* 778.12 *wholesaler*
dealer in real property 440.7 *property man*
deal fairly 799.6 *be honourable*
deal gently 648.3 *be lenient*
deal harshly with 647.5 *be severe*
deal in 340.4 *act;* 778.1 *sell;* 776.1 *trade*
deal in futures 14.5 *invest;* 776.2 *speculate*
dealing 759.1 *exchange;* 746.1 *negotiation;* 778.3 *selling;* 776.4 *trade*
dealing death 382.1 *killing*
deal in generalities 138.27 *make a generalization*
dealing in the marvellous 727.5 *tall story*
dealing out 770.1 *allocation*
dealings 340.2 *deed;* 631.8 *treatment*
dealing with 447.7 *focused*
deal in the marvellous 727.11 *tell a tall story*
deal on inside information 699.25, 700.30 *be fraudulent*
deal out 770.4 *allot;* 377.16 *distribute;* 768.5 *give*
deal underhandedly 699.25 *be fraudulent*
deal with 340.4 *act;* 631.14 *behave towards;* 447.11 *raise the point;* 108.7 *relate to;* 346.9 *take action;* 776.1 *trade*
deal with in depth 722.4 *dissertate*
dean 579.13 *director;* 400.9 *educational leader;* 6.4 *educator;* 396.10 *person of authority;* 7.8 *priest;* 400.6 *religious leader*
deanery 565.4 *official residence;* 7.9 *priesthood;* 7.10 *priestly dwelling*
deanship 7.9 *priesthood*
dear **792.7**; 593.21 *beloved;* 681.3 *costly;* 792.12 *dearly;* 595.4 *likable person;* 593.12 *nicknames for lovers;* 781.3 *opulent;* 467.6 *overestimated*
dear at any price 792.7 *dear*
dear at the price 792.7 *dear*
dear departed 582.13 *the dead*
dear friend 569.6 *close friend*
dear heart 593.12 *nicknames for lovers*
dear love 593.11 *loved one*
dearly **777.16**; **792.12**; 593.30 *lovingly*
dearly beloved 593.11 *loved one*
dearly love 593.23 *love*
dearly loved 593.21 *beloved*
dearly love to 595.9 *like to*
Dearness 792
dearness 792.1 *high price;* 790.1 *price*
dear one 595.4 *likable person*
dearth 98.2 *disappearance;* 206.3 *fewness;* 782.9 *inadequacy;* 563.1 *infertility;* 218.9 *scarcity;* 792.6 *value*
dear to one's heart 593.21 *beloved*
deary 593.12 *nicknames for lovers*
Death 582; 582.2 *death personified*
death **131.3**; **463.5**; **582.1**; 249.1 *adversity;* 798.2 *affliction;* 226.1 *cessation;* 357.6 *destroyer;* 526.4 *disappearance;* 375.1 *disintegration;* 263.1 *ease;* 94.8 *extinction;* 594.7 *hated thing;* 260.2 *illness;* 554.5 *life cycle;* 766.1 *loss;* 288.4 *mishap;* 301.2 *repose*
death and taxes 298.5 *regular thing*
deathbed 582.7 *dying day;* 260.2 *illness;* 287.8 *in time;* 294.11 *late in the day*
deathbed confession 582.7 *dying day;* 808.1 *penitence*
deathbed repentance 582.7 *dying day;* 808.1 *penitence*
deathblow 798.2 *affliction;* 247.2 *defeat;* 131.13 *ender;* 382.5 *execution*
death-bringing 382.23 *deadly*
death by misadventure 382.8 *accidental killing;* 582.5 *ways of dying*
death cell 815.3 *prison cell*
death certificate 744.2 *certificate;* 582.12 *death count;* 743.3 *means of identification*
death chamber 582.4 *death sentence;* 814.16 *instrument of execution*
death count 582.12
death-dealing 382.24 *murderous*
death-defying 615.4 *rash*
death duty 790.7 *tax*
death grip 360.1 *retention*
death house 16.43 *conviction;* 582.4 *death sentence;* 814.16 *instrument of execution*
death instinct 36.22 *libido*
death knell 582.4 *death sentence;* 357.4 *ruin;* 711.1 *warning*
deathless 279.8 *eternal;* 228.9 *stable*
deathlessness 279.3 *life without end;* 228.1 *stability*
deathlike 582.21 *deathly;* 530.8 *drained of colour;* 582.18 *dying;* 506.3 *silent*
deathlike calm 301.2 *repose*
deathlike silence 506.4 *silence*
deathliness 582.1 *death;* 339.1 *inertness;* 301.1 *motionlessness*
deathly **582.21**; 382.23 *deadly;* 530.8 *drained of colour;* 582.18 *dying*
deathly hush 506.4 *silence*
deathly pale 530.8 *drained of colour;* 582.18 *dying*
death metal 18.9 *popular music*
death notice 582.12 *death count*
death on the roads 382.8 *accidental killing*
death penalty 814.13 *capital punishment;* 382.5 *execution*
death personified 582.2
death rate 582.12 *death count*
death rattle 582.7 *dying day*
death ray 587.1 *weapon*
death record 582.12 *death count*
death register 582.12 *death count*
death roll 582.12 *death count*
death row 16.43 *conviction;* 582.4 *death sentence;* 814.16 *instrument of execution;* 815.3 *prison cell*
death scene 582.7 *dying day*
deaths column 582.12 *death count*
death sentence **582.4**; 814.13 *capital punishment;* 16.43 *conviction*
death's-head 582.3 *symbol of death*
death spiral 68.6 *ice-skating*
death stroke 131.13 *ender*
death throes 582.7 *dying day*
death toll 582.12 *death count*
deathtrap 254.5 *danger;* 320.21 *miscellaneous motoring terms;* 700.13 *snare;* 379.1 *trap*
Death Valley 428.14 *desert;* 493.8 *hot place*
death warrant 814.13 *capital punishment;* 16.43 *conviction*
deathwatch 582.7 *dying day*
deathwatch beetle 76.3 *pest*
death wish 602.2 *depression;* 36.22 *libido*
deb 130.14 *beginner*
debacle 247.1 *failure;* 305.4 *fall;* 357.4 *ruin*
debag 552.15 *make nude*
debagged 552.11 *exposed*
de-ball 245.5 *hurt;* 335.9 *make impotent;* 212.4 *take off*
de-balled 335.13 *unsexed*
debar 399.3 *veto*
debark 312.4 *land;* 552.15 *make nude*
debarkation 312.11 *landing*
debarment 399.1 *veto*
debase **367.4**; 623.23 *abase;* 796.19 *corrupt;* 780.25 *demonetize;* 245.3 *make worse;* 412.8 *mix;* 245.6 *pervert;* 678.13 *vilify*
debased 367.21 *degraded;* 800.5 *dishonourable*
debasement **367.15**; 623.10 *abasement;* 245.10 *impairment;* 800.1 *improbity;* 245.8 *perversion;* 678.5 *scorn*
debasing 367.18 *lowering*
debatable 701.10 *arguable;* 447.8 *problematic;* 705.14 *questionable*
debatably 447.13 *problematically;* 705.24 *questionably*
debate **444.3**; **444.13**; 586.40, 751.6 *argue;* 751.2 *argument;* 639.8 *balance;* 734.11 *confer;* 734.4 *conference;* 701.14 *discuss;* 746.3 *discussion;* 4.23 *discuss philosophically;* 705.20 *doubt;* 701.2 *logical argument;* 4.5 *philosophical argument;* 447.11 *raise the point*
debater 444.6, 586.5, 701.6 *arguer*
debating 734.4 *conference*
debauch 601.1 *celebration;* 796.19 *corrupt;* 686.11 *overindulge;* 245.6 *pervert*
debauched 686.7 *dissipated;* 804.12 *immoral;* 796.14 *lecherous*
debauchee 796.8 *immoral man;* 686.5 *self-indulgent person*
debauchery 686.2 *dissipation;* 796.3 *sexual immorality;* 804.2 *vice*
debauching 686.7 *dissipated*
debenture 780.14 *paper money;* 253.2 *promise;* 755.2 *purchase contract*
debenture bond 755.2 *purchase contract*
debilitate 261.6 *fatigue;* 214.5 *make smaller;* 335.7 *remove power from;* 337.7 *weaken*
debilitated 335.12 *impotent;* 337.11 *weakened*
debilitating disease 260.4 *disease*
debilitating illness 335.4 *disability*
debilitation 261.7 *fatigue*
debilitative 214.7 *decrescent*
debility 260.1 *ill health;* 337.3 *poor health*
debit 789.7 *account;* 789.1 *accounts;* 784.1 *debt;* 215.3 *difference;* 766.2 *financial loss*
debit and credit 789.1 *accounts*
debited 789.11 *accounted*
deblossom 44.15 *cultivate*
debouch 315.10 *emerge;* 371.14 *let out;* 313.3 *quit*
deboulé 22.9 *ballet steps*
debris 205.8 *bits and pieces;* 427.9 *grit;* 238.6 *refuse;* 215.1 *remainder;* 316.10 *transferred thing*
debris flow 30.26 *mass movement*
de Broglie wave 326.5 *wave*
Debt 784
debt **784.1**; 783.1 *credit;* 782.6, 786.5 *insolvency;* 772.5 *loan;* 135.2 *need*
debt capital 784.3 *loan*
debt collector 376.35, 769.7 *collector;* 783.5 *lender*
debt-free 785.16 *paid*
debt of honour 784.1 *debt;* 756.1 *promise*
debtor **784.6**; 772.6 *borrower;* 247.5 *failing person;* 786.6 *nonpayer*
debtors budget 789.2 *budgeting*
debtor's prison 815.1 *prison*
debts 378.6 *burden;* 784.1 *debt*
debt to society 814.7 *punishment*
debud 44.15 *cultivate*
debug 40.20 *abort;* 409.19 *tidy*
debugging 40.19 *computing terms*
debunk 367.4 *debase;* 621.6 *deride*
debunked 623.3 *humbled*
debus 312.4 *land*
debut 525.1 *appearance;* 312.10 *arrival;* 353.5 *attempt;* 308.24 *begin;* 308.11, 308.17 *beginning;* 314.1 *entry;* 130.18 *make a beginning;* 654.5 *party;* 130.9 *premiere;* 769.4 *reception;* 21.13 *theatrical performance*
debutant 572.5 *single person*
debutante 130.14 *beginner;* 314.7 *entrant;* 295.8 *new arrival;* 654.6 *social person*
decade 148.8 *measure of time;* 201.6 *ten;* 275.4 *term;* 276.2 *time period*
decadence 245.8 *perversion;* 796.3 *sexual immorality*
decadent 214.7 *decrescent;* 17.16 *literary*
decaf 558.4 *coffee*
decaffeinated coffee 558.4 *coffee*
decagon 176.3 *angled figure;* 27.44 *polygon;* 201.6 *ten*
decagonal 176.9 *angled;* 201.17 *tenth*
decagram 201.6 *ten*
decahedral 176.9 *angled;* 201.17 *tenth*
decahedron 176.3 *angled figure;* 201.6 *ten*
decahydrate 32.10 *salt*
decal 267.4 *adherent*
decalcomania 24.3 *glaze*
Decalogue 810.6 *ethics;* 201.6 *ten;* 16.1 *the law*
decamp 98.18 *abscond;* 526.2 *depart;* 389.5 *escape;* 313.4 *hurry off;* 262.2 *make haste;* 786.7 *not pay;* 313.3 *quit;* 634.8 *run away*
decampment 313.7 *departure;* 389.1 *escape*

decant 368.2 *inject*; 256.15 *purify*; 367.6 *throw down*; 316.11 *transfer*
decantation 316.3 *transmission*
decanter 410.14 *bottle*; 558.10 *drink container*
decapitate 814.5 *execute*; 372.10 *set apart*; 149.10 *shorten*; 212.4 *take off*
decapitated 212.7 *reduced*; 149.8 *shortened*
decapitation 814.13 *capital punishment*; 372.3 *separateness*; 149.2 *shortening*; 212.1 *subtraction*
decapod 201.6 *ten*
decarbonize 255.10, 256.15 *purify*
decathlete 47.3 *athlete*
decathlon 47.2 *field events*; 201.6 *ten*
decay **245.2**; 357.7 *agent of destruction*; 296.3 *antiquity*; 258.10 *be dirty*; 278.4 *be transient*; 236.13 *be worthless*; 582.1 *death*; 214.1 *decrease*; 245.9 *dilapidation*; 258.4 *dirt*; 375.3 *disintegrate*; 375.1 *disintegration*; 296.17 *grow old*; 245.5 *hurt*; 236.10 *poverty*; 28.70 *radioactivity*; 372.9 *separate*; 503.2 *something that makes an unpleasant smell*; 260.15 *ulcer*; 441.1, 441.3 *waste*; 337.1 *weakness*
decayable 214.7 *decrescent*
decay constant 28.70 *radioactivity*
decayed 245.12 *deteriorated*; 337.9 *dilapidated*; 375.5 *disintegrated*; 236.4 *poor*
decaying 214.6 *decreasing*; 245.12 *deteriorated*; 260.23 *diseased*; 375.6 *disintegrating*; 236.4 *poor*; 503.4 *putrid*; 278.6 *transient*
decca phasemeter 323.5 *navigation*
decca system 323.5 *navigation*
decease 131.3, 582.1 *death*; 582.15 *die*
deceased 294.14, 582.19 *dead*; 284.20 *former*
deceit 645.1 *cunning*; 700.1 *deception*; 800.2 *faithlessness*; 700.5 *falseness*; 702.5 *hypocrisy*
deceitful **699.33**; 645.4 *cunning*; 700.35 *deceptive*; 234.8 *exaggerated*; 800.6 *faithless*; 702.10 *hypocritical*; 705.14 *questionable*
deceitfully 645.6 *cunningly*; 800.11 *dishonourably*; 234.14 *distortedly*; 699.40 *falsely*; 702.15 *hypocritically*; 705.24 *questionably*
deceitfulness **699.5**; 234.4 *distortion of the truth*; 736.5 *evasion*; 705.7 *questionableness*
deceive **700.23**; **702.12**; **736.9**; 774.16 *act dishonestly*; 645.5 *be cunning*; 604.8 *be dishonest*; 479.1 *be equivocal*; 699.20, 700.27 *be false*; 699.22 *be hypocritical*; 519.15 *blind*; 705.21 *confuse*; 96.16 *delude*; 189.7 *deviate*; 116.6 *differentiate*; 234.12 *distort the truth*; 700.31 *hoax*; 450.9 *make someone believe*; 737.13 *mystify*; 800.9 *prove false*; 773.10 *take away*; 379.2 *trap*
deceived **604.10**; **700.36**; 465.7 *misjudging*
deceive oneself **700.25**
deceive one's hopes 604.6 *disappoint*
deceiver **700.15**; **718.3**; 736.7 *concealer*; 645.3 *cunning person*; 676.2 *pretender*
deceiving **700.34**; 645.4 *cunning*; 700.1 *deception*; 604.12 *deceptive*; 234.8 *exaggerated*
decelerate 301.8 *be motionless*; 214.4 *decrease*; 245.1 *deteriorate*; 214.5 *make smaller*; 251.8 *restrain*; 333.3 *slow down*
deceleration **333.9**; 214.1 *decrease*; 245.7 *deterioration*; 251.1 *restraint*
decelerometer 26.8 *meter*
December 494.7 *cold weather*
decencies 656.5 *etiquette*
decency 658.1 *courtesy*; 549.1 *elegance*; 795.2 *good morals*; 799.1 *probity*; 801.3 *properness*; 255.1 *purity*; 803.1 *virtue*
decennial 201.17 *tenth*
decennially 201.24 *fivefold*
decennium 201.6 *ten*; 276.2 *time period*
decent 650.6 *benevolent*; 658.7 *courteous*; 810.8 *dutiful*; 799.4 *honourable*; 795.8 *moral*; 255.12 *morally pure*; 235.5 *not bad*; 801.11 *right-minded*; 803.5 *virtuous*
decent chance 107.4 *fair chance*
decent feeling 650.1 *benevolence*
decently 650.10 *benevolently*; 658.14 *courteously*; 658.15 *genteelly*; 799.7 *honourably*; 255.18, 803.9 *virtuously*
Décentralisation Dramatique 21.10 *theatre movements*
decentralization **377.6**; 375.2 *deconstruction*; 398.3 *delegation*; 311.2 *parting*
decentralize **377.15**; 375.4 *deconstruct*; 398.7 *delegate*
decentralized **377.26**; **398.10**
Deception 700
deception **700.1**; 645.1 *cunning*; 189.3 *deviousness*; 774.7 *dishonesty*; 234.4 *distortion of the truth*; 736.5 *evasion*; 699.1 *falsehood*; 700.11 *hoax*; 699.3, 702.5 *hypocrisy*; 465.1 *misjudgment*; 645.2 *stratagem*; 773.3 *taking away*; 379.1 *trap*
deceptive **604.12**; **700.35**; 519.11 *blinding*; 268.15 *crafty*; 189.5 *devious*; 234.8 *exaggerated*; 699.29 *false*; 774.18 *fraudulent*; 699.31, 702.10 *hypocritical*; 525.9 *ostensible*; 705.14 *questionable*; 773.12 *taking*
deceptively 773.13 *avariciously*; 604.13 *disappointingly*; 234.14 *distortedly*; 699.40 *falsely*; 702.15 *hypocritically*; 705.24 *questionably*; 774.19 *thievishly*
deceptiveness 676.1 *affectedness*; 700.1 *deception*; 705.7 *questionableness*
decibel 28.19 *sound propagation*
decidable 27.73 *numerable*
decide 635.12 *choose*; 344.12 *determine*; 131.15 *end*; 16.76, 464.11 *judge*; 452.21 *make certain*; 638.7 *resolve*; 140.13 *rule*; 469.1 *select*; 16.71 *try a case*
decide against 399.3 *veto*
decide beforehand 106.2 *premeditate*
decided **452.3**; 707.14 *assertive*; 131.21 *ended*; 638.1 *resolute*
decidedly 707.24 *truthfully*
decidedness 638.12 *resolution*
decide on 469.1 *select*
decide the issue 344.12 *determine*
decide the outcome 344.12 *determine*
decide the result 344.12 *determine*
deciding 469.14 *selecting*
deciding vote 469.10 *vote*
deciduous 305.16 *descending*; 77.14 *of plants*
deciduous tooth 425.11 *tooth*
deciduous tree 79.1 *tree*
decillion 194.3 *large number*; 201.11 *million*
decimal 27.18 *division*; 196.1 *fraction*; 194.9 *fractional*; 780.22 *monetary*; 194.1 *number*; 27.71 *numerical*; 194.5 *ratio*; 201.17 *tenth*
decimal code 40.10 *character*
decimal coinage 780.9 *British money*
decimal currency 780.1 *money*
decimal fraction 27.18 *division*; 196.1 *fraction*; 194.5 *ratio*
decimalize 27.91 *add*; 201.23 *quintuple*
decimal notation 27.8 *number system*
decimal number 27.8 *number system*
decimal point 27.8 *number system*; 742.1 *sign*
decimal system 194.1 *number*; 27.8 *number system*
decimate 357.8 *destroy*; 814.5 *execute*; 201.23 *quintuple*; 206.8 *reduce*; 382.18 *slaughter*; 212.3 *subtract*; 337.7 *weaken*
decimated 212.7 *reduced*
decimation 357.2 *destroying*; 382.4 *slaughter*; 212.1 *subtraction*
decipher **719.9**; 725.2 *clarify*; 738.3 *reveal*; 5.46, 719.12 *translate*
decipherability 695.10 *simplicity*
decipherable 695.2 *simple*
deciphered 719.15 *interpreted*; 5.40 *translated*
decipherment 719.1 *interpretation*; 5.12, 719.4 *translation*
decision 52.2 *boxing*; 482.4 *formulated intention*; 16.7 *legal trial*; 638.12 *resolution*; 469.6 *selection*; 464.2 *verdict*
decision-making 579.3 *management*
decisive 707.14 *assertive*; 344.13 *causal*; 287.7 *critical*; 222.8 *difficult*; 395.11 *influential*; 638.1 *resolute*; 469.14 *selecting*
decisively 344.14 *causally*; 287.10 *critically*; 395.14 *influentially*; 638.17 *resolutely*
decisive moment 287.3 *critical time*
decisiveness 707.6 *assertiveness*; 638.12 *resolution*
deck 175.1 *base*; 38.21 *bridge*; 367.3 *bring down*; 50.6 *canoeing*; 331.3 *hit*; 411.10 *layer*; 411.2 *level*; 542.12 *ornament*; 50.3 *parts of a sailing boat*; 50.8 *punting*; 410.4 *rack*
deck bridge 38.21 *bridge*
deck chair 23.2 *chair*
decked 50.12 *canoeing*
decked-canoe race 50.6 *canoeing*
decked kayak 50.6 *canoeing*
decked out 547.14 *beautified*; 551.29 *dressed*
deckhand 323.7 *nautical person*
deckhead 50.3 *parts of a sailing boat*
deckle edge 420.6 *roughness*
deckle-edged 420.2 *coarse*
deck out 551.33 *dress up*
deck-stepped 50.10 *sailing*
deck-stepped mast 50.3 *parts of a sailing boat*
deck with flowers 601.18 *salute*
declaim 733.7 *address*; 740.14 *proclaim*
declaimer 733.6 *public speaker*
declamation 733.1 *address*; 729.9 *art of public speaking*
declamatory 729.20 *eloquent*; 733.13 *oratorical*; 542.10 *ornate*
declaration 707.1 *affirmation*; 397.1 *command*; 739.2 *divulgence*; 716.5 *legal evidence*; 396.9 *permission*; 740.1 *publication*; 729.8 *speech*; 729.7 *utterance*
declaration of faith 450.2 *religious belief*
Declaration of Independence 250.3 *independence*
declaration of intent 756.1 *promise*
declaration of truth 707.3 *vow*
declaration of war 661.3 *act of defiance*; 585.4 *belligerency*
declarative 707.10 *affirmative*
declaratory 707.10 *affirmative*; 694.6 *meaningful*; 740.21 *publishing*
declare 707.17 *affirm*; 450.7 *believe*; 397.9 *command*; 739.6 *divulge*; 716.11 *give evidence*; 396.21 *grant authority*; 694.10 *mean*; 740.14 *proclaim*; 4.22 *propound a philosophy*; 140.13 *rule*; 742.12 *signal*; 729.11 *speak*
declare as true 707.18 *vow*
declare Chapter 11 782.13 *lose one's money*
declared 738.14 *manifest*; 740.19 *published*; 707.11 *stated*
declared innocent **805.6**
declare free 390.1 *deliver*
declare independence 85.17 *become a nation*
declare innocent **805.9**
declare one's love 593.26 *court*
declare open 130.24 *open*
declare positively 707.17 *affirm*
declarer 707.9 *affirmer*
declare war 751.6 *argue*; 661.6 *be insubordinate*; 586.36 *combat*; 585.12 *go to war*
declaring war 585.8 *warfare*
declension 224.1 *change*; 305.1 *descent*; 325.14 *deviating course*; 325.13 *deviation*; 5.30 *syntax*
declinable 214.7 *decrescent*
declinate 214.7 *decrescent*
declination 29.5 *celestial sphere*; 305.1 *descent*; 325.13 *deviation*; 311.1 *divergence*; 142.2 *exact location*; 30.45 *magnetic pole*; 26.4 *size*
decline **214.2**; **303.14**; 249.1 *adversity*; 556.17 *age*; 793.12 *be cheap*; 607.7 *become aggravated*; 122.11 *become inferior*; 249.9 *be in trouble*; 708.10 *be negative*; 337.6 *be weak*; 224.8 *cause change*; 131.9 *close*; 214.4 *decrease*; 122.2 *deficiency*; 305.9 *descend*; 305.1 *descent*; 245.1 *deteriorate*; 245.7 *deterioration*; 247.6 *fail*; 247.1 *failure*; 303.1 *go backwards*; 296.17 *grow old*; 350.5 *not use*; 556.5 *old age*; 709.5 *refuse*; 470.1 *reject*; 305.2 *sinkage*; 303.4 *slip back*; 441.1, 441.3 *waste*; 355.2 *withdraw*
declined 470.10, 708.18 *rejected*
decline in fortune 782.13 *lose one's money*
decline in health 249.1 *adversity*; 247.1 *failure*
declining 249.6 *adverse*; 556.12 *ageing*; 793.9 *cheap*; 214.6 *decreasing*; 305.16 *descending*; 245.12 *deteriorated*; 303.23 *receding*; 470.5, 708.2 *rejection*
declining prices **793.2**
declining years 556.5 *old age*
declivitous 305.16 *descending*
declivity 176.2 *obliquity*; 305.6 *slide*
decoagulate 431.23 *dissolve*
decoagulated 431.19 *liquefied*
decoagulation 431.8 *fluidification*
decoct 431.23 *dissolve*; 369.17 *obtain an extract*
decoction 558.2 *drink*; 369.8 *extract*; 394.2 *medicine*; 369.7 *obtaining an extract*; 356.3 *product*; 431.10 *solution*
decode 40.20 *abort*; 719.9 *decipher*; 738.3 *reveal*; 706.20 *solve*; 5.46, 719.12 *translate*
decoded 719.15 *interpreted*; 695.2 *simple*; 706.14 *solved*; 5.40 *translated*
decoder 706.10 *answerer*; 737.4 *brainteaser*; 719.6 *interpreter*
decoding 719.1 *interpretation*; 695.10 *simplicity*; 706.6 *solution*; 5.40 *translated*; 5.12, 719.4 *translation*
decoke 255.10 *purify*
decollate 814.5 *execute*
decollation 814.13 *capital punishment*
décolletage 552.4 *dishabille*; 155.4 *low thing*
décolleté 552.10 *in dishabille*; 155.5 *low*
decolorant 530.4 *colour remover*
decoloration 530.1 *colourlessness*
decolorization 530.1 *colourlessness*
decolorize 531.13 *whiten*
decolorized 531.2 *whitened*
decolour **530.6**
decoloured 530.7 *colourless*
decommission 238.8 *make useless*; 350.6 *stop using*
decommissioned 350.4 *disused*
decompensation 36.19 *defence mechanism*; 36.12 *stress*
decompile 40.20 *abort*
decomposable 375.5 *disintegrated*
decompose 427.27 *come to dust*; 245.2 *decay*; 582.15 *die*; 375.3 *disintegrate*; 377.11 *explode*; 296.17 *grow old*; 245.5 *hurt*; 83.11 *moulder*; 372.9 *separate*
decomposed 245.12 *deteriorated*; 260.23 *diseased*; 375.5 *disintegrated*; 236.4 *poor*; 503.4 *putrid*; 377.20 *separated*
decomposing 375.6 *disintegrating*
decomposition 357.2 *destroying*; 245.9 *dilapidation*; 375.1 *disintegration*; 377.5 *divergence*; 236.10 *poverty*; 427.4 *pulverization*; 372.1 *separation*; 503.2 *something that makes an unpleasant smell*; 258.2 *uncleanness*
decompound 375.4 *deconstruct*
decompressive 214.7 *decrescent*
deconcentrate 377.15 *decentralize*
deconcentrated 377.26 *decentralized*
deconcentration 377.6 *decentralization*
decongestant 37.14 *counteracting*; 37.4 *drug type*
deconstruct **375.4**
deconstructed 375.5 *disintegrated*
deconstruction **375.2**; 719.1 *interpretation*
deconstructionism 403.9 *artistic structure*; 4.7 *school of thought*
deconstructionist 4.11 *follower of a doctrine*
deconstructor 17.15 *literary person*
decontaminate 257.6 *make hygienic*; 255.10, 256.15 *purify*
decontaminated 256.17 *cleaned*
decontamination 256.2 *cleaning*; 257.1 *hygiene*; 28.75 *nuclear accident*; 255.2 *purification*
decontrol 347.3 *counteract*; 767.1 *disposal*; 767.9 *dispose of*; 391.4 *liberate*; 391.1 *liberation*
decor 21.19 *stage set*
decorate **20.19**; 211.6 *add*; 545.8 *beautify*; 164.6 *edge*; 244.1 *improve*; 542.12 *ornament*; 813.9 *reward*; 760.9 *transform*
decorate china 24.11 *make ceramics*
decorated **542.11**; 525.10 *aspectual*; 547.14 *beautified*; 542.10 *ornate*; 20.17 *structured*
decorate pottery 24.11 *make ceramics*
decorating **542.5**
Decoration 542
decoration 211.3 *additional item*; 409.2 *array*; 19.1 *art*; 545.2 *beautiful thing*; 542.4 *honour*; 244.5 *improvement*; 743.4 *insignia*; 744.11 *monument*; 542.1 *ornament*; 813.1 *reward*; 794.1 *trophy*
decorations 601.8 *salute*
decorative 19.26 *artistic*; 525.10 *aspectual*; 211.9 *extra*; 542.10 *ornate*
decorative articles **542.6**
decorative arts 19.1 *art*
decorative glass 24.1 *ceramics*
decoratively 20.20 *architecturally*; 19.31 *artistically*
decorative tile 24.8 *ceramic object*
decorative woodwork **23.9**

decorator **542.8**; 578.2 *artisan*; 224.6 *editor*; 393.12 *repairer*
decorous 407.17 *disciplined*; 160.11, 656.6 *formal*
decorousness 656.1 *formality*
decorticate 552.16 *peel*
decortication 552.6 *peeling*
decorum 549.1 *elegance*; 656.5 *etiquette*; 160.5, 656.1 *formality*; 17.12 *poetic language*
decoy **700.18**; 480.9 *enticement*; 60.3 *hunting equipment*; 363.5, 363.12 *lure*; 700.13, 700.33 *snare*
decoy duck 480.9 *enticement*
Decrease 214
decrease **214.1**; **214.4**; 191.6 *become smaller*; 337.6 *be weak*; 203.2 *certain amount*; 209.6 *change gradually*; 191.1 *contraction*; 305.9 *descend*; 245.1 *deteriorate*; 245.7 *deterioration*; 791.1 *discount*; 766.9 *lose*; 766.1 *loss*; 367.1 *lower*; 367.11 *lowering*; 191.5, 214.5 *make smaller*; 685.4 *moderate*; 685.1 *moderation*; 203.8 *quantify*; 218.9 *scarcity*; 305.2 *sinkage*; 212.3 *subtract*; 212.1 *subtraction*; 441.1, 441.3 *waste*
decreased 214.6 *decreasing*; 367.17 *lowered*; 212.7 *reduced*; 191.7 *smaller*
decrease in size 191.1 *contraction*; 191.5 *make smaller*
decreasing **214.6**; 191.8 *contracting*; 305.16 *descending*; 245.12 *deteriorated*
decreasingly **212.9**; **214.8**; 209.10 *by degrees*; 367.24 *down*
decreasing thing 214.3
decree 397.1, 397.9 *command*; 810.17 *impose a duty*; 635.15 *impose one's will*; 16.76, 464.11 *judge*; 16.3 *law*; 16.68 *legislate*; 713.3 *precept*; 106.5 *predetermination*; 106.1 *predetermine*; 740.1 *publication*; 140.1, 140.13 *rule*; 464.2 *verdict*
decree absolute 397.1 *command*; 571.1 *divorce*; 464.2 *verdict*
decreed 16.46 *legislated*; 106.3 *predetermined*
decree nisi 397.1 *command*; 571.1 *divorce*; 464.2 *verdict*
decree of nullity 571.1 *divorce*
decrement 214.1 *decrease*; 27.31 *differentiation*; 791.1 *discount*; 766.1 *loss*; 212.2 *subtracted item*
decrepit 556.14 *aged*; 245.13 *dilapidated*; 337.10 *ill*; 335.12 *impotent*; 296.11 *old*; 260.21 *unhealthy*
decrepitly 296.18 *venerably*
decrepitude 245.9 *dilapidation*; 296.1 *oldness*; 337.3 *poor health*; 335.1 *powerlessness*
decrescendo 214.1 *decrease*; 214.6 *decreasing*
decrescent **214.7**
decretal 16.45 *legislative*; 579.18 *parliamentary*; 713.3 *precept*
decrial 678.1 *disparagement*; 381.16 *personal attack*
decrier 678.7 *disparager*
decriminalization 347.1 *counteraction*; 16.29 *legalization*
decriminalize 347.3 *counteract*; 16.65 *make legal*; 750.29, 757.3 *permit*
decriminalized 16.44 *legal*; 757.7 *permitted*; 750.18 *permitting*
decry 381.10, 670.17 *criticize*; 678.10 *disparage*
decrying 381.25 *critical*; 678.15 *disparaging*
decumbency 187.1 *horizontality*
decumbent 187.10 *lying*
decuple 201.17 *tenth*
decurrence 305.2 *sinkage*
decurrent 305.16 *descending*; 83.10 *of fungi*
decury 586.16 *army unit*
dedans 63.5 *real tennis*
dedans penthouse 63.5 *real tennis*
dedicate 8.17 *deify*; 768.5 *give*; 752.16 *make an offering*
dedicated 8.15 *deified*; 569.11 *devoted*; 643.2 *earnest*; 632.14 *habituated*; 810.9 *loyal*; 7.15 *religious*; 336.11 *strong in spirit*; 638.2 *tenacious*
dedicated to 663.8 *loyal*
dedicate oneself 638.9 *undertake*
dedicate oneself to 9.7 *worship*
dedicate to 349.1 *use*
dedication 810.3 *allegiance*; 638.13 *concentration*; 8.9 *deification*; 643.5 *earnestness*; 569.3 *familiarity*; 336.2 *healthiness*; 752.6, 768.3 *offering*; 652.1 *philanthropy*; 7.2 *religiousness*; 575.1 *right*; 9.1 *worship*
deduce 701.14 *discuss*; 369.15 *draw out*; 464.12 *estimate*; 443.16, 446.14 *have an idea*; 694.11 *infer*; 719.8 *interpret*; 4.21 *rationalize*; 444.11 *reason*; 476.5 *suppose*; 27.89 *theorize*; 442.12 *think*
deduced 476.8 *supposed*
deduct 210.9 *add*; 791.3 *discount*; 372.10 *set apart*; 212.3 *subtract*; 773.10 *take away*
deducted 212.5 *subtracted*
deductible 790.15 *chargeable*; 214.7 *decrescent*
deduction 476.2 *basis of supposition*; 214.1 *decrease*; 791.1 *discount*; 464.1 *judgment*; 701.2 *logical argument*; 4.4 *philosophical investigation*; 4.8 *philosophical term*; 27.64, 444.2 *reasoning*; 786.2 *stoppage*; 212.1 *subtraction*; 773.3 *taking away*; 790.7 *tax*; 443.1 *thought*; 442.2 *ways of thinking*
deductive 27.86 *logical*; 442.9 *mental*; 444.8 *rational*; 212.6 *subtractive*; 773.12 *taking*
deductively 773.13 *avariciously*; 212.8 *by subtraction*; 212.9 *decreasingly*; 701.19 *logically*; 4.24 *philosophically*
deductive reasoning 444.2 *reasoning*
Dee 90.4 *British rivers*
deed **340.2**; 744.2 *certificate*; 755.1, 755.5 *contract*; 613.8 *courageous act*; 3.14 *historicalness*; 123.2 *important matter*; 485.3 *masterpiece*; 253.2 *promise*; 631.9 *tactics*; 576.2 *task*; 619.3 *wonder-working*
deed of trust 755.2 *purchase contract*
deeds 631.8 *treatment*
deeds of blood 585.8 *warfare*
deejay 692.29 *broadcaster*
deem 450.8 *be of the opinion*; 464.12 *estimate*; 4.22 *propound a philosophy*; 140.13 *rule*
de-emphasis 728.9 *downplaying*
de-emphasize 728.22 *play down*
de-emphasized 728.19 *downplayed*
deep **156.8**; **156.16**; **510.8**; 150.1 *broad*; 529.11 *colourful*; 532.2 *dark*; 523.10 *dark-coloured*; 172.7 *interior*; 4.19 *learned*; 507.6 *loud*; 266.2 *obscure*; 91.7 *oceanic*; 5.43 *phrasal*; 203.6 *quantitative*; 141.13 *spacious*; 152.1 *thick*; 442.11 *thoughtful*; 696.1 *unintelligible*; 156.11, 458.5 *wise*
deep blue 539.1 *blue*
deep blue sea 91.1 *sea*
deep colour 523.3 *dark colour*
deep-coloured 529.11 *colourful*; 523.10 *dark-coloured*
deep-cut 156.8 *deep*
deep depression 31.11 *weather system*
deep-dish 156.8 *deep*
deep diver 55.2 *artificial fly*
deep down 156.16 *deep*
deep-down 156.8 *deep*
deepen **156.14**; 607.6 *aggravate*; 523.13 *become dark*; 532.11 *blacken*; 141.20 *extend*; 213.5 *make bigger*
deepened 607.4 *aggravated*
deepening 607.1 *aggravation*; 156.1 *depth*; 213.1 *increase*
deepening depression 31.11 *weather system*
deeper **156.10**
deepest 156.10 *deeper*
deepest feelings 590.8 *seat of feelings*
deepfreeze 25.4 *kitchen container*; 439.4 *storage*
deep freeze 494.4 *cooler*
deep freezer 494.4 *cooler*
deep-freezing 359.1 *preservation*
deep-fried 25.56 *culinary*
deep frier 25.6 *kitchen equipment*
deep-frozen 416.7 *condensed*
deep-fry 25.55 *cook*
deep frying 25.8 *cooking technique*
deep in debt 784.9 *in debt*
deep-laid 156.8 *deep*; 243.20 *developed*; 485.9 *well-made*
deep-litter house 43.7 *farm building*
deeply 532.12 *blackly*; 156.16 *deep*; 172.16 *inwardly*; 156.17 *profoundly*; 203.7 *quantitatively*; 510.11 *resonantly*; 141.15 *spaciously*; 4.29 *wisely*
deeply felt 590.14 *emotive*
deep-lying 156.8 *deep*
deeply involved 342.18 *active*
deepmost 156.10 *deeper*
deepness **510.3**; 156.1 *depth*; 203.1 *quantity*; 696.11 *unintelligibility*
deep note 510.3 *deepness*
deep ocean 30.12 *ocean*
deep-pan 156.8 *deep*
deep-pitched 510.8 *deep*
deep purple 540.6 *purple*
deep-reaching 156.8 *deep*
deep red 535.1 *red*
deep-rooted 156.9 *deep-seated*; 632.13 *fixed*; 99.6 *intrinsic*; 336.10 *potent*; 228.10 *stabilized*
deep-rootedness 156.2 *intensity*
deep sea 156.4 *deep thing*; 91.1 *sea*
deep-sea 30.51, 91.7 *oceanic*; 156.12 *under*
deep-sea diver 91.6 *oceanographer*; 156.5 *submariner*
deep-sea diving 156.1 *depth*
deep-sea drilling 30.17 *ocean research vessel*
deep-sea fish 55.7 *angle*
deep-sea fisherman 55.6 *angler*; 323.7 *nautical person*
deep-sea fishing 55.1 *angling*; 633.2 *chase*; 74.7 *fishing*
deep-seated **156.9**; 632.13 *fixed*; 99.6 *intrinsic*
deep-seatedness 156.2 *intensity*
deep-sea trolling 55.1 *angling*
deep-set 156.8 *deep*
deep six 582.8 *after death*; 582.17, 583.8 *bury*; 583.6 *grave*
deep-sounding 510.8 *deep*
Deep South Torrid Zone 493.8 *hot place*
deep space 145.1 *distance*; 29.3 *universe*
deep square 53.4 *team*
deep structure 5.29 *grammar*; 694.1 *meaning*; 5.24 *phrasing*
deep thing 156.4
deep thinking **156.7**; 443.2 *intellectual exercise*
deep-throated 515.7 *ululant*
deep tone 532.7 *blackness*
deep-toned 510.8 *deep*
deep-voiced 510.8 *deep*
deep water 156.4 *deep thing*
deep-water 156.12 *under*
deer 60.5 *game*; 332.12 *swift animal*
deer farm 43.6 *farm*
deer hunt 60.2 *hunting*
deer hunter 382.13 *animal killer*; 60.4 *hunter*
deer hunting 382.9 *animal killing*; 60.2 *hunting*
deerlike 71.33 *ungulate*
deer season 292.1 *season*
deer-stalk 633.11 *hunt*; 60.7 *shoot*
deerstalker 551.15 *headgear*; 60.4, 71.24, 633.6 *hunter*
deerstalking 633.2 *chase*; 60.2 *hunting*; 71.23 *mammal hunting*
de-escalate 214.4 *decrease*
de-escalation 214.1 *decrease*; 367.11 *lowering*
def 235.1 *worthy*
deface 548.7 *blemish*; 708.14 *cancel*; 234.11 *deform*; 245.5 *hurt*; 546.5 *make ugly*; 238.8 *make useless*; 358.1 *obliterate*; 357.11 *ruin*
defaced 548.4 *blemished*; 708.20 *cancelled*; 234.7 *deformed*; 546.4 *ugly*
defacement 708.5 *cancellation*; 234.3 *deformity*; 358.3 *obliteration*; 546.1 *ugliness*
defacer **234.5**; 357.6 *destroyer*
de facto 93.13 *real*; 93.22, 95.13 *really*
de facto possession 763.2 *legal terms*
defalcate 786.7 *not pay*
defalcation 786.1 *nonpayment*; 233.2 *omission*
defalcator 786.6 *nonpayer*
defamation **678.3**; 668.1 *disrespect*; 715.2 *false accusation*; 699.6 *lying*; 720.2 *misinterpretation*; 381.16 *personal attack*; 712.3 *vilification*
defamation of character 678.3 *defamation*
defamatorily 715.10 *accusingly*; 712.13 *vituperatively*
defamatory **678.16**; 381.25, 670.27 *critical*; 668.11 *insulting*; 715.9 *perjurious*; 712.9 *vituperative*
defamatory remark 678.4 *aspersion*
defame **678.12**; 715.6 *accuse falsely*; 606.7 *be dissatisfied*; 381.10 *criticize*; 720.1 *misinterpret*; 668.20 *scorn*; 712.6 *vilify*; 670.22 *vituperate*; 802.20 *wrong*
defamed 715.9 *perjurious*
defamer **678.8**
default 233.5 *be incomplete*; 218.5 *be insufficient*; 247.1 *failure*; 233.1 *incompleteness*; 786.1 *nonpayment*; 784.8, 786.7 *not pay*; 233.2 *omission*; 709.1 *refusal*; 709.5 *refuse*
defaulted match 56.2 *golfing terms*
defaulter 784.6 *debtor*; 766.6 *loser*; 786.6 *nonpayer*
defaulting 784.5 *amount owing*; 786.13 *nonpaying*; 784.10 *unable to pay*
defaulting in arrears 233.4 *incomplete*
defeasibility 704.4 *refutability*
defeasible 704.6 *refutable*
defeasibly 704.12 *refutably*
defeat **247.2**; **387.7**; 249.1 *adversity*; 604.2 *bad outcome*; 121.8 *be superior*; 246.9 *be victorious*; 249.11 *cause adversity*; 226.8 *cause to cease*; 470.6 *discarding*; 596.2 *disliked thing*; 236.14 *ill-treat*; 766.1 *loss*; 400.14 *master*; 704.8 *refute*; 226.2 *stop*; 387.1 *subjection*
defeat comprehensively 357.11 *ruin*
defeat easily 246.10 *defeat heavily*
defeated **247.11**; 604.9 *disappointed*; 611.4 *hopeless*; 623.3 *humbled*; 122.18 *outclassed*
defeated candidate 470.9 *rejected person*
defeated player 247.5 *failing person*
defeater 246.5 *victorious person*
defeat heavily 246.10
defeatism 614.1 *cowardice*; 611.1 *hopelessness*; 341.1 *inaction*; 708.1 *negation*; 468.1 *underestimation*
defeatist 388.2 *appeaser*; 614.3 *cowardly*; 611.4 *hopeless*; 611.3 *hopeless person*; 341.3 *inactive*; 708.17 *negative*; 341.2 *nonacting person*; 468.2 *pessimist*; 468.4 *underestimating*
defeat of the enemy 246.2 *victory*
defeat of the prosecution 16.42 *acquittal*
defeat one's hopes 604.6 *disappoint*
defeat the enemy 246.9 *be victorious*
defecate **560.16**; 371.14 *let out*
defecation **560.2**; 256.2 *cleaning*; 260.8 *indigestion*
defect **231.7**; 98.18 *abscond*; 479.3 *apostatize*; 662.15 *be disobedient*; 122.2 *deficiency*; 120.1 *inequality*; 236.8 *inferiority*; 218.8 *insufficiency*; 548.1 *spot*; 804.3 *venial sin*; 254.7 *vulnerability*; 337.1 *weakness*
defected 98.11 *truant*
defection 98.4 *absenteeism*; 479.7 *apostasy*; 662.1 *disobedience*; 800.2 *faithlessness*; 355.3 *relinquishment*
defective **122.17**; 548.4 *blemished*; 802.18 *gone wrong*; 231.1 *imperfect*; 233.4 *incomplete*; 236.2 *inferior*; 120.3 *unequal*; 804.13 *venial*
defective hearing 505.1 *deafness*
defectively 122.21 *badly*; 231.11 *imperfectly*; 120.7 *unequally*
defectiveness 231.5 *imperfection*; 233.1 *incompleteness*
defective sight 519.2 *poor sight*
defect of character 254.7 *vulnerability*
defector 98.6 *absentee*; 355.4 *deserter*; 479.9 *equivocator*
Defence 384
defence **46.10**; **384.1**; **714.2**; 587.3 *arms race*; 585.9 *battle*; 113.5 *conflict*; 347.1 *counteraction*; 704.3 *countercharge*; 706.5 *counterstatement*; 364.7 *deflection*; 444.4 *explanation*; 16.7 *legal trial*; 701.5 *plea*; 252.2, 253.1 *protection*; 64.3 *rugby play*; 585.8 *warfare*; 587.1 *weapon*
Defence Council 584.5 *military staff*
defence cuts 749.1 *pacification*
defenceless 335.11 *unprotected*; 254.3 *vulnerable*; 337.8 *weak*
defencelessly 254.11 *dangerously*; 335.14 *powerlessly*
defencelessness 335.3 *helplessness*; 254.7 *vulnerability*; 337.1 *weakness*
defence mechanism **36.19**; 634.14 *evasion*
defence mechanism camouflage 384.4 *defensiveness*
defence player 58.6 *lacrosse player*
defence reaction 36.19 *defence mechanism*
defences 252.2 *protection*
defence zone 58.3 *ice hockey*
defend **384.17**; **586.39**; 706.18 *answer back*; 585.13 *be at war*; 413.14 *give moral support*; 714.8 *justify*; 113.18 *object*; 701.16 *plead*; 444.14 *premise*; 359.5 *preserve*; 252.10, 550.30 *protect*; 253.10 *secure*

defend against 347.3 *counteract*
defend an action 16.72 *stand trial*
defendant 715.4 *accused person*; 706.10 *answerer*; 444.6 *arguer*; 16.8 *litigant*; 113.11 *opposer*; 705.10 *person questioned*; 716.7 *person who gives evidence*; 704.5 *refuter*
defended **384.30**; 444.10 *causal*; 252.6 *safe*
defender **384.13**; **586.2**; 347.2 *counteracting thing*; 66.3 *football player*; 58.4 *ice hockey player*; 252.3 *protector*; 383.5 *resister*; 64.4 *rugby player*; 45.3 *sportsman*; 413.8 *supporter*; 714.5 *vindicator*
defending **384.29**; 714.11 *vindicatory*; 585.15 *warring*
defend one's attitude 443.16 *have an idea*
defend oneself 715.7 *be accused*; 252.9 *be safe*; 383.8 *revolt*
defenestrate 330.25 *eject*; 371.13 *throw away*
defenestrated 367.19 *fallen*
defenestration 367.12 *downthrow*; 330.4 *ejection*; 371.20 *eviction*
defensible 252.7 *invulnerable*; 714.13 *vindicable*
defensive **364.10**; 701.12 *apologetic*; 634.18 *avoiding*; 444.10 *causal*; 384.29 *defending*; 378.13 *hindering*; 584.8 *military*; 706.13 *retaliatory*; 46.19 *varsity*; 714.11 *vindicatory*
defensive backfield 46.10 *defence*
defensive backs 46.10 *defence*
defensive battle 585.9 *battle*
defensive circle 384.9 *barrier*
defensive coordinator 46.2 *football player*
defensive end 46.10 *defence*
defensive formation 46.10 *defence*
defensive foul 46.13 *penalty*
defensive huddle **46.11**
defensive line 46.10 *defence*; 384.8 *military defences*
defensive lineman 46.10 *defence*
defensively **364.12**; **384.32**; 706.24 *in answer*; 704.11 *in reply*; 714.15 *in vindication*; 584.11 *militarily*; 58.10 *on the field*; 378.16 *with delay*
defensive measure 347.1 *counteraction*
defensive missile 587.5 *missile weapon*
defensive move 384.1 *defence*
defensiveness **384.4**
defensive reaction 634.14 *evasion*
defensive stroke 53.9 *stroke*
defensive tackle 46.10 *defence*
defensive tactic 384.1 *defence*
defensive team 46.10 *defence*
defensive wall 128.3 *exclusion zone*
defensive warfare 585.8 *warfare*
defensive weapon 587.1 *weapon*
defensive weapons 585.1 *war*
defer 294.8 *delay*; 361.12 *interrupt*; 341.4 *not act*; 663.5 *obey*
deference **658.4**; 810.3 *allegiance*; 367.16 *courtesy*; 663.1 *obedience*; 667.3 *respectfulness*; 623.11 *self-abasement*; 664.1 *servility*; 388.1 *submission*
deferent 623.4 *self-abasing*
deferential **658.9**; 367.21 *degraded*; 810.9 *loyal*; 663.7 *obedient*; 664.6 *servile*; 667.9 *showing respect*
deferentially **658.16**; 663.10 *obediently*; 667.22 *respectfully*; 623.28 *subserviently*
deferment 294.3 *delayed action*; 791.1 *discount*; 361.6 *interruption*
defer payment 783.9 *acquire credit*; 791.5 *buy at a discount*
deferral 294.3 *delayed action*
deferred 783.12 *charged*; 294.10 *held up*; 361.9 *interrupted*; 350.1 *unused*
deferred payment 783.1 *credit*; 785.1 *payment*; 777.7 *purchasing*; 786.2 *stoppage*
defer to **658.13**; 664.10 *knuckle under*; 663.5 *obey*; 667.18 *show respect*; 388.3 *submit*
Defiance 661
defiance **661.1**; 660.5 *bravado*; 660.9 *discourtesy*; 662.1 *disobedience*; 113.4 *objection*; 753.1 *protest*; 708.3 *rebuttal*; 383.1 *resistance*
defiance of authority 588.1 *anarchy*
defiance of gravity 415.5 *lightness*; 366.6 *raising*
defiance of orders 662.1 *disobedience*
defiant **661.7**; 381.24 *counterattacking*; 113.24 *discordant*; 660.20 *discourteous*; 662.13 *disobedient*; 708.17 *negative*; 118.12 *nonconformist*; 738.15 *open*; 753.9 *protesting*; 383.10 *resistant*
defiantly **661.9**; 613.18 *courageously*; 753.11 *disapprovingly*; 662.17 *disobediently*; 707.25 *explicitly*; 738.17 *frankly*; 708.22 *negatively*; 113.27 *opposingly*; 383.14 *resistingly*
defiant person **661.4**
deficiency **122.2**; 231.7 *defect*; 98.2 *disappearance*; 206.3 *fewness*; 766.2 *financial loss*; 231.5 *imperfection*; 782.9 *inadequacy*; 233.1 *incompleteness*; 120.1 *inequality*; 218.8 *insufficiency*; 233.2 *omission*; 804.3 *venial sin*
deficiency disease 260.4 *disease*
deficient 122.17 *defective*; 782.4 *inadequate*; 231.2, 233.4 *incomplete*; 218.1, 337.13 *insufficient*; 98.12 *missing*; 120.3 *unequal*; 766.17 *unprofitable*; 804.13 *venial*
deficiently 766.20 *at a loss*; 122.21 *badly*; 233.6 *incompletely*; 120.7 *unequally*
deficit 784.5 *amount owing*; 215.3 *difference*; 766.2 *financial loss*; 218.8 *insufficiency*; 233.2 *omission*
deficit finance 14.1, 780.7 *finance*
deficit financing 13.2 *economy*
deficit spending 13.2 *economy*
defile 798.11 *be evil*; 812.4 *bring into disrepute*; 796.19 *corrupt*; 668.27 *desecrate*; 258.11 *dirty*; 146.3 *gulf*; 245.3 *make worse*; 351.1 *misuse*; 151.6 *narrow place*; 308.7 *passageway*; 678.13 *vilify*
defiled 258.7 *dirty*; 798.7 *evil*; 351.4 *misused*
defilement 258.1 *dirtiness*; 798.1 *evil*; 245.10 *impairment*; 796.2 *indecency*; 351.2 *misuse*; 678.5 *scorn*
defiling 796.12 *indecent*
define **721.16**; 698.31 *be accurate*; 725.2 *clarify*; 722.4 *dissertate*; 719.8 *interpret*; 166.7 *limit*; 4.21 *rationalize*; 136.16, 139.24, 452.22 *specify*; 5.47 *word*
defined 698.21 *accurate*; 520.2 *clear*; 136.12 *conditional*; 719.15 *interpreted*; 738.14 *manifest*; 695.3 *recognizable*
definer 719.6 *interpreter*
defining 99.9 *characteristic*; 719.14 *interpretive*; 137.11 *typical*
definite **707.16**; 452.1 *certain*; 725.3 *clear*; 726.3 *emphatic*; 5.44 *grammatical*; 693.16 *informative*; 695.1 *intelligible*; 166.5 *limited*; 738.14 *manifest*; 452.7 *particular*; 695.3 *recognizable*
definite article 5.35 *part of speech*
definite integral 27.31 *differentiation*
definitely 707.23 *affirmatively*; 452.23 *certainly*; 452.26 *certainly!*; 643.12 *indeed*
definiteness **707.8**; 452.9 *certainty*; 725.1 *clarity*; 695.9 *intelligibility*; 452.18 *particularity*; 695.11 *recognizability*
definition 698.8 *accuracy*; 520.4, 725.1 *clarity*; 719.1 *interpretation*; 166.1 *limitation*; 695.11 *recognizability*; 136.6 *specification*; 692.23 *television reception*; 694.4 *type of meaning*
definitional 136.12 *conditional*; 719.14 *interpretive*
definitive 698.21 *accurate*; 396.12 *authoritative*; 131.20 *ending*; 719.14 *interpretive*; 137.11 *typical*
definitively 131.28 *conclusively*; 137.16 *taxonomically*
deflatability 191.2 *contractibility*
deflatable 191.9 *contractible*
deflate **623.25**; 191.6 *become smaller*; 367.4 *debase*; 621.6 *deride*; 728.21 *detract from*; 367.1 *lower*; 191.5 *make smaller*; 335.8 *overpower*; 704.8 *refute*; 337.7 *weaken*
deflated **728.18**; 337.9 *dilapidated*; 623.3 *humbled*; 367.17 *lowered*; 191.7 *smaller*
deflate one's ego 124.13 *make unimportant*
deflation **728.10**; 191.1 *contraction*; 214.2 *decline*; 793.2 *declining prices*; 214.3 *decreasing thing*; 13.6 *economic factors*; 13.2 *economy*; 14.1, 780.7 *finance*; 623.9 *humiliation*; 367.11 *lowering*; 337.3 *poor health*
deflationary 191.8 *contracting*; 214.7 *decrescent*; 13.13 *economic*; 14.6 *financial*; 780.22 *monetary*
deflationist 214.7 *decrescent*
deflect **325.12**; **481.3**; 189.6 *be oblique*; 144.14 *displace*; 634.6 *evade*; 364.3 *fend off*; 384.24 *parry*; 52.13 *practise judo*
deflected 144.8 *displaced*; 325.21 *indirect*; 189.4 *oblique*
deflection **364.7**; 481.7 *deterrence*; 325.13 *deviation*; 144.1 *displacement*; 377.5 *divergence*; 634.14 *evasion*; 189.1 *obliqueness*; 52.9 *tae kwon do*; 28.15 *wave property*
deflective 325.21 *indirect*; 189.4 *oblique*
defloration 796.3 *sexual immorality*
deflower 796.20 *seduce*; 773.7 *take*
deflowerment 773.1 *taking*
defluxion 305.3 *downflow*; 315.2 *outflow*
defoliant 357.7 *agent of destruction*
defoliate 357.10 *lay waste*
defoliation 357.2 *destroying*; 563.1 *infertility*; 79.10 *tree disease*
deforest 369.12 *displace*; 357.10 *lay waste*; 563.10 *waste*
deforestation 369.2 *displacement*; 79.5 *forestry*; 563.1 *infertility*
deform **234.11**; 548.7 *blemish*; 234.12 *distort the truth*; 38.31 *load*; 161.3 *make shapeless*; 546.5 *make ugly*; 718.4 *misrepresent*; 245.6 *pervert*; 760.9 *transform*
deformation **38.16**; 30.20 *earth movement*; 718.1 *misrepresentation*; 245.8 *perversion*
deformational 30.54 *tectonic*
deformed **231.3**; **234.7**; 548.4 *blemished*; 718.6 *misrepresented*; 546.4 *ugly*
deformity **234.3**; 231.5 *imperfection*; 546.1 *ugliness*
defraud 789.7 *account*; 774.16 *act dishonestly*; 800.10 *be criminal*; 645.5 *be cunning*; 700.30 *be fraudulent*; 351.1 *misuse*; 786.7 *not pay*
defrauder 699.19, 700.17 *cheat*; 774.11 *dishonest person*; 786.6 *nonpayer*
defrauding 786.1 *nonpayment*
defray **777.5**; **785.8**; 787.3 *donate*
defrayal 785.1 *payment*
defraying 785.1 *payment*
defrayment 785.1 *payment*
defray the cost 785.8 *defray*
defrock 371.3 *disbar*; 128.8 *eject*
defrocking 371.18 *dismissal*
defrost 493.14 *be hot*; 431.24 *melt*
defrosted 493.13 *heated*
deft 797.5 *proficient*; 485.6 *skilful*
deft fingers 485.1 *skill*
deftly 485.12 *skilfully*
deftness 797.12 *proficiency*; 485.1, 733.3 *skill*
defunct 582.19 *dead*; 3.18 *in the past*; 94.11 *no more*; 487.2 *not customary*
defuse 343.14 *make inactive*
defy **661.5**; 613.15 *be courageous*; 662.15 *be disobedient*; 638.8 *brace oneself*; 381.8 *counterattack*; 254.9 *face danger*; 113.18 *object*; 753.6 *protest*; 342.14 *push*; 708.11 *rebut*; 383.6 *resist*; 113.20 *withstand*
defy authority 588.4 *be anarchic*
defy comprehension 696.7 *be unintelligible*
defy gravity 415.9 *be light*
defying **661.8**; 661.1 *defiance*
defying comprehension 696.4 *difficult*
defying gravity 304.1 *ascent*
defy orders 662.15 *be disobedient*
defy the law 16.73 *be illegal*
degage 250.13 *informal*
degass 32.29 *absorb*
degassed 32.43 *absorbed*
degassing 32.20 *surface chemistry*
degauss 347.3 *counteract*
degausser 347.2 *counteracting thing*
degeneracy 245.8 *perversion*; 796.3 *sexual immorality*; 804.2 *vice*
degenerate 224.7 *be changed*; 607.7 *become aggravated*; 408.25 *be disordered*; 249.9 *be in trouble*; 760.8 *be transformed*; 214.4 *decrease*; 245.1 *deteriorate*; 245.12 *deteriorated*; 796.16 *do wrong*; 804.12 *immoral*; 796.8 *immoral man*; 804.9 *wicked person*
degenerated 224.12 *changed*; 760.13 *converted*
degenerately 804.20 *immorally*
degenerateness 245.8 *perversion*
degenerating 760.14 *converting*
degeneration 224.1 *change*; 214.1 *decrease*; 760.2 *evolution*; 245.8 *perversion*; 804.2 *vice*
degenerative 245.12 *deteriorated*; 260.23 *diseased*; 236.5 *harmful*
degenerative disease 260.4 *disease*
degenerative joint disease 260.16 *rheumatism*
deglaciation 30.40 *glaciation*
deglutition 557.1 *eating*
degradation 623.10 *abasement*; 367.15 *debasement*; 371.18 *dismissal*; 812.1 *disrespect*; 668.8 *indignity*; 245.8 *perversion*; 678.5 *scorn*; 804.2 *vice*
degrade 623.23 *abase*; 367.4 *debase*; 668.27 *desecrate*; 371.3 *disbar*; 214.5 *make smaller*; 124.13 *make unimportant*; 245.6 *pervert*; 814.1 *punish*; 372.9 *separate*; 32.27 *synthesize*; 678.13 *vilify*
degraded **367.21**; 623.3 *humbled*; 804.12 *immoral*
degrade oneself 812.4 *bring into disrepute*
degrading 812.4 *disreputable*; 668.16 *humiliating*; 814.7 *punishment*
degradingly 367.25 *courteously*
degree **209.1**; 27.27 *equation*; 123.1 *importance*; 407.4 *position*; 136.3 *qualifications*; 108.3 *relative position*; 26.4 *size*
degree of difference 209.3 *gradation*
degrees 324.3 *orientation*
degust 495.9 *taste*
degustation 495.3 *appetizer*
dehisce 80.10 *fruit*; 77.21 *vegetate*
dehiscent 146.7 *cracked*; 80.9 *of a fruit*
dehiscent fruit 80.2 *botanical fruit*
dehorn 43.18 *practise livestock farming*
dehumanization 245.8 *perversion*
dehumanize 804.17 *make wicked*; 245.6 *pervert*
dehumanized 651.11 *cruel*
dehumidification 428.13 *drying*
dehumidifier 428.15 *dryer*
dehumidify 428.17 *dry*
dehydrant 428.15 *dryer*
dehydrate 760.7 *convert into*; 428.17 *dry*; 359.5 *preserve*
dehydrated 428.3 *dried-up*; 617.10 *hungry*; 359.7 *preserved*
dehydrated food 557.7 *food*; 359.3 *preserved thing*
dehydrating 428.9 *drying*
dehydration 760.1 *conversion*; 428.13 *drying*; 359.1 *preservation*; 428.12 *thirst*
dehydrator 428.15 *dryer*
dehydrogenase 33.11 *enzyme*
de-ice 493.14 *be hot*
de-icer 493.3 *heater*
deictic 4.16 *dialectical*
deification **8.9**; 366.7 *lift*; 669.3 *praise*
deified **8.15**; 366.12 *exalted*
deified person **8.10**
deify **8.17**; 9.8 *idolatrize*; 669.14 *praise*; 366.3 *promote*; 667.16 *revere*
deifying 667.10 *reverent*
deign 623.18 *condescend*
deigning 623.15 *condescension*
deil 8.7 *devil*
deism 7.2 *religiousness*; 4.7 *school of thought*
deist 450.5 *believer*; 4.11 *follower of a doctrine*
deistic 8.13 *divine*; 4.14 *of a philosophy*
deity **8.5**; 8.1 *divinity*; 9.3 *idol*; 344.7 *Prime Mover*; 93.7 *self-existence*
déjà vu 518.5 *imagination*; 3.13 *looking back*; 11.10 *psychic phenomenon*; 525.6 *reappearance*; 462.2 *retrospect*
deject 523.14 *make dark*; 626.10 *make sullen*
dejecta 560.4 *excrement*
dejected 523.11 *benighted*; 539.3, 602.6 *depressed*; 604.9 *disappointed*; 611.4 *hopeless*; 623.3 *humbled*; 626.6 *sullen*
dejectedly 611.11 *hopelessly*; 626.13 *sullenly*
dejectedness 602.2 *depression*
dejection 249.1 *adversity*; 560.2 *defecation*; 36.13, 602.2 *depression*; 560.4 *excrement*; 611.1 *hopelessness*; 523.7 *spiritual darkness*; 626.1 *sullenness*
dejecture 560.4 *excrement*
de jure 16.44 *legal*; 16.81 *legally*
de jure possession 763.2 *legal terms*
deke 58.3 *ice hockey*; 58.9 *play hockey*
deked 58.8 *hockey*
deking 58.8 *hockey*
dekko 518.6 *look*
del 27.50 *scalar quantity*
delaminate 411.11 *scale*
delamination 411.6 *layering*
delate 693.13 *inform on*
delator 693.10 *informer*
delay **294.8**; **637.15**; 634.7 *be evasive*;

343.12 *be inactive*; 639.7 *be irresolute*; 666.6 *be neglectful*; 378.9 *block*; 294.3 *delayed action*; 390.2 *deliverance*; 333.2 *hesitate*; 333.12 *hesitation*; 637.8 *hold back*; 343.7 *idleness*; 341.1 *inaction*; 666.2 *indifference*; 361.12 *interrupt*; 361.6 *interruption*; 294.1 *lateness*; 341.4 *not act*; 378.2 *obstacle*; 226.3 *pause*; 333.3 *slow down*; 384.25 *stall*; 631.9 *tactics*; 294.7 *wait*
delayed 333.7; 361.9 *interrupted*; 294.9 *late*
delayed action 294.3
delayed dribble 58.3 *ice hockey*
delayed dribbling 58.3 *ice hockey*
delayed reaction 294.3 *delayed action*
delayer 294.5; 294.4 *latecomer*
delaying 294.12; 341.3 *inactive*; 666.5 *indifferent*; 637.4 *procrastinating*
delaying action 634.15 *evasiveness*
delaying tactics 294.3 *delayed action*
delay of game 46.13 *penalty*
dele 358.1 *obliterate*; 358.3 *obliteration*
delectability 241.9 *tastiness*
delectable 490.6 *pleasant*; 241.4, 495.7 *tasty*
delectation 597.1 *happiness*
d-electron 28.65 *atom*
delegable 398.9 *delegated*
Delegate 398
delegate 398.1; **398.7**; 398.6, 578.3 *agent*; 375.4 *deconstruct*; 768.5 *give*; 396.21 *grant authority*; 579.16 *official*; 469.4 *pick*; 717.8, 748.4 *representative*; 729.10 *speaker*
delegate authority 396.21 *grant authority*
delegated 398.9; 396.13 *elected*
delegated authority 396.1 *authority*
delegation 398.3; 396.3 *acquisition of power*; 375.2 *deconstruction*; 398.2 *representative body*
delegation of power 398.3 *delegation*
delegation of work 398.3 *delegation*
delete 40.20 *abort*; 708.14 *cancel*; 399.4 *censor*; 357.8 *destroy*; 128.8 *eject*; 521.8 *make invisible*; 358.1 *obliterate*; 212.3 *subtract*; 773.10 *take away*
deleted 708.20 *cancelled*; 399.6 *censored*; 128.11 *excluded*; 98.12 *missing*; 358.6 *obliterated*; 212.5 *subtracted*
deleterious 798.9 *detrimental*; 236.5 *harmful*
deleteriously 798.13 *destructively*
deletion 708.5 *cancellation*; 399.2 *censorship*; 357.1 *destruction*; 128.2 *ejection*; 358.3 *obliteration*; 212.1 *subtraction*; 773.3 *taking away*
Delhi belly 560.2 *defecation*
deli 557.17 *food shop*
Delia 10.16 *religious festival*
deliberate 26.15; **106.4**; 713.6 *consult*; 701.14 *discuss*; 446.15 *imagine*; 482.12 *intended*; 580.7 *leisurely*; 694.9 *meant*; 746.5 *negotiate*; 4.20 *philosophize*; 638.1 *resolute*; 443.15 *think about*; 333.5 *unhurried*; 635.6 *willed*
deliberate kicking 66.2 *football play*
deliberately 482.13 *intentionally*; 701.19 *logically*; 446.21 *purposively*; 638.17 *resolutely*; 333.16 *slowly*
deliberateness 482.2 *intentionality*; 333.8 *slowness*
deliberate over 734.11 *confer*
deliberate tripping 66.2 *football play*
deliberation 443.4; 616.1 *caution*; 713.2 *consultation*; 701.2 *logical argument*; 4.4 *philosophical investigation*; 333.8 *slowness*
deliberative 713.7 *advising*; 579.18 *parliamentary*; 443.10 *speculative*; 4.17 *thoughtful*
deliberative assembly 579.10 *legislative body*
deliberative body 579.10 *legislative body*
deliberatively 4.28 *thoughtfully*
delicacies 557.7 *food*; 498.2 *sweetener*
delicacy 488.2 *ability to sense*; 698.8 *accuracy*; 495.3 *appetizer*; 424.2 *brittleness*; 543.1, 549.1 *elegance*; 153.11 *fineness*; 419.12 *gentleness*; 545.1 *gorgeousness*; 404.2 *grain*; 260.1 *ill health*; 466.2 *judiciousness*; 415.5 *lightness*; 241.10 *pleasant thing*; 255.1 *purity*; 591.5 *sensitivity*; 485.1 *skill*; 417.3 *sparseness*; 549.2 *subletly*; 728.3 *subtlety*; 337.1 *weakness*
delicate 404.10; 698.21 *accurate*; 424.1 *brittle*; 466.9 *discriminating*; 543.3 *elegant*; 151.2, 153.4 *fine*; 492.10 *handed*; 415.2 *insubstantial*; 264.12 *problematic*; 549.5 *refined*; 591.1 *sensitive*; 419.6 *soft-hearted*; 529.13 *soft-hued*; 417.1 *sparse*; 728.13 *subtle*; 488.7 *susceptible*; 260.21 *unhealthy*; 254.2 *unsafe*; 337.8 *weak*
delicate eating 557.3
delicate flavour 495.4 *flavour*
delicate health 260.1 *ill health*
delicately 543.5 *elegantly*; 424.5 *fragilely*; 466.16 *judiciously*; 415.11 *lightly*; 264.27 *problematically*; 591.12 *sensitively*; 419.18 *soft-heartedly*; 417.7 *sparsely*; 404.15 *texturally*
delicate move 62.3 *climbing technique*
delicateness 698.8 *accuracy*; 337.1 *weakness*
delicate situation 264.7 *awkward situation*
delicatessen 557.17 *food shop*
delicious 557.27 *edible*; 490.6 *pleasant*; 241.4, 495.7 *tasty*; 235.1 *worthy*
deliciously 557.29 *edibly*; 495.11 *tastily*
deliciousness 495.1 *taste*; 241.9 *tastiness*
delict 806.3 *sin*
delight 597.8 *cause joy*; 241.13, 490.9 *give pleasure*; 597.1 *happiness*; 490.1 *physical pleasure*; 241.11 *pleasant person*; 600.1 *rejoicing*
delighted 597.4 *happy*; 490.7 *pleased*
delightful 597.5; 241.1, 490.6 *pleasant*
delightfulness 241.6 *pleasantness*
delight in 609.7 *be satisfied*; 597.6 *enjoy*; 490.8 *feel pleasure*; 241.14, 595.7 *like*; 593.23 *love*
delimit 770.4 *allot*; 743.10 *identify*; 136.16 *specify*
delimitation 770.1 *allocation*; 136.6 *specification*
delimited 136.12 *conditional*
delineate 99.11 *characterize*; 721.14 *describe*; 703.16 *explain*; 163.5 *outline*; 717.9 *represent*; 139.24 *specify*; 742.9 *use signs*; 17.21 *write*
delineated 703.11 *explanatory*; 19.27 *painted*
delineating 19.3 *drawing*
delineation 721.1 *description*; 19.3, 19.9 *drawing*; 703.3 *explanation*; 163.1 *outline*; 608.6 *profile*; 717.1 *representation*
delineative 163.6 *outlined*
delineator 19.16 *artist*
delineatory 717.13 *representational*
delinquency 804.7 *criminality*; 662.1 *disobedience*; 806.1 *guilt*; 16.38 *lawbreaking*; 802.6 *unlawfulness*; 804.1 *wickedness*
delinquent 804.15 *criminal*; 662.13 *disobedient*; 806.4 *guilty person*; 802.16 *in the wrong*; 16.40 *lawbreaker*; 804.11 *wicked*; 802.10 *wrongdoer*
delinquently 355.8 *apathetically*; 804.21 *criminally*; 662.17 *disobediently*
deliquation 431.8 *fluidification*
deliquesce 375.4 *deconstruct*; 431.24 *melt*; 83.11 *moulder*
deliquescence 375.2 *deconstruction*; 214.1 *decrease*; 377.3 *dilution*; 431.8 *fluidification*
deliquescent 214.7 *decrescent*; 375.6 *disintegrating*; 431.19 *liquefied*; 83.10 *of fungi*
delirious 260.23 *diseased*; 597.4 *happy*; 461.12 *manic*
delirium 461.4 *delusion*; 597.1 *happiness*; 477.6 *reverie*; 260.3 *symptom*
delirium tremens 690.16 *alcoholism*; 461.4 *delusion*; 327.7 *shake*
delish 235.1 *worthy*
deliver 390.1; 649.10 *absolve*; 692.31 *correspond*; 768.5 *give*; 775.4 *give back*; 392.17 *help*; 391.4 *liberate*; 359.5 *preserve*; 252.10 *protect*; 436.5 *provision*; 384.23 *rescue*; 393.3 *restore*; 608.10 *save*; 250.15 *set free*; 316.12, 319.4 *transport*
deliverable 390.4
deliver an address 733.7 *address*
Deliverance 390
deliverance 390.2; 649.3 *absolution*; 16.42 *acquittal*; 608.2 *aid*; 389.1 *escape*; 250.1 *freedom*; 775.1 *giving back*; 391.1 *liberation*; 359.1 *preservation*; 393.9 *restoration*; 252.1 *safety*; 392.2 *support*
deliver a sermon 670.20 *censure*
deliver a speech 729.14 *speak to*
delivered 390.4 *deliverable*; 649.6 *forgiven*
deliverer 390.3; 391.3 *liberator*; 359.4 *preservationist*; 384.15 *rescuer*
deliver oneself 389.5 *escape*
deliver the goods 239.6 *be convenient*; 436.5 *provision*
delivery 53.8; 729.4 *articulation*; 554.4 *biological function*; 130.4 *conception*; 631.1 *conduct*; 390.2 *deliverance*; 768.1 *giving*; 51.2 *grip*; 391.1 *liberation*; 561.7 *obstetrics*; 436.1 *provision*; 63.4 *tennis terms*; 316.2 *transportation*
delivery date 756.1 *promise*
delivery van 316.5 *means of transport*
dell 183.2 *concave land*; 146.3 *gulf*; 92.8 *valley*
dell pony 59.5 *pony*
delocalization 316.1 *transfer*
delocalized 32.35 *combined*
delousing 256.2 *cleaning*; 255.2 *purification*
Delphic oracle 475.8 *oracle*
Delta 29.35 *rocketry*
delta 90.2, 317.11 *channel*; 311.5 *fork*; 92.9 *inlet*; 30.27 *sediment*
deltaic 92.11 *continental*
delta-like 311.8 *fanlike*
delta-shaped 311.8 *fanlike*
deltoid 311.8 *fanlike*; 190.8 *growing*; 199.8 *three-sided*
delude 96.16; 604.8 *be dishonest*; 699.20, 700.27 *be false*; 699.22 *be hypocritical*
deluded 604.10 *deceived*; 461.12 *manic*; 465.7 *misjudging*; 274.17 *mistaken*
delude oneself 700.25 *deceive oneself*
deluder 700.15 *deceiver*
deluge 219.4 *be excessive*; 219.1 *excess*; 376.22 *flood*; 31.25 *rain*; 90.6 *river flow*; 433.29 *water*
deluged 90.11, 433.24 *flooded*
delusion 96.3; **461.4**; 274.6 *fallibility*; 699.1 *falsehood*; 477.5 *fantasy*; 699.3 *hypocrisy*; 700.2 *self-deception*
delusions of grandeur 676.1 *affectedness*; 673.3 *cockiness*; 461.4 *delusion*
delusive 699.29 *false*; 699.31 *hypocritical*; 700.40 *illusory*
delusiveness 700.2 *self-deception*
delusory 96.9, 700.40 *illusory*
de luxe 781.3 *opulent*; 490.6 *pleasant*
delve 44.15 *cultivate*; 43.17 *farm*
delve into 183.9 *make concave*
delve into the supernatural 100.16 *be external*
demagnetization 347.1 *counteraction*
demagnetize 347.3 *counteract*
demagogic 702.8 *cunning*; 733.13 *oratorical*
demagogical 733.13 *oratorical*
demagogically 702.15 *hypocritically*
demagogue 662.8 *agitator*; 579.14 *leader*; 480.14, 483.7 *motivator*; 733.6 *public speaker*; 702.6 *sophist*; 729.10 *speaker*
demagoguery 702.3 *cunning*; 12.1 *government*; 396.7 *type of rule*
demagogy 12.1 *government*; 396.7 *type of rule*
demand 397.2; **397.10**; **474.11**; **710.2**; **710.7**; 790.12 *charge*; 386.6 *compel*; 777.11 *custom*; 617.1, 617.12 *desire*; 369.6 *extortion*; 369.16 *extort*; 790.3 *fee*; 635.15 *impose one's will*; 135.10 *necessitate*; 135.2 *need*; 651.18 *torment*; 349.6 *use*
demand an answer 710.6 *request*
demand assurances 252.9 *be safe*
demand backed by threats 710.2 *demand*
demanded 710.10 *demanding*; 135.4 *required*
demand for payment 710.2 *demand*
demanding 135.6; **710.10**; 280.6 *allowing no delay*; 617.9 *desirous*; 264.10 *difficult*; 261.4 *fatiguing*; 230.2 *perfectionist*; 264.12 *problematic*; 814.21 *punishing*; 264.14 *troublesome*
demanding pity 627.7 *pitiful*
demand payment 710.7 *demand*
demands 474.2 *expectations*
demand tax payment 397.10 *demand*
demand too much 261.6 *fatigue*; 218.7 *make insufficient*
demand with threats 710.7 *demand*
demarcate 770.4 *allot*; 99.11 *characterize*; 466.12 *discriminate*; 166.7 *limit*; 251.8 *restrain*; 136.16 *specify*; 742.9 *use signs*
demarcated 136.12 *conditional*; 466.11 *judged*
demarcation 770.1 *allocation*; 466.1 *discrimination*; 166.1 *limitation*; 251.1 *restraint*; 136.6 *specification*
dematerialization 98.2, 526.4 *disappearance*; 101.2 *unworldliness*
dematerialize 98.18 *abscond*; 526.1 *disappear*; 101.12 *enter a nonmaterial world*; 11.20 *occult*
dematerialized 98.9 *away*; 101.8 *nonmaterial*
dematerializing 101.8 *nonmaterial*
demean 623.23 *abase*
demeaning 367.18 *lowering*
demean oneself 631.13 *behave badly*; 812.4 *bring into disrepute*; 623.18 *condescend*; 623.21 *humble oneself*; 664.10 *knuckle under*
demeanour 631.1 *conduct*; 525.3 *external appearance*; 742.3 *gesture*; 160.6 *nature*
dement 461.15 *make insane*
demented 328.16 *deranged*; 461.11 *insane*; 457.5 *lacking intellect*; 461.12 *manic*
dementedly 461.17 *insanely*
dementia 335.4 *disability*; 457.1 *lack of intellect*; 461.3 *mental deterioration*
dementia praecox 36.11, 461.5 *psychosis*
demerara 534.5 *brown thing*
demerara rum 558.7 *alcoholic drink*
demerara sugar 25.7 *basic ingredient*; 498.2 *sweetener*
demerge 375.4 *deconstruct*
demerger 375.2 *deconstruction*
demerging 375.2 *deconstruction*
demerit 804.3 *venial sin*
demesne 43.6 *farm*; 440.2 *legal terms*
Demeter 562.4 *fertility cult*
demibastion 384.11 *fortification*
demi-column 20.8 *column*
demi-glace 25.15 *sauce*
demigod 8.5 *deity*
demijohn 410.14 *bottle*
demilitarization 335.1 *powerlessness*
demilitarize 749.5 *make peace*; 335.7 *remove power from*
demilune 384.11 *fortification*
demimonde 804.9 *wicked person*
Demiourgos 8.3 *God*
demise 131.3, 582.1 *death*
demised 582.19 *dead*
demisemiquaver 18.17 *notation*
demist 527.12 *make transparent*
demiurge 8.3 *God*
demo 703.6 *mass demonstration*; 376.4 *rally*
demob 377.2 *disbandment*; 377.13 *dismiss*; 584.10 *enlist*; 391.4 *liberate*; 749.1 *pacification*; 589.1 *peace*
demobbed 377.21 *disbanded*
demobilization 377.2 *disbandment*; 391.1 *liberation*; 749.1 *pacification*; 589.1 *peace*
demobilize 377.13 *dismiss*; 584.10 *enlist*; 391.4 *liberate*; 343.14 *make inactive*; 749.5 *make peace*; 372.9 *separate*
demobilized 377.21 *disbanded*
democracy 85.1 *country*; 119.1 *equality*; 469.11 *franchise*; 12.1 *government*; 764.1 *joint possession*; 566.11 *nation*; 396.7 *type of rule*
democracy unlimited 12.1 *government*
democrat 12.6 *political party*
democratic 119.6 *equal*; 12.9, 396.14 *governmental*; 85.16, 86.17, 566.13 *national*
democratically 119.13 *equitably*; 396.24 *ministerially*; 85.19, 86.20 *nationally*; 12.14 *politically*
democratic behaviour 631.1 *conduct*
Democratic Party 12.6 *political party*
democratic republic 86.4 *territorial division*
Democratic Social Centre 12.6 *political party*
democratic state 566.11 *nation*
democratic system 469.11 *franchise*
Democratic whip 400.3 *leader*; 396.10 *person of authority*
democratize 85.17 *become a nation*
Democritean 4.11 *follower of a doctrine*; 4.14 *of a philosophy*
demodulate 692.30 *communicate*
demodulated 692.34 *communicated*
demodulation 692.14 *radio transmission*
demodulator 692.14 *radio transmission*
demographer 1.3 *anthropologist*; 2.11 *sociologist*; 566.6 *studier of mankind*
demographic 1.11 *anthropological*; 2.14 *socioeconomic*
demographically 1.16 *anthropologically*; 2.16 *sociologically*
demographic research 2.2 *sociological research*

demographic survey 2.2 *sociological research*
demographic transition 13.4 *economic development*
demography 1.1 *anthropology*; 2.2 *sociological research*; 2.1 *sociology*; 566.5 *study of mankind*
demolish 357.9; 585.13 *be at war*; 375.4 *deconstruct*; 367.2 *flatten*; 441.2 *lay waste*; 358.1 *obliterate*; 704.8 *refute*
demolished 375.5 *disintegrated*; 367.17 *lowered*; 358.6 *obliterated*
demolisher 357.6 *destroyer*
demolishment 357.2 *destroying*
demolition 375.2 *deconstruction*; 357.2 *destroying*; 245.10 *impairment*; 367.11 *lowering*; 358.3 *obliteration*; 704.1 *refutation*
demon 236.12 *bad person*; 8.7 *devil*; 11.11 *ghost*; 380.4 *violent creature*; 804.9 *wicked person*
demonetize 780.25; 786.12 *devalue the currency*
demonetized 780.22 *monetary*
demonetized coinage 780.15 *false money*
demon for work 342.10 *busy person*
demoniac 651.11 *cruel*; 8.16 *devilish*
demoniacal 651.11 *cruel*
demonic 342.18 *active*; 8.16 *devilish*; 9.10 *idolatrous*; 11.15 *witchlike*
demonical 798.7 *evil*
demonically 8.20 *devilishly*; 11.26 *magically*
demonism 9.2 *idolatry*
demonize 11.21 *bewitch*; 8.18 *devilize*
demonkind 8.7 *devil*
demon-like 8.16 *devilish*
demonstrability 703.5
demonstrable 703.12; 452.1 *certain*
demonstrable existence 93.4
demonstrableness 703.5 *demonstrability*
demonstrably 703.22; 93.22 *really*
demonstrate 703.15; 485.11 *be expert*; 661.6 *be insubordinate*; 725.2 *clarify*; 738.1 *display*; 95.12 *establish reality*; 719.8 *interpret*; 714.8 *justify*; 452.21 *make certain*; 518.18, 520.10 *make visible*; 4.22 *propound a philosophy*; 703.19 *protest*; 454.2 *prove*; 698.30 *prove true*; 342.14 *push*; 4.21 *rationalize*; 701.15 *state*; 27.89 *theorize*
demonstrate against 753.8 *cause mischief*; 709.6 *dissent*
demonstrated 703.9; 452.1 *certain*; 703.11 *explanatory*; 698.20 *proved*; 703.13 *proven*
demonstrate ill will 596.5 *dislike*
demonstrate self-control 473.6 *be disinterested*; 251.10 *restrain oneself*
demonstrate style 724.9 *style*
demonstrating 703.14
Demonstration 703
demonstration 703.1; 661.3 *act of defiance*; 452.13, 698.7 *confirmation*; 738.6 *display*; 709.2 *dissent*; 703.3 *explanation*; 753.3 *gesture of protest*; 719.1 *interpretation*; 16.7 *legal trial*; 520.5 *manifestation*; 27.66, 454.5, 703.4, 716.2 *proof*; 376.4 *rally*
demonstrative 703.10; 716.2 *evidential*; 569.8 *friendly*; 719.14 *interpretive*; 593.17 *loving*; 742.14 *signifying*; 454.9 *verificatory*
demonstratively 703.21; 716.14 *as evidence*; 742.18 *indicatively*; 454.11 *verifiably*
demonstrativeness 703.2; 673.6 *boastfulness*; 593.3 *lovingness*
demonstrator 703.7; 661.4 *defiant person*; 738.12 *displayer*; 662.7, 703.8, 753.4 *protester*
demoralization 245.11 *hurt*; 612.4 *intimidation*
demoralize 796.19 *corrupt*; 245.5 *hurt*; 804.17 *make wicked*
demoralized 612.7 *frightened*; 335.12 *impotent*
demos 566.11 *nation*
demote 15.11 *conduct industrial relations*; 367.4 *debase*; 371.3 *disbar*; 124.13 *make unimportant*; 814.1 *punish*; 144.17 *relegate*; 708.15 *terminate*
demoted 367.21 *degraded*; 305.17 *drooping*; 144.11 *relegated*
demotion 367.15 *debasement*; 305.1 *descent*; 371.18 *dismissal*; 305.4 *fall*; 814.7 *punishment*; 144.4 *relegation*
demulce 419.14 *ease*; 394.19 *remedy*
demulcent 394.5 *analgesic*; 37.4 *drug type*; 685.8 *moderating*; 685.2 *moderator*; 37.7, 268.6 *ointment*; 394.17 *remedial*; 37.16 *soothing*
demur 704.10 *countercharge*; 451.1 *disbelief*; 637.8 *hold back*; 113.18 *object*; 113.4 *objection*; 708.11 *rebut*; 708.3 *rebuttal*; 709.7 *refuse oneself*; 634.4 *shy*; 637.11 *unwillingness*
demure 674.10 *bashful*
demurely 674.17 *modestly*
demureness 674.3 *bashfulness*
demuring 674.10 *bashful*
demurity 674.3 *bashfulness*
demurral 704.3 *countercharge*; 113.4 *objection*; 708.3 *rebuttal*
demurrer 704.3 *countercharge*; 16.5 *litigation*
demurring 709.9 *dissenting*; 637.1 *unwilling*
demystify 719.9 *decipher*
demythologization 719.1 *interpretation*
demythologizer 719.6 *interpreter*
demythologizing 719.14 *interpretive*
den 71.20 *abode of mammals*; 183.2 *concave land*; 565.13 *lair*; 736.6 *privacy*; 565.7 *room*; 550.15 *shelter*; 767.8 *sink*; 655.5 *solitary place*; 577.1 *workshop*
denarius 780.12 *ancient coins*
denary 27.71 *numerical*; 201.17 *tenth*
denationalization 13.1 *economics*
denationalize 245.6 *pervert*
denaturalization 760.2 *evolution*
denaturalize 760.8 *be transformed*; 760.12 *naturalize*; 245.6 *pervert*
denaturalized 760.17 *naturalized*
denature 245.3 *make worse*; 245.6 *pervert*
denaturization 33.9 *protein*
dendriform 311.9 *branched*; 377.24 *divergent*; 79.14 *treelike*
dendritic 311.9 *branched*; 377.24 *divergent*; 79.14 *treelike*
dendrochronology 281.3 *chronology*; 30.42, 275.8 *dating*; 79.3 *timber*
dendroid 84.7 *algal*; 44.16 *horticultural*; 79.14 *treelike*
dendrolater 9.6 *idolater*
dendrolatrous 9.10 *idolatrous*
dendrolatry 9.2 *idolatry*
dendrologic 79.17 *arboricultural*
dendrologically 79.20 *arboriculturally*; 77.25 *botanically*
dendrologist 79.8 *forester*; 77.12 *plant scientist*
dendrologous 79.17 *arboricultural*
dendrology 79.5 *forestry*; 34.1 *life science*; 77.10 *plant science*
dengue 260.7 *tropical disease*
deniably 708.22 *negatively*
denial 704.2; 470.7 *abrogation*; 36.19 *defence mechanism*; 383.4 *desisting*; 634.15 *evasiveness*; 128.1 *exclusion*; 451.3 *incredulity*; 766.1 *loss*; 27.63 *mathematical logic*; 94.3 *negativeness*; 113.4 *objection*; 753.1 *protest*; 708.3 *rebuttal*; 479.8 *recantation*; 709.1 *refusal*; 708.2 *rejection*; 453.10 *suspicion*; 399.1 *veto*
denied 604.9 *disappointed*; 709.9 *dissenting*; 103.4 *forbidden*; 753.9 *protesting*; 708.18 *rejected*; 399.5 *vetoed*
denier 42.1 *fibre*; 404.2 *grain*; 704.5 *refuter*
denigrate 381.10, 670.17 *criticize*; 678.10 *disparage*; 124.13 *make unimportant*; 709.5 *refuse*; 668.20 *scorn*
denigrated 668.18 *undervalued*
denigrating 381.25 *critical*
denigration 678.1 *disparagement*; 381.16 *personal attack*; 709.1 *refusal*
denigratory 678.15 *disparaging*
denim 193.4 *textile*
denims 551.4 *informal dress*; 551.9 *trousers*
denizen 564.1 *inhabitant*
den of iniquity 804.8 *wicked place*
den of vice 804.8 *wicked place*
denominate 139.24 *specify*
denomination 137.8 *genealogy*; 743.1 *identification*; 721.7 *nomenclature*; 7.1 *religion*
denominational 7.16
denominational school 6.12 *educational institution*
denominator 27.18 *division*; 194.5 *ratio*
denotation 698.10 *literalness*; 694.1 *meaning*; 694.4 *type of meaning*
denotative 698.23 *literal*; 694.6 *meaningful*; 742.14 *signifying*
denote 694.10 *mean*; 742.10 *signify*; 717.12 *stand for*; 701.15 *state*
denoted 743.12 *identified*
denouement 17.3 *aspect of fiction*; 739.1 *disclosure*; 345.1 *effect*; 131.10 *ending*; 21.8 *scene*; 289.9 *sequel*; 706.6 *solution*
denounce 715.5 *accuse*; 670.19 *blame*; 381.10 *criticize*; 621.6 *deride*; 594.14 *hate*; 693.13 *inform on*; 10.18 *perform rites*
denounced 715.8 *accusatory*
denouncement 715.1 *accusation*; 670.7 *blame*
denouncer 715.3 *accuser*
denouncing 712.9 *vituperative*
dense 152.2; **416.6**; 267.9 *adhesive*; 376.50 *crowded*; 426.3 *dull*; 414.1 *heavy*; 528.1 *opaque*; 77.13 *plantlike*; 524.8 *stupid*; 152.3 *thick-witted*; 457.6, 528.5 *unintelligent*
dense cloud 31.19 *cloud cover*
dense fog 31.33 *fog*; 524.2 *murk*
densely 416.10; 267.11 *cohesively*; 414.16 *heavily*; 528.13 *opaquely*; 152.9 *thick*
densely arrayed 416.6 *dense*
denseness 152.6; 416.1 *density*; 524.4 *stupidity*; 457.2 *unintelligence*
densify 416.8 *be dense*
densimeter 26.8 *meter*; 416.3 *relative density*
densimetric 26.16 *micrometric*
densimetry 26.2 *micrometry*
densitometer 26.8 *meter*
densitometric 26.16 *micrometric*
Density 416
density 416.1; 152.6 *denseness*; 418.5 *hardness*; 28.9 *mass*; 402.1 *material world*; 528.6 *opaqueness*; 152.5 *thickness*
density current 30.13 *ocean current*
dent 331.13 *blow*; 183.3 *cavity*; 367.14 *depression*; 367.2 *flatten*; 331.3 *hit*; 183.9 *make concave*; 183.4, 183.10 *notch*; 425.7 *sharp point*
dental 35.23
dental auxiliary 35.17 *paramedic*
dental corps 584.4 *military organization*
dental floss 256.10 *cleaning object*
dental hygienist 35.17 *paramedic*
dental powder 256.9 *cleaning agent*
dental record 743.3 *means of identification*
dental surgeon 35.14 *dentist*; 394.15 *healer*
dental surgery 35.4 *dentistry*; 35.9, 394.12 *surgery*
dental surgery assistant 35.17 *paramedic*
dental technician 35.17 *paramedic*
dental therapist 35.17 *paramedic*
dentate 183.7 *notched*; 77.18 *of leaves*
dentately 183.12 *jaggedly*
dented 183.6 *concave*
denticle 425.11 *tooth*
denticulate 425.4 *toothed*
denticulately 183.12 *jaggedly*
denticulation 425.6 *sharpness*
dentiform 425.4 *toothed*
dentifrice 256.9 *cleaning agent*; 394.3 *prophylactic*; 255.3 *purifier*
dentist 35.14; 394.15 *healer*
dentistry 35.4
dentist's chair 413.4 *rest*
dentition 425.6 *sharpness*
denudate 552.15 *make nude*
denudation 766.5 *destruction*; 552.1 *undress*; 30.35 *weathering*
denude 766.13 *destroy*; 739.5 *disclose*; 357.10 *lay waste*; 552.15 *make nude*; 372.10 *set apart*; 212.4 *take off*; 337.7 *weaken*
denuded 552.11 *exposed*
denuder 552.7 *depilation*
denuding 552.1 *undress*
denumerable 27.73 *numerable*
denunciate 715.5 *accuse*; 670.19 *blame*; 712.6 *vilify*
denunciated 715.8 *accusatory*
denunciation 715.1 *accusation*; 621.2 *act of derision*; 670.7 *blame*; 10.5 *Christian rite*; 381.16 *personal attack*; 712.3 *vilification*
denunciatory 715.8 *accusatory*; 670.29 *blaming*; 381.25 *critical*; 712.9 *vituperative*
de-nut 335.9 *make impotent*
de-nutted 335.13 *unsexed*
Denver 87.2 *American cities*
Denver boot 378.4 *restraint*
Denver Stock Show 59.12 *rodeo*
deny 704.9; 634.7 *be evasive*; 708.10 *be negative*; 451.8 *disbelieve*; 4.23 *discuss philosophically*; 128.7 *exclude*; 103.8 *make impossible*; 113.18 *object*; 753.6 *protest*; 708.11 *rebut*; 479.4 *recant*; 709.5 *refuse*; 470.4 *revoke*; 604.7 *thwart*; 399.3 *veto*
deny entry 128.7 *exclude*
denying 383.13 *desisting*; 709.9 *dissenting*; 753.9 *protesting*; 708.19 *rebutting*
denying oneself 709.3 *abnegation*; 383.4 *desisting*
deny oneself 634.3 *abstain*; 684.5 *be self-restrained*; 383.9 *desist*; 709.7 *refuse oneself*; 355.1 *relinquish*; 251.10 *restrain oneself*
deny oneself nothing 686.10 *indulge oneself*
deny the possibility 708.11 *rebut*
deobstruent 37.4 *drug type*
deoch-an-doruis 313.9 *parting*
deodand 814.7 *punishment*
deodorant 501.2; 256.9 *cleaning agent*; 501.4 *deodorizing*; 37.4 *drug type*; 255.3 *purifier*
deodorization 256.2 *cleaning*; 699.14 *façade*; 501.1 *odourlessness*; 255.2 *purification*
deodorize 501.5; 434.20 *aerate*; 699.28 *mask*; 255.10, 256.15 *purify*
deodorized 501.3 *odourless*; 255.14 *purified*
deodorizer 501.2 *deodorant*
deodorizing 501.4
deontic logic 4.6 *branch of philosophy*
deontology 4.6 *branch of philosophy*
Deo volente 8.19 *divinely*
deoxynucleotide 33.10 *nucleoside*
depaganize 7.20 *preach*
de par le Roi 12.14 *politically*
depart 313.1; **526.2**; 98.16 *absent oneself*; 582.15 *die*; 372.13 *diverge*; 389.5 *escape*; 315.9 *exit*; 605.5 *resign*; 634.8 *run away*; 355.2 *withdraw*
departed 313.12; 98.9 *away*; 582.19 *dead*
departed this life 582.19 *dead*
département 86.5 *state*
departer 315.8 *outgoer*
depart from 116.5 *be dissimilar*; 325.1 *deviate*
departing 313.11; 526.6 *disappearing*; 315.15 *outgoing*
department 409.6 *category*; 137.2 *class*; 579.3 *management*; 205.1 *part*; 405.2 *piece*; 6.3 *subject*
départment 86.5 *state*
departmental 405.6 *component*; 205.11 *partial*
departmentalized 205.11 *partial*
departmentally 405.14 *constituently*
Department of Defense 584.4 *military organization*
department store 38.20 *building*; 779.8 *store*
department store account 783.1 *credit*
depart this life 582.15 *die*; 313.2 *withdraw*
Departure 313
departure 313.7; 300.4 *backward motion*; 270.2 *circumlocution*; 131.3, 582.1 *death*; 634.16 *desertion*; 325.13 *deviation*; 98.2, 526.4 *disappearance*; 389.1 *escape*; 139.6 *exception*; 315.1 *exit*; 355.3 *relinquishment*; 605.1 *resignation*; 304.4 *taking off*
departure platform 313.10 *place of departure*
dependability 452.17 *infallibility*; 225.1 *permanence*; 799.1 *probity*
dependable 698.26 *faithful*; 799.4 *honourable*; 452.6 *infallible*; 225.7 *permanent*; 252.6 *safe*; 228.9 *stable*; 638.5 *steady*
dependably 799.7 *honourably*; 228.12 *stably*
dependant 223.9, 289.8 *follower*; 122.6 *inferior*
dependence 450.3 *believing*; 122.1 *inferiority*; 782.6 *insolvency*; 387.1 *subjection*
dependency 396.8 *governmental organization*; 764.1 *joint possession*; 12.5 *political organization*; 763.4 *possession*; 440.1 *property*; 387.1 *subjection*; 86.4 *territorial division*

dependent **387.4**; 664.5 *adherent*; 345.10 *caused*; 267.5 *follower*; 27.77 *given*; 86.17 *national*; 769.5 *recipient*; 664.6 *servile*; 387.9 *subject*; 122.15 *subordinate*; 267.10 *tenacious*; 335.11 *unprotected*
dependently 122.22 *basely*; 691.11 *in a trance*; 335.14 *powerlessly*; 387.11 *under subjection*; 345.12 *with the effect of*
dependent on 345.10 *caused*
dependent on circumstances 222.7 *circumstantial*
dependent relative 289.8 *follower*
dependents 378.6 *burden*
dependent variable 27.29 *mathematical function*
depending on 345.10 *caused*
depend on 452.20 *be certain*; 450.7 *believe*; 387.8 *be subject to*; 345.7 *follow from*
depeople 371.9 *depopulate*
depersonalization 36.16 *dissociation*; 463.1 *oblivion*
depersonalized 463.8 *oblivious*
depict 99.11 *characterize*; 721.14 *describe*; 19.20 *draw*; 703.16 *explain*; 163.5 *outline*; 717.9 *represent*; 139.24 *specify*
depicted 703.11 *explanatory*
depict falsely 720.1 *misinterpret*
depict in glowing terms 727.10 *boast*
depiction 721.1 *description*; 703.3 *explanation*; 163.1 *outline*; 717.1 *representation*
depiction in glowing terms 727.4 *bombast*
depictive 17.18 *descriptive*; 163.6 *outlined*; 717.13 *representational*
depictively 163.7 *essentially*
depilation **552.7**; 547.9 *hair removal*
depilatory 552.7 *depilation*; 37.4 *drug type*; 552.13 *hairless*
deplane 312.4 *land*
deplete 787.2 *consume*; 245.5 *hurt*; 766.12 *lessen*; 218.7 *make insufficient*; 371.11 *void*; 441.1 *waste*; 337.7 *weaken*
depleted 337.9 *dilapidated*; 766.16 *losing*; 787.13 *used*
depleted supply 439.3 *supply*
depletion 245.11 *hurt*; 766.4 *lessening*; 337.3 *poor health*; 371.21 *removal*; 441.3 *waste*
deplorable 798.7 *evil*; 603.5 *lamentable*; 236.4 *poor*
deplorably 798.12 *evilly*
deplore 606.7 *be dissatisfied*; 670.17 *criticize*; 603.6 *lament*
deploy 349.5 *dispose of*; 377.16 *distribute*; 311.11 *move apart*; 143.10 *situate*
deployed 377.22 *distributed*
deployment 377.1 *dispersion*; 311.2 *parting*; 349.6 *use*
deplume 371.3 *disbar*; 552.15 *make nude*
depluming 371.18 *dismissal*
depopulate **371.9**; 377.15 *decentralize*; 357.10 *lay waste*; 98.19 *leave empty*
depopulated 98.14 *unoccupied*
deport 316.14 *bring back*; 128.8 *eject*; 315.13 *emigrate*; 655.13 *ignore*; 371.4 *ostracize*; 814.1 *punish*; 144.16 *replace*
deportation 128.2 *ejection*; 315.4 *emigration*; 371.19 *ostracism*; 814.7 *punishment*; 144.3 *replacement*; 655.3 *separation*; 316.1 *transfer*
deported 655.10 *lonely*; 144.10 *replaced*
deported person 655.7 *outsider*
deportee 144.7 *displaced person*; 371.27 *expellee*; 655.7 *outsider*
deportment 631.1 *conduct*; 525.3 *external appearance*
deport oneself 631.11 *conduct oneself*
depose 707.20 *admit*; 588.4 *be anarchic*; 371.3 *disbar*; 470.2 *discard*; 144.16 *replace*; 708.15 *terminate*
deposed 335.10 *powerless*; 144.10 *replaced*
deposed champion 247.5 *failing person*
deposit **783.3**; **783.10**; 780.26 *bank*; 416.8 *be dense*; 258.4 *dirt*; 215.8 *leave*; 376.26 *mass*; 32.24 *ore*; 205.2 *particular*; 785.1 *payment*; 14.4 *personal finance*; 215.2 *residue*; 30.27 *sediment*; 416.4 *solid body*; 439.1, 439.6 *store*
deposit account 789.1 *accounts*; 783.3 *deposit*; 780.6 *funds*
depositary 780.18 *treasurer*
deposited 789.11 *accounted*; 215.9 *remaining*
deposition 707.5 *admission*; 744.2 *certificate*; 716.5 *legal evidence*; 756.1 *promise*; 144.3 *replacement*; 707.3 *vow*; 30.35 *weathering*
depositional 707.12 *vowed*
depositor **783.6**
depository 410.1 *container*; 780.20 *money store*; 439.4 *storage*
deposits 439.2 *resource*
depot 173.4 *centre of activity*; 312.15 *destination*; 779.7 *emporium*; 321.8 *railway station*; 439.4 *storage*
depot ship 586.24 *warship*
depravation 245.8 *perversion*
deprave 236.13 *be worthless*; 796.19 *corrupt*; 245.6 *pervert*
depraved 236.3 *bad*; 245.12 *deteriorated*; 800.5 *dishonourable*; 798.7 *evil*; 804.12 *immoral*; 796.14 *lecherous*
depraving 796.12 *indecent*
depravity 236.9 *badness*; 798.1 *evil*; 800.1 *improbity*; 796.2 *indecency*; 245.8 *perversion*; 796.3 *sexual immorality*; 804.2 *vice*
deprecate 606.7 *be dissatisfied*; 670.17 *criticize*; 678.10 *disparage*; 113.18 *object*; 728.22 *play down*; 753.6 *protest*; 708.11 *rebut*; 383.6 *resist*
deprecated 708.18 *rejected*
deprecate oneself 674.14 *be modest*; 623.21 *humble oneself*
deprecating 708.19 *rebutting*; 383.10 *resistant*; 674.12 *self-deprecating*; 468.4 *underestimating*
deprecatingly 383.14 *resistingly*
deprecation 713.1 *advice*; 678.1 *disparagement*; 606.1 *dissatisfaction*; 728.9 *downplaying*; 753.1 *protest*; 708.3 *rebuttal*; 383.1 *resistance*; 468.1 *underestimation*
deprecative 708.17 *negative*; 383.10 *resistant*
deprecatively 708.22 *negatively*
deprecatorily 753.11 *disapprovingly*
deprecatory 670.27 *critical*; 678.15 *disparaging*; 753.9 *protesting*
depreciable 214.7 *decrescent*
depreciate 793.12 *be cheap*; 670.17 *criticize*; 214.4 *decrease*; 780.25 *demonetize*; 245.1 *deteriorate*; 728.21 *detract from*; 791.3 *discount*; 678.10 *disparage*; 766.12 *lessen*; 668.20 *scorn*
depreciated 793.9 *cheap*; 728.18 *deflated*; 14.6 *financial*; 780.22 *monetary*
depreciated currency 780.15 *false money*
depreciate the currency 786.12 *devalue the currency*
depreciation **786.4**; 793.2 *declining prices*; 214.1 *decrease*; 728.10 *deflation*; 245.7 *deterioration*; 678.1 *disparagement*; 14.1, 780.7 *finance*; 766.4 *lessening*; 468.1 *underestimation*; 349.6 *use*
depreciative 214.7 *decrescent*
depreciator 678.7 *disparager*
depreciatory 214.7 *decrescent*; 678.15 *disparaging*; 468.4 *underestimating*
depredate 774.14 *plunder*
depredation 357.5 *havoc*; 774.5 *plundering*
depredator 774.9 *plunderer*
depress **602.10**; 481.5 *discourage*; 155.9, 367.1 *lower*; 183.9 *make concave*; 523.14 *make dark*; 214.5 *make smaller*; 626.10 *make sullen*; 475.11 *predict*
depressant 37.4 *drug type*; 37.15 *sedative*
depressed **539.3**; **602.6**; 798.8 *afflicted*; 523.11 *benighted*; 183.6 *concave*; 367.21 *degraded*; 604.9 *disappointed*; 305.17 *drooping*; 611.4 *hopeless*; 563.3 *infertile*; 603.4 *lamenting*; 367.17 *lowered*; 155.7 *lowland*; 461.13 *mentally ill*; 532.6 *sad*; 626.6 *sullen*
depressed arch 20.5 *arch*
depressing 602.7 *distressing*; 603.5 *lamentable*; 367.18 *lowering*; 532.6 *sad*
depressingly 620.8 *boringly*; 798.13 *destructively*; 626.13 *sullenly*
depressing person **602.4**
depression **36.13**; **367.14**; **602.2**; 798.2 *affliction*; 183.1 *concavity*; 214.2 *decline*; 793.2 *declining prices*; 245.7 *deterioration*; 249.2 *economic adversity*; 13.2 *economy*; 611.1 *hopelessness*; 122.5 *inferior state*; 563.1 *infertility*; 782.6 *insolvency*; 367.11 *lowering*; 155.2 *lowlands*; 461.6 *mental breakdown*; 36.10 *neurosis*; 778.5 *sales*; 305.2 *sinkage*; 523.7 *spiritual darkness*; 260.3 *symptom*; 343.6 *unemployment*; 31.11 *weather system*
depressive 214.7 *decrescent*; 367.21 *degraded*; 602.4 *depressing person*; 461.7 *insane person*; 461.13 *mentally ill*
depressively 36.39 *psychologically*
depressive reaction 36.13 *depression*
depress the market 793.13 *make cheap*
deprivation 371.20 *eviction*; 766.1 *loss*; 782.5 *poverty*; 814.7 *punishment*; 218.9 *scarcity*; 372.2 *setting apart*; 773.2 *taking back*
deprive 371.8 *evict*; 782.14 *impoverish*; 766.9 *lose*; 218.7 *make insufficient*; 814.1 *punish*; 773.8 *take back*; 337.7 *weaken*
deprived 766.16 *losing*; 135.5 *necessitous*; 782.1 *poor*
deprived of 135.5 *necessitous*
deprived of strength 337.8 *weak*
deprived of vision 519.8 *blind*
deprive of authority 335.7 *remove power from*
deprive of life 382.16 *kill*
deprive of power 335.7 *remove power from*
deprive of sight 519.15 *blind*
deprive of sleep 261.6 *fatigue*
deprive oneself of 709.7 *refuse oneself*
depriver 371.26 *ejector*
depriving 766.16 *losing*
Depth 156
depth **156.1**; 532.7 *blackness*; 209.1 *degree*; 336.3 *intensity*; 172.1 *interior*; 27.37 *line*; 266.1 *obscurity*; 203.1 *quantity*; 26.4, 158.1 *size*; 141.1 *space*; 152.5 *thickness*; 442.6 *thoughtfulness*
depth charge 587.16 *bomb*; 586.26 *naval mine*
depth indicator 742.5 *indicator*
depth of field 41.8 *composition*; 28.32 *optical instrument*
depth of focus 41.18 *exposure time*; 28.32 *optical instrument*
depth of space 141.1 *space*
depth psychology 36.1 *psychology*
depths 172.2 *inside*
depths of space 145.1 *distance*
depths of winter 494.7 *cold weather*
depth sounder 156.4 *deep thing*
depth sounding 156.6 *bathymetry*; 28.22 *sounding*
depth-sounding 156.13 *bathymetric*
depurate 255.10, 256.15 *purify*
deputation 396.3 *acquisition of power*; 398.3 *delegation*
depute 398.1, 398.7 *delegate*; 762.2 *substitute person*
deputed 398.10 *decentralized*
deputing 398.3 *delegation*; 762.1 *substitution*
deputize 706.23 *answer for*; 762.4 *be a substitute*; 398.7 *delegate*; 396.21 *grant authority*
deputized 398.10 *decentralized*; 396.13 *elected*; 762.8 *substituted*
deputize for 608.11 *assist*
deputizing 398.3 *delegation*; 762.1 *substitution*
deputy **398.4**; 578.3 *agent*; 398.1 *delegate*; 398.9 *delegated*; 392.11, 608.5 *helper*; 122.6 *inferior*; 579.16 *official*; 717.8 *representative*; 762.7 *substitute*; 762.2 *substitute person*
deputy chairman 398.4 *deputy*
deputy chief of staff 584.5 *military staff*
deputy prime minister 398.4 *deputy*
deputy sheriff 398.4 *deputy*
deracinate 357.8 *destroy*; 371.10 *exterminate*; 369.11 *extract*
deracinated 369.19 *dislodged*
deracination 357.2 *destroying*; 369.1 *extraction*
derail 328.9 *disperse*; 144.14 *displace*
derailed 328.14 *dispersed*; 144.8 *displaced*
derailleur 320.11 *bicycle part*
derailment 328.3 *dispersion*; 144.1 *displacement*
derange **328.11**; 375.4 *deconstruct*; 328.8 *disarrange*; 408.21 *disorder*; 245.4 *impair*; 461.15 *make insane*
deranged **328.16**; 328.13 *disarranged*; 408.17 *discomposed*; 408.12 *disordered*; 144.8 *displaced*; 461.11 *insane*
derangement **328.6**; 328.2 *disarrangement*; 375.1 *disintegration*; 408.1 *disorder*; 144.1 *displacement*; 245.10 *impairment*
deration 767.9 *dispose of*
derby 551.15 *headgear*
deregulate 347.3 *counteract*; 767.9 *dispose of*; 391.4 *liberate*
deregulated 391.7 *liberated*
deregulation 347.1 *counteraction*; 391.1 *liberation*
dereism 36.19 *defence mechanism*
derelict 245.13 *dilapidated*; 350.4 *disused*; 355.5 *relinquished*; 767.15 *unclaimed*
derelict house 565.8 *shelter*
dereliction 637.14 *disobedience*; 350.10 *disuse*; 247.1 *failure*; 666.1 *negligence*; 355.3 *relinquishment*
dereliction of duty 758.3 *self-exemption*; 806.3 *sin*
derestrict 347.3 *counteract*; 767.9 *dispose of*
derestriction 347.1 *counteraction*; 393.9 *restoration*
der Führer 400.4 *absolute ruler*
deri 565.8 *shelter*
deride **621.6**; 606.7 *be dissatisfied*; 512.5 *catcall*; 470.3 *exclude*; 660.29, 668.24, 678.14 *ridicule*; 670.23 *show disapproval*
derided 670.35 *hissed*
derider **621.3**
de rigueur 632.12 *established*; 658.8 *good-mannered*; 140.9 *legal*; 810.12 *obligatory*
Derision 621
derision 512.2 *catcall*; 659.1 *discourtesy*; 661.2 *disobedience*; 606.1 *dissatisfaction*; 668.4 *ridicule*; 660.8 *rudeness*; 678.5 *scorn*; 670.9 *show of disapproval*
derisive **621.5**; 512.7 *catcalling*; 661.7 *defiant*; 606.4 *dissatisfied*; 668.14 *ridiculing*; 660.19 *rude*; 678.17 *scornful*
derisively 661.9 *defiantly*; 678.18 *disparagingly*; 668.29 *mockingly*; 659.10, 660.35 *rudely*
derisiveness 621.1 *mockery*
derisory 606.4 *dissatisfied*; 668.14 *ridiculing*; 272.5 *ridiculous*
derisory amount 206.1 *few*
derivation 344.1 *cause*; 369.5 *drawing out*; 345.1 *effect*; 27.64 *reasoning*; 694.4 *type of meaning*
derivation of words 5.1 *linguistics*
derivative 345.10 *caused*; 27.31 *differentiation*; 345.1 *effect*; 125.12 *imitative*; 5.38 *linguistic*
derivatively 125.14 *imitatively*; 345.12 *with the effect of*
derive 344.9 *be the cause of*; 369.15 *draw out*; 27.89 *theorize*
derived 345.10 *caused*
derived authority 396.1 *authority*
derive from 345.7 *follow from*
deriving from 345.10 *caused*
dermapteran 76.10 *insectan*
dermatitis 260.13 *skin disease*
dermatological 35.22 *medical*
dermatological disease 260.4 *disease*
dermatologist 35.13 *medical specialist*
dermatology 35.3 *medical specialty*
dermatophyte 83.5 *fungal association*
dermatophytosis 83.5 *fungal association*
Dermoptera 71.7 *flying mammal*
dermopteran 71.27 *chiropteran*; 71.7 *flying mammal*
dernier cri 553.1 *fashion*
derogate 678.10 *disparage*; 670.18 *find fault*
derogation 678.1 *disparagement*
derogator 678.7 *disparager*
derogatorily 678.18 *disparagingly*
derogatory 678.15 *disparaging*
derrick 38.29 *construction equipment*; 366.9 *lifter*; 154.6 *tall thing*
derriere 168.2 *rear end*
derring-do 613.1 *courage*; 613.8 *courageous act*
derris 44.8 *weedkiller*
derv 437.6 *oil*
dervish 7.7 *monk*
Derwent Water 88.4 *British lakes*
desalinate 255.10, 256.15 *purify*
desalination 256.2 *cleaning*
desalinize 256.15 *purify*
desalt 256.15 *purify*
descale 35.21 *practise dentistry*
descant 722.4 *dissertate*; 722.1 *dissertation*; 18.13, 516.1 *melody*; 18.39 *sing*
descend **305.9**; 122.11 *become inferior*; 414.12 *be heavy*; 300.13 *be in motion*; 156.14 *deepen*; 62.9 *mountaineer*; 303.4 *slip back*
descendant 305.16 *descending*; 215.6 *person remaining*; 289.5 *successor*
descendants 283.2 *future generation*
descended 345.10 *caused*
descend *en rappel* 62.9 *mountaineer*

descendent 367.18 *lowering*
descender 305.8; 62.4 *climbing equipment*
descend from 345.7 *follow from*
descending 305.16; 62.3 *climbing technique*; 305.1 *descent*; 245.12 *deteriorated*; 300.17 *directional*; 367.18 *lowering*
descending *en rappel* 62.3 *climbing technique*
descending from 345.10 *caused*
descending motion 300.6
descending order 132.2 *consecution*; 178.7 *straight line*
descend on 305.12 *drop*
descend to particulars 139.23 *particularize*
descension 305.1 *descent*
Descent 305
descent 289.2; **305.1**; 1.5 *anthropological concept*; 62.3 *climbing technique*; 300.6 *descending motion*; 245.7 *deterioration*; 322.5 *flight*; 137.8 *genealogy*; 623.9 *humiliation*; 132.3 *line*; 367.11 *lowering*
descente 68.1 *skiing*
describe 721.14; 3.20 *chronicle*; 693.12 *communicate*; 703.16 *explain*; 719.8 *interpret*; 717.11 *paint*; 139.24 *specify*; 17.21 *write*
describe a circle 721.17; 306.6 *orbit*
describe briefly 163.5 *outline*
described 3.19 *chronicled*; 703.11 *explanatory*
Description 721
description 721.1; 17.3 *aspect of fiction*; 703.3 *explanation*; 719.1 *interpretation*; 3.7 *narrative*; 721.7 *nomenclature*; 717.1 *representation*
descriptive 17.18; **721.11**; 3.19 *chronicled*; 703.11 *explanatory*; 5.44 *grammatical*; 695.1 *intelligible*; 719.14 *interpretive*; 5.38 *linguistic*; 4.13 *of philosophy*; 163.6 *outlined*; 717.13 *representational*
descriptive grammar 5.29 *grammar*
descriptive linguistics 5.1 *linguistics*
descriptively 17.23; **721.18**; 703.22 *demonstrably*; 5.52 *grammatically*; 5.48 *linguistically*; 3.25 *reportedly*; 717.14 *representationally*
descriptiveness 695.9 *intelligibility*
descriptive statistics 27.53 *statistics*
descriptive writer 721.10
descriptive writing 721.5 *fiction*; 17.4 *nonfiction*
descriptivism 4.7 *school of thought*
descriptivist 4.11 *follower of a doctrine*; 4.14 *of a philosophy*
descry 449.1 *discover*; 695.7 *recognize*; 518.12 *see*
desecrate 668.27; 812.4 *bring into disrepute*; 258.11 *dirty*; 245.3 *make worse*; 351.1 *misuse*
desecrated 351.4 *misused*
desecration 351.2 *misuse*; 804.6 *religious sin*
desecrator 351.3 *abuser*
deselect 470.1 *reject*; 469.5 *vote*
deselected 469.15 *chosen*
deselection 470.6 *discarding*
desensitization 592.4; 36.3 *psychiatric treatment*
desensitize 489.12 *anaesthetize*; 618.13 *make indifferent*; 592.7 *render insensitive*
desensitized 592.2
desensitizing substance 592.6
desert 428.6; **428.14**; **571.8**; 98.18 *abscond*; 479.3 *apostatize*; 614.4 *be a coward*; 760.10 *be converted*; 662.15 *be disobedient*; 150.5 *broad thing*; 141.3 *geographical space*; 357.5 *havoc*; 493.8 *hot place*; 563.3 *infertile*; 563.1 *infertility*; 98.19 *leave empty*; 92.10 *miscellaneous*; 308.8 *open space*; 622.4 *prestige*; 605.5 *resign*; 385.1 *retaliation*; 801.6 *right*; 634.8 *run away*; 421.8 *smooth thing*; 355.2 *withdraw*; 235.6, 803.3 *worth*
desert boots 551.19 *footwear*
desert climate 31.38 *climate*
desert dune 30.37 *dune*
deserted 197.16 *alone*; 571.11 *divorced*; 655.10 *lonely*; 355.5 *relinquished*; 655.11 *secluded*; 98.11 *truant*; 98.14 *unoccupied*; 254.3 *vulnerable*
deserter 355.4; 98.6 *absentee*; 634.17 *avoider*; 614.2 *coward*; 479.9 *equivocator*; 709.4 *refuser*; 633.7 *the hunted*
desertification 31.40 *climatic change*; 563.1 *infertility*
deserting 662.13 *disobedient*; 800.6 *faithless*
deserting husband 634.17 *avoider*
desertion 634.16; 98.4 *absenteeism*; 479.7 *apostasy*; 614.1 *cowardice*; 526.4 *disappearance*; 662.1 *disobedience*; 800.2 *faithlessness*; 355.3 *relinquishment*; 571.2 *separation*
desertion of principles 754.3 *irresolution*
desert island 563.1 *infertility*; 736.6 *privacy*; 655.5 *solitary place*
desert one's principles 754.5 *be irresolute*
deserts 631.1 *conduct*; 385.1 *retaliation*; 814.9 *retribution*; 813.1 *reward*
desert sands 563.1 *infertility*; 92.10 *miscellaneous*
desert war 585.1 *war*
desert warfare 585.8 *warfare*
desert waste 357.5 *havoc*
deserve 575.7 *be entitled to*; 136.14 *be qualified*; 801.13 *be right*; 235.9 *be worthy*
deserved 801.9 *in the right*; 136.9 *qualified*
deservedly 136.17 *capably*; 801.16 *right*
deservedness 136.1 *qualification*
deserved reward 813.1 *reward*
deserved tribute 813.1 *reward*
deserve ill of 631.13 *behave badly*
deserve notice 123.7 *be important*
deserving 617.8 *desirable*; 575.5 *entitled*; 669.21 *praiseworthy*; 235.1 *worthy*
deserving punishment 814.22 *punishable*
déshabillé 657.6 *informal dress*
desiccant 428.9 *drying*
desiccate 428.17 *dry*
desiccated 428.3 *dried-up*; 359.7 *preserved*
desiccation 428.13 *drying*; 359.1 *preservation*
desiccative 428.15 *dryer*; 428.9 *drying*
desiccator 428.15 *dryer*
desiderate 218.6 *be unsatisfied*; 135.8 *miss*
desideratum 617.5 *object of desire*; 135.1 *requirement*
design 19.23; **553.4**; 446.18 *aim*; 409.2 *array*; 19.1 *art*; 403.9 *artistic structure*; 20.18 *be an architect*; 721.14 *describe*; 19.9 *drawing*; 38.30 *engineer*; 160.1, 160.7 *form*; 482.3 *future intention*; 694.12 *intend*; 449.4 *invent*; 449.9 *invention*; 551.35 *make clothing*; 483.1 *motive*; 126.7 *originate*; 717.11 *paint*; 542.3 *pattern*; 484.1, 484.9 *plan*; 484.10 *plan out*; 694.5 *point*; 356.10 *produce*; 356.1 *production*; 446.4 *purpose*; 482.8 *resolve*; 403.14 *structure*; 19.4 *treatment*; 700.8, 700.28 *trick*; 354.2 *undertaking*; 19.6 *work of art*
design a prototype 484.10 *plan out*
designate 99.11 *characterize*; 469.15 *chosen*; 137.13 *class*; 398.7 *delegate*; 743.10 *identify*; 694.10 *mean*; 469.4 *pick*; 139.24 *specify*
designated 474.7 *expected*; 743.12 *identified*
designated hitter 48.2 *baseball player*
designated runner 48.2 *baseball player*
designation 743.1 *identification*; 721.7 *nomenclature*; 469.6 *selection*
design body 11.7 *spirit*
design buildings 20.18 *be an architect*
designed 20.11 *architectural*; 106.4 *deliberate*; 482.12 *intended*; 476.9, 694.9 *meant*; 19.27 *painted*; 484.14 *planned*; 446.12 *purposive*; 20.12 *structural*
designedly 482.13 *intentionally*
designer 20.2 *architect*; 19.16 *artist*; 449.12 *discoverer*; 126.3 *originator*; 484.8 *planner*; 21.27, 356.9 *producer*; 160.10 *prototypical*; 551.31 *styled*
designer drug 394.8, 691.6 *drug*
designer gene 34.12 *molecular biology*
designer label 553.1 *fashion*
designer stubble 420.7 *rough thing*
design houses 20.18 *be an architect*
designing 700.34 *deceiving*; 160.1 *form*; 449.9 *invention*
design school 6.12 *educational institution*
desirability 617.2; 239.3 *convenience*; 593.4 *lovability*; 135.3 *needfulness*; 469.7 *preference*
desirable 617.8; 469.15 *chosen*; 239.1 *convenient*; 617.7 *desired*; 593.22 *lovable*
desirably 617.17; 593.30 *lovingly*
Desire 617
desire 593.5; **617.1**; **617.12**; 610.3 *aspiration*; 610.7 *aspire*; 363.1 *attraction*; 218.6 *be unsatisfied*; 482.3 *future intention*; 595.7, 617.13 *like*; 595.1 *liking*; 593.23 *love*; 135.8 *miss*; 483.1 *motive*; 756.11 *promise oneself*; 710.1, 710.6 *request*; 477.6 *reverie*; 635.1 *will*; 635.11 *wish*
desire concentration 36.28 *cathexis*
desired 617.7; 474.7 *expected*; 710.9 *requesting*; 135.4 *required*
desired object 617.5 *object of desire*
desire for knowledge 644.1, 705.8 *curiosity*
desire knowledge 644.7 *be curious*
desirer 617.6
desires 474.2 *expectations*
desires of the flesh 593.5 *desire*
desiring 617.9 *desirous*; 474.5 *expecting*
desirous 617.9; 593.20 *amorous*; 610.13 *aspirant*; 595.6 *liking*
desirously 617.18; 595.11 *admiringly*
desist 383.9; 226.6 *cease*; 341.4 *not act*
desistance 226.1 *cessation*; 383.4 *desisting*
desisting 383.4; **383.13**
desk 410.3 *cabinet*; 23.4 *table*
desk dictionary 5.28 *dictionary*
desk editor 740.12 *publisher*
desk lamp 522.6 *electric light*
desk sergeant 16.17 *police officer*
desktop publishing 334.9 *electronics*
desk worker 578.1 *worker*
desolate 371.9 *depopulate*; 611.4 *hopeless*; 563.3 *infertile*; 357.10 *lay waste*; 655.10 *lonely*; 602.5 *sad*; 655.11 *secluded*; 563.10 *waste*
desolation 249.1 *adversity*; 357.5 *havoc*; 563.1 *infertility*; 602.1 *sorrow*
desorb 32.29 *absorb*
desorbed 32.43 *absorbed*
desorption 32.20 *surface chemistry*
Despair 611
despair 602.9; 604.5 *be crestfallen*; 611.9 *be hopeless*; 602.2 *depression*; 604.1 *disappointment*; 611.1 *hopelessness*; 341.4 *not act*; 523.7 *spiritual darkness*
despairing 611.4 *hopeless*
despairingly 611.11 *hopelessly*
desperado 651.8 *malefactor*; 382.11 *murderer*; 615.3 *rash person*; 380.4 *violent creature*; 804.9 *wicked person*
desperate 342.18 *active*; 611.4 *hopeless*; 615.4 *rash*; 638.2 *tenacious*; 380.6 *violent*
desperately 611.11 *hopelessly*
desperate move 62.3 *climbing technique*
desperateness 615.1 *rashness*
desperate remedy 352.1 *means*
desperate situation 254.5 *danger*
desperate straits 264.6 *critical situation*
desperation 638.13 *concentration*; 611.1 *hopelessness*; 615.1 *rashness*
despicability 594.4 *hatefulness*
despicable 668.12 *disregardful*; 798.7 *evil*; 594.12 *hated*; 236.4 *poor*; 682.2 *unpleasant*; 804.11 *wicked*
despicableness 236.10 *poverty*
despicably 594.18 *hatefully*
despise 622.28 *disdain*; 596.5 *dislike*; 594.14 *hate*; 660.29 *ridicule*; 668.20 *scorn*
despised 596.9 *disliked*
despising 596.8 *disliking*; 622.23 *prejudiced*
despite 211.10 *additionally*; 668.3 *contempt*; 347.5 *counter*; 670.2 *disrespect*; 751.11 *in disagreement*; 113.31 *opposed to*
despiteful 651.14 *hostile*
despitefulness 594.1 *hate*
despoil 798.11 *be evil*; 668.27 *desecrate*; 766.13 *destroy*; 357.10, 441.2 *lay waste*; 774.14 *plunder*; 773.10 *take away*
despoiler 357.6 *destroyer*; 774.9 *plunderer*; 773.6 *taker*
despoiling 357.5 *havoc*; 774.5 *plundering*; 773.3 *taking away*
despoilment 766.5 *destruction*; 774.5 *plundering*
despoliation 774.5 *plundering*
despond 602.9 *despair*
despondence 708.1 *negation*
despondency 249.1 *adversity*; 602.2 *depression*; 611.1 *hopelessness*; 708.1 *negation*
despondent 539.3, 602.6 *depressed*; 611.4 *hopeless*; 708.17 *negative*
despondently 611.11 *hopelessly*; 708.22 *negatively*
despot 400.4 *absolute ruler*; 396.10 *person of authority*; 647.4 *strict person*
despotic 16.62 *above the law*; 579.17 *managerial*; 400.12 *masterful*; 647.8 *severe*
despotically 16.85 *summarily*
despotism 647.2 *suppression*; 396.7 *type of rule*
despumate 255.10, 256.15 *purify*
desquamate 560.23 *cast*; 552.16 *peel*; 411.11 *scale*
desquamated 560.32 *cast-off*
desquamation 560.12 *dead tissue*; 411.6 *layering*; 552.6 *peeling*
desquamative 552.12 *peeling*
dessert 25.35; **498.3**; 25.9 *dish*; 557.14 *mouthful*
dessertspoon 557.16 *eating utensil*; 410.17 *ladle*
dessert wine 498.5 *sweet drink*; 558.9 *wine*
destabilize 120.5 *be unequal*; 32.25 *solidify*
destabilized 32.32 *solid*
destabilizer 32.3 *phase*
destination 312.15; 131.6 *end point*; 482.6 *objective*
destine 694.12 *intend*; 106.1 *predetermine*
destined 131.23 *annihilated*; 283.11, 756.15 *future*; 452.5 *inevitable*; 694.9 *meant*; 106.3 *predetermined*
destine for 482.9 *intend for*
destiny 344.4 *contributing factor*; 131.5 *fate*; 283.3 *future condition*; 452.16 *inevitability*; 395.1 *influence*; 107.2 *luck*; 106.5 *predetermination*
destitute 135.5 *necessitous*; 249.5 *person in adversity*; 782.1 *poor*
destitution 249.1 *adversity*; 782.5 *poverty*
destrier 586.19 *cavalry*; 59.3 *warhorse*
destroy 357.8; **766.13**; 585.13 *be at war*; 798.11 *be evil*; 708.14 *cancel*; 224.8 *cause change*; 94.13 *cause not to exist*; 526.3 *cause to disappear*; 375.4 *deconstruct*; 246.10 *defeat heavily*; 766.13 *destroy*; 767.9 *dispose of*; 371.10 *exterminate*; 236.14 *ill-treat*; 245.4 *impair*; 131.17, 382.16 *kill*; 441.2 *lay waste*; 238.8 *make useless*; 358.1 *obliterate*; 704.8 *refute*; 372.9 *separate*; 382.18 *slaughter*; 380.8 *use violence*
destroyed 357.15; 131.23 *annihilated*; 245.12 *deteriorated*; 375.5 *disintegrated*; 766.16 *losing*; 94.11 *no more*; 358.6 *obliterated*
destroyer 357.6; **441.7**; 224.6 *editor*; 651.8 *malefactor*; 704.5 *refuter*; 586.24 *warship*
destroyer division 584.4 *military organization*
destroyer escort 586.24 *warship*
destroyer flotilla 584.4 *military organization*
destroy good will 594.16 *cause hate*
destroying 357.2; 37.14 *counteracting*; 357.14 *destructive*; 704.7 *refuting*
destruct 357.8 *destroy*
Destruction 357
destruction 357.1; **441.4**; **766.5**; 798.2 *affliction*; 131.4 *annihilation*; 375.2 *deconstruction*; 245.9 *dilapidation*; 526.5 *disguise*; 236.11 *harmfulness*; 245.10 *impairment*; 382.1 *killing*; 358.3 *obliteration*; 704.1 *refutation*; 382.4 *slaughter*
destructionist 357.6 *destroyer*
destruction of life 382.1 *killing*
destruction of weapons 749.1 *pacification*
destructive 357.14; 249.6 *adverse*; 381.23 *attacking*; 678.16 *defamatory*; 798.9 *detrimental*; 236.5 *harmful*; 382.24 *murderous*; 380.6 *violent*
destructively 357.16; **375.8**; **441.11**; **798.13**; 704.11 *in reply*
destructiveness 357.3; 441.4 *destruction*; 380.1 *violence*
desuetude 767.1 *disposal*; 350.10 *disuse*; 355.3 *relinquishment*
desultorily 224.15, 227.15 *changeably*; 133.18 *disconnectedly*; 299.8 *irregularly*
desultoriness 224.2 *change of mind*; 472.1 *inattention*; 299.1 *irregularity*; 227.2 *irresolution*; 342.7 *restlessness*
desultory 224.11 *changeable*; 133.8 *discontinuous*; 299.4, 408.14 *irregular*; 227.14 *irresolute*; 472.11 *perfunctory*; 325.25 *wandering*
detach 144.18 *disconnect*; 377.12 *disperse*;

268.17 *liquefy*; 100.15, 372.9 *separate*; 197.20 *single out*
detached 4.18; 197.16 *alone*; 144.12 *disconnected*; 473.4 *disinterested*; 472.7 *inattentive*; 250.10 *independent*; 618.7 *indifferent*; 565.16 *manorial*; 463.8 *oblivious*; 100.11 *separate*; 20.12 *structural*; 372.17 *unjoined*; 109.6 *unrelated*; 655.8 *unsociable*
detached house 20.3 *building*; 565.5 *house*
detachedly 144.21 *disconnectedly*
detached retina 519.2 *poor sight*
detachment 4.3; 197.5 *aloneness*; 586.14 *armed forces*; 586.16 *army unit*; 36.13 *depression*; 144.5 *disconnection*; 473.1 *disinterestedness*; 407.8 *harmony*; 472.1 *inattention*; 618.1 *indifference*; 584.4 *military organization*; 463.1 *oblivion*; 100.3 *separateness*; 372.1 *separation*; 655.1 *unsociability*
detach oneself 618.12 *be indifferent*
detail 698.8 *accuracy*; 586.14 *armed forces*; 586.16 *army unit*; 222.6 *aspect*; 770.6 *assign*; 698.31 *be accurate*; 270.5 *be diffuse*; 222.11 *circumstantiate*; 405.1 *component*; 721.16 *define*; 270.1 *diffuseness*; 197.2 *item*; 584.4 *military organization*; 205.2 *particular*; 542.3 *pattern*; 469.4 *pick*; 721.15 *recount*; 124.8 *trifle*
detailed 222.10; 273.5, 698.21 *accurate*; 232.7 *complete*; 721.11 *descriptive*; 270.3 *diffuse*; 576.11 *laborious*
detailed account 721.1 *description*; 270.1 *diffuseness*
detailed description 721.1 *description*
details 721.1 *description*; 139.4 *specifications*; 124.8 *trifle*
detain 251.11; **360.7**; 294.8 *delay*; 378.8 *hinder*; 815.9 *imprison*; 333.3 *slow down*
detained 251.15; 333.7 *delayed*; 294.10 *held up*; 815.8 *imprisoned*; 360.10 *retained*
detainee 309.6 *closed-in person*; 815.5 *prisoner*
detaining 294.12 *delaying*
detainment 378.1 *hindrance*
detect 449.2; 370.12 *draw in*; 142.11 *find*; 743.10 *identify*; 695.7 *recognize*; 488.11 *sense*
detectability 520.3 *visibility*
detectable 449.15 *discoverable*; 518.23, 520.1 *visible*
detected 142.7 *found*
detecting 142.3 *locating*
detection 449.7; 743.1 *identification*
detective 644.3 *curious person*; 449.12 *discoverer*; 16.17 *police officer*; 252.3 *protector*; 705.9 *questioner*
detective novel 721.5 *fiction*
detective story 17.2 *fiction*
detector 449.11; 29.27 *imaging*
détente 749.1 *pacification*
detention 251.4; **360.2**; 294.3 *delayed action*; 333.12 *hesitation*; 378.1 *hindrance*; 815.7 *imprisonment*; 16.6 *legal process*; 814.7 *punishment*
detention centre 815.1 *prison*
detention home 815.1 *prison*
deter 481.2; 378.9 *block*; 596.7 *cause dislike*; 378.8 *hinder*
detergent 256.9 *cleaning agent*; 256.18 *cleansing*; 255.3 *purifier*; 255.15 *purifying*
deteriorate 245.1; 556.17 *age*; 424.4 *be brittle*; 224.7 *be changed*; 607.7 *become aggravated*; 122.11 *become inferior*; 249.9 *be in trouble*; 760.8 *be transformed*; 487.4 *be unaccustomed*; 260.24 *be unhealthy*; 296.17 *grow old*; 766.12 *lessen*; 367.1 *lower*; 245.3 *make worse*; 350.6 *stop using*; 441.1 *waste*
deteriorated 245.12; 224.12 *changed*; 367.17 *lowered*
deteriorating 760.14 *converting*; 245.12 *deteriorated*; 31.46 *seasonal*; 804.11 *wicked*
Deterioration 245
deterioration 245.7; 249.1 *adversity*; 607.1 *aggravation*; 424.2 *brittleness*; 224.1 *change*; 367.15 *debasement*; 303.14 *decline*; 122.2 *deficiency*; 760.2 *evolution*; 247.1 *failure*; 14.1 *finance*; 766.4 *lessening*; 367.11 *lowering*; 487.3 *unaccustomedness*; 441.3 *waste*; 804.1 *wickedness*
determent 378.1 *hindrance*
determinability 26.3 *measurability*
determinable 448.8 *experimental*; 26.14 *measurable*
determinant 344.13 *causal*; 344.1 *cause*; 27.22 *matrix*
determination 228.2; **641.6**; 342.8 *assiduity*; 698.7 *confirmation*; 643.5 *earnestness*; 448.3 *experimentation*; 452.16 *inevitability*; 482.2 *intentionality*; 26.1 *measurement*; 452.18 *particularity*; 640.1 *perseverance*; 454.5, 703.4 *proof*; 638.12 *resolution*; 469.6 *selection*; 136.6 *specification*; 613.3 *steadfastness*; 336.1 *strength*; 267.2 *tenacity*; 635.2 *willpower*
determine 344.12; 210.8 *calculate*; 324.6 *direct*; 27.90 *enumerate*; 448.11 *experiment*; 449.3 *find out*; 635.13 *intend*; 464.11 *judge*; 452.21 *make certain*; 26.10 *measure*; 454.2, 703.17 *prove*; 698.30 *prove true*; 482.8, 638.7 *resolve*; 140.13 *rule*; 469.1 *select*; 136.16, 139.24, 452.22 *specify*
determined 228.11; 342.18 *active*; 136.12 *conditional*; 643.2 *earnest*; 452.5 *inevitable*; 482.12 *intended*; 635.7 *iron-willed*; 26.13 *measured*; 452.7 *particular*; 640.10 *persevering*; 698.20 *proved*; 703.13 *proven*; 638.1 *resolute*; 613.12 *self-reliant*; 336.11 *strong in spirit*; 267.10 *tenacious*; 448.10 *tested*; 641.3 *unyielding*
determined effort 353.5 *attempt*
determinedly 228.13; 267.12 *tenaciously*
determined to 482.11 *intending*
determine to 482.8 *resolve*
determining 210.1 *calculation*; 448.8 *experimental*; 454.9 *verificatory*
determinism 28.81 *causality*; 4.7 *school of thought*
determinist 4.11 *follower of a doctrine*; 4.14 *of a philosophy*
deterministic law 28.81 *causality*
deterrence 481.7
deterrent 378.14 *blocked*; 347.1 *counteraction*; 481.7 *deterrence*; 481.9 *dissuasive*; 378.13 *hindering*; 378.2 *obstacle*; 252.2, 253.1 *protection*; 252.4 *safety device*; 253.6 *secure*; 711.1, 711.8 *warning*; 587.1 *weapon*
detest 596.5 *dislike*; 594.14 *hate*
detestable 798.7 *evil*; 594.12 *hated*; 236.4 *poor*
detestably 798.12 *evilly*
detestation 596.1 *dislike*; 594.1 *hate*
detesting 596.8 *disliking*; 594.10 *hating*
dethrone 588.4 *be anarchic*; 371.3 *disbar*; 144.16 *replace*; 708.15 *terminate*
dethronement 588.1 *anarchy*
detonate 508.5 *bang*; 507.8 *be loud*; 437.11 *fuel*; 330.28 *shoot*
detonation 508.1 *bang*; 380.3 *instance of violence*; 330.7 *shot*
detonator 587.15 *explosive*; 437.2 *lighter*; 330.12 *propellant*
detour 306.8; 224.7 *be changed*; 177.2 *bend*; 224.1 *change*; 179.2, 179.6 *circle*; 177.6 *curve*; 325.1 *deviate*; 325.14 *deviating course*; 317.14 *find one's way*; 306.5 *ringroad*; 317.2 *route*
detoxify 393.6 *cure*; 689.5 *sober up*
detract 678.10 *disparage*; 753.6 *protest*; 372.10 *set apart*
detract from 728.21; 212.3 *subtract*
detracting 468.4 *underestimating*
detraction 728.2; 678.1 *disparagement*; 212.1 *subtraction*; 468.1 *underestimation*
detract nothing 119.11 *equalize*
detractor 451.5 *disbeliever*; 678.7 *disparager*; 468.2 *pessimist*; 753.4 *protester*; 705.9 *questioner*
detractory 678.15 *disparaging*
detrain 312.4 *land*
detribalize 245.6 *pervert*
detriment 236.11 *harmfulness*; 245.10 *impairment*; 240.3 *inconvenience*; 766.1 *loss*
detrimental 798.9; 249.6 *adverse*; 236.5 *harmful*; 240.1 *inconvenient*
detrimentally 249.12 *in adversity*
detrital 427.17 *grainy*; 30.56 *petrographic*
detrited 427.17 *grainy*
detrition 427.4 *pulverization*; 365.2 *wearing away*
detritus 205.8 *bits and pieces*; 427.9 *grit*; 215.2 *residue*; 316.10 *transferred thing*
Detroit 87.2 *American cities*
detrude 367.5 *bear down on*; 371.14 *let out*
detrusion 371.22 *disgorgement*; 367.13 *submergence*
detumesce 214.4 *decrease*
detumescence 214.1 *decrease*
detumescent 214.6 *decreasing*
deuce 69.3 *card game terms*; 111.5 *equality*; 119.2 *equilibrium*; 198.1 *two*
deuced 712.11 *miscellaneous euphemisms*
deus ex machina 21.8 *scene*
deuteragonist 21.23 *role*
deuteranopia 519.2 *poor sight*
deuteranopic 519.9 *weak-sighted*
deuterate 32.26 *react*
deuterogamy 570.3 *types of marriage*
deuteromycetes 83.3 *fungi*
Deuteromycotina 83.3 *fungi*
Deutschmark 780.11 *national coins*
deva 8.5 *deity*
devachan 8.11 *heaven*
devaloka 8.11 *heaven*
devaluated 14.6 *financial*
devaluation 793.2 *declining prices*; 786.4 *depreciation*; 14.1, 780.7 *finance*; 245.8 *perversion*; 212.1 *subtraction*
devalue 780.25 *demonetize*; 793.13 *make cheap*; 238.8 *make useless*; 245.6 *pervert*; 212.3 *subtract*
devalued 793.9 *cheap*; 780.22 *monetary*; 212.7 *reduced*
devalued currency 786.4 *depreciation*; 780.15 *false money*
devalue the currency 786.12
Devanagari 5.13 *letter*
devastate 371.9 *depopulate*; 357.10, 441.2 *lay waste*
devastated 357.15 *destroyed*; 604.9 *disappointed*
devastating 357.14 *destructive*; 380.6 *violent*
devastatingly 357.16, 441.11 *destructively*
Devastation 586.25 *historical naval ships*
devastation 441.4 *destruction*; 357.5 *havoc*; 245.10 *impairment*; 381.14 *siege*
develop 76.17; **243.7**; **302.5**; 765.10 *augment*; 190.6 *become bigger*; 300.13 *be in motion*; 760.8 *be transformed*; 93.18 *come to be*; 6.22 *educate*; 345.7 *follow from*; 302.8 *further*; 244.2 *get better*; 345.8, 555.18 *grow*; 244.1 *improve*; 213.4 *increase*; 190.5, 213.5 *make bigger*; 556.18 *mature*; 41.21 *photograph*; 356.10 *produce*; 738.3 *reveal*; 756.10 *show potential*
developable 190.9 *enlargeable*
develop a habit 632.18 *habituate*
develop a literary style 724.9 *style*
develop a method 352.6 *find means*
develop an attitude 229.4 *tend*
develop a thesis 722.4 *dissertate*
developed 243.20; 556.11 *adult*; 190.7 *bigger*; 345.10 *caused*; 356.11 *productive*
developed countries 13.4 *economic development*
developed world 86.7 *regions of the world*
develop engine trouble 378.9 *block*
developer 41.12 *development*; 190.4 *enlarger*; 356.9 *producer*; 440.7 *property man*
develop from 345.8 *grow*
develop fully 232.5 *be complete*
develop industrially 356.10 *produce*
developing 243.17; 525.7 *appearing*; 760.14 *converting*; 34.26 *developmental*; 130.32 *embryonic*; 190.8, 345.11 *growing*; 233.4 *incomplete*; 555.13 *maturing*; 356.11 *productive*
developing from 345.10 *caused*
developing nations 86.7 *regions of the world*
developing world 12.5 *political organization*
develop into 760.7 *convert into*
develop late 294.6 *be late*
development 41.12; **243.13**; **302.14**; **561.4**; 17.3 *aspect of fiction*; 765.2 *augmentation*; 760.2 *evolution*; 190.1, 345.3 *growth*; 213.1 *increase*; 356.2 *manufacture*; 129.3 *preparation*; 289.9 *sequel*
developmental 34.26; 129.14 *preparatory*
developmental biologist 34.19 *life scientist*
developmental biology 34.15; 34.1 *life science*
developmental psychology 36.1 *psychology*
développés 22.10 *positions at the barre*
develop technical problems 378.9 *block*
devi 8.5 *deity*
deviance 306.2 *circuitousness*; 118.6, 325.13 *deviation*
deviancy 325.13 *deviation*; 274.7 *errancy*
deviant 325.20; 118.17, 802.14 *abnormal*; 325.19 *deviant person*; 189.5 *devious*; 114.5 *diverse*; 118.10 *eccentric*; 274.16 *errant*
deviant person 325.19
deviate 189.7; **325.1**; 224.7 *be changed*; 270.6 *be circuitous*; 751.8 *be different*; 116.5 *be dissimilar*; 114.8 *be diverse*; 118.19 *be independent*; 300.13 *be in motion*; 189.6 *be oblique*; 306.8 *detour*; 325.19 *deviant person*; 311.10, 372.13 *diverge*; 169.8 *move sideways*; 274.20 *transgress*
deviating 270.4 *circumlocutory*; 325.20 *deviant*; 751.10 *different*; 311.6 *divergent*; 100.10 *foreign*; 189.4 *oblique*; 306.9 *orbital*
deviating course 325.14
deviating motion 325.15
Deviation 325
deviation 118.6; **325.13**; 224.1 *change*; 306.2 *circuitousness*; 270.2 *circumlocution*; 751.3 *difference*; 145.1 *distance*; 311.1 *divergence*; 114.1 *diversity*; 479.6 *equivocation*; 36.10 *neurosis*; 189.1 *obliqueness*; 372.1 *separation*
deviationism 118.3 *nonconformism*
deviationist 325.19 *deviant person*; 479.9 *equivocator*; 662.6 *nonconformist*
deviative 325.20 *deviant*
deviatory 224.11 *changeable*; 325.20 *deviant*
device 17.3 *aspect of fiction*; 484.3 *expedient plan*; 743.8 *heraldic device*; 348.2 *instrument*; 449.9 *invention*; 352.1 *means*; 389.2 *means of escape*; 645.2 *stratagem*; 438.1 *tool*; 700.8 *trick*
devil 8.7; 236.12 *bad person*; 25.55 *cook*; 798.6 *evil person*; 594.8 *hated person*; 804.6 *religious sin*; 380.4 *violent creature*; 804.9 *wicked person*
devil dance 22.4 *historic dancing*
devil incarnate 804.9 *wicked person*
devilish 8.16; 651.11 *cruel*; 236.6 *damnable*; 236.5 *harmful*; 804.14 *impious*; 11.15 *witchlike*
devilishly 8.20; 804.20 *immorally*
devilishment 651.1 *malevolence*
devilize 8.18
devilled 25.56 *culinary*
devilled kidneys 25.44 *British dish*
devil-like 8.16 *devilish*
devil-may-care 618.8 *careless*; 459.5 *foolish*; 615.4 *rash*
devil of a lot 208.3 *profuseness*
devilry 798.1 *evil*; 651.1 *malevolence*; 804.6 *religious sin*
devil's advocate 661.4 *defiant person*
devil's food cake 25.36 *cake*
Devil's Island 655.4 *place of confinement*; 815.1 *prison*
devil's tattoo 620.1 *boredom*; 509.1 *drumming*
devil worship 9.2 *idolatry*; 804.6 *religious sin*
devil worshipper 9.6 *idolater*; 804.9 *wicked person*
devil-worshipping 9.10 *idolatrous*
devious 189.5; 645.4 *cunning*; 700.34 *deceiving*; 800.5 *dishonourable*; 812.4 *disreputable*; 325.25 *wandering*
deviously 189.9; 306.12 *circuitously*; 800.11 *dishonourably*
deviousness 189.3; 700.1 *deception*; 325.13 *deviation*; 800.1 *improbity*
devise 645.5 *be cunning*; 93.20 *bring into being*; 403.16 *construct*; 477.14 *imagine*; 478.3 *improvise*; 449.4, 484.11 *invent*; 409.18 *make arrangements*; 126.7 *originate*; 440.9 *own property*; 356.10 *produce*; 700.28 *trick*
devise countermeasures 378.8 *hinder*
devised 106.4 *deliberate*; 477.12 *imaginary*; 356.12 *produced*
devisee 769.6 *beneficiary*
deviser 126.3 *originator*; 484.8 *planner*
devisor 768.4 *giver*
devitalize 335.9 *make impotent*
devitrified 24.10 *ceramic*
devitrified glass 24.9 *industrial ceramics*
devitrify 24.11 *make ceramics*; 528.11 *make opaque*
devoid 94.9 *nonexistent*; 98.13 *vacant*
devoirs 667.7 *respects*
devolution 375.2 *deconstruction*; 398.3 *delegation*
devolve 375.4 *deconstruct*; 398.7 *delegate*
devolved 398.10 *decentralized*
devolvement 398.3 *delegation*
devolve upon 810.14 *be the duty of*

Devonian period 284.3 *geological period*
Devon minnow 55.2 *artificial fly*
devote 768.5 *give*
devoted **569.11**; 593.19 *enamoured*; 632.14 *habituated*; 799.4 *honourable*; 595.6 *liking*; 593.17 *loving*; 663.8, 810.9 *loyal*; 7.15 *religious*; 638.2 *tenacious*; 9.9 *worshipful*
devotedly **569.19**; 799.7 *honourably*; 593.30 *lovingly*; 663.10 *obediently*; 9.12 *worshipfully*
devotedness 342.8 *assiduity*; 638.13 *concentration*; 569.3 *familiarity*; 9.1 *worship*
devoted to 663.8 *loyal*
devotee 450.5 *believer*; 342.10 *busy person*; 632.8 *creature of habit*; 617.6 *desirer*; 7.3 *religious person*; 9.5 *worshipper*
devotee of Bacchus 690.17 *drunkard*
devote oneself 7.19 *be religious*; 638.9 *undertake*
devote oneself to 733.12 *address oneself to*; 354.1 *undertake*
devote to 349.1 *use*
devotion 810.3 *allegiance*; 638.13 *concentration*; 569.3 *familiarity*; 590.5 *good feeling*; 595.1 *liking*; 593.1 *love*; 663.2 *loyalty*; 10.9 *prayer*; 799.1 *probity*; 7.2 *religiousness*; 667.3 *respectfulness*; 9.1 *worship*
devotional 7.15 *religious*; 9.9 *worshipful*; 10.22 *worshipping*
devotionally 9.12 *worshipfully*
devotion to duty 810.4 *sense of duty*
devour 688.5 *be greedy*; 357.12 *consume*; 557.21 *eat*; 557.22 *eat well*; 441.1 *waste*
devoured with jealousy 629.4 *jealous*
devouring 557.2 *appetite*; 557.26 *eating*; 688.6 *gluttonous*
devourment 557.2 *appetite*
devour with one's eyes 518.13 *look*
devout 7.15 *religious*; 10.22 *worshipping*
devoutly 7.23 *religiously*; 10.23 *ritually*
dew **31.37**; **429.6**
Dewar 359.2 *preserver*
dewdrop 31.37 *dew*; 181.3 *round thing*
dewdrops 429.6 *dew*
dewily 295.24 *immaturely*
dewiness 429.7 *bogginess*; 256.1 *cleanness*; 295.3 *immaturity*; 433.3 *wateriness*
dew point 31.37 *dew*; 429.3 *humidity*; 31.6 *weather data*
dew pond 88.2 *small lake*
dewy 256.16 *clean*; 295.12 *immature*; 429.10 *misty*; 290.5 *morning*
dex 691.6 *drug*
dexie 691.6 *drug*
dexo 691.6 *drug*
dexter 743.13 *heraldic*; 743.8 *heraldic device*
dexterity 265.1 *easiness*; 485.1, 733.3 *skill*
dexterous 797.5 *proficient*; 485.6 *skilful*
dexterously 485.12, 797.25 *skilfully*
dexterousness 797.12 *proficiency*; 485.1 *skill*
dexter side 169.1 *side*
dextral 492.10 *handed*
dextrality 492.7 *sense organ*
dextran 431.4 *blood*; 33.4 *polysaccharide*
dextro form 32.13 *structure*
dextrose 498.2 *sweetener*
D-form 32.13 *structure*
d-form 32.13 *structure*
dhal 25.49 *Indian dish*
Dhamma 7.12 *religious text*
dhammaduta 7.8 *priest*
Dhammapada 7.12 *religious text*
dharana 11.10 *psychic phenomenon*
dharani 10.9 *prayer*
dhobi 256.12 *cleaner*
dhobi itch 83.5 *fungal association*; 260.13 *skin disease*; 260.7 *tropical disease*
dhoti 551.25 *accessories*
dhyana 11.10 *psychic phenomenon*
DI 561.3 *propagation*
diabetes 260.4 *disease*
diabetic 260.23 *diseased*; 260.19 *sick person*
diabetic diet 557.6 *nutrition*
diabetic retinopathy 519.2 *poor sight*
diable 8.7 *devil*
diablerie 11.3 *witchcraft*
diablo 8.7 *devil*
diabolic 236.6 *damnable*; 8.16 *devilish*; 9.10 *idolatrous*; 11.15 *witchlike*
diabolical 651.11 *cruel*; 236.6 *damnable*; 8.16 *devilish*; 798.7 *evil*; 9.10 *idolatrous*; 804.14 *impious*; 11.15 *witchlike*
diabolically 8.20 *devilishly*; 798.12 *evilly*; 804.20 *immorally*; 11.26 *magically*
diabolism 9.2 *idolatry*; 804.6 *religious sin*
diabolist 9.6 *idolater*
diabolize 11.21 *bewitch*; 8.18 *devilize*; 804.17 *make wicked*
Diabolus 8.7 *devil*
diachronic 3.15 *historic*; 5.38 *linguistic*; 284.21 *retrospective*
diachronically 3.24 *historically*
diachronic linguistics 5.1 *linguistics*
diacidic 32.36 *acid*
diacidic base 32.9 *base*
diacritic 742.7 *punctuation*
diacritical 5.44 *grammatical*
diacritical mark 5.36 *accent*; 742.7 *punctuation*
diaeresis 5.36 *accent*; 133.5 *caesura*; 17.9 *metre*; 372.5 *separator*
diagnose 739.5 *disclose*; 466.12 *discriminate*; 743.10 *identify*; 35.19 *practise medicine*
diagnosed 466.11 *judged*
diagnosis **35.7**; 739.1 *disclosure*; 466.1 *discrimination*; 448.1 *experiment*; 743.1 *identification*; 260.20 *pathology*
diagnostic **35.24**; 466.9 *discriminating*; 742.14 *signifying*
diagnostically 466.15 *discriminatingly*; 742.18 *indicatively*; 372.22 *in isolation*
diagnostician 713.4 *adviser*; 35.13 *medical specialist*
diagnostic instrument 35.7 *diagnosis*
diagnostic procedure 35.7 *diagnosis*
diagnostic radiology 35.7 *diagnosis*
diagnostics 40.19 *computing terms*; 35.7 *diagnosis*; 719.5 *science of interpretation*
diagnostic test 35.7 *diagnosis*
diagonal 27.37 *line*; 176.8, 189.4 *oblique*; 189.2 *oblique line*; 189.1 *obliqueness*; 68.12 *ski*
diagonal gate 68.3 *ski racing*
diagonally 176.12 *askew*; 325.28 *indirectly*; 189.8 *obliquely*; 68.17 *on a ski run*
diagonal matrix 27.22 *matrix*
diagonal relationship 32.6 *chemical element*
diagonal sidestep 68.2 *cross-country skiing*
diagonal stride 68.2 *cross-country skiing*
diagram 409.8 *chart*; 19.9 *drawing*; 484.5 *map*; 163.1, 163.5 *outline*; 717.11 *paint*; 717.2 *reproduction*
diagrammatic **409.26**; 27.78 *pictorial*; 717.13 *representational*; 721.13 *representing*; 742.14 *signifying*
diagrammatically 742.18 *indicatively*; 409.28 *in place*
dial 167.2, 281.8 *face*; 999; 711.7 *raise the alarm*
dialect **5.26**; 729.1 *faculty of speech*; 5.4 *parent language*; 139.10 *specialized language*
dialectal 5.39 *of language*
dialectic 734.4 *conference*; 701.2 *logical argument*; 4.5 *philosophical argument*
dialectical **4.16**; 444.9 *argumentative*
dialectically 706.24 *in answer*; 701.19 *logically*; 4.24 *philosophically*
dialectical materialism 402.2 *materialization*; 4.7 *school of thought*
dialectical materialist 402.3 *materialist*
dialectician 706.10 *answerer*; 5.2 *linguist*; 4.10 *philosopher*; 444.5 *reasoner*
dialecticism 444.3 *debate*
dialectics 444.3 *debate*
dialectological 5.38 *linguistic*
dialectologist 5.2 *linguist*
dialectology 5.26 *dialect*; 5.1 *linguistics*
dial gauge 26.8 *meter*
dialling **692.11**
dialling code 692.11 *dialling*
dialling tone 692.11 *dialling*
dialogical theology 7.13 *theology*
dialogue 734.1 *conversation*; 729.1 *faculty of speech*; 701.2 *logical argument*; 4.5 *philosophical argument*; 21.2 *play*; 706.3 *question and answer*
dial telephone 692.9 *telephone*
dial tone 692.11 *dialling*
dialyse 35.20 *practise surgery*; 255.10, 256.15 *purify*
dialysis 256.2 *cleaning*; 255.2 *purification*; 394.12 *surgery*; 35.8 *treatment*
diamagnetic 364.9 *abducent*
diamagnetism 28.59 *ferromagnetism*; 364.5 *repulsion*
diamanté 522.16 *bright*; 522.2 *quality of light*
diameter 150.4 *breadth*; 27.42 *circle*; 119.7 *dividing line*; 198.8 *half*; 27.37 *line*; 179.4 *parts of a circle*; 158.1 *size*; 28.7, 141.1 *space*
diametral 27.81 *curvilinear*
diametral pitch 38.7 *gear*
diametric 113.25 *contrary*; 27.81 *curvilinear*
diametrical 113.23 *opposite*
diametrically 113.28 *in opposition*
diametrically opposed 113.25 *contrary*
diametrically opposite 113.23 *opposite*
diamond 176.9 *angled*; 176.3 *angled figure*; 48.1 *baseball*; 69.3 *card game terms*; 65.4 *carom*; 235.8 *exceller*; 418.7 *hard substance*; 27.44 *polygon*
diamond in the rough 161.2 *shapeless thing*
diamond jubilee 601.5 *anniversary*; 298.6 *annually celebrated day*
diamond-like 418.1 *hard*
diamond mine 183.2 *concave land*
Diamond Sculls 50.5 *Henley trophies*
diamond-shaped 27.82 *polygonal*
diamond-studded 781.3 *opulent*
diamond wedding 601.5 *anniversary*
Diana 572.4 *celibate person*; 60.4, 633.6 *hunter*; 29.17 *moon*
Diana complex 36.18 *complex*
dianetics 36.1 *psychology*
diapason 507.1 *loudness*; 18.13 *melody*; 18.16 *musical note*
diapedesis 316.3 *transmission*
diaper 551.23 *children's clothes*
diaphanous 153.4 *fine*; 527.2 *translucent*
diaphanously 527.13 *transparently*
diaphanousness 153.11 *fineness*; 527.6 *translucency*
diaphoresis 315.2 *outflow*; 560.8 *sweat*
diaphoretic 37.4 *drug type*; 37.17 *stimulating*; 560.28 *sweaty*
diaphragm 378.3 *barrier*; 563.3 *birth control*; 41.18 *exposure time*; 21.20 *stage lighting*
diapositive 41.12 *development*
diarist 17.14 *author*; 281.13 *chronicler*; 721.10 *descriptive writer*; 744.9 *recorder*; 275.14 *timekeeper*
diaristic 281.17 *timekeeping*
diarize 281.15 *chronologize*; 220.8 *list*
diarrhoea 560.2 *defecation*; 260.4 *disease*; 260.8 *indigestion*; 260.3 *symptom*
diary 3.5 *chronicle*; 439.5 *collection*; 721.4 *factual account*; 220.5 *list of appointments*; 721.3 *narration*; 17.4 *nonfiction*; 744.6 *record book*; 462.4 *reminder*; 275.13 *timer*; 281.2 *timetable*
Diaspora 100.7 *new arrival*
diaspora 325.18 *diffraction*; 144.3 *replacement*; 377.7 *sprawl*
diastase 33.11 *enzyme*
diastasic 415.4 *leavening*
diaster 34.10 *cell division*
diastole 190.1 *growth*
diastrophic 30.54 *tectonic*
diastrophism 30.20 *earth movement*
diastyle 20.8 *column*
diatessaron 18.16 *musical note*
diathesis 260.1 *ill health*
diatomaceous 84.7 *algal*
diatomaceous earth 84.5 *algal product*
diatomic 32.35 *combined*
diatonic scale 18.20 *key*
diatribe 733.1 *address*; 670.8 *berating*; 729.8 *speech*
diavolo 8.7 *devil*
diazepam 394.8 *drug*
diazotize 32.26 *react*
dib 780.2 *cash*; 44.15 *cultivate*
dibasic 32.36 *acid*
dibasic acid 32.8 *acid*
dibber 44.6, 438.3 *garden tool*
dibble 44.15 *cultivate*; 44.6 *garden tool*
dice **69.5**; 475.10 *cards*; 25.55 *cook*
diced 205.11 *partial*
dice game 69.1 *game*
dice with death 254.9 *face danger*
dicey 107.8 *chance*; 254.1 *dangerous*; 254.2 *unsafe*
dichasial cyme 78.4 *flower head*
dichasium 78.4 *flower head*
dichotomic 198.13 *half*
dichotomize 198.16 *halve*
dichotomous 198.13 *half*; 372.15 *separate*
dichotomously 372.20 *separately*
dichotomy 198.7 *halving*; 4.8 *philosophical term*; 372.3 *separateness*
dichroic 541.6 *variegated*
dichroism 541.1 *variegation*
dick 561.8 *organs of reproduction*; 16.17 *police officer*
dicker 776.3 *bargain*
dickhead 456.5 *ignorant person*
Dick Turpin 774.8 *thief*
dicky 551.8 *shirt*; 254.2 *unsafe*
dicky bow 551.3 *formal dress*; 551.14 *neckwear*
dicotyledon 77.3 *seed plant*
Dicotyledonae 77.3 *seed plant*
dicotyledonous 77.16 *taxonomic*
dictaphone 744.10 *recording instrument*
dictate 713.5 *advise*; 397.1, 397.9 *command*; 386.6 *compel*; 579.2 *direct*; 12.11 *govern*; 400.14 *master*; 135.10 *necessitate*
dictate of conscience 480.11 *motive*
dictate to 396.19 *be authoritarian*; 397.11 *have authority over*
dictating 12.10 *governing*
dictator 400.4 *absolute ruler*; 251.6 *lawmaker*; 579.14 *leader*; 396.10 *person of authority*; 647.4 *strict person*
dictatorial 16.62 *above the law*; 635.9 *autocratic*; 397.14 *commanding*; 386.9 *compelling*; 121.13 *dominant*; 12.9, 396.14 *governmental*; 579.17 *managerial*; 400.12 *masterful*; 647.8 *severe*
dictatorially 397.16 *commandingly*; 400.16 *masterfully*; 12.14 *politically*; 647.11 *severely*; 16.85 *summarily*; 121.16 *superiorly*
dictatorship 85.1 *country*; 579.4 *directorship*; 566.11 *nation*; 647.2 *suppression*; 396.7 *type of rule*
dictatorship of the proletariat 12.1 *government*; 396.7 *type of rule*
diction 729.4 *articulation*; 724.4 *literary style*; 694.1 *meaning*
dictionary **5.28**; **220.3**; 40.11 *application*; 740.6 *book publishing*; 439.5 *collection*; 693.5 *reference book*; 6.14 *school book*
dictionary compiler 5.2 *linguist*
dictionary of dialects 5.28 *dictionary*
dictionary of names 5.28 *dictionary*
dictionary of quotations 5.28 *dictionary*
dictionary of slang 5.28 *dictionary*
dictum 397.1 *command*; 745.1 *maxim*; 707.2 *statement*; 698.4 *truism*; 729.7 *utterance*
dictyopteran 76.10 *insectan*
didactic 713.7 *advising*; 480.19 *persuasive*
didactically 713.9 *advisably*
didacticism 713.1 *advice*
didactic poetry 17.6 *poetry*
didder 327.24 *shake*
diddle 700.10 *fraud*; 593.29 *make love*; 700.8, 700.28 *trick*
diddled 700.36 *deceived*
diddler 700.17 *cheat*; 774.11 *dishonest person*
diddling 593.5 *desire*; 700.7 *tricking*
did you ever 619.14 *wonderful!*
die **582.15**; 249.9 *be in trouble*; 301.8 *be motionless*; 226.6 *cease*; 94.12 *cease to exist*; 69.5 *dice*; 526.1 *disappear*; 315.9 *exit*; 131.19 *expire*; 766.9 *lose*; 20.9 *miscellaneous architectural features*; 341.4 *not act*; 160.2 *prototype*; 313.2 *withdraw*
die a natural death 582.16 *meet one's fate*
die at one's post 640.8 *hold out*
die a violent death 582.16 *meet one's fate*
die away 226.6 *cease*; 94.12 *cease to exist*; 209.6 *change gradually*; 131.18 *come to an end*; 214.4 *decrease*
dieback 83.5 *fungal association*; 44.12 *pests and diseases*; 79.10 *tree disease*
die before one's spouse 571.9 *widow*
die before one's time 582.16 *meet one's fate*
died out 94.11 *no more*
die down 301.8 *be motionless*; 214.4 *decrease*
die fighting 582.16 *meet one's fate*; 638.11 *persist*
die for a cause 752.12 *offer one's life*
die for food 687.5 *fast*

die hard 582.16 *meet one's fate*; 638.11 *persist*
die-hard 225.8 *conservative*; 225.3 *conservative person*; 383.11 *obstinate*; 641.8 *obstinate person*; 113.11 *opposer*; 383.5 *resister*; 640.5 *tenacious person*
die in action 582.16 *meet one's fate*
die in bed 582.16 *meet one's fate*
die in combat 582.16 *meet one's fate*
die in harness 582.16 *meet one's fate*; 640.6 *persevere*
die in one's sleep 582.16 *meet one's fate*
die in poverty 582.16 *meet one's fate*
die in the attempt 353.3 *tackle*
dieldrin 43.14 *pest control*
dielectric 28.48 *insulation*; 39.7 *nonconductor*
dielectric coefficient 28.48 *insulation*
dielectric constant 28.48 *insulation*; 39.7 *nonconductor*
dielectric polarization 28.48 *insulation*
die of embarrassment 674.16 *be self-conscious*
die off 226.6 *cease*
die of love 593.24 *be in love*
die of neglect 582.16 *meet one's fate*
die of old age 582.16 *meet one's fate*
die of shame 674.16 *be self-conscious*
die out 94.12 *cease to exist*; 214.4 *decrease*; 526.1 *disappear*; 131.19 *expire*; 284.14 *pass*
die peacefully 582.16 *meet one's fate*
die prematurely 582.16 *meet one's fate*
dieresis 742.7 *punctuation*
die Roman fashion 382.21 *commit suicide*
diesel 330.13 *fuel*
Diesel cycle 38.13 *engine cycle*; 28.38 *thermodynamics*
diesel-electric 321.4 *locomotive*
diesel-electric propulsion 330.2 *method of propulsion*
diesel engine 38.11 *engine*; 438.5 *machine*
diesel locomotive 321.4 *locomotive*
diesel oil 437.6 *oil*
diesel-propelled 330.19 *propelled*
diesel propulsion 330.2 *method of propulsion*
Dies Irae 583.2 *funeral*
diet **153.10**; 191.6 *become smaller*; 153.14 *become thin*; 684.5 *be self-restrained*; 376.5 *conference*; 579.7 *council*; 687.5 *fast*; 687.1 *fasting*; 766.9 *lose*; 251.5 *means of restraint*; 557.6 *nutrition*; 251.10 *restrain oneself*; 684.1 *self-restraint*; 557.23 *taste*; 394.13 *therapy*
dietary 557.27 *edible*; 557.6 *nutrition*; 394.13 *therapy*
dietary expert 557.19 *dietitian*
dietary plan 557.6 *nutrition*
dieter **766.7**; 557.18 *eater*; 687.4 *fasting person*; 684.4 *self-restrained person*; 153.9 *thin person*
dietetic 557.27 *edible*; 394.17 *remedial*
dietetics 35.6 *health care*; 557.6 *nutrition*
die the death 814.6 *be punished*; 582.16 *meet one's fate*
dietician 557.19 *dietitian*; 394.15 *healer*; 257.3 *hygienist*; 35.17 *paramedic*
dieting 557.3 *delicate eating*; 153.10 *diet*; 687.1 *fasting*; 766.1 *loss*; 557.6 *nutrition*; 251.14, 684.8 *self-restrained*; 684.1 *self-restraint*; 153.3 *slimming*
dietitian 557.19
diet plan 153.10 *diet*
diet programme 153.10 *diet*
diet regimen 557.6 *nutrition*
diet sheet 557.6 *nutrition*
die well 582.16 *meet one's fate*
die with honour 582.16 *meet one's fate*
die without issue 563.7 *be infertile*
die young 582.16 *meet one's fate*
differ 701.13 *argue*; 116.5 *be dissimilar*; 114.8 *be diverse*; 517.11, 751.5 *disagree*
difference **215.3**; **751.3**; 701.1 *argument*; 224.1 *change*; 113.8 *contrariety*; 517.6, 751.1 *disagreement*; 116.1 *dissimilarity*; 234.1 *distortion*; 311.1 *divergence*; 114.1 *diversity*; 100.2 *foreignness*; 743.8 *heraldic device*; 743.10 *identify*; 120.1 *inequality*; 194.4 *mathematical result*; 118.1 *nonconformity*; 706.7 *numerical result*; 372.3 *separateness*; 27.16 *subtraction*; 109.6 *unrelated*; 109.1 *unrelatedness*; 541.1 *variegation*
difference machine 210.5 *computer*
difference of degree 120.1 *inequality*
difference of opinion 751.1 *disagreement*; 242.8 *quarrel*
differencing 743.8 *heraldic device*
different **751.10**; 701.7 *arguing*; 224.11 *changeable*; 113.24 *discordant*; 116.4 *dissimilar*; 311.6 *divergent*; 114.5 *diverse*; 100.10 *foreign*; 118.11 *nonconforming*; 126.5 *novel*; 139.15 *special*; 120.3 *unequal*
differential 27.31 *differentiation*; 466.9 *discriminating*; 194.9 *fractional*; 27.76 *functional*; 209.3 *gradation*; 209.7 *gradational*; 38.8 *machine element*; 210.15 *mathematical*
differential calculus 27.30 *calculus*
differential diagnosis 35.7 *diagnosis*
differential equation 27.31 *differentiation*; 27.27 *equation*
differential focusing 41.13 *framing*
differential geometry 27.34 *geometry*
differentially **209.9**; 466.15 *discriminatingly*
differential operator 27.50 *scalar quantity*
differential psychology 36.1 *psychology*
differentiate **116.6**; 210.9 *add*; 114.8 *be diverse*; 99.11, 139.22 *characterize*; 466.12 *discriminate*; 27.95 *evaluate*; 743.10 *identify*; 209.5 *measure*; 372.10 *set apart*
differentiated 209.7 *gradational*; 466.11 *judged*; 372.17 *unjoined*
differentiation **27.31**; 210.1 *calculation*; 466.1 *discrimination*; 116.1 *dissimilarity*; 209.3 *gradation*; 743.1 *identification*; 464.1 *judgment*; 139.1 *speciality*
differently **751.12**; 701.17 *argumentatively*; 234.13 *asymmetrically*; 224.15 *changeably*; 116.7 *dissimilarly*; 311.16 *divergently*; 114.10 *diversely*; 100.18 *extraneously*; 126.8 *originally*; 120.7 *unequally*
differentness 139.1 *speciality*
different opinions 114.4 *dissension*
Different Time 286
different time 286.1
different wavelength 720.2 *misinterpretation*
differing 751.10 *different*; 751.9 *disagreeing*
differ with 751.5 *disagree*
difficult **222.8**; **264.10**; **696.4**; 249.6 *adverse*; 659.6 *bad-mannered*; 143.8 *circumstantial*; 453.3 *confused*; 254.1 *dangerous*; 576.11 *laborious*; 418.4 *mentally hard*; 737.11 *mysterious*; 266.2 *obscure*; 705.13 *problematic*
difficult character 753.4 *protester*
difficult choice 469.8 *choice*
difficult circumstances 143.3; **222.4**
difficulties 782.5 *poverty*; 221.2 *predicament*
difficultly 222.17; **264.25**
difficult person 264.9
difficult position 264.5 *predicament*
difficult problem 737.5
difficult question 705.4
difficult task 264.3
difficult terrain 264.3 *difficult task*
difficult to comprehend 180.5 *ambiguous*
difficult to handle 264.14 *troublesome*
difficult to hear 505.7 *unheard*
difficult to live with 264.14 *troublesome*
difficult to see 521.2
difficult word 5.17 *word*
Difficulty 264
difficulty **264.1**; 249.1 *adversity*; 231.7 *defect*; 751.1 *disagreement*; 57.1 *gymnastics*; 68.7 *ice-dancing*; 240.3 *inconvenience*; 737.3 *mystification*; 266.1 *obscurity*; 378.2 *obstacle*; 705.1 *question*; 696.11 *unintelligibility*
difficulty in speaking 730.2 *inarticulation*
difficulty of the dive 67.6 *diving*
diffidence 728.5 *reserve*; 655.2, 674.4, 732.3 *shyness*
diffident 728.15 *reserved*; 674.11, 732.1 *shy*
diffidently 728.25 *reservedly*; 674.18, 732.8 *shyly*
diffract 325.12 *deflect*; 377.12 *disperse*
diffracted 325.26 *diffractive*
diffracted wave 326.5 *wave*
diffraction **325.18**; 377.5 *divergence*; 28.29 *optical element*; 326.5 *wave*; 28.15 *wave property*
diffraction grating 28.29 *optical element*
diffractive **325.26**; 377.28 *dispersive*
diffractively 377.29 *dispersively*
diffuse **270.3**; 97.11 *be present*; 138.25 *broadcast*; 325.12 *deflect*; 325.26 *diffractive*; 377.12 *disperse*; 377.19 *dispersed*; 740.13 *make public*; 266.2 *obscure*; 542.10 *ornate*; 5.43 *phrasal*; 311.13 *radiate*; 219.7 *superfluous*; 316.11 *transfer*
diffused 325.26 *diffractive*; 377.22 *distributed*; 524.6 *murky*
diffusely **270.7**; **377.30**; 311.16 *divergently*
diffuse nebula 29.8 *interstellar medium*
diffuseness **270.1**; 542.2 *affectation*; 266.1 *obscurity*; 5.24 *phrasing*; 219.3 *superfluity*
diffuser 316.9 *disease carrier*; 41.15 *lighting*
diffusing filter 41.20 *filter*
diffusion 693.2 *communication*; 325.18 *diffraction*; 270.1 *diffuseness*; 377.1 *dispersion*; 97.2 *omnipresence*; 311.3 *radiation*; 316.3 *transmission*; 28.15 *wave property*
diffusionism 1.5 *anthropological concept*
diffusionist 1.11 *anthropological*
diffusion pump 32.20 *surface chemistry*
diffusive 270.3 *diffuse*; 377.28 *dispersive*; 97.7 *present*
diffusively 270.7 *diffusely*; 377.29 *dispersively*
diffusiveness 270.1 *diffuseness*; 97.2 *omnipresence*
dig 331.13 *blow*; 44.15 *cultivate*; 156.14 *deepen*; 38.30 *engineer*; 284.8 *excavation*; 43.17 *farm*; 331.1 *impel*; 327.9 *jolt*; 183.9 *make concave*; 316.15 *take away*; 668.6 *taunt*; 695.6 *understand*; 576.6 *work*
dig a foundation 413.11 *support*
dig a hole 308.20 *hole*
digamous 570.23 *monogamous*
digamy 570.3 *types of marriage*
dig a pit for 645.5 *be cunning*; 484.13 *plot*
dig at 668.25 *taunt*
dig coal 437.11 *fuel*
dig down 305.15 *tunnel*
Digest 16.1 *the law*
digest 370.13 *absorb*; 409.7 *catalogue*; 409.15 *categorize*; 374.5 *combine*; 191.3 *contracted thing*; 557.21 *eat*; 163.1, 163.5 *outline*; 149.10 *shorten*; 149.3 *shortened version*; 388.4 *succumb*; 723.8 *summarize*; 723.1 *summary*
digested 374.7 *combined*; 149.8 *shortened*
digestible 557.27 *edible*
digestibly 557.29 *edibly*
digestion 370.5 *absorption*; 374.1 *combination*; 557.1 *eating*
digestive 370.17 *absorbent*; 394.6 *purgative*; 394.17 *remedial*
digestive biscuit 25.39 *loaf*
digestive juice 559.2 *secreted substance*
dig for 633.8 *pursue*
digger **183.5**; 38.29 *construction equipment*; 369.10 *excavator*; 308.3 *person who opens*
digging 156.1 *depth*; 305.7 *tunnelling*
digging in one's toes 637.2 *refusing*
digging out 369.3
digging up 369.3 *digging out*
digging up the body 583.7 *inquest*
digging up the past 3.12 *historicism*
dight 551.33 *dress up*
dig in 585.14 *battle*; 384.21 *entrench*; 638.10 *insist*
dig in one's heels 452.20 *be certain*; 383.7 *be obstinate*; 225.5 *be permanent*
dig in one's toes 641.9 *be obstinate*; 640.8 *hold out*
digit 194.1 *number*; 27.9 *numeral*
digital 27.71, 194.7 *numerical*; 194.8 *odd*; 40.21 *on-line*
digital camera 41.16 *camera*
digital circuit 39.13 *circuit*
digital clock 28.87, 281.6 *clock*
digital compact cassette 744.7 *recording*
digital computer 40.3 *computer*
digital display 281.8 *face*
digitalin 33.3 *carbohydrate*
digitally 27.87 *mathematically*; 194.12 *numerically*; 40.22 *on-line*
digital meter 28.82 *measuring instrument*
digital reading 28.82 *measuring instrument*
digital readout 28.82 *measuring instrument*
digital watch 281.7 *watch*
digitizer 40.7 *peripheral*
diglyceride 33.7 *fat*
dignification 8.9 *deification*; 9.1 *worship*
dignified 8.15 *deified*; 543.3 *elegant*; 656.6 *formal*; 123.6 *notable*; 622.18 *prestigious*; 549.5 *refined*; 10.21 *ritualistic*; 631.17 *well-behaved*
dignify 656.10 *celebrate*; 8.17 *deify*; 9.7 *worship*
dignitary 400.3 *leader*
dignities 658.3 *courtesies*
dignity 543.1, 549.1 *elegance*; 656.1 *formality*; 631.2 *good conduct*; 622.4 *prestige*
dig one's heels in 113.20 *withstand*
dig one's toes in 638.10 *insist*
dig one's toes into 360.6 *retain*
dig out **369.13**; 183.9 *make concave*
digraph 5.13 *letter*; 5.16 *spoken letter*
digraphic 5.41 *lettered*
digress 270.6 *be circuitous*; 100.13 *be extraneous*; 189.6 *be oblique*; 109.10 *be unrelated*; 306.8 *detour*; 325.1 *deviate*; 133.15 *lose one's train of thought*
digressing 325.25 *wandering*
digression 17.3 *aspect of fiction*; 133.7 *broken thread*; 306.2 *circuitousness*; 270.2 *circumlocution*; 325.13 *deviation*; 189.1 *obliqueness*; 325.16 *wandering*
digressive **133.11**; 270.4 *circumlocutory*; 189.4 *oblique*; 325.25 *wandering*
digressively 270.8 *circuitously*
digs 565.1 *habitat*
dig up 765.11 *acquire*; 449.2 *detect*; 369.13 *dig out*; 739.5 *disclose*; 583.9 *exhume*
dig up the past 3.21 *antiquarianize*; 284.16 *excavate*
dihedral 322.7 *miscellaneous aviation terms*
dihedral angle 27.39 *angle*
dihydrate 32.10 *salt*
dike 378.3 *barrier*; 317.11 *channel*
dilacerate 372.9 *separate*
dilaceration 372.3 *separateness*
dilapidate 245.5 *hurt*
dilapidated **245.13**; **337.9**; 782.3 *beggarly*; 424.1 *brittle*; 357.15 *destroyed*; 375.5 *disintegrated*; 375.6 *disintegrating*; 254.2 *unsafe*; 349.9 *used*
dilapidation **245.9**; 782.7 *beggary*; 214.1 *decrease*; 357.4 *ruin*; 349.6 *use*; 337.1 *weakness*
dilatability 190.2 *enlargeability*
dilatable 190.9 *enlargeable*; 417.2 *rarefied*
dilatableness 190.2 *enlargeability*
dilatant 190.9 *enlargeable*; 417.2 *rarefied*
dilatation 727.2 *enlargement*; 190.1 *growth*; 417.4 *rarefaction*; 27.48 *transformation*
dilatational 417.2 *rarefied*
dilate 765.10 *augment*; 190.6 *become bigger*; 270.5 *be diffuse*; 150.11 *broaden*; 727.8 *enlarge*; 141.20 *extend*; 213.4 *increase*; 190.5 *make bigger*; 417.6 *make sparse*
dilated 190.7 *bigger*; 727.13 *enlarged*
dilater 190.4 *enlarger*
dilating 190.8 *growing*; 417.2 *rarefied*
dilation 765.2 *augmentation*; 150.4 *breadth*; 727.2 *enlargement*; 190.1 *growth*; 213.1 *increase*; 417.4 *rarefaction*; 27.48 *transformation*
dilational 190.9 *enlargeable*
dilative 190.9 *enlargeable*; 417.2 *rarefied*
dilatometer 26.8 *meter*
dilatometric 26.16 *micrometric*
dilatometry 26.2 *micrometry*
dilator 37.4 *drug type*; 190.4 *enlarger*
dilatorily 294.15 *late*; 333.16 *slowly*
dilatoriness 294.3 *delayed action*; 333.8 *slowness*
dilatory 333.7 *delayed*; 294.9 *late*; 343.3 *not participating*
dilemma 469.8 *choice*; 222.4 *difficult circumstances*; 705.4 *difficult question*; 221.2 *predicament*; 264.4 *problem*
dilettante 466.6 *discriminating person*; 456.5 *ignorant person*; 639.15 *indecisive person*; 549.4 *refined person*; 456.7 *semi-skilled*
dilettantism 456.2 *half-knowledge*; 466.2 *judiciousness*
diligence **471.4**; 342.8 *assiduity*; 665.1 *carefulness*; 640.3 *constancy*

diligent **471.8**; 665.9 *careful*; 342.20 *industrious*; 640.10 *persevering*; 576.10 *working*

diligently 471.15 *attentively*; 665.12 *carefully*

dill 496.5 *herbs*

dill pickle 496.2 *seasoning*

dill water 394.6 *purgative*

dilly 797.17 *good thing*

dilly-dally 639.7 *be irresolute*; 333.2 *hesitate*; 294.7 *wait*

dilly-dallying 333.7 *delayed*; 333.11 *lingering*

diluent 431.9 *solvent*

dilute **377.14**; **377.27**; **433.30**; **497.8**; 224.8 *cause change*; 395.9 *change*; 374.5 *combine*; 367.4 *debase*; 214.5 *make smaller*; 417.6 *make sparse*; 153.16 *make thin*; 412.8 *mix*; 412.12 *mixed*; 728.22 *play down*; 417.2 *rarefied*; 32.32 *solid*; 32.25 *solidify*; 497.5 *tasteless*; 337.7 *weaken*

diluted **433.22**; 377.27 *dilute*; 728.19 *downplayed*; 558.17 *drinkable*; 728.17 *insipid*; 337.13 *insufficient*; 412.12 *mixed*; 417.2 *rarefied*; 497.5 *tasteless*; 153.5 *thinned*

diluter 153.13 *thinner*

dilute solution 32.3 *phase*

dilution **377.3**; **433.5**; **497.1**; 224.1 *change*; 728.9 *downplaying*; 412.1 *mixture*; 417.4 *rarefaction*; 497.1 *tastelessness*; 153.12 *thinning*; 337.1 *weakness*

dim **524.5**; 523.13 *become dark*; 521.7 *become invisible*; 530.7 *colourless*; 523.8, 532.2 *dark*; 530.6 *decolour*; 696.4 *difficult*; 521.2 *difficult to see*; 736.9 *disguise*; 456.6 *ignorant*; 766.12 *lessen*; 523.14 *make dark*; 521.8 *make invisible*; 528.11 *make opaque*; 528.2 *shady*; 524.8 *stupid*; 152.3 *thick-witted*; 457.6, 528.5 *unintelligent*

dim and distant past 3.9 *distant past*

dimbo 459.3 *foolish person*; 456.5 *ignorant person*

dim bulb 456.5 *ignorant person*

dime 780.8 *American money*; 124.8 *trifle*

dime defence 46.10 *defence*

dimension 203.1 *quantity*; 158.1 *size*; 27.35 *space*

dimensional 141.11 *spatial*

dimensions 525.3 *external appearance*; 27.35, 141.1 *space*

dime-store 793.9 *cheap*

dime's worth 691.6 *drug*

dimeter 17.9 *metre*

dimethoate 44.8 *weedkiller*

dimetic 17.20 *metrical*

dimidiate 743.10 *identify*

dimidiation 743.8 *heraldic device*

diminish 623.23 *abase*; 122.11 *become inferior*; 337.6 *be weak*; 209.6 *change gradually*; 214.4 *decrease*; 766.12 *lessen*; 685.4 *moderate*; 728.22 *play down*; 206.8 *reduce*; 608.9 *relieve*; 212.3 *subtract*; 441.1 *waste*; 337.7 *weaken*

diminished 214.6 *decreasing*; 337.9 *dilapidated*; 728.19 *downplayed*; 206.7 *fewer*; 623.3 *humbled*; 122.13 *insignificant*; 212.7 *reduced*; 623.4 *self-abasing*

diminished responsibility 461.1 *insanity*

diminished seventh 201.3 *seven*

diminishing 206.7 *fewer*; 209.7 *gradational*

diminishingly 212.9, 214.8 *decreasingly*

diminishing returns 214.1 *decrease*; 766.2 *financial loss*

diminishment 728.9 *downplaying*; 623.11 *self-abasement*

diminuendo 191.1 *contraction*; 214.1 *decrease*; 214.6 *decreasing*

diminution 214.1 *decrease*; 766.4 *lessening*; 367.11 *lowering*; 685.1 *moderation*; 723.2 *outline*; 218.9 *scarcity*; 212.1 *subtraction*

diminutive 5.44 *grammatical*; 159.7 *little*; 721.8 *name*; 5.35 *part of speech*; 149.7 *short*

diminutively 159.8 *in a small way*; 149.12 *short*

diminutiveness 159.1 *littleness*; 149.1 *shortness*

dim lighting 524.1 *dimness*

dimly **524.12**; 530.9 *colourlessly*; 523.15 *darkly*; 521.9 *invisibly*

dimly lit 524.5 *dim*

dimmed **524.7**

dimmed headlights 522.6 *electric light*

dimmed lights 524.1 *dimness*

dim memory 463.3 *poor memory*

dimmer 39.28 *plug*

dimmer switch 523.2 *darkening*; 524.1 *dimness*

dimming **524.3**; 523.2, 523.9 *darkening*; 214.1 *decrease*; 766.4 *lessening*

dimming switch 39.28 *plug*

Dimness 524

dimness **524.1**; 523.1 *darkness*; 245.7 *deterioration*; 477.5 *fantasy*; 528.6 *opaqueness*; 524.4 *stupidity*; 457.2 *unintelligence*

dimple 183.3 *cavity*

dimpled 183.6 *concave*

dims 522.6 *electric light*

dim sight 519.2 *poor sight*

dim-sighted 519.9 *weak-sighted*

dim sum 25.48 *Chinese dish*

dim view 670.2 *disrespect*

dimwit 459.3 *foolish person*; 457.3 *unintelligent person*

dim-witted 459.5 *foolish*; 456.6 *ignorant*; 337.10 *ill*; 524.8 *stupid*; 457.6, 528.5 *unintelligent*; 486.1 *unskilful*

dim-wittedness 524.4 *stupidity*; 457.2 *unintelligence*

din 507.8 *be loud*; 328.5 *commotion*; 517.2 *dissonant noise*; 507.2 *outcry*; 327.2 *tumult*

dinar 780.11 *national coins*

dine 557.24 *have a meal*; 557.25 *provide food*

dine alfresco 171.12 *be outside*

dined 654.16 *popular*

dine out 654.11 *be sociable*; 557.24 *have a meal*

diner 557.18 *eater*; 557.15 *eating place*; 495.5 *taster*

diner-in 557.18 *eater*

diner-out 557.18 *eater*

Diners' Club™ 783.2 *credit card*

dinette 557.15 *eating place*; 565.7 *room*

ding 50.7 *windsurfing*

dingbat 459.3 *foolish person*

ding-dong 119.8 *on equal terms*; 509.5 *ringing*

ding-dong race 119.2 *equilibrium*

ding-dong theory 5.37 *linguistic theory*

dinghy 50.4 *rowing*; 50.2 *sailing boat*

dinghy racing 50.1 *sailing*

dingily 530.9 *colourlessly*; 524.12 *dimly*

dinginess 258.1 *dirtiness*; 524.2 *murk*

dingle 183.2 *concave land*; 92.8 *valley*

dingleberry 560.5 *faeces*

dingy 530.7 *colourless*; 523.8, 532.2 *dark*; 245.13 *dilapidated*; 524.7 *dimmed*; 258.7 *dirty*; 529.13 *soft-hued*; 544.10 *ugly*

din in 726.6 *emphasize*

dining 557.26 *eating*; 557.4 *eating meals*

dining car 557.15 *eating place*; 321.6 *rolling stock*

dining chair 23.2 *chair*

dining-club member 557.18 *eater*

dining hall 557.15 *eating place*; 565.7 *room*

dining kitchen 565.7 *room*

dining out 557.4 *eating meals*

dining room 557.15 *eating place*; 565.7 *room*; 6.15 *schoolroom*

dining table 23.4 *table*

dining together 569.4 *act of friendship*

din into 112.18 *harp*

dinitro ortho cresol 44.8 *weedkiller*

dinkiness 159.1 *littleness*

dinkum 698.19 *authentic*

dinkum oil 698.1 *truth*

dinky 159.7 *little*; 407.13 *orderly*; 124.4 *trivial*

dinner 557.12 *meal*; 291.5 *night thing*; 654.5 *party*

dinner bell 742.4 *signal*

dinner dance 557.13 *feast*

dinner dress 551.3 *formal dress*; 551.7 *frock*

dinner gong 742.4 *signal*

dinner gown 551.7 *frock*

dinner jacket 551.3, 656.4 *formal dress*

dinner party 654.5 *party*

dinner plate 410.16 *crockery*

dinner service 410.16 *crockery*

dinning 507.6 *loud*

DIN number 41.10 *graininess*

dinoflagellate 75.9 *protozoan*

dinosaur 158.9 *big thing*; 73.6 *extinct reptile*; 284.10 *fossilization*; 296.5 *old thing*; 296.8 *prehistoric animal*; 284.7 *thing of the past*

dint 331.13 *blow*; 331.3 *hit*

diocesan 86.18 *local*; 7.8 *priest*; 7.17 *priestly*

diocese 7.9 *priesthood*; 86.5 *state*

diode **39.18**; 28.55 *circuit*; 28.44 *semiconductor*

diode rectifier 39.18 *diode*

dioecious 78.12 *of flowers*

Diogenes 653.2 *misanthrope*

Dionaea 700.13 *snare*

Dionysia 10.16 *religious festival*

dionysiac dance 22.4 *historic dancing*

dioptric 527.1 *transparent*

dip 256.5 *ablutions*; 256.14 *bathe*; 367.3 *bring down*; 183.2 *concave land*; 367.14 *depression*; 305.5 *dive*; 305.12 *drop*; 368.4 *immerse*; 368.10 *immersion*; 522.5 *incandescent light*; 30.45 *magnetic pole*; 523.14 *make dark*; 524.10 *make dim*; 322.7 *miscellaneous aviation terms*; 25.15 *sauce*; 305.6, 305.14 *slide*; 316.15 *take away*; 774.8 *thief*; 92.8 *valley*; 433.11 *wash*

Dipavamsa 7.12 *religious text*

dip down 305.9 *descend*

dipeptide 33.8 *amino acid*

diphtheria 260.6 *infection*; 260.9 *respiratory disease*

diphthong 5.16 *spoken letter*; 729.7 *utterance*

dip into capital 787.1 *expend*

diplegia 260.17 *nervous disorder*

diploid 44.5 *gardening*; 34.25 *genetic*

diploid number 34.14 *chromosome*

diploidy 34.14 *chromosome*

diploma 744.2 *certificate*; 757.2 *permit*; 136.3 *qualifications*

diplomacy 645.1 *cunning*; 658.2 *good manners*; 748.2 *mediation*; 746.1 *negotiation*; 484.2 *policy*; 12.2 *politics*; 631.9 *tactics*; 631.8 *treatment*

diplomat 398.6 *agent*; 755.4 *contractor*; 645.3 *cunning person*; 398.1 *delegate*; 748.3 *mediator*; 746.4 *negotiator*; 484.8 *planner*

diplomatic 398.9 *delegated*; 658.8 *good-mannered*; 748.6 *mediatory*; 746.8 *negotiated*; 485.6 *skilful*; 458.5 *wise*

diplomatic agent 398.6 *agent*

diplomatically 398.12 *by proxy*; 746.9 *feasibly*; 658.15 *genteelly*; 748.7 *mediatorially*; 398.11 *representatively*; 458.9 *wisely*

diplomatic bag 692.3 *correspondence*

diplomatic code 656.5 *etiquette*

diplomatic corps 398.2 *representative body*

diplomatic excuse 699.11 *half-truth*

diplomatic immunity 758.1 *exemption*; 250.1 *freedom*

diplomatic incident 264.7 *awkward situation*

diplomatic language 5.7 *international language*

diplomatic officer 398.1 *delegate*

diplomatic pouch 410.8 *bag*

diplomatic service 398.2 *representative body*

diplomatic staff 398.2 *representative body*

diplomatist 645.3 *cunning person*; 485.5 *expert*; 748.3 *mediator*

diplopia 519.2 *poor sight*

diplopod 75.4 *arthropod*

Diplopoda 75.4 *arthropod*

dipluran 76.10 *insectan*

dipnoan 74.2 *fish*

dipody 17.9 *metre*

dipole 692.17 *antenna*; 28.50 *electric charge*

dipole antenna 692.17 *antenna*

dipole–dipole interaction 32.11 *chemical bond*

dipole moment 28.50 *electric charge*

dipped 433.24 *flooded*

dipped headlights 522.6 *electric light*

dipped lights 524.1 *dimness*

dipper 523.2 *darkening*; 410.17 *ladle*

dipping 256.5 *ablutions*; 523.9 *darkening*; 305.4 *fall*; 305.18 *falling*

dipping the colours 667.5 *presenting arms*

dippy 461.11 *insane*

dipsomania 690.16 *alcoholism*; 36.15 *compulsion*; 461.4 *delusion*; 558.1 *drinking*

dipsomaniac 690.17 *drunkard*; 690.5 *drunken*

dipsomaniacal 558.16 *drinking*; 690.5 *drunken*

dipstick 26.6 *measuring instrument*; 486.10 *unskilled person*

dip switch 523.2 *darkening*

dipteran 76.10 *insectan*

diptych 198.2 *double*; 19.8 *painting*

Dirac notation 28.80 *quantum theory*

dire 249.6 *adverse*; 798.9 *detrimental*; 612.10 *frightening*; 236.5 *harmful*

direct **140.16**; **255.17**; **324.6**; **324.15**; **579.2**; 340.4 *act*; 631.14 *behave towards*; 150.3 *broad-minded*; 725.3 *clear*; 397.9 *command*; 18.40, 631.15 *conduct*; 324.9 *directly*; 21.38 *dramatize*; 527.4 *easily seen through*; 340.6 *effective*; 716.8 *evidential*; 12.11 *govern*; 5.44 *grammatical*; 396.18 *have authority*; 178.5 *honourable*; 280.5 *immediate*; 395.8 *influence*; 121.10 *lead*; 579.1 *manage*; 400.14 *master*; 483.9 *motivate*; 271.3 *natural*; 426.2 *outspoken*; 356.10 *produce*; 733.10 *send*; 695.2 *simple*; 143.10 *situate*; 68.12 *ski*; 66.5 *soccer*; 178.1 *straight*; 178.2 *straightforward*; 698.18 *truthful*; 354.1 *undertake*; 742.9 *use signs*

directable 324.14 *directed*

direct access 40.19 *computing terms*

direct approach 317.2 *route*

direct belay 62.3 *climbing technique*

direct cannon 65.3 *English billiards*

direct carving 19.12 *sculpture*

direct communication 8.8 *divine manifestation*

direct current 334.7 *electrical power*; 28.51, 39.9 *electric current*

direct debit 785.1 *payment*

direct descent 68.2 *cross-country skiing*

direct dialling 692.11 *dialling*

direct distance dialing 692.11 *dialling*

direct drill 43.17 *farm*

direct dye 42.6 *dye*

directed **324.14**; 21.39 *dramatic*; 452.5 *inevitable*; 483.12 *motivated*

directed energy 576.4 *exertion*

directed number 27.5 *number*

directed towards 324.14 *directed*; 143.6 *situated*

direct evidence 716.5 *legal evidence*

direct free kick 66.2 *football play*

direct hit 51.2 *grip*

directing **324.16**; 579.4 *directorship*; 395.11 *influential*; 16.48 *jurisdictional*; 579.17 *managerial*

direct intuition 8.8 *divine manifestation*

Direction 324

direction **324.1**; 340.1 *action*; 140.8, 396.1 *authority*; 397.1 *command*; 324.5 *directions*; 579.4 *directorship*; 12.3, 396.4 *governance*; 12.1 *government*; 140.4, 579.5 *guide*; 27.37 *line*; 346.4 *management*; 480.11 *motive*; 713.3 *precept*; 21.14 *production*; 317.2 *route*; 27.50 *scalar quantity*; 143.1 *situation*; 631.8 *treatment*

directional **300.17**; **324.13**; 579.17 *managerial*; 483.11 *motivational*; 742.14 *signifying*; 143.7 *situational*

directional antenna 692.17 *antenna*

directional reference 323.5 *navigation*

directional sign 742.1 *sign*

direction finder 324.3 *orientation*

direction-finding 579.5 *guide*

direction indicator 742.5 *indicator*

directions 324.5

directive 397.1 *command*; 397.14 *commanding*; 324.16 *directing*; 16.48 *jurisdictional*; 483.11 *motivational*; 480.19 *persuasive*; 140.1 *rule*

directive therapy 36.3 *psychiatric treatment*

directly **324.9**; 698.39 *accurately*; 426.12 *bluntly*; 725.4 *clearly*; 293.17 *early*; 340.8 *effectively*; 5.52 *grammatically*; 255.20 *homogenously*; 694.13 *meaningfully*; 271.8 *simply*; 293.18 *soon*; 178.12 *straight*; 178.13 *straightforwardly*; 527.13 *transparently*; 698.36 *truthfully*

directly proportional to 27.88 *equal to*

direct mail 480.6 *advertising*

directness **178.8**; 150.6 *broad-mindedness*; 725.1 *clarity*; 280.1 *immediacy*; 271.6 *naturalness*; 426.6 *outspokenness*; 695.10 *simplicity*; 178.6 *straightness*; 698.5 *truthfulness*

direct object 5.35 *part of speech*

direct one's course for 324.7 *take a direction*

direct oneself 324.7 *take a direction*

director **579.13**; 692.17 *antenna*; 400.5 *company leader*; 631.10 *conductor*; 340.3 *doer*; 15.6 *employer*; 395.5 *influential person*; 579.14 *leader*; 346.5 *operator*; 396.10 *person of authority*; 21.27, 356.9 *producer*

directorate 579.6 *governing body*

direct order 397.1 *command*
directorial 579.17 *managerial*
director of studies 579.13 *director*
directors 579.6 *governing body*
directorship 579.4; 12.3 *governance*; 121.2 *leadership*; 396.5 *position of authority*
directory 409.7 *catalogue*; 40.19 *computing terms*; 220.3 *dictionary*; 744.6 *record book*; 693.5 *reference book*
direct primary 469.12 *election*
direct proof 27.66 *proof*
direct proportion 108.2 *interrelatedness*
direct radiation 31.22 *sun*
direct ratio 108.2 *interrelatedness*
directrix 27.42 *circle*
direct tax 788.2 *money received*; 790.7 *tax*
direct tide 91.2 *tide*
direct to 324.6 *direct*
direct vote 469.10 *vote*
direct wave 692.15 *transmitted wave*
dire necessity 782.5 *poverty*
dire straits 254.5 *danger*; 782.5 *poverty*
dirge 583.2 *funeral*; 603.2 *lament*; 17.7 *poem*
dirgeful 583.11 *funeral*
dirgelike 583.11 *funeral*; 603.4 *lamenting*
dirham 780.11 *national coins*
dirigible 322.8 *aircraft*; 324.14 *directed*
dirigisme 12.3 *governance*
dirk 425.8 *sharp-pointed thing*; 587.8 *sharp weapon*
dirndl 551.6 *skirt*
dirofilariasis 75.11 *helminthic disease*
dirt 258.4; 523.3 *dark colour*; 560.5 *faeces*; 796.2 *indecency*; 693.1 *information*; 236.10 *poverty*; 427.5 *powder*; 238.6 *refuse*; 215.2 *residue*
dirt-cheap 793.9 *cheap*
dirt-encrusted 258.7 *dirty*
dirt farmer 43.15 *agriculturist*
dirt farming 43.4 *arable farming*
dirt-free 256.16 *clean*
dirtily 258.12; 427.29 *flakily*; 712.12 *swearingly*
Dirtiness 258
dirtiness 258.1; 245.10 *impairment*; 528.6 *opaqueness*; 236.10 *poverty*; 408.3 *untidiness*
dirt road 317.3, 320.2 *road*; 420.8 *rough ground*
dirt track 59.7 *horseracing*; 420.8 *rough ground*
dirt-track race 61.5 *motorcycle racing*
dirt-track racing 61.5 *motorcycle racing*
dirty 258.7; **258.11**; 782.3 *beggarly*; 532.11 *blacken*; 712.8 *cursing*; 523.10 *dark-coloured*; 524.7 *dimmed*; 796.12 *indecent*; 666.5 *indifferent*; 245.3 *make worse*; 258.9 *obscene*; 91.7 *oceanic*; 236.4 *poor*; 427.15 *powdery*; 528.2 *shady*; 31.48 *stormy*; 524.11 *tarnish*; 408.15 *untidy*
dirty book 258.3 *obscenity*
dirty books 796.2 *indecency*
dirty clothes 256.8 *laundry*
dirty dealings 800.3 *criminality*
dirty dishes 256.8 *laundry*
dirty film 258.3 *obscenity*
dirty habits 258.2 *uncleanness*
dirty hands 806.2 *signs of guilt*
dirty joke 659.3 *act of discourtesy*; 712.1 *curse*; 796.2 *indecency*; 258.3 *obscenity*
dirty language 712.2 *offensive language*
dirty liar 699.18, 700.16 *liar*
dirty lie 699.10 *lie*
dirty linen 256.8 *laundry*
dirty look 670.10 *disapproving look*; 518.6 *look*
dirty magazine 258.3 *obscenity*
dirty mouth 712.1 *curse*
dirty old man 258.6 *dirty person*; 796.8 *immoral man*
dirty person 258.6
dirty snowball 29.19 *comet*
dirty story 796.2 *indecency*; 599.5 *joke*
dirty talk 712.1 *curse*
dirty trick 812.3 *disreputable action*; 800.1 *improbity*; 700.8 *trick*
dirty water 258.5 *swill*
dirty weather 380.5 *violent weather*
dirty weekend 654.3 *meeting*
dirty word 712.1 *curse*
Dis 8.12 *hell*
dis 621.6 *deride*; 678.10 *disparage*
disability 335.4; 231.7 *defect*; 260.2 *illness*; 240.3 *inconvenience*
disable 378.8 *hinder*; 245.5 *hurt*; 103.8 *make impossible*; 343.14 *make inactive*; 238.8 *make useless*; 335.7 *remove power from*; 337.7 *weaken*
disabled 231.3 *deformed*; 335.12 *impotent*; 301.5 *sedentary*
disabled person 260.19 *sick person*
disablement 245.11 *hurt*
disablement benefit 392.4 *social assistance*
disabling 245.11 *hurt*
disablist 466.10 *discriminatory*
disabuse 693.11 *inform*
disaccharide 33.3 *carbohydrate*
disaccord 113.5 *conflict*; 517.6, 751.1 *disagreement*; 118.1 *nonconformity*
disaccordance 118.1 *nonconformity*
disaccustom 487.5; 486.5 *be unskilful*; 481.3 *deflect*; 355.1 *relinquish*
disaccustomed 487.1 *unaccustomed*
disadvantage 240.5 *be inconvenient*; 120.5 *be unequal*; 231.7 *defect*; 122.2 *deficiency*; 240.3 *inconvenience*; 120.1 *inequality*; 766.1 *loss*
disadvantaged 135.5 *necessitous*
disadvantageous 249.6 *adverse*; 236.5 *harmful*; 240.1 *inconvenient*
disaffect 481.4 *put off*
disaffected 596.8 *disliking*; 606.4 *dissatisfied*
disaffection 481.7 *deterrence*; 596.1 *dislike*; 594.1 *hate*
disaffiliated 100.11 *separate*
disaffiliation 100.3 *separateness*
disaffinity 364.5 *repulsion*
disaffirm 704.9 *deny*; 708.11 *rebut*
disaffirmation 704.2 *denial*; 708.3 *rebuttal*; 704.1 *refutation*
disaffirming 708.19 *rebutting*
disagree 372.12; **517.11**; **670.16**; **751.5**; 586.40, 701.13 *argue*; 661.6 *be insubordinate*; 120.5 *be unequal*; 637.6 *be unwilling*; 596.7 *cause dislike*; 451.8 *disbelieve*; 596.5 *dislike*; 114.9, 709.6 *dissent*; 705.20 *doubt*; 694.10 *mean*; 113.18 *object*; 242.11 *quarrel*; 708.11 *rebut*
disagreeable 372.18; 701.8 *argumentative*; 236.3 *bad*; 659.5 *discourteous*; 596.9 *disliked*; 626.7 *irritable*; 499.6 *unpalatable*; 242.1 *unpleasant*
disagreeableness 659.1 *discourtesy*; 242.5 *unpleasantness*
disagreeably 372.23; 701.17 *argumentatively*; 659.9 *discourteously*; 626.14 *irritably*; 242.13 *unpleasantly*
disagreeing 517.8; **670.26**; **751.9**; 661.8 *defying*; 372.18 *disagreeable*; 113.24 *discordant*; 596.9 *disliked*; 596.8 *disliking*; 114.7, 709.9 *dissenting*; 529.12 *gaudy*; 708.19 *rebutting*; 637.2 *refusing*; 120.3 *unequal*
Disagreement 751
disagreement 517.6; **670.4**; **751.1**; 701.1 *argument*; 264.7 *awkward situation*; 113.8 *contrariety*; 451.1 *disbelief*; 596.1 *dislike*; 661.2 *disobedience*; 114.4, 242.7 *dissension*; 118.2, 709.2 *dissent*; 372.4 *disunity*; 118.1 *nonconformity*; 113.4 *objection*; 753.1 *protest*; 708.3 *rebuttal*; 637.11 *unwillingness*
disagree with 113.17 *be against*; 596.7 *cause dislike*; 753.6 *protest*
disallow 708.10 *be negative*; 708.14 *cancel*; 709.6 *dissent*; 128.7 *exclude*; 704.8 *refute*; 470.1 *reject*; 399.3 *veto*; 670.15 *withhold approval*
disallowal 704.1 *refutation*
disallowance 708.5 *cancellation*; 708.2 *rejection*; 399.1 *veto*
disallowed 709.9 *dissenting*; 103.4 *forbidden*; 708.18 *rejected*
disallow payment 786.8 *stop payment*
disambiguate 725.2 *clarify*; 719.8 *interpret*
disappear 526.1; 98.18 *abscond*; 521.7 *become invisible*; 357.13 *be destroyed*; 278.4 *be transient*; 226.6 *cease*; 94.12 *cease to exist*; 736.11 *conceal oneself*; 214.4 *decrease*; 389.5 *escape*; 377.11 *explode*; 195.8 *not exist*; 313.3 *quit*
Disappearance 526
disappearance 98.2; **526.4**; 736.1 *concealment*; 214.1 *decrease*; 377.3 *dilution*; 389.1 *escape*; 521.4 *invisibility*
disappeared 526.7; 98.9 *away*
disappearing 526.6; 526.4 *disappearance*; 278.6 *transient*
disappearing act 526.4 *disappearance*
disappearing trick 389.1 *escape*
disappear into thin air 526.1 *disappear*
disappoint 604.6; **611.10**; 630.11 *amaze*; 218.5 *be insufficient*; 606.6 *dissatisfy*; 247.6 *fail*
disappointed 604.9; 630.7 *amazed*; 670.25 *disapproving*; 606.4 *dissatisfied*
disappointing 604.11; 218.1 *insufficient*; 606.5 *unsatisfactory*
disappointingly 604.13; 218.10 *insufficiently*
Disappointment 604
disappointment 604.1; 630.2 *amazement*; 606.1 *dissatisfaction*; 247.1 *failure*; 611.2 *hopeless situation*; 218.8 *insufficiency*; 627.5 *misfortune*; 495.2 *taste of life*
disapprobation 670.1 *disapproval*; 668.2 *disesteem*; 606.1 *dissatisfaction*; 594.1 *hate*; 113.1 *opposition*; 753.1 *protest*; 624.1 *resentment*
disapprobatory 670.25 *disapproving*
Disapproval 670
disapproval 670.1; 668.2 *disesteem*; 596.1 *dislike*; 606.1 *dissatisfaction*; 594.1 *hate*; 113.1 *opposition*; 753.1 *protest*; 470.5 *rejection*; 624.1 *resentment*
disapprove 670.14; 606.7 *be dissatisfied*; 16.79 *convict*; 596.5 *dislike*; 594.14 *hate*
disapproved 670.31; 16.64 *convicted*; 596.9 *disliked*; 623.3 *humbled*
disapproved of 606.5 *unsatisfactory*
disapprove of 113.17 *be against*; 670.14 *disapprove*; 464.11 *judge*; 753.6 *protest*
disapprover 670.11
disapproving 670.25; 512.7 *catcalling*; 596.8 *disliking*; 606.4 *dissatisfied*; 464.8 *judging*; 113.22 *oppositional*; 753.9 *protesting*; 624.15 *resentful*; 264.14 *troublesome*
disapproving look 670.10
disapprovingly 670.37; **753.11**; 606.8 *discontentedly*; 464.13 *judicially*; 264.29 *perversely*; 624.17 *resentfully*
disarm 685.3 *be moderate*; 627.11 *excite pity*; 589.6, 749.5 *make peace*; 238.8 *make useless*; 685.4 *moderate*; 335.8 *overpower*; 749.4 *pacify*; 335.7 *remove power from*; 337.7 *weaken*
disarmament 749.1 *pacification*; 589.1 *peace*; 335.1 *powerlessness*
disarmament treaty 589.1 *peace*
disarmed 335.11 *unprotected*
disarming 685.8 *moderating*; 749.6 *pacificatory*
disarrange 328.8; 408.21 *disorder*; 144.14 *displace*
disarranged 328.13; 408.12 *disordered*; 144.8 *displaced*
disarrangement 328.2; 408.1 *disorder*; 144.1 *displacement*
disarray 408.1 *disorder*
disarticulate 144.18 *disconnect*
disarticulated 144.12 *disconnected*
disarticulation 144.5 *disconnection*
disassemble 238.8 *make useless*; 372.9 *separate*
disassociate 372.9 *separate*
disassociated 109.6 *unrelated*
disassociate oneself 708.10 *be negative*
disassociation 708.2 *rejection*; 109.1 *unrelatedness*
disassociative 708.17 *negative*
disaster 249.1 *adversity*; 798.2 *affliction*; 604.2 *bad outcome*; 236.11 *harmfulness*; 288.4 *mishap*; 357.4 *ruin*
disaster area 441.4 *destruction*; 357.5 *havoc*
disaster relief 608.4, 652.5 *charity*
disastrous 288.17 *accidental*; 249.6 *adverse*; 357.14 *destructive*; 236.5 *harmful*
disastrously 357.16, 798.13 *destructively*; 249.12 *in adversity*; 288.21 *mistakenly*
disavow 708.10 *be negative*; 704.9 *deny*; 753.6 *protest*; 479.4 *recant*; 470.4 *revoke*
disavowal 470.7 *abrogation*; 704.2 *denial*; 753.1 *protest*; 479.8 *recantation*; 708.2 *rejection*
disavowed 708.18 *rejected*
disbalance 120.5 *be unequal*
disband 375.4 *deconstruct*; 377.13 *dismiss*; 391.4 *liberate*; 372.9 *separate*
disbanded 377.21
disbanding 391.1 *liberation*; 749.1 *pacification*
disbandment 377.2
disbar 371.3; 128.8 *eject*; 655.13 *ignore*
disbarment 128.2 *ejection*
disbarred 128.11 *excluded*; 655.10 *lonely*
Disbelief 451
disbelief 451.1; 708.2 *rejection*; 453.10 *suspicion*
disbelieve 451.8; 708.10 *be negative*; 453.18 *be uncertain*; 705.20 *doubt*
disbelieved 451.7; 708.18 *rejected*
disbeliever 451.5
disbelieving 451.6
disbelievingly 451.10
disburden 390.1 *deliver*; 265.18 *disentangle*; 415.10 *lighten*; 371.12 *unload*
disburdening 415.3 *lightening*
disburdenment 265.8 *disentanglement*
disburse 787.1 *expend*; 785.6 *pay*
disbursed 787.12 *expended*
disbursement 787.4 *expenditure*; 785.1 *payment*
disbursing 785.15 *paying*
disc 504.9 *audio device*; 27.42 *circle*; 179.3 *circular thing*; 43.10 *farm tool*; 187.3 *flat thing*; 29.7 *galaxy*; 744.7 *recording*; 307.6 *rotator*; 411.4 *slice*
discalced 552.11 *exposed*
discard 470.2; 767.9 *dispose of*; 215.8 *leave*; 470.8 *rejected thing*; 355.1 *relinquish*; 350.6 *stop using*; 371.13 *throw away*; 350.11 *unused thing*
discarded 767.12 *disposed*; 350.4 *disused*; 487.2 *not customary*; 470.10 *rejected*; 215.9 *remaining*
discarded matter 238.6 *refuse*
discarding 470.6; 767.1 *disposal*; 350.10 *disuse*
disc camera 41.16 *camera*
discern 425.17 *be mentally sharp*; 458.7 *be wise*; 466.12 *discriminate*; 6.24, 455.11 *know*; 695.7 *recognize*; 518.12 *see*; 372.10 *set apart*; 518.16 *visualize*
discernibility 520.3 *visibility*
discernible 372.19 *separable*; 518.23, 520.1 *visible*
discernibly 520.11 *visibly*
discerning 466.9 *discriminating*; 464.8 *judging*; 464.9 *judicious*; 425.5 *mentally sharp*; 6.20 *refined*; 518.21 *seeing*; 469.14 *selecting*; 156.11 *wise*
discerningly 6.27; 466.16 *judiciously*; 425.18 *sharply*
discernment 442.5 *common sense*; 464.1 *judgment*; 466.2 *judiciousness*; 425.13 *mental sharpness*; 156.3 *profundity*; 6.11 *refinement*; 518.4 *visualization*; 458.1 *wisdom*
disc floret 78.4 *flower head*
discharge 649.3 *absolution*; 649.10 *absolve*; 16.78, 758.10 *acquit*; 16.42, 758.2 *acquittal*; 340.4 *act*; 508.1, 508.5 *bang*; 431.3 *body fluid*; 232.4 *complete*; 39.35 *conduct*; 390.2 *deliverance*; 371.2, 377.13, 580.5, 767.10 *dismiss*; 371.18 *dismissal*; 350.10 *disuse*; 560.15 *excrete*; 560.1 *excretion*; 250.1 *freedom*; 312.4 *land*; 315.12, 389.4 *leak*; 371.14 *let out*; 391.4 *liberate*; 391.1 *liberation*; 663.5 *obey*; 315.2 *outflow*; 785.1 *payment*; 785.7 *pay off*; 560.7 *pus*; 144.17 *relegate*; 144.4 *relegation*; 559.7 *secrete*; 559.1 *secretion*; 330.28 *shoot*; 330.7 *shot*; 350.7 *stop work*; 260.3 *symptom*; 708.15 *terminate*; 708.6 *termination*; 260.15 *ulcer*; 580.3 *unemployment*; 371.12 *unload*; 714.7 *vindicate*; 714.1 *vindication*
discharge a bankrupt 786.10 *forgive a debt*
discharged 16.63, 758.6 *acquitted*; 708.20 *cancelled*; 767.13 *dismissed*; 649.6 *forgiven*; 250.9 *free*; 714.12 *innocent*; 580.7 *leisurely*; 350.3 *not wanted*; 785.16 *paid*; 144.11 *relegated*
discharged bankrupt 786.6 *nonpayer*
discharge of duty 810.5
discharge one's duty 810.16 *do one's duty*
discharge one's obligations 803.8 *be virtuous*
disc harrows 43.10 *farm tool*
disciple 267.5 *follower*; 125.7 *imitator*; 7.3 *religious person*; 413.8 *supporter*
disciplinarian 251.6 *lawmaker*; 579.15 *manager*; 647.4 *strict person*
disciplinary 814.19 *punitive*
disciplinary action 814.7 *punishment*
disciplinary procedure 15.2 *industrial negotiations*
discipline 407.9; 117.10 *assimilate*; 396.19 *be authoritarian*; 647.5 *be severe*; 386.6 *compel*; 15.11 *conduct industrial relations*; 387.7 *defeat*; 387.2 *domination*;

6.22 *educate*; 15.2 *industrial negotiations*; 407.7 *method*; 407.22 *pacify*; 814.1 *punish*; 814.7 *punishment*; 251.8 *restrain*; 251.1 *restraint*; 292.7 *season*; 251.3 *self-restraint*; 647.1 *severity*; 86.14, 447.4 *sphere*; 6.3 *subject*; 631.8 *treatment*
disciplined 407.17; 15.9 *negotiated*; 663.7 *obedient*; 814.20 *punished*; 251.13 *restraining*; 647.8 *severe*
discipline oneself 684.5 *be self-restrained*
discipliner 814.17 *punisher*
disciplining 15.9 *negotiated*
discipular 413.9 *supportive*
disc jockey 692.29 *broadcaster*
disclaim 708.10 *be negative*; 704.9 *deny*; 767.9 *dispose of*; 753.6 *protest*; 479.4 *recant*; 470.4 *revoke*
disclaimed 708.18 *rejected*
disclaimer 704.2 *denial*; 753.1 *protest*; 479.8 *recantation*; 708.2 *rejection*
disclaiming 704.7 *refuting*
disclamation 708.2 *rejection*
disclike 27.83 *spherical*
disclose 739.5; 707.20 *admit*; 703.15 *demonstrate*; 449.2 *detect*; 738.1 *display*; 6.22 *educate*; 740.13 *make public*; 520.10 *make visible*; 308.18 *open*; 525.14 *present*; 741.13 *report*; 738.3 *reveal*; 742.10 *signify*; 729.11 *speak*; 552.14 *undress*
disclosed 739.10; 703.9 *demonstrated*; 738.14 *manifest*; 740.19 *published*; 707.11 *stated*
discloser 739.4; 707.9 *affirmer*
disclosing 739.11; 742.14 *signifying*
Disclosure 739
disclosure 739.1; 707.5 *admission*; 525.1 *appearance*; 703.1 *demonstration*; 449.7 *detection*; 738.10 *manifestation*; 740.1 *publication*
disco 376.10 *dance*; 22.6 *dance hall*; 18.7 *dance music*; 22.1 *dancing*; 654.5 *party*
discobolus 330.14 *thrower*
disco-dance 22.15 *dance*
disco dancer 21.30, 22.5 *dancer*
disco dancing 22.1 *dancing*
discography 220.2 *table*
discoid 179.5 *circular*
discoloration 245.9 *dilapidation*; 529.3 *hue*
discolour 224.8 *cause change*; 529.15 *colour*; 530.6 *decolour*; 541.11 *variegate*
discoloured 530.7 *colourless*; 245.12 *deteriorated*; 529.13 *soft-hued*
discomfit 242.10 *displease*; 328.7 *disturb*
discomfited 408.17 *discomposed*; 328.12 *disturbed*; 623.3 *humbled*
discomfiting 242.1 *unpleasant*
discomfiture 408.1 *disorder*; 328.1 *disturbance*; 242.5 *unpleasantness*
discomfort 798.2 *affliction*; 242.10 *displease*; 240.3 *inconvenience*; 491.1 *pain*; 242.5 *unpleasantness*
discomforting 242.2 *objectionable*
discommode 240.5 *be inconvenient*; 264.23 *cause difficulties*
discommodious 240.1 *inconvenient*
discommodiously 240.6 *inconveniently*
discompose 408.22; 327.22 *agitate*; 328.7 *disturb*
discomposed 408.17; 327.15 *agitated*; 453.3 *confused*; 328.12 *disturbed*
discomposure 327.1 *agitation*; 453.12 *confusion*; 408.1 *disorder*; 328.1 *disturbance*
disconcert 630.11 *amaze*; 408.22 *discompose*; 328.7 *disturb*; 623.17 *humiliate*; 453.20 *make uncertain*; 604.7 *thwart*
disconcerted 630.7 *amazed*; 453.3 *confused*; 604.9 *disappointed*; 408.17 *discomposed*; 328.12 *disturbed*; 623.3 *humbled*
disconcertedness 453.12 *confusion*; 408.1 *disorder*; 328.1 *disturbance*
disconcerting 453.3 *confused*; 328.17 *disturbing*
disconcertingly 328.18 *disturbingly*
disconcertion 453.12 *confusion*
disconcertment 630.2 *amazement*
disconfirm 704.8 *refute*
disconfirmation 704.1 *refutation*
disconnect 133.14; **144.18**; 299.6 *be irregular*; 226.8 *cause to cease*; 39.35 *conduct*; 372.9 *separate*
disconnected 144.12; 133.8 *discontinuous*; 100.8 *extraneous*; 299.4 *irregular*; 36.36 *psychologically disturbed*; 372.15 *separate*; 109.6 *unrelated*
disconnectedly 133.18; **144.21**
disconnectedness 133.1 *discontinuity*; 100.2 *foreignness*
disconnection 144.5; 133.1 *discontinuity*; 36.16 *dissociation*; 299.1 *irregularity*; 372.1 *separation*; 109.1 *unrelatedness*
disconsolate 611.4 *hopeless*; 603.4 *lamenting*; 602.5 *sad*
discontent 604.2 *bad outcome*; 670.1 *disapproval*; 596.1 *dislike*; 606.1 *dissatisfaction*; 606.4 *dissatisfied*; 218.8 *insufficiency*; 626.3 *irritableness*; 626.12 *make irritable*; 753.1 *protest*; 753.9 *protesting*; 624.1 *resentment*; 604.7 *thwart*
discontented 604.9 *disappointed*; 670.25 *disapproving*; 659.5 *discourteous*; 596.8 *disliking*; 606.4 *dissatisfied*; 626.7 *irritable*; 753.9 *protesting*; 624.15 *resentful*; 264.14 *troublesome*; 218.2 *unprovided*
discontentedly 596.10; **606.8**; 659.9 *discourteously*; 626.14 *irritably*; 624.17 *resentfully*
discontentedness 670.1 *disapproval*
discontenting 604.11 *disappointing*
discontentment 670.1 *disapproval*; 606.1 *dissatisfaction*
discontinuance 708.5 *cancellation*; 226.1 *cessation*; 309.1 *closure*; 133.1 *discontinuity*; 247.1 *failure*; 361.6 *interruption*; 355.3 *relinquishment*; 708.6 *termination*; 487.3 *unaccustomedness*
discontinuation 708.5 *cancellation*; 226.1 *cessation*; 133.1 *discontinuity*; 247.1 *failure*; 299.1 *irregularity*
discontinue 133.12; 131.16, 226.6 *cease*; 309.9 *close down*; 247.6 *fail*; 361.12 *interrupt*; 708.15 *terminate*
discontinued 133.9; 350.4 *disused*; 361.9 *interrupted*; 355.5 *relinquished*
Discontinuity 133
discontinuity 133.1; 226.1 *cessation*; 114.1 *diversity*; 30.18 *earth's crust*; 146.1 *interval*; 299.1 *irregularity*; 372.1 *separation*
discontinuous 133.8; 299.4 *irregular*; 276.9 *periodic*; 372.15 *separate*; 146.6 *spaced*
discontinuously 133.17; 146.8 *apart*; 299.8 *irregularly*; 372.20 *separately*
discontinuousness 133.1 *discontinuity*
discord 701.1, 751.2 *argument*; 513.4 *be strident*; 113.5 *conflict*; 751.3 *difference*; 517.6 *disagreement*; 408.1 *disorder*; 242.7 *dissension*; 517.1 *dissonance*; 513.1 *stridency*
discordance 751.1 *disagreement*; 114.4, 242.7 *dissension*; 709.2 *dissent*; 517.1 *dissonance*; 513.1 *stridency*
discordant 113.24; 701.7 *arguing*; 751.10 *different*; 751.9 *disagreeing*; 114.7, 709.9 *dissenting*; 517.7 *dissonant*; 109.8 *distorted*; 529.12 *gaudy*; 507.6 *loud*; 513.7 *strident*; 242.1 *unpleasant*
discordantly 701.17 *argumentatively*; 751.12 *differently*; 109.13 *disproportionately*; 116.7 *dissimilarly*; 517.12 *dissonantly*; 751.11 *in disagreement*; 513.10 *stridently*; 709.11 *uncooperatively*
discotheque 22.6 *dance hall*; 654.5 *party*
Discount 791
discount 791.1; **791.3**; 793.9 *cheap*; 793.1 *cheapness*; 793.13 *make cheap*; 212.3 *subtract*; 212.2 *subtracted item*; 212.1 *subtraction*; 468.3 *underestimate*
discounted 791.6; 212.7 *reduced*
discountenance 113.17 *be against*; 670.14 *disapprove*
discounter 793.7
discounting 212.1 *subtraction*
discount price 790.1 *price*
discount store 793.7 *discounter*
discount ticket 793.4 *bargain*
discourage 481.5; 395.9 *change*; 481.1 *dissuade*; 378.8 *hinder*
discouraged 604.9 *disappointed*; 481.10 *dissuaded*; 611.4 *hopeless*
discouragement 604.1 *disappointment*; 481.6 *dissuasion*; 378.1 *hindrance*; 611.1 *hopelessness*
discouraging 481.9 *dissuasive*; 378.13 *hindering*
discouragingly 481.11 *dissuasively*; 378.16 *with delay*
discourse 733.1, 733.7 *address*; 734.1 *conversation*; 734.9 *converse*; 722.4 *dissertate*; 722.1 *dissertation*; 703.3 *explanation*; 729.1 *faculty of speech*; 701.2 *logical argument*; 17.4 *nonfiction*; 729.14 *speak to*
discourse at length 270.5 *be diffuse*
discourser 734.7 *conversationalist*; 733.6 *public speaker*
discourteous 659.5; **660.20**; **675.8**; 631.18 *badly behaved*; 486.3 *clumsy*; 668.10 *disrespectful*; 544.8 *indecorous*; 242.2 *objectionable*; 672.3 *ungrateful*; 655.8 *unsociable*
discourteously 659.9; **660.36**; 631.20 *badly*; 668.28 *disrespectfully*; 672.7 *ungratefully*; 242.13 *unpleasantly*; 655.14 *unsocially*
discourteousness 659.1 *discourtesy*; 672.1 *ingratitude*
discourteous person 659.4
Discourtesy 659
discourtesy 659.1; **660.9**; 631.4 *bad conduct*; 668.1 *disrespect*; 675.3 *grossness*; 544.2 *impropriety*; 242.6 *objectionability*; 655.1 *unsociability*
discover 449.1; 693.15 *be informed*; 739.5 *disclose*; 142.11 *find*; 633.9 *follow*; 129.18 *forerun*; 455.13 *get to know*; 130.22, 484.11 *invent*; 6.23 *learn*; 293.8 *precede*; 356.10 *produce*; 312.2 *reach*; 738.3 *reveal*; 518.12 *see*; 706.20 *solve*; 630.9 *surprise*
discoverable 449.15; 520.1 *visible*
discover a treasure trove 765.14 *profit*
discovered 449.14; 142.7 *found*; 455.10 *known*; 738.14 *manifest*; 356.12 *produced*; 706.14 *solved*
discoverer 449.12; 739.4 *discloser*; 293.4 *early comer*; 129.8 *precursor*; 356.9 *producer*
discovering 449.13; 142.3 *locating*; 129.14 *preparatory*
Discovery 449
discovery 449.6; 739.1 *disclosure*; 475.2 *divination*; 449.10 *find*; 130.5 *invention*; 738.10 *manifestation*; 129.3 *preparation*; 356.1 *production*; 765.5 *profit*; 439.2 *resource*; 706.6 *solution*
discredit 812.4 *bring into disrepute*; 451.9 *cause disbelief*; 678.12 *defame*; 451.8 *disbelieve*; 812.1 *disrespect*; 594.4 *hatefulness*; 451.3 *incredulity*; 704.8 *refute*
discreditable 236.4 *poor*
discredited 451.7 *disbelieved*; 350.4 *disused*; 594.12 *hated*; 754.7 *irresolute*
discrediting 704.1 *refutation*; 704.7 *refuting*
discreet 616.4 *cautious*; 658.7 *courteous*; 736.17 *noncommittal*; 529.13 *soft-hued*; 458.5 *wise*
discreetly 658.14 *courteously*; 458.9 *wisely*
discrepancy 113.8 *contrariety*; 215.3, 751.3 *difference*; 116.1 *dissimilarity*; 120.1 *inequality*
discrepant 751.10 *different*; 116.4 *dissimilar*
discrepantly 751.12 *differently*; 215.11 *residually*
discrete 133.8 *discontinuous*; 466.11 *judged*; 100.11 *separate*; 377.20 *separated*; 27.70 *universal*; 372.17 *unjoined*; 109.6 *unrelated*
discrete component 39.16 *circuit element*
discrete distribution 27.59 *probability distribution*
discretely 100.18 *extraneously*; 658.15 *genteelly*; 372.22 *in isolation*; 27.87 *mathematically*
discreteness 100.3 *separateness*
discretion 616.1 *caution*; 658.1 *courtesy*; 250.1 *freedom*; 635.4 *free will*; 464.1 *judgment*; 466.2 *judiciousness*; 469.6 *selection*; 736.4 *silence*; 485.1 *skill*; 458.1 *wisdom*
discretional 469.14 *selecting*
discretionary 635.10 *free*; 250.12 *unconditional*
discriminate 466.12; **802.22**; 485.10 *be skilful*; 120.6, 465.11 *be unjust*; 458.7 *be wise*; 116.6 *differentiate*; 6.24 *know*; 469.4 *pick*; 372.10 *set apart*
discriminate against 466.14; 802.22 *discriminate*; 128.7 *exclude*
discriminated against 466.11 *judged*
discriminating 466.9; 99.9 *characteristic*; 464.8 *judging*; 464.9 *judicious*; 4.15 *rational*; 6.20, 549.5 *refined*; 469.14 *selecting*; 728.13 *subtle*; 495.8 *tasteful*
discriminatingly 466.15; 6.27 *discerningly*; 4.29 *wisely*
discriminating person 466.6
Discrimination 466
discrimination 466.1; 116.1 *dissimilarity*; 128.1 *exclusion*; 120.2, 465.3 *injustice*; 464.1 *judgment*; 466.2 *judiciousness*; 466.3 *prejudice*; 6.11 *refinement*; 469.6 *selection*; 372.2 *setting apart*; 485.1 *skill*; 728.3 *subtlety*; 495.2 *taste of life*; 802.1 *unfairness*; 458.1 *wisdom*
discriminatorily 120.8 *unjustly*
discriminatory 466.10; 120.4, 465.8 *unjust*; 802.11 *wrong*
disc-shaped 27.83 *spherical*
discursion 270.2 *circumlocution*; 325.16 *wandering*
discursive 270.4 *circumlocutory*; 722.5 *expository*; 325.25 *wandering*
discursively 325.27 *astray*; 270.8 *circuitously*
discursiveness 325.16 *wandering*
discursive reasoning 444.2 *reasoning*
discus 330.10 *ball*; 179.3 *circular thing*; 47.2 *field events*
discuss 701.14; 639.8 *balance*; 734.11 *confer*; 713.6 *consult*; 722.4 *dissertate*; 705.20 *doubt*; 447.11 *raise the point*
discussing 734.13
discussion 746.3; 734.4 *conference*; 713.2 *consultation*; 722.1 *dissertation*; 137.7 *lecture*; 701.2 *logical argument*; 4.5 *philosophical argument*
discussion group 376.6 *sitting*; 137.6 *students*
discussions 746.1 *negotiation*
discuss philosophically 4.23
discus throw 47.2 *field events*
discus thrower 47.3 *athlete*; 330.14 *thrower*
discus throwing 47.2 *field events*
disc wheel 320.11 *bicycle part*
disdain 622.28; 660.6, 668.3 *contempt*; 661.2 *disobedience*; 470.3 *exclude*; 668.20, 678.5 *scorn*; 622.2 *unapproachability*
disdainful 660.17, 668.13 *contemptuous*; 661.7 *defiant*; 622.15 *unapproachable*
disdainfully 660.34, 668.30 *contemptuously*; 661.9 *defiantly*
disdainfulness 668.3 *contempt*
disease 260.4; 357.7 *agent of destruction*; 245.9 *dilapidation*; 260.2 *illness*; 236.10 *poverty*
disease carrier 316.9
diseased 260.23; 236.4 *poor*
disease prevention 257.1 *hygiene*
disect 27.97 *align*
disedge 426.10 *blunt*
disembark 312.4 *land*; 323.10 *sail*
disembarkation 312.11 *landing*
disembarkment 312.11 *landing*
disembarrass 265.18 *disentangle*
disembarrassment 265.8 *disentanglement*
disembodied 101.8 *nonmaterial*; 11.18 *spiritual*
disembodiment 526.4 *disappearance*; 101.2 *unworldliness*
disembody 526.3 *cause to disappear*; 101.12 *enter a nonmaterial world*
disembogue 371.14 *let out*; 315.11 *run out*
disemboguement 371.22 *disgorgement*
disembowel 372.11 *divide*; 369.14 *suck*; 371.11 *void*
disembowelled 372.15 *separate*
disembowelment 369.4 *sucking*
disemplane 312.4 *land*
disemploy 371.2 *dismiss*
disemployment 470.6 *discarding*
disempower 335.7 *remove power from*
disenable 103.8 *make impossible*
disenchant 604.6 *disappoint*; 481.5 *discourage*
disenchanted 604.9 *disappointed*; 596.8 *disliking*; 481.10 *dissuaded*
disenchantment 604.2 *bad outcome*; 481.7 *deterrence*
disencumber 390.1 *deliver*; 265.18 *disentangle*; 391.4 *liberate*; 415.10 *lighten*; 608.14 *take away*
disencumbering 415.3 *lightening*
disencumberment 390.2 *deliverance*; 265.8 *disentanglement*; 391.1 *liberation*
disendow 782.14 *impoverish*
disenfranchise 387.6 *subject*
disenfranchisement 766.1 *loss*; 387.1 *subjection*
disengage 265.18 *disentangle*; 369.11 *extract*; 54.5 *fence*; 54.3 *fencing movements*; 391.4 *liberate*; 303.2 *retreat*; 372.9 *separate*
disengaged 144.12 *disconnected*; 369.19

dislodged; 54.6 *fencing*; 580.7 *leisurely*; 343.2 *not working*
disengagement 144.5 *disconnection*; 265.8 *disentanglement*; 369.1 *extraction*; 391.1 *liberation*; 303.11 *retreat*
disentangle 265.18; 719.9 *decipher*; 767.9 *dispose of*; 372.9 *separate*; 178.10 *straighten*; 409.19 *tidy*
disentangled 255.16 *simple*; 409.27 *tidied*
disentanglement 265.8
disentitlement 766.1 *loss*
disentomb 369.13 *dig out*; 583.9 *exhume*
disentombment 369.3 *digging out*; 583.7 *inquest*
disequilibrium 227.1 *changeableness*; 120.1 *inequality*
disesteem 668.2; 670.2 *disrespect*
diseur 21.29 *entertainer*
diseuse 21.29 *entertainer*
disfavour 606.7 *be dissatisfied*; 670.1 *disapproval*; 670.14 *disapprove*; 668.2 *disesteem*; 596.1, 596.5 *dislike*; 812.1 *disrespect*; 594.1 *hate*
disfavoured 596.9 *disliked*
disfellowship 371.18 *dismissal*
disfigure 548.7 *blemish*; 234.11 *deform*; 245.5 *hurt*; 743.10 *identify*; 546.5 *make ugly*
disfigured 548.4 *blemished*; 234.7 *deformed*; 546.4 *ugly*
disfigurement 234.3 *deformity*; 548.1 *spot*; 546.1 *ugliness*
disfranchise 387.6 *subject*
disfranchised 335.10 *powerless*
disfranchisement 387.1 *subjection*
disgorge 371.14 *let out*
disgorgement 371.22
disgorger 55.3 *fishing tackle*
disgrace 796.19 *corrupt*; 802.9 *dishonour*; 668.21 *disregard*; 623.13 *disrepute*; 812.1 *disrespect*; 800.1 *improbity*; 236.10 *poverty*; 623.22 *shame*; 712.6 *vilify*
disgraceful 800.5 *dishonourable*; 802.15 *immoral*; 236.4 *poor*; 804.11 *wicked*
disgracefully 800.11 *dishonourably*; 804.18 *wickedly*; 236.15 *worthlessly*
disgrace oneself 804.16 *be wicked*; 812.4 *bring into disrepute*
disgruntled 604.9 *disappointed*; 670.25 *disapproving*; 606.4 *dissatisfied*
disgruntlement 670.1 *disapproval*; 606.1 *dissatisfaction*
disguise 116.3; **526.5**; **550.16**; **700.12**; **700.32**; **736.9**; 699.22 *be hypocritical*; 125.4 *camouflage*; 526.3 *cause to disappear*; 125.2 *copy*; 736.3 *covering up*; 645.1 *cunning*; 116.6 *differentiate*; 699.14 *façade*; 551.5 *fancy dress*; 550.31 *hide*; 699.3 *hypocrisy*; 521.8 *make invisible*; 699.28 *mask*; 389.2 *means of escape*; 702.11 *practise sophistry*; 525.14 *present*; 525.4 *something that appears*; 521.6 *that which makes invisible*
disguised 699.39; **700.41**; **736.15**; 526.7 *disappeared*; 737.11 *mysterious*; 521.3 *private*; 550.37 *protected*
disguised war 585.1 *war*
disguise oneself 526.1 *disappear*
disguise oneself as 525.11 *appear*
disguiser 550.17 *coverer*
disgust 499.9; 364.4 *be repulsive*; 596.7 *cause dislike*; 594.16 *cause hate*; 395.9 *change*; 596.1 *dislike*; 242.10 *displease*; 606.1 *dissatisfaction*; 606.6 *dissatisfy*; 594.1 *hate*; 481.4 *put off*
disgusted 596.8 *disliking*; 606.4 *dissatisfied*
disgustedly 606.8 *discontentedly*
disgusting 596.9 *disliked*; 594.12 *hated*; 236.4 *poor*; 364.8 *repulsive*; 258.8 *unclean*; 499.6 *unpalatable*; 242.1 *unpleasant*
disgustingly 596.11; 546.6 *hideously*
disgustingly rich 781.1 *wealthy*
dish 25.9; 692.17 *antenna*; 545.4 *attractive male*; 567.4 *boyfriend*; 410.16 *crockery*; 557.16 *eating utensil*; 557.14 *mouthful*; 357.11 *ruin*; 316.15 *take away*
dishabille 552.4; 551.4, 657.6 *informal dress*
dish antenna 692.17 *antenna*
disharmonious 751.9 *disagreeing*
disharmoniously 517.12 *dissonantly*; 751.11 *in disagreement*
disharmony 751.1 *disagreement*; 408.1 *disorder*; 242.7 *dissension*; 517.1 *dissonance*
dishcloth 256.11 *cleaning cloth*
dishcloth gourd 256.10 *cleaning object*
dishclout 256.11 *cleaning cloth*
dishearten 602.10 *depress*; 604.6 *disappoint*; 481.5 *discourage*
disheartened 604.9 *disappointed*; 481.10 *dissuaded*; 602.5 *sad*
disheartening 481.9 *dissuasive*
dishearteningly 481.11 *dissuasively*
disheartenment 481.7 *deterrence*
dished 357.15 *destroyed*
dishevel 408.24 *make disordered*
dishevelled 408.15 *untidy*
dishevelment 408.3 *untidiness*
dish of the day 25.9 *dish*; 139.9 *special*
dishonest 236.3 *bad*; 645.4 *cunning*; 700.34 *deceiving*; 604.12, 700.35 *deceptive*; 800.5 *dishonourable*; 699.29 *false*; 699.35, 774.18 *fraudulent*; 702.10 *hypocritical*; 796.11, 802.15 *immoral*; 16.60 *offending*; 453.7 *unreliable*; 804.11 *wicked*
dishonestly 16.83; 645.6 *cunningly*; 800.11 *dishonourably*; 699.40 *falsely*; 702.15 *hypocritically*; 802.28 *immorally*; 774.19 *thievishly*; 453.26 *unreliably*; 804.18 *wickedly*
dishonest person 774.11; 800.4 *dishonourable person*
dishonest politician 351.3 *abuser*
dishonesty 774.7; 236.9 *badness*; 700.1 *deception*; 736.5 *evasion*; 699.1 *falsehood*; 699.8, 700.10 *fraud*; 796.1 *immorality*; 800.1 *improbity*; 16.38 *lawbreaking*; 804.1 *wickedness*
Dishonour 800
dishonour 802.9; 812.4 *bring into disrepute*; 796.19 *corrupt*; 678.12 *defame*; 668.2 *disesteem*; 668.21 *disregard*; 812.1 *disrespect*; 800.1 *improbity*; 754.3 *irresolution*
dishonourable 800.5; 668.12 *disregardful*; 812.4 *disreputable*; 802.15 *immoral*; 754.7 *irresolute*
dishonourable discharge 708.6 *termination*
dishonourable person 800.4
dishonourably 800.11; 754.9 *irresolutely*
dishonour a cheque 786.8 *stop payment*
dishonoured 754.7 *irresolute*
dishonoured cheque 786.3 *bad payment*
dish out 770.4 *allot*; 768.5 *give*; 436.5 *provision*; 785.11 *remunerate*
dishrag 256.11 *cleaning cloth*
dish up 436.5 *provision*
dishware 410.16 *crockery*
dishwasher 410.3 *cabinet*; 256.12 *cleaner*; 401.6 *domestic servant*; 256.7 *washer*
dishwashing liquid 255.3 *purifier*
dishwater 258.5 *swill*; 497.3 *tasteless items*; 337.5 *weak thing*
dishy 363.9 *attractive*
disillusion 604.2 *bad outcome*; 604.6 *disappoint*; 481.5 *discourage*; 606.6 *dissatisfy*; 247.6 *fail*; 693.11 *inform*
disillusioned 604.9 *disappointed*; 596.8 *disliking*; 606.4 *dissatisfied*; 481.10 *dissuaded*
disillusionment 604.2 *bad outcome*; 606.1 *dissatisfaction*
disincarnate 101.12 *enter a nonmaterial world*
disincarnated 101.8 *nonmaterial*
disincarnation 101.2 *unworldliness*
disincentive 481.7 *deterrence*
disinclination 481.7 *deterrence*; 596.1 *dislike*; 637.11 *unwillingness*
disincline 596.7 *cause dislike*; 481.4 *put off*
disinclined 596.8 *disliking*; 637.1 *unwilling*
disinfect 256.13 *clean*; 501.5 *deodorize*; 394.20 *doctor*; 257.6 *make hygienic*; 252.10 *protect*; 255.10, 256.15 *purify*
disinfectant 256.9 *cleaning agent*; 256.18 *cleansing*; 37.14 *counteracting*; 501.2 *deodorant*; 501.4 *deodorizing*; 37.4 *drug type*; 394.3 *prophylactic*; 255.3 *purifier*; 255.15 *purifying*; 394.17 *remedial*; 252.8 *tutelary*
disinfected 256.17 *cleaned*; 257.4 *hygienic*; 501.3 *odourless*; 255.14 *purified*; 252.6 *safe*
disinfection 256.2 *cleaning*; 257.1 *hygiene*; 394.3 *prophylactic*; 255.2 *purification*
disinfestation 256.2 *cleaning*; 255.2 *purification*
disinflation 13.2 *economy*; 14.1, 780.7 *finance*
disinflationary 14.6 *financial*
disinform 718.5 *misinform*
disinformation 234.4 *distortion of the truth*; 736.5 *evasion*; 718.2 *misinformation*; 702.2 *sophism*
disingenuous 645.4 *cunning*; 800.5 *dishonourable*; 699.31, 702.10 *hypocritical*
disingenuously 702.15 *hypocritically*
disingenuousness 699.3, 702.5 *hypocrisy*; 800.1 *improbity*
disinherit 767.9 *dispose of*; 782.14 *impoverish*; 218.7 *make insufficient*; 773.8 *take back*
disinheritance 782.6 *insolvency*; 773.2 *taking back*
disinherited 767.12 *disposed*; 782.2 *insolvent*
disintegrate 375.3; 424.4 *be brittle*; 357.13 *be destroyed*; 408.25 *be disordered*; 427.27 *come to dust*; 245.1 *deteriorate*; 377.11 *explode*; 427.22 *pulverize*; 372.9 *separate*
disintegrated 375.5; 357.15 *destroyed*; 427.18 *pulverized*; 377.20 *separated*
disintegrating 375.6
Disintegration 375
disintegration 375.1; 357.2 *destroying*; 245.9 *dilapidation*; 408.1 *disorder*; 377.5 *divergence*; 28.71 *nuclear reaction*; 427.4 *pulverization*; 372.1 *separation*
disintegration of personality 36.16 *dissociation*
disinter 449.2 *detect*; 369.13 *dig out*; 739.5 *disclose*; 583.9 *exhume*
disinterest 473.1 *disinterestedness*; 618.3 *impartiality*
disinterested 473.4; 620.5 *bored*; 150.3 *broad-minded*; 618.9 *impartial*; 618.7 *indifferent*; 801.7 *right*; 623.5 *submissive*; 803.5 *virtuous*
disinterestedly 473.8; 618.17 *indifferently*
Disinterestedness 473
disinterestedness 473.1; 618.1 *indifference*; 623.12 *submissiveness*; 803.1 *virtue*
disinterment 369.3 *digging out*; 583.7 *inquest*
disinvest 787.1 *expend*
disinvestment 787.6 *extravagance*
disinvolve 265.18 *disentangle*
disinvolvement 265.8 *disentanglement*
disiplinary 15.9 *negotiated*
disjecta membra 205.8 *bits and pieces*
disjoin 133.14 *disconnect*; 372.9 *separate*
disjoint 144.18 *disconnect*
disjointed 144.12 *disconnected*; 133.8 *discontinuous*; 408.12 *disordered*; 372.15 *separate*
disjointedly 133.18, 144.21 *disconnectedly*
disjointedness 144.5 *disconnection*; 133.1 *discontinuity*
disjoint sets 27.21 *set*
disjunct 109.6 *unrelated*
disjunction 133.1 *discontinuity*; 408.1 *disorder*; 27.63 *mathematical logic*; 4.8 *philosophical term*; 372.1 *separation*
disjunctive 372.15 *separate*
disjunctively 372.20 *separately*
disjuncture 372.1 *separation*; 109.1 *unrelatedness*
disk 40.7 *peripheral*; 744.6 *record book*
diskette 40.7 *peripheral*
Diskman™ 40.6 *memory*
disk pack 40.7 *peripheral*
disk reader 40.7 *peripheral*
disk sander 23.11 *woodworking tool*
dislikable 596.9 *disliked*
Dislike 596
dislike 596.1; **596.5**; 590.6 *bad feeling*; 113.17 *be against*; 606.7 *be dissatisfied*; 620.1 *boredom*; 670.1 *disapproval*; 670.14 *disapprove*; 606.1 *dissatisfaction*; 594.1, 594.14 *hate*; 113.1 *opposition*; 620.7 *suffer boredom*; 637.11 *unwillingness*
disliked 596.9; 620.4 *boring*; 594.12 *hated*; 242.1 *unpleasant*
disliked person 596.3
disliked thing 596.2
disliking 596.8
dislocate 144.18 *disconnect*; 328.9 *disperse*; 144.14 *displace*; 372.9 *separate*; 380.8 *use violence*
dislocate circle 57.7 *stationary rings*
dislocated 144.12 *disconnected*; 408.12 *disordered*; 328.14 *dispersed*; 144.8 *displaced*; 57.11 *gymnastic*; 372.15 *separate*
dislocated grip 57.5 *horizontal bar*
dislocation 144.5 *disconnection*; 328.3 *dispersion*; 144.1 *displacement*; 245.11 *hurt*; 380.3 *instance of violence*; 372.1 *separation*
dislocation metamorphism 30.32 *metamorphism*
dislodge 328.9 *disperse*; 144.14, 369.12 *displace*; 371.8 *evict*; 316.15 *take away*
dislodged 369.19; 328.14 *dispersed*; 144.8 *displaced*
dislodgment 328.3 *dispersion*; 144.1, 369.2 *displacement*; 371.20 *eviction*
disloyal 662.13 *disobedient*; 479.11 *equivocating*; 800.6 *faithless*; 227.14 *irresolute*
disloyal friend 479.9 *equivocator*
disloyally 227.15 *changeably*; 800.11 *dishonourably*; 662.17 *disobediently*; 479.13 *perfidiously*
disloyalty 662.1 *disobedience*; 800.2 *faithlessness*; 227.2 *irresolution*; 247.3 *personal fault*
dismal 523.11 *benighted*; 602.6 *depressed*; 626.8 *overcast*; 626.6 *sullen*
dismally 602.12 *joylessly*; 626.13 *sullenly*
dismantle 375.4 *deconstruct*; 357.9 *demolish*; 245.4 *impair*; 343.14 *make inactive*; 238.8 *make useless*; 205.10 *part*; 372.9 *separate*; 350.6 *stop using*
dismantling 375.2 *deconstruction*
dismast 245.4 *impair*; 238.8 *make useless*
dismay 612.2 *fearfulness*; 612.13 *frighten*
dismaying 612.10 *frightening*
dismember 375.4 *deconstruct*; 144.18 *disconnect*; 372.11 *divide*; 814.5 *execute*
dismembered 144.12 *disconnected*; 372.15 *separate*
dismemberment 375.2 *deconstruction*; 144.5 *disconnection*
dismiss 53.19; **371.2**; **377.13**; **580.5**; **767.10**; 649.10 *absolve*; 758.10 *acquit*; 618.12 *be indifferent*; 226.8 *cause to cease*; 526.3 *cause to disappear*; 15.11 *conduct industrial relations*; 470.2 *discard*; 128.8, 364.2 *eject*; 315.13 *emigrate*; 391.4 *liberate*; 343.14 *make inactive*; 704.8 *refute*; 144.17 *relegate*; 608.12 *relieve from duty*; 350.7 *stop work*; 708.15 *terminate*; 714.7 *vindicate*
dismissal 53.11; **371.18**; 377.2 *disbandment*; 470.6 *discarding*; 767.1 *disposal*; 350.10 *disuse*; 128.2 *ejection*; 315.4 *emigration*; 10.6 *Eucharist*; 15.2 *industrial negotiations*; 391.1 *liberation*; 313.9 *parting*; 704.1 *refutation*; 144.4 *relegation*; 364.6 *repulse*; 226.2 *stop*; 708.6 *termination*; 580.3 *unemployment*; 714.1 *vindication*
dismiss charges 16.78 *acquit*
dismissed 767.13; 377.21 *disbanded*; 128.11 *excluded*; 714.12 *innocent*; 580.7 *leisurely*; 15.9 *negotiated*; 350.3 *not wanted*; 470.10 *rejected*; 144.11 *relegated*
dismiss from one's thoughts 649.9 *forgive*
dismissive 364.10 *defensive*
dismissively 364.12 *defensively*; 704.11 *in reply*
dismiss out of hand 470.1 *reject*
dismount 305.9 *descend*; 312.4 *land*; 372.9 *separate*
Disneyland 619.4 *wonder*
Disobedience 662
disobedience 637.14; **661.2**; **662.1**; 588.1 *anarchy*; 113.7 *contrariness*; 118.2 *dissent*; 800.2 *faithlessness*; 408.8 *lawlessness*; 641.5 *obstinacy*; 753.1 *protest*; 708.2 *rejection*; 804.1 *wickedness*
disobedient 662.13; 588.6 *anarchic*; 661.8 *defying*; 408.20 *disorderly*; 800.6 *faithless*; 753.9 *protesting*; 641.2 *refractory*; 264.14 *troublesome*; 113.26 *uncooperative*; 804.11 *wicked*
disobediently 662.17; 588.8 *anarchically*; 753.11 *disapprovingly*; 800.11 *dishonourably*; 661.10 *in defiance*; 264.29 *perversely*; 804.18 *wickedly*
disobey 588.4 *be anarchic*; 662.15 *be disobedient*; 408.26 *be disorderly*; 661.6 *be insubordinate*; 708.10 *be negative*; 118.20 *infringe a law*; 753.6 *protest*; 113.20 *withstand*
disobeyed 708.18 *rejected*
disobeying 662.13 *disobedient*
disoblige 651.16 *be malevolent*
disobliging 651.15 *inconsiderate*
Disorder 408

disorder 161.4; **408.1**; **408.9**; **408.21**; **753.2**; 588.1 *anarchy*; 328.5 *commotion*; 375.4 *deconstruct*; 328.8 *disarrange*; 328.2 *disarrangement*; 133.1 *discontinuity*; 375.1 *disintegration*; 144.14 *displace*; 114.1 *diversity*; 260.2 *illness*; 299.1 *irregularity*; 408.8 *lawlessness*; 412.1 *mixture*; 236.10 *poverty*; 327.2 *tumult*; 662.2 *violation of the law*
disordered 408.12; 328.16 *deranged*; 328.13 *disarranged*; 260.23 *diseased*; 375.5 *disintegrated*; 299.4 *irregular*; 412.12 *mixed*; 236.4 *poor*
disordered personality 36.8
disorderliness 408.1 *disorder*
disorderly 408.20; 588.6 *anarchic*; 675.8 *discourteous*; 662.13 *disobedient*; 299.4 *irregular*; 507.6 *loud*
disorderly behaviour 408.8 *lawlessness*
disorderly house 796.6 *brothel*
disorganization 588.1 *anarchy*; 328.2 *disarrangement*; 408.1 *disorder*; 245.10 *impairment*
disorganize 328.8 *disarrange*; 408.21 *disorder*; 144.14 *displace*; 245.4 *impair*
disorganized 588.6 *anarchic*; 408.16 *confused*; 328.13 *disarranged*; 408.12 *disordered*
disorient 408.22 *discompose*; 328.9 *disperse*
disorientated 328.14 *dispersed*
disorientation 325.13 *deviation*; 328.3 *dispersion*
disoriented 766.18 *at a loss*
disown 634.7 *be evasive*; 708.10 *be negative*; 109.11 *be unconcerned*; 704.9 *deny*; 767.9 *dispose of*
disowned 767.12 *disposed*; 708.18 *rejected*
disowning 704.7 *refuting*
disownment 704.2 *denial*; 708.2 *rejection*
disparage 678.10; 512.5 *catcall*; 381.10, 670.17 *criticize*; 124.13 *make unimportant*; 668.20 *scorn*; 468.3 *underestimate*
disparaged 668.18 *undervalued*
disparagement 678.1; 660.6 *contempt*; 381.16 *personal attack*
disparager 678.7
disparaging 678.15; 660.17 *contemptuous*; 381.25, 670.27 *critical*; 468.4 *underestimating*
disparagingly 678.18; 660.34 *contemptuously*; 468.6 *pessimistically*
disparaging remark 678.4 *aspersion*
disparate 116.4 *dissimilar*; 120.3 *unequal*
disparately 116.7 *dissimilarly*; 120.7 *unequally*
disparity 113.8 *contrariety*; 751.3 *difference*; 116.1 *dissimilarity*; 109.4 *distortion*; 120.1 *inequality*; 118.1 *nonconformity*
dispassion 4.3 *detachment*; 473.1 *disinterestedness*; 618.1 *indifference*
dispassionate 4.18 *detached*; 473.4 *disinterested*; 618.7 *indifferent*; 464.9 *judicious*
dispassionately 473.8 *disinterestedly*; 618.17 *indifferently*; 4.27 *stoically*
dispatch 340.4 *act*; 340.1 *action*; 293.7 *be early*; 631.14 *behave towards*; 693.2 *communication*; 692.31 *correspond*; 357.8 *destroy*; 293.1 *earliness*; 557.22 *eat well*; 382.5 *execution*; 768.5 *give*; 262.4 *haste*; 262.1 *hasten*; 382.16 *kill*; 342.3 *nimbleness*; 741.13 *report*; 733.10 *send*; 300.14 *set in motion*; 332.8 *speed*; 316.12, 319.4 *transport*; 316.2 *transportation*; 342.15 *try*
dispatch box 410.6 *box*; 692.3 *correspondence*
dispatch rider 320.9 *animal transport*
dispel 526.3 *cause to disappear*; 357.8 *destroy*; 377.12 *disperse*; 371.10 *exterminate*; 581.1 *refresh*; 372.9 *separate*
dispensability 124.5 *unimportance*; 238.3 *uselessness*
dispensable 124.1 *unimportant*; 238.1 *useless*; 714.13 *vindicable*
dispensary 35.10, 394.14 *hospital*
dispensation 770.1 *allocation*; 390.2 *deliverance*; 377.1 *dispersion*; 767.1 *disposal*; 128.1 *exclusion*; 758.1 *exemption*; 649.1 *forgiveness*; 757.1 *permission*; 750.8 *permit*
dispense 770.4 *allot*; 377.16 *distribute*; 768.5 *give*
dispensed 377.22 *distributed*
dispensed with 767.12 *disposed*; 350.3 *not wanted*
dispenser 394.16 *druggist*; 37.2 *pharmacologist*
dispense with 390.1 *deliver*; 767.9 *dispose of*; 128.8 *eject*; 350.5 *not use*
dispensing 770.1 *allocation*
dispeople 371.9 *depopulate*
Dispersal 377
dispersal 375.2 *deconstruction*; 526.4 *disappearance*; 377.1 *dispersion*; 372.1 *separation*; 316.3 *transmission*
disperse 328.9; **377.12**; 190.6 *become bigger*; 377.9 *be dispersed*; 316.14 *bring back*; 138.25 *broadcast*; 526.3 *cause to disappear*; 375.4 *deconstruct*; 325.12 *deflect*; 357.8 *destroy*; 408.21 *disorder*; 372.13 *diverge*; 190.5 *make bigger*; 311.13 *radiate*; 206.9 *scatter*; 372.9 *separate*; 300.14 *set in motion*; 32.32 *solid*; 32.25 *solidify*; 367.6 *throw down*; 316.11 *transfer*; 441.1 *waste*
dispersed 328.14; **377.19**; 372.16 *apart*; 190.7 *bigger*; 325.26 *diffractive*; 526.7 *disappeared*; 206.6 *sparse*
dispersed population 377.7 *sprawl*
disperse phase 32.3 *phase*
disperser 190.4 *enlarger*
dispersion 328.3; **377.1**; 325.18 *diffraction*; 526.4 *disappearance*; 145.1 *distance*; 190.1 *growth*; 27.60 *parameter*; 311.3 *radiation*; 372.1 *separation*; 316.3 *transmission*; 441.3 *waste*; 28.15 *wave property*
dispersion force 32.11 *chemical bond*
dispersive 377.28; 190.9 *enlargeable*
dispersively 377.29
dispirit 602.10 *depress*; 481.5 *discourage*
dispirited 602.6 *depressed*; 618.7 *indifferent*; 623.4 *self-abasing*
dispiritedly 618.17 *indifferently*
dispiritedness 602.2 *depression*; 618.1 *indifference*
dispiriting 602.7 *distressing*
displace 144.14; **369.12**; 762.4 *be a substitute*; 328.9 *disperse*; 224.10 *exchange*; 655.13 *ignore*; 372.9 *separate*; 300.14 *set in motion*; 316.15 *take away*; 371.5 *take the place of*
displaceable 316.17 *transferable*
displaced 144.8; 369.19 *dislodged*; 408.12 *disordered*; 328.14 *dispersed*; 118.15 *irregular*; 655.10 *lonely*
displaced person 144.7; 634.17 *avoider*; 100.7 *new arrival*; 655.7 *outsider*; 109.3 *unconnected person*
Displacement 144
displacement 144.1; **369.2**; **414.6**; 156.6 *bathymetry*; 32.14 *chemical reaction*; 36.19 *defence mechanism*; 328.3 *dispersion*; 28.54, 39.11 *electric field*; 224.4 *exchange*; 158.1 *size*; 316.1 *transfer*
displacement activity 342.9 *overactivity*
displacement board 50.7 *windsurfing*
displacement current 28.51 *electric current*
displacement sailing 50.7 *windsurfing*
displacer 371.26 *ejector*
Display 738
display 738.1; **738.6**; 409.12 *arrange*; 409.2 *array*; 525.2 *being in view*; 40.19 *computing terms*; 703.15 *demonstrate*; 703.1 *demonstration*; 376.31 *exhibition*; 518.18, 520.10 *make visible*; 520.5 *manifestation*; 622.9 *ostentation*; 525.14 *present*; 740.8 *public relations*; 692.28 *radar*; 167.3 *show*; 518.7 *view*
display bad manners 659.7 *be discourteous*
display board 740.9 *advertisement*
display cabinet 738.8 *showplace*
display case 738.8 *showplace*; 527.8 *transparent thing*
displayed 738.13; 525.7 *appearing*; 703.9 *demonstrated*; 167.3 *outward*
displayer 738.12
display hauteur 622.28 *disdain*
display of disapproval 670.9 *show of disapproval*
display one's skill 485.11 *be expert*
display something 738.2
display the flag 585.12 *go to war*
displease 242.10; 596.7 *cause dislike*; 606.6 *dissatisfy*
displeased 670.25 *disapproving*; 596.8 *disliking*; 606.4 *dissatisfied*; 624.15 *resentful*
displeasing 242.1 *unpleasant*
displeasure 670.1 *disapproval*; 596.1 *dislike*; 606.1 *dissatisfaction*; 594.1 *hate*; 624.1 *resentment*
displume 371.3 *disbar*
displuming 371.18 *dismissal*
disposability 767.1 *disposal*; 767.2 *disposal of property*; 238.3 *uselessness*
disposable 375.5 *disintegrated*; 238.6 *refuse*; 349.10 *usable*; 237.1 *useful*; 238.1 *useless*
disposable camera 41.16 *camera*
disposable lenses 518.10 *visual aid*
disposable things 767.3
disposably 767.16
Disposal 767
disposal 767.1; 409.1 *arrangement*; 350.10 *disuse*; 778.3 *selling*; 349.6 *use*
disposal of property 767.2
disposal of the dead 583.1 *burial*
dispose 409.12 *arrange*; 137.13 *class*; 395.8 *influence*; 483.9 *motivate*; 407.18 *order*; 480.15 *persuade*; 324.7 *take a direction*
disposed 767.12; 409.20 *arranged*; 482.11 *intending*; 595.6 *liking*; 407.10 *ordered*; 635.6 *willed*; 636.1 *willing*
dispose of 349.5; **767.9**; 131.16 *cease*; 357.8 *destroy*; 704.8 *refute*; 778.1 *sell*
dispose of property 767.11
disposition 409.1 *arrangement*; 229.2 *attitude*; 595.2 *inclination*; 99.4 *nature*; 407.1 *order*; 674.4 *shyness*; 221.4 *state of mind*; 599.8 *temperament*; 635.1 *will*
dispossess 371.8 *evict*; 782.14 *impoverish*; 766.9 *lose*; 608.14 *take away*; 773.8 *take back*
dispossessed 782.2 *insolvent*
dispossession 371.20 *eviction*; 782.6 *insolvency*; 766.1 *loss*; 773.2 *taking back*
dispossessor 371.26 *ejector*
dispraise 670.5 *criticism*; 670.17, 678.11 *criticize*
dispraised 670.33 *criticized*
dispraising 670.27 *critical*
disproof 16.7 *legal trial*; 708.3 *rebuttal*; 704.1 *refutation*
disproportion 120.5 *be unequal*; 234.9 *distort*; 109.4, 234.1 *distortion*; 120.1 *inequality*; 408.2 *irregular order*
disproportionate 109.8, 234.6 *distorted*; 219.6 *excessive*; 408.14 *irregular*; 120.3 *unequal*
disproportionately 109.13; 234.13 *asymmetrically*; 120.7 *unequally*
disproportionation 32.14 *chemical reaction*
disproportioned 120.3 *unequal*
disprovability 704.4 *refutability*
disprovable 704.6 *refutable*
disprovably 704.12 *refutably*
disproval 704.1 *refutation*
disprove 708.11 *rebut*; 704.8 *refute*; 27.89 *theorize*
disproved 708.18 *rejected*
disproving 708.3 *rebuttal*; 704.7 *refuting*
disputability 453.9 *uncertainty*
disputable 701.10 *arguable*; 451.7 *disbelieved*; 16.54 *litigated*; 705.14 *questionable*; 453.1 *uncertain*
disputably 705.24 *questionably*; 451.11 *unbelievably*; 453.23 *uncertainly*
disputant 444.6, 701.6 *arguer*; 113.11 *opposer*
disputation 444.3 *debate*; 701.2 *logical argument*; 113.4 *objection*; 4.5 *philosophical argument*
disputatious 381.21 *aggressive*; 701.8 *argumentative*; 625.4 *irascible*; 16.52 *legalistic*
disputatiousness 625.1 *irascibility*
dispute 586.40, 701.13, 751.6 *argue*; 701.1, 751.2 *argument*; 264.7 *awkward situation*; 585.14 *battle*; 625.6 *be irascible*; 453.18 *be uncertain*; 444.3, 444.13 *debate*; 704.9 *deny*; 451.8 *disbelieve*; 4.23 *discuss philosophically*; 705.20 *doubt*; 16.5 *litigation*; 113.18 *object*
disputed 16.54 *litigated*
disputed area 751.1 *disagreement*
disputedly 701.18 *arguably*; 704.12 *refutably*
disputer 586.5, 701.6 *arguer*; 751.4 *dissenter*
disputes procedure 15.4 *industrial dispute*
disputing 444.9 *argumentative*; 751.9 *disagreeing*; 16.53 *litigating*
disqualification 371.18 *dismissal*; 128.2 *ejection*; 766.1 *loss*; 335.1 *powerlessness*; 47.1 *track events*; 486.8 *unskilfulness*
disqualified 335.10 *powerless*; 486.1 *unskilful*
disqualified athlete 766.6 *loser*
disqualify 371.3 *disbar*; 128.8 *eject*; 103.8 *make impossible*; 238.8 *make useless*; 335.7 *remove power from*
disquiet 327.22 *agitate*; 327.1 *agitation*; 328.7 *disturb*; 328.1 *disturbance*; 612.2 *fearfulness*; 227.2 *irresolution*
disquieted 328.12 *disturbed*; 612.8 *fearful*
disquietingly 328.18 *disturbingly*
disquietude 327.1 *agitation*
disquisition 733.1 *address*; 270.1 *diffuseness*; 722.1 *dissertation*
disquisitional 722.5 *expository*
disregard 668.21; 519.16 *be blind to*; 618.14 *be careless*; 472.12 *be inattentive*; 618.12 *be indifferent*; 661.6 *be insubordinate*; 666.6 *be neglectful*; 472.13 *be thoughtless*; 618.2 *carelessness*; 649.11 *condone*; 668.2 *disesteem*; 661.2 *disobedience*; 728.9 *downplaying*; 128.7 *exclude*; 519.7 *figurative blindness*; 649.2 *forgivingness*; 472.1 *inattention*; 666.1 *negligence*; 341.4 *not act*; 350.5 *not use*; 728.22 *play down*; 470.1 *reject*; 388.3 *submit*; 124.12 *think unimportant*; 472.4 *thoughtlessness*; 463.4 *unthinkingness*
disregarded 728.19 *downplayed*; 128.11 *excluded*; 124.2 *obscure*; 649.8 *overlooked*; 668.18 *undervalued*
disregardful 668.12; 666.4 *negligent*
disregarding 618.8 *careless*; 472.7 *inattentive*; 463.10 *unthinking*
disrelated 100.8 *extraneous*; 109.6 *unrelated*
disrelish 596.1, 596.5 *dislike*; 594.14 *hate*
disrepair 245.9 *dilapidation*
disreputability 812.1 *disrespect*; 236.10 *poverty*
disreputable 812.4; 800.5 *dishonourable*; 668.12 *disregardful*; 236.4 *poor*; 804.11 *wicked*
disreputable action 812.3
disreputable character 812.2
disreputably 594.18 *hatefully*; 804.18 *wickedly*
disrepute 623.13; 668.2 *disesteem*; 670.2 *disrespect*; 594.4 *hatefulness*; 800.1 *improbity*; 804.1 *wickedness*
Disrespect 668
disrespect 668.1; **668.19**; **670.2**; **812.1**; 800.1 *improbity*; 660.11 *sauciness*
disrespected 668.17 *unrespected*
disrespectful 668.10; 670.25 *disapproving*; 659.5, 660.20 *discourteous*; 800.5 *dishonourable*; 660.19 *rude*; 655.8 *unsociable*
disrespectfully 668.28; 660.36 *discourteously*; 800.11 *dishonourably*; 659.10, 660.35 *rudely*; 655.14 *unsocially*
disrespectfulness 660.9 *discourtesy*; 668.1 *disrespect*; 660.8 *rudeness*
disrobe 552.15 *make nude*; 552.14 *undress*
disrobed 552.9 *undressed*
disrobement 552.1 *undress*
disrober 552.8 *nude person*
disrobing 552.1 *undress*
disrupt 328.10; 588.4 *be anarchic*; 240.5 *be inconvenient*; 264.23 *cause difficulties*; 408.21 *disorder*; 144.14 *displace*; 133.16 *interrupt*; 288.6 *take untimely action*
disrupted 328.15; 408.12 *disordered*; 133.10 *interrupted*
disrupting 240.1 *inconvenient*; 288.13 *untimely*
disruption 328.4; 588.1 *anarchy*; 357.2 *destroying*; 408.1, 408.9 *disorder*; 240.3 *inconvenience*; 133.6 *intervention*; 372.1 *separation*; 288.2 *untimeliness*
disruptive 408.20 *disorderly*; 328.17 *disturbing*; 240.1 *inconvenient*; 264.14 *troublesome*
disruptive discharge 39.6 *electric discharge*
disruptively 288.19 *at the wrong time*; 328.18 *disturbingly*; 240.6 *inconveniently*; 264.29 *perversely*; 408.29 *riotously*
disruptiveness 408.8 *lawlessness*
disruptive pupil 264.9 *difficult person*
Dissatisfaction 606
dissatisfaction 606.1; 604.2 *bad outcome*; 620.1 *boredom*; 497.1 *dilution*; 670.1 *disapproval*; 596.1 *dislike*; 233.1 *incompleteness*; 626.3 *irritableness*; 753.1 *protest*; 624.1 *resentment*
dissatisfactory 606.5 *unsatisfactory*
dissatisfied 606.4; 620.5 *bored*; 604.9

disappointed; 670.25 *disapproving*; 596.8 *disliking*; 626.7 *irritable*; 753.9 *protesting*
dissatisfied customer 606.3 *dissatisfied person*; 753.4 *protester*
dissatisfied person 606.3
dissatisfy 606.6; 620.6 *be boring*; 231.9 *be imperfect*; 604.6 *disappoint*; 626.12 *make irritable*
dissave 787.1 *expend*
dissaving 787.6 *extravagance*
dissect 375.4 *deconstruct*; 372.11 *divide*; 205.10 *part*
dissection 34.4 *anatomy*; 375.2 *deconstruction*; 372.1 *separation*
dissemblance 189.3 *deviousness*; 699.14 *façade*; 699.1 *falsehood*
dissemble 340.4 *act*; 479.1 *be equivocal*; 699.20 *be false*; 702.12, 736.9 *deceive*; 189.7 *deviate*; 116.6 *differentiate*; 234.12 *distort the truth*; 699.28 *mask*; 699.24 *pretend*; 800.9 *prove false*
dissembled 699.39 *disguised*
dissembler 736.7 *concealer*; 645.3 *cunning person*; 718.3 *deceiver*
dissembling 189.5 *devious*; 699.29 *false*; 702.10 *hypocritical*; 699.34 *pretending*
disseminate 138.25 *broadcast*; 693.12 *communicate*; 377.16 *distribute*; 740.13 *make public*; 316.11 *transfer*
disseminated 377.22 *distributed*; 740.19 *published*
disseminated sclerosis 260.17 *nervous disorder*
dissemination 693.2 *communication*; 377.1 *dispersion*; 740.1 *publication*; 316.3 *transmission*
disseminative 377.28 *dispersive*
disseminatively 377.29 *dispersively*
dissension 114.4; **242.7**; 113.5 *conflict*; 517.6, 670.4, 751.1 *disagreement*; 662.1 *disobedience*; 372.4 *disunity*
dissent 114.9; **118.2**; **709.2**; **709.6**; 701.13 *argue*; 662.15 *be disobedient*; 661.6 *be insubordinate*; 637.6 *be unwilling*; 444.3, 444.13 *debate*; 372.12, 751.5 *disagree*; 517.6, 751.1 *disagreement*; 451.1 *disbelief*; 451.8 *disbelieve*; 4.23 *discuss philosophically*; 596.1, 596.5 *dislike*; 661.2 *disobedience*; 705.20 *doubt*; 118.18 *not conform*; 637.9 *not cooperate*; 113.18 *object*; 113.4 *objection*; 703.19, 753.1, 753.6 *protest*; 242.11 *quarrel*; 708.11 *rebut*; 708.3 *rebuttal*; 383.6 *resist*; 383.1 *resistance*
dissenter 118.8; **751.4**; 325.19 *deviant person*; 451.5 *disbeliever*; 708.9 *negativist*; 113.11 *opposer*; 703.8, 753.4 *protester*; 705.9 *questioner*; 637.16 *reluctant person*
dissentient 701.7 *arguing*; 751.9 *disagreeing*; 113.24 *discordant*; 118.8, 751.4 *dissenter*; 118.12 *nonconformist*; 113.11 *opposer*; 753.4 *protester*
dissenting 114.7; **709.9**; 701.7 *arguing*; 444.9 *argumentative*; 703.14 *demonstrating*; 372.18 *disagreeable*; 670.26, 751.9 *disagreeing*; 451.6 *disbelieving*; 113.24 *discordant*; 596.8 *disliking*; 662.13 *disobedient*; 250.10 *independent*; 118.12 *nonconformist*; 753.9 *protesting*; 708.19 *rebutting*; 637.2 *refusing*; 637.5 *reluctant*; 383.10 *resistant*
dissentingly 662.17 *disobediently*; 114.10 *diversely*; 751.11 *in disagreement*; 708.22 *negatively*; 383.14 *resistingly*; 709.11 *uncooperatively*
dissentious 701.8 *argumentative*
dissertate 722.4
dissertation 722.1; 270.1 *diffuseness*; 464.1 *judgment*; 17.4 *nonfiction*; 729.8 *speech*
dissertator 722.3
disservice 651.7 *act of malevolence*; 238.3 *uselessness*
dissidence 751.1 *disagreement*; 118.2, 709.2 *dissent*; 113.4 *objection*
dissident 325.19 *deviant person*; 751.9 *disagreeing*; 451.5 *disbeliever*; 113.24 *discordant*; 118.8, 751.4 *dissenter*; 709.9 *dissenting*; 118.12 *nonconformist*; 113.11 *opposer*; 662.7, 703.8, 753.4 *protester*; 709.4 *refuser*; 637.2 *refusing*; 637.16 *reluctant person*
dissidently 709.11 *uncooperatively*
dissilience 383.6 *instance of violence*
dissimilar 116.4; 751.10 *different*; 109.8 *distorted*; 114.5 *diverse*; 718.6 *misrepresented*; 120.3 *unequal*
Dissimilarity 116
dissimilarity 116.1; 751.3 *difference*; 109.4 *distortion*; 114.1 *diversity*; 120.1 *inequality*; 718.1 *misrepresentation*; 126.1 *originality*
dissimilarly 116.7; 751.12 *differently*; 109.13 *disproportionately*; 114.10 *diversely*; 120.7 *unequally*
dissimilation 5.30 *syntax*
dissimilitude 116.1 *dissimilarity*
dissimulate 702.12 *deceive*; 699.28 *mask*; 699.24 *pretend*
dissimulated 699.39 *disguised*
dissimulating 702.10 *hypocritical*; 699.34 *pretending*
dissimulation 125.4 *camouflage*; 340.2 *deed*; 736.5 *evasion*; 699.14 *façade*; 699.7 *pretence*
dissimulator 718.3 *deceiver*
dissipate 766.11 *be wasteful*; 526.3 *cause to disappear*; 357.8 *destroy*; 377.14 *dilute*; 787.1 *expend*; 377.11 *explode*; 766.14 *go to waste*; 686.11 *overindulge*; 441.1, 681.7 *waste*
dissipated 686.7; 377.27 *dilute*; 526.7 *disappeared*; 796.14 *lecherous*; 337.11 *weakened*
dissipated person 766.6 *loser*
dissipating 686.7 *dissipated*
dissipation 686.2; 377.3 *dilution*; 526.4 *disappearance*; 490.1 *physical pleasure*; 337.3 *poor health*; 796.3 *sexual immorality*; 681.5 *unrestrainedness*; 441.3, 766.3 *waste*; 28.15 *wave property*
dissipative 377.28 *dispersive*
dissipatively 377.29 *dispersively*
dissociability 655.1 *unsociability*
dissociable 655.8 *unsociable*
dissociableness 655.1 *unsociability*
dissocial 655.8 *unsociable*
dissociate 32.26 *react*; 372.9 *separate*
dissociated 36.36 *psychologically disturbed*; 100.11 *separate*
dissociate oneself 708.10 *be negative*; 637.9 *not cooperate*
dissociate oneself from 113.17 *be against*
dissociation 36.16; **637.13**; 708.2 *rejection*; 100.3 *separateness*; 113.6 *uncooperativeness*
dissociation energy 32.11 *chemical bond*
dissociation of personality 36.16 *dissociation*
dissociation reaction 36.10 *neurosis*
dissociative 708.17 *negative*
dissociative hysteria 36.12 *stress*
dissoluble 431.21 *liquefiable*; 372.19 *separable*
dissolute 686.7 *dissipated*; 796.14 *lecherous*
dissoluteness 686.2 *dissipation*; 796.3 *sexual immorality*
dissolution 131.4 *annihilation*; 375.2 *deconstruction*; 357.2 *destroying*; 526.4 *disappearance*; 377.2 *disbandment*; 767.1 *disposal*; 431.8 *fluidification*; 372.1 *separation*
dissolutional 431.20 *liquefying*
dissolution of marriage 571.1 *divorce*
dissolvable 431.21 *liquefiable*; 372.19 *separable*
dissolve 431.23; 94.12 *cease to exist*; 209.6 *change gradually*; 375.4 *deconstruct*; 357.8 *destroy*; 377.14, 433.30 *dilute*; 526.1 *disappear*; 377.13 *dismiss*; 767.9 *dispose of*; 131.17 *kill*; 372.9 *separate*; 32.25 *solidify*
dissolved 131.23 *annihilated*; 377.21 *disbanded*; 375.5 *disintegrated*; 571.11 *divorced*; 431.19 *liquefied*; 412.12 *mixed*
dissolve into 760.7 *convert into*
dissolve into chaos 408.25 *be disordered*
dissolvent 431.9 *solvent*
dissolve one's marriage 571.7 *divorce*
dissolver 431.9 *solvent*
dissolving 526.6 *disappearing*; 431.8 *fluidification*; 431.20 *liquefying*
dissolving agent 431.9 *solvent*
Dissonance 517
dissonance 517.1; 507.1 *loudness*; 513.1 *stridency*
dissonant 517.7; 513.7 *strident*
dissonant chord 517.3 *musical dissonance*
dissonantly 517.12
dissonant noise 517.2
dissuade 481.1; 713.5 *advise*; 378.8 *hinder*; 711.5 *warn*
dissuaded 481.10
Dissuasion 481
dissuasion 481.6; 378.1 *hindrance*; 711.1 *warning*
dissuasive 481.9; 713.7 *advising*; 378.13 *hindering*; 711.8 *warning*
dissuasively 481.11; 378.16 *with delay*
distaff 307.4 *axle*; 193.3 *weaving*
distaff side 568.13 *womenfolk*
distal 145.8 *distant*
Distance 145
distance 145.1; **240.4**; 634.10 *avoidance*; 146.1 *interval*; 141.8 *intervening space*; 148.4 *length*; 302.9 *maintain progress*; 524.2 *murk*; 26.4 *size*; 521.6 *that which makes invisible*; 655.1 *unsociability*
distance between 146.1 *interval*
distance event 55.1 *angling*
distance learning 6.2 *educational system*
distance onself 145.6 *keep away*
distant 145.8; **240.2**; 355.6 *apathetic*; 521.2 *difficult to see*; 100.12 *external*; 511.1 *faint-sounding*; 109.7 *illogical*; 337.13 *insufficient*; 294.13 *later*; 524.6 *murky*; 622.15 *unapproachable*; 655.8 *unsociable*
distantly 145.10; 355.8 *apathetically*; 634.21 *away*; 100.18 *extraneously*; 655.14 *unsocially*
distant past 3.9; 296.3 *antiquity*
distant place 145.3
distant time 286.1 *different time*
distaste 670.1 *disapproval*; 596.1 *dislike*
distasteful 596.9 *disliked*; 546.4 *ugly*; 242.1 *unpleasant*
distastefully 242.13 *unpleasantly*
distastefulness 242.5 *unpleasantness*
distemper 19.11 *artist's materials*; 529.15 *colour*; 260.2 *illness*; 529.4 *pigment*; 260.18 *veterinary disease*
distempered 260.23 *diseased*
distend 190.6 *become bigger*; 182.5 *be convex*; 422.8 *be elastic*; 727.8 *enlarge*; 141.20 *extend*; 213.4 *increase*; 190.5 *make bigger*
distended 190.7 *bigger*; 182.4 *convex*; 422.6 *elastic*; 158.16 *fat*
distender 190.4 *enlarger*
distending 422.6 *elastic*
distensibility 190.2 *enlargeability*
distensible 422.6 *elastic*; 190.9 *enlargeable*
distension 182.1 *convexity*; 422.1 *elasticity*; 190.1 *growth*
distensive 190.9 *enlargeable*
distich 198.2 *double*; 17.9 *metre*; 17.8 *part of poem*
distil 432.25 *gasify*; 369.17 *obtain an extract*; 255.10, 256.15 *purify*; 549.6 *refine*; 32.25 *solidify*
distillate 369.8 *extract*; 99.3 *quintessence*
distillation 256.2 *cleaning*; 369.7 *obtaining an extract*; 32.5 *process*; 99.3 *quintessence*; 432.10 *vaporization*
distilled 256.17 *cleaned*; 558.17 *drinkable*; 32.32 *solid*
distilled essence 235.6 *worth*
distilled water 433.1 *water*
distillery 577.1 *workshop*
distinct 520.2, 725.3 *clear*; 185.7 *conspicuous*; 703.12 *demonstrable*; 507.7 *heard*; 123.5 *important*; 466.11 *judged*; 452.7 *particular*; 336.10 *potent*; 695.3 *recognizable*; 695.2 *simple*; 197.14 *singular*; 139.15 *special*; 27.70 *universal*; 372.17 *unjoined*; 518.23, 520.1 *visible*
distinction 137.9; 466.1 *discrimination*; 116.1 *dissimilarity*; 543.1, 549.1 *elegance*; 811.1 *estimation*; 123.1 *importance*; 464.1 *judgment*; 573.3 *nobleness*; 185.1 *prominence*; 695.11 *recognizability*; 549.2 *subtlety*
distinctive 99.9 *characteristic*; 116.4 *dissimilar*; 543.3 *elegant*; 185.6 *eminent*; 139.15 *special*; 137.11 *typical*; 372.17 *unjoined*
distinctive feature 139.3 *characteristic*
distinctively 139.30 *characteristically*; 116.7 *dissimilarly*; 185.11, 811.7 *eminently*; 372.22 *in isolation*; 137.16 *taxonomically*
distinctiveness 743.2 *identity*; 695.11 *recognizability*; 197.4 *singularity*; 139.1 *speciality*
distinctly 336.15 *acutely*; 507.10 *aloud*; 725.4 *clearly*; 466.15 *discriminatingly*; 372.22 *in isolation*; 695.13 *intelligibly*; 185.10 *protuberantly*; 139.28 *specially*; 518.25, 520.11 *visibly*
distinctness 507.3 *audibility*; 725.1 *clarity*; 185.4 *conspicuousness*; 452.18 *particularity*; 695.10 *simplicity*; 520.3 *visibility*
distingué 549.5 *refined*
distinguish 458.7 *be wise*; 99.11, 139.22 *characterize*; 116.6 *differentiate*; 466.12 *discriminate*; 743.10 *identify*; 455.11 *know*; 469.4 *pick*; 695.7 *recognize*; 518.12 *see*; 372.10 *set apart*
distinguishability 695.11 *recognizability*
distinguishable 695.3 *recognizable*; 372.19 *separable*; 520.1 *visible*
distinguished 543.3 *elegant*; 121.15 *excellent*; 139.17 *exceptional*; 123.6 *notable*; 811.3 *reputable*; 235.1 *worthy*
distinguishing 99.9, 139.16 *characteristic*; 743.1 *identification*
distinguishing feature 99.4 *nature*
distort 234.9; **325.6**; 548.7 *blemish*; 224.8 *cause change*; 180.6 *convolute*; 96.16 *delude*; 189.7 *deviate*; 116.6 *differentiate*; 699.26 *falsify*; 274.19 *make a mistake*; 161.3 *make shapeless*; 546.5 *make ugly*; 804.17 *make wicked*; 720.1 *misinterpret*; 465.10 *misjudge*; 718.4 *misrepresent*; 351.1 *misuse*; 245.6 *pervert*; 702.11 *practise sophistry*; 760.9 *transform*
distorted 109.8; **234.6**; 231.3 *deformed*; 189.5 *devious*; 736.15 *disguised*; 274.15 *erroneous*; 699.36 *falsified*; 720.3 *misinterpreted*; 718.6 *misrepresented*; 351.4 *misused*; 325.23 *oblique*; 702.7 *sophistic*; 27.79 *spatial*; 120.3 *unequal*
distorted image 718.1 *misrepresentation*
distortedly 234.14; 351.6 *abusively*; 720.5 *misrepresentedly*
distorted truth 699.11 *half-truth*
distorter 234.5 *defacer*
distorting mirror 718.1 *misrepresentation*; 518.8 *reflection*; 519.5 *visual distortion*
Distortion 234
distortion 109.4; **234.1**; 224.1 *change*; 38.16 *deformation*; 189.3 *deviousness*; 699.9 *falsification*; 231.5 *imperfection*; 120.1 *inequality*; 720.2 *misinterpretation*; 465.1 *misjudgment*; 274.5, 718.1 *misrepresentation*; 351.2 *misuse*; 245.8 *perversion*; 692.19 *radio reception*; 702.1 *sophistry*; 548.1 *spot*; 692.23 *television reception*; 39.14 *terminal*; 325.17 *torsion*
distortion of the truth 234.4
distortive 189.5 *devious*
distort the truth 234.12
distract 328.10 *disrupt*
distracted 328.15 *disrupted*; 472.7 *inattentive*; 463.8 *oblivious*
distractedly 328.19; 463.16 *obliviously*
distracting 328.17 *disturbing*
distraction 328.4 *disruption*; 472.1 *inattention*
distrain 773.8 *take back*
distraint 773.2 *taking back*
distress 249.1 *adversity*; 798.2 *affliction*; 236.9 *badness*; 798.11 *be evil*; 328.7 *disturb*; 261.6 *fatigue*; 612.13 *frighten*; 262.4 *haste*; 236.14 *ill-treat*; 491.1 *pain*; 782.5 *poverty*; 602.1 *sorrow*
distress call 742.6 *word*
distressed 798.8 *afflicted*; 328.12 *disturbed*; 612.8 *fearful*; 491.7 *feeling pain*; 602.5 *sad*; 264.16 *troubled*
distress flare 711.2 *danger signal*
distressing 602.7; 236.3 *bad*; 798.9 *detrimental*; 328.17 *disturbing*; 603.5 *lamentable*; 491.5 *painful*; 627.7 *pitiful*
distressingly 798.13 *destructively*
distress signal 711.2 *danger signal*; 742.4 *signal*
distributary 90.1 *river*
distribute 377.16; 770.4 *allot*; 409.12 *arrange*; 137.13 *class*; 216.10 *make average*; 436.5 *provision*; 740.15 *publish*; 785.11 *remunerate*; 319.4 *transport*
distributed 377.22; 770.7 *allocated*; 740.19 *published*
distributer 319.3 *transporter*
distribution 770.1 *allocation*; 377.1 *dispersion*; 13.6 *economic factors*; 407.1 *order*; 436.1 *provision*; 778.3 *selling*; 319.1 *transport*
distribution network 39.33 *power distribution*
distributive 377.28 *dispersive*
distributively 377.29 *dispersively*; 767.16 *disposably*
distributive operation 27.14 *operation*
distributor 334.7 *electrical power*; 44.6 *garden tool*; 776.10 *trader*
distributor of largess 768.4 *giver*

district 87.7 *city district*; 396.8 *governmental organization*; 86.17 *national*; 205.1 *part*; 733.5 *place of residence*; 12.5 *political organization*; 86.5 *state*
district attorney 715.3 *accuser*; 464.6 *justice*; 251.6 *lawmaker*; 16.10 *law officer*; 16.12 *US law officer*
district council 579.8 *British administrative council*; 16.2 *jurisdiction*
District Court 16.21 *US court*
district court martial 584.6 *military law*
district judge 16.24 *US judge*
district magistrate 16.23 *judge*
district nurse 35.16 *nurse*
district officer 579.16 *official*
district official 15.7 *employee*
distrust **629.2**; **629.8**; 453.18 *be uncertain*; 451.1 *disbelief*; 451.8 *disbelieve*; 705.20 *doubt*; 674.5 *self-deprecation*; 453.10 *suspicion*; 705.6 *uncertainty*
distrustful **629.5**; 451.6 *disbelieving*; 705.15 *sceptical*; 453.1 *uncertain*
distrustfully 451.10 *disbelievingly*; 629.9 *jealously*
distrustfulness 629.2 *distrust*
distrust of mankind 653.1 *misanthropy*
distrust people 653.4 *become a misanthrope*
disturb **328.7**; 327.22 *agitate*; 488.13 *arouse sensation*; 240.5 *be inconvenient*; 264.23 *cause difficulties*; 375.4 *deconstruct*; 408.22 *discompose*; 408.21 *disorder*; 144.14 *displace*; 133.16 *interrupt*; 453.20 *make uncertain*; 288.6 *take untimely action*
Disturbance 328
disturbance **328.1**; 342.1 *activity*; 328.5 *commotion*; 375.1 *disintegration*; 408.1, 408.9 *disorder*; 144.1 *displacement*; 328.4 *disruption*; 240.3 *inconvenience*; 380.3 *instance of violence*; 133.6 *intervention*; 327.13 *tempest*; 327.2 *tumult*; 288.2 *untimeliness*
disturbed **328.12**; 327.15 *agitated*; 328.16 *deranged*; 408.17 *discomposed*; 144.8 *displaced*; 461.11 *insane*; 133.10 *interrupted*; 461.13 *mentally ill*; 36.36 *psychologically disturbed*; 380.6 *violent*
disturbed person 36.8 *disordered personality*
disturbing **328.17**; 144.8 *displaced*; 240.1 *inconvenient*; 288.13 *untimely*
disturbingly **328.18**; 288.19 *at the wrong time*; 375.8 *destructively*
disturb someone's equanimity 624.14 *make angry*
disulphide bond 33.8 *amino acid*
disunion 375.2 *deconstruction*; 372.1 *separation*
disunite 133.14 *disconnect*; 767.9 *dispose of*; 372.9 *separate*
disunited 133.8 *discontinuous*; 372.15 *separate*
disunity **372.4**; 751.1 *disagreement*; 242.7 *dissension*; 372.1 *separation*
disusage 487.3 *unaccustomedness*
disuse **350.10**; 470.6 *discarding*; 767.1 *disposal*; 355.3 *relinquishment*; 350.6 *stop using*; 487.3 *unaccustomedness*
disused **350.4**; 487.2 *not customary*; 470.10 *rejected*
dit 692.8 *data transmission*
ditch 378.3 *barrier*; 317.11 *channel*; 146.2, 146.5 *crack*; 470.2 *discard*; 767.9 *dispose of*; 165.3 *enclosing thing*; 128.3 *exclusion zone*; 184.2 *furrow*; 51.1 *green bowling*; 384.8 *military defences*; 151.6 *narrow place*; 252.2 *protection*; 350.6 *stop using*; 645.2 *stratagem*; 92.8 *valley*; 355.2 *withdraw*; 184.8 *wrinkle*
ditchwater 258.5 *swill*
diterpene 33.20 *terpene*
dither 327.1 *agitation*; 327.21 *be agitated*; 453.19 *hesitate*; 327.25 *pitch*; 326.10, 639.5 *vacillate*
ditherer 639.15 *indecisive person*; 341.2 *nonacting person*
dithering 326.15, 639.1 *vacillating*; 337.12 *weak-willed*
dithyramb 601.1 *celebration*; 17.7 *poem*
dithyrambic 601.10 *celebrative*; 729.20 *eloquent*
dithyrambist 17.14 *author*
ditties 17.6 *poetry*
ditto 112.24 *again*; 111.4, 111.9 *duplicate*; 111.18 *identically*; 125.14 *imitatively*; 112.1 *repetition*
diuretic 37.4 *drug type*; 255.4, 394.6 *purgative*; 37.17 *stimulating*; 560.26 *urinary*
diuretically 560.33 *scatologically*
diurnal 298.12 *cyclic*; 70.15 *of animals*
diurnally 298.16 *cyclically*
diva 21.24 *actor*; 121.6 *paragon*; 485.4 *skilled person*
divagate 325.3 *go astray*
divagation 325.13 *deviation*
divagatory 325.25 *wandering*
divalent 32.35 *combined*
Divali 10.16 *religious festival*
divan 23.6 *bed*; 23.2 *chair*
divaricate 325.1 *deviate*; 311.10 *diverge*; 311.6 *divergent*
divaricating 325.24 *diverging*
divarication 325.13 *deviation*; 311.1 *divergence*
dive **67.10**; **305.5**; 332.9 *acceleration*; 332.4 *be swift*; 156.14 *deepen*; 305.9 *descend*; 67.6 *diving*; 305.12 *drop*; 186.7 *fall vertically*; 322.5 *flight*; 66.4 *play soccer*; 50.16 *row*; 323.10 *sail*; 565.8 *shelter*; 186.1 *verticality*
dive bomber 381.19 *attacker*
dive-bombing 381.13 *air attack*
dive in 130.18 *make a beginning*
dive into 314.13 *fall into*
diver 305.8 *descender*; 72.3 *water bird*
diverge **311.10**; **372.13**; **377.10**; 27.97 *align*; 270.6 *be circuitous*; 751.8 *be different*; 116.5 *be dissimilar*; 114.8 *be diverse*; 189.6 *be oblique*; 150.11 *broaden*; 325.12 *deflect*; 325.1 *deviate*
Divergence 311
divergence **311.1**; **377.5**; 325.13 *deviation*; 751.3 *difference*; 116.1 *dissimilarity*; 145.1 *distance*; 114.1 *diversity*; 189.1 *obliqueness*; 27.50 *scalar quantity*; 372.1 *separation*
divergence zone 30.19 *plate tectonics*
divergency 311.1 *divergence*
divergent **311.6**; **377.24**; 372.16 *apart*; 751.10 *different*; 116.4 *dissimilar*; 325.24 *diverging*; 27.80 *linear*; 189.4 *oblique*
divergently **311.16**; 372.21 *apart*; 751.12 *differently*; 116.7 *dissimilarly*
divergent series 27.20 *sequence*
divergent strabismus 519.2 *poor sight*
diverging **325.24**; 311.6 *divergent*; 114.5 *diverse*
diverging lens 28.29 *optical element*
diverging lines 27.37 *line*
divers 114.6 *assorted*; 207.7 *various*
diverse **114.5**; 701.7 *arguing*; 224.11 *changeable*; 116.4 *dissimilar*; 299.4 *irregular*; 120.3 *unequal*; 207.7 *various*
diversely **114.10**; 701.17 *argumentatively*; 224.15 *changeably*; 116.7 *dissimilarly*; 207.10 *plurally*; 120.7 *unequally*; 541.12 *variedly*
diverse thing 114.3
diversification 224.1 *change*; 114.1 *diversity*; 541.1 *variegation*
diversified 224.12 *changed*; 138.15 *general*
diversiform 114.6 *assorted*; 114.5 *diverse*
diversify 224.7 *be changed*; 114.8 *be diverse*; 224.8 *cause change*; 541.11 *variegate*
diversion 599.2 *amusement*; 224.1 *change*; 325.14 *deviating course*; 325.13 *deviation*; 700.12 *disguise*; 351.2 *misuse*; 318.2 *passing along*; 241.7 *pleasure*; 700.13 *snare*; 700.8 *trick*; 124.8 *trifle*
Diversity 114
diversity **114.1**; 701.1 *argument*; 224.1 *change*; 116.1 *dissimilarity*; 120.1 *inequality*; 299.1 *irregularity*; 207.2 *multiplicity*; 118.1 *nonconformity*; 541.1 *variegation*
diversity of colours 541.1 *variegation*
divert **325.2**; 224.7 *be changed*; 599.13 *be humorous*; 224.8 *cause change*; 325.1 *deviate*; 700.32 *disguise*; 325.7 *misdirect*; 351.1 *misuse*; 786.7 *not pay*; 700.33 *snare*; 700.28 *trick*
divert a river 90.8 *cause to flow*
diverted 351.4 *misused*
diverted call 692.10 *telephone call*
divertimento 21.8 *scene*
diverting 598.2 *cheering*; 599.9 *funny*
divertissement 21.2 *play*; 21.8 *scene*
Dives 781.10 *wealthy person*
Dives and Lazarus 113.3 *opposites*
divest 766.9 *lose*; 355.1 *relinquish*; 773.8 *take back*; 212.4 *take off*; 708.15 *terminate*; 552.14 *undress*
divested 552.11 *exposed*
divestment 766.1 *loss*; 773.2 *taking back*; 552.1 *undress*
dividable 770.7 *allocated*
divide **196.8**; **372.11**; 27.91, 210.9 *add*; 770.4 *allot*; 372.14 *come between*; 375.4 *deconstruct*; 751.5 *disagree*; 466.12 *discriminate*; 377.12 *disperse*; 30.8 *drainage*; 406.9 *itemize*; 216.10 *make average*; 154.4 *mountain range*; 205.10 *part*; 751.7 *pick a fight*; 35.20 *practise surgery*; 203.8 *quantify*; 100.15, 311.12 *separate*; 137.14 *sort*; 469.5 *vote*; 355.2 *withdraw*
divide and rule 12.11 *govern*
divide by four 200.12 *quadrisect*
divide by three 199.11 *trisect*
divide by two 198.16 *halve*
divided 770.7 *allocated*; 406.12 *itemized*; 466.11 *judged*; 205.11 *partial*; 372.15 *separate*
divided by 27.88 *equal to*
divided by two 198.13 *half*
divided into 27.88 *equal to*
divided skirt 551.6 *skirt*
divide in half 198.16 *halve*
divide into four 200.12 *quadrisect*
dividend 27.18 *division*; 59.7 *horseracing*; 764.1 *joint possession*; 205.1 *part*; 770.2 *portion*; 356.7 *produce*; 769.2 *something received*; 215.4 *surplus*
dividends 765.5 *profit*; 14.2 *stock exchange*
divide proportionately 770.4 *allot*
dividers 210.5 *computer*; 27.49 *geometric construction*; 26.6 *measuring instrument*
divide up 770.4 *allot*; 372.11 *divide*
dividing 372.15 *separate*
dividing by four 200.5 *quadrisection*
dividing by three 199.5 *trisection*
dividing by two 198.7 *halving*
dividing line **119.7**; 372.5 *separator*
divination **11.9**; **475.2**; 8.8 *divine manifestation*; 590.2 *impression*; 11.1 *occultism*; 445.2 *precognition*; 719.5 *science of interpretation*
divinatory **11.17**; 445.7 *precognitive*
divine **8.13**; **11.23**; **475.12**; 445.9 *be intuitive*; 283.9 *look ahead*; 593.22 *lovable*; 400.12 *masterful*; 241.1 *pleasant*; 93.14 *self-existent*; 476.5 *suppose*; 7.14 *theologian*; 7.18 *theological*
divine afflatus 477.2 *inspiration*
divine attribute 8.2
Divine Creator 344.7 *Prime Mover*
divine essence 8.1 *divinity*
divine justice 814.9 *retribution*
divine king 400.2 *sovereign*
divinely 8.19
divine manifestation 8.8
divine nature 8.1 *divinity*
divineness 8.1 *divinity*
divine office 10.4 *public worship*
divine principle 8.1 *divinity*
diviner **11.13**; 475.9 *forecaster*; 719.6 *interpreter*; 445.5 *intuitive person*; 283.5 *predictor*; 477.9 *visionary*; 711.4 *warner*
divine revelation 8.8 *divine manifestation*
divine right 396.1 *authority*
divine service 10.4 *public worship*
diving **67.6**; 156.1 *depth*; 305.18 *falling*; 50.4, 50.11 *rowing*
diving bell 156.4 *deep thing*; 305.8 *descender*; 91.5 *oceanography*
diving bird 305.8 *descender*; 72.3 *water bird*
diving board 67.6 *diving*; 422.3 *elastic thing*; 361.5 *projecting object*
diving duck 72.3 *water bird*
diving mask 67.8 *swimwear*
diving position 67.6 *diving*
diving vessel 91.5 *oceanography*
divining 11.9 *divination*
divining rod 449.11 *detector*
divining rods 11.9 *divination*
Divinity 8
divinity **8.1**; 8.5 *deity*; 93.7 *self-existence*; 7.13 *theology*
divinization 8.9 *deification*
divinize 8.17 *deify*
divinized 8.15 *deified*
divisibility 27.18 *division*
divisible **27.74**; 770.7 *allocated*; 372.19 *separable*
division **27.18**; 770.1 *allocation*; 586.16 *army unit*; 374.3 *assembly*; 210.1 *calculation*; 409.6 *category*; 137.2 *class*; 375.2 *deconstruction*; 751.1 *disagreement*; 466.1 *discrimination*; 376.14 *force*; 196.2 *fractional part*; 579.10 *legislative body*; 584.4 *military organization*; 205.1 *part*; 311.2 *parting*; 405.2 *piece*; 372.3 *separateness*; 372.2 *setting apart*; 45.1 *sport*; 86.5 *state*; 35.9 *surgery*; 34.17 *taxonomy*
divisional 466.9 *discriminating*; 196.5 *fractional*; 86.17 *national*
divisional commander 584.5 *military staff*
divisionally 86.20 *nationally*; 406.15 *thematically*
division championship 246.3 *successful thing*
Division I 50.7 *windsurfing*
Division II 50.7 *windsurfing*
Division III 50.7 *windsurfing*
divisionist 19.29 *realist*
division line 147.7 *interface*
divisions 406.5
division sign 27.13 *mathematical symbol*; 742.1 *sign*
divisive 751.9 *disagreeing*
divisively 375.8 *destructively*; 466.15 *discriminatingly*; 751.11 *in disagreement*
divisiveness 751.1 *disagreement*
divisor 27.18 *division*; 205.1 *part*
divorce **571.1**; **571.7**; 767.1 *disposal*; 767.9 *dispose of*; 372.11 *divide*; 372.9 *separate*; 372.1 *separation*; 197.6 *singleness*; 109.1 *unrelatedness*
divorcé 571.4 *divorced person*; 567.5 *single man*; 197.7 *single person*
Divorce and Widowhood 571
divorce case 571.3 *divorce court*
divorce court **571.3**; 16.19 *law court*
divorced **571.11**; 767.12 *disposed*; 655.10 *lonely*; 372.15 *separate*; 197.17 *single*; 109.6 *unrelated*
divorce decree 571.1 *divorce*
divorced man 571.4 *divorced person*
divorced person 571.4
divorced woman 571.4 *divorced person*
divorcée 571.4 *divorced person*; 568.5 *single girl*; 197.7 *single person*
divorcement 571.1 *divorce*; 372.1 *separation*
divorcer 571.4 *divorced person*
divorce settlement 571.3 *divorce court*
divot 56.2 *golfing terms*; 81.2 *grassland*; 205.7 *piece*
divulgation 740.1 *publication*
divulge **739.6**; 449.2 *detect*; 6.22 *educate*; 740.13 *make public*; 738.3 *reveal*
divulged 738.14 *manifest*
divulgence **739.2**; 449.7 *detection*; 740.1 *publication*
divulging 739.11 *disclosing*
divvy 456.5 *ignorant person*
divvying up 770.1 *allocation*
divvy up 770.4 *allot*
Dixie 86.8 *regions of the US*
Dixieland 18.8, 18.33 *jazz*; 86.8 *regions of the US*
DIY 486.4 *bungled*; 646.1 *naive*
DIY type 485.4 *skilled person*
dizzily 227.15 *changeably*
dizziness 472.3 *absent-mindedness*; 690.15 *crapulence*; 690.10 *drunkenness*; 120.1 *inequality*; 337.3 *poor health*; 307.1 *rotation*; 742.1 *sign*; 260.3 *symptom*
dizzy 472.10 *careless*; 690.4 *crapulous*; 154.9 *high*; 227.14 *irresolute*; 307.12 *rotary*; 690.2 *slightly drunk*; 120.3 *unequal*
dizzy round 307.3 *reel*
D-layer 692.15 *transmitted wave*
DML 40.9 *programming language*
DNA 34.9 *cell nucleus*; 34.13 *genetic material*; 33.10 *nucleoside*
DNA double helix 34.12 *molecular biology*
DNA fingerprinting 743.3 *means of identification*
D-notice 399.2 *censorship*; 251.1 *restraint*; 736.4 *silence*
do 340.4 *act*; 342.12 *be active*; 348.4 *be an instrument*; 239.6 *be convenient*; 246.8 *be effective*; 631.14 *behave towards*; 346.7 *be operational*; 601.1 *celebration*; 232.4 *complete*; 631.11 *conduct oneself*; 557.13 *feast*; 792.10 *overcharge*; 356.10 *produce*; 376.9 *social gathering*; 217.4, 609.10 *suffice*; 354.1 *undertake*
do a backward somersault 57.10 *compete in gymnastics*
do a bad job 486.7 *be clumsy*
doable 102.5 *possible*; 346.11 *workable*
do a bunk 98.18 *abscond*; 614.4 *be a coward*; 389.5 *escape*; 634.9 *play truant*

do a cartwheel vault 57.10 *compete in gymnastics*
do a christie 68.14 *ski*
do addition 211.6 *add*
do a favour 650.8 *be benevolent*; 392.22 *improve*
do again 112.16 *repeat*; 761.7 *restore*
do a good deed 652.7 *be charitable*
do a good turn 652.7 *be charitable*; 235.10 *do good*; 392.22 *improve*
do a handspring 57.10 *compete in gymnastics*
do a handstand 57.10 *compete in gymnastics*
do a job 774.12 *steal*
do a kindness 650.8 *be benevolent*
do all one can 576.8 *exert oneself*
do all the talking 735.4 *monopolize the conversation*
do a moonlight flit 389.5 *escape*; 784.8, 786.7 *not pay*; 313.3 *quit*
do an about-turn 761.6 *reverse*
do and no more 217.4 *suffice*
do a nine-to-five 576.6 *work*
do an optional exercise 57.10 *compete in gymnastics*
do a paper on 722.4 *dissertate*
do a poo 560.16 *defecate*
do a portrait 721.14 *describe*
do a prescribed exercise 57.10 *compete in gymnastics*
do a project on 447.11 *raise the point*
do a repeat 112.16 *repeat*
do artistically 543.4 *be elegant*
do a runner 252.9 *be safe*; 526.2 *depart*
do a slow burn 624.12 *become angry*
do as one chooses 250.16 *be independent*
do as one likes 635.14 *follow one's own will*
do as one pleases 588.4 *be anarchic*; 250.16 *be independent*
do as others do 117.8 *comply*
do a swap 776.1 *trade*
do a turn-around 708.12 *renounce*
do a U-turn 224.7 *be changed*; 479.2 *equivocate*; 708.12 *renounce*; 761.6 *reverse*; 773.9 *withdraw a statement*
do away with 708.14 *cancel*; 357.8 *destroy*; 371.10 *exterminate*; 382.16 *kill*
do away with oneself 382.21 *commit suicide*
do a wheelie 61.9 *race*
dob 454.3 *testify*; 716.13 *turn queen's evidence*
do badly 486.7 *be clumsy*; 236.13 *be worthless*; 247.6 *fail*
do battle 585.14 *battle*
dobber 716.7 *person who gives evidence*; 454.7 *verifier*
dobbin 59.1 *horse*
Döbereiner's triads 32.6 *chemical element*
do bird 815.10 *be in prison*; 251.11 *detain*
do boring work 620.7 *suffer boredom*
Dobsonian telescope 29.24 *telescope*
do business 340.4 *act*; 746.5 *negotiate*; 776.1 *trade*
do business with 747.14 *join with*; 776.1 *trade*
doc 35.11 *doctor*; 394.15 *healer*
docent 6.4 *educator*
do charity work 752.11 *volunteer*
do chores 401.8 *serve*
docile 636.3 *amenable*; 407.17 *disciplined*; 265.13 *easy-going*; 6.17 *educable*; 810.9 *loyal*; 663.7 *obedient*; 480.20 *persuadable*; 388.5 *submitting*; 483.13 *suggestible*; 797.4 *well-behaved*
docilely 483.14 *influentially*; 663.10, 797.24 *obediently*; 6.26 *studiously*
docility 636.8 *acquiescence*; 810.3 *allegiance*; 6.10 *educability*; 797.11 *good behaviour*; 663.1 *obedience*; 480.7 *persuadability*; 483.6 *suggestibility*
dock 16.27 *courtroom*; 245.5 *hurt*; 312.4 *land*; 214.5 *make smaller*; 313.10 *place of departure*; 464.3 *place of judgment*; 323.10 *sail*; 372.10 *set apart*; 149.10 *shorten*; 312.16 *stopover*; 439.4 *storage*; 212.4 *take off*; 38.24 *water system*; 577.1 *workshop*
dock at a port 92.12 *be marooned*
docked 233.4 *incomplete*; 212.7 *reduced*; 149.8, 723.7 *shortened*
docker 319.3 *transporter*; 578.1 *worker*
docket 769.3 *acknowledgment of payment*; 220.4 *bill*; 743.10 *identify*; 220.5 *list of appointments*; 743.3 *means of identification*; 757.2 *permit*; 253.2 *promise*; 744.1 *record*; 744.15 *register*
docking 317.13 *flight path*; 312.11 *landing*; 29.35 *rocketry*; 372.3 *separateness*; 149.2 *shortening*; 212.1 *subtraction*
Docklands 87.5 *London*
dockyard 577.1 *workshop*
Doc Martens ™ 551.19 *footwear*
doctor **35.11**; **394.20**; 789.7 *account*; 713.4 *adviser*; 471.6 *attentive person*; 665.7 *caring person*; 224.8 *cause change*; 393.6 *cure*; 6.4 *educator*; 699.26 *falsify*; 394.15 *healer*; 608.5 *helper*; 395.5 *influential person*; 412.8 *mix*; 582.9 *person dealing with the dead*; 35.19 *practise medicine*; 136.8 *qualified person*; 393.12 *repairer*; 392.19 *support*
doctoral 6.21 *curricular*
doctoring 699.9 *falsification*
doctrinaire 452.2 *convinced*; 452.11 *opinionist*; 476.4 *theorist*
doctrinal 450.14 *believed*; 6.21 *curricular*; 7.18 *theological*
doctrinalism 7.13 *theology*
doctrinally 7.23 *religiously*
doctrinarian 4.10 *philosopher*; 476.4 *theorist*
doctrine 4.1 *philosophy*; 7.1 *religion*; 450.2 *religious belief*
doctrine of chance 107.7 *calculation of chance*
doctrinism 7.13 *theology*
docudrama 692.25 *broadcast material*; 721.3 *narration*; 21.2 *play*
document **693.3**; 698.31 *be accurate*; 3.20 *chronicle*; 222.11 *circumstantiate*; 693.12 *communicate*; 716.6 *documentation*; 243.2 *do the groundwork*; 410.5 *packet*; 744.1, 744.13 *record*; 741.13 *report*; 454.1 *verify*
documental 698.21 *accurate*
documentary 698.21 *accurate*; 3.5 *chronicle*; 716.8 *evidential*; 721.4 *factual account*; 721.3 *narration*; 721.12 *narrative*; 741.6 *radio news*; 95.3 *realism*; 744.16 *recorded*
documentary account 721.4 *factual account*
documentary drama 721.3 *narration*; 21.2 *play*
documentary evidence 716.5 *legal evidence*
documentary photography 41.1 *photography*
documentary theatre 21.10 *theatre movements*
documentation **716.6**; 698.8 *accuracy*; 3.5 *chronicle*; 454.6 *evidence*; 318.6 *passport*; 136.3 *qualifications*; 744.1 *record*; 454.4 *verification*
documented 698.21 *accurate*; 136.10 *authorized*; 452.1 *certain*; 3.19 *chronicled*; 716.8 *evidential*; 744.16 *recorded*; 454.8 *verifiable*; 454.10 *verified*
documented fact 273.3 *accurate thing*
documents 454.6 *evidence*; 744.1 *record*
dodder 556.17 *age*; 337.6 *be weak*; 296.17 *grow old*
dodderer 556.7 *older person*
doddering 556.14 *aged*; 296.11 *old*; 327.18 *shaky*
doddle 705.5 *easy question*; 265.6 *easy thing*
dodecagon 201.7 *double figures*
dodecahedron 201.7 *double figures*; 27.46 *polyhedron*
dodecahydrate 32.10 *salt*
dodecaphony 517.4 *atonality*
dodge 645.5 *be cunning*; 479.1 *be equivocal*; 700.30 *be fraudulent*; 736.11 *conceal oneself*; 702.12 *deceive*; 389.6 *elude*; 634.6 *evade*; 634.14 *evasion*; 484.3 *expedient plan*; 700.10 *fraud*; 766.15 *lose someone*; 389.2 *means of escape*; 485.1 *skill*; 702.2 *sophism*; 645.2 *stratagem*; 700.8, 700.28 *trick*; 300.15 *walk*
dodge about 227.12 *be irresolute*
dodger 634.17 *avoider*
dodgery 700.7 *tricking*
dodgily 702.15 *hypocritically*
dodging 700.34 *deceiving*; 699.13 *evasion*; 699.38 *evasive*
dodgy 702.8 *cunning*; 254.1 *dangerous*; 700.34 *deceiving*; 812.4 *disreputable*; 231.1 *imperfect*
dodo 632.8 *creature of habit*; 72.8 *extinct bird*
do down 678.10 *disparage*
do dull work 620.7 *suffer boredom*
do duty for 608.11 *assist*; 762.4 *be a substitute*
doe 568.14 *female animal*; 71.18 *female mammal*; 332.12 *swift animal*
do easily **265.17**
do easy work 576.6 *work*
doer **340.3**; 578.3 *agent*; 342.10 *busy person*; 755.4 *contractor*; 579.15 *manager*; 302.16 *progressive person*
doeskin 550.14 *animal covering*; 435.1 *materials*
do evil 798.11 *be evil*; 236.13 *be worthless*
doff 355.1 *relinquish*; 350.6 *stop using*; 212.4 *take off*; 552.14 *undress*
doffing one's cap 658.4 *deference*
doff one's cap to 667.19 *take off one's hat to*
doff one's hat 658.13 *defer to*
doff one's hat to 669.15 *compliment*
do for 246.9 *be victorious*; 236.13 *be worthless*; 357.8 *destroy*; 382.17 *murder*; 436.5 *provision*; 392.25, 401.8 *serve*
do for oneself 436.5 *provision*
dog **71.9**; 46.11 *defensive huddle*; 633.9 *follow*; 567.16 *male animal*; 71.17 *male mammal*; 46.16 *play defence*; 60.7 *shoot*; 147.17 *stay near*; 546.2 *ugly person*
dog and bone 692.9 *telephone*
dog box 321.6 *rolling stock*
dogbreath 503.2 *something that makes an unpleasant smell*
dog brush 256.10 *cleaning object*
dog collar 179.3 *circular thing*; 551.14 *neckwear*; 7.11 *vestment*
dog days 493.5 *hot weather*; 292.3 *summer*; 31.3 *weather*
dog-ear 184.9 *fold*; 184.1 *wrinkle*
dog-eared 245.13 *dilapidated*; 184.7 *folded*; 548.6 *seedy*; 349.9 *used*
dog-eat-dog 588.6 *anarchic*; 588.1 *anarchy*
dog-end 496.7 *tobacco*
dogfight 585.9 *battle*
dog-fighting 71.23 *mammal hunting*
dogfish 25.18 *sea fish*
dog flea 76.3 *pest*
dog food 557.8 *animal food*; 691.6 *drug*
dog fox 567.16 *male animal*
dogged 640.10 *persevering*; 613.12 *self-reliant*; 638.2 *tenacious*; 641.3 *unyielding*; 635.8 *wilful*
doggedly 641.9 *obstinately*; 640.13 *persistently*; 638.17 *resolutely*
doggedness 641.6 *determination*; 640.1 *perseverance*; 638.12 *resolution*; 635.3 *wilfulness*
dogger 60.4 *hunter*; 633.5 *pursuer*
doggerel 544.9 *inelegant*; 17.19 *narrative*; 697.1 *nonsense*; 17.6 *poetry*
dogging 60.2 *hunting*; 633.1 *pursuit*
doggish 71.28 *carnivorous*
doggone 712.11 *miscellaneous euphemisms*
doggy 71.28 *carnivorous*
doggy-paddling 67.1 *swimming*
dog howling at night 236.11 *harmfulness*
dogie 71.19 *young mammal*
dog in the manger 378.7 *hinderer*; 641.8 *obstinate person*; 683.3 *selfish person*
dog-in-the-manger policy 128.4 *exclusiveness*
dog Latin 5.18 *slang*
dogleg 176.1 *angle*; 325.14 *deviating course*; 189.2 *oblique line*; 325.5 *twist*
doglegged 176.7 *angular*
dogleg hole 56.1 *golf*
doglike 71.28 *carnivorous*
dog lover 70.10 *animal welfarist*
dogma 4.1 *philosophy*; 7.1 *religion*; 450.2 *religious belief*
dogmatic 707.14 *assertive*; 450.11 *believing*; 673.13 *boastful*; 452.2 *convinced*; 466.10 *discriminatory*; 726.3 *emphatic*; 673.14 *opinionated*; 641.4 *set*
dogmatically 450.15 *believingly*; 726.7 *emphatically*; 707.25 *explicitly*; 673.24 *pompously*; 466.17 *prejudicially*; 452.24 *with certainty*
dogmatic theology 7.13 *theology*
dogmatism 452.10 *conviction*; 641.7 *opinionatedness*
dogmatist 466.7 *bigot*; 641.8 *obstinate person*; 452.11 *opinionist*
dogmatize 452.20 *be certain*; 641.9 *be obstinate*
dognap 774.13 *kidnap*
dognapper 774.8 *thief*
dognapping 774.2 *kidnapping*
dog one's every step 633.9 *follow*
dog one's footsteps 633.9 *follow*
do good **235.10**; **797.20**; 652.7 *be charitable*; 239.6 *be convenient*; 237.10 *benefit*; 803.8 *be virtuous*
do-gooder 650.5 *benevolent person*; 340.3 *doer*; 636.12, 652.3 *philanthropist*; 752.8 *volunteer*
do-gooding 652.1 *philanthropy*
dog-paddle 67.9 *swim*; 67.1 *swimming*
dog-paddling 67.11 *swimming*
do great deeds 340.4 *act*
dogsbody 342.10 *busy person*; 401.5 *office assistant*; 578.1 *worker*
dog's breakfast 544.6 *blunder*; 465.2 *mistake*; 546.2 *ugly person*
dog's dinner 486.9 *bungling*; 412.3 *miscellany*
dog show 738.6 *display*
dogsled 320.10 *sled*
dog tag 743.3 *means of identification*
dog the footsteps of 223.16 *attend*
dog tick 76.3 *pest*
dog-tired 261.1 *fatigued*
dogtrot 300.12 *gait*; 333.1 *move slowly*; 333.10 *slow motion*
dogwatch 291.4 *evening thing*
dog-weary 261.1 *fatigued*
do habitually 297.7 *be frequent*
do hard work 576.6 *work*
do homage 667.18 *show respect*; 388.4 *succumb*
do housework 401.8 *serve*
do ill 798.11 *be evil*
doily 256.11 *cleaning cloth*; 550.12 *protective covering*
do in 357.8 *destroy*; 261.6 *fatigue*; 382.17 *murder*
doing 340.5 *acting*; 340.1 *action*; 346.1 *operation*; 356.1 *production*
doing again 112.1 *repetition*
doing away with oneself 382.7 *suicide*
doing business 776.4 *trade*
doing chores 342.19 *busy*
doing fine 765.17 *well-off*
doing great 765.17 *well-off*
doing nicely thank you 781.1 *wealthy*
doing one's best 353.8 *attempting*
doing penance 807.4 *atoning*; 808.7 *penitential*
doing porridge 251.15 *detained*; 815.8 *imprisoned*
doings 340.2 *deed*
doing the right thing 656.1 *formality*
doing time 251.15 *detained*; 815.8 *imprisoned*
doing up 295.5 *fresh start*
doing very nicely 765.17 *well-off*
doing well 248.8 *prosperous*
doing without 383.4 *desisting*
do insider trading 776.2 *speculate*
doit 124.8 *trifle*
do it 561.14 *have sex*
doited 461.11 *insane*
do-it-yourself 486.4 *bungled*; 646.1 *naive*; 393.8 *repair*
do-it-yourselfer 393.12 *repairer*; 485.4 *skilled person*
dojo 52.7 *judo*; 52.8 *karate*
do justice to 557.22 *eat well*; 714.7 *vindicate*
dolally 118.14 *eccentric*; 461.11 *insane*
dolce far niente 341.1 *inaction*; 580.1 *leisure*
doldrums 341.1 *inaction*; 301.2 *repose*; 31.17 *wind system*
dole 218.8 *insufficiency*; 768.3 *offering*; 770.2 *portion*; 392.4 *social assistance*
doleful 603.4 *lamenting*; 602.5 *sad*
dolefully 603.8 *mournfully*; 602.11 *sadly*
dolefulness 603.1 *lamentation*
dole out 770.4 *allot*; 377.16 *distribute*; 768.5 *give*; 26.11 *measure out*; 785.11 *remunerate*
doling out 770.1 *allocation*
doll 717.6 *image*; 159.2 *little thing*; 593.12 *nicknames for lovers*; 568.9 *woman considered as a sex object*
dollar 780.8 *American money*
dollar diplomacy 780.7 *finance*
dollar reserves 780.6 *funds*
dolled up 551.30, 656.7 *dressed-up*
dollop 158.7 *mass*; 205.7 *piece*; 770.2 *portion*
doll's house 159.5 *little space*

doll up 673.17 *be affected;* 551.33, 553.8 *dress up;* 547.16 *make up*
dolly 24.6 *ceramic workshop;* 68.10 *curling;* 320.7 *handcart;* 256.7 *washer*
dolly bird 568.9 *woman considered as a sex object*
dolly mixture 498.4 *confectionery*
dolmades 25.52 *Greek dish*
dolman jacket 551.11 *jacket*
dolmen 583.6 *grave;* 744.11 *monument;* 3.11 *relic;* 284.7 *thing of the past*
dolmen sleeve 551.24 *part of garment*
dolorimetry 26.2 *micrometry*
dolorous 602.5 *sad*
dolour 491.1 *pain;* 602.1 *sorrow*
dolphin 70.5 *aquatic animal;* 654.10 *social animal;* 67.11 *swimming*
dolphinarium 70.8 *animal welfare*
dolphin-butterfly stroke 67.2 *swimming technique*
dolphin kick 67.2 *swimming technique*
dolt 459.3 *foolish person;* 339.2 *inert person;* 646.3 *naive person;* 457.3 *unintelligent person;* 486.10 *unskilled person*
doltish 459.5 *foolish;* 339.5 *inert;* 524.8 *stupid;* 457.6, 528.5 *unintelligent*
dom 567.3 *male title of address*
do magic 619.11 *do wonders*
domain 85.3 *dominion;* 565.2 *environment;* 28.59 *ferromagnetism;* 440.2 *legal terms;* 27.29 *mathematical function;* 440.1 *property;* 86.14, 447.4 *sphere;* 6.3 *subject;* 86.4 *territorial division;* 137.4 *type*
dome 182.3; 20.10 *church architecture;* 356.8 *construction;* 177.3 *curved things;* 20.19 *decorate;* 154.8 *high thing;* 29.23 *observatory;* 550.7 *overhead covering;* 20.6, 550.27 *roof;* 38.27 *superstructure*
domed 20.14 *roofed*
domestic 256.12 *cleaner;* 43.21 *domesticated;* 401.6 *domestic servant;* 392.16 *home help;* 172.8 *internal;* 447.9 *local;* 401.1 *servant;* 655.8 *unsociable;* 578.1 *worker*
domestically 20.20 *architecturally;* 447.12 *topically;* 655.14 *unsocially*
domestic architect 20.2 *architect*
domestic architecture 20.1 *architecture*
domesticate 632.18 *habituate*
domesticated 43.21; 70.15 *of animals;* 301.5 *sedentary*
domesticated animal 70.3
domestic cat 71.10 *cat*
domestic drudge 401.6 *domestic servant*
domestic fowl 72.4 *table bird*
domestic help 256.12 *cleaner;* 392.16 *home help*
domesticity 655.1 *unsociability*
domestic mail 692.2 *postal communication*
domestic science 25.1 *cookery*
domestic servant 401.6; 256.12 *cleaner*
domestic trade 776.5 *commercial trade*
domestic tragedy 21.11 *tragedy*
domestic wiring 39.34 *power supply*
domical 177.4 *curved*
domical vault 20.7 *vault*
domicile 565.1 *habitat;* 733.5 *place of residence;* 564.15 *settle*
domiciled 565.14 *inhabiting;* 564.13 *resident*
domiciliary midwife 35.16 *nurse*
dominance 396.1 *authority;* 34.11 *genetics;* 395.3 *personal influence*
dominant 121.13; **395.13**; 396.12 *authoritative;* 121.14 *best;* 34.25 *genetic;* 18.16 *musical note;* 138.19 *prevailing;* 140.12 *ruling*
dominantly 396.23 *authoritatively;* 121.16 *superiorly*
dominate 395.10 *be a prevailing influence;* 396.19 *be authoritarian;* 154.15 *be high;* 334.10 *be powerful;* 387.7 *defeat;* 140.16 *direct;* 397.11 *have authority over;* 635.15 *impose one's will;* 400.14 *master;* 138.28 *prevail;* 89.9 *tower*
dominating 387.10; 121.13 *dominant;* 154.9 *high;* 400.12 *masterful;* 647.8 *severe*
dominatingly 400.16 *masterfully;* 121.16 *superiorly*
domination 387.2; 140.8, 396.1, 397.3 *authority;* 12.3 *governance;* 395.3 *personal influence;* 121.1 *superiority*
dominations 8.6 *angel*
domineer 396.19 *be authoritarian*
domineering 396.12 *authoritative;* 400.12 *masterful;* 397.15 *self-assured;* 647.8 *severe*
domineeringly 397.16 *commandingly;* 400.16 *masterfully*
dominie 6.4 *educator*
dominion 85.3; 140.8, 397.3 *authority;* 12.3, 396.4 *governance;* 396.8 *governmental organization;* 764.1 *joint possession;* 121.2 *leadership;* 395.3 *personal influence;* 12.5 *political organization;* 763.1, 763.4 *possession;* 129.2 *priority;* 440.1 *property;* 86.4 *territorial division*
dominium 763.2 *legal terms*
domino 550.16, 700.12 *disguise;* 521.6 *that which makes invisible*
dominoes 69.7 *other games*
domino theory 132.4 *repercussion*
do mischief to 798.11 *be evil*
do missionary work 752.11 *volunteer*
do more than enough 219.4 *be excessive*
Don 567.3 *male title of address;* 90.5 *other major rivers*
don 553.8 *dress up;* 400.9 *educational leader;* 6.4 *educator;* 396.11 *expert;* 455.6 *knowledgeable person;* 551.34 *wear*
don a hair shirt 807.6 *apologize*
donate 787.3; 785.8 *defray;* 392.29 *finance;* 679.11 *give;* 768.6 *give to charity;* 750.30 *grant;* 752.16 *make an offering*
donated 750.19 *granted;* 752.19 *sacrificial*
donation 787.7; 608.4, 652.5 *charity;* 392.6 *financial assistance;* 679.7 *gift;* 768.1 *giving;* 750.9, 785.4 *grant;* 752.6, 768.3 *offering;* 785.1 *payment;* 483.5 *positive stimulus*
donative 768.7 *given;* 768.3 *offering*
donator 679.9 *generous person;* 768.4 *giver*
done 253.8 *accomplished;* 232.7 *complete;* 25.56 *culinary;* 700.36 *deceived;* 131.21 *ended;* 632.12 *established;* 284.18 *over;* 354.5 *undertaken*
done by hand 356.12 *produced*
donee 769.5 *recipient*
done for 582.19 *dead;* 357.15 *destroyed;* 245.12 *deteriorated;* 582.18 *dying;* 261.1 *fatigued*
done in 245.12 *deteriorated;* 261.1 *fatigued;* 335.12 *impotent*
done in haste 262.3 *hasty*
done thing 117.5 *convention;* 140.6 *custom*
done to a turn 495.7 *tasty*
done up 261.1 *fatigued;* 295.14 *renewed*
done with 350.4 *disused;* 131.21 *ended*
donga 146.3 *gulf*
donjon 384.12 *fort*
Don Juan 363.6 *charmer;* 700.15 *deceiver;* 699.17 *false person;* 796.8 *immoral man;* 567.7 *libertine;* 593.9 *lover*
donkey 316.6 *beast of burden*
donkey dropper 53.8 *delivery*
donkey-grey 533.1 *grey*
donkey jacket 551.11 *jacket*
donkey's years 277.5 *long duration*
donkey-work 576.1 *work*
Donna 568.3 *female title of address*
donner kebab 25.54 *other dishes*
donnish 455.9 *literate*
donnybrook 701.1, 751.2 *argument;* 408.9 *disorder*
do no evil 803.8 *be virtuous*
do no good 236.13 *be worthless;* 245.5 *hurt*
do no harm 235.10 *do good*
donor 32.11 *chemical bond;* 679.9 *generous person;* 768.4 *giver;* 436.3 *provider*
donor impurity 28.44, 39.4 *semiconductor*
do nothing 343.12 *be inactive;* 335.6 *be powerless;* 341.4 *not act*
do-nothing 341.3 *inactive*
do nothing but 297.7 *be frequent*
do nothing in excess 684.6 *moderate*
do-nothingism 341.1 *inaction*
do no wrong 795.11 *be moral*
Don Quixote 477.9 *visionary*
don't-care 618.9 *impartial*
don't-care attitude 618.3 *impartiality*
don't-know 250.7 *free person;* 639.15 *indecisive person*
don't move 301.11 *stop!*
do number ones 560.17 *urinate*
do number twos 560.16 *defecate*
doodah 124.9 *bauble;* 438.1 *tool*
doodle 696.7 *be unintelligible;* 721.14 *describe;* 19.20 *draw;* 19.9 *drawing*
doodlebug 587.16 *bomb;* 76.5 *larva*
doodler 19.16 *artist*
doodling 19.3 *drawing*
doohickey 438.1 *tool*
dooly 320.6 *litter*
doom 798.11 *be evil;* 582.4 *death sentence;* 131.5 *fate;* 106.5 *predetermination;* 814.9 *retribution;* 357.4 *ruin*
doomed 249.6 *adverse;* 131.23 *annihilated;* 357.15 *destroyed;* 582.18 *dying;* 611.6 *inauspicious;* 106.3 *predetermined*
doom merchant 612.5 *frightener;* 475.8 *oracle*
doomsday 131.5 *fate;* 283.3 *future condition;* 464.4 *judgment day;* 814.9 *retribution;* 357.4 *ruin*
doomster 475.8 *oracle*
doomwatcher 475.8 *oracle*
do one a mischief 236.13 *be worthless*
do one good 392.21 *be helpful;* 257.5 *by hygienic*
do one proud 601.18 *salute*
do one's best 342.15 *try;* 353.2 *try hard*
do one's bidding 663.5 *obey*
do one's bit 810.16 *do one's duty*
do one's damnedest 342.15 *try;* 353.2 *try hard*
do one's duty 810.16; 803.8 *be virtuous;* 768.6 *give to charity;* 663.5 *obey*
do oneself in 382.21 *commit suicide*
do oneself proud 246.6 *be successful*
do one's homework 243.8 *prepare oneself*
do one's job 346.7 *be operational*
do one's own thing 118.19, 250.16 *be independent;* 197.18 *be one;* 100.17 *not conform*
do one's stuff 346.7 *be operational*
do one's thing 346.7 *be operational*
do one's utmost 576.8 *exert oneself*
do one's worst 651.16 *be malevolent*
door 314.6 *means of entry;* 63.5 *real tennis;* 317.2 *route;* 315.6 *way out*
doorbell 742.4 *signal;* 504.8 *something heard;* 510.4 *sources of resonance*
door buzzer 742.4 *signal*
do-or-die 615.4 *rash*
doorframe 403.4 *framework*
doorkeeper 309.5 *person who closes*
door knocker 331.15 *ram;* 742.4 *signal;* 507.4 *sound maker*
doorman 384.14 *guard;* 309.5 *person who closes;* 308.3 *person who opens;* 252.3 *protector;* 21.28 *stagehand*
doormat 388.2 *appeaser;* 256.10 *cleaning object;* 550.9 *floor covering;* 736.2 *hiding place;* 674.7 *modest person;* 732.5 *shy person;* 664.3 *sycophant;* 337.4 *weakling*
doorpost 314.6 *means of entry*
doorstep 304.10 *step;* 152.5 *thickness*
doorstepping 469.12 *election*
doorstop 378.4 *restraint*
doorstopping 741.3 *reporting*
door to door 319.6 *commercially*
door-to-door 319.5 *transportable*
door-to-door salesman 778.10 *salesman*
doorway 314.6 *means of entry;* 308.7 *passageway;* 317.2 *route*
do out of 700.30 *be fraudulent;* 608.14 *take away*
do over 651.18 *torment*
doowop 18.8 *jazz*
doozy 797.17 *good thing*
dopamine 33.16 *hormone*
dopant 39.4 *semiconductor*
dope 489.4 *anaesthetic;* 592.6 *desensitizing substance;* 394.20 *doctor;* 394.8, 691.6 *drug;* 459.3 *foolish person;* 693.1 *information;* 343.14 *make inactive;* 592.7 *render insensitive;* 457.3 *unintelligent person*
doped 691.7 *drugged;* 343.4 *not awake*
dope fiend 691.4 *drug taker*
do penance 808.5; 807.6 *apologize;* 808.4 *be penitent*
dope out 210.8 *calculate;* 194.10 *number*
dopey 592.2 *desensitized;* 261.1 *fatigued;* 343.4 *not awake;* 301.5 *sedentary;* 489.10 *sleepy;* 457.6 *unintelligent*
dopiaza 25.49 *Indian dish*
dopily 691.11 *in a trance;* 343.17 *sleepily;* 261.8 *tiredly*
doping 28.44, 39.4 *semiconductor*
do poorly 221.6 *be in a state of*
do porridge 815.10 *be in prison;* 251.11 *detain*
doppelgänger 750.5 *conformity;* 125.2 *copy;* 115.5 *counterpart;* 96.2 *illusion;* 111.3 *lookalike;* 717.1 *representation;* 762.2 *substitute person;* 198.5 *twin*
do proud 787.1 *expend;* 622.30 *make proud*
do public relations 719.13 *interpret news*
do regularly 632.16 *have a habit*
do repairs 393.1 *repair*
do reverence 367.9 *bow*
Dorian mode 18.20 *key*
Doric 20.16 *columned*
Doric mode 18.20 *key*
Doric order 20.8 *column*
do right by 650.8 *be benevolent*
do-right man 117.6 *conformist*
dormancy 77.8 *bud;* 341.1 *inaction;* 339.1 *inertness;* 361.6 *interruption;* 301.1 *motionlessness;* 343.9 *sleep*
dormant 341.3 *inactive;* 339.5 *inert;* 361.9 *interrupted;* 343.4 *not awake;* 102.6 *potential;* 301.5 *sedentary*
dormantly 301.10 *motionlessly*
dormant volcano 339.3 *inert thing*
dormer 308.7 *passageway*
dormer bungalow 565.5 *house*
dormie side 56.2 *golfing terms*
dormitory 565.7 *room;* 6.15 *schoolroom*
dormitory suburb 87.8 *suburb*
dormitory town 216.8 *middle classes;* 86.11 *settlement*
dormouse 343.11 *sleeper*
dorsal 168.4 *rear*
dorsal fin 74.5 *fish anatomy*
dorsal region 168.2 *rear end*
DOS™ 40.8 *software*
dosage 203.2 *certain amount;* 770.2 *portion;* 26.4 *size*
dose 814.10 *affliction;* 770.4 *allot;* 203.2 *certain amount;* 394.20 *doctor;* 37.3 *drug;* 166.2 *limiting factor;* 394.2 *medicine;* 205.7 *piece;* 770.2 *portion;* 37.5 *prescription;* 260.14 *venereal disease*
dose equivalent 28.70 *radioactivity*
do service 237.9 *be useful;* 663.5 *obey;* 664.11 *pander to;* 401.8 *serve*
dosh 780.2 *cash*
dosimeter 26.8 *meter*
dosimetric 26.16 *micrometric*
dosimetry 26.2 *micrometry*
dosology 37.1 *pharmacology*
do someone a favour 797.20 *do good*
do someone out of 800.10 *be criminal*
do something 340.4 *act;* 392.17 *help*
do something about 353.1 *attempt*
do something for 392.22 *improve*
doss down 301.8 *be motionless;* 565.18 *take up residence*
dosshouse 565.8 *shelter*
dossier 3.5 *chronicle;* 693.3 *document;* 16.7 *legal trial;* 744.1 *record*
do subtraction 212.3 *subtract*
do sums 211.6 *add*
dot 692.8 *data transmission;* 142.2 *exact location;* 159.2 *little thing;* 541.4 *maculation;* 440.6 *marriage settlement;* 742.13 *punctuate;* 206.9 *scatter;* 377.18 *sprinkle;* 541.11 *variegate*
dot about 206.9 *scatter*
dotage 459.1 *folly;* 556.5 *old age;* 296.1 *oldness*
dotard 459.3 *foolish person;* 556.7 *older person*
dote on 593.24 *be in love*
do the bidding of 664.11 *pander to*
do the cleaning 256.13 *clean*
do the deed 340.4 *act*
do the dirty on 800.8 *be dishonourable*
do the fair thing 473.6 *be disinterested*
do the Fosbury flop 47.8 *jump*
do the groundwork 243.2
do the honours 569.15 *be hospitable;* 654.11 *be sociable;* 667.18 *show respect*
do the job 246.8 *be effective*
do the laundry 256.13 *clean*
do the necessary thing 631.14 *behave towards*
do the needful 340.4 *act;* 631.14 *behave towards;* 810.16 *do one's duty;* 785.6 *pay*
do the offices 650.8 *be benevolent*
do the right thing 801.14 *be fair*
do the rounds 318.9 *proceed*
do the splits 57.10 *compete in gymnastics*
do the trick 246.8 *be effective;* 706.22 *be the answer*
do the washing 256.13 *clean*
do the will of 663.5 *obey*
do the work 576.6 *work*
do things backwards 486.5 *be unskilful*
do things by halves 486.5 *be unskilful*

do things halfway 486.5 *be unskilful*
do thoroughly 232.4 *complete*
do time 815.10 *be in prison*
doting 593.19 *enamoured*
dotingly 593.30 *lovingly*
dot-matrix printer 40.7 *peripheral*
dot product 27.50 *scalar quantity*
do transactions 746.5 *negotiate*
dotted 133.8 *discontinuous*; 541.10 *mottled*; 377.23 *sprinkled*
dotted about 377.19 *dispersed*; 206.6 *sparse*
dotting 377.4 *sprinkling*
dottle 215.1 *remainder*
dotty 461.11 *insane*
do twice over 219.5 *be superfluous*
do two jobs 576.6 *work*
double 198.2; **198.12**; **198.15**; 398.5 *alternative*; 48.5 *batting terms*; 115.5 *counterpart*; 68.10 *curling*; 69.6 *darts*; 325.14 *deviating course*; 69.5 *dice*; 479.10 *equivocal*; 184.9 *fold*; 59.7 *horseracing*; 525.5 *impression*; 338.3 *invigorate*; 59.9 *jumping*; 111.3 *lookalike*; 213.5 *make bigger*; 69.10 *play*; 112.16 *repeat*; 112.7 *replica*; 717.1, 721.9 *representation*; 50.11 *rowing*; 762.2 *substitute person*; 550.21 *substitution*; 67.11 *swimming*; 303.5 *turn back*; 303.9 *turn round*; 198.5 *twin*; 198.9 *two*
double agent 198.3 *duality*; 699.17 *false person*; 737.2 *secretiveness*; 700.21 *traitor*
Double-A league 48.1 *baseball*
double-arm 67.11 *swimming*
double-arm movement 67.2 *swimming technique*
double back 303.3 *reverse*; 303.5 *turn back*
double-barrelled 198.11 *double-edged*
double-barrelled gun 587.9 *firearm*
double-barrelled shotgun 330.9 *firearm*
double bed 23.6 *bed*
double bill 21.2 *play*
double-bladed 50.12 *canoeing*
double-bladed paddle 50.6 *canoeing*
double-blade race 50.6 *canoeing*
double-blind trial 448.2 *rehearsal*
double boiler 410.15 *pot*
double-breasted 551.31 *styled*
double-check 454.4 *verification*; 454.1 *verify*
double-checked 454.10 *verified*
double-checking 454.9 *verificatory*
double chin 158.8 *fat*
double-chinned 158.16 *fat*
double coverage 46.10 *defence*
double-cross 645.5 *be cunning*; 268.21 *cheat*; 700.23 *deceive*; 800.9 *prove false*
double-crosser 645.3 *cunning person*; 800.4 *dishonourable person*; 699.17 *false person*; 651.8 *malefactor*; 700.21 *traitor*
double-crossing 645.1 *cunning*; 198.11 *double-edged*; 198.3 *duality*; 800.6 *faithless*; 800.2 *faithlessness*
doubled 112.9 *repeated*; 198.9 *two*
double date 654.3 *meeting*
double-deal 699.21; 268.21 *cheat*; 700.23, 702.12 *deceive*
double-dealer 800.4 *dishonourable person*; 479.9 *equivocator*; 227.6 *fickle person*; 700.21 *traitor*
double-dealing 645.1 *cunning*; 700.34 *deceiving*; 700.1 *deception*; 198.11 *double-edged*; 198.3 *duality*; 699.30 *duplicitous*; 699.2 *duplicity*; 479.11 *equivocating*; 800.6 *faithless*; 800.2 *faithlessness*; 702.5 *hypocrisy*; 702.10 *hypocritical*; 700.38 *treacherous*
double decker 320.19 *bus*
double-decker 198.2 *double*; 411.7 *layered*; 411.5 *layered thing*; 25.11 *sandwich*
double declutch 320.21 *miscellaneous motoring terms*
double-dig 44.15 *cultivate*
doubled over 184.7 *folded*
double dresser 23.5 *cabinet*
double-dribble 49.6 *play basketball*
double-dribbling 49.5 *penalties*
double Dutch 696.12 *unintelligible thing*
double-edged 198.11; 425.3 *sharp-edged*
double-ended 50.12 *canoeing*
double-ended paddle 50.6 *canoeing*
double-ender 50.2 *sailing boat*
double entendre 198.3 *duality*; 479.5 *equivocalness*; 796.2 *indecency*; 599.5 *joke*
double entry 789.1 *accounts*; 744.8 *registration*
double exposure 198.4 *doubling*
double facade 699.2 *duplicity*
double-faced 198.11 *double-edged*
double fault 274.13 *sporting error*
double figures 201.7
double flat 18.16 *musical note*
double for 762.4 *be a substitute*; 550.34 *cover for*
double foul 49.4 *playing terms*
double-fry 25.55 *cook*
double glaze 493.14 *be hot*
double-glazed 493.13 *heated*
double glazing 493.3 *heater*
double-handed 55.8 *angling*
double-handed rod 55.3 *fishing tackle*
double harness 198.14 *pair*; 198.1 *two*
double header 321.7 *train*
double helix 33.10 *nucleoside*
double hook 55.3 *fishing tackle*
double indemnity 775.2 *compensation*
double integral 27.31 *differentiation*
double-jointed 419.2 *pliant*
double kayak race 50.6 *canoeing*
double-leg 57.11 *gymnastic*
double-leg circle 57.6 *pommel horse*
double life 198.3 *duality*; 699.2 *duplicity*
double march 332.11 *swift thing*
double meaning 694.3 *comprehension*; 198.3 *duality*; 479.5 *equivocalness*
double-minded 699.30 *duplicitous*
double-mindedness 699.2 *duplicity*
double negative 274.11 *grammatical error*
doubleness 198.3 *duality*; 699.2 *duplicity*
double-oar 50.11 *rowing*
double-oar rowing 50.4 *rowing*
double one's efforts 640.6 *persevere*; 353.2 *try hard*
double over 184.9 *fold*
double overarm 67.2 *swimming technique*
double paddle 50.17 *canoe*
double-paddle canoeing 50.6 *canoeing*
double parking 320.21 *miscellaneous motoring terms*
double personality 36.8 *disordered personality*; 36.16 *dissociation*
double play 48.6 *fielding terms*
double-pole 68.2 *cross-country skiing*; 68.12, 68.14 *ski*
double-pole with leg kick 68.2 *cross-country skiing*
double punt 50.19 *punt*
double punting 50.8 *punting*
double-quick 332.1 *swift*; 332.14 *swiftly*
double quotes 742.7 *punctuation*
double rainbow 31.27 *rainbow*
double recessiveness 34.11 *genetics*
double rhyme 17.11 *rhyme*
doubles 63.14 *forehand*; 63.4 *tennis terms*
double salt 32.10 *salt*
doubles court 63.8 *squash*; 63.3 *tennis equipment*
double sculling 50.4 *rowing*
Double Sculls 50.5 *Henley trophies*
double sculls 50.4 *rowing*
double sharp 18.16 *musical note*
double-sided 68.12 *ski*; 198.10 *two-sided*
double-sidedness 198.3 *duality*
double-sided skating 68.3 *ski racing*
double somersault 67.6 *diving*
double space 146.1 *interval*
doubles player 63.6 *tennis player*
double star 29.9 *constellation*
double-strength 690.6 *intoxicating*
double stroke 65.4 *carom*
Double Summer Time 275.9 *time zone*
doublet 198.2 *double*; 551.8 *shirt*; 762.3 *substitute thing*; 5.17 *word*
double take-out 68.10 *curling*
double talk 479.1 *be equivocal*; 479.5 *equivocalness*; 699.27 *evade*; 699.13 *evasion*; 5.22 *many words*
doubletalking 699.38 *evasive*
double tenoner 23.11 *woodworking tool*
double throw axel 68.6 *ice-skating*
double-tongue 699.2 *duplicity*; 18.38 *sound*
double-tongued 699.30 *duplicitous*; 479.10 *equivocal*
double top 69.6 *darts*
double up 261.6 *fatigue*
double vision 519.2 *poor sight*
double whammy 594.2 *curse*; 798.4 *evil power*; 712.4 *malediction*
double-wing formation 46.7 *offence*
doubling 198.4; 213.1 *increase*; 112.1 *repetition*; 112.12 *repetitious*; 184.1 *wrinkle*
doubling over 184.1 *wrinkle*
doubly 184.12; 198.19 *twice*
doubt 705.20; 616.5 *be cautious*; 611.9 *be hopeless*; 453.18 *be uncertain*; 616.1 *caution*; 451.1 *disbelief*; 451.8 *disbelieve*; 701.14 *discuss*; 637.13 *dissociation*; 629.2, 629.8 *distrust*; 611.1 *hopelessness*; 105.4 *improbability*; 701.2 *logical argument*; 705.1 *question*; 708.11 *rebut*; 453.10 *suspicion*; 705.6 *uncertainty*; 639.11 *vacillation*
doubter 616.3 *cautious person*; 451.5 *disbeliever*; 705.9 *questioner*; 453.17 *uncertain person*
doubtful 701.10 *arguable*; 616.4 *cautious*; 451.6 *disbelieving*; 629.5 *distrustful*; 105.1 *improbable*; 708.17 *negative*; 705.14 *questionable*; 453.1 *uncertain*; 254.2 *unsafe*; 337.12 *weak-willed*
doubtfully 701.18 *arguably*; 451.10 *disbelievingly*; 105.8 *improbably*; 629.9 *jealously*; 708.22 *negatively*; 705.24 *questionably*; 453.23 *uncertainly*
doubtfulness 451.1 *disbelief*; 105.4 *improbability*; 337.2 *indecisiveness*; 705.7 *questionableness*; 708.3 *rebuttal*; 453.9, 705.6 *uncertainty*
doubtful war 585.1 *war*
doubting 451.6 *disbelieving*; 705.12 *questioning*; 708.19 *rebutting*; 705.15 *sceptical*
doubting Thomas 451.5 *disbeliever*; 705.9 *questioner*; 453.17 *uncertain person*
doubtless 104.11 *probably*
douceur 813.7 *bounty*; 768.2 *gift*
douche 256.6 *bath*; 256.14 *bathe*; 433.34 *hose*; 37.11 *linctus*; 394.6 *purgative*; 433.11 *wash*
dough 25.38 *bread*; 780.2 *cash*; 419.11 *soft thing*
doughboy 586.8 *soldier*
doughiness 419.10 *compressibility*; 430.1 *viscosity*
doughnut 25.36 *cake*
doughnut hole 25.36 *cake*
doughtiness 613.1 *courage*
doughty 613.9 *courageous*
doughy 530.8 *drained of colour*; 419.2 *pliant*
dou louf 25.53 *African dish*
do up 309.7 *close*; 261.6 *fatigue*; 244.1 *improve*; 295.20 *make new*; 393.2 *refurbish*; 551.34 *wear*
dour 651.12 *callous*; 643.1 *solemn*; 626.6 *sullen*; 641.3 *unyielding*
dour ice 68.10 *curling*
dourly 626.13 *sullenly*
dourness 641.5 *obstinacy*; 643.4 *solemnity*
douse 367.3 *bring down*; 523.14 *make dark*; 433.29 *water*
douse the flames 749.4 *pacify*
dove 72.1 *birds*; 805.4 *innocent person*; 748.3 *mediator*; 589.3 *pacifist*; 589.2 *symbol of peace*
dovecote 72.19 *ornithology*; 565.12 *stall*
dove-grey 533.1 *grey*
dovelike 72.21 *avian*; 805.5 *innocent*; 749.6 *pacificatory*; 589.7 *peaceful*
dove of peace 749.2 *peace offering*
Dover sole 25.44 *British dish*; 25.18 *sea fish*
dovetail 23.17 *carpenter*; 368.5 *inset*; 147.8 *interaction*
dovetailed 23.16 *joined*
dovetailing 23.10 *carpenter's term*; 23.16 *joined*
do violence to 351.1 *misuse*; 380.8 *use violence*
do volunteer work 752.11 *volunteer*
dowager 568.2 *female*; 400.1 *master*; 571.6 *surviving spouse*
dowager queen 571.6 *surviving spouse*
dowdy 724.8 *inelegant*; 544.10 *ugly*
dowel 373.8 *fastening*
do well 797.21; 221.6 *be in a state of*; 248.5 *be prosperous*; 485.10 *be skilful*; 246.6 *be successful*; 302.5 *develop*; 244.2 *get better*
do well at 797.19 *be good at*
dower 768.5 *give*; 788.4 *legacy*; 440.6 *marriage settlement*; 440.9 *own property*
dowered 768.7 *given*; 440.8 *propertied*
dowerless 782.2 *insolvent*
do what is expected 810.16 *do one's duty*
do what is necessary 810.16 *do one's duty*
do what is required 340.4 *act*; 217.4 *suffice*
do what one likes 250.16 *be independent*; 635.14 *follow one's own will*
Dow Industrials 14.2 *stock exchange*
do without 634.3 *abstain*; 684.5 *be self-restrained*; 383.9 *desist*; 767.9 *dispose of*; 350.5 *not use*; 709.7 *refuse oneself*
Dow Jones Industrial Index 14.2 *stock exchange*
down 305.19; **367.24**; 602.6 *depressed*; 305.9 *descend*; 305.16 *descending*; 305.1 *descent*; 558.13 *drink*; 367.2 *flatten*; 404.2 *grain*; 611.4 *hopeless*; 603.4 *lamenting*; 415.7 *light thing*; 155.10 *low*; 186.12 *perpendicularly*; 72.17 *plumage*; 28.78 *quantum*; 421.8 *smooth thing*; 419.11 *soft thing*; 238.1 *useless*; 245.14 *worse*
down and down 214.8 *decreasingly*
down-and-out 782.3 *beggarly*; 357.15 *destroyed*; 245.13 *dilapidated*; 766.6 *loser*; 249.5 *person in adversity*; 782.10 *poor person*; 249.7 *unprosperous*
down at heart 305.17 *drooping*
down-at-heel 782.3 *beggarly*; 245.13 *dilapidated*; 548.6 *seedy*; 408.15 *untidy*; 349.9 *used*
down at the mouth 611.4 *hopeless*
downbear 367.5 *bear down on*
downbeat 18.19 *tempo*
down below 305.19 *down*; 155.10 *low*
downbend 305.1 *descent*
downcast 367.21 *degraded*; 539.3, 602.6 *depressed*; 367.12 *downthrow*; 305.17 *drooping*; 367.19 *fallen*; 611.4 *hopeless*
downcome 305.1 *descent*
downcurve 305.1 *descent*; 330.5 *throw*
downdraught 434.4 *air flow*; 31.10 *air movement*; 305.1 *descent*
down-drawn 24.10 *ceramic*
down-drawn kiln 24.6 *ceramic workshop*
downer 249.1 *adversity*; 620.2 *boring thing*; 305.1 *descent*; 691.6 *drug*; 611.2 *hopeless situation*; 685.2 *moderator*; 602.3 *sad person*
downers 592.6 *desensitizing substance*
downfall 249.1 *adversity*; 247.1 *failure*; 305.4 *fall*; 367.11 *lowering*; 31.25 *rain*; 357.4 *ruin*
downfallen 245.12 *deteriorated*
down feathers 72.17 *plumage*
downflow 305.3
downflowing 305.16 *descending*
down-force 61.6 *motor-racing terms*
down for hearing 16.54 *litigated*
downgrade 40.20 *abort*; 367.4 *debase*; 371.3 *disbar*; 305.19 *down*; 214.5 *make smaller*; 814.1 *punish*; 144.17 *relegate*; 305.2 *sinkage*
downgraded 367.21 *degraded*; 144.11 *relegated*
downgrading 367.15 *debasement*; 814.7 *punishment*; 144.4 *relegation*
downhaul 50.3 *parts of a sailing boat*; 50.13 *windsurfing*
downhaul line 50.7 *windsurfing*
downhearted 602.5 *sad*
downheartedness 602.1 *sorrow*
downhill 305.16 *descending*; 305.19 *down*; 265.9 *easy*; 68.17 *on a ski run*; 68.12 *ski*; 245.14 *worse*
downhill all the way 265.9 *easy*
downhill race 68.3 *ski racing*
downhill racing 68.3 *ski racing*
downhill ski 68.5 *ski equipment*
downhill ski run 68.1 *skiing*
downiness 404.2 *grain*; 415.5 *lightness*; 419.9 *smoothness*
downing 557.1 *eating*
Downing Street 396.6 *place of authority*; 201.6 *ten*; 400.8 *the power structure*
down in the dumps 602.6 *depressed*; 611.4 *hopeless*
down in the mouth 305.17 *drooping*
down in the world 245.14 *worse*
downkick 67.2 *swimming technique*
downland 92.11 *continental*; 81.2 *grassland*; 92.7 *upland*
downlight 522.12 *highlight*
down line 321.2 *track*
download 40.20 *abort*; 40.19 *computing terms*

down-market 793.9 *cheap;* 138.21 *common;* 216.3 *mediocre*
down-motion turn 68.4 *skiing technique*
down on one's luck 249.8 *unlucky*
down on one's uppers 135.5 *necessitous*
down on the farm 43.22 *agriculturally*
down payment 205.2 *particular;* 785.1 *payment*
downplay 728.22 *play down*
downplayed 728.19
downplaying 728.9
downpour 305.3 *downflow;* 31.25 *rain;* 380.5 *violent weather*
downright 232.7 *complete;* 232.9 *completely;* 255.17 *direct;* 739.11 *disclosing;* 305.19 *down;* 738.15 *open;* 695.2 *simple;* 698.18 *truthful*
downright lie 699.10 *lie*
downrightness 739.3 *openness;* 695.10 *simplicity;* 698.5 *truthfulness*
downrush 305.3 *downflow*
downrushing 305.16 *descending*
downs 81.2 *grassland;* 154.2 *heights;* 89.1 *mountain;* 92.7 *upland*
down side 56.2 *golfing terms*
downsize 40.19 *computing terms;* 214.5 *make smaller;* 206.8 *reduce*
downsizing 214.1 *decrease*
down south 305.19 *down*
Down's syndrome 461.2 *subnormality*
downstage 21.43 *on stage;* 21.17 *stage*
downstairs 305.19 *down;* 155.10 *low*
downstream 305.19 *down;* 265.9 *easy;* 324.11 *in all directions*
downstreet 305.19 *down*
downsweep method 47.1 *track events*
downswing 56.3 *golf shots*
down the hatch 558.18 *cheers!*
down the middle 198.22 *in half*
downthrow 367.12; 305.1 *descent*
downthrown 367.19 *fallen*
downtime 40.19 *computing terms*
down-to-earth 646.1 *naive;* 95.8 *practical;* 4.15 *rational*
down tools 355.2 *withdraw*
downtown 87.7 *city district;* 324.14 *directed;* 305.19 *down;* 324.11 *in all directions;* 86.18 *local;* 87.14 *urban;* 86.10 *urban area*
downtowner 87.11 *urbanite*
downtrend 245.7 *deterioration*
downturn 214.2, 303.14 *decline;* 305.1 *descent;* 245.7 *deterioration*
downturning 305.16 *descending*
down under 86.7 *regions of the world*
down-unweighting 68.4 *skiing technique*
downward 305.16 *descending;* 300.17 *directional;* 2.14 *socioeconomic*
downward course 245.7 *deterioration*
downward curve 214.2 *decline*
downward mobility 2.7 *social stratification*
downward motion 300.6 *descending motion*
downwards 214.4 *decrease;* 214.8 *decreasingly;* 305.19, 367.24 *down;* 155.10 *low*
downward spiral 214.2 *decline*
downward trend 214.2, 303.14 *decline;* 305.2 *sinkage*
downwash 322.7 *miscellaneous aviation terms*
down-welling 30.13 *ocean current*
downwind 324.14 *directed;* 324.11 *in all directions*
downwind of 500.5 *odorous*
down with 305.19 *down*
downy 404.11 *fluffy;* 415.2 *insubstantial;* 419.3, 421.1 *smooth*
downy mildew 44.12 *pests and diseases*
do wonders 619.11; 246.8 *be effective;* 246.6 *be successful*
do wonders with 393.2 *refurbish*
do worse 245.1 *deteriorate*
do wrong 796.16; **802.21**; 798.11 *be evil;* 16.73 *be illegal;* 804.16 *be wicked;* 236.13 *be worthless;* 412.9 *mix up*
do wrong by 798.11 *be evil*
dowry 392.6 *financial assistance;* 768.1 *giving;* 440.6 *marriage settlement;* 765.5 *profit*
dowse 11.23 *divine*
dowser 449.12 *discoverer;* 11.13 *diviner;* 475.9 *forecaster*
dowsing 11.9, 475.2 *divination*
dowsing rods 11.9 *divination*
doxological 10.21 *ritualistic*
doxologically 10.23 *ritually*
doxology 10.8 *hymn;* 18.5 *sacred music*
doyen 400.5 *company leader;* 485.5 *expert;* 556.7 *older person*
doze 339.4 *be inert;* 489.11 *be unfeeling;* 343.9, 343.13 *sleep;* 263.2 *take it easy;* 489.2 *unconsciousness*
dozen 201.7 *double figures*
dozens 208.2 *multitude*
dozer 38.29 *construction equipment;* 343.11 *sleeper*
dozily 343.17 *sleepily;* 261.8 *tiredly*
doziness 343.9 *sleep*
dozing 343.4 *not awake*
dozy 261.1 *fatigued;* 343.4 *not awake*
DP 40.1 *computing*
DP manager 40.2 *operator*
drab 620.4 *boring;* 523.10 *dark-coloured;* 524.7 *dimmed;* 258.6 *dirty person;* 533.3 *dull;* 529.13 *soft-hued;* 544.10 *ugly*
drabble 258.11 *dirty*
drably 620.8 *boringly;* 524.12 *dimly;* 533.9 *greyly*
drabness 523.3 *dark colour;* 523.1 *darkness;* 533.7 *dullness;* 524.2 *murk;* 544.3 *ugliness*
drachm 414.9 *avoirdupois weight*
drachma 780.11 *national coins*
Draconian 336.10 *potent;* 647.8 *severe*
Draconian measures 647.1 *severity*
draff 258.4 *dirt*
draft 586.14 *armed forces;* 49.2 *basketball player;* 233.5 *be incomplete;* 420.13 *be unfinished;* 386.3 *coercive methods;* 721.14 *describe;* 243.2 *do the groundwork;* 19.20 *draw;* 19.9 *drawing;* 584.10 *enlist;* 386.7 *force;* 160.7 *form;* 585.12 *go to war;* 233.3 *incomplete thing;* 484.6 *outline;* 717.11 *paint;* 780.14 *paper money;* 484.10 *plan out;* 243.10 *preparations;* 717.2 *reproduction;* 420.10 *rough idea;* 476.5 *suppose*
draft-card burner 589.3 *pacifist*
draft dodger 634.17 *avoider;* 589.3 *pacifist;* 709.4 *refuser;* 109.3 *unconnected person*
drafted 584.9 *enlisted;* 586.35 *martial;* 19.27 *painted;* 585.15 *warring*
draftee 585.11 *recruit;* 586.8 *soldier*
draft evader 589.3 *pacifist*
draft exile 589.3 *pacifist*
drafting 19.3 *drawing*
draft pick 49.2 *basketball player;* 46.2 *football player*
draft player 49.2 *basketball player*
draft protester 589.3 *pacifist*
drag 362.12; 363.11 *attract;* 363.1 *attraction;* 395.10 *be a prevailing influence;* 620.6 *be boring;* 378.11 *be inhibited;* 68.16 *bobsled;* 620.3 *boring person;* 620.2 *boring thing;* 347.3 *counteract;* 347.1 *counteraction;* 362.4, 365.1 *friction;* 333.2 *hesitate;* 611.3 *hopeless person;* 59.8 *hunting;* 395.1 *influence;* 166.7 *limit;* 166.2 *limiting factor;* 251.5 *means of restraint;* 322.7 *miscellaneous aviation terms;* 378.2 *obstacle;* 275.15 *pass;* 362.2 *pull;* 251.8 *restrain;* 320.10 *sled;* 496.14 *smoke;* 496.8 *smoking;* 414.8 *weighing down*
drag artist 21.29 *entertainer;* 125.7 *imitator;* 717.5 *performer*
drag-ass 620.3 *boring person*
drag by 275.15 *pass*
drag down 362.12 *drag*
dragée 498.4 *confectionery;* 37.6 *pill*
drag from 386.7 *force*
dragged out 148.1 *long*
dragging 363.8 *attracting;* 68.9 *bobsledding;* 620.4 *boring;* 68.13 *ice-skating;* 333.4 *slow;* 333.10 *slow motion*
dragging out 148.4 *length*
draggle 258.11 *dirty;* 362.12 *drag*
draggletail 258.6 *dirty person*
draggy 620.4 *boring*
draghound 59.8 *hunting*
draghunt 59.8 *hunting*
drag in 368.1 *insert*
drag in the mud 668.21 *disregard*
drag king 568.10 *homosexual*
drag lift 68.1 *skiing*
dragline 38.29 *construction equipment*
dragnet 633.3 *hunting and fishing equipment;* 138.3 *nonspecificness;* 633.1 *pursuit;* 700.13 *snare;* 362.6 *towline*
dragon 625.3 *irascible person;* 70.7 *legendary beast;* 380.4 *violent creature*
drag on 294.6 *be late;* 111.11 *be regular;* 275.15 *pass*
drag one's feet 122.8 *be inferior;* 378.11 *be inhibited;* 294.6 *be late;* 333.2 *hesitate;* 378.8 *hinder;* 637.8 *hold back;* 634.4 *shy*
dragonfly 76.1 *insect;* 541.5 *variegated thing*
dragonnade 381.14 *siege*
dragon's blood 535.6 *red pigment*
dragon's lair 254.5 *danger*
dragon's teeth 379.1 *trap*
dragoon 586.20 *cavalryman;* 386.7 *force;* 59.15 *horse person*
drag out 148.10 *lengthen;* 738.3 *reveal*
drag race 61.1 *motor racing;* 61.9 *race*
drag racer 61.8 *driver*
drag racing 61.1 *motor racing*
drag through the gutter 678.12 *defame*
drag through the mud 678.12 *defame*
drag up 362.12 *drag;* 366.4 *gather up*
drain 90.8 *cause to flow;* 214.1, 214.4 *decrease;* 558.13 *drink;* 428.17 *dry;* 30.63 *ebb;* 349.3 *exploit;* 261.6 *fatigue;* 245.5 *hurt;* 766.12 *lessen;* 766.4 *lessening;* 257.6 *make hygienic;* 218.7 *make insufficient;* 315.7 *outlet;* 308.7 *passageway;* 308.21 *provide passage for;* 255.10, 256.15 *purify;* 238.6 *refuse;* 315.11 *run out;* 767.8 *sink;* 439.4 *storage;* 212.3 *subtract;* 369.14 *suck;* 39.19 *transistor;* 38.22 *tunnel;* 371.11 *void;* 441.1 *waste;* 767.4 *wastebin;* 337.7 *weaken*
drain a bumper 601.17 *congratulate*
drainage 30.8; 256.2 *cleaning;* 371.21 *removal;* 258.5 *swill;* 441.3 *waste*
drainage basin 30.8 *drainage*
drainage channel 30.8 *drainage*
drainage pattern 30.8 *drainage*
drainage system 30.8 *drainage;* 38.24 *water system*
drain away 214.4 *decrease*
drain cleaner 501.2 *deodorant*
drained 245.12 *deteriorated;* 337.9 *dilapidated;* 428.4 *dried-out;* 261.1 *fatigued*
drained of colour 530.8
drain electrode 39.19 *transistor*
draining 245.11 *hurt;* 766.4 *lessening;* 308.15 *providing passage;* 371.21 *removal;* 369.4 *sucking*
draining board 767.8 *sink*
drain of colour 530.6 *decolour*
drain one's glass 558.13 *drink*
drain out 315.11 *run out*
drainpipe 256.10 *cleaning object;* 315.7 *outlet*
drainpipes 551.9 *trousers*
drain the lifeblood of 382.18 *slaughter*
drain tile 24.9 *industrial ceramics*
drain to the dregs 371.11 *void*
drake 70.7 *legendary beast;* 43.8 *livestock;* 567.16 *male animal;* 72.10 *male bird*
DRAM 40.6 *memory*
dram 414.9 *avoirdupois weight;* 690.13 *drink*
Drama 21
drama 21.1; 340.1 *action;* 342.1 *activity;* 340.2 *deed;* 721.3 *narration;* 21.2 *play;* 619.4 *wonder*
drama college 6.12 *educational institution*
drama-documentary 21.2 *play*
drama of fate 21.11 *tragedy*
drama of suspense 21.2 *play*
drama queen 676.2 *pretender;* 673.7 *vain person*
dramatherapist 36.30 *psychiatrist*
drama therapy 36.3 *psychiatric treatment*
dramatic 21.39; 340.5 *acting;* 703.10 *demonstrative;* 18.32 *instrumental;* 17.19 *narrative;* 619.8 *wonderful*
dramatically 21.44; 703.21 *demonstratively;* 17.23 *descriptively*
dramatic art 21.1 *drama*
dramatic conflict 21.9 *dramaturgy*
dramatic convention 21.9 *dramaturgy*
dramatic coup 21.9 *dramaturgy*
dramatic cycle 21.2 *play*
dramatic dance 22.4 *historic dancing*
dramatic entertainment 21.1 *drama;* 21.2 *play*
dramatic form 21.9 *dramaturgy*
dramatic irony 17.3 *aspect of fiction;* 21.9 *dramaturgy*
dramaticism 21.1 *drama*
dramatic monologue 21.2 *play;* 17.7 *poem*
dramatic poet 17.14 *author*
dramatic poetry 17.6 *poetry*
dramatic recital 21.2 *play*
dramatic representation 21.2 *play*
dramatics 673.6 *boastfulness;* 703.2 *demonstrativeness;* 21.1 *drama*
dramatic stroke 21.9 *dramaturgy*
dramatic structure 21.9 *dramaturgy*
dramatic tension 21.9 *dramaturgy*
dramatic unities 21.9 *dramaturgy*
dramatis personae 21.25 *cast;* 220.6 *list of names;* 566.7 *person;* 578.4 *personnel;* 21.23 *role*
dramatist 21.26; 17.14 *author;* 721.10 *descriptive writer;* 356.9 *producer*
dramatization 699.7 *pretence*
dramatize 21.38; 717.10 *act;* 703.18 *appear;* 738.1 *display;* 721.15 *recount;* 17.21 *write*
dramatizer 21.26 *dramatist*
dramaturge 17.14 *author;* 21.26 *dramatist*
dramaturgic 21.39 *dramatic*
dramaturgy 21.9; 619.3 *wonder-working*
Drambuie™ 558.7 *alcoholic drink*
drape 551.32 *dress;* 550.28 *face;* 21.19 *stage set;* 361.10 *suspend;* 361.1 *suspension;* 550.8 *wall covering*
drapeau tricolore 743.7 *flag*
draped 551.29 *dressed*
drape oneself 367.8 *sit*
draper 550.17 *coverer;* 551.26 *fashion designer*
drapery 42.3 *fabric;* 356.7 *produce;* 550.8 *wall covering*
drapes 528.7 *opaque thing*
drastic 336.10 *potent*
drastically 336.15 *acutely*
dratted 236.6 *damnable*
draught 156.6 *bathymetry;* 414.6 *displacement;* 558.2 *drink;* 37.3 *drug;* 394.2 *medicine;* 362.2 *pull;* 369.4 *sucking;* 362.1 *traction*
draught animal 320.9 *animal transport;* 70.3 *domesticated animal*
draught beer 558.7 *alcoholic drink*
draughtboard 541.5 *variegated thing*
draught horse 320.9 *animal transport;* 316.6 *beast of burden;* 59.2 *thoroughbred*
draughtsman 19.16 *artist;* 744.9 *recorder*
draughtsmanship 19.3 *drawing;* 19.4 *treatment*
Dravidian 5.11 *family of languages*
draw 19.20; 363.11 *attract;* 363.1 *attraction;* 780.26 *bank;* 119.10 *be equal;* 51.9 *bowls;* 617.15 *cause desire;* 25.55 *cook;* 721.14 *describe;* 394.20 *doctor;* 107.3 *equal chance;* 111.5 *equality;* 285.4 *equal race;* 119.2 *equilibrium;* 160.7 *form;* 56.3 *golf shots;* 146.3 *gulf;* 58.3 *ice hockey;* 148.10 *lengthen;* 191.5 *make smaller;* 483.9 *motivate;* 151.10 *narrow;* 617.5 *object of desire;* 717.11 *paint;* 46.9 *play;* 58.9 *play hockey;* 436.5 *provision;* 362.2, 362.11 *pull;* 27.96 *represent;* 285.8 *run equally;* 323.10 *sail;* 300.14 *set in motion;* 496.14 *smoke;* 496.8 *smoking;* 226.2 *stop;* 369.14 *suck;* 371.11 *void;* 788.5 *winnings*
draw a bead on 381.2 *fire;* 60.7, 330.28 *shoot*
draw a blank 766.11 *be wasteful;* 247.6 *fail*
draw a blueprint 717.11 *paint*
draw a circle 721.17 *describe a circle;* 179.7 *make circular*
draw a kiln 24.11 *make ceramics*
draw a large income 781.12 *be rich*
draw a match 111.10 *be equal*
draw a meaning 694.11 *infer*
draw a mental picture 476.5 *suppose*
draw an allowance 765.14 *profit*
draw an outline 163.5 *outline*
draw a parallel between 115.11 *make similar*
draw a parallel with 108.8 *be proportionate to*
draw a pay cheque 765.12 *earn*
draw a penalty 58.9 *play hockey*
draw a pension 769.9 *receive*
draw a personal foul 46.18 *be penalized;* 58.9 *play hockey*
draw a red herring 109.10 *be unrelated*
draw a salary 765.12 *earn;* 813.13 *get paid*
draw a shot 51.7 *bowl*
draw a technical foul 58.9 *play hockey*
draw attention 471.13 *attract attention*
draw attention to 738.1 *display;* 738.3 *reveal*

draw attention to oneself 703.18 *appear*
draw a veil over 736.8 *conceal*
drawback 231.7 *defect;* 791.1 *discount;* 240.3 *inconvenience;* 378.2 *obstacle;* 264.8 *snag;* 212.2 *subtracted item*
draw back 612.11 *be afraid;* 362.14 *draw in;* 303.2 *retreat;* 634.4 *shy*
draw back the curtains 522.29 *clarify*
drawbar 321.7 *train;* 373.9 *yoke*
draw blood 491.11 *inflict pain*
draw blueprints 20.18 *be an architect*
draw breath 554.18 *be born;* 581.2 *be refreshed;* 554.16 *live*
drawbridge 38.21, 317.9 *bridge;* 384.12 *fort;* 389.2 *means of escape*
draw close to jack 51.7 *bowl*
drawdown 772.1 *borrowing*
drawee 784.6 *debtor*
drawer 19.16 *artist;* 410.3 *cabinet;* 439.4 *storage;* 362.6 *towline*
drawers 551.18 *underwear*
draw first breath 554.18 *be born*
draw forth 738.3 *reveal*
draw gear 321.7 *train*
draw harrows 43.10 *farm tool*
draw hoe 44.6 *garden tool*
draw in **362.14**; **370.12**; 191.6 *become smaller;* 363.12 *lure;* 191.5 *make smaller*
drawing **19.3**; **19.9**; 20.1 *architecture;* 363.8 *attracting;* 369.1 *extraction;* 334.15 *full of energy;* 27.49 *geometric construction;* 58.3 *ice hockey;* 19.7 *picture;* 721.9 *representation;* 717.2 *reproduction;* 369.4 *sucking;* 394.12 *surgery;* 362.1 *traction;* 362.8 *tractional;* 518.7 *view*
drawing back 596.4 *sign of dislike*
drawing board 484.7 *planning*
drawing frame 19.11 *artist's materials*
drawing in 191.1 *contraction*
drawing off 369.4 *sucking*
drawing on the imagination 727.5 *tall story*
drawing out **369.5**; 620.1 *boredom;* 369.1 *extraction;* 190.1 *growth;* 148.4 *length*
drawing paper 19.11 *artist's materials*
drawing pencil 19.11 *artist's materials*
drawing pin 373.8 *fastening;* 425.8 *sharp-pointed thing*
drawing power 362.5 *magnetism*
drawing room 654.4 *meeting place;* 769.4 *reception;* 565.7 *room*
drawing-room comedy 21.12 *comedy*
drawing together 191.1 *contraction*
draw in one's horns 623.20 *submit*
draw interest 593.25 *be loved;* 765.14 *profit*
drawknife 425.9 *sharp-edged thing;* 421.9 *smoother;* 23.11 *woodworking tool*
drawl 333.2 *hesitate;* 729.3 *mode of speech;* 729.13 *speak in a particular way*
drawling 333.6 *hesitant;* 333.12 *hesitation*
drawn 153.2 *emaciated;* 111.16 *equal;* 58.8 *hockey;* 119.8 *on equal terms;* 19.27 *painted;* 144.9 *removed;* 362.8 *tractional*
drawn battle 119.2 *equilibrium*
draw near 283.7 *be in the future;* 310.9 *converge;* 147.16 *near*
drawn game 119.2 *equilibrium*
draw nigh 283.7 *be in the future;* 147.16 *near*
drawn-in 191.7 *smaller*
drawn match 111.5 *equality;* 119.2 *equilibrium*
drawn out 190.7 *bigger;* 620.4 *boring;* 270.3 *diffuse;* 148.1 *long;* 134.6 *protracted*
drawntogether 191.7 *smaller*
drawn up 484.14 *planned*
draw off 212.3 *subtract;* 369.14 *suck*
draw on 593.26 *court;* 436.5 *provision;* 349.4 *resort to*
draw one's last breath 131.19 *expire*
draw one's pension 605.5 *resign*
draw on one's savings 787.1 *expend*
draw on the imagination 727.11 *tell a tall story*
draw out **369.15**; 344.10 *awaken;* 620.6 *be boring;* 190.6 *become bigger;* 270.5 *be diffuse;* 369.11 *extract;* 148.10 *lengthen;* 190.5 *make bigger;* 134.4 *protract;* 144.15 *remove;* 738.3 *reveal*
draw rein 333.3 *slow down*
draw retirement pay 765.12 *earn*
draw shot 51.2 *grip*
drawstring 373.6 *line*
draw stroke 50.6 *canoeing*
draw stumps 131.16 *cease;* 53.15 *play*
draw the cork 558.13 *drink*
draw the curtains 523.14 *make dark*
draw the line 360.7 *detain;* 251.8 *restrain*
draw the line at 128.7 *exclude;* 166.7 *limit;* 470.1 *reject*
draw the teeth of 426.10 *blunt*
draw to a close 131.18 *come to an end*
draw to a peak 91.10 *billow*
draw together 376.37 *assemble;* 191.5 *make smaller*
draw towards 363.11 *attract*
draw tube 29.25 *mounting*
draw up 312.3 *approach;* 226.6 *cease;* 366.4 *gather up;* 407.24 *line up;* 484.10 *plan out;* 403.14 *structure*
draw up an itinerary 317.14 *find one's way*
draw up a programme 484.10 *plan out*
draw up a schedule 484.10 *plan out*
draw up a will 768.5 *give*
draw up birth charts 11.23 *divine*
draw-weight 51.9 *bowls*
dray 320.9 *animal transport;* 320.10 *sled*
drayage 362.1 *traction;* 316.2 *transportation*
drayhorse 59.2 *thoroughbred*
drayman 316.7 *transferor*
dread 612.11 *be afraid;* 474.8 *expect;* 474.1 *expectation;* 612.1 *fear*
dreaded 474.7 *expected*
dreadful 249.6 *adverse;* 236.3 *bad;* 798.7 *evil;* 612.10 *frightening;* 236.5 *harmful;* 249.13 *too bad!*
dreadfully 798.12 *evilly;* 612.16 *frighteningly;* 249.12 *in adversity*
dreadfulness 236.9 *badness;* 798.1 *evil*
dreading 474.5 *expecting*
dreadlocks 547.8 *haircut;* 420.7 *rough thing*
Dreadnought 586.25 *historical naval ships*
dreadnought 551.12 *coat;* 586.24 *warship*
dreads 547.8 *haircut*
dream 610.3 *aspiration;* 610.7 *aspire;* 545.3 *attractive female;* 105.7 *be improbable;* 474.2 *expectations;* 477.5 *fantasy;* 797.17 *good thing;* 446.6 *ideal;* 96.2 *illusion;* 518.5 *imagination;* 96.13, 446.15, 477.14, 518.17 *imagine;* 482.6 *objective;* 4.20 *philosophize;* 525.4 *something that appears;* 476.5 *suppose*
dreamboat 545.4 *attractive male;* 593.9 *lover*
dream dreams 477.15 *fantasize*
dreamed-up 700.40 *illusory;* 477.12 *imaginary;* 356.12 *produced*
dreamer 634.17 *avoider;* 610.5 *hoper;* 472.6 *inattentive person;* 341.2 *nonacting person;* 343.8 *nonworker;* 446.9 *person of ideas;* 4.10 *philosopher;* 443.7 *thinker;* 96.6 *unrealistic person;* 477.9 *visionary*
dream girl 593.9 *lover*
dreamily 446.22 *imaginatively;* 4.28 *thoughtfully*
dreaming 610.13 *aspirant;* 518.5 *imagination;* 477.10 *imaginative;* 343.4 *not awake;* 4.17 *thoughtful*
dream interpretation 11.9 *divination*
dream interpreter 11.13 *diviner*
dreamland **477.8**; 343.9 *sleep*
dreamlike 96.9 *illusory;* 477.12 *imaginary;* 525.9 *ostensible*
dreamlike thinking 36.19 *defence mechanism*
dream man 545.4 *attractive male;* 593.9 *lover*
dream of 482.10 *aim;* 617.12 *desire*
dream of other worlds 477.15 *fantasize*
dreams 291.5 *night thing*
dream state 36.14 *trance*
dream-symbol interpretation 36.24 *symbolism*
dream up 446.15, 477.14, 518.17 *imagine;* 478.3 *improvise;* 130.22 *invent;* 126.7 *originate;* 356.10 *produce*
dream world 610.3 *aspiration;* 477.8 *dreamland*
dreamy 446.13 *ideal;* 477.12 *imaginary;* 477.10 *imaginative;* 443.10 *speculative*
drearily 620.8 *boringly;* 533.9 *greyly;* 602.12 *joylessly*
dreariness 620.1 *boredom;* 602.2 *depression;* 533.7 *dullness*
dreary 620.5 *bored;* 620.4 *boring;* 602.6 *depressed;* 533.3 *dull;* 544.10 *ugly*
dreary routine 576.1 *work*
dredge 38.29 *construction equipment;* 183.5 *digger;* 362.12 *drag;* 38.30 *engineer;* 369.10 *excavator;* 369.11 *extract;* 427.21 *powder;* 377.18 *sprinkle*
dredger 38.29 *construction equipment;* 183.5 *digger;* 369.10 *excavator;* 366.9 *lifter;* 767.4 *wastebin*
dredge up 366.4 *gather up*
dredging 369.1 *extraction*
D region 434.3 *atmospheric layers*
dregs 258.4 *dirt;* 215.2 *residue;* 131.8 *tail*
dregs of society 804.9 *wicked person*
dreich 620.4 *boring;* 31.49 *cloudy*
drench 256.14 *bathe;* 219.4 *be excessive;* 394.20 *doctor;* 232.6 *fill;* 368.4 *immerse;* 394.2 *medicine;* 43.18 *practise livestock farming;* 433.9 *soaking;* 419.13 *soften;* 433.29 *water*
drenched 219.6 *excessive;* 433.23 *wet*
drenched with sweat 560.28 *sweaty*
drenching 433.9 *soaking*
drenching rain 31.25 *rain*
Dresden 382.15 *slaughterhouse*
Dress 551
dress **551.1**; **551.32**; 268.19 *anoint;* 25.55 *cook;* 394.20 *doctor;* 243.5 *equip;* 438.7 *equipment;* 525.3 *external appearance;* 551.7 *frock;* 244.1 *improve;* 562.7 *make fertile;* 495.10 *make taste;* 365.12 *rub;* 550.25 *wrap*
dress a fly 55.7 *angle*
dressage **59.10**; 59.11 *eventing;* 59.6 *horsemanship*
dressage movement 59.10 *dressage*
dress blues 551.3 *formal dress*
dress circle 21.18 *auditorium;* 518.9 *viewpoint*
dress down 670.20 *censure;* 814.1 *punish*
dressed **551.29**; 55.8 *angling;* 25.56 *culinary;* 243.18 *prepared*
dressed fit to kill 656.7 *dressed-up*
dressed fly 55.2 *artificial fly*
dressed to kill 551.30, 656.7 *dressed-up*
dressed-up **551.30**; **656.7**; 699.39 *disguised;* 211.9 *extra*
dresser 23.5, 410.3 *cabinet;* 35.17 *paramedic;* 21.28 *stagehand;* 551.28 *valet*
dressily **551.36**
dress in 551.34 *wear*
dressing **551.2**; 211.3 *additional item;* 562.3 *fertilizer;* 550.6 *medical covering;* 365.5 *polishing;* 496.2 *seasoning;* 223.5 *side-dish;* 394.10 *surgical dressing*
dressing-down 670.7 *blame;* 814.7 *punishment*
dressing gown 552.4 *dishabille;* 551.4, 657.6 *informal dress;* 551.22 *nightwear;* 551.16 *robe*
dressing room 565.7 *room;* 21.17 *stage*
dressing ship 601.8 *salute*
dressing station 394.14 *hospital*
dressing table 23.4 *table*
dressing-table mirror 518.8 *reflection*
dressing up 551.2 *dressing;* 525.3 *external appearance;* 699.14 *façade*
dressmaker 224.6 *editor;* 551.26 *fashion designer*
dressmaking 551.2 *dressing*
dress rehearsal 243.10 *preparations;* 21.14 *production*
dress shirt 551.8 *shirt*
dress suit 551.3, 656.4 *formal dress;* 551.10 *suit*
dress to kill 551.33 *dress up*
dress uniform 551.3, 656.4 *formal dress*
dress up **551.33**; **553.8**; 673.17 *be affected;* 234.12 *distort the truth;* 244.1 *improve;* 699.28 *mask;* 702.11 *practise sophistry*
dress up as 525.11 *appear*
dress warmly 493.16 *feel hot*
dress whites 551.3 *formal dress*
dressy 553.7 *fashionable;* 551.31 *styled*
drey 71.20 *abode of mammals;* 565.13 *lair*
Dr Fell 594.8 *hated person*
dribble 486.7 *be clumsy;* 203.2 *certain amount;* 90.7 *flow;* 58.1 *hockey;* 58.3 *ice hockey;* 330.27 *kick;* 315.12 *leak;* 315.3 *leakage;* 371.14 *let out;* 49.6 *play basketball;* 58.9 *play hockey;* 49.4 *playing terms;* 560.9 *saliva;* 560.20 *salivate;* 429.16, 433.32 *seep;* 330.5 *throw*
dribble away 766.12 *lessen*
dribbled 58.8 *hockey;* 66.5 *soccer*
dribbler 48.5 *batting terms*
dribbling 486.3 *clumsy;* 66.2 *football play;* 58.1 *hockey;* 58.3 *ice hockey;* 315.3 *leakage;* 49.4 *playing terms;* 560.29 *salivating;* 429.12, 433.25 *seeping*
dribbling away 766.4 *lessening*
dried 428.3 *dried-up;* 359.7 *preserved*
dried-blood meal 43.13 *fertilizer*
dried flower 78.1 *flower*
dried food 557.7 *food;* 359.3 *preserved thing*
dried fruit 80.1 *fruits;* 25.42 *preserve*
dried grass 43.9 *animal feedstuff*
dried milk 558.5 *milk;* 359.3 *preserved thing*
dried-out **428.4**
dried-up **428.3**
dried vegetable 44.11 *vegetable*
drier 31.45 *fine*
drift 131.14 *aim;* 324.2 *bearing;* 793.12 *be cheap;* 343.12 *be inactive;* 250.16 *be independent;* 300.13 *be in motion;* 227.12 *be irresolute;* 415.9 *be light;* 325.15 *deviating motion;* 90.7 *flow;* 30.38 *glacier;* 325.3 *go astray;* 376.26 *mass;* 694.1 *meaning;* 322.7 *miscellaneous aviation terms;* 300.2 *momentum;* 341.4 *not act;* 692.19 *radio reception;* 90.6 *river flow;* 345.4 *significance;* 723.1 *summary;* 104.2, 229.1 *tendency;* 447.1 *topic;* 316.10 *transferred thing;* 300.15 *walk*
driftage 322.7 *miscellaneous aviation terms;* 300.2 *momentum;* 90.6 *river flow*
drift along 302.6 *march on*
drift apart 377.9 *be dispersed*
drifter 343.8 *nonworker;* 323.3 *vessel*
drifting 254.4 *endangered;* 335.12 *impotent;* 300.16 *moving;* 104.6 *probable;* 377.25 *sprawled;* 325.16, 325.25 *wandering*
drifting apart 311.2 *parting*
drifting snow 31.30 *snow*
drift net 74.7 *fishing*
drift off 377.9 *be dispersed*
drift with the current 265.20 *take it easy*
driftwood **377.8**; 316.10 *transferred thing*
drill 117.10 *assimilate;* 396.19 *be authoritarian;* 507.8 *be loud;* 243.6 *brief;* 243.12 *briefing;* 23.17 *carpenter;* 44.15 *cultivate;* 140.6 *custom;* 156.14 *deepen;* 369.13 *dig out;* 6.22 *educate;* 38.30 *engineer;* 576.5, 576.9 *exercise;* 43.17 *farm;* 43.11 *farmland;* 43.10 *farm tool;* 656.3 *formal occasion;* 44.6 *garden tool;* 308.20 *hole;* 38.9 *machine tool;* 308.2 *opener;* 632.6 *procedure;* 307.6 *rotator;* 19.14 *sculptor's materials;* 425.8 *sharp-pointed thing;* 193.4 *textile;* 438.1 *tool;* 425.16 *use a sharp tool;* 438.10 *use tools;* 23.11 *woodworking tool*
drill attention 656.3 *formal occasion*
drilled 308.14 *holed*
driller 183.5 *digger*
drilling 38.29 *construction equipment;* 156.1 *depth;* 369.3 *digging out;* 6.1 *education;* 632.7 *habituation*
drilling machine 38.9 *machine tool*
drilling vessel 30.17 *ocean research vessel*
drillmaster 243.15 *preparer*
drill sergeant 579.13 *director;* 507.5 *loud person;* 243.15 *preparer*
drily **428.24**; 620.8 *boringly;* 599.16 *humorously;* 499.10 *sourly;* 497.10 *without taste*
drink **558.2**; **558.13**; **690.13**; 690.12 *alcohol;* 431.1 *fluid;* 690.8 *get drunk;* 370.11 *ingest;* 581.7 *refreshments;* 495.9 *taste*
drinkable **558.17**; 252.6 *safe;* 495.7 *tasty*
drinkables 436.2 *provisions*
drink container **558.10**
drink deep 690.8 *get drunk*
drinker **558.12**; 690.17 *drunkard;* 43.10 *farm tool;* 495.5 *taster*
drink hard 690.8 *get drunk*
Drinking 558
drinking **558.1**; **558.16**; **690.11**; 370.4 *intake*
drinking bout **690.14**; 601.1 *celebration*
drinking cup 410.13 *drinking vessel*
drinking horn 410.13 *drinking vessel*
drinking place 558.11 *drink provider*
drinking to excess 558.1 *drinking*
drinking vessel **410.13**
drinking water **433.2**; 558.6 *soft drink*
drinking yoghurt 558.5 *milk*

drink in moderation 684.5 *be self-restrained*
drink like a fish 558.13 *drink;* 690.8 *get drunk*
drink moderately 689.3 *be sober*
drink of the gods 558.2 *drink*
drink one's fill 558.13 *drink;* 217.6 *have enough*
drink problem 690.16 *alcoholism*
drink provider 558.11
drinks 223.5 *side-dish*
drinks cabinet 23.5, 410.3 *cabinet*
drink sociably 689.3 *be sober*
drinks party 654.5 *party*
drink the health of 601.17 *congratulate;* 558.14 *drink to*
drink to 558.14; 658.10 *be courteous;* 654.11 *be sociable;* 601.17 *congratulate*
drink up 428.20 *absorb;* 558.13 *drink;* 370.11 *ingest;* 371.11 *void*
drink water 689.3 *be sober*
drip 305.13; 620.3 *boring person;* 314.11 *infiltrate;* 37.12 *injection;* 509.11 *knock;* 315.12 *leak;* 315.3 *leakage;* 394.2 *medicine;* 20.9 *miscellaneous architectural features;* 333.1 *move slowly;* 429.16, 433.32 *seep;* 394.13 *therapy;* 337.4 *weakling*
drip-drop 509.4 *knocking*
drip-dropping 429.12 *seeping*
drip-dry 428.23; 256.13 *clean;* 42.11 *treated*
drip-feed 557.25 *provide food;* 394.13 *therapy*
dripping 25.7 *basic ingredient;* 315.3 *leakage;* 429.12, 433.25 *seeping;* 781.1 *wealthy;* 433.23 *wet*
dripping wet 433.23 *wet*
dripping with 232.8 *full*
dripping with wealth 781.1 *wealthy*
dripstone 20.9 *miscellaneous architectural features*
drip with wealth 781.12 *be rich*
drive 332.9 *acceleration;* 707.6 *assertiveness;* 381.1 *attack;* 63.12 *badminton terms;* 53.17, 330.26, 331.10 *bat;* 707.21 *be assertive;* 338.2 *be full of vigour;* 633.2 *chase;* 386.6 *compel;* 386.1 *compulsion;* 638.13 *concentration;* 726.1 *emphasis;* 342.4 *energy;* 576.4 *exertion;* 261.6 *fatigue;* 376.23 *flock;* 334.11 *give power;* 56.7 *golf;* 51.2 *grip;* 262.4 *haste;* 262.1 *hasten;* 376.43 *herd;* 332.7 *hurry someone up;* 331.1 *impel;* 395.1 *influence;* 483.10 *manipulate;* 381.12 *military attack;* 330.21 *move forward;* 49.6 *play basketball;* 64.5 *play rugby;* 43.18 *practise livestock farming;* 330.20 *propel;* 330.1 *propulsion;* 342.14 *push;* 317.3 *road;* 317.2 *route;* 63.13 *serve;* 300.14 *set in motion;* 60.7 *shoot;* 331.14 *sporting hit;* 53.9 *stroke;* 346.9 *take action;* 63.2 *tennis strokes;* 330.5 *throw;* 349.1 *use;* 338.1 *vigour;* 334.3 *vitality*
drive a bargain 776.3 *bargain*
drive against 381.1 *attack*
drive a hard bargain 13.11 *deal*
drive apart 372.14 *come between*
drive a trade 776.1 *trade*
drive away 364.1 *repel*
drive a wedge between 372.14 *come between*
drive back 364.1 *repel*
driveby shooting 16.39 *crime*
drive crazy 461.15 *make insane*
drive dangerously 254.10 *endanger*
drive-foot landing 47.2 *field events*
drive forward 300.13 *be in motion*
drive headlong 254.10 *endanger*
drive home 726.6 *emphasize*
drive in 368.3 *impact*
drive-in 557.15 *eating place*
drive insane 328.11 *derange*
drive into 480.15 *persuade*
drive into a frenzy 624.14 *make angry*
drive into the open 371.7 *drive out*
drive-in window 557.15 *eating place*
drivel 315.12 *leak;* 697.1 *nonsense;* 560.9 *saliva;* 560.20 *salivate*
drive like leaves 330.21 *move forward*
driveller 731.4 *talker*
drivelling 429.12 *seeping*
drive mad 328.11 *derange;* 461.15 *make insane*
driven 707.14 *assertive;* 334.15 *full of energy;* 262.3 *hasty*
driven snow 494.5 *ice;* 31.30 *snow;* 531.9 *white thing*
drive on 134.8 *go on!;* 331.1 *impel;* 483.9 *motivate;* 302.3 *press on*
drive out 371.7
drive out of baulk 65.8 *play billiards*
drive quickly 332.4 *be swift*
driver 61.8; 631.10 *conductor;* 401.6 *domestic servant;* 56.4 *golf club;* 438.8 *machinist;* 346.5 *operator;* 401.4 *personal attendant;* 330.11 *propeller;* 40.8 *software;* 316.7 *transferor;* 349.8 *user*
drive recklessly 254.10 *endanger*
driverless car 320.4 *personal transport*
drive round the bend 328.11 *derange;* 461.15 *make insane*
drive through 576.8 *exert oneself*
drive to death 382.16 *kill*
drive to despair 611.10 *disappoint*
drive together 376.43 *herd*
drive to the wall 246.10 *defeat heavily*
drive up the wall 328.11 *derange;* 624.14 *make angry;* 461.15 *make insane*
driveway 317.3 *road*
drive wheel 307.6 *rotator*
drive with the bowl 51.7 *bowl*
driving 386.9 *compelling;* 376.2 *herding;* 60.2 *hunting;* 331.17 *impelling;* 320.15 *motor transport;* 300.16 *moving;* 318.2 *passing along;* 330.17 *propulsive;* 31.53 *rainy;* 320.1 *road transport;* 332.8 *speed;* 638.2 *tenacious*
driving ambition 483.1 *motive*
driving force 331.11 *impulsion;* 480.11, 483.1 *motive;* 334.1 *power;* 330.12 *propellant;* 330.1 *propulsion*
driving gloves 551.25 *accessories*
driving iron 56.4 *golf club*
driving licence 320.21 *miscellaneous motoring terms;* 757.2 *permit*
driving licence number 743.3 *means of identification*
driving off 56.3 *golf shots*
driving rain 31.25 *rain*
drizzle 429.15 *be moist;* 305.13 *drip;* 429.2 *mistiness;* 31.25, 31.62 *rain*
drizzling 429.10 *misty;* 31.53 *rainy*
drizzly 429.10 *misty;* 31.53 *rainy*
Dr Johnson's Dictionary 5.28 *dictionary*
drogue 50.3 *parts of a sailing boat;* 252.4 *safety device;* 31.7 *weather instruments*
droit de seigneur 228.4 *stable thing*
droll 599.10 *humorous;* 697.5 *nonsensical;* 272.5 *ridiculous*
drollery 599.1 *humorousness;* 272.4 *joke;* 272.1 *ludicrousness;* 697.3 *tomfoolery*
drolly 599.16 *humorously*
dromedary 316.6 *beast of burden*
drone 111.11 *be regular;* 515.6 *buzz;* 511.4 *faint sound;* 513.2 *hoarseness;* 509.9 *hum;* 509.2 *humming;* 76.16 *infest;* 517.10 *lack harmony;* 343.8 *nonworker;* 333.15 *slow person;* 76.4 *social insect;* 511.8 *sound faint;* 513.5 *sound hoarse;* 18.21 *tone*
drone on 620.6 *be boring;* 731.8 *talk too much*
drongo 611.3 *hopeless person*
droning 511.4 *faint sound;* 513.8 *hoarse;* 509.16, 515.9 *humming;* 515.3 *insect noise;* 517.9 *unmelodious*
drool 557.22 *eat well;* 315.12 *leak;* 371.14 *let out;* 560.20 *salivate;* 429.16 *seep*
drooling 560.29 *salivating;* 429.12 *seeping*
drool over 593.27 *kiss*
droop 305.10; 261.5 *be fatigued;* 260.24 *be unhealthy;* 337.6 *be weak;* 602.9 *despair;* 245.1 *deteriorate;* 247.6 *fail;* 305.2 *sinkage;* 361.10 *suspend;* 361.1 *suspension*
droopiness 602.2 *depression*
drooping 305.17; 261.1 *fatigued;* 260.22 *sick;* 305.2 *sinkage;* 337.8 *weak*
droopy 602.6 *depressed;* 305.17 *drooping*
drop 305.12; 121.3 *advantage;* 495.3 *appetizer;* 486.7 *be clumsy;* 261.5 *be fatigued;* 260.24 *be unhealthy;* 337.6 *be weak;* 214.2, 303.14 *decline;* 214.4 *decrease;* 156.14 *deepen;* 156.1 *depth;* 133.12 *discontinue;* 371.2, 767.10 *dismiss;* 305.5 *dive;* 690.13 *drink;* 305.12 *drop;* 691.10 *drug oneself;* 186.7 *fall vertically;* 71.35 *give birth;* 561.11 *have young;* 814.16 *instrument of execution;* 148.10 *lengthen;* 159.3 *little piece;* 367.11 *lowering;* 205.7 *piece;* 50.19 *punt;* 355.1 *relinquish;* 605.5 *resign;* 181.3 *round thing;* 330.28 *shoot;* 303.4 *slip back;* 21.19 *stage set;* 350.6 *stop using;* 388.4 *succumb;* 367.6 *throw down;* 124.8 *trifle;* 552.14 *undress;* 186.1 *verticality*
drop a brick 486.7 *be clumsy*
drop a catch 486.7 *be clumsy*
drop acid 691.10 *drug oneself*
drop a clanger 247.6 *fail;* 288.9 *make a mistake*
drop a hint 711.5 *warn*
drop a line to 692.31 *correspond;* 316.13 *post*
drop anchor 312.4 *land;* 323.10 *sail;* 565.18 *take up residence*
drop an oar 50.16 *row*
drop a pop-up 486.7 *be clumsy*
drop a sitter 486.7 *be clumsy*
drop ball 66.2 *football play*
drop behind 168.6 *be in the rear*
drop bombs 381.3 *bomb*
drop by 654.12 *visit*
drop by drop 209.10 *by degrees;* 205.12 *partly*
dropcloth 550.9 *floor covering*
drop-crotching 79.6 *tree management*
drop curtain 21.19 *stage set*
drop dead 582.16 *meet one's fate*
drop from the sky 305.12 *drop*
drop from view 463.12 *be forgotten*
drop handlebars 320.11 *bicycle part*
drophead coupé 320.16 *car*
drop in 312.1 *arrive;* 368.1 *insert*
drop in on 654.12 *visit*
drop in the bucket 218.8 *insufficiency;* 124.8 *trifle*
drop in the ocean 218.8 *insufficiency;* 124.8 *trifle*
drop into 314.13 *fall into*
drop it 355.9 *forget it!;* 355.1 *relinquish;* 226.12 *stop!*
drop kick 331.13 *blow;* 331.7 *kick;* 64.3 *rugby play*
drop kick the ball 64.5 *play rugby*
drop-leaf 23.14 *wooden*
drop-leaf table 23.4 *table*
droplet 159.3 *little piece;* 181.3 *round thing*
drop like a stone 186.7 *fall vertically*
drop off 489.11 *be unfeeling;* 305.9 *descend;* 582.15 *die*
drop of the curtain 21.8 *scene*
drop on 305.12 *drop*
drop one 371.16 *belch;* 503.5 *stink*
drop one in it 264.23 *cause difficulties*
drop one's eyes 519.16 *be blind to*
drop one's guard 615.5 *be rash*
drop one's guts 371.16 *belch*
drop one's voice 511.8 *sound faint;* 730.16 *speak in a low voice*
dropout 355.4 *deserter;* 325.19 *deviant person;* 247.5 *failing person;* 118.7 *nonconformist;* 753.4 *protester;* 637.16 *reluctant person;* 64.3 *rugby play;* 109.3 *unconnected person*
drop out 118.19, 250.16 *be independent;* 637.9 *not cooperate;* 355.2 *withdraw*
drop over the side 367.6 *throw down*
drop-pass 58.3 *ice hockey;* 58.9 *play hockey*
drop-passing 58.8 *hockey;* 58.3 *ice hockey*
dropped 554.15 *born;* 68.13 *ice-skating;* 355.5 *relinquished;* 64.6 *rugger*
dropped catch 486.9 *bungling;* 274.13 *sporting error*
dropped goal 64.3 *rugby play*
dropped mohawk 68.7 *ice-dancing*
dropped three 68.7 *ice-dancing*
dropper 37.8 *drops*
dropping 305.4 *fall;* 305.18, 367.20 *falling;* 261.1 *fatigued*
dropping anchor 312.11 *landing*
dropping in 654.3 *meeting*
dropping one's aitches 274.11 *grammatical error*
droppings 258.4 *dirt;* 560.5 *faeces*
drops 37.8
drop scene 21.19 *stage set*
drop scone 25.39 *loaf*
drop-shot 63.12 *badminton terms*
dropsical 190.7 *bigger;* 260.23 *diseased*
drop sprogs 561.10 *reproduce oneself*
dropsy 431.3 *body fluid;* 260.4 *disease;* 190.1 *growth*
drop the bomb 585.13 *be at war*
drop the idea 355.1 *relinquish*
drop the payload 381.3 *bomb*
drop the pilot 313.5 *set out*
dross 411.3 *coat;* 258.4 *dirt;* 238.6 *refuse;* 215.2 *residue*
drossy 411.9 *platelike*
drought 31.28, 428.11 *dryness;* 218.9 *scarcity;* 428.12 *thirst*
drought-stricken 563.3 *infertile*
drought-stricken land 563.1 *infertility*
droughty 428.1 *dry*
drouk 433.29 *water*
drouthy 428.2 *thirsty*
drove 71.21 *assemblage of mammals;* 376.23 *flock;* 43.18 *practise livestock farming;* 208.4 *throng*
drover 43.16 *farm worker;* 59.15 *horse person;* 579.14 *leader*
drown 367.3 *bring down;* 357.12 *consume;* 305.9 *descend;* 357.8 *destroy;* 232.6 *fill;* 582.16 *meet one's fate;* 382.17 *murder;* 358.1 *obliterate;* 506.2 *silence;* 433.29 *water*
drowned 90.11, 433.24 *flooded;* 232.8 *full*
drowning 814.13 *capital punishment;* 305.16 *descending;* 382.2 *murder;* 305.2 *sinkage;* 433.9 *soaking;* 582.5 *ways of dying*
drown oneself 382.21 *commit suicide*
drown one's sorrows 690.8 *get drunk*
drown out 505.10 *muffle*
drown-proofed 67.11 *swimming*
drown-proofing 67.3 *survival swimming;* 67.11 *swimming*
drown the noise 506.2 *silence*
drowse 261.5 *be fatigued;* 489.11 *be unfeeling;* 343.13 *sleep;* 263.2 *take it easy*
drowser 343.11 *sleeper*
drowsily 343.17 *sleepily;* 261.8 *tiredly*
drowsiness 261.7 *fatigue;* 343.9 *sleep*
drowsy 620.5 *bored;* 261.1 *fatigued;* 343.4 *not awake;* 489.10 *sleepy*
Dr. Strangelove 586.6 *militarist*
drub 331.13 *blow;* 246.10 *defeat heavily;* 814.3 *hit;* 331.7 *kick*
drubbing 814.12 *corporal punishment;* 247.2 *defeat*
drudge 342.10 *busy person;* 401.1 *servant;* 576.6 *work;* 578.1 *worker*
drudgery 342.8 *assiduity;* 576.1 *work*
drudging 576.10 *working*
drug 37.3; **394.8**; **691.6**; 489.4 *anaesthetic;* 457.10 *bemuse;* 592.6 *desensitizing substance;* 394.20 *doctor;* 343.14 *make inactive;* 394.2 *medicine;* 592.7 *render insensitive*
drug abuse 691.1 *drug-taking*
drug addict 632.8 *creature of habit;* 691.4 *drug taker;* 260.19 *sick person*
drug addiction 260.4 *disease;* 691.1 *drug-taking*
drug dealer 691.5 *drug pusher*
drug dependence 37.3 *drug;* 691.1 *drug-taking*
drug-dependent 691.8 *addicted*
drug enforcement officer 252.3 *protector*
drugged 691.7; 592.2 *desensitized;* 335.12 *impotent;* 343.4 *not awake*
drugget 256.11 *cleaning cloth;* 550.9 *floor covering*
druggie 691.4 *drug taker*
druggist 394.16; 37.2 *pharmacologist*
drug ice 68.10 *curling*
drug oneself 691.10
drug on the market 793.2 *declining prices*
drug overdose 382.7 *suicide*
drug party 654.5 *party*
drug peddler 691.5 *drug pusher;* 804.9 *wicked person*
drug peddling 804.7 *criminality;* 691.2 *drug pushing*
drug pusher 691.5
drug pushing 691.2
drugs 691.6 *drug*
drug scorer 691.4 *drug taker*
drugs squad 16.15 *British police*
drug store 37.2 *pharmacologist*
drug-store counter 557.15 *eating place*
drug taker 691.4
Drug-Taking 691
drug-taking 691.1; 394.8 *drug*
drug test 47.5 *competition*
drug traffic 776.4 *trade*
drug trafficking 691.2 *drug pushing*
drug treatment 36.3 *psychiatric treatment;* 35.8 *treatment*
drug type 37.4
drug user 691.4 *drug taker*
druid 11.12 *occultist*
druidess 11.12 *occultist*
druidic 7.17 *priestly;* 11.15 *witchlike*
drum 509.8; 20.8 *column;* 509.1 *drumming;* 31.62 *rain;* 112.22 *resound;* 327.24 *shake;* 410.11 *vessel;* 326.9 *vibrate*
drumbeat 509.1 *drumming;* 298.5 *regular thing;* 742.6 *word*

drum-bed sander 23.11 *woodworking tool*
drum corps 584.4 *military organization*
drumhead court martial 16.19 *law court*
drumlin 154.3 *mountain*
drum major 579.14 *leader*
drum majorette 579.14 *leader*
drumming **509.1**; **509.15**; 331.12 *collision;* 31.53 *rainy;* 112.6 *reverberation;* 112.15 *reverberatory;* 326.2 *vibration*
drumming fingers 742.3 *gesture*
drumming out 371.18 *dismissal*
drum 'n' bass 18.9 *popular music*
drum one's fingers 342.12 *be active;* 742.11 *gesture*
drum out 371.3 *disbar;* 371.7 *drive out;* 814.1 *punish*
drum printer 40.7 *peripheral*
drum roll 509.1 *drumming;* 601.8 *salute*
drums 585.2 *glory of war*
drum scale 414.10 *scales*
drumstick 25.28 *poultry*
drunk **690.1**; 690.17 *drunkard;* 686.8 *overindulgent*
drunk and disorderly 690.1 *drunk*
drunkard **690.17**; 558.12 *drinker*
drunk as a fiddler 690.1 *drunk*
drunk as a lord 690.1 *drunk*
drunk as an owl 690.1 *drunk*
drunk as a skunk 690.1 *drunk*
drunk as David's sow 690.1 *drunk*
drunken **690.5**; 558.16 *drinking;* 690.1 *drunk*
drunkenly **690.18**
Drunkenness 690
drunkenness **690.10**; 558.1 *drinking;* 219.2 *overdoing it;* 686.3 *overindulgence;* 245.8 *perversion*
drunken stupor 690.10 *drunkenness*
drupe 80.2 *botanical fruit*
Druse 7.6 *non-Christian*
dry **428.1**; **428.17**; 634.19 *abstaining;* 499.5 *acid;* 463.14 *be forgetful;* 620.4 *boring;* 256.13 *clean;* 225.3 *conservative person;* 243.7 *develop;* 43.21 *domesticated;* 558.17 *drinkable;* 31.45 *fine;* 513.8 *hoarse;* 599.10 *humorous;* 617.10 *hungry;* 563.3 *infertile;* 24.11 *make ceramics;* 257.6 *make hygienic;* 641.8 *obstinate person;* 12.6 *political party;* 359.5 *preserve;* 496.12 *season;* 684.8 *self-restrained;* 684.4 *self-restrained person;* 641.4 *set;* 271.1 *simple;* 689.1 *sober;* 647.4 *strict person;* 497.5 *tasteless;* 428.2 *thirsty*
dryad 8.5 *deity;* 79.13 *tree mythology*
dry air 31.10 *air movement*
dry as a biscuit 428.3 *dried-up*
dry as a bone 428.3 *dried-up;* 428.2 *thirsty*
dry as a mummy 428.3 *dried-up*
dry as a stick 428.3 *dried-up*
dry as dust 620.4 *boring;* 428.3 *dried-up;* 497.5 *tasteless*
dry as parchment 428.3 *dried-up*
dry battery 39.29 *power source;* 439.4 *storage*
dry-cargo 319.5 *transportable*
dry cell 334.7 *electrical power;* 32.19 *electrochemistry;* 39.29 *power source*
dry-clean 256.13 *clean*
dry-cleaner 256.12 *cleaner*
dry-cleaning 256.2 *cleaning;* 42.8 *fabric treatment*
dry climate 31.38 *climate;* 428.14 *desert*
dry county 689.7 *prohibition*
dry cow 43.8 *livestock*
dry dock 312.16 *stopover*
dryer **428.15**
dry farmer 43.15 *agriculturist*
dry farming 43.4 *arable farming*
dry feed 557.8 *animal food*
dry-fly 55.8 *angling*
dry-fly fishing 55.1 *angling*
dry fruit 80.2 *botanical fruit*
dry goods 551.1 *dress;* 13.6 *economic factors;* 778.8 *merchandise*
dry-goods dealer 551.26 *fashion designer*
dry ice 494.5 *ice*
drying **428.9**; **428.13**; 359.1 *preservation*
drying chamber 24.5 *ceramic process*
drying out 689.1 *sober*
drying up 428.13 *drying*
dry land 30.6 *continent*
Dryness 428
dryness **31.28**; **428.11**; 617.3 *appetite;* 620.1 *boredom;* 497.1 *dilution;* 599.1 *humorousness;* 563.1 *infertility;* 271.4 *simplicity;* 499.1 *sourness;* 428.12 *thirst*
dry off 428.17 *dry;* 43.18 *practise livestock farming*
dry out 691.10 *drug oneself;* 428.17 *dry;* 689.5 *sober up*
drypoint 19.15 *engraving*
dry rot 357.7 *agent of destruction;* 258.4 *dirt;* 83.1 *fungus*
dry run 448.2 *rehearsal*
drysalter 436.3 *provider*
dry season 292.1 *season*
dry sherry 558.9 *wine*
dry-shod 428.10 *waterproof*
dry skin **428.16**
dry snow 494.5 *ice*
dry spell 31.28 *dryness*
dry state 689.7 *prohibition*
drysuit 50.7 *windsurfing*
dry throat 617.3 *appetite*
dry up **428.21**; 218.5 *be insufficient;* 214.4 *decrease;* 428.17 *dry;* 506.6 *hush!;* 21.36 *underact;* 441.1 *waste*
dry wine 499.3 *sour thing;* 558.9 *wine*
dry wit 599.3 *wit*
DTP 40.11 *application;* 40.1 *computing*
DT's 690.16 *alcoholism;* 461.4 *delusion*
dual 198.9 *two*
dual carriageway 320.3 *carriageway;* 188.2 *parallel thing;* 317.3 *road*
dualism 198.3 *duality;* 4.7 *school of thought*
dualist 4.11 *follower of a doctrine*
dualistic 4.14 *of a philosophy;* 198.9 *two*
duality **198.3**
dually 198.19 *twice*
dual personality 36.8 *disordered personality;* 198.3 *duality*
dual-purpose 198.10 *two-sided*
Duat 8.12 *hell*
dub 56.6 *golfer*
dubbed shot 56.3 *golf shots*
dubiety 451.1 *disbelief;* 326.3 *vacillation*
dubious 701.10 *arguable;* 451.6 *disbelieving;* 105.1 *improbable;* 705.14 *questionable;* 702.7 *sophistic;* 453.1 *uncertain*
dubiously 451.10 *disbelievingly;* 105.8 *improbably;* 705.24 *questionably;* 702.14 *sophistically;* 453.23 *uncertainly*
dubiousness 451.1 *disbelief;* 705.7 *questionableness;* 453.9 *uncertainty*
dubitable 105.1 *improbable*
Dublin bay prawn 25.19 *shellfish*
dub poetry 17.6 *poetry*
ducal 573.4 *aristocratic*
ducat 780.12 *ancient coins*
Duce 400.4 *absolute ruler;* 579.14 *leader*
duchess 573.1 *nobleman*
duchy 85.3 *dominion;* 396.8 *governmental organization;* 12.5 *political organization;* 86.5 *state*
duck 367.9 *bow;* 367.3 *bring down;* 367.16 *courtesy;* 658.13 *defer to;* 305.5 *dive;* 305.12 *drop;* 634.6 *evade;* 634.14 *evasion;* 72.11 *female bird;* 60.5 *game;* 368.4 *immerse;* 664.10 *knuckle under;* 43.8 *livestock;* 25.20 *meat;* 593.12 *nicknames for lovers;* 814.1 *punish;* 637.2 *refuse;* 53.10 *score;* 367.8 *sit;* 67.11 *swimming;* 300.15 *walk;* 586.24 *warship;* 433.29 *water;* 72.3 *water bird;* 195.1 *zero*
duck and dive 227.12 *be irresolute*
duck and run 389.5 *escape*
duckboard 38.21 *bridge*
duckboards 550.9 *floor covering*
duck dive 67.6 *diving*
ducked 433.24 *flooded*
duck-egg blue 539.1 *blue*
duck farming 43.3 *livestock farming*
duck-fit 624.4 *anger*
duck gybe 50.15 *sail;* 50.1 *sailing*
duck hunter 382.13 *animal killer;* 60.4 *hunter*
duck hunting 382.9 *animal killing;* 60.2 *hunting*
ducking 305.18 *falling;* 368.10 *immersion;* 814.7 *punishment;* 433.9 *soaking;* 367.13 *submergence;* 664.2 *sycophancy*
ducking and diving 227.2 *irresolution*
ducking stool 814.14 *instrument of punishment*
duckling 43.8 *livestock;* 555.4 *young animal;* 72.12 *young bird*
duckpins 51.4 *bowling*
duck responsibility 754.5 *be irresolute*
ducks 53.6 *pad*
duck season 292.1 *season*
duck shoot 633.2 *chase*
duck soup 265.6 *easy thing*
Ducks Unlimited 60.2 *hunting*
duck tack 50.15 *sail;* 50.1 *sailing*
duck the issue 634.7 *be evasive*
ducky 593.12 *nicknames for lovers*
duct 308.1 *opening*
ductile 422.6 *elastic;* 419.2 *pliant;* 362.9 *retractive;* 265.12 *wieldy*
ductility 422.1 *elasticity;* 419.8 *softness*
ductless gland 559.3 *gland*
dud 587.13 *ammunition;* 247.10 *failed;* 247.5 *failing person;* 339.3 *inert thing;* 96.5 *insubstantial person;* 335.10 *powerless;* 247.4 *unsuccessful thing;* 238.1 *useless*
dud cheque 786.3 *bad payment;* 780.15 *false money*
dude 700.22 *dupe;* 567.2 *male;* 486.10 *unskilled person*
dude ranch 43.6 *farm*
dudgeon 624.2 *offence;* 587.8 *sharp weapon*
duds 551.1 *dress*
due 239.1 *convenient;* 324.9 *directly;* 575.2 *entitlement;* 474.7 *expected;* 283.11 *future;* 784.9 *in debt;* 801.9 *in the right;* 785.17 *payable;* 801.6 *right*
due credit 813.1 *reward*
due for demolition 357.15 *destroyed*
duel 54.5 *fence;* 382.4 *slaughter*
dueller 586.1 *combatant;* 54.4 *fencer*
duelling 54.1 *fencing*
duelling pistol 587.10 *historical gun*
duelling sword 54.2 *fencing equipment*
duellist 586.1 *combatant*
due measure 685.1 *moderation*
dueness 631.1 *conduct;* 239.3 *convenience;* 814.8 *penalty;* 136.1 *qualification;* 385.1 *retaliation*
duenna 223.7 *attendant;* 6.4 *educator;* 252.3 *protector*
due north 324.9 *directly*
due payment 785.1 *payment*
due process 277.3 *continuity;* 16.6 *legal process*
due process of law 16.33 *litigation*
due recognition 813.1 *reward*
due respect 667.3 *respectfulness*
dues 790.3 *fee;* 788.2 *money received;* 790.7 *tax*
duet 374.3 *assembly;* 198.2 *double;* 747.9 *team;* 198.1 *two*
due time 239.3 *convenience*
due to 345.10 *caused*
duff 122.14 *poor;* 335.10 *powerless*
duffel 440.4 *possessions*
duffel bag 410.8 *bag*
duffel coat 551.12 *coat*
duffer 56.6 *golfer;* 456.5 *ignorant person;* 486.10 *unskilled person*
dug 308.14 *holed;* 71.2 *mammalian characteristic*
dug in 384.31 *entrenched*
dugout 48.1 *baseball;* 736.2 *hiding place;* 384.8 *military defences;* 252.5 *refuge*
dugout canoe 50.6 *canoeing*
duke 573.1 *nobleman*
dukedom 573.2 *aristocracy;* 85.3 *dominion;* 396.8 *governmental organization;* 12.5 *political organization*
Duke of Perth 22.4 *historic dancing*
dukes 492.7 *sense organ;* 360.3 *tools for gripping*
dulcet 241.3 *comfortable;* 18.30 *harmonic;* 516.6 *melodious;* 490.6 *pleasant*
dulcetly 18.42 *musically*
dulcify 685.4 *moderate*
Dulcinea 593.9 *lover*
dull **426.3**; **533.3**; 620.6 *be boring;* 457.10 *bemuse;* 426.1, 426.10 *blunt;* 620.4 *boring;* 31.49 *cloudy;* 530.7 *colourless;* 530.6 *decolour;* 524.5 *dim;* 524.7 *dimmed;* 261.1 *fatigued;* 459.5 *foolish;* 456.6 *ignorant;* 341.3 *inactive;* 618.7 *indifferent;* 339.5 *inert;* 592.1 *insensitive;* 457.5 *lacking intellect;* 618.13 *make indifferent;* 216.3 *mediocre;* 685.4 *moderate;* 511.7 *mute;* 511.2 *nonresonant;* 343.3 *not participating;* 301.5 *sedentary;* 528.2 *shady;* 529.13 *soft-hued;* 524.8 *stupid;* 524.11 *tarnish;* 497.5 *tasteless;* 152.3 *thick-witted;* 544.10 *ugly;* 528.5 *unintelligent*
dullard 339.2 *inert person;* 457.3 *unintelligent person*
dulled 524.7 *dimmed;* 511.2 *nonresonant*
dull-edged 426.1 *blunt*
dull green 538.1 *green*
dull monotony 620.1 *boredom*
dullness **426.7**; **533.7**; 426.5 *bluntness;* 620.1 *boredom;* 261.7 *fatigue;* 529.3 *hue;* 343.7 *idleness;* 618.1 *indifference;* 339.1 *inertness;* 592.3 *insensitiveness;* 489.1 *lack of feeling;* 524.2 *murk;* 528.6 *opaqueness;* 497.1 *tastelessness*
dull-pointed 426.1 *blunt*
dull sound **511.5**
dull speech 620.2 *boring thing*
dull-witted 152.3 *thick-witted;* 528.5 *unintelligent*
dull-wittedness 528.9 *stupidity*
dully 620.8 *boringly;* 530.9 *colourlessly;* 533.9 *greyly;* 343.16 *impassively;* 426.11 *smoothly;* 497.10 *without taste*
duly 756.16 *as promised*
dumb 70.14 *animalian;* 231.3 *deformed;* 456.6 *ignorant;* 457.8 *nonhuman;* 506.3 *silent;* 732.2 *sparing with words;* 730.11 *speechless;* 152.3 *thick-witted;* 457.6 *unintelligent;* 486.1 *unskilful;* 619.7 *wide-eyed*
dumb animal 70.2 *animal*
dumbbell 456.5 *ignorant person;* 457.3 *unintelligent person*
dumb cluck 456.5 *ignorant person*
dumbfound 630.11 *amaze;* 619.10 *be wonderful;* 604.6 *disappoint;* 730.15 *strike dumb*
dumbfounded 630.7 *amazed;* 506.3 *silent;* 730.11 *speechless;* 619.6 *wondering*
dumbfoundment 619.1 *wonder*
dumb friend 70.2 *animal*
dumbness 732.4 *guarded speech;* 730.5 *mutism;* 506.4 *silence*
dumbo 459.3 *foolish person;* 456.5 *ignorant person;* 457.3 *unintelligent person*
dumbshow 717.3 *acting;* 21.2 *play*
dumbstruck 766.18 *at a loss;* 619.7 *wide-eyed*
dumb waiter 366.10 *elevator*
dumdum 587.13 *ammunition;* 456.5 *ignorant person*
dummy 96.12 *artificial;* 125.2 *copy;* 448.8 *experimental;* 699.12 *fake;* 456.5 *ignorant person;* 717.6 *image;* 461.7 *insane person;* 96.5 *insubstantial person;* 685.2 *moderator;* 343.8 *nonworker;* 160.2 *prototype;* 160.10 *prototypical;* 738.7 *showpiece;* 457.3 *unintelligent person*
dummying 64.3 *rugby play;* 64.6 *rugger*
dummy run 448.2 *rehearsal*
dump 623.23 *abase;* 623.10 *abasement;* 40.20 *abort;* 40.19 *computing terms;* 791.3 *discount;* 767.9 *dispose of;* 408.4 *litter;* 793.13 *make cheap;* 238.6 *refuse;* 778.1 *sell;* 565.8 *shelter;* 767.8 *sink;* 350.6 *stop using;* 439.4 *storage;* 371.12 *unload;* 767.5 *wasteyard;* 355.2 *withdraw*
dumpbin 738.8 *showplace*
dumpcart 320.7 *handcart*
dumpiness 159.1 *littleness;* 149.1 *shortness;* 158.6 *squatness*
dumping 791.2 *bargain;* 767.1 *disposal;* 350.10 *disuse*
dumpling 158.12 *fat person*
dump on 236.14 *ill-treat;* 668.23 *insult*
dump on the market 219.4 *be excessive*
dump truck 38.29 *construction equipment*
dump upon 305.12 *drop*
dumpy 158.16 *fat;* 544.7 *graceless;* 724.8 *inelegant;* 159.7 *little;* 149.7 *short*
dun 534.1 *brown;* 783.8 *credit;* 710.2, 710.7 *demand;* 533.1 *grey;* 59.1 *horse;* 783.5 *lender;* 342.17 *meddle*
dunce 459.3 *foolish person;* 456.5 *ignorant person;* 457.3 *unintelligent person*
dunce cap 551.15 *headgear*
dunce's cap 814.14 *instrument of punishment;* 743.5 *uniform*
Dundee cake 25.36 *cake*
dunderhead 457.3 *unintelligent person*
dune **30.37**; 376.26 *mass;* 154.3 *mountain*
dung 44.15 *cultivate;* 258.4 *dirt;* 560.5 *faeces;* 43.17 *farm;* 43.13, 562.3 *fertilizer;* 437.2 *lighter;* 503.2 *something that makes an unpleasant smell*
dungarees 551.9 *trousers*
dungeon 309.4 *closed place;* 523.4 *dark thing;* 156.4 *deep thing;* 815.1 *prison*
dunghill 767.8 *sink*
dunging 43.5 *cultivation*
dungy 560.25 *faecal;* 258.8 *unclean*

dunk 256.14 *bathe;* 368.4 *immerse;* 49.6 *play basketball;* 49.4 *playing terms;* 433.29 *water*
dunked 433.24 *flooded*
dunking 49.4 *playing terms;* 433.9 *soaking*
dunning 710.2 *demand*
duo 374.3 *assembly;* 18.26 *musical group;* 198.1 *two*
duodecahedron 176.3 *angled figure*
duodecillion 194.3 *large number;* 201.11 *million*
duodecimal 201.7 *double figures;* 201.18 *eleventh*
duodecimal notation 27.8 *number system*
duodecimo 201.7 *double figures;* 159.7 *little;* 159.2 *little thing*
duodenal 172.10 *visceral*
duodenal ulcer 260.8 *indigestion*
duodenary 201.18 *eleventh*
duodenitis 260.8 *indigestion*
duodenum 172.4 *insides*
duodrama 21.2 *play*
duologue 734.1 *conversation;* 21.2 *play*
duomo 10.11 *place of worship*
dupe 700.22; 774.16 *act dishonestly;* 604.8 *be dishonest;* 668.9 *butt;* 111.4 *duplicate;* 247.5 *failing person;* 122.6 *inferior;* 621.4 *laughing stock;* 766.6 *loser;* 450.9 *make someone believe;* 646.3 *naive person;* 249.5 *person in adversity;* 664.3 *sycophant;* 773.10 *take away;* 379.2 *trap;* 700.28 *trick;* 337.4 *weakling*
duped 604.10, 700.36 *deceived*
duper 700.15 *deceiver*
dupery 700.7 *tricking*
duple 198.9 *two*
duple metre 17.9 *metre*
duplex 198.2 *double;* 565.5 *house;* 565.16 *manorial;* 198.9 *two*
duplex apartment 565.5 *house*
duplexity 198.3 *duality*
duplicate 111.4; **111.9**; **111.15**; **125.5**; 219.5 *be superfluous;* 115.2, 125.2, 125.10, 744.5 *copy;* 198.12, 198.15 *double;* 717.6 *image;* 115.12 *imitate;* 213.5 *make bigger;* 743.3 *means of identification;* 561.2 *print;* 112.16 *repeat;* 112.7 *replica;* 717.9 *represent;* 717.1, 721.9 *representation;* 561.9 *reproduce;* 115.8 *simulated;* 198.5 *twin*
duplicate copy 744.5 *copy*
duplicated 198.12 *double;* 112.9 *repeated;* 561.15 *reproduced;* 115.7 *similar;* 115.8 *simulated*
duplicating the cube 737.5 *difficult problem*
duplication 125.2 *copy;* 198.4 *doubling;* 111.4 *duplicate;* 213.1 *increase;* 112.1 *repetition;* 561.2 *reproduction;* 115.1 *similarity;* 219.3 *superfluity*
duplicative 112.12 *repetitious*
duplicator 115.3 *copier;* 125.6 *photocopier*
duplicitous 699.30; 268.15 *crafty;* 699.33 *deceitful;* 700.35 *deceptive;* 198.11 *double-edged;* 800.6 *faithless;* 700.38 *treacherous*
duplicitously 268.24
duplicity 268.9; **699.2**; 645.1 *cunning;* 699.5 *deceitfulness;* 700.1 *deception;* 198.3 *duality;* 736.5 *evasion;* 800.2 *faithlessness;* 700.4 *falseheartedness;* 702.5 *hypocrisy*
durability 277.4 *long-lastingness;* 225.1 *permanence;* 228.1 *stability;* 336.1 *strength;* 423.6 *toughness*
durable 279.8 *eternal;* 277.8 *lasting;* 225.7 *permanent;* 228.9 *stable;* 336.13 *strengthened;* 423.1 *tough*
durable goods 13.6 *economic factors*
durableness 277.4 *long-lastingness*
durables 13.6 *economic factors;* 778.8 *merchandise*
durably 423.12 *toughly*
Duralumin™ 418.7 *hard substance*
duramen 418.7 *hard substance;* 79.3 *timber*
durance 251.4 *detention;* 815.7 *imprisonment*
Duration 277
duration 275.3; **277.1**; 93.6 *continuing existence;* 209.1 *degree;* 141.8 *intervening space;* 148.4 *length*
durbar 579.7 *council*
duress 386.2 *coercion;* 251.1 *restraint*
Durga-puja 10.16 *religious festival*
during 275.26 *all the time*
during the evening 291.7 *evening*
during the past 284.22 *in the past*
durn 712.11 *miscellaneous euphemisms*
durned 712.11 *miscellaneous euphemisms*
dush 238.6 *refuse*
dusk 131.9 *close;* 524.1 *dimness;* 291.1 *evening*
duskily 532.12 *blackly*
duskiness 532.7 *blackness;* 524.1 *dimness*
duskness 258.1 *dirtiness*
dusky 523.8, 532.2 *dark;* 523.10 *dark-coloured;* 524.5 *dim;* 291.6 *evening*
dust 256.13 *clean;* 44.15 *cultivate;* 258.4 *dirt;* 43.13 *fertilizer;* 814.3 *hit;* 415.7 *light thing;* 634.9 *play truant;* 427.5, 427.21 *powder;* 377.18 *sprinkle;* 367.6 *throw down;* 124.8 *trifle;* 541.11 *variegate*
dustball 427.5 *powder*
dustbin 256.10 *cleaning object;* 238.6 *refuse;* 767.8 *sink;* 410.11 *vessel;* 767.4 *wastebin*
dustbin man 767.6 *rubbish collector*
dust bowl 428.14 *desert;* 563.1 *infertility*
dustcart 767.4 *wastebin*
dust cloud 427.5 *powder*
dust cover 256.11 *cleaning cloth;* 165.4 *wrapper*
dust-covered 427.15 *powdery*
dust devil 427.5 *powder;* 31.16 *wind vortex*
dust down 814.1 *punish*
dusted 541.10 *mottled;* 377.23 *sprinkled*
duster 256.11 *cleaning cloth;* 256.10 *cleaning object;* 551.12 *coat;* 358.4 *eraser*
dustheap 238.6 *refuse;* 767.5 *wasteyard*
dustily 428.24 *drily;* 427.29 *flakily*
dustiness 427.1 *powderiness*
dusting 256.2 *cleaning;* 814.12 *corporal punishment;* 427.4 *pulverization;* 157.3 *shallowness;* 377.4 *sprinkling*
dusting down 814.7 *punishment*
dusting off 331.12 *collision*
dusting off the batter 48.4 *pitching terms*
dust jacket 165.4 *wrapper;* 550.4 *wrapping*
dustman 256.12 *cleaner;* 767.6 *rubbish collector;* 578.1 *worker*
dust of antiquity 296.3 *antiquity*
dust off 331.5 *beat*
dust-off 48.4 *pitching terms*
dustpan and brush 256.10 *cleaning object*
dust ruffle 550.10 *bed covering*
dustsheet 256.11 *cleaning cloth;* 165.4 *wrapper*
dust storm 528.7 *opaque thing;* 427.5 *powder;* 380.5 *violent weather;* 31.12 *wind*
dust-up 751.2 *argument;* 408.9 *disorder*
dusty 428.6 *desert;* 524.7 *dimmed;* 258.7 *dirty;* 541.10 *mottled;* 524.6 *murky;* 427.15 *powdery;* 528.2 *shady;* 531.2 *whitened*
dusty air 524.2 *murk*
Dutch 119.6 *equal*
Dutch auction 793.2 *declining prices;* 767.2 *disposal of property;* 778.4 *sale*
Dutch barn 43.7 *farm building*
Dutch cap 378.3 *barrier;* 563.3 *birth control;* 551.15 *headgear*
Dutch courage 690.12 *alcohol;* 613.5 *bold front;* 690.10 *drunkenness*
Dutch elm disease 83.5 *fungal association;* 79.10 *tree disease*
Dutch hoe 44.6 *garden tool*
Dutch oven 493.4 *burner;* 25.5 *cooker*
Dutch rush 82.1 *fern*
Dutch TT 61.5 *motorcycle racing*
Dutch uncle 713.4 *adviser;* 647.4 *strict person*
duteous 810.8 *dutiful;* 663.7 *obedient*
duteously 810.18 *on duty*
duteousness 810.4 *sense of duty*
dutiable 790.15 *chargeable*
dutiful 810.8; 706.16 *answerable;* 803.6 *ethical;* 799.4 *honourable;* 663.7 *obedient;* 667.9 *showing respect;* 797.4 *well-behaved;* 9.9 *worshipful;* 10.22 *worshipping*
dutifully 706.27 *answerably;* 803.10 *ethically;* 799.7 *honourably;* 663.10, 797.24 *obediently;* 810.18 *on duty;* 10.23 *ritually*
dutifulness 797.11 *good behaviour;* 663.1 *obedience;* 810.4 *sense of duty*
Duty 810
duty 810.1; 706.9 *answerability;* 575.2 *entitlement;* 790.8 *levy;* 788.2 *money received;* 480.11 *motive;* 135.3 *needfulness;* 663.1 *obedience;* 205.9 *participation;* 10.1 *ritual;* 803.2 *virtues;* 576.1 *work;* 9.1 *worship*
duty-bound 810.11; 706.16 *answerable*
duty-free 758.8 *tax-free;* 758.13 *with impunity*
duumvirate 12.1 *government;* 747.9 *team*
duvet 550.10 *bed covering;* 493.3 *heater;* 419.11 *soft thing*
DV 8.19 *divinely*
dwarf 11.11 *ghost;* 159.7 *little;* 159.4 *little person;* 149.5 *short person*
dwarf bush tree 44.10 *fruit tree*
dwarfed 159.7 *little*
dwarf elliptical 29.7 *galaxy*
dwarfish 159.7 *little*
dwarfishness 159.1 *littleness*
dwarf pyramid 44.10 *fruit tree*
dwarf tree 79.1 *tree*
dweeb 620.3 *boring person*
dwell 554.17; 93.17 *exist;* 564.14, 565.17 *inhabit;* 97.13 *reside;* 142.10 *settle*
dweller 564.1 *inhabitant*
dwellers 564.2 *inhabitants*
dwell in 565.17 *inhabit;* 763.7 *possess*
dwelling 565.1 *habitat;* 565.14 *inhabiting;* 564.13 *resident*
dwelling place 565.1 *habitat*
dwell on 726.6 *emphasize*
dwell on a mountain 89.10 *climb a mountain*
dwell upon 620.6 *be boring*
dwindle 337.6 *be weak;* 214.4 *decrease;* 526.1 *disappear;* 766.12 *lessen*
dwindle away 526.1 *disappear*
dwindling 214.1 *decrease;* 214.6 *decreasing;* 526.4 *disappearance;* 766.4 *lessening*
DX code 41.10 *graininess*
dyad 198.1 *two*
dyadic 4.16 *dialectical;* 198.9 *two*
dybbuk 8.7 *devil*
dye 42.6; 412.4 *admixture;* 522.28 *bleach;* 28.28, 529.15 *colour;* 412.8 *mix;* 529.4 *pigment;* 42.15 *treat*
dye blue 539.9 *blue*
dyed 529.10 *coloured;* 632.13 *fixed;* 412.12 *mixed;* 42.11 *treated*
dyed-in-the-wool 232.7 *complete;* 225.8 *conservative;* 632.13 *fixed;* 809.3 *impenitent;* 42.11 *treated*
dyed-in-the-wool conservative 225.3 *conservative person*
dyed-in-the-wool sinner 809.2 *impenitent person*
dyed-in-the-yarn 42.11 *treated*
dyeing 42.7; 523.9 *darkening*
dye laser 28.26 *laser*
dyestuff 42.6 *dye;* 529.4 *pigment*
dyestuffs 32.22 *industrial chemistry*
dying 582.18; 582.1 *death;* 526.4 *disappearance;* 526.6 *disappearing;* 260.22 *sick*
dying breath 582.7 *dying day*
dying day 582.7
dying for 617.9 *desirous*
dying for food 687.6 *fasting*
dying out 526.4 *disappearance*
dying patient 582.10 *dying person*
dying person 582.10
dying race 563.1 *infertility*
dying star 29.11 *stellar birth*
dyke 146.2 *crack;* 165.5 *enclose;* 165.3 *enclosing thing;* 568.10 *homosexual;* 30.30 *igneous rock*
dykey 568.15 *female*
Dylan 91.4 *sea god*
dynamic 342.18 *active;* 300.17 *directional;* 334.15 *full of energy;* 331.17 *impelling;* 554.13 *lively;* 28.98 *physical;* 338.4 *vigorous*
dynamically 331.18; 334.19 *energetically;* 300.18 *in motion;* 28.100 *physically*
dynamic belay 62.3 *climbing technique*
dynamic duo 374.3 *assembly*
dynamic energy 342.4 *energy*
dynamic friction 28.10 *force*
dynamic load 38.14 *load*
dynamic memory 40.6 *memory*
dynamic metamorphism 30.32 *metamorphism*
dynamic psychology 36.1 *psychology*
dynamic range 41.10 *graininess*
dynamics 28.2 *classical physics;* 331.11 *impulsion;* 300.1 *motion*
dynamic structure 38.5
dynamic system 38.5 *dynamic structure*
dynamism 342.4 *energy;* 4.7 *school of thought;* 338.1 *vigour;* 334.3 *vitality*
dynamist 4.11 *follower of a doctrine*
dynamistic 4.14 *of a philosophy*
dynamite 357.7 *agent of destruction;* 357.9 *demolish;* 691.6 *drug;* 587.15 *explosive;* 330.13 *fuel;* 379.1 *trap;* 235.1 *worthy*
dynamo 342.10 *busy person;* 437.4 *electricity;* 39.30 *generator;* 438.5 *machine;* 334.6 *source of energy*
dynamometer 26.8 *meter*
dynamometric 26.16 *micrometric*
dynamometry 26.2 *micrometry*
dynamotor 438.5 *machine*
dynastic 12.10 *governing*
dynasty 12.3 *governance;* 132.3 *line;* 573.3 *nobleness;* 396.7 *type of rule*
dyno 691.6 *drug*
dysentery 560.2 *defecation;* 260.8 *indigestion*
dysfunctional 231.1 *imperfect*
dysmenorrhoea 560.11 *menstruation;* 491.2 *painful condition*
dyspepsia 260.8 *indigestion;* 491.2 *painful condition*
dyspeptic 625.4 *irascible;* 626.7 *irritable;* 260.19 *sick person*
dysphasia 730.3 *speech defect*
dysphasic 730.12 *inarticulate*
dysphemia 730.3 *speech defect*
dysphemic 730.12 *inarticulate*
dysphemism 712.1 *curse;* 544.4 *inelegance of speech*
dysphemistic 712.8 *cursing;* 544.9 *inelegant*
dysphemize 712.5 *curse*
dysphonia 730.1 *voicelessness*
dysphonic 730.9 *voiceless*
dyspnoea 260.10 *cardiovascular disease*
dystopia 17.2 *fiction*
Dyu 8.11 *heaven*

E 2.7 *social stratification*
each 139.32 *severally;* 204.6 *whole*
each and every one 138.10 *everyone*
each in his turn 759.8 *in exchange*
each one 138.10 *everyone*
each other 110.2 *interconnection*
each-way bet 59.7 *horseracing*
eager 636.2; 342.18 *active;* 617.9 *desirous;* 643.2 *earnest;* 474.5 *expecting;* 595.6 *liking;* 336.11 *strong in spirit*
eager beaver 342.10 *busy person;* 636.11 *willing worker*
eagerly 342.22 *actively;* 336.15 *acutely;* 595.11 *admiringly;* 617.18 *desirously*
eagerness 636.7; 638.13 *concentration;* 617.1 *desire;* 643.5 *earnestness;* 342.4 *energy;* 595.2 *inclination*
eagle 780.8 *American money;* 304.11 *ascender;* 72.5 *bird of prey;* 518.2 *eye;* 56.2 *golfing terms;* 743.8 *heraldic device;* 742.1 *sign;* 332.12 *swift animal*
eagle eye 518.2 *eye*
eagle-eyed 518.21 *seeing*
eaglet 72.12 *young bird*
eagle-winged 332.1 *swift*
eagre 91.3 *wave*
ear 504.4; 308.4 *body orifice;* 81.4 *cereal grass;* 525.3 *external appearance;* 345.3 *growth;* 28.17 *sound*
earache 504.6 *otology;* 491.2 *painful condition*
ear attachments 504.7
ear clip 504.7 *ear attachments*
ear-cuff 542.7 *jewellery*
ear drops 37.8 *drops;* 504.6 *otology*
eardrum 504.5 *internal ear*
eared 504.12
ear flaps 504.7 *ear attachments*
ear for 485.2 *aptitude*
earful 733.1 *address;* 670.7 *blame;* 504.8 *something heard;* 729.8 *speech*
earhole 504.4 *ear*
earl 573.1 *nobleman*
earldom 573.2 *aristocracy;* 85.3 *dominion*
earldorman 763.6 *lord*
earless 505.4 *deaf*
Earl Grey 558.3 *tea*
earlier 286.3 *another time;* 129.20 *before;* 296.20 *formerly;* 284.17 *past;* 129.11 *prior*
earlies 43.12 *crop*
earliest 293.12 *early;* 129.10 *preceding;* 130.31 *prime*
earliest inhabitant 293.4 *early comer;* 564.1 *inhabitant*
earliest settler 293.4 *early comer*
earliest stage 293.3 *early stage*
earlike 504.12 *eared*
Earliness 293

earliness 293.1; 288.2 *untimeliness*
Earl Marshal 743.9 *herald*
earlobe 504.4 *ear*
Earl's Court 87.5 *London*
early 293.12; **293.17**; 296.21 *archaically*; 130.29 *beginning*; 290.5 *morning*; 284.17 *past*; 296.15 *primal*; 332.1 *swift*
Early American 23.7 *furniture style*
early arrival 293.4 *early comer*
early bird 293.4 *early comer*; 290.2 *morning thing*
early civilizations 566.4 *modern human*
early comer 293.4
early days 130.12 *first move*
early edition 740.4 *newspaper*
early evening 291.1 *evening*
Early Federal 23.7 *furniture style*
early history 293.3 *early stage*
early hour 293.2
early human 566.3
early humanity 566.3 *early human*
early life 555.1 *youth*
early lift 47.2 *field events*
early man 296.7 *ancient people*; 293.3 *early stage*
early maturity 293.5 *prematurity*
early morning 524.1 *dimness*; 293.2 *early hour*
early potatoes 43.12 *crop*
early retirement 15.2 *industrial negotiations*
early riser 293.4 *early comer*
early stage 293.3
early stages 130.12 *first move*
early start 293.1 *earliness*
early time 293.2 *early hour*
early warning 293.3 *early stage*
early warning system 293.3 *early stage*
early wood 79.3 *timber*
earmark 770.4 *allot*; 139.3 *characteristic*; 139.22 *characterize*; 743.10 *identify*; 482.9 *intend for*; 743.3 *means of identification*; 135.10 *necessitate*; 469.4 *pick*; 773.7 *take*
earmarked 743.12 *identified*; 135.4 *required*
earmarking 770.1 *allocation*
earmuffs 551.25 *accessories*; 504.7 *ear attachments*; 252.4 *safety device*
earn 765.12; 575.7 *be entitled to*; 765.9 *gain*; 769.9, 788.7 *receive*
earn a black belt 52.13 *practise judo*
earn a crust 765.12 *earn*
earn a dividend 765.14 *profit*
earn a living 765.12 *earn*
earn an income 813.13 *get paid*
earn a standing ovation 246.6 *be successful*
earn a wage 576.6 *work*
earned income 765.4 *earnings*
earned-run average 48.4 *pitching terms*
earned-run-average leader 48.2 *baseball player*
earner 765.7 *gainer*; 769.5 *recipient*; 578.1 *worker*
earnest 643.2; 156.9 *deep-seated*; 726.3 *emphatic*; 205.2 *particular*; 785.1 *payment*; 638.2 *tenacious*
earnestly 643.11; 726.7 *emphatically*; 638.17 *resolutely*
earnest money 785.1 *payment*
earnestness 643.5; 342.8 *assiduity*; 638.13 *concentration*
earnest of good faith 205.2 *particular*
earn income 765.12 *earn*
earning 785.19 *receiving pay*
earning capacity 237.8 *benefit*
earnings 765.4; 765.1 *gain*; 788.3 *income*; 785.3 *pay*; 813.4 *reward for service*; 769.2 *something received*; 773.5 *takings*
earnings per share 14.2 *stock exchange*
earning status 2.7 *social stratification*
earn interest 213.4 *increase*
earn little or nothing 782.12 *be poor*
ear of corn 81.4 *cereal grass*
EAROM 40.6 *memory*
earphone 504.7 *ear attachments*
earphones 504.9 *audio device*; 769.8 *receiver*
earpiece 504.9 *audio device*; 692.9 *telephone*
ear-piercing 513.9 *shrill*
ear plug 504.7 *ear attachments*; 505.3 *inaudibility*
ear plugs 252.4 *safety device*
ear-rending 507.6 *loud*
earring 504.7 *ear attachments*; 361.3 *suspended object*
ear ring 542.7 *jewellery*
ear-shaped 504.12 *eared*
earshattering 505.6 *deafening*
earshot 504.1 *hearing*; 147.2 *short distance*
ear-splitting 508.8 *banging*; 505.6 *deafening*; 504.14 *hearable*; 507.6 *loud*; 513.7 *strident*
ear-splitting noise 507.1 *loudness*
ear stud 504.7 *ear attachments*
Earth 29.16 *planet*
earth 30.5; 71.20 *abode of mammals*; 175.1 *base*; 39.35 *conduct*; 258.4 *dirt*; 334.7 *electrical power*; 28.52, 39.10 *electric potential*; 59.8 *hunting*; 565.13 *lair*; 252.10 *protect*; 252.4 *safety device*; 30.36 *soil*; 416.4 *solid body*
earth art 19.12 *sculpture*
earthborn 566.12 *human*
earth closet 560.13 *lavatory*; 767.7 *toilet*
earth dam 38.23 *dam*
earthed conductor 39.10 *electric potential*
earthenware 24.1 *ceramics*; 356.7 *produce*
earthenware mark 24.4 *porcelain mark*
earthflow 30.26 *mass movement*
Earth Goddess 562.4 *fertility cult*
earth goddess 8.5 *deity*
earthgrazer 29.16 *planet*
earthling 566.7 *person*
earthlings 566.1 *humankind*
earthly 402.7 *material*
earthly paradise 490.5 *idealized pleasure*
earth matter 95.2 *real world*
Earth Mother 562.4 *fertility cult*
earth movement 30.20
earthmover 38.29 *construction equipment*
earthnut 25.33 *vegetable*
earth orbit 317.13 *flight path*; 29.35 *rocketry*
earth potential 39.10 *electric potential*
earthquake 357.7 *agent of destruction*; 380.3 *instance of violence*; 30.22 *seismic activity*; 379.1 *trap*; 326.5 *wave*
earthquake magnitude 30.22 *seismic activity*
earthquake zone 30.22 *seismic activity*
earth satellite 29.32 *satellite*
earth's atmosphere 31.8 *atmosphere*
Earth Science 30
earth science 30.1
earth's crust 30.18
earth-shaking 123.5 *important*; 395.11 *influential*; 123.6 *notable*; 326.17 *waving*
earthshine 522.4 *natural light*; 29.14 *solar system*
earth's magnetism 28.58 *geomagnetism*
earth's orbit 177.3 *curved things*
earth's surface 30.5 *earth*
earth tremor 30.22 *seismic activity*
earthward 324.10 *clockwise*
earthwork 378.3 *barrier*; 384.12 *fort*; 583.6 *grave*; 742.5 *indicator*; 384.8 *military defences*; 744.11 *monument*; 3.11 *relic*; 284.7 *thing of the past*
earthworm 75.6 *worm*
earthy 30.58
ear trumpet 504.9 *audio device*; 505.1 *deafness*; 504.7 *ear attachments*; 507.4 *sound maker*
ear wax 504.6 *otology*
earwig 76.1 *insect*; 44.12 *pests and diseases*
ear witness 504.2 *hearer*
Ease 263
ease 263.1; **263.3**; **268.20**; **419.14**; **608.1**; 490.10 *comfort*; 222.5 *comfortable circumstances*; 214.4 *decrease*; 265.1 *easiness*; 543.1 *elegance*; 657.4 *freedom*; 250.4 *informality*; 714.8 *justify*; 580.1 *leisure*; 415.10 *lighten*; 265.16 *make easy*; 685.4 *moderate*; 781.7 *opulence*; 749.4 *pacify*; 490.1 *physical pleasure*; 241.7 *pleasure*; 35.19 *practise medicine*; 248.1 *prosperity*; 581.1 *refresh*; 581.5 *refreshment*; 608.9 *relieve*; 394.19 *remedy*; 609.1 *satisfaction*; 485.1 *skill*; 392.2, 392.19 *support*
ease along 333.1 *move slowly*; 330.24 *push*
eased 608.7 *relieved*
easeful 263.4 *at ease*; 490.6 *pleasant*
ease in 368.5 *inset*
easel 19.11 *artist's materials*
easel-painter 19.16 *artist*
easel painting 19.8 *painting*
easement 415.6 *lightening*
ease off 685.3 *be moderate*; 333.3 *slow down*
ease of manner 265.4
ease of viewing 520.4 *clarity*
ease out 767.10 *dismiss*
ease out a line 50.15 *sail*
ease the way 392.28 *further*
ease up 419.15 *be kind*
easier said than done 264.10 *difficult*
easily 265.21; 222.18 *comfortably*; 543.5 *elegantly*; 250.22 *informally*; 648.6 *leniently*; 333.16 *slowly*; 654.18 *sociably*; 419.18 *soft-heartedly*; 263.6 *with ease*
easily detected 527.4 *easily seen through*
easily distinguished 520.1 *visible*
easily excused 649.7 *forgivable*
easily led 483.13 *suggestible*
easily mistaken 696.3 *unrecognizable*
easily roused 625.4 *irascible*
easily seen 185.7 *conspicuous*
easily seen through 527.4
easily tempted 804.13 *venial*
easily understood 695.2 *simple*
Easiness 265
easiness 265.1; 419.12 *gentleness*; 648.1 *leniency*; 757.1 *permission*; 695.10 *simplicity*
easing 265.7; 419.7 *impressionable*; 415.3, 415.6 *lightening*; 685.8 *moderating*; 685.1 *moderation*; 393.11 *recuperation*; 608.8 *relieving*
easing off 333.9 *deceleration*
easing up 419.12 *gentleness*
east 324.4 *compass point*; 324.13 *directional*; 324.12 *north*
East African Safari 61.4 *motor rally*
East African Safari rally 61.1 *motor racing*
East and West 86.7 *regions of the world*
east and west 113.3 *opposites*
eastbound 324.13 *directional*
East End 87.5 *London*
Easter 298.6 *annually celebrated day*; 10.16 *religious festival*; 292.2 *spring*
Easter bonnet 551.15 *headgear*
Easter Island 737.6 *natural mystery*
easterly 324.13 *directional*; 324.12 *north*; 31.15 *wind direction*; 31.47 *windy*
eastern 324.13 *directional*; 86.16 *regional*; 169.6 *side*
Eastern bloc 85.2 *union of nations*
Eastern cut-off style 47.2 *field events*
Eastern Daylight Time 275.9 *time zone*
Easterner 564.10 *US inhabitant*
Eastern Hemisphere 86.7 *regions of the world*
easternmost 324.13 *directional*
Eastern Standard Time 275.9 *time zone*
Easter offering 768.3 *offering*
Easter season 292.1 *season*
Eastertide 10.16 *religious festival*; 292.2 *spring*
easting 324.4 *compass point*
eastings and northings 142.2 *exact location*
Eastlander 564.10 *US inhabitant*
East Side 87.3 *New York*
east side 169.3 *side direction*
eastward 324.4 *compass point*; 324.13 *directional*
eastwardly 324.12 *north*
eastwards 324.12 *north*
east wind 31.15 *wind direction*
easy 265.9; 263.4 *at ease*; 50.21 *avast!*; 222.9, 241.3 *comfortable*; 543.3 *elegant*; 250.13 *informal*; 580.7 *leisurely*; 648.4 *lenient*; 695.2 *simple*; 654.15 *sociable*; 419.6 *soft-hearted*; 333.5 *unhurried*
easy as pie 265.9 *easy*
easy as winking 265.9 *easy*
easy chair 23.2 *chair*; 413.4 *rest*; 419.11 *soft thing*
easy circumstances 781.7 *opulence*
easy come easy go 681.1 *extravagant*; 757.8 *permitting*
easy death 582.5 *ways of dying*
easy does it 265.20 *take it easy*
easy-flowing 265.12 *wieldy*
easy-going 265.13; 657.10 *free*; 618.7 *indifferent*; 250.13 *informal*; 648.4 *lenient*; 241.2 *likable*; 589.7 *peaceful*; 757.8 *permitting*; 301.6 *quiescent*; 654.15 *sociable*; 419.6 *soft-hearted*; 486.1 *unskilful*; 639.4 *unsteady*
easy-going nature 639.14 *apathy*
easy in one's mind 265.14 *relaxed*
easy-listening 504.14 *hearable*; 18.9 *popular music*
easy manner 654.2 *social ambition*
easy mark 668.9 *butt*; 700.22 *dupe*; 335.5 *powerless person*; 337.4 *weakling*
easy meat 265.6 *easy thing*; 335.5 *powerless person*; 337.4 *weakling*
easy money 765.5 *profit*
easy on 263.5 *labour-saving*
easy on the ear 504.14 *hearable*
easy on the eye 525.10 *aspectual*; 518.23 *visible*
easy on the pocket 793.9 *cheap*
easy-paced 333.4 *slow*
easy-peasy 265.9 *easy*
easy pickings 700.22 *dupe*
easy question 705.5
easy ride 265.6 *easy thing*
easy rider 320.14 *cyclist*
easy-running 265.12 *wieldy*
easy stages 333.8 *slowness*
Easy Street 490.5 *idealized pleasure*; 781.7 *opulence*; 248.1 *prosperity*
easy target 265.6 *easy thing*; 254.7 *vulnerability*
easy temper 658.1 *courtesy*
easy terms 793.1 *cheapness*; 749.2 *peace offering*
easy thing 265.6
easy times 248.3 *time of plenty*
easy to comprehend 695.2 *simple*
easy to follow 695.2 *simple*
easy to grasp 695.2 *simple*
easy to read 695.2 *simple*
easy to see 520.2 *clear*
easy to understand 178.2 *straightforward*
easy virtue 796.3 *sexual immorality*
easy word 5.17 *word*
easy work 341.1 *inaction*; 576.1 *work*
eat 557.21; 370.11 *ingest*; 495.9 *taste*; 441.1 *waste*
eatable 557.27 *edible*; 252.6 *safe*
eatables 557.7 *food*; 436.2 *provisions*
eatably 557.29 *edibly*
eat away 214.4 *decrease*; 245.5 *hurt*
eat between meals 557.24 *have a meal*
eat crow 479.4 *recant*; 388.4 *succumb*
eat dirt 623.21 *humble oneself*; 623.20 *submit*; 388.4 *succumb*
eaten up with jealousy 629.4 *jealous*
eater 557.18; 495.5 *taster*
eatery 557.15 *eating place*
eat everything in sight 557.22 *eat well*
eat grass 81.11
eat humble pie 479.4 *recant*; 623.20 *submit*; 388.4 *succumb*; 773.9 *withdraw a statement*
Eating 557
eating 557.1; **557.26**; 370.4 *intake*
eating alone 557.4 *eating meals*
eating crow 479.8 *recantation*
eating for two 561.16 *reproductive*
eating habit 557.5
eating habits 632.5 *tradition*
eating house 557.15 *eating place*
eating in bed 557.4 *eating meals*
eating meals 557.4
eating one's words 479.8 *recantation*
eating on the run 557.4 *eating meals*
eating out 557.4 *eating meals*
eating place 557.15
eating together 557.4 *eating meals*
eating utensil 557.16
eat in moderation 684.5 *be self-restrained*
eat into 314.11 *infiltrate*
eat less 687.5 *fast*; 557.23 *taste*
eat like a horse 688.5 *be greedy*
eat like a pig 557.22 *eat well*
eat no meat 687.5 *fast*
eat nothing 687.5 *fast*
eat one's fill 232.5 *be complete*; 217.6 *have enough*
eat one's hat 479.4 *recant*; 708.12 *renounce*
eat one's head off 688.5 *be greedy*
eat one's heart out 629.6 *be jealous*; 602.8 *grieve*
eat one's words 479.4 *recant*; 708.12 *renounce*; 773.9 *withdraw a statement*
eat out 557.24 *have a meal*
eats 557.7 *food*
eat sparingly 684.5 *be self-restrained*; 687.5 *fast*
eat up 688.5 *be greedy*; 357.12 *consume*; 557.22 *eat well*
eat well 557.22
eau 433.1 *water*

eau de Cologne 502.2 *fragrant thing;* 433.14 *lavender water;* 547.6 *toiletries*
eau-de-nil 538.1 *green*
eau de toilette 502.2 *fragrant thing;* 547.6 *toiletries*
eau potable 558.6 *soft drink*
eavesdrop 644.7 *be curious;* 504.15 *hear*
eavesdropper 504.2 *hearer;* 644.4 *meddler*
eavesdropping 504.1 *hearing*
ebb 30.63; 300.13 *be in motion;* 91.10 *billow;* 303.14 *decline;* 214.1, 214.4 *decrease;* 305.9 *descend;* 245.1 *deteriorate;* 245.7 *deterioration;* 526.1 *disappear;* 526.4 *disappearance;* 90.7 *flow;* 155.3 *lowest point;* 91.7 *oceanic;* 303.12 *reversal;* 303.3 *reverse;* 90.6 *river flow;* 218.9 *scarcity;* 303.4 *slip back;* 441.3 *waste*
ebb and flow 227.11 *be changeable;* 298.7 *be regular;* 91.10 *billow;* 326.8 *oscillate;* 326.1 *oscillation;* 298.1 *regularity;* 91.2 *tide*
ebb away 214.4 *decrease;* 441.1 *waste*
ebbing 214.6 *decreasing;* 245.12 *deteriorated;* 90.10 *fluvial;* 91.7 *oceanic;* 303.23 *receding*
ebb tide 214.3 *decreasing thing;* 155.3 *lowest point;* 298.5 *regular thing;* 91.2 *tide*
ébéniste 23.13 *carpenter*
Eblis 8.7 *devil*
E-boat 586.24 *warship*
ebola virus 260.7 *tropical disease*
ebon 532.1 *black*
ebonite 422.4 *rubber*
ebony 532.1 *black;* 532.9 *black thing;* 523.10 *dark-coloured;* 523.4 *dark thing*
ebriate 690.1 *drunk*
ebriated 690.1 *drunk*
ebriety 690.10 *drunkenness*
ebriose 690.1 *drunk*
ebriosity 690.10 *drunkenness*
EBSIDIC 40.10 *character*
ebullience 597.1 *happiness*
ebullient 597.4 *happy;* 380.6 *violent;* 493.12 *warm-hearted*
ebullition 28.37 *temperature;* 327.3 *turbulence*
eccentric 118.10; **118.14**; 642.1 *capricious;* 642.4 *capricious person;* 139.16 *characteristic;* 27.81 *curvilinear;* 325.20 *deviant;* 325.19 *deviant person;* 751.4 *dissenter;* 459.5 *foolish;* 250.8 *free-thinker;* 250.10 *independent;* 461.7 *insane person;* 100.5 *nonconformist;* 272.3 *object of ridicule;* 459.4 *rash person;* 272.5 *ridiculous;* 696.5 *strange;* 453.7 *unreliable;* 655.6 *unsocial person;* 299.5 *unusual;* 477.9 *visionary*
eccentrically 325.29 *erratically;* 250.20 *freely;* 453.26 *unreliably;* 299.9, 487.8 *unusually*
eccentric circles 27.42 *circle*
eccentricity 642.2 *caprice;* 139.3 *characteristic;* 27.42 *circle;* 231.7 *defect;* 325.13 *deviation;* 459.1 *folly;* 461.1 *insanity;* 272.1 *ludicrousness;* 118.3 *nonconformism;* 29.21 *orbit;* 126.1 *originality;* 453.15 *unreliability;* 299.2 *unusualness*
ecchymose 560.21 *bleed*
ecchymosed 560.30 *bleeding*
ecchymosis 560.10 *bleeding;* 560.1 *excretion*
Eccles cake 25.36 *cake*
ecclesia 579.7 *council;* 16.18 *tribunal*
ecclesiarch 7.8 *priest*
ecclesiastic 7.8 *priest*
ecclesiastical 579.18 *parliamentary;* 7.17 *priestly;* 209.8 *ranked*
ecclesiastical council 579.7 *council*
ecclesiastical court 16.22
ecclesiastical governor 400.6 *religious leader*
ecclesiastical law 16.1 *the law*
ecclesiastically 7.23 *religiously*
ecclesiastical rank 209.2 *rank*
ecclesiastical season 292.1 *season*
ecclesiastical tax 790.7 *tax*
ecclesiasticism 12.1 *government;* 7.9 *priesthood;* 396.7 *type of rule*
ecclesiolater 9.6 *idolater*
ecclesiolatrous 9.10 *idolatrous*
ecclesiolatry 9.2 *idolatry*
ecclesiological 7.18 *theological*
ecclesiologist 7.14 *theologian*
ecclesiology 7.13 *theology*
eccrine 559.5 *of a secretion;* 559.4 *secretory*
eccrine gland 559.3 *gland*
eccrine secretion 559.1 *secretion*
ecdyse 560.23 *cast*
ecdysial 560.32 *cast-off;* 552.12 *peeling*
ecdysiast 21.30 *dancer;* 552.8 *nude person*
ecdysis 560.12 *dead tissue;* 552.6 *peeling*
ECG 35.7 *diagnosis*
echelon 209.2 *rank;* 108.3 *relative position;* 221.1 *state*
echidna 71.6 *insect-eating mammal*
echinoderm 75.3; 70.5 *aquatic animal*
echinodermal 75.17
Echinodermata 75.3 *echinoderm*
echinodermatous 75.17 *echinodermal*
echinoid 75.3 *echinoderm;* 75.17 *echinodermal*
echo 28.21 *architectural acoustics;* 508.5 *bang;* 504.16 *be heard;* 115.10 *be similar;* 198.15 *double;* 509.8 *drum;* 509.1 *drumming;* 750.24 *harmonize;* 750.4 *harmony;* 125.9 *imitate;* 125.1 *imitation;* 692.28 *radar;* 706.19 *react;* 706.4 *reaction;* 112.16 *repeat;* 112.1 *repetition;* 561.9 *reproduce;* 510.1 *resonance;* 510.9 *resonate;* 112.22 *resound;* 112.6 *reverberation;* 504.8 *something heard;* 504.10 *sound quality*
echoed 112.9 *repeated*
echoic 504.14 *hearable;* 125.12 *imitative;* 510.6 *resonant;* 5.42 *worded*
echoic word 5.17 *word*
echoing 750.13 *harmonious;* 504.14 *hearable;* 125.12 *imitative;* 507.6 *loud;* 706.12 *reactive;* 112.12 *repetitious;* 510.6 *resonant*
echoingly 706.24 *in answer*
echolalia 112.1 *repetition*
echolocating 156.13 *bathymetric*
echolocation 504.9 *audio device;* 156.6 *bathymetry*
echo sounder 156.4 *deep thing;* 26.6 *measuring instrument*
echo sounding 156.6 *bathymetry;* 30.17 *ocean research vessel;* 28.22 *sounding*
echt 126.6 *authentic*
eckies 768.2 *gift*
eclair 25.36 *cake*
eclampsia 327.8 *spasm*
eclamptic 327.19 *convulsive*
éclat 338.1 *vigour*
eclectic 138.15 *general;* 412.12 *mixed;* 469.14 *selecting*
eclectically 19.30 *pictorially;* 469.17 *selectively*
eclecticism 138.2 *catholicity;* 412.1 *mixture;* 469.6 *selection*
eclectric 19.29 *realist*
eclipse 121.8 *be superior;* 519.15 *blind;* 519.6 *blinder;* 736.1 *concealment;* 523.2 *darkening;* 523.1 *darkness;* 526.5, 736.9 *disguise;* 550.31 *hide;* 523.14 *make dark;* 521.8 *make invisible;* 29.37 *observe;* 29.21 *orbit;* 521.6 *that which makes invisible*
eclipsed 736.14 *concealed;* 526.7 *disappeared;* 521.1 *invisible*
eclipse of the moon 523.1 *darkness*
eclipse of the sun 523.1 *darkness*
eclipsing 550.1 *covering;* 121.12 *superior*
eclipsing binary 29.9 *constellation*
ecliptic 29.5 *celestial sphere*
eclogue 17.7 *poem*
ecodevelopment 356.2 *manufacture*
ecofarming 43.1 *agriculture*
école 6.12 *educational institution*
Ecole Normale Supérieure 6.13 *university*
Ecole Spéciale Militaire 584.3 *military training*
ecological 1.11 *anthropological;* 34.20 *biological;* 244.16 *improving;* 359.6 *preserving*
ecologically 43.22 *agriculturally;* 34.29 *biologically;* 77.25 *botanically;* 359.8 *preservatively*
ecological psychology 36.1 *psychology*
ecologist 225.4 *conservationist;* 34.19 *life scientist;* 359.4 *preservationist;* 244.12 *reformer*
Ecologists 12.6 *political party*
ecology 34.18; 538.16 *green politics;* 34.1 *life science;* 359.1 *preservation;* 244.11 *reformism*
econometrics 13.3 *economic statistics*
economic 13.13; 789.10 *accounting;* 776.14 *commercial;* 14.6 *financial;* 579.17 *managerial;* 2.14 *socioeconomic*
economic adversity 249.2
economic aid 392.6 *financial assistance*
economical 616.4 *cautious;* 793.9 *cheap;* 684.8 *self-restrained;* 680.4 *thrifty*
economically 13.14; **680.7**; 793.15 *cheaply;* 789.13 *financially;* 579.19 *managerially;* 2.16 *sociologically;* 684.11 *with self-restraint*
economically worded 269.3 *concise*
economical with the truth 234.8 *exaggerated;* 702.7 *sophistic*
economic analysis 13.3 *economic statistics*
economic anthropology 1.1 *anthropology*
economic boom 562.2 *productiveness*
economic botany 77.10 *plant science*
economic decline 563.1 *infertility*
economic determinist 2.11 *sociologist*
economic development 13.4
economic downturn 13.2 *economy*
economic expert 13.9 *economist*
economic factors 13.6
economic geology 30.1 *earth science*
economic growth 13.4 *economic development;* 13.1 *economics*
economic history 3.1 *history*
economic integration 776.5 *commercial trade;* 779.4 *free market*
economic materialism 2.7 *social stratification*
economic migrant 100.7 *new arrival*
economic miracle 393.10 *revival*
economic policy 13.1 *economics*
economic power 2.7 *social stratification*
economic pressure 251.2 *economic restraint*
economic productivity 13.3 *economic statistics*
economic progress 302.12 *advance*
economic prosperity 248.1 *prosperity*
economic recovery 393.10 *revival*
economic restraint 251.2
Economics 13
economics 13.1; 579.3 *management*
economic sanction 13.6 *economic factors*
economic sanctions 585.8 *warfare*
economic stagnation 563.1 *infertility*
economic statistics 13.3
economic status 2.7 *social stratification*
economic system 13.1 *economics*
economic theory 13.1 *economics*
economic union 13.5 *international trade*
economic upturn 13.2 *economy;* 562.2 *productiveness*
economic war 585.1 *war*
economic warfare 585.8 *warfare*
economic zone 776.5 *commercial trade;* 128.3 *exclusion zone;* 779.4 *free market;* 13.5 *international trade;* 86.3 *regional boundary*
economist 13.9
economization 214.1 *decrease*
economize 251.9; 616.5 *be cautious;* 786.11 *be parsimonious;* 684.5 *be self-restrained;* 793.14 *buy cheaply;* 214.5 *make smaller;* 680.6 *save;* 439.6 *store*
economizer 680.3 *saver*
economizing 214.1 *decrease;* 680.4 *thrifty*
economy 13.2; 793.9 *cheap;* 359.1 *preservation;* 436.1 *provision;* 684.1 *self-restraint;* 680.1 *thrift;* 441.3 *waste*
economy-class 793.9 *cheap*
economy drive 680.2 *act of thrift*
economy fare 793.4 *bargain*
economy of words 269.1 *conciseness*
economy price 793.1 *cheapness*
economy size 793.9 *cheap;* 158.3 *large scale*
economy-size 158.15 *big*
economy with the truth 234.4 *distortion of the truth;* 699.11 *half-truth*
ecophysiology 34.18 *ecology*
ecosphere 434.2 *aerosphere;* 30.5 *earth;* 34.2 *living world*
écossaise 22.4 *historic dancing*
ecosystem 34.18 *ecology;* 565.2 *environment*
ecotype 34.18 *ecology*
ecowarrior 753.4 *protester;* 244.12 *reformer*
écrevisse 25.19 *shellfish*
ecru 534.1 *brown;* 533.1 *grey;* 531.1 *white*
EC snake 780.7 *finance*
ecstasis 463.1 *oblivion*
ecstasy 461.4 *delusion;* 593.5 *desire;* 691.6 *drug;* 590.4 *emotion;* 597.1 *happiness;* 477.2 *inspiration;* 463.1 *oblivion;* 593.2 *romantic love*
ecstatic 593.20 *amorous;* 597.4 *happy;* 463.8 *oblivious;* 11.12 *occultist;* 590.13 *passionate;* 600.9 *rejoicing*
ecstatically 463.16 *obliviously;* 600.11 *rejoicingly;* 590.20 *with feeling*
ectoderm 34.15 *developmental biology*
ectodermal 34.26 *developmental*
ectohormone 33.16 *hormone;* 559.2 *secreted substance*
ectomorph 160.6 *nature;* 36.7 *personality type;* 1.9 *physical type;* 153.9 *thin person*
ectomorphic 1.15 *physical;* 153.1 *thin*
ectomorphism 36.7 *personality type*
ectomorphy 36.7 *personality type;* 1.9 *physical type*
ectoparasite 70.4 *type of animal*
ectoparasitic 70.15 *of animals*
ectoplasm 34.7 *cell;* 11.10 *psychic phenomenon;* 525.4 *something that appears*
ectoplasmic 34.23 *cellular*
ectoplasy 11.10 *psychic phenomenon*
ectoproct 75.7 *coelenterate*
Ectoprocta 75.7 *coelenterate*
ectotrophic mycorrhiza 83.5 *fungal association*
ECU 780.7 *finance*
ecumenical 138.15 *general;* 747.18 *joint*
ecumenicalism 138.2 *catholicity;* 747.6 *movement*
ecumenicism 138.2 *catholicity*
ecumenicity 138.2 *catholicity*
ecumenicize 138.23 *generalize*
eczema 260.13 *skin disease*
edacious 688.6 *gluttonous*
edaciously 688.7 *gluttonously*
edaciousness 688.1 *gluttony*
edacity 688.1 *gluttony*
eddy 90.7 *flow;* 90.6 *river flow;* 307.10 *swirl;* 379.1 *trap;* 307.4 *vortex;* 31.16 *wind vortex*
eddy current 28.51, 39.9 *electric current*
edental 426.4 *toothless*
Edentata 71.13 *toothless mammal*
edentate 71.26 *insectivorous;* 426.4 *toothless;* 71.13 *toothless mammal*
edentulous 426.4 *toothless*
Edge 164
edge 163.3; **164.1**; **164.6**; 121.3 *advantage;* 53.17 *bat;* 169.7 *be alongside;* 612.8 *fearful;* 166.3 *furthest point;* 131.7 *limit;* 27.37 *line;* 425.15 *make sharp;* 62.9 *mountaineer;* 176.2 *obliquity;* 169.1 *side;* 53.9 *stroke;* 170.7 *surround*
edge away 637.7 *refuse*
edged 164.8 *edging;* 164.9 *skirting*
edged tool 438.1 *tool*
edgeless 426.1 *blunt;* 421.2 *uniform*
edge of sight 521.6 *that which makes invisible*
edge out 767.10 *dismiss*
edger 44.6 *garden tool*
edge tool 425.9 *sharp-edged thing*
edginess 327.1 *agitation*
edging 164.2; **164.8**; 211.3 *additional item;* 62.3 *climbing technique;* 551.24 *part of garment;* 68.4 *skiing technique*
edging iron 438.3 *garden tool*
edging tool 44.6 *garden tool*
edgy 327.15 *agitated*
EDI 40.14 *data transfer*
edible 557.27; 252.6 *safe;* 495.7 *tasty*
edibles 557.7 *food*
edibly 557.29
edict 397.1 *command;* 16.3 *law;* 740.1 *publication;* 140.1 *rule;* 464.2 *verdict*
edification 797.13 *benefit;* 6.1 *education*
edifice 356.8, 403.6 *construction*
edificial 20.11 *architectural;* 38.32 *structural*
edify 235.10 *do good*
edifying 797.6 *beneficial;* 6.16 *educational;* 795.10 *moralistic;* 237.4 *profitable;* 235.4 *worthwhile*
edifyingly 6.25 *educationally*
Edinburgh 87.4 *British cities*
ediophusikon 21.16 *theatre*
edit 543.4 *be elegant;* 539.10 *blue-pencil;* 224.8 *cause change;* 719.8 *interpret;* 740.15 *publish;* 244.3 *rectify;* 393.1 *repair;* 741.13 *report;* 5.46 *translate*
edit down 214.5 *make smaller*
edited 244.14 *improved;* 719.15 *interpreted;* 358.6 *obliterated;* 5.40 *translated*
edited text 719.1 *interpretation*
editing 256.4 *censorship;* 719.1 *interpretation;* 358.3 *obliteration;* 244.6 *rectification;* 393.8 *repair;* 212.1 *subtraction*
edition 719.1 *interpretation;* 740.4 *news-*

paper; 205.2 *particular*; 561.2 *print*; 244.6 *rectification*; 5.12 *translation*
editor 224.6; **227.4**; 40.11 *application*; 722.3 *dissertator*; 719.6 *interpreter*; 741.4 *journalist*; 464.5 *judge*; 740.11 *newspaperman*; 740.12 *publisher*; 393.12 *repairer*; 244.13 *reviser*; 723.5 *summarizer*
editorial 719.16 *annotative*; 722.2 *article*; 722.5 *expository*; 740.3 *journalism*; 741.14 *journalistic*; 741.9 *news story*
editorial change 358.3 *obliteration*
editorial comment 719.2 *annotation*; 722.2 *article*; 740.3 *journalism*
editorially 741.15 *journalistically*
editorial writer 719.7 *news interpreter*; 740.11 *newspaperman*
editor-in-chief 740.12 *publisher*
edit out 128.8 *eject*; 358.1 *obliterate*; 256.15 *purify*
EDP 40.1 *computing*
educability 6.10
educable 6.17
educatability 6.10 *educability*
educatable 6.17 *educable*
educate 6.22; 243.6 *brief*; 455.14 *cause to know*; 15.11 *conduct industrial relations*; 739.6 *divulge*; 693.11 *inform*; 356.10 *produce*
educated 6.18; 6.19 *knowledgeable*; 4.19 *learned*; 455.9 *literate*; 5.39 *of language*; 356.12 *produced*; 6.20 *refined*
educated palate 557.3 *delicate eating*
educated person 566.4 *modern human*
educate oneself 243.8 *prepare oneself*
educating 324.16 *directing*
Education 6
education 6.1; 243.12 *briefing*; 324.5 *directions*; 244.5 *improvement*; 455.3 *learning*; 6.11 *refinement*
educational 6.16; 693.16 *informative*; 2.12 *sociological*
educational broadcasting 692.25 *broadcast material*
educational institution 6.12; 2.8 *human institution*
educationalist 6.5
educational leader 400.9
educationally 6.25; 2.16 *sociologically*
educationally subnormal 457.7 *intellectually subnormal*; 457.5 *lacking intellect*
educational psychologist 6.5 *educationalist*
educational psychology 36.1 *psychology*
educational status 2.7 *social stratification*
educational system 6.2
educational topic 447.5
Educational Welfare Officer 6.5 *educationalist*
educationist 6.5 *educationalist*
education officer 15.6 *employer*
educative 6.16 *educational*; 395.11 *influential*
educator 6.4; 17.15 *literary person*; 396.10 *person of authority*
educatory 6.16 *educational*
educe 369.15 *draw out*
educible 369.18 *extractive*
eduction 369.5 *drawing out*
eductive 369.18 *extractive*
edulcorate 255.10, 256.15 *purify*
Edwardian 296.14 *historic*
Edward Villella 22.14 *famous ballet dancers*
EEC law 16.1 *the law*
EEG 35.7 *diagnosis*
eel 55.5 *British game fish*; 25.17 *freshwater fish*
eel basket 74.7 *fishing*
eel-like 74.13 *fishlike*
eel pie and mash 25.44 *British dish*
eelworm 44.12 *pests and diseases*
eerie 11.18 *spiritual*
eerily 11.26 *magically*
eeriness 11.2 *the occult*
Eeyore 602.4 *depressing person*; 611.3 *hopeless person*
Eeyorish 602.6 *depressed*
efface 708.14 *cancel*; 357.8 *destroy*; 358.1 *obliterate*
effaced 358.6 *obliterated*
effacement 358.3 *obliteration*
eff and blind 712.5 *curse*
Effect 345
effect 345.1; 340.1 *action*; 348.4 *be an instrument*; 246.6 *be successful*; 344.9 *be the cause of*; 131.12 *end result*; 525.5 *impression*; 348.1 *instrumentality*; 635.13 *intend*; 28.6 *law*; 694.1 *meaning*; 356.10 *produce*; 356.3 *product*; 215.1 *remainder*; 132.4 *repercussion*; 345.5 *show an effect*
effect a change 224.8 *cause change*
effected 345.10 *caused*
effected by 345.10 *caused*
effective 340.6; 164.10 *advantaged*; 525.7 *appearing*; 344.13 *causal*; 232.7 *complete*; 239.1 *convenient*; 726.3 *emphatic*; 395.11 *influential*; 237.3, 348.6 *instrumental*; 346.12 *operative*; 480.19 *persuasive*; 336.10 *potent*; 334.13 *powerful*; 586.8 *soldier*; 246.13 *successful*; 338.4 *vigorous*
effective control 12.3 *governance*
effective dose 37.5 *prescription*
effectively 340.8; 336.15 *acutely*; 164.12 *at an advantage*; 344.14 *causally*; 348.9 *instrumentally*; 204.13 *on the whole*; 346.13 *operationally*; 334.18 *powerfully*; 246.16 *successfully*
effectiveness 334.2 *ability*; 348.1 *instrumentality*; 346.4 *management*; 336.1 *strength*; 121.1 *superiority*
effective procedure 27.28 *algorithm*
effective rate 14.1 *finance*
effectives 586.14 *armed forces*
effect of use 349.6 *use*
effect one's escape 389.5 *escape*
effects 215.5 *estate*; 440.4 *possessions*; 345.2 *visible effect*
effectual 344.13 *causal*; 232.7 *complete*; 239.1 *convenient*; 395.11 *influential*; 237.3, 348.6 *instrumental*; 346.12 *operative*; 334.13 *powerful*
effectuality 334.2 *ability*; 346.4 *management*; 336.1 *strength*
effectually 344.14 *causally*; 99.13 *in essence*; 395.14 *influentially*; 348.9 *instrumentally*; 346.13 *operationally*; 334.18 *powerfully*
effectuate 346.8 *activate*; 344.9 *be the cause of*
effectuation 340.1 *action*; 633.1 *pursuit*
effeminacy 568.1 *female sex*
effeminate 568.15 *female*; 567.17 *male*
effeminize 335.9 *make impotent*
effervesce 327.21 *be agitated*; 434.24 *bubble*; 508.6 *crack*; 512.4 *hiss*
effervescence 432.7 *gaseousness*; 512.1 *hiss*; 415.5 *lightness*; 327.3 *turbulence*; 380.1 *violence*
effervescent 434.18 *bubbly*; 432.21 *gassy*; 512.6 *hissing*; 415.2 *insubstantial*; 327.17 *turbulent*; 380.6 *violent*
effervescently 434.25 *airily*; 415.11 *lightly*; 512.8 *sibilantly*; 432.30 *smokily*
effervescingly 434.25 *airily*; 432.30 *smokily*
effete 245.12 *deteriorated*; 335.13 *unsexed*; 238.1 *useless*; 337.12 *weak-willed*
effeteness 238.3 *uselessness*
efficacious 237.3, 348.6 *instrumental*; 346.12 *operative*; 334.13 *powerful*; 246.13 *successful*
efficaciously 348.9 *instrumentally*; 346.13 *operationally*; 334.18 *powerfully*; 246.16 *successfully*
efficacy 334.2 *ability*; 237.7, 348.1 *instrumentality*; 136.1 *qualification*
efficiency 334.2 *ability*; 265.1 *easiness*; 237.7 *instrumentality*; 346.4 *management*; 797.12 *proficiency*; 136.1 *qualification*; 485.1 *skill*; 38.10 *work*
efficient 485.8 *expert*; 342.20 *industrious*; 237.3, 348.6 *instrumental*; 455.8 *knowledgeable*; 346.12 *operative*; 334.13 *powerful*; 797.5 *proficient*; 136.9 *qualified*; 485.6 *skilful*; 338.4 *vigorous*
efficiently 136.17 *capably*; 348.9 *instrumentally*; 346.13 *operationally*; 334.18 *powerfully*; 485.12 *skilfully*; 237.12 *usefully*
effigy 9.3 *idol*; 717.6 *image*
effing and blinding 712.1 *curse*; 544.4 *inelegance of speech*
effloresce 427.27 *come to dust*; 78.13 *flower*
efflorescence 243.13 *development*; 78.5 *flowering*; 427.5 *powder*; 427.1 *powderiness*; 561.3 *propagation*
efflorescent 78.11 *flowering*; 44.16 *horticultural*
effluence 315.2 *outflow*; 90.6 *river flow*
effluent 560.4 *excrement*; 43.13 *fertilizer*; 90.10 *fluvial*; 315.16 *outflowing*; 90.1 *river*
effluvial 432.18 *miasmic*
effluvium 432.2 *exhalation*; 11.10 *psychic phenomenon*; 503.1 *stench*
efflux 315.2 *outflow*
effluxion 315.2 *outflow*
effort 340.1 *action*; 353.5 *attempt*; 640.2 *commitment*; 264.1 *difficulty*; 576.4 *exertion*; 448.1 *experiment*; 334.1 *power*; 356.1 *production*; 354.2 *undertaking*; 338.1 *vigour*; 38.10 *work*
effortful 264.10 *difficult*
effortless 265.9 *easy*
effortlessly 265.21 *easily*
effortlessness 265.1 *easiness*
effort-wasting 238.2 *futile*
effrontery 167.5 *boldness*; 661.1 *defiance*; 660.1 *insolence*
effulgence 522.2 *quality of light*
effulgent 522.16 *bright*
effuse 270.3 *diffuse*; 315.10 *emerge*; 315.12 *leak*
effused 315.16 *outflowing*
effusion 270.1 *diffuseness*; 371.22 *disgorgement*; 731.2 *effusiveness*; 560.1 *excretion*; 315.3 *leakage*; 315.2 *outflow*
effusive 731.6; 703.10 *demonstrative*; 270.3 *diffuse*; 219.6 *excessive*; 569.8 *friendly*; 315.16 *outflowing*; 590.13 *passionate*
effusively 731.11; 703.21 *demonstratively*; 270.7 *diffusely*; 315.18 *forth*; 569.17 *in friendship*
effusiveness 731.2; 703.2 *demonstrativeness*; 270.1 *diffuseness*; 5.22 *many words*; 219.2 *overdoing it*
effusive welcome 370.2 *receptivity*
EFTPOS 785.1 *payment*
EFTS 40.12 *electronic office*
e.g. 139.31 *namely*
egalitarian 119.6 *equal*; 244.12 *reformer*
egalitarianism 119.1 *equality*; 12.1 *government*; 396.7 *type of rule*
Egeria 713.4 *adviser*
egest 560.15 *excrete*; 371.14 *let out*
egesta 560.4 *excrement*
egestion 560.1 *excretion*; 371.23 *vomiting*
egestive 560.24 *excretory*
egg 72.15 *eggs*; 561.8 *organs of reproduction*; 356.7 *produce*; 181.3 *round thing*; 344.3 *rudiment*; 130.3 *source*
eggbeater 327.14 *agitator*; 322.8 *aircraft*; 307.6 *rotator*
eggcup 410.13 *drinking vessel*
egg drop soup 25.48 *Chinese dish*
egged on 483.12 *motivated*; 480.20 *persuadable*
egg flip 558.7 *alcoholic drink*
egg fu yung 25.48 *Chinese dish*
egghead 400.9 *educational leader*; 396.11, 485.5 *expert*; 442.8 *intellectual person*; 455.6 *knowledgeable person*; 6.7 *learner*; 446.9 *person of ideas*; 4.12 *sage*; 643.7 *serious person*; 443.7 *thinker*
egg-laying mammal 71.3
eggnog 558.7 *alcoholic drink*
egg on 338.3 *invigorate*; 483.10 *manipulate*
egg on one's face 668.8 *indignity*
egg roll 25.48 *Chinese dish*
eggs 72.15; 25.7 *basic ingredient*; 356.7 *produce*
eggs Benedict 25.43 *US dish*
egg-shaped 179.5 *circular*; 181.9 *round*
eggshell 424.3 *brittle thing*; 550.13 *casing*; 72.15 *eggs*; 337.5 *weak thing*
eggshell blue 539.1 *blue*
eggshell glaze 24.3 *glaze*
eggshell porcelain 24.1 *ceramics*
eggspoon 410.17 *ladle*
egg timer 281.9 *hourglass*
egg whisk 307.6 *rotator*
ego 683.2 *egoism*; 139.11 *identity*; 101.6 *internal world*; 36.21 *psyche*; 11.7 *spirit*
ego analysis 36.3 *psychiatric treatment*
ego-centred 683.5 *egoistic*
ego-centredness 683.2 *egoism*
egocentric 683.5 *egoistic*; 172.12 *internalized*; 673.12 *self-interested*
egocentrically 683.9 *egoistically*; 673.22 *selfishly*
egocentricity 683.2 *egoism*
egocentrism 683.2 *egoism*; 172.6 *internalization*
ego-id conflict 36.21 *psyche*
ego ideal 477.4 *ideality*; 36.21 *psyche*
egoism 683.2; 622.3 *conceit*; 653.1 *misanthropy*; 4.7 *school of thought*; 686.4 *self-absorption*; 673.5 *self-interest*
egoist 620.3 *boring person*; 4.11 *follower of a doctrine*; 653.2 *misanthrope*; 622.13 *proud person*; 686.5 *self-indulgent person*; 683.3 *selfish person*
egoistic 683.5; 653.3 *misanthropic*; 4.14 *of a philosophy*; 673.12 *self-interested*
egoistical 683.5 *egoistic*; 673.12 *self-interested*
egoistically 683.9; 653.5 *misanthropically*; 622.32 *proudly*
egoisticalness 673.5 *self-interest*
egomania 36.15 *compulsion*; 467.1 *overestimation*
egomaniac 631.5 *badly behaved person*; 683.3 *selfish person*
ego therapy 36.3 *psychiatric treatment*
egotism 622.3 *conceit*; 683.2 *egoism*; 593.1 *love*; 653.1 *misanthropy*; 673.5 *self-interest*
egotist 620.3 *boring person*; 653.2 *misanthrope*; 683.3 *selfish person*; 673.7 *vain person*
egotistic 683.5 *egoistic*; 686.9 *self-absorbed*; 673.12 *self-interested*
egotistical 683.5 *egoistic*; 653.3 *misanthropic*; 673.12 *self-interested*; 139.18 *subjective*
egotistically 683.9 *egoistically*; 653.5 *misanthropically*; 622.32 *proudly*; 673.22 *selfishly*
egotisticalness 673.5 *self-interest*
ego trip 683.2 *egoism*
egregious 123.6 *notable*
egress 300.4 *backward motion*; 313.7 *departure*; 315.1, 315.9 *exit*; 389.2 *means of escape*; 371.21 *removal*; 90.6 *river flow*; 315.6 *way out*
egression 315.1 *exit*
egressive 315.15 *outgoing*
Egyptian 566.4 *modern human*
Egyptians 284.6 *people of the past*
Egyptological 3.17 *archaeological*
Egyptologist 284.11 *antiquarian*; 3.4 *archaeologist*; 1.4 *palaeoanthropologist*
Egyptology 3.2 *archaeology*; 1.2 *palaeoanthropology*
eiderdown 550.10 *bed covering*; 72.17 *plumage*; 419.11 *soft thing*
eidetic 721.11 *descriptive*; 477.10 *imaginative*; 115.9 *lifelike*
eidetically 115.14 *comparably*
eidetic image 717.6 *image*
Eid-ul-Adha 10.16 *religious festival*
Eid-ul-Fitr 10.16 *religious festival*
Eiffel Tower 154.6 *tall thing*
Eiger 89.6 *other major mountains and ranges*
eight 201.4; 201.15 *eighth*; 27.9 *numeral*
eight all 63.9 *squash terms*
eight ball 65.6 *pool*
eight-beat crawl 67.2 *swimming technique*
eight bells 290.3 *noon*
eight centuries 201.9 *treble figures*
eighteen-hole course 56.1 *golf*
eighteenth 196.4 *less than one*
Eighteenth Amendment 684.1 *self-restraint*; 399.1 *veto*
eighteen-yard 66.5 *soccer*
eighteen-yard box 66.1 *soccer*
eighter 201.4 *eight*
eighter from Decatur 201.4 *eight*
eightfold 201.15 *eighth*
eighth 201.15; 201.4 *eight*; 27.75 *equal*; 196.4 *less than one*; 205.1 *part*
eighth guard 53.4 *fencing movements*
eighth note 18.17 *notation*
eighth part 201.4 *eight*
eightieth 196.4 *less than one*; 201.19 *twentieth*
eight-man 64.6 *rugger*
eight-man shove 64.3 *rugby play*
eights 50.4 *rowing*
eight-sided 27.82 *polygonal*
eightsome reel 22.4 *historic dancing*
eight-step approach 47.2 *field events*
eighty 201.8 *twenty and over*
Einstein theory 141.9 *fourth dimension*
Einstein universe 29.4 *cosmological model*
Eire 85.10 *Ireland*
eisegesis 719.1 *interpretation*
Eisenhower jacket 551.11 *jacket*
either...or 469.17 *selectively*
ejaculate 560.15 *excrete*; 514.14 *hiss*; 371.14 *let out*; 729.11 *speak*
ejaculation 514.7 *cry of disapproval*; 371.22 *disgorgement*; 560.1 *excretion*; 327.8 *spasm*; 729.7 *utterance*

ejaculative 371.29 *expulsive*
ejaculatory 514.19 *hissing*
eject 128.8; 330.25; 364.2; 316.14 *bring back;* 470.2 *discard;* 767.9 *dispose of;* 560.15 *excrete;* 371.1 *expel;* 331.1 *impel;* 144.16 *replace;* 559.7 *secrete;* 372.9 *separate;* 255.11 *simplify;* 350.6 *stop using;* 212.3 *subtract;* 708.15 *terminate*
ejecta 30.25 *eruption;* 560.4 *excrement*
ejectamenta 560.4 *excrement;* 330.8 *missile*
ejected 709.8 *refused;* 372.15 *separate;* 212.5 *subtracted*
ejecting mechanism 371.28 *propellant*
ejection 128.2; 330.4; 470.6 *discarding;* 767.1 *disposal;* 560.1 *excretion;* 371.17 *expulsion;* 144.3 *replacement;* 364.6 *repulse;* 559.1 *secretion;* 372.2 *setting apart;* 330.7 *shot;* 212.1 *subtraction;* 708.6 *termination*
ejective 560.24 *excretory;* 371.29 *expulsive;* 330.18 *projectile*
ejectment 371.17 *expulsion*
ejector 371.26; 330.8 *missile*
ejector seat 330.4 *ejection;* 371.28 *propellant;* 252.4 *safety device*
ejoy 349.5 *dispose of*
eke out 232.4 *complete*
eke out a livelihood 782.12 *be poor*
el 317.10, 321.1 *railway*
elaborate 270.5 *be diffuse;* 543.4 *be elegant;* 222.10 *detailed;* 243.7 *develop;* 243.20 *developed;* 543.3 *elegant;* 244.1 *improve;* 576.11 *laborious;* 542.12 *ornament;* 542.10 *ornate;* 230.5 *perfect;* 403.15 *shape*
elaborately 543.5 *elegantly;* 222.19 *meticulously;* 542.13 *ornately;* 724.10 *stylistically*
elaboration 270.1 *diffuseness;* 543.1 *elegance;* 576.4 *exertion;* 244.5 *improvement*
élan 638.16 *fortitude;* 724.2 *stylishness;* 338.1 *vigour*
élan vital 554.1 *life*
elapse 277.7 *go on;* 275.15, 284.14 *pass*
elasmobranch 74.2 *fish*
elastic 422.6; 190.9 *enlargeable;* 419.2 *pliant;* 303.26 *resilient*
elastically 422.11; 419.17 *softly*
elasticate 422.9 *make elastic*
elastic band 422.3 *elastic thing*
elastic bandage 550.6 *medical covering*
elastic board 57.6 *pommel horse*
elastic fluid 431.1 *fluid;* 432.1 *gas*
Elasticity 422
elasticity 422.1; 334.4 *energy;* 190.2 *enlargeability;* 28.10 *force;* 303.17 *resilience;* 419.8 *softness;* 38.15 *strength of materials*
elasticize 422.9 *make elastic*
elastic scattering 28.71 *nuclear reaction*
elastic strain 38.14 *load*
elastic thing 422.3
elastic tissue 422.3 *elastic thing*
elastomer 422.4 *rubber*
Elastoplast™ 267.3 *adhesive;* 550.6 *medical covering;* 762.3 *substitute thing;* 394.10 *surgical dressing*
elate 622.30 *make proud*
elated 622.22 *boastful;* 597.4 *happy*
elater 82.4 *moss plant*
elation 461.4 *delusion*
E-layer 692.15 *transmitted wave*
Elbe 90.5 *other major rivers*
elbow 331.1 *impel;* 147.19 *meet;* 58.9 *play hockey;* 492.11 *touch*
elbow aside 668.22 *show disrespect*
elbow-cop 384.7 *armour*
elbowed 58.8 *hockey*
elbow grease 576.4 *exertion;* 365.5 *polishing*
elbow guard 54.2 *fencing equipment*
elbowing 262.3 *hasty;* 58.8 *hockey;* 58.3 *ice hockey*
elbow-joint 176.1 *angle*
elbow one's way 576.8 *exert oneself;* 633.13 *follow up;* 342.14 *push*
elbow out 767.10 *dismiss*
elbow pad 58.3 *ice hockey*
elbow protector 53.6 *pad*
elbowroom 141.6 *available space;* 287.2 *opportunity;* 250.5 *scope*
elbow through 318.10 *enter*
elbow to elbow 147.14 *beside*
elbow-to-elbow 147.10 *juxtaposed;* 147.9 *near*
eld 3.8 *past time*
elder 121.15 *excellent;* 400.1 *master;* 400.12 *masterful;* 25.31 *offal;* 296.11 *old;* 556.7 *older person;* 284.17 *past;* 7.8 *priest;* 129.12 *primary;* 121.5 *superior*
elderflower wine 78.8 *flower product*
elderliness 556.5 *old age;* 296.1 *oldness*
elderly 556.14 *aged;* 533.2 *grey-haired;* 296.11 *old*
elders 296.2 *old people*
elders and betters 296.2 *old people*
elder statesman 442.8 *intellectual person*
elder statesmen 579.7 *council*
eldest 129.9 *predecessor*
El Dorado 477.8 *dreamland;* 482.6 *objective;* 756.4 *promised land;* 781.5 *wealth*
eldritch 11.18 *spiritual*
Eleatic 4.11 *follower of a doctrine;* 4.14 *of a philosophy*
Eleaticism 4.7 *school of thought*
elect 469.15 *chosen;* 398.7 *delegate;* 396.21 *grant authority;* 7.21 *ordain;* 469.5 *vote*
elected 396.13; 469.15 *chosen;* 398.9 *delegated*
elected person 398.1 *delegate*
elected representative 398.1 *delegate;* 15.7 *employee*
election 469.12; 396.3 *acquisition of power;* 398.3 *delegation;* 7.9 *priesthood*
electioneer 469.5 *vote*
electioneering 469.12 *election;* 469.16 *elective*
elective 469.16
elector 469.13 *electorate*
electoral 469.16 *elective*
electoral college 469.11 *franchise*
electoral defeat 470.6 *discarding*
electoral district 469.12 *election;* 86.5 *state*
electoral mandate 397.4 *authorization*
electoral roll 469.12 *election;* 220.6 *list of names*
electoral system 469.11 *franchise*
electorate 469.13; 220.6 *list of names;* 86.5 *state;* 16.18 *tribunal*
Electra complex 36.18 *complex;* 593.2 *romantic love*
electric 334.16 *charged;* 39.36 *electronic;* 488.9 *exciting;* 28.98 *physical;* 437.10 *powered;* 332.1 *swift*
electrical 334.16 *charged;* 39.36 *electronic;* 54.6 *fencing;* 28.98 *physical;* 334.17, 437.10 *powered*
electrical conduction 28.43
electrical energy 28.56; 39.26; 28.11, 334.4 *energy*
electrical engineer 578.2 *artisan;* 39.2 *electronics engineer;* 38.2 *engineer*
electrical engineering 39.1 *electronics;* 38.1 *engineering;* 438.6 *mechanics*
electrical épée 54.2 *fencing equipment*
electrical fault 247.4 *unsuccessful thing*
electrical foil 54.2 *fencing equipment*
electrical instrument 39.23
electrically 39.37 *electronically;* 334.19 *energetically;* 28.100 *physically;* 437.12 *powerfully*
electrical oscillation 28.14 *sound wave*
electrical porcelain 24.9 *industrial ceramics*
electrical potential 334.4 *energy*
electrical power 334.7
electrical wheel 24.6 *ceramic workshop*
electric arc 28.46 *electric discharge*
electric battery 437.4 *electricity*
electric blanket 493.3 *heater*
electric blue 539.1 *blue*
electric cable 39.27 *wire*
electric chair 16.43 *conviction;* 582.4 *death sentence;* 437.4 *electricity;* 382.5 *execution;* 814.16 *instrument of execution*
electric charge 28.50; 39.8; 334.7 *electrical power*
electric circuit 28.55, 39.13 *circuit*
electric clock 281.6 *clock*
electric constant 28.50 *electric charge*
electric current 28.51; 39.9; 334.7 *electrical power;* 437.4 *electricity*
electric discharge 28.46; 39.6
electric drill 438.1 *tool*
electric fence 384.9 *barrier;* 43.11 *farmland*
electric fencer 43.10 *farm tool*
electric field 28.54; 39.11
electric field strength 28.54 *electric field*
electric filament 39.27 *wire*
electric fire 493.6 *fire*
electric flux 28.54 *electric field*
electrician 578.2 *artisan;* 39.2 *electronics engineer;* 437.9 *power-worker;* 393.12 *repairer;* 21.28 *stagehand*
electric iron 493.3 *heater;* 421.9 *smoother*
electricity 28.42; 39.3; 437.4; 28.2 *classical physics;* 334.7 *electrical power;* 334.4 *energy;* 330.13, 437.1 *fuel;* 332.11 *swift thing*
electricity meter 437.4 *electricity;* 26.8 *meter*
electricity substation 334.6 *source of energy*
electricity supply 334.7 *electrical power;* 437.4 *electricity*
electric lead 437.4 *electricity*
electric light 522.6; 334.7 *electrical power;* 28.23 *light*
electric locomotive 321.4 *locomotive*
electric meter 39.34 *power supply*
electric mixer 25.6 *kitchen equipment;* 412.6 *mixer*
electric motor 39.31; 28.56 *electrical energy;* 437.4 *electricity*
electric potential 28.52; 39.10
electric power 28.56, 39.26 *electrical energy;* 334.4 *energy*
electric railway 317.10 *railway*
electric shock 334.7 *electrical power*
electric storm 28.47; 31.21 *thunderstorm*
electric switch 437.4 *electricity*
electrification 334.7 *electrical power;* 437.4 *electricity*
electrified 483.12 *motivated*
electrify 630.11 *amaze;* 619.10 *be wonderful;* 437.11 *fuel;* 334.11 *give power;* 338.3 *invigorate;* 483.9 *motivate*
electrifying 488.9 *exciting;* 483.11 *motivational;* 437.10 *powered*
electro 18.9 *popular music*
electroacoustics 28.2 *classical physics*
electroacoustic transducer 39.22 *transformer*
electrobiology 34.1 *life science*
electrocardiography 35.7 *diagnosis*
electrochemical 32.42
electrochemical series 32.19 *electrochemistry*
electrochemist 32.2 *chemist*
electrochemistry 32.19
electroconvulsive shock therapy 36.3 *psychiatric treatment*
electroconvulsive therapy 36.3 *psychiatric treatment;* 394.13 *therapy;* 461.9 *treatment*
electrocute 39.35 *conduct;* 382.19, 814.5 *execute;* 382.17 *murder*
electrocution 814.13 *capital punishment;* 582.4 *death sentence;* 334.7 *electrical power;* 437.4 *electricity;* 382.5 *execution*
electrode 28.43 *electrical conduction;* 334.7 *electrical power;* 39.5 *electrolytic conduction*
electrodeposit 32.28 *electrolyse*
electrodeposited 32.42 *electrochemical*
electrodeposition 32.19 *electrochemistry*
electrode potential 32.19 *electrochemistry*
electrodynamic 39.36 *electronic;* 28.98 *physical*
electrodynamically 39.37 *electronically;* 28.100 *physically*
electrodynamics 28.2 *classical physics;* 334.7 *electrical power*
electroencephalogy 35.7 *diagnosis*
electroform 32.28 *electrolyse*
electroformed 32.42 *electrochemical*
electrolyse 32.28; 375.4 *deconstruct*
electrolysis 375.2 *deconstruction;* 552.7 *depilation;* 28.43 *electrical conduction;* 334.7 *electrical power;* 32.19 *electrochemistry;* 547.9 *hair removal;* 394.12 *surgery*
electrolyte 28.43 *electrical conduction;* 39.3 *electricity;* 32.19 *electrochemistry;* 39.5 *electrolytic conduction*
electrolytic 32.42 *electrochemical;* 39.36 *electronic*
electrolytically 39.37 *electronically;* 375.7 *to pieces*
electrolytic capacitor 39.17 *resistor*
electrolytic cell 28.43 *electrical conduction;* 32.19 *electrochemistry;* 39.5 *electrolytic conduction*
electrolytic conduction 39.5
electrolytic conductor 28.43 *electrical conduction*
electrolytic corrosion 32.19 *electrochemistry*
electrolytic extraction 32.23 *metallurgy*
electrolytic forming 32.19 *electrochemistry*
electrolytic refining 32.19 *electrochemistry*
electromagnet 28.60, 363.3 *magnet*
electromagnetic 39.36 *electronic*
electromagnetically 39.37 *electronically*
electromagnetic conduction 316.3 *transmission*
electromagnetic field 334.4 *energy*
electromagnetic induction 28.49; 28.63 *magnetic phenomenon*
electromagnetic interaction 28.79 *fundamental interaction*
electromagnetic radiation 28.13; 28.62; 334.9 *electronics;* 522.1 *light*
electromagnetic spectrum 28.13, 28.62 *electromagnetic radiation*
electromagnetic theory 28.5 *theory*
electromagnetic wave 28.62 *electromagnetic radiation;* 326.5 *wave*
electromagnetism 28.2 *classical physics;* 334.4 *energy;* 28.57 *magnetism;* 402.6 *natural science*
electromechanical 39.36 *electronic*
electromechanically 39.37 *electronically*
electrometer 28.90 *ammeter;* 39.23 *electrical instrument;* 26.8 *meter*
electrometric 26.16 *micrometric*
electrometry 26.2 *micrometry*
electromotive 32.42 *electrochemical;* 39.36 *electronic*
electromotive force 28.52, 39.10 *electric potential;* 334.4 *energy*
electromotive series 32.19 *electrochemistry*
electron 28.65 *atom;* 28.50 *electric charge;* 28.77 *elementary particle;* 159.2 *little thing;* 402.4 *matter;* 28.44, 39.4 *semiconductor*
electronarcosis 36.3 *psychiatric treatment*
electron conduction 28.44, 39.4 *semiconductor*
electron configuration 28.65 *atom*
electron-deficient 32.35 *combined*
electron-deficient bond 32.11 *chemical bond*
electron-deficient compound 32.7 *chemical compound*
electron emission 39.24
electron gun 39.24 *electron emission*
electronic 39.36; 334.16 *charged;* 438.9 *mechanical;* 348.8 *practical*
electronically 39.37; 334.19 *energetically;* 348.9, 438.11 *instrumentally*
electronic brain 40.3 *computer*
electronic circuit 28.55, 39.13 *circuit*
electronic communication 692.1 *communications*
electronic component 28.55 *circuit*
electronic computer 40.3 *computer*
electronic data processing 210.4 *computing*
electronic device 28.55 *circuit;* 39.16 *circuit element*
electronic flash 41.19 *flash*
electronic instrument 18.25 *musical instrument*
electronic journalism 741.1 *news*
electronic listening device 744.10 *recording instrument*
electronic mail 692.8 *data transmission;* 40.12 *electronic office*
electronic means 348.1 *instrumentality*
electronic media 741.5 *mass communication*
electronic office 40.12; 692.8 *data transmission*
Electronics 39
electronics 39.1; 334.9; 39.13 *circuit;* 438.6 *mechanics*
electronics engineer 39.2
electronics engineering 39.1 *electronics;* 38.1 *engineering*
electronic superhighway 40.14 *data transfer*
electronic surveillance 252.2 *protection*
electronic tube 24.9 *industrial ceramics*
electron lens 39.24 *electron emission*
electron mass 28.97 *fundamental constant*
electron microscope 28.85 *microscope*
electron microscopy 34.6 *cell biology*
electron multiplier 39.24 *electron emission;* 28.93 *radiation detector*
electron physics 334.9 *electronics*
electron shell 28.65 *atom*
electron spectroscopy 32.17 *analysis*

electron-transport chain 33.24 *respiration*
electron tube **39.20**; 39.24 *electron emission*
electro-optical effect 28.33 *photosensitivity*
electro-optics 28.2 *classical physics*
electro-osmosis 32.17 *analysis*
electrophile 32.14 *chemical reaction*
electrophilic 32.38 *reactive*
electrophilic reaction 32.14 *chemical reaction*
electrophoresis 32.17 *analysis*
electrophoretic 32.41 *analytic*
electrophotographic printer 40.7 *peripheral*
electrophotometer 28.32 *optical instrument*
electroplate 550.24 *coat*; 550.3 *coating*; 32.28 *electrolyse*
electroplated 32.42 *electrochemical*
electroplater 550.17 *coverer*
electroplating 32.19 *electrochemistry*; 32.23 *metallurgy*
electrorefining 32.23 *metallurgy*
electroshock 36.3 *psychiatric treatment*
electroshock therapy 36.3 *psychiatric treatment*
electrostatic 39.36 *electronic*
electrostatically 39.37 *electronically*
electrostatic generator 39.30 *generator*
electrostatic induction 28.49 *electromagnetic induction*
electrostatic printer 40.7 *peripheral*
electrostatics 334.7 *electrical power*
electrostriction 28.49 *electromagnetic induction*
electrotechnician 39.2 *electronics engineer*
electrotechnics 39.1 *electronics*
electrotechnology 39.1 *electronics*
electrotherapy 394.13 *therapy*
electrovalent 32.35 *combined*
electrovalent bond 32.11 *chemical bond*
electrovalently 32.46 *chemically*
electrovoltaic 32.42 *electrochemical*
electroweak interaction 28.79 *fundamental interaction*
electrum 780.16 *bullion*; 412.2 *mixed thing*
electrum coinage 780.13 *coinage*
electuary 394.2 *medicine*
eleemosynary 793.11 *free of charge*; 652.6 *philanthropic*
Elegance 543
elegance **543.1**; **549.1**; 553.1 *fashion*; 658.2 *good manners*; 545.1 *gorgeousness*; 5.24 *phrasing*; 6.11 *refinement*; 485.1 *skill*; 724.2 *stylishness*; 728.3 *subtlety*; 495.2 *taste of life*
elegances 658.3 *courtesies*
elegancies 656.5 *etiquette*
elegancy 543.1 *elegance*
elegant **543.3**; 656.6 *formal*; 658.8 *good-mannered*; 545.6 *personable*; 5.43 *phrasal*; 6.20, 549.5 *refined*; 724.7 *stylish*; 728.13 *subtle*; 495.8 *tasteful*; 485.9 *well-made*
elegantly **543.5**; 6.27 *discerningly*; 551.36 *dressily*; 658.15 *genteelly*; 5.51 *phraseologically*; 724.10 *stylistically*; 495.11 *tastily*
elegantly upholstered 781.3 *opulent*
elegant phrase 5.24 *phrasing*
elegiac 583.11 *funeral*; 603.4 *lamenting*; 17.19 *narrative*
elegiacal 583.11 *funereal*
elegiacally 583.12 *funereally*; 17.22 *poetically*
elegiac couplet 17.9 *metre*
elegiac distich 17.9 *metre*
elegiac pentameter 17.9 *metre*
elegiac poem 17.7 *poem*
elegiac poetry 17.6 *poetry*
elegibility 127.1 *inclusion*
elegist 17.14 *author*; 583.3 *funeral director*; 603.3 *lamenter*
elegize 603.6 *lament*; 17.21 *write*
elegy 583.2 *funeral*; 603.2 *lament*; 17.7 *poem*
element 412.4 *admixture*; 169.4, 222.6 *aspect*; 32.6 *chemical element*; 205.4, 405.1 *component*; 565.2 *environment*; 402.4 *matter*; 205.1 *part*; 566.7 *person*; 344.3 *rudiment*; 27.21 *set*; 127.2 *thing included*
elemental **32.34**; 344.13 *causal*; 405.6 *component*; 406.10 *containing*; 31.41 *meteorologic*; 205.11 *partial*; 255.16 *simple*; 11.18 *spiritual*
elementally 405.14 *constituently*; 406.13 *structurally*
elemental spirit 11.11 *ghost*
elementary 344.13 *causal*; 405.6 *component*; 265.9 *easy*; 129.13 *precursory*; 243.16 *preparatory*; 130.35 *rudimentary*; 255.16 *simple*
elementary charge 28.97 *fundamental constant*
elementary particle **28.77**; 402.4 *matter*
elementary unit 402.4 *matter*
elements 406.1 *contents*; 435.1 *materials*; 130.7 *rudiments*; 31.6 *weather data*
elenchus 701.2 *logical argument*; 4.4 *philosophical investigation*
elenctic 4.16 *dialectical*; 701.11 *logical*; 705.12 *questioning*
elephant 316.6 *beast of burden*; 158.9 *big thing*; 154.6 *tall thing*
elephant bird 72.8 *extinct bird*
elephant gun 330.9, 587.9 *firearm*
elephant hunt 633.2 *chase*
elephantiasis 158.4 *gigantism*
elephantine 71.32 *pachydermatous*; 158.17 *stocky*
elephantoid 71.32 *pachydermatous*
elevate 690.9 *be intoxicating*; 415.9 *be light*; 8.17 *deify*; 362.12 *drag*; 302.8 *further*; 244.1 *improve*; 190.5, 213.5 *make bigger*; 186.6 *make vertical*; 366.3 *promote*; 256.15 *purify*; 154.17 *raise*
elevated 190.7 *bigger*; 8.15 *deified*; 690.1 *drunk*; 154.11, 366.12 *exalted*; 154.9 *high*; 89.7 *mountainous*; 321.1 *railway*; 366.11 *raised*; 726.5 *serious*; 622.19 *stately*; 319.5 *transportable*
elevated railway 317.10, 321.1 *railway*
elevate oneself 168.7 *rear up*
elevating 186.2 *making vertical*
elevating oneself 168.3 *rearing up*
elevation 289.4 *accession*; 302.12 *advance*; 403.6 *construction*; 30.6 *continent*; 8.9 *deification*; 690.10 *drunkenness*; 525.3 *external appearance*; 190.1 *growth*; 154.1 *height*; 244.5 *improvement*; 213.1 *increase*; 186.2 *making vertical*; 717.7 *map*; 608.6 *profile*; 366.6 *raising*; 726.2 *seriousness*; 304.2 *upturn*
elevation of the Host 10.6 *Eucharist*
elevator **366.10**; 38.29 *construction equipment*; 304.8 *lift*; 320.4 *personal transport*
elevatory 190.9 *enlargeable*
eleven 201.7 *double figures*; 53.4 *team*
elevenses 557.12 *meal*; 654.3 *meeting*; 290.2 *morning thing*
eleventh **201.18**; 196.4 *less than one*
eleventh hour 287.3 *critical time*; 294.2 *late hour*
eleventh-hour 287.8 *in time*; 294.11 *late in the day*
eleventh-hour rescue 484.3 *expedient plan*
elf 11.11 *ghost*; 70.7 *legendary beast*; 159.4 *little person*; 149.5 *short person*
elfin 159.7 *little*
elicit 344.10 *awaken*; 369.15 *draw out*
elicitation 369.5 *drawing out*
elicitory 369.18 *extractive*
elide 149.10 *shorten*
elided 149.8 *shortened*
eligibility 136.1 *qualification*
eligible 127.8 *included*; 570.22 *marriageable*; 136.9 *qualified*
eligible bachelor 570.4 *marriageability*
eligible party 570.4 *marriageability*
eliminant 560.24 *excretory*; 371.29 *expulsive*
eliminate 708.14 *cancel*; 526.3 *cause to disappear*; 470.2 *discard*; 128.8 *eject*; 560.15 *excrete*; 371.10 *exterminate*; 369.11 *extract*; 131.17 *kill*; 27.92 *manipulate*; 382.17 *murder*; 358.1 *obliterate*; 256.15 *purify*; 32.26 *react*; 206.8 *reduce*; 255.11 *simplify*; 212.3 *subtract*; 371.11 *void*
eliminated 131.23 *annihilated*; 369.19 *dislodged*; 358.6 *obliterated*; 212.5 *subtracted*
eliminate each other 708.16 *cancel out*
eliminate the alternatives 469.1 *select*
elimination 131.4 *annihilation*; 708.5 *cancellation*; 32.14 *chemical reaction*; 357.1 *destruction*; 470.6 *discarding*; 526.5 *disguise*; 128.2 *ejection*; 27.24 *evaluation*; 560.1 *excretion*; 369.1 *extraction*; 358.3 *obliteration*; 255.2 *purification*; 371.21 *removal*; 212.1 *subtraction*
eliminative 560.24 *excretory*
elision 269.1 *conciseness*; 191.1 *contraction*; 723.2 *outline*; 17.12 *poetic language*; 149.2 *shortening*
elite **235.7**; 573.2 *aristocracy*; 797.2 *best*; 123.3 *chief thing*; 469.15 *chosen*; 469.9 *chosen thing*; 128.10 *excluding*; 654.7 *human society*; 797.9 *the best*
elitism 12.1 *government*; 466.4 *social discrimination*
elitist 466.7 *bigot*; 466.10 *discriminatory*
elixir 37.3 *drug*; 369.8 *extract*; 394.2 *medicine*; 99.3 *quintessence*; 394.1 *remedy*
elixir vitae 394.1 *remedy*
Elizabethan 23.7 *furniture style*; 3.15, 296.14 *historic*
Elizabethan Age 3.10 *past age*
Elizabethan theatre 21.16 *theatre*
Elizabethan tragedy 21.11 *tragedy*
elk hunt 633.2 *chase*
ell 211.3 *additional item*
ellipse 27.42 *circle*; 148.6 *oblong*; 306.1 *orbital motion*
ellipsis 133.5 *caesura*; 269.1 *conciseness*; 266.1 *obscurity*; 742.7 *punctuation*; 149.3 *shortened version*; 5.30 *syntax*
ellipsoid 27.45 *curved surface*
ellipsoidal 27.83 *spherical*
elliptic 179.5 *circular*; 269.3 *concise*; 27.81 *curvilinear*
elliptical 306.10 *circular*; 27.81 *curvilinear*; 148.2 *elongated*; 266.2 *obscure*; 149.8 *shortened*
elliptical arch 20.5 *arch*
elliptical galaxy 29.7 *galaxy*
elliptically 179.8 *circularly*; 269.5 *concisely*; 266.4 *obscurely*; 149.12 *short*
elliptically polarized light 28.27 *polarized light*
elliptical orbit 29.21 *orbit*
elocution 729.4 *articulation*
Elohim 8.3 *God*
Elohistic 8.13 *divine*
elongate 148.10 *lengthen*
elongated **148.2**
elongation 38.16 *deformation*; 148.4 *length*
elope 389.5 *escape*; 570.15 *marry*; 313.3 *quit*; 634.8 *run away*
elopement 313.7 *departure*; 634.16 *desertion*; 389.1 *escape*; 570.5 *wedding*
eloper 389.3 *escaper*
elope with 773.10 *take away*
eloquence 542.2 *affectation*; 729.2 *power of speech*; 726.2 *seriousness*; 731.1 *talkativeness*
eloquent **729.20**; 726.3 *emphatic*; 694.6 *meaningful*; 542.10 *ornate*; 731.5 *talkative*
eloquently 729.21 *orally*; 731.10 *talkatively*
elsewhere 98.21 *away*
elucidate 522.29, 725.2 *clarify*; 722.4 *dissertate*; 703.16 *explain*; 719.8 *interpret*; 520.10 *make visible*; 4.21 *rationalize*; 695.5 *simplify*
elucidated 522.22 *enlightened*; 703.11 *explanatory*; 719.15 *interpreted*
elucidation 522.13 *enlightenment*; 703.3 *explanation*; 719.1 *interpretation*
elucidative 719.14 *interpretive*
elucidatory 721.11 *descriptive*; 719.14 *interpretive*
eluctate 391.5 *be liberated*
elude **389.6**; 702.12 *deceive*; 634.6 *evade*; 766.15 *lose someone*; 637.7 *refuse*
elude one 696.7 *be unintelligible*
eluent 32.17 *analysis*
elusion 389.1 *escape*
elusive 634.18 *avoiding*; 702.8 *cunning*; 696.4 *difficult*; 389.8 *escaping*; 96.8 *unreal*
elusively 634.22 *evasively*; 702.15 *hypocritically*
elusiveness 384.4 *defensiveness*; 634.14 *evasion*
elution 32.17 *analysis*
elutriate 255.10, 256.15 *purify*
elver 74.3 *young fish*
Elysia 756.4 *promised land*
Elysian 597.5 *delightful*; 8.14 *heavenly*; 241.1, 490.6 *pleasant*
Elysian Fields 756.4 *promised land*
Elysian fields 8.11 *heaven*; 490.5 *idealized pleasure*; 582.14 *the spiritual world*
Elysium 8.11 *heaven*; 490.5 *idealized pleasure*; 101.1 *nonmaterial world*
Elzevir edition 159.2 *little thing*
emaciate 191.6 *become smaller*; 191.5 *make smaller*; 335.7 *remove power from*; 441.1 *waste*
emaciated **153.2**; 530.8 *drained of colour*; 337.10 *ill*; 191.7 *smaller*; 218.3 *underfed*; 260.21 *unhealthy*
emaciating 191.8 *contracting*
emaciation **153.8**; 191.1 *contraction*; 441.3 *waste*
email 692.8 *data transmission*
emanate 738.5 *be visible*; 315.10 *emerge*; 500.8 *have odour*; 315.12 *leak*; 311.13 *radiate*; 559.7 *secrete*
emanate from 345.7 *follow from*
emanating 315.15 *outgoing*
emanation 560.1 *excretion*; 500.1 *odour*; 315.2 *outflow*; 11.10 *psychic phenomenon*; 311.3 *radiation*; 500.4 *reputation*; 559.1 *secretion*; 525.4 *something that appears*
emanational 559.4 *secretory*
emanative 500.5 *odorous*; 315.15 *outgoing*; 559.4 *secretory*
emanatory 559.4 *secretory*
emancipate 390.1 *deliver*; 391.4 *liberate*; 608.10 *save*; 250.15 *set free*
emancipated 389.8 *escaping*; 250.9 *free*; 391.7 *liberated*
emancipation 608.2 *aid*; 390.2 *deliverance*; 250.1 *freedom*; 391.1 *liberation*
emancipation of the dissonance 517.4 *atonality*
Emancipation Proclamation 250.1 *freedom*; 391.1 *liberation*
emancipator 390.3 *deliverer*; 391.3 *liberator*
emanent 315.15 *outgoing*
emarginate 425.4 *toothed*
emasculate 335.9 *make impotent*; 563.8 *make infertile*; 238.8 *make useless*; 212.4 *take off*
emasculated 335.13 *unsexed*
emasculation 212.1 *subtraction*
embalm 582.17, 583.8 *bury*; 502.6 *perfume*; 359.5 *preserve*
embalmed 583.10 *buried*; 582.22 *postmortem*; 359.7 *preserved*
embalmed body 582.11 *dead person*
embalmer 583.3 *funeral director*; 582.9 *person dealing with the dead*; 359.4 *preservationist*
embalming 582.8 *after death*; 583.1 *burial*; 359.1 *preservation*
embalmment 583.1 *burial*
embank 413.11 *support*
embankment 378.3 *barrier*; 90.2 *channel*; 38.23 *dam*; 376.26 *mass*; 384.8 *military defences*; 317.10 *railway*; 252.4 *safety device*; 38.19 *structure*; 413.2 *supporting part*; 321.2 *track*; 360.4 *wall*
embargo 378.9 *block*; 397.1, 397.9 *command*; 709.2, 709.6 *dissent*; 13.6 *economic factors*; 251.2 *economic restraint*; 128.7 *exclude*; 128.1 *exclusion*; 166.7 *limit*; 166.2 *limiting factor*; 301.9 *make motionless*; 301.1 *motionlessness*; 378.2 *obstacle*; 786.2 *stoppage*; 399.1, 399.3 *veto*
embargoed 397.14 *commanding*; 709.9 *dissenting*; 128.11 *excluded*; 251.13 *restraining*; 399.5 *vetoed*
embark 314.9 *enter*; 313.5 *set out*
embarkation 130.6 *inauguration*; 313.8 *start*
embarkment 313.8 *start*
embark on 130.18 *make a beginning*; 354.1 *undertake*
embark upon office 289.11 *follow in office*
embarras de choix 469.6 *selection*
embarras de richesses 219.1 *excess*; 562.1 *fertility*; 217.8 *plenty*; 469.6 *selection*; 219.3 *superfluity*
embarrass 240.5 *be inconvenient*; 378.11 *be inhibited*; 264.23 *cause difficulties*; 242.10 *displease*; 623.17 *humiliate*; 453.20 *make uncertain*
embarrassed 327.15 *agitated*; 453.3 *confused*; 623.3 *humbled*; 378.15 *inhibitive*; 251.14 *self-restrained*; 674.11 *shy*; 264.16 *troubled*
embarrassing 623.6, 668.16 *humiliating*; 378.15 *inhibitive*; 251.14 *self-restrained*
embarrassingly 453.24 *confusingly*; 378.18 *inhibitively*; 251.17 *with self-restraint*
embarrassing position 264.7 *awkward situation*
embarrassing situation 264.7 *awkward*

situation; 596.2 *disliked thing*; 594.7 *hated thing*
embarrassment 327.1 *agitation*; 453.12 *confusion*; 623.9 *humiliation*; 668.8 *indignity*; 378.5 *inhibition*; 251.3 *self-restraint*; 674.4 *shyness*; 806.2 *signs of guilt*
embarrassment of riches 562.1 *fertility*
embassy 565.4 *official residence*; 398.2 *representative body*
embattled 585.15 *warring*
Embden–Meyerhof pathway 33.24 *respiration*
embed 368.5 *inset*
embedded 368.12 *inserted*
embedment 368.8 *insertion*
embellish 211.6 *add*; 96.16 *delude*; 727.7 *exaggerate*; 244.1 *improve*; 699.28 *mask*; 542.12 *ornament*
embellished 547.14 *beautified*; 699.39 *disguised*; 727.12 *exaggerated*; 542.10 *ornate*
embellishment 727.1 *exaggeration*; 699.14 *façade*; 244.5 *improvement*; 542.1 *ornament*
embers 493.6, 522.8 *fire*
embezzle 774.16 *act dishonestly*; 800.10 *be criminal*; 351.1 *misuse*; 786.7 *not pay*; 773.10 *take away*
embezzlement 800.3 *criminality*; 774.7 *dishonesty*; 351.2 *misuse*; 786.1 *nonpayment*; 773.3 *taking away*
embezzler 774.11 *dishonest person*; 800.4 *dishonourable person*; 786.6 *nonpayer*; 773.6 *taker*
embezzling 800.7 *criminal*
embiopteran 76.10 *insectan*
embitter 594.16 *cause hate*; 499.9 *disgust*; 626.12 *make irritable*; 245.3 *make worse*
embittered 624.15 *resentful*
embitter with disappointment 604.7 *thwart*
emblazon 529.15 *colour*; 743.10 *identify*
emblazoned 743.13 *heraldic*
emblem 743.3 *means of identification*; 163.1 *outline*; 742.1 *sign*; 11.6 *talisman*
emblematic 743.13 *heraldic*; 163.6 *outlined*; 717.13 *representational*; 721.13 *representing*
emblematically 743.14 *identifiably*; 717.14 *representationally*
embodied 525.7 *appearing*; 374.7 *combined*; 550.39 *inclusive*; 402.7 *material*
embodiment 525.1 *appearance*; 374.1 *combination*; 406.1 *contents*; 8.8 *divine manifestation*; 127.1, 550.19 *inclusion*; 402.2 *materialization*; 99.3 *quintessence*; 717.1 *representation*
embody **99.12**; **406.8**; 402.8 *be material*; 374.5 *combine*; 405.11 *consist of*; 127.4, 550.32 *include*; 717.9 *represent*
embodying 405.9 *composing*; 406.10 *containing*
embolden 613.17 *give courage*
embolism 260.10 *cardiovascular disease*; 368.8 *insertion*
embolus 416.4 *solid body*; 309.2 *stopper*
embonpoint 158.5 *fatness*
embosom 593.27 *kiss*
emboss 19.22 *engrave*; 743.10 *identify*; 420.12 *make rough*
embossed 19.28 *sculpted*; 20.17 *structured*
embossing 19.13 *relief-carving*
embossment 608.6 *profile*; 19.13 *relief-carving*
embrace 569.4 *act of friendship*; 267.6 *adhere*; 569.15 *be hospitable*; 593.24 *be in love*; 654.11 *be sociable*; 204.9 *be whole*; 593.14 *communication of love*; 405.11 *consist of*; 99.12 *embody*; 184.11 *enfold*; 184.5 *enfoldment*; 658.12 *greet*; 127.4 *include*; 593.27 *kiss*; 252.10 *protect*; 252.2 *protection*; 360.6 *retain*; 360.1 *retention*; 469.3 *side with*; 658.5 *sign of courtesy*; 147.17 *stay near*; 370.9, 654.9, 654.14 *welcome*
embracing 593.14 *communication of love*
embrasure 384.11 *fortification*
embrocate 268.19 *anoint*
embrocation 394.9 *balm*; 37.7, 268.6 *ointment*
embroider 96.16 *delude*; 234.12 *distort the truth*; 727.7 *exaggerate*; 699.28 *mask*; 542.12 *ornament*; 702.11 *practise sophistry*
embroidered 547.14 *beautified*; 699.39 *disguised*; 727.12 *exaggerated*; 541.6 *variegated*
embroiderer 542.8 *decorator*
embroidery 19.1 *art*; 727.1 *exaggeration*; 699.14 *façade*; 542.1 *ornament*; 542.3 *pattern*
embroilment 327.3 *turbulence*
embrown 534.7 *brown*
embryo 34.15 *developmental biology*; 233.3 *incomplete thing*; 561.7 *obstetrics*; 344.3 *rudiment*; 77.9 *seed*; 130.3 *source*
embryogenesis 34.15 *developmental biology*
embryogeny 34.15 *developmental biology*
embryological 34.20 *biological*; 70.16 *zoological*
embryologically 34.29 *biologically*
embryologist 34.19 *life scientist*; 35.13 *medical specialist*; 70.11 *zoologist*
embryology 70.9 *animal science*; 34.15 *developmental biology*; 34.1 *life science*; 35.3 *medical specialty*
embryonic **130.32**; 344.13 *causal*; 34.26 *developmental*; 295.12 *immature*; 159.7 *little*
embryonically 233.6 *incompletely*
embus 313.5 *set out*
emcee 692.29 *broadcaster*; 579.2 *direct*; 21.27 *producer*
emend 719.8 *interpret*; 244.3 *rectify*; 393.1 *repair*
emendation 224.1 *change*; 719.1 *interpretation*; 244.6 *rectification*; 393.8 *repair*
emendator 719.6 *interpreter*; 393.12 *repairer*
emended 224.12 *changed*; 719.15 *interpreted*
emender 719.6 *interpreter*; 244.13 *reviser*
emerald 538.1 *green*; 538.11 *green thing*
emerge **130.27**; **315.10**; 525.12 *become visible*; 739.9 *be disclosed*; 518.19 *be visible*; 345.7 *follow from*; 312.4 *land*; 389.7 *leak*; 313.5 *set out*
emergence 525.1 *appearance*; 312.10 *arrival*; 130.2 *creation*; 315.1 *exit*
emergency 249.1 *adversity*; 264.6 *critical situation*; 287.3 *critical time*; 254.5 *danger*; 222.4 *difficult circumstances*; 280.1 *immediacy*; 135.3 *needfulness*
emergency aid 608.4 *charity*
emergency buzzer 711.2 *danger signal*
emergency council 713.4 *adviser*
emergency exit 389.2 *means of escape*; 315.6 *way out*
emergency food supply 557.7 *food*
emergency funds 352.5 *reserves*
emergency part 252.4 *safety device*
emergency plan 475.3 *plan*; 484.2 *policy*
emergency procedure 484.2 *policy*
emergency rations 557.7 *food*; 436.1 *provision*
emergency reserves 439.1 *store*
emergent 525.7 *appearing*; 345.10 *caused*; 130.32 *embryonic*; 315.15 *outgoing*
emerging 312.18 *arriving*; 315.1 *exit*; 315.15 *outgoing*
emeritus 284.20, 296.13 *former*; 811.2 *person of repute*; 811.3 *reputable*; 605.7 *resigning*
emersion 315.1 *exit*
emery 425.12 *sharpener*; 421.11 *smooth*
emery board 427.12 *abrasive*; 365.7 *eraser*; 420.7 *rough thing*; 425.12 *sharpener*; 421.9 *smoother*
emery paper 427.12 *abrasive*; 365.7 *eraser*; 420.7 *rough thing*; 425.12 *sharpener*; 421.9 *smoother*
emery wheel 420.7 *rough thing*
emesis 371.23 *vomiting*
emetic 37.4 *drug type*; 371.29 *expulsive*; 371.28 *propellant*; 255.4, 394.6 *purgative*; 394.17 *remedial*; 37.17 *stimulating*
emetically 371.32 *expulsively*
emetocathartic 371.29 *expulsive*
emigrant 100.7 *new arrival*; 315.8 *outgoer*
emigrate **315.13**; 100.14 *be foreign*; 313.3 *quit*
emigration **315.4**; 313.7 *departure*; 377.7 *sprawl*
emigratory 313.13 *outgoing*
émigré 100.7 *new arrival*; 315.8 *outgoer*
eminence 811.1 *estimation*; 154.1, 366.8 *height*; 123.1 *importance*; 185.1 *prominence*; 121.1 *superiority*; 235.6 *worth*
éminence grise 736.7 *concealer*; 398.4 *deputy*; 395.4 *indirect influence*
eminent **185.6**; 154.11, 366.12 *exalted*; 121.15 *excellent*; 123.5 *important*; 123.6 *notable*; 811.3 *reputable*; 235.1 *worthy*
eminent domain 396.1 *authority*
eminently **185.11**; **811.7**; 123.9 *importantly*; 121.16 *superiorly*
emissary 398.6 *agent*; 398.1 *delegate*
emission **28.68**; **371.25**; 560.1 *excretion*; 389.4 *leak*; 315.2 *outflow*; 559.1 *secretion*
emission nebula 29.8 *interstellar medium*
emission spectrum 28.68 *emission*
emissive 371.29 *expulsive*; 559.4 *secretory*
emissivity 371.25 *emission*
emit 767.9 *dispose of*; 560.15 *excrete*; 432.27 *give off*; 315.12 *leak*; 371.14 *let out*; 29.37 *observe*; 559.7 *secrete*
emit rays 371.14 *let out*
emitter 371.28 *propellant*; 39.19 *transistor*
emitter electrode 39.19 *transistor*
emitting 371.29 *expulsive*
Emmanuel 8.4 *God the Son*
emmenagogic 371.29 *expulsive*
emmet 76.4 *social insect*
Emmy 813.2 *prize*
emollient 394.9 *balm*; 241.3 *comfortable*; 268.12 *lubricant*; 685.8 *moderating*; 37.7, 268.6 *ointment*; 749.6 *pacificatory*; 394.17 *remedial*; 37.16 *soothing*
emolument 788.3 *income*; 785.3 *pay*; 765.5 *profit*; 813.4 *reward for service*
emotion **590.4**; 395.1 *influence*; 593.3 *lovingness*; 488.1 *sensation*
emotional 593.20 *amorous*; 395.12 *appealing*; 703.10 *demonstrative*; 36.36 *psychologically disturbed*; 590.12, 591.1 *sensitive*; 478.2 *spontaneous*
emotional instability 590.7 *emotionalism*
emotionalism **590.7**; 703.2 *demonstrativeness*
emotionalist 703.7 *demonstrator*
emotionalistic 703.10 *demonstrative*
emotionality 703.2 *demonstrativeness*; 590.7 *emotionalism*
emotionalize 703.18 *appear*
emotionally **590.21**; 703.21 *demonstratively*; 395.14 *influentially*; 593.30 *lovingly*; 591.13 *oversensitively*; 488.14 *sensationally*
emotionally disturbed person 36.8 *disordered personality*
emotional person 590.9 *feeling person*
emotional strain 36.12 *stress*
emotive **590.14**; 488.9 *exciting*
emotiveness 590.7 *emotionalism*
emotivism 4.7 *school of thought*
emotivist 4.11 *follower of a doctrine*; 4.14 *of a philosophy*
empanada 25.50 *Central American dish*
empanel 744.13 *record*; 744.15 *register*
empanel a jury 16.71 *try a case*
empanelling a jury 16.7 *legal trial*
empanelment 744.8 *registration*
empathetic 650.6 *benevolent*; 764.5 *jointly possessing*; 595.6 *liking*; 590.12, 591.1 *sensitive*; 413.9 *supportive*
empathetically 595.11 *admiringly*; 764.6 *in common*
empathize 650.8 *be benevolent*; 750.21 *be in accord*; 591.11 *be sensitive*; 590.18 *feel for*; 477.16 *have insight*; 627.8 *pity*
empathizer 764.3 *participant*
empathize with 627.8 *pity*
empathizing 750.10 *in accord*
empathy 750.1 *accord*; 590.5 *good feeling*; 477.3 *insight*; 595.1 *liking*; 413.6 *moral support*; 764.2 *participation*; 627.1 *pity*; 591.5 *sensitivity*
Empedoclean 4.11 *follower of a doctrine*; 4.14 *of a philosophy*
emperor 396.10 *person of authority*; 400.2 *sovereign*; 121.5 *superior*
empery 12.3 *governance*
Emphasis 726
emphasis **707.7**; **726.1**; 123.1 *importance*; 336.3 *intensity*; 738.10 *manifestation*; 17.9 *metre*; 729.3 *mode of speech*; 334.1 *power*
emphasize **707.22**; **726.6**; 386.6 *compel*; 738.1 *display*; 123.8 *make important*; 740.16 *publicize*; 742.13 *punctuate*; 738.3 *reveal*; 742.10 *signify*; 695.5 *simplify*; 336.8 *strengthen*
emphasized **707.15**; **726.4**; 738.14 *manifest*
emphatic **726.3**; 707.14 *assertive*; 529.11 *colourful*; 661.7 *defiant*; 738.15 *open*
emphatically **726.7**; 707.23 *affirmatively*; 661.9 *defiantly*
emphatically deny 708.11 *rebut*
emphatic denial 708.3 *rebuttal*
emphysema 260.9 *respiratory disease*
empiracle formula 32.13 *structure*
Empire 23.7 *furniture style*
empire 85.3 *dominion*; 12.3 *governance*; 396.8 *governmental organization*; 12.5 *political organization*; 86.4 *territorial division*
Empire bed 23.6 *bed*
empire building 329.10 *expansionism*
Empire-line 551.31 *styled*
Empire State Building 158.9 *big thing*; 154.6 *tall thing*
empirical 716.8 *evidential*; 448.8 *experimental*; 402.7 *material*; 93.13 *real*; 27.69 *theoretical*
empirically 448.14 *experimentally*
empirical probability 27.62 *probability*; 104.5 *probability theory*
empirical psychology 36.1 *psychology*
empirical sociologist 2.11 *sociologist*
empirical world 402.1 *material world*
empiricism 448.3 *experimentation*; 402.2 *materialization*; 4.7 *school of thought*
empiricist 448.5 *experimenter*; 4.11 *follower of a doctrine*; 4.14 *of a philosophy*
emplace 142.9 *locate*
emplaced 142.6 *located*
emplacement 384.11 *fortification*; 142.4 *placing*
emplane 313.5 *set out*
emplanement 313.8 *start*
employ 237.11 *find useful*; 2.15 *socialize*; 387.6 *subject*; 387.1 *subjection*; 773.7 *take*; 346.9 *take action*; 349.1 *use*; 576.7 *work for*
employability 237.6 *usability*
employable 15.8 *industrial*; 348.6 *instrumental*; 387.9 *subject*; 237.2, 349.10 *usable*
employed 342.19 *busy*; 15.8 *industrial*; 143.6 *situated*; 387.9 *subject*; 349.9 *used*; 576.10 *working*
employee **15.7**; 15.8 *industrial*; 401.5 *office assistant*; 346.5 *operator*; 401.1 *servant*; 387.3 *subordinate*; 578.1 *worker*
employee claim 15.4 *industrial dispute*
employee demands 15.1 *industrial relations*
employee dinner 557.13 *feast*
employee jurisdiction 15.1 *industrial relations*
employee practices 15.1 *industrial relations*
employee relations 15.1 *industrial relations*
employee rights 15.1 *industrial relations*
employees 392.11 *helper*; 578.4 *personnel*
employer **15.6**; 578.3 *agent*; 400.5 *company leader*; 579.13 *director*; 13.9 *economist*; 15.8 *industrial*
employer-employee relations 15.1 *industrial relations*
employer jurisdiction 15.1 *industrial relations*
employer rights 15.1 *industrial relations*
employers 579.6 *governing body*
employer's association 15.1 *industrial relations*
employer's liability 15.2 *industrial negotiations*
employers' organization 15.1 *industrial relations*
employing 15.8 *industrial*
employment **143.4**; 340.1 *action*; 13.6 *economic factors*; 15.8 *industrial*; 348.1 *instrumentality*; 576.3 *job*; 387.1 *subjection*; 773.1 *taking*; 349.6 *use*; 237.5 *usefulness*
employment contract 15.1 *industrial relations*; 755.2 *purchase contract*
employment laws 15.1 *industrial relations*
employment manager 15.6 *employer*
employment relationships 15.1 *industrial relations*
employment rules 15.1 *industrial relations*
employment standards 15.2 *industrial negotiations*
employment status 2.7 *social stratification*

employment training 6.2 *educational system*
employ oneself 340.4 *act*
employ tactics 631.11 *conduct oneself*
emporium 779.7
empower 398.7 *delegate*; 334.11 *give power*; 396.21 *grant authority*; 102.7 *make possible*; 757.3 *permit*; 136.13 *qualify*
empowered 396.12 *authoritative*; 136.10 *authorized*; 334.13 *powerful*
empowerment 396.3 *acquisition of power*; 136.4 *permission*
empress 396.10 *person of authority*; 400.2 *sovereign*
empressement 342.8 *assiduity*
emprise 354.2 *undertaking*
emptily 98.20 *absently*; 699.42 *hypocritically*; 417.7 *sparsely*; 247.12 *unsuccessfully*
emptiness 94.4; **98.3**; 141.2 *empty space*; 699.3 *hypocrisy*; 708.8 *nonexistence*; 335.1 *powerlessness*; 417.3 *sparseness*; 124.5 *unimportance*
emptiness of mind 463.2 *blankness*
emptional 777.13 *bought*
emptor 777.12 *purchaser*
empty 270.3 *diffuse*; 247.10 *failed*; 687.6 *fasting*; 617.10 *hungry*; 699.31 *hypocritical*; 563.3 *infertile*; 415.10 *lighten*; 417.6 *make sparse*; 94.9, 708.21 *nonexistent*; 343.2 *not working*; 702.7 *sophistic*; 141.21 *space*; 417.1 *sparse*; 212.3 *subtract*; 369.14 *suck*; 157.2 *superficial*; 98.14 *unoccupied*; 218.2 *unprovided*; 98.13 *vacant*; 371.11 *void*; 441.1 *waste*
empty bottle 238.6 *refuse*
empty gesture 699.3, 700.3 *hypocrisy*
empty gossip 699.11 *half-truth*
empty-handed 218.2 *unprovided*
empty head 673.7 *vain person*
empty-headed 463.9 *blank*; 459.5 *foolish*; 456.6 *ignorant*; 457.6 *unintelligent*
empty-headedly 457.11 *unintelligently*
empty-headedness 463.2 *blankness*; 459.1 *folly*; 456.1 *ignorance*; 457.2 *unintelligence*
emptying 371.21 *removal*; 369.4 *sucking*
empty larder 782.6 *insolvency*
empty one's pocket 787.1 *expend*; 785.6 *pay*
empty out 371.11 *void*
empty phrase 5.5 *nonstandard language*
empty pride 673.1 *vanity*
empty promises 96.4 *theorization*
empty purse 782.6 *insolvency*
empty set 27.21 *set*
empty shell 98.3 *emptiness*; 215.1 *remainder*
empty space 141.2; 98.3 *emptiness*
empty stomach 617.3 *appetite*
empty talk 542.2 *affectation*; 270.1 *diffuseness*; 697.1 *nonsense*; 5.5 *nonstandard language*; 731.3 *talk*; 96.4 *theorization*
empty the glass 558.13 *drink*
empty threats 335.2 *futile effort*
empty words 5.5 *nonstandard language*; 702.1 *sophistry*
empurple 540.9
empyreal 8.14 *heavenly*
empyrean 8.11 *heaven*; 8.14 *heavenly*; 29.3 *universe*
em rule 742.7 *punctuation*
em space 146.1 *interval*
emu 72.2 *flightless bird*
emulate 125.11; 40.20 *abort*; 117.8 *comply*; 113.19 *confront*; 115.12, 125.9 *imitate*
emulating 125.12 *imitative*
emulation 113.5 *conflict*; 117.1 *conformity*; 125.1 *imitation*
emulative 629.4 *jealous*
emulator 113.12 *competitor*; 40.19 *computing terms*
emulous 629.4 *jealous*
emulously 629.9 *jealously*
emulsifier 557.11 *food content*
emulsify 431.22 *make fluid*; 32.25 *solidify*; 430.11 *thicken*
emulsion 41.11; **430.4**; 32.3 *phase*; 431.10 *solution*
emulsion paint 529.5 *paint*
emulsive 430.8 *viscous*
emulsoid 32.32 *solid*
enable 352.6 *find means*; 334.11 *give power*; 750.30 *grant*; 265.16 *make easy*; 102.7 *make possible*; 757.3 *permit*; 136.13 *qualify*
enabled 136.10 *authorized*; 750.19 *granted*
enablement 136.4 *permission*
enabler 392.11 *helper*
enact 21.34, 340.4, 717.10 *act*; 631.14 *behave towards*; 397.9 *command*; 738.1 *display*; 16.68 *legislate*
enacted 397.14 *commanding*; 21.39 *dramatic*; 16.46 *legislated*
enacting 340.5 *acting*; 16.31 *legislation*
enactment 21.22, 717.3 *acting*; 340.1 *action*; 397.1 *command*; 16.31 *legislation*; 713.3 *precept*; 738.9 *production*; 140.1 *rule*
enamel 550.24 *coat*; 550.3 *coating*; 529.15 *colour*; 24.11 *make ceramics*; 529.4 *pigment*; 421.10 *polish*; 541.11 *variegate*
enamel kiln 24.6 *ceramic workshop*
enamelled 24.10 *ceramic*; 421.4 *polished*
enameller 19.16 *artist*
enamelling 19.1 *art*; 24.10 *ceramic*
enamellist 24.7 *potter*
enamelware 24.1 *ceramics*
enamelwork 541.5 *variegated thing*
enamour 593.28 *win the love of*
enamoured 593.19
enamoured of 593.18 *in love*
enantiomorphic 162.4 *symmetrical*
enantiomorphic figure 27.48 *transformation*
en bloc 232.9 *completely*; 750.31 *in accord*; 204.12 *one and all*
encaenia 10.16 *religious festival*
encamp 565.18 *take up residence*
encapsulate 127.4 *include*; 368.5 *inset*; 149.10 *shorten*; 723.8 *summarize*
encapsulated 149.8 *shortened*
encapsulation 127.1 *inclusion*; 149.2 *shortening*
encase 368.5 *inset*; 550.25 *wrap*
encased 550.37 *protected*
encash 780.26 *bank*; 778.1 *sell*; 13.10 *trade with*
encaustic 24.10 *ceramic*; 19.8 *painting*
encaustically 24.12 *ornamentally*
encaustic tile 24.8 *ceramic object*
enceinte 561.16 *reproductive*
encephalitis 260.6 *infection*
encephalitis lethargica 260.6 *infection*; 260.7 *tropical disease*
encephalopathy 461.3 *mental deterioration*
enchant 11.21 *bewitch*; 619.10 *be wonderful*; 597.8 *cause joy*; 593.28 *win the love of*
enchanted 11.19 *bewitched*; 760.13 *converted*; 593.19 *enamoured*; 597.4 *happy*
enchanter 363.6 *charmer*; 11.4 *witch*
enchanting 597.5 *delightful*; 593.22 *lovable*; 545.6 *personable*; 11.15 *witchlike*
enchantingly 363.14 *attractively*; 593.30 *lovingly*
enchantment 760.1 *conversion*; 597.1 *happiness*; 593.4 *lovability*; 593.2 *romantic love*; 11.3 *witchcraft*
enchantress 363.6 *charmer*; 11.4 *witch*
enchilada 25.50 *Central American dish*
encipher 737.14 *make mysterious*; 696.8 *make unintelligible*
encircle 27.97 *align*; 381.4 *besiege*; 179.6 *circle*; 127.4 *include*; 306.7 *ring*; 170.7 *surround*
encircled 170.5 *surrounded*
encirclement 170.2; 165.1 *enclosure*; 127.1 *inclusion*; 381.14 *siege*
enclave 165.2 *enclosed place*; 655.4 *place of confinement*; 86.5 *state*
enclitic 5.17 *word*; 5.42 *worded*
enclose 165.5; **309.10**; 381.4 *besiege*; 406.6 *contain*; 360.7 *detain*; 184.11 *enfold*; 128.7 *exclude*; 141.20 *extend*; 384.18 *fence*; 127.4 *include*; 252.10 *protect*; 410.21 *put in a container*; 170.7 *surround*; 550.25 *wrap*
enclosed 165.7; **309.15**; 410.20 *containing*; 172.7 *interior*; 550.37 *protected*; 170.5 *surrounded*
enclosed land 43.11 *farmland*
enclosed place 165.2; 309.4 *closed place*
enclosed space 27.35 *space*
enclosement 550.1 *covering*
enclosing 410.20 *containing*; 360.2 *detention*; 165.1 *enclosure*
enclosing thing 165.3
Enclosure 165
enclosure 165.1; 309.4 *closed place*; 165.2 *enclosed place*; 184.5 *enfoldment*; 128.3 *exclusion zone*; 43.11 *farmland*; 127.1 *inclusion*; 86.12 *plot*; 127.2 *thing included*; 585.8 *warfare*
encode 736.9 *disguise*; 737.14 *make mysterious*; 696.8 *make unintelligible*; 11.20 *occult*; 719.12 *translate*
encoded 719.15 *interpreted*; 11.14 *occult*; 696.1 *unintelligible*
encoffin 583.8 *bury*
encomiastic 669.18 *approving*
encomium 669.4 *compliment*; 17.7 *poem*; 729.8 *speech*
encompass 211.6 *add*; 204.9 *be whole*; 405.11 *consist of*; 99.12 *embody*; 141.20 *extend*; 127.4, 550.32 *include*; 179.7 *make circular*; 306.7 *ring*; 170.7 *surround*; 165.6 *wrap*
encompassed 170.5 *surrounded*
encompassing 209.7 *gradational*; 550.39 *inclusive*
encompassment 170.2 *encirclement*
encore 669.5, 669.16 *acclaim*; 112.24 *again*; 669.27 *bravo!*; 112.5 *repeat*; 21.8 *scene*; 198.19 *twice*
encounter 285.6 *be simultaneous*; 331.2 *collide*; 331.12 *collision*; 449.1 *discover*; 449.6 *discovery*; 147.19, 312.8 *meet*; 147.4, 312.14 *meeting*
encounter aliens 11.24 *experience psychic phenomena*
encounter by chance 107.11 *chance upon*
encounter group 36.3 *psychiatric treatment*
encounter unexpectedly 107.11 *chance upon*
encourage 392.23, 713.5 *advise*; 344.10 *awaken*; 650.8 *be benevolent*; 598.8 *cheer*; 6.22 *educate*; 613.17 *give courage*; 413.14 *give moral support*; 244.1 *improve*; 395.8 *influence*; 610.10 *inspire hope*; 483.9 *motivate*
encouraged 483.12 *motivated*; 480.20 *persuadable*
encouragement 613.6; 713.1 *advice*; 344.1 *cause*; 610.4 *comfort*; 480.2 *flattery*; 483.2 *inducement*; 395.1 *influence*; 413.6 *moral support*; 392.9 *patronage*
encouraging 613.14; 713.7 *advising*; 395.12 *appealing*; 756.14 *auspicious*; 598.2, 610.14 *cheering*; 483.11 *motivational*; 480.19 *persuasive*; 392.32, 413.9 *supportive*
encouragingly 756.17 *auspiciously*; 6.25 *educationally*; 610.15 *hopefully*; 395.14, 483.14 *influentially*; 480.21 *persuasively*
Encratism 572.3 *monasticism*; 795.3 *moral purity*
Encratite 572.4 *celibate person*; 572.8 *monastic*; 795.5 *pure person*
encroach 381.4 *besiege*; 314.10 *invade*; 329.5 *transgress*
encroaching 16.60 *offending*; 329.11 *overrun*
encroachment 302.15 *improvement*; 314.3 *inroad*; 16.38 *lawbreaking*; 46.13 *penalty*; 381.14 *siege*; 329.8 *transgression*
encrust 171.11 *be exterior*; 550.28 *face*
encrustation 258.1 *dirtiness*; 550.8 *wall covering*
encrusted 420.2 *coarse*; 258.7 *dirty*
encumber 378.12 *burden*; 378.8 *hinder*; 414.14 *make heavy*
encumbered 378.13 *hindering*; 784.9 *in debt*
encumbering 378.13 *hindering*
encumbrance 211.1 *addition*; 378.6 *burden*; 784.1 *debt*; 378.1 *hindrance*; 414.8 *weighing down*
encyclical 397.1 *command*; 397.14 *commanding*; 740.1 *publication*
encyclopedia 439.5 *collection*; 220.3 *dictionary*; 693.5 *reference book*; 6.14 *school book*
encyclopedic 138.15 *general*; 127.7 *including*; 455.8 *knowledgeable*
encyclopedically 220.13 *inventorially*
End 131
end 131.1; **131.15**; 232.5 *be complete*; 357.13 *be destroyed*; 94.13 *cause not to exist*; 226.8 *cause to cease*; 226.6 *cease*; 94.12 *cease to exist*; 133.2 *cessation*; 309.9 *close down*; 309.1 *closure*; 204.10, 232.4 *complete*; 232.3 *completion*; 582.1 *death*; 312.15 *destination*; 357.8 *destroy*; 526.1 *disappear*; 526.4 *disappearance*; 133.12 *discontinue*; 345.1 *effect*; 305.4 *fall*; 51.1 *green bowling*; 131.25 *hindmost*; 482.6 *objective*; 284.14 *pass*; 694.5 *point*; 446.4 *purpose*; 168.4 *rear*; 168.2 *rear end*; 357.4 *ruin*; 289.9 *sequel*; 226.2 *stop*
end age discrimination 391.6 *treat equally*
end an affair 355.2 *withdraw*
endanger 254.10
endangered 254.4
endangered species 70.1 *animals*; 359.3 *preserved thing*
endangerment 254.5 *danger*
end around 46.9 *play*
endboards 58.3 *ice hockey*
endearing 595.5 *likable*; 593.22 *lovable*
endearingly 593.30 *lovingly*; 595.10 *with great liking*
endearing qualities 593.4 *lovability*
endearment 593.4 *lovability*
endear oneself 593.28 *win the love of*
endeavour 340.1 *action*; 353.5 *attempt*; 334.10 *be powerful*; 576.4 *exertion*; 576.8 *exert oneself*; 448.1 *experiment*; 448.13 *invent*; 334.1 *power*; 356.1 *production*; 353.2 *try hard*; 354.1 *undertake*; 354.2 *undertaking*
ended 131.21; 309.14 *closed down*; 232.7 *complete*; 133.9 *discontinued*; 226.10 *finished*; 3.18 *in the past*; 94.11 *no more*; 284.18 *over*
endemic 172.7 *interior*; 138.17 *widespread*
endemic disease 260.4 *disease*
ender 131.13
en deshabille 552.10 *in dishabille*
end game 69.4 *chess terms*
end-grain wood 23.12 *wood*
end hostilities 589.5 *be at peace*
end in 345.5 *show an effect*
end in a point 425.14 *be sharp*
end in futility 247.8 *miscarry*
ending 131.10; **131.20**; 211.3 *additional item*; 232.3 *completion*; 131.1 *end*; 226.2 *stop*
end in view 482.6 *objective*
end it all 131.19 *expire*
endless 132.11 *continuous*; 202.3 *eternal*; 202.1 *infinite*; 148.1 *long*; 208.8 *numberless*; 217.2 *plentiful*; 134.6 *protracted*
endless band 132.6 *continuum*
endlessly 134.7 *continually*; 132.19 *continuously*; 217.9 *enough*; 202.10 *infinitely*; 148.11 *lengthily*
endlessness 132.5 *continuity*; 279.1 *eternity*; 202.4 *infinity*; 148.4 *length*
endless round 132.6 *continuum*
endless supply 217.8 *plenty*
end line 46.4 *stadium*
end matter 131.10 *ending*; 168.1 *rear*
endmost 131.25 *hindmost*
endocarditis 260.10 *cardiovascular disease*
endocarp 80.3 *fruit structure*
endocrine 34.20 *biological*; 559.5 *of a secretion*
endocrine disease 260.4 *disease*
endocrine gland 559.3 *gland*
endocrinological 34.20 *biological*
endocrinologist 33.2 *biochemist*; 34.19 *life scientist*; 35.13 *medical specialist*
endocrinology 33.1 *biochemistry*; 34.1 *life science*; 35.3 *medical specialty*
endoderm 34.15 *developmental biology*; 172.1 *interior*
endodermal 34.26 *developmental*; 172.7 *interior*
endodermic 172.7 *interior*
endodermis 172.1 *interior*
endodontic 35.23 *dental*
endodontics 35.4 *dentistry*
endodontist 35.14 *dentist*
end of hostilities 589.1 *peace*
end of life 582.1 *death*
end of play 53.1 *cricket match*
end of steel 321.3 *rail*
end of the day 131.9 *close*
end of the line 131.3 *death*; 312.15 *destination*; 131.6 *end point*; 317.10 *railway*; 321.8 *railway station*
end of the pier 21.16 *theatre*
end of the rainbow 145.3 *distant place*; 477.7 *idealism*; 756.4 *promised land*; 781.5 *wealth*
end of the road 131.9 *close*
end of the world 131.5 *fate*; 357.4 *ruin*
end of time 131.5 *fate*; 4.9 *philosophical problem*
end of war 589.1 *peace*
endogamy 570.3 *types of marriage*
endogenous depression 36.13 *depression*
endomitosis 34.10 *cell division*

endomorph 160.6 *nature*; 36.7 *personality type*; 1.9 *physical type*
endomorphic 158.16 *fat*; 1.15 *physical*; 152.1 *thick*
endomorphism 36.7 *personality type*
endomorphy 158.5 *fatness*; 36.7 *personality type*; 1.9 *physical type*
end one's life 582.16 *meet one's fate*
endoparasite 70.4 *type of animal*
endoparasitic 70.15 *of animals*
endoplasm 34.7 *cell*
endoplasmic 34.23 *cellular*
endoplasmic reticulum 34.8 *cell organ*
ENDOR 32.17 *analysis*
endorse 669.12 *accept*; 392.23 *advise*; 707.19 *confirm*; 750.28 *consent*; 755.5 *contract*; 95.12 *establish reality*; 413.14 *give moral support*; 743.11 *identify oneself*; 16.68 *legislate*; 452.21 *make certain*; 757.3 *permit*; 253.11 *promise*; 716.12 *prove*; 469.3 *side with*; 454.1 *verify*
endorse a cheque 780.26 *bank*
endorsed 669.23 *approved*; 750.17 *consenting*; 707.13 *supported*
endorsee 769.5 *recipient*
endorsement 669.1 *approval*; 707.4 *confirmation*; 750.7 *consent*; 743.3 *means of identification*; 320.21 *miscellaneous motoring terms*; 413.6 *moral support*; 757.1 *permission*; 757.2 *permit*; 253.2 *promise*
endorser 707.9 *affirmer*; 755.4 *contractor*
endoscope 35.7 *diagnosis*
endoscopy 35.7 *diagnosis*
endoskeleton 403.7 *skeleton*
endosmosis 370.5 *absorption*; 318.3 *passage into*
endosmotic 370.17 *absorbent*
endosperm 77.9 *seed*
endotrophic mycorrhiza 83.5 *fungal association*
endow 392.29 *finance*; 679.11, 768.5 *give*; 334.11 *give power*; 750.30 *grant*; 781.15 *make rich*; 440.9 *own property*; 436.5 *provision*; 136.13 *qualify*
endowed 485.7 *gifted*; 768.7 *given*; 334.13 *powerful*; 440.8 *propertied*; 136.9 *qualified*
endowing 768.1 *giving*
endowment 136.2, 334.2 *ability*; 485.2 *aptitude*; 392.6 *financial assistance*; 768.1 *giving*; 750.9 *grant*; 136.4 *permission*; 765.5 *profit*
endow with power 334.11 *give power*
endpiece 168.1 *rear*
end play 53.15 *play*
end point **131.6**; 32.18 *gravimetric analysis*
end-product 356.3 *product*
end racial discrimination 391.6 *treat equally*
end result **131.12**; 345.1 *effect*
end rhyme 17.11 *rhyme*
end sexual discrimination 391.6 *treat equally*
ends of the earth 145.3 *distant place*; 131.7 *limit*
end someone's life 382.16 *kill*
end table 23.4 *table*
end to end 147.14 *beside*; 132.20 *in a line*; 148.11 *lengthily*
end-to-end 147.10 *juxtaposed*
end up 345.9 *take effect*
end up in 312.2 *reach*
endurable 413.10 *supportable*
endurance 93.6 *continuing existence*; 277.4 *long-lastingness*; 225.1 *permanence*; 423.8 *physical strength*; 334.1 *power*; 134.2 *protraction*; 640.4 *stamina*; 613.3 *steadfastness*; 336.1 *strength*; 267.2 *tenacity*
endurance event 61.1 *motor racing*
endurance racing 61.1 *motor racing*
endure **640.9**; 413.12 *bear*; 225.5 *be permanent*; 423.10 *be tough*; 93.19 *continue to be*; 277.6 *last*; 554.16 *live*; 638.11 *persist*; 134.4 *protract*; 383.6 *resist*; 649.12 *show mercy*; 388.4 *succumb*; 613.16 *take courage*
endure forever 279.5 *be eternal*
endure hardship 249.9 *be in trouble*
endure longer 765.10 *augment*
enduring 4.18 *detached*; 279.8 *eternal*; 93.12, 277.8 *lasting*; 225.7 *permanent*; 640.10 *persevering*; 423.4 *powerful*; 134.6 *protracted*; 228.9 *stable*; 267.10 *tenacious*
enduringly 134.7 *continually*; 225.9 *permanently*; 423.13 *powerfully*; 228.12 *stably*; 4.27 *stoically*; 267.12 *tenaciously*
endways 148.3 *longitudinal*; 148.12 *longitudinally*; 186.11 *vertically*
endwise 186.11 *vertically*
end zone 46.4 *stadium*
enema 256.2 *cleaning*; 255.4, 394.6 *purgative*; 368.11 *thing inserted*; 433.11 *wash*
enemy 596.3 *disliked person*; 594.8 *hated person*; 113.13 *opponent*
enemy of marriage 572.5 *single person*
energetic 342.18 *active*; 726.3 *emphatic*; 334.15 *full of energy*; 259.1 *healthy*; 342.20 *industrious*; 554.13 *lively*; 336.11 *strong in spirit*; 638.2 *tenacious*; 338.4 *vigorous*; 380.6 *violent*; 576.10 *working*
energetically **334.19**; 336.15 *acutely*; 726.7 *emphatically*; 576.12 *laboriously*; 336.14 *strongly*; 338.6 *with vigour*
energetic person 342.10 *busy person*
energid 34.7 *cell*
energize 334.11 *give power*; 338.3 *invigorate*; 213.5 *make bigger*; 483.9 *motivate*; 336.8 *strengthen*
energized 483.12 *motivated*
energizing 483.11 *motivational*; 480.19 *persuasive*
energy **28.11**; **334.4**; **342.4**; 638.13 *concentration*; 726.1 *emphasis*; 576.4 *exertion*; 259.3 *health*; 336.2 *healthiness*; 554.1 *life*; 330.12 *propellant*; 338.1 *vigour*; 380.1 *violence*; 334.3 *vitality*
energy balance 31.9 *atmospheric process*
energy band 28.44 *semiconductor*
energy charge 36.28 *cathexis*
energy-consuming 441.8 *wasteful*
energy crisis 218.9 *scarcity*
energy depletion 335.1 *powerlessness*
energy gap 28.44 *semiconductor*
energy imparted 28.70 *radioactivity*
Energy Information Administration 334.8 *nuclear power*
energy level 28.65 *atom*
energy-rich bond 33.22 *bioenergetics*
energy-saving 359.6 *preserving*
enervate 261.6 *fatigue*; 612.13 *frighten*; 335.9 *make impotent*; 337.7 *weaken*
enervated 261.1 *fatigued*; 337.11 *weakened*
enervating 612.10 *frightening*
enervation 261.7 *fatigue*; 337.3 *poor health*
en famille 654.18 *sociably*; 657.15 *unaffectedly*
enfant terrible 646.3 *naive person*; 118.7 *nonconformist*
enfeeble 214.5 *make smaller*; 337.7 *weaken*
enfeebled 337.8 *weak*
enfeeblement 214.1 *decrease*; 337.1 *weakness*
enfeoffment 768.1 *giving*
Enfield rifle 587.10 *historical gun*
enfilade 381.2 *fire*; 381.12 *military attack*
enfold **184.11**; 551.32 *dress*; 593.27 *kiss*; 252.10 *protect*; 170.7 *surround*; 165.6, 550.25 *wrap*
enfolded 170.5 *surrounded*
enfoldment **184.5**; 593.14 *communication of love*; 550.1 *covering*; 170.2 *encirclement*
enforce 386.6 *compel*
enforce a speed limit 251.8 *restrain*
enforce civil rights 391.6 *treat equally*
enforced repatriation 144.3 *replacement*
enforcement 386.2 *coercion*
enforcer 251.6 *lawmaker*
enforcing 386.9 *compelling*
enfranchise 250.15 *set free*; 391.6 *treat equally*
enfranchised 469.16 *elective*; 250.9 *free*
enfranchisement 250.3 *independence*
engage 381.1 *attack*; 585.14 *battle*; 810.17 *impose a duty*; 480.15 *persuade*; 293.9 *prepare*; 482.8 *resolve*; 773.7 *take*; 354.1 *undertake*
engaged 288.15, 342.19 *busy*; 810.11 *duty-bound*; 108.5 *interrelated*; 570.22 *marriageable*; 756.12 *promised*; 585.15 *warring*
engaged column 20.8 *column*
engaged couple 593.10 *lovers*
engaged in war 585.15 *warring*
engaged man 567.4 *boyfriend*
engaged person 756.6 *someone promised*
engaged to 593.18 *in love*
engaged tone 692.11 *dialling*
engaged woman 568.4 *girlfriend*
engage in 733.12 *address oneself to*; 354.1 *undertake*
engage in conversation 734.9 *converse*
engage in dialectic 4.23 *discuss philosophically*
engage in fisticuffs 751.6 *argue*; 52.11 *fight*
engage in war 585.13 *be at war*
engagement **21.15**; 585.9 *battle*; 810.7 *commitment*; 354.3, 755.1 *contract*; 482.4 *formulated intention*; 108.2 *interrelatedness*; 593.8 *love affair*; 654.3 *meeting*; 764.2 *participation*; 756.1 *promise*; 773.1 *taking*; 810.2 *task*; 354.2 *undertaking*
engagement book 220.5 *list of appointments*
engagement diary 220.5 *list of appointments*; 462.4 *reminder*
engage oneself 810.15 *be liable*
engagé or ***engagée*** 342.18 *active*
engaging 241.2 *likable*; 593.22 *lovable*
en garde 54.3 *fencing movements*
engender 130.26, 356.10 *produce*; 561.13 *propagate*
engine **38.11**; 405.4 *components*; 38.5 *dynamic structure*; 28.11 *energy*; 321.4 *locomotive*; 438.5 *machine*; 29.35 *rocketry*
engine cycle **38.13**
engine driver 321.9 *railway worker*
engineer **38.2**; **38.30**; 578.2 *artisan*; 344.10 *awaken*; 484.11 *invent*; 438.8 *machinist*; 356.10 *produce*; 356.9 *producer*; 321.9 *railway worker*; 393.12 *repairer*
engineer battalion 584.4 *military organization*
Engineering 38
engineering **38.1**; 356.2 *manufacture*; 438.6 *mechanics*
engineering brick 20.4 *building material*
engineering design 38.1 *engineering*
engineering drawing 38.1 *engineering*
engineering geology 38.1 *engineering*
engine failure 247.4 *unsuccessful thing*
engine lathe 38.9 *machine tool*
engine power 334.4 *energy*
engine trouble 378.2 *obstacle*
England 85.9
English 65.2 *billiards play*
English billiards **65.3**; 65.1 *billiards*
English bond 38.26 *masonry*
English bone china 24.1 *ceramics*
English breakfast 25.44 *British dish*; 557.12 *meal*
English Classics 59.7 *horseracing*
English lakes 88.4 *British lakes*
Englishman 564.9 *British inhabitant*; 85.9 *England*
English mountains 89.5 *British mountains*
English muffin 25.39 *loaf*
English mustard 496.5 *herbs*
Englishness 85.9 *England*
English one-step 22.2 *dance*
English rose 743.6 *national emblem*
English saddle 59.14 *horse-riding terms*
English setter 60.6 *sporting dog*
English sonnet 17.7 *poem*
English-speaking 729.19 *speaking*
English springer 60.6 *sporting dog*
English stroke 50.4 *rowing*
English thoroughbred 59.2 *thoroughbred*
English waltz 22.2 *dance*
engobe 24.2 *raw material*
engorge 688.5 *be greedy*; 557.22 *eat well*; 370.11 *ingest*
engorged 688.6 *gluttonous*
engorgement 557.2 *appetite*; 370.4 *intake*; 219.2 *overdoing it*
engraft 211.6 *add*; 368.6 *plant*
engrail 420.12 *make rough*
engram 36.23 *memory*
en grande tenue 551.30 *dressed-up*
en grande toilette 551.30, 656.7 *dressed-up*
en grand seigneur 622.36 *majestically*
engrave **19.22**; 743.10 *identify*; 744.14 *inscribe*; 228.7 *make stable*; 163.5 *outline*; 717.11 *paint*; 184.8 *wrinkle*
engraved 156.8 *deep*; 19.28 *sculpted*; 228.10 *stabilized*; 184.6 *wrinkly*
engraver **19.18**; 717.4 *person who makes a representation*; 744.9 *recorder*
engraving **19.15**; 19.1 *art*; 163.1 *outline*; 19.7 *picture*; 744.8 *registration*; 19.13 *relief-carving*; 717.2 *reproduction*; 228.4 *stable thing*
engross 370.13 *absorb*; 763.7 *possess*; 777.1 *purchase*
engrossed 471.8 *diligent*; 172.12 *internalized*
engrossment 370.5 *absorption*; 172.6 *internalization*; 763.1 *possession*
engulf 219.4 *be excessive*; 357.12 *consume*; 557.21 *eat*; 90.7 *flow*; 370.11 *ingest*
engulfed 90.11, 433.24 *flooded*
engulfing 370.4 *intake*
engulfment 557.1 *eating*; 370.4 *intake*; 90.6 *river flow*
enhance 607.6 *aggravate*; 726.6 *emphasize*; 727.7 *exaggerate*; 244.1, 392.22 *improve*; 213.5 *make bigger*; 123.8 *make important*; 781.15 *make rich*; 495.10 *make taste*; 542.12 *ornament*; 366.3 *promote*; 738.3 *reveal*
enhanced 607.4 *aggravated*; 726.4 *emphasized*; 727.12 *exaggerated*; 244.14 *improved*; 213.7 *increased*
enhanced radiation bomb 587.16 *bomb*
enhancement 607.1 *aggravation*; 727.1 *exaggeration*; 244.5 *improvement*; 213.1 *increase*
enhancing 37.17 *stimulating*
enharmonic 750.13 *harmonious*
enharmonic scale 18.20 *key*
ENIAC 40.3 *computer*
enigma 705.4 *difficult question*; 479.5 *equivocalness*; 737.3 *mystification*; 266.1 *obscurity*; 619.5 *person of wonder*; 11.2 *the occult*; 453.9 *uncertainty*; 696.12 *unintelligible thing*; 456.3 *unknown thing*
enigmatic 523.11 *benighted*; 453.3 *confused*; 696.4 *difficult*; 528.4 *inscrutable*; 737.11 *mysterious*; 266.2 *obscure*; 11.14 *occult*; 705.13 *problematic*; 745.2 *proverbial*; 696.1 *unintelligible*; 619.8 *wonderful*
enigmatically 453.24 *confusingly*; 266.4 *obscurely*; 11.25 *occultly*; 705.24 *questionably*; 696.13 *unintelligibly*
enigmatic question 696.12 *unintelligible thing*
enjoin 713.5 *advise*; 810.17 *impose a duty*
enjoy **597.6**; 598.7 *be cheerful*; 490.8 *feel pleasure*; 241.14, 595.7 *like*; 763.7 *possess*; 495.9 *taste*
enjoyable 241.1, 490.6 *pleasant*
enjoyably 490.11 *pleasingly*
enjoy company 654.11 *be sociable*
enjoy diplomatic immunity 758.11 *be exempt*
enjoy friendship with 569.13 *befriend*
enjoy good fortune 222.14 *be comfortable*
enjoy good health 259.5 *be healthy*
enjoy His Majesty's hospitality 815.10 *be in prison*
enjoy immunity 758.11 *be exempt*
enjoying 763.8 *possessing*
enjoying liberty 250.10 *independent*
enjoy liberty 250.14 *be free*
enjoy life 338.2 *be full of vigour*
enjoyment 599.2 *amusement*; 597.1 *happiness*; 490.1 *physical pleasure*; 241.7 *pleasure*; 763.1 *possession*; 609.1 *satisfaction*; 654.1 *sociability*; 495.2 *taste of life*; 349.6 *use*
enjoy oneself 490.8 *feel pleasure*
enjoy peace 589.5 *be at peace*; 749.4 *pacify*
enjoy prosperity 248.5 *be prosperous*
enjoy sex 490.8 *feel pleasure*
enjoy success 246.6 *be successful*
enjoy the open air 171.12 *be outside*
enjoy the power of 334.10 *be powerful*
enlace 180.6 *convolute*; 193.8 *interweave*
enlarge **727.8**; 190.6 *become bigger*; 150.11 *broaden*; 111.9 *duplicate*; 190.5, 213.5 *make bigger*; 123.8 *make important*; 158.18 *measure*; 41.21 *photograph*; 717.9 *represent*
enlargeability **190.2**
enlargeable **190.9**
enlarged **727.13**; 607.4 *aggravated*; 190.7 *bigger*; 213.7 *increased*
enlarged heart 260.10 *cardiovascular disease*
enlarged thing **190.3**
enlargement **727.2**; 211.1 *addition*; 41.12 *development*; 270.1 *diffuseness*; 111.4, 125.5 *duplicate*; 190.3 *enlarged thing*; 190.1 *growth*; 213.1 *increase*
enlarger **190.4**; 41.12 *development*
enlarge upon 270.5 *be diffuse*
enlighten 725.2 *clarify*; 8.17 *deify*; 6.22 *educate*; 693.11 *inform*
enlightened **522.22**; 8.13 *divine*; 693.18

informed; 6.19, 455.8 *knowledgeable*; 4.19 *learned*; 652.6 *philanthropic*
enlightening 6.16 *educational*; 693.16 *informative*
Enlightenment 3.10 *past age*
enlightenment 522.13; 8.1 *divinity*; 6.1 *education*; 449.8 *finding out*; 719.1 *interpretation*; 455.1 *knowledge*; 458.1 *wisdom*
enlist 220.9; **584.10**; 314.14 *enrol*; 585.12 *go to war*; 368.7 *install*; 370.10 *introduce*; 213.5 *make bigger*; 483.9 *motivate*; 480.15 *persuade*; 744.15 *register*
enlisted 584.9; 586.35 *martial*
enlisted man 586.8 *soldier*
enlisted person 586.17 *army person*
enlisting 585.7 *war measures*
enlist in one's service 349.4 *resort to*
enlistment 314.1 *entry*; 370.3 *introduction*; 744.8 *registration*
enliven 488.13 *arouse sensation*; 598.6 *bring cheer*; 446.16 *inspire*; 338.3 *invigorate*; 581.1 *refresh*; 393.5 *revive*; 336.8 *strengthen*
enlivened 554.12 *alive*; 581.4 *refreshed*
en masse 232.9 *completely*; 750.31 *in accord*; 208.14 *in crowds*; 204.12 *one and all*; 376.51 *together*
enmesh 700.28 *trick*
enmeshed 700.36 *deceived*
enmeshment 700.7 *tricking*
enmist 31.64 *fog*
enmity 113.5 *conflict*; 751.1 *disagreement*; 596.1 *dislike*; 594.1 *hate*; 651.1 *malevolence*
ennead 201.5 *nine*
enneadic 201.16 *ninth*
enneagon 201.5 *nine*
enneagonal 201.16 *ninth*
enneahedral 201.16 *ninth*
enneahedron 201.5 *nine*
ennoble 8.17 *deify*; 573.5 *make noble*
ennobled 573.4 *aristocratic*; 8.15 *deified*
ennoblement 8.9 *deification*; 575.1 *right*
ennui 620.1 *boredom*
enormity 158.2 *bigness*; 806.3 *sin*; 804.1 *wickedness*
enormous 158.15 *big*; 202.2 *immeasurable*; 141.13 *spacious*
enormously 158.20 *largely*; 203.7 *quantitatively*
enough 217.9; 388.7 *I/we surrender!*; 203.6 *quantitative*; 609.12 *satisfactorily*; 609.6 *satisfactory*; 226.12 *stop!*; 217.7 *sufficiency*; 217.1 *sufficient*
enough and to spare 219.8 *excessively*; 217.2 *plentiful*
enough to get by 217.7 *sufficiency*
enough to go round 217.1 *sufficient*
enough to live on 217.7 *sufficiency*
en passant 318.14 *by the way*; 316.18 *in transit*
enplane 313.5 *set out*
enplanement 313.8 *start*
en plein air 434.26 *out-of-doors*
enprint 41.12 *development*
enrage 596.7 *cause dislike*; 594.16 *cause hate*; 328.11 *derange*; 242.10 *displease*; 624.14 *make angry*; 380.9 *make violent*
enraged 624.16 *angry*; 380.6 *violent*
en rapport 747.19 *associating*; 516.7 *harmonious*; 516.12 *harmoniously*; 750.10, 750.31 *in accord*
enrapture 597.8 *cause joy*; 593.28 *win the love of*
enraptured 593.19 *enamoured*; 597.4 *happy*
enrich 768.5 *give*; 244.1 *improve*; 213.5 *make bigger*; 562.7 *make fertile*; 781.15 *make rich*; 542.12 *ornament*
enriched bread 25.38 *bread*
enriched uranium 437.7 *nuclear power*; 28.73 *nuclear reactor*
enrichment 244.5 *improvement*; 213.1 *increase*
enrich oneself 781.13 *get rich*
enrobe 551.32 *dress*
enrol 130.25; **314.14**; 220.9 *enlist*; 585.12 *go to war*; 368.7 *install*; 370.10 *introduce*; 744.13 *record*; 744.15 *register*
enrolled 130.37; 744.16 *recorded*
Enrolled Nurse 35.16 *nurse*
enrolment 130.8; 314.1 *entry*; 370.3 *introduction*; 744.8 *registration*
en route 318.14 *by the way*; 319.6 *commercially*; 760.18 *convertibly*; 300.18 *in motion*; 316.18 *in transit*
en route to 302.19 *forward*; 317.17 *via*
en rule 373.4 *means of connection*; 742.7 *punctuation*
ens 93.1 *existence*
ensanguined 535.4 *bloody*; 382.24 *murderous*
ensconce 736.8 *conceal*; 142.9 *locate*; 252.10 *protect*
ensconced 142.6 *located*
ensconce oneself 142.10 *settle*
ensemble 21.25 *cast*; 18.26 *musical group*; 551.10 *suit*; 204.5 *unit*; 204.2 *whole thing*
Ens Entium 8.3 *God*
ensepulchre 583.8 *bury*
ensheathe 368.5 *inset*
enshrine 8.17 *deify*; 366.3 *promote*
enshrined 8.15 *deified*; 366.12 *exalted*
enshrinement 8.9 *deification*; 366.7 *lift*
enshroud 31.64 *fog*; 550.25 *wrap*
enshrouded 31.56 *foggy*; 550.37 *protected*
ensiform 425.3 *sharp-edged*
ensign 743.7 *flag*; 50.3 *parts of a sailing boat*; 586.8 *soldier*
ensilage 439.4 *storage*
enslave 647.6 *suppress*; 773.10 *take away*
enslaved 251.15 *detained*; 593.19 *enamoured*; 387.9 *subject*
enslavement 387.1 *subjection*
enslaving 387.9 *subject*
ensnare 630.10 *ambush*; 449.2 *detect*; 633.11 *hunt*; 363.12 *lure*; 483.10 *manipulate*; 484.13 *plot*; 700.33 *snare*; 773.10 *take away*; 480.16 *tempt*; 379.2 *trap*; 700.28 *trick*; 593.28 *win the love of*
ensnared 700.36 *deceived*; 593.19 *enamoured*
ensnarement 700.7 *tricking*
ensnaring 593.20 *amorous*
ensnarl 700.33 *snare*
en space 146.1 *interval*
ensue 289.10 *succeed*
ensuing 345.10 *caused*; 289.12 *succeeding*
ensure 345.7 *follow from*; 452.21 *make certain*; 228.7 *make stable*; 454.1 *verify*
ensure a result 106.2 *premeditate*
ENT 35.3 *medical specialty*; 504.13 *otological*; 504.6 *otology*
entablature 174.3 *architectural summit*; 20.8 *column*
entail 694.12 *intend*; 440.2 *legal terms*
entamoeba 75.10 *parasite*
entangle 696.7 *be unintelligible*; 373.11 *connect*; 373.13 *intercommunicate*; 193.8 *interweave*; 412.9 *mix up*; 700.33 *snare*; 700.28 *trick*
entangled 373.15 *connected*; 700.36 *deceived*; 412.12 *mixed*
entanglement 373.1 *connection*; 193.1 *interweaving*; 593.8 *love affair*; 412.3 *miscellany*; 412.1 *mixture*; 700.7 *tricking*
entanglements 384.9 *barrier*
entangle one's line 55.7 *angle*
entasis 20.8 *column*
entelechial 95.6 *real*
entelechy 99.3 *quintessence*; 95.1 *reality*
entente 750.2, 755.3 *alliance*; 569.2 *friendly relations*; 749.1 *pacification*
entente cordiale 755.3 *alliance*; 569.2 *friendly relations*
enter 314.9; **318.10**; 789.7 *account*; 21.34 *act*; 525.12 *become visible*; 317.14 *find one's way*; 312.5 *get in*; 172.14 *go inside*; 368.2 *inject*; 220.8 *list*; 45.6 *participate*; 744.15 *register*; 127.6 *subsume*
enter a different phase 760.8 *be transformed*
enteral administration 37.13 *administration*
enter a new phase 760.8 *be transformed*
enter a nonmaterial world 101.12
enter as 127.6 *subsume*
entered 127.8 *included*; 220.11 *listed*; 744.16 *recorded*
enter for 314.14 *enrol*
enteric 172.10 *visceral*
enter in a book 744.14 *inscribe*
entering 314.15; 525.7 *appearing*; 312.18 *arriving*
entering the crease area 58.5 *lacrosse*
enter into 127.5 *be included*; 764.4 *have joint possession*
enter into a contract 755.5 *contract*
enter into an agreement 756.7 *promise*
enter into an alliance 755.5 *contract*
enter into argument 444.13 *debate*
enteritis 260.8 *indigestion*
enter names 744.15 *register*
enter one's head 446.14 *have an idea*
enter orbit 29.38 *launch*
enterprise 302.12 *advance*; 776.6 *business*; 342.4 *energy*; 482.3 *future intention*; 477.1 *imagination*; 356.1 *production*; 342.2 *social activity*; 344.6, 354.2 *undertaking*
enterprising 354.6; 342.18 *active*; 353.8 *attempting*; 302.17 *forward*; 477.10 *imaginative*; 448.9 *original*; 338.4 *vigorous*
enterprising businessman 354.4 *volunteer*
enterprisingly 354.9
entertain 569.15 *be hospitable*; 599.13 *be humorous*; 654.11 *be sociable*; 768.5 *give*; 490.9 *give pleasure*; 769.10 *receive someone*
entertained 654.16 *popular*; 769.13 *received*
entertainer 21.29; 22.5 *dancer*
entertain friends 569.15 *be hospitable*
entertaining 598.2 *cheering*; 654.17 *festive*; 599.9 *funny*; 769.4 *reception*; 69.9 *recreational*
entertainingly 69.11 *recreationally*; 654.18 *sociably*
entertainment 599.4; 599.2 *amusement*; 557.4 *eating meals*; 597.2 *fun*; 654.3 *meeting*; 654.5 *party*; 69.8 *pastime*; 490.4 *pleasurable things*; 241.7 *pleasure*; 436.1 *provision*
entertainment industry 21.5 *show business*
entertain respect for 667.15 *respect*
enter the church 7.19 *be religious*
enter the Golden Gate 582.15 *die*
enter the lion's den 254.8 *be in danger*
enter the lists 586.37 *fight*
enter the race 752.13 *be a candidate*
enter the ring 52.11 *fight*
enter upon 289.11 *follow in office*
entêté 641.1 *obstinate*
enthalpy 28.38 *thermodynamics*
enthral 597.8 *cause joy*; 363.12 *lure*; 593.28 *win the love of*
enthralling 597.5 *delightful*
enthrone 601.19 *install*
enthronement 601.3 *ceremony*; 575.1 *right*
enthuse 338.2 *be full of vigour*
enthusiasm 636.7 *eagerness*; 643.5 *earnestness*; 726.1 *emphasis*; 342.4 *energy*; 336.2 *healthiness*; 7.2 *religiousness*; 338.1 *vigour*
enthusiast 342.10 *busy person*; 632.8 *creature of habit*; 21.33 *theatregoer*; 477.9 *visionary*
enthusiastic 342.18 *active*; 636.2 *eager*; 643.2 *earnest*; 726.3 *emphatic*; 477.10 *imaginative*; 336.11 *strong in spirit*; 338.4 *vigorous*
enthusiastically 342.22 *actively*; 336.15 *acutely*; 726.7 *emphatically*
entice 363.12 *lure*; 483.10 *manipulate*; 480.16 *tempt*
enticed 483.12 *motivated*
enticement 480.9; 363.4 *allurement*; 480.2 *flattery*; 483.2 *inducement*; 813.4 *reward for service*
enticing 363.9 *attractive*
entire 232.7 *complete*; 77.18 *of leaves*; 230.1 *perfect*; 203.6 *quantitative*; 255.16 *simple*; 204.7 *uncut*; 197.13 *whole*
entire horse 567.16 *male animal*
entirely 256.20 *clean*; 230.8, 232.9 *completely*; 203.7 *quantitatively*; 204.11 *wholly*
entirety 232.1 *completeness*; 203.4 *total*; 204.2 *whole thing*
entitle 750.29 *permit*; 733.11 *title*
entitled 575.5; 136.10 *authorized*; 801.9 *in the right*; 750.18 *permitting*
entitlement 575.2; 750.8 *permit*; 136.1 *qualification*; 801.6 *right*
entity 93.1 *existence*; 554.1 *life*; 197.1 *one*; 34.3 *organism*; 93.2 *thing*; 204.2 *whole thing*
entomb 582.17, 583.8 *bury*; 309.10 *enclose*; 410.21 *put in a container*
entombed 583.10 *buried*; 410.20 *containing*
entombment 583.1 *burial*
entomological 76.14; 75.18 *arthropodous*
entomologist 76.8; 75.15 *invertebrate zoologist*; 70.11 *zoologist*
entomology 70.9 *animal science*; 75.14 *invertebrate zoology*; 76.7 *study*
entoproct 75.7 *coelenterate*
Entoprocta 75.7 *coelenterate*
entourage 223.10 *attendance*; 289.1 *succession*
entr'acte 21.2 *play*; 21.8 *scene*
entrails 475.10 *cards*; 172.4, 406.3 *insides*
entrain 313.5 *set out*
entrainment 313.8 *start*
entrance 314.5; 21.22 *acting*; 525.1 *appearance*; 312.10 *arrival*; 314.1 *entry*; 167.1, 167.6 *front*; 318.3 *passage into*; 308.7 *passageway*; 370.2 *receptivity*; 317.2 *route*
entranced 11.19 *bewitched*
entrance fee 790.3 *fee*
entrance hall 167.1 *front*; 565.7 *room*
entrancing 597.5 *delightful*; 11.15 *witchlike*
entrant 314.7
entrap 483.10 *manipulate*; 700.33 *snare*; 379.2 *trap*; 700.28 *trick*
entrapment 700.7 *tricking*
entrapped 700.36 *deceived*
entreat 733.8 *appeal to*; 701.16 *plead*; 705.17 *question*; 710.6 *request*
entreating 710.9 *requesting*
entreatingly 710.12 *by request*
entreaty 701.5 *plea*; 705.1 *question*; 710.1 *request*
entrechat 22.9 *ballet steps*
entrée 25.9 *dish*; 314.1 *entry*; 557.14 *mouthful*; 370.2 *receptivity*
entremets 25.9 *dish*; 557.14 *mouthful*
entrench 384.21; 228.7 *make stable*; 252.10 *protect*; 336.8 *strengthen*; 329.5 *transgress*
entrenched 384.31; 225.7 *permanent*; 228.10 *stabilized*
entrenchment 384.8 *military defences*; 225.1 *permanence*
entre nous 737.15 *in secret*
entrepot 779.7 *emporium*; 439.4 *storage*
entrepreneur 353.7 *attempter*; 755.4 *contractor*; 340.3 *doer*; 356.9 *producer*; 354.4 *volunteer*; 778.12 *wholesaler*
entropy 412.1 *mixture*; 28.38 *thermodynamics*
entrust 316.14 *bring back*; 398.7 *delegate*; 768.5 *give*
Entry 314
entry 314.1; 789.1 *accounts*; 67.6 *diving*; 314.5 *entrance*; 59.7 *horseracing*; 368.9 *injection*; 318.3 *passage into*; 370.2 *receptivity*; 744.1 *record*; 744.8 *registration*; 67.11 *swimming*
entry dive 67.6 *diving*
entry into office 289.4 *accession*
Entryphone™ 504.8 *something heard*
entry upon 289.4 *accession*
ENT specialist 504.6 *otology*
entwine 373.11 *connect*; 180.6 *convolute*; 177.6 *curve*; 184.11 *enfold*; 193.8 *interweave*
entwined 180.4 *convolutional*
entwining 184.5 *enfoldment*
enucleate 719.9 *decipher*
E number 557.11 *food content*
enumerable 27.73 *numerable*
enumerate 27.90; 406.9 *itemize*; 220.8 *list*; 194.10, 210.11 *number*; 139.24 *specify*
enumerated 220.11 *listed*
enumerate with 127.6 *subsume*
enumeration 789.3 *accounting*; 210.1 *calculation*; 220.1 *list*; 220.7 *listing*; 27.12 *numeration*
enumeration district 86.5 *state*
enumerative 210.13 *calculative*
enumerator 210.6 *calculator*
enunciate 707.17 *affirm*; 729.11 *speak*
enunciated 729.16 *speech*; 707.11 *stated*
enunciation 729.4 *articulation*; 707.2 *statement*
enunciative 707.10 *affirmative*
enunciator 707.9 *affirmer*
enunciatory 707.10 *affirmative*
enuresis 560.3 *urination*
enuretic 560.26 *urinary*
envelop 171.11 *be exterior*; 357.12 *consume*; 360.7 *detain*; 551.32 *dress*; 184.11 *enfold*; 127.4 *include*; 252.10 *protect*; 170.7 *surround*; 165.6, 550.25 *wrap*
envelope 692.3 *correspondence*; 171.1 *exterior*; 410.5 *packet*; 410.21 *put in a container*; 165.4 *wrapper*; 550.4 *wrapping*
enveloped 410.20 *containing*; 171.6 *exterior*; 170.5 *surrounded*
enveloping 410.20 *containing*

envelopment 550.1 *covering*; 360.2 *detention*; 170.2 *encirclement*; 165.1 *enclosure*; 184.5 *enfoldment*; 54.3 *fencing movements*
envenom 594.16 *cause hate*; 624.14 *make angry*; 626.12 *make irritable*; 245.3 *make worse*
envenomed 651.14 *hostile*; 236.4 *poor*
enviable 617.7 *desired*
envied 617.7 *desired*
envier 617.6 *desirer*
envious 617.9 *desirous*; 538.5 *green-eyed*; 594.10 *hating*; 629.4 *jealous*; 590.13 *passionate*; 624.15 *resentful*; 683.4 *selfish*
enviously 617.18 *desirously*; 594.18 *hatefully*; 629.9 *jealously*; 624.17 *resentfully*; 683.8 *selfishly*
enviousness 629.1 *jealousy*
environ 141.20 *extend*; 170.7 *surround*
environment **565.2**; 222.1 *circumstances*; 142.1 *location*; 19.12 *sculpture*; 170.1 *surroundings*
environmental **538.7**; **565.15**; 222.7 *circumstantial*; 244.16 *improving*; 359.6 *preserving*; 2.12 *sociological*; 170.4 *surrounding*
environmental abuse 351.2 *misuse*
environmental activist 662.7 *protester*
environmental engineering 38.1 *engineering*
environmental health officer 257.3 *hygienist*
environmentalism 538.16 *green politics*; 225.1 *permanence*
environmentalist 225.4 *conservationist*; 359.4 *preservationist*; 244.12 *reformer*
environmentally **565.20**; 359.8 *preservatively*; 222.16 *relatively*; 2.16 *sociologically*
environmental movement 359.1 *preservation*
environment-friendly 538.7 *environmental*; 359.6 *preserving*
environs 86.13 *locality*; 142.1 *location*; 147.5 *near place*; 170.1 *surroundings*
envisage 474.8 *expect*; 446.15, 477.14 *imagine*; 484.12 *plan ahead*
envision 446.15, 477.14 *imagine*
envoi 17.8 *part of poem*
envoy 211.3 *additional item*; 398.6 *agent*; 398.1 *delegate*; 131.10 *ending*; 579.16 *official*; 717.8 *representative*
envoy extraordinary 579.16 *official*
envy 590.6 *bad feeling*; 629.6 *be jealous*; 683.6 *be selfish*; 617.12 *desire*; 538.14 *green-eyed monster*; 594.1, 594.14 *hate*; 629.1 *jealousy*; 624.1 *resentment*; 683.1 *selfishness*; 804.5 *seven deadly sins*
enwrap 550.25 *wrap*
enwrapment 550.1 *covering*
enzyme **33.11**; 32.15 *catalysis*; 224.5 *changer*; 415.8 *leavening*
enzyme class 33.11 *enzyme*
enzymic 33.26 *biochemical*; 415.4 *leavening*
enzymically 33.27 *biochemically*
enzymologist 33.2 *biochemist*
enzymology 33.1 *biochemistry*; 34.1 *life science*
Eocene period 284.3 *geological period*
eolith 3.11 *relic*; 284.7 *thing of the past*
eon 276.3 *geological period*; 30.41 *geological time*
eonothem 30.41 *geological time*
Eos 290.1 *morning*
eosin 42.6 *dye*
EP 744.7 *recording*
eparchy 86.5 *state*
epaulette 743.4 *insignia*
épée 54.6 *fencing*; 54.2 *fencing equipment*; 587.8 *sharp weapon*
épée-fence 54.5 *fence*
épée fencing 54.1 *fencing*
épéeist 54.4 *fencer*
épée prongs 54.2 *fencing equipment*
epeirogenic 30.54 *tectonic*
épergne 542.1 *ornament*
epexegesis 719.1 *interpretation*
ephemera 723.3 *compendium*
ephemeral 227.13 *changeable*; 582.20 *deadly*; 78.2 *flowering plant*; 77.14 *of plants*; 77.2 *plant*; 278.6 *transient*
ephemerality 582.1 *death*; 278.1 *transience*
ephemerally 227.15 *changeably*; 77.24 *herbaceously*; 278.8 *transiently*
ephemeris 323.5 *navigation*; 693.5 *reference book*; 29.6 *star catalogue*
ephemeris time 275.9 *time zone*
ephemeropteran 76.10 *insectan*
ephod 7.11 *vestment*
epic 158.15 *big*; 270.3 *diffuse*; 400.11 *masterpiece*; 721.3 *narration*; 17.19, 721.12 *narrative*; 17.7 *poem*
epicalyx 78.3 *flower part*
epicene 479.10 *equivocal*
epicentral 173.6 *central*
epicentre 173.1 *centre*; 30.22 *seismic activity*
epic length 270.1 *diffuseness*
epic novel 17.2 *fiction*
epic poet 17.14 *author*
epic poetry 17.6 *poetry*
epic simile 17.12 *poetic language*
epic theatre 21.10 *theatre movements*
epicure 466.6 *discriminating person*; 557.18 *eater*; 688.4 *glutton*; 490.3 *pleasure-seeker*; 686.5 *self-indulgent person*; 488.4 *someone or something that feels*; 495.5 *taster*
epicurean 25.56 *culinary*; 466.9 *discriminating*; 4.11 *follower of a doctrine*; 688.4 *glutton*; 688.6 *gluttonous*; 4.14 *of a philosophy*; 241.5 *pleasure-loving*; 241.12 *pleasure-loving person*; 490.3 *pleasure-seeker*; 686.6 *self-indulgent*; 488.4 *someone or something that feels*; 488.7 *susceptible*; 495.7 *tasty*
epicureanism 688.2 *epicurism*; 490.1 *physical pleasure*; 241.7 *pleasure*; 4.7 *school of thought*; 686.1 *self-indulgence*
epicurism **688.2**; 557.3 *delicate eating*
epicycle 179.2 *circle*
epicycloid 27.40 *curve*
epidemic 260.5 *plague*; 138.17 *widespread*
epidemic disease 260.4 *disease*
epidemiological 35.22 *medical*
epidemiologist 35.13 *medical specialist*
epidemiology 34.1 *life science*; 35.3 *medical specialty*; 260.20 *pathology*
epidermal 550.38 *covering*; 171.6 *exterior*; 157.2 *superficial*
epidermic 171.6 *exterior*
epidermis 550.14 *animal covering*; 171.1 *exterior*; 157.4 *shallow thing*; 77.5 *stem*
epidermoid 171.6 *exterior*
epidesis 10.9 *prayer*
epidural 37.12 *injection*; 561.7 *obstetrics*
epigeal 83.10 *of fungi*
epiglottis 729.5 *organ of speech*
epigram 745.1 *maxim*; 795.7 *moral*; 269.2 *outline*; 17.7 *poem*; 697.2 *solecism*
epigrammatic 269.3 *concise*; 745.2 *proverbial*; 723.6 *summary*
epigrammatical 723.6 *summary*
epigrammatically 723.12 *in brief*; 745.4 *proverbially*
epigrammatist 5.2 *linguist*
epigrammatize 745.3 *aphorize*; 269.4 *be concise*; 723.8 *summarize*
epigraph 745.1 *maxim*; 3.11 *relic*
epigrapher 3.4 *archaeologist*; 1.4 *palaeoanthropologist*
epigraphic 1.12 *palaeoanthropological*
epigraphical 3.17 *archaeological*; 1.12 *palaeoanthropological*; 5.40 *translated*
epigraphically 5.48 *linguistically*; 1.17 *palaeoanthropologically*; 3.25 *reportedly*
epigraphist 719.6 *interpreter*; 5.2 *linguist*; 1.4 *palaeoanthropologist*
epigraphy 1.2 *palaeoanthropology*; 744.8 *registration*; 719.5 *science of interpretation*; 5.12 *translation*
epigynous 78.12 *of flowers*
epilepsy 260.4 *disease*; 461.3 *mental deterioration*; 260.17 *nervous disorder*; 327.8 *spasm*
epileptic 327.19 *convulsive*; 260.23 *diseased*
epileptic fit 461.3 *mental deterioration*
epilithic 84.7 *algal*
epilogue 211.3 *additional item*; 131.10 *ending*; 168.1 *rear*; 21.8 *scene*; 289.9 *sequel*
epimenorrhoea 560.11 *menstruation*
epimer 32.13 *structure*
epimeric 32.37 *structural*
epimerism 32.13 *structure*
epiphanic 525.7 *appearing*; 8.13 *divine*; 739.12 *revelatory*
Epiphany 10.15 *holy day*
epiphany 739.1 *disclosure*; 8.8 *divine manifestation*; 738.10 *manifestation*; 402.2 *materialization*; 525.4 *something that appears*
epiphenomenal 107.8 *chance*
epiphenomenalism 4.7 *school of thought*
epiphenomenalist 4.11 *follower of a doctrine*; 4.14 *of a philosophy*
epiphyte 77.2 *plant*
epiphytic 84.7 *algal*; 77.14 *of plants*
epiphytically 84.9 *algologically*; 77.24 *herbaceously*
episcopal 7.17 *priestly*
Episcopalian 7.5 *Christian*; 7.16 *denominational*
episcopal ring 7.11 *vestment*
episcopal vestment 7.11 *vestment*
episcopate 7.9 *priesthood*
episode 17.3 *aspect of fiction*; 3.14 *historicalness*; 222.2 *occurrence*; 205.2 *particular*; 21.8 *scene*
episodic 133.8 *discontinuous*
epispastic 37.4 *drug type*
epistemologically 4.24 *philosophically*
epistemology 4.6 *branch of philosophy*
Epistle 10.6 *Eucharist*
Epistles 7.12 *religious text*
epistolary 692.33 *communicational*
epistolary novel 17.2 *fiction*
epistrophe 17.12 *poetic language*; 509.7 *repeated word*; 112.1 *repetition*
epistyle 174.3 *architectural summit*
epitaph 583.4 *funeral objects*; 5.25 *inscription*; 313.9 *parting*
epitaphic 583.11 *funeral*; 5.43 *phrasal*
epitaphist 583.3 *funeral director*
epithalamium 570.6 *general terms*; 17.7 *poem*
epitheca 84.3 *plant body*
epithelioma 260.12 *cancer*
epithet 745.1 *maxim*; 721.8 *name*
epitome 191.3 *contracted thing*; 446.6 *ideal*; 163.1, 269.2 *outline*; 99.3 *quintessence*; 717.1 *representation*; 149.3 *shortened version*; 723.1 *summary*; 5.12 *translation*
epitomical 269.3 *concise*; 446.13 *ideal*
epitomization 149.2 *shortening*
epitomize **446.19**; 269.4 *be concise*; 99.12 *embody*; 163.5 *outline*; 717.9 *represent*; 149.10 *shorten*; 723.8 *summarize*
epitomized 149.8 *shortened*
epitomizer 723.5 *summarizer*
e pluribus unum 114.2 *assortment*
epoch 281.3 *chronology*; 276.3 *geological period*; 30.41 *geological time*; 275.4 *term*; 276.2 *time period*
epoch-making 123.6 *notable*
epode 17.8 *part of poem*; 17.7 *poem*
eponym 721.8 *name*
eponymy 721.7 *nomenclature*
EPOS 40.12 *electronic office*
epos 17.7 *poem*; 17.6 *poetry*
epoxide resin 32.21 *polymer*
epoxy 435.1 *materials*
epoxy resin 267.3 *adhesive*
Epsom salts 394.6 *purgative*
equable 4.18 *detached*; 119.6 *equal*; 685.6 *moderate*
equably 119.13 *equitably*; 685.9 *moderately*; 4.27 *stoically*
equal **27.75**; **111.16**; **119.5**; **119.6**; **285.11**; 111.10 *be equal*; 235.9 *be worthy*; 750.14 *conforming*; 188.6 *correlate*; 188.4 *correlated*; 27.93 *equate*; 108.5 *interrelated*; 801.7 *right*; 228.9 *stable*; 217.1 *sufficient*; 162.4 *symmetrical*; 194.11, 210.10 *total*
equal chance **107.3**
equal exchange 111.2 *equivalence*; 110.1 *interchange*
equal footing 119.1 *equality*
Equality **119**
equality **27.26**; **111.5**; **119.1**; 801.1 *fairness*; 14.1 *finance*; 108.2 *interrelatedness*; 188.1 *parallelism*; 115.1 *similarity*; 228.1 *stability*; 162.1 *symmetry*
equalization **119.3**; 504.10 *sound quality*
equalization fund 14.1, 780.7 *finance*
equalize **119.11**; 111.10 *be equal*; 108.8 *be proportionate to*; 708.16 *cancel out*; 110.9 *correlate*; 27.93 *equate*; 750.24 *harmonize*; 216.10 *make average*; 187.7 *make horizontal*; 115.11 *make similar*; 228.7 *make stable*; 750.26 *make uniform*; 162.6 *symmetrize*
equalized 708.20 *cancelled*; 119.6 *equal*
equalizing 708.7 *cancelling out*
equally **111.19**; **119.12**; **162.8**; **801.19**; 115.14 *comparably*; 27.87 *mathematically*; 110.10 *reciprocally*; 108.10 *relevantly*; 228.12 *stably*; 222.15 *under the circumstances*; 750.34 *uniformly*
equally divided 119.8 *on equal terms*
equalness 801.1 *fairness*
equal opportunity **391.2**; 111.5, 119.1 *equality*
equal race **285.4**
equal rights 111.5, 119.1 *equality*; 391.2 *equal opportunity*; 568.1 *female sex*; 250.2 *free speech*
equal sign 27.13 *mathematical symbol*; 742.1 *sign*
equal standing 111.5 *equality*
equal status 391.2 *equal opportunity*
equal swap 754.1 *compromise*
equal the best 235.9 *be worthy*
equal to **27.88**; 334.13 *powerful*; 217.1 *sufficient*
equal value 111.5 *equality*
equal weight 708.7 *cancelling out*
equal with **285.14**
equanimity 167.4 *assurance*; 4.3 *detachment*; 685.1 *moderation*; 609.1 *satisfaction*
equanimous 4.18 *detached*
equate **27.93**; 108.8 *be proportionate to*; 119.11 *equalize*; 216.10 *make average*; 111.8 *make the same*; 706.20 *solve*
equation **27.27**; 210.1 *calculation*; 119.3 *equalization*; 28.6 *law*; 706.7 *numerical result*; 27.65 *theory*
equation of state 28.6 *law*; 28.38 *thermodynamics*
equation of time 275.9 *time zone*
equator 34.10 *cell division*; 179.3 *circular thing*; 119.7 *dividing line*; 86.2 *geographical region*; 198.8 *half*; 493.8 *hot place*
equatorial 493.11 *warm*
equatorially 86.19 *geographically*
equatorial mounting 29.25 *mounting*
equatorial rainforest 493.8 *hot place*
equatorial rainy zone 31.39 *climatic zone*
equestrian 59.17 *equine*; 59.15 *horse person*
equestrian director 21.31 *circus performer*
equestrianism 59.6 *horsemanship*
equestrian painter 19.16 *artist*
equestrian painting 19.10 *art subject*
equestrienne 59.15 *horse person*
equidistance 188.1 *parallelism*
equidistant 111.16, 119.6 *equal*; 27.80 *linear*; 188.3 *parallel*
equidistantly 119.13 *equitably*
equilateral 119.6 *equal*; 27.80 *linear*; 162.4 *symmetrical*
equilaterally 162.7 *symmetrically*
equilateral triangle 176.3 *angled figure*; 27.43 *triangle*
equilibrate 111.10 *be equal*; 750.24 *harmonize*; 162.6 *symmetrize*
equilibrated 32.38 *reactive*
equilibration 111.5 *equality*; 119.3 *equalization*
equilibrist 21.31 *circus performer*
equilibrium **119.2**; 32.14 *chemical reaction*; 28.10 *force*; 750.4 *harmony*; 301.1 *motionlessness*; 111.6 *regularity*; 132.7 *stability*; 162.1 *symmetry*
equilibrium constant 32.14 *chemical reaction*
equilizer **119.4**
equine **59.17**; 71.33 *ungulate*
equine distemper 260.18 *veterinary disease*
equine species 59.1 *horse*
equinoctial 91.7 *oceanic*; 292.9 *seasonal*
equinoctially 292.18 *seasonally*
equinoctial tide 154.8 *high thing*; 91.2 *tide*
equinox 29.5 *celestial sphere*
equip **243.5**; 6.22 *educate*; 352.6 *find means*; 551.35 *make clothing*; 436.5 *provision*; 136.13 *qualify*
equipment **438.7**; 243.11 *fitting out*; 348.2 *instrument*; 136.4 *permission*; 436.1 *provision*; 136.1 *qualification*; 352.2 *supplies*
equipoise 119.2 *equilibrium*; 301.1 *motionlessness*
equipollence 750.5 *conformity*; 119.3 *equalization*; 111.2 *equivalence*
equipollent 750.14 *conforming*; 119.6 *equal*; 111.13 *equivalent*
equiponderance 111.5, 119.1 *equality*
equiponderant 111.16 *equal*
equiponderate 111.10 *be equal*
equip oneself 439.6 *store*

equipose 162.1 *symmetry*
equipped 243.18 *prepared*; 436.8 *provisional*; 136.9 *qualified*
equipper 243.15 *preparer*
equipping 436.1 *provision*; 436.7 *provisioning*
equisetum 82.1 *fern*
equitable 473.4 *disinterested*; 119.6 *equal*; 799.4 *honourable*; 801.7 *right*
equitableness 473.1 *disinterestedness*; 801.1 *fairness*
equitably 119.13; 473.8 *disinterestedly*
equitation 59.6 *horsemanship*; 300.2 *momentum*
equity 801.1 *fairness*; 799.1 *probity*
equity law 16.1 *the law*
equivalence 111.2; 750.5 *conformity*; 110.3 *correlation*; 706.8 *correspondence*; 27.26, 119.1 *equality*; 27.63 *mathematical logic*; 4.8 *philosophical term*; 115.1 *similarity*; 762.1 *substitution*; 694.4 *type of meaning*
equivalence point 32.18 *gravimetric analysis*
equivalence relation 27.63 *mathematical logic*
equivalency 119.1 *equality*
equivalent 111.13; 32.41 *analytic*; 750.14 *conforming*; 110.6 *correlative*; 706.15 *correspondent*; 115.5 *counterpart*; 119.6 *equal*; 111.2 *equivalence*; 759.1 *exchange*; 759.6 *in exchange*; 27.86 *logical*; 694.6 *meaningful*; 115.7 *similar*; 762.7 *substitute*; 762.1 *substitution*; 719.17 *translational*
equivalent circuit 39.13 *circuit*
equivalently 115.14 *comparably*; 110.11 *correlatively*; 706.26 *correspondingly*; 119.12 *equally*; 111.18 *identically*; 759.8 *in exchange*; 762.9 *instead*
equivalent meaning 694.4 *type of meaning*
equivalent triangles 27.43 *triangle*
equivocal 479.10; 180.5 *ambiguous*; 634.18 *avoiding*; 645.4 *cunning*; 189.5 *devious*; 696.4 *difficult*; 699.38 *evasive*; 453.6 *indeterminate*; 694.6 *meaningful*; 266.2 *obscure*; 705.14 *questionable*; 702.9 *quibbling*; 702.7 *sophistic*; 639.1 *vacillating*; 5.42 *worded*
equivocality 736.5 *evasion*
equivocally 479.12; 180.8 *circularly*; 189.9 *deviously*; 634.22 *evasively*; 453.25 *indeterminately*; 639.16 *irresolutely*; 5.50 *lexically*; 266.4 *obscurely*; 705.24 *questionably*; 702.14 *sophistically*
equivocalness 479.5; 270.2 *circumlocution*; 694.3 *comprehension*; 736.5 *evasion*; 453.14 *indeterminacy*; 5.22 *many words*; 720.2 *misinterpretation*; 266.1 *obscurity*; 696.11 *unintelligibility*
equivocal passage 694.3 *comprehension*
equivocate 479.2; **736.13**; 180.7 *be ambiguous*; 479.1 *be equivocal*; 634.7 *be evasive*; 189.7 *deviate*; 699.27 *evade*; 453.19 *hesitate*; 720.1 *misinterpret*; 702.13 *quibble*; 639.5 *vacillate*
equivocating 479.11; 479.10 *equivocal*; 702.9 *quibbling*
Equivocation 479
equivocation 479.6; 189.3 *deviousness*; 479.5 *equivocalness*; 699.13, 736.5 *evasion*; 634.15 *evasiveness*; 699.11 *half-truth*; 227.2 *irresolution*; 702.1 *sophistry*; 326.3, 639.11 *vacillation*
equivocator 479.9; 699.18, 700.16 *liar*; 702.6 *sophist*
equivoque 479.5 *equivocalness*
equotidian 138.21 *common*
ERA 391.2 *equal opportunity*
era 281.3 *chronology*; 276.3 *geological period*; 30.41 *geological time*; 275.4 *term*; 276.2 *time period*
eradicable 369.18 *extractive*; 212.6 *subtractive*
eradicably 212.9 *decreasingly*
eradicate 195.9 *annihilate*; 94.13 *cause not to exist*; 357.8 *destroy*; 128.8 *eject*; 371.10 *exterminate*; 369.11 *extract*; 358.1 *obliterate*; 212.3 *subtract*; 773.10 *take away*
eradicated 358.6 *obliterated*; 212.5 *subtracted*
eradication 357.2 *destroying*; 128.2 *ejection*; 369.1 *extraction*; 358.3 *obliteration*; 212.1 *subtraction*; 773.3 *taking away*
eradicative 369.18 *extractive*
erasable 40.21 *on-line*
erase 40.20 *abort*; 708.14 *cancel*; 526.3 *cause to disappear*; 256.13 *clean*; 357.8 *destroy*; 365.14 *erode*; 371.10 *exterminate*; 521.8 *make invisible*; 358.1 *obliterate*; 212.3 *subtract*; 773.10 *take away*
erased 358.6 *obliterated*; 212.5 *subtracted*
erased from the record 649.8 *overlooked*
erase from one's memory 463.13 *forget*
eraser 358.4; **365.7**; 256.10 *cleaning object*; 357.6 *destroyer*; 521.6 *that which makes invisible*
erasing 358.3 *obliteration*
ERA supporter 391.3 *liberator*
erasure 357.1 *destruction*; 526.5 *disguise*; 358.3 *obliteration*; 212.1 *subtraction*; 773.3 *taking away*; 365.2 *wearing away*
erathem 30.41 *geological time*
Erebus 8.12 *hell*
erect 154.18; 20.18 *be an architect*; 403.16 *construct*; 38.30 *engineer*; 344.11 *inaugurate*; 405.13 *make*; 213.5 *make bigger*; 228.7 *make stable*; 186.6 *make vertical*; 77.14 *of plants*; 356.10 *produce*; 376.44 *put together*; 366.1 *raise*; 622.15 *unapproachable*; 186.8 *vertical*
erected 366.11 *raised*; 20.12 *structural*
erectile 366.11 *raised*
erecting 186.2 *making vertical*
erection 20.3 *building*; 182.2 *bulge*; 403.6 *construction*; 186.2 *making vertical*; 356.2 *manufacture*; 376.33 *putting together*; 366.6 *raising*; 186.1 *verticality*
erectly 622.32 *proudly*; 186.11 *vertically*
erectness 186.1 *verticality*
E region 434.3 *atmospheric layers*
eremite 118.9 *hermit*; 197.8 *loner*; 655.6 *unsocial person*
Erewhon 610.3 *aspiration*; 477.8 *dreamland*; 756.4 *promised land*
erg 334.5 *unit of work*; 38.10 *work*
ergo 750.36 *accordingly*; 345.12 *with the effect of*
ergonomics 576.4 *exertion*
ergotism 83.5 *fungal association*
Erie 88.3 *US lakes*
Erin 85.10 *Ireland*
Eris 585.3 *gods and goddesses of war*
eristic 701.6 *arguer*; 701.9 *hostile*; 701.2 *logical argument*; 4.5 *philosophical argument*
ERM 780.7 *finance*
ermine 550.14 *animal covering*; 743.13 *heraldic*; 743.8 *heraldic device*
ermines 743.8 *heraldic device*
erminites 743.8 *heraldic device*
erminois 743.8 *heraldic device*
ERNIE 227.3 *changeable thing*; 40.3 *computer*
erode 365.14; 375.3 *disintegrate*; 245.5 *hurt*; 766.12 *lessen*; 212.3 *subtract*; 441.1 *waste*; 427.28 *weather*
eroded 526.7 *disappeared*; 563.3 *infertile*; 212.7 *reduced*; 30.59 *weathered*
erogenous 593.20 *amorous*
Eros 593.16 *gods and goddesses of love*; 36.22 *libido*
erosion 357.7 *agent of destruction*; 214.1 *decrease*; 245.9 *dilapidation*; 526.4 *disappearance*; 375.1 *disintegration*; 28.10 *force*; 766.4 *lessening*; 427.4 *pulverization*; 212.1 *subtraction*; 441.3 *waste*; 365.2 *wearing away*; 30.35 *weathering*
erosive 365.10 *frictional*
erotic 593.20 *amorous*; 796.12 *indecent*; 490.6 *pleasant*
erotica 796.2 *indecency*; 552.2 *nudity*
erotic dancer 21.30 *dancer*
erotic desire 36.22 *libido*
eroticism 593.5 *desire*; 36.22 *libido*; 490.1 *physical pleasure*; 796.3 *sexual immorality*
erotic literature 796.2 *indecency*
erotic novel 17.2 *fiction*
erotic poetry 17.6 *poetry*
erotomania 461.4 *delusion*; 593.5 *desire*
err 486.5 *be unskilful*; 804.16 *be wicked*; 796.16 *do wrong*; 325.3 *go astray*; 274.19, 288.9 *make a mistake*; 720.1 *misinterpret*; 802.23 *sin*; 274.20 *transgress*
errancy 274.7
errand boy 401.5 *office assistant*
errant 274.16; 325.25 *wandering*
errantry 325.16 *wandering*
erratic 642.1 *capricious*; 133.8 *discontinuous*; 114.5 *diverse*; 30.38 *glacier*; 299.4, 408.14 *irregular*; 300.16 *moving*; 453.17 *uncertain person*; 453.7 *unreliable*; 299.5 *unusual*; 325.25 *wandering*
erratically 325.29; 642.6 *capriciously*; 408.27 *in disorder*; 114.11, 299.8 *irregularly*; 453.26 *unreliably*
erraticism 227.2 *irresolution*
erratum 274.12 *typing error*
erring 274.16 *errant*; 288.16 *mistaken*; 804.11 *wicked*
erroneous 274.15; 699.29 *false*; 802.12 *incorrect*; 288.16 *mistaken*; 702.7 *sophistic*
erroneously 274.21; 699.40 *falsely*; 288.21, 720.4 *mistakenly*; 702.14 *sophistically*; 802.26 *wrong*
erroneousness 274.3; 699.1 *falsehood*; 231.5 *imperfection*; 802.2 *incorrectness*
Error 274
error 459.2 *act of folly*; 51.5 *bowling delivery*; 486.9 *bungling*; 231.7 *defect*; 247.1 *failure*; 699.1 *falsehood*; 477.5 *fantasy*; 231.5 *imperfection*; 472.5 *inattentive act*; 240.3 *inconvenience*; 802.2 *incorrectness*; 288.3 *lost chance*; 720.2 *misinterpretation*; 274.1, 465.2 *mistake*; 27.66 *proof*; 28.83 *sensitivity*; 325.16 *wandering*; 802.8 *wrongdoing*
error of law 16.4 *bad law*
ersatz 772.11 *borrowed*; 125.13 *imitation*; 115.8 *simulated*
erstwhile 294.14 *dead*; 296.13 *former*; 129.11 *prior*
eruct 371.16, 508.7 *belch*; 371.14 *let out*
eructate 371.16 *belch*
eructation 371.24, 432.5, 508.4 *belch*
eructative 371.31
erudite 6.18 *educated*; 442.10 *intelligent*; 4.19 *learned*; 17.16 *literary*; 455.9 *literate*; 458.5 *wise*
erudition 442.4 *cleverness*; 6.9 *learnedness*; 455.3 *learning*; 17.1 *literature*; 458.1 *wisdom*
erupt 130.27, 315.10 *emerge*; 371.14 *let out*; 308.18 *open*
erupting 315.15 *outgoing*
eruption 30.25; 371.22 *disgorgement*; 315.1 *exit*; 380.3 *instance of violence*; 260.13 *skin disease*
eruptive 371.29 *expulsive*; 315.15 *outgoing*; 380.6 *violent*; 30.55 *volcanic*
eruptively 371.32 *expulsively*; 315.18 *forth*
eruptiveness 371.22 *disgorgement*
erysipelas 260.13 *skin disease*
erysipelatous 260.23 *diseased*
erythema 260.13 *skin disease*
erythrocyte 431.4 *blood*
ESA 29.31 *space travel*
escalade 381.9 *attack successfully*; 304.14 *climb*; 314.10 *invade*; 381.14 *siege*
escalader 381.19 *attacker*; 586.1 *combatant*
escalate 765.10 *augment*; 792.9 *be dear*; 213.4 *increase*; 213.5 *make bigger*; 366.2 *send up*
escalated 366.11 *raised*
escalating 213.6 *increasing*; 304.23 *rising*
escalation 765.2 *augmentation*; 213.1 *increase*; 366.6 *raising*
escalator 366.10 *elevator*; 304.8 *lift*; 316.5 *means of transport*
escalier 304.7 *means of ascent*
escapable 634.20 *avoidable*
escapade 642.3 *whim*
Escape 389
escape 389.1; **389.5**; 98.18 *abscond*; 250.14 *be free*; 252.9 *be safe*; 390.2 *deliverance*; 526.2 *depart*; 313.7 *departure*; 526.4 *disappearance*; 372.13 *diverge*; 315.10 *emerge*; 634.6 *evade*; 634.14 *evasion*; 758.12 *exempt oneself*; 391.4 *liberate*; 391.1 *liberation*; 766.15 *lose someone*; 246.7 *overcome obstacles*; 77.2 *plant*; 313.3 *quit*; 634.8 *run away*; 384.28 *survive*
escape artist 21.29 *entertainer*
escape character 40.10 *character*
escape clause 746.2 *basis for negotiations*; 136.7 *condition*; 389.2 *means of escape*; 252.1 *safety*
escaped 634.18 *avoiding*; 389.8 *escaping*; 250.9 *free*; 77.15 *wild*
escape detection 389.6 *elude*
escaped prisoner 389.3 *escaper*
escapee 634.17 *avoider*; 526.4 *disappearance*; 389.3 *escaper*; 250.7 *free person*; 391.3 *liberator*; 633.7 *the hunted*
escape from jail 389.5 *escape*
escape hatch 389.2 *means of escape*; 252.4 *safety device*; 315.6 *way out*
escape lane 320.3 *carriageway*
escape notice 674.15; 521.7 *become invisible*; 389.6 *elude*
escape one 696.7 *be unintelligible*
escaper 389.3; 634.17 *avoider*
escape route 315.6 *way out*
escape sequence 40.10 *character*
escape velocity 29.35 *rocketry*
escape wheel 307.6 *rotator*
escaping 389.8; 526.6 *disappearing*
escapism 36.19 *defence mechanism*; 389.1 *escape*; 477.6 *reverie*; 758.3 *self-exemption*; 634.12 *shyness*
escapist 634.17 *avoider*; 36.8 *disordered personality*; 389.3 *escaper*; 477.9 *visionary*
escapologist 21.29 *entertainer*; 389.3 *escaper*
escapology 526.4 *disappearance*; 389.1 *escape*
escargot 25.19 *shellfish*
escargots 25.45 *French dish*
escarp 384.11 *fortification*
escarpment 154.2 *heights*; 176.2 *obliquity*; 186.3 *vertical thing*
eschar 550.14 *animal covering*
eschatological 131.20 *ending*; 482.12 *intended*; 7.18 *theological*
eschatologist 7.14 *theologian*
eschatology 131.5 *fate*; 482.5 *final intention*; 283.4 *looking to the future*; 7.13 *theology*
escheat 814.7 *punishment*
eschew 634.1 *avoid*; 684.5 *be self-restrained*
eschewal 684.1 *self-restraint*
eschew artifice 646.4 *be naive*
escort 223.15; 223.7 *attendant*; 567.4 *boyfriend*; 631.15 *conduct*; 631.10 *conductor*; 593.26 *court*; 579.2 *direct*; 568.4 *girlfriend*; 384.14 *guard*; 223.14 *keep company with*; 593.9 *lover*; 223.12 *partner*; 252.10 *protect*; 252.2 *protection*
escorted 223.20 *accompanied*
escribed figure 27.41 *geometric figure*
escrime 54.1 *fencing*
escritoire 410.3 *cabinet*; 23.4 *table*
escudo 780.11 *national coins*
escuela 6.12 *educational institution*
esculent 557.27 *edible*; 495.7 *tasty*
escutcheon 743.8 *heraldic device*
esker 154.4 *mountain range*
Eskimo 494.6 *Arctic*
Eskimo roll 50.6 *canoeing*
Esky 410.6 *box*; 494.4 *cooler*
ESN 6.17 *educable*
esoteric 523.11 *benighted*; 139.17 *exceptional*; 737.11 *mysterious*; 266.2 *obscure*; 11.14 *occult*; 11.12 *occultist*; 4.13 *of philosophy*; 264.12 *problematic*; 696.1 *unintelligible*
esoterica 737.7 *esotericism*; 11.2 *the occult*
esoterically 11.25 *occultly*; 4.25 *theoretically*; 696.13 *unintelligibly*
esotericism 737.7; 11.1 *occultism*; 696.11 *unintelligibility*
esoterics 11.1 *occultism*
esoteric sense 694.4 *type of meaning*
esotropia 519.2 *poor sight*
ESP 488.1 *sensation*; 101.3 *spiritual world*
espadrilles 551.19 *footwear*
espalier 193.2 *braid*; 44.10 *fruit tree*; 193.8 *interweave*
especial 139.15 *special*
especially 139.28 *specially*; 121.16 *superiorly*
Esperanto 5.7 *international language*
espionage 518.3 *observation*; 737.2 *secretiveness*; 662.3 *subversion*
esplanade 317.7 *arcade*; 187.3 *flat thing*; 167.1 *front*
espousal 593.8 *love affair*; 570.5 *wedding*
espouse 570.15 *marry*; 756.7 *promise*; 469.3 *side with*
espouse a theory 4.22 *propound a philosophy*
espoused 570.21 *married*; 570.8 *spouse*
espouser 570.8 *spouse*
espresso café 557.15 *eating place*
esprit de corps 750.1 *accord*; 747.2 *fellowship*; 569.2 *friendly relations*
esprit d'escalier 294.3 *delayed action*
espy 449.1 *discover*; 518.12 *see*
Esq. 567.3 *male title of address*
esquire 567.3 *male title of address*
ESR 32.17 *analysis*
Essay 722
essay 353.1, 353.5 *attempt*; 722.1 *disser-*

tation; 448.1, 448.11 *experiment*; 721.3 *narration*; 17.4 *nonfiction*
essayed 448.10 *tested*
essayer 353.7 *attempter*
essaying 353.8 *attempting*
essayist 721.10 *descriptive writer*; 722.3 *dissertator*
esse 93.1 *existence*
Essence 99
essence 99.1; 123.3 *chief thing*; 406.1 *contents*; 369.8 *extract*; 160.1 *form*; 502.2 *fragrant thing*; 701.4 *gist*; 446.1 *idea*; 694.1 *meaning*; 93.3 *nature*; 230.3 *perfection*; 37.5 *prescription*; 356.3 *product*; 255.8 *simplicity*; 797.9 *the best*; 447.1 *topic*; 235.6 *worth*
Essene 7.6 *non-Christian*
essential 99.5; 175.3 *base*; 405.8 *belonging*; 797.2 *best*; 123.3 *chief thing*; 386.1 *compulsion*; 406.10 *containing*; 123.5 *important*; 93.11 *intrinsic*; 135.4 *required*; 135.1 *requirement*
essential amino acid 33.8 *amino acid*
essential clause 746.2 *basis for negotiations*
essential content 99.2
essential element 33.15
essential facts 139.4 *specifications*
essential fatty acid 33.7 *fat*
essentialism 4.7 *school of thought*
essentialist 4.11 *follower of a doctrine*; 4.14 *of a philosophy*
essentiality 123.1 *importance*; 135.3 *needfulness*
essentialize 369.17 *obtain an extract*
essentially 163.7; 175.5 *basically*; 405.14 *constituently*; 99.13 *in essence*; 135.12 *in need*; 204.13 *on the whole*; 93.22 *really*; 406.13 *structurally*; 447.14 *thematically*
essential nature 93.3 *nature*
essential oil 502.2 *fragrant thing*; 547.6 *toiletries*
essential part 123.3 *chief thing*; 205.5 *largest part*; 554.1 *life*
essentials 139.4 *specifications*
Essex man 574.1 *plebeian*
Est 36.3 *psychiatric treatment*
establish 175.4 *base*; 130.17 *begin*; 707.19 *confirm*; 243.2 *do the groundwork*; 95.12 *establish reality*; 743.10 *identify*; 130.23, 344.11 *inaugurate*; 16.68 *legislate*; 142.9 *locate*; 452.21 *make certain*; 225.6, 279.7 *make permanent*; 228.7 *make stable*; 356.10 *produce*; 454.2, 703.17 *prove*; 698.30 *prove true*; 140.13 *rule*; 701.15 *state*
establish a connection 108.7 *relate to*
establish a mean 216.10 *make average*
establish an interrelationship 110.8 *interrelate*
established 632.12; 216.1 *average*; 452.1 *certain*; 452.3 *decided*; 743.12 *identified*; 142.6 *located*; 296.12 *olden*; 334.14 *operative*; 225.7 *permanent*; 440.8 *propertied*; 698.20 *proved*; 1.14 *societal*; 228.10 *stabilized*; 707.13 *supported*
established custom 632.4 *custom*
established practice 10.1 *ritual*
established ways 632.3 *way*
establisher 356.9 *producer*
establishing 743.1 *identification*; 130.34 *inaugural*; 454.9 *verificatory*
establishment 452.13, 698.7, 707.4 *confirmation*; 403.6 *construction*; 743.1 *identification*; 130.6 *inauguration*; 356.2 *manufacture*; 225.1 *permanence*; 142.4 *placing*; 454.5 *proof*; 779.8 *store*
establish reality 95.12
establish residence 142.10 *settle*
establish the trend 395.8 *influence*
estate 215.5; 320.16 *car*; 43.6 *farm*; 565.4 *official residence*; 763.4 *possession*; 440.1 *property*; 143.5 *rank*; 221.1 *state*; 781.5 *wealth*; 635.5 *will*
estate agent 440.7 *property man*; 778.12 *wholesaler*
estate and effects 440.4 *possessions*
estate duty 790.7 *tax*
estate management 43.1 *agriculture*
esteem 669.2 *admiration*; 669.11 *approve*; 450.8 *be of the opinion*; 464.12 *estimate*; 811.1 *estimation*; 595.7 *like*; 593.23 *love*; 123.8 *make important*; 185.1 *prominence*; 667.1, 667.15 *respect*; 9.1, 9.7 *worship*; 235.6 *worth*
esteemed 593.21 *beloved*; 185.6 *eminent*; 667.12 *respected*; 9.11 *worshipped*; 235.1 *worthy*
esterify 32.26 *react*
estimable 210.14 *calculable*; 26.14 *measurable*; 669.21 *praiseworthy*; 667.13 *respectable*; 235.1 *worthy*
estimably 210.16 *mathematically*
estimate 464.12; 789.7 *account*; 713.1 *advice*; 210.8 *calculate*; 693.3 *document*; 27.93 *equate*; 448.11 *experiment*; 719.8 *interpret*; 719.1 *interpretation*; 464.1 *judgment*; 26.10, 209.5 *measure*; 26.1 *measurement*; 474.9 *predict*; 790.1 *price*; 790.7 *tax*; 446.17 *theorize*
estimated 26.13 *measured*; 448.10 *tested*; 446.10 *theoretical*
estimated position 323.5 *navigation*
estimated value 28.83 *sensitivity*
estimation 811.1; 210.1 *calculation*; 448.3 *experimentation*; 446.1 *idea*; 464.1 *judgment*; 26.1 *measurement*; 27.66 *proof*
estimative 210.13 *calculative*
estimator 713.4 *adviser*; 210.6 *calculator*; 16.23 *judge*; 26.9 *measurer*
estrange 594.16 *cause hate*; 372.11 *divide*
estranged 571.11 *divorced*
estrangement 751.1 *disagreement*; 594.4 *hatefulness*; 571.2 *separation*
estuarial 92.11 *continental*
estuarine 91.7 *oceanic*
estuary 317.11 *channel*; 92.9 *inlet*
Estuary English 5.26 *dialect*
esurient 688.6 *gluttonous*
E.T. 100.6 *outsider*
et al. 207.12 *et cetera*
etc. 207.12 *et cetera*; 127.9 *inclusively*
et cetera 207.12; 211.10 *additionally*; 127.9 *inclusively*
etch 19.22 *engrave*; 743.10 *identify*; 744.14 *inscribe*; 163.5 *outline*; 717.11 *paint*; 184.8 *wrinkle*
etched 184.6 *wrinkly*
etcher 19.18 *engraver*; 717.4 *person who makes a representation*
etching 19.1 *art*; 19.15 *engraving*; 163.1 *outline*; 542.3 *pattern*; 717.2 *reproduction*
etching point 19.15 *engraving*
eternal 202.3; **279.8**; 8.13 *divine*; 275.21 *lasting through time*; 101.8 *nonmaterial*; 225.7, 277.9 *permanent*; 134.6 *protracted*
eternal damnation 8.12 *hell*
eternal fire 283.3 *future condition*
eternalization 279.4
eternalize 279.6
eternal life 554.5 *life cycle*; 101.1 *nonmaterial world*; 756.4 *promised land*
eternally 202.12; **279.11**; 275.30 *chronologically*; 134.7 *continually*; 8.19 *divinely*; 277.12 *everlastingly*; 101.13 *metaphysically*; 225.9 *permanently*
eternal peace 263.1 *ease*
eternal rest 582.1 *death*; 279.3 *life without end*; 301.2 *repose*
eternal return 112.4 *return*
eternal triangle 796.4 *illicit love*; 629.1 *jealousy*; 593.8 *love affair*
eternal verities 698.1 *truth*
eternal youth 756.4 *promised land*
Eternity 279
eternity 202.7; **279.1**; 8.2 *divine attribute*; 554.5 *life cycle*; 101.1 *nonmaterial world*; 225.1 *permanence*
ether 434.1 *air*; 489.4 *anaesthetic*; 417.5, 432.1 *gas*; 154.8 *high thing*; 415.7 *light thing*
ethereal 432.17, 434.12 *airy*; 8.14 *heavenly*; 154.9 *high*; 477.12 *imaginary*; 415.2 *insubstantial*; 101.8 *nonmaterial*; 417.1 *sparse*; 11.18 *spiritual*; 96.8 *unreal*
etherealism 432.9 *aeriness*
ethereality 434.9 *airiness*; 415.5 *lightness*; 417.3 *sparseness*; 96.1 *unreality*
etherealization 417.4 *rarefaction*; 432.10 *vaporization*
etherealize 417.6 *make sparse*; 11.20 *occult*
etherealized 417.2 *rarefied*
ethereally 432.28 *aerily*; 415.11 *lightly*; 101.13 *metaphysically*; 417.7 *sparsely*
ethereal world 101.1 *nonmaterial world*
etheriability 432.9 *aeriness*
etheric body 11.7 *spirit*
etherification 432.10 *vaporization*
etherify 432.25 *gasify*
ethering 43.5 *cultivation*
etherism 489.2 *unconsciousness*
etherize 432.26 *aerate*; 489.12 *anaesthetize*
etherized 489.7 *anaesthetized*
Ethernet 40.15 *network*
ethical 803.6; 810.8 *dutiful*; 799.4 *honourable*; 795.8, 801.10 *moral*; 4.13 *of philosophy*; 631.17 *well-behaved*
ethical drug 37.3 *drug*; 394.2 *medicine*
ethically 803.10; 799.7 *honourably*; 795.13 *morally*; 810.18 *on duty*; 4.25 *theoretically*; 631.19 *well*
ethicalness 795.1 *morality*
ethical self 36.21 *psyche*
ethical system 4.2 *philosophical system*
ethics 810.6; 4.6 *branch of philosophy*; 795.1 *morality*; 799.1 *probity*; 7.1 *religion*; 803.2 *virtues*
Ethiopian 566.4 *modern human*
Ethiopians 284.6 *people of the past*
ethnic 566.12 *human*; 564.12 *native*; 1.13 *racial*; 1.14 *societal*
ethnically 566.15 *humanly*; 1.18 *societally*; 2.16 *sociologically*
ethnic cleansing 382.3 *homicide*; 144.3 *replacement*; 382.4 *slaughter*; 466.4 *social discrimination*; 585.1 *war*; 585.8 *warfare*
ethnic group 566.9 *group*; 2.6 *social group*; 1.7 *society*
ethnic minority 566.9 *group*
ethnic music 18.10 *world music*
ethnic origin 1.6 *race*
ethnobiological 34.20 *biological*
ethnobiologist 34.19 *life scientist*
ethnobiology 34.1 *life science*
ethnobotanical 77.20 *botanical*
ethnobotanist 77.12 *plant scientist*
ethnobotany 1.1 *anthropology*; 77.10 *plant science*
ethnocentric 466.10 *discriminatory*
ethnocentrically 466.17 *prejudicially*
ethnocentricity 466.4 *social discrimination*
ethnocide 382.4 *slaughter*; 466.4 *social discrimination*
ethnogenic 1.11 *anthropological*
ethnogenist 1.3 *anthropologist*
ethnogeny 1.1 *anthropology*
ethnographer 1.3 *anthropologist*; 566.6 *studier of mankind*
ethnographic 1.11 *anthropological*
ethnographical 566.12 *human*
ethnographically 1.16 *anthropologically*; 566.15 *humanly*
ethnography 1.1 *anthropology*; 566.5 *study of mankind*
ethnological 1.11 *anthropological*
ethnologically 1.16 *anthropologically*
ethnologist 1.3 *anthropologist*
ethnology 1.1 *anthropology*; 566.5 *study of mankind*
ethnomusicologist 1.3 *anthropologist*
ethnomusicology 1.1 *anthropology*
ethnoscientific 1.11 *anthropological*
ethnoscientific studies 1.1 *anthropology*
ethological 631.16 *behaving*; 70.16 *zoological*
ethologist 70.11 *zoologist*
ethology 70.9 *animal science*; 36.1 *psychology*
ethos 795.1 *morality*; 4.2 *philosophical system*; 631.6 *way of life*
ethylene 33.17 *plant hormone*
ethylene glycol 493.3 *heater*
etiolate 530.6 *decolour*; 531.13 *whiten*
etiolated 530.7 *colourless*; 335.12 *impotent*
etiolation 530.1 *colourlessness*; 531.7 *whiteness*
etiological 344.13 *causal*
etiology 344.1 *cause*; 260.20 *pathology*
etiquette 549.3; **656.5**; 117.4 *conventionalism*; 160.5, 656.1 *formality*; 631.2 *good conduct*; 658.2 *good manners*; 801.3 *properness*; 632.5 *tradition*
Etna 493.8 *hot place*
Eton collar 551.14 *neckwear*
Eton crop 547.8 *haircut*
Eton jacket 551.11 *jacket*
étrier 62.4 *climbing equipment*
Etruscan 296.14 *historic*; 19.29 *realist*
Etruscans 284.6 *people of the past*
etymological 5.38 *linguistic*; 694.6 *meaningful*
etymologically 5.48 *linguistically*
etymologist 5.2 *linguist*
etymology 344.1 *cause*; 5.1 *linguistics*; 694.4 *type of meaning*
etymon 5.35 *part of speech*; 344.3 *rudiment*; 5.17 *word*
EU 85.2 *union of nations*
eucalyptus 502.3 *incense*
Eucharist 10.6; 10.5 *Christian rite*; 671.2 *thanks*
eucharistial 10.14 *sacred object*
eucharistic 10.21 *ritualistic*
euchromosome 34.14 *chromosome*
Euclidean geometry 27.34 *geometry*
Euclidean space 27.35 *space*
Euclidian 4.11 *follower of a doctrine*; 4.14 *of a philosophy*
eudaemonia 263.1 *ease*
eudaemonic 263.4 *at ease*
eudaemonism 4.7 *school of thought*
eudaemonist 4.11 *follower of a doctrine*
eudaemonistic 4.14 *of a philosophy*
eudiometer 432.15 *vaporimeter*
eugenics 34.11 *genetics*; 35.3 *medical specialty*; 561.3 *propagation*
euglena 159.2 *little thing*
euhemerism 719.1 *interpretation*; 4.7 *school of thought*
euhemerist 4.11 *follower of a doctrine*; 719.6 *interpreter*
euhemeristic 719.14 *interpretive*; 4.14 *of a philosophy*
eukaryote 34.3 *organism*
eukaryotic 34.23 *cellular*
eukaryotic cell 34.7 *cell*
eulogia 10.9 *prayer*
eulogist 583.3 *funeral director*; 669.9 *praiser*
eulogistic 669.18 *approving*; 583.11 *funeral*
eulogistical 583.11 *funeral*
eulogistically 583.12 *funereally*
eulogize 582.17 *bury*; 669.15 *compliment*
eulogizer 583.3 *funeral director*; 669.9 *praiser*
eulogy 582.8 *after death*; 669.4 *compliment*; 583.2 *funeral*; 729.8 *speech*
cumitosis 34.10 *cell division*
Eumycota 83.3 *fungi*
eunuch 567.12; 572.4 *celibate person*
eupepsia 259.3 *health*
eupeptic 259.1 *healthy*
euphemism 676.1 *affectedness*; 189.3 *deviousness*; 542.1 *ornament*; 255.1 *purity*; 795.4 *self-righteousness*
euphemisms 712.16
euphemistic 676.3 *affected*; 189.5 *devious*; 795.10 *moralistic*; 255.12 *morally pure*; 542.10 *ornate*
euphemistically 189.9 *deviously*
euphemize 685.4 *moderate*; 542.12 *ornament*
euphonic 750.13 *harmonious*; 516.6 *melodious*
euphonically 750.33 *harmoniously*
euphonious 543.3 *elegant*; 750.13 *harmonious*; 516.6 *melodious*; 490.6 *pleasant*
euphoniously 543.5 *elegantly*; 750.33 *harmoniously*; 516.11 *melodiously*
euphoniousness 750.4 *harmony*; 516.3 *melodiousness*
euphony 543.1 *elegance*; 750.4 *harmony*; 516.3 *melodiousness*; 18.13 *melody*; 17.12 *poetic language*
euphoria 597.1 *happiness*; 490.1 *physical pleasure*
euphoric 597.4 *happy*; 490.7 *pleased*; 600.9 *rejoicing*
euphorically 600.11 *rejoicingly*
Euphrates 90.5 *other major rivers*
euphuism 676.1 *affectedness*; 542.1 *ornament*
euphuist 542.9 *phrasemonger*; 543.2 *stylist*
euphuistic 542.10 *ornate*
euphuize 542.12 *ornament*
Eurasia 92.1 *continent*
Eurasian 412.5 *hybrid*
eureka 446.25 *got it!*
eurhythmic 162.5 *even*
eurhythmical 162.5 *even*
eurhythmics 22.1 *dancing*; 576.5 *exercise*; 244.9 *physical improvement*
eurhythmy 162.3 *evenness*
Euripidean tragedy 21.11 *tragedy*
Eurobond market 780.7 *finance*
Eurocheque 780.14 *paper money*
Eurocrat 579.16 *official*
Eurocurrency market 780.7 *finance*
euro-disco 18.7 *dance music*
Eurodollar 780.7 *finance*
Eurodollar market 14.1, 780.7 *finance*

Euromarket 776.5 *commercial trade;* 780.7 *finance;* 779.4 *free market;* 13.5 *international trade*
Euro-MP 579.16 *official*
Euronet 40.15 *network*
Europe 92.1 *continent*
European Bank 780.7 *finance;* 771.4 *lending institution*
European Boxing Union 52.2 *boxing*
European commissioner 579.16 *official*
European Community 776.5 *commercial trade;* 779.4 *free market;* 566.9 *group;* 764.1 *joint possession*
European Community law 16.1 *the law*
European Cup 66.1 *soccer*
European Cup Winners' Cup 66.1 *soccer*
European Currency Unit 14.1 *finance*
European Economic Area 779.4 *free market*
European Economic Community 776.5 *commercial trade;* 779.4 *free market;* 566.9 *group;* 13.5 *international trade*
European Free Trade Association 776.5 *commercial trade;* 779.4 *free market;* 13.5 *international trade*
European Games 47.5 *competition*
Europeanize 760.12 *naturalize*
Europeanized 760.17 *naturalized*
European Luge Championships 68.9 *bobsledding*
European Monetary System 14.1, 780.7 *finance*
European Parliament 579.10 *legislative body*
European Parliament member 579.16 *official*
European sea bass 55.5 *British game fish*
European Southern Observatory 29.23 *observatory*
European Union 776.5 *commercial trade;* 779.4 *free market;* 13.5 *international trade;* 764.1 *joint possession*
Europe class 50.2 *sailing boat*
Europhile 12.6 *political party*
Eurosceptic 12.6 *political party*
Eurus 31.15 *wind direction*
Euryale 11.4 *witch*
eurypterid 75.4 *arthropod*
Eustachian tube 504.5 *internal ear*
eutectic 32.7 *chemical compound;* 32.3 *phase;* 32.32 *solid*
Eutelsat™ 692.7 *satellite communication*
euthanasia 382.1 *killing;* 582.5 *ways of dying*
Eutheria 71.5 *placental mammal*
eutherian 71.25 *mammalian;* 71.5 *placental mammal*
eutherian characteristic 71.5 *placental mammal*
eutrophication 84.1 *alga*
evacuant 255.4 *purgative*
evacuate 560.16 *defecate;* 315.10 *emerge;* 98.19 *leave empty;* 371.11 *void;* 313.2, 355.2 *withdraw*
evacuated 144.10 *replaced*
evacuation 560.2 *defecation;* 313.7 *departure;* 315.1 *exit;* 355.3 *relinquishment;* 371.21 *removal;* 144.3 *replacement*
evacuation service 584.4 *military organization*
evacuee 144.7 *displaced person;* 655.7 *outsider*
evade 634.6; 699.27; 800.8 *be dishonourable;* 479.1 *be equivocal;* 736.11 *conceal oneself;* 702.12 *deceive;* 189.7 *deviate;* 389.6 *elude;* 736.13 *equivocate;* 639.6 *hesitate;* 766.15 *lose someone*
evade liability 758.12 *exempt oneself*
evade one's creditors 786.7 *not pay*
evade one's responsibilities 754.5 *be irresolute;* 758.12 *exempt oneself*
evader 634.17 *avoider;* 736.7 *concealer;* 389.3 *escaper*
evade tax 13.12 *cheat*
evade taxes 774.16 *act dishonestly;* 389.6 *elude;* 786.7 *not pay;* 709.5 *refuse*
evaginate 192.3 *invert*
evagination 192.1 *inversion*
evaluate 27.95; 719.11 *criticize;* 27.90 *enumerate;* 464.12 *estimate;* 26.10, 209.5 *measure;* 790.11 *price;* 4.21 *rationalize*
evaluation 27.24; 464.1 *judgment;* 26.1 *measurement;* 27.66 *proof*
evaluation of returns 469.12 *election*
evanesce 278.4 *be transient;* 214.4 *decrease;* 526.1 *disappear*
evanescence 214.1 *decrease;* 526.4 *disappearance;* 278.1 *transience*
evanescent 214.6 *decreasing;* 526.6 *disappearing;* 278.6 *transient*
evanescently 526.8 *fleetingly*
evangelical 7.5 *Christian;* 7.15 *religious*
evangelism 760.3 *persuasion;* 393.10 *revival*
evangelist 7.5 *Christian;* 760.5 *converter*
evangelization 760.3 *persuasion*
evangelize 450.9 *make someone believe;* 760.11 *persuade;* 7.20 *preach*
evangelized 760.16 *influenced*
evaporability 432.8 *volatility*
evaporable 432.23 *volatile*
evaporate 416.8 *be dense;* 278.4 *be transient;* 94.12 *cease to exist;* 214.4 *decrease;* 357.8 *destroy;* 377.14 *dilute;* 526.1 *disappear;* 428.23 *drip-dry;* 428.17 *dry;* 30.63 *ebb;* 377.11 *explode;* 432.25 *gasify;* 766.12 *lessen;* 32.25 *solidify;* 441.1 *waste*
evaporated 31.43 *atmospheric;* 377.27 *dilute;* 428.4 *dried-out;* 32.32 *solid*
evaporated milk 558.5 *milk*
evaporating 526.6 *disappearing*
evaporation 31.9 *atmospheric process;* 214.1 *decrease;* 377.3 *dilution;* 526.4 *disappearance;* 766.4 *lessening;* 315.2 *outflow;* 32.3 *phase;* 28.37 *temperature;* 432.10 *vaporization;* 441.3 *waste;* 30.10 *water cycle*
evaporative 428.9 *drying;* 432.23 *volatile*
evaporator 428.15 *dryer*
evaporimeter 26.8 *meter*
evasion 634.14; 699.13; 736.5; 645.1 *cunning;* 189.3 *deviousness;* 479.5 *equivocalness;* 389.1 *escape;* 484.3 *expedient plan;* 702.5 *hypocrisy;* 645.2 *stratagem;* 52.9 *tae kwon do*
evasion of responsibility 754.3 *irresolution;* 758.3 *self-exemption*
evasive 699.38; 634.18 *avoiding;* 702.8 *cunning;* 189.5 *devious;* 479.10 *equivocal;* 389.8 *escaping;* 234.8 *exaggerated;* 754.7 *irresolute;* 736.17 *noncommittal;* 732.2 *sparing with words;* 639.1 *vacillating*
evasive action 634.14 *evasion*
evasively 634.22; 234.14 *distortedly;* 479.12 *equivocally;* 702.15 *hypocritically;* 754.9 *irresolutely;* 52.16 *professionally*
evasiveness 634.15; 736.5 *evasion;* 732.3 *shyness*
Eve 568.2 *female;* 480.13 *tempter*
eve 291.1 *evening*
even 162.5; 698.39 *accurately;* 750.14 *conforming;* 119.11 *equalize;* 187.8 *horizontal;* 187.7 *make horizontal;* 27.71 *numerical;* 194.8 *odd;* 119.8 *on equal terms;* 298.14 *orderly;* 111.17, 298.11 *regular;* 421.1, 421.11 *smooth;* 162.6 *symmetrize;* 421.2 *uniform*
even as 285.15 *as*
even break 111.5 *equality;* 119.2 *equilibrium;* 801.1 *fairness*
even chance 104.4 *chance;* 107.3 *equal chance;* 102.3 *strong possibility*
even deal 801.1 *fairness*
even-handed 801.7 *right*
even handedness 801.1 *fairness*
even if 476.11 *supposing*
evening 291.1; 291.6; 291.7; 131.9 *close*
evening bag 410.8 *bag*
evening class 291.4 *evening thing*
evening damp 429.6 *dew*
evening dress 551.3, 656.4 *formal dress*
evening gloves 551.25 *accessories*
evening gown 551.3, 656.4 *formal dress;* 551.7 *frock*
evening light 524.1 *dimness*
evening meal 557.12 *meal*
evening news 291.4 *evening thing;* 741.6 *radio news*
evening of one's life 556.5 *old age*
evening paper 740.4 *newspaper*
evening prayers 10.4 *public worship*
evening primrose 291.4 *evening thing*
evenings 291.7 *evening;* 111.20 *regularly*
evening service 10.4 *public worship*
evening shirt 551.8 *shirt*
evening star 291.4 *evening thing;* 29.10 *star*
evening thing 291.4
evening time 291.1 *evening*
evening twilight 291.1 *evening*
evening up 119.3 *equalization*
even keel 119.2 *equilibrium*
even less 214.8 *decreasingly*
evenly 750.35 *consistently;* 119.12, 162.8 *equally;* 187.11 *horizontally;* 298.17 *orderly;* 111.20, 298.15 *regularly;* 421.14 *smoothly*
evenly matched 119.8 *on equal terms*
even money 111.5, 119.1 *equality*
even more 121.17 *supremely*
even more so 213.8 *increasingly*
evenness 162.3; 119.1 *equality;* 119.2 *equilibrium;* 187.1 *horizontality;* 298.4 *orderliness;* 111.6 *regularity;* 421.7 *smoothness*
even number 194.2 *kind of number;* 27.5 *number*
even out 216.10 *make average;* 750.26 *make uniform*
even pace 111.6 *regularity*
evens 59.7 *horseracing;* 102.3 *strong possibility*
even-sided 119.6 *equal;* 162.5 *even;* 162.4 *symmetrical*
even-sidedly 162.8 *equally*
even sides 162.1 *symmetry*
evensong 291.1 *evening;* 10.4 *public worship*
even Stevens 162.8 *equally*
event 345.1 *effect;* 27.58 *frequency distribution;* 3.14 *historicalness;* 222.2 *occurrence;* 45.1 *sport*
even temper 658.1 *courtesy;* 4.3 *detachment*
even-tempered 658.7 *courteous;* 4.18 *detached*
eventer 59.15 *horse person*
eventful 342.19 *busy;* 222.7 *circumstantial;* 123.6 *notable*
event horizon 29.11 *stellar birth*
eventide 291.1 *evening*
eventing 59.11; 59.6 *horsemanship*
even-toed 71.33 *ungulate*
even-toed ungulate 71.15 *hoofed mammal*
events 447.3 *matter of interest*
eventual 345.10 *caused;* 222.7 *circumstantial;* 283.11, 756.15 *future;* 131.24 *limiting;* 102.6 *potential*
eventuality 222.1 *circumstances;* 102.1 *possibility*
eventually 131.26 *finally;* 283.14 *in the future;* 102.11, 756.18 *potentially;* 222.16 *relatively;* 345.12 *with the effect of*
eventuate in 345.5 *show an effect*
even up 119.11 *equalize;* 111.8 *make the same;* 162.6 *symmetrize*
even with 211.10 *additionally*
ever 275.26 *all the time*
ever and anon 297.1 *frequently*
ever-changing 224.11, 227.13 *changeable*
Everest 154.3 *mountain;* 89.6 *other major mountains and ranges;* 121.4 *summit*
evergreen 279.8 *eternal;* 538.4 *fresh;* 538.8 *greenness;* 277.8 *lasting;* 77.14 *of plants;* 225.7 *permanent;* 77.2 *plant;* 228.9 *stable;* 79.1 *tree;* 79.14 *treelike*
evergreen copy 741.10 *copy*
ever higher 304.26 *up*
ever-increasing 213.6 *increasing*
everlasting 279.10 *continuing forever;* 202.3, 279.8 *eternal;* 275.21 *lasting through time;* 225.7, 277.9 *permanent;* 134.6 *protracted*
Everlasting Father 8.3 *God*
everlasting flower 78.1 *flower*
everlastingly 277.12; 134.7 *continually;* 225.9 *permanently*
everlastingness 202.7, 279.1 *eternity;* 225.1 *permanence*
ever less 214.8 *decreasingly*
evermore 279.11 *eternally*
eversion 224.1 *change*
ever so many 208.6 *many*
evert 224.8 *cause change*
ever-victorious 246.15 *victorious*
ever-welcome 654.16 *popular*
every 289.12 *succeeding;* 204.6 *whole*
every afternoon 291.7 *evening*
every bit 204.11 *wholly*
everybody 204.4 *all;* 138.10 *everyone;* 566.1 *humankind*
everybody's fool 668.9 *butt*
everybody under the sun 138.10 *everyone*
everyday 117.15; 216.1 *average;* 138.21 *common;* 632.10 *familiar;* 632.9 *habitual;* 5.39 *of language;* 298.14 *orderly;* 231.4 *ordinary;* 271.1 *simple;* 349.9 *used*
every day 298.16 *cyclically*
everyday knowledge 485.1 *skill*
everyday occurrence 297.4 *frequency*
everyday speech 271.4 *simplicity*
everyday work 576.1 *work*
every evening 291.7 *evening*
every inch 232.10 *fully;* 204.11 *wholly*
every inch a king 121.15 *excellent*
every living soul 566.1 *humankind*
everyman 138.9; 216.7 *average person;* 566.7 *person;* 574.1 *plebeian*
every man for himself 588.1 *anarchy;* 683.1 *selfishness*
every man Jack 138.10 *everyone*
every month 298.16 *cyclically*
every morning 290.8 *in the morning*
every mother's son 376.20 *crowd;* 138.10 *everyone*
every night 298.16 *cyclically;* 291.7 *evening*
every now and again 299.8 *irregularly;* 297.2 *sometimes*
everyone 138.10; 204.4 *all;* 566.1 *humankind*
everyone and everything 204.4 *all*
every other 289.12 *succeeding*
every other day 298.16 *cyclically*
every other month 298.16 *cyclically*
every other night 298.16 *cyclically*
every other week 298.16 *cyclically*
every other year 298.16 *cyclically*
every second 289.12 *succeeding*
every so often 146.8 *apart;* 297.2 *sometimes*
everything 204.4 *all;* 138.10 *everyone*
everything being equal 464.14 *considering*
every way 324.11 *in all directions*
every week 298.16 *cyclically*
everywhere 377.31; 141.16 *extensively;* 97.15 *here;* 324.11 *in all directions;* 97.7 *present;* 138.32 *universally*
every which way 408.28 *anyhow;* 141.16 *extensively;* 324.11 *in all directions;* 114.11 *irregularly*
every whit 232.10 *fully*
everywoman 216.7 *average person;* 138.9 *everyman;* 566.7 *person*
every year 298.16 *cyclically*
evict 371.8; 128.8 *eject;* 766.9 *lose;* 144.16 *replace;* 773.8 *take back*
evicted 128.11 *excluded;* 144.10 *replaced*
eviction 371.20; 128.2 *ejection;* 766.1 *loss;* 144.3 *replacement;* 773.2 *taking back*
evictor 371.26 *ejector*
Evidence 716
evidence 454.6; 716.1; 715.1 *accusation;* 476.2 *basis of supposition;* 452.9 *certainty;* 452.13, 698.7 *confirmation;* 16.7 *legal trial;* 701.3 *line of argument;* 738.10 *manifestation;* 694.10 *mean;* 396.9 *permission;* 703.4 *proof;* 703.17 *prove;* 738.3 *reveal;* 742.1 *sign;* 520.3 *visibility*
evidence in chief 716.5 *legal evidence*
evident 716.9; 525.7 *appearing;* 703.12 *demonstrable;* 527.4 *easily seen through;* 738.14 *manifest;* 308.13 *opened up;* 104.6 *probable;* 518.23, 520.1 *visible*
evidential 716.8; 703.13 *proven;* 742.14 *signifying;* 454.9 *verificatory*
evidentially 742.18 *indicatively*
evidently 716.15; 525.15 *apparently;* 738.16 *manifestly;* 308.25 *obviously;* 518.25, 520.11 *visibly*
evidentness 716.3
Evil 798
evil 798.1; 798.7; 351.5 *abusive;* 249.1 *adversity;* 236.3 *bad;* 236.9 *badness;* 523.11 *benighted;* 532.5 *black-hearted;* 8.16 *devilish;* 800.5 *dishonourable;* 236.5 *harmful;* 796.11 *immoral;* 796.1 *immorality;* 802.16 *in the wrong;* 651.10 *malevolent;* 351.2 *misuse;* 523.7 *spiritual darkness;* 804.11 *wicked;* 804.1 *wickedness*
evil act 651.7 *act of malevolence*
evil deed 802.8 *wrongdoing*
evil disposition 651.1 *malevolence*
evildoer 236.12 *bad person;* 340.3 *doer;* 798.6 *evil person;* 651.8 *malefactor;* 804.9 *wicked person*
evildoing 804.11 *wicked;* 804.1 *wickedness*
evil eye 594.2 *curse;* 518.6 *look;* 11.5 *spell*
evil genius 236.12 *bad person;* 798.6 *evil person*
evil intent 651.1 *malevolence*
evilly 798.12; 351.6 *abusively;* 804.18 *wickedly*

evil-minded 651.10 *malevolent*
evil nature 796.1 *immorality*
evilness 236.9 *badness;* 798.1 *evil;* 800.1 *improbity;* 651.1 *malevolence;* 802.5 *unrighteousness*
evil omen 711.1 *warning*
evil person 798.6
evil plight 798.5 *evil thing*
evil portent 711.1 *warning*
evil power 798.4
evil ruler 798.6 *evil person*
evil-smelling 503.3 *stinking*
evil speaking 712.3 *vilification*
evil-speaking 594.13 *angry*
evil spell 594.2 *curse;* 798.4 *evil power*
evil spirit 236.12 *bad person;* 8.7 *devil*
evil star 249.3 *bad fortune;* 798.3 *bad luck;* 236.11 *harmfulness*
evil thing 798.5
evil wish 798.5 *evil thing*
evince 452.21 *make certain;* 454.2, 703.17 *prove;* 738.3 *reveal;* 701.15 *state*
evirate 335.9 *make impotent*
eviscerate 245.5 *hurt;* 369.14 *suck;* 371.11 *void*
evisceration 369.4 *sucking*
evocation 344.1 *cause;* 34.15 *developmental biology;* 369.5 *drawing out;* 462.1 *memory;* 717.1 *representation;* 11.5 *spell*
evocative 721.11 *descriptive;* 369.18 *extractive;* 694.6 *meaningful;* 462.7 *memorable;* 717.13 *representational*
evocatively 369.22 *expressively*
evocative psychotherapy 36.3 *psychiatric treatment*
evoke 344.10 *awaken;* 115.10 *be similar;* 11.22 *conjure;* 369.15 *draw out;* 483.9 *motivate;* 721.15 *recount;* 717.9 *represent*
evolute 27.40 *curve*
evolution 34.16; 760.2; 340.1 *action;* 210.1 *calculation;* 93.8 *creation;* 340.2 *deed;* 302.14 *development;* 34.1 *life science;* 300.3 *motion towards;* 554.8 *theories of life*
evolutionary 34.27; 34.20 *biological*
evolutionist 34.19 *life scientist*
evolve 300.13 *be in motion;* 760.8 *be transformed;* 209.6 *change gradually;* 93.18 *come to be;* 302.5 *develop;* 345.7 *follow from;* 244.2 *get better;* 356.10 *produce;* 403.15 *shape;* 756.10 *show potential*
evolved 345.10 *caused;* 93.15 *created*
evolve into 760.7 *convert into*
evolving 760.14 *converting;* 760.2 *evolution*
evolving from 345.10 *caused*
evulse 369.11 *extract*
evulsion 369.1 *extraction*
ewe 568.14 *female animal;* 71.18 *female mammal;* 43.8 *livestock*
ewe-lamb 568.14 *female animal*
ewer 24.8 *ceramic object;* 410.11 *vessel;* 433.16 *water carrier*
ex 284.20 *former;* 129.11 *prior*
exacerbate 607.6 *aggravate;* 594.16 *cause hate;* 727.7 *exaggerate;* 213.5 *make bigger;* 626.12 *make irritable;* 380.9 *make violent;* 245.3 *make worse*
exacerbated 607.4 *aggravated;* 245.12 *deteriorated;* 727.12 *exaggerated*
exacerbation 607.1 *aggravation;* 727.1 *exaggeration;* 245.10 *impairment;* 213.1 *increase*
exact 273.5, 698.21 *accurate;* 665.9 *careful;* 790.12 *charge;* 725.3 *clear;* 269.3 *concise;* 801.8 *correct;* 397.10, 710.7 *demand;* 222.10 *detailed;* 369.16 *extort;* 386.7 *force;* 656.6 *formal;* 115.9 *lifelike;* 230.1 *perfect;* 647.8 *severe*
exacta 59.7 *horseracing*
exact amount 217.7 *sufficiency*
exact a penalty 814.2 *penalize*
exact compensation 385.3 *retaliate*
exact image 717.6 *image*
exacting 369.20; 135.6 *demanding;* 264.10 *difficult;* 261.4 *fatiguing;* 230.2 *perfectionist;* 264.12 *problematic;* 647.8 *severe*
exactingly 369.21 *away;* 647.11 *severely*
exaction 710.2 *demand;* 369.6 *extorsion;* 790.8 *levy*
exaction of penalty 814.8 *penalty*
exactitude 273.1, 698.8 *accuracy;* 665.4 *fastidiousness*
exactive 369.20 *exacting*
exact likeness 717.1 *representation*
exact location 142.2
exactly 273.8, 698.39 *accurately;* 725.4 *clearly;* 115.14 *comparably;* 269.5 *concisely;* 324.9 *directly;* 222.19 *meticulously;* 230.7 *perfectly;* 139.28 *specially*
exactly enough 217.9 *enough*
exactness 273.1, 698.8 *accuracy;* 665.1 *carefulness;* 725.1 *clarity;* 269.1 *conciseness;* 230.3 *perfection*
exact picture 717.6 *image*
exact retribution 814.2 *penalize*
exact revenge 651.19 *be pitiless*
exact science 28.1 *physics*
exact time 275.7 *time measurement*
exaggerate 329.4; 727.7; 607.6 *aggravate;* 219.4 *be excessive;* 234.12 *distort the truth;* 477.15 *fantasize;* 477.14 *imagine;* 213.5 *make bigger;* 123.8 *make important;* 720.1 *misinterpret;* 718.4 *misrepresent;* 467.4 *overestimate*
exaggerated 234.8; 329.13; 727.12; 707.15 *emphasized;* 219.6 *excessive;* 699.36 *falsified;* 477.10 *imaginative;* 231.2 *incomplete;* 720.3 *misinterpreted;* 718.6 *misrepresented;* 542.10 *ornate;* 467.6 *overestimated;* 699.34 *pretending;* 681.2 *unrestrained*
exaggerated lengths 727.1 *exaggeration*
exaggeratedly 727.16; 720.5 *misrepresentedly*
exaggerating 727.1 *exaggeration*
Exaggeration 727
exaggeration 727.1; 542.2 *affectation;* 607.1 *aggravation;* 234.4 *distortion of the truth;* 219.1 *excess;* 329.9 *excessiveness;* 477.4 *ideality;* 213.1 *increase;* 720.2 *misinterpretation;* 718.1 *misrepresentation;* 467.1 *overestimation;* 699.7 *pretence;* 740.8 *public relations;* 681.5 *unrestrainedness*
exaggerator 727.6; 467.3 *optimist*
exalt 8.17 *deify;* 213.5 *make bigger;* 123.8 *make important;* 10.19 *offer worship;* 667.17, 669.14 *praise;* 366.3 *promote;* 154.17 *raise;* 9.7 *worship*
exaltation 72.13 *assemblage of birds;* 8.9 *deification;* 597.1 *happiness;* 154.1 *height;* 213.1 *increase;* 366.7 *lift;* 669.3 *praise;* 10.3 *rite of worship;* 9.1 *worship*
exalted 154.11; 366.12; 8.15 *deified;* 185.6 *eminent;* 123.6 *notable*
exaltedly 185.11 *eminently*
exaltedness 185.1 *prominence*
exalting 575.1 *right*
examination 471.2 *close attention;* 722.1 *dissertation;* 448.3 *experimentation;* 734.6 *interview;* 16.7 *legal trial;* 518.3 *observation;* 4.4 *philosophical investigation;* 705.3 *questionnaire*
examinational 705.13 *problematic*
examination paper 6.14 *school book*
examinations 136.3 *qualifications*
examine 464.12 *estimate;* 448.11 *experiment;* 518.14 *inspect;* 705.18 *interrogate;* 4.20 *philosophize;* 35.19 *practise medicine;* 705.17 *question;* 471.11 *take note of;* 16.71 *try a case*
examined 705.16 *questioned*
examinee 705.10 *person questioned*
examiner 471.6 *attentive person;* 734.7 *conversationalist;* 644.3 *curious person;* 464.5 *judge;* 705.9 *questioner*
examiner of accounts 789.6 *accountant*
examine the accounts 789.8 *audit*
examining 705.12 *questioning*
example 631.1 *conduct;* 703.3 *explanation;* 446.6 *ideal;* 719.1 *interpretation;* 205.2 *particular;* 129.4, 140.5 *precedent;* 713.3 *precept;* 160.2 *prototype;* 814.7 *punishment;* 717.8 *representative;* 738.7 *showpiece;* 711.1 *warning*
exam success 246.3 *successful thing*
exanimate 582.19 *dead*
exasperate 607.8 *annoy;* 264.22 *cause trouble;* 261.6 *fatigue;* 380.9 *make violent;* 624.9 *offend*
exasperated 624.15 *resentful*
exasperating 607.5 *aggravating;* 264.13 *inconvenient*
exasperatingly 624.17 *resentfully*
exasperation 607.2 *annoyance;* 624.1 *resentment*
ex cathedra 707.14 *assertive;* 396.23 *authoritatively;* 707.25 *explicitly*
excavate 284.16; 3.21 *antiquarianize;* 156.14 *deepen;* 369.13 *dig out;* 38.30 *engineer;* 308.20 *hole;* 183.9 *make concave;* 305.15 *tunnel*
excavated 308.14 *holed*
excavate the past 284.16 *excavate*
excavation 284.8; 183.2 *concave land;* 38.29 *construction equipment;* 156.1 *depth;* 449.7 *detection;* 369.3 *digging out;* 3.12 *historicism;* 308.5 *hole;* 305.7 *tunnelling*
excavation site 577.1 *workshop*
excavator 369.10; 38.29 *construction equipment;* 183.5 *digger;* 308.3 *person who opens;* 578.1 *worker*
exceed 329.3; 121.8 *be superior;* 213.4 *increase*
exceeding 121.12 *superior*
exceedingly 121.16 *superiorly*
exceeding the law 16.55 *illegal*
exceed one's authority 16.74 *be lawless*
exceed requirements 219.5 *be superfluous*
excel 139.25; 797.19 *be good at;* 485.10 *be skilful;* 121.8 *be superior;* 235.9 *be worthy;* 329.3 *exceed*
excellence 137.9 *distinction;* 797.8 *good;* 123.1 *importance;* 230.3 *perfection;* 485.1 *skill;* 121.1 *superiority;* 235.6, 803.3 *worth;* 622.8 *worthiness*
excellent 121.15; 400.13; 797.1 *good;* 123.6 *notable;* 230.1 *perfect;* 485.6 *skilful;* 619.8 *wonderful;* 235.1, 803.7 *worthy*
excellently 400.16 *masterfully;* 230.7 *perfectly;* 121.16 *superiorly;* 797.22 *well;* 235.11, 803.11 *worthily*
exceller 235.8; 485.3 *masterpiece;* 485.4 *skilled person*
excelsior 304.26 *up*
excelsior figure 304.11 *ascender*
except 212.8 *by subtraction;* 128.7, 470.3 *exclude;* 128.12 *exclusively;* 758.9 *exempt;* 215.8 *leave;* 372.10 *set apart;* 250.15 *set free;* 212.3 *subtract;* 222.15 *under the circumstances*
excepted 128.11 *excluded;* 758.5 *exempt;* 250.9 *free;* 212.5 *subtracted;* 372.17 *unjoined*
except for 128.12 *exclusively*
excepting 212.8 *by subtraction;* 128.12 *exclusively*
exception 139.6; 118.6 *deviation;* 670.4 *disagreement;* 114.1 *diversity;* 128.1 *exclusion;* 758.1 *exemption;* 250.1 *freedom;* 470.5 *rejection;* 372.2 *setting apart;* 212.1 *subtraction*
exceptional 139.17; 114.5 *diverse;* 118.14 *eccentric;* 105.2 *questionable;* 299.5 *unusual;* 619.8 *wonderful*
exceptionality 118.4 *unusualness*
exceptionally 139.30 *characteristically;* 114.10 *diversely;* 105.10 *rarely;* 299.9 *unusually*
exceptionalness 299.2 *unusualness*
exceptional person 619.5 *person of wonder*
exception to the rule 114.1 *diversity;* 139.6 *exception*
excerpt 723.9 *compile;* 469.4 *pick*
excerpts 469.9 *chosen thing;* 723.3 *compendium*
Excess 219
excess 219.1; 215.3 *difference;* 270.1 *diffuseness;* 329.9 *excessiveness;* 213.1 *increase;* 250.6 *liberality;* 342.9 *overactivity;* 686.3 *overindulgence;* 217.8 *plenty;* 219.7 *superfluous;* 215.4, 215.10 *surplus;* 250.12 *unconditional;* 380.1 *violence*
excessive 219.6; 329.12; 792.7 *dear;* 270.3 *diffuse;* 727.12 *exaggerated;* 727.14 *extravagant;* 686.8 *overindulgent;* 215.10 *surplus;* 250.12 *unconditional;* 681.2 *unrestrained;* 238.1 *useless;* 380.6 *violent*
excessive bureaucracy 219.2 *overdoing it*
excessive charge 790.3 *fee;* 792.2 *unfair price*
excessive consumption 557.2 *appetite*
excessive drinking 690.11 *drinking*
excessive frankness 659.1 *discourtesy*
excessive interest 784.4 *interest*
excessive loyalty 727.4 *bombast*
excessively 219.8; 250.21; 329.16; 727.17; 792.12 *dearly;* 681.9 *extravagantly;* 215.11 *residually;* 686.12 *self-indulgently*
excessiveness 329.9; 727.1 *exaggeration;* 219.1 *excess;* 727.3 *extravagance;* 686.3 *overindulgence*
excessive praise 677.1 *flattery*
excessive speed 332.8 *speed*
excessive zeal 636.7 *eagerness*
excess of freedom 250.6 *liberality*
excess profit 13.7 *corporation*
excess profits tax 790.7 *tax*
Exchange 759
exchange 224.4; 224.10; 759.1; 759.5; 780.26 *bank;* 119.3 *equalization;* 780.7 *finance;* 762.6 *give a substitute;* 110.1 *interchange;* 779.1 *market;* 746.1 *negotiation;* 692.12 *public telephone system;* 706.3 *question and answer;* 706.19 *react;* 110.7 *reciprocate;* 778.1 *sell;* 778.3 *selling;* 14.2 *stock exchange;* 762.1 *substitution;* 762.5 *take a substitute;* 776.1, 776.4 *trade;* 316.1, 316.11 *transfer*
exchangeable 224.14; 759.6 *in exchange;* 776.13 *mercantile;* 746.8 *negotiated;* 110.4 *reciprocal;* 316.17 *transferable*
exchangeably 706.24 *in answer;* 316.18 *in transit*
exchange control 780.7 *finance*
exchanged 759.7; 110.4 *reciprocal;* 762.8 *substituted*
exchanged vow 755.1 *contract*
exchange for 759.5 *exchange;* 762.5 *take a substitute*
exchange force 28.79 *fundamental interaction*
exchange gifts 224.10 *exchange*
exchange goods 224.10 *exchange*
exchange ideas 4.23 *discuss philosophically*
exchange letters 692.31 *correspond*
exchange meaningful looks 730.14 *have difficulty speaking*
exchange of blows 331.12 *collision*
exchange of gases 434.8 *respiration*
exchange of gifts 224.4 *exchange*
exchange of goods 224.4 *exchange;* 776.4 *trade*
exchange of views 734.4 *conference;* 713.2 *consultation;* 746.3 *discussion*
exchange of vows 756.1 *promise*
exchange opinions 444.13 *debate;* 701.14 *discuss*
exchange pleasantries 734.9 *converse*
exchange premium 14.1 *finance*
exchanger 227.4 *editor*
exchange rate 13.6 *economic factors;* 14.1, 780.7 *finance*
Exchange Rate Mechanism 14.1 *finance;* 13.5 *international trade*
exchange rate parity 780.7 *finance*
exchange signals 742.12 *signal*
exchange student 759.4 *person who exchanges*
exchange value 119.3 *equalization;* 790.2 *value*
exchange views 734.11 *confer*
exchange vows 756.7 *promise*
exchange words 734.9 *converse*
exchanging 776.13 *mercantile*
exchanging favours 747.3 *mutual relationship*
exchequer 780.6 *funds;* 439.4 *storage;* 780.19 *treasury*
excipient 37.5 *prescription*
excise 369.13 *dig out;* 790.8 *levy;* 35.20 *practise surgery;* 212.4 *take off*
excise duty 13.6 *economic factors*
exciseman 769.7 *collector*
excise officer 769.7 *collector*
excision 369.3 *digging out;* 212.1 *subtraction;* 35.9 *surgery*
excitability 590.7 *emotionalism;* 615.1 *rashness;* 342.7 *restlessness*
excitable 342.18 *active;* 590.13 *passionate*
excitant 691.6 *drug*
excitation 342.1 *activity;* 690.10 *drunkenness;* 28.67 *excited atom*
excitation energy 28.67 *excited atom*
excite 327.22 *agitate;* 488.13 *arouse sensation;* 344.10 *awaken;* 690.9 *be intoxicating;* 593.25 *be loved;* 496.13 *be piquant;* 617.15 *cause desire;* 490.9 *give pleasure;* 338.3 *invigorate;* 483.9 *motivate*
excited 593.20 *amorous;* 474.5 *expecting;* 490.7 *pleased;* 327.16 *restless;* 488.7 *susceptible*
excited atom 28.67
excitedly 727.16 *exaggeratedly;* 593.30 *lovingly*
excited state 28.67 *excited atom*
excite expectations 475.11 *predict*
excite hate 596.7 *cause dislike;* 594.16 *cause hate*
excite love 619.10 *be wonderful*
excitement 727.1 *exaggeration;* 488.1 *sensation;* 327.2 *tumult;* 338.1 *vigour*
excite pity 627.11
excite the attention of 471.13 *attract attention*

exciting 488.9; 721.11 *descriptive*; 690.6 *intoxicating*; 338.5 *invigorating*; 480.19 *persuasive*; 496.10 *stimulating*
excitingly 488.14 *sensationally*
exclaim 514.14 *hiss*; 729.11 *speak*; 729.12 *speak loudly*
exclamation 514.7 *cry of disapproval*; 619.2 *sign of wonderment*; 729.7 *utterance*
exclamation mark 742.7 *punctuation*; 619.2 *sign of wonderment*
exclamatory 514.19 *hissing*
exclave 86.5 *state*
exclude 128.7; **470.3**; 233.5 *be incomplete*; 758.9 *exempt*; 655.13 *ignore*; 215.8 *leave*; 166.7 *limit*; 103.8 *make impossible*; 371.4 *ostracize*; 251.8 *restrain*; 372.10 *set apart*; 255.11 *simplify*; 212.3 *subtract*; 399.3 *veto*; 670.15 *withhold approval*
excluded 128.11; 670.31 *disapproved*; 758.5 *exempt*; 98.12 *missing*; 709.8 *refused*; 470.10 *rejected*; 212.5 *subtracted*; 372.17 *unjoined*
excluded person 128.5
excluding 128.10; 212.8 *by subtraction*; 128.12 *exclusively*
Exclusion 128
exclusion 128.1; 371.18 *dismissal*; 758.1 *exemption*; 166.1 *limitation*; 371.19 *ostracism*; 470.5 *rejection*; 655.3 *separation*; 372.2 *setting apart*; 212.1 *subtraction*; 399.1 *veto*
exclusionary 128.10 *excluding*
exclusion order 128.1 *exclusion*
exclusion zone 128.3; 86.3 *regional boundary*
exclusive 128.10 *excluding*; 166.5 *limited*; 741.9 *news story*; 763.9 *possessed*; 763.8 *possessing*; 741.3 *reporting*; 251.13 *restraining*; 655.8 *unsociable*; 792.8 *valuable*; 399.5 *vetoed*; 235.1 *worthy*
exclusively 128.12; 399.7 *by veto*; 197.24 *once*; 763.10 *possessively*; 251.16 *under restraints*; 655.14 *unsocially*; 792.13 *valuably*
exclusiveness 128.4
exclusive of 212.8 *by subtraction*; 128.12 *exclusively*
exclusive possession 763.1 *possession*
exclusive rights 251.1 *restraint*
exclusive sale 778.3 *selling*
exclusivity 128.4 *exclusiveness*; 251.1 *restraint*; 655.1 *unsociability*
exclusory 128.10 *excluding*
excogitate 477.14 *imagine*; 4.20 *philosophize*
excogitation 4.4 *philosophical investigation*
excommunicate 16.79 *convict*; 371.3 *disbar*; 128.8 *eject*; 10.18 *perform rites*; 399.3 *veto*; 712.7 *wish ill*
excommunicated 712.10 *maledictive*; 10.21 *ritualistic*; 399.5 *vetoed*
excommunication 10.5 *Christian rite*; 371.18 *dismissal*; 128.2 *ejection*; 712.4 *malediction*; 399.1 *veto*
ex-con 250.7 *free person*
ex-convict 250.7 *free person*
excoriate 552.16 *peel*
excoriation 552.6 *peeling*
excrement 560.4; 431.3 *body fluid*; 258.4 *dirt*; 215.2 *residue*; 503.2 *something that makes an unpleasant smell*
excremental 560.25 *faecal*; 258.8 *unclean*
excrementary 560.25 *faecal*
excrementitious 258.8 *unclean*
excrescence 182.1 *convexity*; 219.3 *superfluity*
excrescent 182.4 *convex*
excrescently 182.6 *convexly*
excreta 560.4 *excrement*
excrete 560.15; 315.12 *leak*; 371.14 *let out*; 559.7 *secrete*
Excretion 560
excretion 560.1; 256.2 *cleaning*; 371.22 *disgorgement*; 767.1 *disposal*; 315.2 *outflow*; 34.5 *physiology*; 559.1 *secretion*; 258.2 *uncleanness*
excretionary 560.24 *excretory*
excretive 560.24 *excretory*
excretory 560.24; 315.17 *leaky*; 34.22 *physiological*; 559.4 *secretory*
excruciate 491.11 *inflict pain*
excruciating 491.5 *painful*
excruciatingly 491.13 *painfully*
exculpate 649.10 *absolve*; 16.78, 758.10 *acquit*; 805.9 *declare innocent*; 714.7 *vindicate*
exculpated 16.63 *acquitted*; 805.6 *declared innocent*; 649.6 *forgiven*
exculpating 714.11 *vindicatory*
exculpation 649.3 *absolution*; 16.42 *acquittal*; 805.2 *legal innocence*; 714.1 *vindication*
exculpatory 714.11 *vindicatory*
excurse 325.3 *go astray*
excursion 793.9 *cheap*; 306.2 *circuitousness*; 270.2 *circumlocution*; 329.7 *crossing*; 325.13 *deviation*
excursion fare 793.4 *bargain*
excursive 270.4 *circumlocutory*
excursus 270.2 *circumlocution*; 325.16 *wandering*
excusable 649.7 *forgivable*; 801.9 *in the right*; 714.13 *vindicable*
excusatory 714.11 *vindicatory*
excuse 758.10 *acquit*; 758.2 *acquittal*; 807.2 *apology*; 714.2 *defence*; 390.1 *deliver*; 390.2 *deliverance*; 128.7 *exclude*; 444.4 *explanation*; 649.9 *forgive*; 649.1 *forgiveness*; 483.1 *motive*; 701.5 *plea*; 444.14 *premise*; 344.5 *reason*; 250.15 *set free*; 645.2 *stratagem*; 714.7 *vindicate*
excused 758.6 *acquitted*; 444.10 *causal*; 128.11 *excluded*; 649.6 *forgiven*
excuse-me dance 22.2 *dance*
excuse oneself 758.12 *exempt oneself*
excuser 714.5 *vindicator*
excusing 384.29 *defending*; 649.4 *forgiving*; 714.11 *vindicatory*
excusing the liberty 667.23 *saving your grace*
exec 400.7 *military leader*; 396.10 *person of authority*
execrable 236.3 *bad*; 236.6 *damnable*; 594.12 *hated*
execrableness 236.9 *badness*
execrate 594.14 *hate*; 712.6 *vilify*; 670.22 *vituperate*
execration 670.8 *berating*; 594.1 *hate*; 712.3 *vilification*
execrative 594.10 *hating*; 712.10 *maledictive*
execratively 712.14 *damningly*; 594.18 *hatefully*
execratory 670.27 *critical*
executant 340.3 *doer*; 578.1 *worker*
execute 382.19; **814.5**; 340.4 *act*; 631.14 *behave towards*; 633.14 *carry on*; 232.4 *complete*; 230.5 *perfect*; 356.10 *produce*; 647.6 *suppress*; 346.9 *take action*; 354.1 *undertake*
execute a contract 755.5 *contract*
execute a gymnastic movement 57.10 *compete in gymnastics*
execute a sentence 814.2 *penalize*
execute a will 768.5 *give*
executed 814.20 *punished*; 647.9 *suppressed*; 354.5 *undertaken*
execute justice 814.2 *penalize*
execution 382.5; 340.1 *action*; 814.13 *capital punishment*; 582.4 *death sentence*; 67.6 *diving*; 57.1 *gymnastics*; 382.1 *killing*; 16.7 *legal trial*; 346.1 *operation*; 356.1 *production*; 633.1 *pursuit*; 485.1 *skill*; 647.2 *suppression*
execution chamber 16.43 *conviction*
executioner 382.12; 357.6 *destroyer*; 382.10 *killer*; 814.17 *punisher*; 380.4 *violent creature*
execution of judgment 16.7 *legal trial*; 464.2 *verdict*
execution of justice 814.8 *penalty*
execution of sentence 814.8 *penalty*
executive 578.3 *agent*; 400.5 *company leader*; 340.3 *doer*; 340.6 *effective*; 15.6 *employer*; 579.6 *governing body*; 12.1 *government*; 12.9 *governmental*; 16.48 *jurisdictional*; 579.15 *manager*; 579.17 *managerial*; 400.12 *masterful*; 346.5 *operator*; 396.10 *person of authority*; 121.5 *superior*; 578.1 *worker*
executive assistant 398.4 *deputy*; 401.5 *office assistant*; 578.1 *worker*
executively 16.86 *jurisdictionally*; 400.16 *masterfully*
executive office 577.1 *workshop*
executive officer 400.7 *military leader*; 396.10 *person of authority*
executor 578.3 *agent*; 340.3 *doer*; 579.15 *manager*
executrix 578.3 *agent*
exegesis 719.2 *annotation*; 722.1 *dissertation*; 703.3 *explanation*; 719.1 *interpretation*; 5.12 *translation*
exegete 722.3 *dissertator*; 719.6 *interpreter*; 5.2 *linguist*
exegetic 703.11 *explanatory*; 719.14 *interpretive*
exegetical 722.5 *expository*; 719.14 *interpretive*; 5.40 *translated*
exegetically 703.22 *demonstrably*; 719.18 *in other words*; 5.48 *linguistically*
exegetics 719.5 *science of interpretation*; 5.12 *translation*
exegetist 703.7 *demonstrator*; 719.6 *interpreter*
exemplar 446.6 *ideal*; 717.1 *representation*
exemplary 446.13 *ideal*; 719.14 *interpretive*; 230.1 *perfect*; 160.10 *prototypical*; 717.13 *representational*; 711.8 *warning*; 235.1, 803.7 *worthy*
exemplification 703.3 *explanation*; 719.1 *interpretation*
exemplificatory 703.11 *explanatory*
exemplified 703.11 *explanatory*
exemplify 446.19 *epitomize*; 703.16 *explain*; 719.8 *interpret*; 4.21 *rationalize*; 717.12 *stand for*
exemplifying 703.11 *explanatory*
exempt 758.5; **758.9**; 16.78 *acquit*; 16.63 *acquitted*; 390.1 *deliver*; 389.8 *escaping*; 128.7, 470.3 *exclude*; 128.11 *excluded*; 649.9 *forgive*; 250.9 *free*; 391.4 *liberate*; 750.29, 757.3 *permit*; 750.18 *permitting*; 250.15 *set free*; 372.17 *unjoined*
exempted 16.63 *acquitted*; 128.11 *excluded*; 758.5 *exempt*; 391.7 *liberated*; 750.18 *permitting*
exemptibility 391.1 *liberation*
exemptible 391.7 *liberated*; 714.13 *vindicable*
Exemption 758
exemption 758.1; 16.42 *acquittal*; 390.2 *deliverance*; 767.1 *disposal*; 389.1 *escape*; 128.1 *exclusion*; 649.1 *forgiveness*; 250.1 *freedom*; 391.1 *liberation*; 757.1 *permission*; 750.8 *permit*; 470.5 *rejection*; 372.2 *setting apart*
exemptive 128.10 *excluding*
exempt oneself 758.12
exequies 583.2 *funeral*
exercise 576.5; **576.9**; 340.4 *act*; 300.11 *bodily movement*; 243.6 *brief*; 243.12 *briefing*; 57.10 *compete in gymnastics*; 340.2 *deed*; 257.1 *hygiene*; 346.1 *operation*; 244.9 *physical improvement*; 243.8 *prepare oneself*; 576.2 *task*; 354.2 *undertaking*; 349.1, 349.6 *use*; 353.6 *venture*
exercise a pull 363.11 *attract*
exercise book 6.14 *school book*
exercised 349.9 *used*
exercised in arms 585.17 *military*
exercise discretion 485.10 *be skilful*
exercise influence 395.8 *influence*
exercise judgment 16.76 *judge*
exercise one's discretion 469.1 *select*
exercise one's intellect 443.12 *think*
exercise power 334.10 *be powerful*; 396.18 *have authority*
exercise self-control 684.5 *be self-restrained*
exercising 576.10 *working*
exercising choice 469.16 *selecting*
exert authority 647.5 *be severe*; 12.11 *govern*
exert energy 334.10 *be powerful*
exert influence 334.10 *be powerful*; 395.8 *influence*
exertion 576.4; 340.1 *action*; 640.2 *commitment*; 261.7 *fatigue*; 334.1 *power*; 338.1 *vigour*
exert no authority 588.5 *misgovern*
exert oneself 576.8; 338.2 *be full of vigour*; 342.15 *try*; 353.2 *try hard*
exert pressure 483.10 *manipulate*
exert sovereignty 85.18
exert weight 414.12 *be heavy*
exes 765.5 *profit*
exfiltrate 315.12 *leak*
exfiltration 315.3 *leakage*
exfoliate 552.16 *peel*; 411.11 *scale*
exfoliation 411.6 *layering*; 552.6 *peeling*
exfoliatory 552.12 *peeling*
ex gratia payment 768.2 *gift*; 785.3 *pay*
exhalation 432.2; 524.2 *murk*; 500.1 *odour*; 434.8 *respiration*; 503.1 *stench*; 432.10 *vaporization*
exhale 432.27 *give off*; 500.8 *have odour*; 315.12 *leak*; 371.14 *let out*; 434.21 *respire*
exhaling 434.19 *respiratory*
exhaust 226.8 *cause to cease*; 787.2 *consume*; 261.6 *fatigue*; 245.5 *hurt*; 371.14 *let out*; 218.7 *make insufficient*; 417.6 *make sparse*; 238.8 *make useless*; 315.2 *outflow*; 335.7 *remove power from*; 349.1 *use*; 371.11 *void*; 441.1, 681.7 *waste*
exhausted 245.12 *deteriorated*; 245.13 *dilapidated*; 261.1 *fatigued*; 335.12 *impotent*; 284.18 *over*; 260.21 *unhealthy*; 349.9, 787.13 *used*; 337.11 *weakened*
exhaust fan 501.2 *deodorant*
exhaust fumes 503.2 *something that makes an unpleasant smell*
exhausting 264.10 *difficult*; 261.4 *fatiguing*; 576.11 *laborious*; 814.21 *punishing*
exhaustingly 261.9 *tiringly*
exhausting work 576.1 *work*
exhaustion 214.1 *decrease*; 335.4 *disability*; 261.7 *fatigue*; 245.11 *hurt*; 766.4 *lessening*; 337.3 *poor health*; 371.21 *removal*; 349.6 *use*; 441.3 *waste*
exhaustion of supplies 245.7 *deterioration*
exhaustive 232.7 *complete*
exhaustively 156.17 *profoundly*
exhaust the possibilities of 349.3 *exploit*
exhibit 439.5 *collection*; 703.15 *demonstrate*; 738.1 *display*; 738.2 *display something*; 743.10 *identify*; 716.5 *legal evidence*; 518.18, 520.10 *make visible*; 525.14 *present*; 4.22 *propound a philosophy*; 738.7 *showpiece*; 520.6 *visible thing*
exhibited 703.9 *demonstrated*; 738.13 *displayed*
exhibition 376.31; 676.1 *affectedness*; 525.2 *being in view*; 439.5 *collection*; 703.1 *demonstration*; 738.6 *display*; 779.2 *fair*; 813.3 *grant*; 520.5 *manifestation*; 740.8 *public relations*; 21.13 *theatrical performance*; 518.7 *view*
exhibitional 703.9 *demonstrated*
exhibition centre 738.8 *showplace*
exhibitioner 769.5 *recipient*
exhibition game 46.1 *football*
exhibition hall 738.8 *showplace*
exhibitionism 673.6 *boastfulness*; 703.2 *demonstrativeness*; 552.1 *undress*
exhibitionist 703.10 *demonstrative*; 703.7 *demonstrator*; 738.12 *displayer*; 552.8 *nude person*; 452.11 *opinionist*; 676.2 *pretender*; 673.7 *vain person*
exhibitionistic 673.13 *boastful*; 703.10 *demonstrative*
exhibitor 738.12 *displayer*; 21.27 *producer*
exhilarate 690.9 *be intoxicating*; 598.6 *bring cheer*; 446.16 *inspire*; 338.3 *invigorate*; 581.1 *refresh*
exhilarated 598.1 *cheerful*; 690.1 *drunk*; 581.4 *refreshed*
exhilarating 690.6 *intoxicating*; 338.5 *invigorating*; 581.3 *refreshing*
exhilaratingly 581.8 *refreshingly*
exhilaration 598.3 *cheerfulness*; 690.10 *drunkenness*; 597.1 *happiness*; 581.5 *refreshment*; 338.1 *vigour*
exhort 713.5 *advise*; 613.17 *give courage*; 483.9 *motivate*
exhortation 480.4; 613.6 *encouragement*; 733.2 *salutation*; 729.8 *speech*
exhorted 483.12 *motivated*
exhumation 369.3 *digging out*; 3.12 *historicism*; 583.7 *inquest*
exhume 583.9; 3.21 *antiquarianize*; 369.13 *dig out*; 284.16 *excavate*
exhusband 567.5 *single man*
ex hypothesi 476.10 *supposedly*; 4.25 *theoretically*
exigency 264.6 *critical situation*; 222.4 *difficult circumstances*; 280.1 *immediacy*; 135.3 *needfulness*
exigent 280.6 *allowing no delay*; 135.6 *demanding*; 222.8 *difficult*
exigently 369.21 *away*; 222.17 *difficultly*
exiguity 206.3 *fewness*; 151.7 *fineness*; 159.1 *littleness*
exiguous 151.2 *fine*; 159.7 *little*; 206.6 *sparse*
exiguously 206.11 *sparsely*
exile 144.7 *displaced person*; 128.8 *eject*; 128.2 *ejection*; 315.13 *emigrate*; 315.4 *emigration*; 128.5 *excluded person*; 655.13 *ignore*; 100.7 *new arrival*; 371.19 *ostracism*;

371.4 *ostracize*; 315.8 *outgoer*; 655.7 *outsider*; 814.1 *punish*; 814.7 *punishment*; 144.16 *replace*; 655.3 *separation*
exiled 128.11 *excluded*; 655.10 *lonely*; 144.10 *replaced*
exilement 371.19 *ostracism*
exist 93.17; 77.22 *be dormant*; 402.8 *be material*; 97.11, 282.5 *be present*; 95.10 *be real*; 554.16 *live*
Existence 93
existence 93.1; 282.3 *actuality*; 525.2 *being in view*; 554.1 *life*; 554.10 *lifestyle*; 402.1 *material world*; 97.1 *presence*; 698.2 *reality*
existence of god 4.9 *philosophical problem*
existent 554.12 *alive*; 93.10 *existing*; 97.7, 282.6 *present*
existentialism 93.1 *existence*; 4.7 *school of thought*
existentialist 4.11 *follower of a doctrine*; 4.14 *of a philosophy*
existentially 93.22 *really*
existential psychology 36.1 *psychology*
existential quantifier 27.63 *mathematical logic*
existential theology 7.13 *theology*
existential therapy 36.3 *psychiatric treatment*
existing 93.10; **698.16**; 554.1 *life*; 97.7, 282.6 *present*; 95.6 *real*
existing conditions 222.1 *circumstances*
existing together 285.1 *same time*
exist outside 100.16 *be external*
exist simultaneously 285.6 *be simultaneous*
exist together 285.6 *be simultaneous*
Exit 315
exit 315.1; **315.9**; 98.16 *absent oneself*; 21.34 *act*; 21.22 *acting*; 300.4 *backward motion*; 317.11 *channel*; 736.11 *conceal oneself*; 131.3, 582.1 *death*; 313.7 *departure*; 526.4 *disappearance*; 389.2 *means of escape*; 308.7 *passageway*; 373.5 *road*; 315.6 *way out*; 313.2 *withdraw*
ex-libris 743.3 *means of identification*
exobiology 29.1 *astronomy*; 34.1 *life science*
exocarp 80.3 *fruit structure*
Exocet™ 330.8 *missile*; 587.5 *missile weapon*
exocrine 559.5 *of a secretion*
exocrine gland 559.3 *gland*
exode 21.8 *scene*
exodontic 35.23 *dental*
exodontics 35.4 *dentistry*
exodontist 35.14 *dentist*
exodus 313.7 *departure*; 315.1 *exit*; 21.8 *scene*
ex officio 396.12 *authoritative*; 579.19 *managerially*
exogamy 570.3 *types of marriage*
exon 34.13 *genetic material*
exonerate 649.10 *absolve*; 16.78, 758.10 *acquit*; 805.9 *declare innocent*; 714.7 *vindicate*
exonerated 16.63, 758.6 *acquitted*; 805.6 *declared innocent*; 649.6 *forgiven*
exonerating 649.4 *forgiving*; 714.11 *vindicatory*
exoneration 649.3 *absolution*; 16.42, 758.2 *acquittal*; 805.2 *legal innocence*; 714.1 *vindication*
exonerative 714.11 *vindicatory*
exorbitance 727.1 *exaggeration*; 219.1 *excess*; 727.3 *extravagance*; 792.2 *unfair price*
exorbitant 681.3 *costly*; 792.7 *dear*; 325.20 *deviant*; 727.12 *exaggerated*; 219.6, 329.12 *excessive*; 727.14 *extravagant*
exorbitantly 792.12 *dearly*; 727.17 *excessively*
exorbitant price 792.2 *unfair price*
exorbitation 325.13 *deviation*
exorcise 371.10 *exterminate*; 10.18 *perform rites*
exorcised 10.21 *ritualistic*
exorcism 10.5 *Christian rite*
exorcist 11.12 *occultist*
exorcizer 11.12 *occultist*
exordium 130.10 *introduction*
exoskeletal 171.6 *exterior*
exoskeleton 171.1 *exterior*; 403.7 *skeleton*
exosmosis 370.5 *absorption*
exosmotic 370.17 *absorbent*
exosphere 31.8 *atmosphere*; 434.3 *atmospheric layers*; 154.8 *high thing*; 174.1 *summit*
exoteric 695.2 *simple*
exotic 145.8 *distant*; 118.14 *eccentric*; 139.17 *exceptional*; 171.10 *extraneous*; 100.10 *foreign*; 44.19 *ornamental*; 77.2 *plant*; 109.6 *unrelated*; 77.15 *wild*; 619.8 *wonderful*
exotically 100.18 *extraneously*; 77.24 *herbaceously*; 44.20 *horticulturally*; 109.12 *irrelevantly*
exotic dancer 21.30 *dancer*; 552.8 *nude person*
exoticness 100.2 *foreignness*
exotropia 519.2 *poor sight*
expand 211.6 *add*; 765.10 *augment*; 190.6 *become bigger*; 270.5 *be diffuse*; 422.8 *be elastic*; 138.24, 150.11 *broaden*; 209.6 *change gradually*; 727.8 *enlarge*; 141.20 *extend*; 345.8 *grow*; 213.4 *increase*; 190.5, 213.5 *make bigger*; 417.6 *make sparse*; 27.92 *manipulate*
expandable 190.9 *enlargeable*
expanded 190.7 *bigger*; 270.3 *diffuse*; 727.13 *enlarged*; 213.7 *increased*; 417.2 *rarefied*
expanded palette 529.5 *paint*
expanded polystyrene 32.21 *polymer*
expander 190.4 *enlarger*
expanding 190.8, 345.11 *growing*; 213.6 *increasing*; 417.2 *rarefied*
expanding bullet 587.13 *ammunition*
expanding economy 248.1 *prosperity*
expanding universe 29.4 *cosmological model*
expanse 150.4 *breadth*; 141.3 *geographical space*; 158.1 *size*; 141.1 *space*
expansibility 190.2 *enlargeability*
expansible 190.9 *enlargeable*
expansile 190.9 *enlargeable*
Expansion 190
expansion 28.39; 765.2 *augmentation*; 270.1 *diffuseness*; 727.2 *enlargement*; 27.24 *evaluation*; 12.3 *governance*; 190.1, 345.3 *growth*; 213.1 *increase*; 417.4 *rarefaction*; 141.1 *space*
expansionary 190.9 *enlargeable*
expansion coefficient 28.39 *expansion*
expansionism 329.10; 585.5 *bellicosity*; 566.11 *nation*; 314.4 *right of entry*
expansionist 586.6 *militarist*
expansionistic 586.33 *combative*
expansive 765.18 *acquisitional*; 158.15 *big*; 150.1 *broad*; 703.10 *demonstrative*; 731.6 *effusive*; 190.9 *enlargeable*; 127.7 *including*; 417.2 *rarefied*; 141.13 *spacious*
expansively 703.21 *demonstratively*; 731.11 *effusively*; 765.20 *gainfully*; 190.10 *largely*; 141.15 *spaciously*; 417.7 *sparsely*
expansiveness 158.2 *bigness*; 150.4 *breadth*; 703.2 *demonstrativeness*; 141.4 *spaciousness*
expat 655.7 *outsider*
expatiate 270.5 *be diffuse*; 731.8 *talk too much*
expatiation 270.1 *diffuseness*
expatriate 128.8 *eject*; 315.13 *emigrate*; 100.7 *new arrival*; 371.4 *ostracize*; 315.8 *outgoer*; 655.7 *outsider*; 313.3 *quit*; 109.3 *unconnected person*
expatriation 128.2 *ejection*; 315.4 *emigration*; 371.19 *ostracism*
expect 283.10; **474.8**; 610.7 *aspire*; 575.7 *be entitled to*; 243.3 *be prepared*; 810.17 *impose a duty*; 482.7 *intend*; 484.12 *plan ahead*; 293.9 *prepare*; 104.10 *think likely*
expectance 474.1 *expectation*
expectancy 474.1 *expectation*; 283.4 *looking to the future*
expectant 474.6; **610.12**; 474.4 *expectant person*; 474.5 *expecting*; 561.16 *reproductive*
expectantly 474.12; 610.15 *hopefully*
expectant mother 474.4 *expectant person*
expectant person 474.4
Expectation 474
expectation 474.1; **610.2**; 450.3 *believing*; 575.2 *entitlement*; 283.4 *looking to the future*; 475.1 *prediction*; 293.5 *prematurity*; 104.1 *probability*
expectation neurosis 36.10 *neurosis*
expectations 474.2; 610.2 *expectation*
expectative 293.16 *premature*
expect better 604.4 *be disappointed*
expected 474.7; 283.13 *foreseen*; 476.9 *meant*; 104.6 *probable*
expectedly 474.13; 104.11 *probably*
expected soon 293.13 *imminent*
expected value 27.60 *parameter*
expecting 474.5; 474.6, 610.12 *expectant*; 561.16 *reproductive*
expecting a baby 561.16 *reproductive*
expecting a happy event 561.16 *reproductive*
expecting better 604.9 *disappointed*
expecting more 604.9 *disappointed*
expecting otherwise 604.9 *disappointed*
expect it of 810.17 *impose a duty*
expect more 604.4 *be disappointed*
expectorant 37.4 *drug type*; 394.6 *purgative*; 560.29 *salivating*; 37.17 *stimulating*
expectorate 560.15 *excrete*; 560.20 *salivate*
expectoration 560.1 *excretion*; 560.9 *saliva*
expect otherwise 604.4 *be disappointed*
expect the worst 474.8 *expect*
expect too much 218.7 *make insufficient*
expedience 239.3 *convenience*; 617.2 *desirability*
expediency 239.3 *convenience*; 237.5 *usefulness*
expedient 713.8 *advisable*; 392.34 *beneficial*; 239.5 *convenience*; 239.1 *convenient*; 617.8 *desirable*; 484.3 *expedient plan*; 750.16 *fitting*; 348.2 *instrument*; 352.1 *means*; 95.8 *practical*; 645.2 *stratagem*; 762.1 *substitution*; 237.1 *useful*
expediential 239.1 *convenient*
expediently 239.7 *conveniently*; 617.17 *desirably*; 750.38 *fittingly*
expedient plan 484.3
expedite 348.4 *be an instrument*; 293.7 *be early*; 332.4 *be swift*; 392.28 *further*; 262.1 *hasten*; 265.16 *make easy*; 316.12 *transport*
expedite one's end 239.6 *be convenient*
expediting 265.7 *easing*; 392.8 *furtherance*
expedition 293.1 *earliness*; 262.4 *haste*; 342.3 *nimbleness*; 332.8 *speed*; 585.8 *warfare*
expeditionary force 586.14 *armed forces*
expeditious 342.18 *active*; 293.12 *early*; 262.3 *hasty*; 332.1 *swift*
expeditiously 293.17 *early*; 332.14 *swiftly*
expeditiousness 262.4 *haste*; 332.8 *speed*
expel 371.1; 316.14 *bring back*; 526.3 *cause to disappear*; 371.3 *disbar*; 470.2 *discard*; 369.12 *displace*; 128.8, 330.25, 364.2 *eject*; 315.13 *emigrate*; 560.15 *excrete*; 655.13 *ignore*; 331.1 *impel*; 814.1 *punish*; 144.16 *replace*; 372.9 *separate*; 255.11 *simplify*; 212.3 *subtract*
expelled 128.11 *excluded*; 655.10 *lonely*; 144.10 *replaced*; 372.15 *separate*; 212.5 *subtracted*
expellee 371.27; 315.8 *outgoer*
expellent 371.29 *expulsive*
expeller 371.26 *ejector*
expend 787.1; 349.5 *dispose of*; 785.6 *pay*; 777.2 *shop*; 349.1 *use*; 441.1 *waste*
expendability 124.5 *unimportance*; 238.3 *uselessness*
expendable 124.1 *unimportant*; 238.1 *useless*
expended 787.12; 315.16 *outflowing*
expending 787.10; 785.15 *paying*
Expenditure 787
expenditure 787.4; 790.5 *cost*; 315.5 *export*; 766.2 *financial loss*; 785.1 *payment*; 777.8 *shopping*; 441.3 *waste*
expense 787.5; 766.2 *financial loss*; 441.3 *waste*
expense account 789.1 *accounts*; 787.5 *expense*; 768.2 *gift*; 765.5 *profit*; 813.4 *reward for service*
expenses 790.5 *cost*; 787.5 *expense*
expensive 681.3 *costly*; 792.7 *dear*; 781.3 *opulent*; 467.6 *overestimated*; 235.3 *valuable*
expensively 777.16, 792.12 *dearly*
expensiveness 792.1 *high price*
experience 590.15 *feel*; 590.1 *feeling*; 455.13 *get to know*; 3.14 *historicalness*; 455.3 *learning*; 556.3 *maturity*; 136.3 *qualifications*; 488.1 *sensation*; 488.11 *sense*; 485.1 *skill*; 495.9 *taste*; 495.2 *taste of life*; 458.1 *wisdom*
experienced 556.11 *adult*; 645.4 *cunning*; 400.13 *excellent*; 485.8 *expert*; 6.19, 455.8 *knowledgeable*; 243.18 *prepared*; 136.9 *qualified*
experienced hand 485.5 *expert*
experience growth 765.10 *augment*
experience psychic phenomena 11.24
experiences 3.6 *biography*
experiential 27.69 *theoretical*
Experiment 448
experiment 448.1; **448.11**; 449.9 *invention*; 243.10 *preparations*; 353.4 *test*; 353.6 *venture*
experimental 448.8; 616.4 *cautious*; 486.3 *clumsy*; 449.13 *discovering*; 487.2 *not customary*; 448.9 *original*; 705.15 *sceptical*; 353.9 *tentative*; 28.99 *theoretical*; 453.5 *uncertified*
experimental animal 70.3 *domesticated animal*
experimentalism 448.3 *experimentation*
experimentalist 448.5 *experimenter*
experimentalize 448.11 *experiment*
experimentally 448.14; 353.10 *ambitiously*; 448.15 *inventively*; 449.16 *originally*; 705.23 *questioningly*; 487.8 *unusually*
experimental method 631.7 *way*
experimental physics 28.4
experimental psychology 36.1 *psychology*
experimental scientist 476.4 *theorist*
experimental taxonomy 34.17 *taxonomy*
experimental theatre 21.1 *drama*
experimentation 448.3; 448.4 *originality*
experimented upon 448.10 *tested*
experimentee 448.7
experimenter 448.5; 353.7 *attempter*; 703.7 *demonstrator*; 705.9 *questioner*; 476.4 *theorist*
experimenting 448.8 *experimental*
experiment on 382.22 *kill animals*
expert 396.11; **396.17**; **400.10**; **485.5**; **485.8**; 713.4 *adviser*; 123.4 *bigwig*; 340.3 *doer*; 6.16 *educational*; 6.4 *educator*; 400.13 *excellent*; 464.5 *judge*; 455.8 *knowledgeable*; 455.6 *knowledgeable person*; 4.19 *learned*; 121.6 *paragon*; 230.1 *perfect*; 230.4 *perfectionist*; 797.5 *proficient*; 136.9 *qualified*; 136.8 *qualified person*; 4.12 *sage*; 485.6 *skilful*; 485.4 *skilled person*; 139.14 *specialist*; 139.21 *specialized*
expertise 455.2 *information*; 230.3 *perfection*; 797.12 *proficiency*; 136.3 *qualifications*; 485.1, 733.3 *skill*; 139.7 *special skill*
expertly 396.26; 6.25 *educationally*; 400.16 *masterfully*; 485.12, 797.25 *skilfully*; 4.29 *wisely*
expertly made 485.9 *well-made*
expert mechanic 230.4 *perfectionist*
expertness 485.1, 733.3 *skill*
expert system 40.17 *artificial intelligence*
expiate 807.5 *atone*; 752.14 *offer reparation*; 609.11 *recompense*
expiation 807.1 *atonement*; 752.6 *offering*; 394.1 *remedy*; 609.2 *reparation*; 762.1 *substitution*
expiator 807.3 *atoner*
expiatory 807.4 *atoning*; 752.19 *sacrificial*
expiatory offering 807.2 *apology*
expiration 131.2 *cessation*; 232.3 *completion*; 131.3, 582.1 *death*; 434.8 *respiration*
expire 131.19; 94.12 *cease to exist*; 582.15 *die*; 526.1 *disappear*; 371.14 *let out*; 284.14 *pass*; 434.21 *respire*
expired 3.18 *in the past*
expiring 582.18 *dying*
expiry 131.2 *cessation*; 582.1 *death*
explain 703.16; 721.16 *define*; 738.1 *display*; 722.4 *dissertate*; 719.8 *interpret*; 714.8 *justify*; 265.16 *make easy*; 701.16 *plead*; 444.14 *premise*; 4.21 *rationalize*; 738.3 *reveal*; 695.5 *simplify*; 706.20 *solve*
explainable 714.13 *vindicable*
explained 701.12 *apologetic*; 703.11 *explanatory*; 719.15 *interpreted*; 695.2 *simple*; 706.14 *solved*
explainer 703.7 *demonstrator*; 719.6 *interpreter*

explaining 719.14 *interpretive*
explain wrongly 720.1 *misinterpret*
explanation 444.4; 703.3; 714.2 *defence;* 721.1 *description;* 739.1 *disclosure;* 722.1 *dissertation;* 719.1 *interpretation;* 4.1 *philosophy;* 701.5 *plea;* 344.5 *reason;* 695.10 *simplicity;* 706.6 *solution;* 476.1 *supposition;* 694.4 *type of meaning*
explanatory 703.11; 719.16 *annotative;* 344.13, 444.10 *causal;* 721.11 *descriptive;* 695.1 *intelligible;* 719.14 *interpretive;* 739.12 *revelatory;* 742.14 *signifying;* 706.14 *solved;* 714.11 *vindicatory*
explanatory remark 719.2 *annotation*
expletive 514.7 *cry of disapproval;* 712.1 *curse;* 270.1 *diffuseness;* 219.3 *superfluity;* 5.19 *swearword*
explicability 695.9 *intelligibility*
explicable 701.12 *apologetic;* 695.1 *intelligible*
explicably 701.20 *apologetically*
explicate 725.2 *clarify;* 719.8 *interpret;* 4.21 *rationalize;* 695.5 *simplify*
explication 719.1 *interpretation*
explicative 719.14 *interpretive*
explicator 703.7 *demonstrator*
explicatory 721.11 *descriptive;* 703.11 *explanatory;* 695.1 *intelligible;* 719.14 *interpretive;* 739.12 *revelatory*
explicit 707.14 *assertive;* 150.3 *broad-minded;* 725.3 *clear;* 703.9 *demonstrated;* 27.77 *given;* 693.16 *informative;* 694.6 *meaningful;* 308.16, 738.15 *open;* 695.2 *simple*
explicitly 707.25; 725.4 *clearly;* 695.13 *intelligibly;* 694.13 *meaningfully;* 552.17 *nakedly;* 308.26 *openly*
explicitness 707.6 *assertiveness;* 150.6 *broad-mindedness;* 725.1 *clarity;* 694.3 *comprehension;* 308.9 *openness;* 695.10 *simplicity*
explode 377.11; 508.5 *bang;* 342.12 *be active;* 424.4 *be brittle;* 624.12 *become angry;* 507.8 *be loud;* 514.10 *cry out;* 357.9 *demolish;* 375.3 *disintegrate;* 590.17 *feel deeply;* 437.11 *fuel;* 308.18 *open;* 704.8 *refute;* 330.28 *shoot;* 304.17 *spring up*
exploded 451.7 *disbelieved*
exploding 508.8 *banging;* 704.7 *refuting*
exploit 349.3; 340.4 *act;* 797.19 *be good at;* 485.10 *be skilful;* 613.8 *courageous act;* 340.2 *deed;* 466.14 *discriminate against;* 123.2 *important matter;* 244.1 *improve;* 485.3 *masterpiece;* 351.1 *misuse;* 356.10 *produce;* 387.6 *subject;* 647.6 *suppress;* 287.5 *take the opportunity;* 619.3 *wonder-working*
exploitable 349.10 *usable*
exploitation 351.2 *misuse;* 485.1 *skill;* 647.2 *suppression;* 349.6 *use*
exploitative 351.5 *abusive;* 647.8 *severe*
exploitatively 351.6 *abusively*
exploited 466.11 *judged;* 351.4 *misused;* 647.9 *suppressed;* 349.9 *used*
exploiter 349.8 *user*
exploration 448.3 *experimentation;* 449.9 *invention;* 129.3 *preparation*
exploratory 449.13 *discovering;* 448.8 *experimental;* 293.15 *precursory;* 129.14 *preparatory;* 705.12 *questioning*
explore 448.11 *experiment;* 129.18 *forerun;* 449.4 *invent;* 30.65 *map;* 4.20 *philosophize;* 130.21 *pioneer;* 293.8 *precede*
explored 455.10 *known*
explorer 644.3 *curious person;* 449.12 *discoverer;* 293.4 *early comer;* 227.7 *person who moves around;* 129.8 *precursor*
explore underwater 91.9 *sail the high seas*
explosion 624.4 *anger;* 508.1 *bang;* 375.1 *disintegration;* 357.5 *havoc;* 380.3 *instance of violence;* 507.1 *loudness*
explosive 587.15; 357.7 *agent of destruction;* 508.3 *banger;* 508.8 *banging;* 424.1 *brittle;* 254.1 *dangerous;* 371.29 *expulsive;* 437.2 *lighter;* 315.15 *outgoing;* 437.10 *powered;* 330.18 *projectile;* 371.28 *propellant;* 380.6 *violent*
explosive device 587.16 *bomb;* 330.12 *propellant*
explosively 508.10; 375.8 *destructively;* 371.32 *expulsively;* 315.18 *forth;* 330.34 *forward;* 424.5 *fragilely;* 437.12 *powerfully*
explosives 32.22 *industrial chemistry*
expo 703.1 *demonstration;* 738.6 *display*
exponent 703.7 *demonstrator;* 722.3 *dissertator;* 719.6 *interpreter;* 27.17 *multiplication;* 194.6 *power*
exponential 194.9 *fractional;* 27.76 *functional*
exponential distribution 27.59 *probability distribution*
exponential function 27.29 *mathematical function*
exponentially 27.87, 210.16 *mathematically*
exponential series 27.20 *sequence*
exponentiation 27.17 *multiplication*
export 315.5; 13.13 *economic;* 315.13 *emigrate;* 436.5 *provision;* 13.10 *trade with;* 316.12, 319.4 *transport;* 316.2 *transportation*
export and import 776.5 *commercial trade;* 776.1 *trade*
exportation 315.5 *export;* 316.2 *transportation*
exporter 13.9 *economist;* 776.10 *trader;* 316.7 *transferor;* 778.12 *wholesaler*
exporting 13.2 *economy;* 315.5 *export*
exporting and importing 776.5 *commercial trade*
exposable 552.11 *exposed*
expose 434.20 *aerate;* 703.15 *demonstrate;* 449.2 *detect;* 739.5 *disclose;* 738.1 *display;* 740.13 *make public;* 518.18, 520.10 *make visible;* 308.18 *open;* 41.21 *photograph;* 525.14 *present;* 704.8 *refute;* 738.3 *reveal;* 552.14 *undress;* 337.7 *weaken*
exposé 721.2 *brief description;* 739.2 *divulgence*
exposed 552.11; 434.12 *airy;* 525.7 *appearing;* 520.2 *clear;* 703.9 *demonstrated;* 739.10 *disclosed;* 449.14 *discovered;* 738.14 *manifest;* 308.12 *open;* 740.19 *published;* 335.11 *unprotected;* 520.1 *visible;* 254.3 *vulnerable*
exposed flank 254.7 *vulnerability*
exposed part 254.7 *vulnerability*
exposed to view 520.2 *clear*
expose oneself 254.9 *face danger;* 525.14 *present;* 552.14 *undress*
exposer 739.4 *discloser;* 552.8 *nude person*
expose the trick 645.5 *be cunning*
expose to danger 254.10 *endanger*
expose to sunlight 428.19 *bake*
expose to view 738.1 *display*
exposing 552.1 *undress*
exposing oneself 796.7 *sexual assault*
exposition 703.1 *demonstration;* 738.6 *display;* 722.1 *dissertation;* 703.3 *explanation;* 779.2 *fair;* 719.1 *interpretation;* 520.5 *manifestation*
expositional 703.9 *demonstrated*
expositive 721.11 *descriptive;* 719.14 *interpretive*
expositor 703.7 *demonstrator;* 722.3 *dissertator;* 5.2 *linguist;* 733.6 *public speaker*
expository 722.5; 703.9 *demonstrated;* 721.11 *descriptive;* 693.16 *informative;* 719.14 *interpretive;* 739.12 *revelatory*
expository prose 17.5 *prose*
expository scene 21.8 *scene*
ex post facto 284.23 *before now*
expostulate 481.1 *dissuade;* 113.18 *object;* 753.6 *protest*
expostulation 481.6 *dissuasion;* 113.4 *objection;* 753.1 *protest;* 711.1 *warning*
expostulatory 481.9 *dissuasive*
exposure 525.1 *appearance;* 494.3 *chill;* 520.4 *clarity;* 449.7 *detection;* 41.12 *development;* 739.1 *disclosure;* 520.5, 738.10 *manifestation;* 434.5 *open air;* 552.1 *undress;* 254.7 *vulnerability*
exposure meter 522.11 *photoelectricity*
exposure of infants 382.3 *homicide*
exposure scene 21.8 *scene*
exposure time 41.18
expound 722.4 *dissertate;* 703.16 *explain;* 719.8 *interpret;* 4.22 *propound a philosophy;* 4.21 *rationalize*
expounded 703.11 *explanatory*
expounder 703.7 *demonstrator;* 722.3 *dissertator;* 719.6 *interpreter;* 733.6 *public speaker*
expounding 703.3 *explanation*
express 707.14 *assertive;* 703.9 *demonstrated;* 369.12 *displace;* 703.16 *explain;* 160.7 *form;* 694.10 *mean;* 694.6 *meaningful;* 316.13 *post;* 738.3 *reveal;* 729.11 *speak;* 139.15 *special;* 724.9 *style;* 332.1 *swift;* 332.11 *swift thing;* 321.7 *train;* 319.5 *transportable;* 5.45 *use language;* 17.21 *write*
express acknowledgments 671.6 *be grateful*
expressage 316.2 *transportation*
express contempt 660.29 *ridicule*
express delivery 692.2 *postal communication*
express disapprobation 670.14 *disapprove*
express disapproval 670.14 *disapprove;* 113.18 *object*
express doubts 709.6 *dissent;* 708.11 *rebut*
expressed 724.6 *styled*
expressed desire 710.1 *request*
express gratitude 671.6 *be grateful*
expressible 738.13 *displayed*
expressing 369.7 *obtaining an extract*
express in words 724.9 *style*
expression 27.25 *algebraic expression;* 369.2 *displacement;* 525.3 *external appearance;* 160.4 *forming;* 738.10 *manifestation;* 694.1 *meaning;* 160.6 *nature;* 729.7 *utterance*
expressionism 21.10 *theatre movements*
expressionist 21.42 *activist;* 19.29 *realist*
expressionistically 19.30 *pictorially*
expressionless 696.1 *unintelligible*
expressionlessly 696.13 *unintelligibly*
expression of dissatisfaction 606.2
expression of ideas 724.4 *literary style*
expression of regret 807.2 *apology*
expressive 17.18, 721.11 *descriptive;* 543.3 *elegant;* 160.9 *formed;* 693.16 *informative;* 694.6 *meaningful;* 742.14 *signifying*
expressively 369.22; 703.21 *demonstratively;* 17.23 *descriptively;* 543.5 *elegantly;* 160.13 *formatively;* 742.18 *indicatively;* 695.13 *intelligibly*
expressly 698.39 *accurately;* 139.28 *specially*
express mail 692.2 *postal communication*
expressman 316.8 *messenger*
express messenger 332.13 *swift person*
expressness 707.6 *assertiveness*
express one's condolences 627.9 *sorrow*
express one's feelings 624.13 *vent one's anger*
express one's regrets 807.6 *apologize*
express one's remorse 807.6 *apologize*
express pain 491.12
express pithily 269.4 *be concise;* 723.8 *summarize*
express regret 807.6 *apologize*
express regrets 658.10 *be courteous;* 808.4 *be penitent*
express speed 332.8 *speed*
express sympathy for 627.9 *sorrow*
express thanks 671.6 *be grateful*
express train 332.11 *swift thing*
expressway 317.3, 320.2, 373.5 *road*
expropriate 371.8 *evict;* 766.9 *lose;* 351.1 *misuse;* 773.8 *take back*
expropriation 371.20 *eviction;* 766.1 *loss;* 814.7 *punishment;* 372.2 *setting apart;* 773.2 *taking back*
expropriator 773.6 *taker*
expropriatory 773.12 *taking*
expugnable 254.3 *vulnerable*
Expulsion 371
expulsion 371.17; 470.6 *discarding;* 369.2 *displacement;* 128.2, 330.4 *ejection;* 315.4 *emigration;* 334.4 *energy;* 560.1 *excretion;* 814.7 *punishment;* 255.2 *purification;* 144.3 *replacement;* 364.6 *repulse;* 655.3 *separation;* 372.2 *setting apart;* 212.1 *subtraction;* 708.6 *termination;* 316.1 *transfer*
expulsive 371.29; 315.15 *outgoing;* 330.18 *projectile*
expulsively 371.32
expunction 358.3 *obliteration*
expunge 708.14 *cancel;* 357.8 *destroy;* 358.1 *obliterate*
expunged 358.6 *obliterated*
expurgate 128.8 *eject;* 245.5 *hurt;* 255.10, 256.15 *purify;* 212.3 *subtract;* 647.6 *suppress*
expurgated 256.17 *cleaned;* 795.10 *moralistic;* 647.9 *suppressed*
expurgation 256.4 *censorship;* 128.2 *ejection;* 255.1 *purity;* 795.4 *self-righteousness;* 212.1 *subtraction;* 647.2 *suppression*
exquisite 545.5 *beautiful;* 543.3 *elegant;* 797.1 *good;* 491.5 *painful;* 490.6 *pleasant;* 619.8 *wonderful;* 235.1 *worthy*
exquisitely 797.22 *well*
exquisite manners 658.2 *good manners*
exquisiteness 545.1 *gorgeousness*
exsection 369.3 *digging out*
ex-serviceman 586.11 *former soldier*
ex-servicewoman 586.11 *former soldier*
exsiccant 428.9 *drying*
exsiccate 428.17 *dry*
exsiccated 428.3 *dried-up*
exsiccation 428.13 *drying*
exsiccative 428.15 *dryer;* 428.9 *drying*
exsiccator 428.15 *dryer*
ex-slave 250.7 *free person*
expiration 432.2 *exhalation*
exsuction 369.4 *sucking*
extant 554.12 *alive;* 93.10 *existing;* 97.7, 282.6 *present*
extemporaneous 478.1 *improvised*
extemporaneously 478.7 *extempore*
extemporary 478.1 *improvised*
extempore 478.7; 478.1 *improvised*
extemporization 478.4 *improvisation*
extemporize 478.3 *improvise*
extemporizer 478.6 *improviser*
extend 141.20; 211.6 *add;* 27.97 *align;* 150.9 *be broad;* 190.6 *become bigger;* 270.5 *be diffuse;* 422.8 *be elastic;* 219.4 *be excessive;* 148.9 *be long;* 138.24 *broaden;* 132.14 *continue;* 294.8 *delay;* 148.10 *lengthen;* 190.5, 213.5 *make bigger;* 417.6 *make sparse;* 308.19 *open up;* 134.4 *protract;* 203.8 *quantify;* 145.7 *reach*
extendability 190.2 *enlargeability*
extendable 190.9 *enlargeable*
extend credit 783.8 *credit*
extended 190.7 *bigger;* 270.3 *diffuse;* 422.6 *elastic;* 294.10 *held up;* 213.7 *increased;* 148.1 *long;* 694.6 *meaningful;* 308.13 *opened up;* 134.6 *protracted;* 203.6 *quantitative;* 417.2 *rarefied;* 141.13 *spacious*
extended family 376.17 *family*
extendedly 294.15 *late*
extended meaning 694.3 *comprehension*
extender 62.4 *climbing equipment*
extendibility 190.2 *enlargeability;* 419.8 *softness*
extendible 190.9 *enlargeable;* 419.2 *pliant*
extending 422.6 *elastic;* 190.8 *growing;* 417.2 *rarefied*
extend to 232.6 *fill;* 145.7 *reach*
extensibility 422.1 *elasticity;* 190.2 *enlargeability;* 419.8 *softness*
extensible 422.6 *elastic;* 190.9 *enlargeable;* 419.2 *pliant*
extensibleness 190.2 *enlargeability*
extensile 190.9 *enlargeable;* 419.2 *pliant*
extensin 33.4 *polysaccharide*
extension 211.1 *addition;* 203.2 *certain amount;* 294.3 *delayed action;* 270.1 *diffuseness;* 422.1 *elasticity;* 190.3 *enlarged thing;* 190.1 *growth;* 213.1 *increase;* 148.4 *length;* 134.2 *protraction;* 417.4 *rarefaction;* 158.1 *size;* 141.1 *space;* 692.9 *telephone*
extensional 190.9 *enlargeable*
extension ladder 304.9 *ladder*
extension sling 62.4 *climbing equipment*
extensive 141.12; 158.15 *big;* 150.1 *broad;* 190.9 *enlargeable;* 138.18 *far-reaching;* 138.15 *general;* 209.7 *gradational;* 127.7 *including;* 148.1 *long;* 308.13 *opened up;* 417.2 *rarefied;* 138.17 *widespread*
extensive farming 43.1 *agriculture*
extensively 141.16; 150.7 *broadly;* 209.9 *differentially;* 190.10 *largely;* 148.11 *lengthily;* 308.25 *obviously;* 156.17 *profoundly;* 417.7 *sparsely;* 138.32 *universally*
extensiveness 158.2 *bigness;* 150.4 *breadth;* 141.4 *spaciousness;* 138.4 *widespreadness*
extensor 190.4 *enlarger*
extent 150.4 *breadth;* 209.1 *degree;* 275.3 *duration;* 156.2 *intensity;* 148.4 *length;* 131.7 *limit;* 166.2 *limiting factor;* 203.1 *quantity;* 26.4, 158.1 *size;* 27.35, 141.1 *space;* 27.38 *surface*
extenuate 714.8 *justify;* 214.5 *make smaller;* 685.4 *moderate;* 136.15 *modify;* 337.7 *weaken*
extenuating 384.29 *defending;* 714.11 *vindicatory*

extenuating circumstances 714.2 *defence*; 136.5 *modification*
extenuatingly 714.15 *in vindication*
extenuation 214.1 *decrease*; 714.2 *defence*
extenuatory 714.11 *vindicatory*
exterior 171.1; **171.6**; 19.10 *art subject*; 100.12 *external*; 525.3 *external appearance*; 525.8 *outer*; 27.35 *space*; 169.2 *surface*; 520.6 *visible thing*
exterior angle 27.39 *angle*
exteriority 171.1 *exterior*; 100.4 *externality*
exteriorization 171.4 *externalization*
exteriorize 171.14 *externalize*
exteriorized 171.9 *externalized*
exteriorized protoplasm 11.10 *psychic phenomenon*
exterminate 371.10; 94.13 *cause not to exist*; 357.8 *destroy*; 131.17 *kill*; 382.22 *kill animals*; 358.1 *obliterate*; 382.18 *slaughter*
exterminated 131.23 *annihilated*; 358.6 *obliterated*
extermination 382.9 *animal killing*; 131.4 *annihilation*; 357.1 *destruction*; 358.3 *obliteration*; 382.4 *slaughter*
exterminator 357.6 *destroyer*
external 100.12; 171.1, 171.6 *exterior*; 525.8 *outer*; 372.17 *unjoined*; 520.1 *visible*
external appearance 525.3
external application 394.10 *surgical dressing*
external-combustion engine 38.11 *engine*
external evidence 716.5 *legal evidence*
external gear 38.7 *gear*
externality 100.4; 171.1 *exterior*
externalization 171.4; 100.4 *externality*
externalize 171.14; 100.16 *be external*; 402.8 *be material*
externalized 171.9; 100.12 *external*
externalizing 100.12 *external*
externally 171.15; 525.15 *apparently*; 100.18 *extraneously*; 372.22 *in isolation*; 738.16 *manifestly*; 520.11 *visibly*
externally acting hormone 33.16 *hormone*
externalness 171.1 *exterior*
external respiration 33.24 *respiration*
externals 525.3 *external appearance*
external secretion 559.2 *secreted substance*
external work 28.38 *thermodynamics*
externment 371.18 *dismissal*
extinct 582.19 *dead*; 526.7 *disappeared*; 341.3, 343.1 *inactive*; 3.18 *in the past*; 94.11 *no more*; 284.18 *over*
extinct arthropod 75.4 *arthropod*
extinct bird 72.8
extinction 94.8; 131.4 *annihilation*; 582.1 *death*; 214.1 *decrease*; 357.1 *destruction*; 526.4 *disappearance*; 343.5 *inactivity*
extinct reptile 73.6
extinct volcano 339.3 *inert thing*
extinguish 121.8 *be superior*; 94.13 *cause not to exist*; 357.8 *destroy*; 481.5 *discourage*; 131.17 *kill*; 523.14 *make dark*; 343.14 *make inactive*
extinguisher 357.6 *destroyer*
extinguishing 523.9 *darkening*
extinguishment 523.2 *darkening*
extirpate 357.8 *destroy*; 371.8 *evict*; 358.1 *obliterate*; 212.3 *subtract*
extirpated 358.6 *obliterated*
extirpation 357.2 *destroying*; 358.3 *obliteration*; 212.1 *subtraction*
extirpative 212.6 *subtractive*
extol 10.19 *offer worship*; 667.17, 669.14 *praise*; 740.16 *publicize*; 9.7 *worship*
extolled 10.21 *ritualistic*; 9.11 *worshipped*
extoller 669.9 *praiser*
extolment 669.3 *praise*; 9.1 *worship*
extorsion 369.6
extort 369.16; 397.10, 710.7 *demand*; 386.7 *force*; 771.5 *lend*; 792.10 *overcharge*; 647.6 *suppress*; 773.10 *take away*
extorted 710.10 *demanding*
extorting 710.10 *demanding*; 773.3 *taking away*
extortion 792.4; 386.3 *coercive methods*; 397.2, 710.2 *demand*; 774.7 *dishonesty*; 790.3 *fee*; 771.1 *lending*; 647.2 *suppression*; 773.3 *taking away*; 662.2 *violation of the law*
extortionary 369.20 *exacting*
extortionate 681.3 *costly*; 792.7 *dear*; 369.20 *exacting*; 771.6 *loaned*; 773.12 *taking*
extortionately 773.13 *avariciously*; 792.12 *dearly*
extortionate price 792.2 *unfair price*
extortioner 773.6 *taker*
extortionist 386.4 *coercive person*; 662.9 *criminal*; 783.5 *lender*; 792.5 *overcharger*; 710.4 *requester*; 773.6 *taker*
extortive 710.10 *demanding*; 369.20 *exacting*
extort protection money 774.16 *act dishonestly*; 773.10 *take away*
extra 211.4; **211.9**; 21.24 *actor*; 211.10 *additionally*; 270.1 *diffuseness*; 128.11 *excluded*; 100.8 *extraneous*; 790.3 *fee*; 295.5 *fresh start*; 120.1 *inequality*; 741.5 *mass communication*; 740.4 *newspaper*; 741.9 *news story*; 765.5 *profit*; 295.14 *renewed*; 252.4 *safety device*; 53.10 *score*; 219.3 *superfluity*; 219.7 *superfluous*; 215.10 *surplus*; 350.1 *unused*; 350.11 *unused thing*; 238.1 *useless*
extrachromosomal genetic element 34.13 *genetic material*
extract 32.30; **369.8**; **369.11**; 390.1 *deliver*; 394.20 *doctor*; 349.3 *exploit*; 431.2 *juice*; 205.2 *particular*; 35.21 *practise dentistry*; 356.10 *produce*; 356.3 *product*; 436.5 *provision*; 99.3 *quintessence*; 144.15 *remove*; 738.3 *reveal*; 212.3 *subtract*; 773.10 *take away*
extract a root 27.91 *add*
extracted 369.19 *dislodged*; 144.9 *removed*; 212.5 *subtracted*
extracting 394.12 *surgery*
Extraction 369
extraction 369.1; 390.2 *deliverance*; 35.4 *dentistry*; 137.8 *genealogy*; 32.23 *metallurgy*; 369.7 *obtaining an extract*; 144.2 *removal*; 212.1 *subtraction*; 773.3 *taking away*
extraction of roots 210.1 *calculation*; 27.17 *multiplication*
extractive 369.18; 32.45 *metallurgical*
extractor 369.9
extractor fan 501.2 *deodorant*; 307.6 *rotator*
extract roots 210.9 *add*
extracts 723.3 *compendium*
extracurricular 6.21 *curricular*
extradite 316.14 *bring back*; 128.8 *eject*; 775.4 *give back*; 371.4 *ostracize*
extradition 128.2 *ejection*; 775.1 *giving back*; 371.19 *ostracism*; 316.1 *transfer*
extrados 20.9 *miscellaneous architectural features*
extra edition 740.4 *newspaper*
extra-embryonic membrane 34.15 *developmental biology*
extragalactic 29.36 *astronomical*
extragalactically 29.39 *astronomically*
extra help 211.4 *extra*
extra-high-voltage a.c. transmission 39.33 *power distribution*
extra innings 48.1 *baseball*; 211.4 *extra*
extrajudicial 16.56 *unauthorized*
extrajudicial execution 382.5 *execution*
extra large 158.15 *big*
extra load 211.1 *addition*
extramarital relations 796.4 *illicit love*
extra money 765.5 *profit*
extra mouth to feed 211.5 *extra person*
extramundane 29.36 *astronomical*; 8.13 *divine*; 101.8 *nonmaterial*; 11.18 *spiritual*
extramural 6.21 *curricular*; 171.7 *outside*
extraneous 100.8; **171.10**; 128.11 *excluded*; 109.6 *unrelated*
extraneously 100.18; 109.12 *irrelevantly*
extraneousness 100.1; **171.5**; 116.1 *dissimilarity*; 109.1 *unrelatedness*
extraordinariness 118.4 *unusualness*
extraordinary 139.16 *characteristic*; 118.14 *eccentric*; 105.2 *questionable*; 619.8 *wonderful*
extra pair of hands 211.5 *extra person*
extra person 211.5
extra point 46.6 *scoring*
extrapolate 210.9 *add*; 27.93 *equate*
extrapolation 210.1 *calculation*; 27.66 *proof*
extra power 334.1 *power*
extras 787.5 *expense*; 211.4 *extra*; 215.4 *surplus*
extrasensory 101.9 *parapsychological*; 445.7 *precognitive*; 11.16 *psychic*
extrasensory perception 590.2 *impression*; 11.1 *occultism*; 445.2 *precognition*; 488.1 *sensation*; 442.2 *ways of thinking*
extraterrestrial 29.36 *astronomical*; 100.12 *external*; 11.11 *ghost*; 100.6 *outsider*; 11.18 *spiritual*
extraterrestrially 29.39 *astronomically*
extra time 211.4 *extra*
extra-time victory 246.2 *victory*
Extravagance 681
extravagance 681.4; **727.3**; **787.6**; 542.2 *affectation*; 459.1 *folly*; 351.2 *misuse*; 686.3 *overindulgence*; 217.8 *plenty*; 441.3 *waste*
extravagant 681.1; **727.14**; 351.5 *abusive*; 792.7 *dear*; 477.11 *fantastical*; 542.10 *ornate*; 686.8 *overindulgent*; 217.2 *plentiful*; 787.11 *spendthrift*; 441.8 *wasteful*
extravagantly 681.9; 351.6 *abusively*; 792.12 *dearly*; 727.17 *excessively*; 787.14 *generously*; 542.13 *ornately*; 441.10 *wastefully*
extravaganza 477.4 *ideality*; 21.7 *show*
extravagation 329.7 *crossing*
extravasate 560.21 *bleed*; 560.4 *excrement*; 560.15 *excrete*; 315.12 *leak*; 371.14 *let out*
extravasated 315.16 *outflowing*
extravasation 371.22 *disgorgement*; 560.4 *excrement*; 560.1 *excretion*; 315.3 *leakage*
extravasation of blood 560.10 *bleeding*
extravehicular activity 29.31 *space travel*
extra weight 414.4 *heaviness*
extra work 576.2 *task*
extreme 156.9 *deep-seated*; 145.8 *distant*; 164.8 *edging*; 727.12 *exaggerated*; 219.1 *excess*; 219.6 *excessive*; 166.6 *furthest*; 244.16 *improving*; 131.7 *limit*; 131.24 *limiting*; 491.5 *painful*; 230.3 *perfection*; 336.10 *potent*; 681.2 *unrestrained*; 380.6 *violent*
extremely 336.15 *acutely*; 727.17 *excessively*; 164.11 *marginally*; 121.16 *superiorly*; 209.11 *to a degree*
extreme penalty 814.13 *capital punishment*
extremes 727.1 *exaggeration*; 219.1 *excess*; 113.2 *oppositeness*; 681.5 *unrestrainedness*
extreme unction 10.5 *Christian rite*; 582.7 *dying day*
extremism 727.1 *exaggeration*; 244.11 *reformism*
extremist 325.19 *deviant person*; 727.6 *exaggerator*; 244.16 *improving*; 244.12 *reformer*; 662.10 *seditionist*
extremity 164.1 *edge*; 166.3 *furthest point*; 131.7 *limit*; 174.1 *summit*
extricable 390.4 *deliverable*
extricably 390.6
extricate 390.1 *deliver*; 265.18 *disentangle*; 369.11 *extract*; 391.4 *liberate*; 144.15 *remove*; 250.15 *set free*
extricated 369.19 *dislodged*; 144.9 *removed*
extricate oneself 391.5 *be liberated*
extrication 390.2 *deliverance*; 265.8 *disentanglement*; 369.1 *extraction*; 391.1 *liberation*; 144.2 *removal*
extrinsic 100.12 *external*; 109.7 *illogical*; 372.17 *unjoined*
extrinsicality 100.4 *externality*
extrinsically 100.18 *extraneously*; 372.22 *in isolation*
extroversion 171.4 *externalization*; 36.7 *personality type*
extroversive 36.35 *extroverted*
extrovert 171.4 *externalization*; 36.35 *extroverted*; 36.7 *personality type*; 654.15 *sociable*; 338.4 *vigorous*
extroverted 36.35; 171.9 *externalized*; 338.4 *vigorous*
extrovertedness 36.7 *personality type*
extrudable 42.9 *spun*
extrude 560.15 *excrete*; 371.14 *let out*; 42.13 *spin*
extruded 42.9 *spun*
extruder 42.2 *spinning*
extrusion 371.22 *disgorgement*; 560.1 *excretion*; 315.1 *exit*; 30.29 *petrogenesis*; 42.2 *spinning*
extrusive 30.56 *petrographic*
extrusive rock 30.30 *igneous rock*
exuberance 270.1 *diffuseness*; 219.1 *excess*; 562.1 *fertility*; 597.1 *happiness*
exuberant 270.3 *diffuse*; 219.6 *excessive*; 562.5 *fertile*; 597.4 *happy*
exuberate 217.5 *about*
exudate 433.4; 560.4 *excrement*; 315.12 *leak*; 560.8 *sweat*
exudation 560.4 *excrement*; 560.1 *excretion*; 433.4 *exudate*; 315.2 *outflow*; 559.1 *secretion*; 560.8 *sweat*
exudative 560.24 *excretory*; 315.17 *leaky*; 559.4 *secretory*
exude 560.15 *excrete*; 315.12 *leak*; 559.7 *secrete*; 429.16, 433.32 *seep*; 560.19 *sweat*
exult 600.5 *rejoice*
exultant 600.9 *rejoicing*
exultation 600.1 *rejoicing*
exultet 10.8 *hymn*
exult in 622.25 *be proud of*
exurb 87.8 *suburb*
exurban 87.14 *urban*
exurbia 86.11 *settlement*; 87.8 *suburb*
exuviae 560.12 *dead tissue*; 258.4 *dirt*
exuvial 560.32 *cast-off*; 552.12 *peeling*
exuviate 552.16 *peel*
exuviation 552.6 *peeling*
ex-wife 568.12 *woman in the family*
eyas 72.12 *young bird*
eye 518.2; 525.3 *external appearance*; 55.3 *fishing tackle*; 308.5 *hole*; 28.23 *light*; 518.13 *look*
eyeball 518.2 *eye*; 518.14 *inspect*
eyeball to eyeball 113.29 *at odds*; 147.14 *beside*; 113.24 *discordant*; 518.24 *visually*
eyeball-to-eyeball 147.10 *juxtaposed*
eyebath 410.12 *bath*; 37.11 *linctus*; 268.7 *pomade*
eyebrow 518.2 *eye*
eyebrow plucking 547.9 *hair removal*
eye-catching 520.2 *clear*; 185.7 *conspicuous*; 738.14 *manifest*; 518.23 *visible*
eye clinic 519.3 *aid for poor sight*
eyed 518.21 *seeing*
eye disease 519.2 *poor sight*
eye drops 519.3 *aid for poor sight*; 37.8 *drops*
eye for 485.2 *aptitude*
eye for an eye 807.1 *atonement*; 759.1 *exchange*
eye-for-eye 110.4 *reciprocal*
eyeful 518.7 *view*
eyeglass 527.8 *transparent thing*; 518.10 *visual aid*
eyehole 308.5 *hole*
eye hospital 519.3 *aid for poor sight*
eyelash 518.2 *eye*
eyeless 519.8 *blind*; 233.4 *incomplete*
eyelessness 519.1 *blindness*
eyelet 373.8 *fastening*; 308.5 *hole*
eyelid 550.14 *animal covering*; 518.2 *eye*
eyelike 518.20 *visual*
eye-liner 547.4 *cosmetics*
eye lotion 268.7 *pomade*
eye make-up 547.4 *cosmetics*
eye muscle 518.2 *eye*
eye of the hurricane 342.1 *activity*; 173.2 *central thing*; 301.2 *repose*
eye of the storm 31.16 *wind vortex*
eye-opener 449.7 *detection*; 630.4 *surprising thing*; 518.7 *view*; 619.4 *wonder*
eye-opening 6.16 *educational*; 518.23 *visible*
eyepatch 519.6 *blinder*
eyepiece 28.30 *lens system*; 29.25 *mounting*
eye rhyme 17.11 *rhyme*
eyeshade 550.12 *protective covering*; 523.6 *shade*; 518.10 *visual aid*
eye-shadow 529.9 *complexion*; 547.4 *cosmetics*
eyeshot 518.9 *viewpoint*; 520.3 *visibility*
eyesight 520.3 *visibility*; 518.1 *vision*
eyesocket 518.2 *eye*
eyes on stalks 619.2 *sign of wonderment*
eyesore 548.3 *blot on the landscape*; 20.3 *building*; 546.3 *ugly place*; 518.7 *view*
eyespot 84.3 *plant body*
eyestrain 519.2 *poor sight*
eye test 35.7 *diagnosis*
eye to eye 518.24 *visually*
eyetooth 425.11 *tooth*
eye up 518.13 *look*
eyewash 519.3 *aid for poor sight*; 394.9 *balm*; 37.8 *drops*; 677.1 *flattery*; 699.15 *nonsense*; 268.7 *pomade*
eyewitness 707.9 *affirmer*; 693.9 *informant*; 518.11 *observer*; 716.7 *person who gives evidence*; 97.5 *someone present*; 454.7 *verifier*

eyewitness account 693.2 *communication*; 741.2 *news event*
Eyre 88.5 *other major lakes*
Eyre of Justice 16.20 *British court*
eyrie 154.8 *high thing*; 565.13 *lair*; 72.14 *nest*
Ezekiel 711.4 *warner*

F1 car 61.1 *motor racing*
fab 797.1 *good*; 797.27 *great!*; 619.14 *wonderful!*; 235.1 *worthy*
Fabian 341.3 *inactive*; 12.6 *political party*; 244.12 *reformer*; 333.5 *unhurried*
Fabianism 12.1 *government*; 341.1 *inaction*; 244.11 *reformism*; 333.8 *slowness*
Fabian policy 341.1 *inaction*
fable 699.9 *falsification*; 699.26 *falsify*; 17.2 *fiction*; 477.7 *idealism*; 699.10 *lie*; 721.3 *narration*
fabled 575.5 *entitled*; 699.36 *falsified*; 477.12 *imaginary*; 811.3 *reputable*; 476.8 *supposed*
fabler 17.14 *author*
fabliau 17.2 *fiction*
fabric **42.3**; **403.2**; 99.1 *essence*; 435.1 *materials*; 402.4 *matter*; 356.7 *produce*; 30.28 *rock*; 193.4, 404.5 *textile*; 42.10 *woven*
fabricate **96.17**; 234.12 *distort the truth*; 699.26 *falsify*; 477.14 *imagine*; 405.13 *make*; 356.10 *produce*; 376.44 *put together*; 403.15 *shape*
fabricated 234.8 *exaggerated*; 699.36 *falsified*; 477.12 *imaginary*; 38.32 *structural*
fabricating 699.33 *deceitful*
fabrication 234.4 *distortion of the truth*; 699.9 *falsification*; 477.5 *fantasy*; 403.3 *form*; 699.6 *lying*; 356.2 *manufacture*; 376.33 *putting together*
fabricator 699.18, 700.16 *liar*; 356.9 *producer*
fabric dealer 551.26 *fashion designer*
Fabrics and Dyeing 42
fabric treatment 42.8
fabula 21.2 *play*
fabulist 17.14 *author*; 721.10 *descriptive writer*; 699.18, 700.16 *liar*
fabulous 17.17 *fictional*; 797.1 *good*; 477.12 *imaginary*; 103.2 *unbelievable*; 235.1 *worthy*
fabulous bird 72.9
fabulously 797.22 *well*; 619.13 *wonderfully*
faburden 516.4 *harmonics*
façade **699.14**; 519.6 *blinder*; 171.1 *exterior*; 525.3 *external appearance*; 167.2 *face*; 167.1 *front*; 167.3 *show*; 169.2 *surface*; 520.6 *visible thing*
face **167.2**; **281.8**; **550.28**; 169.7 *be alongside*; 613.15 *be courageous*; 171.11 *be exterior*; 167.10 *be in front*; 113.15 *be opposite*; 638.8 *brace oneself*; 660.2 *cheek*; 113.19 *confront*; 474.8 *expect*; 171.1 *exterior*; 525.3 *external appearance*; 699.14 *façade*; 56.1 *golf*; 56.4 *golf club*; 411.10 *layer*; 130.18 *make a beginning*; 699.28 *mask*; 551.27 *model*; 160.6 *nature*; 185.3 *protuberance*; 27.38 *surface*; 5.15 *type style*; 186.3 *vertical thing*
face about 303.9, 325.11 *turn round*
face a total loss 766.9 *lose*
face bankruptcy 766.10 *have a financial loss*
face both ways 479.2 *equivocate*
face card 69.3 *card game terms*
face-centred 32.33 *crystalline*
face-centred-cubic crystal 32.4 *crystal*
facecloth 256.11 *cleaning cloth*
face cream 394.9 *balm*; 256.9 *cleaning agent*; 268.7 *pomade*
faced 411.8 *coated*; 550.36 *covered*
face danger **254.9**; 613.15 *be courageous*; 661.5 *defy*
face death 254.9 *face danger*
face defeat 766.9 *lose*
face difficulties 264.20 *be in difficulty*
face disaster 486.5 *be unskilful*
face disqualification 766.9 *lose*
face down 187.10 *lying*
face flannel 256.11 *cleaning cloth*
faceguard 46.18 *be penalized*; 58.5 *lacrosse*; 53.6 *pad*
faceguarding 46.13 *penalty*
face heavy odds 254.9 *face danger*
face in the crowd 736.7 *concealer*
face-lift 244.5 *improvement*; 547.2 *plastic surgery*; 393.8 *repair*
face like a tombstone 602.6 *depressed*
facemask 46.18 *be penalized*; 365.7 *eraser*; 58.3 *ice hockey*; 46.3 *uniform*
face-off 58.8 *hockey*; 58.3 *ice hockey*; 58.9 *play hockey*
face-off circle 58.3 *ice hockey*
face pack 547.3 *beauty treatment*
face powder 427.5 *powder*
facer 630.3 *shock*
face reality 388.3 *submit*
face-saving measures 135.3 *needfulness*
facet 169.4, 222.6 *aspect*; 405.1 *component*; 171.1 *exterior*; 525.3 *external appearance*
faceted 176.9 *angled*; 171.6 *exterior*
face the ball 58.9 *play hockey*
face the cameras 21.34 *act*
face the facts 388.3 *submit*
face the issue 638.8 *brace oneself*
face the music 613.15 *be courageous*; 814.6 *be punished*
face the odds 613.15 *be courageous*; 638.8 *brace oneself*
face the other way 325.11 *turn round*
facetiae 796.2 *indecency*
facetious 599.10 *humorous*
facetiously 599.16 *humorously*
facetiousness 599.1 *humorousness*
face to face 113.29 *at odds*; 147.14 *beside*; 113.24 *discordant*; 738.17 *frankly*
face-to-face 147.10 *juxtaposed*; 113.23 *opposite*
face up to 167.10 *be in front*
face value 525.5 *impression*; 790.2 *value*
facial 547.3 *beauty treatment*; 365.6 *massage*; 167.7 *outward*
facial distortion 234.2
facial expression 525.3 *external appearance*
facially 525.15 *apparently*
facial massage 365.6 *massage*
facial scrub 365.7 *eraser*
facies 525.3 *external appearance*; 30.28 *rock*
facile 265.9 *easy*
facilely 265.21 *easily*
facileness 265.2 *simplicity*
facilitate 352.6 *find means*; 392.28 *further*; 719.8 *interpret*; 265.16 *make easy*; 757.3 *permit*; 250.15 *set free*; 695.5 *simplify*; 480.16 *tempt*
facilitated 265.11 *made easy*
facilitating 265.10 *feasible*; 392.30 *helping*
facilitation 265.7 *easing*; 392.8 *furtherance*
facilitative 392.30 *helping*
facilitator 392.11 *helper*
facilities 239.5 *convenience*; 352.1 *means*
facility 136.2 *ability*; 392.7 *convenience*; 265.1 *easiness*; 102.2 *possibleness*; 695.10 *simplicity*; 485.1 *skill*
facing 411.3 *coat*; 171.6 *exterior*; 525.3 *external appearance*; 113.23 *opposite*; 421.10 *polish*; 169.6 *side*; 169.2 *surface*; 550.8 *wall covering*
facing both ways 479.10 *equivocal*
facing death 254.4 *endangered*
facing the ball 58.5 *lacrosse*
facing the firing squad 254.4 *endangered*
facsimile 115.2, 125.2 *copy*; 111.4, 125.5 *duplicate*; 40.12 *electronic office*; 561.2 *print*; 717.1, 721.9 *representation*
facsimile machine 115.3 *copier*; 125.6 *photocopier*
facsimile transmission 692.8 *data transmission*
fact **93.5**; 222.6 *aspect*; 3.14 *historicalness*; 95.1 *reality*; 452.12 *something certain*; 698.1 *truth*
fact-find 705.17 *question*
fact-finding 705.12 *questioning*
facticity 93.4 *demonstrable existence*
faction 692.25 *broadcast material*; 721.3 *narration*; 205.1 *part*; 376.16 *party*; 405.2 *piece*; 7.1 *religion*; 662.3 *subversion*; 113.10 *the opposition*
factional 376.49 *grouped*; 721.12 *narrative*; 662.14 *subversive*
factious 701.8 *argumentative*
factitious 699.32 *spurious*
factitiously 699.41 *spuriously*
factitiousness 699.4 *spuriousness*
fact of the matter 93.5 *fact*
factor 222.6 *aspect*; 143.2 *circumstances*; 405.1 *component*; 344.4 *contributing factor*; 34.13 *genetic material*; 34.11 *genetics*; 348.2 *instrument*; 579.15 *manager*; 194.4 *mathematical result*; 402.4 *matter*; 27.17 *multiplication*; 205.1 *part*; 127.2 *thing included*
factorage 776.4 *trade*
factor analysis 27.55 *statistical methods*
factorial 34.25 *genetic*; 27.17 *multiplication*
factorization 27.17 *multiplication*
factorize 27.91 *add*; 372.11 *divide*
factors 406.1 *contents*
factorship 776.4 *trade*
factory 38.20 *building*; 2.8 *human institution*; 356.2 *manufacture*; 577.1 *workshop*
factory discount price 790.1 *price*
factory farm 43.6 *farm*
factory farming 43.1 *agriculture*; 356.2 *manufacture*
factory floor 376.13 *workforce*
factory-gate price 790.1 *price*
factory hand 578.1 *worker*
factory-made 356.12 *produced*
factory mark 24.4 *porcelain mark*
factory of lies 699.11 *half-truth*
factory price 790.1 *price*
factory worker 578.1 *worker*
factotum 342.10 *busy person*; 401.1 *servant*; 578.1 *worker*
facts 452.13, 698.7 *confirmation*; 716.1 *evidence*; 455.2, 693.1 *information*; 741.1 *news*; 698.3 *the truth*
facts and figures 693.1 *information*
facts of life 561.3 *propagation*; 95.5 *realities*; 698.3 *the truth*
facts of the matter 698.3 *the truth*
factual 452.1 *certain*; 3.19 *chronicled*; 273.6 *correct*; 716.8 *evidential*; 721.12 *narrative*; 93.13, 95.6 *real*; 698.15 *true*
factual account 721.4
factuality 452.9 *certainty*; 93.4 *demonstrable existence*; 95.1 *reality*
factualize 93.20 *bring into being*; 95.11 *make real*
factually 716.14 *as evidence*; 698.35 *truly*
factually proven 698.20 *proved*
factualness 3.14 *historicalness*
facula 29.15 *sun*
faculty 136.2, 334.2 *ability*; 485.2 *aptitude*; 6.6 *instructorship*; 455.4 *intellect*; 485.1 *skill*; 6.3 *subject*
faculty of judgment 464.1 *judgment*
faculty of sight 518.1 *vision*
faculty of speech 729.1
faculty psychology 36.1 *psychology*
FAD 33.12 *coenzyme*
fad 115.2 *copy*; 595.3 *likes*; 295.2 *trendiness*; 642.3 *whim*
faddiness 665.4 *fastidiousness*
faddish 642.1 *capricious*; 295.10 *new*
faddishness 642.2 *caprice*
faddism 642.2 *caprice*
faddist 295.9 *modern person*
faddy 642.1 *capricious*; 665.9 *careful*
fade 521.7 *become invisible*; 524.9 *be dim*; 278.4 *be transient*; 337.6 *be weak*; 522.28 *bleach*; 209.6 *change gradually*; 529.15 *colour*; 530.6 *decolour*; 214.4 *decrease*; 245.1 *deteriorate*; 526.1 *disappear*; 56.7 *golf*; 56.3 *golf shots*; 296.17 *grow old*; 530.5 *lose colour*; 524.10 *make dim*; 320.21 *miscellaneous motoring terms*; 441.1 *waste*; 531.13 *whiten*
fadeaway 48.4 *pitching terms*
fade away 521.7 *become invisible*; 260.24 *be unhealthy*; 226.6 *cease*; 94.12 *cease to exist*; 131.18 *come to an end*; 214.4 *decrease*; 526.1 *disappear*
faded 530.7 *colourless*; 245.12 *deteriorated*; 524.7 *dimmed*; 428.3 *dried-up*; 522.21 *light*; 529.13 *soft-hued*; 531.2 *whitened*
faded hue 529.3 *hue*
fade from one's memory 463.12 *be forgotten*
fade from sight 214.4 *decrease*
fade in 525.12 *become visible*
fade into the background 388.3 *submit*
fade out 524.9 *be dim*; 226.6 *cease*; 209.6 *change gradually*; 131.18 *come to an end*; 526.1 *disappear*; 766.12 *lessen*
fade-out 523.2 *darkening*; 214.1 *decrease*; 526.4 *disappearance*
fading 530.7 *colourless*; 530.1 *colourlessness*; 214.1 *decrease*; 214.6 *decreasing*; 245.7 *deterioration*; 526.4 *disappearance*; 526.6 *disappearing*; 428.13 *drying*; 582.18 *dying*; 209.7 *gradational*; 692.19 *radio reception*; 278.6 *transient*
fading away 526.4 *disappearance*
fading fast 582.18 *dying*
fading out 526.4 *disappearance*; 209.7 *gradational*; 766.4 *lessening*
faecal **560.25**; 258.8 *unclean*
faeces **560.5**; 258.4 *dirt*
fag 342.10 *busy person*; 261.6 *fatigue*; 567.9 *offensive terms for homosexual*; 387.3 *subordinate*; 496.7 *tobacco*; 576.1, 576.6 *work*; 578.1 *worker*
fag end 215.1 *remainder*; 131.8 *tail*; 496.7 *tobacco*
fagged 261.1 *fatigued*
fagged out 261.1 *fatigued*
faggot 437.2 *lighter*; 435.1 *materials*; 567.9 *offensive terms for homosexual*; 79.3 *timber*
faggots 25.20 *meat*
fag out 261.6 *fatigue*
Fahrenheit scale 493.2 *heat measurement*
faience 24.1 *ceramics*
fail **247.6**; 486.7 *be clumsy*; 357.13 *be destroyed*; 604.4 *be disappointed*; 261.5 *be fatigued*; 231.9 *be imperfect*; 122.8 *be inferior*; 563.7 *be infertile*; 218.5 *be insufficient*; 249.9 *be in trouble*; 335.6 *be powerless*; 786.9 *be unable to pay*; 260.24 *be unhealthy*; 486.5 *be unskilful*; 238.7 *be useless*; 337.6 *be weak*; 453.21 *change*; 214.4 *decrease*; 245.1 *deteriorate*; 604.6 *disappoint*; 305.10 *droop*; 802.24 *go wrong*; 38.31 *load*; 766.9 *lose*; 247.9 *malfunction*; 226.7 *stop working*
failed **247.10**; 122.17 *defective*; 563.6 *having no effect*; 766.16 *losing*; 486.1 *unskilful*; 337.11 *weakened*
failing 556.14 *aged*; 231.7 *defect*; 122.17 *defective*; 122.2 *deficiency*; 357.15 *destroyed*; 245.12 *deteriorated*; 247.10 *failed*; 247.1 *failure*; 218.10 *insufficiently*; 766.16 *losing*; 247.3 *personal fault*; 804.13 *venial*; 804.3 *venial sin*; 254.7 *vulnerability*
failing grade 166.2 *limiting factor*
failing health 247.1 *failure*; 260.1 *ill health*
failing person 247.5
failing sight 519.2 *poor sight*
fail in health 247.6 *fail*
fail in one's duties 247.6 *fail*
fail in one's duty 758.12 *exempt oneself*
fail-safe 252.7 *invulnerable*
fail-safe device 252.4 *safety device*
fail-safe system 252.4 *safety device*
fail the test 231.9 *be imperfect*
fail to act 618.12 *be indifferent*; 341.4 *not act*
fail to appear 98.15 *be absent*; 526.2 *depart*
fail to appreciate 672.6 *be ungrateful*
fail to deliver 604.6 *disappoint*
fail to fulfil 233.5 *be incomplete*
fail to hear 505.8 *be deaf*
fail to heed 618.14 *be careless*
fail to inspire 618.16 *be mediocre*
fail to interest 620.6 *be boring*
fail to move 618.12 *be indifferent*; 618.16 *be mediocre*
fail to retract 707.19 *confirm*
fail to score 247.7 *be defeated*
fail to see 457.9 *lack intellect*
Failure 247
failure **247.1**; 303.21 *backslider*; 604.2 *bad outcome*; 486.9 *bungling*; 214.1 *decrease*; 122.2 *deficiency*; 38.16 *deformation*; 596.2 *disliked thing*; 247.5 *failing person*; 305.4 *fall*; 238.4 *futility*; 611.3 *hopeless person*; 231.5 *imperfection*; 122.6 *inferior*; 786.5 *insolvency*; 218.8 *insufficiency*; 766.6 *loser*; 766.1 *loss*; 337.3 *poor health*; 470.8 *rejected thing*; 357.4 *ruin*; 806.3 *sin*; 226.2 *stop*; 495.2 *taste of life*; 21.13 *theatrical performance*; 486.10 *unskilled person*
failure of credit 786.5 *insolvency*
failure to act 341.1 *inaction*
failure to hear 505.1 *deafness*
failure to pay 247.1 *failure*
fainéant 343.8 *nonworker*
faint 261.5 *be fatigued*; 593.24 *be in love*; 335.6 *be powerless*; 489.11 *be unfeeling*; 260.24 *be unhealthy*; 337.6 *be weak*; 530.7 *colourless*; 521.2 *difficult to see*; 335.4 *disability*; 511.1 *faint-sounding*; 261.7 *fatigue*; 261.1 *fatigued*; 337.10 *ill*; 728.16 *imperceptible*; 453.6 *indeterminate*; 337.13 *insufficient*; 766.9 *lose*; 730.10 *low-voiced*;

524.6 *murky*; 506.3 *silent*; 388.4 *succumb*; 489.2 *unconsciousness*; 505.7 *unheard*
faint-coloured 530.8 *drained of colour*
faint heart 614.1 *cowardice*
faint-hearted 614.3 *cowardly*; 639.3 *timid*
faint-heartedly 614.5 *cravenly*
faint-heartedness 614.1 *cowardice*; 637.13 *dissociation*; 639.13 *timidity*
faint hope 610.1 *hope*; 705.7 *questionableness*; 102.4 *remote possibility*
fainting 261.7 *fatigue*; 261.1 *fatigued*; 260.3 *symptom*
faintly 511.10; 530.9 *colourlessly*; 524.12 *dimly*; 728.27 *imperceptibly*; 453.25 *indeterminately*; 506.5 *silently*; 337.14 *weakly*
Faintness 511
faintness 524.1 *dimness*; 261.7 *fatigue*; 728.7 *imperceptibility*; 505.3 *inaudibility*; 453.14 *indeterminacy*; 521.4 *invisibility*; 511.3 *mutedness*; 530.2 *paleness*; 337.3 *poor health*; 506.4 *silence*; 696.11 *unintelligibility*
faint praise 728.2 *detraction*; 678.1 *disparagement*
faint resemblance 115.1 *similarity*
faint smell 500.1 *odour*
faint sound 511.4; 505.3 *inaudibility*
faint-sounding 511.1
fair 779.2; 756.14 *auspicious*; 545.5 *beautiful*; 601.1 *celebration*; 658.7 *courteous*; 473.4 *disinterested*; 738.6 *display*; 767.2 *disposal of property*; 119.6 *equal*; 31.45 *fine*; 799.4 *honourable*; 618.9 *impartial*; 464.9 *judicious*; 797.3 *kind*; 522.21 *light*; 216.3, 618.10 *mediocre*; 685.6 *moderate*; 795.8 *moral*; 235.5 *not bad*; 428.5 *rainless*; 4.15 *rational*; 801.7 *right*; 609.6 *satisfactory*; 493.11 *warm*; 531.3 *white-haired*
fair and foul 113.3 *opposites*
fair and square 178.5, 799.4 *honourable*
fair ball 48.5 *batting terms*
fair catch 64.3 *rugby play*; 46.12 *special team*
fair chance 107.4
fair copy 125.2 *copy*
fair dealing 178.8 *directness*
fair-dealing 799.4 *honourable*
fair dinkum 698.40 *right!*
faired 426.1 *blunt*
fair exchange 119.3 *equalization*; 110.1 *interchange*; 776.4 *trade*
fair expectation 104.4 *chance*
fair fighter 799.3 *honourable person*
fair game 668.9 *butt*; 700.22 *dupe*
fair hair 537.6 *yellowness*
fair-haired 531.3 *white-haired*; 537.3 *yellow-haired*
fairing 768.2 *gift*
fairish 216.3 *mediocre*
fairishness 216.6 *mediocrity*
Fair Isle 551.13 *sweater*
fairlead 50.3 *parts of a sailing boat*
fairly 473.8 *disinterestedly*; 801.19 *equally*; 119.13 *equitably*; 391.8 *free*; 799.7 *honourably*; 618.19 *impartially*; 685.9 *moderately*; 4.26 *rationally*; 4.27 *stoically*; 209.11 *to a degree*; 618.20 *unexceptionally*
fair-minded 473.4 *disinterested*; 801.7 *right*; 458.5 *wise*
fair-mindedness 473.1 *disinterestedness*; 801.1 *fairness*
fairness 801.1; 178.8 *directness*; 473.1 *disinterestedness*; 119.1 *equality*; 795.2 *good morals*; 545.1 *gorgeousness*; 618.3 *impartiality*; 797.10 *kindness*; 522.14 *light colour*; 685.1 *moderation*; 799.1 *probity*; 531.7 *whiteness*
fair offer 752.3 *business offer*; 749.2 *peace offering*
fair play 801.1 *fairness*; 795.2 *good morals*
fair price 119.3 *equalization*
fair sex 568.1 *female sex*
fair shake 119.2 *equilibrium*
fair share 770.2 *portion*
fair size 158.3 *large scale*
fair-size 158.15 *big*
fair-skinned 531.1 *white*
fair territory 48.1 *baseball*
fair to middling 259.1 *healthy*; 216.3 *mediocre*; 685.6 *moderate*; 235.5 *not bad*
fair trade laws 13.1 *economics*
fair trial 16.7 *legal trial*
fair value 119.3 *equalization*; 790.2 *value*
fairway 56.1 *golf*
fair way 145.2 *great distance*
fair-weather friend 642.4 *capricious person*; 699.19 *cheat*; 700.19 *hypocrite*
fair-weather sailor 323.7 *nautical person*; 486.10 *unskilled person*
fair wind 392.1 *help*
fair words 658.1 *courtesy*
fairy 11.11 *ghost*; 159.4 *little person*; 11.18 *spiritual*
fairy cycle 320.12 *bicycle*
fairy godmother 8.6 *angel*; 392.15 *benefactor*; 679.9 *generous person*; 768.4 *giver*; 619.5 *person of wonder*; 252.3 *protector*; 413.8 *supporter*
fairyland 477.8 *dreamland*; 619.4 *wonder*
fairy lights 522.6 *electric light*
fairy ring 83.2 *mushroom*; 11.6 *talisman*
fairy shrimp 75.4 *arthropod*
fairy tale 17.2 *fiction*; 477.4 *ideality*; 699.10 *lie*; 721.3 *narration*
fairy-tale ending 246.1 *success*
fait accompli 93.5 *fact*
faith 450.3 *believing*; 452.10 *conviction*; 610.2 *expectation*; 698.13 *faithfulness*; 253.1 *protection*; 799.2 *purity*; 7.1 *religion*; 450.2 *religious belief*; 252.1 *safety*; 803.2 *virtues*
faith cure 394.13 *therapy*
faithful 698.26; 698.21 *accurate*; 450.11 *believing*; 273.6 *correct*; 569.11 *devoted*; 803.6 *ethical*; 799.4 *honourable*; 452.6 *infallible*; 115.9 *lifelike*; 593.17 *loving*; 663.8 *loyal*; 255.12 *morally pure*; 640.10 *persevering*; 95.7 *realistic*; 7.15 *religious*; 267.10 *tenacious*; 5.40 *translated*; 719.17 *translational*
faithful copy 125.2 *copy*
faithful likeness 115.1 *similarity*
faithful love 593.2 *romantic love*
faithfully 273.8 *accurately*; 450.15 *believingly*; 115.14 *comparably*; 569.19 *devotedly*; 803.10 *ethically*; 799.7 *honourably*; 593.30 *lovingly*; 663.10 *obediently*; 7.23 *religiously*; 267.12 *tenaciously*; 255.18 *virtuously*
faithfully rendered 698.25 *lifelike*
faithfulness 698.13; 698.8 *accuracy*; 273.2 *correctness*; 663.2 *loyalty*; 799.1 *probity*; 7.2 *religiousness*
faithful rendering 698.12 *realism*
faithful servant 664.3 *sycophant*
faithful spouse 570.8 *spouse*
faithful translation 5.12, 719.4 *translation*
faith-heal 11.24 *experience psychic phenomena*
faith healer 35.12, 394.15 *healer*; 11.12 *occultist*; 393.12 *repairer*
faith healing 394.11 *medical art*; 35.2 *natural medicine*; 11.1 *occultism*
faithless 800.6; 451.6 *disbelieving*; 700.38 *treacherous*
faithlessly 800.11 *dishonourably*
faithlessness 800.2; 662.1 *disobedience*
fake 699.12; **699.37**; 96.12 *artificial*; 96.7 *artificiality*; 699.25 *be fraudulent*; 772.11 *borrowed*; 772.9 *borrow illegally*; 699.19 *cheat*; 125.2, 125.10 *copy*; 699.33 *deceitful*; 702.12 *deceive*; 700.15 *deceiver*; 699.39 *disguised*; 234.12 *distort the truth*; 234.8 *exaggerated*; 699.14 *façade*; 699.36 *falsified*; 699.26 *falsify*; 699.35 *fraudulent*; 702.10 *hypocritical*; 58.3 *ice hockey*; 772.3, 774.6 *illegal borrowing*; 125.13 *imitation*; 700.39 *imitative*; 699.28 *mask*; 58.9 *play hockey*; 46.15 *play offence*
fake a confession 715.6 *accuse falsely*
fake book 736.2 *hiding place*
fake bottom 700.12 *disguise*
fake conduct 699.5 *deceitfulness*
fake confession 715.2 *false accusation*
faked 699.36 *falsified*; 58.8 *hockey*
fake kick 46.12 *special team*
faker 699.19 *cheat*; 125.8 *copier*; 700.15 *deceiver*; 702.6 *sophist*
fakery 699.8 *fraud*; 702.5 *hypocrisy*
fake someone out 700.28 *trick*
fake suicide 382.7 *suicide*
fake the evidence 715.6 *accuse falsely*
faking 699.9 *falsification*; 699.8 *fraud*; 702.10 *hypocritical*; 58.3 *ice hockey*
fakir 7.7 *monk*; 11.12 *occultist*; 7.3 *religious person*
Falak al Aflak 8.11 *heaven*
Falangists 12.6 *political party*
falchion 587.8 *sharp weapon*
falcon 72.5 *bird of prey*; 743.8 *heraldic device*; 633.6 *hunter*
falconer 633.6 *hunter*
falconet 587.12 *historical guns*
falconry 633.2 *chase*
fall 305.4; 249.1 *adversity*; 292.4 *autumn*; 793.12 *be cheap*; 357.13 *be destroyed*; 254.8 *be in danger*; 337.6 *be weak*; 804.16 *be wicked*; 214.2, 303.14 *decline*; 793.2 *declining prices*; 214.4 *decrease*; 156.14 *deepen*; 156.1 *depth*; 245.1 *deteriorate*; 305.5 *dive*; 796.16 *do wrong*; 305.12 *drop*; 247.6 *fail*; 247.1 *failure*; 90.7 *flow*; 367.11 *lowering*; 582.16 *meet one's fate*; 29.20 *meteor*; 31.62 *rain*; 298.5 *regular thing*; 561.10 *reproduce oneself*; 303.4 *slip back*; 274.20 *transgress*; 305.11 *trip*; 186.1 *verticality*; 52.5 *wrestling*
fall about 600.8 *laugh*
fallacious 700.35 *deceptive*; 274.15 *erroneous*; 699.29 *false*; 802.12 *incorrect*; 702.7 *sophistic*
fallaciously 699.40 *falsely*; 702.14 *sophistically*
fallaciousness 274.3 *erroneousness*; 699.1 *falsehood*; 700.5 *falseness*; 802.2 *incorrectness*; 702.1 *sophistry*
fallacy 96.3 *delusion*; 274.3 *erroneousness*; 699.1 *falsehood*; 700.5 *falseness*; 274.4 *faulty reasoning*; 465.1 *misjudgment*; 702.2 *sophism*; 702.1 *sophistry*
fall apart 278.4 *be transient*; 245.1 *deteriorate*; 375.3 *disintegrate*; 372.9 *separate*
fall asleep 489.11 *be unfeeling*; 582.15 *die*; 226.9 *pause*
fall away 372.13 *diverge*
fallback 303.11 *retreat*
fall back 303.2 *retreat*
fall back on 349.4 *resort to*; 384.28 *survive*
fall behind 122.8 *be inferior*; 303.2 *retreat*
fall below 122.8 *be inferior*; 218.5 *be insufficient*
fall by the wayside 238.7 *be useless*; 247.6 *fail*
fall colours 534.5 *brown thing*
fall down 305.10 *droop*; 305.12 *drop*; 305.11 *trip*
fall down before 667.19 *take off one's hat to*
fallen 367.19; 357.15 *destroyed*; 8.16 *devilish*; 796.13 *unchaste*; 804.11 *wicked*
fallen angel 8.6 *angel*; 8.7 *devil*; 766.6 *loser*; 804.9 *wicked person*
fallen by the wayside 245.12 *deteriorated*; 766.16 *losing*
fallen nature 804.1 *wickedness*
fallen woman 796.9 *immoral woman*; 804.9 *wicked person*
faller 305.8 *descender*
fall flat 247.8 *miscarry*
fall for 700.24 *be deceived*; 593.24 *be in love*; 450.7 *believe*; 483.8 *be motivated*; 480.18 *be persuaded*
fall foul of 249.9 *be in trouble*
fall from favour 812.4 *bring into disrepute*
fall from grace 249.9 *be in trouble*; 804.16 *be wicked*; 812.4 *bring into disrepute*; 802.23 *sin*
fall guy 668.9 *butt*; 700.22 *dupe*; 621.4 *laughing stock*; 766.6 *loser*; 272.3 *object of ridicule*; 762.2 *substitute person*
fall headlong 367.7 *lean*; 305.11 *trip*
fall heir to 765.14 *profit*
fallibility 274.6; 247.1 *failure*; 231.5 *imperfection*; 465.1 *misjudgment*; 453.15 *unreliability*
fallible 274.16 *errant*; 231.1 *imperfect*; 465.7 *misjudging*; 453.7 *unreliable*
fallibly 465.13 *misguidedly*; 453.26 *unreliably*
fall ill 260.24 *be unhealthy*; 245.1 *deteriorate*
fall in 376.41 *band together*; 424.4 *be brittle*; 191.6 *become smaller*; 750.25 *conform*; 305.10 *droop*; 132.17, 407.24 *line up*
falling 305.18; **367.20**; 793.9 *cheap*; 214.6 *decreasing*; 245.12 *deteriorated*; 305.4 *fall*; 305.18 *falling*; 14.6 *financial*; 90.10 *fluvial*; 120.3 *unequal*
falling apart 357.15 *destroyed*; 245.13 *dilapidated*; 375.6 *disintegrating*
falling away 303.14 *decline*
falling birth rate 563.1 *infertility*
falling down 357.15 *destroyed*
falling exchange rate 14.1, 780.7 *finance*
falling hair 552.7 *depilation*
falling in love 593.18 *in love*; 593.8 *love affair*
falling leaves 742.1 *sign*
falling off 214.2 *decline*; 245.12 *deteriorated*; 245.7 *deterioration*; 766.4 *lessening*
falling-out 701.1, 751.2 *argument*
falling pressure 31.6 *weather data*
falling price 214.3 *decreasing thing*
falling rocks 62.2 *climbing dangers*
falling short 604.11 *disappointing*; 233.1 *incompleteness*; 120.3 *unequal*
falling sickness 260.4 *disease*; 260.17 *nervous disorder*; 327.8 *spasm*
falling star 29.20 *meteor*; 522.4 *natural light*
falling to pieces 245.13 *dilapidated*; 254.2 *unsafe*
fall in price 793.12 *be cheap*
fall into 314.13
fall into a gorge 92.12 *be marooned*
fall into a habit 632.18 *habituate*
fall into a routine 111.11 *be regular*
fall into arrears 786.9 *be unable to pay*
fall into a trap 630.12 *be surprised*
fall into confusion 408.25 *be disordered*
fall into disarray 408.25 *be disordered*
fall into disuse 487.4 *be unaccustomed*
fall into evil ways 804.16 *be wicked*
fall into line 664.13 *conform*
fall into one's hands 769.9 *receive*
fall into place 407.24 *line up*
fall into quicksand 92.12 *be marooned*
fall into ruin 357.13 *be destroyed*
fall in with 310.10 *come together*; 117.8 *comply*
fall-line 68.1 *skiing*
fall off 303.14 *decline*; 305.9 *descend*; 245.1 *deteriorate*; 303.1 *go backwards*
fall of the leaf 292.4 *autumn*
fall on 484.11 *invent*
fall on bad days 249.9 *be in trouble*
fall on deaf ears 505.11 *be unheard*
fall on hard times 249.9 *be in trouble*; 782.13 *lose one's money*
fall on one's feet 248.6 *be fortunate*
fall on one's knees 627.12 *ask for mercy*; 664.10 *knuckle under*; 667.19 *take off one's hat to*
fall on one's sword 382.21 *commit suicide*
fall on the ear 504.16 *be heard*
Fallopian tubes 561.8 *organs of reproduction*
fallout 371.25 *emission*; 28.75 *nuclear accident*; 334.8 *nuclear power*; 427.5 *powder*; 356.3 *product*
fall out 701.13 *argue*; 345.9 *take effect*
fallout shelter 252.5 *refuge*; 384.10 *shelter*
fall out with 751.5 *disagree*
fall over 664.8 *be servile*; 305.11 *trip*
fallow 43.20 *farmable*; 341.3 *inactive*; 339.5 *inert*; 563.3 *infertile*; 343.2 *not working*; 350.1 *unused*; 537.1 *yellow*
fallowness 339.1 *inertness*; 563.1 *infertility*
fall prostrate 305.11 *trip*
falls 90.2 *channel*
fall short 604.4 *be disappointed*; 231.9 *be imperfect*; 233.5 *be incomplete*; 122.8 *be inferior*; 218.5 *be insufficient*; 120.5 *be unequal*; 604.6 *disappoint*; 247.6 *fail*; 766.10 *have a financial loss*
fall short of perfection 231.9 *be imperfect*
fall sick 260.24 *be unhealthy*
fall silent 506.1 *be silent*
fall through the air 305.12 *drop*
fall to 810.14 *be the duty of*; 557.22 *eat well*; 130.18 *make a beginning*; 354.1 *undertake*
fall to bits 427.27 *come to dust*
fall to leeward 323.9 *navigate*
fall to one 788.7 *receive*
fall to one's lot 107.10 *chance*; 769.9 *receive*
fall to one's share 769.9 *receive*
fall to pieces 424.4 *be brittle*; 278.4 *be transient*; 375.3 *disintegrate*; 247.9 *malfunction*
fall upon 312.2 *reach*; 381.5 *strike*
fall vertically 186.7
fall victim to 700.24 *be deceived*
false 699.29; 96.12 *artificial*; 700.35 *deceptive*; 699.39 *disguised*; 479.11 *equivocating*; 274.15 *erroneous*; 234.8 *exaggerated*; 800.6 *faithless*; 54.6 *fencing*; 699.35 *fraudulent*; 700.37, 702.10 *hypocritical*; 802.12 *incorrect*; 27.86 *logical*; 718.6 *misrepresented*; 115.8 *simulated*

false accusation 715.2
false air 699.14 *façade*
false alarm 711.3
false alert 711.3 *false alarm*
false arch 20.5 *arch*
false arrest 16.4 *bad law*
false attack 54.3 *fencing movements*
false beard 550.16 *disguise*
false charge 715.2 *false accusation*
false colour 699.14 *façade*
false colours 700.12 *disguise*
false conclusion 274.1 *mistake*
false conduct 699.1 *falsehood*
false construction 720.2 *misinterpretation*
false dawn 604.3 *mirage*; 290.1 *morning*; 96.4 *theorization*
false depiction 720.2 *misinterpretation*
false dew 31.37, 429.6 *dew*
false display 676.1 *affectedness*
false evidence 736.5 *evasion*; 715.2 *false accusation*
false expectation 604.1 *disappointment*
false face 700.3 *hypocrisy*
false-faced 700.37 *hypocritical*
false friend 699.19 *cheat*; 700.19 *hypocrite*
false front 542.2 *affectation*; 700.12 *disguise*; 699.14 *façade*; 700.3 *hypocrisy*
false-fronted 700.37 *hypocritical*
false fruit 80.2 *botanical fruit*
false gold 780.16 *bullion*
false hair 551.15 *headgear*; 547.10 *wig*
false-hearted 699.33 *deceitful*; 700.38 *treacherous*
falseheartedness 700.4; 699.5 *deceitfulness*
Falsehood 699
falsehood 699.1; 700.1 *deception*; 234.4 *distortion of the truth*; 477.4 *ideality*; 800.1 *improbity*; 718.1 *misrepresentation*
false hope 610.1 *hope*
false hopes 604.1 *disappointment*
false idea 720.2 *misinterpretation*
false image 718.1 *misrepresentation*
false impression 96.3 *delusion*; 274.6 *fallibility*; 720.2 *misinterpretation*
false imprisonment 774.2 *kidnapping*
false information 718.2 *misinformation*
false light 699.14 *façade*; 720.2 *misinterpretation*; 718.1 *misrepresentation*
falsely 699.40; 115.14 *comparably*; 800.11 *dishonourably*; 234.14 *distortedly*; 720.4 *mistakenly*; 702.14 *sophistically*; 718.8 *unrepresentatively*; 802.26 *wrong*
falsely coloured 699.39 *disguised*
falsely colouring 699.14 *façade*
falsely pious 699.31 *hypocritical*
falsely swearing 699.33 *deceitful*
false modesty 255.1 *purity*; 795.4 *self-righteousness*; 468.1 *underestimation*
false money 780.15
false move 274.1 *mistake*
false name 721.8 *name*
falseness 700.5; 700.1 *deception*; 274.3 *erroneousness*; 800.2 *faithlessness*; 699.1 *falsehood*; 700.3 *hypocrisy*; 802.2 *incorrectness*; 699.4 *spuriousness*
false person 699.17
false piety 699.3 *hypocrisy*
false political promises 645.1 *cunning*
false pregnancy 711.3 *false alarm*
false pride 622.3 *conceit*
false reading 234.4 *distortion of the truth*; 720.2 *misinterpretation*; 465.1 *misjudgment*
false reasoning 702.1 *sophistry*
false report 711.3 *false alarm*
false reputation 700.5 *falseness*
false root 5.17 *word*
false rumour 711.3 *false alarm*; 699.11 *half-truth*
false scent 238.5 *waste of effort*
false scorpion 76.2 *arachnid*
false sense 720.2 *misinterpretation*
false shame 795.4 *self-righteousness*
false show 542.2 *affectation*; 699.14 *façade*; 700.3 *hypocrisy*
false start 46.13 *penalty*; 130.11 *starting point*; 47.1 *track events*
false step 274.1 *mistake*
false swearing 699.6 *lying*
false thing 699.16
false tooth 425.11 *tooth*
falsetto 18.32 *instrumental*; 513.3 *shrillness*
false warning 711.3 *false alarm*
false witness 715.3 *accuser*; 699.18, 700.16 *liar*; 699.6 *lying*
falsies 551.25 *accessories*
falsification 699.9; 720.2 *misinterpretation*; 274.5, 718.1 *misrepresentation*
falsified 699.36; 274.15 *erroneous*; 720.3 *misinterpreted*
falsifier 699.18, 700.16 *liar*
falsify 699.26; 800.8 *be dishonourable*; 699.20 *be false*; 699.25 *be fraudulent*; 234.12 *distort the truth*; 274.19 *make a mistake*; 720.1 *misinterpret*; 718.4 *misrepresent*; 702.11 *practise sophistry*
falsifying 699.9 *falsification*
falsify the accounts 789.7 *account*
falsity 676.1 *affectedness*; 234.4 *distortion of the truth*; 274.3 *erroneousness*; 800.2 *faithlessness*; 699.1 *falsehood*; 699.8 *fraud*; 27.63 *mathematical logic*; 27.64 *reasoning*
Falstaff 158.12 *fat person*
faltboat 50.6 *canoeing*
falter 227.11 *be changeable*; 333.2, 453.19 *hesitate*; 732.7 *keep quiet*; 327.25 *pitch*; 327.7, 327.24 *shake*; 327.11 *stagger*
faltering 453.2 *irresolute*; 453.11 *irresoluteness*; 327.6 *shaking*; 327.18 *shaky*; 333.4 *slow*
falteringly 333.16 *slowly*
fame 462.5 *day to remember*; 797.8 *good*; 248.1 *prosperity*; 740.7 *publicity*; 575.1 *right*; 246.1 *success*
fame and fortune 248.1 *prosperity*; 246.1 *success*
famed 740.20 *well-known*
familiar 569.10; **632.10**; **657.9**; 660.15 *audacious*; 216.1 *average*; 569.6 *close friend*; 138.21 *common*; 659.5 *discourteous*; 668.10 *disrespectful*; 117.15 *everyday*; 632.14 *habituated*; 250.13 *informal*; 6.19 *knowledgeable*; 447.9 *local*; 112.13 *monotonous*; 11.6 *talisman*
familiarity 569.3; **657.3**; 216.4 *average*; 632.1 *habit*; 250.4 *informality*; 455.1 *knowledge*; 112.3 *repetitiveness*; 654.1 *sociability*
familiarize oneself with 455.13 *get to know*
familiarly 657.13 *casually*; 250.22 *informally*; 569.18 *intimately*
familiar name 721.8 *name*
familiar spirit 11.11 *ghost*; 11.6 *talisman*
familiar with 455.8 *knowledgeable*
family 376.17; 409.6 *category*; 27.40 *curve*; 289.2 *descent*; 137.8 *genealogy*; 566.9 *group*; 2.8 *human institution*; 654.7 *human society*; 564.2 *inhabitants*; 137.3 *kingdom*; 205.1 *part*; 2.4 *social organization*; 34.17 *taxonomy*; 204.5 *unit*
family allowance 392.4 *social assistance*
family benefit 392.4 *social assistance*
family car 320.16 *car*; 216.8 *middle classes*
family circle 654.7 *human society*
family concern 779.8 *store*
family court 16.21 *US court*
family court judge 16.24 *US judge*
family credit 392.4 *social assistance*
family doctor 35.11 *doctor*
family farm 43.6 *farm*
family group 2.6 *social group*
family history 284.12 *genealogy*
family likeness 115.1 *similarity*
family man 567.13 *man in the family*
family meal 557.12 *meal*
family member 373.3 *associate*
family name 721.8 *name*
family of languages 5.11
family-oriented 654.18 *sociably*
family pet 593.11 *loved one*
family planning 563.3 *birth control*
family plot 583.5 *cemetery*
family practitioner 35.11 *doctor*
family punt 50.8 *punting*
family relationship 108.1 *relatedness*
family resemblance 111.3 *lookalike*; 115.1 *similarity*
family responsibilities 378.6 *burden*
family reunion 654.3 *meeting*
family room 565.7 *room*
family secret 737.1 *secrecy*
family size 158.3 *large scale*
family-size 158.15 *big*
family therapy 36.3 *psychiatric treatment*
family training 36.3 *psychiatric treatment*
family tree 289.2 *descent*; 79.12 *figurative usage*; 284.12 *genealogy*; 132.3 *line*
famine 617.3 *appetite*; 782.7 *beggary*; 563.1 *infertility*; 218.9, 557.10 *scarcity*
famine relief 608.4 *charity*
famine-stricken 218.3 *underfed*
famish 687.5 *fast*
famished 687.6 *fasting*; 617.10 *hungry*; 218.3 *underfed*
famishing 687.6 *fasting*
famishment 687.2 *short rations*
famous 3.19 *chronicled*; 575.5 *entitled*; 797.1 *good*; 455.10 *known*; 738.14 *manifest*; 248.8 *prosperous*; 811.3 *reputable*; 246.13 *successful*; 740.20 *well-known*; 235.1 *worthy*
famous ballet dancers 22.14
famous dancers 22.6
famous friendships 569.7
famously 248.9 *prosperously*; 797.22 *well*; 235.11 *worthily*
famousness 740.7 *publicity*; 246.1 *success*
famous tennis players 63.7
fan 669.8 *admirer*; 190.6 *become bigger*; 434.22 *blow*; 494.4 *cooler*; 632.8 *creature of habit*; 267.5 *follower*; 311.5 *fork*; 593.9 *lover*; 190.5 *make bigger*; 494.12 *make cold*; 311.11 *move apart*; 330.11 *propeller*; 256.15 *purify*; 581.1 *refresh*; 413.8 *supporter*; 21.33 *theatregoer*; 434.7 *ventilator*; 9.5 *worshipper*
fanatic 466.7 *bigot*; 342.10 *busy person*; 325.19 *deviant person*; 118.8 *dissenter*; 727.6 *exaggerator*; 465.5 *misjudging person*; 641.8 *obstinate person*; 452.11 *opinionist*; 7.4 *religionist*
fanatical 342.18 *active*; 452.2 *convinced*; 466.10 *discriminatory*; 636.2 *eager*; 590.13 *passionate*; 7.15 *religious*; 641.4 *set*; 465.8 *unjust*
fanatically 466.17 *prejudicially*; 7.23 *religiously*; 465.14 *unjustly*
fanatical worker 342.10 *busy person*
fanaticism 452.10 *conviction*; 636.7 *eagerness*; 590.4 *emotion*; 465.3 *injustice*; 641.7 *opinionatedness*; 7.2 *religiousness*; 466.4 *social discrimination*
fanciable 477.13 *imaginable*; 617.11 *lustful*
fancied 593.21 *beloved*; 96.9 *illusory*; 477.12 *imaginary*; 476.8 *supposed*
fancied up 551.30 *dressed-up*
fancier 617.6 *desirer*; 485.5 *expert*; 72.20 *ornithologist*
fanciful 642.1 *capricious*; 477.11 *fantastical*; 446.11 *ideational*; 96.9 *illusory*; 477.12 *imaginary*; 697.5 *nonsensical*; 105.2 *questionable*; 443.10 *speculative*; 476.8 *supposed*; 96.10 *theoretical*; 94.10 *unreal*
fancifully 642.6 *capriciously*; 477.17 *imaginatively*
fancifulness 477.1 *imagination*
fan club 669.8 *admirer*
fancy 450.8 *be of the opinion*; 469.15 *chosen*; 792.7 *dear*; 617.1, 617.12 *desire*; 477.5 *fantasy*; 443.6 *idea*; 446.6 *ideal*; 477.4 *ideality*; 96.2 *illusion*; 477.1 *imagination*; 446.15, 477.14, 518.17 *imagine*; 590.2 *impression*; 595.7, 617.13 *like*; 595.3 *likes*; 593.23 *love*; 542.10 *ornate*; 469.2 *prefer*; 469.7 *preference*; 593.2 *romantic love*; 476.5 *suppose*; 476.1 *supposition*; 67.11 *swimming*; 446.2 *theory*; 642.3 *whim*; 635.1 *will*
fancy diving 67.6 *diving*
fancy dress 551.5
fancy dress dance 22.1 *dancing*
fancy-dress party 654.5 *party*
fancy-free 572.6 *celibate*; 250.10 *independent*; 618.7 *indifferent*; 109.6 *unrelated*
fancy-led 477.10 *imaginative*
fancy price 792.1 *high price*
fancy up 551.33 *dress up*
fancywork 542.3 *pattern*
fan dance 22.2 *dance*
fandango 22.4 *historic dancing*
fane 10.11 *place of worship*
fanfare 600.2; 507.1 *loudness*; 510.2 *ringing*; 601.8 *salute*; 742.6 *word*
fanfaron 727.6 *exaggerator*
fanfaronade 699.14 *façade*; 601.8 *salute*
fang 425.11 *tooth*
fanged 425.4 *toothed*
fanglike 425.4 *toothed*
fangs 360.3 *tools for gripping*; 425.11 *tooth*
fan heater 493.3 *heater*
fanlight 308.7 *passageway*; 522.10 *window*
fanlike 311.8; 190.8 *growing*
fanned 190.7 *bigger*; 20.15 *vaulted*; 434.17 *ventilated*
fanned out 190.7 *bigger*
fanning 190.8 *growing*; 190.1 *growth*; 311.2 *parting*; 434.6 *ventilation*
fanning out 325.18 *diffraction*; 377.5 *divergence*; 190.1 *growth*; 311.2 *parting*
fanny 561.8 *organs of reproduction*; 168.2 *rear end*
fanon 7.11 *vestment*
fan out 190.6 *become bigger*; 377.10 *diverge*; 190.5 *make bigger*; 311.11 *move apart*
fan oven 25.5 *cooker*
fan palm 79.1 *tree*
fan scale 414.10 *scales*
fan-shaped 311.8 *fanlike*; 190.8 *growing*; 199.8 *three-sided*
fan-shaped backboard 49.3 *basketball equipment*
fantail 20.9 *miscellaneous architectural features*
fantasia 477.6 *reverie*
fantasist 477.9 *visionary*
fantasize 477.15; 96.13, 446.15 *imagine*
fantast 477.9 *visionary*
fantastic 642.1 *capricious*; 477.11 *fantastical*; 446.13 *ideal*; 96.9 *illusory*; 103.2 *unbelievable*; 619.8 *wonderful*; 235.1 *worthy*
fantastic! 235.12
fantastical 477.11; 94.10 *unreal*; 681.2 *unrestrained*
fantasticality 477.1 *imagination*
fantastically 446.22 *imaginatively*; 619.13 *wonderfully*
fantasy 477.5; 610.3 *aspiration*; 36.19 *defence mechanism*; 446.6 *ideal*; 477.4 *ideality*; 96.2 *illusion*; 477.1, 518.5 *imagination*; 699.10 *lie*; 721.3 *narration*; 94.5 *nonreality*; 619.4 *wonder*
fantasy novel 17.2 *fiction*
fantoccini 717.6 *image*; 21.7 *show*
fan-trained tree 44.10 *fruit tree*
fan vault 20.7 *vault*
fan vaulting 20.7 *vault*
FAQ 40.16 *Internet*
far 145.8 *distant*; 145.10 *distantly*; 47.10 *fast*; 166.6 *furthest*; 148.1 *long*; 169.6 *side*
far above 116.4 *dissimilar*
Faraday constant 28.97 *fundamental constant*
far afield 145.10 *distantly*
far and away 121.17 *supremely*
far and near 145.10 *distantly*
farandole 22.4 *historic dancing*
far and wide 145.10 *distantly*; 141.16 *extensively*
far away 145.8 *distant*; 145.10 *distantly*; 329.15 *out of reach*
far below 116.4 *dissimilar*
farce 621.2 *act of derision*; 21.12 *comedy*; 599.4 *entertainment*; 21.2 *play*; 272.2 *slapstick comedy*; 697.3 *tomfoolery*; 124.8 *trifle*
farcer 21.24 *actor*
farceur 697.4 *buffoon*; 21.26 *dramatist*
farceuse 21.26 *dramatist*
farcical 621.5 *derisive*; 599.10 *humorous*; 697.5 *nonsensical*; 272.5 *ridiculous*; 21.40 *tragic*
farcically 599.16 *humorously*
far cry 145.2 *great distance*
farcy 260.18 *veterinary disease*
fare 221.6 *be in a state of*; 557.21 *eat*; 790.3 *fee*; 557.7 *food*; 316.10 *transferred thing*
Far East 145.3 *distant place*; 86.7 *regions of the world*
farewell 313.11 *departing*; 313.14 *goodbye!*; 313.9 *parting*
fare well 222.14 *be comfortable*; 248.5 *be prosperous*
farewell address 313.9 *parting*; 729.8 *speech*
farewell oration 729.8 *speech*
farewell performance 21.13 *theatrical performance*
far-fetched 451.7 *disbelieved*; 329.13, 727.12 *exaggerated*; 109.7 *illogical*; 105.1 *improbable*; 272.5 *ridiculous*
far-flung 145.8 *distant*; 141.12 *extensive*; 138.18 *far-reaching*
far from it 116.4 *dissimilar*; 708.23, 709.12 *no!*
far gone 245.12 *deteriorated*; 582.18 *dying*
farina 427.8 *meal*
farinaceous 81.8 *grasslike*; 44.16 *horticultural*; 427.16 *mealy*

far infrared 28.13 *electromagnetic radiation*
farl 25.39 *loaf*
farm 43.6; **43.17**; 43.19 *agricultural*; 243.7 *develop*; 168.8 *nurture*; 356.10 *produce*; 440.1 *property*; 319.5 *transportable*; 577.1 *workshop*
farmable 43.20
farm agent 43.16 *farm worker*
farm animal 70.3 *domesticated animal*
farm belt 43.11 *farmland*
farm bike 43.10 *farm tool*
farm bottom land 92.12 *be marooned*
farmboy 43.16 *farm worker*
farm building 43.7
farm business 43.1 *agriculture*
farm club 48.1 *baseball*
farmed 43.20 *farmable*
farmer 43.15 *agriculturist*; 564.5 *countryman*; 557.20 *food provider*; 243.15 *preparer*; 356.9 *producer*; 578.1 *worker*
farmer's almanac 439.5 *collection*
farmer's lung 83.5 *fungal association*
farmers' market 779.1 *market*
farm-gate sale 43.1 *agriculture*
farmhand 43.16 *farm worker*; 401.1 *servant*; 578.1 *worker*
farmhouse 43.19 *agricultural*; 43.7 *farm building*; 565.5 *house*; 25.39 *loaf*
farm implement 43.10 *farm tool*
farming 43.19 *agricultural*; 43.1 *agriculture*; 356.2 *manufacture*
farmland 43.11; 538.8 *greenness*
farm machinery 43.10 *farm tool*
farm manager 43.16 *farm worker*; 579.15 *manager*
farm office 43.7 *farm building*
farm pond 88.2 *small lake*
farm road 320.2 *road*
farmstead 43.6 *farm*
farm tool 43.10
farmtoun 43.6 *farm*
farm track 320.2 *road*
farmwork 576.1 *work*
farm worker 43.16; 578.1 *worker*
farmyard 43.7 *farm building*
farmyard manure 43.13, 562.3 *fertilizer*
farmyard smells 503.2 *something that makes an unpleasant smell*
farnesol 33.20 *terpene*
farness 145.1 *distance*; 166.3 *furthest point*
far off 145.8 *distant*; 145.10 *distantly*
far out 118.14 *eccentric*; 487.2 *not customary*
farrago 412.3 *miscellany*
far-ranging 138.18 *far-reaching*
far-reaching 138.18; 141.12 *extensive*; 148.1 *long*
farrier 59.15 *horse person*
farriery 59.14 *horse-riding terms*
farrow 71.35 *give birth*; 561.11 *have young*; 555.4 *young animal*
farrowing crate 43.7 *farm building*
farrowing house 43.7 *farm building*
farse 10.10 *religious manual*
far-seeing 518.21 *seeing*
farside 169.3 *side direction*
far sight 519.2 *poor sight*; 518.1 *vision*
far-sighted 518.22 *bespectacled*; 458.6 *intelligent*; 518.21 *seeing*; 519.9 *weak-sighted*
far-sightedness 519.2 *poor sight*; 518.4 *visualization*; 458.1 *wisdom*
fart 371.16, 371.24, 432.5, 508.4, 508.7 *belch*; 503.2 *something that makes an unpleasant smell*; 503.5 *stink*
farther 145.8 *distant*; 145.10 *distantly*
farthermost 145.8 *distant*
farthest 145.8 *distant*
farthing 780.10 *former British money*
farthingale 551.18 *underwear*
farting 371.24 *belch*
far ultraviolet 28.13 *electromagnetic radiation*
Far West 145.3 *distant place*
fascia 411.3 *coat*; 525.3 *external appearance*; 743.3 *means of identification*; 20.9 *miscellaneous architectural features*
fascial 20.17 *structured*
fasciate 541.8 *checked*
fasciately 541.12 *variedly*
fascicled 376.49 *grouped*
fascicular 376.49 *grouped*
fascicule 205.2 *particular*
fascinate 395.10 *be a prevailing influence*; 363.12 *lure*; 483.9 *motivate*; 593.28 *win the love of*
fascinated 11.19 *bewitched*; **593.19** *enamoured*; 595.6 *liking*; 619.6 *wondering*
fascinating 395.12 *appealing*; **363.9** *attractive*; 595.5 *likable*; 483.11 *motivational*; 480.19 *persuasive*; 11.15 *witchlike*
fascinatingly 483.14 *influentially*; 595.10 *with great liking*
fascination 363.4 *allurement*; 617.1 *desire*; 480.3 *incentive*; 483.2 *inducement*; 395.1 *influence*; 595.1 *liking*; 593.1 *love*; 593.2 *romantic love*; 619.1 *wonder*
fascioliasis 75.11 *helminthic disease*
Fascism 12.1 *government*; 647.2 *suppression*; 396.7 *type of rule*
fascism 466.4 *social discrimination*
Fascist 12.9, 396.14 *governmental*; 647.8 *severe*
fascist 466.7 *bigot*; 466.10 *discriminatory*
Fascists 12.6 *political party*
Fashion 553
fashion 553.1; **553.9**; 631.1 *conduct*; 117.5 *convention*; 115.2 *copy*; 632.4 *custom*; 721.14 *describe*; 551.2 *dressing*; 525.3 *external appearance*; 160.7, 403.3 *form*; 160.5 *formality*; 405.13 *make*; 356.10 *produce*; 403.15 *shape*; 221.1 *state*; 724.1 *style*; 229.1 *tendency*; 317.1 *way*
fashionable 553.7; 525.10 *aspectual*; 295.16 *avant-garde*; 221.9 *conditionally*; 551.30, 656.7 *dressed-up*; 632.12 *established*; 160.11 *formal*; 221.8 *in a state of*; 622.21 *ostentatious*; 282.6 *present*; 724.7 *stylish*
fashionable élite 553.6
fashionableness 553.2
fashionable set 295.6 *avant-garde*
fashionably 553.10; 160.14 *conventionally*; 551.36 *dressily*; 295.23 *trendily*
fashion artist 19.16 *artist*
fashion boots 551.19 *footwear*
fashion business 553.3
fashion designer 551.26
fashion designing 551.2 *dressing*
fashioned 160.9 *formed*
fashioning 160.4 *forming*
fashion model 553.5; 551.27 *model*
fashion photography 41.1 *photography*
fashion plate 553.5 *fashion model*
fashion reporter 741.4 *journalist*
fashion show 738.6 *display*
fashion victim 115.4 *person who copies*
Fass 814.15 *instrument of torture*
fast 47.10; **253.9**; **687.5**; 342.18 *active*; 342.22 *actively*; 807.6 *apologize*; 684.5 *be self-restrained*; 53.13 *bowling*; 51.9 *bowls*; 529.10 *coloured*; 569.11 *devoted*; 293.12 *early*; 687.3 *fast day*; 687.1 *fasting*; 262.6 *hastily*; 262.3 *hasty*; 280.5 *immediate*; 218.8 *insufficiency*; 766.9 *lose*; 251.5 *means of restraint*; 280.7 *prepared for immediate use*; 32.38 *reactive*; 251.10 *restrain oneself*; 360.10 *retained*; 684.1 *self-restraint*; 332.1 *swift*; 796.13 *unchaste*; 9.7 *worship*
fast asleep 343.4 *not awake*
fast ball 48.4 *pitching terms*; 330.5 *throw*
fast bowler 53.4 *team*
fast break offence 49.4 *playing terms*
fast-breeder reactor 334.8, 437.7 *nuclear power*; 28.73 *nuclear reactor*
fast by 147.12 *near*
fast colour 228.4 *stable thing*
fast day 687.3; 601.5 *anniversary*; 10.15 *holy day*
fast delivery 53.8 *delivery*
fast dye 42.6 *dye*; 529.4 *pigment*
fasten 309.7 *close*; 373.11 *connect*; 361.10 *suspend*
fasten down 228.7 *make stable*
fastened 309.12 *closed*; 373.15 *connected*
fastener 373.8 *fastening*
fastening 373.8; 373.1 *connection*; 360.3 *tools for gripping*
fasten on 123.8 *make important*; 360.6 *retain*
fasten one's seatbelt 243.4 *prepare for action*
faster 807.3 *atoner*; 766.7 *dieter*; 687.4 *fasting person*; 300.19 *go!*; 262.8 *hurry up!*; 684.4 *self-restrained person*
faster race 765.2 *augmentation*
faster than sound 332.1 *swift*
fast film 41.10 *graininess*
fast food 557.7 *food*
fast-food chef 25.2 *cook*
fast-food counter 557.15 *eating place*
fast-food restaurant 557.15 *eating place*
fast foxtrot 22.2 *dance*
fast friendship 569.3 *familiarity*
fast green 51.1 *green bowling*
fastidious 665.9 *careful*; 256.16 *clean*; 471.8 *diligent*; 466.9 *discriminating*; 670.28 *fault-finding*; 656.6 *formal*; 799.4 *honourable*; 230.2 *perfectionist*; 549.5 *refined*; 647.8 *severe*; 728.13 *subtle*; 264.14 *troublesome*
fastidiously 471.15 *attentively*; 466.16 *judiciously*; 647.11 *severely*
fastidiousness 665.4; 273.1, 698.8 *accuracy*; 471.3 *carefulness*; 256.1 *cleanness*; 670.6 *fault-finding*; 656.1 *formality*; 466.2 *judiciousness*; 799.1 *probity*; 469.6 *selection*; 647.1 *severity*; 728.3 *subtlety*
fastigiate 425.1 *sharp*
fastigium 174.3 *architectural summit*
Fasting 687
fasting 687.1; **687.6**; 807.2 *apology*; 782.7 *beggary*; 218.8 *insufficiency*; 766.1 *loss*; 251.14, 684.8 *self-restrained*; 684.1 *self-restraint*; 218.3 *underfed*; 9.1 *worship*
fasting person 687.4
fast lane 320.3 *carriageway*
fast-liver 686.5 *self-indulgent person*
fast living 686.2 *dissipation*
fast-living 686.7 *dissipated*
fastly 253.17; 569.19 *devotedly*
fast motion 332.8 *speed*
fastness 384.12 *fort*; 252.5 *refuge*; 332.8 *speed*
Fastnet Race 50.1 *sailing*
Fast of Av 10.16 *religious festival*
fast operator 755.4 *contractor*
fast patrol boat 586.24 *warship*
fast rate 332.8 *speed*
fast reaction 32.14 *chemical reaction*
fast reactor 28.73 *nuclear reactor*
fast talker 645.3 *cunning person*
fast transport ship 586.24 *warship*
fast wicket 53.5 *wicket*
fat 33.7; **158.8**; **158.16**; 25.7 *basic ingredient*; 190.6 *become bigger*; 43.21 *domesticated*; 562.5 *fertile*; 557.11 *food content*; 414.1 *heavy*; 33.6 *lipid*; 781.4 *lush*; 190.5 *make bigger*; 219.2 *overdoing it*; 217.2 *plentiful*; 217.8 *plenty*; 248.8 *prosperous*; 268.13 *slippery*; 152.1 *thick*; 152.5 *thickness*; 181.10 *well-rounded*
fatal 382.23, 582.20 *deadly*; 357.14 *destructive*; 236.5 *harmful*
fatal accident 382.8 *accidental killing*; 582.5 *ways of dying*
fatal blow 357.4 *ruin*
fatal car crash 382.8 *accidental killing*
fatal disease 582.5 *ways of dying*
fatal flaw 804.3 *venial sin*; 254.7 *vulnerability*
fatal gift 700.14
fatal illness 260.2 *illness*
fatalism 4.7 *school of thought*; 388.1 *submission*
fatalist 4.11 *follower of a doctrine*; 341.2 *nonacting person*
fatalistic 4.14 *of a philosophy*; 388.5 *submitting*
fatalities 582.12 *death count*
fatality 798.2 *affliction*; 582.11 *dead person*; 582.5 *ways of dying*
fatality list 582.12 *death count*
fatally 582.23; 357.16, 798.13 *destructively*; 382.25 *lethally*
fatal move 247.2 *defeat*
fatal plane crash 382.8 *accidental killing*
fatal train crash 382.8 *accidental killing*
Fata Morgana 477.5 *fantasy*; 96.2 *illusion*; 518.5 *imagination*
fat-arsed 158.16 *fat*
fat as a pig 158.16 *fat*; 152.1 *thick*
fat cat 765.7 *gainer*; 248.4 *prosperous person*; 781.10 *wealthy person*
fat cattle 43.8 *livestock*
fat chance 105.4 *improbability*; 708.24 *never!*; 107.6 *poor chance*
fat clay 24.2 *raw material*
fate 131.5; 344.4 *contributing factor*; 283.3 *future condition*; 452.16 *inevitability*; 395.1 *influence*; 107.2 *luck*; 106.5 *predetermination*
fated 131.23 *annihilated*; 582.18 *dying*; 283.11, 756.15 *future*; 452.5 *inevitable*; 106.3 *predetermined*
fateful 123.5 *important*; 452.5 *inevitable*; 475.15 *presageful*
fatefully 452.25 *inevitably*; 475.16 *predictively*
fatefulness 452.16 *inevitability*
fate of Icarus 305.4 *fall*
fat-free diet 557.6 *nutrition*
fathead 50.7 *windsurfing*
Father 8.3 *God*; 567.3 *male title of address*; 344.7 *Prime Mover*
father 344.9 *be the cause of*; 556.8 *man*; 567.13 *man in the family*; 7.8 *priest*; 344.7 *Prime Mover*; 130.26 *produce*; 356.9 *producer*; 561.13 *propagate*; 561.5 *propagator*
Father Christmas 679.9 *generous person*; 768.4 *giver*
father complex 36.18 *complex*
fathered 554.15 *born*
father figure 762.2 *substitute person*; 36.25 *surrogate*
father fixation 36.17 *fixation*
fatherhood 554.4 *biological function*; 561.4 *development*; 567.13 *man in the family*
father image 36.25 *surrogate*; 36.24 *symbolism*
fatherland 565.3 *home*; 85.6 *native land*; 86.4 *territorial division*
fatherly 650.6 *benevolent*; 556.13 *middle-aged*
fatherly eye 252.2 *protection*
Father of Lies 699.18, 700.16 *liar*
father of the chapel 15.7 *employee*
Father of the House 12.8 *politician*
Father's Day 298.6 *annually celebrated day*
father substitute 762.2 *substitute person*
father symbol 36.24 *symbolism*
Father Time 245.9 *dilapidation*; 296.2 *old people*
fathom 458.7 *be wise*; 156.14 *deepen*; 26.10 *measure*; 4.21 *rationalize*; 695.6 *understand*
fathomable 695.1 *intelligible*; 26.14 *measurable*
fathomableness 695.9 *intelligibility*
fathomer 156.4 *deep thing*
Fathometer™ 156.4 *deep thing*
fathomless 156.8 *deep*
fathomlessness 156.1 *depth*
fatidic 475.13 *predicting*
fatigue 261.6; **261.7**; 620.6 *be boring*; 620.1 *boredom*; 335.4 *disability*; 351.1 *misuse*; 337.3 *poor health*; 260.3 *symptom*; 810.2 *task*; 349.1 *use*; 576.1 *work*; 576.7 *work for*
fatigued 261.1; 620.5 *bored*; 335.12 *impotent*; 260.21 *unhealthy*; 337.11 *weakened*
fatigue duty 576.1 *work*
fatigues 551.3, 656.4 *formal dress*
fatiguing 261.4; 236.3 *bad*; 264.10 *difficult*
fat lamb 43.8 *livestock*
fatling 43.8 *livestock*
fatly 158.20 *largely*
fatness 158.5; 414.4 *heaviness*; 268.3 *oiliness*; 181.2 *round body*; 152.5 *thickness*
fat of the land 557.7 *food*; 781.7 *opulence*; 217.8 *plenty*; 248.1 *prosperity*
fat part 21.23 *role*
fat person 158.12
fatso 158.12 *fat person*
fatstock 43.8 *livestock*
fatted 190.7 *bigger*
fatten 152.8; 190.6 *become bigger*; 213.4 *increase*; 190.5 *make bigger*; 43.18 *practise livestock farming*; 557.25 *provide food*
fattened 190.7 *bigger*
fattened-up 168.5 *bred*
fattening 557.27 *edible*; 190.1 *growth*; 213.1 *increase*
fattening house 43.7 *farm building*
fatten on 557.22 *eat well*; 664.15 *sponge*
fatten up 168.8 *nurture*; 557.25 *provide food*
fatter 190.7 *bigger*
fattiness 268.3 *oiliness*; 219.2 *overdoing it*
fattishness 158.5 *fatness*
fattism 466.4 *social discrimination*
fatty 158.12 *fat person*; 268.13 *slippery*
fatty acid 33.7 *fat*
fatty-acid ester 33.7 *fat*
fatuity 272.1 *ludicrousness*; 457.2 *unintelligence*
fatuous 459.5 *foolish*; 697.5 *nonsensical*; 272.5 *ridiculous*; 457.6 *unintelligent*
fatuously 457.11 *unintelligently*
fatuousness 459.1 *folly*; 272.1 *ludicrousness*
faucet 309.2 *stopper*
fault 63.12 *badminton terms*; 146.2 *crack*; 670.17 *criticize*; 231.7 *defect*; 122.2 *deficiency*; 30.20 *earth movement*; 236.8 *inferi-*

ority; 133.4 *interruption;* 59.9 *jumping;* 92.10 *miscellaneous;* 274.1 *mistake;* 308.1 *opening;* 806.3 *sin;* 63.4 *tennis terms;* 804.3 *venial sin*
fault-block mountain 30.21 *mountain building*
fault-finder 670.12 *critic;* 659.4 *discourteous person;* 596.3 *disliked person*
fault-finding 670.6; 670.28; 678.1 *disparagement;* 264.14 *troublesome*
faultily 274.22 *wrongly*
faultiness 122.2 *deficiency;* 231.5 *imperfection;* 236.8 *inferiority*
faulting 30.20 *earth movement*
faultless 698.21 *accurate;* 232.7 *complete;* 805.5 *innocent;* 230.1 *perfect;* 795.9 *pure;* 204.7 *uncut*
faultlessly 805.11 *innocently;* 230.7 *perfectly*
faultlessness 698.8 *accuracy;* 805.1 *innocence;* 795.3 *moral purity;* 230.3 *perfection;* 255.1 *purity*
fault line 30.20 *earth movement*
faulty 486.4 *bungled;* 122.17 *defective;* 274.15 *erroneous;* 231.1 *imperfect;* 236.2 *inferior;* 337.13 *insufficient;* 704.6 *refutable;* 702.7 *sophistic*
faulty logic 702.1 *sophistry*
faulty reasoning 274.4
faulty syntax 5.29 *grammar;* 274.11 *grammatical error*
faulty vision 519.2 *poor sight*
faun 8.5 *deity*
fauna 70.1 *animals*
fauteuil 21.18 *auditorium*
Fauvist 19.29 *realist*
fauxbourdon 516.4 *harmonics*
faux de mieux 762.9 *instead*
faux pas 274.10, 544.6 *blunder;* 486.9 *bungling;* 806.3 *sin;* 247.4 *unsuccessful thing*
favonian 31.47 *windy*
favour 669.2 *admiration;* 121.3 *advantage;* 248.7 *be auspicious;* 648.3 *be lenient;* 650.4 *benevolent act;* 757.4 *be permissive;* 115.10 *be similar;* 635.12 *choose;* 617.12 *desire;* 466.12, 802.22 *discriminate;* 235.10 *do good;* 811.1 *estimation;* 302.8, 392.28 *further;* 768.2 *gift;* 413.14 *give moral support;* 248.2 *good fortune;* 797.17 *good thing;* 575.3 *honours;* 392.22 *improve;* 595.2 *inclination;* 395.4 *indirect influence;* 648.1 *leniency;* 627.3 *mercy;* 413.6 *moral support;* 469.2, 595.8 *prefer;* 469.7 *preference;* 710.1 *request;* 667.1, 667.15 *respect;* 813.1 *reward;* 392.2, 669.13 *support*
favourable 569.12; 669.18 *approving;* 756.14 *auspicious;* 392.34 *beneficial;* 610.14 *cheering;* 222.9 *comfortable;* 569.8 *friendly;* 797.1 *good;* 475.15 *presageful;* 248.8 *prosperous;* 246.13 *successful;* 413.9 *supportive;* 287.6 *timely;* 235.4 *worthwhile*
favourable attitude 595.1 *liking*
favourable auspices 756.3 *potential*
favourable chance 107.5 *good chance*
favourable critic 669.7 *advocate*
favourableness 797.8 *good;* 287.1 *timeliness*
favourable opportunity 287.2 *opportunity*
favourable outcome 27.62 *probability;* 246.1 *success*
favourable prospect 104.4 *chance*
favourable review 669.4 *compliment;* 719.3 *criticism*
favourable towards 595.6 *liking*
favourable verdict 16.42 *acquittal;* 16.7 *legal trial*
favourable wind 31.15 *wind direction*
favourably 569.20; 595.11 *admiringly;* 756.17 *auspiciously;* 222.18 *comfortably;* 392.36 *helpfully;* 569.17 *in friendship;* 287.9 *opportunely;* 248.9 *prosperously;* 246.16 *successfully;* 121.16 *superiorly*
favourably disposed 392.35 *benevolent*
favoured 669.23 *approved;* 595.5 *likable*
favoured by 811.3 *reputable*
favoured suitor 593.11 *loved one*
favouring 392.30 *helping;* 595.6 *liking;* 469.14 *selecting;* 115.7 *similar;* 802.11 *wrong*
favourite 593.21 *beloved;* 123.4 *bigwig;* 363.6 *charmer;* 469.15 *chosen;* 235.8 *exceller;* 569.10 *familiar;* 173.8 *focal;* 59.7 *horseracing;* 9.4 *idolized person;* 593.11 *loved one;* 622.12 *object of pride;* 566.7 *person;* 811.2 *person of repute;* 121.12 *superior*
favourite of the gods 248.4 *prosperous person*
favouritism 466.5; 569.1 *friendship;* 465.3 *injustice;* 469.7 *preference;* 802.1 *unfairness*
favours 593.6 *courtship*
favour with 768.5 *give*
favus 83.5 *fungal association*
fawn 664.9; 677.11 *be sycophantic;* 534.1 *brown;* 555.4 *young animal;* 71.19 *young mammal*
fawner 677.7 *sycophant*
fawning 667.9 *showing respect;* 664.2, 677.5 *sycophancy;* 664.7, 677.16 *sycophantic*
fawningly 664.17 *sycophantically*
fawn on 677.11 *be sycophantic;* 658.13 *defer to*
fawn over 471.14 *be solicitous*
fax 693.12 *communicate;* 693.2 *communication;* 692.31 *correspond;* 692.8 *data transmission;* 111.4, 111.9, 125.5 *duplicate;* 40.12 *electronic office;* 115.12 *imitate;* 40.15 *network;* 316.13 *post;* 717.1 *representation*
faxed 111.15 *duplicate*
fax machine 692.8 *data transmission*
fax number 692.8 *data transmission*
fay 11.11 *ghost*
faze 619.10 *be wonderful;* 453.20 *make uncertain*
fazed 619.6 *wondering*
f-block 32.6 *chemical element*
Fea 585.3 *gods and goddesses of war*
fealty 667.2 *admiration;* 810.3 *allegiance;* 663.2 *loyalty*
Fear 612
fear 612.1; 612.11 *be afraid;* 254.5 *danger;* 596.1, 596.5 *dislike;* 474.8 *expect;* 474.1 *expectation;* 594.7 *hated thing;* 619.1, 619.9 *wonder*
fear and trembling 612.1 *fear*
feared 596.9 *disliked;* 474.7 *expected*
fear for 612.14 *worry*
fearful 612.8; 614.3 *cowardly;* 596.8 *disliking;* 612.10 *frightening;* 619.8 *wonderful*
fearfully 612.15; 614.5 *cravenly;* 619.13 *wonderfully*
fearfulness 612.2; 614.1 *cowardice*
fear God 799.6 *be honourable;* 7.19 *be religious;* 9.7 *worship*
fearing 596.8 *disliking;* 612.7 *frightened*
fearless 613.9 *courageous*
fearlessly 613.18 *courageously*
fearlessness 613.1 *courage*
fearnought 551.12 *coat*
fear of animals 70.13
fear of God 7.2 *religiousness*
fearsome 596.9 *disliked;* 612.10 *frightening*
fear-stricken 612.7 *frightened*
feasibility 102.2 *possibleness;* 265.3 *wieldiness*
feasible 265.10; 746.8 *negotiated;* 102.5 *possible;* 95.9 *realizable*
feasibly 746.9; 102.11 *potentially*
feast 557.13; 688.3 *act of gluttony;* 601.1 *celebration;* 557.24 *have a meal;* 10.15 *holy day;* 654.5 *party;* 490.4 *pleasurable things;* 217.8 *plenty;* 557.25 *provide food;* 600.5 *rejoice;* 600.1 *rejoicing;* 10.16 *religious festival*
feast and famine 113.3 *opposites*
feast day 601.5 *anniversary;* 10.15 *holy day;* 600.1 *rejoicing*
feaster 557.18 *eater*
feasting 557.2 *appetite;* 557.4 *eating meals*
Feast of Circumcision 10.16 *religious festival*
Feast of Tabernacles 10.16 *religious festival*
Feast of the Annunciation 10.16 *religious festival*
Feast of the Dedication 10.16 *religious festival*
Feast of Weeks 10.16 *religious festival*
feast one's eyes on 518.13 *look*
feat 613.8 *courageous act;* 340.2 *deed;* 484.3 *expedient plan;* 485.3 *masterpiece;* 246.1 *success;* 576.2 *task;* 354.2 *undertaking;* 619.3 *wonder-working*
feather 639.15 *indecisive person;* 415.7 *light thing;* 72.17 *plumage;* 50.16 *row;* 419.11 *soft thing;* 124.8 *trifle;* 137.4 *type*
feather ball 56.5 *golf ball*
featherbed 490.10 *comfort;* 15.11 *conduct industrial relations;* 419.13 *soften*
feather bed 23.6 *bed;* 490.4 *pleasurable things;* 419.11 *soft thing*
featherbedded 15.9 *negotiated*
featherbedding 15.1 *industrial relations;* 15.9 *negotiated*
featherbrain 642.4 *capricious person*
featherbrained 642.1 *capricious;* 639.2 *changeable;* 408.16 *confused;* 124.4 *trivial*
feather duster 256.10 *cleaning object*
feathered friend 72.1 *birds*
featherheaded 124.4 *trivial*
featheriness 419.9 *smoothness*
feathering 322.7 *miscellaneous aviation terms;* 50.4, 50.11 *rowing*
feather in one's cap 246.1 *success;* 794.1 *trophy*
feather one's nest 248.5 *be prosperous;* 683.6 *be selfish;* 490.8 *feel pleasure;* 781.13 *get rich*
feather palm 79.1 *tree*
feathers 550.14 *animal covering;* 72.16 *avian anatomy;* 63.11 *badminton equipment;* 542.6 *decorative articles;* 72.17 *plumage*
feather star 75.3 *echinoderm*
featherweight 586.3 *athlete;* 52.4 *boxer;* 52.3 *boxing weight divisions;* 52.14 *combat;* 414.1 *heavy;* 415.1 *light;* 159.4 *little person;* 414.7 *weighing*
feathery 415.2 *insubstantial;* 419.3 *smooth*
feathery cloud 31.20 *cloud appearance*
feat of creation 400.11 *masterpiece*
feat of endurance 613.8 *courageous act*
feat of skill 485.3 *masterpiece*
feature 169.4 *aspect;* 139.3 *characteristic;* 405.1 *component;* 223.4 *concomitant;* 738.1 *display;* 21.38 *dramatize;* 726.6 *emphasize;* 525.3 *external appearance;* 740.16 *publicize;* 139.9 *special;* 127.2 *thing included;* 520.6 *visible thing*
feature article 741.9 *news story*
feature copy 741.10 *copy*
featured 738.13 *displayed*
feature film 356.5 *work of art*
featureless 132.11 *continuous;* 298.11 *regular;* 161.5 *shapeless;* 639.4 *unsteady;* 98.13 *vacant*
featurelessness 161.1 *shapelessness*
feature news 741.9 *news story*
features 406.1 *contents;* 525.3 *external appearance;* 160.6 *nature*
features editor 740.11 *newspaperman*
feature story 693.4 *mass communication;* 741.9 *news story*
feature writer 693.9 *informant*
featuring 406.10 *containing;* 21.41 *stagestruck*
febrifugal 37.14 *counteracting;* 394.17 *remedial*
febrifuge 394.4 *antidote;* 37.4 *drug type*
febrile 260.23 *diseased*
febrile disease 260.4 *disease*
febrile seizure 260.4 *disease*
February 494.7 *cold weather;* 149.4 *short thing*
feckless 642.1 *capricious;* 486.1 *unskilful;* 238.1 *useless*
fecklessness 642.2 *caprice;* 238.3 *uselessness*
feculence 258.4 *dirt;* 560.5 *faeces*
feculent 560.25 *faecal*
fecund 562.5 *fertile;* 477.10 *imaginative;* 781.4 *lush;* 356.11 *productive*
fecundate 562.7 *make fertile;* 561.13 *propagate*
fecundated 561.16 *reproductive*
fecundation 562.2 *productiveness;* 561.3 *propagation*
fecundity 562.1 *fertility;* 217.8 *plenty*
fedayeen 586.9 *guerrilla*
federal 12.9, 396.14 *governmental;* 85.16 *national*
Federal Bureau of Investigation 16.16 *US police*
Federal Communications Commission 692.24 *television broadcasting*
federal council 579.7 *council*
Federal Court 16.21 *US court*
federal debt 784.2 *national debt*
federal depository 780.20 *money store*
federal election 469.12 *election*
federalism 12.1 *government;* 747.5 *joint control;* 396.7 *type of rule*
federalization 377.6 *decentralization*
federalized 377.26 *decentralized*
federal judge 16.24 *US judge*
federally 750.32 *in alliance;* 85.19 *nationally*
federal marshal 16.12 *US law officer*
federal post 396.5 *position of authority*
federal prison 815.1 *prison*
Federal Reserve System 780.19 *treasury*
federate 374.6 *come together;* 747.16 *join*
federated 374.8 *cooperative*
federation 750.2 *alliance;* 376.15 *association;* 374.2 *cooperation;* 396.8 *governmental organization;* 747.5 *joint control;* 764.1 *joint possession;* 12.5 *political organization;* 747.9 *team;* 85.2 *union of nations*
Fédération Internationale de Gymnastique 57.4 *gymnastic organization*
Fédération Internationale de Hockey 58.1 *hockey*
Fédération Internationale de l'Automobile 61.7 *racing governing body*
Fédération Internationale d'Escrime 54.1 *fencing*
Fédération Internationale de Ski 68.1 *skiing*
Fédération Internationale Motocycliste 61.7 *racing governing body*
Fédération Internationale des Sociétés d'Aviron 50.4 *rowing*
fedora 551.15 *headgear*
fed-up 620.5 *bored*
fed up with 261.2 *bored*
fee 790.3; 765.4 *earnings;* 787.5 *expense;* 768.2 *gift;* 440.3 *historic property terms;* 763.3 *medieval ownership;* 785.3 *pay;* 813.4 *reward for service*
feeble 122.17 *defective;* 337.10 *ill;* 335.12 *impotent;* 524.6 *murky;* 497.5 *tasteless;* 804.13 *venial;* 337.8 *weak*
feeble-minded 459.5 *foolish;* 337.10 *ill;* 457.7 *intellectually subnormal;* 457.5 *lacking intellect*
feeble-mindedly 457.11 *unintelligently*
feeble-mindedness 459.1 *folly;* 457.1 *lack of intellect;* 461.2 *subnormality*
feebleness 497.1 *tastelessness;* 337.1 *weakness*
feebly 122.21 *badly;* 335.14 *powerlessly;* 337.14 *weakly*
feed 43.9 *animal feedstuff;* 557.8 *animal food;* 557.21 *eat;* 21.29 *entertainer;* 38.9 *machine tool;* 562.7 *make fertile;* 81.12 *manage grassland;* 43.18 *practise livestock farming;* 359.5 *preserve;* 557.25 *provide food;* 436.1, 436.5 *provision;* 581.1 *refresh;* 21.23 *role;* 554.20 *support life*
feedback 39.15 *circuit function;* 761.5 *reply*
feedback inhibition 33.11 *enzyme*
feedbin 43.10 *farm tool*
feeder 557.18 *eater;* 43.10 *farm tool;* 39.33 *power distribution;* 436.3 *provider;* 90.1 *river;* 21.23 *role*
feeder line 317.10 *railway*
feeder road 320.3 *carriageway*
feeding 557.1, 557.26 *eating;* 557.27 *edible;* 44.5 *gardening;* 436.1 *provision*
feeding frenzy 688.3 *act of gluttony*
feeding organ 557.16 *eating utensil*
feedlot 43.7 *farm building*
feed on 664.15 *sponge*
feed oneself full 557.22 *eat well*
feed one's face 557.22 *eat well*
feed one's tapeworm 557.22 *eat well*
feedstore 43.10 *farm tool*
feedstuff 557.8 *animal food*
fee faw fum 11.5 *spell*
feel 590.15; 445.9 *be intuitive;* 492.13 *be touched by;* 139.3 *characteristic;* 446.15 *imagine;* 466.2 *judiciousness;* 4.22 *propound a philosophy;* 624.8 *resent;* 488.11 *sense;* 404.1 *texture;* 492.1, 492.11 *touch*
feel an aversion for 596.5 *dislike*
feel an obligation 671.6 *be grateful*
feel at home 250.17 *be informal;* 657.11 *not stand on ceremony*
feel at liberty 250.17 *be informal*
feel bad 260.24 *be unhealthy*
feel cheap 623.24 *be humiliated*
feel cheated 218.6 *be unsatisfied*
feel concern for 644.7 *be curious*
feel confident 610.6 *hope*
feel contrite 808.4 *be penitent*
feel deeply 590.17; 591.11 *be sensitive*
feel discontented 624.8 *resent*
feel disgust 596.5 *dislike*
feel dissatisfied 218.6 *be unsatisfied*
feel dizzy 261.5 *be fatigued*
feeler 205.4 *component;* 448.1 *experiment;*

492.7 *sense organ;* 752.2 *tentative offer;* 360.3 *tools for gripping*
feeler gauge 26.6 *measuring instrument*
feel fear 596.5 *dislike*
feel fine 259.5 *be healthy*
feel fondness for 595.7 *like*
feel for 590.18; 591.11 *be sensitive;* 593.23 *love;* 627.8 *pity*
feel free 250.17 *be informal*
feel giddy 261.5 *be fatigued*
feel good 259.5 *be healthy;* 490.8 *feel pleasure*
feel great 259.5 *be healthy*
feel guilty 806.9 *appear guilty;* 808.4 *be penitent*
feel helpless 335.6 *be powerless*
feel hot 493.16
feel hungry 218.6 *be unsatisfied*
feel hurt 624.10 *be offended*
feel ill 260.24 *be unhealthy*
feeling 590.1; **590.10**; 170.3 *atmosphere;* 450.1 *belief;* 631.1 *conduct;* 726.1 *emphasis;* 446.1 *idea;* 445.3 *insight;* 445.1 *intuition;* 593.3 *lovingness;* 4.1 *philosophy;* 627.1 *pity;* 475.1 *prediction;* 488.1 *sensation;* 488.5 *sensible;* 590.12, 591.1 *sensitive;* 446.2 *theory;* 492.1 *touch*
feeling fine 259.1 *healthy*
feeling for 485.2 *aptitude*
feeling for language 724.4 *literary style*
feeling good 259.1 *healthy;* 490.1 *physical pleasure*
feeling great 259.1 *healthy*
feeling guilty 806.6 *appearing guilty*
feeling hot 493.9 *hot*
feelingly 488.14 *sensationally;* 591.12 *sensitively;* 590.20 *with feeling*
feeling of frustration 604.1 *disappointment*
feeling pain 491.7
feeling person 590.9; 445.5 *intuitive person*
Feelings 590
feelings 590.3; 488.2 *ability to sense*
feeling the pinch 135.5 *necessitous*
feeling well 259.1 *healthy*
feel in one's bones 590.16
feel instinctively 590.16 *feel in one's bones*
feel insulted 624.8 *resent*
feel like hell 260.24 *be unhealthy*
feel like oneself again 259.6 *get healthy*
feel no friction 421.12 *go smoothly*
feel no obligation 672.6 *be ungrateful*
feel no remorse 809.5 *be impenitent*
feel nothing 809.5 *be impenitent*
feel offended 624.8 *resent*
feel oneself again 581.2 *be refreshed*
feel one's way 519.14 *be blind;* 616.5 *be cautious*
feel pain 491.9; 249.9 *be in trouble*
feel pique 624.10 *be offended*
feel piqued 624.8 *resent*
feel pity 627.8 *pity*
feel pleasure 490.8
feel pride 622.29; 673.16 *show off*
feel refreshed 581.2 *be refreshed*
feel remorse 808.4 *be penitent*
feel resentment 624.8 *resent*
feel rotten 260.24 *be unhealthy*
feel shame 808.4 *be penitent;* 674.16 *be self-conscious*
feel sick 260.24 *be unhealthy*
feel sick at 596.5 *dislike*
feel small 623.24 *be humiliated*
feel something is missing 218.6 *be unsatisfied*
feel sore 624.8 *resent*
feel sorrow for 627.8 *pity*
feel sorry 808.4 *be penitent*
feel sorry for 627.8 *pity*
feel sure 452.20 *be certain*
feel the draught 249.10 *need money*
feel the lack 218.6 *be unsatisfied*
feel the need for 135.7 *require*
feel the pinch 264.20 *be in difficulty;* 782.12 *be poor;* 249.10 *need money*
feel the pulse 448.11 *experiment*
feel the spirit 7.19 *be religious*
feel the urge 483.8 *be motivated;* 480.18 *be persuaded*
feel unfulfilled 218.6 *be unsatisfied*
feel up 492.11 *touch*
feel well 259.5 *be healthy*
fees 788.3 *income*
fee simple 440.2, 763.2 *legal terms*
fee tail 440.2 *legal terms*
feet of clay 231.7 *defect;* 700.5 *falseness;* 254.7 *vulnerability;* 337.1 *weakness*
Fehling's test 33.5 *sugar test*
feign 340.4 *act;* 702.12 *deceive;* 699.24 *pretend*
feigning 702.10 *hypocritical;* 699.7 *pretence;* 699.34 *pretending*
feint 52.2 *boxing;* 54.5 *fence;* 54.3 *fencing movements;* 52.11 *fight;* 699.7 *pretence;* 699.24 *pretend;* 645.2 *stratagem;* 700.8, 700.28 *trick*
feinting 52.2 *boxing;* 52.14 *combat;* 700.34 *deceiving;* 54.6 *fencing*
feisty 336.9 *physically strong;* 338.4 *vigorous*
feldspar 30.34 *mineral;* 24.2 *raw material*
f-electron 28.65 *atom*
felicitate 601.15 *celebrate*
felicitation 669.4 *compliment*
felicitous 543.3 *elegant;* 597.4 *happy;* 248.8 *prosperous;* 287.6 *timely;* 485.9 *well-made*
felicitously 543.5 *elegantly;* 248.9 *prosperously*
felicity 543.1 *elegance;* 597.1 *happiness;* 490.1 *physical pleasure;* 248.1 *prosperity*
felid 71.8 *flesh-eating mammal*
Felidae 71.8 *flesh-eating mammal*
feline 71.28 *carnivorous;* 71.10 *cat;* 645.4 *cunning;* 71.8 *flesh-eating mammal*
fell 550.14 *animal covering;* 382.23 *deadly;* 357.9 *demolish;* 367.2 *flatten;* 154.2 *heights;* 187.7 *make horizontal;* 79.18 *manage trees;* 89.1 *mountain;* 330.28 *shoot*
fella 593.9 *lover*
fell boots 551.19 *footwear*
felling 79.6 *tree management*
felling licence 79.6 *tree management*
felling saw 79.7 *timber production*
fellow 223.11 *companion;* 747.10 *cooperator;* 115.5 *counterpart;* 400.9 *educational leader;* 6.4 *educator;* 119.5 *equal;* 569.5 *friend;* 567.2 *male;* 567.3 *male title of address;* 405.5 *member;* 769.5 *recipient*
fellow citizen 564.8 *national*
fellow countryman 564.8 *national*
fellow creature 569.5 *friend;* 566.7 *person*
fellow feeling 650.1 *benevolence;* 747.2 *fellowship;* 569.2 *friendly relations;* 590.5 *good feeling;* 593.1 *love;* 764.2 *participation;* 627.1 *pity*
fellows 747.9 *team*
fellowship 747.2; 750.2 *alliance;* 376.15 *association;* 223.3 *companionship;* 392.6 *financial assistance;* 569.1 *friendship;* 768.2 *gift;* 654.8 *good company;* 813.3 *grant;* 788.3 *income;* 6.6 *instructorship;* 764.2 *participation;* 765.5 *profit;* 769.2 *something received*
fellowship winner 769.5 *recipient*
fellow student 6.7 *learner*
fellow tenant 764.3 *participant*
fellow traveller 223.11 *companion;* 700.20 *plotter;* 413.8 *supporter*
fellow worker 578.5 *partner*
fell pony 59.5 *pony*
fell walker 62.7 *mountaineer*
fell walking 62.1 *mountaineering*
felo de se 814.11 *penance;* 382.7 *suicide*
felon 800.4 *dishonourable person;* 806.4 *guilty person;* 16.40 *lawbreaker;* 651.8 *malefactor;* 804.9 *wicked person;* 802.10 *wrongdoer*
felonious 800.7, 804.15 *criminal;* 802.16 *in the wrong;* 16.60 *offending*
feloniously 804.21 *criminally*
felony 16.39 *crime;* 800.3, 804.7 *criminality;* 806.3 *sin;* 662.2 *violation of the law;* 802.8 *wrongdoing*
felsic rock 30.30 *igneous rock*
felt 435.1 *materials;* 42.14 *weave*
felted 42.10 *woven*
felt hat 551.15 *headgear*
Female 568
female 568.2; **568.15**; 78.12 *of flowers*
female animal 568.14
female bird 72.11
female circumcision 10.7 *non-Christian ritual*
female condom 563.3 *birth control*
female genital mutilation 10.7 *non-Christian ritual*
female impersonator 21.29 *entertainer;* 125.7 *imitator;* 717.5 *performer;* 227.8 *person who changes costume*
female mammal 71.18
female person 568.2 *female*
female sex 568.1
female sex organs 561.8 *organs of reproduction*
female title of address 568.3
female transvestite 568.10 *homosexual*
female warrior 586.10 *woman soldier*
feme covert 570.11 *married woman*
femidom 563.3 *birth control*
feminality 568.1 *female sex*
feminine 568.15 *female;* 5.44 *grammatical*
feminine gender 568.1 *female sex*
feminine intuition 445.1 *intuition*
feminineness 568.1 *female sex*
feminine rhyme 17.11 *rhyme*
femininity 568.1 *female sex*
feminism 391.2 *equal opportunity;* 568.1 *female sex;* 244.11 *reformism*
feminist 568.15 *female;* 568.11 *liberated woman;* 622.23 *prejudiced;* 244.12 *reformer*
feministic 568.15 *female*
feminist theatre 21.10 *theatre movements*
feminist theology 7.13 *theology*
feminist therapy 36.3 *psychiatric treatment*
femme de chambre 401.6 *domestic servant*
femme fatale 545.3 *attractive female;* 363.6 *charmer;* 568.6 *loose woman;* 593.9 *lover;* 483.7 *motivator;* 480.13 *tempter*
femme sole 572.5 *single person*
fen 92.3, 429.8 *marsh*
fence 54.5; **384.18**; 378.3, 384.9 *barrier;* 800.10 *be criminal;* 479.1 *be equivocal;* 634.7 *be evasive;* 378.9 *block;* 372.6 *boundary;* 166.4 *boundary marker;* 331.2 *collide;* 774.11 *dishonest person;* 165.5 *enclose;* 165.3 *enclosing thing;* 736.13 *equivocate;* 699.27 *evade;* 59.11 *eventing;* 128.3 *exclusion zone;* 43.11 *farmland;* 586.37 *fight;* 59.9 *jumping;* 44.3 *ornamental garden;* 384.24 *parry;* 769.9 *receive;* 769.5 *recipient;* 776.1 *trade;* 776.10 *trader;* 360.4 *wall;* 778.12 *wholesaler*
fenced-in 378.14 *blocked;* 165.7 *enclosed;* 360.10 *retained*
fence in 360.7 *detain;* 165.5 *enclose;* 252.10 *protect*
fence off 128.7 *exclude*
fencer 54.4; 586.3 *athlete;* 59.2 *thoroughbred*
fence round 252.10 *protect*
fences 59.7 *horseracing*
fence-sitter 618.6 *indifferent person*
fencible 586.8 *soldier*
Fencing 54
fencing 54.1; **54.6**; 699.13 *evasion;* 699.38 *evasive*
fencing area 54.1 *fencing*
fencing assault 54.1 *fencing*
fencing association 54.1 *fencing*
fencing bout 54.1 *fencing*
fencing clothes 54.2 *fencing equipment*
fencing equipment 54.2
fencing movements 54.3
fencing sword 587.8 *sharp weapon*
fencing weapon 54.2 *fencing equipment*
fender 384.2 *safeguard*
fend for oneself 250.16 *be independent*
fend off 364.3; 384.24 *parry*
fenestella 20.9 *miscellaneous architectural features*
fenestra 20.9 *miscellaneous architectural features*
fenestrated 20.17 *structured*
fenestrated cupola 20.9 *miscellaneous architectural features*
fenland 92.3 *marsh*
fennel 496.5 *herbs*
fenny 92.11 *continental;* 429.11 *marshy*
Fens 86.9 *regions of Britain*
Fensalir 8.11 *heaven*
fenugreek 496.5 *herbs*
feodal 440.8 *propertied*
feral 70.15 *of animals*
fermata 133.5 *caesura;* 226.3 *pause*
ferment 434.11 *aeration;* 624.4 *anger;* 327.21 *be agitated;* 434.24 *bubble;* 224.8 *cause change;* 224.5 *changer;* 328.5 *commotion;* 408.5 *confusion;* 760.1 *conversion;* 760.7 *convert into;* 415.8 *leavening;* 415.10 *lighten;* 83.11 *moulder;* 32.26 *react;* 499.8 *sour;* 760.9 *transform;* 327.3 *turbulence;* 380.1 *violence*
fermentation 434.11 *aeration;* 224.1 *change;* 760.1 *conversion;* 366.10 *elevator;* 432.7 *gaseousness;* 415.8 *leavening;* 327.3 *turbulence*
fermentation vat 760.4 *medium of conversion*
fermentative 415.4 *leavening*
fermented 558.17 *drinkable;* 83.9 *fungal;* 499.6 *unpalatable*
fermented drink 558.7 *alcoholic drink*
fermenting 760.14 *converting;* 415.4 *leavening;* 356.1 *production*
ferment into 760.7 *convert into*
fermion 28.77 *elementary particle*
fern 82.1
fern ally 82.1 *fern*
fernlike 82.5
fernlike plant 82.1 *fern*
fern plant 82.2
Ferns and Mosses 82
fern seed 82.2 *fern plant*
ferny 82.5 *fernlike*
féroce 25.51 *West Indian dish*
ferocious 651.11 *cruel;* 380.6 *violent*
ferociously 380.10 *violently*
ferociousness 651.2 *cruelness*
ferocity 651.2 *cruelness;* 380.1 *violence*
ferreting 633.2 *chase;* 71.23 *mammal hunting*
ferreting out 449.7 *detection*
ferret out 449.2 *detect*
ferriage 316.2 *transportation*
ferric 32.34 *elemental*
ferriferous plumbous 32.34 *elemental*
ferrimagnetism 28.59 *ferromagnetism*
Ferris wheel 307.6 *rotator*
ferrite 28.60 *magnet*
ferroconcrete 20.4, 435.2 *building material;* 418.7 *hard substance*
ferromagnetic core 28.60 *magnet*
ferromagnetic material 28.59 *ferromagnetism*
ferromagnetism 28.59
ferrosoferric 32.34 *elemental*
ferrous 32.34 *elemental*
ferrovitreous 20.17 *structured*
ferrovitreous construction 20.4 *building material*
ferruginous 534.1 *brown*
ferrule 55.3 *fishing tackle*
ferry 90.2 *channel;* 316.12 *transport;* 323.3 *vessel*
ferry bridge 38.21 *bridge*
ferry crossing 323.2 *waterway*
ferrying 323.11 *nautical*
ferryman 323.8 *boatman;* 316.7 *transferor*
ferry terminal 226.4 *stopping place*
fertile 562.5; 270.3 *diffuse;* 43.20 *farmable;* 80.6 *fruiting;* 477.10 *imaginative;* 781.4 *lush;* 217.2 *plentiful;* 356.11 *productive;* 765.19 *yielding*
fertile imagination 477.1 *imagination;* 562.2 *productiveness*
fertilely 765.20 *gainfully*
fertile nuclide 28.72 *nuclear fission*
fertile soil 344.2 *source*
Fertility 562
fertility 562.1; 554.4 *biological function;* 270.1 *diffuseness;* 217.8 *plenty*
fertility cult 562.4
fertility dance 22.4 *historic dancing*
fertility drug 562.3 *fertilizer*
fertility god 8.5 *deity*
fertility rite 562.4 *fertility cult;* 10.7 *non-Christian ritual*
fertility symbol 562.4 *fertility cult;* 36.24 *symbolism*
fertilization 562.2 *productiveness;* 561.3 *propagation*
fertilize 44.15 *cultivate;* 43.17 *farm;* 338.3 *invigorate;* 562.7 *make fertile;* 81.12 *manage grassland;* 561.13 *propagate*
fertilized 561.16 *reproductive*
fertilizer 43.13; **44.7**; **562.3**; 561.5 *propagator*
fertilizers 32.22 *industrial chemistry*
fertilizer spreader 43.10 *farm tool*
fertilizing 43.5 *cultivation*
ferule 814.14 *instrument of punishment*
fervent 342.18 *active;* 726.3 *emphatic;* 593.19 *enamoured;* 262.3 *hasty;* 590.13 *passionate;* 336.10 *potent;* 7.15 *religious;* 380.6 *violent*
fervently 336.15 *acutely;* 726.7 *emphatically;* 593.30 *lovingly;* 590.20 *with feeling*
fervent patriotism 585.5 *bellicosity*
fervid 336.10 *potent*
fervour 636.7 *eagerness;* 590.4 *emotion;*

726.1 *emphasis*; 342.4 *energy*; 7.2 *religiousness*; 593.2 *romantic love*
fescue 43.12 *crop*
fesse point 743.8 *heraldic device*
festa 601.1 *celebration*
festal 10.21 *ritualistic*
festal cheer 557.9 *plenty*
festally 10.23 *ritually*
fester **560.18**; 258.10 *be dirty*; 245.2 *decay*
festering 260.23 *diseased*; 260.6 *infection*; 560.27 *purulent*; 560.7 *pus*; 260.15 *ulcer*; 258.8 *unclean*
festina lente 333.8 *slowness*
festival 600.1 *rejoicing*; 10.16 *religious festival*; 376.9 *social gathering*
Festival of Lights 10.16 *religious festival*
festive **654.17**; 601.10 *celebrative*; 10.21 *ritualistic*
festive board 557.9 *plenty*
festive gathering 557.13 *feast*
festively 654.18 *sociably*
festive occasion 601.1 *celebration*
festivities 601.1 *celebration*; 600.1 *rejoicing*
festivity 601.1 *celebration*; 654.5 *party*; 600.1 *rejoicing*; 10.16 *religious festival*; 654.1 *sociability*; 376.9 *social gathering*
festoon 542.12 *ornament*
festoon blind 523.6 *shade*
FET 39.19 *transistor*
fetal 34.26 *developmental*; 130.32 *embryonic*
fetch 316.14 *bring back*; 790.13 *cost*; 11.11 *ghost*; 96.2 *illusion*; 312.2 *reach*; 50.15 *sail*; 700.8, 700.28 *trick*
fetch a blow 381.5 *strike*
fetch a good price 778.2 *be sold*
fetch and carry 316.14 *bring back*; 664.10 *knuckle under*; 664.11 *pander to*
fetch breath 554.18 *be born*
fetch down 367.2 *flatten*
fetching 363.9 *attractive*
fetch up in 312.2 *reach*
fête **600.6**; 601.15, 656.10 *celebrate*; 601.1 *celebration*; 656.3 *formal occasion*; 658.12 *greet*; 557.25 *provide food*; 601.18 *salute*
fête champêtre 19.10 *art subject*; 557.13 *feast*; 654.5 *party*
fêted 654.16 *popular*
fetid 236.4 *poor*; 503.3 *stinking*; 258.8 *unclean*
fetidness 503.1 *stench*
fetish 8.5 *deity*; 9.3 *idol*; 10.14 *sacred object*; 11.6 *talisman*
fetishism 461.4 *delusion*; 9.2 *idolatry*; 10.7 *non-Christian ritual*; 11.3 *witchcraft*
fetishist 9.6 *idolater*
fetishistic 9.10 *idolatrous*; 10.21 *ritualistic*; 11.15 *witchlike*
fetishization 8.9 *deification*
fetishize 9.8 *idolatrize*
fetish-like 9.10 *idolatrous*
fetor 236.10 *poverty*; 503.1 *stench*; 258.2 *uncleanness*
fetoscope 35.7 *diagnosis*
fetoscopy 35.7 *diagnosis*
fetter 373.12 *bind*; 251.12 *gag*; 373.4 *means of connection*; 378.10 *restrain*; 378.4 *restraint*; 252.4 *safety device*
fettered 373.16 *bound*
fetters 814.14 *instrument of punishment*; 251.5 *means of restraint*
fettle 259.3 *health*; 24.11 *make ceramics*; 160.6 *nature*; 221.5 *physical state*; 221.1 *state*; 221.4 *state of mind*
fettling 24.5 *ceramic process*
fetus 34.15 *developmental biology*; 561.7 *obstetrics*; 344.3 *rudiment*
feu 440.3 *historic property terms*
feud 701.13, 751.6 *argue*; 701.1, 751.2 *argument*; 440.3 *historic property terms*; 763.3 *medieval ownership*; 242.8, 242.11 *quarrel*
feudal 12.9 *governmental*; 296.14 *historic*; 440.8 *propertied*; 387.9 *subject*
feudal court 16.19 *law court*
feudalism 12.1 *government*; 387.1 *subjection*
feudality 12.1 *government*; 440.3 *historic property terms*; 763.3 *medieval ownership*
feudal lord 252.3 *protector*
feudal tax 790.9 *historical taxes*
feudatory 440.8 *propertied*
feuding 701.9 *hostile*
feuilleton 740.4 *newspaper*
fever 493.1 *heat*; 260.6 *infection*; 327.5, 342.7 *restlessness*; 742.1 *sign*; 260.3 *symptom*; 260.7 *tropical disease*; 327.2 *tumult*
fevered 260.23 *diseased*; 535.2 *red-faced*; 327.16 *restless*; 493.12 *warm-hearted*
feverish 342.18 *active*; 260.23 *diseased*; 262.3 *hasty*; 535.2 *red-faced*; 327.16 *restless*; 260.22 *sick*; 493.12 *warm-hearted*
feverish haste 262.4 *haste*
feverishly 327.27 *agitatedly*; 262.6 *hastily*; 493.17 *warmly*
feverishness 493.1 *heat*; 327.5 *restlessness*; 260.3 *symptom*
Few 206
few **206.1**; **206.5**; 203.2 *certain amount*; 207.6 *plural*; 203.6 *quantitative*; 153.6 *scant*; 218.4 *scarce*; 452.8 *unspecified*
few and far between 377.19 *dispersed*; 218.4 *scarce*; 206.6 *sparse*
fewer **206.7**
few in number 153.6 *scant*
fewness **206.3**; 203.2 *certain amount*; 122.3 *inferior numbers*; 153.12 *thinning*
few words 269.1 *conciseness*
fey 582.18 *dying*; 590.11 *intuitive*; 11.18 *spiritual*
Feydeau farce 21.12 *comedy*
feyness 11.8 *psychic power*
fez 551.15 *headgear*
fiancé 567.4 *boyfriend*; 593.9 *lover*; 756.6 *someone promised*
fiancée 568.4 *girlfriend*; 593.9 *lover*; 756.6 *someone promised*
Fianna Fáil 12.6 *political party*
fiasco 798.2 *affliction*; 604.2 *bad outcome*; 247.1 *failure*
fiat 397.1 *command*; 140.1 *rule*
fiat money 780.14 *paper money*
fib 105.7 *be improbable*; 105.6 *implausibility*; 699.10 *lie*; 718.1 *misrepresentation*
fibber 699.18, 700.16 *liar*
fibbery 699.6 *lying*
fibbing 699.33 *deceitful*; 699.6 *lying*
fibre **42.1**; **404.6**; 557.11 *food content*; 373.6 *line*; 435.1 *materials*
fibreboard 435.4 *board*
fibre cable 692.6 *telecommunication*
fibreglass 527.9 *glass*; 435.1 *materials*; 550.12 *protective covering*
fibre-optic cable 692.6 *telecommunication*
fibre optics 40.14 *data transfer*; 28.34 *photometry*
fibre-optics transmission 28.34 *photometry*
fibre paper 435.3 *paper*
fibre pole 47.2 *field events*
fibres 32.22 *industrial chemistry*
fibrescope 35.7 *diagnosis*
fibrin 33.9 *protein*
fibrosis 260.4 *disease*
fibrositis 260.16 *rheumatism*
fibrous 423.3 *hard*; 404.8 *rough*; 75.22 *spongelike*
fibrously 404.15 *texturally*
fibrous protein 33.9 *protein*
fibrous root 77.7 *root*
fibrous-rooted 77.19 *of roots*
fibster 699.18, 700.16 *liar*
ficelle 700.8 *trick*
fichu 551.14 *neckwear*
fickle 453.8, 642.1 *capricious*; 224.11, 639.2 *changeable*; 479.11 *equivocating*; 227.14 *irresolute*
fickleness 642.2 *caprice*; 453.16 *capriciousness*; 224.2 *change of mind*; 639.12 *inconstancy*; 227.2 *irresolution*
fickle person **227.6**
fictile 160.9 *formed*
fiction **17.2**; **721.5**; 234.4 *distortion of the truth*; 699.9 *falsification*; 477.4 *ideality*; 356.4 *mental product*; 721.3 *narration*; 699.7 *pretence*; 96.4 *theorization*
fictional **17.17**; 699.36 *falsified*; 477.12 *imaginary*; 477.10 *imaginative*; 721.12 *narrative*; 96.10 *theoretical*
fictional biography 17.2, 721.5 *fiction*
fictional horse 59.1 *horse*
fictionalization 699.7 *pretence*
fictionalize 477.15 *fantasize*; 721.15 *recount*
fictionalized 699.36 *falsified*; 17.17 *fictional*
fiction editor 740.12 *publisher*
fictionist 721.10 *descriptive writer*
fiction writer 17.14 *author*; 721.10 *descriptive writer*
fictitious 234.8 *exaggerated*; 477.12 *imaginary*; 702.7 *sophistic*; 96.10 *theoretical*
fictive 477.12 *imaginary*
fiddle 789.7 *account*; 800.10 *be criminal*; 700.30 *be fraudulent*; 13.12 *cheat*; 800.3 *criminality*; 774.7 *dishonesty*; 484.3 *expedient plan*; 699.9 *falsification*; 699.26 *falsify*; 700.10 *fraud*; 342.17 *meddle*; 786.1 *nonpayment*; 18.38 *sound*; 774.12 *steal*; 492.11 *touch*
fiddle one's income tax 786.7 *not pay*
fiddler 774.11 *dishonest person*
fiddler crab 75.4 *arthropod*
fiddle with 224.8 *cause change*; 492.11 *touch*
fiddling 774.18 *fraudulent*; 576.11 *laborious*; 342.21 *meddling*; 342.7 *restlessness*; 774.1 *stealing*; 124.4 *trivial*
fideism 452.10 *conviction*
fidelity 698.8 *accuracy*; 640.3 *constancy*; 273.2 *correctness*; 698.13 *faithfulness*; 452.17 *infallibility*; 663.2 *loyalty*; 799.1 *probity*; 267.2 *tenacity*
fidget 227.12 *be irresolute*; 342.10 *busy person*; 262.4 *haste*; 262.2 *make haste*; 327.24 *shake*
fidgetiness 327.5, 342.7 *restlessness*
fidgeting 227.2 *irresolution*
fidgety 342.18 *active*; 639.2 *changeable*; 227.14 *irresolute*; 327.16 *restless*
Fido 71.9 *dog*
fiducial point 29.21 *orbit*; 27.36 *point*
fiduciary 780.22 *monetary*
fiduciary currency 780.14 *paper money*
fiduciary heir 769.6 *beneficiary*
fief 440.3 *historic property terms*; 763.3 *medieval ownership*
fiefdom 440.3 *historic property terms*
field **53.16**; 27.23 *algebra*; 40.19 *computing terms*; 165.2 *enclosed place*; 43.11 *farmland*; 28.10 *force*; 81.2 *grassland*; 743.8 *heraldic device*; 58.8 *hockey*; 633.6 *hunter*; 92.6 *lowland*; 27.1 *mathematics*; 141.7 *range*; 27.21 *set*; 139.8 *specialization*; 86.14, 447.4 *sphere*; 45.2 *sportsground*; 46.4 *stadium*; 6.3 *subject*; 692.21 *television*; 47.9 *track*
field army 586.14 *armed forces*; 584.4 *military organization*
field army commander 584.5 *military staff*
field beans 43.12 *crop*
field day 601.5 *anniversary*; 656.3 *formal occasion*; 600.1 *rejoicing*
field desorb 32.29 *absorb*
field desorption 32.20 *surface chemistry*
field emission 39.24 *electron emission*
field-emission microscope 28.85 *microscope*
fielder 48.2 *baseball player*; 53.4 *team*
field events **47.2**
field frequency 692.21 *television*
field general 46.7 *offence*
field general court martial 584.6 *military law*
field glasses 28.32 *optical instrument*; 518.10 *visual aid*
field goal 49.4 *playing terms*; 46.6 *scoring*; 246.3 *successful thing*
field-goal kicker 46.12 *special team*
field grade officer 584.5 *military staff*
field gun 587.11 *guns*
field hockey 58.1 *hockey*
fielding 53.12 *cricketing*; 64.3 *rugby play*
fielding side 53.4 *team*
fielding terms **48.6**
field ionize 32.29 *absorb*
field-ion microscope 28.85 *microscope*
field judge 47.3 *athlete*; 46.2 *football player*
field magnet 363.3 *magnet*
field marshal 400.7 *military leader*; 397.6 *person in command*
field mushroom 83.2 *mushroom*; 25.33 *vegetable*
field of battle 585.10 *battleground*; 382.15 *slaughterhouse*
field of blood 585.10 *battleground*; 382.6 *ritual killing*
field of conflict 585.10 *battleground*
field of force 334.4 *energy*; 28.10 *force*
field of inquiry 447.4 *sphere*
field of study 447.5 *educational topic*
field of view 28.32 *optical instrument*; 29.28 *resolution*; 520.6 *visible thing*
field of vision 518.9 *viewpoint*; 520.6 *visible thing*
field peas 43.12 *crop*
field piece 587.11 *guns*
fieldsman 53.4 *team*
field sports 60.2 *hunting*
field station 448.6 *place of experimentation*; 31.5 *weather station*
field stop 28.32 *optical instrument*
field strength 39.11 *electric field*
field trial 60.2 *hunting*
fieldwork 384.8 *military defences*; 576.1 *work*
fiend 8.7 *devil*; 804.9 *wicked person*
fiendish 651.11 *cruel*; 8.16 *devilish*; 804.14 *impious*; 11.15 *witchlike*
fiendishly 8.20 *devilishly*; 804.20 *immorally*
fiendishness 651.2 *cruelness*
fiendlike 651.11 *cruel*; 8.16 *devilish*
fierce 342.18 *active*; 624.16 *angry*; 493.9 *hot*; 336.10 *potent*; 380.6 *violent*; 585.16 *warlike*
fiercely 336.14 *strongly*; 380.10 *violently*
fierceness 380.1 *violence*
fierily 493.17 *warmly*
fiery 522.16 *bright*; 726.3 *emphatic*; 493.9 *hot*; 590.13 *passionate*; 535.2 *red-faced*; 380.6 *violent*
fiery cross 711.2 *danger signal*; 742.1 *sign*; 585.7 *war measures*
fiery temper 625.1 *irascibility*
fiesta 601.1 *celebration*; 10.16 *religious festival*; 376.9 *social gathering*
fifteen 201.7 *double figures*
fifteenth 201.18 *eleventh*; 196.4 *less than one*
fifth **201.12**; 27.75 *equal*; 201.1 *five*; 201.24 *fivefold*; 196.4 *less than one*; 18.16 *musical note*
Fifth Avenue 551.2 *dressing*
fifth column 588.1 *anarchy*; 662.3 *subversion*
fifth columnism 662.3 *subversion*
fifth columnist 588.3 *anarchist*; 479.9 *equivocator*; 693.10 *informer*; 700.20 *plotter*; 662.10 *seditionist*
fifth guard 54.3 *fencing movements*
fifthly 201.24 *fivefold*
fifth part 201.1 *five*
fifth wheel 219.3 *superfluity*
fiftieth 196.4 *less than one*; 201.19 *twentieth*
fifty 53.10 *score*; 201.8 *twenty and over*
fifty cents 780.8 *American money*
fifty-dollar bill 780.8 *American money*
fifty-fifty 111.16 *equal*; 107.3 *equal chance*; 111.19 *equally*; 198.22 *in half*; 216.2 *medium*; 412.12 *mixed*; 235.5 *not bad*; 119.8 *on equal terms*
fifty-fifty split 111.5 *equality*
fifty pence 780.9 *British money*
fifty percent 198.8 *half*; 198.22 *in half*
fig 221.5 *physical state*
fight **52.11**; **331.9**; **586.37**; 701.13, 751.6 *argue*; 701.1, 751.2 *argument*; 585.9, 585.14 *battle*; 624.11 *be angry*; 613.15 *be courageous*; 662.16 *be subversive*; 381.20 *bout*; 52.2 *boxing*; 113.5 *conflict*; 751.5 *disagree*; 408.9 *disorder*; 585.12 *go to war*; 113.18 *object*; 58.9 *play hockey*; 242.11, 624.5 *quarrel*; 596.6 *react against*; 637.7 *refuse*
fight a defensive battle 384.26 *act on the defensive*
fight against 347.3 *counteract*; 113.14 *oppose*
fight a guerrilla war 753.8 *cause mischief*
fight as a heavyweight 52.11 *fight*
fight back 381.8 *counterattack*; 384.26 *retaliate*
fighter 586.3 *athlete*; 353.7 *attempter*; 52.4 *boxer*; 586.1 *combatant*; 586.31 *military aircraft*; 242.9 *unpleasant person*
fighter-bomber 586.31 *military aircraft*
fighter pilot 586.32 *airman*; 381.19 *attacker*
fight fire with fire 385.3 *retaliate*
fight for 384.22 *plead for*
fight for freedom 391.5 *be liberated*
fighting 381.23 *attacking*; 52.2 *boxing*; 52.14 *combat*; 52.1 *combat sports*; 113.5 *conflict*; 751.9 *disagreeing*; 751.1 *disagreement*; 242.7 *dissension*; 701.9 *hostile*; 58.3 *ice hockey*; 584.8 *military*; 585.8 *warfare*; 585.15 *warring*
fighting animal **586.4**
fighting bird 586.4 *fighting animal*
fighting chance 107.4 *fair chance*

fighting cock 613.7 *courageous person;* 586.4 *fighting animal*
fighting dog 586.4 *fighting animal*
fighting drunk 690.1 *drunk*
fighting fish 586.4 *fighting animal*
fighting fit 259.1 *healthy*
fighting forces 586.14 *armed forces*
fighting mad 624.16 *angry*
fighting man 586.1 *combatant;* 586.8 *soldier*
fighting seat 55.1 *angling*
fighting skill 52.1 *combat sports*
fighting spirit 585.5 *bellicosity;* 613.1 *courage*
fighting sport 52.1 *combat sports*
fight it out 585.14 *battle*
fight off 384.24 *parry;* 383.8 *revolt*
fight on! 383.16
fight one's way 633.13 *follow up*
fight shy 634.4 *shy*
fight the good fight 585.14 *battle;* 795.11 *be moral;* 803.8 *be virtuous;* 7.20 *preach*
fight to the death 638.11 *persist*
fight to the finish 585.14 *battle;* 638.11 *persist*
fig leaf 551.25 *accessories*
figment 699.9 *falsification;* 477.4 *ideality;* 96.2 *illusion;* 518.5 *imagination;* 356.4 *mental product*
figmental 96.9 *illusory*
figment of the imagination 477.4 *ideality;* 356.4 *mental product*
figural 194.7 *numerical*
figurant 21.30 *dancer*
figurante 21.30 *dancer*
figurate 194.7 *numerical*
figuration 717.1 *representation*
figurative 694.6 *meaningful;* 542.10 *ornate;* 19.29 *realist;* 717.13 *representational;* 721.13 *representing*
figurative blindness 519.7
figurative dark thing 523.5
figurative language 17.12 *poetic language*
figuratively 694.13 *meaningfully;* 542.13 *ornately;* 19.30 *pictorially;* 717.14 *representationally*
figurative meaning 694.4 *type of meaning*
figurativeness 542.1 *ornament*
figure 210.8 *calculate;* 139.3 *characteristic;* 525.3 *external appearance;* 553.9 *fashion;* 160.1, 160.7 *form;* 27.41 *geometric figure;* 36.26 *gestalt;* 516.4 *harmonics;* 68.13 *ice-skating;* 717.6 *image;* 160.6 *nature;* 194.1 *number;* 27.9 *numeral;* 790.1 *price;* 19.12 *sculpture;* 163.2 *shadow;* 780.5 *sum*
figured bass 516.4 *harmonics*
figure eight 177.3 *curved things*
figure-ground 36.26 *gestalt*
figurehead 167.1 *front;* 124.10 *nonentity;* 335.5 *powerless person*
figure-hugging 267.9 *adhesive;* 151.1 *narrow*
figure of eight 179.2 *circle;* 201.4 *eight;* 322.5 *flight*
figure of fun 668.9 *butt;* 621.4 *laughing stock;* 272.3 *object of ridicule*
figure of speech 542.1 *ornament*
figure out 210.8 *calculate;* 194.10 *number;* 4.21 *rationalize*
figures 27.1 *mathematics;* 210.2 *statistics*
figure-skate 68.15 *ice-skate*
figure-skating 68.6 *ice-skating*
figure-watching 766.1 *loss*
figure work 210.1 *calculation*
figurine 24.8 *ceramic object;* 717.6 *image;* 19.12 *sculpture;* 794.1 *trophy*
figuring 210.1 *calculation;* 27.12 *numeration;* 19.12 *sculpture*
figurist 19.17 *sculptor*
Fijian 5.11 *family of languages*
filament 42.1, 404.6 *fibre;* 78.3 *flower part;* 29.7 *galaxy;* 28.25 *light source;* 435.1 *materials;* 151.8 *narrow thing;* 29.15 *sun*
filamentary cloud 31.20 *cloud appearance*
filament lamp 28.25 *light source*
filamentous 84.7 *algal;* 151.2 *fine*
filariasis 75.11 *helminthic disease*
filch 774.12 *steal;* 774.1 *stealing*
filched 16.59 *stolen*
filcher 774.8 *thief*
filching 774.1 *stealing*
file 427.12 *abrasive;* 586.16 *army unit;* 410.6 *box;* 409.7 *catalogue;* 409.15 *categorize;* 3.5, 3.20 *chronicle;* 439.5 *collection;* 40.19 *computing terms;* 132.2 *consecution;* 294.8 *delay;* 693.3 *document;* 365.7 *eraser;* 427.25 *grate;* 365.15 *grind;* 406.9 *itemize;* 132.17 *line up;* 220.8 *list;* 425.15 *make sharp;* 191.5 *make smaller;* 584.4 *military organization;* 410.5 *packet;* 132.8 *procession;* 744.1, 744.13 *record;* 420.7 *rough thing;* 425.12 *sharpener;* 421.9 *smoother;* 439.6 *store;* 220.2 *table*
file a brief 16.70 *litigate*
file a claim 16.70 *litigate*
file a suit 16.70 *litigate*
file charges 715.5 *accuse*
filed 409.24 *categorized;* 3.19 *chronicled;* 220.11 *listed;* 744.16 *recorded*
file down 421.11 *smooth;* 212.3 *subtract*
file for divorce 571.7 *divorce*
file past 132.17 *line up*
file server 40.15 *network*
filet steak 25.22 *beef*
filial love 593.1 *love*
filiated 750.11 *allied*
filibeg 551.6 *skirt*
filibuster 378.9 *block;* 294.8 *delay;* 294.3 *delayed action;* 378.7 *hinderer;* 378.2 *obstacle;* 637.12 *opposition;* 731.9 *out-talk;* 702.13 *quibble*
filibusterer 294.5 *delayer;* 113.11 *opposer*
Filicinae 82.1 *fern*
filicopsid 82.1 *fern*
Filicopsida 82.1 *fern*
filiform 151.2 *fine*
filigree 193.2 *braid;* 193.8 *interweave;* 542.3 *pattern*
filing 409.5 *categorization;* 191.1 *contraction;* 365.3 *grinding;* 220.7 *listing;* 159.3 *little piece;* 744.8 *registration*
filing cabinet 410.3 *cabinet*
filing clerk 744.9 *recorder*
filings 205.8 *bits and pieces;* 427.6 *crumb;* 215.2 *residue*
filing system 220.2 *table*
fill 232.6; 219.4 *be excessive;* 97.11 *be present;* 394.20 *doctor;* 213.4 *increase;* 35.21 *practise dentistry;* 393.1 *repair;* 436.6 *replenish;* 609.8 *satisfy;* 439.6 *store;* 406.7 *stuff;* 38.28 *substructure;* 217.4 *suffice*
fill a gap 232.4 *complete*
fill a need 392.26 *be useful;* 232.4 *complete*
fill a post 12.11 *govern*
fill a space 211.6 *add;* 232.6 *fill*
filled 217.3; 232.8 *full*
fille de joie 490.3 *pleasure-seeker*
filled to overflowing 219.6 *excessive*
filled up 232.8 *full*
filled with holes 308.14 *holed*
filler 270.1 *diffuseness;* 20.9 *miscellaneous architectural features;* 406.4 *stuffing*
fillet 373.10 *band;* 25.55 *cook;* 551.15 *headgear;* 371.11 *void*
fill in 762.4 *be a substitute;* 725.2 *clarify;* 232.4 *complete;* 550.34 *cover for;* 693.11 *inform;* 213.5 *make bigger;* 393.1 *repair*
fill-in 762.2 *substitute person;* 550.21 *substitution*
filling 232.2 *fullness;* 213.6 *increasing;* 112.2 *iteration;* 609.5 *satisfying;* 406.4 *stuffing;* 394.12 *surgery;* 368.11 *thing inserted*
filling depression 31.11 *weather system*
fillings 35.4 *dentistry*
filling station 437.6 *oil;* 439.4 *storage*
filling the bill 217.1 *sufficient*
filling up 232.2 *fullness*
fill-in light 41.15 *lighting*
fill in the cracks 393.1 *repair*
fill in the gaps 218.5 *be insufficient*
fillip 331.13 *blow;* 480.8 *incentive;* 483.3 *stimulus*
fillness 510.3 *deepness*
fill oneself 688.5 *be greedy*
fill one's lungs 581.2 *be refreshed*
fill one's stomach 557.22 *eat well*
fill out 190.6 *become bigger;* 232.5 *be complete;* 232.4 *complete;* 152.8 *fatten;* 213.4 *increase;* 213.5 *make bigger;* 181.11 *make round*
fill space 158.19 *be big*
fill the air 507.8 *be loud*
fill the bill 239.6 *be convenient;* 246.8 *be effective;* 237.9 *be useful;* 750.27 *fit;* 217.4 *suffice*
fill the gap 211.6 *add*
fill the port 68.16 *bobsled*
fill to capacity 232.6 *fill*
fill up 232.6 *fill;* 437.11 *fuel;* 213.5 *make bigger;* 436.6 *replenish;* 439.6 *store;* 406.7 *stuff;* 217.4 *suffice*
fill-up 232.2 *fullness*
fill up again 393.3 *restore*
fill with conceit 673.18 *make conceited*
fill with desire 617.15 *cause desire*
fill with distaste 481.4 *put off*
fill with holes 308.20 *hole*
fill with longing 617.15 *cause desire*
filly 568.14 *female animal;* 71.18 *female mammal;* 59.1 *horse;* 555.4 *young animal;* 71.19 *young mammal*
film 41.9; 411.3 *coat;* 550.3 *coating;* 153.11 *fineness;* 524.10 *make dim;* 524.2 *murk;* 528.7 *opaque thing;* 738.9 *production;* 744.13 *record;* 744.7 *recording;* 717.9 *represent;* 717.2 *reproduction;* 157.4 *shallow thing;* 521.6 *that which makes invisible;* 527.8 *transparent thing;* 518.7 *view;* 356.5 *work of art*
film actor 21.24 *actor*
film actress 21.24 *actor*
film advance 41.18 *exposure time*
film camera 41.16 *camera*
film classification 399.2 *censorship*
film directing 21.6 *cinema*
film director 356.9 *producer*
filmed 744.16 *recorded*
filmgoer 21.33 *theatregoer*
film horse 59.1 *horse*
filminess 404.2 *grain;* 524.2 *murk;* 528.6 *opaqueness;* 527.6 *translucency*
filmography 220.2 *table*
film over 524.9 *be dim*
film plane 41.18 *exposure time*
film producer 356.9 *producer*
film review 719.3 *criticism*
film rewind 41.18 *exposure time*
films 21.3
film school 6.12 *educational institution*
film speed 41.10 *graininess*
film star 21.24 *actor;* 235.8 *exceller*
filmy 404.10 *delicate;* 521.2 *difficult to see;* 524.6 *murky;* 411.9 *platelike;* 528.2 *shady;* 527.2 *translucent*
Filofax™ 220.5 *list of appointments*
filo pastry 25.37 *pastry*
filoplume 72.17 *plumage*
filter 41.20; 320.3 *carriageway;* 28.55 *circuit;* 256.10 *cleaning object;* 325.1 *deviate;* 315.12 *leak;* 24.11 *make ceramics;* 308.6 *porous thing;* 39.34 *power supply;* 255.3 *purifier;* 255.10, 256.15 *purify;* 40.8 *software;* 32.25 *solidify;* 39.22 *transformer*
filter cloth 24.6 *ceramic workshop*
filter coffee 558.4 *coffee*
filtered 256.17 *cleaned;* 32.32 *solid*
filtered water 558.6 *soft drink*
filter-feeder 70.4 *type of animal*
filter in 314.11 *infiltrate*
filtering 39.15 *circuit function;* 315.3 *leakage*
filter press 24.6 *ceramic workshop*
filter pressing 24.5 *ceramic process*
filter pump 32.20 *surface chemistry*
filter through 97.11 *be present*
filter-tip 496.7, 496.11 *tobacco*
filth 712.1 *curse;* 258.4 *dirt;* 594.7 *hated thing;* 796.2 *indecency;* 236.10 *poverty*
filthiness 258.1 *dirtiness;* 796.2 *indecency;* 236.10 *poverty*
filthy 712.8 *cursing;* 258.7 *dirty;* 796.12 *indecent;* 258.9 *obscene;* 236.4 *poor;* 675.9 *ribald;* 408.15 *untidy*
filthy language 712.2 *offensive language*
filthy lucre 780.2 *cash;* 781.6 *money;* 765.5 *profit*
filthy rich 781.1 *wealthy;* 765.17 *well-off*
filthy talk 796.2 *indecency*
filtrable virus 34.3 *organism*
filtrate 315.12 *leak*
filtration 256.2 *cleaning;* 315.3 *leakage;* 32.5 *process*
fin 205.4 *component;* 119.4 *equilizer;* 74.5 *fish anatomy;* 201.1 *five;* 228.3 *stabilizer;* 67.1 *swimming;* 50.7 *windsurfing*
finagle 800.8 *be dishonourable*
final 313.11 *departing;* 131.20 *ending;* 47.1 *track events*
final arguments 16.7 *legal trial*
final attempt 353.5 *attempt*
final cause 482.5 *final intention*
final curtain 131.10 *ending;* 21.8 *scene*
final decision 482.4 *formulated intention*
final defeat 247.2 *defeat*
final demand 397.2, 710.2 *demand;* 711.1 *warning*
finale 131.1 *end;* 131.10 *ending;* 21.8 *scene*
final intention 482.5
final invoice 711.1 *warning*
finality 131.11; 582.7 *dying day;* 225.1 *permanence*
finalization 232.3 *completion*
finalize 204.10, 232.4 *complete;* 131.15 *end;* 225.6 *make permanent*
finalize accounts 789.9 *settle accounts*
finalized 232.7 *complete;* 131.21 *ended*
finally 131.26; **226.11**; **309.17**
final notice 710.2 *demand;* 711.1 *warning*
final objective 482.6 *objective*
final offer 752.3 *business offer*
final rest 263.1 *ease*
final resting place 583.5 *cemetery;* 226.5, 301.3 *resting place*
final result 345.1 *effect*
final say 395.1 *influence*
Final Solution 814.13 *capital punishment;* 382.4 *slaughter*
final stage 131.9 *close*
final stroke 382.5 *execution*
final touch 232.1 *completeness;* 244.5 *improvement*
final warning 397.2 *demand;* 711.1 *warning*
final word 482.4 *formulated intention*
final words 582.7 *dying day*
Finance 14
finance 14.1; **392.29**; **780.7**; 13.11 *deal;* 777.5, 785.8 *defray;* 787.3 *donate;* 787.7 *donation;* 352.6 *find means;* 679.11, 768.5 *give;* 14.5 *invest;* 413.13 *support financially*
finance a purchase 772.7 *borrow*
finance company 783.4 *bank;* 771.4 *lending institution*
finance house 783.4 *bank*
financer 768.4 *giver*
finances 352.4 *financial resources;* 780.6 *funds*
financial 14.6; 789.10 *accounting;* 776.14 *commercial;* 13.13 *economic;* 780.22 *monetary;* 87.14 *urban*
financial accounting 789.1 *accounts;* 14.1 *finance*
financial adviser 14.3 *stockbroker*
financial affairs 14.1 *finance*
financial aid 413.7 *financial support*
financial assistance 392.6; 768.2 *gift*
financial backing 392.6 *financial assistance*
financial circles 780.7 *finance*
financial collapse 782.6 *insolvency*
financial company 780.19 *treasury*
financial consultant 713.4 *adviser*
financial control 396.1 *authority;* 14.1, 780.7 *finance*
financial crisis 786.5 *insolvency*
financial dealing 759.1 *exchange*
financial disaster 249.2 *economic adversity*
financial district 87.7 *city district*
financial embarrassment 264.7 *awkward situation;* 782.6 *insolvency*
financial escape 389.1 *escape*
financial forecaster 475.9 *forecaster*
financial house 780.19 *treasury*
financial institution 771.4 *lending institution*
financial loss 766.2
financially 780.28; **789.13**; 13.14 *economically;* 788.8 *profitably*
financially embarrassed 782.2 *insolvent*
financially rewarding 246.14, 813.15 *rewarding*
financially ruined 782.2 *insolvent*
financially sound 781.2 *solvent*
financially stable 781.2 *solvent*
financially worthwhile 765.15 *gainful*
financial plan 484.1 *plan*
financial power 781.5 *wealth*
financial provision 780.6 *funds*
financial records 789.1 *accounts*
financial resources 352.4
financial reverse 249.2 *economic adversity*
financial reward 813.1 *reward*
financial ruin 249.2 *economic adversity;* 782.6, 786.5 *insolvency*
financial sector 13.2 *economy*
financial security 13.6 *economic factors*
financial setback 249.2 *economic adversity*

financial soundness 781.8 *solvency*
financial stability 781.8 *solvency*
financial statement 693.3 *document*
financial support 413.7; 788.3 *income*
Financial Times-Stock Exchange 100 Index; 14.2 *stock exchange*
financial unsoundness 782.6 *insolvency*
financial upturn 393.10 *revival*
financial world 780.7 *finance*
financial year 14.1 *finance*
financier 780.17; 771.3 *lender*; 14.3 *stockbroker*; 780.18 *treasurer*; 778.12 *wholesaler*
financing 772.1 *borrowing*
finch 72.6 *songbird*
finchlike 72.21 *avian*
find 142.11; **449.10**; 449.1 *discover*; 211.4 *extra*; 352.6 *find means*; 797.17 *good thing*; 464.11 *judge*; 29.20 *meteor*; 356.10 *produce*; 765.5 *profit*; 436.5 *provision*; 777.6 *purchase*; 312.2 *reach*; 140.13 *rule*; 16.71 *try a case*
find a bargain 791.5 *buy at a discount*
findable 449.15 *discoverable*
find a clue 449.2 *detect*
find against 16.79 *convict*; 464.11 *judge*
find agreement 748.1 *mediate*
find a husband for 570.17 *matchmake*
find a loophole 246.7 *overcome obstacles*
find a mate for 570.17 *matchmake*
find-and-destroy mission 381.12 *military attack*
find an opening 308.23
find an out 714.8 *justify*
find a remedy 347.3 *counteract*
find a resolution 719.9 *decipher*
find a solution 719.9 *decipher*
find a use for 237.11 *find useful*
find a way 348.5, 352.6 *find means*; 317.14 *find one's way*; 484.11 *invent*
find a way out 246.7 *overcome obstacles*
find a way round 347.3 *counteract*; 246.7 *overcome obstacles*
find a wife for 570.17 *matchmake*
find bargains 793.14 *buy cheaply*
find credence 450.10 *be believed*
find difficult 264.18
find engaged 288.6 *take untimely action*
finder 449.12 *discoverer*; 29.25 *mounting*
find fault 670.18; 264.23 *cause difficulties*; 264.24 *create difficulties*; 678.11 *criticize*
find fault with 606.7 *be dissatisfied*
find favour 669.17 *meet with approval*
find for 16.78 *acquit*; 464.11 *judge*
find freedom 389.5 *escape*
find guilty 16.79 *convict*
find hard to understand 696.9 *find unintelligible*
find indispensable 135.9 *find necessary*
finding 449.13 *discovering*; 449.6 *discovery*; 16.7 *legal trial*; 142.3 *locating*; 765.5 *profit*; 464.2 *verdict*
finding again 393.9 *restoration*
finding a penny 475.6 *good-luck sign*
finding of innocence 805.2 *legal innocence*
finding out 449.8
finding the spot 142.3 *locating*
find innocent 805.9 *declare innocent*
find intolerable 624.8 *resent*
find liable 16.79 *convict*
find loathsome 594.14 *hate*
find means 348.5; **352.6**; 344.10 *awaken*
find necessary 135.9
find no common ground 372.12 *disagree*
find no fault 669.11 *approve*
find not guilty 16.78 *acquit*; 805.9 *declare innocent*
find one's bearings 323.9 *navigate*
find one's El Dorado 781.13 *get rich*
find one's feet again 393.4 *be restored*
find one's level 407.24 *line up*
find one's match 385.4 *serve one right*
find one's way 317.14
find one's way into 314.9 *enter*
find out 449.3; 455.13 *get to know*; 6.23 *learn*; 452.21 *make certain*
find out about 449.3 *find out*
find peace and quiet 263.2 *take it easy*
find problems 264.23 *cause difficulties*; 264.24 *create difficulties*
find relief 389.5 *escape*
find room for 127.4 *include*
find safety 252.9 *be safe*
find space for 127.4 *include*
find the key to 719.9 *decipher*
find the meaning 719.9 *decipher*
find the means 344.10 *awaken*
find the philosopher's stone 781.13 *get rich*
find the sense of 719.9 *decipher*
find the spot 142.11 *find*
find time for 580.4 *have leisure*
find too difficult 696.9 *find unintelligible*
find to one's cost 604.4 *be disappointed*
find unintelligible 696.9
find useful 237.11; **392.27**; 349.3 *exploit*
find words for 729.11 *speak*; 5.47 *word*
find words to express 729.11 *speak*; 724.9 *style*
fine 31.45; **151.2**; **153.4**; 698.21 *accurate*; 801.12 *all right*; 545.5 *beautiful*; 24.10 *ceramic*; 386.3 *coercive methods*; 16.43 *conviction*; 543.3 *elegant*; 797.1 *good*; 259.1 *healthy*; 790.8 *levy*; 159.7 *little*; 622.21 *ostentatious*; 814.1 *punish*; 814.7 *punishment*; 428.5 *rainless*; 251.1 *restraint*; 698.40 *right!*; 404.9 *smooth*; 417.1 *sparse*; 527.2 *translucent*; 235.1 *worthy*; 42.10 *woven*
fine adjustment 698.8 *accuracy*; 273.3 *accurate thing*
fine and dandy 797.1 *good*
fine art 717.2 *reproduction*
fine arts 19.1 *art*
fine blade 587.8 *sharp weapon*
fine chemicals 32.22 *industrial chemistry*
fine china 24.1 *ceramics*
fined 814.20 *punished*
fine detail 273.3 *accurate thing*
fine distinction 273.3 *accurate thing*
fine-drawn 404.10 *delicate*; 151.2 *fine*
fine fettle 407.5 *orderliness*; 221.5 *physical state*; 221.4 *state of mind*
fine fryer 568.9 *woman considered as a sex object*
Fine Gael 12.6 *political party*
fine grain 41.10 *graininess*
fine-grained 404.9 *smooth*
fine-grained texture 30.28 *rock*
fine kettle of fish 264.5 *predicament*
fine line 273.3 *accurate thing*
finely 159.8 *in a small way*; 417.7 *sparsely*; 404.15 *texturally*
finely adjusted 698.21 *accurate*
fine mess 264.5 *predicament*
fineness 151.7; **153.11**; 698.8 *accuracy*; 404.2 *grain*; 159.1 *littleness*; 417.3 *sparseness*; 527.6 *translucency*
fineness of grain 404.2 *grain*
fine opportunity 287.2 *opportunity*
fine print 139.4 *specifications*
fine qualities 803.2 *virtues*
finer 121.12 *superior*
fine rain 31.25 *rain*
fine reaching 50.1 *sailing*
finer feelings 590.3 *feelings*; 591.5 *sensitivity*
finer points 273.3 *accurate thing*
finery 551.1 *dress*; 656.4 *formal dress*
fines herbes 496.5 *herbs*
finespun 404.10 *delicate*; 151.2 *fine*
finesse 645.5 *be cunning*; 69.3 *card game terms*; 645.1 *cunning*; 466.2 *judiciousness*; 69.10 *play*; 485.1 *skill*; 728.3 *subtlety*
fine-structure constant 28.97 *fundamental constant*
fine-toned 516.6 *melodious*
fine-tune 244.3 *rectify*
fine tuning 273.1, 591.10 *accuracy*
fine-weave 42.10 *woven*
fine workmanship 485.1 *skill*
fine-woven 404.9 *smooth*
fine writer 724.5 *stylist*
finger 690.13 *drink*; 742.5 *indicator*; 205.7 *piece*; 492.7 *sense organ*; 488.4 *someone or something that feels*; 360.3 *tools for gripping*; 492.11 *touch*; 349.1 *use*; 742.9 *use signs*
finger alphabet 505.1 *deafness*
finger bowl 410.16 *crockery*
fingerbreadth 147.2 *short distance*
fingering 492.2 *touching*
finger-licking 557.27 *edible*
finger-lickin' good 495.7 *tasty*
fingerling 159.4 *little person*; 74.3 *young fish*
fingermark 744.12 *vestige*
fingernail 418.7 *hard substance*; 492.7 *sense organ*; 425.9 *sharp-edged thing*
fingernails 360.3 *tools for gripping*
finger painter 19.16 *artist*
finger painting 19.2, 19.8 *painting*
finger post 742.5 *indicator*
fingerprint 743.10 *identify*; 743.3 *means of identification*; 215.1 *remainder*; 742.1 *sign*; 742.9 *use signs*; 345.2 *visible effect*
fingerprinted 743.12 *identified*
finger puppet 717.6 *image*
fingers 151.8 *narrow thing*; 360.3 *tools for gripping*
finger sandwich 25.11 *sandwich*
finger's-breadth 147.2 *short distance*
fingerstall 394.10 *surgical dressing*
finger's width 147.2 *short distance*
fingertip 492.7 *sense organ*; 488.4 *someone or something that feels*
finial 174.3 *architectural summit*
finickiness 471.2 *close attention*; 469.6 *selection*
finicky 222.10 *detailed*; 264.14 *troublesome*
fining 814.7 *punishment*
finis 131.1 *end*
finish 211.3 *additional item*; 232.5 *be complete*; 226.6 *cease*; 133.2 *cessation*; 309.9 *close down*; 309.1 *closure*; 57.10 *compete in gymnastics*; 204.10, 232.4 *complete*; 232.1 *completeness*; 232.3 *completion*; 312.15 *destination*; 133.12 *discontinue*; 543.1, 549.1 *elegance*; 131.1, 131.15 *end*; 131.10 *ending*; 57.5 *horizontal bar*; 59.7 *horseracing*; 551.35 *make clothing*; 284.14 *pass*; 230.5 *perfect*; 230.3 *perfection*; 50.16 *row*; 50.4 *rowing*; 485.1 *skill*; 421.11 *smooth*; 421.7 *smoothness*; 226.2 *stop*; 404.1 *texture*
finished 226.10; 309.14 *closed down*; 232.7 *complete*; 582.19 *dead*; 133.9 *discontinued*; 543.3 *elegant*; 131.21 *ended*; 400.13 *excellent*; 485.8 *expert*; 103.3 *hopeless*; 3.18 *in the past*; 94.11 *no more*; 284.18 *over*; 230.1 *perfect*; 50.11 *rowing*; 485.6 *skilful*; 485.9 *well-made*
finished article 356.3 *product*
finished state 232.1 *completeness*
finisher 340.3 *doer*; 131.13 *ender*; 551.26 *fashion designer*
finish first 47.7 *race*
finish halfway 231.10 *leave imperfect*
finishing 232.3 *completion*; 131.20 *ending*; 47.1 *track events*
finishing line 482.6 *objective*
finishing off 232.3 *completion*
finishing school 6.12 *educational institution*
finishing stroke 131.13 *ender*
finishing tape 482.6 *objective*
finishing touch 211.3 *additional item*; 232.1 *completeness*; 244.5 *improvement*
finish off 131.16 *cease*; 131.15 *end*
finish one's preparations 243.4 *prepare for action*
finish tape 47.1 *track events*
finish the job 576.6 *work*
finish the race 312.2 *reach*
finite 27.72 *complex*; 194.9 *fractional*; 166.5 *limited*; 203.6 *quantitative*
finitely 27.87 *mathematically*; 203.7 *quantitatively*
finite number 27.7 *natural number*
finite quantity 166.2 *limiting factor*
finite sequence 27.20 *sequence*
finite set 27.21 *set*
fink 715.5 *accuse*; 715.3 *accuser*; 693.10 *informer*
fin keel 50.3 *parts of a sailing boat*
finnan haddock 25.16 *fish dish*; 74.8 *food fish*
Finn class 50.2 *sailing boat*
Finno-Ugric 5.11 *family of languages*
fiord 92.9 *inlet*
fipples 692.23 *television reception*
fir cone 79.2 *tree part*
fire 381.2; **493.6**; **522.8**; 633.19 *after him!*; 357.7 *agent of destruction*; 428.19 *bake*; 585.14 *battle*; 493.15 *burn*; 226.8 *cause to cease*; 15.11 *conduct industrial relations*; 371.2, 580.5, 767.10 *dismiss*; 128.8 *eject*; 590.4 *emotion*; 726.1 *emphasis*; 586.37 *fight*; 381.15 *firing*; 437.11 *fuel*; 522.24 *light*; 507.1 *loudness*; 24.11 *make ceramics*; 343.14 *make inactive*; 380.9 *make violent*; 535.7 *red thing*; 144.17 *relegate*; 608.12 *relieve from duty*; 60.7, 330.28 *shoot*; 742.4 *signal*; 350.7 *stop work*; 708.15 *terminate*; 331.4 *throw*
fire alarm 711.2 *danger signal*; 252.4 *safety device*; 742.4 *signal*
firearm 330.9; **587.9**; 508.3 *banger*
fire a salute 658.12 *greet*; 667.20 *salute*
fire a salvo 601.18 *salute*
fire a shot 51.7 *bowl*
fire at 381.2 *fire*; 330.28 *shoot*
fire a volley 330.28 *shoot*
fire a warning flare 711.7 *raise the alarm*
fire a warning shot 742.12 *signal*
fire away 130.18 *make a beginning*
fireball 493.6, 522.8 *fire*; 29.20 *meteor*
fire bell 711.2 *danger signal*; 510.4 *sources of resonance*
fire blanket 252.4 *safety device*
fireblight 44.12 *pests and diseases*
firebomb 587.16 *bomb*; 493.6 *fire*; 437.2 *lighter*
firebomber 493.7 *fireman*; 437.9 *powerworker*
firebox 493.6 *fire*; 321.5 *locomotive part*
firebrand 662.8 *agitator*; 586.5 *arguer*; 493.6 *fire*; 437.2 *lighter*; 480.14, 483.7 *motivator*; 380.4 *violent creature*
firebreak 146.1 *interval*
fire-breathing 493.12 *warm-hearted*
firebrick 24.9 *industrial ceramics*
firebug 493.7 *fireman*
firecracker 508.3 *banger*
fire curtain 550.12 *protective covering*; 21.19 *stage set*
fired 708.20 *cancelled*; 24.10 *ceramic*; 767.13 *dismissed*; 226.10 *finished*; 493.13 *heated*; 580.7 *leisurely*; 15.9 *negotiated*; 350.3 *not wanted*
firedamp 432.3 *miasma*
fired employee 470.9 *rejected person*
fire door 252.4 *safety device*
fired porcelain 24.1 *ceramics*
firedrake 70.7 *legendary beast*
fire-eater 21.31 *circus performer*; 586.1 *combatant*; 380.4 *violent creature*
fire engine 433.13 *irrigator*; 535.7 *red thing*
fire-engine siren 742.4 *signal*
fire escape 304.7 *means of ascent*; 389.2 *means of escape*; 252.4 *safety device*; 315.6 *way out*
fire extinguisher 252.4 *safety device*
fire fighter 493.7 *fireman*; 252.3 *protector*
firefly 522.9
fireglow 535.7 *red thing*
firehouse 87.13 *municipal building*
fire insurance 252.2 *protection*
firelight 522.8 *fire*
firelighter 522.8 *fire*; 437.2 *lighter*
firelit 522.18 *lit*
fireman 493.7; 252.3 *protector*; 321.9 *railway worker*; 742.8 *signer*
fireman's ladder 317.2 *route*
fire off 330.28 *shoot*
fire of love 593.5 *desire*
fire on 381.2 *fire*
fire one's imagination 446.16 *inspire*
fireplace 493.6 *fire*
fireproof 252.7 *invulnerable*; 423.11 *make tough*; 423.1 *tough*
fireproof clothing 384.6 *protective clothing*
firer 24.7 *potter*
fire raiser 493.7 *fireman*; 380.4 *violent creature*
fire-raising 357.3 *destructiveness*
fire sale 791.2 *bargain*; 778.4 *sale*
fire ship 437.2 *lighter*; 586.24 *warship*
fireside 565.3 *home*
fireside chat 734.2 *chat*
fire station 87.13 *municipal building*
firestorm 493.6 *fire*
fire the first shot 381.1 *attack*
fire the parting shot 706.18 *answer back*
fire the starting gun 47.7 *race*
fire tongs 360.3 *tools for gripping*
firetrap 379.1 *trap*
fire up 437.11 *fuel*; 338.3 *invigorate*; 380.9 *make violent*
fire wall 252.4 *safety device*
firewatcher 252.3 *protector*
firewood 437.2 *lighter*; 79.3 *timber*
fireworks 587.15 *explosive*; 522.8 *fire*; 485.3 *masterpiece*; 601.8 *salute*
fire worship 9.2 *idolatry*
fire worshipper 9.6 *idolater*
fire-worshipping 9.10 *idolatrous*
firing 381.15; 51.9 *bowls*; 24.5 *ceramic*

process; 371.18 *dismissal*; 767.1 *disposal*; 128.2 *ejection*; 15.2 *industrial negotiations*; 330.6 *shooting*; 226.2 *stop*; 708.6 *termination*
firing line 585.10 *battleground*
firing on all cylinders 338.6 *with vigour*
firing shot 51.2 *grip*
firing squad 16.43 *conviction*; 582.4 *death sentence*; 382.5 *execution*; 814.16 *instrument of execution*
firing squad member 382.12 *executioner*
firkin 410.11 *vessel*
firm 776.7 *company*; 13.7 *corporation*; 416.6 *dense*; 569.11 *devoted*; 726.3 *emphatic*; 423.3 *hard*; 452.6 *infallible*; 418.4 *mentally hard*; 383.11 *obstinate*; 225.7 *permanent*; 336.10 *potent*; 360.9 *retentive*; 647.8 *severe*; 418.10 *solidify*; 228.9 *stable*; 638.5 *steady*; 779.8 *store*; 336.11 *strong in spirit*; 418.2 *tough*; 641.3 *unyielding*; 577.1 *workshop*
firm advice 713.3 *precept*
firmament 8.11 *heaven*; 29.3 *universe*
firm attachment 593.1 *love*
firm control 647.1 *severity*
firm date 756.1 *promise*
firm fixture 228.4 *stable thing*
firm foundation 228.4 *stable thing*
firm hand 647.1 *severity*
firm hold 360.1 *retention*
firming up 228.1 *stability*
firmly 336.15 *acutely*; 452.23 *certainly*; 416.10 *densely*; 569.19 *devotedly*; 418.13 *inflexibly*; 225.9 *permanently*; 383.14 *resistingly*; 647.11 *severely*; 228.12 *stably*; 360.11 *tenaciously*; 423.12 *toughly*
firmness 569.3 *familiarity*; 418.5 *hardness*; 452.17 *infallibility*; 383.2 *obstinacy*; 225.1 *permanence*; 647.1 *severity*; 228.1 *stability*; 336.1 *strength*; 423.6 *toughness*; 638.15 *will*
firmness of purpose 635.2 *willpower*
firm-packed 416.6 *dense*
firm price 752.3 *business offer*
firm principle 140.4 *guide*
firm up 416.9 *make dense*; 228.7 *make stable*; 152.7 *thicken*
firn 62.5 *rock face*
first 129.21; 130.40; 130.29, 308.17 *beginning*; 121.14, 235.2 *best*; 293.12, 293.17 *early*; 27.75 *equal*; 167.1 *front*; 295.10 *new*; 295.21 *newly*; 197.11 *one*; 126.4 *original*; 126.8 *originally*; 129.10 *preceding*; 129.23 *primarily*; 129.12 *primary*; 246.5 *victorious person*
first aid 392.5 *medical assistance*; 394.17 *remedial*; 394.13 *therapy*
first-aid station 394.14 *hospital*
First Amendment 250.2 *free speech*
first among equals 121.5 *superior*
first and foremost 129.21, 130.40 *first*
first and last 197.14 *singular*
first appearance 525.1 *appearance*; 130.9 *premiere*
first arrival 293.4 *early comer*
first attack 58.6 *lacrosse player*
first attempt 353.5 *attempt*
first base 48.1 *baseball*; 130.12 *first move*
first-baseman 48.2 *baseball player*
first-baseman's glove 48.3 *baseball equipment*
first-base umpire 48.2 *baseball player*
first beginnings 130.2 *creation*
firstborn 129.9 *predecessor*
First Cause 8.3 *God*
first cause 4.9 *philosophical problem*
first choice 123.3 *chief thing*; 469.9 *chosen thing*
first-class 573.4 *aristocratic*; 235.2 *best*; 121.15 *excellent*; 797.1, 797.8 *good*; 781.3 *opulent*; 235.1 *worthy*
first-class cricket 53.1 *cricket match*
first-class mail 692.2 *postal communication*
first-class stamp 692.3 *correspondence*
first comer 564.1 *inhabitant*
first communion 10.5 *Christian rite*
first concern 129.2 *priority*
first course 25.9 *dish*; 130.12 *first move*; 557.14 *mouthful*
first crack 293.2 *early hour*
first crack of dawn 293.2 *early hour*
first cuckoo 292.2 *spring*
first defence 58.6 *lacrosse player*
first-degree burn 493.1 *heat*
first-degree murder 382.2 *murder*
first derivative 27.31 *differentiation*
first draft 484.6 *outline*; 243.10 *preparations*
first early 43.12 *crop*
first echelon 586.14 *armed forces*
first edition 126.2 *original*
first fiddle 123.4 *bigwig*; 485.4 *skilled person*
first finger 492.7 *sense organ*
first floor 175.2 *foot*
first gallery 63.5 *real tennis*
first go 353.5 *attempt*
first guard 54.3 *fencing movements*
first-hand 126.4 *original*
first house 21.13 *theatrical performance*
first importance 123.1 *importance*
first impression 525.5 *impression*
first innings 130.12 *first move*
first in the field 126.4 *original*
first lady 121.6 *paragon*
first lap 130.12 *first move*
first law 28.38 *thermodynamics*
first leg 130.12 *first move*
first light 524.1 *dimness*; 290.1 *morning*; 304.3 *sunrise*
first love 593.2 *romantic love*
firstly 293.17 *early*; 130.40 *first*; 295.21 *newly*
first move 130.12
first name 721.8 *name*
first night 525.1 *appearance*; 295.4 *beginning*; 130.9 *premiere*; 21.13 *theatrical performance*
first-nighter 21.33 *theatregoer*
first-night nerves 21.22 *acting*
first object ball 65.4 *carom*
first of all 130.40 *first*; 121.17 *supremely*
first officer 322.3 *aircraft personnel*
first-order 32.38 *reactive*
first-past-the-post system 469.11 *franchise*
first payment 785.1 *payment*
first-person narrative 17.3 *aspect of fiction*
first place 129.2 *priority*; 121.1 *superiority*
first-place finisher 246.5 *victorious person*
first principle 402.4 *matter*; 344.3 *rudiment*
first principles 130.7 *rudiments*; 27.65 *theory*
first priority 123.3 *chief thing*
first prize 794.1 *trophy*
first quarter 29.17 *moon*
first-rate 235.2 *best*; 121.15, 400.13 *excellent*; 797.1 *good*; 123.6 *notable*; 485.6 *skilful*; 235.1 *worthy*
first-rater 235.8 *exceller*; 246.4 *successful person*; 797.16 *superior person*
first refusal 777.7 *purchasing*
first round 130.12 *first move*
first school 6.12 *educational institution*
first screening 525.1 *appearance*
first secretary 579.16 *official*
first see the light 554.18 *be born*
first slip 53.4 *team*
first stage 130.12 *first move*
first step 293.3 *early stage*; 130.12 *first move*; 344.3 *rudiment*
first steps 130.4 *conception*
first-string 485.4 *skilled person*; 235.1 *worthy*
first-string player 485.4 *skilled person*
first-team player 49.2 *basketball player*
first thing 293.17 *early*; 130.40 *first*; 344.3 *rudiment*
first time 130.9 *premiere*
first tooth 425.11 *tooth*
first violin 579.14 *leader*
first wicket down 53.4 *team*
First World War 585.1 *war*
firth 92.9 *inlet*
Firth of Forth 92.9 *inlet*
fiscal 789.10 *accounting*; 776.14 *commercial*; 13.13 *economic*; 14.6 *financial*; 780.22 *monetary*
fiscal competence 781.8 *solvency*
fiscal incompetence 782.6 *insolvency*
fiscally 13.14 *economically*; 780.28, 789.13 *financially*
fiscal policy 13.6 *economic factors*; 13.1 *economics*
fiscal year 276.4 *period of activity*
fish 74.2; 74.15; 55.7 *angle*; 70.5 *aquatic animal*; 369.11 *extract*; 74.1 *fishes*; 633.11 *hunt*; 382.22 *kill animals*; 70.4 *type of animal*
fishability 74.7 *fishing*
fish anatomy 74.5
fish and chips 25.44 *British dish*; 25.16 *fish dish*
fish-and-chip shop 557.15 *eating place*
fish ball 25.16 *fish dish*
fishbowl 74.6 *study of fish*
fish breeding 74.6 *study of fish*
fishcake 25.16 *fish dish*
fish course 25.9 *dish*; 557.14 *mouthful*
fish day 687.3 *fast day*; 684.1 *self-restraint*
fish dish 25.16
fish eagle 74.11 *fishing animal*
fished 55.8 *angling*
fisher 74.10; 55.6 *angler*
fisherfolk 74.10 *fisher*
fisherman 55.6 *angler*; 74.10 *fisher*; 557.20 *food provider*; 633.6 *hunter*; 323.7 *nautical person*
fisherman's jersey 551.13 *sweater*
fisherman's tale 727.5 *tall story*
fisherman's yarn 699.10 *lie*
fishery 74.7 *fishing*
Fishes 74
fishes 74.1
fisheye lens 41.17 *lens*; 518.8 *reflection*
fish farm 43.6 *farm*; 74.6 *study of fish*
fish farmer 74.10 *fisher*
fish farming 74.7 *fishing*; 43.3 *livestock farming*
fish-finder 74.7 *fishing*
fish finger 25.16 *fish dish*
fish food 557.8 *animal food*
fish for 633.8 *pursue*
fish for compliments 673.15 *be vain*
fish for invitations 654.11 *be sociable*
fish fork 557.16 *eating utensil*
fishgig 74.7 *fishing*
fish glue 267.3 *adhesive*; 74.9 *fish product*
fish-hold 74.7 *fishing*
fish-hook 74.7 *fishing*; 55.3 *fishing tackle*; 425.8 *sharp-pointed thing*; 700.13 *snare*
fishiness 189.3 *deviousness*
Fishing 55
fishing 74.7; 55.1, 55.8 *angling*; 633.2 *chase*; 369.1 *extraction*; 633.16 *hunting*
fishing animal 74.11
fishing bank 74.7 *fishing*
fishing bird 72.3 *water bird*
fishing boat 323.3 *vessel*
fishing cat 74.11 *fishing animal*
fishing fleet 74.7 *fishing*
fishing ground 74.7 *fishing*
fishing licence 757.2 *permit*
fishing line 74.7 *fishing*; 633.3 *hunting and fishing equipment*
fishing net 633.3 *hunting and fishing equipment*
fishing pole 55.3 *fishing tackle*; 633.3 *hunting and fishing equipment*
fishing rod 55.3 *fishing tackle*; 633.3 *hunting and fishing equipment*
fishing season 292.1 *season*
fishing tackle 55.3
fishing the water 55.1 *angling*
fishing to the rise 55.1 *angling*
fishing with bait 55.1 *angling*
fish in the sea 566.1 *humankind*
fish in troubled waters 264.21 *get into trouble*
fish joint 23.10 *carpenter's term*; 321.3 *rail*
fish kettle 410.15 *pot*
fish knife 557.16 *eating utensil*; 425.10 *knife*
fish ladder 74.7 *fishing*
fishlike 74.13
fish line 74.7 *fishing*
fish-liver oil 74.9 *fish product*
fish louse 75.4 *arthropod*; 75.10 *parasite*
fish lover 74.12 *ichthyologist*
fishman 74.10 *fisher*
fish market 779.1 *market*
fishmeal 43.9 *animal feedstuff*; 43.13, 44.7, 562.3 *fertilizer*; 74.9 *fish product*
fishmonger 74.10 *fisher*; 557.20 *food provider*; 557.17 *food shop*; 436.3 *provider*; 778.13 *retailer*
fishnet 193.2 *braid*; 74.7 *fishing*; 633.3 *hunting and fishing equipment*
fishnet tights 551.20 *legwear*
fish out 369.11 *extract*
fish out of water 325.19 *deviant person*; 144.7 *displaced person*; 751.4 *dissenter*; 118.7 *nonconformist*; 109.2 *unrelated thing*; 655.6 *unsocial person*
fish pie 25.16 *fish dish*
fishplate 321.3 *rail*
fishpond 88.2 *small lake*; 74.6 *study of fish*
fish product 74.9
fish roe 74.9 *fish product*
fish seller 74.10 *fisher*
fishskin disease 428.16 *dry skin*
fish soup 25.13 *soup*
fish stick 25.16 *fish dish*
fish store 557.17 *food shop*
fish story 699.10 *lie*; 727.5 *tall story*
fishtail 67.11 *swimming*
fishtail kick 67.2 *swimming technique*
fishtank 565.12 *stall*; 74.6 *study of fish*
fish the water 55.7 *angle*
fish to the rise 55.7 *angle*
fishtrap 74.7 *fishing*
fish up 366.4 *gather up*
fish way 74.7 *fishing*
fish weir 74.7 *fishing*
fishwife 74.10 *fisher*; 625.3 *irascible person*
fish with a pole 55.7 *angle*
fish with a rod 55.7 *angle*
fish with bait 55.7 *angle*
fishy 800.7 *criminal*; 189.5 *devious*; 74.13 *fishlike*
fishy transaction 800.3 *criminality*; 700.7 *tricking*
fissile 424.1 *brittle*; 146.7 *cracked*; 372.19 *separable*
fissile nuclide 28.72 *nuclear fission*
fissility 424.2 *brittleness*
fission 375.4 *deconstruct*; 375.2 *deconstruction*; 28.72 *nuclear fission*; 334.8 *nuclear power*; 372.1 *separation*
fissionable 372.19 *separable*
fissionable material 587.15 *explosive*
fissionable nuclide 28.72 *nuclear fission*
fission energy 28.11 *energy*
fission product 28.72 *nuclear fission*
fission reaction 32.14 *chemical reaction*; 28.72 *nuclear fission*
fissure 146.2 *crack*; 184.2 *furrow*; 308.20 *hole*; 133.4 *interruption*; 308.1 *opening*; 372.3 *separateness*; 30.24 *volcanic activity*; 184.8 *wrinkle*
fissured 146.7 *cracked*; 308.12 *open*
fissure sealing 35.4 *dentistry*
fist 742.3 *gesture*; 742.7 *punctuation*; 492.7 *sense organ*; 360.3 *tools for gripping*; 587.1 *weapon*
fistfight 408.9 *disorder*
fistful 815.4 *prison sentence*
fisticuffs 701.1, 751.2 *argument*; 52.2 *boxing*; 331.12 *collision*; 408.9 *disorder*; 380.3 *instance of violence*; 242.8, 624.5 *quarrel*
fistula 260.15 *ulcer*
fit 750.27; 119.9 *adequate*; 267.6 *adhere*; 801.12 *all right*; 239.6 *be convenient*; 108.8 *be proportionate to*; 136.14 *be qualified*; 706.22 *be the answer*; 381.20 *bout*; 117.7 *conform*; 239.1 *convenient*; 119.11 *equalize*; 243.5 *equip*; 259.1 *healthy*; 260.2 *illness*; 380.3 *instance of violence*; 551.35 *make clothing*; 117.9 *make conform*; 461.3 *mental deterioration*; 342.3 *nimbleness*; 160.12 *on form*; 17.8 *part of poem*; 276.1 *period*; 336.9 *physically strong*; 334.13 *powerful*; 136.9 *qualified*; 204.8 *sound*; 327.8 *spasm*; 221.1 *state*; 287.6 *timely*; 237.2 *usable*; 642.3 *whim*
fit a beam 23.17 *carpenter*
fit a mould 221.6 *be in a state of*
fit and ready 259.1 *healthy*
fit as a fiddle 259.1 *healthy*; 336.9 *physically strong*
fit as a flea 336.9 *physically strong*
fit badly 751.8 *be different*
fit for habitation 565.14 *inhabiting*
fit for legislation 16.47 *liable to law*
fit for marriage 570.22 *marriageable*
fit for nothing 238.1 *useless*
fit for release 390.4 *deliverable*
fit for use 243.19 *in hand*; 237.2 *usable*
fitful 453.8, 642.1 *capricious*; 227.13 *changeable*; 327.19 *convulsive*; 133.8 *discontinuous*; 114.5 *diverse*; 299.4 *irregular*; 276.9 *periodic*
fitfully 453.27, 642.6 *capriciously*; 227.15 *changeably*; 133.17 *discontinuously*; 276.14 *for short periods*; 114.11, 299.8 *irregularly*
fitfulness 642.2 *caprice*; 453.16 *capriciousness*; 133.1 *discontinuity*; 114.1 *diversity*; 299.1 *irregularity*; 227.2 *irresolution*
fit in 117.8 *comply*; 117.9 *make conform*

fit into a category 108.9 *have a relative position*
fit like a glove 267.6 *adhere*
fitly 287.9 *opportunely*
fitness 334.2 *ability;* 485.2 *aptitude;* 239.3 *convenience;* 706.8 *correspondence;* 259.3 *health;* 336.2 *healthiness;* 160.6 *nature;* 243.14 *preparedness;* 136.1 *qualification;* 257.2 *salubrity;* 287.1 *timeliness*
fitness for marriage 570.4 *marriageability*
fit of anger 624.4 *anger*
fit of temper 594.5, 624.4 *anger*
fit of terror 612.1 *fear*
fit of the sulks 626.2 *sign of sullenness*
fit out 243.5 *equip;* 352.6 *find means;* 551.35 *make clothing;* 436.5 *provision*
fits and starts 327.1 *agitation;* 299.1 *irregularity*
fitted 405.7 *modular;* 136.9 *qualified*
fitted carpet 550.9 *floor covering*
fittedness 136.1 *qualification*
fitted sheet 550.10 *bed covering*
fitted unit 410.3 *cabinet*
fitter 578.2 *artisan;* 551.26 *fashion designer;* 438.8 *machinist;* 38.4 *mechanical engineer;* 243.15 *preparer*
fit the bill 617.16 *be desirable*
fit the occasion 287.4 *be timely*
fit tight 267.6 *adhere*
fitting 750.16; 239.1 *convenient;* 706.15 *correspondent;* 617.8 *desirable;* 543.3 *elegant;* 136.9 *qualified;* 217.1 *sufficient;* 287.6 *timely*
fittingly 750.38; 136.17 *capably;* 239.7 *conveniently;* 706.26 *correspondingly;* 287.9 *opportunely;* 801.18 *properly*
fittingness 543.1 *elegance*
fitting out 243.11; 436.1 *provision*
fitting retribution 814.9 *retribution;* 714.4 *revenge*
fittings 438.7 *equipment*
fitting the circumstances 222.7 *circumstantial*
fitting together 147.8 *interaction;* 376.33 *putting together*
fit to bust 232.8 *full*
fit to drop 261.1 *fatigued*
fit together 374.5 *combine;* 405.13 *make;* 376.44 *put together*
fit up 484.13 *plot*
fit-up 484.4 *plot*
five 201.1; 201.12 *fifth;* 27.9 *numeral*
five-act play 21.2 *play*
five-and-dime 124.4 *trivial*
Five and Over 201
five-and-ten 793.9 *cheap*
five and twenty 201.8 *twenty and over*
five-a-side 201.1 *five*
five-barred gate 43.11 *farmland*
five-by-five 201.1 *five*
five cents 780.8 *American money*
five centuries 201.9 *treble figures*
five C's 201.9 *treble figures*
five-dollar bill 780.8 *American money;* 201.1 *five*
five-figure 201.21 *thousandth*
five-finger 201.1 *five*
five fingers 815.4 *prison sentence*
fivefold 201.24; 201.12 *fifth*
five hundred 201.9 *treble figures*
five hundred and one 69.6 *darts*
five-man defence 49.4 *playing terms*
five-metre platform 67.6 *diving*
five-minute penalty 58.3 *ice hockey*
five-nations championship 64.2 *championship*
five o'clock 290.4 *afternoon;* 557.12 *meal*
five-o'clock shadow 420.7 *rough thing*
five pence 780.9 *British money*
five-pound note 780.9 *British money;* 201.1 *five*
fiver 780.8 *American money;* 780.9 *British money;* 201.1 *five*
five shillings 780.10 *former British money*
five-sided 27.82 *polygonal*
fivesome 201.1 *five*
five-spot 201.1 *five*
fivestones 201.1 *five*
five-year plan 484.1 *plan*
fix 550.33; 175.4 *base;* 700.30 *be fraudulent;* 137.13 *class;* 143.3, 222.4 *difficult circumstances;* 324.6 *direct;* 691.6 *drug;* 699.9 *falsification;* 699.26 *falsify;* 700.10 *fraud;* 142.9 *locate;* 452.21 *make certain;* 335.9 *make impotent;* 225.6 *make permanent;* 228.7 *make stable;* 814.2 *penalize;* 221.2, 264.5 *predicament;* 106.2 *premeditate;* 243.4 *prepare for action;* 703.17 *prove;* 801.15 *put right;* 203.8 *quantify;* 244.3 *rectify;* 394.19 *remedy;* 393.1 *repair;* 638.7 *resolve;* 143.10 *situate;* 139.24 *specify;* 212.4 *take off*
fix a fight 52.11 *fight*
fix a position 50.15 *sail*
fixated 471.8 *diligent;* 461.13 *mentally ill*
fixation 36.17; 34.6 *cell biology;* 461.4 *delusion;* 471.4 *diligence;* 632.1 *habit;* 301.1 *motionlessness;* 142.4 *placing;* 465.4 *prejudgment*
fixation neurosis 36.10 *neurosis*
fixation of affect 36.17 *fixation*
fixative 267.3 *adhesive;* 19.11 *artist's materials;* 502.2 *fragrant thing;* 529.4 *pigment*
fixed 632.13; 700.35 *deceptive;* 452.3 *decided;* 106.4 *deliberate;* 119.6 *equal;* 253.9 *fast;* 335.12 *impotent;* 452.5 *inevitable;* 142.6 *located;* 301.4 *motionless;* 452.7 *particular;* 225.7 *permanent;* 5.43 *phrasal;* 440.8 *propertied;* 393.13 *repaired;* 228.10 *stabilized;* 465.8 *unjust*
fixed array 692.28 *radar*
fixed assets 13.7 *corporation;* 440.5 *personal estate*
fixed bridge 38.21 *bridge*
fixed costs 13.7 *corporation*
fixed day 275.11 *date*
fixed expression 5.24 *phrasing*
fixed fight 52.2 *boxing*
fixed-focus lens 41.17 *lens*
fixed form 17.10 *verse form*
fixed-head coupé 320.16 *car*
fixed idea 465.4 *prejudgment*
fixedly 253.17 *fastly;* 301.10 *motionlessly;* 225.9 *permanently*
fixedness 225.1 *permanence;* 228.1 *stability*
fixed point 27.36 *point*
fixed-point notation 27.8 *number system*
fixed position 384.8 *military defences*
fixed price 790.1 *price*
fixed resolve 638.12 *resolution*
fixed seat 50.4 *rowing*
fixed-seat 50.11 *rowing*
fixed-seat rowing 50.4 *rowing*
fixed-spool 55.8 *angling*
fixed-spool reel 55.3 *fishing tackle*
fixed star 29.10 *star*
fixed term 275.3 *duration*
fixed ways 632.3 *way*
fixer 550.18; 41.12 *development;* 393.12 *repairer*
fixing 550.20; 62.8 *mountaineering;* 452.18 *particularity;* 142.4 *placing;* 393.8 *repair;* 212.1 *subtraction*
fixing point 62.5 *rock face*
fixing solution 41.12 *development*
fix in one's mind 462.11 *memorize*
fixity 641.6 *determination;* 277.4 *longlastingness;* 301.1 *motionlessness;* 225.1 *permanence;* 228.1 *stability*
fixity of purpose 638.13 *concentration*
fix on 324.7 *take a direction*
fix one's teeth into 360.6 *retain*
fix the date 281.14 *keep time*
fix the day 281.14 *keep time*
fix the game 645.5 *be cunning*
fix the price of 790.11 *price*
fix the time 281.14 *keep time*
fix to 253.14 *make fast*
fixture 223.4 *concomitant;* 438.7 *equipment;* 228.4 *stable thing*
fixtures 438.7 *equipment*
fixtures and fittings 440.4 *possessions*
fix up 409.17 *come to an arrangement;* 244.1 *improve;* 436.5 *provision;* 393.2 *refurbish*
fix upon 471.12 *scrutinize*
fizz 434.24 *bubble;* 512.4 *hiss;* 558.6 *soft drink*
fizziness 432.7 *gaseousness*
fizzing 512.1 *hiss*
fizzle 508.6 *crack;* 512.4 *hiss*
fizzle out 131.18 *come to an end;* 247.6 *fail*
fizzling 512.6 *hissing*
fizzy 434.18 *bubbly;* 558.17 *drinkable;* 432.21 *gassy;* 512.6 *hissing*
fizzy drink 558.6 *soft drink*
fizzy water 433.2 *drinking water;* 558.6 *soft drink*
fjord 30.7 *landform*
flab 158.8 *fat*
flabbergast 630.11 *amaze;* 619.10 *be wonderful*
flabbergasted 630.7 *amazed;* 619.6 *wondering*
flabbiness 158.5 *fatness;* 419.8 *softness;* 152.5 *thickness*
flabby 158.16 *fat;* 419.1 *soft;* 152.1 *thick*
flabellate 190.8 *growing*
flabelliform 190.8 *growing*
flaccid 339.5 *inert;* 419.1 *soft;* 337.8 *weak*
flaccidity 419.8 *softness;* 337.1 *weakness*
flaccidly 419.17 *softly*
flaccidness 419.8 *softness*
flack 738.12 *displayer;* 693.9 *informant;* 483.7 *motivator;* 719.7 *news interpreter;* 740.10 *publicizer*
flackery 480.6 *advertising;* 740.8 *public relations*
flacon 502.2 *fragrant thing*
flag 743.7; 261.5 *be fatigued;* 260.24 *be unhealthy;* 337.6 *be weak;* 435.2 *building material;* 602.9 *despair;* 247.6 *fail;* 56.2 *golfing terms;* 741.12 *headline;* 333.2 *hesitate;* 50.3 *parts of a sailing boat*
flag day 601.5 *anniversary;* 652.5 *charity;* 768.3 *offering*
flag down 742.11 *gesture*
flagellant 807.3 *atoner;* 808.3 *penitent person*
flagellate 84.7 *algal;* 814.3 *hit;* 75.9 *protozoan;* 75.23 *protozoan*
flagellate oneself 807.6 *apologize;* 808.5 *do penance*
flagellate protozoan 75.9 *protozoan*
flagellation 807.2 *apology;* 814.12 *corporal punishment;* 808.2 *type of penance*
flagellator 814.17 *punisher*
flagellum 34.8 *cell organ*
flagging 333.9 *deceleration;* 261.1 *fatigued;* 337.3 *poor health;* 260.22 *sick;* 333.4 *slow*
flagitious 804.11 *wicked*
flagitiousness 804.1 *wickedness*
flagman 711.4 *warner*
flag of convenience 484.3 *expedient plan;* 743.7 *flag;* 645.2 *stratagem*
flag officer 584.5 *military staff*
flag of surrender 743.7 *flag*
flag of truce 743.7 *flag;* 749.2 *peace offering;* 589.2 *symbol of peace*
flagon 410.14 *bottle*
flagpole 743.7 *flag*
flagrancy 660.3 *audacity;* 673.3 *cockiness;* 738.10 *manifestation;* 804.1 *wickedness*
flagrant 660.15 *audacious;* 738.14 *manifest;* 804.13 *venial;* 740.20 *well-known;* 804.11 *wicked*
flagrantly 660.32 *audaciously;* 738.16 *manifestly;* 804.18 *wickedly*
flags 601.8 *salute*
flagship 586.24 *warship*
flag signals 692.27 *signalling*
flagstaff 743.7 *flag;* 154.6 *tall thing*
flagstick 56.2 *golfing terms*
flagstone 175.1 *base;* 435.2 *building material;* 550.11 *paving;* 317.4 *road surface;* 421.8 *smooth thing*
flag waving 742.3 *gesture;* 601.9 *rejoicing*
flail 331.5 *beat;* 814.3 *hit;* 381.5 *strike;* 331.16 *weapons*
flailing 381.23 *attacking*
flail mower 43.10 *farm tool*
flair 136.2, 334.2 *ability;* 485.2 *aptitude;* 442.4 *cleverness;* 466.2 *judiciousness;* 724.2 *stylishness*
flak 587.13 *ammunition;* 670.5, 678.2 *criticism*
flak-catcher 480.12 *persuader*
flake 424.4 *be brittle;* 427.6 *crumb;* 427.23 *crumble;* 552.16 *peel;* 205.7 *piece;* 62.5 *rock face;* 411.11 *scale;* 372.10 *set apart;* 411.4 *slice;* 496.7 *tobacco*
flaked maize 43.9 *animal feedstuff*
flaked out 261.1 *fatigued;* 343.4 *not awake*
flake off 552.16 *peel;* 411.11 *scale*
flake out 261.5 *be fatigued*
flake white 531.8 *whitener*
flakily 427.29
flakiness 424.2 *brittleness;* 427.2 *crumbliness;* 411.6 *layering*
flaking 424.1 *brittle;* 427.4 *pulverization*
flak jacket 384.6 *protective clothing;* 46.3 *uniform*
flaky 424.1 *brittle;* 427.19 *crumbly;* 411.9 *platelike*
flaky pastry 25.37 *pastry*
flam 699.10 *lie*
flambeau 522.7 *lantern*
flamboyance 673.3 *cockiness;* 703.2 *demonstrativeness;* 727.3 *extravagance*
flamboyant 522.16 *bright;* 703.10 *demonstrative;* 727.14 *extravagant;* 542.10 *ornate*
flamboyantly 673.21 *cockily;* 703.21 *demonstratively;* 727.17 *excessively;* 522.30 *lightly;* 542.13 *ornately*
flame 493.15 *burn;* 593.5 *desire;* 493.6, 522.8 *fire;* 522.25 *light up;* 535.7 *red thing*
flame-coloured 536.1 *orange;* 535.1 *red*
flame gun 44.6 *garden tool*
flamen 7.8 *priest*
flamenco 22.4 *historic dancing*
flameout 322.7 *miscellaneous aviation terms*
flameproof 42.15 *treat;* 42.11 *treated*
flameproofing 42.8 *fabric treatment*
flames 493.6 *fire*
flames of love 593.5 *desire*
flamethrower 493.6 *fire;* 587.11 *guns*
flame with passion 593.24 *be in love*
flaming 522.16 *bright;* 40.16 *Internet;* 493.10 *on fire;* 380.6 *violent*
flaming June 493.5 *hot weather*
flamingo 72.3 *water bird*
flammability 493.6 *fire*
flammable 254.1 *dangerous;* 493.10 *on fire;* 437.10 *powered*
flan 25.36 *cake*
flanch 743.8 *heraldic device*
flan dish 25.6 *kitchen equipment*
flâneur 343.8 *nonworker*
flange 163.3 *edge;* 38.27 *superstructure*
flank 169.7 *be alongside;* 25.22 *beef;* 252.10 *protect;* 306.7 *ring;* 169.1 *side*
flanker 46.7 *offence;* 64.4 *rugby player*
flanking 169.6 *side*
flanking attack 381.12 *military attack*
flannel 677.2, 677.9 *blarney;* 256.11 *cleaning cloth;* 193.4 *textile*
flannelette 193.4 *textile*
flannels 551.9 *trousers*
flan ring 25.6 *kitchen equipment*
flap 211.3 *additional item;* 327.1 *agitation;* 751.2 *argument;* 327.21 *be agitated;* 227.11 *be changeable;* 550.2 *cover;* 327.4 *fuss;* 262.4 *haste;* 411.1 *layer;* 551.24 *part of garment;* 326.12 *wave*
flapjack 25.39 *loaf*
flare 150.9 *be broad;* 190.6 *become bigger;* 150.4 *breadth;* 493.15 *burn;* 41.8 *composition;* 711.2 *danger signal;* 522.8 *fire;* 322.5 *flight;* 190.1 *growth;* 522.25 *light up;* 190.5 *make bigger;* 587.5 *missile weapon;* 522.2 *quality of light;* 50.10 *sailing;* 742.4 *signal*
flared 190.7 *bigger;* 150.1 *broad*
flared skirt 551.6 *skirt*
flare gybe 50.15 *sail;* 50.1 *sailing*
flare pass 46.9 *play*
flare path 522.6 *electric light*
flares 551.9 *trousers*
flare star 29.12 *variable star*
flare up 624.12 *become angry;* 213.4 *increase;* 522.25 *light up*
flare-up 624.4 *anger;* 380.3 *instance of violence*
flaring 522.16 *bright;* 529.12 *gaudy;* 190.8 *growing;* 190.1 *growth;* 493.10 *on fire*
flash 41.19; 227.11 *be changeable;* 738.1 *display;* 327.12, 327.26 *flicker;* 445.3 *insight;* 280.3 *instant;* 88.1 *lake;* 522.25 *light up;* 522.4 *natural light;* 525.14 *present;* 522.2 *quality of light;* 478.5 *spontaneity;* 552.14 *undress*
flashback 3.13 *looking back;* 462.2 *retrospect*
flashbulb 41.19 *flash;* 522.7 *lantern*
flash by 332.6 *accelerate;* 318.8 *pass*
flash cube 41.19 *flash*
flash desorption 32.20 *surface chemistry*
flasher 552.8 *nude person;* 796.10 *sex offender*
flash flood 90.6 *river flow;* 379.1 *trap;* 380.5 *violent weather*
flashgun 41.19 *flash;* 522.7 *lantern*
flashiness 673.3 *cockiness;* 703.2 *demonstrativeness*
flashing 522.16 *bright;* 552.11 *exposed;* 522.15 *lucent;* 522.2 *quality of light;* 796.7 *sexual assault;* 742.16 *signalling;* 332.1 *swift;* 552.1 *undress*
flashing light 711.2 *danger signal;* 522.6 *electric light;* 742.4 *signal*

flash in the pan 711.3 *false alarm;* 149.4 *short thing;* 246.1 *success;* 278.2 *transient thing*
flashlamp 522.7 *lantern*
flashlight 522.7 *lantern*
flashlit 522.18 *lit*
flash note 780.15 *false money*
flash of inspiration 443.6 *idea*
flash on the mind 739.9 *be disclosed*
flash out with 478.3 *improvise*
flash photography 41.1 *photography*
flash point 493.1 *heat*
flashy 522.16 *bright;* 703.10 *demonstrative;* 529.12 *gaudy;* 542.10 *ornate*
flask 410.14 *bottle;* 558.10 *drink container*
flask fungi 83.3 *fungi*
flat 426.1 *blunt;* 620.4 *boring;* 92.11 *continental;* 245.12 *deteriorated;* 261.1 *fatigued;* 187.8 *horizontal;* 187.11 *horizontally;* 187.2 *horizontal surface;* 565.5 *house;* 782.2 *insolvent;* 27.80 *linear;* 155.7 *lowland;* 92.3 *marsh;* 18.16 *musical note;* 511.2 *nonresonant;* 298.14 *orderly;* 440.1 *property;* 111.17, 298.11 *regular;* 301.5 *sedentary;* 157.4 *shallow thing;* 191.7 *smaller;* 529.13 *soft-hued;* 27.79, 141.11 *spatial;* 21.19 *stage set;* 513.7 *strident;* 157.2 *superficial;* 497.5 *tasteless;* 421.2 *uniform;* 517.9 *unmelodious*
flat as a pancake 187.8 *horizontal*
flat-bed plotter 40.7 *peripheral*
flatboard 50.7 *windsurfing*
flat broke 782.2 *insolvent;* 135.5 *necessitous;* 249.7 *unprosperous*
flat chest 153.7 *thinness*
flat-chested 153.1 *thin*
flatcoat retriever 60.6 *sporting dog*
flat contradiction 708.3 *rebuttal*
flat country 92.6 *lowland*
flat denial 708.3 *rebuttal*
flat fare 790.3 *fee*
flatfish 74.2 *fish;* 187.3 *flat thing;* 74.8 *food fish;* 25.18 *sea fish*
flatfoot 16.17 *police officer;* 253.3 *security officer*
flatiron 187.4 *flattener;* 421.9 *smoother*
flat land 187.3 *flat thing*
flatly 620.8 *boringly;* 187.11 *horizontally;* 298.17 *orderly;* 111.20, 298.15 *regularly;* 421.14, 426.11 *smoothly;* 497.10 *without taste*
flatmate 223.11 *companion;* 564.3 *householder;* 764.3 *participant*
flatness 426.5 *bluntness;* 620.1 *boredom;* 191.1 *contraction;* 497.1 *dilution;* 187.1 *horizontality;* 122.5 *inferior state;* 155.2 *lowlands;* 517.3 *musical dissonance;* 298.4 *orderliness;* 111.6 *regularity;* 421.7 *smoothness;* 27.38 *surface*
flat on one's back 187.11 *horizontally*
flat out 217.9 *enough;* 261.1 *fatigued;* 187.10 *lying;* 332.14 *swiftly;* 338.6 *with vigour*
flat-out 332.1 *swift*
flat-out speed 332.8 *speed*
flat racing 59.7 *horseracing*
flat rate 790.3 *fee*
flat refusal 709.1 *refusal*
flat roll 43.10 *farm tool*
flat roof 550.7 *overhead covering;* 20.6 *roof*
flats 187.3 *flat thing;* 92.6 *lowland;* 155.2 *lowlands;* 155.4 *low thing;* 157.4 *shallow thing*
flat screen 40.7 *peripheral*
flat-sharing 764.5 *jointly possessing*
flat shoes 551.19 *footwear*
flat spin 322.5 *flight*
flat surface 187.3 *flat thing;* 27.38 *surface*
flatten **367.2**; 426.10 *blunt;* 246.10 *defeat heavily;* 357.9 *demolish;* 155.9 *lower;* 187.7 *make horizontal;* 298.10 *make regular;* 191.5 *make smaller;* 111.8 *make the same;* 153.16 *make thin;* 357.11 *ruin;* 404.13, 421.11 *smooth*
flatten down 421.11 *smooth*
flattened **187.9**; 426.1 *blunt;* 155.5 *low;* 367.17 *lowered;* 153.5 *thinned;* 421.2 *uniform*
flattener **187.4**; 421.9 *smoother*
flattening 191.1 *contraction;* 357.2 *destroying;* 367.12 *downthrow;* 155.1 *lowness*
flatten oneself 367.8 *sit*
flatten out 298.10 *make regular;* 178.10 *straighten*
flatter **677.8**; 658.10 *be courteous;* 645.5 *be cunning;* 699.22 *be hypocritical;* 727.10 *boast;* 664.9 *fawn;* 599.15 *humour;* 125.9 *imitate;* 718.4 *misrepresent;* 483.9 *motivate;* 669.14 *praise;* 593.28 *win the love of*
flattered 727.12 *exaggerated;* 483.12 *motivated*
flatterer **677.6**; 117.6 *conformist;* 645.3 *cunning person;* 483.7 *motivator;* 599.7 *person who humours*
flattering **677.12**; 669.18 *approving;* 593.6 *courtship;* 645.4 *cunning;* 479.11 *equivocating;* 658.8 *good-mannered;* 599.11 *humouring;* 699.31 *hypocritical;* 483.2 *inducement;* 718.1 *misrepresentation;* 718.6 *misrepresented;* 664.7 *sycophantic*
flatteringly **677.17**
flatter oneself 673.15 *be vain;* 622.29 *feel pride*
flatter to deceive 677.9 *blarney*
Flattery 677
flattery **480.2**; **677.1**; 727.4 *bombast;* 593.14 *communication of love;* 658.1 *courtesy;* 645.1 *cunning;* 699.3 *hypocrisy;* 718.1 *misrepresentation;* 241.10 *pleasant thing;* 483.5 *positive stimulus;* 669.3 *praise*
flat thing 187.3
flatties 551.19 *footwear;* 155.4 *low thing*
flat-toned 517.9 *unmelodious*
flattop 586.24 *warship*
flat tyre 187.3 *flat thing;* 378.2 *obstacle*
flatulence 542.2 *affectation;* 371.24, 432.5, 508.4 *belch;* 260.8 *indigestion*
flatulency 371.24, 432.5 *belch*
flatulent **432.20**; 434.14 *aerial;* 270.3 *diffuse;* 371.31 *eructative*
flatulous 371.31 *eructative*
flat universe 29.4 *cosmological model*
flatuosity 371.24, 432.5 *belch*
flatus 371.24, 432.5 *belch;* 260.8 *indigestion;* 503.2 *something that makes an unpleasant smell*
flatware 187.3 *flat thing*
flatways 187.11 *horizontally*
flatwise 187.11 *horizontally*
flatworm 75.6 *worm*
flaunt 703.15 *demonstrate;* 738.1 *display*
flaunted 738.13 *displayed*
flaunter 738.12 *displayer*
flaunting 529.12 *gaudy;* 738.15 *open;* 622.21 *ostentatious;* 326.4 *rock;* 796.13 *unchaste*
flavescent 537.2 *yellowish*
flavone 33.18 *pigment*
flavonoid 33.18 *pigment*
flavonol 33.18 *pigment*
flavoprotein 33.12 *coenzyme;* 33.9 *protein*
Flavour 496
flavour **495.4**; 211.6 *add;* 412.4 *admixture;* 139.3 *characteristic;* 25.55 *cook;* 495.10 *make taste;* 496.12 *season*
flavour enhancer 495.4 *flavour;* 557.11 *food content*
flavourful 496.9 *piquant;* 241.4, 495.7 *tasty*
flavouring 211.3 *additional item;* 495.4 *flavour;* 496.2 *seasoning*
flavourless 728.17 *insipid;* 497.5 *tasteless*
flavourlessness 728.8 *insipidness*
flaw 548.7 *blemish;* 146.2 *crack;* 231.7 *defect;* 236.8 *inferiority;* 378.2 *obstacle;* 308.1 *opening;* 548.1 *spot;* 804.3 *venial sin;* 254.7 *vulnerability*
flawed 548.4 *blemished;* 274.15 *erroneous;* 231.1 *imperfect;* 233.4 *incomplete;* 236.2 *inferior;* 704.6 *refutable;* 702.7 *sophistic*
flawed argument 702.2 *sophism*
flawed logic 274.4 *faulty reasoning*
flawless 698.21 *accurate;* 797.2 *best;* 543.3 *elegant;* 230.1 *perfect;* 204.7 *uncut;* 235.1 *worthy*
flawlessly 230.7 *perfectly*
flawlessness 698.8 *accuracy;* 230.3 *perfection;* 255.1 *purity;* 797.9 *the best;* 235.6 *worth*
flawless performance 230.3 *perfection*
flax 43.12 *crop*
flaxen 522.21 *light*
flaxen-haired 531.3 *white-haired;* 537.3 *yellow-haired*
flaxseed 77.9 *seed*
flay 814.5 *execute;* 814.3 *hit;* 552.15 *make nude;* 372.10 *set apart*
flay alive 814.5 *execute*
F-layer 692.15 *transmitted wave*
flaying alive 814.13 *capital punishment*
flay one's back 814.3 *hit*
flea 258.4 *dirt;* 76.3 *pest*
fleabag 565.8 *shelter*
flea beetle 44.12 *pests and diseases*
fleabite 124.8 *trifle*
flea-bitten 245.13 *dilapidated;* 258.8 *unclean;* 76.12 *verminous*
flea circus 21.7 *show*
flea-flicker 46.9 *play*
flea in one's ear 670.7 *blame;* 729.8 *speech*
fleam 425.8 *sharp-pointed thing*
flea market 793.7 *discounter;* 779.1 *market*
fleapit 245.9 *dilapidation;* 21.16 *theatre*
flèche 20.10 *church architecture;* 54.3 *fencing movements;* 425.8 *sharp-pointed thing;* 154.6 *tall thing*
fléchette 587.6 *historical missile weapon*
fleck 159.3 *little piece;* 541.4 *maculation*
flection 184.1 *wrinkle*
flectional 184.7 *folded*
fled 98.9 *away*
fledge 243.7 *develop*
fledged 243.20 *developed*
fledgling 130.15 *baby;* 295.8 *new arrival;* 555.11 *young;* 555.4 *young animal;* 72.12 *young bird*
flee 98.18 *abscond;* 614.4 *be a coward;* 526.2 *depart;* 389.5 *escape;* 313.4 *hurry off;* 634.8 *run away*
fleece 774.16 *act dishonestly;* 550.14 *animal covering;* 700.30 *be fraudulent;* 782.14 *impoverish;* 552.15 *make nude;* 792.10 *overcharge;* 372.10 *set apart;* 419.11 *soft thing;* 773.10 *take away;* 212.4 *take off*
fleeced 782.2 *insolvent*
fleeciness 421.7 *smoothness*
fleecy 419.3, 421.1 *smooth*
fleecy cloud 31.20 *cloud appearance*
flee one's homeland 100.14 *be foreign*
fleer 389.3 *escaper*
fleet 374.3 *assembly;* 376.14 *force;* 262.3 *hasty;* 92.9 *inlet;* 584.4 *military organization;* 586.23 *naval unit;* 586.22 *navy;* 332.1 *swift;* 208.4 *throng*
Fleet Admiral 400.7 *military leader;* 323.7 *nautical person;* 397.6 *person in command*
Fleet Air Arm 586.29 *air force;* 586.23 *naval unit*
fleet arm 586.22 *navy*
fleet auxiliary vessels 586.24 *warship*
fleet blockade 585.8 *warfare*
fleet chief petty officer 586.27 *naval man*
fleeting 526.6 *disappearing;* 262.3 *hasty;* 300.16 *moving;* 278.6 *transient;* 96.8 *unreal*
fleetingly **526.8**; 278.8 *transiently*
fleetly 332.14 *swiftly*
fleetness 332.8 *speed*
fleet of foot 332.1 *swift*
Fleet Street 740.3 *journalism*
Flemish bond 38.26 *masonry*
flesh 80.3 *fruit structure;* 566.2 *human nature;* 402.4 *matter;* 25.20 *meat*
flesh and blood 402.4 *matter;* 402.5 *object;* 566.7 *person*
flesh-coloured 535.1 *red*
flesh-eater 557.18 *eater;* 70.4 *type of animal*
flesh-eating 71.28 *carnivorous;* 557.26 *eating;* 557.5 *eating habit*
flesh-eating mammal 71.8
fleshiness 158.5 *fatness;* 181.2 *round body*
fleshings 551.20 *legwear*
fleshliness 796.3 *sexual immorality*
fleshly 566.12 *human;* 796.14 *lecherous;* 402.7 *material*
flesh one's sword 585.13 *be at war*
flesh-pink 535.1 *red*
fleshpots 781.7 *opulence;* 490.4 *pleasurable things;* 557.9 *plenty;* 248.1 *prosperity*
flesh show 21.7 *show*
fleshy 158.16 *fat;* 80.9 *of a fruit;* 181.10 *well-rounded*
fleur-de-lis 743.8 *heraldic device*
fleur pastry 25.37 *pastry*
fleury 743.13 *heraldic*
flex 422.8 *be elastic;* 422.1 *elasticity;* 334.7 *electrical power;* 437.4 *electricity;* 39.27 *wire*
flex defence 46.10 *defence*
flexed 422.6 *elastic;* 184.7 *folded*
flexibility 422.2 *adaptability;* 453.16 *capriciousness;* 227.1 *changeableness;* 422.1 *elasticity;* 117.3 *pliancy;* 102.2 *possibleness;* 485.1 *skill;* 419.8 *softness;* 265.3 *wieldiness*
flexible 422.7 *adaptive;* 453.8 *capricious;* 117.11 *conformable;* 422.6 *elastic;* 419.2 *pliant;* 102.5 *possible;* 485.6 *skilful;* 639.4 *unsteady;* 265.12 *wieldy*
flexibly 117.16, 422.12 *adaptably;* 453.27 *capriciously;* 422.11 *elastically;* 419.17 *softly*
flexile 419.2 *pliant*
flexing 422.6 *elastic*
flexitime 15.2 *industrial negotiations;* 13.8 *industrial relations*
flex one's muscles 423.10 *be tough;* 243.8 *prepare oneself*
flexuous 184.7 *folded*
flexuously 184.12 *doubly*
flexure 325.14 *deviating course;* 184.1 *wrinkle*
flic 16.17 *police officer*
flick 331.13 *blow;* 327.26 *flicker;* 362.3 *jerk;* 58.9 *play hockey;* 66.4 *play soccer;* 492.3 *press;* 362.13 *pull at;* 331.6 *tap;* 492.11 *touch*
flicked 58.8 *hockey*
flicker **327.12**; **327.26**; 227.11 *be changeable;* 299.6 *be irregular;* 299.1 *irregularity;* 522.25 *light up;* 522.2 *quality of light;* 326.9 *vibrate*
flickering **327.20**; 227.13 *changeable;* 299.4 *irregular;* 299.1 *irregularity;* 522.15 *lucent;* 522.2 *quality of light;* 326.14 *vibrating;* 326.2 *vibration*
flickeringly 299.8 *irregularly*
flickery 327.20 *flickering;* 522.15 *lucent*
flicking 58.1 *hockey*
flick knife 425.10 *knife;* 587.8 *sharp weapon*
flicks 21.3 *films*
flick stroke 58.1 *hockey*
flier 740.9 *advertisement;* 70.6 *flying animal*
flies 21.17 *stage*
flight **322.5**; 586.30 *air force unit;* 72.13 *assemblage of birds;* 322.1 *aviation;* 53.18 *bowl;* 69.6 *darts;* 36.19 *defence mechanism;* 53.8 *delivery;* 313.7 *departure;* 634.16 *desertion;* 526.4 *disappearance;* 389.1 *escape;* 584.4 *military organization;* 300.2 *momentum;* 366.2 *send up;* 208.4 *throng*
flight attendant 401.3 *attendant*
flight bag 410.9 *baggage*
flight control 322.6
flight engineer 322.3 *aircraft personnel*
flight feather 72.17 *plumage*
flight formation 322.5 *flight*
flightiness 642.2 *caprice;* 472.2 *impetuosity;* 227.2 *irresolution*
flight lane 317.13 *flight path;* 317.2 *route*
flightless 72.21 *avian*
flightless bird 72.2
flight level 322.5 *flight*
flight-lieutenant 586.32 *airman*
flight line 322.4 *airport*
flight of fancy 477.4 *ideality;* 96.2 *illusion;* 727.5 *tall story*
flight of stairs 304.7 *means of ascent;* 317.2 *route*
flight path 317.13
flight reaction 36.10 *neurosis*
flight recorder 744.10 *recording instrument*
flight sergeant 586.32 *airman*
flight sergeant aircrew 586.32 *airman*
flight strip 317.13 *flight path*
flight test 448.2 *rehearsal*
flight-test 448.12 *rehearse*
flighty 642.1 *capricious;* 472.10 *careless;* 639.2 *changeable;* 227.14 *irresolute*
flimflam 645.5 *be cunning;* 604.8 *be dishonest;* 700.30 *be fraudulent;* 699.33 *deceitful;* 774.7 *dishonesty;* 700.10 *fraud;* 699.10 *lie;* 699.15 *nonsense;* 645.2 *stratagem;* 700.28 *trick;* 700.7 *tricking*
flimflam man 700.17 *cheat;* 645.3 *cunning person;* 774.11 *dishonest person*
flimflammed 700.36 *deceived*
flimflammer 700.17 *cheat*
flimflammery 700.7 *tricking*
flimsily 424.5 *fragilely;* 415.11 *lightly;* 419.17 *softly;* 527.13 *transparently*
flimsiness 424.2 *brittleness;* 153.11 *fineness;* 415.5 *lightness;* 417.3 *sparseness;* 527.6 *translucency*
flimsy 424.1 *brittle;* 153.4 *fine;* 415.2 *insubstantial;* 337.13 *insufficient;* 419.1 *soft;* 417.1 *sparse;* 157.2 *superficial;* 527.2 *translucent;* 124.4 *trivial;* 96.8 *unreal*

flimsy item 337.5 *weak thing*
flinch 612.11 *be afraid;* 732.6 *be shy;* 491.9 *feel pain;* 637.7 *refuse;* 634.4 *shy*
flinch at 709.5 *refuse*
flinching 634.18 *avoiding;* 634.12 *shyness*
fling 448.1 *experiment;* 22.4 *historic dancing;* 377.17 *sow;* 330.5, 330.23, 331.4 *throw;* 367.6 *throw down*
fling down 367.6 *throw down*
flinger 330.14 *thrower*
flinging 330.3 *throwing*
fling money around 787.1 *expend*
fling off 313.1 *depart;* 371.10 *exterminate*
fling wide the gates 601.18 *salute;* 370.9 *welcome*
flint 418.7 *hard substance;* 437.2 *lighter;* 24.2 *raw material*
flint axe 3.11 *relic*
flint chisel 438.4 *prehistoric tool*
flint glass 527.9 *glass*
flint-hearted 651.12 *callous*
flintiness 628.1 *pitilessness*
flintlock 587.10 *historical gun*
flint pebbles 24.2 *raw material*
flint tool 3.11 *relic*
flinty 651.12 *callous;* 30.57 *chalky;* 418.1 *hard;* 628.4 *pitiless*
flip 331.13 *blow;* 25.55 *cook;* 731.6 *effusive;* 660.13 *insolent;* 362.3 *jerk;* 362.13 *pull at;* 331.6 *tap;* 330.5, 330.23 *throw*
flip-flop 642.5 *be capricious;* 224.7 *be changed;* 224.11 *changeable;* 224.2 *change of mind;* 39.13 *circuit;* 40.19 *computing terms;* 642.3 *whim*
flip-flops 551.19 *footwear*
flip of the coin 107.3 *equal chance*
flip one's lid 624.12 *become angry*
flippancy 459.1 *folly;* 599.1 *humorousness;* 660.10 *impudence;* 615.1 *rashness;* 124.7 *triviality*
flippant 459.5 *foolish;* 599.10 *humorous;* 660.21 *impudent;* 615.4 *rash*
flippantly 660.30 *insolently*
flipper 205.4 *component;* 53.8 *delivery;* 492.7 *sense organ;* 21.19 *stage set;* 67.1 *swimming*
flippers 67.8 *swimwear*
flip the switch 346.8 *activate*
flirt 642.5 *be capricious;* 471.14 *be solicitous;* 642.4 *capricious person;* 593.26 *court;* 479.9 *equivocator;* 362.3 *jerk;* 593.9 *lover;* 362.13 *pull at*
flirtation 593.6 *courtship;* 593.8 *love affair;* 642.3 *whim*
flirtatious 593.20 *amorous;* 642.1 *capricious*
flirtatiously 593.30 *lovingly*
flirtatiousness 642.2 *caprice;* 593.6 *courtship;* 593.4 *lovability*
flirting 593.6 *courtship*
flirty 593.20 *amorous*
flit 227.12 *be irresolute;* 332.4 *be swift;* 278.4 *be transient;* 313.7 *departure;* 634.16 *desertion;* 389.1 *escape;* 327.12 *flicker;* 634.9 *play truant;* 313.3 *quit*
flitch 25.30 *bacon;* 79.3 *timber*
flitched 23.16 *joined*
flitched joint 23.10 *carpenter's term*
flitter 227.12 *be irresolute*
float 227.12 *be irresolute;* 415.9 *be light;* 352.6 *find means;* 55.3 *fishing tackle;* 421.12 *go smoothly;* 304.20 *hover;* 130.23 *inaugurate;* 14.5 *invest;* 415.7 *light thing;* 84.3 *plant body;* 330.33 *start;* 67.3 *survival swimming;* 67.9 *swim;* 67.1 *swimming;* 776.1 *trade;* 326.12 *wave*
floatability 415.5 *lightness*
floatable 415.2 *insubstantial*
float a loan 772.7 *borrow;* 771.5 *lend*
floated 67.11 *swimming*
floater 330.10 *ball;* 50.7 *windsurfing*
float fishing 55.1 *angling*
floating 227.13 *changeable;* 691.7 *drugged;* 14.6 *financial;* 250.9 *free;* 415.2 *insubstantial;* 415.5 *lightness;* 780.22 *monetary;* 323.11 *nautical;* 304.23 *rising;* 67.1, 67.11 *swimming;* 109.6 *unrelated*
floating bridge 317.9 *bridge*
floating currency 14.1 *finance*
floating debt 784.1 *debt*
floating device 67.3 *survival swimming*
floating diver 55.2 *artificial fly*
floating exchange rate 780.7 *finance*
floating island 25.35 *dessert;* 92.2 *island*
floating plug 55.2 *artificial fly*
floating-point notation 27.8 *number system*
floating point operation 40.19 *computing terms*
floating thing 415.7 *light thing*
floating up 304.1 *ascent*
floating vote 639.11 *vacillation*
floating voter 250.7 *free person;* 639.15 *indecisive person*
float in the air 304.20 *hover*
float rod 55.3 *fishing tackle*
float tackle 55.3 *fishing tackle*
float to the surface 415.9 *be light*
float up 304.17 *spring up*
floaty 415.2 *insubstantial*
floccinaucinihilipilification 195.3 *nothingness*
floccose 411.9 *platelike*
flocculate 32.25 *solidify*
flocculence 419.9 *smoothness*
flocculent 420.3 *barbed;* 411.9 *platelike;* 427.15 *powdery;* 419.3 *smooth*
flocculent colloidal 32.32 *solid*
flocculently 411.12 *in layers*
flocculent precipitate 32.3 *phase*
floccus 411.4 *slice*
flock **376.23**; 72.13 *assemblage of birds;* 71.21 *assemblage of mammals;* 208.11 *crowd;* 411.4 *slice;* 208.4 *throng;* 10.17 *worshipper*
flock together 376.39 *come together*
floe 30.39 *iceberg*
flog 331.5 *beat;* 767.11 *dispose of property;* 262.1 *hasten;* 814.3 *hit;* 491.11 *inflict pain;* 778.1 *sell*
flog a dead horse 219.5 *be superfluous;* 238.9 *waste effort*
flogger 814.17 *punisher*
flogging 331.12 *collision;* 814.12 *corporal punishment;* 331.17 *impelling;* 491.1 *pain*
flood **376.22**; 357.7 *agent of destruction;* 219.4 *be excessive;* 302.11 *course;* 208.11, 376.40 *crowd;* 219.1 *excess;* 90.7, 431.25 *flow;* 550.31 *hide;* 154.8 *high thing;* 368.4 *immerse;* 314.2 *influx;* 380.3 *instance of violence;* 315.2 *outflow;* 329.1 *overstep;* 329.6 *overstepping;* 217.8 *plenty;* 31.26 *raininess;* 90.6 *river flow;* 315.11 *run out;* 21.20 *stage lighting;* 91.2 *tide;* 380.5 *violent weather;* 433.29 *water*
flood-control system 38.24 *water system*
flooded **90.11**; **433.24**; 429.11 *marshy;* 329.11 *overrun*
floodgate 315.7 *outlet;* 38.24 *water system*
flood in **314.12**
flooding 219.6 *excessive;* 329.11 *overrun;* 329.6 *overstepping;* 433.9 *soaking*
flooding over 550.1 *covering*
floodlight 522.6 *electric light;* 522.24 *light;* 41.15 *lighting;* 21.20 *stage lighting*
floodlit 317.15 *accessible;* 522.18 *lit*
flood of words 266.1 *obscurity*
flood out 315.11 *run out*
flood plain 30.7 *landform;* 92.6 *lowland;* 429.8 *marsh*
flood proof 428.10 *waterproof*
flood the market 219.4 *be excessive;* 793.13 *make cheap*
flood the tanks 323.10 *sail*
flood tide 154.8 *high thing;* 213.3 *increasing thing;* 91.2 *tide*
floor 630.11 *amaze;* 175.1 *base;* 367.3 *bring down;* 203.2 *certain amount;* 790.3 *fee;* 187.3 *flat thing;* 122.5 *inferior state;* 411.2 *level;* 155.4 *low thing;* 410.4 *rack;* 704.8 *refute;* 357.11 *ruin*
floorboards 550.9 *floor covering*
floor covering **550.9**; 175.1 *base*
floorer 704.1 *refutation*
floor exercises **57.8**
flooring 175.1 *base;* 38.21 *bridge*
floor leader 579.14 *leader*
floor plan 484.5 *map*
floor polish 256.9 *cleaning agent;* 421.10 *polish*
floor polisher 421.9 *smoother*
floors 50.8 *punting*
floor show 21.7 *show*
floor tile 24.9 *industrial ceramics*
flop 778.2 *be sold;* 337.6 *be weak;* 486.9 *bungling;* 245.1 *deteriorate;* 305.10 *droop;* 247.6 *fail;* 247.5 *failing person;* 305.4 *fall;* 47.2 *field events;* 766.6 *loser;* 470.8 *rejected thing;* 419.13 *soften;* 21.13 *theatrical performance;* 247.4 *unsuccessful thing*
flop down 305.10 *droop*
flophouse 565.8 *shelter*
floppiness 268.2 *runniness;* 419.8 *softness;* 337.1 *weakness*
flopping 305.18 *falling*
floppy 40.7 *peripheral;* 419.1 *soft;* 337.8 *weak*
floppy disk 28.64 *magnetic recording;* 40.7 *peripheral;* 307.6 *rotator*
flops 40.19 *computing terms*
flora 77.11 *herbarium;* 77.1 *plants*
flora and fauna 34.2 *living world*
floral **78.10**; 502.4 *fragrant;* 44.16 *horticultural*
floral arrangement 542.1 *ornament*
floral charge 743.8 *heraldic device*
floral dance 78.9 *figurative usage*
floral diagram 78.3 *flower part*
floral envelope 78.3 *flower part*
floral formula 78.3 *flower part*
Floralia 10.16 *religious festival*
floral leaf 77.6 *leaf*
florally **78.14**; 502.7 *fragrantly;* 44.20 *horticulturally*
floral marquetry 23.9 *decorative woodwork*
floreate 78.10 *floral*
Florence Nightingale 35.16 *nurse*
florescence 243.13 *development;* 78.5 *flowering;* 345.3 *growth;* 561.3 *propagation*
florescent 243.20 *developed;* 78.11 *flowering;* 44.16 *horticultural*
floret 78.1 *flower*
floriate 78.10 *floral*
floricultural 44.16 *horticultural*
floriculture 78.7 *flower culture;* 44.1 *horticulture*
floriculturist 78.7 *flower culture;* 44.13 *horticulturist*
florid 529.11 *colourful;* 78.10 *floral;* 259.1 *healthy;* 542.10 *ornate;* 535.2 *red-faced;* 541.6 *variegated*
floridly 78.14 *florally;* 542.13 *ornately;* 535.10 *ruddily;* 541.12 *variedly*
floridness 542.1 *ornament;* 535.5 *redness*
florid style 543.1 *elegance*
florilegium 77.11 *herbarium*
florin 780.10 *former British money*
florist 78.7 *flower culture;* 778.13 *retailer*
floristic 78.10 *floral*
floristically 78.14 *florally*
floristics 78.7 *flower culture*
flossiness 419.9 *smoothness*
flossy 419.3 *smooth*
flotation 130.9 *premiere;* 243.9 *preparation*
flotilla 374.3 *assembly;* 584.4 *military organization;* 586.23 *naval unit*
flotilla leader 586.24 *warship*
flotsam 767.3 *disposable things;* 655.7 *outsider;* 316.10 *transferred thing*
flotsam and jetsam 205.8 *bits and pieces;* 767.3 *disposable things;* 377.8 *driftwood;* 655.7 *outsider*
flounce 542.6 *decorative articles;* 164.2 *edging;* 362.3 *jerk;* 327.25 *pitch;* 184.3, 184.10 *pleat;* 362.13 *pull at;* 327.11 *stagger*
flounce off 313.1 *depart*
flounder 55.4 *American game fish;* 486.7 *be clumsy;* 264.20 *be in difficulty;* 187.3 *flat thing;* 264.19 *have difficulty;* 327.25 *pitch;* 25.18 *sea fish;* 327.11 *stagger;* 307.10 *swirl;* 326.12 *wave*
flounderer 766.6 *loser*
floundering 766.18 *at a loss*
flour 25.7 *basic ingredient;* 427.24 *grind;* 427.8 *meal;* 427.21 *powder;* 377.18 *sprinkle;* 531.9 *white thing*
flour dredger 25.6 *kitchen equipment*
flouriness 427.1 *powderiness*
flourish 327.22 *agitate;* 190.6 *become bigger;* 222.14 *be comfortable;* 562.6 *be fertile;* 259.5 *be healthy;* 248.5 *be prosperous;* 246.6 *be successful;* 703.15 *demonstrate;* 738.1 *display;* 797.21 *do well;* 543.1 *elegance;* 78.13 *flower;* 213.4 *increase;* 507.1 *loudness;* 83.12 *mushroom;* 542.1 *ornament;* 542.3 *pattern;* 18.22 *phrase;* 510.2 *ringing;* 77.21 *vegetate;* 326.12 *wave;* 742.6 *word*
flourished 738.13 *displayed*
flourishing 562.5 *fertile;* 78.11 *flowering;* 538.4 *fresh;* 190.8 *growing;* 190.1 *growth;* 259.1 *healthy;* 77.13 *plantlike;* 248.8 *prosperous;* 326.4 *rock;* 246.13 *successful;* 338.4 *vigorous*
floury 427.16 *mealy*
flout 661.5 *defy*
flout authority 662.15 *be disobedient*
flout etiquette 659.7 *be discourteous*
flouting 668.15 *taunting*
flow **90.7**; **431.6**; **431.25**; 217.5 *about;* 342.12 *be active;* 270.5 *be diffuse;* 219.4 *be excessive;* 300.13 *be in motion;* 134.3 *continue;* 134.1 *continuity;* 376.40 *crowd;* 270.1 *diffuseness;* 30.63 *ebb;* 543.1 *elegance;* 560.1 *excretion;* 265.19 *go easily;* 302.6 *march on;* 300.2 *momentum;* 275.15 *pass;* 132.7 *stability;* 289.1 *succession;* 91.2 *tide;* 28.8 *time*
flowage 90.6 *river flow*
flow back 90.7 *flow;* 303.3 *reverse*
flow between 372.14 *come between*
flow by 275.15 *pass*
flow chart 409.8 *chart;* 484.5 *map*
flow down 305.13 *drip*
flower **78.1**; **78.13**; 765.10 *augment;* 190.6 *become bigger;* 248.5 *be prosperous;* 246.6 *be successful;* 235.7 *elite;* 502.2 *fragrant thing;* 44.9 *garden plant;* 79.19, 345.8, 555.18 *grow;* 345.3 *growth;* 561.11 *have young;* 213.4 *increase;* 556.18 *mature;* 77.2 *plant;* 356.7 *produce;* 99.3 *quintessence;* 797.9 *the best;* 77.21 *vegetate*
flowerage 78.5 *flowering*
flower arrangement 409.2 *array;* 78.1 *flower;* 542.1 *ornament*
flower basket 410.7 *basket*
flowerbed 44.3 *ornamental garden*
flower bud 77.8 *bud*
flower child 78.9 *figurative usage;* 118.7 *nonconformist*
flower cluster 78.4 *flower head*
flower culture **78.7**
flowered 78.10 *floral*
flowerer 78.2 *flowering plant*
floweret 78.1 *flower*
flower garden 502.2 *fragrant thing;* 44.2 *garden;* 44.3 *ornamental garden*
flower girl 570.7 *bridal party;* 78.7 *flower culture*
flower grower 78.7 *flower culture;* 44.13 *horticulturist*
flower growing 78.7 *flower culture;* 44.1 *horticulture*
flower head **78.4**; 205.6 *branch*
floweriness 542.1 *ornament*
flowering **78.5**; **78.11**; 243.20 *developed;* 243.13 *development;* 190.8, 345.11 *growing;* 190.1 *growth;* 555.13 *maturing;* 561.3 *propagation;* 77.16 *taxonomic*
flowering plant **78.2**; 77.3 *seed plant*
flower-like 78.10 *floral*
flower market 779.1 *market*
flower painter 19.16 *artist*
flower painting 19.10 *art subject*
flower part **78.3**
flowerpot 44.4 *nursery*
flower power 78.9 *figurative usage*
flower product **78.8**
Flowers 78
flowers 78.1 *flower;* 583.4 *funeral objects;* 427.5 *powder*
flower seller 78.7 *flower culture*
flower selling 78.7 *flower culture*
flowers of speech 542.1 *ornament*
flowers of sulphur 427.5 *powder*
flower stalk 77.5 *stem*
flowery 78.10 *floral;* 502.4 *fragrant;* 44.16 *horticultural;* 542.10 *ornate;* 815.3 *prison cell;* 292.10 *spring*
flowery speaker 542.9 *phrasemonger*
flowery speech 729.2 *power of speech*
flowery writer 542.9 *phrasemonger*
flow from 345.7 *follow from*
flow in 91.10 *billow;* 314.12 *flood in;* 90.7 *flow*
flowing **431.15**; 227.13 *changeable;* 134.5 *continual;* 270.3 *diffuse;* 219.6 *excessive;* 90.10 *fluvial;* 300.16 *moving;* 90.6 *river flow*
flowing bowl 690.13 *drink*
flowing on 302.18 *ongoing*
flowing river 90.1 *river*
flowing together 90.6 *river flow*
flowmeter **431.12**; 28.88 *barometer*
flown 98.9 *away*
flow of electricity 28.51 *electric current*
flow of ideas 443.5 *creative thought*
flow of time 277.2 *time*
flow of traffic 300.2 *momentum*
flow of words 731.1 *talkativeness*
flow on 302.6 *march on;* 433.29 *water*
flow onwards 275.15 *pass*

flow out 219.4 *be excessive;* 91.10 *billow;* 90.7 *flow;* 389.7 *leak;* 315.11 *run out;* 304.17 *spring up;* 441.1 *waste*
flow over 90.7 *flow*
flow sheet 409.8 *chart*
flow together 173.9 *centre;* 90.7 *flow*
flu 260.6 *infection;* 260.9 *respiratory disease*
flub 486.9 *bungling*
flubbed 231.1 *imperfect*
fluctuant 326.13 *oscillating*
fluctuate 642.5 *be capricious;* 227.11 *be changeable;* 224.7 *be changed;* 299.6 *be irregular;* 120.5 *be unequal;* 453.21 *change;* 326.8 *oscillate;* 326.10, 639.5 *vacillate*
fluctuating 453.8 *capricious;* 224.11, 227.13 *changeable;* 300.17 *directional;* 299.4 *irregular;* 326.13 *oscillating*
fluctuating currency 780.1 *money*
fluctuation 453.16 *capriciousness;* 224.1 *change;* 227.1 *changeableness;* 300.5 *circuition;* 776.5 *commercial trade;* 639.12 *inconstancy;* 299.1 *irregularity;* 326.1 *oscillation*
flue 493.6 *fire;* 308.7 *passageway*
fluency 265.1 *easiness;* 543.1 *elegance;* 431.6 *flow;* 57.1 *gymnastics;* 729.2 *power of speech;* 90.6 *river flow;* 731.1 *talkativeness*
fluent 270.3 *diffuse;* 543.3 *elegant;* 431.15 *flowing;* 90.10 *fluvial;* 300.16 *moving;* 729.19 *speaking;* 731.5 *talkative*
fluently 90.13; 543.5 *elegantly;* 431.26 *fluidly;* 724.10 *stylistically;* 731.10 *talkatively*
fluent tongue 731.1 *talkativeness*
fluff 434.10 *air bubble;* 486.7 *be clumsy;* 274.10 *blunder;* 486.9 *bungling;* 404.2 *grain;* 517.10 *lack harmony;* 415.10 *lighten;* 415.7 *light thing;* 427.5 *powder;* 419.13 *soften;* 419.11 *soft thing;* 21.36 *underact*
fluffily 415.11 *lightly;* 419.17 *softly*
fluffiness 404.2 *grain;* 415.5 *lightness;* 419.9 *smoothness*
fluff one's lines 463.14 *be forgetful;* 486.5 *be unskilful*
fluff up 419.13 *soften*
fluffy 404.11; 415.2 *insubstantial;* 419.3 *smooth*
Fluid 431
fluid 431.1; **431.14**; 453.8 *capricious;* 227.13 *changeable;* 543.3 *elegant;* 268.10 *slippery;* 419.1 *soft;* 433.1 *water;* 433.21 *watery*
fluidal 431.14 *fluid*
fluid extract 431.1 *fluid*
fluidic 431.14 *fluid*
fluidification 431.8
fluidify 431.22 *make fluid*
fluid intake 558.1 *drinking;* 370.4 *intake*
fluidity 431.5; 453.16 *capriciousness;* 227.1 *changeableness;* 543.1 *elegance;* 268.2 *runniness*
fluidize 432.26 *aerate;* 431.22 *make fluid*
fluidly 431.26; 453.27 *capriciously;* 227.15 *changeably;* 268.22 *slimily;* 419.17 *softly;* 433.35 *wetly*
fluid mechanics 431.13; 28.2 *classical physics*
fluidmeter 431.12 *flowmeter*
fluidness 431.5 *fluidity*
fluke 107.2 *luck;* 75.10 *parasite;* 425.8 *sharp-pointed thing;* 105.5 *unexpectedness;* 75.6 *worm*
fluke! 107.16
fluky 107.8 *chance;* 105.3 *unexpected;* 75.20 *wormlike*
flume 146.3 *gulf;* 315.7 *outlet*
flummox 457.10 *bemuse;* 696.7 *be unintelligible;* 453.20 *make uncertain*
flummoxed 696.6 *confused*
flunk 247.6 *fail*
flunked 247.10 *failed*
flunkey 387.3 *subordinate*
flunky 122.6 *inferior;* 401.1 *servant;* 578.1 *worker*
fluoresce 522.25 *light up*
fluorescence 522.1 *light;* 28.24 *light emission*
fluorescent 522.16 *bright;* 522.15 *lucent*
fluorescent clothing 520.7 *that which makes visible*
fluorescent lamp 39.20 *electron tube*
fluorescent light 522.6 *electric light;* 28.25 *light source*
fluorescent paint 520.7 *that which makes visible*
fluorescent tube 24.9 *industrial ceramics;* 28.25 *light source*
fluoric 32.34 *elemental*
fluoridate 252.10 *protect;* 32.26 *react*
fluoridated 32.34 *elemental*
fluoridation 35.6 *health care*
fluoride 394.3 *prophylactic*
fluorinate 252.10 *protect*
fluorinated 32.34 *elemental*
fluormate 32.26 *react*
fluorocarbon 435.1 *materials*
fluorometer 26.8 *meter*
fluorometric 26.16 *micrometric*
fluorometry 26.2 *micrometry*
flurried 327.15 *agitated*
flurry 327.4 *fuss;* 262.4 *haste;* 494.5 *ice;* 342.3 *nimbleness;* 31.25 *rain;* 31.30 *snow;* 332.8 *speed*
flush 674.16 *be self-conscious;* 674.2 *blushing;* 69.3 *card game terms;* 256.13 *clean;* 529.9 *complexion;* 324.9 *directly;* 119.6 *equal;* 493.16 *feel hot;* 217.3 *filled;* 90.7 *flow;* 232.8 *full;* 493.1 *heat;* 187.8 *horizontal;* 187.11 *horizontally;* 633.11 *hunt;* 187.7 *make horizontal;* 622.30 *make proud;* 529.16 *make up;* 255.10 *purify;* 535.9 *redden;* 535.5 *redness;* 90.6 *river flow;* 60.7 *shoot;* 68.12 *ski;* 421.1 *smooth;* 781.1 *wealthy;* 765.17 *well-off*
flushed 674.9 *blushing;* 690.1 *drunk;* 535.2 *red-faced;* 493.12 *warm-hearted*
flushed with pride 622.22 *boastful*
flushed with rage 624.16 *angry*
flushed with victory 246.15 *victorious*
flush gate 68.3 *ski racing*
flushing 674.2 *blushing;* 255.2 *purification;* 535.2 *red-faced*
flushing out 256.2 *cleaning*
flushly 421.14 *smoothly*
flushness 187.1 *horizontality;* 421.7 *smoothness*
flush out 256.13 *clean;* 255.10, 256.15 *purify*
flush with anger 624.12 *become angry*
fluster 327.22 *agitate;* 328.7 *disturb;* 327.4 *fuss*
flustered 327.15 *agitated;* 328.12 *disturbed;* 327.16 *restless;* 690.2 *slightly drunk*
flute 20.8 *column;* 20.19 *decorate;* 184.2 *furrow;* 18.39 *sing;* 729.13 *speak in a particular way;* 184.8 *wrinkle*
fluted 20.16 *columned;* 184.6 *wrinkly*
fluted armour 384.7 *armour*
fluting 20.8 *column;* 542.3 *pattern*
flutter 327.22 *agitate;* 517.5 *atmospheric dissonance;* 327.21 *be agitated;* 327.10 *beat;* 227.11 *be changeable;* 612.12 *be fearful;* 327.12, 327.26 *flicker;* 322.5 *flight;* 262.4 *haste;* 326.11 *rock;* 67.11 *swimming;* 326.9 *vibrate;* 326.2 *vibration;* 326.12 *wave*
flutteration 327.4 *fuss*
flutter down 305.12 *drop*
fluttering 327.16 *restless;* 488.3 *stimulus*
fluttering eyelashes 742.3 *gesture*
flutter kick 67.2 *swimming technique*
flutter one's eyelashes 742.11 *gesture;* 518.13 *look*
flutter someone's heart 593.28 *win the love of*
fluttery 327.16 *restless*
fluvial 90.10
fluviomarine 90.10 *fluvial*
fluvioterrestrial 90.12 *hydrological*
flux 227.1 *changeableness;* 560.2 *defecation;* 39.11 *electric field;* 560.1 *excretion;* 431.6 *flow;* 28.10 *force;* 431.24 *melt;* 300.2 *momentum;* 90.6 *river flow;* 431.10 *solution;* 431.9 *solvent;* 289.1 *succession;* 91.2 *tide*
flux and reflux 326.1 *oscillation;* 91.2 *tide*
flux collector 29.24 *telescope*
flux density 28.10 *force*
fluxibility 431.8 *fluidification*
fluxible 431.15 *flowing*
fluxile 431.15 *flowing*
fluxility 431.6 *flow;* 431.5 *fluidity*
fluxion 27.31 *differentiation;* 431.6 *flow*
fluxional 431.15 *flowing*
fluxionary 431.15 *flowing*
fluxive 431.15 *flowing*
fluxure 431.5 *fluidity*
fly 72.25; **322.10**; 98.18 *abscond;* 48.5 *batting terms;* 342.12 *be active;* 154.15 *be high;* 332.4 *be swift;* 278.4 *be transient;* 645.4 *cunning;* 526.2 *depart;* 389.5 *escape;* 317.14 *find one's way;* 743.7 *flag;* 70.6 *flying animal;* 633.3 *hunting and fishing equipment;* 76.1 *insect;* 262.2 *make haste;* 551.24 *part of garment;* 275.15 *pass;* 634.8 *run away;* 700.13 *snare;* 304.19 *take off;* 316.12, 319.4 *transport;* 300.15 *walk;* 326.12 *wave*
fly about 740.17 *be published*
fly a flag 327.22 *agitate*
fly against 381.1 *attack*
fly a kite 740.13 *make public;* 353.4 *test*
fly aloft 304.19 *take off*
fly apart 377.11 *explode*
fly at 625.6 *be irascible*
fly away 278.4 *be transient*
fly ball 48.5 *batting terms*
flyblow 76.16 *infest*
flyblown 258.8 *unclean;* 76.12 *verminous*
fly-boy 585.11 *recruit*
flyby 29.35 *rocketry*
fly by 275.15 *pass*
fly-by-light 322.6 *flight control*
fly-by-night 634.18 *avoiding;* 645.3 *cunning person;* 247.5 *failing person*
fly-by-wire 519.7 *figurative blindness;* 322.6 *flight control*
flycatcher 72.6 *songbird*
fly dick 16.17 *police officer*
fly down 305.12 *drop*
flyer 740.9 *advertisement;* 322.3 *aircraft personnel*
fly-fish 55.7 *angle;* 74.15 *fish;* 633.11 *hunt*
fly-fisher 55.6 *angler*
fly-fishing 55.1 *angling;* 633.2 *chase;* 74.7 *fishing*
fly floor 21.17 *stage*
fly gallery 21.17 *stage*
fly in 436.5 *provision*
fly in all directions 377.11 *explode*
flying 322.1 *aviation;* 71.27 *chiropteran;* 154.9 *high;* 300.16 *moving;* 318.2 *passing along;* 332.1 *swift;* 278.6 *transient*
flying animal 70.6
flying axel 68.6 *ice-skating*
flying back kick 52.9 *tae kwon do*
flying boat 586.31 *military aircraft*
flying bomb 587.16 *bomb*
flying buttress 20.10 *church architecture;* 20.8 *column;* 413.2 *supporting part;* 360.4 *wall*
flying circus 322.1 *aviation*
flying column 586.14 *armed forces*
flying corps 586.29 *air force*
flying doctor 322.1 *aviation;* 394.15 *healer*
Flying Dutchman 323.7 *nautical person*
Flying Dutchman class 50.2 *sailing boat*
flying fish 74.2 *fish;* 70.6 *flying animal*
flying fox 70.6 *flying animal*
flying insect 70.6 *flying animal*
flying kick 52.9 *tae kwon do*
flying lap 61.6 *motor-racing terms*
flying mammal 71.7; 70.6 *flying animal*
flying mare 52.5 *wrestling*
flying officer 586.32 *airman*
flying picket 15.4 *industrial dispute*
flying reptile 73.6 *extinct reptile*
flying reverse crescent kick 52.9 *tae kwon do*
flying saucer 29.34 *SETI*
flying saucers 737.6 *natural mystery*
flying squad 16.15 *British police*
flying start 332.9 *acceleration;* 121.3, 164.4 *advantage;* 130.11 *starting point*
flying up 304.4 *taking off*
fly in the ointment 231.7 *defect;* 378.2 *obstacle*
fly into a passion 624.12 *become angry*
fly into a rage 624.12 *become angry*
flyman 21.28 *stagehand*
fly off 311.15 *change direction;* 325.8 *sidestep*
fly off the handle 624.12 *become angry*
fly one's flag 585.12 *go to war*
fly out 48.7 *play baseball*
fly-out 48.6 *fielding terms*
flyover 317.15 *accessible;* 38.21 *bridge;* 318.5 *crossing point;* 317.3, 373.5 *road*
flypaper 267.3 *adhesive;* 700.13 *snare*
flypast 656.3 *formal occasion;* 322.7 *miscellaneous aviation terms;* 667.5 *presenting arms;* 601.8 *salute*
fly pattern 46.9 *play*
fly rod 55.3 *fishing tackle*
fly spoon 55.2 *artificial fly*
fly-spotted 541.10 *mottled*
fly the nest 98.18 *abscond*
fly to arms 585.12 *go to war*
flytrap 700.13 *snare*
fly up 304.17 *spring up*
flyweight 586.3 *athlete;* 52.4 *boxer;* 52.3 *boxing weight divisions;* 52.14 *combat;* 414.7 *weighing*
flywheel 307.6 *rotator*
FM transmitter 692.16 *transmitter*
f-number 41.18 *exposure time;* 28.31 *lens element*
foal 71.35 *give birth;* 561.11 *have young;* 59.1 *horse;* 555.4 *young animal;* 71.19 *young mammal*
foaled 554.15 *born*
foam 434.10 *air bubble;* 124.9 *bauble;* 91.10 *billow;* 434.24 *bubble;* 415.7 *light thing;* 560.9 *saliva;* 419.11 *soft thing;* 91.3 *wave*
foam at the mouth 327.21 *be agitated;* 624.11 *be angry*
foam-filled 419.4 *compressible*
foam-filling 419.11 *soft thing*
foam-flecked 531.2 *whitened*
foam glass 24.9 *industrial ceramics*
foamily 531.14 *whitely*
foaminess 415.5 *lightness*
foaming 624.16 *angry;* 415.2 *insubstantial;* 560.29 *salivating;* 531.2 *whitened*
foaming at the mouth 624.16 *angry;* 461.12 *manic*
foam rubber 422.4 *rubber*
foamy 434.18 *bubbly;* 415.2 *insubstantial*
fob 281.7 *watch*
f.o.b. 793.11 *free of charge*
fob off 762.6 *give a substitute*
fob off on 386.7 *force*
focal 173.8; 121.14 *best;* 310.7 *convergent;* 27.81 *curvilinear*
focalization 173.3 *centrality;* 310.5 *focus*
focalize 173.9 *centre*
focalized 173.7 *centralized*
focalizing 173.3 *centrality*
focal length 41.17 *lens;* 28.31 *lens element*
focal plane 28.31 *lens element*
focal point 173.1 *centre;* 363.7 *centre of attraction;* 173.5 *focus;* 28.31 *lens element*
focus 173.5; **310.5**; **310.11**; 173.1, 173.9 *centre;* 363.7 *centre of attraction;* 27.42 *circle;* 520.4 *clarity;* 41.8 *composition;* 99.2 *essential content;* 447.2 *issue;* 41.17 *lens;* 28.31 *lens element;* 518.13 *look;* 520.10 *make visible;* 41.21 *photograph;* 243.4 *prepare for action;* 30.22 *seismic activity*
focused 447.7; 310.7 *convergent;* 695.1 *intelligible*
focusing 173.3 *centrality;* 310.7 *convergent;* 28.32 *optical instrument*
focusing screen 41.18 *exposure time*
focus on 447.10; 482.10 *aim;* 173.9 *centre;* 520.10 *make visible*
fodder 43.9 *animal feedstuff;* 557.8 *animal food;* 81.11 *eat grass;* 435.1 *materials;* 43.18 *practise livestock farming*
fodder beet 43.12 *crop*
fodder crop 43.12 *crop*
fodder grass 81.1 *grass*
fodder peas 43.12 *crop*
fodder rape 43.12 *crop*
Fodor 693.5 *reference book*
foe 594.8 *hated person;* 113.13 *opponent*
foetid 432.18 *miasmic*
foetid air 432.3 *miasma*
fog 31.33; **31.64**; 528.10 *be opaque;* 41.8 *composition;* 736.9 *disguise;* 521.4 *invisibility;* 524.10 *make dim;* 161.3 *make shapeless;* 453.20 *make uncertain;* 429.2 *mistiness;* 524.2 *murk;* 528.7 *opaque thing;* 32.3 *phase;* 161.1 *shapelessness;* 521.6 *that which makes invisible;* 433.3 *wateriness;* 432.4 *water vapour*
fog band 429.2 *mistiness*
fog bank 31.33 *fog*
fogbound 251.15 *detained;* 31.56 *foggy*
fogbow 31.27 *rainbow*
fog drip 31.37, 429.6 *dew*
foggily 524.12 *dimly;* 533.9 *greyly;* 453.25 *indeterminately;* 31.65 *meteorologically;* 528.13 *opaquely;* 161.6 *shapelessly*
fogginess 453.14 *indeterminacy;* 521.4 *invisibility;* 429.2 *mistiness;* 524.2 *murk;* 266.1 *obscurity;* 528.6 *opaqueness;* 161.1 *shapelessness;* 31.35 *visibility*
foggy 31.56; 416.7 *condensed;* 696.4 *difficult;* 521.2 *difficult to see;* 533.3 *dull;* 453.6 *indeterminate;* 429.10 *misty;* 524.6

murky; 266.2 *obscure;* 528.2 *shady;* 432.19 *smoky*
foghorn 711.2 *danger signal;* 579.5 *guide;* 742.4 *signal*
fog lamp 522.6 *electric light*
fog level 41.10 *graininess*
fogou 583.6 *grave;* 3.11 *relic;* 284.7 *thing of the past*
fog signal 711.2 *danger signal;* 321.2 *track*
foible 231.7 *defect;* 247.3 *personal fault;* 804.3 *venial sin*
foil 634.2 *avert;* 426.9 *blunt instrument;* 411.3 *coat;* 113.21 *counteract;* 364.7 *deflection;* 21.29 *entertainer;* 54.6 *fencing;* 54.2 *fencing equipment;* 378.8 *hinder;* 621.4 *laughing stock;* 587.8 *sharp weapon;* 604.7 *thwart;* 165.4 *wrapper;* 550.4 *wrapping*
foil button 54.2 *fencing equipment*
foiled 604.9 *disappointed*
foil-fence 54.5 *fence*
foil fencing 54.1 *fencing*
foil grip 54.2 *fencing equipment*
foil guard 54.2 *fencing equipment*
foiling 378.1 *hindrance*
foilsman 586.3 *athlete;* 54.4 *fencer*
foin 381.18 *hit*
foison 217.8 *plenty*
foist on 386.7 *force*
fold 30.64; 184.9; 69.3 *card game terms;* 226.6 *cease;* 309.4 *closed place;* 30.20 *earth movement;* 309.10 *enclose;* 165.2 *enclosed place;* 247.6 *fail;* 43.7 *farm building;* 593.27 *kiss;* 411.1 *layer;* 551.35 *make clothing;* 420.12 *make rough;* 551.24 *part of garment;* 69.10 *play;* 307.9 *roll;* 565.12 *stall;* 10.17 *worshipper;* 184.1 *wrinkle*
foldable 191.9 *contractible*
fold around 184.9 *fold*
foldaway 23.14 *wooden*
foldaway bed 23.6 *bed*
fold-belt mountain 30.21 *mountain building*
foldboat 50.6 *canoeing*
folded 184.7; 551.31 *styled*
folded arms 742.3 *gesture*
folded dipole 692.17 *antenna*
folded over 184.7 *folded*
folder 439.5 *collection;* 410.5 *packet;* 165.4 *wrapper*
fold-hinge 30.20 *earth movement*
fold in 25.55 *cook*
folding 30.20 *earth movement;* 43.3 *livestock farming;* 23.14 *wooden*
folding cabbage 780.2 *cash*
folding canoe 50.6 *canoeing*
folding chair 23.2 *chair*
folding cycle 320.12 *bicycle*
folding green 780.2 *cash*
folding ladder 304.9 *ladder*
folding money 780.2 *cash*
fold mountain 30.21 *mountain building*
fold one's arms 742.11 *gesture*
fold over 184.9 *fold*
fold to one's heart 593.27 *kiss*
fold up 191.6 *become smaller;* 131.16, 226.6 *cease;* 184.9 *fold;* 439.6 *store*
foliage 205.6 *branch;* 538.8 *greenness;* 77.6 *leaf*
foliage bud 77.8 *bud*
foliar feed 44.7 *fertilizer*
foliate 77.14 *of plants;* 411.9 *platelike*
foliated 411.7 *layered;* 30.56 *petrographic*
foliated rock 30.33 *metamorphic rock*
foliation 411.6 *layering;* 30.29 *petrogenesis*
folic acid 33.13 *vitamin*
folie à deux 461.4 *delusion*
folio 205.2 *particular*
foliose 84.8 *lichenoid*
foliose lichen 84.6 *lichen*
folium 27.40 *curve*
folk 566.9 *group;* 566.1 *humankind;* 18.33 *jazz;* 1.14 *societal;* 1.7 *society*
folk art 1.8 *tradition*
folk ballad 18.11 *folk music*
folk costume 551.3 *formal dress*
folk dance 22.4 *historic dancing*
folk dancing 22.1 *dancing*
Folketing 579.10 *legislative body*
folk etymology 274.11 *grammatical error;* 5.1 *linguistics*
folk history 3.7 *narrative;* 1.8 *tradition*
folk literature 17.1 *literature*
folklore 632.4 *custom;* 450.2 *religious belief;* 566.5 *study of mankind;* 1.8, 296.6 *tradition*
folklorist 566.6 *studier of mankind*
folk medicine 394.11 *medical art;* 35.2 *natural medicine*
folkmoot 579.7 *council*
folk motif 1.8 *tradition*
folk music 18.11
folk play 21.2 *play*
folk poetry 17.6 *poetry*
folk psychology 36.1 *psychology*
folk rock 18.11 *folk music;* 18.9 *popular music*
folks 376.17 *family*
folksiness 657.3 *familiarity*
folk society 2.5 *society*
folksong 18.11 *folk music;* 516.2 *song;* 1.8 *tradition*
folk story 17.2 *fiction*
folksy 657.9 *familiar;* 18.33 *jazz*
folk tale 17.2 *fiction;* 721.3 *narration;* 3.7 *narrative;* 1.8 *tradition*
foller 191.4 *contractor*
follicle 80.2 *botanical fruit*
Follies 21.7 *show*
follow 122.10; 633.9; 664.14; 223.16 *attend;* 168.6 *be in the rear;* 117.8 *comply;* 750.25 *conform;* 125.11 *emulate;* 345.7 *follow from;* 125.9 *imitate;* 4.22 *propound a philosophy;* 4.21 *rationalize;* 401.8 *serve;* 139.27 *specialize;* 147.17 *stay near;* 289.10 *succeed;* 695.6 *understand;* 349.1 *use*
follow a course 631.11 *conduct oneself*
follow advice 713.6 *consult*
follow a pattern 298.7 *be regular*
follow a plan 484.12 *plan ahead*
follow at heel 664.14 *follow*
follow a trend 221.6 *be in a state of*
follow bad advice 604.4 *be disappointed*
follow custom 658.11 *have good manners*
followed 633.17 *pursued*
follower 223.9; 267.5; 289.8; 664.5 *adherent;* 669.8 *admirer;* 117.6 *conformist;* 387.4 *dependent;* 125.7 *imitator;* 122.6 *inferior;* 593.9 *lover;* 633.5 *pursuer;* 401.1 *servant;* 413.8 *supporter;* 9.5, 10.17 *worshipper*
follower of a doctrine 4.11
follower of fashion 115.4 *person who copies*
follow from 345.7
follow in a series 132.13 *be consecutive*
following 223.10 *attendance;* 345.10 *caused;* 132.9 *consecutive;* 294.12 *delaying;* 125.1 *imitation;* 125.12 *imitative;* 633.15 *pursuing;* 633.1 *pursuit;* 300.10 *regular movement;* 115.7 *similar;* 289.12 *succeeding;* 289.1 *succession*
following from 345.10 *caused*
following spot 21.20 *stage lighting*
following the letter 698.23 *literal;* 698.10 *literalness*
following upon 345.12 *with the effect of*
following wind 434.4 *air flow;* 392.1 *help;* 330.12 *propellant;* 31.15 *wind direction*
follow in office 289.11
follow in sequence 289.10 *succeed*
follow in the wake 168.6 *be in the rear*
follow like sheep 125.11 *emulate;* 663.5 *obey*
follow on 132.13 *be consecutive;* 125.11 *emulate*
follow one's bent 250.16 *be independent*
follow one's career 631.11 *conduct oneself*
follow one's conscience 483.8 *be motivated;* 803.8 *be virtuous*
follow one's hunch 445.9 *be intuitive*
follow one's instincts 483.8 *be motivated*
follow one's nose 500.7 *smell;* 324.7 *take a direction*
follow one's own will 635.14
follow on from 345.7 *follow from*
follow orders 663.5 *obey*
follow protocol 160.8, 656.11 *be formal*
follow separate paths 372.13 *diverge*
follow suit 117.8 *comply;* 125.11 *emulate*
follow that car 633.19 *after him!*
follow the beaten path 117.8 *comply*
follow the book 663.5 *obey*
follow the chase 633.11 *hunt*
follow the crowd 750.25 *conform;* 664.14 *follow*
follow the example of 125.11 *emulate*
follow the fashion 117.8 *comply*
follow the golden mean 685.3 *be moderate*
follow the herd 125.11 *emulate*
follow the law 16.67
follow the letter 698.32 *be literal*
follow the party line 663.5 *obey;* 140.17 *obey orders*
follow the rising star 479.3 *apostatize*
follow the scent 633.9 *follow;* 60.7 *shoot;* 500.7 *smell*
follow the trail 633.9 *follow*
follow the trend 295.18 *be trendy;* 117.8 *comply*
follow through 134.3 *continue;* 640.7 *maintain*
follow-through 51.10 *bowling;* 51.5 *bowling delivery;* 51.9 *bowls;* 56.3 *golf shots;* 51.2 *grip;* 63.2 *tennis strokes*
follow up 633.13; 35.19 *practise medicine;* 134.4 *protract*
follow-up 134.1 *continuity;* 35.6 *health care;* 289.9 *sequel*
Folly 459
folly 459.1; 356.8 *construction;* 456.1 *ignorance;* 272.1 *ludicrousness;* 615.1 *rashness;* 457.2 *unintelligence*
foment 344.10 *awaken;* 394.20 *doctor;* 380.9 *make violent*
fomentation 344.1 *cause;* 493.3 *heater;* 37.7 *ointment;* 394.10 *surgical dressing;* 394.13 *therapy*
fomenter 344.8 *contributor*
fond 617.9 *desirous;* 593.17 *loving;* 590.12 *sensitive*
fondant 498.4 *confectionery;* 25.41 *sweet*
fond farewell 658.3 *courtesies*
fond feeling 595.1 *liking*
fond illusion 700.2 *self-deception*
fondle 593.14 *communication of love;* 490.9 *give pleasure;* 492.4, 593.27 *kiss;* 492.11 *touch*
fondling 593.14 *communication of love;* 492.2 *touching*
fond look 593.14 *communication of love*
fondly 593.30 *lovingly*
fondness 617.1 *desire;* 590.5 *good feeling;* 595.1 *liking;* 593.1 *love*
fondness for company 654.1 *sociability*
fondness for society 654.1 *sociability*
fondness for the bottle 690.11 *drinking*
fond of 593.18 *in love*
fond of a drink 690.5 *drunken*
fond of company 654.15 *sociable*
fondue 25.45 *French dish;* 25.15 *sauce;* 25.34 *vegetarian dish*
fondue fork 557.16 *eating utensil*
fondus 22.10 *positions at the barre*
fons et origo 344.2 *source*
font 10.12 *church;* 5.15 *type style*
food 557.7; 554.3 *life requirements;* 435.1 *materials;* 436.2 *provisions;* 581.7 *refreshments*
food aid 768.3 *offering*
food chain 34.18 *ecology*
food-combining diet 557.6 *nutrition*
food content 557.11
food department 557.17 *food shop*
food fish 74.8; 74.2 *fish*
food for powder 586.17 *army person*
food for the body 557.7 *food*
food for the mind 557.7 *food*
food for the spirit 557.7 *food*
food for worms 582.11 *dead person*
food hall 557.17 *food shop*
foodie 557.18 *eater;* 688.4 *glutton;* 495.5 *taster*
food mixer 25.6 *kitchen equipment*
food mountain 376.25 *assemblage;* 557.9 *plenty;* 439.1 *store*
food of the gods 557.7 *food*
food orgy 688.3 *act of gluttony*
food parcel 768.3 *offering*
food plant 77.2 *plant*
food poisoning 260.2 *illness;* 260.8 *indigestion;* 260.6 *infection*
food preparation 25.1 *cookery*
food processing 25.1 *cookery*
food processor 327.14 *agitator;* 25.6 *kitchen equipment;* 431.11 *liquidizer;* 412.6 *mixer;* 427.11 *pulverizer;* 307.6 *rotator*
food provider 557.20
food pyramid 34.18 *ecology*
food rations 436.1 *provision*
food shop 557.17
food stamp 768.3 *offering*
food stamps 436.1 *provision;* 652.4 *welfare state*
food store 84.3 *plant body*
foodstuffs 557.7 *food;* 436.2 *provisions*
food supply 436.1 *provision*
food web 34.18 *ecology*
fool 697.8; 697.4 *buffoon;* 668.9 *butt;* 21.32 *clown;* 25.35 *dessert;* 700.22 *dupe;* 459.3 *foolish person;* 456.5 *ignorant person;* 465.5 *misjudging person;* 646.3 *naive person;* 272.3 *object of ridicule;* 21.23 *role;* 773.10 *take away;* 700.28 *trick;* 457.3 *unintelligent person;* 486.10 *unskilled person*
fool around 340.4 *act;* 697.8 *fool;* 593.27 *kiss*
fooled 700.36 *deceived*
foolery 459.2 *act of folly*
foolhardiness 613.4 *adventurousness;* 472.2 *impetuosity;* 615.1 *rashness*
foolhardy 613.13 *adventurous;* 459.5 *foolish;* 615.4 *rash*
fooling 700.7 *tricking*
fooling around 593.6 *courtship;* 796.3 *sexual immorality*
foolish 459.5; 465.9 *misjudged;* 697.5 *nonsensical;* 615.4 *rash;* 272.5 *ridiculous;* 157.2 *superficial;* 124.4 *trivial;* 457.6 *unintelligent;* 486.1 *unskilful*
foolish hope 105.4 *improbability*
foolishly 459.8; 465.13 *misguidedly;* 697.9 *nonsensically;* 615.6 *rashly;* 457.11 *unintelligently;* 486.11 *unskilfully*
foolishness 459.1 *folly;* 272.1 *ludicrousness;* 457.2 *unintelligence*
foolish person 459.3
foolproof 252.7 *invulnerable;* 265.12 *wieldy*
foolscap 435.3 *paper*
fool's errand 766.3 *waste;* 238.5 *waste of effort*
fool's gold 780.16 *bullion;* 711.3 *false alarm;* 699.16 *false thing;* 700.6 *imitation;* 604.3 *mirage;* 238.5 *waste of effort*
fool's paradise 610.3 *aspiration;* 604.3 *mirage;* 465.1 *misjudgment;* 467.2 *overestimate;* 96.4 *theorization*
fool with 486.7 *be clumsy;* 245.4 *impair*
foot 175.2; 586.17 *army person;* 205.4 *component;* 155.4 *low thing;* 148.7 *measure of length;* 17.9 *metre;* 82.4 *moss plant;* 17.8 *part of poem*
footage 148.4 *length*
foot-and-mouth disease 260.18 *veterinary disease*
football 46.1; 330.10 *ball;* 410.19 *inflatable;* 66.1 *soccer*
Football Association 66.1 *soccer*
Football Association Challenge Cup 66.1 *soccer*
football boots 551.19 *footwear*
football championship 66.1 *soccer*
football club 66.1 *soccer*
football coach 66.3 *football player*
footballer 336.5 *athlete*
Footballer of the Year 66.3 *football player*
football fan 66.3 *football player*
football field 66.1 *soccer*
football game 46.1 *football;* 66.1 *soccer*
football ground 66.1 *soccer*
football helmet 252.4 *safety device*
football kit 66.1 *soccer*
Football League 66.1 *soccer*
football manager 66.3 *football player*
football match 66.1 *soccer*
football organization 66.1 *soccer*
football pitch 66.1 *soccer*
football play 66.2
football player 46.2; 66.3; 336.5 *athlete*
football referee 66.3 *football player*
football season 292.1 *season*
football side 66.1 *soccer*
football stadium 66.1 *soccer*
football team 66.1 *soccer*
football trainer 66.3 *football player*
football uniform 66.1 *soccer*
footbath 256.6, 410.12 *bath*
footboard 23.6 *bed*
footbridge 38.21, 317.9 *bridge*
foot-dragger 333.15 *slow person*
foot-dragging 333.6 *hesitant;* 333.12 *hesitation;* 378.5 *inhibition;* 378.15 *inhibitive;* 113.6 *uncooperativeness*
foot fault 51.2 *grip;* 63.4 *tennis terms*
footgear 551.19 *footwear*
Foot Guard 586.12 *ceremonial troops*
foothill 89.1 *mountain;* 185.2 *projection*
foothills 154.2 *heights;* 155.2 *lowlands*
foothold 308.10 *opportunity;* 360.1 *retention;* 62.5 *rock face*

footing 175.1 *base;* 143.2, 222.1 *circumstances;* 395.1 *influence;* 209.2 *rank;* 360.1 *retention;* 221.1 *state;* 38.28 *substructure*
footlicking 664.2 *sycophancy;* 664.7 *sycophantic*
footlights 522.6 *electric light;* 21.20 *stage lighting*
foot line 68.10 *curling*
footling 124.4 *trivial*
footloose 250.10 *independent;* 325.25 *wandering*
footloose and fancy free 250.10 *independent;* 325.25 *wandering*
footman 401.6 *domestic servant*
footnote 211.3 *additional item;* 719.10 *annotate;* 719.2 *annotation;* 175.2 *foot*
footpath 318.4 *access;* 317.6 *path*
footplate 321.5 *locomotive part*
foot-pound 334.5 *unit of work*
footprint 183.3 *cavity;* 716.4 *indication;* 743.3 *means of identification;* 322.7 *miscellaneous aviation terms;* 215.1 *remainder;* 744.12 *vestige;* 345.2 *visible effect*
foot regiment 586.16 *army unit*
footrest 413.4 *rest;* 304.10 *step*
foot rule 26.6 *measuring instrument*
foots 21.20 *stage lighting*
Footsie 14.2 *stock exchange*
footsie 593.14 *communication of love;* 742.3 *gesture*
footslogger 586.17 *army person*
foot soldier 586.17 *army person*
footsore 261.1 *fatigued*
foot spot 65.4 *carom;* 65.6 *pool*
foot steering 50.7 *windsurfing*
footstep 304.10 *step;* 744.12 *vestige*
footstone 583.4 *funeral objects*
footstool 413.4 *rest;* 664.3 *sycophant*
footstrap 50.7 *windsurfing*
foot string 65.4 *carom*
foot the bill 785.8 *defray*
foot transport 320.1 *road transport*
foot-warmer 493.3 *heater*
footway 317.6 *path*
footwear **551.19**
footweary 261.1 *fatigued*
footwork 52.2 *boxing*
foozle 486.7 *be clumsy;* 486.9 *bungling*
foozled 486.4 *bungled*
fop 551.27 *model;* 673.7 *vain person*
foppish 673.11 *cocky*
foppishly 673.21 *cockily*
foppishness 551.2 *dressing*
for **482.14**; 398.12 *by proxy;* 669.19 *supporting*
for a beginning 130.40 *first*
forage 557.8 *animal food;* 81.11 *eat grass;* 774.14 *plunder;* 436.5 *provision*
forage cap 551.15 *headgear*
forage harvester 43.10 *farm tool*
foraging 774.5 *plundering;* 774.17 *stolen*
for a kick-off 130.40 *first*
for all ages 237.1 *useful*
for all one knows 456.12 *ignorantly;* 107.14 *perchance;* 102.9 *possibly*
for all practical purposes 99.13 *in essence;* 147.13 *nearly*
for all that 211.10 *additionally*
for all to see 520.2 *clear;* 716.15 *evidently;* 703.20, 738.16 *manifestly;* 740.22 *publicly*
for a long time 277.11 *long*
for always 275.30 *chronologically;* 279.11 *eternally;* 360.11 *tenaciously;* 131.27 *to the end*
foraminiferan 75.9 *protozoan*
for a moment 278.8 *transiently*
for a purpose 482.14 *for;* 482.12 *intended*
for a reason 482.12 *intended*
for a season 275.26 *all the time*
for a song 777.14 *buying;* 793.15 *cheaply*
for a start 130.40 *first*
for a time 275.26 *all the time*
for a while 282.10 *for the present*
foray 381.1 *attack;* 774.14 *plunder;* 774.5 *plundering*
for aye 279.11 *eternally*
forbear 634.3 *abstain;* 648.3 *be lenient;* 684.5 *be self-restrained;* 383.9 *desist;* 634.24 *hands off!;* 350.5 *not use;* 627.10, 649.12 *show mercy*
forbearance 634.11 *abstinence;* 383.4 *desisting;* 649.2 *forgivingness;* 657.4 *freedom;* 648.1 *leniency;* 627.3 *mercy;* 350.8 *nonuse;* 684.1 *self-restraint*
forbearant 627.6 *pitying*
forbearer 383.5 *resister*
forbearing 383.4, 383.13 *desisting;* 648.4 *lenient;* 649.5 *merciful;* 684.8 *self-restrained*
forbearingly 383.15 *abstemiously;* 684.11 *with self-restraint*
for better or worse 279.11 *eternally*
forbid 709.6 *dissent;* 128.7 *exclude;* 378.8 *hinder;* 16.75 *make illegal;* 103.8 *make impossible;* 704.8 *refute;* 399.3 *veto*
forbiddance 128.1 *exclusion*
forbidden **103.4**; 128.11 *excluded;* 16.55 *illegal;* 329.15 *out of reach;* 399.5 *vetoed*
forbidden fruit 80.5 *figurative usage;* 796.4 *illicit love;* 617.5 *object of desire*
forbidden love 796.4 *illicit love;* 593.8 *love affair*
forbidding 523.11 *benighted;* 655.8 *unsociable;* 399.1 *veto*
forbiddingly 655.14 *unsocially*
force **28.10**; **376.14**; **386.7**; 340.1 *action;* 374.3 *assembly;* 344.10 *awaken;* 53.17 *bat;* 395.10 *be a prevailing influence;* 334.10 *be powerful;* 344.1 *cause;* 90.2 *channel;* 386.2 *coercion;* 243.7 *develop;* 726.1 *emphasis;* 334.4 *energy;* 576.4 *exertion;* 365.1 *friction;* 302.8 *further;* 236.14 *ill-treat;* 635.15 *impose one's will;* 331.11 *impulsion;* 395.1 *influence;* 348.2 *instrument;* 483.10 *manipulate;* 694.1 *meaning;* 351.1, 351.2 *misuse;* 346.1 *operation;* 698.11 *pedantry;* 480.15 *persuade;* 334.1 *power;* 796.20 *seduce;* 336.1 *strength;* 376.12 *team;* 380.8 *use violence;* 338.1 *vigour;* 380.1 *violence*
force a card 700.30 *be fraudulent*
force a confrontation 738.4 *show oneself*
force a passage 318.10 *enter*
force a surrender 246.9 *be victorious*
forced 262.3 *hasty;* 109.7 *illogical;* 44.19 *ornamental*
forced entry 314.3 *inroad*
forced labour 386.3 *coercive methods;* 815.7 *imprisonment;* 576.1 *work*
forced landing 305.5 *dive*
forced march 262.4 *haste;* 332.11 *swift thing*
forced out 48.6 *fielding terms;* 605.7 *resigning*
forced reconciliation 749.1 *pacification*
forced resignation 588.1 *anarchy;* 605.1 *resignation*
forced saving 790.8 *levy*
forced vibration 28.14 *sound wave*
force eight 31.14 *windiness*
force-feed 386.7 *force;* 557.25 *provide food*
force-feeding 386.3 *coercive methods*
forceful 351.5 *abusive;* 342.18 *active;* 164.10 *advantaged;* 707.14 *assertive;* 386.9 *compelling;* 721.11 *descriptive;* 340.6 *effective;* 726.3 *emphatic;* 395.11 *influential;* 698.24 *pedantic;* 480.19 *persuasive;* 336.10 *potent;* 334.13 *powerful;* 638.2 *tenacious;* 338.4 *vigorous;* 380.6 *violent*
forcefully 351.6 *abusively;* 342.22 *actively;* 381.26 *aggresively;* 164.12 *at an advantage;* 386.11 *compellingly;* 331.18 *dynamically;* 340.8 *effectively;* 726.7 *emphatically;* 330.34 *forward;* 395.14 *influentially;* 480.21 *persuasively;* 334.18 *powerfully;* 336.14 *strongly;* 380.10 *violently;* 338.6 *with vigour*
forcefulness 707.6 *assertiveness;* 726.1 *emphasis;* 334.1 *power;* 338.1 *vigour;* 380.1 *violence*
forceful person 386.4 *coercive person*
force in 368.3 *impact*
force into a mould 117.9 *make conform*
force into oblivion 358.1 *obliterate*
force majeure 386.2 *coercion;* 452.16 *inevitability*
force nine 31.14 *windiness*
force of gravity 334.4 *energy;* 414.5 *gravity;* 363.2 *pulling power*
force of habit 632.1 *habit*
force of inertia 334.4 *energy*
force oneself 637.10 *grudge*
force one's way 576.8 *exert oneself;* 633.13 *follow up*
force open 380.8 *use violence*
force out 371.7 *drive out;* 369.16 *extort;* 48.7 *play baseball*
forcep 55.3 *fishing tackle*
force play 48.6 *fielding terms*
forceps 369.10 *excavator;* 360.3 *tools for gripping*
forceps delivery 561.7 *obstetrics*
for certain 454.12 *assuredly*
forces 38.14 *load*
force someone's hand 386.6 *compel*
force someone to strip 552.15 *make nude*
force ten 31.14 *windiness*
force to accept 386.7 *force*
force to resign 588.4 *be anarchic*
force to step down 704.8 *refute*
force to the wall 264.23 *cause difficulties*
force upon 386.7 *force*
forcible 386.9 *compelling;* 710.10 *demanding;* 334.13 *powerful;* 338.4 *vigorous;* 380.6 *violent*
forcible demand 710.2 *demand*
forcible removal 144.3 *replacement*
forcible wedlock 570.5 *wedding*
forcibly 710.12 *by request;* 386.11 *compellingly;* 334.18 *powerfully;* 336.14 *strongly;* 380.10 *violently;* 338.6 *with vigour*
forcing 386.2 *coercion*
forcing a card 700.10 *fraud*
forcing a run 48.4 *pitching terms*
forcing bag 25.6 *kitchen equipment*
forcing bed 44.4 *nursery*
forcing house 44.4 *nursery*
ford 38.21 *bridge;* 90.2 *channel;* 318.11 *cross;* 318.5 *crossing point;* 151.6 *narrow place;* 157.4 *shallow thing*
for dear life 342.22 *actively*
fore 167.1, 167.6 *front;* 711.10 *look out!*
fore and aft 232.9 *completely;* 50.10 *sailing*
fore-and-aft sail 50.3 *parts of a sailing boat*
forearm 243.3 *be prepared;* 205.4 *component;* 711.5 *warn*
forearmed 474.5 *expecting;* 243.18 *prepared;* 711.9 *warned*
forebear 129.9 *predecessor;* 709.7 *refuse oneself*
forebears 296.2 *old people*
forebode 254.10 *endanger;* 475.11 *predict*
foreboding 254.1 *dangerous;* 474.1 *expectation;* 612.2 *fearfulness;* 445.3 *insight;* 475.13 *predicting;* 475.1 *prediction;* 711.1, 711.8 *warning*
forecaddie 56.6 *golfer*
forecast **31.57**; **129.19**; 11.23 *divine;* 474.2 *expectations;* 283.4 *looking to the future;* 484.12 *plan ahead;* 484.2 *policy;* 474.9, 475.11 *predict;* 475.14 *predicted;* 475.1 *prediction;* 104.1 *probability;* 31.4 *weather forecast*
forecaster **475.9**; 11.13 *diviner;* 283.5 *predictor*
forecasting 11.9 *divination;* 475.1 *prediction*
forecastle 167.1 *front*
forecheck 58.3 *ice hockey;* 58.9 *play hockey*
forechecker 58.4 *ice hockey player*
forechecking 58.3 *ice hockey*
foreclose 309.9 *close down;* 773.8 *take back*
foreclosed 784.10 *unable to pay*
foreclosing 773.2 *taking back*
foreclosure 784.5 *amount owing;* 309.1 *closure;* 773.2 *taking back*
foreconscious 36.21 *psyche*
forecourt 167.1 *front*
foredeck 167.1 *front*
forefather 293.4 *early comer;* 129.9 *predecessor*
forefathers 582.13 *the dead*
forefinger 742.5 *indicator;* 492.7 *sense organ*
forefront 167.1 *front;* 129.2 *priority*
foregoer 129.8 *precursor*
foregoing 284.19 *antiquarian;* 129.11 *prior*
foregone conclusion 465.4 *prejudgment;* 106.6 *premeditation;* 452.12 *something certain*
foreground 167.1, 167.6 *front;* 147.5 *near place*
forehand **63.14**; 51.9 *bowls;* 293.17 *early;* 293.16 *premature;* 293.20 *prematurely*
forehand drive 63.2 *tennis strokes*
forehand grip 51.2 *grip*
forehand volley 63.2 *tennis strokes*
forehead 525.3 *external appearance;* 185.3 *protuberance*
foreign **100.10**; 128.11 *excluded;* 171.10 *extraneous;* 594.12 *hated;* 372.17 *unjoined;* 109.6 *unrelated*
foreign accent 729.3 *mode of speech*
foreign body 128.6 *thing excluded*
foreign coins 780.11 *national coins*
foreign correspondent 693.9 *informant;* 741.4 *journalist;* 740.11 *newspaperman*
foreign currency reserves 14.1 *finance*
foreign editor 741.4 *journalist*
foreigner 295.8 *new arrival;* 100.6, 655.7 *outsider;* 109.3 *unconnected person*
foreigners 171.5 *extraneousness*
foreign exchange dealer 778.12 *wholesaler*
foreign exchange market 14.1, 780.7 *finance*
foreign influx 314.4 *right of entry*
foreign language dictionary 5.28 *dictionary*
foreign-language student 5.2 *linguist*
foreign-language study 5.1 *linguistics*
foreign loan 771.2 *loan*
foreign-made 100.12 *external*
foreignness **100.2**; 171.5 *extraneousness;* 109.1 *unrelatedness*
foreign product 100.4 *externality*
foreign rule 12.3 *governance*
foreign sector 13.2 *economy*
foreign service 398.2 *representative body*
foreign trade 776.5 *commercial trade*
forejudge 466.13 *prejudge*
foreknowledge 455.1 *knowledge;* 283.4 *looking to the future*
foreland 92.5 *peninsula*
forelimb 205.4 *component*
forelock-tugging 667.11 *in a respectful stance*
foreman 579.15 *manager;* 121.5 *superior*
foreman of the jury 16.26, 464.7 *jury*
foremast 167.1 *front*
foremost 121.14 *best;* 130.30 *front;* 123.5 *important;* 129.12 *primary*
foremother 129.9 *predecessor*
forename 721.8 *name*
forenamed 129.11 *prior*
forenoon 290.1, 290.5 *morning*
forensic 16.49 *judicatory;* 35.22 *medical*
forensic medicine 35.3 *medical specialty*
forensic pathologist 35.13 *medical specialist*
forensic pathology 260.20 *pathology*
foreordain 106.1 *predetermine*
foreordained 106.3 *predetermined*
foreordination 106.5 *predetermination*
fore rib 25.22 *beef*
forerun **129.18**; 475.11 *predict*
forerunner 579.13 *director;* 449.12 *discoverer;* 475.5 *omen;* 140.5 *precedent;* 129.8 *precursor*
foresail 50.3 *parts of a sailing boat*
foresee 11.23 *divine;* 518.17 *imagine;* 482.7 *intend;* 283.9 *look ahead;* 484.12 *plan ahead;* 474.9, 475.11 *predict;* 293.9 *prepare;* 104.10 *think likely;* 518.16 *visualize*
foreseeable 474.7 *expected;* 756.15 *future;* 283.12 *predictable;* 475.14 *predicted*
foreseeably 474.13 *expectedly;* 475.16 *predictively*
foreseeing 475.13 *predicting*
foreseen **283.13**; 474.7 *expected*
foreshadow 475.11 *predict*
fore shank 25.23 *beef;* 25.27 *lamb*
foreshock 30.22 *seismic activity*
foreshorten 19.23 *design;* 149.10 *shorten*
foreshortened 19.27 *painted;* 149.8 *shortened*
foreshortening 149.2 *shortening;* 19.4 *treatment*
foreshow 475.11 *predict*
foresight 616.1 *caution;* 455.1 *knowledge;* 283.4 *looking to the future;* 484.2 *policy;* 475.1 *prediction;* 293.5 *prematurity;* 243.9 *preparation;* 11.8 *psychic power;* 518.10 *visual aid;* 518.4 *visualization;* 458.1 *wisdom*
foresighted 293.16 *premature*
foresightedly 293.20 *prematurely*
foreskin 561.8 *organs of reproduction*
forest 77.1 *plants;* 416.4 *solid body;* 79.4 *trees*
forestage 21.17 *stage*
forestal 79.16 *wooded*
forestall 128.7 *exclude;* 283.10 *expect;* 378.8 *hinder;* 763.7 *possess;* 293.9 *prepare*
forestalled 128.11 *excluded*
forestalling 378.1 *hindrance;* 777.7 *purchasing*
forestalment 763.1 *possession*

forestay 50.3 *parts of a sailing boat*
forested 77.13 *plantlike;* 79.16 *wooded*
forester 79.8; 359.4 *preservationist;* 252.3 *protector*
forest fire 493.6 *fire*
forest green 538.1 *green*
forest manager 79.8 *forester*
forest of 208.4 *throng*
forest ranger 79.8 *forester*
forestry 79.5; 43.4 *arable farming;* 77.10 *plant science*
forest spirit 8.5 *deity*
foretaste 205.2 *particular;* 129.6 *preview*
foretell 11.23 *divine;* 129.19 *forecast;* 283.9 *look ahead;* 475.11 *predict*
foreteller 11.13 *diviner*
foretelling 475.13 *predicting;* 475.1 *prediction*
for eternity 101.13 *metaphysically*
forethought 616.1 *caution;* 484.2 *policy;* 243.9 *preparation;* 458.1 *wisdom*
foretime 3.8 *past time*
foretoken 475.5 *omen;* 475.11 *predict*
foretold 283.13 *foreseen;* 475.14 *predicted*
foretopman 304.11 *ascender;* 323.7 *nautical person*
forever 275.26 *all the time;* 275.30 *chronologically;* 134.7 *continually;* 202.3 *eternal;* 202.12, 279.11 *eternally;* 202.7 *eternity;* 277.10 *for the duration;* 232.10 *fully;* 101.13 *metaphysically;* 225.9 *permanently;* 360.11 *tenaciously*
for ever and ever 279.11 *eternally;* 225.9 *permanently*
forever in one's memory 462.7 *memorable*
for evermore 279.11 *eternally;* 277.10 *for the duration*
forever tired 261.1 *fatigued*
for everyday use 237.1 *useful*
for everyone 695.2 *simple*
forewarn 616.6 *caution;* 283.10 *expect;* 475.11 *predict;* 711.5 *warn*
forewarned 474.5 *expecting;* 243.18 *prepared;* 711.9 *warned*
forewarning 475.5 *omen;* 475.13 *predicting;* 475.1 *prediction;* 711.1 *warning*
foreword 167.1 *front;* 130.10 *introduction;* 129.5 *preface;* 729.8 *speech*
forfeit 766.9 *lose;* 766.1 *loss;* 814.1 *punish;* 814.7 *punishment;* 355.1 *relinquish;* 355.3 *relinquishment;* 212.2 *subtracted item*
forfeit one's reputation 812.4 *bring into disrepute*
forfeiture 766.1 *loss;* 814.7 *punishment*
forfeiture of deposit 470.6 *discarding*
for free 768.9 *as a gift;* 793.11 *free of charge;* 752.20 *persuasively*
for fun 599.17 *jokingly*
forgather 376.39 *come together*
forgathering 376.1 *assembly*
forge 699.25, 700.30 *be fraudulent;* 125.10 *copy;* 234.12 *distort the truth;* 699.26 *falsify;* 553.9 *fashion;* 493.6 *fire;* 160.7 *form;* 780.24 *monetize;* 356.10 *produce;* 577.1 *workshop*
forge ahead 302.3 *press on*
forged 699.36 *falsified;* 699.35 *fraudulent;* 125.13 *imitation;* 700.39 *imitative;* 699.32 *spurious*
forged note 780.15 *false money*
forged passport 699.16 *false thing*
forger 578.2 *artisan;* 699.19 *cheat;* 125.8 *copier;* 774.11 *dishonest person;* 780.17 *financier;* 115.4 *person who copies;* 717.4 *person who makes a representation*
forgery 125.2 *copy;* 774.7 *dishonesty;* 780.15 *false money;* 699.9 *falsification;* 699.8, 700.10 *fraud;* 699.4 *spuriousness*
forget 358.2; 463.13; 648.3 *be lenient;* 412.11 *be mixed up;* 666.6 *be neglectful;* 672.6 *be ungrateful;* 649.9 *forgive;* 766.9 *lose*
forgetful 463.9 *blank;* 472.7 *inattentive;* 412.13 *mixed-up;* 666.4 *negligent;* 489.6 *unfeeling;* 672.3 *ungrateful*
forgetfully 472.14 *inattentively;* 463.16 *obliviously;* 672.7 *ungratefully*
Forgetfulness 463
forgetfulness 358.5; 463.2 *blankness;* 472.1 *inattention;* 672.1 *ingratitude;* 666.1 *negligence*
forgetful person 463.7
forget grievances 749.5 *make peace*
forget it 708.24 *never!;* 618.21 *never mind!;* 355.1 *relinquish;* 226.12 *stop!*
forget it! 355.9
forget-me-not 539.6 *blue thing*
forget one's differences 589.5 *be at peace*
forget oneself 624.12 *become angry*
forget one's lines 463.14 *be forgetful*
forget one's manners 706.18 *answer back*
forget one's place 660.22 *be rude;* 660.28 *get above oneself*
forget one's principles 800.8 *be dishonourable*
forget one's problems 263.2 *take it easy*
forget one's words 486.5 *be unskilful*
forgettable 463.11 *forgotten;* 124.1 *unimportant*
forgetting 463.9 *blank;* 358.5 *forgetfulness;* 36.23 *memory*
forget work 263.2 *take it easy*
forging 403.5 *structuring*
forgivable 649.7; 801.9 *in the right;* 124.1 *unimportant;* 714.13 *vindicable*
forgivably 714.15 *in vindication*
forgive 463.15; 649.9; 16.78, 758.10 *acquit;* 650.8 *be benevolent;* 648.3 *be lenient;* 627.10 *show mercy*
forgive a debt 786.10
forgive and forget 463.15, 649.9 *forgive;* 749.5 *make peace*
forgiven 649.6; 16.63 *acquitted;* 648.5 *given consideration*
Forgiveness 649
forgiveness 649.1; 16.42 *acquittal;* 463.6 *amnesty;* 650.1 *benevolence;* 648.1 *leniency;* 391.1 *liberation;* 627.3 *mercy;* 589.1 *peace;* 749.2 *peace offering*
forgiveness of debts 786.1 *nonpayment*
forgiveness of sin 649.1 *forgiveness*
forgiveness of sins 391.1 *liberation*
forgive one's sins 649.9 *forgive*
forgiving 649.4; 650.6 *benevolent;* 648.4 *lenient;* 627.6 *pitying*
forgivingly 16.88; 649.14; 650.10 *benevolently;* 749.7 *pacifically*
forgiving nature 649.2 *forgivingness*
forgivingness 649.2
forgo 684.5 *be self-restrained;* 767.9 *dispose of;* 355.1 *relinquish;* 605.5 *resign*
forgoing 767.1 *disposal;* 355.3 *relinquishment*
forgone 767.12 *disposed;* 355.5 *relinquished*
for good 131.28 *conclusively;* 279.11 *eternally;* 277.10 *for the duration;* 232.10 *fully;* 225.9 *permanently;* 360.11 *tenaciously*
for good and all 131.28 *conclusively;* 279.11 *eternally;* 277.10 *for the duration;* 232.10 *fully;* 225.9 *permanently;* 360.11 *tenaciously*
forgo repayment 783.9 *acquire credit*
forgo sex 572.10 *be continent;* 795.11 *be moral*
forgotten 463.11; 766.16 *losing;* 358.6 *obliterated;* 672.4 *unthanked*
forgotten anniversary 472.5 *inattentive act*
forgotten birthday 472.5 *inattentive act*
forgotten man 128.5 *excluded person*
forgotten name 472.5 *inattentive act*
for humane reasons 627.13 *pitifully*
fork 311.5; 176.1, 176.11 *angle;* 320.11 *bicycle part;* 311.14 *branch;* 69.4 *chess terms;* 44.15 *cultivate;* 377.10 *diverge;* 557.16 *eating utensil;* 44.6, 438.3 *garden tool;* 198.8 *half;* 198.16 *halve;* 330.24 *push;* 90.1 *river;* 425.8 *sharp-pointed thing;* 316.15 *take away;* 79.2 *tree part;* 425.16 *use a sharp tool*
fork bender 11.12 *occultist*
fork bending 11.1 *occultism*
forked 176.7 *angular;* 311.9 *branched;* 198.13 *half*
forked tongue 645.3 *cunning person;* 699.2 *duplicity*
for keeps 202.12, 279.11 *eternally;* 360.11 *tenaciously*
for kicks 490.11 *pleasingly*
fork in 557.22 *eat well*
forking 311.9 *branched;* 311.4 *branching;* 377.24 *divergent;* 198.7 *halving*
forklift 366.9 *lifter*
fork lightning 31.21 *thunderstorm*
forklike 311.9 *branched*
fork out 787.1 *expend;* 768.5 *give;* 785.6 *pay*
fork supper 557.12 *meal*
for long 277.11 *long*
forlorn 611.4 *hopeless;* 655.10 *lonely;* 602.5 *sad*
forlorn hope 604.1 *disappointment*
Form 160
form 160.1; 160.7; 403.3; 71.20 *abode of mammals;* 34.4 *anatomy;* 93.20 *bring into being;* 117.5 *convention;* 32.4 *crystal;* 140.6 *custom;* 721.14 *describe;* 553.4 *design;* 67.6 *diving;* 6.22 *educate;* 525.3 *external appearance;* 656.1 *formality;* 36.26 *gestalt;* 259.3 *health;* 59.7 *horseracing;* 743.1 *identification;* 130.22 *invent;* 160.3 *kind;* 16.34 *legal formality;* 405.13 *make;* 117.9 *make conform;* 407.18 *order;* 717.11 *paint;* 484.10 *plan out;* 713.3 *precept;* 356.10 *produce;* 608.6 *profile;* 160.2 *prototype;* 744.1 *record;* 10.1 *ritual;* 19.21 *sculpt;* 163.2 *shadow;* 403.15 *shape;* 221.1 *state;* 137.6 *students;* 34.17 *taxonomy;* 632.5 *tradition;* 19.4 *treatment;* 137.4 *type;* 349.1 *use;* 317.1 *way*
formable 419.7 *impressionable*
form a cartel 755.5 *contract;* 251.9 *economize*
form a community 2.15 *socialize*
form a core 416.8 *be dense*
form a crocodile 132.17 *line up*
form a government 12.12 *take authority*
form a hypothesis 476.5 *suppose*
form a kernel 416.8 *be dense*
formal 160.11; 656.6; 117.14 *conformist;* 551.3 *formal dress;* 160.9 *formed;* 658.8 *good-mannered;* 544.9 *inelegant;* 17.16 *literary;* 5.39 *of language;* 407.10 *ordered;* 403.12 *organic;* 251.14 *self-restrained;* 647.8 *severe;* 27.69 *theoretical;* 407.14 *well-ordered*
formal agreement 669.1 *approval;* 755.1 *contract*
formal argument 444.3 *debate*
formal attire 656.4 *formal dress*
formal cause 344.1 *cause*
formal clothes 551.1 *dress*
formal contract 755.1 *contract*
formaldehyde 359.2 *preserver*
formal dining 557.4 *eating meals*
formal dinner 557.13 *feast*
formal dress 551.3; 656.4
formal expression 27.65 *theory*
formal garden 44.2 *garden*
form a line 132.17 *line up*
formalism 656.2; 117.4 *conventionalism;* 407.1 *order;* 10.2 *ritualism;* 21.10 *theatre movements*
formalist 21.42 *activist;* 117.6 *conformist;* 7.4 *religionist*
formalistic 656.6 *formal;* 407.10 *ordered;* 7.15 *religious*
formalistically 407.25 *in order*
formalities 658.3 *courtesies;* 656.5 *etiquette*
Formality 656
formality 160.5; 656.1; 117.4 *conventionalism;* 705.5 *easy question;* 658.2 *good manners;* 16.34 *legal formality;* 10.1 *ritual;* 251.3 *self-restraint;* 647.1 *severity;* 632.5 *tradition*
formalization 407.1 *order*
formalize 656.9; 160.7 *form;* 16.68 *legislate*
formalized 407.10 *ordered*
formal language 5.29 *grammar;* 5.6 *official language*
formal logic 4.6 *branch of philosophy;* 27.63 *mathematical logic*
formally 656.12; 160.13 *formatively;* 658.15 *genteelly;* 5.52 *grammatically;* 647.11 *severely;* 251.17 *with self-restraint*
formally dressed 656.7 *dressed-up*
formal meal 557.12 *meal*
formalness 656.1 *formality*
formal occasion 656.3; 557.13 *feast*
formal reasoning 442.2 *ways of thinking*
formal speech 733.1 *address*
formal usage 5.29 *grammar*
formal visit 654.3 *meeting*
form an alliance 750.22; 373.13 *intercommunicate*
form an image of 477.14 *imagine*
form a partnership 755.5 *contract;* 570.19 *merge*
form a picket line 378.9 *block*
form a queue 132.17 *line up*
form a scab 393.6 *cure*
format 40.20 *abort;* 40.19 *computing terms;* 525.3 *external appearance;* 160.1, 160.7, 403.3 *form;* 160.2 *prototype*
formation 525.1 *appearance;* 160.1, 403.3 *form;* 130.5 *invention;* 407.1 *order;* 64.3 *rugby play;* 403.5 *structuring*
formational 409.22 *organizational*
formative 130.29 *beginning;* 344.13 *causal;* 405.6 *component;* 160.9 *formed;* 5.44 *grammatical;* 419.7 *impressionable;* 5.35 *part of speech;* 356.11 *productive*
formatively 160.13
form a whole 204.9 *be whole*
form criticism 719.3 *criticism*
formed 160.9; 20.17 *structured*
form engraver 23.13 *carpenter*
former 284.20; 296.13; 294.14 *dead;* 3.15 *historic;* 129.11 *prior;* 605.7 *resigning*
former British coinage 780.10 *former British money*
former British money 780.10
for mercy's sake 627.14 *have pity!*
formerly 294.18; 296.20; 129.20 *before;* 605.10 *by resigning;* 3.24 *historically;* 284.22 *in the past*
former soldier 586.11
former time 286.1 *different time*
former times 3.8, 284.1 *past time*
Formica™ 411.5 *layered thing;* 435.1 *materials;* 550.12 *protective covering*
formication 327.5 *restlessness;* 260.13 *skin disease;* 488.3 *stimulus*
formidable 264.10 *difficult;* 612.10 *frightening;* 123.6 *notable;* 336.10 *potent*
formidably 264.26 *arduously*
forming 160.4; 160.1 *form;* 356.1 *production*
formless 408.14 *irregular;* 161.5 *shapeless*
formlessly 161.6 *shapelessly*
formlessness 161.1 *shapelessness*
form letters 5.47 *word*
form of government 12.1 *government*
form of law 160.5 *formality;* 16.34 *legal formality*
form of speech 724.4 *literary style*
form of worship 10.4 *public worship;* 10.1 *ritual*
for money 765.20 *gainfully*
form part of 405.10 *compose*
formroom 6.15 *schoolroom*
Formschneider 23.13 *carpenter*
form teacher 6.4 *educator*
formula 16.34 *legal formality;* 745.1 *maxim;* 27.14 *operation;* 5.23 *phrase;* 484.2 *policy;* 140.5 *precedent;* 713.3 *precept;* 37.5 *prescription;* 160.2 *prototype;* 394.1 *remedy;* 10.1 *ritual;* 32.13 *structure;* 27.65 *theory*
Formula 1 car 61.1 *motor racing*
Formula 1 driver 61.8 *driver*
Formula 1 race 61.2; 61.1 *motor racing*
Formula 1 racer 61.8 *driver*
Formula 1 racing 61.1 *motor racing*
Formula 2 racing 61.1 *motor racing*
Formula 3 61.1 *motor racing*
Formula 40 class 50.2 *sailing boat*
Formula 3000 61.1 *motor racing*
formulaic 10.21 *ritualistic*
formulary 656.6 *formal;* 713.3 *precept;* 10.1 *ritual*
Formula Super Vee racing 61.1 *motor racing*
formulate 745.3 *aphorize;* 553.9 *fashion;* 160.7 *form;* 446.15 *imagine;* 484.11 *invent;* 356.10 *produce;* 738.3 *reveal;* 403.15 *shape;* 729.11 *speak;* 724.9 *style;* 5.45 *use language*
formulated 18.31 *composed*
formulated intention 482.4
formulation 160.4 *forming;* 738.10 *manifestation;* 356.1 *production*
Formula Vauxhall Lotus 61.1 *motor racing*
fornicate 796.17 *be sexually immoral;* 593.29 *make love*
fornication 593.5 *desire;* 796.3 *sexual immorality*
for nickels and dimes 793.15 *cheaply*
for noble reasons 803.9 *virtuously*
for nothing 793.15 *cheaply;* 793.11 *free of charge;* 768.7 *given*
for now 275.26 *all the time*
for one's benefit 237.4 *profitable*
for oneself 641.9 *obstinately*
for one's own part 139.29 *personally*
for one's own sake 683.8 *selfishly*
for one's service 813.19 *rewardingly*
for peanuts 793.9 *cheap*
for pennies 793.15 *cheaply*
for pity's sake 627.14 *have pity!*
for private ends 683.8 *selfishly*

for profit 776.15 *profitable*; 683.8 *selfishly*
for public notice 738.16 *manifestly*
forrard 302.19 *forward*
forray 381.12 *military attack*
for real 93.13 *real*
for recreation 67.12 *by swimming*
for rent 752.17 *offered*
for revenge 798.12 *evilly*
forsake 479.2 *equivocate*; 98.19 *leave empty*; 800.9 *prove false*; 355.2 *withdraw*
forsaken 197.16 *alone*; 355.5 *relinquished*; 98.14 *unoccupied*
forsakenly 355.7 *on hold*
forsake one's duties 355.2 *withdraw*
for sale **767.14**; 768.7 *given*; 752.17 *offered*; 778.18 *on sale*; 752.20 *persuasively*
for short periods **276.14**
forsooth 698.35 *truly*
for specified periods **276.13**
for sport 599.17 *jokingly*
for starters 130.40 *first*
for sure 454.12 *assuredly*
forswear 634.3 *abstain*; 767.9 *dispose of*; 479.4 *recant*; 355.1 *relinquish*; 708.12 *renounce*
forswearer 479.9 *equivocator*
forswearing 634.11 *abstinence*; 699.33 *deceitful*; 767.1 *disposal*; 699.6 *lying*; 708.19 *rebutting*; 479.8 *recantation*; 708.4 *renunciation*
forsworn 767.12 *disposed*
fort **384.12**; 356.8 *construction*; 252.5 *refuge*
fortalice 384.12 *fort*
forte 455.2 *information*; 507.6 *loud*; 507.9 *loudly*; 507.1 *loudness*; 485.1 *skill*; 139.7 *special skill*; 86.14 *sphere*; 235.6 *worth*
Fortean animals 737.6 *natural mystery*
Forth 90.4 *British rivers*
forth **315.18**; 302.19 *forward*
for that reason 750.36 *accordingly*
forthcoming 243.17 *developing*; 739.11 *disclosing*; 283.11 *future*; 293.13 *imminent*; 147.9 *near*; 315.15 *outgoing*
forthcoming event 283.6 *future event*
for the asking 768.7 *given*
for the better 244.17 *better*
for the chop 357.15 *destroyed*
for the count 52.16 *professionally*
for the duration **277.10**; 275.26 *all the time*
for the first time 448.15 *inventively*
for the general public 695.13 *intelligibly*; 695.2 *simple*
for the interim 275.26 *all the time*
for the layman 695.13 *intelligibly*; 695.2 *simple*
for the moment 282.10 *for the present*
for the most part 140.18 *as a rule*; 99.13 *in essence*; 216.11 *on average*; 204.13 *on the whole*; 138.31 *overall*
for the nonce 282.10 *for the present*; 278.9 *for the time being*
for the occasion 282.10 *for the present*; 287.9 *opportunely*; 287.6 *timely*
for the present **282.10**
for the price of 790.16 *at a price*
for the public good 652.8 *philanthropically*; 237.12 *usefully*
for the sake of 392.37 *in aid of*
for the time being **278.9**; 275.26 *all the time*; 282.10 *for the present*
for the worse 245.14 *worse*
for this occasion 282.10 *for the present*
forthright 324.9 *directly*; 527.4 *easily seen through*; 271.3 *natural*; 738.15 *open*; 695.2 *simple*; 698.18 *truthful*
forthrightly 738.17 *frankly*; 739.13 *openly*
forthrightness 527.10 *openness*; 695.10 *simplicity*; 698.5 *truthfulness*
forthwith 293.17 *early*; 280.8 *immediately*
fortieth 196.4 *less than one*; 201.19 *twentieth*
fortification **384.11**; 585.6 *art of war*; 707.4 *confirmation*; 185.2 *projection*; 252.5 *refuge*; 336.1 *strength*
fortified 384.30 *defended*; 418.3 *hardened*; 581.4 *refreshed*; 336.13 *strengthened*; 707.13 *supported*
fortified line 384.8 *military defences*
fortified wine 558.9 *wine*
fortifier 707.9 *affirmer*
fortify 707.19 *confirm*; 253.14 *make fast*; 412.8 *mix*; 252.10 *protect*; 581.1 *refresh*; 384.20 *reinforce*; 336.8 *strengthen*
fortifying 581.3 *refreshing*; 336.4 *strengthening*
fortissimo 507.6 *loud*; 507.9 *loudly*; 507.1 *loudness*
fortitude **638.16**; 640.4 *stamina*; 613.3 *steadfastness*; 803.2 *virtues*
Fort Knox 780.20 *money store*
fortnight 201.7 *double figures*; 275.4 *term*; 276.2 *time period*
fortnightly 298.12 *cyclic*; 298.16 *cyclically*; 740.5 *journal*
fortress 356.8 *construction*; 384.12 *fort*; 252.5 *refuge*
Fortress America 585.1 *war*
fortuitous 107.8 *chance*; 105.3 *unexpected*
fortuitously 107.13 *by chance*; 105.11 *luckily*
fortuitousness 107.1 *chance*
fortuity 107.1 *chance*
fortunate 756.14 *auspicious*; 107.8 *chance*; 475.15 *presageful*; 248.8 *prosperous*; 246.13 *successful*; 287.6 *timely*
Fortunate Isles 477.8 *dreamland*
fortunately 756.17 *auspiciously*; 107.13 *by chance*; 287.9 *opportunely*; 248.9 *prosperously*; 246.16 *successfully*
fortune **780.3**; 227.3 *changeable thing*; 248.2 *good fortune*; 107.2 *luck*; 475.1 *prediction*; 248.1 *prosperity*; 246.1 *success*; 781.5 *wealth*
fortune's favourite 248.4 *prosperous person*
fortunes of war 585.1 *war*
fortune teller 101.7 *believer in a nonmaterial world*; 11.13 *diviner*; 475.9 *forecaster*; 283.5 *predictor*
fortune-telling 11.9, 475.2 *divination*; 283.4 *looking to the future*; 11.1 *occultism*; 475.13 *predicting*
forty 201.8 *twenty and over*
forty-ninth parallel 147.7 *interface*
forty-one 65.6 *pool*
fortysomething 556.13 *middle-aged*
forty winks 263.1 *ease*; 343.9 *sleep*
forum 173.4 *centre of activity*; 87.7 *city district*; 734.4 *conference*; 779.6 *marketplace*; 398.2 *representative body*; 16.18 *tribunal*
for want of 218.10 *insufficiently*
forward **302.17**; **302.19**; **330.34**; 659.6 *bad-mannered*; 49.2 *basketball player*; 239.6 *be convenient*; 692.31 *correspond*; 668.10 *disrespectful*; 167.6 *front*; 302.8, 392.28 *further*; 413.14 *give moral support*; 300.19 *go!*; 57.11 *gymnastic*; 58.2 *hockey player*; 58.4 *ice hockey player*; 244.1 *improve*; 167.11 *in front*; 265.16 *make easy*; 316.13 *post*; 293.16 *premature*; 64.4 *rugby player*; 50.10 *sailing*; 733.10 *send*; 316.12, 319.4 *transport*
forwardal 302.10 *forward motion*
forward bow stroke 50.6 *canoeing*
forward dislocate circle 57.7 *stationary rings*
forward dive 67.6 *diving*
forwarded 319.5 *transportable*
forwarded mail 692.2 *postal communication*
forwarder 79.7 *timber production*
forwarding 302.10 *forward motion*; 392.8 *furtherance*; 319.1 *transport*; 319.5 *transportable*
forward line 167.1 *front*
forward-looking 302.17 *forward*
forwardly 293.20 *prematurely*
forward march 302.10 *forward motion*
forward mast 50.3 *parts of a sailing boat*
Forward Motion 302
forward motion **302.10**; 289.1 *succession*
forward movement 289.1 *succession*
forward pass 330.5 *throw*
forward planning 475.3 *plan*
forward progress 46.7 *offence*
forwards 57.12 *competitively*; 302.19 *forward*
forward somersault 57.8 *floor exercises*; 57.5 *horizontal bar*
forward uprise 57.7 *stationary rings*
forward upstart 57.7 *stationary rings*
for what purpose? 237.12 *usefully*
for what reason? 705.25 *what?*
for your ears only 737.15 *in secret*
Fosbury flop 47.2 *field events*
fosse 183.2 *concave land*; 165.3 *enclosing thing*; 384.8 *military defences*
fossil **30.43**; 582.11 *dead person*; 284.10 *fossilization*; 296.5 *old thing*; 34.3 *organism*; 359.3 *preserved thing*; 3.11 *relic*; 215.1 *remainder*
fossil algae 84.5 *algal product*
fossil animal 30.43 *fossil*
fossil bird 72.8 *extinct bird*
fossil fish **74.4**
fossil footprint 30.43 *fossil*
fossil fuel 284.10 *fossilization*; 437.1 *fuel*; 334.6 *source of energy*
fossiliferous 30.61 *fossilized*
fossilization **284.10**; 416.2 *concentration*; 30.43 *fossil*; 418.6 *solidification*
fossilize 416.8 *be dense*; 30.62 *lithify*; 418.10 *solidify*
fossilized **30.61**; 284.19 *antiquarian*; 418.3 *hardened*; 582.22 *postmortem*
fossilized remains 284.7 *thing of the past*
fossil man 30.43 *fossil*
fossilology 3.2 *archaeology*
fossil plant 30.43 *fossil*
fossil record 34.16 *evolution*; 30.43 *fossil*; 284.10 *fossilization*
fossil reptile 73.6 *extinct reptile*
fossil track 30.43 *fossil*
foster 392.23 *advise*; 762.4 *be a substitute*; 550.34 *cover for*; 344.12 *determine*; 6.22 *educate*; 302.8 *further*; 413.14 *give moral support*; 244.1 *improve*; 359.5 *preserve*; 252.10 *protect*; 550.40 *substitutive*
fosterage 392.9 *patronage*
foster child 387.4 *dependent*
fostering 392.32 *supportive*
foster parent 762.2 *substitute person*; 550.21 *substitution*
fou as a coot 690.1 *drunk*
fou as a wulk 690.1 *drunk*
fouetté 22.9 *ballet steps*
fouetté en tournant 22.9 *ballet steps*
foul 51.10 *bowling*; 52.2 *boxing*; 65.4 *carom*; 331.2 *collide*; 804.15 *criminal*; 712.8 *cursing*; 560.16 *defecate*; 258.7, 258.11 *dirty*; 596.9 *disliked*; 798.7 *evil*; 52.11 *fight*; 66.2 *football play*; 58.5 *lacrosse*; 245.3 *make worse*; 323.9 *navigate*; 48.7 *play baseball*; 49.6 *play basketball*; 58.9 *play hockey*; 49.4 *playing terms*; 66.4 *play soccer*; 236.4 *poor*; 364.8 *repulsive*; 802.7 *sense of wrong*; 31.48 *stormy*; 258.8 *unclean*; 804.11 *wicked*
foul ball 48.5 *batting terms*
fouled 258.7 *dirty*; 66.5 *soccer*
fouled-up 486.4 *bungled*; 408.19 *mixed-up*
fouling 66.2 *football play*
foul language 712.2 *offensive language*
foul line 48.1 *baseball*; 51.4 *bowling*
foul mouth 712.1 *curse*; 594.6 *swearing*
foul-mouthed 594.13 *angry*; 659.6 *bad-mannered*; 712.8 *cursing*
foul-mouthing 712.1 *curse*
foulness 258.1 *dirtiness*; 798.1 *evil*; 236.10 *poverty*; 258.2 *uncleanness*
foul off 48.7 *play baseball*
foul out 49.6 *play basketball*
foul play 651.7 *act of malevolence*; 16.39 *crime*; 804.7 *criminality*; 645.1 *cunning*; 340.2 *deed*; 812.3 *disreputable action*; 798.5 *evil thing*; 700.10 *fraud*; 800.1 *improbity*; 465.3 *injustice*; 381.16 *personal attack*; 466.3 *prejudice*; 802.7 *sense of wrong*; 802.6 *unlawfulness*
foul shooter 49.2 *basketball player*
foul shot 49.4 *playing terms*
foul-smelling 503.3 *stinking*
foul stroke 65.3 *English billiards*
foul taste 499.2 *unpalatability*
foul-tasting 499.6 *unpalatable*
foul territory 48.1 *baseball*
foul the line 325.3 *go astray*
foul tip 48.5 *batting terms*
foul-tongued 712.8 *cursing*
foul up 486.7 *be clumsy*; 258.10 *be dirty*; 408.23 *confuse*; 378.8 *hinder*; 274.19 *make a mistake*
foul-up 274.10 *blunder*; 486.9 *bungling*; 408.6 *mix-up*; 378.2 *obstacle*
foul weather 380.5 *violent weather*
found **142.7**; 175.4 *base*; 449.14 *discovered*; 243.2 *do the groundwork*; 129.18 *forerun*; 160.7 *form*; 130.23, 344.11 *inaugurate*; 228.7 *make stable*; 356.10 *produce*; 393.13 *repaired*
foundation 175.1 *base*; 130.6 *inauguration*; 129.3 *preparation*; 243.10 *preparations*; 344.3 *rudiment*; 38.28 *substructure*; 413.2 *supporting part*; 447.1 *topic*
foundational 344.13 *causal*; 130.34 *inaugural*; 129.14 *preparatory*; 38.32 *structural*; 413.9 *supportive*
foundation garment 551.18 *underwear*
foundations 403.6 *construction*; 38.28 *substructure*
foundation stone 413.2 *supporting part*
founded 447.7 *focused*
founded on a rock 252.7 *invulnerable*
founder 357.13 *be destroyed*; 414.12 *be heavy*; 249.9 *be in trouble*; 156.14 *deepen*; 305.9 *descend*; 449.12 *discoverer*; 582.16 *meet one's fate*; 327.25 *pitch*; 484.8 *planner*; 344.7 *Prime Mover*; 356.9 *producer*
foundering 305.16 *descending*
founder member 356.9 *producer*
found guilty 806.5 *guilty*
founding 129.14 *preparatory*
founding father 129.8 *precursor*; 356.9 *producer*
found innocent 805.6 *declared innocent*
foundling 655.7 *outsider*
found not guilty 805.6 *declared innocent*
found object 19.12 *sculpture*
foundry 760.4 *medium of conversion*; 577.1 *workshop*
foundryman 578.2 *artisan*
found wanting 218.1 *insufficient*; 670.32 *unsatisfactory*
fount 439.2 *resource*; 344.2 *source*; 5.15 *type style*
fountain 304.12 *geyser*; 44.3 *ornamental garden*; 315.2 *outflow*; 439.2 *resource*; 344.2 *source*; 304.17 *spring up*; 304.2 *upturn*; 433.1 *water*
fountainhead 90.2 *channel*; 130.3, 344.2 *source*
Fountain of Youth 482.6 *objective*; 756.4 *promised land*
fountain syringe 433.11 *wash*
Four 200
four **200.1**; **200.7**; 27.9 *numeral*; 53.10 *score*
four and twenty 201.8 *twenty and over*
four-ball match 56.1 *golf*
four-beat trudgen crawl 67.2 *swimming technique*
four bits 780.8 *American money*
four by four 200.14 *in fours*
four centred arch 20.5 *arch*
four-dimensional continuum 28.7 *space*
four-dimensional space 27.35, 28.7 *space*
four-eyed 518.22 *bespectacled*
four-figure 201.21 *thousandth*
four-flusher 699.19 *cheat*; 700.15 *deceiver*
fourfold 200.7 *four*; 200.13 *four times*
fourfoldness 200.4 *quadruplication*
four-footed 200.9 *tetramerous*
four-handed 200.10 *quartered*
four humours **599.12**
four hundred 201.9 *treble figures*
Fourier series 27.20 *sequence*
four-in-hand 200.3 *foursome*; 551.14 *neckwear*
four-leaf clover 200.3 *foursome*; 475.6 *good-luck sign*; 11.6 *talisman*
four-legged 200.9 *tetramerous*
four-legged friend 70.2 *animal*
four-letter 712.8 *cursing*; 5.39 *of language*
four-letter word 712.1 *curse*; 200.3 *foursome*; 5.19 *swearword*
four-man bobsled 68.9 *bobsledding*
four-man kayak race 50.6 *canoeing*
four-minute warning 281.10 *signal*
four of a kind 69.3 *card game terms*
four-part 200.10 *quartered*
four-parted 200.10 *quartered*
four-poster 200.3 *foursome*
four-poster bed 23.6 *bed*
fours 51.9 *bowls*; 50.4 *rowing*
fourscore 201.8 *twenty and over*
fourscore and ten 201.8 *twenty and over*
four seasons 200.3 *foursome*
four-sided 27.82 *polygonal*; 200.8 *quadrilateral*
fours match 51.1 *green bowling*
foursome **200.3**; 200.1 *four*; 56.1 *golf*
foursome reel 22.4 *historic dancing*
foursquare 200.13 *four times*; 200.8 *quadrilateral*
four-step 51.10 *bowling*

four-step delivery 51.5 *bowling delivery*
four-stroke 200.10 *quartered*
four-stroke cycle 38.13 *engine cycle*
fourteen 201.7 *double figures*
fourteenth 201.18 *eleventh*; 196.4 *less than one*
fourth 200.15; 27.75 *equal*; 200.7 *four*; 196.4 *less than one*; 18.16 *musical note*; 200.6 *quarter*
fourth-class mail 692.2 *postal communication*
fourth dimension 141.9
fourth-dimensional 141.11 *spatial*
fourth estate 740.3 *journalism*; 741.1 *news*
fourth finger 492.7 *sense organ*
fourth guard 54.3 *fencing movements*
fourthly 200.15 *fourth*
Fourth of July 601.5 *anniversary*; 298.6 *annually celebrated day*
fourth part 200.6 *quarter*
fourth power 27.17 *multiplication*
four times 200.13
four winds 200.3 *foursome*
foutou 25.53 *African dish*
fowl 72.1 *birds*; 633.11 *hunt*; 43.8 *livestock*
fowler 633.6 *hunter*
fowling 633.2 *chase*
fowling piece 587.9 *firearm*; 633.3 *hunting and fishing equipment*
fowl of the air 72.1 *birds*
FOX 692.24 *television broadcasting*
fox 645.3 *cunning person*; 59.8 *hunting*; 332.12 *swift animal*; 541.11 *variegate*
foxdog 59.8 *hunting*
foxglove 540.3 *purple thing*
foxhole 183.2 *concave land*; 736.2 *hiding place*; 384.8 *military defences*; 308.7 *passageway*; 252.5 *refuge*
foxhound 633.6 *hunter*; 59.8 *hunting*
fox hunt 633.2 *chase*; 59.8 *hunting*
fox-hunter 382.13 *animal killer*; 71.24, 633.6 *hunter*; 59.2 *thoroughbred*
fox-hunting 382.9 *animal killing*; 59.8 *hunting*; 71.23 *mammal hunting*
foxiness 645.1, 702.3 *cunning*
foxing 541.4 *maculation*
fox in the henhouse 378.2 *obstacle*
foxlike 71.28 *carnivorous*
foxtrot 22.2, 22.15 *dance*
foxtrotter 22.5 *dancer*
foxy 534.1 *brown*; 71.28 *carnivorous*; 645.4, 702.8 *cunning*; 800.5 *dishonourable*
foxy lady 363.6 *charmer*
foyer 21.18 *auditorium*; 167.1 *front*; 314.6 *means of entry*; 565.7 *room*
fracas 701.1, 751.2 *argument*; 328.5 *commotion*; 380.3 *instance of violence*
fracastorius 730.7 *voiceless person*
fractal 27.28 *algorithm*; 27.41 *geometric figure*
Fraction 196
fraction 196.1; 203.2 *certain amount*; 27.6 *complex number*; 27.18 *division*; 233.3 *incomplete thing*; 32.22 *industrial chemistry*; 205.1 *part*; 405.2 *piece*; 194.5 *ratio*; 124.8 *trifle*
fractional 194.9; **196.5**; 405.6 *component*; 27.71 *numerical*; 205.11 *partial*; 203.6 *quantitative*
fractional crystallization 32.5 *process*
fractional currency 780.13 *coinage*
fractional distillation 32.22 *industrial chemistry*; 32.5 *process*
fractionalize 372.11 *divide*
fractionally 196.7; 405.14 *constituently*; 205.12 *partly*; 203.7 *quantitatively*
fractional part 196.2
fractionate 372.11 *divide*; 432.25 *gasify*; 32.25 *solidify*
fractionation 32.22 *industrial chemistry*; 437.6 *oil*; 432.10 *vaporization*
fractionize 372.11 *divide*
fractious 701.8 *argumentative*; 625.4 *irascible*; 113.26 *uncooperative*
fractiousness 113.7 *contrariness*; 637.14 *disobedience*; 625.1 *irascibility*
fracture 424.4 *be brittle*; 146.2, 146.5 *crack*; 38.16 *deformation*; 30.20 *earth movement*; 30.64 *fold*; 491.11 *inflict pain*; 491.3 *injury*; 380.3 *instance of violence*; 133.4 *interruption*; 38.31 *load*; 308.18 *open*; 308.1 *opening*; 372.9 *separate*; 380.8 *use violence*
fractured 146.7 *cracked*; 491.6 *injured*; 308.12 *open*
fractureproof 423.1 *tough*
fragile 424.1 *brittle*; 151.2 *fine*; 278.7 *impermanent*; 337.8 *weak*
fragile as an eggshell 424.1 *brittle*
fragile item 337.5 *weak thing*
fragilely 424.5
fragileness 424.2 *brittleness*
fragility 424.2 *brittleness*; 151.7 *fineness*; 335.1 *powerlessness*; 337.1 *weakness*
fragment 196.3; 424.4 *be brittle*; 427.6 *crumb*; 196.8, 372.11 *divide*; 377.11 *explode*; 159.3 *little piece*; 205.1, 205.10 *part*; 405.2 *piece*; 427.22 *pulverize*
fragmentary 196.5 *fractional*; 231.2, 233.4 *incomplete*; 205.11 *partial*
fragmentation 377.5 *divergence*; 427.4 *pulverization*; 372.1 *separation*
fragmentation bomb 587.16 *bomb*
fragmented 133.8 *discontinuous*; 205.11 *partial*; 377.20 *separated*
fragments 215.1 *remainder*
Fragrance 502
fragrance 502.1; 500.1 *odour*; 490.1 *physical pleasure*; 498.1 *sweetness*
fragrance-free 501.3 *odourless*
fragrancy 502.1 *fragrance*
fragrant 502.4; 78.10 *floral*; 500.5 *odorous*; 490.6, 498.7 *pleasant*
fragrantly 502.7; 78.14 *florally*; 498.9 *sweetly*
fragrant thing 502.2
frail 424.1 *brittle*; 153.2 *emaciated*; 337.10 *ill*; 335.12 *impotent*; 796.13 *unchaste*; 254.2 *unsafe*; 804.13 *venial*
frailly 424.5 *fragilely*
frailty 424.2 *brittleness*; 153.8 *emaciation*; 231.5 *imperfection*; 556.5 *old age*; 337.3 *poor health*; 335.1 *powerlessness*; 804.3 *venial sin*
framboesia 260.13 *skin disease*; 260.7 *tropical disease*
frame 715.6 *accuse falsely*; 320.11 *bicycle part*; 51.4 *bowling*; 23.17 *carpenter*; 410.1 *container*; 41.12 *development*; 715.2 *false accusation*; 699.9 *falsification*; 699.26 *falsify*; 175.2 *foot*; 160.1, 160.7 *form*; 403.4 *framework*; 368.5 *inset*; 402.4 *matter*; 44.4 *nursery*; 163.1, 163.5 *outline*; 484.10 *plan out*; 484.13 *plot*; 106.2 *premeditate*; 243.10 *preparations*; 356.10 *produce*; 160.2 *prototype*; 163.2 *shadow*; 403.15 *shape*; 65.5 *snooker*; 136.16 *specify*; 724.9 *style*; 38.27 *superstructure*; 413.11 *support*; 413.2 *supporting part*; 170.7 *surround*; 692.21 *television*; 137.4 *type*; 165.6 *wrap*; 165.4 *wrapper*
framed 106.4 *deliberate*; 23.16 *joined*; 715.9 *perjurious*
frame frequency 692.21 *television*
frame of mind 590.4 *emotion*; 221.4 *state of mind*
frame of reference 746.2 *basis for negotiations*; 27.33 *coordinates*; 136.6 *specification*
framer 484.8 *planner*
frames 518.10 *visual aid*
frame-up 715.2 *false accusation*; 699.9 *falsification*; 699.8 *fraud*; 484.4 *plot*; 106.6 *premeditation*
framework 403.4; 243.10 *preparations*; 163.2 *shadow*; 413.2 *supporting part*; 165.4 *wrapper*
framing 41.13; 23.10 *carpenter's term*; 41.8 *composition*; 403.4 *framework*; 23.16 *joined*
franc 780.11 *national coins*
franchise 469.11; 758.4 *licence*; 250.15 *set free*
franchised 250.9 *free*
franchisement 250.3 *independence*
Franciscan 782.10 *poor person*
Francophobe 594.9 *hater*
Francophobia 594.3 *race hatred*
Francophobic 594.11 *racist*
franc-tireur 586.8 *soldier*
frangibility 424.2 *brittleness*
frangible 424.1 *brittle*
frangibleness 424.2 *brittleness*
frangipani 502.3 *incense*
Franglais 5.26 *dialect*
frank 150.3 *broad-minded*; 692.31 *correspond*; 703.10 *demonstrative*; 739.11 *disclosing*; 527.4 *easily seen through*; 731.6 *effusive*; 178.5, 799.4 *honourable*; 250.13 *informal*; 646.1 *naive*; 271.3 *natural*; 308.16, 738.15 *open*; 426.2 *outspoken*; 733.10 *send*; 698.18 *truthful*
frankalmoign 440.3 *historic property terms*; 763.3 *medieval ownership*
Frankenstein's monster 554.6 *things brought to life*
Frankfurt Book Fair 740.6 *book publishing*
frankfurter 25.29 *sausage*
Frankfurt School 4.7 *school of thought*
frankincense 502.3 *incense*
franking machine 692.3 *correspondence*
frankly 738.17; 426.12 *bluntly*; 703.21 *demonstratively*; 731.11 *effusively*; 799.7 *honourably*; 250.22 *informally*; 646.5 *naively*; 308.26, 739.13 *openly*; 271.8 *simply*; 178.13 *straightforwardly*; 698.36 *truthfully*
frankness 703.2 *demonstrativeness*; 731.2 *effusiveness*; 250.4 *informality*; 646.2 *naivety*; 271.6 *naturalness*; 308.9, 527.10, 739.3 *openness*; 426.6 *outspokenness*; 799.1 *probity*; 698.5 *truthfulness*
frantic 342.18 *active*; 461.12 *manic*; 380.6 *violent*
frantic haste 342.3 *nimbleness*
frappé 558.7 *alcoholic drink*; 494.8 *cold*
frascati 558.9 *wine*
frat 569.14 *seek the friendship of*
fraternal 750.11 *allied*; 747.19 *associating*; 650.6 *benevolent*; 569.8 *friendly*; 593.17 *loving*
fraternalism 747.2 *fellowship*; 569.1 *friendship*
fraternally 650.10 *benevolently*; 569.17 *in friendship*
fraternal twins 198.6 *twins*
fraternity 376.15 *association*; 747.2 *fellowship*; 569.1 *friendship*; 654.8 *good company*; 566.9 *group*; 747.9 *team*
fraternity house 6.15 *schoolroom*
fraternization 569.1 *friendship*; 654.1 *sociability*
fraternize 654.13; 374.6 *come together*; 750.22 *form an alliance*
fraternizer 700.20 *plotter*
fraternize with 569.13 *befriend*
fraternizing 750.11 *allied*
fratricide 651.7 *act of malevolence*; 382.3 *homicide*; 382.11 *murderer*
fratting 654.1 *sociability*
Frau 568.3 *female title of address*
fraud 699.8; **700.10**; 699.19 *cheat*; 16.39 *crime*; 800.3 *criminality*; 645.3 *cunning person*; 700.15, 718.3 *deceiver*; 774.7 *dishonesty*; 800.4 *dishonourable person*; 812.3 *disreputable action*; 485.5 *expert*; 699.17 *false person*; 16.38 *lawbreaking*; 351.2 *misuse*; 645.2 *stratagem*
fraud squad 16.15 *British police*
fraudulence 800.3 *criminality*; 699.5 *deceitfulness*; 700.1 *deception*; 189.3 *deviousness*; 699.8, 700.10 *fraud*
fraudulency 800.3 *criminality*; 700.1 *deception*
fraudulent 699.35; **774.18**; 351.5 *abusive*; 800.7 *criminal*; 699.33 *deceitful*; 700.35 *deceptive*; 189.5 *devious*; 812.4 *disreputable*; 702.10 *hypocritical*; 16.60 *offending*
fraudulently 351.6 *abusively*; 16.83 *dishonestly*; 800.11 *dishonourably*; 774.19 *thievishly*
fraught 232.8 *full*
fraught with danger 254.1 *dangerous*
fraught with difficulties 378.14 *blocked*
Fraulein 568.3 *female title of address*
Fraunhofer lines 29.15 *sun*
fray 342.1 *activity*; 701.1 *argument*; 328.5 *commotion*; 245.1 *deteriorate*; 408.9 *disorder*; 365.14 *erode*; 576.4 *exertion*; 245.5 *hurt*
frayed 245.13 *dilapidated*
frazzle 365.14 *erode*; 245.5 *hurt*
frazzled 493.10 *on fire*
freak 642.4 *capricious person*; 325.19 *deviant person*; 751.4 *dissenter*; 114.1 *diversity*; 691.4 *drug taker*; 118.10 *eccentric*; 619.5 *person of wonder*; 642.3 *whim*
freak accident 105.5 *unexpectedness*
freaked out 691.7 *drugged*
freakish 642.1 *capricious*; 114.5 *diverse*; 118.14 *eccentric*; 630.8 *surprising*; 105.3 *unexpected*
freakishly 114.10 *diversely*
freakishness 642.2 *caprice*; 461.1 *insanity*; 118.4 *unusualness*
freak out 624.12 *become angry*; 691.10 *drug oneself*; 590.17 *feel deeply*
freaky 118.14 *eccentric*; 630.8 *surprising*
freckle 534.3 *brownness*; 541.4 *maculation*; 260.13 *skin disease*; 377.18 *sprinkle*; 541.11 *variegate*
freckled 541.10 *mottled*; 377.23 *sprinkled*
freckling 541.4 *maculation*; 377.4 *sprinkling*
Frederick Ashton 22.14 *famous ballet dancers*
Fred Perry 63.7 *famous tennis players*
free 250.9; **391.8**; **635.10**; **657.10**; 649.10 *absolve*; 16.78, 758.10 *acquit*; 16.63, 758.6 *acquitted*; 768.9 *as a gift*; 65.9 *billiard*; 150.3 *broad-minded*; 572.6 *celibate*; 390.1 *deliver*; 390.4 *deliverable*; 265.18 *disentangle*; 767.9 *dispose of*; 389.8 *escaping*; 369.11 *extract*; 390.6 *extricably*; 250.20 *freely*; 793.11 *free of charge*; 768.7 *given*; 57.11 *gymnastic*; 68.13 *ice-skating*; 758.7 *independent*; 580.6 *leisure*; 580.7 *leisurely*; 391.4 *liberate*; 391.7 *liberated*; 268.17 *liquefy*; 265.16 *make easy*; 62.8 *mountaineering*; 350.3 *not wanted*; 343.2 *not working*; 738.15 *open*; 308.13 *opened up*; 308.19 *open up*; 393.3 *restore*; 608.10 *save*; 372.15 *separate*; 268.10 *slippery*; 5.40 *translated*; 719.17 *translational*; 109.6 *unrelated*; 714.7 *vindicate*
free admission 793.6 *absence of charge*
free agent 46.2 *football player*; 250.7 *free person*
free-and-easiness 657.4 *freedom*
free-and-easy 569.10 *familiar*; 657.10 *free*; 250.13 *informal*; 615.4 *rash*; 654.15 *sociable*
free as a bird 250.10 *independent*
free as air 250.10 *independent*
free association 36.27 *association of ideas*
free-association test 36.5 *psychological test*
free as the wind 250.10 *independent*
free ball 65.5 *snooker*
freebase 691.10 *drug oneself*
freebasing 691.1 *drug-taking*
freebie 793.6 *absence of charge*; 211.4 *extra*; 768.2 *gift*; 752.1 *offer*; 483.5 *positive stimulus*; 765.5 *profit*
freeboard 146.1 *interval*
free board 793.6 *absence of charge*
freeboot 774.14 *plunder*
freebooter 710.5 *beggar*; 586.6 *militarist*; 774.9 *plunderer*
freebooting 774.5 *plundering*
freeborn 250.9 *free*
free citizen 250.7 *free person*
free city 12.5 *political organization*
free climbing 62.1 *mountaineering*
free country 85.1 *country*
freed 767.12 *disposed*; 649.6 *forgiven*; 250.9 *free*; 391.7 *liberated*
free-dancing 68.7 *ice-dancing*
free delivery 793.6 *absence of charge*
freed from blame 758.6 *acquitted*
freedman 250.7 *free person*
Freedom 250
freedom 250.1; **657.4**; 16.42, 758.2 *acquittal*; 150.6 *broad-mindedness*; 390.2 *deliverance*; 389.1 *escape*; 580.1 *leisure*; 391.1 *liberation*; 757.1 *permission*; 265.5 *smoothness*; 109.1 *unrelatedness*
freedom fighter 586.9 *guerrilla*; 383.5 *resister*; 753.5 *seditionist*
freedom from artifice 646.2 *naivety*
freedom from blame 805.1 *innocence*
freedom from dirt 256.1 *cleanness*
freedom from fear 250.2 *free speech*
freedom from sin 805.1 *innocence*
freedom from want 250.2 *free speech*
freedom from war 749.1 *pacification*; 589.1 *peace*
freedom of action 250.1, 657.4 *freedom*
freedom of choice 250.1 *freedom*; 635.4 *free will*; 352.1 *means*; 469.6 *selection*
freedom of movement 250.1 *freedom*
freedom of religion 250.2 *free speech*
freedom of the press 250.2 *free speech*
freedom of thought 250.1 *freedom*
freedom of worship 250.2 *free speech*
free drink 793.6 *absence of charge*
free duty 13.6 *economic factors*
freedwoman 250.7 *free person*
free economy 776.5 *commercial trade*
free enterprise 776.5 *commercial trade*; 250.1 *freedom*
free entry 793.6 *absence of charge*
free exchange rate 780.7 *finance*
free exercises 57.1 *gymnastics*
free fall 29.31 *space travel*

free-faller 305.8 *descender*
free fight 250.6 *liberality*
free-floating anxiety 36.12 *stress*
Freefone™ 793.6 *absence of charge*
Freefone™ call 692.10 *telephone call*
free-for-all 408.9 *disorder*; 250.6 *liberality*; 250.12 *unconditional*
free for the asking 793.11 *free of charge*
free from 255.13 *pure*
free from blame 714.7 *vindicate*
free from guile 646.1 *naive*
free from impurities 255.10, 256.15 *purify*
free from sin 805.5 *innocent*
free gift 793.6 *absence of charge*; 211.4 *extra*; 768.2 *gift*; 765.5 *profit*
free goods 13.6 *economic factors*
free hand 635.4 *free will*; 250.6 *liberality*; 757.1 *permission*
freehand drawing 19.3 *drawing*; 721.9 *representation*
free hit 58.1 *hockey*
freehold 564.11 *inhabited*; 763.1, 763.4 *possession*; 440.8 *propertied*; 440.1 *property*
freeholder 564.3 *householder*; 440.7 *property man*
freeing 649.3 *absolution*; 265.8 *disentanglement*; 767.1 *disposal*; 391.1 *liberation*; 372.1 *separation*
free kick 66.2 *football play*; 64.3 *rugby play*; 46.12 *special team*
freelance 250.16 *be independent*; 250.10 *independent*; 586.6 *militarist*; 741.13 *report*; 576.6 *work*; 578.1 *worker*
freelance pay 788.3 *income*
freelancer 250.7 *free person*; 693.9 *informant*; 586.6 *militarist*; 740.11 *newspaperman*; 578.1 *worker*
freelance reporter 693.9 *informant*; 741.4 *journalist*
freelance writer 741.4 *journalist*
free-liver 686.5 *self-indulgent person*
free living 686.2 *dissipation*
free-living 686.7 *dissipated*
free-living flatworm 75.6 *worm*
freeload 654.11 *be sociable*; 793.14 *buy cheaply*; 710.8 *solicit money*
freeloader 793.8 *bargain hunter*; 710.5 *beggar*; 343.8 *nonworker*; 782.10 *poor person*; 664.3 *sponger*
freeloading 710.11 *begging*; 710.3 *solicitation*; 664.7 *sycophantic*
free lodging 793.6 *absence of charge*
free love 250.6 *liberality*; 757.1 *permission*; 593.2 *romantic love*; 796.3 *sexual immorality*; 570.3 *types of marriage*
free lunch 793.6 *absence of charge*; 490.4 *pleasurable things*
freely **250.20**; 150.7 *broadly*; 572.12 *celibately*; 265.21 *easily*; 16.88 *forgivingly*; 391.8 *free*; 389.9 *fugitively*; 679.12 *generously*; 250.22 *informally*; 109.12 *irrelevantly*; 739.13 *openly*; 372.20 *separately*; 758.13 *with impunity*
freeman 250.7 *free person*; 87.11 *urbanite*
free market **779.4**; 250.1 *freedom*; 314.4 *right of entry*
free-market economy 776.5 *commercial trade*; 13.2 *economy*
Freemason 736.7 *concealer*; 737.7 *esotericism*
Freemasonry 737.7 *esotericism*
freemasonry 747.2 *fellowship*; 569.1 *friendship*
free meal 768.3 *offering*
free mentally 391.4 *liberate*
free-minded 250.10 *independent*
free-mindedly 250.20 *freely*
free moments 580.1 *leisure*
free of charge **793.11**
free oneself 391.5 *be liberated*; 372.13 *diverge*
free pardon 649.1 *forgiveness*
free pass 793.6 *absence of charge*
free person **250.7**
free play 58.5 *lacrosse*; 250.5 *scope*
free port 793.6 *absence of charge*; 13.6 *economic factors*; 779.7 *emporium*; 250.1 *freedom*; 314.4 *right of entry*
free position 58.5 *lacrosse*
Freepost™ 793.6 *absence of charge*; 692.2 *postal communication*
free postage 793.6 *absence of charge*
free quarters 793.6 *absence of charge*
free radical 227.3 *changeable thing*
free range 250.5 *scope*
free-range 250.11 *ranging*
free-range hen 43.8 *livestock*
free ride 793.6 *absence of charge*
free-rider 343.8 *nonworker*
free sail 50.18 *windsurf*
free sailing 50.7 *windsurfing*
free scope 250.5 *scope*
free seat 793.6 *absence of charge*
free service 793.6 *absence of charge*
freesheet 793.6 *absence of charge*; 740.4 *newspaper*
free shot 49.4 *playing terms*
free-skate 68.15 *ice-skate*
free-skating 68.6 *ice-skating*
free-skating movement 68.6 *ice-skating*
free socage 440.3 *historic property terms*; 763.3 *medieval ownership*
free space 28.7 *space*
free-speaking 250.13 *informal*; 729.19 *speaking*
free speech **250.2**; 657.4 *freedom*
free spirit 250.7 *free person*; 635.4 *free will*; 118.7 *nonconformist*
free-spirited 250.10 *independent*
free-spoken 646.1 *naive*
freestyle 59.10 *dressage*; 52.16 *professionally*; 68.12 *ski*; 67.11 *swimming*; 50.13 *windsurfing*; 52.15 *wrestling*
freestyle event 67.1 *swimming*
freestyle sailing 50.7 *windsurfing*
freestyle skiing 68.1 *skiing*
freestyle wrestler 586.3 *athlete*; 52.6 *wrestler*
freestyle wrestling 52.5 *wrestling*
free-thinker **250.8**; 150.6 *broad-mindedness*; 451.5 *disbeliever*; 118.7 *nonconformist*
free thinking 250.1 *freedom*
free-thinking 150.3 *broad-minded*; 250.10 *independent*; 118.13 *unconventional*
free thought 657.4 *freedom*
free throw 49.4 *playing terms*
free-throw lane 49.1 *basketball*
free ticket 793.6 *absence of charge*
free time 263.1 *ease*; 580.1 *leisure*
free to choose 250.10 *independent*
free trade 793.6 *absence of charge*; 776.5 *commercial trade*; 250.1 *freedom*; 13.5 *international trade*; 314.4 *right of entry*
free-trade area 776.5 *commercial trade*; 250.1 *freedom*; 779.4 *free market*
free-trader 250.7 *free person*
free-trade zone 13.5 *international trade*
free translation 5.12, 719.4 *translation*
free union 570.3 *types of marriage*
free verse 17.10 *verse form*
freeway 317.3, 320.2, 373.5 *road*
freewheel 265.17 *do easily*; 265.19 *go easily*; 421.12 *go smoothly*; 341.4 *not act*; 300.15 *walk*
freewheeling 250.10 *independent*
free will **635.4**; 250.1, 657.4 *freedom*; 4.9 *philosophical problem*; 469.6 *selection*
freewoman 250.7 *free person*
free world 12.5 *political organization*
freezable 494.9 *heat-resistant*
freeze **31.32**; 267.6 *adhere*; 489.12 *anaesthetize*; 494.10 *be cold*; 494.11 *become cold*; 416.8 *be dense*; 339.4 *be inert*; 301.8 *be motionless*; 226.8 *cause to cease*; 68.10 *curling*; 251.2 *economic restraint*; 418.9 *harden*; 494.12 *make cold*; 301.9 *make motionless*; 228.7 *make stable*; 301.1 *motionlessness*; 359.5 *preserve*; 592.7 *render insensitive*; 31.63 *snow*; 32.25 *solidify*; 786.2 *stoppage*; 786.8 *stop payment*; 350.6 *stop using*
freeze-dried 494.9 *heat-resistant*; 252.7 *invulnerable*; 359.7 *preserved*
freeze-dried food 557.7 *food*; 359.3 *preserved thing*
freeze-dry 428.17 *dry*; 494.12 *make cold*; 359.5 *preserve*
freeze-drying 359.1 *preservation*
freeze in one's tracks 226.6 *cease*
freeze onto 267.6 *adhere*
freeze out 371.7 *drive out*; 470.3 *exclude*; 655.13 *ignore*
freeze over 494.11 *become cold*
freeze pay 251.9 *economize*
freeze prices 251.9 *economize*; 166.7 *limit*
freezer 410.3 *cabinet*; 494.4 *cooler*; 28.35 *heat*; 25.4 *kitchen container*; 359.2 *preserver*; 439.4 *storage*
freezer bag 410.8 *bag*
freezer stock 557.7 *food*
freeze the ball 49.6 *play basketball*
freeze to death 494.11 *become cold*
freeze-up 31.32 *freeze*; 494.5 *ice*
freeze with horror 612.11 *be afraid*
freezing **494.2**; 539.2 *bluish*; 494.8 *cold*; 416.7 *condensed*; 31.55 *cool*; 494.9 *heat-resistant*; 32.3 *phase*; 49.4 *playing terms*; 359.1 *preservation*; 28.37 *temperature*; 31.47 *windy*
freezing cold 494.2 *freezing*
freezing fog 31.33 *fog*
freezing point 28.37 *temperature*
freezing rain 31.29 *hail*
Fregean 4.14 *of a philosophy*
F region 434.3 *atmospheric layers*
freight 406.6 *contain*; 414.6 *displacement*; 232.6 *fill*; 406.2 *load*; 778.8 *merchandise*; 319.2 *thing transported*; 316.10 *transferred thing*; 316.12, 319.4 *transport*; 319.5 *transportable*; 316.2 *transportation*
freightage 790.6 *business costs*; 316.10 *transferred thing*; 316.2 *transportation*
freight car 321.6 *rolling stock*
freight carriage 319.1 *transport*
freight charges 790.6 *business costs*
freighted 232.8 *full*
freighter 316.5 *means of transport*; 316.7 *transferor*; 323.3 *vessel*
freightliner 321.6 *rolling stock*
freight train 410.10 *cart*; 316.5 *means of transport*; 321.7 *train*
French art nouveau glass 24.1 *ceramics*
French billiards 65.1 *billiards*; 65.4 *carom*
French blue 539.5 *blueness*
French bread 25.39 *loaf*
French-Canadian dialect 5.26 *dialect*
French dip sandwich 25.11 *sandwich*
French dish **25.45**
French door 314.6 *means of entry*
French dressing 25.15 *sauce*; 496.2 *seasoning*
French farce 21.12 *comedy*
French fleur-de-lis 743.6 *national emblem*
French GP at Bandol 61.2 *Formula 1 race*
Frenchified 760.17 *naturalized*
Frenchify 760.12 *naturalize*
French kiss 593.14 *communication of love*
French knickers 551.18 *underwear*
French leave 98.4 *absenteeism*; 634.16 *desertion*; 389.1 *escape*
French letter 563.3 *birth control*
French mustard 496.5 *herbs*
French navy 539.1 *blue*
French Open 63.1 *tennis*
French perfume 502.2 *fragrant thing*
French polish 421.10 *polish*
French provincial 23.7 *furniture style*
French stick 25.39 *loaf*
French toast 25.38 *bread*
frenetic 342.18 *active*; 461.12 *manic*; 380.6 *violent*
frenzied 342.18 *active*; 624.16 *angry*; 381.23 *attacking*; 461.12 *manic*; 380.6 *violent*
frenzy 342.1 *activity*; 461.4 *delusion*; 342.4 *energy*; 477.2 *inspiration*; 477.6 *reverie*; 327.8 *spasm*; 327.2 *tumult*; 380.1 *violence*
Freon™ 432.11 *vaporizer*
frequence 297.4 *frequency*
Frequency 297
frequency **297.4**; 209.1 *degree*; 334.7 *electrical power*; 28.51, 39.9 *electric current*; 27.58 *frequency distribution*; 326.1 *oscillation*; 298.1 *regularity*; 28.8 *time*; 326.5 *wave*; 28.16 *waveform*
frequency allocation 692.14 *radio transmission*
frequency band 297.6 *radio frequency*; 692.14 *radio transmission*; 326.5 *wave*; 28.16 *waveform*
frequency distribution **27.58**
frequency-division multiplex 692.14 *radio transmission*
frequency function 27.59 *probability distribution*
frequency modulation 297.6 *radio frequency*; 692.14 *radio transmission*
frequency response 28.83 *sensitivity*
frequency spectrum 297.6 *radio frequency*; 326.5 *wave*; 28.16 *waveform*
frequent **297.3**; **297.8**; **349.2**; **565.19**; 97.12 *attend*; 209.7 *gradational*; 632.14 *habituated*; 632.16 *have a habit*; 223.14 *keep company with*; 134.4 *protract*; 298.11 *regular*
frequentation 654.3 *meeting*
frequenter 632.8 *creature of habit*; 97.5 *someone present*
frequenter of restaurants 557.18 *eater*
frequenting **297.5**; 654.3 *meeting*; 97.2 *omnipresence*
frequently **297.1**; 209.9 *differentially*; 298.15 *regularly*; 112.23 *repeatedly*
frequentness 297.4 *frequency*
frequent occurrence 297.4 *frequency*
frequent patron 632.8 *creature of habit*
fresco 19.8 *painting*
fresh **538.4**; 434.15 *breezy*; 256.16 *clean*; 494.8 *cold*; 668.10 *disrespectful*; 130.32 *embryonic*; 211.9 *extra*; 31.45 *fine*; 259.1 *healthy*; 295.12 *immature*; 295.24 *immaturely*; 660.21 *impudent*; 338.5 *invigorating*; 290.5 *morning*; 350.2 *new*; 235.5 *not bad*; 126.5 *novel*; 501.3 *odourless*; 498.7 *pleasant*; 359.7 *preserved*; 255.14 *purified*; 581.3 *refreshing*; 487.1 *unaccustomed*; 434.17 *ventilated*; 538.2 *verdant*; 31.47 *windy*
fresh air 501.1 *odourlessness*; 434.5 *open air*; 257.2 *salubrity*
fresh-air fiend 257.3 *hygienist*
fresh as a daisy 256.16 *clean*; 259.1 *healthy*; 295.12 *immature*; 255.14 *purified*
fresh as paint 295.12 *immature*
fresh blood 289.5 *successor*
fresh breeze 31.13 *wind strength*
fresh coffee 502.2 *fragrant thing*
freshen 434.20 *aerate*; 31.58 *blow*; 256.13 *clean*; 501.5 *deodorize*; 338.3 *invigorate*; 494.12 *make cold*; 257.6 *make hygienic*; 255.10, 256.15 *purify*; 581.1 *refresh*; 393.5 *revive*
freshened 256.17 *cleaned*
freshened up 581.4 *refreshed*; 295.14 *renewed*
freshener 256.9 *cleaning agent*
freshening 256.2 *cleaning*; 501.4 *deodorizing*
freshening up 581.5 *refreshment*
freshen up 256.13 *clean*; 244.1 *improve*; 295.20 *make new*; 581.1 *refresh*; 393.2 *refurbish*
fresher 130.14 *beginner*; 295.8 *new arrival*
freshet 90.1 *river*; 90.6 *river flow*
fresh fields 130.13 *new beginnings*
fresh fish 25.16 *fish dish*
fresh fruit 25.35 *dessert*
freshly 538.18 *greenly*; 295.24 *immaturely*; 350.13 *newly*; 501.7 *odourlessly*; 126.8 *originally*; 581.8 *refreshingly*; 498.9 *sweetly*
freshly ground coffee 558.4 *coffee*
freshman 130.14 *beginner*; 6.7 *learner*; 295.8 *new arrival*
fresh milk 558.5 *milk*
freshness 256.1 *cleanness*; 494.1 *coldness*; 295.3 *immaturity*; 660.10 *impudence*; 350.9 *newness*; 501.1 *odourlessness*; 126.1 *originality*; 255.1 *purity*; 581.5 *refreshment*; 660.11 *sauciness*; 498.1 *sweetness*; 338.1 *vigour*; 555.2 *youthfulness*
fresh news 741.9 *news story*
fresh smell 500.1 *odour*
fresh spurt 393.10 *revival*
fresh start **295.5**; 130.13 *new beginnings*
fresh water 433.1 *water*
freshwater bait fishing 55.1 *angling*
freshwater fish **25.17**; 74.1 *fishes*
freshwater fishing 633.2 *chase*
freshwater lake 88.1 *lake*
freshwater sailor 486.10 *unskilled person*
fresh wind 31.14 *windiness*
fret 624.4 *anger*; 342.12 *be active*; 624.11 *be angry*; 625.6 *be irascible*; 626.9 *be sullen*; 514.13 *cry*; 20.19 *decorate*; 365.15 *grind*; 743.8 *heraldic device*; 245.5 *hurt*; 262.2 *make haste*; 31.34 *mist*; 624.9 *offend*; 342.7 *restlessness*; 612.14 *worry*
fretful 342.18 *active*; 642.1 *capricious*; 625.4 *irascible*
fretfully 625.9 *irascibly*
fretfulness 642.2 *caprice*; 625.1 *irascibility*
fretsaw 438.1 *tool*
fretting 365.3 *grinding*; 365.11 *rough*; 612.9 *worried*; 612.3 *worry*
fret vapour 524.2 *murk*
fretwork 193.2 *braid*

Freud 36.29 *psychologist*
Freudian 36.33
Freudian analysis 36.3 *psychiatric treatment*
Freudian fixation 36.17 *fixation*
Freudianism 36.1 *psychology*
Freudian psychology 36.1 *psychology*
Freudian slip 697.2 *solecism;* 274.9 *trivial error*
Freya 593.16 *gods and goddesses of love*
friability 424.2 *brittleness;* 427.2 *crumbliness*
friable 424.1 *brittle;* 427.19 *crumbly;* 268.10 *slippery*
friableness 424.2 *brittleness;* 427.2 *crumbliness*
friable rock 62.2 *climbing dangers*
friar 7.7 *monk*
friary 7.10 *priestly dwelling*
fribbler 124.10 *nonentity*
fricassée 25.32 *meat dish*
frication 365.1 *friction*
fricative 5.41 *lettered;* 5.16 *spoken letter*
Friction 365
friction 362.4; 365.1; 331.12 *collision;* 113.5 *conflict;* 347.1 *counteraction;* 333.9 *deceleration;* 751.1 *disagreement;* 242.7 *dissension;* 334.4 *energy;* 28.10 *force;* 365.10 *frictional;* 378.1 *hindrance;* 513.2 *hoarseness*
frictional 365.10; 347.4 *counteracting*
frictional electricity 28.42 *electricity*
frictionize 365.13 *abrade*
frictionless 750.10 *in accord;* 5.41 *lettered;* 421.1 *smooth;* 265.12 *wieldy*
frictionless continuant 5.16 *spoken letter*
friction match 522.8 *fire*
Friday 687.3 *fast day*
fridge 410.3 *cabinet;* 494.4 *cooler;* 25.4 *kitchen container;* 359.2 *preserver;* 439.4 *storage*
fridge-freezer 410.3 *cabinet;* 494.4 *cooler;* 439.4 *storage*
fried 25.56 *culinary;* 690.1 *drunk*
fried bread 25.38 *bread*
fried catfish 25.43 *US dish*
fried fish 25.16 *fish dish*
fried noodles 25.48 *Chinese dish*
fried rice 25.48 *Chinese dish*
Friend 7.5 *Christian*
friend 569.5; 713.4 *adviser;* 373.3 *associate;* 223.11 *companion;* 285.5 *contemporary;* 590.9 *feeling person;* 797.15 *good person;* 595.4 *likable person;* 654.6 *social person;* 413.8 *supporter*
friend at court 395.4 *indirect influence*
friend in need 569.5 *friend;* 392.13 *supporter*
friendless 197.16 *alone;* 655.10 *lonely;* 335.11 *unprotected*
friendlessness 197.5 *aloneness*
friendlike 569.8 *friendly*
friendlily 797.23 *nicely*
friendliness 241.8 *amiability;* 658.1 *courtesy;* 569.1 *friendship;* 590.5 *good feeling;* 250.4 *informality;* 797.10 *kindness;* 595.1 *liking;* 749.2 *peace offering;* 654.1 *sociability*
friendly 569.8; 747.19 *associating;* 392.35, 650.6 *benevolent;* 658.7 *courteous;* 797.3 *kind;* 241.2, 595.5 *likable;* 593.17 *loving;* 749.6 *pacificatory;* 589.7 *peaceful;* 590.12 *sensitive;* 654.15 *sociable*
friendly approach 749.2 *peace offering*
friendly critic 392.13 *supporter*
friendly match 66.1 *soccer*
friendly relations 569.2
friendly society 783.4 *bank;* 771.4 *lending institution*
friendly takeover 13.7 *corporation*
friendly talk 734.2 *chat*
friendly with 569.9 *friends with*
friend of the family 569.6 *close friend*
friends and acquaintances 654.7 *human society*
friends and relations 654.7 *human society*
Friendship 569
friendship 569.1; 650.1 *benevolence;* 223.3 *companionship;* 152.6 *denseness;* 747.2 *fellowship;* 654.8 *good company;* 595.1 *liking;* 593.1 *love;* 413.6 *moral support;* 589.1 *peace;* 108.1 *relatedness;* 2.3 *social environment*
Friends of the Earth 538.16 *green politics;* 359.1 *preservation;* 244.11 *reformism*
friends with 569.9
frier 25.6 *kitchen equipment*
frieze 174.3 *architectural summit;* 20.9 *miscellaneous architectural features*
frig 62.9 *mountaineer*
frigate 586.24 *warship*
frigate bird 72.3 *water bird*
Frigg 570.14 *gods and goddesses of marriage*
frigging 62.3 *climbing technique*
fright 612.1 *fear;* 612.13 *frighten;* 630.3 *shock;* 546.2 *ugly person;* 518.7 *view*
frighten 612.13; 647.5 *be severe;* 619.10 *be wonderful;* 596.7 *cause dislike;* 711.7 *raise the alarm;* 630.9 *surprise;* 651.18 *torment*
frighten away 481.2 *deter*
frightened 612.7; 614.3 *cowardly;* 674.11 *shy*
frightened person 612.6
frightened to death 612.7 *frightened*
frightener 612.5
frightening 612.10; 254.1 *dangerous;* 612.4 *intimidation;* 711.8 *warning;* 619.8 *wonderful*
frighteningly 612.16
frighten off 481.2 *deter*
frightful 612.10 *frightening*
frightfully 612.16 *frighteningly*
fright neurosis 36.10 *neurosis*
frigid 494.8 *cold;* 31.55 *cool;* 618.7 *indifferent;* 592.1 *insensitive;* 795.9 *pure;* 655.8 *unsociable*
frigidarium 494.6 *Arctic*
frigidity 494.2 *freezing;* 795.3 *moral purity;* 655.1 *unsociability*
frigidly 494.13 *coldly;* 655.14 *unsocially*
frigid zone 494.6 *Arctic*
frigorific 494.9 *heat-resistant*
frill 211.3 *additional item;* 542.6 *decorative articles;* 72.17 *plumage;* 219.3 *superfluity*
frills 542.1 *ornament*
fringe 211.3 *additional item;* 171.11 *be exterior;* 542.6 *decorative articles;* 163.3, 164.1, 164.6 *edge;* 164.2 *edging;* 171.1 *exterior;* 547.8 *haircut;* 131.7 *limit;* 15.9 *negotiated;* 361.3 *suspended object;* 118.13 *unconventional*
fringe adjustments 15.2 *industrial negotiations*
fringe benefit 765.5 *profit;* 769.2 *something received*
fringe benefits 813.4 *reward for service*
fringed 164.9 *skirting*
fringe medicine 35.2 *natural medicine*
fringe theatre 21.1 *drama*
fringilline 72.21 *avian*
fringing 131.24 *limiting*
frippery 124.9 *bauble;* 793.5 *cheap item;* 542.6 *decorative articles;* 551.1 *dress*
frisky 342.18 *active*
frisson 327.10 *beat;* 488.3 *stimulus*
frit 612.7 *frightened*
fritted glaze 24.3 *glaze*
fritter 25.36 *cake;* 351.1 *misuse;* 441.1, 681.7 *waste*
fritter away 766.11 *be wasteful;* 787.1 *expend;* 681.7 *waste*
frittering 441.3 *waste*
Frivolity 642
frivolity 472.3 *absent-mindedness;* 642.2 *caprice;* 459.1 *folly;* 615.1 *rashness;* 124.7 *triviality*
frivolous 642.1 *capricious;* 459.5 *foolish;* 615.4 *rash;* 157.2 *superficial;* 124.4 *trivial*
frivolously 642.6 *capriciously*
frivolousness 642.2 *caprice;* 124.7 *triviality*
frizz 547.8 *haircut*
frizzy 420.3 *barbed*
frock 551.7; 551.1 *dress;* 7.21 *ordain;* 7.11 *vestment*
frock coat 551.12 *coat*
frocked 551.29 *dressed*
Froebel system 6.2 *educational system*
frog 373.8 *fastening;* 321.3 *rail;* 67.11 *swimming*
froggy 73.13 *amphibian*
frog in the throat 513.2 *hoarseness*
frog kick 67.2 *swimming technique*
froglet 73.8 *young amphibian*
frog-like 73.13 *amphibian*
frogman 305.8 *descender*
frogmarch 331.1 *impel*
frogs legs 25.45 *French dish*
frogspawn 73.8 *young amphibian*
frog spit 84.1 *alga*
frolic 22.15, 600.7 *dance*
frolic about 340.4 *act*
from 315.19 *out of*
from a biased standpoint 229.6 *probably*
from a distance 100.18 *extraneously*
from age to age 279.11 *eternally*
from a historical perspective 3.24 *historically*
from all directions 550.42 *inclusively*
from a selfish standpoint 653.5 *misanthropically*
from A to Z 232.9 *completely;* 127.9 *inclusively*
from bad to worse 607.9; 249.12 *in adversity*
from before the Flood 296.12 *olden*
from beginning to end 232.9 *completely*
from behind 120.7 *unequally*
from coast to coast 232.9 *completely;* 141.17 *from end to end*
from day to day 275.26 *all the time*
from door to door 316.18 *in transit*
from end to end 141.17; 232.9 *completely*
from every place 141.18 *from everywhere*
from every quarter 324.11 *in all directions*
from everywhere 141.18
from experience 284.24 *retrospectively*
from far and near 232.9 *completely*
from first to last 232.9 *completely*
from generation to generation 279.11 *eternally*
from hand to hand 316.18 *in transit*
from head to foot 232.9 *completely*
from hell to breakfast 141.17 *from end to end*
from here to eternity 141.17 *from end to end*
from instinct 457.12 *nonhumanly*
from its birth 130.39 *from the beginning*
from its inception 130.39 *from the beginning*
from loyalty 569.19 *devotedly*
from north to south 141.17 *from end to end*
from now on 283.15 *after*
from outer space 100.18 *extraneously*
from past experience 284.24 *retrospectively*
from personal motives 683.8 *selfishly*
from pillar to post 300.18 *in motion;* 316.18 *in transit;* 639.16 *irresolutely;* 326.18 *to and fro*
from pole to pole 141.17 *from end to end*
from scratch 295.22 *again;* 130.39 *from the beginning*
from sea to sea 232.9 *completely*
from side to side 298.15 *regularly*
from stem to stern 232.9 *completely*
from that angle 222.15 *under the circumstances*
from the beginning 130.39; 112.24, 295.22 *again*
from the context 694.13 *meaningfully*
from the first 130.39 *from the beginning*
from the foundations 130.39 *from the beginning*
from the four winds 324.11 *in all directions*
from the grapevine 693.19 *reportedly*
from the ground up 295.22 *again*
from the heart 652.8 *philanthropically*
from the rear 120.7 *unequally*
from the start 295.22 *again*
from the top 295.22 *again;* 761.13 *reversibly*
from the word go 130.39 *from the beginning*
from this moment on 283.15 *after*
from this time forth 283.15 *after*
from time immemorial 3.24 *historically;* 284.22 *in the past*
from time to time 275.28, 297.2 *sometimes*
from top to bottom 232.9 *completely;* 141.17 *from end to end*
from top to toe 232.9 *completely*
from wall to wall 232.9 *completely*
from what place? 705.25 *what?*
frond 82.2 *fern plant;* 77.6 *leaf;* 84.3 *plant body*
Frondeur 662.6 *nonconformist*
Front 167
front 130.30; 167.1; 167.6; 31.10 *air movement;* 585.10 *battleground;* 171.11 *be exterior;* 167.10 *be in front;* 167.5 *boldness;* 51.9 *bowls;* 113.19 *confront;* 551.1 *dress;* 171.1, 171.6 *exterior;* 525.3 *external appearance;* 699.14 *façade;* 550.28 *face;* 121.10 *lead;* 147.5 *near place;* 129.15 *precede;* 129.2 *priority;* 169.2 *surface;* 521.6 *that which makes invisible*
frontage 167.1 *front;* 143.1 *situation*
frontal 31.44; 130.30, 167.6 *front*
frontal system 31.11 *weather system*
front bowls 51.2 *grip*
front court 49.1 *basketball*
front crawl 67.1 *swimming*
front door 167.1 *front;* 314.6 *means of entry*
front elevation 167.1 *front*
front-end loader 38.29 *construction equipment;* 43.10 *farm tool*
frontier 372.6 *boundary;* 164.1 *edge;* 166.3 *furthest point;* 147.3 *juxtaposition;* 131.7 *limit;* 131.24 *limiting*
frontier post 318.5 *crossing point*
frontiersman 564.5 *countryman;* 129.8 *precursor*
fronting 167.6 *front*
frontispiece 174.3 *architectural summit;* 167.1 *front;* 130.10 *introduction;* 129.5 *preface*
front kick 52.9 *tae kwon do*
front line 586.14 *armed forces;* 585.10 *battleground;* 167.1 *front*
front-line troops 586.14 *armed forces*
front matter 167.1 *front;* 130.10 *introduction;* 129.5 *preface*
front of house 21.18 *auditorium*
front-of-house staff 21.28 *stagehand*
front of the queue 129.2 *priority*
front page 167.1 *front*
front-page 693.17 *newsworthy;* 123.6 *notable*
front-point 62.9 *mountaineer*
front-pointing 62.3 *climbing technique;* 62.8 *mountaineering*
front position 129.2 *priority*
front room 565.7 *room*
front row 64.4 *rugby player*
front rows 21.18 *auditorium*
frontrunner 129.8 *precursor*
front scale 57.6 *pommel horse*
frontstage 21.43 *on stage;* 21.17 *stage*
front stalls 21.18 *auditorium*
front-surfaced 28.29 *optical element*
front tooth 425.11 *tooth*
front up to 167.10 *be in front*
frost 31.36; 550.24 *coat;* 494.2 *freezing;* 533.8 *grey;* 494.5 *ice;* 528.11 *make opaque;* 31.63 *snow;* 498.8 *sweeten;* 174.7 *top;* 531.13 *whiten;* 531.9 *white thing*
frostbite 494.3 *chill;* 62.2 *climbing dangers*
frost-bitten 494.8 *cold*
frost-covered 31.55 *cool*
frost damage 31.36 *frost*
frosted 494.8 *cold;* 31.55 *cool;* 524.6 *murky;* 527.3 *semitransparent;* 528.2 *shady;* 498.6 *sweet;* 174.6 *topped;* 531.2 *whitened*
frosted glass 527.9 *glass;* 524.2 *murk;* 528.7 *opaque thing;* 522.10 *window*
frost hollow 31.36 *frost;* 494.5 *ice*
frostily 494.13 *coldly;* 31.65 *meteorologically*
frostiness 494.5 *ice;* 655.1 *unsociability*
frosting 550.3 *coating;* 498.3 *dessert;* 494.5 *ice;* 427.4 *pulverization;* 174.4 *top layer*
frosty 494.8 *cold;* 31.55 *cool;* 618.7 *indifferent;* 655.8 *unsociable;* 531.2 *whitened*
froth 434.10 *air bubble;* 124.9 *bauble;* 91.10 *billow;* 434.24 *bubble;* 258.4 *dirt;* 415.7 *light thing;* 560.9 *saliva;* 91.3 *wave*
froth at the mouth 560.20 *salivate*
froth-blower 690.17 *drunkard*
froth flotation 32.23 *metallurgy*
frothily 434.25 *airily*
frothiness 415.5 *lightness*
frothing 560.29 *salivating*
frothy 434.18 *bubbly;* 415.2 *insubstantial;* 542.10 *ornate;* 124.4 *trivial*
frottage 365.1 *friction;* 19.7 *picture*
froufrou 512.1 *hiss*
froward 641.1 *obstinate*
frown 625.7; 659.3 *act of discourtesy;* 624.11 *be angry;* 626.11 *be irritable;* 643.8 *be serious;* 670.10 *disapproving look;* 234.2 *facial distortion;* 742.3, 742.11 *gesture;* 659.8 *get angry;* 234.10 *make faces;* 670.23 *show disapproval;* 624.6 *sign of anger;*

596.4 *sign of dislike;* 625.2 *sign of irascibility;* 626.4 *sign of irritableness*
frown down 623.26 *outdo*
frowning 626.7 *irritable;* 625.5 *showing irascibility;* 643.1 *solemn*
frown on 670.14 *disapprove;* 655.13 *ignore*
frowns of fortune 249.3 *bad fortune*
frowstiness 503.1 *stench*
frowsty 503.3 *stinking*
frowziness 503.1 *stench*
frowzy 258.7 *dirty;* 503.3 *stinking*
frozen 489.7 *anaesthetized;* 494.8 *cold;* 416.7 *condensed;* 592.2 *desensitized;* 350.4 *disused;* 418.3 *hardened;* 341.3 *inactive;* 252.7 *invulnerable;* 166.5 *limited;* 301.4 *motionless;* 359.7 *preserved;* 440.8 *propertied;* 251.13 *restraining;* 32.32 *solid;* 228.9 *stable*
frozen assets 784.5 *amount owing;* 440.5 *personal estate*
frozen balance 784.5 *amount owing*
frozen ball 65.2 *billiards play*
frozen collocation 5.23 *phrase*
frozen corn snow 68.1 *skiing*
frozen food 557.7 *food;* 359.3 *preserved thing*
frozen like a statue 228.9 *stable*
frozen-out 655.10 *lonely*
frozen over 418.3 *hardened*
frozen rain 494.5 *ice*
frozen shoulder 260.16 *rheumatism*
frozen solid 494.8 *cold;* 418.3 *hardened*
fructan 33.4 *polysaccharide*
fructiferous 562.5 *fertile;* 80.6 *fruiting*
fructiferously 80.11
fructification 243.13 *development;* 562.2 *productiveness;* 561.3 *propagation*
fructify 562.6 *be fertile;* 80.10 *fruit;* 244.2 *get better;* 561.11 *have young;* 562.7 *make fertile*
fructose 557.11 *food content;* 498.2 *sweetener*
fructuous 80.6 *fruiting*
fructuously 80.11 *fructiferously*
frugal 616.4 *cautious;* 684.8 *self-restrained;* 680.4 *thrifty*
frugality 359.1 *preservation;* 684.1 *self-restraint;* 680.1 *thrift*
frugally 680.7 *economically;* 684.11 *with self-restraint*
frugivore 80.4 *fruit eating*
frugivorous 557.26 *eating;* 80.8 *fruit-eating*
frugivorousness 557.5 *eating habit;* 80.4 *fruit eating*
fruit 80.10; 25.9 *dish;* 44.10 *fruit tree;* 345.3 *growth;* 561.11 *have young;* 356.7 *produce;* 498.2 *sweetener;* 79.9 *tree product;* 765.6 *yield*
fruitage 44.1 *horticulture*
fruitarian 80.4 *fruit eating*
fruitarianism 80.4 *fruit eating*
fruit basket 410.7 *basket*
fruit bat 80.4 *fruit eating*
fruit-bearing 562.5 *fertile;* 80.6 *fruiting;* 345.11 *growing*
fruit belt 43.11 *farmland*
fruitcake 25.36 *cake;* 498.3 *dessert;* 118.10 *eccentric;* 461.7 *insane person*
fruit crush 498.5 *sweet drink*
fruit cup 25.35 *dessert;* 498.5 *sweet drink*
fruit diet 557.6 *nutrition*
fruit drop 44.12 *pests and diseases*
fruit-eater 80.4 *fruit eating*
fruit eating 80.4
fruit-eating 80.8
fruit-eating animal 80.4 *fruit eating*
fruit-eating person 80.4 *fruit eating*
fruiter 44.13 *horticulturist;* 79.1 *tree*
fruiterer 80.4 *fruit eating*
fruit farm 43.6 *farm;* 44.2 *garden*
fruit farmer 43.15 *agriculturist;* 44.13 *horticulturist*
fruit farming 43.4 *arable farming*
fruit flan 25.35 *dessert*
fruitful 43.20 *farmable;* 562.5 *fertile;* 80.6 *fruiting;* 356.11 *productive;* 237.4 *profitable;* 246.13 *successful;* 765.19 *yielding*
fruitfully 562.8; 43.22 *agriculturally;* 80.11 *fructiferously;* 765.20 *gainfully;* 356.13 *productively;* 246.16 *successfully*
fruitfulness 237.8 *benefit;* 562.1 *fertility*
fruit grower 44.13 *horticulturist*
fruit growing 80.4 *fruit eating;* 44.1 *horticulture*
fruit gum 498.4 *confectionery*
fruitily 80.11 *fructiferously*
fruitiness 500.1 *odour*
fruiting 80.6; 243.20 *developed*
fruiting body 80.2 *botanical fruit;* 83.4 *fungal body*
fruition 232.3 *completion;* 243.13 *development;* 561.3 *propagation*
fruit juice 558.6 *soft drink;* 498.5 *sweet drink*
fruitless 247.10 *failed;* 238.2 *futile;* 563.3 *infertile;* 672.5 *thankless*
fruitlessly 672.7 *ungratefully;* 563.11 *unproductively;* 247.12 *unsuccessfully*
fruitlessness 238.4 *futility;* 563.1 *infertility;* 766.3 *waste*
fruitlike 80.7
fruit of someone's loins 561.6 *progeny*
fruit picker 43.16 *farm worker;* 44.13 *horticulturist*
Fruits 80
fruits 80.1
fruit salad 25.35 *dessert*
fruit seller 80.4 *fruit eating*
fruit selling 80.4 *fruit eating*
fruits of the earth 80.1 *fruits*
fruit squash 498.5 *sweet drink*
fruit stall 557.17 *food shop*
fruit structure 80.3
fruit tea 558.3 *tea*
fruit tree 44.10; 79.1 *tree*
fruit wall 80.3 *fruit structure*
fruity 44.17 *botanical;* 502.4 *fragrant;* 80.7 *fruitlike;* 796.12 *indecent*
frumpish 408.15 *untidy*
frumpy 724.8 *inelegant*
frustrate 113.21, 347.3 *counteract;* 378.8 *hinder;* 604.7 *thwart*
frustrated 604.9 *disappointed*
frustrated expectations 604.1 *disappointment*
frustrating 347.4 *counteracting;* 604.11 *disappointing*
frustratingly 604.13 *disappointingly*
frustration 347.1 *counteraction;* 604.1 *disappointment;* 247.1 *failure;* 335.2 *futile effort;* 378.1 *hindrance;* 36.12 *stress*
frustration test 36.5 *psychological test*
frustrator 378.7 *hinderer*
frustule 84.3 *plant body*
frustum 27.45 *curved surface;* 20.9 *miscellaneous architectural features;* 27.46 *polyhedron;* 215.1 *remainder*
fruticose 84.8 *lichenoid*
fruticose lichen 84.6 *lichen*
fry 70.5 *aquatic animal;* 493.14 *be hot;* 25.55 *cook;* 555.4 *young animal;* 74.3 *young fish*
frying 25.8 *cooking technique*
frying in hell 16.64 *convicted*
frying pan 25.6 *kitchen equipment;* 410.15 *pot*
fry over lightly 25.55 *cook*
fry sunny side up 25.55 *cook*
fry-up 412.2 *mixed thing*
F star 29.13 *luminosity*
f-stop 41.18 *exposure time*
FTP 40.16 *Internet*
fuchsia 540.6 *purple;* 535.1 *red*
fuchsine 42.6 *dye*
fuck 561.14 *have sex;* 593.29 *make love;* 712.15 *miscellaneous swearwords*
fuck all 195.2 *nothing*
fucked 357.15 *destroyed;* 335.10 *powerless*
fucked-up 486.4 *bungled;* 408.19 *mixed-up;* 335.10 *powerless;* 238.1 *useless*
fucking 593.5 *desire*
fucking hell 712.15 *miscellaneous swearwords*
fuck it 712.15 *miscellaneous swearwords*
fuck me 712.15 *miscellaneous swearwords*
fuck off 313.1 *depart;* 313.15 *go!;* 371.33 *go away!;* 712.15 *miscellaneous swearwords*
fuck up 486.7 *be clumsy;* 408.23 *confuse;* 245.4 *impair;* 274.19 *make a mistake;* 351.1 *misuse*
fuck-up 274.10 *blunder;* 408.6 *mix-up;* 378.2 *obstacle*
fuckwit 459.3 *foolish person;* 456.5 *ignorant person*
fuck with 245.4 *impair*
fuckwitted 456.6 *ignorant*
fuck you 712.15 *miscellaneous swearwords*
fucoid 84.7 *algal*
fucoxanthin 33.18 *pigment;* 84.3 *plant body*
fuddle 690.9 *be intoxicating;* 457.10 *bemuse;* 690.8 *get drunk*
fuddled 690.2 *slightly drunk*
fudge 789.7 *account;* 479.1 *be equivocal;* 634.7 *be evasive;* 498.4 *confectionery;* 96.16 *delude;* 702.11 *practise sophistry;* 25.41 *sweet;* 700.28 *trick*
fudge cake 25.36 *cake*
fudge the issue 699.27 *evade*
fudging the issue 699.13 *evasion*
Fuel 437
fuel 330.13; **437.1**; **437.11**; 334.12 *generate power;* 28.35 *heat;* 213.5 *make bigger;* 435.1 *materials;* 436.5 *provision;* 439.6 *store*
fuel assembly 28.73 *nuclear reactor*
fuel cell 28.43 *electrical conduction;* 334.7 *electrical power;* 437.4 *electricity;* 32.19 *electrochemistry;* 39.29 *power source*
fuel-efficient 437.10 *powered*
fuel element 28.73 *nuclear reactor*
fuel filter 256.10 *cleaning object*
fuel injection 437.6 *oil*
fuel rod 334.8, 437.7 *nuclear power;* 28.73 *nuclear reactor*
fuel ship 586.24 *warship*
fuel stop 61.6 *motor-racing terms*
fuel to the flame 436.1 *provision*
fuel up 439.6 *store*
fug 493.1 *heat;* 503.1 *stench*
fugacious 278.6 *transient*
fugacity 278.1 *transience*
fugal 125.12 *imitative*
fuggy 493.9 *hot;* 503.3 *stinking*
fugitate 371.4 *ostracize*
fugitation 371.19 *ostracism*
fugitive 372.16 *apart;* 634.17 *avoider;* 634.18 *avoiding;* 526.6 *disappearing;* 389.3 *escaper;* 389.8 *escaping;* 633.7 *the hunted;* 278.6 *transient;* 96.8 *unreal*
fugitively 389.9; 526.8 *fleetingly*
fugleman 579.14 *leader;* 121.5 *superior*
fugue 125.1 *imitation;* 333.13 *slow thing;* 36.14 *trance*
fugue state 36.14 *trance*
Führer 400.4 *absolute ruler;* 579.14 *leader*
Fujiyama 10.13 *shrine*
fulcrum 307.4 *axle;* 173.1 *centre;* 123.3 *chief thing;* 413.2 *supporting part*
fulfil 340.4 *act;* 309.9 *close down;* 204.10, 232.4 *complete;* 230.5 *perfect;* 609.8 *satisfy;* 217.4 *suffice*
fulfil expectations 706.22 *be the answer*
fulfilled 622.20; 230.1 *perfect;* 609.4 *satisfied*
fulfilling 609.5 *satisfying*
fulfilment 312.17 *achievement;* 309.1 *closure;* 232.1 *completeness;* 232.3 *completion;* 609.1, 622.7 *satisfaction;* 217.7 *sufficiency*
fulfil one's duty 810.16 *do one's duty*
fulguration 380.5 *violent weather*
fuliginous 532.1 *black;* 533.1 *grey*
full 232.8; 150.1 *broad;* 510.8 *deep;* 416.6 *dense;* 721.11 *descriptive;* 222.10 *detailed;* 324.9 *directly;* 557.26 *eating;* 219.6 *excessive;* 158.16 *fat;* 217.3 *filled;* 406.11 *loaded;* 507.6 *loud;* 516.6 *melodious;* 230.1 *perfect;* 609.4 *satisfied;* 309.13 *stopped;* 204.6 *whole*
full armour 384.7 *armour*
fullback 66.3 *football player;* 58.2 *hockey player;* 46.7 *offence;* 64.4 *rugby player*
full-ball 65.9 *billiard*
full-ball aim 65.2 *billiards play*
full-bellied 158.16 *fat*
full blast 507.9 *loudly;* 507.1 *loudness*
full bloom 78.5 *flowering*
full blow 78.5 *flowering*
full-blown 158.15 *big;* 190.7 *bigger;* 232.7 *complete*
full-bodied 152.2 *dense;* 558.17 *drinkable*
full-bodied wine 558.9 *wine*
full-bosomed 158.16 *fat*
full capacity 232.2 *fullness*
full career 332.8 *speed*
full chorus 507.9 *loudly;* 507.1 *loudness*
full circle 179.2 *circle;* 306.3 *orbit;* 307.1 *rotation*
full-coloured 529.11 *colourful*
full complement 232.2 *fullness;* 127.1 *inclusion*
full course 204.3 *whole situation*
full coverage 127.1 *inclusion*
full crew 232.2 *fullness*
full cycle 179.2 *circle*
full details 739.3 *openness*
full dress 551.3, 656.4 *formal dress*
full-dress uniform 551.3 *formal dress*
full extent 232.2 *fullness*
full-face 525.3 *external appearance*
full-faced 158.16 *fat;* 167.6 *front*
full-face picture 167.2 *face*
full-face portrait 19.10 *art subject*
full-fledged 190.7 *bigger;* 232.7 *complete*
full-frontal 167.6 *front*
full gale 31.14 *windiness*
full-grown 556.11 *adult;* 158.15 *big;* 190.7 *bigger;* 232.7 *complete;* 243.20 *developed*
full growth 158.2 *bigness*
full head of steam 334.4 *energy*
full house 69.3 *card game terms;* 232.2 *fullness;* 21.33 *theatregoer;* 21.13 *theatrical performance*
full length 232.2 *fullness;* 148.4 *length*
full-length 148.1 *long*
full-length mirror 28.29 *optical element;* 518.8 *reflection*
full-length novel 356.5 *work of art*
full-length portrait 19.10 *art subject*
full lick 332.8 *speed*
full list 204.5 *unit*
full load 232.2 *fullness*
full meal 557.12 *meal*
full measure 232.2 *fullness;* 217.7 *sufficiency*
full military rites 583.1 *burial*
full moon 29.17 *moon;* 522.4 *natural light*
full name 721.8 *name*
full nelson 360.1 *retention;* 52.5 *wrestling*
fullness 232.2; 150.4 *breadth;* 158.5 *fatness;* 217.8 *plenty;* 152.5 *thickness;* 204.1 *whole*
full of 232.8 *full*
full of beans 342.18 *active;* 259.1 *healthy;* 338.4 *vigorous*
full of difficult words 266.2 *obscure*
full of energy 334.15
full of flavour 495.11 *tastily*
full of forgiveness 627.6 *pitying*
full of grace 8.13 *divine*
full of guilt 808.6 *penitent*
full of hate 594.10 *hating;* 651.10 *malevolent;* 624.15 *resentful*
full of holes 183.6 *concave*
full of hope 756.14 *auspicious;* 756.17 *auspiciously;* 474.5 *expecting;* 610.11 *hopeful*
full of joy 597.4 *happy*
full of labour 576.11 *laborious*
full of loathing 651.10 *malevolent*
full of malice 594.10 *hating*
full of meaning 694.6 *meaningful*
full of mercy 627.6 *pitying*
full of news 741.14 *journalistic*
full of noise 507.6 *loud*
full of Old Nick 236.5 *harmful*
full of oneself 673.11 *cocky*
full of pep 338.4 *vigorous*
full of potential 756.14 *auspicious*
full of praises 9.9 *worshipful*
full of promise 756.14 *auspicious;* 756.17 *auspiciously*
full of regrets 808.6 *penitent*
full of remorse 808.6 *penitent*
full of revenge 651.13 *merciless*
full of ruses 645.4 *cunning*
full of sin 804.11 *wicked*
full of snares 645.4 *cunning*
full of stamina 342.20 *industrious*
full of steam 259.1 *healthy*
full of surprises 630.8 *surprising*
full of the devil 236.5 *harmful*
full of vitality 342.18 *active;* 259.1 *healthy;* 423.4 *powerful*
full of years 296.11 *old*
full opportunity 250.5 *scope*
full out 232.10 *fully*
full pardon 649.1 *forgiveness;* 749.2 *peace offering*
full particulars 222.1 *circumstances*
full pelt 332.8 *speed;* 338.6 *with vigour*
full play 250.5 *scope*
full pressure 576.4 *exertion*
full quota 232.2 *fullness;* 127.1 *inclusion*
full radiator 28.40 *heating effect*
full report 739.2 *divulgence*
full sail 332.8 *speed*
full satisfaction 785.1 *payment*
full-scale 158.15 *big;* 232.7 *complete*
full scope 250.5 *scope*
full set 127.1 *inclusion*
full settlement 785.1 *payment*

full size 158.2 *bigness*; 232.2 *fullness*
full-size 158.15 *big*
full skirt 551.6 *skirt*
full speed 332.8 *speed*
full speed ahead 638.18 *here goes!*; 332.14 *swiftly*
full steam ahead 338.6 *with vigour*
full stop 301.1 *motionlessness*; 742.7 *punctuation*; 372.5 *separator*
full stride 47.1 *track events*
full-throated 510.8 *deep*; 507.6 *loud*; 515.7 *ululant*; 514.16 *vociferous*
full tide 91.2 *tide*
full tilt 342.22 *actively*; 324.9 *directly*
full to bursting 232.8 *full*
full-toned 516.6 *melodious*
full to overflowing 232.8 *full*
full toss 53.8 *delivery*; 330.5 *throw*
full to the brim 232.8 *full*
full turn 57.5 *horizontal bar*
full up 557.26 *eating*; 217.3 *filled*; 232.8 *full*; 609.4 *satisfied*
full value 232.2 *fullness*
full view 204.3 *whole situation*
full volume 232.2 *fullness*
full-wave rectifier 39.21 *rectifier*
fully **232.10**; 416.10 *densely*; 406.14 *internally*; 222.19 *meticulously*; 204.11 *wholly*
fully armed 243.18 *prepared*
fully charged 232.8 *full*
fully comprehensive 138.15 *general*; 204.6 *whole*
fully developed 190.7 *bigger*
fully dressed 243.18 *prepared*
fully engaged 342.19 *busy*
fully fashioned 551.31 *styled*
fully fledged 190.7 *bigger*; 232.7 *complete*; 243.20 *developed*
fully furnished 243.18 *prepared*
fully grown 190.7 *bigger*; 232.7 *complete*
fully laden 232.8 *full*
fully mature 230.1 *perfect*
fully occupied 342.19 *busy*
fully occupied person 342.10 *busy person*
fully restored 204.8 *sound*
fully ripe 230.1 *perfect*
fully trained 243.18 *prepared*
fulmar 72.3 *water bird*
fulminate 624.11 *be angry*; 507.8 *be loud*; 330.30 *blow up*; 712.6 *vilify*
fulmination 712.3 *vilification*
fulsome 669.18 *approving*; 658.9 *deferential*
fulsomely 658.16 *deferentially*
fulsomeness 658.4 *deference*
Fulton Street 779.1 *market*
fulvous 534.1 *brown*; 537.2 *yellowish*
fumble 486.7 *be clumsy*; 486.9 *bungling*; 46.9 *play*; 492.11 *touch*
fumbler 486.10 *unskilled person*
fumbling 486.3 *clumsy*
fume 342.12 *be active*; 624.11 *be angry*; 493.15 *burn*; 432.27 *give off*; 371.14 *let out*; 262.2 *make haste*; 327.3 *turbulence*
fumigant 394.3 *prophylactic*
fumigate 432.26 *aerate*; 501.5 *deodorize*; 257.6 *make hygienic*; 255.10, 256.15 *purify*
fumigated 501.3 *odourless*
fumigation 256.2 *cleaning*; 257.1 *hygiene*; 501.1 *odourlessness*; 255.2 *purification*; 432.10 *vaporization*
fumigator 501.2 *deodorant*
fuming 624.16 *angry*; 432.18 *miasmic*; 327.17 *turbulent*; 380.6 *violent*
fumurole 30.25 *eruption*
fumy 432.18 *miasmic*
fun **597.2**; 599.2 *amusement*; 598.3 *cheerfulness*; 654.17 *festive*; 490.1 *physical pleasure*; 490.6 *pleasant*; 69.9 *recreational*
funambulist 336.5 *athlete*
funboard 50.7 *windsurfing*
funboard storm sail 50.7 *windsurfing*
function 340.4 *act*; 348.4 *be an instrument*; 407.23 *be in order*; 346.7 *be operational*; 237.9 *be useful*; 601.1 *celebration*; 601.3 *ceremony*; 40.19 *computing terms*; 348.1 *instrumentality*; 16.2 *jurisdiction*; 27.29 *mathematical function*; 205.9 *participation*; 4.8 *philosophical term*; 446.4 *purpose*; 376.9 *social gathering*; 810.2 *task*; 237.6 *usability*; 349.6 *use*
functional **27.76**; 340.6 *effective*; 27.29 *mathematical function*; 346.10 *operational*; 95.8, 348.8 *practical*; 446.12 *purposive*; 237.1 *useful*
functional analysis 27.30 *calculus*
functional calculus 27.63 *mathematical logic*
functional disease 260.4 *disease*
functional equation 27.27 *equation*
functionalism 1.5 *anthropological concept*; 4.7 *school of thought*; 237.5 *usefulness*
functionalist 1.11 *anthropological*; 4.11 *follower of a doctrine*; 4.14 *of a philosophy*
functionality 348.1 *instrumentality*
functionally 340.8 *effectively*; 27.87 *mathematically*; 346.13 *operationally*; 446.21 *purposively*
functional nervous disorder 36.9 *psychological disorder*
functional psychology 36.1 *psychology*
functional psychosis 36.11 *psychosis*
functionary 578.3 *agent*; 400.3 *leader*; 579.16 *official*
functioning 340.1 *action*; 346.10 *operational*; 348.8 *practical*; 446.12 *purposive*; 349.10 *usable*; 349.6 *use*
functionless 238.1 *useless*
fund 376.25 *assemblage*; 652.5 *charity*; 785.8 *defray*; 392.29 *finance*; 352.6 *find means*; 679.11 *give*; 14.5 *invest*; 439.1, 439.6 *store*; 413.13 *support financially*; 780.19 *treasury*
fundament 175.1 *base*; 168.2 *rear end*
fundamental 175.3 *base*; 405.8 *belonging*; 344.13 *causal*; 123.5 *important*; 93.11, 99.6, 172.11 *intrinsic*; 28.20 *musical note*; 130.35 *rudimentary*; 647.8 *severe*; 255.16 *simple*; 27.70 *universal*
fundamental constant **28.97**
fundamental interaction **28.79**
fundamentalism 7.2 *religiousness*; 647.1 *severity*; 466.4 *social discrimination*
fundamentalist 466.7 *bigot*; 7.5 *Christian*; 7.16 *denominational*; 466.10 *discriminatory*; 7.6 *non-Christian*; 7.15 *religious*
fundamentally 99.14 *at heart*; 175.5 *basically*; 344.14 *causally*; 405.14 *constituently*; 255.20 *homogenously*; 27.87 *mathematically*; 130.42 *principally*; 93.22 *really*; 647.11 *severely*
fundamental nature 93.3 *nature*
fundamental note 18.16 *musical note*
fundamental particle 28.77 *elementary particle*; 402.4 *matter*
fundamentals 123.3 *chief thing*; 95.5 *realities*; 344.3 *rudiment*; 139.4 *specifications*
funded 439.7 *stored*
funded debt 784.2 *national debt*
funder 768.4 *giver*
fund-holder 35.11 *doctor*
fund-holding 789.2 *budgeting*; 35.1 *medicine*
funding 392.6 *financial assistance*
fund-raiser 772.6 *borrower*; 652.5 *charity*; 765.7 *gainer*; 710.4 *requester*; 413.8 *supporter*
fund-raising 710.11 *begging*; 772.1 *borrowing*; 765.1 *gain*; 765.15 *gainful*; 710.3 *solicitation*
funds **780.6**; 352.4 *financial resources*; 440.5 *personal estate*
funds for investment 780.6 *funds*
funds in hand 780.6 *funds*
fundus 175.1 *base*
funebrial 583.11 *funeral*
funeral **583.2**; **583.11**; 582.8 *after death*; 656.3 *formal occasion*
funeral ceremony 583.2 *funeral*
funeral colour 540.1 *purpleness*
funeral dance 22.4 *historic dancing*
funeral director **583.3**; 582.9 *person dealing with the dead*
funeral hymn 583.2 *funeral*
funeral march 333.13 *slow thing*
funeral objects **583.4**
funeral oration 583.2 *funeral*; 603.2 *lament*; 313.9 *parting*
funeral parlour 582.8 *after death*; 583.2 *funeral*
funeral pile 583.1 *burial*
funeral procession 583.2 *funeral*; 132.8 *procession*; 333.13 *slow thing*
funeral pyre 493.6 *fire*
funeral rites 582.7 *dying day*; 583.2 *funeral*
funeral sermon 583.2 *funeral*
funeral service 583.2 *funeral*
funeral urn 583.4 *funeral objects*
funerary 583.11 *funeral*
funerary sculpture 19.12 *sculpture*
funereal 523.10 *dark-coloured*; 583.11 *funeral*; 582.22 *postmortem*; 10.21 *ritualistic*; 532.6 *sad*
funereally **583.12**
fungal **83.9**
fungal antibiotic **83.6**
fungal association **83.5**
fungal body **83.4**
fungal constituent 84.6 *lichen*
fungal disease 83.5 *fungal association*
Fungi **83**; 83.3 *fungi*
fungi **83.3**; 554.9 *classifications of life*
fungicidal 37.14 *counteracting*; 44.18 *herbicidal*
fungicide 83.7 *antifungal agent*; 37.4 *drug type*; 43.14 *pest control*; 382.14 *plant killer*; 44.8 *weedkiller*
fungiform 83.9 *fungal*
fungistat 83.7 *antifungal agent*
fungoid 83.9 *fungal*
fungology 34.1 *life science*
fungosity 83.1 *fungus*
fungous 83.9 *fungal*
fungus **83.1**; 258.4 *dirt*; 375.1 *disintegration*; 77.4 *lower plant*
funicle 77.9 *seed*; 77.5 *stem*
funicular 317.12 *cableway*; 366.10 *elevator*; 304.8 *lift*; 321.1 *railway*; 68.1 *skiing*
funk 614.4 *be a coward*; 612.12 *be fearful*; 614.2 *coward*; 614.1 *cowardice*; 612.1 *fear*; 634.4 *shy*
funker 639.15 *indecisive person*
funk hole 252.5 *refuge*
funkster 18.24 *musician*
fun-loving 490.7 *pleased*
funnel 310.9 *converge*; 579.2 *direct*; 321.5 *locomotive part*; 310.6 *narrowing*; 308.7 *passageway*; 308.21 *provide passage for*; 61.9 *race*; 316.11 *transfer*
funnelling 61.6 *motor-racing terms*
funnily 599.16 *humorously*
funniness 599.1 *humorousness*
funny **599.9**; 598.1 *cheerful*; 118.14 *eccentric*; 599.10 *humorous*; **461.11** *insane*; 600.10 *laughing*; 697.5 *nonsensical*; 272.5 *ridiculous*
funny farm 461.8 *mental hospital*
funny ha-ha 272.5 *ridiculous*
funny house 461.8 *mental hospital*
funny money 780.15 *false money*
funny place 461.8 *mental hospital*
funny side 169.4 *aspect*
funny story 599.5 *joke*
fun time 490.2 *good time*
fur 550.14 *animal covering*; 551.12 *coat*; 258.4 *dirt*; 743.8 *heraldic device*; 71.2 *mammalian characteristic*; 551.14 *neckwear*; 356.7 *produce*; 419.11 *soft thing*
furanose 33.3 *carbohydrate*
furbelow 542.6 *decorative articles*; 164.6 *edge*; 164.2 *edging*
furbish 365.12 *rub*
furcate 311.14 *branch*; 311.9 *branched*
furcation 311.4 *branching*
fur coat 493.3 *heater*
furcula 311.5 *fork*
furculum 311.5 *fork*
furfuraceous 427.16 *mealy*; 411.9 *platelike*
furfuraceously 411.12 *in layers*
fur hat 493.3 *heater*
furious **540.8**; 594.13, 624.16 *angry*; 236.5 *harmful*; 262.3 *hasty*; 380.6 *violent*
furiously 624.18 *angrily*
furious rage 624.4 *anger*
furl 184.9 *fold*; 307.9 *roll*; 184.1 *wrinkle*
furl a sail 50.15 *sail*
fur-lined 493.13 *heated*
furlough 371.2 *dismiss*; 371.18 *dismissal*; 263.1 *ease*; 98.5 *leave of absence*; 757.2 *permit*; 708.6 *termination*; 580.2 *time off*
furnace 24.6 *ceramic workshop*; 493.6 *fire*; 28.35 *heat*; 379.1 *trap*; 577.1 *workshop*
furnish 243.5 *equip*; 352.6 *find means*; 356.10 *produce*; 436.5 *provision*; 752.11 *volunteer*
furnish a good excuse 714.8 *justify*
furnished 243.18 *prepared*; 436.8 *provisional*
furnishing 438.7 *equipment*; 243.11 *fitting out*; 436.1 *provision*; 436.7 *provisioning*
furnishings 211.3 *additional item*; 23.1 *furniture*
furniture **23.1**; 438.7 *equipment*; 440.4 *possessions*
Furniture and Woodwork **23**
furniture cover 550.12 *protective covering*
furniture-designing 23.1 *furniture*
furniture factory 23.1 *furniture*
furniture-maker 23.13 *carpenter*
furniture-making 23.1 *furniture*
furniture polish 256.9 *cleaning agent*; 550.3 *coating*; 421.10 *polish*
furniture store 23.1 *furniture*
furniture style **23.7**
furore 328.5 *commotion*; 327.2 *tumult*
furred up 258.7 *dirty*
furrier 550.17 *coverer*; 551.26 *fashion designer*
furriness 419.9 *smoothness*
furrow **184.2**; 146.2, 146.5 *crack*; 43.11 *farmland*; 420.12 *make rough*; 184.3, 184.10 *pleat*; 420.8 *rough ground*; 184.8 *wrinkle*
furrowed 420.2 *coarse*; 146.7 *cracked*; 184.6 *wrinkly*
furry 420.3 *barbed*; 419.3 *smooth*
furry friend 70.2 *animal*
further **302.8**; **392.28**; 211.8 *additional*; 211.10 *additionally*; 145.8 *distant*; 145.10 *distantly*; 413.14 *give moral support*; 244.1 *improve*; 265.16 *make easy*; 134.4 *protract*
furtherance **392.8**; 302.12 *advance*; 302.14 *development*; 244.5 *improvement*; 413.6 *moral support*; 134.2 *protraction*
further education college 6.12 *educational institution*
furthering 302.12 *advance*; 392.33 *helpful*
furthermore 211.10 *additionally*
furthermost 145.8 *distant*
further oneself 302.7 *make one's way*
further one's purpose 237.9 *be useful*
further promote 6.22 *educate*
further reflection 244.7 *reconsideration*
further throw 765.2 *augmentation*
furthest **166.6**; 145.8 *distant*; 131.24 *limiting*
furthest point **166.3**
furtive 700.34 *deceiving*; 189.5 *devious*; 737.10 *secretive*
furtively 189.9 *deviously*; 737.16 *stealthily*
furtiveness 700.1 *deception*; 189.3 *deviousness*; 737.2 *secretiveness*
Fury 357.7 *agent of destruction*
fury 594.5, 624.4 *anger*; 590.6 *bad feeling*; 625.3 *irascible person*; 380.1 *violence*; 380.4 *violent creature*; 651.9 *vixen*
fuscous 534.1 *brown*
fuse 197.19 *become one*; 493.14 *be hot*; 374.5 *combine*; 39.35 *conduct*; 587.15 *explosive*; 747.16 *join*; 437.2 *lighter*; 431.24 *melt*; 412.8 *mix*; 39.28 *plug*; 252.4 *safety device*
fused 374.7 *combined*; 412.12 *mixed*
fusible 431.21 *liquefiable*
fusiform 83.10 *of fungi*; 425.1 *sharp*; 151.3 *tapered*
fusil 743.8 *heraldic device*; 587.10 *historical gun*
fusilier 586.13 *historical soldiery*
fusillade 381.2 *fire*; 381.15 *firing*; 330.7 *shot*
fusing 431.8 *fluidification*; 431.20 *liquefying*
fusion 747.7 *association*; 374.1 *combination*; 431.8 *fluidification*; 18.8 *jazz*; 412.2 *mixed thing*; 412.1 *mixture*; 28.72 *nuclear fission*; 334.8 *nuclear power*; 18.9 *popular music*; 28.37 *temperature*
fusion bomb 334.8 *nuclear power*
fusion energy 28.11 *energy*
fusion reaction 28.72 *nuclear fission*
fusion reactor **28.76**
fuss **327.4**; 751.6 *argue*; 751.2 *argument*; 342.12 *be active*; 327.21 *be agitated*; 328.5 *commotion*; 408.9 *disorder*; 727.7 *exaggerate*; 727.1 *exaggeration*; 262.4 *haste*; 342.3 *nimbleness*; 113.4 *objection*; 467.2 *overestimate*
fuss and bother 342.3 *nimbleness*
fuss-budget 342.11 *meddler*
fussily 222.19 *meticulously*
fussiness 244.5 *improvement*
fussing 670.6 *fault-finding*; 327.16 *restless*
fussing over 471.5 *solicitude*
fuss over 471.14 *be solicitous*
fusspot 466.6 *discriminating person*; 342.11 *meddler*
fussy 342.18 *active*; 222.10 *detailed*; 576.11 *laborious*; 542.10 *ornate*; 230.2 *perfectionist*; 264.14 *troublesome*

fussy eater 264.9 difficult person; 557.18 eater
fust 503.1 stench
fustian 542.2 affectation; 727.15 bombastic; 270.3 diffuse; 542.10 ornate
fustigate 814.3 hit
fustily 503.6 stinkingly
fustiness 503.1 stench
fusty 258.7 dirty; 503.3 stinking
futhark 5.14 alphabet
futile **238.2**; **611.7**; 247.10 failed; 486.1 unskilful; 238.1 useless; 236.1 worthless
futile activity 342.9 overactivity
futile effort **335.2**; 247.1 failure
futile exploit 335.2 futile effort
futilely 247.12 unsuccessfully
futilitarianism 238.5 waste of effort
futility **238.4**; 247.1 failure; 335.1 powerlessness; 238.3 uselessness; 236.7 worthlessness
futon 23.6 bed
future **283.11**; **756.15**; 474.7 expected; 283.1 future time; 294.13 later; 593.11 loved one; 102.6 potential; 5.34 tense
future condition 283.3
future event 283.6
future generation 283.2
future generations 289.6 posterity
future intention 482.3
future interrogative 705.11 question mark
future perfect 5.34 tense
future state 283.3 future condition; 554.5 life cycle; 582.14 the spiritual world
Future Time 283
future time **283.1**; 286.1 different time
future years 283.1 future time
futurism 295.2 trendiness
futurist 295.9 modern person
futuristic 17.16 literary; 295.10 new
futuristically 295.21 newly
futurity 283.1 future time
futurologist 475.9 forecaster
fuzz 415.7 light thing
fuzzily 453.25 indeterminately; 266.4 obscurely; 161.6 shapelessly; 404.15 texturally
fuzziness 404.2 grain; 453.14 indeterminacy; 521.4 invisibility; 524.2 murk; 266.1 obscurity; 528.6 opaqueness; 161.1 shapelessness
fuzzy 420.3 barbed; 696.4 difficult; 521.2 difficult to see; 404.11 fluffy; 453.6 indeterminate; 524.6 murky; 266.2 obscure; 528.2 shady; 161.5 shapeless; 489.10 sleepy
fuzzy logic 40.17 artificial intelligence
fuzzy tongue 690.15 crapulence
fylfot 743.6 national emblem; 11.6 talisman
fylker 86.5 state

G 414.5 gravity; 201.10 thousand
gab 731.7 be talkative; 731.3 talk
gabber 731.4 talker
gabbiness 731.1 talkativeness
gabble 731.7 be talkative; 731.3 talk; 697.6 talk nonsense
gabbling 731.5 talkative
gabby 731.5 talkative
gabelle 790.9 historical taxes
gaberdine coat 551.12 coat
gabion 384.11 fortification
gabionade 384.11 fortification
gable 174.3 architectural summit; 20.9 miscellaneous architectural features; 361.5 projecting object
gable end 20.9 miscellaneous architectural features
gable roof 550.7 overhead covering
Gabriel 8.6 angel
Gadarene swine 382.9 animal killing
gadget 484.3 expedient plan; 348.2 instrument; 402.5 object; 438.1 tool
gadget play 46.9 play
gadoid 74.13 fishlike
Gael 564.9 British inhabitant
Gaelic Athletic Association 58.7 hurling
gaff 55.3 fishing tackle; 50.3 parts of a sailing boat; 425.8 sharp-pointed thing; 587.8 sharp weapon; 425.16 use a sharp tool
gaffe 459.2 act of folly; 274.10, 544.6 blunder; 486.9 bungling; 657.5 nonobservance
gaffer 579.15 manager; 121.5 superior
gaff rig 50.3 parts of a sailing boat
gaff-rigged 50.10 sailing
gaffsail 50.3 parts of a sailing boat
gag **251.12**; 599.5 joke; 251.5 means of restraint; 506.2 silence; 697.2 solecism; 730.15 strike dumb; 697.6 talk nonsense; 371.15 vomit
gaga 556.14 aged; 328.16 deranged; 459.5 foolish; 457.7 intellectually subnormal
gage 691.6 drug
gagged 251.15 detained; 730.11 speechless
gagging 371.23 vomiting
gaggle 72.13 assemblage of birds; 515.5 sing
gag man 21.26 dramatist
gagster 599.6 humorist
gag writer 21.26 dramatist; 599.6 humorist
Gaia 30.5 earth
gaiety 601.1 celebration; 598.3 cheerfulness; 597.1 happiness; 654.1 sociability
gaily 598.9 cheerfully; 597.9 joyfully
gain **765.1**; **765.9**; **813.14**; 312.9 achieve; 302.12 advance; 392.21 be helpful; 237.8, 237.10, 797.13 benefit; 39.15 circuit function; 797.21 do well; 211.4 extra; 781.13 get rich; 345.8 grow; 345.3 growth; 213.1, 213.4 increase; 788.2 money received; 356.7 produce; 765.5 profit; 436.1 provision; 769.9, 788.7 receive; 778.1 sell; 776.1 trade; 813.5 turnover; 781.5 wealth
gain acceptance 450.10 be believed
gain access 308.19 open up
gain admittance 314.9 enter
gain a flying start 293.7 be early
gain a foothold 308.23 find an opening
gain a footing 395.8 influence
gain a hearing 395.8 influence
gain altitude 304.19 take off
gain a reward 813.12 be rewarded
gain ascendancy over 623.26 outdo
gain credit 669.17 meet with approval
gained 769.13, 788.6 received
gainer 765.7
gain from 237.11 find useful
gainful **765.15**; 392.34 beneficial; 237.4 profitable; 788.6 received; 246.14, 813.15 rewarding
gain full play 395.10 be a prevailing influence
gainfully **765.20**; 788.8, 813.20 profitably; 246.16 successfully
gainfulness 765.1 gain
gain ground 765.10 augment; 213.4 increase; 302.3 press on
gain height 765.10 augment; 302.3 press on; 304.19 take off
gain immortality 202.9 be infinite
gaining 765.18 acquisitional; 765.1 gain
gaining altitude 304.4 taking off
gaining ground 765.2 augmentation
gaining height 304.1 ascent; 765.2 augmentation; 304.23 rising
gaining on 765.2 augmentation
gaining time 765.2 augmentation
gaining weight 765.2 augmentation
gain in value 765.10 augment; 765.2 augmentation; 213.4 increase
gain mastery 395.10 be a prevailing influence
gain on 332.6 accelerate; 765.10 augment; 302.9 maintain progress
gain one's end 246.6 be successful
gain one's freedom 391.5 be liberated
gain one's goal 246.6 be successful
gain one's spurs 669.17 meet with approval
gain power 334.10 be powerful; 12.12 take authority
gains 765.5 profit; 781.5 wealth
gainsay 701.13 argue; 704.9 deny; 709.6 dissent; 113.18 object; 753.6 protest; 708.11 rebut
gainsayer 708.9 negativist; 113.11 opposer; 709.4 refuser
gainsaying 709.2 dissent; 753.1 protest; 708.3 rebuttal; 708.19 rebutting
gain self-determination 85.17 become a nation
gain strength 213.4 increase
gain the friendship of 569.13 befriend
gain the upper hand 395.10 be a prevailing influence; 623.26 outdo; 396.20 take authority
gain the weather gauge 323.9 navigate
gain time 765.10 augment; 293.7 be early; 294.8 delay; 302.4 make good time
gain weight 765.10 augment; 190.6 become bigger; 414.12 be heavy
gait **300.12**; 59.10 dressage
gaiter 68.5 ski equipment
gaiters 551.20 legwear
gal 568.2 female
gala 601.1 celebration; 656.3 formal occasion; 654.5 party; 376.9 social gathering
galactic 29.36 astronomical; 138.16 universal
galactically 29.39 astronomically
galactic centre 29.7 galaxy
galactic latitude 29.5 celestial sphere
galactic longitude 29.5 celestial sphere
galactic nebula 29.7 galaxy
gala day 601.5 anniversary
Galahad 572.4 celibate person; 799.3 honourable person
gala night 21.13 theatrical performance
gala performance 656.3 formal occasion
galaxy **29.7**; 376.28 cluster; 208.4 throng
gale 332.11 swift thing; 379.1 trap; 380.5 violent weather; 31.13 wind strength
gale-force 31.47 windy
Galen 394.15 healer
Galenic 394.18 medical
galenical 394.2 medicine; 37.5 prescription
gale warning 711.2 danger signal
Galilean satellite 29.18 satellite
Galilean telescope 29.24 telescope
galilee porch 20.10 church architecture
Galina Ulanova 22.14 famous ballet dancers
gall 651.4 bitterness; 660.2 cheek; 365.15 grind; 236.11 harmfulness; 594.1 hate; 625.1 irascibility; 624.1 resentment; 559.2 secreted substance; 499.2 unpalatability
gall and wormwood 596.1 dislike; 499.3 sour thing
gallant 613.10 chivalrous; 613.9 courageous; 658.7 courteous; 658.6 courteous person; 593.19 enamoured; 593.9 lover; 471.9 solicitous
gallant company 586.17 army person
gallantly 658.14 courteously
gallantry 613.8 courageous act; 658.1 courtesy; 593.6 courtship; 613.2 heroism; 471.5 solicitude
galleass 586.25 historical naval ships
galleon 586.25 historical naval ships
gallery 317.7 arcade; 21.18 auditorium; 439.5 collection; 376.31 exhibition; 565.7 room; 738.8 showplace; 21.33 theatregoer; 518.9 viewpoint
gallery forest 79.4 trees
galley 25.3 kitchen; 565.7 room
galleys 814.7 punishment
galley salve 387.5 subjected person
galley slave 323.8 boatman; 342.10 busy person; 401.7 slave; 578.1 worker
galliard 22.4 historic dancing
Gallicism 5.26 dialect
galliform 72.21 avian
galligaskins 551.20 legwear; 551.9 trousers
gallimaufry 412.3 miscellany
gallinaceous 72.21 avian
galling 365.3 grinding; 365.11 rough
gallium arsenide 39.4 semiconductor
gallop 332.9 acceleration; 332.4 be swift; 300.12 gait; 59.16 ride; 300.15 walk
gallop at 381.1 attack
galloper 332.12 swift animal
galloping 332.1 swift
galloping guns 587.11 guns
galloping rhythm 260.10 cardiovascular disease
galloway 59.5 pony
gallows 382.5 execution; 361.4 hanger; 814.16 instrument of execution
gallows humour 599.3 wit
Gallup poll™ 469.10 vote
gally 660.14 cheeky
galop 22.4 historic dancing
galore 208.9 ample; 217.8 plenty
galoshes 551.19 footwear
galumph 486.7 be clumsy
galvanic electricity 334.7 electrical power
galvanize 488.13 arouse sensation; 331.1 impel; 338.3 invigorate; 483.9 motivate
galvanized 483.12 motivated
galvanizing 483.11 motivational
galvanometer 28.90 ammeter; 39.23 electrical instrument; 26.8 meter
galvanometric 26.16 micrometric
galvanometry 26.2 micrometry
gambit 353.5 attempt; 448.1 experiment; 130.10 introduction; 631.9 tactics; 700.8 trick
gamble 615.5 be rash; 107.1 chance; 476.3 conjecture; 475.12 divine; 254.10 endanger; 254.9 face danger; 448.13 invent; 102.7 make possible; 69.10 play; 615.2 rash move; 453.22 risk; 776.2 speculate; 476.5 suppose; 353.3 tackle; 107.12 take a chance; 104.10 think likely; 453.15 unreliability
gambler 475.9 forecaster; 615.3 rash person; 476.4 theorist
gambling 107.7 calculation of chance; 476.3 conjecture; 254.5 danger; 107.3 equal chance; 299.3 irregular thing; 776.8 speculation; 354.2 undertaking
gambling chance 107.4 fair chance
gambling den 804.8 wicked place
gambling game 69.1 game
gamboge 537.7 yellow pigment
gambol 22.15 dance
gambrel roof 20.6 roof
game **60.5**; **69.1**; 613.13 adventurous; 70.1 animals; 353.8 attempting; 668.9 butt; 700.11 hoax; 337.10 ill; 640.12 indomitable; 576.3 job; 25.20 meat; 482.6 objective; 484.4 plot; 45.1 sport; 645.2 stratagem; 631.9 tactics; 63.4 tennis terms; 633.7 the hunted; 638.4 undaunted; 636.1 willing
game bag 410.8 bag
game bird 72.4 table bird
game birds 60.5 game
gamecock 586.4 fighting animal
game fish 74.2 fish; 74.8 food fish; 25.17 freshwater fish
game fishing 55.1 angling; 633.2 chase; 74.7 fishing
game fowl 72.4 table bird
gamekeeper 252.3, 384.15 protector
game licence 60.2 hunting
gameness 613.4 adventurousness; 640.4 stamina; 636.6 willingness
game of chance 107.3 equal chance
game of golf 56.1 golf
game of tenpins 51.4 bowling
game plan 46.14 miscellaneous terms; 631.9 tactics
game-playing 40.17 artificial intelligence
game reserve 70.8 animal welfare; 359.1 preservation
game rules 631.9 tactics
games 47.5 competition; 576.5 exercise
Games and Pastimes 69
games computer 40.3 computer
game, set, and match 246.2 victory
game shooting 60.2 hunting
game show 692.25 broadcast material; 21.7 show
game-show host 21.29 entertainer
game show presenter 705.9 questioner
gamesmanship 645.1 cunning; 631.9 tactics
games room 565.7 room
gamete 34.7 cell; 84.4 reproductive body
game terms 63.5 real tennis
game theory 40.17 artificial intelligence; 4.7 school of thought
game time 46.5
gametophyte 82.4 moss plant
game to the last 640.12 indomitable
game warden 70.10 animal welfarist
game-winning 246.15 victorious
gaminess 496.1 piquancy; 503.2 something that makes an unpleasant smell
gaming 107.3 equal chance
gaming table 23.4 table
gamma 41.10 graininess
gamma camera 41.16 camera
gammadion 11.6 talisman
gamma distribution 27.59 probability distribution
gamma function 27.29 mathematical function
gamma-ray astronomy 29.1 astronomy
gamma rays 28.13 electromagnetic radiation; 28.70 radioactivity
gammon 25.30 bacon; 699.15 nonsense
gammy 337.10 ill
gamut 132.2 consecution; 18.20 key; 18.16 musical note; 141.7 range
gamy 496.9 piquant; 503.4 putrid
gander 43.8 livestock; 518.6 look; 567.16 male animal; 72.10 male bird
gandery 542.6 decorative articles
gandy 675.7 vulgar
gandy dancer 321.9 railway worker
ganef 774.11 dishonest person
gang 750.2 alliance; 376.1 assembly; 376.11 group; 578.4 personnel
gang along 313.1 depart
gangbang 796.7 sexual assault

ganger 579.15 *manager*; 578.1 *worker*
Ganges 90.5 *other major rivers*
ganging up 750.11 *allied*
gangland 804.7 *criminality*
gangliness 153.7 *thinness*
gangling 486.3 *clumsy*; 154.12 *tall*; 153.1 *thin*
gangly 154.12 *tall*
gang member 662.9 *criminal*; 774.11 *dishonest person*; 798.6 *evil person*; 382.11 *murderer*
gang murder 382.2 *murder*
Gangotri 10.13 *shrine*
gangplank 38.21 *bridge*; 317.2 *route*
gang rape 380.2 *physical violence*; 774.5 *plundering*; 796.7 *sexual assault*
gangrene 258.10 *be dirty*; 245.2 *decay*; 245.9 *dilapidation*; 375.3 *disintegrate*; 375.1 *disintegration*; 260.6 *infection*; 260.15 *ulcer*
gangrenous 260.23 *diseased*; 375.5 *disintegrated*; 375.6 *disintegrating*
gangrenously 375.8 *destructively*
gang rule 16.41 *lawlessness*
gangsta rap 18.9 *popular music*
gangster 662.9 *criminal*; 774.11 *dishonest person*; 800.4 *dishonourable person*; 340.3 *doer*; 691.6 *drug*; 651.8 *malefactor*; 382.11 *murderer*; 804.9 *wicked person*
gang together 747.14 *join with*
gangue 32.24 *ore*
gang up 376.41 *band together*; 750.22 *form an alliance*; 223.14 *keep company with*
gang up with 654.13 *fraternize*; 747.14 *join with*
gang warfare 662.2 *violation of the law*
gangway 38.21 *bridge*; 308.7 *passageway*; 317.2 *route*
gangway ladder 304.9 *ladder*
ganja 691.6 *drug*
gannet 557.18 *eater*; 688.4 *glutton*; 72.3 *water bird*
gannet-like 557.26 *eating*
ganoid scale 74.5 *fish anatomy*
gantry crane 366.9 *lifter*
Ganymede 316.7 *transferor*
gap 183.2 *concave land*; 231.7 *defect*; 94.4, 98.3 *emptiness*; 133.4 *interruption*; 146.1 *interval*; 141.8 *intervening space*; 135.2 *need*; 233.2 *omission*; 308.1 *opening*; 226.3 *pause*; 372.3 *separateness*
gape 146.5 *crack*; 156.14 *deepen*; 146.3 *gulf*; 518.6, 518.13 *look*; 308.18 *open*; 308.1 *opening*; 619.9 *wonder*
gaper 518.11 *observer*
gaping 146.7 *cracked*; 156.8 *deep*; 308.12 *open*; 619.7 *wide-eyed*
gapingly 308.27 *cavernously*
gap in the market 135.2 *need*
gappy 146.7 *cracked*; 133.8 *discontinuous*
garage 38.20 *building*; 320.21 *miscellaneous motoring terms*; 18.9 *popular music*; 359.5 *preserve*; 252.10 *protect*; 410.21 *put in a container*; 565.7 *room*; 439.4 *storage*
garaged 410.20 *containing*
garage sale 791.2 *bargain*; 793.7 *discounter*; 767.2 *disposal of property*; 778.4 *sale*
garaging 320.21 *miscellaneous motoring terms*
Garamond type 5.15 *type style*
garance 42.6 *dye*
Garand rifle 587.11 *guns*
garb 551.1, 551.32 *dress*; 525.3 *external appearance*
garbage 258.4 *dirt*; 767.3 *disposable things*; 58.8 *hockey*; 408.4 *litter*; 441.5 *waste product*
garbage can 767.4 *wastebin*
garbage goal 58.3 *ice hockey*
garbage man 767.6 *rubbish collector*
garbed 551.29 *dressed*
garble 789.7 *account*; 699.9 *falsification*; 699.26 *falsify*; 696.8 *make unintelligible*; 718.5 *misinform*; 720.1 *misinterpret*; 720.2 *misinterpretation*; 212.3 *subtract*; 697.6 *talk nonsense*
garbled 233.4 *incomplete*; 718.7 *misinformed*; 720.3 *misinterpreted*; 264.12 *problematic*; 696.1 *unintelligible*
garbling 699.9 *falsification*; 718.2 *misinformation*; 720.2 *misinterpretation*
gardant 743.13 *heraldic*
garden **44.2**; 62.9 *mountaineer*; 44.14 *practise horticulture*
garden centre 44.2 *garden*
garden chair 44.3 *ornamental garden*
garden city 87.4 *British cities*; 44.2 *garden*; 86.10 *urban area*
gardener 401.6 *domestic servant*; 44.13 *horticulturist*; 356.9 *producer*; 578.1 *worker*
garden flower 78.1 *flower*
garden gate 201.4 *eight*
garden gnome 44.3 *ornamental garden*
garden hose 433.13 *irrigator*
gardenia 502.2 *fragrant thing*
gardening **44.5**; 62.3 *climbing technique*; 44.1 *horticulture*; 62.8 *mountaineering*
garden line 44.6 *garden tool*
Garden of Eden 477.8 *dreamland*; 44.2 *garden*
garden of remembrance 583.5 *cemetery*; 44.2 *garden*
garden of rest 583.5 *cemetery*; 44.2 *garden*
Garden of the Hesperides 44.2 *garden*
garden party 654.5 *party*
garden path 44.3 *ornamental garden*; 317.2 *route*
garden plant **44.9**; 77.2 *plant*
garden roller 187.4 *flattener*; 421.9 *smoother*
garden room 565.7 *room*
garden sculpture 19.12 *sculpture*
garden seat 44.3 *ornamental garden*
garden shed 44.4 *nursery*
garden shop 44.2 *garden*
garden suburb 44.2 *garden*; 87.8 *suburb*
garden tool **44.6**; **438.3**; 438.1 *tool*
garden-variety 271.1 *simple*
garden work 576.1 *work*
Gargantua 158.10 *big person*
Gargantuan 158.15 *big*
gargle 256.9 *cleaning agent*; 37.11 *linctus*; 394.3 *prophylactic*; 255.3 *purifier*
gargoyle 717.6 *image*; 315.7 *outlet*; 546.2 *ugly person*
gari 25.53 *African dish*
garish 522.16 *bright*; 520.2 *clear*; 529.12 *gaudy*; 544.10 *ugly*; 675.7 *vulgar*
garishly 529.18 *colourfully*
garishness 544.3 *ugliness*
garland 78.1 *flower*; 658.12 *greet*; 743.8 *heraldic device*; 743.4 *insignia*; 601.18 *salute*; 794.1 *trophy*
garlic 496.2 *seasoning*; 503.2 *something that makes an unpleasant smell*; 11.6 *talisman*
garlic dip 25.15 *sauce*
garlic salt 496.2 *seasoning*
garlic sausage 25.29 *sausage*
garment 551.1, 551.32 *dress*
Garment District 551.2 *dressing*
garment-maker 551.26 *fashion designer*
garment-making 551.2 *dressing*
garmentworker 551.26 *fashion designer*
garner 439.4 *storage*; 439.6 *store*
garnering 439.4 *storage*
garnet 535.7 *red thing*; 373.7 *tackle*
garnish 211.6 *add*; 211.3 *additional item*; 25.55 *cook*; 495.10 *make taste*; 542.1, 542.12 *ornament*; 496.2 *seasoning*
garnished 542.10 *ornate*
garnishing 211.3 *additional item*
garniture 551.24 *part of garment*
garret 154.8 *high thing*; 565.7 *room*
garrison 586.14 *armed forces*; 384.21 *entrench*; 384.14 *guard*; 252.10 *protect*; 252.3 *protector*
garrisoned 252.6 *safe*
garron 59.5 *pony*
garrotte 814.13 *capital punishment*; 382.19, 814.5 *execute*; 814.16 *instrument of execution*; 382.17 *murder*; 335.8 *overpower*
garrotter 382.11 *murderer*; 814.17 *punisher*
garrotting 382.2 *murder*
garrulity 731.1 *talkativeness*
garrulous 739.11 *disclosing*; 731.5 *talkative*
garrulously 731.10 *talkatively*
garrulousness 731.1 *talkativeness*
garter 373.8 *fastening*; 542.4 *honour*; 551.20 *legwear*; 794.1 *trophy*
garter belt 551.18 *underwear*
garuda 72.9 *fabulous bird*
Gas 432
gas **417.5**; **432.1**; **437.3**; 434.1 *air*; 371.24, 432.5 *belch*; 731.7 *be talkative*; 814.13 *capital punishment*; 366.10 *elevator*; 382.19, 814.5 *execute*; 330.13, 437.1 *fuel*; 437.3 *gas*; 260.8 *indigestion*; 814.16 *instrument of execution*; 435.1 *materials*; 320.21 *miscellaneous motoring terms*; 382.17 *murder*; 334.6 *source of energy*; 503.1 *stench*; 382.7 *suicide*; 731.3 *talk*; 96.4 *theorization*
gas analysis 32.18 *gravimetric analysis*
gasbag 734.8 *chatterer*; 410.19 *inflatable*; 731.4 *talker*
gas balloon **432.13**
gas burner 437.3 *gas*
gas chamber 16.43 *conviction*; 582.4 *death sentence*; 382.5 *execution*; 814.16 *instrument of execution*; 382.15 *slaughterhouse*
gas-cooled reactor 437.7 *nuclear power*; 28.73 *nuclear reactor*
gas discharge 28.46, 39.6 *electric discharge*
gas-discharge tube 28.46, 39.6 *electric discharge*; 39.20 *electron tube*; 28.25 *light source*
gaseity 432.7 *gaseousness*
gaseous **432.16**; 415.2 *insubstantial*; 437.10 *powered*; 32.32 *solid*; 417.1 *sparse*
gaseous medium 434.1 *air*
gaseous nebula 29.8 *interstellar medium*
gaseousness **432.7**; 415.5 *lightness*; 417.3 *sparseness*
gaseous state 432.7 *gaseousness*
gasfield 437.3 *gas*; 439.2 *resource*
gas fire 493.6 *fire*
gas-fired 493.13 *heated*; 437.10 *powered*
gas-fitter 437.9 *power-worker*
gas gangrene 432.6 *aerogastria*
gas gun 43.14 *pest control*
gas-guzzling 437.10 *powered*
gash 146.2, 146.5 *crack*; 308.20 *hole*; 491.11 *inflict pain*; 491.3 *injury*; 183.4, 183.10 *notch*; 372.9 *separate*; 372.3 *separateness*
gas heater 493.3 *heater*
gashed 308.14 *holed*
gasholder 437.3 *gas*; 432.14 *gasworks*; 439.4 *storage*
gasification 432.10 *vaporization*
gasified 432.16 *gaseous*
gasiform 432.16 *gaseous*
gasify **432.25**; 415.10 *lighten*; 417.6 *make sparse*
gas jet 493.6 *fire*; 522.5 *incandescent light*
gasket 50.3 *parts of a sailing boat*
gaslamp 432.14 *gasworks*; 522.5 *incandescent light*
gas laser 28.26 *laser*
gas leakage 389.4 *leak*
gaslight 432.14 *gasworks*; 522.5 *incandescent light*; 28.23 *light*
gaslike 432.16 *gaseous*
gas main 437.3 *gas*
gasman 578.2 *artisan*; 437.9 *power-worker*
gas mantle 522.5 *incandescent light*
gas mask 359.2 *preserver*; 384.6 *protective clothing*; 252.4 *safety device*
gas meter 437.3 *gas*; 26.8 *meter*; 432.15 *vaporimeter*
gas oil 437.6 *oil*
gasolier 432.14 *gasworks*; 522.5 *incandescent light*
gasoline 437.6 *oil*
gasometer 437.3 *gas*; 432.14 *gasworks*; 439.4 *storage*; 432.15 *vaporimeter*
gas oneself 382.21 *commit suicide*
gas oven 493.6 *fire*; 382.15 *slaughterhouse*
gasp 261.5 *be fatigued*; 514.13 *cry*; 514.6 *cry of pain*; 491.12 *express pain*; 513.5 *sound hoarse*; 729.13 *speak in a particular way*; 729.7 *utterance*; 619.9 *wonder*
gasping 261.7 *fatigue*
gasping for breath 261.3 *panting*
gas pipe 437.3 *gas*
gas plant 432.14 *gasworks*
gasp of admiration 619.2 *sign of wonderment*
gas poker 437.3 *gas*
gasproof 252.7 *invulnerable*
gas-propelled 330.19 *propelled*
gas propulsion 330.2 *method of propulsion*
gasp with admiration 619.9 *wonder*
gas ring 493.4 *burner*; 25.5 *cooker*
gasser 734.8 *chatterer*; 731.4 *talker*
gas shell 587.5 *missile weapon*
gassiness 432.7 *gaseousness*; 731.1 *talkativeness*
gassing oneself 382.7 *suicide*
gassy **432.21**; 432.20 *flatulent*; 432.16 *gaseous*; 503.3 *stinking*; 731.5 *talkative*
gas tank 437.3 *gas*
Gastarbeiter 100.7 *new arrival*
gas thermometer 28.89 *thermometer*
gastralgia 260.8 *indigestion*
gastric 559.5 *of a secretion*; 172.10 *visceral*
gastric juice 559.2 *secreted substance*
gastric ulcer 260.8 *indigestion*
gastrin 33.11 *enzyme*
gastritis 260.8 *indigestion*
gastroenteritis 260.4 *disease*; 260.6 *infection*
gastroenterologist 35.13 *medical specialist*
gastroenterology 35.3 *medical specialty*
gastrointestinal disease 260.4 *disease*
gastronome 688.4 *glutton*
gastronomic 25.56 *culinary*; 688.6 *gluttonous*
gastronomically 25.57 *culinarily*; 688.7 *gluttonously*
gastronomy 25.1 *cookery*; 688.2 *epicurism*
gastropod 75.5 *mollusc*; 70.4 *type of animal*
Gastropoda 75.5 *mollusc*
gastropodan 75.19 *molluscan*
gastropodous 75.19 *molluscan*
gastroscope 35.7 *diagnosis*
gastroscopy 35.7 *diagnosis*
gastrotrich 75.6 *worm*
Gastrotricha 75.6 *worm*
gastrula 34.15 *developmental biology*
gastrulation 34.15 *developmental biology*
gas turbine 437.3 *gas*; 38.12 *turbine*
gas vapour 32.3 *phase*
gas vent 30.25 *eruption*
gas warfare 585.8 *warfare*
gasworks **432.14**; 437.3 *gas*; 577.1 *workshop*
gat 587.9 *firearm*; 587.11 *guns*
gate 50.6 *canoeing*; 39.13 *circuit*; 765.4 *earnings*; 43.11 *farmland*; 384.12 *fort*; 59.9 *jumping*; 314.6 *means of entry*; 788.2 *money received*; 308.7 *passageway*; 313.10 *place of departure*; 814.1 *punish*; 68.3 *ski racing*; 39.19 *transistor*; 315.6 *way out*
gateau 25.36 *cake*; 498.3 *dessert*
gate-crash 100.16 *be external*; 654.11 *be sociable*; 314.10 *invade*; 751.7 *pick a fight*; 564.15 *settle*
gate-crasher 793.8 *bargain hunter*; 751.4 *dissenter*; 378.7 *hinderer*; 564.6 *illegal occupant*; 100.8, 314.8 *intruder*; 654.6 *social person*; 109.3 *unconnected person*
gate-crashing 100.12 *external*; 100.4 *externality*
gated 308.15 *providing passage*; 814.20 *punished*
gated crossing 321.2 *track*
gate electrode 39.19 *transistor*
gatehouse 384.12 *fort*
gatekeeper 741.4 *journalist*; 309.5 *person who closes*
gate-leg 23.14 *wooden*
gate-leg table 23.4 *table*
gate money 765.4 *earnings*; 788.2 *money received*; 769.2 *something received*
gate of ivory 699.11 *half-truth*
gate post 314.6 *means of entry*
gateway 40.19 *computing terms*; 314.6 *means of entry*; 40.15 *network*
gather 376.37 *assemble*; 190.6 *become bigger*; 310.10 *come together*; 43.17 *farm*; 504.15 *hear*; 551.35 *make clothing*; 191.5 *make smaller*; 312.8 *meet*; 184.3, 184.10 *pleat*; 300.14 *set in motion*; 439.6 *store*; 31.59 *storm*; 476.5 *suppose*
gather dust 778.2 *be sold*; 341.4 *not act*
gathered 376.46 *assembled*; 191.7 *smaller*; 551.31 *styled*
gathered to one's fathers 582.19 *dead*
gatherer 376.35 *collector*; 765.7 *gainer*
gather food 436.5 *provision*
gather in 765.11 *acquire*; 765.9 *gain*
Gathering 376
gathering 765.3 *acquisition*; 376.1 *assembly*; 734.4 *conference*; 191.8 *contracting*; 191.1 *contraction*; 190.8 *growing*; 376.3, 654.3 *meeting*; 439.4 *storage*; 260.15 *ulcer*; 10.17 *worshipper*
gathering clouds 249.1 *adversity*; 475.7 *bad-luck sign*; 254.6 *danger signal*; 711.1 *warning*
gathering in 765.1 *gain*
gathering of the clans 376.9 *social gathering*
gathering storm 254.6 *danger signal*; 711.1 *warning*

gather momentum 332.6 *accelerate*
gather notes 243.2 *do the groundwork*
gather round 376.39 *come together*
gather speed 332.6 *accelerate*
gather together 765.11 *acquire*; 376.39 *come together*
gather up 366.4
gather way 300.13 *be in motion*; 323.9 *navigate*; 302.3 *press on*
gating 814.7 *punishment*
Gatling gun 587.12 *historical guns*
gator 73.5 *crocodilian*
GATT 755.3 *alliance*; 776.9 *bargaining*
gauche 486.3 *clumsy*; 497.6 *coarse*; 675.8 *discourteous*; 544.7 *graceless*; 456.6 *ignorant*; 487.2 *not customary*; 538.3 *raw*
gauchely 497.11 *tastelessly*
gaucheness 497.4 *bad taste*; 544.1 *inelegance*
gaucherie 544.6 *blunder*; 456.1 *ignorance*; 544.1 *inelegance*; 657.5 *nonobservance*; 486.8 *unskilfulness*
gaucho 43.16 *farm worker*; 59.15 *horse person*
gaud 793.5 *cheap item*
gaudily 529.18 *colourfully*
gaudiness 520.4 *clarity*; 793.3 *shoddiness*; 675.1 *tastelessness*; 544.3 *ugliness*
gaudy 529.12; 520.2 *clear*; 497.6 *coarse*; 738.14 *manifest*; 793.10 *shoddy*; 544.10 *ugly*
gauge 150.4 *breadth*; 210.5 *computer*; 464.12 *estimate*; 742.5 *indicator*; 42.5 *knitting*; 26.10, 158.18 *measure*; 28.82 *measuring instrument*; 26.8 *meter*; 210.11 *number*; 324.3 *orientation*; 321.3 *rail*; 317.10 *railway*; 744.10 *recording instrument*; 158.1 *size*; 332.8 *speed*
gaugeable 26.14 *measurable*
gauged 26.13 *measured*
gauger 26.9 *measurer*
gauging 26.1 *measurement*
gauleiter 400.4 *absolute ruler*
gauminess 430.1 *viscosity*
gaumy 430.8 *viscous*
gaunt 153.2 *emaciated*; 563.3 *infertile*
gauntlet 384.7 *armour*
gauntlets 551.25 *accessories*; 384.6 *protective clothing*
gauntness 153.8 *emaciation*
Gaussian distribution 27.59 *probability distribution*
gauze 153.11 *fineness*; 21.19 *stage set*; 394.10 *surgical dressing*; 527.8 *transparent thing*
gauziness 153.11 *fineness*; 527.6 *translucency*
gauzy 153.4 *fine*; 527.2 *translucent*
gavel 743.4 *insignia*
gavotte 22.4 *historic dancing*
gawk 518.13 *look*; 619.9 *wonder*
gawkiness 544.1 *inelegance*; 153.7 *thinness*
gawkish 486.3 *clumsy*; 544.7 *graceless*
gawkishness 544.1 *inelegance*
gawky 486.3 *clumsy*; 544.7 *graceless*; 153.1 *thin*
gawp 518.13 *look*; 619.9 *wonder*
gawper 518.11 *observer*
gay 601.10 *celebrative*; 598.1 *cheerful*; 529.11 *colourful*; 597.4 *happy*; 567.8, 568.10 *homosexual*; 567.17 *male*
gayatri 10.9 *prayer*
gay dog 567.2 *male*
Gay Gordons 22.4 *historic dancing*
gay liberation 391.2 *equal opportunity*; 250.1 *freedom*
gaze 659.7 *be discourteous*; 742.11 *gesture*; 518.6, 518.13 *look*
gaze and gaze 619.9 *wonder*
gazebo 44.3 *ornamental garden*; 565.7 *room*; 518.9 *viewpoint*
gazehound 518.2 *eye*
gazelle 332.12 *swift animal*
gazer 518.11 *observer*
gazette 740.5 *journal*
gazetteer 409.7 *catalogue*; 220.3 *dictionary*; 693.5 *reference book*
gazpacho 25.13 *soup*
gazump 776.3 *bargain*; 13.12 *cheat*
gazunder 776.3 *bargain*; 13.12 *cheat*; 560.14, 767.7 *toilet*
gear 38.7; 320.11 *bicycle part*; 551.1 *dress*; 438.7 *equipment*; 551.5 *fancy dress*; 243.11 *fitting out*; 438.5 *machine*; 38.8 *machine element*; 763.4 *possession*; 440.4 *possessions*; 61.9 *race*; 307.6 *rotator*
gear drive 38.6 *simple machine*
gearing 438.5 *machine*; 61.6 *motor-racing terms*
gear oneself up 243.8 *prepare oneself*
gears 438.5 *machine*
gear tooth 38.7 *gear*
gear train 38.7 *gear*
gear up 243.4 *prepare for action*
gearwheel 38.8 *machine element*; 307.6 *rotator*
Gebratene Huhnerleber 25.46 *German dish*
gecko 73.2 *lizard*
gedan-barai 52.8 *karate*
gee 325.8 *sidestep*
geegaw 124.9 *bauble*
gee-gee 59.1 *horse*
gee whillikers 712.16 *euphemisms*
gee whiz 712.16 *euphemisms*
gefilte fish 25.16 *fish dish*
gegenschein 522.4 *natural light*; 29.14 *solar system*
Gehenna 8.12 *hell*
Geiger counter 26.8 *meter*; 28.93 *radiation detector*
Geiger–Müller counter 28.93 *radiation detector*
geisha 21.30 *dancer*
geisha girl 21.30 *dancer*
geist 11.7 *spirit*
gel 430.6 *gelatin*; 32.3 *phase*; 37.6 *pill*; 32.25 *solidify*; 21.20 *stage lighting*; 152.7 *thicken*
gelatin 430.6; 41.11 *emulsion*; 33.9 *protein*; 21.20 *stage lighting*
gelatine 25.7 *basic ingredient*; 416.5 *condenser*
gelatinity 430.1 *viscosity*
gelatinization 416.2 *concentration*
gelatinize 416.8 *be dense*; 430.11 *thicken*
gelatinous 430.9
gelatinousness 430.1 *viscosity*
geld 335.9 *make impotent*; 563.8 *make infertile*; 212.4 *take off*
gelded 563.5 *rendered infertile*; 335.13 *unsexed*
gelding 59.1 *horse*; 563.2 *making infertile*; 567.16 *male animal*
gel filtration 32.17 *analysis*
gelid 494.8 *cold*
gelidity 494.2 *freezing*
gelignite 587.15 *explosive*
gelled 32.32 *solid*
gelt 780.2 *cash*
gem 235.8 *exceller*; 797.17 *good thing*
Gemara 7.12 *religious text*
Gemeinschaft 2.4 *social organization*
gem engraver 19.18 *engraver*
gem engraving 19.15 *engraving*
geminate 198.12, 198.15 *double*
geminated 198.12 *double*
gemination 198.4 *doubling*
Gemini 198.6 *twins*
gemma 77.8 *bud*; 82.4 *moss plant*
gemma cup 82.4 *moss plant*
gemmate 77.21 *vegetate*
gemmation 77.8 *bud*
gemmulation 77.8 *bud*
gemmule 77.8 *bud*
Gemusesuppe 25.46 *German dish*
gen 716.1 *evidence*; 693.1 *information*
gendarmerie 16.14 *police*
gender 137.3 *kingdom*; 2.3 *social environment*; 5.30 *syntax*
gene 34.25 *genetic*; 34.13 *genetic material*; 34.11 *genetics*; 554.2 *living matter*
genealogical tree 79.12 *figurative usage*
genealogy 137.8; **284.12**; 132.3 *line*
gene cloning 34.12 *molecular biology*
genecology 34.11 *genetics*
gene complement 34.13 *genetic material*
gene complex 34.11 *genetics*
gene flow 34.11 *genetics*
gene frequency 34.11 *genetics*
Gene Kelly 22.6 *famous dancers*
gene manipulation 561.3 *propagation*
gene mutation 34.13 *genetic material*
gene pool 34.11 *genetics*
gene probe 34.12 *molecular biology*
general 138.15; 586.17 *army person*; 216.1 *average*; 117.15 *everyday*; 127.7 *including*; 453.6 *indeterminate*; 764.5 *jointly possessing*; 400.7 *military leader*; 566.13 *national*; 397.6 *person in command*; 121.5 *superior*; 27.70 *universal*; 204.6 *whole*
general anaesthesia 394.5 *analgesic*
general anaesthetic 394.5 *analgesic*
general applicability 138.1 *generality*
general aptitude test battery 36.5 *psychological test*
general audit 13.7 *corporation*
general benefit 237.8 *benefit*
general court martial 584.6 *military law*
general delivery 692.2 *postal communication*
general dictionary 5.28 *dictionary*
general election 469.12 *election*
general fiction 740.6 *book publishing*
general headquarters 173.4 *centre of activity*
general hospital 35.10 *hospital*
general idea 138.8 *generalization*
general instruction 713.3 *precept*
generalissimo 400.7 *military leader*
Generality 138
generality 138.1; 216.4 *average*; 566.9 *group*; 127.1 *inclusion*; 452.19, 453.14 *indeterminacy*; 204.1 *whole*
generalization 138.8; 274.2 *inaccuracy*; 444.2 *reasoning*; 27.65 *theory*; 204.1 *whole*
generalize 138.23; 138.27 *make a generalization*; 216.10 *make average*; 444.11 *reason*; 27.89 *theorize*
generalized 138.20
general knowledge 455.2 *information*
general levy 586.14 *armed forces*
general linguistics 5.1 *linguistics*
generally 138.29; 140.18 *as a rule*; 150.7 *broadly*; 297.1 *frequently*; 127.9 *inclusively*; 453.25 *indeterminately*; 27.87 *mathematically*; 216.11 *on average*; 204.13 *on the whole*
generally speaking 138.29 *generally*; 147.13 *nearly*; 216.11 *on average*
general manager 340.3 *doer*
general market 779.7 *emporium*
general medicine 35.1 *medicine*
general officer 584.5 *military staff*
general outlook 31.4 *weather forecast*
general paralysis 260.17 *nervous disorder*
general paresis 260.17 *nervous disorder*
general policy 584.1 *military affairs*
general population 566.9 *group*
general practice 35.1 *medicine*
general practitioner 35.11 *doctor*
general principle 27.65 *theory*
general proposition 27.65 *theory*
general public 138.11; 566.9 *group*; 564.2 *inhabitants*
general-purpose 348.8 *practical*
general relativity 29.4 *cosmological model*
general rule 138.5 *averageness*
general run 138.6 *average*
general semantics 694.1 *meaning*
general servant 401.1 *servant*
generalship 585.6 *art of war*; 121.2 *leadership*; 209.2 *rank*; 631.9 *tactics*
general staff 584.5 *military staff*
general strike 15.4 *industrial dispute*; 13.8 *industrial relations*; 226.2 *stop*
general studies 6.3 *subject*
general surgeon 35.13 *medical specialist*
general surgery 35.9, 394.12 *surgery*
general synopsis 31.4 *weather forecast*
general tendency 104.2 *tendency*
general terms 570.6
general theory of relativity 141.9 *fourth dimension*; 28.5 *theory*
general union 15.3 *organized labour*
general war 585.1 *war*
generate 295.19 *begin*; 344.9 *be the cause of*; 39.35 *conduct*; 554.19 *give birth to*; 130.22 *invent*; 562.7 *make fertile*; 126.7 *originate*; 356.10 *produce*; 561.13 *propagate*; 27.96 *represent*
generate power 334.12
generating 295.4 *beginning*
generating station 437.4 *electricity*; 39.32 *power station*; 334.6 *source of energy*
generation 376.18; 295.4 *beginning*; 344.1 *cause*; 561.3 *propagation*; 276.2 *time period*
generations 277.5 *long duration*
generations of man 566.1 *humankind*
generative 344.13 *causal*; 562.5 *fertile*; 561.16 *reproductive*
generator 39.30; 28.56 *electrical energy*; 437.4 *electricity*; 438.5 *machine*; 39.32 *power station*; 334.6 *source of energy*
gene replacement therapy 35.8 *treatment*
generic 216.1 *average*; 138.20 *generalized*; 160.10 *prototypical*; 34.28 *taxonomic*; 137.11 *typical*
generically 34.29 *biologically*; 160.13 *formatively*; 137.16 *taxonomically*
generic drug 394.2 *medicine*
generic name 37.3 *drug*
Generosity 679
generosity 679.5; 650.2 *charity*; 658.1 *courtesy*; 787.7 *donation*; 768.1 *giving*; 797.10 *kindness*; 652.1 *philanthropy*; 473.2 *unselfishness*; 803.1 *virtue*
generous 679.1; 392.35 *benevolent*; 158.15 *big*; 650.7 *charitable*; 658.7 *courteous*; 787.10 *expending*; 569.8 *friendly*; 768.8, 813.18 *giving*; 797.3 *kind*; 648.4 *lenient*; 652.6 *philanthropic*; 627.6 *pitying*; 490.6 *pleasant*; 217.2 *plentiful*; 473.5 *unselfish*; 803.5 *virtuous*
generous endowment 781.5 *wealth*
generous giver 768.4 *giver*
generous giving 768.1 *giving*
generous-hearted 769.12 *receptive*
generously 679.12; **787.14**; 768.9 *as a gift*; 650.11 *charitably*; 658.14 *courteously*; 658.15 *genteelly*; 569.17 *in friendship*; 158.20 *largely*; 648.6 *leniently*; 797.23 *nicely*; 652.8 *philanthropically*; 627.13 *pitifully*; 473.9 *unselfishly*; 803.9 *virtuously*
generous nature 768.1 *giving*
generousness 158.2 *bigness*; 650.2 *charity*; 648.1 *leniency*
generous person 679.9
gene sequence 34.13 *genetic material*
gene sequencing 34.12 *molecular biology*
genesis 130.2 *creation*; 561.3 *propagation*
gene splicing 34.13 *genetic material*; 34.12 *molecular biology*
gene string 34.14 *chromosome*
gene structure 34.12 *molecular biology*
gene therapy 35.8 *treatment*
genetic 34.25; 34.20 *biological*; 344.13 *causal*; 345.10 *caused*; 561.16 *reproductive*
genetically 34.29 *biologically*; 344.14 *causally*; 561.18 *reproductively*
genetic code 34.13 *genetic material*
genetic constitution 34.11 *genetics*
genetic counselling 35.6 *health care*
genetic drift 34.11 *genetics*
genetic element 34.13 *genetic material*
genetic engineering 34.11 *genetics*; 34.1 *life science*; 34.12 *molecular biology*; 561.3 *propagation*
genetic fingerprinting 743.3 *means of identification*; 34.12 *molecular biology*
geneticist 34.19 *life scientist*
genetic likeness 115.1 *similarity*
genetic mapping 34.12 *molecular biology*
genetic material 34.13
genetic psychology 36.1 *psychology*
genetics 34.11; 34.1 *life science*; 554.7 *studies of life*
genetic screening 35.7 *diagnosis*
Geneva Bible 7.12 *religious text*
genial 650.6 *benevolent*; 598.1 *cheerful*; 658.7 *courteous*; 569.8 *friendly*; 241.2 *likable*; 654.15 *sociable*
geniality 241.8 *amiability*; 650.1 *benevolence*; 598.3 *cheerfulness*; 569.1 *friendship*; 654.1 *sociability*
genially 569.17 *in friendship*; 241.15 *pleasantly*; 654.18 *sociably*
genic 34.25 *genetic*
genie 392.15 *benefactor*
genie of the lamp 348.3 *assistant*
genital 561.16 *reproductive*
genitalia 561.8 *organs of reproduction*; 344.2 *source*
genitally 561.18 *reproductively*
genitals 561.8 *organs of reproduction*
genitive 5.31 *case*
genitourinary 35.22 *medical*
genitourinary medicine 35.3 *medical specialty*
genius 136.2 *ability*; 485.2 *aptitude*; 19.5 *artistry*; 229.2 *attitude*; 442.4 *cleverness*; 8.5 *deity*; 235.8 *exceller*; 396.11, 400.10 *expert*; 11.11 *ghost*; 477.2 *inspiration*; 458.4 *intellectual*; 442.8 *intellectual person*; 458.2 *intelligence*; 455.6 *knowledgeable person*; 121.6 *paragon*; 619.5 *person of wonder*; 4.12 *sage*; 485.4 *skilled person*; 139.7 *special skill*; 797.16 *superior person*; 443.7 *thinker*
genius for 485.2 *aptitude*
genned up 693.18 *informed*; 6.19 *knowledgeable*
Genoa 50.3 *parts of a sailing boat*

genocidal 382.24 *murderous*
genocide 651.7 *act of malevolence*; 814.13 *capital punishment*; 357.2 *destroying*; 382.3 *homicide*; 382.4 *slaughter*
Genoese pastry 25.37 *pastry*
genome 34.13 *genetic material*
genomic 34.25 *genetic*
genotype 34.11 *genetics*; 34.12 *molecular biology*
genotypic 34.25 *genetic*
genre 160.3 *kind*; 721.6 *sort*; 137.4 *type*
genre painter 19.16 *artist*
genre painting 19.10 *art subject*
genro 579.7 *council*
gent 567.2 *male*; 573.1 *nobleman*
genteel 658.8 *good-mannered*; 795.10 *moralistic*; 549.5 *refined*
genteelism 795.4 *self-righteousness*
genteelly **658.15**
genteelness 658.2 *good manners*
gentian 496.5 *herbs*
gentian blue 539.5 *blueness*
gentian violet 540.2 *purple pigment*
gentilities 658.3 *courtesies*
gentility 543.1 *elegance*; 658.2 *good manners*; 566.9 *group*; 573.3 *nobleness*
gentle 658.7 *courteous*; 511.1 *faint-sounding*; 805.5 *innocent*; 415.2 *insubstantial*; 648.4 *lenient*; 685.6 *moderate*; 627.6 *pitying*; 265.14 *relaxed*; 419.6 *soft-hearted*; 333.5 *unhurried*
gentle as a lamb 685.6 *moderate*
gentle breeze 31.13 *wind strength*
gentlefolk 573.2 *aristocracy*
gentle handling 631.8 *treatment*
gentleman 658.6 *courteous person*; 401.6 *domestic servant*; 567.2 *male*; 567.3 *male title of address*; 566.10 *member of society*; 566.4 *modern human*; 573.1 *nobleman*; 549.4 *refined person*; 631.3 *well-behaved person*
gentleman farmer 43.15 *agriculturist*
gentlemanliness 658.2 *good manners*
gentlemanly 573.4 *aristocratic*; 658.8 *good-mannered*; 799.4 *honourable*; 567.17 *male*; 549.5 *refined*; 631.17 *well-behaved*
gentlemanly behaviour 631.2 *good conduct*
gentleman of the road 118.7 *nonconformist*
gentleman's agreement 810.7 *commitment*; 755.1 *contract*; 756.1 *promise*
gentleman's club 645.1 *cunning*
gentleman's gentleman 401.6 *domestic servant*
Gentlemen 767.7 *toilet*
gentlemen's agreement 354.3 *contract*
gentleness **419.12**; 658.1 *courtesy*; 648.1 *leniency*; 415.5 *lightness*; 685.1 *moderation*; 627.1 *pity*
gentle sex 568.1 *female sex*
gentlewoman 573.1 *nobleman*; 549.4 *refined person*
gently 658.14 *courteously*; 648.6 *leniently*; 415.11 *lightly*; 685.9 *moderately*; 627.13 *pitifully*; 333.16 *slowly*; 419.18 *soft-heartedly*
gentrification 87.1 *city*
gentrified 87.14 *urban*
gentrify 295.20 *make new*; 393.2 *refurbish*; 87.15 *urbanize*
gentry 573.2 *aristocracy*; 235.7 *elite*; 654.7 *human society*
gents 560.13 *lavatory*
genuflect 367.9 *bow*; 367.16 *courtesy*; 623.21 *humble oneself*; 10.19 *offer worship*; 663.6 *show obeisance to*; 667.19 *take off one's hat to*; 9.7 *worship*
genuflection 667.4 *mark of respect*; 663.3 *obeisance*; 623.11 *self-abasement*; 388.1 *submission*; 9.1 *worship*
genuine 126.6, 698.19 *authentic*; 3.19 *chronicled*; 801.8 *correct*; 643.2 *earnest*; 16.51 *legitimate*; 95.7 *realistic*; 396.15 *true*
genuinely 396.25, 698.37 *authentically*; 801.20 *correctly*; 643.11 *earnestly*; 3.25 *reportedly*; 454.11 *verifiably*
genuineness 698.6 *authenticity*; 801.2 *correctness*; 3.14 *historicalness*; 16.30 *legitimacy*; 126.1 *originality*
genus 137.3 *kingdom*; 205.1 *part*; 34.17 *taxonomy*; 137.4 *type*
geocentric 29.36 *astronomical*; 173.6 *central*
geochemical 30.48 *geological*
geochemist 32.2 *chemist*; 30.3 *geologist*
geochemistry 32.1 *chemistry*; 30.1 *earth science*
geochronological 30.48 *geological*
geochronological unit 30.41 *geological time*
geochronologist 30.3 *geologist*
geochronology 30.1 *earth science*
geodesic 27.37 *line*; 20.17 *structured*
geodesic dome 20.6 *roof*; 38.27 *superstructure*
geodesist 30.3 *geologist*; 210.7 *mathematician*; 26.9 *measurer*
geodesy 30.1 *earth science*; 26.1 *measurement*; 142.5 *topography*
geodetic 30.48 *geological*; 142.8 *locational*; 26.12 *metrical*
geodetically 30.66 *geographically*; 26.17 *measurably*; 142.13 *topographically*
geodetics 26.1 *measurement*
geographic 1.11 *anthropological*
geographical 1.11 *anthropological*; 142.8 *locational*; 86.16 *regional*; 143.7 *situational*
geographical feature 30.7 *landform*
geographically **30.66**; **86.19**; **143.11**; 1.16 *anthropologically*; 142.13 *topographically*
geographical region **86.2**
geographical space **141.3**
geographical unit 86.1 *region*
geography 30.1 *earth science*; 143.1 *situation*; 142.5 *topography*
geoid 30.5 *earth*
geolinguist 5.2 *linguist*
geolinguistic 5.38 *linguistic*
geolinguistics 5.1 *linguistics*
geological **30.48**
geological epoch 284.3 *geological period*
geological fold 184.1 *wrinkle*
geologically 30.66 *geographically*
geological period **276.3**; **284.3**; 275.4 *term*
geological time **30.41**
geological time scale 30.41 *geological time*
geological time unit 30.41 *geological time*
geologist **30.3**
geology 30.1 *earth science*
geomagnetic 30.49 *geophysical*
geomagnetic field 30.44 *geomagnetism*
geomagnetic pole 30.45 *magnetic pole*
geomagnetics 30.2 *geophysics*
geomagnetism **28.58**; **30.44**; 30.2 *geophysics*
geomagnetist 30.4 *geophysicist*
geomancer 11.13 *diviner*; 283.5 *predictor*
geomancy 11.9, 475.2 *divination*
geometer 210.7 *mathematician*
geometric 210.15 *mathematical*; 194.8 *odd*; 19.24 *pictorial*
geometrical 27.68 *mathematical*
geometrically 210.16 *mathematically*; 194.12 *numerically*; 19.30 *pictorially*
geometric construction **27.49**
geometric figure **27.41**
geometrician 27.2, 210.7 *mathematician*
geometric instrument 27.49 *geometric construction*
geometric mean 27.60 *parameter*
geometric optics 28.2 *classical physics*
geometric perspective 19.4 *treatment*
geometric progression 302.10 *forward motion*; 27.20 *sequence*
geometric series 27.20 *sequence*
geometric shape 27.41 *geometric figure*
geometry **27.34**; 176.4 *angular measurement*; 210.1 *calculation*; 27.1 *mathematics*
geomorphic feature 30.7 *landform*
geomorphological 30.48 *geological*
geomorphologically 30.66 *geographically*
geomorphologist 403.10 *anatomist*; 30.3 *geologist*
geomorphology 30.1 *earth science*; 403.8 *science of structure*
geophysical **30.49**
geophysical satellite 29.32 *satellite*
geophysicist **30.4**; 402.3 *materialist*
geophysics **30.2**; 28.4 *experimental physics*; 402.6 *natural science*
geopolitical 30.48 *geological*
geopolitics 30.1 *earth science*
geoponic 43.19 *agricultural*
geoponics 43.1 *agriculture*
Geordie 564.9 *British inhabitant*
Geordie dialect 5.26 *dialect*
George 235.1 *worthy*
George Balanchine 22.14 *famous ballet dancers*
George Cross 743.4 *insignia*; 794.1 *trophy*
George Washington 698.14 *truthful person*
Georgian 23.7 *furniture style*; 296.14 *historic*
georgic 43.19 *agricultural*; 17.7 *poem*
geoscience 30.1 *earth science*
geosphere 30.5 *earth*
geospheric 30.50 *terrestrial*
geostationary orbit 29.32 *satellite*
geostationary satellite 692.7 *satellite communication*
geostrophic 31.43 *atmospheric*
geostrophic force 31.9 *atmospheric process*
geostrophic wind 31.12 *wind*
geosynchronous orbit 29.32 *satellite*
geotechnical engineering 38.17 *civil engineering*
geothermal 334.17, 437.10 *powered*
geothermal energy 28.11 *energy*; 437.8 *renewable energy*
geothermal power 334.6 *source of energy*
geothermal power station 39.32 *power station*
geraniol 33.20 *terpene*
geranium 535.7 *red thing*
gerbil food 557.8 *animal food*
geriatric 556.14 *aged*; 556.15 *age-related*; 35.22, 394.18 *medical*; 556.7 *older person*
geriatrician 556.6 *gerontology*; 35.13 *medical specialist*
geriatric medicine 556.6 *gerontology*
geriatric patient 260.19 *sick person*
geriatrics 35.3 *medical specialty*
germ 34.26 *developmental*; 34.15 *developmental biology*; 260.6 *infection*; 159.2 *little thing*; 34.3 *organism*; 344.3 *rudiment*; 130.3 *source*
German 57.11 *gymnastic*
German chocolate cake 25.36 *cake*
German dish **25.46**
germane 750.16 *fitting*; 108.4 *related*
germanely 108.10 *relevantly*
germaneness 108.1 *relatedness*
German GP at Hockenheim 61.2 *Formula 1 race*
German gymnastics 57.1 *gymnastics*
Germanic 5.11 *family of languages*
germanic 32.34 *elemental*
germanium 39.4 *semiconductor*
Germanize 760.12 *naturalize*
Germanized 760.17 *naturalized*
German measles 260.6 *infection*
germanous 32.34 *elemental*
German short-haired pointer 60.6 *sporting dog*
German silver 700.6 *imitation*
germ-carrier 260.6 *infection*
germ cell 34.7 *cell*
germen 34.7 *cell*
germ-free 257.4 *hygienic*
germicidal 37.14 *counteracting*; 255.15 *purifying*
germicide 382.13 *animal killer*; 37.4 *drug type*; 394.3 *prophylactic*
germinal 344.13 *causal*; 34.26 *developmental*; 130.32 *embryonic*; 159.7 *little*; 561.16 *reproductive*
germinant 34.26 *developmental*
germinate 190.6 *become bigger*; 562.6 *be fertile*; 130.27 *emerge*; 345.8 *grow*; 561.11 *have young*; 83.12 *mushroom*; 130.26 *produce*; 77.21 *vegetate*
germinating 34.26 *developmental*; 190.8 *growing*
germinating seed 77.9 *seed*
germination 34.15 *developmental biology*; 190.1 *growth*; 561.3 *propagation*; 77.9 *seed*
germinative 34.26 *developmental*
germ layer 34.15 *developmental biology*
germ plasm 34.7 *cell*
germ warfare 585.8 *warfare*
Geronimo 633.19 *after him!*
gerontocracy 12.1 *government*
gerontologic 556.15 *age-related*
gerontologist 556.6 *gerontology*; 35.13 *medical specialist*
gerontology **556.6**; 35.3 *medical specialty*
gerrymander 645.5 *be cunning*
gerrymandered 700.35 *deceptive*
gerrymandering 645.1 *cunning*; 700.10 *fraud*
Gesellschaft 2.4 *social organization*
Gesell's development schedule 36.5 *psychological test*
gesso 19.11 *artist's materials*
Gestalt **36.26**; 160.1 *form*; 4.8 *philosophical term*; 204.2 *whole thing*
Gestaltism 36.1 *psychology*
Gestalt psychology 36.1 *psychology*
Gestalt theory 36.1 *psychology*
Gestalt therapy 36.3 *psychiatric treatment*; 394.13 *therapy*
Gestalt whole 160.1 *form*
gestate 243.7 *develop*
gestation 243.13 *development*; 561.3 *propagation*
gestatory 130.32 *embryonic*
geste 17.2 *fiction*
gesticulate 631.11 *conduct oneself*; 742.11 *gesture*; 730.14 *have difficulty speaking*; 300.15 *walk*
gesticulation 729.4 *articulation*; 300.11 *bodily movement*; 631.1 *conduct*; 340.2 *deed*; 742.3 *gesture*; 730.6 *silent speech*
gesticulative 742.15 *gestural*
gesticulator 742.8 *signer*
gestural **742.15**
gesture **742.3**; **742.11**; 693.7 *advice*; 729.4 *articulation*; 300.11 *bodily movement*; 631.1 *conduct*; 631.11 *conduct oneself*; 340.2 *deed*; 21.9 *dramaturgy*; 742.11 *gesture*; 730.14 *have difficulty speaking*; 660.7 *insult*; 5.5 *nonstandard language*; 730.6 *silent speech*; 742.9 *use signs*; 300.15 *walk*
gesture of equality 631.1 *conduct*
gesture of protest **753.3**
gesturer 742.8 *signer*
get 316.14 *bring back*; 755.6 *catch*; 760.7 *convert into*; 369.15 *draw out*; 765.9 *gain*; 313.15 *go!*; 446.14 *have an idea*; 777.1 *purchase*; 769.9, 788.7 *receive*; 773.7 *take*; 695.6 *understand*
get a bad name 670.24 *be open to criticism*
get a bad press 670.24 *be open to criticism*
get a bearing 142.11 *find*
get about 654.11 *be sociable*
get above oneself **660.28**; 673.15 *be vain*
get a break 248.6 *be fortunate*; 308.23 *find an opening*
get a corner on 763.7 *possess*
get acquainted 569.13 *befriend*
get across 695.4 *be intelligible*; 694.10 *mean*
get a firm hold 360.6 *retain*
get a fix 142.11 *find*
get a foothold 62.9 *mountaineer*; 360.6 *retain*
get after 638.9 *undertake*
get agitated about 590.17 *feel deeply*
get a half-nelson on 360.6 *retain*
get ahead **121.11**; **293.11**; 312.9 *achieve*; 246.6 *be successful*; 302.9 *maintain progress*
get a headlock on 360.6 *retain*
get ahead of 121.8 *be superior*; 293.8 *precede*
get a head start 293.7 *be early*; 121.11 *get ahead*
get a hold on 12.12 *take authority*
get all snarled up 264.18 *find difficult*
get all tangled up 264.18 *find difficult*
get along 313.1 *depart*; 302.1 *go forward*
get along with 654.13 *fraternize*
get along without 767.9 *dispose of*
get a medal 813.12 *be rewarded*; 765.14 *profit*
get a middle-aged spread 556.17 *age*
get a move on 332.6 *accelerate*; 332.4 *be swift*; 262.8 *hurry up!*; 302.9 *maintain progress*; 342.23 *rise and shine!*; 638.9 *undertake*
get an earful 504.15 *hear*
get angry **659.8**; 624.12 *become angry*; 625.6 *be irascible*
get a receipt 785.6 *pay*
get a reprieve 389.5 *escape*
get a reward 813.12 *be rewarded*
get around 740.17 *be published*; 485.10 *be skilful*
get a running start 121.11 *get ahead*
get a second wind 121.11 *get ahead*
get a share 770.5 *get one's allotment*
get a stranglehold on 360.6 *retain*
get-at-able 312.20 *attainable*; 147.9 *near*; 492.8 *touchable*
get a tan 493.16 *feel hot*
get a tight grip 360.6 *retain*

get a toehold 360.6 *retain*
get at the truth 698.31 *be accurate*
getaway 332.3 *accelerating;* 332.9 *acceleration;* 313.7 *departure;* 389.1 *escape*
get away 391.5 *be liberated;* 313.1 *depart;* 372.13 *diverge;* 389.5 *escape*
get away with it 757.5 *be permitted;* 389.5 *escape;* 758.12 *exempt oneself*
get away with murder 757.5 *be permitted;* 758.12 *exempt oneself*
get a wiggle on 293.10 *hasten*
get back 706.17 *answer;* 347.3 *counteract*
get back at 761.7 *restore*
get back to normal 393.4 *be restored*
get behind 392.24 *back*
get behindhand 786.9 *be unable to pay*
get better **244.2**; 224.7 *be changed;* 393.4 *be restored;* 797.21 *do well;* 756.10 *show potential;* 304.21 *upturn*
get by 216.9 *be average;* 221.6 *be in a state of;* 618.16 *be mediocre*
get by any means 352.6 *find means*
get by on 349.5 *dispose of*
get caught red-handed 806.8 *be guilty*
get changed 551.34 *wear*
get chummy with 569.13 *befriend*
get close 147.16 *near*
get cold feet 614.4 *be a coward;* 612.12 *be fearful;* 479.2 *equivocate*
get cracking 340.4 *act;* 332.4 *be swift;* 130.18 *make a beginning*
get credit 784.7 *be in debt*
get cross 624.12 *become angry*
get crow's-feet 556.17 *age*
get cut down 582.16 *meet one's fate*
get dirty 258.10 *be dirty*
get divorced 571.7 *divorce*
get done 346.9 *take action*
get down 305.9 *descend;* 305.12 *drop;* 557.21 *eat;* 312.4 *land;* 367.8 *sit;* 354.1 *undertake*
get down to 353.3 *tackle;* 638.9 *undertake*
get down to it 576.6 *work*
get dressed 551.34 *wear*
get drunk **690.8**; 558.13 *drink*
get engaged 705.22 *pop the question*
get engaged to 756.7 *promise*
get even 785.13 *retaliate*
get even with 814.2 *penalize;* 385.3 *retaliate*
get fat 190.6 *become bigger;* 248.5 *be prosperous*
get fatter 765.10 *augment*
get fired 315.14 *be dismissed;* 580.4 *have leisure*
get for a song 791.5 *buy at a discount*
get free 250.14 *be free;* 391.5 *be liberated;* 372.13 *diverge;* 389.5 *escape*
get fresh 660.22 *be rude*
get frostbite 494.11 *become cold*
get going 340.4 *act;* 248.5 *be prosperous;* 313.15 *go!;* 130.18 *make a beginning;* 342.23 *rise and shine!;* 638.9 *undertake*
get healthy **259.6**
get hitched 570.15 *marry*
get hold of 765.9 *gain;* 773.7 *take;* 695.6 *understand*
get hot 147.16 *near*
get huffy 624.10 *be offended*
get ideas 446.18 *aim*
get in **312.5**; 314.9 *enter*
get in advance 765.12 *earn*
get in a mess 264.20 *be in difficulty*
get in a pickle 222.13 *get into difficulties*
get in a rut 111.11 *be regular*
get in back of 392.24 *back*
get in early 293.11 *get ahead*
get in line 132.17 *line up*
get in one's corner 480.15 *persuade*
get in print 740.17 *be published*
get in the way 486.7 *be clumsy;* 378.9 *block*
get into a fix 221.7 *be in a predicament;* 222.13 *get into difficulties*
get into a habit 632.18 *habituate*
get into a jam 221.7 *be in a predicament;* 222.13 *get into difficulties*
get into character 21.37 *rehearse*
get into debt 786.9 *be unable to pay*
get into difficulties **222.13**; 264.20 *be in difficulty*
get into gear 243.4 *prepare for action*
get into hot water 222.13 *get into difficulties;* 264.21 *get into trouble*
get into mischief 662.15 *be disobedient*
get into one's head 476.5 *suppose*
get into one's stride 632.18 *habituate*
get into the final 136.13 *qualify*
get into the papers 740.18 *become famous*
get into trouble **264.21**; 798.11 *be evil;* 222.13 *get into difficulties*
get in touch 692.30 *communicate*
get involved 354.1 *undertake*
get it 449.3 *find out*
get it bad 483.8 *be motivated;* 480.18 *be persuaded*
get it wrong 274.18 *be in error*
get job satisfaction 813.12 *be rewarded*
get killed 582.16 *meet one's fate*
get laid off 580.4 *have leisure*
get laryngitis 506.1 *be silent*
get light 522.26 *grow light*
get loose 372.13 *diverge*
get lost 254.8 *be in danger;* 313.15 *go!;* 325.3 *go astray;* 371.33 *go away!*
get lower 305.9 *descend*
get lower and lower 305.9 *descend*
get lucky 222.14 *be comfortable;* 246.6 *be successful*
get mad 624.12 *become angry*
get married 570.15 *marry*
get miffed 624.10 *be offended*
get mileage out of 349.3 *exploit*
get mixed up in 340.4 *act*
get moving 130.19 *start off*
get near 147.16 *near*
get nearer 765.10 *augment*
get no better 245.1 *deteriorate*
get no results 247.6 *fail*
get nowhere 335.6 *be powerless;* 238.9 *waste effort*
get nowhere fast 333.1 *move slowly*
get off 16.78 *acquit;* 391.5 *be liberated;* 390.1 *deliver;* 305.9 *descend;* 389.5 *escape;* 312.4 *land;* 313.5 *set out;* 226.12 *stop!*
get off lightly 389.5 *escape*
get off scot-free 391.5 *be liberated;* 758.12 *exempt oneself*
get off the subject 270.6 *be circuitous*
get old 556.17 *age*
get on 556.17 *age;* 221.6 *be in a state of;* 246.6 *be successful;* 302.5 *develop;* 304.15 *mount*
get on credit 772.10 *buy on credit*
get one by 217.4 *suffice*
get one's allotment **770.5**
get one's ass moving 638.9 *undertake*
get one's back up 624.12 *become angry;* 624.9 *offend*
get one's blood up 624.12 *become angry*
get one's breath back 581.2 *be refreshed*
get one's call-up papers 585.12 *go to war*
get one's clothes on 551.34 *wear*
get one's comeuppance 814.6 *be punished;* 813.12 *be rewarded*
get one's dander up 624.12 *become angry*
get one's deserts 814.6 *be punished;* 813.12 *be rewarded;* 385.4 *serve one right*
get oneself done up 553.8 *dress up*
get oneself killed 382.21 *commit suicide*
get one's feet wet 130.18 *make a beginning*
get one's finger out 332.4 *be swift;* 293.10 *hasten*
get one's fingers on 765.9 *gain*
get one's footing 360.6 *retain*
get one's goat 596.7 *cause dislike*
get one's gorge up 624.12 *become angry*
get one's hands dirty 576.6 *work*
get one's head down 343.13 *sleep;* 354.1 *undertake*
get one's head in 64.5 *play rugby*
get one's Irish up 624.12 *become angry*
get one's mind into 354.1 *undertake*
get one's money's worth 349.3 *exploit;* 777.1 *purchase*
get one's monkey up 624.12 *become angry*
get one's own back 761.7 *restore;* 385.3, 785.13 *retaliate*
get one's sea legs 323.10 *sail*
get one's second wind 581.2 *be refreshed*
get one's share 770.5 *get one's allotment*
get one's teeth into 557.22 *eat well;* 354.1 *undertake*
get one wrong 720.1 *misinterpret*
get on in years 556.17 *age*
get on one's nerves 596.7 *cause dislike;* 624.9 *offend*
get on one's soapbox 707.21 *be assertive*
get on swimmingly 248.5 *be prosperous*
get on the cuff 772.10 *buy on credit*
get on the road 130.19 *start off*
get on the stick 638.9 *undertake*
get on tick 772.10 *buy on credit*
get on well 248.5 *be prosperous*
get on well with 654.13 *fraternize*
get on with 340.4 *act*
get out 739.9 *be disclosed;* 391.5 *be liberated;* 390.1 *deliver;* 389.5 *escape;* 315.9 *exit;* 369.11 *extract;* 313.15 *go!;* 371.33 *go away!;* 740.13 *make public*
get-out 389.1 *escape*
get out of 391.5 *be liberated;* 634.5 *shirk*
get out of control 408.26 *be disorderly*
get out of hand 408.26 *be disorderly*
get out of here 371.33 *go away!*
get out of line 118.18 *not conform*
get out of practice 486.5 *be unskilful*
get over 300.13 *be in motion;* 393.4 *be restored*
get over a snag 246.7 *overcome obstacles*
get overheated 493.16 *feel hot*
get over the hump 246.7 *overcome obstacles*
get over the worst 224.7 *be changed;* 244.2 *get better*
get paid **813.13**; 765.12 *earn*
get pally with 569.13 *befriend*
get past 318.8 *pass*
get personal 660.22 *be rude*
get pinned 593.26 *court*
get pissed 558.13 *drink*
get pregnant 561.10 *reproduce oneself*
get promoted 246.6 *be successful*
get ready 243.1 *prepare;* 243.8 *prepare oneself;* 436.5 *provision*
get ready for action 243.8 *prepare oneself*
get religion 7.19 *be religious*
get results 246.6 *be successful*
get rich **781.13**; 248.5 *be prosperous;* 246.6 *be successful;* 797.21 *do well*
get rid of 526.3 *cause to disappear;* 357.8 *destroy;* 470.2 *discard;* 767.9 *dispose of;* 128.8 *eject;* 389.6 *elude;* 371.10 *exterminate;* 382.16 *kill;* 355.1 *relinquish;* 778.1 *sell;* 255.11 *simplify;* 371.13 *throw away*
get ripped off 792.11 *overpay*
get round 677.10 *cajole*
get round someone 483.10 *manipulate*
get round the table 734.11 *confer;* 746.5 *negotiate*
get sacked 46.15 *play offence*
get satisfaction 385.3 *retaliate*
get shot of 372.13 *diverge;* 371.13 *throw away*
get sidetracked 270.6 *be circuitous;* 109.10 *be unrelated;* 325.3 *go astray*
get some kick 780.26 *bank*
get some shuteye 263.2 *take it easy*
get something for nothing 765.14 *profit*
get something through 746.5 *negotiate*
get somewhere 312.9 *achieve;* 302.7 *make one's way*
get sore 624.12 *become angry*
get spliced 570.15 *marry*
get stale 261.5 *be fatigued*
get started 130.18 *make a beginning*
get steamed up 624.12 *become angry*
gettable 769.14 *receivable;* 492.8 *touchable*
getter 32.29 *absorb;* 769.5 *recipient*
gettering 32.20 *surface chemistry*
getter-ion pump 32.20 *surface chemistry*
get the better of 121.8 *be superior;* 623.26 *outdo*
get the bird 315.14 *be dismissed*
get the boot 315.14 *be dismissed*
get the bullet 708.15 *terminate*
get thee hence 313.15 *go!;* 371.33 *go away!*
get the feel of 632.18 *habituate*
get the full particulars 222.11 *circumstantiate*
get the giggles 600.8 *laugh*
get the gist of 695.6 *understand*
get the hang of 632.18 *habituate;* 6.24 *know;* 400.15 *learn;* 695.6 *understand*
get the hungries 557.22 *eat well*
get the idea 695.6 *understand*
get the job done 217.4 *suffice*
get the jump on 121.8 *be superior*
get the knack of 632.18 *habituate*
get the lead out 342.12 *be active;* 342.23 *rise and shine!*
get the new look 295.18 *be trendy*
get the picture 695.6 *understand*
get there 312.9 *achieve;* 246.6 *be successful;* 312.2 *reach*
get there early 293.7 *be early*
get there first 293.7 *be early*
get the sack 315.14 *be dismissed;* 580.4 *have leisure*
get the whip hand 12.12, 396.20 *take authority*
get the wrong idea 696.9 *find unintelligible*
get through 787.2 *consume;* 314.11 *infiltrate;* 318.8 *pass;* 136.13 *qualify*
getting 765.1 *gain;* 769.1 *receiving;* 773.1 *taking*
getting ahead **293.6**; 302.15 *improvement*
getting a middle-aged spread 556.12 *ageing*
getting back 393.9, 761.2 *restoration*
getting crow's-feet 556.12 *ageing*
getting down 557.1 *eating*
getting drunk 690.11 *drinking*
getting even 814.9 *retribution*
getting hitched 570.1 *marriage*
getting hold of 765.1 *gain*
getting in early 293.6 *getting ahead*
getting old 556.12 *ageing*
getting on 556.12 *ageing;* 296.11 *old*
getting one's hands dirty 576.1 *work*
getting one's leg over 593.5 *desire*
getting on for 283.14 *in the future*
getting on in years 556.12 *ageing;* 296.11 *old*
getting pinned 593.6 *courtship*
getting ready 243.9 *preparation*
getting rid of 767.1 *disposal*
getting round 677.3 *cajolery*
gettings 765.5 *profit*
getting well 259.1 *healthy*
getting worse 245.12 *deteriorated*
get to 765.10 *augment;* 145.7, 312.2 *reach*
get together 765.11 *acquire;* 376.41 *band together;* 654.11 *be sociable;* 310.10 *come together;* 747.14 *join with;* 749.5 *make peace*
get-together 654.3 *meeting;* 376.9 *social gathering*
get together with 747.14 *join with*
get to grips with 353.3 *tackle*
get to hear of 693.15 *be informed*
get to know **455.13**; 569.13 *befriend;* 695.6 *understand*
get too dear 792.9 *be dear*
get to one 624.9 *offend*
get to the top 312.9 *achieve*
get tough 647.5 *be severe*
get tough with 647.6 *suppress*
get under one's feet 378.9 *block*
get under way 323.9 *navigate;* 313.5 *set out;* 130.19 *start off*
get up 366.5 *arise;* 342.12 *be active;* 393.4 *be restored;* 186.5 *be vertical;* 31.58 *blow;* 403.16 *construct;* 356.10 *produce;* 304.16 *stand up*
get-up 551.1 *dress;* 403.3 *form;* 160.6 *nature*
get-up-and-go 707.6 *assertiveness;* 342.4 *energy;* 338.1 *vigour;* 334.3 *vitality*
get up one's nose 596.7 *cause dislike;* 499.9 *disgust;* 242.10 *displease*
get up steam 323.9 *navigate*
get up to date 295.17 *become new*
get used to 632.18 *habituate*
get warm 449.2 *detect;* 147.16 *near*
get weaving 130.18 *make a beginning;* 638.9 *undertake*
get well 393.4 *be restored;* 259.6 *get healthy*
get what one deserves 385.4 *serve one right*
get what was coming 385.4 *serve one right*
get what was due 385.4 *serve one right*
get wind of 693.15 *be informed;* 449.2 *detect;* 500.7 *smell*
get wise to 455.13 *get to know;* 695.6 *understand*
get with it 295.18 *be trendy*
get working 393.1 *repair*
get worse 607.7 *become aggravated;* 122.11 *become inferior;* 260.24 *be unhealthy;* 245.1 *deteriorate*
get wrong 412.11 *be mixed up;* 696.9

find unintelligible; 720.1 *misinterpret;* 465.10 *misjudge*
get you gone 371.33 *go away!*
geullah 10.9 *prayer*
gewgaw 124.9 *bauble;* 793.5 *cheap item*
gewgaws 542.6 *decorative articles*
geyser **304.12**; 30.25 *eruption;* 493.3 *heater;* 493.8 *hot place;* 92.10 *miscellaneous*
G-force 414.5 *gravity*
G-force loading 61.6 *motor-racing terms*
ghastliness 236.9 *badness*
ghastly 236.3 *bad;* 582.21 *deathly;* 530.8 *drained of colour;* 612.10 *frightening;* 531.4 *pale*
ghat 146.3 *gulf*
Ghazi 586.6 *militarist*
ghazi 7.4 *religionist*
ghee 25.7 *basic ingredient;* 431.2 *juice*
gherkin 496.2 *seasoning*
ghetto 87.7 *city district;* 309.4 *closed place;* 128.3 *exclusion zone;* 566.9 *group;* 655.4 *place of confinement;* 372.2 *setting apart;* 86.10 *urban area*
ghetto blaster 504.9 *audio device;* 692.18 *radio;* 507.4 *sound maker*
ghettoization 128.1 *exclusion;* 466.4 *social discrimination*
ghettoize 128.7 *exclude*
ghettoized 86.18 *local*
ghetto resident 782.10 *poor person*
ghost **11.11**; 477.5 *fantasy;* 612.5 *frightener;* 97.6 *ghostly presence;* 96.2 *illusion;* 518.5 *imagination;* 525.4 *something that appears;* 101.3 *spiritual world*
ghostbuster 11.12 *occultist*
ghost dance 10.7 *non-Christian ritual;* 11.1 *occultism*
ghost-fire 24.11 *make ceramics*
ghost firing 24.5 *ceramic process*
ghostlike 530.8 *drained of colour*
ghostliness 11.2 *the occult;* 101.2 *unworldliness*
ghostly 582.21 *deathly;* 530.8 *drained of colour;* 101.8 *nonmaterial;* 97.7 *present;* 11.18 *spiritual;* 96.8 *unreal*
ghostly presence 97.6
ghost of a chance 105.4 *improbability*
ghost-ridden 11.19 *bewitched*
ghosts 737.6 *natural mystery;* 582.14 *the spiritual world*
ghost story 17.2, 721.5 *fiction*
ghost town 339.3 *inert thing;* 86.11 *settlement;* 87.9 *town*
ghost word 5.17 *word*
ghostwrite 762.4 *be a substitute;* 550.34 *cover for*
ghostwriter 398.5 *alternative;* 721.10 *descriptive writer;* 740.12 *publisher;* 762.2 *substitute person;* 550.21 *substitution*
ghoul 11.11 *ghost;* 804.9 *wicked person*
ghoulish 651.11 *cruel*
ghoulishly 11.26 *magically*
GI 585.11 *recruit;* 586.8 *soldier*
giant 158.15 *big;* 158.10 *big person;* 158.9 *big thing;* 29.13 *luminosity;* 336.6 *muscleman;* 154.12 *tall;* 154.7, 158.11 *tall person*
giant cartwheel vault 57.6 *pommel horse*
giant circles 57.5 *horizontal bar*
giant elliptical 29.7 *galaxy*
giantess 158.10 *big person*
giantism 158.4 *gigantism*
giant planet 29.16 *planet*
giant reptile 72.6 *extinct reptile*
giant size 158.3 *large scale*
giant-size 158.15 *big*
giant slalom race 68.3 *ski racing*
giant slalom racing 68.3 *ski racing*
giant slalom ski 68.5 *ski equipment*
giant sloth 296.8 *prehistoric animal*
giant spiral 29.7 *galaxy*
giant star 29.13 *luminosity*
giardia 75.10 *parasite*
giardiasis 75.12 *protozoal disease*
gib 71.10 *cat*
gibber 731.7 *be talkative;* 696.7 *be unintelligible;* 515.4 *cry*
gibbering 696.1 *unintelligible*
gibberish 697.1 *nonsense;* 5.5 *nonstandard language;* 696.12 *unintelligible thing*
gibbet 814.5 *execute;* 382.5 *execution;* 361.4 *hanger;* 814.16 *instrument of execution*
gibbous 182.4 *convex;* 181.9 *round*
gibbous moon 29.17 *moon*
gibbousness 182.1 *convexity;* 181.1 *roundness*
Gibbs function 28.38 *thermodynamics*
giberellin 33.17 *plant hormone*
GI bride 570.8 *spouse*
giddiness 642.2 *caprice;* 690.15 *crapulence;* 459.1 *folly;* 337.3 *poor health;* 307.1 *rotation*
giddy 642.1 *capricious;* 639.2 *changeable;* 690.4 *crapulous;* 154.9 *high;* 227.14 *irresolute;* 327.16 *restless;* 307.12 *rotary;* 690.2 *slightly drunk;* 120.3 *unequal;* 486.1 *unskilful*
Gideon Bible 7.12 *religious text*
GIFT 561.3 *propagation*
gift **679.7**; **768.2**; 136.2, 334.2 *ability;* 793.6 *absence of charge;* 229.3, 485.2 *aptitude;* 797.13 *benefit;* 813.7 *bounty;* 608.4, 652.5 *charity;* 768.5 *give;* 750.9 *grant;* 752.6 *offering;* 483.5 *positive stimulus;* 797.12 *proficiency;* 765.5 *profit;* 769.2 *something received;* 139.7 *special skill;* 316.10 *transferred thing*
gifted **485.7**; 442.10, 458.6 *intelligent;* 455.8 *knowledgeable;* 334.13 *powerful;* 797.5 *proficient;* 136.9 *qualified;* 485.6 *skilful*
gifted child 235.8 *exceller;* 485.4 *skilled person*
giftedly 797.25 *skilfully*
gifting 768.1 *giving*
gift of healing 394.11 *medical art*
gift of life 554.4 *biological function*
gift of pleasing 593.4 *lovability*
gift of the gab 729.2 *power of speech;* 731.1 *talkativeness*
gift tax 790.7 *tax*
gift token 768.2 *gift*
gift voucher 768.2 *gift*
giftwrap 525.14 *present;* 550.25 *wrap*
giftwrapper 550.17 *coverer*
giftwrapping 550.4 *wrapping*
gig 21.15 *engagement;* 18.27 *performance*
gigabyte 40.19 *computing terms;* 201.10 *thousand*
gigantesque 158.15 *big*
gigantic 158.15 *big;* 154.12 *tall*
gigantism 158.4
giggle 514.2 *cry of joy;* 514.11, 599.14, 600.8 *laugh;* 600.3 *laughter;* 597.7 *show joy*
giggler 600.4 *rejoicer*
giggling 514.17 *cheering;* 600.10 *laughing;* 600.3 *laughter*
gigolo 796.8 *immoral man;* 567.7 *libertine;* 593.9 *lover;* 664.3 *sponger*
gigue 22.4 *historic dancing*
GI Joe 216.7 *average person;* 564.10 *US inhabitant*
Gilbert and Sullivan 21.4 *musical drama*
gild 550.24 *coat;* 529.15 *colour;* 96.16 *delude;* 699.14 *façade;* 24.11 *make ceramics;* 537.10 *make yellow;* 542.12 *ornament;* 702.11 *practise sophistry*
gilded 24.10 *ceramic;* 699.39 *disguised;* 781.3 *opulent;* 542.10 *ornate;* 537.1 *yellow*
gilded decoration 24.3 *glaze*
gilder 542.8 *decorator*
gilding 542.3 *pattern*
gilding the lily 727.1 *exaggeration*
gild the lily 219.5 *be superfluous;* 727.7 *exaggerate;* 244.1 *improve;* 718.4 *misrepresent;* 542.12 *ornament*
gild the pill 490.9 *give pleasure;* 480.16 *tempt*
gill 74.5 *fish anatomy;* 83.4 *fungal body;* 593.9 *lover;* 90.1 *river*
gill cover 74.5 *fish anatomy*
gill net 74.7 *fishing;* 700.13 *snare*
gills 434.8 *respiration*
gill slit 74.5 *fish anatomy*
gilt 568.14 *female animal;* 71.18 *female mammal;* 43.8 *livestock;* 699.28 *mask;* 542.3 *pattern;* 537.1 *yellow*
gilt-edged 253.7 *guaranteed;* 235.3 *valuable*
gilt-edged security 253.2 *promise*
gimbal 307.4 *axle;* 50.3 *parts of a sailing boat*
gimcrack 124.9 *bauble;* 424.1 *brittle;* 793.5 *cheap item;* 124.4 *trivial;* 254.2 *unsafe;* 337.8 *weak*
gimlet 425.8 *sharp-pointed thing*
gimlet eye 518.2 *eye*
gimlet-eyed 518.21 *seeing*
Gimli 8.11 *heaven*
gimmick 484.3 *expedient plan;* 295.7 *new thing;* 485.1 *skill;* 700.8 *trick*
gimmickry 295.1 *newness*
gimmicky 700.35 *deceptive;* 295.10 *new*
gimp 164.2 *edging*
gimpy 337.10 *ill*
gin 700.13, 700.33 *snare;* 379.1 *trap*
gin and It 558.8 *mixed drink*
gin and Jaguar belt 86.11 *settlement*
gin and tonic 558.8 *mixed drink*
ginger 496.5 *herbs;* 554.1 *life;* 536.1 *orange*
ginger ale 558.6 *soft drink*
ginger beer 558.6 *soft drink*
gingerbread 25.36 *cake*
gingerbread man 717.6 *image*
ginger group 480.14, 483.7 *motivator*
ginger-haired 535.3 *red-haired*
gingerly 665.12 *carefully;* 616.4 *cautious;* 616.7 *cautiously*
gingernob 535.7 *red thing*
ginger up 338.3 *invigorate*
gingery 554.13 *lively*
ginned 700.42 *trapped*
ginned up 690.1 *drunk*
ginormous 158.15 *big*
ginseng 394.7 *tonic*
gin sling 558.8 *mixed drink*
gin-sodden 690.5 *drunken*
gintrap 43.14 *pest control*
gippo 431.2 *juice*
giraffe 71.15 *hoofed mammal;* 154.6 *tall thing*
gird 306.7 *ring*
girded 170.5 *surrounded*
girder 20.4 *building material;* 373.4 *means of connection;* 38.27 *superstructure;* 413.2 *supporting part*
girder bridge 38.21 *bridge*
girdle 373.10 *band;* 179.3 *circular thing;* 251.12 *gag;* 179.7 *make circular;* 251.5 *means of restraint;* 306.7 *ring;* 413.5 *supporting garment;* 551.18 *underwear*
girdle the earth 306.7 *ring*
gird one's loins 336.7 *be strong*
gird up one's loins 243.8 *prepare oneself*
girl 555.9 *child;* 401.6 *domestic servant;* 691.6 *drug;* 568.2 *female;* 568.4 *girlfriend;* 593.9 *lover;* 566.7 *person;* 568.12 *woman in the family;* 555.8 *young woman*
girl Friday 398.4 *deputy;* 392.11, 608.5 *helper;* 578.1 *worker*
girlfriend **568.4**; 569.6 *close friend;* 593.9 *lover;* 223.12 *partner*
girlhood 555.1 *youth*
girlie magazine 796.2 *indecency*
girlish 568.15 *female;* 153.1 *thin;* 555.11 *young*
girlish figure 153.7 *thinness*
girlishly 555.14 *youthfully*
girlishness 568.1 *female sex;* 555.2 *youthfulness*
girllike 555.11 *young*
girl next door 138.9 *everyman*
girly show 21.7 *show*
girn 234.2 *facial distortion;* 234.10 *make faces*
giro cheque 780.14 *paper money*
Girondists 12.6 *political party*
girth 373.10 *band;* 158.1 *size*
GI's 560.2 *defecation*
gisarme 587.8 *sharp weapon*
Giselle 22.11 *classical ballets*
gist **701.4**; 123.3 *chief thing;* 406.1 *contents;* 99.2 *essential content;* 205.5 *largest part;* 694.1 *meaning;* 723.1 *summary;* 447.1 *topic*
git 631.5 *badly behaved person;* 313.15 *go!;* 594.8 *hated person;* 682.6 *nasty person*
give **679.11**; **768.5**; 422.8 *be elastic;* 635.16 *bequeath;* 785.8 *defray;* 787.3 *donate;* 422.1 *elasticity;* 750.30 *grant;* 440.9 *own property;* 813.11 *pay;* 356.10 *produce;* 436.5 *provision;* 419.8 *softness;* 752.11 *volunteer;* 419.16 *yield*
give a bear hug 360.6 *retain*
give a big hand 669.16 *acclaim*
give a birthday present 768.5 *give*
give a black mark 670.20 *censure*
giveable 768.7 *given*
give a bonus 671.6 *be grateful*
give a boost to 213.5 *make bigger*
give a bouquet 669.15 *compliment*
give a break 581.1 *refresh;* 627.10 *show mercy*
give a breather 581.1 *refresh*
give a catcall 753.7 *complain;* 742.11 *gesture*
give access to 773.11 *be hospitable*
give a chance to 102.7 *make possible*
give a Christmas present 768.5 *give*
give a come-hither look 593.26 *court*
give a commission 585.12 *go to war*
give a concession 791.3 *discount*
give a deserved reward 813.9 *reward*
give a direction 397.9 *command*
give admittance to 370.7 *admit*
give a dressing-down 670.20 *censure;* 814.1 *punish*
give a drubbing 246.10 *defeat heavily*
give advice 713.5 *advise*
give a face-lift to 244.1 *improve;* 393.2 *refurbish*
give a false alarm 711.7 *raise the alarm*
give a false idea 720.1 *misinterpret*
give a false impression 700.23 *deceive;* 720.1 *misinterpret*
give a false reading 234.12 *distort the truth*
give a false show 699.28 *mask*
give a firm date 756.7 *promise*
give a flawless performance 230.6 *be perfect*
give a free hand 250.15 *set free*
give a French kiss 593.27 *kiss*
give a good hiding 331.5 *beat*
give a good reason 714.8 *justify*
give a gratuity 768.5 *give*
give a guided tour 738.1 *display*
give a hand 671.6 *be grateful;* 392.17 *help*
give a hand-signal 742.11 *gesture*
give a hearing 504.15 *hear;* 16.76 *judge*
give a hero's welcome 658.12 *greet*
give a hiding 814.3 *hit*
give a Judas kiss 699.23 *be deceitful*
give a knee-jerk reaction 445.10 *be instinctive*
give a last chance 627.10 *show mercy*
give a lead 483.9 *motivate*
give a leg-up 392.22 *improve;* 366.3 *promote*
give a lesson 814.1 *punish*
give a lethal injection 382.19, 814.5 *execute*
give a lift 366.3 *promote*
give allegiance to 663.5 *obey*
give alms 768.6 *give to charity;* 10.18 *perform rites*
give a long-term loan 771.5 *lend*
give a look 742.11 *gesture*
give a loose translation 5.46 *translate*
give a mandate 397.9 *command*
give a miss 634.4 *shy*
give an advantage 239.6 *be convenient*
give a name to 743.10 *identify*
give an anniversary gift 768.5 *give*
give an assist 392.17 *help*
give an audition 705.17 *question*
give and go 58.3 *ice hockey;* 58.9 *play hockey*
give and take 754.4 *compromise;* 755.1, 755.5 *contract;* 759.5 *exchange;* 110.1 *interchange;* 685.1 *moderation;* 110.7, 747.12 *reciprocate;* 385.3 *retaliate;* 761.4, 761.8 *return*
give-and-take 754.1 *compromise;* 754.6 *compromising;* 759.1 *exchange;* 748.2 *mediation;* 747.3 *mutual relationship;* 110.4 *reciprocal*
give an earful 670.20 *censure*
give an edge to 338.3 *invigorate*
give an encore 112.17 *iterate*
give an equal exchange 110.7 *reciprocate*
give an equivalent 759.5 *exchange*
give an example 719.8 *interpret*
give an impetus to 331.1 *impel*
give an impression 171.13 *appear outwardly*
give an intentional walk 48.7 *play baseball*
give an order 397.9 *command*
give an outline of 723.8 *summarize*
give a password 742.9 *use signs*
give a prison sentence 16.79 *convict*
give a prize 768.5 *give*
give a raspberry 753.7 *complain*
give a rebel yell 661.6 *be insubordinate*
give a receipt 769.9 *receive*
give a reference for 669.13 *support*
give a roasting 670.21 *berate*
give a rough idea 420.13 *be unfinished*
give a ruling 397.11 *have authority over*
give a scholarship 813.10 *grant*
give a second chance 627.10 *show mercy*
give a sense to 719.8 *interpret*
give a short-term loan 771.5 *lend*

give a shot 394.20 *doctor*
give a spin 719.13 *interpret news*
give assistance 392.17 *help*
give assurances 252.10 *protect*
give a standing ovation 669.16 *acclaim*
give a start 330.33 *start*
give a substitute 762.6
give a sworn statement 707.18 *vow*
give asylum to 773.11 *be hospitable*
give a talk 733.7 *address*
give a ticket to 370.7 *admit*
give a true report 698.31 *be accurate*
give attention to details 698.31 *be accurate*
give a twist to 720.1 *misinterpret*
give authority 396.21 *grant authority*
give a verbatim account 698.32 *be literal*
giveaway 793.6 *absence of charge*; 793.9 *cheap*; 739.2 *divulgence*; 211.4 *extra*; 793.11 *free of charge*; 765.15 *gainful*; 768.2 *gift*; 768.7 *given*; 740.4 *newspaper*; 768.3 *offering*; 765.5 *profit*
give away 679.10 *be generous*; 739.7 *betray*; 768.5 *give*; 570.16 *join in marriage*; 793.13 *make cheap*; 738.3 *reveal*
giveaway price 793.1 *cheapness*
give a wide berth 252.9 *be safe*
give a wigging 670.20 *censure*
give a wolf whistle 742.11 *gesture*
give a written guarantee 756.8 *guarantee*
give a wrong idea 96.16 *delude*
give back 775.4; 393.3, 761.7 *restore*
give back one's position 775.4 *give back*
give battle 585.14 *battle*
give birth 71.35; 562.6 *be fertile*; 130.26 *produce*; 561.10 *reproduce oneself*
give birth to 554.19; 295.19 *begin*; 356.10 *produce*
give blow for blow 759.5 *exchange*; 110.7 *reciprocate*
give by will 768.5 *give*
give carte blanche to 757.4 *be permissive*
give chase 633.10 *chase*
give consideration 658.10 *be courteous*
give constructive criticism 719.11 *criticize*
give counsel 713.5 *advise*
give courage 613.17
give credit 671.6 *be grateful*; 783.8 *credit*; 771.5 *lend*
give criticism 719.11 *criticize*
give details of 139.23 *particularize*
give diplomatic immunity 250.15 *set free*
give directions 324.6 *direct*
give dispensation 757.3 *permit*
give ear 504.15 *hear*
give enlightenment 719.8 *interpret*
give evidence 716.11; 16.72 *stand trial*; 454.3 *testify*
give evidence of 742.10 *signify*
give fair warning 711.5 *warn*
give false evidence 715.6 *accuse falsely*
give false information 718.5 *misinform*
give feedback 761.9 *reply*
give final notice 397.10 *demand*
give financial reward 813.9 *reward*
give financial support 650.9 *be charitable*
give first aid 394.20 *doctor*
give fitting retribution 714.10 *avenge*
give food and drink 581.1 *refresh*
give forgiveness 649.9 *forgive*
give free 768.5 *give*
give freely 650.9 *be charitable*; 679.10 *be generous*; 768.6 *give to charity*
give free rein 391.4 *liberate*
give free rein to 250.15 *set free*
give generously 679.10 *be generous*; 473.7 *be unselfish*; 768.6 *give to charity*
give ground 303.2 *retreat*
give heart to 338.3 *invigorate*
give her ten 50.21 *avast!*
give his comeuppance 814.2 *penalize*
give hope 554.21 *invigorate*; 475.11 *predict*
give in 483.8 *be motivated*; 226.6 *cease*; 388.3 *submit*; 355.2 *withdraw*; 419.16 *yield*
give in exchange 759.5 *exchange*; 762.6 *give a substitute*; 110.7 *reciprocate*
give in marriage 570.16 *join in marriage*
give in return 759.5 *exchange*
give insight 719.8 *interpret*
give instances 703.16 *explain*
give in to 122.9 *yield to*
give it a go 353.1 *attempt*; 448.13 *invent*
give it a shot 353.11 *here goes!*
give it a try 353.1 *attempt*
give it a whirl 353.1 *attempt*
give it one's all 353.2 *try hard*
give it some welly 338.2 *be full of vigour*; 334.11 *give power*
give it straight 269.4 *be concise*; 799.6 *be honourable*
give it the gun 338.2 *be full of vigour*; 334.11 *give power*
give job satisfaction 813.9 *reward*
give laws 16.68 *legislate*
give laws to 12.11 *govern*
give leave 750.29 *permit*
give life to 554.19 *give birth to*; 561.13 *propagate*
give light 522.24 *light*
give lines 814.1 *punish*
give lip 660.25 *answer back*
give money 787.3 *donate*
give moral support 413.14
given 27.77; **768.7**; 452.1 *certain*; 222.7 *circumstantial*; 793.11 *free of charge*; 632.14 *habituated*; 436.8 *provisional*; 769.11 *receiving*; 476.8 *supposed*
given a bad press 670.33 *criticized*
given away 793.11 *free of charge*; 768.7 *given*
given consideration 648.5
give new life to 392.19 *support*
give news coverage to 550.33 *fix*
given free 793.11 *free of charge*
given name 721.8 *name*
given notice to quit 767.13 *dismissed*
give no clue 696.10 *be unexplained*
give no credit 672.6 *be ungrateful*
given one's marching orders 767.13 *dismissed*
give no quarter 628.6 *be pitiless*; 647.5 *be severe*; 382.18 *slaughter*
give nothing away 737.12 *keep secret*
give notice 767.10 *dismiss*; 475.11 *predict*; 605.5 *resign*; 711.5 *warn*
give no trouble 265.15 *be easy*
given out 377.22 *distributed*
given permission 648.5 *given consideration*
given status 108.6 *ranked*
given that 222.15 *under the circumstances*
given the boot 767.13 *dismissed*
given the chop 767.13 *dismissed*
given the heave-ho 767.13 *dismissed*
given the red light 709.8 *refused*
given the sack 767.13 *dismissed*
given the third degree 705.16 *questioned*
given the thumbs down 709.8 *refused*
given to drink 690.5 *drunken*
given up 133.9 *discontinued*
give occasion for 344.9 *be the cause of*
give off 432.27; 560.15 *excrete*; 559.7 *secrete*
give one a bellyful 620.6 *be boring*
give one a fright 630.9 *surprise*
give one a loan 771.5 *lend*
give one a necklace 814.5 *execute*
give one a turn 630.9 *surprise*
give one his head 250.15 *set free*
give one leeway 250.15 *set free*
give one pause 481.2 *deter*
give one's all 576.8 *exert oneself*
give one's assent 669.12 *accept*
give one's best regards 658.10 *be courteous*
give one's best wishes 658.10 *be courteous*
give one's blessing 669.12 *accept*; 650.8 *be benevolent*; 750.28 *consent*; 413.14 *give moral support*; 757.3 *permit*
give one's cards 144.17 *relegate*
give one's consent 669.12 *accept*
give oneself airs 622.26 *be too proud*; 673.15 *be vain*
give oneself to 638.9 *undertake*
give oneself up 388.3 *submit*
give one's IOU 772.7 *borrow*; 756.8 *guarantee*; 253.11 *promise*
give one's marching orders 371.2 *dismiss*; 144.17 *relegate*
give one's money back 775.5 *compensate*
give one's oath 707.18 *vow*
give one's quietus 382.19 *execute*
give one's walking papers 144.17 *relegate*
give one's word 253.11, 756.7 *promise*; 707.18 *vow*
give one the bird 668.25 *taunt*
give one the giggles 272.7 *make one laugh*
give one the slip 389.6 *elude*; 634.6 *evade*
give one trouble 264.17 *be difficult*
give one what for 670.21 *berate*
give out 739.6 *divulge*; 768.5 *give*; 371.14 *let out*; 740.13 *make public*; 441.1 *waste*
give over 226.6 *cease*; 768.5 *give*; 226.12 *stop!*
give peace to 749.4 *pacify*
give permission 396.21 *grant authority*; 757.3 *permit*
give personal recognizance 253.11 *promise*
give personal reward 813.9 *reward*
give place 303.2 *retreat*
give pleasure 241.13; **490.9**
give points to 120.5 *be unequal*
give power 334.11
give praise to 768.5 *give*
give priority 129.17
give quarter 648.3 *be lenient*; 627.10 *show mercy*
giver 768.4; 436.3 *provider*
give recognition 783.11 *recognize*
give refuge to 370.9 *welcome*
give relief to 392.19 *support*
give renewed strength to 581.1 *refresh*
give respect 658.10 *be courteous*
give respite 627.10 *show mercy*
give rise to 344.9 *be the cause of*
give sanctuary to 773.11 *be hospitable*; 370.9 *welcome*
give satisfaction 807.5 *atone*; 752.14 *offer reparation*
give scope 265.16 *make easy*; 250.15 *set free*
give security 253.12 *certify*
give shelter to 773.11 *be hospitable*
give some lip 706.18 *answer back*
give someone a bell 692.32 *telephone*
give someone a buzz 692.32 *telephone*
give someone a call 692.32 *telephone*
give someone a chance 757.4 *be permissive*; 750.30 *grant*
give someone a fright 612.13 *frighten*
give someone a refill 558.15 *provide drink*
give someone a tinkle 692.32 *telephone*
give someone carte blanche 250.15 *set free*
give someone his head 757.4 *be permissive*
give someone lip 659.7 *be discourteous*; 661.5 *defy*
give someone the axe 708.15 *terminate*
give someone the bird 753.7 *complain*; 364.1 *repel*
give someone the blues 626.10 *make sullen*
give someone the boot 767.10 *dismiss*
give someone the chop 767.10 *dismiss*; 708.15 *terminate*
give someone the finger 753.7 *complain*
give someone the heave-ho 767.10 *dismiss*; 708.15 *terminate*
give someone the once-over 518.14 *inspect*
give someone the pip 626.10 *make sullen*
give someone the slip 766.15 *lose someone*; 313.3 *quit*
give strength to 336.8 *strengthen*
give stripes 814.3 *hit*
give strokes 814.3 *hit*
give suck 558.15 *provide drink*; 557.25 *provide food*
give support 392.23 *advise*
give supportive evidence 714.8 *justify*
give sworn testimony 707.18 *vow*
give teeth 334.11 *give power*
give temporarily 771.5 *lend*
give terms 749.4 *pacify*
give thanks 671.7; 671.6 *be grateful*; 600.7 *dance*; 10.19 *offer worship*; 10.20 *pray*; 9.7 *worship*
give the alarm 711.7 *raise the alarm*
give the all clear 750.28 *consent*; 757.3 *permit*
give the axe 371.2 *dismiss*
give the battle cry 661.6 *be insubordinate*
give the big E 128.8 *eject*; 144.17 *relegate*
give the boot 371.2 *dismiss*
give the brown envelope 144.17 *relegate*
give the bum's rush 371.1 *expel*
give the cat 814.3 *hit*
give the cold shoulder 668.23 *insult*; 371.4 *ostracize*; 670.15 *withhold approval*
give the elbow 128.8 *eject*; 144.17 *relegate*
give the freedom of 250.15 *set free*
give the game away 739.7 *betray*
give the go-ahead 669.12 *accept*; 750.28 *consent*; 757.3 *permit*
give the go-by 634.1 *avoid*; 668.23 *insult*
give the green light 669.12 *accept*; 757.3 *permit*
give the heave-ho 144.17 *relegate*
give the hook 371.2 *dismiss*
give the lie to 708.11 *rebut*
give the nod 750.28 *consent*; 757.3 *permit*
give the OK 669.12 *accept*; 750.28 *consent*; 757.3 *permit*; 714.7 *vindicate*
give the old heave-ho 371.1 *expel*
give the red light 670.15 *withhold approval*
give the run of 250.15 *set free*
give the sack 371.2, 767.10 *dismiss*
give the silent treatment 371.4 *ostracize*
give the third degree 814.4 *torture*
give the thumbs down 399.3 *veto*; 670.15 *withhold approval*
give the thumbs up 669.12 *accept*; 750.28 *consent*
give the true story 698.29 *be truthful*
give the V-sign 753.7 *complain*; 742.11 *gesture*
give the word 707.17 *affirm*
give the works 814.4 *torture*
give the wrong answer 802.19 *be wrong*
give three cheers 669.16 *acclaim*; 671.6 *be grateful*; 514.12, 598.8 *cheer*
give thumbs up 757.3 *permit*
give tit for tat 759.5 *exchange*; 110.7 *reciprocate*; 785.13 *retaliate*
give to 349.1 *use*
give to charity 768.6; 787.3 *donate*
give to eat 557.25 *provide food*
give tongue 507.8 *be loud*; 515.4 *cry*
give to understand 693.11 *inform*
give trouble 264.22 *cause trouble*
give two cheers 728.21 *detract from*
give umbrage 624.9 *offend*
give undivided attention to 471.11 *take note of*
give up 611.9 *be hopeless*; 456.9 *be ignorant*; 480.18 *be persuaded*; 684.5 *be self-restrained*; 226.6 *cease*; 639.10 *compromise*; 487.5 *disaccustom*; 470.2 *discard*; 133.12 *discontinue*; 767.9 *dispose of*; 128.7 *exclude*; 768.5 *give*; 341.4 *not act*; 355.1 *relinquish*; 605.5 *resign*; 559.7 *secrete*; 350.6 *stop using*; 388.3 *submit*; 355.2 *withdraw*
give up alcohol 689.4
give up arms 685.3 *be moderate*
give up drinking 689.4 *give up alcohol*
give up eating 687.5 *fast*
give up everything for 638.9 *undertake*
give up hope 611.9 *be hopeless*
give up one's friends 655.12 *be unsocial*
give up the crown 605.5 *resign*
give up the ghost 582.15 *die*; 131.19 *expire*
give up the idea 355.1 *relinquish*
give up work 580.4 *have leisure*
give utterance to 729.11 *speak*
give vent to 739.6 *divulge*; 371.14 *let out*
give voice 707.17 *affirm*; 514.15 *sing out*
give vows 252.10 *protect*
give warning 475.11 *predict*
give way 424.4 *be brittle*; 337.6 *be weak*; 639.10 *compromise*; 602.9 *despair*; 305.10 *droop*; 303.2 *retreat*; 388.3 *submit*; 419.16 *yield*
give weight to 123.8 *make important*
give what for 814.2 *penalize*

give what is due 813.11 *pay*
give with both hands 679.10 *be generous*
Giving 768
giving 768.1; **768.8**; **813.18**; 650.7 *charitable*; 787.7 *donation*; 422.6 *elastic*; 679.1 *generous*; 771.1 *lending*; 419.2 *pliant*
giving away 742.14 *signifying*
Giving Back 775
giving back 775.1; 393.9, 761.2 *restoration*
giving credit 771.1 *lending*; 671.5 *thanking*
giving in 388.1 *submission*
giving light 522.3 *lightening*
giving notice 605.1 *resignation*
giving out 377.1 *dispersion*
giving temporarily 771.1 *lending*
giving up 767.1 *disposal*; 355.3 *relinquishment*
giving up the fort 388.1 *submission*
giving way 388.1 *submission*
gizmo 484.3 *expedient plan*; 348.2 *instrument*; 438.1 *tool*
gizzard 72.16 *avian anatomy*
glabrous 552.13 *hairless*; 421.1 *smooth*
glacé 522.17 *lustrous*; 421.4 *polished*; 421.11 *smooth*
glacé fruit 498.2 *sweetener*
glacial 494.8 *cold*; 30.60 *glaciated*; 296.15 *primal*
glacial advance 30.40 *glaciation*
glacial deposit 30.27 *sediment*
glacial erosion 30.35 *weathering*
glacial lake 88.1 *lake*
glacial maximum 30.40 *glaciation*
glacial period 284.3 *geological period*; 30.40 *glaciation*
glacial recession 30.40 *glaciation*
glacial surge 30.40 *glaciation*
glacial valley 30.7 *landform*
glaciate 416.8 *be dense*; 494.12 *make cold*; 418.10 *solidify*
glaciated 30.60
glaciation 30.40; 31.40 *climatic change*; 416.2 *concentration*; 418.6 *solidification*
glacier 30.38; 31.32 *freeze*; 494.5 *ice*; 62.5 *rock face*
glacier milk 30.38 *glacier*
glaciological 30.48 *geological*
glaciologist 30.3 *geologist*
glaciology 30.1 *earth science*
glacis 384.11 *fortification*; 62.5 *rock face*
glad 598.1 *cheerful*; 597.4 *happy*
gladden 598.6 *bring cheer*; 597.8 *cause joy*; 490.9 *give pleasure*
glade 141.3 *geographical space*; 308.8 *open space*; 79.4 *trees*
glad eye 518.6 *look*
glad-hand 654.13 *fraternize*
gladiator 586.3 *athlete*
gladiatorial 586.35 *martial*; 584.8 *military*
gladiatorial combat 382.4 *slaughter*
gladly 598.9 *cheerfully*; 597.9 *joyfully*; 636.16 *willingly*
gladness 597.1 *happiness*
glad rags 551.1 *dress*
gladsome 597.4 *happy*
Gladstone bag 410.9 *baggage*
glair 430.3 *paste*
glaive 587.8 *sharp weapon*
glamorize 545.8, 547.15 *beautify*
glamorous 545.5 *beautiful*; 553.7 *fashionable*
glamorously 551.36 *dressily*; 553.10 *fashionably*
glamour 545.1 *gorgeousness*; 11.5 *spell*
glance 492.12 *abut*; 53.17, 330.26 *bat*; 311.15 *change direction*; 325.2 *divert*; 742.3, 742.11 *gesture*; 522.25 *light up*; 518.6, 518.13 *look*; 147.19 *meet*; 147.4 *meeting*; 53.9 *stroke*
glancing 742.15 *gestural*; 147.11 *meeting*; 492.9 *touching*
glancing light 541.5 *variegated thing*
glancingly 518.26 *watchfully*
gland 559.3; 172.4 *insides*
glanders 260.18 *veterinary disease*
glandular 559.5 *of a secretion*; 559.4 *secretory*; 172.10 *visceral*
glandular fever 260.6 *infection*
glandularly 559.8
glandulous 559.5 *of a secretion*
glandulously 559.8 *glandularly*
glans penis 561.8 *organs of reproduction*
glare 624.11 *be angry*; 626.11 *be irritable*; 643.8 *be serious*; 670.10 *disapproving look*; 522.25 *light up*; 518.6, 518.13 *look*; 522.2 *quality of light*; 31.61 *shine*; 624.6 *sign of anger*; 625.2 *sign of irascibility*; 626.4 *sign of irritableness*
glaring 522.16 *bright*; 520.2 *clear*; 529.12 *gaudy*; 738.14 *manifest*; 518.21 *seeing*; 336.12 *strong to the senses*; 740.20 *well-known*
glaring error 274.10 *blunder*
Glasgow 87.4 *British cities*
Glashem 8.11 *heaven*
glasnost 738.11 *openness*
glass 527.9; 20.18 *be an architect*; 424.3 *brittle thing*; 20.4 *building material*; 203.3 *container*; 32.4 *crystal*; 558.2 *drink*; 558.10 *drink container*; 410.13 *drinking vessel*; 24.9 *industrial ceramics*; 24.11 *make ceramics*; 435.1 *materials*; 518.8 *reflection*; 421.8 *smooth thing*; 527.8 *transparent thing*; 337.5 *weak thing*; 31.7 *weather instruments*
glass-blower 578.2 *artisan*
glass case 527.8 *transparent thing*
glass ceiling 466.4 *social discrimination*
glass electrode 32.19 *electrochemistry*
glasses 519.3 *aid for poor sight*; 28.29 *optical element*; 527.8 *transparent thing*; 518.10 *visual aid*
glass eye 519.3 *aid for poor sight*
glass fibre 38.25 *construction material*; 24.9 *industrial ceramics*
glasshouse 424.3 *brittle thing*; 44.4 *nursery*; 565.7 *room*; 815.2 *the inside*; 527.8 *transparent thing*
glassiness 522.2 *quality of light*; 421.7 *smoothness*; 527.5 *transparency*
glass-like 527.1 *transparent*
glasspaper 427.12 *abrasive*; 365.7 *eraser*; 420.7 *rough thing*; 425.12 *sharpener*; 421.9 *smoother*
glass sculpture 19.12 *sculpture*
glass snake 73.2 *lizard*
glassware 24.1 *ceramics*; 410.16 *crockery*; 527.9 *glass*
glassy 530.8 *drained of colour*; 418.1 *hard*; 522.17 *lustrous*; 528.3 *mirror-like*; 421.4 *polished*; 268.10 *slippery*; 527.1 *transparent*
glassy-eyed 690.2 *slightly drunk*
glassy rock 30.30 *igneous rock*
Glaswegian 564.9 *British inhabitant*
glaucoma 519.1 *blindness*; 260.7 *tropical disease*
glaucomatous 519.8 *blind*
glaucous 538.1 *green*
glaze 24.3; **522.27**; 550.24 *coat*; 550.3 *coating*; 494.5 *ice*; 24.11 *make ceramics*; 524.10 *make dim*; 430.3 *paste*; 529.4 *pigment*; 421.10 *polish*; 421.11 *smooth*; 498.8 *sweeten*
glazed 24.10 *ceramic*; 494.8 *cold*; 550.36 *covered*; 421.4 *polished*; 690.2 *slightly drunk*; 498.6 *sweet*
glazed frost 31.29 *hail*
glazed ware 24.1 *ceramics*
glaze-fire 24.11 *make ceramics*
glaze firing 24.5 *ceramic process*
glaze ice 31.29 *hail*
glaze kiln 24.6 *ceramic workshop*
glaze over 524.9 *be dim*
glazer 24.7 *potter*
glazing 24.10 *ceramic*; 24.5 *ceramic process*
GLC 32.17 *analysis*
gleam 522.25 *light up*; 522.2 *quality of light*
gleaming 522.17 *lustrous*; 421.4 *polished*
gleamingly 522.30 *lightly*
glean 765.11 *acquire*; 369.15 *draw out*; 43.17 *farm*; 469.4 *pick*; 439.6 *store*
gleaner 256.12 *cleaner*; 376.35 *collector*; 765.7 *gainer*
gleaning 765.3 *acquisition*
gleanings 469.9 *chosen thing*; 765.4 *earnings*; 774.4 *stolen goods*; 773.5 *takings*; 765.6 *yield*
glebe 43.11 *farmland*
glee 597.1 *happiness*; 516.2 *song*
gleefully 597.9 *joyfully*
gleefulness 597.1 *happiness*
gleet 431.3 *body fluid*; 560.7 *pus*
gleg 342.18 *active*
glen 183.2 *concave land*; 92.8 *valley*
glengarry 551.15 *headgear*
glib 658.9 *deferential*; 265.9 *easy*; 421.6 *smooth-mannered*; 731.5 *talkative*
glibly 658.16 *deferentially*; 421.16 *suavely*; 731.10 *talkatively*
glibness 658.4 *deference*; 265.2 *simplicity*; 731.1 *talkativeness*
glib tongue 645.3 *cunning person*
glide 53.17 *bat*; 415.9 *be light*; 736.11 *conceal oneself*; 54.5 *fence*; 54.3 *fencing movements*; 90.7 *flow*; 322.10 *fly*; 265.19 *go easily*; 421.12 *go smoothly*; 73.15 *live as a reptile*; 30.26 *mass movement*; 341.4 *not act*; 305.6, 305.14 *slide*; 268.16 *slip*; 53.9 *stroke*
glide path 322.5 *flight*
glide plane 162.2 *symmetry operation*
glider 322.8 *aircraft*
glide reflection 27.48 *transformation*
glider pilot 322.3 *aircraft personnel*
gliding 322.1 *aviation*; 305.18 *falling*
glimmer 522.25 *light up*; 31.61 *shine*
glimmering 522.15 *lucent*
glimpse 449.1 *discover*; 449.6 *discovery*; 518.6 *look*; 518.12 *see*
glint 522.25 *light up*; 522.2 *quality of light*
glinting 522.16 *bright*
glissade 22.9 *ballet steps*; 62.9 *mountaineer*; 305.6, 305.14 *slide*; 268.16 *slip*
glissading 62.3 *climbing technique*; 62.8 *mountaineering*
glissando 305.6 *slide*
glissées 22.10 *positions at the barre*
glisten 522.25 *light up*
glistening 522.17 *lustrous*; 522.2 *quality of light*
glister 522.2 *quality of light*
glitch 236.8 *inferiority*; 378.2 *obstacle*; 226.2 *stop*; 274.14 *technical error*
Glitnir 8.11 *heaven*
glitter 522.25 *light up*; 522.2 *quality of light*
glitterati 765.8 *wealthy people*
glittering 522.16 *bright*; 781.3 *opulent*
glittery 522.16 *bright*
glitz 520.4 *clarity*; 675.1 *tastelessness*
glitzy 520.2 *clear*; 656.7 *dressed-up*; 781.3 *opulent*; 675.7 *vulgar*
GLM 68.1 *skiing*
gloaming 524.1 *dimness*; 291.1 *evening*
gloating 651.3 *callousness*
gloating pleasure 651.3 *callousness*
glob 158.7 *mass*
global 141.12 *extensive*; 127.7 *including*; 764.5 *jointly possessing*; 30.50 *terrestrial*; 138.16 *universal*; 204.6 *whole*
global approach 127.1 *inclusion*
globality 138.1 *generality*
globalize 138.23 *generalize*
globally 141.16 *extensively*; 127.9 *inclusively*; 764.6 *in common*
global outlook 85.5 *internationalism*
global view 138.7
global village 764.1 *joint possession*
global war 585.1 *war*
global warming 31.40 *climatic change*; 493.5 *hot weather*
globe 163.4, 717.7 *map*; 181.3 *round thing*; 204.2 *whole thing*
globose 181.9 *round*
globosely 181.13 *roundly*
globosity 181.1 *roundness*
globous 181.9 *round*
globular 181.9 *round*
globular cloud 31.20 *cloud appearance*
globular cluster 29.9 *constellation*
globularity 181.1 *roundness*
globularly 181.13 *roundly*
globular protein 33.9 *protein*
globule 181.3 *round thing*
globulin 431.4 *blood*; 33.9 *protein*
glomerate 376.48 *cumulate*
glom on to 765.9 *gain*
gloom 523.1 *darkness*; 602.2 *depression*; 611.1 *hopelessness*; 643.4 *solemnity*; 523.7 *spiritual darkness*
gloom and doom 249.1 *adversity*; 611.1 *hopelessness*
gloomily 532.12 *blackly*; 523.15 *darkly*; 533.9 *greyly*; 611.11 *hopelessly*; 602.12 *joylessly*; 626.13 *sullenly*
gloominess 523.1 *darkness*; 602.2 *depression*; 533.7 *dullness*; 611.1 *hopelessness*
gloomy 249.6 *adverse*; 523.11 *benighted*; 31.49 *cloudy*; 523.8 *dark*; 539.3, 602.6 *depressed*; 524.7 *dimmed*; 533.3 *dull*; 611.4 *hopeless*; 532.6 *sad*; 626.6 *sullen*
gloomy day 249.4 *time of adversity*
glop 430.7 *slime*
Gloria 10.6 *Eucharist*; 10.8 *hymn*
Gloria in Excelsis 10.8 *hymn*
Gloria Patri 10.8 *hymn*
glorification 8.9 *deification*; 213.1 *increase*; 669.3 *praise*; 575.1 *right*; 10.3 *rite of worship*; 9.1 *worship*
glorified 8.15 *deified*; 10.21 *ritualistic*; 9.11 *worshipped*
glorify 8.17 *deify*; 213.5 *make bigger*; 123.8 *make important*; 10.19 *offer worship*; 667.17, 669.14 *praise*; 740.16 *publicize*; 9.7 *worship*
gloriole 522.12 *highlight*
glorious 185.6 *eminent*; 600.9 *rejoicing*; 10.21 *ritualistic*; 235.1 *worthy*
gloriously 185.11 *eminently*; 235.11 *worthily*
gloriously drunk 690.1 *drunk*
glory 600.2 *fanfare*; 669.3 *praise*; 185.1 *prominence*; 248.1 *prosperity*; 600.5 *rejoice*; 575.1 *right*
glory hole 565.7 *room*
glory in 622.25 *be proud of*
glory of war 585.2
gloss 719.10 *annotate*; 719.2 *annotation*; 5.28 *dictionary*; 700.12, 700.32 *disguise*; 722.4 *dissertate*; 722.1 *dissertation*; 699.14 *façade*; 265.16 *make easy*; 699.28 *mask*; 421.10 *polish*; 702.11 *practise sophistry*; 522.2 *quality of light*; 421.11 *smooth*; 5.46 *translate*
glossarial 719.16 *annotative*; 722.5 *expository*; 220.12 *inventorial*; 5.42 *worded*
glossarially 220.13 *inventorially*; 5.50 *lexically*
glossarist 722.3 *dissertator*; 719.6 *interpreter*
glossary 5.28, 220.3 *dictionary*; 406.5 *divisions*
glossator 719.6 *interpreter*
glossed 699.39, 700.41 *disguised*; 719.15 *interpreted*
glosseme 5.17 *word*
gloss finish 41.12 *development*
glossiness 421.7 *smoothness*
glossolalia 514.3 *cry of praise*; 5.5 *nonstandard language*; 729.2 *power of speech*; 7.2 *religiousness*; 11.5 *spell*
glossological 5.38 *linguistic*
glossologist 5.2 *linguist*
glossology 5.1 *linguistics*
gloss over 736.8 *conceal*; 699.28 *mask*
gloss paint 529.5 *paint*
glossy 522.17 *lustrous*; 421.4 *polished*
glossy magazine 740.5 *journal*
glossy paper 435.3 *paper*
glottal stop 5.16 *spoken letter*
glottis 729.5 *organ of speech*
glottochronological 5.38 *linguistic*
glottochronology 5.1 *linguistics*
glottological 5.38 *linguistic*
glove 551.32 *dress*; 58.1 *hockey*; 58.5 *lacrosse*; 53.6 *pad*
gloved 551.29 *dressed*
glove puppet 717.6 *image*
glover 551.26 *fashion designer*
gloves 551.25 *accessories*; 384.6 *protective clothing*; 68.5 *ski equipment*; 66.1 *soccer*
glow 545.7 *be beautiful*; 493.14 *be hot*; 529.9 *complexion*; 726.1 *emphasis*; 726.6 *emphasize*; 493.6, 522.8 *fire*; 522.25 *light up*; 529.16 *make up*; 522.2 *quality of light*; 535.9 *redden*; 535.5 *redness*; 560.19 *sweat*
glow discharge 28.46, 39.6 *electric discharge*
glower 624.11 *be angry*; 626.11 *be irritable*; 643.8 *be serious*; 659.8 *get angry*; 518.6, 518.13 *look*; 624.6 *sign of anger*; 625.2 *sign of irascibility*; 626.4 *sign of irritableness*
glowering 626.7 *irritable*; 626.8 *overcast*; 625.5 *showing irascibility*
glower lour 625.7 *frown*
glowing 529.11 *colourful*; 726.3 *emphatic*; 259.1 *healthy*; 493.9 *hot*; 522.15 *lucent*; 535.2 *red-faced*; 560.28 *sweaty*
glowing health 259.3 *health*
glowingly 522.30 *lightly*
glowing terms 669.4 *compliment*
glow lamp 39.20 *electron tube*
glow-worm 522.9 *firefly*; 76.5 *larva*; 75.6 *worm*
glucocorticoid 33.16 *hormone*
glucose 557.11 *food content*; 498.2 *sweetener*
glucoside 33.3 *carbohydrate*
glue 267.3, 430.2 *adhesive*; 267.7 *cause to adhere*; 373.11 *connect*; 360.6 *retain*; 430.10 *stick*; 360.3 *tools for gripping*
glued 373.15 *connected*; 360.10 *retained*
glue ear 260.9 *respiratory disease*
gluelike 360.9 *retentive*; 430.8 *viscous*
gluelikeness 430.1 *viscosity*

glue onto 211.6 *add*
glue-sniffing 691.1 *drug-taking*
glue together 211.6 *add;* 393.1 *repair*
gluey 267.9 *adhesive;* 360.9 *retentive;* 430.8 *viscous*
glueyness 430.1 *viscosity*
gluhwein 498.5 *sweet drink*
glulam timber 38.25 *construction material*
glum 539.3, 602.6 *depressed;* 643.1 *solemn;* 626.6 *sullen*
glume 81.3 *grass plant*
glumly 602.12 *joylessly;* 643.10 *solemnly;* 626.13 *sullenly*
glumness 602.2 *depression;* 626.1 *sullenness*
glut 620.6 *be boring;* 219.4 *be excessive;* 688.5 *be greedy;* 793.2 *declining prices;* 219.1 *excess;* 217.8 *plenty;* 562.2 *productiveness;* 219.3 *superfluity;* 215.4 *surplus*
gluten 430.2 *adhesive;* 33.9 *protein*
glutenous 430.8 *viscous*
glutinose 430.8 *viscous*
glutinosity 430.1 *viscosity*
glutinous 430.8 *viscous*
glutinousness 430.1 *viscosity*
glut oneself 688.5 *be greedy;* 217.4 *suffice*
glutted 217.3 *filled*
glut the market 793.13 *make cheap*
glutting 688.6 *gluttonous*
glutton **688.4**; 617.6 *desirer;* 557.18 *eater;* 686.5 *self-indulgent person*
glutton for punishment 342.10 *busy person*
glutton for work 342.10 *busy person*
gluttonize 688.5 *be greedy;* 557.22 *eat well*
gluttonizing 688.6 *gluttonous*
gluttonous **688.6**; 617.9 *desirous;* 557.26 *eating;* 686.8 *overindulgent*
gluttonously **688.7**; 557.28 *carnivorously*
Gluttony 688
gluttony **688.1**; 557.2 *appetite;* 219.2 *overdoing it;* 686.3 *overindulgence;* 804.5 *seven deadly sins*
glycan 33.4 *polysaccharide*
glyceride 33.7 *fat*
glycerinate 268.18 *lubricate*
glycerine 33.3 *carbohydrate;* 268.5 *lubricant;* 498.2 *sweetener*
glycerinize 268.18 *lubricate*
glycerol 33.3 *carbohydrate*
glycerolate 268.18 *lubricate*
glycerophosphatide 33.6 *lipid*
glycogen 33.4 *polysaccharide*
glycolipid 33.6 *lipid*
glycolysis 34.6 *cell biology;* 33.24 *respiration*
glycolytic 33.26 *biochemical*
glycoprotein 33.9 *protein*
glycosaminoglycan 33.4 *polysaccharide*
glycoside 33.3 *carbohydrate*
glyph 19.13 *relief-carving*
glyptic 19.25 *sculptural*
glyptography 19.15 *engraving*
gnarl 404.12 *coarsen;* 420.12 *make rough;* 79.2 *tree part*
gnarled 420.2 *coarse;* 416.7 *condensed;* 79.14 *treelike*
gnarly 420.2 *coarse*
gnash 557.21 *eat*
gnashing 624.16 *angry;* 557.1 *eating;* 380.6 *violent*
gnashing the teeth 624.4 *anger*
gnash one's teeth 335.6 *be powerless;* 742.11 *gesture*
gnat 76.1 *insect*
gnat's piss 690.12 *alcohol*
gnaw 365.13 *abrade;* 491.10 *be painful;* 557.21 *eat;* 245.5 *hurt;* 372.9 *separate;* 441.1 *waste*
gnaw at the roots 245.5 *hurt*
gnaw away 365.13 *abrade*
gnawing 365.10 *frictional;* 491.5 *painful;* 71.30 *rodent-like*
gnawing mammal 71.12
gneissic 30.57 *chalky*
gneissoid 30.57 *chalky*
gneissose 30.57 *chalky*
gnome 11.11 *ghost;* 70.7 *legendary beast;* 159.4 *little person;* 745.1 *maxim;* 149.5 *short person*
gnomic 745.2 *proverbial*
gnomic formula 745.1 *maxim*
gnomon 281.8 *face*
gnomonic projection 717.7 *map*
gnosiology 4.6 *branch of philosophy*
gnosis 737.7 *esotericism;* 455.1 *knowledge*
gnostic 6.18 *educated;* 266.2 *obscure;* 696.1 *unintelligible*
Gnosticism 4.7 *school of thought*
gnotobiotic 34.20 *biological*
gnotobiotically 43.22 *agriculturally*
gnotobiotics 34.1 *life science;* 43.3 *livestock farming*
GNP 765.4 *earnings*
go 707.6 *assertiveness;* 353.5 *attempt;* 246.8 *be effective;* 300.13 *be in motion;* 407.23 *be in order;* 346.7 *be operational;* 298.2 *cycle;* 313.1, 526.2 *depart;* 342.4 *energy;* 560.15 *excrete;* 315.9 *exit;* 448.1 *experiment;* 141.8 *intervening space;* 276.4 *period of activity;* 318.9 *proceed;* 145.7 *reach;* 393.7 *resort;* 634.8 *run away;* 324.7 *take a direction;* 338.1 *vigour;* 355.2 *withdraw*
go! 300.19; **313.15**
go aboard 314.9 *enter;* 304.15 *mount;* 313.5 *set out*
go about 306.6 *orbit;* 50.15 *sail;* 354.1 *undertake*
go absent without leave 389.5 *escape;* 634.8 *run away;* 355.2 *withdraw*
go across 318.11 *cross*
goad 607.8 *annoy;* 496.13 *be piquant;* 262.4 *haste;* 262.1 *hasten;* 331.1 *impel;* 480.8 *incentive;* 380.9 *make violent;* 483.10 *manipulate;* 624.9 *offend;* 752.9 *offer;* 425.8 *sharp-pointed thing;* 483.3, 488.3 *stimulus;* 425.16 *use a sharp tool*
goaded 483.12 *motivated*
go adrift 325.3 *go astray*
go after 316.14 *bring back;* 633.8 *pursue;* 638.9 *undertake*
go against 113.16 *be contrary;* 347.3 *counteract*
go against the grain 404.14; 751.8 *be different;* 118.19 *be independent;* 596.7 *cause dislike;* 420.12 *make rough*
go ahead 452.26 *certainly!;* 302.11 *course;* 302.9 *maintain progress;* 130.18 *make a beginning;* 302.3 *press on*
go-ahead 669.1 *approval;* 750.7 *consent;* 354.6 *enterprising;* 302.17 *forward;* 538.15 *green light;* 338.4 *vigorous*
go ahead of 129.15 *precede*
goal 131.14 *aim;* 312.15 *destination;* 324.1 *direction;* 58.1 *hockey;* 58.7 *hurling;* 58.3 *ice hockey;* 58.5 *lacrosse;* 480.11, 483.1 *motive;* 482.6 *objective;* 617.5 *object of desire;* 49.4 *playing terms;* 446.4 *purpose;* 64.1 *rugger;* 66.1 *soccer;* 246.3 *successful thing;* 353.6 *venture*
goal area 58.5 *lacrosse;* 66.1 *soccer*
goal crease 58.3 *ice hockey;* 58.5 *lacrosse*
goal-directed 446.12 *purposive*
goalie 58.2 *hockey player;* 58.4 *ice hockey player*
goalkeeper 66.3 *football player;* 58.2 *hockey player;* 58.4 *ice hockey player;* 384.15 *protector*
goalkeeper's protective clothing 58.1 *hockey;* 58.3 *ice hockey*
goalkeeper's stick 58.3 *ice hockey*
goal kick 66.2 *football play*
goal line 64.1 *rugger;* 66.1 *soccer;* 46.4 *stadium*
go all out 332.4 *be swift;* 576.8 *exert oneself;* 250.19 *liberalize;* 353.2 *try hard*
go all out for 446.18 *aim*
goalminder 58.4 *ice hockey player*
go along with 750.21 *be in accord;* 636.13 *be willing;* 117.8 *comply;* 747.15 *concur;* 663.5 *obey;* 388.3 *submit*
goal-oriented 483.12 *motivated;* 480.20 *persuadable*
goal post 66.1 *soccer*
goal posts 64.1 *rugger;* 46.4 *stadium*
goalscorer 66.3 *football player*
goal-tend 49.6 *play basketball*
goaltender 58.2 *hockey player;* 58.4 *ice hockey player*
goal-tending 49.5 *penalties*
go amiss 240.5 *be inconvenient;* 247.8 *miscarry*
go and get 316.14 *bring back*
go and return 298.8 *be cyclic*
go ape 461.14 *become insane*
go around 306.6 *orbit*
go around with 569.13 *befriend*
go as 717.10 *act*
go astern 323.9 *navigate;* 50.15 *sail*
go astray 325.3; 254.8 *be in danger;* 796.16 *do wrong;* 802.23 *sin*
goat 43.8 *livestock;* 25.20 *meat*
goatee 420.7 *rough thing*
goatherd 43.16 *farm worker*
goathide 435.1 *materials*
goatish 796.14 *lecherous*
go at it 130.18 *make a beginning*
go at liberty 391.5 *be liberated*
goatlike 71.33 *ungulate*
goatskin 435.1 *materials*
goat's milk 558.5 *milk*
go away 313.1, 526.2 *depart;* 372.13 *diverge;* 313.15 *go!*
go away! 371.33
go AWOL 98.18 *abscond;* 662.15 *be disobedient;* 391.5 *be liberated;* 526.2 *depart;* 355.2 *withdraw*
go awry 247.8 *miscarry*
gob 308.4 *body orifice;* 203.2 *certain amount;* 158.7 *mass*
go back 112.19 *return to;* 761.6 *reverse;* 303.5 *turn back;* 325.11 *turn round*
go back and forth 298.7 *be regular;* 639.5 *vacillate*
go back in time 296.16 *be old*
go back on 479.4 *recant*
go backwards 303.1; 168.7 *rear up*
go bad 258.10 *be dirty;* 245.2 *decay;* 245.1 *deteriorate;* 499.8 *sour*
go bail for 784.7 *be in debt;* 391.4 *liberate;* 252.10 *protect*
go ballistic 624.12 *become angry*
go bananas 590.17 *feel deeply*
go bankrupt 786.9 *be unable to pay;* 247.6 *fail;* 782.13 *lose one's money;* 249.10 *need money;* 226.7 *stop working*
gobbet 557.14 *mouthful;* 205.2 *particular;* 205.7 *piece*
gobble 688.5 *be greedy;* 557.22 *eat well;* 56.3 *golf shots;* 370.11 *ingest;* 515.5 *sing*
gobbledegook 479.5 *equivocalness;* 729.1 *faculty of speech;* 697.1 *nonsense;* 5.5 *nonstandard language;* 266.1 *obscurity*
gobbler 557.18 *eater;* 688.4 *glutton;* 72.10 *male bird*
gobble up 357.12 *consume;* 441.1 *waste*
gobbling 557.2 *appetite;* 688.6 *gluttonous*
go before 129.15, 293.8 *precede;* 475.11 *predict;* 243.1 *prepare;* 370.8 *show in*
go begging 219.5 *be superfluous;* 238.7 *be useless*
go belly up 786.9 *be unable to pay;* 582.15 *die;* 247.6 *fail;* 766.10 *have a financial loss;* 782.13 *lose one's money;* 249.10 *need money;* 226.7 *stop working*
go below 155.8 *be low*
go berserk 624.11 *be angry;* 380.7 *be violent;* 381.5 *strike*
go-between 398.6, 578.3 *agent;* 348.3 *assistant;* 570.13 *matchmaker;* 748.3 *mediator;* 746.4 *negotiator*
go beyond 329.1 *overstep*
go beyond belief 105.7 *be improbable*
Gobi 428.14 *desert;* 493.8 *hot place*
go big-game hunting 633.11 *hunt;* 60.7 *shoot*
go blank 21.36 *underact*
goblet 410.13 *drinking vessel*
goblin 11.11 *ghost;* 70.7 *legendary beast*
go blind 519.14 *be blind*
gobo 21.20 *stage lighting*
go bond for 756.8 *guarantee*
go broke 766.10 *have a financial loss;* 782.13 *lose one's money*
gobs 158.7 *mass*
gobsmack 630.11 *amaze;* 730.15 *strike dumb*
gobsmacked 630.7 *amazed;* 766.18 *at a loss;* 730.11 *speechless;* 619.6 *wondering*
gobstopper 25.41 *sweet*
go bust 786.9 *be unable to pay;* 247.6 *fail;* 766.10 *have a financial loss;* 782.13 *lose one's money;* 776.2 *speculate*
go busted 782.13 *lose one's money*
go by 117.8 *comply*
go by the board 247.8 *miscarry*
go by the book 273.7 *be accurate;* 799.6 *be honourable;* 140.17 *obey orders*
go by the card 323.9 *navigate*
go cap in hand 710.6 *request*
go cart 320.8 *baby carriage*
go catting 639.9 *change sides*
go chase yourself 371.33 *go away!*
go clubbing 654.11 *be sociable*
go cold turkey 691.10 *drug oneself;* 355.1 *relinquish*
go contemporary 295.18 *be trendy*
go courting 593.26 *court*
God 8.3; 130.16 *originator;* 344.7 *Prime Mover;* 356.9 *producer*
god 8.5 *deity;* 9.3 *idol*
go dancing 22.15 *dance*
goddaughter 568.12 *woman in the family*
goddess 8.5 *deity;* 593.9 *lover*
goddess of health 259.3 *health*
go dead slow 333.1 *move slowly*
go deaf 505.8 *be deaf*
godfather 123.4 *bigwig;* 567.13 *man in the family*
God-fearing 7.15 *religious*
God forbid 708.24 *never!*
godforsaken 145.8 *distant;* 804.14 *impious;* 655.10 *lonely;* 98.14 *unoccupied*
godforsaken hole 655.5 *solitary place*
godforsaken place 145.3 *distant place*
God-given 768.7 *given*
godhead 8.1 *divinity*
godhood 8.1 *divinity*
go directly 324.7 *take a direction*
go dirt-cheap 793.12 *be cheap*
God knows 456.13 *who knows?*
God knows where 145.3 *distant place*
godless 804.14 *impious*
godlike 8.13 *divine;* 93.14 *self-existent*
godliness 8.1 *divinity;* 799.2 *purity;* 801.4 *righteousness;* 803.1 *virtue*
godly 8.13 *divine;* 801.10 *moral;* 230.1 *perfect;* 799.5 *pure;* 7.15 *religious;* 803.5 *virtuous*
god-making 366.7 *lift*
godmother 568.12 *woman in the family*
go down 191.6 *become smaller;* 357.13 *be destroyed;* 214.4 *decrease*
go downhill 357.13 *be destroyed;* 249.9 *be in trouble;* 305.9 *descend;* 245.1 *deteriorate*
go down the drain 766.14 *go to waste;* 441.1 *waste*
go down the tubes 303.1 *go backwards*
go down well 450.10 *be believed*
go down with 260.24 *be unhealthy*
go down with flying 638.11 *persist*
go dry 684.5 *be self-restrained;* 689.4 *give up alcohol*
gods 518.9 *viewpoint*
God's acre 583.5 *cemetery*
God's answer to 235.1 *worthy*
God's country 85.6 *native land*
God's creation 566.7 *person*
godsend 797.17 *good thing*
God's gift to women 673.7 *vain person*
godship 8.1 *divinity*
God's image 566.7 *person*
God's in heaven 201.3 *seven*
godson 567.13 *man in the family*
God's own 469.15 *chosen;* 235.1 *worthy*
God's peace 589.9 *peace!*
God's plenty 217.8 *plenty*
God's purpose 482.5 *final intention*
God's truth 698.3 *the truth*
God the Father 8.3 *God*
God the Son 8.4
go Dutch 119.10 *be equal;* 654.11 *be sociable;* 754.4 *compromise;* 198.17 *go halves;* 764.4 *have joint possession;* 216.10 *make average;* 785.9 *pay one's way*
go easily 265.19
go easy 685.3 *be moderate;* 265.20 *take it easy*
go easy on 648.3 *be lenient;* 627.10 *show mercy*
goer 568.6 *loose woman;* 315.8 *outgoer;* 59.2 *thoroughbred*
go even-Stephen 764.4 *have joint possession*
go far 248.5 *be prosperous*
go fast 302.9 *maintain progress;* 262.2 *make haste*
go faster 262.2 *make haste*
go fell walking 62.9 *mountaineer*
gofer 388.2 *appeaser;* 342.10 *busy person;* 392.11 *helper;* 122.6 *inferior;* 663.4 *obedient person;* 401.5 *office assistant;* 387.3 *subordinate;* 578.1 *worker*
go fifty-fifty 111.10 *be equal;* 754.4 *compromise;* 198.17 *go halves;* 764.4 *have joint possession;* 216.10 *make average*
go first 129.15 *precede*
go fishing 633.11 *hunt*
go flat 245.2 *decay*
go flat out 250.19 *liberalize;* 353.2 *try hard*
go for 482.10 *aim;* 381.1 *attack;* 316.14

bring back; 593.23 *love;* 381.5 *strike;* 324.7 *take a direction*
go for a burton 582.15 *die;* 305.11 *trip*
go for a song 793.12 *be cheap*
go for broke 638.8 *brace oneself;* 353.2 *try hard*
go for help 392.17 *help*
go for it 638.8 *brace oneself;* 353.11, 638.18 *here goes!*
go for the jack 51.7 *bowl*
go forward 302.1; 302.1 *go forward*
go free 250.14 *be free;* 391.5 *be liberated*
go full bat 332.4 *be swift*
go full belt at 381.1 *attack*
go full pelt 332.4 *be swift*
go full steam 332.4 *be swift*
go full tilt 332.4 *be swift*
go get it 638.9 *undertake*
go-getter 342.10 *busy person;* 340.3 *doer;* 484.8 *planner;* 302.16 *progressive person;* 354.4 *volunteer*
go-getting 342.18 *active;* 302.12 *advance;* 610.13 *aspirant;* 302.17 *forward;* 338.4 *vigorous*
goggle 518.13 *look*
goggle at 619.9 *wonder*
goggled 62.8 *mountaineering*
goggle-eyed 518.21 *seeing*
goggles 62.4 *climbing equipment;* 384.6 *protective clothing;* 68.5 *ski equipment;* 67.8 *swimwear;* 518.10 *visual aid*
go-go 332.1 *swift*
go-go dancer 21.30, 22.5 *dancer*
go great guns 246.6 *be successful*
go grey 556.17 *age;* 533.8 *grey*
gogsee 68.10 *curling*
go half and half 754.4 *compromise*
go halfway 216.10 *make average*
go halves 198.17; 119.10 *be equal;* 770.5 *get one's allotment;* 764.4 *have joint possession;* 216.10 *make average*
go hand in hand 285.7 *synchronize*
go home 303.5 *turn back*
go hungry 687.5 *fast*
go hunting 633.11 *hunt;* 60.7 *shoot*
go in 314.9 *enter;* 53.15 *play*
go in a huddle 734.10 *chat*
go in for 733.12 *address oneself to;* 632.16 *have a habit;* 139.27 *specialize;* 354.1, 638.9 *undertake*
going 342.18 *active;* 313.7 *departure;* 526.4 *disappearance;* 526.6 *disappearing;* 582.18 *dying;* 300.1 *motion;* 300.16 *moving;* 346.10 *operational;* 315.15 *outgoing;* 355.3 *relinquishment*
going after 633.1 *pursuit*
going around the corner 48.6 *fielding terms*
going away 313.7 *departure;* 526.4 *disappearance*
going back 303.10 *backward motion;* 313.7 *departure;* 479.11 *equivocating;* 761.1 *reversion*
going backwards 168.3 *rearing up*
going before 129.1 *precedence*
going belly up 766.2 *financial loss*
going blind 519.1 *blindness*
going cheap 793.9 *cheap*
going down 16.43 *conviction;* 214.6 *decreasing;* 305.1 *descent*
going down fighting 640.12 *indomitable*
going downhill 245.12 *deteriorated*
going down the tubes 303.19 *backsliding*
going Dutch 119.1 *equality*
going for a song 793.9 *cheap*
going forward 302.10 *forward motion*
going grey 556.12 *ageing*
going halves 119.1 *equality*
going home 377.2 *disbandment*
going on 233.4 *incomplete;* 302.20 *in progress*
going on and on 279.10 *continuing forever;* 270.3 *diffuse*
going on board 313.8 *start*
going on the rampage 624.4 *anger*
going out 593.6 *courtship;* 315.1 *exit*
going-out-of-business sale 791.2 *bargain;* 778.4 *sale*
going over 479.7 *apostasy*
going over again 112.2 *iteration*
going rate 790.3 *fee*
goings-on 447.3 *matter of interest*
going steady 593.6 *courtship*
going the rounds 741.14 *journalistic*
going through the roof 681.3 *costly;* 792.7 *dear*
going to extremes 727.3 *extravagance*
going together 593.6 *courtship*
going to law 16.53 *litigating;* 16.5 *litigation*
going too far 727.3 *extravagance*
going to pot 245.12 *deteriorated*
going to the head 690.6 *intoxicating*
going to the root 123.5 *important*
going to the wall 766.2 *financial loss*
going up 304.6 *mounting*
going with 593.6 *courtship*
going without 634.19 *abstaining;* 687.6 *fasting*
go in opposition 113.14 *oppose*
go inside 172.14
go into 722.4 *dissertate*
go into a decline 260.24 *be unhealthy*
go into a huddle 376.39 *come together*
go into a partnership 755.5 *contract*
go into a tailspin 214.4 *decrease*
go into a trance 11.24 *experience psychic phenomena*
go into debt 782.13 *lose one's money*
go into detail 270.5 *be diffuse;* 222.11 *circumstantiate;* 139.23 *particularize*
go into details 273.7 *be accurate*
go into ecstasies over 590.17 *feel deeply*
go into exile 128.9 *be excluded*
go into hiding 521.7 *become invisible*
go into league with 755.5 *contract*
go into liquidation 786.9 *be unable to pay;* 226.7 *stop working*
go into mourning for 603.6 *lament*
go into orbit 179.6 *circle;* 306.6 *orbit;* 307.8 *rotate*
go into overdrive 334.11 *give power;* 262.2 *make haste*
go into particulars 273.7 *be accurate*
go into partnership 374.6 *come together;* 747.14 *join with*
go into purdah 521.7 *become invisible*
go into receivership 226.7 *stop working*
go into recession 214.4 *decrease*
go into retirement 655.12 *be unsocial;* 526.2 *depart;* 580.4 *have leisure;* 605.5 *resign*
go into retreat 526.2 *depart*
go into reverse 303.3 *reverse*
go into seclusion 655.12 *be unsocial*
go into the red 783.9 *acquire credit;* 784.7 *be in debt;* 766.10 *have a financial loss;* 792.11 *overpay*
go into training 6.23 *learn*
go into voluntary exile 128.9 *be excluded*
go in with 747.14 *join with*
go it alone 250.16 *be independent;* 197.18 *be one*
goitre 260.4 *disease*
go kaput 802.24 *go wrong;* 247.9 *malfunction*
Go-Karting™ 61.1 *motor racing*
go lame 337.6 *be weak;* 333.2 *hesitate*
Golconda 781.5 *wealth*
gold 780.16 *bullion;* 173.2 *central thing;* 235.8 *exceller;* 780.1 *money;* 47.9 *track;* 537.1 *yellow;* 537.8 *yellow thing*
gold and silver standard 780.7 *finance*
goldarn 712.11 *miscellaneous euphemisms*
gold bar 780.16 *bullion*
gold-based 780.22 *monetary*
gold brick 634.17 *avoider;* 634.5 *shirk;* 333.15 *slow person;* 700.8 *trick*
gold bricker 634.17 *avoider*
gold coinage 780.13 *coinage*
gold cup 794.1 *trophy*
gold decoration 24.3 *glaze*
gold-digger 765.7 *gainer;* 593.9 *lover*
gold-digging 765.16 *greedy*
golden 756.14 *auspicious;* 292.12 *autumn;* 610.14 *cheering;* 536.1 *orange;* 589.7 *peaceful;* 248.8 *prosperous;* 235.3 *valuable;* 537.1 *yellow*
golden age 222.5 *comfortable circumstances;* 805.3 *naivety;* 284.1 *past time;* 248.3 *time of plenty*
golden apple 483.5 *positive stimulus*
golden-brown algae 84.2 *algae*
golden calf 9.3 *idol*
golden days 248.3 *time of plenty*
golden dream 477.6 *reverie*
golden goose 781.5 *wealth*
golden-haired 531.3 *white-haired;* 537.3 *yellow-haired*
golden handcuffs 785.3 *pay;* 813.4 *reward for service*
golden handshake 211.4 *extra;* 768.2 *gift;* 313.9 *parting;* 785.3 *pay;* 765.5 *profit;* 671.3 *recognition;* 813.4 *reward for service;* 708.6 *termination*
golden hello 785.3 *pay;* 813.4 *reward for service*
golden jubilee 601.5 *anniversary*
goldenly 537.11 *yellowly*
golden mean 216.5 *medium;* 684.2, 685.1 *moderation;* 27.44 *polygon;* 19.4 *treatment*
golden oldie 556.7 *older person*
golden opportunity 287.2, 308.10 *opportunity;* 752.2 *tentative offer*
golden parachute 785.3 *pay;* 765.5 *profit;* 813.4 *reward for service*
golden rectangle 27.44 *polygon*
golden retriever 60.6 *sporting dog*
golden rule 713.3 *precept*
golden section 27.44 *polygon;* 19.4 *treatment*
Golden Temple of Amritsar 10.13 *shrine*
golden time 248.3 *time of plenty*
golden times 589.1 *peace*
golden-toned 516.6 *melodious*
golden touch 781.5 *wealth*
golden wedding 601.5 *anniversary*
golden wedding anniversary 298.6 *annually celebrated day*
golden years 556.5 *old age*
golden-yellow 537.1 *yellow*
goldfish 536.3 *orange thing*
goldfish bowl 527.8 *transparent thing*
gold leaf 542.3 *pattern*
gold medal 47.5 *competition;* 57.1 *gymnastics;* 743.4 *insignia;* 794.1 *trophy*
gold-medal 121.14, 235.2 *best;* 123.6 *notable*
gold medallist 47.3, 336.5 *athlete;* 485.4 *skilled person*
gold mine 183.2 *concave land;* 439.2 *resource;* 781.5 *wealth*
gold plate 550.3 *coating*
gold reserves 780.6 *funds*
gold-rimmed glasses 518.10 *visual aid*
gold-sheet inlay 23.9 *decorative woodwork*
goldsmith 578.2 *artisan*
gold sovereign 780.10 *former British money*
gold standard 14.1, 780.7 *finance*
gold star 542.4 *honour*
Goldstein-Sheerer test 36.6 *intelligence test*
gold tooth 425.11 *tooth*
gold vault 439.4 *storage*
gold watch 671.3 *recognition*
Goldwynism 274.11 *grammatical error*
Golf 56
golf 56.1; **56.7**
golf bag 410.8 *bag*
golf ball 56.5; 330.10 *ball;* 56.2 *golfing terms*
golfball printer 40.7 *peripheral*
golf bodies 56.1 *golf*
golf club 56.4
golf club part 56.4 *golf club*
golf course 56.1 *golf*
golfer 56.6
golf game 56.1 *golf*
golfing 56.1 *golf*
golfing terms 56.2
golf match 56.1 *golf*
golf rules 56.2 *golfing terms*
golf shots 56.3
golf widow 571.6 *surviving spouse*
Golgi apparatus 34.8 *cell organ*
Golgi body 34.8 *cell organ*
Golgi complex 34.8 *cell organ*
Golgi vesicle 34.8 *cell organ*
golgotha 583.5 *cemetery*
goliard 21.29 *entertainer*
Goliath 158.10 *big person;* 336.6 *muscleman;* 154.7 *tall person*
go light 742.4 *signal*
go like a rocket 262.2 *make haste*
go like clockwork 407.23 *be in order;* 265.19 *go easily*
go like gangbusters 338.2 *be full of vigour*
golliwog 717.6 *image*
go looking for trouble 751.7 *pick a fight*
go lower 156.14 *deepen*
go mad 461.14 *become insane;* 459.6 *be foolish;* 590.17 *feel deeply*
go missing 98.18 *abscond*
go modern 295.18 *be trendy*
go mouldy 499.8 *sour*
go mountaineering 62.9 *mountaineer*
gonadotrophic hormone 33.16 *hormone*
gonadotrophin 562.3 *fertilizer;* 33.16 *hormone*
go native 657.11 *not stand on ceremony*
gondola 317.12 *cableway;* 321.6 *rolling stock*
gondola lift 68.1 *skiing*
gondolier 323.8 *boatman;* 316.7 *transferor*
Gondwana 30.19 *plate tectonics*
gone 98.9 *away;* 582.19 *dead;* 690.3 *dead drunk;* 313.12 *departed;* 526.7 *disappeared;* 463.11 *forgotten;* 103.3 *hopeless;* 341.3 *inactive;* 3.18 *in the past;* 195.7 *null;* 284.18 *over;* 611.5 *past hope*
gone away 313.12 *departed;* 526.7 *disappeared*
gone bad 245.12 *deteriorated;* 236.4 *poor*
gone before 582.19 *dead*
gone but not forgotten 582.19 *dead*
gone by the board 766.16 *losing*
gone down the drain 766.16 *losing*
gone for a burton 582.19 *dead*
gone forever 766.16 *losing;* 284.18 *over*
gone for good 766.16 *losing;* 284.18 *over*
gone missing 766.16 *losing;* 144.13 *misplaced*
gone off 313.12 *departed;* 245.12 *deteriorated*
goner 582.10 *dying person;* 611.3 *hopeless person*
gone to Elysium 582.19 *dead*
gone to ground 526.7 *disappeared*
gone to pot 782.3 *beggarly;* 556.13 *middle-aged*
gone to ruin 782.3 *beggarly*
gone to seed 44.17 *botanical;* 77.13 *plantlike*
gone wrong 802.18
gonfalon 743.7 *flag*
gong 542.4 *honour;* 575.3 *honours;* 743.4 *insignia;* 281.10 *signal;* 507.4 *sound maker;* 510.4 *sources of resonance;* 794.1 *trophy*
gonidium 84.4 *reproductive body*
go nightclubbing 654.11 *be sociable*
goniometer 176.4 *angular measurement;* 26.8 *meter*
goniometric 26.16 *micrometric*
goniometry 176.4 *angular measurement;* 26.2 *micrometry*
gonion 176.1 *angle*
gonorrhoea 260.4 *disease;* 260.14 *venereal disease*
goo 258.4 *dirt;* 430.7 *slime*
Good 797
good 797.1; **797.8**; 756.14 *auspicious;* 392.34 *beneficial;* 650.6 *benevolent;* 617.8 *desirable;* 557.27 *edible;* 543.3 *elegant;* 799.4 *honourable;* 805.5 *innocent;* 595.5 *likable;* 795.8 *moral;* 663.7 *obedient;* 237.4 *profitable;* 252.6 *safe;* 485.6 *skilful;* 237.6 *usability;* 237.2 *usable;* 349.6 *use;* 237.5 *usefulness;* 803.5 *virtuous;* 631.17 *well-behaved;* 235.4 *worthwhile;* 235.1 *worthy*
good acquaintance 595.4 *likable person*
good and bad 231.1 *imperfect*
good and early 293.12, 293.17 *early*
good and evil 113.3 *opposites*
good and mad 624.16 *angry*
good and tired 620.5 *bored*
good as gold 803.5 *virtuous;* 235.1 *worthy*
good as new 295.14 *renewed*
good as one's word 235.1 *worthy*
good at 400.13 *excellent;* 455.8 *knowledgeable;* 485.6 *skilful*
good bargain 777.6 *purchase*
good behaviour 797.11; 631.2 *good conduct;* 658.2 *good manners;* 663.2 *loyalty;* 803.1 *virtue*
good books 669.2 *admiration*
good break 248.2 *good fortune*
good breeding 549.1 *elegance;* 658.2 *good manners;* 573.3 *nobleness*
good buy 793.4 *bargain;* 787.4 *expenditure;* 777.6 *purchase*
goodbye 313.9 *parting*
goodbye! 313.14
good chance 107.5; 104.4 *chance;* 287.2 *opportunity;* 102.3 *strong possibility*
good character 799.1 *probity*
good cheer 598.3 *cheerfulness;* 557.7 *food;* 654.1 *sociability*

good child 631.3 *well-behaved person*
good citizenship 652.2 *public spiritedness*
good climate 257.2 *salubrity*
good clip 332.8 *speed*
good colour 811.1 *estimation*
good companion 654.6 *social person*
good company **654.8**; 241.8 *amiability*; 654.6 *social person*
good condition 259.3 *health*; 407.5 *orderliness*; 221.5 *physical state*
good conduct **631.2**
good conscience 803.1 *virtue*
good constitution 259.3 *health*
good credit risk 783.1 *credit*
good deal 793.4 *bargain*
good debt 784.1 *debt*
good deed 650.4 *benevolent act*; 340.2 *deed*; 392.2 *support*
good deportment 658.2 *good manners*
good ear 504.1 *hearing*
good eater 688.4 *glutton*
good English 5.29 *grammar*
good enough 235.5 *not bad*; 609.6 *satisfactory*
good example 803.4 *virtuous person*
good excuse 714.2 *defence*
good eyesight 518.1 *vision*
good faith 663.2 *loyalty*; 799.1 *probity*
good feeling **590.5**
good fellow 654.6 *social person*
good fellowship 654.8 *good company*
good food 557.7 *food*
good for it 781.2 *solvent*
good form 656.5 *etiquette*; 160.5 *formality*
good-for-nothing 800.5 *dishonourable*; 800.4 *dishonourable person*; 766.6 *loser*; 124.2 *obscure*; 335.10 *powerless*; 238.1 *useless*; 804.9 *wicked person*
good-for-nothingness 800.1 *improbity*
good for one 259.2 *healthful*
good fortune **248.2**; 222.5 *comfortable circumstances*; 107.2 *luck*
Good Friday 687.3 *fast day*; 10.15 *holy day*
good giver 768.4 *giver*
good graces 669.2 *admiration*
good grammar 5.29 *grammar*
good grounds 714.2 *defence*
good head for 485.2 *aptitude*
good health 259.3 *health*
good-hearted 650.6 *benevolent*
good-heartedly 650.10 *benevolently*
good heavens! **630.14**
good host 654.6 *social person*
good housekeeping 680.1 *thrift*
good humour 598.3 *cheerfulness*; 658.1 *courtesy*; 221.4 *state of mind*
good-humoured 650.6 *benevolent*; 598.1 *cheerful*; 658.7 *courteous*; 221.8 *in a state of*
good-humouredly 221.9 *conditionally*; 658.14 *courteously*
good husbandry 680.1 *thrift*
good idea 443.6 *idea*
goodies 557.7 *food*
goodies and baddies 113.3 *opposites*
good influence 224.6 *editor*; 244.5 *improvement*
good in law 16.46 *legislated*
good in parts 231.1 *imperfect*
good intention 482.1 *intention*
good intentions 631.1 *conduct*
good lady 570.11 *married woman*
good light 522.10 *window*
good likeness 115.1 *similarity*
goodliness 797.10 *kindness*; 797.14 *largeness*
good listener 591.8 *sensitive person*
good-looking 363.9 *attractive*; 545.5 *beautiful*
good looks 525.3 *external appearance*; 545.1 *gorgeousness*
good loser 799.3 *honourable person*
good luck 248.2 *good fortune*; 797.17 *good thing*; 107.2 *luck*; 287.2 *opportunity*
good luck! **248.10**
good-luck charm 475.6 *good-luck sign*; 359.2 *preserver*; 11.6 *talisman*
good-luck sign **475.6**
good lungs 507.4 *sound maker*
goodly 158.15 *big*; 797.3 *kind*; 797.7 *large*; 803.9 *virtuously*
goodman 567.3 *male title of address*; 570.10 *married man*
good management 680.1 *thrift*
good-mannered **658.8**
good manners **658.2**; 549.1 *elegance*; 656.5 *etiquette*; 797.11 *good behaviour*; 631.2 *good conduct*; 654.2 *social ambition*
good match 570.4 *marriageability*
good memory 462.1 *memory*; 360.5 *retentiveness*
good mixer 654.6 *social person*
good morals **795.2**
good move 246.3 *successful thing*
good-natured 650.6 *benevolent*; 598.1 *cheerful*; 797.3 *kind*; 241.2 *likable*; 589.7 *peaceful*; 639.4 *unsteady*
good-naturedly 650.10 *benevolently*; 797.23 *nicely*
good-naturedness 650.1 *benevolence*; 797.10 *kindness*
good neighbour 650.5 *benevolent person*; 797.15 *good person*; 595.4 *likable person*; 652.3 *philanthropist*; 654.6 *social person*; 392.13 *supporter*
goodness 650.1 *benevolence*; 797.8 *good*; 631.2 *good conduct*; 795.2 *good morals*; 259.4 *healthfulness*; 805.1 *innocence*; 663.1 *obedience*; 799.1 *probity*; 485.1 *skill*; 803.1 *virtue*; 235.6 *worth*
goodness and mercy 650.1 *benevolence*
goodness gracious 619.14 *wonderful!*
goodness-of-fit test 27.54 *hypothesis testing*
Good News Bible 7.12 *religious text*
good nick 407.5 *orderliness*
goodnight 313.14 *goodbye!*; 313.9 *parting*
good nose 500.2 *sense of smell*
good notice 669.4 *compliment*
good nutrition 257.2 *salubrity*
good occasion 287.1 *timeliness*
good odds 107.5 *good chance*
good odour 500.4 *reputation*
good offices 650.4 *benevolent act*; 748.2 *mediation*; 749.1 *pacification*; 252.2 *protection*; 392.2 *support*
good old days 3.8, 284.1 *past time*
good old summertime 292.3 *summer*
good omen 475.5 *omen*; 756.3 *potential*
good opinion 669.2 *admiration*; 667.1 *respect*
good opportunity 287.2 *opportunity*; 102.3 *strong possibility*
good pair of lungs 507.4 *sound maker*
good part 21.23 *role*
good person **797.15**; 799.3 *honourable person*; 805.4 *innocent person*; 595.4 *likable person*; 803.4 *virtuous person*
good piste 68.1 *skiing*
good point 235.6 *worth*
good policy 239.3 *convenience*
good press 669.4 *compliment*
good prospects 756.3 *potential*
good quality 797.8 *good*; 235.6 *worth*; 235.1 *worthy*
good reason 714.2 *defence*
good reference 811.1 *estimation*
good report 811.1 *estimation*
good review 719.3 *criticism*
good riddance 390.2 *deliverance*; 766.1 *loss*
good right arm 608.5 *helper*
good role model 340.3 *doer*
goods 13.6 *economic factors*; 13.2 *economy*; 778.8 *merchandise*; 440.5 *personal estate*; 356.7 *produce*; 319.2 *thing transported*; 316.10 *transferred thing*; 319.5 *transportable*
good sales 778.5 *sales*
Good Samaritan 650.5 *benevolent person*; 679.9 *generous person*; 768.4 *giver*; 797.15 *good person*; 595.4 *likable person*; 652.3 *philanthropist*; 591.8 *sensitive person*; 392.13 *supporter*; 803.4 *virtuous person*; 752.8 *volunteer*
goods and chattels 440.4 *possessions*
goods and services 356.7 *produce*
good sense 458.2 *intelligence*; 460.2 *rationality*
good shot 633.6 *hunter*; 330.15 *shooter*; 246.3 *successful thing*
good size 158.3 *large scale*
good-size 158.15 *big*
goods on approval 778.8 *merchandise*
goods on assignment 778.8 *merchandise*
good sort 799.3 *honourable person*
good spirits 598.3 *cheerfulness*; 221.4 *state of mind*
good sport 799.3 *honourable person*
good stead 237.5 *usefulness*
goods train 316.5 *means of transport*; 321.7 *train*
good sword 586.1 *combatant*
good table 557.9 *plenty*
good taste 543.1, 549.1 *elegance*; 795.2 *good morals*; 466.2 *judiciousness*; 255.1 *purity*; 728.3 *subtlety*; 495.2 *taste of life*
good temper 4.3 *detachment*
good-tempered 4.18 *detached*
good terms 569.2 *friendly relations*
good thing **797.17**
good things to come 756.3 *potential*
good time **490.2**
good time coming 283.3 *future condition*
good-time girl 490.3 *pleasure-seeker*
good times 781.7 *opulence*; 248.3 *time of plenty*
good times coming 477.7 *idealism*
good trim 407.5 *orderliness*
good try 353.5 *attempt*
good turn 650.4 *benevolent act*; 797.10 *kindness*; 392.2 *support*
good understanding 569.2 *friendly relations*
good usage 349.6 *use*
good value 793.1 *cheapness*
good-value 793.9 *cheap*
good visibility 31.35 *visibility*
good way 145.2 *great distance*
good wheeze 443.6 *idea*
goodwife 568.3 *female title of address*; 570.11 *married woman*
goodwill **636.9**; 650.1 *benevolence*; 569.1 *friendship*; 392.10 *helpfulness*; 652.1 *philanthropy*
goodwill towards man 650.1 *benevolence*
good wishes 667.7 *respects*
good with money 680.4 *thrifty*
good word 669.4 *compliment*
good work 650.4 *benevolent act*; 622.7 *satisfaction*
good works 650.2, 652.5 *charity*; 2.10 *social services*
goody 568.3 *female title of address*; 570.11 *married woman*
goody-goody 650.5 *benevolent person*; 699.17 *false person*; 699.31 *hypocritical*; 805.5 *innocent*; 805.4 *innocent person*; 255.5 *pure person*; 803.4 *virtuous person*
goody-goodyism 656.2 *formalism*
gooey 360.9 *retentive*
gooeyness 430.1 *viscosity*
goof 274.10 *blunder*; 456.5 *ignorant person*
go off 258.10 *be dirty*; 507.8 *be loud*; 245.2 *decay*; 311.11 *move apart*; 325.8 *sidestep*; 499.8 *sour*
go off half-cocked 293.10 *hasten*
go off one's head 461.14 *become insane*
go off sick 260.24 *be unhealthy*
go offside 64.5 *play rugby*; 66.4 *play soccer*
go offsides 58.9 *play hockey*
go off the air 505.11 *be unheard*; 526.1 *disappear*
go off the point 109.10 *be unrelated*; 133.15 *lose one's train of thought*
goofing off 333.11 *lingering*
goof off 333.2 *hesitate*
goof-off 333.15 *slow person*
googly 53.8 *delivery*; 700.9 *sleight of hand*
googol 194.3 *large number*; 201.11 *million*
googolplex 194.3 *large number*; 201.11 *million*
goo-goo eyes 593.6 *courtship*
gook 430.7 *slime*
goolies 561.8 *organs of reproduction*
go on **277.7**; 297.7 *be frequent*; 300.13 *be in motion*; 132.14, 134.3 *continue*; 313.1 *depart*; 640.7 *maintain*; 619.14 *wonderful!*
go on! **134.8**
go on a bender 690.8 *get drunk*; 686.11 *overindulge*
go on a binge 688.5 *be greedy*; 600.5 *rejoice*
go on a blind 690.8 *get drunk*
go on about 112.18 *harp*; 795.12 *moralize*
go on active service 585.13 *be at war*
go on a diet 684.5 *be self-restrained*; 687.5 *fast*
go on a furlough 580.4 *have leisure*; 263.2 *take it easy*
go on and on 620.6 *be boring*; 270.5 *be diffuse*; 202.9 *be infinite*; 731.7 *be talkative*; 112.18 *harp*
go on a pilgrimage 7.19 *be religious*; 9.7 *worship*
go on a pub-crawl 690.8 *get drunk*
go on a rampage 507.8 *be loud*
go on as before 393.4 *be restored*
go on a spree 654.11 *be sociable*; 690.8 *get drunk*
go on at 112.18 *harp*
go on board 304.15 *mount*
go one better 645.5 *be cunning*; 121.8 *be superior*
go one-on-one 58.9 *play hockey*
go one's own way 118.19, 250.16 *be independent*; 641.9 *be obstinate*; 635.14 *follow one's own will*
go one's separate ways 377.9 *be dispersed*
go on forever 620.6 *be boring*; 279.5 *be eternal*
go on furlough 98.17 *take leave of absence*
go on holiday 98.17 *take leave of absence*
go on honeymoon 570.15 *marry*
go on hunger strike 753.8 *cause mischief*
go on leave 581.2 *be refreshed*; 758.12 *exempt oneself*; 263.2 *take it easy*; 98.17 *take leave of absence*
go on location 98.17 *take leave of absence*
go on oiled wheels 265.19 *go easily*
go on one's feelings 445.9 *be intuitive*
go on relief 782.12 *be poor*
go on sabbatical 98.17 *take leave of absence*
go onside 66.4 *play soccer*
go on strike 753.8 *cause mischief*; 709.5 *refuse*; 226.7 *stop working*
go on the air 504.16 *be heard*
go on the attack 381.1 *attack*
go on the blink 802.24 *go wrong*
go on the dole 782.12 *be poor*
go on the fuddle 690.8 *get drunk*
go on the lam 391.5 *be liberated*; 252.9 *be safe*; 736.11 *conceal oneself*; 634.6 *evade*
go on the parish 782.12 *be poor*
go on the pill 563.9 *practise birth control*
go on the rampage 381.9 *attack successfully*; 408.26 *be disorderly*; 380.7 *be violent*
go on the rocks 357.13 *be destroyed*; 249.9 *be in trouble*; 247.6 *fail*
go on the wagon 634.3 *abstain*; 684.5 *be self-restrained*; 689.4 *give up alcohol*; 251.10 *restrain oneself*
go on the warpath 585.13 *be at war*; 380.7 *be violent*; 751.7 *pick a fight*
go onto the offensive 381.1 *attack*
go on trial 715.7 *be accused*
go on vacation 263.2 *take it easy*; 98.17 *take leave of absence*
go on welfare 782.12 *be poor*
goose 593.14 *communication of love*; 72.11 *female bird*; 60.5 *game*; 742.3 *gesture*; 512.3 *hisser*; 492.4 *kiss*; 43.8 *livestock*; 25.20 *meat*; 492.11 *touch*; 72.3 *water bird*
goose barnacle 75.4 *arthropod*
gooseberry 109.3 *unconnected person*
gooseberry bush 561.7 *obstetrics*
gooseberry sawfly 44.12 *pests and diseases*
gooseboy 43.16 *farm worker*
goose bumps 612.2 *fearfulness*; 420.7 *rough thing*
goose egg 195.1 *zero*
goose fair 779.1 *market*
goose flesh 612.2 *fearfulness*; 420.7 *rough thing*; 488.3 *stimulus*
goosefoot family 77.3 *seed plant*
goosegirl 43.16 *farm worker*
gooselike 72.21 *avian*
gooseneck 50.3 *parts of a sailing boat*
goosenecked 50.10 *sailing*
goose pimples 420.7 *rough thing*; 488.3 *stimulus*
goose someone 742.11 *gesture*
goosestep 300.12 *gait*
goosewing 50.15 *sail*
goosing 492.2 *touching*
goosy 72.21 *avian*
go OTT 304.14 *climb*; 329.4 *exaggerate*
go out 523.13 *become dark*; 654.11 *be sociable*; 131.18 *come to an end*; 315.9 *exit*
go out for trade 776.1 *trade*
go out of business 226.7 *stop working*
go out of commission 802.24 *go wrong*
go out of print 526.1 *disappear*

go out of style 296.17 *grow old*
go out of town 98.17 *take leave of absence*
go out of use 526.1 *disappear*
go out with 593.26 *court*; 223.14 *keep company with*; 569.14 *seek the friendship of*
go over 479.3 *apostatize*; 246.6 *be successful*; 639.9 *change sides*; 355.2 *withdraw*
go over again 112.17 *iterate*
go over big 246.6 *be successful*
go overboard 219.4 *be excessive*
go over one's head 696.7 *be unintelligible*
go over the hill 391.4 *liberate*
go over the limit 329.4 *exaggerate*
go over the top 381.1 *attack*; 585.14 *battle*; 219.4 *be excessive*; 304.14 *climb*; 329.4 *exaggerate*
go over the wall 389.5 *escape*; 391.4 *liberate*
go partners 747.14 *join with*
go partying 654.11 *be sociable*
gopher 40.16 *Internet*
go phut 802.24 *go wrong*
go pitapat 327.24 *shake*; 326.9 *vibrate*
go postal 624.12 *become angry*
go pubbing 654.11 *be sociable*
go pub-crawling 654.11 *be sociable*
go public 739.5 *disclose*; 740.13 *make public*
go quietly 685.3 *be moderate*
Gordian knot 737.5 *difficult problem*; 264.4 *problem*
gore 425.14 *be sharp*; 431.4 *blood*; 551.24 *part of garment*; 535.7 *red thing*
gored skirt 551.6 *skirt*
go regularly 632.16 *have a habit*
gorge 219.4 *be excessive*; 688.5 *be greedy*; 183.2 *concave land*; 146.3 *gulf*; 30.7 *landform*; 686.11 *overindulge*; 308.7 *passageway*; 217.4 *suffice*; 92.8 *valley*
gorged 219.6 *excessive*; 232.8 *full*; 688.6 *gluttonous*
gorge oneself 557.22 *eat well*
gorgeous 545.5 *beautiful*; 597.5 *delightful*; 235.1 *worthy*
gorgeousness **545.1**
gorger 688.4 *glutton*
gorgerin 174.3 *architectural summit*
gorget 384.7 *armour*
gorging 557.2 *appetite*; 688.6 *gluttonous*
Gorgon 518.2 *eye*
go right through one 513.4 *be strident*
goriness 431.5 *fluidity*
goring 381.18 *hit*
gormandize 688.5 *be greedy*; 557.22 *eat well*; 490.8 *feel pleasure*
gormandizer 688.4 *glutton*
gormandizing 557.2 *appetite*
gormless 459.5 *foolish*
go round 300.13 *be in motion*; 179.6 *circle*; 317.14 *find one's way*; 307.8 *rotate*; 170.7 *surround*
go round in circles 639.7 *be irresolute*; 306.6 *orbit*; 238.9 *waste effort*
go round the bend 461.14 *become insane*
go rusty 486.5 *be unskilful*
gory 431.18, 535.4 *bloody*; 382.24 *murderous*
Gosain 7.8 *priest*
go scot-free 391.5 *be liberated*; 389.5 *escape*
go separate ways 372.13 *diverge*; 311.12 *separate*
go septic 245.2 *decay*
gosh 712.16 *euphemisms*; 619.14 *wonderful!*
go shares 119.10 *be equal*; 654.11 *be sociable*; 770.5 *get one's allotment*; 764.4 *have joint possession*; 216.10 *make average*
goshawk 72.5 *bird of prey*
goshdarn 712.16 *euphemisms*; 712.11 *miscellaneous euphemisms*
goshdarned 712.11 *miscellaneous euphemisms*
Goshen 756.4 *promised land*
go shooting 633.11 *hunt*; 60.7 *shoot*
go shopping 777.2 *shop*
go short and wide 51.7 *bowl*
go sidewards 300.13 *be in motion*
go sideways 169.8 *move sideways*
gosling 43.8 *livestock*; 72.12 *young bird*
go slow 753.8 *cause mischief*; 15.12 *have an industrial dispute*; 333.1 *move slowly*; 576.6 *work*
go-slow 753.3 *gesture of protest*; 333.12 *hesitation*; 15.4 *industrial dispute*; 13.8 *industrial relations*
go smoothly **421.12**; 265.19 *go easily*
go solo 197.18 *be one*
go sour 245.2 *decay*; 499.8 *sour*
go spare 624.12 *become angry*
gospel 10.6 *Eucharist*; 18.5 *sacred music*; 698.3 *the truth*; 698.15 *true*
gospel music 18.5 *sacred music*
Gospels 7.12 *religious text*
gospel song 10.8 *hymn*
gossamer 404.10 *delicate*; 153.4 *fine*; 153.11 *fineness*; 415.7 *light thing*; 527.8 *transparent thing*; 124.8 *trifle*; 337.5 *weak thing*
gossameriness 404.2 *grain*
gossamer thread 337.5 *weak thing*
gossamery 404.10 *delicate*; 415.2 *insubstantial*
gossip 693.7 *advice*; 644.7 *be curious*; 734.2, 734.10 *chat*; 734.8 *chatterer*; 678.3 *defamation*; 678.8 *defamer*; 693.10 *informer*; 740.13 *make public*; 447.3 *matter of interest*; 644.4 *meddler*; 644.2 *prying*; 740.1 *publication*; 504.8 *something heard*; 729.10 *speaker*; 731.3 *talk*; 731.4 *talker*; 678.13 *vilify*
gossip column 740.3 *journalism*; 741.9 *news story*
gossip columnist 678.8 *defamer*; 721.10 *descriptive writer*; 693.9 *informant*; 741.4 *journalist*; 740.11 *newspaperman*
gossiper 678.8 *defamer*; 729.10 *speaker*
gossiping 678.16 *defamatory*
gossipmonger 644.4 *meddler*
gossip writer 693.9 *informant*
gossipy 734.14 *conversational*; 731.6 *effusive*; 693.16 *informative*; 447.9 *local*; 644.6 *prying*
go stale 245.2 *decay*
go steady with 593.26 *court*
go straight 803.8 *be virtuous*; 244.2 *get better*; 324.7 *take a direction*
Gotham 87.3 *New York*; 86.10 *urban area*
go the pretty way 306.8 *detour*
go the round 306.7 *ring*
go the rounds 740.17 *be published*
go the whole hog 638.6 *be resolute*; 342.15 *try*
Gothic 23.7 *furniture style*; 296.14 *historic*; 5.41 *lettered*; 19.29 *realist*
Gothic horror 17.2 *fiction*
Gothic novel 17.2, 721.5 *fiction*
Gothic type 5.15 *type style*
go through 631.14 *behave towards*; 787.2 *consume*; 349.5 *dispose of*; 590.15 *feel*; 349.1 *use*; 681.7 *waste*
go through hell 491.9 *feel pain*
go through phases 227.11 *be changeable*
go through the books 789.8 *audit*
go through the ceiling 792.9 *be dear*
go through the roof 213.4 *increase*
Goths 284.6 *people of the past*
got it! **446.25**
goto 40.19 *computing terms*
go to 145.7 *reach*
go to a funeral 583.8 *bury*
go to all lengths 638.6 *be resolute*
go to and fro 298.7 *be regular*; 639.5 *vacillate*
go to any length 638.6 *be resolute*
go to any lengths 576.8 *exert oneself*
go to arbitration 754.4 *compromise*
go to bat for 392.24 *back*
go to bed 301.8 *be motionless*; 263.2 *take it easy*
go to bed late 342.13 *be busy*
go to blazes 357.13 *be destroyed*
go to church 7.19 *be religious*
go to confession 807.6 *apologize*; 808.4 *be penitent*
go to court 751.6 *argue*
go to earth 736.11 *conceal oneself*
go to exaggerated lengths 727.7 *exaggerate*
go to extremes 727.9 *be extravagant*
go together 223.13 *accompany*; 439.6 *store*
go together with 223.13 *accompany*
go to glory 582.15 *die*
go to ground 526.1 *disappear*
go to heaven 8.17 *deify*; 101.12 *enter a nonmaterial world*
go to hell 357.13 *be destroyed*; 101.12 *enter a nonmaterial world*
go to hospital 260.24 *be unhealthy*
go to it 130.18 *make a beginning*; 638.9 *undertake*
go to law 16.70 *litigate*
go to meet 312.8 *meet*
go too far 727.9 *be extravagant*; 250.19 *liberalize*; 329.1 *overstep*
go to one's corner 52.11 *fight*
go to one's head 690.9 *be intoxicating*; 673.16 *show off*
go to one's reward 582.15 *die*
go to parties 654.11 *be sociable*
go to pieces 357.13 *be destroyed*; 245.1 *deteriorate*; 375.3 *disintegrate*
go topless 552.14 *undress*
go to pot 556.17 *age*; 357.13 *be destroyed*; 249.9 *be in trouble*; 245.1 *deteriorate*; 796.16 *do wrong*; 766.14 *go to waste*; 782.13 *lose one's money*; 441.1 *waste*
go to press 740.15 *publish*
go to ruin 245.1 *deteriorate*; 782.13 *lose one's money*; 441.1 *waste*
go to school 6.23 *learn*
go to seed 556.17 *age*; 245.1 *deteriorate*; 766.14 *go to waste*
go to sleep 489.11 *be unfeeling*; 263.2 *take it easy*
go to the bad 804.16 *be wicked*; 796.16 *do wrong*; 802.23 *sin*
go to the block 778.2 *be sold*
go to the bog 608.13 *relieve oneself*
go to the country 469.5 *vote*
go to the devil 245.1 *deteriorate*
go to the dogs 357.13 *be destroyed*; 249.9 *be in trouble*; 804.16 *be wicked*; 245.1 *deteriorate*; 796.16 *do wrong*; 247.6 *fail*; 766.14 *go to waste*; 802.23 *sin*
go to the john 608.13 *relieve oneself*
go to the polls 469.5 *vote*
go to the toilet 560.15 *excrete*
go to the wall 357.13 *be destroyed*; 264.20 *be in difficulty*; 786.9 *be unable to pay*; 247.6 *fail*; 766.10 *have a financial loss*; 782.13 *lose one's money*
go to war **585.12**; 701.13, 751.6 *argue*
go to waste **766.14**; 357.13 *be destroyed*; 238.7 *be useless*; 441.1 *waste*
got rid of 767.12 *disposed*
gotten 788.6 *received*
Götterdämmerung 131.5 *fate*
gouache 19.11 *artist's materials*; 529.5 *paint*; 19.8 *painting*
gouge 183.4, 183.10 *notch*; 792.10 *overcharge*; 52.12 *wrestle*; 52.5 *wrestling*
gouged 30.59 *weathered*
gouge out 369.13 *dig out*; 183.9 *make concave*
gouging 792.7 *dear*; 792.4 *extortion*; 52.5 *wrestling*
goulash 25.32 *meat dish*; 412.2 *mixed thing*
go under 357.13 *be destroyed*; 264.20 *be in difficulty*; 305.9 *descend*
go underground 588.4 *be anarchic*; 252.9 *be safe*; 736.11 *conceal oneself*; 305.15 *tunnel*
go under water 305.9 *descend*
go unnoticed 216.9 *be average*
go unpunished 389.5 *escape*
go up 304.13 *ascend*
go up in flames 493.15 *burn*
go up in smoke 766.14 *go to waste*; 247.8 *miscarry*
go up Salt River 582.15 *die*
go upstairs 304.15 *mount*
go up the spout 766.14 *go to waste*
go up the wall 624.12 *become angry*
gourd 410.14 *bottle*
Gourlay 56.5 *golf ball*
gourmand 557.18 *eater*; 688.4 *glutton*; 241.5 *pleasure-loving*; 490.3 *pleasure-seeker*; 686.5 *self-indulgent person*; 495.5 *taster*
gourmandise 688.2 *epicurism*
gourmandising 686.3 *overindulgence*; 686.8 *overindulgent*; 490.1 *physical pleasure*
gourmandism 557.2 *appetite*; 557.3 *delicate eating*; 688.2 *epicurism*
gourmet 466.6 *discriminating person*; 557.18 *eater*; 688.4 *glutton*; 241.5 *pleasure-loving*; 490.3 *pleasure-seeker*; 686.5 *self-indulgent person*; 495.5 *taster*
gout 260.16 *rheumatism*
gouty 260.23 *diseased*; 690.5 *drunken*
govern **12.11**; 334.10 *be powerful*; 140.16 *direct*; 396.18 *have authority*; 397.11 *have authority over*; 579.1 *manage*; 400.14 *master*; 685.4 *moderate*; 407.22 *pacify*
governance **12.3**; **396.4**; 396.1 *authority*; 579.3 *management*; 334.1 *power*; 631.9 *tactics*
governess 6.4 *educator*; 401.4 *personal attendant*; 252.3 *protector*
governing **12.10**; 396.12 *authoritative*; 121.13 *dominant*; 579.17 *managerial*
governing body **12.4**; **579.6**; 6.5 *educationalist*
government **12.1**; 397.3 *authority*; 396.4 *governance*; 579.10 *legislative body*; 579.3 *management*; 334.1 *power*
governmental **12.9**; **396.14**; 631.16 *behaving*; 397.14 *commanding*; 579.17 *managerial*; 566.13 *national*
governmental architecture 20.1 *architecture*
governmental committee 713.4 *adviser*
governmental funds 780.19 *treasury*
governmentally 397.16 *commandingly*; 12.14 *politically*; 2.16 *sociologically*
governmental organization **396.8**
governmental power 12.3 *governance*
Government and Politics **12**
government by estates 12.1 *government*
Government Communications Headquarters 584.4 *military organization*
government debt 784.2 *national debt*
government documents 693.3 *document*
government institution 2.8 *human institution*
government man 815.5 *prisoner*
government office 579.3 *management*
government offices 577.1 *workshop*
government papers 744.1 *record*
government post 396.5 *position of authority*
government servant 579.16 *official*
governor **12.7**; 579.13 *director*; 6.5 *educationalist*; 400.9 *educational leader*; 38.11 *engine*; 400.3, 579.14 *leader*; 567.3 *male title of address*; 400.1 *master*; 251.5 *means of restraint*; 396.10 *person of authority*; 378.4 *restraint*; 121.5 *superior*
governor general 579.13 *director*; 400.3 *leader*
governorship 396.5 *position of authority*
governor's mansion 565.4 *official residence*
go west 357.13 *be destroyed*; 582.15 *die*
go with 223.13 *accompany*; 147.17 *stay near*
go without 687.5 *fast*; 709.7 *refuse oneself*
go without food 687.5 *fast*
go without saying 738.5 *be visible*
go with the crowd 216.9 *be average*
go with the flow 117.8 *comply*; 750.25 *conform*
go with the stream 117.8 *comply*; 664.14 *follow*; 302.6 *march on*
go with the tide 265.20 *take it easy*
gown 551.32 *dress*; 551.5 *fancy dress*; 551.7 *frock*; 551.16 *robe*; 7.11 *vestment*
gowned 551.29 *dressed*
go wrong **802.24**; 238.7 *be useless*; 604.6 *disappoint*; 796.16 *do wrong*; 247.9 *malfunction*; 247.8 *miscarry*
GPO 692.2 *postal communication*
grab 320.21 *miscellaneous motoring terms*; 360.6 *retain*; 773.7 *take*; 773.10 *take away*; 774.3 *theft*; 492.11 *touch*
grab away 633.10 *chase*
grab bag 114.3 *diverse thing*; 412.3 *miscellany*
grabber 773.6 *taker*
grabbing 360.1 *retention*; 773.1 *taking*; 773.3 *taking away*
grab bucket 38.29 *construction equipment*
grabby 765.16 *greedy*
grab one 446.14 *have an idea*
grab one's opportunity 287.5 *take the opportunity*
grace 650.1 *benevolence*; 543.1, 549.1 *elegance*; 649.1 *forgiveness*; 768.2 *gift*; 545.1 *gorgeousness*; 797.10 *kindness*; 627.3 *mercy*; 18.16 *musical note*; 542.12 *ornament*; 652.1 *philanthropy*; 10.9 *prayer*; 485.1 *skill*; 724.2 *stylishness*; 671.2 *thanks*; 803.2 *virtues*
grace-and-favour 793.11 *free of charge*

grace-and-favour flat 793.6 *absence of charge*
grace before meals 671.2 *thanks*
graceful 658.7 *courteous;* 543.3 *elegant;* 593.22 *lovable;* 549.5 *refined;* 724.7 *stylish*
graceful gesture 658.5 *sign of courtesy*
gracefully 658.14 *courteously;* 8.19 *divinely;* 543.5 *elegantly;* 724.10 *stylistically*
gracefulness 658.1 *courtesy;* 543.1 *elegance;* 545.1 *gorgeousness*
graceless 544.7; 486.3 *clumsy;* 546.4 *ugly*
gracelessly 546.6 *hideously;* 544.11 *inelegantly*
gracelessness 544.1 *inelegance;* 546.1 *ugliness*
grace note 18.16 *musical note*
grace of God 650.1 *benevolence*
graces 658.3 *courtesies*
grace the occasion 97.12 *attend*
gracile 545.5 *beautiful;* 543.3 *elegant;* 153.1 *thin*
gracility 153.7 *thinness*
gracious 658.7 *courteous;* 569.8 *friendly;* 636.4 *helpful;* 797.3 *kind;* 648.4 *lenient;* 652.6 *philanthropic;* 627.6 *pitying;* 667.9 *showing respect;* 657.8 *sociable;* 631.17 *well-behaved*
gracious host 631.3 *well-behaved person*
gracious living 549.1 *elegance*
graciously 658.14 *courteously;* 569.17 *in friendship;* 648.6 *leniently;* 627.13 *pitifully;* 667.22 *respectfully;* 631.19 *well*
gracious manners 631.2 *good conduct*
graciousness 658.1 *courtesy;* 631.2 *good conduct;* 636.9 *goodwill;* 797.10 *kindness;* 648.1 *leniency;* 657.2 *sociability*
gradation 209.3; 409.5 *categorization;* 407.3 *hierarchy;* 5.30 *syntax*
gradational 209.7; 407.12 *hierarchical*
grade 409.15 *categorize;* 409.6 *category;* 466.12 *discriminate;* 187.7 *make horizontal;* 26.10, 158.18, 209.5 *measure;* 189.1 *obliqueness;* 407.4 *position;* 209.2 *rank;* 137.5 *social class;* 137.14 *sort;* 137.6 *students;* 407.19 *systematize*
grade crossing 317.10 *railway*
graded 409.24 *categorized;* 137.12 *classed;* 209.7 *gradational;* 407.12 *hierarchical;* 466.11 *judged*
grade school 6.12 *educational institution*
gradient 27.37 *line;* 27.50 *scalar quantity;* 321.2 *track;* 304.2 *upturn*
gradient post 321.2 *track*
gradient wind 31.12 *wind*
Grading 209
grading 409.5 *categorization;* 137.1 *classification;* 38.29 *construction equipment;* 209.3 *gradation;* 209.2 *rank*
Gradual 10.6 *Eucharist;* 10.8 *hymn*
gradual 209.7 *gradational;* 333.5 *unhurried*
gradualism 209.1 *degree;* 244.11 *reformism;* 333.8 *slowness*
gradualist 244.12 *reformer*
gradually 209.10 *by degrees;* 205.12 *partly;* 333.16 *slowly*
gradualness 209.1 *degree*
graduate 246.6 *be successful;* 601.20 *come out;* 6.21 *curricular;* 466.12 *discriminate;* 400.10 *expert;* 244.2 *get better;* 26.10, 158.18, 209.5 *measure;* 136.8 *qualified person;* 485.4 *skilled person;* 246.4 *successful person*
graduated 209.7 *gradational;* 466.11 *judged;* 26.13 *measured*
graduated scale 26.6, 28.82 *measuring instrument*
graduate school 6.12 *educational institution*
graduation 409.5 *categorization;* 601.3 *ceremony;* 466.1 *discrimination;* 656.3 *formal occasion;* 209.3 *gradation;* 244.5 *improvement*
gradus 5.28 *dictionary*
Graeco-Roman 52.15 *wrestling*
Graeco-Roman wrestler 586.3 *athlete;* 52.6 *wrestler*
Graeco-Roman wrestling 52.5 *wrestling*
graffiti 744.4 *inscription*
graffito 19.9 *drawing*
graft 373.11 *connect;* 373.1 *connection;* 800.3 *criminality;* 44.15 *cultivate;* 774.7 *dishonesty;* 211.4 *extra;* 44.5 *gardening;* 368.8 *insertion;* 368.6 *plant;* 561.13 *propagate;* 774.4 *stolen goods;* 394.12 *surgery*
grafted 368.12 *inserted;* 44.19 *ornamental*
grafting 44.5 *gardening;* 368.8 *insertion;* 35.9, 394.12 *surgery*
graft union 44.5 *gardening*
grain 404.2; **427.7**; 557.8 *animal food;* 229.2 *attitude;* 81.4 *cereal grass;* 404.12 *coarsen;* 80.1 *fruits;* 80.3 *fruit structure;* 427.24 *grind;* 159.2 *little thing;* 435.1 *materials;* 529.4 *pigment;* 77.9 *seed;* 137.4 *type*
grain bin 43.10 *farm tool*
grain drier 43.10 *farm tool*
grained 404.8 *rough*
grain elevator 43.7 *farm building*
grain farm 43.6 *farm*
grain farming 43.4 *arable farming*
graininess 41.10; **427.3**; 404.2 *grain*
grain of sand 159.2 *little thing;* 30.27 *sediment*
Grain scan 35.7 *diagnosis*
grains of sand 566.1 *humankind*
grain weevil 76.3 *pest*
grainy 427.17; 420.2 *coarse;* 404.8 *rough*
grainy picture 692.23 *television reception*
gram 414.9 *avoirdupois weight*
gramercy 671.9 *thank you!*
graminaceous 81.8 *grasslike*
graminaceous plant 81.1 *grass*
Gramineae 81.1 *grass*
gramineous 81.8 *grasslike*
graminiferous 81.8 *grasslike*
graminivore 81.6 *grass eater*
graminivorous 557.26 *eating;* 81.10 *grass-eating*
graminivorousness 557.5 *eating habit*
grammar 5.29; 6.14 *school book*
grammar book 6.14 *school book*
grammarian 5.2 *linguist*
grammatical 5.44; 5.38 *linguistic*
grammatical analysis 5.30 *syntax*
grammatical error 274.11
grammatically 5.52; 5.48 *linguistically*
grammatical meaning 694.4 *type of meaning*
grammaticalness 5.29 *grammar*
grammatical rules 5.29 *grammar*
grammatical studies 5.30 *syntax*
grammatic character 5.13 *letter*
grammatologist 5.2 *linguist*
grammatology 5.1 *linguistics*
gramophone record 744.7 *recording;* 307.6 *rotator*
Grampian Mountains 89.5 *British mountains*
gramyre 11.3 *witchcraft*
granary 43.7 *farm building;* 439.4 *storage*
granary bread 25.38 *bread*
grand 158.15 *big;* 780.3 *fortune;* 123.5 *important;* 565.16 *manorial;* 622.21 *ostentatious;* 726.5 *serious;* 622.19 *stately;* 201.10 *thousand;* 235.1 *worthy*
Grand Canyon 92.8 *valley*
grand-champion 235.2 *best*
granddaughter 568.12 *woman in the family*
grand design 204.3 *whole situation*
grand duchy 85.3 *dominion*
grand duke 573.1 *nobleman*
grande dame 622.13 *proud person*
grandee 123.4 *bigwig*
grandes épreuves 61.2 *Formula 1 race*
grandeur 158.2 *bigness;* 543.1 *elegance;* 622.6 *majesty;* 726.2 *seriousness*
grandfather 556.8 *man;* 567.13 *man in the family*
grandfather clock 281.6 *clock*
grand fellow 235.8 *exceller*
Grand Guignol 21.9 *dramaturgy;* 21.2 *play*
grandiloquence 542.2 *affectation;* 727.4 *bombast;* 544.4 *inelegance of speech;* 729.2 *power of speech;* 726.2 *seriousness;* 673.1 *vanity*
grandiloquent 727.15 *bombastic;* 729.20 *eloquent;* 329.13 *exaggerated;* 544.9 *inelegant;* 542.10 *ornate;* 726.5 *serious*
grandiloquently 726.7 *emphatically;* 727.16 *exaggeratedly;* 729.21 *orally;* 542.13 *ornately;* 673.24 *pompously*
grandiose 329.13 *exaggerated;* 727.14 *extravagant;* 542.10 *ornate*
grandiosity 622.6 *majesty*
grand jury 16.26, 464.7 *jury*
Grand Lama 7.8 *priest*
grand larceny 774.1 *stealing*
grandly 622.34 *imposingly*
grand mal 461.3 *mental deterioration;* 260.17 *nervous disorder*
grand master 400.10 *expert*
grandmother 556.9 *woman;* 568.12 *woman in the family*
grandmother clock 281.6 *clock*
Grand National 59.7 *horseracing*
grandness 158.2 *bigness*
Grand Old Party 12.6 *political party*
grand opening 295.4 *beginning*
grand opening sale 791.2 *bargain;* 778.4 *sale*
grand opera 18.4 *opera*
grand panjandrum 123.4 *bigwig*
grandparents 296.2 *old people*
Grand Prix 61.2 *Formula 1 race*
Grand Prix car 61.1 *motor racing*
Grand Prix driver 61.8 *driver*
Grand Prix race 61.5 *motorcycle racing;* 61.1 *motor racing*
Grand Prix racer 61.8 *driver*
Grand Prix racing 61.1 *motor racing*
Grand Prix World Championship 61.1 *motor racing*
Grand Prix yacht racing 50.1 *sailing*
grands battements 22.10 *positions at the barre*
Grandsire Triple 18.6 *campanology*
grand slam 69.3 *card game terms;* 246.3 *successful thing*
grand-slam home run 48.5 *batting terms*
grand-slammer 48.5 *batting terms*
grandson 567.13 *man in the family*
grandstand 518.9 *viewpoint*
grand strategy 585.6 *art of war;* 584.1 *military affairs*
grand theft 774.1 *stealing*
grand toilette 656.4 *formal dress*
grand view 204.3 *whole situation*
grand vizier 579.16 *official*
grange 43.7 *farm building;* 565.4 *official residence*
granger 43.15 *agriculturist*
granita 25.35 *dessert*
granite 20.4, 435.2 *building material;* 418.1 *hard;* 418.7 *hard substance;* 38.26 *masonry;* 19.14 *sculptor's materials*
granite moss 82.3 *moss*
granite rock 228.4 *stable thing*
granitic 30.57 *chalky;* 418.1 *hard*
granny 556.9 *woman*
granny-bash 466.14 *discriminate against*
granny-basher 466.7 *bigot*
granny-bashing 466.4 *social discrimination*
granny flat 565.5 *house*
granny glasses 518.10 *visual aid*
granny knot 373.6 *line*
Gran Premio de Barcelona 61.5 *motorcycle racing*
grant 750.9; **750.30**; **785.4**; **813.3**; **813.10**; 396.3 *acquisition of power;* 739.8 *admit;* 43.2 *Common Agricultural Policy;* 783.8 *credit;* 392.6 *financial assistance;* 413.7 *financial support;* 768.2 *gift;* 768.5 *give;* 768.1 *giving;* 396.21 *grant authority;* 788.3 *income;* 771.5 *lend;* 771.1 *lending;* 440.9 *own property;* 757.2 *permit;* 765.5 *profit;* 388.3 *submit;* 413.13 *support financially*
grant absolution 758.10 *acquit;* 649.9 *forgive*
grant a final decree 571.7 *divorce*
grant a loan 783.8 *credit*
grant amnesty to 758.10 *acquit;* 648.3 *be lenient;* 649.9 *forgive*
grant an annulment 571.7 *divorce*
grant an armistice 749.4 *pacify*
grant a pardon 627.10 *show mercy*
grant a respite 16.78 *acquit*
grant asylum 252.10 *protect;* 370.9 *welcome*
grant a truce 749.4 *pacify*
grant authority 396.21
grant a visa to 773.11 *be hospitable*
grant bail to 391.4 *liberate*
grant clemency 749.4 *pacify*
granted 750.19; 396.13 *elected;* 768.7 *given;* 788.6 *received;* 476.8 *supposed*
granted amnesty 649.6 *forgiven;* 648.5 *given consideration*
grantee 769.5 *recipient*
grant equality to 391.6 *treat equally*
grant equal rights to 391.6 *treat equally*
Granth 7.12 *religious text*
grant immunity 758.9 *exempt;* 649.9 *forgive;* 757.3 *permit;* 250.15 *set free*
grant impunity 758.9 *exempt*
grant-in-aid 768.2 *gift;* 785.4 *grant*
granting 768.1, 768.8 *giving;* 222.15 *under the circumstances*
granting a visa 773.4 *taking in*
grant-maintained school 6.12 *educational institution*
grantor 768.4 *giver*
grant peace 749.4 *pacify*
grant permission 669.12 *accept*
grant remission 714.7 *vindicate*
granular 427.17 *grainy;* 159.7 *little;* 404.8 *rough*
granularity 427.3 *graininess*
granularly 427.29 *flakily*
granular snow 494.5 *ice;* 31.30 *snow*
granular texture 404.2 *grain*
granulate 404.12 *coarsen;* 427.27 *come to dust;* 427.24 *grind;* 420.12 *make rough;* 418.10 *solidify*
granulated 420.2 *coarse;* 418.3 *hardened;* 427.18 *pulverized;* 404.8 *rough*
granulated sugar 25.7 *basic ingredient;* 498.2 *sweetener*
granulation 404.2 *grain;* 427.3 *graininess;* 427.4 *pulverization;* 420.6 *roughness;* 418.6 *solidification*
granule 43.13 *fertilizer;* 427.7 *grain;* 159.2 *little thing;* 29.15 *sun*
granules 30.27 *sediment*
granulet 427.7 *grain*
granulization 427.4 *pulverization*
granulize 427.24 *grind*
grape 330.8 *missile*
grapefruit juice 558.6 *soft drink*
grapeshot 587.14 *historical ammunition;* 330.8 *missile*
grapevine 80.5 *figurative usage;* 504.8 *something heard;* 693.8 *source of information*
graph 27.32; 409.8 *chart;* 19.9 *drawing;* 125.5 *duplicate;* 163.1, 163.5 *outline;* 27.96 *represent;* 717.2 *reproduction*
grapheme 5.13 *letter;* 5.16 *spoken letter*
graphemics 5.1 *linguistics*
graphic 17.18, 721.11 *descriptive;* 409.26 *diagrammatic;* 726.3 *emphatic;* 695.1 *intelligible;* 5.41 *lettered;* 115.9 *lifelike;* 40.21 *on-line;* 19.24, 27.78 *pictorial;* 95.7 *realistic;* 717.13 *representational*
graphically 115.14 *comparably;* 721.18 *descriptively;* 5.48 *linguistically;* 40.22 *on-line;* 19.30 *pictorially;* 717.14 *representationally*
graphic artist 19.16 *artist;* 717.4 *person who makes a representation*
graphic arts 19.1 *art*
graphic character 40.10 *character*
graphic equalizer 504.10 *sound quality*
graphicness 695.9 *intelligibility*
graphic representation 27.32 *graph*
graphics 717.2 *reproduction*
graphite 256.9 *cleaning agent;* 268.5 *lubricant*
graphitic 32.34 *elemental*
graphology 719.5 *science of interpretation*
graph paper 27.32 *graph*
grapnel 252.4 *safety device;* 360.3 *tools for gripping*
grapple 381.9 *attack successfully;* 586.37 *fight;* 360.6 *retain;* 79.7 *timber production;* 52.12 *wrestle;* 52.5 *wrestling;* 373.9 *yoke*
grappler 586.3 *athlete;* 52.6 *wrestler*
grapple with 267.6 *adhere;* 113.19 *confront;* 381.5 *strike;* 638.9 *undertake*
grappling iron 252.4 *safety device;* 360.3 *tools for gripping;* 373.9 *yoke*
graptolite 30.43 *fossil*
Grasmere 88.4 *British lakes*
grasp 334.2 *ability;* 267.6 *adhere;* 458.7 *be wise;* 455.13 *get to know;* 446.14 *have an idea;* 455.1 *knowledge;* 400.15 *learn;* 763.1 *possession;* 359.5 *preserve;* 252.2 *protection;* 141.7 *range;* 4.21 *rationalize;* 360.6 *retain;* 360.1 *retention;* 773.7 *take;* 492.11 *touch;* 695.6 *understand;* 695.12 *understanding*
grasped 360.10 *retained*
grasping 765.16 *greedy;* 360.9 *retentive;* 773.1, 773.12 *taking;* 492.2 *touching*
graspingly 773.13 *avariciously*
grasping nature 773.1 *taking*
grasp the meaning 695.6 *understand*
grasp the nettle 354.1, 638.9 *undertake*
grass 81.1; 715.5 *accuse;* 715.3 *accuser;* 557.8 *animal food;* 739.7 *betray;* 739.4 *discloser;* 691.6 *drug;* 479.9 *equivocator;* 81.2 *grassland;* 71.37 *graze;* 538.8 *greenness;* 51.2 *grip;* 693.10 *informer;* 693.13 *inform on;* 81.12 *manage grassland;* 716.7 *person*

who gives evidence; 731.4 *talker*; 454.3 *testify*; 454.7 *verifier*
grass-covered 81.9 *grassy*
grass cutter 81.5; 425.9 *sharp-edged thing*
grass eater 81.6
grass-eating 81.10
Grasses 81
grasses 77.3 *seed plant*
grass family 81.1 *grass*
grass flower 81.3 *grass plant*
grass-green 81.9 *grassy*; 538.1 *green*
grasshopper 76.1 *insect*
grassland 81.2; 43.11 *farmland*; 141.3 *geographical space*; 538.8 *greenness*; 92.6 *lowland*; 77.1 *plants*
grassless 428.6 *desert*
grasslike 81.8
grasslike plant 81.1 *grass*
grass on 716.13 *turn queen's evidence*
grass over 81.12 *manage grassland*
grass plant 81.3
grass roots 123.3 *chief thing*; 81.7 *figurative usage*; 138.11 *general public*; 123.5 *important*; 574.2 *the common people*
grass silage 43.9 *animal feedstuff*
grass-skiing 68.1 *skiing*
grass skirt 551.6 *skirt*
grasstrack racing 61.1 *motor racing*
grass up 716.13 *turn queen's evidence*
grass widow 571.4 *divorced person*; 81.7 *figurative usage*; 571.6 *surviving spouse*
grass widower 571.6 *surviving spouse*
grass widowerhood 571.1 *divorce*; 571.5 *widowhood*
grass widowhood 571.1 *divorce*; 571.5 *widowhood*
grassy 81.9; 44.17 *botanical*; 419.4 *compressible*; 77.13 *plantlike*; 538.2 *verdant*
grate 427.25; 513.4 *be strident*; 515.6 *buzz*; 596.7 *cause dislike*; 594.16 *cause hate*; 25.55 *cook*; 493.6 *fire*; 365.15 *grind*; 517.10 *lack harmony*; 420.12 *make rough*; 308.6 *porous thing*; 513.5 *sound hoarse*
grated 420.2 *coarse*; 427.18 *pulverized*
grateful 671.4; 669.18 *approving*
gratefully 671.8
gratefulness 671.1 *gratitude*
grateful thanks 671.2 *thanks*
grate on one's ears 513.4 *be strident*
grater 427.13; 25.6 *kitchen equipment*; 420.7 *rough thing*
gratification 648.1 *leniency*; 490.1 *physical pleasure*; 609.1 *satisfaction*
gratified 648.5 *given consideration*; 671.4 *grateful*; 490.7 *pleased*; 609.4 *satisfied*
gratify 648.3 *be lenient*; 241.13, 490.9 *give pleasure*; 599.15 *humour*; 622.30 *make proud*; 609.8 *satisfy*
gratifying 241.1, 490.6 *pleasant*; 609.5 *satisfying*
gratifyingly 648.6 *leniently*
gratin dish 25.6 *kitchen equipment*
grating 517.7 *dissonant*; 544.9 *inelegant*; 365.9 *irritation*; 28.29 *optical element*; 427.4 *pulverization*; 50.8 *punting*; 365.11 *rough*; 513.7 *strident*
gratis 768.9 *as a gift*; 793.11 *free of charge*; 768.7 *given*
Gratitude 671
gratitude 671.1; 669.2 *admiration*; 813.1 *reward*
gratuit 793.6 *absence of charge*
gratuitous 793.11 *free of charge*; 765.15 *gainful*; 768.7 *given*; 660.18 *insulting*; 476.7 *suppositional*
gratuitously 768.9 *as a gift*; 765.20 *gainfully*
gratuitousness 793.6 *absence of charge*
gratuity 793.6 *absence of charge*; 813.7 *bounty*; 211.4 *extra*; 768.2 *gift*; 785.3 *pay*; 483.5 *positive stimulus*; 765.5 *profit*; 671.3 *recognition*
gravadlax 25.16 *fish dish*
gravamen 715.1 *accusation*; 99.2 *essential content*
grave 583.6; 5.36 *accent*; 582.8 *after death*; 309.4 *closed place*; 183.2 *concave land*; 156.4 *deep thing*; 19.22 *engrave*; 656.6 *formal*; 123.5 *important*; 795.10 *moralistic*; 226.5, 301.3 *resting place*; 726.5 *serious*; 643.1 *solemn*; 622.19 *stately*
grave accent 742.7 *punctuation*
grave affair 123.2 *important matter*
grave clothes 551.17; 583.4 *funeral objects*
grave digger 183.5 *digger*; 583.3 *funeral director*
gravel 435.2 *building material*; 427.9 *grit*; 38.26 *masonry*; 550.11 *paving*; 30.27 *sediment*; 30.36 *soil*; 550.29 *surface*
gravelliness 427.3 *graininess*
gravelly 420.2 *coarse*; 30.58 *earthy*; 427.17 *grainy*; 418.1 *hard*; 513.8 *hoarse*
gravel road 317.3 *road*
gravely 726.7 *emphatically*; 643.10 *solemnly*; 622.33 *with dignity*
graven 19.25 *sculptural*
graveness 795.4 *self-righteousness*
graven image 9.3 *idol*; 717.6 *image*
grave note 510.3 *deepness*
graveolent 503.3 *stinking*
grave pit 583.6 *grave*
graver 19.15 *engraving*; 23.11 *woodworking tool*
grave-robber 774.9 *plunderer*
grave-robbing 369.3 *digging out*; 774.5 *plundering*; 774.17 *stolen*
graveside service 583.2 *funeral*
graveside services 582.8 *after death*
gravestone 550.2 *cover*; 583.4 *funeral objects*; 744.11 *monument*
grave-wax 375.1 *disintegration*
graveyard 582.8 *after death*; 583.5 *cemetery*; 226.5, 301.3 *resting place*
gravid 474.6 *expectant*; 561.16 *reproductive*
gravimetric 32.41 *analytic*; 30.49 *geophysical*
gravimetric analysis 32.18
gravimetry 30.2 *geophysics*; 32.18 *gravimetric analysis*
gravitas 643.4 *solemnity*
gravitate 414.12 *be heavy*; 305.9 *descend*
gravitate towards 229.4 *tend*
gravitation 229.2 *attitude*; 414.5 *gravity*; 334.1 *power*; 305.2 *sinkage*
gravitational 363.10 *magnetic*
gravitational collapse 29.11 *stellar birth*
gravitational constant 29.4 *cosmological model*
gravitational force 29.4 *cosmological model*; 28.10 *force*
gravitational interaction 28.79 *fundamental interaction*
gravitational pull 414.5 *gravity*
gravitational redshift 29.7 *galaxy*
gravity 414.5; 656.1 *formality*; 123.1, 643.6 *importance*; 395.1 *influence*; 622.6 *majesty*; 402.1 *material world*; 334.1 *power*; 363.2 *pulling power*; 203.1 *quantity*; 795.4 *self-righteousness*; 726.2 *seriousness*; 643.4 *solemnity*
gravity dam 38.23 *dam*
gravity geophysics 30.2 *geophysics*
gravity-operated railway 317.10 *railway*
gravy 780.2 *cash*; 768.2 *gift*; 431.2 *juice*; 765.5 *profit*; 25.15 *sauce*
gravy boat 410.16 *crockery*
grayhound 332.4 *be swift*
grayling 55.5 *British game fish*; 25.17 *freshwater fish*
Gray Panther 533.6 *figurative usage*; 556.7 *older person*
graze 71.37; 365.13 *abrade*; 492.12 *abut*; 688.5 *be greedy*; 157.6 *be shallow*; 557.21 *eat*; 81.11 *eat grass*; 557.24 *have a meal*; 491.11 *inflict pain*; 491.3 *injury*; 147.19 *meet*; 147.4 *meeting*; 43.18 *practise livestock farming*; 492.3 *press*; 557.25 *provide food*; 157.4 *shallow thing*; 492.11 *touch*
grazed 43.20 *farmable*; 491.6 *injured*
grazer 81.6 *grass eater*; 70.4 *type of animal*
grazier 43.15 *agriculturist*; 356.9 *producer*
grazing 557.26 *eating*; 557.5 *eating habit*; 557.4 *eating meals*; 43.11 *farmland*; 81.10 *grass-eating*; 81.2 *grassland*; 43.3 *livestock farming*; 147.11 *meeting*; 365.4 *scraping*
grazing-incidence telescope 29.26 *radio telescope*
grease 25.7 *basic ingredient*; 258.11 *dirty*; 768.2 *gift*; 268.5 *lubricant*; 268.18 *lubricate*; 265.16 *make easy*; 421.10 *polish*; 421.11 *smooth*; 419.13 *soften*
greased 421.4 *polished*
greased lightning 332.11 *swift thing*
greased palm 480.9 *enticement*
grease gun 268.8 *lubricator*; 421.10 *polish*
grease job 268.1 *slipperiness*
grease leather 268.18 *lubricate*
grease monkey 578.2 *artisan*
greasepaint 547.4 *cosmetics*; 21.1 *drama*; 551.5 *fancy dress*; 21.21 *stage requisite*
greaseproof paper 25.6 *kitchen equipment*; 435.3 *paper*
greaser 320.14 *cyclist*
grease the palm 480.17 *bribe*; 768.5 *give*; 813.11 *pay*
grease the ways 265.16 *make easy*
grease the wheels 392.28 *further*; 265.16 *make easy*; 480.16 *tempt*
greasily 268.23 *oilily*
greasiness 268.3 *oiliness*; 421.7 *smoothness*
greasy 258.7 *dirty*; 421.4 *polished*; 268.13 *slippery*; 677.15 *unctuous*
greasy junkie 691.4 *drug taker*
greasy rock 62.2 *climbing dangers*
greasy spoon 557.15 *eating place*
great 158.15 *big*; 235.12 *fantastic!*; 797.1 *good*; 414.1 *heavy*; 123.5 *important*; 395.11 *influential*; 400.12 *masterful*; 217.2 *plentiful*; 336.10 *potent*; 334.13 *powerful*; 141.13 *spacious*; 235.1 *worthy*
great! 797.27
great and small 113.3 *opposites*
great auk 72.8 *extinct bird*
Great Australian Bight 92.9 *inlet*
Great Barrier Reef 92.2 *island*
Great Bear 88.5 *other major lakes*
great big 158.15 *big*
great bloodshed 382.4 *slaughter*
Great Britain 85.8
great catch 123.4 *bigwig*
great circle 27.42 *circle*; 198.8 *half*
great-circle sailing 323.5 *navigation*
greatcoat 551.12 *coat*
great day 601.5 *anniversary*; 123.2 *important matter*; 600.1 *rejoicing*
great distance 145.2
Great Divide 154.4 *mountain range*
great doings 342.1 *activity*; 123.2 *important matter*
greaten 190.6 *become bigger*
greater 27.75 *equal*; 203.6 *quantitative*; 121.12 *superior*
greater and greater 213.8 *increasingly*
greater city 87.1 *city*
greater doxology 10.8 *hymn*
greater good 469.8 *choice*
Greater London 87.5 *London*
Greater New York 87.3 *New York*
greater number 207.3 *majority*
greater part 205.5 *largest part*; 207.3 *majority*
greater proportion 207.3 *majority*
greater than 27.88 *equal to*
greatest 121.14 *best*; 27.75 *equal*
greatest elongation 29.16 *planet*
greatest number 207.3 *majority*
great expectations 610.3 *aspiration*; 283.4 *looking to the future*
great gun 587.11 *guns*
great house 356.8 *construction*
great hundred 201.9 *treble figures*
greatly 414.16 *heavily*; 158.20 *largely*; 235.11 *worthily*
great man 123.4 *bigwig*
Great Mogul 400.2 *sovereign*
Great Mother 8.3 *God*
greatness 396.2 *authoritativeness*; 158.2 *bigness*; 797.8 *good*; 123.1 *importance*; 395.1 *influence*; 334.1 *power*; 336.1 *strength*; 121.1 *superiority*; 235.6 *worth*
great news 123.2 *important matter*
great number 208.2 *multitude*
great quantity 203.2 *certain amount*; 219.1 *excess*; 217.8 *plenty*
great respect 667.2 *admiration*
Great Salt Lake 88.3 *US lakes*
great seal 743.3 *means of identification*
Great Slave 88.5 *other major lakes*
great speed 332.8 *speed*
great success 246.1 *success*
great thing 123.3 *chief thing*
great unwashed 574.2 *the common people*
Great Vowel Shift 5.37 *linguistic theory*
Great Wall of China 378.3, 384.9 *barrier*
great waters 91.1 *sea*
great way 145.2 *great distance*
great work 356.6
great work of literature 485.3 *masterpiece*
great worth 792.6 *value*
greave 384.7 *armour*
grebe 72.3 *water bird*
grebo 18.9 *popular music*
Grecian couch 23.2 *chair*
greed 557.2 *appetite*; 617.1 *desire*; 329.9 *excessiveness*; 765.1 *gain*; 688.1 *gluttony*; 686.3 *overindulgence*; 683.1 *selfishness*; 773.1 *taking*
greedily 773.13 *avariciously*; 557.28 *carnivorously*; 329.16 *excessively*; 765.20 *gainfully*; 688.7 *gluttonously*; 683.8 *selfishly*
greediness 688.1 *gluttony*
greedy 765.16; 617.9 *desirous*; 557.26 *eating*; 688.6 *gluttonous*; 686.8 *overindulgent*; 683.4 *selfish*; 773.12 *taking*; 218.2 *unprovided*
greedy guts 688.4 *glutton*
greedy person 688.4 *glutton*; 773.6 *taker*
greedy pig 617.6 *desirer*; 688.4 *glutton*
Greek 5.41 *lettered*; 566.4 *modern human*
Greek alphabet 5.14 *alphabet*
Greek chorus 21.23 *role*
Greek cross plan 20.10 *church architecture*
Greek dish 25.52
Greek drama 21.2 *play*
Greek fire 587.16 *bomb*; 493.6 *fire*
Greek gift 700.14 *fatal gift*; 645.2 *stratagem*
Greek meeting Greek 119.8 *on equal terms*
Greek meets Greek 119.2 *equilibrium*
Greek salad 25.52 *Greek dish*
Greek theatre 21.16 *theatre*
Greek tragedy 21.11 *tragedy*
Green 12.9 *governmental*
green 538.1; **538.17**; 499.5 *acid*; 780.2 *cash*; 28.28 *colour*; 225.4 *conservationist*; 538.7 *environmental*; 187.3 *flat thing*; 56.1 *golf*; 81.2 *grassland*; 81.9 *grassy*; 51.1 *green bowling*; 538.8 *greenness*; 51.2 *grip*; 450.12 *gullible*; 456.6 *ignorant*; 295.12, 555.12 *immature*; 629.4 *jealous*; 646.1, 805.7 *naive*; 77.14 *of plants*; 77.13 *plantlike*; 359.4 *preservationist*; 359.6 *preserving*; 538.3 *raw*; 538.6 *sick*; 45.2 *sportsground*; 487.1 *unaccustomed*; 260.21 *unhealthy*; 486.2 *unskilled*; 538.2 *verdant*
green about the gills 337.10 *ill*
green algae 84.2 *algae*
green and blacks 592.6 *desensitizing substance*
green apple 499.3 *sour thing*
green around the gills 260.22, 538.6 *sick*
greenback 780.8 *American money*; 538.12 *figurative usage*
green bacon 25.30 *bacon*
green ball 65.5 *snooker*
Green Bay 538.12 *figurative usage*
green bean 538.9 *greenstuff*
green belt 141.3 *geographical space*; 538.8 *greenness*; 86.6 *regions*; 87.8 *suburb*; 170.1 *surroundings*
Green Berets 538.12 *figurative usage*
green-blue 539.1 *blue*
green bowling 51.1
green card 538.11 *green thing*; 320.21 *miscellaneous motoring terms*; 757.2 *permit*
green dragon 691.6 *drug*; 538.11 *green thing*
green envy 538.14 *green-eyed monster*
greenery 538.8 *greenness*; 77.6 *leaf*; 77.1 *plants*
green-eyed 538.5; 594.10 *hating*; 629.4 *jealous*
green-eyed jealousy 629.1 *jealousy*
green-eyed monster 538.14; 629.1 *jealousy*
greenfinch 538.11 *green thing*
green-fingered 485.6 *skilful*
green fingers 136.2 *ability*; 485.2 *aptitude*; 44.5 *gardening*; 538.8 *greenness*
greenfly 538.11 *green thing*; 76.3 *pest*; 44.12 *pests and diseases*
greengage 538.9 *greenstuff*
greengrocer 557.20 *food provider*; 557.17 *food shop*; 80.4 *fruit eating*; 538.9 *greenstuff*; 436.3 *provider*; 778.13 *retailer*
greenheart 538.11 *green thing*
greenhorn 130.14 *beginner*; 700.22 *dupe*; 456.5 *ignorant person*; 805.4 *innocent person*; 646.3 *naive person*; 100.7, 295.8 *new arrival*; 486.10 *unskilled person*; 538.13 *young thing*
green hornet 691.6 *drug*; 538.11 *green thing*
greenhouse 424.3 *brittle thing*; 538.12 *figurative usage*; 493.8 *hot place*; 44.4 *nursery*; 565.7 *room*; 344.2 *source*; 527.8 *transparent thing*
greenhouse effect 31.40 *climatic change*; 538.12 *figurative usage*; 493.5 *hot weather*

greenhouse gases 493.5 *hot weather*
green ice 538.11 *green thing*
greening 538.16 *green politics*
greenish 538.1 *green*
greenish-yellow 537.1 *yellow*
greenkeeper 538.8 *greenness*
green labelling 538.16 *green politics*
Greenland 538.12 *figurative usage*
Greenland Sea 538.12 *figurative usage*
green leek 538.9 *greenstuff*
greenlet 538.11 *green thing*
green light **538.15**; 669.1 *approval*; 750.7 *consent*; 522.6 *electric light*; 742.4 *signal*
greenly **538.18**; 555.15 *immaturely*
greenmail 776.9 *bargaining*; 538.12 *figurative usage*; 777.7 *purchasing*
green man 522.6 *electric light*
green manure 43.12 *crop*; 43.13 *fertilizer*
green monkey disease 260.7 *tropical disease*
Green Mountains 538.12 *figurative usage*
green movement 359.1 *preservation*
Greenness 538
greenness **538.8**; 295.3, 555.3 *immaturity*; 646.2, 805.3 *naivety*; 499.1 *sourness*; 486.8 *unskilfulness*
green old age 556.5 *old age*
green paper 693.3 *document*; 538.11 *green thing*
Green Party 538.16 *green politics*; 12.6 *political party*
Green Party member 225.4 *conservationist*
Greenpeace 538.16 *green politics*; 359.1 *preservation*; 244.11 *reformism*
Greenpeace member 359.4 *preservationist*
green pepper 538.9 *greenstuff*
green pigment **538.10**
green plant 77.2 *plant*
green plants 77.1 *plants*
green politics **538.16**
green porphyry 538.11 *green thing*
green pound 43.2 *Common Agricultural Policy*; 538.12 *figurative usage*; 14.1, 780.7 *finance*
Green Revolution 43.4 *arable farming*; 562.1 *fertility*
Green River 538.12 *figurative usage*
greenroom 538.12 *figurative usage*; 21.17 *stage*
green run 68.1 *skiing*
Greens 538.16 *green politics*
greens 538.9 *greenstuff*; 25.33 *vegetable*
green salad 25.14 *salad*
greensand 538.11 *green thing*
greenshank 538.11 *green thing*
greensick 538.6 *sick*
green snake 538.11 *green thing*
greenstick fracture 538.13 *young thing*
greenstone 538.11 *green thing*
greenstuff **538.9**; 780.2 *cash*
greensward 81.2 *grassland*
green tea 558.3 *tea*; 538.13 *young thing*
green the desert 562.7 *make fertile*
green thing **538.11**
greentop 53.5 *wicket*
green turtle 538.11 *green thing*
green vegetable 25.33, 44.11 *vegetable*
green vegetables 80.1 *fruits*
Greenwich Mean Time 275.9 *time zone*
Greenwich Village 87.3 *New York*
green with envy 538.5 *green-eyed*; 624.15 *resentful*
greenwood 538.8 *greenness*; 79.4 *trees*
greet **658.12**; 733.9 *approach*; 569.15 *be hospitable*; 742.11 *gesture*; 769.10 *receive someone*; 667.20 *salute*; 654.14 *welcome*
greeting **667.6**; 312.12, 769.4 *reception*; 733.2 *salutation*; 658.5 *sign of courtesy*; 729.7 *utterance*; 654.9 *welcome*
greetings 514.4 *cry of greeting*; 733.15 *hail!*; 667.7 *respects*; 312.24 *welcome!*
gregarious 654.15 *sociable*
gregariously 654.18 *sociably*
gregariousness 654.1 *sociability*
Gregorian calendar 281.3 *chronology*; 275.13 *timer*
Gregorian chant 10.8 *hymn*
Gregorian mode 18.20 *key*
greige 533.1 *grey*; 533.4 *greyness*; 531.1 *white*
gremlin 11.11 *ghost*; 236.11 *harmfulness*; 378.7 *hinderer*; 322.7 *miscellaneous aviation terms*
gremlins 274.14 *technical error*
grenade 508.3 *banger*; 587.16 *bomb*
grenadier 586.13 *historical soldiery*
Grenadier Guard 586.12 *ceremonial troops*
grenadine 558.7 *alcoholic drink*
Gresham's law 245.7 *deterioration*
Gretna Green wedding 570.5 *wedding*
grey **533.1**; **533.8**; 556.17 *age*; 31.49 *cloudy*; 530.7 *colourless*; 117.6, 117.14 *conformist*; 602.6 *depressed*; 524.5 *dim*; 59.1 *horse*; 216.3 *mediocre*; 296.11 *old*; 531.3 *white-haired*
grey area 533.6 *figurative usage*
greybeard 533.6 *figurative usage*; 556.8 *man*; 556.7 *older person*
grey-black 532.1 *black*
grey-blue 539.1 *blue*
grey colour 533.4 *greyness*
grey eminence 395.4 *indirect influence*
Grey Friar 533.5 *grey thing*; 782.10 *poor person*
grey-green 538.1 *green*
grey hair 533.5 *grey thing*
grey-haired **533.2**; 556.14 *aged*; 296.11 *old*; 531.3 *white-haired*
grey-headed 533.2 *grey-haired*
greyhen 72.11 *female bird*; 533.5 *grey thing*
greyhound 533.5 *grey thing*; 332.12 *swift animal*
greying 556.12 *ageing*; 533.2 *grey-haired*
greyish 533.1 *grey*
greyishness 533.4 *greyness*
grey knight 533.6 *figurative usage*
greylag 533.5 *grey thing*
greyly **533.9**; 296.18 *venerably*
grey man 533.6 *figurative usage*
grey market 533.6 *figurative usage*; 779.3 *sellers' market*
grey matter 442.7 *brain*; 533.6 *figurative usage*; 458.2 *intelligence*
grey mould 44.12 *pests and diseases*
grey mullet 55.5 *British game fish*
Greyness 533
greyness **533.4**; 524.2 *murk*; 556.5 *old age*; 531.7 *whiteness*
grey pigment 533.4 *greyness*
grey population 533.6 *figurative usage*
grey squirrel 533.5 *grey thing*
grey thing **533.5**
greywacke 533.5 *grey thing*
grey whale 533.5 *grey thing*
grey wolf 533.5 *grey thing*
gribble 75.4 *arthropod*
gricer 321.10 *miscellaneous*
grid 193.2 *braid*; 334.7 *electrical power*; 39.20 *electron tube*; 61.6 *motor-racing terms*; 21.17 *stage*
griddle 493.4 *burner*; 25.55 *cook*; 25.5 *cooker*
gridiron 187.3 *flat thing*; 46.4 *stadium*; 21.17 *stage*
gridlock 320.21 *miscellaneous motoring terms*; 301.1 *motionlessness*; 132.8 *procession*; 226.2 *stop*
grid reference 142.2 *exact location*
grief 798.2 *affliction*; 602.1 *sorrow*
grief-stricken 798.8 *afflicted*; 602.5 *sad*
grievance 15.4 *industrial dispute*; 802.7 *sense of wrong*
grievance procedure 15.4 *industrial dispute*
grieve **602.8**; 249.9 *be in trouble*; 582.17 *bury*; 627.11 *excite pity*; 603.6 *lament*; 624.9 *offend*; 627.9 *sorrow*
grieve for 590.18 *feel for*; 627.9 *sorrow*
griever 603.3 *lamenter*
grieving 603.1 *lamentation*; 603.4 *lamenting*
grievous 798.8 *afflicted*; 602.7 *distressing*; 627.7 *pitiful*; 236.4 *poor*
grievous bodily harm 651.7 *act of malevolence*; 331.12 *collision*; 381.16 *personal attack*
grievously 798.13 *destructively*; 249.12 *in adversity*
griffin 72.9 *fabulous bird*; 743.8 *heraldic device*; 70.7 *legendary beast*
grill 493.14 *be hot*; 534.7 *brown*; 493.4 *burner*; 25.55 *cook*; 25.5 *cooker*; 705.18 *interrogate*; 25.32 *meat dish*
grille 308.6 *porous thing*; 63.5 *real tennis*
grilled 534.2 *browned*; 25.56 *culinary*; 705.16 *questioned*
grille penthouse 63.5 *real tennis*
grilling 25.8 *cooking technique*; 705.2 *questioning*
grill room 557.15 *eating place*
grilse 74.3 *young fish*
grim 236.3 *bad*; 523.11 *benighted*; 651.12 *callous*; 659.5 *discourteous*; 612.10 *frightening*; 643.1 *solemn*; 638.3 *strong-willed*; 626.6 *sullen*; 641.3 *unyielding*
grimace 626.11 *be irritable*; 234.2 *facial distortion*; 625.7 *frown*; 742.3, 742.11 *gesture*; 518.6, 518.13 *look*; 234.10 *make faces*; 596.6 *react against*; 625.2 *sign of irascibility*; 626.4 *sign of irritableness*
grimacing 742.15 *gestural*; 625.5 *showing irascibility*
grimalkin 71.10 *cat*
grim determination 638.12 *resolution*
grime 523.3 *dark colour*; 258.4 *dirt*; 258.11 *dirty*
griminess 258.1 *dirtiness*
grimly 523.15 *darkly*; 659.9 *discourteously*; 626.13 *sullenly*
Grimm's law 5.37 *linguistic theory*
grimness 236.9 *badness*; 651.3 *callousness*; 641.6 *determination*; 643.4 *solemnity*; 523.7 *spiritual darkness*; 626.1 *sullenness*
grim-visaged war 585.1 *war*
grimy 523.10 *dark-coloured*; 258.7 *dirty*; 528.2 *shady*
grin 598.7 *be cheerful*; 597.7 *show joy*
grin and bear it 598.7 *be cheerful*; 638.11 *persist*; 388.4 *succumb*; 613.16 *take courage*
grind **365.15**; **427.24**; 491.10 *be painful*; 513.4 *be strident*; 25.55 *cook*; 357.9 *demolish*; 557.21 *eat*; 24.11 *make ceramics*; 425.15 *make sharp*; 191.5 *make smaller*; 372.9 *separate*; 513.5 *sound hoarse*; 632.3 *way*; 576.1, 576.6 *work*
grind down 660.26 *oppress*
grinder 191.4 *contractor*; 25.6 *kitchen equipment*; 38.9 *machine tool*; 427.11 *pulverizer*; 25.11 *sandwich*; 425.11 *tooth*
grinding **365.3**; 24.5 *ceramic process*; 191.1 *contraction*; 357.2 *destroying*; 491.5 *painful*; 427.4 *pulverization*; 365.11 *rough*; 576.10 *working*
grind into the dust 357.9 *demolish*
grindstone 620.2 *boring thing*; 427.11 *pulverizer*; 425.12 *sharpener*; 576.1 *work*
grind to a halt 226.6 *cease*
grind to dust 357.9 *demolish*
grind to powder 357.9 *demolish*
grind underfoot 357.9 *demolish*
grind under one's heel 357.9 *demolish*
grinning 598.1 *cheerful*
grip **51.2**; 267.6 *adhere*; 410.8 *bag*; 410.9 *baggage*; 491.10 *be painful*; 373.12 *bind*; 373.8 *fastening*; 362.4 *friction*; 742.3 *gesture*; 56.4 *golf club*; 12.3, 396.4 *governance*; 395.1 *influence*; 763.1 *possession*; 252.2 *protection*; 360.6 *retain*; 360.1 *retention*; 485.1 *skill*; 327.8 *spasm*; 438.1 *tool*; 360.3 *tools for gripping*; 492.11 *touch*
gripe 606.7 *be dissatisfied*; 753.7 *complain*; 606.2 *expression of dissatisfaction*; 113.18 *object*; 360.6 *retain*; 802.7 *sense of wrong*
griper 606.3 *dissatisfied person*
gripes 260.8 *indigestion*
grip of iron 360.1 *retention*
grip of steel 360.1 *retention*
gripped 373.16 *bound*; 360.10 *retained*
gripping 395.12 *appealing*; 491.5 *painful*; 360.9 *retentive*; 492.2 *touching*
grips 491.2 *painful condition*
grisaille 533.4 *greyness*; 19.8 *painting*
griseous 533.1 *grey*
grisette 568.2 *female*
grisly 546.4 *ugly*
grist 435.1 *materials*; 427.8 *meal*
gristle 418.7 *hard substance*; 416.4 *solid body*; 423.7 *tough thing*
gristly 418.1, 423.3 *hard*
grist to the mill 765.1 *gain*; 436.1 *provision*
grit **427.9**; 613.1 *courage*; 638.16 *fortitude*; 404.2 *grain*; 418.7 *hard substance*; 640.4 *stamina*; 336.1 *strength*
grit one's teeth 638.8 *brace oneself*; 742.11 *gesture*; 640.8 *hold out*
grits 25.40 *breakfast cereal*; 25.43 *US dish*
gritstone 62.5 *rock face*
gritted teeth 638.16 *fortitude*
gritter 320.21 *miscellaneous motoring terms*
grittily 427.29 *flakily*; 418.12 *toughly*
grittiness 404.2 *grain*; 427.3 *graininess*; 418.5 *hardness*
gritting 320.21 *miscellaneous motoring terms*
gritty 427.17 *grainy*; 418.1 *hard*; 404.8 *rough*
grizzle 541.11 *variegate*; 531.13 *whiten*
grizzled 533.2 *grey-haired*; 541.10 *mottled*; 296.11 *old*; 531.3 *white-haired*
grizzly 533.2 *grey-haired*
groan 753.7 *complain*; 514.13 *cry*; 514.6 *cry of pain*; 491.12 *express pain*; 753.3 *gesture of protest*; 603.2 *lament*
groaning 514.18 *crying*
groaning board 217.8, 557.9 *plenty*
groat 780.10 *former British money*
groats 427.8 *meal*
grocer 557.20 *food provider*; 436.3 *provider*; 778.13 *retailer*
groceries 557.7 *food*; 436.2 *provisions*
grocer's 557.17 *food shop*
grocery 557.17 *food shop*
groceryman 778.13 *retailer*
grog 690.12 *alcohol*; 558.7 *alcoholic drink*
grog-blossom 690.16 *alcoholism*
grogginess 592.4 *desensitization*
groggy 592.2 *desensitized*; 337.10 *ill*; 301.5 *sedentary*; 260.22 *sick*
groin 311.5 *fork*; 20.9 *miscellaneous architectural features*
groin vault 20.7 *vault*
grommet 504.7 *ear attachments*; 743.7 *flag*
groom 567.4 *boyfriend*; 570.7 *bridal party*; 243.6 *brief*; 256.13 *clean*; 401.6 *domestic servant*; 43.16 *farm worker*; 59.15 *horse person*; 43.18 *practise livestock farming*; 59.16 *ride*; 570.8 *spouse*; 407.21 *tidy*
groomed 551.30 *dressed-up*; 407.13 *orderly*; 243.18 *prepared*; 421.1 *smooth*
grooming 59.14 *horse-riding terms*
grooming kit 59.14 *horse-riding terms*
groove 146.2, 146.5 *crack*; 140.6 *custom*; 184.2 *furrow*; 183.4 *notch*; 317.6 *path*; 62.5 *rock face*; 181.6 *round*; 632.3 *way*; 184.8 *wrinkle*
grooved 146.7 *cracked*; 184.6 *wrinkly*
groover 597.3 *joyful person*
groovy 553.7 *fashionable*; 235.1 *worthy*
grope 519.14 *be blind*; 486.7 *be clumsy*; 593.14 *communication of love*; 492.4 *kiss*; 492.11 *touch*
grope one's way 333.2 *hesitate*
groping 486.3 *clumsy*; 593.14 *communication of love*; 333.6 *hesitant*; 492.2 *touching*
gross 236.3 *bad*; 659.6 *bad-mannered*; 765.13 *be profitable*; 497.6 *coarse*; 158.16 *fat*; 765.15 *gainful*; 804.12 *immoral*; 544.8 *indecorous*; 765.5 *profit*; 769.9, 788.7 *receive*; 203.4 *total*; 201.9 *treble figures*; 546.4 *ugly*; 675.7 *vulgar*; 204.6 *whole*
gross behaviour 659.2 *bad manners*
gross domestic product 13.3 *economic statistics*; 356.7 *produce*
gross indecency 796.7 *sexual assault*
grossly 792.12 *dearly*; 546.6 *hideously*; 544.11 *inelegantly*; 659.10 *rudely*
gross national product 13.3 *economic statistics*; 356.7 *produce*
grossness **675.3**; 659.2 *bad manners*; 236.9 *badness*; 158.5 *fatness*; 544.2 *impropriety*; 796.2 *indecency*
gross out 596.7 *cause dislike*
gross-out 804.10 *bad person*
gross profit 13.7 *corporation*; 813.5 *turnover*
gross profits 788.2 *money received*; 765.5 *profit*
gross receipts 765.4 *earnings*; 788.2 *money received*; 769.2 *something received*
gross return 765.4 *earnings*
gross revenue 765.4 *earnings*
gross score 56.2 *golfing terms*
gross someone out 804.16 *be wicked*
gross structure 34.4 *anatomy*
gross weight 414.7 *weighing*
grotesque 234.7 *deformed*; 118.14 *eccentric*; 477.11 *fantastical*; 544.9 *inelegant*; 718.6 *misrepresented*; 619.8 *wonderful*
grotesquely 234.13 *asymmetrically*
grotesqueness 118.4 *unusualness*
grotesquerie 234.3 *deformity*; 718.1 *misrepresentation*; 118.4 *unusualness*
grottiness 236.10 *poverty*
grotto 44.3 *ornamental garden*
grotty 666.5 *indifferent*; 236.4 *poor*; 260.22 *sick*; 124.4 *trivial*; 546.4 *ugly*; 258.8 *unclean*
grouch 626.11 *be irritable*; 659.4 *dis-*

courteous person; 625.3 *irascible person;* 670.13 *pessimist;* 626.5 *sullen person*
grouchily 625.9 *irascibly;* 626.14 *irritably*
grouchiness 625.1 *irascibility;* 626.3 *irritableness*
grouchy 701.8 *argumentative;* 625.4 *irascible;* 626.7 *irritable*
ground 53.2; 55.8 *angling;* 19.11 *artist's materials;* 175.1, 175.3, 175.4 *base;* 143.2 *circumstances;* 39.35 *conduct;* 30.6 *continent;* 25.56 *culinary;* 357.15 *destroyed;* 6.22 *educate;* 334.7 *electrical power;* 28.52 *electric potential;* 367.2 *flatten;* 312.4 *land;* 452.21 *make certain;* 205.11 *partial;* 427.18 *pulverized;* 814.1 *punish;* 344.5 *reason;* 86.1 *region;* 323.10 *sail;* 45.2 *sportsground;* 413.9 *supportive*
ground-attack aircraft 586.31 *military aircraft*
ground bait 55.1 *angling;* 700.13 *snare*
ground ball 48.5 *batting terms*
ground-based observatory 29.23 *observatory*
ground bass 516.4 *harmonics*
groundbreaker 129.8 *precursor*
ground-breaking 129.14 *preparatory*
ground clearance 61.6 *motor-racing terms*
ground control 322.6 *flight control*
ground cover 44.9 *garden plant*
groundcrew 322.3 *aircraft personnel*
ground drive 63.2 *tennis strokes*
grounded 143.8 *circumstantial;* 335.12 *impotent;* 6.19 *knowledgeable;* 367.17 *lowered;* 814.20 *punished;* 228.10 *stabilized*
ground engineer 322.3 *aircraft personnel*
grounder 48.5 *batting terms*
ground floor 175.2 *foot*
ground fog 31.33 *fog*
ground-force attack 381.12 *military attack*
ground forces 584.2 *the military*
ground frost 31.36 *frost*
ground gained 302.12 *advance;* 765.2 *augmentation*
ground game 46.9 *play*
ground glass 527.9 *glass;* 528.7 *opaque thing*
Groundhog Day 31.3 *weather*
groundhog hunting 633.2 *chase*
grounding 367.12 *downthrow;* 814.7 *punishment;* 64.6 *rugger*
grounding the ball 64.3 *rugby play*
grounding the club 56.3 *golf shots*
ground intentionally 46.18 *be penalized*
groundless 107.9 *causeless;* 704.6 *refutable;* 702.7 *sophistic*
groundlessly 704.12 *refutably;* 702.14 *sophistically*
groundlessness 704.4 *refutability*
ground-level 175.3 *base*
groundling 322.3 *aircraft personnel;* 21.33 *theatregoer*
ground meat 25.20 *meat*
ground money 59.12 *rodeo*
groundnut meal 43.9 *animal feedstuff*
groundnuts 43.12 *crop*
ground out 48.7 *play baseball*
ground pine 82.1 *fern*
ground plan 484.5 *map;* 163.1 *outline*
groundreflected wave 692.15 *transmitted wave*
ground rent 790.3 *fee*
ground run 322.5 *flight*
grounds 136.7 *condition;* 452.13 *confirmation;* 714.2 *defence;* 258.4 *dirt;* 716.1 *evidence;* 444.4 *explanation;* 701.3 *line of argument;* 480.11, 483.1 *motive;* 440.1 *property;* 344.5 *reason;* 215.2 *residue*
grounds for dismissal 15.2 *industrial negotiations*
grounds for divorce 571.3 *divorce court*
groundsheet 550.9 *floor covering*
groundspeed 322.5 *flight;* 332.8 *speed*
ground staff 586.32 *airman*
ground state 28.67 *excited atom*
ground station 31.5 *weather station*
ground stroke 63.2 *tennis strokes*
ground swell 327.13 *tempest*
ground to dust 427.18 *pulverized*
ground under repair 56.1 *golf*
groundwater 30.9
ground wave 692.15 *transmitted wave*
groundwork 409.11 *arrangements;* 129.3 *preparation;* 243.10 *preparations;* 344.3 *rudiment;* 130.7 *rudiments;* 413.2 *supporting part;* 326.5 *wave*
group 376.11; **376.38**; **566.9**; 27.23 *algebra;* 750.2 *alliance;* 586.16 *army unit;* 409.12 *arrange;* 376.25 *assemblage;* 376.37 *assemble;* 374.3, 376.1 *assembly;* 409.15 *categorize;* 409.6 *category;* 32.6 *chemical element;* 137.2, 137.13 *class;* 374.5 *combine;* 376.39 *come together;* 19.23 *design;* 158.18 *measure;* 584.4 *military organization;* 205.1 *part;* 19.12 *sculpture;* 27.21 *set;* 137.5 *social class;* 2.4 *social organization;* 407.19 *systematize;* 169.5 *team*
group activity 654.1 *sociability;* 342.2 *social activity*
group behaviour 2.6 *social group*
group captain 586.32 *airman*
group dynamics 36.3 *psychiatric treatment*
grouped 376.49; **407.11**; 409.20 *arranged;* 409.24 *categorized;* 137.12 *classed*
groupie 669.8 *admirer;* 632.8 *creature of habit;* 223.9, 267.5, 289.8 *follower;* 122.6 *inferior;* 593.9 *lover;* 9.5 *worshipper;* 555.6 *young person*
group influence 395.6
grouping 407.2; 409.1 *arrangement;* 374.3, 376.1 *assembly;* 409.5 *categorization;* 137.2 *class;* 137.1 *classification;* 376.11 *group;* 19.4 *treatment*
group interaction 2.6 *social group*
Group of Seven 13.5 *international trade*
group participation 764.2 *participation*
group photograph 41.4 *portrait*
group practice 35.1 *medicine*
group psychology 36.1 *psychology*
group psychotherapy 36.3 *psychiatric treatment*
group relations training 36.3 *psychiatric treatment*
group solidarity 2.6 *social group*
group test 36.5 *psychological test*
group therapy 394.13 *therapy*
group together 376.37 *assemble*
grouse 606.7 *be dissatisfied;* 626.11 *be irritable;* 753.7 *complain;* 60.5 *game;* 25.20 *meat;* 113.18 *object;* 802.7 *sense of wrong;* 72.4 *table bird*
grouse moor 92.6 *lowland*
grouser 659.4 *discourteous person;* 606.3 *dissatisfied person;* 670.13 *pessimist;* 753.4 *protester;* 626.5 *sullen person*
grouse season 292.1 *season*
grouse shoot 633.2 *chase*
grouse shooter 382.13 *animal killer*
grouse shooting 382.9 *animal killing;* 60.2 *hunting*
grousing 626.7 *irritable*
grout 267.3 *adhesive;* 550.28 *face;* 38.26 *masonry;* 550.8 *wall covering*
grouts 258.4 *dirt*
grovel 187.6 *be horizontal;* 155.8 *be low;* 471.14 *be solicitous;* 387.8 *be subject to;* 367.9 *bow;* 664.9 *fawn;* 663.6 *show obeisance to;* 623.20 *submit;* 388.4 *succumb;* 307.10 *swirl;* 667.19 *take off one's hat to*
groveller 388.2 *appeaser;* 664.3 *sycophant*
grovelling 367.15 *debasement;* 367.21 *degraded;* 663.3 *obeisance;* 388.1 *submission;* 664.2 *sycophancy;* 664.7 *sycophantic*
groves of academe 455.7 *academia*
grow 79.19; **345.8**; **555.18**; 765.10 *augment;* 190.6 *become bigger;* 760.8 *be transformed;* 209.6 *change gradually;* 93.18 *come to be;* 243.7 *develop;* 43.17 *farm;* 302.8 *further;* 213.4 *increase;* 213.5 *make bigger;* 556.18 *mature;* 43.18 *practise livestock farming;* 356.10 *produce;* 154.16 *rise;* 77.21 *vegetate*
grow bag 44.4 *nursery;* 344.2 *source*
grow better 244.2 *get better*
grow dark 523.13 *become dark;* 31.60 *cloud*
grow dim 524.9 *be dim;* 214.4 *decrease*
grower 43.15 *agriculturist;* 243.15 *preparer;* 356.9 *producer*
grow fat 248.5 *be prosperous*
grow from 345.8 *grow*
grow fruit 44.14 *practise horticulture*
growing 190.8; **345.11**; 760.14 *converting;* 209.7 *gradational;* 213.6 *increasing;* 356.2 *manufacture;* 555.13 *maturing;* 77.13 *plantlike;* 338.4 *vigorous*
growing apart 372.1 *separation*
growing medium 344.2 *source*
growing old 556.12 *ageing*
growing pains 555.2 *youthfulness*
growing plants 44.5 *gardening*
growing season 292.3 *summer*
growing soft 214.1 *decrease*
growing together 374.1 *combination*
grow in profusion 217.5 *about*
growl 515.1 *animal cry;* 624.11 *be angry;* 626.11 *be irritable;* 515.4 *cry;* 625.7 *frown;* 659.8 *get angry;* 624.6 *sign of anger;* 625.2 *sign of irascibility;* 626.4 *sign of irritableness;* 729.13 *speak in a particular way*
grow larger 213.4 *increase*
growler 30.39 *iceberg*
grow less 214.4 *decrease*
grow light 522.26
grow like a weed 190.6 *become bigger*
growling 624.16 *angry;* 659.6 *bad-mannered;* 659.5 *discourteous;* 625.5 *showing irascibility*
grow moss 245.2 *decay*
grown 190.7 *bigger;* 168.5 *bred;* 243.20 *developed;* 356.12 *produced*
grown old 556.14 *aged*
grown up 243.20 *developed*
grown-up 556.11 *adult;* 556.7 *older person*
grow old 296.17; 556.17 *age;* 245.1 *deteriorate*
grow on one 632.17 *become a habit*
grow pale 524.9 *be dim;* 522.28 *bleach*
grow plants 168.8 *nurture*
grow rank 258.10 *be dirty*
grow rich 248.5 *be prosperous;* 213.4 *increase*
grow rusty 487.4 *be unaccustomed*
grow smaller 214.4 *decrease*
grow soft 214.4 *decrease*
grow stale 245.2 *decay*
growth 190.1; **345.3**; 765.2 *augmentation;* 260.12 *cancer;* 32.4 *crystal;* 302.14, 561.4 *development;* 760.2 *evolution;* 213.1 *increase;* 356.2 *manufacture;* 34.5 *physiology;* 77.1 *plants;* 260.3 *symptom*
growth ring 79.3 *timber*
growth study 1.10 *measurement*
growth substance 33.17 *plant hormone*
grow together 267.6 *adhere;* 374.5 *combine*
grow up 556.17 *age;* 304.13 *ascend;* 190.6 *become bigger;* 213.4 *increase;* 304.18 *jump;* 556.18 *mature*
grow vegetables 44.14 *practise horticulture*
grow weak 260.24 *be unhealthy;* 337.6 *be weak*
groyne 252.4 *safety device;* 38.24 *water system*
GRP 50.10 *sailing*
GRP board 50.7 *windsurfing*
GRP hull 50.3 *parts of a sailing boat*
grub 557.7 *food;* 76.5 *larva;* 79.18 *manage trees;* 436.2 *provisions;* 555.4 *young animal*
grubbily 258.12 *dirtily*
grubbiness 258.1 *dirtiness;* 236.10 *poverty;* 408.3 *untidiness*
grubby 258.7 *dirty;* 236.4 *poor;* 408.15 *untidy;* 76.12 *verminous*
grub out 369.11 *extract*
grub's on! 25.58
grub's up 25.58 *grub's on!*
grudge 637.10; **682.8**; 590.6 *bad feeling;* 651.4 *bitterness;* 594.1 *hate;* 218.7 *make insufficient;* 624.1 *resentment*
grudging 594.10 *hating;* 682.1 *mean;* 624.15 *resentful;* 264.14 *troublesome*
grudging apology 808.1 *penitence*
grudgingly 594.18 *hatefully;* 682.9 *meanly;* 624.17 *resentfully*
grudging service 637.14 *disobedience*
grudging thanks 672.1 *ingratitude*
gruel 25.40 *breakfast cereal;* 497.3 *tasteless items*
gruelling 264.10 *difficult;* 261.4 *fatiguing;* 576.11 *laborious;* 814.21 *punishing*
gruesome 236.3 *bad;* 546.4 *ugly*
gruff 149.9 *abrupt;* 651.12 *callous;* 659.5 *discourteous;* 513.8 *hoarse;* 625.4 *irascible;* 626.7 *irritable*
gruffly 659.9 *discourteously;* 625.9 *irascibly;* 626.14 *irritably*
gruffness 149.6 *abruptness;* 659.1 *discourtesy;* 513.2 *hoarseness;* 625.1 *irascibility;* 626.3 *irritableness;* 732.3 *shyness*
Grumbacher red 535.6 *red pigment*
grumble 606.7 *be dissatisfied;* 626.11 *be irritable;* 753.7 *complain;* 509.8 *drum*
grumbler 606.3 *dissatisfied person;* 753.4 *protester;* 626.5 *sullen person*
grumbling 659.6 *bad-mannered;* 509.1 *drumming;* 626.7 *irritable*
grump 625.3 *irascible person;* 626.5 *sullen person*
grumpily 625.9 *irascibly;* 626.14 *irritably;* 499.11 *splenetically*
Grumpiness 625
grumpiness 625.1 *irascibility;* 626.3 *irritableness*
grumpishness 626.1 *sullenness*
grumpy 625.4 *irascible;* 626.7 *irritable;* 499.7 *splenetic*
Grundyism 255.1 *purity;* 795.4 *self-righteousness*
grunge 258.4 *dirt;* 18.9 *popular music*
grungy 236.4 *poor*
grunt 388.2 *appeaser;* 261.5 *be fatigued;* 515.4 *cry;* 513.2 *hoarseness;* 73.16 *live as an amphibian;* 513.5 *sound hoarse;* 387.3 *subordinate*
grunt-and-groan 52.15 *wrestling*
grunt-and-groaner 586.3 *athlete;* 52.6 *wrestler*
grunting 513.8 *hoarse*
gruntled 490.7 *pleased*
grylloblatodean 76.10 *insectan*
GSC 32.17 *analysis*
G star 29.13 *luminosity*
G-string 551.25 *accessories;* 552.4 *dishabille*
G-suit 551.10 *suit*
guacamole 25.50 *Central American dish*
guanine 34.12 *molecular biology;* 33.10 *nucleoside*
guano 258.4 *dirt;* 560.5 *faeces;* 562.3 *fertilizer*
guarantee 452.14; **756.2**; **756.8**; 354.3 *contract;* 392.29 *finance;* 452.21 *make certain;* 253.2, 253.11 *promise;* 252.10 *protect;* 252.1 *safety;* 454.1 *verify;* 707.3, 707.18 *vow*
guaranteed 253.7; **452.4**; 253.7 *guaranteed;* 756.13 *guaranteeing;* 252.6 *safe;* 707.12 *vowed*
guaranteed annual income 392.4 *social assistance*
guaranteed loan 784.3 *loan*
guaranteeing 756.13
guarantee payments 15.2 *industrial negotiations*
guarantor 452.15; 707.9 *affirmer;* 784.6 *debtor;* 756.5 *promise-maker*
guaranty 784.3 *loan*
guard 384.14; 223.7 *attendant;* 49.2 *basketball player;* 665.11 *care for;* 68.10 *curling;* 384.17, 586.39 *defend;* 251.11 *detain;* 223.15 *escort;* 54.5 *fence;* 54.3 *fencing movements;* 518.11 *observer;* 46.7 *offence;* 49.6 *play basketball;* 359.5 *preserve;* 252.10, 550.30 *protect;* 252.2 *protection;* 252.3 *protector;* 321.9 *railway worker;* 253.10 *secure;* 711.4 *warner;* 665.8 *watchful person*
guard against 243.3 *be prepared;* 471.11 *take note of*
guard cell 77.6 *leaf*
guard dog 71.9 *dog;* 252.3 *protector;* 384.5 *self-defence*
guard-duty 665.5 *watchfulness*
guarded 223.20 *accompanied;* 616.4 *cautious;* 252.6 *safe;* 732.2 *sparing with words*
guardedness 616.1 *caution;* 665.5 *watchfulness*
guarded speech 732.4
guardhouse 815.1 *prison*
guardian 252.3, 384.15 *protector;* 413.8 *supporter;* 413.9 *supportive;* 252.8 *tutelary;* 665.8 *watchful person*
guardian angel 8.6 *angel;* 392.15 *benefactor;* 586.2 *defender;* 252.3 *protector;* 413.8 *supporter;* 665.8 *watchful person*
Guardian Angels 252.3 *protector*
guardian of morality 795.6 *moralist*
guardianship 252.2 *protection*
guarding 665.9 *careful;* 251.4 *detention;* 49.4 *playing terms;* 252.8 *tutelary;* 665.5 *watchfulness*
guard of honour 667.5 *presenting arms*
guard one's pride 622.31 *save face*
guard one's reputation 799.6 *be honourable*
guardrail 252.4 *safety device*
Guards 586.14 *armed forces*

guard ship 586.24 *warship*
Guardsman 586.12 *ceremonial troops*; 586.8 *soldier*
guard's van 321.6 *rolling stock*
guar gum 430.2 *adhesive*
gubernatorial 12.9, 396.14 *governmental*; 579.17 *managerial*
guck 430.7 *slime*
guddle 633.11 *hunt*
guddler 633.6 *hunter*
gudgeon 307.4 *axle*
guellemin 655.6 *unsocial person*
guerdon 813.1, 813.9 *reward*
Guernsey 551.13 *sweater*
guerrilla 586.9; 588.3 *anarchist*; 381.19 *attacker*; 382.10 *killer*; 753.10 *lawbreaking*; 385.2 *revenger*; 662.10 *seditionist*
guerrilla attack 381.16 *terrorist attack*
guerrilla force 586.14 *armed forces*
guerrilla tactics 588.1 *anarchy*
guerrilla war 753.2 *disorder*
guerrilla warfare 383.3 *resistance movement*; 662.4 *revolution*; 585.8 *warfare*
guess 450.8 *be of the opinion*; 476.3 *conjecture*; 705.20 *doubt*; 464.12 *estimate*; 448.11 *experiment*; 464.1 *judgment*; 475.11 *predict*; 476.5 *suppose*; 96.14, 446.17 *theorize*; 446.2 *theory*; 453.9 *uncertainty*
guess at 590.16 *feel in one's bones*
guessed 476.8 *supposed*
guesser 476.4 *theorist*
guessing 476.3 *conjecture*; 705.15 *sceptical*; 476.7 *suppositional*
guesstimate 210.8 *calculate*; 476.3 *conjecture*; 475.11 *predict*; 476.5 *suppose*; 446.17 *theorize*
guesstimated 446.10 *theoretical*
guesstimating 476.7 *suppositional*
guesswork 476.3 *conjecture*; 475.2 *divination*; 448.3 *experimentation*; 274.2 *inaccuracy*; 464.1 *judgment*; 96.4 *theorization*; 453.9, 705.6 *uncertainty*; 456.3 *unknown thing*
guest 314.7 *entrant*; 564.3 *householder*; 763.5 *possessor*; 654.6 *social person*; 575.4 *titleholder*
guest house 565.10 *hotel*
guest of His Majesty 815.5 *prisoner*
guest pass 793.6 *absence of charge*
guest rope 373.6 *line*
guest soap 256.9 *cleaning agent*
guest ticket 793.6 *absence of charge*
guest worker 100.7 *new arrival*
guff 731.3 *talk*
guffaw 514.2 *cry of joy*; 514.11, 599.14 *laugh*; 597.7 *show joy*
guidable 324.14 *directed*
guidance 713.1 *advice*; 324.5 *directions*; 579.4 *directorship*; 6.1 *education*; 392.2 *support*; 631.8 *treatment*
guidance counsellor 713.4 *adviser*
guide 140.4; **579.5**; 392.23, 713.5 *advise*; 392.14, 713.4 *adviser*; 53.17 *bat*; 631.15 *conduct*; 631.10 *conductor*; 140.16, 324.6, 579.2 *direct*; 579.13 *director*; 6.22 *educate*; 223.15 *escort*; 396.11, 400.10 *expert*; 742.5 *indicator*; 395.8 *influence*; 62.7 *mountaineer*; 130.21 *pioneer*; 129.15 *precede*; 713.3 *precept*; 129.8 *precursor*; 742.9 *use signs*; 223.8 *usher*
guidebook 740.6 *book publishing*; 220.3 *dictionary*; 693.5 *reference book*
guided 223.20 *accompanied*; 6.19 *knowledgeable*
guided missile 587.5 *missile weapon*
guided-missile destroyer 586.24 *warship*
guide dog 519.3 *aid for poor sight*; 71.9 *dog*
guided wave 326.5 *wave*
guideless 254.3 *vulnerable*
guideline 140.4 *guide*; 713.3 *precept*
guide number 41.15 *lighting*
guidepost 742.5 *indicator*
guide telescope 29.25 *mounting*
guiding 324.16 *directing*; 324.5 *directions*; 6.16 *educational*; 395.11 *influential*; 579.17 *managerial*; 129.14 *preparatory*
guiding light 480.11, 483.1 *motive*
guiding principle 480.11, 483.1 *motive*
guiding spirit 8.5 *deity*
guiding star 522.13 *enlightenment*; 742.5 *indicator*; 483.1 *motive*
guidon 743.7 *flag*
guild 750.2 *alliance*; 376.15 *association*; 15.3 *organized labour*
guilder 780.11 *national coins*
guildsman 776.11 *chamber of commerce member*
guild socialism 12.1 *government*
guile 645.1 *cunning*; 699.5 *deceitfulness*; 700.1 *deception*; 702.5 *hypocrisy*
guileful 645.4 *cunning*; 699.33 *deceitful*; 700.34 *deceiving*
guilefully 645.6 *cunningly*
guileless 527.4 *easily seen through*; 646.1, 805.7 *naive*; 271.3 *natural*; 698.18 *truthful*
guilelessly 805.12 *naively*
guilelessness 646.2, 805.3 *naivety*; 527.10 *openness*; 698.5 *truthfulness*
guillotine 226.8 *cause to cease*; 582.4 *death sentence*; 382.19, 814.5 *execute*; 382.5 *execution*; 814.16 *instrument of execution*; 226.2 *stop*
guillotining 814.13 *capital punishment*
Guilt 806
guilt 806.1; 804.7 *criminality*; 16.38 *lawbreaking*; 808.1 *penitence*
guilt complex 806.2 *signs of guilt*
guilt feelings 808.1 *penitence*
guiltily 16.89; **806.11**; 804.21 *criminally*; 808.8 *penitently*
guiltiness 274.7 *errancy*; 806.1 *guilt*
guiltless 16.63 *acquitted*; 805.5 *innocent*; 230.1 *perfect*; 803.5 *virtuous*
guiltlessly 16.88 *forgivingly*; 805.11 *innocently*; 803.9 *virtuously*
guiltlessness 805.1 *innocence*; 230.3 *perfection*; 803.1 *virtue*
guilt-offering 762.3 *substitute thing*
guilty 806.5; 670.36 *blameworthy*; 16.64 *convicted*; 804.15 *criminal*; 274.16 *errant*; 802.16 *in the wrong*; 16.7 *legal trial*; 16.60 *offending*; 808.6 *penitent*
guilty act 804.7 *criminality*; 806.3 *sin*; 802.8 *wrongdoing*
guilty behaviour 806.2 *signs of guilt*
guilty conscience 808.1 *penitence*; 806.2 *signs of guilt*
guilty feelings 806.2 *signs of guilt*
guilty love 796.4 *illicit love*
guilty party 715.4 *accused person*; 806.4 *guilty person*
guilty person 806.4
guimpe 551.14 *neckwear*
guinea 780.10 *former British money*
guinea cock 72.10 *male bird*
guinea fowl 72.4 *table bird*
guinea pig 448.7 *experimentee*
guinea worm 75.10 *parasite*
guisard 700.15 *deceiver*
guise 171.3 *appearance*; 631.1 *conduct*; 551.5 *fancy dress*; 525.4 *something that appears*; 221.1 *state*; 317.1 *way*
guiser 700.15 *deceiver*
Gulag 815.1 *prison*; 814.7 *punishment*
gulch 146.3 *gulf*
gules 743.13 *heraldic*; 743.8 *heraldic device*; 535.1 *red*
gulf 146.3; 317.11 *channel*; 183.2 *concave land*; 156.4 *deep thing*; 92.9 *inlet*; 90.6 *river flow*
Gulf of Alaska 92.9 *inlet*
Gulf of California 92.9 *inlet*
Gulf of Campeche 92.9 *inlet*
Gulf of Guinea 92.9 *inlet*
Gulf of Mexico 92.9 *inlet*
Gulf of Saint Lawrence 92.9 *inlet*
Gulf Stream 493.8 *hot place*; 30.13 *ocean current*
gull 700.30 *be fraudulent*; 700.22 *dupe*; 72.3 *water bird*
gullet 557.16 *eating utensil*
gullibility 450.3 *believing*; 465.1 *misjudgment*; 646.2 *naivety*
gullible 450.12; 450.11 *believing*; 465.7 *misjudging*; 646.1 *naive*; 538.3 *raw*
gullibly 450.15 *believingly*; 465.13 *misguidedly*; 646.5 *naively*
gullied 62.8 *mountaineering*
gully 183.2 *concave land*; 146.3 *gulf*; 151.6 *narrow place*; 62.5 *rock face*; 53.4 *team*; 92.8 *valley*
gully washer 380.5 *violent weather*
gulp 688.5 *be greedy*; 558.2, 558.13 *drink*; 557.21 *eat*; 370.11 *ingest*; 370.4 *intake*
gulp down 558.13 *drink*; 557.21 *eat*; 370.11 *ingest*
gulping 558.1 *drinking*; 557.1 *eating*; 688.6 *gluttonous*; 370.4 *intake*
gum 267.4 *adherent*; 267.3, 430.2 *adhesive*; 267.7 *cause to adhere*; 422.3 *elastic thing*; 360.6 *retain*; 559.2 *secreted substance*; 430.10 *stick*; 25.41 *sweet*; 360.3 *tools for gripping*; 79.9 *tree product*
gum arabic 33.4 *polysaccharide*
gumball 691.6 *drug*
gumbo 412.2 *mixed thing*; 25.13 *soup*; 430.8 *viscous*
gumbolike 430.8 *viscous*
gumdrop 498.4 *confectionery*; 25.41 *sweet*
gum elastic 422.4 *rubber*
gumlike 430.8 *viscous*
gumlikeness 430.1 *viscosity*
gummed 360.10 *retained*
gumminess 430.1 *viscosity*
gummosity 430.1 *viscosity*
gummous 430.8 *viscous*
gummy 267.9 *adhesive*; 360.9 *retentive*; 430.8 *viscous*
gum print 41.12 *development*
gumption 458.2 *intelligence*
gumshoe 449.12 *discoverer*
gumshoes 551.19 *footwear*
gum turpentine 79.9 *tree product*
gum up 378.9 *block*; 430.10 *stick*
gum up the works 378.9 *block*
gun 357.7 *agent of destruction*; 508.3 *banger*; 330.9, 587.9 *firearm*; 633.6 *hunter*; 633.3 *hunting and fishing equipment*; 382.2 *murder*; 330.28 *shoot*; 330.15 *shooter*; 50.7 *windsurfing*
gunbarrel 68.1 *skiing*
gunbearer 316.7 *transferor*
gunboat 586.24 *warship*
gunboat diplomacy 748.2 *mediation*; 586.22 *navy*; 585.1 *war*
guncarriage 587.11 *guns*
guncotton 587.15 *explosive*; 330.13 *fuel*
gundog 71.9 *dog*; 633.6 *hunter*; 60.6 *sporting dog*
gun down 586.37 *fight*; 382.17 *murder*; 330.28 *shoot*; 382.18 *slaughter*
gun emplacement 384.11 *fortification*; 587.11 *guns*
gunfire 381.15 *firing*; 507.1 *loudness*; 330.7 *shot*
gun for 330.28 *shoot*
gunge 258.4 *dirt*; 430.7 *slime*
gungeon 691.6 *drug*
gung-ho 586.33 *combative*; 636.2 *eager*; 584.8 *military*; 85.16 *national*; 638.2 *tenacious*; 585.16 *warlike*
gung-ho attitude 342.8 *assiduity*; 584.7 *miscellaneous terms*
gung-ho nationalism 85.4 *nationalism*
gungy 236.4 *poor*
gunk 258.4 *dirt*; 430.7 *slime*
gunky 236.4 *poor*
gunman 386.4 *coercive person*; 586.1 *combatant*; 774.11 *dishonest person*; 651.8 *malefactor*; 382.11 *murderer*; 330.15 *shooter*
gunmetal 533.5 *grey thing*
gunner 586.32 *airman*; 586.17 *army person*; 330.15 *shooter*
gunnery 587.2 *arms*; 585.6 *art of war*; 381.15 *firing*; 330.6 *shooting*
gunning 633.2 *chase*; 60.2 *hunting*
gun park 587.11 *guns*
gunpowder 357.7 *agent of destruction*; 587.15 *explosive*; 330.13 *fuel*; 558.3 *tea*
gun rack 587.4 *arsenal*
gunroom 587.4 *arsenal*; 439.4 *storage*
gun-running 587.3 *arms race*
guns 587.11
gunshot 254.6 *danger signal*; 147.2 *short distance*; 330.7 *shot*
gunsight 518.10 *visual aid*
gunsmith 578.2 *artisan*
gunstock 587.9 *firearm*
gunter rig 50.3 *parts of a sailing boat*
gunter-rigged 50.10 *sailing*
Gunter's chain 26.6 *measuring instrument*
gunwale 50.6 *canoeing*; 50.4 *rowing*
gurge 307.10 *swirl*; 307.4 *vortex*
gurgle 434.24 *bubble*; 90.7 *flow*
gurk 371.16 *belch*
Gurkha 586.6 *militarist*
guru 400.9 *educational leader*; 6.4 *educator*; 485.5 *expert*; 442.8 *intellectual person*; 579.14 *leader*; 396.10 *person of authority*; 7.8 *priest*; 400.6 *religious leader*; 4.12 *sage*; 458.3 *wise man*
gush 270.5 *be diffuse*; 270.1 *diffuseness*; 731.2 *effusiveness*; 90.7, 431.25 *flow*; 389.7 *leak*; 315.2 *outflow*; 90.6 *river flow*; 315.11 *run out*; 213.2 *spread*; 304.17 *spring up*; 731.8 *talk too much*; 304.2 *upturn*
gusher 304.12 *geyser*; 315.2 *outflow*; 439.2 *resource*
gushiness 731.2 *effusiveness*
gushing 270.3 *diffuse*; 731.6 *effusive*; 219.6 *excessive*; 90.10 *fluvial*; 5.22 *many words*; 315.2 *outflow*
gushingly 731.11 *effusively*
gush out 315.11 *run out*
gusset 551.24 *part of garment*
gusseted 551.31 *styled*
gussied up 551.30 *dressed-up*
gussy up 551.33 *dress up*
gust 434.4 *air flow*; 31.58, 434.22 *blow*; 31.12 *wind*
gustation 495.3 *appetizer*
gustiness 31.14 *windiness*
gusto 726.1 *emphasis*; 495.4 *flavour*; 597.1 *happiness*; 338.1 *vigour*
gusty 434.15 *breezy*; 31.47 *windy*
gut 25.55 *cook*; 92.9 *inlet*; 357.10 *lay waste*; 410.18 *stomach*; 369.14 *suck*; 371.11 *void*; 441.1 *waste*
gut-ache 491.2 *painful condition*
gutless 614.3 *cowardly*; 339.5 *inert*; 337.12 *weak-willed*
gutlessness 337.2 *indecisiveness*; 339.1 *inertness*
gut reaction 590.2 *impression*; 445.4 *instinct*
guts 405.4 *components*; 613.1 *courage*; 557.16 *eating utensil*; 638.16 *fortitude*; 172.4, 406.3 *insides*; 590.8 *seat of feelings*; 640.4 *stamina*; 336.1 *strength*; 338.1 *vigour*
gutsiness 640.4 *stamina*
gutsy 613.9 *courageous*; 640.12 *indomitable*
gutta 56.5 *golf ball*
guttae 37.8 *drops*
guttapercha 422.4 *rubber*
guttapercha ball 56.5 *golf ball*
guttation 429.6 *dew*; 34.5 *physiology*; 559.1 *secretion*
gutter 227.11 *be changeable*; 524.9 *be dim*; 51.4, 51.10 *bowling*; 327.26 *flicker*; 184.2 *furrow*; 315.7 *outlet*; 767.8 *sink*; 184.8 *wrinkle*
gutteral 513.8 *hoarse*
gutteral consonant 5.16 *spoken letter*
gutteralize 513.5 *sound hoarse*
gutterally 513.10 *stridently*
gutteralness 513.2 *hoarseness*
gutteral sound 513.2 *hoarseness*
gutter ball 51.5 *bowling delivery*
guttering 327.20 *flickering*
gutter press 740.3 *journalism*; 741.5 *mass communication*
gutter shot 51.5 *bowling delivery*
gutting 369.4 *sucking*
guttural 5.41 *lettered*; 5.39 *of language*; 729.18 *phonetic*; 5.16 *spoken letter*
guttural accent 5.26 *dialect*
guv 567.3 *male title of address*
guvnor 567.3 *male title of address*; 400.1 *master*
guy 621.6 *deride*; 717.6 *image*; 373.6 *line*; 567.2 *male*; 720.1 *misinterpret*; 465.6 *misjudged person*; 718.4 *misrepresent*; 718.1 *misrepresentation*; 50.3 *parts of a sailing boat*; 566.7 *person*; 660.29, 678.14 *ridicule*; 373.7 *tackle*; 668.25 *taunt*
guy derrick 38.29 *construction equipment*
Guy Fawkes 717.6 *image*; 700.20 *plotter*; 662.10 *seditionist*
Guy Fawkes Day 298.6 *annually celebrated day*
guyot 30.16 *ocean floor*
guy rope 373.6 *line*
guy wires 57.5 *horizontal bar*
guzzle 688.5 *be greedy*; 557.22 *eat well*; 690.8 *get drunk*
guzzler 558.12 *drinker*; 688.4 *glutton*
guzzling 557.2 *appetite*; 690.5 *drunken*; 557.26 *eating*; 688.6 *gluttonous*
gyaku-zuki 52.8 *karate*
gybe 323.9 *navigate*; 50.15 *sail*; 50.1 *sailing*
gymkhana 59.6 *horsemanship*
gymnasium 57.1 *gymnastics*; 6.15 *schoolroom*
gymnast 336.5 *athlete*; 485.4 *skilled person*
gymnastic 57.11; 45.5 *sporting*; 576.10 *working*
gymnastically 45.7 *sportingly*
gymnastic apparatus 57.3
gymnastic clothing 57.2
gymnastic mat 57.3 *gymnastic apparatus*

gymnastic organization 57.4
gymnastic routine 57.1 *gymnastics*
Gymnastics 57
gymnastics 57.1; 300.11 *bodily movement*; 576.5 *exercise*
gymnastics association 57.4 *gymnastic organization*
gymnastics club 57.4 *gymnastic organization*
gymnastics coach 57.9 *gymnasts*
gymnastic scoring 57.1 *gymnastics*
gymnastic shoes 57.2 *gymnastic clothing*
gymnastics judge 57.9 *gymnasts*
gymnasts 57.9
gymnosophical 552.9 *undressed*
gymnosophist 552.8 *nude person*
gymnosophy 552.1 *undress*
gymnosperm 77.3 *seed plant*
Gymnospermae 77.3 *seed plant*
gym pants 551.9 *trousers*
gym shoes 49.3 *basketball equipment*; 551.19 *footwear*
gymslip 551.7 *frock*
gynaeceum 593.13 *abode of love*
gynaecocracy 12.1 *government*
gynaecological 35.22, 394.18 *medical*
gynaecologist 35.13 *medical specialist*; 561.7 *obstetrics*
gynaecology 568.1 *female sex*; 35.3 *medical specialty*
gynarchy 568.1 *female sex*; 12.1 *government*
gyniatrics 568.1 *female sex*
gyniatry 568.1 *female sex*
gynocracy 568.1 *female sex*; 12.1 *government*
gynoecium 78.3 *flower part*; 561.8 *organs of reproduction*
gynography 568.1 *female sex*
gyp 700.30 *be fraudulent*; 700.17 *cheat*; 700.10 *fraud*
gypper 700.17 *cheat*
gyppy tummy 260.8 *indigestion*
gypsum 435.1 *materials*; 24.2 *raw material*
gypsy 11.13 *diviner*; 100.10 *foreign*; 100.5 *nonconformist*; 778.11 *pedlar*
gypsy dance 22.4 *historic dancing*
gypsy signs 742.1 *sign*
gyrate 300.13 *be in motion*; 307.8 *rotate*
gyrating 300.17 *directional*; 306.11 *orbiting*; 307.11 *rotating*
gyration 300.5 *circuition*; 307.1 *rotation*
gyrational 300.17 *directional*; 307.12 *rotary*
gyratory 306.10 *circular*; 300.17 *directional*; 307.12 *rotary*
gyre 8.7 *devil*; 30.13 *ocean current*; 306.6 *orbit*; 306.1 *orbital motion*; 307.8 *rotate*
gyre upward 304.19 *take off*
gyring 306.1 *orbital motion*; 306.11 *orbiting*
gyring up 304.4 *taking off*
gyro 307.6 *rotator*
gyrocompass 28.84 *altimeter*; 579.5 *guide*; 323.5 *navigation*; 307.6 *rotator*
gyron 743.8 *heraldic device*
gyroplane 307.6 *rotator*
gyroscope 28.84 *altimeter*; 307.6 *rotator*
gyroscopic 307.12 *rotary*
gyrostabilizer 307.6 *rotator*
gyrostat 28.84 *altimeter*
gyrostatic 307.12 *rotary*
gyrostatics 307.7 *science of rotation*

H 691.6 *drug*
H_2O 433.1 *water*
haar 524.2 *murk*
habanera 22.2 *dance*
habeas corpus 397.2 *demand*; 16.6 *legal process*
haberdasher 551.26 *fashion designer*; 778.13 *retailer*
habergeon 384.7 *armour*
habilimentation 551.2 *dressing*
habilimented 551.29 *dressed*
habiliments 551.1 *dress*
Habit 632
habit 632.1; 138.5 *averageness*; 750.6 *convention*; 32.4 *crystal*; 140.6 *custom*; 59.10 *dressage*; 691.1 *drug-taking*; 160.5 *formality*; 407.7 *method*; 112.3 *repetitiveness*; 10.1 *ritual*; 474.3 *the expected thing*; 1.8 *tradition*; 349.6 *use*; 7.11 *vestment*
habit and repute 713.3 *precept*
Habitat 565
habitat 565.1; 565.2 *environment*; 142.1 *location*; 733.5 *place of residence*
habitation 356.8 *construction*; 565.1 *habitat*; 733.5 *place of residence*; 97.3 *residence*
habited 551.29 *dressed*
habit-forming 632.15; 395.12 *appealing*; 690.6 *intoxicating*; 480.19 *persuasive*
habits 795.1 *morality*; 631.6 *way of life*
habitual 407.15; **632.9**; 216.1 *average*; 138.21 *common*; 750.15 *conventional*; 140.10 *customary*; 160.11 *formal*; 297.3 *frequent*; 632.14 *habituated*; 112.13 *monotonous*
habitual action 632.1 *habit*
habitual drunkard 690.17 *drunkard*
habitual liar 699.18, 700.16 *liar*
habitually 632.19; 140.18 *as a rule*; 160.14, 750.37 *conventionally*; 297.1 *frequently*; 691.11 *in a trance*; 216.11 *on average*; 138.30 *usually*
habitually drunk 690.5 *drunken*
habitual lying 699.6 *lying*
habitualness 138.5 *averageness*; 297.4 *frequency*
habituate 632.18; 632.16 *have a habit*; 750.26 *make uniform*
habituated 632.14; 97.8 *attendant*; 641.4 *set*
habituation 632.7
habitude 632.2 *tendency*
habitué 632.8 *creature of habit*; 654.6 *social person*; 97.5 *someone present*
háček 5.36 *accent*; 742.7 *punctuation*
hacienda 43.6 *farm*; 440.1 *property*
hack 320.18 *cab*; 68.10 *curling*; 721.10 *descriptive writer*; 59.1 *horse*; 68.13 *ice-skating*; 693.9 *informant*; 741.4 *journalist*; 420.12 *make rough*; 740.11 *newspaperman*; 183.4, 183.10 *notch*; 308.18 *open*; 49.6 *play basketball*; 61.9 *race*; 59.4 *saddle horse*; 372.9 *separate*; 486.10 *unskilled person*; 578.1 *worker*
hackbut 587.10 *historical gun*
hacked 420.3 *barbed*; 308.12 *open*
hacker 40.2 *operator*
hackette 741.4 *journalist*
hacking 61.6 *motor-racing terms*; 49.5 *penalties*
hacking jacket 551.11 *jacket*
hackle 743.4 *insignia*
Hackney 87.5 *London*
hackney 59.1 *horse*; 59.2 *thoroughbred*
hackney cab 320.18 *cab*
hackneyed 138.22 *commonplace*; 632.10 *familiar*; 112.13 *monotonous*; 745.2 *proverbial*; 349.9 *used*; 5.42 *worded*
hackneyed expression 5.21 *catchword*
hackneyed phrase 745.1 *maxim*
hack weight 68.10 *curling*
hack work 576.1 *work*
had 700.36 *deceived*
hadal 30.51 *oceanic*
had best 810.14 *be the duty of*
had better 810.14 *be the duty of*
haddock 74.8 *food fish*; 25.18 *sea fish*
Hades 8.12 *hell*; 101.1 *nonmaterial world*; 582.14 *the spiritual world*; 804.8 *wicked place*
Hadith 7.12 *religious text*
Hadrian's Wall 378.3, 384.9 *barrier*; 147.7 *interface*
hadron 28.77 *elementary particle*
Haeckel's law 34.16 *evolution*
haem 33.24 *respiration*
haemal 431.18 *bloody*
haematemesis 560.10 *bleeding*
haematologist 35.13 *medical specialist*
haematology 35.3 *medical specialty*
haematopoietic disease 260.4 *disease*
haematuria 560.10 *bleeding*
haemic 431.18 *bloody*
haemogenic 431.18 *bloody*
haemoglobin 431.4 *blood*; 33.18 *pigment*; 33.24 *respiration*
haemolytic anaemia 260.11 *blood disease*
haemophilia 560.10 *bleeding*; 260.11 *blood disease*; 431.5 *fluidity*
haemophiliac 260.19 *sick person*
haemophilic 431.18 *bloody*; 260.23 *diseased*
haemoprotein 33.9 *protein*
haemoptysis 560.10 *bleeding*
haemorrhage 560.21 *bleed*; 560.10 *bleeding*; 260.11 *blood disease*; 431.6 *flow*; 766.12 *lessen*; 766.4 *lessening*; 315.2 *outflow*
haemorrhaging 560.30 *bleeding*
haemorrhoea 560.10 *bleeding*
haemostasis 416.2 *concentration*
haemostatic 416.6 *dense*
haft 438.1 *tool*
hag 651.9 *vixen*
hagbut 587.10 *historical gun*
haggard 582.21 *deathly*; 153.2 *emaciated*; 261.1 *fatigued*
haggardness 153.8 *emaciation*
haggis 25.44 *British dish*; 25.32 *meat dish*; 25.29 *sausage*
haggle 776.3 *bargain*; 793.14 *buy cheaply*; 752.10 *offer to buy*
haggler 777.12 *purchaser*; 776.10 *trader*
haggling 776.9 *bargaining*; 777.14 *buying*; 746.8 *negotiated*; 746.1 *negotiation*
hagiographer 721.10 *descriptive writer*
hagiographical 7.18 *theological*
hagiography 721.4 *factual account*; 677.1 *flattery*; 17.4 *nonfiction*; 7.13 *theology*
hagiological 7.18 *theological*
hagiologist 7.14 *theologian*
hagiology 7.13 *theology*
hag-ridden 11.19 *bewitched*
ha-ha 372.6 *boundary*; 146.2 *crack*; 165.3 *enclosing thing*; 44.3 *ornamental garden*
haiku 269.2 *outline*; 17.7 *poem*
hail 31.29; 669.16 *acclaim*; 733.9 *approach*; 514.4 *cry of greeting*; 376.22 *flood*; 658.12 *greet*; 312.23 *hello!*; 494.5 *ice*; 31.24 *precipitation*; 733.2 *salutation*; 742.12 *signal*; 31.63 *snow*; 208.4 *throng*; 742.6 *word*
hail! 733.15
hailer 742.8 *signer*
hail-fellow-well-met 569.10 *familiar*; 654.15 *sociable*
hailing 742.16 *signalling*
Hail Mary 10.9 *prayer*
hail-Mary 46.9 *play*
hailstone 494.5 *ice*; 31.24 *precipitation*
hailstorm 31.29 *hail*; 494.5 *ice*; 380.5 *violent weather*
hair 550.14 *animal covering*; 71.2 *mammalian characteristic*; 151.8 *narrow thing*; 425.8 *sharp-pointed thing*; 421.8 *smooth thing*; 419.11 *soft thing*
hairband 179.3 *circular thing*
hairbreadth escape 254.5 *danger*; 389.1 *escape*
hairbrush 256.10 *cleaning object*; 814.14 *instrument of punishment*; 421.9 *smoother*
hair colour 547.7 *hairdressing*
hair conditioner 268.7 *pomade*
haircut 547.8; 552.7 *depilation*
hair cutting 547.7 *hairdressing*
hair-do 547.8 *haircut*
hairdresser 547.13 *beautician*; 256.12 *cleaner*; 401.4 *personal attendant*
hairdressers 547.11 *hairdressing salon*
hairdressing 547.7
hairdressing salon 547.11
hair-dryer 428.15 *dryer*
hair dyeing 547.7 *hairdressing*
hair extension 547.10 *wig*
hairgrip 373.8 *fastening*
hair hygrometer 433.19 *measuring instrument*
hairiness 420.6 *roughness*
hairless 552.13; 421.1 *smooth*
hairlessness 552.5 *baldness*
hairlike 151.2 *fine*
hairline crack 146.2 *crack*; 308.1 *opening*
hair moss 82.3 *moss*
hair of the dog 690.13 *drink*
hair on end 711.2 *danger signal*
hairpiece 551.15 *headgear*
hairpin 373.8 *fastening*; 61.6 *motor-racing terms*; 68.12 *ski*; 68.3 *ski racing*; 325.5 *twist*
hairpin bend 176.1 *angle*; 320.3 *carriageway*; 325.14 *deviating course*
hairpin curve 189.2 *oblique line*
hair-pulling 52.5 *wrestling*
hair-raising 488.9 *exciting*; 612.10 *frightening*
hair removal 547.9
hair remover 552.7 *depilation*
hair removing 552.13 *hairless*
hair's-breadth 147.2 *short distance*
hair shirt 807.2 *apology*; 808.1 *penitence*; 551.8 *shirt*
hair space 146.1 *interval*
hair-splitter 273.4 *accurate person*; 466.6 *discriminating person*; 702.6 *sophist*
hair-splitting 273.1 *accuracy*; 273.5 *accurate*; 466.9 *discriminating*; 670.6, 670.28 *fault-finding*; 466.2 *judiciousness*; 702.4, 702.9 *quibbling*
hairspring 438.5 *machine*; 422.5 *spring*
hair standing on end 612.1 *fear*
hair straightening 547.8 *haircut*
hairstyle 547.8 *haircut*
hair styling 547.7 *hairdressing*
hair-stylist 547.13 *beautician*
hair transplant 551.15 *headgear*
hair-trigger 332.1 *swift*
hairy 420.3 *barbed*; 378.14 *blocked*; 254.1 *dangerous*; 264.12 *problematic*; 404.8 *rough*
hajj 9.1 *worship*
hajji 450.5 *believer*; 7.3 *religious person*; 9.5 *worshipper*
haka 22.4 *historic dancing*
hakam 7.8 *priest*
hake 25.18 *sea fish*
hakim 35.12, 394.15 *healer*
halal 255.14 *purified*
halberd 587.8 *sharp weapon*
halberdier 586.13 *historical soldiery*
halcyon 589.7 *peaceful*; 248.8 *prosperous*; 301.6 *quiescent*
halcyon days 222.5 *comfortable circumstances*; 597.2 *fun*; 797.17 *good thing*; 248.3 *time of plenty*; 31.3 *weather*
hale 259.1 *healthy*; 160.12 *on form*; 336.9 *physically strong*; 362.11 *pull*; 204.8 *sound*; 338.4 *vigorous*
hale and hearty 259.1 *healthy*; 336.9 *physically strong*; 204.8 *sound*; 338.4 *vigorous*
haleness 259.3 *health*
Hale Observatories 29.23 *observatory*
Hale Telescope 29.24 *telescope*
half 198.8; **198.13**; 49.1 *basketball*; 196.5 *fractional*; 196.7 *fractionally*; 46.5 *game time*; 233.4 *incomplete*; 233.6 *incompletely*; 198.22 *in half*; 196.4 *less than one*; 205.1 *part*; 205.12 *partly*
half a chance 107.6 *poor chance*; 102.3 *strong possibility*
half-a-crown 780.10 *former British money*
half-a-dozen 201.2 *six*
half a gale 31.14 *windiness*
half a hundred 201.8 *twenty and over*
half a mo 280.3 *instant*; 278.3 *short duration*
half and half 216.2 *medium*; 216.12 *mediumly*; 205.12 *partly*
half-and-half 111.16 *equal*; 198.22 *in half*; 412.12 *mixed*; 119.8 *on equal terms*
half-and-half split 111.5 *equality*
half a sec 280.3 *instant*
half-asleep 261.1 *fatigued*; 343.4 *not awake*
half-assed 486.4 *bungled*
half a tick 280.3 *instant*
half-awake 261.1 *fatigued*
halfback 58.2 *hockey player*; 46.7 *offence*; 64.4 *rugby player*
half-bagged 690.2 *slightly drunk*
half-baked 486.4 *bungled*; 293.16 *premature*; 456.7 *semiskilled*
half-ball 65.9 *billiard*
half-ball stroke 65.2 *billiards play*
half-believe 451.8 *disbelieve*
half-blood 412.5 *hybrid*
half-blooded 412.12 *mixed*
half-bred 43.21 *domesticated*
half-breed 412.5 *hybrid*; 412.12 *mixed*; 1.6 *race*; 1.13 *racial*
half-butt cue 65.3 *English billiards*
half-butt rest 65.3 *English billiards*
half-caste 412.5 *hybrid*; 412.12 *mixed*; 1.6 *race*; 1.13 *racial*
half cell 32.19 *electrochemistry*
half century 201.8 *twenty and over*
half circle 179.2 *circle*
half-clothed 552.10 *in dishabille*
half-cocked 293.16 *premature*
half-crown 780.10 *former British money*
half-cut 690.2 *slightly drunk*
half-dark 524.5 *dim*
half-dead 582.18 *dying*; 261.1 *fatigued*; 341.3 *inactive*
half-dollar 780.8 *American money*
half-done 233.4 *incomplete*; 666.5 *indifferent*
half-dressed 552.10 *in dishabille*
half-face 525.3 *external appearance*
half fare 793.4 *bargain*
half-fed 218.3 *underfed*
half-filled 231.2 *incomplete*

half-finished 231.2, 233.4 *incomplete;* 205.11 *partial*
half-gone 341.3 *inactive*
half-hardy 44.17 *botanical;* 77.15 *wild*
half-heard 511.1 *faint-sounding*
half-hearted 637.3 *cautious;* 233.4 *incomplete;* 618.7 *indifferent;* 728.17 *insipid;* 337.12 *weak-willed*
half-hearted attempt 353.5 *attempt*
half-heartedly 618.17 *indifferently;* 728.26 *insipidly;* 685.9 *moderately;* 637.17 *unwillingly;* 337.14 *weakly*
half-heartedness 639.14 *apathy;* 637.13 *dissociation;* 233.1 *incompleteness;* 618.1 *indifference;* 728.8 *insipidness*
half-hearted thanks 672.1 *ingratitude*
half-holiday 580.2 *time off*
half-hose 551.20 *legwear*
half-hunter 281.7 *watch*
half-knowledge **456.2**; 455.2 *information*
half-length portrait 19.10 *art subject*
half-lie 699.11 *half-truth*
half-life 28.70 *radioactivity*
half-light 524.1 *dimness;* 529.3 *hue*
half line 17.8 *part of poem*
halfling 159.4 *little person*
half-lit 524.5 *dim*
half-mast 367.10 *lower the flag*
half-measure **754.2**; 754.6 *compromising;* 216.6 *mediocrity*
half measures 486.9 *bungling;* 218.8 *insufficiency;* 238.5 *waste of effort*
half-moon 177.3 *curved things;* 29.17 *moon*
half-moon glasses 518.10 *visual aid*
half-nelson 360.1 *retention;* 52.5 *wrestling*
half pay 788.3 *income*
halfpenny 780.10 *former British money*
half-pint 159.4 *little person;* 149.5 *short person*
half-pint glass 410.13 *drinking vessel*
half-point 324.4 *compass point*
half-price 793.9 *cheap*
half rations 218.8 *insufficiency*
half relief 19.13 *relief-carving*
half-remembered 463.11 *forgotten*
half rhyme 17.11 *rhyme*
half-seas over 690.1 *drunk*
half-seen 521.2 *difficult to see*
half-shot 690.2 *slightly drunk*
half-shove 50.19 *punt;* 50.8 *punting*
half-skilled 486.2 *unskilled*
half-slip 551.18 *underwear*
half sovereign 780.10 *former British money*
half space 146.1 *interval*
half standard 44.10 *fruit tree*
half starve 684.5 *be self-restrained;* 687.5 *fast*
half-starved 687.6 *fasting;* 617.10 *hungry;* 218.3 *underfed*
half the battle 123.3 *chief thing*
half-timbered building 20.3 *building*
half-timbering 356.8 *construction*
half-time 49.1 *basketball;* 46.5 *game time;* 276.4 *period of activity*
half-tone 522.12 *highlight;* 529.3 *hue;* 41.3 *photograph*
half-tonner 50.10 *sailing*
half-tonner class 50.2 *sailing boat*
half-true 699.36 *falsified*
half-truth **699.11**
half-turn 57.8 *floor exercises*
half-volley 63.5 *real tennis*
half volte 59.10 *dressage*
half-war 585.1 *war*
half-wave rectifier 39.21 *rectifier*
halfway 754.1 *compromise;* 754.6 *compromising;* 754.8 *compromisingly;* 198.13 *half;* 216.2 *medium;* 216.12 *mediumly;* 64.6 *rugger;* 66.5 *soccer*
halfway house 216.5 *medium;* 685.1 *moderation;* 815.1 *prison;* 565.11 *retreat*
halfway line 64.1 *rugger;* 66.1 *soccer*
halfway point 216.5 *medium*
half-white 531.1 *white*
halfwit 459.3 *foolish person;* 457.3 *unintelligent person*
halibut 74.8 *food fish;* 25.18 *sea fish*
halitosis 503.2 *something that makes an unpleasant smell*
hall 504.3 *auditorium;* 356.8 *construction;* 565.4 *official residence;* 565.7 *room;* 317.2 *route;* 6.15 *schoolroom;* 738.8 *showplace;* 21.16 *theatre*
hallelujah 514.3 *cry of praise;* 600.2 *fanfare;* 600.12 *hurrah!;* 10.8 *hymn;* 601.7 *thanksgiving*
hallelujah chorus 600.2 *fanfare*
Halley's Comet 522.4 *natural light;* 298.5 *regular thing*
hallmark 139.3 *characteristic;* 743.10 *identify;* 743.3 *means of identification;* 721.8 *name;* 742.1 *sign*
hallmarked 698.19 *authentic;* 743.12 *identified*
hallmarked silver 698.6 *authenticity*
halloa 59.8 *hunting*
hall of mirrors 519.5 *visual distortion*
hall of residence 6.15 *schoolroom*
halloo 633.19 *after him!;* 633.10 *chase;* 514.5 *hunting cry*
hallow 601.16 *commemorate;* 8.17 *deify;* 9.7 *worship*
hallowed 8.13 *divine*
hallowed by custom 632.12 *established*
hallowedness 8.1 *divinity*
Hallowe'en 298.6 *annually celebrated day;* 10.16 *religious festival;* 11.3 *witchcraft*
halls of death 582.14 *the spiritual world*
hallucinate 700.25 *deceive oneself;* 11.24 *experience psychic phenomena;* 96.13, 477.14, 518.17 *imagine*
hallucinating 461.12 *manic*
hallucination 461.4 *delusion;* 274.6 *fallibility;* 700.5 *falseness;* 477.5 *fantasy;* 96.2 *illusion;* 518.5 *imagination;* 11.10 *psychic phenomenon;* 525.4 *something that appears*
hallucinatory 96.9, 700.40 *illusory;* 525.9 *ostensible*
hallucinogen 691.6 *drug;* 37.4 *drug type*
hallucinogenic 691.9 *addictive;* 37.17 *stimulating*
hallux 492.7 *sense organ*
hallway 308.7 *passageway;* 317.2 *route*
halo 179.3 *circular thing;* 29.7 *galaxy;* 522.12 *highlight;* 31.22 *sun*
haloed 8.15 *deified;* 522.17 *lustrous*
halogen 32.6 *chemical element*
halogenate 32.26 *react*
halogen light 522.6 *electric light*
halothane 489.4 *anaesthetic*
halt 301.8 *be motionless;* 337.6 *be weak;* 131.16, 226.6 *cease;* 131.2, 133.2 *cessation;* 231.3 *deformed;* 294.8 *delay;* 294.3 *delayed action;* 133.12 *discontinue;* 247.1 *failure;* 333.2 *hesitate;* 301.1 *motionlessness;* 321.8 *railway station;* 264.8 *snag;* 226.2 *stop;* 301.11 *stop!;* 312.16 *stopover;* 226.4 *stopping place*
halted 133.9 *discontinued;* 294.10 *held up*
halter 814.16 *instrument of execution;* 251.5 *means of restraint;* 551.8 *shirt;* 373.9 *yoke*
halt hostilities 749.5 *make peace*
halting 233.4 *incomplete;* 299.4 *irregular;* 333.4 *slow*
haltingly 299.8 *irregularly;* 333.16 *slowly*
halt one's progress 481.3 *deflect*
halt the arms race 589.6 *make peace;* 749.4 *pacify*
halvah 25.54 *other dishes*
halve **198.16**; 372.11 *divide;* 216.10 *make average*
halved 198.13 *half;* 372.15 *separate*
halved hole 56.2 *golfing terms*
halving **198.7**
halyard 743.7 *flag;* 50.3 *parts of a sailing boat;* 373.7 *tackle*
ham 21.24 *actor;* 25.30 *bacon;* 21.9 *dramaturgy;* 727.7 *exaggerate;* 21.35 *overact;* 486.2 *unskilled;* 486.10 *unskilled person*
ham acting 21.22 *acting*
hamadryad 8.5 *deity;* 79.13 *tree mythology*
ham and cheese sandwich 25.11 *sandwich*
hamartia 21.11 *tragedy*
ham-bone soup 25.43 *US dish*
hamburger 25.20 *meat;* 25.11 *sandwich*
hamburger place 557.15 *eating place*
ham-fisted 611.8 *bad;* 544.7 *graceless*
ham-fistedness 264.2 *awkwardness*
ham-handed 486.3 *clumsy*
ham-handedness 486.8 *unskilfulness*
Hamitic 5.11 *family of languages*
Hamito-Semitic 5.11 *family of languages*
ham it up 486.5 *be unskilful;* 727.7 *exaggerate;* 21.35 *overact*
hamlet 87.1 *city;* 86.11 *settlement;* 87.10 *village*
hammed up 21.40 *tragic*
hammer 330.10 *ball;* 331.5, 427.26 *beat;* 507.8 *be loud;* 121.8 *be superior;* 587.7 *blunt weapon;* 62.4 *climbing equipment;* 331.2 *collide;* 47.2 *field events;* 418.7 *hard substance;* 504.5 *internal ear;* 331.15 *ram;* 112.22 *resound;* 381.5 *strike;* 438.1 *tool;* 438.10 *use tools*
hammer and sickle 742.1 *sign*
hammer and tongs 331.12 *collision;* 576.12 *laboriously;* 380.10 *violently;* 338.6 *with vigour*
hammer at 576.8 *exert oneself*
hammer away at 112.18 *harp;* 640.6 *persevere*
hammer blows 380.2 *physical violence*
hammer glove 47.2 *field events*
hammerhead 331.15 *ram*
hammer home 726.6 *emphasize*
hammer in 368.3 *impact*
hammering 331.12 *collision;* 112.6 *reverberation;* 112.15 *reverberatory*
hammer into 112.18 *harp*
hammerlock 360.1 *retention*
hammer out 553.9 *fashion;* 160.7 *form*
hammerstone 331.15 *ram*
hammer throw 47.2 *field events*
hammer-thrower 47.3 *athlete*
hammer-throwing 47.2 *field events*
hamming 21.22 *acting;* 727.1 *exaggeration*
hamming it up 21.22 *acting*
hammock 23.6 *bed;* 301.3 *resting place;* 361.3 *suspended object*
hammy 21.40 *tragic*
hamper 410.7 *basket;* 264.23 *cause difficulties;* 378.8 *hinder;* 245.5 *hurt;* 166.7 *limit;* 414.14 *make heavy;* 604.7 *thwart*
hampered 604.9 *disappointed*
hampering 378.1 *hindrance*
Hampstead 87.5 *London*
ham sandwich 25.11 *sandwich*
hamse 742.7 *punctuation*
hamster food 557.8 *animal food*
hamstring 245.5 *hurt;* 335.8 *overpower;* 357.11 *ruin*
hamzah 5.36 *accent*
hand 669.5 *acclaim;* 348.3 *assistant;* 69.3 *card game terms;* 205.4 *component;* 69.2 *contest;* 340.3 *doer;* 392.1 *help;* 346.6 *operative;* 566.7 *person;* 25.24 *pork;* 742.7 *punctuation;* 492.7 *sense organ;* 360.3 *tools for gripping;* 578.1 *worker*
hand back 775.4 *give back;* 393.3 *restore*
handbag 410.8 *bag;* 780.20 *money store;* 316.10 *transferred thing*
handball 422.3 *elastic thing;* 66.2 *football play*
handbarrow 320.7 *handcart*
hand beater 25.6 *kitchen equipment*
handbell 18.6 *campanology;* 510.4 *sources of resonance*
handbill 740.9 *advertisement*
handbook 693.5 *reference book;* 6.14 *school book*
handbrake turn 320.21 *miscellaneous motoring terms*
handbreadth 150.4 *breadth*
handcart **320.7**; 410.10 *cart*
handclap 669.5 *acclaim*
handclapping 669.5 *acclaim*
handclasp 569.4 *act of friendship;* 658.5 *sign of courtesy;* 654.9 *welcome*
hand cream 255.3 *purifier*
handcuff 373.12 *bind;* 251.12 *gag;* 309.11 *restrain*
handcuffed 373.16 *bound*
handcuffs 373.8 *fastening;* 251.5 *means of restraint;* 309.3 *restrainer*
hand down 635.16 *bequeath*
hand down a judgment 140.13 *rule*
handed **492.10**
handed down 1.14 *societal*
handfork 44.6 *garden tool*
handful 203.3 *container;* 662.9 *criminal;* 264.9 *difficult person;* 264.3 *difficult task;* 206.1 *few;* 815.4 *prison sentence;* 662.5 *troublemaker*
hand grenade 587.16 *bomb*
handgrip 55.3 *fishing tackle*
handgun 587.9 *firearm*
handhold 360.1 *retention*
handicap 121.3 *advantage;* 240.5 *be inconvenient;* 120.5 *be unequal;* 378.6, 378.12 *burden;* 231.7 *defect;* 122.2 *deficiency;* 56.2 *golfing terms;* 59.7 *horseracing;* 260.2 *illness;* 240.3 *inconvenience;* 120.1 *inequality;* 414.14 *make heavy;* 50.10 *sailing;* 414.8 *weighing down*
handicapped 378.14 *blocked;* 231.3 *deformed;* 414.3 *ponderous*
handicap race 50.1 *sailing*
handicap score 56.2 *golfing terms*
handicap stroke 56.3 *golf shots*
handicraft 19.1 *art;* 340.2 *deed*
handicraftsman 578.2 *artisan;* 340.3 *doer*
handicraftswoman 578.2 *artisan*
handicraft worker 340.3 *doer*
handily 239.7 *conveniently;* 348.9 *instrumentally;* 485.12 *skilfully;* 237.12 *usefully*
hand in 63.9 *squash terms*
handiness 97.4 *availability;* 239.3 *convenience;* 348.1 *instrumentality;* 159.1 *littleness;* 147.1 *nearness;* 797.12 *proficiency;* 485.1 *skill;* 237.5 *usefulness;* 265.3 *wieldiness*
handing back 775.1 *giving back*
handing in one's notice 605.1 *resignation*
hand in glove 747.20 *cooperatively;* 223.22 *hand in hand;* 569.18 *intimately*
hand-in-glove 223.19 *associated;* 747.19 *associating;* 569.10 *familiar;* 492.9 *touching*
handing over 355.3 *relinquishment*
hand in hand **223.22**; 747.20 *cooperatively;* 750.32 *in alliance;* 569.18 *intimately;* 654.18 *sociably*
hand-in-hand 569.10 *familiar;* 169.10 *laterally;* 147.9 *near;* 492.9 *touching*
hand in one's notice 605.5 *resign*
hand in one's resignation 605.5 *resign*
hand it to 669.15 *compliment*
handiwork 340.2 *deed;* 356.1 *production;* 345.2 *visible effect*
handkerchief 551.25 *accessories;* 256.11 *cleaning cloth*
hand-knit sweater 551.13 *sweater*
handle 631.14 *behave towards;* 550.33 *fix;* 579.1 *manage;* 721.8 *name;* 575.1 *right;* 50.4 *rowing;* 778.1 *sell;* 346.9 *take action;* 438.1 *tool;* 492.11 *touch;* 776.1 *trade;* 349.1 *use*
handle a consignment 319.4 *transport*
handlebars 320.11 *bicycle part;* 420.7 *rough thing*
handle cargo 319.4 *transport*
handled 66.5 *soccer*
handler 550.18 *fixer;* 346.5 *operator*
handle tenderly 648.3 *be lenient*
handle the ball 64.5 *play rugby*
handle with kid gloves 648.3 *be lenient*
handling 340.1 *action;* 550.20 *fixing;* 66.2 *football play;* 346.4, 579.3 *management;* 492.2 *touching;* 631.8 *treatment;* 349.6 *use*
hand loom 42.4, 193.3 *weaving*
hand lotion 256.9 *cleaning agent;* 268.7 *pomade;* 255.3 *purifier*
handmade 356.12 *produced*
handmaid 348.3 *assistant;* 401.6 *domestic servant*
handmaiden 401.6 *domestic servant*
hand-me-down 551.1 *dress;* 349.9 *used*
hand-me-downs 552.4 *dishabille*
hand-milk 43.18 *practise livestock farming*
hand mirror 28.29 *optical element;* 518.8 *reflection*
hand of death 582.1 *death*
handoff 46.9 *play;* 46.15 *play offence*
hand of friendship 749.2 *peace offering*
hand on 316.14 *bring back*
hand-operated 492.10 *handed;* 348.8 *practical*
hand-out 740.9 *advertisement;* 652.5 *charity;* 392.6 *financial assistance;* 679.7 *gift;* 693.4 *mass communication;* 741.9 *news story;* 768.3 *offering;* 483.5 *positive stimulus;* 436.5 *provision;* 63.9 *squash terms*
hand out a sample 752.9 *offer*
hand out bouquets 813.9 *reward*
hand out brickbats 670.17 *criticize*
hand over 318.11 *cross;* 768.5 *give;* 355.1 *relinquish;* 316.11 *transfer;* 316.12 *transport;* 316.2 *transportation*
hand over fist 304.26 *up*
hand over one's sword 388.3 *submit*
hand over the baton 47.7 *race*
hand-paint 24.11 *make ceramics*
hand-painted 24.10 *ceramic*
hand-painted decorations 24.3 *glaze*
hand-pick 469.4 *pick;* 212.3 *subtract*
hand-picked 469.15 *chosen;* 235.1 *worthy*

handprop 21.21 *stage requisite*
hand round 436.5 *provision*
hands 281.8 *face*; 392.11 *helper*; 578.4 *personnel*
hands across the sea 569.2 *friendly relations*
hands down 265.21 *easily*
handsel 768.2 *gift*; 785.1 *payment*
handset 504.9 *audio device*; 692.9 *telephone*
handshake 569.4 *act of friendship*; 40.19 *computing terms*; 40.14 *data transfer*; 664.9 *fawn*; 742.3 *gesture*; 756.1 *promise*; 312.12 *reception*; 658.5 *sign of courtesy*; 654.9 *welcome*
handshaking 664.2 *sycophancy*; 664.7 *sycophantic*
hand signal 742.3 *gesture*
hands in pockets 742.3 *gesture*
hands off 341.1 *inaction*; 341.3 *inactive*
hands off! 634.24
handsome 545.5 *beautiful*; 679.1 *generous*
handsome fortune 781.5 *wealth*
handsomenesss 545.1 *gorgeousness*
hands-on 492.10 *handed*
hands on hips 742.3 *gesture*
handspike 438.1 *tool*
handspring 57.8 *floor exercises*; 192.1 *inversion*; 192.3 *invert*; 304.5 *jump*; 57.6 *pommel horse*
handstand 57.5 *horizontal bar*; 57.7 *stationary rings*; 67.11 *swimming*
handstand dive 67.6 *diving*
handstand position 57.5 *horizontal bar*
handstrap 57.2 *gymnastic clothing*
hand's turn 576.2 *task*
hand to hand 319.6 *commercially*; 492.17 *manually*
hand-to-mouth 782.1 *poor*; 217.1 *sufficient*
hand-to-mouth existence 782.5 *poverty*
hand tool 438.1 *tool*
hand towel 256.11 *cleaning cloth*
hand-turn 24.11 *make ceramics*
hand-turned 24.10 *ceramic*
hand-turned wheel 24.6 *ceramic workshop*
handwoven 193.6 *interwoven*
handy 97.10 *available*; 239.1 *convenient*; 392.33 *helpful*; 348.6 *instrumental*; 415.1 *light*; 159.7 *little*; 147.9 *near*; 797.5 *proficient*; 485.6 *skilful*; 492.8 *touchable*; 237.1 *useful*; 265.12 *wieldy*
handyman 342.10 *busy person*; 393.12 *repairer*; 401.1 *servant*; 485.4 *skilled person*; 578.1 *worker*
hang 57.10 *compete in gymnastics*; 382.19, 814.5 *execute*; 304.20 *hover*; 582.16 *meet one's fate*; 43.14 *pest control*; 57.7 *stationary rings*; 361.10 *suspend*; 361.1 *suspension*
hang about 343.12 *be inactive*; 147.17 *stay near*; 294.7 *wait*
hang a picture 738.2 *display something*
hangar 322.4 *airport*; 565.7 *room*
hang around 97.12 *attend*; 147.17 *stay near*; 294.7 *wait*
hang around with 654.13 *fraternize*; 223.14 *keep company with*
hang back 616.5 *be cautious*; 378.11 *be inhibited*; 674.15 *escape notice*; 453.19 *hesitate*; 637.8 *hold back*; 634.4 *shy*; 294.7 *wait*
hang by a thread 254.8 *be in danger*
hang by the neck 814.5 *execute*
hangdog 806.6 *appearing guilty*; 623.3 *humbled*; 664.7 *sycophantic*
hangdog look 623.9 *humiliation*; 626.2 *sign of sullenness*
hang down 305.10 *droop*; 361.10 *suspend*
hang, draw, and quarter 814.5 *execute*
hang 'em high 382.26 *no quarter!*; 814.24 *string him up!*
hanger 361.4; 49.4 *playing terms*; 587.8 *sharp weapon*; 438.1 *tool*
hanger-on 664.5 *adherent*; 710.5 *beggar*; 387.4 *dependent*; 223.9, 267.5, 289.8 *follower*; 677.7 *sycophant*
hang fire 343.12 *be inactive*; 339.4 *be inert*; 563.7 *be infertile*; 301.8 *be motionless*; 637.8 *hold back*; 341.4 *not act*; 226.9 *pause*; 294.7 *wait*
hang glide 361.10 *suspend*
hang-glider 322.8 *aircraft*; 305.8 *descender*
hang in 638.11 *persist*
hanging 814.13 *capital punishment*; 582.4 *death sentence*; 382.5 *execution*; 382.2 *murder*; 21.19 *stage set*; 361.7 *suspended*; 361.11 *suspension*; 550.8 *wall covering*; 337.8 *weak*
hanging back 378.5 *inhibition*; 453.2 *irresolute*
hanging ball 56.2 *golfing terms*
hanging basket 44.3 *ornamental garden*
hanging by a thread 582.18 *dying*; 254.2 *unsafe*
hanging by the wrists 814.12 *corporal punishment*
hanging, drawing, and quartering 814.13 *capital punishment*
hanging garden 44.2 *garden*
Hanging Gardens of Babylon 44.2 *garden*
hanging in there 640.10 *persevering*
hanging judge 16.23 *judge*; 814.17 *punisher*; 647.4 *strict person*
hanging object 361.3 *suspended object*
hanging offence 804.7 *criminality*
hanging on 360.1 *retention*
hanging oneself 382.7 *suicide*
hanging out 297.5 *frequenting*
hanging rope 814.16 *instrument of execution*
hanging together 750.14 *conforming*
hanging up 226.2 *stop*
hanging valley 30.7 *landform*
hang it up 350.7 *stop work*; 388.3 *submit*
hang like a millstone 414.13 *weigh on*
hang loose 419.14 *ease*; 226.9 *pause*
hangman 357.6 *destroyer*; 382.12 *executioner*; 382.10 *killer*; 814.17 *punisher*; 380.4 *violent creature*
hang on 267.8 *be tenacious*; 294.8 *delay*; 664.14 *follow*; 640.8 *hold out*; 277.6 *last*; 134.4 *protract*; 360.6 *retain*
hang oneself 382.21 *commit suicide*
hang one's head 623.24 *be humiliated*
hang one's lip 626.9 *be sullen*
hang on in there 277.6 *last*; 134.4 *protract*
hang on someone's words 504.15 *hear*
hang on to 683.6 *be selfish*; 439.6 *store*
hangout 565.2 *environment*
hang out 97.12 *attend*; 428.23 *drip-dry*
hang out a signal 742.12 *signal*
hang out at 297.8, 565.19 *frequent*
hang out the flags 601.18 *salute*
hang out to dry 428.23 *drip-dry*
hang out with 654.13 *fraternize*; 223.14 *keep company with*
hangover 690.15 *crapulence*
hang over 333.2 *hesitate*; 361.11 *project*
Hang Seng Index 14.2 *stock exchange*
hang technique 47.2 *field events*
hang time 46.12 *special team*
hang together 267.6 *adhere*; 750.25 *conform*; 747.13 *work together*
hang tough 423.10 *be tough*
hang up 226.6 *cease*; 350.6 *stop using*; 361.10 *suspend*; 692.32 *telephone*
hang-up 231.7 *defect*; 471.4 *diligence*; 378.2 *obstacle*
hang upon 345.7 *follow from*
hang up on 730.15 *strike dumb*
hang up one's hat 565.18 *take up residence*
hang up one's spikes 350.7 *stop work*
hang weights on 414.14 *make heavy*
hank 376.27 *bundle*; 50.3 *parts of a sailing boat*
hanker after 617.12 *desire*; 595.7 *like*
hankering 617.1 *desire*; 595.1, 595.6 *liking*
hanky-panky 812.3 *disreputable action*; 593.8 *love affair*; 700.7 *tricking*
Hannukah 10.16 *religious festival*
Hanoverian 296.14 *historic*
Hansard 744.1 *record*
Hansen's disease 260.7 *tropical disease*
ha'penny 780.10 *former British money*
haphazard 453.8 *capricious*; 107.8 *chance*; 486.3 *clumsy*; 114.5 *diverse*; 262.3 *hasty*; 299.4, 408.14 *irregular*
haphazardly 107.13 *by chance*; 408.27 *in disorder*; 114.11, 299.8 *irregularly*
haphazardness 114.1 *diversity*; 299.1 *irregularity*; 408.2 *irregular order*
hapless 249.8 *unlucky*
haploid 34.25 *genetic*
haploid number 34.14 *chromosome*
haploidy 34.14 *chromosome*
haplomitosis 34.10 *cell division*
haply 102.9 *possibly*
happen 340.4 *act*; 95.10 *be real*; 107.10 *chance*; 525.13 *occur*; 345.5 *show an effect*; 345.9 *take effect*
happen again 112.21 *be repeated*
happen every day 297.7 *be frequent*
happening 340.5 *acting*; 340.1 *action*; 282.3 *actuality*; 525.2 *being in view*; 345.1 *effect*; 3.14 *historicalness*; 222.2 *occurrence*; 21.2 *play*; 93.2 *thing*; 447.6 *topical*
happening late 294.9 *late*
happenings 447.3 *matter of interest*
happen often 297.7 *be frequent*
happen upon 449.1 *discover*
happen yearly 298.8 *be cyclic*
happily 598.9 *cheerfully*; 597.9 *joyfully*; 105.11 *luckily*; 287.9 *opportunely*; 490.11 *pleasingly*; 248.9 *prosperously*; 609.13 *with satisfaction*
happily in love 593.18 *in love*
Happiness 598
happiness 597.1; 797.13 *benefit*; 598.3 *cheerfulness*; 490.1 *physical pleasure*; 248.1 *prosperity*; 600.1 *rejoicing*; 609.1 *satisfaction*; 246.1 *success*
happy 597.4; 598.1 *cheerful*; 690.1 *drunk*; 749.6 *pacificatory*; 490.7 *pleased*; 248.8 *prosperous*; 600.9 *rejoicing*; 609.4 *satisfied*; 287.6 *timely*; 485.9 *well-made*
happy as a sandboy 597.4 *happy*
happy chance 287.2 *opportunity*
happy coincidence 287.1 *timeliness*
happy dreams 263.1 *ease*
happy either way 618.9 *impartial*
happy ending 797.17 *good thing*; 246.1 *success*
happy event 561.3 *propagation*
happy family 750.1 *accord*
happy few 121.7 *the best people*
happy fortune 248.2 *good fortune*
happy-go-lucky 615.4 *rash*; 486.1 *unskilful*
happy hour 490.2 *good time*
happy hunting ground 8.11 *heaven*; 101.1 *nonmaterial world*; 301.3 *resting place*
happy hunting grounds 582.14 *the spiritual world*
happy medium 754.1 *compromise*; 216.5 *medium*; 684.2, 685.1 *moderation*
happy release 582.5 *ways of dying*
happy thought 484.3 *expedient plan*
Happy Valley 477.8 *dreamland*
hapteron 84.3 *plant body*
har 31.35 *visibility*
hara-kiri 10.7 *non-Christian ritual*; 814.11 *penance*; 382.7 *suicide*
harangue 733.1, 733.7 *address*; 270.5 *be diffuse*; 722.4 *dissertate*; 722.1 *dissertation*; 795.12 *moralize*; 729.14 *speak to*; 729.8 *speech*
haranguer 729.10 *speaker*
harass 798.11 *be evil*; 236.13 *be worthless*; 466.14 *discriminate against*; 328.7 *disturb*; 261.6 *fatigue*; 236.14 *ill-treat*; 342.17 *meddle*; 624.9 *offend*; 633.8 *pursue*; 647.6 *suppress*; 651.18 *torment*; 612.14 *worry*
harassed 647.9 *suppressed*; 264.16 *troubled*; 612.9 *worried*
harassing 651.10 *malevolent*
harassment 381.11 *attack*; 236.11 *harmfulness*; 651.5 *intolerance*; 607.3 *nuisance*; 647.2 *suppression*
harbinger 475.5 *omen*; 129.8 *precursor*; 475.11 *predict*
harbour 312.15 *destination*; 165.2 *enclosed place*; 252.10 *protect*; 226.4 *stopping place*; 38.24 *water system*
harbour a design 482.8 *resolve*
hard 418.1; **423.3**; 499.5 *acid*; 249.6 *adverse*; 651.12 *callous*; 24.10 *ceramic*; 228.11 *determined*; 264.10 *difficult*; 558.17 *drinkable*; 809.3 *impenitent*; 592.1 *insensitive*; 690.6 *intoxicating*; 576.11 *laborious*; 266.2 *obscure*; 383.11 *obstinate*; 628.4 *pitiless*; 814.21 *punishing*; 647.8 *severe*; 228.9 *stable*; 638.3 *strong-willed*; 152.4 *thick-skinned*; 338.6 *with vigour*
hard and fast rule 140.4 *guide*
hard as a rock 418.1 *hard*
hard as iron 418.1 *hard*; 638.3 *strong-willed*
hard as nails 418.1 *hard*; 647.8 *severe*; 641.3 *unyielding*
hard-ass 641.8 *obstinate person*
hard as steel 418.1 *hard*
hard as stone 418.1 *hard*
hard at it 342.19 *busy*; 576.10 *working*
hard at work 342.19 *busy*
hardback 740.6 *book publishing*
hard bargaining 776.9 *bargaining*; 746.1 *negotiation*
hard blow 249.1 *adversity*
hardboard 435.4 *board*; 23.12 *wood*
hard-boil 418.9 *harden*
hard-boiled 423.3 *hard*; 418.3 *hardened*; 418.4 *mentally hard*; 423.5 *mentally tough*; 641.3 *unyielding*
hard breathing 261.7 *fatigue*
hard by 147.12 *near*
hard case 809.2 *impenitent person*; 628.3 *pitiless person*
hard cash 780.2 *cash*
hard centre 418.5 *hardness*
hard cheese 107.15 *hard luck!*
hard coal 435.1 *materials*
hardcore 435.2 *building material*; 38.25 *construction material*; 418.5 *hardness*; 18.9 *popular music*; 383.10 *resistant*; 416.4 *solid body*; 641.3 *unyielding*
hard-core pornography 796.2 *indecency*
hard-core supporter 640.5 *tenacious person*
hard corn 260.15 *ulcer*
hard currency 780.1 *money*
hard disk 28.64 *magnetic recording*; 40.7 *peripheral*
hard dose 814.10 *affliction*
hard drink 690.12 *alcohol*
hard drinker 558.12 *drinker*; 690.17 *drunkard*
hard drinking 690.11 *drinking*; 690.5 *drunken*
hard driving 332.8 *speed*
hard drug 691.6 *drug*
hard ECU 780.7 *finance*
harden 418.9; 792.9 *be dear*; 416.8 *be dense*; 618.12 *be indifferent*; 228.6 *be stable*; 423.10 *be tough*; 243.7 *develop*; 632.18 *habituate*; 423.11 *make tough*; 292.7 *season*; 336.8 *strengthen*; 152.7 *thicken*
hardened 418.3; 651.12 *callous*; 243.20 *developed*; 632.14 *habituated*; 809.3 *impenitent*; 592.1 *insensitive*; 628.4 *pitiless*; 292.15 *seasoned*; 423.2 *toughened*; 622.15 *unapproachable*; 489.6 *unfeeling*; 641.3 *unyielding*; 804.11 *wicked*
hardened face 660.3 *audacity*
hardened sinner 809.2 *impenitent person*
hardening 416.1 *density*; 243.13 *development*; 632.7 *habituation*; 418.6 *solidification*; 228.1 *stability*; 336.4 *strengthening*
hardening of the arteries 260.10 *cardiovascular disease*; 245.9 *dilapidation*; 335.4 *disability*; 418.6 *solidification*
harden one's heart 809.5 *be impenitent*; 618.12 *be indifferent*; 628.6 *be pitiless*; 709.5 *refuse*
harden up 50.15 *sail*
hard facts 123.3 *chief thing*
hard fate 249.3 *bad fortune*
hard feelings 590.6 *bad feeling*; 594.1 *hate*; 624.1 *resentment*
hard-fire 24.11 *make ceramics*
hard firing 24.5 *ceramic process*
hard-fought 576.11 *laborious*
hard freeze 31.32 *freeze*
hard frost 31.36 *frost*; 494.5 *ice*
hard furrow to plough 264.3 *difficult task*
hard going 264.3 *difficult task*
hard graft 264.3 *difficult task*
hard-grained 79.15 *woody*
hard hand 647.1 *severity*
hard hat 550.5 *body covering*; 551.15 *headgear*
hard-head 641.8 *obstinate person*; 383.5 *resister*
hard-headed 95.8 *practical*; 383.10 *resistant*; 647.8 *severe*; 641.3 *unyielding*
hard-headedly 383.14 *resistingly*
hardhearted 651.12 *callous*; 809.3 *impenitent*; 418.4 *mentally hard*; 423.5 *mentally tough*; 628.4 *pitiless*; 647.8 *severe*; 804.11 *wicked*
hardheartedly 809.6 *impenitently*; 418.13 *inflexibly*; 647.11 *severely*; 423.14 *single-mindedly*; 804.18 *wickedly*
hardheartedness 651.3 *callousness*; 489.313 *heedlessness*; 809.1 *impenitence*; 418.8 *mental hardness*; 423.9 *mental toughness*; 628.1 *pitilessness*
hardhearted person 809.2 *impenitent person*

hard-hitting 638.2 tenacious
hard house 18.9 popular music
hardihood 613.1 courage
hardily 423.13 powerfully; 336.14 strongly
hardiness 613.1 courage; 423.8 physical strength
hard labour 814.7 punishment; 576.1 work
hard landing 29.35 rocketry
hard lenses 518.10 visual aid
hard life 249.1 adversity; 264.6 critical situation
hard light 41.15 lighting
hardline 586.33 combative; 383.11 obstinate; 641.4 set
hard line 641.6 determination
hardliner 225.3 conservative person; 632.8 creature of habit; 586.6 militarist; 641.8 obstinate person; 12.6 political party; 383.5 resister; 647.4 strict person
hard lines 814.10 affliction; 107.15 hard luck!
hard luck 249.3 bad fortune; 288.3 lost chance
hard luck! 107.15
hardly 264.25 difficultly; 151.11 narrowly; 206.11 sparsely
hardly a chance 105.4 improbability
hardly any 206.5 few
hardly breathing 341.3 inactive
hardly ever 105.10 rarely
hardly like 116.4 dissimilar
hardly possible 619.8 wonderful
hard master 647.4 strict person
hard-mouthed 641.2 refractory
Hardness 418
hardness 418.5; 651.3 callousness; 416.1 density; 228.2, 641.6 determination; 264.1 difficulty; 404.2 grain; 489.313 heedlessness; 809.1 impenitence; 592.3 insensitiveness; 383.2 obstinacy; 628.1 pitilessness; 647.1 severity; 638.14 tenacity; 423.6 toughness
hardness of heart 809.1 impenitence; 418.8 mental hardness; 628.1 pitilessness; 804.1 wickedness
hard news 741.1 news; 741.9 news story
hard-nose 641.8 obstinate person
hard-nosed 423.5 mentally tough; 383.10 resistant; 641.3 unyielding
hardnut 592.5 insensitive person
hard nut to crack 737.5 difficult problem; 264.4 problem; 696.12 unintelligible thing
hard of hearing 505.4 deaf
hard of heart 651.12 callous
hard pad 260.18 veterinary disease
hard palate 729.5 organ of speech
hardpan 175.1 base; 416.4 solid body
hard-paste 24.10 ceramic
hard-paste porcelain 24.1 ceramics
hard pitch 48.4 pitching terms
hard porn 796.2 indecency
hard-pressed 262.3 hasty; 782.2 insolvent
hard pruning 44.5 gardening
hard pull 264.3 difficult task
hard put to it 782.2 insolvent
hard return 40.19 computing terms
hard-right 225.8 conservative
hard road to travel 264.3 difficult task
hard rock 18.9 popular music
hard roe 74.5 fish anatomy; 25.16 fish dish
hard row 814.10 affliction
hard row of stumps 264.3 difficult task
hard row to hoe 264.3 difficult task
hard rubber 422.4 rubber
hard sector 40.19 computing terms
hard sell 480.6 advertising; 483.2 inducement; 778.6 salesmanship
hard selling 480.5 propaganda
hard-shell 383.10 resistant
hard-shelled 641.4 set
hardship 249.1 adversity; 264.6 critical situation; 782.5 poverty
hard shoulder 320.3 carriageway; 164.1 edge
hard standing 322.4 airport; 320.21 miscellaneous motoring terms
hard steel 418.7 hard substance
hard substance 418.7
hard-surface 68.12 ski
hard-surface snow 68.1 skiing
hard tack 557.7 food
hard task 264.3 difficult task; 354.2 undertaking
hard thinking 443.2 intellectual exercise
hard tick 76.2 arachnid
hard times 264.7 awkward situation; 264.6 critical situation; 782.6 insolvency; 249.4 time of adversity
hard to believe 451.7 disbelieved; 105.2 questionable
hard to catch 634.18 avoiding
hard to come by 218.4 scarce
hard to decode 696.1 unintelligible
hard to get 218.4 scarce
hard to pin down 476.7 suppositional
hard to please 264.14 troublesome
hard to satisfy 264.14 troublesome
hard to swallow 105.2 questionable
hard to understand 696.4 difficult
hard up 782.2 insolvent; 782.1 poor; 249.7 unprosperous; 218.2 unprovided
hard usage 349.6 use
hard vacuum 32.20 surface chemistry
hardware 418.7 hard substance; 356.7 produce
hard water 433.1 water
hard-wearing 336.13 strengthened; 423.1 tough
hard winter 31.31 coldness
hardwire 40.20 abort
hard-won 576.11 laborious
hardwood 418.7 hard substance; 79.1 tree; 23.12 wood; 79.15 woody
hardwood paddle 50.6 canoeing
hard word 5.17 word
hard words 266.1 obscurity
hard work 342.8 assiduity; 640.2 commitment; 264.3 difficult task; 576.1 work
hard worker 342.10 busy person; 354.4 volunteer
hard-working 342.20 industrious; 576.10 working
hardy 44.17 botanical; 613.9 courageous; 259.1 healthy; 336.9 physically strong; 423.4 powerful; 338.4 vigorous; 77.15 wild
hare 25.20 meat; 332.12 swift animal; 300.15 walk
harebrained 459.5 foolish; 615.4 rash
hare coursing 71.23 mammal hunting
hare hunting 59.8, 60.2 hunting
harelike 71.31 rabbit-like
harem 593.13 abode of love; 568.13 womenfolk
hare off 332.4 be swift
hare's fur glaze 24.3 glaze
hark 633.10 chase; 504.15 hear; 504.18 hear hear!
hark back 284.15, 303.8 look back; 3.22, 462.12 remember; 761.6 reverse
harking-back 3.13, 303.15 looking back
Harlem 87.3 New York
Harlequin 21.32 clown; 21.23 role; 541.5 variegated thing
harlequinade 21.2 play
Harlequin and Columbine 593.10 lovers
harlot 796.9 immoral woman; 568.7 prostitute
harlotry 796.5 prostitution; 796.3 sexual immorality
harlot's trade 796.5 prostitution
harm 651.7 act of malevolence; 798.2 affliction; 798.11 be evil; 240.5 be inconvenient; 766.13 destroy; 766.5 destruction; 236.11 harmfulness; 245.5, 245.11 hurt; 240.3 inconvenience; 351.1, 351.2 misuse; 651.18 torment; 337.7 weaken; 802.20 wrong; 802.8 wrongdoing
harmed 245.12 deteriorated
harmful 236.5; 351.5 abusive; 249.6 adverse; 254.1 dangerous; 357.14 destructive; 245.12 deteriorated; 798.9 detrimental; 240.1 inconvenient; 802.16 in the wrong
harmfully 351.6 abusively; 798.13 destructively; 249.12 in adversity
harmfulness 236.11; 798.2 affliction
harmless 623.1 humble; 257.4 hygienic; 805.5 innocent; 685.6 moderate; 589.7 peaceful; 252.6 safe; 335.11 unprotected; 235.4 worthwhile
harmless joke 124.8 trifle
harmlessly 805.11 innocently; 335.14 powerlessly
harmlessness 335.3 helplessness; 805.1 innocence; 252.1 safety; 337.1 weakness
harmonic 18.30; 27.85 cyclic; 516.7, 750.13 harmonious; 18.16, 28.20 musical note; 326.13 oscillating; 18.21 tone
harmonically 18.42 musically
harmonic minor scale 18.20 key
harmonic progression 516.4 harmonics; 27.20 sequence
harmonics 18.14; 516.4
harmonic scale 18.20 key
harmonious 407.16; 516.7; 750.13; 747.19 associating; 529.11 colourful; 117.12 conforming; 374.8 cooperative; 188.4 correlated; 543.3 elegant; 111.13 equivalent; 162.5 even; 569.8 friendly; 18.30 harmonic; 750.10 in accord; 516.6 melodious; 589.7 peaceful; 162.4 symmetrical; 140.11 uniform
harmoniously 516.12; 750.33; 117.17 conformingly; 747.20 cooperatively; 543.5 elegantly; 111.18 identically; 750.31 in accord; 374.10 in combination; 569.17 in friendship; 18.42 musically
harmoniousness 516.3 melodiousness
harmonist 516.5 melodist
harmonization 516.4 harmonics; 750.4 harmony; 412.1 mixture
harmonize 18.34; 407.20; 516.8; 750.24; 111.7 be the same; 374.6 come together; 747.15 concur; 117.7 conform; 188.6 correlate; 111.8 make the same; 412.8 mix; 749.4 pacify; 516.9 set to music; 18.39 sing; 162.6 symmetrize
harmonized 374.7 combined; 412.12 mixed
harmonizing 18.30 harmonic; 516.7 harmonious
harmonograph 326.6 measuring instrument
harmony 407.8; 750.4; 750.1 accord; 232.1 completeness; 117.1 conformity; 374.2 cooperation; 543.1 elegance; 111.2 equivalence; 162.3 evenness; 747.2 fellowship; 57.8 floor exercises; 569.2 friendly relations; 569.1 friendship; 545.1 gorgeousness; 516.3 melodiousness; 18.13 melody; 412.2 mixed thing; 18.1 music; 188.1 parallelism; 589.1 peace; 162.1 symmetry; 140.7 uniformity
harness 55.1 angling; 384.7 armour; 373.12 bind; 62.4 climbing equipment; 438.7 equipment; 251.12 gag; 251.5 means of restraint; 43.18 practise livestock farming; 373.7 tackle; 50.7 windsurfing; 373.9 yoke
harnessed 373.16 bound; 384.30 defended
harness line 50.7 windsurfing
harp 112.18
harping 112.12 repetitious
harp on 620.6 be boring; 111.11 be regular; 134.3 continue; 112.18 harp
harpoon 587.6 historical missile weapon; 425.8 sharp-pointed thing; 587.8 sharp weapon; 425.16 use a sharp tool
harpy 72.9 fabulous bird; 70.7 legendary beast
harridan 625.3 irascible person
harrier 47.3 athlete; 72.5 bird of prey; 332.13 swift person
harrow 43.17 farm; 491.11 inflict pain; 425.8 sharp-pointed thing; 421.11 smooth; 421.9 smoother; 425.16 use a sharp tool
harrowed 421.2 uniform
harrowing 43.5 cultivation; 602.7 distressing; 491.5 painful
harrows 43.10 farm tool
harry 381.1 attack; 633.8 pursue; 651.18 torment
harrying 381.23 attacking
Harry Tate 201.4 eight
harsh 651.12 callous; 659.5 discourteous; 517.7 dissonant; 529.12 gaudy; 236.5 harmful; 504.14 hearable; 628.4 pitiless; 647.8 severe; 499.7 splenetic; 513.7 strident; 499.6 unpalatable; 380.6 violent
harshly 365.17 abrasively; 659.9 discourteously; 517.12 dissonantly; 651.20 malevolently; 628.7 pitilessly; 647.11 severely; 499.10 sourly; 499.11 splenetically; 513.10 stridently; 380.10 violently
harshness 651.3 callousness; 659.1 discourtesy; 517.1 dissonance; 236.11 harmfulness; 647.1 severity; 496.4 stimulation; 513.1 stridency; 380.1 violence
Harsh Sound 513
harsh sound 513.1 stridency
harsh treatment 647.1 severity
harsh voice 730.2 inarticulation
harsh words 670.8 berating
hart 567.16 male animal; 71.17 male mammal
hartshorn 394.7 tonic
harum-scarum 408.28 anyhow; 408.20 disorderly; 114.11 irregularly
haruspex 11.13 diviner; 475.9 forecaster; 7.8 priest
haruspical 11.17 divinatory; 475.15 presageful
haruspicate 283.9 look ahead
haruspication 11.9 divination
haruspicy 11.9, 475.2 divination
Harvard-Yale race 50.4 rowing
harvest 765.11 acquire; 292.4 autumn; 43.17 farm; 345.8 grow; 345.3 growth; 356.7 produce; 439.1, 439.6 store; 765.6 yield
harvest dance 22.4 historic dancing
harvested 765.19 yielding
harvester 376.35 collector; 43.10 farm tool
Harvest Festival 10.16 religious festival
harvest home 557.13 feast; 601.7 thanksgiving
harvesting 43.5 cultivation
harvestman 76.2 arachnid
harvest mite 76.3 pest
harvest moon 292.4 autumn; 29.17 moon; 522.4 natural light
harvest supper 557.13 feast
harvest time 292.4 autumn
Harvey Smith salute 742.3 gesture; 668.7 sign of disrespect
has-been 247.5 failing person; 3.18 in the past
hash 408.23 confuse; 691.6 drug; 408.4 litter; 25.32 meat dish; 412.3 miscellany; 412.2 mixed thing; 408.6 mix-up
hashish 691.6 drug
hash mark 743.4 insignia; 46.4 stadium
Hasidic 7.16 denominational
hasp 373.8 fastening; 309.3 restrainer
hassle 607.8 annoy; 751.6 argue; 751.2 argument; 264.17 be difficult; 240.5 be inconvenient; 647.5 be severe; 408.22 discompose; 328.7 disturb; 576.4 exertion; 670.18 find fault; 262.4 haste; 378.8 hinder; 342.17 meddle; 342.3 nimbleness; 607.3 nuisance
hassock 376.27 bundle; 81.2 grassland
hastate 77.18 of leaves; 425.1 sharp
Haste 262
haste 262.4; 293.1 earliness; 342.3 nimbleness; 293.5 prematurity; 615.1 rashness; 332.8 speed
hasten 262.1; 293.10; 344.10 awaken; 342.12 be active; 293.7 be early; 332.4 be swift; 302.8, 392.28 further; 332.7 hurry someone up; 265.16 make easy; 262.2 make haste
hasten away 262.2 make haste
hastening 265.7 easing; 262.4 haste; 262.3 hasty
hasten off 313.4 hurry off
hasten someone's end 382.16 kill
hastily 262.6; 293.17 early; 293.20 prematurely; 615.6 rashly; 332.14 swiftly
hastiness 262.5; 293.1 earliness; 293.5 prematurity; 615.1 rashness; 332.8 speed
hasty 262.3; 486.3 clumsy; 293.12 early; 293.16 premature; 615.4 rash; 157.2 superficial; 332.1 swift
hasty retreat 389.1 escape
hat 550.5 body covering; 551.15 headgear
hat brim 361.5 projecting object
hatch 76.17, 243.7 develop; 19.20 draw; 72.15 eggs; 96.17 fabricate; 561.11 have young; 477.14 imagine; 484.11 invent; 523.14 make dark; 314.6 means of entry; 72.24 nest; 484.13 plot; 356.10 produce; 561.13 propagate; 72.12 young bird
hatch a plot 484.13 plot
hatchback 320.16 car
hatcheck girl 401.3 attendant
hatched 554.15 born; 356.12 produced
hatcher 484.8 planner
hatchery 72.14 nest; 72.19 ornithology; 344.2 source
hatches, matches, and dispatches 693.4 mass communication
hatchet 425.9 sharp-edged thing; 587.8 sharp weapon; 79.7 timber production
hatchet face 153.7 thinness
hatchet-faced 153.1 thin
hatchet job 678.2 criticism; 357.2 destroying
hatchet man 357.6 destroyer; 678.7 disparager; 651.8 malefactor; 382.11 murderer; 814.17 punisher
hatching 523.2 darkening; 243.17 developing; 243.13 development; 561.3 propagation

hatchment 583.4 *funeral objects;* 743.8 *heraldic device*
hatchway 314.6 *means of entry*
Hate 594
hate 594.1; 594.14; 113.17 *be against;* 651.16 *be malevolent;* 751.5 *disagree;* 596.1, 596.5 *dislike;* 651.1 *malevolence;* 113.1 *opposition*
hated 594.12
hated person 594.8
hated thing 594.7
hate evil 803.8 *be virtuous*
hateful 751.9 *disagreeing;* 596.8 *disliking;* 798.7 *evil;* 594.12 *hated;* 594.10 *hating;* 651.10 *malevolent;* 236.4 *poor;* 242.1 *unpleasant*
hatefully 594.18; 798.12 *evilly;* 751.11 *in disagreement;* 651.20 *malevolently*
hatefulness 594.4; 812.1 *disrespect;* 798.1 *evil;* 651.1 *malevolence*
hate mankind 653.4 *become a misanthrope*
hate men 653.4 *become a misanthrope*
hate one's guts 594.14 *hate*
hater 594.9
hater of man 653.2 *misanthrope*
hater of mankind 653.2 *misanthrope*
hater of women 653.2 *misanthrope*
hate the world 653.4 *become a misanthrope*
hating 594.10; 751.9 *disagreeing;* 596.8 *disliking;* 651.10 *malevolent*
hatless 552.10 *in dishabille*
hatmaking 551.2 *dressing*
hatpin 373.8 *fastening;* 542.7 *jewellery;* 425.8 *sharp-pointed thing*
hat rack 361.4 *hanger*
hatred 590.6 *bad feeling;* 751.1 *disagreement;* 596.1 *dislike;* 594.1 *hate;* 651.1 *malevolence;* 113.1 *opposition*
hatred of mankind 653.1 *misanthropy*
hatted 551.29 *dressed*
hatter 551.26 *fashion designer*
hatting 551.2 *dressing*
hat trick 53.8 *delivery;* 485.3 *masterpiece;* 246.3 *successful thing;* 199.2 *trident*
hat waving 742.3 *gesture*
hauberk 384.7 *armour*
haughtily 660.33 *arrogantly;* 655.14 *unsocially*
haughtiness 660.4 *arrogance;* 622.3 *conceit;* 655.1 *unsociability*
haughty 660.16 *arrogant;* 622.17 *conceited;* 668.13 *contemptuous;* 655.8 *unsociable*
haul 765.3 *acquisition;* 38.30 *engineer;* 323.9 *navigate;* 362.2, 362.11 *pull;* 300.14 *set in motion;* 774.4 *stolen goods;* 16.36 *stolen property;* 773.5 *takings;* 316.12, 319.4 *transport;* 576.6 *work*
haulage 362.1 *traction;* 319.1 *transport;* 316.2 *transportation*
haul ass 332.4 *be swift*
haul before the court 16.70 *litigate*
haul down 367.10 *lower the flag*
haul down the flag 388.3 *submit*
hauled before the court 16.54 *litigated*
hauled up 715.8 *accusatory*
hauler 38.29 *construction equipment;* 362.6 *towline;* 316.7 *transferor*
haulier 362.6 *towline*
haul in 55.7 *angle;* 251.11 *detain*
hauling 38.29 *construction equipment;* 362.1 *traction;* 362.8 *tractional;* 316.2 *transportation*
hauling freightage 319.1 *transport*
hauling over the coals 670.7 *blame*
haulm 81.3 *grass plant*
haul over the coals 670.20 *censure*
haul up 715.5 *accuse;* 366.4 *gather up*
haunch 20.9 *miscellaneous architectural features*
haunches 168.2 *rear end*
haunt 97.12 *attend;* 565.2 *environment;* 297.8, 565.19 *frequent;* 632.16 *have a habit;* 86.13 *locality;* 142.1 *location;* 134.4 *protract;* 462.13 *remind;* 612.14 *worry*
haunted 11.19 *bewitched;* 97.7 *present;* 612.9 *worried*
haunter 97.5 *someone present*
haunting 297.3 *frequent;* 297.5 *frequenting;* 632.15 *habit-forming;* 462.7 *memorable;* 112.14 *recurrent*
hauntingly 297.1 *frequently*
Haurvatat 8.6 *angel*
hausfrau 578.1 *worker*
haustorium 83.4 *fungal body*
haute couture 551.2 *dressing;* 553.1 *fashion*
haute cuisine 25.1 *cookery*
haute école 59.6 *horsemanship*
hauteur 622.5 *stateliness*
haut monde 235.7 *elite*
Havana 496.7 *tobacco*
have 127.4 *include;* 763.7 *possess;* 695.6 *understand*
have a baby 561.10 *reproduce oneself*
have a bachelor's apartment 572.9 *be celibate*
have a bachelor's flat 572.9 *be celibate*
have a bad conscience 806.9 *appear guilty*
have a bad liver 625.6 *be irascible*
have a bad outcome 604.4 *be disappointed*
have a bad result 604.4 *be disappointed*
have a bad temper 625.6 *be irascible*
have a bad time 249.9 *be in trouble*
have a ball 490.8 *feel pleasure;* 600.5 *rejoice*
have a bath 256.14 *bathe*
have a bearing on 108.7 *relate to*
have a bellyful 217.4 *suffice*
have a bent 229.4 *tend*
have a bias 469.2 *prefer*
have a big appetite 688.5 *be greedy*
have a big heart 650.8 *be benevolent;* 473.7 *be unselfish*
have a big mouth 731.8 *talk too much*
have a birdie 56.7 *golf*
have a birthday 298.9 *commemorate*
have a birthmark 743.11 *identify oneself*
have a bite 55.7 *angle*
have a blank cheque 757.5 *be permitted;* 250.19 *liberalize*
have a blind spot 519.14 *be blind;* 696.9 *find unintelligible*
have a bogey 56.7 *golf*
have a bowel movement 560.16 *defecate*
have a brainwave 443.16 *have an idea*
have a break 133.13 *pause*
have a breakdown 378.9 *block*
have a bright future 756.10 *show potential*
have a bumper crop 765.11 *acquire*
have a bumpy face 420.11 *be rough*
have a butcher's 518.14 *inspect*
have a buyer 778.2 *be sold*
have a cameo role 21.36 *underact*
have a cash-flow crisis 786.9 *be unable to pay*
have a catnap 263.2 *take it easy*
have a chance 107.12 *take a chance*
have a change 581.2 *be refreshed*
have a cheek 661.5 *defy*
have a cheque bounce 249.10 *need money*
have a chinwag 734.10 *chat*
have a choice 469.1 *select*
have a circulation 740.18 *become famous*
have a claim to 801.13 *be right*
have a classification 108.9 *have a relative position*
have a clear conscience 805.8 *be innocent*
have a close call 389.5 *escape*
have a closed mind 641.9 *be obstinate*
have a close shave 389.5 *escape*
have acne 420.11 *be rough*
have a cockup 378.9 *block*
have a comedown 249.9 *be in trouble*
have a complaint 260.24 *be unhealthy*
have a connection with 108.7 *relate to*
have a conservative outlook 378.11 *be inhibited*
have a constitution 12.13 *be governed*
have a corner 58.9 *play hockey*
have a cosy chat 734.10 *chat*
have a crack 231.9 *be imperfect*
have a crack at 353.1 *attempt*
have a credibility gap 751.8 *be different*
have a credit facility 772.10 *buy on credit*
have a crush on 593.24 *be in love;* 595.7 *like*
have a cut at 381.6 *stab*
have a date 593.26 *court*
have a dekko 518.14 *inspect*
have a dilemma 221.7 *be in a predicament*
have a discussion 746.5 *negotiate*
have a distinctive appearance 695.8 *be recognizable*
have a donnybrook 751.6 *argue*
have a double meaning 479.1 *be equivocal*
have a down on 594.14 *hate*
have a drink 558.13 *drink*
have a dust-up 751.6 *argue*
have a falling-out 751.5 *disagree*
have a false front 700.32 *disguise*
have a false start 46.18 *be penalized*
have a fancy for 593.23 *love*
have a fault 231.9 *be imperfect*
have a feed 557.24 *have a meal*
have a feeling about 445.9 *be intuitive*
have a fencing bout 54.5 *fence*
have a financial loss 766.10
have a financial reverse 249.10 *need money*
have a financial setback 249.10 *need money*
have a finger in 340.4 *act;* 764.4 *have joint possession*
have a flair 334.10 *be powerful;* 485.10 *be skilful*
have a flat 378.9 *block*
have a fling 448.13 *invent;* 686.11 *overindulge*
have a fling at 381.5 *strike*
have a flying start 164.7 *have an advantage*
have a fondness for 593.23 *love*
have a foul mouth 594.17 *anger*
have a foursome 56.7 *golf*
have a free hand 757.5 *be permitted;* 250.18 *have scope;* 250.19 *liberalize*
have a free kick 66.4 *play soccer*
have a free mind 250.14 *be free*
have a fresh start 295.17 *become new*
have a gainful occupation 813.13 *get paid*
have a generous heart 650.8 *be benevolent*
have a generous nature 768.5 *give*
have a genius for 229.4 *tend*
have a gift 334.10 *be powerful;* 229.4 *tend*
have a gift for 797.19 *be good at;* 485.10 *be skilful*
have a go 353.1 *attempt;* 298.7 *be regular;* 353.11 *here goes!;* 448.13 *invent*
have a goal kick 66.4 *play soccer*
have a go at 456.10 *know little;* 381.5 *strike*
have a good appetite 557.22 *eat well*
have a good ear 504.15 *hear*
have a good effect 235.10 *do good*
have a good idea 443.16 *have an idea*
have a good memory 360.8 *remember*
have a good reputation 811.5 *have repute*
have a good style 543.4 *be elegant*
have a good time 597.6 *enjoy;* 248.10 *good luck!*
have a grand opening 295.19 *begin*
have a grasping nature 773.7 *take*
have a grudge against 596.5 *dislike*
have a habit 632.16
have a haemorrhage 624.12 *become angry*
have a hairbreadth escape 389.5 *escape*
have a hand in 340.4 *act;* 348.4 *be an instrument;* 344.12 *determine;* 392.28 *further;* 764.4 *have joint possession*
have a head start 164.7 *have an advantage*
have a heart 627.14 *have pity!*
have a heart attack 260.24 *be unhealthy*
have a heart-to-heart 734.10 *chat*
have a hiccup 378.9 *block*
have a high profile 520.8 *be visible*
have a hold over 395.10 *be a prevailing influence*
have a hopeless case 335.6 *be powerless*
have a house-warming 295.19 *begin*
have a hunch 590.16 *feel in one's bones;* 476.5 *suppose;* 446.17 *theorize*
have a jagged edge 425.14 *be sharp*
have a Jimmy Riddle 560.17 *urinate*
have a kind heart 593.23 *love*
have a kindness for 593.23 *love*
have a knack for 485.10 *be skilful*
have a knees-up 600.5 *rejoice*
have a knock-down-drag-out fight 751.6 *argue*
have a leaning 229.4 *tend*
have a liberated mind 250.14 *be free*
have a light touch 543.4 *be elegant*
have a little chat 734.10 *chat*
have all the luck 248.6 *be fortunate*
have all the virtues 803.8 *be virtuous*
have all to oneself 763.7 *possess*
have a long face 626.9 *be sullen*
have a look at 518.14 *inspect*
have a look of 525.11 *appear*
have a look-see 518.14 *inspect*
have a low IQ 457.9 *lack intellect*
have a lucky break 248.6 *be fortunate;* 248.5 *be prosperous*
have a malignant growth 345.8 *grow*
have a market 778.2 *be sold*
have a mash on 593.24 *be in love*
have ambition 683.6 *be selfish*
have a meal 557.24
have a meaning 694.10 *mean*
have a meltdown 437.11 *fuel*
have a mental block 358.2 *forget*
have a method 317.14 *find one's way*
have a mild manner 658.10 *be courteous*
have a mind to 636.13 *be willing;* 482.8 *resolve*
have a mishap 249.9 *be in trouble;* 378.9 *block*
have a monotonous job 620.7 *suffer boredom*
have a motive 482.8 *resolve*
have a mutual dependence 387.8 *be subject to*
have a mutual relationship 108.8 *be proportionate to*
have an accident 249.9 *be in trouble;* 378.9 *block*
have an account with 783.9 *acquire credit;* 784.7 *be in debt*
have an active interest 342.16 *be sociable*
have an advantage 164.7; 765.9 *gain*
have an affair 804.16 *be wicked*
have an affinity 374.5 *combine*
have an affinity for 595.7 *like*
have an affliction 260.24 *be unhealthy*
have an ague 327.24 *shake*
have an anniversary 298.9 *commemorate*
have an aptitude 229.4 *tend*
have a narrow escape 389.5 *escape*
have a narrow outlook 166.7 *limit*
have a narrow squeak 389.5 *escape*
have an athletic build 423.10 *be tough*
have an attachment for 595.7 *like*
have an attack 260.24 *be unhealthy*
have an attraction 363.11 *attract*
have an auction 767.11 *dispose of property*
have and hold 763.7 *possess*
have an ear for 485.10 *be skilful;* 504.15 *hear*
have an edge 425.14 *be sharp*
have a need for 710.6 *request*
have an effect 344.12 *determine;* 345.5 *show an effect*
have an emergency 222.13 *get into difficulties*
have an empty stomach 687.5 *fast*
have a nervous breakdown 590.17 *feel deeply*
have an estate 440.9 *own property*
have a new look 295.17 *become new*
have a new start 295.17 *become new*
have an expense account 765.14 *profit*
have an eye for 485.10 *be skilful*
have an eye to 283.8, 482.7 *intend*
have a nice day 313.14 *goodbye!*
have an idea 443.16; 446.14; 476.5 *suppose*
have an illness 249.9 *be in trouble*
have an impact with 483.9 *motivate*
have an in 314.9 *enter*
have an income 769.9 *receive*
have an independent mind 391.4 *liberate*
have an industrial dispute 15.12
have an infatuation 593.24 *be in love*
have an inkling 476.5 *suppose*
have an inspiration 477.14 *imagine*
have an instinct 229.4 *tend*
have an iron grip 360.6 *retain*
have an open day 654.11 *be sociable*
have an orgasm 490.8 *feel pleasure*
have another 558.13 *drink*
have another thing coming 274.18 *be in error*
have a notion 476.5 *suppose*
have an overdraft 772.7 *borrow*

have an ulterior motive 645.5 *be cunning*
have an uncontrollable temper 625.6 *be irascible*
have an unfair advantage 765.9 *gain*
have a party 600.5 *rejoice*
have a penalty stroke 56.7 *golf*
have a photographic memory 360.8 *remember*
have a piece of 764.4 *have joint possession*
have a place 12.11 *govern*
have a point 425.14 *be sharp*; 108.7 *relate to*
have a policy 484.12 *plan ahead*
have a poor appetite 557.23 *taste*
have a poor ear 504.15 *hear*
have a poor return 766.10 *have a financial loss*
have a portfolio 440.9 *own property*
have a powwow with 713.6 *consult*
have a practice 394.20 *doctor*
have a predicament 221.7 *be in a predicament*
have a predisposition 229.4 *tend*
have a preference 469.2, 595.8 *prefer*
have a premonition 283.9 *look ahead*
have a price war 778.1 *sell*
have a prior engagement 288.8 *be busy*
have a private income 765.12 *earn*
have a prizefight 52.11 *fight*
have a problem 221.7 *be in a predicament*; 264.20 *be in difficulty*
have a prominent feature 185.8 *protrude*
have a propensity 595.8 *prefer*; 229.4 *tend*
have aptitude 334.10 *be powerful*
have a purpose 482.8 *resolve*
have a rapid heartbeat 298.7 *be regular*
have a red face 623.24 *be humiliated*
have a refill 558.13 *drink*
have a relationship 108.7 *relate to*
have a relative position **108.9**
have a rest 581.2 *be refreshed*; 263.2 *take it easy*
have a reversal 766.9 *lose*
have a rough surface 420.11 *be rough*
have a route 317.14 *find one's way*
have artistic licence 250.14 *be free*
have a run-in 751.6 *argue*
have a sale 767.11 *dispose of property*
have a say 469.5 *vote*
have a say in 395.8 *influence*
have a say-so 250.14 *be free*
have a screw loose 461.14 *become insane*
have a seat 312.24 *welcome!*
have a second childhood 556.17 *age*
have a second meaning 479.1 *be equivocal*
have a sense 694.10 *mean*
have a setback 766.9 *lose*
have a set-to 701.13, 751.6 *argue*
have a sharp tongue 625.6 *be irascible*
have a shit 560.16 *defecate*
have a shopping list 777.2 *shop*
have a short fuse 625.6 *be irascible*
have a short memory 463.14 *be forgetful*
have a short temper 625.6 *be irascible*
have a shot at 353.1 *attempt*
have a shower 256.14 *bathe*
have a side effect 345.6 *have a visible effect*; 345.5 *show an effect*
have a simple answer 265.15 *be easy*
have a sit-down strike 709.5 *refuse*
have a slanging match 751.6 *argue*; 712.6 *vilify*
have a slash 560.17 *urinate*
have a social conscience 652.7 *be charitable*
have a stab at 353.1 *attempt*; 448.13 *invent*
have a stake in 764.4 *have joint possession*
have a standing 221.6 *be in a state of*
have a stroke 260.24 *be unhealthy*
have a sudden brainwave 478.3 *improvise*
have a summit meeting 746.5 *negotiate*
have a suspicion 453.18 *be uncertain*; 619.12 *wonder whether*
have a sweet tongue 658.10 *be courteous*
have a talk 734.9 *converse*
have a tantrum 624.11 *be angry*
have a temper 625.6 *be irascible*
have a tendency 632.16 *have a habit*; 229.4 *tend*
have a tête-à-tête with 713.6 *consult*
have a theory 476.5 *suppose*
have a thick skin 618.12 *be indifferent*
have a thing about 593.18 *in love*
have a tiff 624.11 *be angry*
have at one's command 397.12 *be available to one*; 349.5 *dispose of*; 763.7 *possess*
have at one's disposal 397.12 *be available to one*; 349.5 *dispose of*; 763.7 *possess*
have at one's elbow 713.6 *consult*
have at one's mercy 387.6 *subject*
have a touchback 46.17 *kick*
have a turn 298.7 *be regular*
have a use for 237.11 *find useful*
have authority **396.18**; 250.16 *be independent*; 334.10 *be powerful*; 12.11 *govern*
have authority over **397.11**
have authorization 757.5 *be permitted*
have a vacancy for 135.7 *require*
have a vantage point 121.11 *get ahead*
have a vicelike grip 360.6 *retain*
have a visible effect **345.6**
have a voice 395.8 *influence*; 469.1 *select*; 469.5 *vote*
have a voice in 764.4 *have joint possession*
have a vote 469.5 *vote*
have a walkover 265.17 *do easily*
have a way with 579.1 *manage*
have a weakness for 593.23 *love*
have a whip-round 768.6 *give to charity*
have a word with 734.9 *converse*
have bad breath 503.5 *stink*
have bad luck 247.6 *fail*
have bad taste **497.9**
have balls 338.2 *be full of vigour*
have barefaced cheek 661.5 *defy*
have being 554.16 *live*
have belongings 440.9 *own property*
have bills to pay 784.7 *be in debt*
have BO 503.5 *stink*
have bought it 357.13 *be destroyed*
have bought the farm 357.13 *be destroyed*
have brains 458.8 *be intelligent*
have buoyancy 422.10 *be adaptable*
have by the throat 360.6 *retain*
have cancer 345.8 *grow*
have capital gains 765.14 *profit*
have carte blanche 250.19 *liberalize*
have certain status 108.9 *have a relative position*
have charge of 579.1 *manage*; 252.10 *protect*
have charisma 334.10 *be powerful*; 395.8 *influence*
have children 561.10 *reproduce oneself*
have chutzpah 661.5 *defy*
have clean hands 805.8 *be innocent*
have clearance 757.5 *be permitted*
have clout 185.9 *be prominent*; 396.18 *have authority*; 395.8 *influence*
have cold feet 244.4 *reconsider*
have compassion 419.15 *be kind*; 648.3 *be lenient*
have composure 684.7 *be calm*
have consequence 345.5 *show an effect*
have continuity 297.7 *be frequent*
have coverage 46.16 *play defence*
have currency 138.28 *prevail*
have dealings with 569.13 *befriend*; 776.1 *trade*
have debts 378.12 *burden*
have decency 799.6 *be honourable*
have deep understanding 156.15 *be profound*
have defective sight 519.14 *be blind*
have dependents to support 378.12 *burden*
have designs 595.7 *like*; 484.13 *plot*
have designs on 482.10 *aim*; 756.11 *promise oneself*
have differences with 751.5 *disagree*; 242.11 *quarrel*
have different opinions 114.9 *dissent*
have difficulties 221.7 *be in a predicament*; 249.9 *be in trouble*
have difficulty **264.19**
have difficulty speaking **730.14**
have diminishing returns 766.10 *have a financial loss*
have discord 114.9 *dissent*
have dissention 372.12 *disagree*
have distinction 185.9 *be prominent*
have done with 350.6 *stop using*
have doubts about 451.8 *disbelieve*
have drive 334.10 *be powerful*
have elbowroom 250.18 *have scope*
have encroachment 46.18 *be penalized*
have enough **217.6**; 232.5 *be complete*
have every intention 283.8 *intend*; 482.8 *resolve*
have everything 232.5 *be complete*
have excess 219.4 *be excessive*
have exclusive possession of 763.7 *possess*
have exclusive rights to 763.7 *possess*
have experience 485.11 *be expert*
have expertise 396.22 *be an authority on*
have expired 284.13 *be past*
have extra money 765.14 *profit*
have eyes for 593.23 *love*
have faith 610.8 *be optimistic*; 7.19 *be religious*
have faith in 452.20 *be certain*; 450.7 *believe*
have false piety 699.22 *be hypocritical*
have family responsibilities 378.12 *burden*
have fatigue 247.6 *fail*
have feet of clay 700.27 *be false*; 231.9 *be imperfect*
have fish to fry 354.1 *undertake*
have flexibility 422.8 *be elastic*
have fond illusions 700.25 *deceive oneself*
have for sale 778.1 *sell*
have forty winks 339.4 *be inert*; 343.13 *sleep*; 263.2 *take it easy*
have freedom of choice 250.14 *be free*
have free time 580.4 *have leisure*; 341.4 *not act*
have free will 250.14 *be free*; 469.1 *select*
have friends 569.13 *befriend*; 654.13 *fraternize*
have from 769.9 *receive*
have fun 598.7 *be cheerful*; 597.6 *enjoy*; 490.8 *feel pleasure*; 654.13 *fraternize*; 248.10 *good luck!*
have gainful employment 765.12 *earn*
have gangrene 258.10 *be dirty*
have G-force loading 61.9 *race*
have good breeding 658.11 *have good manners*
have good hang time 46.17 *kick*
have good manners **658.11**
have good prospects 756.10 *show potential*
have gooseflesh 494.10 *be cold*; 492.13 *be touched by*; 488.11 *sense*
have goose-pimples 488.11 *sense*
have got to 386.8 *be compelled*
have ground clearance 61.9 *race*
have grounds for 801.13 *be right*
have growing pains 555.18 *grow*
have guilt feelings 808.4 *be penitent*
have guts 613.15 *be courageous*
have had a bellyful 217.6 *have enough*
have had enough 217.6 *have enough*; 388.3 *submit*
have had it 357.13 *be destroyed*
have had one's chips 582.15 *die*
have had one's day 556.17 *age*; 284.13 *be past*
have had one's lesson 385.4 *serve one right*
have had too much 690.7 *be drunk*
have halitosis 503.5 *stink*
have hard feelings towards 594.14 *hate*
have heartburn 629.6 *be jealous*
have high hopes 610.7 *aspire*
have high regard for 595.7 *like*
have histrionics 727.7 *exaggerate*
have hoped better of 604.4 *be disappointed*
have hoped for better 604.4 *be disappointed*
have horns 425.14 *be sharp*
have hysterics 590.17 *feel deeply*
have illegal motion 46.18 *be penalized*
have impact 345.5 *show an effect*
have importance 395.8 *influence*
have independent means 250.16 *be independent*
have inferior rank 387.8 *be subject to*
have influence 395.8 *influence*
have in hand 360.7 *detain*; 763.7 *possess*
have in mind 450.8 *be of the opinion*; 482.7 *intend*; 694.10 *mean*; 756.11 *promise oneself*
have in mind to 283.8 *intend*
have in one's book 631.14 *behave towards*
have in one's charge 579.1 *manage*
have in one's grasp 763.7 *possess*
have in one's grip 763.7 *possess*
have in one's name 763.7 *possess*
have in one's possession 763.7 *possess*
have in one's power 395.10 *be a prevailing influence*
have in prospect 474.8 *expect*
have in reserve 350.5 *not use*
have insight **477.16**; 695.6 *understand*
have integrity 255.9 *be pure*
have intercourse 593.29 *make love*
have in the bag 253.13 *secure one's objective*
have in view 482.7 *intend*
have it all 232.5 *be complete*
have it away 561.14 *have sex*
have it bad 593.24 *be in love*
have it both ways **198.18**; 702.12 *deceive*; 699.21 *double-deal*
have it easy 248.5 *be prosperous*; 265.17 *do easily*
have it from 693.15 *be informed*
have it in for 596.5 *dislike*; 594.14 *hate*; 651.18 *torment*
have it made 248.5 *be prosperous*
have it off 561.14 *have sex*; 593.29 *make love*
have it over one 121.8 *be superior*
have it soft 265.17 *do easily*
have its roots in 345.7 *follow from*
have joint possession **764.4**
have jurisdiction over **16.69**
have kittens 612.12 *be fearful*
have know 693.11 *inform*
have know-how 334.10 *be powerful*
have laws 12.13 *be governed*
have leisure **580.4**
have life 554.16 *live*
have little in common 116.5 *be dissimilar*
have little weight 415.9 *be light*
have long ears 504.15 *hear*
have losses 766.10 *have a financial loss*
have love for 593.23 *love*
have luck 248.6 *be fortunate*; 107.12 *take a chance*
have many dates 593.25 *be loved*
have mercy 627.14 *have pity!*
have mercy on 627.10 *show mercy*
have merit 235.9 *be worthy*
have misgivings 705.20 *doubt*
have mobility 300.13 *be in motion*
have money 781.12 *be rich*
have money coming in 765.12 *earn*
have money to burn 781.12 *be rich*
have morals 255.9 *be pure*
have more than enough 264.20 *be in difficulty*
haven 312.15 *destination*; 655.4 *place of confinement*; 252.2 *protection*; 301.3 *resting place*; 565.11 *retreat*
have natural talent 229.4 *tend*
have need of 135.7 *require*
have nerve 661.5 *defy*
have never felt better 259.5 *be healthy*
have nine lives 252.9 *be safe*; 554.16 *live*
have no affectations 646.4 *be naive*
have no alibi 806.8 *be guilty*
have no ambition 341.4 *not act*
have no answer 696.10 *be unexplained*
have no aspirations 618.16 *be mediocre*
have no bearing on 109.10 *be unrelated*
have no bounds 202.8 *have no limit*
have no censorship 250.14 *be free*
have no chance 335.6 *be powerless*; 238.7 *be useless*
have no choice 386.8 *be compelled*
have no clout 124.11 *be unimportant*
have no concern with 109.11 *be unconcerned*
have no conscience 809.5 *be impenitent*
have no control 335.6 *be powerless*
have no desire for 596.5 *dislike*
have no doubt 452.20 *be certain*
have no doubts about 450.7 *believe*
have no ear 504.15 *hear*
have no ear for 505.8 *be deaf*

have no end 279.5 *be eternal*
have no enjoyment from 620.7 *suffer boredom*
have no excuse 806.8 *be guilty*
have no existence 708.13 *be nothing*
have no faults 255.9 *be pure*
have no feelings 628.6 *be pitiless*; 423.10 *be tough*
have no fight left 388.3 *submit*
have no function 341.4 *not act*
have no grasp of 696.9 *find unintelligible*
have no guile 646.4, 805.10 *be naive*
have no guilt 805.8 *be innocent*
have no guts 614.4 *be a coward*
have no hand in 634.1 *avoid*
have no hang-ups 646.4 *be naive*
have no heart 628.6 *be pitiless*
have no heart for 596.5 *dislike*
have no hope 341.4 *not act*
have no inclination for 596.5 *dislike*
have no influence 335.6 *be powerless*
have no interest in 109.11 *be unconcerned*
have no issue 563.7 *be infertile*
have no law 16.74 *be lawless*
have no liability 758.11 *be exempt*
have no life 341.4 *not act*
have no liking for 596.5 *dislike*
have no limit 202.8
have no love for 594.14 *hate*
have no luck 249.9 *be in trouble*
have no manners 659.7 *be discourteous*
have no meaning 697.7 *be nonsense*
have no mercy 628.6, 651.19 *be pitiless*
have no money 249.10 *need money*
have no morals 618.14 *be careless*; 800.8 *be dishonourable*; 796.17 *be sexually immoral*
have no more 766.9 *lose*
have no objection 750.21 *be in accord*
have no offers 572.9 *be celibate*
have no offspring 563.7 *be infertile*
have no option 386.8 *be compelled*
have no pity 628.6 *be pitiless*
have no point 100.13 *be extraneous*
have no power 335.6 *be powerless*
have no prejudice 618.15 *be impartial*
have no prospects 782.12 *be poor*
have no pull 124.11 *be unimportant*
have no purpose 238.7 *be useless*
have no ready cash 786.9 *be unable to pay*
have no recollection of 463.13 *forget*
have no regard for 670.14 *disapprove*; 668.19 *disrespect*
have no regrets 809.5 *be impenitent*
have no relation to 100.13 *be extraneous*
have no relevance 100.13 *be extraneous*
have no remorse 809.5 *be impenitent*
have no resistance 335.6 *be powerless*
have no respect for 670.14 *disapprove*; 668.19 *disrespect*
have no responsibility 758.11 *be exempt*
have no say 335.6 *be powerless*
have no secrets 695.4 *be intelligible*; 738.4 *show oneself*
have no self-doubt 673.15 *be vain*
have no sex 572.10 *be continent*
have no shame 738.4 *show oneself*
have no sin 255.9 *be pure*
have no smell 501.6
have no solution 696.10 *be unexplained*
have no stomach for 614.4 *be a coward*; 637.6 *be unwilling*; 596.5 *dislike*
have no strength left 261.5 *be fatigued*
have no taste 497.7 *be tasteless*
have no taste for 618.12 *be indifferent*
have nothing in common 116.5 *be dissimilar*
have nothing on 122.9 *yield to*
have nothing to add 232.4 *complete*
have nothing to confess 805.8 *be innocent*
have nothing to declare 805.8 *be innocent*
have nothing to do 341.4 *not act*
have nothing to hide 805.8 *be innocent*
have no time for 659.7 *be discourteous*; 596.5 *dislike*; 668.19 *disrespect*
have no tricks 646.4 *be naive*
have no truck with 637.9 *not cooperate*
have nots 574.2 *the common people*
have no use 219.5 *be superfluous*; 238.7 *be useless*
have no use for 596.5 *dislike*; 350.5 *not use*
have no value 236.13 *be worthless*
have no weight 124.11 *be unimportant*
have occasion for 135.7 *require*
have odour 500.8
have offspring 561.11 *have young*
have on 551.34 *wear*
have one's birth 561.11 *have young*
have one's conviction overturned 389.5 *escape*
have one's doubts 453.18 *be uncertain*; 705.20 *doubt*
have one's eye on 617.12 *desire*; 756.11 *promise oneself*
have one's eyes opened 695.6 *understand*
have one's fill 232.5 *be complete*
have one's fling 342.12 *be active*; 250.19 *liberalize*
have one's foibles 804.16 *be wicked*
have one's hand in 485.10 *be skilful*
have one's hands full 342.13 *be busy*; 264.20 *be in difficulty*
have one's head 250.18 *have scope*
have one's head for 814.1 *punish*
have one's heart's desire 609.7 *be satisfied*
have one's knife in 596.6 *react against*
have one's nativity 554.18 *be born*
have one's nerves stretched 488.12 *awake*
have one's own way 635.15 *impose one's will*
have one's palm greased 813.13 *get paid*
have one's period 298.8 *be cyclic*; 560.22 *menstruate*
have one's plans ruined 604.4 *be disappointed*
have one's plate full 342.13 *be busy*
have one's pride 622.24 *be proud*
have one's reward 813.12 *be rewarded*
have one's say 707.17 *affirm*; 707.21 *be assertive*; 729.11 *speak*
have one's self-respect 622.24 *be proud*
have one's senses 488.11 *sense*
have one's way 250.16 *be independent*
have one's way with 593.29 *make love*; 796.20 *seduce*
have one's weak side 804.16 *be wicked*
have one too many 690.8 *get drunk*
have on offer 778.1 *sell*; 13.10 *trade with*
have on one's hands 219.5 *be superfluous*
have on one's plate 631.14 *behave towards*
have on the carpet 814.1 *punish*
have on the side 350.5 *not use*
have openness 308.22 *be open*
have over a barrel 396.18 *have authority*
have overall responsibility 579.2 *direct*
have passion for 595.7 *like*
have perfect pitch 504.15 *hear*
have permission 757.5 *be permitted*
have persistence 360.6 *retain*
have personal motives 683.6 *be selfish*
have physical strength 423.10 *be tough*
have pity 648.3 *be lenient*; 627.10 *show mercy*
have pity! 627.14
have pity for 627.8 *pity*
have play 250.18 *have scope*
have plenty of rope 250.18 *have scope*
have plenty of time 580.4 *have leisure*
have poor health 260.24 *be unhealthy*
have possession 46.15 *play offence*
have possibilities 756.10 *show potential*
have power 334.10 *be powerful*; 12.11 *govern*; 396.18 *have authority*
have power over 395.10 *be a prevailing influence*; 397.11 *have authority over*
have precedence 129.16 *take precedence*
have priority 123.7 *be important*; 129.16 *take precedence*
have progeny 561.11 *have young*
have prongs 425.14 *be sharp*
have prospects 283.10 *expect*
have pull 395.8 *influence*
have pulling power 395.8 *influence*
have quality 235.9 *be worthy*
have qualms 612.12 *be fearful*
have quick wits 425.17 *be mentally sharp*
have ready 243.4 *prepare for action*
have recourse 393.7 *resort*
have recourse to 349.4 *resort to*
have regard for 650.8 *be benevolent*
have regrets 808.4 *be penitent*
have regular wages 765.12 *earn*
have relevance 108.7 *relate to*
have repute 811.5
have reservations 451.8 *disbelieve*
have resilience 422.10 *be adaptable*
have resources 440.9 *own property*
have responsibility 579.2 *direct*
have room to breathe 250.18 *have scope*
have round 773.11 *be hospitable*
haversack 410.9 *baggage*
have saving grace 803.8 *be virtuous*
have scope 250.18
have scruples 637.6 *be unwilling*
have second sight 518.17 *imagine*
have second thoughts 443.14; 616.5 *be cautious*; 808.4 *be penitent*; 639.6 *hesitate*; 244.4 *reconsider*
have seen better days 556.17 *age*; 249.9 *be in trouble*; 245.1 *deteriorate*
have self-control 166.7 *limit*
have self-reliance 250.16 *be independent*
have self-restraint 166.7 *limit*
have sex 561.14; 593.29 *make love*
have sexual intercourse 561.14 *have sex*
have sharp wits 425.17 *be mentally sharp*
have simplicity 647.7 *be unadorned*
have small chance 107.12 *take a chance*
have someone on 700.28 *trick*
have someone's blessing 757.5 *be permitted*
have someone's ear 504.15 *hear*
have something extra 121.11 *get ahead*
have something in hand 121.11 *get ahead*
have something in reserve 121.11 *get ahead*
have some use 237.9 *be useful*
have sovereignty 85.17 *become a nation*
have spare time 580.4 *have leisure*
have stamina 334.10 *be powerful*
have staying power 334.10 *be powerful*
have sticky fingers 774.12 *steal*
have substance 440.9 *own property*
have success 246.6 *be successful*; 765.9 *gain*
have superiority 120.5 *be unequal*
have survivability 423.10 *be tough*
have sway 395.10 *be a prevailing influence*; 334.10 *be powerful*
have sway over 397.11 *have authority over*
have taped 579.1 *manage*
have taste 543.4 *be elegant*
have tea 557.24 *have a meal*
have teething troubles 378.9 *block*
have temerity 661.5 *defy*
have tenacity 423.10 *be tough*; 360.6 *retain*
have tenure of 763.7 *possess*
have the advantage 120.5 *be unequal*
have the appearance of 525.11 *appear*
have the audacity 660.22 *be rude*
have the best intentions 650.8 *be benevolent*; 805.8 *be innocent*
have the blarney 645.5 *be cunning*
have the blues 626.9 *be sullen*
have the brass neck 660.22 *be rude*
have the casting vote 395.10 *be a prevailing influence*; 344.12 *determine*
have the cheek 660.22 *be rude*
have the common touch 658.10 *be courteous*
have the curse 560.22 *menstruate*
have the deed for 763.7 *possess*
have the desired effect 239.6 *be convenient*
have the disadvantage 120.5 *be unequal*
have the ear of 395.8 *influence*
have the edge on 121.8 *be superior*
have the effect of 344.9 *be the cause of*
have the final say 706.18 *answer back*; 395.10 *be a prevailing influence*
have the freedom of 250.18 *have scope*
have the gall 660.22 *be rude*
have the golden touch 781.12 *be rich*
have the habit of 632.16 *have a habit*
have the hots for 796.17 *be sexually immoral*; 617.13 *like*
have the inside track 121.11 *get ahead*; 164.7 *have an advantage*
have the jump on 164.7 *have an advantage*
have the knack 797.19 *be good at*; 136.14 *be qualified*; 485.10 *be skilful*
have the know-how 396.22 *be an authority on*; 485.11 *be expert*
have the knowledge 485.11 *be expert*
have the last laugh 121.8 *be superior*
have the last word 706.18 *answer back*; 707.21 *be assertive*; 294.8 *delay*; 704.8 *refute*
have the law on 16.70 *litigate*
have the lion's share 121.11 *get ahead*
have the makings of 104.8 *be probable*
have the means 352.6 *find means*; 217.6 *have enough*
have the measure of 579.1 *manage*
have the Midas touch 765.14 *profit*
have the nerve 660.22 *be rude*
have the pip 626.9 *be sullen*
have the pole position 121.11 *get ahead*
have the right connections 395.8 *influence*
have the right touch 485.10 *be skilful*
have the run of 250.18 *have scope*
have the runs 560.16 *defecate*
have the same meaning 694.10 *mean*
have the say-so 396.18 *have authority*
have the shivers 494.10 *be cold*
have the talent for 334.10 *be powerful*
have the trick of 485.10 *be skilful*
have the upper hand 396.18 *have authority*
have the use of 349.5 *dispose of*
have the usufruct 349.5 *dispose of*
have the verdict read 16.71 *try a case*
have the vote 469.5 *vote*
have the whip hand 121.8 *be superior*; 396.18 *have authority*
have time for 768.5 *give*
have time to kill 620.7 *suffer boredom*
have time to spare 293.7 *be early*
have title to 763.7 *possess*
have to 386.8 *be compelled*
have to dinner 557.25 *provide food*
have to do with 340.4 *act*; 631.14 *behave towards*; 764.4 *have joint possession*; 108.7 *relate to*
have tone 422.8 *be elastic*
have too much 690.8 *get drunk*
have to one's name 440.9 *own property*
have to repay 784.7 *be in debt*
have to spare 349.5 *dispose of*
have trouble 249.9 *be in trouble*; 264.19 *have difficulty*
have two meanings 479.1 *be equivocal*
have under one's belt 253.13 *secure one's objective*
have under one's thumb 395.10 *be a prevailing influence*; 396.18 *have authority*
have understanding 477.16 *have insight*; 695.6 *understand*
have up 16.70 *litigate*
have virtue 799.6 *be honourable*; 255.9 *be pure*
have visions 4.20 *philosophize*
have visitors 560.22 *menstruate*
have vitality 334.10 *be powerful*
have wealth 781.12 *be rich*; 765.12 *earn*
have weight 414.12 *be heavy*
have what it takes 334.10 *be powerful*; 336.7 *be strong*; 640.9 *endure*
have withdrawal symptoms 691.10 *drug oneself*
have words 701.13 *argue*
have x-ray eyes 527.12 *make transparent*; 518.12 *see*
have young 561.11
have zest 338.2 *be full of vigour*
having 127.7 *including*; 763.8 *possessing*
having a closed mind 528.5 *unintelligent*
having a light touch 415.1 *light*
having and holding 763.8 *possessing*
having an excuse 714.13 *vindicable*
having a part 764.1 *joint possession*
having a prior engagement 288.15 *busy*
having a share 764.1 *joint possession*
having a weaker side 804.13 *venial*

having bad taste 497.6 *coarse*; 495.8 *tasteful*
having ears 504.12 *eared*
having flavour 495.7 *tasty*
having full play 250.11 *ranging*
having good taste 495.8 *tasteful*
having had it 582.18 *dying*
having had too much 690.1 *drunk*
having in view 482.11 *intending*
having it good 248.1 *prosperity*
having it off 593.5 *desire*
having meaning 694.6 *meaningful*
having motion 300.16 *moving*
having no case 16.64 *convicted*
having no effect **563.6**
having no legal protection 16.56 *unauthorized*
having no regrets 809.3 *impenitent*
having no remorse 809.3 *impenitent*
having no sorrow 809.3 *impenitent*
having nothing to eat 687.5 *fast*
having one's foibles 804.13 *venial*
having poor sight 519.9 *weak-sighted*
having possessions 763.8 *possessing*
having sense 694.6 *meaningful*
having tea 557.4 *eating meals*
having teeth 334.14 *operative*
having weight 414.1 *heavy*
havoc **357.5**; 441.4 *destruction*; 245.10 *impairment*; 381.14 *siege*
haw 325.8 *sidestep*
Hawes Water 88.4 *British lakes*
hawk 381.19 *attacker*; 72.5 *bird of prey*; 767.11 *dispose of property*; 518.2 *eye*; 633.11 *hunt*; 633.6 *hunter*; 586.6 *militarist*; 710.6 *request*; 560.20 *salivate*; 778.1 *sell*; 513.5 *sound hoarse*; 647.4 *strict person*
hawk about 740.13 *make public*
hawker 514.9 *crier*; 633.6 *hunter*; 778.11 *pedlar*
hawk-eyed 518.21 *seeing*
hawking 633.2 *chase*
hawkish 72.21 *avian*; 381.22 *militant*; 585.16 *warlike*
hawkishness 585.5 *bellicosity*
hawser 373.6 *line*; 50.3 *parts of a sailing boat*
hay 43.9 *animal feedstuff*; 557.8 *animal food*; 22.4 *historic dancing*
haybarn 43.7 *farm building*
haybox 493.4 *burner*
haycock 43.10 *farm tool*; 439.1 *store*
Hay Diet™ 557.6 *nutrition*
hay fever 260.1 *ill health*
hayfield 43.11 *farmland*
haylage 43.9 *animal feedstuff*
hayloft 43.7 *farm building*
haymaker 331.14 *sporting hit*
haymaking 43.5 *cultivation*; 292.3 *summer*
haymish 657.9 *familiar*
hayrack 43.10 *farm tool*
hayrick 376.27 *bundle*; 43.10 *farm tool*; 439.1 *store*
hayseed 564.5 *countryman*; 646.3 *naive person*; 87.12 *rural dweller*; 77.9 *seed*
haystack 376.27 *bundle*; 43.10 *farm tool*; 439.1 *store*
hay turner 43.10 *farm tool*
haywain 43.10 *farm tool*
haywire 408.18 *muddled*
hazard 65.2 *billiards play*; 107.1 *chance*; 254.5 *danger*; 254.10 *endanger*; 254.9 *face danger*; 378.2 *obstacle*; 453.22 *risk*; 107.12 *take a chance*; 379.1 *trap*; 453.15 *unreliability*
hazard a guess 476.5 *suppose*; 619.12 *wonder whether*
hazarding 254.5 *danger*
hazardous 378.14 *blocked*; 254.1 *dangerous*; 453.7 *unreliable*
hazardously 254.11 *dangerously*; 378.17 *in the way*; 453.26 *unreliably*
hazardousness 254.5 *danger*
hazard side 63.5 *real tennis*
haze 31.64 *fog*; 521.4 *invisibility*; 453.20 *make uncertain*; 31.34 *mist*; 524.2 *murk*; 528.7 *opaque thing*; 521.6 *that which makes invisible*; 527.8 *transparent thing*; 433.3 *wateriness*
hazel 534.1 *brown*
hazily 524.12 *dimly*; 453.25 *indeterminately*; 521.9 *invisibly*; 31.65 *meteorologically*; 161.6 *shapelessly*
haziness 453.14 *indeterminacy*; 521.4 *invisibility*; 524.2 *murk*; 528.6 *opaqueness*; 161.1 *shapelessness*; 31.35 *visibility*
hazy 696.4 *difficult*; 521.2 *difficult to see*; 31.56 *foggy*; 453.6 *indeterminate*; 541.10 *mottled*; 524.6 *murky*; 528.2 *shady*; 161.5 *shapeless*; 96.8 *unreal*
hazy recollection 463.3 *poor memory*
hazzan 7.8 *priest*
H-beam 38.27 *superstructure*
H-bomb 587.16 *bomb*
H-D curve 41.10 *graininess*
he 567.2 *male*
head **174.2**; 19.10 *art subject*; 167.10 *be in front*; 123.4 *bigwig*; 51.10 *bowling*; 442.7 *brain*; 475.10 *cards*; 409.6 *category*; 90.2 *channel*; 123.3 *chief thing*; 137.2 *class*; 400.5 *company leader*; 579.2 *direct*; 579.13 *director*; 691.4 *drug taker*; 400.9 *educational leader*; 334.4 *energy*; 173.8 *focal*; 173.5 *focus*; 66.2 *football play*; 130.30 *front*; 56.4 *golf club*; 51.2 *grip*; 741.12 *headline*; 717.6 *image*; 560.13 *lavatory*; 121.10 *lead*; 400.14 *master*; 400.12 *masterful*; 92.5 *peninsula*; 566.7 *person*; 396.10 *person of authority*; 130.21 *pioneer*; 66.4 *play soccer*; 129.15 *precede*; 356.7 *produce*; 19.12 *sculpture*; 794.2 *spoils*; 121.5 *superior*; 324.7 *take a direction*; 767.7 *toilet*; 174.5, 174.7 *top*; 433.17 *water cycle*
headache 491.2 *painful condition*; 264.4 *problem*; 260.3 *symptom*
headachy 260.22 *sick*
head-and-shoulders 167.6 *front*
head-and-shoulders above 121.12 *superior*
head-and-shoulders shot 167.2 *face*
head an institution 400.14 *master*
head a school 400.14 *master*
headband 373.10 *band*; 179.3 *circular thing*; 551.15 *headgear*
headboard 23.6 *bed*
head bobbing 67.1 *swimming*
head boy 121.5 *superior*
headcase 118.10 *eccentric*; 461.7 *insane person*
head coach 48.2 *baseball player*; 49.2 *basketball player*; 46.2 *football player*
head cold 501.1 *odourlessness*; 260.9 *respiratory disease*
head count 210.3 *count*; 220.6 *list of names*
head cushion 65.4 *carom*
head doctor 461.10 *psychiatrist*
headdress 551.15 *headgear*; 7.11 *vestment*
headed 66.5 *soccer*; 174.6 *topped*
headed for 324.14 *directed*; 452.5 *inevitable*
header 40.19 *computing terms*; 305.5 *dive*; 305.4 *fall*; 38.26 *masonry*
header forward straight 67.6 *diving*
header forward with tuck 67.6 *diving*
head first 615.6 *rashly*; 380.10 *violently*
head for 446.18 *aim*; 323.9 *navigate*; 393.7 *resort*; 324.7 *take a direction*
head foremost 380.10 *violently*
headgear **551.15**
head guard 384.6 *protective clothing*
head honcho 400.5 *company leader*; 396.10 *person of authority*; 121.5 *superior*
head-hunter 633.6 *hunter*; 382.10 *killer*
head-hunting 382.24 *murderous*
headily 500.10 *odorously*
heading 324.2 *bearing*; 721.2 *brief description*; 409.6 *category*; 137.2 *class*; 743.7 *flag*; 322.5 *flight*; 66.2 *football play*; 174.2 *head*
heading for 283.14 *in the future*
heading up 579.17 *managerial*; 50.1 *sailing*
head in the clouds 472.3 *absent-mindedness*; 463.8 *oblivious*; 477.6 *reverie*
head in the sand 341.1 *inaction*
head into 130.18 *make a beginning*
head into the wind 323.9 *navigate*
headlamp 522.6 *electric light*
headland 43.11 *farmland*; 92.5 *peninsula*; 185.2 *projection*
headless 205.11 *partial*; 212.7 *reduced*
headlight 522.6 *electric light*
headline **741.12**; 738.1 *display*; 740.3 *journalism*; 123.8 *make important*; 693.17 *newsworthy*; 740.16 *publicize*
head linesman 46.2 *football player*
headlock 360.1 *retention*; 52.5 *wrestling*
headlong 262.3 *hasty*; 615.4 *rash*; 615.6 *rashly*; 332.1 *swift*; 332.14 *swiftly*; 380.10 *violently*
headlong plunge 332.9 *acceleration*
headlong rush 332.9 *acceleration*
head louse 76.3 *pest*
headman 579.13 *director*; 400.3 *leader*; 58.9 *play hockey*
headmanning 58.8 *hockey*
headmanning the puck 58.3 *ice hockey*
headmaster 579.13 *director*; 400.9 *educational leader*; 6.4 *educator*; 396.10 *person of authority*; 121.5 *superior*
headmistress 400.9 *educational leader*; 6.4 *educator*; 396.10 *person of authority*; 121.5 *superior*
headmost 121.14 *best*; 129.12 *primary*
head nurse 35.16 *nurse*
head of department 400.9 *educational leader*; 15.6 *employer*
head off 481.3 *deflect*; 364.3 *fend off*; 364.1 *repel*
head office 577.1 *workshop*
head of pressure 433.17 *water cycle*
head of sixth-form 400.9 *educational leader*
head of state 579.13 *director*; 400.3 *leader*; 397.6 *person in command*
head of the household 579.13 *director*; 564.3 *householder*
head-on 113.24 *discordant*
head-on collision 331.12 *collision*
head over heels 232.9 *completely*; 192.4 *inversely*; 408.18 *muddled*; 307.13 *round*
head-over-heels 192.2 *inverted*
head patting 742.3 *gesture*
headphones 504.9 *audio device*; 769.8 *receiver*; 692.9 *telephone*
headpiece 174.2 *head*
head pin 51.4 *bowling*
headquarter 173.9 *centre*
headquarters 173.4 *centre of activity*; 584.1 *military affairs*; 484.7 *planning*
headrest 413.4 *rest*
headroom 141.6 *available space*; 146.1 *interval*
headsail 50.3 *parts of a sailing boat*
heads and tails 113.3 *opposites*
head scanner 394.14 *hospital*
headscarf 551.15 *headgear*
headset 504.9 *audio device*; 769.8 *receiver*; 692.9 *telephone*
headship 121.2 *leadership*; 396.5 *position of authority*
headshrinker 394.15 *healer*; 36.30, 461.10 *psychiatrist*
headsman 814.17 *punisher*
headsman's axe 814.16 *instrument of execution*
head spot 65.4 *carom*; 65.6 *pool*
headstand 192.1 *inversion*
head start 121.3, 164.4 *advantage*; 293.1 *earliness*
headstock 307.4 *axle*
heads together 713.2 *consultation*
headstone 174.3 *architectural summit*; 583.4 *funeral objects*; 20.9 *miscellaneous architectural features*
head straight on 324.7 *take a direction*
headstream 90.2 *channel*
head string 65.4 *carom*; 65.6 *pool*
headstrong 588.6 *anarchic*; 459.5 *foolish*; 641.1 *obstinate*; 264.14 *troublesome*; 380.6 *violent*; 635.8 *wilful*
headstrongness 267.2 *tenacity*
heads will roll 814.24 *string him up!*
head teacher 400.9 *educational leader*; 6.4 *educator*
head-to-wind 50.10 *sailing*
head up 579.2 *direct*; 129.15 *precede*; 50.15 *sail*
head waiter 401.3 *attendant*; 436.4 *caterer*
headwaters 90.2 *channel*; 344.2 *source*
headway 765.2 *augmentation*; 141.6 *available space*; 302.10 *forward motion*; 244.5 *improvement*; 300.3 *motion towards*
headwind 434.4 *air flow*; 347.2 *counteracting thing*; 322.5 *flight*; 31.15 *wind direction*
headwork 443.2 *intellectual exercise*
heady 588.6 *anarchic*; 502.4 *fragrant*; 690.6 *intoxicating*; 500.5 *odorous*; 336.12 *strong to the senses*
heady scent 500.1 *odour*
heal 393.6 *cure*; 259.7 *make healthy*; 749.4 *pacify*; 35.19 *practise medicine*; 394.19 *remedy*
heal-all 394.1 *remedy*
healed 393.15 *cured*; 259.1 *healthy*
healer **35.12**; **394.15**; 393.12 *repairer*
healing 394.11 *medical art*; 35.2 *natural medicine*; 393.11 *recuperation*; 394.17 *remedial*; 393.16 *restorative*; 35.25 *therapeutic*
healing agent 37.3 *drug*
healing art 394.13 *therapy*
healing gift 394.1 *remedy*
healing over 393.11 *recuperation*
healing quality 394.1 *remedy*
healing touch 394.11 *medical art*
heal itself 393.6 *cure*
heal over 393.6 *cure*
Health 259
health **259.3**; 558.2 *drink*; 160.6 *nature*; 257.2 *salubrity*; 601.6 *tribute*; 338.1 *vigour*; 235.6 *worth*
health and safety representative 15.7 *employee*
health and strength 259.3 *health*
health and wealth 248.1 *prosperity*
health care **35.6**; 35.1 *medicine*; 650.3 *welfare*
health centre 35.10 *hospital*
health club 257.1 *hygiene*
health diet 687.1 *fasting*
health education 35.6 *health care*
health farm 257.1 *hygiene*
health food 557.7 *food*; 257.2 *salubrity*
health-food restaurant 557.15 *eating place*
health-food shop 557.17 *food shop*
healthful **259.2**; 257.4 *hygienic*
healthfully 259.8 *healthily*; 257.7 *hygienically*
healthfulness **259.4**; 257.2 *salubrity*
health-giving 259.2 *healthful*; 257.4 *hygienic*; 394.17 *remedial*
healthily **259.8**; 160.13 *formatively*; 257.7 *hygienically*
healthiness **336.2**; 797.8 *good*; 259.3 *health*; 257.2 *salubrity*
health inspector 257.3 *hygienist*
health insurance 253.1 *protection*; 392.4 *social assistance*
health officer 35.11 *doctor*
health promotion 35.6 *health care*
health resort 257.1 *hygiene*
health salts 394.6 *purgative*
health spa 257.1 *hygiene*
health visitor 35.16 *nurse*
healthy **259.1**; 801.12 *all right*; 158.15 *big*; 393.15 *cured*; 797.1 *good*; 257.4 *hygienic*; 338.5 *invigorating*; 160.12 *on form*; 336.9 *physically strong*; 204.8 *sound*; 338.4 *vigorous*; 235.4 *worthwhile*
healthy diet 257.2 *salubrity*
healthy eating 557.6 *nutrition*
healthy food 557.7 *food*
healthy hue 529.9 *complexion*
healthy state 259.3 *health*
heap 765.11 *acquire*; 765.3 *acquisition*; 376.37 *assemble*; 320.16 *car*; 203.2 *certain amount*; 158.7, 376.26 *mass*; 205.7 *piece*; 439.1, 439.6 *store*
heap abuse upon 712.6 *vilify*
heaped 376.47 *collected*; 439.7 *stored*
heaped cloud 31.20 *cloud appearance*
heaped up 374.9 *assembled*
heaping coals of fire 385.1 *retaliation*
heap on 211.6 *add*
heaps 208.3 *profuseness*
heaps of money 780.3 *fortune*; 781.6 *money*
heap up 374.5 *combine*
hear **504.15**; 693.15 *be informed*; 464.11 *judge*; 705.17 *question*; 488.11 *sense*
hearable **504.14**; 507.7 *heard*
hearably 504.17 *aurally*
hear a case 16.69 *have jurisdiction over*; 16.76 *judge*; 16.71 *try a case*
hear a cause 16.69 *have jurisdiction over*; 16.71 *try a case*
hear a complaint 16.69 *have jurisdiction over*
hear both sides 801.14 *be fair*
heard **507.7**; 692.34 *communicated*; 769.13 *received*
heard of 455.10 *known*
hearer **504.2**; 769.5 *recipient*
hear from 504.15 *hear*
hear hear! **504.18**; 669.27 *bravo!*
Hearing 504
hearing **504.1**; 504.11 *aural*; 554.4 *biological function*; 579.7 *council*; 16.7 *legal trial*; 705.3 *questionnaire*; 448.2 *rehearsal*; 488.1 *sensation*
hearing aid 504.9 *audio device*; 505.1 *deafness*; 504.7 *ear attachments*; 507.4 *sound maker*; 28.18 *source of sound*
hearing distance 504.1 *hearing*

hearing-impaired 505.4 *deaf*
hearing impairment 505.1 *deafness*
hearing loss 505.1 *deafness*
hearing of evidence 16.7 *legal trial*
hearing specialist 504.6 *otology*
hearing test 35.7 *diagnosis*
hearken 504.15 *hear*
hearkener 504.2 *hearer*
hear of 504.15 *hear*
hear on the grapevine 504.15 *hear*
hear out 504.15 *hear*
hearsay 222.7 *circumstantial*; 740.1 *publication*; 504.8 *something heard*
hearsay evidence 716.5 *legal evidence*; 504.8 *something heard*
hearse 583.4 *funeral objects*
hear sentence 16.72 *stand trial*
heart 69.3 *card game terms*; 173.1 *centre*; 123.3 *chief thing*; 99.2 *essential content*; 172.5 *inner nature*; 172.2 *inside*; 172.4, 406.3 *insides*; 554.3 *life requirements*; 25.31 *offal*; 356.7 *produce*; 590.8 *seat of feelings*
heartache 602.1 *sorrow*
heart and soul 232.9 *completely*; 204.11 *wholly*
heart attack 260.10 *cardiovascular disease*; 335.4 *disability*
heartbeat 298.5 *regular thing*; 326.2 *vibration*
heartbreak 602.1 *sorrow*
heartbreaker 567.7 *libertine*; 593.9 *lover*
heartbreaking 602.7 *distressing*; 627.7 *pitiful*
heartbroken 604.9 *disappointed*; 602.5 *sad*
heartburn 260.8 *indigestion*; 629.1 *jealousy*; 491.2 *painful condition*
heartburning 629.1 *jealousy*; 624.1 *resentment*
heart condition 260.10 *cardiovascular disease*
heart disease 260.10 *cardiovascular disease*; 260.4 *disease*
hear tell 504.15 *hear*
hear tell of 504.15 *hear*
hearten 598.6 *bring cheer*; 613.17 *give courage*; 338.3 *invigorate*; 392.19 *support*
heartening 610.14 *cheering*; 613.6 *encouragement*; 613.14 *encouraging*; 392.32 *supportive*
heart failure 260.10 *cardiovascular disease*
heartfelt 156.9 *deep-seated*; 590.14 *emotive*
heartfelt apology 808.1 *penitence*
hearth 493.6 *fire*; 565.3 *home*; 252.5 *refuge*
hearth and home 565.3 *home*
hear the call 480.18 *be persuaded*
hear the case 464.11 *judge*
hear things 504.15 *hear*; 96.13 *imagine*
hearth rug 550.9 *floor covering*
hearthstone 256.9 *cleaning agent*; 493.6 *fire*
heartily 336.15 *acutely*; 160.13 *formatively*; 259.8 *healthily*; 569.17 *in friendship*; 576.12 *laboriously*; 654.18 *sociably*
heartiness 569.1 *friendship*; 259.3 *health*
heartland 172.3 *inland*; 86.6 *regions*
heartless 651.12 *callous*; 809.3 *impenitent*; 592.1 *insensitive*; 418.4 *mentally hard*; 628.4 *pitiless*
heartlessly 651.20 *malevolently*; 628.7 *pitilessly*; 592.8 *unfeelingly*
heartlessness 651.3 *callousness*; 489.313 *heedlessness*; 592.3 *insensitiveness*; 628.1 *pitilessness*
heart-lung machine 394.14 *hospital*
heart of flint 651.3 *callousness*; 628.1 *pitilessness*
heart of gold 650.1 *benevolence*
heart of marble 651.3 *callousness*
heart of oak 613.7 *courageous person*; 418.7 *hard substance*
heart of stone 651.3 *callousness*; 809.1 *impenitence*; 628.1 *pitilessness*
heart of the matter 123.3 *chief thing*; 447.1 *topic*
heart pain 261.7 *fatigue*; 491.2 *painful condition*
heart-rending 627.7 *pitiful*
heart rot 44.12 *pests and diseases*; 79.10 *tree disease*
heart's blood 554.3 *life requirements*
heart's desire 482.6 *objective*
heartsmitten 593.19 *enamoured*
hearts of oak 638.16 *fortitude*
heart-stopping 254.2 *unsafe*
heart surgeon 35.13 *medical specialist*
heart surgery 35.9, 394.12 *surgery*
heart-throb 593.9 *lover*; 326.2 *vibration*
heart-to-heart 734.2 *chat*; 738.15 *open*
heart trouble 260.10 *cardiovascular disease*
heart urchin 75.3 *echinoderm*
heart-warming 598.2 *cheering*; 490.6 *pleasant*; 493.12 *warm-hearted*
heartwood 418.7 *hard substance*; 79.3 *timber*; 23.12 *wood*
hearty 569.8 *friendly*; 259.1 *healthy*; 323.7 *nautical person*; 160.12 *on form*; 654.15 *sociable*; 489.5 *unfeeling person*
hearty assent 750.7 *consent*
hearty eater 557.18 *eater*; 688.4 *glutton*
hearty thanks 671.2 *thanks*
hearty welcome 654.9 *welcome*
hear voices 504.15 *hear*
Heat 493
heat 28.35; **31.23**; **493.1**; 624.4 *anger*; 493.14 *be hot*; 28.2 *classical physics*; 25.55 *cook*; 428.14 *desert*; 590.4 *emotion*; 334.4 *energy*; 334.12 *generate power*; 418.9 *harden*; 205.3 *stage*; 47.1 *track events*
heat capacity 28.36 *heat flow*
heated 493.13; 590.13 *passionate*; 380.6 *violent*
heatedly 624.18 *angrily*
heated pool 67.7 *swimming pool*
heated up 493.13 *heated*
heat-engine cycle 38.13 *engine cycle*
heater 493.3; 28.35 *heat*; 334.6 *source of energy*
heat exchange 28.36 *heat flow*
heat exchanger 334.6 *source of energy*
heat exhaustion 493.5 *hot weather*
heat flow 28.36
heat flow rate 28.36 *heat flow*
heath 81.2 *grassland*; 92.6 *lowland*
heat haze 493.5 *hot weather*; 31.34 *mist*
Heathcliff and Cathy 593.10 *lovers*
heathcock 72.10 *male bird*
heathen 451.5 *disbeliever*; 451.6 *disbelieving*; 9.6 *idolater*; 9.10 *idolatrous*
heathenism 9.2 *idolatry*; 451.4 *unbelief*
heathenize 9.8 *idolatrize*
heathenry 9.2 *idolatry*
heather 540.3 *purple thing*
heathering 43.5 *cultivation*
heath hen 72.11 *female bird*
Heath Robinson 477.11 *fantastical*
heating 493.9 *hot*
heating device 28.35 *heat*
heating effect 28.40
heating element 493.3 *heater*
heating system 28.35 *heat*
heat lamp 493.6 *fire*
heat measurement 493.2
heat-proof 494.9 *heat-resistant*
heat rash 493.5 *hot weather*; 260.13 *skin disease*
heat-resistant 494.9
heat retention 359.1 *preservation*
heat-seeking missile 330.8 *missile*
heatstroke 493.5 *hot weather*
heat the boiler 243.4 *prepare for action*
heat through 493.14 *be hot*
heat transfer 31.9 *atmospheric process*; 28.36 *heat flow*
heat transport 31.9 *atmospheric process*
heat-treat 418.9 *harden*
heat-treated 418.3 *hardened*
heat treatment 394.13 *therapy*
heat unit 493.2 *heat measurement*
heat up 493.14 *be hot*; 593.25 *be loved*; 25.55 *cook*; 213.5 *make bigger*
heat wave 31.23 *heat*; 493.5 *hot weather*; 326.5 *wave*
heat with solar power 437.11 *fuel*
heave 91.10 *billow*; 331.13 *blow*; 576.4 *exertion*; 331.1 *impel*; 362.2, 362.11 *pull*; 366.1 *raise*; 366.6 *raising*; 330.5, 330.23, 331.4 *throw*; 316.12 *transport*; 326.9 *vibrate*; 371.15 *vomit*; 91.3 *wave*; 576.6 *work*
heave a brick 381.7 *stone*
heaved 366.11 *raised*
heave in sight 520.9 *appear*; 525.12 *become visible*
Heaven 756.4 *promised land*
heaven 8.11; 21.18 *auditorium*; 597.2 *fun*; 283.3 *future condition*; 154.8 *high thing*; 490.5 *idealized pleasure*; 554.5 *life cycle*; 279.3 *life without end*; 101.1 *nonmaterial world*; 395.2 *occult influence*; 241.6 *pleasantness*; 301.3 *resting place*; 174.1 *summit*; 582.14 *the spiritual world*
heaven be praised 671.9 *thank you!*
heavenly 8.14; 29.36 *astronomical*; 597.5 *delightful*; 101.8 *nonmaterial*; 241.1 *pleasant*; 235.1 *worthy*
heavenly being 8.6 *angel*
heavenly body 29.10 *star*
heavenly host 8.6 *angel*
heavenly kingdom 101.1 *nonmaterial world*
heaven on earth 490.5 *idealized pleasure*
heavens 141.2 *empty space*; 154.8 *high thing*; 174.1 *summit*; 29.3 *universe*
heaven-sent 797.1 *good*; 287.6 *timely*
heavenward 324.10 *clockwise*; 154.20 *higher*; 304.26 *up*
heave out 371.1 *expel*
heaver 330.14 *thrower*
heave the lead 156.14 *deepen*; 323.9 *navigate*
heave to 50.15, 323.10 *sail*
heavier-than-air craft 322.8 *aircraft*
heavily 414.16; 620.8 *boringly*; 416.10 *densely*; 301.10 *motionlessly*; 203.7 *quantitatively*
heavily built 158.17 *stocky*
Heaviness 414
heaviness 414.4; 620.1 *boredom*; 724.3 *inelegance*; 203.1 *quantity*; 343.9 *sleep*; 158.6 *squatness*; 152.5 *thickness*
heaving 50.10 *sailing*; 330.3 *throwing*; 362.1 *traction*; 371.23 *vomiting*
heaving line 50.3 *parts of a sailing boat*
heaving stomach 596.4 *sign of dislike*
Heaviside layer 434.3 *atmospheric layers*
heavy 414.1; 223.7 *attendant*; 158.10 *big person*; 620.4 *boring*; 31.49 *cloudy*; 68.10 *curling*; 416.6 *dense*; 264.10 *difficult*; 414.16 *heavily*; 31.52 *humid*; 123.5 *important*; 724.8 *inelegant*; 339.5 *inert*; 576.11 *laborious*; 741.5 *mass communication*; 336.6 *muscleman*; 511.2 *nonresonant*; 91.7 *oceanic*; 203.6 *quantitative*; 31.53 *rainy*; 21.23 *role*; 301.5 *sedentary*; 726.5 *serious*; 158.17 *stocky*; 152.1 *thick*; 430.8 *viscous*
heavy-armed 384.30 *defended*
heavy-armed soldier 586.8 *soldier*
heavy artillery 587.11 *guns*
heavy as a horse 414.1 *heavy*
heavy as lead 414.1 *heavy*
heavy bombardment 381.12 *military attack*
heavy bomber 586.31 *military aircraft*
heavy brigade 586.16 *army unit*
heavy build 158.6 *squatness*
heavy cavalry 586.19 *cavalry*
heavy clothing 62.4 *climbing equipment*
heavy dragoon 586.20 *cavalryman*; 59.15 *horse person*
heavy drinker 558.12 *drinker*
heavy-duty 336.13 *strengthened*
heavy eater 557.18 *eater*; 688.4 *glutton*
heavy-eyed 261.1 *fatigued*; 343.4 *not awake*
heavy father 21.23 *role*
heavy food 557.7 *food*
heavy-footed 486.3 *clumsy*; 544.7 *graceless*
heavy-going 264.11 *rough*
heavy gun 587.11 *guns*
heavy-handed 486.3 *clumsy*; 544.7 *graceless*; 492.10 *handed*; 724.8 *inelegant*; 414.3 *ponderous*; 647.8 *severe*; 489.6 *unfeeling*; 380.6 *violent*
heavy-handedly 492.15 *insensitively*; 647.11 *severely*
heavy-handedness 724.3 *inelegance*; 489.1 *lack of feeling*; 486.8 *unskilfulness*
heavyhearted 602.5 *sad*
heavyheartedness 602.1 *sorrow*
heavy hog 43.8 *livestock*
heavy industry 356.2 *manufacture*
heavy-laden 378.14 *blocked*; 232.8 *full*
heavy-lidded 261.1 *fatigued*
heavy metal 32.6 *chemical element*; 587.11 *guns*; 18.9 *popular music*
heavy scene 123.2 *important matter*
heavy sea 327.13 *tempest*; 91.3 *wave*
heavyset 158.17 *stocky*
heavy sledding 264.3 *difficult task*
heavy sleep 343.9 *sleep*
heavy sleeper 339.2 *inert person*
heavy socks 62.4 *climbing equipment*
heavy sound 511.5 *dull sound*
heavy swell 91.3 *wave*
heavy traffic 342.6 *business*
heavy water 433.1 *water*
heavyweight 586.3 *athlete*; 123.4 *bigwig*; 52.4 *boxer*; 52.3 *boxing weight divisions*; 52.14 *combat*; 158.12 *fat person*; 414.1 *heavy*; 643.7 *serious person*; 414.7 *weighing*
heavyweight champion 52.4 *boxer*
heavy wet snow 68.1 *skiing*
heavy wine 558.9 *wine*
heavy with 562.5 *fertile*; 561.16 *reproductive*
heavy woman 21.23 *role*
heavy work 576.1 *work*
hebdomadal 298.12 *cyclic*
hebdomadary 298.12 *cyclic*
hebephrenia 36.11, 461.5 *psychosis*
hebetude 426.7 *dullness*; 528.9 *stupidity*; 457.2 *unintelligence*
hebetudinous 426.3 *dull*
Hebraist 284.11 *antiquarian*
Hebrew 7.16 *denominational*; 566.4 *modern human*
Hebrew alphabet 5.14 *alphabet*
Hecate 11.4 *witch*
hecatomb 357.5 *havoc*; 752.6 *offering*
heckle 378.8 *hinder*; 670.23 *show disapproval*; 668.25 *taunt*
heckler 378.7 *hinderer*; 113.11 *opposer*
heck of a lot 208.3 *profuseness*
hectic 342.19 *busy*; 535.2 *red-faced*
hectic flush 535.5 *redness*
hectograph copy 111.4 *duplicate*
hector 727.6 *exaggerator*; 660.26 *oppress*
hectoring 612.4 *intimidation*
hedge 616.5 *be cautious*; 479.1 *be equivocal*; 634.7 *be evasive*; 372.6 *boundary*; 166.4 *boundary marker*; 189.7 *deviate*; 165.3 *enclosing thing*; 736.13 *equivocate*; 43.11 *farmland*; 384.18 *fence*; 44.3 *ornamental garden*; 702.13 *quibble*
hedge clipper 438.3 *garden tool*
hedgecutter 43.10 *farm tool*
hedgehog 425.8 *sharp-pointed thing*
hedgehop 322.10 *fly*
hedgehopping 322.5 *flight*
hedge-laying 43.5 *cultivation*
hedge one's bets 616.5 *be cautious*; 252.9 *be safe*; 746.6 *make conditions*
hedgerow 165.3 *enclosing thing*; 43.11 *farmland*
hedgerow tree 79.1 *tree*
hedge trimmer 44.6 *garden tool*
hedging 43.5 *cultivation*; 189.5 *devious*; 189.3 *deviousness*; 702.4, 702.9 *quibbling*
hedonism 688.1 *gluttony*; 490.1 *physical pleasure*; 241.7 *pleasure*; 4.7 *school of thought*; 686.1 *self-indulgence*
hedonist 4.11 *follower of a doctrine*; 241.12 *pleasure-loving person*; 490.3 *pleasure-seeker*; 686.5 *self-indulgent person*
hedonistic 688.6 *gluttonous*; 4.14 *of a philosophy*; 490.7 *pleased*; 241.5 *pleasure-loving*; 686.6 *self-indulgent*
hedonize 688.5 *be greedy*
hedontics 36.1 *psychology*
heebie-jeebies 327.1 *agitation*; 690.16 *alcoholism*; 488.3 *stimulus*
heed 665.10 *be careful*; 471.3, 665.1 *carefulness*; 616.1 *caution*; 504.15 *hear*; 504.1 *hearing*; 663.5 *obey*; 471.12 *scrutinize*; 667.18 *show respect*
heedful 665.9 *careful*; 616.4 *cautious*; 471.7 *watchful*
heedfully 616.7 *cautiously*
heedfulness 616.1 *caution*
heeding 504.1 *hearing*
heedless 618.8 *careless*; 459.5 *foolish*; 262.3 *hasty*; 472.7 *inattentive*; 651.15 *inconsiderate*; 666.4 *negligent*; 615.4 *rash*; 489.6 *unfeeling*; 672.3 *ungrateful*; 505.5 *unhearing*; 463.10 *unthinking*
heedlessly 618.18 *carelessly*; 472.14 *inattentively*; 463.16 *obliviously*; 262.7, 615.6 *rashly*; 672.7 *ungratefully*
heedlessness 489.313; 618.2 *carelessness*; 505.1 *deafness*; 459.1 *folly*; 472.1 *inattention*; 651.6 *inconsiderateness*; 666.1 *negligence*; 615.1 *rashness*; 463.4 *unthinkingness*
heed the call 483.8 *be motivated*
hee-haw 515.1 *animal cry*
heel 120.5 *be unequal*; 325.1 *deviate*; 175.2 *foot*; 56.4 *golf club*; 168.1 *rear*; 393.1 *repair*; 50.15 *sail*
heel-hook 62.3 *climbing technique*; 62.9 *mountaineer*
heel in 44.15 *cultivate*
heeling 393.8 *repair*; 64.3 *rugby play*; 64.6 *rugger*; 120.3 *unequal*

heel over 323.10 *sail*
heel piece 168.1 *rear*
heels over head 307.13 *round*
heeltaps 215.2 *residue*
heel the ball 64.5 *play rugby*
heft 414.4 *heaviness;* 366.1 *raise;* 414.15 *weigh*
heftiness 414.4 *heaviness;* 158.6 *squatness*
hefting 414.7 *weighing*
hefty 264.10 *difficult;* 414.1 *heavy;* 158.17 *stocky*
Hegelian 101.7 *believer in a nonmaterial world;* 4.11 *follower of a doctrine;* 101.10 *idealistic;* 4.14 *of a philosophy*
Hegelian dialectic 4.5 *philosophical argument*
Hegelianism 101.5 *idealism;* 4.7 *school of thought*
hegemonic 121.14 *best;* 579.17 *managerial;* 334.13 *powerful*
hegemony 396.1 *authority;* 121.2 *leadership;* 395.3 *personal influence;* 334.1 *power*
Hegira 313.7 *departure*
he-goat 567.16 *male animal*
Heidelberg man 296.7 *ancient people*
heifer 568.14 *female animal;* 71.18 *female mammal;* 43.8 *livestock*
Height 154
height 154.1; 366.8; 209.1 *degree;* 148.4 *length;* 27.37 *line;* 203.1 *quantity;* 26.4, 158.1 *size;* 28.7, 141.1 *space;* 121.4 *summit*
heighten 607.6 *aggravate;* 727.8 *enlarge;* 190.5, 213.5 *make bigger;* 366.3 *promote;* 154.17 *raise*
heighten awareness 488.13 *arouse sensation*
heightened 607.4 *aggravated;* 190.7 *bigger;* 727.13 *enlarged;* 213.7 *increased*
heightener 488.3 *stimulus*
heightening 607.1 *aggravation;* 727.2 *enlargement;* 190.8 *growing;* 190.1 *growth;* 213.1 *increase*
height measure 154.5
height of perfection 230.3 *perfection*
heights 154.2; 89.1 *mountain;* 92.7 *upland*
height-weight ratio 1.10 *measurement*
heinous 236.3 *bad;* 532.5 *black-hearted;* 651.11 *cruel;* 16.60 *offending;* 806.7 *sinful;* 804.11 *wicked*
heinousness 236.9 *badness;* 651.2 *cruelness;* 804.1 *wickedness*
heir 769.6 *beneficiary;* 474.4 *expectant person;* 765.7 *gainer;* 215.6 *person remaining;* 392.12 *recipient;* 289.5 *successor;* 781.10 *wealthy person*
heir apparent 769.6 *beneficiary;* 289.5 *successor*
heir-at-law 769.6 *beneficiary*
heirdom 763.1 *possession*
heiress 769.6 *beneficiary;* 474.4 *expectant person;* 765.7 *gainer;* 289.5 *successor;* 781.10 *wealthy person*
heirloom 296.5 *old thing;* 440.5 *personal estate;* 769.1 *receiving;* 3.11 *relic*
heir presumptive 769.6 *beneficiary;* 289.5 *successor*
heirs 283.2 *future generation*
heirship 763.1 *possession;* 769.1 *receiving*
heir to a fortune 781.10 *wealthy person*
Heisenberg uncertainty principle 28.81 *causality*
heist 366.1 *raise;* 774.12 *steal;* 773.10 *take away;* 773.3 *taking away;* 774.3 *theft*
Hel 8.12 *hell*
held 410.20 *containing;* 58.8 *hockey;* 763.9 *possessed;* 360.10 *retained;* 252.6 *safe;* 228.9 *stable;* 439.7 *stored*
held back 378.13 *hindering;* 166.5 *limited*
held ball 49.4 *playing terms*
held in 360.10 *retained*
held in low esteem 668.17 *unrespected*
held in respect 667.12 *respected*
held position 57.6 *pommel horse*
held together 750.14 *conforming*
held up 294.10; 333.7 *delayed;* 378.13 *hindering*
Heley 56.5 *golf ball*
heliacal 29.36 *astronomical;* 306.10 *circular*
helical 180.4 *convolutional;* 27.81 *curvilinear*
helical gear 38.7 *gear*
helically 180.8 *circularly*
Helicon 17.13 *poetic genius*
helicopter 322.8 *aircraft;* 586.31 *military aircraft*
helicopter gunship 586.31 *military aircraft*
helicopter skiing 68.1 *skiing*
heliocentric 29.36 *astronomical;* 173.6 *central*
heliocentrically 29.39 *astronomically*
heliograph 692.8 *data transmission;* 742.4 *signal*
heliographer 742.8 *signer*
heliographic 742.16 *signalling*
heliolater 9.6 *idolater*
heliolatrous 9.10 *idolatrous*
heliolatry 9.2 *idolatry*
heliometer 26.8 *meter*
heliometric 26.16 *micrometric*
heliometry 26.2 *micrometry*
Helios 29.15 *sun*
heliostat 29.24 *telescope*
heliotrope 540.6 *purple;* 540.3 *purple thing*
heliport 312.15 *destination*
helium 366.10 *elevator;* 330.13 *fuel;* 415.7 *light thing*
helium balloon 322.8 *aircraft;* 366.10 *elevator;* 432.13 *gas balloon*
helium-neon laser 28.26 *laser*
helix 27.40 *curve;* 306.1 *orbital motion*
hell 8.12; 249.1 *adversity;* 408.5 *confusion;* 156.4 *deep thing;* 283.3 *future condition;* 493.8 *hot place;* 101.1 *nonmaterial world;* 491.1 *pain;* 582.14 *the spiritual world;* 804.8 *wicked place*
Helladic 296.14 *historic*
hellbent 459.5 *foolish;* 482.11 *intending;* 638.1 *resolute*
hell-born 8.16 *devilish*
hellcat 380.4 *violent creature;* 651.9 *vixen*
hell-driver 332.13 *swift person*
Hellenic 5.11 *family of languages;* 296.14 *historic*
Hellenistic 3.15, 296.14 *historic;* 19.29 *realist*
Hellenistic Age 3.10 *past age*
Hellespont 92.9 *inlet*
hellfire 283.3 *future condition;* 493.8 *hot place*
hell for leather 332.14 *swiftly*
hell-hag 651.9 *vixen*
hellhound 380.4 *violent creature*
hellish 651.11 *cruel;* 236.6 *damnable;* 8.16 *devilish;* 804.11 *wicked;* 11.15 *witchlike*
hellishly 8.20 *devilishly*
hellishness 804.1 *wickedness*
hello 514.4 *cry of greeting;* 733.15 *hail!;* 312.12 *reception*
hello! 312.23
hell of a lot 208.3 *profuseness*
hell on earth 491.1 *pain*
hell-raiser 380.4 *violent creature*
hell-raising 408.20 *disorderly*
Hell's Angel 586.1 *combatant*
Hell's Kitchen 87.3 *New York*
hell to pay 814.9 *retribution*
hell west and crooked 141.16 *extensively*
helm 384.7 *armour;* 579.5 *guide;* 323.5 *navigation;* 50.3 *parts of a sailing boat;* 438.1 *tool*
helmet 384.7 *armour;* 62.4 *climbing equipment;* 551.15 *headgear;* 743.8 *heraldic device;* 58.1 *hockey;* 58.3 *ice hockey;* 58.5 *lacrosse;* 53.6 *pad;* 384.6 *protective clothing;* 46.3 *uniform*
Helmholtz function 28.38 *thermodynamics*
helminth 75.10 *parasite;* 75.6 *worm*
helminthic 75.20 *wormlike*
helminthic disease 75.11
helminthoid 75.20 *wormlike*
helminthological 75.20 *wormlike*
helminthologist 75.15 *invertebrate zoologist;* 70.11 *zoologist*
helminthology 70.9 *animal science;* 75.14 *invertebrate zoology*
helmsman 579.13 *director;* 323.7 *nautical person;* 50.9 *sailor*
helmsmanship 324.1 *direction;* 579.4 *directorship;* 323.5 *navigation*
Heloise and Abelard 593.10 *lovers*
helot 664.3 *sycophant*
helotism 664.1 *servility*
Help 392
help 392.1; 392.17; 340.4 *act;* 608.2 *aid;* 608.11 *assist;* 348.3 *assistant;* 348.4 *be an instrument;* 652.7 *be charitable;* 239.6 *be convenient;* 569.16 *be favourable;* 237.9 *be useful;* 256.12 *cleaner;* 40.19 *computing terms;* 636.14, 747.11 *cooperate;* 747.1 *cooperation;* 658.1 *courtesy;* 344.12 *determine;* 235.10, 797.20 *do good;* 768.2 *gift;* 413.14 *give moral support;* 768.6 *give to charity;* 392.16 *home help;* 348.1 *instrumentality;* 265.16 *make easy;* 413.6 *moral support;* 394.1, 394.19 *remedy;* 401.1 *servant;* 401.8 *serve;* 265.5 *smoothness;* 773.10 *take away;* 390.5 *to the rescue!;* 237.5 *usefulness;* 578.1 *worker*
help a lame duck 392.22 *improve*
help along 392.28 *further;* 265.16 *make easy*
help decide 344.12 *determine*
helper 392.11; 608.5; 713.4 *adviser;* 348.3 *assistant;* 344.8 *contributor;* 747.10 *cooperator;* 398.4 *deputy;* 768.4 *giver;* 797.15 *good person;* 652.3 *philanthropist;* 387.3 *subordinate;* 413.8 *supporter*
helpful 392.33; 636.4; 650.6 *benevolent;* 239.1 *convenient;* 747.17 *cooperative;* 6.16 *educational;* 569.12 *favourable;* 265.10 *feasible;* 123.5 *important;* 348.6 *instrumental;* 797.3 *kind;* 608.8 *relieving;* 394.17 *remedial;* 413.9 *supportive;* 237.1 *useful*
helpful act 650.4 *benevolent act*
helpfully 392.36; 650.10 *benevolently;* 608.15 *comfortingly;* 6.25 *educationally;* 569.20 *favourably;* 348.9 *instrumentally;* 797.23 *nicely;* 237.12 *usefully*
helpful neighbour 658.6 *courteous person*
helpfulness 392.10; 650.1 *benevolence;* 239.3 *convenience;* 747.1 *cooperation;* 636.9 *goodwill;* 797.10 *kindness;* 652.1 *philanthropy;* 237.5 *usefulness*
helpful person 595.4 *likable person*
help fund 768.6 *give to charity*
helping 392.30; 348.6 *instrumental;* 557.14 *mouthful;* 205.7 *piece;* 770.2 *portion;* 436.1 *provision;* 608.8 *relieving;* 401.9 *serving*
helping hand 608.2 *aid;* 392.1 *help;* 392.11 *helper;* 652.3 *philanthropist;* 413.8 *supporter;* 636.11 *willing worker*
helpless 335.12 *impotent;* 254.3 *vulnerable;* 337.8 *weak*
helplessly 254.11 *dangerously;* 335.14 *powerlessly;* 337.14 *weakly*
helplessness 335.3; 254.7 *vulnerability;* 337.1 *weakness*
helpmate 707.9 *affirmer;* 608.5 *helper;* 570.8 *spouse;* 392.13, 413.8 *supporter*
helpmeet 608.5 *helper;* 570.8 *spouse;* 392.13 *supporter*
help on 265.16 *make easy*
help out 392.29 *finance;* 392.17 *help*
help up 366.1 *raise*
help with money 768.6 *give to charity*
help yourself 452.26 *certainly!;* 312.24 *welcome!*
helter-skelter 408.28 *anyhow;* 262.6 *hastily;* 114.11 *irregularly;* 332.14 *swiftly*
helve 438.1 *tool*
Helvellyn 89.5 *British mountains*
hem 164.6 *edge;* 164.2 *edging;* 513.5 *sound hoarse*
he-man 613.7 *courageous person;* 567.6 *macho man;* 336.6 *muscleman;* 380.4 *violent creature*
hemeralopia 519.2 *poor sight*
hemeralopic 519.9 *weak-sighted*
hemiacetal 33.3 *carbohydrate*
hemicellulose 33.4 *polysaccharide*
Hemichordata 75.2 *protochordate*
hemichordate 75.16 *invertebrate;* 75.2 *protochordate;* 75.6 *worm*
hemidemisemiquaver 18.17 *notation*
hemihydrate 32.10 *salt*
hemiketal 33.3 *carbohydrate*
hem in 381.4 *besiege;* 165.5 *enclose;* 251.8 *restrain*
hemiplegia 335.4 *disability;* 260.17 *nervous disorder*
hemiplegic 335.12 *impotent;* 260.19 *sick person*
hemipteran 76.10 *insectan*
hemisphere 198.8 *half;* 205.1 *part;* 181.3 *round thing*
hemispherical 181.9 *round*
hemistich 17.8 *part of poem*
hemline 164.2 *edging;* 551.24 *part of garment*
hemlock 814.16 *instrument of execution*
hemmed 551.31 *styled*
hemmed-in 165.7 *enclosed;* 170.5 *surrounded*
hemp 691.6 *drug*
hempen collar 814.16 *instrument of execution*
hen 568.14 *female animal;* 72.11 *female bird;* 43.8 *livestock*
hence 750.36 *accordingly;* 345.12 *with the effect of*
henceforth 283.15 *after*
henceforward 283.15 *after*
henchman 384.13 *defender;* 392.11 *helper;* 122.6 *inferior;* 401.4 *personal attendant;* 401.1 *servant*
hen coop 43.7 *farm building*
hendecagon 201.7 *double figures*
hendecagonal 201.18 *eleventh*
hendecahedron 201.7 *double figures*
hendecasyllabic 17.20 *metrical*
henhouse 43.7 *farm building;* 565.12 *stall*
Henley stewart 50.9 *sailor*
Henley trophies 50.5
henna 536.2 *orangeness;* 535.6 *red pigment*
hen party 654.5 *party;* 376.9 *social gathering;* 568.13 *womenfolk*
henpeck 670.18 *find fault;* 387.6 *subject*
henpecked 387.9 *subject*
henpecked husband 570.10 *married man;* 663.4 *obedient person*
henpecking 670.6 *fault-finding*
hen run 43.7 *farm building*
Henry Kissinger 589.4 *Nobel Peace Prize*
hepatic 82.6 *mosslike*
Hepaticae 82.3 *moss*
Hepaticopsida 82.3 *moss*
heptad 201.3 *seven*
heptadic 201.14 *seventh*
heptagon 176.3 *angled figure;* 27.44 *polygon;* 201.3 *seven*
heptagonal 176.9 *angled;* 27.82 *polygonal;* 201.14 *seventh*
heptahedral 201.14 *seventh*
heptahedron 201.3 *seven*
heptahydrate 32.10 *salt*
heptameter 17.9 *metre;* 201.3 *seven*
heptangular 201.14 *seventh*
heptastich 17.8 *part of poem*
Heptateuch 201.3 *seven*
heptathlete 47.3 *athlete*
heptathlon 47.2 *field events*
heptatonic 201.14 *seventh*
heptavalent 32.35 *combined*
heptose 33.3 *carbohydrate*
her 568.2 *female*
Hera 570.14 *gods and goddesses of marriage*
Heraclitean 4.11 *follower of a doctrine;* 4.14 *of a philosophy*
herald 743.9; 449.12 *discoverer;* 129.19 *forecast;* 693.9 *informant;* 449.4 *invent;* 475.5 *omen;* 129.8 *precursor;* 475.11 *predict;* 740.14 *proclaim;* 740.10 *publicizer;* 742.12 *signal*
herald extraordinary 743.9 *herald*
heraldic 743.13
heraldically 743.14 *identifiably*
heraldic bird 72.9 *fabulous bird*
heraldic colour 529.1 *colour*
heraldic device 743.8
heraldic official 743.9 *herald*
heraldic register 743.9 *herald*
heraldic tincture 743.8 *heraldic device*
heralding 475.13 *predicting*
heraldist 743.9 *herald*
herb 412.4 *admixture;* 25.7 *basic ingredient;* 44.9 *garden plant;* 394.2 *medicine;* 77.2 *plant;* 44.11 *vegetable*
herbaceous 44.16 *horticultural;* 77.14 *of plants;* 77.13 *plantlike*
herbaceous border 44.3 *ornamental garden*
herbaceously 77.24
herbaceous perennial 77.2 *plant*
herbaceous plant 77.2 *plant*
herbage 81.2 *grassland;* 77.1 *plants*
herbal 77.11 *herbarium;* 44.16 *horticultural;* 394.18 *medical;* 77.13 *plantlike*
herbalism 35.2 *natural medicine;* 35.8 *treatment*
herbalist 35.12, 394.15 *healer;* 77.12 *plant scientist*
herbal remedy 394.2 *medicine*
herbal tea 558.3 *tea*
herbarium 77.11
herb doctor 394.15 *healer*

herb garden 502.2 *fragrant thing;* 44.2 *garden*
herbicidal 44.18
herbicide 43.14 *pest control;* 382.14 *plant killer;* 44.8 *weedkiller*
herbivore 557.18 *eater;* 81.6 *grass eater;* 70.4 *type of animal*
herbivorous 557.26 *eating;* 81.10 *grass-eating;* 70.15 *of animals*
herbivorously 81.13; 557.28 *carnivorously*
herbivorousness 557.5 *eating habit*
herbs 496.5; 502.2 *fragrant thing;* 500.2 *sense of smell*
herb sausage 25.29 *sausage*
herb tea 394.7 *tonic*
herby 500.5 *odorous;* 496.9 *piquant*
Herculean 264.10 *difficult;* 576.11 *laborious;* 336.9 *physically strong*
Herculean task 264.3 *difficult task*
Hercules 158.10 *big person;* 336.6 *muscleman*
herd 376.43; 71.21 *assemblage of mammals;* 117.6 *conformist;* 376.23 *flock;* 43.18 *practise livestock farming*
herded 376.46 *assembled*
herder 43.16 *farm worker*
herding 376.2; 43.3 *livestock farming*
herd manager 43.16 *farm worker*
herdsman 376.34 *assembler;* 43.16 *farm worker;* 579.14 *leader*
here 97.15; 282.8 *available;* 312.22 *on arrival;* 142.12 *where*
hereabouts 147.12 *near;* 142.12 *where*
hereafter 283.15 *after;* 464.4 *judgment day;* 101.1 *nonmaterial world;* 582.14 *the spiritual world*
here and there 377.30 *diffusely;* 133.17 *discontinuously;* 206.10 *in ones and twos;* 317.17 *via;* 142.12 *where*
hereat 142.12 *where*
hereditament 215.5 *estate;* 440.2 *legal terms;* 769.1 *receiving;* 345.2 *visible effect*
hereditarily 440.10 *proprietarily;* 769.15 *receptively*
hereditary 345.10 *caused;* 34.25 *genetic;* 440.8 *propertied;* 769.14 *receivable;* 788.6 *received;* 215.9 *remaining*
hereditary character 34.11 *genetics*
heredity 34.11 *genetics*
here goes! 353.11; 638.18
hereinafter 283.15 *after*
here lies 583.4 *funeral objects*
here's health 558.18 *cheers!*
here's looking at you 558.18 *cheers!*
here's to you 558.18 *cheers!*
heresy 274.7 *errancy;* 118.3 *nonconformism;* 451.4 *unbelief*
heresy-hunt 7.20 *preach*
heresy-hunting 7.2 *religiousness;* 466.4 *social discrimination*
here, there, and everywhere 114.11 *irregularly;* 141.16 *extensively*
heretic 325.19 *deviant person;* 451.5 *disbeliever;* 118.8 *dissenter;* 594.8 *hated person*
heretical 451.6 *disbelieving;* 274.16 *errant;* 118.12 *nonconformist*
here today gone tomorrow 526.6 *disappearing*
heretofore 284.23 *before now*
herewith 348.9 *instrumentally*
heritable 440.8 *propertied*
heritably 440.10 *proprietarily*
heritage 788.4 *legacy;* 763.1 *possession;* 769.1 *receiving*
heritor 769.6 *beneficiary*
herky-jerky 299.4 *irregular*
her ladyship 568.3 *female title of address*
herm 19.12 *sculpture*
Her Majesty's Loyal Opposition 113.10 *the opposition*
hermaphrodite 335.5 *powerless person*
hermeneutic 719.14 *interpretive;* 701.2 *logical argument;* 5.40 *translated*
hermeneutically 5.48 *linguistically*
hermeneutics 719.5 *science of interpretation;* 5.12 *translation*
Hermes 507.5 *loud person;* 316.8 *messenger;* 332.13 *swift person*
hermetic 11.14 *occult*
hermetically 309.16 *impermeably*
hermetically seal 417.6 *make sparse*
hermetically sealed 309.12 *closed;* 252.7 *invulnerable*
hermeticism 11.1 *occultism*
hermetics 11.1 *occultism*
hermetism 11.1 *occultism*
hermit 118.9; 572.4 *celibate person;* 736.7 *concealer;* 355.4 *deserter;* 325.19 *deviant person;* 197.8 *loner;* 7.7 *monk;* 109.3 *unconnected person;* 655.6 *unsocial person*
hermitage 7.10 *priestly dwelling;* 252.5 *refuge*
hermit crab 75.4 *arthropod*
hermit-like 7.15 *religious*
hernia 491.2 *painful condition*
hero 613.7 *courageous person;* 340.3 *doer;* 235.8 *exceller;* 9.4 *idolized person;* 593.11 *loved one;* 619.5 *person of wonder;* 21.23 *role;* 25.11 *sandwich;* 586.8 *soldier;* 246.4 *successful person*
Hero and Leander 593.10 *lovers*
Herod 380.4 *violent creature*
heroic 340.5 *acting;* 613.10 *chivalrous;* 613.9 *courageous;* 296.14 *historic;* 18.32 *instrumental;* 576.11 *laborious;* 586.35 *martial;* 17.19, 721.12 *narrative;* 1.14 *societal;* 638.4 *undaunted*
heroic age 284.5 *historical period;* 3.10 *past age*
heroically 613.18 *courageously;* 586.42 *martially*
heroic couplet 17.9 *metre*
heroic drama 21.2 *play*
heroic exploit 613.8 *courageous act*
heroic poetry 17.6 *poetry*
heroic qualities 803.2 *virtues*
heroics 673.6 *boastfulness;* 613.8 *courageous act*
heroin 394.8, 691.6 *drug*
heroine 613.7 *courageous person;* 340.3 *doer;* 9.4 *idolized person;* 593.11 *loved one;* 619.5 *person of wonder;* 21.23 *role;* 246.4 *successful person;* 586.10 *woman soldier*
heroism 613.2
heron 72.3 *water bird*
hero's welcome 601.4 *reception*
hero worship 667.2 *admiration;* 9.2 *idolatry;* 593.1 *love;* 669.3 *praise;* 619.1 *wonder*
hero-worship 9.8 *idolatrize;* 669.14 *praise;* 667.16 *revere;* 619.9 *wonder*
hero-worshipper 669.8 *admirer;* 593.9 *lover;* 9.5 *worshipper*
hero-worshipping 669.18 *approving;* 667.10 *reverent;* 9.9 *worshipful*
herpes 260.13 *skin disease;* 260.14 *venereal disease*
herpes simplex 260.4 *disease;* 260.14 *venereal disease*
herpes zoster 260.13 *skin disease*
herpetological 73.14
herpetologist 73.10; 70.11 *zoologist*
herpetology 73.9; 70.9 *animal science;* 73.14 *herpetological*
Herr 567.3 *male title of address*
herring 74.8 *food fish;* 25.18 *sea fish*
herringbone 68.2 *cross-country skiing;* 23.16 *joined;* 68.4 *skiing technique*
herringbone strutting 23.10 *carpenter's term*
herring-like 74.13 *fishlike*
herring pond 91.1 *sea*
herring roe 74.9 *fish product*
herself 568.2 *female;* 139.12 *I*
Hershey bar 743.4 *insignia*
hertz 297.6 *radio frequency;* 28.16 *waveform*
Hertzsprung–Russell diagram 29.13 *luminosity*
hesitance 616.1 *caution;* 337.2 *indecisiveness*
hesitancy 616.1 *caution;* 451.1 *disbelief;* 639.11 *vacillation*
hesitant 333.6; 616.4, 637.3 *cautious;* 451.6 *disbelieving;* 453.2 *irresolute;* 326.15, 639.1 *vacillating;* 337.12 *weak-willed*
hesitantly 616.7 *cautiously;* 451.10 *disbelievingly;* 639.16 *irresolutely;* 634.23 *shyly;* 453.23 *uncertainly;* 637.17 *unwillingly*
hesitate 333.2; 453.19; 639.6; 616.5 *be cautious;* 227.12 *be irresolute;* 451.8 *disbelieve;* 705.20 *doubt;* 674.15 *escape notice;* 637.8 *hold back;* 326.10 *vacillate*
hesitating 227.14, 453.2 *irresolute;* 705.15 *sceptical;* 639.1 *vacillating*
hesitatingly 705.24 *questionably*
hesitation 333.12; 616.1 *caution;* 451.1 *disbelief;* 637.13 *dissociation;* 453.11 *irresoluteness;* 227.2, 754.3 *irresolution;* 705.6 *uncertainty;* 326.3, 639.11 *vacillation*
hesitation waltz 22.2 *dance*
hesitator 616.3 *cautious person;* 341.2 *nonacting person*
hesperidium 80.2 *botanical fruit*
Hesperus 291.4 *evening thing;* 29.10 *star*
Hessian 586.6 *militarist*
heterochromatin 34.9 *cell nucleus*
heterochromosome 34.14 *chromosome*
heteroclite 5.44 *grammatical*
heterocyclic 32.7 *chemical compound;* 32.35 *combined*
heterodox 118.12 *nonconformist*
heterodoxy 274.7 *errancy;* 118.3 *nonconformism*
heterogeneity 116.1 *dissimilarity;* 114.1 *diversity;* 120.1 *inequality;* 412.1 *mixture;* 109.1 *unrelatedness*
heterogeneous 2.13 *communal;* 114.5 *diverse;* 412.12 *mixed*
heterogeneous catalysis 32.15 *catalysis*
heterogeneously 114.10 *diversely;* 412.14 *in the midst;* 2.16 *sociologically*
heterogenous 138.15 *general;* 109.6 *unrelated*
heterolyse 32.26 *react*
heterolysis 32.14 *chemical reaction*
heterolytic 32.38 *reactive*
heterolytic fission 32.14 *chemical reaction*
heteromorphism 114.2 *assortment*
heteromorphous 114.6 *assorted*
heteronomy 12.3 *governance;* 396.7 *type of rule*
heterophony 516.4 *harmonics*
heteropolar bond 32.11 *chemical bond*
heteropolysaccharide 33.4 *polysaccharide*
heteropteran 76.10 *insectan*
heterosexism 622.11 *prejudice;* 466.4 *social discrimination*
heterosexist 466.10 *discriminatory*
heterosexual 178.9 *straight person;* 178.4 *traditional*
heterosome 34.14 *chromosome*
heterothallic 83.10 *of fungi*
heterotropia 519.2 *poor sight*
hetoheptose 33.3 *carbohydrate*
het up 624.16 *angry*
heuristic 4.16 *dialectical;* 449.15 *discoverable;* 701.11 *logical;* 701.2 *logical argument;* 27.69 *theoretical*
heuristic solution 27.64 *reasoning*
hew 553.9 *fashion;* 367.2 *flatten;* 160.7 *form;* 308.18 *open;* 372.9 *separate*
hew down 367.2 *flatten*
hewn 308.12 *open*
hex 798.11 *be evil;* 11.21 *bewitch;* 249.11 *cause adversity;* 594.2 *curse;* 798.4 *evil power;* 712.4 *malediction;* 11.5 *spell;* 712.7 *wish ill*
hexacanth 75.13 *invertebrate larva*
hexachord 201.2 *six*
hexad 201.2 *six*
hexadecimal 201.7 *double figures;* 201.18 *eleventh*
hexadecimal code 40.10 *character*
hexadecimal notation 27.8 *number system*
hexadic 201.13 *sixth*
hexagon 176.3 *angled figure;* 27.44 *polygon;* 201.2 *six*
hexagonal 176.9 *angled;* 32.33 *crystalline;* 27.82 *polygonal;* 201.13 *sixth*
hexagonal close packed 32.33 *crystalline*
hexagonal close packing 32.4 *crystal*
hexagonal crystal 32.4 *crystal*
hexagram 176.3 *angled figure;* 27.44 *polygon;* 201.2 *six*
hexagrammoid 176.9 *angled*
hexahedral 27.84 *cubic;* 201.13 *sixth*
hexahedron 27.46 *polyhedron;* 201.2 *six*
hexahydrate 32.10 *salt*
hexameter 17.9 *metre;* 201.2 *six*
hexangular 201.13 *sixth*
hexapod 201.2 *six*
Hexapoda 76.1 *insect*
hexastich 17.8 *part of poem*
hexastyle 20.8 *column*
Hexateuch 201.2 *six*
hexatonic 201.13 *sixth*
hexavalent 32.35 *combined*
hexed 11.19 *bewitched;* 798.10 *inauspicious;* 712.10 *maledictive*
hexentric 62.8 *mountaineering*
hexentric nut 62.4 *climbing equipment*
hexose 33.3 *carbohydrate*
heyday 275.5 *indefinite period;* 248.3 *time of plenty*
heyday of the blood 555.1 *youth*
Hey rube 742.6 *word*
H-hour 275.11 *date*
hi 733.15 *hail!;* 312.23 *hello!*
hiatus 133.5 *caesura;* 146.1 *interval;* 141.8 *intervening space*
hibernacle 494.6 *Arctic*
hibernaculum 494.6 *Arctic*
hibernal 292.13 *winter*
hibernate 343.13 *sleep;* 292.6 *spend the season*
hibernating 339.5 *inert;* 343.4 *not awake*
hibernation 339.1 *inertness;* 343.9 *sleep;* 292.5 *winter*
hibernator 343.11 *sleeper*
Hibernia 85.10 *Ireland*
Hibernicism 5.26 *dialect*
hiccup 690.7 *be drunk;* 371.16, 371.24, 432.5, 508.4, 508.7 *belch;* 690.10 *drunkenness;* 236.8 *inferiority;* 378.2 *obstacle*
hiccupping 690.10 *drunkenness;* 690.2 *slightly drunk*
hic jacet 583.4 *funeral objects*
hick 564.5 *countryman;* 122.13 *insignificant;* 646.3 *naive person;* 574.1 *plebeian;* 486.10 *unskilled person;* 87.14 *urban*
hickdom 86.6 *regions*
Hickling Broad 88.4 *British lakes*
Hickstead 59.11 *eventing*
hick town 122.7 *inferior thing;* 655.5 *solitary place;* 87.10 *village*
hidden 519.13; 634.18 *avoiding;* 523.11 *benighted;* 736.14 *concealed;* 526.7 *disappeared;* 700.41 *disguised;* 172.12 *internalized;* 737.11 *mysterious;* 521.3 *private;* 550.37 *protected;* 655.11 *secluded;* 696.1 *unintelligible;* 696.3 *unrecognizable*
hidden camera 521.5 *invisible thing*
hidden cause 344.4 *contributing factor*
hidden cave 736.2 *hiding place*
hidden hand 579.13 *director;* 395.4 *indirect influence*
hidden income 813.4 *reward for service*
hidden influence 395.4 *indirect influence*
hidden meaning 694.4 *type of meaning*
hidden panel 389.2 *means of escape;* 550.15 *shelter*
hidden persuader 740.10 *publicizer*
hidden power 396.1 *authority*
hidden self 139.11 *identity*
hide 550.31; 550.14 *animal covering;* 521.7 *become invisible;* 645.5 *be cunning;* 252.9 *be safe;* 732.6 *be shy;* 526.3 *cause to disappear;* 736.8 *conceal;* 526.1 *disappear;* 389.6 *elude;* 634.6 *evade;* 814.3 *hit;* 172.15 *keep inside;* 737.12 *keep secret;* 521.8 *make invisible;* 435.1 *materials;* 11.20 *occult;* 359.5 *preserve;* 356.7 *produce;* 252.10 *protect;* 550.15 *shelter;* 439.6 *store;* 521.6 *that which makes invisible*
hide-and-seek 634.14 *evasion;* 521.5 *invisible thing*
hideaway 736.2 *hiding place;* 565.11 *retreat;* 550.15 *shelter*
hide away 736.8 *conceal;* 521.8 *make invisible;* 252.10 *protect*
hidebound 166.5 *limited;* 641.4 *set;* 465.8 *unjust*
hideboundness 656.1 *formality*
hide from 736.11 *conceal oneself*
hide one's abilities 563.7 *be infertile*
hide one's face 623.24 *be humiliated*
hideosity 546.1 *ugliness*
hideous 234.7 *deformed;* 612.10 *frightening;* 364.8 *repulsive;* 546.4 *ugly*
hideously 546.6; 234.13 *asymmetrically;* 612.16 *frighteningly;* 364.11 *repulsively*
hideousness 234.3 *deformity;* 546.1 *ugliness*
hideout 736.2 *hiding place;* 252.5 *refuge;* 550.15 *shelter;* 655.5 *solitary place*
hide out 736.11 *conceal oneself;* 550.30 *protect*
hider 736.7 *concealer;* 645.3 *cunning person*
hide under a bushel 521.8 *make invisible*
hiding 634.18 *avoiding;* 519.11 *blinding;* 331.12 *collision;* 736.1 *concealment;* 814.12 *corporal punishment;* 550.1 *covering;* 247.2 *defeat;* 526.6 *disappearing;* 526.5 *disguise;* 521.4 *invisibility;* 246.2 *victory*
hiding place 736.2; 252.5 *refuge;* 550.15 *shelter;* 655.5 *solitary place;* 439.1 *store;* 521.6 *that which makes invisible*

hidrotic 37.4 *drug type;* 37.17 *stimulating*
hidy-hole 736.2 *hiding place;* 252.5 *refuge;* 521.6 *that which makes invisible*
hie 332.4 *be swift*
hiemal 292.13 *winter*
hierarch 7.8 *priest*
hierarchic 209.8 *ranked*
hierarchical 407.12; 409.25 *categorical;* 137.10 *classificatory;* 209.8 *ranked*
hierarchical database 40.11 *application*
hierarchically 209.9 *differentially;* 407.25 *in order;* 137.16 *taxonomically*
hierarchy 407.3; 409.5 *categorization;* 137.1 *classification;* 12.1 *government;* 209.2 *rank;* 289.1 *succession*
hierarchy of authority 2.7 *social stratification*
hieratical 7.17 *priestly*
hierocracy 12.1 *government;* 7.9 *priesthood*
hierocratic 7.17 *priestly*
hieroglyph 5.13 *letter;* 742.1 *sign*
hieroglyphic 5.41 *lettered;* 717.13 *representational*
hieroglyphically 5.48 *linguistically*
hieroglyphics 737.4 *brain-teaser;* 717.1 *representation;* 742.1 *sign*
hierographical 7.18 *theological*
hierography 7.13 *theology*
hierological 7.18 *theological*
hierologist 7.14 *theologian*
hierology 7.13 *theology*
hieromancer 11.13 *diviner*
hieromancy 11.9 *divination*
hieromarch 7.7 *monk*
Hieronymite 655.6 *unsocial person*
hierophant 7.8 *priest*
hierophantic 7.17 *priestly*
hieroscopy 11.9 *divination*
hi-fi 591.10 *accuracy*
hi-fi enthusiast 504.2 *hearer*
hi-fi unit 410.3 *cabinet*
higgle 776.3 *bargain*
higgledy-piggledy 408.28 *anyhow;* 412.14 *in the midst;* 114.11 *irregularly;* 408.4 *litter;* 412.12 *mixed;* 408.18 *muddled*
higgling 776.9 *bargaining*
high 154.9; **154.19**; 598.1 *cheerful;* 375.5 *disintegrated;* 691.7 *drugged;* 690.1 *drunk;* 47.10 *fast;* 597.2 *fun;* 123.5 *important;* 148.1 *long;* 89.7 *mountainous;* 89.11 *on the mountain;* 490.7 *pleased;* 503.4 *putrid;* 203.6 *quantitative;* 600.9 *rejoicing;* 513.9 *shrill;* 141.13 *spacious;* 499.6 *unpalatable;* 31.11 *weather system;* 31.47 *windy*
high achiever 340.3 *doer;* 797.16 *superior person*
high-altitude wind 31.12 *wind*
high and dry 428.1 *dry;* 228.9 *stable*
high and low 232.9 *completely;* 141.16 *extensively;* 113.3 *opposites*
high-and-mightiness 673.3 *cockiness*
high-and-mighty 622.19 *stately*
high antiquity 284.1 *past time*
high approval 123.1 *importance*
high as a kite 597.4 *happy;* 490.7 *pleased*
highball 558.8 *mixed drink;* 321.2 *track*
highball glass 410.13 *drinking vessel*
highball it 332.5 *run like a shot*
high birth rate 562.2 *productiveness*
high blood pressure 260.10 *cardiovascular disease;* 260.3 *symptom*
high boots 551.19 *footwear*
high-born 573.4 *aristocratic*
highboy 23.5, 410.3 *cabinet*
highbrow 6.18 *educated;* 400.9 *educational leader;* 400.13 *excellent;* 396.11, 485.5 *expert;* 442.8 *intellectual person;* 455.6 *knowledgeable person;* 4.19 *learned;* 455.9 *literate;* 443.11 *reasoning;* 4.12 *sage;* 643.7 *serious person;* 443.7 *thinker;* 458.5 *wise*
high calibre 121.1 *superiority*
high-calorie 557.27 *edible*
high camp 21.12 *comedy*
high-caste 573.4 *aristocratic*
high casualties 382.4 *slaughter*
highchair 23.2 *chair;* 154.8 *high thing*
High-Church 7.16 *denominational*
high-class 573.4 *aristocratic;* 797.1 *good*
high cloud 31.18 *cloud*
high collar 551.14 *neckwear*
high colour 535.7 *red thing*
high-coloured 529.11 *colourful*
high comedy 21.12 *comedy*
high commissioner 398.1 *delegate;* 400.3 *leader;* 396.10 *person of authority*
high-cost 792.7 *dear*
high country 92.7 *upland*
High Court 16.20 *British court;* 16.19 *law court;* 464.3 *place of judgment*
High Court of Justiciary 16.20 *British court*
high day 601.5 *anniversary*
high days and holidays 600.1 *rejoicing*
high definition 692.23 *television reception*
high-definition 520.2 *clear*
high-definition television 692.21 *television*
high-density 208.10 *crowded*
high diving 67.6 *diving*
high dudgeon 624.2 *offence*
high endeavour 353.6 *venture*
high-energy radiation 28.70 *radioactivity*
higher 154.10; **154.20**; 27.75 *equal;* 101.8 *nonmaterial;* 121.12 *superior*
higher arithmetic 27.4 *simple arithmetic*
higher criticism 719.3 *criticism*
higher education 6.2 *educational system*
higher interest rate account 780.6 *funds*
higher jump 765.2 *augmentation*
higher mathematics 27.1 *mathematics*
higher position 129.2 *priority*
higher rank 129.2 *priority*
higher-up 121.5 *superior*
higher-ups 396.4 *governance;* 400.8 *the power structure*
highest 121.14 *best;* 27.75 *equal;* 154.10 *higher;* 89.7 *mountainous;* 174.5 *top*
highest bidder 777.12 *purchaser*
highest common factor 27.17 *multiplication*
highest level 174.1 *summit*
highest point 174.1 *summit*
high executioner 814.17 *punisher*
high explosive 587.15 *explosive;* 437.2 *lighter*
high-falutin 542.10 *ornate;* 622.18 *prestigious*
high-falutin ways 673.3 *cockiness*
high fashion 551.2 *dressing;* 553.1 *fashion;* 295.2 *trendiness*
high-fibre 257.4 *hygienic*
high-fibre food 557.7 *food*
high fidelity 591.10, 698.8 *accuracy;* 273.2 *correctness*
high-fidelity 273.6 *correct*
high finance 14.1, 780.7 *finance*
high-flier 340.3 *doer;* 121.6 *paragon;* 622.4 *prestige*
high-flown 366.12 *exalted;* 477.10 *imaginative;* 542.10 *ornate*
high flyer 246.4 *successful person;* 797.16 *superior person*
high-flying 542.10 *ornate;* 622.18 *prestigious*
Highgate 87.5 *London*
high-geared 332.1 *swift*
high-grade rock 30.33 *metamorphic rock*
high ground 334.1 *power;* 121.4 *summit*
high-handed 396.12 *authoritative;* 397.15 *self-assured;* 647.8 *severe;* 622.19 *stately*
high-handedly 396.23 *authoritatively;* 397.16 *commandingly;* 647.11 *severely;* 380.10 *violently*
high hat 551.15 *headgear*
high-hatted 622.14 *proud*
high heels 551.19 *footwear;* 154.8 *high thing*
high hopes 610.3 *aspiration*
high ideals 799.1 *probity*
high income 781.5 *wealth*
high-inside 54.6 *fencing;* 54.3 *fencing movements;* 54.7 *on guard*
high interest 784.4 *interest*
high IQ 458.2 *intelligence*
high jinks 601.1 *celebration;* 697.3 *tomfoolery*
high jump 47.2 *field events;* 304.5 *jump;* 814.7 *punishment*
high jumper 47.3, 336.5 *athlete*
high jumping 47.2 *field events*
high key 41.8 *composition*
high-kicker 22.5 *dancer*
high kicks 22.2 *dance*
highland 92.11 *continental;* 89.7 *mountainous;* 86.16 *regional;* 92.7 *upland*
high land 304.2 *upturn*
Highland dancing 22.1 *dancing*
Highlander 564.5 *countryman;* 85.11 *Scotland*
Highland fling 22.4 *historic dancing*
highlands 154.2 *heights;* 29.17 *moon;* 89.1 *mountain;* 86.6 *regions*
high-level 123.5 *important;* 579.17 *managerial*
high-level bombing 381.13 *air attack*
high-level language 40.9 *programming language*
high-level talks 746.3 *discussion;* 734.5 *talks*
high-level waste 28.74 *nuclear waste*
highlight 522.12; 139.22 *characterize;* 123.3 *chief thing;* 726.6 *emphasize;* 99.2 *essential content;* 522.24 *light;* 123.8 *make important;* 520.10 *make visible;* 738.10 *manifestation;* 469.4 *pick;* 525.14 *present;* 740.16 *publicize;* 738.3 *reveal;* 742.10 *signify*
highlighted 520.2 *clear;* 726.4 *emphasized;* 522.18 *lit;* 738.14 *manifest*
highlighter 520.7 *that which makes visible*
highlights 41.8 *composition*
high-liver 686.5 *self-indulgent person*
high living 686.2 *dissipation*
high-living 686.7 *dissipated*
highly 366.13; 203.7 *quantitatively*
highly capable 458.6 *intelligent*
highly coloured 721.11 *descriptive;* 727.12 *exaggerated;* 695.1 *intelligible*
highly-coloured imagination 477.1 *imagination*
highly considered 667.12 *respected*
highly flavoured 496.9 *piquant;* 336.12 *strong to the senses*
highly productive 562.5 *fertile*
highly qualified 485.8 *expert;* 455.9 *literate;* 485.6 *skilful*
highly regarded 667.12 *respected*
highly seasoned 496.9 *piquant;* 336.12 *strong to the senses*
highly strung 612.8 *fearful;* 625.4 *irascible;* 591.2 *oversensitive;* 590.12 *sensitive*
highly thought of 811.3 *reputable;* 667.12 *respected*
highly wrought 243.20 *developed*
High Mass 10.6 *Eucharist*
high-minded 799.4 *honourable;* 795.8 *moral;* 255.12 *morally pure;* 622.19 *stately;* 473.5 *unselfish*
high-mindedly 799.7 *honourably;* 473.9 *unselfishly;* 255.18 *virtuously*
high-mindedness 799.1 *probity;* 255.1 *purity;* 473.2 *unselfishness*
high moral tone 255.1 *purity*
high muck-a-muck 123.4 *bigwig*
highness 154.1 *height*
high noon 290.3 *noon*
high-noon 290.6 *noon*
high-nosed 622.19 *stately*
high note 513.3 *shrillness;* 18.21 *tone*
high-octane 437.10 *powered*
high office 396.5 *position of authority*
high official 579.16 *official*
high on the hog 248.8 *prosperous;* 248.9 *prosperously;* 781.16 *wealthily*
high opinion 667.1 *respect*
high-outside 54.6 *fencing;* 54.3 *fencing movements;* 54.7 *on guard*
high-pass filter 39.22 *transformer*
high pitch 513.3 *shrillness;* 18.21 *tone*
high-pitched 542.10 *ornate;* 513.9 *shrill*
highpockets 158.11 *tall person*
high point 99.2 *essential content*
high post 49.4 *playing terms*
high-powered 336.10 *potent;* 60.8 *shooting*
high-powered rifle 60.3 *hunting equipment*
high-pressure 386.9 *compelling*
high-pressure worker 342.10 *busy person*
high price 792.1
high-price 792.7 *dear*
high-priced 681.3 *costly;* 792.7 *dear*
high priest 579.14 *leader;* 7.8 *priest;* 400.6 *religious leader*
high-principled 803.6 *ethical;* 799.4 *honourable;* 801.10 *moral*
high principles 799.1 *probity;* 803.2 *virtues*
high-priority 123.5 *important*
high productivity 562.2 *productiveness*
high profile 520.4 *clarity*
high-profile 520.2 *clear*
high-ranking 123.6 *notable*
high rate 790.3 *fee*
high regard 667.2 *admiration*
high relief 608.6 *profile;* 19.13 *relief-carving;* 520.7 *that which makes visible;* 520.6 *visible thing*
high resolution 372.1 *separation*
high-resolution 372.19 *separable*
high-rise 154.9 *high;* 565.16 *manorial;* 20.12 *structural*
high-rise building 20.3, 38.20 *building;* 356.8 *construction*
high-rise flats 565.6 *apartment block;* 154.6 *tall thing*
high road 317.3 *road*
high saturation 28.28 *colour*
high school 6.12 *educational institution;* 59.6 *horsemanship*
high-school football 46.1 *football*
high seas 250.1 *freedom;* 91.1 *sea*
high sign 742.1 *sign*
high society 573.2 *aristocracy;* 553.6 *fashionable élite;* 654.7 *human society*
high-sounding 507.6 *loud;* 542.10 *ornate*
high-sounding words 542.2 *affectation*
high-speed 332.1 *swift*
high-speed steel 38.9 *machine tool*
high-spirited 598.1 *cheerful;* 221.8 *in a state of;* 622.14 *proud*
high spirits 598.3 *cheerfulness;* 342.4 *energy;* 597.1 *happiness;* 221.4 *state of mind*
high spot 123.3 *chief thing*
high standard of living 248.1 *prosperity*
high standing 123.1 *importance;* 667.1 *respect*
high-stepper 59.2 *thoroughbred*
highstick 58.9 *play hockey*
highsticked 58.8 *hockey*
highsticking 58.1, 58.8 *hockey;* 58.3 *ice hockey*
high street 342.6 *business;* 87.7 *city district;* 317.3 *road*
high-street 87.14 *urban*
high summer 493.5 *hot weather;* 292.3 *summer*
high table 165.2 *enclosed place*
high tackle 64.3 *rugby play*
hightail 313.4 *hurry off*
high tar 496.7 *tobacco*
high-tar 496.11 *tobacco*
high tax bracket 781.5 *wealth*
high tea 557.12 *meal;* 654.3 *meeting*
high tech 352.1 *means;* 438.6 *mechanics*
high-tech 356.11 *productive*
high technology 356.2 *manufacture;* 352.1 *means;* 438.6 *mechanics*
high-technology 356.11 *productive*
high-tech war 585.1 *war*
high temperature 493.1 *heat;* 260.3 *symptom*
high-temperature gas-cooled reactor 28.73 *nuclear reactor*
high-temperature superconductor 28.45 *superconductivity*
high-tensile steel 323.4 *shipbuilding*
high tension 334.4 *energy*
high-tension 334.16 *charged*
high thing 154.8
high tide 154.8 *high thing;* 30.15, 91.2 *tide*
high time 239.3 *convenience;* 294.2 *late hour*
high tone 542.2 *affectation*
high tragedy 21.11 *tragedy*
high treason 753.2 *disorder;* 800.2 *faithlessness;* 662.3 *subversion*
high turnout 208.4 *throng*
high up 154.9, 154.19 *high;* 89.11 *on the mountain*
high vacuum 32.20 *surface chemistry*
high value 792.6 *value*
high-value 792.8 *valuable*
high-velocity 332.1 *swift*
high-voltage a.c. transmission 39.33 *power distribution*
high-voltage d.c. transmission 39.33 *power distribution*
high volume 507.1 *loudness*
high water 154.8 *high thing;* 91.2 *tide*
high-water mark 166.2 *limiting factor;* 26.6 *measuring instrument*
highway 318.2 *passing along;* 317.3, 320.2, 373.5 *road*
highway engineering 38.17 *civil engineering*
highwayman 774.8 *thief*

highway patrolman 253.3 *security officer*
highway ramp 373.5 *road*
highway restaurant 226.4 *stopping place*
highway robber 774.8 *thief*
highway robbery 774.1 *stealing;* 792.2 *unfair price*
highways and by-ways 317.3 *road*
highway sign 742.5 *indicator;* 742.1 *sign*
high wind 31.14 *windiness*
high-wire artist 21.31 *circus performer*
high yellow 412.5 *hybrid*
high-yielding 562.5 *fertile;* 356.11 *productive*
HII region 29.8 *interstellar medium*
hijack 700.33 *snare;* 774.12 *steal;* 773.10 *take away*
hijacked 774.17 *stolen;* 700.42 *trapped*
hijacker 386.4 *coercive person;* 773.6 *taker;* 774.8 *thief*
hijacking 700.13 *snare;* 774.1 *stealing;* 774.17 *stolen;* 773.3 *taking away*
hike 190.5 *make bigger;* 366.1 *raise*
hiked 213.7 *increased*
hike up 338.3 *invigorate;* 190.5, 213.5 *make bigger*
hiking 190.1 *growth*
hiking trail 317.6 *path*
hilarious 599.9 *funny;* 600.10 *laughing;* 272.5 *ridiculous*
hilariously 599.16 *humorously;* 272.8 *ridiculously*
hilarity 599.2 *amusement;* 600.3 *laughter*
hill 30.7 *landform;* 89.1, 154.3 *mountain;* 176.2 *obliquity;* 305.6 *slide;* 304.2 *upturn*
hill and dale 113.3 *opposites*
hillbilly 564.5 *countryman;* 89.3 *mountaineer;* 646.3 *naive person;* 574.1 *plebeian*
hillbilly music 18.11 *folk music*
hill climb 61.1 *motor racing*
hill climbing 61.1 *motor racing;* 62.1 *mountaineering;* 304.6 *mounting*
hill-dweller 89.3 *mountaineer*
hill-dwelling 89.7, 154.13 *mountainous*
hill farm 43.6 *farm*
hill farmer 43.15 *agriculturist*
hill fog 31.33 *fog*
hill mist 31.34 *mist*
hillock 182.3 *dome;* 155.2 *lowlands;* 89.1, 154.3 *mountain*
hillocky 154.13 *mountainous*
hillside 169.1 *side*
hilltop 154.2 *heights;* 89.1 *mountain;* 174.1 *summit*
hilly 89.7, 154.13 *mountainous;* 176.8 *oblique*
hilum 77.9 *seed*
him 567.2 *male*
Himalayan 89.7, 154.13 *mountainous*
Himalayas 154.4 *mountain range;* 89.6 *other major mountains and ranges*
himation 551.16 *robe*
himbo 456.5 *ignorant person*
himself 139.12 *I;* 567.2 *male*
hind 568.14 *female animal;* 71.18 *female mammal;* 168.4 *rear*
hinder **378.8**; 634.2 *avert;* 662.15 *be disobedient;* 240.5 *be inconvenient;* 218.5 *be insufficient;* 238.7 *be useless;* 264.23 *cause difficulties;* 226.8 *cause to cease;* 347.3 *counteract;* 294.8 *delay;* 328.10 *disrupt;* 245.5 *hurt;* 166.7 *limit;* 414.14 *make heavy;* 383.6 *resist;* 251.8 *restrain;* 333.3 *slow down;* 309.8 *stop;* 604.7 *thwart;* 113.20 *withstand*
hindered 604.9 *disappointed;* 328.15 *disrupted;* 294.10 *held up;* 378.13 *hindering;* 218.2 *unprovided*
hinderer **378.7**
hindering **378.13**; 294.12 *delaying;* 378.1 *hindrance;* 240.1 *inconvenient;* 113.26 *uncooperative*
hindlimb 205.4 *component*
hindmost **131.25**; 168.4 *rear*
hindquarters 168.2 *rear end*
hindrance **378.1**; 634.10 *avoidance;* 309.1 *closure;* 347.1 *counteraction;* 231.7 *defect;* 294.3 *delayed action;* 662.1 *disobedience;* 328.4 *disruption;* 481.6 *dissuasion;* 378.7 *hinderer;* 240.3 *inconvenience;* 166.2 *limiting factor;* 637.12 *opposition;* 251.1 *restraint;* 264.8 *snag;* 226.2 *stop*
hind shank 25.23 *beef;* 25.27 *lamb*
hindsight 462.1 *memory*
Hindu 7.16 *denominational;* 7.6 *non-Christian*
Hindu text 7.12 *religious text*
hindward 303.28 *backwards*
hinge 307.4 *axle;* 373.11 *connect;* 373.8 *fastening;* 373.4 *means of connection;* 307.8 *rotate*
hinged 373.15 *connected*
hingle 307.4 *axle*
Hinman Cup 50.1 *sailing*
hinny 568.3 *female title of address;* 412.5 *hybrid*
hint 693.7, 713.1 *advice;* 713.5 *advise;* 476.2 *basis of supposition;* 739.6 *divulge;* 739.2 *divulgence;* 206.1 *few;* 590.2 *impression;* 483.10 *manipulate;* 475.3 *plan;* 475.11 *predict;* 476.6 *propound;* 446.2 *theory;* 693.14 *tip;* 711.5 *warn;* 711.1 *warning*
hint at 694.10 *mean;* 742.10 *signify*
hinter 480.14 *motivator*
hinterland 141.3 *geographical space;* 172.3 *inland;* 171.2 *outside;* 168.1 *rear;* 86.6 *regions*
hinting 476.7 *suppositional;* 711.8 *warning*
hip 553.7 *fashionable;* 6.19 *knowledgeable;* 20.9 *miscellaneous architectural features;* 169.1 *side*
hip bath 256.6, 410.12 *bath*
hip boots 551.19 *footwear*
hip flask 410.14 *bottle;* 558.10 *drink container*
hip, hip, hooray 600.12 *hurrah!*
hip-hip hurrah 514.3 *cry of praise*
hip-hop 18.9 *popular music*
hip-huggers 551.9 *trousers*
hipped 20.14 *roofed*
hipped on 593.18 *in love*
hipped roof 20.6 *roof*
hippie 250.8 *free-thinker;* 100.5, 118.7 *nonconformist;* 753.4 *protester;* 118.13 *unconventional*
hippiedom 118.3 *nonconformism*
hippo 158.12 *fat person*
hippocras 558.7 *alcoholic drink*
Hippocrates 394.15 *healer*
Hippocratic 35.22, 394.18 *medical*
Hippocratic oath 810.6 *ethics;* 35.1 *medicine*
Hippocrene 17.13 *poetic genius*
hippodrome 21.16 *theatre*
hippogriff 70.7 *legendary beast*
hippopotamus 158.9 *big thing;* 71.15 *hoofed mammal;* 71.14 *pachyderm*
hippy 158.16 *fat*
hip roof 20.6 *roof*
hipsters 551.9 *trousers*
hircine 71.33 *ungulate*
hire 15.11 *conduct industrial relations;* 790.3 *fee*
hire car 320.18 *cab*
hired 15.9 *negotiated;* 785.19 *receiving pay*
hired assassin 651.8 *malefactor;* 382.11 *murderer*
hired gun 382.11 *murderer*
hired hand 401.1 *servant*
hired help 392.16 *home help;* 401.1 *servant*
hired killer 382.11 *murderer;* 804.9 *wicked person*
hired mourner 583.3 *funeral director*
HI region 29.8 *interstellar medium*
hireling 122.6 *inferior;* 401.1 *servant*
hire personnel 352.6 *find means*
hire purchase 772.4, 783.1 *credit;* 777.7 *purchasing;* 786.2 *stoppage*
hire-purchase dealer 771.3 *lender*
hire-purchase payment 785.1 *payment*
hiring 15.9 *negotiated*
hiring practices 15.2 *industrial negotiations*
Hiroshima 382.15 *slaughterhouse*
hirple 333.1 *move slowly*
hirsute 420.3 *barbed*
Hirudinea 75.6 *worm*
hirudinean 75.6 *worm;* 75.20 *wormlike*
hirundine 72.21 *avian*
His Excellency 400.3 *leader*
His Highness 123.4 *bigwig;* 400.2 *sovereign*
his Honour 16.23 *judge*
His Lordship 464.6 *justice;* 567.3 *male title of address*
his nibs 123.4 *bigwig;* 16.23 *judge;* 622.13 *proud person*
hispid 420.3 *barbed;* 420.2 *coarse;* 425.2 *spiked*
hispidity 420.6 *roughness*
His Royal Highness 400.2 *sovereign*
hiss **512.1**; **512.4**; **514.14**; 515.1 *animal cry;* 517.5 *atmospheric dissonance;* 606.7 *be dissatisfied;* 515.2 *bird song;* 753.7 *complain;* 515.4 *cry;* 514.7 *cry of disapproval;* 606.2 *expression of dissatisfaction;* 742.3, 742.11 *gesture;* 753.3 *gesture of protest;* 730.14 *have difficulty speaking;* 73.15 *live as a reptile;* 692.19 *radio reception;* 670.23 *show disapproval;* 670.9 *show of disapproval;* 668.6, 668.25 *taunt;* 730.4 *whispering*
His Satanic Majesty 8.7 *devil*
hissed **670.35**
hisser **512.3**
hissing **512.6**; **514.19**; 512.1 *hiss;* 730.12 *inarticulate;* 507.1 *loudness;* 753.9 *protesting;* 670.9 *show of disapproval;* 73.12 *snakelike;* 668.15 *taunting*
hissingly 517.12 *dissonantly*
Hissing Sound 512
hist 504.18 *hear hear!;* 512.9 *sh!*
histochemistry 34.6 *cell biology*
histogram 27.58 *frequency distribution;* 27.32 *graph*
histological 34.20 *biological*
histologically 34.29 *biologically*
histologist 403.10 *anatomist;* 34.19 *life scientist*
histology 34.4 *anatomy;* 34.6 *cell biology;* 34.1 *life science;* 403.8 *science of structure*
histone 33.9 *protein*
histoplasmosis 83.5 *fungal association*
historian **3.3**; 17.14 *author;* 281.13 *chronicler;* 721.10 *descriptive writer;* 396.11 *expert;* 744.9 *recorder*
historic **3.15**; **296.14**; 284.17 *past*
historical **3.16**; 452.1 *certain;* 3.19 *chronicled;* 296.14 *historic;* 3.18 *in the past;* 284.17 *past;* 93.13, 95.6 *real*
historical ammunition 587.14
historical documents 744.1 *record*
historical geology 3.2 *archaeology;* 30.1 *earth science*
historical gun 587.10
historical guns 587.12
historical linguistics 5.1 *linguistics*
historically **3.24**; 296.21 *archaically;* 284.24 *retrospectively*
historical map 163.4 *map*
historical materialism 3.1 *history*
historical method 3.12 *historicism*
historical methodology 3.1 *history*
historical missile weapon 587.6
historical naval ships 586.25
historicalness 3.14
historical novel 17.2, 721.5 *fiction*
historical painter 19.16 *artist*
historical painting 19.10 *art subject*
historical period 284.5
historical record 3.5 *chronicle;* 744.1 *record*
historical soldiery 586.13
historical taxes 790.9
historic building 296.5 *old thing*
historic dancing 22.4
Historic District 296.5 *old thing*
historic fencing 54.1 *fencing*
historicism 3.12
historicity 452.9 *certainty;* 93.4 *demonstrable existence;* 3.14 *historicalness;* 95.1 *reality*
historic present 5.34 *tense*
historic property terms 440.3
historiographer 17.14 *author;* 281.13 *chronicler;* 721.10 *descriptive writer;* 3.3 *historian*
historiographical 3.16 *historical;* 17.19 *narrative*
historiography 3.1 *history;* 17.4 *nonfiction*
History 3
history **3.1**; 3.5 *chronicle;* 631.1 *conduct;* 554.11 *life story;* 721.3 *narration;* 17.4 *nonfiction;* 3.8, 284.1 *past time;* 136.3 *qualifications;* 744.1 *record;* 462.2 *retrospect*
history of ideas 3.1 *history*
history of illness 260.2 *illness*
history of science 3.1 *history*
histricomorphs 71.12 *gnawing mammal*
histrionic 676.3 *affected;* 703.10 *demonstrative;* 21.39 *dramatic;* 727.12 *exaggerated*
histrionical 727.12 *exaggerated*
histrionically 676.5 *affectedly;* 703.21 *demonstratively;* 21.44 *dramatically;* 727.16 *exaggeratedly*
histrionic art 21.1 *drama*
histrionics 21.22 *acting;* 676.1 *affectedness;* 673.6 *boastfulness;* 703.2 *demonstrativeness;* 21.1 *drama;* 727.1 *exaggeration*
histrionism 21.1 *drama*
his Worship 16.23 *judge;* 464.6 *justice*
hit **331.3**; **381.18**; **814.3**; 312.1 *arrive;* 331.10 *bat;* 48.5 *batting terms;* 331.13 *blow;* 52.14 *combat;* 814.12 *corporal punishment;* 691.6 *drug;* 235.8 *exceller;* 54.5 *fence;* 54.3 *fencing movements;* 586.37 *fight;* 797.17 *good thing;* 51.2 *grip;* 236.14 *ill-treat;* 491.11 *inflict pain;* 491.3 *injury;* 485.3 *masterpiece;* 147.19 *meet;* 619.5 *person of wonder;* 48.7 *play baseball;* 58.9 *play hockey;* 18.9 *popular music;* 492.3 *press;* 596.6 *react against;* 330.28 *shoot;* 331.14 *sporting hit;* 381.5 *strike;* 246.1 *success;* 246.4 *successful person;* 246.3 *successful thing;* 21.13 *theatrical performance;* 492.11 *touch;* 380.8 *use violence*
hit a bad patch 249.9 *be in trouble*
hit a clinker 517.10 *lack harmony*
hit a fly 48.7 *play baseball*
hit a grand-slammer 48.7 *play baseball*
hit a grounder 48.7 *play baseball*
hit a home run 48.7 *play baseball*
hit and miss 448.1 *experiment*
hit-and-miss 615.4 *rash*
hit-and-run accident 320.21 *miscellaneous motoring terms*
hit-and-run play 48.5 *batting terms*
hit an iceberg 92.12 *be marooned*
hit a receiver 46.15 *play offence*
hit a reef 92.12 *be marooned*
hit a sandbar 92.12 *be marooned*
hit a snag 378.9 *block*
hit a straight 61.9 *race*
hit back 385.3 *retaliate*
hit below the belt 802.21 *do wrong;* 52.11 *fight*
hit bottom 602.9 *despair*
hitch 604.2 *bad outcome;* 362.3 *jerk;* 378.2 *obstacle;* 43.18 *practise livestock farming;* 362.13 *pull at;* 50.15 *sail;* 264.8 *snag;* 226.2 *stop;* 274.14 *technical error*
hitch and hike 326.8 *oscillate;* 326.18 *to and fro*
hitched 570.21 *married*
hitch-hike 22.2 *dance*
hitchhiker 320.21 *miscellaneous motoring terms*
hitchhiking 320.21 *miscellaneous motoring terms*
hitchkick technique 47.2 *field events*
hitch to 211.6 *add*
hitch up to 211.6 *add*
hit for 324.7 *take a direction*
hit hard 338.2 *be full of vigour*
hit hard times 264.20 *be in difficulty*
hitherto 284.23 *before now;* 3.24 *historically*
hit in 58.9 *play hockey*
hit-in 58.1, 58.8 *hockey*
hit it 246.6 *be successful*
hit it off 246.6 *be successful*
hit it off with 569.13 *befriend;* 750.21 *be in accord*
Hitler 400.4 *absolute ruler;* 236.12 *bad person;* 798.6 *evil person;* 594.8 *hated person*
Hitler diaries 699.16 *false thing*
hit man 804.10 *bad person;* 586.1 *combatant;* 357.6 *destroyer;* 651.8 *malefactor;* 382.11 *murderer;* 814.17 *punisher*
hit one 446.14 *have an idea*
hit or miss 274.2 *inaccuracy*
hit-or-miss 472.10 *careless;* 107.8 *chance;* 408.14 *irregular*
hit over the head 331.8 *club;* 331.3 *hit*
hit rock bottom **195.10**; 249.9 *be in trouble;* 602.9 *despair*
hit someone up 772.7 *borrow*
hitter 48.2 *baseball player*
hit the batter 48.7 *play baseball*
hit the big time 248.5 *be prosperous*
hit the bottle 690.8 *get drunk*
hit the crossbar 47.8 *jump;* 46.17 *kick*
hit the finish tape 47.7 *race*
hit the headlines 740.18 *become famous*
hit the jackpot 246.6 *be successful;* 781.13 *get rich;* 765.14 *profit*
hit the mark 246.6 *be successful*
hit the puck 58.9 *play hockey*
hit the road 736.11 *conceal oneself;* 313.5 *set out;* 130.19 *start off*
hit the roof 624.12 *become angry;* 590.17 *feel deeply;* 659.8 *get angry;* 213.4 *increase*
hit the shops 777.2 *shop*

hit the skids 122.11 *become inferior;* 245.1 *deteriorate*
hit the spot 239.6 *be convenient*
hit the target 381.3 *bomb*
hitting 52.14 *combat;* 814.12 *corporal punishment;* 58.1 *hockey*
hitting below the belt 52.2 *boxing;* 800.1 *improbity*
hitting on 142.3 *locating*
hitting up 772.1 *borrowing;* 691.1 *drug-taking;* 773.1 *taking*
Hittite 566.4 *modern human*
hit town 312.1 *arrive*
hit tune 18.9 *popular music*
hit up 773.7 *take*
hit upon 107.11 *chance upon;* 449.1 *discover;* 305.12 *drop;* 142.11 *find;* 484.11 *invent;* 312.2 *reach*
hit upon an idea 449.4 *invent*
hit wicket 53.11 *dismissal;* 274.13 *sporting error*
HIV 260.6 *infection*
hive 342.6 *business;* 76.4 *social insect;* 439.4 *storage;* 439.6 *store;* 208.4 *throng*
hived off 372.17 *unjoined*
hive of activity 342.6 *business*
hive off 377.12 *disperse;* 372.10 *set apart*
hive of industry 342.6 *business;* 577.1 *workshop*
hives 260.13 *skin disease*
hiya 312.23 *hello!*
hoagie 25.11 *sandwich*
hoar 494.8 *cold;* 31.36 *frost;* 533.2 *grey-haired;* 531.9 *white thing*
hoard **682.7**; 765.11 *acquire;* 765.3 *acquisition;* 376.25 *assemblage;* 376.37 *assemble;* 252.10 *protect;* 436.5 *provision;* 777.1 *purchase;* 439.1 *store*
hoarded 376.47 *collected;* 439.7 *stored*
hoarder **376.36**; 665.6 *careful person;* 765.7 *gainer;* 682.5 *miser;* 777.12 *purchaser*
hoarding 740.9 *advertisement;* 738.8 *showplace*
hoard supplies 243.3 *be prepared*
hoar frost 31.36 *frost;* 31.29 *hail;* 494.5 *ice*
hoarily 556.16 *maturely*
hoariness 556.5 *old age;* 531.7 *whiteness*
hoarse **513.8**; 730.10 *low-voiced*
hoarsely 517.12 *dissonantly;* 730.17 *voicelessly*
hoarseness **513.2**; 517.1 *dissonance;* 730.2 *inarticulation;* 260.3 *symptom*
hoary 556.14 *aged;* 533.2 *grey-haired;* 296.11 *old;* 531.3 *white-haired;* 531.2 *whitened*
hoary age 296.1 *oldness*
hoax **700.11**; **700.31**; 699.25 *be fraudulent;* 711.3 *false alarm;* 699.8 *fraud*
hoaxed 700.36 *deceived*
hoaxer 700.15, 718.3 *deceiver;* 699.17 *false person*
hob 493.4 *burner;* 25.5 *cooker*
Hobbism 4.7 *school of thought*
Hobbist 4.11 *follower of a doctrine;* 4.14 *of a philosophy*
hobbit 159.4 *little person*
hobble 251.12 *gag;* 378.8 *hinder;* 251.5 *means of restraint;* 333.1 *move slowly;* 335.8 *overpower;* 264.5 *predicament;* 357.11 *ruin;* 333.10 *slow motion*
hobble skirt 551.6 *skirt*
hobbling 245.11 *hurt;* 337.10 *ill;* 333.4 *slow*
hobby 633.4 *activity;* 595.3 *likes;* 69.8 *pastime;* 342.2 *social activity*
hobbyhorse 320.12 *bicycle*
hobgoblin 11.11 *ghost*
hobnail boots 551.19 *footwear*
hobnob 654.13 *fraternize;* 223.14 *keep company with*
hobnobbing 654.1 *sociability*
hobnob with 569.13 *befriend*
hobo 710.5 *beggar;* 258.6 *dirty person;* 118.7 *nonconformist;* 343.8 *nonworker;* 227.7 *person who moves around;* 782.10 *poor person*
Hobson's choice 469.8 *choice;* 386.1 *compulsion;* 705.4 *difficult question*
hock 772.7 *borrow;* 25.24, 25.25 *pork;* 558.9 *wine*
hocked 253.7 *guaranteed*
hockey **58.1**; **58.8**
hockey association 58.1 *hockey*
hockey ball 330.10 *ball;* 58.1 *hockey*
hockey clothing 58.1 *hockey*
hockey player **58.2**; 58.4 *ice hockey player*
hockey stick 58.1 *hockey;* 58.3 *ice hockey;* 331.15 *ram*
hockey stop 68.4 *skiing technique*
hockey technique 58.1 *hockey*
hocking 772.1 *borrowing;* 771.1 *lending*
hock shop 771.4 *lending institution*
hocus-pocus 700.40 *illusory;* 700.9 *sleight of hand;* 11.5 *spell*
hodden 404.8 *rough*
hodgepodge 114.2 *assortment;* 408.4 *litter*
Hodgkin's disease 260.11 *blood disease*
hoe 256.10 *cleaning object;* 44.15 *cultivate;* 43.17 *farm;* 44.6, 438.3 *garden tool;* 438.10 *use tools*
hoed 44.19 *ornamental*
hoedown 22.4 *historic dancing;* 654.5 *party*
hoe one's own row 197.18 *be one*
hog 683.6 *be selfish;* 557.18 *eater;* 688.4 *glutton;* 43.8 *livestock;* 567.16 *male animal;* 763.7 *possess;* 683.3 *selfish person*
hogahn 10.7 *non-Christian ritual*
hogback 154.4 *mountain range*
hog caller 507.5 *loud person*
hogg 43.8 *livestock*
hogget 43.8 *livestock*
hoggish 688.6 *gluttonous;* 258.8 *unclean;* 71.33 *ungulate*
hoggishly 688.7 *gluttonously*
hoggishness 688.1 *gluttony*
hog line 68.10 *curling*
hog's back 59.9 *jumping;* 154.4 *mountain range*
hogshead 410.11 *vessel*
hog-wallow 258.5 *swill*
hogwash 699.15 *nonsense;* 702.2 *sophism;* 258.5 *swill*
hoick 366.1 *raise*
hoick back 61.9 *race*
hoicking back 61.6 *motor-racing terms*
hoick out 212.3 *subtract*
hoi polloi 216.7 *average person;* 342.6 *business;* 138.11 *general public;* 566.9 *group;* 122.6 *inferior;* 574.2 *the common people;* 675.6 *vulgar herd*
hoist 38.29 *construction equipment;* 38.30 *engineer;* 743.7 *flag;* 366.9 *lifter;* 154.17, 366.1 *raise;* 366.6 *raising*
hoisted 366.11 *raised*
hoisting 38.29 *construction equipment*
hoisting one's flag over 763.1 *possession*
hoist sail 323.9 *navigate*
hoist the Blue Peter 313.5 *set out*
hoity-toity 622.14 *proud*
hoke 699.15 *nonsense*
hokey 125.13 *imitation*
hokey cokey 22.2 *dance*
hoki 25.18 *sea fish*
hoking 21.22 *acting*
hoking it up 21.22 *acting*
hokum 699.15 *nonsense;* 702.2 *sophism*
Holborn 87.5 *London*
hold 267.6 *adhere;* 450.7, 590.19 *believe;* 46.18 *be penalized;* 228.6 *be stable;* 69.3 *card game terms;* 226.8 *cause to cease;* 57.10 *compete in gymnastics;* 406.6 *contain;* 93.19 *continue to be;* 294.8 *delay;* 251.11 *detain;* 691.10 *drug oneself;* 141.20 *extend;* 175.2 *foot;* 12.3, 396.4 *governance;* 58.1 *hockey;* 68.7 *ice-dancing;* 127.4 *include;* 395.4 *indirect influence;* 395.1 *influence;* 69.10 *play;* 58.9 *play hockey;* 66.4 *play soccer;* 763.7 *possess;* 763.1 *possession;* 359.5 *preserve;* 360.6 *retain;* 360.1 *retention;* 62.5 *rock face;* 701.15 *state;* 301.11 *stop!;* 439.4 *storage;* 439.6 *store;* 773.10 *take away;* 492.11 *touch;* 695.6 *understand*
hold a boxing match 52.11 *fight*
hold a brief for 392.23 *advise;* 384.22 *plead for*
hold a certain position 108.9 *have a relative position*
hold a charity event 710.8 *solicit money*
hold a clearance sale 778.1 *sell*
hold a conference 734.11 *confer;* 746.5 *negotiate*
hold a confidential discussion 713.6 *consult*
hold a consultation 713.6 *consult*
hold a conversation 734.9 *converse*
hold a court case 715.5 *accuse*
hold a demonstration 661.6 *be insubordinate*
hold a directorship 400.14 *master*
hold a fire sale 778.1 *sell*
hold a going-out-of-business sale 778.1 *sell*
hold a heading 324.7 *take a direction*
hold a healthy lead 121.10 *lead*
holdall 410.8 *bag;* 410.9 *baggage;* 439.4 *storage*
hold all the aces 395.10 *be a prevailing influence;* 396.19 *be authoritarian;* 121.8 *be superior*
hold all the cards 395.10 *be a prevailing influence;* 121.8 *be superior*
hold all the trumps 265.17 *do easily*
hold a meeting 376.42 *call together*
hold an advantage 121.11 *get ahead*
hold an election 469.5 *vote*
hold an exhibition 738.2 *display something*
hold an opinion 4.22 *propound a philosophy*
hold a position 57.10 *compete in gymnastics*
hold a protest meeting 753.8 *cause mischief*
hold a public inquiry 713.6 *consult*
hold a referendum 469.5 *vote*
hold a responsible position 579.2 *direct*
hold a sale 778.1 *sell*
hold a séance 11.22 *conjure*
hold as hostage 236.14 *ill-treat*
hold a special sale 752.9 *offer*
hold a subordinate position 387.8 *be subject to*
hold a summit 734.11 *confer;* 746.5 *negotiate*
hold a symposium 722.4 *dissertate*
hold at bay 384.24 *parry;* 251.8 *restrain*
hold a trial 715.5 *accuse*
hold a wake 583.8 *bury*
hold a wrestling match 52.12 *wrestle*
hold back **637.8**; 634.3 *abstain;* 616.5 *be cautious;* 684.5 *be self-restrained;* 386.6 *compel;* 481.3 *deflect;* 294.8 *delay;* 378.8 *hinder;* 218.7 *make insufficient;* 226.9 *pause;* 251.8 *restrain;* 251.10 *restrain oneself;* 333.3 *slow down*
hold centre stage 738.5 *be visible*
hold cheap 668.19 *disrespect;* 124.12 *think unimportant;* 468.3 *underestimate*
hold court 16.69 *have jurisdiction over;* 16.76 *judge*
hold dear 595.7 *like;* 593.23 *love;* 667.15 *respect*
hold down 367.5 *bear down on;* 360.7 *detain;* 251.8 *restrain;* 387.6 *subject*
hold down inflation 251.9 *economize*
holder 410.1 *container;* 763.5 *possessor;* 440.7 *property man;* 769.5 *recipient;* 46.12 *special team;* 439.4 *storage;* 575.4 *titleholder*
holder of dual nationality 564.8 *national*
hold exclusive rights 251.8 *restrain*
holdfast 373.8 *fastening;* 84.3 *plant body*
hold fast 267.6 *adhere;* 640.8 *hold out;* 638.10 *insist;* 492.11 *touch*
hold for 482.9 *intend for*
hold for questioning 705.18 *interrogate*
hold for ransom 774.13 *kidnap*
hold forth 733.7 *address;* 795.12 *moralize;* 729.14 *speak to;* 731.8 *talk too much*
hold forth without interruption 735.4 *monopolize the conversation*
hold good 698.27 *be true*
hold hard 301.11 *stop!*
hold in 360.7 *detain;* 166.7 *limit*
hold in abeyance 350.5 *not use*
hold in affection 593.23 *love*
hold in captivity 251.11 *detain*
hold in check 251.8 *restrain;* 333.3 *slow down*
hold in common 764.4 *have joint possession*
hold incommunicado 251.11 *detain*
hold in contempt 660.22 *be rude;* 670.14 *disapprove;* 668.19 *disrespect;* 594.14 *hate;* 668.20 *scorn*
hold in disgust 594.14 *hate*
holding 410.20 *containing;* 691.2 *drug pushing;* 43.6 *farm;* 57.8 *floor exercises;* 66.2 *football play;* 58.1, 58.8 *hockey;* 58.3 *ice hockey;* 127.7 *including;* 406.11 *loaded;* 46.13 *penalty;* 49.4 *playing terms;* 86.12 *plot;* 763.8 *possessing;* 763.1 *possession;* 440.1 *property;* 360.1 *retention;* 439.1 *store;* 492.2 *touching*
holding back 360.2 *detention*
holding good 698.15 *true*
holding hands 569.4 *act of friendship*
holding in 360.2 *detention*
holding on 267.2 *tenacity*
holding one's own 259.1 *healthy*
holdings 376.25 *assemblage*
holding the faith 7.15 *religious*
holding the reins 579.17 *managerial*
holding the sceptre 12.10 *governing*
holding together 267.1 *adhesion*
holding true 698.15 *true*
holding up 413.1 *support;* 698.15 *true*
holding water 698.15 *true*
hold in high esteem 667.15 *respect*
hold in high regard 669.11 *approve;* 667.15 *respect*
hold in low esteem 670.14 *disapprove;* 668.19 *disrespect*
hold in one's mind 462.11 *memorize;* 360.8 *remember*
hold in reverence 667.16 *revere*
hold in solution 431.23 *dissolve*
hold in thrall 593.28 *win the love of*
hold it 301.11 *stop!*
hold mass executions 814.5 *execute*
hold no brief for 341.4 *not act*
hold off 634.1 *avoid;* 350.5 *not use;* 384.24 *parry;* 383.6 *resist*
hold office 579.2 *direct;* 12.11 *govern;* 396.18 *have authority*
hold off the wet 428.22 *keep dry*
hold on 267.8 *be tenacious;* 294.8 *delay;* 492.11 *touch*
hold one back 378.8 *hinder;* 166.7 *limit*
hold one's breath 339.4 *be inert;* 301.8 *be motionless;* 506.1 *be silent;* 619.9 *wonder*
hold oneself back 251.10 *restrain oneself*
hold oneself erect 622.24 *be proud*
hold oneself in readiness 243.8 *prepare oneself*
hold oneself straight 186.5 *be vertical*
hold oneself up 366.5 *arise*
hold one's fire 339.4 *be inert*
hold one's ground 585.13 *be at war;* 638.10 *insist*
hold one's hand out 814.6 *be punished*
hold one's head 622.24 *be proud*
hold one's head up 366.5 *arise*
hold one's horses 339.4 *be inert;* 294.8 *delay;* 226.9 *pause*
hold one's lead 302.9 *maintain progress*
hold one's liquor 689.3 *be sober*
hold one's nose 501.6 *have no smell*
hold one's own 119.10 *be equal;* 384.28 *survive;* 113.20 *withstand*
hold one's tongue 506.1, 736.12 *be silent;* 730.13 *be voiceless;* 732.7 *keep quiet;* 737.12 *keep secret*
hold on life 554.5 *life cycle*
hold on to 360.7 *detain*
hold open house 654.11 *be sociable*
hold opposite opinions 114.9 *dissent*
hold opposite views 751.5 *disagree*
hold out **640.8**; 336.7 *be strong;* 277.6 *last;* 752.9 *offer;* 638.11 *persist;* 228.8 *show determination;* 113.20 *withstand*
hold out a carrot 480.17 *bribe;* 483.9 *motivate*
hold out an incentive 752.9 *offer*
hold out for 776.3 *bargain;* 640.8 *hold out*
hold out hopes 475.11 *predict*
hold out hopes for 756.9 *be auspicious*
hold out one's hand 742.11 *gesture;* 749.4 *pacify;* 710.8 *solicit money*
hold out one's own 638.11 *persist*
hold over 294.8 *delay*
hold over one's head 254.10 *endanger*
hold power 579.2 *direct;* 396.18 *have authority*
hold prisoner 236.14 *ill-treat*
hold responsible 670.19 *blame*
hold someone's hand 392.20 *sustain*
hold someone up 774.12 *steal*
hold steady 324.7 *take a direction*
hold surgery 35.19 *practise medicine*
hold sway 140.15 *be the rule;* 12.11 *govern;* 396.18 *have authority*
hold sway over 140.16 *direct*
hold talks 734.11 *confer;* 746.5 *negotiate*
hold the ball 49.6 *play basketball*
hold the edge 121.11 *get ahead*
hold the faith 7.19 *be religious*
hold the floor 707.21 *be assertive*
hold the fort 762.4 *be a substitute*
hold the helm 323.9 *navigate*
hold the lead 121.10 *lead*

hold the line 294.8 *delay;* 324.7 *take a direction*
hold the L position 57.10 *compete in gymnastics*
hold the portfolio 579.1 *manage*
hold the purse strings 14.5 *invest;* 579.1 *manage*
hold the reins 579.2 *direct;* 12.11 *govern;* 579.1 *manage*
hold the road 119.11 *equalize;* 228.8 *show determination*
hold the scales 16.76 *judge*
hold the tiller 579.2 *direct*
hold the trump hand 121.11 *get ahead*
hold the upper hand 121.11 *get ahead*
hold the whip hand 395.10 *be a prevailing influence;* 121.11 *get ahead*
hold tight 360.6 *retain*
hold together 267.6 *adhere;* 267.7 *cause to adhere;* 750.25 *conform;* 747.13 *work together*
hold to ransom 386.7 *force;* 651.18 *torment*
hold true 698.27 *be true*
holdup 294.3 *delayed action;* 333.12 *hesitation;* 226.2 *stop;* 774.3 *theft*
hold up 228.6 *be stable;* 336.7 *be strong;* 698.27 *be true;* 226.8 *cause to cease;* 226.6 *cease;* 294.8 *delay;* 360.7 *detain;* 361.12 *interrupt;* 415.10 *lighten;* 792.10 *overcharge;* 226.9 *pause;* 154.17, 366.1 *raise;* 413.11 *support*
hold-up man 774.11 *dishonest person*
hold up one's hands 388.3 *submit*
hold up to view 739.5 *disclose*
hold water 444.12 *be reasonable;* 698.27 *be true*
hold with 669.11 *approve*
hold within 172.15 *keep inside*
hold your tongue 506.6 *hush!*
hole **308.5**; **308.20**; 183.2 *concave land;* 146.2 *crack;* 156.4 *deep thing;* 222.4 *difficult circumstances;* 94.4 *emptiness;* 56.1, 56.7 *golf;* 56.2 *golfing terms;* 368.1 *insert;* 565.13 *lair;* 159.5 *little space;* 142.1 *location;* 308.1 *opening;* 264.5 *predicament;* 252.5 *refuge;* 28.44, 39.4 *semiconductor;* 372.3 *separateness;* 565.8 *shelter*
hole conduction 28.44, 39.4 *semiconductor*
holed **308.14**
hole-high ball 56.2 *golfing terms*
hole in one 273.3 *accurate thing;* 56.3 *golf shots;* 246.3 *successful thing*
hole in the wall 410.2 *compartment*
hole out 56.3 *golf shots*
holey 245.13 *dilapidated*
Holi 10.16 *religious festival*
holiday 263.4 *at ease;* 298.7 *be regular;* 601.1 *celebration;* 601.2 *commemoration;* 263.1 *ease;* 597.2 *fun;* 10.15 *holy day;* 98.5 *leave of absence;* 226.3, 226.9 *pause;* 757.2 *permit;* 241.10 *pleasant thing;* 581.6 *refresher;* 298.5 *regular thing;* 600.1 *rejoicing;* 580.2 *time off;* 248.3 *time of plenty*
holidays 15.2 *industrial negotiations*
holiday town 87.1 *city*
holier-than-thou 805.5 *innocent;* 795.10 *moralistic;* 622.14 *proud;* 7.15 *religious*
holiness 8.1 *divinity;* 799.2 *purity;* 803.1 *virtue*
holism 4.7 *school of thought;* 204.1 *whole*
holistic 204.6 *whole*
holistically 204.11 *wholly*
holistic approach 204.1 *whole*
holistic medicine 394.11 *medical art;* 35.2 *natural medicine*
hollandaise sauce 25.15 *sauce*
holler 514.1 *cry;* 514.10 *cry out*
hollow 232.9 *completely;* 183.6 *concave;* 183.2 *concave land;* 367.14 *depression;* 367.2 *flatten;* 308.20 *hole;* 700.37 *hypocritical;* 233.4 *incomplete;* 337.13 *insufficient;* 155.2 *lowlands;* 183.9 *make concave;* 308.1 *opening;* 510.6 *resonant;* 699.32 *spurious;* 96.8 *unreal;* 98.13 *vacant*
hollow-cheeked 153.2 *emaciated*
hollow cheeks 153.8 *emaciation*
hollow-chisel mortiser 23.11 *woodworking tool*
hollowed 308.14 *holed*
hollow-eyed 153.2 *emaciated;* 261.1 *fatigued*
hollow eyes 153.8 *emaciation*
hollowly 98.20 *absently;* 183.11 *concavely*
hollow man 96.5 *insubstantial person*
hollowness 183.1 *concavity;* 98.3 *emptiness;* 700.3 *hypocrisy;* 233.1 *incompleteness;* 510.1 *resonance;* 699.4 *spuriousness*
hollow out 183.9 *make concave*
hollow tile 24.9 *industrial ceramics*
hollow tree 736.2 *hiding place*
Hollywood 87.2 *American cities;* 21.3 *films;* 21.5 *show business*
Hollywood costume 551.5 *fancy dress*
holm 92.2 *island*
holocaust 493.6 *fire;* 357.5 *havoc;* 382.4 *slaughter*
Holocene period 284.3 *geological period*
holocephalan 74.2 *fish*
holocrine 559.4 *secretory*
holocrine secretion 559.1 *secretion*
holoenzyme 33.11 *enzyme*
hologram 111.4 *duplicate;* 522.12 *highlight;* 717.6 *image;* 525.4 *something that appears;* 41.5 *stereoscopic image*
holograph 126.2 *original*
holographic 111.15 *duplicate*
holographically 111.18 *identically;* 41.23 *photographically*
holographic image 41.5 *stereoscopic image*
holography 522.12 *highlight;* 41.1 *photography*
holophrastic 5.39 *of language*
holothurian 75.3 *echinoderm;* 75.17 *echinodermal*
holster 587.4 *arsenal*
holt 565.13 *lair;* 79.4 *trees*
Holtzman inkblot technique 36.5 *psychological test*
holy 8.13 *divine;* 7.15 *religious;* 803.5 *virtuous*
Holy Bible 7.12 *religious text*
Holy City 8.11 *heaven*
Holy Communion 10.6 *Eucharist*
holy cow 619.14 *wonderful!*
holy cross 10.14 *sacred object*
holy day **10.15**; 601.5 *anniversary;* 298.6 *annually celebrated day*
holy fear 9.1 *worship*
Holy Grail 482.6 *objective;* 756.4 *promised land;* 10.14 *sacred object*
Holy Joe 7.8 *priest*
holy mackerel 619.14 *wonderful!*
holyman 7.3 *religious person*
Holy Mary 8.10 *deified person*
holy matrimony 10.5 *Christian rite;* 755.1 *contract;* 570.1 *marriage*
holy Moses 619.14 *wonderful!*
Holy Office 16.22 *ecclesiastical court*
holy of holies 165.2 *enclosed place;* 252.5 *refuge;* 10.13 *shrine*
holy orders 10.5 *Christian rite;* 572.3 *monasticism;* 7.9 *priesthood*
holy place 173.4 *centre of activity;* 10.13 *shrine*
holy rite 10.5 *Christian rite*
holy roller 7.5 *Christian*
Holy Roman Empire 85.3 *dominion;* 3.10 *past age*
holy shit 619.14 *wonderful!*
holy smoke 619.14 *wonderful!*
holystone 256.13 *clean;* 256.9 *cleaning agent*
holy terror 798.6 *evil person;* 380.4 *violent creature*
Holy Trinity 8.3 *God*
holy war 585.1 *war*
holy warrior 381.19 *attacker*
holy water **433.15**; 10.14 *sacred object*
holy wedlock 570.1 *marriage*
Holy Writ 698.3 *the truth*
homage 667.2 *admiration;* 810.3 *allegiance;* 663.3 *obeisance;* 388.1 *submission;* 9.1 *worship*
homaloid 187.2 *horizontal surface*
homaloidal 187.8 *horizontal*
homburg 551.15 *headgear*
home **565.3**; 312.15 *destination;* 172.14 *go inside;* 565.1 *habitat;* 172.2 *inside;* 172.8 *internal;* 312.4 *land;* 85.6 *native land;* 147.9 *near;* 312.22 *on arrival;* 733.5 *place of residence;* 252.5 *refuge;* 301.3 *resting place;* 344.2 *source*
home again 312.22 *on arrival*
home and dry 252.6 *safe;* 246.13 *successful*
home and hosed 252.6 *safe*
home base 48.1 *baseball*
homebody 655.6 *unsocial person*
home brew 690.12 *alcohol*
home circle 654.7 *human society*
homecoming 303.20, 312.13 *return*
homecoming queen 235.8 *exceller*
home computer 40.3 *computer*
Home Counties 216.8 *middle classes;* 86.9 *regions of Britain*
home economics 25.1 *cookery;* 579.3 *management*
home farm 43.6 *farm*
home for the dying 394.14 *hospital*
home free 252.6 *safe;* 246.13 *successful*
home furnishings 23.1 *furniture*
home ground 565.2 *environment;* 85.6 *native land*
home-grown food 557.7 *food*
Home Guard 586.15 *army;* 586.2 *defender;* 252.3 *protector;* 584.2 *the military*
Home Guardsman 586.8 *soldier*
home help **392.16**; 256.12 *cleaner;* 578.1 *worker*
home in 310.11 *focus*
home in on 173.9 *centre;* 142.11 *find*
homeland 565.3 *home;* 85.6 *native land;* 655.4 *place of confinement;* 86.4 *territorial division*
home learning 6.2 *educational system*
homeless 782.3 *beggarly;* 227.13 *changeable;* 100.10 *foreign;* 144.10 *replaced;* 249.7 *unprosperous;* 109.6 *unrelated*
homelessness 249.1 *adversity;* 782.7 *beggary;* 109.1 *unrelatedness*
homeless person 258.6 *dirty person;* 144.7 *displaced person;* 100.7 *new arrival;* 655.7 *outsider;* 249.5 *person in adversity;* 782.10 *poor person*
homeless shelter 252.2 *protection*
homelife 655.1 *unsociability*
homelike 172.8 *internal*
homeliness 525.3 *external appearance;* 657.3 *familiarity;* 271.4 *simplicity;* 546.1 *ugliness*
home-loving 301.5 *sedentary*
homely 525.10 *aspectual;* 657.9 *familiar;* 271.1 *simple;* 546.4 *ugly*
home-made 486.4 *bungled;* 646.1 *naive;* 356.12 *produced*
home movie 41.14 *cine film*
home nurse 35.16 *nurse*
Home Office 16.2 *jurisdiction*
homeopath 35.12, 394.15 *healer*
homeopathic 35.22 *medical*
homeopathy 35.2 *natural medicine;* 35.8 *treatment*
homeostasis 119.2 *equilibrium;* 111.6 *regularity;* 228.1 *stability*
homeostatic 119.6 *equal;* 111.17 *regular;* 228.9 *stable*
home page 40.16 *Internet*
home-plate umpire 48.2 *baseball player*
homer 246.3 *successful thing*
Homeric 158.15 *big;* 17.19 *narrative*
Homeric epithet 17.12 *poetic language*
Homeric hymn 10.8 *hymn*
Homeric simile 17.12 *poetic language*
home rule 12.1 *government;* 250.3 *independence;* 396.7 *type of rule*
home run 48.5 *batting terms;* 331.14 *sporting hit;* 246.3 *successful thing*
home-run hitter 48.2 *baseball player*
home-run leader 48.2 *baseball player*
homesick 617.9 *desirous*
homesickness 617.1 *desire*
home side 169.5 *team*
homespun 255.17 *direct;* 646.1 *naive;* 356.12 *produced;* 404.8 *rough;* 420.7 *rough thing;* 271.1 *simple;* 193.4 *textile*
homestead 43.6 *farm;* 565.3 *home;* 440.1 *property*
home stretch 131.9 *close*
home-sweet-home 565.3 *home*
home-thrust 381.18 *hit*
home town 565.3 *home*
home towner 564.8 *national*
home trade 776.5 *commercial trade*
home truth 271.6 *naturalness;* 738.11 *openness*
home truths 670.7 *blame;* 95.5 *realities;* 698.3 *the truth*
home tutor 6.4 *educator*
home visit 35.6 *health care*
homeward 312.19 *approaching;* 324.10 *clockwise*
homeward-bound 312.19 *approaching;* 303.27 *returning*
homeward journey 303.20 *return*
homework 243.10 *preparations;* 576.1 *work*
homeyness 657.3 *familiarity;* 271.4 *simplicity*
homicidal 651.11 *cruel;* 382.24 *murderous*
homicidally 382.25 *lethally*
homicidal mania 461.4 *delusion*
homicidal maniac 798.6 *evil person;* 461.7 *insane person;* 651.8 *malefactor;* 382.11 *murderer;* 380.4 *violent creature*
homicide **382.3**; 651.7 *act of malevolence;* 16.39 *crime;* 382.11 *murderer;* 380.2 *physical violence;* 662.2 *violation of the law*
homilist 6.4 *educator*
homily 733.1 *address;* 722.1 *dissertation;* 795.7 *moral;* 17.4 *nonfiction;* 729.8 *speech*
homing 314.15 *entering;* 303.27 *returning*
homing in on 142.3 *locating*
homing pigeon 316.8 *messenger*
hominid 296.7 *ancient people;* 30.43 *fossil;* 566.1 *humankind;* 71.34 *primate*
Hominidae 71.16 *primate*
hominids 71.16 *primate*
hominoid 566.12 *human*
homo 567.17 *male;* 567.9 *offensive terms for homosexual*
homocentric 173.7 *centralized*
homocyclic 32.7 *chemical compound;* 32.35 *combined*
homoeopathic 394.18 *medical*
homoeopathy 394.11 *medical art*
Homo erectus 296.7 *ancient people;* 566.3 *early human*
homogeneity 750.5 *conformity;* 111.2 *equivalence;* 111.6 *regularity;* 255.8 *simplicity;* 2.5 *society*
homogeneous 111.13 *equivalent;* 111.12 *same;* 115.7 *similar;* 255.16 *simple*
homogeneous catalysis 32.15 *catalysis*
homogeneously 115.14 *comparably*
homogenetic 750.14 *conforming*
homogenize 115.11 *make similar;* 111.8 *make the same;* 750.26 *make uniform*
homogenized milk 558.5 *milk*
homogenous 750.14 *conforming;* 111.17 *regular*
homogenously **255.20**; 111.18 *identically*
homograph 111.2 *equivalence;* 5.17 *word*
homographic 111.13 *equivalent;* 5.42 *worded*
homoiotherm 71.1 *mammal*
homoiothermic 71.25 *mammalian;* 493.12 *warm-hearted*
homoiousia 111.2 *equivalence*
homoiousian 111.13 *equivalent*
homologous 750.14 *conforming;* 119.6 *equal;* 108.5 *interrelated*
homologous chromosome 34.14 *chromosome*
homology 750.5 *conformity;* 108.2 *interrelatedness;* 108.1 *relatedness*
homolysis 32.14 *chemical reaction*
homolytic 32.38 *reactive*
homolytic fission 32.14 *chemical reaction*
Homo neanderthalensis 566.3 *early human*
homonym 111.2 *equivalence;* 5.17 *word*
homonymic 111.13 *equivalent;* 5.42 *worded*
homonymous 479.10 *equivocal;* 694.6 *meaningful*
homonymy 115.1 *similarity*
homoousia 111.1 *sameness*
homoousian 111.12 *same*
homophobe 466.7 *bigot;* 594.9 *hater;* 465.5 *misjudging person*
homophobia 465.3 *injustice;* 466.4 *social discrimination*
homophobic 466.10 *discriminatory;* 465.8 *unjust*
homophobically 466.17 *prejudicially*
homophone 111.2 *equivalence;* 5.17 *word*
homophonic 111.13 *equivalent;* 18.30 *harmonic;* 516.7, 750.13 *harmonious;* 5.42 *worded*
homophonically 750.33 *harmoniously*
homophony 516.4 *harmonics;* 750.4 *harmony;* 18.13 *melody*
homophyllic 111.14 *lookalike*
homophyly 111.3 *lookalike*
homopolar bond 32.11 *chemical bond*
homopolymer 32.21 *polymer*
homopolysaccharide 33.4 *polysaccharide*
homopteran 76.10 *insectan*
Homo sapiens 296.7 *ancient people;* 566.1 *humankind*

homosexual 567.8; 568.10; 567.17 *male*
homosexual marriage 570.3 *types of marriage*
homosexual neurosis 36.10 *neurosis*
homothallic 83.10 *of fungi*
homothety 27.48 *transformation*
homunculus 159.4 *little person*
homy 172.8 *internal*; 271.1 *simple*
hon 593.12 *nicknames for lovers*
honcho 579.2 *direct*; 252.10 *protect*
hone 273.7 *be accurate*; 425.15 *make sharp*; 425.12 *sharpener*
honed 425.3 *sharp-edged*
honest 255.17 *direct*; 803.6 *ethical*; 178.5, 799.4 *honourable*; 797.3 *kind*; 16.50 *law-abiding*; 795.8, 801.10 *moral*; 646.1 *naive*; 271.3 *natural*; 308.16, 738.15 *open*; 454.13 *really!*; 698.18 *truthful*; 473.5 *unselfish*
honest John 698.14 *truthful person*
honestly 95.14 *certainly*; 643.11 *earnestly*; 803.10 *ethically*; 738.17 *frankly*; 255.20 *homogenously*; 799.7 *honourably*; 797.23 *nicely*; 308.26 *openly*; 126.8 *originally*; 454.13 *really!*; 178.13 *straightforwardly*; 698.36 *truthfully*; 473.9 *unselfishly*
honest money 780.1 *money*
honest person 799.3 *honourable person*; 803.4 *virtuous person*
honest sweat 560.8 *sweat*
honest to God 707.26 *as God is my witness!*; 95.14 *certainly*
honest-to-God 698.19 *authentic*; 738.15 *open*; 93.13 *real*; 698.15 *true*
honest-to-goodness 698.19 *authentic*; 738.15 *open*; 698.15 *true*
honesty 178.8 *directness*; 795.2 *good morals*; 797.10 *kindness*; 646.2 *naivety*; 271.6 *naturalness*; 308.9, 739.3 *openness*; 799.1 *probity*; 801.3 *properness*; 255.1 *purity*; 698.5 *truthfulness*; 473.2 *unselfishness*; 803.2 *virtues*
honey 430.6 *gelatin*; 593.12 *nicknames for lovers*; 76.4 *social insect*; 498.8 *sweeten*; 498.2 *sweetener*; 568.9 *woman considered as a sex object*; 537.8 *yellow thing*
honeybee 76.4 *social insect*
honey-blond 537.3 *yellow-haired*
honeybunch 593.12 *nicknames for lovers*
honey child 593.12 *nicknames for lovers*
honey-coloured 537.1 *yellow*
honeycomb 183.3 *cavity*; 308.20 *hole*; 245.5 *hurt*; 183.9 *make concave*; 308.6 *porous thing*; 439.4 *storage*; 498.2 *sweetener*
honeycombed 245.12 *deteriorated*; 308.14 *holed*
honeydew 559.2 *secreted substance*; 498.2 *sweetener*
honeyed 677.13; 516.6 *melodious*; 498.6 *sweet*
honeyed phrases 677.2 *blarney*
honeyed tongue 658.1 *courtesy*
honeyed words 677.2 *blarney*; 593.14 *communication of love*; 480.2 *flattery*
honey fungus 44.12 *pests and diseases*
honeying 593.6 *courtship*
honeymoon 130.8 *enrolment*; 570.6 *general terms*; 570.15 *marry*; 241.10 *pleasant thing*; 593.28 *win the love of*
honeymoon cottage 593.13 *abode of love*
honeymooners 570.9 *married couple*
honeymoon period 597.2 *fun*; 248.3 *time of plenty*
honeymoon suite 593.13 *abode of love*; 570.6 *general terms*
honeypot 410.15 *pot*
honeysuckle 502.2 *fragrant thing*
honey-tongued 658.8 *good-mannered*; 677.13 *honeyed*
Hong Kong 87.6 *other cities*
honk 711.2 *danger signal*; 507.1 *loudness*; 711.7 *raise the alarm*; 742.12 *signal*; 515.5 *sing*
honorarium 768.2 *gift*; 785.3 *pay*; 765.5 *profit*; 813.4 *reward for service*
honorary 793.11 *free of charge*
honorary degree 813.1 *reward*
honorary title 813.1 *reward*
honorary treasurer 780.18 *treasurer*
honorific 667.8 *respectful*
honorifically 9.12 *worshipfully*
Honour 799
honour 542.4; 669.2 *admiration*; 7.19 *be religious*; 656.10 *celebrate*; 462.14, 601.16 *commemorate*; 600.6 *fête*; 413.14 *give moral support*; 56.3 *golf shots*; 795.2 *good morals*; 658.12 *greet*; 123.8 *make important*; 480.11 *motive*; 10.19 *offer worship*; 785.7 *pay off*; 241.10 *pleasant thing*; 669.3, 669.14 *praise*; 622.4 *prestige*; 622.1 *pride*; 799.1 *probity*; 253.2 *promise*; 801.3 *properness*; 255.1 *purity*; 7.2 *religiousness*; 667.1 *respect*; 667.16 *revere*; 813.1, 813.9 *reward*; 575.1 *right*; 10.3 *rite of worship*; 794.1 *trophy*; 803.1 *virtue*; 9.1, 9.7 *worship*
honour a bill 785.7 *pay off*
honourable 178.5; 799.4; 601.11 *commemorative*; 255.17 *direct*; 810.8 *dutiful*; 698.26 *faithful*; 797.3 *kind*; 795.8, 801.10 *moral*; 255.12 *morally pure*; 622.14 *proud*; 811.3 *reputable*; 473.5 *unselfish*; 803.5 *virtuous*
honourable discharge 708.6 *termination*
honourable mention 669.4 *compliment*
honourableness 797.10 *kindness*; 799.1 *probity*; 473.2 *unselfishness*
honourable person 799.3
honourably 799.7; 811.7 *eminently*; 255.20 *homogenously*; 178.13 *straightforwardly*; 473.9 *unselfishly*; 255.18, 803.9 *virtuously*; 9.12 *worshipfully*
honour and glory 248.1 *prosperity*
honoured 542.11 *decorated*; 811.3 *reputable*; 667.12 *respected*; 575.4 *titleholder*; 575.6 *worshipful*; 9.11 *worshipped*
honour graduate 246.4 *successful person*
honouring 601.2 *commemoration*
honour point 743.8 *heraldic device*
honours 575.3; 542.4 *honour*; 813.1 *reward*
honours list 794.1 *trophy*
honour system 56.2 *golfing terms*
honour the dead 298.9 *commemorate*
honour with 768.5 *give*
honour with a title 813.9 *reward*
honour with one's presence 97.12 *attend*
hooch 690.12 *alcohol*; 558.7 *alcoholic drink*
hood 804.10 *bad person*; 68.9 *bobsledding*; 550.5 *body covering*; 662.9 *criminal*; 551.32 *dress*; 551.15 *headgear*; 550.31 *hide*; 523.14 *make dark*; 651.8 *malefactor*; 523.6 *shade*; 7.11 *vestment*
hooded 736.14 *concealed*; 551.29 *dressed*; 550.37 *protected*
hoodlum 586.1 *combatant*; 662.9 *criminal*; 774.11 *dishonest person*; 651.8 *malefactor*; 804.9 *wicked person*
hoodoo 798.4 *evil power*; 236.11 *harmfulness*; 11.3 *witchcraft*
hoodooed 798.10 *inauspicious*
hoodwink 519.15 *blind*; 700.28 *trick*
hoodwinking 700.7 *tricking*
hooey 697.1, 699.15 *nonsense*; 702.2 *sophism*
hoof and horn 562.3 *fertilizer*
hoof-and-horn meal 43.13 *fertilizer*
hoof-and-mouth disease 260.18 *veterinary disease*
hoofed 71.33 *ungulate*
hoofed mammal 71.15
hoofer 21.30, 22.5 *dancer*
hoof it 22.15 *dance*
hook 55.7 *angle*; 53.17 *bat*; 51.5 *bowling delivery*; 373.11 *connect*; 325.2 *divert*; 373.8 *fastening*; 56.7 *golf*; 56.3 *golf shots*; 361.4 *hanger*; 58.1 *hockey*; 633.11 *hunt*; 18.13 *melody*; 92.5 *peninsula*; 58.9 *play hockey*; 796.18 *prostitute*; 425.8 *sharp-pointed thing*; 700.13, 700.33 *snare*; 331.14 *sporting hit*; 53.9 *stroke*; 438.1 *tool*; 360.3 *tools for gripping*; 425.16 *use a sharp tool*; 438.10 *use tools*; 373.9 *yoke*
hookah 496.7 *tobacco*
hook and eye 373.8 *fastening*; 551.24 *part of garment*
hooked 691.8 *addicted*; 176.7 *angular*; 51.10 *bowling*; 373.15 *connected*; 58.8 *hockey*; 593.18 *in love*; 570.21 *married*; 700.42 *trapped*
hooked-in 50.13 *windsurfing*
hooked rug 550.9 *floor covering*
hooker 804.10 *bad person*; 796.9 *immoral woman*; 64.4 *rugby player*
Hooker's green 538.10 *green pigment*
hookey 634.16 *desertion*
hook in 700.33 *snare*; 50.18 *windsurf*
hooking 58.1, 58.8 *hockey*; 58.3 *ice hockey*
hooking off 61.6 *motor-racing terms*
hook, line, and sinker 232.9 *completely*; 204.11 *wholly*
hook off 61.9 *race*
Hook of Holland 92.5 *peninsula*
hook over 176.11 *angle*
hook pass 46.9 *play*; 49.4 *playing terms*
hooks 360.3 *tools for gripping*
hook shot 49.4 *playing terms*
hook up 747.16 *join*; 361.10 *suspend*
hook-up 570.2 *alliance*; 747.7 *association*; 322.7 *miscellaneous aviation terms*
hook up to 211.6 *add*
hook up with 654.13 *fraternize*; 570.15 *marry*; 570.19 *merge*
hookwinked 700.36 *deceived*
hookworm 75.10 *parasite*
hookworm disease 75.11 *helminthic disease*; 260.7 *tropical disease*
hooky 98.4 *absenteeism*; 389.1 *escape*; 355.3 *relinquishment*
hooligan 804.10 *bad person*; 586.1 *combatant*; 662.9 *criminal*; 234.5 *defacer*; 651.8 *malefactor*; 615.3 *rash person*; 408.11 *troublemaker*; 242.9 *unpleasant person*; 380.4 *violent creature*
hooliganism 16.41, 408.8 *lawlessness*; 380.2 *physical violence*
hoop 179.3 *circular thing*; 373.4 *means of connection*; 551.18 *underwear*
hoop skirt 551.6 *skirt*
hooray 514.3 *cry of praise*; 600.12 *hurrah!*
hoosegow 815.2 *the inside*
hoot 72.18, 515.2 *bird song*; 512.2, 512.5 *catcall*; 514.7 *cry of disapproval*; 514.2 *cry of joy*; 742.3, 742.11 *gesture*; 514.14 *hiss*; 514.11, 599.14 *laugh*; 72.26, 515.5 *sing*; 668.6, 668.25 *taunt*
hootchy-kootchy show 21.7 *show*
hooter 185.3 *protuberance*; 500.2 *sense of smell*; 281.10, 742.4 *signal*; 507.4 *sound maker*
hooting 512.7 *catcalling*; 507.2 *outcry*; 668.15 *taunting*
hoot owl 72.5 *bird of prey*
Hoover™ 256.10 *cleaning object*
hoover 256.13 *clean*
hoovering 256.2 *cleaning*
hop 22.15, 376.10 *dance*; 22.1 *dancing*; 300.12 *gait*; 304.5, 304.18 *jump*; 73.16 *live as an amphibian*; 654.5 *party*
hop aboard 304.15 *mount*
hop about 327.21 *be agitated*
HOPE 394.14 *hospital*
Hope 610
hope 610.1; 610.6; 450.3 *believing*; 617.1 *desire*; 474.8 *expect*; 474.1 *expectation*; 482.3 *future intention*; 102.7 *make possible*; 483.1 *motive*; 756.3 *potential*; 253.1 *protection*; 102.4 *remote possibility*; 756.10 *show potential*; 803.2 *virtues*
hope against hope 610.6 *hope*
hope and a prayer 610.1 *hope*
hope and pray 610.6 *hope*
hope chest 23.5 *cabinet*
hoped for 474.7 *expected*; 283.13 *foreseen*; 756.15 *future*
hope for 617.12 *desire*; 474.8 *expect*; 283.9 *look ahead*
hope for the best 610.8 *be optimistic*
hopeful 610.11; 756.14 *auspicious*; 617.9 *desirous*; 474.5 *expecting*; 610.5 *hoper*; 482.11 *intending*
hopefully 610.15; 756.17 *auspiciously*; 474.12 *expectantly*
hopefulness 474.1 *expectation*; 610.1 *hope*
hopeless 103.3; 611.4; 611.8 *bad*; 604.9 *disappointed*; 582.18 *dying*; 247.10 *failed*; 238.2 *futile*; 809.3 *impenitent*; 766.16 *losing*; 804.11 *wicked*
hopeless case 582.10 *dying person*; 247.5 *failing person*; 611.3 *hopeless person*; 809.2 *impenitent person*
hopeless failure 247.1 *failure*
hopeless loss 766.1 *loss*
hopelessly 103.12; 611.11; 766.19 *irrecoverably*; 247.12 *unsuccessfully*
hopelessness 103.6; 611.1; 604.1 *disappointment*; 238.4 *futility*; 341.1 *inaction*
hopeless person 611.3
hopeless situation 611.2
hope on 640.8 *hold out*
hoper 610.5; 617.6 *desirer*
hopes 474.2 *expectations*
hopes unrealized 604.1 *disappointment*
hope to God 610.6 *hope*
hop garden 44.2 *garden*
hop grower 44.13 *horticulturist*
hophead 691.4 *drug taker*
hop in 304.15 *mount*
hoping 617.9 *desirous*; 610.1 *hope*; 610.11 *hopeful*
hoping for conquest 593.6 *courtship*
hoplite 586.8 *soldier*
Hop-o'-my-thumb 159.4 *little person*
hop on 313.5 *set out*
hopped-up 332.1 *swift*
hopper 48.5 *batting terms*; 76.1 *insect*; 410.11 *vessel*
hoppercar 321.6 *rolling stock*
hop picker 43.16 *farm worker*; 44.13 *horticulturist*
hopping 327.15 *agitated*; 624.16 *angry*; 47.2 *field events*; 304.24 *leaping*; 327.5 *restlessness*; 47.9 *track*
hopping mad 624.16 *angry*
hops 558.7 *alcoholic drink*
hop, skip, and jump 304.5 *jump*
hop, step, and jump 47.2 *field events*; 47.8 *jump*
hop the twig 582.15 *die*
hop to it 293.10 *hasten*
hop up 213.5 *make bigger*
Horatian 17.19 *narrative*
Horatian ode 17.7 *poem*
horde 586.18 *army of people*; 376.20, 376.40 *crowd*; 208.4 *throng*
horizon 29.5 *celestial sphere*; 177.3 *curved things*; 526.4 *disappearance*; 145.3 *distant place*; 163.3 *edge*; 187.3 *flat thing*; 521.6 *that which makes invisible*; 520.3 *visibility*
horizontal 187.8; 57.11 *gymnastic*; 187.2 *horizontal surface*; 27.80 *linear*; 178.1 *straight*; 421.2 *uniform*
horizontal angle 187.2 *horizontal surface*
horizontal axis 187.2 *horizontal surface*
horizontal bar 57.5; 57.3 *gymnastic apparatus*
Horizontality 187
horizontality 187.1; 421.7 *smoothness*
horizontal line 187.2 *horizontal surface*; 178.7 *straight line*
horizontally 187.11; 421.14 *smoothly*; 178.12 *straight*
horizontal machine 38.9 *machine tool*
horizontal member 38.27 *superstructure*
horizontalness 187.1 *horizontality*
horizontal scale 57.6 *pommel horse*
horizontal surface 187.2
Horlicks™ 558.5 *milk*
hormic psychology 36.1 *psychology*
hormogonium 84.4 *reproductive body*
hormonal 33.26 *biochemical*; 559.5 *of a secretion*
hormonally 33.27 *biochemically*
hormone 33.16; 394.8 *drug*; 559.2 *secreted substance*
hormone-like substance 33.16 *hormone*
hormone replacement therapy 394.13 *therapy*; 35.8 *treatment*
hormone therapy 394.13 *therapy*
horn 5.36 *accent*; 181.5 *cone*; 711.2 *danger signal*; 410.13 *drinking vessel*; 418.7 *hard substance*; 425.8 *sharp-pointed thing*; 742.4 *signal*; 403.7 *skeleton*; 507.4 *sound maker*; 510.4 *sources of resonance*
horn antenna 692.17 *antenna*
horned 425.4 *toothed*
horned liverwort 82.3 *moss*
horned moon 29.17 *moon*
horned owl 72.5 *bird of prey*
hornet's nest 379.1 *trap*
Horney 36.29 *psychologist*
Horneyan 36.33 *Freudian*
Horneyan psychology 36.1 *psychology*
hornified 418.3 *hardened*
horn in 314.10 *invade*
horniness 593.5 *desire*
horn inlay 23.9 *decorative woodwork*
horn lantern 522.7 *lantern*
hornlike 425.4 *toothed*
horn of plenty 562.1 *fertility*; 217.8 *plenty*; 25.33 *vegetable*
hornpipe 22.4 *historic dancing*
horn-rimmed glasses 518.10 *visual aid*
horns of a dilemma 453.11 *irresoluteness*

hornswoggle 700.28 *trick*
hornswoggling 700.7 *tricking*
hornwort 82.3 *moss*
horny 593.20 *amorous*; 418.1 *hard*; 796.14 *lecherous*
horny-handed 576.10 *working*
horologe 281.5 *timekeeper*; 275.13 *timer*
horological 275.21 *lasting through time*; 281.17 *timekeeping*
horologically 281.18
horologist 281.12 *chronologist*; 275.14 *timekeeper*
horology 281.4; 275.10 *chronometry*
horoscope 11.9 *divination*; 283.4 *looking to the future*; 395.2 *occult influence*; 475.1 *prediction*
horoscopy 11.9, 475.2 *divination*
horrendous 236.3 *bad*; 612.10 *frightening*
horrible 236.3 *bad*; 798.15 *bad luck!*; 798.7 *evil*; 612.10 *frightening*; 364.8 *repulsive*; 242.1 *unpleasant*
horribleness 798.1 *evil*
horribly 798.12 *evilly*; 612.16 *frighteningly*; 364.11 *repulsively*
horrid 236.3 *bad*; 594.12 *hated*; 242.1 *unpleasant*
horrida bella 585.1 *war*
horridness 236.9 *badness*
horrific 236.3 *bad*; 612.10 *frightening*
horrifically 612.16 *frighteningly*
horrification 612.1 *fear*
horrified 612.7 *frightened*
horrifingly 612.16 *frighteningly*
horrify 242.10 *displease*; 612.13 *frighten*
horrifying 612.10 *frightening*
horripilate 420.11 *be rough*; 488.11 *sense*
horripilation 420.6 *roughness*; 488.3 *stimulus*
horror 236.9 *badness*; 596.1 *dislike*; 612.1 *fear*; 630.3 *shock*; 546.2 *ugly person*
horror story 17.2 *fiction*
horror-struck 612.7 *frightened*
hors de combat 335.12 *impotent*; 238.1 *useless*
hors d'oeuvre 25.12; 495.3 *appetizer*; 25.9 *dish*; 557.14 *mouthful*; 129.5 *preface*
horse 59.1; 320.9 *animal transport*; 342.10 *busy person*; 586.19 *cavalry*; 691.6 *drug*; 57.3 *gymnastic apparatus*; 59.15 *horse person*; 815.6 *prison officer*
horse about 697.8 *fool*
horse around 408.26 *be disorderly*
horse artillery 586.19 *cavalry*; 587.10 *historical gun*; 59.15 *horse person*
horse blanket 550.14 *animal covering*
horse box 59.14 *horse-riding terms*
horsecloth 59.14 *horse-riding terms*
horse coper 700.17 *cheat*
horse doctor 394.15 *healer*; 59.15 *horse person*; 35.15 *veterinarian*
horse-drawn 362.8 *tractional*
horse fair 779.1 *market*
horseflesh 59.1 *horse*
Horse Guard 586.12 *ceremonial troops*
horsehair 59.14 *horse-riding terms*; 420.7 *rough thing*
horsehair worm 75.6 *worm*
Horsehead nebula 29.8 *interstellar medium*
horsehide 550.14 *animal covering*; 48.3 *baseball equipment*; 435.1 *materials*
horse lacking quality 59.1 *horse*
horse latitudes 86.2 *geographical region*; 301.2 *repose*; 31.17 *wind system*
horse laugh 514.2 *cry of joy*
horseleech 35.15 *veterinarian*
horselike 71.33 *ungulate*
horse litter 320.6 *litter*
horseman 586.20 *cavalryman*; 59.15 *horse person*
horsemanship 59.6
horse marine 486.10 *unskilled person*
horse mushroom 25.33 *vegetable*
horse person 59.15
horse pistol 587.10 *historical gun*
horseplay 697.3 *tomfoolery*
horsepower 334.4 *energy*; 576.4 *exertion*
horseracing 59.7; 59.6 *horsemanship*
horseradish 496.5 *herbs*
horseradish sauce 25.15 *sauce*; 496.2 *seasoning*
horse railway 317.10 *railway*
horse rider 59.15 *horse person*
horse riding 59.6 *horsemanship*
Horse Riding and Racing 59
horse-riding terms 59.14
horse sense 442.5 *common sense*; 4.3 *detachment*; 458.2 *intelligence*
horseshoe 177.3 *curved things*; 475.6 *good-luck sign*; 59.14 *horse-riding terms*; 11.6 *talisman*
horseshoe arch 20.5 *arch*
horseshoe crab 75.4 *arthropod*
horseshoe magnet 28.60, 363.3 *magnet*
horse show 59.6 *horsemanship*
horse soldier 586.20 *cavalryman*; 59.15 *horse person*
horsetail 82.1 *fern*
horse-trader 700.17 *cheat*; 776.10 *trader*
horse-trading 776.9 *bargaining*; 59.14 *horse-riding terms*; 746.1 *negotiation*
horse transport 320.1 *road transport*
horsewhip 814.3 *hit*; 59.14 *horse-riding terms*; 814.14 *instrument of punishment*
horsewhipping 814.12 *corporal punishment*
horsewomanship 59.6 *horsemanship*
horsy 71.33 *ungulate*
hortative 713.7 *advising*; 483.11 *motivational*
hortatively 713.9 *advisably*; 483.14 *influentially*
hortatorily 713.9 *advisably*; 483.14 *influentially*
hortatory 713.7 *advising*; 483.11 *motivational*; 480.19 *persuasive*
horticultural 44.16
horticulturally 44.20; 77.25 *botanically*
Horticulture 44
horticulture 44.1; 77.10 *plant science*
horticulturist 44.13
hortus siccus 77.11 *herbarium*
Horus 72.9 *fabulous bird*
hosanna 514.3 *cry of praise*; 600.2 *fanfare*; 600.12 *hurrah!*; 10.8 *hymn*; 601.7 *thanksgiving*
hose 433.34; 44.6 *garden tool*; 551.20 *legwear*; 308.7 *passageway*; 429.14 *sprinkle*
hose down 433.34 *hose*
hosel 56.4 *golf club*
hosepipe 433.13 *irrigator*
hosier 551.26 *fashion designer*
hosiery 551.2 *dressing*; 551.20 *legwear*; 356.7 *produce*
hosing 429.5 *sprinkle*; 433.8 *watering*
hosing down 433.8 *watering*
hospice 35.10, 394.14 *hospital*; 565.11 *retreat*
hospitable 650.7 *charitable*; 569.8 *friendly*; 679.1 *generous*; 370.15 *receptive*; 654.15 *sociable*; 312.21 *welcoming*
hospitably 650.11 *charitably*; 569.17 *in friendship*; 370.18 *receptively*; 654.18 *sociably*
hospital 35.10; **394.14**; 38.20 *building*; 356.8 *construction*; 226.5 *resting place*
hospital administrator 35.17 *paramedic*
hospital bed 394.14 *hospital*
hospital case 260.19 *sick person*
hospital doctor 35.11 *doctor*
hospitality 650.2 *charity*; 557.4 *eating meals*; 569.1 *friendship*; 679.5 *generosity*; 654.8 *good company*; 312.12 *reception*; 370.2 *receptivity*; 654.1 *sociability*; 773.4 *taking in*
hospitalize 394.20 *doctor*
hospitalized 260.22 *sick*
hospital patient 260.19 *sick person*
hospital ship 394.14 *hospital*; 586.24 *warship*
hospital social worker 35.17 *paramedic*
hospital train 394.14 *hospital*
hospital ward 35.10, 394.14 *hospital*
host 586.18 *army of people*; 654.11 *be sociable*; 692.29 *broadcaster*; 436.4 *caterer*; 376.20 *crowd*; 579.2 *direct*; 34.18 *ecology*; 21.29 *entertainer*; 376.23 *flock*; 260.6 *infection*; 769.10 *receive someone*; 208.4 *throng*; 70.4 *type of animal*
hostage 251.7 *charge*; 227.10 *person who is exchanged*; 815.5 *prisoner*; 387.5 *subjected person*
hostage taking 381.16 *terrorist attack*
hostel 565.10 *hotel*
hostelry 565.10 *hotel*
hostess 401.3 *attendant*
hostile 651.14; **701.9**; 249.6 *adverse*; 381.21 *aggressive*; 586.33 *combative*; 347.4 *counteracting*; 364.10 *defensive*; 372.18 *disagreeable*; 670.26, 751.9 *disagreeing*; 596.8 *disliking*; 594.10 *hating*; 629.4 *jealous*; 113.22 *oppositional*; 753.9 *protesting*
hostile attack 381.12 *military attack*
hostile critic 678.7 *disparager*
hostile criticism 670.5, 678.2 *criticism*
hostile jury 16.43 *conviction*
hostilely 347.5 *counter*; 372.23 *disagreeably*; 753.11 *disapprovingly*; 594.18 *hatefully*; 751.11 *in disagreement*; 629.9 *jealously*
hostile personality 36.8 *disordered personality*
hostile takeover 13.7 *corporation*
hostile verdict 16.43 *conviction*
hostile witness 715.3 *accuser*
hostilities 585.4 *belligerency*
hostility 381.11 *attack*; 347.1 *counteraction*; 670.4, 751.1 *disagreement*; 596.1 *dislike*; 372.4 *disunity*; 236.11 *harmfulness*; 594.1 *hate*; 629.1 *jealousy*; 651.1 *malevolence*; 113.1 *opposition*; 753.1 *protest*
hostler 43.16 *farm worker*
hot 31.51; **493.9**; 796.14 *lecherous*; 147.9 *near*; 496.9 *piquant*; 428.5 *rainless*; 16.59, 774.17 *stolen*; 336.12 *strong to the senses*; 380.6 *violent*
hot air 727.4 *bombast*; 366.10 *elevator*; 415.7 *light thing*; 467.2 *overestimate*; 731.3 *talk*; 96.4 *theorization*
hot-air balloon 322.8 *aircraft*; 366.10 *elevator*
hot-air current 493.8 *hot place*
hot-air vent 493.3 *heater*
hot and bothered 327.16 *restless*; 493.12 *warm-hearted*
hot and cold 113.3 *opposites*
hot as hell 493.10 *on fire*
hot bath 256.6 *bath*
hotbed 173.4 *centre of activity*; 562.1 *fertility*; 493.8 *hot place*; 260.6 *infection*; 44.4 *nursery*; 344.2 *source*; 379.1 *trap*
hot-blooded 625.4 *irascible*; 488.7 *susceptible*; 380.6 *violent*; 493.12 *warm-hearted*
hot-bloodedly 625.9 *irascibly*
hot body 28.35 *heat*
hotbox 307.4 *axle*
hot chocolate 558.5 *milk*; 498.5 *sweet drink*
hotchpotch 114.2 *assortment*; 376.32 *miscellany*
hot climate 31.38 *climate*
hot corner 48.6 *fielding terms*
hot dog 25.11 *sandwich*
hot-dog 68.14 *ski*
hot-dogging 68.12 *ski*; 68.1 *skiing*
hot-dog stand 557.15 *eating place*
hotel 565.10; 38.20 *building*; 226.5 *resting place*
hotelier 436.4 *caterer*
hotelkeeper 436.4 *caterer*
hotel manager 436.4 *caterer*
hot flush 493.1 *heat*
hotfoot 262.6 *hastily*; 262.3 *hasty*
hotfoot it 332.4 *be swift*
hot for 617.11 *lustful*
hot goods 774.4 *stolen goods*; 773.5 *takings*
hot gospeller 7.5 *Christian*
hot grog 558.7 *alcoholic drink*
hothead 590.9 *feeling person*; 625.3 *irascible person*; 459.4, 615.3 *rash person*; 626.5 *sullen person*
hotheaded 459.5 *foolish*; 262.3 *hasty*; 590.13 *passionate*; 615.4 *rash*; 380.6 *violent*
hotheadedness 615.1 *rashness*
hothouse 493.8 *hot place*; 44.4 *nursery*; 344.2 *source*
hothouse plant 77.2 *plant*
hot item 16.36 *stolen property*
hot line 692.12 *public telephone system*
hotly 31.65 *meteorologically*; 493.17 *warmly*
hot-metal printing 561.1 *reproduction*
hot money 780.6 *funds*
hotness 28.35, 493.1 *heat*
hot news 741.9 *news story*
hot off the press 741.14 *journalistic*; 295.10 *new*; 447.6 *topical*
hot on the trail 60.9 *on the trail*; 633.18 *pursuant to*
hot pants 552.4 *dishabille*; 617.4 *sexual desire*; 551.9 *trousers*
hot place 493.8
hotplate 493.4 *burner*; 25.5 *cooker*
hot press 421.9 *smoother*
hot-press 421.11 *smooth*
hot property 774.4 *stolen goods*; 773.5 *takings*
hot pursuit 633.2 *chase*
hot-rod race 61.1 *motor racing*
hot-rod racing 61.1 *motor racing*
hot-shoe 41.19 *flash*
hot shot 691.6 *drug*
hot-shot 691.10 *drug oneself*
hot shower 256.6 *bath*
hot spell 31.23 *heat*; 493.5 *hot weather*
hot spot 493.8 *hot place*
hot spring 30.25 *eruption*; 493.8 *hot place*; 92.10 *miscellaneous*
hot springs 394.14 *hospital*; 257.1 *hygiene*
hotspur 380.4 *violent creature*
hot substance 28.35 *heat*
hotted-up 332.1 *swift*
hot-tempered 625.4 *irascible*; 493.12 *warm-hearted*
hotter 31.50 *warm*
hottie 493.3 *heater*
hotting 774.3 *theft*
hot toddy 558.7 *alcoholic drink*; 498.5 *sweet drink*
hot tub 256.6 *bath*
hot under the collar 624.16 *angry*
hot up 213.5 *make bigger*
hot war 585.1 *war*
hot water 256.9 *cleaning agent*; 143.3 *difficult circumstances*; 221.2, 264.5 *predicament*; 255.3 *purifier*
hot-water bottle 410.14 *bottle*; 493.3 *heater*
hot-water crust pastry 25.37 *pastry*
hot-water pipes 493.3 *heater*
hot-water tank 493.3 *heater*
hot weather 493.5; 31.23 *heat*
hot-wire 774.12 *steal*
hot-wiring 320.21 *miscellaneous motoring terms*; 774.3 *theft*
Houdini 389.3 *escaper*
hound 71.9 *dog*; 633.6 *hunter*; 59.8 *hunting*; 651.18 *torment*
hounded 633.17 *pursued*
hounding 633.2 *chase*; 633.1 *pursuit*
hound of Hell 380.4 *violent creature*
Hound of the Baskervilles 380.4 *violent creature*
hounds 633.6 *hunter*
hound's tooth check 541.2 *check*
houngan 11.12 *occultist*; 7.8 *priest*
hour 281.3 *chronology*; 148.8 *measure of time*; 222.2 *occurrence*; 275.4 *term*; 276.2 *time period*
hour angle 29.5 *celestial sphere*
hour by hour 298.16 *cyclically*
hourglass 281.9; 191.3 *contracted thing*
hourglass figure 191.3 *contracted thing*; 153.7 *thinness*
hour hand 742.5 *indicator*
hourly 298.12 *cyclic*; 298.16 *cyclically*; 276.13 *for specified periods*; 297.1 *frequently*; 275.22 *periodic*; 111.17 *regular*; 111.20 *regularly*
hour of decision 222.3 *critical moment*
hours worked 15.2 *industrial negotiations*
House 12.4 *governing body*; 579.12 *US government*
house 565.5; 38.20 *building*; 376.19 *clique*; 356.8, 403.6 *construction*; 68.10 *curling*; 314.7 *entrant*; 565.1 *habitat*; 504.2 *hearer*; 733.5 *place of residence*; 18.9 *popular music*; 440.1 *property*; 252.10, 550.30 *protect*; 779.8 *store*; 21.16 *theatre*; 21.33 *theatregoer*
house agent 778.12 *wholesaler*
house arrest 251.4 *detention*; 814.7 *punishment*
houseboat 565.9 *mobile home*
housebound 251.15 *detained*; 301.5 *sedentary*
house boy 401.6 *domestic servant*
housebreak 774.12 *steal*
housebreaker 662.9 *criminal*; 314.8 *intruder*; 16.40 *lawbreaker*; 774.8 *thief*
housebreaking 314.3 *inroad*; 774.1 *stealing*
housebuilder 578.2 *artisan*
house built on sand 337.5 *weak thing*
housecarl 586.12 *ceremonial troops*
house cat 71.10 *cat*
housecleaner 256.12 *cleaner*
housecleaning 256.2 *cleaning*
housecoat 552.4 *dishabille*; 551.4, 657.6 *informal dress*; 551.16 *robe*
house curtain 21.19 *stage set*

housed 565.14 *inhabiting*; 23.16 *joined*
house divided against itself 751.1 *disagreement*
housed joint 23.10 *carpenter's term*
house fire 493.6 *fire*
household 216.1 *average*; 117.15 *everyday*; 632.10 *familiar*; 376.17 *family*; 564.2 *inhabitants*
Household Cavalry 586.14 *armed forces*
householder 564.3; 763.5 *possessor*; 440.7 *property man*
household gods 8.5 *deity*
household insurance 252.2 *protection*
household management 579.3 *management*
household servant 401.1 *servant*
household troops 586.14 *armed forces*
household words 271.4 *simplicity*
househusband 579.15 *manager*; 567.13 *man in the family*; 570.10 *married man*
housekeeper 436.4 *caterer*; 401.6 *domestic servant*; 392.16 *home help*; 579.15 *manager*
housekeeping 579.3 *management*
houseless 144.10 *replaced*
house lights 522.6 *electric light*; 21.20 *stage lighting*
house magazine 740.5 *journal*
housemaid 256.12 *cleaner*; 401.6 *domestic servant*
housemaid's knee 260.16 *rheumatism*
House majority leader 579.14 *leader*; 12.8 *politician*
houseman 35.11 *doctor*
housemaster 400.9 *educational leader*
House minority leader 579.14 *leader*; 12.8 *politician*
housemistress 400.9 *educational leader*
housemother 400.1 *master*
house music 18.9 *popular music*
house number 733.5 *place of residence*
house of cards 424.3 *brittle thing*; 337.5 *weak thing*
House of Commons 579.11 *British government*; 12.4 *governing body*
house of correction 815.1 *prison*; 244.10 *reformatory*
house of detention 815.1 *prison*
house of God 10.11 *place of worship*
house of ill repute 796.6 *brothel*
House of Lords 16.20 *British court*; 579.11 *British government*; 12.4 *governing body*
House of Peers 579.11 *British government*; 12.4 *governing body*
house of prayer 10.11 *place of worship*
house of prostitution 804.8 *wicked place*
House of Representatives 12.4 *governing body*; 579.12 *US government*
house organ 740.5 *journal*
housepainting 542.5 *decorating*
house party 654.5 *party*
house pet 70.3 *domesticated animal*
house physician 35.11 *doctor*
house plant 77.2 *plant*
house-proud 622.14 *proud*
house-raising 654.5 *party*
house rent 790.3 *fee*
house rules 632.5 *tradition*
house-sharing 764.5 *jointly possessing*
house steward 401.6 *domestic servant*
house surgeon 35.11 *doctor*
housetop 174.3 *architectural summit*; 550.7 *overhead covering*
house-trained 560.26 *urinary*
house-tree-person projective test 36.5 *psychological test*
house-warming 295.4 *beginning*; 130.8 *enrolment*; 654.5 *party*; 376.9 *social gathering*
housewife 436.4 *caterer*; 579.15 *manager*; 570.11 *married woman*; 568.12 *woman in the family*; 578.1 *worker*
housewifery 579.3 *management*
housework 576.1 *work*
housing 550.12 *protective covering*
housing benefit 392.4 *social assistance*
housing estate 565.6 *apartment block*; 87.7 *city district*
Houston 87.2 *American cities*
Houyhnhnm 59.1 *horse*
hovel 565.8 *shelter*
hover 304.20; 227.12 *be irresolute*; 415.9 *be light*; 72.25 *fly*; 333.2 *hesitate*; 361.11 *project*
hovering 154.9 *high*
hover mower 44.6 *garden tool*
hover on the brink 254.8 *be in danger*
hover over 471.10 *be attentive*; 154.15 *be high*; 147.17 *stay near*
how 317.16
how? 705.25 *what?*
how about that 619.14 *wonderful!*
how are you? 312.23 *hello!*
how dare you! 661.11
how do you do? 312.23 *hello!*
how-do-you-do 264.5 *predicament*
however 317.16 *how*
however little 209.10 *by degrees*
however much 209.10 *by degrees*
how it goes 222.1 *circumstances*
how it is 143.2 *circumstances*; 221.3 *state of affairs*; 698.3 *the truth*
howitzer 587.11 *guns*
howl 507.8 *be loud*; 513.4 *be strident*; 31.58 *blow*; 753.7 *complain*; 514.13, 515.4 *cry*; 514.6 *cry of pain*; 491.12 *express pain*; 753.3 *gesture of protest*; 602.8 *grieve*; 603.2 *lament*; 599.14 *laugh*; 507.2 *outcry*; 513.1 *stridency*; 603.7 *weep*
howler 274.10, 544.6 *blunder*; 272.4 *joke*; 465.2 *mistake*; 697.2 *solecism*; 546.2 *ugly person*
howling 515.1 *animal cry*; 514.18 *crying*; 513.7 *strident*; 515.7 *ululant*; 380.6 *violent*
howling gale 31.14 *windiness*
howlingly 515.10
howling success 246.1 *success*
how much? 705.25 *what?*
how's that! 53.21
how things stack up 221.3 *state of affairs*
how things stand 143.2 *circumstances*; 221.3 *state of affairs*
howzat 53.21 *how's that!*
hoyden 555.8 *young woman*
hoydenish 646.1 *naive*
HPLC 32.17 *analysis*
HTML 40.16 *Internet*
http 40.16 *Internet*
huaca 8.5 *deity*
hub 307.4 *axle*; 173.1 *centre*; 123.3 *chief thing*; 310.5 *focus*; 38.8 *machine element*
hubbie 223.12 *partner*
hubble-bubble 496.7 *tobacco*
Hubble classification 29.7 *galaxy*
Hubble constant 29.7 *galaxy*
Hubble Space Telescope 29.24 *telescope*
hub brake 320.11 *bicycle part*
hubbub 328.5 *commotion*; 408.5 *confusion*; 514.1 *cry*; 517.2 *dissonant noise*; 507.2 *outcry*; 327.2 *tumult*
hubby 570.10 *married man*
hub gear 320.11 *bicycle part*
hubris 660.3 *audacity*; 622.3 *conceit*; 467.1 *overestimation*; 21.11 *tragedy*
hubristic 622.16 *oppressive*; 467.5 *overestimating*
huckster 776.3 *bargain*; 727.10 *boast*; 778.11 *pedlar*
huckstering 727.4 *bombast*
huddle 46.8; 191.6 *become smaller*; 376.39 *come together*; 734.4 *conference*; 713.6 *consult*; 713.2 *consultation*; 376.21 *scrum*
huddled 191.7 *smaller*
Hudibrastic verse 17.6 *poetry*
Hudson 90.3 *US rivers*
Hudson Bay 92.9 *inlet*
hue 529.3; 412.4 *admixture*; 28.28 *colour*; 99.4 *nature*; 137.4 *type*
hue and cry 633.2 *chase*; 711.2 *danger signal*; 514.5 *hunting cry*; 467.2 *overestimate*; 742.6 *word*
hueless 530.7 *colourless*
huff 434.22 *blow*; 624.14 *make angry*; 624.2 *offence*; 624.9 *offend*; 50.8 *punting*
huffed 624.16 *angry*
huffiness 625.1 *irascibility*
huffy 625.4 *irascible*
hug 569.4 *act of friendship*; 267.6 *adhere*; 654.11 *be sociable*; 490.10 *comfort*; 593.14 *communication of love*; 184.11 *enfold*; 184.5 *enfoldment*; 742.3, 742.11 *gesture*; 490.9 *give pleasure*; 658.12 *greet*; 359.5 *preserve*; 360.6 *retain*; 360.1 *retention*; 658.5 *sign of courtesy*; 147.17 *stay near*; 654.9 *welcome*
huge 158.15 *big*
hugely 158.20 *largely*; 203.7 *quantitatively*
hugeness 158.2 *bigness*
huggable 593.22 *lovable*
huggermugger 114.11 *irregularly*; 737.16 *stealthily*
hugging 593.14 *communication of love*
hug oneself 622.29 *feel pride*; 673.16 *show off*
Huguenot 7.5 *Christian*
hula 22.2 *dance*
hula-hula 22.2 *dance*
hulk 486.7 *be clumsy*; 158.10 *big person*; 336.6 *muscleman*; 486.10 *unskilled person*; 380.4 *violent creature*
hulkiness 158.6 *squatness*
hulking 264.15, 486.3 *clumsy*; 240.1 *inconvenient*; 158.17 *stocky*
hulky 158.17 *stocky*
hull 550.13 *casing*; 171.1 *exterior*; 50.3 *parts of a sailing boat*; 50.7 *windsurfing*
hullabaloo 328.5 *commotion*; 408.5 *confusion*; 514.1 *cry*; 517.2 *dissonant noise*; 507.2 *outcry*
hum 509.9; 342.13 *be busy*; 111.11 *be regular*; 31.58 *blow*; 342.6 *business*; 515.6 *buzz*; 208.11 *crowd*; 509.2 *humming*; 692.19 *radio reception*; 510.9 *resonate*; 511.8 *sound faint*; 503.1 *stench*; 503.5 *stink*
human 566.12; 566.7 *person*; 627.6 *pitying*; 804.13 *venial*
human being 554.1 *life*; 566.7 *person*
human beings 566.1 *humankind*
human cannonball 21.31 *circus performer*
human communications 2.3 *social environment*
Human Cry 514
human development 2.9 *social change*
hum and haw 639.8 *balance*
human dynamo 342.10 *busy person*
humane 650.6 *benevolent*; 648.4 *lenient*; 652.6 *philanthropic*; 627.6 *pitying*
human ecologist 1.3 *anthropologist*
human ecology 1.1 *anthropology*; 34.18 *ecology*; 2.1 *sociology*
humanely 650.10 *benevolently*; 648.6 *leniently*; 652.8 *philanthropically*; 627.13 *pitifully*
humaneness 650.1 *benevolence*; 648.1 *leniency*; 652.1 *philanthropy*
human error 274.6 *fallibility*
human failing 566.2 *human nature*; 254.7 *vulnerability*
human fallibility 566.2 *human nature*
human flea 76.3 *pest*
human frailty 566.2 *human nature*; 804.3 *venial sin*
human garbage can 688.4 *glutton*
human geography 1.1 *anthropology*; 30.1 *earth science*
human institution 2.8
human interaction 2.3 *social environment*
humanism 244.11 *reformism*; 4.7 *school of thought*; 566.5 *study of mankind*
humanist 4.11 *follower of a doctrine*; 250.8 *free-thinker*; 250.10 *independent*; 402.3 *materialist*; 244.12 *reformer*; 566.6 *studier of mankind*
humanistic 566.12 *human*; 250.10 *independent*; 17.16 *literary*; 4.14 *of a philosophy*
humanistically 566.15 *humanly*
humanistic psychology 36.1 *psychology*
humanistic therapy 36.3 *psychiatric treatment*
humanitarian 650.5 *benevolent person*; 679.9 *generous person*; 679.2 *magnanimous*; 652.6 *philanthropic*; 652.3 *philanthropist*; 752.18 *voluntary*; 752.8 *volunteer*
humanitarianism 650.1 *benevolence*; 652.1 *philanthropy*; 652.2 *public spiritedness*; 566.5 *study of mankind*
humanities 554.7 *studies of life*; 6.3 *subject*
humanity 650.1 *benevolence*; 566.1 *humankind*; 654.7 *human society*; 648.1 *leniency*; 652.1 *philanthropy*; 627.1 *pity*
humanize 566.14 *make human*
Humankind 566
humankind 566.1; 654.7 *human society*; 554.1 *life*
human life 554.1 *life*
humanlike 566.12 *human*
humanlike machine 566.8
humanly 566.15; 2.16 *sociologically*
human nature 566.2
human object 402.5 *object*
humanoid 296.7 *ancient people*; 566.12 *human*; 566.8 *humanlike machine*
human palaeontology 3.2 *archaeology*
human race 566.1 *humankind*
human relations 579.3 *management*
human resources 352.3
human rights 250.2 *free speech*
human sacrifice 752.7 *martyr*
human scientist 1.3 *anthropologist*
human social behaviour 2.3 *social environment*
human society 654.7
human species 566.1 *humankind*
human studies 1.1 *anthropology*
human weakness 566.2 *human nature*; 804.3 *venial sin*
Humber 90.4 *British rivers*
humble 623.1; 658.7 *courteous*; 367.4 *debase*; 623.17 *humiliate*; 674.8 *modest*; 663.9 *obeisant*; 124.2 *obscure*; 7.15 *religious*; 667.9 *showing respect*; 732.1 *shy*; 271.1 *simple*; 387.6 *subject*; 388.5 *submitting*; 122.15 *subordinate*; 604.7 *thwart*; 468.4 *underestimating*; 473.5 *unselfish*; 9.9 *worshipful*
humble apology 808.1 *penitence*
humble confession 808.1 *penitence*
humbled 623.3; 604.9 *disappointed*; 122.18 *outclassed*; 9.9 *worshipful*
humbleness 623.7 *humility*; 122.1 *inferiority*; 667.3 *respectfulness*; 271.4 *simplicity*
humble oneself 623.21; 7.19 *be religious*; 9.7 *worship*
humble person 623.16
humble pie 479.8 *recantation*
humble servant 401.1 *servant*
humble submission 388.1 *submission*
humbling 604.2 *bad outcome*
humbling oneself 9.1 *worship*
humbly 623.27; 122.22 *basely*; 367.25, 658.14 *courteously*; 674.17 *modestly*; 468.6 *pessimistically*; 7.23 *religiously*; 667.22 *respectfully*; 732.8 *shyly*; 473.9 *unselfishly*; 388.6 *with humility*; 9.12 *worshipfully*
humbug 699.19 *cheat*; 700.15 *deceiver*; 699.17 *false person*; 700.11 *hoax*; 702.5 *hypocrisy*; 456.5 *ignorant person*; 699.15 *nonsense*; 676.2 *pretender*; 699.32 *spurious*; 699.4 *spuriousness*
humbuggery 699.15 *nonsense*; 699.4 *spuriousness*
humdinger 158.9 *big thing*; 235.8 *exceller*; 797.17 *good thing*
humdrum 620.1 *boredom*; 620.4 *boring*; 112.13 *monotonous*; 112.3 *repetitiveness*; 271.1 *simple*; 497.5 *tasteless*
humdrumness 620.1 *boredom*
humect 429.13 *moisten*
humectant 37.4 *drug type*; 429.9 *moist*; 433.26 *wetting*
humectate 429.13 *moisten*
humectation 429.1 *moisture*
Hume's Law 4.8 *philosophical term*
humid 31.52; 429.9 *moist*; 493.11 *warm*
humid climate 31.38 *climate*
humidification 429.3 *humidity*
humidify 429.13 *moisten*
humidity 429.3; 31.23 *heat*; 31.6 *weather data*
humidly 31.65 *meteorologically*; 429.17 *moistly*
humidness 31.23 *heat*; 429.3 *humidity*
humidor 433.19 *measuring instrument*; 496.7 *tobacco*
humiliate 623.17; 249.11 *cause adversity*; 367.4 *debase*; 668.27 *desecrate*; 124.13 *make unimportant*; 387.6 *subject*; 604.7 *thwart*
humiliated 367.21 *degraded*; 604.9 *disappointed*; 623.3 *humbled*; 122.18 *outclassed*; 808.7 *penitential*
humiliate oneself 812.4 *bring into disrepute*; 808.5 *do penance*
humiliating 623.6; **668.16**; 367.18 *lowering*; 808.7 *penitential*
humiliatingly 808.8 *penitently*
humiliation 623.9; 249.1 *adversity*; 604.2 *bad outcome*; 367.15 *debasement*; 305.4 *fall*; 668.8 *indignity*
Humility 623
humility 623.7; 658.1 *courtesy*; 122.1 *inferiority*; 674.1 *modesty*; 663.3 *obeisance*; 7.2 *religiousness*; 667.3 *respectfulness*; 732.3 *shyness*; 388.1 *submission*; 468.1 *underestimation*; 473.2 *unselfishness*; 9.1 *worship*

Humism 4.7 *school of thought*
Humist 4.11 *follower of a doctrine*
humming **509.2**; **509.16**; **515.9**; 342.19 *busy*; 511.4 *faint sound*; 515.3 *insect noise*; 510.1 *resonance*; 510.6 *resonant*
humming top 307.6 *rotator*
hummock 182.3 *dome*; 155.2 *lowlands*; 89.1, 154.3 *mountain*
hummocky 154.13 *mountainous*
hummus 25.52 *Greek dish*; 25.12 *hors d'oeuvre*; 25.34 *vegetarian dish*
hum of activity 342.6 *business*
humongous 158.15 *big*
humoral 431.16 *rheumy*
humorist **599.6**; 697.4 *buffoon*; 21.29 *entertainer*
humorous **599.10**; 600.10 *laughing*; 697.5 *nonsensical*
humorously **599.16**; 697.9 *nonsensically*
humorousness **599.1**
Humour **599**
humour **599.15**; 229.2 *attitude*; 648.3 *be lenient*; 431.3 *body fluid*; 599.1 *humorousness*; 429.1 *moisture*; 99.4 *nature*; 221.4 *state of mind*; 599.8 *temperament*; 642.3 *whim*
humour column 741.9 *news story*
humouring **599.11**; 648.1 *leniency*
humourless 620.4 *boring*; 643.1 *solemn*
humourless comedian 620.3 *boring person*
humourlessness 643.4 *solemnity*
humourous 272.5 *ridiculous*
humoursome 642.1 *capricious*
hump 182.5 *be convex*; 182.2 *bulge*; 182.3 *dome*; 154.3 *mountain*; 316.12 *transport*; 576.6 *work*
humpback bridge 38.21, 317.9 *bridge*
humped 182.4 *convex*
humping 593.5 *desire*; 316.2 *transportation*
Hun 357.6 *destroyer*; 651.8 *malefactor*
hunch 476.2 *basis of supposition*; 367.16 *courtesy*; 590.2 *impression*; 445.3 *insight*; 475.1 *prediction*; 367.8 *sit*; 478.5 *spontaneity*; 446.2 *theory*
hunchback 234.3 *deformity*
hunchbacked 234.7 *deformed*
hunch down 367.8 *sit*
hunched 367.23 *sedentary*
hundred 208.7 *myriad*; 86.5 *state*; 201.9 *treble figures*
hundred and forty-four 201.9 *treble figures*
hundred and twenty 201.9 *treble figures*
hundredfold 201.24 *fivefold*; 201.20 *hundredth*
hundred percent 201.9 *treble figures*
hundreds 208.2 *multitude*
hundreds and hundreds 201.9 *treble figures*
hundreds and thousands 208.2 *multitude*; 201.9 *treble figures*
hundreds of thousands 208.2 *multitude*
hundreds place 27.8 *number system*
hundredth **201.20**; 196.4 *less than one*
hundred thousand 201.10 *thousand*
hundred-to-one chance 105.4 *improbability*
hundredweight 414.9 *avoirdupois weight*; 201.9 *treble figures*
hung 361.7 *suspended*
Hungarian goulash 412.2 *mixed thing*; 25.54 *other dishes*
Hungarian GP at Hungaroring 61.2 *Formula 1 race*
hunger 557.2, 617.3 *appetite*; 782.7 *beggary*; 617.14 *be hungry*; 617.1 *desire*; 557.22 *eat well*; 687.5 *fast*; 687.2 *short rations*
hunger for 617.12 *desire*
hunger pains 491.2 *painful condition*
hunger strike 753.3 *gesture of protest*
hunger striker 687.4 *fasting person*
hunger striking 687.2 *short rations*
hunging 692.10 *telephone call*
hung jury 119.2 *equilibrium*; 16.7 *legal trial*
hung over 690.4 *crapulous*
hung parliament 119.2 *equilibrium*
hungrily **617.19**; 687.7 *abstemiously*; 557.28 *carnivorously*; 688.7 *gluttonously*
hungriness 617.3 *appetite*
hungry **617.10**; 782.3 *beggarly*; 557.26 *eating*; 687.6 *fasting*; 135.5 *necessitous*; 218.3 *underfed*
hungry as a bear 218.3 *underfed*
hungry for knowledge 6.17 *educable*
hung-up 328.16 *deranged*; 471.8 *diligent*
hunk 545.4 *attractive male*; 567.4 *boyfriend*; 203.2 *certain amount*; 363.6 *charmer*; 158.7 *mass*; 336.6 *muscleman*; 205.7 *piece*
hunkers 168.2 *rear end*
hunk of a man 336.6 *muscleman*
hunky 363.9 *attractive*
hunky-dory 797.1 *good*; 235.1 *worthy*
Huns 284.6 *people of the past*
hunt **633.11**; 381.1 *attack*; 633.2 *chase*; 449.2 *detect*; 449.7 *detection*; 59.15 *horse person*; 59.8, 60.2 *hunting*; 382.22 *kill animals*; 705.17 *question*; 59.16 *ride*; 60.7 *shoot*
hunt ball 376.10 *dance*; 654.5 *party*
hunt button 59.8 *hunting*
hunt down 647.6 *suppress*
hunted 634.18 *avoiding*; 633.17 *pursued*
hunter **60.4**; **71.24**; **633.6**; 382.13 *animal killer*; 330.16 *archer*; 59.1 *horse*; 59.15 *horse person*; 59.8 *hunting*; 59.2 *thoroughbred*; 281.7 *watch*
hunter-killer 586.24 *warship*
hunter's moon 292.4 *autumn*; 29.17 *moon*
hunter trials 59.8 *hunting*
hunt for 633.8 *pursue*; 60.7 *shoot*
hunting **59.8**; **60.2**; **633.16**; 382.9 *animal killing*; 633.2 *chase*; 449.7 *detection*; 322.5 *flight*; 633.1 *pursuit*; 60.8 *shooting*
hunting accessories 60.3 *hunting equipment*
hunting and fishing equipment **633.3**
Hunting and Shooting **60**
hunting association 60.2 *hunting*
hunting at force 60.2 *hunting*
hunting boots 60.3 *hunting equipment*
hunting cap 59.8 *hunting*
hunting clothes 60.3 *hunting equipment*
hunting cry **514.5**
hunting dance 22.4 *historic dancing*
hunting dog 71.9 *dog*; 60.6 *sporting dog*
Huntingdon's chorea 260.17 *nervous disorder*
hunting equipment **60.3**
hunting horn 59.8 *hunting*
hunting jacket 60.3 *hunting equipment*; 551.11 *jacket*
hunting knife 425.10 *knife*
hunting licence 60.2 *hunting*
hunting limit 60.2 *hunting*
hunting lodge 60.2 *hunting*
hunting party 60.2 *hunting*
hunting rifle 633.3 *hunting and fishing equipment*; 60.3 *hunting equipment*
hunting season 60.2 *hunting*; 292.1 *season*
hunting, shooting, and fishing 633.2 *chase*
hunt livery 59.8 *hunting*
hunt master 59.15 *horse person*; 59.8 *hunting*
hunt out 371.7 *drive out*
huntress 60.4, 633.6 *hunter*
hunt sab 70.10 *animal welfarist*
hunt saboteur 70.10 *animal welfarist*
hunt secretary 59.15 *horse person*
hunt servant 59.15 *horse person*
huntsman 382.13 *animal killer*; 514.9 *crier*; 59.15 *horse person*; 633.6 *hunter*; 579.15 *manager*
hunt terrier 59.8 *hunting*
hunt the facts 705.17 *question*
hurdle 304.14 *climb*; 43.11 *farmland*; 304.5, 304.18 *jump*; 378.2 *obstacle*; 47.7 *race*; 264.8 *snag*; 47.1 *track events*
hurdler 47.3 *athlete*; 59.2 *thoroughbred*
hurdle racing 59.7 *horseracing*
hurdles 59.7 *horseracing*; 47.9 *track*; 47.1 *track events*
hurdling 304.5 *jump*
hurl 330.5, 330.23, 331.4 *throw*
hurl at 381.7 *stone*
hurl defiance at 661.5 *defy*
hurler 330.14 *thrower*
hurley 58.7 *hurling*
hurling **58.7**; 330.3 *throwing*
hurling association 58.7 *hurling*
hurling ball 58.7 *hurling*
hurling stick 58.7 *hurling*
hurl oneself 380.7 *be violent*
hurly-burly 328.5 *commotion*; 408.9 *disorder*; 327.2 *tumult*
Huron 88.3 *US lakes*
hurrah 669.27 *bravo!*; 514.12, 598.8 *cheer*; 514.3 *cry of praise*; 600.2 *fanfare*
hurrah! **600.12**
hurray 514.12 *cheer*
hurricane 420.9 *broken water*; 332.11 *swift thing*; 379.1 *trap*; 380.5 *violent weather*; 31.13 *wind strength*; 31.16 *wind vortex*
hurricane-force 31.47 *windy*
hurricane lamp 522.5 *incandescent light*
hurricane warning 711.2 *danger signal*; 711.1 *warning*; 31.4 *weather forecast*
hurried 293.12 *early*; 262.3 *hasty*; 332.1 *swift*
hurriedly 293.17 *early*; 262.6 *hastily*
hurriedness 293.1 *earliness*
hurry 342.12 *be active*; 293.7 *be early*; 332.4 *be swift*; 293.1 *earliness*; 262.4 *haste*; 262.1 *hasten*; 262.2 *make haste*; 483.9 *motivate*; 342.3 *nimbleness*; 332.8 *speed*
hurrying 332.1 *swift*
hurryingly 332.14 *swiftly*
hurry off **313.4**
hurry-scurry 262.4 *haste*; 342.3 *nimbleness*
hurry someone up **332.7**
hurry up! **262.8**
hurry-up offence 46.7 *offence*
hurst 79.4 *trees*
hurt **245.5**; **245.11**; 651.7 *act of malevolence*; 798.8 *afflicted*; 798.2 *affliction*; 798.11 *be evil*; 240.5 *be inconvenient*; 242.12, 491.10 *be painful*; 236.13 *be worthless*; 245.12 *deteriorated*; 491.7 *feeling pain*; 491.9 *feel pain*; 236.11 *harmfulness*; 240.3 *inconvenience*; 491.11 *inflict pain*; 624.2 *offence*; 624.9 *offend*; 491.1 *pain*; 814.1 *punish*; 624.15 *resentful*; 651.18 *torment*; 337.7 *weaken*; 802.20 *wrong*; 802.8 *wrongdoing*
hurtful 798.9 *detrimental*; 236.5 *harmful*; 240.1 *inconvenient*; 491.8 *inflicting pain*; 802.16 *in the wrong*; 682.2 *unpleasant*
hurtfully 798.13 *destructively*; 491.13 *painfully*; 624.17 *resentfully*
hurtfulness 798.2 *affliction*; 236.11 *harmfulness*; 491.1 *pain*; 682.4 *unpleasantness*
hurting 491.7 *feeling pain*; 491.8 *inflicting pain*; 782.2 *insolvent*; 491.5 *painful*
hurtle 332.4 *be swift*; 380.7 *be violent*; 331.2 *collide*; 331.4 *throw*
hurtless 235.4 *worthwhile*
hurtling 332.1 *swift*
hurt one's pocket 792.9 *be dear*
hurt pride 623.9 *humiliation*
hurt the ears 517.10 *lack harmony*
husband 680.5 *be thrifty*; 556.8 *man*; 567.13 *man in the family*; 570.10 *married man*; 400.1 *master*; 223.12 *partner*; 439.6 *store*
husbandhood 570.1 *marriage*
husbandless 572.6 *celibate*; 571.12 *widowed*
husbandly 570.20 *matrimonial*
husbandman 43.15 *agriculturist*; 574.1 *plebeian*
husband one's resources 680.5 *be thrifty*
husbandry 43.1 *agriculture*; 579.3 *management*
hush 512.4 *hiss*; 214.5 *make smaller*; 685.4 *moderate*; 511.7 *mute*; 301.2 *repose*; 506.2, 506.4 *silence*; 730.15 *strike dumb*
hush! **506.6**
hushed 511.1 *faint-sounding*; 301.6 *quiescent*; 506.3 *silent*
hush-hush 123.5 *important*; 737.9 *secret*
hushing 512.1 *hiss*
hush money 768.2 *gift*; 790.8 *levy*; 483.5 *positive stimulus*; 813.8 *secret money*
Hush Puppies™ 551.19 *footwear*
hush puppies 25.38 *bread*
hush up 737.12 *keep secret*
husk 550.13 *casing*; 81.4 *cereal grass*; 98.3 *emptiness*; 171.1 *exterior*; 80.3 *fruit structure*; 215.1 *remainder*
huskily 730.17 *voicelessly*
huskiness 513.2 *hoarseness*; 730.2 *inarticulation*
husks 238.6 *refuse*; 215.2 *residue*
husky 316.6 *beast of burden*; 513.8 *hoarse*; 730.10 *low-voiced*
hussar 586.20 *cavalryman*; 59.15 *horse person*
Hussite 7.5 *Christian*
hussy 660.12 *impudent person*; 568.6 *loose woman*; 804.9 *wicked person*; 555.8 *young woman*
hustings 469.12 *election*; 740.7 *publicity*
hustle 342.12 *be active*; 332.4 *be swift*; 331.13 *blow*; 262.4 *haste*; 262.1 *hasten*; 331.1 *impel*; 327.23 *jolt*; 262.2 *make haste*; 483.9 *motivate*; 330.21 *move forward*; 342.3 *nimbleness*; 796.18 *prostitute*; 710.6 *request*; 300.14 *set in motion*; 774.12 *steal*
hustle and bustle 342.3 *nimbleness*
hustle away 262.1 *hasten*
hustle out 371.1 *expel*
hustler 342.10 *busy person*; 796.8 *immoral man*; 302.16 *progressive person*; 710.4 *requester*; 332.13 *swift person*
hustling 342.19 *busy*; 774.1 *stealing*; 332.1 *swift*
hut 565.8 *shelter*
hutch 71.20 *abode of mammals*; 309.4 *closed place*; 309.10 *enclose*; 43.7 *farm building*; 565.8 *shelter*
Huygens' principle 326.5 *wave*
huzzah 669.5, 669.16 *acclaim*; 514.3 *cry of praise*; 600.2 *fanfare*
hyacinth 539.6 *blue thing*
hyacinthine 539.1 *blue*; 540.6 *purple*
hyaenid 71.8 *flesh-eating mammal*
Hyaenidae 71.8 *flesh-eating mammal*
hyalin 527.8 *transparent thing*
hyaline 527.1 *transparent*
hyalite 527.8 *transparent thing*
hyaloplasm 34.7 *cell*
hyancinth 540.3 *purple thing*
hybrid **412.5**; 374.4 *compound*; 412.12 *mixed*; 5.17 *word*
hybrid computer 40.3 *computer*
hybrid expression 5.17 *word*
hybrid flower 412.5 *hybrid*
hybridization 412.1 *mixture*; 32.12 *valence*
hybridize 412.8 *mix*
hybrid language 5.26 *dialect*
hybrid orbital 32.12 *valence*
hybrid rose 412.5 *hybrid*
hydathode 559.3 *gland*
hydatid 75.13 *invertebrate larva*
Hyde Park 87.5 *London*
hydragogue 37.4 *drug type*; 431.9 *solvent*
hydra-headed 561.15 *reproduced*
hydrant 433.13 *irrigator*
hydrate **433.6**; 374.5 *combine*; 32.26 *react*; 32.10 *salt*; 433.29 *water*
hydrated 32.36 *acid*; 433.21 *watery*
hydration 433.6 *hydrate*
hydraulic 438.9 *mechanical*; 433.21 *watery*
hydraulically **433.36**; 438.11 *instrumentally*
hydraulic lift 366.9 *lifter*
hydraulic power 334.4 *energy*
hydraulic press 38.6 *simple machine*
hydraulics 431.13 *fluid mechanics*; 433.18 *hydrography*; 438.6 *mechanics*
hydraulic tailgate 366.9 *lifter*
hydro 394.14 *hospital*
hydrocele 431.3 *body fluid*; 260.4 *disease*
hydrocephalic 260.23 *diseased*
hydrocephalous 260.23 *diseased*
hydrodynamic 28.98 *physical*; 433.21 *watery*
hydrodynamically 433.36 *hydraulically*; 28.100 *physically*
hydrodynamics 28.2 *classical physics*; 431.13 *fluid mechanics*; 433.18 *hydrography*; 438.6 *mechanics*
hydroelectric 39.36 *electronic*; 334.17, 437.10 *powered*
hydroelectrically 437.12 *powerfully*
hydroelectricity 437.4 *electricity*; 334.6 *source of energy*
hydroelectric power 334.4 *energy*
hydroelectric power station 39.32 *power station*
hydroelectric station 334.6 *source of energy*
hydrogen 366.10 *elevator*; 33.15 *essential element*; 330.13 *fuel*; 417.5 *gas*

hydrogenate 432.26 *aerate*; 32.26 *react*
hydrogen balloon 366.10 *elevator*; 432.13 *gas balloon*
hydrogen bomb 587.16 *bomb*; 334.8 *nuclear power*
hydrogen bond 32.11 *chemical bond*
hydrogen electrode 32.19 *electrochemistry*
hydrogenous 32.34 *elemental*
hydrogen peroxide 530.4 *colour remover*; 394.3 *prophylactic*
hydrogen sulphide 503.2 *something that makes an unpleasant smell*
hydrogeology 431.13 *fluid mechanics*
hydrograph 433.19 *measuring instrument*
hydrographer 433.20 *hydrologist*; 91.6 *oceanographer*
hydrographic 30.49 *geophysical*; 91.8 *oceanographic*
hydrographically 91.12 *oceanographically*
hydrography **433.18**; 91.5 *oceanography*; 30.17 *ocean research vessel*
hydroid 75.21 *coelenterate*
hydrokinetics 431.13 *fluid mechanics*; 433.18 *hydrography*
hydrol 433.1 *water*
hydrolase 33.11 *enzyme*
hydrolic cement 24.9 *industrial ceramics*
hydrologic 90.12 *hydrological*
hydrological **90.12**; 30.48 *geological*
hydrological cycle 30.10 *water cycle*
hydrologically 90.13 *fluently*; 30.66 *geographically*
hydrologic cycle 433.17 *water cycle*
hydrologist **433.20**; 30.3 *geologist*
hydrology 30.1 *earth science*; 431.13 *fluid mechanics*; 433.18 *hydrography*
hydrolyse 375.4 *deconstruct*; 32.26 *react*
hydrolysis 375.2 *deconstruction*; 433.6 *hydrate*
hydrolytically 375.7 *to pieces*
hydromancy 11.9, 475.2 *divination*; 433.15 *holy water*
hydromechanics 433.18 *hydrography*; 438.6 *mechanics*
hydrometeor 31.24 *precipitation*; 433.17 *water cycle*
hydrometeorologic 31.54 *pluvial*
hydrometeorology 31.1 *meteorology*
hydrometer 28.88 *barometer*; 431.12 *flowmeter*; 26.8 *meter*; 416.3 *relative density*
hydrometric 26.16 *micrometric*; 433.21 *watery*
hydrometrically 433.36 *hydraulically*
hydrometry 431.13 *fluid mechanics*; 433.18 *hydrography*; 26.2 *micrometry*
hydropathy 433.7 *hydrotherapeutics*
hydrophilic 32.32 *solid*
hydrophilic colloid 32.3 *phase*
hydrophobia 260.6 *infection*; 461.3 *mental deterioration*
hydrophobic 32.32 *solid*
hydrophobic colloid 32.3 *phase*
hydrophyte 77.2 *plant*
hydrophytic 77.14 *of plants*
hydroponic 44.16 *horticultural*
hydroponically 43.22 *agriculturally*; 44.20 *horticulturally*
hydroponic food 557.7 *food*
hydroponics 43.4 *arable farming*; 44.5 *gardening*; 433.18 *hydrography*
hydroscopically 433.36 *hydraulically*
hydrosol 32.3 *phase*
hydrosphere 30.5 *earth*; 433.17 *water cycle*
hydrospheric 90.12 *hydrological*; 30.50 *terrestrial*
hydrostat 433.19 *measuring instrument*
hydrostatic 90.12 *hydrological*; 433.21 *watery*
hydrostatically 433.36 *hydraulically*
hydrostatic head 433.17 *water cycle*
hydrostatics 431.13 *fluid mechanics*; 433.18 *hydrography*
hydrotherapeutic 433.27 *cleansing*
hydrotherapeutics 433.7
hydrotherapy 433.7 *hydrotherapeutics*; 394.13 *therapy*
hydrothermal water 433.1 *water*
hydrous 433.21 *watery*
Hydrozoa 75.7 *coelenterate*
hydrozoan 75.7, 75.21 *coelenterate*
hyena 557.18 *eater*; 688.4 *glutton*; 651.8 *malefactor*
hyetographic 31.54 *pluvial*
hyetography 31.1 *meteorology*
Hygeia 259.3 *health*
Hygiene 257
hygiene **257.1**; 256.5 *ablutions*; 256.2 *cleaning*; 35.6 *health care*; 259.4 *healthfulness*; 359.1 *preservation*; 394.3 *prophylactic*; 252.2 *protection*
hygienic **257.4**; 256.16 *clean*; 256.18 *cleansing*; 259.2 *healthful*; 359.6 *preserving*; 255.15 *purifying*; 394.17 *remedial*; 252.6 *safe*; 252.8 *tutelary*
hygienically **257.7**; 256.19 *cleanly*; 259.8 *healthily*; 255.19 *purely*; 252.11 *safely*
hygienics 257.1 *hygiene*
hygienist **257.3**; 35.17 *paramedic*
hygric 433.28
hygrodeik 433.19 *measuring instrument*
hygrograph 433.19 *measuring instrument*; 31.7 *weather instruments*
hygrographic 31.42 *barometric*
hygrometer 28.88 *barometer*; 433.19 *measuring instrument*; 26.8 *meter*; 31.7 *weather instruments*
hygrometric 31.42 *barometric*; 433.28 *hygric*; 26.16 *micrometric*
hygrometry 433.18 *hydrography*; 26.2 *micrometry*
hygrophilous 433.28 *hygric*
hygroscope 433.19 *measuring instrument*
hygroscopic 433.28 *hygric*
hygrothermagraph 433.19 *measuring instrument*
hygrothermal 433.28 *hygric*
hylomorphism 4.7 *school of thought*
hylozoism 4.7 *school of thought*
Hymen 570.14 *gods and goddesses of marriage*
hymeneal 570.6 *general terms*; 570.20 *matrimonial*
hymeneal rites 570.5 *wedding*
hymenium 83.4 *fungal body*
hymenopteran 76.10 *insectan*
Hymettus honey 498.2 *sweetener*
hymn **10.8**; 600.2 *fanfare*; 17.7 *poem*; 18.5 *sacred music*; 516.2 *song*; 671.2 *thanks*
hymnal 10.8 *hymn*; 18.32 *instrumental*
hymnary 10.8 *hymn*
hymning 10.8 *hymn*
hymnody 18.5 *sacred music*
hymnographical 10.21 *ritualistic*
hymnography 10.8 *hymn*
hymnological 10.21 *ritualistic*
hymnology 10.8 *hymn*; 18.5 *sacred music*
hymn-singing 10.8 *hymn*; 10.3 *rite of worship*; 9.1 *worship*
hymn tune 18.5 *sacred music*
hymn writer 18.24 *musician*
hypabyssal intrusion 30.30 *igneous rock*
hype 480.6 *advertising*; 727.10 *boast*; 727.4 *bombast*; 669.15 *compliment*; 691.4 *drug taker*; 727.7 *exaggerate*; 727.1 *exaggeration*; 677.8 *flatter*; 677.1 *flattery*; 244.1 *improve*; 467.4 *overestimate*; 467.1 *overestimation*; 740.16 *publicize*; 740.8 *public relations*
hyped 727.12 *exaggerated*
hyped up 488.7 *susceptible*
hyper 342.18 *active*
hyperacidity 260.8 *indigestion*
hyperactive 342.18 *active*; 488.7 *susceptible*
hyperactive child 342.10 *busy person*
hyperactivity 342.9 *overactivity*
hyperaesthesia 488.2 *ability to sense*
hyperbaton 542.1 *ornament*
hyperbola 177.2 *bend*; 27.42 *circle*
hyperbole 542.2 *affectation*; 727.1 *exaggeration*; 329.9 *excessiveness*; 467.1 *overestimation*; 699.7 *pretence*; 681.5 *unrestrainedness*
hyperbolic 177.4 *curved*; 27.81 *curvilinear*; 329.13, 727.12 *exaggerated*; 542.10 *ornate*; 699.34 *pretending*; 681.2 *unrestrained*
hyperbolically 177.7 *curvedly*; 727.16 *exaggeratedly*; 329.16 *excessively*; 542.13 *ornately*; 467.7 *overoptimistically*; 699.41 *spuriously*
hyperbolic cosine 27.52 *trigonometric function*
hyperbolic function 27.52 *trigonometric function*
hyperbolic orbit 29.21 *orbit*
hyperbolic sine 27.52 *trigonometric function*
hyperbolic spiral 27.40 *curve*
hyperbolic tangent 27.52 *trigonometric function*
hyperbolism 727.1 *exaggeration*
hyperbolize 727.7 *exaggerate*
hyperboloid 27.45 *curved surface*; 27.83 *spherical*
hyperborean 324.13 *directional*; 145.8 *distant*
hypercathexis 36.28 *cathexis*
hypercritical 670.28 *fault-finding*; 264.14 *troublesome*
hypercriticalness 670.6 *fault-finding*
hypercriticism 670.6 *fault-finding*
hypercube 27.35 *space*
hyperfocal distance 41.18 *exposure time*
Hyperion 29.15 *sun*
hypermarket 557.17 *food shop*; 779.8 *store*
hypermetropia 519.2 *poor sight*
hypermetropic 519.9 *weak-sighted*
hyperphysical 11.16 *psychic*
hyperphysics 11.1 *occultism*
hyperplasia 158.4 *gigantism*
hyperpyrexia 260.3 *symptom*
hypersensitive 590.12 *sensitive*
hypersensitization 41.10 *graininess*
hypersonic 332.1 *swift*
hypersonically 332.14 *swiftly*
hypersonic speed 332.8 *speed*
hyperspace 27.35 *space*
hypersphere 27.35 *space*
hypertension 260.10 *cardiovascular disease*; 260.3 *symptom*
hypertext link 40.16 *Internet*
hyperthermia 260.3 *symptom*
hyperthermy 260.3 *symptom*
hyperthyroidism 260.4 *disease*; 342.9 *overactivity*
hypertrophied 190.7 *bigger*
hypertrophy 190.6 *become bigger*; 158.4 *gigantism*; 190.1 *growth*; 190.5 *make bigger*
hype up 669.15 *compliment*
hypha 83.4 *fungal body*
hyphal 83.10 *of fungi*
hyphen 373.4 *means of connection*; 742.7 *punctuation*; 372.5 *separator*
hyphenate 742.13 *punctuate*
hyphenated 373.15 *connected*; 742.17 *punctuated*
hyping 727.15 *bombastic*
hypnosis 489.4 *anaesthetic*; 394.5 *analgesic*; 592.4 *desensitization*; 463.1 *oblivion*; 11.10 *psychic phenomenon*; 343.9 *sleep*
hypnospore 84.4 *reproductive body*
hypnotherapeutic 36.32 *psychological*
hypnotherapist 36.30 *psychiatrist*
hypnotherapy 36.3 *psychiatric treatment*; 394.13 *therapy*
hypnotic 489.9 *anaesthetic*; 395.12 *appealing*; 386.9 *compelling*; 37.4 *drug type*; 685.8 *moderating*; 483.11 *motivational*; 463.8 *oblivious*; 480.19 *persuasive*; 608.3 *reliever*; 608.8 *relieving*; 394.17 *remedial*; 37.15 *sedative*; 11.15 *witchlike*
hypnotically 363.13 *attractionally*; 386.11 *compellingly*; 395.14, 483.14 *influentially*; 463.16 *obliviously*; 11.25 *occultly*
hypnotic suggestion 36.3 *psychiatric treatment*
hypnotic trance 11.10 *psychic phenomenon*; 36.14 *trance*
hypnotism 395.2 *occult influence*; 11.1 *occultism*; 363.2 *pulling power*
hypnotist 21.29 *entertainer*; 394.15 *healer*; 483.7 *motivator*; 11.12 *occultist*; 393.12 *repairer*
hypnotize 489.12 *anaesthetize*; 395.10 *be a prevailing influence*; 11.21 *bewitch*; 363.12 *lure*; 483.10 *manipulate*; 592.7 *render insensitive*
hypnotized 489.7 *anaesthetized*; 11.19 *bewitched*; 483.12 *motivated*; 343.4 *not awake*
hypnotizer 483.7 *motivator*
hypo 41.12 *development*
hypocaust 493.3 *heater*
hypochondria 461.4 *delusion*; 260.1 *ill health*; 36.10 *neurosis*
hypochondriac 700.15 *deceiver*; 461.7 *insane person*; 260.19 *sick person*; 260.21 *unhealthy*; 337.4 *weakling*
hypochondriacal 36.36 *psychologically disturbed*
hypocrisy **699.3**; **700.3**; **702.5**; 645.1 *cunning*; 700.4 *falseheartedness*; 677.1 *flattery*; 800.1 *improbity*
hypocrite **700.19**; 699.19 *cheat*; 645.3 *cunning person*; 700.15 *deceiver*; 234.5 *defacer*; 774.11 *dishonest person*; 699.17 *false person*; 227.6 *fickle person*; 125.7 *imitator*; 676.2 *pretender*; 702.6 *sophist*
hypocritical **699.31**; **700.37**; **702.10**; 645.4 *cunning*; 800.5 *dishonourable*; 198.11 *double-edged*; 479.11 *equivocating*; 677.12 *flattering*
hypocritically **699.42**; **702.15**; 800.11 *dishonourably*; 234.14 *distortedly*; 699.40 *falsely*
hypocriticalness 699.3, 700.3 *hypocrisy*
hypocycloid 27.40 *curve*
hypodermic 155.6 *lower*
hypodermic needle 308.2 *opener*; 425.8 *sharp-pointed thing*
hypogastric 155.6 *lower*
hypogeal 156.12 *under*
hypogene 156.12 *under*
hypogeous 156.12 *under*
hypogeum 156.4 *deep thing*
hypoglycaemic shock therapy 36.3 *psychiatric treatment*
hypogynous 78.12 *of flowers*
hypolimnion 155.4 *low thing*
hypomania 461.4 *delusion*
hypomaniac 461.7 *insane person*
hypomenorrhoea 560.11 *menstruation*
hypotaxis 5.30 *syntax*
hypotension 260.10 *cardiovascular disease*; 260.3 *symptom*
hypotenuse 27.43 *triangle*
hypotheca 84.3 *plant body*
hypothecator 4.10 *philosopher*
hypothermia 494.3 *chill*; 260.3 *symptom*
hypothesis 450.1 *belief*; 444.4 *explanation*; 443.6 *idea*; 28.6 *law*; 701.3 *line of argument*; 4.8 *philosophical term*; 4.1 *philosophy*; 344.3 *rudiment*; 476.1 *supposition*; 96.4 *theorization*; 27.65, 446.2 *theory*
hypothesist 4.10 *philosopher*; 476.4 *theorist*
hypothesis testing 27.54
hypothesize 443.16 *have an idea*; 4.20 *philosophize*; 701.15 *state*; 476.5 *suppose*; 27.89, 96.14, 446.17 *theorize*
hypothesized 476.8 *supposed*
hypothesizer 4.10 *philosopher*
hypothetical 450.14 *believed*; 477.12 *imaginary*; 701.11 *logical*; 4.13 *of philosophy*; 476.7 *suppositional*; 27.69, 28.99, 96.10, 446.10 *theoretical*; 453.1 *uncertain*
hypothetical argument 476.1 *supposition*
hypothetically 701.18 *arguably*; 450.16 *believably*; 96.18 *ideally*; 476.10 *supposedly*; 4.25, 446.20 *theoretically*
hypsographic 154.14 *altimetric*
hypsography 154.5 *height measure*
hypsometer 154.5 *height measure*; 26.8 *meter*
hypsometric 154.14 *altimetric*; 26.16 *micrometric*
hypsometry 154.5 *height measure*; 26.2 *micrometry*
hyracoid 71.15 *hoofed mammal*; 71.33 *ungulate*
Hyracoidea 71.15 *hoofed mammal*
hyrax-like 71.33 *ungulate*
Hyrcanian wood 737.5 *difficult problem*
hyssop 496.5 *herbs*
hysterectomy 563.2 *making infertile*; 394.12 *surgery*
hysteresis 333.12 *hesitation*; 28.63 *magnetic phenomenon*
hysteretic 333.7 *delayed*
hysteria 461.4 *delusion*; 461.6 *mental breakdown*; 36.10 *neurosis*; 36.12 *stress*
hysteric 461.7 *insane person*
hysterical 642.1 *capricious*; 599.9 *funny*; 461.12 *manic*; 590.13 *passionate*; 380.6 *violent*
hysterically 36.39 *psychologically*; 590.20 *with feeling*
hysterical personality 36.8 *disordered personality*
hysterical trance 36.14 *trance*
hysterics 36.12 *stress*

I 139.12; 566.7 *person*
IAA 33.17 *plant hormone*
iamb 17.9 *metre*
iambic 17.20 *metrical*
iambic pentameter 17.9 *metre*
I and I 139.12 *I*
iatric 35.22 *medical*
iatrochemistry 32.1 *chemistry*

iatrogenic 260.23 *diseased*
I-beam 38.27 *superstructure*
ibid 111.18 *identically*
ibidem 111.18 *identically*
ibis 72.3 *water bird*
ibuprofen 394.5 *analgesic*
ice 494.5; 550.24 *coat*; 31.32 *freeze*; 359.2 *preserver*; 68.1 *skiing*; 421.8 *smooth thing*; 31.63 *snow*; 498.8 *sweeten*; 174.7 *top*; 527.8 *transparent thing*; 433.1 *water*
ice age 31.40 *climatic change*; 494.7 *cold weather*; 284.3 *geological period*; 30.40 *glaciation*
ice axe 62.4 *climbing equipment*
ice bag 494.4 *cooler*
ice bar 55.1 *angling*
iceberg 30.39; 494.6 *Arctic*; 592.5 *insensitive person*; 92.2 *island*; 655.6 *unsocial person*
ice blue 539.1 *blue*
ice-bound 494.8 *cold*
icebox 494.4 *cooler*; 25.4 *kitchen container*; 815.3 *prison cell*; 439.4 *storage*
icebreaker 586.24 *warship*
ice bucket 494.4 *cooler*
icecap 30.38 *glacier*; 494.5 *ice*
ice cloud 31.18 *cloud*
ice-cold 494.8 *cold*
ice-covered 531.2 *whitened*
ice cream 25.35, 498.3 *dessert*
ice-cream parlour 557.15 *eating place*
ice-cream scoop 410.17 *ladle*
ice-cream soda 498.5 *sweet drink*
ice crystal 31.24 *precipitation*
ice cube 494.5 *ice*
iced 494.8 *cold*; 58.8 *hockey*; 359.7 *preserved*; 498.6 *sweet*; 174.6 *topped*
ice-dance 68.13 *ice-skating*
ice-dance music 68.7 *ice-dancing*
ice-dancer 68.11 *skier*
ice-dancing 68.7
ice-dancing move 68.7 *ice-dancing*
iced tea 558.3 *tea*
iced up 494.8 *cold*
ice erosion 30.35 *weathering*
icefall 30.38 *glacier*
ice field 30.38 *glacier*; 494.5 *ice*
ice fish 55.7 *angle*; 633.11 *hunt*
ice fishing 55.1 *angling*; 633.2 *chase*
ice floe 494.5 *ice*; 30.39 *iceberg*; 92.2 *island*
ice hammer 62.4 *climbing equipment*
ice hockey 58.3
ice hockey association 58.3 *ice hockey*
ice hockey clothing 58.3 *ice hockey*
ice hockey player 58.4
ice hockey skates 58.3 *ice hockey*
ice hockey stick 58.3 *ice hockey*
ice hockey tactics 58.3 *ice hockey*
ice hole 55.1 *angling*
ice house 494.4 *cooler*
Icelandic low 31.11 *weather system*
ice machine 494.4 *cooler*
ice milk 558.5 *milk*
ice over 494.11 *become cold*; 31.63 *snow*
ice pack 494.4 *cooler*; 30.39 *iceberg*
icepick 425.8 *sharp-pointed thing*
ice queen 592.5 *insensitive person*
ice raft 30.39 *iceberg*
ice rink 58.3 *ice hockey*; 421.8 *smooth thing*
ice sculpture 424.3 *brittle thing*
ice sheet 30.38 *glacier*; 494.5 *ice*
ice shelf 30.38 *glacier*
ice show 21.7 *show*
ice-skate 68.15; 421.12 *go smoothly*
ice-skater 68.11 *skier*
ice-skating 68.6; **68.13**
ice spoon 55.1 *angling*
ice surf 50.18 *windsurf*
ice surfer 50.9 *sailor*
ice surfing 50.7 *windsurfing*
ice the puck 58.9 *play hockey*
ice tongue 30.38 *glacier*
ice up 494.11 *become cold*
I Ching 11.9, 475.2 *divination*
ichor 431.3 *body fluid*; 560.7 *pus*
ichorous 431.16 *rheumy*
ichthyic 74.13 *fishlike*
ichthyoid 74.13 *fishlike*
ichthyological 74.14
ichthyologist 74.12; 70.11 *zoologist*
ichthyology 70.9 *animal science*; 74.6 *study of fish*
ichthyomancy 11.9 *divination*
ichthyomorphic 74.13 *fishlike*
ichthyophagy 557.5 *eating habit*
ichthyophile 74.12 *ichthyologist*
ichthyopterygian 73.6 *extinct reptile*
ichthyosaur 73.6 *extinct reptile*
ichthyosaurus 296.8 *prehistoric animal*
ichthyosis 428.16 *dry skin*
icicle 424.3 *brittle thing*; 494.5 *ice*; 592.5 *insensitive person*; 361.3 *suspended object*
icily 494.13 *coldly*; 418.12 *toughly*; 655.14 *unsocially*
iciness 494.2 *freezing*; 655.1 *unsociability*
icing 550.3 *coating*; 498.3 *dessert*; 494.2 *freezing*; 58.8 *hockey*; 58.3 *ice hockey*; 322.7 *miscellaneous aviation terms*; 174.4 *top layer*
icing on the cake 211.3 *additional item*; 232.1 *completeness*; 244.5 *improvement*
icing sugar 25.7 *basic ingredient*; 498.2 *sweetener*
icon 21.24 *actor*; 40.19 *computing terms*; 9.3 *idol*; 717.6 *image*; 19.8 *painting*; 10.14 *sacred object*
I confess 808.9 *sorry!*
iconic 19.24 *pictorial*; 717.13 *representational*; 721.13 *representing*
iconoclasm 357.3 *destructiveness*; 118.3 *nonconformism*
iconoclast 357.6 *destroyer*; 118.8 *dissenter*; 7.4 *religionist*
iconoclastic 118.12 *nonconformist*
iconographer 742.8 *signer*
iconography 742.2 *symbolism*
iconolater 9.6 *idolater*
iconolatrous 9.10 *idolatrous*
iconolatry 9.2 *idolatry*
iconologist 742.8 *signer*
iconology 742.2 *symbolism*
icon painter 19.16 *artist*
icosahedron 27.46 *polyhedron*
ICR 40.13 *character recognition*
icterus 537.6 *yellowness*
icthyomancer 11.13 *diviner*
icy 494.8 *cold*; 31.55 *cool*; 418.3 *hardened*; 638.3 *strong-willed*; 655.8 *unsociable*; 31.47 *windy*
icy fingers 612.1 *fear*
ID 744.2 *certificate*; 743.3 *means of identification*; 318.6 *passport*
id 139.11 *identity*; 101.6 *internal world*; 36.21 *psyche*; 11.7 *spirit*
i.d. 716.6 *documentation*
Idea 446
idea 443.6; **446.1**; 450.1 *belief*; 484.3 *expedient plan*; 160.1 *form*; 701.4 *gist*; 477.4 *ideality*; 717.6 *image*; 590.2 *impression*; 449.9 *invention*; 694.1 *meaning*; 356.4 *mental product*; 4.1 *philosophy*; 446.3 *plan*; 694.5 *point*; 344.5 *reason*; 478.5 *spontaneity*; 476.1 *supposition*; 446.2 *theory*; 447.1 *topic*; 642.3 *whim*
idea behind 344.5 *reason*
idea conveyed 694.1 *meaning*
ideal 446.6; **446.13**; 232.1 *completeness*; 477.4 *ideality*; 477.12 *imaginary*; 480.11, 483.1 *motive*; 617.5 *object of desire*; 4.13 *of philosophy*; 230.1 *perfect*; 96.10 *theoretical*; 344.6 *undertaking*
idealism 101.5; **446.7**; **477.7**; 467.1 *overestimation*; 244.11 *reformism*; 4.7 *school of thought*; 96.4 *theorization*; 473.2 *unselfishness*; 803.1 *virtue*
idealist 353.7 *attempter*; 101.7 *believer in a nonmaterial world*; 466.6 *discriminating person*; 4.11 *follower of a doctrine*; 610.5 *hoper*; 101.10 *idealistic*; 467.3 *optimist*; 446.9 *person of ideas*; 652.3 *philanthropist*; 4.10 *philosopher*; 244.12 *reformer*; 96.6 *unrealistic person*; 477.9 *visionary*
idealistic 101.10; 446.13 *ideal*; 477.10 *imaginative*; 244.16 *improving*; 4.14 *of a philosophy*; 652.6 *philanthropic*; 96.11 *unrealistic*; 473.5 *unselfish*; 803.5 *virtuous*
idealistically 244.17 *better*; 446.22, 477.17 *imaginatively*; 467.7 *overoptimistically*; 652.8 *philanthropically*; 101.14 *subjectively*; 4.25 *theoretically*; 473.9 *unselfishly*; 803.9 *virtuously*
ideality 477.4; 446.7 *idealism*; 476.1 *supposition*
idealization 446.7 *idealism*; 477.4 *ideality*; 27.65 *theory*
idealize 96.15; 477.15 *fantasize*; 9.8 *idolatrize*; 446.15 *imagine*; 4.20 *philosophize*
idealized 446.13 *ideal*
idealized pleasure 490.5
ideally 96.18; **446.23**; 795.13 *morally*; 4.25 *theoretically*
idealness 446.7 *idealism*; 230.3 *perfection*
ideals 446.5 *ideology*; 795.1 *morality*; 803.2 *virtues*; 631.6 *way of life*
ideas 446.5 *ideology*
ideas person 446.9 *person of ideas*
ideate 446.15 *imagine*; 442.12, 443.12 *think*
ideation 443.2 *intellectual exercise*
ideational 446.11; 4.13 *of philosophy*
ideatum 446.1 *idea*
idée fixe 641.7 *opinionatedness*; 465.4 *prejudgment*
idem 111.12 *same*; 111.1 *sameness*
identical 750.14 *conforming*; 110.6 *correlative*; 27.75, 119.6 *equal*; 694.6 *meaningful*; 111.12 *same*; 115.7 *similar*
identically 111.18; 115.14 *comparably*; 110.11 *correlatively*; 119.12 *equally*; 750.34 *uniformly*
identicalness 111.1 *sameness*
identical twins 198.6 *twins*
identifiability 520.3 *visibility*
identifiable 449.15 *discoverable*; 743.12 *identified*; 738.14 *manifest*; 695.3 *recognizable*; 520.1 *visible*
identifiably 743.14; 449.16 *originally*
Identification 743
identification 743.1; 36.19 *defence mechanism*; 449.6 *discovery*; 590.5 *good feeling*; 462.1 *memory*; 721.7 *nomenclature*
identification papers 743.3 *means of identification*
identification sign 742.1 *sign*
identified 743.12
identify 743.10; 99.11, 139.22 *characterize*; 449.1 *discover*; 455.11 *know*; 469.4 *pick*; 695.7 *recognize*; 462.12 *remember*
identifying 742.14 *signifying*
identifying sign 742.1 *sign*
identifying with 750.10 *in accord*
identify oneself 743.11
identify with 750.21 *be in accord*; 110.9 *correlate*
Identikit™ 117.15 *everyday*; 743.3 *means of identification*; 717.2 *reproduction*
identity 139.11; **743.2**; 750.1 *accord*; 110.3 *correlation*; 27.26 *equality*; 139.2 *personality*; 4.8 *philosophical term*; 27.21 *set*; 197.4 *singularity*; 694.4 *type of meaning*
identity card 716.6 *documentation*; 743.3 *means of identification*
identity element 27.21 *set*
identity matrix 27.22 *matrix*
identity number 743.3 *means of identification*
ideogram 5.13 *letter*
ideograph 5.13 *letter*
ideographic 5.41 *lettered*
ideological 446.13 *ideal*; 4.13 *of philosophy*; 443.11 *reasoning*
ideologically 446.24; 4.25 *theoretically*
ideological war 585.1 *war*
ideologist 446.9 *person of ideas*; 652.3 *philanthropist*; 443.7 *thinker*
ideologue 446.9 *person of ideas*; 4.10 *philosopher*
ideology 446.5; 4.2 *philosophical system*; 450.2 *religious belief*
Ides 275.11 *date*
id est 703.22 *demonstrably*; 719.18 *in other words*
idiochromosome 34.14 *chromosome*
idiocy 459.1 *folly*; 461.1 *insanity*; 457.1 *lack of intellect*; 461.2 *subnormality*
idioglossia 5.5 *nonstandard language*
idiolect 729.1 *faculty of speech*; 724.4 *literary style*; 5.5 *nonstandard language*; 139.10 *specialized language*; 696.12 *unintelligible thing*
idiom 5.26 *dialect*; 729.1 *faculty of speech*; 271.4 *simplicity*; 139.10 *specialized language*; 5.3 *spoken language*; 724.1 *style*; 694.4 *type of meaning*
idiomatic 139.16 *characteristic*; 543.3 *elegant*; 694.6 *meaningful*; 5.39 *of language*
idiomatically 5.49 *colloquially*; 724.10 *stylistically*
idiomatic speech 729.1 *faculty of speech*; 5.3 *spoken language*
idiophone 18.25 *musical instrument*
idioplasm 34.7 *cell*
idiosyncrasy 118.5; 229.2 *attitude*; 139.3 *characteristic*; 231.7 *defect*; 126.1 *originality*; 724.1 *style*; 632.2 *tendency*; 642.3 *whim*
idiosyncratic 642.1 *capricious*; 99.9, 139.16 *characteristic*; 118.14 *eccentric*; 299.5 *unusual*
idiosyncratically 724.10 *stylistically*
idiot 459.3 *foolish person*; 461.7 *insane person*; 272.3 *object of ridicule*; 457.3 *unintelligent person*
idiot box 692.22 *television set*
idiotic 459.5 *foolish*; 457.7 *intellectually subnormal*; 457.5 *lacking intellect*; 697.5 *nonsensical*
idiotically 459.8 *foolishly*; 457.11 *unintelligently*
idiot savant 461.7 *insane person*; 619.5 *person of wonder*
I disagree 704.13 *no!*
idle 263.4 *at ease*; 343.12 *be inactive*; 301.8 *be motionless*; 346.7 *be operational*; 238.2 *futile*; 341.3 *inactive*; 339.5 *inert*; 580.7 *leisurely*; 333.1 *move slowly*; 341.4 *not act*; 343.3 *not participating*; 350.3 *not wanted*; 343.2 *not working*; 301.5 *sedentary*; 157.2 *superficial*; 333.5 *unhurried*; 350.1 *unused*
idle fancy 477.7 *idealism*
idle gossip 734.2 *chat*; 731.3 *talk*
idle hours 341.1 *inaction*
idle moments 580.1 *leisure*
idleness 343.7; 350.10 *disuse*; 263.1 *ease*; 238.4 *futility*; 341.1 *inaction*; 339.1 *inertness*; 580.1 *leisure*
idler 634.17 *avoider*; 294.4 *latecomer*; 666.3 *negligent person*; 341.2 *nonacting person*; 343.8 *nonworker*; 333.15 *slow person*
idle rich 341.2 *nonacting person*; 343.8 *nonworker*
idler wheel 307.6 *rotator*
idle talk 734.2 *chat*
idly 339.7 *inertly*; 350.12 *out of use*; 333.16 *slowly*; 341.5 *without action*
idol 9.3; 21.24 *actor*; 8.5 *deity*; 235.8 *exceller*; 717.6 *image*; 593.11 *loved one*; 619.5 *person of wonder*
idolater 9.6; 804.9 *wicked person*
idolatrize 9.8; 667.16 *revere*
idolatrous 9.10; 669.18 *approving*
idolatrously 9.12 *worshipfully*
idolatry 9.2; 593.1 *love*; 669.3 *praise*; 804.6 *religious sin*
idolism 9.2 *idolatry*
idolization 667.2 *admiration*; 8.9 *deification*; 9.2 *idolatry*; 593.1 *love*
idolize 8.17 *deify*; 9.8 *idolatrize*; 593.23 *love*; 669.14 *praise*; 667.16 *revere*; 619.9 *wonder*
idolized 8.15 *deified*; 9.11 *worshipped*
idolized person 9.4
idolizer 9.6 *idolater*; 9.5 *worshipper*
idolizing 667.10 *reverent*
I don't believe it 630.14 *good heavens!*; 619.14 *wonderful!*
idyll 17.7 *poem*
idyllic 17.19 *narrative*; 241.1, 490,6 *pleasant*
i.e. 719.18 *in other words*; 139.31 *namely*
if 476.11 *supposing*; 222.15 *under the circumstances*
iffy 107.8 *chance*; 254.1 *dangerous*; 812.4 *disreputable*
if not 222.15 *under the circumstances*
I-formation 46.7 *offence*
if possible 102.9 *possibly*
if so 222.15 *under the circumstances*
I give up 456.13 *who knows?*
igloo 494.6 *Arctic*
igneous 493.10 *on fire*; 30.56 *petrographic*
igneous rock 30.30; 30.28 *rock*
ignis fatuus 522.9 *firefly*; 96.2 *illusion*; 518.5 *imagination*
ignite 624.12 *become angry*; 493.15 *burn*; 522.24 *light*
ignition 493.6, 522.8 *fire*
ignition system 437.2 *lighter*
ignoble 800.5 *dishonourable*
ignobly 800.11 *dishonourably*
ignominious 812.4 *disreputable*; 712.9 *vituperative*
ignominiously 712.13 *vituperatively*
ignominy 812.1 *disrespect*
ignoramus 456.5 *ignorant person*; 457.3 *unintelligent person*
Ignorance 456
ignorance 456.1; 519.7 *figurative blindness*; 459.1 *folly*; 489.1 *lack of feeling*; 646.2 *naivety*; 641.7 *opinionatedness*; 523.7 *spiritual darkness*; 457.2 *unintelligence*; 486.8 *unskilfulness*
ignorant 456.6; 523.11 *benighted*; 519.12 *blind to*; 459.5 *foolish*; 646.1 *naive*; 457.6 *unintelligent*; 486.2 *unskilled*

ignorantly 456.12; 487.6 *unaccustomedly*; 457.11 *unintelligently*
ignorant of 487.1 *unaccustomed*
ignorant person 456.5
ignore 655.13; 634.1 *avoid*; 519.16 *be blind to*; 505.8 *be deaf*; 659.7 *be discourteous*; 472.12 *be inattentive*; 661.6 *be insubordinate*; 666.6 *be neglectful*; 641.9 *be obstinate*; 472.13 *be thoughtless*; 489.11 *be unfeeling*; 672.6 *be ungrateful*; 649.11 *condone*; 668.21 *disregard*; 128.7 *exclude*; 341.4 *not act*; 350.5 *not use*; 470.1 *reject*; 388.3 *submit*
ignored 668.18 *undervalued*; 672.4 *unthanked*
ignore formalities 262.2 *make haste*
ignore instructions 662.15 *be disobedient*
ignore the consequences 615.5 *be rash*
ignoring 128.12 *exclusively*; 472.4 *thoughtlessness*
iguana 73.2 *lizard*
ikat weave 42.10 *woven*
ikkyo 52.10 *aikido*
ilk 137.8 *genealogy*; 721.6 *sort*; 137.4 *type*
ill 337.10; 249.6 *adverse*; 798.8 *afflicted*; 264.25 *difficultly*; 798.12 *evilly*; 236.11 *harmfulness*; 260.22 *sick*; 260.21 *unhealthy*; 236.15 *worthlessly*
ill-advised 486.4 *bungled*; 459.5 *foolish*; 240.1 *inconvenient*; 465.9 *misjudged*; 615.4 *rash*
ill-balanced 120.3 *unequal*
ill-behaved 264.14 *troublesome*
ill-bred 631.18 *badly behaved*; 659.6 *bad-mannered*; 646.1 *naive*; 675.7 *vulgar*
ill-breeding 631.4 *bad conduct*; 659.2 *bad manners*; 675.3 *grossness*
ill-considered 486.4 *bungled*; 459.5 *foolish*; 262.3 *hasty*; 240.1 *inconvenient*; 615.4 *rash*; 486.1 *unskilful*
ill-contrived 486.4 *bungled*; 240.1 *inconvenient*
ill-defined 486.4 *bungled*; 521.2 *difficult to see*; 138.20 *generalized*; 524.6 *murky*; 161.5 *shapeless*
ill-devised 486.4 *bungled*
ill-disciplined 686.8 *overindulgent*
ill-disposed 236.5 *harmful*; 651.10 *malevolent*
ill disposition 651.1 *malevolence*
ill-dressed 525.10 *aspectual*
illegal 16.55; 236.3 *bad*; 804.15 *criminal*; 796.11 *immoral*; 802.16 *in the wrong*; 752.17 *offered*; 335.10 *powerless*; 806.7 *sinful*; 399.5 *vetoed*
illegal alien 295.8 *new arrival*
illegal bodycheck 58.5 *lacrosse*
illegal borrowing 772.3; **774.6**
illegal entry 314.3 *inroad*
illegal execution 814.13 *capital punishment*
illegal gain 765.5 *profit*
illegal hold 52.5 *wrestling*
illegal hooking 64.3 *rugby play*
illegal immigrant 564.6 *illegal occupant*
illegality 16.35; 236.9 *badness*; 804.7 *criminality*; 806.1 *guilt*; 806.3 *sin*; 802.6 *unlawfulness*; 399.1 *veto*
illegalize 16.75 *make illegal*
illegally 16.82; 399.7 *by veto*; 804.21 *criminally*; 16.89 *guiltily*; 752.20 *persuasively*; 335.14 *powerlessly*
illegally ground the ball 46.18 *be penalized*
illegal motion 46.13 *penalty*
illegal occupant 564.6
illegal offer 752.4
illegal speed 332.8 *speed*
illegal use of hands 46.13 *penalty*
illegibility 358.3 *obliteration*; 696.11 *unintelligibility*
illegible 358.6 *obliterated*; 264.12 *problematic*; 696.1 *unintelligible*
illegibly 696.13 *unintelligibly*
illegitimacy 16.35 *illegality*; 699.4 *spuriousness*; 802.6 *unlawfulness*; 399.1 *veto*
illegitimate 16.55 *illegal*; 802.16 *in the wrong*; 699.32 *spurious*; 399.5 *vetoed*
illegitimately 399.7 *by veto*; 16.82 *illegally*
illegitimize 16.75 *make illegal*
ill-equipped 335.11 *unprotected*; 218.2 *unprovided*
ill-fated 249.8 *unlucky*
ill-favoured 546.4 *ugly*
ill feeling 651.4 *bitterness*; 596.1 *dislike*; 594.1 *hate*
ill feelings 624.1 *resentment*
ill fortune 249.3 *bad fortune*; 798.3 *bad luck*; 288.3 *lost chance*; 107.2 *luck*
ill-furnished 218.2 *unprovided*
ill-gotten 774.17 *stolen*
ill-gotten gains 765.5 *profit*; 769.2 *something received*; 774.4 *stolen goods*; 773.5 *takings*
Ill Health 260
ill health 260.1; 231.5 *imperfection*
ill humour 624.1 *resentment*; 626.1 *sullenness*
ill-humoured 625.4 *irascible*; 624.15 *resentful*; 626.6 *sullen*
ill-humouredly 625.9 *irascibly*; 626.13 *sullenly*
illiberality 641.7 *opinionatedness*
illicit 700.35 *deceptive*; 699.35 *fraudulent*; 16.55 *illegal*; 802.16 *in the wrong*; 399.5 *vetoed*
illicit love 796.4; 250.6 *liberality*; 593.8 *love affair*
illicitly 399.7 *by veto*; 16.82 *illegally*; 802.28 *immorally*
illicitness 16.35 *illegality*; 802.6 *unlawfulness*; 399.1 *veto*
illicit practice 699.8, 700.10 *fraud*
illimitability 202.4 *infinity*
illimitable 202.1 *infinite*
illimitably 202.10 *infinitely*
ill-intentioned 651.10 *malevolent*
illiteracy 456.1 *ignorance*
illiterate 456.6 *ignorant*; 456.5 *ignorant person*; 5.39 *of language*
illiterately 5.49 *colloquially*
illiterate speech 5.5 *nonstandard language*
ill-judged 486.4 *bungled*
ill-lit 523.8 *dark*; 524.5 *dim*
ill luck 288.3 *lost chance*
ill-made 234.7 *deformed*
ill-mannered 631.18 *badly behaved*; 659.6 *bad-mannered*; 486.3 *clumsy*; 672.3 *ungrateful*
ill-mannered person 631.5 *badly behaved person*
ill-matched 570.21 *married*; 120.3 *unequal*
ill nature 594.1 *hate*; 651.1 *malevolence*; 626.1 *sullenness*
ill-natured 594.10 *hating*; 651.10 *malevolent*; 626.6 *sullen*
ill-naturedly 594.18 *hatefully*; 626.14 *irritably*
illness 260.2; 249.1 *adversity*; 798.2 *affliction*; 245.9 *dilapidation*; 594.7 *hated thing*; 260.1 *ill health*
illogical 109.7; 274.15 *erroneous*; 103.1 *impossible*; 702.7 *sophistic*; 457.6 *unintelligent*
illogicality 103.5 *impossibility*; 702.1 *sophistry*; 457.2 *unintelligence*; 109.1 *unrelatedness*
illogically 103.11 *impossibly*; 702.14 *sophistically*; 457.11 *unintelligently*
illogicalness 702.1 *sophistry*
ill-omened 611.6 *inauspicious*; 288.13 *untimely*; 711.8 *warning*
ill-planned 240.1 *inconvenient*
ill-prepared 486.4 *bungled*
ill-proportioned 544.7 *graceless*
ill-repute 812.1 *disrespect*
ill service 651.7 *act of malevolence*
ill-sorted 120.3 *unequal*
ill-sounding 544.9 *inelegant*
ill-spent 238.2 *futile*
ill-starred 611.6 *inauspicious*; 249.8 *unlucky*; 288.13 *untimely*
ill-supplied 218.2 *unprovided*
ill temper 626.3 *irritableness*
ill-tempered 626.7 *irritable*
ill-timed 486.4 *bungled*; 240.1 *inconvenient*; 465.9 *misjudged*; 288.13 *untimely*
ill-treat 236.14; 351.1 *misuse*; 651.18 *torment*; 380.8 *use violence*; 802.20 *wrong*
ill-treated 351.4 *misused*
ill-treatment 651.7 *act of malevolence*; 236.11 *harmfulness*; 351.2 *misuse*; 349.6 *use*
ill turn 651.7 *act of malevolence*
illuminance 28.24 *light emission*
illuminate 725.2 *clarify*; 529.15 *colour*; 738.1 *display*; 6.22 *educate*; 703.16 *explain*; 719.8 *interpret*; 522.24 *light*; 520.10 *make visible*; 19.19 *paint*; 4.21 *rationalize*; 738.3 *reveal*
illuminated 520.2 *clear*; 522.22 *enlightened*; 703.11 *explanatory*; 522.18 *lit*; 19.27 *painted*
illuminated sign 522.6 *electric light*
illuminati 455.7 *academia*; 522.13 *enlightenment*; 442.8 *intellectual person*
illuminating 721.11 *descriptive*; 6.16 *educational*; 703.11 *explanatory*; 722.5 *expository*; 693.16 *informative*; 719.14 *interpretive*; 522.15 *lucent*
illuminatingly 703.22 *demonstrably*; 6.25 *educationally*; 522.30 *lightly*
illumination 6.1 *education*; 522.13 *enlightenment*; 703.3 *explanation*; 449.8 *finding out*; 719.1 *interpretation*; 455.1 *knowledge*; 522.1 *light*; 28.24 *light emission*; 522.3 *lightening*; 19.2 *painting*; 542.3 *pattern*; 19.7 *picture*; 717.2 *reproduction*; 520.7 *that which makes visible*
illuminations 601.8 *salute*
illuminator 19.16 *artist*; 542.8 *decorator*
illumine 522.24 *light*
ill-use 236.14 *ill-treat*; 351.1, 351.2 *misuse*; 802.20 *wrong*
illusion 96.2; 461.4 *delusion*; 274.6 *fallibility*; 700.5 *falseness*; 477.5 *fantasy*; 518.5 *imagination*; 11.10 *psychic phenomenon*; 700.9 *sleight of hand*; 525.4 *something that appears*
illusionary 518.20 *visual*
illusionism 96.3 *delusion*; 19.4 *treatment*
illusionist 125.7 *imitator*; 19.24 *pictorial*
illusive 700.40 *illusory*; 477.12 *imaginary*
illusorily 101.13 *metaphysically*
illusory 96.9; **700.40**; 477.12 *imaginary*; 101.8 *nonmaterial*; 525.9 *ostensible*; 702.7 *sophistic*; 94.10 *unreal*; 518.20 *visual*
illustrate 721.14 *describe*; 703.16 *explain*; 719.8 *interpret*; 520.10 *make visible*; 163.5 *outline*; 717.11 *paint*; 454.2 *prove*; 4.21 *rationalize*
illustrated 703.11 *explanatory*; 719.15 *interpreted*
illustrated dictionary 5.28 *dictionary*
illustration 703.3 *explanation*; 719.1 *interpretation*; 163.1 *outline*; 542.3 *pattern*; 19.7 *picture*; 454.5 *proof*; 717.2 *reproduction*; 520.6 *visible thing*
illustrative 19.26 *artistic*; 17.18, 721.11 *descriptive*; 703.11 *explanatory*; 695.1 *intelligible*; 719.14 *interpretive*; 717.13 *representational*; 454.9 *verificatory*
illustratively 19.31 *artistically*; 703.22 *demonstrably*; 721.18 *descriptively*; 719.18 *in other words*; 717.14 *representationally*; 454.11 *verifiably*
illustrator 19.16 *artist*; 542.8 *decorator*; 703.7 *demonstrator*; 717.4 *person who makes a representation*
illustrious 575.5 *entitled*
ill will 590.6 *bad feeling*; 596.1 *dislike*; 798.1 *evil*; 594.1 *hate*; 651.1 *malevolence*
ill-willed 651.10 *malevolent*
ill wind 249.1 *adversity*; 798.3 *bad luck*; 236.11 *harmfulness*
ill-wisher 596.3 *disliked person*
ill wishes 594.1 *hate*; 712.4 *malediction*
ill-wishing 651.10 *malevolent*
image 717.6; 171.3 *appearance*; 96.7 *artificiality*; 125.2 *copy*; 115.5 *counterpart*; 477.4 *ideality*; 9.3 *idol*; 27.29 *mathematical function*; 41.3 *photograph*; 19.7 *picture*; 518.8 *reflection*; 717.9 *represent*; 742.1 *sign*; 525.4 *something that appears*; 36.24 *symbolism*
image blur 41.8 *composition*
image-building 477.1 *imagination*
image distance 28.31 *lens element*
image-maker 740.10 *publicizer*
image recorder 518.8 *reflection*
imagery 477.1 *imagination*; 17.12 *poetic language*
imaginable 477.13; 102.5 *possible*; 476.8 *supposed*
imaginably 102.11 *potentially*
imaginal 171.8 *apparent*
imaginary 477.12; 171.8 *apparent*; 27.72 *complex*; 96.9 *illusory*; 101.8 *nonmaterial*; 194.8 *odd*; 525.9 *ostensible*; 476.8 *supposed*; 96.10 *theoretical*; 94.10 *unreal*; 518.20 *visual*; 619.8 *wonderful*
imaginary number 27.6 *complex number*; 194.2 *kind of number*
imaginary part 27.6 *complex number*
imaginary world 477.4 *ideality*; 101.1 *nonmaterial world*
Imagination 477
imagination 446.8; **477.1**; **518.5**; 645.1 *cunning*; 699.9 *falsification*; 94.5 *nonreality*; 126.1 *originality*; 518.4 *visualization*
imaginative 477.10; 19.26 *artistic*; 645.4 *cunning*; 699.36 *falsified*; 446.11 *ideational*; 721.12 *narrative*; 697.5 *nonsensical*; 126.4 *original*; 518.21 *seeing*
imaginative exercise 477.4 *ideality*
imaginative journalism 234.4 *distortion of the truth*
imaginatively 446.22; **477.17**; 19.31 *artistically*; 721.18 *descriptively*; 126.8 *originally*
imaginativeness 446.8, 477.1 *imagination*; 562.2 *productiveness*
imagine 96.13; **446.15**; **477.14**; **518.17**; 450.8 *be of the opinion*; 699.26 *falsify*; 126.7 *originate*; 356.10 *produce*; 721.15 *recount*; 476.5 *suppose*; 443.12 *think*; 518.16 *visualize*
imagined 446.11 *ideational*; 700.40 *illusory*; 477.12 *imaginary*; 356.12 *produced*; 476.8 *supposed*
imaging 29.27
imaging system 29.27 *imaging*
imago 446.1 *idea*; 76.5 *larva*; 36.24 *symbolism*
I'm all right Jack 686.4 *self-absorption*
imam 7.8 *priest*; 400.6 *religious leader*; 121.5 *superior*
imbalance 227.1 *changeableness*; 234.9 *distort*; 109.4, 234.1 *distortion*; 120.1 *inequality*
imbalanced 227.13 *changeable*; 109.8 *distorted*
imbecile 459.3 *foolish person*; 337.10 *ill*; 461.7 *insane person*; 457.3 *unintelligent person*
imbecilic 459.5 *foolish*; 457.7 *intellectually subnormal*; 457.5 *lacking intellect*
imbecility 459.1 *folly*; 457.1 *lack of intellect*; 461.2 *subnormality*
imbibe 558.13 *drink*; 370.11 *ingest*
imbibing 558.1, 558.16 *drinking*
imbibition 558.1 *drinking*; 370.4 *intake*
imbibitory 370.17 *absorbent*
imbricate 550.26 *overlie*; 20.14 *roofed*
imbricated roof 20.6 *roof*
imbrication 550.1 *covering*
imbroglio 412.3 *miscellany*; 264.4 *problem*
imbrue 529.15 *colour*; 433.29 *water*
imbruement 433.9 *soaking*
imbue 117.10 *assimilate*; 97.11 *be present*; 529.15 *colour*; 374.5 *combine*; 632.18 *habituate*; 368.2 *inject*; 412.8 *mix*; 433.31 *steep*
imbued 632.13 *fixed*
I'm done for 582.24 *I'm dying!*
I'm dying! 582.24
I'm guilty 808.9 *sorry!*
imino acid 33.8 *amino acid*
imitate 115.12; **125.9**; 21.34 *act*; 525.11 *appear*; 762.4 *be a substitute*; 111.7 *be the same*; 772.9 *borrow illegally*; 117.8 *comply*; 111.9 *duplicate*; 96.17 *fabricate*; 742.11 *gesture*; 774.15 *infringe*; 699.24 *pretend*; 112.16 *repeat*; 717.9 *represent*; 668.24 *ridicule*; 773.10 *take away*
imitated 772.11 *borrowed*; 477.12 *imaginary*; 125.12 *imitative*; 115.8 *simulated*
imitating 772.3, 774.6 *illegal borrowing*; 668.14 *ridiculing*
Imitation 125
imitation 125.1; **125.13**; **700.6**; 96.12 *artificial*; 96.7 *artificiality*; 117.1 *conformity*; 115.2, 125.2 *copy*; 699.39 *disguised*; 111.4 *duplicate*; 699.12 *fake*; 772.3, 774.6 *illegal borrowing*; 700.39 *imitative*; 525.5 *impression*; 699.7 *pretence*; 112.1 *repetition*; 717.1, 721.9 *representation*; 668.4 *ridicule*; 115.1 *similarity*; 115.8 *simulated*; 773.3 *taking away*; 457.2 *unintelligence*
imitative 125.12; **700.39**; 699.39 *disguised*; 699.37 *fake*; 112.9 *repeated*; 717.13 *representational*; 115.8 *simulated*; 457.6 *unintelligent*
imitatively 125.14; 398.12 *by proxy*; 115.14 *comparably*; 111.18 *identically*; 457.11 *unintelligently*
imitativeness 457.2 *unintelligence*
imitator 125.7; 772.6 *borrower*; 117.6 *conformist*; 774.10 *infringer*; 115.4 *person who copies*
immaculacy 805.1 *innocence*; 795.3 *moral purity*; 230.3 *perfection*; 255.1 *purity*
immaculate 256.16 *clean*; 805.5 *inno-*

cent; 230.1 *perfect;* 255.13, 531.5, 795.9 *pure;* 803.5 *virtuous*
Immaculate Conception 795.3 *moral purity*
immaculately 805.11 *innocently;* 230.7 *perfectly;* 255.19 *purely;* 803.9 *virtuously*
immaculateness 256.1 *cleanness;* 795.3 *moral purity;* 230.3 *perfection*
immanent 99.6 *intrinsic*
immaterial 100.8 *extraneous;* 109.7 *illogical;* 618.11 *insignificant;* 521.1 *invisible;* 101.8 *nonmaterial;* 417.1 *sparse;* 11.18 *spiritual;* 124.1 *unimportant*
immaterialism 96.1 *unreality;* 101.2 *unworldliness*
immaterialist 101.8 *nonmaterial*
immaterialistic 101.8 *nonmaterial*
immateriality 100.1 *extraneousness;* 618.5 *insignificance;* 417.3 *sparseness;* 124.5 *unimportance;* 96.1 *unreality;* 101.2 *unworldliness*
immaterialize 101.12 *enter a nonmaterial world;* 11.20 *occult*
immaterially 100.18 *extraneously;* 101.13 *metaphysically*
immaterialness 101.2 *unworldliness*
immature **76.13**; **295.12**; **555.12**; 499.5 *acid;* 231.2, 233.4 *incomplete;* 646.1, 805.7 *naive;* 538.3 *raw;* 487.1 *unaccustomed;* 457.6 *unintelligent;* 486.2 *unskilled;* 288.13 *untimely*
immature amphibian 73.8 *young amphibian*
immaturely **295.24**; **555.15**; 805.12 *naively;* 487.6 *unaccustomedly;* 457.11 *unintelligently*
immature personality 36.8 *disordered personality*
immature thing 538.13 *young thing*
immaturity **295.3**; **555.3**; 231.5 *imperfection;* 233.1 *incompleteness;* 646.2, 805.3 *naivety;* 457.2 *unintelligence;* 486.8 *unskilfulness;* 288.2 *untimeliness;* 555.1 *youth*
immeasurability **202.5**
immeasurable **202.2**; 8.13 *divine;* 208.8 *numberless*
immeasurably **202.11**; 208.13 *numerously*
Immediacy 280
immediacy **280.1**; 97.4 *availability;* 293.1 *earliness;* 262.4 *haste;* 147.1 *nearness*
immediate **280.5**; 97.10 *available;* 324.15 *direct;* 293.12 *early;* 262.3 *hasty;* 147.9 *near;* 332.1 *swift;* 447.6 *topical*
immediate circle 97.4 *availability*
immediate constituent analysis 5.30 *syntax*
immediately **280.8**; 293.17 *early;* 262.6 *hastily;* 93.23 *now;* 332.14 *swiftly*
immediateness 280.1 *immediacy*
Immelann turn 322.5 *flight*
immemorial 279.9 *agelong;* 275.21 *lasting through time;* 296.12 *olden;* 1.14 *societal*
immemorially 296.21 *archaically*
immemorial wisdom 1.8 *tradition*
immense 158.15 *big;* 202.2 *immeasurable;* 141.13 *spacious*
immensely 202.11 *immeasurably;* 158.20 *largely;* 141.15 *spaciously*
immenseness 158.2 *bigness;* 202.6 *vastness*
immensity 158.2 *bigness;* 141.4 *spaciousness;* 202.6 *vastness*
immerge 368.4 *immerse*
immerse **368.4**; 156.14 *deepen;* 433.29 *water*
immersed **368.14**; 433.24 *flooded;* 156.12 *under*
immerse oneself in 368.4 *immerse*
immersion **368.10**; 10.5 *Christian rite;* 156.1 *depth;* 433.15 *holy water;* 305.2 *sinkage;* 433.9 *soaking*
immersion heater 493.3 *heater*
immigrant 312.18 *arriving;* 314.15 *entering;* 314.7 *entrant;* 100.7, 295.8 *new arrival;* 564.13 *resident;* 564.7 *settler*
immigrate 100.14 *be foreign;* 314.14 *enrol;* 564.15 *settle*
immigration 314.4 *right of entry*
imminent **293.13**; 312.19 *approaching;* 474.7 *expected;* 283.11 *future*
imminently 283.14 *in the future;* 293.18 *soon*
immiscibility 372.3 *separateness*
immiscible 372.17 *unjoined*
immission 370.1 *admittance*
immix 412.8 *mix*
immobile 341.3, 343.1 *inactive;* 339.5 *inert;* 301.4 *motionless;* 225.7 *permanent;* 228.9 *stable*
immobility 341.1 *inaction;* 343.5 *inactivity;* 339.1 *inertness;* 301.1 *motionlessness;* 225.1 *permanence;* 228.1 *stability*
immobilization 228.1 *stability*
immobilization techniques 52.10 *aikido*
immobilize 343.14 *make inactive;* 301.9 *make motionless;* 225.6 *make permanent;* 52.13 *practise judo*
immobilized 52.15 *wrestling*
immoderate 219.6 *excessive;* 686.8 *overindulgent;* 250.12 *unconditional;* 681.2 *unrestrained;* 380.6 *violent*
immoderately 219.8, 250.21 *excessively;* 681.9 *extravagantly;* 686.12 *self-indulgently*
immoderation 250.6 *liberality;* 219.2 *overdoing it;* 686.3 *overindulgence;* 681.5 *unrestrainedness*
immodest 738.15 *open;* 796.13 *unchaste;* 673.8 *vain*
immodestly 796.21 *immorally;* 673.19 *vainly*
immodesty 796.3 *sexual immorality;* 673.1 *vanity*
immolate 382.20 *kill ritually*
immolation 382.6 *ritual killing*
immoral **796.11**; **802.15**; **804.12**; 236.3 *bad;* 800.5 *dishonourable;* 662.13 *disobedient;* 812.4 *disreputable;* 798.7 *evil;* 675.9 *ribald*
immoralist 631.5 *badly behaved person*
Immorality 796
immorality **796.1**; 236.9 *badness;* 662.1 *disobedience;* 798.1 *evil;* 800.1 *improbity;* 245.8 *perversion;* 804.2 *vice*
immorally **796.21**; **802.28**; **804.20**; 800.11 *dishonourably;* 662.17 *disobediently;* 798.12 *evilly*
immoral man **796.8**
immoral woman **796.9**
immortal 121.14 *best;* 8.13 *divine;* 202.3, 279.8 *eternal;* 225.7, 277.9 *permanent*
immortality 8.2 *divine attribute;* 202.7 *eternity;* 554.5 *life cycle;* 279.3 *life without end;* 225.1 *permanence*
immortalization 8.9 *deification*
immortalize 8.17 *deify;* 279.6 *eternalize;* 225.6 *make permanent*
immortalized 8.15 *deified*
immortal life 554.5 *life cycle*
immortally 202.12 *eternally;* 225.9 *permanently*
immotive 301.4 *motionless*
immovability 641.6 *determination;* 418.8 *mental hardness;* 228.1 *stability*
immovable 253.9 *fast;* 301.4 *motionless;* 225.7 *permanent;* 440.8 *propertied;* 228.9 *stable;* 638.5 *steady;* 641.3 *unyielding*
immovables 440.2 *legal terms*
immovably 253.17 *fastly*
immune 16.63 *acquitted;* 389.8 *escaping;* 758.5 *exempt;* 250.9 *free;* 257.4 *hygienic;* 592.1 *insensitive;* 252.7 *invulnerable;* 253.6 *secure*
immunity 389.1 *escape;* 758.1 *exemption;* 649.1 *forgiveness;* 250.1 *freedom;* 257.1 *hygiene;* 253.1 *protection;* 252.1 *safety*
immunization 35.6 *health care;* 257.1 *hygiene;* 394.3 *prophylactic;* 252.2 *protection*
immunize 394.20 *doctor;* 257.6 *make hygienic;* 35.19 *practise medicine;* 252.10 *protect*
immunized 257.4 *hygienic;* 252.6 *safe*
immunizing 257.4 *hygienic*
immunoglobulin 33.9 *protein*
immunological 34.20 *biological*
immunologically 34.29 *biologically*
immunologist 34.19 *life scientist;* 35.13 *medical specialist*
immunology 34.1 *life science;* 35.3 *medical specialty*
immunosuppressant 394.4 *antidote*
immunosuppressive 37.14 *counteracting;* 37.4 *drug type*
immunotherapy 394.13 *therapy;* 35.8 *treatment*
immure 309.10 *enclose;* 815.9 *imprison*
immurement 251.4 *detention;* 815.7 *imprisonment*
immutability 225.1 *permanence;* 228.1 *stability*
immutable 279.8 *eternal;* 418.4 *mentally hard;* 225.7 *permanent;* 228.9 *stable*
immutable law 228.4 *stable thing*
immutably 418.13 *inflexibly;* 225.9 *permanently;* 228.12 *stably*
IMP 771.4 *lending institution*
imp 642.4 *capricious person;* 8.7 *devil;* 11.11 *ghost;* 368.6 *plant;* 662.5 *troublemaker*
impact **368.3**; 492.12 *abut;* 331.2 *collide;* 331.12 *collision;* 345.1 *effect;* 525.5 *impression;* 395.1 *influence*
impacted 368.12 *inserted*
impaction 368.8 *insertion*
impactment 368.8 *insertion*
impact printer 40.7 *peripheral*
impact upon 345.5 *show an effect*
impair **245.4**; 486.7 *be clumsy;* 798.11 *be evil;* 236.13 *be worthless;* 548.7 *blemish;* 224.8 *cause change;* 395.9 *change;* 234.11 *deform;* 766.13 *destroy;* 378.8 *hinder;* 218.7 *make insufficient;* 546.5 *make ugly;* 238.8 *make useless;* 342.17 *meddle;* 351.1 *misuse;* 194.8 *odd;* 329.5 *transgress;* 441.1 *waste;* 337.7 *weaken*
impaired 245.12 *deteriorated;* 233.4 *incomplete*
impaired visibility 524.2 *murk*
impaired vision 519.2 *poor sight*
impairment **245.10**; 122.2 *deficiency;* 766.5 *destruction;* 233.1 *incompleteness;* 337.1 *weakness*
impale 814.5 *execute;* 743.10 *identify;* 491.11 *inflict pain;* 381.6 *stab*
impalement 814.13 *capital punishment;* 743.8 *heraldic device;* 381.18 *hit*
impaling 743.8 *heraldic device*
impalpability 159.1 *littleness;* 96.1 *unreality;* 101.2 *unworldliness*
impalpable 728.16 *imperceptible;* 159.7 *little;* 101.8 *nonmaterial;* 96.8 *unreal*
impalpably 101.13 *metaphysically;* 159.9 *microscopically*
impanation 10.6 *Eucharist*
imparity 120.1 *inequality*
impart 693.12 *communicate;* 6.22 *educate;* 768.5 *give;* 729.11 *speak*
impartable 768.7 *given*
impartation 768.1 *giving*
imparter 768.4 *giver*
impartial **618.9**; 150.3 *broad-minded;* 473.4 *disinterested;* 111.16, 119.6 *equal;* 799.4 *honourable;* 4.15 *rational;* 801.7 *right;* 458.5 *wise*
impartiality **618.3**; 150.6 *broad-mindedness;* 473.1 *disinterestedness;* 111.5 *equality;* 801.1 *fairness;* 685.1 *moderation;* 799.1 *probity*
impartially **618.19**; 473.8 *disinterestedly;* 111.19, 801.19 *equally;* 119.13 *equitably;* 799.7 *honourably;* 4.26 *rationally*
impartial observer 618.6 *indifferent person*
impartial person **473.3**
imparting 768.1, 768.8 *giving*
imparting of life 554.1 *life*
impart life 554.19 *give birth to*
impart momentum 332.6 *accelerate*
impart odour to **500.9**
impassability 309.1 *closure*
impassable 264.11 *rough;* 309.13 *stopped*
impassably 309.16 *impermeably*
impasse 309.1 *closure;* 103.7, 378.2 *obstacle;* 264.8 *snag*
impassioned 726.3 *emphatic;* 590.13 *passionate;* 380.6 *violent*
impassive 341.3 *inactive;* 618.7 *indifferent;* 339.5 *inert;* 592.1 *insensitive;* 343.3 *not participating;* 628.4 *pitiless;* 301.6 *quiescent;* 489.6 *unfeeling;* 696.1 *unintelligible*
impassively **343.16**; 618.17 *indifferently;* 339.7 *inertly;* 301.10 *motionlessly;* 628.7 *pitilessly;* 696.13 *unintelligibly;* 341.5 *without action*
impassivity 489.313 *heedlessness;* 343.7 *idleness;* 341.1 *inaction;* 339.1 *inertness;* 592.3 *insensitiveness;* 696.11 *unintelligibility*
impasto 19.8 *painting*
impatience 659.2 *bad manners;* 262.5 *hastiness;* 625.1 *irascibility;* 615.1 *rashness*
impatient 659.5 *discourteous;* 262.3 *hasty;* 625.4 *irascible;* 615.4 *rash;* 624.15 *resentful*
impatiently 659.9 *discourteously;* 625.9 *irascibly;* 262.7, 615.6 *rashly*
impeach 715.5 *accuse;* 670.19 *blame;* 16.70 *litigate*
impeachability 806.1 *guilt*
impeachable 715.8 *accusatory;* 670.36 *blameworthy;* 806.5 *guilty*
impeached 715.8 *accusatory*
impeacher 715.3 *accuser*
impeachment 715.1 *accusation;* 670.7 *blame;* 16.5 *litigation*
impeccability 805.1 *innocence;* 230.3 *perfection*
impeccable 805.5 *innocent;* 230.1 *perfect;* 803.5 *virtuous*
impeccably 805.11 *innocently;* 230.7 *perfectly;* 803.9 *virtuously*
impeccancy 230.3 *perfection*
impeccant 230.1 *perfect*
impecuniosity 782.5 *poverty*
impecunious 782.1 *poor;* 249.7 *unprosperous*
impecuniously 782.15 *poorly*
impecuniousness 782.5 *poverty*
impedance 28.53, 39.12 *resistance*
impede 378.9 *block;* 378.8 *hinder;* 251.8 *restrain;* 333.3 *slow down;* 399.3 *veto*
impeded 333.7 *delayed;* 378.13 *hindering*
impeder 378.7 *hinderer*
impediment 604.2 *bad outcome;* 378.1 *hindrance;* 240.3 *inconvenience;* 378.2 *obstacle;* 251.1 *restraint;* 571.2 *separation;* 399.1 *veto*
impedimenta 438.7 *equipment;* 440.4 *possessions;* 316.10 *transferred thing*
impeding 378.13 *hindering*
impel **331.1**; 344.10 *awaken;* 386.6 *compel;* 262.1 *hasten;* 483.9 *motivate;* 480.15 *persuade;* 330.20 *propel;* 342.14 *push;* 300.14 *set in motion*
impelled 483.12 *motivated*
impellent 331.17 *impelling;* 331.11 *impulsion*
impeller 330.11 *propeller;* 307.6 *rotator*
impelling **331.17**; 344.13 *causal;* 334.15 *full of energy;* 300.16 *moving*
impelling force 331.11 *impulsion*
impend 104.8 *be probable*
impending 312.19 *approaching;* 243.17 *developing;* 474.7 *expected;* 283.11 *future;* 293.13 *imminent*
impending disaster 254.5 *danger*
impenetrability 309.1 *closure;* 152.6 *denseness;* 416.1 *density;* 418.5 *hardness;* 103.6 *hopelessness;* 528.6 *opaqueness;* 336.1 *strength;* 696.11 *unintelligibility*
impenetrable 152.2, 416.6 *dense;* 103.3 *hopeless;* 528.1 *opaque;* 264.12 *problematic;* 264.11 *rough;* 309.13 *stopped;* 696.1 *unintelligible*
impenetrably 309.16 *impermeably;* 528.13 *opaquely;* 696.13 *unintelligibly*
impenitence **809.1**
impenitent **809.3**
impenitently **809.6**
impenitentness 809.1 *impenitence*
impenitent person **809.2**
imperative 280.6 *allowing no delay;* 396.12 *authoritative;* 397.14 *commanding;* 386.9 *compelling;* 135.6 *demanding;* 99.5 *essential;* 123.5 *important;* 5.33 *mood;* 810.12 *obligatory;* 4.8 *philosophical term*
imperatively 397.16 *commandingly;* 386.11 *compellingly;* 135.12 *in need*
imperativeness 396.2 *authoritativeness*
imperceptibility **728.7**; 521.4 *invisibility;* 159.1 *littleness*
imperceptible **728.16**; 511.1 *faint-sounding;* 337.13 *insufficient;* 521.1 *invisible;* 159.7 *little;* 333.5 *unhurried*
imperceptibleness 728.7 *imperceptibility*
imperceptibly **728.27**; 489.13 *insensibly;* 521.9 *invisibly;* 159.9 *microscopically;* 337.14 *weakly*
imperceptive 519.12 *blind to;* 592.1 *insensitive*
imperceptively 426.13 *obtusely;* 457.11 *unintelligently*
impercipience 426.7 *dullness*
impercipient 592.1 *insensitive*
imperfect **231.1**; 548.4 *blemished;* 486.4 *bungled;* 122.17 *defective;* 234.7 *deformed;* 233.4 *incomplete;* 236.2 *inferior;* 78.12 *of flowers;* 205.11 *partial;* 5.34 *tense;* 804.13 *venial*
imperfect cadence 517.4 *atonality*
imperfect fungi 83.3 *fungi*
Imperfection 231

imperfection 231.5; 122.2 *deficiency*; 234.3 *deformity*; 233.1 *incompleteness*; 236.8 *inferiority*; 218.8 *insufficiency*; 646.2 *naivety*; 548.1 *spot*; 804.3 *venial sin*; 254.7 *vulnerability*
imperfect item 231.6
imperfectly 231.11; 234.13 *asymmetrically*; 122.21 *badly*; 486.11 *unskilfully*; 804.19 *vulnerably*
imperfectness 231.5 *imperfection*
imperia 20.9 *miscellaneous architectural features*
imperial 121.13 *dominant*; 12.10 *governing*; 396.14 *governmental*; 26.12 *metrical*
Imperial Defence College 584.3 *military training*
imperialism 85.3 *dominion*; 329.10 *expansionism*; 12.3 *governance*; 566.11 *nation*; 396.7 *type of rule*
imperialist 586.6 *militarist*
imperialistic 586.33 *combative*; 85.16 *national*
imperialistically 586.41 *aggressively*; 85.19 *nationally*
imperialist war 585.1 *war*
imperial paper 435.3 *paper*
imperial purple 540.1 *purpleness*
imperial system 26.5 *measuring system*
imperial wood pulp 435.3 *paper*
imperil 254.10 *endanger*
imperilment 254.5 *danger*
imperious 396.12 *authoritative*; 400.12 *masterful*; 397.15 *self-assured*; 622.19 *stately*
imperiously 397.16 *commandingly*; 400.16 *masterfully*
imperiousness 396.2 *authoritativeness*
imperishability 279.1 *eternity*; 225.1 *permanence*
imperishable 279.8 *eternal*; 225.7 *permanent*; 228.9 *stable*
imperishably 225.9 *permanently*; 228.12 *stably*
imperium 121.2 *leadership*
imperium in imperio 12.1 *government*
impermanence 227.1 *changeableness*; 278.1 *transience*
impermanent 278.7; 227.13 *changeable*
impermanently 227.15 *changeably*; 278.8 *transiently*
impermeability 309.1 *closure*; 416.1 *density*; 528.6 *opaqueness*
impermeable 309.12 *closed*; 416.6 *dense*; 528.1 *opaque*
impermeably 309.16; 528.13 *opaquely*
impermissibility 16.35 *illegality*
impermissible 16.55 *illegal*; 399.5 *vetoed*
impermissibly 399.7 *by veto*
impersonal 473.4 *disinterested*; 618.7 *indifferent*; 402.7 *material*
impersonally 473.8 *disinterestedly*; 618.17 *indifferently*; 402.9 *materially*
impersonate 21.34, 717.10 *act*; 125.9 *imitate*; 699.28 *mask*; 699.24 *pretend*; 717.9 *represent*
impersonating 717.3 *acting*
impersonation 21.22, 717.3 *acting*; 125.1 *imitation*; 125.3 *mockery*; 699.7 *pretence*; 717.1 *representation*; 668.4 *ridicule*
impersonator 699.19 *cheat*; 700.15 *deceiver*; 21.29 *entertainer*; 125.7 *imitator*; 717.5 *performer*; 227.8 *person who changes costume*; 115.4 *person who copies*
impertinence 661.1 *defiance*; 668.1 *disrespect*; 660.10 *impudence*; 660.1 *insolence*; 242.6 *objectionability*; 660.11 *sauciness*
impertinent 659.6 *bad-mannered*; 661.7 *defiant*; 668.10 *disrespectful*; 660.21 *impudent*; 660.13 *insolent*; 242.2 *objectionable*
impertinently 661.9 *defiantly*; 668.28 *disrespectfully*; 660.30 *insolently*; 659.10 *rudely*
imperturbability 4.3 *detachment*; 228.2 *determination*; 301.2 *repose*
imperturbable 4.18 *detached*; 228.11 *determined*; 301.6 *quiescent*
imperturbably 228.13 *determinedly*; 4.27 *stoically*
impervious 309.12 *closed*; 416.6 *dense*; 103.3 *hopeless*; 592.1 *insensitive*; 528.1 *opaque*; 641.4 *set*; 489.6 *unfeeling*
imperviously 416.10 *densely*; 309.16 *impermeably*; 528.13 *opaquely*
imperviousness 309.1 *closure*; 416.1 *density*; 103.6 *hopelessness*; 528.6 *opaqueness*
impetigo 260.13 *skin disease*
impetrate 10.20 *pray*
impetration 10.9 *prayer*
impetrational 10.21 *ritualistic*
impetuosity 472.2; 262.5 *hastiness*; 293.5 *prematurity*; 615.1 *rashness*; 380.1 *violence*
impetuous 262.3 *hasty*; 590.13 *passionate*; 293.16 *premature*; 615.4 *rash*; 478.2 *spontaneous*; 380.6 *violent*
impetuously 472.14 *inattentively*; 293.20 *prematurely*; 262.7, 615.6 *rashly*
impetuousness 262.5 *hastiness*; 615.1 *rashness*
impetus 332.9 *acceleration*; 334.4 *energy*; 331.11 *impulsion*; 300.2 *momentum*; 480.11, 483.1 *motive*; 330.1 *propulsion*; 338.1 *vigour*
impiety 351.2 *misuse*; 804.6 *religious sin*
impinge 492.12 *abut*; 147.19 *meet*; 329.5 *transgress*
impingement 147.4 *meeting*
impinge upon 331.2 *collide*
impinging 147.11 *meeting*
impious 804.14; 351.5 *abusive*
impiously 351.6 *abusively*; 804.20 *immorally*
impish 236.5 *harmful*
implacability 628.2 *inflexibility*; 638.14 *tenacity*
implacable 594.13 *angry*; 628.5 *inflexible*; 638.3 *strong-willed*; 641.3 *unyielding*
implant 37.19 *administer*; 117.10 *assimilate*; 632.18 *habituate*; 368.2 *inject*; 37.12 *injection*; 368.6 *plant*
implantation 368.9 *injection*; 368.8 *insertion*
implanted 632.13 *fixed*; 368.13 *injected*
implausibility 105.6; 705.7 *questionableness*; 451.2 *unbelievability*
implausible 451.7 *disbelieved*; 105.2, 705.14 *questionable*
implausibly 705.24 *questionably*; 451.11 *unbelievably*
implead 16.70 *litigate*
implement 340.4 *act*; 348.4 *be an instrument*; 348.2 *instrument*; 356.10 *produce*; 346.9 *take action*; 438.1 *tool*
implementation 340.1 *action*; 346.1 *operation*
implicate 715.5 *accuse*; 127.4 *include*
implicated 715.8 *accusatory*; 806.5 *guilty*; 108.4 *related*
implication 715.1 *accusation*; 806.1 *guilt*; 127.1 *inclusion*; 27.63 *mathematical logic*; 694.1 *meaning*; 108.1 *relatedness*
implication sign 27.13 *mathematical symbol*
implicative 742.14 *signifying*
implicit 27.77 *given*; 694.6 *meaningful*
implied 222.7 *circumstantial*; 694.6 *meaningful*; 694.9 *meant*
implied consent 757.1 *permission*
implied sense 694.4 *type of meaning*
implode 191.6 *become smaller*; 191.5 *make smaller*
implore 10.20 *pray*; 710.6 *request*
imploring 710.1 *request*
implosion 191.1 *contraction*
implosive 191.8 *contracting*
imply 716.10 *make evident*; 694.10 *mean*; 742.10 *signify*; 701.15 *state*; 693.14 *tip*
impolite 631.18 *badly behaved*; 659.5 *discourteous*; 668.10 *disrespectful*; 544.8 *indecorous*; 242.2 *objectionable*; 655.8 *unsociable*
impolitely 631.20 *badly*; 659.9 *discourteously*; 655.14 *unsocially*
impoliteness 659.1 *discourtesy*; 668.1 *disrespect*; 242.6 *objectionability*
impolitic 240.1 *inconvenient*; 486.1 *unskilful*
imponderability 415.5 *lightness*; 159.1 *littleness*; 101.2 *unworldliness*
imponderable 415.1 *light*; 159.7 *little*; 101.8 *nonmaterial*
imponderableness 415.5 *lightness*
imponderably 415.11 *lightly*; 101.13 *metaphysically*; 159.9 *microscopically*
imponderous 415.1 *light*
import 370.7 *admit*; 370.1 *admittance*; 100.16 *be external*; 123.7 *be important*; 13.13 *economic*; 314.1 *entry*; 123.1, 643.6 *importance*; 368.1 *insert*; 368.8 *insertion*; 694.10 *mean*; 694.1 *meaning*; 436.5 *provision*; 345.4, 694.2 *significance*; 13.10 *trade with*; 316.12 *transport*; 316.2 *transportation*
importable 316.17 *transferable*
Importance 123
importance 123.1; **643.6**; 262.4 *haste*; 395.1 *influence*; 129.2 *priority*; 185.1 *prominence*; 726.2 *seriousness*; 694.2 *significance*
important 123.5; **643.3**; 667.14 *awe-inspiring*; 235.2 *best*; 185.6 *eminent*; 121.15 *excellent*; 395.11 *influential*; 579.17 *managerial*; 346.12 *operative*; 726.5 *serious*; 694.7 *significant*
important figure 566.7 *person*
importantly 123.9; 185.11 *eminently*; 395.14 *influentially*; 346.13 *operationally*; 121.16 *superiorly*
important matter 123.2
important occasion 123.2 *important matter*
important person 123.4 *bigwig*; 566.7 *person*
importation 370.1 *admittance*; 100.4 *externality*; 368.8 *insertion*; 314.4 *right of entry*; 316.2 *transportation*
import duty 13.6 *economic factors*
imported 314.15 *entering*; 100.12 *external*; 368.12 *inserted*
imported word 5.17 *word*
importer 13.9 *economist*; 776.10 *trader*; 316.7 *transferor*; 778.12 *wholesaler*
importing 370.1 *admittance*; 13.2 *economy*; 100.12 *external*; 694.6 *meaningful*; 314.4 *right of entry*
import levy 788.2 *money received*
import momentum 331.1 *impel*
importunate 280.6 *allowing no delay*
importune 342.17 *meddle*; 796.18 *prostitute*
importuning 796.5 *prostitution*
importunity 710.1 *request*
impose 211.6 *add*; 667.21 *command respect*; 386.6 *compel*; 397.10 *demand*; 397.11 *have authority over*; 814.1 *punish*
impose a ban 397.9 *command*; 399.3 *veto*
impose a curfew 251.11 *detain*
impose a duty 810.17; 386.6 *compel*
impose a fine 251.8 *restrain*
impose an embargo 397.9 *command*; 251.9 *economize*
impose a penalty 814.2 *penalize*
impose a tariff 251.9 *economize*
impose conditions 746.6 *make conditions*
imposed peace 749.1 *pacification*; 589.1 *peace*
impose martial law 647.5 *be severe*
impose on 349.4 *resort to*
impose one's will 635.15
impose order upon 298.10 *make regular*
impose peace 749.4 *pacify*
imposing 667.14 *awe-inspiring*; 158.15 *big*; 123.6 *notable*; 622.19 *stately*
imposingly 622.34
imposition 211.1 *addition*; 814.10 *affliction*; 810.1 *duty*; 790.8 *levy*
imposition on one's time 342.6 *business*
Impossibility 103
impossibility 103.5; 103.6 *hopelessness*; 107.6 *poor chance*; 27.62 *probability*; 451.2 *unbelievability*
impossibility of discovery 696.11 *unintelligibility*
impossible 103.1; 264.10 *difficult*; 451.7 *disbelieved*; 611.7 *futile*; 709.12 *no!*; 619.8 *wonderful*
impossible! 103.13
impossibleness 103.5 *impossibility*
impossible to explain 696.1 *unintelligible*
impossibly 103.11
impost 20.8 *column*; 790.8 *levy*; 20.9 *miscellaneous architectural features*
imposter 699.19 *cheat*; 700.15 *deceiver*; 699.17 *false person*; 125.7 *imitator*; 486.10 *unskilled person*
impostor 762.2 *substitute person*
impostrous 699.35 *fraudulent*; 699.32 *spurious*
imposture 645.1 *cunning*; 700.5 *falseness*; 699.8, 700.10 *fraud*; 125.1 *imitation*; 699.4 *spuriousness*
impotence 588.1 *anarchy*; 341.1 *inaction*; 563.1 *infertility*; 124.6 *obscurity*; 335.1 *powerlessness*; 486.8 *unskilfulness*; 238.3 *uselessness*; 337.1 *weakness*
impotent 335.12; 341.3 *inactive*; 563.3 *infertile*; 124.2 *obscure*; 486.1 *unskilful*; 238.1 *useless*; 337.8 *weak*
impotent fury 335.2 *futile effort*
impotently 335.14 *powerlessly*; 563.11 *unproductively*; 337.14 *weakly*
impound 251.11 *detain*; 309.10 *enclose*; 815.9 *imprison*; 773.8 *take back*
impounding 773.2 *taking back*
impoundment 38.23 *dam*; 251.4 *detention*
impoverish 782.14; 767.9 *dispose of*; 766.12 *lessen*; 218.7 *make insufficient*; 214.5 *make smaller*; 441.1 *waste*; 337.7 *weaken*
impoverished 245.12 *deteriorated*; 782.2 *insolvent*; 124.2 *obscure*; 766.17 *unprofitable*; 337.11 *weakened*
impoverishment 214.1 *decrease*; 245.7 *deterioration*; 766.4 *lessening*; 337.3 *poor health*; 782.5 *poverty*
impracticability 103.6 *hopelessness*; 238.3 *uselessness*
impracticable 264.10 *difficult*; 238.1 *useless*
impractical 477.11 *fantastical*; 103.3 *hopeless*; 446.13 *ideal*; 109.7 *illogical*; 4.13 *of philosophy*; 350.1 *unused*; 238.1 *useless*
impracticality 103.6 *hopelessness*; 446.7 *idealism*; 238.3 *uselessness*
impractically 103.12 *hopelessly*; 446.22 *imaginatively*; 350.12 *out of use*; 238.10 *uselessly*
imprecate 712.7 *wish ill*
imprecation 712.1 *curse*; 712.4 *malediction*
imprecatory 712.10 *maledictive*
imprecise 138.20 *generalized*; 802.12 *incorrect*; 453.6 *indeterminate*; 266.2 *obscure*
imprecisely 453.25 *indeterminately*; 266.4 *obscurely*; 802.26 *wrong*; 274.22 *wrongly*
impreciseness 266.1 *obscurity*
imprecision 274.2 *inaccuracy*; 452.19, 453.14 *indeterminacy*; 138.3 *nonspecificness*; 266.1 *obscurity*
impregnability 253.1 *protection*; 252.1 *safety*; 336.1 *strength*
impregnable 252.7 *invulnerable*; 253.6 *secure*
impregnably 252.11 *safely*; 253.16 *surely*
impregnate 97.11 *be present*; 374.5 *combine*; 368.2 *inject*; 562.7 *make fertile*; 412.8 *mix*; 561.13 *propagate*; 433.31 *steep*
impregnated 374.7 *combined*; 368.13 *injected*; 561.16 *reproductive*
impregnation 368.9 *injection*; 412.1 *mixture*; 561.3 *propagation*; 433.10 *steeping*
impresario 738.12 *displayer*; 21.27 *producer*
impress 630.11 *amaze*; 488.13 *arouse sensation*; 619.10 *be wonderful*; 667.21 *command respect*; 19.22 *engrave*; 584.10 *enlist*; 386.7 *force*; 743.10 *identify*; 395.8 *influence*; 774.13 *kidnap*; 183.9 *make concave*; 743.3 *means of identification*; 483.9 *motivate*; 419.13 *soften*; 345.2 *visible effect*
impressed 630.7 *amazed*; 619.6 *wondering*
impressed with oneself 673.10 *self-admiring*
impressibility 639.14 *apathy*; 480.7 *persuadability*; 591.5 *sensitivity*; 419.8 *softness*; 483.6 *suggestibility*
impressible 419.2 *pliant*; 591.1 *sensitive*; 483.13 *suggestible*
impression 525.5; **590.2**; 171.3 *appearance*; 450.1 *belief*; 183.1 *concavity*; 111.4 *duplicate*; 477.4 *ideality*; 395.1 *influence*; 445.3 *insight*; 717.1, 721.9 *representation*; 488.1 *sensation*; 492.1 *touch*; 176.5 *viewpoint*
impressionability 639.14 *apathy*; 591.5 *sensitivity*
impressionable 419.7; 760.15 *convertible*; 6.17 *educable*; 590.10 *feeling*; 227.14 *irresolute*; 591.1 *sensitive*; 488.7 *susceptible*; 639.4 *unsteady*
impressionably 227.15 *changeably*; 419.18 *soft-heartedly*
impressional 171.8 *apparent*
impressionist 21.29 *entertainer*; 18.32 *instrumental*; 19.29 *realist*
impressionistic 721.11 *descriptive*; 163.6 *outlined*; 717.13 *representational*; 721.13 *representing*
impressionistically 19.30 *pictorially*
impressionist music 18.3 *classical music*

impressive 525.7 *appearing*; 667.14 *awe-inspiring*; 450.13 *believable*; 185.6 *eminent*; 488.9 *exciting*; 797.1 *good*; 395.11 *influential*; 123.6 *notable*; 480.19 *persuasive*; 622.18 *prestigious*; 726.5 *serious*; 619.8 *wonderful*
impressive effort 576.4 *exertion*
impressively 185.11 *eminently*; 395.14 *influentially*; 480.21 *persuasively*; 797.22 *well*
impressiveness 185.1 *prominence*; 726.2 *seriousness*
impressment 386.3 *coercive methods*; 774.2 *kidnapping*; 584.1 *military affairs*
impress on 726.6 *emphasize*
impress upon 345.6 *have a visible effect*
imprimatur 669.1 *approval*; 757.2 *permit*
imprint 345.6 *have a visible effect*; 743.10 *identify*; 183.9 *make concave*; 743.3 *means of identification*; 742.1 *sign*; 345.2 *visible effect*
imprinted 743.12 *identified*
imprinter 742.8 *signer*
imprison **815.9**; 251.11, 360.7 *detain*; 165.5, 309.10 *enclose*; 655.13 *ignore*; 172.15 *keep inside*; 252.10 *protect*; 814.1 *punish*
imprisoned **815.8**; 251.15 *detained*; 165.7, 309.15 *enclosed*; 814.20 *punished*; 360.10 *retained*; 252.6 *safe*
imprisoning 360.2 *detention*
imprisonment **815.7**; 251.4 *detention*; 814.7 *punishment*
Improbability 105
improbability **105.4**; 453.13 *indemonstrability*; 107.6 *poor chance*; 705.7 *questionableness*; 630.1 *surprise*; 451.2 *unbelievability*
improbable **105.1**; 451.7 *disbelieved*; 109.7 *illogical*; 453.4 *indemonstrable*; 705.14 *questionable*; 619.8 *wonderful*
improbably **105.8**; 705.24 *questionably*; 453.26 *unreliably*
improbity **800.1**; 479.7 *apostasy*; 645.1 *cunning*; 699.5 *deceitfulness*; 798.1 *evil*; 699.1 *falsehood*; 16.38 *lawbreaking*; 786.1 *nonpayment*; 804.1 *wickedness*
impromptu 478.7 *extempore*; 478.1 *improvised*
impromptu talk 478.4 *improvisation*
improper **802.13**; 240.1 *inconvenient*; 796.12 *indecent*; 544.8 *indecorous*; 236.4 *poor*; 804.11 *wicked*
improper fraction 196.1 *fraction*; 194.5 *ratio*
improperly **802.27**; 233.6 *incompletely*; 240.6 *inconveniently*
impropriety **544.2**; **802.3**; 675.3 *grossness*; 240.3 *inconvenience*; 236.10 *poverty*; 806.3 *sin*; 804.3 *venial sin*
improvable **244.15**; 765.18 *acquisitional*; 760.15 *convertible*
improvably 244.17 *better*
improve **244.1**; **392.22**; 765.10 *augment*; 224.7 *be changed*; 760.8 *be transformed*; 224.8 *cause change*; 395.9 *change*; 235.10, 797.20 *do good*; 797.21 *do well*; 6.22 *educate*; 302.8 *further*; 244.2 *get better*; 213.4 *increase*; 781.15 *make rich*; 136.15 *modify*; 230.5 *perfect*; 484.10 *plan out*; 393.2 *refurbish*; 756.10 *show potential*; 304.21 *upturn*
improved **244.14**; 765.18 *acquisitional*; 547.14 *beautified*; 224.12 *changed*; 760.13 *converted*; 136.11 *modified*; 393.13 *repaired*
improved mileage 765.2 *augmentation*
improved productivity 13.4 *economic development*
improved relations 749.1 *pacification*
improved technology 13.4 *economic development*
improved version 244.8 *better thing*
improve living conditions 2.15 *socialize*
Improvement 244
improvement **244.5**; **302.15**; 765.2 *augmentation*; 797.13 *benefit*; 224.1 *change*; 760.2 *evolution*; 14.1 *finance*; 392.1 *help*; 213.1 *increase*; 136.5 *modification*; 547.1 *transfiguration*
improve on 121.8 *be superior*
improve oneself 244.2 *get better*
improve on nature 244.1 *improve*
improver 224.6 *editor*; 302.16 *progressive person*; 244.13 *reviser*
improve the occasion 287.5 *take the opportunity*
improve upon 244.1 *improve*
improvidence 681.4 *extravagance*; 615.1 *rashness*; 441.3 *waste*
improvident 681.1 *extravagant*; 615.4 *rash*; 441.8 *wasteful*
improvidently 441.10 *wastefully*
improving **244.16**; 797.6 *beneficial*; 760.14 *converting*; 6.16 *educational*
improvingly 6.25 *educationally*
Improvisation 478
improvisation **478.4**; 21.22 *acting*; 484.3 *expedient plan*; 477.5 *fantasy*; 18.2 *music making*; 21.2 *play*
improvisatore 478.6 *improviser*
improvisatrice 478.6 *improviser*
improvise **478.3**; 717.10 *act*; 243.2 *do the groundwork*; 477.14 *imagine*; 21.35 *overact*; 18.36 *play*
improvised **478.1**; 18.31 *composed*; 21.39 *dramatic*
improvised drama 21.2 *play*
improviser **478.6**; 21.24 *actor*
improvising 21.22 *acting*
imprudence 459.1 *folly*; 240.3 *inconvenience*; 615.1 *rashness*
imprudent 739.11 *disclosing*; 459.5 *foolish*; 240.1 *inconvenient*; 615.4 *rash*
imprudently 459.8 *foolishly*
impudence **660.10**; 659.2 *bad manners*; 661.1 *defiance*; 668.1 *disrespect*; 660.1 *insolence*; 660.11 *sauciness*
impudent **660.21**; 659.6 *bad-mannered*; 661.7 *defiant*; 668.10 *disrespectful*; 660.13 *insolent*; 738.15 *open*
impudently 661.9 *defiantly*; 668.28 *disrespectfully*; 660.30 *insolently*; 659.10 *rudely*
impudent person **660.12**
impudent talk 661.3 *act of defiance*
impugn 705.20 *doubt*; 113.18 *object*; 708.11 *rebut*
impugnation 113.4 *objection*; 708.3 *rebuttal*
impugning 708.19 *rebutting*
impugnment 113.4 *objection*
impulse 332.9 *acceleration*; 617.1 *desire*; 590.2 *impression*; 331.11 *impulsion*; 395.1 *influence*; 445.3 *insight*; 480.11, 483.1 *motive*; 478.5 *spontaneity*; 642.3 *whim*
impulse-reaction turbine 38.12 *turbine*
impulse turbine 38.12 *turbine*
Impulsion 331
impulsion **331.11**; 344.1 *cause*; 36.15 *compulsion*; 262.4 *haste*; 300.2 *momentum*; 330.1 *propulsion*
impulsive 262.3 *hasty*; 331.17 *impelling*; 590.11 *intuitive*; 615.4 *rash*; 478.2 *spontaneous*; 486.1 *unskilful*
impulsively 331.18 *dynamically*; 330.34 *forward*; 472.14 *inattentively*; 262.7, 615.6 *rashly*
impulsiveness 262.5 *hastiness*; 472.2 *impetuosity*; 615.1 *rashness*; 478.5 *spontaneity*
impunity 16.42 *acquittal*; 389.1 *escape*; 758.1 *exemption*
impure 804.12 *immoral*; 796.12 *indecent*; 258.8 *unclean*; 250.12 *unconditional*
impurely 250.21 *excessively*
impureness 245.8 *perversion*
impure thoughts 796.2 *indecency*
impurity 245.8 *perversion*; 128.6 *thing excluded*; 258.2 *uncleanness*; 804.2 *vice*
impurity atom 28.44, 39.4 *semiconductor*
imputation 715.1 *accusation*
imputative 715.8 *accusatory*
impute 715.5 *accuse*
I myself 139.12 *I*
in **53.20**; **314.17**; **368.15**; 97.17 *at home*; 53.12 *cricketing*; 632.12 *established*; 815.8 *imprisoned*; 314.18 *into*; 295.10 *new*; 63.4 *tennis terms*
in A1 condition 259.1 *healthy*
in a bad humour 626.7 *irritable*
in a bad mood 221.8 *in a state of*
in a bad temper 594.13 *angry*
in a bad way 249.6 *adverse*; 245.12 *deteriorated*; 254.4 *endangered*; 260.22 *sick*
in a beeline 324.9 *directly*
in a belligerent way 661.10 *in defiance*
in abeyance 341.3 *inactive*; 339.7 *inertly*; 355.7 *on hold*; 335.10 *powerless*; 339.6 *suspended*; 350.1 *unused*
in a big way 158.20 *largely*
inability 247.1 *failure*; 335.1 *powerlessness*; 486.8 *unskilfulness*; 238.3 *uselessness*
inability to act 341.1 *inaction*
inability to pay 784.5 *amount owing*; 247.1 *failure*; 786.5 *insolvency*
inability to see 519.7 *figurative blindness*
inability to wait 262.5 *hastiness*
in a bind 254.4 *endangered*
in a black hole 602.6 *depressed*
in a blissful manner 248.9 *prosperously*
in a blue funk 612.7 *frightened*
in a body 223.21, 376.51 *together*
in Abraham's bosom 582.19 *dead*
in a brown study 472.8 *absent-minded*; 477.10 *imaginative*; 443.10 *speculative*; 4.17 *thoughtful*
in absentia 98.20 *absently*
in abundance 208.9 *ample*
in a carefree manner 263.6 *with ease*
in a catch-22 situation 254.4 *endangered*; 639.16 *irresolutely*
inaccessibility 145.1, 240.4 *distance*; 103.6 *hopelessness*; 655.1 *unsociability*
inaccessible 145.8 *distant*; 103.3 *hopeless*; 655.8 *unsociable*
inaccessibly 655.14 *unsocially*
in accord **750.10**; **750.31**; 117.12 *conforming*; 117.17 *conformingly*; 516.12 *harmoniously*
in accordance 117.17 *conformingly*
inaccuracy **274.2**; 802.2 *incorrectness*; 453.14 *indeterminacy*; 266.1 *obscurity*
inaccurate 274.15 *erroneous*; 802.12 *incorrect*; 453.6 *indeterminate*; 718.6 *misrepresented*; 266.2 *obscure*
inaccurately 453.25 *indeterminately*; 266.4 *obscurely*; 718.8 *unrepresentatively*; 802.26 *wrong*; 274.22 *wrongly*
in accusation 715.10 *accusingly*
in a certain state 221.9 *conditionally*; 221.8 *in a state of*
in a circle 307.13 *round*
in a clear style 695.13 *intelligibly*
in a cold sweat 612.7 *frightened*
in a coma 260.22 *sick*; 489.8 *unconscious*
in a constrained manner 728.28 *moderately*
in a context 108.10 *relevantly*
in a controversial way 751.11 *in disagreement*; 709.11 *uncooperatively*
in a corner 378.14 *blocked*; 378.17 *in the way*; 264.16 *troubled*
in a courageous way 661.9 *defiantly*
in a cowardly way 337.14 *weakly*
in a critical condition 582.18 *dying*
in a critical way 753.11 *disapprovingly*
in a crocodile 132.20 *in a line*; 223.21 *together*
Inaction 341
inaction **341.1**; 343.5 *inactivity*; 339.1 *inertness*; 301.1 *motionlessness*; 634.13 *shirking*
in action 340.5 *acting*; 342.18 *active*
inactivate 343.14 *make inactive*
inactive **341.3**; **343.1**; 634.18 *avoiding*; 620.4 *boring*; 618.7 *indifferent*; 339.5 *inert*; 580.7 *leisurely*; 301.4 *motionless*; 350.3 *not wanted*; 663.7 *obedient*; 32.38 *reactive*
inactively **343.15**; 620.8 *boringly*; 618.17 *indifferently*; 339.7 *inertly*; 301.10 *motionlessly*; 663.10 *obediently*
inactive volcano 30.24 *volcanic activity*
Inactivity 343
inactivity **343.5**; 620.1 *boredom*; 350.10 *disuse*; 263.1 *ease*; 341.1 *inaction*; 618.1 *indifference*; 339.1 *inertness*; 580.1 *leisure*; 301.1 *motionlessness*; 663.1 *obedience*; 634.13 *shirking*; 388.1 *submission*; 219.3 *superfluity*
in actuality 95.13 *really*
in addition 211.10 *additionally*; 213.8 *increasingly*
in a dead heat 285.14 *equal with*
in a decline 260.22 *sick*
in a delicate condition 561.16 *reproductive*
inadequacy **782.9**; 231.5 *imperfection*; 233.1 *incompleteness*; 122.3 *inferior numbers*; 218.8 *insufficiency*; 238.3 *uselessness*
inadequate **782.4**; 604.11 *disappointing*; 231.2, 233.4 *incomplete*; 218.1, 337.13 *insufficient*; 159.7 *little*; 205.11 *partial*; 120.3 *unequal*; 670.32 *unsatisfactory*; 486.1 *unskilful*; 238.1 *useless*
inadequately **782.17**; 233.6 *incompletely*; 218.10 *insufficiently*; 205.12 *partly*; 120.7 *unequally*; 487.7 *unskilfully*; 337.14 *weakly*
in a destructive manner 798.13 *destructively*
in a different class 121.12 *superior*
in a different way 751.12 *differently*
in a dilemma 705.13 *problematic*; 264.16 *troubled*
in a direct fashion 255.20 *homogenously*
in a direct line 324.9 *directly*
in a dishonest way 774.19 *thievishly*
in a disorderly manner 299.8 *irregularly*
in a dither 327.27 *agitatedly*
inadmissible 128.11 *excluded*; 240.1 *inconvenient*
inadmissible evidence 716.5 *legal evidence*
in a downward curve 212.9 *decreasingly*
in a dream 463.16 *obliviously*
in a drunken stupor 690.3 *dead drunk*; 690.18 *drunkenly*
in advance 785.21 *cash down*; 293.17 *early*; 129.21 *first*; 167.11 *in front*
in adverse circumstances 249.12 *in adversity*; 249.7 *unprosperous*
in adversity **249.12**
inadvertent 107.9 *causeless*
inadvertently 107.13 *by chance*
inadvisability 240.3 *inconvenience*
inadvisable 240.1 *inconvenient*
inadvisably 240.6 *inconveniently*
in a fair way 119.13 *equitably*
in a false light 718.8 *unrepresentatively*
in a few words 723.12 *in brief*
in a firm grip 360.11 *tenaciously*
in a fix 378.14 *blocked*; 222.8 *difficult*; 264.16 *troubled*
in a fixed position 253.17 *fastly*
in a flap 327.16 *restless*
in a flash 262.6 *hastily*; 280.9 *in the shortest possible time*
in a foreign country 100.18 *extraneously*
in a frame-up 715.10 *accusingly*
in a friendly fashion 654.18 *sociably*
in a friendly spirit 569.17 *in friendship*
in a friendly way 569.17 *in friendship*
in a funk 612.7 *frightened*
in a generous-hearted manner 769.15 *receptively*
in a gentlemanly manner 631.19 *well*
in agony 491.7 *feeling pain*
in a good mood 221.8 *in a state of*
in a gracious manner 648.6 *leniently*
in a greedy fashion 773.13 *avariciously*
in agreement 117.12 *conforming*; 374.8 *cooperative*; 749.7 *pacifically*
in a groove 111.20 *regularly*
in a gruff manner 625.9 *irascibly*
in a harmless way 805.11 *innocently*
in a hateful manner 594.18 *hatefully*; 751.11 *in disagreement*
in a helpful manner 650.10 *benevolently*
in a high-handed manner 647.11 *severely*
in a hole-and-corner way 737.16 *stealthily*
in a huff 624.16 *angry*
in a humble manner 473.9 *unselfishly*
in a hurry 262.3 *hasty*
in a hurtful manner 624.17 *resentfully*
in aid of **392.37**
in a jam 222.8 *difficult*; 254.4 *endangered*; 264.16 *troubled*
in a jumble 408.27 *in disorder*
in a kind-hearted way 627.13 *pitifully*
in a lather 327.15 *agitated*
in a liberating atmosphere 391.8 *free*
inalienable 99.5 *essential*; 250.9 *free*
inalienable rights 250.2 *free speech*
in a line **132.20**; 148.12 *longitudinally*
in all 232.9 *completely*
in all areas 141.16 *extensively*
in all conscience 799.7 *honourably*; 643.12 *indeed*; 707.24 *truthfully*
in all directions **324.11**; 377.31 *everywhere*
in all haste 262.3 *hasty*
in alliance **750.32**
in all innocence 805.11 *innocently*; 799.8 *purely*; 255.18, 803.9 *virtuously*
in all lands 141.16 *extensively*
in all likelihood 703.22 *demonstrably*; 102.11 *potentially*; 104.11 *probably*; 95.13 *really*
in all places 141.16 *extensively*
in all probability 104.11 *probably*
in all quarters 377.31 *everywhere*

in all respects 698.39 *accurately;* 232.9 *completely*
in all seriousness 643.11 *earnestly;* 707.24 *truthfully*
in all truth 204.13 *on the whole*
inalterable 228.9 *stable*
in a manipulative way 773.13 *avariciously*
in a mass 376.51 *together*
in amazement 619.13 *wonderfully*
in ambush 521.1 *invisible*
in a measure 209.11 *to a degree*
in amends 775.7 *redemptively*
in a mess 408.27 *in disorder;* 264.16 *troubled;* 408.15 *untidy*
in a minority 206.7 *fewer*
in a moment 278.8 *transiently*
in a muddle 408.27 *in disorder*
in an abusive manner 712.13 *vituperatively*
in an accommodating manner 754.8 *compromisingly*
in an active manner 346.13 *operationally*
in an affectionate way 593.30 *lovingly*
in an aggressive way 751.11 *in disagreement*
in an alien way 372.22 *in isolation*
in an amusing way 654.18 *sociably*
in an antagonistic way 594.18 *hatefully*
in an aside 511.10 *faintly*
in a natural way 402.9 *materially*
in ancient times 296.19 *anciently*
in and out 224.15, 227.15 *changeably;* 326.18 *to and fro*
inane 459.5 *foolish;* 457.6 *unintelligent*
in a negative manner 378.18 *inhibitively*
in an egotistical manner 653.5 *misanthropically*
in an elaborate manner 222.19 *meticulously*
inanely 457.11 *unintelligently*
in a nervous state 625.9 *irascibly*
in an evasive manner 754.9 *irresolutely*
in an everyday manner 298.17 *orderly*
in an excellent manner 803.11 *worthily*
in an expert manner 396.26 *expertly*
in an explicit way 150.7 *broadly*
in anger 624.18 *angrily*
in an ill humour 626.13 *sullenly*
inanimate 582.19 *dead;* 343.1 *inactive;* 457.8 *nonhuman*
inanimately 582.23 *fatally;* 343.15 *inactively;* 457.12 *nonhumanly*
inanimate nature 457.4 *nonhuman existence*
inanimate object 339.3 *inert thing;* 402.5 *object*
inanimate objects 457.4 *nonhuman existence*
in an indecent manner 712.12 *swearingly*
in an inferior place 122.19 *inferiorly*
in an inferior state 122.19 *inferiorly*
in an informal way 250.22 *informally*
in an inhibited way 378.18 *inhibitively*
in an instant 280.9 *in the shortest possible time;* 278.8 *transiently*
in an interesting condition 561.16 *reproductive*
in an intimate fashion 569.18 *intimately*
in an intrusive manner 378.16 *with delay*
in an irritable mood 625.9 *irascibly*
inanity 459.1 *folly;* 457.2 *unintelligence*
in a noble manner 400.16 *masterfully*
in an obscene manner 804.20 *immorally*
in an offensive way 659.10 *rudely*
in an offhand manner 478.7 *extempore*
in an open-minded way 769.15 *receptively*
in an optimistic way 756.17 *auspiciously*
in answer 706.24; 701.20 *apologetically;* 704.11 *in reply*
in anticipation 129.22; 243.22 *in preparation;* 104.11 *probably*
in an uncompromising way 641.9 *obstinately*
in an undertone 511.10 *faintly;* 737.15 *in secret;* 730.17 *voicelessly*
in an ungentlemanly manner 631.20 *badly*
in an unpleasant manner 659.9 *discourteously*
in a nutshell 269.3 *concise;* 269.5 *concisely;* 159.8 *in a small way;* 723.12 *in brief;* 745.4 *proverbially;* 149.12 *short*
in any case 317.16 *how*
in any event 317.16 *how;* 107.14 *perchance*
in a paddy 624.18 *angrily;* 624.16 *angry*
in a passionate moment 595.11 *admiringly*
in a patriotic way 85.19 *nationally*
in a peaceful way 589.8 *peacefully*
in a perfect way 805.11 *innocently;* 121.17 *supremely;* 255.18 *virtuously*
in a perfect world 446.23 *ideally*
in a permissive fashion 757.9 *with permission*
in a persuasive manner 752.20 *persuasively*
in a pet 624.15 *resentful*
in a pickle 378.14 *blocked;* 222.8 *difficult;* 264.16 *troubled*
in a pinch 135.12 *in need*
in a pleasing way 595.10 *with great liking*
in a polite manner 658.14 *courteously*
in a political context 396.24 *ministerially*
in a possessive manner 629.9 *jealously*
inappetence 618.1 *indifference*
inappetency 618.1 *indifference*
inappetent 618.7 *indifferent*
in apple-pie order 407.13 *orderly*
inapplicability 100.1 *extraneousness;* 109.1 *unrelatedness;* 238.3 *uselessness*
inapplicable 100.8 *extraneous;* 109.6 *unrelated;* 238.1 *useless*
inapplicably 100.18 *extraneously;* 109.12 *irrelevantly*
inapposite 109.6 *unrelated*
inappositely 109.12 *irrelevantly*
inappositeness 109.1 *unrelatedness*
inappreciability 159.1 *littleness*
inappreciable 521.1 *invisible;* 159.7 *little;* 124.1 *unimportant*
inappreciably 159.8 *in a small way*
inapprehensibility 696.11 *unintelligibility*
inapprehensible 696.1 *unintelligible*
inappropriate 802.13 *improper;* 240.1 *inconvenient;* 109.6 *unrelated;* 288.13 *untimely*
inappropriately 288.19 *at the wrong time;* 802.27 *improperly;* 109.12 *irrelevantly*
inappropriateness 240.3 *inconvenience;* 109.1 *unrelatedness;* 288.2 *untimeliness*
in a predicament 264.16 *troubled*
in a profitable way 569.20 *favourably*
inapt 802.13 *improper;* 109.6 *unrelated;* 288.13 *untimely;* 238.1 *useless*
inaptitude 240.3 *inconvenience;* 109.1 *unrelatedness;* 238.3 *uselessness*
inaptly 109.12 *irrelevantly*
inaptness 109.1 *unrelatedness*
in a quandary 453.3 *confused;* 453.24 *confusingly;* 264.16 *troubled*
in a race 61.11
in a rage 624.16 *angry*
in a receptive way 769.15 *receptively*
in a relative way 222.16 *relatively*
in a repressive way 399.7 *by veto*
in a resolute manner 228.13 *determinedly*
in a respectful stance 667.11
in armour 243.18 *prepared*
in arms 555.11 *young*
in a roundabout way 270.8, 306.12 *circuitously*
in a row 132.20 *in a line;* 289.14 *in succession*
in arrears 233.6 *incompletely;* 784.11 *insolvently;* 786.13 *nonpaying;* 215.12 *with a remainder;* 786.15 *without paying*
inarticulacy 732.4 *guarded speech*
inarticulate 730.12; 646.1 *naive;* 674.11 *shy;* 732.2 *sparing with words;* 730.11 *speechless;* 696.1 *unintelligible;* 619.7 *wide-eyed*
inarticulately 696.13 *unintelligibly*
inarticulateness 730.2 *inarticulation*
inarticulation 730.2
inartistic 486.4 *bungled;* 646.1 *naive*
in a rush 262.3 *hasty*
in a rut 111.20 *regularly*
in a safe manner 253.16 *surely*
in ascendancy 121.12 *superior*
in a scrape 264.16 *troubled*
in a secret manner 399.8 *under censorship*
in a sense 694.13 *meaningfully*
in a series 132.18 *consecutively*
in a serious mood 626.13 *sullenly*
in a sharp tone 659.9 *discourteously;* 625.9 *irascibly*
in a short time 293.18 *soon*
in a short while 293.18 *soon*
in a shy manner 655.14 *unsocially*
in a similar situation 115.13 *similarly*
in a small way 159.8
in a sour disposition 625.9 *irascibly*
in a Spartan manner 687.7 *abstemiously*
in a speculative way 476.10 *supposedly*
in a spin 327.16 *restless;* 307.13 *round*
in a spiteful manner 714.16 *vindictively*
in association 374.8 *cooperative*
in association with 223.24, 747.22 *with*
in a standoffish mood 145.11 *reservedly*
in a state of 221.8; 221.9 *conditionally*
in a stew 624.16 *angry*
in astonishment 619.13 *wonderfully*
in a strange way 116.7 *dissimilarly;* 100.18 *extraneously*
in a strop 624.16 *angry*
in a stubborn manner 418.13 *inflexibly*
in a suggestive manner 742.18 *indicatively*
in a swinging motion 298.15 *regularly*
in a sympathetic manner 595.11 *admiringly*
in a tangle 264.16 *troubled*
in a temper 624.16 *angry*
in a temporary manner 754.8 *compromisingly*
in a tense manner 418.12 *toughly*
in a tight corner 254.4 *endangered*
in a tight spot 264.16 *troubled*
in a tizzy 327.27 *agitatedly;* 328.12 *disturbed*
in atonement 775.7 *redemptively*
in a trance 691.11; 477.10 *imaginative;* 463.16 *obliviously*
in a trice 280.9 *in the shortest possible time;* 278.8 *transiently*
in a trickle 206.10 *in ones and twos*
in attendance 97.8 *attendant;* 282.8 *available*
Inattention 472
inattention 472.1; 486.9 *bungling;* 618.2 *carelessness;* 505.1 *deafness;* 659.1 *discourtesy;* 666.1 *negligence;* 615.1 *rashness;* 342.7 *restlessness;* 463.4 *unthinkingness*
inattentive 472.7; 618.8 *careless;* 659.5 *discourteous;* 459.5 *foolish;* 666.4 *negligent;* 615.4 *rash;* 505.5 *unhearing;* 486.1 *unskilful;* 463.10 *unthinking;* 325.25 *wandering*
inattentive act 472.5
inattentively 472.14; 618.18 *carelessly;* 659.9 *discourteously;* 463.16 *obliviously*
inattentiveness 472.1 *inattention*
inattentive person 472.6
in at the death 382.25 *lethally*
in at the kill 382.25 *lethally*
in a twinkling 280.9 *in the shortest possible time;* 278.8 *transiently*
inaudibility 505.3; 506.4 *silence;* 28.17 *sound;* 696.11 *unintelligibility*
inaudible 511.1 *faint-sounding;* 337.13 *insufficient;* 730.10 *low-voiced;* 506.3 *silent;* 505.7 *unheard;* 696.1 *unintelligible*
inaudibly 505.12 *deafly;* 506.5 *silently;* 696.13 *unintelligibly;* 337.14 *weakly*
inaugural 130.34; 308.17 *beginning;* 129.13 *precursory*
inaugural address 130.9 *premiere;* 733.2 *salutation*
inaugurate 130.23; **344.11**; 295.19, 308.24 *begin;* 129.18 *forerun;* 368.7, 601.19 *install;* 370.10 *introduce*
inaugurated 295.13; 130.37 *enrolled*
inauguration 130.6; 289.4 *accession;* 295.4, 308.11 *beginning;* 601.3 *ceremony;* 656.3 *formal occasion;* 370.3 *introduction;* 243.9 *preparation*
inauguratory 130.34 *inaugural*
inauspicious 611.6; **798.10**; 249.6 *adverse;* 105.1 *improbable;* 475.15 *presageful;* 288.13 *untimely*
inauspiciously 798.14; 288.19 *at the wrong time;* 249.12 *in adversity;* 475.16 *predictively*
inauspiciousness 798.3 *bad luck;* 288.2 *untimeliness*
in authority 396.23 *authoritatively;* 121.13 *dominant;* 395.11 *influential*
in autumn 292.18 *seasonally*
in a vacuum 417.7 *sparsely*
in a vindictive way 798.12 *evilly*
in a warmhearted manner 627.13 *pitifully*
in a way 115.13 *similarly;* 209.11 *to a degree*
in awe 667.10 *reverent;* 619.13 *wonderfully*
in a while 294.17 *later;* 293.18 *soon*
in a whirl 307.13 *round*
in a whisper 737.15 *in secret;* 730.17 *voicelessly*
in a wicked way 662.17 *disobediently*
in a word 269.5 *concisely;* 723.12 *in brief;* 149.12 *short*
in back of 168.9 *in the rear*
in bad condition 221.8 *in a state of*
in bad form 221.9 *conditionally;* 221.8 *in a state of*
in bad health 260.22 *sick*
in bad nick 260.22 *sick*
in bad spirits 221.9 *conditionally;* 221.8 *in a state of*
in bad taste 544.8 *indecorous;* 675.9 *ribald;* 544.10 *ugly*
in battle 701.9 *hostile;* 585.15 *warring*
in baulk 65.9 *billiard*
in bed 260.22 *sick*
in behalf of 550.43 *alternatively;* 398.12 *by proxy*
in being 97.7 *present*
in between 216.12 *mediumly*
in bits 372.21 *apart;* 375.5 *disintegrated;* 205.11 *partial;* 372.20 *separately*
in bits and pieces 245.13 *dilapidated*
in black 603.8 *mournfully*
in black and white 744.17 *on the record;* 744.16 *recorded*
in bliss 248.8 *prosperous*
in bloom 78.11 *flowering;* 44.16 *horticultural;* 555.13 *maturing*
in blossom 78.11 *flowering*
in blue water 91.11 *nautically*
in bold relief 520.2 *clear;* 738.14 *manifest*
in bondage 387.9 *subject*
in bonds 251.15 *detained;* 401.9 *serving;* 387.9 *subject*
inborn 99.6 *intrinsic*
inborn aptitude 485.2 *aptitude*
inbound 312.19 *approaching;* 314.15 *entering*
in brackets 368.15 *in*
inbred 374.7 *combined;* 43.21 *domesticated;* 99.6 *intrinsic*
in brief 723.12; 269.5 *concisely;* 163.7 *essentially;* 149.12 *short*
in broad daylight 716.15 *evidently;* 703.20, 738.16 *manifestly*
in bulk 204.12 *one and all*
in business 776.20 *in trade*
Inca 566.4 *modern human*
in cahoots 747.19 *associating;* 750.32 *in alliance;* 747.21 *in cooperation*
incalculability 202.5 *immeasurability*
incalculable 107.8 *chance;* 202.2 *immeasurable;* 208.8 *numberless*
incalculably 202.11 *immeasurably;* 208.13 *numerously*
in camera 737.15 *in secret;* 521.9 *invisibly;* 521.3 *private*
incandesce 522.25 *light up*
incandescence 493.1 *heat;* 28.40 *heating effect;* 522.1 *light;* 28.24 *light emission*
incandescent 493.9 *hot;* 522.15 *lucent*
incandescent lamp 28.25 *light source*
incandescent light 522.5
incandescently 522.30 *lightly*
incant 11.21 *bewitch;* 10.20 *pray;* 710.6 *request*
incantation 5.22 *many words;* 710.1 *request;* 11.5 *spell*
incantational 710.9 *requesting;* 11.15 *witchlike*
incantatory 11.15 *witchlike*
incapability 335.1 *powerlessness*
incapable 218.1 *insufficient;* 335.10 *powerless;* 486.1 *unskilful*
incapably 487.7 *unskilfully*
incapacitate 378.8 *hinder;* 343.14 *make inactive;* 335.7 *remove power from*

incapacitated 691.7 *drugged;* 335.12 *impotent*
incapacity 247.1 *failure;* 335.1 *powerlessness;* 486.8 *unskilfulness*
in captivity 251.15 *detained;* 815.8 *imprisoned;* 401.10 *obediently;* 401.9 *serving;* 387.9 *subject;* 387.11 *under subjection*
incarcerate 251.11 *detain;* 309.10 *enclose;* 815.9 *imprison;* 814.1 *punish*
incarcerated 251.15 *detained;* 815.8 *imprisoned*
incarceration 251.4 *detention;* 814.7 *punishment*
incarnadine 535.4 *bloody;* 535.9 *redden*
incarnate 554.12 *alive;* 525.7 *appearing;* 402.8 *be material;* 8.13 *divine;* 99.12 *embody;* 402.7 *material;* 717.9 *represent*
incarnation 525.1 *appearance;* 8.8 *divine manifestation;* 738.10 *manifestation;* 402.2 *materialization;* 99.3 *quintessence;* 717.1 *representation*
Incas 284.6 *people of the past*
in cash 781.2 *solvent*
incautious 459.5 *foolish;* 615.4 *rash;* 478.2 *spontaneous*
incautiousness 615.1 *rashness*
incendiary 357.14 *destructive;* 493.7 *fireman;* 493.10 *on fire;* 437.10 *powered*
incendiary bomb 587.16 *bomb;* 493.6 *fire*
incense **502.3**; 594.16 *cause hate;* 624.9 *offend;* 752.6 *offering;* 10.14 *sacred object*
incensed 624.16 *angry*
incensory 10.14 *sacred object*
incentive **480.3**; **480.8**; 791.2 *bargain;* 331.11 *impulsion;* 483.2 *inducement;* 483.11 *motivational;* 480.19 *persuasive;* 813.4 *reward for service*
incentive pay 768.2 *gift*
inception 295.4, 308.11 *beginning;* 130.6 *inauguration*
inceptive 308.17 *beginning;* 344.13 *causal;* 130.34 *inaugural*
inceptively 344.14 *causally*
incertitude 453.9 *uncertainty*
incessancy 132.5 *continuity;* 297.4 *frequency*
incessant 342.18 *active;* 134.5 *continual;* 279.10 *continuing forever;* 132.11 *continuous;* 509.15 *drumming;* 297.3 *frequent;* 277.9 *permanent;* 112.14 *recurrent*
incessantly 134.7 *continually;* 132.19 *continuously;* 277.12 *everlastingly;* 297.1 *frequently;* 112.23, 509.19 *repeatedly*
incest 796.7 *sexual assault*
incestuous 796.15 *unlawful*
inch 92.2 *island;* 92.6 *lowland;* 148.7 *measure of length;* 147.2 *short distance*
in chains 387.9 *subject*
inch along 333.1 *move slowly*
in character 139.16 *characteristic;* 632.11 *normal*
in charge 396.23 *authoritatively;* 12.10 *governing;* 579.17 *managerial;* 579.19 *managerially*
inch by inch 209.10 *by degrees;* 333.16 *slowly*
in check 166.5 *limited;* 251.13 *restraining*
inches taller 622.17 *conceited*
inch forward 302.7 *make one's way*
inchmeal 209.10 *by degrees*
inchoate 130.32 *embryonic;* 295.12 *immature;* 130.34 *inaugural*
inchoation 130.6 *inauguration*
inchoative 130.34 *inaugural*
in chorus 516.7 *harmonious;* 516.12, 750.33 *harmoniously;* 285.13 *synchronously*
incident 17.3 *aspect of fiction;* 3.14 *historicalness;* 222.2 *occurrence*
incidental 223.17 *accompanying;* 222.6 *aspect;* 107.8 *chance;* 222.7 *circumstantial;* 222.10 *detailed;* 100.8 *extraneous;* 109.7 *illogical;* 124.3 *secondary*
incidentally 100.18 *extraneously;* 109.12 *irrelevantly;* 222.19 *meticulously;* 222.16 *relatively;* 124.14 *unimportantly*
incidentalness 100.1 *extraneousness*
incinerate 493.15 *burn;* 583.8 *bury;* 357.12 *consume*
incineration 583.1 *burial;* 357.2 *destroying*
incinerator 493.6 *fire;* 767.4 *wastebin*
incipience 130.6 *inauguration*
incipient 130.34 *inaugural;* 159.7 *little*
incircle 27.42 *circle*
in circles 307.13 *round*
in circulation 740.19 *published*
incise 146.5 *crack;* 19.22 *engrave;* 744.14 *inscribe;* 183.10 *notch;* 35.20 *practise surgery*
incised 156.8 *deep*
incision 146.2 *crack;* 183.4 *notch;* 372.3 *separateness;* 35.9 *surgery*
incisive 164.10 *advantaged;* 707.14 *assertive;* 269.3 *concise;* 726.3 *emphatic*
incisively 164.12 *at an advantage;* 269.5 *concisely;* 726.7 *emphatically*
incisiveness 707.6 *assertiveness;* 442.4 *cleverness;* 269.1 *conciseness;* 726.1 *emphasis*
incisor 425.11 *tooth*
incisural 183.7 *notched*
incisure 183.4 *notch*
incite 713.5 *advise;* 344.10 *awaken;* 613.17 *give courage;* 262.1 *hasten;* 331.1 *impel;* 380.9 *make violent;* 483.10 *manipulate*
incited 483.12 *motivated;* 480.20 *persuadable*
incitement 613.6 *encouragement;* 480.2 *flattery;* 331.11 *impulsion*
inciting 483.11 *motivational*
incitive 483.11 *motivational*
incivility 659.1 *discourtesy;* 668.1 *disrespect;* 675.3 *grossness;* 660.1 *insolence;* 242.6 *objectionability*
in civvies 589.7 *peaceful*
inclemency 494.7 *cold weather;* 628.1 *pitilessness;* 647.1 *severity*
inclement 494.8 *cold;* 647.8 *severe;* 31.48 *stormy*
inclement weather 380.5 *violent weather*
inclination **595.2**; 485.2 *aptitude;* 229.2 *attitude;* 324.2 *bearing;* 593.7 *choice;* 617.1 *desire;* 30.45 *magnetic pole;* 667.4 *mark of respect;* 189.1 *obliqueness;* 29.21 *orbit;* 469.7 *preference;* 305.6 *slide;* 495.2 *taste of life;* 635.1 *will*
inclinational 189.4 *oblique*
inclination of balance 120.1 *inequality*
incline 176.11 *angle;* 189.6 *be oblique;* 243.2 *do the groundwork;* 154.2 *heights;* 367.7 *lean;* 483.9 *motivate;* 480.15 *persuade;* 469.2 *prefer;* 305.14 *slide;* 324.7 *take a direction;* 229.4 *tend;* 304.2 *upturn*
inclined 482.11 *intending;* 176.8, 189.4 *oblique;* 636.1 *willing*
inclined fold 30.20 *earth movement*
inclined plane 38.6 *simple machine;* 27.38 *surface*
inclined railway 321.1 *railway*
inclined towards 595.6 *liking;* 229.5 *tending to*
incline one's head 367.9 *bow*
incline the head 667.19 *take off one's hat to*
incline towards 229.4 *tend*
inclining 189.4 *oblique;* 229.5 *tending to*
inclining towards 229.5 *tending to*
in clover 490.7 *pleased;* 248.8 *prosperous;* 248.9 *prosperously;* 781.16 *wealthily;* 781.1 *wealthy*
include **127.4**; **550.32**; 211.6 *add;* 370.7 *admit;* 405.11 *consist of;* 99.12, 406.8 *embody;* 447.10 *focus on;* 368.1 *insert*
included **127.8**; 211.8 *additional;* 368.12 *inserted*
include out 128.7 *exclude*
including **127.7**; 211.10 *additionally;* 405.9 *composing;* 406.10 *containing*
Inclusion 127
inclusion **127.1**; **550.19**; 211.1 *addition;* 370.1 *admittance;* 764.2 *participation;* 127.2 *thing included;* 368.11 *thing inserted*
inclusive **550.39**; 211.8 *additional;* 406.10 *containing;* 138.15 *general;* 127.7 *including*
inclusive language 127.1 *inclusion*
inclusively **127.9**; **550.42**; 405.14 *constituently;* 406.14 *internally*
inclusiveness 138.1 *generality;* 127.1 *inclusion;* 204.1 *whole*
inclusive of 211.10 *additionally;* 405.9 *composing*
incognito 700.15 *deceiver;* 700.12 *disguise;* 700.41, 736.15 *disguised;* 737.15 *in secret;* 737.11 *mysterious*
incognizable 696.3 *unrecognizable*
incognizance 456.1 *ignorance*
incognizant 456.6 *ignorant*
incoherence 133.1 *discontinuity;* 408.1 *disorder;* 453.14 *indeterminacy;* 461.1 *insanity*
incoherent 408.16 *confused;* 270.3 *diffuse;* 133.8 *discontinuous;* 453.6 *indeterminate;* 457.7 *intellectually subnormal;* 696.1 *unintelligible;* 299.5 *unusual*
incoherently 453.25 *indeterminately;* 696.13 *unintelligibly*
in cold blood 618.17 *indifferently;* 482.13 *intentionally;* 628.7 *pitilessly;* 592.8 *unfeelingly*
in cold storage 294.10 *held up;* 339.7 *inertly*
in collaboration 211.10 *additionally;* 747.21 *in cooperation*
in collaboration with 747.22 *with*
in collusion 747.21 *in cooperation*
in colour 529.10 *coloured*
in combat 381.26 *aggresively*
in combination 374.10
income **788.3**; 765.4 *earnings;* 13.6 *economic factors;* 352.4 *financial resources;* 785.3 *pay;* 440.5 *personal estate;* 356.7 *produce;* 813.4 *reward for service;* 769.2 *something received;* 781.5 *wealth*
incomer 314.7 *entrant;* 128.5 *excluded person;* 289.8 *follower;* 295.8 *new arrival;* 564.7 *settler*
income support 392.4 *social assistance;* 652.4 *welfare state*
income tax 13.6 *economic factors;* 768.2 *gift;* 790.7 *tax*
income-tax haven 484.3 *expedient plan*
income-tax return 744.1 *record*
in comfort 248.9 *prosperously*
incoming 312.19 *approaching;* 312.18 *arriving;* 314.15 *entering;* 314.1 *entry;* 100.12 *external;* 100.4 *externality*
incomings 788.2 *money received*
incoming tide 298.5 *regular thing;* 379.1 *trap*
in command 396.23 *authoritatively;* 579.19 *managerially*
in commemoration of 601.21 *in honour of*
incommensurability 116.2 *unlikeness*
incommensurable 116.4 *dissimilar;* 27.74 *divisible;* 109.7 *illogical*
incommensurate 116.4 *dissimilar*
incommensurately 116.7 *dissimilarly*
in commerce 776.20 *in trade*
in committee 734.13 *discussing*
incommode 240.5 *be inconvenient*
incommodious 240.1 *inconvenient;* 151.1 *narrow*
incommodiously 240.6 *inconveniently*
incommodiousness 240.3 *inconvenience;* 151.5 *narrowness*
in common **764.6**; 764.5 *jointly possessing*
in common parlance 271.8 *simply*
incommunicability 696.11 *unintelligibility*
incommunicable 696.1 *unintelligible*
incommunicado 736.14 *concealed*
incommunicative 732.1 *shy*
incommunicatively 732.8 *shyly*
incommunicativeness 732.3 *shyness*
in communion 750.11 *allied*
incommutable 228.9 *stable*
in-company union 15.3 *organized labour*
in company with 223.24 *with*
incomparability 121.1 *superiority*
incomparable 121.14, 235.2 *best;* 116.4 *dissimilar;* 126.5 *novel*
incomparably 116.7 *dissimilarly;* 126.8 *originally;* 121.17 *supremely*
in comparison 108.10 *relevantly*
incompatibility 701.1 *argument;* 751.3 *difference;* 751.1 *disagreement;* 571.3 *divorce court;* 118.1 *nonconformity;* 27.64 *reasoning;* 116.2 *unlikeness;* 655.1 *unsociability*
incompatible 701.7 *arguing;* 113.25 *contrary;* 751.10 *different;* 751.9 *disagreeing;* 116.4 *dissimilar;* 27.86 *logical;* 655.10 *lonely;* 118.11 *nonconforming*
incompatibly 701.17 *argumentatively;* 751.12 *differently;* 116.7 *dissimilarly;* 751.11 *in disagreement;* 655.14 *unsocially*
in compensation 775.7 *redemptively;* 813.19 *rewardingly*
incompetence 236.8 *inferiority;* 218.8 *insufficiency;* 335.1 *powerlessness;* 486.8 *unskilfulness;* 238.3 *uselessness*
incompetent 611.8 *bad;* 236.2 *inferior;* 218.1 *insufficient;* 766.6 *loser;* 335.10 *powerless;* 486.1 *unskilful;* 486.10 *unskilled person;* 238.1 *useless*
incompetently 218.10 *insufficiently;* 335.14 *powerlessly;* 486.11, 487.7 *unskilfully;* 238.10 *uselessly*
in competition 67.12 *by swimming*
incomplete **231.2**; **233.4**; 196.5 *fractional;* 666.5 *indifferent;* 218.1 *insufficient;* 27.86 *logical;* 205.11 *partial;* 161.5 *shapeless;* 420.5 *unfinished*
incompletely **233.6**; **420.15**; 231.11 *imperfectly;* 205.12 *partly*
Incompleteness 233
incompleteness **233.1**; 231.5 *imperfection;* 218.8 *insufficiency;* 420.10 *rough idea;* 161.1 *shapelessness*
incomplete pass 46.9 *play*
incomplete set 231.6 *imperfect item*
incomplete thing 233.3
incompletion 161.1 *shapelessness*
in compliance with 663.10 *obediently*
incomprehensibility 202.5 *immeasurability;* 266.1 *obscurity;* 696.11 *unintelligibility*
incomprehensible 202.2 *immeasurable;* 266.2 *obscure;* 696.1 *unintelligible*
incomprehensibly 266.4 *obscurely;* 696.13 *unintelligibly*
incomprehension 456.1 *ignorance;* 457.2 *unintelligence*
incompressibility 416.1 *density*
incompressible 416.6 *dense*
inconceivability 103.5 *impossibility;* 696.11 *unintelligibility*
inconceivable 103.1 *impossible;* 696.1 *unintelligible;* 619.8 *wonderful*
inconceivably 103.11 *impossibly;* 696.13 *unintelligibly*
in concert 750.13 *harmonious;* 750.33 *harmoniously;* 750.10, 750.31 *in accord;* 374.10 *in combination;* 747.21 *in cooperation;* 285.13 *synchronously;* 747.22 *with*
in conclusion 706.25 *conclusively;* 131.26 *finally*
inconclusive 337.13 *insufficient;* 704.6 *refutable*
inconclusively 704.12 *refutably;* 337.14 *weakly*
in concord 516.7 *harmonious;* 516.12 *harmoniously*
in condition 259.1 *healthy;* 221.8 *in a state of*
in conference 734.13 *discussing*
in confidence 737.15 *in secret*
in confinement 814.20 *punished*
in conflict 701.17 *argumentatively;* 753.11 *disapprovingly;* 113.31 *opposed to*
in conformity with 663.10 *obediently*
in confrontation 113.29 *at odds*
in confusion 408.27 *in disorder;* 114.11 *irregularly*
in Congress 398.11 *representatively*
incongruent 109.8 *distorted;* 120.3 *unequal*
incongruently 109.13 *disproportionately*
incongruity 751.3 *difference;* 114.1 *diversity;* 118.1 *nonconformity;* 116.2 *unlikeness*
incongruous 751.10 *different;* 116.4 *dissimilar;* 114.5 *diverse;* 802.13 *improper;* 118.11 *nonconforming;* 299.5 *unusual*
incongruously 751.12 *differently;* 116.7 *dissimilarly;* 766.21 *out of place;* 118.21 *unconformably*
incongruousness 299.2 *unusualness*
in conjunction with 211.10 *additionally;* 747.21 *in cooperation;* 223.24, 747.22 *with*
in connection with 373.17
in consent 516.7 *harmonious;* 516.12 *harmoniously*
inconsequence 618.5 *insignificance;* 124.5 *unimportance*
in consequence 345.12 *with the effect of*
inconsequential 618.11 *insignificant;* 702.7 *sophistic;* 124.1 *unimportant*
inconsequentially 124.14 *unimportantly*
inconsiderable 122.13 *insignificant;* 159.7 *little;* 124.1 *unimportant*
inconsiderably 159.8 *in a small way;* 122.20 *insignificantly*
inconsiderate **651.15**; 631.18 *badly behaved;* 519.12 *blind to;* 659.5 *discourteous;* 615.4 *rash;* 472.9 *thoughtless;* 672.3 *ungrateful*
inconsiderate driver 631.5 *badly behaved person*
inconsiderately 631.20 *badly;* 659.9 *dis-*

courteously; 472.14 inattentively; 651.20 malevolently; 672.7 ungratefully
inconsiderateness **651.6**; 659.1 discourtesy; 672.1 ingratitude
inconsideration 651.6 inconsiderateness; 615.1 rashness; 472.4 thoughtlessness
inconsistency 642.2 caprice; 224.1 change; 227.1 changeableness; 113.8 contrariety; 751.3 difference; 114.1 diversity; 479.6 equivocation; 274.4 faulty reasoning; 299.1 irregularity; 118.1 nonconformity; 27.64 reasoning; 702.1 sophistry; 453.15 unreliability
inconsistent 642.1 capricious; 224.11, 227.13 changeable; 113.25 contrary; 751.10 different; 114.5 diverse; 274.15 erroneous; 299.4 irregular; 27.86 logical; 118.11 nonconforming; 702.7 sophistic; 453.7 unreliable
inconsistently 224.15, 227.15 changeably; 751.12 differently; 114.10 diversely; 299.8 irregularly; 702.14 sophistically; 118.21 unconformably; 453.26 unreliably
inconsolable 602.5 sad
inconspicuous 521.2 difficult to see; 728.16 imperceptible
inconspicuously 728.27 imperceptibly
inconspicuousness 728.7 imperceptibility
inconstancy **639.12**; 642.2 caprice; 453.16 capriciousness; 224.1 change; 227.1 changeableness; 299.1 irregularity
inconstant 453.8, 642.1 capricious; 224.11, 227.13, 639.2 changeable; 114.5 diverse; 299.4 irregular; 700.38 treacherous
inconstantly 453.27 capriciously; 224.15, 227.15 changeably; 114.10 diversely; 299.8 irregularly
in constant use 349.9 used
in contact 147.14 beside; 373.14 connective; 147.10 juxtaposed
in contempt of 751.11 in disagreement
incontestable 738.14 manifest
incontinence 335.4 disability; 767.1 disposal; 250.6 liberality; 686.3 overindulgence; 796.3 sexual immorality; 560.3 urination
incontinent 335.12 impotent; 796.14 lecherous; 686.8 overindulgent; 250.12 unconditional; 560.26 urinary
incontinently 250.21 excessively; 686.12 self-indulgently
in contradiction 708.22 negatively; 709.11 uncooperatively
in contrast 347.5 counter; 113.31 opposed to; 108.10 relevantly
in control 396.23 authoritatively; 579.19 managerially
incontrovertible 750.20 agreeable; 452.3 decided; 228.9 stable
Inconvenience 240
inconvenience **240.3**; 240.5 be inconvenient; 378.9 block; 378.6, 378.12 burden; 264.23 cause difficulties; 328.10 disrupt; 328.4 disruption; 378.2 obstacle; 264.8 snag; 288.2 untimeliness; 238.3 uselessness
inconvenienced 328.15 disrupted; 264.16 troubled
inconvenient **240.1**; **264.13**; 378.14 blocked; 465.9 misjudged; 288.13 untimely; 238.1 useless
inconveniently **240.6**; 288.19 at the wrong time; 264.28 awkwardly; 328.18 disturbingly; 378.17 in the way; 238.10 uselessly
in conversation 706.24 in answer
in convoy 223.21 together
in cooperation **747.21**; 764.6 in common; 747.22 with
incorporate 370.13 absorb; 374.5 combine; 405.11 consist of; 99.12 embody; 127.4, 550.32 include; 101.8 nonmaterial; 776.1 trade
incorporated 374.7 combined; 776.19 corporate; 550.39 inclusive
incorporated company 776.7 company; 13.7 corporation
incorporating 405.9 composing; 127.7 including
incorporation 370.5 absorption; 747.7 association; 374.1 combination; 127.1, 550.19 inclusion
incorporative 127.7 including
incorporator 550.17 coverer
incorporeal 101.8 nonmaterial; 417.1 sparse; 11.18 spiritual; 96.8 unreal
incorporeality 417.3 sparseness; 96.1 unreality
incorporeally 101.13 metaphysically
incorporealness 101.2 unworldliness
incorporeity 101.2 unworldliness
incorrect **802.12**; 274.15 erroneous; 802.13 improper; 544.9 inelegant; 27.86 logical; 718.6 misrepresented
incorrectly 718.8 unrepresentatively; 802.26 wrong; 274.22 wrongly
incorrectness **802.2**; 274.3 erroneousness; 675.3 grossness; 544.4 inelegance of speech; 657.5 nonobservance
incorrect spelling 5.27 spelling
incorrect usage 5.29 grammar; 274.11 grammatical error
incorrigibility 809.1 impenitence; 641.5 obstinacy
incorrigible 809.3 impenitent; 766.16 losing; 611.5 past hope; 641.2 refractory; 804.11 wicked
incorrigibly 804.18 wickedly
incorrupt 805.5 innocent
incorruptedness 805.1 innocence
incorruptibility 279.1 eternity; 259.3 health; 805.1 innocence; 799.1 probity
incorruptible 279.8 eternal; 799.4 honourable; 805.5 innocent
incorruption 259.3 health; 805.1 innocence
in court 16.87 in litigation; 16.81 legally
incrassate 190.7 bigger; 152.1 thick; 430.11 thicken; 430.8 viscous
incrassation 430.1 viscosity
Increase 213
increase **213.1**; **213.4**; 211.1 addition; 607.6 aggravate; 765.10 augment; 765.2 augmentation; 190.6 become bigger; 203.2 certain amount; 209.6 change gradually; 219.1 excess; 244.2 get better; 345.8 grow; 190.1, 345.3 growth; 244.5 improvement; 148.10 lengthen; 190.5, 213.5 make bigger; 207.4 multiplication; 207.9 pluralize; 356.7 produce; 436.1 provision; 203.8 quantify; 366.2 send up; 439.6 store; 304.2 upturn
increased **213.7**; 607.4 aggravated; 190.7 bigger; 207.8 multiplicative; 203.6 quantitative
increased output 356.2 manufacture
increase fourfold 200.11 quadruple
increase in size 190.6 become bigger; 190.1 growth; 190.5 make bigger
increase numbers 213.5 make bigger
increase one's demands 218.6 be unsatisfied
increaser 190.4 enlarger
increase the chances 104.9 make probable
increase the odds 104.9 make probable
increase threefold 199.10 triple
increasing **213.6**; 209.7 gradational; 190.8, 345.11 growing; 244.14 improved; 207.8 multiplicative
increasingly **213.8**; 209.10 by degrees; 190.10 largely
increasing thing **213.3**
incredibility 105.6 implausibility; 451.2 unbelievability
incredible 451.7 disbelieved; 105.2 questionable; 103.2 unbelievable; 619.8 wonderful; 619.14 wonderful!
incredibly 103.11 impossibly; 105.8 improbably; 451.11 unbelievably
in credit **783.13**; 789.13 financially
incredulity **451.3**; 630.2 amazement; 453.10 suspicion
incredulous 451.6 disbelieving
incredulously 451.10 disbelievingly
increment 211.1 addition; 765.2 augmentation; 27.31 differentiation; 213.1 increase; 813.4 reward for service
incremental 211.8 additional
incriminate 715.5 accuse; 670.19 blame
incriminated 715.8 accusatory
incriminating evidence 716.5 legal evidence
incrimination 715.1 accusation
incriminator 715.3 accuser
incriminatory 715.8 accusatory
in-crowd 295.6 avant-garde; 376.19 clique
in crowds **208.14**
incrusted 418.1 hard
incubate 243.7 develop; 168.8 nurture; 561.13 propagate
incubating 243.17 developing
incubation 243.13 development; 561.3 propagation
incubator 359.2 preserver; 344.2 source
incubus 8.7 devil; 414.8 weighing down
inculcate 374.5 combine; 6.22 educate
inculpability 805.1 innocence
inculpable 805.5 innocent
inculpate 715.5 accuse
inculpated 806.5 guilty
inculpation 806.1 guilt
incumbent 564.1 inhabitant
incumbent on 810.12 obligatory; 414.3 ponderous
incurable 382.23 deadly; 611.5 past hope; 236.4 poor; 260.22 sick; 641.3 unyielding
incurably 611.11 hopelessly
incur a duty 810.15 be liable; 579.2 direct
incur a penalty 766.9 lose
incur a responsibility 810.15 be liable
incur blame 596.7 cause dislike
incur costs 787.1 expend
incur expenses 787.1 expend
incuriosity 472.1 inattention; 618.1 indifference
incurious 472.7 inattentive; 618.7 indifferent
incuriously 472.14 inattentively; 618.17 indifferently
incuriousness 618.1 indifference
incur liabilities 772.10 buy on credit
incur loss 766.9 lose
incur losses 766.10 have a financial loss
incurred 354.5 undertaken
incursion 314.3 inroad; 381.14 siege; 329.8 transgression; 585.8 warfare
incursive 314.16 invasive
incursively 314.17 in
incur upon 381.9 attack successfully
incurvate 183.6 concave
incurvation 183.1 concavity
incurvature 177.1 curvature
incus 504.5 internal ear
in custody 251.15 detained; 252.6 safe
in danger 254.4 endangered; 254.3 vulnerable
in date order 275.25 of known date
in Davy Jones' locker 367.24 down
in days gone by 3.24 historically
in days of yore 284.22 in the past
in debt **784.9**; 378.14 blocked; 789.13 financially; 782.2 insolvent; 784.11 insolvently; 786.15 without paying
indebted 378.14 blocked; 671.4 grateful; 784.9 in debt; 782.2 insolvent; 786.13 nonpaying
indebtedness 784.1 debt; 782.6 insolvency
indecency **796.2**; 497.4 bad taste; 800.1 improbity; 258.3 obscenity; 236.10 poverty; 804.2 vice
indecent **539.4**; **796.12**; 497.6 coarse; 712.8 cursing; 800.5 dishonourable; 804.12 immoral; 258.9 obscene; 236.4 poor; 675.9 ribald
indecent assault 381.16 personal attack; 380.2 physical violence; 796.7 sexual assault
indecent exposure 796.7 sexual assault; 552.1 undress
indecently 258.12 dirtily; 800.11 dishonourably; 796.21, 804.20 immorally; 552.17 nakedly; 712.12 swearingly; 497.11 tastelessly
indecently assault 796.20 seduce
indecently dressed 552.11 exposed
indecipherable 264.12 problematic
indecision 337.2 indecisiveness; 339.1 inertness; 453.11 irresoluteness; 326.3, 639.11 vacillation
indecisive 224.11 changeable; 339.5 inert; 453.2 irresolute; 639.1 vacillating; 337.12 weak-willed
indecisively 224.15 changeably; 639.16 irresolutely; 453.23 uncertainly; 337.14 weakly
indecisiveness **337.2**; 339.1 inertness; 453.11 irresoluteness
indecisive person **639.15**
in decline 214.8 decreasingly; 245.12 deteriorated
indecorous **544.8**; 802.13 improper; 804.13 venial
indecorously 802.27 improperly; 544.11 inelegantly; 804.19 vulnerably
indecorousness 802.3 impropriety
indecorum 804.3 venial sin
in deduction 212.8 by subtraction
indeed **643.12**; 454.12 assuredly; 698.37 authentically; 95.14 certainly; 698.35 truly
in deep 484.15 planning
in deep water 264.16 troubled
indefatigability 342.8 assiduity; 640.2 commitment
indefatigable 342.20 industrious; 423.4 powerful; 640.11 steady; 638.2 tenacious
in default 233.4 incomplete; 233.6 incompletely; 218.10 insufficiently; 215.12 with a remainder
in default of 762.9 instead
indefeasible 228.9 stable
indefectability 230.3 perfection
indefectible 230.1 perfect
in defence 701.12 apologetic; 701.20 apologetically; 384.32 defensively; 706.24 in answer; 704.11 in reply
indefensible 335.11 unprotected
indefensibly 335.14 powerlessly
in defiance **661.10**; 753.11 disapprovingly; 751.11 in disagreement
indefinable 696.1 unintelligible
indefinableness 696.11 unintelligibility
indefinite 521.2 difficult to see; 138.20 generalized; 5.44 grammatical; 453.6 indeterminate; 528.4 inscrutable; 266.2 obscure; 161.5 shapeless; 96.8 unreal; 696.3 unrecognizable; 452.8 unspecified
indefinite article 5.35 part of speech
indefinite integral 27.31 differentiation
indefinitely 453.25 indeterminately; 202.10 infinitely; 521.9 invisibly; 266.4 obscurely; 161.6 shapelessly
indefiniteness 479.5 equivocalness; 453.14 indeterminacy; 266.1 obscurity
indefinite period **275.5**
indefinite time 275.5 indefinite period
indehiscent 80.9 of a fruit
indehiscent fruit 80.2 botanical fruit
indelible 462.7 memorable; 228.9 stable
indelible ink 532.8 black pigment; 228.4 stable thing
indelibly 228.12 stably
indelicacy 544.2 impropriety; 796.2 indecency
indelicate 712.8 cursing; **796.12** indecent; 544.8 indecorous; 546.4 ugly
indelicate language 712.2 offensive language
indelicately 544.11 inelegantly; 712.12 swearingly
in demand 669.24 admired; 617.7 desired; 135.4 required; 778.16 sold
indemnification 807.1 atonement; 775.2, 813.6 compensation
indemnificatory 807.4 atoning; 813.17 compensatory; 775.6 restoring
indemnify 807.5 atone; 775.5 compensate; 649.9 forgive; 813.11 pay; 785.10 pay back; 253.11 promise; 609.11 recompense
indemnifying 775.6 restoring
indemnity 807.1 atonement; 775.2, 813.6 compensation; 649.1 forgiveness; 785.4 grant; 253.2 promise; 609.2 reparation; 785.2 repayment
indemonstrability **453.13**
indemonstrable **453.4**
in denial 708.22 negatively
indent 755.5 contract; 397.10, 710.2, 710.7 demand; 183.9 make concave; 420.12 make rough; 135.10 necessitate; 183.10 notch; 742.13 punctuate; 135.1 requirement; 773.7 take; 773.1 taking
indentation 183.1 concavity; 367.14 depression; 404.3 nap; 183.4 notch
indented 183.6 concave; 183.7 notched; 742.17 punctuated
indention 183.1 concavity; 742.7 punctuation; 773.1 taking
indenture 387.6 subject
indentured 387.9 subject
indentured servant 387.5 subjected person
indentureship 387.1 subjection
independence **250.3**; 758.2 acquittal; 572.1 celibacy; 657.4 freedom; 635.4 free will; 12.1 government; 126.1 originality; 100.3 separateness; 781.8 solvency; 622.2 unapproachability; 109.1 unrelatedness
Independence Day 601.5 anniversary; 298.6 annually celebrated day
independent **250.10**; **758.7**; 572.6 celibate; 635.10, 657.10 free; 250.7 free person; 27.77 given; 12.9, 396.14 governmental; 639.15 indecisive person; 85.16 national; 118.7 nonconformist; 100.11 separate; 197.15 solo; 622.15 unapproachable;

118.13 *unconventional*; 15.10 *unionized*; 109.6 *unrelated*
Independent Broadcasting Authority 692.24 *television broadcasting*
independently 197.21 *alone*; 572.12 *celibately*; 100.18 *extraneously*; 250.20 *freely*; 15.13 *industrially*; 109.12 *irrelevantly*; 396.24 *ministerially*; 85.19 *nationally*; 118.22 *out of step*
independent means 250.3 *independence*
independent mind 391.1 *liberation*
independent-minded 391.7 *liberated*
independent referee 713.4 *adviser*
independent rule 250.3 *independence*
independent school 6.12 *educational institution*
independent state 85.1 *country*
independent television 692.24 *television broadcasting*
Independent Television Authority 692.24 *television broadcasting*
Independent Television Commission 692.24 *television broadcasting*
independent union 15.3 *organized labour*
independent variable 27.29 *mathematical function*
independent voter 250.7 *free person*
independent worker 578.1 *worker*
in deposit 439.7 *stored*
in depth 156.17 *profoundly*
in-depth reporting 741.3 *reporting*
in descending order 214.8 *decreasingly*
indescribable 619.8 *wonderful*
indescribably 619.13 *wonderfully*
indestructibility 225.1 *permanence*; 228.1 *stability*
indestructible 225.7 *permanent*; 228.9 *stable*; 418.2, 423.1 *tough*
indestructibly 225.9 *permanently*; 228.12 *stably*; 423.12 *toughly*
in detail 665.12 *carefully*; 270.7 *diffusely*; 205.12 *partly*; 156.17 *profoundly*; 139.32 *severally*
in detention 815.8 *imprisoned*
indeterminable 107.8 *chance*; 202.2 *immeasurable*
indeterminableness 202.5 *immeasurability*
indeterminably 202.11 *immeasurably*
indeterminacy **452.19**; **453.14**; 28.81 *causality*; 107.1 *chance*
indeterminate **453.6**; 138.20 *generalized*; 96.8 *unreal*; 452.8 *unspecified*
indeterminately **453.25**
indetermination 107.1 *chance*
index 409.7 *catalogue*; 409.15 *categorize*; 406.5 *divisions*; 167.2 *face*; 742.5 *indicator*; 406.9 *itemize*; 220.8 *list*; 27.17 *multiplication*; 194.6 *power*; 742.7 *punctuation*; 744.13 *record*; 744.6 *record book*; 693.5 *reference book*; 137.14 *sort*; 407.19 *systematize*; 220.2 *table*
index card 744.6 *record book*
indexed 409.24 *categorized*; 407.11 *grouped*; 743.12 *identified*; 406.12 *itemized*; 220.11 *listed*; 744.16 *recorded*
indexes 210.2 *statistics*
index finger 742.5 *indicator*; 492.7 *sense organ*
index fossil 30.43 *fossil*
indexical 137.10 *classificatory*; 407.11 *grouped*
indexically 409.28 *in place*; 406.15 *thematically*
indexing 409.5 *categorization*; 407.2 *grouping*; 220.7 *listing*; 744.8 *registration*
Index Librorum Prohibitorum 399.2 *censorship*
India 92.1 *continent*
Indian 564.1 *inhabitant*; 1.6 *race*; 1.13 *racial*
Indian dish **25.49**
Indian horse 59.1 *horse*
Indian ink 532.8 *black pigment*
Indianize 760.12 *naturalize*
Indian mode 18.20 *key*
Indian red 535.6 *red pigment*
Indian summer 31.23 *heat*; 493.5 *hot weather*; 393.10 *revival*; 292.3 *summer*; 31.3 *weather*
Indian tea 558.3 *tea*
Indian temple dance 22.4 *historic dancing*
Indian yellow 537.7 *yellow pigment*
India paper 435.3 *paper*
india rubber 422.4 *rubber*
indicate 324.6, 579.2 *direct*; 738.1 *display*; 446.19 *epitomize*; 703.16 *explain*; 743.10 *identify*; 716.10 *make evident*; 520.10 *make visible*; 694.10 *mean*; 129.15 *precede*; 475.11 *predict*; 738.3 *reveal*; 742.10 *signify*; 452.22 *specify*; 701.15 *state*; 693.14 *tip*; 742.9 *use signs*
indicated 452.7 *particular*
indicated value 28.82 *measuring instrument*
indicating 743.1 *identification*; 693.16 *informative*; 694.6 *meaningful*
indicating instrument 28.82 *measuring instrument*
indication **716.4**; 693.7 *advice*; 721.2 *brief description*; 223.4 *concomitant*; 703.3 *explanation*; 743.1 *identification*; 738.10 *manifestation*; 721.7 *nomenclature*; 475.5 *omen*; 452.18 *particularity*; 27.64 *reasoning*; 717.1 *representation*; 742.1 *sign*; 260.3 *symptom*; 446.2 *theory*; 711.1 *warning*
indicative 35.24 *diagnostic*; 716.8 *evidential*; 703.11 *explanatory*; 738.14 *manifest*; 694.6 *meaningful*; 5.33 *mood*; 475.13 *predicting*; 742.14 *signifying*; 446.10 *theoretical*
indicatively **742.18**; 716.14 *as evidence*; 703.22 *demonstrably*; 743.14 *identifiably*; 446.21 *purposively*
indicator **742.5**; 522.6 *electric light*; 32.18 *gravimetric analysis*; 716.4 *indication*; 26.8 *meter*; 742.1 *sign*; 711.1 *warning*
indicator light 522.6 *electric light*
indicatory 742.14 *signifying*
indict 715.5 *accuse*; 16.70 *litigate*
indictability 806.1 *guilt*
indictable 715.8 *accusatory*
indictable offence 16.39 *crime*
indicted 715.8 *accusatory*
indicter 715.3 *accuser*
indictment 715.1 *accusation*
indie 18.9 *popular music*
Indifference **618**
indifference **618.1**; **666.2**; 639.14 *apathy*; 620.1 *boredom*; 505.1 *deafness*; 36.13 *depression*; 497.1 *dilution*; 473.1 *disinterestedness*; 637.13 *dissociation*; 343.7 *idleness*; 341.1 *inaction*; 472.1 *inattention*; 339.1 *inertness*; 657.1 *informality*; 592.3 *insensitiveness*; 216.6 *mediocrity*; 301.1 *motionlessness*; 589.1 *peace*; 605.2 *stoicism*; 472.4 *thoughtlessness*; 655.1 *unsociability*; 463.4 *unthinkingness*
indifference to art 646.2 *naivety*
indifferent **618.7**; **666.5**; 355.6 *apathetic*; 620.4 *boring*; 473.4 *disinterested*; 341.3 *inactive*; 250.10 *independent*; 339.5 *inert*; 657.7 *informal*; 592.1 *insensitive*; 216.3 *mediocre*; 685.6 *moderate*; 235.5 *not bad*; 343.3 *not participating*; 605.8 *resigned*; 301.5 *sedentary*; 497.5 *tasteless*; 505.1 *unhearing*; 655.8 *unsociable*; 639.4 *unsteady*; 463.10 *unthinking*
in different directions 116.7 *dissimilarly*
indifferentism 618.1 *indifference*
indifferentist 618.6 *indifferent person*
indifferently **618.17**; 355.8 *apathetically*; 620.8 *boringly*; 473.8 *disinterestedly*; 250.20 *freely*; 343.16 *impassively*; 472.14 *inattentively*; 339.7 *inertly*; 463.16 *obliviously*; 605.9 *stoically*; 592.8 *unfeelingly*; 655.14 *unsocially*; 341.5 *without action*
indifferent person **618.6**
in different ways 114.10 *diversely*
in difficulties 249.6 *adverse*; 784.9 *in debt*; 782.2 *insolvent*; 264.16 *troubled*
indigence 782.5 *poverty*
indigene 564.1 *inhabitant*
indigenous 564.12 *native*; 293.15 *precursory*; 1.13 *racial*; 77.15 *wild*
indigenously 293.19 *primevally*
indigenous race 1.6 *race*
indigent 782.1 *poor*; 782.10 *poor person*
indigestibility 423.6 *toughness*
indigestible 423.3 *hard*
indigestibly 423.12 *toughly*
indigestion **260.8**; 491.2 *painful condition*
indignant 624.16 *angry*; 670.25 *disapproving*; 624.15 *resentful*
indignantly 624.18 *angrily*; 624.17 *resentfully*
indignation 670.1 *disapproval*
indignity **668.8**; 624.2 *offence*
indigo 539.1 *blue*; 539.5 *blueness*; 28.28 *colour*; 529.4 *pigment*; 540.6 *purple*
in diplomatic language 746.9 *feasibly*
indirect **325.21**; 270.4 *circumlocutory*; 222.7 *circumstantial*; 700.34 *deceiving*; 189.5 *devious*; 5.44 *grammatical*; 189.4 *oblique*; 266.2 *obscure*; 306.9 *orbital*; 66.5 *soccer*
indirect authority 396.1 *authority*
indirect cannon 65.3 *English billiards*
indirect costs 13.7 *corporation*
indirect course 325.14 *deviating course*
in-directed 36.34 *introverted*
indirect election 469.12 *election*
indirect evidence 716.5 *legal evidence*
indirect free kick 66.2 *football play*
indirect influence **395.4**
indirection 306.2 *circuitousness*; 700.1 *deception*; 325.13 *deviation*; 189.3 *deviousness*; 189.1 *obliqueness*
indirectly **325.28**; 398.12 *by proxy*; 270.8, 306.12 *circuitously*; 189.9 *deviously*; 5.52 *grammatically*; 266.4 *obscurely*; 222.16 *relatively*
indirect motion 325.15 *deviating motion*
indirectness 270.2 *circumlocution*; 189.1 *obliqueness*; 266.1 *obscurity*
indirect object 5.35 *part of speech*
indirect proof 27.66 *proof*
indirect question 5.23 *phrase*; 705.11 *question mark*
indirect radiation 31.22 *sun*
indirect speech 5.23 *phrase*
indirect tax 788.2 *money received*; 790.7 *tax*
indirect wave 692.15 *transmitted wave*
in dire straits 784.9 *in debt*; 249.7 *unprosperous*
in disagreement **751.11**
in disarray 408.12 *disordered*; 408.27 *in disorder*
indiscernibility 521.4 *invisibility*
indiscernible 521.1 *invisible*; 159.7 *little*
indiscernibly 521.9 *invisibly*; 159.9 *microscopically*
indiscipline 588.1 *anarchy*; 662.1 *disobedience*; 686.3 *overindulgence*
indiscreet 486.3 *clumsy*; 739.11 *disclosing*; 693.16 *informative*; 615.4 *rash*; 804.13 *venial*
indiscreetly 739.13 *openly*; 804.19 *vulnerably*
indiscretion 486.9 *bungling*; 459.1 *folly*; 739.3 *openness*; 615.1 *rashness*; 806.3 *sin*; 804.3 *venial sin*
indiscriminate 618.9 *impartial*
indiscriminate bombing 381.13 *air attack*
indiscriminately 618.19 *impartially*; 408.27 *in disorder*
indiscriminating 486.3 *clumsy*
indiscrimination 618.3 *impartiality*
in disequilibrium 120.3 *unequal*
in disguise 526.8 *fleetingly*
in dishabille **552.10**
in disorder **408.27**; 408.12 *disordered*
indispensability 135.3 *needfulness*
indispensable 99.5 *essential*; 123.5 *important*; 135.4 *required*
indispensably 135.12 *in need*
indispose 481.4 *put off*
indisposed 260.22 *sick*; 637.1 *unwilling*
indisposition 260.1 *ill health*; 260.2 *illness*; 637.11 *unwillingness*
indisputability 452.9 *certainty*
indisputable 707.16 *definite*; 703.12 *demonstrable*; 93.13 *real*; 228.9 *stable*
indisputably 707.23 *affirmatively*; 454.12 *assuredly*; 228.12 *stably*
in disrepair 245.13 *dilapidated*
indissolubility 416.1 *density*; 197.3 *oneness*
indissoluble 416.7 *condensed*; 360.9 *retentive*; 228.9 *stable*; 197.13 *whole*
indissolubly 228.12 *stably*; 360.11 *tenaciously*
indistinct 521.2 *difficult to see*; 511.1 *faint-sounding*; 519.13 *hidden*; 728.16 *imperceptible*; 453.6 *indeterminate*; 524.6 *murky*; 266.2 *obscure*; 696.3 *unrecognizable*
indistinctly 524.12 *dimly*; 728.27 *imperceptibly*; 453.25 *indeterminately*; 521.9 *invisibly*; 266.4 *obscurely*
indistinctness 453.14 *indeterminacy*; 521.4 *invisibility*; 524.2 *murk*; 511.3 *mutedness*; 266.1 *obscurity*
indistinguishability 750.5 *conformity*; 521.4 *invisibility*; 111.1 *sameness*
indistinguishable 750.14 *conforming*; 521.1 *invisible*; 524.6 *murky*; 111.12 *same*; 696.3 *unrecognizable*
indistinguishably 111.18 *identically*; 521.9 *invisibly*; 750.34 *uniformly*
in distress 782.1 *poor*
individual 232.7 *complete*; 114.5 *diverse*; 118.14 *eccentric*; 566.12 *human*; 250.10 *independent*; 554.1 *life*; 126.5 *novel*; 197.1, 197.11 *one*; 34.3 *organism*; 452.7 *particular*; 139.13, 566.7 *person*; 742.14 *signifying*; 197.14 *singular*; 139.15 *special*; 109.6 *unrelated*; 299.5 *unusual*; 204.6 *whole*
individualism 250.3 *independence*; 4.7 *school of thought*; 683.1 *selfishness*
individualist 4.11 *follower of a doctrine*; 250.7 *free person*; 68.11 *skier*
individualistic 118.14 *eccentric*; 250.10 *independent*; 4.14 *of a philosophy*; 683.4 *selfish*; 139.15 *special*; 139.18 *subjective*
individualistically 250.20 *freely*; 683.8 *selfishly*
individuality 114.1 *diversity*; 743.2 *identity*; 250.3 *independence*; 402.1 *material world*; 126.1 *originality*; 197.4 *singularity*; 139.1 *speciality*; 109.1 *unrelatedness*; 118.4 *unusualness*
individualize 139.26 *personalize*
individualized 139.20 *personalized*
individually 114.10 *diversely*; 250.20 *freely*; 566.15 *humanly*; 742.18 *indicatively*; 109.12 *irrelevantly*; 197.22 *one by one*; 126.8 *originally*; 139.29 *personally*
individual project 447.5 *educational topic*
individual psychology 36.1 *psychology*
individual retirement account 13.6 *economic factors*
individual test 36.5 *psychological test*
indivisibility 267.1 *adhesion*; 416.1 *density*; 197.3 *oneness*; 255.8 *simplicity*; 204.1 *whole*
indivisible 267.9 *adhesive*; 416.6 *dense*; 27.74 *divisible*; 99.7 *integral*; 255.16 *simple*; 197.13 *whole*
indivisibly 267.11 *cohesively*; 197.23 *wholly*
indocile 641.2 *refractory*
indocility 637.14 *disobedience*; 641.5 *obstinacy*
indoctrinate 117.10 *assimilate*; 6.22 *educate*; 632.18 *habituate*; 450.9 *make someone believe*; 480.15, 760.11 *persuade*
indoctrination 6.1 *education*; 632.7 *habituation*; 760.3 *persuasion*; 480.5 *propaganda*
indoctrinator 760.5 *converter*
Indo-European 5.11 *family of languages*
Indo-Germanic 5.11 *family of languages*
Indo-Iranian 5.11 *family of languages*
indolence 343.7 *idleness*; 341.1 *inaction*; 339.1 *inertness*; 93.9 *mere existence*; 301.1 *motionlessness*; 333.8 *slowness*
indolent 341.3 *inactive*; 339.5 *inert*; 343.3 *not participating*; 301.5 *sedentary*; 333.5 *unhurried*; 93.16 *vegetating*
indolently 343.16 *impassively*; 339.7 *inertly*; 333.16 *slowly*
indomitable **640.12**; 613.9 *courageous*; 638.4 *undaunted*
indoor 165.7 *enclosed*; 58.8 *hockey*; 172.8 *internal*; 67.11 *swimming*
indoor game 69.1 *game*
indoor garden 44.2 *garden*
indoor gardening 44.1 *horticulture*
indoor hockey 58.1 *hockey*
indoors 172.2 *inside*
indoor sport 45.4 *sporting activity*
indoor swimming pool 67.7 *swimming pool*
indoor track events 47.1 *track events*
in double harness 570.21 *married*; 570.24 *matrimonially*
in double jeopardy 254.4 *endangered*
in double-quick time 332.14 *swiftly*
in double-time 332.14 *swiftly*
in doubt 705.14 *questionable*; 705.24 *questionably*
Indra 585.3 *gods and goddesses of war*
in draft 484.14 *planned*
indraught 314.2 *influx*; 370.4 *intake*
indrawal 314.2 *influx*; 370.4 *intake*
indrawing 314.2 *influx*
in dribs and drabs 133.17 *discontinuously*; 206.10 *in ones and twos*; 205.12 *partly*
indubitability 452.9 *certainty*; 707.8 *definiteness*

indubitable 452.3 *decided;* 707.16 *definite;* 104.6 *probable*
indubitableness 707.8 *definiteness*
indubitably 707.23 *affirmatively;* 698.37 *authentically;* 95.14, 452.23 *certainly;* 104.11 *probably*
induce 363.11 *attract;* 344.10 *awaken;* 701.14 *discuss;* 369.15 *draw out;* 483.9 *motivate;* 752.9 *offer;* 480.15 *persuade;* 35.20 *practise surgery;* 444.11 *reason;* 442.12 *think*
induced 483.12 *motivated;* 480.20 *persuadable*
induced current 28.51, 39.9 *electric current*
induced electricity 334.7 *electrical power*
induced sweat 560.8 *sweat*
inducement **483.2**; 768.2 *gift;* 480.8 *incentive;* 480.1 *persuasion;* 363.2 *pulling power;* 813.4 *reward for service*
inducing 480.19 *persuasive*
inducing secretion **559.6**
induct 130.25, 314.14 *enrol;* 130.23 *inaugurate;* 368.7, 601.19 *install*
inductance 334.7 *electrical power;* 28.53, 39.12 *resistance*
induction 476.2 *basis of supposition;* 34.15 *developmental biology;* 334.7 *electrical power;* 130.8 *enrolment;* 314.1 *entry;* 370.3 *introduction;* 701.2 *logical argument;* 4.4 *philosophical investigation;* 7.9 *priesthood;* 27.64, 444.2 *reasoning;* 35.9 *surgery;* 442.2 *ways of thinking*
induction coil 39.17 *resistor*
induction motor 39.31 *electric motor*
induction training 15.2 *industrial negotiations*
inductive 39.36 *electronic;* 27.86 *logical;* 363.10 *magnetic;* 444.8 *rational*
inductively 701.19 *logically*
inductive reasoning 444.2 *reasoning*
inductor 28.55 *circuit;* 39.17 *resistor*
in due course 283.14 *in the future;* 294.17 *later*
in due form 656.12 *formally*
indulge 650.8 *be benevolent;* 648.3 *be lenient;* 757.4 *be permissive;* 471.14 *be solicitous;* 558.13 *drink;* 490.9 *give pleasure;* 599.15 *humour;* 392.22 *improve;* 609.8 *satisfy*
indulged 649.6 *forgiven;* 648.5 *given consideration*
indulge in 340.4 *act;* 631.11 *conduct oneself;* 686.10 *indulge oneself*
indulge in wishful thinking 700.25 *deceive oneself*
indulgence 649.1 *forgiveness;* 649.2 *forgivingness;* 657.4 *freedom;* 648.1 *leniency;* 757.1 *permission;* 245.8 *perversion;* 490.1 *physical pleasure;* 471.5 *solicitude*
indulgent 392.35, 650.6 *benevolent;* 265.13 *easy-going;* 657.10 *free;* 648.4 *lenient;* 649.5 *merciful;* 757.8 *permitting;* 471.9 *solicitous*
indulgently 650.10 *benevolently;* 649.14 *forgivingly;* 648.6 *leniently;* 490.11 *pleasingly;* 757.9 *with permission*
indulge one's appetite 688.5 *be greedy*
indulge oneself **686.10**; 588.4 *be anarchic;* 688.5 *be greedy;* 683.6 *be selfish;* 490.8 *feel pleasure*
indulge one's fancy 469.4 *pick*
indulging 599.11 *humouring*
in duplicate 111.18 *identically;* 561.17 *repeatedly*
indurate 809.5 *be impenitent;* 418.3 *hardened*
indurated 418.3 *hardened*
induration 809.1 *impenitence*
indurative 809.3 *impenitent*
indusium 82.2 *fern plant*
industrial **15.8**; 24.10 *ceramic;* 2.13 *communal;* 356.11 *productive;* 776.17 *professional*
industrial action 15.4 *industrial dispute;* 703.6 *mass demonstration;* 709.1 *refusal;* 226.2 *stop*
industrial archaeology 284.9 *antiquarianism;* 3.2 *archaeology*
industrial architect 20.2 *architect*
industrial architecture 20.1 *architecture*
industrial area 577.1 *workshop*
industrial art 19.1 *art*
industrial artist 19.16 *artist*
industrial ceramics **24.9**
industrial chemistry **32.22**; 32.1 *chemistry*
industrial city 87.1 *city*
industrial conflict 15.4 *industrial dispute*
industrial design 19.1 *art*
industrial designer 19.16 *artist*
industrial dispute **15.4**
industrial engineering 38.3 *mechanical engineering*
industrial espionage 737.2 *secretiveness*
industrial estate 577.1 *workshop*
industrial institution 2.8 *human institution*
industrialist 578.3 *agent;* 356.9 *producer*
industrialization 13.4 *economic development;* 356.2 *manufacture*
industrialize 356.10 *produce;* 2.15 *socialize*
industrialized 2.13 *communal;* 356.11 *productive*
industrialized society 2.5 *society*
industrializing governmental 2.13 *communal*
industrial law 15.5 *labour law*
industrially **15.13**; 20.20 *architecturally;* 24.12 *ornamentally;* 2.16 *sociologically*
industrial medicine 35.1 *medicine*
industrial negotiations **15.2**
industrial organization 2.4 *social organization*
industrial psychologist 36.29 *psychologist*
industrial psychology 36.1 *psychology*
industrial relations **13.8**
Industrial Relations **15**
industrial relations **15.1**
Industrial Relations Act 15.5 *labour law*
Industrial Revolution 13.6 *economic factors;* 284.5 *historical period*
industrial rock 18.9 *popular music*
industrial safety 13.8 *industrial relations*
industrial spy 753.5 *seditionist*
industrial strife 15.4 *industrial dispute*
industrial town 577.1 *workshop*
industrial tribunal 15.1 *industrial relations*
industrial union 15.3 *organized labour*
industrial unionism 15.1 *industrial relations*
industries fair 779.2 *fair*
industrious **342.20**; 340.5 *acting;* 640.10 *persevering;* 576.10 *working*
industriously 342.22 *actively*
industriousness 342.8 *assiduity;* 640.2 *commitment*
industry 342.8 *assiduity;* 342.6, 776.6 *business;* 356.2 *manufacture;* 576.1 *work*
industry-wide 15.10 *unionized*
industry-wide strike 15.4 *industrial dispute*
in Dutch 264.16 *troubled*
indweller 564.1 *inhabitant*
indwelt 564.11 *inhabited*
IndyCar racing 61.1 *motor racing*
in earnest 638.17 *resolutely;* 707.24 *truthfully*
in easy circumstances 781.1 *wealthy*
inebriant 690.6 *intoxicating*
inebriate 690.9 *be intoxicating;* 690.17 *drunkard;* 690.5 *drunken*
inebriated 690.1 *drunk*
inebriating 690.6 *intoxicating*
inebriation 690.10 *drunkenness*
inebriative 690.6 *intoxicating*
inebriety 690.10 *drunkenness*
inedibility 423.6 *toughness*
inedible 423.3 *hard;* 242.3, 499.6 *unpalatable*
inedibly 499.10 *sourly*
ineffability 696.11 *unintelligibility*
ineffable 8.13 *divine;* 103.2 *unbelievable;* 696.1 *unintelligible;* 456.8 *unknown;* 619.8 *wonderful*
ineffably 8.19 *divinely;* 619.13 *wonderfully*
in effect 93.10 *existing;* 204.13 *on the whole;* 95.13 *really*
ineffective 247.10 *failed;* 563.6 *having no effect;* 233.4 *incomplete;* 335.10 *powerless;* 238.1 *useless*
ineffectively 233.6 *incompletely;* 335.14 *powerlessly;* 247.12 *unsuccessfully;* 238.10 *uselessly*
ineffectiveness 247.1 *failure;* 233.1 *incompleteness;* 335.1 *powerlessness;* 238.3 *uselessness*
ineffectual 247.10 *failed;* 233.4 *incomplete;* 335.10 *powerless;* 639.3 *timid;* 124.1 *unimportant;* 486.1 *unskilful;* 238.1 *useless;* 337.8 *weak*
ineffectuality 233.1 *incompleteness;* 337.2 *indecisiveness;* 335.1 *powerlessness;* 486.8 *unskilfulness*
ineffectually 233.6 *incompletely;* 335.14 *powerlessly;* 124.14 *unimportantly;* 247.12 *unsuccessfully;* 238.10 *uselessly;* 337.14 *weakly*
ineffectualness 238.3 *uselessness*
inefficacious 247.10 *failed;* 335.10 *powerless*
inefficaciously 247.12 *unsuccessfully*
inefficacy 238.3 *uselessness*
inefficiency 247.1 *failure;* 236.8 *inferiority;* 335.1 *powerlessness;* 486.8 *unskilfulness;* 238.3 *uselessness*
inefficient 236.2 *inferior;* 335.10 *powerless;* 486.1 *unskilful;* 238.1 *useless*
inefficiently 335.14 *powerlessly;* 486.11 *unskilfully*
inelastic 424.1 *brittle;* 416.6 *dense;* 423.3 *hard;* 418.2 *tough;* 641.3 *unyielding*
inelasticity 424.2 *brittleness;* 641.6 *determination;* 418.5 *hardness;* 383.2 *obstinacy*
inelastic scattering 28.71 *nuclear reaction*
inelastic strain 38.14 *load*
Inelegance **544**
inelegance **544.1**; **675.4**; **724.3**; 497.4 *bad taste;* 266.1 *obscurity;* 546.1 *ugliness*
inelegance of speech **544.4**
inelegancy 544.1 *inelegance*
inelegant **544.9**; **724.8**; 486.3 *clumsy;* 497.6 *coarse;* 544.7 *graceless;* 266.2 *obscure;* 546.4 *ugly;* 675.7 *vulgar*
inelegantly **544.11**; 546.6 *hideously;* 266.4 *obscurely;* 497.11 *tastelessly*
ineligible 240.1 *inconvenient;* 470.10 *rejected*
ineligible athlete 470.9 *rejected person*
ineligible receiver 46.13 *penalty*
ineluctability 452.16 *inevitability*
ineluctable 386.10 *compulsory;* 452.5 *inevitable*
ineluctably 452.25 *inevitably*
in embryo 243.17 *developing;* 233.4 *incomplete;* 130.41 *in the bud*
in employment 401.9 *serving*
inept 611.8 *bad;* 459.5 *foolish;* 240.1 *inconvenient;* 335.10 *powerless;* 486.1 *unskilful;* 238.1 *useless*
ineptitude 459.1 *folly;* 335.1 *powerlessness;* 486.8 *unskilfulness;* 238.3 *uselessness*
ineptly 335.14 *powerlessly;* 486.11 *unskilfully*
ineptness 486.8 *unskilfulness*
inequal 420.1 *rough*
Inequality **120**
inequality **120.1**; 751.3 *difference;* 109.4 *distortion;* 114.1 *diversity;* 27.26 *equality;* 465.3 *injustice;* 299.1 *irregularity;* 420.6 *roughness*
inequally 420.14 *roughly*
in equal measures 754.8 *compromisingly*
in equal parts 754.8 *compromisingly*
in equilibrium 119.12 *equally;* 750.13 *harmonious*
inequitable 466.10 *discriminatory;* 120.4 *unjust;* 802.11 *wrong*
inequitably 466.17 *prejudicially;* 120.8 *unjustly*
inequity 120.2 *injustice;* 466.3 *prejudice;* 802.1 *unfairness*
ineradicable 99.7 *integral;* 228.9 *stable*
inerrantist 7.4 *religionist*
in error 274.21 *erroneously;* 465.13 *misguidedly;* 465.7 *misjudging;* 274.17 *mistaken;* 720.4 *mistakenly*
inert **339.5**; 634.18 *avoiding;* 592.2 *desensitized;* 32.34 *elemental;* 341.3, 343.1 *inactive;* 618.7 *indifferent;* 301.5 *sedentary;* 333.5 *unhurried;* 93.16 *vegetating*
inert gas 32.6 *chemical element*
inertia 341.1 *inaction;* 343.5 *inactivity;* 618.1 *indifference;* 339.1 *inertness;* 28.9 *mass;* 93.9 *mere existence;* 301.1 *motionlessness;* 333.8 *slowness*
inertial navigation 323.5 *navigation*
inertly **339.7**; 343.15 *inactively;* 618.17 *indifferently;* 301.10 *motionlessly;* 341.5 *without action*
Inertness **339**
inertness **339.1**; 639.14 *apathy;* 341.1 *inaction;* 343.5 *inactivity;* 301.1 *motionlessness;* 333.8 *slowness*
inert person **339.2**
inert thing **339.3**
inescapable 452.5 *inevitable;* 810.12 *obligatory*
inescapableness 452.16 *inevitability*
inescapably 452.25 *inevitably*
in essence **99.13**; 204.13 *on the whole;* 406.13 *structurally;* 447.14 *thematically*
inessential 100.8 *extraneous;* 124.8 *trifle;* 124.1 *unimportant*
inessentiality 100.1 *extraneousness;* 124.5 *unimportance*
inestimable 202.2 *immeasurable;* 235.3, 792.8 *valuable*
inestimably 202.11 *immeasurably;* 792.13 *valuably*
in estrangement 571.13 *without one's spouse*
inevasible 452.5 *inevitable*
inevasibleness 452.16 *inevitability*
in everyday use 349.9 *used*
in every detail 698.39 *accurately*
in every direction 324.11 *in all directions*
in every place 141.16 *extensively*
in every quarter 141.16 *extensively;* 324.11 *in all directions*
in every respect 204.11 *wholly*
in every way 232.9 *completely*
in evidence 716.14 *as evidence;* 703.22 *demonstrably*
inevitability **452.16**
inevitable **452.5**; 386.9 *compelling*
inevitableness 452.16 *inevitability*
inevitably **452.25**; 386.11 *compellingly*
inexact 486.3 *clumsy;* 274.15 *erroneous;* 138.20 *generalized;* 453.6 *indeterminate;* 666.5 *indifferent;* 266.2 *obscure*
inexactitude 274.2 *inaccuracy;* 666.2 *indifference;* 138.3 *nonspecificness*
inexactly 266.4 *obscurely;* 274.22 *wrongly*
inexactness 274.2 *inaccuracy;* 452.19, 453.14 *indeterminacy;* 465.1 *misjudgment;* 266.1 *obscurity*
in excess 686.12 *self-indulgently*
in excess of requirements 219.8 *excessively*
in exchange **759.6**; **759.8**; 110.10 *reciprocally*
in exchange for 759.8 *in exchange*
inexcitability 4.3 *detachment;* 618.1 *indifference;* 339.1 *inertness*
inexcitable 618.7 *indifferent;* 301.6 *quiescent*
inexcusable 806.5 *guilty;* 802.17 *unforgivable;* 804.11 *wicked*
inexcusably 806.11 *guiltily;* 804.18 *wickedly*
inexhaustible 208.8 *numberless;* 217.2 *plentiful;* 134.6 *protracted*
inexhaustibly 134.7 *continually;* 217.9 *enough;* 681.9 *extravagantly*
inexistence 98.1 *absence*
in existence 97.14 *in person*
inexistent 98.8 *absent*
inexorability 452.16 *inevitability;* 638.14 *tenacity*
inexorable 452.5 *inevitable;* 628.5 *inflexible;* 302.18 *ongoing;* 638.3 *strong-willed;* 641.3 *unyielding*
inexorableness 628.2 *inflexibility*
inexorably 452.25 *inevitably;* 641.9 *obstinately*
inexpectant 619.6 *wondering*
in expectation 474.5 *expecting*
inexpedience 240.3 *inconvenience;* 288.2 *untimeliness;* 238.3 *uselessness*
inexpediency 240.3 *inconvenience;* 238.3 *uselessness*
inexpedient 240.1 *inconvenient;* 288.13 *untimely;* 238.1 *useless*
inexpediently 288.19 *at the wrong time;* 240.6 *inconveniently*
inexpensive 793.9 *cheap*
inexpensively 777.15, 793.15 *cheaply*
inexpensiveness 793.1 *cheapness*
inexperience 456.2 *half-knowledge;* 295.3, 555.3 *immaturity;* 646.2, 805.3 *naivety;* 487.3 *unaccustomedness;* 486.8 *unskilfulness*
inexperienced 295.12, 555.12 *imma-*

ture; 646.1, 805.7 *naive;* 538.3 *raw;* 456.7 *semiskilled;* 487.1 *unaccustomed;* 486.2 *unskilled*
inexpert 538.3 *raw;* 456.7 *semiskilled;* 486.2 *unskilled*
inexpertly 486.11, 487.7 *unskilfully*
inexpertness 456.2 *half-knowledge;* 486.8 *unskilfulness*
inexpiable 804.11 *wicked*
in explanation 719.18 *in other words;* 714.15 *in vindication*
inexplicability 107.1 *chance;* 696.11 *unintelligibility*
inexplicable 107.9 *causeless;* 696.1 *unintelligible*
inexplicably 107.13 *by chance;* 696.13 *unintelligibly*
inexpressibility 696.11 *unintelligibility*
inexpressible 696.1 *unintelligible;* 619.8 *wonderful*
inexpugnable 252.7 *invulnerable*
inextensibility 418.5 *hardness*
in extenso 270.7 *diffusely;* 148.11 *lengthily*
inextinguishable 228.9 *stable;* 380.6 *violent*
in extremis 582.18 *dying;* 727.17 *excessively*
inextricable 267.9 *adhesive*
inextricably 267.11 *cohesively*
in fact 93.22, 95.13 *really;* 698.35 *truly*
in fair condition 235.5 *not bad*
in fair health 259.1 *healthy*
in fairness 801.17 *by rights*
infallibility 452.17; 230.3 *perfection*
infallible 452.6; 230.1 *perfect*
infamous 812.4 *disreputable;* 802.15 *immoral;* 455.10 *known;* 738.14 *manifest;* 740.20 *well-known;* 804.11 *wicked*
infamy 812.1 *disrespect;* 740.7 *publicity;* 804.1 *wickedness*
infancy 130.4 *conception;* 335.3 *helplessness;* 555.1 *youth*
infant 130.15 *baby;* 555.9 *child;* 130.32 *embryonic;* 805.4 *innocent person;* 730.9 *voiceless;* 730.7 *voiceless person;* 337.4 *weakling;* 555.11 *young*
infanticide 651.7 *act of malevolence;* 382.3 *homicide;* 382.11 *murderer;* 10.7 *non-Christian ritual*
infantile 457.6 *unintelligent;* 555.11 *young*
infantile fixation 36.17 *fixation*
infantile paralysis 260.17 *nervous disorder*
infant prodigy 619.5 *person of wonder*
infantry 586.16 *army unit*
infantry assault 381.12 *military attack*
infantry battalion 584.4 *military organization*
infantry division 584.4 *military organization*
infantry engagement 585.9 *battle*
infantryman 586.17 *army person;* 585.11 *recruit*
infantry regiment 584.4 *military organization*
infantry service 585.8 *warfare*
infant school 6.12 *educational institution*
infants' wear 551.23 *children's clothes*
infarct 309.2 *stopper*
infarction 260.10 *cardiovascular disease*
in fashion 221.9 *conditionally;* 632.12 *established;* 282.6 *present;* 295.23 *trendily*
infatuated 593.19 *enamoured;* 595.6 *liking*
infatuated with 593.18 *in love*
infatuating 595.5 *likable*
infatuatingly 595.10 *with great liking*
infatuation 595.3 *likes;* 595.1 *liking;* 593.2 *romantic love*
in favour 569.9 *friends with;* 669.19 *supporting;* 636.1 *willing*
in favour of 762.9 *instead*
in favour with 811.3 *reputable*
in fear and trembling 612.7 *frightened*
in fear of 612.15 *fearfully*
infect 412.10 *become mixed;* 236.13 *be worthless;* 395.9 *change;* 258.11 *dirty;* 245.3 *make worse;* 483.10 *manipulate;* 316.11 *transfer*
infected 260.23 *diseased;* 236.4 *poor*
infection 260.6; 249.1 *adversity;* 245.10 *impairment;* 395.1 *influence;* 412.1 *mixture;* 260.5 *plague;* 236.10 *poverty;* 316.3 *transmission;* 258.2 *uncleanness*
infectious 395.12 *appealing;* 254.1 *dangerous;* 260.23 *diseased;* 236.5 *harmful;* 316.17 *transferable;* 258.8 *unclean*
infectious disease 260.4 *disease;* 316.10 *transferred thing*
infectiously 395.14 *influentially;* 412.14 *in the midst;* 316.18 *in transit*
infectious mononucleosis 260.6 *infection*
infectiousness 260.6 *infection*
infectious person 316.9 *disease carrier*
infective hepatitis 260.6 *infection*
infecund 563.3 *infertile*
infecundity 563.1 *infertility*
infelicitous 288.17 *accidental;* 486.4 *bungled;* 240.1 *inconvenient*
infelicity 486.9 *bungling*
infer 694.11; 693.15 *be informed;* 464.12 *estimate;* 443.16 *have an idea;* 719.8 *interpret;* 4.21 *rationalize;* 444.11 *reason;* 476.5 *suppose;* 27.89 *theorize*
inference 693.7 *advice;* 476.2 *basis of supposition;* 345.1 *effect;* 464.1 *judgment;* 4.4 *philosophical investigation;* 4.8 *philosophical term;* 27.64, 444.2 *reasoning*
inferential 222.7 *circumstantial;* 27.86 *logical;* 444.8 *rational*
inferentially 222.16 *relatively*
inferior 122.6; **122.12**; **236.2**; 611.8 *bad;* 604.11 *disappointing;* 116.4 *dissimilar;* 231.1 *imperfect;* 218.1 *insufficient;* 155.6 *lower;* 216.3 *mediocre;* 124.10 *nonentity;* 401.1 *servant;* 793.10 *shoddy;* 387.9 *subject;* 289.7, 289.13, 387.3 *subordinate;* 124.4 *trivial;* 120.3 *unequal*
Inferiority 122
inferiority 122.1; **236.8**; 231.5 *imperfection;* 120.1 *inequality;* 218.8 *insufficiency;* 155.1 *lowness;* 216.6 *mediocrity;* 793.3 *shoddiness;* 387.1 *subjection;* 289.3 *subordination;* 124.7 *triviality*
inferiority complex 36.18 *complex*
inferiorly 122.19
inferior numbers 122.3
inferior personality 36.8 *disordered personality*
inferior planet 29.16 *planet*
inferior rank 387.1 *subjection*
inferior standing 122.1 *inferiority*
inferior state 122.5
inferior status 122.1 *inferiority;* 387.1 *subjection*
inferior thing 122.7
inferior version 231.6 *imperfect item*
infernal 651.11 *cruel;* 236.6 *damnable;* 8.16 *devilish;* 804.14 *impious*
infernally 8.20 *devilishly*
infernal machine 587.16 *bomb*
inferno 408.5 *confusion;* 8.12 *hell;* 493.8 *hot place*
inferred 694.6 *meaningful;* 476.8 *supposed*
infertile 563.3; 335.13 *unsexed*
Infertility 563
infertility 563.1; 335.4 *disability;* 218.9 *scarcity*
infest 76.16; 208.12 *overcrowd;* 329.5 *transgress*
infestation 329.8 *transgression*
infested 232.8 *full;* 329.11 *overrun;* 76.12 *verminous*
infeudation 768.1 *giving*
infidel 451.5 *disbeliever;* 7.6 *non-Christian*
infidelity 800.2 *faithlessness;* 796.4 *illicit love;* 227.2 *irresolution;* 593.8 *love affair;* 451.4 *unbelief*
infield 48.1 *baseball*
infielder 48.2 *baseball player*
infielder's glove 48.3 *baseball equipment*
infield fly 48.6 *fielding terms*
infield fly rule 48.6 *fielding terms*
infighting 751.1 *disagreement*
in file 132.20 *in a line*
infiltrate 314.11; 370.13 *absorb;* 412.10 *become mixed;* 97.11 *be present;* 662.16 *be subversive;* 318.10 *enter;* 433.31 *steep*
infiltrating 318.13 *penetrating*
infiltration 314.3 *inroad;* 412.1 *mixture;* 318.3 *passage into;* 433.10 *steeping;* 662.3 *subversion*
infiltrator 662.10 *seditionist*
in fine feather 551.30, 656.7 *dressed-up;* 259.1 *healthy*
in fine fettle 221.9 *conditionally;* 259.1 *healthy;* 221.8 *in a state of;* 160.12 *on form;* 407.13 *orderly;* 336.9 *physically strong;* 204.8 *sound*
in fine form 259.1 *healthy*
in fine trim 259.1 *healthy*
infinite 202.1; 29.36 *astronomical;* 158.15 *big;* 27.72 *complex;* 8.13 *divine;* 279.8 *eternal;* 141.12 *extensive;* 194.9 *fractional;* 208.8 *numberless;* 97.7 *present;* 203.6 *quantitative*
infinitely 202.10; 29.39 *astronomically;* 8.19 *divinely;* 158.20 *largely;* 27.87 *mathematically;* 208.13 *numerously;* 203.7 *quantitatively*
infiniteness 202.4 *infinity*
infinite number 27.11 *infinity;* 27.7 *natural number*
infinite regress 303.10 *backward motion*
infinite sequence 27.20 *sequence*
infinite set 27.21 *set*
infinitesimal 27.72 *complex;* 521.2 *difficult to see;* 159.7 *little;* 196.6 *small;* 195.6 *zero*
infinitesimal calculus 27.30 *calculus*
infinitesimally 27.87 *mathematically;* 159.9 *microscopically*
infinitesimal number 27.10 *zero*
infinite space 141.2 *empty space;* 202.6 *vastness*
infinite supply 202.4 *infinity*
infinitive 5.33 *mood*
infinitude 279.1 *eternity;* 27.11, 202.4 *infinity*
Infinity 202
infinity 27.11; **202.4**; 145.1 *distance;* 8.2 *divine attribute;* 141.2 *empty space;* 279.1 *eternity;* 41.18 *exposure time;* 194.3 *large number;* 148.4 *length;* 208.1 *multiplicity;* 203.5 *numbers*
infirm 337.10 *ill;* 260.21 *unhealthy;* 453.7 *unreliable;* 804.13 *venial*
infirmary 35.10, 394.14 *hospital*
infirmity 260.1 *ill health;* 260.2 *illness;* 231.5 *imperfection;* 556.5 *old age;* 337.3 *poor health;* 453.15 *unreliability;* 804.3 *venial sin*
infirmity of purpose 639.11 *vacillation*
in fits 327.29 *jerkily*
in fits and starts 133.17 *discontinuously*
infix 211.6 *add;* 211.3 *additional item;* 368.5 *inset;* 5.35 *part of speech*
infixed 368.12 *inserted*
infixion 368.8 *insertion*
in flagrante delicto 340.7 *actively;* 806.11 *guiltily*
inflame 607.6 *aggravate;* 593.25 *be loved;* 338.3 *invigorate;* 380.9 *make violent;* 624.9 *offend*
inflamed 260.23 *diseased;* 483.12 *motivated;* 590.13 *passionate;* 380.6 *violent*
in flames 493.10 *on fire*
inflaming 483.11 *motivational;* 480.19 *persuasive;* 493.12 *warm-hearted*
inflammability 493.6 *fire*
inflammable 254.1 *dangerous;* 493.10 *on fire;* 437.10 *powered*
inflammation 493.1 *heat;* 491.1 *pain;* 260.3 *symptom;* 260.15 *ulcer*
inflammatory 483.11 *motivational*
inflatable 410.19; 190.9 *enlargeable;* 190.3 *enlarged thing*
inflate 765.10 *augment;* 190.6 *become bigger;* 727.10 *boast;* 209.6 *change gradually;* 780.25 *demonetize;* 727.8 *enlarge;* 190.5, 213.5 *make bigger;* 673.18 *make conceited;* 720.1 *misinterpret;* 792.10 *overcharge*
inflated 434.14 *aerial;* 190.7 *bigger;* 622.22 *boastful;* 727.13 *enlarged;* 727.12 *exaggerated;* 720.3 *misinterpreted;* 542.10 *ornate*
inflatedness 727.4 *bombast*
inflater 190.4 *enlarger*
inflating 727.15 *bombastic*
inflation 765.2 *augmentation;* 790.5 *cost;* 13.6 *economic factors;* 13.3 *economic statistics;* 13.2 *economy;* 727.2 *enlargement;* 14.1, 780.7 *finance;* 190.1 *growth;* 213.3 *increasing thing;* 792.3 *inflationary price;* 720.2 *misinterpretation;* 219.3 *superfluity*
inflationary 765.18 *acquisitional;* 681.3 *costly;* 792.7 *dear;* 13.13 *economic;* 190.9 *enlargeable;* 14.6 *financial;* 780.22 *monetary*
inflationary pressure 792.3 *inflationary price*
inflationary price 792.3
inflationary spiral 13.6 *economic factors;* 14.1, 780.7 *finance;* 792.3 *inflationary price*
inflationary universe 29.4 *cosmological model*
inflator 190.4 *enlarger*
inflect 224.8 *cause change*
inflected 5.44 *grammatical;* 5.39 *of language*
inflected language 5.10 *language type*
inflection 211.3 *additional item;* 224.1 *change;* 729.3 *mode of speech;* 5.35 *part of speech;* 5.16 *spoken letter;* 5.30 *syntax*
inflectional 5.44 *grammatical;* 5.42 *worded*
inflectionally 5.50 *lexically*
inflexibility 628.2; 228.2, 641.6 *determination;* 418.5 *hardness;* 418.8 *mental hardness;* 423.9 *mental toughness;* 383.2 *obstinacy;* 647.1 *severity;* 228.1 *stability;* 638.14 *tenacity*
inflexible 628.5; 228.11 *determined;* 452.5 *inevitable;* 418.4 *mentally hard;* 423.5 *mentally tough;* 383.11 *obstinate;* 647.8 *severe;* 228.9 *stable;* 638.3 *strong-willed;* 418.2 *tough;* 641.3 *unyielding*
inflexibly 418.13; 228.13 *determinedly;* 383.14 *resistingly;* 647.11 *severely;* 423.14 *single-mindedly;* 228.12 *stably*
inflict 386.7 *force;* 814.1 *punish*
inflicting pain 491.8
infliction 814.10 *affliction*
inflict pain 491.11; 814.1 *punish;* 814.4 *torture*
inflict punishment 814.1 *punish;* 385.3 *retaliate*
in flight 389.9 *fugitively*
in-flight magazine 740.5 *journal*
inflood 314.12 *flood in*
in flood 90.11 *flooded;* 90.13 *fluently*
inflooding 314.2 *influx;* 314.16 *invasive*
inflorescence 78.4 *flower head*
inflorescent 78.11 *flowering*
inflow 314.12 *flood in;* 314.2 *influx;* 90.6 *river flow*
in flower 243.20 *developed;* 78.11 *flowering*
inflowing 314.16 *invasive*
Influence 395
influence 395.1; **395.8**; 340.4 *act;* 340.1 *action;* 346.8 *activate;* 363.11 *attract;* 140.8, 396.1 *authority;* 344.10 *awaken;* 348.4 *be an instrument;* 123.7 *be important;* 334.10 *be powerful;* 224.8 *cause change;* 344.4 *contributing factor;* 579.13 *director;* 129.18 *forerun;* 396.18 *have authority;* 123.1 *importance;* 483.2 *inducement;* 348.2 *instrument;* 237.7, 348.1 *instrumentality;* 450.9 *make someone believe;* 579.1 *manage;* 483.9 *motivate;* 480.14 *motivator;* 480.15, 760.11 *persuade;* 480.1 *persuasion;* 334.1 *power;* 476.6 *propound;* 121.1 *superiority;* 229.4 *tend;* 229.1 *tendency*
influenceable 760.15 *convertible*
influenced 760.16; 483.12 *motivated*
influence negatively 395.9 *change*
influence of alcohol 690.10 *drunkenness*
influence pedlar 395.5 *influential person*
influence positively 395.9 *change*
influencing 483.11 *motivational*
influential 395.11; 396.12 *authoritative;* 344.13, 348.7 *causal;* 386.9 *compelling;* 340.6 *effective;* 363.10 *magnetic;* 483.11 *motivational;* 123.6 *notable;* 346.12 *operative;* 480.19 *persuasive;* 334.13 *powerful;* 140.12 *ruling*
influentially 395.14; **483.14**; 363.14 *attractively;* 344.14 *causally;* 386.11 *compellingly;* 340.8 *effectively;* 348.9 *instrumentally;* 346.13 *operationally;* 334.18 *powerfully*
influential person 395.5; 123.4 *bigwig*
influenza 260.4 *disease;* 260.6 *infection;* 260.9 *respiratory disease*
influx 314.2
info 693.1 *information*
in focus 520.2 *clear;* 520.1 *visible*
in force 93.10 *existing;* 334.14, 346.12 *operative;* 336.14 *strongly*
in foreign lands 100.18 *extraneously*
in foreign parts 100.18 *extraneously*
inform 693.11; 713.5 *advise;* 243.6 *brief;* 455.14 *cause to know;* 99.11 *characterize;* 3.20 *chronicle;* 692.30 *communicate;* 739.6 *divulge;* 6.22 *educate;* 719.8 *interpret;* 740.13 *make public;* 694.10 *mean;* 742.12 *signal;* 454.3 *testify;* 716.13 *turn queen's evidence;* 711.5 *warn*
in form 221.8 *in a state of*
inform against 715.5 *accuse*
informal 250.13; **657.7**; 734.14 *conversational;* 666.5 *indifferent;* 5.39 *of language;* 551.31 *styled;* 16.56 *unauthorized*
informal agreement 755.1 *contract*

informal clothes 551.1 *dress*
informal dress **551.4**; **657.6**; 552.4 *dishabille*
Informality 657
informality **250.4**; **657.1**; 552.4 *dishabille*; 666.2 *indifference*
informal language 5.3 *spoken language*
informally **250.22**; **657.12**; 5.49 *colloquially*; 734.15 *conversationally*; 551.36 *dressily*; 552.17 *nakedly*
informally dressed 552.10 *in dishabille*
informal meal 557.12 *meal*
informalness 657.1 *informality*
informal speech 5.3 *spoken language*
informant **693.9**; 692.29 *broadcaster*; 739.4 *discloser*; 716.7 *person who gives evidence*; 454.7 *verifier*; 711.4 *warner*
Information 693
information **455.2**; **693.1**; 713.1 *advice*; 3.5 *chronicle*; 716.1 *evidence*; 741.1 *news*; 711.1 *warning*
informational 6.16 *educational*; 693.16 *informative*
information centre 693.8 *source of information*
information office 693.8 *source of information*
information processing 210.4 *computing*; 693.6 *information technology*
information retrieval 210.4 *computing*; 693.6 *information technology*
information superhighway 40.14 *data transfer*
information technology **693.6**; 40.1, 210.4 *computing*
information theory 693.6 *information technology*
informative **693.16**; 713.7 *advising*; 734.14 *conversational*; 721.11 *descriptive*; 739.11 *disclosing*; 6.16 *educational*; 392.33 *helpful*; 695.1 *intelligible*; 741.14 *journalistic*; 711.8 *warning*
informatively 713.9 *advisably*; 6.25 *educationally*; 741.15 *journalistically*; 3.25 *reportedly*
informativeness 695.9 *intelligibility*
informatory 693.16 *informative*
informed **693.18**; 716.8 *evidential*; 455.8 *knowledgeable*; 4.19 *learned*
informedly 6.25 *educationally*
informer **693.10**; 715.3 *accuser*; 739.4 *discloser*; 479.9 *equivocator*; 699.17 *false person*; 693.9 *informant*; 16.8 *litigant*; 731.4 *talker*; 700.21 *traitor*; 454.7 *verifier*
inform on **693.13**; 739.7 *betray*
in fours **200.14**
infracostal 155.6 *lower*
infraction 118.2 *dissent*; 329.8 *transgression*; 802.6 *unlawfulness*; 662.2 *violation of the law*; 802.8 *wrongdoing*
infractor 802.10 *wrongdoer*
infra dig 544.8 *indecorous*; 574.4 *ordinary*; 675.7 *vulgar*
infra dignitatem 544.8 *indecorous*; 675.7 *vulgar*
infrangibility 423.6 *toughness*
infrangible 267.9 *adhesive*; 416.6 *dense*; 423.1 *tough*
infrangibly 423.12 *toughly*
infrared astronomy 29.1 *astronomy*
infrared film 41.9 *film*
infrared observatory 29.23 *observatory*
infrared photography 41.1 *photography*
infrared radiation 28.13 *electromagnetic radiation*; 522.1 *light*
infrared spectrometry 32.17 *analysis*
infrared spectrum 28.68 *emission*
infrared telescope 29.24 *telescope*
infrasound 28.17 *sound*
infrastructural 403.11 *structural*
infrastructure 403.6 *construction*; 175.2 *foot*
infrequency 299.1 *irregularity*; 206.4 *rarity*
infrequent 377.19 *dispersed*; 299.4 *irregular*; 275.23 *occasional*; 218.4 *scarce*; 206.6 *sparse*; 792.8 *valuable*
infrequently 377.30 *diffusely*; 133.17 *discontinuously*; 218.10 *insufficiently*; 299.8 *irregularly*; 275.28 *sometimes*; 206.11 *sparsely*; 792.13 *valuably*
in friendship **569.17**; 654.18 *sociably*
infringe **774.15**; 662.15 *be disobedient*; 100.16 *be external*; 381.4 *besiege*; 802.21 *do wrong*; 329.5 *transgress*
infringe a copyright 772.9 *borrow illegally*; 773.7 *take*
infringe a law **118.20**
infringed 772.11 *borrowed*; 774.18 *fraudulent*
infringement 118.2 *dissent*; 100.4 *externality*; 16.38 *lawbreaking*; 381.14 *siege*; 329.8 *transgression*; 662.2 *violation of the law*; 802.8 *wrongdoing*
infringement of copyright 772.3, 774.6 *illegal borrowing*; 773.1 *taking*
infringer **774.10**; 773.6 *taker*
infringing 100.12 *external*; 802.16 *in the wrong*; 16.60 *offending*
in front **167.11**; 329.17 *ahead*; 145.10 *distantly*; 129.21 *first*
in full 270.7 *diffusely*; 232.10 *fully*; 222.19 *meticulously*
in full bloom 556.11 *adult*; 78.11 *flowering*; 556.16 *maturely*
in full blow 78.11 *flowering*
in full career 332.14 *swiftly*
in full control 334.13 *powerful*
in full cry 507.9 *loudly*; 633.18 *pursuant to*; 633.15 *pursuing*
in full dress 551.30, 656.7 *dressed-up*
in full gallop 332.14 *swiftly*
in full sail 332.14 *swiftly*
in full swing 342.19 *busy*
in full view 738.16 *manifestly*; 740.22 *publicly*; 520.1 *visible*
in full war-paint 243.18 *prepared*
in fun 599.17 *jokingly*
in funds 781.2 *solvent*
infuriate 624.14 *make angry*; 380.9 *make violent*
infuriated 624.16 *angry*; 380.6 *violent*
infuriatingly 624.18 *angrily*
infuse 37.19 *administer*; 374.5 *combine*; 431.23 *dissolve*; 368.2 *inject*; 412.8 *mix*; 369.17 *obtain an extract*; 433.31 *steep*
infused 368.13 *injected*
infuse new blood into 244.1 *improve*
infusible 416.7 *condensed*
infusion 37.13 *administration*; 412.4 *admixture*; 558.2 *drink*; 369.8 *extract*; 368.9 *injection*; 394.2 *medicine*; 412.2 *mixed thing*; 412.1 *mixture*; 369.7 *obtaining an extract*; 431.10 *solution*; 433.10 *steeping*; 394.7 *tonic*
in future 283.14 *in the future*
ingathering 376.1 *assembly*
in general 138.29 *generally*; 216.11 *on average*; 204.13 *on the whole*
ingenious 645.4 *cunning*; 446.11 *ideational*; 477.10 *imaginative*; 484.15 *planning*; 485.6 *skilful*
ingeniously 484.17 *conspiratorially*; 446.22, 477.17 *imaginatively*; 485.12 *skilfully*
ingenious plan 484.3 *expedient plan*
ingenue 805.4 *innocent person*; 646.3 *naive person*; 21.23 *role*; 450.6 *trusting person*
ingenuity 645.1 *cunning*; 446.8, 477.1 *imagination*; 485.1, 733.3 *skill*
ingenuous 527.4 *easily seen through*; 295.12, 555.12 *immature*; 646.1, 805.7 *naive*; 271.3 *natural*; 308.16 *open*; 538.3 *raw*; 698.18 *truthful*
ingenuously 646.5, 805.12 *naively*; 308.26 *openly*
ingenuousness 295.3, 555.3 *immaturity*; 646.2, 805.3 *naivety*; 308.9, 527.10 *openness*; 698.5 *truthfulness*
ingenuous person 646.3 *naive person*
ingest **370.11**; 37.19 *administer*; 557.21 *eat*
ingesting 557.1 *eating*
ingestion 557.1 *eating*; 370.4 *intake*
ingestive 370.17 *absorbent*
inglenook 410.2 *compartment*; 493.6 *fire*; 565.3 *home*
in glowing terms 726.7 *emphatically*
in-goal 64.6 *rugger*
in-goal area 64.1 *rugger*
ingoing 314.15 *entering*; 314.1 *entry*; 36.34 *introverted*
ingoingness 36.7 *personality type*
in good condition 259.1 *healthy*; 221.8 *in a state of*; 235.5 *not bad*; 160.12 *on form*; 407.13 *orderly*
in good faith 799.7 *honourably*
in good form 221.9 *conditionally*; 221.8 *in a state of*
in good health 801.12 *all right*; 259.1 *healthy*; 336.9 *physically strong*; 204.8 *sound*
in good heart 259.1 *healthy*
in good nick 259.1 *healthy*; 160.12 *on form*; 407.13 *orderly*; 336.9 *physically strong*
in good odour 669.24 *admired*; 811.3 *reputable*
in good order 407.13 *orderly*
in good shape 259.1 *healthy*; 336.9 *physically strong*
in good spirits 598.1 *cheerful*; 221.9 *conditionally*; 221.8 *in a state of*
in good time 293.17 *early*
in good trim 407.13 *orderly*
in good trust 569.19 *devotedly*
ingot 780.16 *bullion*; 435.1 *materials*
ingraft 632.18 *habituate*; 368.6 *plant*
ingrained 374.7 *combined*; 632.13 *fixed*; 99.6 *intrinsic*; 228.10 *stabilized*
ingrate 672.2 *thankless person*
ingratiate 421.13 *smooth over*
ingratiate oneself 677.10 *cajole*; 658.13 *defer to*; 664.9 *fawn*; 593.28 *win the love of*
ingratiating 677.14 *cajoling*; 658.9 *deferential*; 599.11 *humouring*; 667.9 *showing respect*; 421.6 *smooth-mannered*; 664.7 *sycophantic*
ingratiatingly 658.16 *deferentially*; 664.17 *sycophantically*
ingratiation 677.3 *cajolery*; 658.4 *deference*; 664.2 *sycophancy*
Ingratitude 672
ingratitude **672.1**; 463.4 *unthinkingness*
ingredient 211.3 *additional item*; 412.4 *admixture*; 205.4, 405.1, 405.6 *component*; 402.4 *matter*; 127.2 *thing included*
ingredients 406.1 *contents*
ingress 314.5 *entrance*; 314.1 *entry*; 368.9 *injection*; 300.3 *motion towards*; 318.3 *passage into*; 90.6 *river flow*; 381.14 *siege*
ingression 314.1 *entry*
ingressive 314.15 *entering*
in-group 295.6 *avant-garde*; 376.19 *clique*
ingrowing 314.16 *invasive*
inguen 311.5 *fork*
ingurgitate 557.21 *eat*; 370.11 *ingest*
ingurgitation 557.1 *eating*; 370.4 *intake*
inhabit **564.14**; **565.17**; 554.17 *dwell*; 93.17 *exist*; 97.13 *reside*; 142.10 *settle*
inhabitance 97.3 *residence*
Inhabitant 564
inhabitant **564.1**
inhabitants **564.2**; 566.9 *group*
inhabited **564.11**
inhabiter 564.1 *inhabitant*
inhabiting **565.14**
inhalant **37.10**
inhalation 37.13 *administration*; 314.2 *influx*; 370.4 *intake*; 434.8 *respiration*; 500.2 *sense of smell*
inhale 37.19 *administer*; 370.12 *draw in*; 434.21 *respire*; 500.7 *smell*; 496.14 *smoke*
inhalement 370.4 *intake*
in half **198.22**
inhaling 434.19 *respiratory*
in halves 198.22 *in half*; 372.20 *separately*
in hand **243.19**; 243.22 *in preparation*; 403.19 *in production*; 439.7 *stored*; 350.1 *unused*
in-handle turn 68.10 *curling*
in harbour 252.6 *safe*
inharmonious 517.7 *dissonant*; 513.7 *strident*
in harmony 117.17 *conformingly*; 374.8 *cooperative*; 516.7 *harmonious*; 516.12 *harmoniously*
in harness 340.5 *acting*; 342.19 *busy*; 243.18 *prepared*; 387.9 *subject*
in haste 262.3 *hasty*
in health 259.1 *healthy*
in heaps 208.14 *in crowds*
in heat 292.17 *in season*; 593.30 *lovingly*
in hell 16.64 *convicted*; 8.20 *devilishly*
in hellfire 8.20 *devilishly*
inhere 405.12 *be one of*
inherent 175.3 *base*; 405.8 *belonging*; 127.8 *included*; 93.11, 99.6, 172.11 *intrinsic*
inherent ability 485.2 *aptitude*
inherently 405.14 *constituently*; 127.9 *inclusively*; 93.22 *really*
inherit 345.7 *follow from*; 781.13 *get rich*; 345.6 *have a visible effect*; 440.9 *own property*; 765.14 *profit*; 769.9, 788.7 *receive*; 246.12 *succeed to*; 773.7 *take*
inheritable 767.14 *for sale*
inheritance 289.4 *accession*; 215.5 *estate*; 34.11 *genetics*; 768.2 *gift*; 788.4 *legacy*; 440.5 *personal estate*; 763.1 *possession*; 765.5 *profit*; 769.1 *receiving*; 773.1 *taking*; 345.2 *visible effect*; 635.5 *will*
inheritance of acquired characteristics 34.16 *evolution*
inheritance tax 790.7 *tax*
inherited 345.10 *caused*; 765.15 *gainful*; 769.13, 788.6 *received*
inheriting 765.15 *gainful*; 773.12 *taking*
inheriting from 345.10 *caused*
inheritor 769.6 *beneficiary*; 474.4 *expectant person*; 215.6 *person remaining*; 289.5 *successor*
inheritors 283.2 *future generation*
inheritress 769.6 *beneficiary*
inhibit 347.3 *counteract*; 166.7 *limit*; 399.3 *veto*
inhibited 251.14 *self-restrained*; 36.37 *subconscious*
inhibitedly 36.39 *psychologically*
inhibiting 37.14 *counteracting*; 166.5 *limited*; 251.14 *self-restrained*; 399.5 *vetoed*
inhibition **378.5**; 36.19 *defence mechanism*; 33.11 *enzyme*; 166.1 *limitation*; 251.3 *self-restraint*
inhibitive **378.15**
inhibitively **378.18**
inhibitor 347.1 *counteraction*; 37.4 *drug type*
in hiding 526.8 *fleetingly*; 389.9 *fugitively*; 521.9 *invisibly*
in high 332.14 *swiftly*
in high cotton 781.1 *wealthy*
in high dudgeon 624.16 *angry*
in high esteem 669.24 *admired*
in high gear 332.14 *swiftly*
in high hopes 474.5 *expecting*
in high relief 520.2 *clear*
in high spirits 598.1 *cheerful*
in his prime 226.11 *finally*
in hock 253.7 *guaranteed*; 784.9 *in debt*; 782.2 *insolvent*; 784.11 *insolvently*; 135.5 *necessitous*
in holes 245.13 *dilapidated*
in holy wedlock 570.24 *matrimonially*
in honour of **601.21**
inhospitable 651.15 *inconsiderate*
inhospitably 655.14 *unsocially*
in hospital 260.22 *sick*; 260.25 *unhealthily*
inhospitality 655.1 *unsociability*
in hot blood 624.18 *angrily*
in hot pursuit 60.9 *on the trail*; 633.18 *pursuant to*; 633.15 *pursuing*
in hot water 264.16 *troubled*
in-house 172.8 *internal*; 97.9 *resident*
in-house magazine 740.5 *journal*
inhuman 651.11 *cruel*; 236.5 *harmful*; 653.3 *misanthropic*; 804.11 *wicked*
inhumane 651.11 *cruel*; 647.8 *severe*
inhumanely 647.11 *severely*
inhumaneness 651.2 *cruelness*
inhumanity 651.2 *cruelness*; 236.11 *harmfulness*; 653.1 *misanthropy*; 628.1 *pitilessness*; 647.1 *severity*; 804.1 *wickedness*
inhumanly 653.5 *misanthropically*; 804.18 *wickedly*
inhumation 583.1 *burial*
inhume 583.8 *bury*
inhumed 583.10 *buried*
in hysterics 380.6 *violent*
in ICU 260.22 *sick*
in ignorance 456.12 *ignorantly*
inimical 381.21 *aggressive*; 586.33 *combative*; 347.4 *counteracting*; 372.18 *disagreeable*; 751.9 *disagreeing*; 596.8 *disliking*; 701.9 *hostile*; 113.22 *oppositional*
inimically 586.41 *aggressively*; 701.17 *argumentatively*; 347.5 *counter*; 372.23 *disagreeably*; 751.11 *in disagreement*; 113.27 *opposingly*
inimitability 698.6 *authenticity*; 121.1 *superiority*
inimitable 698.19 *authentic*; 121.14 *best*; 139.17 *exceptional*; 126.5 *novel*
inimitably 126.8 *originally*; 121.17 *supremely*
in imitation of 398.12 *by proxy*
in Indian file 132.20 *in a line*
in instalments 785.21 *cash down*; 233.6 *incompletely*; 772.13 *on loan*; 205.12 *partly*
in intensive care 582.18 *dying*; 260.22 *sick*
in inverted order 192.2 *inverted*
iniquitous 798.7 *evil*; 804.11 *wicked*
iniquitously 804.18 *wickedly*

iniquity 798.1 *evil;* 806.3 *sin;* 804.1 *wickedness*
in irons 251.15 *detained;* 50.10 *sailing*
in isolation 372.22
in italics 726.4 *emphasized*
initial 130.29, 308.17 *beginning;* 743.11 *identify oneself;* 5.13 *letter;* 5.41 *lettered;* 129.13 *precursory;* 742.9 *use signs;* 5.47 *word*
initially 130.38 *in the beginning*
initial rhyme 17.11 *rhyme*
initials 744.4 *inscription;* 743.3 *means of identification*
initial teaching alphabet 5.14 *alphabet*
initiate 130.17, 295.19, 308.24 *begin;* 130.14 *beginner;* 631.14 *behave towards;* 130.25, 314.14 *enrol;* 737.7 *esotericism;* 129.18 *forerun;* 130.23, 344.11 *inaugurate;* 368.7, 601.19 *install;* 370.10 *introduce;* 6.7 *learner;* 483.9 *motivate;* 126.7 *originate;* 354.1 *undertake*
initiate a buyout 776.3 *bargain*
initiated 130.37 *enrolled;* 295.13 *inaugurated*
initiation 295.4, 308.11 *beginning;* 344.1 *cause;* 601.3 *ceremony;* 130.8 *enrolment;* 314.1 *entry;* 656.3 *formal occasion;* 370.3 *introduction;* 126.1 *originality;* 769.4 *reception*
initiation ceremony 130.8 *enrolment*
initiation rite 10.7 *non-Christian ritual*
initiative 130.29 *beginning;* 342.4 *energy;* 250.1 *freedom;* 370.16 *introductory;* 130.11 *starting point*
initiator 130.16 *originator*
initiatory 130.29 *beginning;* 344.13 *causal;* 130.36, 370.16 *introductory;* 129.13 *precursory*
in its infancy 130.41 *in the bud*
in its own way 139.30 *characteristically*
inject 368.2; 37.19 *administer;* 394.20 *doctor;* 308.20 *hole;* 433.34 *hose;* 35.19 *practise medicine;* 433.31 *steep*
injected 368.13; 308.14 *holed*
injecting 691.1 *drug-taking*
injection 37.12; **368.9**; 814.13 *capital punishment;* 394.2 *medicine;* 29.35 *rocketry;* 433.10 *steeping*
inject oneself 691.10 *drug oneself*
in jeopardy 254.4 *endangered*
injudicial 16.56 *unauthorized*
injudicious 459.5 *foolish;* 240.1 *inconvenient;* 615.4 *rash*
injudiciously 240.6 *inconveniently*
injunction 397.2, 710.2 *demand;* 378.1 *hindrance;* 15.4 *industrial dispute;* 16.6 *legal process;* 713.3 *precept;* 135.1 *requirement;* 251.1 *restraint;* 140.1 *rule;* 399.1 *veto*
injunctive 397.14 *commanding;* 710.10 *demanding;* 140.9 *legal;* 251.13 *restraining;* 15.10 *unionized;* 399.5 *vetoed*
injunctively 399.7 *by veto*
injure 798.11 *be evil;* 236.13 *be worthless;* 249.11 *cause adversity;* 766.13 *destroy;* 245.5 *hurt;* 491.11 *inflict pain;* 351.1 *misuse;* 651.18 *torment;* 337.7 *weaken;* 802.20 *wrong*
injured 491.6; 798.8 *afflicted;* 245.12 *deteriorated*
injured husband 570.10 *married man;* 21.23 *role*
injured pride 623.9 *humiliation*
injurious 351.5 *abusive;* 659.6 *bad-mannered;* 678.16 *defamatory;* 357.14 *destructive;* 245.12 *deteriorated;* 798.9 *detrimental;* 236.5 *harmful;* 802.16 *in the wrong*
injuriously 351.6 *abusively;* 659.10 *rudely*
injuriousness 245.11 *hurt*
injury 491.3; 249.1 *adversity;* 798.2, 814.10 *affliction;* 766.5 *destruction;* 236.11 *harmfulness;* 594.7 *hated thing;* 245.11 *hurt;* 351.2 *misuse;* 802.7 *sense of wrong;* 806.3 *sin;* 802.8 *wrongdoing*
injury time 211.4 *extra*
injustice 120.2; **465.3**; 16.4 *bad law;* 236.9 *badness;* 798.1 *evil;* 800.1 *improbity;* 381.16 *personal attack;* 802.7 *sense of wrong;* 806.3 *sin;* 802.1 *unfairness*
in juxtaposition 147.14 *beside*
ink 19.11 *artist's materials;* 532.11 *blacken;* 532.8 *black pigment;* 532.9 *black thing;* 523.4 *dark thing*
inkblot test 36.5 *psychological test*
inked 19.27 *painted*
in keeping 117.12 *conforming;* 117.17 *conformingly;* 750.38 *fittingly*
in key 18.41 *in tune*
inkily 532.12 *blackly*
ink in 532.11 *blacken;* 19.19 *paint*
in kind 759.8 *in exchange*
in kindness 650.10 *benevolently*
inkiness 532.7 *blackness*
ink-jet printer 40.7 *peripheral*
inkling 476.2 *basis of supposition;* 443.6 *idea;* 590.2 *impression;* 455.2 *information;* 728.6 *suggestion*
inky 532.1 *black;* 523.10 *dark-coloured*
in labour 561.16 *reproductive*
inlaid 541.8 *checked;* 368.12 *inserted;* 23.14 *wooden*
inlaid decoration 23.1 *furniture*
inlaid tile 24.8 *ceramic object*
inland 172.3; **172.9**; 319.5 *transportable*
inland navigation 323.1 *water travel*
inland post 692.2 *postal communication*
Inland Revenue 13.6 *economic factors;* 790.7 *tax*
inlands 172.3 *inland*
inland sea 88.1 *lake*
inland waterway 323.2 *waterway*
inlay 541.2 *check;* 368.5 *inset;* 368.11 *thing inserted;* 541.11 *variegate;* 23.18 *work wood*
in layers 411.12; 411.7 *layered*
in league 374.8 *cooperative;* 750.32 *in alliance;* 374.10 *in combination;* 747.21 *in cooperation*
in left field 461.11 *insane*
in length 148.11 *lengthily*
inlet 92.9; 317.11 *channel;* 183.2 *concave land;* 314.5 *entrance*
in lieu 706.27 *answerably;* 144.20 *out of place*
in lieu of 762.9 *instead*
in life 554.12 *alive*
in like manner 115.13 *similarly;* 750.34 *uniformly*
in limbo 350.4 *disused*
in line 117.12 *conforming;* 117.17 *conformingly;* 289.14 *in succession*
in line with 324.9 *directly*
in liquidation 357.15 *destroyed*
in liquor 690.1 *drunk*
in litigation 16.87
in loads 208.14 *in crowds*
in lock step 285.10 *synchronized*
in loco 239.1 *convenient;* 142.12 *where*
in loco parentis 762.9 *instead*
in lots 205.12 *partly*
in love 593.18
in love with 593.18 *in love*
in low gear 333.17 *in slow motion*
in luck 248.8 *prosperous*
in luxury 248.8 *prosperous*
in majority 207.11
in malice 236.15 *worthlessly*
in masses 208.14 *in crowds*
inmate 251.7 *charge;* 309.6 *closed-in person;* 564.1 *inhabitant;* 815.5 *prisoner;* 387.5 *subjected person*
in memoriam 583.12 *funereally;* 462.16 *memorably*
in memory of 601.21 *in honour of;* 462.16 *memorably*
in mid air 361.13 *pendulously*
in mid-progress 302.20 *in progress*
in mid-stream 316.18 *in transit*
inmigrant 314.7 *entrant*
inmigration 314.4 *right of entry*
in miniature 159.8 *in a small way*
in mint condition 393.13 *repaired*
in moderation 685.9 *moderately;* 251.17 *with self-restraint*
in mortal fear 612.15 *fearfully*
inmost 172.12 *internalized*
in mothballs 439.7 *stored*
in motion 300.18; 300.16 *moving*
in mourning 603.8 *mournfully*
inn 565.10 *hotel*
innaccessible 240.2 *distant*
in name only 96.19 *apparently;* 699.41 *spuriously*
in nappies 555.11 *young*
innards 405.4 *components;* 172.4, 406.3 *insides*
innate 445.8 *instinctive;* 93.11, 99.6, 172.11 *intrinsic*
innate ability 136.2 *ability;* 485.2 *aptitude*
innately 172.16 *inwardly*
innateness 93.3 *nature*
innate reaction 445.4 *instinct*
in nature's garb 552.9 *undressed*
in need 135.12; 233.4 *incomplete;* 135.5 *necessitous;* 782.1 *poor;* 782.15 *poorly*
in need of repair 802.18 *gone wrong*
inner 127.8 *included;* 172.7 *interior;* 139.19 *personal*
inner being 11.7 *spirit*
inner block 52.9 *tae kwon do*
inner cabinet 579.6 *governing body;* 579.3 *management*
inner child 36.21 *psyche*
inner circle 376.7 *committee;* 128.4 *exclusiveness*
inner city 87.7 *city district;* 86.10 *urban area*
inner-city 565.15 *environmental*
inner-city ghetto 245.9 *dilapidation*
inner-directed 250.10 *independent*
inner ear 504.5 *internal ear*
inner form 160.1 *form*
inner layer 172.1 *interior*
inner life 172.5 *inner nature*
inner man 139.11 *identity;* 172.5 *inner nature*
inner mind 11.7 *spirit*
innermost 172.11 *intrinsic*
innermost being 172.5 *inner nature*
innermost thought 443.3 *thoughtfulness*
inner nature 172.5
inner part 172.2 *inside*
inner person 172.5 *inner nature*
inner product 27.50 *scalar quantity*
inner self 139.11 *identity*
inner sense 11.8 *psychic power*
inner side 172.1 *interior*
inner ski turn 68.4 *skiing technique*
inner surface 172.1 *interior*
inner tube 432.13 *gas balloon;* 410.19 *inflatable;* 67.3 *survival swimming*
inner voice 810.4 *sense of duty*
inner wall 172.1 *interior*
inner workings 406.3 *insides*
inning 48.1 *baseball;* 65.1 *billiards;* 276.4 *period of activity*
innings 53.1 *cricket match;* 276.4 *period of activity*
innkeeper 436.4 *caterer*
in no case 708.23 *no!*
Innocence 805
innocence 805.1; 16.42 *acquittal;* 335.3 *helplessness;* 456.1 *ignorance;* 295.3 *immaturity;* 795.3 *moral purity;* 646.2 *naivety;* 230.3 *perfection;* 255.1, 799.2 *purity;* 803.1 *virtue;* 254.7 *vulnerability;* 337.1 *weakness*
innocent 714.12; **805.5**; 16.63 *acquitted;* 700.22 *dupe;* 450.12 *gullible;* 456.6 *ignorant;* 295.12 *immature;* 805.4 *innocent person;* 255.12 *morally pure;* 646.1 *naive;* 646.3 *naive person;* 589.7 *peaceful;* 230.1 *perfect;* 795.9, 799.5 *pure;* 538.3 *raw;* 252.6 *safe;* 450.6 *trusting person;* 487.1 *unaccustomed;* 335.11 *unprotected;* 572.7 *virginal;* 803.5 *virtuous;* 235.4 *worthwhile;* 555.11 *young*
innocent as a child 805.7 *naive*
innocent as a dove 805.5 *innocent*
innocent as a lamb 805.5 *innocent;* 252.6 *safe*
innocent intentions 805.1 *innocence*
innocently 805.11; 16.88 *forgivingly;* 646.5 *naively;* 335.14 *powerlessly;* 799.8 *purely;* 487.6 *unaccustomedly;* 255.18, 803.9 *virtuously;* 555.14 *youthfully*
innocentness 805.1 *innocence*
innocent party 805.4 *innocent person*
innocent person 805.4
innocent tumour 260.12 *cancer*
innocuous 257.4 *hygienic;* 805.5 *innocent;* 252.6 *safe;* 235.4 *worthwhile*
innocuously 805.11 *innocently*
in no place 94.16 *nowhere*
in nothing flat 332.14 *swiftly*
in no time 280.9 *in the shortest possible time;* 332.14 *swiftly*
in no uncertain terms 726.7 *emphatically;* 695.13 *intelligibly*
innovate 295.18 *be trendy;* 224.8 *cause change;* 116.6 *differentiate;* 129.18 *forerun;* 130.22, 448.13 *invent;* 126.7 *originate;* 356.10 *produce*
innovation 224.1 *change;* 130.5 *invention;* 295.1 *newness;* 126.1, 448.4 *originality;* 129.3 *preparation;* 356.1 *production*
innovational 224.11 *changeable*
innovative 224.11 *changeable;* 354.6 *enterprising;* 477.10 *imaginative;* 130.33 *inventive;* 295.10 *new;* 126.4, 448.9 *original;* 129.14 *preparatory;* 356.11 *productive*
innovatively 224.15 *changeably;* 354.9 *enterprisingly;* 448.15 *inventively;* 295.21 *newly;* 126.8 *originally;* 356.13 *productively*
innovator 224.6 *editor;* 448.5 *experimenter;* 478.6 *improviser;* 126.3 *originator;* 129.8 *precursor;* 356.9 *producer;* 354.4 *volunteer*
innovatory 129.14 *preparatory*
in no way 195.11 *none;* 94.14 *not at all*
innoxious 257.4 *hygienic*
inn sign 743.3 *means of identification*
innuendo 678.4 *aspersion*
innumerability 202.5 *immeasurability;* 208.1 *multiplicity*
innumerable 202.2 *immeasurable;* 208.8 *numberless*
innumerably 202.11 *immeasurably;* 208.13 *numerously*
in numerical order 194.12 *numerically*
in obedience to 663.10 *obediently*
in oblivion 618.17 *indifferently*
in occupation 97.9 *resident*
inoculate 37.19 *administer;* 374.5 *combine;* 394.20 *doctor;* 368.2 *inject;* 257.6 *make hygienic;* 35.19 *practise medicine;* 252.10 *protect*
inoculated 257.4 *hygienic;* 368.13 *injected;* 252.6 *safe*
inoculation 35.6 *health care;* 257.1 *hygiene;* 368.9 *injection;* 394.3 *prophylactic;* 252.2 *protection*
inodorous 501.3 *odourless*
inodorousness 501.1 *odourlessness*
in-off 65.3 *English billiards*
inoffensive 623.1 *humble;* 805.5 *innocent;* 589.7 *peaceful;* 235.4 *worthwhile*
inoffensively 805.11 *innocently*
inoffensiveness 805.1 *innocence*
in oils 19.30 *pictorially*
in olden days 296.19 *anciently*
in olden times 3.24 *historically*
in on 693.18 *informed;* 764.5 *jointly possessing*
in one piece 204.6 *whole*
in one's absence 98.20 *absently*
in ones and twos 206.10
in one's bad book 596.9 *disliked*
in one's behalf 762.9 *instead*
in one's birthday suit 552.17 *nakedly;* 552.9 *undressed*
in one's control 387.9 *subject*
in one's cups 690.1 *drunk*
in one's debt 671.4 *grateful*
in one's employ 401.9 *serving*
in one's grasp 763.9 *possessed*
in one's hands 763.9 *possessed*
in one's head 446.11 *ideational;* 446.20 *theoretically*
in one's infancy 555.11 *young;* 555.14 *youthfully*
in one's name 763.9 *possessed;* 763.10 *possessively*
in one's old age 556.16 *maturely*
in one's opinion 446.24 *ideologically*
in one's own time 580.8 *leisurely*
in one's pay 401.9 *serving*
in one's place 762.9 *instead*
in one's pocket 387.9 *subject*
in one's power 387.9 *subject*
in one's prime 556.11 *adult;* 556.16 *maturely*
in one's right mind 393.15 *cured;* 460.4 *sane*
in one's second childhood 457.5 *lacking intellect*
in one's shell 618.7 *indifferent;* 655.8 *unsociable*
in one's shirtsleeves 263.4 *at ease;* 552.10 *in dishabille;* 552.17 *nakedly*
in one's shoes 762.9 *instead*
in one's sleep 489.13 *insensibly*
in one's spare time 580.8 *leisurely*
in one's stride 632.19 *habitually;* 485.12 *skilfully*
in one's teens 201.18 *eleventh;* 555.11 *young;* 555.14 *youthfully*
in one's thoughts 447.12 *topically*
in open court 738.16 *manifestly;* 740.22 *publicly*
in open rebellion 661.10 *in defiance*
inoperability 103.6 *hopelessness*
inoperable 382.23 *deadly;* 103.3 *hopeless;* 611.5 *past hope;* 260.22 *sick*
inoperably 103.12 *hopelessly*

in operation 340.5 *acting;* 346.10 *operational;* 349.10 *usable*
inoperational 350.1 *unused*
inoperative 341.3 *inactive;* 335.10 *powerless;* 238.1 *useless*
inopportune 240.1 *inconvenient;* 288.13 *untimely*
inopportunely 288.19 *at the wrong time;* 240.6 *inconveniently*
inopportune moment 288.2 *untimeliness*
inopportuneness 240.3 *inconvenience;* 288.2 *untimeliness*
in opposition 113.28; 249.6 *adverse;* 753.11 *disapprovingly;* 113.24 *discordant;* 703.23 *in protest;* 708.22 *negatively*
in opposition to 347.5 *counter;* 113.31 *opposed to*
in orbit 154.19 *high*
in order 407.25; 409.20 *arranged;* 132.9 *consecutive;* 132.18 *consecutively;* 407.12 *hierarchical;* 221.8 *in a state of;* 409.28 *in place;* 289.14 *in succession;* 220.13 *inventorially;* 407.26 *orderly*
in orderly fashion 407.26 *orderly*
in order to 482.14 *for*
in order to influence 483.14 *influentially*
in order to oppress 400.16 *masterfully*
in order to prevent 399.7 *by veto*
in order to provoke 751.11 *in disagreement*
inordinacy 727.1 *exaggeration;* 727.3 *extravagance*
inordinancy 686.3 *overindulgence*
inordinate 727.12 *exaggerated;* 219.6 *excessive;* 727.14 *extravagant;* 686.8 *overindulgent;* 681.2 *unrestrained*
inordinately 727.17 *excessively;* 681.9 *extravagantly*
inordinateness 686.3 *overindulgence*
inorganic 32.31 *chemical;* 32.35 *combined;* 457.8 *nonhuman*
inorganic base 32.9 *base*
inorganic chemist 32.2 *chemist*
inorganic chemistry 32.1 *chemistry;* 402.6 *natural science*
inorganic compound 32.7 *chemical compound*
inorganic pigment 529.4 *pigment*
inorganic sediment 30.27 *sediment*
inosilicate 30.34 *mineral*
inositol 33.3 *carbohydrate*
in other words 719.18; 703.22 *demonstrably;* 694.13 *meaningfully*
in outline 525.15 *apparently;* 269.5 *concisely;* 163.7 *essentially;* 163.6 *outlined*
in over one's head 784.11 *insolvently;* 335.14 *powerlessly*
in pain 798.8 *afflicted*
in pairs 198.9 *two;* 198.20 *two by two*
in pantomime 742.18 *indicatively*
in par 111.19 *equally*
in Paradise 582.19 *dead*
in parallel 188.7; 706.26 *correspondingly;* 39.37 *electronically*
in parenthesis 368.15 *in*
in Parliament 398.11 *representatively*
in part 233.6 *incompletely;* 205.12 *partly*
in particular 139.28 *specially*
in partnership 374.8 *cooperative;* 750.32 *in alliance;* 374.10 *in combination*
in parts 205.12 *partly;* 375.7 *to pieces*
in passage to 317.17 *via*
in passing 316.18 *in transit*
in pastels 19.30 *pictorially*
in past times 284.22 *in the past*
in-patient 35.18 *patient;* 260.19 *sick person*
in peace 589.8 *peacefully*
in peak condition 259.1 *healthy*
in pencil 19.30 *pictorially*
in perfect condition 230.1 *perfect*
in perfect health 230.1 *perfect*
in perfect order 407.13 *orderly*
in peril 254.4 *endangered*
in perpetuity 202.12 *eternally*
in person 97.14; 139.29 *personally*
in phase 111.20 *regularly;* 326.5 *wave*
in pieces 372.16, 372.21 *apart;* 375.5 *disintegrated;* 205.11 *partial;* 372.20 *separately*
in place 409.28; 706.27 *answerably;* 117.17 *conformingly;* 143.11 *geographically;* 97.16 *on the spot;* 142.12 *where*
in place of 762.9 *instead;* 144.20 *out of place*
in places 377.30 *diffusely;* 206.10 *in ones and twos;* 142.12 *where*
in plain English 799.7 *honourably;* 719.18 *in other words;* 695.13 *intelligibly;* 265.11 *made easy*
in plain terms 695.13 *intelligibly*
in plain view 520.11 *visibly*
in plain words 799.7 *honourably;* 719.18 *in other words;* 694.13 *meaningfully;* 308.26 *openly;* 271.8 *simply*
in play 346.10 *operational*
in-play wall 63.9 *squash terms*
in plenty 208.9 *ample*
in point of fact 93.22 *really;* 698.35 *truly*
in pole position 61.11 *in a race*
in poor condition 260.22 *sick*
in poor health 249.6 *adverse;* 260.22 *sick*
in poor shape 249.6 *adverse;* 260.22 *sick*
in port 252.6 *safe*
in position 143.11 *geographically*
in possession 763.8 *possessing*
inpouring 314.16 *invasive*
in power 396.23 *authoritatively;* 12.10 *governing*
in practice 243.18 *prepared;* 95.13 *really;* 349.9 *used*
in preparation 243.22; 243.17 *developing;* 129.22 *in anticipation;* 233.4 *incomplete*
in pretence 702.10 *hypocritical*
in print 740.19 *published*
in prison 815.8 *imprisoned*
in private 521.9 *invisibly;* 736.18 *privately;* 655.14 *unsocially*
in production 403.19
in profit 788.8 *profitably*
in profusion 208.9 *ample*
in progress 302.20; 134.5 *continual;* 243.17 *developing;* 233.4 *incomplete*
in proof 716.14 *as evidence;* 703.22 *demonstrably;* 484.14 *planned*
in proportion 27.74 *divisible*
in proportion to 108.10 *relevantly*
in propria persona 97.14 *in person*
in prose 271.8 *simply*
in protest 703.23
in public 703.20, 738.16 *manifestly;* 520.11 *visibly*
in purdah 655.10 *lonely*
in puris naturalibus 552.9 *undressed*
in pursuance of 482.14 *for;* 633.18 *pursuant to*
in pursuit 633.18 *pursuant to;* 633.15 *pursuing*
input 40.20 *abort;* 40.19 *computing terms;* 39.35 *conduct;* 314.1 *entry;* 135.2 *need;* 744.13 *record;* 744.16 *recorded*
input impedance 39.12 *resistance*
input-output device 40.7 *peripheral*
input signal 39.14 *terminal*
input terminal 39.14 *terminal*
input voltage 39.14 *terminal*
in queer street 782.2 *insolvent*
inquest 583.7; 582.8 *after death;* 16.7 *legal trial;* 705.2 *questioning*
in question 701.10 *arguable;* 701.18 *arguably;* 254.1 *dangerous;* 447.13 *problematically;* 705.14 *questionable;* 705.24 *questionably;* 453.23 *uncertainly*
in quest of 633.18 *pursuant to;* 633.15 *pursuing*
in quick succession 297.1 *frequently*
inquietude 327.1 *agitation;* 227.2 *irresolution*
inquire 644.7 *be curious;* 701.14 *discuss;* 448.11 *experiment;* 4.20 *philosophize;* 705.17 *question;* 447.11 *raise the point*
inquire after 644.7 *be curious*
inquire into 722.4 *dissertate*
inquirer 706.10 *answerer;* 353.7 *attempter;* 734.7 *conversationalist;* 644.3 *curious person;* 448.5 *experimenter;* 4.10 *philosopher;* 710.4 *requester*
inquiring 644.5 *curious;* 448.8 *experimental;* 705.12 *questioning;* 353.9 *tentative*
inquiring mind 644.1, 705.8 *curiosity*
inquiry 644.1 *curiosity;* 722.1 *dissertation;* 448.1 *experiment;* 16.7 *legal trial;* 701.2 *logical argument;* 705.2 *questioning;* 354.2 *undertaking*
Inquisition 16.22 *ecclesiastical court*
inquisition 644.1 *curiosity;* 16.7 *legal trial;* 705.2 *questioning;* 647.2 *suppression*
inquisitional 464.8 *judging;* 16.49 *judicatory*
inquisitive 644.5 *curious;* 6.17 *educable;* 705.12 *questioning*
inquisitively 644.8 *curiously;* 705.23 *questioningly*
inquisitiveness 644.1, 705.8 *curiosity;* 6.10 *educability*
inquisitive person 342.11 *meddler*
inquisitor 644.3 *curious person;* 814.17 *punisher;* 705.9 *questioner;* 647.4 *strict person*
inquisitorial 644.5 *curious;* 647.8 *severe*
inquisitorially 644.8 *curiously*
inquorate 206.7 *fewer*
in rags 782.3 *beggarly;* 245.13 *dilapidated;* 408.15 *untidy*
in rapid succession 297.1 *frequently*
in rapport 750.10 *in accord*
in readiness 243.22 *in preparation;* 243.18 *prepared*
in reality 95.13 *really;* 698.35 *truly*
in rebellion 662.14 *subversive*
in rebellion against 753.11 *disapprovingly*
in receipt 788.8 *profitably*
in receivership 357.15 *destroyed*
in recess 226.10 *finished*
in recession 245.12 *deteriorated*
in recompense 775.7 *redemptively*
in redemption 775.7 *redemptively*
in reduced circumstances 782.1 *poor;* 782.15 *poorly*
in regard to 108.10 *relevantly*
in relation to 373.17 *in connection with;* 108.10 *relevantly*
in relief 738.14 *manifest;* 19.30 *pictorially*
in remembrance of 601.21 *in honour of*
in repentance 807.8 *penitently*
in reply 704.11; 706.24 *in answer*
in repose 301.10 *motionlessly*
in reprisal 385.5 *retaliatory*
in requital 775.7 *redemptively;* 385.6 *with vengeance*
in reserve 339.7 *inertly;* 439.7 *stored;* 339.6 *suspended;* 350.1 *unused*
in residence 97.17 *at home;* 565.14 *inhabiting;* 97.9 *resident*
in response 701.20 *apologetically;* 706.24 *in answer;* 704.11 *in reply*
in restitution 775.7 *redemptively*
in retaliation 385.5 *retaliatory*
in retirement 605.10 *by resigning;* 580.7 *leisurely;* 605.7 *resigning*
in retreat 247.11 *defeated*
in return 759.8 *in exchange*
in reverse 303.29; 303.28 *backwards;* 192.4 *inversely*
inroad 314.3; 381.14 *siege*
inroads 441.3 *waste*
in round numbers 147.13 *nearly*
in round terms 5.51 *phraseologically*
in ruins 357.15 *destroyed;* 245.13 *dilapidated;* 375.5 *disintegrated*
inrun 314.2 *influx*
in running order 346.10 *operational*
inrush 314.12 *flood in;* 314.2 *influx*
inrushing 314.16 *invasive*
in sackcloth and ashes 603.8 *mournfully;* 808.8 *penitently*
in safe hands 252.6 *safe*
in safe keeping 252.6 *safe*
in safety 252.6 *safe;* 252.11 *safely*
insalubrious 382.23 *deadly;* 260.23 *diseased;* 236.5 *harmful;* 796.12 *indecent;* 258.8 *unclean*
insalubrity 236.11 *harmfulness*
ins and outs 222.1 *circumstances;* 139.4 *specifications;* 50.7 *windsurfing*
insane 461.11; 328.16 *deranged;* 593.19 *enamoured;* 459.5 *foolish;* 457.5 *lacking intellect;* 380.6 *violent*
insane asylum 461.8 *mental hospital*
insanely 461.17; 328.19 *distractedly;* 459.8 *foolishly;* 457.11 *unintelligently*
insane person 461.7
insanitary 258.8 *unclean*
Insanity 461
insanity 461.1; 328.6 *derangement;* 459.1 *folly;* 457.1 *lack of intellect*
insatiability 688.1 *gluttony*
insatiable 617.9 *desirous;* 688.6 *gluttonous;* 218.2 *unprovided*
insatiable curiosity 705.8 *curiosity*
in scale 209.7 *gradational*
inscape 160.3 *kind*
inscribe 744.14; 27.97 *align;* 719.10 *annotate;* 314.14 *enrol;* 743.11 *identify oneself;* 370.10 *introduce;* 744.13 *record;* 5.47 *word*
inscribed 5.43 *phrasal;* 744.16 *recorded*
inscribed figure 27.41 *geometric figure*
inscribing 744.8 *registration*
inscription 5.25; **744.4**; 719.2 *annotation;* 583.4 *funeral objects;* 3.11 *relic*
inscrutability 528.8 *obscurity;* 696.11 *unintelligibility*
inscrutable 528.4; 523.11 *benighted;* 696.4 *difficult;* 737.11 *mysterious;* 696.1 *unintelligible*
inscrutably 523.15 *darkly;* 528.13 *opaquely;* 696.13 *unintelligibly*
in search of 633.18 *pursuant to*
in season 292.17; 561.16 *reproductive;* 292.9 *seasonal*
in second place 289.15 *as follows*
in secrecy 737.16 *stealthily*
in secret 737.15; 736.18 *privately*
insect 76.1; 55.1 *angling;* 75.4 *arthropod;* 70.4 *type of animal;* 75.6 *worm*
Insecta 75.4 *arthropod;* 76.1 *insect*
insectan 76.10
insect-eating mammal 71.6
insecticidal 44.18 *herbicidal*
insecticide 382.13 *animal killer;* 37.4 *drug type;* 43.14 *pest control;* 394.3 *prophylactic;* 44.8 *weedkiller*
insectiform 76.10 *insectan*
insectile 75.18 *arthropodous;* 76.10 *insectan*
Insectivora 71.6 *insect-eating mammal*
insectivore 557.18 *eater;* 71.6 *insect-eating mammal;* 70.4 *type of animal*
insectivorous 71.26; 557.26 *eating;* 70.15 *of animals;* 77.14 *of plants*
insectivorously 557.28 *carnivorously*
insectivorousness 557.5 *eating habit*
insect larva 75.6 *worm*
insect-like 75.18 *arthropodous;* 76.10 *insectan*
insect noise 515.3
Insects and Arachnids 76
insecure 453.7 *unreliable;* 254.2 *unsafe*
insecurely 453.26 *unreliably*
insecurity 254.5 *danger;* 453.15 *unreliability;* 254.7 *vulnerability*
in security 252.6 *safe*
inselberg 154.3 *mountain*
in self-defence 384.32 *defensively;* 52.16 *professionally;* 385.5 *retaliatory*
in self-reproach 808.8 *penitently*
inseminate 562.7 *make fertile;* 561.13 *propagate*
insemination 561.3 *propagation*
insensate 592.1 *insensitive*
Insensibility 489
insensibility 36.13 *depression;* 261.7 *fatigue;* 456.1 *ignorance;* 341.1 *inaction;* 618.1 *indifference;* 339.1 *inertness;* 592.3 *insensitiveness;* 260.17 *nervous disorder;* 463.1 *oblivion;* 301.2 *repose;* 477.6 *reverie;* 343.9 *sleep;* 260.3 *symptom*
insensible 489.7 *anaesthetized;* 691.7 *drugged;* 335.12 *impotent;* 341.3 *inactive;* 618.7 *indifferent;* 339.5 *inert;* 592.1 *insensitive;* 343.4 *not awake;* 463.8 *oblivious;* 301.6 *quiescent;* 394.17 *remedial*
insensibly 489.13; 691.11 *in a trance;* 618.17 *indifferently;* 339.7 *inertly;* 343.17 *sleepily*
insensitive 592.1; 497.6 *coarse;* 659.5 *discourteous;* 426.3 *dull;* 651.15 *inconsiderate;* 618.7 *indifferent;* 418.4 *mentally hard;* 152.4 *thick-skinned;* 472.9 *thoughtless;* 489.6 *unfeeling;* 505.5 *unhearing*
insensitively 492.15; 659.9 *discourteously;* 618.17 *indifferently;* 489.13 *insensibly;* 426.13 *obtusely;* 497.11 *tastelessly;* 592.8 *unfeelingly*
insensitiveness 592.3; 426.7 *dullness;* 489.1 *lack of feeling*
insensitive person 592.5
Insensitivity 592
insensitivity 497.4 *bad taste;* 505.1 *deafness;* 659.1 *discourtesy;* 426.7 *dullness;* 651.6 *inconsiderateness;* 618.1 *indifference;* 472.4 *thoughtlessness*
in sentences 5.51 *phraseologically*
insentient 489.6 *unfeeling*
inseparability 267.1 *adhesion;* 416.1 *density;* 569.3 *familiarity;* 147.1 *nearness*
inseparable 267.9 *adhesive;* 223.19 *associated;* 416.6 *dense;* 569.10 *familiar;* 99.7 *integral;* 147.9 *near;* 197.13 *whole*
inseparables 569.6 *close friend*

inseparably 267.11 cohesively; 569.18 intimately; 223.21 together
in sequence 289.14 in succession; 220.13 inventorially
in series 39.37 electronically; 407.25 in order; 220.13 inventorially
insert 368.1; 211.6 add; 37.19 administer; 370.7 admit; 740.9 advertisement; 314.11 infiltrate; 406.7 stuff; 368.11 thing inserted
inserted 368.12; 211.8 additional
Insertion 368
insertion 368.8; 211.1 addition; 370.1 admittance; 740.9 advertisement; 314.3 inroad; 205.7 piece; 393.8 repair; 29.35 rocketry; 368.11 thing inserted
in service 401.9 serving; 349.9 used
in-service training 6.2 educational system
in servitude 401.10 obediently; 401.9 serving
inset 368.5; 368.11 thing inserted
in-set 295.6 avant-garde
in set form 656.12 formally
in set phrases 5.51 phraseologically
in set terms 5.51 phraseologically
in seventh heaven 597.4 happy; 174.8 on top
in shallow water 254.4 endangered
in shape 160.12 on form
inshore 147.9 near
inshore fishing 633.2 chase
in short 269.5 concisely; 723.12 in brief; 149.12 short; 447.14 thematically
in short supply 218.4 scarce
in shreds 245.13 dilapidated
in sickness 260.25 unhealthily
Inside 172
inside 172.2; 815.8 imprisoned; 368.15 in; 127.9 inclusively; 406.3 insides; 172.7 interior; 406.14 internally; 172.16 inwardly; 27.35 space
in side 63.12 badminton terms
inside agent 693.10 informer
inside and out 141.16 extensively
inside home 58.6 lacrosse player
inside information 693.7 advice
inside job 484.4 plot
inside left 66.3 football player
inside out 761.13 reversibly
inside-out 192.2 inverted
inside-out and back-to-front 192.2 inverted
insider 127.3 person included
insider dealing 699.8, 700.10 fraud; 484.4 plot; 776.8 speculation
inside right 66.3 football player
insider trading 484.4 plot; 776.8 speculation
inside run 46.9 play
insides 172.4; 406.3; 405.4 components
inside ski 68.5 ski equipment
inside the boom 50.20 offshore
inside-the-park home run 48.5 batting terms
inside track 121.3, 164.4 advantage
insidious 645.4, 702.8 cunning; 700.35 deceptive; 357.14 destructive
insidiously 702.15 hypocritically
insidiousness 702.3 cunning; 700.1 deception; 357.1 destruction
insight 445.3; 477.3; 522.13 enlightenment; 590.2 impression; 719.1 interpretation; 445.1 intuition; 466.2 judiciousness; 156.3 profundity; 11.8 psychic power; 6.11 refinement; 518.4 visualization; 442.2 ways of thinking; 458.1 wisdom
in sight 525.7 appearing; 520.1 visible; 520.11 visibly; 518.24 visually
insightful 466.9 discriminating; 719.14 interpretive; 445.6 intuitive; 6.20 refined
insightfully 6.27 discerningly; 466.16 judiciously
in sight of 302.20 in progress
insignia 743.4; 520.6 visible thing
insignificance 618.5; 100.1 extraneousness; 122.1 inferiority; 124.5 unimportance; 236.7 worthlessness
insignificant 122.13; 618.11; 100.8 extraneous; 159.7 little; 196.6 small; 124.1 unimportant; 236.1 worthless
insignificantly 122.20; 100.18 extraneously; 159.8 in a small way; 618.20 unexceptionally; 124.14 unimportantly
insignificant matter 124.8 trifle
in sign language 742.18 indicatively
in silence 506.5 silently
insincere 645.4 cunning; 800.5 dishonourable; 677.12 flattering; 699.31, 700.37, 702.10 hypocritical
insincerely 800.11 dishonourably; 699.42, 702.15 hypocritically
insincere praise 677.1 flattery
insincerity 645.1 cunning; 677.1 flattery; 699.3, 700.3, 702.5 hypocrisy; 800.1 improbity
in single file 132.20 in a line; 148.12 longitudinally
insinuate 715.5 accuse; 314.11 infiltrate; 368.1 insert; 483.10 manipulate; 693.14 tip; 678.13 vilify
insinuated 368.12 inserted
insinuate oneself 677.11 be sycophantic; 664.9 fawn
insinuating 678.16 defamatory; 693.16 informative; 483.11 motivational
insinuatingly 483.14 influentially
insinuation 715.1 accusation; 693.7 advice; 678.4 aspersion; 314.3 inroad; 368.8 insertion
insipid 728.17; 620.4 boring; 530.8 drained of colour; 337.13 insufficient; 497.5 tasteless; 639.3 timid
insipidity 620.1 boredom; 728.8 insipidness; 497.1 tastelessness
insipidly 728.26; 620.8 boringly; 337.14 weakly; 497.10 without taste
insipidness 728.8; 497.1 tastelessness
insist 638.10; 707.21 be assertive; 641.9 be obstinate; 386.6 compel; 726.6 emphasize; 480.15 persuade; 710.6 request
insistence 707.6 assertiveness; 726.1 emphasis; 123.1 importance; 640.1 perseverance; 480.1 persuasion; 710.1 request; 638.14 tenacity
insistent 707.14 assertive; 509.15 drumming; 726.3 emphatic; 710.9 requesting; 638.2 tenacious
insistently 710.12 by request; 726.7 emphatically; 707.25 explicitly; 509.19 repeatedly
insister 707.9 affirmer
insist on 386.6 compel; 397.10, 474.11 demand
in situ 143.11 geographically; 97.16 on the spot; 142.12 where
in slavery 401.10 obediently; 401.9 serving; 387.9 subject; 387.11 under subjection
in slight measure 209.10 by degrees
in slow motion 333.17
in smithereens 205.11 partial
insobriety 690.10 drunkenness
insolate 428.19 bake
insolated 428.8 baked
insolation 428.13 drying
Insolence 660
insolence 660.1; 706.1 answer; 659.2 bad manners; 622.3 conceit; 661.1 defiance; 668.1 disrespect
insolent 660.13; 706.11 answering; 659.6 bad-mannered; 622.17 conceited; 661.7 defiant; 668.10 disrespectful
insolently 660.30; 661.9 defiantly; 668.28 disrespectfully; 706.24 in answer; 659.10 rudely
insolent person 659.4 discourteous person
in solitary 815.8 imprisoned
in solitary confinement 815.8 imprisoned
insoluble 416.7 condensed; 27.73 numerable; 696.2 unexplained
insolubly 416.10 densely
in solution 431.19 liquefied
insolvable 27.73 numerable
insolvency 782.6; 786.5; 247.1 failure; 766.2 financial loss; 218.8 insufficiency; 357.4 ruin
insolvent 782.2; 784.6 debtor; 247.10 failed; 247.5 failing person; 786.13 nonpaying; 782.10 poor person; 784.10 unable to pay; 766.17 unprofitable
insolvent debtor 786.6 nonpayer
insolvently 784.11; 247.12 unsuccessfully; 786.15 without paying
in some degree 108.10 relevantly
in some measure 205.12 partly; 209.11 to a degree
in someone's bad books 594.12 hated
in someone's black books 594.12 hated
in someone's wake 223.21 together
in some sense 694.13 meaningfully
in some way 317.16 how
insomnia 342.7 restlessness
insomniac 488.6 conscious; 260.19 sick person
insouciance 265.4 ease of manner; 618.1 indifference; 666.1 negligence
insouciant 618.11 indifferent; 666.4 negligent
insouciantly 618.17 indifferently
in spasms 327.29 jerkily
in spate 90.11 flooded
inspect 518.14; 665.11 care for; 464.12 estimate; 705.17 question
inspect accounts 789.8 audit
inspected 705.16 questioned
inspection 464.1 judgment; 518.3 observation; 705.2 questioning; 665.5 watchfulness
inspection of accounts 789.3 accounting
inspection of books 789.3 accounting
inspector 464.5 judge; 579.15 manager; 518.11 observer; 705.9 questioner; 321.9 railway worker
inspector of accounts 789.6 accountant
inspectorship 396.5 position of authority
inspiration 477.2; 344.1 cause; 443.5 creative thought; 8.5 deity; 726.1 emphasis; 484.3 expedient plan; 446.8 imagination; 395.1 influence; 370.4 intake; 458.2 intelligence; 445.1 intuition; 449.9 invention; 483.1 motive; 17.13 poetic genius; 356.1 production; 434.8 respiration; 478.5 spontaneity; 338.1 vigour; 442.2 ways of thinking
inspirational 395.12 appealing; 344.13 causal; 590.11 intuitive
inspirationally 344.14 causally; 446.22 imaginatively; 395.14, 483.14 influentially; 4.29 wisely
inspiration from the muse 477.2 inspiration
inspire 446.16; 344.10 awaken; 370.12 draw in; 613.17 give courage; 338.3 invigorate; 483.9 motivate; 434.21 respire
inspire awe 619.10 be wonderful
inspired 270.3 diffuse; 726.3 emphatic; 446.11 ideational; 477.10 imaginative; 445.6 intuitive; 483.12 motivated; 480.20 persuadable
inspire hope 610.10
inspirer 480.14 motivator; 344.7 Prime Mover
inspire respect 667.21 command respect
inspiring 395.12 appealing; 344.13 causal; 386.9 compelling; 338.5 invigorating
inspiringly 344.14 causally; 4.29 wisely
inspirit 613.17 give courage; 446.16 inspire; 483.9 motivate
inspissate 416.8 be dense; 430.11 thicken; 430.8 viscous
inspissation 430.1 viscosity
in spite 651.20 malevolently
in spite of 211.10 additionally; 347.5 counter; 264.25 difficultly; 751.11 in disagreement; 113.31 opposed to
in spite of oneself 637.17 unwillingly
in spitting distance 147.12 near
in splendid isolation 372.22 in isolation
in sport 599.17 jokingly
in spots 133.17 discontinuously; 206.10 in ones and twos; 299.8 irregularly; 142.12 where
in spring 292.18 seasonally
instability 642.2 caprice; 227.1 changeableness; 38.16 deformation; 328.6 derangement; 114.1 diversity; 299.1 irregularity; 278.1 transience; 453.15 unreliability; 254.7 vulnerability; 337.1 weakness
install 368.7; 601.19; 130.25 enrol; 130.23 inaugurate; 370.10 introduce; 142.9 locate; 143.10 situate
installation 130.8 enrolment; 130.6 inauguration; 370.3 introduction; 142.4 placing; 19.12 sculpture; 577.1 workshop
installed 130.37 enrolled; 142.6 located
instalment 772.11 borrowed; 772.4 credit; 205.2 particular; 785.1 payment
instalment buying 783.1 credit
instalment loan 771.2 loan
instalment plan 772.4, 783.1 credit; 786.2 stoppage
instalment-plan payment 785.1 payment
Instamatic™ 41.16 camera
instance 222.11 circumstantiate; 222.2 occurrence
instance of violence 380.3
instant 280.3; 342.18 active; 275.11 date; 280.5 immediate; 280.4 point in time; 282.6 present; 243.21 ready-made; 278.3 short duration; 276.2 time period
instantaneity 280.1 immediacy; 332.8 speed
instantaneous 280.5 immediate; 332.1 swift
instantaneous current 39.9 electric current
instantaneously 280.8 immediately; 332.14 swiftly
instantaneousness 280.1 immediacy; 332.8 speed
instantaneous voltage 39.10 electric potential
instant coffee 558.4 coffee
instant dislike 596.1 dislike
instantly 280.8 immediately
instate 368.7, 601.19 install
instatement 370.3 introduction
in statu quo 225.9 permanently
instead 762.9; 706.27 answerably; 144.20 out of place
instead of 762.9 instead
in step 117.12 conforming; 285.10 synchronized; 285.13 synchronously
instigate 130.23, 344.11 inaugurate; 483.9 motivate; 480.15 persuade
instigating 483.11 motivational
instigation 344.1 cause; 130.6 inauguration
instigative 130.34 inaugural; 483.11 motivational
instigator 480.14, 483.7 motivator; 344.7 Prime Mover; 356.9 producer
instigatory 130.34 inaugural
instil 37.19 administer; 117.10 assimilate; 374.5 combine; 6.22 educate; 368.2 inject; 412.8 mix
instillation 412.1 mixture
instinct 445.4; 229.3 aptitude; 476.2 basis of supposition; 590.2 impression; 457.4 nonhuman existence; 478.5 spontaneity; 632.2 tendency; 442.2 ways of thinking
instinctive 445.8; 590.11 intuitive; 442.9 mental; 457.8 nonhuman; 478.2 spontaneous
instinctive dislike 596.1 dislike
instinctive feeling 590.2 impression
instinctively 478.7 extempore; 445.11 intuitively; 442.14 mentally; 457.12 nonhumanly
instinctual 445.8 instinctive; 457.8 nonhuman
instinctually 457.12 nonhumanly
in stir 815.8 imprisoned
institute 6.12 educational institution; 130.25 enrol; 130.23, 344.11 inaugurate; 356.10 produce
instituted 632.12 established
institute legal proceedings 16.70 litigate
institution 750.6 convention; 632.4 custom; 130.6 inauguration; 7.9 priesthood; 10.1 ritual; 16.1 the law
institutional 750.15 conventional
institutional building 38.20 building
institutionalization 632.7 habituation
institutionalize 750.26 make uniform
institutionalized 750.15 conventional; 632.12 established
institutionary 130.34 inaugural
in stock 778.18 on sale; 436.7 provisioning; 439.7 stored
in storage 439.7 stored
in store 243.19 in hand; 763.9 possessed; 439.7 stored
in strips 411.12 in layers
instruct 713.5 advise; 117.10 assimilate; 243.6 brief; 455.14 cause to know; 397.9 command; 738.1 display; 6.22 educate; 703.16 explain; 693.11 inform; 400.14 master
instructable 6.17 educable
instructed 485.8 expert; 455.8 knowledgeable; 243.18 prepared
instructing 324.16 directing
instruction 713.1 advice; 243.12 briefing; 397.1 command; 693.2 communication; 324.5 directions; 6.1 education; 140.4 guide; 455.3 learning; 713.3 precept
instructional 6.16 educational; 693.16 informative
instructional ski 68.5 ski equipment
instructions 703.3 explanation
instructive 713.7 advising; 6.16 educational; 395.11 influential; 693.16 informative; 814.19 punitive; 711.8 warning

instructively 713.9 *advisably;* 6.25 *educationally*
instructor 703.7 *demonstrator;* 579.13 *director;* 400.9 *educational leader;* 6.4 *educator*
instructorship 6.6
instrument 348.2; 409.16 *adapt;* 578.3 *agent;* 700.22 *dupe;* 12.1 *government;* 392.1 *help;* 122.6 *inferior;* 352.1 *means;* 28.82 *measuring instrument;* 124.10 *nonentity;* 664.3 *sycophant;* 438.1 *tool*
instrumental 18.32; 237.3; 348.6; 348.7 *causal;* 448.8 *experimental;* 392.30 *helping;* 438.9 *mechanical;* 349.9 *used*
instrumentalism 448.3 *experimentation;* 4.7 *school of thought*
instrumentalist 4.11 *follower of a doctrine;* 18.24 *musician;* 4.14 *of a philosophy*
Instrumentality 348
instrumentality 237.7; 348.1
instrumentally 348.9; 438.11; 18.42 *musically;* 349.11 *usefully*
instrumentate 18.35 *compose*
instrumentation 516.4 *harmonics;* 348.1 *instrumentality;* 28.82 *measuring instrument;* 409.9 *musical arrangement;* 18.2 *music making*
instrument of execution 814.16
instrument of punishment 814.14
instrument of torture 814.15
instrument transformer 39.22 *transformer*
in style 221.9 *conditionally*
in subjection 387.9 *subject*
insubordinate 588.6 *anarchic;* 662.13 *disobedient;* 408.20 *disorderly;* 668.10 *disrespectful;* 753.10 *lawbreaking*
insubordinately 588.8 *anarchically;* 753.11 *disapprovingly;* 662.17 *disobediently*
insubordination 588.1 *anarchy;* 661.2, 662.1 *disobedience*
in substance 99.14 *at heart;* 204.13 *on the whole*
insubstantial 415.2; 434.12 *airy;* 424.1 *brittle;* 153.4 *fine;* 700.40 *illusory;* 477.12 *imaginary;* 233.4 *incomplete;* 218.1, 337.13 *insufficient;* 521.1 *invisible;* 101.8 *nonmaterial;* 417.1 *sparse;* 11.18 *spiritual;* 527.2 *translucent;* 124.4 *trivial;* 124.1 *unimportant;* 96.8 *unreal;* 453.7 *unreliable;* 673.8 *vain*
insubstantiality 700.5 *falseness;* 153.11 *fineness;* 233.1 *incompleteness;* 521.4 *invisibility;* 417.3 *sparseness;* 527.6 *translucency;* 124.5 *unimportance;* 453.15 *unreliability;* 101.2 *unworldliness;* 673.1 *vanity*
insubstantialize 101.12 *enter a nonmaterial world*
insubstantially 424.5 *fragilely;* 233.6 *incompletely;* 218.10 *insufficiently;* 415.11 *lightly;* 101.13 *metaphysically;* 417.7 *sparsely;* 527.13 *transparently;* 453.26 *unreliably*
insubstantial person 96.5
insubstantial thing 337.5 *weak thing*
in succession 289.14; 132.18 *consecutively*
insufferable 596.9 *disliked*
insufficience 120.1 *inequality*
Insufficiency 218
insufficiency 218.8; 122.2 *deficiency;* 98.2 *disappearance;* 247.1 *failure;* 766.2 *financial loss;* 231.5 *imperfection;* 782.9 *inadequacy;* 233.1 *incompleteness;* 120.1 *inequality;* 135.2 *need;* 233.2 *omission;* 27.64 *reasoning*
insufficient 218.1; 337.13; 604.11 *disappointing;* 247.10 *failed;* 782.4 *inadequate;* 231.2, 233.4 *incomplete;* 205.11 *partial;* 120.3 *unequal;* 766.17 *unprofitable;* 670.32 *unsatisfactory;* 486.1 *unskilful*
insufficient diet 557.10 *scarcity;* 687.2 *short rations*
insufficient evidence 16.7 *legal trial*
insufficient funds 784.5 *amount owing;* 782.6 *insolvency*
insufficient income 782.5 *poverty*
insufficiently 218.10; 766.20 *at a loss;* 231.11 *imperfectly;* 782.17 *inadequately;* 233.6 *incompletely;* 120.7 *unequally;* 247.12 *unsuccessfully;* 337.14 *weakly*
insular 197.16 *alone;* 92.11 *continental;* 466.10 *discriminatory;* 86.18 *local;* 86.16 *regional;* 372.17 *unjoined;* 465.8 *unjust*
insularism 466.3 *prejudice*
insularity 197.5 *aloneness;* 465.3 *injustice;* 100.3 *separateness;* 372.2 *setting apart;* 109.1 *unrelatedness*
insularly 92.13 *continentally*
insulate 493.14 *be hot;* 39.35 *conduct;* 24.11 *make ceramics;* 505.10 *muffle;* 252.10, 550.30 *protect;* 372.10 *set apart*
insulated 493.13 *heated;* 494.9 *heat-resistant*
insulating material 39.7 *nonconductor*
insulation 28.48; 493.3 *heater;* 39.7 *nonconductor;* 359.1 *preservation;* 550.12 *protective covering*
insulator 28.43 *electrical conduction;* 334.7 *electrical power;* 28.48 *insulation;* 39.7 *nonconductor*
insulin 394.8 *drug;* 33.9 *protein*
insulin shock therapy 36.3 *psychiatric treatment*
insult 660.7; 668.5; 668.23; 661.3 *act of defiance;* 659.3 *act of discourtesy;* 706.18 *answer back;* 659.7 *be discourteous;* 661.6 *be insubordinate;* 245.10 *impairment;* 624.2 *offence;* 624.9 *offend;* 242.11 *quarrel;* 678.5 *scorn*
insulted 624.15 *resentful*
insulting 660.18; 668.11; 678.16 *defamatory;* 661.7 *defiant*
insultingly 661.9 *defiantly*
in sum 204.12 *one and all*
in summer 292.18 *seasonally*
in Sunday best 551.30, 656.7 *dressed-up*
in Sunday go-to-meeting clothes 551.30 *dressed-up*
insuperability 103.6 *hopelessness*
insuperable 103.3 *hopeless*
insuperably 103.12 *hopelessly*
in support 569.19 *devotedly;* 714.15 *in vindication*
insurable 768.7 *given*
insurance 616.2; 107.7 *calculation of chance;* 452.14 *guarantee;* 253.2 *promise;* 252.2 *protection*
insurance certificate 744.2 *certificate*
insurance papers 744.2 *certificate*
insurance policy 616.2 *insurance;* 253.2 *promise;* 755.2 *purchase contract*
insurance premium 756.2 *guarantee*
insurance spraying 43.5 *cultivation*
insure 243.3 *be prepared;* 253.12 *certify;* 756.8 *guarantee;* 253.11 *promise*
insured 253.7, 452.4 *guaranteed;* 252.6 *safe*
insured mail 692.2 *postal communication*
insurer 452.15 *guarantor*
insurgence 16.41 *lawlessness;* 383.3 *resistance movement;* 662.4 *revolution*
insurgency 753.2 *disorder;* 662.4 *revolution*
insurgent 753.10 *lawbreaking;* 16.61 *lawless;* 383.12 *resisting;* 662.10 *seditionist;* 662.14 *subversive*
insurmountability 103.6 *hopelessness*
insurmountable 103.3 *hopeless*
insurmountable debt 786.5 *insolvency*
insurmountably 103.12 *hopelessly*
insurrection 661.3 *act of defiance;* 753.2 *disorder;* 383.3 *resistance movement;* 662.4 *revolution*
insurrectional 662.14 *subversive*
insurrectionary 753.10 *lawbreaking;* 662.14 *subversive*
insurrectionist 662.10 *seditionist*
in suspense 474.12 *expectantly;* 474.5 *expecting;* 339.7 *inertly;* 361.13 *pendulously*
in suspension 431.19 *liquefied*
in swarms 208.14 *in crowds*
inswinger 53.8 *delivery*
in sworn testimony 707.24 *truthfully*
in sympathy 627.13 *pitifully*
in sync 750.13 *harmonious;* 516.12 *harmoniously;* 285.10 *synchronized;* 285.13 *synchronously*
intact 232.7 *complete;* 230.1 *perfect;* 359.7 *preserved;* 252.6 *safe;* 204.7 *uncut;* 572.7 *virginal*
intaglio 19.13 *relief-carving*
intaglio rilievo 19.13 *relief-carving*
in tails 551.30, 656.7 *dressed-up*
intake 370.4; 314.7 *entrant;* 314.2 *influx;* 135.2 *need*
in tandem 747.21 *in cooperation;* 148.12 *longitudinally*
in tandem with 223.24 *with*
intangibility 159.1 *littleness;* 96.1 *unreality;* 101.2 *unworldliness*
intangible 159.7 *little;* 101.8 *nonmaterial;* 440.8 *propertied;* 11.18 *spiritual;* 96.8 *unreal*
intangible assets 440.5 *personal estate*
intangibles 440.5 *personal estate*
intangibly 101.13 *metaphysically;* 159.9 *microscopically*
intarsia 23.9 *decorative woodwork*
in tatters 357.15 *destroyed;* 245.13 *dilapidated*
in Technicolor™ 529.10 *coloured;* 529.18 *colourfully*
integer 27.6 *complex number;* 194.2 *kind of number;* 197.1 *one;* 204.2 *whole thing*
integers 203.5 *numbers*
integral 99.7; 405.8 *belonging;* 232.7 *complete;* 405.6 *component;* 27.31 *differentiation;* 194.9 *fractional;* 27.76 *functional;* 210.15 *mathematical;* 405.7 *modular;* 27.71 *numerical;* 197.13, 204.6 *whole*
integral calculus 27.30 *calculus*
integral equation 27.31 *differentiation;* 27.27 *equation*
integrality 232.1 *completeness;* 197.3 *oneness;* 204.1 *whole*
integrally 405.14 *constituently;* 197.23, 204.11 *wholly*
integral part 405.1 *component*
integral sign 27.13 *mathematical symbol*
integrant 405.1, 405.6 *component*
integrate 210.9 *add;* 412.10 *become mixed;* 197.19 *become one;* 204.9 *be whole;* 374.5 *combine;* 232.4 *complete;* 119.11 *equalize;* 27.95 *evaluate;* 127.4 *include;* 412.8 *mix*
integrated 374.7 *combined;* 127.8 *included;* 99.7 *integral;* 412.12 *mixed;* 204.6 *whole*
integrated circuit 39.13 *circuit;* 334.9 *electronics;* 159.2 *little thing*
integration 747.7 *association;* 210.1 *calculation;* 374.1 *combination;* 27.31 *differentiation;* 127.1 *inclusion;* 412.1 *mixture;* 244.11 *reformism;* 204.1 *whole*
integrationist 244.12 *reformer*
integrity 795.2 *good morals;* 197.3 *oneness;* 799.1 *probity;* 801.3 *properness;* 255.1 *purity;* 801.4 *righteousness;* 803.1 *virtue;* 204.1 *whole*
integument 550.13 *casing;* 171.1 *exterior*
integumental 550.38 *covering;* 171.6 *exterior*
Intellect 442
intellect 455.4; 442.8 *intellectual person;* 442.3, 458.2 *intelligence;* 101.6 *internal world;* 444.1 *reason*
intellectual 458.4; 156.7 *deep thinking;* 6.18 *educated;* 400.9 *educational leader;* 400.13 *excellent;* 396.11, 396.17, 485.5 *expert;* 446.11 *ideational;* 442.8 *intellectual person;* 455.6 *knowledgeable person;* 4.19 *learned;* 455.9 *literate;* 442.9 *mental;* 444.5 *reasoner;* 443.11, 444.7 *reasoning;* 4.12 *sage;* 643.7 *serious person;* 485.4 *skilled person;* 443.7 *thinker;* 443.8 *thoughtful;* 458.5 *wise;* 578.1 *worker*
intellectual exercise 443.2
intellectualism 458.2 *intelligence;* 442.1 *mind*
intellectuality 6.9 *learnedness;* 442.1 *mind*
intellectualize 443.17 *philosophize;* 4.21 *rationalize*
intellectually 396.26 *expertly;* 455.15 *knowledgeably;* 400.16 *masterfully;* 442.14 *mentally;* 4.24 *philosophically;* 6.26 *studiously*
intellectually subnormal 457.7
intellectually weak 457.5 *lacking intellect*
intellectual person 442.8
intellectual subnormality 36.9 *psychological disorder;* 461.2 *subnormality*
intellectual weakness 457.1 *lack of intellect*
intelligence 442.3; 458.2; 713.1 *advice;* 645.1 *cunning;* 6.10 *educability;* 716.1 *evidence;* 693.1 *information;* 455.4 *intellect;* 455.3 *learning;* 425.13 *mental sharpness;* 741.1 *news;* 460.2 *rationality;* 444.1 *reason;* 711.1 *warning*
intelligence quotient 36.6 *intelligence test*
intelligence service 737.2 *secretiveness*
intelligence staff 584.5 *military staff*
intelligence test 36.6; 36.5 *psychological test*
intelligence testing 36.4 *psychometrics*
intelligent 442.10; 458.6; 645.4 *cunning;* 6.17 *educable;* 522.22 *enlightened;* 455.8 *knowledgeable;* 4.19 *learned;* 425.5 *mentally sharp;* 460.5 *rational;* 443.11, 444.7 *reasoning;* 485.6 *skilful*
intelligently 442.15; 458.10; 455.15 *knowledgeably;* 425.18 *sharply;* 485.12 *skilfully;* 6.26 *studiously*
intelligentsia 455.7 *academia*
Intelligibility 695
intelligibility 695.9; 725.1 *clarity;* 460.2 *rationality;* 265.2, 271.4 *simplicity;* 694.4 *type of meaning*
intelligible 695.1; 725.3 *clear;* 265.9 *easy;* 738.14 *manifest;* 694.6 *meaningful;* 460.5 *rational;* 255.16 *simple;* 407.14 *well-ordered*
intelligibly 695.13; 725.4 *clearly;* 694.13 *meaningfully;* 271.8 *simply*
Intelsat™ 692.7 *satellite communication*
intemperance 690.11 *drinking;* 329.9 *excessiveness;* 727.3 *extravagance;* 688.1 *gluttony;* 250.6 *liberality;* 219.2 *overdoing it;* 686.3 *overindulgence*
intemperate 690.5 *drunken;* 727.14 *extravagant;* 688.6 *gluttonous;* 686.8 *overindulgent;* 250.12 *unconditional;* 380.6 *violent*
intemperately 250.21, 727.17 *excessively;* 686.12 *self-indulgently*
in tempo 18.41 *in tune*
intend 283.8; 482.7; 635.13; 694.12; 446.18 *aim;* 474.8 *expect;* 694.10 *mean;* 484.9 *plan;* 106.1 *predetermine;* 595.8 *prefer;* 638.7 *resolve*
intendant 579.16 *official*
intended 482.12; 593.11 *loved one;* 476.9, 694.9 *meant;* 484.14 *planned*
intend for 482.9
intending 482.11; 595.6 *liking;* 229.5 *tending to*
intense 529.11 *colourful;* 156.9 *deep-seated;* 590.13 *passionate;* 336.10 *potent;* 726.5 *serious;* 338.4 *vigorous;* 380.6 *violent*
intensely 336.15 *acutely;* 380.10 *violently;* 590.20 *with feeling*
intensification 607.1 *aggravation;* 727.1 *exaggeration;* 213.1 *increase*
intensified 607.4 *aggravated;* 152.2 *dense;* 727.12 *exaggerated;* 213.7 *increased*
intensify 607.6 *aggravate;* 727.7 *exaggerate;* 338.3 *invigorate;* 213.5 *make bigger;* 152.7 *thicken*
intensity 156.2; 336.3; 209.1 *degree;* 152.6 *denseness;* 590.4 *emotion;* 726.1 *emphasis;* 529.3 *hue;* 338.1 *vigour;* 380.1 *violence*
intensive 5.44 *grammatical;* 5.35 *part of speech;* 5.17 *word;* 5.42 *worded*
intensive farming 43.1 *agriculture*
intensively 5.50 *lexically*
intensive therapy 35.8 *treatment*
intensive therapy unit 35.10 *hospital*
intent 131.14 *aim;* 643.2 *earnest;* 482.1 *intention;* 694.5 *point;* 638.1 *resolute;* 635.1, 638.15 *will*
Intention 482
intention 482.1; 131.14 *aim;* 610.3 *aspiration;* 595.2 *inclination;* 480.11, 483.1 *motive;* 446.3, 484.1 *plan;* 694.5 *point;* 10.9 *prayer;* 106.6 *premeditation;* 756.1 *promise;* 638.12 *resolution;* 694.4 *type of meaning;* 353.6 *venture;* 635.1 *will*
intentional 106.4 *deliberate;* 482.12 *intended;* 484.14 *planned;* 446.12 *purposive;* 635.6 *willed*
intentional bias 482.5 *final intention*
intentional grounding 46.13 *penalty*
intentionality 482.2
intentional knock-on 64.3 *rugby play*
intentionally 482.13; 484.16 *as planned;* 446.21 *purposively*
intentional pass 48.4 *pitching terms*
intentions 631.1 *conduct*
intently 638.17 *resolutely*
intentness 342.8 *assiduity*
intent on 482.11 *intending*
intent upon 638.1 *resolute*
inter 583.8 *bury;* 736.8 *conceal;* 156.14 *deepen;* 368.4 *immerse*
interact 108.8 *be proportionate to;* 342.16 *be sociable;* 706.19 *react;* 110.7, 747.12 *reciprocate;* 2.15 *socialize*
interacting 110.1 *interchange;* 108.5 *interrelated;* 110.4 *reciprocal;* 162.4 *symmetrical*
interaction 147.8; 340.1 *action;* 110.1 *interchange;* 108.2 *interrelatedness;* 346.2 *joint operation;* 747.3 *mutual relationship;*

706.3 *question and answer*; 342.2 *social activity*; 2.3 *social environment*; 162.1 *symmetry*
interactive 340.5 *acting*; 342.18 *active*; 747.18 *joint*; 706.12 *reactive*; 2.12 *sociological*
interactively 706.24 *in answer*; 2.16 *sociologically*
inter alia 412.14 *in the midst*
inter alios 412.14 *in the midst*
interalliance 108.2 *interrelatedness*
interallied 108.5 *interrelated*
interassociate 108.8 *be proportionate to*; 110.8 *interrelate*
interassociated 108.5 *interrelated*
interassociation 108.2 *interrelatedness*
interbraiding 42.2 *spinning*
interbred 412.12 *mixed*
interbreed 412.10 *become mixed*; 412.8 *mix*
interbreeding 412.1 *mixture*
intercalary 275.24 *between times*
intercalate 368.1 *insert*
intercalated 275.24 *between times*; 368.12 *inserted*
intercalation 368.8 *insertion*
intercalative 368.12 *inserted*
intercallation compound 32.7 *chemical compound*
intercaste marriage 570.3 *types of marriage*
intercede 392.23 *advise*; 413.14 *give moral support*; 748.1 *mediate*; 753.6 *protest*
intercede for 348.4 *be an instrument*
interceder 748.3 *mediator*
intercept 27.32 *graph*; 504.15 *hear*; 378.8 *hinder*
intercepted pass 46.9 *play*
interception 378.1 *hindrance*; 64.3 *rugby play*
interceptor 586.31 *military aircraft*
intercession 348.1 *instrumentality*; 748.2 *mediation*; 413.6 *moral support*; 10.9 *prayer*; 753.1 *protest*; 392.2 *support*
intercessional 348.7 *causal*; 748.6 *mediatory*; 413.9 *supportive*
intercessor 748.3 *mediator*; 746.4 *negotiator*
intercessory 748.6 *mediatory*
interchange **110.1**; 111.7 *be the same*; 193.9 *cross*; 193.5 *crossroads*; 119.3 *equalization*; 224.4, 224.10, 759.1, 759.5 *exchange*; 762.6 *give a substitute*; 108.2 *interrelatedness*; 706.3 *question and answer*; 706.19 *react*; 110.7 *reciprocate*; 373.5 *road*; 316.1, 316.11 *transfer*; 300.15 *walk*
interchangeability 750.5 *conformity*; 119.3 *equalization*; 111.2 *equivalence*; 110.1 *interchange*
interchangeable 750.14 *conforming*; 111.13 *equivalent*; 224.14 *exchangeable*; 759.6 *in exchange*; 110.4 *reciprocal*; 316.17 *transferable*
interchangeably 706.24 *in answer*; 759.8 *in exchange*; 193.10 *interlacedly*; 316.18 *in transit*; 110.10 *reciprocally*
interchanged 759.7 *exchanged*; 108.5 *interrelated*; 110.4 *reciprocal*
interchanging 193.7 *crossing*; 108.2 *interrelatedness*
intercollegiate 50.11 *rowing*
intercollegiate rowing 50.4 *rowing*
Intercollegiate Yacht Racing Association 50.1 *sailing*
intercolumniation 20.8 *column*
intercom 504.9 *audio device*; 692.9 *telephone*
intercommunicate **373.13**; 147.19 *meet*
intercommunicating 147.10 *juxtaposed*
intercommunication 373.2 *association*; 734.1 *conversation*; 108.2 *interrelatedness*; 193.1 *interweaving*; 147.4 *meeting*; 746.1 *negotiation*; 654.1 *sociability*
intercommunicative 746.8 *negotiated*
intercommunion 654.1 *sociability*
interconnect 108.8 *be proportionate to*; 373.11 *connect*; 134.3 *continue*; 110.8 *interrelate*
interconnected **110.5**; 373.15 *connected*; 134.5 *continual*; 108.5 *interrelated*
interconnected circuits 28.55 *circuit*
interconnectedness 162.1 *symmetry*
interconnecting 193.7 *crossing*
interconnection **110.2**; 373.1 *connection*; 134.1 *continuity*; 108.2 *interrelatedness*; 373.4 *means of connection*; 108.1 *relatedness*
interconnective 373.14 *connective*
intercontinental ballistic missile 587.5 *missile weapon*
intercourse 373.2 *association*; 734.1 *conversation*; 108.2 *interrelatedness*; 654.1 *sociability*; 2.3 *social environment*
intercrop 193.8 *interweave*
intercrossing 318.5 *crossing point*
interdepend 110.8 *interrelate*
interdependence 110.2 *interconnection*; 108.2 *interrelatedness*; 162.1 *symmetry*
interdependent 110.5 *interconnected*; 108.5 *interrelated*; 162.4 *symmetrical*
interdependently 110.10 *reciprocally*; 108.10 *relevantly*
interdict 397.1, 397.9 *command*; 397.2, 397.10 *demand*; 709.2, 709.6 *dissent*; 128.7 *exclude*; 251.12 *gag*; 251.8 *restrain*; 251.1 *restraint*; 399.1, 399.3 *veto*
interdicted 397.14 *commanding*
interdiction 709.2 *dissent*; 128.1 *exclusion*; 378.1 *hindrance*; 399.1 *veto*
interdictive 709.9 *dissenting*; 251.13 *restraining*; 399.5 *vetoed*
interdictively 399.7 *by veto*; 709.11 *uncooperatively*; 251.16 *under restraints*
interdictor 586.31 *military aircraft*
interdictory 128.10 *excluding*
interdigitate 193.8 *interweave*
interdigitated 193.6 *interwoven*
interdigitation 193.1 *interweaving*
interdisciplinary education 6.3 *subject*
interest **784.4**; 633.4 *activity*; 123.7 *be important*; 797.13 *benefit*; 496.13 *be piquant*; 644.1 *curiosity*; 211.4 *extra*; 123.1 *importance*; 213.3 *increasing thing*; 395.1 *influence*; 788.2 *money received*; 483.9 *motivate*; 356.7 *produce*; 765.5 *profit*; 108.7 *relate to*; 342.2 *social activity*; 86.14 *sphere*; 447.1 *topic*
interest-bearing 356.11 *productive*
interested 644.5 *curious*
interesting 593.22 *lovable*; 447.8 *problematic*; 496.10 *stimulating*
interestingly 447.13 *problematically*; 496.16 *stimulatingly*
interest oneself in 342.16 *be sociable*
interest rate 14.1 *finance*
interface **147.7**; 40.20 *abort*; 492.12 *abut*; 40.19 *computing terms*; 492.6 *contiguity*; 373.13 *intercommunicate*; 147.19 *meet*; 147.4 *meeting*; 39.28 *plug*
interfaced 373.15 *connected*
interfacing 492.9 *touching*
interfaith 412.12 *mixed*
interfaith marriage 412.2 *mixed thing*; 570.3 *types of marriage*
interfere 340.4 *act*; 46.18 *be penalized*; 328.10 *disrupt*; 378.8 *hinder*; 342.17 *meddle*; 748.1 *mediate*; 58.9 *play hockey*; 399.3 *veto*
interfered 58.8 *hockey*
interfered with 328.15 *disrupted*
interference 517.5 *atmospheric dissonance*; 48.5 *batting terms*; 347.1 *counteraction*; 328.4 *disruption*; 378.1 *hindrance*; 58.1 *hockey*; 58.3 *ice hockey*; 505.3 *inaudibility*; 348.1 *instrumentality*; 58.5 *lacrosse*; 342.9 *overactivity*; 692.19 *radio reception*; 692.23 *television reception*; 521.6 *that which makes invisible*; 399.1 *veto*; 326.5 *wave*; 28.15 *wave property*
interference pattern 28.28 *colour*
interferer 378.7 *hinderer*; 342.11 *meddler*
interfere with 224.8 *cause change*; 347.3 *counteract*; 412.8 *mix*; 796.20 *seduce*
interfering 348.7 *causal*; 347.4 *counteracting*; 378.13 *hindering*; 58.8 *hockey*; 395.11 *influential*; 342.21 *meddling*; 342.9 *overactivity*
interfering so-and-so 378.7 *hinderer*
interferometer 28.92 *light meter*; 26.8 *meter*; 28.32 *optical instrument*
interferometric 26.16 *micrometric*
interferometry 29.27 *imaging*; 26.2 *micrometry*; 28.96 *microscopy*
interferon 394.4 *antidote*; 33.9 *protein*
interfile 193.8 *interweave*
interfuse 193.8 *interweave*
interfusion 193.1 *interweaving*; 412.1 *mixture*
intergalactic 29.36 *astronomical*; 141.12 *extensive*
intergalactically 29.39 *astronomically*; 141.16 *extensively*
intergalactic space 141.2 *empty space*
interglacial 275.24 *between times*; 31.40 *climatic change*; 30.60 *glaciated*; 30.40 *glaciation*
interglaciation 31.40 *climatic change*
intergression 314.1 *entry*
interim 275.24 *between times*; 263.1 *ease*; 133.3, 275.6 *interval*; 282.7 *occasional*; 226.3 *pause*
interim period 275.6 *interval*; 226.3 *pause*
interior **172.1**; **172.7**; 19.10 *art subject*; 127.8 *included*; 172.9 *inland*; 27.35 *space*; 169.2 *surface*
interior angle 27.39 *angle*
interior decorating 542.5 *decorating*
interior decoration 542.1 *ornament*
interior decorator 393.12 *repairer*
interior design 542.5 *decorating*
interiority 172.1 *interior*
interior light 522.6 *electric light*
interior monologue 17.3 *aspect of fiction*; 735.1 *soliloquy*
interjacence 370.1 *admittance*
interject 211.6 *add*; 706.18 *answer back*; 368.1 *insert*; 133.16 *interrupt*; 729.11 *speak*
interjected 706.13 *retaliatory*
interjecting 706.13 *retaliatory*
interjection 211.1 *addition*; 370.1 *admittance*; 706.5 *counterstatement*; 514.7 *cry of disapproval*; 368.8 *insertion*; 133.6 *intervention*; 5.35 *part of speech*; 733.2 *salutation*; 729.7 *utterance*
interjectional 5.44 *grammatical*
interlace 193.8 *interweave*; 412.8 *mix*
interlaced 193.6 *interwoven*; 412.12 *mixed*
interlacedly **193.10**
interlaced scanning 692.21 *television*
interlacement 193.1 *interweaving*
interlacing 108.2 *interrelatedness*; 193.1 *interweaving*
interlard 412.8 *mix*
interlay 193.8 *interweave*; 412.8 *mix*
interleave 114.8 *be diverse*; 412.8 *mix*
interline 193.8 *interweave*
interlineally 193.10 *interlacedly*
interlinearly 193.10 *interlacedly*
interlineation 211.3 *additional item*; 193.1 *interweaving*
interlining 411.1 *layer*; 406.4 *stuffing*
interlink 108.8 *be proportionate to*; 110.8 *interrelate*
interlinkage 108.2 *interrelatedness*
interlinked 110.5 *interconnected*; 108.5 *interrelated*
interlock 108.8 *be proportionate to*; 110.8 *interrelate*; 193.8 *interweave*
interlocked 108.5 *interrelated*
interlocking 110.5 *interconnected*; 108.2 *interrelatedness*; 193.1 *interweaving*
interlock stitch 42.5 *knitting*
interlocute 706.19 *react*
interlocution 734.1 *conversation*; 734.6 *interview*; 4.5 *philosophical argument*; 706.3 *question and answer*
interlocutor 706.10 *answerer*; 734.7 *conversationalist*; 705.9 *questioner*; 729.10 *speaker*
interlocutory 734.12 *conversing*; 706.12 *reactive*
interlope 100.16 *be external*
interloper 128.5 *excluded person*; 100.8 *intruder*
interloping 100.12 *external*; 100.4 *externality*
interlude 211.3 *additional item*; 21.12 *comedy*; 275.6 *interval*; 226.3 *pause*; 21.2 *play*; 21.8 *scene*
interlunar 275.24 *between times*
intermarriage 412.1 *mixture*; 570.3 *types of marriage*
intermarried 412.12 *mixed*
intermarry 412.10 *become mixed*; 570.15 *marry*
intermeddle 342.17 *meddle*; 748.1 *mediate*
intermeddler 342.11 *meddler*
intermeddling 748.2 *mediation*
intermediacy 348.1 *instrumentality*
intermediary 398.6 *agent*; 348.3 *assistant*; 398.1 *delegate*; 398.9 *delegated*; 748.3 *mediator*; 216.2 *medium*; 746.4 *negotiator*; 589.3 *pacifist*; 729.10 *speaker*
intermediate 348.4 *be an instrument*; 275.24 *between times*; 348.7 *causal*; 748.1 *mediate*; 216.2 *medium*
intermediate bond 32.11 *chemical bond*
intermediate-frequency amplifier 692.18 *radio*
intermediate host 70.4 *type of animal*
intermediate-level waste 28.74 *nuclear waste*
intermediately 748.7 *mediatorially*; 216.12 *mediumly*
intermediateness 348.1 *instrumentality*
intermediate rock 30.30 *igneous rock*
intermediate technology 356.2 *manufacture*
intermediation 748.2 *mediation*
intermediator 748.3 *mediator*
intermedium 373.4 *means of connection*; 216.5 *medium*
interment 583.1 *burial*; 156.1 *depth*; 368.10 *immersion*; 358.3 *obliteration*
intermeshed 108.5 *interrelated*
intermeshing 108.2 *interrelatedness*
intermetallic compound 32.7 *chemical compound*
intermezzo 211.3 *additional item*; 18.4 *opera*; 21.2 *play*; 21.8 *scene*
interminability 202.4 *infinity*; 148.4 *length*
interminable 279.10 *continuing forever*; 132.11 *continuous*; 202.1 *infinite*; 148.1 *long*; 134.6 *protracted*
interminably 134.7 *continually*; 217.9 *enough*; 202.10 *infinitely*; 148.11 *lengthily*
intermingle 193.8 *interweave*; 412.8 *mix*; 2.15 *socialize*
intermingled 412.12 *mixed*
intermingling 412.1 *mixture*
intermission 133.3 *interval*; 141.8 *intervening space*; 21.8 *scene*
intermit 299.6 *be irregular*; 298.7 *be regular*
intermittence 133.1 *discontinuity*; 299.1 *irregularity*; 206.4 *rarity*
intermittent 133.8 *discontinuous*; 299.4 *irregular*; 275.23 *occasional*; 276.9 *periodic*; 206.6 *sparse*
intermittently 453.27 *capriciously*; 133.17 *discontinuously*; 299.8 *irregularly*; 275.28 *sometimes*
intermittent showers 31.25 *rain*
intermix 114.8 *be diverse*; 412.8 *mix*
intermixed 412.12 *mixed*
intermixture 412.1 *mixture*
intermodal transportation 319.1 *transport*
intern 251.11 *detain*; 35.11 *doctor*; 6.4 *educator*; 309.10 *enclose*; 815.9 *imprison*; 814.1 *punish*
internal **101.11**; **172.8**; 172.1, 172.7 *interior*; 521.3 *private*; 172.10 *visceral*
internal bleeding 260.11 *blood disease*
internal-combustion engine 38.11 *engine*; 438.5 *machine*
internal ear **504.5**
internal energy 334.4 *energy*; 28.38 *thermodynamics*
internal evidence 716.5 *legal evidence*
internal examination 35.6 *health care*
internal friction 365.1 *friction*
internal gear 38.7 *gear*
internality 172.1 *interior*
internalization **172.6**
internalize 370.13 *absorb*; 172.15 *keep inside*; 443.17 *philosophize*
internalized **172.12**
internally **406.14**; 521.9 *invisibly*; 172.16 *inwardly*; 101.14 *subjectively*
internal medicine 35.3 *medical specialty*; 35.1 *medicine*
internalness 172.1 *interior*
internal organs 172.4 *insides*
internal resistance 39.12 *resistance*
internal respiration 34.6 *cell biology*; 33.24 *respiration*
Internal Revenue 13.6 *economic factors*
internal rhyme 17.11 *rhyme*
internal secretion 559.2 *secreted substance*
internal world 101.6
international 395.13 *dominant*; 764.5 *jointly possessing*; 85.16, 566.13 *national*; 61.10 *racing*; 138.16 *universal*; 204.6 *whole*
international agreement 755.3 *alliance*
International Atomic Energy Agency 334.8 *nuclear power*
International Badminton Federation 63.10 *badminton*

International Boxing Federation 52.2 *boxing*
International Canoe Federation 50.6 *canoeing*
International Casting Federation 55.1 *angling*
International Challenge Cup 50.6 *canoeing*
international code 692.11 *dialling*
international cooperation 566.9 *group*
international date line 166.4 *boundary marker*
International Date Line 281.3 *chronology;* 275.9 *time zone*
International Development Association 13.4 *economic development*
international direct dialling 692.11 *dialling*
Internationaler Deutscher Skimarathon in Hirschau 68.2 *cross-country skiing*
international fair 779.2 *fair*
international finance 14.1 *finance*
International Finance Corporation 13.4 *economic development;* 780.7 *finance*
international government 12.1 *government*
International Hockey Board 58.1 *hockey*
International Ice Hockey Federation 58.3 *ice hockey*
internationalism 85.5; 138.1 *generality*
internationalist 85.15; 652.3 *philanthropist*
internationality 85.5 *internationalism*
internationalize 764.4 *have joint possession;* 760.12 *naturalize*
internationalized 760.17 *naturalized*
International Labour Organisation 13.8 *industrial relations*
international language 5.7
international law 16.1 *the law*
international loan 771.2 *loan*
International Luge Federation 68.9 *bobsledding*
internationally 566.15 *humanly;* 61.11 *in a race;* 764.6 *in common;* 395.14 *influentially;* 85.19, 86.20 *nationally;* 138.32 *universally*
international mail 692.2 *postal communication*
International Monetary Fund 13.4 *economic development;* 14.1, 780.7 *finance*
international organization 764.1 *joint possession*
international pact 755.3 *alliance*
international paper 740.4 *newspaper*
International Phonetic Alphabet 5.14 *alphabet*
international police 16.14 *police*
international racing 61.1 *motor racing*
International Red Cross 589.2 *symbol of peace*
international sailing 50.1 *sailing*
International Scientific Vocabulary 5.7 *international language*
international show jumping 59.9 *jumping*
International Skating 135 Union; 68.6 *ice-skating*
International Socialists 12.6 *political party*
international society 566.9 *group*
International Swimming Federation 67.5 *swimming association*
international trade 13.5; 776.5 *commercial trade*
international union organization 15.3 *organized labour*
International Yacht Racing Union 50.1 *sailing*
internecine 357.14 *destructive;* 382.24 *murderous*
internecine war 585.1 *war*
interned 815.8 *imprisoned*
internee 309.6 *closed-in person*
Internet 40.16
Internet Explorer™ 40.16 *Internet*
Internetworking 40.15 *network*
internment 251.4 *detention;* 815.7 *imprisonment;* 814.7 *punishment;* 585.7 *war measures*
internode 77.5 *stem*
interpellant 705.12 *questioning*
interpellate 705.17 *question*
interpellation 705.2 *questioning;* 733.2 *salutation*
interpellator 734.7 *conversationalist;* 705.9 *questioner*
interpenetrate 108.8 *be proportionate to;* 314.11 *infiltrate;* 193.8 *interweave*
interpenetration 314.3 *inroad;* 147.8 *interaction;* 108.2 *interrelatedness;* 193.1 *interweaving;* 318.3 *passage into*
interpenetratively 193.10 *interlacedly*
interpersonal relations 2.3 *social environment*
interphase 34.10 *cell division*
interplanetary 29.36 *astronomical*
interplanetary space 141.2 *empty space;* 29.14 *solar system*
interplay 108.8 *be proportionate to;* 759.1 *exchange;* 110.1 *interchange;* 747.3 *mutual relationship;* 110.7, 747.12 *reciprocate*
interplaying 108.2 *interrelatedness;* 110.4 *reciprocal*
Interpol 16.14 *police*
interpolate 210.9, 211.6 *add;* 27.93 *equate;* 368.1 *insert;* 133.16 *interrupt*
interpolated 211.8 *additional;* 368.12 *inserted*
interpolation 211.3 *additional item;* 210.1 *calculation;* 368.8 *insertion;* 133.6 *intervention;* 205.7 *piece;* 27.66 *proof*
interpolative 368.12 *inserted*
interpose 211.6 *add;* 348.4 *be an instrument;* 372.14 *come between;* 378.8 *hinder;* 133.16 *interrupt;* 342.17 *meddle;* 748.1 *mediate*
interposition 211.1 *addition;* 378.1 *hindrance;* 348.1 *instrumentality;* 748.2 *mediation*
interpret 719.8; 409.16 *adapt;* 224.8 *cause change;* 725.2 *clarify;* 721.16 *define;* 466.12 *discriminate;* 722.4 *dissertate;* 265.16 *make easy;* 18.36 *play;* 4.21 *rationalize;* 738.3 *reveal;* 695.5 *simplify;* 706.20 *solve;* 760.9 *transform;* 5.46, 719.12 *translate*
interpretability 695.9 *intelligibility*
interpretable 695.1 *intelligible*
Interpretation 719
interpretation 719.1; 21.22 *acting;* 224.1 *change;* 760.1 *conversion;* 466.1 *discrimination;* 722.1 *dissertation;* 409.9 *musical arrangement;* 695.10 *simplicity;* 706.6 *solution;* 694.4 *type of meaning*
interpretational 466.9 *discriminating;* 719.14 *interpretive;* 706.14 *solved*
interpretative 722.5 *expository;* 695.1 *intelligible;* 719.14 *interpretive;* 694.6 *meaningful*
interpretatively 719.18 *in other words*
interpret dreams 11.23, 475.12 *divine*
interpreted 719.15; 21.39 *dramatic;* 466.11 *judged;* 695.2 *simple;* 706.14 *solved*
interpreted language 40.9 *programming language*
interpreter 719.6; 722.3 *dissertator;* 5.2 *linguist;* 40.8 *software*
interpreter of dreams 475.9 *forecaster*
interpreting dreams 475.2 *divination*
interpretive 719.14; 721.11 *descriptive;* 722.5 *expository;* 695.1 *intelligible;* 17.16 *literary;* 694.6 *meaningful;* 739.12 *revelatory;* 742.14 *signifying*
interpretively 742.18 *indicatively;* 719.18 *in other words*
interpretive reporting 741.3 *reporting*
interpret news 719.13
interpret the part 21.37 *rehearse*
interpret the scriptures 7.22 *theologize*
interquartile range 27.60 *parameter*
interracial 412.12 *mixed;* 566.13 *national*
interracially 412.14 *in the midst*
interracial marriage 412.2 *mixed thing;* 570.3 *types of marriage*
Interrail Card™ 793.4 *bargain*
interred 583.10 *buried;* 368.14 *immersed*
interregnum 588.1 *anarchy;* 12.1 *government;* 275.6 *interval*
interrelate 110.8; 750.25 *conform;* 134.3 *continue;* 747.12 *reciprocate*
interrelated 108.5; 750.14 *conforming;* 134.5 *continual;* 110.5 *interconnected*
interrelatedness 108.2; 134.1 *continuity*
interrelating 747.18 *joint*
interrelation 134.1 *continuity;* 162.1 *symmetry*
interrelationship 110.2 *interconnection*
interrobang 742.7 *punctuation*
interrogate 705.18; 644.7 *be curious*
interrogated 705.16 *questioned*
interrogation 734.6 *interview;* 705.2 *questioning*
interrogation mark 705.11 *question mark*
interrogation point 705.11 *question mark*
interrogative 705.12 *questioning*
interrogative clause 705.11 *question mark*
interrogative pronoun 705.11 *question mark*
interrogator 734.7 *conversationalist;* 705.9 *questioner*
interrupt 133.16; **361.12**; 659.7 *be discourteous;* 233.5 *be incomplete;* 226.8 *cause to cease;* 328.10 *disrupt;* 378.8 *hinder;* 314.10 *invade;* 342.17 *meddle;* 226.9 *pause;* 729.11 *speak;* 288.6 *take untimely action*
interrupted 133.10; **361.9**; 328.15 *disrupted;* 226.10 *finished;* 233.4 *incomplete;* 372.15 *separate*
interrupted state 233.1 *incompleteness*
interrupter 378.7 *hinderer*
interrupting 288.13 *untimely*
interruption 133.4; **361.6**; 659.2 *bad manners;* 328.4 *disruption;* 378.1 *hindrance;* 146.1 *interval;* 141.8 *intervening space;* 133.6 *intervention;* 342.9 *overactivity;* 226.3 *pause;* 226.2 *stop;* 288.2 *untimeliness*
intersect 492.12 *abut;* 27.97 *align;* 176.11 *angle;* 310.9 *converge;* 193.9 *cross*
intersecting 193.7 *crossing;* 27.80 *linear;* 20.17 *structured;* 492.9 *touching*
intersecting lines 27.37 *line*
intersecting road 373.5 *road*
intersecting vault 20.7 *vault*
intersection 176.1 *angle;* 311.4 *branching;* 320.3 *carriageway;* 492.6 *contiguity;* 318.5 *crossing point;* 193.5 *crossroads;* 317.3 *road;* 27.21 *set*
intersectional 193.7 *crossing*
interspace 146.1 *interval;* 146.4 *space*
interspaced 146.6 *spaced*
interspatial 146.6 *spaced*
interspatially 146.8 *apart;* 193.10 *interlacedly*
intersperse 114.8 *be diverse;* 412.8 *mix*
interspersed 412.12 *mixed*
interstate 373.5 *road;* 319.5 *transportable*
interstate commerce 13.1 *economics*
interstate highway 317.3, 320.2 *road*
interstellar 29.36 *astronomical;* 141.12 *extensive*
interstellar dust 29.8 *interstellar medium*
interstellar gas 29.8 *interstellar medium*
interstellar medium 29.8
interstellar molecule 29.8 *interstellar medium*
interstellar space 141.2 *empty space*
interstice 146.2 *crack*
interstitial 146.6 *spaced*
interstitial compound 32.7 *chemical compound*
interstitially 146.8 *apart*
intertextual 17.16 *literary*
intertexture 193.1 *interweaving;* 404.1 *texture*
intertidal 30.52 *coastal;* 91.7 *oceanic*
intertidal zone 30.15 *tide*
intertropical convergence zone 31.17 *wind system*
intertwine 374.5 *combine;* 184.11 *enfold;* 193.8 *interweave;* 412.8 *mix*
intertwined 374.7 *combined;* 108.5 *interrelated;* 193.6 *interwoven;* 412.12 *mixed*
intertwinement 193.1 *interweaving*
intertwining 108.2 *interrelatedness;* 193.1 *interweaving;* 42.2 *spinning*
intertwiningly 193.10 *interlacedly*
intertwist 412.8 *mix*
intertwisted 412.12 *mixed*
interurban 87.14 *urban*
Interval 146
interval 133.3; **146.1**; **209.4**; **275.6**; 263.1 *ease;* 94.4 *emptiness;* 141.8 *intervening space;* 18.16 *musical note;* 18.17 *notation;* 233.2 *omission;* 308.1 *opening;* 226.3 *pause;* 276.1 *period;* 21.8 *scene;* 292.1 *season;* 28.8 *time;* 31.3 *weather*
intervallic 275.24 *between times;* 146.6 *spaced*
interval scale 27.56 *nonparametric methods*
intervene 340.4 *act;* 348.4 *be an instrument;* 378.9 *block;* 328.10 *disrupt;* 251.9 *economize;* 378.8 *hinder;* 133.16 *interrupt;* 342.17 *meddle;* 748.1 *mediate;* 275.15 *pass;* 776.1 *trade*
intervener 16.8 *litigant*
intervening 348.7 *causal;* 378.13 *hindering;* 318.13 *penetrating*
intervening space 141.8; 146.1 *interval*
intervention 133.6; 776.5 *commercial trade;* 328.4 *disruption;* 13.6 *economic factors;* 251.2 *economic restraint;* 378.1 *hindrance;* 348.1 *instrumentality;* 748.2 *mediation;* 378.2 *obstacle;* 318.3 *passage into;* 585.1 *war*
interventional 378.14 *blocked;* 348.7 *causal;* 378.13 *hindering;* 251.13 *restraining*
interventionalist 251.6 *lawmaker*
interventionally 378.17 *in the way*
interventionism 776.5 *commercial trade;* 251.2 *economic restraint*
interview 734.6; 654.3 *meeting;* 705.17 *question;* 706.3 *question and answer;* 705.3 *questionnaire;* 706.19 *react;* 741.13 *report*
interviewee 706.10 *answerer;* 705.10 *person questioned*
interviewer 734.7 *conversationalist;* 705.9 *questioner*
interwar 275.24 *between times*
interweave 193.8; 374.5 *combine;* 373.11 *connect;* 412.8 *mix*
Interweaving 193
interweaving 193.1; 108.2 *interrelatedness;* 42.4 *weaving*
interwork 108.8 *be proportionate to;* 193.1 *interweaving*
interworking 108.5 *interrelated;* 108.2 *interrelatedness*
interwoven 193.6; 374.7 *combined;* 373.15 *connected;* 108.5 *interrelated;* 412.12 *mixed*
intestate 358.6 *obliterated*
intestinal 308.15 *providing passage;* 172.10 *visceral*
intestinal gland 559.3 *gland*
intestinally 308.27 *cavernously*
intestines 180.3 *convoluted thing;* 557.16 *eating utensil;* 172.4 *insides;* 308.7 *passageway*
in that case 750.36 *accordingly;* 222.15 *under the circumstances*
in that place 142.12 *where*
in that way 750.36 *accordingly*
in the abstract 4.25 *theoretically*
in the act 340.7 *actively;* 806.11 *guiltily*
in the affirmative 750.39 *with consent*
in the afternoon 291.7 *evening*
in the aggregate 204.12 *one and all*
in the air 170.6 *atmospheric;* 154.19 *high;* 740.19 *published*
in the altogether 552.17 *nakedly;* 552.9 *undressed*
in the army 585.15 *warring*
in the ascendant 304.22 *ascending;* 395.11 *influential;* 121.12 *superior*
in the background 344.14 *causally;* 145.10 *distantly;* 168.9 *in the rear*
in the bag 253.8 *accomplished;* 410.20 *containing*
in the bank 763.9 *possessed*
in the bargain bin 791.7 *at a discount*
in the beginning 130.38
in the big house 251.15 *detained;* 815.8 *imprisoned*
in the black 765.20 *gainfully;* 783.13 *in credit;* 785.16 *paid;* 781.2 *solvent;* 765.17 *well-off*
in the book 744.16 *recorded*
in the boondocks 145.10 *distantly*
in the boonies 145.10 *distantly*
in the bud 130.41; 34.26 *developmental;* 130.32 *embryonic*
in the buff 552.17 *nakedly;* 552.9 *undressed*
in the business 342.21 *meddling*
in the cannon's mouth 586.42 *martially*
in the case 222.15 *under the circumstances*
in the centre of 173.10 *centrally*
in the chair 579.17 *managerial;* 579.19 *managerially*
in the chips 781.1 *wealthy*
in the circumstances 221.9 *conditionally*
in the clear 16.63 *acquitted;* 805.5 *innocent;* 252.6 *safe*
in the clink 252.6 *safe*
in the clouds 154.19 *high;* 89.11 *on the mountain*

in the club 561.16 *reproductive*
in the clutches of 387.9 *subject*
in the cooler 815.8 *imprisoned*
in the course of 275.26 *all the time*
in the cradle 555.11 *young*; 555.14 *youthfully*
in the crease area 58.10 *on the field*
in the current mode 295.23 *trendily*
in the dark 519.12 *blind to*; 523.15 *darkly*; 456.6 *ignorant*
in the database 744.16 *recorded*
in the days of 275.29 *one day*
in the deepfreeze 339.7 *inertly*
in the depths 602.6 *depressed*
in the direction of 317.17 *via*
in the dirt 367.24 *down*
in the distance 145.10 *distantly*
in the doctor's hands 260.25 *unhealthily*
in the doldrums 602.6 *depressed*; 611.4 *hopeless*
in the dough 781.1 *wealthy*
in the driving seat 396.23 *authoritatively*; 395.13 *dominant*; 579.17 *managerial*; 579.19 *managerially*
in the dust 623.3 *humbled*
in the embryonic stage 243.17 *developing*
in the end 706.25 *conclusively*; 131.26, 226.11, 309.17 *finally*; 452.25 *inevitably*
in the evening 291.7 *evening*
in the event 222.15 *under the circumstances*
in the event that 476.11 *supposing*
in the expected way 620.8 *boringly*
in the face of 661.9 *defiantly*; 753.11 *disapprovingly*; 97.16 *on the spot*; 113.31 *opposed to*
in the family way 474.6 *expectant*; 561.16 *reproductive*
in the file 744.16 *recorded*
in the final analysis 131.26 *finally*
in the first place 130.40 *first*
in the flesh 554.12 *alive*; 97.14 *in person*; 402.7 *material*; 139.29 *personally*
in the foreground 738.14 *manifest*
in the fourth place 200.15 *fourth*
in the freezer 359.7 *preserved*
in the fresh air 501.3 *odourless*; 501.7 *odourlessly*
in the future **283.14**; 286.3 *another time*; 294.17 *later*
in the gaseous state 432.16 *gaseous*
in the gloaming 524.12 *dimly*
in the grave 583.10 *buried*; 582.19 *dead*
in the gravy 781.1 *wealthy*
in the grip of 360.10 *retained*
in the habit 632.14 *habituated*
in the hands of 763.9 *possessed*; 387.9 *subject*
in the headlines 740.20 *well-known*
in the hoosegow 252.6 *safe*
in the hot seat 254.4 *endangered*; 579.19 *managerially*
in the index 744.16 *recorded*
in the interim 275.26 *all the time*; 282.10 *for the present*
in the know 693.18 *informed*; 6.19, 455.8 *knowledgeable*
in the large 158.20 *largely*
in the lead 329.17 *ahead*; 167.11 *in front*; 329.14 *surpassing*
in the lee of 252.11 *safely*
in the limelight 738.14 *manifest*; 740.22 *publicly*
in the lion's den 254.4 *endangered*
in the long run 131.26 *finally*; 216.11 *on average*; 138.31 *overall*
in the lowest position 122.19 *inferiorly*
in the L position 57.12 *competitively*
in the main 140.18 *as a rule*; 123.9 *importantly*; 99.13 *in essence*; 204.13 *on the whole*; 138.31 *overall*; 121.16 *superiorly*
in the majority 207.11 *in majority*
in the marketplace 776.20 *in trade*
in the mass 204.12 *one and all*
in the meantime 275.26 *all the time*; 282.10 *for the present*; 278.9 *for the time being*
in the melting pot 412.12 *mixed*
in the middle 216.12 *mediumly*
in the middle of 173.10 *centrally*; 412.14 *in the midst*; 764.5 *jointly possessing*
in the midst 412.14
in the midst of 340.7 *actively*; 173.10 *centrally*; 412.14 *in the midst*
in the mind 446.11 *ideational*; 446.20 *theoretically*; 447.12 *topically*
in the mind's eye 446.11 *ideational*; 477.17 *imaginatively*; 446.20 *theoretically*
in the minutes 744.16 *recorded*
in the mode 632.12 *established*
in the money 780.28 *financially*; 248.8 *prosperous*; 781.1 *wealthy*
in the morning 290.8
in the name of 396.23 *authoritatively*; 392.37 *in aid of*; 12.14 *politically*
in the negative 708.22 *negatively*
in the neighbourhood 565.20 *environmentally*; 147.9, 147.12 *near*; 170.8 *round*
in the news 740.19 *published*; 447.6 *topical*; 447.12 *topically*
in the nick 815.8 *imprisoned*
in the night 523.15 *darkly*
in the nude 552.17 *nakedly*; 552.9 *undressed*
in the offing 243.17 *developing*; 145.10 *distantly*; 283.14 *in the future*
in the open 171.15 *externally*; 738.14 *manifest*; 308.25 *obviously*; 739.13 *openly*; 434.26 *out-of-doors*; 740.19 *published*
in the open air 171.15 *externally*; 434.26 *out-of-doors*
in the open water 67.12 *by swimming*
in theory 96.18 *ideally*; 476.10 *supposedly*; 446.20 *theoretically*
in the ownership of 763.9 *possessed*
in the past 3.18; **284.22**; 286.3 *another time*
in the pay of 387.9 *subject*; 387.11 *under subjection*
in the picture 693.18 *informed*; 455.8 *knowledgeable*; 488.5 *sensible*
in the pink 801.12 *all right*; 259.1 *healthy*; 160.12 *on form*; 407.13 *orderly*; 230.1 *perfect*; 336.9 *physically strong*; 490.7 *pleased*; 535.10 *ruddily*
in the pipeline 319.6 *commercially*; 233.4 *incomplete*
in the pits 61.11 *in a race*
in the plural 207.6 *plural*
in the possession of 763.9 *possessed*; 763.10 *possessively*
in the poverty trap 135.5 *necessitous*; 782.1 *poor*; 782.15 *poorly*
in the presence of 97.16 *on the spot*
in the present case 221.9 *conditionally*
in the public eye 520.2 *clear*; 740.22 *publicly*; 740.20 *well-known*
in the pudding club 561.16 *reproductive*
in the raw 552.17 *nakedly*; 552.9 *undressed*
in the rear 168.9
in the red 766.20 *at a loss*; 783.12 *charged*; 784.9 *in debt*; 782.2 *insolvent*; 784.11 *insolvently*; 766.17 *unprofitable*; 786.15 *without paying*
in the refrigerator 359.7 *preserved*
in the right 801.9; **801.21**
in the ring 52.16 *professionally*
in the rough 325.21 *indirect*; 420.14 *roughly*
in the saddle 396.23 *authoritatively*; 579.19 *managerially*; 243.18 *prepared*
in the sale 791.7 *at a discount*
in the same boat 764.5 *jointly possessing*; 115.13 *similarly*
in the same breath 280.9 *in the shortest possible time*
in the same category 115.13 *similarly*
in the same class 127.8 *included*
in the same league 127.8 *included*
in the same place 111.18 *identically*
in the same way 115.14 *comparably*; 111.18 *identically*; 750.34 *uniformly*
in the same words 698.38 *literally*
in the second place 289.15 *as follows*; 198.21 *second*
in the Senate 398.11 *representatively*
in the sense that 694.13 *meaningfully*
in the service of 392.37 *in aid of*
in the shade 523.15 *darkly*
in the shops 778.18 *on sale*
in the singular 197.22 *one by one*
in the small hours 293.17 *early*; 291.7 *evening*
in the soup 254.4 *endangered*; 264.16 *troubled*
in the spotlight 21.43 *on stage*
in the stars 283.16 *predictably*
in the sticks 145.10 *distantly*
in the sun 434.26 *out-of-doors*
in the swim 248.9 *prosperously*
in the teeth of 661.9 *defiantly*; 264.25 *difficultly*
in the thick of 340.7 *actively*
in the third place 199.14 *third*
in the twilight 524.12 *dimly*
in the usual course 138.30 *usually*
in the vanguard 167.11 *in front*
in the vernacular 271.8 *simply*
in the vicinity 565.20 *environmentally*; 147.9, 147.12 *near*; 239.8 *nearby*; 170.8 *round*
in the way 378.17; 378.14 *blocked*
in the wind 283.14 *in the future*
in the wind's eye 324.11 *in all directions*
in the wings 21.43 *on stage*
in the wrong 802.16; 806.5 *guilty*
in the wrong place 144.20 *out of place*; 144.10 *replaced*
in the year of 275.29 *one day*
in this vicinity 142.12 *where*
in this way 317.16 *how*; 222.15 *under the circumstances*
in threes 199.13
inti 780.11 *national coins*
intimacy 593.5 *desire*; 569.3 *familiarity*; 595.1 *liking*; 147.1 *nearness*; 654.1 *sociability*
intimate 569.6 *close friend*; 569.10 *familiar*; 172.12 *internalized*; 595.5 *likable*; 694.10 *mean*; 147.9 *near*; 139.19 *personal*; 737.9 *secret*; 742.10 *signify*; 693.14 *tip*
intimate friend 569.6 *close friend*; 595.4 *likable person*
intimately 569.18; 172.16 *inwardly*; 595.10 *with great liking*
intimate review 21.7 *show*
intimation 693.7 *advice*; 476.2 *basis of supposition*; 590.2 *impression*; 455.2 *information*; 475.3 *plan*; 728.6 *suggestion*
in time 287.8; **287.11**; 293.17 *early*; 18.41 *in tune*; 294.17 *later*; 285.10 *synchronized*; 285.13 *synchronously*
in times gone by 284.22 *in the past*
intimidate 647.5 *be severe*; 387.7 *defeat*; 481.2 *deter*; 254.10 *endanger*; 386.7 *force*; 612.13 *frighten*; 480.15 *persuade*; 651.18 *torment*
intimidated 612.7 *frightened*
intimidating 387.10 *dominating*; 612.10 *frightening*
intimidation 612.4; 651.7 *act of malevolence*; 381.11 *attack*; 386.2 *coercion*; 481.7 *deterrence*; 387.2 *domination*; 651.5 *intolerance*; 585.1 *war*
intimidatory 651.10 *malevolent*
intinction 10.6 *Eucharist*
in tip-top condition 259.1 *healthy*
into 314.18; 342.18 *active*
in token of 742.18 *indicatively*
intolerable 236.3 *bad*; 596.9 *disliked*; 491.5 *painful*
intolerance 651.5; 590.6 *bad feeling*; 347.1 *counteraction*; 236.11 *harmfulness*; 465.3 *injustice*; 641.7 *opinionatedness*; 628.1 *pitilessness*; 466.3 *prejudice*; 647.1 *severity*
intolerant 347.4 *counteracting*; 466.10 *discriminatory*; 236.5 *harmful*; 651.10 *malevolent*; 647.8 *severe*; 465.8 *unjust*
intolerantly 347.5 *counter*; 651.20 *malevolently*; 466.17 *prejudicially*; 647.11 *severely*; 465.14 *unjustly*
intonation 729.3 *mode of speech*
intone 18.39 *sing*
in torment 8.20 *devilishly*
into sight 525.15 *apparently*; 520.11 *visibly*
into the bargain 211.10 *additionally*
into the black 783.15
into the red 783.15 *into the black*
in toto 232.9 *completely*; 204.11 *wholly*
in touch 693.18 *informed*; 6.19 *knowledgeable*; 64.6 *rugger*
into view 520.11 *visibly*
in tow 223.21 *together*
intoxicant 394.8 *drug*; 690.6 *intoxicating*
intoxicate 597.8 *cause joy*; 338.3 *invigorate*
intoxicated 690.1 *drunk*; 597.4 *happy*
intoxicated person 690.17 *drunkard*
intoxicating 690.6; 336.12 *strong to the senses*
intoxicating liquor 690.12 *alcohol*
intoxication 690.10 *drunkenness*; 597.1 *happiness*; 245.10 *impairment*; 245.8 *perversion*
intractability 662.1 *disobedience*; 628.2 *inflexibility*; 418.8 *mental hardness*; 383.2, 641.5 *obstinacy*
intractable 347.4 *counteracting*; 662.13 *disobedient*; 628.5 *inflexible*; 418.4 *mentally hard*; 383.11 *obstinate*; 641.2 *refractory*; 264.14 *troublesome*
intractably 347.5 *counter*; 662.17 *disobediently*; 418.13 *inflexibly*; 383.14 *resistingly*
intractile 418.4 *mentally hard*
intracutaneous injection 37.12 *injection*
in trade 776.20
intradermal injection 37.12 *injection*
intrados 20.9 *miscellaneous architectural features*
in training 486.2 *unskilled*
intramural 6.21 *curricular*; 165.7 *enclosed*
intramurally 165.8 *confinedly*
intramuscular injection 37.12 *injection*
intransigence 641.6 *determination*; 418.8 *mental hardness*; 635.3 *wilfulness*
intransigent 418.4 *mentally hard*; 113.11 *opposer*; 638.3 *strong-willed*; 641.3 *unyielding*; 635.8 *wilful*
intransigently 418.13 *inflexibly*; 641.9 *obstinately*
in transit 316.18; 318.14 *by the way*; 319.6 *commercially*; 760.18 *convertibly*; 300.18 *in motion*; 302.20 *in progress*; 144.20 *out of place*
in transition 760.18 *convertibly*
intransitive 5.44 *grammatical*
intransitively 5.52 *grammatically*
intransitive verb 5.35 *part of speech*
in transit to 317.17 *via*
intransmutable 228.9 *stable*
intrauterine 172.10 *visceral*
intravenous 172.7 *interior*
intravenous injection 37.12 *injection*; 394.13 *therapy*
intravenous pyelogram 35.7 *diagnosis*
intrepid 613.12 *self-reliant*
intrepidity 613.3 *steadfastness*
intrepidly 613.18 *courageously*
intricacy 180.2 *coil*; 180.1 *convolution*; 264.1 *difficulty*; 737.3 *mystification*
intricate 180.4 *convolutional*; 737.11 *mysterious*; 264.12 *problematic*
intricately 180.8 *circularly*; 264.27 *problematically*
intricateness 180.1 *convolution*
intrigant 484.8 *planner*; 700.20 *plotter*
intrigue 645.5 *be cunning*; 496.13 *be piquant*; 645.1 *cunning*; 796.4 *illicit love*; 593.8 *love affair*; 483.9 *motivate*; 342.9 *overactivity*; 484.4, 484.13 *plot*; 737.2 *secretiveness*; 662.3 *subversion*
intriguer 645.3 *cunning person*; 342.11 *meddler*; 484.8 *planner*; 700.20 *plotter*
intriguing 645.4 *cunning*; 593.22 *lovable*; 342.21 *meddling*; 484.15 *planning*; 496.10 *stimulating*
intriguingly 484.17 *conspiratorially*; 496.16 *stimulatingly*
in trim 259.1 *healthy*
intrinsic 93.11; **99.6**; **172.11**; 405.8 *belonging*; 344.13 *causal*; 127.8 *included*; 255.16 *simple*; 139.15 *special*; 698.17 *truistic*
intrinsicality 172.5 *inner nature*
intrinsically 344.14 *causally*; 255.20 *homogenously*; 127.9 *inclusively*; 99.13 *in essence*; 172.16 *inwardly*
intrinsic truth 698.4 *truism*
in triplicate 111.18 *identically*; 561.17 *repeatedly*; 199.12 *thrice*
in triumph 246.16 *successfully*
introception 370.1 *admittance*
introceptive 370.14 *admissive*
introduce 370.10; 211.6 *add*; 658.10 *be courteous*; 569.15 *be hospitable*; 167.10 *be in front*; 579.2 *direct*; 314.14 *enrol*; 129.19 *forecast*; 368.2 *inject*; 368.1 *insert*; 243.1 *prepare*; 370.8 *show in*
introduce a red herring 700.32 *disguise*
introduced 368.12 *inserted*; 77.15 *wild*
introduce oneself 654.13 *fraternize*
introduction 130.10; **370.3**; 525.1 *appearance*; 658.3 *courtesies*; 314.1 *entry*; 167.1 *front*; 368.8 *insertion*; 129.5 *preface*; 21.8 *scene*
introductive 370.16 *introductory*
introductorily 243.23 *preparatorily*
introductory 130.36; **370.16**; 308.17 *beginning*; 129.13 *precursory*; 243.16 *preparatory*
introit 10.6 *Eucharist*; 18.5 *sacred music*
introject 368.1 *insert*

introjected 368.12 *inserted*
introjection 368.8 *insertion*
intromission 370.1 *admittance*; 368.8 *insertion*
intromissive 370.14 *admissive*
intromit 370.7 *admit*; 368.1 *insert*
intromittent 370.14 *admissive*
intromittent organ 561.8 *organs of reproduction*
intron 34.13 *genetic material*
introspect 4.20, 443.17 *philosophize*; 705.17 *question*
introspection 463.1 *oblivion*; 4.4 *philosophical investigation*; 443.3 *thoughtfulness*
introspection psychology 36.1 *psychology*
introspective 463.8 *oblivious*; 705.12 *questioning*; 443.10 *speculative*; 4.17 *thoughtful*
introspectively 705.23 *questioningly*; 4.28, 443.18 *thoughtfully*
in trouble 249.6 *adverse*; 264.16 *troubled*
introversion 378.5 *inhibition*; 172.6 *internalization*; 192.1 *inversion*; 36.7 *personality type*; 251.3 *self-restraint*; 655.2 *shyness*
introversive 378.15 *inhibitive*; 36.34 *introverted*; 251.14 *self-restrained*
introvert 378.7 *hinderer*; 172.6 *internalization*; 36.34 *introverted*; 192.3 *invert*; 728.11 *modest person*; 36.7 *personality type*
introverted 36.34; 172.12 *internalized*; 655.9 *shy*
introvertedness 36.7 *personality type*
intrude 100.16 *be external*; 328.10 *disrupt*; 342.17 *meddle*; 751.7 *pick a fight*; 288.6 *take untimely action*; 329.5 *transgress*
intruder 100.8; **314.8**; 751.4 *dissenter*; 128.5 *excluded person*; 378.7 *hinderer*
intrusion 328.4 *disruption*; 100.4 *externality*; 314.3 *inroad*; 30.29 *petrogenesis*; 329.8 *transgression*; 288.2 *untimeliness*
intrusive 100.12 *external*; 378.13 *hindering*; 314.16 *invasive*; 342.21 *meddling*; 329.11 *overrun*; 30.56 *petrographic*; 288.13 *untimely*
intrusively 288.19 *at the wrong time*; 328.18 *disturbingly*; 329.16 *excessively*; 100.18 *extraneously*; 314.17 *in*; 378.16 *with delay*
intrusiveness 342.9 *overactivity*
intrusive person 713.4 *adviser*
in truth 454.12 *assuredly*; 95.14 *certainly*; 799.7 *honourably*; 698.35 *truly*
intubation 37.12 *injection*
intuit 445.9 *be intuitive*; 458.7 *be wise*; 11.23 *divine*; 590.16 *feel in one's bones*; 446.14 *have an idea*; 476.5 *suppose*; 442.12 *think*
Intuition 445
intuition 445.1; 476.2 *basis of supposition*; 450.1 *belief*; 476.3 *conjecture*; 443.6 *idea*; 590.2 *impression*; 455.1 *knowledge*; 4.4 *philosophical investigation*; 11.8 *psychic power*; 478.5 *spontaneity*; 446.2 *theory*; 442.2 *ways of thinking*; 458.1 *wisdom*
intuitionism 4.7 *school of thought*
intuitive 445.6; **590.11**; 442.9 *mental*; 478.2 *spontaneous*; 476.7 *suppositional*
intuitively 445.11; 442.14 *mentally*; 443.18 *thoughtfully*
intuitiveness 445.1 *intuition*
intuitive person 445.5
intuitive reasoning 445.1 *intuition*
intumesce 213.4 *increase*
intumescence 190.1 *growth*; 213.2 *spread*
in tune 18.41; 18.30 *harmonic*; 516.7, 750.13 *harmonious*; 516.12 *harmoniously*
in turmoil 114.11 *irregularly*
in turn 68.16 *bobsled*; 132.18 *consecutively*; 407.25 *in order*; 139.32 *severally*
in twain 198.22 *in half*; 372.20 *separately*
in two 184.12 *doubly*; 198.22 *in half*; 372.20 *separately*
in twos 198.9 *two*; 198.20 *two by two*
in twos and threes 206.10 *in ones and twos*
inulin 33.4 *polysaccharide*
inunction 268.4 *anointment*; 268.6 *ointment*
inunctum 268.6 *ointment*
inundant 90.10 *fluvial*
inundate 219.4 *be excessive*; 90.7 *flow*; 550.31 *hide*; 315.11 *run out*; 433.29 *water*
inundated 90.11, 433.24 *flooded*; 329.11 *overrun*
inundation 357.7 *agent of destruction*; 219.1 *excess*; 315.2 *outflow*; 329.6 *overstepping*; 90.6 *river flow*; 433.9 *soaking*
inundatorily 90.13 *fluently*
in unfinished form 420.15 *incompletely*
in unison 267.11 *cohesively*; 516.7 *harmonious*; 516.12, 750.33 *harmoniously*; 285.13 *synchronously*; 223.21 *together*
inurbane 659.5 *discourteous*
inurbanity 659.1 *discourtesy*
inure 243.7 *develop*; 632.18 *habituate*; 292.7 *season*
inured 489.7 *anaesthetized*; 632.14 *habituated*; 292.15 *seasoned*
inurement 243.13 *development*; 632.7 *habituation*
in use 346.10 *operational*; 349.9 *used*
inutile 238.1 *useless*
inutility 335.1 *powerlessness*; 219.3 *superfluity*; 124.7 *triviality*; 238.3 *uselessness*
invade 314.10; 381.9 *attack successfully*; 585.13 *be at war*; 100.16 *be external*; 586.38 *conquer*; 245.5 *hurt*; 76.16 *infest*; 329.5 *transgress*
invader 381.19 *attacker*; 128.5 *excluded person*; 564.6 *illegal occupant*; 314.8 *intruder*
invading 381.23 *attacking*; 100.12 *external*
invaginate 192.3 *invert*
invagination 192.1 *inversion*
in vain 238.2 *futile*; 247.12 *unsuccessfully*; 238.10 *uselessly*
invalid 708.20 *cancelled*; 802.12 *incorrect*; 337.13 *insufficient*; 27.86 *logical*; 35.18 *patient*; 335.10 *powerless*; 335.5 *powerless person*; 355.5 *relinquished*; 260.19 *sick person*; 702.7 *sophistic*; 260.21 *unhealthy*; 238.1 *useless*; 337.4 *weakling*
invalid argument 27.64 *reasoning*
invalidate 708.10 *be negative*; 708.14 *cancel*; 94.13 *cause not to exist*; 347.3 *counteract*; 357.8 *destroy*; 704.8 *refute*; 335.7 *remove power from*; 708.12 *renounce*; 27.89 *theorize*; 337.7 *weaken*; 355.2 *withdraw*
invalidated 708.20 *cancelled*; 335.10 *powerless*; 708.18 *rejected*
invalidating 347.4 *counteracting*; 704.7 *refuting*
invalidation 708.5 *cancellation*; 347.1 *counteraction*; 335.1 *powerlessness*; 704.1 *refutation*; 708.2 *rejection*; 708.4 *renunciation*
invalided 260.22 *sick*
invalidism 260.1 *ill health*
invalidity 335.4 *disability*; 802.2 *incorrectness*; 27.64 *reasoning*; 702.1 *sophistry*
invalidly 708.22 *negatively*; 355.7 *on hold*
invaluable 237.4 *profitable*; 235.3, 792.8 *valuable*
invaluableness 792.6 *value*
invaluably 792.13 *valuably*
invariability 111.6 *regularity*; 112.3 *repetitiveness*; 228.1 *stability*
invariable 620.4 *boring*; 750.14 *conforming*; 27.77 *given*; 632.9 *habitual*; 112.13 *monotonous*; 225.7 *permanent*; 111.17 *regular*; 228.9 *stable*; 228.4 *stable thing*
invariable quantity 228.4 *stable thing*
invariably 620.8 *boringly*; 750.35 *consistently*; 632.19 *habitually*; 225.9 *permanently*; 111.20 *regularly*; 138.32 *universally*; 138.30 *usually*
invariant 27.25 *algebraic expression*; 111.17 *regular*; 111.6 *regularity*
invasion 100.4 *externality*; 314.3 *inroad*; 381.14 *siege*; 329.8 *transgression*; 585.8 *warfare*
invasive 314.16; 100.12 *external*; 329.11 *overrun*
invasively 329.16 *excessively*; 314.17 *in*
invective 733.1 *address*; 712.1 *curse*; 712.8 *cursing*; 729.8 *speech*
inveigh against 381.10 *criticize*; 712.6 *vilify*
inveigle 677.10 *cajole*; 483.10 *manipulate*; 480.16 *tempt*; 379.2 *trap*
inveiglement 677.3 *cajolery*
inveigler 677.6 *flatterer*
inveigling 677.14 *cajoling*
invent 130.22; **448.13**; **449.4**; **484.11**; 344.9 *be the cause of*; 295.18 *be trendy*; 93.20 *bring into being*; 224.8 *cause change*; 96.17 *fabricate*; 699.26 *falsify*; 129.18 *forerun*; 443.16 *have an idea*; 446.15, 477.14 *imagine*; 478.3 *improvise*; 126.7 *originate*; 356.10 *produce*; 738.3 *reveal*; 403.14 *structure*
invented 699.36 *falsified*; 477.12 *imaginary*; 356.12 *produced*
invention 130.5; **449.9**; 19.5 *artistry*; 344.1 *cause*; 224.1 *change*; 484.3 *expedient plan*; 699.9 *falsification*; 477.1 *imagination*; 478.4 *improvisation*; 295.1 *newness*; 126.2 *original*; 446.3 *plan*; 356.1 *production*
inventive 130.33; 344.13 *causal*; 224.11 *changeable*; 645.4 *cunning*; 449.13 *discovering*; 562.5 *fertile*; 446.11 *ideational*; 477.10 *imaginative*; 478.1 *improvised*; 295.10 *new*; 126.4, 448.9 *original*; 356.11 *productive*; 443.10 *speculative*
inventively 448.15; 344.14 *causally*; 224.15 *changeably*; 562.8 *fruitfully*; 446.22, 477.17 *imaginatively*; 295.21 *newly*; 126.8, 449.16 *originally*; 356.13 *productively*; 443.18 *thoughtfully*
inventiveness 443.5 *creative thought*; 645.1 *cunning*; 446.8, 477.1 *imagination*; 126.1, 448.4 *originality*; 562.2 *productiveness*
inventive power 443.5 *creative thought*
inventor 449.12 *discoverer*; 448.5 *experimenter*; 478.6 *improviser*; 126.3, 130.16 *originator*; 446.9 *person of ideas*; 484.8 *planner*; 129.8 *precursor*; 344.7 *Prime Mover*; 356.9 *producer*
inventorial 220.12; 789.10 *accounting*
inventorially 220.13
inventoried 220.11 *listed*
inventorize 721.16 *define*
inventory 789.8 *audit*; 409.7 *catalogue*; 409.15 *categorize*; 439.5 *collection*; 210.3 *count*; 406.5 *divisions*; 220.1, 220.8 *list*; 210.11 *number*; 744.1 *record*; 204.5 *unit*
inveracious 699.29 *false*
inveracity 699.1 *falsehood*
Inverness 87.4 *British cities*
inverse 27.74 *divisible*; 27.18 *division*; 27.22 *matrix*; 113.23 *opposite*; 113.2 *oppositeness*; 27.21 *set*
inverse cosine 27.52 *trigonometric function*
inverse function 27.29 *mathematical function*
inversely 192.4; 113.28 *in opposition*
inversely proportional to 27.88 *equal to*
inverse proportion 108.2 *interrelatedness*
inverse ratio 108.2 *interrelatedness*
inverse sine 27.52 *trigonometric function*
inverse tangent 27.52 *trigonometric function*
inverse trigonometric function 27.52 *trigonometric function*
Inversion 192
inversion 192.1; 210.1 *calculation*; 224.1 *change*; 113.2 *oppositeness*; 17.12 *poetic language*; 303.12 *reversal*; 32.13 *structure*; 162.2 *symmetry operation*
invert 192.3; 113.15 *be opposite*; 224.8 *cause change*; 357.9 *demolish*; 20.9 *miscellaneous architectural features*; 32.26 *react*
invertebrate 75.1; **75.16**; 70.15 *of animals*; 70.4 *type of animal*
invertebrate chordate 75.1 *invertebrate*
invertebrate larva 75.13
Invertebrates 75
invertebrate zoologist 75.15; 70.11 *zoologist*
invertebrate zoology 75.14; 70.9 *animal science*
inverted 192.2; 57.11 *gymnastic*; 113.23 *opposite*
inverted comma 742.7 *punctuation*
inverted grip 57.5 *horizontal bar*
inverted hang 57.7 *stationary rings*
invertedly 761.13 *reversibly*
inverted order 192.1 *inversion*
inverted snobbery 622.3 *conceit*
inverter 39.34 *power supply*
invert sugar 32.13 *structure*
invest 14.5; **780.27**; 585.13 *be at war*; 381.4 *besiege*; 551.32 *dress*; 130.25 *enrol*; 787.1 *expend*; 368.7 *install*; 370.10 *introduce*; 7.21 *ordain*; 136.13 *qualify*; 776.2 *speculate*; 439.6 *store*
invested 551.29 *dressed*; 787.12 *expended*; 439.7 *stored*
investigate 464.12 *estimate*; 448.11 *experiment*; 4.20 *philosophize*; 705.17 *question*
investigated 705.16 *questioned*
investigation 448.1 *experiment*; 448.3 *experimentation*; 734.6 *interview*; 4.4 *philosophical investigation*; 705.2 *questioning*
investigation into first causes 4.4 *philosophical investigation*
investigative 448.8 *experimental*; 705.12 *questioning*
investigative journalism 739.2 *divulgence*
investigative journalist 739.4 *discloser*; 740.11 *newspaperman*
investigatively 448.14 *experimentally*; 705.23 *questioningly*
investigative reporting 741.3 *reporting*
investigator 644.3 *curious person*; 739.4 *discloser*; 448.5 *experimenter*; 4.10 *philosopher*; 705.9 *questioner*
invest in 14.5 *invest*; 777.1 *purchase*
investing 777.14 *buying*
investiture 551.2 *dressing*; 130.8 *enrolment*; 768.1 *giving*; 750.9 *grant*; 370.3 *introduction*; 7.9 *priesthood*
investment 551.2 *dressing*; 787.5 *expense*; 14.1 *finance*; 768.1 *giving*; 136.4 *permission*; 381.14 *siege*; 776.8 *speculation*; 439.1 *store*; 585.8 *warfare*
investment account 781.5 *wealth*
investment capital 352.4 *financial resources*
investment portfolio 352.4 *financial resources*
investments 352.4 *financial resources*; 781.5 *wealth*
investor 783.6 *depositor*; 440.7 *property man*; 777.12 *purchaser*; 787.8 *spender*; 14.3 *stockbroker*
invest with 768.5 *give*; 750.30 *grant*
invest with power 334.11 *give power*
inveteracy 632.1 *habit*
inveterate 632.14 *habituated*; 809.3 *impenitent*; 296.12 *olden*
inveterately 296.21 *archaically*
inveterate sinner 809.2 *impenitent person*
invidious 594.12 *hated*; 629.4 *jealous*; 242.1 *unpleasant*
invidiously 629.9 *jealously*
in view 97.10 *available*; 518.23, 520.1 *visible*; 520.11 *visibly*
invigilate 665.11 *care for*; 579.1 *manage*; 518.15 *watch*
invigilation 665.5 *watchfulness*
invigilator 518.11 *observer*
invigorate 338.3; **554.21**; 488.13 *arouse sensation*; 213.5 *make bigger*; 581.1 *refresh*; 393.5 *revive*; 336.8 *strengthen*
invigorated 581.4 *refreshed*
invigorating 338.5; 494.8 *cold*; 31.45 *fine*; 259.2 *healthful*; 581.3 *refreshing*; 37.17 *stimulating*; 336.4 *strengthening*
invigoratingly 581.8 *refreshingly*
invigoration 213.1 *increase*; 581.5 *refreshment*; 336.4 *strengthening*; 338.1 *vigour*
invincibility 336.1 *strength*
invincible 121.14 *best*; 383.12 *resisting*; 246.15 *victorious*
invincible ignorance 519.7 *figurative blindness*
invincibly 383.14 *resistingly*; 246.16 *successfully*; 121.17 *supremely*
in vindication 714.15
inviolability 336.1 *strength*
inviolable 225.7 *permanent*
inviolable place 252.5 *refuge*
inviolably 225.9 *permanently*
inviolate 204.7 *uncut*
Invisibility 521
invisibility 521.4; 736.1 *concealment*; 526.4 *disappearance*; 159.1 *littleness*; 696.11 *unintelligibility*
invisible 521.1; 526.7 *disappeared*; 519.13 *hidden*; 337.13 *insufficient*; 159.7 *little*; 696.1 *unintelligible*
invisible earnings 776.5 *commercial trade*
invisible goods 776.5 *commercial trade*
invisible imports 521.5 *invisible thing*
invisible ink 521.5 *invisible thing*
invisible man 737.8 *anonymity*
invisible mending 393.8 *repair*
invisibles 776.5 *commercial trade*
invisible thing 521.5

invisible trade 776.5 *commercial trade;* 13.5 *international trade*
invisibly **521.9**; 526.8 *fleetingly;* 159.9 *microscopically;* 737.16 *stealthily*
invitation 370.1 *admittance;* 397.1 *command;* 658.3 *courtesies;* 480.2 *flattery;* 483.2 *inducement;* 752.1 *offer;* 710.1 *request;* 742.6 *word*
invitational 710.9 *requesting*
invitatory 370.15 *receptive*
invite 658.10 *be courteous;* 654.11 *be sociable;* 397.9 *command;* 710.6 *request;* 370.9 *welcome*
invite difficulties 264.19 *have difficulty*
invite offers 752.9 *offer*
invite over 557.25 *provide food*
inviter 742.8 *signer*
inviting 617.8 *desirable;* 483.11 *motivational;* 752.17 *offered;* 480.19 *persuasive;* 241.1, 490.6 *pleasant;* 370.15 *receptive;* 710.9 *requesting;* 742.16 *signalling;* 654.15 *sociable;* 495.7 *tasty;* 312.21 *welcoming*
invitingly 483.14 *influentially;* 480.21 *persuasively;* 370.18 *receptively*
invocation 10.9 *prayer;* 710.1 *request;* 733.2 *salutation;* 11.5 *spell*
invocational 710.9 *requesting;* 10.21 *ritualistic;* 11.15 *witchlike*
invocatory 733.14 *vocative*
in vogue 551.36 *dressily;* 632.12 *established*
invoice 220.4, 790.4 *bill;* 710.7 *demand;* 220.8 *list;* 743.3 *means of identification;* 744.1 *record;* 789.9 *settle accounts;* 789.4 *statement*
invoiced 789.11 *accounted*
invoke 733.8 *appeal to;* 11.22 *conjure;* 10.20 *pray;* 710.6 *request;* 729.14 *speak to*
invoke a blessing 10.20 *pray*
involucre 78.3 *flower part;* 77.6 *leaf;* 550.4 *wrapping*
involuntarily 386.11 *compellingly;* 478.7 *extempore;* 387.11 *under subjection*
involuntariness 478.5 *spontaneity*
involuntary 386.9 *compelling;* 478.2 *spontaneous;* 387.9 *subject*
involuntary saving 790.8 *levy*
involuntary servitude 387.1 *subjection*
involute 27.40 *curve*
involution 210.1 *calculation;* 180.1 *convolution*
involutional 180.4 *convolutional*
involutional melancholia 36.13 *depression;* 461.6 *mental breakdown*
involve 405.11 *consist of;* 127.4 *include;* 694.12 *intend;* 373.13 *intercommunicate;* 135.10 *necessitate*
involved 342.18 *active;* 180.5 *ambiguous;* 764.5 *jointly possessing;* 412.12 *mixed;* 266.2 *obscure;* 484.15 *planning;* 264.12 *problematic;* 108.4 *related*
involved in 412.12 *mixed*
involved style 266.1 *obscurity*
involved with 590.12 *sensitive*
involvement 373.1 *connection;* 590.5 *good feeling;* 127.1 *inclusion;* 412.1 *mixture;* 764.2 *participation;* 108.1 *relatedness*
involve oneself 764.4 *have joint possession*
involving effort 576.11 *laborious*
invulnerability 253.1 *protection;* 252.1 *safety;* 336.1 *strength*
invulnerable **252.7**; 384.31 *entrenched;* 257.4 *hygienic;* 253.6 *secure;* 228.9 *stable*
invulnerably 252.11 *safely;* 228.12 *stably;* 336.14 *strongly;* 253.16 *surely*
in want 135.12 *in need;* 135.5 *necessitous;* 782.1 *poor*
inward 314.15 *entering;* 314.17 *in;* 172.7 *interior;* 172.8 *internal;* 172.12 *internalized;* 521.3 *private;* 67.11 *swimming*
inwardbound 312.19 *approaching*
inward dive 67.6 *diving*
inwardly **172.16**; 526.8 *fleetingly;* 314.17 *in;* 521.9 *invisibly*
inwardness 172.1 *interior;* 172.6 *internalization*
inwards 314.17 *in;* 521.9 *invisibly*
in water colours 19.30 *pictorially*
inweave 193.8 *interweave*
in what position? 705.25 *what?*
in what way? 705.25 *what?*
in-wick 68.10 *curling;* 68.13 *ice-skating*
in winter 292.18 *seasonally*
in with 569.9 *friends with*
in wonder 619.13 *wonderfully*
in wonderment 619.6 *wondering*
in working order 243.19 *in hand;* 346.10 *operational;* 95.8 *practical*
I object 704.13 *no!*
I/O device 40.7 *peripheral*
iodic 32.34 *elemental*
iodine 33.15 *essential element;* 394.3 *prophylactic*
iodometric 26.16 *micrometric*
iodometry 26.2 *micrometry*
iodous 32.34 *elemental*
iomáin 58.7 *hurling*
ion **28.66**; 28.50 *electric charge;* 39.5 *electrolytic conduction;* 159.2 *little thing;* 402.4 *matter*
ion-exchange chromatography 32.17 *analysis*
ion gauge 32.20 *surface chemistry*
Ionian mode 18.20 *key*
ionic 32.35 *combined;* 17.9 *metre*
ionically 32.46 *chemically*
ionic bond 32.11 *chemical bond*
ionic compound 32.7 *chemical compound*
Ionic order 20.8 *column*
ionization 32.14 *chemical reaction;* 28.66 *ion*
ionization chamber 28.93 *radiation detector*
ionization energy 28.66 *ion*
ionization potential 28.66 *ion*
ionize 32.26 *react*
ionizing radiation 28.70 *radioactivity*
ionographic printer 40.7 *peripheral*
ionosphere 31.8 *atmosphere;* 434.3 *atmospheric layers;* 692.15 *transmitted wave*
ionospheric 31.43 *atmospheric*
ionospheric disturbance 692.15 *transmitted wave*
ionospheric reflection 692.15 *transmitted wave*
ionospheric storm 692.15 *transmitted wave*
ionospheric wave 692.15 *transmitted wave*
ion pump 32.20 *surface chemistry*
iota 196.3 *fragment;* 159.3 *little piece;* 728.6 *suggestion;* 124.8 *trifle*
IOU 756.2 *guarantee;* 772.5 *loan;* 780.14 *paper money;* 253.2 *promise;* 755.2 *purchase contract*
ipecacuanha 394.6 *purgative*
ipse dixit 707.2 *statement*
ipsissima verba 111.1 *sameness*
ipso facto 93.22 *really*
IQ 442.3 *intelligence*
IQ meter 36.4 *psychometrics*
IQ test 36.6 *intelligence test*
IRA 586.14 *armed forces*
Ira 624.7 *gods and goddesses of anger*
IRA member 586.9 *guerrilla;* 662.10, 753.5 *seditionist*
Irangate 736.5 *evasion*
Iraqi Republican Guards 586.14 *armed forces*
irascibility **625.1**; 149.6 *abruptness;* 642.2 *caprice;* 751.1 *disagreement;* 626.3 *irritableness;* 365.9 *irritation;* 591.6 *oversensitivity*
irascible **625.4**; 149.9 *abrupt;* 701.8 *argumentative;* 659.6 *bad-mannered;* 642.1 *capricious;* 751.9 *disagreeing;* 626.7 *irritable;* 591.2 *oversensitive;* 641.2 *refractory*
irascible person **625.3**
irascibly **625.9**; 751.11 *in disagreement;* 626.14 *irritably;* 659.10 *rudely*
irate 594.13, 624.16 *angry*
irately 624.18 *angrily*
ire 594.5, 624.4 *anger*
ireful 624.16 *angry*
Ireland **85.10**
Irene and Vernon Castle 22.6 *famous dancers*
irenic 749.6 *pacificatory;* 589.7 *peaceful*
irenical 749.6 *pacificatory*
irenically 749.7 *pacifically*
irenicon 749.2 *peace offering*
irenics 749.1 *pacification;* 589.1 *peace*
irenic theology 589.1 *peace*
I repent 808.9 *sorry!*
iridesce 522.25 *light up*
iridescence 227.1 *changeableness;* 28.28 *colour;* 522.2 *quality of light;* 541.1 *variegation*
iridescent **541.7**; 227.13 *changeable;* 522.17 *lustrous*
iridescent cloud 31.20 *cloud appearance*
iridescently 227.15 *changeably;* 541.12 *variedly*
iridic 32.34 *elemental*
iridous 32.34 *elemental*
irimi nage 52.10 *aikido*
Iris 316.8 *messenger;* 332.13 *swift person*
iris 539.6 *blue thing;* 518.2 *eye;* 21.20 *stage lighting*
iris diaphragm 41.18 *exposure time;* 21.20 *stage lighting*
Irish accent 5.26 *dialect*
Irish bull 274.11 *grammatical error*
Irish dancing 22.1 *dancing*
Irish government 12.4 *governing body*
Irish Guard 586.12 *ceremonial troops*
Irish hockey 58.7 *hurling*
Irishism 5.26 *dialect;* 85.10 *Ireland*
Irish jig 22.4 *historic dancing*
Irishman 85.10 *Ireland*
Irish moss 82.3 *moss*
Irishness 85.10 *Ireland*
Irish setter 60.6 *sporting dog*
Irish shamrock 743.6 *national emblem*
Irish stew 25.44 *British dish;* 412.2 *mixed thing*
Irish wake 582.8 *after death;* 583.2 *funeral*
Irish water spaniel 60.6 *sporting dog*
Irish whiskey 558.7 *alcoholic drink*
irk 620.6 *be boring;* 240.5 *be inconvenient;* 264.22 *cause trouble;* 328.7 *disturb;* 261.6 *fatigue*
irksome 620.4 *boring;* 261.4 *fatiguing;* 240.1, 264.13 *inconvenient;* 242.1 *unpleasant*
irksomeness 620.1 *boredom*
iron 256.13 *clean;* 33.15 *essential element;* 28.59 *ferromagnetism;* 187.4 *flattener;* 557.11 *food content;* 638.16 *fortitude;* 56.4 *golf club;* 533.5 *grey thing;* 418.1 *hard;* 418.7 *hard substance;* 493.3 *heater;* 187.7 *make horizontal;* 365.16 *massage;* 421.11 *smooth;* 421.9 *smoother;* 638.3 *strong-willed;* 394.7 *tonic*
Iron Age 3.10 *past age;* 284.4 *prehistoric age*
Iron-Age 296.15 *primal*
Iron-Age man 296.7 *ancient people*
iron boot 814.15 *instrument of torture*
ironbound 420.2 *coarse*
ironbound coast 92.4 *coast;* 379.1 *trap*
ironclad 384.30 *defended;* 586.25 *historical naval ships*
iron club 56.4 *golf club*
iron constitution 259.3 *health*
Iron Cross 743.4 *insignia*
Iron Curtain 378.3 *barrier;* 372.6 *boundary;* 128.3 *exclusion zone;* 147.7 *interface*
Iron Curtain country 85.1 *country*
ironed 256.17 *cleaned;* 187.9 *flattened;* 421.2 *uniform*
iron-grey 533.1 *grey*
iron grip 360.1 *retention*
iron hand 647.2 *suppression;* 631.8 *treatment*
iron horse 320.12 *bicycle;* 321.4 *locomotive*
ironic 676.3 *affected;* 198.11 *double-edged;* 599.10 *humorous;* 668.14 *ridiculing*
ironical 676.3 *affected*
ironically 599.16 *humorously*
ironist 599.6 *humorist;* 676.2 *pretender*
iron lung 394.14 *hospital;* 359.2 *preserver*
Iron Maiden 814.15 *instrument of torture*
iron meteorite 29.20 *meteor*
ironmonger 778.13 *retailer*
ironmongery 356.7 *produce*
iron nerve 228.2 *determination*
iron-nerved 228.11 *determined*
iron out 265.16 *make easy;* 365.16 *massage;* 404.13, 421.11 *smooth;* 178.10 *straighten;* 409.19 *tidy*
iron out problems 713.6 *consult*
iron rations 557.7 *food;* 218.8 *insufficiency;* 436.1 *provision;* 687.2 *short rations*
iron rule 647.2 *suppression*
irons 814.14 *instrument of punishment;* 251.5 *means of restraint*
iron shot 56.3 *golf shots*
iron sickle 438.4 *prehistoric tool*
Ironsides 586.20 *cavalryman;* 59.15 *horse person*
ironstone 24.1 *ceramics*
iron sway 12.3 *governance*
iron throat 507.4 *sound maker*
ironware 356.7 *produce*
iron will 228.2 *determination;* 638.15 *will;* 635.2 *willpower*
iron-willed **635.7**; 228.11 *determined;* 638.3 *strong-willed*
irony 676.1 *affectedness;* 198.3 *duality;* 17.12 *poetic language;* 668.4 *ridicule;* 599.3 *wit*
irradiate 522.24 *light;* 359.5 *preserve;* 32.26 *react*
irradiation 359.1 *preservation*
irrational 27.72 *complex;* 27.6 *complex number;* 27.74 *divisible;* 103.1 *impossible;* 457.5 *lacking intellect;* 457.8 *nonhuman;* 194.8 *odd;* 702.7 *sophistic*
irrationality 461.1 *insanity;* 457.1 *lack of intellect;* 457.4 *nonhuman existence;* 702.1 *sophistry*
irrationally 103.11 *impossibly;* 457.12 *nonhumanly;* 702.14 *sophistically;* 457.11 *unintelligently*
irrational number 27.6 *complex number;* 194.2 *kind of number*
irreclaimable 809.3 *impenitent;* 766.16 *losing;* 804.11 *wicked*
irreclaimably 766.19 *irrecoverably*
irreconcilability 751.1 *disagreement*
irreconcilable 113.25 *contrary;* 751.9 *disagreeing*
irreconcilably 751.11 *in disagreement*
irrecoverable 103.3 *hopeless;* 766.16 *losing;* 284.18 *over*
irrecoverably **766.19**; 103.12 *hopelessly*
irredeemability 236.9 *badness*
irredeemable 236.3 *bad;* 809.3 *impenitent;* 766.16 *losing;* 611.5 *past hope;* 786.14 *unpaid;* 804.11 *wicked*
irredeemably 611.11 *hopelessly;* 766.19 *irrecoverably;* 804.18 *wickedly*
irreducible 255.16 *simple;* 723.6 *summary*
irreducibly 255.20 *homogenously*
irreflexive relation 27.63 *mathematical logic*
irrefutable 452.3 *decided*
irregardless 317.16 *how*
irregular **118.15**; **299.4**; **408.14**; 802.14 *abnormal;* 227.13 *changeable;* 32.33 *crystalline;* 300.17 *directional;* 133.8 *discontinuous;* 234.6 *distorted;* 584.9 *enlisted;* 657.10 *free;* 5.44 *grammatical;* 231.1 *imperfect;* 78.12 *of flowers;* 276.9 *periodic;* 420.1 *rough;* 586.8 *soldier;* 27.79 *spatial;* 16.56 *unauthorized;* 120.3 *unequal;* 453.7 *unreliable*
irregular forces 584.2 *the military*
irregular galaxy 29.7 *galaxy*
Irregularity 299
irregularity **299.1**; 802.4 *abnormality;* 227.1 *changeableness;* 133.1 *discontinuity;* 234.1 *distortion;* 114.1 *diversity;* 139.6 *exception;* 657.4 *freedom;* 16.35 *illegality;* 231.5 *imperfection;* 120.1 *inequality;* 408.2 *irregular order;* 420.6 *roughness;* 453.15 *unreliability*
irregularly **114.11**; **299.8**; 234.13 *asymmetrically;* 227.15 *changeably;* 133.17 *discontinuously;* 276.14 *for short periods;* 5.52 *grammatically;* 231.11 *imperfectly;* 408.27 *in disorder;* 420.14 *roughly;* 120.7 *unequally;* 453.26 *unreliably*
irregular motion 300.5 *circuition*
irregular order **408.2**
irregular polyhedron 27.46 *polyhedron*
irregulars 584.2 *the military*
irregular thing **299.3**
irregular union 796.4 *illicit love*
irrelation 109.1 *unrelatedness*
irrelative 100.8 *extraneous*
irrelatively 109.12 *irrelevantly*
irrelevance 270.2 *circumlocution;* 100.1 *extraneousness;* 618.5 *insignificance;* 124.5 *unimportance;* 109.1 *unrelatedness*
irrelevancy 100.1 *extraneousness;* 124.5 *unimportance;* 109.1 *unrelatedness*
irrelevant 270.4 *circumlocutory;* 100.8 *extraneous;* 618.11 *insignificant;* 124.1 *unimportant;* 109.6 *unrelated*
irrelevantly **109.12**; 100.18 *extraneously;* 618.20 *unexceptionally;* 124.14 *unimportantly*
irreligion 451.4 *unbelief*
irreligionist 451.5 *disbeliever*
irreligious 804.14 *impious*
irreligiously 804.20 *immorally*
irremediable 611.5 *past hope;* 236.4 *poor*
irremissible 804.11 *wicked*
irremovable 253.9 *fast;* 641.3 *unyielding*
irreparable 103.3 *hopeless;* 611.5 *past hope*
irreparable loss 766.1 *loss*

irreparably 103.12 *hopelessly*
irreplaceability 123.1 *importance*
irreplaceable 123.5 *important;* 235.3 *valuable*
irreprehensible 805.5 *innocent*
irrepressible 641.2 *refractory;* 380.6 *violent*
irreproachability 805.1 *innocence;* 230.3 *perfection;* 803.1 *virtue*
irreproachable 805.5 *innocent;* 230.1 *perfect;* 803.5 *virtuous*
irreproachably 805.11 *innocently;* 230.7 *perfectly;* 803.9 *virtuously*
irresistibility 386.1 *compulsion*
irresistible 395.12 *appealing;* 363.9 *attractive;* 386.9 *compelling;* 483.11 *motivational;* 480.19 *persuasive;* 334.13 *powerful*
irresistible force 386.1 *compulsion;* 331.11 *impulsion*
irresistible progress 302.15 *improvement*
irresistibly 363.13 *attractionally;* 386.11 *compellingly;* 395.14, 483.14 *influentially;* 480.21 *persuasively;* 334.18 *powerfully*
irresolute 227.14; 453.2; 754.7; 479.11 *equivocating;* 335.12 *impotent;* 339.5 *inert;* 757.8 *permitting;* 639.1 *vacillating;* 337.12 *weak-willed*
irresolutely 639.16; 754.9; 227.15 *changeably;* 335.14 *powerlessly;* 453.23 *uncertainly;* 337.14 *weakly;* 757.9 *with permission*
irresoluteness 453.11
irresolution 227.2; 754.3; 479.6 *equivocation;* 337.2 *indecisiveness;* 339.1 *inertness;* 453.11 *irresoluteness;* 326.3, 639.11 *vacillation*
irresponsibility 588.1 *anarchy;* 642.2 *caprice;* 459.1 *folly;* 639.12 *inconstancy;* 615.1 *rashness*
irresponsible 588.6 *anarchic;* 453.8, 642.1 *capricious;* 639.2 *changeable;* 615.4 *rash*
irresponsibly 588.8 *anarchically;* 453.27 *capriciously;* 615.6 *rashly*
irretrievable 766.16 *losing;* 611.5 *past hope*
irretrievable breakdown 357.4 *ruin*
irretrievable loss 766.1 *loss*
irretrievably 766.19 *irrecoverably*
irreverence 668.1 *disrespect*
irreverent 668.10 *disrespectful*
irreverential 668.10 *disrespectful*
irreverently 668.28 *disrespectfully*
irreversibility 641.6 *determination;* 302.15 *improvement;* 228.1 *stability*
irreversible 324.15 *direct;* 302.18 *ongoing;* 611.5 *past hope;* 32.38 *reactive;* 228.9 *stable;* 641.3 *unyielding*
irreversible reaction 32.14 *chemical reaction*
irreversibly 228.12 *stably*
irrevocability 452.16 *inevitability*
irrevocable 103.3 *hopeless;* 611.5 *past hope;* 228.9 *stable*
irrevocably 103.12 *hopelessly;* 452.25 *inevitably;* 228.12 *stably*
irrigate 90.8 *cause to flow;* 43.17 *farm;* 562.7 *make fertile;* 433.29 *water*
irrigation 43.5 *cultivation;* 433.7 *hydrotherapeutics;* 433.8 *watering*
irrigational 433.26 *wetting*
irrigation system 38.24 *water system*
irrigator 433.13; 43.10 *farm tool*
irriguous 433.26 *wetting*
irritability 488.2 *ability to sense;* 625.1 *irascibility;* 626.3 *irritableness;* 591.6 *oversensitivity*
irritable 626.7; 701.8 *argumentative;* 625.4 *irascible;* 591.2 *oversensitive;* 488.7 *susceptible*
irritableness 626.3
irritably 626.14; 701.17 *argumentatively;* 625.9 *irascibly;* 591.13 *oversensitively*
irritant 365.10 *frictional;* 408.11 *troublemaker*
irritate 607.8 *annoy;* 240.5 *be inconvenient;* 328.7 *disturb;* 261.6 *fatigue;* 365.15 *grind;* 625.8 *make irascible;* 626.12 *make irritable;* 380.9 *make violent;* 245.3 *make worse;* 342.17 *meddle;* 624.9 *offend*
irritated 328.12 *disturbed;* 624.15 *resentful;* 488.7 *susceptible*
irritating 607.5 *aggravating;* 240.1 *inconvenient;* 342.21 *meddling*
irritatingly 365.17 *abrasively;* 607.10 *annoyingly;* 328.18 *disturbingly;* 240.6 *inconveniently;* 624.17 *resentfully*
irritation 365.9; 607.2 *annoyance;* 240.3 *inconvenience;* 491.1 *pain;* 624.1 *resentment*
irrupt 314.10 *invade;* 329.1 *overstep*
irruption 314.3 *inroad;* 329.6 *overstepping;* 381.14 *siege*
irruptive 314.16 *invasive*
isangoma 11.4 *witch*
ISBN 743.3 *means of identification*
ISDN 40.14 *data transfer*
I see 446.25 *got it!*
isidium 84.6 *lichen*
isinglass 74.9 *fish product*
Isis 90.4 *British rivers*
I-ski 68.5 *ski equipment*
Islamic 7.16 *denominational*
Islamic text 7.12 *religious text*
Islamize 7.20 *preach*
island 92.2; 318.5 *crossing point;* 92.2 *island;* 185.2 *projection;* 86.1 *region*
island arc 30.20 *earth movement*
island chain 92.2 *island*
island continent 92.2 *island*
islander 92.11 *continental*
island group 92.2 *island*
island universe 29.7 *galaxy*
isle 92.2 *island*
Isle of Man TT 61.5 *motorcycle racing*
Isles of the Blest 477.8 *dreamland;* 8.11 *heaven*
islet 92.2 *island;* 86.1 *region*
isleted 92.11 *continental*
ism 450.2 *religious belief*
ISO-7 40.10 *character*
isoantibody 431.4 *blood*
isobar 31.4 *weather forecast*
isobaric 31.42 *barometric*
isochronal 298.11 *regular;* 285.10 *synchronized*
isochronally 285.13 *synchronously*
isochronism 285.3 *synchronism*
isochronous 298.11 *regular;* 285.10 *synchronized*
isochronously 285.13 *synchronously*
isocracy 12.1 *government*
isogamy 84.4 *reproductive body*
isogesis 719.1 *interpretation*
isogete 719.6 *interpreter*
isogloss 5.26 *dialect*
isokont 84.2 *algae*
isolate 128.7 *exclude;* 655.13 *ignore;* 257.6 *make hygienic;* 469.4 *pick;* 100.15 *separate;* 372.10 *set apart;* 197.20 *single out*
isolated 197.16 *alone;* 36.34 *introverted;* 655.10 *lonely;* 655.11 *secluded;* 737.9 *secret;* 100.11 *separate;* 118.16 *solitary;* 372.17 *unjoined;* 254.3 *vulnerable*
isolated case 197.2 *item*
isolated instance 139.6 *exception;* 197.2 *item*
isolate oneself 197.18 *be one*
isolation 197.5 *aloneness;* 36.19 *defence mechanism;* 128.3 *exclusion zone;* 257.1 *hygiene;* 394.3 *prophylactic;* 252.2 *protection;* 100.3 *separateness;* 655.3 *separation;* 372.2 *setting apart;* 109.1 *unrelatedness*
isolation block 46.9 *play*
isolationism 197.5 *aloneness;* 250.1 *freedom;* 566.11 *nation;* 85.4 *nationalism;* 4.7 *school of thought;* 372.3 *separateness;* 634.12 *shyness;* 109.1 *unrelatedness*
isolationist 197.16 *alone;* 4.11 *follower of a doctrine;* 250.9 *free;* 250.7 *free person;* 118.9 *hermit;* 197.8 *loner;* 85.14 *nationalist;* 4.14 *of a philosophy;* 372.8 *person who separates*
isolationist nation 85.1 *country*
isolation ward 35.10, 394.14 *hospital*
isolex 5.26 *dialect*
isomer 32.13 *structure*
isomerase 33.11 *enzyme*
isomeric 32.37 *structural*
isomerism 32.13 *structure*
isometric drawing 717.2 *reproduction*
isometric projection 717.2 *reproduction;* 27.48 *transformation*
isometrics 576.5 *exercise*
isomorphic 160.9 *formed*
isomorphism 160.1 *form*
isomorphous 160.9 *formed*
isophone 5.26 *dialect*
isopod 75.4 *arthropod*
isoprene rubber 32.21 *polymer*
isoprene unit 33.20 *terpene*
isopteran 76.10 *insectan*
ISO rating 41.10 *graininess*
isosceles 162.4 *symmetrical*
isosceles triangle 176.3 *angled figure;* 27.43 *triangle*
isospin 28.78 *quantum*
isostacy 30.18 *earth's crust*
isostatic 30.53 *solid-earth*
isostatic equilibrium 30.18 *earth's crust*
isotactic 32.44 *polymeric*
isotactic polymer 32.21 *polymer*
isotherm 31.4 *weather forecast*
isothermal 31.43 *atmospheric;* 31.42 *barometric*
isothermal change 28.39 *expansion*
isothermal layer 434.3 *atmospheric layers*
isotope 28.69; 402.4 *matter*
isotope effect 32.14 *chemical reaction*
isotrophic 111.12 *same*
isotrophically 111.18 *identically*
isotrophy 111.1 *sameness*
isotropic 750.14 *conforming*
isotropy 750.5 *conformity;* 119.3 *equalization*
I-spy 518.3 *observation*
Israel 756.4 *promised land*
Israfel 8.6 *angel*
issuance 377.1 *dispersion;* 315.1 *exit*
issue 447.2; 525.1 *appearance;* 525.12 *become visible;* 123.3 *chief thing;* 780.13 *coinage;* 377.16 *distribute;* 345.1 *effect;* 130.27, 315.10 *emerge;* 131.12 *end result;* 99.2 *essential content;* 315.1 *exit;* 701.4 *gist;* 389.4, 389.7 *leak;* 701.3 *line of argument;* 16.5 *litigation;* 780.24 *monetize;* 205.2 *particular;* 525.14 *present;* 356.3 *product;* 740.15 *publish;* 705.1 *question;* 741.13 *report;* 313.5 *set out;* 345.5 *show an effect;* 706.6 *solution;* 14.2 *stock exchange*
issue a caveat 711.5 *warn*
issue a command 397.9 *command*
issue a counterorder 708.16 *cancel out*
issue a D-notice 399.4 *censor*
issue a flat contradiction 708.11 *rebut*
issue a flat denial 708.11 *rebut*
issue a manifesto 707.17 *affirm;* 397.9 *command*
issue an edict 397.9 *command*
issue an injunction 397.10 *demand;* 251.8 *restrain*
issue an ultimatum 710.7 *demand*
issue a press release 707.17 *affirm*
issue a publication 740.15 *publish*
issue a public warning 711.5 *warn*
issue a statement 397.9 *command*
issue a suit 710.6 *request*
issue a supportive statement 707.19 *confirm*
issue a warning notice 397.10 *demand*
issue a warrant 397.10 *demand*
issued 377.22 *distributed;* 780.22 *monetary*
issue forth 130.27, 315.10 *emerge;* 313.5 *set out*
issue from 345.7 *follow from*
issue price 14.2 *stock exchange*
issuing 315.15 *outgoing;* 706.14 *solved*
issuing forth 525.1 *appearance*
isthmian 92.11 *continental;* 151.4 *narrow-leaved*
isthmus 191.3 *contracted thing;* 373.4 *means of connection;* 151.6 *narrow place;* 92.5 *peninsula*
I swear 454.13 *really!*
IT 693.6 *information technology*
it 698.6 *authenticity;* 480.3 *incentive;* 126.2 *original*
Italian dish 25.47
Italian friction hitch 62.3 *climbing technique*
Italian GP at Monza 61.2 *Formula 1 race*
Italian ryegrass 43.12 *crop*
Italian sonnet 17.7 *poem*
Italic 5.11 *family of languages*
italic 5.41 *lettered*
italicize 726.6 *emphasize;* 742.13 *punctuate*
italicized 742.17 *punctuated*
italics 726.1 *emphasis*
italic type 5.15 *type style*
itch 363.1 *attraction;* 492.13 *be touched by;* 617.1 *desire;* 488.11 *sense;* 327.24 *shake;* 260.13 *skin disease;* 488.3 *stimulus*
itch for 617.12 *desire*
itchiness 327.5 *restlessness;* 591.7 *soreness*
itching 593.5 *desire;* 327.5 *restlessness*
itching for 617.9 *desirous*
itch mite 76.3 *pest*
itchy 488.9 *exciting;* 327.16 *restless;* 591.3 *sore*
itchy feet 342.7 *restlessness*
item 197.2; 789.1 *accounts;* 222.6 *aspect;* 405.1 *component;* 447.2 *issue;* 402.5 *object;* 197.1 *one;* 205.2 *particular;* 356.3 *product;* 744.1 *record;* 21.8 *scene;* 93.2 *thing;* 127.2 *thing included*
itemization 220.1 *list;* 220.7 *listing*
itemize 406.9; 222.11 *circumstantiate;* 721.16 *define;* 703.16 *explain;* 220.8 *list;* 744.15 *register;* 139.24 *specify*
itemized 406.12; 789.10 *accounting;* 220.11 *listed*
itemized account 220.4 *bill*
items 406.5 *divisions;* 211.4 *extra;* 220.1 *list*
iterate 112.17; 276.10 *be periodical;* 111.11 *be regular;* 640.6 *persevere*
iterated 112.10; 640.11 *steady*
iteration 112.2; 27.28 *algorithm;* 640.3 *constancy;* 726.1 *emphasis;* 276.5 *recurrent period*
iterative 726.3 *emphatic;* 276.8 *periodical;* 112.12 *repetitious*
it follows that 750.36 *accordingly;* 345.12 *with the effect of*
I think not 708.23 *no!*
itinerary 220.5 *list of appointments;* 475.3 *plan;* 693.5 *reference book;* 317.2 *route*
it's all over 582.24 *I'm dying!*
it's curtains 582.24 *I'm dying!*
itself 139.12 *I*
it serves you right 385.7 *revenge!*
itsy-bitsy 159.7 *little*
itty-bitty 159.7 *little*
ITV 692.24 *television broadcasting*
IUCD 563.3 *birth control*
IUD 563.3 *birth control*
Ivan Lendl 63.7 *famous tennis players*
I've had it 582.24 *I'm dying!*
IVF 561.3 *propagation*
ivories 18.16 *musical note;* 425.11 *tooth*
ivory 418.7 *hard substance;* 522.21 *light;* 522.14 *light colour;* 421.8 *smooth thing;* 531.1 *white;* 531.9 *white thing*
ivory black 532.8 *black pigment*
ivory-carving 19.12 *sculpture*
ivory tower 736.6 *privacy;* 252.5 *refuge;* 655.5 *solitary place*
Ivy League 6.13 *university*
I/we surrender! 388.7
Ixion's wheel 307.6 *rotator*

jab 353.5 *attempt;* 331.13 *blow;* 52.11 *fight;* 331.3, 381.18 *hit;* 491.11 *inflict pain;* 491.3 *injury;* 394.2 *medicine;* 492.3 *press;* 331.14 *sporting hit;* 52.9 *tae kwon do;* 492.11 *touch*
jabbed 52.14 *combat*
jabber 731.7 *be talkative;* 52.4 *boxer;* 5.5 *nonstandard language;* 731.3 *talk*
jabberer 731.4 *talker*
jabbering 731.3 *talk;* 731.5 *talkative*
jabbing 52.2 *boxing;* 52.14 *combat*
jabot 551.14 *neckwear*
jack 780.2 *cash;* 743.7 *flag;* 51.1 *green bowling;* 366.9 *lifter;* 567.16 *male animal;* 71.17 *male mammal;* 320.21 *miscellaneous motoring terms;* 438.1 *tool*
jackal 664.3 *sycophant*
jackass 459.3 *foolish person;* 71.17 *male mammal*
jackboot 647.2 *suppression;* 631.8 *treatment*
jackboots 551.19 *footwear*
Jack Buchanan 22.6 *famous dancers*
jackdaw 72.6 *songbird*
jackdaw in peacock's feathers 700.15 *deceiver;* 486.10 *unskilled person*
jacket 551.11; 550.5 *body covering;* 550.13 *casing;* 410.5 *packet*
Jack Frost 31.36 *frost;* 494.5 *ice*
jack-high 51.9 *bowls*
Jack-in-office 660.12 *impudent person;* 579.16 *official*
jack-in-office 400.4 *absolute ruler*
jack it in 605.5 *resign;* 355.2 *withdraw*
Jack Ketch 814.17 *punisher*
jackknife 425.10 *knife*
jack of all trades 342.10 *busy person;* 485.4 *skilled person;* 578.1 *worker*
jack-o'-lantern 522.9 *firefly;* 96.2 *illusion*
jack plane 23.11 *woodworking tool*
jackpot 813.2 *prize;* 765.5 *profit*
jack-pudding 21.32 *clown*

jackscrew 366.9 *lifter*
Jack shit 195.2 *nothing*
jackstraw 96.5 *insubstantial person*
Jack Tar 323.7 *nautical person*
jack up 213.5 *make bigger;* 366.1 *raise*
Jacobean 23.7 *furniture style;* 296.14 *historic*
Jacobean tragedy 21.11 *tragedy*
Jacobin 662.6 *nonconformist*
Jacobins 12.6 *political party*
Jacob's ladder 304.9 *ladder*
Jacquard loom 42.4 *weaving*
Jacques Cousteau 91.6 *oceanographer*
jactation 327.5 *restlessness*
jactitate 327.21 *be agitated*
jactitation 327.5 *restlessness*
jaculate 330.20 *propel*
jaculation 330.1 *propulsion;* 330.3 *throwing*
jaculatory 330.18 *projectile*
Jacuzzi™ 256.6, 410.12 *bath;* 493.8 *hot place;* 365.6 *massage;* 433.11 *wash*
jade 620.6 *be boring;* 596.7 *cause dislike;* 261.6 *fatigue;* 538.1 *green;* 538.11 *green thing;* 59.1 *horse;* 568.8 *nasty woman;* 59.4 *saddle horse*
jaded 261.2, 620.5 *bored;* 138.22 *commonplace*
jadedness 261.7 *fatigue*
jag 690.14 *drinking bout*
jagged 420.2 *coarse;* 183.7 *notched;* 425.4 *toothed*
jagged edge 425.7 *sharp point*
jaggedly 183.12; 420.14 *roughly*
jaggedness 420.6 *roughness*
jaggy 420.2 *coarse;* 183.7 *notched*
jaguar 541.5 *variegated thing*
Jah 8.3 *God*
jahannan 8.12 *hell*
jail 309.4 *closed place;* 386.3 *coercive methods;* 309.10 *enclose;* 655.13 *ignore;* 815.9 *imprison;* 172.2 *inside;* 814.14 *instrument of punishment;* 172.15 *keep inside;* 655.4 *place of confinement;* 815.1 *prison;* 814.1 *punish;* 226.5 *resting place*
jailbird 251.7 *charge;* 806.4 *guilty person;* 16.40 *lawbreaker;* 815.5 *prisoner*
jailbreak 389.1 *escape*
jail-breaker 389.3 *escaper*
jail cell 815.3 *prison cell*
jailed 309.15 *enclosed*
jailer 251.6 *lawmaker;* 397.6 *person in command;* 309.5 *person who closes;* 815.6 *prison officer*
jail fever 260.6 *infection*
jailhouse 815.1 *prison*
jailhouse lawyer 444.6 *arguer*
Jain 7.6 *non-Christian*
Jainist text 7.12 *religious text*
jainpan 320.6 *litter*
jakes 560.5 *faeces;* 767.7 *toilet*
jalopy 320.16 *car*
jam 226.6 *cease;* 208.11 *crowd;* 294.8 *delay;* 294.3 *delayed action;* 143.3, 222.4 *difficult circumstances;* 232.6 *fill;* 430.6 *gelatin;* 478.3 *improvise;* 301.9 *make motionless;* 191.5 *make smaller;* 247.9 *malfunction;* 62.9 *mountaineer;* 505.10 *muffle;* 378.2 *obstacle;* 221.2, 264.5 *predicament;* 25.42 *preserve;* 359.3 *preserved thing;* 376.21 *scrum;* 406.7 *stuff;* 498.2 *sweetener;* 18.37 *syncopate;* 208.4 *throng*
Jamaican ganja 691.6 *drug*
Jamaica rum 558.7 *alcoholic drink*
jambalaya 25.43 *US dish*
jamboree 601.1 *celebration;* 490.4 *pleasurable things*
jam doughnut 25.36 *cake*
James 36.29 *psychologist*
James-Lange theory 36.3 *psychiatric treatment*
jam in 314.12 *flood in;* 368.3 *impact*
jamjar 410.15 *pot*
jammed 317.15 *accessible;* 208.10 *crowded;* 152.2 *dense;* 232.8 *full;* 294.10 *held up;* 309.13 *stopped*
jammed tight 232.8 *full*
jamming 50.12 *canoeing;* 62.3 *climbing technique;* 505.3 *inaudibility;* 18.2 *music making;* 50.10 *sailing;* 521.6 *that which makes invisible*
jamming cleat 50.3 *parts of a sailing boat*
jamming stroke 50.6 *canoeing*
jammy 430.9 *gelatinous;* 235.1 *worthy*
jammy swine 107.16 *fluke!*
jam-packed 208.10, 376.50 *crowded;* 232.8 *full*
jam sandwich 320.17 *police car;* 25.11 *sandwich*
jam session 22.1 *dancing;* 478.4 *improvisation*
jam tart 25.36 *cake*
jam tomorrow 283.3 *future condition;* 477.7 *idealism;* 480.8 *incentive*
JANET 40.15 *network*
jangle 513.4 *be strident;* 517.10 *lack harmony;* 510.10 *ring*
jangling 517.1 *dissonance;* 517.7 *dissonant*
janissary 586.12 *ceremonial troops*
janitor 401.3 *attendant;* 518.11 *observer*
Janrt 36.29 *psychologist*
January 494.7 *cold weather*
Janus 198.3 *duality;* 479.9 *equivocator*
Janus-faced 699.30 *duplicitous*
Janus-like 198.11 *double-edged*
japan 532.11 *blacken;* 532.8 *black pigment;* 550.24 *coat;* 550.3 *coating*
Japanese garden 44.2 *garden*
Japanese GP at Suzuka 61.2 *Formula 1 race*
Japanese rising sun 743.6 *national emblem*
japanning 23.1 *furniture*
jape 599.5 *joke*
japer 697.4 *buffoon*
jar 513.4 *be strident;* 596.7 *cause dislike;* 594.16 *cause hate;* 24.8 *ceramic object;* 203.3 *container;* 558.2 *drink;* 327.9, 327.23 *jolt;* 517.10 *lack harmony;* 359.2 *preserver;* 410.11 *vessel*
jardinière 44.4 *nursery*
jargon 729.1 *faculty of speech;* 5.20 *jargon word;* 139.10 *specialized language;* 5.3 *spoken language;* 694.4 *type of meaning*
jargonal 5.39 *of language*
jargonish 5.39 *of language*
jargonistic 5.39 *of language*
jargonize 5.45 *use language*
jargon word 5.20
jarhead 586.28 *marines;* 585.11 *recruit*
jarring 327.19 *convulsive;* 517.1 *dissonance;* 517.7 *dissonant;* 544.9 *inelegant;* 513.7 *strident*
jasmine 502.2 *fragrant thing*
jasmine tea 558.3 *tea*
Jason 323.7 *nautical person*
jaspé 541.9 *striped*
jasper 541.5 *variegated thing*
Jataka 7.12 *religious text*
jaundice 465.12 *bias;* 629.1 *jealousy;* 466.3 *prejudice;* 537.6 *yellowness*
jaundiced 466.10 *discriminatory;* 629.4 *jealous;* 260.21 *unhealthy;* 465.8 *unjust;* 537.4 *yellow-faced*
jaundiced eye 465.3 *injustice;* 629.1 *jealousy*
jaundiced look 629.1 *jealousy*
jaundiced view 629.1 *jealousy*
jaundice-eyed 629.4 *jealous*
jauntily 598.9 *cheerfully*
jauntiness 598.3 *cheerfulness*
jaunty 598.1 *cheerful*
java 558.4 *coffee*
Java man 296.7 *ancient people;* 566.3 *early human*
javelin 330.10 *ball;* 47.2 *field events;* 587.6 *historical missile weapon;* 587.8 *sharp weapon*
javelin carrying 47.2 *field events*
javelin throw 47.2 *field events*
javelin thrower 47.3 *athlete;* 330.14 *thrower*
javelin throwing 47.2 *field events*
jaw 731.7 *be talkative;* 525.3 *external appearance;* 169.1 *side;* 731.3 *talk*
jawbreaker 498.4 *confectionery;* 418.7 *hard substance;* 5.17 *word*
jawbreaking 264.12 *problematic*
jaw-jaw 731.3 *talk*
jawless fish 74.2 *fish*
jaws 557.16 *eating utensil*
jaws of death 254.5 *danger;* 582.1 *death*
jaws of life 320.21 *miscellaneous motoring terms*
jay 731.4 *talker*
Jaycee 776.11 *chamber of commerce member;* 13.9 *economist*
jazz 18.8; 18.33
jazz band 18.26 *musical group*
jazzed up 213.7 *increased*
jazz-funk 18.9 *popular music*
jazzman 18.24 *musician*
jazz up 213.5 *make bigger*
JCB™ 38.29 *construction equipment;* 369.10 *excavator*
JCL 40.9 *programming language*
J-cloth™ 256.11 *cleaning cloth*
jealous 629.4; 593.20 *amorous;* 538.5 *green-eyed;* 594.10 *hating;* 590.13 *passionate;* 624.15 *resentful;* 683.4 *selfish*
jealously 629.9; 594.18 *hatefully;* 593.30 *lovingly;* 624.17 *resentfully;* 683.8 *selfishly*
jealousness 629.1 *jealousy*
Jealousy 629
jealousy 629.1; 590.6 *bad feeling;* 538.14 *green-eyed monster;* 594.1 *hate;* 624.1 *resentment;* 593.2 *romantic love;* 683.1 *selfishness*
Jean Lafitte 774.9 *plunderer*
jeans 657.6 *informal dress;* 551.9 *trousers*
jeepers 712.11 *miscellaneous euphemisms*
jeepers-creepers 712.16 *euphemisms*
jeer 659.3 *act of discourtesy;* 512.2, 512.5 *catcall;* 753.7 *complain;* 514.7 *cry of disapproval;* 753.3 *gesture of protest;* 514.14 *hiss;* 660.29 *ridicule;* 670.23 *show disapproval;* 670.9 *show of disapproval;* 668.6, 668.25 *taunt*
jeer at 621.6 *deride*
jeer capstan 366.9 *lifter*
jeered 670.35 *hissed*
jeering 512.7 *catcalling;* 659.1 *discourtesy;* 514.19 *hissing;* 621.1 *mockery;* 753.9 *protesting;* 668.15 *taunting*
jeeringly 659.10 *rudely*
jeers 366.9 *lifter*
Jehovah 8.3 *God*
Jehovah's Witness 7.5 *Christian*
Jehu 332.13 *swift person*
jejunal 172.10 *visceral*
jejune 218.1 *insufficient;* 497.5 *tasteless*
jejuneness 497.1 *dilution*
jejunum 172.4 *insides*
Jekyll and Hyde 198.3 *duality;* 113.3 *opposites*
jell 416.8 *be dense;* 418.10 *solidify*
jelled 416.7 *condensed;* 430.9 *gelatinous*
jellied 430.9 *gelatinous*
jellied eel 25.16 *fish dish;* 74.8 *food fish*
jellification 430.1 *viscosity*
jellify 416.8 *be dense;* 430.11 *thicken*
jelling 416.7 *condensed*
jelly 25.35 *dessert;* 430.6 *gelatin;* 25.42 *preserve;* 359.3 *preserved thing;* 359.2 *preserver;* 498.2 *sweetener;* 430.11 *thicken*
jelly bean 25.41 *sweet*
jellyfish 70.5 *aquatic animal;* 614.2 *coward;* 161.2 *shapeless thing;* 337.4 *weakling*
jelly fungi 83.3 *fungi*
jelly-like 430.9 *gelatinous*
jelly-likeness 430.1 *viscosity*
jelly mould 410.16 *crockery*
jemmy 438.1 *tool*
jennet 59.4 *saddle horse*
jenny 71.18 *female mammal*
jeopardize 254.10 *endanger*
jeopardy 107.1 *chance;* 254.5 *danger*
jeremiad 733.1 *address*
jerid 587.8 *sharp weapon*
jerk 362.3; 327.21 *be agitated;* 299.6 *be irregular;* 420.11 *be rough;* 22.2 *dance;* 459.3 *foolish person;* 331.1 *impel;* 299.1 *irregularity;* 327.9, 327.23 *jolt;* 362.13 *pull at;* 327.24 *shake;* 330.23 *throw;* 486.10 *unskilled person*
jerkily 327.29; 299.8 *irregularly*
jerkin 551.11 *jacket*
jerkiness 327.1 *agitation;* 133.1 *discontinuity;* 299.1 *irregularity*
jerking 299.4 *irregular*
jerkwater 122.13 *insignificant;* 124.4 *trivial;* 87.14 *urban*
jerkwater engine 321.4 *locomotive*
jerkwater town 122.7 *inferior thing;* 655.5 *solitary place;* 87.10 *village*
jerky 327.19 *convulsive;* 133.8 *discontinuous;* 299.4 *irregular*
jeroboam 410.14 *bottle*
jerry 560.14, 767.7 *toilet*
jerry-built 424.1 *brittle;* 486.4 *bungled;* 231.2 *incomplete;* 122.14 *poor;* 124.4 *trivial;* 254.2 *unsafe;* 337.8 *weak*
jerry-built house 424.3 *brittle thing*
jerrycan 320.21 *miscellaneous motoring terms*
jersey 49.3 *basketball equipment;* 551.13 *sweater;* 46.3 *uniform*
Jerusalem 173.4 *centre of activity;* 10.13 *shrine*
Jerusalem Bible 7.12 *religious text*
Jesse James 774.8 *thief*
jest 599.13 *be humorous;* 668.9 *butt;* 599.5 *joke;* 124.8 *trifle*
jester 697.4 *buffoon;* 21.32 *clown;* 599.6 *humorist*
jester's cap 551.15 *headgear*
jesting 599.3 *wit*
Jesuit 702.6 *sophist*
jesuitic 702.7 *sophistic*
jesuitically 702.14 *sophistically*
Jesuitism 699.4 *spuriousness*
jesuitry 702.1 *sophistry*
Jesus 8.4 *God the Son*
Jesus boots 551.19 *footwear*
Jesus Christ 8.4 *God the Son;* 712.15 *miscellaneous swearwords*
Jesus freak 450.5 *believer;* 7.5 *Christian*
Jesus wept 712.15 *miscellaneous swearwords*
JET 334.8 *nuclear power*
jet 532.1 *black;* 532.9 *black thing;* 523.4 *dark thing;* 371.22 *disgorgement;* 334.4 *energy;* 371.14 *let out;* 315.2 *outflow;* 330.12 *propellant;* 61.9 *race;* 315.11 *run out;* 68.4 *skiing technique;* 304.17 *spring up;* 332.11 *swift thing;* 304.2 *upturn*
jet-black 532.1 *black;* 523.10 *dark-coloured*
jeté 22.9 *ballet steps*
jet engine 38.11 *engine*
jet flight 332.11 *swift thing*
jet lag 322.1 *aviation*
jet-lagged 261.1 *fatigued*
jet-propelled 330.19 *propelled;* 332.1 *swift*
jet propulsion 334.4 *energy;* 330.2 *method of propulsion*
jetsam 767.3 *disposable things;* 316.10 *transferred thing*
jet set 573.2 *aristocracy;* 295.6 *avant-garde;* 235.7 *elite;* 553.6 *fashionable élite*
jet-setter 342.10 *busy person;* 553.6 *fashionable élite;* 490.3 *pleasure-seeker*
jetstream 434.4 *air flow;* 31.10 *air movement*
jetting 61.6 *motor-racing terms*
jettison 470.2 *discard;* 767.9 *dispose of;* 371.20 *eviction;* 415.10 *lighten;* 355.1 *relinquish;* 350.6 *stop using;* 371.13 *throw away*
jettisoned 350.4 *disused;* 355.5 *relinquished*
jet turn 68.4 *skiing technique*
jetty 378.3 *barrier;* 532.1 *black;* 185.2 *projection;* 38.24 *water system*
jeu de paume 63.1 *tennis*
jeune premier 21.24 *actor*
jeune première 21.23 *role*
jeunesse dorée 781.11 *the rich*
Jew 7.6 *non-Christian*
jewel 545.3 *attractive female;* 307.4 *axle;* 235.8 *exceller;* 797.17 *good thing;* 485.3 *masterpiece*
jewel in the crown 593.11 *loved one;* 622.12 *object of pride;* 738.7 *showpiece;* 797.9 *the best*
jeweller 578.2 *artisan;* 542.8 *decorator*
jewellery 542.7
jewellery box 410.6 *box*
Jewish 7.16 *denominational*
Jewish ghetto 87.7 *city district*
Jewish text 7.12 *religious text*
Jewtown 87.7 *city district*
jib 639.6 *hesitate;* 50.3 *parts of a sailing boat;* 637.7 *refuse;* 303.6 *shrink back;* 634.4 *shy;* 325.8 *sidestep*
jib at 709.5 *refuse*
jibbering 266.2 *obscure;* 731.5 *talkative*
jibberish 266.1 *obscurity*
jibbing 634.12 *shyness*
jibe 750.27 *fit;* 668.6 *taunt*
jibe at 668.25 *taunt*
jibing 668.15 *taunting*
jiffy 280.3 *instant*
jig 55.2 *artificial fly;* 22.15 *dance;* 22.4 *historic dancing;* 362.3 *jerk;* 327.9 *jolt;* 160.2 *prototype;* 362.13 *pull at;* 21.8 *scene;* 327.24 *shake;* 700.13 *snare*
jig about 22.15 *dance*
jigger 24.6 *ceramic workshop;* 410.13 *drinking vessel;* 321.4 *locomotive;* 24.11 *make ceramics;* 76.3 *pest;* 327.24 *shake*
jiggery-pokery 702.4 *quibbling;* 700.7 *tricking*
jigget 327.9 *jolt;* 327.24 *shake*
jiggle 362.3 *jerk;* 362.13 *pull at;* 327.24 *shake*
jiggler 327.14 *agitator*

jigsaw 374.2 *cooperation;* 438.1 *tool;* 23.11 *woodworking tool*
jigsaw piece 405.3 *unit*
jihad 585.1 *war*
jill 71.18 *female mammal*
jillion 194.3 *large number;* 201.11 *million;* 208.7 *myriad*
jillions 208.2 *multitude*
jilt 479.9 *equivocator;* 604.7 *thwart;* 355.2 *withdraw*
jilted 604.9 *disappointed;* 596.9 *disliked;* 594.12 *hated;* 355.5 *relinquished*
jilter 355.4 *deserter*
jim-dandy 797.1 *good;* 797.17 *good thing*
jimjams 690.16 *alcoholism*
Jimmy 564.9 *British inhabitant;* 567.3 *male title of address*
Jimmy Connors 63.7 *famous tennis players*
Jimmy Hix 201.2 *six*
Jimmy Riddle 560.3 *urination*
jingle 510.10 *ring;* 510.2 *ringing*
jingles 17.6 *poetry*
jingling 510.7 *ringing*
jingo 466.7 *bigot;* 5.21 *catchword*
jingoism 585.5 *bellicosity;* 566.11 *nation;* 85.4 *nationalism;* 466.4 *social discrimination*
jingoist 466.7 *bigot;* 586.6 *militarist;* 85.14 *nationalist*
jingoistic 586.33 *combative;* 466.10 *discriminatory;* 85.16 *national;* 5.39 *of language*
jingoistically 586.41 *aggressively;* 85.19 *nationally;* 466.17 *prejudicially*
jinn 70.7 *legendary beast*
jinni 11.11 *ghost*
jinx 798.11 *be evil;* 11.21 *bewitch;* 249.11 *cause adversity;* 798.4 *evil power;* 236.11 *harmfulness;* 712.4 *malediction;* 11.5 *spell*
jinxed 11.19 *bewitched;* 798.10 *inauspicious;* 712.10 *maledictive*
jinxed again 798.15 *bad luck!*
jitterbug 22.2, 22.15 *dance;* 22.5 *dancer;* 591.9 *oversensitive person*
jitteriness 639.13 *timidity*
jitters 327.1 *agitation*
jittery 327.15 *agitated;* 612.8 *fearful;* 639.3 *timid*
jive 22.2, 22.15 *dance;* 18.8 *jazz*
jiver 22.5 *dancer*
jo 593.9 *lover*
Joan of Arc 586.10 *woman soldier*
Job 782.10 *poor person*
job 576.3; 346.3, 776.6 *business;* 40.19 *computing terms;* 340.2 *deed;* 143.4 *employment;* 308.10 *opportunity;* 576.2 *task;* 774.3 *theft;* 354.2 *undertaking*
job allocation 770.1 *allocation*
jobber 755.4 *contractor;* 776.10 *trader;* 778.12 *wholesaler*
jobbery 645.1 *cunning*
jobbing 776.4 *trade*
job description 15.2 *industrial negotiations*
job due yesterday 262.4 *haste*
job flexibility 15.2 *industrial negotiations*
jobless 341.3 *inactive;* 580.7 *leisurely;* 350.3 *not wanted;* 343.2 *not working*
joblessness 341.1 *inaction;* 580.3 *unemployment*
job lot 412.3 *miscellany*
job of work 576.2 *task*
job satisfaction 813.1 *reward*
Job's comforter 602.4 *depressing person;* 611.3 *hopeless person*
jobseeker's allowance 392.4 *social assistance*
job-share 398.7 *delegate*
job sharing 770.1 *allocation;* 398.3 *delegation*
jobsworth 579.16 *official*
job training 6.2 *educational system*
job well done 622.7 *satisfaction*
Jock 564.9 *British inhabitant;* 567.3 *male title of address*
jockette 59.15 *horse person*
jockey 645.5 *be cunning;* 631.11 *conduct oneself;* 59.15 *horse person*
jockey cap 551.15 *headgear*
jockeying 631.9 *tactics*
jockeying for position 631.9 *tactics*
jockey's colours 743.5 *uniform*
jockey shorts 551.18 *underwear*
jockstrap 551.25 *accessories;* 552.4 *dishabille;* 47.4 *sports equipment;* 413.5 *supporting garment;* 551.18 *underwear*
jocose 599.10 *humorous*
jocular 599.10 *humorous;* 697.5 *nonsensical*
jodan-uke 52.8 *karate*
jodhpurs 551.9 *trousers*
Jodrell Bank 29.23 *observatory*
joe 566.7 *person*
Joe Bloggs 216.7 *average person;* 138.9 *everyman;* 566.7 *person*
Joe Public 216.7 *average person;* 138.9 *everyman;* 566.9 *group;* 574.1 *plebeian*
Joe Six-Pack 138.9 *everyman*
Joe Soap 216.7 *average person;* 566.7 *person*
joey 71.19 *young mammal*
jog 331.13 *blow;* 576.9 *exercise;* 300.12 *gait;* 742.11 *gesture;* 331.1 *impel;* 362.3 *jerk;* 327.9, 327.23 *jolt;* 483.9 *motivate;* 362.13 *pull at;* 333.10 *slow motion;* 300.15 *walk*
joggers 551.9 *trousers*
jogging 576.5 *exercise;* 257.1 *hygiene;* 244.9 *physical improvement*
jogging suit 47.4 *sports equipment;* 551.10 *suit*
joggle 331.13 *blow;* 331.1 *impel;* 362.3 *jerk;* 327.9, 327.23 *jolt;* 362.13 *pull at*
joggling 327.18 *shaky*
jog on 302.6 *march on*
jog one's memory 462.13 *remind*
jog suit 551.10 *suit*
jog trot 300.12 *gait;* 333.10 *slow motion*
jog-trot 333.1 *move slowly*
john 560.13 *lavatory;* 767.7 *toilet*
John Barleycorn 690.12 *alcohol;* 558.7 *alcoholic drink*
John Brown 662.10 *seditionist*
John Bull 564.9 *British inhabitant;* 85.9 *England;* 574.1 *plebeian*
John Doe 138.9 *everyman;* 566.7 *person;* 456.4 *unknown person*
John McEnroe 63.7 *famous tennis players*
John Newcombe 63.7 *famous tennis players*
Johnny 567.3 *male title of address*
johnny 563.3 *birth control*
Johnny-come-lately 294.4 *latecomer;* 295.8 *new arrival*
Johnny on the spot 293.4 *early comer*
John Q. Public 216.7 *average person;* 138.9 *everyman*
John Smith and Pocahontas 569.7 *famous friendships*
Johnsonese 542.2 *affectation;* 266.1 *obscurity*
Johnsonian 266.2 *obscure;* 542.10 *ornate*
John Thomas 561.8 *organs of reproduction*
joie de vivre 597.1 *happiness;* 490.1 *physical pleasure*
join 747.16; 492.12 *abut;* 211.6 *add;* 197.19 *become one;* 267.7 *cause to adhere;* 374.5 *combine;* 232.4 *complete;* 405.10 *compose;* 132.15 *concatenate;* 373.11 *connect;* 314.14 *enrol;* 764.4 *have joint possession;* 570.16 *join in marriage;* 147.18 *juxtapose;* 111.8 *make the same;* 312.8 *meet;* 376.44 *put together;* 393.1 *repair;* 211.7 *support*
join a charmed circle 251.8 *restrain*
join a consortium 755.5 *contract*
join a shooting party 60.7 *shoot*
join battle 585.14 *battle;* 113.19 *confront*
joined 23.16; 211.8 *additional;* 223.19 *associated;* 374.7 *combined;* 373.15 *connected;* 376.48 *cumulate;* 127.8 *included;* 147.10 *juxtaposed;* 570.21 *married;* 405.7 *modular;* 108.4 *related;* 197.13 *whole*
joiner 578.2 *artisan;* 23.13 *carpenter;* 654.6 *social person*
joinery 23.8 *woodwork*
join forces 376.41 *band together;* 747.14 *join with*
join forces with 374.6 *come together*
join hands 374.6 *come together*
join hands with 747.14 *join with*
join in 97.12 *attend;* 342.16, 654.11 *be sociable;* 764.4 *have joint possession;* 45.6 *participate;* 69.10 *play;* 2.15 *socialize;* 747.13 *work together*
joining 211.1 *addition;* 373.1 *connection;* 492.6 *contiguity;* 23.16 *joined;* 147.3 *juxtaposition*
joining of forces 747.4 *joint operation*
joining together 376.1 *assembly;* 374.1 *combination*
joining up 585.7 *war measures*
join in holy wedlock 570.16 *join in marriage*
join in marriage 570.16
join one's fortunes to 747.14 *join with*
joint 747.18; 750.11 *allied;* 23.10 *carpenter's term;* 374.7 *combined;* 373.14 *connective;* 492.6 *contiguity;* 691.6 *drug;* 30.20 *earth movement;* 764.5 *jointly possessing;* 373.4 *means of connection;* 565.8 *shelter*
joint action 747.4 *joint operation;* 764.2 *participation*
joint bank account 764.1 *joint possession*
Joint Chiefs of Staff 584.5 *military staff*
joint consultation committee 15.4 *industrial dispute*
joint control 747.5
joint dominion 12.3 *governance*
jointed 55.8 *angling;* 176.7 *angular;* 75.18 *arthropodous;* 23.16 *joined*
jointed plugs 55.2 *artificial fly*
joint effort 747.4 *joint operation*
jointer 23.11 *woodworking tool*
Joint European Torus 28.94 *particle accelerator*
joint government 764.1 *joint possession*
join the angels 582.15 *die*
join the army 585.12 *go to war*
join the chain gang 815.10 *be in prison*
join the choir invisible 582.15 *die*
join the colours 584.10 *enlist*
join the dance 22.15 *dance*
joint heir 769.6 *beneficiary*
join the majority 582.15 *die*
join the opposition 479.3 *apostatize*
join the rat race 342.13 *be busy*
join the traffic 318.9 *proceed*
jointing 30.20 *earth movement*
jointly 211.10 *additionally;* 747.20 *cooperatively;* 374.10 *in combination;* 764.6 *in common;* 373.17 *in connection with*
jointly possessed 764.5 *jointly possessing*
jointly possessing 764.5
jointly with 747.22 *with*
joint-master 59.15 *horse person*
join together 374.5 *combine*
joint operation 346.2; **747.4**; 585.8 *warfare*
joint owner 764.3 *participant*
joint ownership 764.1 *joint possession*
joint possession 764.1
joint regulations 15.1 *industrial relations*
joint rule 12.3 *governance*
joint stock 764.1 *joint possession*
joint tenancy 764.1 *joint possession*
jointure 440.2 *legal terms*
joint venture 346.2 *joint operation*
join up 376.41 *band together;* 584.10 *enlist;* 585.12 *go to war*
join up with 747.14 *join with*
join Weightwatchers 687.5 *fast*
join with 747.14; 750.22 *form an alliance*
joist 23.17 *carpenter;* 23.10 *carpenter's term;* 228.3 *stabilizer;* 38.27 *superstructure;* 23.12 *wood*
joisted 23.16 *joined*
jo kata 52.10 *aikido*
joke 272.4; **599.5**; 621.2 *act of derision;* 599.13 *be humorous;* 668.9 *butt;* 700.11 *hoax;* 697.2 *solecism;* 697.6 *talk nonsense;* 124.8 *trifle;* 486.10 *unskilled person*
joker 697.4 *buffoon;* 69.3 *card game terms;* 621.3 *derider;* 599.6 *humorist;* 567.2 *male;* 378.2 *obstacle;* 700.8 *trick*
joker in the pack 325.19 *deviant person*
jokesmith 21.26 *dramatist;* 599.6 *humorist*
joke writer 21.26 *dramatist*
jokey 599.10 *humorous*
jokiness 599.1 *humorousness*
joking 599.10 *humorous;* 599.3 *wit*
jokingly 599.17
jollification 601.1 *celebration;* 600.1 *rejoicing*
jolliness 600.1 *rejoicing*
jollity 601.1 *celebration;* 598.3 *cheerfulness;* 654.1 *sociability*
jolly 24.10 *ceramic;* 24.6 *ceramic workshop;* 598.1 *cheerful;* 586.28 *marines;* 600.9 *rejoicing;* 654.15 *sociable*
jolly a cup 24.11 *make ceramics*
jolly along 598.6 *bring cheer*
Jolly Roger 743.7 *flag*
jolt 327.9; **327.23**; 420.11 *be rough;* 331.13 *blow;* 331.2 *collide;* 331.12 *collision;* 331.1 *impel;* 362.3 *jerk;* 380.9 *make violent;* 483.9 *motivate;* 362.13 *pull at;* 630.3 *shock;* 630.9 *surprise*
joltiness 133.1 *discontinuity;* 420.6 *roughness;* 327.3 *turbulence*
jolting 420.4 *bumpy;* 327.19 *convulsive*
jolty 327.19 *convulsive;* 133.8 *discontinuous*
Jonah 602.4 *depressing person*
jones 691.4 *drug taker*
jongleur 17.14 *author;* 21.29 *entertainer*
Jonsonian comedy 21.12 *comedy*
Jophiel 8.6 *angel*
Jordan 90.5 *other major rivers*
Joseph Rotblat 589.4 *Nobel Peace Prize*
Joseph's coat 541.5 *variegated thing*
Joseph Surface 699.19 *cheat;* 700.19 *hypocrite*
josh 599.13 *be humorous*
joshing 599.3 *wit*
joss 9.3 *idol*
joss stick 502.3 *incense*
jostle 331.13 *blow;* 331.1 *impel;* 327.9, 327.23 *jolt;* 147.19 *meet;* 668.22 *show disrespect*
jostling crowd 342.6 *business*
jo suburi 52.10 *aikido*
jot 196.3 *fragment;* 744.14 *inscribe;* 159.3 *little piece;* 728.6 *suggestion;* 124.8 *trifle*
jot down 744.14 *inscribe*
jotter 744.6 *record book*
jottings 744.3 *notes*
joule 493.2 *heat measurement;* 334.5 *unit of work*
jounce 327.9, 327.23 *jolt*
jour maigre 687.3 *fast day*
journal 740.5; 789.5 *account book;* 307.4 *axle;* 220.4 *bill;* 3.5 *chronicle;* 721.4 *factual account;* 38.8 *machine element;* 721.3 *narration;* 17.4 *nonfiction;* 276.7 *periodical;* 744.6 *record book;* 281.2 *timetable*
journal box 307.4 *axle*
journalese 5.20 *jargon word;* 741.9 *news story*
journalism 740.3; 721.4 *factual account;* 693.4 *mass communication;* 741.1 *news*
journalist 741.4; 644.3 *curious person;* 721.10 *descriptive writer;* 722.3 *dissertator;* 550.18 *fixer;* 693.9 *informant;* 719.7 *news interpreter;* 740.11 *newspaperman;* 705.9 *questioner;* 744.9 *recorder;* 578.1 *worker*
journalistic 741.14; 5.39 *of language;* 705.15 *sceptical*
journalistically 741.15; 5.49 *colloquially*
journalize 789.7 *account*
journals 693.4 *mass communication*
journey 318.1 *passage;* 318.9 *proceed*
journeyman 578.2 *artisan*
journey's end 312.15 *destination;* 131.6 *end point;* 301.3 *resting place*
journeywork 576.1 *work*
journo 741.4 *journalist*
joust 586.37 *fight*
jouster 586.3 *athlete*
jousting armour 384.7 *armour*
jovial 598.1 *cheerful;* 654.15 *sociable*
joviality 598.3 *cheerfulness;* 654.1 *sociability*
jovially 621.7 *mockingly*
Jovian 29.36 *astronomical*
Jovian planet 29.16 *planet*
jowl 169.1 *side*
Joy 597
joy 598.3 *cheerfulness;* 597.2 *fun;* 597.1 *happiness;* 241.11 *pleasant person;* 600.1 *rejoicing*
joyful 598.1 *cheerful;* 597.4 *happy;* 600.9 *rejoicing*
joyfully 597.9; 598.9 *cheerfully;* 600.11 *rejoicingly*
joyfulness 597.1 *happiness;* 600.1 *rejoicing*
joyful person 597.3
joyless 602.6 *depressed*
joylessly 602.12
joylessness 602.2 *depression*
joyous 654.17 *festive;* 597.4 *happy*
joyously 654.18 *sociably*
joyousness 597.1 *happiness*
joy-ride 772.9 *borrow illegally;* 774.6 *illegal borrowing;* 774.15 *infringe;* 774.12 *steal*
joyrider 774.10 *infringer*
joyriding 774.18 *fraudulent;* 772.3, 774.6 *illegal borrowing;* 774.3 *theft*
joystick 579.5 *guide;* 40.7 *peripheral*

J stroke 50.6 *canoeing*
jubbah 551.16 *robe*
jubilant 597.4 *happy*; 600.9 *rejoicing*
jubilantly 600.11 *rejoicingly*
jubilate 601.16 *commemorate*; 600.5 *rejoice*
Jubilate Deo 10.8 *hymn*
jubilation 601.1 *celebration*; 600.1 *rejoicing*
jubilee 601.5 *anniversary*; 298.6 *annually celebrated day*; 601.1 *celebration*; 601.2 *commemoration*; 600.1 *rejoicing*; 201.8 *twenty and over*
jubilize 601.16 *commemorate*
Judaeo-Christian 7.16 *denominational*
Judaic 7.16 *denominational*
Judaize 7.20 *preach*
Judas 800.4 *dishonourable person*; 479.9 *equivocator*; 651.8 *malefactor*; 700.21 *traitor*; 804.9 *wicked person*
Judas Iscariot 699.17 *false person*; 700.21 *traitor*
Judas kiss 699.5 *deceitfulness*; 800.2 *faithlessness*
judas-window 518.9 *viewpoint*
judder 327.9, 327.23 *jolt*; 320.21 *miscellaneous motoring terms*; 327.7, 327.24 *shake*
juddering 327.6 *shaking*; 327.18 *shaky*
judge 16.23; **16.76**; **464.5**; **464.11**; 713.4 *adviser*; 47.3 *athlete*; 458.7 *be wise*; 466.12 *discriminate*; 466.6 *discriminating person*; 464.12 *estimate*; 397.11 *have authority over*; 16.69 *have jurisdiction over*; 473.3 *impartial person*; 719.8 *interpret*; 464.6 *justice*; 52.8 *karate*; 6.24 *know*; 58.6 *lacrosse player*; 251.6 *lawmaker*; 16.10 *law officer*; 16.13 *lawyer*; 400.3 *leader*; 748.1 *mediate*; 748.3 *mediator*; 685.4 *moderate*; 685.2 *moderator*; 397.6 *person in command*; 396.10 *person of authority*; 372.8 *person who separates*; 4.22 *propound a philosophy*; 814.17 *punisher*; 444.11 *reason*; 140.13 *rule*; 469.1 *select*; 52.9 *tae kwon do*; 275.16 *time*; 16.71 *try a case*
judge advocate 464.6 *justice*; 16.10 *law officer*
judge advocate general 16.23 *judge*; 464.6 *justice*
judge and jury 16.18 *tribunal*
judge by eye 464.12 *estimate*
judged 464.10; **466.11**
Judge Jeffreys 16.23 *judge*
Judge Roy Bean 16.23 *judge*
judgeship 396.5 *position of authority*
judging 464.8; 464.1 *judgment*
judgingly 16.81 *legally*
Judgment 464
judgment 464.1; 450.1 *belief*; 16.43 *conviction*; 482.4 *formulated intention*; 442.3 *intelligence*; 719.1 *interpretation*; 466.2 *judiciousness*; 16.7 *legal trial*; 16.33 *litigation*; 579.3 *management*; 748.2 *mediation*; 4.1 *philosophy*; 713.3 *precept*; 444.1 *reason*; 6.11 *refinement*; 814.9 *retribution*; 469.6 *selection*; 464.2 *verdict*; 458.1 *wisdom*
judgmental 670.29 *blaming*; 464.8 *judging*; 444.7 *reasoning*
judgmentally 6.27 *discerningly*; 466.16 *judiciously*; 748.7 *mediatorially*; 4.29 *wisely*
Judgment Day 283.3 *future condition*; 16.18 *tribunal*
judgment day 464.4
judgment seat 16.27 *courtroom*; 464.3 *place of judgment*; 16.18 *tribunal*
judicative 16.49 *judicatory*
judicatorial 16.49 *judicatory*; 16.48 *jurisdictional*
judicatory 16.49; 464.9 *judicious*; 16.48 *jurisdictional*; 16.18 *tribunal*
judicature 16.2 *jurisdiction*
judicial 16.49 *judicatory*; 464.9 *judicious*; 579.17 *managerial*
judicial assembly 16.18 *tribunal*
judicially 464.13; 16.81 *legally*
judicial murder 814.13 *capital punishment*; 382.5 *execution*
judicial oath 707.3 *vow*
judicial officer 579.16 *official*
judicial separation 571.2 *separation*
judiciary 16.23 *judge*; 16.48 *jurisdictional*
judicious 464.9; 713.8 *advisable*; 616.4 *cautious*; 239.1 *convenient*; 466.9 *discriminating*; 16.49 *judicatory*; 685.6 *moderate*; 4.15 *rational*; 6.20 *refined*; 442.11 *thoughtful*; 458.5 *wise*
judiciously 466.16; 713.9 *advisably*; 616.7 *cautiously*; 6.27 *discerningly*; 442.15 *intelligently*; 464.13 *judicially*; 685.9 *moderately*; 4.29, 458.9 *wisely*
judiciousness 466.2; 616.1 *caution*; 685.1 *moderation*; 442.6 *thoughtfulness*; 458.1 *wisdom*
judo 52.7; 52.1 *combat sports*; 384.5 *self-defence*; 52.15 *wrestling*
judo club 52.7 *judo*
judo grade 52.7 *judo*
judoist 586.3 *athlete*; 52.7 *judo*
judoka 52.7 *judo*
judo kata 52.7 *judo*
judo mat 52.7 *judo*
judo match 52.7 *judo*
judo practitioner 52.7 *judo*
judo referee 52.7 *judo*
judo technique 52.7 *judo*
jug 24.8 *ceramic object*; 815.9 *imprison*; 815.2 *the inside*; 410.11 *vessel*; 433.16 *water carrier*
jug-eared 504.12 *eared*
jug ears 504.4 *ear*
Juggernaut 9.3 *idol*
juggernaut 357.7 *agent of destruction*; 316.5 *means of transport*
juggle 700.29; 645.5 *be cunning*; 699.25 *be fraudulent*; 702.11 *practise sophistry*
juggled 700.40 *illusory*
juggled figures 699.8 *fraud*
juggler 21.31 *circus performer*; 645.3 *cunning person*
jugglery 645.1 *cunning*; 700.9 *sleight of hand*
juggling 699.9 *falsification*; 700.9 *sleight of hand*
jug kettle 410.15 *pot*
juice 431.2; 690.12 *alcohol*; 28.51, 39.9 *electric current*; 369.8 *extract*
juiced 690.3 *dead drunk*
juice extractor 369.9 *extractor*; 431.11 *liquidizer*
juice head 690.17 *drunkard*
juiceless 428.3 *dried-up*
juice of the grape 558.9 *wine*
juicer 25.6 *kitchen equipment*
juicily 431.26 *fluidly*
juiciness 431.7; 431.5 *fluidity*; 555.2 *youthfulness*
juicy 419.4 *compressible*; 431.15 *flowing*; 490.6 *pleasant*; 292.10 *spring*; 241.4 *tasty*; 235.1 *worthy*
juicy part 21.23 *role*
jujitsuist 586.3 *athlete*
juju 10.14 *sacred object*; 11.6 *talisman*
jujube 25.41 *sweet*
jujuism 11.3 *witchcraft*
juke house 796.6 *brothel*
julep 558.8 *mixed drink*; 558.6 *soft drink*
Julian calendar 281.3 *chronology*; 275.13 *timer*
julienne 25.13 *soup*
Juliet cap 551.15 *headgear*
jumble 114.8 *be diverse*; 793.5 *cheap item*; 408.5 *confusion*; 161.4, 408.21 *disorder*; 767.3 *disposable things*; 245.4 *impair*; 408.4 *litter*; 376.32, 412.3 *miscellany*; 412.1 *mixture*; 412.9 *mix up*; 215.2 *residue*
jumbled 408.12 *disordered*; 412.12 *mixed*; 412.13 *mixed-up*; 408.18 *muddled*; 264.12 *problematic*
jumble sale 791.2 *bargain*; 779.10 *bazaar*; 793.7 *discounter*; 767.2 *disposal of property*; 778.4 *sale*
jumbo 158.15 *big*; 158.9 *big thing*; 319.5 *transportable*
jump 47.8; **304.5**; **304.18**; 332.9 *acceleration*; 121.3 *advantage*; 327.21 *be agitated*; 630.12 *be surprised*; 332.4 *be swift*; 57.10 *compete in gymnastics*; 329.7 *crossing*; 54.3 *fencing movements*; 47.2 *field events*; 57.8 *floor exercises*; 300.12 *gait*; 68.15 *ice-skate*; 68.6 *ice-skating*; 146.1 *interval*; 327.9, 327.23 *jolt*; 64.5 *play rugby*; 57.6 *pommel horse*; 59.16 *ride*; 630.3 *shock*; 68.1 *skiing*; 213.2 *spread*; 302.13 *step*; 381.5 *strike*
jump about 327.21 *be agitated*
jump ahead 332.6 *accelerate*
jump at 636.13 *be willing*; 633.10 *chase*
jump at the chance 293.11 *get ahead*
jump a wave 50.18 *windsurf*
jump bail 389.5 *escape*; 634.8 *run away*
jump ball 49.4 *playing terms*
jump down someone's throat 625.6 *be irascible*; 624.13 *vent one's anger*
jumped ball 65.6 *pool*
jumped ship 98.11 *truant*
jumper 47.3 *athlete*; 22.5 *dancer*; 551.7 *frock*; 64.4 *rugby player*; 320.10 *sled*; 551.13 *sweater*; 59.2 *thoroughbred*
jumpers 551.23 *children's clothes*
jump forward 54.5 *fence*
jump higher 765.10 *augment*
jump in 67.10 *dive*; 304.15 *mount*
jumpiness 327.1 *agitation*; 342.7 *restlessness*; 639.13 *timidity*
jumping 59.9; 327.19 *convulsive*; 47.2 *field events*; 57.8 *floor exercises*; 304.24 *leaping*; 57.6 *pommel horse*; 47.9 *track*
jumping at the chance 293.6 *getting ahead*
jumping jack 422.3 *elastic thing*; 522.8 *fire*
jumping lane 59.9 *jumping*
jumping-off place 87.10 *village*
jumping-off point 313.10 *place of departure*
jumping with 232.8 *full*
jump in time 133.3 *interval*
jump jet 586.31 *military aircraft*
jump jockey 59.15 *horse person*
jump-off 59.9 *jumping*; 130.11 *starting point*
jump on 313.5 *set out*
jump on the bandwagon 479.3 *apostatize*; 117.8 *comply*; 750.25 *conform*; 664.14 *follow*
jump out 315.10 *emerge*
jump overboard 382.21 *commit suicide*
jumps 59.7 *horseracing*
jump ship 98.18 *abscond*; 479.3 *apostatize*; 639.9 *change sides*
jump shot 49.4 *playing terms*
jump suit 551.10 *suit*
jump the gun 293.7 *be early*; 293.10 *hasten*; 288.5 *mistime*
jump the wall 391.5 *be liberated*
jump to it 293.10 *hasten*; 342.14 *push*
jump to one's feet 366.5 *arise*
jump turn 68.4 *skiing technique*
jump up 366.5 *arise*; 304.17 *spring up*
jumpy 342.18 *active*; 327.19 *convulsive*; 612.8 *fearful*; 625.4 *irascible*; 591.2 *oversensitive*; 488.7 *susceptible*; 639.3 *timid*
juncaceous 77.16 *taxonomic*
junction 176.1 *angle*; 376.1 *assembly*; 492.6 *contiguity*; 318.5 *crossing point*; 312.15 *destination*; 147.3 *juxtaposition*; 373.4 *means of connection*; 310.4 *meeting place*; 317.10 *railway*
junction box 334.7 *electrical power*
juncture 143.2 *circumstances*; 275.11 *date*; 209.4 *interval*; 147.1 *nearness*; 222.2 *occurrence*; 280.4 *point in time*
Jung 36.29 *psychologist*
Jungian 36.33 *Freudian*
Jungian psychology 36.1 *psychology*
jungle 493.8 *hot place*; 77.1 *plants*; 18.9 *popular music*; 408.7 *tangle*; 79.4 *trees*
jungle green 538.1 *green*
jungle telegraph 504.8 *something heard*
jungle warfare 585.8 *warfare*
junior 387.4 *dependent*; 122.6 *inferior*; 387.9 *subject*; 122.15 *subordinate*; 555.11 *young*; 555.6 *young person*
junior chamber of commerce 776.5 *commercial trade*; 13.7 *corporation*
junior high 6.12 *educational institution*
juniority 387.1 *subjection*
junior judo 52.7 *judo*
junior-lightweight 52.3 *boxing weight divisions*; 52.14 *combat*
junior minister 579.16 *official*; 12.8 *politician*
junior officer 584.5 *military staff*
junior rank 387.1 *subjection*
junior school 6.12 *educational institution*
junior technician 586.32 *airman*
juniper 496.5 *herbs*
junk 793.5 *cheap item*; 470.2 *discard*; 767.3 *disposable things*; 691.6 *drug*; 699.12 *fake*; 236.8 *inferiority*; 238.6 *refuse*; 355.1 *relinquish*; 215.2 *residue*; 350.6 *stop using*; 371.13 *throw away*
junked 350.4 *disused*
junket 601.15 *celebrate*; 557.13 *feast*
junk food 557.7 *food*
junkie 691.4 *drug taker*
junk mail 693.4 *mass communication*
junkman 778.11 *pedlar*; 767.6 *rubbish collector*
junk pile 767.5 *wasteyard*
junk room 565.7 *room*
junk sale 778.4 *sale*
junk shop 793.7 *discounter*
junky 699.37 *fake*; 236.2 *inferior*
junkyard 767.5 *wasteyard*
Juno 570.14 *gods and goddesses of marriage*
Junoesque 545.5 *beautiful*
junta 376.16 *party*
jun-zuki 52.8 *karate*
Jupiter 29.16 *planet*
jural 16.49 *judicatory*
jurally 16.81 *legally*
Jurassic period 284.3 *geological period*
jurat 16.26 *jury*
juridical 464.9 *judicious*; 16.48 *jurisdictional*
jurisdiction 16.2; 396.4 *governance*; 121.2 *leadership*; 16.6 *legal process*; 16.33 *litigation*; 86.14 *sphere*
jurisdictional 16.48; 396.14 *governmental*; 16.49 *judicatory*
jurisdictionally 16.86; 16.81 *legally*
jurisdictive 16.49 *judicatory*; 16.48 *jurisdictional*
jurisprudence 16.32; 140.2 *canon*
jurisprudential 16.49 *judicatory*; 16.45 *legislative*
jurisprudently 16.81 *legally*
jurist 444.6 *arguer*; 464.5 *judge*; 16.26 *jury*; 16.13 *lawyer*
juristically 16.81 *legally*
juror 16.26, 464.7 *jury*
juror's panel 16.26 *jury*
jury 16.26; **464.7**; 464.5 *judge*; 464.7 *jury*; 16.13 *lawyer*; 50.10 *sailing*; 52.9 *tae kwon do*
jury box 16.27 *courtroom*; 464.3 *place of judgment*
jury list 16.26, 464.7 *jury*; 744.1 *record*
juryman 16.26, 464.7 *jury*
jury mast 252.4 *safety device*
jury member 473.3 *impartial person*
jury panel 16.26 *jury*
jury poll 469.10 *vote*
jury rig 50.3 *parts of a sailing boat*; 252.4 *safety device*
jury-rig 50.15 *sail*
jury-rigged 478.1 *improvised*
jurywoman 16.26, 464.7 *jury*
jus canonicum 16.1 *the law*
jus gentium 16.1 *the law*
jus naturale 16.1 *the law*
jussive 5.33 *mood*
just 273.8 *accurately*; 473.4 *disinterested*; 119.6 *equal*; 803.6 *ethical*; 250.9 *free*; 799.4 *honourable*; 618.9 *impartial*; 464.9 *judicious*; 16.44 *legal*; 685.6 *moderate*; 795.8 *moral*; 295.21 *newly*; 801.7 *right*; 458.5 *wise*
just a bit 209.10 *by degrees*
just about 147.13 *nearly*; 216.11 *on average*
just a few 206.1 *few*
just a minute 278.3 *short duration*
just around the corner 147.12 *near*
just as 285.15 *as*; 115.13 *similarly*
just a second 278.3 *short duration*
just a tick 278.3 *short duration*
just cause 714.2 *defence*
just deserts 385.1 *retaliation*; 814.9 *retribution*; 813.1 *reward*
just do 217.4 *suffice*
juste milieu 216.5 *medium*
just enough 217.9 *enough*
just happen 107.10 *chance*
just here 142.12 *where*
justice 464.6; 473.1 *disinterestedness*; 111.5, 119.1 *equality*; 801.1 *fairness*; 795.2 *good morals*; 618.3 *impartiality*; 110.1 *interchange*; 16.23 *judge*; 400.3 *leader*; 16.28 *legality*; 16.33 *litigation*; 685.1 *moderation*; 799.1 *probity*; 385.1 *retaliation*; 814.9 *retribution*; 813.1 *reward*; 803.2 *virtues*
Justice Department 16.2 *jurisdiction*
justice of the peace 16.23 *judge*; 464.6 *justice*; 16.10 *law officer*; 400.3 *leader*; 579.16 *official*; 396.10 *person of authority*
justiceship 16.23 *judge*
justice under the law 16.33 *litigation*
justiciable 16.48 *jurisdictional*; 16.47 *liable to law*; 16.54 *litigated*; 16.58 *unjust*
justiciary 16.23 *judge*; 16.49 *judicatory*; 16.48 *jurisdictional*; 814.17 *punisher*
justifiable 701.12 *apologetic*; 801.9 *in the right*; 714.13 *vindicable*
justifiable homicide 16.39 *crime*
justifiably 701.20 *apologetically*; 703.22 *demonstrably*; 4.26 *rationally*

justification 649.3 *absolution*; 16.42 *acquittal*; 714.2 *defence*; 444.4 *explanation*; 480.11 *motive*; 396.9 *permission*; 4.1 *philosophy*; 701.5 *plea*; 703.4 *proof*
justified 701.12 *apologetic*; 444.10 *causal*; 649.6 *forgiven*; 801.9 *in the right*; 703.13 *proven*
justifier 714.5 *vindicator*
justify **714.8**; 16.78 *acquit*; 649.11 *condone*; 701.16 *plead*; 444.14 *premise*; 703.17 *prove*; 4.21 *rationalize*
justifying 649.4 *forgiving*; 714.11 *vindicatory*
justifyingly 714.15 *in vindication*
Justinian's Code 228.4 *stable thing*
just in time 287.11 *in time*
just know 445.9 *be intuitive*
just lie there 339.4 *be inert*
just like that 265.21 *easily*
just lose 766.9 *lose*
justly 801.17 *by rights*; 473.8 *disinterestedly*; 801.19 *equally*; 119.13 *equitably*; 803.10 *ethically*; 250.20 *freely*; 799.7 *honourably*; 618.19 *impartially*; 16.81 *legally*
just miss 247.7 *be defeated*
justness 685.1 *moderation*
just now 282.9 *at present*; 295.21 *newly*
just once 197.24 *once*
just out 295.10 *new*
just price 119.3 *equalization*
just punishment 714.4 *revenge*
just retribution 814.9 *retribution*
just revenge 385.1 *retaliation*
just right 698.25 *lifelike*; 230.1 *perfect*; 217.1 *sufficient*
just round the corner 283.11 *future*; 293.13 *imminent*; 283.14 *in the future*
just sit there 339.4 *be inert*
just so 273.8 *accurately*; 222.19 *meticulously*; 407.26 *orderly*; 230.1 *perfect*
just stand there 339.4 *be inert*
just the same 111.18 *identically*
just the thing 797.17 *good thing*
just the ticket 490.2 *good time*
just the time 287.1 *timeliness*
just this once 197.24 *once*
just when 285.15 *as*
jut 315.10 *emerge*; 550.26 *overlie*; 361.11 *project*
jute 193.4 *textile*
jut out 185.8 *protrude*
jutting 525.7 *appearing*; 361.8 *projecting*
juttingly 185.10 *protuberantly*
jutting out 185.5 *protuberant*
juvenescence 555.2 *youthfulness*
juvenescent 555.11 *young*
juvenile 34.26 *developmental*; 34.15 *developmental biology*; 555.11 *young*; 555.6 *young person*
juvenile court 16.19 *law court*
juvenile delinquency 804.7 *criminality*
juvenile delinquent 802.10 *wrongdoer*
juvenile detention centre 244.10 *reformatory*
juvenile fiction 740.6 *book publishing*
juvenile home 244.10 *reformatory*
juvenile lead 21.24 *actor*; 21.23 *role*
juvenilely 555.14 *youthfully*
juvenilia 555.2 *youthfulness*
juvenility 555.2 *youthfulness*
juxtapose **147.18**; 108.7 *relate to*
juxtaposed **147.10**
juxtaposition **147.3**; 239.4 *nearness*
juxtapositional 147.10 *juxtaposed*
juxtapositive 147.10 *juxtaposed*

K 201.10 *thousand*
K2 89.6 *other major mountains and ranges*
ka 115.5 *counterpart*; 111.3 *lookalike*
Kaaba 10.13 *shrine*
kaboom 508.1 *bang*
Kabuki 22.4 *historic dancing*; 21.2 *play*
Kabuki costume 551.5 *fancy dress*
Kailasa 8.11 *heaven*
Kaiser 400.2 *sovereign*
Kaiserin 400.2 *sovereign*
kaiten nage 52.10 *aikido*
kala-azar 260.7 *tropical disease*
Kalahari 428.14 *desert*; 493.8 *hot place*
kalashnikov 587.11 *guns*
Kalbshaxe 25.46 *German dish*
kale 43.12 *crop*
kaleidoscope 227.3 *changeable thing*; 224.5 *changer*; 114.3 *diverse thing*; 412.3 *miscellany*; 541.5 *variegated thing*
kaleidoscopic 114.6 *assorted*; 522.16 *bright*; 224.11, 227.13 *changeable*; 529.10 *coloured*; 412.12 *mixed*; 541.6 *variegated*
kaleidoscopically 224.15 *changeably*; 114.10 *diversely*; 412.14 *in the midst*; 541.12 *variedly*
kalidin 33.8 *amino acid*
Kalif 7.8 *priest*
kalogeros 7.7 *monk*
kalophonic chant 10.8 *hymn*
Kama 593.16 *gods and goddesses of love*
Kamaloka 8.11 *heaven*
kamarupa 11.7 *spirit*
Kamavachara 8.11 *heaven*
kame 154.4 *mountain range*
kamikaze 382.7 *suicide*
kamikaze bombing 381.13 *air attack*
kampong 88.7 *lake dwelling*
kanga 551.16 *robe*
kangaroo court 16.19 *law court*; 16.41 *lawlessness*; 464.3 *place of judgment*; 633.1 *pursuit*
Kanji 5.13 *letter*
kanon 10.8 *hymn*
Kantian 101.7 *believer in a nonmaterial world*; 4.11 *follower of a doctrine*; 101.10 *idealistic*; 4.14 *of a philosophy*
Kantianism 101.5 *idealism*; 4.7 *school of thought*
kaolin 24.2 *raw material*
kaon 28.77 *elementary particle*
kapok 419.11 *soft thing*
kapow 508.1 *bang*
kappelmeister 18.24 *musician*
kaput 582.19 *dead*; 357.15 *destroyed*; 245.13 *dilapidated*; 247.10 *failed*; 802.18 *gone wrong*; 94.11 *no more*; 335.10 *powerless*; 350.1 *unused*; 238.1 *useless*
karabiner 62.4 *climbing equipment*
Karaoke 18.9 *popular music*
karate **52.8**; 52.1 *combat sports*; 384.5 *self-defence*
karate club 52.8 *karate*
karate combatant 52.8 *karate*
karate expert 586.3 *athlete*; 52.8 *karate*
karate grade 52.8 *karate*
karate mat 52.8 *karate*
karate referee 52.8 *karate*
karate styles 52.8 *karate*
karate technique 52.8 *karate*
Kariba 88.5 *other major lakes*
karma 106.5 *predetermination*
karmic body 11.7 *spirit*
karoo 428.14 *desert*
Kartikeya 585.3 *gods and goddesses of war*
karting 61.1 *motor racing*
karyokinesis 34.10 *cell division*
karyomitosis 34.10 *cell division*
karyoplasm 34.9 *cell nucleus*
karyosome 34.9 *cell nucleus*
karyotin 34.9 *cell nucleus*
kashmiri 25.49 *Indian dish*
katabatic 50.10 *sailing*
katabatic wind 50.1 *sailing*; 31.12 *wind*
katame-waza 52.7 *judo*
Kavannah 7.2 *religiousness*
kayak 50.17 *canoe*; 50.6 *canoeing*
kayo 131.17 *kill*
Kazam 508.1 *bang*
kebab house 557.15 *eating place*
kebabs 25.54 *other dishes*
kedge 362.11 *pull*; 252.4 *safety device*; 50.2 *sailing boat*
kedgeree 25.16 *fish dish*
keel 72.16 *avian anatomy*; 50.6 *canoeing*; 175.2 *foot*; 50.3 *parts of a sailing boat*; 228.3 *stabilizer*
keel arch 20.5 *arch*
keelboat 50.2 *sailing boat*
keelhaul 814.1 *punish*
keelhauling 814.7 *punishment*
keel lock 50.6 *canoeing*
keel over 323.10 *sail*
keel row 22.4 *historic dancing*
keel-stepped 50.10 *sailing*
keema nan 25.49 *Indian dish*
Keemun 558.3 *tea*
keen 342.18 *active*; 164.10 *advantaged*; 583.8 *bury*; 627.2 *condolence*; 514.13 *cry*; 644.5 *curious*; 617.9 *desirous*; 636.2 *eager*; 726.3 *emphatic*; 488.9 *exciting*; 583.2 *funeral*; 603.2, 603.6 *lament*; 425.5 *mentally sharp*; 425.3 *sharp-edged*; 336.11 *strong in spirit*; 338.4 *vigorous*; 31.47 *windy*
keen appetite 617.3 *appetite*
keen as a razor 425.3 *sharp-edged*
keen as mustard 636.2 *eager*
keen-edged 425.3 *sharp-edged*
keener 583.3 *funeral director*; 603.3 *lamenter*
keen eye 518.2 *eye*
keening 514.6 *cry of pain*; 603.1 *lamentation*; 603.4 *lamenting*
keenly 336.15 *acutely*; 164.12 *at an advantage*; 644.8 *curiously*; 425.18 *sharply*
keen-minded 425.5 *mentally sharp*
keenness 636.7 *eagerness*; 726.1 *emphasis*; 336.2 *healthiness*; 425.13 *mental sharpness*; 338.1 *vigour*
keen nose 500.2 *sense of smell*
keen on 593.18 *in love*
keen-scented 500.5 *odorous*
keen sense of hearing 504.1 *hearing*
keen to learn 644.5 *curious*
keen-witted 442.10 *intelligent*
keen-wittedness 442.4 *cleverness*
keep 601.16 *commemorate*; 384.17 *defend*; 360.7 *detain*; 384.12 *fort*; 225.6 *make permanent*; 350.5 *not use*; 10.18 *perform rites*; 46.15 *play offence*; 359.1 *preservation*; 359.5 *preserve*; 252.10 *protect*; 436.5 *provision*; 252.5 *refuge*; 360.6 *retain*; 439.6 *store*; 413.13 *support financially*; 392.20 *sustain*; 392.3 *sustenance*
keep abreast with 119.10 *be equal*
keep accounts 789.7 *account*; 210.12 *check*
keep a clear head 689.3 *be sober*
keep a count 210.8 *calculate*
keep a date 312.8 *meet*
keep a diary 3.20 *chronicle*
keep afloat 323.10 *sail*
keep a happy medium 684.6 *moderate*
keep a journal 281.15 *chronologize*
keep a light rein 648.3 *be lenient*
keep alive 134.3 *continue*; 359.5 *preserve*; 554.20 *support life*
keep a look out 616.5 *be cautious*; 518.15 *watch*
keep a low profile 521.7 *become invisible*; 736.11 *conceal oneself*; 674.15 *escape notice*
keep a mistress 796.17 *be sexually immoral*
keep an even pace 111.11 *be regular*
keep an eye on 616.5 *be cautious*; 665.11 *care for*; 252.10 *protect*; 471.11 *take note of*
keep an open mind 150.12 *be broadminded*; 473.6 *be disinterested*; 250.14 *be free*; 453.19 *hesitate*
keep apart 372.14 *come between*; 372.11 *divide*; 145.6 *keep away*; 100.15 *separate*; 146.4 *space*
keep a safe distance 252.9 *be safe*
keep a Spartan regimen 687.5 *fast*
keep a stock 436.5 *provision*
keep a straight face 643.8 *be serious*; 736.12 *be silent*
keep at a distance 145.6 *keep away*
keep a tally of 220.10 *score*
keep at arm's length 634.1 *avoid*; 364.3 *fend off*; 655.13 *ignore*; 145.6 *keep away*; 384.24 *parry*; 383.6 *resist*
keep at bay 364.3 *fend off*; 383.6 *resist*
keep a tight rein 647.5 *be severe*
keep at it 640.6 *persevere*; 134.4 *protract*; 576.6 *work*
keep away **145.6**; 98.15 *be absent*; 709.5 *refuse*
keep away from 634.1 *avoid*; 145.6 *keep away*
keep a whole skin 252.9 *be safe*
keep bachelor's hall 572.9 *be celibate*
keep back 481.3 *deflect*; 360.7 *detain*; 737.12 *keep secret*; 333.3 *slow down*; 439.6 *store*
keep behind bars 251.11 *detain*; 252.10 *protect*
keep busy 342.13 *be busy*
keep by 439.6 *store*
keep calm 251.10 *restrain oneself*
keep clean 256.13 *clean*
keep clear 634.1 *avoid*
keep clear of 145.6 *keep away*
keep close 737.12 *keep secret*
keep close to 147.17 *stay near*
keep coming 112.21 *be repeated*
keep company with **223.14**; 569.13 *befriend*; 654.13 *fraternize*
keep cool 473.6 *be disinterested*
keep costs down 680.6 *save*
keep count 220.10 *score*
keep dark 737.12 *keep secret*; 523.14 *make dark*
keep down 367.5 *bear down on*; 357.8 *destroy*; 387.6 *subject*
keep dry **428.22**
keeper 223.7 *attendant*; 28.60 *magnet*; 579.15 *manager*; 46.9 *play*; 815.6 *prison officer*; 252.3, 384.15 *protector*; 53.4 *team*
keeper of the purse 780.18 *treasurer*
keep faith 799.6 *be honourable*
keep fit 259.5 *be healthy*; 257.5 *by hygienic*; 576.5, 576.9 *exercise*
keep for 482.9 *intend for*
keep for later 294.8 *delay*
keep for oneself 683.6 *be selfish*; 763.7 *possess*
keep fresh 359.5 *preserve*
keep from 634.1 *avoid*
keep from laughing 643.8 *be serious*
keep from sleep 261.6 *fatigue*
keep going 300.13 *be in motion*; 134.3 *continue*; 134.8 *go on!*; 640.7 *maintain*; 359.5 *preserve*
keep hands off 250.15 *set free*
keep holy 601.16 *commemorate*
keep in 360.7 *detain*; 309.10 *enclose*; 814.1 *punish*; 170.7 *surround*
keep incomplete 161.3 *make shapeless*
keep in custody 252.10 *protect*
keeping 117.1 *conformity*; 252.2 *protection*; 360.1 *retention*; 252.8 *tutelary*
keeping alive 359.1 *preservation*
keeping a Spartan regimen 687.6 *fasting*
keeping clean 256.1 *cleanness*
keeping cool 473.1 *disinterestedness*
keeping down 367.13 *submergence*
keeping fit 576.5 *exercise*; 257.1 *hygiene*
keeping for oneself 683.1 *selfishness*
keeping fresh 359.1 *preservation*
keeping healthy 257.1 *hygiene*
keeping in 360.2 *detention*; 814.7 *punishment*
keeping Lent 687.6 *fasting*
keeping long hours 342.20 *industrious*
keeping one's fast 687.6 *fasting*
keeping one's own company 655.1 *unsociability*
keep in good repair 359.5 *preserve*
keeping to oneself 655.1 *unsociability*
keeping to one side 372.2 *setting apart*
keeping under 367.13 *submergence*
keeping up appearances 549.3 *etiquette*
keeping within the law 16.28 *legality*
keep in hand 360.7 *detain*; 350.5 *not use*; 439.6 *store*
keep in one's place 388.4 *succumb*
keep in purdah 655.13 *ignore*
keep in reserve 350.5 *not use*
keep inside **172.15**
keep in sight 520.10 *make visible*
keep in step 119.10 *be equal*; 117.8 *comply*; 285.7 *synchronize*
keep in the background 736.11 *conceal oneself*; 674.15 *escape notice*
keep in the dark 523.14 *make dark*; 456.11 *make ignorant*; 737.13 *mystify*
keep in time 285.7 *synchronize*
keep in touch 492.12 *abut*
keep in view 520.10 *make visible*
keep it up 134.8 *go on!*
keep late hours 294.6 *be late*
keep law and order 12.11 *govern*
keep Lent 687.5 *fast*
keep locked up 252.10 *protect*
keep moving 342.13 *be busy*; 134.8 *go on!*
keep mum 506.1, 736.12 *be silent*; 730.13 *be voiceless*; 737.12 *keep secret*; 341.4 *not act*
keepnet 55.3 *fishing tackle*; 633.3 *hunting and fishing equipment*
keep off 634.24 *hands off!*; 145.6 *keep away*; 384.24 *parry*
keep off liquor 689.3 *be sober*
keep on 342.13 *be busy*; 134.3 *continue*; 640.7 *maintain*; 302.3 *press on*; 134.4 *protract*
keep one guessing 696.7 *be unintelligible*
keep one's balance 228.6 *be stable*
keep one's chin up 613.16 *take courage*
keep one's cool 228.6 *be stable*; 251.10 *restrain oneself*
keep one's counsel 732.7 *keep quiet*; 737.12 *keep secret*
keep one's distance 634.1 *avoid*; 655.12 *be unsocial*; 145.6 *keep away*
keep one's ears open 504.15 *hear*
keep oneself to oneself 634.1 *avoid*; 732.7 *keep quiet*
keep one's eye in 518.12 *see*
keep one's eyes on 518.15 *watch*

keep one's eyes skinned 518.15 *watch*
keep one's fingers crossed 610.9 *be hopeful*
keep one's hair on 251.10 *restrain oneself*
keep one's hand in 632.18 *habituate*
keep one's hands clean 634.1 *avoid*
keep one's hat on 668.22 *show disrespect*
keep one's head down 521.7 *become invisible*
keep one's health 259.5 *be healthy*
keep one's hopes up 610.9 *be hopeful*
keep one's mouth shut 736.12 *be silent*; 732.7 *keep quiet*; 737.12 *keep secret*
keep one's nose clean 140.17 *obey orders*
keep one's offer open 752.9 *offer*
keep one's powder dry 243.8 *prepare oneself*
keep one's promise 799.6 *be honourable*
keep one's shirt on 251.10 *restrain oneself*
keep one's trap shut 732.7 *keep quiet*
keep one's wallet shut 786.11 *be parsimonious*
keep one's wool 251.10 *restrain oneself*
keep one's word 799.6 *be honourable*
keep on ice 359.5 *preserve*
keep on keeping on 342.13 *be busy*; 134.3 *continue*; 640.6 *persevere*
keep on one's legs 259.5 *be healthy*
keep on the go 342.13 *be busy*
keep on trying 640.6 *persevere*
keep open house 679.10 *be generous*; 769.10 *receive someone*
keep order 396.18 *have authority*; 579.1 *manage*; 407.22 *pacify*; 252.10 *protect*; 251.8 *restrain*; 253.10 *secure*
keep out 128.7 *exclude*; 251.8 *restrain*
keep out of 634.1 *avoid*; 341.4 *not act*
keep out of mischief 631.12 *behave well*
keep out of trouble 589.5 *be at peace*
keep out of war 589.5 *be at peace*
keep pace with 119.10 *be equal*; 285.7 *synchronize*
keep pointed 324.7 *take a direction*
keep posted 693.11 *inform*; 721.15 *recount*
keep private 655.13 *ignore*
keep quiet 732.7; 301.8 *be motionless*; 506.1 *be silent*; 730.13 *be voiceless*; 341.4 *not act*; 251.10 *restrain oneself*; 388.3 *submit*
keep running 359.5 *preserve*
keep safe 359.5 *preserve*; 252.10 *protect*
keep safe and sound 253.10 *secure*
keepsake 768.2 *gift*; 462.3, 794.3 *memento*
keep score 220.10 *score*
keep secret 737.12; 360.7 *detain*
keep shtoom 730.13 *be voiceless*; 732.7 *keep quiet*
keep sight of 520.10 *make visible*
keep silent 506.1 *be silent*
keep smiling 610.9 *be hopeful*
keep someone guessing 453.20 *make uncertain*
keep stable 228.7 *make stable*
keep steadfast 799.6 *be honourable*
keep-stepped mast 50.3 *parts of a sailing boat*
keep still 301.8 *be motionless*
keep stored away 350.5 *not use*
keep straight 803.8 *be virtuous*
keep supplied 436.5 *provision*
keep sweet 685.4 *moderate*
keep tabs on 616.5 *be cautious*; 665.11 *care for*; 743.10 *identify*
keep the ball rolling 134.3 *continue*; 640.7 *maintain*
keep the books 789.7 *account*
keep the faith 663.6 *show obeisance to*
keep the field 585.13 *be at war*
keep the golden mean 684.6 *moderate*
keep the law 663.5 *obey*
keep the nose down 324.7 *take a direction*
keep the peace 589.5 *be at peace*; 685.3 *be moderate*; 749.4 *pacify*; 589.9 *peace!*
keep the pot boiling 342.13 *be busy*; 134.3 *continue*; 640.7 *maintain*
keep the same beat 285.7 *synchronize*
keep the score 210.8 *calculate*
keep things moving 134.3 *continue*
keep time 281.14; 281.16 *measure time*; 275.16 *time*
keep time with 223.13 *accompany*; 285.7 *synchronize*
keep together 747.13 *work together*
keep to oneself 655.12 *be unsocial*; 360.7 *detain*; 737.12 *keep secret*
keep to one side 360.7 *detain*
keep to the point 178.11 *be straight*
keep under 367.5 *bear down on*
keep under cover 550.31 *hide*; 359.5 *preserve*; 252.10 *protect*
keep under observation 518.15 *watch*
keep under one's hat 737.12 *keep secret*
keep under one's thumb 387.6 *subject*
keep under wraps 736.8 *conceal*; 737.12 *keep secret*
keep up 134.3 *continue*; 640.7 *maintain*; 225.6 *make permanent*; 359.5 *preserve*
keep up with 119.10 *be equal*; 654.12 *visit*
keep warm 493.16 *feel hot*
keep watertight 428.22 *keep dry*
keep well 259.5 *be healthy*
keep wicket 53.16 *field*
keep within bounds 684.6, 685.4 *moderate*; 251.8 *restrain*
keep within limits 685.4 *moderate*
keep within the law 16.67 *follow the law*
keep your distance 634.24 *hands off!*
keep your mouth shut 506.6 *hush!*
keep your trap shut 506.6 *hush!*
kef 691.6 *drug*
kefta 25.52 *Greek dish*
keg 410.11 *vessel*
keg beer 558.7 *alcoholic drink*
keister 168.2 *rear end*
kelp 84.1 *alga*
kempt 407.13 *orderly*
ken 455.11 *know*; 455.1 *knowledge*; 695.7 *recognize*
kendo 54.1 *fencing*
kennel 309.4 *closed place*; 309.10 *enclose*; 376.23 *flock*; 565.12 *stall*
kennel huntsman 59.15 *horse person*
kennel man 59.15 *horse person*
kenning 17.12 *poetic language*
ken no kamae 52.10 *aikido*
kenosis 623.9 *humiliation*
Kensington 87.5 *London*
ken suburi 52.10 *aikido*
Kent mental test 36.6 *intelligence test*
Kentucky Derby 59.7 *horseracing*
Kentucky Fried Chicken™ 25.43 *US dish*
kepi 551.15 *headgear*
Keplerian telescope 29.24 *telescope*
Kepler's laws 29.14 *solar system*
kept 359.7 *preserved*; 360.10 *retained*
kept back 709.8 *refused*
kept by 439.7 *stored*
kept in 360.10 *retained*
kept on a lead 251.13 *restraining*
kept under constraint 251.13 *restraining*
kept woman 568.4 *girlfriend*; 796.9 *immoral woman*; 593.11 *loved one*
keratin 33.9 *protein*; 403.7 *skeleton*
kerb 164.1 *edge*; 317.4 *road surface*
kerb crawling 796.5 *prostitution*
kerb market 779.3 *sellers' market*
kerbside parking 318.2 *passing along*
kerbstone 317.4 *road surface*
kerchief 551.14 *neckwear*
kerf 183.4, 183.10 *notch*
kermes 535.6 *red pigment*
kern 586.8 *soldier*
kernel 173.1 *centre*; 123.3 *chief thing*; 99.2 *essential content*; 80.3 *fruit structure*; 406.3 *insides*; 77.9 *seed*
kernels 80.1 *fruits*
kernmantel rope 62.4 *climbing equipment*
kerplunk 324.9 *directly*
kestrel 72.5 *bird of prey*
ketchup 496.2 *seasoning*
ketohexose 33.3 *carbohydrate*
ketooctose 33.3 *carbohydrate*
ketopentose 33.3 *carbohydrate*
ketose 33.3 *carbohydrate*
ketotetrose 33.3 *carbohydrate*
ketotriose 33.3 *carbohydrate*
kettle 493.4 *burner*; 25.5 *cooker*; 410.15 *pot*
kettle of fish 143.2 *circumstances*
kevel 427.26 *beat*
Kew Gardens 44.2 *garden*
kewpie doll 813.2 *prize*
key 18.20; 173.6 *central*; 287.7 *critical*; 209.1 *degree*; 173.8 *focal*; 123.5 *important*; 719.1 *interpretation*; 92.2 *island*; 308.2 *opener*; 346.12 *operative*; 344.5 *reason*; 252.4 *safety device*; 742.1 *sign*; 719.4 *translation*
keyboard 18.16 *musical note*; 40.7 *peripheral*
keyboarder 744.9 *recorder*
keyboard instrument 18.25 *musical instrument*
key card 308.2 *opener*
key centre 18.21 *tone*
keyed up 243.18 *prepared*
key figure 173.5 *focus*
keyhole 308.5 *hole*
keyhole surgery 35.9 *surgery*
key man 485.5 *expert*
Keyneseanism 4.7 *school of thought*
Keynesian 4.11 *follower of a doctrine*; 4.14 *of a philosophy*
Keynesian economics 13.1 *economics*
keynote 123.3 *chief thing*; 140.4 *guide*; 18.16 *musical note*; 447.1 *topic*
key person 123.4 *bigwig*; 579.15 *manager*
key point 287.3 *critical time*; 123.2 *important matter*
keys 743.4 *insignia*; 18.16 *musical note*
key signature 18.17 *notation*
keystone 174.3 *architectural summit*; 99.2 *essential content*; 413.2 *supporting part*
keystone combination 48.2 *baseball player*
Key West 92.2 *island*
KGB 737.2 *secretiveness*
khaddar 193.4 *textile*
khaki 534.1 *brown*; 656.4 *formal dress*
khakis 551.3 *formal dress*
khaki uniform 551.3 *formal dress*
khan 400.2 *sovereign*
khazi 560.13 *lavatory*; 767.7 *toilet*
Khshathra Vairya 8.6 *angel*
kibble 427.26 *beat*
kibbutz 43.6 *farm*; 764.1 *joint possession*
kibbutznik 43.15 *agriculturist*; 764.3 *participant*
kibe 260.15 *ulcer*
kibitzer 342.11, 644.4 *meddler*
kick 46.17; 330.27; 331.7; 342.1 *activity*; 693.7 *advice*; 331.13 *blow*; 347.1 *counteraction*; 487.5 *disaccustom*; 66.2 *football play*; 597.2 *fun*; 742.3, 742.11 *gesture*; 381.18 *hit*; 113.18 *object*; 496.1 *piquancy*; 64.5 *play rugby*; 66.4 *play soccer*; 492.3 *press*; 330.20 *propel*; 330.1 *propulsion*; 753.1, 753.6 *protest*; 470.5 *rejection*; 355.1 *relinquish*; 64.3 *rugby play*; 488.3 *stimulus*; 381.5 *strike*; 67.2 *swimming technique*; 330.5 *throw*; 492.11 *touch*; 338.1 *vigour*; 52.12 *wrestle*; 52.5 *wrestling*
kick against the pricks 753.6 *protest*
kick-ahead 64.3 *rugby play*
kick around 387.6 *subject*
kick ass 585.13 *be at war*; 381.5 *strike*
kick at goal 64.3 *rugby play*
kickback 480.10 *bribe*; 347.1 *counteraction*; 768.2 *gift*; 752.4 *illegal offer*; 483.5 *positive stimulus*; 706.4 *reaction*; 813.8 *secret money*
kick back 347.3 *counteract*; 706.19 *react*; 385.3 *retaliate*; 761.8 *return*
kick downstairs 371.3 *disbar*; 470.2 *discard*; 144.17 *relegate*
kicked around 387.9 *subject*
kicker 69.3 *card game terms*; 46.12 *special team*
kick in 768.5 *give*
kicking 381.23 *attacking*; 66.2 *football play*; 46.19 *varsity*; 380.6 *violent*; 52.5, 52.15 *wrestling*
kicking against the pricks 753.1 *protest*
kicking ass 814.7 *punishment*
kicking downstairs 144.4 *relegation*
kicking out 371.17 *expulsion*
kicking strap 50.3 *parts of a sailing boat*
kicking team 46.12 *special team*
kicking tee 46.12 *special team*
kicking the ball 49.5 *penalties*
kicking upstairs 144.4 *relegation*
kick in the ass 631.8 *treatment*
kick in the pants 631.8 *treatment*
kick in the teeth 709.2 *dissent*
kick it 582.15 *die*
kickoff 66.2 *football play*; 64.3 *rugby play*; 46.12 *special team*; 130.11 *starting point*
kick off 46.17 *kick*; 130.18 *make a beginning*; 66.4 *play soccer*; 330.33 *start*
kick one's heels 343.12 *be inactive*; 341.4 *not act*; 294.7 *wait*
kick out 470.2 *discard*; 371.2, 767.10 *dismiss*; 128.8 *eject*; 371.1 *expel*; 144.17 *relegate*
kick over 357.9 *demolish*
kick over the traces 662.16 *be subversive*; 804.16 *be wicked*; 118.18 *not conform*
kick pleat 551.24 *part of garment*
kickshaw 793.5 *cheap item*
kickstand 320.11 *bicycle part*
kick-start 130.20 *activate*
kickstool 304.10 *step*
kick the air 814.6 *be punished*
kick the bucket 94.12 *cease to exist*; 582.15 *die*
kick the habit 634.3 *abstain*; 689.4 *give up alcohol*
kick turn 68.2 *cross-country skiing*; 68.4 *skiing technique*
kick under the table 693.7 *advice*; 742.3 *gesture*; 711.5 *warn*; 711.1 *warning*
kick up a row 751.6 *argue*; 624.11 *be angry*; 408.26 *be disorderly*; 380.7 *be violent*
kick up a shindig 380.7 *be violent*
kick up a shindy 751.6 *argue*; 342.12 *be active*; 507.8 *be loud*
kick up bobsy-die 751.6 *argue*
kick up dirt 624.11 *be angry*
kick up one's heels 597.6 *enjoy*
kick up shit 624.12 *become angry*
kick upstairs 371.2 *dismiss*; 244.5 *improvement*; 573.5 *make noble*; 144.17 *relegate*
kick wheel 24.6 *ceramic workshop*
kid 550.14 *animal covering*; 599.13 *be humorous*; 555.9 *child*; 43.8 *livestock*; 561.6 *progeny*; 700.28 *trick*; 555.4 *young animal*; 71.19 *young mammal*; 555.7 *young man*; 555.6 *young person*
kidder 700.15 *deceiver*
kiddie 555.9 *child*
kidding 700.7 *tricking*; 599.3 *wit*
kid-glove 648.4 *lenient*
kid gloves 551.25 *accessories*; 648.1 *leniency*; 631.8 *treatment*
kid-glove treatment 648.1 *leniency*
kidnap 774.13; 251.11 *detain*; 386.7 *force*; 806.10 *sin*; 700.33 *snare*; 773.10 *take away*
kidnapped 251.15 *detained*; 774.17 *stolen*; 700.42 *trapped*
kidnapper 386.4 *coercive person*; 798.6 *evil person*; 251.6 *lawmaker*; 773.6 *taker*; 774.8 *thief*
kidnapping 774.2; 386.3 *coercive methods*; 251.4 *detention*; 700.13 *snare*; 774.17 *stolen*; 773.3 *taking away*; 381.16 *terrorist attack*
kidney 172.4 *insides*; 25.31 *offal*; 721.6 *sort*; 137.4 *type*
kidney donor 768.4 *giver*
kidney machine 394.14 *hospital*
kids 555.10 *the young*
kid's stuff 265.6 *easy thing*
Kierkegaardian 4.11 *follower of a doctrine*; 4.14 *of a philosophy*
Kilimanjaro 89.6 *other major mountains and ranges*
kill 131.17; 382.16; 651.17; 381.9 *attack successfully*; 585.13 *be at war*; 798.11 *be evil*; 708.14 *cancel*; 94.13 *cause not to exist*; 226.8 *cause to cease*; 399.4 *censor*; 586.38 *conquer*; 357.8 *destroy*; 814.5 *execute*; 441.2 *lay waste*; 335.8 *overpower*; 90.1 *river*; 60.7 *shoot*; 212.4 *take off*; 330.5 *throw*
kill animals 382.22
killed 708.20 *cancelled*; 582.19 *dead*; 60.8 *shooting*
killer 382.10; 381.19 *attacker*; 586.1 *combatant*; 662.9 *criminal*; 69.6 *darts*; 357.6, 441.7 *destroyer*; 798.6 *evil person*; 797.17 *good thing*; 651.8 *malefactor*; 382.11 *murderer*; 804.9 *wicked person*
killer-diller 797.17 *good thing*
killer disease 260.4 *disease*
killer dog 382.10 *killer*
killian 68.7 *ice-dancing*; 68.13 *ice-skating*
killian hold 68.7 *ice-dancing*
killick 252.4 *safety device*
kill in cold blood 651.17 *kill*
Killing 382
killing 382.1; 582.6; 651.7 *act of malev-*

olence; 382.23 *deadly;* 357.2 *destroying;* 236.5 *harmful;* 60.2 *hunting;* 576.11 *laborious;* 765.5 *profit;* 246.1 *success*
killing field 585.10 *battleground*
killing fields 382.15 *slaughterhouse*
killing oneself 382.7 *suicide*
killjoy 620.3 *boring person;* 481.8 *cautionary person;* 602.4 *depressing person;* 378.7 *hinderer;* 685.2 *moderator;* 341.2 *nonacting person;* 670.13 *pessimist*
kill off 131.16 *cease*
kill oneself 382.21 *commit suicide;* 582.16 *meet one's fate*
kill ritually 382.20
kill the fatted calf 654.11 *be sociable;* 490.8 *feel pleasure;* 601.18 *salute*
kill time 343.12 *be inactive;* 341.4 *not act*
kill with kindness 245.5 *hurt*
kiln 428.19 *bake;* 24.6 *ceramic workshop;* 493.6 *fire*
kilner jar 25.6 *kitchen equipment;* 410.11 *vessel*
kiln furniture 24.6 *ceramic workshop*
kilo 414.9 *avoirdupois weight;* 201.10 *thousand*
kilobyte 40.19 *computing terms;* 201.10 *thousand*
kilocalorie 493.2 *heat measurement*
kilogram 414.9 *avoirdupois weight;* 201.10 *thousand*
kilohertz 297.6 *radio frequency*
kilometre 148.7 *measure of length;* 201.10 *thousand*
kilometres per hour 332.8 *speed*
kilowatt 334.5 *unit of work*
kilt 551.3 *formal dress;* 551.6 *skirt;* 743.5 *uniform*
kilter 221.5 *physical state*
kimono 552.4 *dishabille;* 551.16 *robe*
kin 373.3 *associate;* 137.8 *genealogy*
kind 160.3; 797.3; 392.35, 650.6 *benevolent;* 658.7 *courteous;* 569.8 *friendly;* 648.4 *lenient;* 241.2 *likable;* 593.17 *loving;* 649.5 *merciful;* 652.6 *philanthropic;* 627.6 *pitying;* 419.6 *soft-hearted;* 721.6 *sort;* 137.4 *type;* 473.5 *unselfish;* 235.4 *worthwhile*
kind act 650.4 *benevolent act;* 797.10 *kindness*
kind deed 650.4 *benevolent act*
kindergarten 6.12 *educational institution*
kindest regards 667.7 *respects*
kind-hearted 650.6 *benevolent;* 652.6 *philanthropic;* 627.6 *pitying;* 419.6 *soft-hearted*
kind-heartedly 650.10 *benevolently;* 652.8 *philanthropically;* 627.13 *pitifully*
kind-heartedness 650.1 *benevolence;* 652.1 *philanthropy*
kindle 344.10 *awaken;* 624.12 *become angry;* 493.15 *burn;* 437.11 *fuel;* 71.35 *give birth;* 338.3 *invigorate;* 522.24 *light*
kindliness 241.8 *amiability;* 650.1 *benevolence;* 658.1 *courtesy;* 569.1 *friendship;* 797.10 *kindness;* 648.1 *leniency*
kindling 437.2 *lighter;* 79.3 *timber*
kindly 392.35 *benevolent;* 392.38, 650.10 *benevolently;* 658.7 *courteous;* 658.14 *courteously;* 649.14 *forgivingly;* 569.8 *friendly;* 569.17 *in friendship;* 648.4 *lenient;* 648.6 *leniently;* 241.2 *likable;* 593.30 *lovingly;* 652.6 *philanthropic;* 627.13 *pitifully;* 413.9 *supportive;* 473.9 *unselfishly*
kindly disposition 650.1 *benevolence*
kindness 797.10; 650.1 *benevolence;* 650.4 *benevolent act;* 658.1 *courtesy;* 649.2 *forgivingness;* 569.1 *friendship;* 419.12 *gentleness;* 392.10 *helpfulness;* 648.1 *leniency;* 593.3 *lovingness;* 652.1 *philanthropy;* 627.1 *pity;* 654.1 *sociability;* 392.2 *support;* 473.2 *unselfishness*
kind of 209.11 *to a degree*
kind offices 392.2 *support*
kind of number 194.2
kind person 650.5 *benevolent person;* 768.4 *giver;* 595.4 *likable person;* 652.3 *philanthropist*
kindred 108.4 *related*
kindred spirit 115.5 *counterpart*
kind regards 667.7 *respects*
kind remembrances 658.3 *courtesies*
kinematic 300.17 *directional;* 28.98 *physical*
kinematically 28.100 *physically*
kinematics 28.2 *classical physics;* 300.1 *motion*
kinesiatrics 300.1 *motion*
kinesics 742.3 *gesture*
kinesipathic 300.17 *directional*
kinesipathy 300.1 *motion*
kinesis 300.1 *motion*
kinesitherapy 300.1 *motion*
kinesodic 300.17 *directional*
kinetic 32.31 *chemical;* 300.17 *directional;* 334.15 *full of energy;* 483.11 *motivational;* 28.98 *physical*
kinetically 300.18 *in motion;* 28.100 *physically*
kinetic art 19.1 *art*
kinetic energy 28.11, 334.4 *energy;* 300.1 *motion*
kineticist 32.2 *chemist*
kinetics 32.14 *chemical reaction;* 32.1 *chemistry;* 300.1 *motion*
kinetic sculpture 19.12 *sculpture*
kinetic theory 28.5 *theory*
kinetochore 34.14 *chromosome*
kinetosome 34.8 *cell organ*
king 69.4 *chess terms;* 396.10 *person of authority;* 76.4 *social insect;* 400.2 *sovereign;* 121.5 *superior*
king bolt 321.7 *train*
kingdom 137.3; 85.3 *dominion;* 396.8 *governmental organization;* 566.11 *nation;* 12.5 *political organization;* 34.17 *taxonomy;* 86.4 *territorial division*
kingdom come 283.3 *future condition;* 8.11 *heaven*
Kingdom of God 8.11 *heaven*
kin-geri 52.8 *karate*
kingfish 400.5 *company leader;* 25.18 *sea fish*
kingfisher 305.8 *descender;* 74.11 *fishing animal;* 72.3 *water bird*
kingfisher blue 539.1 *blue*
King James' Bible 7.12 *religious text*
King Kong 158.9 *big thing*
kinglike 12.10 *governing;* 396.14 *governmental*
kingliness 573.3 *nobleness*
kingly 12.10 *governing;* 396.14 *governmental;* 622.19 *stately*
kingmaker 579.13 *director;* 395.4 *indirect influence*
king of arms 743.9 *herald*
King of Death 582.2 *death personified*
King of Kings 8.3 *God*
King of Terrors 582.2 *death personified*
King of the Jews 8.4 *God the Son*
king pair 53.10 *score*
kingpin 123.4 *bigwig;* 123.3 *chief thing;* 400.5 *company leader;* 373.8 *fastening;* 579.15 *manager*
king post 413.2 *supporting part*
king-post truss 23.10 *carpenter's term*
kingprawn 25.19 *shellfish*
King's Bench 16.20 *British court*
King's Colour 743.7 *flag*
King's highway 317.3 *road*
kingship 12.1 *government;* 121.2 *leadership*
king-size 158.15 *big;* 158.3 *large scale;* 496.7, 496.11 *tobacco*
king-size bed 23.6 *bed*
King's Proctor 16.11 *British law officer*
king's ransom 781.6 *money*
King Tutankhamen's tomb 583.6 *grave;* 284.7 *thing of the past*
kinin 33.8 *amino acid*
kink 180.2 *coil;* 231.7 *defect;* 118.5 *idiosyncrasy;* 420.12 *make rough;* 420.7 *rough thing;* 642.3 *whim*
kinkiness 461.1 *insanity*
kinky 461.11 *insane*
kinorhynch 75.6 *worm*
Kinorhyncha 75.6 *worm*
kinship 750.1 *accord;* 1.5 *anthropological concept;* 2.8 *human institution;* 108.1 *relatedness;* 115.1 *similarity*
kinship group 566.9 *group*
kinsman 373.3 *associate*
kiosk 779.9 *stall*
kip 780.11 *national coins;* 343.9, 343.13 *sleep*
kip down 263.2 *take it easy*
kiphouse 565.8 *shelter*
kipper 428.17 *dry;* 25.16 *fish dish;* 74.8 *food fish;* 359.5 *preserve;* 496.12 *season*
kippered 496.9 *piquant*
kippered fish 25.16 *fish dish*
kippered herring 25.16 *fish dish*
kippers 25.44 *British dish*
kir 558.8 *mixed drink*
kirk 10.11 *place of worship*
Kirlian photography 11.1 *occultism*
Kirov Ballet 22.12 *ballet companies*
kir rose 558.8 *mixed drink*
kirtle 551.6 *skirt*
kismet 106.5 *predetermination*
kiss 492.4; 593.27; 492.12 *abut;* 569.4 *act of friendship;* 593.14 *communication of love;* 658.12 *greet;* 147.19 *meet;* 658.5 *sign of courtesy;* 492.11 *touch;* 654.9, 654.14 *welcome*
kissable 593.22 *lovable*
kiss and make up 649.9 *forgive;* 749.5 *make peace*
kiss-and-tell confession 17.4 *nonfiction*
kisser 308.4 *body orifice;* 167.2 *face*
kiss goodbye 766.9 *lose*
kiss hands 367.9 *bow*
kissing 593.14 *communication of love*
kissing disease 260.6 *infection*
kissing hands 367.16 *courtesy*
kissing someone's hand 658.4 *deference*
kissing the hem 667.4 *mark of respect*
kiss off 708.15 *terminate*
kiss of life 67.3 *survival swimming*
kiss of peace 10.5 *Christian rite*
kiss shot 65.4 *carom*
kiss someone's hand 658.13 *defer to*
kiss the book 707.18 *vow*
kiss the ring of 667.19 *take off one's hat to*
kiss the rod 388.4 *succumb*
kit 71.10 *cat;* 551.1 *dress;* 438.7 *equipment;* 243.11 *fitting out;* 204.5 *unit;* 71.19 *young mammal*
kitbag 410.8 *bag*
kitchen 25.3; 565.7 *room;* 577.1 *workshop*
kitchen boy 401.6 *domestic servant*
kitchen cabinet 579.7 *council*
kitchen container 25.4
kitchen equipment 25.6
kitchenette 565.7 *room*
kitchen garden 44.2 *garden*
kitchen knife 425.10 *knife*
kitchen maid 401.6 *domestic servant*
kitchen police 584.4 *military organization*
kitchen range 493.4 *burner;* 25.5 *cooker*
kitchen scales 414.10 *scales*
kitchen sink 410.12 *bath;* 767.8 *sink*
kitchen-sink 721.12 *narrative*
kitchen-sink drama 721.3 *narration;* 21.2 *play;* 95.3 *realism;* 21.10 *theatre movements*
kitchen table 23.4 *table*
kitchen unit 410.3 *cabinet*
kitchenware 356.7 *produce*
kitchen work 576.1 *work*
kite 322.8 *aircraft;* 72.5 *bird of prey;* 780.15 *false money;* 304.19 *take off*
kite a check 780.24 *monetize*
kith 373.3 *associate*
kith and kin 376.17 *family*
kit out 243.5 *equip;* 436.5 *provision*
kitsch 122.4 *poor quality;* 793.3 *shoddiness*
kitted out 551.29 *dressed*
kitten 71.10 *cat;* 71.35 *give birth;* 561.11 *have young;* 337.4 *weakling;* 555.4 *young animal;* 71.19 *young mammal*
kittenish 71.28 *carnivorous*
kittens 427.5 *powder*
Kitt Peak National Observatory 29.23 *observatory*
kitty 51.1 *green bowling;* 764.1 *joint possession;* 813.2 *prize;* 439.1 *store*
kitty-cornered 189.4 *oblique;* 189.8 *obliquely*
kiwi 72.2 *flightless bird*
Klansman 736.7 *concealer;* 737.7 *esotericism*
klaxon 711.2 *danger signal;* 507.4 *sound maker*
Kleenex™ 256.11 *cleaning cloth*
Klein 36.29 *psychologist*
Klein bottle 132.6 *continuum;* 27.47 *topology*
Kleinian 36.33 *Freudian*
kleptomania 461.4 *delusion;* 774.1 *stealing*
kleptomaniac 386.5 *compulsive person;* 461.7 *insane person;* 774.17 *stolen;* 774.8 *thief*
kletterschuh 62.4 *climbing equipment*
klieg light 522.6 *electric light;* 21.20 *stage lighting*
klister 68.12 *ski*
klister wax 68.5 *ski equipment*
kloof 146.3 *gulf*
klutz 457.3 *unintelligent person*
klutziness 544.1 *inelegance;* 236.8 *inferiority*
klutzy 544.7 *graceless;* 236.2 *inferior;* 457.6 *unintelligent*
klystron 39.20 *electron tube*
K meson 28.77 *elementary particle*
kmukamtch 8.7 *devil*
knack 136.2 *ability;* 485.2 *aptitude;* 645.1 *cunning;* 484.3 *expedient plan;* 352.1 *means;* 632.2 *tendency*
knacker 382.13 *animal killer*
knackered 261.1 *fatigued*
knacker's yard 382.15 *slaughterhouse*
knackery 382.9 *animal killing*
knackwurst 25.29 *sausage*
knap 154.2 *heights*
knapsack 410.9 *baggage;* 316.10 *transferred thing*
knapsack sprayer 44.6 *garden tool*
knave 645.3 *cunning person;* 800.4 *dishonourable person;* 804.9 *wicked person*
knavery 645.1 *cunning;* 800.1 *improbity;* 804.1 *wickedness*
knavish 645.4 *cunning;* 804.11 *wicked*
knead 427.26 *beat;* 25.55 *cook;* 160.7 *form;* 365.16 *massage;* 412.8 *mix;* 419.13 *soften;* 492.11 *touch*
kneading 365.6 *massage*
knee 331.7 *kick;* 58.9 *play hockey;* 50.8 *punting*
knee breeches 551.9 *trousers*
kneecap 814.4 *torture*
kneed 58.8 *hockey*
knee-deep 156.8 *deep;* 157.1 *shallow*
knee guard 49.3 *basketball equipment*
knee-high 159.7 *little;* 155.5 *low;* 154.12 *tall;* 555.11 *young*
knee-high to a grasshopper 155.5 *low;* 555.11 *young*
knee-hole 23.14 *wooden*
knee-hole desk 23.4 *table*
kneeing 58.8 *hockey;* 58.3 *ice hockey*
knee-jerk 445.4 *instinct;* 445.8 *instinctive;* 478.2 *spontaneous*
knee-jerk journalism 741.3 *reporting*
knee-jerk reaction 478.5 *spontaneity*
knee-joint 176.1 *angle*
kneel 367.9 *bow;* 658.13 *defer to;* 664.10 *knuckle under;* 10.19 *offer worship;* 663.6 *show obeisance to;* 388.4 *succumb;* 667.19 *take off one's hat to;* 9.7 *worship*
knee-length 148.1 *long*
knee-length socks 551.20 *legwear*
kneeling 367.16 *courtesy;* 367.21 *degraded;* 667.11 *in a respectful stance;* 667.4 *mark of respect;* 663.3 *obeisance;* 663.9 *obeisant;* 388.1 *submission;* 388.5 *submitting;* 9.1 *worship*
kneel on 331.7 *kick*
kneel to 710.6 *request*
knee pad 58.3 *ice hockey*
knees-up 376.10 *dance;* 22.1 *dancing;* 654.5 *party*
knell 582.4 *death sentence;* 583.2 *funeral;* 603.2 *lament;* 711.7 *raise the alarm;* 510.10 *ring;* 510.2 *ringing;* 357.4 *ruin;* 742.4 *signal;* 711.1 *warning*
knickerbocker glory 25.35 *dessert*
knickerbockers 551.9 *trousers*
knickers 551.9 *trousers;* 551.18 *underwear*
knick-knack 124.9 *bauble;* 793.5 *cheap item*
knick-knacks 542.6 *decorative articles*
knife 425.10; 62.4 *climbing equipment;* 557.16 *eating utensil;* 308.20 *hole;* 60.3 *hunting equipment;* 491.11 *inflict pain;* 382.2, 382.17 *murder;* 308.2 *opener;* 587.8 *sharp weapon;* 381.6 *stab;* 438.1 *tool;* 425.16 *use a sharp tool*
knifeblade piton 62.4 *climbing equipment*
knife block 52.9 *tae kwon do*
knifed 308.14 *holed*
knife edge 164.3 *cutting edge;* 151.8 *narrow thing;* 62.5 *rock face;* 425.7 *sharp point*
knife-edged 425.3 *sharp-edged*
knife-grinder 578.2 *artisan;* 393.12 *repairer*
knifelike 425.3 *sharp-edged*
knife pleat 184.3 *pleat*
knife point 425.7 *sharp point*
knife sharpener 425.12 *sharpener*
knife-thrower 330.14 *thrower*
knifing 381.18 *hit;* 382.2 *murder*

knight 586.20 *cavalryman*; 69.4 *chess terms*; 586.1 *combatant*; 613.7 *courageous person*; 658.6 *courteous person*; 384.13 *defender*; 59.15 *horse person*; 573.5 *make noble*; 573.1 *nobleman*; 575.4 *titleholder*
knighted 542.11 *decorated*
knight errant 586.1 *combatant*; 384.13 *defender*; 59.15 *horse person*; 477.9 *visionary*
knight errantry 477.4 *ideality*
knighthood 575.1 *right*
knighting 575.1 *right*
knight in shining armour 613.7 *courageous person*; 799.3 *honourable person*; 252.3 *protector*; 255.5 *pure person*; 803.4 *virtuous person*
knightliness 613.2 *heroism*
knightly 613.10 *chivalrous*; 658.14 *courteously*; 585.17 *military*
knightly deed 613.8 *courageous act*
knight of the road 778.10 *salesman*
Knightsbridge 87.5 *London*
knight's-move 325.15 *deviating motion*
knight's-move thought 36.16 *dissociation*
knit 191.6 *become smaller*; 193.8 *interweave*; 42.5 *knitting*; 191.5 *make smaller*; 356.10 *produce*; 551.13 *sweater*; 42.14 *weave*; 184.8 *wrinkle*
knit one's brows 626.11 *be irritable*
knitted 191.7 *smaller*; 42.10 *woven*; 184.6 *wrinkly*
knitted brow 184.4 *wrinkled thing*
knitted fabric 42.3 *fabric*
knitted sweater 551.13 *sweater*
knitter 193.3 *weaving*
knitting **42.5**; 193.2 *braid*; 191.1 *contraction*; 160.4 *forming*
knitting machine 42.5 *knitting*
knitting needle 425.8 *sharp-pointed thing*
knit together 393.6 *cure*
knob 182.2 *bulge*; 404.12 *coarsen*; 361.4 *hanger*; 154.3 *mountain*; 561.8 *organs of reproduction*; 62.5 *rock face*
knobbliness 420.6 *roughness*
knobbly 420.2 *coarse*
knobby 420.2 *coarse*
knobkerrie 587.7 *blunt weapon*
knobstick 587.7 *blunt weapon*
knock **509.11**; 507.8 *be loud*; 331.13 *blow*; 508.2 *crack*; 670.5 *criticism*; 670.17, 678.11 *criticize*; 561.14 *have sex*; 331.3, 381.18 *hit*; 327.9 *jolt*; 492.3 *press*; 330.5 *throw*; 492.11 *touch*
knockabout 272.5 *ridiculous*; 272.2 *slapstick comedy*; 21.40 *tragic*
knock about 351.1 *misuse*
knockabout farce 21.12 *comedy*
knock about with 569.13 *befriend*
knock at the door 312.3 *approach*
knock back 558.13 *drink*
knock back a few 690.8 *get drunk*
knock cold 331.3 *hit*
knockdown 52.2 *boxing*; 793.9 *cheap*; 52.14 *combat*
knock down 357.9 *demolish*; 791.3 *discount*; 52.11, 331.9 *fight*; 155.9 *lower*; 793.13 *make cheap*; 187.7 *make horizontal*; 335.8 *overpower*; 704.8 *refute*; 381.5 *strike*
knock down a hurdle 47.7 *race*
knockdown argument 704.1 *refutation*
knock-down-drag-out 751.9 *disagreeing*
knock-down-drag-out fight 751.2 *argument*
knock down pins 51.8 *bowl*
knockdown price 791.2 *bargain*; 793.1 *cheapness*
knockdown punch 52.2 *boxing*
knock down to 778.1 *sell*
knocked down 155.5 *low*; 187.10 *lying*
knocked flat 155.5 *low*; 187.10 *lying*
knocked off course 144.8 *displaced*
knocked out 489.7 *anaesthetized*; 52.14 *combat*; 247.11 *defeated*; 489.8 *unconscious*
knocked over 155.5 *low*
knocked up 261.1 *fatigued*
knocker 670.12 *critic*; 678.7 *disparager*; 331.15 *ram*
knockers 182.2 *bulge*
knock flat 155.9 *lower*; 187.7 *make horizontal*; 357.11 *ruin*
knock for a loop 630.11 *amaze*
knock-for-knock 320.21 *miscellaneous motoring terms*
knock for six 630.11 *amaze*
knock galley-west 408.22 *discompose*
knock hard 507.8 *be loud*
knock heads together 331.2 *collide*
knock in 368.3 *impact*
knocking **509.4**; 678.2 *criticism*; 678.15 *disparaging*; 509.17 *rattling*
knocking down 357.2 *destroying*
knocking knees 612.1 *fear*
knocking off course 144.1 *displacement*
knocking on wood 475.6 *good-luck sign*
knocking shop 796.6 *brothel*
knock into 312.8 *meet*
knock into shape 117.10 *assimilate*; 553.9 *fashion*; 160.7 *form*; 760.9 *transform*
knock it off 506.1 *be silent*; 506.6 *hush!*; 226.12 *stop!*
knock-kneed 310.7 *convergent*
knock-knock 509.4 *knocking*
knock off 791.3 *discount*; 561.14 *have sex*; 774.12 *steal*; 212.4 *take off*
knock off course 144.14 *displace*
knock off one's perch 623.23 *abase*
knock-on 132.10 *repercussive*; 64.3 *rugby play*
knock-on effect 132.4 *repercussion*
knockout 52.2 *boxing*; 52.14 *combat*; 131.13 *ender*; 235.8 *exceller*; 797.17 *good thing*; 619.5 *person of wonder*; 45.1 *sport*; 246.2 *victory*
knock out 489.12 *anaesthetize*; 457.10 *bemuse*; 246.10 *defeat heavily*; 52.11, 331.9 *fight*; 131.17 *kill*; 343.14 *make inactive*; 335.8 *overpower*; 356.10 *produce*; 592.7 *render insensitive*; 357.11 *ruin*
knockout blow 131.13 *ender*; 357.4 *ruin*
knockout drops 489.4 *anaesthetic*; 592.6 *desensitizing substance*
knock out of shape 161.3 *make shapeless*
knockout punch 52.2 *boxing*; 357.4 *ruin*; 331.14 *sporting hit*
knock over 357.9 *demolish*; 155.9 *lower*
knock senseless 592.7 *render insensitive*
knock the bottom out 49.6 *play basketball*
knock the cover off 53.17 *bat*
knock together 405.13 *make*
knock up 261.6 *fatigue*; 561.13 *propagate*; 366.2 *send up*
knoll 154.3 *mountain*
knot 182.2 *bulge*; 376.27 *bundle*; 373.11 *connect*; 193.8 *interweave*; 373.6 *line*; 420.12 *make rough*; 148.7 *measure of length*; 323.6 *nautical speed*; 378.4 *restraint*; 420.7 *rough thing*; 416.4 *solid body*; 332.8 *speed*; 27.47 *topology*; 79.2 *tree part*
knot garden 44.2 *garden*
knothole 308.5 *hole*
knotted 420.2 *coarse*; 416.7 *condensed*; 373.15 *connected*
knotted score 119.2 *equilibrium*
knottiness 264.1 *difficulty*
knotting 193.2 *braid*; 27.47 *topology*
knotty 420.2 *coarse*; 416.7 *condensed*; 737.11 *mysterious*; 264.12, 705.13 *problematic*
knotty problem 737.5 *difficult problem*; 705.4 *difficult question*; 264.4 *problem*; 696.12 *unintelligible thing*
knout 814.14 *instrument of punishment*
know **6.24**; **455.11**; 396.22 *be an authority on*; 452.20 *be certain*; 485.11 *be expert*; 693.15 *be informed*; 458.8 *be intelligent*; 450.7 *believe*; 579.1 *manage*; 695.6 *understand*
knowability 695.9 *intelligibility*
knowable 695.1 *intelligible*; 455.10 *known*; 695.3 *recognizable*
know again 462.12 *remember*
know-all 442.8 *intellectual person*; 455.6 *knowledgeable person*; 4.12 *sage*; 673.7 *vain person*
know all about 396.22 *be an authority on*
know all the answers 645.5 *be cunning*; 485.10 *be skilful*; 455.12 *know by heart*; 400.15 *learn*
know back to front 396.22 *be an authority on*
know backwards 485.11 *be expert*; 6.24 *know*; 455.12 *know by heart*
know by heart **455.12**; 6.24 *know*
know by instinct 590.16 *feel in one's bones*
know for sure 452.20 *be certain*
know forward and backward 485.11 *be expert*; 455.12 *know by heart*
know full well 455.12 *know by heart*
know how 136.14 *be qualified*
know-how 136.2, 334.2 *ability*; 485.2 *aptitude*; 645.1 *cunning*; 455.2 *information*; 352.1 *means*; 317.1 *way*
know how to 400.15 *learn*
know how to mix 654.11 *be sociable*
knowing 645.4 *cunning*; 590.10 *feeling*; 455.1 *knowledge*; 455.8 *knowledgeable*; 458.5 *wise*
knowingly 482.13 *intentionally*; 455.15 *knowledgeably*
knowing no better 805.7 *naive*
knowing no wrong 805.7 *naive*
knowing one's place 667.9 *showing respect*
knowing person 485.5 *expert*
know inside out 396.22 *be an authority on*; 6.24 *know*; 455.12 *know by heart*
know-it-all 673.13 *boastful*; 442.8 *intellectual person*; 673.7 *vain person*
Knowledge 455
knowledge **455.1**; 396.2 *authoritativeness*; 452.9 *certainty*; 645.1 *cunning*; 522.13 *enlightenment*; 590.1 *feeling*; 693.1 *information*; 352.1 *means*; 485.1 *skill*; 695.12 *understanding*; 458.1 *wisdom*
knowledgeable **6.19**; **455.8**; 396.12 *authoritative*; 645.4 *cunning*; 396.17 *expert*; 442.10 *intelligent*; 4.19 *learned*; 444.7 *reasoning*; 139.21 *specialized*; 156.11, 458.5 *wise*
knowledgeableness 442.4 *cleverness*
knowledgeable person **455.6**
knowledgeably **455.15**; 396.23 *authoritatively*; 396.26 *expertly*; 442.15 *intelligently*; 485.12 *skilfully*; 4.29 *wisely*
knowledge of law 16.32 *jurisprudence*
knowledge of the enemy 585.6 *art of war*
knowledge-seeking 705.12 *questioning*
know like a book 6.24 *know*
know little **456.10**
known **455.10**; 452.1 *certain*; 632.10 *familiar*; 27.77 *given*; 743.12 *identified*; 349.9 *used*
known as 743.12 *identified*
known attitudes 631.1 *conduct*
known by 743.12 *identified*
know no better 659.7 *be discourteous*; 646.4, 805.10 *be naive*
know no bounds 219.4 *be excessive*
know no law 16.74 *be lawless*
know no limit 202.8 *have no limit*
know nothing 456.9 *be ignorant*
Know-Nothings 737.7 *esotericism*
know no wrong 805.10 *be naive*
know one's job 136.14 *be qualified*
know one's onions 485.11 *be expert*
know one's own mind 638.6 *be resolute*; 635.14 *follow one's own will*
know one's place 674.14 *be modest*; 750.25 *conform*; 388.4 *succumb*
know one's stuff 396.22 *be an authority on*; 485.11 *be expert*; 455.12 *know by heart*
know the real world 698.28 *bring into existence*
know the right people 395.8 *influence*
know the ropes 396.22 *be an authority on*; 485.11 *be expert*; 6.24 *know*; 455.12 *know by heart*
know the score 458.7 *be wise*; 6.24 *know*
know what's what 442.13 *be intelligent*; 485.10 *be skilful*; 458.7 *be wise*; 6.24 *know*
know when to stop 684.5 *be self-restrained*; 251.10 *restrain oneself*
knub 404.3 *nap*
knuckle ball 48.4 *pitching terms*; 330.5 *throw*
knuckle-duster 587.7 *blunt weapon*; 331.16 *weapons*
knuckle sandwich 492.7 *sense organ*
knuckle under **664.10**; 623.20 *submit*; 388.4 *succumb*; 122.9 *yield to*
knurled 420.2 *coarse*
KO 246.10 *defeat heavily*; 335.8 *overpower*; 357.11 *ruin*; 246.3 *successful thing*; 246.2 *victory*
kobold 11.11 *ghost*
KO'd 247.11 *defeated*
koheleth 7.8 *priest*
kohen 7.8 *priest*
kohl 547.4 *cosmetics*
koine 5.7 *international language*
koji 7.7 *monk*
kolkhoz 43.6 *farm*; 764.1 *joint possession*
kol nidre 10.9 *prayer*
kombu 84.5 *algal product*
kominuter 427.11 *pulverizer*
Komodo dragon 73.2 *lizard*
konimeter 427.14 *koniology*
koniology **427.14**
kontakion 10.8 *hymn*
kook 461.7 *insane person*
kooky 118.14 *eccentric*
kop 154.3 *mountain*
kopeck 780.4 *change*
kopje 154.3 *mountain*
Koran 7.12 *religious text*
korma 25.49 *Indian dish*
Korsakoff's psychosis 36.11, 461.5 *psychosis*
kosher 256.16 *clean*; 117.14 *conformist*; 255.14 *purified*
koshi-waza 52.7 *judo*
kote gaeshi 52.10 *aikido*
kowtow 367.9 *bow*; 367.16 *courtesy*; 658.13 *defer to*; 664.10 *knuckle under*; 667.4 *mark of respect*; 663.3 *obeisance*; 663.6 *show obeisance to*; 388.1 *submission*; 388.4 *succumb*; 667.19 *take off one's hat to*
kowtower 664.3 *sycophant*
kowtowing 658.4 *deference*; 658.9 *deferential*; 367.21 *degraded*; 667.9 *showing respect*; 664.7 *sycophantic*
kraken 70.7 *legendary beast*
K rations 436.1 *provision*; 687.2 *short rations*
Krebs cycle 34.6 *cell biology*; 33.24 *respiration*
Kreis 86.5 *state*
krill 70.5 *aquatic animal*
kris 425.10 *knife*; 587.8 *sharp weapon*
krona 780.11 *national coins*
krone 780.11 *national coins*
Kshatriya 586.6 *militarist*
K star 29.13 *luminosity*
kudos 669.4 *compliment*; 185.1 *prominence*
Ku Klux Klan 737.7 *esotericism*
kukri 587.8 *sharp weapon*
kulfi 25.49 *Indian dish*
Kumbum 10.13 *shrine*
kumi jo 52.10 *aikido*
kumiss 558.5 *milk*
kumi tachi 52.10 *aikido*
Künstlerroman 17.2 *fiction*
kur 59.10 *dressage*
Kuril Trench 30.16 *ocean floor*
kurtosis 27.59 *probability distribution*
kuru 461.3 *mental deterioration*
kuting 68.10 *curling*
kuting stone 68.10 *curling*
kvetch 606.7 *be dissatisfied*; 606.3 *dissatisfied person*
kwashiorkor 260.4 *disease*; 260.7 *tropical disease*
kwela 18.10 *world music*
Kyle of Lochalsh 92.9 *inlet*
kymograph 326.6 *measuring instrument*
Kyōgen 21.2 *play*
Kyokushinkai 52.8 *karate*
Kyrie Eleison 10.9 *prayer*
Kyries 10.6 *Eucharist*
Kyu grade 52.7 *judo*

laager 384.9 *barrier*; 384.12 *fort*
lab 448.6 *place of experimentation*; 577.1 *workshop*
labarum 743.7 *flag*
label 139.22 *characterize*; 137.13 *class*; 743.8 *heraldic device*; 743.10 *identify*; 743.3 *means of identification*; 721.8 *name*; 738.8 *showplace*; 137.4 *type*
labelled 743.12 *identified*
labelling 743.1 *identification*
labial 5.41 *lettered*; 5.16 *spoken letter*
labia majora 561.8 *organs of reproduction*
labia minora 561.8 *organs of reproduction*
labiate 77.16 *taxonomic*
labile 227.13 *changeable*
labiodental 5.16 *spoken letter*
labionasal 5.16 *spoken letter*
laboratory 760.4 *medium of conversion*; 448.6 *place of experimentation*; 6.15 *schoolroom*; 577.1 *workshop*
laboratory animal 70.3 *domesticated animal*; 448.7 *experimentee*
laboratory test 35.7 *diagnosis*
Labor Day 298.6 *annually celebrated day*
laborious **576.11**; 264.10 *difficult*; 261.4

fatiguing; 342.20 *industrious*; 814.21 *punishing*
laboriously 576.12; 264.26 *arduously*; 261.9 *tiringly*
laboriousness 342.8 *assiduity*; 264.1 *difficulty*
labor union 776.5 *commercial trade*; 13.8 *industrial relations*
labor union member 776.11 *chamber of commerce member*; 13.9 *economist*
Labour 12.9 *governmental*
labour 340.4 *act*; 340.1 *action*; 342.8 *assiduity*; 109.10 *be unrelated*; 264.3 *difficult task*; 727.7 *exaggerate*; 112.18 *harp*; 15.8 *industrial*; 15.1 *industrial relations*; 123.8 *make important*; 561.7 *obstetrics*; 578.4 *personnel*; 327.25 *pitch*; 353.2 *try hard*; 576.1, 576.6 *work*
labour camp 386.3 *coercive methods*; 815.1 *prison*; 814.7 *punishment*
labour costs 13.8 *industrial relations*
labour dispute 15.4 *industrial dispute*
laboured 243.20 *developed*; 727.12 *exaggerated*; 109.7 *illogical*; 544.9 *inelegant*; 576.11 *laborious*
laboured breathing 261.7 *fatigue*
labourer 216.7 *average person*; 346.6 *operative*; 356.9 *producer*; 401.1 *servant*; 578.1 *worker*
labour force 13.4 *economic development*; 13.8, 15.1 *industrial relations*; 578.4 *personnel*
labouring 727.1 *exaggeration*; 342.20 *industrious*; 576.10 *working*
labour in vain 486.6 *act foolishly*; 766.11 *be wasteful*; 441.1 *waste*; 238.9 *waste effort*
Labourite 12.6 *political party*
labour law 15.5; 13.8 *industrial relations*
labour-management body 15.1 *industrial relations*
Labour Management Relations Act 15.5 *labour law*
labour of love 793.6 *absence of charge*; 650.4 *benevolent act*; 768.1 *giving*; 354.2 *undertaking*; 636.10 *voluntary work*; 576.1 *work*
labour of Sisyphus 335.2 *futile effort*; 766.3 *waste*; 238.5 *waste of effort*
labour on behalf of 392.25 *serve*
labour pains 561.7 *obstetrics*; 491.2 *painful condition*
Labour Party 12.6 *political party*
labour pool 578.4 *personnel*
labour relations 15.1 *industrial relations*
labour resources 352.3 *human resources*
labour-saving 263.5; 265.10 *feasible*; 580.7 *leisurely*; 438.9 *mechanical*; 680.4 *thrifty*
labour-saving device 392.7 *convenience*
labour the obvious 219.5 *be superfluous*; 695.5 *simplify*; 238.9 *waste effort*
labour under 221.7 *be in a predicament*; 260.24 *be unhealthy*
labour under a disadvantage 264.19 *have difficulty*
labour under difficulties 264.19 *have difficulty*
labour union 15.3 *organized labour*
Labrador 60.6 *sporting dog*
lab rat 448.7 *experimentee*
labyrinth 737.4 *brain-teaser*; 180.3 *convoluted thing*; 504.5 *internal ear*; 408.7 *tangle*
labyrinthine 180.4 *convolutional*; 325.21 *indirect*; 408.18 *muddled*; 737.11 *mysterious*; 264.12 *problematic*
labyrinthitis 504.6 *otology*
Lacan 36.29 *psychologist*
Lacanian 36.33 *Freudian*
Lacanian psychology 36.1 *psychology*
laccolith 30.30 *igneous rock*; 30.28 *rock*
lace 193.2 *braid*; 373.11 *connect*; 153.11 *fineness*; 193.8 *interweave*; 373.6 *line*; 412.8 *mix*; 542.3 *pattern*; 193.4 *textile*; 527.8 *transparent thing*; 42.4 *weaving*
laced 373.15 *connected*; 193.6 *interwoven*; 551.31 *styled*
lace into 381.5 *strike*
lace maker 542.8 *decorator*
lace making 193.2 *braid*
lacerate 372.9 *separate*
lacerated 491.6 *injured*
laceration 491.3 *injury*; 372.3 *separateness*
Lacertilia 73.2 *lizard*
lacertilian 73.2 *lizard*; 73.11 *reptilian*
lace up 551.34 *wear*
lace-ups 551.19 *footwear*
lacework 193.2 *braid*; 542.3 *pattern*
lachrymal 431.16 *rheumy*
lachrymator 37.4 *drug type*
lachrymatory 431.16 *rheumy*
lachrymose 603.4 *lamenting*
laciness 193.2 *braid*; 153.11 *fineness*
lacing 193.1 *interweaving*; 42.4 *weaving*
lack 122.11 *become inferior*; 233.5 *be incomplete*; 218.5 *be insufficient*; 782.12 *be poor*; 231.7 *defect*; 98.2 *disappearance*; 206.3 *fewness*; 231.5 *imperfection*; 782.9 *inadequacy*; 233.1 *incompleteness*; 135.2 *need*; 233.2 *omission*; 782.5 *poverty*; 710.6 *request*; 135.7 *require*; 218.9 *scarcity*
lackadaisical 618.7, 666.5 *indifferent*; 472.11 *perfunctory*
lackadaisicalness 618.1 *indifference*
lack bias 473.6 *be disinterested*; 698.29 *be truthful*
lack candour 699.22 *be hypocritical*
lack compassion 628.6 *be pitiless*
lack conviction 754.5 *be irresolute*
lack courage 614.4 *be a coward*
lack courtesy 668.22 *show disrespect*
lack definition 161.3 *make shapeless*
lack discipline 250.19 *liberalize*
lack disguise 698.29 *be truthful*
lack emotion 684.7 *be calm*; 473.6 *be disinterested*
lack equality 420.11 *be rough*
lack experience 805.10 *be naive*
lackey 348.3 *assistant*; 401.1 *servant*; 387.3 *subordinate*
lack fairness 120.6 *be unjust*
lack harmony 517.10; 372.12 *disagree*
lack honesty 800.8 *be dishonourable*
lack hope 611.9 *be hopeless*
lackie 664.3 *sycophant*
lack information 456.9 *be ignorant*
lacking 782.4 *inadequate*; 231.2, 233.4 *incomplete*; 218.1, 337.13 *insufficient*; 766.16 *losing*; 98.12 *missing*; 135.5 *necessitous*; 94.9 *nonexistent*; 195.7 *null*; 135.4 *required*; 218.2 *unprovided*
lacking application 350.1 *unused*
lacking definition 161.5 *shapeless*
lacking emotion 684.10 *calm*
lacking intellect 457.5
lacking nothing 232.7 *complete*
lacking refinement 497.6 *coarse*
lacking self-control 335.12 *impotent*
lacking sight 519.8 *blind*
lacking strength 337.8 *weak*
lacking style 495.8 *tasteful*
lacking substance 477.12 *imaginary*
lacking taste 497.6 *coarse*
lack integrity 699.20 *be false*
lack intellect 457.9
lack interest 620.6 *be boring*
lack light 523.12 *be dark*
lacklustre 530.7 *colourless*; 602.6 *depressed*; 524.7 *dimmed*; 530.8 *drained of colour*
lack maturity 805.10 *be naive*
lack mercy 647.5 *be severe*
lack of ability 486.8 *unskilfulness*
lack of action 341.1 *inaction*
lack of advantage 238.4 *futility*
lack of ambition 341.1 *inaction*
lack of appetite 557.3 *delicate eating*; 618.1 *indifference*; 260.3 *symptom*
lack of appreciation 672.1 *ingratitude*
lack of assumption 698.5 *truthfulness*
lack of attention 505.1 *deafness*
lack of authority 335.1 *powerlessness*
lack of awareness 489.1 *lack of feeling*
lack of benefit 238.4 *futility*
lack of betterment 245.7 *deterioration*
lack of bias 473.1 *disinterestedness*; 801.1 *fairness*; 698.5 *truthfulness*
lack of bite 426.8 *toothlessness*
lack of brains 457.1 *lack of intellect*
lack of care 651.6 *inconsiderateness*
lack of censorship 250.2 *free speech*
lack of ceremony 657.1 *informality*
lack of clarity 694.3 *comprehension*; 511.3 *mutedness*; 266.1 *obscurity*; 696.11 *unintelligibility*
lack of colour 271.5 *unadornment*
lack of commitment 355.3 *relinquishment*; 639.11 *vacillation*
lack of committal 754.3 *irresolution*
lack of communication 626.1 *sullenness*
lack of concealment 520.3 *visibility*
lack of concentration 342.7 *restlessness*
lack of concern 651.6 *inconsiderateness*
lack of confession 809.1 *impenitence*
lack of confinement 250.1 *freedom*
lack of conscience 800.1 *improbity*
lack of consent 709.2 *dissent*; 709.1 *refusal*
lack of consideration 659.1 *discourtesy*; 519.7 *figurative blindness*
lack of continuity 133.1 *discontinuity*
lack of contrition 809.1 *impenitence*
lack of convention 657.1 *informality*
lack of conviction 754.3 *irresolution*
lack of courage 614.1 *cowardice*
lack of credit 672.1 *ingratitude*
lack of danger 252.1 *safety*
lack of decoration 271.5 *unadornment*
lack of definition 161.1 *shapelessness*
lack of delay 280.1 *immediacy*
lack of democracy 120.2 *injustice*
lack of depth 157.3 *shallowness*
lack of deviation 698.9 *uniformity*
lack of discernment 519.7 *figurative blindness*
lack of discipline 408.8 *lawlessness*; 250.6 *liberality*
lack of disguise 698.5 *truthfulness*
lack of drive 639.12 *inconstancy*
lack of ease 264.2 *awkwardness*
lack of emotion 684.3 *calmness*; 473.1 *disinterestedness*
lack of enjoyment 620.1 *boredom*
lack of enlightenment 519.7 *figurative blindness*
lack of exaggeration 698.5 *truthfulness*
lack of expectation 630.1 *surprise*; 619.1 *wonder*
lack of expression 696.11 *unintelligibility*
lack of fairness 120.2 *injustice*
lack of feeling 489.1; 592.3 *insensitiveness*
lack of finesse 544.1 *inelegance*
lack of fitness 260.1 *ill health*
lack of flattery 698.5 *truthfulness*
lack of food 557.10 *scarcity*
lack of formality 657.1 *informality*
lack of function 238.3 *uselessness*
lack of grace 264.2 *awkwardness*
lack of gratitude 672.1 *ingratitude*
lack of harmony 372.4 *disunity*
lack of haste 333.8 *slowness*
lack of heat 494.1 *coldness*
lack of hindrance 265.5 *smoothness*
lack of hope 611.1 *hopelessness*
lack of humanity 651.1 *malevolence*
lack of importance 100.1 *extraneousness*
lack of improvement 245.7 *deterioration*
lack of incisiveness 426.8 *toothlessness*
lack of integrity 699.1 *falsehood*; 800.1 *improbity*
lack of intellect 457.1
lack of intelligence 524.4 *stupidity*
lack of interest 620.1 *boredom*; 618.1 *indifference*
lack of knowledge 456.1 *ignorance*; 457.2 *unintelligence*
lack of light 523.1 *darkness*
lack of maintenance 245.9 *dilapidation*
lack of manners 659.2 *bad manners*
lack of meaning 696.11 *unintelligibility*
lack of mercy 647.1 *severity*
lack of moral fibre 614.1 *cowardice*
lack of morals 796.1 *immorality*; 800.1 *improbity*
lack of naturalness 266.1 *obscurity*
lack of ornamentation 271.5 *unadornment*
lack of oxygen 62.2 *climbing dangers*
lack of perception 519.7 *figurative blindness*
lack of pigment 531.7 *whiteness*
lack of pity 628.1 *pitilessness*
lack of planning 240.3 *inconvenience*
lack of polish 544.1 *inelegance*
lack of politeness 659.2 *bad manners*
lack of power 335.1 *powerlessness*
lack of practice 487.3 *unaccustomedness*; 486.8 *unskilfulness*
lack of prejudice 150.6 *broad-mindedness*; 473.1 *disinterestedness*
lack of pretence 698.5 *truthfulness*
lack of pretension 698.5 *truthfulness*
lack of principle 804.3 *venial sin*
lack of principles 796.1 *immorality*; 800.1 *improbity*
lack of professionalism 486.8 *unskilfulness*
lack of proficiency 486.8 *unskilfulness*
lack of profit 766.2 *financial loss*
lack of progress 341.1 *inaction*
lack of protection 335.3 *helplessness*; 254.7 *vulnerability*
lack of protocol 240.3 *inconvenience*
lack of purpose 238.4 *futility*
lack of reason 457.1 *lack of intellect*
lack of refinement 497.4 *bad taste*; 724.3 *inelegance*
lack of repair 245.9 *dilapidation*
lack of resolution 754.3 *irresolution*; 639.11 *vacillation*
lack of respect 668.1 *disrespect*
lack of restraint 250.1 *freedom*
lack of retraction 707.4 *confirmation*
lack of risk 252.1 *safety*
lack of satisfaction 218.8 *insufficiency*
lack of self-confidence 674.5 *self-deprecation*
lack of self-respect 664.1 *servility*
lack of sensation 489.1 *lack of feeling*
lack of sense 696.11 *unintelligibility*
lack of seriousness 124.7 *triviality*
lack of sex 572.2 *virginity*
lack of sight 519.1 *blindness*
lack of skill 264.2 *awkwardness*; 236.8 *inferiority*; 486.8 *unskilfulness*; 238.3 *uselessness*
lack of smell 501.1 *odourlessness*
lack of solidity 417.3 *sparseness*
lack of spirit 614.1 *cowardice*
lack of strength 260.1 *ill health*; 337.1 *weakness*
lack of style 544.1 *inelegance*; 495.2 *taste of life*
lack of substance 417.3 *sparseness*; 124.5 *unimportance*
lack of success 247.1 *failure*
lack of talent 486.8 *unskilfulness*
lack of talk 626.1 *sullenness*
lack of taste 497.4 *bad taste*
lack of thoroughness 231.5 *imperfection*
lack of transparency 266.1 *obscurity*
lack of understanding 457.2 *unintelligence*; 696.11 *unintelligibility*
lack of unity 372.4 *disunity*
lack of use 350.8 *nonuse*; 238.3 *uselessness*
lack of value 236.7 *worthlessness*
lack of variation 620.1 *boredom*
lack of veneration 668.1 *disrespect*
lack of ventilation 503.1 *stench*
lack of warning 630.1 *surprise*
lack of weight 415.5 *lightness*
lack of willpower 639.12 *inconstancy*
lack of wisdom 457.2 *unintelligence*
lack of wit 457.2 *unintelligence*
lack of zeal 637.13 *dissociation*
lack prejudice 150.12 *be broad-minded*; 473.6 *be disinterested*
lack reason 457.9 *lack intellect*
lack refinement 497.9 *have bad taste*
lack regularity 299.6 *be irregular*; 420.11 *be rough*
lack resolution 754.5 *be irresolute*
lack restraint 250.14 *be free*; 250.19 *liberalize*
lack skill 486.5 *be unskilful*
lack sophistication 805.10 *be naive*
lack talent 486.5 *be unskilful*
lack taste 497.9 *have bad taste*
lack uniformity 420.11 *be rough*
lack unity 372.12 *disagree*
lack variation 620.6 *be boring*
lack variety 620.6 *be boring*
lack weight 415.9 *be light*
laconic 269.3 *concise*; 732.2 *sparing with words*; 723.6 *summary*
laconically 269.5 *concisely*; 723.11 *summarily*
laconicism 269.1 *conciseness*; 732.4 *guarded speech*; 723.4 *summariness*
laconicness 732.4 *guarded speech*
laconism 269.1 *conciseness*; 732.4 *guarded speech*; 723.4 *summariness*
lacquer 550.24 *coat*; 550.3 *coating*; 529.15 *colour*; 529.4 *pigment*; 23.18 *work wood*
lacquered 421.4 *polished*; 23.14 *wooden*
lacquered furniture 23.1 *furniture*
lacquering 23.1 *furniture*
lacrimal 559.5 *of a secretion*
lacrimal gland 559.3 *gland*
lacrimate 559.7 *secrete*
lacrimation 559.1 *secretion*

lacrimatory 559.6 *inducing secretion;* 559.5 *of a secretion;* 559.4 *secretory*
lacrosse 58.5
lacrosse association 58.5 *lacrosse*
lacrosse ball 58.5 *lacrosse*
lacrosse player 58.6
lacrosse stick 58.5 *lacrosse*
lacrosse techniques 58.5 *lacrosse*
lactase 33.11 *enzyme*
lactate 71.36; 559.7 *secrete*
lactating 559.4 *secretory*
lactation 431.3 *body fluid;* 431.7 *juiciness;* 559.1 *secretion*
lactational 559.4 *secretory*
lactationally 559.8 *glandularly*
lacteal 431.17 *milky;* 559.5 *of a secretion*
lacteally 431.26 *fluidly;* 559.8 *glandularly*
lacteous 431.17 *milky*
lactescence 431.7 *juiciness;* 531.7 *whiteness*
lactescent 431.17 *milky;* 559.4 *secretory;* 531.1 *white*
lactic 558.17 *drinkable;* 431.17 *milky*
lactiferous 431.17 *milky;* 559.4 *secretory*
lactifugal 37.14 *counteracting*
lactifuge 37.4 *drug type*
lactogenic 559.6 *inducing secretion*
lactose 557.11 *food content;* 498.2 *sweetener*
lacuna 133.5 *caesura;* 231.7 *defect;* 94.4 *emptiness;* 146.1 *interval;* 141.8 *intervening space;* 135.2 *need;* 233.2 *omission;* 226.3 *pause*
lacuscular 88.9 *lakelike*
lacustral 88.9 *lakelike*
lacustrian 88.6 *lake dweller;* 88.9 *lakelike*
lacustrine 88.9 *lakelike*
lacustrine dweller 88.6 *lake dweller*
lacustrine dwelling 88.7 *lake dwelling*
lacy 153.4 *fine;* 193.6 *interwoven*
lad 555.9 *child;* 567.2 *male;* 567.3 *male title of address;* 555.7 *young man*
ladder 304.9; 132.2 *consecution;* 154.8 *high thing;* 373.4 *means of connection;* 389.2 *means of escape;* 317.2 *route;* 372.9 *separate;* 372.3 *separateness*
ladder-back 23.14 *wooden*
ladder-back chair 23.2 *chair*
ladder climbing 304.6 *mounting*
ladder-like 304.25
laddie 555.9 *child;* 555.7 *young man*
laddish 408.20 *disorderly;* 567.17 *male*
laddishness 408.8 *lawlessness;* 567.1 *male sex*
lade 406.6 *contain;* 232.6 *fill;* 414.14 *make heavy*
laden 232.8 *full;* 406.11, 414.2 *loaded*
laden weight 414.9 *avoirdupois weight*
ladies 560.13 *lavatory;* 767.7 *toilet*
ladies' man 363.6 *charmer;* 227.6 *fickle person;* 567.7 *libertine;* 593.9 *lover*
ladies of the chorus 21.25 *cast*
Ladies Plate 50.5 *Henley trophies*
ladies' room 560.13 *lavatory*
lading 414.6 *displacement;* 406.2 *load*
ladle 410.17; 25.6 *kitchen equipment;* 316.15 *take away*
ladled 410.20 *containing*
Ladoga 88.5 *other major lakes*
la dolce vita 490.1 *physical pleasure*
Lady 568.3 *female title of address*
lady 658.6 *courteous person;* 568.2 *female;* 568.3 *female title of address;* 570.11 *married woman;* 400.1 *master;* 566.10 *member of society;* 566.4 *modern human;* 573.1 *nobleman;* 575.4 *titleholder;* 631.3 *well-behaved person*
Lady Bountiful 679.9 *generous person;* 768.4 *giver*
Lady chapel 10.11 *place of worship*
Lady Chatterley's Lover 796.2 *indecency*
Lady Day 10.15 *holy day*
lady in amorata 593.9 *lover*
lady-in-waiting 401.6 *domestic servant*
lady-killer 593.9 *lover*
ladylike 573.4 *aristocratic;* 568.15 *female;* 658.8 *good-mannered;* 549.5 *refined;* 631.17 *well-behaved*
ladylike behaviour 631.2 *good conduct*
ladylikeness 658.2 *good manners*
lady luck 107.2 *luck*
Lady Mayor 400.3 *leader*
Lady Muck 573.1 *nobleman*
lady of the bedchamber 401.6 *domestic servant*
lady of the house 400.1 *master*
lady of the manor 400.1 *master*
lady of the night 568.7 *prostitute*
Lady Poverty 782.5 *poverty*
lady's maid 401.6 *domestic servant;* 551.28 *valet*
lady with a lamp 35.16 *nurse*
laevo form 32.13 *structure*
lag 493.14 *be hot;* 122.8 *be inferior;* 815.10 *be in prison;* 294.6 *be late;* 251.11 *detain;* 251.4 *detention;* 333.2 *hesitate;* 294.1 *lateness;* 16.40 *lawbreaker;* 65.6 *pool;* 815.4 *prison sentence;* 550.30 *protect;* 454.3 *testify;* 716.13 *turn queen's evidence*
lag behind 168.6 *be in the rear;* 294.6 *be late;* 288.5 *mistime*
lager glass 410.13 *drinking vessel*
laggard 294.4 *latecomer;* 343.3 *not participating;* 333.15 *slow person*
lagged 493.13 *heated*
lagger 716.7 *person who gives evidence;* 454.7 *verifier*
lagging 65.4 *carom;* 294.12 *delaying;* 493.3 *heater;* 333.6 *hesitant;* 294.1 *lateness;* 333.11 *lingering;* 550.12 *protective covering*
lagging behind 294.12 *delaying*
lagniappe 211.4 *extra;* 768.2 *gift;* 765.5 *profit;* 219.3 *superfluity*
lagomorph 71.12 *gnawing mammal*
Lagomorpha 71.12 *gnawing mammal*
lagomorphic 71.31 *rabbit-like*
lagomorphous 71.31 *rabbit-like*
lagoon 30.11 *coast;* 92.2 *island;* 88.1 *lake*
lahar 30.26 *mass movement*
laid 554.15 *born*
laid-back 263.4 *at ease;* 618.7 *indifferent;* 419.6 *soft-hearted*
laid bare 337.9 *dilapidated;* 739.10 *disclosed;* 552.11 *exposed*
laid into 670.34 *censured*
laid low 623.3 *humbled;* 155.5 *low;* 337.11 *weakened*
laid off 708.20 *cancelled;* 767.13 *dismissed;* 341.3 *inactive;* 580.7 *leisurely;* 15.9 *negotiated;* 350.3 *not wanted;* 343.2 *not working;* 144.11 *relegated*
laid out 787.12 *expended*
laid to rest 583.10 *buried*
laid up 337.9 *dilapidated;* 350.4 *disused;* 343.2 *not working;* 335.10 *powerless;* 260.22 *sick;* 439.7 *stored*
laid up in lavender 359.7 *preserved*
Laing 36.29 *psychologist*
Laingian 36.33 *Freudian*
lair 565.13; 71.20 *abode of mammals;* 736.6 *privacy;* 550.15 *shelter*
laird 763.6 *lord;* 400.1 *master*
laissez aller 341.1 *inaction*
laissez faire 776.5 *commercial trade;* 13.6 *economic factors;* 250.1 *freedom;* 341.1 *inaction;* 666.2 *indifference;* 648.1 *leniency;* 757.8 *permitting*
laissez-faire attitude 757.1 *permission*
laissez passer 318.6 *passport;* 757.2 *permit*
lake 88.1; 203.2 *certain amount;* 28.28 *colour;* 42.6 *dye;* 323.2 *waterway*
lake dweller 88.6
lake dwelling 88.7
lake fog 31.33 *fog*
lake house 88.7 *lake dwelling*
lakelet 88.2 *small lake*
lakelike 88.9
lake lodge 88.7 *lake dwelling*
lake naphthol 42.6 *dye*
lake poet 17.14 *author*
laker 88.6 *lake dweller*
Lakes 88
lake sediment 30.27 *sediment*
lakeside dweller 88.6 *lake dweller*
lakeside house 88.7 *lake dwelling*
lakeside village 88.7 *lake dwelling*
lake trout 55.4 *American game fish*
lakh 201.10 *thousand*
lakhs 780.3 *fortune*
Lallans 5.26 *dialect*
lallation 730.3 *speech defect*
lam 313.4 *hurry off*
lama 7.8 *priest*
Lamarckian 34.27 *evolutionary*
Lamarckism 34.16 *evolution*
lamasery 7.10 *priestly dwelling*
lamb 25.26; **25.27**; 71.35 *give birth;* 561.11 *have young;* 805.4 *innocent person;* 43.8 *livestock;* 25.20 *meat;* 646.3 *naive person;* 593.12 *nicknames for lovers;* 43.18 *practise livestock farming;* 589.2 *symbol of peace;* 555.4 *young animal;* 71.19 *young mammal*
lambada 22.2 *dance*
lambast 670.21 *berate*
lambaste 331.5 *beat;* 814.3 *hit*
lambasted 670.34 *censured*
lambasting 670.8 *berating*
lambent 522.15 *lucent*
Lambeth 87.5 *London*
Lambeth Palace 7.10 *priestly dwelling*
Lambeth Walk 22.2 *dance*
lambing house 43.7 *farm building*
lambkin 555.4 *young animal;* 71.19 *young mammal*
lambkins 593.12 *nicknames for lovers*
lamblike 805.5 *innocent*
Lamb of God 8.4 *God the Son*
lambrequin 743.8 *heraldic device*
lamb's liver 25.31 *offal*
lamb to the slaughter 762.3 *substitute thing;* 450.6 *trusting person*
lame 231.3 *deformed;* 245.5 *hurt;* 337.10 *ill;* 233.4 *incomplete;* 238.8 *make useless;* 335.8 *overpower;* 337.7 *weaken*
lamebrain 457.3 *unintelligent person*
lame dog 766.6 *loser;* 337.4 *weakling*
lame duck 766.6 *loser;* 786.6 *nonpayer;* 249.5 *person in adversity;* 337.4 *weakling*
lamella 411.3 *coat;* 83.4 *fungal body*
lamellar 411.9 *platelike*
lamellar compound 32.7 *chemical compound*
lamellate 411.9 *platelike*
lamellated 411.9 *platelike*
lamellation 411.6 *layering*
lamellibranch 75.5 *mollusc*
lamelliform 411.9 *platelike*
lameness 245.11 *hurt;* 231.5 *imperfection;* 337.3 *poor health*
lament 603.2; **603.6**; 582.17, 583.8 *bury;* 627.2 *condolence;* 514.13 *cry;* 583.2 *funeral;* 602.8 *grieve;* 627.9 *sorrow*
lamentable 603.5; 611.8 *bad;* 602.7 *distressing;* 236.4 *poor*
Lamentation 603
lamentation 603.1; 582.8 *after death;* 514.6 *cry of pain;* 583.2 *funeral;* 603.2 *lament*
lamented 582.19 *dead*
lamenter 603.3
lamenting 603.4; 583.11 *funeral;* 603.1 *lamentation;* 808.6 *penitent*
lame verse 17.6 *poetry*
lamia 70.7 *legendary beast;* 11.4 *witch*
lamina 424.3 *brittle thing;* 411.3 *coat;* 77.6 *leaf;* 84.3 *plant body;* 27.38 *surface;* 23.11 *woodworking tool*
laminate 411.10 *layer;* 411.7 *layered;* 411.5 *layered thing;* 24.11 *make ceramics;* 23.18 *work wood*
laminated 411.8 *coated;* 411.7 *layered*
laminated furniture 23.1 *furniture*
laminated glass 527.9 *glass;* 24.9 *industrial ceramics;* 411.5 *layered thing*
laminated paper 435.3 *paper*
laminated wood 411.5 *layered thing*
lamination 411.6 *layering*
Lammas 10.15 *holy day*
lamp 522.5 *incandescent light;* 28.25 *light source*
lampblack 532.8 *black pigment*
lampholder 522.6 *electric light*
lamping 633.2 *chase*
lamplight 522.5 *incandescent light*
lamplighter 522.7 *lantern*
lamplit 522.18 *lit*
lampoon 621.2 *act of derision;* 599.13 *be humorous;* 621.6 *deride;* 599.4 *entertainment;* 668.4, 678.6, 678.14 *ridicule*
lampooner 621.3 *derider;* 599.6 *humorist;* 678.9 *ridiculer*
lampoonist 621.3 *derider;* 678.9 *ridiculer*
lamppost 522.6 *electric light;* 154.6 *tall thing*
lampshade 524.1 *dimness;* 550.12 *protective covering*
lampshell 75.5 *mollusc*
lamp-standard 522.6 *electric light*
LAN 40.15 *network*
Län 86.5 *state*
lanate 420.3 *barbed*
Lancashire hotpot 25.44 *British dish*
lance 586.37 *fight;* 44.6 *garden tool;* 308.20 *hole;* 382.17 *murder;* 308.2 *opener;* 425.8 *sharp-pointed thing;* 587.8 *sharp weapon;* 381.6 *stab;* 330.23 *throw;* 425.16 *use a sharp tool*
lance-corporal 586.17 *army person*
lanced 308.14 *holed*
lancelet 75.2 *protochordate*
Lancelot 255.5 *pure person*
Lancelot and Guinevere 593.10 *lovers*
lanceolate 77.18 *of leaves;* 425.1 *sharp*
lancer 586.20 *cavalryman;* 586.13 *historical soldiery;* 59.15 *horse person*
lance rest 384.7 *armour*
Lancers 22.2 *dance*
lance-shaped 425.1 *sharp*
lancet 20.13 *arched;* 308.2 *opener;* 425.8 *sharp-pointed thing*
lancet arch 20.5 *arch*
lancet window 20.9 *miscellaneous architectural features*
lancinating 491.5 *painful*
lancination 491.1 *pain*
Land 86.5 *state*
land 312.4; 301.8 *be motionless;* 57.10 *compete in gymnastics;* 30.6 *continent;* 85.1 *country;* 305.12 *drop;* 322.10 *fly;* 47.8 *jump;* 77.14 *of plants;* 440.1 *property;* 86.1 *region;* 323.10 *sail*
land a blow 52.11 *fight*
land and sea 113.3 *opposites*
land a rabbit punch 52.11 *fight*
land attack 381.12 *military attack*
land breeze 50.1 *sailing;* 31.12 *wind*
land bridge 30.16 *ocean floor;* 92.5 *peninsula*
land crab 75.4 *arthropod*
landed 763.8 *possessing;* 440.8 *propertied*
landed estate 763.4 *possession;* 440.1 *property*
landed gentry 573.2 *aristocracy*
landed property 440.1 *property*
lander 29.33 *planetary probe*
landfall 312.11 *landing*
landfill 238.6 *refuse;* 767.8 *sink;* 439.4 *storage*
landfill site 767.5 *wasteyard*
land forces 584.2 *the military*
landform 30.7
land-grabber 700.17 *cheat*
landholding 763.1 *possession*
landing 312.11; 174.3 *architectural summit;* 305.5 *dive;* 47.2 *field events;* 322.5 *flight;* 57.5 *horizontal bar;* 411.2 *level;* 304.7 *means of ascent;* 565.7 *room;* 47.9 *track*
landing area 47.2 *field events*
landing beam 322.6 *flight control*
landing craft 586.24 *warship*
landing field 322.4 *airport;* 317.13 *flight path*
landing on one's feet 246.1 *success*
landing stage 304.7 *means of ascent*
landing strip 322.4 *airport*
land in the cooler 815.10 *be in prison*
landlady 436.4 *caterer;* 400.1 *master*
landlocked 172.9 *inland;* 88.9 *lakelike*
landlocked water 88.2 *small lake*
landlord 436.4 *caterer;* 400.1 *master;* 763.5 *possessor;* 575.4 *titleholder*
landlubber 486.10 *unskilled person*
landmark 99.2 *essential content;* 123.2 *important matter;* 742.5 *indicator;* 520.6 *visible thing*
landmass 30.6, 92.1 *continent;* 86.1 *region*
landmine 587.16 *bomb*
land-office business 248.1 *prosperity*
Land of Liberty 85.7 *United States*
land of Nod 343.9 *sleep*
land of our fathers 86.4 *territorial division*
land of promise 756.4 *promised land*
land on a beach 92.12 *be marooned*
land one in trouble 236.13 *be worthless*
land on one's feet 252.9 *be safe;* 246.7 *overcome obstacles*
land operations 585.8 *warfare*
landowner 400.1 *master;* 763.5 *possessor;* 440.7 *property man;* 575.4 *titleholder*
landownership 763.1 *possession*
landowning 763.8 *possessing;* 763.1 *possession*
land pirate 700.17 *cheat*
lands 440.1 *property*
landscape 19.10 *art subject;* 30.6 *continent;* 41.4 *portrait;* 44.14 *practise horticulture;* 518.7 *view*
landscape architect 20.2 *architect;* 44.13 *horticulturist*
landscape architecture 20.1 *architecture;* 44.1 *horticulture*
landscaped 44.19 *ornamental*
landscape gardener 44.13 *horticulturist*
landscape gardening 44.1 *horticulture*
landscape painter 19.16 *artist*

landscape photography 41.1 *photography*
landscapist 44.13 *horticulturist*
land shark 700.17 *cheat*
landside 322.4 *airport*
landslide 357.7 *agent of destruction*; 305.3 *downflow*; 30.26 *mass movement*
landslide victory 246.2 *victory*
landslip 357.7 *agent of destruction*; 305.3 *downflow*
land station 31.5 *weather station*
land tenure 763.1 *possession*
land travel 300.2 *momentum*
land-use planning 38.17 *civil engineering*
landward 324.10 *clockwise*
lane 320.3 *carriageway*; 317.11 *channel*; 317.3, 373.5 *road*; 317.2 *route*; 47.1 *track events*
Lange 36.29 *psychologist*
Langlauf 68.2 *cross-country skiing*; 68.1 *skiing*
langouste 25.19 *shellfish*
language 729.1 *faculty of speech*; 724.4 *literary style*; 40.9 *programming language*; 40.8 *software*; 6.3 *subject*
Language and Linguistics 5
language group 5.11 *family of languages*
language laboratory 6.15 *schoolroom*
language of confusion 5.5 *nonstandard language*
language student 5.2 *linguist*
language type 5.10
langue 729.1 *faculty of speech*; 5.3 *spoken language*
languid 261.1 *fatigued*; 337.10 *ill*; 339.5 *inert*; 343.3 *not participating*; 301.5 *sedentary*; 333.5 *unhurried*
languidly 343.16 *impassively*; 339.7 *inertly*; 301.10 *motionlessly*; 333.16 *slowly*; 337.14 *weakly*
languish 261.5 *be fatigued*; 260.24 *be unhealthy*; 337.6 *be weak*; 602.8 *grieve*
languisher 602.3 *sad person*
languishing 593.19 *enamoured*; 602.5 *sad*; 260.22 *sick*
languishing look 593.14 *communication of love*
languishment 261.7 *fatigue*; 602.1 *sorrow*
languor 620.1 *boredom*; 261.7 *fatigue*; 343.7 *idleness*; 339.1 *inertness*; 301.1 *motionlessness*; 333.8 *slowness*
languorous 620.4 *boring*; 261.1 *fatigued*; 301.5 *sedentary*; 333.5 *unhurried*
languorously 620.8 *boringly*; 301.10 *motionlessly*; 333.16 *slowly*
lank 544.10 *ugly*
lankiness 154.1 *height*; 153.7 *thinness*
lanky 154.12 *tall*; 153.1 *thin*
lanolin 394.9 *balm*; 268.7 *pomade*
lantern 522.7; 154.8 *high thing*; 20.9 *miscellaneous architectural features*
lantern cupola 20.9 *miscellaneous architectural features*
lantern-jawed 153.1 *thin*
lantern jaws 153.7 *thinness*
lanternslide 41.12 *development*
lanthanoid 32.6 *chemical element*
lanyard 50.3 *parts of a sailing boat*; 373.7 *tackle*
laodicean 618.6 *indifferent person*
lap 332.6 *accelerate*; 179.2, 179.6 *circle*; 298.2 *cycle*; 558.13 *drink*; 329.3 *exceed*; 90.7 *flow*; 184.9 *fold*; 411.1 *layer*; 61.6 *motor-racing terms*; 181.12 *move round*; 306.3 *orbit*; 550.26 *overlie*; 47.7, 61.9 *race*; 252.5 *refuge*; 306.7 *ring*; 90.6 *river flow*; 181.6 *round*; 205.3 *stage*; 67.1 *swimming*; 204.3 *whole situation*
laparoscope 35.7 *diagnosis*
laparoscopy 35.7 *diagnosis*
laparotomy 394.12 *surgery*
lapdog 117.6 *conformist*; 71.9 *dog*; 664.3 *sycophant*
lapel 211.3 *additional item*; 551.24 *part of garment*
lapel pin 743.5 *uniform*
lap fence 44.3 *ornamental garden*
lapidary 19.18 *engraver*; 583.11 *funeral*; 5.43 *phrasal*
lapidary inscription 5.25 *inscription*
lapidary phrases 583.4 *funeral objects*
lapidate 814.5 *execute*; 381.7 *stone*; 330.23 *throw*
lapidation 814.13 *capital punishment*; 381.18 *hit*
lapideous 418.1 *hard*
lapidification 418.6 *solidification*
lapis lazuli 539.6 *blue thing*
lap joint 23.10 *carpenter's term*
lap of luxury 222.5 *comfortable circumstances*; 248.1 *prosperity*
lapped 332.3 *accelerating*; 61.10 *racing*
lappet 211.3 *additional item*
lapping 332.3 *accelerating*; 332.9 *acceleration*; 558.1 *drinking*; 61.10 *racing*; 90.6 *river flow*
lap robe 550.5 *body covering*
Lapsang Souchong 558.3 *tea*
lapse 303.19 *backsliding*; 487.4 *be unaccustomed*; 804.16 *be wicked*; 245.1 *deteriorate*; 245.7 *deterioration*; 451.8 *disbelieve*; 796.16 *do wrong*; 303.1 *go backwards*; 472.5 *inattentive act*; 141.8 *intervening space*; 274.19 *make a mistake*; 806.3 *sin*; 305.2 *sinkage*; 141.21 *space*; 274.20 *transgress*; 274.9 *trivial error*; 325.16 *wandering*
lapsed 245.12 *deteriorated*; 3.18 *in the past*
lapse into disorder 408.25 *be disordered*
lapse into oblivion 122.10 *follow*
lapse into unconsciousness 335.6 *be powerless*
lapse of memory 463.3 *poor memory*
lapse of time 275.2 *passage of time*; 277.2 *time*
lapsing 303.23 *receding*
lapsus calami 274.9 *trivial error*
lapsus linguae 274.9 *trivial error*
laptop 40.3 *computer*
lap up 558.13 *drink*; 370.11 *ingest*
Laputan 477.11 *fantastical*
lapwing 72.3 *water bird*
larcenist 774.8 *thief*
larcenous 774.17 *stolen*
larcenously 774.19 *thievishly*
larceny 774.1 *stealing*
lard 268.19 *anoint*; 25.7 *basic ingredient*; 25.55 *cook*; 158.8 *fat*; 268.18 *lubricate*
lardaceous 268.13 *slippery*
larder 25.3 *kitchen*; 25.4 *kitchen container*; 565.7 *room*; 439.4 *storage*
larder-fridge 25.4 *kitchen container*
larding needle 25.6 *kitchen equipment*
lardy 268.13 *slippery*
lardy cake 25.36 *cake*
large 797.7; 158.15, 679.4 *big*; 414.1 *heavy*
large amount 203.2 *certain amount*; 208.2 *multitude*
large-animal practice 35.5 *veterinary medicine*
large as life 158.15 *big*
large-format camera 41.16 *camera*
large-hearted 652.6 *philanthropic*
large inheritance 781.5 *wealth*
large-lettered 5.41 *lettered*
largely 158.20; **190.10**; 414.16 *heavily*; 123.9 *importantly*; 204.13 *on the whole*; 138.31 *overall*
largemouth black bass 55.4 *American game fish*
largeness 797.14; 158.2 *bigness*
large number 194.3
large numbers 208.2 *multitude*
large office 577.1 *workshop*
large order 264.3 *difficult task*
large-print book 519.3 *aid for poor sight*
larger 190.7 *bigger*
larger than life 158.15 *big*
large scale 158.3
large-scale 158.15 *big*
large size 797.14 *largeness*; 158.3 *large scale*
large-size 158.15 *big*; 797.7 *large*
largess 768.1 *giving*; 768.3 *offering*
largest 27.75 *equal*
largest part 205.5
large turnout 208.4 *throng*
larghetto 333.16 *slowly*
largo 333.16 *slowly*
lariat 373.9 *yoke*
lark 304.11 *ascender*; 597.2 *fun*; 599.5 *joke*; 72.6 *songbird*
lark about 697.8 *fool*
lark around 340.4 *act*
larrikin 651.8 *malefactor*
larrup 814.3 *hit*
larva 76.5; 70.5 *aquatic animal*; 34.15 *developmental biology*; 344.3 *rudiment*; 555.4 *young animal*
larval 34.26 *developmental*; 76.13 *immature*
laryngitis 491.2 *painful condition*; 260.9 *respiratory disease*; 506.4 *silence*
larynx 729.5 *organ of speech*; 507.4 *sound maker*
lascivious 593.20 *amorous*; 796.14 *lecherous*; 617.11 *lustful*; 258.9 *obscene*
lasciviously 258.12 *dirtily*; 593.30 *lovingly*; 617.20 *lustfully*
lasciviousness 593.5 *desire*; 258.3 *obscenity*; 796.3 *sexual immorality*
laser 28.26; 334.9 *electronics*; 522.12 *highlight*; 587.1 *weapon*
laser copy 744.5 *copy*
laser printer 115.3 *copier*; 40.7 *peripheral*
laser show 522.12 *highlight*; 21.7 *show*
laser surgery 35.9 *surgery*
laser targeting 381.13 *air attack*
lash 331.5 *beat*; 670.21 *berate*; 331.13 *blow*; 373.11 *connect*; 262.1 *hasten*; 814.3 *hit*; 814.14 *instrument of punishment*; 380.9 *make violent*; 483.10 *manipulate*; 483.4 *negative stimulus*
lashed 373.15 *connected*
lashing 373.6 *line*
lashings 217.8 *plenty*
lash into a fury 380.9 *make violent*
lash out at 381.5 *strike*
lass 555.9 *child*; 568.3 *female title of address*; 593.9 *lover*; 555.8 *young woman*
Lassa fever 260.7 *tropical disease*
lassi 25.49 *Indian dish*; 558.5 *milk*
lassie 555.9 *child*; 568.2 *female*; 568.3 *female title of address*; 555.8 *young woman*
lassitude 261.7 *fatigue*
lasso 373.12 *bind*; 587.6 *historical missile weapon*; 373.9 *yoke*
lassoed 373.16 *bound*
lasso lift 68.6 *ice-skating*
last 277.6; 289.15 *as follows*; 225.5 *be permanent*; 423.10 *be tough*; 93.19 *continue to be*; 313.11 *departing*; 131.20 *ending*; 131.24 *limiting*; 554.16 *live*; 129.11 *prior*; 134.4 *protract*; 289.12 *succeeding*
last act 131.10 *ending*
last agony 582.7 *dying day*
last an eternity 225.5 *be permanent*
last a round 52.12 *wrestle*
last arrival 294.1 *lateness*
last arriver 294.4 *latecomer*
last ball 131.9 *close*
last bid 353.5 *attempt*
last breath 131.3 *death*; 582.7 *dying day*
last cent 131.8 *tail*
last challenge 353.5 *attempt*
last-ditcher 641.8 *obstinate person*; 113.11 *opposer*
last-ditch stand 294.3 *delayed action*
last forever 279.5 *be eternal*; 202.9 *be infinite*; 225.5 *be permanent*
last frontier 131.7 *limit*
last gallery 63.5 *real tennis*
last gasp 131.3 *death*; 582.7 *dying day*; 352.1 *means*
last handshake 313.9 *parting*
last hope 610.1 *hope*; 352.1 *means*
last hour 582.7 *dying day*
lasting 93.12; **277.8**; 554.12 *alive*; 279.10 *continuing forever*; 632.11 *normal*; 225.7 *permanent*; 134.6 *protracted*; 423.1 *tough*
lastingly 134.7 *continually*; 225.9 *permanently*; 423.12 *toughly*
lastingness 423.6 *toughness*
lasting peace 589.1 *peace*
lasting power 423.8 *physical strength*
lasting through time 275.21
last innings 131.9 *close*
last in the field 289.8 *follower*
Last Judgment 283.3 *future condition*; 464.4 *judgment day*
last judgment 131.5 *fate*
last lap 131.9 *close*; 312.15 *destination*
last laugh 131.10 *ending*
lastly 289.15 *as follows*; 131.26 *finally*
last man in 289.8 *follower*
last minute 287.3 *critical time*; 294.2 *late hour*
last-minute 262.3 *hasty*; 287.8 *in time*; 294.11 *late in the day*; 254.2 *unsafe*
last-minute preparations 294.3 *delayed action*
last-minute rescue 484.3 *expedient plan*
last-minute rush 262.4 *haste*
last moment 195.4 *zero level*
last month 284.22 *in the past*; 284.1 *past time*
last name 721.8 *name*
last night 284.1 *past time*
last one out 215.6 *person remaining*
last orders 131.11 *finality*
last out 277.6 *last*
last outpost 166.3 *furthest point*
last over 131.9 *close*
last penny 131.8 *tail*
last place 289.3 *subordination*
last post 583.2 *funeral*; 603.2 *lament*; 313.9 *parting*; 742.6 *word*
last quarter 29.17 *moon*
last resort 239.5 *convenience*; 484.3 *expedient plan*; 352.1 *means*; 252.5 *refuge*
last rest 301.3 *resting place*
last rites 10.5 *Christian rite*; 582.7 *dying day*; 603.1 *lamentation*
last round 131.9 *close*
last season 284.22 *in the past*
last-second 254.2 *unsafe*
last shot 353.5 *attempt*
last stage 131.9 *close*
last stop 312.15 *destination*; 131.6 *end point*
last straw 378.6 *burden*; 624.3 *cause of offence*; 219.2 *overdoing it*
last throw 352.1 *means*
last time of asking 710.2 *demand*
last touch 232.1 *completeness*
last try 353.5 *attempt*
last waltz 22.2 *dance*
last week 284.22 *in the past*; 284.1 *past time*
last will and testament 768.1 *giving*; 253.2 *promise*; 635.5 *will*
last word 713.4 *adviser*; 752.3 *business offer*; 706.5 *counterstatement*; 294.3 *delayed action*; 131.10 *ending*; 235.8 *exceller*; 244.5 *improvement*; 230.3 *perfection*
last words 131.3 *death*; 582.7 *dying day*; 313.9 *parting*
last year 284.22 *in the past*; 284.1 *past time*
Las Vegas 87.2 *American cities*
Las Vegas wedding 570.5 *wedding*
latch 373.12 *bind*; 309.7 *close*; 373.8 *fastening*; 309.3 *restrainer*
latched 373.16 *bound*; 309.12 *closed*
latch on to 664.14 *follow*; 695.6 *understand*
late 294.9; **294.15**; 294.14, 582.19 *dead*; 333.7 *delayed*; 291.7 *evening*; 284.20 *former*; 129.11 *prior*; 605.7 *resigning*; 289.12 *succeeding*
late arrival 294.1 *lateness*
late arriver 294.4 *latecomer*
late at night 291.7 *evening*
late bloomer 294.4 *latecomer*
latecomer 294.4; 289.8 *follower*; 295.8 *new arrival*
late developer 294.4 *latecomer*
late edition 740.4 *newspaper*
late evening 524.1 *dimness*
late extra 740.4 *newspaper*
late hour 294.2
late in the day 294.11
late lamented 294.14, 582.19 *dead*
late lift 47.2 *field events*
lately 605.10 *by resigning*; 294.18 *formerly*; 284.22 *in the past*; 294.15 *late*; 295.21 *newly*
latency 645.1 *cunning*; 339.1 *inertness*; 521.4 *invisibility*; 301.1 *motionlessness*; 484.4 *plot*; 694.4 *type of meaning*
Lateness 294
lateness 294.1; 262.4 *haste*; 288.2 *untimeliness*
late-night review 21.7 *show*
latent 634.18 *avoiding*; 736.15 *disguised*; 339.5 *inert*; 521.1 *invisible*; 11.14 *occult*; 301.5 *sedentary*
latent heat 493.2 *heat measurement*; 28.38 *thermodynamics*
latent image 41.11 *emulsion*
latently 339.7 *inertly*; 301.10 *motionlessly*
latent meaning 694.4 *type of meaning*
later 294.13; **294.17**; 286.3 *another time*; 283.11 *future*; 283.14 *in the future*; 289.12 *succeeding*
lateral 46.9 *play*; 46.15 *play offence*; 169.6 *side*
lateral bud 77.8 *bud*
laterality 169.1 *side*
lateral line 74.5 *fish anatomy*
laterally 169.10
lateral movement 30.13 *ocean current*
lateral root 77.7 *root*
laterals 336.1 *strength*
lateral thinking 476.2 *basis of supposition*; 443.5 *creative thought*
lateral water hazard 56.1 *golf*

later generations 289.6 *posterity*
late riser 294.4 *latecomer*
lateritic soil 30.36 *soil*
later on 283.14 *in the future;* 294.17 *later*
later time 286.1 *different time*
late-running 294.12 *delaying*
latest 295.10 *new;* 289.12 *succeeding*
latest news 741.9 *news story*
late wood 79.3 *timber*
latex 431.2 *juice;* 435.1 *materials;* 422.4 *rubber;* 559.2 *secreted substance*
lath 23.17 *carpenter;* 153.11 *fineness;* 435.1 *materials;* 411.4 *slice;* 23.12 *wood*
lath and plaster 435.2 *building material*
lathe 23.17 *carpenter;* 38.9 *machine tool;* 760.4 *medium of conversion;* 23.11 *woodworking tool*
lather 434.10 *air bubble;* 256.14 *bathe;* 814.3 *hit;* 268.5 *lubricant;* 268.18 *lubricate*
lathering 256.5 *ablutions*
lathery 531.2 *whitened*
lathi 587.7 *blunt weapon*
lathing 23.12 *wood*
laths 23.10 *carpenter's term*
lathwork 23.12 *wood*
laticifer 559.3 *gland*
laticiferous 559.4 *secretory*
Latin American Integration Association 779.4 *free market;* 13.5 *international trade*
Latinate 542.10 *ornate*
Latin cross plan 20.10 *church architecture*
Latino 1.6 *race*
latitude 27.39 *angle;* 141.6 *available space;* 166.4 *boundary marker;* 150.4 *breadth;* 657.4 *freedom;* 86.2 *geographical region;* 250.5 *scope;* 143.1 *situation;* 26.4 *size*
latitude and longitude 142.2 *exact location*
latitudinal 166.6 *furthest;* 86.16 *regional*
latitudinal line 119.7 *dividing line*
latitudinally 86.19 *geographically*
latitudinarian 250.8 *free-thinker;* 250.10 *independent;* 648.2 *lenient person*
latitudinarianism 250.1 *freedom*
latrine 560.13 *lavatory;* 503.2 *something that makes an unpleasant smell;* 767.7 *toilet*
latter 168.4 *rear;* 289.12 *succeeding*
latter days 283.3 *future condition*
Latter-Day Saint 7.5 *Christian*
latter end 168.2 *rear end*
latterly 295.21 *newly*
lattice 193.2 *braid;* 32.4 *crystal;* 403.4 *framework;* 308.6 *porous thing*
latticework 403.4 *framework*
laud 10.19 *offer worship;* 667.17, 669.3, 669.14 *praise;* 9.7 *worship*
laudable 617.8 *desirable;* 669.21 *praiseworthy;* 667.13 *respectable;* 235.1 *worthy*
laudably 235.11 *worthily*
laudanum 489.4 *anaesthetic;* 394.5 *analgesic;* 685.2 *moderator*
laudation 669.3 *praise;* 10.3 *rite of worship;* 9.1 *worship*
laudational 10.21 *ritualistic*
laudator 669.9 *praiser*
laudatory 669.18 *approving;* 677.12 *flattering*
lauds 10.4 *public worship*
laugh **514.11**; **599.14**; **600.8**; 598.7 *be cheerful;* 507.8 *be loud;* 514.2 *cry of joy;* 742.3, 742.11 *gesture;* 600.3 *laughter;* 597.7 *show joy;* 697.2 *solecism*
laughable 599.9 *funny;* 600.10 *laughing;* 697.5 *nonsensical;* 272.5 *ridiculous*
laughableness 272.1 *ludicrousness*
laughably 599.16 *humorously;* 272.8 *ridiculously*
laugh at 621.6 *deride;* 470.3 *exclude;* 668.25 *taunt*
laugh at an offer 218.6 *be unsatisfied*
laugh at danger 613.15 *be courageous*
laugher 600.4 *rejoicer*
laughing **600.10**; 598.1 *cheerful;* 514.17 *cheering;* 742.15 *gestural*
laughing gas 394.5 *analgesic*
laughingly 621.7 *mockingly*
laughing stock **621.4**; 668.9 *butt;* 751.4 *dissenter;* 700.22 *dupe*
laugh in someone's face 661.6 *be insubordinate*
laugh like a drain 599.14 *laugh*
laugh line 184.1 *wrinkle*
laugh one's head off 599.14 *laugh*
laugh out of court 660.29 *ridicule*
laughter **600.3**; 599.2 *amusement;* 598.3 *cheerfulness;* 514.2 *cry of joy;* 507.1 *loudness*
laughter and tears 113.3 *opposites*
laugh till one cries 599.14 *laugh*
launch **29.38**; 130.20 *activate;* 525.1 *appearance;* 295.19, 308.24 *begin;* 130.1, 308.11 *beginning;* 130.23, 344.11 *inaugurate;* 130.6 *inauguration;* 601.19 *install;* 323.9 *navigate;* 130.9 *premiere;* 525.14 *present;* 330.20 *propel;* 50.15 *sail;* 330.33 *start;* 304.19 *take off;* 331.4 *throw;* 354.1 *undertake*
launch a balloon d'essai 353.4 *test*
launch an appeal 765.9 *gain;* 768.6 *give to charity;* 710.8 *solicit money*
launch an attack 381.1 *attack*
launch a trial balloon 740.13 *make public;* 353.4 *test*
launched 130.37 *enrolled;* 295.13 *inaugurated;* 323.11 *nautical*
launched into eternity 582.19 *dead*
launcher 29.35 *rocketry*
launching 295.4 *beginning;* 130.9 *premiere;* 243.9 *preparation;* 323.4 *shipbuilding*
launching ceremony 323.4 *shipbuilding*
launching pad 587.5 *missile weapon*
launching site 317.13 *flight path*
launch into 354.1 *undertake*
launch into eternity 382.16 *kill*
launch out at 381.5 *strike*
launch vehicle 29.35 *rocketry*
launder 256.13 *clean;* 421.11 *smooth*
laundered 256.17 *cleaned*
laundered money 813.8 *secret money*
launderer 256.12 *cleaner*
laundering 42.8 *fabric treatment*
laundress 256.12 *cleaner*
laundrette 256.7 *washer*
laundry **256.8**; 256.2 *cleaning;* 577.1 *workshop*
laundry basket 410.7 *basket*
laundry maid 401.6 *domestic servant*
laundryman 256.12 *cleaner*
laundry room 565.7 *room;* 577.1 *workshop*
Laurasia 30.19 *plate tectonics*
laureate 121.6 *paragon*
laurels 482.6 *objective;* 794.1 *trophy*
laurel wreath 794.1 *trophy*
lav 565.7 *room*
lava 30.25 *eruption;* 493.8 *hot place*
lavabo 10.6 *Eucharist*
lava flow 30.25 *eruption*
lavage 256.5 *ablutions*
laval 30.55 *volcanic*
lavation 256.5 *ablutions*
lavatory **560.13**; 565.7 *room;* 767.7 *toilet*
lavatory attendant 256.12 *cleaner*
lavatory bowl 767.7 *toilet*
lavatory paper 256.11 *cleaning cloth*
lave 433.34 *hose;* 255.10, 256.15 *purify*
lavender 502.2 *fragrant thing;* 540.6 *purple;* 540.3 *purple thing*
lavender bag 502.2 *fragrant thing*
lavender sachet 502.2 *fragrant thing*
lavender water **433.14**; 78.8 *flower product;* 502.2 *fragrant thing*
laver 25.33 *vegetable*
laver bread 84.5 *algal product;* 25.33 *vegetable*
laverock 304.11 *ascender*
laving 433.11 *wash*
lavish 679.3 *abundant;* 219.4 *be excessive;* 727.9 *be extravagant;* 681.1, 727.14 *extravagant;* 679.1 *generous;* 781.3 *opulent;* 217.2 *plentiful;* 441.1, 681.7 *waste;* 441.8 *wasteful*
lavishly 727.17 *excessively;* 681.9 *extravagantly;* 679.12 *generously;* 441.10 *wastefully;* 781.16 *wealthily*
lavishness 681.4, 727.3 *extravagance;* 781.7 *opulence;* 441.3 *waste*
lavish upon 219.4 *be excessive;* 768.5 *give*
Law 16
law **16.3**; **28.6**; 396.1 *authority;* 397.1 *command;* 407.9 *discipline;* 745.1 *maxim;* 298.4 *orderliness;* 757.1 *permission;* 713.3 *precept;* 140.1 *rule;* 16.1 *the law;* 27.65 *theory;* 632.5 *tradition;* 464.2 *verdict*
law-abiding **16.50**; 117.14 *conformist;* 407.17 *disciplined;* 799.4 *honourable;* 663.7 *obedient;* 589.7 *peaceful;* 801.11 *right-minded;* 388.5 *submitting;* 631.17 *well-behaved*
law-abiding citizen 663.4 *obedient person;* 631.3 *well-behaved person*
law and equity 16.1 *the law*
law and order 407.9 *discipline;* 589.1 *peace*
lawbreaker **16.40**; 662.9 *criminal;* 800.4 *dishonourable person;* 651.8 *malefactor;* 804.9 *wicked person;* 802.10 *wrongdoer*
lawbreaking **16.38**; **753.10**; 800.7, 804.15 *criminal;* 800.3, 804.7 *criminality;* 662.13 *disobedient;* 662.2 *violation of the law*
law consultancy 16.32 *jurisprudence*
law court **16.19**; 16.7 *legal trial;* 464.3 *place of judgment*
law courts 16.27 *courtroom*
law-enforcer 16.17 *police officer*
lawful 396.12 *authoritative;* 407.17 *disciplined;* 16.44 *legal;* 698.24 *pedantic;* 757.7 *permitted*
lawful authority 396.1 *authority*
lawfully 396.23 *authoritatively;* 16.86 *jurisdictionally;* 16.81 *legally;* 757.9 *with permission*
lawfulness 16.28 *legality;* 698.11 *pedantry*
lawful possession 763.1 *possession*
lawgiver 579.13 *director;* 12.7 *governor;* 16.9 *lawmaker*
lawgiving 16.31 *legislation;* 16.45 *legislative*
lawless **16.61**; 588.6 *anarchic;* 662.13 *disobedient;* 408.20 *disorderly;* 802.16 *in the wrong;* 753.10 *lawbreaking*
lawlessly **16.84**; 588.8 *anarchically;* 753.11 *disapprovingly;* 662.17 *disobediently*
lawlessness **16.41**; **408.8**; 588.1 *anarchy;* 753.2 *disorder;* 802.6 *unlawfulness;* 662.2 *violation of the law*
Law Lord 16.9 *lawmaker*
lawmaker **16.9**; **251.6**; 579.13 *director;* 12.7 *governor*
lawmaking 16.31 *legislation;* 16.45 *legislative;* 579.3 *management*
lawn 81.2 *grassland;* 538.8 *greenness;* 44.3 *ornamental garden;* 421.8 *smooth thing*
lawn bowls 51.1 *green bowling*
lawn grass 81.1 *grass*
lawn meet 59.8 *hunting*
lawn mower 44.6, 438.3 *garden tool;* 81.5 *grass cutter;* 425.9 *sharp-edged thing*
lawn party 654.5 *party*
lawn rake 44.6 *garden tool*
lawn tennis 63.1 *tennis*
law of averages 104.5 *probability theory;* 140.3 *rule of nature*
law of commerce 16.1 *the law*
law of contract 16.1 *the law*
law of crime 16.1 *the law*
law of diminishing returns 245.7 *deterioration*
law officer **16.10**
law of nations 16.1 *the law*
law of the air 16.1 *the law*
law of the jungle 588.1 *anarchy;* 140.3 *rule of nature*
law of the land 16.1 *the law*
law of the sea 16.1 *the law*
law reports 16.7 *legal trial*
laws 12.5 *political organization*
law school 6.12 *educational institution*
laws of motion 28.6 *law;* 300.1 *motion*
laws of nature 402.1 *material world*
laws of reflection 28.6 *law*
laws of refraction 28.6 *law*
laws of thermodynamics 28.6 *law*
lawsuit 715.1 *accusation;* 340.1 *action;* 16.5, 16.33 *litigation*
lawyer **16.13**; 713.4 *adviser;* 398.6 *agent;* 586.5, 701.6 *arguer;* 471.6 *attentive person;* 644.3 *curious person;* 395.5 *influential person;* 483.7 *motivator;* 746.4 *negotiator;* 705.9 *questioner*
lax 650.6 *benevolent;* 618.8 *careless;* 657.10 *free;* 453.6 *indeterminate;* 666.5 *indifferent;* 339.5 *inert;* 648.4 *lenient;* 343.3 *not participating;* 757.8 *permitting;* 268.10 *slippery;* 419.1 *soft;* 419.6 *soft-hearted;* 250.12 *unconditional;* 804.13 *venial*
laxation 419.12 *gentleness*
laxative 256.2 *cleaning;* 37.4 *drug type;* 371.29 *expulsive;* 560.25 *faecal;* 371.28 *propellant;* 255.4, 394.6 *purgative;* 394.17 *remedial;* 37.17 *stimulating*
laxity 618.2 *carelessness;* 657.4 *freedom;* 419.12 *gentleness;* 274.2 *inaccuracy;* 453.14 *indeterminacy;* 339.1 *inertness;* 648.1 *leniency;* 250.6 *liberality;* 796.3 *sexual immorality;* 804.3 *venal sin*
laxly 419.18 *soft-heartedly;* 419.17 *softly;* 757.9 *with permission*
laxness 419.12 *gentleness;* 250.6 *liberality*
lay 324.2 *bearing;* 38.30 *engineer;* 561.14 *have sex;* 561.11 *have young;* 411.10 *layer;* 187.7 *make horizontal;* 17.7 *poem;* 456.7 *semiskilled;* 516.2 *song;* 486.2 *unskilled*
lay a block 51.7 *bowl*
lay aboard 381.9 *attack successfully*
layabout 341.2 *nonacting person;* 343.8 *nonworker*
lay about one 381.5 *strike*
lay a cornerstone 413.11 *support*
lay a false scent 700.27 *be false;* 736.11 *conceal oneself*
lay a foundation stone 413.11 *support*
lay a hand on 798.11 *be evil*
lay an embargo on 301.9 *make motionless*
lay aside 470.2 *discard;* 350.6 *stop using;* 316.15 *take away*
lay at one's feet 752.11 *volunteer*
lay a trap for 700.33 *snare*
layaway 62.8 *mountaineering*
lay away 439.6 *store*
layaway move 62.3 *climbing technique*
laybacking 62.3 *climbing technique;* 62.8 *mountaineering*
lay-back spin 68.6 *ice-skating*
lay bare 449.2 *detect;* 739.5 *disclose;* 520.10 *make visible;* 738.3 *reveal;* 552.14 *undress*
lay before 752.9 *offer*
lay bricks 550.28 *face*
lay by 439.6 *store*
lay-by 318.2 *passing along;* 226.4 *stopping place;* 321.2 *track*
lay disciple 7.7 *monk*
lay down 411.10 *layer;* 367.1 *lower;* 187.7 *make horizontal;* 4.22 *propound a philosophy;* 140.13 *rule;* 476.5 *suppose*
lay down a cellar 558.15 *provide drink*
lay down guidelines 166.7 *limit*
lay down one's arms 749.5 *make peace;* 388.3 *submit*
lay down one's life 582.16 *meet one's fate*
lay down the law 707.21 *be assertive;* 396.19 *be authoritarian;* 452.20 *be certain;* 397.9 *command;* 660.27 *dare;* 12.11 *govern;* 140.13 *rule*
lay eggs 381.3 *bomb*
Layer 411
layer **411.1**; **411.10**; 434.3 *atmospheric layers;* 550.24 *coat;* 550.3 *coating;* 44.15 *cultivate;* 187.3 *flat thing;* 184.9 *fold;* 43.8 *livestock;* 561.13 *propagate;* 410.4 *rack;* 184.1 *wrinkle*
layer cake 411.5 *layered thing*
layer cloud 31.20 *cloud appearance*
layered **411.7**
layered thing **411.5**
layering **411.6**; 44.5 *gardening*
layer-on of hands 394.15 *healer*
layette 551.23 *children's clothes*
lay eyes on 518.12 *see*
lay for 324.7 *take a direction*
lay hands on 765.9 *gain;* 492.11 *touch*
lay in 439.6 *store*
lay in ashes 357.10 *lay waste*
lay in a stock 436.5 *provision*
lay in drink 558.15 *provide drink*
laying bare 552.1 *undress*
laying claim to 763.1 *possession*
laying hen 43.8 *livestock*
laying into 670.8 *berating*
laying it on 658.4 *deference*
laying off 371.18 *dismissal;* 15.2 *industrial negotiations*
laying on 550.1 *covering*
laying one's hands on 142.3 *locating*
laying on of hands 10.5 *Christian rite;* 394.11 *medical art;* 492.2 *touching*
laying open 738.10 *manifestation*
laying siege 593.6 *courtship*
laying the first stone 130.9 *premiere*
laying waste 357.5 *havoc;* 381.14 *siege*
lay in ruins 357.10 *lay waste*
lay in the dust 357.9 *demolish*
lay in the grave 583.8 *bury*
lay into 670.21 *berate;* 557.22 *eat well;* 381.5 *strike*

lay it on 727.10 *boast;* 658.13 *defer to;* 557.22 *eat well;* 677.8 *flatter*
lay it on thick 219.4 *be excessive;* 727.10 *boast;* 677.8 *flatter;* 480.15 *persuade*
lay low 155.9 *lower;* 381.5 *strike*
layman 456.5 *ignorant person*
lay off 226.8 *cause to cease;* 15.11 *conduct industrial relations;* 371.2, 580.5, 767.10 *dismiss;* 343.14 *make inactive;* 144.17 *relegate;* 608.12 *relieve from duty;* 226.12, 301.11 *stop!;* 350.7 *stop work;* 708.15 *terminate*
lay-off 15.2 *industrial negotiations;* 144.4 *relegation;* 226.2 *stop;* 708.6 *termination;* 343.6, 580.3 *unemployment*
lay of the land 143.2, 222.1 *circumstances*
lay on 211.6 *add;* 550.23 *cover*
lay one's back open 814.3 *hit*
lay oneself open to 254.9 *face danger*
lay one's hands on 142.11 *find;* 773.7 *take*
lay on hands 10.18 *perform rites*
lay on the lash 814.3 *hit*
lay on the scale 414.15 *weigh*
lay on the table 294.8 *delay*
lay open 739.5 *disclose;* 738.3 *reveal;* 552.14 *undress*
layout 409.2 *array;* 143.2 *circumstances;* 484.5 *map;* 407.1 *order;* 163.1 *outline*
lay out 409.12 *arrange;* 367.3 *bring down;* 583.8 *bury;* 19.23 *design;* 787.1 *expend;* 160.7 *form;* 407.18 *order;* 163.5 *outline;* 785.6 *pay;* 484.10 *plan out;* 141.21 *space;* 742.9 *use signs;* 441.1 *waste*
lay over 550.23 *cover;* 133.13 *pause*
lay siege to 381.4 *besiege;* 586.36 *combat;* 593.26 *court*
lay the blame on 715.5 *accuse*
lay the cornerstone 484.10 *plan out*
lay the first stone 130.24 *open*
lay the foundation 484.10 *plan out*
lay the foundations 243.2 *do the groundwork;* 344.11 *inaugurate*
lay the foundation stone 130.24 *open*
lay to 323.10 *sail*
lay to rest 583.8 *bury*
lay traps 633.11 *hunt*
lay up 374.5 *combine;* 343.14 *make inactive;* 238.8 *make useless;* 49.4 *playing terms;* 372.10 *set apart;* 350.6 *stop using;* 439.6 *store*
lay up a sailboat 50.15 *sail*
lay up in lavender 502.6 *perfume*
lay upon 397.10 *demand*
lay waste **357.10**; **441.2**; 381.9 *attack successfully;* 585.13 *be at war;* 245.4 *impair;* 238.8 *make useless;* 563.10 *waste*
Laza 8.12 *hell*
lazar 782.10 *poor person*
lazaretto 394.14 *hospital*
lazar-house 394.14 *hospital*
Lazarus 554.5 *life cycle;* 782.10 *poor person*
laze 343.12 *be inactive;* 333.1 *move slowly;* 263.2 *take it easy*
laze around 339.4 *be inert*
lazily 343.16 *impassively;* 339.7 *inertly;* 333.16 *slowly;* 341.5 *without action*
laziness 637.15 *delay;* 343.7 *idleness;* 341.1 *inaction;* 666.2 *indifference;* 339.1 *inertness;* 333.8 *slowness*
lazy 263.4 *at ease;* 341.3 *inactive;* 666.5 *indifferent;* 339.5 *inert;* 343.3 *not participating;* 637.4 *procrastinating;* 333.5 *unhurried*
lazy river 90.1 *river*
lazzo 21.12 *comedy*
lbw 53.11 *dismissal*
LCD 522.11 *photoelectricity*
lea 43.11 *farmland;* 81.2 *grassland;* 92.6 *lowland*
leach 431.23 *dissolve;* 315.12 *leak;* 255.10, 256.15 *purify;* 433.29 *water*
leaching 431.8 *fluidification;* 315.3 *leakage;* 433.9 *soaking*
lead **121.10**; 21.24 *actor;* 121.3 *advantage;* 631.14 *behave towards;* 167.10 *be in front;* 18.40, 631.15 *conduct;* 156.4 *deep thing;* 140.16, 324.6, 579.2 *direct;* 334.7 *electrical power;* 223.15 *escort;* 55.3 *fishing tackle;* 251.12 *gag;* 12.11 *govern;* 533.5 *grey thing;* 396.18 *have authority;* 395.8 *influence;* 579.1 *manage;* 400.14 *master;* 251.5 *means of restraint;* 209.5 *measure;* 26.6 *measuring instrument;* 483.9 *motivate;* 323.5 *navigation;* 130.21 *pioneer;* 129.15 *precede;* 129.4 *precedent;* 47.7 *race;* 309.3 *restrainer;* 378.4 *restraint;* 21.23 *role;* 252.4 *safety device;* 742.1 *sign;* 68.11 *skier;* 324.7 *take a direction;* 174.7 *top;* 414.11 *weight;* 39.27 *wire;* 373.9 *yoke*
lead a bad life 631.13 *behave badly*
leadable 324.14 *directed*
lead a boring life 620.7 *suffer boredom*
lead a charmed life 248.6 *be fortunate*
lead a cloistered life 655.12 *be unsocial*
lead a coup 588.4 *be anarchic;* 662.16 *be subversive;* 773.7 *take;* 396.20 *take authority*
lead a good life 631.12 *behave well*
lead an uprising 753.8 *cause mischief*
lead a putsch 753.8 *cause mischief*
lead a rebellion 662.16 *be subversive*
lead astray 796.19 *corrupt;* 804.17 *make wicked;* 483.10 *manipulate*
lead balloon 414.11 *weight*
lead block 46.9 *play;* 46.15 *play offence*
lead by the nose 395.10 *be a prevailing influence;* 396.19 *be authoritarian;* 387.6 *subject*
lead captive 387.7 *defeat*
lead crystal 24.1 *ceramics;* 527.9 *glass*
leaden 620.4 *boring;* 530.7 *colourless;* 523.10 *dark-coloured;* 524.5 *dim;* 533.3 *dull;* 533.1 *grey;* 414.1 *heavy;* 301.5 *sedentary*
leaden hours 620.2 *boring thing*
leadenly 414.16 *heavily*
leadenness 523.1 *darkness*
leader **400.3**; **579.14**; 722.2 *article;* 123.4 *bigwig;* 51.3 *bowls player;* 40.19 *computing terms;* 631.10 *conductor;* 740.3 *journalism;* 741.9 *news story;* 396.10 *person of authority;* 129.8 *precursor;* 139.9 *special;* 121.5 *superior;* 79.2 *tree part;* 223.8 *usher*
leader of the opposition 661.4 *defiant person*
leader of the Opposition 579.14 *leader;* 12.8 *politician*
leader of the orchestra 579.14 *leader*
leadership **121.2**; 396.1 *authority;* 579.4 *directorship;* 556.3 *maturity;* 395.3 *personal influence;* 209.2 *rank;* 631.8 *treatment*
leader writer 722.3 *dissertator;* 741.4 *journalist;* 719.7 *news interpreter;* 740.11 *newspaperman*
lead glass 527.9 *glass*
lead-in 130.10 *introduction*
leading 396.12 *authoritative;* 324.16 *directing;* 324.5 *directions;* 130.30 *front;* 12.10 *governing;* 123.5 *important;* 395.11 *influential;* 579.17 *managerial;* 400.12 *masterful;* 123.6 *notable;* 129.10 *preceding;* 129.14 *preparatory;* 129.12 *primary;* 209.8 *ranked;* 121.12 *superior;* 229.5 *tending to;* 174.5 *top*
leading aircraftman 586.32 *airman*
leading article 722.2 *article;* 740.3 *journalism*
leading case 713.3 *precept*
leading item 139.9 *special*
leading lady 21.24 *actor*
leading light 123.4 *bigwig;* 522.13 *enlightenment*
leading man 21.24 *actor*
leading note 18.16 *musical note*
leading part 395.1 *influence*
leading question 705.4 *difficult question*
leading role 21.23 *role*
leading sense 694.4 *type of meaning*
leading to 229.5 *tending to*
lead into temptation 483.10 *manipulate;* 480.16 *tempt*
lead in triumph 387.7 *defeat*
lead line 156.4 *deep thing;* 323.5 *navigation*
lead-off man 48.2 *baseball player*
lead on 593.26 *court;* 579.2 *direct;* 363.12 *lure*
lead one a dance 634.6 *evade*
lead one to expect 104.8 *be probable*
lead over 579.2 *direct*
lead poisoning 260.2 *illness*
lead role 21.23 *role*
lead runner 129.8 *precursor*
lead sinker 55.3 *fishing tackle*
leadsman 323.7 *nautical person*
lead the dance 129.18 *forerun;* 121.10 *lead*
lead the way 579.2 *direct;* 130.21 *pioneer;* 243.1 *prepare*
lead the way to 449.4 *invent*
lead the worship 752.15 *offer worship*
lead through 579.2 *direct*
lead to 344.9 *be the cause of;* 145.7 *reach;* 229.4 *tend*
lead to the altar 570.15 *marry;* 593.28 *win the love of*
lead up to 243.1 *prepare*
lead vocalist 18.23 *singer*
leaf **77.6**; 205.6 *branch;* 411.3 *coat;* 82.2 *fern plant;* 81.3 *grass plant;* 205.2 *particular;* 356.7 *produce;* 79.2 *tree part;* 77.21 *vegetate*
leaf blade 77.6 *leaf*
leaf bud 77.8 *bud*
leaf cast 79.10 *tree disease*
leaf curl 44.12 *pests and diseases;* 79.10 *tree disease*
leaf cutting 44.5 *gardening*
leaf fall 77.6 *leaf*
leaf-green 538.1 *green*
leaf-hopper 76.1 *insect;* 44.12 *pests and diseases*
leafless 552.12 *peeling*
leaflet 740.9 *advertisement;* 205.6 *branch;* 82.2 *fern plant;* 77.6 *leaf*
leaflike 411.9 *platelike*
leaflike part 77.6 *leaf*
leaf litter 79.4 *trees*
leaf miner 44.12 *pests and diseases*
leaf mould 44.12 *pests and diseases;* 79.4 *trees*
leaf out 79.19 *grow*
leaf spot 44.12 *pests and diseases*
leaf spring 422.5 *spring*
leafstalk 77.6 *leaf;* 77.5 *stem*
leaf sweeper 44.6 *garden tool*
leaf tissue 77.6 *leaf*
leafy 77.14 *of plants;* 77.13 *plantlike;* 538.2 *verdant*
leafy liverwort 82.3 *moss*
league 750.2, 755.3 *alliance;* 374.2 *cooperation;* 137.5 *social class;* 45.1 *sport;* 747.9 *team;* 137.4 *type*
league championship 246.3 *successful thing*
league cricket 53.1 *cricket match*
leagued 374.8 *cooperative*
League match 66.1 *soccer*
League of Nations 579.7 *council*
league with 374.6 *come together;* 755.5 *contract*
leak **315.12**; **389.4**; **389.7**; 693.7 *advice;* 231.9 *be imperfect;* 231.7 *defect;* 449.7 *detection;* 767.9 *dispose of;* 739.6 *divulge;* 739.2 *divulgence;* 315.3 *leakage;* 766.12 *lessen;* 429.16 *seep;* 560.3 *urination;* 441.1 *waste*
leakage **315.3**; 214.1 *decrease;* 314.3 *inroad;* 389.4 *leak;* 766.4 *lessening;* 441.3 *waste*
leak air 389.7 *leak*
leak away 389.7 *leak*
leak detector 32.20 *surface chemistry*
leaked 739.10 *disclosed*
leak gas 389.7 *leak*
leak in 314.11 *infiltrate*
leaking 245.13 *dilapidated;* 232.8 *full;* 315.3 *leakage*
leaking tyre 512.3 *hisser*
leak out 739.9 *be disclosed;* 315.12 *leak*
leakproof 252.7 *invulnerable;* 428.10 *waterproof*
leaky **315.17**; 739.11 *disclosing;* 308.14 *holed;* 231.1 *imperfect;* 254.2 *unsafe*
leal 663.8 *loyal*
lean **367.7**; 176.11 *angle;* 189.6 *be oblique;* 120.5 *be unequal;* 423.4 *powerful;* 469.2 *prefer;* 229.4 *tend;* 153.1 *thin;* 218.3 *underfed*
lean and hungry look 153.8 *emaciation*
lean backwards 168.7 *rear up*
lean-burn engine 438.5 *machine*
lean clay 24.2 *raw material*
lean cuisine 25.1 *cookery;* 687.1 *fasting*
lean forwards 367.7 *lean*
leaning 229.2 *attitude;* 617.1 *desire;* 595.2 *inclination;* 595.6 *liking;* 189.4 *oblique;* 189.1 *obliqueness;* 469.7 *preference;* 632.2 *tendency;* 229.5 *tending to;* 120.3 *unequal*
leaning backwards 168.3 *rearing up*
leaning over backwards 727.1 *exaggeration*
leaning to one side 802.11 *wrong*
leaning towards 229.5 *tending to*
lean-limbed 153.1 *thin*
leanly 423.13 *powerfully*
leanness 423.8 *physical strength;* 218.9 *scarcity;* 153.7 *thinness*
lean on 386.6 *compel*
lean over backwards 636.13 *be willing;* 727.7 *exaggerate;* 367.7 *lean*
lean period 249.4 *time of adversity*
lean-to 565.7 *room;* 565.8 *shelter*
lean to one side 802.22 *discriminate*
lean towards 802.22 *discriminate;* 595.8 *prefer;* 229.4 *tend*
leap 332.9 *acceleration;* 71.21 *assemblage of mammals;* 353.5 *attempt;* 332.4 *be swift;* 22.15 *dance;* 300.12 *gait;* 59.7 *horseracing;* 146.1 *interval;* 47.8, 304.5, 304.18 *jump;* 129.3 *preparation;* 213.2 *spread;* 302.13 *step;* 300.15 *walk*
leap at 636.13 *be willing;* 633.10 *chase*
leap for joy 600.5 *rejoice*
leapfrog 329.7 *crossing;* 304.5 *jump;* 326.8 *oscillate;* 329.1 *overstep*
leaping **304.24**; 327.15 *agitated*
leap in the dark 254.5 *danger;* 615.2 *rash move*
leap into 469.3 *side with*
leap out 695.8 *be recognizable*
leaps and bounds 302.13 *step*
leap to one's feet 366.5 *arise*
leap up 366.5 *arise;* 304.17 *spring up*
leap year 298.5 *regular thing*
learn **6.23**; **400.15**; 693.15 *be informed;* 449.3 *find out;* 244.2 *get better;* 455.13 *get to know;* 504.15 *hear;* 462.11 *memorize;* 695.6 *understand*
learn a habit 632.18 *habituate*
learn a trade 400.15 *learn*
learn by experience 244.2 *get better*
learn by heart 400.15 *learn;* 462.11 *memorize*
learn by rote 455.12 *know by heart;* 462.11 *memorize*
learned **4.19**; 6.18 *educated;* 442.10 *intelligent;* 17.16 *literary;* 458.5 *wise*
learned in the law 16.45 *legislative*
learned journal 276.7 *periodical*
learnedness **6.9**
learned person 485.5 *expert*
learner **6.7**; 578.2 *artisan;* 130.14 *beginner;* 387.3 *subordinate;* 486.10 *unskilled person*
learner's dictionary 5.28 *dictionary*
learn from 713.6 *consult*
learn from experience 808.4 *be penitent*
learning **6.8**; **455.3**; 243.17 *developing;* 449.8 *finding out;* 17.1 *literature;* 695.12 *understanding;* 458.1 *wisdom*
learning by heart 462.1 *memory*
learning difficulties 461.2 *subnormality*
learn obedience 388.4 *succumb*
learn one's lesson 808.4 *be penitent;* 711.6 *be warned*
learn one's lines 21.37 *rehearse*
learnt by heart 462.9 *memorized*
learn to live together 749.5 *make peace*
lease 564.14 *inhabit;* 763.1 *possession;* 755.2 *purchase contract*
leased 564.11 *inhabited*
leasehold 763.1 *possession;* 440.8 *propertied;* 440.1 *property*
leaseholder 564.3 *householder;* 763.5 *possessor;* 440.7 *property man*
leash 373.12 *bind;* 251.12 *gag;* 251.5 *means of restraint;* 309.11, 378.10 *restrain;* 309.3 *restrainer;* 378.4 *restraint;* 373.9 *yoke*
leashed 378.14 *blocked;* 373.16 *bound*
leasing contract 755.2 *purchase contract*
least **206.2**; 203.2 *certain amount;* 27.75 *equal;* 206.7 *fewer;* 122.12 *inferior;* 203.6 *quantitative*
least bit 124.8 *trifle*
least one can do 217.7 *sufficiency*
leather 550.14 *animal covering;* 331.5 *beat;* 256.11 *cleaning cloth;* 814.3 *hit;* 435.1 *materials;* 356.7 *produce;* 423.7 *tough thing*
leather chair 23.2 *chair*
leatheriness 423.6 *toughness*
leathering 331.12 *collision*
leatherjacket 76.5 *larva;* 44.12 *pests and diseases*
leather jacket 551.11 *jacket*
leather leg-guard 58.3 *ice hockey*
leatherlike 423.3 *hard*
leatherneck 586.28 *marines*
leather punch 308.2 *opener*
leather shoes 551.19 *footwear*
leathery 418.1, 423.3 *hard*
leave **215.8**; 98.16 *absent oneself;* 634.1

avoid; 315.14 *be dismissed*; 635.16 *bequeath*; 316.14 *bring back*; 750.7 *consent*; 313.1 *depart*; 571.8 *desert*; 372.13 *diverge*; 263.1 *ease*; 128.7 *exclude*; 315.9 *exit*; 657.4 *freedom*; 768.5 *give*; 98.5 *leave of absence*; 648.1 *leniency*; 758.4 *licence*; 313.9 *parting*; 757.1 *permission*; 757.2 *permit*; 581.6 *refresher*; 605.5 *resign*; 634.8 *run away*; 350.6 *stop using*; 439.6 *store*; 388.3 *submit*; 580.2 *time off*; 355.2 *withdraw*
leave a clean plate 557.22 *eat well*
leave a deposit 253.15 *reserve*
leave a fingerprint 345.6 *have a visible effect*
leave a footprint 345.6 *have a visible effect*
leave a gap 218.5 *be insufficient*
leave ajar 308.18 *open*
leave a lacuna 218.5 *be insufficient*
leave alone 341.4 *not act*; 350.5 *not use*
leave a loophole 746.6 *make conditions*
leave a remainder 120.5 *be unequal*
leave a runner stranded 48.7 *play baseball*
leave a trace 345.6 *have a visible effect*
leave behind 332.6 *accelerate*; 765.10 *augment*; 329.3 *exceed*; 463.13 *forget*; 215.8 *leave*; 766.15 *lose someone*; 302.9 *maintain progress*
leave dangling 233.5 *be incomplete*
leave destitute 782.14 *impoverish*
leave empty 98.19
leave fingerprints 743.11 *identify oneself*
leave footprints 743.11 *identify oneself*
leave for 393.7 *resort*
leave half-done 666.6 *be neglectful*
leave hanging 233.5 *be incomplete*
leave holding the baby 700.30 *be fraudulent*
leave hold of 355.1 *relinquish*
leave home 313.3 *quit*
leave imperfect 231.10
leave in high dudgeon 313.1 *depart*
leave in suspense 639.7 *be irresolute*
leave in the air 233.5 *be incomplete*
leave in the lurch 700.30 *be fraudulent*; 604.6 *disappoint*
leave it to chance 107.12 *take a chance*
leave it to fate 107.12 *take a chance*
leave land behind 313.5 *set out*
leaven 434.11 *aeration*; 25.7 *basic ingredient*; 224.8 *cause change*; 395.9 *change*; 224.5 *changer*; 344.4 *contributing factor*; 760.1 *conversion*; 760.7 *convert into*; 244.1 *improve*; 415.8 *leavening*; 415.10 *lighten*; 292.8 *mitigate*; 760.9 *transform*
leavened 292.16 *mitigated*
leavening 415.4; **415.8**; 434.11 *aeration*; 224.1 *change*; 760.14 *converting*
leavening agent 224.5 *changer*
leave no address 736.11 *conceal oneself*
leave no choice 386.6 *compel*
leave no escape 386.6 *compel*
leave no loose ends 204.10 *complete*
leave no option 386.6 *compel*
leave no remainder 119.11 *equalize*
leave no space 97.11 *be present*
leave no stone unturned 576.8 *exert oneself*
leave no survivors 358.1 *obliterate*
leave nothing out 232.4 *complete*
leave nothing to chance 616.5 *be cautious*; 232.4 *complete*
leave no trace 94.12 *cease to exist*; 358.1 *obliterate*; 313.3 *quit*
leave of absence 98.5; 758.4 *licence*; 757.2 *permit*
leave off 226.6 *cease*; 133.12 *discontinue*; 226.12 *stop!*; 350.6 *stop using*
leave one cold 620.6 *be boring*
leave one's bills unpaid 784.8 *not pay*
leave one's body 11.24 *experience psychic phenomena*
leave one's calling card 654.12 *visit*
leave one's job 226.7 *stop working*
leave one's post 605.5 *resign*
leave on one side 318.8 *pass*
leave out 128.7 *exclude*; 758.9 *exempt*; 215.8 *leave*; 720.1 *misinterpret*; 141.21 *space*; 212.3 *subtract*
leave over 215.8 *leave*
leaver 315.8 *outgoer*
leaves 538.8 *greenness*; 77.6 *leaf*; 238.6 *refuse*
leave senseless 331.9 *fight*
leave speechless 630.11 *amaze*
leave standing 332.6 *accelerate*; 329.3 *exceed*
leave stranded 355.2 *withdraw*
leavetaking 313.11 *departing*; 313.9 *parting*
leave the beaten path 118.19 *be independent*
leave the country 313.3 *quit*
leave the door open 752.9 *offer*
leave the earth 304.19 *take off*
leave the field 53.15 *play*
leave the ground 304.19 *take off*
leave the neighbourhood 313.3 *quit*
leave the nest 556.18 *mature*; 313.3 *quit*
leave the options open 746.6 *make conditions*
leave the pocket 46.15 *play offence*
leave the scene 98.16 *absent oneself*
leave the stage 313.2 *withdraw*
leave unavenged 649.12 *show mercy*
leave undecided 639.7 *be irresolute*
leave undeveloped 161.3 *make shapeless*
leave undone 233.5 *be incomplete*; 666.6 *be neglectful*
leave unfinished 233.5 *be incomplete*; 420.13 *be unfinished*; 231.10 *leave imperfect*; 238.9 *waste effort*
leave unsatisfied 604.6 *disappoint*
leave work 313.2 *withdraw*
leaving 313.11 *departing*; 313.7 *departure*; 768.1 *giving*; 315.15 *outgoing*; 355.3 *relinquishment*
leaving behind 765.2 *augmentation*
leaving ground 304.19 *taking off*
leaving present 671.3 *recognition*
leavings 205.8 *bits and pieces*; 258.4 *dirt*; 122.7 *inferior thing*; 356.3 *product*; 238.6 *refuse*; 215.2 *residue*
Leavisite 722.3 *dissertator*; 719.6 *interpreter*; 17.15 *literary person*
Lebensraum 141.6 *available space*; 85.3 *dominion*; 566.11 *nation*; 250.5 *scope*; 204.2 *whole thing*
lech 796.17 *be sexually immoral*; 617.6 *desirer*
lecher 617.6 *desirer*; 796.8 *immoral man*; 593.9 *lover*; 804.9 *wicked person*
lecherous 796.14; 617.11 *lustful*
lecherously 617.20 *lustfully*
lecherousness 617.4 *sexual desire*; 796.3 *sexual immorality*
lechery 617.4 *sexual desire*; 796.3 *sexual immorality*
leching 292.17 *in season*
Lech Wałesa 589.4 *Nobel Peace Prize*
lecithin 33.6 *lipid*
Leclanché cell 32.19 *electrochemistry*
lectern 10.12 *church*; 23.4 *table*
lection 719.1 *interpretation*
lectionary 10.10 *religious manual*
lecture 137.7; 733.1, 733.7 *address*; 670.7 *blame*; 670.20 *censure*; 722.1 *dissertation*; 703.16 *explain*; 703.3 *explanation*; 480.2 *flattery*; 795.12 *moralize*; 21.7 *show*; 729.14 *speak to*; 729.8 *speech*
lecture course 447.5 *educational topic*
lecture hall 6.15 *schoolroom*
lecturer 703.7 *demonstrator*; 722.3 *dissertator*; 400.9 *educational leader*; 6.4 *educator*; 733.6 *public speaker*; 729.10 *speaker*
lectureship 6.6 *instructorship*
LED 522.11 *photoelectricity*
led 223.20 *accompanied*
led by the nose 387.9 *subject*
lederhosen 551.9 *trousers*; 743.5 *uniform*
ledge 187.3 *flat thing*; 411.2 *level*; 185.2 *projection*; 62.5 *rock face*; 68.1 *skiing*
ledged 62.8 *mountaineering*; 68.12 *ski*
ledger 789.5 *account book*; 220.4 *bill*; 744.6 *record book*
ledgering 55.1 *angling*
ledger line 18.17 *notation*
ledger rod 55.3 *fishing tackle*
leeboards 50.3 *parts of a sailing boat*
leech 267.4 *adherent*; 35.11 *doctor*; 394.15 *healer*; 343.8 *nonworker*; 75.10 *parasite*; 664.3 *sponger*; 773.6 *taker*; 75.6 *worm*
leechcraft 394.11 *medical art*
leechlike 664.7 *sycophantic*; 75.20 *wormlike*
Leeds 87.4 *British cities*
leek-green 538.1 *green*
leer 234.2 *facial distortion*; 742.3, 742.11 *gesture*; 518.6, 518.13 *look*; 234.10 *make faces*
lees 258.4 *dirt*; 215.2 *residue*; 131.8 *tail*
lee shore 379.1 *trap*
lee side 169.3 *side direction*
leeward 324.10 *clockwise*
lee-wave cloud 31.20 *cloud appearance*
leeway 141.6 *available space*; 325.15 *deviating motion*; 657.4 *freedom*; 146.1 *interval*; 250.5 *scope*
left 52.14 *combat*; 313.12 *departed*; 12.6 *political party*; 28.78 *quantum*; 215.9 *remaining*; 169.6 *side*; 331.14 *sporting hit*; 372.17 *unjoined*
left behind 215.9 *remaining*; 767.15 *unclaimed*
left centre three-quarter 64.4 *rugby player*
left defence 58.4 *ice hockey player*
left field centre field 48.1 *baseball*
left fielder 48.2 *baseball player*
left half 66.3 *football player*
left hand 169.1 *side*
left-hand 61.10 *racing*
left-handed 486.3 *clumsy*; 479.10 *equivocal*; 492.10 *handed*; 668.11 *insulting*; 492.5 *toucher*
left-handed compliment 668.5 *insult*
left-handed hitter 48.2 *baseball player*
left-handed marriage 570.3 *types of marriage*
left-handedness 492.7 *sense organ*; 486.8 *unskilfulness*
left-hander 61.6 *motor-racing terms*
left-hand kink 61.6 *motor-racing terms*
left-hand side 169.3 *side direction*
left hanging 233.4 *incomplete*
left high and dry 254.3 *vulnerable*
left hook 52.2 *boxing*
leftie 12.6 *political party*; 662.11 *rebel*
left in the air 233.4 *incomplete*
leftist 12.6 *political party*
left jab 52.2 *boxing*
left-luggage office 321.8 *railway station*
left of centre 685.7 *politically moderate*
left out 128.11 *excluded*; 98.12 *missing*
leftover 211.3 *additional item*; 350.3 *not wanted*; 219.7 *superfluous*; 215.10 *surplus*; 441.9 *waste*
leftovers 258.4 *dirt*; 122.7 *inferior thing*; 238.6 *refuse*; 215.2 *residue*; 219.3 *superfluity*; 215.4 *surplus*; 441.5 *waste product*
left side 169.3 *side direction*
left stick 58.3 *ice hockey*
left to right 326.18 *to and fro*
left to rot 350.1 *unused*
left unfinished 233.4 *incomplete*
left uppercut 52.2 *boxing*
leftward 324.10 *clockwise*
left wing 58.4 *ice hockey player*; 58.6 *lacrosse player*
left-winger 12.6 *political party*
left wing three-quarter 64.4 *rugby player*
left without words 619.7 *wide-eyed*
leg 25.22 *beef*; 205.4 *component*; 25.26, 25.27 *lamb*; 25.25 *pork*; 53.14 *positioned*; 25.28 *poultry*; 205.3 *stage*; 47.1 *track events*
legacy 788.4; 768.2 *gift*; 440.5 *personal estate*; 765.5 *profit*; 769.1 *receiving*; 316.10 *transferred thing*; 345.2 *visible effect*; 635.5 *will*
legal 16.44; **140.9**; 396.12 *authoritative*; 298.14 *orderly*; 698.24 *pedantic*; 757.7 *permitted*; 750.18 *permitting*; 705.15 *sceptical*
legal action 340.1 *action*; 16.5, 16.33 *litigation*
legal administration 16.2 *jurisdiction*
legal administrator 16.10 *law officer*
legal advice 16.32 *jurisprudence*
legal adviser 713.4 *adviser*; 16.13 *lawyer*
legal agreement 755.1 *contract*
legal argument 444.3 *debate*
legal authority 16.2 *jurisdiction*
legal beagle 16.13 *lawyer*
legal case 16.5 *litigation*
legal chicanery 700.10 *fraud*
legal claim 763.1 *possession*
legal code 16.1 *the law*
legal competence 16.2 *jurisdiction*
legal costs 790.6 *business costs*
legal counsel 713.4 *adviser*
legal debt 814.8 *penalty*
legal defence 714.2 *defence*
legal dispute 16.5 *litigation*
legal eagle 16.13 *lawyer*
legalese 5.20 *jargon word*; 5.6 *official language*
legal estate 440.1 *property*
legal ethics 4.6 *branch of philosophy*
legal evidence 716.5
legal flaw 16.4 *bad law*
legal force 386.2 *coercion*
legal formality 16.34
legal government 12.1 *government*
legal heir 769.6 *beneficiary*
legal history 3.1 *history*
legal innocence 805.2
legalism 16.28 *legality*
legal issue 16.5 *litigation*
legalistic 16.52; 656.6 *formal*
legality 16.28; 396.1 *authority*; 12.1 *government*; 698.11 *pedantry*; 757.1 *permission*
legalization 16.29
legalize 396.21 *grant authority*; 16.65 *make legal*; 750.29, 757.3 *permit*
legalized 396.16 *authorized*; 16.44 *legal*; 757.7 *permitted*; 750.18 *permitting*
legalized killing 814.13 *capital punishment*; 582.4 *death sentence*; 382.5 *execution*
legal learning 16.32 *jurisprudence*
legal liability 814.8 *penalty*
legally 16.81; 396.23 *authoritatively*; 16.86 *jurisdictionally*; 298.17 *orderly*; 757.9 *with permission*
legally separated 571.11 *divorced*
legally sound 16.46 *legislated*
legal obligation 814.8 *penalty*
legal order 397.1 *command*; 397.2 *demand*
legal possession 763.1 *possession*
legal power 396.1 *authority*
legal practitioner 16.13 *lawyer*
legal precedent 632.5 *tradition*
legal procedure 16.6 *legal process*
legal proceeding 340.1 *action*
legal proceedings 16.6 *legal process*
legal process 16.6; 16.33 *litigation*
legal punishment 814.8 *penalty*
legal quibble 273.3 *accurate thing*
legal remedy 16.5 *litigation*
legal representative 16.13 *lawyer*
legal restraint 251.1 *restraint*
legal rights 250.2 *free speech*
legal separation 571.2 *separation*
legal tender 780.1 *money*
legal terms 440.2; **763.2**
legal trial 16.7
legate 398.6 *agent*; 398.1 *delegate*
legatee 769.6 *beneficiary*
legatine 398.9 *delegated*
legation 398.2 *representative body*
legationary 398.9 *delegated*
legator 768.4 *giver*
leg break 53.13 *bowling*; 53.8 *delivery*; 325.15 *deviating motion*
leg bye 53.10 *score*
leg cutter 53.8 *delivery*
legend 719.2 *annotation*; 721.2 *brief description*; 699.9 *falsification*; 17.2 *fiction*; 5.25, 744.4 *inscription*; 721.3 *narration*; 3.7 *narrative*; 1.8, 296.6 *tradition*
legendary 3.19 *chronicled*; 699.36 *falsified*; 17.17 *fictional*; 477.12 *imaginary*; 1.14 *societal*
legendary beast 70.7
legendary horse 59.1 *horse*
legendary serpent 73.3 *snake*
legerdemain 700.9 *sleight of hand*
leg fillet 25.24 *pork*
leggings 551.20 *legwear*
leg glance 53.9 *stroke*
leg glide 53.9 *stroke*
leggy 154.12 *tall*
legibility 695.10 *simplicity*
legible 695.2 *simple*
legion 586.18 *army of people*; 586.16 *army unit*; 376.14 *force*; 208.5 *multitudinous*; 208.4 *throng*
legionary 586.11 *former soldier*
Légion d'Honneur 794.1 *trophy*
legionnaire 586.11 *former soldier*; 585.11 *recruit*
legionnaire's disease 260.9 *respiratory disease*
legislate 16.68; 340.4 *act*; 397.9 *command*; 396.18 *have authority*; 579.1 *manage*
legislated 16.46
legislate for 12.11 *govern*
legislation 16.31; 397.1 *command*; 579.3 *management*; 713.10 *precept*; 464.2 *verdict*
legislational 16.45 *legislative*
legislative 16.45; 397.14 *commanding*; 579.17 *managerial*; 579.18 *parliamentary*
legislative assembly 579.10 *legislative body*
legislative body 579.10

legislative branch 579.10 *legislative body*
legislator 579.13 *director;* 12.7 *governor;* 16.9, 251.6 *lawmaker*
legislatorial 16.45 *legislative*
legislatorship 16.31 *legislation*
legislature 376.5 *conference;* 16.31 *legislation;* 579.10 *legislative body*
legit 21.1 *drama;* 16.44 *legal;* 757.7 *permitted*
legitimacy **16.30**; 698.6 *authenticity;* 396.1 *authority;* 801.2 *correctness;* 16.28 *legality;* 698.11 *pedantry*
legitimate **16.51**; 698.19 *authentic;* 396.12 *authoritative;* 801.8 *correct;* 16.44 *legal;* 698.24 *pedantic;* 757.7 *permitted;* 396.15 *true*
legitimately 396.25, 698.37 *authentically;* 396.23 *authoritatively;* 16.81 *legally;* 698.38 *literally;* 757.9 *with permission*
legitimateness 16.28 *legality*
legitimate succession 396.3 *acquisition of power*
legitimate theatre 21.1 *drama*
legitimatize 396.21 *grant authority;* 16.65 *make legal*
legitimatized 16.44 *legal*
legitimization 16.29 *legalization*
legitimize 16.65 *make legal;* 757.3 *permit*
legitimized 16.44 *legal*
legless 690.3 *dead drunk;* 231.3 *deformed;* 233.4 *incomplete;* 205.11 *partial*
legless lizard 73.2 *lizard*
Lego™ 405.3 *unit*
leg-of-mutton sleeve 551.24 *part of garment*
leg-pull 700.11 *hoax;* 599.5 *joke*
leg-puller 700.15 *deceiver*
legroom 141.6 *available space*
legs eleven 201.7 *double figures*
leg show 21.7 *show*
leg slip 53.4 *team*
leg theory 53.8 *delivery*
leg trap 53.8 *delivery*
legume 80.2 *botanical fruit;* 25.33, 44.11 *vegetable*
legumes 80.1 *fruits*
leguminous 80.6 *fruiting;* 44.16 *horticultural;* 77.16 *taxonomic*
leg-up 302.12 *advance;* 392.1 *help;* 366.7 *lift*
legwarmers 551.20 *legwear*
legwear 551.20
legwork 741.3 *reporting;* 576.1 *work*
Leibnitzian 4.11 *follower of a doctrine;* 4.14 *of a philosophy*
Leibnitz's Law 4.8 *philosophical term*
leishmania 75.10 *parasite*
leishmaniasis 75.12 *protozoal disease*
Leisure 580
leisure **580.1**; **580.6**; 263.1 *ease;* 341.1 *inaction;* 226.3 *pause*
leisured 263.4 *at ease;* 341.3 *inactive;* 580.7 *leisurely;* 301.6 *quiescent*
leisured class 781.11 *the rich*
leisured classes 341.2 *nonacting person;* 343.8 *nonworker*
leisureliness 333.8 *slowness*
leisurely **580.7**; **580.8**; 263.4 *at ease;* 26.15 *deliberate;* 341.3 *inactive;* 294.15 *late;* 265.14 *relaxed;* 333.16 *slowly;* 333.5 *unhurried*
leisurely gait 333.10 *slow motion*
leisurely progress 333.8 *slowness*
leisure pool 67.7 *swimming pool*
leisure pursuit 633.4 *activity*
leisure suit 551.10 *suit*
leisure time 226.3 *pause*
leisure wear 551.4, 657.6 *informal dress*
leitmotiv 17.3 *aspect of fiction;* 516.1 *melody;* 18.4 *opera;* 447.1 *topic*
lek 780.11 *national coins;* 72.14 *nest*
Le Mans 24-hour race 61.3 *sports-car race*
Le Mans start 50.7 *windsurfing*
lemma 81.3 *grass plant;* 27.65 *theory*
lemming-like 117.13 *compliant*
lemmings 382.9 *animal killing*
lemniscate 27.40 *curve*
lemon 247.5 *failing person;* 80.5 *figurative usage;* 122.7 *inferior thing;* 499.3 *sour thing;* 247.4 *unsuccessful thing;* 537.8 *yellow thing*
lemonade 558.6 *soft drink;* 498.5 *sweet drink*
lemon chicken 25.48 *Chinese dish*
lemon grove 44.2 *garden*
lemon meringue pie 25.36 *cake*
lemon sole 25.18 *sea fish*
lemon squeezer 369.9 *extractor;* 80.5 *figurative usage;* 25.6 *kitchen equipment*
lemon tea 558.3 *tea*
lemon thyme 496.5 *herbs*
lemon verbena 496.5 *herbs*
lemony 499.5 *acid*
lemon yellow 537.7 *yellow pigment*
lemon-yellow 537.1 *yellow*
lemures 11.11 *ghost*
lend **771.5**; 783.8 *credit;* 392.29 *finance;* 768.5 *give;* 436.5 *provision;* 752.11 *volunteer*
lend a hand 636.14 *cooperate;* 392.17 *help*
lend a helping hand 413.14 *give moral support;* 752.11 *volunteer*
lend an ear 504.15 *hear*
lend at interest 771.5 *lend*
lender **771.3**; **783.5**; 436.3 *provider;* 778.12 *wholesaler*
lender of last resort 783.5 *lender*
lend force to 336.8 *strengthen*
Lending 771
lending **771.1**; 784.3 *loan;* 771.6 *loaned;* 436.1 *provision*
lending at interest 771.1 *lending*
lending institution 771.4
lending money 771.1 *lending*
lending on collateral 771.1 *lending*
lending on security 771.1 *lending*
lend itself 392.26 *be useful*
lend-lease 771.2 *loan*
lend money 771.5 *lend*
lend one's backing to 669.13 *support*
lend oneself 392.23 *advise;* 747.12 *reciprocate*
lend oneself to 348.4 *be an instrument*
lend on security 771.5 *lend*
lend wings to 392.28 *further;* 332.7 *hurry someone up*
Length 148
length **148.4**; 27.37 *line;* 205.7 *piece;* 203.1 *quantity;* 26.4, 158.1 *size;* 28.7, 141.1 *space*
lengthen **148.10**; 190.6 *become bigger;* 270.5 *be diffuse;* 141.20 *extend;* 190.5, 213.5 *make bigger*
lengthened 190.7 *bigger;* 148.1 *long;* 134.6 *protracted*
lengthener 190.4 *enlarger*
lengthening 190.8 *growing;* 190.1 *growth;* 148.4 *length*
lengthily 148.11
lengthiness 148.4 *length*
lengthman 321.9 *railway worker*
length of time 277.2 *time*
lengthways 187.11 *horizontally;* 148.3 *longitudinal;* 148.12 *longitudinally*
lengthwise 187.11 *horizontally*
lengthy 270.3 *diffuse;* 148.1 *long*
lenience 648.1 *leniency*
Leniency 648
leniency **648.1**; 419.12 *gentleness;* 627.3 *mercy;* 749.2 *peace offering;* 757.1 *permission;* 631.8 *treatment*
lenient **648.4**; 650.6 *benevolent;* 658.7 *courteous;* 265.13 *easy-going;* 649.5 *merciful;* 757.8 *permitting;* 627.6 *pitying;* 419.6 *soft-hearted*
leniently **648.6**; 658.14 *courteously;* 16.88 *forgivingly;* 749.7 *pacifically;* 419.18 *soft-heartedly;* 757.9 *with permission*
lenient person 648.2
Leninism 12.1 *government;* 396.7 *type of rule*
Leninist 12.9 *governmental*
lenitive 268.12 *lubricant;* 685.8 *moderating;* 685.2 *moderator;* 268.6 *ointment;* 749.6 *pacificatory;* 394.17 *remedial*
lenity 649.2 *forgivingness;* 648.1 *leniency*
lens **41.17**; 182.2 *bulge;* 518.2 *eye;* 24.9 *industrial ceramics;* 28.29 *optical element;* 527.8 *transparent thing*
lens aperture 28.31 *lens element*
lens attachment 41.17 *lens*
lens cap 41.17 *lens*
lens cover 41.17 *lens*
lens element 28.31
lenses 518.10 *visual aid*
lens hood 41.17 *lens*
lens mount 41.17 *lens*
lens system **28.30**; 41.17 *lens*
Lent 687.3 *fast day;* 10.16 *religious festival*
lent 771.6 *loaned*
Lenten 687.6 *fasting;* 684.8 *self-restrained*
Lenten fare 687.1 *fasting;* 218.8 *insufficiency;* 684.1 *self-restraint*
lenticular 182.4 *convex;* 27.81 *curvilinear*
lenticular cloud 31.20 *cloud appearance*
lenticular galaxy 29.7 *galaxy*
lentiform 182.4 *convex*
lentitude 333.8 *slowness*
lentivirus 260.6 *infection*
lentivirus disease 260.4 *disease*
lentor 430.1 *viscosity*
leonine 71.28 *carnivorous*
Leopard 586.21 *armoured cavalry*
leopard 541.5 *variegated thing*
leopardess 71.18 *female mammal*
leotard 57.2 *gymnastic clothing;* 551.10 *suit*
leper 655.7 *outsider*
leper asylum 394.14 *hospital*
leper colony 394.14 *hospital*
lepidopteran 76.10 *insectan*
lepidopterist 76.8 *entomologist*
leporid 71.31 *rabbit-like*
leporids 71.12 *gnawing mammal*
leporine 71.31 *rabbit-like*
leprechaun 11.11 *ghost;* 159.4 *little person*
leprosy 260.13 *skin disease;* 260.7 *tropical disease*
leprous 260.23 *diseased;* 258.8 *unclean*
leptocephalic 151.4 *narrow-leaved*
lepton 28.77 *elementary particle*
leptophyllous 151.4 *narrow-leaved*
leptorrhine 151.4 *narrow-leaved*
leptosome 153.9 *thin person*
leptosomic 153.1 *thin*
les 568.10 *homosexual*
lesbian 568.15 *female;* 568.10 *homosexual*
lesbian marriage 570.3 *types of marriage*
lese-majesty 662.3 *subversion*
lesion 491.3 *injury*
less 212.8 *by subtraction;* 203.2 *certain amount;* 206.7 *fewer;* 122.19 *inferiorly;* 206.2 *least*
less and less 209.10 *by degrees;* 212.9, 214.8 *decreasingly*
lessee 564.3 *householder;* 763.5 *possessor;* 440.7 *property man;* 769.5 *recipient*
lessen **766.12**; 191.6 *become smaller;* 214.4 *decrease;* 419.14 *ease;* 244.1 *improve;* 191.5 *make smaller;* 685.4 *moderate;* 608.9 *relieve;* 337.7 *weaken*
lessened 212.7 *reduced*
lessening **766.4**; 191.8 *contracting;* 191.1 *contraction;* 214.1 *decrease;* 685.1 *moderation*
lesser 27.75 *equal;* 122.12 *inferior*
lesser creation 122.6 *inferior*
lesser doxology 10.8 *hymn*
lesser evil 469.8 *choice*
lesser importance 289.3 *subordination*
lesser of two evils 469.8 *choice*
less important 289.13 *subordinate*
Lesson 10.6 *Eucharist*
lesson 670.7 *blame;* 722.1 *dissertation;* 137.7 *lecture;* 795.7 *moral;* 814.7 *punishment;* 711.1 *warning*
less so 214.8 *decreasingly*
less than 27.88 *equal to;* 122.19 *inferiorly*
less than one 196.4
less than one's hopes 604.11 *disappointing*
less than perfect 231.1 *imperfect*
less than somewhat 218.10 *insufficiently*
Les Sylphides 22.11 *classical ballets*
let 63.12 *badminton terms;* 309.1 *closure;* 564.11 *inhabited;* 757.3 *permit;* 763.7 *possess;* 476.5 *suppose;* 63.4 *tennis terms*
let alone 211.10 *additionally;* 634.1 *avoid;* 134.3 *continue;* 128.12 *exclusively;* 225.6 *make permanent;* 341.4 *not act*
let an opportunity slip 288.7 *lose one's chance*
let be 134.3 *continue;* 225.6 *make permanent*
let bygones be bygones 463.15, 649.9 *forgive;* 749.5 *make peace*
letdown 623.10 *abasement;* 604.2 *bad outcome;* 247.1 *failure;* 611.2 *hopeless situation*
let down 604.6 *disappoint;* 604.9 *disappointed;* 623.3 *humbled;* 148.10 *lengthen;* 367.1 *lower;* 800.9 *prove false*
let down one's side 800.9 *prove false*
let drop 739.6 *divulge;* 367.6 *throw down*
let fall 486.7 *be clumsy;* 739.6 *divulge;* 367.6 *throw down*
let fly 624.12 *become angry;* 381.2 *fire;* 50.15 *sail;* 330.28 *shoot;* 503.5 *stink;* 331.4 *throw*
let fly at 381.5 *strike*
let go 16.78, 758.10 *acquit;* 16.63 *acquitted;* 618.12 *be indifferent;* 390.1 *deliver;* 371.2 *dismiss;* 767.9 *dispose of;* 355.9 *forget it!;* 250.19 *liberalize;* 144.17 *relegate;* 608.12 *relieve from duty;* 250.15 *set free;* 367.6 *throw down*
let go free 391.4 *liberate*
let go no further 737.12 *keep secret*
let go of 391.4 *liberate;* 355.1 *relinquish;* 605.5 *resign*
lethal 382.23, 582.20 *deadly;* 357.14 *destructive*
lethal chamber 814.16 *instrument of execution*
lethal injection 582.4 *death sentence;* 382.5 *execution;* 814.16 *instrument of execution*
lethally **382.25**; 357.16 *destructively*
lethargic 261.1 *fatigued;* 618.7 *indifferent;* 343.3 *not participating;* 333.5 *unhurried*
lethargically 343.16 *impassively;* 261.8 *tiredly*
lethargy 36.13 *depression;* 261.7 *fatigue;* 343.7 *idleness;* 618.1 *indifference;* 333.8 *slowness;* 388.1 *submission*
let have it 331.3 *hit*
Lethean 463.9 *blank*
let in 211.6 *add;* 370.7 *admit*
let in daylight 739.5 *disclose*
let it be known 740.13 *make public*
let it go 649.11 *condone;* 649.9 *forgive*
let it pass 649.9 *forgive*
let it rip 332.6 *accelerate*
let know 693.11 *inform*
let loose 391.4 *liberate*
let loose of 767.9 *dispose of*
let off 649.10 *absolve;* 16.78, 758.10 *acquit;* 16.63, 758.6 *acquitted;* 390.1 *deliver;* 649.6 *forgiven;* 250.15 *set free;* 330.28 *shoot;* 503.5 *stink*
let-off 16.42 *acquittal;* 390.2 *deliverance*
let off scot-free 758.10 *acquit*
let off steam 432.27 *give off*
let off the hook 16.78 *acquit;* 16.63 *acquitted;* 648.3 *be lenient;* 649.6 *forgiven;* 391.4 *liberate*
let on 739.6 *divulge*
let one in on 739.6 *divulge*
let one's breath out 371.14 *let out*
let oneself go 588.4 *be anarchic;* 270.5 *be diffuse;* 245.1 *deteriorate;* 250.19 *liberalize*
let oneself in 314.9 *enter*
let oneself in for 264.19 *have difficulty;* 354.1 *undertake*
let one's hair down 250.17 *be informal;* 250.19 *liberalize;* 657.11 *not stand on ceremony*
let or hindrance 378.1 *hindrance*
let out **371.14**; 390.1 *deliver;* 739.5 *disclose;* 371.2 *dismiss;* 767.9 *dispose of;* 739.6 *divulge;* 391.4 *liberate*
let-out 16.4 *bad law;* 390.2 *deliverance;* 352.1 *means;* 389.2 *means of escape*
let-out clause 746.2 *basis for negotiations*
le tout ensemble 204.4 *all*
let out on bail 391.4 *liberate*
let pass 649.11 *condone;* 341.4 *not act*
let rip 371.16 *belch*
let sleeping dogs lie 134.3 *continue;* 225.6 *make permanent;* 341.4 *not act;* 250.15 *set free*
let slip 739.5 *disclose;* 465.10 *misjudge;* 367.6 *throw down*
let some light in 739.5 *disclose*
let someone down 247.6 *fail*
let someone have it 381.5 *strike*
letter **5.13**; 692.3 *correspondence;* 721.4 *factual account;* 743.10 *identify;* 742.1 *sign;* 5.47 *word*
letter bomb 587.16 *bomb;* 700.13 *snare*
letter bombing 381.16 *terrorist attack*
letterbox 692.3 *correspondence*
letter by letter 273.8 *accurately*
letter carrier 316.8 *messenger;* 692.4 *postal worker*
lettered **5.41**; 743.12 *identified;* 4.19 *learned;* 17.16 *literary*
lettered player 485.4 *skilled person*
letterer 742.8 *signer*
letter for letter 125.14 *imitatively;* 5.48 *linguistically;* 698.38 *literally*
letterhead 743.3 *means of identification*

lettering 5.13 *letter*; 5.41 *lettered*; 542.3 *pattern*
letterman 336.5 *athlete*
letter of credit 783.2 *credit card*; 780.14 *paper money*
letter of introduction 743.3 *means of identification*; 669.6 *recommendation*
letter of the law 16.34 *legal formality*; 647.1 *severity*
letter post 692.2 *postal communication*
letterpress printing 561.1 *reproduction*
letter-quality printer 40.7 *peripheral*
letter *s* 512.3 *hisser*
letters 455.3 *learning*; 17.1 *literature*; 455.5 *science*; 316.10 *transferred thing*
letters a foot high 740.8 *public relations*
letters after one's name 743.3 *means of identification*; 813.1 *reward*
letters of fire 740.8 *public relations*
letters patent 397.4 *authorization*; 757.2 *permit*
letters to the editor 740.3 *journalism*; 693.4 *mass communication*
letter writer 692.5 *correspondent*
let the side down 479.3 *apostatize*
letting go 767.1 *disposal*
letting off 627.3 *mercy*
lettuce 538.9 *greenstuff*
let up 226.6 *cease*; 133.13, 226.9 *pause*; 333.3 *slow down*; 226.12 *stop!*; 263.2 *take it easy*
let-up 263.1 *ease*; 133.3 *interval*; 685.1 *moderation*; 226.3 *pause*
let well alone 341.4 *not act*
let well enough alone 225.6 *make permanent*
leucocyte 431.4 *blood*
leucoderma 260.13 *skin disease*; 531.7 *whiteness*
leucoplast 34.8 *cell organ*
leucorrhoea 431.3 *body fluid*; 560.7 *pus*
leucotomy 36.3 *psychiatric treatment*
leukaemia 260.11 *blood disease*; 260.12 *cancer*; 260.4 *disease*
leukaemic 260.23 *diseased*
levant 784.8, 786.7 *not pay*
levee 378.3 *barrier*; 90.2 *channel*
level 411.2; 409.6 *category*; 38.17 *civil engineering*; 750.14 *conforming*; 357.9 *demolish*; 111.16, 285.11 *equal*; 119.11 *equalize*; 381.2 *fire*; 367.2 *flatten*; 209.7 *gradational*; 187.8 *horizontal*; 187.11 *horizontally*; 187.2 *horizontal surface*; 122.5 *inferior state*; 209.4 *interval*; 92.6 *lowland*; 216.10 *make average*; 187.7 *make horizontal*; 298.10 *make regular*; 111.8 *make the same*; 750.26 *make uniform*; 119.8 *on equal terms*; 298.14 *orderly*; 410.4 *rack*; 209.2 *rank*; 111.17, 298.11 *regular*; 108.3 *relative position*; 421.11 *smooth*; 137.5 *social class*; 504.10 *sound quality*; 421.2 *uniform*
level-action 60.8 *shooting*
level-action rifle 60.3 *hunting equipment*
level crossing 318.5 *crossing point*; 317.10 *railway*; 321.2 *track*
level-green 51.9 *bowls*
level-green bowls 51.1 *green bowling*
level ground 187.3 *flat thing*; 155.2 *lowlands*
level-headed 4.18 *detached*; 95.8 *practical*; 460.5 *rational*; 458.5 *wise*
level-headedness 4.3 *detachment*; 458.1 *wisdom*
levelled 187.9 *flattened*; 367.17 *lowered*
Leveller 244.12 *reformer*
leveller 357.6 *destroyer*
levelling 367.12 *downthrow*; 367.11 *lowering*
levelling off 191.1 *contraction*; 214.2 *decline*
levelling out 214.2 *decline*
levelling up 119.3 *equalization*
levelly 209.9 *differentially*; 111.19 *equally*; 111.20 *regularly*; 421.14 *smoothly*
levelness 119.1 *equality*; 187.1 *horizontality*; 298.4 *orderliness*; 111.6 *regularity*; 421.7 *smoothness*
level off 214.4 *decrease*
level of meaning 694.4 *type of meaning*
level out 214.4 *decrease*; 187.7 *make horizontal*; 298.10 *make regular*
level pegged 285.14 *equal with*; 119.8 *on equal terms*
level pegging 111.16, 285.11 *equal*; 111.5, 119.1 *equality*; 285.4 *equal race*; 147.9 *near*; 147.2 *short distance*
level up 119.11 *equalize*; 216.10 *make average*
level with 799.6 *be honourable*; 285.14 *equal with*; 232.8 *full*
leven 366.10 *elevator*
lever 369.10 *excavator*; 395.4 *indirect influence*; 366.9 *lifter*; 330.11 *propeller*; 50.19 *punt*; 366.1 *raise*; 38.6 *simple machine*; 57.7 *stationary rings*; 438.1 *tool*; 438.10 *use tools*
leverage 395.1 *influence*; 784.3 *loan*; 250.5 *scope*; 121.1 *superiority*; 438.1 *tool*
leveraged 776.18 *contractual*
leveraged buyout 13.7 *corporation*
levered 50.14 *punting*
leveret 71.19 *young mammal*
levering 50.8 *punting*
lever out 369.12 *displace*
leviathan 158.9 *big thing*
levigate 427.22 *pulverize*; 365.12 *rub*; 421.11 *smooth*
levigated 427.18 *pulverized*
levigation 365.3 *grinding*; 427.4 *pulverization*; 421.7 *smoothness*
levigator 427.11 *pulverizer*
levirate 570.3 *types of marriage*
leviration 570.3 *types of marriage*
Levi's™ 551.9 *trousers*
levitate 304.13 *ascend*; 415.9 *be light*; 11.24 *experience psychic phenomena*; 304.20 *hover*; 366.1 *raise*
levitated 366.11 *raised*
levitating 415.2 *insubstantial*; 415.5 *lightness*
levitation 304.1 *ascent*; 415.5 *lightness*; 11.1 *occultism*; 366.6 *raising*
levitational 415.2 *insubstantial*
levitative 415.2 *insubstantial*
Levite 7.8 *priest*
levity 642.2 *caprice*; 598.3 *cheerfulness*; 639.12 *inconstancy*; 415.5 *lightness*; 615.1 *rashness*
levy 790.8; 586.14 *armed forces*; 790.12 *charge*; 43.2 *Common Agricultural Policy*; 397.2, 397.10, 710.7 *demand*; 773.8 *take back*; 773.5 *takings*
levying 773.2 *taking back*
lewd 796.12 *indecent*; 796.14 *lecherous*; 258.9 *obscene*; 675.9 *ribald*
lewdly 258.12 *dirtily*
lewdness 796.2 *indecency*; 258.3 *obscenity*
Lewis acid 32.8 *acid*
Lewis base 32.9 *base*
Lewis Carroll and Alice 569.7 *famous friendships*
Lewis gun 587.12 *historical guns*
lexical 694.8 *semantic*; 5.42 *worded*
lexically 5.50
lexical meaning 694.4 *type of meaning*
lexicographer 396.11 *expert*; 719.6 *interpreter*; 5.2 *linguist*
lexicographical 5.41 *lettered*; 5.38 *linguistic*
lexicographically 5.48 *linguistically*
lexicography 5.28 *dictionary*; 5.1 *linguistics*; 719.5 *science of interpretation*
lexicological 5.38 *linguistic*
lexicologist 5.2 *linguist*
lexicology 5.1 *linguistics*
lexicon 5.28, 220.3 *dictionary*; 6.14 *school book*
lexicostatistical 5.38 *linguistic*
lexicostatistics 5.1 *linguistics*
lexigraphy 5.13 *letter*
lex mercatoria 16.1 *the law*
lex non scripta 16.1 *the law*
lex scripta 16.1 *the law*
ley 81.2 *grassland*
ley grass 81.1 *grass*
lez 568.10 *homosexual*
L-form 32.13 *structure*
***l*-form** 32.13 *structure*
LGM 29.34 *SETI*
Lha 8.6 *angel*
liability 706.9 *answerability*; 229.2 *attitude*; 784.1 *debt*; 810.1 *duty*; 806.1 *guilt*; 814.8 *penalty*; 104.1 *probability*; 254.7 *vulnerability*
liable 810.10; 706.16 *answerable*; 16.64 *convicted*; 784.9 *in debt*; 104.6 *probable*; 814.22 *punishable*; 254.3 *vulnerable*
liableness 104.1 *probability*
liable to 229.5 *tending to*
liable to illness 260.21 *unhealthy*
liable to law 16.47
liable to prosecution 715.8 *accusatory*
liable to the law 16.48 *jurisdictional*
liaise 373.13 *intercommunicate*
liaise with 108.7 *relate to*
liaising 373.14 *connective*
liaison 373.2 *association*; 796.4 *illicit love*; 593.8 *love affair*; 748.3 *mediator*; 108.1 *relatedness*
liana 77.2 *plant*
liar 699.18; **700.16**; 645.3 *cunning person*; 700.15, 718.3 *deceiver*; 234.5 *defacer*; 774.11 *dishonest person*; 727.6 *exaggerator*; 699.17 *false person*; 702.6 *sophist*
liar dice 69.5 *dice*
libation 371.22 *disgorgement*; 558.2, 690.13 *drink*
libational 10.21 *ritualistic*
libationary 10.21 *ritualistic*
libations 690.12 *alcohol*
libation to Bacchus 690.13 *drink*
libel 715.6 *accuse falsely*; 381.10 *criticize*; 678.3 *defamation*; 678.12 *defame*; 715.2 *false accusation*; 236.11 *harmfulness*; 236.14 *ill-treat*; 699.6 *lying*; 720.1 *misinterpret*; 720.2 *misinterpretation*; 381.16 *personal attack*; 712.3 *vilification*; 712.6 *vilify*
libellant 715.3 *accuser*; 16.8 *litigant*
libelled 715.9 *perjurious*
libellee 16.8 *litigant*
libeller 715.3 *accuser*; 678.8 *defamer*
libelling 699.33 *deceitful*
libellous 381.25 *critical*; 678.16 *defamatory*; 699.36 *falsified*; 720.3 *misinterpreted*; 715.9 *perjurious*; 712.9 *vituperative*
libellously 715.10 *accusingly*; 678.18 *disparagingly*; 720.5 *misrepresentedly*; 712.13 *vituperatively*
Liberal 12.9 *governmental*
liberal 150.3 *broad-minded*; 650.7 *charitable*; 6.21 *curricular*; 787.10 *expending*; 250.9 *free*; 250.7 *free person*; 138.15 *general*; 679.1 *generous*; 768.8, 813.18 *giving*; 648.2 *lenient person*; 589.7 *peaceful*; 652.6 *philanthropic*; 217.2 *plentiful*; 685.7 *politically moderate*; 244.12 *reformer*
Liberal Democrat Party 12.6 *political party*
liberal education 6.2 *educational system*
liberalism 250.1 *freedom*; 244.11 *reformism*; 650.3 *welfare*
liberality 250.6; 150.6 *broad-mindedness*; 650.2 *charity*; 787.7 *donation*; 679.5 *generosity*; 768.1 *giving*; 652.1 *philanthropy*
liberalization 391.1 *liberation*
liberalize 250.19; 391.4 *liberate*
liberalized 391.7 *liberated*
liberally 768.9 *as a gift*; 650.11 *charitably*; 679.12, 787.14 *generously*
Liberals 12.6 *political party*
liberal thinking 391.1 *liberation*
liberate 391.4; 16.78, 758.10 *acquit*; 390.1 *deliver*; 265.18 *disentangle*; 767.9 *dispose of*; 369.11 *extract*; 393.3 *restore*; 608.10 *save*; 559.7 *secrete*; 372.9 *separate*; 250.15 *set free*; 714.7 *vindicate*
liberated 391.7; 16.63, 758.6 *acquitted*; 390.4 *deliverable*; 369.19 *dislodged*; 767.12 *disposed*; 389.8 *escaping*; 250.9 *free*; 372.15 *separate*; 250.12 *unconditional*
liberated man 567.14
liberated mind 250.1 *freedom*
liberated spirit 391.1 *liberation*
liberated woman 568.11; 250.7 *free person*
liberating 767.1 *disposal*; 391.7 *liberated*; 372.1 *separation*
Liberation 391
liberation 391.1; 16.42, 758.2 *acquittal*; 608.2 *aid*; 390.2 *deliverance*; 767.1 *disposal*; 389.1 *escape*; 369.1 *extraction*; 250.1 *freedom*
liberation theology 7.13 *theology*
liberator 391.3; 390.3 *deliverer*
libertarian 250.9 *free*; 250.8 *free-thinker*
libertarianism 250.1 *freedom*
libertinage 593.5 *desire*
libertine 567.7; 617.6 *desirer*; 250.8 *free-thinker*; 796.8 *immoral man*; 796.14 *lecherous*; 593.9 *lover*; 490.3 *pleasure-seeker*
libertinism 250.6 *liberality*; 796.3 *sexual immorality*
liberty 758.2 *acquittal*; 750.7 *consent*; 250.1 *freedom*; 580.1 *leisure*
Liberty Bell 250.3 *independence*
Liberty Hall 250.6 *liberality*
liberty horse 59.1 *horse*
libidinal energy 36.22 *libido*
libidinal object 36.22 *libido*
libidinous 796.14 *lecherous*; 617.11 *lustful*
libidinously 617.20 *lustfully*
libidinousness 617.4 *sexual desire*
libido 36.22; 593.5 *desire*; 617.4 *sexual desire*; 796.3 *sexual immorality*
libido analogue 36.22 *libido*
libido arrest 36.17 *fixation*
libido fixation 36.17 *fixation*
librarian 579.15 *manager*; 740.12 *publisher*
library 740.6 *book publishing*; 439.5 *collection*; 376.31 *exhibition*; 736.6 *privacy*; 565.7 *room*; 6.15 *schoolroom*; 577.1 *workshop*
library school 6.12 *educational institution*
library table 23.4 *table*
libration 29.17 *moon*; 326.1 *oscillation*
libratory 326.13 *oscillating*
librettist 17.14 *author*; 721.10 *descriptive writer*; 21.26 *dramatist*; 18.24 *musician*
libretto 18.4 *opera*; 21.2 *play*
licence 758.4; 669.1 *approval*; 250.1, 657.4 *freedom*; 16.29 *legalization*; 250.6 *liberality*; 396.9, 757.1 *permission*; 750.8, 757.2 *permit*; 136.3 *qualifications*
licenced 396.16 *authorized*
license 669.12 *accept*; 396.21 *grant authority*; 16.65 *make legal*; 750.29, 757.3 *permit*; 136.13 *qualify*
licensed 136.10 *authorized*; 16.50 *law-abiding*; 16.44 *legal*; 757.7 *permitted*; 750.18 *permitting*
Licensed Practical Nurse 35.16 *nurse*
licensed premises 558.11 *drink provider*
licensee 436.4 *caterer*; 769.5 *recipient*
license plate number 743.3 *means of identification*
licentiate 136.3 *qualifications*
licentious 686.7 *dissipated*; 16.61 *lawless*; 796.14 *lecherous*; 258.9 *obscene*; 490.7 *pleased*; 250.12 *unconditional*
licentiously 250.21 *excessively*
licentiousness 593.5 *desire*; 686.2 *dissipation*; 250.6 *liberality*; 258.3 *obscenity*; 796.3 *sexual immorality*
lichen 84.6; 84.1 *alga*; 83.5 *fungal association*; 77.4 *lower plant*; 82.3 *moss*
lichened 84.8 *lichenoid*
licheniform 84.8 *lichenoid*
lichenized 84.8 *lichenoid*
lichenoid 84.8
lichenological 84.8 *lichenoid*
lichenologist 84.6 *lichen*; 77.12 *plant scientist*
lichenology 84.6 *lichen*; 77.10 *plant science*
lichenometry 84.6 *lichen*
lichenose 84.8 *lichenoid*
lichenous 84.8 *lichenoid*
licit 16.44 *legal*; 757.7 *permitted*; 750.18 *permitting*
licitly 16.81 *legally*
licitness 16.28 *legality*
lick 256.5 *ablutions*; 331.5 *beat*; 121.8 *be superior*; 246.10 *defeat heavily*; 300.12 *gait*; 18.13 *melody*; 557.23 *taste*
licked 247.11 *defeated*
lickerish 796.14 *lecherous*
lickerishness 796.3 *sexual immorality*
lickety-split 262.6 *hastily*; 332.14 *swiftly*
licking 331.12 *collision*; 247.2 *defeat*; 557.3 *delicate eating*; 246.2 *victory*
lick into shape 243.6 *brief*; 160.7 *form*; 407.21 *tidy*; 760.9 *transform*
lick one's lips 617.14 *be hungry*
lickspittle 664.9 *fawn*; 664.3 *sycophant*
lick the arse of 664.9 *fawn*
lick the boots of 388.4 *succumb*
lick the dust 664.10 *knuckle under*; 623.20 *submit*; 388.4 *succumb*
lick the feet of 664.9 *fawn*
lick the platter clean 557.22 *eat well*
lick the shoes of 664.9 *fawn*
lid 550.2 *cover*; 551.15 *headgear*; 523.6 *shade*; 309.2 *stopper*
lie 699.10; 324.2 *bearing*; 800.8 *be dishonourable*; 699.20 *be false*; 187.6 *be horizontal*; 105.7 *be improbable*; 221.6 *be in a state of*; 339.4 *be inert*; 143.9 *be situated*; 57.10 *compete in gymnastics*; 702.12 *deceive*; 234.4 *distortion of the truth*; 234.12 *distort the truth*; 736.5 *evasion*; 105.6 *implausibility*; 800.1 *improbity*; 718.4 *misrepresent*; 718.1 *misrepresentation*; 645.2 *stratagem*
lie-abed 343.11 *sleeper*
lie ahead 283.7 *be in the future*

lie around 343.12 *be inactive;* 170.7 *surround*
lie a sailboat 50.15 *sail*
lie back 263.2 *take it easy*
lie below the surface 172.13 *be interior*
lie beneath 172.13 *be interior*
lied 516.2 *song*
lie dead 341.4 *not act*
lieder singer 516.5 *melodist*
lie detector 449.11 *detector;* 36.4 *psychometrics*
lie doggo 339.4 *be inert;* 736.11 *conceal oneself*
lie dormant 343.13 *sleep*
lie down 187.6 *be horizontal;* 155.8 *be low;* 367.8 *sit;* 263.2 *take it easy*
lie fallow 563.7 *be infertile;* 341.4 *not act;* 350.6 *stop using*
lie flat 187.6 *be horizontal*
liege 400.1 *master;* 387.5 *subjected person*
liege lord 400.1 *master;* 252.3 *protector*
liegeman 401.1 *servant*
lie heavy upon 414.14 *make heavy*
lie idle 339.4 *be inert;* 341.4 *not act;* 350.6 *stop using*
lie in one's power 334.10 *be powerful*
lie in the future 283.7 *be in the future*
lie in the grave 582.15 *die*
lie in wait 339.4 *be inert;* 379.2 *trap*
lie low 521.7 *become invisible;* 645.5 *be cunning;* 155.8 *be low;* 252.9 *be safe;* 736.11 *conceal oneself;* 526.1 *disappear;* 389.6 *elude*
lientery 560.2 *defecation*
lie of the ball 56.2 *golfing terms*
lie of the land 222.1 *circumstances;* 324.1 *direction*
lie on one's back 187.6 *be horizontal*
lie on the ball 64.5 *play rugby*
lie on velvet 248.5 *be prosperous*
lie opposite 113.15 *be opposite*
lie over 550.26 *overlie*
lie parallel 188.5 *parallel*
lierne vault 20.7 *vault*
lie still 339.4 *be inert*
lie to 323.10 *sail*
lieutenant 586.17 *army person;* 398.4 *deputy;* 392.11 *helper;* 586.27 *naval man*
lieutenant-colonel 586.17 *army person*
lieutenant-commander 586.27 *naval man*
lieutenant general 586.17 *army person;* 397.6 *person in command*
lieutenant governor 400.3 *leader*
lie within 172.13 *be interior*
Life 554
life 554.1; 342.1 *activity;* 3.6 *biography;* 342.4 *energy;* 93.1 *existence;* 17.4 *nonfiction;* 815.4 *prison sentence;* 338.1 *vigour*
life activity 554.4 *biological function*
life a curfew 391.4 *liberate*
life after death 283.3 *future condition;* 101.1 *nonmaterial world*
life-and-death 643.3 *important*
life assurance 252.2 *protection;* 392.4 *social assistance*
life belt 415.7 *light thing;* 359.2 *preserver;* 550.12 *protective covering;* 252.4 *safety device;* 67.3 *survival swimming*
lifeblood 431.4 *blood;* 99.2 *essential content;* 554.3 *life requirements*
lifeboat 390.3 *deliverer;* 252.4 *safety device*
lifeboatman 390.3 *deliverer*
life buoy 415.7 *light thing;* 252.4 *safety device;* 67.3 *survival swimming*
life cycle 554.5; 298.2 *cycle;* 760.2 *evolution*
life everlasting 279.3 *life without end*
life expectancy 554.5 *life cycle*
life force 554.1 *life*
life-giving 554.12 *alive;* 561.16 *reproductive*
Life Guard 586.12 *ceremonial troops*
lifeguard 384.14 *guard;* 359.4 *preservationist;* 252.3 *protector;* 253.3 *security officer;* 67.4 *swimmer*
lifeguarding 67.3 *survival swimming*
life instinct 36.22 *libido*
life insurance 252.2 *protection*
life jacket 415.7 *light thing;* 359.2 *preserver;* 550.12 *protective covering;* 252.4 *safety device;* 67.3 *survival swimming*
lifeless 582.19 *dead;* 343.1 *inactive;* 339.5 *inert;* 301.5 *sedentary;* 497.5 *tasteless*
lifelessly 582.23 *fatally;* 343.15 *inactively;* 339.7 *inertly;* 301.10 *motionlessly*
lifelessness 497.1 *dilution;* 637.13 *dissociation;* 343.5 *inactivity;* 339.1 *inertness*
lifelike 115.9; 698.25; 273.6 *correct;* 95.7 *realistic*
lifeline 373.6 *line;* 50.3 *parts of a sailing boat;* 359.2 *preserver;* 252.4 *safety device*
lifelong 554.12 *alive;* 277.8 *lasting*
lifelong dream 482.6 *objective*
lifelong friend 569.6 *close friend*
lifemanship 631.9 *tactics*
life of abstinence 572.2 *virginity*
life of ease 222.5 *comfortable circumstances;* 248.1 *prosperity*
life of Riley 781.7 *opulence;* 248.1 *prosperity*
life of the party 654.6 *social person*
life on earth 554.1 *life*
life peer 573.1 *nobleman;* 579.16 *official;* 12.8 *politician*
life preserver 587.7 *blunt weapon;* 415.7 *light thing;* 67.3 *survival swimming*
lifer 815.5 *prisoner*
life raft 252.4 *safety device*
life requirements 554.3
life-saver 390.3 *deliverer;* 359.4 *preservationist;* 252.3 *protector;* 67.4 *swimmer*
life-saving 390.4 *deliverable;* 390.2 *deliverance;* 67.3 *survival swimming*
Life Science 34
life science 34.1
life sciences 554.7 *studies of life*
life scientist 34.19
life senses 554.4 *biological function*
life size 158.2 *bigness*
life-size 158.15 *big*
life space 204.2 *whole thing*
life span 556.1 *age;* 275.3 *duration;* 554.5 *life cycle*
life story 554.11; 3.6 *biography;* 721.4 *factual account;* 17.4 *nonfiction*
lifestyle 554.10; 221.1 *state;* 632.3 *way;* 631.6 *way of life*
life-support system 394.14 *hospital;* 554.5 *life cycle;* 359.2 *preserver*
life-threatening 254.1 *dangerous;* 382.23 *deadly;* 357.14 *destructive*
lifetime 556.1 *age;* 554.5 *life cycle;* 148.8 *measure of time*
life to come 283.3 *future condition;* 554.5 *life cycle*
life vest 252.4 *safety device;* 67.3 *survival swimming*
life without end 279.3
lift 304.8; 366.7; 302.12 *advance;* 434.1 *air;* 304.13 *ascend;* 331.10 *bat;* 68.16 *bobsled;* 53.8 *delivery;* 767.9 *dispose of;* 362.12 *drag;* 366.10 *elevator;* 576.4 *exertion;* 47.2 *field events;* 302.8 *further;* 154.1 *height;* 68.6 *ice-skating;* 244.5 *improvement;* 774.15 *infringe;* 366.9 *lifter;* 316.5 *means of transport;* 50.3 *parts of a sailing boat;* 320.4 *personal transport;* 154.17, 366.1 *raise;* 68.1 *skiing;* 774.12 *steal;* 392.2, 392.19 *support;* 774.3 *theft;* 316.12 *transport;* 576.6 *work*
lift a finger 340.4 *act*
lift an oar 50.16 *row*
lift bridge 38.21 *bridge*
lift controls 391.4 *liberate*
lifted 68.13 *ice-skating;* 366.11 *raised*
lifter 366.9; 774.8 *thief*
lift front legs 168.7 *rear up*
lifting 68.9 *bobsledding;* 68.13 *ice-skating;* 774.6 *illegal borrowing;* 366.6 *raising;* 304.23 *rising;* 774.1 *stealing*
lifting front legs 168.3 *rearing up*
liftoff 313.8 *start;* 304.4 *taking off*
lift off 304.27 *alley-oop!;* 304.19 *take off*
lift oneself 366.5 *arise*
lift restrictions 767.9 *dispose of*
lift the ban on 757.3 *permit*
lift the roof 513.4 *be strident*
lift the veil 739.5 *disclose*
lift the veil on 449.2 *detect*
lift up 154.17, 366.1 *raise*
ligament 373.6 *line;* 403.7 *skeleton*
ligand 32.11 *chemical bond*
ligase 33.11 *enzyme*
ligate 373.11 *connect*
ligature 373.6 *line*
ligger 710.5 *beggar*
Light 522
light 28.23; 415.1; 522.1; 522.21; 522.24; 531.6; 531.12; 434.12 *airy;* 520.2 *clear;* 68.10 *curling;* 711.2 *danger signal;* 553.4 *design;* 558.17 *drinkable;* 265.9 *easy;* 28.13 *electromagnetic radiation;* 334.9 *electronics;* 153.4 *fine;* 437.11 *fuel;* 334.12 *generate power;* 527.9 *glass;* 337.13 *insufficient;* 719.1 *interpretation;* 28.25 *light source;* 522.18 *lit;* 520.10 *make visible;* 203.6 *quantitative;* 304.23 *rising;* 529.13 *soft-hued;* 206.6, 417.1 *sparse;* 221.1 *state;* 157.2 *superficial;* 520.7 *that which makes visible;* 796.13 *unchaste;* 124.1 *unimportant;* 520.6 *visible thing;* 326.5 *wave*
light air 31.13 *wind strength*
light-armed soldier 586.8 *soldier*
light artillery 587.11 *guns*
light as a fairy 415.1 *light*
light as a feather 415.1 *light*
light as air 415.1 *light*
light as day 522.19 *sunny*
light as thistledown 415.1 *light*
light beam 28.24 *light emission*
light blue 539.1 *blue*
lightboard 21.17 *stage;* 21.20 *stage lighting*
light bomber 586.31 *military aircraft*
light breeze 31.13 *wind strength*
light brigade 586.16 *army unit*
light bulb 522.6 *electric light;* 24.9 *industrial ceramics;* 28.25 *light source*
light buoy 522.6 *electric light*
light cavalry 586.19 *cavalry*
light coat 551.12 *coat*
light colour 522.14
light-coloured 522.21 *light*
light comedian 21.24 *actor*
light comedy 21.12 *comedy*
light-complexioned 531.1 *white*
light cruiser 586.24 *warship*
light dragoon 586.20 *cavalryman;* 59.15 *horse person*
light drinker 558.12 *drinker*
light eater 557.18 *eater*
light emission 28.24
light-emitting diode 39.18 *diode;* 28.25 *light source*
lighten 415.10; 522.28 *bleach;* 598.6 *bring cheer;* 265.18 *disentangle;* 522.26 *grow light;* 522.24 *light;* 685.4 *moderate;* 31.61 *shine*
lightened 522.21 *light;* 522.18 *lit*
lightener 366.10 *elevator*
light engine 321.4 *locomotive*
lightening 415.3; 415.6; 522.3; 522.15 *lucent*
lighten ship 415.10 *lighten*
lighter 437.2; 522.8 *fire*
lighterage 790.6 *business costs;* 316.2 *transportation*
lighter fuel 437.3 *gas*
lighter in one's purse 787.10 *expending*
lighter-than-air 434.12 *airy;* 415.1 *light*
lighter-than-air craft 322.8 *aircraft*
light filter 524.1 *dimness*
light-fingered 800.7 *criminal;* 415.1 *light;* 774.17 *stolen*
light-fingeredness 774.1 *stealing*
light fingers 800.3 *criminality;* 774.1 *stealing*
light fitting 522.6 *electric light*
light-flyweight 52.3 *boxing weight divisions;* 52.14 *combat*
light-footed 342.18 *active;* 415.1 *light;* 332.1 *swift*
light-gathering power 29.28 *resolution*
light-grey 533.1 *grey*
light guide 28.29 *optical element*
light hand 648.1 *leniency*
light-handed 492.10 *handed;* 415.1 *light*
light-handedly 492.16 *sensitively*
light-headed 227.14 *irresolute*
light-hearted 598.1 *cheerful*
light-heartedly 598.9 *cheerfully*
light-heartedness 598.3 *cheerfulness;* 597.1 *happiness*
light-heavyweight 52.3 *boxing weight divisions;* 52.14 *combat;* 414.7 *weighing*
light horse 586.19 *cavalry;* 59.1 *horse;* 59.15 *horse person*
lighthouse 522.6 *electric light;* 579.5 *guide;* 742.5 *indicator;* 323.5 *navigation;* 736.6 *privacy;* 252.4 *safety device;* 154.6 *tall thing;* 186.3 *vertical thing*
lighthouse beacon 742.4 *signal*
lighthouse-keeper 711.4 *warner*
lighthouse operator 742.8 *signer*
light industry 356.2 *manufacture*
light infantry 586.16 *army unit*
lighting 41.15; 522.5 *incandescent light;* 28.25 *light source;* 522.15 *lucent*
lighting board 21.20 *stage lighting*
lighting desk 21.20 *stage lighting*
lighting man 21.28 *stagehand*
lighting plot 21.20 *stage lighting*
lighting-up time 522.6 *electric light;* 291.1 *evening;* 320.21 *miscellaneous motoring terms*
lightish 522.21 *light*
lightless 523.8 *dark*
light lunch 557.12 *meal*
lightly 415.11; 522.30; 434.25 *airily;* 203.7 *quantitatively;* 157.8 *shallowly;* 206.11, 417.7 *sparsely;* 337.14 *weakly;* 531.14 *whitely*
lightly built 1.15 *physical*
light machine gun 587.11 *guns*
light meal 557.12 *meal*
light meter 28.92; 41.18 *exposure time*
light microscopy 34.6 *cell biology*
light-middleweight 52.3 *boxing weight divisions;* 52.14 *combat*
light-minded 642.1 *capricious;* 639.2 *changeable;* 227.14 *irresolute;* 486.1 *unskilful*
light-mindedness 642.2 *caprice;* 227.2 *irresolution*
light music 18.9 *popular music*
Lightness 415
lightness 415.5; 434.9 *airiness;* 153.11 *fineness;* 120.1 *inequality;* 522.14 *light colour;* 530.2 *paleness;* 203.1 *quantity;* 796.3 *sexual immorality;* 157.3 *shallowness;* 417.3 *sparseness*
lightning 334.7 *electrical power;* 28.47 *electric storm;* 522.4 *natural light;* 31.59 *storm;* 332.11 *swift thing;* 31.21 *thunderstorm;* 15.10 *unionized*
lightning arrester 28.47 *electric storm*
lightning conductor 334.7 *electrical power;* 28.47 *electric storm;* 252.4 *safety device;* 31.21 *thunderstorm*
lightning flash 332.11 *swift thing;* 31.21 *thunderstorm*
lightning sketch 19.9 *drawing*
lightning speed 332.8 *speed*
lightning strike 15.4 *industrial dispute;* 31.21 *thunderstorm*
light of love 593.2 *romantic love*
light of one's life 593.11 *loved one*
light on 218.1 *insufficient*
light on one's feet 415.1 *light*
light pen 40.7 *peripheral;* 522.11 *photoelectricity*
light pipe 28.29 *optical element*
light pocket 782.6 *insolvency*
light pollution 29.23 *observatory*
lightproof 309.12 *closed;* 523.8 *dark;* 528.1 *opaque*
light railway 317.10, 321.1 *railway*
light rain 31.25 *rain*
light ray 522.1 *light*
light reaction 33.23 *photosynthesis*
light red oxide 535.6 *red pigment*
light rein 648.1 *leniency*
light relief 21.12 *comedy*
light rum 558.7 *alcoholic drink*
lights 320.3 *carriageway;* 21.20 *stage lighting;* 321.2 *track*
light-sensitive 522.23 *photoelectric*
light-sensitive cell 518.2 *eye*
light-sensitive material 28.33 *photosensitivity*
lightship 522.6 *electric light;* 579.5 *guide;* 742.5 *indicator;* 323.5 *navigation;* 252.4 *safety device*
light show 522.12 *highlight;* 21.7 *show*
light shower 31.25 *rain*
light signal 522.6 *electric light*
light-skinned 530.8 *drained of colour*
light sleep 343.9 *sleep*
light socket 522.6 *electric light*
lightsome 342.18 *active*
light source 28.25; 522.5 *incandescent light;* 41.15 *lighting*
lights out 523.2 *darkening;* 742.6 *word*
light switch 437.4 *electricity;* 522.6 *electric light*
light the fuse 130.20 *activate*
light the touchpaper 437.11 *fuel*
light thing 415.7
light-tight 523.8 *dark;* 528.1 *opaque*
light up 522.25; 522.24 *light*
light upon 107.11 *chance upon;* 305.12 *drop;* 765.14 *profit;* 312.2 *reach*
light verse 17.6 *poetry*
light vessel 579.5 *guide*
light water reactor 334.8 *nuclear power*
light wave 522.1 *light*
lightweight 586.3 *athlete;* 52.3 *boxing weight divisions;* 52.14 *combat;* 414.1 *heavy;* 122.13 *insignificant;* 415.1 *light;*

159.4 *little person*; 124.10 *nonentity*; 157.5 *shallow person*; 157.2 *superficial*; 124.4 *trivial*; 337.8 *weak*; 337.4 *weakling*; 414.7 *weighing*
light-welterweight 52.3 *boxing weight divisions*; 52.14 *combat*
light wine 558.9 *wine*
light year 29.22 *astronomical unit*; 148.7 *measure of length*
light years 145.1 *distance*
ligneous 423.3 *hard*; 437.10 *powered*; 79.15 *woody*
ligniform 79.15 *woody*
lignin 34.7 *cell*; 33.4 *polysaccharide*; 79.3 *timber*
lignite 534.5 *brown thing*; 437.5 *coal*
lignitic 437.10 *powered*
lignocaine 489.4 *anaesthetic*
lignography 19.15 *engraving*; 23.8 *woodwork*
ligule 81.3 *grass plant*; 77.6 *leaf*
likability 593.4 *lovability*
likable **241.2**; **595.5**; 617.8 *desirable*; 593.22 *lovable*; 490.6 *pleasant*
likable person **595.4**
likable trait 235.6 *worth*
like **241.14**; **595.7**; **617.13**; 669.11 *approve*; 750.14 *conforming*; 617.12 *desire*; 317.16 *how*; 111.14 *lookalike*; 593.1, 593.23 *love*; 717.13 *representational*; 115.7 *similar*; 115.13 *similarly*; 229.4 *tend*; 750.34 *uniformly*
like a battering ram 380.10 *violently*
like a bird 332.1 *swift*
like a bitch 625.9 *irascibly*
like a bomb 342.22 *actively*
like a boor 659.10 *rudely*
like a brother 650.10 *benevolently*
like a diplomat 398.12 *by proxy*; 746.9 *feasibly*
like a drowned rat 433.23 *wet*
like a father 650.10 *benevolently*
like a fossil 215.12 *with a remainder*
like a giant refreshed 581.4 *refreshed*
like a Good Samaritan 752.20 *persuasively*
like a hog 688.7 *gluttonously*
like a horse 688.7 *gluttonously*; 414.16 *heavily*
like a kid again 581.4 *refreshed*
like a lead balloon 414.16 *heavily*
like a leech 664.18 *parasitically*
like a limpet 267.11 *cohesively*
like a lord 622.36 *majestically*
like a machine 485.12 *skilfully*
like a mad bull 380.6 *violent*
like a mad dog 380.6 *violent*
like a man 638.17 *resolutely*
like a master 485.12 *skilfully*
like a maze 180.4 *convolutional*
like a monk 572.12 *celibately*
like a mother 650.10 *benevolently*
like a mule 641.9 *obstinately*
like an acrobat 419.17 *softly*
like an ambassador 398.11 *representatively*
like an ape 125.14 *imitatively*
like an athlete 419.17 *softly*
like an eagle 332.1 *swift*
like a nerd 659.10 *rudely*
like a new man 581.4 *refreshed*
like an expert 485.12 *skilfully*
like an illusion 101.13 *metaphysically*
like an innocent child 805.12 *naively*
like a nomad 100.18 *extraneously*
like a nun 572.12 *celibately*
like a parrot 125.14 *imitatively*
like a penitent 808.8 *penitently*
like a photograph 115.14 *comparably*
like a pig 688.7 *gluttonously*
like a pirate 774.19 *thievishly*
like a predator 773.13 *avariciously*; 774.19 *thievishly*
like a Puritan 255.18 *virtuously*
like a raging bull 380.6 *violent*
like a relic 215.12 *with a remainder*
like a rocket 262.6 *hastily*
like a sailor 323.12 *nautically*
like a servant 387.11 *under subjection*
like a shot 636.17 *spontaneously*
like a shrew 625.9 *irascibly*
like a torrent 90.13 *fluently*
like a vice 360.11 *tenaciously*
like a vixen 625.9 *irascibly*
like a volcano 92.13 *continentally*
like a war 661.10 *in defiance*
like a wolf 688.7 *gluttonously*
like a yob 659.10 *rudely*
like best 469.2 *prefer*
like better 469.2 *prefer*
like cats and dogs 751.9 *disagreeing*; 751.11 *in disagreement*
like clockwork 265.21 *easily*; 111.20, 298.15 *regularly*
like crazy 338.6 *with vigour*
liked 593.21 *beloved*; 595.5 *likable*; 654.16 *popular*
like death warmed up 260.22 *sick*
like double Dutch 696.1 *unintelligible*
like father like son 115.13 *similarly*
like for like 385.1 *retaliation*; 385.5 *retaliatory*
like friends 654.18 *sociably*
like Gadarene swine 380.10 *violently*
like gangbusters 338.6 *with vigour*
like glue 360.11 *tenaciously*
like gold dust 792.8 *valuable*
like grains of sand 268.10 *slippery*
like greased lightning 262.6 *hastily*; 280.8 *immediately*; 332.1 *swift*
like hell 709.12 *no!*; 338.6 *with vigour*
like ivy 267.11 *cohesively*
like lead 414.16 *heavily*
likelihood 703.5 *demonstrability*; 474.1 *expectation*; 107.5 *good chance*; 283.4 *looking to the future*; 102.1 *possibility*; 27.62, 104.1 *probability*
likeliness 104.1 *probability*
likely 756.14 *auspicious*; 450.13 *believable*; 703.22 *demonstrably*; 474.7 *expected*; 102.5 *possible*; 283.12 *predictable*; 283.16 *predictably*; 104.6 *probable*; 104.11 *probably*; 95.9 *realizable*; 229.5 *tending to*
like mad 380.10 *violently*; 338.6 *with vigour*
like magic 619.8 *wonderful*
like man and wife 570.24 *matrimonially*
like-minded 750.10 *in accord*
like-mindedness 750.1 *accord*
liken 108.8 *be proportionate to*; 115.11 *make similar*; 750.26 *make uniform*
likeness 117.1, 750.5 *conformity*; 125.2 *copy*; 119.1 *equality*; 717.6 *image*; 525.5 *impression*; 19.7 *picture*; 518.8 *reflection*; 717.1, 721.9 *representation*; 115.1 *similarity*
like new 393.15 *cured*; 295.21 *newly*; 393.13 *repaired*
like no other 139.30 *characteristically*
like nothing 265.21 *easily*
like parchment 424.1 *brittle*
likes **595.3**
like sheep 750.31 *in accord*
like so 222.15 *under the circumstances*
like stroke 56.2 *golfing terms*
like that 750.36 *accordingly*; 222.15 *under the circumstances*
like the curate's egg 122.17 *defective*; 231.1 *imperfect*
like the spitting image 115.13 *similarly*
like this 222.15 *under the circumstances*
like to **595.9**
likewise 111.18 *identically*; 115.13 *similarly*; 750.34 *uniformly*
Liking **595**
liking **595.1**; **595.6**; 669.2 *admiration*; 229.2 *attitude*; 617.1 *desire*; 590.5 *good feeling*; 593.1 *love*; 469.7 *preference*; 495.2 *taste of life*
lilac 540.6 *purple*; 540.3 *purple thing*
liliaceous 77.16 *taxonomic*
Lilliputian 159.7 *little*; 149.5 *short person*
lilt 120.5 *be unequal*; 516.10 *sing*; 516.2 *song*
lilting 516.6 *melodious*
lily 502.2 *fragrant thing*; 531.9 *white thing*
lily family 77.3 *seed plant*
lily-livered 537.5, 614.3 *cowardly*; 337.12 *weak-willed*
lily pond 44.3 *ornamental garden*
lily-white 531.1 *white*
limation 365.3 *grinding*; 427.4 *pulverization*
limb 205.6 *branch*; 205.4 *component*; 79.2 *tree part*
limber 587.11 *guns*; 419.2 *pliant*
limberly 419.17 *softly*
limberness 419.8 *softness*
limber up 419.14 *ease*; 576.9 *exercise*; 243.8 *prepare oneself*
limb from limb 372.21 *apart*
limbless 233.4 *incomplete*; 205.11 *partial*; 212.7 *reduced*
limbless amphibian 73.7 *amphibian*
limbo 350.10 *disuse*; 94.4 *emptiness*; 8.12 *hell*
lime 267.3 *adhesive*; 530.4 *colour remover*; 43.13, 562.3 *fertilizer*; 538.9 *greenstuff*; 700.33 *snare*; 499.3 *sour thing*
lime-green 538.1 *green*
limekiln 24.6 *ceramic workshop*
limelight 522.6 *electric light*; 740.7 *publicity*; 21.20 *stage lighting*
limerick 17.7 *poem*
limestone 43.13 *fertilizer*; 38.26 *masonry*
lime twig 700.13 *snare*
limewater 433.1 *water*
Limey 564.9 *British inhabitant*
limey 80.5 *figurative usage*; 586.27 *naval man*
Limeyland 85.8 *Great Britain*
Limit **166**
limit **131.7**; **166.7**; 770.4 *allot*; 218.5 *be insufficient*; 372.6 *boundary*; 69.3 *card game terms*; 203.2 *certain amount*; 27.31 *differentiation*; 164.1 *edge*; 128.7 *exclude*; 378.8 *hinder*; 743.10 *identify*; 166.1 *limitation*; 191.5, 214.5 *make smaller*; 27.29 *mathematical function*; 685.4 *moderate*; 151.10 *narrow*; 203.8 *quantify*; 251.8 *restrain*; 251.1 *restraint*; 158.1 *size*; 136.16 *specify*; 174.1 *summit*
limitability 191.2 *contractibility*
limitable 191.9 *contractible*
limitation **166.1**; 191.1 *contraction*; 214.1 *decrease*; 231.7 *defect*; 209.1 *degree*; 128.1 *exclusion*; 378.1 *hindrance*; 440.2 *legal terms*; 151.5 *narrowness*; 251.1 *restraint*; 136.6 *specification*; 212.2 *subtracted item*; 804.3 *venial sin*
limitations 251.1 *restraint*
limited **166.5**; 136.12 *conditional*; 776.19 *corporate*; 128.10 *excluding*; 209.7 *gradational*; 378.13 *hindering*; 218.1 *insufficient*; 159.7 *little*; 86.18 *local*; 684.9, 685.6 *moderate*; 151.1 *narrow*; 440.8 *propertied*; 203.6 *quantitative*; 251.13 *restraining*; 191.7 *smaller*; 124.4 *trivial*
limited choice 469.8 *choice*
limited company 776.7 *company*; 13.7 *corporation*
limited nuclear warfare 585.8 *warfare*
limited offer 483.5 *positive stimulus*
limited options 469.8 *choice*
limited-over match 53.1 *cricket match*
limited period 275.3 *duration*
limited war 585.1 *war*
limiting **131.24**; 136.12 *conditional*; 191.8 *contracting*; 684.9 *moderate*; 251.13 *restraining*
limiting condition 136.7 *condition*
limiting factor **166.2**; 251.1 *restraint*
limiting magnitude 29.28 *resolution*
limitless 158.15 *big*; 202.1 *infinite*; 208.8 *numberless*
limitlessly 202.10 *infinitely*; 158.20 *largely*
limitlessness 202.4 *infinity*
limitless resources 781.5 *wealth*
limit of endurance 261.7 *fatigue*
limit oneself 684.5 *be self-restrained*
limit one's speed 166.7 *limit*
limits 164.1 *edge*
limn 721.14 *describe*; 19.20 *draw*; 163.5 *outline*
limner 19.16 *artist*
limnetic zone 88.8 *limnology*
limning 19.3 *drawing*; 163.1 *outline*
limnograph 88.8 *limnology*
limnologic 88.9 *lakelike*
limnologically **88.10**
limnologist 88.8 *limnology*
limnology **88.8**
limnometer 88.8 *limnology*
limnophilous 88.9 *lakelike*
limo 320.16 *car*
limonene 33.20 *terpene*
limousine 320.16 *car*
limp 337.6 *be weak*; 339.5 *inert*; 333.1 *move slowly*; 333.10 *slow motion*; 419.1 *soft*; 337.8 *weak*
limpet 267.4 *adherent*
limpet mine 587.16 *bomb*
limpid 725.3 *clear*; 695.2 *simple*; 527.1 *transparent*
limpidity 725.1 *clarity*; 695.10 *simplicity*; 527.5 *transparency*
limpidly 725.4 *clearly*; 527.13 *transparently*
limpidness 527.5 *transparency*
limping 337.10 *ill*; 233.4 *incomplete*; 333.4 *slow*
limply 339.7 *inertly*; 419.17 *softly*
limpness 419.8 *softness*; 337.1 *weakness*
limp-wristed 337.12 *weak-willed*
limulus 75.4 *arthropod*
linchpin 123.3 *chief thing*; 373.8 *fastening*
Lincoln 87.4 *British cities*
Lincoln green 538.1 *green*
linctus **37.11**; 394.2 *medicine*; 412.2 *mixed thing*
Lindy-hop 22.2 *dance*
line **27.37**; **132.3**; **373.6**; 733.4 *approach*; 586.14 *armed forces*; 586.16 *army unit*; 132.16 *arrange consecutively*; 324.2 *bearing*; 493.14 *be hot*; 166.4 *boundary marker*; 117.1 *conformity*; 132.2 *consecution*; 324.1 *direction*; 232.6 *fill*; 55.3 *fishing tackle*; 137.8 *genealogy*; 56.3 *golf shots*; 209.3 *gradation*; 411.10 *layer*; 26.6 *measuring instrument*; 18.13, 516.1 *melody*; 778.8 *merchandise*; 151.8 *narrow thing*; 323.5 *navigation*; 573.3 *nobleness*; 18.17 *notation*; 17.8 *part of poem*; 215.6 *person remaining*; 148.5 *piece*; 132.8 *procession*; 317.10 *railway*; 393.1 *repair*; 317.2 *route*; 139.8 *specialization*; 86.14 *sphere*; 541.3 *striping*; 289.1 *succession*; 631.9 *tactics*; 692.21 *television*; 19.4 *treatment*; 137.4 *type*; 317.1 *way*; 184.8 *wrinkle*
lineage 289.2 *descent*; 137.8, 284.12 *genealogy*; 132.3 *line*; 573.3 *nobleness*; 215.6 *person remaining*
lineal 132.9 *consecutive*; 27.80 *linear*
lineament 160.6 *nature*; 608.6 *profile*
lineaments 525.3 *external appearance*
linear **27.80**; 132.9 *consecutive*; 27.76 *functional*; 148.3 *longitudinal*; 26.12 *metrical*; 77.18 *of leaves*; 19.24 *pictorial*; 178.1 *straight*
linear accelerator 334.8 *nuclear power*; 28.94 *particle accelerator*
linear algebra 27.23 *algebra*
linear build 1.9 *physical type*
linear circuit 39.13 *circuit*
linear equation 27.27 *equation*
linear extent 27.37 *line*
linearity 27.37 *line*; 178.6 *straightness*
linearly 27.87 *mathematically*
linear measurement 27.37 *line*
linear motion 28.8 *time*
linear perspective 19.4 *treatment*
linear response 28.83 *sensitivity*
linear scale 27.32 *graph*
linear strain 38.14 *load*
linebacker 46.10 *defence*
line call 46.8 *huddle*
lined 211.8 *additional*; 556.14 *aged*; 411.8 *coated*; 493.13 *heated*; 406.11 *loaded*; 541.9 *striped*; 184.6 *wrinkly*
line drawing 19.9 *drawing*
line drive 48.5 *batting terms*; 331.14 *sporting hit*
line engraving 19.15 *engraving*
line graph 163.1 *outline*
line infantry 586.16 *army unit*
line integral 27.31 *differentiation*
line in the sand 166.4 *boundary marker*
line judge 46.2 *football player*
line management 15.1 *industrial relations*
line manager 15.6 *employer*
linen 551.1 *dress*; 42.12 *natural*; 193.4 *textile*
line of action 631.1 *conduct*; 317.1 *way*
line of advance 317.2 *route*
line of argument **701.3**
line of attack 54.3 *fencing movements*; 317.1 *way*
line of battle 585.9 *battle*
line of business 576.3 *job*
line of credit 783.1 *credit*; 352.4 *financial resources*
line of descent 289.2 *descent*
line of direction 324.1 *direction*
line of duty 810.2 *task*
line of least resistance 388.1 *submission*
line of reasoning 701.3 *line of argument*
line of retreat 317.2 *route*
line of sight 324.2 *bearing*; 520.3 *visibility*
line-of-sight transmission 692.15 *transmitted wave*
line of succession 769.1 *receiving*
line of symmetry 27.41 *geometric figure*
line of tenpins 51.4 *bowling*
line of work 576.3 *job*

line one's pocket 248.5 *be prosperous;* 781.13 *get rich;* 765.14 *profit*
line-out 64.3 *rugby play*
line printer 40.7 *peripheral*
liner 323.3 *vessel*
lines 160.1 *form;* 21.2 *play;* 814.7 *punishment*
line segment 27.37 *line*
linesman 66.3 *football player;* 58.4 *ice hockey player;* 692.13 *telephoner;* 63.6 *tennis player*
linesman's chair 63.3 *tennis equipment*
line spectrum 28.68 *emission*
lines per frame 692.21 *television*
line up **132.17**; **407.24**; 27.97 *align;* 409.12 *arrange;* 132.16 *arrange consecutively;* 750.25 *conform;* 407.18 *order*
line-up 409.1 *arrangement;* 132.1 *consecutiveness;* 220.6 *list of names;* 407.1 *order;* 65.6 *pool*
line up with 747.14 *join with*
lingam 562.4 *fertility cult;* 9.3 *idol*
linga sharira 11.7 *spirit*
linger 333.2 *hesitate;* 294.7 *wait*
lingerer 333.15 *slow person*
lingerie 551.18 *underwear*
lingering **333.11**; 333.7 *delayed;* 510.6 *resonant*
lingeringly 333.16 *slowly*
lingering note 510.1 *resonance*
lingo 729.1 *faculty of speech;* 5.20 *jargon word;* 5.4 *parent language*
lingua 5.3 *spoken language*
lingua franca 5.26 *dialect;* 5.7 *international language*
lingual 5.38 *linguistic;* 729.16 *speech*
linguist **5.2**; 719.6 *interpreter*
linguistic **5.38**; 694.8 *semantic;* 729.16 *speech*
linguistically **5.48**; 729.21 *orally;* 724.10 *stylistically*
linguistic analysis 5.1 *linguistics*
linguistic analyst 5.2 *linguist*
linguistic distribution 5.1 *linguistics*
linguistic geographer 5.2 *linguist*
linguistic geography 5.1 *linguistics*
linguistician 5.2 *linguist*
linguistics **5.1**; 694.1 *meaning;* 729.6 *phonetics;* 719.5 *science of interpretation*
linguistic scholar 5.2 *linguist*
linguistic science 5.1 *linguistics*
linguistic scientist 5.2 *linguist*
linguistic structure 5.1 *linguistics*
linguistic theory **5.37**
linguistic typology 5.1 *linguistics*
liniment 394.9 *balm;* 37.7 *ointment*
lining 211.3 *additional item;* 411.1 *layer;* 406.4 *stuffing*
link 570.2 *alliance;* 374.5 *combine;* 405.1 *component;* 132.15 *concatenate;* 373.11 *connect;* 522.7 *lantern;* 373.4 *means of connection;* 570.19 *merge;* 746.4 *negotiator;* 108.1 *relatedness;* 150.10 *span*
linkage 267.1 *adhesion;* 34.10 *cell division;* 108.1 *relatedness*
link-boy 522.7 *lantern*
linked 317.15 *accessible;* 267.9 *adhesive;* 750.11 *allied;* 374.7 *combined;* 373.15 *connected;* 127.8 *included;* 405.7 *modular;* 108.4 *related*
linking 36.27 *association of ideas;* 373.1 *connection;* 147.10 *juxtaposed*
links 56.1 *golf;* 45.2 *sportsground*
linksman 56.6 *golfer*
link up 492.12 *abut;* 376.41 *band together;* 692.30 *communicate*
link with 108.7 *relate to*
linn 90.2 *channel;* 88.2 *small lake*
Linnaean system 34.17 *taxonomy*
lino 550.9 *floor covering*
linocut 19.15 *engraving*
linoleum 175.1 *base;* 550.9 *floor covering*
linseed 43.12 *crop;* 77.9 *seed*
linseed meal 43.9 *animal feedstuff*
linsey-woolsey 412.3 *miscellany;* 404.8 *rough;* 420.7 *rough thing*
lint 427.5 *powder;* 394.10 *surgical dressing*
lintel 174.3 *architectural summit;* 314.6 *means of entry;* 20.9 *miscellaneous architectural features;* 413.2 *supporting part*
lint remover 256.10 *cleaning object*
lion 123.4 *bigwig;* 613.7 *courageous person;* 743.8 *heraldic device;* 567.16 *male animal;* 654.10 *social animal*
lion couchant 743.8 *heraldic device*
lioness 568.14 *female animal;* 71.18 *female mammal*
lion-hearted 613.9 *courageous*
lion-heartedness 613.1 *courage*
lion hunt 633.2 *chase*
lion hunter 633.6 *hunter*
lionization 8.9 *deification;* 366.7 *lift;* 669.3 *praise;* 575.1 *right*
lionize 600.6 *fête;* 9.8 *idolatrize;* 123.8 *make important;* 669.14 *praise;* 366.3 *promote;* 667.16 *revere;* 601.18 *salute*
lionized 366.12 *exalted;* 9.11 *worshipped*
lionizer 9.5 *worshipper*
lionizing 669.18 *approving*
lion-like 71.28 *carnivorous*
lion rampant 743.8 *heraldic device*
lion's mouth 254.5 *danger*
lion's share 121.3 *advantage;* 219.1 *excess;* 205.5 *largest part;* 207.3 *majority*
lion tamer 21.31 *circus performer*
lip 660.25 *answer back;* 659.2 *bad manners;* 660.2 *cheek;* 661.1 *defiance;* 164.1 *edge;* 18.38 *sound*
lipase 33.11 *enzyme*
lipid **33.6**
lipoamide 33.12 *coenzyme*
lip off 706.18 *answer back*
lipoic acid 33.13 *vitamin*
lipolysis 33.7 *fat*
lipoprotein 33.6 *lipid;* 33.9 *protein*
liposuction 547.2 *plastic surgery*
Lippizaner stallion 59.10 *dressage*
lippy 659.6 *bad-mannered;* 731.6 *effusive*
lip-read 505.8 *be deaf;* 719.12 *translate*
lip-reader 505.1 *deafness;* 719.6 *interpreter*
lip-reading 505.1 *deafness;* 719.4 *translation*
lips 525.3 *external appearance;* 729.5 *organ of speech*
lip service 699.3, 700.3 *hypocrisy*
lipstick 529.9 *complexion;* 547.4 *cosmetics;* 551.5 *fancy dress;* 535.6 *red pigment*
lip-sync 285.3 *synchronism*
liquate 431.22 *make fluid*
liquefacient 431.19 *liquefied;* 431.9 *solvent*
liquefaction 375.2 *deconstruction;* 377.3 *dilution;* 431.8 *fluidification;* 431.5 *fluidity;* 28.37 *temperature;* 441.3 *waste*
liquefactive 431.20 *liquefying*
liquefiable **431.21**
liquefied **431.19**; 377.27 *dilute;* 375.5 *disintegrated*
liquefy **268.17**; 527.11 *be transparent;* 375.4 *deconstruct;* 377.14 *dilute;* 431.22 *make fluid;* 419.13 *soften;* 32.25 *solidify;* 441.1 *waste*
liquefying **431.20**
liquesce 431.22 *make fluid*
liquescence 431.8 *fluidification*
liquescency 431.8 *fluidification*
liquescent 431.19 *liquefied*
liqueur 558.7 *alcoholic drink;* 498.5 *sweet drink*
liqueur glass 410.13 *drinking vessel*
liquid 431.1, 431.14 *fluid;* 5.41 *lettered;* 32.3 *phase;* 440.8 *propertied;* 268.2 *runniness;* 268.10 *slippery;* 32.32 *solid;* 5.16 *spoken letter;* 527.1 *transparent;* 433.1 *water;* 433.21 *watery*
liquid assets 780.6 *funds;* 440.5 *personal estate;* 781.5 *wealth*
liquidate 780.26 *bank;* 526.3 *cause to disappear;* 357.8 *destroy;* 371.10 *exterminate;* 131.17 *kill;* 358.1 *obliterate;* 785.7 *pay off;* 382.18 *slaughter*
liquidated 131.23 *annihilated;* 358.6 *obliterated;* 785.16 *paid*
liquidation 131.4 *annihilation;* 13.7 *corporation;* 357.1 *destruction;* 358.3 *obliteration;* 785.1 *payment;* 382.4 *slaughter*
liquidator 769.7 *collector;* 357.6 *destroyer*
liquid conductor 28.43 *electrical conduction;* 39.3 *electricity*
liquid diet 687.1 *fasting;* 557.6 *nutrition*
liquidescence 431.5 *fluidity*
liquid extract 431.1 *fluid*
liquid fuel 29.35 *rocketry*
liquidity 352.4 *financial resources;* 431.5 *fluidity;* 780.6 *funds;* 268.2 *runniness*
liquidity ratio 783.1 *credit*
liquidization 431.8 *fluidification*
liquidize 25.55 *cook;* 431.22 *make fluid*
liquidizer **431.11**; 25.6 *kitchen equipment;* 412.6 *mixer*
liquidly 431.26 *fluidly;* 433.35 *wetly*
liquidness 431.5 *fluidity*
liquid oxygen 494.4 *cooler;* 437.3 *gas*
liquid state 431.1 *fluid*
liquifier 431.9 *solvent*
liquiform 431.14 *fluid*
liquor 690.12 *alcohol;* 558.7 *alcoholic drink;* 431.1 *fluid*
liquor cabinet 23.5 *cabinet*
liquored up 690.1 *drunk*
liquorice 498.4 *confectionery;* 496.5 *herbs;* 394.6 *purgative;* 25.41 *sweet*
liquorice allsort 25.41 *sweet*
liquor store 558.11 *drink provider*
liquor up 690.8 *get drunk*
lira 780.11 *national coins*
Lisbon 87.6 *other cities*
lisible 695.2 *simple*
lisle stockings 551.20 *legwear*
lisp 730.14 *have difficulty speaking;* 512.4 *hiss*
lisping 512.1 *hiss;* 730.12 *inarticulate;* 729.3 *mode of speech;* 730.3 *speech defect*
lissom 419.2 *pliant*
lissomly 419.17 *softly*
List 220
list **220.1**; **220.8**; 789.8 *audit;* 189.6 *be oblique;* 120.5 *be unequal;* 409.7 *catalogue;* 409.15 *categorize;* 137.2 *class;* 406.5 *divisions;* 120.1 *inequality;* 406.9 *itemize;* 210.11 *number;* 189.1 *obliqueness;* 744.1, 744.13 *record;* 744.15 *register;* 323.10 *sail;* 469.6 *selection;* 305.14 *slide;* 139.24 *specify;* 127.6 *subsume;* 289.1 *succession;* 281.2 *timetable;* 42.4 *weaving*
listed **220.11**; 409.24 *categorized;* 407.11 *grouped;* 127.8 *included;* 406.12 *itemized;* 744.16 *recorded;* 20.12 *structural*
listed building 20.3 *building;* 296.5 *old thing;* 359.3 *preserved thing*
listen 504.15 *hear;* 504.18 *hear hear!*
listenability 504.10 *sound quality*
listenable 504.14 *hearable*
listener 504.2 *hearer;* 769.5 *recipient*
listener in 504.2 *hearer*
listen in 692.30 *communicate;* 504.15 *hear*
listening 504.11 *aural;* 504.1 *hearing*
listening in 504.1 *hearing*
listening post 504.3 *auditorium*
listen to 713.6 *consult;* 504.15 *hear*
listen with deaf ears 466.13 *prejudge*
listing **220.7**; 409.5 *categorization;* 137.2 *class;* 407.2 *grouping;* 220.1 *list;* 189.4 *oblique;* 744.8 *registration;* 120.3 *unequal*
listless 602.6 *depressed;* 261.1 *fatigued;* 472.7 *inattentive;* 618.7 *indifferent;* 343.3 *not participating;* 333.5 *unhurried*
listlessly 343.16 *impassively;* 618.17 *indifferently;* 602.12 *joylessly;* 261.8 *tiredly*
listlessness 639.14 *apathy;* 261.7 *fatigue;* 343.7 *idleness;* 618.1 *indifference*
list of appointments **220.5**
list of characters 566.7 *person*
list of names **220.6**
list price 790.1 *price*
list requirements 251.8 *restrain*
lit **522.18**; 317.15 *accessible;* 520.2 *clear*
litany 10.9 *prayer*
literacy 6.9 *learnedness;* 455.3 *learning*
literae humaniores 17.1 *literature*
literal **698.23**; 273.6 *correct;* 5.41 *lettered;* 694.6 *meaningful;* 646.1 *naive;* 5.40 *translated;* 719.17 *translational;* 274.12 *typing error*
literalism 273.2 *correctness;* 125.1 *imitation;* 698.10 *literalness*
literality 698.10 *literalness;* 694.4 *type of meaning*
literally **698.38**; 273.8 *accurately;* 125.14 *imitatively;* 5.48 *linguistically;* 694.13 *meaningfully;* 230.7 *perfectly*
literal meaning 698.10 *literalness;* 694.4 *type of meaning*
literal-minded 646.1 *naive;* 698.24 *pedantic*
literal-mindedness 698.11 *pedantry*
literalness **698.10**; 273.2 *correctness;* 7.2 *religiousness*
literal translation 5.12, 719.4 *translation*
literarily 5.48 *linguistically*
literary **17.16**; 6.18 *educated;* 5.39 *of language*
literary agent 398.6 *agent;* 740.12 *publisher*
literary composition 356.1 *production;* 356.5 *work of art*
literary conversion 316.4 *translation*
literary critic 719.6 *interpreter;* 17.15 *literary person*
literary criticism 719.3 *criticism*
literary language 5.6 *official language*
literary magazine 740.5 *journal*
literary person **17.15**; 721.10 *descriptive writer*
literary scholar 17.15 *literary person*
literary style **724.4**
literary theft 774.6 *illegal borrowing*
literary work 356.1 *production;* 356.5 *work of art*
literate **455.9**; 6.18 *educated;* 4.19 *learned*
literati 455.7 *academia*
literatim 125.14 *imitatively*
Literature 17
literature **17.1**; 6.14 *school book;* 455.5 *science*
lithagogue 37.4 *drug type*
lithe 419.2 *pliant*
lithely 419.17 *softly*
litheness 419.8 *softness*
lithesome 419.2 *pliant*
lithic 418.1 *hard;* 30.56 *petrographic*
lithification 30.29 *petrogenesis*
lithified sediment 30.31 *sedimentary rock*
lithify **30.62**
lithograph 19.15 *engraving;* 721.9 *representation;* 717.2 *reproduction*
lithography 19.1 *art*
lithoid 418.1 *hard*
lithosphere 30.18 *earth's crust*
lithospheric 30.53 *solid-earth*
lithospheric plate 30.19 *plate tectonics*
litigable 16.54 *litigated*
litigant **16.8**; 715.3 *accuser;* 586.5 *arguer;* 16.53 *litigating;* 113.11 *opposer*
litigate **16.70**; 715.5 *accuse;* 444.13 *debate;* 113.18 *object*
litigated **16.54**
litigating **16.53**
litigation **16.5**; **16.33**; 715.1 *accusation;* 444.3 *debate;* 160.5 *formality*
litigator 444.6 *arguer;* 16.8 *litigant*
litigious 715.8 *accusatory;* 381.21 *aggressive;* 444.9, 586.34, 701.8 *argumentative;* 160.11 *formal;* 16.52 *legalistic;* 16.53 *litigating*
litigiously 715.10 *accusingly;* 586.41 *aggressively;* 160.14 *conventionally;* 16.87 *in litigation*
litigiousness 16.5 *litigation*
litigious person 16.8 *litigant*
litmus 32.18 *gravimetric analysis*
litmus paper 32.18 *gravimetric analysis*
litotes 468.1 *underestimation*
litter **320.6**; **408.4**; 376.24 *brace;* 258.4 *dirt;* 71.35 *give birth;* 561.11 *have young;* 316.5 *means of transport;* 238.6 *refuse;* 215.2 *residue;* 377.17 *sow;* 441.5 *waste product;* 555.4 *young animal*
littérateur 442.8 *intellectual person*
litter bearer 316.7 *transferor*
litter bin 256.10 *cleaning object;* 410.11 *vessel;* 767.4 *wastebin*
litterbug 258.6 *dirty person;* 408.10 *slattern*
littered 554.15 *born;* 258.7 *dirty*
litter lout 258.6 *dirty person;* 408.10 *slattern*
litter picker 767.6 *rubbish collector*
little **159.7**; 206.1, 206.5 *few;* 337.13 *insufficient;* 149.7 *short;* 206.6 *sparse;* 206.11 *sparsely;* 124.1 *unimportant*
little angel 555.9 *child*
Little Bighorn 382.15 *slaughterhouse*
little bit 124.8 *trifle*
little black dress 523.4 *dark thing;* 551.7 *frock*
little black number 551.7 *frock*
little boy 567.2 *male*
little boys' room 560.13 *lavatory;* 767.7 *toilet*
little by little 209.10 *by degrees;* 205.12 *partly;* 333.16 *slowly*
little cherub 555.9 *child*
little extra 211.4 *extra*
little few 218.8 *insufficiency*
little finger 492.7 *sense organ*
little game 631.9 *tactics*
little girl 568.2 *female*
little girls' room 560.13 *lavatory;* 767.7 *toilet*
little green man 100.6 *outsider*
little green men 11.11 *ghost;* 538.11 *green thing*
little grey cells 458.2 *intelligence*
Little Hitler 400.4 *absolute ruler*
little imp 555.9 *child*
Little Italy 87.3 *New York*

little jobs 560.6 *urine*
Little League baseball 48.1 *baseball*
Little League World Series 48.1 *baseball*
little mama 568.9 *woman considered as a sex object*
little man 138.9 *everyman*; 574.1 *plebeian*
little monkey 555.9 *child*; 662.5 *troublemaker*
littleness 159.1; 122.3 *inferior numbers*; 683.1 *selfishness*; 149.1 *shortness*
little one 555.9 *child*
little person 159.4
little piece 159.3
little school 815.2 *the inside*
little ships 586.23 *naval unit*
little something extra 164.4 *advantage*
little space 159.5
little theatre 21.16 *theatre*
little thing 159.2
little toe 492.7 *sense organ*
little way 147.2 *short distance*
little worth 289.3 *subordination*
littoral 30.52 *coastal*; 92.11 *continental*; 164.1 *edge*; 164.8 *edging*; 91.7 *oceanic*; 70.15 *of animals*
lit up 690.1 *drunk*; 522.18 *lit*
liturgic 656.8 *ceremonious*
liturgical 18.32 *instrumental*; 10.21 *ritualistic*
liturgical drama 21.2 *play*
liturgical east end 20.10 *church architecture*
liturgical garment 7.11 *vestment*
liturgically 10.23 *ritually*
liturgical music 18.5 *sacred music*
liturgics 10.2 *ritualism*
liturgism 10.2 *ritualism*
liturgology 10.2 *ritualism*
liturgy 601.3 *ceremony*; 656.3 *formal occasion*; 10.4 *public worship*; 10.1 *ritual*
live 554.16; 342.18 *active*; 554.12 *alive*; 97.11, 282.5 *be present*; 51.9 *bowls*; 28.52 *electric potential*; 39.36 *electronic*; 93.17 *exist*; 334.15 *full of energy*; 97.14 *in person*; 34.21 *living*; 62.8 *mountaineering*
live a certain way 221.6 *be in a state of*
live again 393.4 *be restored*
Live Aid 768.3 *offering*
live alone 572.9 *be celibate*
live ammunition 587.13 *ammunition*; 181.8 *round*
live and let live 473.6 *be disinterested*; 225.6 *make permanent*; 341.4 *not act*; 250.15 *set free*
live-and-let-live 648.4 *lenient*
live apart 571.7 *divorce*
live as an amphibian 73.16
live as a reptile 73.15
live a simple life 646.4 *be naive*
live a spartan life 647.7 *be unadorned*
live at 554.17 *dwell*
live ball 49.4 *playing terms*
live-bearing 561.16 *reproductive*
live beyond one's means 681.8 *overspend*
live bowl 51.2 *grip*
live by a creed 707.17 *affirm*
live by one's wits 645.5 *be cunning*; 800.8 *be dishonourable*; 485.10 *be skilful*
live cartridge 587.13 *ammunition*
live circuit 39.10 *electric potential*
live conductor 39.10 *electric potential*
live coverage 692.25 *broadcast material*; 741.3 *reporting*
lived in 564.11 *inhabited*
live for the day 282.5 *be present*
live for today 282.5 *be present*
live frugally 684.5 *be self-restrained*
live honourably 255.9 *be pure*
live immoderately 250.19 *liberalize*
live in 93.17 *exist*; 564.14, 565.17 *inhabit*; 97.13 *reside*; 401.8 *serve*
live-in 97.9 *resident*
live in another land 100.14 *be foreign*
live in a whirl 342.13 *be busy*
live in cloud-cuckoo land 700.25 *deceive oneself*
live in clover 248.5 *be prosperous*
live in hope 610.6 *hope*
live in ignorance 646.4 *be naive*
live-in lover 567.13 *man in the family*; 223.12, 570.12 *partner*; 568.12 *woman in the family*
live-in maid 401.6 *domestic servant*
live in peace 749.4 *pacify*
live in poverty 135.11 *be needy*; 782.12 *be poor*
live in single blessedness 572.9 *be celibate*
live in the past 284.15 *look back*; 286.4 *mistime*
live in the present 282.5 *be present*
live it up 654.13 *fraternize*; 248.10 *good luck!*
live jack 51.2 *grip*
livelihood 143.4 *employment*; 392.3 *sustenance*
live like a Christian 799.6 *be honourable*
live like a hermit 572.11 *be monastic*
live like a monk 572.11 *be monastic*; 255.9 *be pure*; 251.10 *restrain oneself*
live like a nun 572.11 *be monastic*; 255.9 *be pure*
live like a Puritan 255.9 *be pure*
liveliness 422.2 *adaptability*; 598.3 *cheerfulness*; 726.1 *emphasis*; 342.4 *energy*; 336.2 *healthiness*; 554.1 *life*; 332.10 *quickness of mind*; 496.4 *stimulation*; 338.1 *vigour*; 334.3 *vitality*
live load 38.14 *load*; 414.7 *weighing*
lively 554.13; 342.18 *active*; 422.7 *adaptive*; 342.19 *busy*; 598.1 *cheerful*; 726.3 *emphatic*; 334.15 *full of energy*; 477.10 *imaginative*; 332.2 *mentally quick*; 654.15 *sociable*; 496.10 *stimulating*; 338.4 *vigorous*; 554.22 *vitally*
lively imagination 477.1 *imagination*
liven 554.19 *give birth to*; 554.16 *live*
live off 664.15 *sponge*
live on 462.15 *be remembered*; 93.19 *continue to be*; 134.4 *protract*
live on a budget 680.5 *be thrifty*
live on air 687.5 *fast*
live on a pittance 135.11 *be needy*; 782.12 *be poor*
live on capital 787.1 *expend*
live on credit 784.7 *be in debt*
live on Easy Street 248.5 *be prosperous*; 781.12 *be rich*
live one's life 554.16 *live*
live one's own life 100.17 *not conform*
live on immoral earnings 796.18 *prostitute*
live on rations 687.5 *fast*
live on the breadline 135.11 *be needy*
live on the road 100.14 *be foreign*
live or die 638.17 *resolutely*
live out one's time 134.4 *protract*
live plainly 684.5 *be self-restrained*
live poorly 782.12 *be poor*
live purely 255.9 *be pure*
liver 172.4 *insides*; 626.3 *irritableness*; 25.31 *offal*
liver-coloured 534.1 *brown*
live relay 692.25 *broadcast material*
liver fluke 75.10 *parasite*; 260.18 *veterinary disease*; 75.6 *worm*
liveried 551.29 *dressed*
liverish 690.5 *drunken*
liverishness 260.8 *indigestion*
live rope 62.4 *climbing equipment*
Liverpool 87.4 *British cities*
Liverpudlian 564.9 *British inhabitant*
liver sausage 25.29 *sausage*
liverwort 82.3 *moss*
livery 551.3, 656.4 *formal dress*; 743.5 *uniform*
liveryman 776.11 *chamber of commerce member*; 13.9 *economist*
livery stable 59.14 *horse-riding terms*
live separately 571.7 *divorce*
live shot 587.13 *ammunition*
live show 21.7 *show*
live side by side 2.15 *socialize*
live simply 684.5 *be self-restrained*; 709.7 *refuse oneself*
livestock 43.8; 70.3 *domesticated animal*
livestock farm 43.6 *farm*
livestock farmer 43.15 *agriculturist*
livestock farming 43.3; 43.1 *agriculture*
livestock market 779.1 *market*
live theatre 21.1 *drama*
live through 393.4 *be restored*; 590.15 *feel*
live to eat 688.5 *be greedy*
live together 570.18; 223.14 *keep company with*; 570.15 *marry*
liveware 210.6 *calculator*; 40.2 *operator*
live well 248.5 *be prosperous*
live wire 342.10 *busy person*; 340.3 *doer*; 334.7 *electrical power*; 302.16 *progressive person*
live with 223.14 *keep company with*
live within one's means 680.5 *be thrifty*; 793.14 *buy cheaply*
livid 540.7; 624.16 *angry*; 539.2 *bluish*; 523.10 *dark-coloured*; 582.21 *deathly*; 524.5 *dim*; 530.8 *drained of colour*; 540.8 *furious*; 531.4 *pale*
lividity 539.8 *bluishness*; 540.5 *lividness*
lividly 624.18 *angrily*
lividness 540.5; 539.8 *bluishness*; 523.1 *darkness*
living 34.21; 554.12 *alive*; 93.10 *existing*; 565.14 *inhabiting*; 554.1 *life*; 115.9 *lifelike*; 5.39 *of language*; 440.1 *property*; 392.3 *sustenance*
living apart 571.11 *divorced*; 571.2 *separation*
living area 769.4 *reception*
living being 554.1 *life*; 34.3 *organism*
living fossil 75.4 *arthropod*; 74.4 *fossil fish*
living hell 249.1 *adversity*
living image 115.5 *counterpart*; 111.3 *lookalike*
living in 564.13 *resident*
living in cloud-cuckoo-land 700.2 *self-deception*
living in clover 248.1 *prosperity*
living issue 447.2 *issue*
living language 729.1 *faculty of speech*; 5.3 *spoken language*
living matter 554.2
living off one's capital 787.6 *extravagance*
living on borrowed time 556.14 *aged*
living on capital 787.11 *spendthrift*
living on immoral earnings 796.5 *prostitution*
living organism 34.3 *organism*
living person 554.1 *life*
living quarters 565.1 *habitat*
living room 769.4 *reception*; 565.7 *room*; 250.5 *scope*
living soul 554.1 *life*; 566.7 *person*
living space 141.6 *available space*; 250.5 *scope*
living thing 34.3 *organism*
living things 554.1 *life*
living tissue 554.2 *living matter*
living wage 217.7 *sufficiency*
living will 710.1 *request*
living world 34.2
lixiviate 431.23 *dissolve*; 315.12 *leak*; 255.10, 256.15 *purify*; 433.29 *water*
lixiviation 431.8 *fluidification*; 315.3 *leakage*; 433.9 *soaking*
lixivium 431.10 *solution*
lizard 73.2
lizard-like 73.11 *reptilian*
lizard-like reptile 73.2 *lizard*
llama 316.6 *beast of burden*
llano 81.2 *grassland*; 92.6 *lowland*
llyn 88.1 *lake*
load 38.14; **38.31**; **330.32**; **406.2**; 40.20 *abort*; 211.6 *add*; 211.1 *addition*; 249.1 *adversity*; 699.25 *be fraudulent*; 203.2 *certain amount*; 406.6 *contain*; 414.6 *displacement*; 232.6 *fill*; 414.14 *make heavy*; 778.8 *merchandise*; 219.2 *overdoing it*; 439.1, 439.6 *store*; 39.14 *terminal*; 319.2 *thing transported*; 316.10 *transferred thing*; 319.4 *transport*; 38.10 *work*
load-bearing capacity 336.1 *strength*
load-bearing wall 20.9 *miscellaneous architectural features*
loaded 406.11; **414.2**; 211.8 *additional*; 690.3 *dead drunk*; 106.4 *deliberate*; 691.7 *drugged*; 232.8 *full*; 439.7 *stored*; 319.5 *transportable*; 781.1 *wealthy*; 765.17 *well-off*
loaded dice 699.8 *fraud*; 120.1 *inequality*
loaded table 217.8, 557.9 *plenty*
loader 243.15 *preparer*; 319.3 *transporter*
load factor 322.7 *miscellaneous aviation terms*
loading 414.6 *displacement*; 322.7 *miscellaneous aviation terms*; 318.2 *passing along*; 243.9 *preparation*; 319.1 *transport*; 319.5 *transportable*
loading the bases 48.4 *pitching terms*
load line 742.5 *indicator*; 26.6 *measuring instrument*
load of old rubbish 238.6 *refuse*
loads 208.3 *profuseness*
load the bases 48.7 *play baseball*
load the dice 700.30 *be fraudulent*; 106.2 *premeditate*
load the gun 243.4 *prepare for action*
load tightly 416.9 *make dense*
load with ornament 542.12 *ornament*
loaf 25.39; 343.12 *be inactive*; 341.4 *not act*
loafer 341.2 *nonacting person*; 343.8 *nonworker*
loafers 551.19 *footwear*
loafing 341.1 *inaction*; 343.3 *not participating*
loam 258.4 *dirt*; 30.36 *soil*
loamy 419.4 *compressible*; 30.58 *earthy*
loan 771.2; **772.5**; **784.3**; 650.4 *benevolent act*; 783.1, 783.8 *credit*; 392.29 *finance*; 392.6 *financial assistance*; 771.5 *lend*; 752.11 *volunteer*
loan agreement 772.1 *borrowing*
loan applicant 784.6 *debtor*
loan application 772.1 *borrowing*
loan capital 784.3 *loan*
loaned 771.6; 772.11 *borrowed*
loanee 784.6 *debtor*
loaner 771.3 *lender*
loaning 771.1 *lending*
loan-maker 783.5 *lender*
loan office 771.4 *lending institution*
loan officer 771.3 *lender*
loan repayment 784.3 *loan*
loan shark 771.3, 783.5 *lender*; 792.5 *overcharger*; 628.3 *pitiless person*
loan-sharking 792.4 *extortion*; 771.1 *lending*
loan transaction 772.1 *borrowing*
loan translation 5.17 *word*
loan word 5.17 *word*
loath 596.8 *disliking*; 637.1 *unwilling*
loathe 651.16 *be malevolent*; 596.5 *dislike*; 594.14 *hate*
loathed 594.12 *hated*
loathing 596.1 *dislike*; 596.8 *disliking*; 594.1 *hate*; 594.10 *hating*; 651.1 *malevolence*
loathingly 594.18 *hatefully*
loathness 637.11 *unwillingness*
loathsome 596.9 *disliked*; 594.12 *hated*; 236.4 *poor*; 364.8 *repulsive*; 242.1 *unpleasant*
loathsomeness 812.1 *disrespect*; 594.4 *hatefulness*
lob 366.2 *send up*; 63.13 *serve*; 63.2 *tennis strokes*; 330.5, 330.23, 331.4 *throw*
lobbed 366.11 *raised*
lobbied 483.12 *motivated*
lobbing 330.3 *throwing*
lobby 167.1 *front*; 395.6 *group influence*; 395.8 *influence*; 483.10 *manipulate*; 314.6 *means of entry*; 480.14, 483.7 *motivator*; 480.15 *persuade*; 769.4 *reception*; 565.7 *room*; 317.2 *route*
lobby correspondent 741.4 *journalist*
lobbyer 480.14 *motivator*
lobbying 483.2 *inducement*; 480.1 *persuasion*
lobbyist 353.7 *attempter*; 340.3 *doer*; 395.5 *influential person*; 480.14, 483.7 *motivator*; 710.4 *requester*
lobed 77.18 *of leaves*
lobe-finned fish 74.2 *fish*
lobotomy 394.12 *surgery*
lobster 75.4 *arthropod*; 25.19 *shellfish*
lobster bisque 25.13 *soup*
lobstertails 260.14 *venereal disease*
lobster thermidor 25.45 *French dish*
local 86.18; **447.9**; 565.15 *environmental*; 565.10 *hotel*; 564.1 *inhabitant*; 172.8 *internal*; 85.13, 564.12 *native*; 147.9 *near*; 143.7 *situational*; 87.14 *urban*; 87.11 *urbanite*
local anaesthesia 394.5 *analgesic*
local anaesthetic 394.5 *analgesic*
local authority 16.2 *jurisdiction*
local call 692.10 *telephone call*
local climate 31.38 *climate*
local code 692.11 *dialling*
local colour 17.3 *aspect of fiction*; 19.4 *treatment*
locale 565.2 *environment*; 86.13 *locality*; 142.1 *location*; 143.1 *situation*; 170.1 *surroundings*
local election 469.12 *election*
local exchange 692.12 *public telephone system*
local government 12.1 *government*
local-government election 469.12 *election*
Local Group 29.7 *galaxy*

local history 3.1 *history*
local-history topic 447.5 *educational topic*
local-interest 447.9 *local*
localism 5.26 *dialect*
locality **86.13**; 565.2 *environment*; 142.1 *location*; 147.5 *near place*; 143.1 *situation*
localization 377.6 *decentralization*
localize 377.15 *decentralize*; 251.8 *restrain*
localized 377.26 *decentralized*; 86.18 *local*
localized war 585.1 *war*
local jurisdiction 16.2 *jurisdiction*
locally 565.20 *environmentally*; 143.11 *geographically*; 87.16 *municipally*; 86.20 *nationally*; 147.12 *near*; 447.12 *topically*
local newspaper 741.5 *mass communication*
local paper 740.4 *newspaper*
local pronunciation 5.26 *dialect*
local radio 692.20 *radio broadcasting*
local road 317.3 *road*
local tax 790.7 *tax*
local television 692.24 *television broadcasting*
local time 281.3 *chronology*; 275.9 *time zone*
local wind 31.12 *wind*
local worthy 123.4 *bigwig*
locatable 142.7 *found*
locate **142.9**; 409.12 *arrange*; 173.9 *centre*; 449.1 *discover*; 142.10 *settle*; 143.10 *situate*
located **142.6**; 449.14 *discovered*; 142.7 *found*; 143.6 *situated*
locating **142.3**; 173.3 *centrality*; 142.4 *placing*
Location 142
location **142.1**; 409.1 *arrangement*; 324.1 *direction*; 449.6 *discovery*; 733.5 *place of residence*; 27.36 *point*; 143.1 *situation*
locational **142.8**; 2.14 *socioeconomic*
locational theory 2.2 *sociological research*
locative 5.31 *case*
loch 88.1 *lake*
Loch Leven 88.4 *British lakes*
Loch Lomond 88.4 *British lakes*
Loch Ness 88.4 *British lakes*
Loch Ness monster 700.11 *hoax*; 70.7 *legendary beast*; 737.6 *natural mystery*
Loch Rannoch 88.4 *British lakes*
Loch Tay 88.4 *British lakes*
lock 373.12 *bind*; 317.11 *channel*; 309.7 *close*; 373.8 *fastening*; 587.9 *firearm*; 301.9 *make motionless*; 320.21 *miscellaneous motoring terms*; 301.1 *motionlessness*; 309.3 *restrainer*; 360.6 *retain*; 360.1 *retention*; 64.4 *rugby player*; 252.4 *safety device*; 38.24 *water system*
lock and key 373.8 *fastening*
lock away 252.10 *protect*; 253.10 *secure*
lockbox 253.5 *safe*
locked 373.16 *bound*; 309.12 *closed*
locked away 253.6 *secure*
locked up 410.20 *containing*; 815.8 *imprisoned*; 253.6 *secure*
locker 410.6 *box*; 50.8 *punting*
lock horns 751.6 *argue*
lock in 360.7 *detain*
locking in 360.2 *detention*
locking karabiner 62.4 *climbing equipment*
locking the blade 50.6 *canoeing*
lockjaw 260.6 *infection*
lockout 128.1 *exclusion*; 13.8 *industrial relations*; 378.2 *obstacle*; 709.1 *refusal*; 226.2 *stop*
lock out 378.9 *block*; 226.8 *cause to cease*; 15.12 *have an industrial dispute*; 709.5 *refuse*
locksmith 578.2 *artisan*; 308.3 *person who opens*
lock step 285.4 *equal race*
lock, stock, and barrel 232.9 *completely*; 203.4 *total*; 204.11 *wholly*
lock the blade 50.17 *canoe*
lockup 815.1 *prison*
lock up 309.7 *close*; 736.8 *conceal*; 384.17 *defend*; 309.10 *enclose*; 815.9 *imprison*; 814.1 *punish*; 253.10 *secure*
loco 461.11 *insane*; 321.4 *locomotive*
Locomotion 321.10 *miscellaneous*
locomotion 300.1 *motion*; 34.5 *physiology*
locomotive **321.4**; 334.15 *full of energy*; 300.16 *moving*; 362.6 *towline*
locomotive part 321.5
locomotory 34.22 *physiological*
Locrian mode 18.20 *key*
locum 398.5 *alternative*; 35.11 *doctor*; 211.5 *extra person*; 608.5 *helper*; 762.2 *substitute person*; 550.21 *substitution*; 550.40 *substitutive*
locum tenens 608.5 *helper*; 762.2 *substitute person*
locus 27.36 *point*
locust 557.18 *eater*; 688.4 *glutton*; 76.1 *insect*; 76.3 *pest*; 773.6 *taker*
locusts 357.7 *agent of destruction*
locution 5.24 *phrasing*; 729.7 *utterance*
locutionary 5.43 *phrasal*
lode 411.1 *layer*; 32.24 *ore*; 439.2 *resource*
loden 551.11 *jacket*
loden green 538.1 *green*
lodestar 579.5 *guide*; 742.5 *indicator*; 363.3 *magnet*; 483.1 *motive*
lodestone 475.6 *good-luck sign*; 28.60, 362.7, 363.3 *magnet*
lodestuff 32.24 *ore*
lodge 71.20 *abode of mammals*; 376.19 *clique*; 554.17 *dwell*; 737.7 *esotericism*; 564.14 *inhabit*; 301.9 *make motionless*; 565.4 *official residence*; 565.18 *take up residence*
lodge a complaint 715.5 *accuse*
lodged 565.14 *inhabiting*
lodger 564.3 *householder*; 763.5 *possessor*
lodging 565.1 *habitat*; 226.5 *resting place*
lodgings 565.1 *habitat*
lodicule 81.3 *grass plant*
loess 215.2 *residue*; 30.27 *sediment*; 316.10 *transferred thing*
loft 53.17, 330.26 *bat*; 154.8 *high thing*; 565.7 *room*; 366.2 *send up*; 439.4 *storage*
lofted shot 56.3 *golf shots*
loftily 660.33 *arrogantly*; 622.34 *imposingly*; 473.9 *unselfishly*
loftiness 542.2 *affectation*; 660.4 *arrogance*; 673.3 *cockiness*; 668.3 *contempt*; 154.1, 366.8 *height*; 726.2 *seriousness*; 622.5 *stateliness*; 121.1 *superiority*; 473.2 *unselfishness*
loft ladder 304.9 *ladder*
lofty 660.16 *arrogant*; 668.13 *contemptuous*; 366.12 *exalted*; 154.9 *high*; 89.7 *mountainous*; 542.10 *ornate*; 726.5 *serious*; 141.13 *spacious*; 622.19 *stately*; 473.5 *unselfish*
lofty ground 121.4 *summit*
log 3.5, 3.20 *chronicle*; 437.2 *lighter*; 27.19 *logarithm*; 79.18 *manage trees*; 435.1 *materials*; 26.6 *measuring instrument*; 323.5 *navigation*; 194.6 *power*; 744.13 *record*; 744.6 *record book*; 332.8 *speed*; 79.3 *timber*; 23.12 *wood*
loganberry 412.5 *hybrid*
logan stone 326.7 *oscillator*
logarithm **27.19**; 210.1 *calculation*; 194.6 *power*
logarithmic 194.9 *fractional*; 27.76 *functional*; 210.15 *mathematical*
logarithmically 27.87, 210.16 *mathematically*
logarithmic function 27.29 *mathematical function*
logarithmic paper 27.32 *graph*
logarithmic scale 27.32 *graph*; 27.19 *logarithm*
logarithmic series 27.20 *sequence*
logarithmic spiral 27.40 *curve*
logarithm tables 27.19 *logarithm*
log basket 410.7 *basket*
logbook 3.5 *chronicle*; 320.21 *miscellaneous motoring terms*; 744.6 *record book*
log cabin 565.5 *house*
loge 21.18 *auditorium*
logged 3.19 *chronicled*; 744.16 *recorded*
logger 79.8 *forester*
loggia 317.7 *arcade*; 20.9 *miscellaneous architectural features*
logging 79.6 *tree management*
logic 4.6 *branch of philosophy*; 698.7 *confirmation*; 701.2 *logical argument*; 444.2 *reasoning*; 442.2 *ways of thinking*
logical **27.86**; **701.11**; 442.9 *mental*; 4.15, 444.8 *rational*; 443.11 *reasoning*
logical argument 701.2
logical connective 27.63 *mathematical logic*
logical empiricism 4.7 *school of thought*
logical empiricist 4.11 *follower of a doctrine*
logical expression 27.63 *mathematical logic*
logical formula 27.63 *mathematical logic*
logical impossibility 103.5 *impossibility*
logicalize 4.21 *rationalize*; 444.11 *reason*
logically **701.19**; 698.37 *authentically*; 442.15 *intelligently*; 27.87 *mathematically*; 4.24 *philosophically*; 4.26 *rationally*; 444.15 *reasonably*; 443.18 *thoughtfully*
logically demonstrated 698.20 *proved*
logically proven 698.20 *proved*
logical operation 27.63 *mathematical logic*; 27.14 *operation*
logical operator 27.63 *mathematical logic*; 27.13 *mathematical symbol*
logical order 407.3 *hierarchy*
logical outcome 345.1 *effect*
logical positivism 4.7 *school of thought*
logical positivist 4.11 *follower of a doctrine*
logical process 444.2 *reasoning*
logical product 27.63 *mathematical logic*
logical proposition 27.63 *mathematical logic*
logical reasoning 27.64 *reasoning*
logical sum 27.63 *mathematical logic*
logical thinker 443.7 *thinker*
logical thought 444.2 *reasoning*
logical value 27.63 *mathematical logic*
logic bomb 40.19 *computing terms*
logic-chopper 645.3 *cunning person*; 702.6 *sophist*
logic-chopping 702.7 *sophistic*; 702.1 *sophistry*
logic circuit 39.13 *circuit*
logician 701.6 *arguer*; 4.10 *philosopher*; 444.5 *reasoner*
logicize 701.14 *discuss*; 4.21 *rationalize*
login 40.20 *abort*; 40.19 *computing terms*
logistic 27.40 *curve*
logistics 585.6 *art of war*; 243.11 *fitting out*; 584.1 *military affairs*; 436.1 *provision*; 631.9 *tactics*
log jam 294.3 *delayed action*; 119.2 *equilibrium*; 341.1 *inaction*; 378.2 *obstacle*; 264.8 *snag*; 226.2 *stop*
log-jammed 294.10 *held up*
log-line knot 323.6 *nautical speed*
logo 743.3 *means of identification*
logoff 40.20 *abort*; 40.19 *computing terms*
logomachize 701.14 *discuss*; 4.23 *discuss philosophically*
logomachy 4.5 *philosophical argument*
logomancy 11.9 *divination*
logomania 731.1 *talkativeness*
logometric 194.9 *fractional*
logon 40.20 *abort*; 40.19 *computing terms*
logophile 5.2 *linguist*
logorrhoea 270.1 *diffuseness*; 729.2 *power of speech*; 731.1 *talkativeness*
Logos 5.17 *word*
logotherapy 36.3 *psychiatric treatment*
logotype 743.3 *means of identification*
logout 40.20 *abort*; 40.19 *computing terms*
log paper 27.32 *graph*
logroll 759.5 *exchange*
logrolling 759.1 *exchange*; 747.3 *mutual relationship*
log table 210.5 *computer*
log tables 27.19 *logarithm*
loin 25.26, 25.27 *lamb*; 25.24, 25.25 *pork*
loin chop 25.27 *lamb*
loincloth 551.25 *accessories*
loins 561.4 *development*
loipe 68.1 *skiing*
loiter 333.2 *hesitate*; 294.7 *wait*
loiterer 333.15 *slow person*
loitering 333.7 *delayed*; 333.11 *lingering*
loiteringly 333.16 *slowly*
Lokayata 4.7 *school of thought*
Loki 700.15 *deceiver*; 8.7 *devil*
loll 263.2 *take it easy*
lollapalooza 235.8 *exceller*; 797.17 *good thing*
Lollard 7.5 *Christian*
lolling 343.3 *not participating*
lollipop 498.4 *confectionery*; 25.41 *sweet*
lolly 780.2 *cash*
lollygag 333.2 *hesitate*; 593.27 *kiss*
lollygagging 593.6 *courtship*; 333.7 *delayed*; 333.11 *lingering*
lomentum 80.2 *botanical fruit*
London **87.5**; 87.4 *British cities*; 86.10 *urban area*
Londoner 564.9 *British inhabitant*
lone 197.16 *alone*; 197.11 *one*; 118.16 *solitary*
loneliness 197.5 *aloneness*; 655.3 *separation*; 372.2 *setting apart*
lonely **655.10**; 197.16 *alone*; 372.17 *unjoined*
lonely hearts club 570.13 *matchmaker*
lonely hearts column 570.13 *matchmaker*
lonely pride 655.1 *unsociability*
loneness 197.5 *aloneness*
lone pair 32.11 *chemical bond*
loner **197.8**; 325.19 *deviant person*; 250.8 *free-thinker*; 118.9 *hermit*; 655.6 *unsocial person*
lonesome 197.16 *alone*; 655.10 *lonely*
lonesomeness 197.5 *aloneness*
lone wolf 736.7 *concealer*; 325.19 *deviant person*; 250.8 *free-thinker*; 118.9 *hermit*; 197.8 *loner*; 655.6 *unsocial person*
lone woman 572.5 *single person*
long **148.1**; **277.11**; 610.7 *aspire*; 270.3 *diffuse*; 57.11 *gymnastic*; 595.7 *like*; 203.6 *quantitative*; 141.13 *spacious*
long ago 3.24 *historically*; 284.22 *in the past*; 3.8 *past time*
long arm 12.3 *governance*
long-awaited 474.7 *expected*
longbow 357.7 *agent of destruction*; 330.9 *firearm*; 587.6 *historical missile weapon*
long bread 781.6 *money*
long-butt cue 65.3 *English billiards*
longcase clock 281.6 *clock*
long chalk 145.2 *great distance*
long circuit 61.6 *motor-racing terms*
long-course 67.11 *swimming*
long-course pool 67.7 *swimming pool*
long-distance 145.8 *distant*; 68.13 *ice-skating*; 67.11 *swimming*; 47.9 *track*
long-distance call 692.10 *telephone call*
long-distance communication 692.1 *communications*
long-distance hitter 48.2 *baseball player*
long-distance race 47.1 *track events*
long-distance racing 68.8 *speed-skating*; 47.1 *track events*
long-distance runner 47.3 *athlete*
long-distance running 47.1 *track events*
long-distance swimmer 67.4 *swimmer*
long-distance swimming 67.1 *swimming*
long division 27.18 *division*
long dozen 201.7 *double figures*
long-drawn-out 270.3 *diffuse*; 148.1 *long*
long dress 656.4 *formal dress*
long drink 558.2 *drink*
long drink of water 154.7, 158.11 *tall person*; 153.9 *thin person*
long duration **277.5**; 134.2 *protraction*
long-eared 504.12 *eared*
longed for 617.7 *desired*
longer endurance 765.2 *augmentation*
long established 296.12 *olden*
longevity 259.3 *health*; 554.5 *life cycle*; 556.5 *old age*
long face 626.2 *sign of sullenness*; 643.4 *solemnity*
long-faced 602.6 *depressed*; 643.1 *solemn*
long-focus lens 41.17 *lens*
long for 593.24 *be in love*; 218.6 *be unsatisfied*; 617.12 *desire*; 135.8 *miss*
long game 56.3 *golf shots*
long gloves 551.25 *accessories*
long gone 582.19 *dead*
long green 781.6 *money*
long habit 632.1 *habit*
long haul 145.2 *great distance*
long home 583.6 *grave*
long hop 53.8 *delivery*
long hot summer 493.5 *hot weather*
longing 593.20 *amorous*; 610.13 *aspirant*; 610.3 *aspiration*; 593.5, 617.1 *desire*; 595.1, 595.6 *liking*
longing for 617.9 *desirous*; 135.5 *necessitous*
longingly 595.11 *admiringly*
long in-off 65.2 *billiards play*
long in the tooth 556.13 *middle-aged*
longitude 27.39 *angle*; 166.4 *boundary marker*; 86.2 *geographical region*; 148.4 *length*; 143.1 *situation*; 26.4 *size*
longitudinal **148.3**; 166.6 *furthest*; 86.16 *regional*
longitudinal dune 30.37 *dune*
longitudinal line 119.7 *dividing line*

longitudinally 148.12; 86.19 *geographically*
longitudinal strain 38.14 *load*
longitudinal wave 28.12, 326.5 *wave*
long johns 493.3 *heater*; 551.18 *underwear*
long jump 47.2 *field events*
long jumper 47.3 *athlete*
long jumping 47.2 *field events*
long-lasting 277.8 *lasting*; 275.21 *lasting through time*; 225.7 *permanent*; 228.9 *stable*; 423.1 *tough*
long-lastingness 277.4
long-legged 154.12 *tall*
longlegs 154.7, 158.11 *tall person*
long life 259.3 *health*
long-life food 557.7 *food*; 359.3 *preserved thing*
long-life milk 558.5 *milk*; 359.3 *preserved thing*
long-limbed 154.12 *tall*
long-lived 554.12 *alive*; 277.8 *lasting*
long loser 65.2 *billiards play*
long-lost 766.16 *losing*
Long Melford 331.14 *sporting hit*
long moss 82.3 *moss*
long-necked 154.12 *tall*
longness 148.4 *length*
long note 18.19 *tempo*
long odds 107.5 *good chance*; 105.4 *improbability*; 102.4 *remote possibility*
long off 53.4 *team*
long on 53.4 *team*
long on-off 65.2 *billiards play*
long pants 551.9 *trousers*
long past 284.19 *antiquarian*
long period 32.6 *chemical element*
long range 145.1 *distance*
long-range 145.8 *distant*; 319.5 *transportable*
long-range forecast 31.4 *weather forecast*
long-range plan 475.3 *plan*
long run 145.2 *great distance*; 21.13 *theatrical performance*
long shot 105.4 *improbability*; 107.6 *poor chance*; 41.4 *portrait*; 102.4 *remote possibility*
long sight 519.2 *poor sight*; 518.1 *vision*
long-sighted 518.22 *bespectacled*; 519.9 *weak-sighted*
long-sightedness 519.2 *poor sight*
long since 3.24 *historically*; 284.22 *in the past*
long ski 68.5 *ski equipment*
long sleeve 551.24 *part of garment*
long-sleeved 551.31 *styled*
long-sleeved shirt 551.8 *shirt*
longstanding 277.8 *lasting*; 296.12 *olden*; 225.7 *permanent*
long-standing client 632.8 *creature of habit*
longstop 53.4 *team*
long story made short 163.1 *outline*
long string 65.6 *pool*
long-suffering 649.2 *forgivingness*; 648.4 *lenient*; 649.5 *merciful*; 627.3 *mercy*
long suit 235.6 *worth*
long sword 22.4 *historic dancing*
long-term 277.8 *lasting*
long-term forecast 31.4 *weather forecast*
long-term loan 771.2 *loan*
long-term soldier 586.8 *soldier*
long to 595.9 *like to*
long trail 145.2 *great distance*
long trousers 551.9 *trousers*
longueur 620.1 *boredom*
long underwear 551.18 *underwear*
long use 349.6 *use*
long wave 297.6 *radio frequency*; 692.14 *radio transmission*
long way 145.2 *great distance*
long way round 325.14 *deviating course*; 306.5 *ringroad*
longways 148.3 *longitudinal*; 148.12 *longitudinally*
long-winded 620.4 *boring*; 270.3 *diffuse*; 148.1 *long*; 731.5 *talkative*
long-windedly 620.8 *boringly*; 270.7 *diffusely*
long-windedness 620.1 *boredom*; 270.1 *diffuseness*; 544.4 *inelegance of speech*; 729.2 *power of speech*; 731.1 *talkativeness*
long-winded speaker 620.3 *boring person*
long-wire antenna 692.17 *antenna*
long word 5.17 *word*
long-worded 542.10 *ornate*
long words 542.2 *affectation*
Longworth trap 700.13 *snare*
loo 560.13 *lavatory*; 565.7 *room*; 767.7 *toilet*
looby 486.10 *unskilled person*
loofah 256.10 *cleaning object*
loofie 68.10 *curling*
look 518.6; **518.13**; 693.7 *advice*; 525.11 *appear*; 171.13 *appear outwardly*; 631.1 *conduct*; 525.3 *external appearance*; 553.1 *fashion*; 742.3 *gesture*; 160.6 *nature*
look after 579.1 *manage*; 35.19 *practise medicine*; 359.5 *preserve*; 252.10 *protect*; 392.25, 401.8 *serve*; 392.19 *support*
look after number one 197.18 *be one*; 686.10 *indulge oneself*
look after oneself 259.5 *be healthy*
look aghast 619.9 *wonder*
look ahead 283.9; 484.12 *plan ahead*
lookalike 111.3; **111.14**; 21.24 *actor*; 750.5 *conformity*; 115.5 *counterpart*; 525.5 *impression*; 717.1 *representation*; 762.7 *substitute*; 762.2 *substitute person*; 198.5 *twin*
look alike 111.7 *be the same*
look ashamed 806.9 *appear guilty*
look askance 518.13 *look*; 596.6 *react against*
look askance at 606.7 *be dissatisfied*
look at 474.8 *expect*; 518.13 *look*
look away 519.16 *be blind to*
look back 284.15; **303.8**; 3.21 *antiquarianize*; 462.12 *remember*; 761.6 *reverse*
look before one leaps 616.5 *be cautious*; 637.8 *hold back*
look black 624.11 *be angry*; 626.11 *be irritable*; 475.11 *predict*
look blank 604.5 *be crestfallen*; 736.12 *be silent*; 696.7 *be unintelligible*
look blue 604.5 *be crestfallen*
look closely at 518.14 *inspect*
look daggers 624.11 *be angry*; 742.11 *gesture*; 518.13 *look*
look deadpan 696.7 *be unintelligible*
look down on 154.15 *be high*; 670.14 *disapprove*; 622.28 *disdain*; 668.20 *scorn*
look down one's nose 518.13 *look*
look down upon 89.9 *tower*
looked for 283.13 *foreseen*; 756.15 *future*
look embarrassed 806.9 *appear guilty*
looker 545.3 *attractive female*; 545.4 *attractive male*; 518.11 *observer*
looker-on 518.11 *observer*; 97.5 *someone present*
look expressionless 696.7 *be unintelligible*
look foolish 623.24 *be humiliated*
look for 243.3 *be prepared*; 474.8 *expect*; 482.7 *intend*; 633.8 *pursue*; 104.10 *think likely*
look for a disagreement 751.7 *pick a fight*
look for a welcome 312.3 *approach*
look for trouble 751.7 *pick a fight*
look forward 283.9 *look ahead*
look forward to 610.7 *aspire*; 474.8 *expect*; 756.11 *promise oneself*
look guilty 806.9 *appear guilty*
look in 314.9 *enter*
look-in 287.2 *opportunity*
look inferior 116.5 *be dissimilar*
looking 742.15 *gestural*; 518.21 *seeing*
looking after number one 683.1 *selfishness*
looking ahead 283.4 *looking to the future*
looking back 3.13; **303.15**; 284.2 *retrospection*; 284.21 *retrospective*; 761.2 *reversion*
looking for 633.1 *pursuit*
looking glass 518.8 *reflection*
looking guilty 806.6 *appearing guilty*
looking to the future 283.4
looking true 698.25 *lifelike*
looking up 244.14 *improved*
look in mint condition 393.4 *be restored*
look in on 97.12 *attend*
look in one's eyes 631.1 *conduct*
look in the face 613.15 *be courageous*
look into 4.20 *philosophize*
look into a crystal 283.9 *look ahead*
look in vain for 766.9 *lose*
look kindly on 248.7 *be auspicious*
look like 525.11 *appear*; 750.25 *conform*; 717.9 *represent*
look like new 393.4 *be restored*
look like rain 523.13 *become dark*
look like thunder 624.11 *be angry*
look natural 736.12 *be silent*
look of power 397.5 *self-assurance*
look of reality 698.12 *realism*
look ominous 475.11 *predict*
look on 97.12 *attend*; 335.6 *be powerless*; 341.4 *not act*
lookout 518.11 *observer*; 252.3 *protector*; 711.4 *warner*; 665.5 *watchfulness*
look out 616.5 *be cautious*; 68.18 *danger!*
look out! 711.10
look out for 665.11 *care for*; 474.10 *wait*
lookout man 323.7 *nautical person*
look out the window 341.4 *not act*
look over 518.14 *inspect*
look over one's shoulder 637.8 *hold back*; 284.15, 303.8 *look back*
look right through 659.7 *be discourteous*
looks 525.3 *external appearance*
look-see 518.3 *observation*
look serious 643.8 *be serious*
look sheepish 806.9 *appear guilty*
look sideways 518.13 *look*
look straight at 518.13 *look*
look superior 116.5 *be dissimilar*
look the other way 634.1 *avoid*; 519.16 *be blind to*; 618.12 *be indifferent*
look through rosecoloured glasses 610.8 *be optimistic*
look to 810.17 *impose a duty*
look to be 525.11 *appear*
look to one's profits 776.1 *trade*
look true 698.33 *seem lifelike*
look twice 616.5 *be cautious*
look up 654.12 *visit*
look up to 155.8 *be low*; 9.8 *idolatrize*; 667.15 *respect*; 667.16 *revere*
look volumes 742.11 *gesture*
look where you're going 711.10 *look out!*
look young 259.5 *be healthy*
loom 520.9 *appear*; 158.19 *be big*; 525.12 *become visible*; 254.10 *endanger*; 304.20 *hover*; 50.4 *rowing*; 42.4, 193.3 *weaving*; 577.1 *workshop*
loomed 193.6 *interwoven*
looming 293.13 *imminent*
loom large 158.19 *be big*; 95.10 *be real*; 518.19, 738.5 *be visible*
loom over 304.20 *hover*
loom up 518.19 *be visible*
loon 461.7 *insane person*; 72.3 *water bird*
loony 36.8 *disordered personality*; 118.10 *eccentric*; 461.7 *insane person*; 457.6 *unintelligent*
loony bin 461.8 *mental hospital*
loony school 461.8 *mental hospital*
loony tune 461.7 *insane person*
loop 40.20 *abort*; 177.2 *bend*; 563.3 *birth control*; 68.16 *bobsled*; 179.2 *circle*; 180.2 *coil*; 40.19 *computing terms*; 180.6 *convolute*; 177.6 *curve*; 373.8 *fastening*; 322.5 *flight*; 322.10 *fly*; 68.6 *ice-skating*; 306.3 *orbit*; 306.7 *ring*; 321.2 *track*; 373.9 *yoke*
loop antenna 692.17 *antenna*
looped 306.10 *circular*; 177.4 *curved*; 42.10 *woven*
looper 76.5 *larva*
loophole 16.4 *bad law*; 231.7 *defect*; 484.3 *expedient plan*; 384.11 *fortification*; 389.2 *means of escape*; 315.6 *way out*
loopholed 384.30 *defended*
looping 64.3 *rugby play*; 64.6 *rugger*
looping the loop 322.5 *flight*
loop jump 68.6 *ice-skating*
loopy 461.11 *insane*
loose 227.13 *changeable*; 274.15 *erroneous*; 389.8 *escaping*; 657.10 *free*; 138.20 *generalized*; 453.6 *indeterminate*; 391.4 *liberate*; 268.17 *liquefy*; 265.16 *make easy*; 757.8 *permitting*; 355.1 *relinquish*; 64.6 *rugger*; 372.9, 372.15 *separate*; 250.15 *set free*; 268.10 *slippery*; 419.1 *soft*; 377.25 *sprawled*; 5.40 *translated*; 719.17 *translational*; 796.13 *unchaste*; 250.12 *unconditional*; 325.25 *wandering*; 337.8 *weak*
loose a rope 50.15 *sail*
loose ball 49.4 *playing terms*
loose bowels 560.2 *defecation*
loosebox 43.7 *farm building*
loose-footed 50.10 *sailing*
loose-footed sail 50.3 *parts of a sailing boat*
loose forward 64.4 *rugby player*
loose impediments 56.1 *golf*
loose in the attic 461.11 *insane*
loose in the head 461.11 *insane*
loose-knit 270.3 *diffuse*
loose-limbed 419.2 *pliant*
loosely 250.21 *excessively*; 138.29 *generally*; 453.25 *indeterminately*; 372.20 *separately*; 419.17 *softly*; 757.9 *with permission*; 274.22 *wrongly*
loose morals 796.3 *sexual immorality*; 804.2 *vice*
loosen 263.3, 419.14 *ease*; 391.4 *liberate*; 268.17 *liquefy*; 372.9 *separate*; 419.13 *soften*; 337.7 *weaken*
loosened 372.15 *separate*
looseness 427.2 *crumbliness*; 657.4 *freedom*; 274.2 *inaccuracy*; 453.14 *indeterminacy*; 138.3 *nonspecificness*; 268.2 *runniness*; 419.8 *softness*; 337.1 *weakness*
loosening 372.1 *separation*
loosen one's grip 355.1 *relinquish*
loosen up 419.14 *ease*
loose off 330.28 *shoot*
loose rocks 62.2 *climbing dangers*
loose screw 231.7 *defect*
loose scrum 64.3 *rugby play*
loose talk 796.2 *indecency*
loose translation 5.12, 719.4 *translation*
loose woman 568.6; 796.9 *immoral woman*
loosing 391.1 *liberation*; 372.1 *separation*
loot 780.2 *cash*; 357.10, 441.2 *lay waste*; 774.14 *plunder*; 794.2 *spoils*; 774.4 *stolen goods*; 773.10 *take away*; 408.11 *troublemaker*
loot and pillage 774.14 *plunder*
looter 357.6 *destroyer*; 773.6 *taker*
looting 441.4 *destruction*; 357.5 *havoc*; 774.5 *plundering*; 774.17 *stolen*; 773.3 *taking away*
looting and pillaging 774.5 *plundering*
lop 44.15 *cultivate*; 79.18 *manage trees*; 372.10 *set apart*; 149.10 *shorten*; 212.4 *take off*
lope 332.4 *be swift*; 300.12 *gait*; 300.15 *walk*
lop-eared 504.12 *eared*
lopolith 30.28 *rock*
lopped 233.4 *incomplete*; 212.7 *reduced*
lopper 44.6, 438.3 *garden tool*; 430.11 *thicken*
loppering 430.1 *viscosity*
lopping 212.1 *subtraction*; 79.6 *tree management*
lopsided 486.3 *clumsy*; 234.6 *distorted*; 120.3 *unequal*
lopsidedly 234.13 *asymmetrically*
lopsidedness 234.1 *distortion*; 120.1 *inequality*
loquacious 734.12 *conversing*; 270.3 *diffuse*; 739.11 *disclosing*; 693.16 *informative*; 729.19 *speaking*; 731.5 *talkative*; 5.42 *worded*
loquaciously 734.15 *conversationally*; 270.7 *diffusely*; 5.50 *lexically*; 731.10 *talkatively*
loquaciousness 731.1 *talkativeness*
loquacity 270.1 *diffuseness*; 5.22 *many words*; 729.2 *power of speech*; 731.1 *talkativeness*
loran 322.6 *flight control*
loran-A system 323.5 *navigation*
loran-B system 323.5 *navigation*
loran system 323.5 *navigation*
Lord 8.3 *God*; 567.3 *male title of address*
lord 763.6; 400.1 *master*; 573.1 *nobleman*; 575.4 *titleholder*
Lord Advocate 16.11 *British law officer*
lord and master 763.6 *lord*; 570.10 *married man*; 400.1 *master*
Lord Chancellor 16.25 *British judge*; 16.11 *British law officer*
Lord Chancellor's Court 16.20 *British court*
Lord Chief Justice 16.25 *British judge*
lord-in-waiting 401.6 *domestic servant*
lord it 660.27 *dare*; 660.28 *get above oneself*
lord it over 396.19 *be authoritarian*; 622.28 *disdain*; 400.14 *master*
Lord Jesus 8.4 *God the Son*
lordliness 396.2 *authoritativeness*; 622.6 *majesty*
lordly 573.4 *aristocratic*; 396.12 *authoritative*; 12.10 *governing*; 400.12 *masterful*; 397.15 *self-assured*; 622.19 *stately*; 575.6 *worshipful*
Lord Lyon 743.9 *herald*
Lord Mayor 16.11 *British law officer*; 400.3 *leader*
Lord Mayor's show 656.3 *formal occasion*

Lord Muck 573.1 *nobleman;* 622.13 *proud person*
Lord of Appeal 16.25 *British judge*
Lord of Creation 566.7 *person;* 622.13 *proud person*
Lord of Lords 8.3 *God*
lord of misrule 408.11 *troublemaker*
lord of the bedchamber 401.6 *domestic servant*
Lord of the Flies 8.7 *devil*
Lord of the manor 123.4 *bigwig;* 763.6 *lord;* 400.1 *master;* 440.7 *property man*
lord paramount 400.1 *master*
lord provost 16.11 *British law officer*
Lord's 53.2 *ground*
Lord's Day 10.15 *holy day*
Lord's day 263.1 *ease*
lordship 573.2 *aristocracy;* 121.2 *leadership;* 763.1 *possession*
Lords Spiritual 12.4 *governing body;* 579.16 *official*
Lord's Supper 10.6 *Eucharist*
Lords Temporal 12.4 *governing body;* 579.16 *official*
lore 645.1 *cunning;* 632.4 *custom;* 455.3 *learning;* 17.1 *literature;* 1.8, 296.6 *tradition*
Lorelei 480.13 *tempter*
lorelei 11.4 *witch*
lorgnette 518.10 *visual aid*
lorica 550.14 *animal covering;* 384.7 *armour*
loriner 59.15 *horse person*
lorn 655.10 *lonely*
lorry 410.10 *cart;* 316.5 *means of transport;* 319.5 *transportable;* 320.20 *truck*
lorryload 203.3 *container*
Los Angeles 87.2 *American cities*
lose 766.9; 247.7 *be defeated;* 249.9 *be in trouble;* 214.4 *decrease;* 357.8 *destroy;* 144.19 *misplace;* 355.1 *relinquish;* 778.1 *sell*
lose a battle 387.8 *be subject to*
lose a chance 766.9 *lose*
lose an opportunity 288.7 *lose one's chance*
lose badly 247.7 *be defeated*
lose by a whisker 247.7 *be defeated;* 766.9 *lose*
lose colour 530.5; 522.28 *bleach*
lose consciousness 335.6 *be powerless;* 766.9 *lose*
lose contact with 766.9 *lose*
lose control 624.12 *become angry;* 380.7 *be violent;* 245.1 *deteriorate*
lose currency 296.17 *grow old*
lose earnings 766.10 *have a financial loss*
lose everything 782.13 *lose one's money*
lose face 486.6 *act foolishly;* 122.9 *yield to*
lose feathers 552.16 *peel*
lose flavour 245.2 *decay*
lose ground 245.1 *deteriorate;* 303.1 *go backwards;* 333.3 *slow down*
lose handle 68.10 *curling*
lose hands down 247.7 *be defeated*
lose health 245.1 *deteriorate*
lose heart 611.9 *be hopeless;* 602.9 *despair*
lose heat 494.11 *become cold*
lose height 305.9 *descend*
lose hope 611.9 *be hopeless;* 602.9 *despair*
lose interest 618.12 *be indifferent;* 497.7 *be tasteless;* 355.1 *relinquish*
lose interest in 766.12 *lessen*
lose it 486.5 *be unskilful*
lose leaves 79.19 *grow*
lose momentum 333.3 *slow down*
lose money 766.10 *have a financial loss*
lose money on 778.1 *sell*
lose not a moment 262.2 *make haste*
lose no time 293.10 *hasten;* 262.2 *make haste*
lose one 696.7 *be unintelligible*
lose one's bearings 325.3 *go astray*
lose one's bottle 614.4 *be a coward*
lose one's chance 288.7; 294.7 *wait*
lose one's cunning 486.5 *be unskilful*
lose one's feel 486.5 *be unskilful*
lose one's fortune 249.10 *need money*
lose one's freedom 387.8 *be subject to;* 766.9 *lose*
lose one's head 459.6 *be foolish;* 486.5 *be unskilful*
lose one's hearing 505.8 *be deaf*
lose one's heart 593.24 *be in love;* 593.26 *court*
lose one's husband 571.10 *be widowed*
lose one's inheritance 249.10 *need money*
lose one's life 582.15 *die*
lose one's marbles 461.14 *become insane*
lose one's memory 766.9 *lose*
lose one's money 782.13
lose one's nerve 614.4 *be a coward;* 486.5 *be unskilful*
lose one's rag 624.12 *become angry*
lose one's rights 387.8 *be subject to;* 766.9 *lose*
lose one's self-respect 664.8 *be servile*
lose one's sight 519.14 *be blind*
lose one's skill 486.5 *be unskilful*
lose one's temper 624.12 *become angry;* 659.8 *get angry*
lose one's tongue 730.14 *have difficulty speaking*
lose one's touch 486.5 *be unskilful*
lose one's voice 506.1 *be silent;* 214.4 *decrease;* 730.14 *have difficulty speaking*
lose one's way 325.3 *go astray*
lose one's wits 461.14 *become insane*
lose out 247.7 *be defeated;* 486.5 *be unskilful;* 247.6 *fail;* 766.9 *lose*
lose out on love 249.9 *be in trouble*
lose patience 624.12 *become angry*
lose power 247.9 *malfunction*
lose profits 766.10 *have a financial loss*
loser 766.6; 247.5 *failing person;* 611.3 *hopeless person;* 122.6 *inferior;* 249.5 *person in adversity;* 470.9 *rejected person;* 387.5 *subjected person;* 486.10 *unskilled person*
lose repute 812.4 *bring into disrepute*
lose shine 524.11 *tarnish*
lose sight of 521.7 *become invisible;* 766.9 *lose*
lose someone 766.15; 332.6 *accelerate*
lose someone's attention 618.16 *be mediocre*
lose speed 333.3 *slow down*
lose strength 260.24 *be unhealthy*
lose taste 497.7 *be tasteless;* 245.2 *decay*
lose the baby 563.7 *be infertile*
lose the ball 58.9 *play hockey*
lose the battle 247.7 *be defeated;* 249.9 *be in trouble;* 766.12 *lessen;* 766.9 *lose*
lose the day 766.9 *lose*
lose the election 247.7 *be defeated;* 766.9 *lose*
lose the game 247.7 *be defeated;* 249.9 *be in trouble*
lose the match 247.7 *be defeated;* 249.9 *be in trouble;* 766.9 *lose*
lose the race 247.7 *be defeated*
lose the scent 501.6 *have no smell*
lose the thread 109.10 *be unrelated;* 325.4 *lose track of*
lose the upper hand 122.9 *yield to*
lose the vote 247.7 *be defeated*
lose the war 247.7 *be defeated;* 249.9 *be in trouble*
lose time 294.6 *be late;* 288.6 *take untimely action*
lose track of 325.4; 766.9 *lose;* 144.19 *misplace*
lose value 245.1 *deteriorate*
lose water 389.7 *leak*
lose weight 191.6 *become smaller;* 153.14 *become thin;* 684.5 *be self-restrained;* 687.5 *fast;* 415.10 *lighten;* 766.9 *lose;* 214.5 *make smaller*
losing 766.16; 766.1 *loss;* 144.6 *misplacement*
losing balance 120.3 *unequal*
losing battle 766.3 *waste*
losing candidate 469.13 *electorate*
losing game 247.2 *defeat*
losing general 247.5 *failing person*
losing ground 245.7 *deterioration*
losing hazard 65.3 *English billiards*
losing it 486.3 *clumsy*
losing move 247.2 *defeat*
losing one's feel 486.3 *clumsy*
losing one's touch 486.3 *clumsy*
losing person 247.5 *failing person*
losings 766.2 *financial loss*
losing weight 191.1 *contraction;* 687.1 *fasting;* 557.6 *nutrition*
Loss 766
loss 766.1; 814.10 *affliction;* 214.1 *decrease;* 247.2 *defeat;* 215.3 *difference;* 98.2 *disappearance;* 526.5 *disguise;* 315.5 *export;* 238.4 *futility;* 245.10 *impairment;* 389.4 *leak;* 233.2 *omission;* 357.4 *ruin;* 212.2 *subtracted item;* 441.3 *waste*
losses 766.2 *financial loss*
loss leader 791.2, 793.4 *bargain;* 480.9 *enticement;* 766.2 *financial loss;* 778.8 *merchandise;* 483.5 *positive stimulus*
loss-leading 766.17 *unprofitable*
loss-making 214.7 *decrescent;* 238.2 *futile;* 766.17, 776.16 *unprofitable*
loss of ball 58.5 *lacrosse*
loss of battle 387.1 *subjection*
loss of condition 260.1 *ill health*
loss of consciousness 335.4 *disability;* 261.7 *fatigue;* 766.1 *loss;* 260.3 *symptom*
loss of control 335.4 *disability*
loss of earnings 766.2 *financial loss*
loss of face 668.8 *indignity*
loss of faith 451.4 *unbelief*
loss of fortune 782.6 *insolvency*
loss of freedom 766.1 *loss;* 387.1 *subjection*
loss of hope 611.1 *hopelessness*
loss of innocence 804.1 *wickedness*
loss of interest 766.3 *waste*
loss of life 582.1 *death*
loss of memory 463.2 *blankness;* 358.5 *forgetfulness*
loss of morale 245.11 *hurt*
loss of nerve 639.13 *timidity*
loss of profit 766.2 *financial loss*
loss of rights 766.1 *loss;* 387.1 *subjection*
loss of strength 337.3 *poor health*
loss of value 214.1 *decrease*
loss of vision 519.1 *blindness*
loss of voice 730.1 *voicelessness*
loss of weight 766.1 *loss*
lost 98.9 *away;* 16.64 *convicted;* 247.11 *defeated;* 526.7 *disappeared;* 463.11 *forgotten;* 809.3 *impenitent;* 233.4 *incomplete;* 325.21 *indirect;* 766.16 *losing;* 144.13 *misplaced;* 611.5 *past hope*
lost and gone 284.18 *over*
lost art 766.8 *lost thing*
lost at sea 766.16 *losing*
lost battle 249.1 *adversity;* 247.2 *defeat;* 766.8 *lost thing*
lost bet 247.4 *unsuccessful thing*
lost cause 247.2 *defeat;* 611.2 *hopeless situation;* 809.2 *impenitent person;* 766.8 *lost thing;* 470.8 *rejected thing*
lost chance 288.3; 766.8 *lost thing*
lost child 633.7 *the hunted*
lost connection 133.7 *broken thread*
lost election 470.6 *discarding;* 766.8 *lost thing;* 247.4 *unsuccessful thing*
lost forever 284.18 *over*
lost fortune 249.2 *economic adversity*
lost from view 766.16 *losing*
lost game 249.1 *adversity;* 766.8 *lost thing*
Lost Generation 766.8 *lost thing*
lost ground 766.8 *lost thing*
lost hope 766.8 *lost thing*
lost in amazement 766.18 *at a loss;* 619.6 *wondering*
lost inheritance 249.2 *economic adversity*
lost in the distance 521.2 *difficult to see*
lost in thought 472.8 *absent-minded;* 766.18 *at a loss;* 443.9 *concentrating;* 4.17 *thoughtful*
lost in wonder 619.6 *wondering*
lost labour 486.9 *bungling;* 247.1 *failure;* 766.8 *lost thing;* 342.9 *overactivity;* 238.5 *waste of effort*
lost language 5.9 *ancient language*
lost leader 479.9 *equivocator*
lost life 766.8 *lost thing*
lost love 249.1 *adversity;* 766.8 *lost thing*
lost match 249.1 *adversity*
lost melody 516.1 *melody*
lost memory 766.8 *lost thing*
lost opportunity 288.3 *lost chance;* 766.8 *lost thing*
lost sheep 766.6 *loser;* 804.9 *wicked person*
lost shot 352.1 *means*
lost soul 8.7 *devil;* 766.6 *loser;* 804.9 *wicked person*
lost thing 766.8
lost time 766.8 *lost thing*
lost to 618.7 *indifferent*
lost to oblivion 463.11 *forgotten*
lost to sight 526.7 *disappeared*
lost tribes 766.8 *lost thing*
lost war 249.1 *adversity;* 247.2 *defeat;* 766.8 *lost thing*
lost-wax casting 19.12 *sculpture*
lost youth 766.8 *lost thing*
lot 475.10 *cards;* 203.2 *certain amount;* 166.2 *limiting factor;* 107.2 *luck;* 86.12 *plot;* 770.2 *portion;* 106.5 *predetermination;* 440.1 *property;* 221.1 *state*
Lothario 363.6 *charmer;* 593.9 *lover*
lotion 394.9 *balm;* 37.7, 268.6 *ointment;* 255.3 *purifier*
lots 208.2 *multitude;* 217.8 *plenty*
lots of luck 248.10 *good luck!*
lottery 107.3 *equal chance;* 788.5 *winnings*
Lotus-123 40.11 *application*
lotus-eater 80.5 *figurative usage;* 343.8 *nonworker;* 490.3 *pleasure-seeker;* 477.9 *visionary*
lotus-eating 301.1 *motionlessness*
louche 796.12 *indecent*
loud 507.6; 509.15 *drumming;* 529.12 *gaudy;* 504.14 *hearable;* 738.14 *manifest;* 542.10 *ornate;* 510.7 *ringing;* 513.7 *strident;* 336.12 *strong to the senses;* 544.10 *ugly;* 514.16 *vociferous;* 675.7 *vulgar*
loud breathing 507.1 *loudness*
loud cry 514.1 *cry*
loud drunk 631.5 *badly behaved person*
loud-hailer 504.9 *audio device;* 740.1 *publication;* 507.4 *sound maker*
loud instrument 507.4 *sound maker*
loud laughter 507.1 *loudness*
loudly 507.9; 336.15 *acutely;* 513.10 *stridently;* 514.20 *vociferously*
loudmouth 351.3 *abuser;* 659.4 *discourteous person;* 596.3 *disliked person*
loudmouthed 507.6 *loud;* 514.16 *vociferous*
Loudness 507
loudness 507.1; 529.3 *hue;* 28.17 *sound;* 544.3 *ugliness*
loudness level 28.19 *sound propagation*
loud noise 507.1 *loudness*
loud pedal 507.4 *sound maker*
loud person 507.5
loud report 507.1 *loudness*
loudspeaker 504.9 *audio device;* 740.1 *publication;* 692.18 *radio;* 507.4 *sound maker;* 28.18 *source of sound;* 39.22 *transformer*
loudspeaker van 504.9 *audio device*
loud-speaking 729.19 *speaking*
loud-spoken 729.19 *speaking*
lough 88.1 *lake*
Lough Neagh 88.4 *British lakes*
Louis Quatorze 23.7 *furniture style*
Louis Quinze 23.7 *furniture style*
Louis Seize 23.7 *furniture style*
Louisville slugger 48.3 *baseball equipment*
lounge 343.12 *be inactive;* 565.7 *room;* 263.2 *take it easy;* 767.7 *toilet*
lounge chair 23.2 *chair*
lounger 343.8 *nonworker*
lounge suit 656.4 *formal dress;* 551.4 *informal dress;* 551.10 *suit*
loungewear 657.6 *informal dress*
lounging pyjamas 551.4 *informal dress*
lounging robe 551.16 *robe*
loupe 518.10 *visual aid*
lour 624.11 *be angry;* 523.13 *become dark;* 524.9 *be dim;* 626.11 *be irritable;* 659.8 *get angry;* 625.2 *sign of irascibility;* 626.4 *sign of irritableness;* 711.5 *warn*
Lourdes 173.4 *centre of activity;* 737.6 *natural mystery;* 482.6 *objective*
louring 523.8 *dark;* 524.5 *dim;* 626.7 *irritable;* 626.8 *overcast;* 625.5 *showing irascibility*
louse 804.10 *bad person;* 258.4 *dirt;* 76.3 *pest*
louse up 274.10 *blunder;* 378.8 *hinder;* 274.19 *make a mistake*
lousiness 236.10 *poverty*
lousy 798.7 *evil;* 236.4 *poor;* 793.10 *shoddy;* 258.8 *unclean;* 76.12 *verminous*
lousy with 232.8 *full*
lousy with money 781.1 *wealthy*
lout 631.5 *badly behaved person;* 659.4 *discourteous person;* 651.8 *malefactor;* 242.9 *unpleasant person;* 486.10 *unskilled person;* 675.5 *vulgar person*
loutish 659.6 *bad-mannered*
loutishly 659.10 *rudely*
loutishness 659.2 *bad manners;* 675.3 *grossness*
louvre 20.9 *miscellaneous architectural features*
lovability 593.4
lovable 593.22; 595.5 *likable;* 490.6 *pleasant*
lovableness 593.4 *lovability*

lovably 593.30 *lovingly*; 595.10 *with great liking*
lovage 496.5 *herbs*
Love 593
love 593.1; **593.23**; 669.2 *admiration*; 650.8 *be benevolent*; 658.10 *be courteous*; 650.1 *benevolence*; 658.3 *courtesies*; 617.1 *desire*; 8.2 *divine attribute*; 569.1 *friendship*; 590.5 *good feeling*; 595.4 *likable person*; 595.7, 617.13 *like*; 595.1 *liking*; 593.11 *loved one*; 593.12 *nicknames for lovers*; 94.2 *nothingness*; 803.2 *virtues*; 619.1 *wonder*; 195.1 *zero*
love affair 593.8
love-all 111.16 *equal*; 119.2 *equilibrium*
love-all score 111.5 *equality*
love a party 654.11 *be sociable*
lovebirds 593.10 *lovers*
lovebite 593.14 *communication of love*
love charm 11.5 *spell*
love company 654.11 *be sociable*
loved 593.21 *beloved*
love deuce 63.4 *tennis terms*
loved one 593.11
loved ones 582.13 *the dead*
love feast 10.16 *religious festival*
love food 688.5 *be greedy*
love for one's country 593.1 *love*
love game 246.2 *victory*
love good 803.8 *be virtuous*
love-hate relationship 593.2 *romantic love*
love-in 490.4 *pleasurable things*
love interest 21.23 *role*
love item 593.15
loveless 596.8 *disliking*; 594.12 *hated*
love letter 593.15 *love item*
loveliness 545.1 *gorgeousness*; 593.4 *lovability*; 490.1 *physical pleasure*; 241.6 *pleasantness*
lovelorn 593.19 *enamoured*; 594.12 *hated*
lovelornness 593.3 *lovingness*
lovely 545.3 *attractive female*; 545.5 *beautiful*; 597.5 *delightful*; 595.5 *likable*; 593.22 *lovable*; 241.1, 490.6 *pleasant*; 235.1 *worthy*
love lyric 593.15 *love item*
lovemaking 593.5 *desire*
love match 570.3 *types of marriage*
love names 593.12 *nicknames for lovers*
love nest 593.13 *abode of love*; 565.5 *house*; 654.4 *meeting place*
love of mankind 650.1 *benevolence*
love of war 585.5 *bellicosity*
love oneself 683.7 *be egoistic*
love one's job 576.8 *exert oneself*
love poem 593.15 *love item*
love potion 490.4 *pleasurable things*; 11.5 *spell*
lover 593.9; 471.6 *attentive person*; 567.4 *boyfriend*; 568.4 *girlfriend*; 595.4 *likable person*; 593.12 *nicknames for lovers*; 223.12 *partner*; 710.4 *requester*
lover boy 567.4 *boyfriend*
lovers 593.10
love scene 21.8 *scene*
love seat 23.2 *chair*
lovesick 593.19 *enamoured*
lovesickness 593.3 *lovingness*
love slap 593.14 *communication of love*
lovesome 593.22 *lovable*
love song 593.15 *love item*; 516.2 *song*
love sonnet 593.15 *love item*
love story 17.2, 721.5 *fiction*
love to 595.9 *like to*
love to distraction 593.23 *love*
love to eat 688.5 *be greedy*
love token 593.15 *love item*; 794.3 *memento*
loveworthy 593.22 *lovable*
lovey 593.12 *nicknames for lovers*
lovie 21.24 *actor*
loving 593.17; 650.6 *benevolent*; 803.6 *ethical*; 595.6 *liking*
loving care 665.2 *consideration*
loving couple 593.10 *lovers*
loving cup 558.10 *drink container*; 410.13 *drinking vessel*; 794.1 *trophy*
loving kindness 650.1 *benevolence*
loving looks 593.14 *communication of love*
lovingly 593.30; 595.11 *admiringly*; 650.10 *benevolently*; 803.10 *ethically*
lovingness 593.3
loving touch 593.14 *communication of love*
loving words 593.14 *communication of love*
low 155.5; **155.10**; 793.9 *cheap*; 515.4 *cry*; 510.8 *deep*; 602.6 *depressed*; 668.12 *disregardful*; 511.1 *faint-sounding*; 513.8 *hoarse*; 122.5 *inferior state*; 337.13 *insufficient*; 367.18 *lowering*; 623.2 *lowly*; 730.10 *low-voiced*; 5.39 *of language*; 236.4 *poor*; 793.10 *shoddy*; 149.7 *short*; 388.5 *submitting*; 157.2 *superficial*; 730.17 *voicelessly*; 31.11 *weather system*
low attendance 206.1 *few*
low birth rate 563.1 *infertility*
low blood pressure 260.10 *cardiovascular disease*; 260.3 *symptom*
low-born 574.3 *common*; 623.2 *lowly*
lowboy 23.5, 410.3 *cabinet*
low-brow 456.6 *ignorant*
low-budget 793.9 *cheap*
low-built 155.5 *low*
low-calorie 557.27 *edible*
low-calorie drink 558.6 *soft drink*
low camp 21.12 *comedy*
low-caste 574.3 *common*; 122.12 *inferior*
low-cholesterol diet 557.6 *nutrition*
Low-Church 7.16 *denominational*
low-class 122.12 *inferior*
low cloud 31.18 *cloud*
low comedian 21.24 *actor*
low comedy 21.12 *comedy*
low cunning 699.5 *deceitfulness*
low-cut 552.10 *in dishabille*; 155.5 *low*
low-cut neckline 155.4 *low thing*
low definition 521.4 *invisibility*; 524.2 *murk*
low-definition 521.2 *difficult to see*; 524.6 *murky*
low-density 206.6 *sparse*
low down 155.10 *low*
low-down 574.3 *common*; 800.5 *dishonourable*; 693.1 *information*
low ebb 122.5 *inferior state*
lower 155.6; **155.9**; **367.1**; 623.23 *abase*; 209.6 *change gradually*; 156.14 *deepen*; 305.9 *descend*; 668.27 *desecrate*; 791.3 *discount*; 27.75 *equal*; 122.12 *inferior*; 524.10 *make dim*; 214.5 *make smaller*; 511.7 *mute*; 245.6 *pervert*; 475.11 *predict*; 168.4 *rear*; 2.14 *socioeconomic*; 387.6, 387.9 *subject*; 675.10 *vulgarize*
lower animal 75.1 *invertebrate*
lower atmosphere 434.3 *atmospheric layers*
lower back 168.2 *rear end*
lower bound 27.21 *set*
lower-case 5.41 *lettered*
lower-case letter 5.15 *type style*
Lower Chamber 579.11 *British government*; 12.4 *governing body*; 579.12 *US government*
lower charges 793.13 *make cheap*
lower class 566.9 *group*; 122.1 *inferiority*; 2.7 *social stratification*
lower classes 122.6 *inferior*
lower criticism 719.3 *criticism*
lower deck 175.2 *foot*
lower depths 156.4 *deep thing*
lowered 367.17; 623.3 *humbled*; 155.5 *low*
lower ground floor 175.2 *foot*
Lower House 579.11 *British government*; 12.4 *governing body*; 579.12 *US government*
Lowering 367
lowering 367.11; **367.18**; 156.1 *depth*; 305.16 *descending*; 305.1 *descent*; 155.1 *lowness*; 305.2 *sinkage*
lowering oneself 623.15 *condescension*
lowering the body 583.2 *funeral*
lower limit 203.2 *certain amount*; 27.31 *differentiation*; 166.2 *limiting factor*
Lower Lough Erne 88.4 *British lakes*
lower merit 289.3 *subordination*
lower middle class 566.9 *group*
lower oneself 812.4 *bring into disrepute*; 623.18 *condescend*
lower one's sights 355.1 *relinquish*
lower one's tone 623.20 *submit*
lower orders 122.6 *inferior*; 574.2 *the common people*
lower plant 77.4
lower standards 367.4 *debase*
lower status 387.1 *subjection*
lower the body 583.8 *bury*
lower the flag 367.10
lower the price 793.13 *make cheap*
lower the standard 367.10 *lower the flag*
lower the tone 675.10 *vulgarize*
lower world 8.12 *hell*; 101.1 *nonmaterial world*
lowest 175.3 *base*; 156.10 *deeper*; 27.75 *equal*; 122.12 *inferior*; 155.6 *lower*
lowest common denominator 138.6 *average*; 695.10 *simplicity*
lowest common multiple 27.17 *multiplication*
low esteem 668.3 *contempt*; 670.2 *disrespect*
lowest level 175.1 *base*; 155.3 *lowest point*
lowest of the low 122.6 *inferior*
lowest point 155.3; 175.1 *base*; 122.5 *inferior state*; 195.4 *zero level*
low-fat 557.27 *edible*; 257.4 *hygienic*
low-fat diet 557.6 *nutrition*
low-fat food 557.7 *food*
low gear 333.10 *slow motion*
low grade 236.8 *inferiority*
low-grade 122.12, 236.2 *inferior*; 793.10 *shoddy*
low-grade rock 30.33 *metamorphic rock*
low-heeled 155.5 *low*
low heels 155.4 *low thing*
low-hung 155.5 *low*
low income 782.5 *poverty*
low-inside 54.6 *fencing*; 54.3 *fencing movements*; 54.7 *on guard*
low in tone 532.2 *dark*
low IQ 459.1 *folly*; 457.1 *lack of intellect*
low key 41.8 *composition*
low-key 685.6 *moderate*
lowland 92.6; **155.7**; 92.11 *continental*; 86.16 *regional*
Lowlander 85.11 *Scotland*
lowlander 564.5 *countryman*
lowlands 155.2; 86.6 *regions*
low language 5.19 *swearword*
low-level 155.5 *low*; 124.3 *secondary*
low-level bombing 381.13 *air attack*
low-level flying 322.5 *flight*
low-level language 40.9 *programming language*
low-level waste 28.74 *nuclear waste*
lowlife 804.10 *bad person*; 812.2 *disreputable character*; 122.6 *inferior*; 122.15 *subordinate*
lowlihood 623.8 *lowliness*
lowliness 623.8; 122.1 *inferiority*; 271.4 *simplicity*; 682.4 *unpleasantness*
low-loader 321.6 *rolling stock*
lowly 623.2; 124.2 *obscure*; 271.1 *simple*; 388.5 *submitting*; 682.2 *unpleasant*
low-lying 155.7 *lowland*
Low Mass 10.6 *Eucharist*
low mental age 457.1 *lack of intellect*
low-necked 552.10 *in dishabille*; 155.5 *low*
Lowness 155
lowness 155.1; 510.3 *deepness*; 602.2 *depression*; 513.2 *hoarseness*; 122.5 *inferior state*; 511.3 *mutedness*; 236.10 *poverty*; 793.3 *shoddiness*; 149.1 *shortness*
low note 510.3 *deepness*; 18.21 *tone*
low on 218.1 *insufficient*
low opinion 668.3 *contempt*; 670.2 *disrespect*
low-outside 54.6 *fencing*; 54.3 *fencing movements*; 54.7 *on guard*
lowpaid 782.1 *poor*
low-pass filter 39.22 *transformer*
low pay 218.8 *insufficiency*; 782.5 *poverty*
low pitch 18.21 *tone*
low point 122.5 *inferior state*
low post 49.4 *playing terms*
low pressure 417.3 *sparseness*
low-pressure 417.1 *sparse*
low-priced 793.9 *cheap*; 124.4 *trivial*
low price tag 793.1 *cheapness*
low profile 521.4 *invisibility*
low-profile 521.2 *difficult to see*; 728.15 *reserved*
low quality 236.8 *inferiority*
low-quality 236.2 *inferior*; 793.10 *shoddy*
low rate 790.3 *fee*
low reading age 457.1 *lack of intellect*
low relief 608.6 *profile*; 19.13 *relief-carving*
low resolution 372.1 *separation*
low-resolution 372.19 *separable*
low-rise 155.5 *low*; 20.12 *structural*
low-rise building 20.3 *building*
Lowry–Brønsted acid 32.8 *acid*
Lowry–Brønsted base 32.9 *base*
low-salt 257.4 *hygienic*
low-salt food 557.7 *food*
low saturation 28.28 *colour*
low-set 155.5 *low*
low-slung 155.5 *low*
low-spirited 221.8 *in a state of*
low spirits 602.2 *depression*; 221.4 *state of mind*
low standard 231.5 *imperfection*; 236.8 *inferiority*
low-standard 236.2 *inferior*
low tar 496.7 *tobacco*
low-tar 496.11 *tobacco*
low tech 438.6 *mechanics*
low-tech 356.11 *productive*
low technology 356.2 *manufacture*; 438.6 *mechanics*
low-technology 356.11 *productive*
low temperature 494.1 *coldness*
low-temperature physics 28.3 *modern physics*
low thing 155.4
low tide 155.3 *lowest point*; 157.4 *shallow thing*; 30.15, 91.2 *tide*
low-toned 532.2 *dark*
low turnout 206.1 *few*
low vacuum 32.20 *surface chemistry*
low visibility 524.2 *murk*
low voice 510.3 *deepness*; 730.4 *whispering*
low-voiced 730.10
low water 782.6 *insolvency*; 155.3 *lowest point*; 218.9 *scarcity*; 157.4 *shallow thing*; 91.2 *tide*
low-water mark 166.2 *limiting factor*
low-weight 415.1 *light*
low yield 563.1 *infertility*
low-yield 563.3 *infertile*
lox 494.4 *cooler*; 25.16 *fish dish*; 437.3 *gas*
loyal 663.8; **810.9**; 569.11 *devoted*; 698.26 *faithful*; 799.4 *honourable*; 452.6 *infallible*; 593.17 *loving*; 267.10 *tenacious*
loyal customer 777.12 *purchaser*
loyal devotion 595.1 *liking*
loyalist 117.6 *conformist*; 663.4 *obedient person*
loyally 569.19 *devotedly*; 799.7 *honourably*; 663.10 *obediently*; 810.18 *on duty*; 267.12 *tenaciously*
loyal party member 663.4 *obedient person*
loyal support 569.1 *friendship*
loyal supporter 640.5 *tenacious person*
loyalty 663.2; 810.3 *allegiance*; 698.13 *faithfulness*; 452.17 *infallibility*; 593.1 *love*; 799.1 *probity*; 667.3 *respectfulness*; 267.2 *tenacity*
loyalty card 791.1 *discount*
loyalty oath 707.3 *vow*
lozenge 176.3 *angled figure*; 743.8 *heraldic device*; 394.2 *medicine*; 37.6 *pill*; 27.44 *polygon*
LP 744.7 *recording*
L position 57.7 *stationary rings*
LSD 691.6 *drug*
LSI 39.13 *circuit*
lubber 486.10 *unskilled person*
lubber line 324.3 *orientation*
lubberliness 486.8 *unskilfulness*
lubberly 486.3 *clumsy*
lube 268.1 *slipperiness*
lubricant 268.5; **268.12**; 421.10 *polish*
lubricate 268.18; 265.16 *make easy*; 421.11 *smooth*; 419.13 *soften*
lubricated 268.11; 421.4 *polished*; 265.12 *wieldy*
lubricating 268.12 *lubricant*; 685.8 *moderating*; 268.1 *slipperiness*
lubricating agent 268.5 *lubricant*
lubricating oil 268.5 *lubricant*
lubrication 268.1 *slipperiness*; 421.7 *smoothness*
lubricational 268.12 *lubricant*
lubricative 268.12 *lubricant*
lubricator 268.8; 268.5 *lubricant*; 421.10 *polish*
lubricatory 268.12 *lubricant*
lubricious 796.12 *indecent*; 421.4 *polished*
lubricitate 268.18 *lubricate*
lubricity 796.3 *sexual immorality*; 268.1 *slipperiness*; 421.7 *smoothness*

lubrification 268.1 *slipperiness*
lubrify 268.18 *lubricate*
lubritorium 320.21 *miscellaneous motoring terms*
lucency 522.1 *light*
lucent 522.15; 527.2 *translucent*
lucerne 557.8 *animal food;* 43.12 *crop*
lucid 520.2, 725.3 *clear;* 527.4 *easily seen through;* 522.22 *enlightened;* 694.6 *meaningful;* 4.15, 460.5 *rational;* 695.2 *simple*
lucidity 725.1 *clarity;* 4.3 *detachment;* 527.10 *openness;* 460.2 *rationality;* 265.2, 695.10 *simplicity*
lucidly 725.4 *clearly;* 695.13 *intelligibly;* 4.26 *rationally;* 460.7 *sanely*
Lucifer 8.6 *angel;* 8.7 *devil;* 29.10 *star*
lucifer 522.8 *fire;* 437.2 *lighter*
luck 107.2; 227.3 *changeable thing;* 222.5 *comfortable circumstances;* 248.2 *good fortune;* 287.2 *opportunity;* 102.3 *strong possibility;* 246.1 *success*
luckily 105.11; 107.13 *by chance;* 222.18 *comfortably;* 287.9 *opportunely;* 248.9 *prosperously;* 246.16 *successfully*
luckiness 222.5 *comfortable circumstances*
luckless 249.8 *unlucky*
luck of the draw 248.2 *good fortune;* 107.2 *luck*
luck on one's side 107.2 *luck*
luck piece 11.6 *talisman*
lucky 107.8 *chance;* 222.9 *comfortable;* 797.1 *good;* 248.8 *prosperous;* 246.13 *successful;* 287.6 *timely*
lucky bean 11.6 *talisman*
lucky break 248.2 *good fortune;* 287.2, 308.10 *opportunity;* 246.1 *success*
lucky charm 11.6 *talisman*
lucky devil 248.4 *prosperous person*
lucky dip 114.3 *diverse thing;* 107.3 *equal chance;* 412.3 *miscellany;* 788.5 *winnings*
lucky dog 107.16 *fluke!;* 248.4 *prosperous person*
lucky draw 788.5 *winnings*
lucky fellow 248.4 *prosperous person*
lucky find 211.4 *extra;* 449.10 *find*
lucky man 593.11 *loved one;* 756.6 *someone promised*
lucky shot 248.2 *good fortune;* 107.2 *luck;* 105.5 *unexpectedness*
lucky strike 248.2 *good fortune;* 107.2 *luck*
lucky stroke 246.1 *success*
lucrative 562.5 *fertile;* 765.15 *gainful;* 356.11 *productive;* 237.4, 785.18 *profitable;* 246.14, 813.15 *rewarding*
lucrative deal 765.1 *gain*
lucratively 765.20 *gainfully;* 813.20 *profitably;* 246.16 *successfully*
lucre 780.2 *cash;* 781.6 *money;* 765.5 *profit*
Lucretia 572.4 *celibate person*
Lucretian 4.11 *follower of a doctrine;* 4.14 *of a philosophy*
lucubration 722.1 *dissertation*
Lucullan banquet 688.3 *act of gluttony;* 557.13 *feast*
Lucullus 557.18 *eater;* 688.4 *glutton*
Luddite 357.6 *destroyer;* 662.10 *seditionist*
ludicrous 459.5 *foolish;* 544.9 *inelegant;* 697.5 *nonsensical*
ludicrously 459.8 *foolishly*
ludicrousness 272.1; 459.1 *folly*
luff 323.9 *navigate*
luffing 50.1, 50.10 *sailing*
luff-tackle 366.9 *lifter*
luff up 50.15 *sail*
Luftseilbahn 68.1 *skiing*
lug 308.4 *body orifice;* 504.4 *ear;* 362.2, 362.11 *pull;* 438.1 *tool;* 316.12 *transport*
luge 68.16 *bobsled;* 68.9 *bobsledding;* 320.10 *sled*
lugeing 68.9 *bobsledding;* 68.13 *ice-skating*
luge race 68.9 *bobsledding*
luge racing 68.9 *bobsledding*
luge techniques 68.9 *bobsledding*
luggage 410.9 *baggage;* 440.4 *possessions;* 319.2 *thing transported;* 316.10 *transferred thing*
luggage label 743.3 *means of identification*
luggage rack 410.10 *cart*
luggage trolley 320.7 *handcart*
luggage van 321.6 *rolling stock*
lugger 50.2 *sailing boat*
lughole 504.4 *ear*
lugsail 50.3 *parts of a sailing boat*
lugubrious 602.6 *depressed*
lugubriously 602.12 *joylessly*
lukewarm 637.3 *cautious;* 618.7 *indifferent;* 754.7 *irresolute;* 216.3 *mediocre*
lukewarmly 754.9 *irresolutely*
lukewarmness 639.14 *apathy;* 493.1 *heat;* 618.1 *indifference;* 754.3 *irresolution*
lukewarm room-temperature 493.9 *hot*
lukewarm support 678.1 *disparagement*
lull 609.9 *comfort;* 294.3 *delayed action;* 263.1, 608.1 *ease;* 343.5 *inactivity;* 133.3, 275.6 *interval;* 301.9 *make motionless;* 685.4 *moderate;* 301.1 *motionlessness;* 749.1 *pacification;* 226.3 *pause;* 581.6 *refresher;* 301.2 *repose;* 506.2, 506.4 *silence*
lullaby 685.2 *moderator;* 516.2 *song*
lull in hostilities 589.1 *peace*
lulu 545.3 *attractive female*
Luma white 531.8 *whitener*
lumbago 491.2 *painful condition;* 260.16 *rheumatism*
lumbar 168.4 *rear*
lumbar puncture 35.7 *diagnosis*
lumbar region 168.2 *rear end*
lumber 486.7 *be clumsy;* 38.25 *construction material;* 367.2 *flatten;* 408.4 *litter;* 79.18 *manage trees;* 238.6 *refuse;* 215.2 *residue;* 79.3 *timber;* 23.12 *wood*
lumbered with 378.14 *blocked*
lumberer 79.8 *forester*
lumbering 264.15, 486.3 *clumsy;* 240.1 *inconvenient;* 333.4 *slow;* 333.10 *slow motion;* 158.17 *stocky;* 79.6 *tree management*
lumberjack 79.8 *forester;* 551.11 *jacket;* 437.9 *power-worker*
lumber-jacket 551.11 *jacket*
lumber room 565.7 *room*
lumber yard 79.7 *timber production*
lumbricoid 75.20 *wormlike*
luminance 28.24 *light emission*
luminary 29.10 *star*
luminescence 522.1 *light;* 28.24 *light emission*
luminosity 29.13; 529.3 *hue;* 522.1, 531.12 *light*
luminosity class 29.13 *luminosity*
luminous 695.1 *intelligible;* 531.6 *light;* 522.15 *lucent*
luminous efficacy 28.24 *light emission*
luminous efficiency 28.24 *light emission*
luminous flux 28.24 *light emission*
luminous glaze 529.4 *pigment*
luminous intensity 28.24 *light emission*
luminously 522.30 *lightly;* 531.14 *whitely*
luminousness 522.1 *light*
lump 345.3 *growth;* 418.7 *hard substance;* 414.4 *heaviness;* 158.7 *mass;* 205.7 *piece;* 416.4 *solid body;* 260.3 *symptom;* 486.10 *unskilled person*
lumpfish caviar 25.16 *fish dish*
lumpily 420.14 *roughly*
lumpiness 418.5 *hardness;* 414.4 *heaviness;* 420.6 *roughness;* 158.6 *squatness*
lumpish 414.1 *heavy;* 339.5 *inert;* 158.17 *stocky*
lumpishness 724.3 *inelegance;* 158.6 *squatness*
lump it 388.4 *succumb*
lump sum 780.5 *sum*
lump together 374.5 *combine*
lumpy 420.2 *coarse;* 416.7 *condensed;* 418.1 *hard;* 414.1 *heavy;* 158.17 *stocky*
lumpy cloud 31.20 *cloud appearance*
lunacy 459.1 *folly;* 461.1 *insanity*
lunar 29.36 *astronomical;* 177.4 *curved;* 91.7 *oceanic*
lunar base 29.31 *space travel*
lunar eclipse 523.1 *darkness;* 29.17 *moon*
lunar landscape 563.1 *infertility*
lunar module 29.30 *spacecraft*
lunar month 29.17 *moon;* 275.4 *term*
lunar motion 326.1 *oscillation*
lunar tide 91.2 *tide*
lunate 27.81 *curvilinear*
lunatic 36.8 *disordered personality;* 459.5 *foolish;* 461.7 *insane person*
lunatic asylum 461.8 *mental hospital*
lunatic fringe 325.19 *deviant person*
lunch 557.24 *have a meal;* 557.12 *meal*
lunch counter 557.15 *eating place*
luncheon 557.12 *meal*
luncheonette 557.15 *eating place*
luncher 557.18 *eater*
lunching 557.4 *eating meals*
lunchroom 557.15 *eating place*
lune 27.42 *circle*
lunette 384.8 *military defences;* 20.9 *miscellaneous architectural features*
lung 172.4 *insides;* 434.8 *respiration*
lung cancer 260.12 *cancer;* 260.9 *respiratory disease;* 496.8 *smoking*
lunge 332.4 *be swift;* 54.5 *fence;* 54.3 *fencing movements;* 381.18 *hit;* 381.6 *stab*
lunge punch 52.9 *tae kwon do*
lungi 551.25 *accessories*
lunging 54.6 *fencing*
lungs 507.4 *sound maker*
lungs of brass 507.4 *sound maker*
lunker 158.9 *big thing*
Lun-yu 7.12 *religious text*
Lupercalia 10.16 *religious festival*
lupin 43.12 *crop*
lupine 71.28 *carnivorous*
lupus 260.13 *skin disease*
lurch 690.7 *be drunk;* 299.6 *be irregular;* 299.1 *irregularity;* 327.25 *pitch;* 326.4, 326.11 *rock;* 50.16 *row;* 327.11 *stagger;* 305.11 *trip*
lurcher 71.9 *dog*
lurching 305.18 *falling;* 299.4 *irregular;* 299.1 *irregularity;* 326.16 *rocking*
lure 363.5; **363.12**; 55.2 *artificial fly;* 617.15 *cause desire;* 593.26 *court;* 480.9 *enticement;* 480.3 *incentive;* 483.2 *inducement;* 395.8 *influence;* 483.10 *manipulate;* 617.5 *object of desire;* 752.9 *offer;* 483.5 *positive stimulus;* 813.4 *reward for service;* 700.13, 700.33 *snare;* 480.16 *tempt*
lured 483.12 *motivated*
Lurex™ 522.16 *bright;* 522.2 *quality of light*
lurid 522.16 *bright;* 520.2 *clear;* 530.8 *drained of colour;* 529.12 *gaudy*
lurk 521.7 *become invisible;* 645.5 *be cunning;* 339.4 *be inert;* 526.1 *disappear*
lurker 645.3 *cunning person*
lurking 521.1 *invisible*
lurk in the shadows 523.12 *be dark*
Lüscher colour test 36.5 *psychological test*
luscious 490.6 *pleasant;* 241.4 *tasty*
lusciousness 241.9 *tastiness*
lush 781.4; 545.5 *beautiful;* 558.12 *drinker;* 690.14 *drinking bout;* 562.5 *fertile;* 690.8 *get drunk;* 77.13 *plantlike;* 490.6 *pleasant;* 217.2 *plentiful*
lushed 690.3 *dead drunk*
lushness 562.1 *fertility;* 217.8 *plenty*
lust 593.5, 617.1 *desire;* 593.2 *romantic love;* 804.5 *seven deadly sins;* 617.4 *sexual desire;* 796.3 *sexual immorality;* 804.2 *vice*
lust after 617.12 *desire;* 617.13 *like*
lustful 617.11; 593.20 *amorous;* 804.12 *immoral;* 796.14 *lecherous*
lustfully 617.20; 804.20 *immorally;* 593.30 *lovingly*
lustily 336.15 *acutely;* 576.12 *laboriously;* 507.9 *loudly;* 338.6 *with vigour*
lustiness 338.1 *vigour*
lusting 292.17 *in season*
lustral 807.4 *atoning;* 256.18 *cleansing;* 255.15 *purifying*
lustrate 255.10, 256.15 *purify*
lustration 807.2 *apology;* 10.5 *Christian rite;* 255.2 *purification;* 256.3 *religious cleansing*
lustrational 807.4 *atoning*
lustrative 807.4 *atoning*
lustre 522.1 *light;* 522.2 *quality of light;* 421.7 *smoothness*
lustreless 530.7 *colourless;* 524.7 *dimmed;* 528.2 *shady*
lustreware 24.1 *ceramics*
lustrous 522.17
lusty 259.1 *healthy;* 507.6 *loud;* 336.9 *physically strong;* 158.17 *stocky;* 338.4 *vigorous*
lute 267.3 *adhesive;* 267.7 *cause to adhere;* 24.11 *make ceramics*
luteal 559.5 *of a secretion*
luteolin 537.7 *yellow pigment*
luteous 537.2 *yellowish*
Lutheran 7.5 *Christian*
Lutine bell 742.4 *signal*
luting 24.5 *ceramic process*
luxate 144.18 *disconnect*
luxation 144.5 *disconnection*
luxuriance 219.1 *excess;* 562.1 *fertility;* 217.8 *plenty*
luxuriant 416.6 *dense;* 219.6 *excessive;* 562.5 *fertile;* 542.10 *ornate;* 77.13 *plantlike;* 490.6 *pleasant;* 217.2 *plentiful*
luxuriantly 217.9 *enough*
luxuriate 217.5 *about;* 219.4 *be excessive;* 490.8 *feel pleasure*
luxuriate in 686.10 *indulge oneself*
luxuriating 217.2 *plentiful*
luxuries 557.7 *food*
luxurious 781.3 *opulent;* 490.6 *pleasant;* 248.8 *prosperous*
luxuriously 490.11 *pleasingly;* 248.9 *prosperously;* 781.16 *wealthily*
luxuriousness 219.3 *superfluity*
luxury 792.7 *dear;* 781.7 *opulence;* 490.1 *physical pleasure;* 241.10 *pleasant thing;* 241.7 *pleasure;* 217.8 *plenty;* 248.1 *prosperity;* 686.1 *self-indulgence;* 246.1 *success;* 219.3 *superfluity;* 219.7 *superfluous*
luxury article 219.3 *superfluity*
luxury car 219.3 *superfluity*
luxury coach 320.19 *bus*
luxury flat 219.3 *superfluity*
luxury goods 490.4 *pleasurable things*
luxury hotel 219.3 *superfluity*
luxury price 792.1 *high price*
LW transmitter 692.16 *transmitter*
lyase 33.11 *enzyme*
lycée 6.12 *educational institution*
lyceum 6.12 *educational institution*
lychgate 314.6 *means of entry*
lycopod 82.1 *fern*
lycopodium 82.1 *fern*
lycopsid 82.1 *fern*
Lycra™ 422.3 *elastic thing*
lyddite 587.15 *explosive*
Lydian mode 18.20 *key*
lye 431.10 *solution*
lying 187.10; **699.6**; 699.33 *deceitful;* 699.5 *deceitfulness;* 700.1 *deception;* 800.5 *dishonourable;* 234.8 *exaggerated;* 187.1 *horizontality;* 702.10 *hypocritical;* 720.2 *misinterpretation;* 57.6 *pommel horse*
lying down 155.5 *low;* 155.1 *lowness;* 187.10 *lying;* 388.5 *submitting*
lying flat 187.10 *lying*
lying-in 561.7 *obstetrics*
lying-in-state 583.2 *funeral*
lying in wait 379.1 *trap*
lying on the ball 64.3 *rugby play*
lymph 431.3 *body fluid*
lymphocyte 431.4 *blood*
lymphogram 35.7 *diagnosis*
lymphography 35.7 *diagnosis*
lymphoma 260.11 *blood disease*
lynch 382.19, 814.5 *execute;* 670.23 *show disapproval*
lyncher 814.17 *punisher*
lynch him 814.24 *string him up!*
lynching 814.13 *capital punishment;* 382.5 *execution*
lynch law 588.1 *anarchy;* 814.13 *capital punishment;* 16.41 *lawlessness*
lynx 518.2 *eye*
lynx-eyed 629.4 *jealous;* 518.21 *seeing*
Lyon King of Arms 743.9 *herald*
Lyonnesse 477.8 *dreamland*
lyophilic 32.32 *solid*
lyophilic colloid 32.3 *phase*
lyophobic 32.32 *solid*
lyophobic colloid 32.3 *phase*
lyrenaic philosophy 4.7 *school of thought*
lyric 18.30 *harmonic;* 17.7 *poem;* 516.2 *song*
lyrical 516.6 *melodious;* 17.19 *narrative*
lyrically 516.11 *melodiously;* 17.22 *poetically*
lyricist 17.14 *author;* 516.5 *melodist;* 18.24 *musician*
lyric poet 17.14 *author*
lyric poetry 17.6 *poetry*
Lysenkoism 34.16 *evolution*
lysosome 34.8 *cell organ*
lysozyme 33.11 *enzyme*

M 691.6 *drug*
M1A1 586.21 *armoured cavalry*
M-1 rifle 587.11 *guns*
M25 306.5 *ringroad*
M-60 machine gun 587.11 *guns*
ma'am 568.3 *female title of address*
maarib 10.4 *public worship*
Mab 11.11 *ghost*
Mac 567.3 *male title of address*
mac 551.12 *coat*
macadam 435.2 *building material;* 550.11 *paving;* 25.51 *West Indian dish*
macadamize 550.29 *surface*

macaroni cheese 25.34 *vegetarian dish*
macaronics 17.6 *poetry*
macaroon 25.36 *cake*
macassar 268.6 *ointment*
Macau Grand Prix 61.5 *motorcycle racing*
McCarthyism 633.1 *pursuit*; 466.4 *social discrimination*
McDonald's™ 557.15 *eating place*
Mace 347.2 *counteracting thing*; 384.5 *self-defence*
mace 587.7 *blunt weapon*; 496.5 *herbs*; 743.4 *insignia*; 331.16 *weapons*
macebearer 16.10 *law officer*
macedoine 25.14 *salad*
macerate 419.13 *soften*; 433.31 *steep*
macerated 218.3 *underfed*
maceration 807.2 *apology*; 433.10 *steeping*
Mach 1 28.19 *sound propagation*
macher 123.4 *bigwig*
machete 425.10 *knife*; 587.8 *sharp weapon*
Machiavelli 645.3 *cunning person*; 484.8 *planner*
Machiavellian 645.4 *cunning*; 699.29 *false*; 484.15 *planning*
Machiavellianism 645.1 *cunning*; 699.1 *falsehood*
machicolated 384.30 *defended*
machicolation 384.11 *fortification*
machinate 484.13 *plot*; 702.11 *practise sophistry*; 700.28 *trick*
machination 702.3 *cunning*; 700.4 *false-heartedness*; 484.4 *plot*; 645.2 *stratagem*; 700.7 *tricking*
machinator 700.20 *plotter*
machine **438.5**; 40.3 *computer*; 38.5 *dynamic structure*; 28.11 *energy*; 348.2 *instrument*; 356.2 *manufacture*; 356.10 *produce*; 438.1 *tool*
machine code 5.8 *artificial language*; 40.9 *programming language*
machine-design engineering 38.3 *mechanical engineering*
machine element **38.8**
machine gun 357.7 *agent of destruction*; 587.11 *guns*
machine-gun fire 381.15 *firing*
machine-gunner 586.17 *army person*
machine knitting 42.5 *knitting*
machine loom 42.4 *weaving*
machine-made 356.12 *produced*
machine-milk 43.18 *practise livestock farming*
machine-minded 438.9 *mechanical*
machine-minder 438.8 *machinist*
machine part 38.8 *machine element*
machinery 405.4 *components*; 38.5 *dynamic structure*; 438.5 *machine*; 356.2 *manufacture*; 352.2 *supplies*
machine tool **38.9**; 438.1 *tool*
machining 356.2 *manufacture*
machinist **438.8**; 578.2 *artisan*; 346.6 *operative*; 21.28 *stagehand*
machismo 673.6 *boastfulness*; 567.1 *male sex*
Mach number 28.19 *sound propagation*; 332.8 *speed*
macho 567.17 *male*
macho man **567.6**
machzor 10.10 *religious manual*
Mackenzie 90.5 *other major rivers*
mackerel 55.4 *American game fish*; 55.5 *British game fish*; 74.8 *food fish*; 25.18 *sea fish*
mackerel sky 31.20 *cloud appearance*; 541.5 *variegated thing*
mackerel spinner 55.2 *artificial fly*
Mackinaw coat 551.11 *jacket*
McKinley 154.3 *mountain*
mackintosh 551.12 *coat*
McLeod gauge 32.20 *surface chemistry*
McNaghten Rules 461.1 *insanity*
macramé 193.2 *braid*; 193.8 *interweave*
macrobiotic diet 557.6 *nutrition*
macroclimate 31.38 *climate*
macrocosm 29.3 *universe*; 204.2 *whole thing*
macroeconomics 13.1 *economics*
macro lens 41.17 *lens*
macrometeorology 31.1 *meteorology*
macromolecular structure 34.12 *molecular biology*
macromolecule 554.2 *living matter*; 34.12 *molecular biology*; 32.21 *polymer*
macron 5.36 *accent*; 742.7 *punctuation*
macronucleus 34.9 *cell nucleus*
macronutrient 33.15 *essential element*
macrophotography 41.1 *photography*
macroscopic 158.15 *big*
macroseism 30.22 *seismic activity*
macrosociology 2.1 *sociology*
macula 541.4 *maculation*; 260.13 *skin disease*
macular 541.10 *mottled*
maculate 258.11 *dirty*; 541.10 *mottled*; 541.11 *variegate*
maculation **541.4**
macumba 18.10 *world music*
mad 624.16 *angry*; 642.1 *capricious*; 328.16 *deranged*; 593.19 *enamoured*; 459.5 *foolish*; 461.11 *insane*; 697.5 *nonsensical*; 380.6 *violent*
mad about 593.18 *in love*
Madam 568.3 *female title of address*
madam 796.9 *immoral woman*; 400.1 *master*
madame 568.3 *female title of address*; 660.12 *impudent person*
Madame Tussaud's™ 439.5 *collection*
mad as a hatter 461.11 *insane*
mad as a hornet 624.16 *angry*
madcap 615.4 *rash*; 459.4, 615.3 *rash person*; 380.4 *violent creature*
mad-cow disease 461.3 *mental deterioration*; 260.18 *veterinary disease*
mad dash 342.3 *nimbleness*
madden 624.14 *make angry*; 461.15 *make insane*; 380.9 *make violent*
maddened 380.6 *violent*
maddeningly 624.17 *resentfully*
madder 42.6 *dye*; 529.4 *pigment*; 535.6 *red pigment*
madding crowd 342.6 *business*
mad doctor 36.30, 461.10 *psychiatrist*
mad dog 380.4 *violent creature*
made 93.15 *created*; 160.9 *formed*; 356.12 *produced*
made a joke of 700.36 *deceived*
made easier 265.11 *made easy*
made easy **265.11**; 695.2 *simple*
made in heaven 252.7 *invulnerable*
madeira 558.9 *wine*
Madeira cake 25.36 *cake*
made law 16.46 *legislated*
made legal 396.16 *authorized*
madeleine 25.36 *cake*
made light of 728.19 *downplayed*
made man 302.16 *progressive person*
made man and wife 570.21 *married*
mademoiselle 568.3 *female title of address*; 555.8 *young woman*
made of money 781.1 *wealthy*
made one 570.21 *married*
made public 703.9 *demonstrated*; 738.13 *displayed*; 740.19 *published*
made ready 243.18 *prepared*
made redundant 767.13 *dismissed*
made simple 695.2 *simple*
made sport of 700.36 *deceived*
made to grovel 387.9 *subject*
made-to-measure 139.20 *personalized*; 551.31 *styled*
made-to-order 551.31 *styled*
made-up 406.10 *containing*; 25.56 *culinary*; 699.36 *falsified*; 96.10 *theoretical*
made up of 127.7 *including*
madhouse 408.5 *confusion*; 461.8 *mental hospital*
Madison Avenue 480.6 *advertising*
madly 461.17 *insanely*; 593.30 *lovingly*
madman 461.7 *insane person*; 380.4 *violent creature*
madness 328.6 *derangement*; 459.1 *folly*; 461.1 *insanity*
Madonna 8.10 *deified person*
mad race 342.3 *nimbleness*
madras 25.49 *Indian dish*; 496.2 *seasoning*; 193.4 *textile*
Madrid 87.6 *other cities*
madrigal 18.3 *classical music*; 17.7 *poem*; 181.7 *round*; 516.2 *song*
mad round 654.3 *meeting*
mad scramble 342.3 *nimbleness*
Madura foot 83.5 *fungal association*
madwoman 461.7 *insane person*
mae-geri 52.8 *karate*
Maelstrom 90.6 *river flow*
maelstrom 342.1 *activity*; 90.6 *river flow*; 379.1 *trap*; 327.2 *tumult*; 307.4 *vortex*
maenad 690.17 *drunkard*
maestà 19.10 *art subject*
maestro 6.4 *educator*; 396.11, 400.10 *expert*; 18.24 *musician*; 230.4 *perfectionist*; 485.4 *skilled person*
Mae West 415.7 *light thing*; 252.4 *safety device*; 67.3 *survival swimming*
maffick 601.15 *celebrate*
mafficking 601.9 *rejoicing*
Mafia 737.7 *esotericism*
Mafia hit man 382.11 *murderer*
Mafia member 662.9 *criminal*
mafic rock 30.30 *igneous rock*
Mafioso 662.9 *criminal*
mafioso 736.7 *concealer*; 737.7 *esotericism*; 798.6 *evil person*
maftir 7.8 *priest*
magazine 587.4 *arsenal*; 587.9 *firearm*; 740.5 *journal*; 276.7 *periodical*; 439.4 *storage*
magazine rifle 587.9 *firearm*
magazines 693.4 *mass communication*
magazine section 740.4 *newspaper*
magdalen 808.3 *penitent person*
mage 11.4 *witch*
magenta 28.28 *colour*; 540.6 *purple*; 535.1 *red*
maggid 7.8 *priest*
maggot 55.1 *angling*; 477.4 *ideality*; 76.5 *larva*; 642.3 *whim*
maggoty 258.8 *unclean*; 76.12 *verminous*
magianism 11.3 *witchcraft*
magic 760.1 *conversion*; 96.3 *delusion*; 700.40 *illusory*; 395.2 *occult influence*; 11.1 *occultism*; 334.1 *power*; 700.9 *sleight of hand*; 11.3 *witchcraft*; 619.14 *wonderful!*; 619.3 *wonder-working*; 235.1 *worthy*
magical 700.40 *illusory*; 11.15 *witchlike*; 619.8 *wonderful*
magically **11.26**
magical power 334.1 *power*
magic belt 11.6 *talisman*
magic carpet 332.11 *swift thing*; 11.6 *talisman*; 554.6 *things brought to life*
magic circle 11.6 *talisman*
magician 224.6, 227.4 *editor*; 21.29 *entertainer*; 630.5 *surpriser*; 11.4 *witch*
magic lantern 41.12 *development*; 518.8 *reflection*
magic mushroom 691.6 *drug*; 83.2 *mushroom*
magic ring 11.6 *talisman*
magic show 21.7 *show*
magic spell 395.2 *occult influence*; 11.5 *spell*
magic sword 11.6 *talisman*
magic symbol 742.1 *sign*
magic words 11.5 *spell*
Maginot Line 384.9 *barrier*; 147.7 *interface*
magism 11.3 *witchcraft*
magisterial 121.13 *dominant*; 12.10 *governing*; 16.49 *judicatory*; 400.12 *masterful*; 485.6 *skilful*
magisterially 622.34 *imposingly*; 121.16 *superiorly*
magistracy 16.23 *judge*; 16.2 *jurisdiction*; 396.5 *position of authority*
magistral 400.12 *masterful*
magistrality 396.1 *authority*
magistrate 16.23 *judge*; 464.6 *justice*; 16.13 *lawyer*; 400.3 *leader*; 579.16 *official*; 396.10 *person of authority*; 814.17 *punisher*
magistrates' court 16.20 *British court*; 464.3 *place of judgment*
magma 493.8 *hot place*; 412.2 *mixed thing*; 30.24 *volcanic activity*
magma chamber 30.24 *volcanic activity*
magmatic 30.56 *petrographic*
magmatic rock 30.30 *igneous rock*
magmatism 30.29 *petrogenesis*
magmatite 30.34 *mineral*
Magna Carta 16.1 *the law*
magnanimity **679.6**; 650.2 *charity*; 649.2 *forgivingness*; 648.1 *leniency*; 473.2 *unselfishness*; 803.1 *virtue*
magnanimous **679.2**; 650.7 *charitable*; 648.4 *lenient*; 649.5 *merciful*; 473.5 *unselfish*; 803.5 *virtuous*
magnanimously 650.11 *charitably*; 649.14 *forgivingly*; 648.6 *leniently*; 473.9 *unselfishly*; 803.9 *virtuously*
magnate 123.4 *bigwig*; 780.17 *financier*; 765.7 *gainer*; 781.10 *wealthy person*
magnesium 33.15 *essential element*
magnesium alloy 38.25 *construction material*
magnet **28.60**; **362.7**; **363.3**; 267.3 *adhesive*
magnetic **362.10**; **363.10**; 395.12 *appealing*; 334.16 *charged*; 483.11 *motivational*; 480.19 *persuasive*; 28.98 *physical*
magnetic alloy 28.59 *ferromagnetism*
magnetically **362.16**; 363.13 *attractionally*; 334.19 *energetically*; 28.100 *physically*
magnetic anomaly 30.44 *geomagnetism*
magnetic attaction 28.57 *magnetism*
magnetic card 28.64 *magnetic recording*
magnetic compass 323.5 *navigation*
magnetic constant 28.61 *magnetic quantity*
magnetic damping 28.63 *magnetic phenomenon*
magnetic declination 28.58 *geomagnetism*
magnetic deflection 28.63 *magnetic phenomenon*
magnetic dip 28.58 *geomagnetism*
magnetic dipole moment 28.61 *magnetic quantity*
magnetic disk 28.64 *magnetic recording*
magnetic epoch 28.58 *geomagnetism*
magnetic equator 28.58 *geomagnetism*; 30.45 *magnetic pole*
magnetic field 334.4 *energy*; 28.61 *magnetic quantity*
magnetic field strength 28.61 *magnetic quantity*
magnetic flux 28.61 *magnetic quantity*
magnetic focusing 28.63 *magnetic phenomenon*
magnetic force 334.4 *energy*
magnetic hysteresis 28.63 *magnetic phenomenon*
magnetic induction 28.61 *magnetic quantity*
magnetic ink 28.64 *magnetic recording*
magnetic ink character recognition 28.64 *magnetic recording*
magnetic iron ore 28.60 *magnet*
magnetic lens 28.63 *magnetic phenomenon*
magnetic levitation 28.63 *magnetic phenomenon*
magnetic memory 28.64 *magnetic recording*
magnetic meridian 28.58 *geomagnetism*
magnetic mine 587.16 *bomb*
magnetic mirror 28.63 *magnetic phenomenon*
magnetic moment 28.61 *magnetic quantity*
magnetic monopole 28.60 *magnet*
magnetic needle 579.5 *guide*; 742.5 *indicator*; 363.3 *magnet*; 323.5 *navigation*
magnetic North 324.4 *compass point*; 28.58 *geomagnetism*
magnetic North Pole 28.58 *geomagnetism*
magnetic personality 483.2 *inducement*; 395.3 *personal influence*
magnetic phenomenon **28.63**
magnetic pole **30.45**
magnetic potential difference 28.61 *magnetic quantity*
magnetic quantity **28.61**
magnetic recording **28.64**
magnetic repulsion 28.57 *magnetism*; 364.5 *repulsion*
magnetic resonance imaging 28.64 *magnetic recording*
magnetic reversal 28.58, 30.44 *geomagnetism*
magnetics 28.2 *classical physics*
magnetic separating 24.5 *ceramic process*
magnetic South 28.58 *geomagnetism*
magnetic South Pole 28.58 *geomagnetism*
magnetic storage 28.64 *magnetic recording*
magnetic storm 28.58, 30.44 *geomagnetism*; 327.13 *tempest*; 380.5 *violent weather*
magnetic stripe 28.64 *magnetic recording*
magnetic tape 28.64 *magnetic recording*; 744.6 *record book*; 744.7 *recording*
magnetic track 28.64 *magnetic recording*
magnetic variable 28.61 *magnetic quantity*
magnetism **28.57**; **362.5**; 28.2 *classical physics*; 334.4 *energy*; 480.3 *incentive*; 483.2 *inducement*; 395.1 *influence*; 363.2 *pulling power*
magnetite 28.60, 363.3 *magnet*
magnetization 28.61 *magnetic quantity*; 363.2 *pulling power*

magnetize 363.11 *attract;* 334.11 *give power;* 362.15 *pull towards*
magnetized 363.10 *magnetic*
magnetized iron 363.3 *magnet*
magnetizer 362.7 *magnet*
magnetizing coil 28.60 *magnet*
magneto 437.4 *electricity;* 39.30 *generator;* 334.6 *source of energy*
magnetohydrodynamic 28.98 *physical*
magnetohydrodynamically 28.100 *physically*
magnetohydrodynamics 28.3 *modern physics*
magnetometer 28.90 *ammeter;* 26.8 *meter*
magnetometric 26.16 *micrometric*
magnetometry 26.2 *micrometry*
magnetomotive force 28.61 *magnetic quantity*
magneton 28.61 *magnetic quantity*
magneto-optical effect 28.63 *magnetic phenomenon*
magnetopause 30.44 *geomagnetism*
magnetosphere 28.58, 30.44 *geomagnetism;* 29.16 *planet*
magnetostriction 28.63 *magnetic phenomenon*
magnetron 39.20 *electron tube*
magnifiable 190.9 *enlargeable*
Magnificat 10.8 *hymn;* 671.2 *thanks*
magnification 607.1 *aggravation;* 8.9 *deification;* 727.2 *enlargement;* 190.1 *growth;* 213.1 *increase;* 28.32 *optical instrument;* 10.3 *rite of worship;* 518.10 *visual aid;* 9.1 *worship*
magnificence 797.8 *good;* 545.1 *gorgeousness;* 235.6 *worth*
magnificent 797.1 *good;* 235.1 *worthy*
magnificently 797.22 *well*
magnified 607.4 *aggravated;* 190.7 *bigger;* 8.15 *deified;* 727.13 *enlarged;* 213.7 *increased;* 681.2 *unrestrained*
magnifier 518.10 *visual aid*
magnify 607.6 *aggravate;* 190.6 *become bigger;* 8.17 *deify;* 727.8 *enlarge;* 190.5, 213.5 *make bigger;* 123.8 *make important;* 10.19 *offer worship;* 669.14 *praise;* 9.7 *worship*
magnifying glass 518.10 *visual aid*
magnifying mirror 518.8 *reflection*
magnifying power 28.32 *optical instrument*
magniloquence 542.2 *affectation;* 727.4 *bombast;* 729.2 *power of speech;* 726.2 *seriousness*
magniloquent 727.15 *bombastic;* 270.3 *diffuse;* 729.20 *eloquent;* 542.10 *ornate;* 726.5 *serious*
magniloquently 726.7 *emphatically;* 727.16 *exaggeratedly;* 729.21 *orally;* 542.13 *ornately*
magnitude 209.1 *degree;* 123.1 *importance;* 395.1 *influence;* 29.13 *luminosity;* 203.1 *quantity;* 27.50 *scalar quantity;* 26.4, 158.1 *size*
magnolia 531.1 *white*
magnox reactor 437.7 *nuclear power;* 28.73 *nuclear reactor*
magnum 410.14 *bottle*
magnum opus 356.6 *great work;* 400.11, 485.3 *masterpiece*
magpie 376.36 *hoarder;* 72.6 *songbird;* 731.4 *talker*
magsman 700.17 *cheat*
magus 11.4 *witch*
maharajah 579.14 *leader;* 400.2 *sovereign*
mahatma 11.12 *occultist*
Mahavastu 7.12 *religious text*
Mahdi 579.14 *leader*
mahlstick 19.11 *artist's materials*
mahogany 534.1 *brown;* 421.8 *smooth thing*
maid 401.3 *attendant;* 256.12 *cleaner;* 401.6 *domestic servant;* 255.5 *pure person;* 572.5 *single person;* 578.1 *worker;* 555.8 *young woman*
maiden 130.29 *beginning;* 572.6 *celibate;* 53.8 *delivery;* 568.2 *female;* 44.5 *gardening;* 59.7 *horseracing;* 295.12 *immature;* 814.16 *instrument of execution;* 255.5, 795.5 *pure person;* 568.5 *single girl;* 572.5 *single person;* 79.1 *tree;* 555.8 *young woman*
maiden aunt 197.7, 572.5 *single person*
maidenhead 795.3 *moral purity;* 572.2 *virginity*
maidenhood 250.3 *independence;* 795.3 *moral purity;* 572.2 *virginity;* 555.1 *youth*
maiden lady 572.5 *single person*
maidenliness 555.2 *youthfulness*
maidenly 572.6 *celibate;* 568.15 *female;* 295.24 *immaturely;* 795.9 *pure;* 572.7 *virginal;* 555.11 *young*
maiden name 721.8 *name*
maiden over 53.8 *delivery*
maiden race 59.7 *horseracing*
maiden speech 130.9 *premiere*
maiden voyage 295.4 *beginning;* 130.9 *premiere*
maid-in-waiting 401.6 *domestic servant*
maid of all work 342.10 *busy person;* 578.1 *worker*
maid of honour 570.7 *bridal party;* 569.6 *close friend*
maidservant 401.6 *domestic servant*
maids of honour 25.36 *cake*
maieusis 739.4 *discloser*
maieutic 348.7 *causal;* 739.11 *disclosing;* 701.2 *logical argument*
mail 384.7 *armour;* 692.31 *correspond;* 692.3 *correspondence;* 316.13 *post;* 550.12 *protective covering;* 252.4 *safety device;* 733.10 *send;* 319.2 *thing transported;* 316.10 *transferred thing;* 587.1 *weapon*
mailable 316.17 *transferable*
mailbag 692.3 *correspondence*
mailbomb 587.16 *bomb*
mailbombing 381.16 *terrorist attack*
mailbox 692.3 *correspondence;* 40.12 *electronic office*
mail carrier 316.8 *messenger;* 692.4 *postal worker*
mail-clad 384.30 *defended*
mailcoach 321.6 *rolling stock*
mailed 384.30 *defended*
mailed fist 647.2 *suppression*
mailing 316.2 *transportation*
mailing list 693.4 *mass communication*
mail-in vote 469.10 *vote*
maillot 551.21 *beachwear*
mailman 316.8 *messenger;* 692.4 *postal worker*
mail pouch 692.3 *correspondence*
mailsack 692.3 *correspondence*
mailshot 693.4 *mass communication*
mail train 321.7 *train*
mail van 321.6 *rolling stock*
mailwoman 692.4 *postal worker*
maim 245.5 *hurt;* 335.8 *overpower;* 337.7 *weaken*
maimed 231.3 *deformed;* 233.4 *incomplete*
main 317.15 *accessible;* 121.14 *best;* 173.8 *focal;* 123.5 *important;* 400.12 *masterful;* 91.1 *sea;* 767.8 *sink;* 319.5 *transportable*
main attraction 123.3 *chief thing*
main body 586.14 *armed forces;* 205.5 *largest part*
main chance 104.4 *chance;* 123.3 *chief thing;* 107.5 *good chance*
main course 25.9 *dish;* 557.14 *mouthful*
maincrop potatoes 43.12 *crop*
main drag 317.5 *crossing*
Maine lobster 25.43 *US dish*
main entrance 167.1 *front*
main feature 123.3 *chief thing;* 139.9 *special*
main force 386.2 *coercion;* 334.1 *power*
mainframe 40.3 *computer*
main interest 173.5 *focus*
mainland 30.6 *continent*
mainline 691.10 *drug oneself*
main line 317.10 *railway;* 321.2 *track*
mainliner 691.4 *drug taker*
main-line railway 321.1 *railway*
main-line station 321.8 *railway station*
mainlining 691.1 *drug-taking*
mainly 140.18 *as a rule;* 123.9 *importantly;* 99.13 *in essence;* 216.11 *on average;* 204.13 *on the whole;* 138.31 *overall;* 130.42 *principally;* 121.16 *superiorly*
mainmast 50.3 *parts of a sailing boat*
main meaning 694.4 *type of meaning*
main memory 40.6 *memory*
main office 173.4 *centre of activity;* 577.1 *workshop*
main part 123.3 *chief thing;* 219.1 *excess;* 205.5 *largest part*
main place 173.4 *centre of activity*
main point 123.3 *chief thing;* 447.1 *topic*
main reaction 32.14 *chemical reaction*
main road 317.3, 320.2, 373.5 *road*
mainsail 50.3 *parts of a sailing boat*
main sequence 29.11 *stellar birth*
main-sequence star 29.13 *luminosity*
main shock 30.22 *seismic activity*
mainspring 438.5 *machine;* 480.11 *motive;* 344.2 *source;* 422.5 *spring*
mains supply 39.34 *power supply*
mainstay 123.3 *chief thing;* 253.1 *protection;* 252.5 *refuge;* 392.13 *supporter;* 413.2 *supporting part*
mainstream 18.33 *jazz*
mainstream jazz 18.8 *jazz*
main street 87.7 *city district;* 317.3, 373.5 *road;* 87.14 *urban*
maintain **640.7**; 450.7, 590.19 *believe;* 134.3 *continue;* 360.7 *detain;* 279.6 *eternalize;* 35.20 *practise surgery;* 359.5 *preserve;* 4.22 *propound a philosophy;* 134.4 *protract;* 436.5 *provision;* 393.1 *repair;* 701.15 *state;* 413.13 *support financially;* 554.20 *support life;* 392.20 *sustain;* 346.9 *take action*
maintain a certain footing 221.6 *be in a state of*
maintain control 334.10 *be powerful*
maintain course 50.15 *sail*
maintained 450.14 *believed*
maintainer 413.8 *supporter*
maintain firm control 647.5 *be severe*
maintaining 413.9 *supportive*
maintaining one's distance 655.1 *unsociability*
maintain one's grip 640.8 *hold out*
maintain one's ground 640.8 *hold out*
maintain one's hold 360.6 *retain*
maintain one's status 221.6 *be in a state of*
maintain progress **302.9**
maintain supply 436.5 *provision*
maintain the status quo 225.6 *make permanent*
maintain tradition 160.8 *be formal*
maintenance 640.3 *constancy;* 134.1 *continuity;* 16.39 *crime;* 360.2 *detention;* 571.3 *divorce court;* 765.4 *earnings;* 413.7 *financial support;* 788.3 *income;* 346.4 *management;* 440.6 *marriage settlement;* 359.1 *preservation;* 436.1 *provision;* 393.8 *repair;* 392.4 *social assistance;* 769.2 *something received;* 392.3 *sustenance*
maintenance service 584.4 *military organization*
main thing 123.3 *chief thing*
main topic 123.3 *chief thing*
main wall 63.5 *real tennis*
maisonette 565.5 *house*
maître d' 401.3 *attendant*
maître d'hôtel 401.3 *attendant;* 436.4 *caterer*
maize 43.12 *crop*
maize silage 43.9 *animal feedstuff*
majesterial 622.19 *stately*
majestic 8.13 *divine;* 543.3 *elegant;* 12.10 *governing;* 396.14 *governmental;* 400.12 *masterful;* 726.5 *serious;* 622.19 *stately;* 575.6 *worshipful*
majestically **622.36**; 8.19 *divinely;* 726.7 *emphatically*
majestic progress 302.15 *improvement*
majesty **622.6**; 396.2 *authoritativeness;* 8.2 *divine attribute*
Majlis 579.10 *legislative body*
majolica painter 24.7 *potter*
major 586.17 *army person;* 121.15 *excellent;* 123.5 *important;* 400.12 *masterful;* 485.1 *skill;* 139.8 *specialization*
major axis 27.42 *circle*
major championships 56.1 *golf*
major-domo 401.6 *domestic servant*
major earthquake 30.22 *seismic activity*
major element 33.15 *essential element*
major general 586.17 *army person;* 397.6 *person in command*
major golf courses 56.1 *golf*
major in 6.23 *learn;* 139.27 *specialize*
major interval 18.16 *musical note*
majority **207.3**; 203.2 *certain amount;* 209.7 *gradational;* 209.4 *interval;* 205.5 *largest part;* 205.1 *part;* 207.6 *plural;* 203.6 *quantitative;* 121.1 *superiority*
majority rule 12.1 *government;* 396.7 *type of rule*
majority verdict 16.7 *legal trial*
majority vote 469.10 *vote*
majority whip 579.15 *manager;* 12.8 *politician*
major key 18.20 *key*
major league baseball 48.1 *baseball*
major part 205.5 *largest part*
major planet 29.16 *planet*
major poet 17.14 *author*
major scale 18.20 *key*
major subject 485.1 *skill*
major suit 485.1 *skill*
major surgery 35.9 *surgery*
major term 4.8 *philosophical term*
major third 199.6 *third*
major war 585.1 *war*
majuscule 5.41 *lettered;* 5.15 *type style*
make **405.13**; 344.10 *awaken;* 344.9 *be the cause of;* 93.20 *bring into being;* 386.6 *compel;* 243.7 *develop;* 160.7 *form;* 765.9 *gain;* 244.1 *improve;* 356.10 *produce;* 376.44 *put together;* 403.15 *shape;* 194.11, 210.10 *total;* 137.4 *type*
make a 180-degree turn 708.12 *renounce*
make a bad buy 777.1 *purchase*
make a bad match 570.15 *marry*
make a bad move 247.6 *fail*
make a balls-up of 245.4 *impair*
make a bank shot 65.8 *play billiards*
make a beeline for 324.7 *take a direction*
make a beginning **130.18**
make a bequest 768.5 *give*
make a bid 353.1 *attempt;* 776.3 *bargain;* 13.11 *deal;* 746.6 *make conditions*
make a bid for 752.10 *offer to buy*
make a blocking kick 52.13 *practise judo*
make a bloomer 802.19 *be wrong*
make a bomb 781.13 *get rich*
make a boo-boo 288.9 *make a mistake*
make a bow 367.9 *bow*
make a break 224.7 *be changed;* 65.8 *play billiards*
make a break for 324.7 *take a direction*
make abstruse 266.3 *make obscure*
make a bundle 781.13 *get rich*
make a burnt offering 752.16 *make an offering*
make a buy 777.1 *purchase*
make a buyout 777.1 *purchase*
make a call 692.32 *telephone*
make a change 224.8 *cause change*
make a changeover 47.7 *race*
make a charity appeal 710.8 *solicit money*
make a choice 469.1 *select*
make a circle 179.6 *circle*
make a circuit 306.6 *orbit*
make a clean sweep 256.13 *clean;* 371.11 *void*
make a comeback 393.4 *be restored;* 244.2 *get better*
make a commotion 727.7 *exaggerate*
make a compact 755.5 *contract*
make a conquest 593.28 *win the love of*
make a contract 756.8 *guarantee*
make a copy 316.16 *translate*
make a copy of 561.9 *reproduce*
make a corner in 777.1 *purchase*
make acquaintance 654.13 *fraternize*
make a crossing 318.11 *cross*
make a cynosure of 740.16 *publicize*
make a date 593.26 *court;* 654.13 *fraternize*
make addresses 593.26 *court*
make a dead reckoning 50.15 *sail*
make a deal 776.3 *bargain;* 409.17 *come to an arrangement;* 754.4 *compromise;* 749.5 *make peace;* 746.5 *negotiate*
make a dent in 441.1 *waste*
make a deposit 791.5 *buy at a discount;* 783.10 *deposit*
make a deposition 707.18 *vow*
make adequate provision 217.4 *suffice*
make a detour 179.6 *circle;* 306.8 *detour*
make a diagram 717.11 *paint*
make a diagram of 721.14 *describe*
make adjustments 754.4 *compromise*
make a double play 48.7 *play baseball*
make a down payment 785.6 *pay*
make a draught 434.22 *blow*
make advances 593.26 *court;* 569.14 *seek the friendship of*
make a face 596.6 *react against*
make a fair catch 46.17 *kick*
make a fair exchange 776.1 *trade*
make a fair offer 752.9 *offer*
make a false attack 54.5 *fence*
make a false image 718.4 *misrepresent*
make a false start 47.7 *race*
make a faux pas 486.7 *be clumsy*
make a feint 54.5 *fence*
make a final demand 710.7 *demand*
make a find 777.1 *purchase*
make a flying kick 52.13 *practise judo*

make a fool of 349.3 *exploit*; 623.22 *shame*; 773.10 *take away*; 700.28 *trick*
make a forced march 262.2 *make haste*
make a fortune 248.5 *be prosperous*; 781.13 *get rich*; 765.14 *profit*
make a fresh start 130.28 *begin again*; 808.4 *be penitent*
make a fuel stop 61.9 *race*
make a fuss 113.18 *object*
make a fuss about 123.8 *make important*; 467.4 *overestimate*
make a generalization 138.27
make a gentleman's agreement 756.7 *promise*
make a getaway 389.5 *escape*
make a gift 768.5 *give*
make a good buy 777.1 *purchase*
make a good living 765.14 *profit*
make a good match 570.15 *marry*
make a good start 302.2 *start*
make a go of 246.6 *be successful*
make a guess 476.5 *suppose*
make a habit of 632.16 *have a habit*
make a hash of 486.7 *be clumsy*; 408.23 *confuse*; 247.6 *fail*
make a high tackle 64.5 *play rugby*
make a hit 246.6 *be successful*; 593.28 *win the love of*
make a hostage of 387.7 *defeat*
make a house call 35.19 *practise medicine*
make a killing 246.6 *be successful*; 791.5 *buy at a discount*; 781.13 *get rich*; 765.14 *profit*; 778.1 *sell*; 776.2 *speculate*; 776.1 *trade*
make a kiss shot 65.8 *play billiards*
make a landfall 312.4 *land*; 323.10 *sail*
make a last-ditch stand 294.8 *delay*
make a legal defence 714.8 *justify*
make a lip 626.9 *be sullen*
make a list 220.8 *list*
make all clear for 265.16 *make easy*
make all-out war 751.6 *argue*
make allowances 136.15 *modify*
make allowances for 649.12 *show mercy*; 714.7 *vindicate*
make a loan application 772.7 *borrow*
make a loss 247.6 *fail*
make a man of 235.10 *do good*
make a match 570.17 *matchmake*
make amends 785.14 *atone*; 808.5 *do penance*; 752.14 *offer reparation*; 813.11 *pay*; 609.11 *recompense*; 393.3 *restore*; 9.7 *worship*
make amends for 807.5 *atone*; 775.5 *compensate*
make a mess 258.11 *dirty*
make a mess of 486.7 *be clumsy*
make a mint 781.13 *get rich*
make a mistake 274.19; **288.9**; 486.5 *be unskilful*; 804.16 *be wicked*; 802.19 *be wrong*
make a mockery of 621.6 *deride*
make a move 130.19 *start off*; 300.15 *walk*
make an addition to 211.7 *support*
make an alliance 374.6 *come together*
make an appearance 312.1 *arrive*; 525.12 *become visible*
make an arrest 251.11 *detain*
make an ass of 700.28 *trick*
make an attempt 353.1 *attempt*
make an educated guess 475.11 *predict*
make an effort 340.4 *act*; 576.8 *exert oneself*; 342.15 *try*
make an empty gesture 700.26 *be a hypocrite*; 699.22 *be hypocritical*
make an end of 131.16 *cease*
make an entrance 21.34 *act*; 520.9 *appear*; 314.9 *enter*; 312.5 *get in*
make an error 699.20 *be false*
make a nest egg 439.6 *store*
make a net profit 765.14 *profit*
make a new version 719.12 *translate*
make an example of 814.1 *punish*
make an exception 128.7 *exclude*; 212.3 *subtract*
make an exit 315.9 *exit*
make angry 624.14; 625.8 *make irascible*
make an idol of 9.8 *idolatrize*
make an impression 338.2 *be full of vigour*; 123.7 *be important*; 462.15 *be remembered*; 738.5 *be visible*; 111.9 *duplicate*
make an impression in 419.13 *soften*
make an incision 35.20 *practise surgery*
make an offer 776.3 *bargain*; 752.9 *offer*; 777.1 *purchase*
make an offer for 752.10 *offer to buy*
make an offering 752.16
make a note 462.13 *remind*
make an outward show 699.28 *mask*
make an overture 752.9 *offer*
make an unlawful entry 774.12 *steal*
make an unsecured loan 771.5 *lend*
make a packet 781.13 *get rich*
make a pact 374.6 *come together*
make a pass 66.4 *play soccer*
make a pass at 381.6 *stab*
make a patsy of 349.3 *exploit*
make a pawn of 349.3 *exploit*
make a payment 785.6 *pay*
make a peace offering 752.16 *make an offering*
make a pile 781.13 *get rich*
make a pit stop 61.9 *race*
make a plan 484.9 *plan*
make a point 476.6 *propound*; 447.11 *raise the point*
make a point of 386.6 *compel*
make a poor likeness 718.4 *misrepresent*
make apparent 525.14 *present*
make appointments 12.12 *take authority*
make a prediction 475.11 *predict*
make a preliminary sketch 420.13 *be unfinished*
make a presentation 768.5 *give*
make a present of 768.5 *give*
make a press announcement 707.17 *affirm*
make a pretense of 699.24 *pretend*
make a prisoner 773.10 *take away*
make a profit 248.5 *be prosperous*; 797.21 *do well*; 765.9 *gain*; 781.13 *get rich*; 765.14 *profit*; 778.1 *sell*; 776.1 *trade*; 13.10 *trade with*
make a prognosis 475.11 *predict*
make a promise 756.7 *promise*
make a purchase 777.1 *purchase*
make a reference to 108.7 *relate to*
make a report on 464.12 *estimate*
make a request 710.6 *request*
make a requital 385.3 *retaliate*
make a reservation 253.15 *reserve*
make a resolution 638.7 *resolve*
make a résumé 723.8 *summarize*
make a rough copy 420.13 *be unfinished*
make a rough sketch 243.2 *do the groundwork*
make a round trip 179.6 *circle*; 306.6 *orbit*; 761.8 *return*
make arrangements 409.18
make a rude remark 661.6 *be insubordinate*
make a ruling 140.13 *rule*
make a run 68.16 *bobsled*
make a running attack 54.5 *fence*
make a sacrifice 473.7 *be unselfish*
make a sacrificial offering 752.16 *make an offering*
make a sale 778.1 *sell*
make a scene 624.11 *be angry*
make a secured loan 771.5 *lend*
make a shindy 624.11 *be angry*
make a show of 738.1 *display*; 699.24 *pretend*
make a side move 169.8 *move sideways*
make as if 699.24 *pretend*
make a signal 742.12 *signal*
make a sortie 381.8 *counterattack*
make a space 146.4 *space*
make a special request 710.6 *request*
make a speech 733.7 *address*
make a splash 219.4 *be excessive*
make a stand 585.14 *battle*; 384.21 *entrench*; 383.6 *resist*
make a start 130.18 *make a beginning*
make a statement 707.17 *affirm*; 721.15 *recount*
make a stir 123.7 *be important*; 123.8 *make important*
make a straight thrust 54.5 *fence*
make a strike 51.8 *bowl*
make a success of 246.6 *be successful*
make a suggestion 476.6 *propound*
make a sweeping statement 138.27 *make a generalization*
make a synopsis of 723.8 *summarize*
make a takeover bid 776.3 *bargain*
make a thumbnail sketch 163.5 *outline*
make a toast 569.15 *be hospitable*
make a to-do 727.7 *exaggerate*
make a tool of 349.3 *exploit*
make a treaty 746.5 *negotiate*
make a trial of 353.4 *test*
make a true representation 698.31 *be accurate*
make a U-turn 303.9 *turn round*
make available to all 695.5 *simplify*
make average 216.10
make a V sign 660.29 *ridicule*
make a wally of 700.28 *trick*
make a way 317.14 *find one's way*
make away with 357.8 *destroy*; 382.16 *kill*
make away with oneself 382.21 *commit suicide*
make a weak effort 231.10 *leave imperfect*
make a whole 232.5 *be complete*
make a widow 571.9 *widow*
make a widower 571.9 *widow*
make a will 768.5 *give*
make a word-for-word translation 5.46 *translate*
make a wry face 626.11 *be irritable*
make bad blood 596.7 *cause dislike*
make badly 236.13 *be worthless*
make barren 335.9 *make impotent*; 238.8 *make useless*
make basic plans 243.2 *do the groundwork*
make believe 700.25 *deceive oneself*; 477.14 *imagine*
make-believe 477.5 *fantasy*; 700.40 *illusory*; 477.12 *imaginary*; 94.5 *nonreality*; 700.2 *self-deception*; 96.10 *theoretical*
make better 224.8 *cause change*; 395.9 *change*; 235.10, 797.20 *do good*; 244.1 *improve*
make bigger 190.5; **213.5**
make bitter 626.12 *make irritable*
make blind 519.15 *blind*
make bold 659.7 *be discourteous*; 660.22 *be rude*
make bold to 250.19 *liberalize*
make both ends meet 680.5 *be thrifty*
make bright 421.11 *smooth*
make by hand 356.10 *produce*
make capital out of 349.3 *exploit*; 237.11 *find useful*; 244.2 *get better*; 765.14 *profit*
make captive 251.11 *detain*
make ceramics 24.11
make certain 452.21; 616.5 *be cautious*; 253.11 *promise*; 252.10 *protect*; 454.1 *verify*
make cheap 793.13
make circular 179.7
make claims upon 397.10 *demand*
make clean 256.13 *clean*
make clear 725.2 *clarify*; 703.16 *explain*; 719.8 *interpret*; 265.16 *make easy*; 4.21 *rationalize*; 244.3 *rectify*; 695.5 *simplify*
make clothing 551.35
make coarse 245.6 *pervert*
make cold 494.12
make comfortable 490.10 *comfort*
make common cause 747.13 *work together*
make complete 232.4 *complete*
make complex 180.7 *be ambiguous*
make concave 183.9
make conceited 673.18
make concessions 757.3 *permit*
make concise 244.3 *rectify*
make concrete 402.8 *be material*
make conditions 746.6
make conform 117.9
make consistent 298.10 *make regular*; 162.6 *symmetrize*
make constant 298.10 *make regular*
make contact 492.12 *abut*; 692.30 *communicate*; 147.18 *juxtapose*; 243.1 *prepare*
make content 749.4 *pacify*
make continual 298.10 *make regular*
make corrections 244.3 *rectify*
make crystal-clear 695.5 *simplify*
make dark 523.14
make deaf 505.9 *deafen*
make deliveries 436.5 *provision*
make demands 397.10 *demand*; 746.6 *make conditions*; 135.10 *necessitate*
make dense 416.9
make dependent 387.6 *subject*
make different 224.8 *cause change*
make difficulties 113.20 *withstand*
make dim 524.10
make dirty 258.11 *dirty*
make disappear 278.5 *make transient*
make disordered 408.24
make disproportionate 120.5 *be unequal*
make dissimilar 718.4 *misrepresent*
make diverse 114.8 *be diverse*
make do 216.9 *be average*; 680.5 *be thrifty*; 478.3 *improvise*
make do with 349.5 *dispose of*; 762.5 *take a substitute*
make drunk 690.9 *be intoxicating*
make due provision 436.5 *provision*
make easier 265.16 *make easy*
make easily understood 695.5 *simplify*
make easy 265.16; 695.5 *simplify*
make elastic 422.9
make ends meet 786.11 *be parsimonious*; 554.20 *support life*
make enemies 594.16 *cause hate*; 372.11 *divide*
make equal 708.16 *cancel out*
make even 298.10 *make regular*
make every second count 262.2 *make haste*
make evident 716.10
make exception 136.15 *modify*
make excuses 634.5 *shirk*
make excuses for 714.8 *justify*
make exempt 16.78 *acquit*
make extra demands 261.6 *fatigue*
make eyes 593.26 *court*
make eyes at 518.13 *look*
make faces 234.10
make faces at 668.26 *cock a snook*
make famous 740.16 *publicize*
make fast 253.14; 228.7 *make stable*; 50.15 *sail*
make fertile 562.7
make few demands 648.3 *be lenient*
make fine 698.31 *be accurate*
make fine adjustments 698.31 *be accurate*
make firm 253.14 *make fast*
make fluid 431.22
make for 302.8, 392.28 *further*; 323.9 *navigate*; 324.7 *take a direction*
make fragrant 498.8 *sweeten*
make free with 659.7 *be discourteous*; 660.22 *be rude*; 250.19 *liberalize*
make fresh 256.13 *clean*
make friendly overtures to 569.14 *seek the friendship of*
make friends 569.13 *befriend*; 654.13 *fraternize*; 749.5 *make peace*
make friends with 569.13 *befriend*; 374.6 *come together*
make full 406.7 *stuff*
make fun of 599.13 *be humorous*; 668.24, 678.14 *ridicule*; 700.28 *trick*
make glow 338.3 *invigorate*
make good 312.9 *achieve*; 807.5 *atone*; 248.5 *be prosperous*; 246.6 *be successful*; 775.5 *compensate*; 119.11 *equalize*; 244.2 *get better*; 244.3 *rectify*; 393.1 *repair*; 436.6 *replenish*; 385.3 *retaliate*; 454.1 *verify*; 714.7 *vindicate*
make good one's escape 389.5 *escape*
make good progress 302.2 *start*
make good time 302.4
make green 538.17 *green*
make happen 346.8 *activate*; 344.9 *be the cause of*
make happy 749.4 *pacify*
make hard 418.9 *harden*
make haste 262.2
make hay of 349.3 *exploit*
make headway 765.10 *augment*; 244.2 *get better*; 302.1 *go forward*
make headway against 246.7 *overcome obstacles*
make healthy 259.7; 244.1 *improve*
make heavy 414.14
make heavy weather of 264.18 *find difficult*
make hell freeze over 103.10 *attempt the impossible*
make history 340.4 *act*; 462.15 *be remembered*
make horizontal 187.7
make human 566.14
make hygienic 257.6
make ignorant 456.11
make ill 249.11 *cause adversity*
make illegal 16.75; 16.79 *convict*; 399.3 *veto*
make illegible 358.1 *obliterate*
make immaculate 256.13 *clean*

make immovable 253.14 *make fast*
make immune 16.78 *acquit*
make impatient 625.8 *make irascible*
make important **123.8**; 738.3 *reveal*
make impossible 103.8; 708.10 *be negative*
make impotent **335.9**
make improvements 244.1 *improve*; 244.3 *rectify*
make inactive **343.14**; 245.4 *impair*; 238.8 *make useless*
make incumbent 810.17 *impose a duty*
make indifferent **618.13**
make inferior 387.6 *subject*
make infertile **563.8**
make initial progress 302.2 *start*
make inoperative 245.4 *impair*
make inroads 329.5 *transgress*
make inroads on 441.1 *waste*
make insane **461.15**
make insensitive 618.13 *make indifferent*
make insufficient **218.7**
make into 760.9 *transform*
make into a novel 17.21 *write*
make into a play 17.21 *write*
make into a whole 232.4 *complete*
make invisible **521.8**
make irascible **625.8**
make irritable **626.12**
make it 312.9 *achieve*; 248.5 *be prosperous*; 246.6 *be successful*; 244.2 *get better*; 781.13 *get rich*; 312.2 *reach*
make it all square 119.10 *be equal*; 216.10 *make average*
make it big 123.7 *be important*; 244.2 *get better*
make it easy for 757.4 *be permissive*
make it one's aim 353.1 *attempt*
make it one's duty 810.15 *be liable*; 756.8 *guarantee*
make it tough for 264.23 *cause difficulties*
make It up 649.9 *forgive*; 749.5 *make peace*
make it with 593.29 *make love*
make jealous 629.7 *arouse jealousy*
make known 693.12 *communicate*; 739.5 *disclose*; 740.13 *make public*
make lame 238.8 *make useless*
make larger 190.5 *make bigger*
make law 397.9 *command*
make laws 16.68 *legislate*
make leeway 302.3 *press on*
make legal **16.65**; 396.21 *grant authority*; 579.1 *manage*; 757.3 *permit*
make less 214.5 *make smaller*
make light 415.10 *lighten*
make lighter 415.10 *lighten*
make light of 265.17 *do easily*; 728.22 *play down*; 468.3 *underestimate*
make light work of 265.17 *do easily*
make like 115.12 *imitate*; 699.24 *pretend*
make likely 104.9 *make probable*
make like new 393.3 *restore*
make little of 468.3 *underestimate*
make love **593.29**; 561.14 *have sex*
make love to 490.9 *give pleasure*
make mad 624.14 *make angry*; 380.9 *make violent*
make matters up 807.5 *atone*
make merry 490.8 *feel pleasure*; 600.5 *rejoice*
make mincemeat of 357.9 *demolish*; 357.11 *ruin*
make mincemeat of someone 121.8 *be superior*
make mischief 662.15 *be disobedient*; 379.2 *trap*
make money 785.12 *be profitable*; 248.5 *be prosperous*; 246.6 *be successful*; 797.21 *do well*; 765.9 *gain*; 781.13 *get rich*
make money by 765.12 *earn*
make more 213.5 *make bigger*
make motionless **301.9**
make much ado 123.8 *make important*
make much of 727.10 *boast*; 593.23 *love*; 123.8 *make important*; 740.16 *publicize*; 601.18 *salute*
make music 18.36 *play*
make mute 730.15 *strike dumb*
make mutual concessions 754.4 *compromise*
make mysterious **737.14**
make neat 256.13 *clean*; 244.1 *improve*
make neutral 708.16 *cancel out*
make new **295.20**
make noble **573.5**
make no bones about 707.21 *be assertive*; 738.4 *show oneself*
make no comment 737.12 *keep secret*
make no confession 809.5 *be impenitent*
make no demands 265.15 *be easy*; 648.3 *be lenient*
make no difference 119.11 *equalize*
make no impact upon 618.16 *be mediocre*
make no impression 124.11 *be unimportant*
make no mistake 695.7 *recognize*
make no mystery 738.4 *show oneself*
make no noise 506.1 *be silent*
make no point 270.6 *be circuitous*
make no profit 766.10 *have a financial loss*
make no secret of 738.4 *show oneself*
make no sign 737.12 *keep secret*
make notes 744.14 *inscribe*
make nothing of 696.9 *find unintelligible*
make no use of 441.1 *waste*
make no waves 388.3 *submit*
make nude **552.15**
make null and void 16.77 *annul*; 708.14 *cancel*
make obeisance 367.9 *bow*; 658.13 *defer to*; 664.10 *knuckle under*; 667.19 *take off one's hat to*
make obligatory 397.10 *demand*
make obscure **266.3**
make obvious 738.3 *reveal*
make off 313.4 *hurry off*; 634.8 *run away*
make off-limits 399.3 *veto*
make off with 774.12 *steal*
make one 197.19 *become one*; 570.16 *join in marriage*; 255.11 *simplify*
make one eat dirt 623.17 *humiliate*
make one fed-up 620.6 *be boring*
make one feel small 623.17 *humiliate*
make one jump 630.9 *surprise*
make one laugh **272.7**
make one look silly 700.28 *trick*
make one more 211.7 *support*
make one of us 480.15 *persuade*
make one's adieus 313.6 *part*
make one's apologies 807.6 *apologize*
make one's contribution 211.6 *add*
make one's daily round 298.8 *be cyclic*
make one's debut 130.27 *emerge*
make one's defence 16.72 *stand trial*
make oneself 637.10 *grudge*
make oneself at home 250.17 *be informal*; 657.11 *not stand on ceremony*; 654.12 *visit*
make oneself attractive 593.28 *win the love of*
make oneself felt 395.8 *influence*
make oneself liable 810.15 *be liable*
make oneself responsible 784.7 *be in debt*
make oneself scarce 98.16 *absent oneself*; 389.5 *escape*; 313.4 *hurry off*; 262.2 *make haste*; 634.8 *run away*
make oneself useful 237.9 *be useful*; 392.17 *help*; 401.8 *serve*
make oneself welcome 654.12 *visit*
make one's excuses 709.5 *refuse*
make one's exit 313.2 *withdraw*
make one's eyes open 619.10 *be wonderful*
make one's fortune 248.5 *be prosperous*; 781.13 *get rich*
make one's gorge rise 364.4 *be repulsive*
make one's head spin 457.10 *bemuse*
make one's head swim 690.9 *be intoxicating*; 696.7 *be unintelligible*; 619.10 *be wonderful*
make one sick 596.7 *cause dislike*
make one's mark 248.5 *be prosperous*; 246.6 *be successful*
make one's mouth water 617.15 *cause desire*; 480.16 *tempt*
make one's name 740.16 *publicize*
make one's nest 565.18 *take up residence*
make one's own 765.9 *gain*; 139.26 *personalize*
make one's plle 248.5 *be prosperous*; 765.14 *profit*
make one's point 483.9 *motivate*
make one's presence felt 97.12 *attend*
make one's quarry 633.12 *aim at*
make one's rounds 306.7 *ring*
make one's submission 476.6 *propound*
make one's voice heard 395.8 *influence*
make one's way **302.7**; 300.13 *be in motion*; 244.2 *get better*
make one tired 620.6 *be boring*
make one yawn 620.6 *be boring*
make opaque **528.11**
make operate 346.8 *activate*
make operational 346.8 *activate*; 243.4 *prepare for action*
make ordinary 298.10 *make regular*
make or mar 344.9 *be the cause of*; 395.9 *change*
make out 221.6 *be in a state of*; 719.9 *decipher*; 593.27 *kiss*; 695.7 *recognize*; 518.12 *see*
make-out artist 593.9 *lover*
make over 768.5 *give*; 393.2 *refurbish*; 316.11 *transfer*
make overtures 569.13 *befriend*; 746.5 *negotiate*
make overtures to 710.6 *request*
make overweight 414.14 *make heavy*
make passes 593.26 *court*
make peace **589.6**; **749.5**; 649.9 *forgive*; 749.4 *pacify*; 226.9 *pause*
make periodical **276.11**
make permanent **225.6**; **279.7**
make plain 738.3 *reveal*; 695.5 *simplify*
make play with 349.3 *exploit*
make pleasant 498.8 *sweeten*
make pointed 425.15 *make sharp*
make poor 782.14 *impoverish*
make porous 308.20 *hole*
make port 312.4 *land*; 323.10 *sail*
make possible **102.7**; 265.16 *make easy*; 757.3 *permit*
make pregnant 561.13 *propagate*
make preparations 243.1 *prepare*
make probable **104.9**
make progress 342.13 *be busy*; 134.3 *continue*; 244.2 *get better*; 302.1 *go forward*
make proposals 746.6 *make conditions*
make proud **622.30**
make provision 436.5 *provision*
make public **740.13**
make quiet 506.2 *silence*
Maker 344.7 *Prime Mover*
maker 578.3 *agent*; 130.16 *originator*; 356.9 *producer*
make rapid strides 765.10 *augment*
make ready 6.22 *educate*; 352.6 *find means*; 243.1 *prepare*; 243.4 *prepare for action*; 436.5 *provision*
make real **95.11**; 402.8 *be material*
make red 535.9 *redden*
make redress 775.5 *compensate*
make redundant 226.8 *cause to cease*; 15.11 *conduct industrial relations*; 371.2, 580.5, 767.10 *dismiss*; 128.8 *eject*; 144.17 *relegate*; 350.7 *stop work*
make reference to 738.3 *reveal*
make regular **298.10**
make reparation 813.11 *pay*
make reparation for 801.15 *put right*
make reparations 775.5 *compensate*
make restitution 775.4 *give back*; 761.7 *restore*
make rich **781.15**
make right 807.5 *atone*
make rivers run uphill 103.10 *attempt the impossible*
make room 146.4 *space*
make room for 141.21 *space*
make rough **420.12**
make round **181.11**; 179.7 *make circular*
make routine 298.10 *make regular*
make safe 252.10 *protect*; 253.10 *secure*
make sane 460.6 *be sane*
make sense 695.4 *be intelligible*; 444.12 *be reasonable*
make sense of 719.8 *interpret*
make shallow **157.7**
make shapeless **161.3**
make sharp **425.15**
makeshift 484.3 *expedient plan*; 231.6 *imperfect item*; 478.1 *improvised*; 231.2 *incomplete*; 218.8 *insufficiency*; 352.1 *means*; 122.14 *poor*; 243.16 *preparatory*; 762.7 *substitute*; 217.1 *sufficient*; 349.9 *used*
make shift to 353.1 *attempt*
make shift with 349.5 *dispose of*
make shipshape 244.1 *improve*; 178.10 *straighten*
make short shrift of 628.6 *be pitiless*
make short work of 265.17 *do easily*; 557.22 *eat well*; 262.2 *make haste*; 357.11 *ruin*; 342.15 *try*; 576.6 *work*
make silent 506.2 *silence*
make similar **115.11**
make simple 271.7 *be simple*; 255.11 *simplify*
make small 245.5 *hurt*
make smaller **191.5**; **214.5**; 416.9 *make dense*
make smell like roses 699.28 *mask*
make someone 593.29 *make love*; 740.16 *publicize*
make someone believe **450.9**
make someone eat dust 262.2 *make haste*
make someone jump 612.13 *frighten*
make someone's blood boil 624.14 *make angry*
make someone's ears burn 504.15 *hear*
make someone's hackles rise 492.12 *abut*
make someone's mouth water 483.9 *motivate*
make something happen 638.10 *insist*
make sore 624.14 *make angry*
make sound 253.14 *make fast*
make sparse **417.6**
make speeches 729.14 *speak to*
make spherical 181.11 *make round*
make stable **228.7**
make steadfast 253.14 *make fast*
make straight 178.10 *straighten*
make strides 302.3 *press on*
make strong 336.8 *strengthen*
make sullen **626.10**
make sure 616.5 *be cautious*; 452.21 *make certain*; 228.7 *make stable*
make taboo 399.4 *censor*
make tangible 698.28 *bring into existence*
make taste **495.10**
make terms 750.23 *arrange*; 755.5 *contract*
make the air blue 712.5 *curse*
make the big time 246.6 *be successful*
make the desert bloom 562.7 *make fertile*
make the effort 353.1 *attempt*
make the first move 130.21 *pioneer*
make the front page 740.18 *become famous*
make the grade 312.9 *achieve*; 246.6 *be successful*; 244.2 *get better*; 217.4 *suffice*
make the most of 340.4 *act*; 349.5 *dispose of*; 349.3 *exploit*; 244.1 *improve*; 467.4 *overestimate*
make the point 705.20 *doubt*
make the rubble bounce 381.3 *bomb*
make the running 332.6 *accelerate*; 329.3 *exceed*
make the same **111.8**
make the sparks fly 342.15 *try*
make the supreme sacrifice 582.16 *meet one's fate*
make the welkin ring 507.8 *be loud*
make thin **153.16**
make things awkward 264.23 *cause difficulties*
make things difficult 264.24 *create difficulties*; 103.8 *make impossible*
make things easy for 483.9 *motivate*; 480.16 *tempt*
make things hum 342.15 *try*
make things worse 264.23 *cause difficulties*; 245.3 *make worse*
make tidy 256.13 *clean*
make time for 768.5 *give*
make to order 551.35 *make clothing*
make tough **423.11**
make tracks 332.4 *be swift*; 313.1 *depart*; 262.2 *make haste*; 634.8 *run away*
make transient **278.5**
make transparent **527.12**
make trouble 408.26 *be disorderly*; 586.36 *combat*; 751.7 *pick a fight*
make ugly **546.5**; 245.5 *hurt*
make unbreakable 423.11 *make tough*
make uncertain **453.20**
make unclean 258.11 *dirty*; 245.3 *make worse*; 351.1 *misuse*
make uniform **750.26**; 698.31 *be accurate*; 298.10 *make regular*; 255.11 *simplify*; 162.6 *symmetrize*
make unimportant **124.13**
make unintelligible **696.8**
make unlike 116.6 *differentiate*

make unwelcome 659.7 *be discourteous*; 472.13 *be thoughtless*; 470.3 *exclude*; 364.3 *fend off*; 371.4 *ostracize*
make up 529.16; **547.16**; 127.5 *be included*; 93.20 *bring into being*; 374.5 *combine*; 232.4 *complete*; 405.10 *compose*; 116.3 *disguise*; 406.8 *embody*; 96.17 *fabricate*; 477.14 *imagine*; 244.1 *improve*; 405.13 *make*; 356.10 *produce*; 436.6 *replenish*
make-up 125.4 *camouflage*; 529.9 *complexion*; 374.4 *compound*; 406.1 *contents*; 547.4 *cosmetics*; 551.5 *fancy dress*; 403.3 *form*; 160.4 *forming*; 127.1 *inclusion*; 99.4 *nature*; 139.2 *personality*; 21.21 *stage requisite*
make up an account 789.7 *account*
make-up artist 547.13 *beautician*; 21.28 *stagehand*
make-up box 547.5
make up for 807.5 *atone*
make up leeway 302.4 *make good time*
make-up man 21.28 *stagehand*
make up one's mind 638.7 *resolve*; 469.1 *select*
make up the numbers 211.7 *support*
make up the shortfall 211.6 *add*
make uptight 625.8 *make irascible*
make up time 332.6 *accelerate*
make up to 677.10 *cajole*; 664.9 *fawn*; 569.14 *seek the friendship of*
make useless 238.8
make use of 237.11 *find useful*; 664.15 *sponge*; 349.1 *use*
make vertical 186.6
make violent 380.9
make visible 518.18; **520.10**
make war 585.13 *be at war*
make waves 123.7 *be important*; 118.18 *not conform*
make way 323.9 *navigate*
make way for 634.1 *avoid*; 265.16 *make easy*; 325.8 *sidestep*; 388.3 *submit*
make weak 337.7 *weaken*
makeweight 119.4 *equilizer*; 232.2 *fullness*; 414.10 *scales*
make welcome 654.11 *be sociable*; 769.10 *receive someone*
make well 393.6 *cure*; 259.7 *make healthy*; 749.4 *pacify*
make whole 232.4 *complete*; 393.3 *restore*
make whoopee 593.27 *kiss*; 600.5 *rejoice*
make wicked 804.17
make work 346.8 *activate*; 342.15 *try*; 576.6 *work*
make-work 15.9 *negotiated*
make-work rules 15.2 *industrial negotiations*
make worse 245.3; 607.6 *aggravate*
make yellow 537.10
make young 555.17
make yourself at home 312.24 *welcome!*
making 312.17 *achievement*; 243.13 *development*; 356.2 *manufacture*; 356.1 *production*; 403.5 *structuring*
making a break 65.3 *English billiards*
making amends 807.1 *atonement*; 807.4 *atoning*; 775.2 *compensation*
making a prisoner 773.3 *taking away*
making a profit 237.4 *profitable*
making arrangements 409.11 *arrangements*
making dim 524.3 *dimming*
making equal 708.7 *cancelling out*
making friends 569.1 *friendship*
making good 807.1 *atonement*; 775.2 *compensation*; 244.6 *rectification*
making infertile 563.2
making it with 593.5 *desire*
making light 522.3 *lightening*
making light of 728.9 *downplaying*
making like new 393.8 *repair*
making love 593.5 *desire*
making much of 727.4 *bombast*
making one's own 763.1 *possession*
making out 593.6 *courtship*
making progress 550.22 *progression*
making ready 243.9 *preparation*
making right 807.1 *atonement*
makings 765.4 *earnings*; 765.1 *gain*
making sense 695.1 *intelligible*
making smooth 421.7 *smoothness*
making someone 593.5 *desire*
making terms 746.1 *negotiation*
making tracks 332.8 *speed*
making up for 807.1 *atonement*
making up one's mind 469.6 *selection*
making vertical 186.2
making war 585.8 *warfare*
making whoopee 593.6 *courtship*
malachite 538.11 *green thing*
malacologist 75.15 *invertebrate zoologist*; 70.11 *zoologist*
malacology 70.9 *animal science*; 75.14 *invertebrate zoology*
malacostracan 75.4 *arthropod*
maladjusted 328.16 *deranged*
maladjusted personality 36.8 *disordered personality*
maladminister 486.5 *be unskilful*; 351.1 *misuse*
maladministered 486.4 *bungled*
maladministration 486.9 *bungling*; 351.2 *misuse*
maladroit 486.3 *clumsy*
malady 260.2 *illness*
mala fide 800.11 *dishonourably*
malaise 798.2 *affliction*; 602.2 *depression*; 491.1 *pain*; 260.3 *symptom*
malamute 316.6 *beast of burden*
malapert 660.13 *insolent*
malapropism 5.29 *grammar*; 274.11 *grammatical error*; 272.4 *joke*; 351.2 *misuse*; 697.2 *solecism*
malapropos 288.19 *at the wrong time*; 240.1 *inconvenient*; 288.13 *untimely*
malaria 260.6 *infection*; 432.3 *miasma*; 75.12 *protozoal disease*; 260.7 *tropical disease*
malarial fever 260.6 *infection*; 260.7 *tropical disease*
Malathion™ 44.8 *weedkiller*
Malawi 88.5 *other major lakes*
Malay 5.11 *family of languages*
malaya 25.49 *Indian dish*
Malayo-Polynesian 5.11 *family of languages*
malcological 75.19 *molluscan*
malcontent 264.9 *difficult person*; 606.4 *dissatisfied*; 606.3 *dissatisfied person*; 662.6 *nonconformist*; 753.4 *protester*; 753.9 *protesting*
malcontented 606.4 *dissatisfied*
Male 567
male 567.2; **567.17**; 78.12 *of flowers*
male animal 567.16
male bird 72.10
male chauvinism 567.1 *male sex*; 466.4 *social discrimination*
male chauvinist 466.7 *bigot*; 653.2 *misanthrope*
male chauvinist pig 466.7 *bigot*; 567.6 *macho man*; 653.2 *misanthrope*
malediction 712.4; 798.4 *evil power*; 236.11 *harmfulness*; 594.1 *hate*
maledictive 712.10; 594.10 *hating*
maledictively 594.18 *hatefully*
maledictory 712.10 *maledictive*
male-dominated society 567.1 *male sex*
male exclusiveness 567.1 *male sex*
malefactor 651.8; 340.3 *doer*; 798.6 *evil person*; 806.4 *guilty person*; 16.40 *lawbreaker*; 804.9 *wicked person*; 802.10 *wrongdoer*
male feminist 567.14 *liberated man*
malefic 236.5 *harmful*; 651.10 *malevolent*
maleficence 798.1 *evil*; 651.1 *malevolence*
maleficent 798.7 *evil*; 804.11 *wicked*
male mammal 71.17
male member 561.8 *organs of reproduction*
male menopause 556.4 *middle age*
male model 738.12 *displayer*; 551.27 *model*
male nurse 35.16 *nurse*
male person 567.2 *male*
male pill 563.3 *birth control*
male prostitute 796.8 *immoral man*; 567.7 *libertine*
male rape 380.2 *physical violence*
male sex 567.1
male sex organs 561.8 *organs of reproduction*
male stripper 552.8 *nude person*
male title of address 567.3
Malevolence 651
malevolence 651.1; 798.1 *evil*; 236.11 *harmfulness*; 594.1 *hate*; 653.1 *misanthropy*; 395.2 *occult influence*; 804.1 *wickedness*
malevolent 651.10; 798.7 *evil*; 236.5 *harmful*; 594.10 *hating*; 714.14 *vindictive*; 804.11 *wicked*
malevolently 651.20; 798.12 *evilly*; 594.18 *hatefully*; 714.16 *vindictively*; 804.18 *wickedly*
malfeasance 16.39 *crime*
malfeasant 651.8 *malefactor*
malform 234.11 *deform*
malformation 234.3 *deformity*
malformed 234.7 *deformed*
malfunction 247.9; 238.7 *be useless*; 378.9 *block*; 802.24 *go wrong*; 378.2 *obstacle*
malfunctioning 378.14 *blocked*; 802.18 *gone wrong*
malice 798.1 *evil*; 236.11 *harmfulness*; 594.1 *hate*; 651.1 *malevolence*; 624.1 *resentment*
malice aforethought 594.1 *hate*; 651.1 *malevolence*
malicious 798.7 *evil*; 236.5 *harmful*; 594.10 *hating*; 651.10 *malevolent*; 624.15 *resentful*; 714.14 *vindictive*
malicious gossip 678.3 *defamation*
maliciously 798.12 *evilly*; 594.18 *hatefully*; 651.20 *malevolently*; 624.17 *resentfully*; 714.16 *vindictively*
maliciousness 651.1 *malevolence*
malign 381.10 *criticize*; 678.12 *defame*; 236.5 *harmful*; 651.10 *malevolent*; 802.20 *wrong*
malignance 651.1 *malevolence*
malignancy 798.2 *affliction*; 236.11 *harmfulness*
malignant 382.23 *deadly*; 798.9 *detrimental*; 798.7 *evil*; 236.5 *harmful*; 594.10 *hating*; 651.10 *malevolent*
malignant growth 345.3 *growth*
malignantly 594.18 *hatefully*; 382.25 *lethally*
malignant tumour 260.12 *cancer*
malign influence 249.3 *bad fortune*; 798.4 *evil power*; 395.2 *occult influence*
maligning 381.25 *critical*
malignity 798.1 *evil*; 236.11 *harmfulness*; 594.1 *hate*; 651.1 *malevolence*; 523.7 *spiritual darkness*
malinger 699.23 *be deceitful*; 634.5 *shirk*
malingerer 700.15 *deceiver*; 260.19 *sick person*
malingering 699.33 *deceitful*; 699.5 *deceitfulness*
malison 712.4 *malediction*
mall 173.4 *centre of activity*; 779.7 *emporium*
malleability 6.10 *educability*; 663.1 *obedience*; 117.3 *pliancy*; 419.8 *softness*; 483.6 *suggestibility*
malleable 117.11 *conformable*; 6.17 *educable*; 227.14 *irresolute*; 663.7 *obedient*; 419.2 *pliant*; 388.5 *submitting*; 483.13 *suggestible*; 265.12 *wieldy*
malleably 117.16 *adaptably*; 6.26 *studiously*
mallet 331.15 *ram*; 19.14 *sculptor's materials*
malleus 504.5 *internal ear*
mallophagan 76.10 *insectan*
malnourished 153.2 *emaciated*; 260.21 *unhealthy*
malnutrition 260.4 *disease*; 153.8 *emaciation*; 218.8 *insufficiency*; 557.10 *scarcity*
maloccio 712.4 *malediction*
malodorous 503.3 *stinking*; 258.8 *unclean*
malodorously 503.6 *stinkingly*
malodorousness 503.1 *stench*
malodour 503.1 *stench*
malpractice 16.39 *crime*; 351.2 *misuse*; 806.3 *sin*
malt bread 25.38 *bread*
malt culms 43.9 *animal feedstuff*
malted milk 558.5 *milk*
malt house 577.1 *workshop*
Malthusianism 245.7 *deterioration*
malting 577.1 *workshop*
malt liquor 558.7 *alcoholic drink*
maltreat 798.11 *be evil*; 236.14 *ill-treat*; 351.1 *misuse*; 651.18 *torment*; 802.20 *wrong*
maltreated 351.4 *misused*
maltreatment 651.7 *act of malevolence*; 236.11 *harmfulness*; 351.2 *misuse*
malt vinegar 25.7 *basic ingredient*
Malvern Hills 89.5 *British mountains*
mamaloi 7.8 *priest*
mamba 73.3 *snake*
mambo 22.2 *dance*
Mameluke 586.6 *militarist*
mamilla 182.2 *bulge*; 71.2 *mammalian characteristic*
mamma 71.2 *mammalian characteristic*
mammal 71.1; 70.4 *type of animal*
mammal hunting 71.23
Mammalia 71.1 *mammal*
mammalian 71.25
mammalian characteristic 71.2
mammal-like 71.25 *mammalian*
mammal-like reptile 73.6 *extinct reptile*
Mammals 71
mammals 554.9 *classifications of life*
mammary 559.5 *of a secretion*
mammary gland 559.3 *gland*; 71.2 *mammalian characteristic*
mammogram 35.7 *diagnosis*
mammography 35.7 *diagnosis*
mammologist 71.22; 70.11 *zoologist*
mammology 70.9 *animal science*; 71.1 *mammal*
mammon 780.2 *cash*; 781.6 *money*
Mammonism 9.2 *idolatry*
Mammonist 9.6 *idolater*
Mammonistic 9.10 *idolatrous*
mammonolater 9.6 *idolater*
mammonolatrous 9.10 *idolatrous*
mammonolatry 9.2 *idolatry*
mammoth 158.15 *big*; 158.9 *big thing*; 284.10 *fossilization*
mammothermography 35.7 *diagnosis*
mammy 252.3 *protector*
man 556.8; 664.5 *adherent*; 401.6 *domestic servant*; 384.21 *entrench*; 243.5 *equip*; 566.1 *humankind*; 567.2 *male*; 567.1 *male sex*; 567.3 *male title of address*; 566.7 *person*; 436.5 *provision*; 664.3 *sycophant*; 346.9 *take action*
mana 8.5 *deity*; 334.1 *power*
man about the house 567.13 *man in the family*
man about town 485.5 *expert*; 654.6 *social person*
manacle 373.12 *bind*; 251.12 *gag*
manacled 373.16 *bound*
manacles 373.8 *fastening*; 251.5 *means of restraint*
manage 579.1; 340.4 *act*; 344.10 *awaken*; 631.14 *behave towards*; 221.6 *be in a state of*; 334.10 *be powerful*; 140.16 *direct*; 12.11 *govern*; 396.18 *have authority*; 121.10 *lead*; 409.18 *make arrangements*; 400.14 *master*; 407.18 *order*; 246.7 *overcome obstacles*; 346.9 *take action*; 354.1 *undertake*
manageability 265.3 *wieldiness*
manageable 636.3 *amenable*; 793.9 *cheap*; 663.7 *obedient*; 413.10 *supportable*; 265.12 *wieldy*; 346.11 *workable*
managed 14.6 *financial*; 15.8 *industrial*
managed currency 14.1, 780.7 *finance*; 780.1 *money*
manage grassland 81.12
Management 579
management 346.4; **579.3**; 340.1 *action*; 140.8 *authority*; 396.4 *governance*; 579.6 *governing body*; 12.1 *government*; 15.1 *industrial relations*; 121.2 *leadership*; 631.8 *treatment*; 349.6 *use*
management accounting 789.1 *accounts*
management buyout 13.7 *corporation*; 777.7 *purchasing*
management by objectives 484.1 *plan*
management consultant 713.4 *adviser*
management demands 15.1 *industrial relations*
management-employee relations 15.1 *industrial relations*
management engineering 38.1 *engineering*
management lock-out 15.4 *industrial dispute*
management practices 15.1 *industrial relations*
management review 484.2 *policy*
management study 579.3 *management*
manager 579.15; 578.3 *agent*; 48.2 *baseball player*; 52.4 *boxer*; 400.5 *company leader*; 579.13 *director*; 340.3 *doer*; 15.6 *employer*; 395.5 *influential person*; 480.14, 483.7 *motivator*; 346.5 *operator*; 396.10 *person of authority*; 484.8 *planner*; 21.27 *producer*; 121.5 *superior*
manageress 579.15 *manager*
managerial 579.17; 340.6 *effective*; 354.6 *enterprising*; 396.14 *governmental*; 15.8 *industrial*; 400.12 *masterful*

managerial control 579.4 *directorship*
managerially **579.19**; 15.13 *industrially*; 400.16 *masterfully*
managers 579.6 *governing body*
managership 579.3 *management*
manage trees **79.18**
managing 324.5 *directions*; 15.8 *industrial*; 579.3 *management*; 579.17 *managerial*
managing director 340.3 *doer*; 15.6 *employer*; 579.15 *manager*
managing editor 741.4 *journalist*; 740.12 *publisher*
mañana 286.3 *another time*; 294.3 *delayed action*; 283.1 *future time*
mañana attitude 637.15 *delay*
man and beast 113.3 *opposites*
man and wife 570.9 *married couple*
man a ship 323.9 *navigate*
man-at-arms 586.17 *army person*; 586.20 *cavalryman*; 586.1 *combatant*; 586.8 *soldier*
man at the top 566.7 *person*
man at the wheel 323.7 *nautical person*
Manchester 87.4 *British cities*
Manchu 5.11 *family of languages*
man-crazy 796.13 *unchaste*
Mancunian 564.9 *British inhabitant*
mandala 179.2 *circle*; 742.1 *sign*; 11.6 *talisman*
mandamus 16.6 *legal process*
mandarin 123.4 *bigwig*; 400.3 *leader*; 579.16 *official*; 536.3 *orange thing*
Mandarin collar 551.14 *neckwear*
mandate 669.1 *approval*; 397.4 *authorization*; 397.13 *authorize*; 386.2 *coercion*; 386.6 *compel*; 85.3 *dominion*; 85.18 *exert sovereignty*; 12.1 *government*; 396.8 *governmental organization*; 16.2 *jurisdiction*; 757.1 *permission*; 484.2 *policy*; 12.5 *political organization*; 713.3 *precept*; 136.6 *specification*; 86.4 *territorial division*
mandated 85.16 *national*; 397.15 *self-assured*
mandated territory 85.3 *dominion*; 12.1 *government*; 12.5 *political organization*
mandatory 397.14 *commanding*; 386.10 *compulsory*; 136.12 *conditional*; 85.3 *dominion*; 99.5 *essential*; 140.9 *legal*; 810.12 *obligatory*
mandibles 557.16 *eating utensil*
mandrel 307.4 *axle*
manducate 557.21 *eat*
manducation 557.1 *eating*
man-eater 363.6 *charmer*; 557.18 *eater*; 633.6 *hunter*; 382.10 *killer*
man-eating 557.26 *eating*; 557.5 *eating habit*; 382.24 *murderous*
manège 59.6 *horsemanship*
manes 11.11 *ghost*
man Friday 348.3 *assistant*; 392.11 *helper*; 401.5 *office assistant*
man from Mars 100.6 *outsider*
manfully 638.17 *resolutely*
manganese 33.15 *essential element*
manganic 32.34 *elemental*
manganous 32.34 *elemental*
mange 260.13 *skin disease*; 260.18 *veterinary disease*
mangels 43.12 *crop*
manginess 260.1 *ill health*
mangle 256.13 *clean*; 191.4 *contractor*; 428.23 *drip-dry*; 428.15 *dryer*; 369.9 *extractor*; 187.4 *flattener*; 491.11 *inflict pain*; 421.11 *smooth*; 421.9 *smoother*
mangled 428.4 *dried-out*; 233.4 *incomplete*; 236.2 *inferior*
mangonel 330.9 *firearm*; 587.6 *historical missile weapon*
mangrove sudd 92.3 *marsh*
mangy 260.23 *diseased*; 236.4 *poor*; 793.10 *shoddy*; 258.8 *unclean*; 260.21 *unhealthy*
manhandle 351.1 *misuse*; 316.15 *take away*; 316.12 *transport*
man-hater 594.9 *hater*; 653.2 *misanthrope*
man-hating 653.3 *misanthropic*
Manhattan 558.8 *mixed drink*; 87.3 *New York*
manhole 308.7 *passageway*
manhood 556.2 *adulthood*; 567.1 *male sex*
manhood suffrage 469.11 *franchise*
man-hour 276.4 *period of activity*
man-hours 576.2 *task*
manhunt 633.1 *pursuit*
mania 36.15 *compulsion*; 461.4 *delusion*; 590.4 *emotion*; 632.1 *habit*; 595.3 *likes*
maniac 461.7 *insane person*
manic **461.12**; 342.18 *active*; 590.13 *passionate*
manic-depressive 227.5 *changeable person*; 461.7 *insane person*
manic-depressive psychosis 36.11, 461.5 *psychosis*
Manichaeism 4.7 *school of thought*
manicure 547.3 *beauty treatment*
manicured 543.3 *elegant*
manicure set 547.5 *make-up box*
manicurist 547.13 *beautician*
manifest **738.14**; 520.9 *appear*; 525.7 *appearing*; 220.4 *bill*; 703.15 *demonstrate*; 703.9 *demonstrated*; 739.5 *disclose*; 738.1 *display*; 527.4 *easily seen through*; 716.9 *evident*; 93.10 *existing*; 178.5 *honourable*; 520.10 *make visible*; 308.13 *opened up*; 97.7 *present*; 717.9 *represent*; 738.3 *reveal*; 789.4 *statement*; 518.23, 520.1 *visible*; 740.20 *well-known*
manifestation **520.5**; **738.10**; 525.1 *appearance*; 703.1 *demonstration*; 449.7 *detection*; 739.1 *disclosure*; 716.3 *evidentness*; 11.11 *ghost*; 97.6 *ghostly presence*; 402.2 *materialization*; 97.1 *presence*; 740.7 *publicity*; 717.1 *representation*; 742.4 *signal*
manifested 738.13 *displayed*
manifesting 739.12 *revelatory*
manifestly **703.20**; **738.16**; 525.15 *apparently*; 716.15 *evidently*; 308.25 *obviously*; 449.16 *originally*; 93.22 *really*; 518.25, 520.11 *visibly*
manifestness 738.10 *manifestation*; 97.1 *presence*
manifesto 397.1 *command*; 469.12 *election*; 4.2 *philosophical system*; 484.2 *policy*; 740.1 *publication*; 450.2 *religious belief*; 707.2 *statement*
manifold 114.5 *diverse*; 207.8 *multiplicative*; 208.5 *multitudinous*; 27.47 *topology*
manikin 717.6 *image*; 159.4 *little person*
man in the family **567.13**
man in the moon 29.17 *moon*
man in the street 216.7 *average person*; 138.9 *everyman*; 566.7 *person*
man-in-the-street 574.1 *plebeian*
maniple 586.16 *army unit*; 7.11 *vestment*
manipulatable 346.11 *workable*
manipulate **27.92**; **483.10**; 340.4 *act*; 631.14 *behave towards*; 631.11 *conduct oneself*; 394.20 *doctor*; 699.26 *falsify*; 396.18 *have authority*; 579.1 *manage*; 484.13 *plot*; 702.11 *practise sophistry*; 346.9 *take action*; 773.10 *take away*; 492.11 *touch*; 700.28 *trick*; 349.1 *use*
manipulated 700.36 *deceived*; 699.36 *falsified*
manipulate market prices 776.2 *speculate*
manipulate the truth 720.1 *misinterpret*
manipulating 702.8 *cunning*; 492.2 *touching*
manipulation 396.1 *authority*; 702.3 *cunning*; 27.24 *evaluation*; 699.9 *falsification*; 346.4, 579.3 *management*; 720.2 *misinterpretation*; 351.2 *misuse*; 484.4 *plot*; 773.3 *taking away*; 394.13 *therapy*; 631.8 *treatment*; 700.7 *tricking*
manipulative 699.33 *deceitful*; 773.12 *taking*
manipulatively 773.13 *avariciously*
manipulative treatment 35.8 *treatment*
manipulator 340.3 *doer*; 395.5 *influential person*; 480.14, 483.7 *motivator*
Manitoba 88.5 *other major lakes*
manitou 8.5 *deity*
mankind 566.1 *humankind*; 654.7 *human society*; 554.1 *life*; 567.1 *male sex*
mankind-hater 653.2 *misanthrope*
manky 236.4 *poor*; 258.8 *unclean*
manlike 567.17 *male*
manliness 613.2 *heroism*; 567.1 *male sex*; 336.1 *strength*
manly 545.5 *beautiful*; 613.10 *chivalrous*; 567.17 *male*; 336.9 *physically strong*
man-mad 796.13 *unchaste*
man-made 96.12 *artificial*; 125.13 *imitation*; 700.39 *imitative*; 356.12 *produced*
man-made lake 700.6 *imitation*; 88.1 *lake*
man-management 579.3 *management*
man mountain 158.10 *big person*
manna 557.7 *food*; 554.3 *life requirements*; 768.3 *offering*; 392.3 *sustenance*
mannan 33.4 *polysaccharide*
manned crossing 321.2 *track*
manned flight 29.31 *space travel*
mannequin 738.12 *displayer*; 553.5 *fashion model*
manner 631.1 *conduct*; 525.3 *external appearance*; 352.1 *means*; 221.1 *state*; 724.1 *style*; 137.4 *type*; 317.1 *way*
mannered 676.3 *affected*; 544.9 *inelegant*
mannerism 139.3 *characteristic*; 743.1 *identification*; 118.5 *idiosyncrasy*; 724.1 *style*; 632.2 *tendency*
mannerist 19.29 *realist*
mannerless brat 596.3 *disliked person*
mannerless imp 659.4 *discourteous person*
mannerliness 658.2 *good manners*
mannerly 407.17 *disciplined*
manner of speaking 724.4 *literary style*
manner of working 317.1 *way*
manners 631.1 *conduct*; 795.1 *morality*; 632.5 *tradition*; 631.6 *way of life*
manners and customs 632.4 *custom*
mannish 567.17 *male*
mannishness 567.1 *male sex*
mannitol 33.3 *carbohydrate*
manoeuvrability 250.5 *scope*; 265.3 *wieldiness*
manoeuvrable 250.11 *ranging*; 265.12 *wieldy*; 346.11 *workable*
manoeuvre 340.4 *act*; 585.13 *be at war*; 645.5 *be cunning*; 631.11 *conduct oneself*; 340.2 *deed*; 322.5 *flight*; 579.1 *manage*; 484.13 *plot*; 645.2 *stratagem*; 631.9 *tactics*; 346.9 *take action*; 492.11 *touch*; 349.1 *use*; 300.15 *walk*
manoeuvrer 645.3 *cunning person*; 480.14, 483.7 *motivator*; 484.8 *planner*
manoeuvres 585.6 *art of war*; 631.9 *tactics*
manoeuvring 645.1 *cunning*; 346.4 *management*; 631.9 *tactics*
man of action 342.10 *busy person*; 340.3 *doer*; 302.16 *progressive person*
man of blood 382.10 *killer*; 380.4 *violent creature*
man of dishonour 800.4 *dishonourable person*
man of genius 619.5 *person of wonder*
man of goodwill 650.5 *benevolent person*
man of high standing 811.2 *person of repute*
man of his word 799.3 *honourable person*
man of honour 799.3 *honourable person*; 811.2 *person of repute*
man of impulse 642.4 *capricious person*
man of letters 721.10 *descriptive writer*; 17.15 *literary person*
man of means 248.4 *prosperous person*; 781.10 *wealthy person*
man of peace 589.3 *pacifist*
man of prayer 450.5 *believer*; 7.3 *religious person*
man of property 763.6 *lord*; 440.7 *property man*; 248.4 *prosperous person*
man of straw 639.15 *indecisive person*; 96.5 *insubstantial person*; 124.10 *nonentity*; 335.5 *powerless person*; 157.5 *shallow person*; 337.4 *weakling*
man of substance 763.6 *lord*; 248.4 *prosperous person*
man of taste 549.4 *refined person*
man of the cloth 7.8 *priest*
man of the house 400.1 *master*; 440.7 *property man*
man of the match 246.4 *successful person*
man of the world 485.5 *expert*; 567.7 *libertine*; 556.8 *man*
man of the year 246.4 *successful person*
man-of-war 586.24 *warship*
manometer 26.8 *meter*; 432.15 *vaporimeter*
manometric 26.16 *micrometric*
manometry 26.2 *micrometry*
man on the make 593.9 *lover*
manor 86.13 *locality*; 142.1 *location*; 440.1 *property*
manor house 565.4 *official residence*
manorial **565.16**; 440.8 *propertied*
manorial court 16.19 *law court*
man overboard 390.5 *to the rescue!*
manpower 334.4 *energy*; 576.4 *exertion*; 352.3 *human resources*; 578.4 *personnel*; 334.1 *power*; 376.13 *workforce*
manqué 233.4 *incomplete*
mansard 154.8 *high thing*
mansard roof 20.6 *roof*
man's best friend 71.9 *dog*
manse 565.4 *official residence*; 7.10 *priestly dwelling*
manservant 401.6 *domestic servant*
man's evening dress 523.4 *dark thing*
mansion 356.8 *construction*; 565.4 *official residence*; 440.1 *property*
Mansion House 565.4 *official residence*
man-size 158.15 *big*
manslaughter 382.8 *accidental killing*; 16.39 *crime*; 382.1 *killing*; 382.2 *murder*
mansuetude 658.1 *courtesy*
mantelet 384.7 *armour*
mantelpiece 361.5 *projecting object*; 413.2 *supporting part*
mantelshelf 62.5 *rock face*
manteltree 79.12 *figurative usage*
man the breach 384.21 *entrench*
man the defences 384.21 *entrench*
man the fort 384.21 *entrench*
man the guns 384.21 *entrench*
mantic 475.13 *predicting*
manticore 70.7 *legendary beast*
mantilla 551.15 *headgear*
mantis 76.1 *insect*
mantissa 27.19 *logarithm*; 194.6 *power*
mantis shrimp 75.4 *arthropod*
mantle 551.25 *accessories*; 551.32 *dress*; 30.18 *earth's crust*; 535.9 *redden*; 7.11 *vestment*
mantled 551.29 *dressed*
mantle of snow 31.30 *snow*
mantling 743.8 *heraldic device*
mantology 11.9 *divination*
man-to-man 58.8 *hockey*
man-to-man assignment 58.3 *ice hockey*
man-to-man defence 46.10 *defence*; 49.4 *playing terms*
mantra 10.8 *hymn*; 745.1 *maxim*; 10.9 *prayer*
mantua 551.7 *frock*
manual 492.10 *handed*; 15.8 *industrial*; 18.16 *musical note*; 348.8 *practical*; 693.5 *reference book*; 6.14 *school book*
manual labour 576.1 *work*
manually **492.17**; 15.13 *industrially*; 348.9 *instrumentally*; 576.12 *laboriously*
manual skill 485.1 *skill*
manual work 576.1 *work*
manual worker 216.7 *average person*; 340.3 *doer*; 15.7 *employee*; 438.8 *machinist*; 578.1 *worker*
manubrium 84.4 *reproductive body*
manufacture **356.2**; 340.1 *action*; 243.13 *development*; 96.17 *fabricate*; 356.10 *produce*; 356.3 *product*; 376.33 *putting together*; 376.44 *put together*; 403.15 *shape*
manufactured 356.12 *produced*
manufactured item 356.3 *product*
manufacturer 578.3 *agent*; 356.9 *producer*
manufacturing 13.2 *economy*; 356.2 *manufacture*; 356.11 *productive*
manufacturing plant 577.1 *workshop*
manufacturing town 577.1 *workshop*
manumission 391.1 *liberation*
manumit 391.4 *liberate*; 250.15 *set free*
manumitter 391.3 *liberator*
manure 44.15 *cultivate*; 258.4 *dirt*; 560.5 *faeces*; 43.17 *farm*; 43.13, 44.7, 562.3 *fertilizer*; 562.7 *make fertile*
manure heap 43.10 *farm tool*
manuscript 126.2 *original*; 3.11 *relic*
manuscript editor 740.12 *publisher*
Man/Woman of the Year 813.2 *prize*
many **208.6**; 297.3 *frequent*; 208.2 *multitude*; 207.6 *plural*; 207.1 *plurality*; 203.6 *quantitative*; 452.8 *unspecified*
many a time 297.1 *frequently*
many-celled invertebrate 75.1 *invertebrate*
many-coloured 529.10 *coloured*; 541.6 *variegated*
many-hued 541.6 *variegated*
many-one 27.76 *functional*
many-sided 169.6 *side*; 485.6 *skilful*; 207.7 *various*
many-sidedness 207.2 *multiplicity*; 485.1 *skill*
many thanks 671.9 *thank you!*
many times 297.1 *frequently*
many times over 112.23 *repeatedly*
many-tongued 507.6 *loud*

many voices 114.4 *dissension*
many words 5.22
MAO inhibitor 37.4 *drug type*
Maoism 12.1 *government*
Mao jacket 551.11 *jacket*
Maori 284.6 *people of the past*
maoz tzur 10.8 *hymn*
map 30.65; **163.4**; **484.5**; **717.7**; 62.4 *climbing equipment*; 38.30 *engineer*; 142.2 *exact location*; 324.3 *orientation*; 717.11 *paint*; 693.5 *reference book*
maple syrup 498.2 *sweetener*
mapmaker 717.4 *person who makes a representation*
mapmaking 717.7 *map*
map of the heavens 717.7 *map*
map out 129.18 *forerun*; 484.10 *plan out*
map out a course 484.10 *plan out*
mapped 26.13 *measured*
mapping 38.17 *civil engineering*; 27.29 *mathematical function*
map reference 142.2 *exact location*
maquette 19.12 *sculpture*
Maquis 586.14 *armed forces*; 586.9 *guerrilla*
mar 486.7 *be clumsy*; 548.7 *blemish*; 395.9 *change*; 245.4 *impair*; 412.8 *mix*; 357.11 *ruin*; 337.7 *weaken*
Mara 8.7 *devil*
marabenta 18.10 *world music*
marabi 18.10 *world music*
marabout 118.9 *hermit*; 197.8 *loner*; 7.3 *religious person*; 655.6 *unsocial person*
Maracaibo 88.5 *other major lakes*
marae 10.13 *shrine*
marasmic 153.2 *emaciated*
marasmus 191.1 *contraction*; 245.9 *dilapidation*; 260.4 *disease*; 153.8 *emaciation*
marathon 68.2 *cross-country skiing*; 145.2 *great distance*; 47.9 *track*
marathoner 47.3 *athlete*
marathon group 36.3 *psychiatric treatment*
marathon race 47.1 *track events*
marathon racing 47.1 *track events*
marathon runner 47.3, 336.5 *athlete*
maraud 586.38 *conquer*
marauder 586.6 *militarist*; 774.9 *plunderer*; 773.6 *taker*
marauding 774.17 *stolen*; 773.3 *taking away*
marble 20.4, 435.2 *building material*; 418.1 *hard*; 418.7 *hard substance*; 38.26 *masonry*; 181.3 *round thing*; 19.14 *sculptor's materials*; 19.12 *sculpture*; 421.8 *smooth thing*; 541.11 *variegate*; 531.1 *white*; 531.9 *white thing*
marbled 541.9 *striped*
marbled paper 541.5 *variegated thing*
marbled ware 24.1 *ceramics*
marble-hearted 651.12 *callous*
marbling 541.3 *striping*; 19.4 *treatment*
marbly 541.9 *striped*
march 661.3 *act of defiance*; 585.6 *art of war*; 585.13 *be at war*; 661.6 *be insubordinate*; 302.11 *course*; 54.5 *fence*; 54.3 *fencing movements*; 300.12 *gait*; 703.6 *mass demonstration*; 703.19 *protest*; 86.6 *regions*; 317.2 *route*; 300.15 *walk*
march against 381.1 *attack*
march away 313.5 *set out*
Märchen 17.2 *fiction*
marcher 661.4 *defiant person*; 662.7, 753.4 *protester*
Marches 86.9 *regions of Britain*
marches 86.3 *regional boundary*
march for 703.19 *protest*
marching 703.14 *demonstrating*; 300.1 *motion*
marching and countermarching 631.9 *tactics*
marching band 18.26 *musical group*
marching orders 397.1 *command*; 767.1 *disposal*; 144.4 *relegation*; 708.6 *termination*
march in lock step 285.7 *synchronize*
march in slow-time 333.1 *move slowly*
marchioness 573.1 *nobleman*
march off 313.5 *set out*
march of time 302.11 *course*; 277.2 *time*
march on 302.6; 134.4 *protract*
march out 315.9 *exit*; 313.3 *quit*
march past 656.3 *formal occasion*; 132.17 *line up*; 132.8 *procession*; 601.8 *salute*
march to war 585.13 *be at war*
Marconi rig 50.3 *parts of a sailing boat*
Marconi-rigged 50.10 *sailing*
Marcopole™ 692.7 *satellite communication*
Mardi Gras 601.1 *celebration*; 10.15 *holy day*
mare 568.14 *female animal*; 71.18 *female mammal*; 59.1 *horse*; 29.17 *moon*
Marengo 59.3 *warhorse*
mare's milk 558.5 *milk*
mare's-tail 31.20 *cloud appearance*
Margaret Smith 63.7 *famous tennis players*
margarine 25.7 *basic ingredient*
margarita 558.8 *mixed drink*
margin 141.6 *available space*; 215.3 *difference*; 791.1 *discount*; 163.3, 164.1 *edge*; 657.4 *freedom*; 166.3 *furthest point*; 146.1 *interval*; 219.3 *superfluity*
marginal 325.19 *deviant person*; 164.8 *edging*; 163.6 *outlined*; 50.7, 50.13 *windsurfing*
marginal constituency 469.12 *election*
marginal costs 13.7 *corporation*
marginalia 211.3 *additional item*; 719.2 *annotation*; 744.3 *notes*
marginalize 164.6 *edge*
marginally 164.11; 163.7 *essentially*; 196.7 *fractionally*
marginal note 211.3 *additional item*
margin notes 744.3 *notes*
margin of profit 813.5 *turnover*
Margot Fonteyn 22.14 *famous ballet dancers*
margrave 573.1 *nobleman*
margravine 573.1 *nobleman*
mariage de convenance 570.3 *types of marriage*
Mariana Trench 156.4 *deep thing*; 30.16 *ocean floor*; 91.1 *sea*
Maria Taglioni 22.14 *famous ballet dancers*
Maria Tallchief 22.14 *famous ballet dancers*
Marie Rambert 22.14 *famous ballet dancers*
marigold 536.3 *orange thing*
marijuana 691.6 *drug*
marina 165.2 *enclosed place*; 167.1 *front*
marinade 359.2 *preserver*; 496.2 *seasoning*
marinate 369.17 *obtain an extract*; 359.5 *preserve*; 496.12 *season*; 419.13 *soften*
marinated 359.7 *preserved*
marinating 243.17 *developing*; 369.7 *obtaining an extract*
marination 359.1 *preservation*
marine 586.28 *marines*; 323.11 *nautical*; 323.7 *nautical person*; 30.51, 91.7 *oceanic*; 70.15 *of animals*; 585.11 *recruit*
marine animal 70.5 *aquatic animal*
marine archaeology 3.2 *archaeology*
marine biologist 34.19 *life scientist*; 91.6 *oceanographer*; 70.11 *zoologist*
marine biology 70.9 *animal science*; 34.1 *life science*; 91.5 *oceanography*
marine engineering 38.3 *mechanical engineering*
marine fish 74.1 *fishes*
marine geology 30.1 *earth science*
marine mammal 71.11; 70.5 *aquatic animal*
marine painter 19.16 *artist*
marine painting 19.10 *art subject*
marine park 565.12 *stall*
Mariner 29.33 *planetary probe*
mariner 579.13 *director*; 323.7 *nautical person*; 586.27 *naval man*
marine reptile 73.6 *extinct reptile*
marines 586.28; 586.14 *armed forces*; 253.4 *security forces*; 584.2 *the military*
marine scientist 323.7 *nautical person*
marine sextant 323.5 *navigation*
marine's uniform 743.5 *uniform*
Mariology 7.13 *theology*
marionette 717.6 *image*
marionette show 21.7 *show*
marital 570.20 *matrimonial*
marital infidelity 796.4 *illicit love*
maritally 570.24 *matrimonially*
marital relations 593.5 *desire*
maritime 30.51, 91.7 *oceanic*
maritime climate 31.38 *climate*
maritime meteorology 31.1 *meteorology*
marjoram 496.5 *herbs*
mark 224.8 *cause change*; 139.3 *characteristic*; 99.11, 139.22 *characterize*; 601.16 *commemorate*; 231.7 *defect*; 234.11 *deform*; 234.3 *deformity*; 258.4 *dirt*; 811.1 *estimation*; 209.3 *gradation*; 345.6 *have a visible effect*; 245.5 *hurt*; 743.10 *identify*; 123.1 *importance*; 716.4 *indication*; 24.11 *make ceramics*; 743.3 *means of identification*; 209.5 *measure*; 780.11 *national coins*; 482.6 *objective*; 757.2 *permit*; 185.1 *prominence*; 742.1 *sign*; 548.1 *spot*; 471.11 *take note of*; 137.4 *type*; 742.9 *use signs*; 744.12 *vestige*; 345.2 *visible effect*; 5.47 *word*
mark as one's prey 633.12 *aim at*
markdown 793.9 *cheap*; 793.1 *cheapness*
mark down 791.3 *discount*; 744.14 *inscribe*; 793.13 *make cheap*; 469.4 *pick*; 468.3 *underestimate*
mark down for 482.9 *intend for*
marked 548.5; 317.15 *accessible*; 139.16 *characteristic*; 234.7 *deformed*; 726.4 *emphasized*; 121.15 *excellent*; 743.12 *identified*; 231.1 *imperfect*; 738.14 *manifest*; 336.10 *potent*
marked down 793.9 *cheap*; 791.6 *discounted*
markedly 139.30 *characteristically*
marked man 715.4 *accused person*
marked out for destruction 357.15 *destroyed*
marked trail 68.1 *skiing*
marker 65.7 *billiards player*; 51.3 *bowls player*; 56.6 *golfer*; 742.1 *sign*; 742.8 *signer*
marker's box 63.5 *real tennis*
Market 779
market 778.7; **779.1**; 87.7 *city district*; 738.6 *display*; 13.6 *economic factors*; 557.17 *food shop*; 244.1 *improve*; 759.2 *place of exchange*; 778.1 *sell*; 777.2 *shop*; 14.2 *stock exchange*; 776.1 *trade*; 13.10 *trade with*
marketability 778.7 *market*
marketable 13.13 *economic*; 776.13 *mercantile*; 778.15 *saleable*
marketably 778.17
market cross 779.6 *marketplace*
marketer 776.10 *trader*; 778.12 *wholesaler*
market garden 44.2 *garden*; 44.14 *practise horticulture*
market gardener 44.13 *horticulturist*
market gardening 43.4 *arable farming*; 80.4 *fruit eating*; 44.1 *horticulture*; 356.2 *manufacture*
marketing 777.14 *buying*; 13.2 *economy*; 778.3 *selling*
marketing board 43.2 *Common Agricultural Policy*
market maker 14.3 *stockbroker*; 776.10 *trader*; 778.12 *wholesaler*
marketplace 779.6; 342.6 *business*; 173.4 *centre of activity*; 87.7 *city district*; 759.2 *place of exchange*
market price 790.1 *price*
market research 778.7 *market*; 705.2 *questioning*
market researcher 705.9 *questioner*
market square 87.7 *city district*
market town 173.4 *centre of activity*; 779.6 *marketplace*; 86.11 *settlement*; 87.9 *town*
market trader 778.11 *pedlar*; 778.14 *street trader*
marking 525.3 *external appearance*
marking one's territory 763.1 *possession*
markings 743.4 *insignia*; 721.8 *name*
marking the occasion 601.2 *commemoration*
markka 780.11 *national coins*
mark of authority 743.4 *insignia*
mark off 743.10 *identify*; 26.10 *measure*
mark of recognition 658.3 *courtesies*
mark of respect 667.4
mark out 721.17 *describe a circle*; 469.4 *pick*; 372.10 *set apart*; 742.9 *use signs*
mark out a course 484.10 *plan out*
mark paid 788.7 *receive*
marksman 633.6 *hunter*; 330.15 *shooter*
markswoman 633.6 *hunter*; 330.15 *shooter*
mark the cards 700.30 *be fraudulent*
mark the occasion 462.14, 601.16 *commemorate*
mark the way 742.9 *use signs*
mark time 301.8 *be motionless*; 281.16 *measure time*; 141.21 *space*; 275.16 *time*
mark up 792.10 *overcharge*
marl 562.3 *fertilizer*; 562.7 *make fertile*; 24.2 *raw material*
marlin 55.4 *American game fish*
marlinespike 425.8 *sharp-pointed thing*
marlin fishing 633.2 *chase*
marm 568.3 *female title of address*
marmalade 536.3 *orange thing*; 25.42 *preserve*; 359.3 *preserved thing*; 498.2 *sweetener*
marmoreal 19.25 *sculptural*
marmot 654.10 *social animal*
maroon 534.1 *brown*; 767.9 *dispose of*; 372.11 *divide*; 540.6 *purple*; 535.1 *red*
marooned 92.11 *continental*
marooned person 655.6 *unsocial person*
marplot 378.7 *hinderer*; 486.10 *unskilled person*
marque 743.3 *means of identification*; 137.4 *type*
marquee 550.7 *overhead covering*
marquess 573.1 *nobleman*
Marquess of Queensberry rules 52.2 *boxing*
marqueteur 23.13 *carpenter*
marquetried 23.14 *wooden*
marquetried furniture 23.1 *furniture*
marquetry 541.2 *check*; 23.9 *decorative woodwork*; 23.1 *furniture*
marquetry worker 23.13 *carpenter*
marquis 573.1 *nobleman*
marquise 25.35 *dessert*; 573.1 *nobleman*
marred 122.17 *defective*; 233.4 *incomplete*
Marriage 570
marriage 570.1; 10.5 *Christian rite*; 223.3 *companionship*; 374.2 *cooperation*; 412.2 *mixed thing*; 2.3 *social environment*
marriageability 570.4
marriageable 570.22
marriageable age 570.4 *marriageability*
marriageableness 570.4 *marriageability*
marriage act 593.5 *desire*
marriage adviser 713.4 *adviser*; 570.13 *matchmaker*; 748.3 *mediator*
marriage banns 742.6 *word*
marriage bed 570.1 *marriage*
marriage broker 570.13 *matchmaker*; 748.3 *mediator*
marriage bureau 570.13 *matchmaker*
marriage by proxy 570.3 *types of marriage*
marriage certificate 744.2 *certificate*; 743.3 *means of identification*
marriage contract 755.1 *contract*; 756.1 *promise*
marriage counsellor 748.3 *mediator*
marriage encounter 36.3 *psychiatric treatment*
marriage feast 570.6 *general terms*
marriage guidance 36.3 *psychiatric treatment*
marriage guidance counsellor 713.4 *adviser*; 570.13 *matchmaker*; 748.3 *mediator*
marriage licence 570.6 *general terms*
marriage lines 570.6 *general terms*
marriage of convenience 570.3 *types of marriage*
marriage on the rocks 571.1 *divorce*
marriage partner 570.8 *spouse*
marriage portion 440.6 *marriage settlement*
marriage procession 570.6 *general terms*
marriage relationship 108.1 *relatedness*
marriage service 10.5 *Christian rite*
marriage settlement 440.6
marriage song 570.6 *general terms*
marriage tie 570.1 *marriage*
marriage toast 570.6 *general terms*
marriage vows 570.5 *wedding*
married 570.21; 223.19 *associated*
married couple 570.9
married love 593.2 *romantic love*
married man 570.10; 567.13 *man in the family*
married name 721.8 *name*
married state 570.1 *marriage*
married status 570.1 *marriage*
married woman 570.11; 568.12 *woman in the family*
marrow 173.1 *centre*; 99.2 *essential content*; 172.5 *inner nature*; 406.3 *insides*
marry 570.15; 374.6 *come together*; 755.5 *contract*; 630.14 *good heavens!*; 454.13 *really!*; 593.28 *win the love of*
marry into money 570.15 *marry*
marry off 767.9 *dispose of*; 570.16 *join in marriage*
marry well 570.15 *marry*

Mars 585.3 *gods and goddesses of war;* 29.16 *planet;* 535.7 *red thing*
marsala 558.9 *wine*
marsh **92.3**; **429.8**; 88.2 *small lake;* 419.11 *soft thing;* 379.1 *trap*
marshal 409.12 *arrange;* 376.42 *call together;* 223.15 *escort;* 743.10 *identify;* 400.3 *leader;* 579.16 *official;* 407.18 *order;* 396.10 *person of authority;* 223.8 *usher*
marshalled 223.20 *accompanied;* 409.20 *arranged*
marshalling 409.1 *arrangement;* 243.11 *fitting out;* 743.8 *heraldic device;* 376.2 *herding*
marshalling yard 317.10 *railway;* 321.8 *railway station*
marsh bird 72.3 *water bird*
marshiness 429.7 *bogginess;* 419.10 *compressibility*
marshland 92.3 *marsh*
marshlight 522.9 *firefly*
marshmallow 25.41 *sweet*
marshy **429.11**; 419.4 *compressible;* 92.11 *continental;* 88.9 *lakelike*
Mars orange 536.2 *orangeness*
marsupial 71.25 *mammalian;* 71.4 *pouched mammal*
marsupial characteristic 71.4 *pouched mammal*
Marsupialia 71.4 *pouched mammal*
marsupialian 71.25 *mammalian*
marsupium 71.4 *pouched mammal*
mart 173.4 *centre of activity;* 87.7 *city district;* 779.1 *market*
Martello tower 384.12 *fort;* 154.6 *tall thing*
Martha Graham 22.14 *famous ballet dancers*
martial **586.35**; 381.22, 613.11 *militant;* 584.8, 585.17 *military*
martial art 52.1 *combat sports*
martial arts 384.5 *self-defence*
martial law 12.1 *government;* 647.1 *severity;* 396.7 *type of rule*
martially **586.42**; 584.11 *militarily*
martial music 585.2 *glory of war*
martial race 586.7 *militarist nation*
Martian 29.36 *astronomical;* 11.11 *ghost;* 100.6 *outsider*
Martina Navratilova 63.7 *famous tennis players*
martinet 400.4 *absolute ruler;* 647.4 *strict person*
Martini™ 558.9 *wine*
martini 558.8 *mixed drink*
Martin Luther King 589.4 *Nobel Peace Prize*
Martinmas 10.15 *holy day*
martlet 72.9 *fabulous bird;* 743.8 *heraldic device*
martyr **752.7**; 661.4 *defiant person;* 8.10 *deified person;* 491.11 *inflict pain;* 382.20 *kill ritually;* 249.5 *person in adversity;* 7.3 *religious person;* 814.4 *torture;* 466.8 *victim of discrimination;* 803.4 *virtuous person*
martyrdom 814.13 *capital punishment;* 582.4 *death sentence;* 752.6 *offering;* 491.1 *pain;* 382.6 *ritual killing;* 473.2 *unselfishness*
martyred 582.19 *dead;* 8.15 *deified;* 491.7 *feeling pain;* 752.19 *sacrificial;* 473.5 *unselfish*
martyrization 814.13 *capital punishment;* 382.6 *ritual killing*
martyrize 382.20 *kill ritually;* 814.4 *torture*
martyrology 582.12 *death count*
martyr to ill health 260.19 *sick person*
marvel 525.4 *something that appears;* 619.4, 619.9 *wonder*
marvelling 630.7 *amazed;* 619.6 *wondering*
marvellous 597.5 *delightful;* 619.8 *wonderful;* 235.1 *worthy*
marvellously 246.16 *successfully;* 619.13 *wonderfully*
Marxism 244.11 *reformism;* 4.7 *school of thought;* 2.7 *social stratification;* 396.7 *type of rule*
Marxism-Leninism 12.1 *government*
Marxist 451.5 *disbeliever;* 4.11 *follower of a doctrine;* 12.9, 396.14 *governmental;* 402.3 *materialist;* 4.14 *of a philosophy;* 244.12 *reformer;* 2.14 *socioeconomic;* 2.11 *sociologist*
Marxist history 3.1 *history*
Marxists 12.6 *political party*
Mary Ann 691.6 *drug*
Mary Jane 691.6 *drug*
Maryland Hunt Cup 59.7 *horseracing*
Mary Warner 691.6 *drug*
Mary Whitehouse 255.6 *prude*
marzipan 498.3 *dessert;* 25.41 *sweet*
masala dosa 25.49 *Indian dish*
mascara 547.4 *cosmetics*
mascon 29.17 *moon*
mascot 475.6 *good-luck sign;* 359.2 *preserver;* 11.6 *talisman*
masculine 5.44 *grammatical;* 567.17 *male*
masculine gender 567.1 *male sex*
masculine rhyme 17.11 *rhyme*
masculinity 567.1 *male sex*
maser 28.26 *laser;* 39.21 *rectifier*
MASH 394.14 *hospital*
mash 427.26 *beat;* 412.8 *mix;* 372.9 *separate;* 419.13 *soften;* 497.3 *tasteless items*
mashed 412.12 *mixed*
mashed potato 22.2 *dance*
masher 593.9 *lover;* 427.11 *pulverizer*
mashie 56.4 *golf club*
mashie iron 56.4 *golf club*
mashie niblick 56.4 *golf club*
mashing 427.4 *pulverization*
mash tun 410.11 *vessel*
mashy 419.4 *compressible*
masjid 10.11 *place of worship*
mask **699.28**; 519.15 *blind;* 736.8 *conceal;* 736.3 *covering up;* 550.16, 700.12, 700.32 *disguise;* 699.14 *façade;* 551.5 *fancy dress;* 550.31 *hide;* 521.8 *make invisible;* 546.5 *make ugly;* 702.11 *practise sophistry;* 252.4 *safety device;* 167.3 *show;* 521.6 *that which makes invisible*
masked 548.4 *blemished;* 736.14 *concealed;* 700.41 *disguised;* 521.3 *private;* 550.37 *protected*
masked ball 736.3 *covering up;* 22.1 *dancing;* 654.5 *party*
masker 550.17 *coverer*
masking 519.11 *blinding;* 736.3 *covering up*
masking tape 267.3 *adhesive;* 521.6 *that which makes invisible*
masochism 388.1 *submission*
masochist 388.2 *appeaser*
masochistic 388.5 *submitting*
mason 20.2 *architect;* 578.2 *artisan*
Mason-Dixon Line 372.6 *boundary;* 147.7 *interface*
masonry **38.26**; 435.2 *building material*
Masorah 7.12 *religious text*
masque 700.12 *disguise;* 654.5 *party;* 21.2 *play*
masquerade 717.10 *act;* 717.3 *acting;* 22.1 *dancing;* 702.12, 736.9 *deceive;* 550.16, 700.12, 700.32 *disguise;* 699.14 *façade;* 551.5 *fancy dress;* 550.31 *hide;* 699.28 *mask;* 654.5 *party*
masquerader 736.7 *concealer;* 550.17 *coverer;* 700.15 *deceiver*
masquerading 700.41 *disguised;* 699.34 *pretending*
Mass 10.5 *Christian rite;* 10.6 *Eucharist*
mass **28.9**; **158.7**; **376.26**; 586.18 *army of people;* 376.37 *assemble;* 203.2 *certain amount;* 208.11, 376.20, 376.40 *crowd;* 416.1 *density;* 414.4 *heaviness;* 205.5 *largest part;* 207.3 *majority;* 416.9 *make dense;* 402.4 *matter;* 205.7 *piece;* 203.1 *quantity;* 18.5 *sacred music;* 158.1 *size;* 416.4 *solid body;* 439.1 *store;* 152.5 *thickness;* 208.4 *throng*
massacre 651.7 *act of malevolence;* 814.13 *capital punishment;* 586.38 *conquer;* 357.8 *destroy;* 357.2 *destroying;* 814.5 *execute;* 651.17 *kill;* 382.4, 382.18 *slaughter*
massacred 582.19 *dead*
Massacre of the Innocents 382.4 *slaughter*
mass action 747.4 *joint operation*
massage **365.6**; **365.16**; 394.20 *doctor;* 419.14 *ease;* 419.13 *soften;* 394.13 *therapy;* 492.11 *touch*
massage parlour 796.6 *brothel*
massager 492.5 *toucher*
massage the accounts 789.7 *account*
massaging 365.6 *massage;* 492.2 *touching*
massagist 492.5 *toucher*
mass book 10.10 *religious manual*
mass burial 583.1 *burial*
mass communication **693.4**; **741.5**; 692.1 *communications;* 740.2 *mass media*
mass demonstration **703.6**
mass destruction 357.2 *destroying*
massed 376.47 *collected;* 208.10 *crowded;* 416.6 *dense*
massed attack 381.12 *military attack*
mass energy 334.4 *energy*
masses 216.7 *average person;* 138.11 *general public*
massé shot 65.2 *billiards play*
masses of 208.4 *throng*
masseur **365.8**; 394.15 *healer;* 401.4 *personal attendant;* 492.5 *toucher*
masseuse 394.15 *healer;* 365.8 *masseur;* 401.4 *personal attendant;* 492.5 *toucher*
mass execution 814.13 *capital punishment*
mass grave 583.6 *grave*
massicot 537.7 *yellow pigment*
massif 89.1 *mountain;* 154.4 *mountain range*
massive 158.15 *big;* 416.6 *dense;* 414.1 *heavy;* 402.7 *material;* 203.6 *quantitative;* 152.1 *thick;* 79.15 *woody;* 235.1 *worthy*
massively 416.10 *densely;* 414.16 *heavily;* 158.20 *largely;* 203.7 *quantitatively*
massiveness 158.2 *bigness;* 414.4 *heaviness;* 152.5 *thickness*
mass media **740.2**; 692.1 *communications;* 693.4, 741.5 *mass communication*
mass meeting 376.4 *rally*
mass movement **30.26**; 342.5 *activism*
mass murder 651.7 *act of malevolence;* 814.13 *capital punishment;* 357.2 *destroying;* 382.2 *murder*
mass murderer 798.6 *evil person;* 651.8 *malefactor;* 382.11 *murderer;* 380.4 *violent creature*
mass number 28.69 *isotope*
mass of 208.4 *throng*
massotherapist 365.8 *masseur*
massotherapy 365.6 *massage*
mass-produce 111.8 *make the same;* 356.10 *produce;* 561.9 *reproduce*
mass-produced 356.12 *produced*
mass production 356.2 *manufacture;* 562.2 *productiveness;* 111.6 *regularity;* 561.1 *reproduction*
mass screening 35.7 *diagnosis*
mass spectrograph 28.91 *spectrometer*
mass spectrometer 28.91 *spectrometer*
mass spectrometry 32.17 *analysis*
mass strike 15.4 *industrial dispute*
mass suicide 382.7 *suicide*
mass X-ray 35.7 *diagnosis*
massy 158.15 *big;* 416.6 *dense;* 414.1 *heavy;* 402.7 *material*
mast 50.3 *parts of a sailing boat;* 154.6 *tall thing*
mastaba 583.6 *grave*
mastectomy 394.12 *surgery*
Master 400
master **400.1**; **400.14**; 578.2 *artisan;* 19.16 *artist;* 395.10 *be a prevailing influence;* 797.19 *be good at;* 387.7 *defeat;* 579.13 *director;* 400.9 *educational leader;* 6.4 *educator;* 121.15, 400.13 *excellent;* 400.10 *expert;* 442.8 *intellectual person;* 6.24, 455.11 *know;* 763.6 *lord;* 567.3 *male title of address;* 323.7 *nautical person;* 246.11 *overmaster;* 230.4 *perfectionist;* 485.4 *skilled person;* 139.14 *specialist;* 121.5 *superior;* 695.6 *understand*
master aircrew 586.32 *airman*
master builder 20.2 *architect*
MasterCard™ 772.4 *credit;* 783.2 *credit card*
master carpenter 400.10 *expert*
masterful **400.12**; 396.12 *authoritative;* 797.5 *proficient;* 136.9 *qualified;* 140.12 *ruling;* 485.6 *skilful*
masterfully **400.16**; 136.17 *capably;* 797.25 *skilfully*
masterfulness 396.2 *authoritativeness;* 797.12 *proficiency*
master key 308.2 *opener*
masterliness 797.12 *proficiency*
masterly 400.13 *excellent;* 396.17 *expert;* 396.26 *expertly;* 230.1 *perfect;* 797.5 *proficient;* 485.6 *skilful;* 246.13 *successful;* 121.16 *superiorly*
master mariner 323.7 *nautical person*
master mason 20.2 *architect;* 578.2 *artisan*
mastermind 631.14 *behave towards;* 631.11 *conduct oneself;* 455.6 *knowledgeable person;* 579.1 *manage;* 121.6 *paragon;* 484.8 *planner;* 485.4 *skilled person*
masterminding 631.8 *treatment*
master of ceremonies 692.29 *broadcaster;* 738.12 *displayer;* 579.14 *leader;* 21.27 *producer*
master of hounds 514.9 *crier;* 579.15 *manager*
master of the house 400.1 *master*
Master of the Rolls 16.25 *British judge*
master of the violin 396.11, 400.10 *expert*
master painter 230.4 *perfectionist*
masterpiece **400.11**; **485.3**; 545.3 *attractive female;* 545.2 *beautiful thing;* 340.2 *deed;* 235.8 *exceller;* 797.17 *good thing;* 356.6 *great work;* 230.3 *perfection;* 619.4 *wonder;* 19.6 *work of art*
master plan 484.1 *plan*
mastership 121.2 *leadership;* 485.1 *skill*
master spirit 123.4 *bigwig*
masterstroke 484.3 *expedient plan;* 797.17 *good thing;* 485.3 *masterpiece;* 619.4 *wonder*
master thief 400.10 *expert;* 230.4 *perfectionist*
masterwork 356.6 *great work;* 400.11, 485.3 *masterpiece;* 19.6 *work of art*
mastery 136.2 *ability;* 19.5 *artistry;* 140.8, 396.1, 397.3 *authority;* 387.2 *domination;* 12.3 *governance;* 455.1 *knowledge;* 455.3 *learning;* 230.3 *perfection;* 485.1 *skill;* 246.1 *success;* 695.12 *understanding*
masthead 174.2 *head;* 741.12 *headline;* 154.8 *high thing;* 743.3 *means of identification;* 814.1 *punish*
masthead light 522.6 *electric light*
masthead sloop 50.2 *sailing boat*
mastic 430.2 *adhesive*
masticate 557.21 *eat;* 419.13 *soften*
mastication 557.1 *eating*
Mastigomycotina 83.3 *fungi*
Mastigophora 75.9 *protozoan*
mastigophoran 75.9 *protozoan*
mastodon 158.9 *big thing;* 296.8 *prehistoric animal*
masturbation 490.1 *physical pleasure*
mat 84.1 *alga;* 24.10 *ceramic;* 256.11 *cleaning cloth;* 550.9 *floor covering;* 51.1 *green bowling;* 38.28 *substructure;* 42.14 *weave*
matador 382.13 *animal killer;* 586.3 *athlete*
Mata Hari 480.13 *tempter*
match 706.21 *answer to;* 525.11 *appear;* 111.10 *be equal;* 108.8 *be proportionate to;* 115.10 *be similar;* 111.7 *be the same;* 381.20 *bout;* 117.7, 750.25 *conform;* 750.5 *conformity;* 69.2 *contest;* 110.9 *correlate;* 110.3 *correlation;* 706.8 *correspondence;* 113.21 *counteract;* 119.5 *equal;* 522.8 *fire;* 516.8 *harmonize;* 525.5 *impression;* 373.13 *intercommunicate;* 437.2 *lighter;* 111.3 *lookalike;* 570.1 *marriage;* 570.17 *matchmake;* 158.18 *measure;* 198.14 *pair;* 45.1 *sport;* 63.4 *tennis terms*
match abandoned 53.1 *cricket match*
match against 113.19 *confront*
matchbox 410.6 *box;* 437.2 *lighter*
matched 111.14 *lookalike;* 570.21 *married;* 119.8 *on equal terms;* 198.9 *two*
matched in age 285.9 *simultaneous*
matched pair 115.6 *couple*
matchet 587.8 *sharp weapon*
match fishing 55.1 *angling*
match in cunning 645.5 *be cunning*
matching 529.11 *colourful;* 750.14 *conforming;* 110.6 *correlative;* 706.15 *correspondent;* 516.7 *harmonious;* 111.14 *lookalike;* 115.7 *similar;* 551.31 *styled*
matching set 115.6 *couple*
matchless 121.14, 235.2, 797.2 *best;* 116.4 *dissimilar*
matchlessly 121.17 *supremely*
matchlock 587.10 *historical gun*
matchlockman 586.13 *historical soldiery*
matchmake **570.17**; 746.7 *act as a go-between;* 198.14 *pair*
matchmaker **570.13**; 398.6 *agent;* 748.3 *mediator;* 746.4 *negotiator*
match play 56.1 *golf*
match point 222.3 *critical moment*
match poorly 751.8 *be different*
matchstick 337.5 *weak thing*
matchstick man 163.1 *outline*
match up with 119.10 *be equal*
match-winning 246.15 *victorious*
matchwood 424.3 *brittle thing;* 337.5 *weak thing*
mate 69.4 *chess terms;* 374.6 *come together;* 223.11 *companion;* 115.5 *counterpart;*

119.5 *equal*; 569.5 *friend*; 392.11 *helper*; 595.4 *likable person*; 593.29 *make love*; 567.3 *male title of address*; 570.17 *matchmake*; 198.14 *pair*; 578.5 *partner*; 654.6 *social person*; 558.3 *tea*
mated 570.21 *married*; 198.9 *two*
mateless 572.6 *celibate*
matelot 323.7 *nautical person*
mater 568.12 *woman in the family*
materfamilias 568.12 *woman in the family*
material 402.7; 525.7 *appearing*; 406.10 *containing*; 406.1 *contents*; 99.1 *essence*; 42.3 *fabric*; 123.5 *important*; 93.11 *intrinsic*; 435.1 *materials*; 402.4 *matter*; 97.7 *present*; 95.6 *real*; 352.2 *supplies*; 193.4, 404.5 *textile*; 492.8 *touchable*; 520.1 *visible*
material existence 402.1 *material world*; 95.1 *reality*
materialism 402.2 *materialization*; 4.7 *school of thought*; 683.1 *selfishness*
materialist 402.3; 451.5 *disbeliever*; 4.11 *follower of a doctrine*; 4.14 *of a philosophy*
materialistic 402.7 *material*; 683.4 *selfish*
materialistically 683.8 *selfishly*
materiality 123.1 *importance*; 402.1 *material world*; 402.4 *matter*; 93.3 *nature*; 97.1 *presence*; 95.1 *reality*
materialization 402.2; 525.1 *appearance*; 93.8 *creation*; 8.8 *divine manifestation*; 11.11 *ghost*; 738.10 *manifestation*
materialize 520.9, 703.18 *appear*; 525.12 *become visible*; 402.8 *be material*; 97.11 *be present*; 93.18 *come to be*; 95.11 *make real*; 738.4 *show oneself*
materialized 93.15 *created*; 402.7 *material*
materially 402.9; 123.9 *importantly*; 99.13 *in essence*; 97.14 *in person*; 406.13 *structurally*
materialness 123.1 *importance*; 402.1 *material world*; 97.1 *presence*
Materials 435
materials 435.1; 403.2 *fabric*; 402.4 *matter*; 352.2 *supplies*
materials budget 789.2 *budgeting*
material things 440.4 *possessions*
Material World 402
material world 402.1
materia medica 394.2 *medicine*; 37.1 *pharmacology*
maternal 650.6 *benevolent*
maternal love 593.1 *love*
maternally 650.10 *benevolently*
maternity 561.4 *development*; 568.12 *woman in the family*
maternity allowance 392.4 *social assistance*
maternity benefit 392.4 *social assistance*
maternity dress 551.7 *frock*
maternity grant 392.4 *social assistance*
maternity hospital 35.10 *hospital*
maternity wear 551.1 *dress*
matey 569.8 *friendly*; 654.15 *sociable*
mateyness 223.3 *companionship*; 569.1 *friendship*
math 27.1 *mathematics*
math co-processor 40.5 *processor*
mathematical 27.68; **210.15**; 789.10 *accounting*; 698.21 *accurate*; 28.99 *theoretical*
mathematical addition 211.2
mathematical biology 27.3 *applied mathematics*
mathematical biophysics 27.3 *applied mathematics*
mathematical computing 27.3 *applied mathematics*
mathematical ecology 27.3 *applied mathematics*
mathematical exactness 698.8 *accuracy*
mathematical function 27.29
mathematical geography 27.3 *applied mathematics*
mathematical logic 27.63; 27.1 *mathematics*
mathematically 27.87; **210.16**; 203.7 *quantitatively*
mathematically exact 698.21 *accurate*
mathematical model 27.65 *theory*
mathematical notation 717.1 *representation*; 742.1 *sign*
mathematical physics 27.3 *applied mathematics*
mathematical precision 273.1 *accuracy*
mathematical probability 107.7 *calculation of chance*; 27.62 *probability*; 104.5 *probability theory*
mathematical reasoning 27.64 *reasoning*
mathematical result 194.4
mathematical symbol 27.13
mathematical theorem 476.1 *supposition*
mathematician 27.2; **210.7**; 706.10 *answerer*
Mathematics 27
mathematics 27.1
maths 27.1 *mathematics*
matin 290.5 *morning*
matinal 290.5 *morning*
matinée 290.4 *afternoon*; 21.13 *theatrical performance*
matinée coat 551.23 *children's clothes*
matinée idol 21.24 *actor*; 593.11 *loved one*
mating 593.5 *desire*
mating call 515.1 *animal cry*
matins 290.1 *morning*; 10.4 *public worship*
matriarch 400.1 *master*; 568.12 *woman in the family*
matriarchal 556.14 *aged*; 12.9, 396.14 *governmental*; 400.12 *masterful*
matriarchally 556.16 *maturely*
matriarchate 12.1 *government*
matriarchy 568.1 *female sex*; 12.1 *government*
matricide 651.7 *act of malevolence*; 382.3 *homicide*; 382.11 *murderer*
matriculate 220.9 *enlist*
matrimonial 570.20; 755.7 *contractual*; 10.21 *ritualistic*
matrimonial agent 570.13 *matchmaker*
matrimonial cause 571.3 *divorce court*
matrimonially 570.24; 755.8 *contractually*
matrimony 755.1 *contract*; 570.1 *marriage*
matrix 27.22; 160.2 *prototype*
matrix mechanics 28.3 *modern physics*; 28.80 *quantum theory*
matrix printer 40.7 *peripheral*
matron 568.2 *female*; 579.15 *manager*; 570.11 *married woman*; 400.1 *master*; 35.16 *nurse*; 556.9 *woman*
matronage 568.13 *womenfolk*
matronliness 556.2 *adulthood*
matronly 568.15 *female*; 400.12 *masterful*; 570.20 *matrimonial*; 556.13 *middle-aged*
matronymic 721.8 *name*
matt 524.7 *dimmed*; 528.2 *shady*; 529.13 *soft-hued*
matted 420.3 *barbed*; 416.7 *condensed*; 258.7 *dirty*
matted hair 420.7 *rough thing*
matter 402.4; 123.7 *be important*; 431.3 *body fluid*; 346.3 *business*; 406.1 *contents*; 258.4 *dirt*; 99.1 *essence*; 560.18 *fester*; 123.1 *importance*; 435.1 *materials*; 694.1 *meaning*; 430.5 *mucus*; 560.7 *pus*; 203.1 *quantity*; 95.1 *reality*; 447.1 *topic*; 260.15 *ulcer*; 344.6 *undertaking*
matter for discussion 447.2 *issue*
matter for judgment 16.5 *litigation*
Matterhorn 154.3 *mountain*; 89.6 *other major mountains and ranges*
mattering 560.27 *purulent*; 560.7 *pus*
matter in hand 354.2 *undertaking*
matter of course 632.1 *habit*
matter of fact 93.5 *fact*; 3.14 *historicalness*; 95.1 *reality*
matter-of-fact 618.7 *indifferent*; 646.1 *naive*; 95.8 *practical*; 4.15 *rational*; 271.1 *simple*
matter-of-factly 618.17 *indifferently*; 646.5 *naively*; 271.8 *simply*
matter-of-factness 646.2 *naivety*; 271.4 *simplicity*
matter of indifference 124.8 *trifle*
matter of interest 447.3
matt finish 41.12 *development*; 524.2 *murk*
matt glaze 24.3 *glaze*
matting 550.9 *floor covering*
mattock 438.3 *garden tool*; 425.9 *sharp-edged thing*
mattress 736.2 *hiding place*; 780.20 *money store*; 413.4 *rest*
mattress cover 550.10 *bed covering*
maturation 556.2 *adulthood*; 243.13 *development*; 190.1 *growth*; 632.7 *habituation*
mature 556.18; 556.11 *adult*; 556.17 *age*; 760.8 *be transformed*; 190.7 *bigger*; 232.7 *complete*; 243.7 *develop*; 243.20 *developed*; 244.2 *get better*; 555.18 *grow*; 244.1 *improve*; 556.13 *middle-aged*; 296.11 *old*; 230.1, 230.5 *perfect*; 292.7 *season*; 419.13 *soften*
matured 243.20 *developed*; 485.8 *expert*; 230.1 *perfect*; 292.15 *seasoned*
mature into 760.7 *convert into*
maturely 556.16; 296.18 *venerably*
matureness 556.3 *maturity*
maturing 555.13; 760.14 *converting*; 243.17 *developing*; 632.7 *habituation*
maturity 556.3; 556.2 *adulthood*; 556.4 *middle age*; 296.1 *oldness*; 230.3 *perfection*; 243.14 *preparedness*; 287.1 *timeliness*
matutinal 290.5 *morning*
maudlin 590.12 *sensitive*; 690.2 *slightly drunk*
maul 236.14 *ill-treat*; 245.4 *impair*; 491.11 *inflict pain*; 492.4 *kiss*; 64.5 *play rugby*; 64.3 *rugby play*; 381.5 *strike*; 492.11 *touch*
mauling 491.3 *injury*
maulstick 19.11 *artist's materials*
maumet 9.3 *idol*
Mauna Kea Observatory 29.23 *observatory*
maunder 270.6 *be circuitous*
Maundy money 768.3 *offering*
Maundy Thursday 10.15 *holy day*
Maureen Connolly 63.7 *famous tennis players*
Mauritius hurricane 31.16 *wind vortex*
mausoleum 356.8 *construction*; 583.6 *grave*; 744.11 *monument*; 301.3 *resting place*
mauvaise honte 795.4 *self-righteousness*
mauve 540.6 *purple*
mauveine 42.6 *dye*; 540.2 *purple pigment*
maverick 250.10 *independent*; 100.5, 118.7, 662.6 *nonconformist*; 118.13 *unconventional*
maw 308.4 *body orifice*; 557.16 *eating utensil*
mawashi-geri 52.8 *karate*
mawkish 590.12 *sensitive*
mawkishly 590.21 *emotionally*
mawkishness 590.7 *emotionalism*
max 121.14 *best*
maxidress 551.7 *frock*
Maxim 745
maxim 745.1; 5.21 *catchword*; 810.6 *ethics*; 140.4 *guide*; 795.7 *moral*; 269.2 *outline*; 4.1 *philosophy*; 713.3 *precept*; 707.2 *statement*; 698.4 *truism*
maximal 121.14 *best*; 27.75 *equal*; 174.5 *top*
Maxim gun 587.12 *historical guns*
maximization 727.2 *enlargement*
maximize 727.8 *enlarge*; 349.3 *exploit*; 213.5 *make bigger*; 27.94 *order*; 467.4 *overestimate*
maximized 727.13 *enlarged*
maximum 121.14 *best*; 232.2 *fullness*; 174.1 *summit*; 174.5 *top*
maximum-acceleration 61.10 *racing*
maximum-acceleration event 61.1 *motor racing*
maximum and minimun thermometer 28.89 *thermometer*
maximum likelihood 27.62 *probability*
maximum pressure 576.4 *exertion*
maximum-security prison 655.4 *place of confinement*; 815.1 *prison*
maximum speed 332.8 *speed*
maximum-speed event 61.1 *motor racing*
maxiskirt 551.6 *skirt*
maya 11.10 *psychic phenomenon*
Maya Plisetskaya 22.14 *famous ballet dancers*
Mayas 284.6 *people of the past*
maybe 102.9 *possibly*
may blossom 78.1 *flower*
May Day 298.6 *annually celebrated day*; 292.2 *spring*
Mayday 742.6 *word*
mayday 711.2 *danger signal*
Mayfair 87.5 *London*
mayfly 55.1 *angling*
mayhem 357.5 *havoc*
mayonnaise 25.15 *sauce*; 496.2 *seasoning*
mayor 16.10 *law officer*; 400.3 *leader*; 579.16 *official*; 396.10 *person of authority*; 121.5 *superior*
mayoralty 16.2 *jurisdiction*; 396.5 *position of authority*
mayor-council system 579.9 *US administrative council*
mayoress 400.3 *leader*; 396.10 *person of authority*
maypole 154.6 *tall thing*
maypole dance 22.4 *historic dancing*
May Queen 235.8 *exceller*
Maytime 292.2 *spring*
maze 737.4 *brain-teaser*; 180.3 *convoluted thing*; 264.4 *problem*; 408.7 *tangle*
mazurka 22.4 *historic dancing*
mazy 325.21 *indirect*
mbaqanga 18.10 *world music*
MC 21.27 *producer*
MCC 53.2 *ground*
MD 123.4 *bigwig*; 18.24 *musician*
ME 260.6 *infection*
me 139.12 *I*; 737.15 *in secret*; 101.6 *internal world*
mea culpa 807.2 *apology*; 808.9 *sorry!*
mead 43.11 *farmland*; 81.2 *grassland*; 92.6 *lowland*; 498.5 *sweet drink*
meadow 43.11 *farmland*; 81.2 *grassland*; 92.6 *lowland*; 308.8 *open space*
meadow grass 81.1 *grass*
meadow land 81.2 *grassland*
meadowy 81.9 *grassy*
meads of asphodel 582.14 *the spiritual world*
meagre 782.4 *inadequate*; 233.4 *incomplete*; 218.1 *insufficient*; 159.7 *little*; 153.6 *scant*; 206.6 *sparse*; 680.4 *thrifty*
meagre diet 557.10 *scarcity*
meagrely 782.17 *inadequately*; 206.11 *sparsely*; 153.17 *thin*
meagreness 206.3 *fewness*; 782.9 *inadequacy*; 122.3 *inferior numbers*; 218.8 *insufficiency*; 159.1 *littleness*; 153.12 *thinning*
meagre resources 782.5 *poverty*
meal 427.8; **557.12**; 25.7 *basic ingredient*
mealiness 427.3 *graininess*
meal ticket 768.3 *offering*
mealtime 25.56 *culinary*
mealworm 76.5 *larva*
mealy 427.16; 530.8 *drained of colour*
mealy bug 44.12 *pests and diseases*
mealy-mouth 699.19 *cheat*; 700.19 *hypocrite*; 664.3 *sycophant*
mealy-mouthed 699.31, 700.37 *hypocritical*; 795.10 *moralistic*; 664.7 *sycophantic*; 337.12 *weak-willed*
mealy-mouthedly 699.42 *hypocritically*
mealy-mouthedness 699.3, 700.3 *hypocrisy*; 795.4 *self-righteousness*
mealymouthing 664.2 *sycophancy*
mean 682.1; **694.10**; 782.3 *beggarly*; 123.7 *be important*; 173.6 *central*; 173.1 *centre*; 446.19 *epitomize*; 798.7 *evil*; 651.14 *hostile*; 127.4 *include*; 218.1 *insufficient*; 482.7 *intend*; 625.4 *irascible*; 623.2 *lowly*; 216.2, 216.5 *medium*; 786.13 *nonpaying*; 203.5 *numbers*; 242.2 *objectionable*; 124.2 *obscure*; 27.60 *parameter*; 236.4 *poor*; 683.4 *selfish*; 793.10 *shoddy*; 742.10 *signify*; 717.12 *stand for*
mean business 638.6 *be resolute*
meander 189.6 *be oblique*; 90.2 *channel*; 180.6 *convolute*; 306.8 *detour*; 90.7 *flow*; 325.5 *twist*
meandering 306.2 *circuitousness*; 180.2 *coil*; 180.4 *convolutional*; 90.10 *fluvial*; 325.21 *indirect*; 189.4 *oblique*; 189.1 *obliqueness*; 306.9 *orbital*
meandering river 90.1 *river*
mean deviation 27.60 *parameter*
me and you 198.1 *two*
mean error 27.60 *parameter*
meanie 682.5 *miser*; 682.6 *nasty person*
Meaning 694
meaning 694.1; 123.3 *chief thing*; 482.1 *intention*; 719.1 *interpretation*; 5.1 *linguistics*; 446.4 *purpose*; 742.1 *sign*; 345.4 *significance*; 5.17 *word*
meaningful 694.6; 123.5 *important*; 695.1 *intelligible*; 446.12 *purposive*; 742.14 *signifying*; 5.42 *worded*
meaningful look 730.6 *silent speech*
meaningful looks 729.4 *articulation*
meaningfully 694.13; 742.18 *indicatively*; 5.50 *lexically*; 446.21 *purposively*
meaningfulness 695.9 *intelligibility*; 694.1 *meaning*; 694.4 *type of meaning*
meaning harm 651.10 *malevolent*
meaningless 694.6 *meaningful*; 697.5

nonsensical; 157.2 *superficial*; 696.1 *unintelligible*
meaningless act 340.2 *deed*
meaninglessly 697.9 *nonsensically*; 696.13 *unintelligibly*
meaninglessness 696.11 *unintelligibility*
meaningly 694.13 *meaningfully*
mean life 28.70 *radioactivity*
mean little 124.11 *be unimportant*
meanly **682.9**; **782.16**; 625.9 *irascibly*; 651.20 *malevolently*; 683.8 *selfishly*
mean-minded 683.4 *selfish*
mean-mindedness 683.1 *selfishness*
Meanness 682
meanness 782.7 *beggary*; 798.1 *evil*; 122.3 *inferior numbers*; 218.8 *insufficiency*; 625.1 *irascibility*; 623.8 *lowliness*; 651.1 *malevolence*; 242.6 *objectionability*; 124.6 *obscurity*; 236.10 *poverty*; 683.1 *selfishness*; 793.3 *shoddiness*
mean no harm 589.5 *be at peace*; 805.8 *be innocent*
mean nothing 697.7 *be nonsense*; 696.7 *be unintelligible*
mean old stick 682.5 *miser*
Means 352
means **352.1**; 222.1 *circumstances*; 239.5 *convenience*; 780.6 *funds*; 348.2 *instrument*; 348.1 *instrumentality*; 435.1 *materials*; 440.5 *personal estate*; 317.1 *way*; 781.5 *wealth*
means-ends analysis 40.17 *artificial intelligence*
mean seriously 476.6 *propound*
means of access 317.2 *route*
means of ascent 304.7
means of communication 692.1 *communications*
means of connection 373.4
means of entry 314.6
means of escape **389.2**; 352.1 *means*; 252.1 *safety*; 252.4 *safety device*
means of identification 743.3
means of protection 252.2 *protection*
means of restraint 251.5
means of safety 252.4 *safety device*
means of transport 316.5
mean something 694.10 *mean*
mean something else 694.10 *mean*
mean-spirited 683.4 *selfish*
mean-spiritedness 683.1 *selfishness*
means to an end 392.1 *help*
meant **476.9**; **694.9**; 482.12 *intended*; 484.14 *planned*
mean the opposite 694.10 *mean*
mean the reverse 694.10 *mean*
mean the same thing 694.10 *mean*
meantime 278.9 *for the time being*; 275.6 *interval*
mean to 283.8 *intend*; 482.8 *resolve*
mean to say 694.10 *mean*
mean well 650.8 *be benevolent*
mean what one says 178.11 *be straight*; 707.22 *emphasize*
meanwhile 275.26 *all the time*; 282.10 *for the present*; 278.9 *for the time being*
measles 260.6 *infection*
measly 786.13 *nonpaying*; 124.2 *obscure*; 236.4 *poor*; 206.6 *sparse*
meassure 298.1 *regularity*
measurability 26.3
measurable **26.14**; 210.14 *calculable*; 27.73 *numerable*
measurably **26.17**; 210.16 *mathematically*
measure **26.10**; **158.18**; **209.5**; 770.4 *allot*; 216.4 *average*; 340.2 *deed*; 209.1 *degree*; 27.90 *enumerate*; 156.2 *intensity*; 148.4 *length*; 166.2 *limiting factor*; 551.35 *make clothing*; 352.1 *means*; 26.1 *measurement*; 516.1 *melody*; 17.9 *metre*; 18.17 *notation*; 210.11 *number*; 346.1 *operation*; 452.18 *particularity*; 17.8 *part of poem*; 148.5 *piece*; 770.2 *portion*; 436.1 *provision*; 203.8 *quantify*; 203.1 *quantity*; 158.1 *size*; 706.6 *solution*; 706.20 *solve*; 141.1 *space*; 452.22 *specify*; 18.19 *tempo*; 414.15 *weigh*
measured **26.13**; 106.4 *deliberate*; 209.7 *gradational*; 17.20 *metrical*; 684.9, 685.6 *moderate*; 203.6 *quantitative*; 298.11 *regular*; 706.14 *solved*; 217.1 *sufficient*
measured quantity 28.82 *measuring instrument*; 203.1 *quantity*
measured value 28.82 *measuring instrument*
measure for measure 807.1 *atonement*; 759.1 *exchange*; 110.1 *interchange*; 385.1 *retaliation*
measureless 202.2 *immeasurable*; 208.8 *numberless*
measurelessly 202.11 *immeasurably*
measurelessness 202.5 *immeasurability*
Measurement 26
measurement **1.10**; **26.1**; 209.3 *gradation*; 28.82 *measuring instrument*; 27.12 *numeration*; 203.1 *quantity*; 158.1 *size*
measure off 26.10 *measure*
measure of length 148.7
measure of time 148.8
measure one's length 305.11 *trip*
measure out **26.11**; 768.5 *give*; 166.7 *limit*; 26.10 *measure*; 141.21 *space*
measure public opinion 469.5 *vote*
measurer **26.9**; 51.3 *bowls player*
measures 340.1 *action*; 352.1 *means*; 484.2 *policy*; 243.10 *preparations*
measure time **281.16**; 275.16 *time*
measure up 26.10 *measure*
measure up to 111.10, 119.10 *be equal*; 334.10 *be powerful*; 217.4 *suffice*
measuring 26.1 *measurement*; 26.12 *metrical*; 203.6 *quantitative*; 203.1 *quantity*
measuring device 28.82 *measuring instrument*
measuring instrument **26.6**; **28.82**; **326.6**; **433.19**
measuring jug 25.6 *kitchen equipment*
measuring rod 26.6 *measuring instrument*
measuring system 26.5
measuring tape 47.2 *field events*
meat **25.20**; 406.1 *contents*; 99.2 *essential content*; 557.7 *food*; 80.3 *fruit structure*; 435.1 *materials*; 356.7 *produce*; 447.1 *topic*
meat-and-bone meal 43.9 *animal feedstuff*; 43.13 *fertilizer*
meatballs 25.20 *meat*
meat compartment 25.4 *kitchen container*
meat dish 25.32
meat-eater 557.18 *eater*; 70.4 *type of animal*
meat-eating 557.26 *eating*; 557.5 *eating habit*
meathead 459.3 *foolish person*; 592.5 *insensitive person*; 336.6 *muscleman*
meathooks 360.3 *tools for gripping*
meatiness 158.6 *squatness*
meat juice 431.2 *juice*
meatless day 687.3 *fast day*
meat market 779.1 *market*
meatpacker 578.1 *worker*
meat safe 25.4 *kitchen container*
meat substitute 25.21
meaty 726.3 *emphatic*; 694.7 *significant*; 158.17 *stocky*
Mecca 173.4 *centre of activity*; 482.6 *objective*; 10.13 *shrine*
Meccano™ 405.3 *unit*
mechanic 578.2 *artisan*; 438.8 *machinist*; 38.4 *mechanical engineer*; 320.21 *miscellaneous motoring terms*; 346.5 *operator*; 393.12 *repairer*
mechanical **438.9**; 334.16 *charged*; 28.98 *physical*; 348.8 *practical*; 38.32 *structural*
mechanical advantage 438.6 *mechanics*; 38.10 *work*
mechanical aid 438.1 *tool*
mechanical device 38.5 *dynamic structure*; 438.5 *machine*; 438.1 *tool*
mechanical digger 369.10 *excavator*
mechanical drawing 19.3 *drawing*; 721.9 *representation*; 717.2 *reproduction*
mechanical energy 334.4 *energy*
mechanical engineer **38.4**; 578.2 *artisan*; 38.2 *engineer*
mechanical engineering **38.3**; 38.1 *engineering*; 438.6 *mechanics*
mechanical instrument 18.25 *musical instrument*
mechanically 632.19 *habitually*; 348.9, 438.11 *instrumentally*; 28.100 *physically*; 38.33 *structurally*
mechanically precise 698.21 *accurate*
mechanical malfunction 247.4 *unsuccessful thing*
mechanical means 348.1 *instrumentality*
mechanical oscillation 28.14 *sound wave*
mechanical power 438.6 *mechanics*
mechanical precision 698.8 *accuracy*
mechanical solidarity 2.5 *society*
mechanical strength 336.1 *strength*
mechanical wave 326.5 *wave*
mechanical weathering 30.35 *weathering*
mechanician 438.8 *machinist*
mechanics **438.6**; 331.11 *impulsion*; 402.6 *natural science*
mechanism 32.14 *chemical reaction*; 405.4 *components*; 38.5 *dynamic structure*; 348.2 *instrument*; 438.5 *machine*; 4.7 *school of thought*
mechanist 4.11 *follower of a doctrine*; 438.8 *machinist*
mechanistic 438.9 *mechanical*; 4.14 *of a philosophy*
mechanization 348.1 *instrumentality*
mechanize 356.10 *produce*; 438.10 *use tools*
mechanized 334.16 *charged*; 438.9 *mechanical*; 356.11 *productive*
mechanized battalion 584.4 *military organization*
mechanized division 584.4 *military organization*
mecopteran 76.10 *insectan*
medal 47.5 *competition*; 542.4 *honour*; 575.3 *honours*; 743.4 *insignia*; 744.11 *monument*; 813.2 *prize*; 19.13 *relief-carving*; 794.1 *trophy*
medallion 542.7 *jewellery*; 19.13 *relief-carving*; 11.6 *talisman*; 794.1 *trophy*
medallist 47.3 *athlete*; 246.5 *victorious person*
medal play 56.1 *golf*
meddle **342.17**; 340.4 *act*; 486.7 *be clumsy*; 644.7 *be curious*; 378.8 *hinder*; 245.4 *impair*; 748.1 *mediate*
meddler **342.11**; **644.4**; 713.4 *adviser*; 378.7 *hinderer*; 748.3 *mediator*
meddlesome 342.21 *meddling*; 644.6 *prying*
meddlesomeness 342.9 *overactivity*
meddle with 224.8 *cause change*; 412.8 *mix*
meddling **342.21**; 378.13 *hindering*; 378.1 *hindrance*; 395.11 *influential*; 748.2 *mediation*; 342.9 *overactivity*; 644.2, 644.6 *prying*
meddling person 342.11 *meddler*
Medea 11.4 *witch*
media blitz 740.8 *public relations*
media event 740.8 *public relations*
media hype 741.9 *news story*; 740.8 *public relations*
medial 216.2 *medium*
medially 216.12 *mediumly*
median 173.6 *central*; 173.1 *centre*; 117.15 *everyday*; 216.2, 216.5 *medium*; 235.5 *not bad*; 231.4 *ordinary*; 27.60 *parameter*; 27.43 *triangle*
medianly 216.12 *mediumly*
mediant 18.16 *musical note*
median triangle 27.43 *triangle*
media personality 692.29 *broadcaster*
mediate **748.1**; 348.4 *be an instrument*; 15.12 *have an industrial dispute*; 589.6 *make peace*; 685.4 *moderate*; 749.4 *pacify*
mediated 746.8 *negotiated*; 15.10 *unionized*
mediately 748.7 *mediatorially*
mediating 15.10 *unionized*
Mediation 748
mediation **748.2**; 755.1 *contract*; 15.4 *industrial dispute*; 348.1 *instrumentality*; 746.1 *negotiation*; 749.1 *pacification*
mediative 348.7 *causal*
mediator **748.3**; 398.6, 578.3 *agent*; 348.3 *assistant*; 755.4 *contractor*; 15.6 *employer*; 464.5 *judge*; 570.13 *matchmaker*; 685.2 *moderator*; 746.4 *negotiator*; 589.3, 749.3 *pacifist*; 729.10 *speaker*
mediatorial 748.6 *mediatory*
mediatorially **748.7**; 749.7 *pacifically*
mediatory **748.6**; 749.6 *pacificatory*
medic 35.11 *doctor*; 394.15 *healer*; 608.5 *helper*
medicable 394.18 *medical*; 393.14 *repairable*
Medicaid 35.1 *medicine*; 252.1 *safety*
medical **35.22**; **394.18**; 35.6 *health care*
medical advice 394.11 *medical art*
medical adviser 713.4 *adviser*
medical art 394.11
medical assistance 392.5
medical assistant 35.17 *paramedic*
medical attendant 35.17 *paramedic*
medical auxiliary 35.17 *paramedic*
medical care 35.1 *medicine*; 394.13 *therapy*; 35.8 *treatment*
medical centre 173.4 *centre of activity*
medical consultation 35.6 *health care*
medical corps 586.16 *army unit*; 584.4 *military organization*
medical covering 550.6
medical doctor 35.11 *doctor*
medical ethics 4.6 *branch of philosophy*; 35.1 *medicine*
medical examination 35.6 *health care*
medical examiner 35.13 *medical specialist*
medical genetics 35.3 *medical specialty*
medical history 35.6 *health care*
medical insurance 35.1 *medicine*
medical intervention 35.8 *treatment*
medical jurisprudence 35.1 *medicine*
medically **35.26**; 394.21 *remedially*
medical officer 35.11 *doctor*; 257.3 *hygienist*
medical physics 28.4 *experimental physics*
medical practice 394.11 *medical art*; 35.1 *medicine*
medical practitioner 35.11 *doctor*
medical profession 35.1 *medicine*
medical registrar 35.11 *doctor*
medical report 693.3 *document*
medical school 6.12 *educational institution*
medical science 35.3 *medical specialty*
medical service 584.4 *military organization*
medical specialist 35.13
medical specialty 35.3
medical student 35.11 *doctor*
medical technician 35.17 *paramedic*
medical test 35.7 *diagnosis*
medical treatment 394.13 *therapy*; 35.8 *treatment*
medicament 394.2 *medicine*
Medicare 35.1 *medicine*; 253.1 *protection*; 252.1 *safety*
medicate 393.6 *cure*; 394.20 *doctor*; 35.19 *practise medicine*
medicated 393.16 *restorative*
medication 37.3 *drug*; 394.2 *medicine*; 35.8 *treatment*
medicinal 37.3 *drug*; 394.17 *remedial*; 393.16 *restorative*; 496.10 *stimulating*; 35.25 *therapeutic*
medicinal compound 412.2 *mixed thing*
medicinal drink 496.6 *cordial*
medicinal herb 394.2 *medicine*; 77.2 *plant*
medicinal leech 75.6 *worm*
medicinally 496.15 *piquantly*; 394.21 *remedially*
medicinal plant 77.2 *plant*
medicinal value 394.1 *remedy*
Medicine 35
medicine **35.1**; **394.2**; 37.3 *drug*; 394.11 *medical art*; 392.5 *medical assistance*
medicine bottle 394.2 *medicine*
medicine cabinet 394.2 *medicine*
medicine chest 394.2 *medicine*
medicine man 394.15 *healer*; 711.4 *warner*; 11.4 *witch*
medicine show 740.8 *public relations*; 21.7 *show*
medico 394.15 *healer*
medicopsychology 36.2 *psychiatry*
Medieval 3.15 *historic*
medieval 296.14 *historic*
medieval costume 551.5 *fancy dress*
medieval dance 22.4 *historic dancing*
medieval government 12.1 *government*
medievalism 284.9, 296.4 *antiquarianism*; 3.12 *historicism*
medievalist 284.11, 296.9 *antiquarian*
medieval ownership 763.3
Medieval times 3.10 *past age*
mediocre **216.3**; **618.10**; 685.6 *moderate*; 235.5 *not bad*; 122.16, 231.4 *ordinary*; 124.4 *trivial*
mediocreness 216.6 *mediocrity*
mediocrity **216.6**; **618.4**; 122.5 *inferior state*; 124.10 *nonentity*; 231.8 *ordinariness*; 157.5 *shallow person*; 124.7 *triviality*
meditate 482.7 *intend*; 443.12 *think*; 619.12 *wonder whether*; 9.7 *worship*
meditation 443.3 *thoughtfulness*; 36.14 *trance*; 9.1 *worship*
meditational 9.9 *worshipful*
meditative 443.10 *speculative*; 4.17 *thoughtful*; 9.9 *worshipful*

meditatively 4.28 *thoughtfully*; 9.12 *worshipfully*
meditativeness 443.3 *thoughtfulness*
meditative trance 463.1 *oblivion*
Mediterranean 493.8 *hot place*
Mediterranean climate 31.38 *climate*
medium **158.14**; **216.2**; **216.5**; 19.11 *artist's materials*; 101.7 *believer in a non-material world*; 99.1 *essence*; 348.2 *instrument*; 348.1 *instrumentality*; 719.6 *interpreter*; 445.5 *intuitive person*; 352.1 *means*; 685.6 *moderate*; 11.12 *occultist*; 475.8 *oracle*; 529.5 *paint*; 21.20 *stage lighting*
medium-grained texture 30.28 *rock*
mediumism 11.1 *occultism*
mediumistic 11.16 *psychic*
mediumistic trance 11.10 *psychic phenomenon*
mediumly **216.12**
medium of conversion **760.4**
medium of exchange 780.1 *money*
medium-pace bowler 53.4 *team*
medium-range 319.5 *transportable*
medium shot 41.4 *portrait*
medium-size 158.14 *medium*
medium steel 323.4 *shipbuilding*
medium-term forecast 31.4 *weather forecast*
medium wave 297.6 *radio frequency*; 692.14 *radio transmission*
medley 114.2 *assortment*; 376.32, 412.3 *miscellany*; 67.11 *swimming*
medley of colour 541.1 *variegation*
medley race 67.1 *swimming*
medley relay 47.9 *track*
medley relay race 47.1 *track events*
medulla 77.5 *stem*
medullary 419.4 *compressible*
Medusa 11.4 *witch*
medusa 75.7 *coelenterate*
medusoid 75.21 *coelenterate*
meed 813.1 *reward*
meek 623.1 *humble*; 674.8 *modest*; 663.7 *obedient*; 388.5 *submitting*; 335.11 *unprotected*
meekly 623.27 *humbly*; 674.17 *modestly*; 663.10 *obediently*; 388.6 *with humility*
meekness 335.3 *helplessness*; 623.7 *humility*; 674.1 *modesty*; 663.1 *obedience*
meerschaum 496.7 *tobacco*
meet **147.19**; **312.8**; 492.12 *abut*; 331.2 *collide*; 310.10, 376.39 *come together*; 117.7 *conform*; 449.1 *discover*; 59.7 *horseracing*; 59.8 *hunting*; 373.13 *intercommunicate*; 376.3 *meeting*; 785.7 *pay off*; 45.1 *sport*; 609.10 *suffice*
meet a crosscurrent 113.15 *be opposite*
meet a deadline 262.2 *make haste*
meet a demand 778.2 *be sold*; 436.5 *provision*
meet adversity 249.9 *be in trouble*
meet a headwind 113.15 *be opposite*
meet an order 436.5 *provision*
meet a sticky end 582.16 *meet one's fate*
meet by accident 107.11 *chance upon*
meet by chance 312.8 *meet*
meet contractual obligations 15.11 *conduct industrial relations*
meet God 7.19 *be religious*
meet halfway 639.10, 754.4 *compromise*; 749.5 *make peace*
meet head-on 113.15 *be opposite*; 113.19 *confront*
meeting **147.4**; **147.11**; **312.14**; **376.3**; **654.3**; 331.12 *collision*; 734.4 *conference*; 373.1 *connection*; 492.6 *contiguity*; 310.1 *convergence*; 310.7 *convergent*; 579.7 *council*; 449.6 *discovery*; 45.1 *sport*; 492.9 *touching*
meeting halfway 754.1 *compromise*
meetinghouse 10.11 *place of worship*
meeting in camera 737.1 *secrecy*
meeting of minds 750.1 *accord*; 713.2 *consultation*
meeting one's friends 654.3 *meeting*
meeting place **310.4**; **654.4**; 492.6 *contiguity*; 312.14 *meeting*
meeting point 492.6 *contiguity*; 147.7 *interface*
meeting the cost 785.1 *payment*
meeting with God 8.8 *divine manifestation*
meet one's death 582.15 *die*
meet one's end 582.15 *die*
meet one's fate **582.16**; 582.15 *die*
meet one's Maker 582.15 *die*
meet one's match 385.4 *serve one right*
meet on the battlefield 585.14 *battle*
meet requirements 217.4 *suffice*
meet reward 814.9 *retribution*
meet Saint Peter 582.15 *die*
meet the cost 785.8 *defray*; 787.1 *expend*
meet the eye 520.9 *appear*
meet the needs of 609.10 *suffice*
meet with 713.6 *consult*; 449.1 *discover*
meet with a loss 766.9 *lose*
meet with approbation 669.17 *meet with approval*
meet with approval **669.17**
meet with disapproval 670.24 *be open to criticism*
meet with success 246.6 *be successful*
mega 158.15 *big*
megabucks 780.3 *fortune*; 781.6 *money*
megabyte 40.19 *computing terms*
Megaera 624.7 *gods and goddesses of anger*
megahertz 297.6 *radio frequency*
megalith 744.11 *monument*; 3.11 *relic*; 284.7 *thing of the past*
megalithic 158.15 *big*
megalomania 36.15 *compulsion*; 461.4 *delusion*; 467.1 *overestimation*; 673.1 *vanity*
megalomaniac 386.5 *compulsive person*; 461.7 *insane person*; 467.3 *optimist*; 673.8 *vain*
megalopolis 87.1 *city*; 86.10 *urban area*
megalopteran 76.10 *insectan*
meganucleus 34.9 *cell nucleus*
megaphone 504.9 *audio device*; 507.4 *sound maker*; 28.18 *source of sound*
megaphyll 77.6 *leaf*
megastar 9.4 *idolized person*; 811.2 *person of repute*
megastore 779.8 *store*
megaton bomb 587.16 *bomb*
megawatt 334.5 *unit of work*
megrim 491.2 *painful condition*; 642.3 *whim*
megrims 327.8 *spasm*; 260.18 *veterinary disease*
mein 160.6 *nature*
meiosis 34.10 *cell division*
meiotic 34.25 *genetic*
me-ism 673.5 *self-interest*
Meissen's crossed swords 24.4 *porcelain mark*
Meistersinger 17.14 *author*; 516.5 *melodist*
meke 22.4 *historic dancing*
Mekong 90.5 *other major rivers*
melamine formaldehyde 435.1 *materials*
melancholia 36.13 *depression*; 461.6 *mental breakdown*; 36.10 *neurosis*
melancholic 602.6 *depressed*; 602.4 *depressing person*; 599.12 *four humours*; 611.4 *hopeless*; 611.3 *hopeless person*; 461.7 *insane person*; 461.13 *mentally ill*; 36.7 *personality type*; 626.6 *sullen*
melancholy 620.1 *boredom*; 620.4 *boring*; 539.3 *depressed*; 602.2 *depression*; 611.1 *hopelessness*; 236.4 *poor*; 236.10 *poverty*; 626.6 *sullen*; 626.1 *sullenness*
Melanesian 5.11 *family of languages*; 1.6 *race*; 1.13 *racial*
mélange 412.2 *mixed thing*
melanic 523.10 *dark-coloured*
melanin 532.8 *black pigment*; 534.3 *brownness*
melanism 532.7 *blackness*
melanistic 532.2 *dark*
melanoma 260.12 *cancer*; 260.13 *skin disease*
melanosis 532.7 *blackness*
melanous 523.10 *dark-coloured*
Melba toast 25.38 *bread*
Melbourne 87.6 *other cities*
mêlée 408.9 *disorder*
melifluous 18.30 *harmonic*
melifluously 516.11 *melodiously*
melinite 587.15 *explosive*
meliorable 244.15 *improvable*
meliorate 244.1 *improve*
melioration 6.1 *education*; 244.5 *improvement*
meliorative 244.16 *improving*
meliorism 244.11 *reformism*
meliorist 244.12 *reformer*
mellifluent 516.6 *melodious*
mellifluous 543.3 *elegant*; 516.6 *melodious*; 490.6 *pleasant*
mellifluously 543.5 *elegantly*
mellow 556.17 *age*; 760.8 *be transformed*; 529.15 *colour*; 241.3 *comfortable*; 510.8 *deep*; 243.7 *develop*; 243.20 *developed*; 419.14 *ease*; 244.2 *get better*; 18.30 *harmonic*; 556.18 *mature*; 516.6 *melodious*; 296.11 *old*; 419.13 *soften*; 419.6 *soft-hearted*; 529.13 *soft-hued*
mellow into 760.7 *convert into*
mellowly 296.18 *venerably*
mellowness 419.12 *gentleness*; 556.4 *middle age*; 296.1 *oldness*; 243.14 *preparedness*
melodic 750.13 *harmonious*; 516.6 *melodious*
melodically 750.33 *harmoniously*; 516.11 *melodiously*; 18.42 *musically*
melodic line 516.1 *melody*
melodics 18.14 *harmonics*
melodic scale 18.20 *key*
melodious **516.6**; 510.8 *deep*; 18.30 *harmonic*; 750.13 *harmonious*; 498.7 *pleasant*
melodiously **516.11**; 18.42 *musically*; 498.9 *sweetly*
melodiousness **516.3**; 18.1 *music*; 498.1 *sweetness*
melodist **516.5**
melodize 18.34, 750.24 *harmonize*; 516.9 *set to music*
melodrama 727.1 *exaggeration*; 21.2 *play*; 21.11 *tragedy*
melodramatic 21.39 *dramatic*; 727.12 *exaggerated*; 590.13 *passionate*
melodramatically 21.44 *dramatically*; 727.16 *exaggeratedly*; 488.14 *sensationally*
melodramatist 21.26 *dramatist*
melodramatize 21.38 *dramatize*
melody **18.13**; **516.1**; 750.4 *harmony*; 18.1 *music*
melon 80.5 *figurative usage*
Melpomene 21.11 *tragedy*
melt **431.24**; 493.14 *be hot*; 278.4 *be transient*; 94.12 *cease to exist*; 760.7 *convert into*; 375.4 *deconstruct*; 526.1 *disappear*; 627.11 *excite pity*; 268.17 *liquefy*; 32.3 *phase*; 31.30, 31.63 *snow*; 419.13 *soften*; 32.25 *solidify*; 30.24 *volcanic activity*; 441.1 *waste*
meltable 431.21 *liquefiable*
meltage 31.30 *snow*
melt away 278.4 *be transient*; 209.6 *change gradually*; 214.4 *decrease*; 526.2 *depart*; 441.1 *waste*
meltdown 28.75 *nuclear accident*; 357.4 *ruin*
melt down 493.14 *be hot*; 431.24 *melt*; 369.17 *obtain an extract*
melted 375.5 *disintegrated*; 431.19 *liquefied*; 32.32 *solid*
melted out 782.3 *beggarly*
melting 593.20 *amorous*; 227.13 *changeable*; 760.1 *conversion*; 760.14 *converting*; 375.2 *deconstruction*; 526.4 *disappearance*; 375.6 *disintegrating*; 431.8 *fluidification*; 493.5 *hot weather*; 431.20 *liquefying*; 32.3 *phase*; 419.2 *pliant*; 28.37 *temperature*; 441.3 *waste*
melting look 518.6 *look*
meltingly 526.8 *fleetingly*
melting point 493.1 *heat*; 28.37 *temperature*
melting pot 760.4 *medium of conversion*; 412.6 *mixer*; 566.11 *nation*
melt into 209.6 *change gradually*; 760.7 *convert into*
melt into thin air 94.12 *cease to exist*
melts 25.31 *offal*
melt the heart 627.11 *excite pity*
meltwater 30.38 *glacier*; 31.30 *snow*; 433.1 *water*
member **405.5**; 205.4 *component*; 764.3 *participant*; 127.3 *person included*; 27.21 *set*
member of Congress 579.16 *official*; 12.8 *politician*
member of parliament 398.1 *delegate*; 251.6 *lawmaker*; 579.16 *official*; 12.8 *politician*
member of society **566.10**
member of staff 405.5 *member*
member of the establishment 123.4 *bigwig*
member of the resistance 385.2 *revenger*
member of the underground 385.2 *revenger*
membership 127.1 *inclusion*; 764.2 *participation*; 654.1 *sociability*
members only 128.4 *exclusiveness*
membrane 411.3 *coat*; 521.6 *that which makes invisible*
membraneously 411.12 *in layers*
membranophone 18.25 *musical instrument*
membranous 411.9 *platelike*
memento **462.3**; **794.3**; 768.2 *gift*; 744.11 *monument*; 3.11 *relic*
memento mori 582.3 *symbol of death*
memo 744.1 *record*; 462.4 *reminder*
memoir 722.1 *dissertation*; 17.4 *nonfiction*; 744.1 *record*
memoirs 3.6 *biography*; 721.4 *factual account*; 554.11 *life story*; 462.2 *retrospect*
memo pad 744.6 *record book*
memorabilia 462.3 *memento*; 744.1 *record*; 3.11 *relic*; 215.1 *remainder*
memorability 123.1 *importance*
memorable **462.7**; 123.6 *notable*
memorably **462.16**; 123.9 *importantly*; 215.11 *residually*
memorandum 123.2 *important matter*; 462.4 *reminder*
memorial **462.10**; 601.11 *commemorative*; 583.11 *funeral*; 583.4 *funeral objects*; 583.6 *grave*; 462.3 *memento*; 744.11 *monument*
memorial arch 744.11 *monument*
Memorial Day 298.6 *annually celebrated day*
memorial inscription 744.11 *monument*
memorialization 601.2 *commemoration*; 279.4 *eternalization*
memorialize 462.14, 601.16 *commemorate*; 279.6 *eternalize*
memorially 3.25 *reportedly*
memorial service 601.2 *commemoration*; 583.2 *funeral*; 10.4 *public worship*
memorization 632.7 *habituation*; 462.1 *memory*; 360.5 *retentiveness*
memorize **462.11**; 455.12 *know by heart*; 400.15 *learn*; 21.37 *rehearse*; 360.8 *remember*
memorized **462.9**
memorizing 360.5 *retentiveness*
Memory 462
memory **36.23**; **40.6**; **462.1**; 601.2 *commemoration*; 40.4 *computer*; 462.5 *day to remember*; 446.1 *idea*; 215.1 *remainder*; 439.4 *storage*
memory artist 21.29 *entertainer*
memory gap 358.5 *forgetfulness*
memory trace 36.23 *memory*
memsahib 568.3 *female title of address*
Men 767.7 *toilet*
men 586.14 *armed forces*; 566.1 *humankind*; 567.15 *menfolk*; 578.4 *personnel*
menace 651.7 *act of malevolence*; 798.11 *be evil*; 254.5 *danger*; 254.10 *endanger*; 612.13 *frighten*; 594.8 *hated person*; 475.11 *predict*; 651.18 *torment*; 711.5 *warn*; 711.1 *warning*
menacing 523.11 *benighted*; 254.1 *dangerous*; 612.10 *frightening*; 651.10 *malevolent*; 711.8 *warning*
menacingly 254.11 *dangerously*; 612.16 *frighteningly*
ménage 564.2 *inhabitants*
ménage à trois 796.4 *illicit love*; 593.8 *love affair*; 199.2 *trident*
menagerie 439.5 *collection*; 376.31 *exhibition*; 412.3 *miscellany*; 565.12 *stall*
menaion 10.10 *religious manual*
menarche 560.11 *menstruation*; 562.2 *productiveness*
mend 244.2 *get better*; 259.6 *get healthy*; 244.1 *improve*; 801.15 *put right*; 244.3 *rectify*; 394.19 *remedy*; 393.1, 393.8 *repair*
mendable 393.14 *repairable*
mendaceous 699.29 *false*
mendacious 234.8 *exaggerated*; 702.10 *hypocritical*
mendaciously 234.14 *distortedly*; 699.40 *falsely*
mendaciousness 699.1 *falsehood*
mendacity 234.4 *distortion of the truth*; 699.1 *falsehood*; 702.5 *hypocrisy*
mended 393.13 *repaired*
Mendelian 34.25 *genetic*
Mendelian genetics 34.11 *genetics*
Mendel's laws 34.11 *genetics*
mender 393.12 *repairer*; 244.13 *reviser*
mendicancy 782.7 *beggary*; 710.3 *solicitation*
mendicant 710.5 *beggar*; 782.3 *beggarly*; 710.11 *begging*; 7.7 *monk*; 782.10 *poor person*

mendicant friar 710.5 *beggar;* 782.10 *poor person*
mending 244.6 *rectification;* 393.11 *recuperation;* 393.8 *repair*
Mendip Hills 89.5 *British mountains*
mend one's ways 244.2 *get better*
menfolk 567.15
menhir 583.6 *grave;* 744.11 *monument;* 3.11 *relic;* 284.7 *thing of the past*
menial 388.2 *appeaser;* 122.6 *inferior;* 401.1 *servant;* 664.6 *servile;* 401.9 *serving;* 388.5 *submitting;* 578.1 *worker*
menially 401.10 *obediently;* 664.16 *with servility*
menialness 664.1 *servility*
meningitis 260.6 *infection*
men in white coats 36.30, 461.10 *psychiatrist*
meniscal 177.4 *curved*
meniscoid 182.4 *convex*
meniscus 177.2 *bend;* 27.42 *circle;* 182.1 *convexity*
Mennonite 7.5 *Christian*
men of today 285.5 *contemporary*
menopausal 560.31 *menstrual;* 556.13 *middle-aged*
menopause 563.1 *infertility;* 560.11 *menstruation;* 556.4 *middle age*
menorah 10.14 *sacred object*
menorrhagia 560.11 *menstruation*
mensal 25.56 *culinary*
Mensa member 458.4 *intellectual*
men's clothing 551.1 *dress*
menses 298.2 *cycle;* 560.11 *menstruation*
Mensheviks 12.6 *political party*
men's magazine 796.2 *indecency;* 740.5 *journal*
mens rea 482.1 *intention*
Men's Room 767.7 *toilet*
mens sana 460.1 *sanity*
mens sana in corpore sano 259.3 *health*
menstrual 560.31; 298.12 *cyclic*
menstrual cycle 298.2 *cycle;* 276.5 *recurrent period*
menstrual flow 431.3 *body fluid;* 560.11 *menstruation*
menstruate 560.22; 298.8 *be cyclic*
menstruating 560.31 *menstrual*
menstruation 560.11; 298.2 *cycle;* 562.2 *productiveness;* 276.5 *recurrent period*
menstruum 431.9 *solvent*
mensurability 26.3 *measurability*
mensurable 210.14 *calculable;* 26.14 *measurable;* 27.73 *numerable*
mensural 26.12 *metrical*
mensuration 28.95; 26.1 *measurement*
mensurational 26.12 *metrical*
mensurative 26.12 *metrical*
menswear 551.1 *dress*
mental 442.9; 446.11 *ideational;* 461.11 *insane;* 101.11 *internal;* 443.8 *thoughtful*
mental activity 443.1 *thought*
mental affliction 798.2 *affliction*
mental agility 332.10 *quickness of mind*
mental agitation 327.1 *agitation*
mental and physical distress 261.7 *fatigue*
mental arithmetic 27.12 *numeration*
mental asylum 394.14 *hospital*
mental attitude 631.1 *conduct*
mental block 463.2 *blankness;* 358.5 *forgetfulness*
mental body 11.7 *spirit*
mental breakdown 461.6; 36.10 *neurosis*
mental case 461.7 *insane person;* 260.19 *sick person*
mental chemistry 36.1 *psychology*
mental cruelty 571.3 *divorce court*
mental decay 335.4 *disability*
mental deficiency 457.1 *lack of intellect;* 461.2 *subnormality*
mental derangement 328.6 *derangement*
mental deterioration 461.3
mental disorder 328.6 *derangement;* 260.4 *disease;* 36.9 *psychological disorder*
mental entities 4.9 *philosophical problem*
mental equilibrium 460.1 *sanity*
mental fatigue 261.7 *fatigue*
mental fluctuation 326.3 *vacillation*
mental freedom 391.1 *liberation*
mental handicap 335.4 *disability;* 457.1 *lack of intellect;* 461.2 *subnormality*
mental hardness 418.8
mental health 460.1 *sanity*
mental home 461.8 *mental hospital*
mental hospital 461.8; 394.14 *hospital;* 36.31 *psychiatric hospital*
mental illness 798.2 *affliction;* 461.1 *insanity*
mental image 446.1 *idea;* 477.4 *ideality;* 717.6 *image*
mental impairment 461.2 *subnormality*
mental instability 461.1 *insanity*
mental institution 461.8 *mental hospital*
mentalism 4.7 *school of thought*
mentality 442.3 *intelligence;* 442.1 *mind*
mentally 442.14; 101.14 *subjectively;* 446.20 *theoretically*
mentally defective personality 36.8 *disordered personality*
mentally deficient 457.7 *intellectually subnormal;* 457.5 *lacking intellect*
mentally deranged 328.16 *deranged*
mentally handicapped 457.7 *intellectually subnormal;* 457.5 *lacking intellect*
mentally hard 418.4
mentally ill 461.13
mentally quick 332.2
mentally retarded 457.5 *lacking intellect*
mentally sharp 425.5
mentally sound 460.4 *sane*
mentally strong 423.5 *mentally tough*
mentally subnormal 457.7 *intellectually subnormal*
mentally tough 423.5
mentally weak 457.5 *lacking intellect*
mental object 446.1 *idea*
mental philosophy 4.6 *branch of philosophy*
mental picture 446.1 *idea;* 477.4 *ideality*
mental process 443.1 *thought*
mental product 356.4
mental quickness 332.10 *quickness of mind*
mental reservation 479.5 *equivocalness*
mental retardation 457.1 *lack of intellect*
mental sharpness 425.13
mental shock 36.12 *stress*
mental skill 485.1 *skill*
mental specialist 36.30 *psychiatrist*
mental strength 423.9 *mental toughness*
mental stress 36.12 *stress*
mental subnormality 36.9 *psychological disorder;* 461.2 *subnormality*
mental test 36.5 *psychological test;* 36.4 *psychometrics*
mental toughness 423.9
mental treatment 394.13 *therapy*
mental weakness 457.1 *lack of intellect*
menthol 33.20 *terpene;* 496.7 *tobacco*
mention 721.16 *define;* 740.13 *make public;* 693.4 *mass communication;* 738.3 *reveal;* 729.11 *speak;* 139.24 *specify*
mentionable 795.10 *moralistic*
mentioned 738.13 *displayed*
mentor 392.14, 713.4 *adviser;* 579.13 *director;* 400.9 *educational leader;* 6.4 *educator;* 396.10 *person of authority;* 446.9 *person of ideas;* 252.3 *protector;* 4.12 *sage*
menu 220.4 *bill;* 40.19 *computing terms;* 220.2 *table*
meow 515.1 *animal cry;* 515.4 *cry*
MEP 400.3 *leader;* 579.16 *official;* 396.10 *person of authority*
meperidine 394.5 *analgesic*
Mephisto 8.7 *devil*
Mephistophelean 8.16 *devilish*
Mephistopheles 8.7 *devil;* 804.6 *religious sin*
Mephistophelian 804.14 *impious*
mephitic 432.18 *miasmic;* 503.3 *stinking*
mephitis 432.3 *miasma;* 503.1 *stench*
mercantile 776.13; 13.13 *economic*
mercantile system 13.6 *economic factors*
mercantile system tariff 251.2 *economic restraint*
mercantilism 251.2 *economic restraint*
mercantilist 251.6 *lawmaker*
Mercator projection 163.4 *map*
Mercator's projection 717.7 *map*
mercenaries 586.14 *armed forces*
mercenary 586.35 *martial;* 586.6 *militarist;* 585.17 *military;* 585.11 *recruit*
mercenary army 586.15 *army*
mercenary forces 584.2 *the military*
mercer 551.26 *fashion designer;* 778.13 *retailer*
mercerize 423.11 *make tough*
merchandise 778.8; 438.7 *equipment;* 440.5 *personal estate;* 356.7 *produce;* 778.1 *sell;* 439.1 *store;* 776.1 *trade;* 13.10 *trade with*
merchandiser 13.9 *economist;* 776.10 *trader;* 778.12 *wholesaler*
merchandising 778.3 *selling;* 776.4 *trade*
merchant 578.3 *agent;* 13.9 *economist;* 778.13 *retailer;* 776.10 *trader;* 319.5 *transportable;* 778.12 *wholesaler*
merchantable 776.13 *mercantile;* 778.15 *saleable*
merchant bank 780.19 *treasury*
merchant jack 743.7 *flag*
merchant-like 776.13 *mercantile*
merchantman 323.3 *vessel*
merchant marine 586.22 *navy*
merchant navy 586.22 *navy*
merchant prince 778.12 *wholesaler*
merchant ship 323.3 *vessel*
merchant venturer 778.12 *wholesaler*
merciful 649.5; 648.4 *lenient;* 627.6 *pitying*
mercifully 16.88, 649.14 *forgivingly;* 648.6 *leniently;* 749.7 *pacifically;* 627.13 *pitifully*
mercifulness 649.2 *forgivingness;* 648.1 *leniency;* 627.3 *mercy;* 627.1 *pity*
merciless 651.13; 647.8 *severe;* 638.3 *strong-willed;* 641.3 *unyielding*
mercilessly 628.7 *pitilessly;* 647.11 *severely*
mercilessness 628.1 *pitilessness*
MERCOSUR 779.4 *free market*
mercurial 453.8, 642.1 *capricious;* 639.2 *changeable;* 227.14 *irresolute;* 332.2 *mentally quick;* 300.16 *moving;* 590.13 *passionate*
mercurially 300.18 *in motion*
Mercurian 29.36 *astronomical*
mercuric 32.34 *elemental*
Mercurochrome™ 394.3 *prophylactic*
mercurous 32.34 *elemental*
Mercury 316.8 *messenger;* 29.16 *planet;* 332.13 *swift person*
mercury 227.3 *changeable thing*
mercury barometer 28.88 *barometer;* 31.7 *weather instruments*
Mercurycard™ 692.9 *telephone*
mercury thermometer 28.89 *thermometer*
mercury-vapour lamp 522.6 *electric light;* 39.20 *electron tube;* 28.25 *light source*
mercy 627.3; 650.1 *benevolence;* 8.2 *divine attribute;* 388.7 *I/we surrender!;* 648.1 *leniency;* 749.2 *peace offering*
mercy flight 322.1 *aviation*
mercy killer 382.10 *killer*
mercy killing 382.1 *killing*
mercy seat 16.27 *courtroom*
mere 255.16 *simple;* 88.2 *small lake*
mere existence 93.9; 782.5 *poverty*
mere handful 206.1 *few*
merely exist 93.21
merengue 18.10 *world music*
mere nothing 124.8 *trifle*
mere notion 476.3 *conjecture*
mere rhetoric 702.1 *sophistry*
meretricious 676.3 *affected;* 727.14 *extravagant;* 699.31 *hypocritical;* 542.10 *ornate;* 544.10 *ugly;* 796.13 *unchaste;* 675.7 *vulgar*
meretriciousness 699.3 *hypocrisy*
mere wreck 245.9 *dilapidation*
merganser 305.8 *descender*
merge 570.19; 197.19 *become one;* 127.5 *be included;* 111.7 *be the same;* 374.5 *combine;* 373.11 *connect;* 750.24 *harmonize;* 747.16 *join;* 111.8 *make the same;* 412.8 *mix;* 773.7 *take*
merged 750.11 *allied;* 374.9 *assembled;* 373.15 *connected;* 776.19 *corporate;* 750.13 *harmonious;* 127.8 *included;* 412.12 *mixed;* 108.4 *related;* 111.12 *same;* 773.12 *taking*
merge in 405.10 *compose*
merge into 760.7 *convert into*
mergence 111.1 *sameness*
merger 570.2 *alliance;* 747.7 *association;* 776.9 *bargaining;* 752.3 *business offer;* 374.1 *combination;* 373.1 *connection;* 13.7 *corporation;* 346.2 *joint operation;* 412.1 *mixture;* 108.1 *relatedness;* 773.1 *taking*
merge with 747.14 *join with*
merging 747.7 *association;* 111.12 *same*
meridian 29.5 *celestial sphere;* 86.2 *geographical region;* 290.3, 290.6 *noon;* 86.16 *regional;* 174.1 *summit;* 174.5 *top*
meridional 324.13 *directional;* 174.5 *top*
meringue 434.10 *air bubble*
merino 193.4 *textile*
merit 136.14 *be qualified;* 801.13 *be right;* 235.9 *be worthy;* 137.9 *distinction;* 797.8 *good;* 123.1 *importance;* 622.4 *prestige;* 237.6 *usability;* 235.6, 803.3 *worth;* 622.8 *worthiness*
merited 136.9 *qualified*
meritedness 136.1 *qualification*
meritocracy 235.7 *elite;* 12.1 *government;* 396.7 *type of rule*
meritocrat 235.7 *elite*
meritocratic 12.9 *governmental*
meritorious 617.8 *desirable;* 575.5 *entitled;* 797.1 *good;* 669.21 *praiseworthy;* 235.1, 803.7 *worthy*
meritoriously 617.17 *desirably;* 803.11 *worthily*
meritoriousness 617.2 *desirability*
Merle Park 22.14 *famous ballet dancers*
Merlin 11.4 *witch*
merlon 384.11 *fortification*
mermaid 91.4 *sea god;* 11.4 *witch*
merman 91.4 *sea god*
merocrine 559.4 *secretory*
merocrine secretion 559.1 *secretion*
merrily 598.9 *cheerfully;* 597.9 *joyfully;* 600.11 *rejoicingly;* 654.18 *sociably*
Merrimack 586.25 *historical naval ships*
merriment 599.2 *amusement;* 601.1 *celebration;* 598.3 *cheerfulness;* 597.1 *happiness;* 600.1 *rejoicing;* 654.1 *sociability*
merry 601.10 *celebrative;* 598.1 *cheerful;* 690.1 *drunk;* 597.4 *happy;* 599.10 *humorous;* 697.5 *nonsensical;* 490.7 *pleased;* 600.9 *rejoicing;* 654.15 *sociable*
merry-andrew 21.32 *clown*
merry dancers 522.4 *natural light*
merrymake 601.15 *celebrate*
merrymaker 597.3 *joyful person;* 600.4 *rejoicer*
merrymaking 601.1 *celebration;* 598.3 *cheerfulness;* 597.2 *fun;* 600.1 *rejoicing;* 654.1 *sociability*
merry men 586.17 *army person*
merry widow 21.23 *role;* 571.6 *surviving spouse*
Mersey 90.4 *British rivers*
mesa 154.2 *heights;* 92.7 *upland*
mésalliance 109.5 *misconnection;* 570.3 *types of marriage*
mescaline 691.6 *drug*
mesh 193.2 *braid;* 108.2 *interrelatedness;* 193.8 *interweave;* 747.12 *reciprocate;* 700.13 *snare*
meshed 700.42 *trapped*
mesh together 193.8 *interweave*
mesiad 216.2 *medium*
mesial 216.2 *medium*
mesivta 6.12 *educational institution*
mesmeric 395.12 *appealing;* 386.9 *compelling;* 685.8 *moderating;* 483.11 *motivational;* 480.19 *persuasive*
mesmerically 363.13 *attractionally;* 11.25 *occultly*
mesmerism 395.2 *occult influence;* 11.1 *occultism;* 363.2 *pulling power*
mesmerize 489.12 *anaesthetize;* 395.10 *be a prevailing influence;* 11.21 *bewitch;* 363.12 *lure;* 483.10 *manipulate*
mesmerized 11.19 *bewitched;* 483.12 *motivated*
mesne profits 788.2 *money received*
mesocarp 80.3 *fruit structure*
mesoderm 34.15 *developmental biology*
mesodermal 34.26 *developmental*
meso-form 32.13 *structure*
Mesolithic 296.15 *primal*
Mesolithic period 284.4 *prehistoric age*
mesomitosis 34.10 *cell division*
mesomorph 160.6 *nature;* 36.7 *personality type;* 1.9 *physical type*
mesomorphic 1.15 *physical*
mesomorphism 36.7 *personality type*
mesomorphy 36.7 *personality type;* 1.9 *physical type*
meson 28.77 *elementary particle;* 159.2 *little thing;* 402.4 *matter*
mesophyll 77.6 *leaf*
mesosome 34.8 *cell organ*
mesosphere 154.8 *high thing*
mesozoan 75.1, 75.16 *invertebrate*
Mesozoic 296.15 *primal*
Mesozoic era 284.3 *geological period*
mess 486.9 *bungling;* 203.2 *certain*

amount; 408.23 confuse; 408.5 confusion; 247.1 failure; 557.24 have a meal; 408.4 litter; 412.3 miscellany; 408.6 mix-up; 264.5 predicament; 565.7 room
message 693.2 communication; 694.1 meaning; 795.7 moral; 742.4 signal; 447.1 topic; 316.10 transferred thing
message conveyed 694.1 meaning
message-receiver 769.5 recipient
messed-up 486.4 bungled; 408.19 mixed-up
messenger 316.8; 398.1 delegate; 398.4 deputy; 693.9 informant; 401.5 office assistant; 475.5 omen; 692.4 postal worker; 129.8 precursor; 740.10 publicizer; 742.8 signer; 332.13 swift person
messenger of God 8.6 angel
messenger of the gods 332.13 swift person
messenger RNA 34.13 genetic material
messer 557.18 eater
Messiah 8.4 God the Son; 579.14 leader
messianic 8.13 divine
messianically 8.19 divinely
Messier Catalogue 29.6 star catalogue
messily 258.12 dirtily
messiness 258.1 dirtiness; 666.2 indifference; 408.3 untidiness
messing 557.4 eating meals
mess jacket 551.11 jacket
mess kit 551.3, 656.4 formal dress
messmate 557.18 eater; 569.5 friend
mess room 557.15 eating place; 565.7 room
messuage 440.2 legal terms
mess up 486.7 be clumsy; 258.11 dirty; 245.4 impair; 408.24 make disordered; 412.9 mix up
mess with 224.8 cause change
messy 486.4 bungled; 258.7 dirty; 666.5 indifferent; 408.15 untidy
mestizo 412.5 hybrid
metabolic 33.26 biochemical; 34.22 physiological; 224.13 transformative
metabolically 33.27 biochemically
metabolic pathway 33.21 metabolism
metabolism 33.21; 34.5 physiology; 224.3 transformation
metabolite 33.21 metabolism
metabolize 33.25; 224.9 transform
metachronism 288.1 wrong time
metachronistic 288.10 mistimed
metachronistically 288.18 out of chronological order
metaethics 4.6 branch of philosophy
metafiction 17.2 fiction
metage 26.1 measurement
metal 32.6 chemical element; 418.7 hard substance; 743.8 heraldic device; 435.1 materials; 32.23 metallurgy
metalanguage 5.7 international language
metal clip 62.4 climbing equipment
metal conductor 28.43 electrical conduction
metal detector 449.11 detector
metal engraver 19.18 engraver
metal engraving 19.15 engraving
metal fatigue 38.16 deformation
metal furniture 23.1 furniture
metal inlay 23.9 decorative woodwork
metallic 32.34 elemental; 513.7 strident
metallic bond 32.11 chemical bond
metallic conductor 39.3 electricity
metallic currency 780.13 coinage
metallic pigment 529.4 pigment
metalloid 32.6 chemical element; 32.34 elemental; 32.23 metallurgy
metalloprotein 33.9 protein
metallurgical 32.45; 32.31 chemical
metallurgical engineering 38.1 engineering
metallurgically 32.46 chemically
metallurgist 32.2 chemist
metallurgy 32.23; 32.1 chemistry; 38.1 engineering
metal ore 435.1 materials
metal poisoning 260.2 illness
metals 321.3 rail
metal sculptor 19.17 sculptor
metal sculpture 19.12 sculpture
metal ski 68.5 ski equipment
metal spike 62.4 climbing equipment
metalwork 19.1 art
metalworker 578.2 artisan
metalworks 577.1 workshop
metamathematics 27.1 mathematics
metamitosis 34.10 cell division
metamorphic 30.56 petrographic; 224.13 transformative
metamorphic grade 30.32 metamorphism
metamorphic rock 30.33; 30.28 rock
metamorphism 30.32
metamorphose 227.11 be changeable; 760.7 convert into; 76.17 develop; 224.9, 760.9 transform
metamorphosed 760.13 converted
metamorphosis 227.1 changeableness; 760.1 conversion; 34.15 developmental biology; 76.5 larva; 30.29 petrogenesis; 224.3 transformation; 73.8 young amphibian
metamorphous 224.13 transformative
metanarrative 17.3 aspect of fiction; 4.2 philosophical system
metaphase 34.10 cell division
metaphor 111.2 equivalence; 719.1 interpretation; 721.3 narration; 542.1 ornament; 5.24 phrasing; 17.12 poetic language; 115.1 similarity; 762.3 substitute thing; 694.4 type of meaning
metaphorical 111.13 equivalent; 694.6 meaningful; 542.10 ornate; 5.43 phrasal
metaphorically 111.18 identically; 694.13 meaningfully; 542.13 ornately; 5.51 phraseologically; 115.13 similarly
metaphorical meaning 694.4 type of meaning
metaphrastic 719.17 translational
metaphysical 17.16 literary; 101.8 nonmaterial; 4.13 of philosophy; 7.18 theological
metaphysical idealism 101.5 idealism
metaphysically 101.13; 11.25 occultly; 4.24 philosophically
metaphysical poet 17.14 author
metaphysical poetry 17.6 poetry
metaphysical world 101.1 nonmaterial world
metaphysician 11.12 occultist; 4.10 philosopher
metaphysicist 11.12 occultist
metaphysics 4.6 branch of philosophy; 93.1 existence; 11.1 occultism; 36.1 psychology
metaphysics of presence 93.1 existence; 97.1 presence
metapsychic 11.16 psychic
metapsychical 11.16 psychic
metapsychism 11.1 occultism
metapsychist 11.12 occultist
metapsychology 36.1 psychology
metapsychosis 11.8 psychic power
metastable 32.35 combined
metastable equilibrium 28.10 force
metastable state 28.67 excited atom
metastasis 316.3 transmission
metastasize 316.11 transfer
metastatic 316.17 transferable
metastatically 316.18 in transit
Metatheria 71.4 pouched mammal
metatherian 71.25 mammalian; 71.4 pouched mammal
metathesis 316.1 transfer
metathesize 316.11 transfer
metathetic 316.17 transferable
Metazoa 75.1 invertebrate
metazoa 554.9 classifications of life
metazoan 75.1, 75.16 invertebrate
metempsychosis 402.2 materialization; 316.1 transfer; 224.3 transformation
meteor 29.20; 522.4 natural light; 278.2 transient thing
meteoric 29.36 astronomical; 332.1 swift; 278.6 transient
meteorically 29.39 astronomically; 332.14 swiftly
meteorite 29.20 meteor
meteorite crater 29.20 meteor
meteoritic 29.36 astronomical
meteoroid 29.20 meteor
meteorologic 31.41
meteorological 30.49 geophysical; 31.41 meteorologic
meteorologically 31.65; 30.66 geographically
Meteorological Office 31.4 weather forecast
meteorological satellite 29.32 satellite
meteorologist 31.2; 475.9 forecaster; 30.4 geophysicist
meteorology 31.1; 28.4 experimental physics; 30.2 geophysics
Meteorology and Climatology 31
meteor shower 29.20 meteor
meteor swarm 29.20 meteor
mete out 770.4 allot; 768.5 give; 26.11 measure out
meter 26.8; 26.10 measure; 28.82 measuring instrument
meterable 26.14 measurable
metered 26.13 measured
metered mail 692.2 postal communication
metereomancy 11.9 divination
metermaid 318.7 traffic controller
meter-reader 437.9 power-worker
meter reading 28.82 measuring instrument
methadone 691.6 drug
methane 437.3 gas
method 407.7; 733.4 approach; 750.6 convention; 140.6 custom; 352.1 means; 409.3 organization; 27.66 proof; 317.1, 631.7 way
method act 21.37 rehearse
method acting 21.22 acting
method actor 21.24 actor
methodical 140.10 customary; 656.6 formal; 298.14 orderly; 409.22 organizational; 484.14 planned; 333.5 unhurried; 407.14 well-ordered
methodically 407.27; 484.16 as planned; 409.28 in place; 140.19 to rule
methodicalness 407.6; 333.8 slowness
Methodist 7.5 Christian
methodization 409.3 organization
methodize 409.13 organize; 484.9 plan; 407.19 systematize
methodized 409.21 organized
method of operating 631.7 way
method of payment 15.2 industrial negotiations
method of propulsion 330.2
methodology 407.6 methodicalness; 317.1 way
methods 352.1 means
methods and resources 352.1 means
meths 437.6 oil
Methuselah 556.7 older person; 296.2 old people
methuselah 410.14 bottle
methylated spirits 437.6 oil
methylene blue 539.5 blueness
methyl orange 32.18 gravimetric analysis
methyl red 32.18 gravimetric analysis
methyl violet 540.2 purple pigment
meticulous 273.5, 698.21 accurate; 665.9 careful; 222.10 detailed; 471.8 diligent; 466.9 discriminating; 656.6 formal; 799.4 honourable; 230.2 perfectionist; 647.8 severe; 333.5 unhurried; 407.14 well-ordered
meticulously 222.19; 471.15 attentively; 799.7 honourably; 466.16 judiciously; 647.11 severely
meticulousness 273.1, 698.8 accuracy; 471.3, 665.1 carefulness; 466.2 judiciousness; 407.6 methodicalness; 799.1 probity; 647.1 severity; 333.8 slowness
métier 776.6 business; 455.2 information; 576.3 job; 485.1 skill; 139.7 special skill; 86.14 sphere
métis 412.5 hybrid
Metonic 298.13 anniversary
Metonic cycle 298.12 cyclic
metonym 5.17 word
metonymy 17.12 poetic language
metrazol shock therapy 36.3 psychiatric treatment
metre 17.9; 148.7 measure of length; 275.12 musical time; 298.5 regular thing; 18.19 tempo
metric 26.12 metrical
metrical 17.20; **26.12**; 298.14 orderly
metrically 26.17 measurably; 17.22 poetically
metrical unit 17.9 metre
metrics 17.9 metre; 729.6 phonetics
metric system 26.5 measuring system
metritis 321.1 railway
metro 317.10, 321.1 railway
métro 317.10 railway; 317.8 tunnel
metrological 26.12 metrical
metrologically 26.17 measurably
metrology 26.1 measurement; 28.95 mensuration
metronome 273.3 accurate thing; 326.7 oscillator; 298.5 regular thing; 18.19 tempo
metropolis 87.1 city; 86.10 urban area
metropolitan 565.15 environmental; 86.17 national; 564.12 native; 564.4 townsman; 87.14 urban
metropolitan area 87.1 city; 86.10 urban area
metropolitan district 86.5 state
Metropolitan Police 16.15 British police
mettle 613.1 courage; 638.16 fortitude; 338.1 vigour
mettled 613.9 courageous
mettlesome 342.18 active; 613.9 courageous; 338.4 vigorous
mew 515.1 animal cry; 515.4 cry; 72.14 nest
mewl 514.13, 515.4 cry
mews 317.3 road
Mexican mud 691.6 drug
Mexico City 87.6 other cities
meze 25.52 Greek dish
mezuzah 10.14 sacred object
mezzanine 21.18 auditorium; 565.7 room
mezze 25.12 hors d'oeuvre
mezzocerchio 54.3 fencing movements
mezzo rilievo 608.6 profile; 19.13 relief-carving
mezzotint 19.15 engraving; 529.3 hue
MI5 737.2 secretiveness
MI6 737.2 secretiveness
Miami 87.2 American cities
miasma 432.3; 236.11 harmfulness; 260.6 infection; 524.2 murk; 503.1 stench
miasmal 236.5 harmful; 432.18 miasmic; 524.6 murky; 503.3 stinking
miasmatic 432.18 miasmic
miasmic 432.18; 382.23 deadly; 524.6 murky; 503.3 stinking
mica 30.34 mineral
mica capacitor 39.17 resistor
Michael 8.6 angel
Michaelmas 292.4 autumn; 10.15 holy day
Michelangelo virus 40.19 computing terms
Michelin 693.5 reference book
Michigan 88.3 US lakes
Mickey Finn 489.4 anaesthetic; 592.6 desensitizing substance; 412.2 mixed thing
Mickey Mouse 265.9 easy; 124.4 trivial; 238.1 useless
MICR 40.13 character recognition
micro 40.3 computer
microbe 159.2 little thing; 34.3 organism
microbial 159.7 little; 34.21 living
microbial genetics 34.11 genetics
microbic 159.7 little
microbiological 34.20 biological
microbiologist 34.19 life scientist; 35.13 medical specialist
microbiology 34.1 life science; 35.3 medical specialty
microcard 744.6 record book
microcentrum 34.8 cell organ
microchip 39.13 circuit; 159.2 little thing
microcircuit 39.13 circuit; 334.9 electronics
microclimate 31.38 climate
microcomputer 40.3 computer
microcopied 111.15 duplicate
microcopy 111.4 duplicate; 41.6 microphotograph
microcosm 159.2 little thing; 204.2 whole thing
microcosmic 159.7 little
microcosmically 159.9 microscopically
microcrystal 32.4 crystal
microcrystalline 32.33 crystalline
microdiskette 40.7 peripheral
microdot 159.2 little thing
microeconomics 13.1 economics
microelectronics 39.1, 334.9 electronics
microfibril 34.8 cell organ
microfiche 159.2 little thing; 41.6 microphotograph; 744.6 record book
microfilaria 75.13 invertebrate larva
microfilm 159.2 little thing; 41.6 microphotograph; 744.6 record book
microfilm reader 518.10 visual aid
microfloppy 40.7 peripheral
micrography 159.1 littleness
microgravity 29.31 space travel
microhabitat 565.2 environment
microlith 3.11 relic; 284.7 thing of the past
micrometeorite 29.20 meteor
micrometeorology 31.1 meteorology
micrometer 273.3 accurate thing; 28.84 altimeter; 159.1 littleness; 26.8 meter
micrometer calliper 26.8 meter
micrometer gauge 26.8 meter
micrometric 26.16

micrometry 26.2; 698.8 *accuracy*
microminiaturization 159.1 *littleness*
Micronesian 5.11 *family of languages*
micronization 427.4 *pulverization*
micronize 427.22 *pulverize*
micronucleus 34.9 *cell nucleus*
micronutrient 33.15 *essential element*
microorganism 159.2 *little thing*; 34.3 *organism*
micropalaeontological 3.17 *archaeological*
micropalaeontologist 3.4 *archaeologist*
micropalaeontology 3.2 *archaeology*
microphone 504.9 *audio device*; 507.4 *sound maker*; 692.9 *telephone*; 39.22 *transformer*
microphotograph 41.6; 159.2 *little thing*
microphotography 41.1 *photography*
microphyll 77.6 *leaf*
microphyte 159.2 *little thing*; 34.3 *organism*
microprocessor 334.9 *electronics*; 40.5 *processor*
micropyle 78.3 *flower part*; 77.9 *seed*
microreader 518.10 *visual aid*
microscope 28.85; 159.1 *littleness*; 28.32 *optical instrument*; 520.7 *that which makes visible*; 518.10 *visual aid*
microscopic 698.21 *accurate*; 521.2 *difficult to see*; 159.7 *little*; 518.20 *visual*
microscopical examination 34.6 *cell biology*
microscopically 159.9
microscopic detail 698.8 *accuracy*
microscopy 28.96; 159.1 *littleness*; 518.10 *visual aid*
microsecond 275.4 *term*; 276.2 *time period*
microseism 30.22 *seismic activity*
microskirt 552.4 *dishabille*; 551.6 *skirt*
microskirted 552.10 *in dishabille*
microsome 34.8 *cell organ*
microspore 427.10 *spore*
microtubule 34.8 *cell organ*
microvillus 34.7 *cell*
microwave 25.55 *cook*; 25.5 *cooker*
microwave amplifier 39.21 *rectifier*
microwave background 29.4 *cosmological model*
microwave cooking 25.1 *cookery*
microwave food 557.7 *food*
microwave generator 39.20 *electron tube*
microwave link 692.14 *radio transmission*
microwave oscillator 39.21 *rectifier*
microwave oven 493.4 *burner*
microwaves 28.13 *electromagnetic radiation*; 692.14 *radio transmission*
microwave spectroscopy 32.17 *analysis*
microwave spectrum 28.68 *emission*
microwire 62.4 *climbing equipment*
micturate 560.17 *urinate*
micturation 560.3 *urination*
mid 198.13 *half*; 216.5 *medium*; 53.14 *positioned*
mid- 216.2 *medium*
Midas 781.10 *wealthy person*
Midas touch 248.2 *good fortune*; 781.5 *wealth*
Mid-Atlantic accent 5.26 *dialect*
Mid-Atlantic Ridge 30.16 *ocean floor*
midchannel 90.2 *channel*
midday 290.6 *noon*
mid-day 290.3 *noon*
midday sun 493.5 *hot weather*
midden 43.10 *farm tool*; 408.4 *litter*; 238.6 *refuse*; 767.8 *sink*
middle 173.6 *central*; 173.1 *centre*; 198.13 *half*; 172.2 *inside*; 216.2, 216.5 *medium*; 2.14 *socioeconomic*; 5.32 *voice*
middle age 556.4; 556.2 *adulthood*; 554.5 *life cycle*
middle-aged 556.13
Middle Ages 284.5 *historical period*; 3.10 *past age*
Middle America 216.8 *middle classes*
Middle American 117.6 *conformist*
middlebrow 216.1 *average*; 138.21 *common*
middle class 654.7 *human society*; 2.7 *social stratification*
middle classes 216.8; 566.9 *group*; 574.2 *the common people*
Middle Comedy 21.12 *comedy*
middle course 754.1 *compromise*; 216.5 *medium*
middle cut 25.30 *bacon*
middle-distance 68.13 *ice-skating*; 47.9 *track*
middle-distance race 47.1 *track events*
middle-distance racing 68.8 *speed-skating*; 47.1 *track events*
middle-distance runner 47.3 *athlete*
middle-distance running 47.1 *track events*
middle ear 504.5 *internal ear*
Middle-earth 477.8 *dreamland*
Middle East 86.7 *regions of the world*
middle finger 492.7 *sense organ*
middle-finger gesture 742.3 *gesture*
middle ground 754.1 *compromise*; 216.5 *medium*
middle-income earner 216.8 *middle classes*
middle lamella 34.7 *cell*
middle life 556.4 *middle age*
middleman 398.6, 578.3 *agent*; 398.1 *delegate*; 748.3 *mediator*; 746.4 *negotiator*; 436.3 *provider*; 778.13 *retailer*; 778.12 *wholesaler*
middle manager 216.8 *middle classes*
middlemost 216.2 *medium*; 216.12 *mediumly*
middle name 721.8 *name*
middle neck 25.26 *lamb*
middle of the day 290.3 *noon*
middle-of-the-road 138.21 *common*; 216.2 *medium*; 235.5 *not bad*; 231.4 *ordinary*; 685.7 *politically moderate*
middle-of-the-roader 618.6 *indifferent person*; 216.8 *middle classes*
middle position 48.2 *baseball player*
middle school 6.12 *educational institution*
middle term 216.5 *medium*
middleware 40.19 *computing terms*
middle way 754.1 *compromise*; 618.3 *impartiality*; 684.2, 685.1 *moderation*
middleweight 586.3 *athlete*; 52.4 *boxer*; 52.3 *boxing weight divisions*; 52.14 *combat*; 414.1 *heavy*; 414.7 *weighing*
Middle West 86.8 *regions of the US*
middle years 556.4 *middle age*
middling 117.15 *everyday*; 216.3, 618.10 *mediocre*; 216.2 *medium*; 685.6 *moderate*; 235.5 *not bad*; 122.16, 231.4 *ordinary*
middlingly 122.20 *insignificantly*; 618.20 *unexceptionally*
middy blouse 551.8 *shirt*
midfield 66.5 *soccer*
midfield player 58.6 *lacrosse player*
midfield striker 66.3 *football player*
midfield stripe 46.4 *stadium*
midge 76.1 *insect*; 76.3 *pest*; 149.5 *short person*
midget 159.7 *little*; 159.4 *little person*; 149.5 *short person*
midget-car race 61.1 *motor racing*
midget-car racing 61.1 *motor racing*
MIDI 40.11 *application*
midicoat 551.11 *jacket*
midinette 568.2 *female*
midiron 56.4 *golf club*
midiskirt 551.6 *skirt*
midland 172.9 *inland*
Midlands 86.9 *regions of Britain*
midlife crisis 556.4 *middle age*
mid mashie 56.4 *golf club*
midmost 173.6 *central*; 216.2 *medium*; 216.12 *mediumly*
midnight 291.3
midnight blue 539.1 *blue*; 523.3 *dark colour*
Midnight Mass 10.6 *Eucharist*
midnight sun 29.15 *sun*
midoceanic ridge 30.16 *ocean floor*; 30.19 *plate tectonics*
mid off 53.4 *team*
mid on 53.4 *team*
midpoint 173.6 *central*; 173.1 *centre*; 216.5 *medium*; 27.36 *point*
mid-range zoom 41.17 *lens*
midriff 173.2 *central thing*; 410.18 *stomach*
midsection 216.5 *medium*
midshipman 586.27 *naval man*
midst of things 342.1 *activity*
midstream 90.2 *channel*
midsummer 493.5 *hot weather*; 292.3, 292.11 *summer*
Midsummer Day 292.3 *summer*
midterm 216.5 *medium*
midtown 87.7 *city district*; 87.14 *urban*
midway 198.13 *half*; 216.2 *medium*; 216.12 *mediumly*
Midwest accent 5.26 *dialect*
midwife 348.3 *assistant*; 35.16 *nurse*; 561.7 *obstetrics*; 35.17 *paramedic*
midwifery 35.6 *health care*; 348.1 *instrumentality*; 561.7 *obstetrics*
midwinter 292.5, 292.13 *winter*
mien 171.3 *appearance*; 631.1 *conduct*; 525.3 *external appearance*
miff 624.2 *offence*; 624.9 *offend*
might 396.1 *authority*; 395.1 *influence*; 334.1 *power*; 336.1 *strength*; 380.1 *violence*
might and main 576.4 *exertion*
might as well 469.2 *prefer*
might be 102.8 *be possible*
might do worse 469.2 *prefer*
mightily 158.20 *largely*; 334.18 *powerfully*
mightiness 396.2 *authoritativeness*; 395.1 *influence*; 334.1 *power*
might is right 585.5 *bellicosity*
mighty 396.12 *authoritative*; 158.15 *big*; 395.11 *influential*; 336.10 *potent*; 334.13 *powerful*; 622.18 *prestigious*; 380.6 *violent*
mighty effort 576.4 *exertion*
mignonette 538.1 *green*
migraine 491.2 *painful condition*; 260.3 *symptom*
migrant 72.1 *birds*; 100.10 *foreign*; 315.8 *outgoer*
migrant worker 100.7 *new arrival*
migrate 315.13 *emigrate*
migration 313.7 *departure*; 315.4 *emigration*; 300.1 *motion*
migratory bird 72.1 *birds*
mikado 400.2 *sovereign*
mike 504.9 *audio device*; 507.4 *sound maker*
Mikhail Baryshnikov 22.14 *famous ballet dancers*
Mikhail Gorbachev 589.4 *Nobel Peace Prize*
mikvah 10.7 *non-Christian ritual*
mil 196.4 *less than one*
milady 568.3 *female title of address*
milah 10.7 *non-Christian ritual*
milanese sauce 25.15 *sauce*
milch cow 562.1 *fertility*; 43.8 *livestock*; 439.3 *supply*
mild 558.7 *alcoholic drink*; 658.7 *courteous*; 493.9 *hot*; 648.4 *lenient*; 685.6 *moderate*; 589.7 *peaceful*; 419.6 *soft-hearted*; 497.5 *tasteless*; 31.50, 493.11 *warm*
mild as milk 685.6 *moderate*
milder 31.45 *fine*
mildew 357.7 *agent of destruction*; 258.10 *be dirty*; 245.2 *decay*; 245.9 *dilapidation*; 258.4 *dirt*; 83.1 *fungus*; 245.5 *hurt*; 83.11 *moulder*; 44.12 *pests and diseases*; 79.10 *tree disease*
mildewed 245.13 *dilapidated*; 83.9 *fungal*
mildewy 44.17 *botanical*; 83.9 *fungal*
mildly 658.14 *courteously*; 648.6 *leniently*; 31.65 *meteorologically*; 419.18 *softheartedly*; 497.10 *without taste*
mild manner 658.1 *courtesy*
mild-mannered 658.7 *courteous*; 589.7 *peaceful*
mildness 658.1 *courtesy*; 419.12 *gentleness*; 648.1 *leniency*; 685.1 *moderation*; 497.1 *tastelessness*
mile 148.7 *measure of length*
mileage 148.4 *length*; 320.21 *miscellaneous motoring terms*
mileometer 742.5 *indicator*; 26.8 *meter*; 332.8 *speed*
milepost 742.5 *indicator*
miler 47.3 *athlete*
miles away 145.2 *great distance*; 463.8 *oblivious*; 443.10 *speculative*
miles gloriosus 586.1 *combatant*; 21.23 *role*
miles per hour 332.8 *speed*
milestone 99.2 *essential content*; 123.2 *important matter*; 742.5 *indicator*; 209.4 *interval*; 26.6 *measuring instrument*; 222.2 *occurrence*
miliaria 260.13 *skin disease*
miliary fever 260.7 *tropical disease*
milieu 170.3 *atmosphere*; 222.1 *circumstances*
militancy 340.1 *action*; 342.5 *activism*; 585.5 *bellicosity*; 585.4 *belligerency*
militant 381.22; **613.11**; 340.5 *acting*; 342.18 *active*; 381.19 *attacker*; 342.10 *busy person*; 586.33 *combative*; 661.4 *defiant person*; 661.8 *defying*; 751.9 *disagreeing*; 340.3 *doer*; 586.6 *militarist*; 584.8 *military*; 7.15 *religious*; 380.4 *violent creature*; 585.16 *warlike*; 585.15 *warring*
militant Christian 7.5 *Christian*; 586.6 *militarist*
militantly 586.41 *aggressively*; 661.10 *in defiance*; 585.18 *to war*
militant scene 342.5 *activism*
militarily 584.11; 2.16 *sociologically*; 585.18 *to war*
militarism 585.5 *bellicosity*; 584.7 *miscellaneous terms*; 647.2 *suppression*
militarist 586.6; 586.1 *combatant*; 647.4 *strict person*
militaristic 586.33 *combative*; 381.22 *militant*; 647.8 *severe*; 585.16 *warlike*
militaristically 586.41 *aggressively*; 585.18 *to war*
militarist nation 586.7
militarize 585.12 *go to war*
military 584.8; **585.17**; 2.12 *sociological*
military academy 585.6 *art of war*; 6.12 *educational institution*; 584.3 *military training*
Military Affairs 584
military affairs 584.1
military aircraft 586.31
military architect 20.2 *architect*
military architecture 20.1 *architecture*
military arm 584.2 *the military*
military attack 381.12
military band 585.2 *glory of war*; 584.7 *miscellaneous terms*; 18.26 *musical group*
military base 396.6 *place of authority*
military bearing 584.7 *miscellaneous terms*
military branch 584.2 *the military*
military burial 583.1 *burial*
military canteen 557.15 *eating place*
military cap 551.15 *headgear*
military cemetery 583.5 *cemetery*
military citation 794.1 *trophy*
military conduct 632.5 *tradition*
military conflict 585.1 *war*
military court 16.7 *legal trial*
military decoration 794.1 *trophy*
military defeat 247.2 *defeat*
military defences 384.8
military discharge 589.1 *peace*
military discipline 632.5 *tradition*
military duty 585.7 *war measures*
military equipment 584.1 *military affairs*
military evolutions 585.6 *art of war*
military experience 585.6 *art of war*
military flag 743.7 *flag*
military forces 586.14 *armed forces*; 584.2 *the military*
military government 12.1 *government*; 584.7 *miscellaneous terms*; 396.7 *type of rule*
military governor 400.3 *leader*; 396.10 *person of authority*
military headquarters staff 584.5 *military staff*
military honours 584.7 *miscellaneous terms*
military–industrial complex 584.2 *the military*
military insignia 743.4 *insignia*
military installations 584.1 *military affairs*
military judge 16.23 *judge*
military justice 16.7 *legal trial*
military law 584.6
military leader 400.7
military leadership 585.6 *art of war*
military man 586.8 *soldier*
military markings 743.4 *insignia*
military medal 794.1 *trophy*
military mess 557.15 *eating place*
military music 584.7 *miscellaneous terms*
military officer 400.7 *military leader*; 396.10 *person of authority*
military operation 585.1 *war*
military orders 585.8 *warfare*
military organization 584.4
Military Police 584.6 *military law*
military police 584.6 *military law*; 16.14 *police*
military police corps 584.6 *military law*; 584.4 *military organization*
military prison 815.1 *prison*
military radar 692.28 *radar*

military rank 396.5 *position of authority*; 209.2 *rank*
military rations 687.2 *short rations*
military ribbon 794.1 *trophy*
military salute 584.7 *miscellaneous terms*
military sanctions 585.8 *warfare*
military schottische 22.4 *historic dancing*
military science 584.1 *military affairs*
military service 584.1 *military affairs*; 585.8 *warfare*
military service number 743.3 *means of identification*
military spirit 585.5 *bellicosity*; 584.7 *miscellaneous terms*
military staff 584.5
military strategy 584.1 *military affairs*
military tactics 584.1 *military affairs*
military tradition 585.5 *bellicosity*; 584.7 *miscellaneous terms*
military training 584.3
military two-step 22.2 *dance*
military uniform 551.3 *formal dress*; 743.5 *uniform*
military unit 584.4 *military organization*; 396.6 *place of authority*
military victory 246.2 *victory*
militate against 340.4 *act*; 113.16 *be contrary*; 240.5 *be inconvenient*; 395.9 *change*; 347.3 *counteract*
militate for 340.4 *act*
militia 586.15 *army*; 252.3 *protector*; 584.2 *the military*
militiaman 586.8 *soldier*
milk 558.5; 431.3 *body fluid*; 349.3 *exploit*; 431.2 *juice*; 71.36 *lactate*; 71.2 *mammalian characteristic*; 43.18 *practise livestock farming*; 356.7 *produce*; 436.5 *provision*; 559.2 *secreted substance*; 369.14 *suck*; 773.10 *take away*; 531.9 *white thing*
milk and honey 557.9 *plenty*; 248.1 *prosperity*
milk and water 337.5 *weak thing*
milk-and-water 337.13 *insufficient*; 685.6 *moderate*; 497.5 *tasteless*
milk bar 557.15 *eating place*
milk bottle 410.14 *bottle*; 349.7 *reused product*
milk chocolate 498.4 *confectionery*
milk dry 441.1 *waste*
milked 43.21 *domesticated*
milker 43.8 *livestock*
milkiness 431.7 *juiciness*; 528.6 *opaqueness*; 527.7 *semitransparency*; 531.7 *whiteness*
milking 369.4 *sucking*
milking machine 43.10 *farm tool*
milking parlour 43.7 *farm building*
milking stool 23.2 *chair*
milk it 21.35 *overact*
milkmaid 43.16 *farm worker*
milkman 557.20 *food provider*; 436.3 *provider*; 778.12 *wholesaler*
milk of human kindness 650.1 *benevolence*
milk of magnesia 394.6 *purgative*
milk punch 558.7 *alcoholic drink*
milk shake 558.5 *milk*
milksop 614.2 *coward*; 337.4 *weakling*
milk tank 43.10 *farm tool*
milk tooth 425.11 *tooth*
milk train 321.7 *train*
milk-white 531.1 *white*
milky 431.17; 530.7 *colourless*; 558.17 *drinkable*; 524.6 *murky*; 527.3 *semitransparent*; 528.2 *shady*; 531.1 *white*
milky drink 558.5 *milk*
Milky Way 522.4 *natural light*
mill 208.11, 376.40 *crowd*; 427.24 *grind*; 420.12 *make rough*; 356.10 *produce*; 427.11 *pulverizer*; 577.1 *workshop*
mill around 327.21 *be agitated*; 376.40 *crowd*; 307.10 *swirl*
millboard 435.4 *board*
millenarian 244.16 *improving*; 244.12 *reformer*; 201.21 *thousandth*
millenarianism 244.11 *reformism*
millenary 276.8 *periodical*; 201.10 *thousand*; 201.21 *thousandth*
millenial 201.21 *thousandth*
millenium 148.8 *measure of time*
millenium virus 40.19 *computing terms*
millennial 279.9 *agelong*; 298.13 *anniversary*; 276.8 *periodical*
millennially 298.16 *cyclically*
millennium 279.2 *a long time*; 298.3 *anniversary*; 477.7 *idealism*; 464.4 *judgment day*; 275.4 *term*; 201.10 *thousand*; 276.2 *time period*; 201.9 *treble figures*
millet 43.12 *crop*
milliard 194.3 *large number*; 201.11 *million*
milliardaire 201.11 *million*
milligram 414.9 *avoirdupois weight*; 201.10 *thousand*
millilitre 201.10 *thousand*
millimetre 148.7 *measure of length*; 147.2 *short distance*; 201.10 *thousand*
milliner 551.26 *fashion designer*; 778.13 *retailer*
millinery 551.2 *dressing*; 551.15 *headgear*
milling 376.50 *crowded*; 427.4 *pulverization*
milling machine 38.9 *machine tool*
million 201.11; 194.3 *large number*; 208.7 *myriad*
millionaire 765.7 *gainer*; 201.11 *million*; 619.5 *person of wonder*; 248.4 *prosperous person*; 781.10 *wealthy person*
millionairess 781.10 *wealthy person*
million million 201.11 *million*
millions 780.3 *fortune*; 208.2 *multitude*
millionth 201.22; 196.4 *less than one*
million-to-one chance 105.4 *improbability*
millipede 201.10 *thousand*
millisecond 148.8 *measure of time*; 275.4 *term*; 276.2 *time period*
millpond 88.2 *small lake*; 421.8 *smooth thing*
millrace 90.6 *river flow*
Mills & Boon™ 740.6 *book publishing*; 17.2 *fiction*
millstone 427.11 *pulverizer*; 414.8 *weighing down*
millstone round one's neck 378.6 *burden*
millstream 90.1 *river*; 90.6 *river flow*
mill wheel 307.6 *rotator*
milquetoast 614.2 *coward*
Miltonic 17.19 *narrative*
mimamsa 4.7 *school of thought*
MIME 40.16 *Internet*
mime 21.34, 717.10 *act*; 717.3 *acting*; 742.11 *gesture*, 125.9 *imitate*; 125.3 *mockery*; 717.5 *performer*; 21.2 *play*
mime artist 717.5 *performer*
Mimeograph™ 115.2, 125.10 *copy*; 111.4, 111.9, 125.5 *duplicate*; 115.12 *imitate*
mimeographed 111.15 *duplicate*
mimesis 21.22 *acting*; 125.1 *imitation*
mimetic 21.39 *dramatic*; 125.12 *imitative*
mimic 21.34, 717.10 *act*; 112.8 *creature of habit*; 621.3 *derider*; 21.29 *entertainer*; 742.11 *gesture*; 115.12, 125.9 *imitate*; 125.7 *imitator*; 717.5 *performer*; 227.8 *person who changes costume*; 115.4 *person who copies*; 112.16 *repeat*
mimicked 115.8 *simulated*
mimicking 21.22 *acting*; 115.1 *similarity*
mimicry 21.22, 717.3 *acting*; 125.4 *camouflage*; 125.3 *mockery*
miming 21.22 *acting*
mimographer 21.26 *dramatist*
minaret 154.6 *tall thing*
minatory 711.8 *warning*
mince 25.55 *cook*; 427.24 *grind*; 25.20 *meat*; 333.1 *move slowly*; 372.9 *separate*; 300.15 *walk*
minced 25.56 *culinary*; 205.11 *partial*
minced meat 25.20 *meat*
mince no words 271.7 *be simple*
mince pie 25.36 *cake*
mincer 25.6 *kitchen equipment*
minchah 10.4 *public worship*
mincing no words 271.6 *naturalness*
mincing steps 333.10 *slow motion*
mind 442.1; 665.10 *be careful*; 624.10 *be offended*; 596.5 *dislike*; 223.15 *escort*; 504.15 *hear*; 504.1 *hearing*; 595.2 *inclination*; 455.4 *intellect*; 442.3, 458.2 *intelligence*; 101.6 *internal world*; 663.5 *obey*; 252.10 *protect*; 36.21 *psyche*; 444.1 *reason*; 11.7 *spirit*; 635.1 *will*
mind-blowing 691.9 *addictive*; 619.8 *wonderful*
mind-body problem 4.9 *philosophical problem*
mind boggler 705.4 *difficult question*
mind-boggling 202.2 *immeasurable*; 619.8 *wonderful*
mind cure 36.3 *psychiatric treatment*
minded 223.20 *accompanied*
minder 223.7 *attendant*; 586.2 *defender*; 438.8 *machinist*; 252.3 *protector*
mindful 650.6 *benevolent*; 665.9 *careful*; 616.4 *cautious*; 455.8 *knowledgeable*; 462.8 *remembering*; 471.9 *solicitous*
mindfully 471.15 *attentively*; 650.10 *benevolently*
mindfulness 471.1 *attention*; 650.1 *benevolence*; 665.1 *carefulness*; 665.2 *consideration*; 671.1 *gratitude*
mindful of obligations 671.4 *grateful*
mindless 457.5 *lacking intellect*
mindlessly 457.11 *unintelligently*
mindlessness 457.1 *lack of intellect*
mind like a sieve 463.3 *poor memory*
mind made up 465.4 *prejudgment*; 638.12 *resolution*
mind of one's own 641.5 *obstinacy*
mind one's health 259.5 *be healthy*
mind one's manners 160.8 *be formal*; 658.11 *have good manners*
mind one's own business 473.6 *be disinterested*; 618.12 *be indifferent*
mind over matter 394.5 *analgesic*; 635.2 *willpower*
mind reader 101.7 *believer in a nonmaterial world*; 21.29 *entertainer*; 11.12 *occultist*
mind reading 11.1 *occultism*
mind set 229.2 *attitude*
mind's eye 462.1 *memory*; 518.4 *visualization*
mind the gap 711.10 *look out!*
mind your step 711.10 *look out!*
mine 587.16 *bomb*; 183.2 *concave land*; 156.14 *deepen*; 156.4 *deep thing*; 357.9 *demolish*; 369.13 *dig out*; 384.18 *fence*; 308.5 *hole*; 245.5 *hurt*; 183.9 *make concave*; 30.65 *map*; 384.8 *military defences*; 356.10 *produce*; 439.2 *resource*; 700.13, 700.33 *snare*; 344.2 *source*; 773.10 *take away*; 379.1 *trap*; 305.15 *tunnel*; 781.5 *wealth*; 577.1 *workshop*
mine coal 437.11 *fuel*
mined 700.42 *trapped*
minefield 379.1 *trap*
mine host 436.4 *caterer*; 654.6 *social person*
minelayer 586.24 *warship*
minenwerfer 587.11 *guns*
mine of information 455.6 *knowledgeable person*
miner 578.2 *artisan*; 309.6 *closed-in person*; 183.5 *digger*; 369.10 *excavator*; 586.13 *historical soldiery*; 308.3 *person who opens*; 356.9 *producer*; 156.5 *submariner*
mineral 30.34; 435.1 *materials*; 402.4 *matter*; 457.8 *nonhuman*
mineral acid 32.8 *acid*
mineral aggregate 30.28 *rock*
mineral deposit 439.2 *resource*
mineral dye 42.6 *dye*
mineralization 30.43 *fossil*
mineralize 30.62 *lithify*
mineralized 30.61 *fossilized*
mineralized bone 30.43 *fossil*
mineralized shell 30.43 *fossil*
mineralocorticoid 33.16 *hormone*
mineralogical 30.48 *geological*
mineralogically 30.66 *geographically*
mineralogist 30.3 *geologist*
mineralogy 30.1 *earth science*
mineral oil 437.6 *oil*
mineral rights 763.1 *possession*
minerals 557.11 *food content*
mineral water 433.2 *drinking water*; 558.6 *soft drink*; 433.1 *water*
miner's lamp 522.7 *lantern*
mineshaft 308.5 *hole*
minestrone 25.47 *Italian dish*; 25.13 *soup*
minesweeper 586.24 *warship*
mine-thrower 587.11 *guns*
minginess 682.3 *parsimony*
mingle 342.16 *be sociable*; 374.5 *combine*; 412.8 *mix*; 2.15 *socialize*
mingled 374.7 *combined*; 412.12 *mixed*
mingle with 654.11 *be sociable*
mingling 374.1 *combination*; 412.1 *mixture*; 342.2 *social activity*
mingy 682.1 *mean*
mini 40.3 *computer*; 159.7 *little*; 159.2 *little thing*
miniature 159.7 *little*; 159.2 *little thing*; 19.8 *painting*; 19.7 *picture*
miniature camera 41.16 *camera*
miniaturist 19.16 *artist*
miniaturization 191.1 *contraction*; 159.1 *littleness*
miniaturize 191.5 *make smaller*
miniaturized 159.7 *little*; 191.7 *smaller*
minibike 320.12 *bicycle*
minicab 320.18 *cab*
minicomputer 40.3 *computer*
minidisc 744.7 *recording*
minidiskette 40.7 *peripheral*
minidress 551.7 *frock*
minifloppy 40.7 *peripheral*
minim 159.3 *little piece*; 18.17 *notation*
minimal 27.75 *equal*; 206.7 *fewer*; 122.13 *insignificant*; 159.7 *little*; 728.14 *simple*; 206.6 *sparse*
minimalism 728.4 *simplicity*
minimalist 18.32 *instrumental*; 19.29 *realist*
minimalist music 18.3 *classical music*
minimally 159.8 *in a small way*; 122.19 *inferiorly*; 19.30 *pictorially*; 728.24 *simply*
minimal sculpture 19.12 *sculpture*
minimization 468.1 *underestimation*; 728.1 *understatement*
minimize 678.10 *disparage*; 214.5 *make smaller*; 27.94 *order*; 468.3 *underestimate*; 728.20 *understate*
minimized 728.12 *understated*
minimizer 468.2 *pessimist*
minimizing 678.15 *disparaging*; 468.4 *underestimating*
minimum 206.7 *fewer*; 122.5 *inferior state*; 122.13 *insignificant*; 206.2 *least*; 217.7 *sufficiency*
minimum allowance 218.8 *insufficiency*
minimum hours 15.2 *industrial negotiations*
minimum lending rate 14.1, 780.7 *finance*; 784.3 *loan*
minimum requirement 231.5 *imperfection*; 217.7 *sufficiency*
minimum-security prison 815.1 *prison*
minimum wages 15.2 *industrial negotiations*
mining 156.1 *depth*; 369.3 *digging out*; 305.7 *tunnelling*
mining engineer 578.2 *artisan*
mining engineering 38.1 *engineering*
minion 401.1 *servant*; 387.3 *subordinate*; 664.3 *sycophant*
minipill 563.3 *birth control*
miniseries 692.25 *broadcast material*
miniskirt 552.4 *dishabille*; 149.4 *short thing*; 551.6 *skirt*
miniskirted 552.10 *in dishabille*
minister 392.14 *adviser*; 398.6, 578.3 *agent*; 760.5 *converter*; 398.1 *delegate*; 583.3 *funeral director*; 400.3 *leader*; 579.1 *manage*; 752.15 *offer worship*; 579.16 *official*; 10.18 *perform rites*; 12.8 *politician*; 7.8 *priest*
minister designate 469.13 *electorate*
ministerial 398.9 *delegated*; 12.9, 396.14 *governmental*; 7.17 *priestly*
ministerially 396.24; 398.12 *by proxy*; 12.14 *politically*; 398.11 *representatively*
ministering 401.9 *serving*; 392.32 *supportive*
ministering angel 35.16 *nurse*; 392.13 *supporter*
ministering spirits 8.6 *angel*
minister of state 400.3 *leader*; 396.10 *person of authority*
minister plenipotentiary 398.6 *agent*
minister to 348.4 *be an instrument*; 394.20 *doctor*; 663.5 *obey*; 35.19 *practise medicine*; 401.8 *serve*; 392.19 *support*; 576.7 *work for*
ministrant 392.32 *supportive*
ministration 392.2 *support*
ministrative 392.32 *supportive*
ministress 7.8 *priest*
ministry 579.3 *management*; 392.2 *support*
Ministry of Defence 584.4 *military organization*
minium 535.6 *red pigment*
mink 550.14 *animal covering*; 551.12 *coat*
mink farming 43.3 *livestock farming*
minnesinger 17.14 *author*; 516.5 *melodist*
Minnesota multiphasic personality inventory 36.5 *psychological test*
Minnesota pre-school scale 36.6 *intelligence test*
Minnie 587.11 *guns*

minnow 55.1 *angling;* 159.4 *little person*
minor 122.6 *inferior;* 124.3 *secondary;* 122.15 *subordinate;* 555.11 *young;* 555.6 *young person*
minor axis 27.42 *circle*
minor-counties cricket 53.1 *cricket match*
minor deity 8.5 *deity*
minor detail 222.6 *aspect*
minor earthquake 30.22 *seismic activity*
minority 203.2 *certain amount;* 206.7 *fewer;* 209.7 *gradational;* 122.3 *inferior numbers;* 209.4 *interval;* 206.2 *least;* 205.1 *part;* 2.14 *socioeconomic;* 113.10 *the opposition;* 555.1 *youth*
minority group 206.2 *least*
minority rights 391.2 *equal opportunity*
minority rule 12.1 *government*
minority voice 703.8 *protester*
minority whip 579.15 *manager;* 12.8 *politician*
minor key 18.20 *key*
minor league baseball 48.1 *baseball*
minor offence 804.3 *venial sin*
minor planet 29.16 *planet*
minor poet 17.14 *author*
minor role 21.23 *role*
minor scale 18.20 *key*
minor surgery 35.9 *surgery*
minor term 4.8 *philosophical term*
minor third 199.6 *third*
minotaur 70.7 *legendary beast*
minster 10.11 *place of worship*
minstrel 17.14 *author;* 21.29 *entertainer;* 516.5 *melodist;* 18.24 *musician*
minstrel show 21.7 *show*
mint 160.7 *form;* 496.5 *herbs;* 780.24 *monetize;* 356.10 *produce;* 577.1 *workshop*
mint condition 295.10 *new;* 295.1, 350.9 *newness;* 230.3 *perfection*
minted 780.22 *monetary*
minted coinage 780.13 *coinage*
minter 780.17 *financier;* 780.18 *treasurer*
minting 780.13 *coinage*
mint julep 558.8 *mixed drink*
mint master 780.17 *financier;* 780.18 *treasurer*
mint money 781.13 *get rich*
mint of money 780.3 *fortune;* 781.6 *money*
mint sauce 25.15 *sauce;* 496.2 *seasoning*
minty 496.9 *piquant*
minuend 212.2 *subtracted item;* 27.16 *subtraction*
minuet 22.4 *historic dancing*
minus 212.8 *by subtraction;* 27.88 *equal to;* 233.6 *incompletely;* 784.9 *in debt;* 122.19 *inferiorly;* 98.12 *missing;* 94.9 *nonexistent;* 212.7 *reduced;* 212.1 *subtraction*
minuscule 5.41 *lettered;* 159.7 *little;* 5.15 *type style*
minus sign 27.13 *mathematical symbol;* 742.1 *sign*
minute 3.20 *chronicle;* 222.10 *detailed;* 270.3 *diffuse;* 159.7 *little;* 148.8 *measure of time;* 275.4 *term;* 276.2 *time period*
minute book 3.5 *chronicle;* 744.6 *record book*
minuted 3.19 *chronicled*
minute gun 281.10, 742.4 *signal*
minute hand 742.5 *indicator*
minutely 270.7 *diffusely;* 159.8 *in a small way;* 222.19 *meticulously*
minuteness 270.1 *diffuseness;* 159.1 *littleness;* 402.4 *matter*
minutes 3.5 *chronicle;* 744.1 *record*
minutia 222.6 *aspect;* 159.3 *little piece*
minutiae 139.4 *specifications;* 124.8 *trifle*
minx 660.12 *impudent person;* 568.8 *nasty woman;* 555.8 *young woman*
minyn 10.17 *worshipper*
Miocene period 284.3 *geological period*
Mir 29.30 *spacecraft*
mirabile dictu 619.13 *wonderfully*
miracidium 75.13 *invertebrate larva*
miracle 525.4 *something that appears;* 105.5 *unexpectedness;* 619.4 *wonder*
miracle drug 394.8 *drug*
miracle-monger 727.6 *exaggerator*
miracle play 21.2 *play*
miracle-worker 619.5 *person of wonder;* 630.5 *surpriser*
miracle-working 619.3 *wonder-working*
miraculous 103.2 *unbelievable;* 619.8 *wonderful*
miraculously 619.13 *wonderfully*
miraculousness 11.2 *the occult;* 105.5 *unexpectedness*
mirador 518.9 *viewpoint*
mirage **604.3**; 700.5 *falseness;* 699.16 *false thing;* 477.5 *fantasy;* 96.2 *illusion;* 518.5 *imagination;* 525.4 *something that appears*
Mira variable 29.12 *variable star*
mire 258.4 *dirt;* 92.3, 429.8 *marsh*
miriness 258.1 *dirtiness*
mirror 525.11 *appear;* 115.10 *be similar;* 475.10 *cards;* 750.25 *conform;* 198.15 *double;* 125.9 *imitate;* 125.1 *imitation;* 518.18 *make visible;* 28.29 *optical element;* 518.8 *reflection;* 112.16 *repeat;* 717.9 *represent;* 421.8 *smooth thing*
mirror aperture 28.31 *lens element*
mirror cabinet 23.5 *cabinet*
mirrored 528.3 *mirror-like;* 525.8 *outer;* 112.9 *repeated*
mirror image 717.6 *image;* 525.5 *impression;* 518.8 *reflection;* 717.1 *representation;* 27.48 *transformation*
mirroring 125.1 *imitation;* 528.3 *mirror-like;* 528.6 *opaqueness;* 525.8 *outer*
mirror lens 41.17 *lens*
mirror-like **528.3**; 421.4 *polished;* 518.20 *visual*
mirror plane 162.2 *symmetry operation*
mirror symmetry 27.41 *geometric figure*
mirror system 28.30 *lens system*
mirth 599.2 *amusement;* 598.3 *cheerfulness*
miru 84.5 *algal product*
miry 92.11 *continental;* 258.7 *dirty*
misaddress 325.7 *misdirect*
misadventure 249.1 *adversity;* 288.4 *mishap*
misalign 751.8 *be different*
misaligned 751.10 *different*
misaligning 751.3 *difference*
misalliance 109.5 *misconnection;* 570.3 *types of marriage*
misandrist 466.7 *bigot;* 466.10 *discriminatory;* 594.9 *hater;* 653.2 *misanthrope;* 572.5 *single person*
misandrous 572.6 *celibate;* 466.10 *discriminatory;* 653.3 *misanthropic*
misandry 572.1 *celibacy;* 651.1 *malevolence;* 653.1 *misanthropy;* 466.4 *social discrimination*
misanthrope **653.2**; 594.9 *hater;* 682.5 *miser*
misanthropic 653.3
misanthropically 653.5
misanthropism 653.1 *misanthropy*
misanthropist 594.9 *hater;* 653.2 *misanthrope*
Misanthropy 653
misanthropy **653.1**; 651.1 *malevolence*
misapplication 486.9 *bungling;* 109.5 *misconnection;* 720.2 *misinterpretation;* 351.2 *misuse;* 702.1 *sophistry;* 441.3 *waste*
misapplied 486.4 *bungled;* 240.1 *inconvenient;* 109.9 *misconnected;* 702.7 *sophistic*
misapply 486.5 *be unskilful;* 351.1 *misuse;* 702.11 *practise sophistry;* 441.1 *waste*
misapprehend 274.18 *be in error;* 720.1 *misinterpret*
misapprehension 720.2 *misinterpretation;* 274.1 *mistake*
misappropriate 351.1 *misuse*
misappropriated 774.18 *fraudulent;* 351.4 *misused*
misappropriation 774.6 *illegal borrowing;* 351.2 *misuse*
misappropriation of funds 774.7 *dishonesty*
misbegotten 546.4 *ugly*
misbehave 662.15 *be disobedient;* 631.13 *behave badly;* 804.16 *be wicked*
misbehaved 662.13 *disobedient;* 804.11 *wicked*
misbehaving 804.11 *wicked*
misbehaviour 631.4 *bad conduct;* 662.1 *disobedience;* 806.3 *sin;* 804.1 *wickedness*
misbelief 451.4 *unbelief*
miscalculate 604.4 *be disappointed;* 274.19 *make a mistake;* 465.10 *misjudge;* 467.4 *overestimate;* 468.3 *underestimate*
miscalculated 468.5 *underestimated*
miscalculation 604.1 *disappointment;* 465.1 *misjudgment;* 274.1 *mistake;* 467.1 *overestimation;* 630.1 *surprise;* 468.1 *underestimation*
miscarriage 563.1 *infertility;* 247.4 *unsuccessful thing*
miscarriage of justice 16.4 *bad law;* 465.3 *injustice*
miscarried 604.11 *disappointing;* 247.10 *failed*
miscarry **247.8**; 486.7 *be clumsy;* 563.7 *be infertile;* 249.9 *be in trouble;* 94.13 *cause not to exist*
miscarrying 247.10 *failed*
miscast 21.40 *tragic*
miscegenate 570.15 *marry*
miscegenation 412.1 *mixture;* 570.3 *types of marriage*
miscegenetic 412.12 *mixed;* 570.23 *monogamous*
miscellanea 205.8 *bits and pieces;* 723.3 *compendium;* 114.3 *diverse thing;* 376.32, 412.3 *miscellany*
miscellaneous 114.6 *assorted;* 138.15 *general;* 412.12 *mixed*
miscellaneous architectural features 20.9
miscellaneous aviation terms 322.7
miscellaneous collection 412.3 *miscellany*
miscellaneous euphemisms 712.11
miscellaneous expenses 787.5 *expense*
miscellaneously 114.10 *diversely;* 412.14 *in the midst*
miscellaneous motoring terms 320.21
miscellaneous swearwords 712.15
miscellany **376.32**; **412.3**; 114.2 *assortment;* 723.3 *compendium;* 114.1 *diversity*
mischance 249.3 *bad fortune;* 288.3 *lost chance*
mischief 651.7 *act of malevolence;* 631.4 *bad conduct;* 642.2 *caprice;* 798.1 *evil;* 236.11 *harmfulness;* 245.11 *hurt;* 802.8 *wrongdoing*
mischief-maker 798.6 *evil person;* 378.7 *hinderer;* 753.4 *protester;* 662.5 *troublemaker;* 242.9 *unpleasant person*
mischief-making 662.1 *disobedience;* 662.13 *disobedient;* 236.5 *harmful*
mischievous 631.18 *badly behaved;* 642.1 *capricious;* 357.14 *destructive;* 798.7 *evil;* 236.5 *harmful;* 802.16 *in the wrong*
mischievously 798.12 *evilly*
mischievousness 798.1 *evil;* 236.11 *harmfulness*
miscibility 412.1 *mixture*
miscible 412.12 *mixed*
miscite 699.26 *falsify*
misciting 699.9 *falsification*
miscomputate 720.1 *misinterpret*
miscomputation 720.2 *misinterpretation*
misconceive 234.12 *distort the truth;* 720.1 *misinterpret;* 465.10 *misjudge*
misconceived 720.3 *misinterpreted*
misconception 96.3 *delusion;* 700.5 *falseness;* 720.2 *misinterpretation;* 465.1 *misjudgment;* 274.1 *mistake*
misconduct 631.4 *bad conduct;* 659.2 *bad manners;* 486.5 *be unskilful;* 486.9 *bungling;* 806.3 *sin*
misconduct penalty 58.3 *ice hockey*
misconnected 109.9
misconnection 109.5
misconstruction 234.4 *distortion of the truth;* 720.2 *misinterpretation;* 465.1 *misjudgment;* 274.1 *mistake*
misconstrue 234.12 *distort the truth;* 274.19 *make a mistake;* 720.1 *misinterpret;* 465.10 *misjudge;* 702.11 *practise sophistry*
misconstrued 720.3 *misinterpreted;* 465.9 *misjudged*
miscreant 16.40 *lawbreaker;* 651.8 *malefactor;* 804.11 *wicked;* 804.9 *wicked person;* 802.10 *wrongdoer*
miscue 65.2 *billiards play;* 274.19 *make a mistake;* 65.8 *play billiards;* 274.13 *sporting error;* 274.9 *trivial error*
miscued 65.9 *billiard*
misdate 286.4 *mistime*
misdated 288.14 *anachronistic;* 288.10 *mistimed;* 286.2 *occurring at a different time*
misdating 286.1 *different time;* 288.1 *wrong time*
misdeal 69.3 *card game terms;* 69.10 *play*
misdeed 16.39 *crime;* 274.8 *moral error;* 806.3 *sin;* 802.8 *wrongdoing*
misdemeanour 16.39 *crime;* 804.7 *criminality;* 806.3 *sin;* 802.8 *wrongdoing*
misdiagnose 720.1 *misinterpret*
misdiagnosis 720.2 *misinterpretation*
misdirect **325.7**; 700.27 *be false;* 486.5 *be unskilful;* 483.10 *manipulate;* 351.1 *misuse*
misdirected 700.36 *deceived;* 325.20 *deviant;* 351.4 *misused*
misdirection 325.13 *deviation;* 700.5 *falseness;* 351.2 *misuse;* 46.9 *play*
misdoing 806.3 *sin;* 802.8 *wrongdoing*
misdoubt 629.2, 629.8 *distrust*
misdoubtful 629.5 *distrustful*
mise 755.1 *contract*
miseducate 720.1 *misinterpret*
mise-en-scène 21.14 *production;* 21.19 *stage set*
misemploy 351.1 *misuse*
misemployed 351.4 *misused*
misemployment 351.2 *misuse*
miser **682.5**; 793.8 *bargain hunter;* 665.6 *careful person;* 376.36 *hoarder;* 786.6 *nonpayer*
miserable 249.6 *adverse;* 798.8 *afflicted;* 603.4 *lamenting;* 124.2 *obscure;* 491.5 *painful;* 236.4 *poor;* 602.5 *sad*
miserably 798.13 *destructively;* 249.12 *in adversity;* 602.11 *sadly*
misericord 587.8 *sharp weapon*
miserliness 682.3 *parsimony;* 683.1 *selfishness*
miserly 218.1 *insufficient;* 682.1 *mean;* 786.13 *nonpaying;* 683.4 *selfish*
misery 249.1 *adversity;* 798.2 *affliction;* 620.3 *boring person;* 602.4 *depressing person;* 491.1 *pain;* 670.13 *pessimist;* 236.10 *poverty;* 602.1 *sorrow*
miseryguts 602.4 *depressing person*
misevaluate 718.5 *misinform*
misevaluation 718.2 *misinformation*
misfeasance 16.39 *crime*
misfield 274.19 *make a mistake*
misfire 486.9 *bungling;* 247.9 *malfunction*
misfiring 320.21 *miscellaneous motoring terms*
misfit 751.8 *be different;* 325.19 *deviant person;* 751.10 *different;* 751.4 *dissenter;* 247.5 *failing person;* 118.7 *nonconformist;* 109.3 *unconnected person;* 116.2 *unlikeness;* 655.6 *unsocial person*
misfitting 751.3 *difference*
misform 161.3 *make shapeless*
misfortune **627.5**; 651.7 *act of malevolence;* 249.1 *adversity;* 249.3 *bad fortune;* 798.3 *bad luck;* 604.2 *bad outcome;* 245.7 *deterioration;* 247.1 *failure;* 288.3 *lost chance*
misgiving 451.1 *disbelief;* 705.6 *uncertainty*
misgivings 612.2 *fearfulness*
misgovern **588.5**; 486.5 *be unskilful;* 351.1 *misuse;* 647.6 *suppress*
misgovernment 588.1 *anarchy;* 486.9 *bungling;* 12.1 *government*
misguidance 700.5 *falseness*
misguide 700.27 *be false;* 234.12 *distort the truth*
misguided 486.4 *bungled;* 700.36 *deceived;* 234.8 *exaggerated;* 465.7 *misjudging*
misguidedly 465.13
mishandle 486.5 *be unskilful;* 236.14 *ill-treat;* 351.1 *misuse;* 647.6 *suppress*
mishandled 486.4 *bungled;* 351.4 *misused*
mishandling 486.9 *bungling;* 351.2 *misuse*
mishap **288.4**; 249.1 *adversity;* 472.5 *inattentive act;* 378.2 *obstacle*
mishit 486.7 *be clumsy;* 486.9 *bungling;* 274.19 *make a mistake;* 274.13 *sporting error*
mishmash 408.4 *litter;* 412.3 *miscellany*
Mishnah 7.12 *religious text;* 1.8 *tradition*
misinform **718.5**; 700.27 *be false;* 234.12 *distort the truth;* 456.11 *make ignorant;* 325.7 *misdirect;* 702.11 *practise sophistry*
misinformation **718.2**; 234.4 *distortion of the truth;* 736.5 *evasion;* 700.5 *falseness;* 702.2 *sophism*
misinformed **718.7**; 700.36 *deceived;* 234.8 *exaggerated;* 456.6 *ignorant;* 802.12 *incorrect;* 702.7 *sophistic*
misinterpret **720.1**; 699.26 *falsify;* 274.19 *make a mistake;* 718.5 *misinform;* 465.10 *misjudge;* 760.9 *transform*
Misinterpretation 720
misinterpretation **720.2**; 760.1 *conversion;* 699.9 *falsification;* 699.11 *half-truth;*

718.2 *misinformation*; 465.1 *misjudgment*; 274.1 *mistake*
misinterpreted 720.3; 718.7 *misinformed*; 465.9 *misjudged*
misjudge 465.10; 604.4 *be disappointed*; 696.9 *find unintelligible*; 274.19, 288.9 *make a mistake*; 720.1 *misinterpret*; 351.1 *misuse*; 467.4 *overestimate*; 288.6 *take untimely action*; 468.3 *underestimate*
misjudged 465.9; 467.6 *overestimated*; 468.5 *underestimated*
misjudged person 465.6
misjudging 465.7; 288.16 *mistaken*
misjudging person 465.5
Misjudgment 465
misjudgment 465.1; 459.2 *act of folly*; 16.4 *bad law*; 486.9 *bungling*; 604.1 *disappointment*; 288.3 *lost chance*; 720.2 *misinterpretation*; 274.1 *mistake*; 351.2 *misuse*; 467.1 *overestimation*; 630.1 *surprise*; 468.1 *underestimation*
mislaid 766.16 *losing*; 144.13 *misplaced*; 98.12 *missing*
mislay 766.9 *lose*; 144.19 *misplace*
mislaying 766.1 *loss*; 144.6 *misplacement*
mislead 604.8 *be dishonest*; 479.1 *be equivocal*; 700.27 *be false*; 736.9 *deceive*; 96.16 *delude*; 234.12 *distort the truth*; 456.11 *make ignorant*; 804.17 *make wicked*; 483.10 *manipulate*; 325.7 *misdirect*; 702.11 *practise sophistry*
misleader 700.15 *deceiver*
misleading 519.11 *blinding*; 700.34 *deceiving*; 604.12, 700.35 *deceptive*; 479.10 *equivocal*; 234.8 *exaggerated*; 700.5 *falseness*; 702.7 *sophistic*
misleadingly 604.13 *disappointingly*
misled 604.10, 700.36 *deceived*; 456.6 *ignorant*; 465.7 *misjudging*
mislike 596.5 *dislike*
mislocate 144.19 *misplace*
mislocated 144.13 *misplaced*
mislocation 144.6 *misplacement*
mismanage 486.5 *be unskilful*; 588.5 *misgovern*; 351.1 *misuse*
mismanaged 486.4 *bungled*
mismanagement 486.9 *bungling*; 351.2 *misuse*
mismanager 486.10 *unskilled person*
mismarry 570.15 *marry*
mismatch 751.8 *be different*
mismatched 751.10 *different*; 120.3 *unequal*
mismatching 751.3 *difference*
misnaming 721.7 *nomenclature*
misogamic 572.6 *celibate*
misogamist 594.9 *hater*; 572.5 *single person*
misogamy 572.1 *celibacy*
misogynist 466.7 *bigot*; 466.10 *discriminatory*; 594.9 *hater*; 653.2 *misanthrope*; 572.5 *single person*
misogynous 572.6 *celibate*; 466.10 *discriminatory*; 653.3 *misanthropic*
misogyny 572.1 *celibacy*; 567.1 *male sex*; 651.1 *malevolence*; 653.1 *misanthropy*; 466.4 *social discrimination*
misperception 486.9 *bungling*
misplace 144.19; 766.9 *lose*
misplaced 144.13; 408.12 *disordered*; 118.15 *irregular*; 766.16 *losing*
misplacement 144.6
misplacing 766.1 *loss*
misprint 274.19 *make a mistake*; 274.12 *typing error*
misprision 16.39 *crime*
misprize 668.19 *disrespect*; 468.3 *underestimate*
mispronounce 274.19 *make a mistake*
mispronunciation 544.5; 274.11 *grammatical error*; 729.3 *mode of speech*
misput 144.19 *misplace*; 144.13 *misplaced*
misputting 144.6 *misplacement*
misquotation 718.2 *misinformation*; 720.2 *misinterpretation*; 274.5 *misrepresentation*
misquote 699.9 *falsification*; 699.26 *falsify*; 274.19 *make a mistake*; 718.5 *misinform*; 720.1 *misinterpret*; 702.11 *practise sophistry*
misquoted 718.7 *misinformed*; 720.3 *misinterpreted*
misread 720.1 *misinterpret*; 720.3 *misinterpreted*; 465.10 *misjudge*
misreading 720.2 *misinterpretation*
misreckon 465.10 *misjudge*
misreference 109.5 *misconnection*
misreferred 109.9 *misconnected*
misrelation 109.5 *misconnection*
misremember 463.14 *be forgetful*
misreport 699.26 *falsify*
misreporting 699.9 *falsification*
misrepresent 718.4; 715.6 *accuse falsely*; 96.16 *delude*; 116.6 *differentiate*; 234.12 *distort the truth*; 699.26 *falsify*; 274.19 *make a mistake*; 720.1 *misinterpret*; 702.11 *practise sophistry*
Misrepresentation 718
misrepresentation 274.5; **718.1**; 116.3 *disguise*; 234.4 *distortion of the truth*; 715.2 *false accusation*; 699.9 *falsification*; 720.2 *misinterpretation*; 717.1 *representation*
misrepresented 718.6; 234.8 *exaggerated*; 699.36 *falsified*; 720.3 *misinterpreted*; 715.9 *perjurious*
misrepresentedly 720.5
misrepresenting 718.6 *misrepresented*
misrule 588.1 *anarchy*; 486.5 *be unskilful*; 486.9 *bungling*; 588.5 *misgovern*; 351.1, 351.2 *misuse*; 647.6 *suppress*
Miss 568.3 *female title of address*
miss 135.8; 505.8 *be deaf*; 233.5 *be incomplete*; 120.5 *be unequal*; 218.6 *be unsatisfied*; 65.2 *billiards play*; 486.9 *bungling*; 617.12 *desire*; 389.6 *elude*; 128.7 *exclude*; 247.6 *fail*; 247.1 *failure*; 66.2 *football play*; 463.13 *forget*; 766.9 *lose*; 465.10 *misjudge*; 65.8 *play billiards*; 66.4 *play soccer*; 274.13 *sporting error*; 555.8 *young woman*
Missa bassa 10.6 *Eucharist*
Missa brevis 10.6 *Eucharist*
missal 10.10 *religious manual*
Miss America 235.8 *exceller*
miss an opportunity 247.6 *fail*; 766.9 *lose*
Missa solemnis 10.6 *Eucharist*
Miss Clever 673.7 *vain person*
missed 65.9 *billiard*; 233.4 *incomplete*; 66.5 *soccer*
missed chance 249.3 *bad fortune*; 486.9 *bungling*
missed opportunity 288.3 *lost chance*
missed out 128.11 *excluded*
missed third strike 48.5 *batting terms*
misshape 548.7 *blemish*; 234.9 *distort*; 231.6 *imperfect item*; 161.3 *make shapeless*; 546.5 *make ugly*
misshapen 234.6 *distorted*; 408.14 *irregular*; 546.4 *ugly*
misshapenly 234.13 *asymmetrically*
misshapenness 234.3 *deformity*; 408.2 *irregular order*
missile 330.8; 587.13 *ammunition*; 587.5 *missile weapon*; 330.18 *projectile*; 332.11 *swift thing*
missile battalion 584.4 *military organization*
missilery 587.2 *arms*
missile strike 381.13 *air attack*
missile weapon 587.5
missing 98.12; 98.9 *away*; 526.7 *disappeared*; 128.11 *excluded*; 233.4 *incomplete*; 766.16 *losing*; 144.13 *misplaced*; 94.9 *nonexistent*; 195.7 *null*; 135.4 *required*
missing link 133.7 *broken thread*; 231.6 *imperfect item*; 233.2 *omission*
missing person 98.6 *absentee*; 526.4 *disappearance*; 633.7 *the hunted*
mission 576.3 *job*; 10.11 *place of worship*; 713.3 *precept*; 398.2 *representative body*; 810.2 *task*; 354.2 *undertaking*; 585.8 *warfare*
missionary 760.5 *converter*; 652.3 *philanthropist*; 7.4 *religionist*; 7.15 *religious*; 752.8 *volunteer*
missionary spirit 7.2 *religiousness*
mission worker 652.3 *philanthropist*
missis 570.11 *married woman*
Mississippi 90.3 *US rivers*
Mississippi mud pie 25.35 *dessert*
miss nothing 471.11 *take note of*
miss one's cue 486.5 *be unskilful*; 21.36 *underact*
miss one's deadline 262.2 *make haste*
miss one's footing 305.11 *trip*
Missouri 90.3 *US rivers*
miss out 233.5 *be incomplete*; 128.7 *exclude*
misspell 274.19 *make a mistake*; 720.1 *misinterpret*; 5.47 *word*
misspelling 274.11 *grammatical error*; 720.2 *misinterpretation*; 5.27 *spelling*
misspelt 720.3 *misinterpreted*
misspend 441.1, 681.7 *waste*
misspent youth 766.8 *lost thing*
miss stays 50.15 *sail*
misstate 699.26 *falsify*; 274.19 *make a mistake*; 718.5 *misinform*
misstated 718.7 *misinformed*
misstatement 699.9 *falsification*; 718.2 *misinformation*; 274.5 *misrepresentation*
miss the beat 286.4 *mistime*
miss the boat 247.6 *fail*; 288.7 *lose one's chance*; 294.7 *wait*
miss the bus 288.7 *lose one's chance*
miss the moment 286.4 *mistime*
miss the point 100.13 *be extraneous*; 109.10 *be unrelated*; 325.4 *lose track of*
Miss Universe 235.8 *exceller*
missus 568.3 *female title of address*
missy 555.8 *young woman*
mist 31.34; 528.10 *be opaque*; 31.64 *fog*; 521.4 *invisibility*; 524.10 *make dim*; 524.2 *murk*; 528.7 *opaque thing*; 32.3 *phase*; 433.33 *sprinkle*; 433.12 *sprinkler*; 521.6 *that which makes invisible*; 527.8 *transparent thing*; 433.3 *wateriness*; 432.4 *water vapour*
mistake 274.1; **465.2**; 459.2 *act of folly*; 486.9 *bungling*; 231.7 *defect*; 247.1 *failure*; 472.5 *inattentive act*; 802.2 *incorrectness*; 272.4 *joke*; 288.3 *lost chance*; 720.1 *misinterpret*; 720.2 *misinterpretation*; 465.10 *misjudge*; 412.9 *mix up*; 806.3 *sin*; 802.8 *wrongdoing*
mistaken 274.17; **288.16**; 802.12 *incorrect*; 720.3 *misinterpreted*; 465.9 *misjudged*; 465.7 *misjudging*; 412.13 *mixed-up*
mistakenly 288.21; **720.4**; 274.21 *erroneously*; 465.13 *misguidedly*; 802.26 *wrong*
mistakenness 802.2 *incorrectness*
mistake of law 16.4 *bad law*
mistaking 288.16 *mistaken*
mistaught 718.7 *misinformed*
misteach 718.5 *misinform*; 720.1 *misinterpret*; 245.6 *pervert*
misteaching 718.2 *misinformation*; 720.2 *misinterpretation*
misted 528.2 *shady*
mister 567.3 *male title of address*
Mister Charlie 567.3 *male title of address*
mister fix-it 578.2 *artisan*; 401.1 *servant*
misthrow 486.7 *be clumsy*; 486.9 *bungling*
mistily 524.12 *dimly*; 533.9 *greyly*; 453.25 *indeterminately*; 31.65 *meteorologically*; 528.13 *opaquely*; 161.6 *shapelessly*; 432.30 *smokily*; 527.13 *transparently*
mistime 286.4; **288.5**; 751.8 *be different*; 465.10 *misjudge*; 288.6 *take untimely action*
mistimed 288.10; 751.10 *different*; 286.2 *occurring at a different time*
mistiming 751.3 *difference*; 286.1 *different time*; 288.2 *untimeliness*; 288.1 *wrong time*
mistiness 429.2; 453.14 *indeterminacy*; 521.4 *invisibility*; 524.2 *murk*; 527.7 *semitransparency*; 161.1 *shapelessness*; 31.35 *visibility*
mist over 524.9 *be dim*
mistranslate 720.1 *misinterpret*
mistranslated 720.3 *misinterpreted*
mistranslation 720.2 *misinterpretation*
mistreat 798.11 *be evil*; 236.14 *ill-treat*; 351.1 *misuse*
mistreatment 351.2 *misuse*
mistress 6.4 *educator*; 568.3 *female title of address*; 568.4 *girlfriend*; 763.6 *lord*; 593.11 *loved one*; 593.9 *lover*; 400.1 *master*; 490.3 *pleasure-seeker*
mistress of the house 400.1 *master*
mistrial 465.3 *injustice*
mistrust 453.18 *be uncertain*; 451.1 *disbelief*; 451.8 *disbelieve*; 629.2, 629.8 *distrust*; 705.20 *doubt*; 453.10 *suspicion*; 705.6 *uncertainty*
mistrustful 451.6 *disbelieving*; 629.5 *distrustful*; 453.1 *uncertain*
mistrustfully 451.10 *disbelievingly*; 629.9 *jealously*
mistrustfulness 629.2 *distrust*
misty 429.10; 696.4 *difficult*; 521.2 *difficult to see*; 533.3 *dull*; 31.56 *foggy*; 453.6 *indeterminate*; 524.6 *murky*; 527.3 *semitransparent*; 528.2 *shady*; 161.5 *shapeless*; 432.19 *smoky*
misunderstand 274.18 *be in error*; 412.11 *be mixed up*; 751.5 *disagree*; 696.9 *find unintelligible*; 720.1 *misinterpret*; 465.10 *misjudge*
misunderstanding 701.1 *argument*; 751.1 *disagreement*; 720.2 *misinterpretation*; 465.1 *misjudgment*; 274.1 *mistake*
misunderstood 701.10 *arguable*; 720.3 *misinterpreted*; 465.9 *misjudged*
misusage 274.11 *grammatical error*
Misuse 351
misuse 351.1; **351.2**; 651.7 *act of malevolence*; 486.5 *be unskilful*; 486.9 *bungling*; 766.13 *destroy*; 349.3 *exploit*; 236.14 *ill-treat*; 245.8 *perversion*; 245.6 *pervert*; 349.6 *use*; 441.1, 441.3, 766.3 *waste*
misused 351.4
misuse of words 720.2 *misinterpretation*; 351.2 *misuse*
misuse power 351.1 *misuse*
misuse words 351.1 *misuse*
mitch 634.9 *play truant*
mite 76.2 *arachnid*; 555.9 *child*; 218.8 *insufficiency*; 159.4 *little person*; 76.3 *pest*
mite box 768.3 *offering*
mitelike 76.11 *arachnidan*
mithridate 394.4 *antidote*
mitigate 292.8; 419.14 *ease*; 244.1 *improve*; 714.8 *justify*; 166.7 *limit*; 214.5 *make smaller*; 685.4 *moderate*; 136.15 *modify*; 608.9 *relieve*; 421.13 *smooth over*
mitigated 292.16; 136.11 *modified*
mitigating 714.11 *vindicatory*
mitigating circumstances 714.2 *defence*
mitigation 214.1 *decrease*; 714.2 *defence*; 608.1 *ease*; 244.5 *improvement*; 166.1 *limitation*; 627.3 *mercy*; 685.1 *moderation*; 136.5 *modification*
mitigative 714.11 *vindicatory*
mitigatory 136.11 *modified*
Mitla 10.13 *shrine*
mitochondrial 34.23 *cellular*
mitochondrion 34.8 *cell organ*
mitosis 34.10 *cell division*
mitotic 34.25 *genetic*
mitraille 587.14 *historical ammunition*
mitrailleuse 587.12 *historical guns*
mitral stenosis 260.10 *cardiovascular disease*
mitre 176.11 *angle*; 23.17 *carpenter*; 7.11 *vestment*
mitred 176.7 *angular*; 23.16 *joined*
mitre joint 176.1 *angle*; 23.10 *carpenter's term*
mittens 551.25 *accessories*; 62.4 *climbing equipment*
mittimus 397.2 *demand*
mitts 551.25 *accessories*; 360.3 *tools for gripping*
mitzvah 650.4 *benevolent act*
mix 412.8; 327.22 *agitate*; 114.8 *be diverse*; 342.16 *be sociable*; 374.1 *combination*; 374.5 *combine*; 25.55 *cook*; 24.11 *make ceramics*; 412.2 *mixed thing*; 307.10 *swirl*
mix and match 412.8 *mix*
mixed 412.12; 114.6 *assorted*; 374.7 *combined*; 1.13 *racial*
mixed bag 114.3 *diverse thing*; 376.32 *miscellany*
mixed blessing 240.3 *inconvenience*; 216.6 *mediocrity*
mixed cloud 31.18 *cloud*
mixed drink 558.8; 558.2 *drink*
mixed economy 13.1 *economics*
mixed farm 43.6 *farm*
mixed farming 43.1 *agriculture*
mixed foursome 56.1 *golf*
mixed glyceride 33.7 *fat*
mixed grill 25.44 *British dish*; 25.32 *meat dish*
mixed herbs 496.5 *herbs*
mixed indicator 32.18 *gravimetric analysis*
mixed lot 376.32 *miscellany*
mixed marriage 570.3 *types of marriage*
mixed meeting 59.7 *horseracing*
mixed number 27.6 *complex number*
mixed party 654.5 *party*
mixed race 1.6 *race*
mixed salad 25.14 *salad*
mixed set 61.6 *motor-racing terms*
mixed thing 412.2
mixed-up 408.19; **412.13**; 412.12 *mixed*
mixer 412.6; 558.8 *mixed drink*; 412.7 *person who mixes*; 654.6 *social person*; 558.6 *soft drink*
mix in 211.6 *add*
mixing 374.1 *combination*; 412.1 *mixture*; 342.2 *social activity*
mixing bowl 410.16 *crockery*; 25.6 *kitchen equipment*; 412.6 *mixer*

mixing it up 52.14 *combat*
mixing tank 24.6 *ceramic workshop*
mix it 594.16 *cause hate*
mixologist 412.7 *person who mixes*
mixolydian 18.20 *key*
mixte frame 320.11 *bicycle part*
mix together 412.10 *become mixed*; 374.5 *combine*
Mixture 412
mixture 412.1; 114.2 *assortment*; 374.1 *combination*; 374.4 *compound*; 245.10 *impairment*; 394.2 *medicine*; 376.32 *miscellany*; 412.2 *mixed thing*; 32.3 *phase*
mix up 412.9; 408.23 *confuse*; 408.21 *disorder*; 378.8 *hinder*; 266.3 *make obscure*; 412.8 *mix*
mix-up 408.6; 378.2 *obstacle*
mix-up in dates 288.1 *wrong time*
mix with 211.6 *add*; 654.11 *be sociable*; 211.7 *support*
mix with water 374.5 *combine*
Miya-zaki-jingu 10.13 *shrine*
mizzen 168.4 *rear*
mizzenmast 50.3 *parts of a sailing boat*; 168.1 *rear*
mizzle 429.15 *be moist*; 429.2 *mistiness*; 31.62 *rain*
mizzly 429.10 *misty*
MK skates™ 68.6 *ice-skating*
MMR vaccine 394.3 *prophylactic*
mnemonic 462.7 *memorable*; 462.4 *reminder*
mnemonically 462.16 *memorably*
Mnemosyne 462.1 *memory*
mo 280.3 *instant*
moa 72.8 *extinct bird*
moan 606.7 *be dissatisfied*; 626.9 *be sullen*; 31.58 *blow*; 753.7 *complain*; 514.13 *cry*; 514.6 *cry of pain*; 491.12 *express pain*; 742.3, 742.11 *gesture*; 602.8 *grieve*; 603.2 *lament*; 113.18 *object*; 626.2 *sign of sullenness*; 511.8 *sound faint*
moaner 606.3 *dissatisfied person*; 670.13 *pessimist*; 753.4 *protester*
moaning 514.18 *crying*; 511.4 *faint sound*; 742.15 *gestural*
moaning Minnie 753.4 *protester*
moat 378.3 *barrier*; 183.2 *concave land*; 146.2 *crack*; 165.5 *enclose*; 165.3 *enclosing thing*; 128.3 *exclusion zone*; 384.18 *fence*; 384.12 *fort*; 384.8 *military defences*; 252.2 *protection*
moated 384.30 *defended*
mob 633.12 *aim at*; 750.2 *alliance*; 586.18 *army of people*; 408.26 *be disorderly*; 208.11, 376.20 *crowd*; 219.1 *excess*; 138.11 *general public*; 601.18 *salute*; 670.23 *show disapproval*; 208.4 *throng*
mobbed 208.10 *crowded*
mobcap 551.15 *headgear*
mobile 32.41 *analytic*; 453.8 *capricious*; 227.13 *changeable*; 300.16 *moving*; 19.12 *sculpture*; 2.14 *socioeconomic*
Mobile Army Surgical Hospital 584.4 *military organization*
mobile belt 30.20 *earth movement*
mobile camera 692.21 *television*
mobile crane 38.29 *construction equipment*
mobile home 565.9
mobile phase 32.17 *analysis*
mobile phone 504.9 *audio device*; 692.16 *transmitter*
mobile radio 692.18 *radio*
mobile radio station 692.20 *radio broadcasting*
mobile station 692.24 *television broadcasting*
mobile telephone 504.9 *audio device*; 692.9 *telephone*
mobile unit 692.20 *radio broadcasting*
mobile warfare 585.8 *warfare*
mobility 453.16 *capriciousness*; 227.1 *changeableness*; 300.1 *motion*; 2.7 *social stratification*
mobilization 376.1 *assembly*; 584.1 *military affairs*; 300.2 *momentum*; 243.9 *preparation*; 585.7 *war measures*
mobilize 376.42 *call together*; 584.10 *enlist*; 585.12 *go to war*; 243.4 *prepare for action*; 300.14 *set in motion*
mobilized 376.46 *assembled*; 243.18 *prepared*; 585.15 *warring*
Möbius strip 132.6 *continuum*; 27.47 *topology*
mob law 588.1 *anarchy*; 12.1 *government*; 16.41 *lawlessness*; 396.7 *type of rule*
mob member 774.11 *dishonest person*
mobocracy 588.2 *anarchism*; 12.1 *government*; 396.7 *type of rule*
mobocrat 588.3 *anarchist*
mobocratic 588.7 *anarchistic*
mob rule 588.1 *anarchy*; 408.9 *disorder*; 12.1 *government*; 396.7 *type of rule*
mobster 804.10 *bad person*; 662.9 *criminal*; 774.11 *dishonest person*; 800.4 *dishonourable person*; 798.6 *evil person*; 651.8 *malefactor*
moccasins 551.19 *footwear*
mocha 534.1 *brown*; 558.4 *coffee*
mock 96.12 *artificial*; 700.27 *be false*; 599.13 *be humorous*; 699.22 *be hypocritical*; 621.6 *deride*; 451.8 *disbelieve*; 470.3 *exclude*; 448.8 *experimental*; 699.12, 699.37 *fake*; 125.9 *imitate*; 125.13 *imitation*; 700.39 *imitative*; 124.13 *make unimportant*; 668.24, 678.14 *ridicule*; 115.8 *simulated*; 668.6, 668.25 *taunt*; 700.28 *trick*
mocked 700.36 *deceived*; 115.8 *simulated*
mocker 451.5 *disbeliever*; 678.9 *ridiculer*
mockery 125.3; **621.1**; 621.2 *act of derision*; 659.1 *discourtesy*; 700.5 *falseness*; 699.3 *hypocrisy*; 668.4 *ridicule*
mock-heroic 17.19 *narrative*
mock-heroic poetry 17.6 *poetry*
mocking 699.31 *hypocritical*; 668.14 *ridiculing*; 678.17 *scornful*; 668.15 *taunting*
mockingly 621.7; **668.29**; 125.14 *imitatively*; 659.10 *rudely*
mock up 420.13 *be unfinished*; 448.12 *rehearse*
mock-up 125.2 *copy*; 448.2 *rehearsal*; 420.10 *rough idea*; 738.7 *showpiece*
modal 221.8 *in a state of*
modality 4.8 *philosophical term*; 221.1 *state*
modal logic 4.6 *branch of philosophy*
modal scale 18.20 *key*
mode 733.4 *approach*; 553.4 *design*; 553.1 *fashion*; 18.20 *key*; 352.1 *means*; 27.60 *parameter*; 221.1 *state*; 724.1 *style*; 317.1 *way*
model 475.4; **551.27**; 19.11 *artist's materials*; 216.4 *average*; 125.2 *copy*; 738.1 *display*; 738.12 *displayer*; 111.4, 125.5 *duplicate*; 446.19 *epitomize*; 448.8 *experimental*; 703.3 *explanation*; 553.9 *fashion*; 553.5 *fashion model*; 160.7 *form*; 446.6, 446.13 *ideal*; 717.6 *image*; 525.5 *impression*; 28.6 *law*; 159.7 *little*; 159.2 *little thing*; 743.3 *means of identification*; 126.2 *original*; 484.6 *outline*; 230.1 *perfect*; 230.3 *perfection*; 129.4, 140.5 *precedent*; 160.2 *prototype*; 160.10 *prototypical*; 448.2 *rehearsal*; 448.12 *rehearse*; 19.21 *sculpt*; 19.12 *sculpture*; 738.7 *showpiece*; 26.7 *standard*; 476.1 *supposition*
model after 125.9 *imitate*
model builder 476.4 *theorist*
modelled 160.9 *formed*; 19.28 *sculpted*
modeller 717.4 *person who makes a representation*; 19.17 *sculptor*
modelling 160.4 *forming*; 36.3 *psychiatric treatment*; 19.12 *sculpture*
modelling clay 19.14 *sculptor's materials*; 419.11 *soft thing*
modelling tool 19.14 *sculptor's materials*
model maker 717.4 *person who makes a representation*
model oneself upon 125.9 *imitate*
modem 40.14 *data transfer*; 40.12 *electronic office*; 40.7 *peripheral*
mode of behaviour 631.1 *conduct*
mode of expression 724.4 *literary style*; 694.1 *meaning*
mode of operation 317.1 *way*
mode of speech 729.3
mode of use 349.6 *use*
moderate 684.6; **684.9**; **685.4**; **685.6**; 634.3 *abstain*; 634.19 *abstaining*; 648.3 *be lenient*; 793.9 *cheap*; 347.3 *counteract*; 214.4 *decrease*; 4.18 *detached*; 263.3 *ease*; 265.9 *easy*; 250.9 *free*; 250.7 *free person*; 618.9 *impartial*; 244.1 *improve*; 618.6 *indifferent person*; 648.4 *lenient*; 166.7 *limit*; 748.1 *mediate*; 216.3 *mediocre*; 216.2 *medium*; 216.8 *middle classes*; 292.8 *mitigate*; 136.15 *modify*; 231.4 *ordinary*; 728.22 *play down*; 12.6 *political party*; 244.12 *reformer*; 608.9 *relieve*; 251.14 *self-restrained*; 333.3 *slow down*; 178.9 *straight person*; 178.4 *traditional*; 468.4 *underestimating*; 333.5 *unhurried*; 31.50 *warm*
moderate breeze 31.13 *wind strength*
moderate climate 31.38 *climate*
moderated 728.19 *downplayed*; 292.16 *mitigated*; 136.11 *modified*
moderate drinker 689.8 *sober person*
moderate frost 31.36 *frost*
moderately 684.12; **685.9**; **728.28**; 634.21 *away*; 793.15 *cheaply*; 250.20 *freely*; 648.6 *leniently*; 216.12 *mediumly*; 749.7 *pacifically*; 205.12 *partly*; 468.6 *pessimistically*; 333.16 *slowly*; 4.27 *stoically*; 251.17 *with self-restraint*
moderateness 216.5 *medium*; 684.2, 685.1 *moderation*
moderate one's hunger 685.5
moderate one's language 685.4 *moderate*
moderating 685.8; 347.4 *counteracting*
moderating influence 748.3 *mediator*
Moderation 685
moderation 684.2; **685.1**; 634.11 *abstinence*; 347.1 *counteraction*; 214.1 *decrease*; 214.6 *decreasing*; 4.3 *detachment*; 728.9 *downplaying*; 618.3 *impartiality*; 244.5 *improvement*; 648.1 *leniency*; 166.1 *limitation*; 748.2 *mediation*; 216.5 *medium*; 749.1 *pacification*; 393.11 *recuperation*; 251.3 *self-restraint*
moderator 685.2; 394.9 *balm*; 579.13 *director*; 473.3 *impartial person*; 748.3 *mediator*; 334.8 *nuclear power*; 28.73 *nuclear reactor*; 394.1 *remedy*
modern 23.7 *furniture style*; 295.10 *new*; 448.9 *original*; 282.6 *present*
modern ballet 22.8 *ballet*
modern dance 22.8 *ballet*; 22.1 *dancing*
modern dance music 18.7 *dance music*
modern-dress production 21.14 *production*
modern human 566.4
modernism 295.1 *newness*; 448.4 *originality*; 4.7 *school of thought*; 295.2 *trendiness*; 282.4 *up-to-dateness*
modernist 17.14 *author*; 4.11 *follower of a doctrine*; 295.9 *modern person*; 448.9 *original*
modernistic 295.10 *new*
modernistically 295.21 *newly*
modernity 295.1 *newness*; 282.4 *up-to-dateness*
modernization 224.1 *change*; 295.5 *fresh start*; 244.5 *improvement*; 15.2 *industrial negotiations*
modernize 224.7 *be changed*; 282.5 *be present*; 224.8 *cause change*; 15.11 *conduct industrial relations*; 302.8 *further*; 244.1 *improve*; 295.20 *make new*; 393.2 *refurbish*
modernized 224.12 *changed*; 244.14 *improved*; 15.9 *negotiated*; 295.14 *renewed*
modernizing 15.9 *negotiated*
modern jazz 18.8 *jazz*
modern man 566.4 *modern human*; 295.9 *modern person*
modern master 19.16 *artist*
modern music 18.3 *classical music*
modern person 295.9
modern physics 28.3
modern poet 17.14 *author*
modern production 21.14 *production*
modern times 282.2 *the present day*
modern warfare 585.1 *war*
modern woman 568.11 *liberated woman*; 566.4 *modern human*
modest 674.8; 637.3 *cautious*; 793.9 *cheap*; 623.1 *humble*; 685.6 *moderate*; 255.12 *morally pure*; 646.1 *naive*; 795.9 *pure*; 728.15 *reserved*; 251.14 *self-restrained*; 732.1 *shy*; 271.1, 728.14 *simple*; 468.4 *underestimating*; 473.5 *unselfish*
modestly 674.17; 793.15 *cheaply*; 623.27 *humbly*; 468.6 *pessimistically*; 728.25 *reservedly*; 732.8 *shyly*; 473.9 *unselfishly*; 255.18 *virtuously*; 251.17 *with self-restraint*
modest person 674.7; **728.11**
Modesty 674
modesty 674.1; 637.13 *dissociation*; 623.7 *humility*; 795.3 *moral purity*; 646.2 *naivety*; 255.1 *purity*; 728.5 *reserve*; 251.3 *self-restraint*; 655.2, 732.3 *shyness*; 271.4, 728.4 *simplicity*; 468.1 *underestimation*; 473.2 *unselfishness*
modicum 412.4 *admixture*
modifiability 114.1 *diversity*
modification 136.5; 224.1 *change*; 760.1 *conversion*
modified 136.11; 224.12 *changed*
modified leaf 77.6 *leaf*
modifier 224.5 *changer*; 5.35 *part of speech*
modify 136.15; 224.7 *be changed*; 224.8 *cause change*; 116.6 *differentiate*; 760.9 *transform*
modifying 5.44 *grammatical*
modish 295.16 *avant-garde*; 551.30, 656.7 *dressed-up*; 632.12 *established*; 553.7 *fashionable*
modishly 551.36 *dressily*; 295.23 *trendily*
modiste 551.26 *fashion designer*
modular 405.7
modular arithmetic 27.4 *simple arithmetic*
modulate 224.8 *cause change*; 692.30 *communicate*; 750.24 *harmonize*; 276.11 *make periodical*; 685.4 *moderate*; 136.15 *modify*
modulated 692.34 *communicated*; 18.31 *composed*; 750.13 *harmonious*; 136.11 *modified*
modulated carrier 692.14 *radio transmission*
modulating 750.13 *harmonious*
modulation 224.1 *change*; 750.4 *harmony*; 18.20 *key*; 729.3 *mode of speech*; 685.1 *moderation*; 136.5 *modification*; 692.14 *radio transmission*
modulator 692.14 *radio transmission*
module 20.9 *miscellaneous architectural features*; 44.4 *nursery*; 197.1 *one*; 29.30 *spacecraft*; 6.3 *subject*; 405.3 *unit*
modulus 27.6 *complex number*
modulus of elasticity 38.15 *strength of materials*
modus operandi 221.1 *state*; 317.1, 631.7 *way*
modus vivendi 754.1 *compromise*; 221.1 *state*; 762.1 *substitution*; 317.1 *way*; 631.6 *way of life*
mog 71.10 *cat*
Mogul 566.4 *modern human*; 400.2 *sovereign*
mogul 123.4 *bigwig*; 68.12 *ski*; 68.1 *skiing*
moguled 68.12 *ski*
moguled piste 68.1 *skiing*
Mogul Empire 85.3 *dominion*
mogul skiing 68.1 *skiing*
mohair 193.4 *textile*
Mohammedan 7.6 *non-Christian*
mohican 547.8 *haircut*
Mohorovičić discontinuity 30.18 *earth's crust*
moiety 198.8 *half*; 205.1 *part*
moil 307.10 *swirl*; 327.2 *tumult*; 576.6 *work*
moiler 578.1 *worker*
Moine Thrust 30.20 *earth movement*
moiré 541.7 *iridescent*; 541.5 *variegated thing*; 541.1 *variegation*
moist 429.9; 431.15 *flowing*; 433.21 *watery*
moist air 31.10 *air movement*
moisten 429.13; 367.6 *throw down*; 433.29 *water*
moistening 433.26 *wetting*
moistiness 429.1 *moisture*
moistly 429.17; 431.26 *fluidly*; 31.65 *meteorologically*; 433.35 *wetly*
moistness 429.1 *moisture*; 433.3 *wateriness*
Moisture 429
moisture 429.1; 431.7 *juiciness*; 433.1 *water*; 31.6 *weather data*
moistureless 428.1 *dry*
moistureproof 428.10 *waterproof*
moisturizer 394.9 *balm*
moisty 429.9 *moist*
mojo 236.11 *harmfulness*; 742.1 *sign*; 11.6 *talisman*
moke 316.6 *beast of burden*
molar 425.11 *tooth*
molar gas constant 28.97 *fundamental constant*
molar heat capacity 28.36 *heat flow*
molasses 267.4 *adherent*; 43.9 *animal feedstuff*; 498.2 *sweetener*
mole 378.3 *barrier*; 519.4 *blind people*; 534.3 *brownness*; 449.12 *discoverer*; 165.3 *enclosing thing*; 693.10 *informer*; 644.4 *meddler*; 716.7 *person who gives evidence*; 185.2 *projection*; 252.4 *safety device*; 737.2 *secretiveness*; 260.13 *skin disease*; 711.4 *warner*; 38.24 *water system*
mole-catcher 382.13 *animal killer*; 633.6 *hunter*

mole-catching 633.2 *chase;* 71.23 *mammal hunting*
molecular 32.35 *combined;* 159.7 *little;* 405.7 *modular;* 205.11 *partial*
molecular biologist 34.19 *life scientist*
molecular biology 34.12; 34.1 *life science*
molecular cloud 29.11 *stellar birth*
molecular formula 32.13 *structure*
molecular genetics 34.11 *genetics;* 34.12 *molecular biology*
molecular orbital 32.12 *valence*
molecular-orbital theory 32.12 *valence*
molecular weight 414.9 *avoirdupois weight*
molecule 205.4 *component;* 159.2 *little thing;* 402.4 *matter;* 405.3 *unit*
molehill 155.2 *lowlands*
molehole 308.7 *passageway*
mole poblano 25.50 *Central American dish*
moleskin 193.4 *textile*
molest 798.11 *be evil;* 328.10 *disrupt;* 236.14 *ill-treat;* 351.1 *misuse;* 651.18 *torment*
molestation 328.4 *disruption;* 236.11 *harmfulness;* 351.2 *misuse*
molested 328.15 *disrupted*
molester 651.8 *malefactor*
mole trap 43.14 *pest control;* 700.13 *snare*
Molewyn Mountains 89.5 *British mountains*
Molisch's test 33.5 *sugar test*
moll 568.9 *woman considered as a sex object*
mollification 608.1 *ease;* 419.12 *gentleness;* 685.1 *moderation;* 749.1 *pacification*
mollified 419.7 *impressionable;* 292.16 *mitigated;* 608.7 *relieved*
mollifier 685.2 *moderator;* 608.3 *reliever*
mollify 419.14 *ease;* 292.8 *mitigate;* 685.4 *moderate;* 749.4 *pacify;* 608.9 *relieve*
mollifying 419.12 *gentleness;* 419.7 *impressionable*
mollusc 75.5; 70.4 *type of animal*
Mollusca 75.5 *mollusc*
molluscan 75.19
molluscicide 43.14 *pest control*
mollusc-like invertebrate 75.5 *mollusc*
mollycoddle 490.10 *comfort*
mollycoddled 490.7 *pleased*
Molotov cocktail 587.16 *bomb*
molten 375.5 *disintegrated;* 493.13 *heated;* 493.9 *hot;* 431.19 *liquefied;* 32.32 *solid;* 30.55 *volcanic*
molybdenous 32.34 *elemental*
molybdenum 33.15 *essential element*
molybdic 32.34 *elemental*
molybdous 32.34 *elemental*
mom 568.12 *woman in the family*
mom and pop store 779.8 *store*
moment 275.11 *date;* 28.10 *force;* 123.1, 643.6 *importance;* 331.11 *impulsion;* 280.3 *instant;* 222.2 *occurrence;* 280.4 *point in time;* 278.3 *short duration;* 276.2 *time period*
momentarily 278.8 *transiently*
momentariness 278.1 *transience*
momentary 278.6 *transient*
momentary success 246.1 *success*
moment of force 331.11 *impulsion*
moment of inertia 28.9 *mass*
moment of truth 287.3 *critical time*
momentous 287.7 *critical;* 123.5, 643.3 *important;* 395.11 *influential*
momentously 287.10 *critically;* 395.14 *influentially*
momentousness 643.6 *importance*
momentum 300.2; 334.4 *energy;* 331.11 *impulsion;* 28.9 *mass;* 330.1 *propulsion*
monachal 572.8 *monastic*
monad 159.2 *little thing;* 402.4 *matter;* 197.1 *one;* 34.3 *organism;* 93.2 *thing*
Monadhliath Mountains 89.5 *British mountains*
monadic 4.16 *dialectical;* 197.11 *one*
monadism 93.1 *existence*
monandry 570.3 *types of marriage*
monarch 396.10 *person of authority;* 400.2 *sovereign*
monarchal 396.14 *governmental*
monarchical 12.10 *governing;* 12.9 *governmental*
monarchical absolutism 12.1 *government*
monarchical government 12.1 *government*
monarchist 662.12 *reactionary*
monarchy 85.1 *country;* 12.1 *government;* 396.7 *type of rule*
monastery 165.2 *enclosed place;* 7.10 *priestly dwelling;* 736.6 *privacy;* 252.5 *refuge*
monastic 572.8; 572.4 *celibate person;* 165.7 *enclosed;* 7.7 *monk;* 7.15 *religious*
monastically 572.12 *celibately;* 165.8 *confinedly*
monasticism 572.3
monastic order 572.3 *monasticism*
monatomic 32.35 *combined*
monclinic 32.33 *crystalline*
monetarism 4.7 *school of thought*
monetarist 4.11 *follower of a doctrine;* 251.6 *lawmaker;* 4.14 *of a philosophy*
monetary 780.22; 776.14 *commercial;* 13.13 *economic;* 14.6 *financial*
monetary aid 392.6 *financial assistance*
monetary denomination 780.1 *money*
monetary policy 13.1 *economics*
monetary unit 780.1 *money*
monetary value 790.2 *value*
monetize 780.24
Money 780
money 780.1; **781.6**; 352.4 *financial resources;* 785.1 *payment;* 483.5 *positive stimulus;* 759.3 *something in exchange;* 781.5 *wealth*
moneybag 780.20 *money store;* 439.4 *storage*
moneybags 781.10 *wealthy person*
money belt 410.9 *baggage;* 780.20 *money store*
moneybox 410.6 *box;* 780.20 *money store;* 439.4 *storage*
moneybroker 771.3 *lender*
moneychanger 780.17 *financier;* 759.4 *person who exchanges;* 778.12 *wholesaler*
money coming in 765.4 *earnings;* 788.2 *money received*
money-dealer 780.17 *financier*
money dealings 14.1, 780.7 *finance*
money drawer 439.4 *storage*
moneyed 781.1 *wealthy*
moneyed class 781.11 *the rich*
moneyer 780.17 *financier*
money-grubber 765.7 *gainer;* 682.5 *miser;* 683.3 *selfish person*
money-grubbing 765.1 *gain;* 765.16 *greedy;* 682.1 *mean;* 683.4 *selfish*
money in the bank 780.6 *funds*
moneylender 780.17 *financier;* 771.3 *lender;* 436.3 *provider;* 778.12 *wholesaler*
moneylending 771.1 *lending*
moneyless 782.1 *poor*
moneymaker 765.7 *gainer;* 781.10 *wealthy person*
moneymaking 765.1 *gain;* 765.15 *gainful;* 785.18 *profitable;* 813.15 *rewarding;* 781.5 *wealth*
money man 780.17 *financier*
money management 14.1 *finance*
money market 14.1, 780.7 *finance*
money of account 780.1 *money*
money order 692.3 *correspondence;* 780.14 *paper money*
money power 14.1, 780.7 *finance*
money-raising 772.11 *borrowed;* 772.1 *borrowing*
money received 788.2; 769.2 *something received*
money-saving 680.4 *thrifty*
money-spinner 765.7 *gainer;* 781.10 *wealthy person*
money-spinning 765.15 *gainful*
money store 780.20
money supply 13.6 *economic factors*
money's worth 793.1 *cheapness;* 790.2 *value*
money to burn 219.3 *superfluity*
monger 778.13 *retailer*
Mongolic 5.11 *family of languages*
Mongoloid 1.13 *racial*
Mongoloid race 1.6 *race*
mongrel 71.9 *dog;* 412.5 *hybrid;* 412.12 *mixed*
mongrelism 412.1 *mixture*
mongrelize 412.8 *mix*
Monica Seles 63.7 *famous tennis players*
monies 780.6 *funds*
moniker 721.8 *name*
moniliasis 83.5 *fungal association*
monism 4.7 *school of thought*
monist 4.11 *follower of a doctrine;* 4.14 *of a philosophy*
monition 711.1 *warning*
Monitor 586.25 *historical naval ships*
monitor 713.4 *adviser;* 504.15 *hear;* 504.2 *hearer;* 281.14 *keep time;* 73.2 *lizard;* 518.11 *observer;* 579.16 *official;* 40.7 *peripheral;* 252.10 *protect;* 275.16 *time;* 518.15 *watch*
monitory 713.7 *advising;* 481.9 *dissuasive;* 693.16 *informative;* 475.13 *predicting;* 711.8 *warning*
monk 7.7; 450.5 *believer;* 572.4 *celibate person;* 797.15 *good person;* 255.5, 795.5 *pure person;* 655.6 *unsocial person;* 803.4 *virtuous person*
monkey 780.9 *British money;* 668.9 *butt;* 642.4 *capricious person;* 700.22 *dupe;* 71.16 *primate;* 331.15 *ram;* 201.9 *treble figures*
monkey about with 645.5 *be cunning*
monkey around 697.8 *fool*
monkey business 645.1 *cunning;* 700.7 *tricking*
monkey jacket 551.11 *jacket*
monkey on one's back 378.6 *burden*
monkey's cousin 201.7 *double figures*
monkey shines 662.1 *disobedience*
monkey tricks 662.1 *disobedience*
monkey up 304.14 *climb*
monkey with 245.4 *impair*
monkish 572.8 *monastic*
mono 260.6 *infection;* 197.11 *one*
monoacidic 32.36 *acid*
monoacidic base 32.9 *base*
monobasic 32.36 *acid*
monobasic acid 32.8 *acid*
monocarpellary 80.9 *of a fruit*
monocarpic 80.9 *of a fruit*
monochasial cyme 78.4 *flower head*
monochasium 78.4 *flower head*
monochromatic 529.10 *coloured;* 197.12 *one-sided*
monochromatic light 522.1 *light*
monochromatic radiation 28.26 *laser*
monochromator 28.91 *spectrometer*
monochrome 529.1 *colour;* 19.8 *painting;* 28.98 *physical*
monochrome television 692.21 *television*
monocle 197.10 *single thing;* 518.10 *visual aid*
monoclinic crystal 32.4 *crystal*
monoclonal antibody 394.4 *antidote*
monocotyledon 77.3 *seed plant*
Monocotyledonae 77.3 *seed plant*
monocotyledonous 77.16 *taxonomic*
monocropping 43.4 *arable farming*
monoculture 43.4 *arable farming*
monocycle 320.12 *bicycle*
monodic 516.7 *harmonious*
monodist 735.2 *soliloquist*
monodrama 21.2 *play;* 735.1 *soliloquy*
monodramatic 735.5 *soliloquizing*
monody 516.4 *harmonics;* 18.13 *melody;* 17.7 *poem;* 735.1 *soliloquy*
monoecious 78.12 *of flowers*
monofilament 42.1 *fibre*
monogamist 570.10 *married man*
monogamous 570.23
monogamously 570.24 *matrimonially*
monogamy 570.3 *types of marriage*
monoglot 729.19 *speaking*
monoglyceride 33.7 *fat*
monogram 5.13 *letter;* 24.11 *make ceramics;* 743.3 *means of identification;* 24.4 *porcelain mark*
monogrammatic 5.41 *lettered*
monograph 722.1 *dissertation*
monogynist 570.10 *married man*
monogyny 570.3 *types of marriage*
monohull 197.10 *single thing*
monohydrate 32.10 *salt*
monokini 551.21 *beachwear;* 67.8 *swimwear*
monolingual 197.12 *one-sided;* 729.19 *speaking*
monolingual dictionary 5.28 *dictionary*
monolith 744.11 *monument;* 3.11 *relic*
monolithic 416.6 *dense;* 255.16 *simple*
monolithic column 20.8 *column*
monologic 735.5 *soliloquizing*
monological 735.5 *soliloquizing*
monologist 21.29 *entertainer;* 735.2 *soliloquist;* 197.9 *soloist;* 729.10 *speaker*
monologize 735.3 *soliloquize;* 729.15 *talk to oneself*
monologue 21.2 *play;* 21.8 *scene;* 735.1 *soliloquy;* 197.9 *soloist;* 729.8 *speech*
monology 735.1 *soliloquy*
monomania 36.15 *compulsion;* 461.4 *delusion*
monomaniac 386.5 *compulsive person;* 461.7 *insane person*
monomer 32.21 *polymer*
monomeric 32.44 *polymeric*
monometallism 780.7 *finance*
monometer 32.20 *surface chemistry*
monomolecular 32.38 *reactive*
monophonic 516.7 *harmonious*
monophonic sound 504.10 *sound quality*
monophony 516.4 *harmonics*
monopolist 251.6 *lawmaker;* 683.3 *selfish person;* 778.12 *wholesaler*
monopolistic 395.13 *dominant;* 763.8 *possessing;* 251.13 *restraining;* 683.4 *selfish*
monopolistically 763.10 *possessively*
monopolization 763.1 *possession*
monopolize 395.10 *be a prevailing influence;* 683.6 *be selfish;* 360.7 *detain;* 251.9 *economize;* 166.7 *limit;* 763.7 *possess;* 777.1 *purchase;* 13.10 *trade with*
monopolized by 763.9 *possessed*
monopolizer 763.5 *possessor*
monopolize the conversation 735.4; 731.8 *talk too much*
monopoly 13.6 *economic factors;* 251.2 *economic restraint;* 128.4 *exclusiveness;* 166.2 *limiting factor;* 763.1 *possession;* 778.3 *selling*
monorail 317.12 *cableway;* 321.1 *railway;* 319.5 *transportable*
monosaccharide 33.3 *carbohydrate*
monosemous 694.6 *meaningful*
monosemy 694.3 *comprehension*
monosodium glutamate 495.4 *flavour;* 557.11 *food content*
monostich 269.2 *outline;* 17.8 *part of poem*
monosyllabic 269.3 *concise;* 5.39 *of language;* 732.2 *sparing with words*
monosyllabically 5.48 *linguistically*
monosyllabic language 5.10 *language type*
monosyllabism 269.1 *conciseness*
monosyllable 5.17 *word*
monoterpene 33.20 *terpene*
monotone 112.13 *monotonous;* 41.3 *photograph;* 18.21 *tone*
monotonous 112.13; 620.4 *boring;* 750.14 *conforming;* 132.11 *continuous;* 119.6 *equal;* 261.4 *fatiguing;* 509.16 *humming;* 111.17 *regular;* 497.5 *tasteless*
monotonously 620.8 *boringly;* 119.13 *equitably;* 111.20 *regularly;* 112.23, 509.19 *repeatedly;* 261.9 *tiringly;* 497.10 *without taste*
monotonousness 111.6 *regularity*
monotonous work 342.8 *assiduity*
monotony 620.1 *boredom;* 620.2 *boring thing;* 132.5 *continuity;* 497.1 *dilution;* 111.6 *regularity;* 112.3 *repetitiveness*
Monotremata 71.3 *egg-laying mammal*
monotrematous 71.25 *mammalian*
monotreme 71.3 *egg-laying mammal*
monounsaturated fat 33.7 *fat*
monovalent 32.35 *combined*
monsieur 567.3 *male title of address*
monsignor 7.8 *priest*
monsoon 434.4 *air flow;* 31.17 *wind system*
monsoon season 31.26 *raininess*
monster 158.15 *big;* 158.9 *big thing;* 118.10 *eccentric;* 619.5 *person of wonder;* 546.2 *ugly person;* 380.4 *violent creature;* 804.9 *wicked person*
monster man 158.10 *big person*
monstrance 10.14 *sacred object*
monstrosity 619.5 *person of wonder*
monstrous 158.15 *big;* 651.11 *cruel;* 118.14 *eccentric;* 236.5 *harmful;* 546.4 *ugly;* 619.8 *wonderful*
monstrous lie 699.10 *lie*
monstrously 158.20 *largely*
monstrousness 651.2 *cruelness;* 118.4 *unusualness*
montage 19.7 *picture;* 376.33 *putting together*
Mont Blanc 154.3 *mountain;* 89.6 *other major mountains and ranges*
mont-de-piété 771.4 *lending institution*
Monte Carlo 61.4 *motor rally*
Monte Carlo rally 61.1 *motor racing*
monteria 25.50 *Central American dish*

Montessori system 6.2 *educational system*
Montezeuma pie 25.50 *Central American dish*
Montezuma's revenge 560.2 *defecation*; 260.8 *indigestion*
month 148.8 *measure of time*; 275.4 *term*; 276.2 *time period*
monthlies 560.11 *menstruation*
monthly 298.12 *cyclic*; 298.16 *cyclically*; 276.13 *for specified periods*; 632.9 *habitual*; 740.5 *journal*; 560.31 *menstrual*; 275.22 *periodic*; 276.7, 276.8 *periodical*; 111.17 *regular*; 111.20 *regularly*
monthly bills 787.5 *expense*
monthly discharge 560.11 *menstruation*
months of the year 298.5 *regular thing*
monticule 89.1, 154.3 *mountain*
monticulous 89.7 *mountainous*
montura 59.1 *horse*
monument 744.11; 356.8 *construction*; 583.4 *funeral objects*; 742.5 *indicator*; 462.3 *memento*; 154.6 *tall thing*; 284.7 *thing of the past*
monumental 158.15 *big*; 3.15 *historic*; 89.7 *mountainous*; 123.6 *notable*; 19.25 *sculptural*; 154.12 *tall*
monumentally 3.25 *reportedly*
monumental mason 19.17 *sculptor*
monumental sculptor 19.17 *sculptor*
monumental sculpture 19.12 *sculpture*
monument mason 583.3 *funeral director*
Monza 1,000 kilometres 61.3 *sports-car race*
moo 515.1 *animal cry*; 515.4 *cry*
mooch 343.12 *be inactive*; 710.8 *solicit money*; 773.7 *take*
mooch around 333.1 *move slowly*
moocher 710.5 *beggar*
mooching 55.1 *angling*; 710.11 *begging*; 710.3 *solicitation*; 773.1 *taking*
mood 5.33; 17.3 *aspect of fiction*; 229.2 *attitude*; 631.1 *conduct*; 590.4 *emotion*; 99.4 *nature*; 221.4 *state of mind*; 5.30 *syntax*; 642.3 *whim*
moodily 227.15 *changeably*; 626.13 *sullenly*; 299.9 *unusually*
moodiness 227.2 *irresolution*; 626.1 *sullenness*; 299.2 *unusualness*
moody 642.1 *capricious*; 602.6 *depressed*; 227.14 *irresolute*; 624.15 *resentful*; 626.6 *sullen*; 264.14 *troublesome*; 299.5 *unusual*
moody person 227.5 *changeable person*
moolah 780.2 *cash*
moon 29.17; 227.3 *changeable thing*; 668.26 *cock a snook*; 522.4 *natural light*; 306.4 *orbiting body*; 29.18 *satellite*; 552.14 *undress*
moon base 29.31 *space travel*
moonbeam 522.4 *natural light*
moon-faced 158.16 *fat*
moon goddess 8.5 *deity*
Moonie 7.5 *Christian*
mooning 593.20 *amorous*; 552.11 *exposed*; 796.7 *sexual assault*; 668.7 *sign of disrespect*; 552.1 *undress*
moonless 523.8 *dark*
moonlight 389.6 *elude*; 28.23 *light*; 29.17 *moon*; 522.4 *natural light*; 576.6 *work*
moonlight flit 313.7 *departure*; 389.1 *escape*
moonlighting 389.1 *escape*
moonlit 522.18 *lit*
moonrise 291.1 *evening*; 522.4 *natural light*; 304.3 *sunrise*
moonset 291.1 *evening*
moonshine 690.12 *alcohol*; 558.7 *alcoholic drink*; 522.4 *natural light*; 699.15 *nonsense*; 702.1 *sophistry*
moor 373.12 *bind*; 81.2 *grassland*; 154.2 *heights*; 312.4 *land*; 92.6 *lowland*; 92.3 *marsh*; 323.10 *sail*
moored 228.10 *stabilized*
Moore turn 57.6 *pommel horse*
mooring 312.11 *landing*; 50.10 *sailing*
mooring line 50.3 *parts of a sailing boat*
moorings 373.6 *line*
moorish 92.11 *continental*
moorland 141.3 *geographical space*; 81.2 *grassland*; 154.2 *heights*; 92.6 *lowland*
moose 60.5 *game*
moot 701.10 *arguable*; 453.18 *be uncertain*; 579.7 *council*; 701.14 *discuss*; 746.3 *discussion*; 705.20 *doubt*; 447.8 *problematic*; 476.6 *propound*; 705.14 *questionable*; 476.7 *suppositional*; 453.1 *uncertain*
mooted 243.17 *developing*; 447.8 *problematic*; 476.8 *supposed*
mooter 691.6 *drug*
moot point 705.4 *difficult question*; 447.2 *issue*
mop 428.20 *absorb*; 256.13 *clean*; 256.10 *cleaning object*; 428.15 *dryer*
mopboard 175.2 *foot*
mope 626.9 *be sullen*; 602.9 *despair*
moped 320.13 *motorcycle*
moper 620.3 *boring person*; 602.4 *depressing person*; 606.3 *dissatisfied person*; 611.3 *hopeless person*
mopiness 626.1 *sullenness*
moping 593.20 *amorous*; 602.6 *depressed*
mopishness 655.1 *unsociability*
mop one's brow 581.2 *be refreshed*
moppet 555.9 *child*
mopping-up 256.2 *cleaning*; 428.13 *drying*
mop up 428.20 *absorb*; 256.13 *clean*
mopy 655.8 *unsociable*
morainal 30.60 *glaciated*
moraine 205.8 *bits and pieces*; 30.38 *glacier*; 154.4 *mountain range*; 215.2 *residue*; 316.10 *transferred thing*
morainic 30.60 *glaciated*
moral 795.7; **795.8**; **801.10**; 713.7 *advising*; 5.21 *catchword*; 810.8 *dutiful*; 701.4 *gist*; 799.4 *honourable*; 797.3 *kind*; 745.1 *maxim*; 255.12 *morally pure*; 4.13 *of philosophy*; 713.3 *precept*; 803.5 *virtuous*
moral badness 796.1 *immorality*
moral climate 795.1 *morality*
moral code 4.2 *philosophical system*; 7.1 *religion*
moral delinquency 796.1 *immorality*
moral dilemma 705.4 *difficult question*
morale 747.2 *fellowship*; 584.7 *miscellaneous terms*; 221.4 *state of mind*
morale-boosting 392.32 *supportive*
moral education 6.2 *educational system*
moral error 274.8
moral fibre 638.16 *fortitude*; 799.1 *probity*
moral goodness 803.1 *virtue*
moral guardian 255.6 *prude*
moral guideline 713.3 *precept*
moral imperative 810.4 *sense of duty*
moral injunction 713.1 *advice*
moralist 795.6; 4.10 *philosopher*; 631.3 *well-behaved person*
moralistic 795.10; 464.8 *judging*; 801.10 *moral*; 745.2 *proverbial*
moralistically 795.13 *morally*; 4.25 *theoretically*
Morality 795
morality 795.1; 805.1 *innocence*; 797.10 *kindness*; 799.1 *probity*; 255.1 *purity*; 803.1 *virtue*
morality play 21.2 *play*
moralize 795.12; 713.5 *advise*; 745.3 *aphorize*; 4.22 *propound a philosophy*
moralizing 713.1 *advice*; 713.7 *advising*; 795.10 *moralistic*; 745.2 *proverbial*
moral laws 803.2 *virtues*
morally 795.13; 713.9 *advisably*; 799.7 *honourably*; 797.23 *nicely*; 810.18 *on duty*; 4.25 *theoretically*; 255.18, 803.9 *virtuously*
morally pure 255.12
morally weak 804.13 *venial*
morally wrong 796.11 *immoral*
Moral Majority 795.6 *moralist*
moralness 795.1 *morality*
moral obligation 810.4 *sense of duty*
moral philosophy 4.6 *branch of philosophy*
moral purity 795.3; 255.1 *purity*
Moral Rearmament 795.2 *good morals*
moral rectitude 255.1 *purity*; 803.1 *virtue*
moral relativism 4.9 *philosophical problem*
moral rule 713.3 *precept*
morals 810.6 *ethics*; 446.5 *ideology*; 795.1 *morality*; 4.2 *philosophical system*; 799.1 *probity*; 255.1 *purity*; 7.1 *religion*; 803.2 *virtues*; 631.6 *way of life*
moral sense 810.4 *sense of duty*
moral sensibility 477.3 *insight*; 554.1 *life*
moral standards 795.1 *morality*
moral strength 803.1 *virtue*
moral support 413.6; 392.2 *support*
moral tone 803.1 *virtue*
moral turpitude 796.1 *immorality*; 800.1 *improbity*; 804.2 *vice*
moral virtues 803.2 *virtues*
moral weakness 804.3 *venial sin*
morass 264.6 *critical situation*; 92.3 *marsh*
moratorium 294.3 *delayed action*; 361.6 *interruption*; 749.1 *pacification*; 226.3 *pause*; 786.2 *stoppage*
moratorium on nuclear testing 749.1 *pacification*
morbid 260.23 *diseased*; 236.4 *poor*
morbid curiosity 644.2 *prying*
morbidity 260.1 *ill health*; 236.10 *poverty*
morbidly 260.25 *unhealthily*
morbid psychology 36.1 *psychology*
morbific 260.23 *diseased*
mordacious 651.14 *hostile*
mordacity 651.4 *bitterness*
mordancy 651.4 *bitterness*; 726.1 *emphasis*
mordant 42.6 *dye*; 726.3 *emphatic*; 651.14 *hostile*; 529.4 *pigment*; 336.12 *strong to the senses*
mordent 18.16 *musical note*
more 211.8 *additional*; 211.10 *additionally*; 669.27 *bravo!*; 203.2 *certain amount*; 207.11 *in majority*; 207.3 *majority*; 207.6 *plural*; 207.1 *plurality*
more and more 209.10 *by degrees*; 213.8 *increasingly*
more bricks than bouquets 470.5 *rejection*
more convenient time 286.1 *different time*
more dead than alive 261.1 *fatigued*
more detail 124.8 *trifle*
moreish 557.27 *edible*; 495.7 *tasty*
more kicks than ha'pence 470.5 *rejection*
morel 25.33 *vegetable*
more often than not 140.18 *as a rule*; 297.1 *frequently*
more or less 147.13 *nearly*; 216.11 *on average*; 203.6 *quantitative*; 203.7 *quantitatively*
moreover 211.10 *additionally*
mores 632.4 *custom*; 656.5 *etiquette*; 795.1 *morality*; 2.3 *social environment*; 803.2 *virtues*; 631.6 *way of life*
more so 213.8 *increasingly*; 121.12 *superior*
more than enough 679.3 *abundant*; 217.9 *enough*; 219.2 *overdoing it*; 217.2 *plentiful*; 217.8 *plenty*
more than ever 121.17 *supremely*
more than half 207.3 *majority*
more than is fair 219.1 *excess*
more than is needed 219.3 *superfluity*
more than one 207.6 *plural*; 207.1 *plurality*
more than satisfy 217.4 *suffice*
morganatic 570.23 *monogamous*
morganatically 570.24 *matrimonially*
morganatic marriage 570.3 *types of marriage*
morgue 582.8 *after death*; 583.1 *burial*
moribund 556.14 *aged*; 556.12 *ageing*; 582.18 *dying*; 260.22 *sick*
moribundly 582.23 *fatally*; 556.16 *maturely*
morion 384.7 *armour*
MORI poll™ 469.10 *vote*
Mormon 7.5 *Christian*; 570.10 *married man*
Mormonism 570.3 *types of marriage*
morn 290.1 *morning*; 304.3 *sunrise*
morning 290.1; **290.5**; 130.2 *creation*; 304.3 *sunrise*
morning after 690.15 *crapulence*
morning-after pill 563.3 *birth control*
morning coat 551.3 *formal dress*; 551.11 *jacket*
morning dress 551.3, 656.4 *formal dress*
morning-fresh 290.5 *morning*
morning glory 290.2 *morning thing*
morning light 290.1 *morning*
morning, noon, and night 297.1 *frequently*
morning paper 740.4 *newspaper*
morning prayers 10.4 *public worship*
mornings 290.8 *in the morning*; 111.20 *regularly*
morning service 10.4 *public worship*
morning sickness 290.2 *morning thing*
morning star 290.2 *morning thing*; 29.10 *star*
morning thing 290.2
morning time 290.1 *morning*
morocco 550.14 *animal covering*
moron 459.3 *foolish person*; 461.7 *insane person*; 457.3 *unintelligent person*
moronic 459.5 *foolish*; 457.7 *intellectually subnormal*; 457.5 *lacking intellect*
moronically 457.11 *unintelligently*
morose 602.6 *depressed*; 499.7 *splenetic*; 626.6 *sullen*; 655.8 *unsociable*
morosely 499.11 *splenetically*; 626.13 *sullenly*; 655.14 *unsocially*
moroseness 499.4 *spleen*; 626.1 *sullenness*; 655.1 *unsociability*
morph 691.6 *drug*
morpheme 5.35 *part of speech*; 5.17 *word*
morphemeic 5.44 *grammatical*
morphemically 5.52 *grammatically*
Morpheus 343.9 *sleep*
morphia 394.5 *analgesic*
morphine 33.19 *alkaloid*; 394.5 *analgesic*; 394.8, 691.6 *drug*; 343.10 *soporific*
morphogenesis 160.4 *forming*
morphogenetic resonance 510.1 *resonance*
morphogenic 160.9 *formed*
morphologic 160.9 *formed*
morphological 34.20 *biological*; 5.38 *linguistic*; 403.12 *organic*; 5.42 *worded*
morphologically 34.29 *biologically*; 160.13 *formatively*; 5.50 *lexically*; 403.18 *structurally*
morphological unit 5.17 *word*
morphologist 403.10 *anatomist*; 34.19 *life scientist*; 5.2 *linguist*
morphology 34.4 *anatomy*; 160.1, 403.3 *form*; 34.1 *life science*; 5.1 *linguistics*; 403.8 *science of structure*
morphophonemic 5.38 *linguistic*
morphophonemics 5.1 *linguistics*
morphophonology 5.1 *linguistics*
Morris chair 23.2 *chair*
morris dance 22.4 *historic dancing*
morris dancing 22.1 *dancing*
morrow 290.1 *morning*
Mors 582.2 *death personified*
Morse code 5.8 *artificial language*; 692.8 *data transmission*; 742.4 *signal*; 692.27 *signalling*
morsel 495.3 *appetizer*; 196.3 *fragment*; 159.3 *little piece*; 557.14 *mouthful*; 205.7 *piece*
mortal 382.23, 582.20 *deadly*; 357.14 *destructive*; 798.9 *detrimental*; 566.12 *human*; 278.7 *impermanent*; 566.7 *person*; 806.7 *sinful*
mortal blow 798.2 *affliction*; 131.13 *ender*
mortal fear 612.1 *fear*
mortal horror 596.1 *dislike*
mortal illness 582.5 *ways of dying*
mortality 582.1 *death*; 582.12 *death count*; 566.2 *human nature*
mortality rate 582.12 *death count*
mortality table 582.12 *death count*
mortally 798.13 *destructively*; 566.15 *humanly*; 804.20 *immorally*; 382.25 *lethally*
mortally ill 260.22 *sick*
mortal remains 582.11 *dead person*; 215.1 *remainder*
mortal sin 247.3 *personal fault*; 804.4 *sin*
mortar 267.3 *adhesive*; 435.2 *building material*; 38.25 *construction material*; 550.28 *face*; 587.12 *historical guns*; 38.26 *masonry*; 330.8 *missile*; 550.8 *wall covering*
mortar attack 381.12 *military attack*
mortarboard 551.15 *headgear*; 743.5 *uniform*
mortgage 783.9 *acquire credit*; 378.6 *burden*; 253.12 *certify*; 783.1 *credit*; 772.5, 784.3 *loan*; 253.2 *promise*
mortgage arrears 249.2 *economic adversity*
mortgage company 771.4 *lending institution*
mortgaged 772.11 *borrowed*; 253.7 *guaranteed*; 784.9 *in debt*
mortgage deed 755.2 *purchase contract*
mortgaged to the hilt 784.9 *in debt*
mortgagee 771.3, 783.5 *lender*; 763.5 *possessor*
mortgage holder 771.3 *lender*
mortgage one's house 772.7 *borrow*; 378.12 *burden*
mortgage repayment 784.3 *loan*
mortgage shark 700.17 *cheat*
mortgaging 772.1 *borrowing*
mortgagor 772.6 *borrower*; 784.6 *debtor*

mortician 583.3 *funeral director;* 582.9 *person dealing with the dead*
mortification 807.2 *apology;* 582.1 *death;* 604.1 *disappointment;* 375.1 *disintegration;* 623.13 *disrepute;* 623.9 *humiliation;* 668.8 *indignity;* 808.2 *type of penance*
mortification of the flesh 808.2 *type of penance*
mortified 604.9 *disappointed;* 623.3 *humbled*
mortify 258.10 *be dirty;* 375.3 *disintegrate;* 623.17 *humiliate;* 623.22 *shame*
mortifying 623.6, 668.16 *humiliating*
mortify oneself 807.6 *apologize*
mortify one's flesh 807.6 *apologize;* 808.5 *do penance*
mortify the flesh 684.5 *be self-restrained*
mortise 23.17 *carpenter;* 23.10 *carpenter's term*
mortise and tenon 23.10 *carpenter's term*
mortised 23.16 *joined*
mortise lock 373.8 *fastening*
mortiser 23.11 *woodworking tool*
mortmain 440.2 *legal terms*
mortuary 582.8 *after death;* 583.1 *burial;* 583.11 *funeral*
morula 34.15 *developmental biology*
mosaic 24.8 *ceramic object;* 541.2 *check;* 374.2 *cooperation;* 114.3 *diverse thing;* 412.3 *miscellany;* 542.3 *pattern;* 44.12 *pests and diseases;* 19.24 *pictorial;* 19.7 *picture;* 79.10 *tree disease*
mosaic gold 700.6 *imitation*
mosasaur 73.6 *extinct reptile*
Moscow 87.6 *other cities*
Moselle 90.5 *other major rivers;* 558.9 *wine*
Moses 372.8 *person who separates*
Moses basket 410.7 *basket*
mosey along 313.1 *depart;* 333.1 *move slowly*
MOSFET 39.19 *transistor*
mosiacs 19.1 *art*
mosque 10.11 *place of worship*
mosquito 76.1 *insect;* 76.3 *pest*
mosquito net 308.6 *porous thing*
mosquito netting 550.7 *overhead covering*
moss 82.3; 538.8 *greenness;* 92.3 *marsh*
moss ally 82.3 *moss*
moss-covered 82.6 *mosslike*
moss-grown 82.6 *mosslike*
moss killer 44.8 *weedkiller*
mosslike 82.6
mosslike plant 82.3 *moss*
moss plant 82.4
moss stitch 42.5 *knitting*
mosstrooper 586.9 *guerrilla;* 774.9 *plunderer*
mossy 44.17 *botanical;* 419.4 *compressible;* 82.6 *mosslike*
most 121.14 *best;* 203.2 *certain amount;* 219.1 *excess;* 207.11 *in majority;* 207.3 *majority;* 207.6 *plural;* 203.6 *quantitative*
most certainly 454.12 *assuredly*
most desirable 235.1 *worthy*
most important 123.5 *important*
most likely 104.11 *probably*
mostly 140.18 *as a rule;* 99.13 *in essence;* 216.11 *on average;* 204.13 *on the whole;* 138.31 *overall*
MOS transistor 39.19 *transistor*
most recent 295.10 *new*
MOT 320.21 *miscellaneous motoring terms*
mot 745.1 *maxim*
MOT certificate 757.2 *permit*
mote 258.4 *dirt;* 427.7 *grain;* 415.7 *light thing;* 159.3 *little piece*
motel 565.10 *hotel;* 320.21 *miscellaneous motoring terms;* 226.5 *resting place*
motet 10.8 *hymn;* 18.5 *sacred music*
moth 357.7 *agent of destruction;* 76.1 *insect*
moth and rust 245.9 *dilapidation*
mothball 294.8 *delay;* 359.2 *preserver;* 350.6 *stop using;* 439.6 *store*
mothballed 350.4 *disused;* 294.10 *held up;* 335.10 *powerless;* 359.7 *preserved*
mothball fleet 586.22 *navy*
mothballing 294.3 *delayed action*
moth-eaten 284.19 *antiquarian;* 245.13 *dilapidated;* 296.12 *olden;* 548.6 *seedy;* 76.12 *verminous*
mother 650.8 *be benevolent;* 490.10 *comfort;* 5.39 *of language;* 359.5 *preserve;* 344.7 *Prime Mover;* 130.26 *produce;* 356.9 *producer;* 561.5 *propagator;* 252.10 *protect;* 392.20 *sustain;* 556.9 *woman;* 568.12 *woman in the family*
Mother Carey's chickens 711.1 *warning*
mother complex 36.18 *complex*
mother country 85.6 *native land;* 86.4 *territorial division*
mother earth 30.5 *earth;* 562.1 *fertility*
mothered 554.15 *born*
mother figure 762.2 *substitute person;* 36.25 *surrogate*
mother fixation 36.17 *fixation*
motherhood 554.4 *biological function;* 561.4 *development;* 568.12 *woman in the family*
Mother Hubbard 551.7 *frock*
mothering 392.3 *sustenance*
motherland 565.3 *home;* 85.6 *native land;* 86.4 *territorial division*
motherly 650.6 *benevolent;* 593.17 *loving;* 556.13 *middle-aged*
Mother Nature 8.3 *God;* 356.9 *producer*
mother of all battles 585.1 *war*
Mother of God 8.10 *deified person*
Mother of Parliaments 579.11 *British government;* 12.4 *governing body*
mother-of-pearl 541.5 *variegated thing*
mother-of-pearl inlay 23.9 *decorative woodwork*
Mother of the Muses 462.1 *memory*
Mother's Day 298.6 *annually celebrated day*
mother's milk 431.3 *body fluid;* 558.5 *milk*
mother's ruin 558.7 *alcoholic drink*
mother's skirt 736.2 *hiding place*
mother substitute 762.2 *substitute person*
mother superior 400.1 *master;* 7.7 *monk*
mother surrogate 36.25 *surrogate*
mother symbol 36.24 *symbolism*
Mother Teresa 650.5 *benevolent person;* 589.4 *Nobel Peace Prize*
mother-to-be 474.4 *expectant person;* 561.7 *obstetrics*
mother tongue 729.1 *faculty of speech;* 5.4 *parent language;* 695.10 *simplicity*
mother wit 442.5 *common sense;* 458.2 *intelligence*
mothproof 252.7 *invulnerable*
mothy 76.12 *verminous*
motif 17.3 *aspect of fiction;* 516.1 *melody;* 447.1 *topic*
motile 84.7 *algal;* 300.16 *moving*
motility 300.1 *motion*
Motion 300
motion 300.1; 340.1 *action;* 342.1 *activity;* 713.1 *advice;* 631.1 *conduct;* 560.2 *defecation;* 144.1 *displacement;* 560.5 *faeces;* 742.11 *gesture;* 447.2 *issue;* 346.1 *operation;* 484.1 *plan;* 710.1 *request;* 752.2 *tentative offer;* 28.8 *time;* 300.15 *walk*
motion after 300.10 *regular movement*
motional 300.16 *moving*
motion from 303.11 *retreat*
motion in front 300.10 *regular movement*
motion into 300.3 *motion towards*
motionless 301.4; 341.3, 343.1 *inactive;* 339.5 *inert*
motionlessly 301.10; 343.15 *inactively;* 339.7 *inertly*
Motionlessness 301
motionlessness 301.1; 341.1 *inaction;* 339.1 *inertness*
motion out of 300.4 *backward motion*
motion picture 738.9 *production*
motion-picture film 744.7 *recording*
motion-picture rating 399.2 *censorship*
motion round 300.5 *circuition*
motion sickness 320.21 *miscellaneous motoring terms*
motion towards 300.3
motivate 483.9; 340.4 *act;* 346.8 *activate;* 344.10 *awaken;* 617.15 *cause desire;* 349.5 *dispose of;* 331.1 *impel;* 395.8 *influence;* 579.1 *manage;* 480.15 *persuade;* 476.6 *propound;* 300.14 *set in motion*
motivated 483.12; 6.17 *educable;* 480.20 *persuadable*
motivates 123.7 *be important*
motivating 395.12 *appealing;* 483.11 *motivational;* 480.19 *persuasive*
motivation 344.1 *cause;* 6.10 *educability;* 395.1 *influence;* 579.3 *management;* 300.2 *momentum;* 480.11, 483.1 *motive*
motivational 483.11; 300.16 *moving*
motivationally 300.18 *in motion*
motivator 480.14; **483.7**; 713.4 *adviser;* 579.13 *director;* 449.12 *discoverer;* 340.3 *doer;* 344.7 *Prime Mover*
Motive 483
motive 176.6; **480.11**; **483.1**; 342.4 *energy;* 444.4 *explanation;* 334.15 *full of energy;* 331.17 *impelling;* 395.1 *influence;* 482.1 *intention;* 300.16 *moving;* 330.17 *propulsive;* 344.5 *reason*
motive force 36.22 *libido*
motiveless 642.1 *capricious*
motivelessness 642.2 *caprice*
motive power 334.4 *energy;* 331.11 *impulsion;* 300.1 *motion;* 330.1 *propulsion*
motivity 300.1 *motion*
mot juste 273.3 *accurate thing;* 543.1 *elegance*
motley 114.6 *assorted;* 114.2 *assortment;* 21.32 *clown;* 21.12 *comedy;* 551.5 *fancy dress;* 412.3 *miscellany;* 412.12 *mixed;* 541.6 *variegated;* 541.5 *variegated thing;* 541.1 *variegation*
motley collection 114.3 *diverse thing*
motley crew 412.3 *miscellany*
motocross 61.5 *motorcycle racing*
motocrosser 61.8 *driver*
motocross racer 320.14 *cyclist*
motor 320.16 *car;* 38.5 *dynamic structure;* 438.5 *machine;* 300.16 *moving;* 334.6 *source of energy*
motorbicycle 320.13 *motorcycle*
motorbike 320.13 *motorcycle;* 61.5 *motorcycle racing*
motorbike and sidecar 320.13 *motorcycle*
motorbike race 61.5 *motorcycle racing*
motorbike racing 61.5 *motorcycle racing*
motorcade 320.21 *miscellaneous motoring terms;* 132.8 *procession*
motorcar 320.16 *car;* 321.5 *locomotive part*
motor coach 320.19 *bus*
motorcycle 320.13; 316.5 *means of transport;* 61.5 *motorcycle racing*
motorcycle class 61.5 *motorcycle racing*
motorcycle courier 320.14 *cyclist*
motorcycle race 61.5 *motorcycle racing*
motorcycle racer 61.8 *driver*
motorcycle racing 61.5
motorcycling 320.1 *road transport*
motorcycling association 61.7 *racing governing body*
motorcyclist 320.14 *cyclist;* 61.8 *driver*
motordrive 41.18 *exposure time*
motor haulage 320.1 *road transport*
motoring 320.15 *motor transport*
motor inn 565.10 *hotel*
motorized 438.9 *mechanical*
motorized division 584.4 *military organization*
motorized sled 320.10 *sled*
motorman 321.9 *railway worker*
motor-mouth 731.4 *talker*
motor mower 438.3 *garden tool*
motor neurone disease 260.17 *nervous disorder*
motor oil 268.5 *lubricant*
motor race 61.1 *motor racing;* 61.9 *race*
motor racer 61.8 *driver*
Motor Racing 61
motor racing 61.1
motor-racing terms 61.6
motor rally 61.4; 61.1 *motor racing*
motorscooter 320.13 *motorcycle*
motor show 738.6 *display;* 779.2 *fair*
motor sport 61.1 *motor racing*
motor torpedo boat 586.24 *warship*
motor transport 320.15; 320.1 *road transport*
motor trial 61.1 *motor racing*
motorway 318.2 *passing along;* 317.3, 320.2, 373.5 *road;* 68.1 *skiing;* 319.5 *transportable*
motorway restaurant 557.15 *eating place*
motorway services 226.4 *stopping place*
motorway sign 742.5 *indicator;* 742.1 *sign*
motory 300.16 *moving*
motte 154.3 *mountain*
mottle 541.4 *maculation;* 79.10 *tree disease;* 541.11 *variegate*
mottled 541.10; 412.12 *mixed;* 531.3 *white-haired*
mottled effect 412.3 *miscellany*
mottlement 541.4 *maculation*
mottling 541.4 *maculation*
motto 5.21 *catchword;* 743.8 *heraldic device;* 745.1 *maxim;* 795.7 *moral*
motzi 10.9 *prayer*
moue 234.2 *facial distortion;* 742.3, 742.11 *gesture;* 626.2 *sign of sullenness*
mould 139.3 *characteristic;* 20.19 *decorate;* 553.4 *design;* 245.9 *dilapidation;* 258.4 *dirt;* 375.1 *disintegration;* 111.4, 111.9 *duplicate;* 6.22 *educate;* 550.28 *face;* 553.9 *fashion;* 160.7, 403.3 *form;* 30.43 *fossil;* 83.1 *fungus;* 25.6 *kitchen equipment;* 24.11 *make ceramics;* 117.9 *make conform;* 99.4 *nature;* 126.2 *original;* 717.11 *paint;* 356.10 *produce;* 160.2 *prototype;* 19.21 *sculpt;* 403.15 *shape;* 419.13 *soften;* 221.1 *state;* 760.9 *transform;* 137.4 *type;* 499.2 *unpalatability;* 349.1 *use;* 550.8 *wall covering*
mouldable 419.2 *pliant*
mould-breaking 295.11 *unfamiliar*
mould clay 24.11 *make ceramics*
moulded 111.15 *duplicate;* 160.9 *formed;* 50.10 *sailing;* 19.28 *sculpted;* 19.25 *sculptural;* 20.17 *structured*
moulded hull 50.3 *parts of a sailing boat*
moulder 83.11; 258.10 *be dirty;* 245.2 *decay;* 375.3 *disintegrate;* 296.17 *grow old;* 19.17 *sculptor;* 499.8 *sour*
mouldering 245.13 *dilapidated;* 375.5 *disintegrated;* 375.1 *disintegration;* 296.12 *olden*
mouldiness 245.9 *dilapidation;* 258.1 *dirtiness;* 236.10 *poverty*
moulding 267.9 *adhesive;* 111.4 *duplicate;* 160.4 *forming;* 542.3 *pattern;* 356.1 *production;* 19.12 *sculpture;* 403.5 *structuring*
mould the figure 267.6 *adhere*
mouldy 44.17 *botanical;* 258.7 *dirty;* 83.9 *fungal;* 296.12 *olden;* 236.4 *poor;* 499.6 *unpalatable*
moult 560.23 *cast;* 552.16 *peel;* 552.6 *peeling*
moulted 552.12 *peeling*
moulting 560.32 *cast-off;* 560.12 *dead tissue;* 552.6, 552.12 *peeling*
mound 376.37 *assemble;* 182.3 *dome;* 583.6 *grave;* 376.26 *mass;* 384.8 *military defences;* 744.11 *monument;* 154.3 *mountain*
mount 304.15; 304.13 *ascend;* 792.9 *be dear;* 300.13 *be in motion;* 304.14 *climb;* 89.10 *climb a mountain;* 314.9 *enter;* 59.1 *horse;* 213.4 *increase;* 368.5 *inset;* 89.1, 154.3 *mountain;* 304.6 *mounting;* 366.1 *raise;* 59.16 *ride;* 154.16 *rise;* 59.4 *saddle horse;* 313.5 *set out*
mountain 89.1; **154.3**; 765.3 *acquisition;* 203.2 *certain amount;* 30.7 *landform;* 158.7, 376.26 *mass;* 185.2 *projection;* 420.8 *rough ground;* 228.4 *stable thing*
mountain artillery 587.11 *guns*
mountain belt 30.20 *earth movement*
mountain bike 320.12 *bicycle*
mountain building 30.21
mountain circuit 61.6 *motor-racing terms*
mountain climate 31.38 *climate*
mountain-climb 62.9 *mountaineer*
mountain climber 304.11 *ascender;* 89.3 *mountaineer*
mountain climbing 89.1 *mountain;* 62.1 *mountaineering*
Mountain Daylight Time 275.9 *time zone*
mountain dew 558.7 *alcoholic drink*
mountain-dweller 89.3 *mountaineer*
mountain-dwelling 89.7, 154.13 *mountainous*
mountained 89.7 *mountainous*
mountaineer 62.7; **62.9**; **89.3**; 304.11 *ascender;* 89.10 *climb a mountain*
mountaineering 62.1; **62.8**; 89.1 *mountain;* 304.6 *mounting*
Mountaineering and Climbing 62
mountaineering association 62.6
mountain hypothermia 62.2 *climbing dangers*
mountain infantry 586.16 *army unit*
mountain lake 88.1 *lake*
mountain lion 60.5 *game*
mountain man 89.3 *mountaineer*
mountain mist 31.34 *mist*
mountain of money 780.3 *fortune;* 781.6 *money*
mountainous 89.7; **154.13**; 765.18 *acquisitional;* 158.15 *big;* 203.6 *quantitative*

mountain range 154.4; 299.3 *irregular thing;* 89.1 *mountain*
Mountains 89
mountain skiing 68.1 *skiing*
mountain ski touring 68.2 *cross-country skiing*
Mountain Standard Time 275.9 *time zone*
mountain stream 90.1 *river*
mountaintop 154.2 *heights;* 89.1 *mountain;* 736.6 *privacy;* 62.5 *rock face;* 174.1 *summit*
mountain torrent 90.6 *river flow*
mountain warfare 585.8 *warfare*
mountain wind 31.12 *wind*
Mount Cook 89.6 *other major mountains and ranges*
mountebank 699.19 *cheat;* 700.15 *deceiver;* 21.29 *entertainer;* 125.7 *imitator;* 702.6 *sophist;* 486.10 *unskilled person*
mountebankery 702.5 *hypocrisy;* 699.4 *spuriousness*
mounted 59.17 *equine;* 366.11 *raised*
mounted band 18.26 *musical group*
mounted infantry 586.19 *cavalry*
mounted infantryman 586.20 *cavalryman*
mounted police 586.19 *cavalry;* 59.15 *horse person;* 16.14 *police*
mounted rifles 586.19 *cavalry;* 59.15 *horse person*
mounted soldier 586.20 *cavalryman*
mounted troops 586.19 *cavalry;* 59.15 *horse person*
mount guard 252.10 *protect*
Mountie 59.15 *horse person;* 16.17 *police officer*
Mounties 16.14 *police*
mounting 29.25; **304.6**; 300.7 *ascending motion;* 792.7 *dear;* 300.17 *directional;* 154.9 *high;* 89.7 *mountainous;* 21.14 *production;* 304.23 *rising;* 413.2 *supporting part*
mounting costs 792.3 *inflationary price*
Mount Logan 89.6 *other major mountains and ranges*
Mount McKinley 89.4 *US mountains*
mount money 59.12 *rodeo*
Mount Olympus 89.6 *other major mountains and ranges*
Mount Omei 10.13 *shrine*
Mount Palomar 89.4 *US mountains*
Mount Tai 10.13 *shrine*
mount the barricades 662.16 *be subversive*
mount the throne 12.12, 396.20 *take authority*
Mount Whitney 89.4 *US mountains*
Mount Wilson 89.4 *US mountains*
mourn 582.17, 583.8 *bury;* 602.8 *grieve;* 603.6 *lament*
mourner 583.3 *funeral director;* 603.3 *lamenter;* 627.4 *pitying person*
mourn for 603.6 *lament*
mournful 523.11 *benighted;* 583.11 *funeral;* 603.4 *lamenting;* 532.6, 602.5 *sad*
mournfully 603.8; 523.15 *darkly;* 602.11 *sadly*
mournfulness 603.1 *lamentation*
mourning 582.8 *after death;* 627.2 *condolence;* 583.2, 583.11 *funeral;* 603.1 *lamentation;* 603.4 *lamenting;* 532.6 *sad;* 602.1 *sorrow*
mourning black 656.4 *formal dress*
mourning clothes 532.9 *black thing;* 523.4 *dark thing;* 551.3 *formal dress;* 743.5 *uniform*
mourning colour 540.1 *purpleness*
mourn one's husband 571.10 *be widowed*
mouse 388.2 *appeaser;* 614.2 *coward;* 612.6 *frightened person;* 623.16 *humble person;* 633.11 *hunt;* 159.4 *little person;* 674.7, 728.11 *modest person;* 591.9 *oversensitive person;* 40.7 *peripheral;* 732.5 *shy person*
mouse-coloured 533.1 *grey*
mousehole 308.7 *passageway*
mouselike 623.1 *humble;* 71.30 *rodent-like;* 674.11 *shy*
mouser 71.10 *cat;* 633.6 *hunter*
mousetrap 43.14 *pest control;* 700.13 *snare*
moussaka 25.52 *Greek dish*
mousse 434.10 *air bubble;* 25.35 *dessert;* 415.7 *light thing;* 419.11 *soft thing*
moustache 420.7 *rough thing;* 425.8 *sharp-pointed thing*
moustached 420.3 *barbed*
mousy 530.7 *colourless;* 530.8 *drained of colour;* 533.1 *grey;* 71.30 *rodent-like;* 732.1 *shy;* 544.10 *ugly*
mouth 699.22 *be hypocritical;* 308.4 *body orifice;* 660.2 *cheek;* 557.21 *eat;* 557.16 *eating utensil;* 314.5 *entrance;* 525.3 *external appearance;* 92.9 *inlet;* 729.5 *organ of speech*
mouthbrooder 74.2 *fish*
mouthful 557.14; 733.1 *address;* 495.3 *appetizer;* 203.3 *container;* 729.8 *speech*
mouthguard 46.3 *uniform*
mouthing 699.3 *hypocrisy*
mouth off 706.18 *answer back*
mouthpiece 52.2 *boxing;* 693.9 *informant;* 719.7 *news interpreter;* 748.4 *representative;* 692.9 *telephone*
mouth-to-mouth 67.11 *swimming*
mouth-to-mouth resuscitation 67.3 *survival swimming*
mouthwash 256.9 *cleaning agent;* 501.2 *deodorant;* 37.11 *linctus;* 394.3 *prophylactic;* 255.3 *purifier*
mouthwatering 617.8 *desirable;* 557.27 *edible;* 490.6 *pleasant;* 241.4, 495.7 *tasty*
mouthwateringly 495.11 *tastily*
mouthy 676.3 *affected;* 660.14 *cheeky;* 731.6 *effusive*
movability 300.1 *motion*
movable 300.16 *moving;* 440.8 *propertied;* 316.17 *transferable;* 319.5 *transportable*
movable bridge 38.21 *bridge*
movableness 300.1 *motion*
movables 440.2 *legal terms*
movably 300.18 *in motion*
move 340.4 *act;* 340.1 *action;* 713.5 *advise;* 327.22 *agitate;* 353.5 *attempt;* 363.11 *attract;* 342.12 *be active;* 300.13 *be in motion;* 224.8 *cause change;* 453.21 *change;* 760.7 *convert into;* 340.2 *deed;* 560.16 *defecate;* 144.14 *displace;* 144.1 *displacement;* 627.11 *excite pity;* 302.1 *go forward;* 331.1 *impel;* 483.9 *motivate;* 480.15 *persuade;* 69.10 *play;* 330.20 *propel;* 476.6 *propound;* 710.6 *request;* 300.14 *set in motion;* 142.10 *settle;* 645.2 *stratagem;* 631.9 *tactics;* 346.9 *take action;* 316.15 *take away;* 319.4 *transport*
move across 318.11 *cross*
move along 318.9 *proceed*
move apart 311.11; 377.9 *be dispersed*
move back 303.2 *retreat*
move close 147.16 *near*
moved 144.8 *displaced;* 483.12 *motivated*
move fast 342.12 *be active;* 332.4 *be swift;* 313.4 *hurry off;* 302.9 *maintain progress;* 262.2 *make haste*
move forward 330.21
move freely 250.14 *be free*
move heaven and earth 576.8 *exert oneself;* 640.6 *persevere*
move house 313.3 *quit;* 142.10 *settle;* 300.15 *walk*
move in 142.10, 564.15 *settle;* 565.18 *take up residence*
move into 763.7 *possess*
move it 300.19 *go!;* 262.8 *hurry up!*
movement 747.6; 340.1 *action;* 342.1 *activity;* 760.1 *conversion;* 560.2 *defecation;* 144.1 *displacement;* 21.9 *dramaturgy;* 57.8 *floor exercises;* 300.1 *motion;* 346.1 *operation;* 376.16 *party;* 318.1 *passage;* 7.1 *religion;* 316.1 *transfer*
move off 313.5 *set out*
move on 277.7 *go on;* 330.21 *move forward*
move one's bowels 560.16 *defecate*
move out 355.2 *withdraw*
move over 300.13 *be in motion;* 300.15 *walk*
mover 713.4 *adviser;* 340.3 *doer;* 480.14 *motivator*
mover and shaker 340:3 *doer*
move round 181.12
movers and shakers 480.14 *motivator*
move sideways 169.8
move slowly 333.1; 620.6 *be boring;* 580.4 *have leisure*
move the goalposts 227.12 *be irresolute;* 479.2 *equivocate*
move through 318.8 *pass*
move to and fro 326.8 *oscillate*
move to compassion 627.11 *excite pity*
move together 62.9 *mountaineer*
move to tears 627.11 *excite pity*
move up 147.16 *near*
move with the times 224.7 *be changed;* 295.18 *be trendy;* 302.5 *develop;* 293.11 *get ahead*
movie 356.5 *work of art*
movies 21.3 *films*
movie theatre 21.16 *theatre*
moving 300.16; 342.18 *active;* 395.12 *appealing;* 721.11 *descriptive;* 144.8 *displaced;* 590.14 *emotive;* 334.15 *full of energy;* 331.17 *impelling;* 300.1 *motion;* 302.18 *ongoing;* 318.12 *passing;* 627.7 *pitiful;* 316.1 *transfer*
moving apart 311.2 *parting;* 372.1 *separation*
moving pavement 316.5 *means of transport;* 320.4 *personal transport*
moving spirit 483.7 *motivator*
moving staircase 366.10 *elevator*
moving target 482.6 *objective*
moving together 62.3 *climbing technique*
moving with the times 293.6 *getting ahead*
mow 44.15 *cultivate;* 43.17 *farm;* 81.12 *manage grassland;* 149.10 *shorten;* 626.4 *sign of irritableness;* 421.11 *smooth;* 439.1, 439.6 *store;* 438.10 *use tools*
mow down 585.13 *be at war;* 357.9 *demolish;* 367.2 *flatten;* 382.18 *slaughter*
mowed 149.8 *shortened*
mower 43.10 *farm tool;* 81.5 *grass cutter*
mowing 149.2 *shortening*
mowing grass 81.1 *grass*
mowing machine 43.10 *farm tool;* 81.5 *grass cutter*
mown 149.8 *shortened*
moxie 342.4 *energy;* 638.16 *fortitude;* 640.4 *stamina*
mozzy 76.1 *insect*
MP 400.3 *leader;* 396.10 *person of authority*
Mr 567.3 *male title of address*
Mr and Mrs 570.9 *married couple*
Mr Average 216.7 *average person;* 138.9 *everyman*
Mr Big 123.4 *bigwig;* 121.5 *superior*
Mr Clever 673.7 *vain person*
MRI 35.7 *diagnosis*
mRNA 33.10 *nucleoside*
Mr Nobody 574.1 *plebeian;* 456.4 *unknown person*
Mr Normal 460.3 *sane person*
Mrs 568.3 *female title of address*
MR scanner 394.14 *hospital*
Mrs Grundy 620.3 *boring person;* 117.6 *conformist;* 795.6 *moralist;* 255.6 *prude*
Mrs Mary Whitehouse 795.6 *moralist*
Mrs Mop 256.12 *cleaner;* 401.6 *domestic servant;* 392.16 *home help*
Mrs Spend Spend Spend 681.6 *spendthrift*
Mrs Warren's profession 796.5 *prostitution*
Mr Universe 336.6 *muscleman*
Mr X 456.4 *unknown person*
Ms 568.3 *female title of address*
MSDOS™ 40.8 *software*
M star 29.13 *luminosity*
MTI switch 692.28 *radar*
MTU 40.7 *peripheral*
much ado 342.1 *activity*
much ado about nothing 486.9 *bungling;* 467.2 *overestimate*
much greater than 27.88 *equal to*
much later on 294.17 *later*
much less than 27.88 *equal to*
much-married man 570.10 *married man*
much obliged 671.4 *grateful;* 671.9 *thank you!*
much of a muchness 231.4 *ordinary;* 115.7 *similar*
much the same 119.6 *equal;* 115.7 *similar*
much up 258.11 *dirty*
mucilage 268.5 *lubricant*
mucilaginous 430.8 *viscous*
mucilaginousness 430.1 *viscosity*
mucin 33.9 *protein*
muck 44.15 *cultivate;* 258.4 *dirt;* 560.5 *faeces;* 43.17 *farm;* 43.13 *fertilizer;* 238.6 *refuse*
mucked-up 408.19 *mixed-up*
muckfork 43.10 *farm tool*
muckheap 43.10 *farm tool*
muckiness 258.1 *dirtiness*
mucking about 697.3 *tomfoolery*
mucking out 59.14 *horse-riding terms*
muck out 256.13 *clean;* 43.18 *practise livestock farming;* 59.16 *ride*
muckrake 678.12 *defame*
muckraker 678.8 *defamer;* 741.4 *journalist*
muckraking 43.5 *cultivation;* 678.3 *defamation;* 741.3 *reporting*
muckspreader 43.10 *farm tool*
muckspreading 43.5 *cultivation*
muck up 245.4 *impair*
mucky 258.7 *dirty*
mucoid 559.5 *of a secretion;* 268.13 *slippery*
mucopolysaccharide 33.4 *polysaccharide*
mucoprotein 33.9 *protein*
mucopus 560.7 *pus*
mucor 431.3 *body fluid*
mucous 559.5 *of a secretion;* 560.29 *salivating*
mucronate 425.1 *sharp*
mucronation 425.6 *sharpness*
mucus 430.5; 431.3 *body fluid;* 258.4 *dirt;* 268.5 *lubricant;* 560.9 *saliva;* 559.2 *secreted substance*
mud 258.4 *dirt;* 92.3, 429.8 *marsh;* 30.27 *sediment;* 419.11 *soft thing*
muda 10.3 *rite of worship;* 9.1 *worship*
mudbank 157.4 *shallow thing*
mud brick 24.9 *industrial ceramics*
mudder 59.7 *horseracing*
muddied 528.2 *shady*
muddily 92.13 *continentally;* 88.10 *limnologically*
muddiness 429.7 *bogginess;* 258.1 *dirtiness;* 266.1 *obscurity;* 528.6 *opaqueness*
muddle 457.10 *bemuse;* 408.23 *confuse;* 408.5 *confusion;* 328.8 *disarrange;* 328.2 *disarrangement;* 736.9 *disguise;* 161.4, 408.21 *disorder;* 408.4 *litter;* 266.3 *make obscure;* 412.3 *miscellany;* 412.1 *mixture;* 412.9 *mix up;* 266.1 *obscurity;* 264.5 *predicament*
muddled 408.18; 328.13 *disarranged;* 408.12 *disordered;* 465.7 *misjudging;* 412.13 *mixed-up;* 266.2 *obscure;* 690.2 *slightly drunk*
muddleheaded 408.16 *confused*
muddle through 302.7 *make one's way;* 246.7 *overcome obstacles*
muddling 328.17 *disturbing*
mud-dried 258.7 *dirty*
muddy 419.4 *compressible;* 92.11 *continental;* 696.4 *difficult;* 258.7, 258.11 *dirty;* 88.9 *lakelike;* 266.3 *make obscure;* 528.11 *make opaque;* 429.11 *marshy;* 266.2 *obscure;* 528.2 *shady;* 524.11 *tarnish*
muddy pool 88.2 *small lake*
muddy the waters 327.22 *agitate;* 645.5 *be cunning;* 736.9 *disguise*
muddy water 528.7 *opaque thing*
muddy waters 521.6 *that which makes invisible*
mud flap 320.11 *bicycle part*
mud flat 92.3 *marsh;* 157.4 *shallow thing*
mudflow 30.26 *mass movement*
mudguard 320.11 *bicycle part*
mud hen 72.3 *water bird*
mudhole 92.3 *marsh*
mudlark 258.6 *dirty person*
mud shoe 50.8 *punting*
mudslinger 678.8 *defamer*
mudslinging 678.3 *defamation;* 678.16 *defamatory*
mud-wrestler 258.6 *dirty person*
muesli 25.40 *breakfast cereal*
muezzin 7.8 *priest;* 742.8 *signer*
muezzin's call 742.6 *word*
muezzin's cry 10.4 *public worship*
muff 551.25 *accessories;* 486.7 *be clumsy;* 274.10 *blunder;* 486.9 *bungling;* 274.19 *make a mistake;* 486.10 *unskilled person*
muffer 486.10 *unskilled person*
muffin 25.39 *loaf*
muffle 505.10; 736.8 *conceal;* 357.8 *destroy;* 511.7 *mute;* 506.2 *silence;* 730.15 *strike dumb;* 337.7 *weaken*
muffled 511.1 *faint-sounding;* 337.13 *insufficient;* 730.10 *low-voiced;* 511.2 *nonresonant*
muffled drum 583.2 *funeral;* 742.4 *signal*
muffled voice 730.4 *whispering*
muffle kiln 24.6 *ceramic workshop*
muffler 551.14 *neckwear*
muffuletta 25.11 *sandwich*
mufti 551.4, 657.6 *informal dress*
mug 668.9 *butt;* 24.8 *ceramic object;*

558.10 *drink container*; 410.13 *drinking vessel*; 700.22 *dupe*; 167.2 *face*; 774.12 *steal*; 381.5 *strike*; 608.14 *take away*; 380.8 *use violence*
MUGA scan 35.7 *diagnosis*
mugger 381.19 *attacker*; 386.4 *coercive person*; 662.9 *criminal*; 16.40 *lawbreaker*; 651.8 *malefactor*; 773.6 *taker*; 774.8 *thief*; 380.4 *violent creature*
mugginess 429.3 *humidity*
mugging 381.16 *personal attack*; 774.1 *stealing*
muggles 691.6 *drug*
muggy 31.52 *humid*; 429.9 *moist*; 493.11 *warm*
muggy spell 31.23 *heat*
muggy weather 31.23 *heat*
mughlai 25.49 *Indian dish*
mug shot 167.2 *face*; 41.4 *portrait*
mug up 21.37 *rehearse*
mugwump 250.7 *free person*
mugwumpish 685.7 *politically moderate*
Muharram 10.16 *religious festival*
mujtahid 7.8 *priest*
mukdam 7.8 *priest*
mulatto 412.5 *hybrid*; 1.6 *race*; 1.13 *racial*
mulberry 540.6 *purple*; 535.7 *red thing*
mulch 550.2 *cover*; 44.15 *cultivate*; 43.17 *farm*; 44.7, 562.3 *fertilizer*; 562.7 *make fertile*
mulct 814.1 *punish*; 814.7 *punishment*
mulctable 814.22 *punishable*
mule 342.10 *busy person*; 412.5 *hybrid*; 641.8 *obstinate person*
mules 551.19 *footwear*
mule train 320.9 *animal transport*
muliebrity 568.1 *female sex*
mulish 641.1 *obstinate*; 71.33 *ungulate*; 635.8 *wilful*
mulishly 641.9 *obstinately*
mulishness 641.5 *obstinacy*; 635.3 *wilfulness*
mull 92.5 *peninsula*; 498.8 *sweeten*
mullah 6.4 *educator*; 7.8 *priest*
mulled wine 558.7 *alcoholic drink*; 498.5 *sweet drink*
muller 427.11 *pulverizer*
mullet 547.8 *haircut*; 743.8 *heraldic device*; 25.18 *sea fish*
mulligatawny 25.13 *soup*
mullock 258.4 *dirt*; 238.6 *refuse*
mull over 443.13 *concentrate*
multiangular 27.82 *polygonal*
multicellular 34.23 *cellular*
multicentre bond 32.11 *chemical bond*
multicolour 529.2 *colourfulness*
multicoloured 114.6 *assorted*; 529.10 *coloured*; 541.6 *variegated*
multicolour yawn 371.23 *vomiting*
multicultural 412.12 *mixed*
multiemployer agreement 15.1 *industrial relations*
multifaceted 114.6 *assorted*; 169.6 *side*; 207.7 *various*
multifacial 27.84 *cubic*
multifarious 114.6 *assorted*; 208.5 *multitudinous*; 207.7 *various*
multifariously 208.13 *numerously*; 207.10 *plurally*
multifariousness 207.2 *multiplicity*
multiflagellate 84.7 *algal*
multiflorous 44.16 *horticultural*
multifold 207.8 *multiplicative*; 208.5 *multitudinous*
multifoldness 208.1 *multiplicity*
multiform 114.6 *assorted*; 116.4 *dissimilar*; 207.7 *various*
multiformity 114.2 *assortment*; 116.1 *dissimilarity*; 207.2 *multiplicity*
multigravida 561.7 *obstetrics*
multihull 50.10 *sailing*
multihull racing 50.1 *sailing*
multilateral 755.7 *contractual*; 207.7 *various*
multilateralism 207.2 *multiplicity*
multilateralist 207.5 *pluralist*
multilaterally 755.8 *contractually*; 207.10 *plurally*
multilingual 5.2 *linguist*; 5.38 *linguistic*; 729.19 *speaking*; 719.17 *translational*; 207.7 *various*
multilingual dictionary 5.28 *dictionary*
multilingualism 5.1 *linguistics*
multilingually 5.48 *linguistically*
multiloquence 731.1 *talkativeness*
multiloquent 731.5 *talkative*
multiloquy 731.1 *talkativeness*
multimillion 201.11 *million*
multimillionaire 201.11 *million*; 248.4 *prosperous person*; 781.10 *wealthy person*
multinational 395.13 *dominant*; 207.7 *various*
multinational company 395.6 *group influence*
multinomial 27.76 *functional*
multinucleate 34.24 *nuclear*
multiparous 562.5 *fertile*
multipartite 372.15 *separate*
multiple 27.17, 207.4 *multiplication*; 207.8 *multiplicative*; 208.5 *multitudinous*; 207.6 *plural*
multiple collision 331.12 *collision*
multiple fruit 80.2 *botanical fruit*
multiple image 41.4 *portrait*
multiple personality 36.8 *disordered personality*; 36.16 *dissociation*; 207.2 *multiplicity*
multiple sclerosis 260.17 *nervous disorder*; 418.6 *solidification*
multiple span 38.21 *bridge*
multiple star 29.9 *constellation*
multiple store 779.8 *store*
multiplexing 40.19 *computing terms*; 40.14 *data transfer*
multiplex transmission 692.14 *radio transmission*
multipliable 190.9 *enlargeable*
multiplicand 27.17, 207.4 *multiplication*
multiplication 27.17; **207.4**; 210.1 *calculation*; 190.1 *growth*; 213.1 *increase*; 561.1 *reproduction*
multiplication sign 27.13 *mathematical symbol*; 742.1 *sign*
multiplication table 210.5 *computer*; 207.4 *multiplication*
multiplication tables 27.17 *multiplication*
multiplicative 207.8
multiplicity 207.2; **208.1**; 114.2 *assortment*; 114.1 *diversity*
multiplied 207.8 *multiplicative*
multiplied by 27.88 *equal to*
multiplier 27.17, 207.4 *multiplication*
multiplier reel 55.3 *fishing tackle*
multiply 561.12; 27.91, 210.9 *add*; 190.6 *become bigger*; 562.6 *be fertile*; 213.4 *increase*; 213.5 *make bigger*; 83.12 *mushroom*; 208.13 *numerously*; 207.9 *pluralize*; 207.10 *plurally*; 356.10 *produce*
multiply by four 200.11 *quadruple*
multiply by three 199.10 *triple*
multiply by two 198.15 *double*
multiplying 190.8 *growing*
multiplying by three 199.4 *triplication*
multiply out 27.91 *add*
multipoint tool 38.9 *machine tool*
multipurpose 114.6 *assorted*; 237.1 *useful*; 207.7 *various*
multiracial 412.12 *mixed*; 207.7 *various*
multiracial state 566.11 *nation*
multirole 207.7 *various*
multisonous 507.6 *loud*
multistage 411.7 *layered*
multistage rocket 29.35 *rocketry*
multistorey 154.9 *high*; 565.16 *manorial*; 20.12 *structural*
multistorey building 20.3, 38.20 *building*
multistorey car park 154.6 *tall thing*
multistranded wire 39.27 *wire*
multitasking 40.15 *network*
Multitude 208
multitude 208.2; 586.18 *army of people*; 376.20 *crowd*; 138.11 *general public*; 207.2 *multiplicity*; 203.1 *quantity*; 208.4 *throng*
multitudinal 208.5 *multitudinous*
multitudinous 208.5; 217.3 *filled*; 297.3 *frequent*; 207.6 *plural*
multitudinously 297.1 *frequently*; 208.13 *numerously*; 207.10 *plurally*
multitudinousness 297.4 *frequency*; 207.2, 208.1 *multiplicity*
multivariate analysis 27.55 *statistical methods*
multivocal 694.3 *comprehension*; 694.6 *meaningful*
multiwire cable 692.6 *telecommunication*
multure 427.4 *pulverization*
mum 732.1 *shy*; 506.3 *silent*; 730.11 *speechless*; 568.12 *woman in the family*
mumble 511.4 *faint sound*; 511.8 *sound faint*; 730.16 *speak in a low voice*; 729.13 *speak in a particular way*; 730.4 *whispering*
mumbled 511.1 *faint-sounding*
mumbling 511.4 *faint sound*; 730.10 *low-voiced*; 696.11 *unintelligibility*
mumbo jumbo 266.1 *obscurity*; 700.9 *sleight of hand*; 11.5 *spell*
mumbo-jumbo 700.40 *illusory*; 266.2 *obscure*
Mu metal™ 28.59 *ferromagnetism*
mummer 21.24 *actor*; 700.15 *deceiver*
mummers' play 21.2 *play*
mummery 21.22 *acting*; 601.3 *ceremony*; 700.12 *disguise*; 699.3 *hypocrisy*
mummification 583.1 *burial*; 428.13 *drying*; 359.1 *preservation*
mummified 583.10 *buried*; 428.3 *dried-up*; 582.22 *postmortem*; 359.7 *preserved*
mummifier 359.4 *preservationist*
mummify 583.8 *bury*; 428.21 *dry up*; 359.5 *preserve*
mummy 582.11 *dead person*; 359.3 *preserved thing*; 568.12 *woman in the family*
mummy-case 583.1 *burial*
mummy chamber 583.6 *grave*
mummy's boy 567.9 *offensive terms for homosexual*; 337.4 *weakling*
mummy wrapping 583.4 *funeral objects*
mumpish 626.7 *irritable*
mumpishness 626.1 *sullenness*
mumps 260.6 *infection*
mum's the word 506.6 *hush!*
munch 557.21 *eat*
muncheel 320.6 *litter*
munching 557.1 *eating*
mundane 750.15 *conventional*; 112.13 *monotonous*; 111.17 *regular*; 271.1 *simple*
mundaneness 683.1 *selfishness*; 271.4 *simplicity*
mundunugu 11.4 *witch*
municipal 16.48 *jurisdictional*; 86.17 *national*; 87.14 *urban*
municipal building 87.13
municipal council 579.8 *British administrative council*
municipal court 16.21 *US court*
municipal court judge 16.24 *US judge*
municipal garden 44.2 *garden*
municipal hospital 35.10 *hospital*
municipality 87.1 *city*; 16.2 *jurisdiction*; 86.11 *settlement*
municipally 87.16; 16.86 *jurisdictionally*; 86.20 *nationally*
municipal tax 790.7 *tax*
munificence 679.5 *generosity*; 652.1 *philanthropy*; 473.2 *unselfishness*
munificent 679.1 *generous*; 652.6 *philanthropic*; 473.5 *unselfish*
munificently 652.8 *philanthropically*; 473.9 *unselfishly*
munificentness 652.1 *philanthropy*
muniments 744.2 *certificate*
munitions 587.2 *arms*; 352.2 *supplies*
muon 28.77 *elementary particle*; 159.2 *little thing*
mural 19.8 *painting*
mural painter 19.16 *artist*
murder 382.2; **382.17**; 651.7 *act of malevolence*; 72.13 *assemblage of birds*; 662.15 *be disobedient*; 94.13 *cause not to exist*; 226.8 *cause to cease*; 16.39 *crime*; 804.7 *criminality*; 357.8 *destroy*; 357.2 *destroying*; 798.5 *evil thing*; 814.5 *execute*; 380.3 *instance of violence*; 382.16, 651.17 *kill*; 382.1, 582.6 *killing*; 441.2 *lay waste*; 380.2 *physical violence*; 806.10 *sin*; 662.2 *violation of the law*
murdered 582.19 *dead*
murderer 382.11; 381.19 *attacker*; 662.9 *criminal*; 357.6, 441.7 *destroyer*; 798.6 *evil person*; 594.8 *hated person*; 382.10 *killer*; 16.40 *lawbreaker*; 651.8 *malefactor*; 814.17 *punisher*; 380.4 *violent creature*; 804.9 *wicked person*
murderers' row 48.5 *batting terms*
murderess 382.11 *murderer*
murdering the Queen's English 274.11 *grammatical error*
murder most foul 382.2 *murder*
murderous 382.24; 651.11 *cruel*; 582.20 *deadly*; 806.7 *sinful*; 380.6 *violent*
murderously 382.25 *lethally*
murderousness 380.1 *violence*
murder weapon 382.2 *murder*
murex 535.6 *red pigment*
muricate 420.1 *rough*; 425.4 *toothed*
murine 71.30 *rodent-like*
murk 524.2; 523.1 *darkness*; 533.7 *dullness*; 523.7 *spiritual darkness*
murkily 533.9 *greyly*; 266.4 *obscurely*
murkiness 523.1 *darkness*; 524.2 *murk*; 266.1 *obscurity*; 528.6 *opaqueness*
murky 524.6; 523.11 *benighted*; 416.7 *condensed*; 523.8, 532.2 *dark*; 696.4 *difficult*; 258.7 *dirty*; 533.3 *dull*; 266.2 *obscure*; 528.2 *shady*
murmur 31.58 *blow*; 90.7 *flow*; 509.9 *hum*; 509.2 *humming*; 511.8 *sound faint*; 730.16 *speak in a low voice*; 729.13 *speak in a particular way*; 729.7 *utterance*; 730.4 *whispering*
murmuration 511.4 *faint sound*
murmured 511.1 *faint-sounding*
murmuring 511.4 *faint sound*; 730.10 *low-voiced*
murmur of discontent 711.1 *warning*
Murphy's law 140.3 *rule of nature*
murrain 260.18 *veterinary disease*
murrey 743.13 *heraldic*; 743.8 *heraldic device*; 540.6 *purple*; 535.1 *red*
musaph 10.4 *public worship*
Muscadet 558.9 *wine*
muscatel 498.5 *sweet drink*
Musci 82.3 *moss*
muscle 223.7 *attendant*; 182.2 *bulge*; 576.4 *exertion*; 373.6 *line*; 334.1 *power*; 336.1 *strength*
muscle-bound 418.2 *tough*
muscle cell 34.7 *cell*
muscle in 334.10 *be powerful*; 314.10 *invade*
muscleman 336.6; 567.6 *macho man*
muscle power 334.4 *energy*; 576.4 *exertion*
muscle relaxant 394.4 *antidote*; 37.4 *drug type*
muscles 423.8 *physical strength*
muscovado 534.5 *brown thing*
muscular 567.17 *male*; 336.9 *physically strong*; 423.4 *powerful*; 418.2 *tough*
muscular dystrophy 260.17 *nervous disorder*
muscularity 423.8 *physical strength*; 336.1 *strength*
muscularly 423.13 *powerfully*
muscular rheumatism 260.16 *rheumatism*
musculature 336.1 *strength*
musculoskeletal disease 260.4 *disease*
Muse 17.13 *poetic genius*
muse 8.5 *deity*; 477.15 *fantasize*; 477.2 *inspiration*; 4.20 *philosophize*; 619.12 *wonder whether*
muse of dancing 22.1 *dancing*
museum 439.5 *collection*; 376.31 *exhibition*; 738.8 *showplace*
museum piece 235.8 *exceller*; 296.5 *old thing*; 3.11 *relic*; 738.7 *showpiece*; 284.7 *thing of the past*; 19.6 *work of art*
mush 25.40 *breakfast cereal*; 593.2 *romantic love*
mushroom 83.2; **83.12**; 765.10 *augment*; 190.6 *become bigger*; 562.6 *be fertile*; 534.1 *brown*; 83.4 *fungal body*; 213.4 *increase*; 25.33, 44.11 *vegetable*; 531.1 *white*
mushroom bulb 522.6 *electric light*
mushroom cloud 587.16 *bomb*; 83.2 *mushroom*; 587.1 *weapon*
mushroom eating 83.8 *study of fungi*
mushroom farm 43.6 *farm*; 83.8 *study of fungi*
mushroom farmer 83.8 *study of fungi*
mushroom grower 44.13 *horticulturist*; 83.8 *study of fungi*
mushroom growing 44.1 *horticulture*
mushrooming 190.8 *growing*; 304.4 *taking off*
mushroom soup 25.13 *soup*
Music 18
music 18.1; 374.2 *cooperation*; 59.8 *hunting*; 28.17 *sound*
musica ficta 516.4 *harmonics*
musical 18.29; 504.11 *aural*; 21.39 *dramatic*; 516.6 *melodious*; 21.4 *musical drama*; 738.9 *production*
musical arrangement 409.9
musical comedy 599.4 *entertainment*; 21.4 *musical drama*
musical composition 356.1 *production*; 356.5 *work of art*
musical cry 514.8
musical director 18.24 *musician*
musical dissonance 517.3
musical drama 21.4
musical ear 504.1 *hearing*

musical genius 396.11, 400.10 *expert*
musical group 18.26
musical instrument 18.25; 28.18 *source of sound*
musical interval 28.20 *musical note*
musicality 504.1 *hearing*; 516.3 *melodiousness*; 18.1 *music*
musically 18.42
musicalness 516.3 *melodiousness*; 18.1 *music*
musical notation 717.1 *representation*; 742.1 *sign*
musical note 18.16; **28.20**; 18.17 *notation*
musical quality 516.3 *melodiousness*
musical repetition 509.6
musical scale 28.20 *musical note*
musical structure 403.9 *artistic structure*
musical texture 516.3 *melodiousness*
musical time 275.12
music drama 18.4 *opera*
music hall 21.7 *show*; 21.5 *show business*; 21.16 *theatre*
musician 18.24; 356.9 *producer*; 485.4 *skilled person*; 578.1 *worker*
musicianly 18.29 *musical*
musicianship 18.1 *music*; 356.1 *production*
music loving 18.29 *musical*
music making 18.2
music master 18.24 *musician*
musicography 18.14 *harmonics*
musicology 18.14 *harmonics*
musicophile 18.29 *musical*
music review 719.3 *criticism*
music room 504.3 *auditorium*; 6.15 *schoolroom*
music school 6.12 *educational institution*
music stand 413.2 *supporting part*
music teacher 18.24 *musician*
music theory 18.14 *harmonics*
musing 4.4 *philosophical investigation*; 443.10 *speculative*; 4.17 *thoughtful*; 443.3 *thoughtfulness*
musique concrète 18.3 *classical music*
musi-yaki 25.54 *other dishes*
musk 502.1 *fragrance*; 502.3 *incense*; 559.2 *secreted substance*
muskellunge 55.4 *American game fish*
musket 330.9 *firearm*; 587.10 *historical gun*
musketeer 586.13 *historical soldiery*; 330.15 *shooter*
musketry 587.2 *arms*; 381.15 *firing*; 330.6 *shooting*
musketry practice 585.6 *art of war*
musk gland 71.2 *mammalian characteristic*
muskily 502.7 *fragrantly*
muskiness 502.1 *fragrance*
musky 502.4 *fragrant*
Muslim 7.16 *denominational*; 7.6 *non-Christian*
muslin 153.11 *fineness*; 524.2 *murk*; 193.4 *textile*; 527.8 *transparent thing*
mussel 25.19 *shellfish*
mussel shrimp 75.4 *arthropod*
Mussulman 7.6 *non-Christian*
must 386.8 *be compelled*; 810.14 *be the duty of*; 83.1 *fungus*
mustang 59.1 *horse*; 59.4 *saddle horse*
mustard 43.12 *crop*; 496.5 *herbs*; 537.1 *yellow*; 537.8 *yellow thing*
mustard and cress 77.9 *seed*
mustard family 77.3 *seed plant*
mustard plaster 394.10 *surgical dressing*
mustard seed 159.2 *little thing*
mustard-yellow 537.1 *yellow*
mustelid 71.8 *flesh-eating mammal*
Mustelidae 71.8 *flesh-eating mammal*
musteline 71.28 *carnivorous*
muster 376.1 *assembly*; 376.42 *call together*
mustered 376.46 *assembled*
muster out 377.13 *dismiss*
muster roll 220.6 *list of names*
must have 135.9 *find necessary*
mustily 258.12 *dirtily*; 503.6 *stinkingly*; 296.18 *venerably*
mustiness 258.1 *dirtiness*; 503.1 *stench*
musty 258.7 *dirty*; 83.9 *fungal*; 296.12 *olden*; 503.3 *stinking*
muscular dystrophy 260.4 *disease*
mutability 453.16 *capriciousness*; 224.1 *change*; 227.1 *changeableness*
mutable 453.8 *capricious*; 224.11, 227.13 *changeable*
mutably 224.15 *changeably*
mutant 118.17 *abnormal*; 118.10 *eccentric*; 34.25 *genetic*
mutate 114.8 *be diverse*; 453.21 *change*; 760.7 *convert into*; 224.9 *transform*
mutated 760.13 *converted*
mutating 760.14 *converting*
mutation 760.1 *conversion*; 234.3 *deformity*; 118.6 *deviation*; 114.1 *diversity*; 224.3 *transformation*
mutational 34.25 *genetic*
mutatis mutandis 224.15 *changeably*
mutative 224.13 *transformative*
mute 511.7; **730.8**; 231.3 *deformed*; 583.3 *funeral director*; 505.3 *inaudibility*; 505.10 *muffle*; 506.2 *silence*; 511.6 *silencer*; 506.3 *silent*; 732.2 *sparing with words*; 730.11 *speechless*; 730.15 *strike dumb*; 730.7 *voiceless person*; 337.7 *weaken*
mute button 505.3 *inaudibility*
muted 511.1 *faint-sounding*; 337.13 *insufficient*; 730.10 *low-voiced*; 524.6 *murky*; 511.2 *nonresonant*; 506.3 *silent*; 529.13 *soft-hued*; 505.7 *unheard*; 696.1 *unintelligible*
mutedness 511.3; 506.4 *silence*
muteness 732.4 *guarded speech*; 730.5 *mutism*; 506.4 *silence*; 696.11 *unintelligibility*
mutilate 548.7 *blemish*; 245.5 *hurt*; 546.5 *make ugly*; 357.11 *ruin*; 212.3 *subtract*; 814.4 *torture*
mutilated 231.3 *deformed*; 233.4 *incomplete*; 212.7 *reduced*; 546.4 *ugly*
mutilation 245.11 *hurt*; 233.1 *incompleteness*; 212.1 *subtraction*; 546.1 *ugliness*
mutineer 588.3 *anarchist*; 662.11 *rebel*
mutineering 662.1 *disobedience*
mutinous 588.6 *anarchic*; 662.13 *disobedient*; 408.20 *disorderly*; 753.10 *lawbreaking*; 16.61 *lawless*; 383.12 *resisting*; 662.14 *subversive*
mutinously 588.8 *anarchically*; 753.11 *disapprovingly*; 662.17 *disobediently*; 383.14 *resistingly*; 662.18 *subversively*
mutinousness 662.1 *disobedience*; 662.4 *revolution*
mutiny 588.1 *anarchy*; 588.4 *be anarchic*; 662.16 *be subversive*; 753.8 *cause mischief*; 662.1 *disobedience*; 753.2 *disorder*; 16.41 *lawlessness*; 753.1, 753.6 *protest*; 383.3 *resistance movement*; 383.8 *revolt*; 662.4 *revolution*
mutism 730.5
mutt 71.9 *dog*
mutter 626.11 *be irritable*; 509.9 *hum*; 509.2 *humming*; 511.8 *sound faint*; 730.16 *speak in a low voice*; 729.13 *speak in a particular way*; 729.7 *utterance*; 730.4 *whispering*
muttered 511.1 *faint-sounding*
muttering 511.4 *faint sound*; 730.10 *low-voiced*; 711.1 *warning*
mutton 25.44 *British dish*; 25.20 *meat*
muttonchops 420.7 *rough thing*
mutual 759.6 *in exchange*; 110.5 *interconnected*; 108.5 *interrelated*; 747.18 *joint*; 764.5 *jointly possessing*
mutual affection 593.1 *love*
mutual affinity 595.1 *liking*
mutual agreement 755.1 *contract*
mutual approach 310.1 *convergence*
mutual assistance 747.3 *mutual relationship*
mutual attraction 363.1 *attraction*; 593.1 *love*
mutual concession 754.1 *compromise*; 685.1 *moderation*
mutual conductance 28.53, 39.12 *resistance*
mutual consultation 713.2 *consultation*
mutual-defence treaty 755.3 *alliance*
mutual dependence 110.2 *interconnection*; 387.1 *subjection*
mutual friend 569.5 *friend*
mutual friends 569.6 *close friend*
mutual good will 569.2 *friendly relations*
mutual hatred 596.1 *dislike*
mutual inductance 28.53, 39.12 *resistance*
mutual induction 28.63 *magnetic phenomenon*
mutual influence 110.2 *interconnection*
mutualism 34.18 *ecology*; 110.2 *interconnection*; 747.3 *mutual relationship*; 764.2 *participation*
mutuality 750.1 *accord*; 759.1 *exchange*; 110.2 *interconnection*; 108.2 *interrelatedness*; 747.3 *mutual relationship*; 108.1 *relatedness*
mutualization 110.2 *interconnection*
mutual love 595.1 *liking*; 593.1 *love*
mutual lovers 593.10 *lovers*
mutually 310.12 *convergently*; 759.8 *in exchange*; 110.10 *reciprocally*; 108.10 *relevantly*
mutually approaching 310.8 *advancing*
mutually assured destruction 119.2 *equilibrium*; 589.1 *peace*
mutualness 747.3 *mutual relationship*
mutual pledge 756.1 *promise*
mutual regard 569.2 *friendly relations*
mutual relationship 747.3; 110.2 *interconnection*
mutual repulsion 364.5 *repulsion*
mutual respect 569.2 *friendly relations*
mutual support 569.2 *friendly relations*
mutual transfer 316.1 *transfer*
mutual understanding 750.1 *accord*; 593.1 *love*
muu-muu 551.7 *frock*
muzzily 524.12 *dimly*
muzzle 357.8 *destroy*; 587.9 *firearm*; 251.12 *gag*; 251.5 *means of restraint*; 335.8 *overpower*; 309.11 *restrain*; 309.3 *restrainer*; 506.2 *silence*
muzzled 251.15 *detained*
muzzleloader 587.10 *historical gun*
muzzy 524.6 *murky*; 690.2 *slightly drunk*
MVP 246.4 *successful person*
MW transmitter 692.16 *transmitter*
myalgia 491.2 *painful condition*; 260.16 *rheumatism*
myalisma 450.2 *religious belief*
myasthenia 260.17 *nervous disorder*
myasthenia gravis 260.17 *nervous disorder*
mycelial 83.10 *of fungi*
mycelium 83.4 *fungal body*
mycetoma 83.5 *fungal association*
mycobiont 83.5 *fungal association*; 84.6 *lichen*
mycologic 83.10 *of fungi*
mycologist 77.12 *plant scientist*; 83.8 *study of fungi*
mycology 77.10 *plant science*; 83.8 *study of fungi*
mycophagist 83.8 *study of fungi*
mycophagy 83.8 *study of fungi*
mycoplasma 34.3 *organism*
mycorrhiza 83.5 *fungal association*
mycosis 83.5 *fungal association*
mycotic 83.10 *of fungi*
my dear man 567.3 *male title of address*
my dear woman 568.3 *female title of address*
my good lady 568.3 *female title of address*
my good man 567.3 *male title of address*
my humble self 139.12 *I*
Mylai 382.15 *slaughterhouse*
my lord 567.3 *male title of address*
my lud 16.23 *judge*
my man 569.5 *friend*
mynah bird 72.7 *cagebird*
myocardial infarction 260.10 *cardiovascular disease*
myocarditis 260.10 *cardiovascular disease*
myoglobin 33.9 *protein*; 33.24 *respiration*
myology 403.8 *science of structure*
myomorphs 71.12 *gnawing mammal*
myopia 519.2 *poor sight*
myopic 519.9 *weak-sighted*
Myoskinji 10.13 *shrine*
myriad 208.7; 202.2 *immeasurable*; 201.10 *thousand*
myriads 208.2 *multitude*
myriapod 75.4 *arthropod*
Myriapoda 75.4 *arthropod*
myrmidon 586.6 *militarist*
myrrh 583.1 *burial*; 496.5 *herbs*; 502.3 *incense*
myself 139.12 *I*; 101.6 *internal world*
mystagogue 579.14 *leader*; 11.12 *occultist*
mysterious 737.11; 523.11 *benighted*; 696.4 *difficult*; 266.2 *obscure*; 11.14 *occult*; 705.13 *problematic*; 103.2 *unbelievable*; 696.1 *unintelligible*; 456.8 *unknown*; 619.8 *wonderful*
mysteriously 523.15 *darkly*; 266.4 *obscurely*; 11.25 *occultly*; 696.13 *unintelligibly*; 619.13 *wonderfully*; 9.12 *worshipfully*
mysterious message 696.12 *unintelligible thing*
mysteriousness 266.1 *obscurity*; 11.2 *the occult*
mysterious stranger 737.8 *anonymity*
mystery 705.4 *difficult question*; 737.7 *esotericism*; 737.3 *mystification*; 11.1 *occultism*; 11.2 *the occult*; 696.11 *unintelligibility*; 696.12 *unintelligible thing*; 456.3 *unknown thing*
mystery play 21.2 *play*
mystery story 17.2 *fiction*
mystery tour 456.3 *unknown thing*
mystic 450.5 *believer*; 523.11 *benighted*; 4.11 *follower of a doctrine*; 11.12 *occultist*; 4.14 *of a philosophy*; 7.15 *religious*; 7.3 *religious person*; 696.1 *unintelligible*
mystical 8.13 *divine*; 103.2 *unbelievable*; 696.1 *unintelligible*
mystical experience 8.8 *divine manifestation*
mystical intuition 8.8 *divine manifestation*
mystically 8.19 *divinely*; 11.25 *occultly*; 9.12 *worshipfully*
mysticism 11.1 *occultism*; 7.2 *religiousness*; 4.7 *school of thought*; 696.11 *unintelligibility*
mystification 737.3; 702.3 *cunning*; 736.5 *evasion*; 11.1 *occultism*; 696.11 *unintelligibility*
mystified 696.6 *confused*; 264.16 *troubled*
mystify 737.13; 457.10 *bemuse*; 696.7 *be unintelligible*; 264.23 *cause difficulties*; 705.21 *confuse*; 456.11 *make ignorant*; 453.20 *make uncertain*; 528.12 *obscure*; 11.20 *occult*; 702.11 *practise sophistry*
mystifying 702.8 *cunning*; 528.4 *inscrutable*; 737.11 *mysterious*
myth 699.9 *falsification*; 17.2 *fiction*; 477.7 *idealism*; 721.3 *narration*; 3.7 *narrative*; 1.8, 296.6 *tradition*
mythical 3.19 *chronicled*; 17.17 *fictional*; 477.12 *imaginary*; 96.10 *theoretical*
mythical hero 336.6 *muscleman*
mythically 3.25 *reportedly*; 1.18 *societally*
mythical seaman 323.7 *nautical person*
mythic heaven 582.14 *the spiritual world*
mythic hell 582.14 *the spiritual world*
myth-maker 477.9 *visionary*
mythological 17.17 *fictional*; 477.12 *imaginary*; 721.12 *narrative*; 1.14 *societal*
mythological bird 72.9 *fabulous bird*
mythologically 1.18 *societally*
mythologist 17.14 *author*; 566.6 *studier of mankind*
mythologize 699.26 *falsify*; 721.15 *recount*
mythologized 699.36 *falsified*
mythology 17.2 *fiction*; 566.5 *study of mankind*; 1.8, 296.6 *tradition*
mythomania 699.6 *lying*
mythomaniac 700.16 *liar*
mythopoeia 17.2 *fiction*
myxomatosis 260.18 *veterinary disease*
myxomycetes 83.3 *fungi*
Myxomycota 83.3 *fungi*

Naafi 557.15 *eating place*
nab 251.11 *detain*; 700.33 *snare*; 773.10 *take away*; 492.11 *touch*
nabbing 773.2 *taking back*
nabla 27.50 *scalar quantity*
nabob 400.2 *sovereign*; 781.10 *wealthy person*
nacho 25.50 *Central American dish*
nacre 541.5 *variegated thing*
nacreous 541.7 *iridescent*
nacreously 541.12 *variedly*
NAD 33.12 *coenzyme*
nada 195.2 *nothing*
nadir 175.1 *base*; 29.5 *celestial sphere*; 156.4 *deep thing*; 122.5 *inferior state*; 155.3 *lowest point*; 29.21 *orbit*; 195.4 *zero level*
NADP 33.12 *coenzyme*
naff 236.2 *inferior*; 238.1 *useless*
naff off 313.15 *go!*; 371.33 *go away!*; 226.12 *stop!*
nag 670.18 *find fault*; 112.18 *harp*; 59.1 *horse*; 625.3 *irascible person*; 483.10 *manipulate*; 568.8 *nasty woman*; 242.11 *quarrel*; 59.4 *saddle horse*
Nagari 5.13 *letter*
Nagasaki 382.15 *slaughterhouse*
nage-waza 52.7 *judo*
nagging 670.6, 670.28 *fault-finding*

nag into 480.15 *persuade*
nagual 8.5 *deity*
nagware 40.19 *computing terms*
naiad 8.5 *deity*
naïf 295.12, 555.12 *immature;* 646.1 *naive*
nail 373.11 *connect;* 373.8 *fastening;* 361.4 *hanger;* 418.7 *hard substance;* 425.8 *sharp-pointed thing;* 438.1 *tool;* 438.10 *use tools*
nailbomb 587.16 *bomb*
nailbrush 256.10 *cleaning object;* 420.7 *rough thing*
nail down 95.12 *establish reality;* 253.14 *make fast*
nailed 373.15 *connected*
nailfile 427.12 *abrasive;* 365.7 *eraser;* 421.9 *smoother*
nail in one's coffin 247.1 *failure*
nail polish 547.4 *cosmetics;* 535.6 *red pigment*
nails 360.3 *tools for gripping;* 587.1 *weapon*
nail varnish 547.4 *cosmetics*
naira 780.11 *national coins*
naive **646.1**; **805.7**; 450.12 *gullible;* 456.6 *ignorant;* 295.12, 555.12 *immature;* 308.16 *open;* 538.3 *raw;* 19.29 *realist;* 721.13 *representing;* 698.18 *truthful;* 487.1 *unaccustomed;* 254.3 *vulnerable*
naively **646.5**; **805.12**; 254.11 *dangerously;* 308.26 *openly;* 487.6 *unaccustomedly*
naive person **646.3**
Naivety **646**
naivety **646.2**; **805.3**; 456.1 *ignorance;* 295.3, 555.3 *immaturity;* 308.9 *openness;* 698.5 *truthfulness;* 254.7 *vulnerability*
naked 520.2 *clear;* 255.17 *direct;* 738.15 *open;* 271.1 *simple;* 552.9 *undressed;* 254.3 *vulnerable*
naked as a jaybird 552.9 *undressed*
naked eye 520.3 *visibility*
naked force 647.2 *suppression*
naked lady 552.8 *nude person*
nakedly **552.17**
nakedness 552.2 *nudity;* 271.4 *simplicity;* 254.7 *vulnerability*
naked person 552.8 *nude person*
naked steel 587.8 *sharp weapon*
namby-pamby 614.3 *cowardly;* 337.4 *weakling;* 337.12 *weak-willed*
name **721.8**; 721.16 *define;* 743.10 *identify;* 743.2 *identity;* 743.3 *means of identification;* 575.1 *right;* 139.24 *specify;* 246.1 *success;* 5.17 *word*
name and address 692.3 *correspondence;* 743.3 *means of identification*
name badge 743.3 *means of identification*
name calling 701.1 *argument*
namechild 5.2 *linguist*
named 743.12 *identified;* 452.7 *particular;* 5.42 *worded*
name day 601.5 *anniversary;* 275.11 *date*
namegiver 5.2 *linguist*
name in lights 740.8 *public relations*
namely **139.31**; 719.18 *in other words*
name names 739.7 *betray;* 139.24 *specify*
name of the game 99.2 *essential content*
name part 21.23 *role*
nameplate 743.3 *means of identification*
namer 5.2 *linguist*
name recognition 246.1 *success*
namesake 721.8 *name*
name tag 742.1 *sign*
nametape 743.3 *means of identification*
name up in lights 246.1 *success*
naming 743.1 *identification;* 721.7 *nomenclature*
naming ceremony 721.7 *nomenclature*
namtar 8.7 *devil*
nan 25.38 *bread*
nan bread 25.49 *Indian dish*
nancy 567.9 *offensive terms for homosexual*
nanny 401.6 *domestic servant;* 401.4 *personal attendant;* 252.3 *protector*
nanny goat 568.14 *female animal;* 71.18 *female mammal;* 43.8 *livestock*
nanny state 252.1 *safety;* 652.4 *welfare state*
nanosecond 275.4 *term;* 276.2 *time period*
naos 20.9 *miscellaneous architectural features;* 10.13 *shrine*
nap **404.3**; 263.1 *ease;* 226.3, 226.9 *pause;* 343.9, 343.13 *sleep;* 263.2 *take it easy;* 489.2 *unconsciousness;* 42.14 *weave;* 42.4 *weaving*
napalm bomb 587.16 *bomb*
naphtha 437.6 *oil*
Napierian logarithm 27.19 *logarithm*
Napier's bones 27.67 *calculator;* 40.3, 210.5 *computer*
Naples yellow 537.7 *yellow pigment*
Napoleon and Josephine 593.10 *lovers*
Napoleonic code 16.1 *the law*
nappe 90.2 *channel;* 305.3 *downflow*
napped 42.10 *woven*
nappy 551.23 *children's clothes*
Naraka 8.12 *hell*
narcism 673.4 *self-admiration*
narcissism 683.2 *egoism;* 593.1 *love;* 686.4 *self-absorption;* 673.4 *self-admiration*
narcissist 686.5 *self-indulgent person;* 683.3 *selfish person*
narcissistic 683.5 *egoistic;* 686.9 *self-absorbed;* 673.10 *self-admiring*
Narcissus 673.7 *vain person*
narcoanalysis 36.3 *psychiatric treatment*
narcohypnosis 36.3 *psychiatric treatment*
narcosis 592.4 *desensitization;* 335.4 *disability;* 463.1 *oblivion*
narcotherapist 36.30 *psychiatrist*
narcotherapy 36.3 *psychiatric treatment*
narcotic 691.9 *addictive;* 489.4, 489.9 *anaesthetic;* 592.6 *desensitizing substance;* 394.8, 691.6 *drug;* 37.4 *drug type;* 685.8 *moderating;* 394.17 *remedial;* 37.15 *sedative;* 343.10 *soporific*
narcotically 691.11 *in a trance*
narcotics 691.6 *drug*
narcotization 592.4 *desensitization*
narcotize 489.12 *anaesthetize;* 343.14 *make inactive;* 592.7 *render insensitive*
narcotized 343.4 *not awake*
nard 268.6 *ointment*
narghile 496.7 *tobacco*
naris 500.2 *sense of smell*
nark 715.5 *accuse;* 715.3 *accuser;* 693.10 *informer;* 716.7 *person who gives evidence;* 716.13 *turn queen's evidence;* 454.7 *verifier*
Narnia 477.8 *dreamland*
narrate 3.20 *chronicle;* 693.12 *communicate;* 744.13 *record;* 721.15 *recount*
narrated 3.19 *chronicled*
narration **721.3**; 693.2 *communication;* 3.7 *narrative*
narrative **3.7**; **17.19**; **721.12**; 17.3 *aspect of fiction;* 340.2 *deed;* 721.3 *narration;* 744.1 *record*
narrative fiction 17.2 *fiction*
narrative poem 721.3 *narration;* 17.7 *poem*
narrative poetry 17.6 *poetry*
narrative voice 17.3 *aspect of fiction*
narrative writing 721.3 *narration*
narratology 17.3 *aspect of fiction*
narrator 21.24 *actor;* 693.9 *informant;* 729.10 *speaker*
narrow **151.1**; **151.10**; 191.6 *become smaller;* 68.10 *curling;* 128.10 *excluding;* 166.5 *limited;* 191.5 *make smaller;* 251.13 *restraining;* 191.7 *smaller;* 465.8 *unjust*
narrow-beaked 151.4 *narrow-leaved*
narrow boat 323.3 *vessel*
narrowcast 740.13 *make public*
narrowcasting 740.2 *mass media*
narrow defeat 247.2 *defeat*
narrowed 191.7 *smaller*
narrow escape 254.5 *danger;* 389.1 *escape*
narrow gauge 151.8 *narrow thing;* 321.3 *rail*
narrow-gauge 151.4 *narrow-leaved*
narrow-gauged 151.4 *narrow-leaved*
narrow house 583.6 *grave*
narrowing **151.9**; **310.6**; 191.8 *contracting;* 191.1 *contraction;* 310.7 *convergent*
narrowing gap 310.2 *approach;* 310.6 *narrowing*
narrow-leaved **151.4**
narrowly **151.11**; 128.12 *exclusively*
narrow means 782.5 *poverty*
narrow mind 465.3 *injustice*
narrow-minded 452.2 *convinced;* 466.10 *discriminatory;* 795.10 *moralistic;* 465.8 *unjust*
narrow-mindedly 466.17 *prejudicially;* 465.14 *unjustly*
narrow-mindedness 452.10 *conviction;* 465.3 *injustice;* 641.7 *opinionatedness;* 466.3 *prejudice;* 795.4 *self-righteousness*
Narrowness **151**
narrowness **151.5**; 466.3 *prejudice*
narrow-nosed 151.4 *narrow-leaved*
narrow outlook 166.2 *limiting factor*
narrow-petalled 151.4 *narrow-leaved*
narrow place **151.6**
narrows 151.6 *narrow place*
narrow-skulled 151.4 *narrow-leaved*
narrow squeak 389.1 *escape;* 147.2 *short distance*
narrow the gap 310.9 *converge*
narrow thing **151.8**
narrow victory 246.2 *victory*
narrow waist 153.7 *thinness*
narrow-waisted 153.1 *thin*
narthex 20.10 *church architecture*
nary a one 94.6 *absence*
NASA 29.31 *space travel*
nasal 5.41 *lettered;* 500.6 *olfactory;* 729.18 *phonetic;* 5.16 *spoken letter*
nasal cavity 308.4 *body orifice;* 729.5 *organ of speech;* 500.2 *sense of smell*
nasal congestion 501.1 *odourlessness*
nasality 513.2 *hoarseness;* 729.3 *mode of speech*
nasally 500.10 *odorously*
nasal mucus 258.4 *dirt*
nasal tone 513.2 *hoarseness*
nascent 130.32 *embryonic*
Nashville 87.2 *American cities;* 18.12 *Tin Pan Alley*
Nassau scoring 56.2 *golfing terms*
nastily 659.9 *discourteously;* 242.13 *unpleasantly;* 236.15 *worthlessly*
nastiness 236.9 *badness;* 659.1 *discourtesy;* 798.1 *evil;* 796.2 *indecency;* 651.1 *malevolence;* 242.5, 682.4 *unpleasantness*
nasty 236.3 *bad;* 254.1 *dangerous;* 659.5 *discourteous;* 798.7 *evil;* 594.12 *hated;* 651.14 *hostile;* 258.8 *unclean;* 499.6 *unpalatable;* 242.1, 682.2 *unpleasant*
nasty person **682.6**
nasty piece of work 651.8 *malefactor*
nasty taste 499.2 *unpalatability*
nasty type 804.9 *wicked person*
nasty woman **568.8**
natality 561.3 *propagation*
natation 67.1 *swimming*
natational 67.11 *swimming*
natatorium 256.6 *bath;* 67.7 *swimming pool*
natatory 323.11 *nautical;* 67.11 *swimming*
nation **566.11**; 85.1 *country;* 396.8 *governmental organization;* 1.7 *society;* 86.4 *territorial division*
national **85.16**; **86.17**; **564.8**; **566.13**; 250.9 *free;* 396.14 *governmental;* 172.8 *internal;* 85.13 *native;* 5.39 *of language;* 1.14 *societal;* 138.16 *universal*
National Anglers Council 55.1 *angling*
national anthem 516.2 *song*
National Assembly 579.10 *legislative body*
National Basketball Association 49.1 *basketball*
national code 692.11 *dialling*
national coins **780.11**
national colours 743.7 *flag*
national consciousness 566.11 *nation;* 85.4 *nationalism*
national costume 551.3 *formal dress*
national credit 784.2 *national debt*
National Curriculum 6.3 *subject*
national debt **784.2**; 13.3 *economic statistics*
national defence 253.4 *security forces;* 584.2 *the military*
national defence headquarters 584.4 *military organization*
national device 743.6 *national emblem*
national dress 551.3 *formal dress;* 743.5 *uniform*
national election 469.12 *election*
national emblem **743.6**
national entity 566.11 *nation*
national flag 743.7 *flag*
National Front 12.6 *political party*
National Front member 586.1 *combatant;* 662.10 *seditionist*
national government 12.1 *government*
national grid 334.7 *electrical power;* 437.4 *electricity;* 39.33 *power distribution*
National Health Service 35.1 *medicine;* 253.1 *protection;* 252.1 *safety;* 392.4 *social assistance*
National Hockey League 58.3 *ice hockey*
National Hot Rod Association 61.7 *racing governing body*
National Hunt racing 59.7 *horseracing*
national income 765.4 *earnings;* 788.3 *income*
National Insurance 790.7 *tax*
national insurance 253.1 *protection;* 392.4 *social assistance*
National Insurance number 743.3 *means of identification*
nationalism **85.4**; 566.11 *nation;* 86.15 *regionalism;* 4.7 *school of thought;* 372.3 *separateness*
nationalist **85.14**; 4.11 *follower of a doctrine;* 4.14 *of a philosophy*
nationalistic 85.16 *national*
nationalistically 85.19, 86.20 *nationally*
Nationalists 12.6 *political party*
nationality 566.11 *nation;* 85.4 *nationalism;* 1.7 *society*
nationalization 776.5 *commercial trade;* 13.1 *economics;* 764.1 *joint possession;* 773.1 *taking*
nationalize 764.4 *have joint possession;* 773.7 *take;* 776.1 *trade;* 13.10 *trade with*
nationalized 776.19 *corporate;* 13.13 *economic*
National Labor Relations Act 15.5 *labour law*
National Labor Relations Board 15.5 *labour law*
national language 5.4 *parent language*
National League 48.1 *baseball*
nationally **85.19**; **86.20**; 566.15 *humanly;* 396.24 *ministerially;* 1.18 *societally;* 138.32 *universally*
national military college 584.3 *military training*
national monument 744.11 *monument*
national newspaper 741.5 *mass communication*
national official 15.7 *employee*
national paper 740.4 *newspaper*
national planning 484.1 *plan*
National Public Radio 692.20 *radio broadcasting*
national security 736.4 *silence*
national service 585.7 *war measures*
National Socialism 12.1 *government;* 396.7 *type of rule*
national status 250.3 *independence*
national union organization 15.3 *organized labour*
nationhood 85.1 *country;* 250.3 *independence*
nation in arms 586.7 *militarist nation*
nation state 566.11 *nation;* 12.5 *political organization;* 86.4 *territorial division*
nationwide 138.16 *universal*
nationwide circulation 740.7 *publicity*
native **85.13**; **564.12**; 32.34 *elemental;* 564.1 *inhabitant;* 646.1 *naive;* 5.39 *of language;* 1.6 *race;* 1.13 *racial;* 77.15 *wild*
native accent 729.3 *mode of speech*
native American 1.6 *race*
native custom 632.4 *custom*
native land **85.6**; 565.3 *home;* 86.4 *territorial division*
native language 5.4 *parent language*
native people 1.6 *race*
native population 564.2 *inhabitants*
native quarter 655.4 *place of confinement*
native soil 85.6 *native land*
native tongue 729.1 *faculty of speech;* 5.4 *parent language*
native wit 334.2 *ability;* 442.5 *common sense*
Nativity 10.16 *religious festival*
nativity 19.10 *art subject;* 554.4 *biological function;* 130.4 *conception;* 561.3 *propagation*
NATO 755.3 *alliance*
natriuretic 37.4 *drug type;* 37.17 *stimulating*
natron 583.1 *burial*
natter 731.7 *be talkative;* 734.2, 734.10 *chat;* 729.1 *faculty of speech*
natterer 734.8 *chatterer*
nattily 551.36 *dressily*
natty 256.16 *clean;* 551.30 *dressed-up;* 551.31 *styled*
natural **42.12**; **271.3**; 55.8 *angling;* 126.6 *authentic;* 118.10 *eccentric;* 543.3 *elegant;* 657.9 *familiar;* 93.11 *intrinsic;* 115.9 *lifelike;* 34.21 *living;* 402.7 *material;* 18.16 *musical note;* 646.1, 805.7 *naive;* 632.11 *normal;* 95.7 *realistic;* 478.2 *spontaneous*

natural affection 593.1 *love*
natural bent 485.2 *aptitude*
natural cement 24.9 *industrial ceramics*
natural childbirth 561.7 *obstetrics*
natural colour 529.1 *colour;* 529.9 *complexion*
natural death 582.5 *ways of dying*
natural deposit 439.2 *resource*
natural disaster 249.1 *adversity;* 357.7 *agent of destruction*
natural dye 42.6 *dye;* 529.4 *pigment*
natural fabric 42.3 *fabric*
natural feature 30.7 *landform*
natural fibre 42.1 *fibre*
natural fly 55.1 *angling*
natural fly-fishing 55.1 *angling*
natural gas 437.3 *gas;* 435.1 *materials;* 334.6 *source of energy*
natural harbour 92.9 *inlet*
natural history 34.1 *life science*
natural idiom 271.4 *simplicity*
naturalism 273.2 *correctness;* 95.3, 698.12 *realism;* 4.7 *school of thought;* 21.10 *theatre movements*
naturalist 21.42 *activist;* 4.11 *follower of a doctrine;* 34.19 *life scientist;* 77.12 *plant scientist;* 19.29 *realist*
naturalistic 273.6 *correct;* 721.11 *descriptive;* 698.25 *lifelike;* 17.16 *literary;* 4.14 *of a philosophy;* 95.7 *realistic;* 717.13 *representational*
naturalistically 19.30 *pictorially*
naturalization 760.2 *evolution;* 632.7 *habituation;* 370.3 *introduction;* 117.3 *pliancy*
naturalize **760.12**; 117.10 *assimilate;* 760.8 *be transformed;* 632.18 *habituate;* 370.9 *welcome*
naturalized **760.17**; 760.13 *converted;* 632.14 *habituated;* 564.13 *resident;* 77.15 *wild*
naturalized citizen 564.8 *national*
natural lake 88.1 *lake*
natural language 5.3 *spoken language*
natural-language understanding 40.17 *artificial intelligence*
natural law 140.3 *rule of nature;* 16.1 *the law*
natural light **522.4**; 41.15 *lighting*
natural logarithm 27.19 *logarithm;* 194.6 *power*
naturally **657.14**; 698.37 *authentically;* 452.26 *certainly!;* 115.14 *comparably;* 543.5 *elegantly;* 402.9 *materially;* 805.12 *naively;* 55.9 *on the water;* 126.8 *originally;* 485.12 *skilfully;* 345.12 *with the effect of*
naturally gifted 485.7 *gifted*
naturally-occurring 32.40 *synthetic*
natural magic 11.3 *witchcraft*
natural medicine **35.2**
natural mystery **737.6**
naturalness **271.6**; 543.1 *elegance;* 657.3 *familiarity;* 646.2, 805.3 *naivety;* 698.12 *realism*
natural number **27.7**
natural philosophy 4.6 *branch of philosophy;* 28.1 *physics*
natural politeness 656.5 *etiquette*
natural power 136.2 *ability*
natural resource 439.2 *resource*
natural resources 13.4 *economic development;* 352.2 *supplies*
natural rubber 422.4 *rubber*
natural satellite 29.18 *satellite*
natural science **402.6**; 34.1 *life science;* 28.1 *physics;* 455.5 *science*
natural scientist 34.19 *life scientist*
natural selection 34.16 *evolution*
natural talent 229.3, 485.2 *aptitude*
natural theology 7.13 *theology*
natural virtues 803.2 *virtues*
natural weapon 587.1 *weapon*
natural world 34.2 *living world;* 95.2 *real world*
Nature 356.9 *producer*
nature **93.3**; **99.4**; **160.6**; 34.2 *living world;* 402.1 *material world;* 139.2 *personality;* 137.4 *type*
nature cure 394.11 *medical art;* 394.13 *therapy*
nature of meaning 4.9 *philosophical problem*
nature of the beast 99.4 *nature*
nature of time 4.9 *philosophical problem*
nature reserve 359.1 *preservation*
nature's bounty 562.1 *fertility*
nature topic 447.5 *educational topic*
naturism 552.1 *undress*
naturist 552.8 *nude person*
naturistic 552.9 *undressed*
naturopath 35.12, 394.15 *healer*
naturopathy 394.11 *medical art;* 35.2 *natural medicine;* 35.8 *treatment*
naught 195.2 *nothing;* 94.2 *nothingness*
naught beside 197.1 *one*
naughtily 631.20 *badly;* 800.11 *dishonourably;* 662.17 *disobediently;* 712.12 *swearingly*
naughtiness 631.4 *bad conduct;* 662.1 *disobedience;* 806.3 *sin;* 804.1 *wickedness*
naughty 631.18 *badly behaved;* 712.8 *cursing;* 662.13 *disobedient;* 796.12 *indecent;* 264.14 *troublesome;* 796.13 *unchaste;* 804.11 *wicked*
naughty child 631.5 *badly behaved person;* 662.5 *troublemaker*
naughty story 796.2 *indecency*
naughty word 712.1 *curse;* 5.19 *swearword*
nauplius 75.13 *invertebrate larva*
nausea 260.8 *indigestion;* 742.1 *sign;* 596.4 *sign of dislike;* 260.3 *symptom;* 371.23 *vomiting*
nauseant 255.4, 394.6 *purgative*
nauseate 364.4 *be repulsive;* 596.7 *cause dislike;* 594.16 *cause hate;* 499.9 *disgust;* 242.10 *displease*
nauseated 596.8 *disliking;* 260.22, 538.6 *sick;* 371.30 *vomiting*
nauseating 596.9 *disliked;* 219.6 *excessive;* 594.12 *hated;* 236.4 *poor;* 364.8 *repulsive;* 258.8 *unclean;* 499.6 *unpalatable;* 242.1 *unpleasant*
nauseatingly 499.10 *sourly*
nauseous 596.8 *disliking;* 594.12 *hated;* 236.4 *poor;* 258.8 *unclean*
nautch 22.4 *historic dancing*
nautch-girl 21.30 *dancer*
nautical **323.11**; 91.7 *oceanic*
nautical almanac 323.5 *navigation;* 693.5 *reference book*
nautically **91.11**; **323.12**
nautical mile 148.7 *measure of length*
nautical mile per hour 323.6 *nautical speed*
nautical person **323.7**
nautical speed **323.6**
nautilus 180.3 *convoluted thing*
naval 586.35 *martial;* 584.8, 585.17 *military;* 323.11 *nautical*
naval airman 586.27 *naval man*
naval architect 323.7 *nautical person*
naval architecture 323.4 *shipbuilding*
naval armament 586.22 *navy*
naval engagement 585.9 *battle*
naval engineering 38.1 *engineering;* 323.4 *shipbuilding*
naval man **586.27**; 323.7 *nautical person*
naval mine **586.26**
naval officer 323.7 *nautical person;* 586.27 *naval man*
naval operations 585.8 *warfare*
naval reservist 586.27 *naval man*
naval service 586.22 *navy;* 585.8 *warfare*
naval unit **586.23**
naval warfare 585.8 *warfare*
navar 322.6 *flight control*
nave 317.7 *arcade;* 307.4 *axle;* 173.2 *central thing;* 10.12 *church*
navel 173.2 *central thing*
navigable 319.5 *transportable*
navigable river 317.11 *channel;* 90.1 *river*
navigable water 323.2 *waterway*
navigate **323.9**; 631.15 *conduct;* 325.1 *deviate;* 579.2 *direct;* 142.11 *find;* 324.7 *take a direction*
navigated 319.5 *transportable*
navigation **323.5**; 324.1 *direction;* 142.5 *topography;* 323.1 *water travel*
navigational 142.8 *locational;* 579.17 *managerial;* 319.5 *transportable*
navigational aid 579.5 *guide;* 323.5 *navigation*
navigational beacon 692.27 *signalling*
navigational instrument 323.5 *navigation*
navigational radar 323.5 *navigation*
navigational satellite 323.5 *navigation;* 29.32 *satellite*
navigation laws 323.5 *navigation*
navigation lights 522.6 *electric light*
navigator 322.3 *aircraft personnel;* 586.32 *airman;* 579.13 *director;* 323.7 *nautical person*
NAVSTAR Global Positioning System 323.5 *navigation*
navvy 578.1 *worker*
navy **586.22**; 586.14 *armed forces;* 539.1 *blue;* 376.14 *force;* 253.4 *security forces;* 584.2 *the military*
navy blue 539.1 *blue;* 523.3 *dark colour*
navy man 323.7 *nautical person;* 586.27 *naval man;* 585.11 *recruit*
navy staff 584.5 *military staff*
navy uniform 743.5 *uniform*
nay 708.1 *negation;* 704.13, 708.23 *no!;* 753.1 *protest;* 469.10 *vote*
naysay 708.10 *be negative;* 704.9 *deny*
naysayer 113.11 *opposer;* 704.5 *refuter*
naysaying 708.1 *negation;* 704.1 *refutation*
Nazi 466.7 *bigot;* 466.10 *discriminatory;* 12.9, 396.14 *governmental;* 465.5 *misjudging person;* 12.6 *political party*
Nazi SA 586.14 *armed forces*
Nazism 12.1 *government;* 466.4 *social discrimination;* 647.2 *suppression;* 396.7 *type of rule*
Nazi swastika 743.6 *national emblem*
NBA Championship 49.1 *basketball*
NBA Most Valuable Player 49.2 *basketball player*
NBC 692.24 *television broadcasting*
NCAA swimming 67.5 *swimming association*
NCAA wrestler 52.6 *wrestler*
NCCA Baseball Championship 48.1 *baseball*
NCCA Basketball Championship 49.1 *basketball*
NCK 40.14 *data transfer*
n-dimensional space 27.35 *space*
Neanderthal 380.4 *violent creature*
Neanderthaler 284.6 *people of the past*
Neanderthal man 296.7 *ancient people;* 566.3 *early human;* 284.6 *people of the past*
neap 91.7 *oceanic*
neap tide 214.3 *decreasing thing;* 155.3 *lowest point;* 298.5 *regular thing;* 30.15, 91.2 *tide*
near **147.9**; **147.12**; **147.16**; 97.10 *available;* 569.10 *familiar;* 283.11 *future;* 147.10 *juxtaposed;* 682.1 *mean;* 169.6 *side;* 115.7 *similar;* 289.12 *succeeding*
near and far 141.16 *extensively*
near at hand 283.11 *future;* 293.13 *imminent;* 147.12 *near;* 97.16 *on the spot*
near beer 558.6 *soft drink*
nearby **239.2**; **239.8**; 97.10, 282.8 *available;* 86.18, 447.9 *local;* 86.20 *nationally;* 147.9, 147.12 *near*
near death 260.22 *sick*
near enough 147.13 *nearly*
nearer 147.9 *near*
nearest 97.10 *available;* 147.9 *near*
nearest the top 154.10 *higher*
near extinction 206.6 *sparse*
near failure 604.1 *disappointment*
near gale 31.13 *wind strength*
near infrared 28.13 *electromagnetic radiation*
nearing 312.19 *approaching;* 147.9 *near*
near likeness 115.1 *similarity*
nearly **147.13**; 115.14 *comparably;* 151.11 *narrowly;* 204.13 *on the whole;* 203.7 *quantitatively*
nearly all 205.5 *largest part*
nearly the same 115.7 *similar*
near miss 254.5 *danger;* 389.1 *escape;* 247.1 *failure;* 147.2 *short distance*
nearness **147.1**; **239.4**; 97.4 *availability;* 280.2 *closeness;* 569.3 *familiarity;* 147.3 *juxtaposition;* 115.1 *similarity*
near place **147.5**
near rhyme 17.11 *rhyme*
nearside 320.21 *miscellaneous motoring terms;* 169.3 *side direction*
near sight 519.2 *poor sight;* 518.1 *vision*
near-sighted 518.22 *bespectacled;* 519.9 *weak-sighted*
near-sightedness 519.2 *poor sight*
near the bone 796.12 *indecent*
near the knuckle 539.4, 796.12 *indecent;* 258.9 *obscene*
near the surface 157.8 *shallowly*
near the wind 324.11 *in all directions*
near thing 254.5 *danger;* 389.1 *escape;* 147.2 *short distance*
near tragedy 254.5 *danger*
near-truth 699.11 *half-truth*
near ultraviolet 28.13 *electromagnetic radiation*
near vacuum 417.5 *gas*
neat 665.9 *careful;* 256.16 *clean;* 543.3 *elegant;* 492.10 *handed;* 690.6 *intoxicating;* 407.13 *orderly;* 255.13 *pure;* 271.1 *simple;* 485.6 *skilful;* 336.12 *strong to the senses;* 409.27 *tidied;* 235.1 *worthy*
neat and tidy 407.13 *orderly*
neat as a button 407.13 *orderly*
neaten 256.13 *clean;* 244.1 *improve;* 178.10 *straighten;* 407.21, 409.19 *tidy*
neatened 409.27 *tidied*
neath 155.10 *low*
neatly 256.19 *cleanly;* 543.5 *elegantly;* 409.28 *in place;* 407.26 *orderly;* 485.12 *skilfully*
neatly put 543.3 *elegant*
neatly wrought 543.3 *elegant*
neatness 543.1 *elegance;* 665.4 *fastidiousness;* 407.5 *orderliness;* 271.4 *simplicity;* 485.1, 733.3 *skill*
neat weight 414.7 *weighing*
Nebenstimme 223.6 *accompanier*
nebula 376.28 *cluster;* 29.8 *interstellar medium*
nebulizer 37.10 *inhalant*
nebulous 696.4 *difficult;* 31.56 *foggy;* 138.20 *generalized;* 524.6 *murky;* 96.8 *unreal*
nebulous star 29.10 *star*
necessaries 135.1 *requirement*
necessarily 386.11 *compellingly;* 99.13 *in essence;* 135.12 *in need;* 93.22 *really;* 345.12 *with the effect of*
necessary 452.1 *certain;* 386.9 *compelling;* 386.10 *compulsory;* 617.7 *desired;* 99.5 *essential;* 93.10 *existing;* 123.5 *important;* 452.5 *inevitable;* 27.86 *logical;* 135.4 *required;* 135.1 *requirement*
necessary and sufficient condition 27.64 *reasoning*
necessary truth 4.8 *philosophical term*
necessitate **135.10**; 386.6 *compel*
necessities 135.1 *requirement*
necessitous **135.5**; 782.1 *poor*
necessitousness 135.3 *needfulness;* 782.5 *poverty*
necessity 452.9 *certainty;* 386.1 *compulsion;* 93.4 *demonstrable existence;* 452.16 *inevitability;* 135.3 *needfulness;* 4.8 *philosophical term;* 782.5 *poverty;* 135.1 *requirement*
neck 25.22 *beef;* 191.3 *contracted thing;* 56.4 *golf club;* 593.27 *kiss;* 373.4 *means of connection;* 20.9 *miscellaneous architectural features;* 151.8 *narrow thing;* 551.24 *part of garment;* 92.5 *peninsula;* 57.6 *pommel horse*
neck and crop 232.9 *completely;* 380.10 *violently*
neck and neck 111.19, 119.12 *equally;* 285.14 *equal with*
neck-and-neck 111.16, 285.11 *equal;* 285.4 *equal race;* 147.9 *near;* 119.8 *on equal terms*
neck-and-neck race 111.5 *equality;* 119.2 *equilibrium*
neckband 373.10 *band;* 179.3 *circular thing;* 551.14 *neckwear*
neckcloth 551.14 *neckwear*
neckerchief 551.14 *neckwear*
necking 174.3 *architectural summit;* 593.14 *communication of love;* 593.6 *courtship*
necklace 179.3 *circular thing;* 814.5 *execute;* 814.16 *instrument of execution;* 542.7 *jewellery;* 551.14 *neckwear*
neck of the womb 561.8 *organs of reproduction*
neck of the woods 86.13 *locality;* 142.1 *location*
neck or nothing 638.17 *resolutely*
neckpiece 551.14 *neckwear*
neck slice 25.27 *lamb*
neckstrap 59.14 *horse-riding terms*
neck sweetbread 25.31 *offal*
necktie 551.14 *neckwear*
neckwear **551.14**
necrolater 9.6 *idolater*
necrolatrous 9.10 *idolatrous*
necrolatry 9.2 *idolatry*
necrological 583.11 *funeral*
necrologically 583.12 *funereally*
necrologist 583.3 *funeral director*
necrology 582.12 *death count*
necromancer 11.13 *diviner;* 11.4 *witch*

necromancy 11.9, 475.2 *divination;* 11.3 *witchcraft*
necromania 461.4 *delusion*
necromantic 11.15 *witchlike*
necromantically 11.26 *magically*
necropolis 583.5 *cemetery*
necropsy 582.8 *after death;* 583.7 *inquest*
necrose 375.3 *disintegrate*
necrosis 582.1 *death;* 375.1 *disintegration*
necrotic 375.6 *disintegrating*
necrotically 375.8 *destructively*
nectar 558.2 *drink;* 78.8 *flower product;* 490.4 *pleasurable things;* 559.2 *secreted substance;* 498.2 *sweetener*
nectared 498.6 *sweet*
nectareous 498.6 *sweet*
nectarine 536.3 *orange thing*
nectary 78.3 *flower part;* 559.3 *gland*
need 135.2; 233.5 *be incomplete;* 218.5 *be insufficient;* 782.12 *be poor;* 218.6 *be unsatisfied;* 386.1 *compulsion;* 474.11 *demand;* 617.1, 617.12 *desire;* 249.2 *economic adversity;* 392.27 *find useful;* 231.5 *imperfection;* 233.1 *incompleteness;* 233.2 *omission;* 782.5 *poverty;* 135.7 *require;* 218.9 *scarcity;* 349.6 *use*
need a break 261.5 *be fatigued*
need a change 261.5 *be fatigued*
need a holiday 261.5 *be fatigued*
need an interpreter 696.7 *be unintelligible*
need a rest 261.5 *be fatigued*
need a vacation 261.5 *be fatigued*
need badly 135.8 *miss*
needed 617.7 *desired;* 135.4 *required*
need few words 269.4 *be concise*
need for 135.3 *needfulness*
needful 135.4 *required*
needfulness 135.3
need help 221.7 *be in a predicament*
neediness 135.3 *needfulness;* 782.5 *poverty*
needing 617.9 *desirous;* 233.4 *incomplete;* 135.5 *necessitous;* 218.2 *unprovided*
needing water 428.1 *dry*
need kid-glove treatment 591.11 *be sensitive*
needle 425.14 *be sharp;* 19.15 *engraving;* 579.5 *guide;* 742.5 *indicator;* 42.5 *knitting;* 77.6 *leaf;* 483.10 *manipulate;* 28.82 *measuring instrument;* 323.5 *navigation;* 624.9 *offend;* 308.2 *opener;* 425.8 *sharp-pointed thing;* 79.2 *tree part*
needle bath 433.11 *wash*
needle bearing 307.4 *axle*
needle candy 691.6 *drug*
needle cast 79.10 *tree disease*
needlegun 587.10 *historical gun*
needle-like 425.1 *sharp*
needle-pointed 425.1 *sharp*
needle-sharp 425.1 *sharp*
needless 219.7 *superfluous*
needlessly 219.8 *excessively*
needless risk 615.2 *rash move*
needlewoman 578.2 *artisan;* 551.26 *fashion designer*
needlework 542.3 *pattern*
needleworker 551.26 *fashion designer*
need money 249.10
needs 135.1 *requirement*
needy 135.5 *necessitous;* 782.1 *poor*
needy person 782.10 *poor person*
ne'er a one 94.6 *absence*
ne'er-do-well 812.2 *disreputable character;* 766.6 *loser;* 804.9 *wicked person*
nefarious 532.5 *black-hearted;* 800.5 *dishonourable;* 812.4 *disreputable;* 798.7 *evil;* 16.60 *offending;* 804.11 *wicked*
nefariously 798.12 *evilly*
negate 708.10 *be negative;* 708.14 *cancel;* 94.13 *cause not to exist;* 347.3 *counteract;* 357.8 *destroy;* 451.8 *disbelieve;* 4.23 *discuss philosophically;* 767.9 *dispose of;* 103.8 *make impossible;* 113.18 *object;* 479.4 *recant;* 709.5 *refuse;* 704.8 *refute;* 470.4 *revoke*
negated 708.20 *cancelled;* 708.18 *rejected*
negating 753.9 *protesting;* 709.8 *refused;* 704.7 *refuting*
Negation 708
negation 708.1; 470.7 *abrogation;* 708.5 *cancellation;* 347.1 *counteraction;* 36.19 *defence mechanism;* 704.2 *denial;* 27.63 *mathematical logic;* 94.3 *negativeness;* 4.8 *philosophical term;* 753.1 *protest;* 479.8 *recantation;* 709.1 *refusal;* 704.1 *refutation*
negative 708.17; 357.14 *destructive;* 41.12 *development;* 111.4, 111.15, 125.5 *duplicate;* 334.7 *electrical power;* 39.36 *electronic;* 611.4 *hopeless;* 378.15 *inhibitive;* 708.1 *negation;* 94.9 *nonexistent;* 27.71 *numerical;* 194.8 *odd;* 753.9 *protesting;* 709.8 *refused;* 383.10 *resistant;* 527.8 *transparent thing;* 113.26 *uncooperative*
negative acceleration 333.9 *deceleration*
negative answer 709.1 *refusal*
negative attitude 708.1 *negation*
negative balance of payments 784.2 *national debt*
negative charge 28.50 *electric charge*
negative command 397.1 *command*
negative correlation 27.61 *correlation*
negative electrode 334.7 *electrical power*
negative equity 249.2 *economic adversity*
negative feedback 39.15 *circuit function;* 385.1 *retaliation*
negative ion 28.66 *ion*
negatively 708.22; 753.11 *disapprovingly;* 39.37 *electronically;* 611.11 *hopelessly;* 378.18 *inhibitively;* 704.11 *in reply;* 27.87 *mathematically;* 383.14 *resistingly;* 709.11 *uncooperatively*
negativeness 94.3; 708.1 *negation;* 383.1 *resistance;* 113.6 *uncooperativeness*
negative number 27.5 *number*
negative outlook 468.1 *underestimation*
negative reaction 385.1 *retaliation*
negative reinforcement 36.20 *conditioning*
negative resistance 39.15 *circuit function*
negative result 247.1 *failure*
negative review 719.3 *criticism*
negative stimulus 483.4
negative transference 36.27 *association of ideas*
negative veto 670.3 *nonacceptance*
negative vote 469.10 *vote*
negativism 36.19 *defence mechanism;* 611.1 *hopelessness;* 378.5 *inhibition;* 708.1 *negation*
negativist 708.9; 378.7 *hinderer;* 611.3 *hopeless person;* 113.11 *opposer*
negativistic 611.4 *hopeless*
negativity 708.1 *negation;* 94.3 *negativeness;* 753.1 *protest;* 704.1 *refutation;* 113.6 *uncooperativeness*
negator 704.5 *refuter*
neglect 233.5 *be incomplete;* 666.6 *be neglectful;* 672.6 *be ungrateful;* 618.2 *carelessness;* 637.15 *delay;* 245.9 *dilapidation;* 668.2 *disesteem;* 668.21 *disregard;* 247.1 *failure;* 463.13 *forget;* 341.1 *inaction;* 350.8 *nonuse;* 341.4 *not act;* 350.5 *not use;* 637.7 *refuse;* 463.4 *unthinkingness;* 408.3 *untidiness*
neglected 486.4 *bungled;* 350.4 *disused;* 233.4 *incomplete;* 124.2 *obscure;* 668.18 *undervalued;* 672.4 *unthanked*
neglectful 472.10 *careless;* 668.12 *disregardful;* 247.10 *failed;* 341.3 *inactive;* 666.4 *negligent;* 637.4 *procrastinating;* 463.10 *unthinking;* 408.15 *untidy*
neglectfully 233.6 *incompletely;* 666.7 *negligently;* 247.12 *unsuccessfully*
neglectfulness 666.1 *negligence*
negligée 551.22 *nightwear;* 551.16 *robe*
Negligence 666
negligence 666.1; 618.2 *carelessness;* 637.15 *delay;* 245.9 *dilapidation;* 247.1 *failure;* 262.5 *hastiness;* 274.2 *inaccuracy;* 341.1 *inaction;* 233.1 *incompleteness;* 350.8 *nonuse;* 615.1 *rashness;* 806.3 *sin;* 408.3 *untidiness*
negligent 666.4; 472.10, 618.8 *careless;* 486.3 *clumsy;* 668.12 *disregardful;* 247.10 *failed;* 262.3 *hasty;* 341.3 *inactive;* 637.4 *procrastinating;* 615.4 *rash;* 463.10 *unthinking;* 408.15 *untidy*
negligent dress 552.4 *dishabille*
negligently 666.7; 618.18 *carelessly;* 233.6 *incompletely;* 463.16 *obliviously;* 486.11 *unskilfully;* 247.12 *unsuccessfully;* 341.5 *without action*
negligently dressed 552.10 *in dishabille*
negligent person 666.3
negligible 159.7 *little;* 124.1 *unimportant*
negligibly 159.8 *in a small way;* 124.14 *unimportantly*
negotiability 754.1 *compromise*
negotiable 754.6 *compromising;* 755.7 *contractual;* 15.9, 746.8 *negotiated;* 316.17 *transferable;* 346.11 *workable*
negotiable instrument 780.14 *paper money*
negotiate 750.23 *arrange;* 776.3 *bargain;* 754.4 *compromise;* 734.11 *confer;* 713.6 *consult;* 755.5 *contract;* 318.11 *cross;* 13.11 *deal;* 15.12 *have an industrial dispute;* 748.1 *mediate;* 752.10 *offer to buy*
negotiate a loan 772.7 *borrow;* 771.5 *lend*
negotiate a trade-off 785.6 *pay*
negotiate a treaty 755.5 *contract*
negotiated 15.9; **746.8**; 750.12 *arranged;* 755.7, 776.18 *contractual;* 749.6 *pacificatory*
negotiated points 15.2 *industrial negotiations*
negotiated release 252.1 *safety*
negotiate peace 748.1 *mediate*
negotiating 750.12 *arranged;* 755.7 *contractual;* 15.9 *negotiated*
negotiating body 398.2 *representative body*
negotiating rights 15.2 *industrial negotiations*
Negotiation 746
negotiation 746.1; 776.9 *bargaining;* 754.1 *compromise;* 755.1 *contract;* 15.1 *industrial relations;* 748.2 *mediation*
negotiations 713.2 *consultation;* 15.4 *industrial dispute;* 746.1 *negotiation;* 734.5 *talks*
negotiation session 713.2 *consultation*
negotiator 746.4; 398.6 *agent;* 755.4 *contractor;* 398.1 *delegate;* 748.3 *mediator;* 749.3 *pacifist;* 776.10 *trader*
Negrillo 1.6 *race*
Negrito 1.6 *race*
Negro 532.2 *dark;* 1.6 *race*
Negroid 532.2 *dark;* 1.13 *racial*
Negroid race 1.6 *race*
Negroism 532.7 *blackness*
negro spiritual 18.5 *sacred music*
negus 558.7 *alcoholic drink*
Nehru jacket 551.11 *jacket*
neigh 515.1 *animal cry;* 515.4 *cry*
neighbour 147.6; 147.18 *juxtapose*
neighbourhood 97.4 *availability;* 565.2 *environment;* 565.15 *environmental;* 566.9 *group;* 564.2 *inhabitants;* 86.13 *locality;* 147.5 *near place;* 170.4 *surrounding;* 170.1 *surroundings*
neighbourhood watch 16.17 *police officer*
Neighbourhood Watch 252.3 *protector;* 253.4 *security forces*
neighbourhood watch 665.5 *watchfulness*
neighbourhood watchman 665.8 *watchful person*
neighbouring 86.18 *local;* 147.9 *near;* 239.2 *nearby*
neighbourliness 569.1 *friendship;* 654.1 *sociability*
neighbourly 392.35, 650.6 *benevolent;* 569.8 *friendly;* 654.15 *sociable*
nein! 708.23 *no!*
neither confirm nor deny 737.12 *keep secret*
neither good nor bad 216.3 *mediocre;* 235.5 *not bad*
neither here nor there 98.21 *away;* 100.18 *extraneously;* 109.7 *illogical;* 216.12 *mediumly;* 94.16 *nowhere*
neither hide nor hair 94.7 *not any*
neither more no less 119.6 *equal*
neither more nor less 698.39 *accurately;* 111.16 *equal*
nekton 70.5 *aquatic animal*
nelson 53.10 *score*
Nematoda 75.6 *worm*
nematode 75.6 *worm*
nematomorph 75.6 *worm*
Nematomorpha 75.6 *worm*
nembutsu 10.9 *prayer*
nem. con. 750.31 *in accord*
Nemertea 75.6 *worm*
nemertean 75.6 *worm*
Nemesis 714.6 *avenger;* 624.7 *gods and goddesses of anger;* 385.1 *retaliation;* 814.9 *retribution*
neoclassical 19.29 *realist*
neoclassic costume 551.5 *fancy dress*
neocolonialism 12.3 *governance*
neo-Darwinian 34.27 *evolutionary*
neo-Darwinism 34.16 *evolution*
neo-Darwinist 34.19 *life scientist*
neodymium-glass laser 28.26 *laser*
neoexpressionist 19.29 *realist*
neoimpressionist 19.29 *realist*
neo-Lamarckian 34.27 *evolutionary*
neo-Lamarckism 34.16 *evolution*
neolith 3.11 *relic*
Neolithic 296.15 *primal*
Neolithic period 284.4 *prehistoric age*
neological 295.10 *new*
neologically 295.21 *newly*
neologism 295.1 *newness;* 5.17 *word*
neologist 5.2 *linguist;* 295.9 *modern person*
neologistic 295.10 *new*
neologistical 295.10 *new;* 5.42 *worded*
neologistically 5.50 *lexically;* 295.21 *newly*
neologize 5.45 *use language*
neology 295.1 *newness*
neomycin 83.6 *fungal antibiotic*
neo-Nazi 586.1 *combatant*
neon lamp 28.25 *light source*
neon light 522.6 *electric light;* 39.20 *electron tube*
neon lighting 522.6 *electric light*
neophilia 295.1 *newness*
neophiliac 295.9 *modern person*
neophyte 130.14 *beginner;* 760.6 *convert;* 6.7 *learner;* 295.8 *new arrival;* 7.3 *religious person*
neophytic 295.10 *new*
neoplasm 260.12 *cancer*
neoplastic disease 260.4 *disease*
Neo-Platonic 101.10 *idealistic*
Neo-Platonically 101.14 *subjectively*
Neo-Platonism 101.5 *idealism;* 4.7 *school of thought*
Neo-Platonist 101.7 *believer in a nonmaterial world;* 4.11 *follower of a doctrine;* 4.14 *of a philosophy*
neoprene 422.4 *rubber*
neoromantic 19.29 *realist*
neosilicate 30.34 *mineral*
neotenous 73.13 *amphibian;* 34.26 *developmental*
neotenous amphibian 73.8 *young amphibian*
neoteny 34.15 *developmental biology;* 73.8 *young amphibian*
neoteric 295.9 *modern person*
nepenthe 394.5 *analgesic;* 343.10 *soporific*
nepenthes 592.6 *desensitizing substance*
nephanalysis 31.1 *meteorology*
nephew 567.13 *man in the family*
nephological 31.49 *cloudy*
nephology 31.1 *meteorology*
nephrologist 35.13 *medical specialist*
nephrology 35.3 *medical specialty*
ne plus ultra 232.1 *completeness;* 235.8 *exceller;* 230.3 *perfection*
nepotism 466.5 *favouritism;* 465.3 *injustice*
nepotistic 466.10 *discriminatory*
Neptune 323.7 *nautical person;* 29.16 *planet;* 91.4 *sea god*
Neptunian 29.36 *astronomical*
nerd 620.3 *boring person;* 659.4 *discourteous person;* 456.5 *ignorant person;* 486.10 *unskilled person;* 337.4 *weakling*
nerdy 456.6 *ignorant*
Nereid 8.5 *deity;* 91.4 *sea god*
Nereus 91.4 *sea god*
neritic 30.52 *coastal*
nerval 488.10 *sensory*
nerve 167.5 *boldness;* 660.2 *cheek;* 613.1 *courage;* 661.1 *defiance;* 228.2 *determination;* 492.7 *sense organ;* 488.4 *someone or something that feels;* 336.1 *strength*
nerve cell 488.4 *someone or something that feels*
nerve centre 173.4 *centre of activity;* 488.4 *someone or something that feels*
nerved 228.11 *determined*
nerve-ending 492.7 *sense organ;* 488.4 *someone or something that feels*
nerve fibre 488.4 *someone or something that feels*
nerveless 335.12 *impotent;* 639.3 *timid;* 489.6 *unfeeling;* 337.12 *weak-willed*
nervelessness 337.2 *indecisiveness*
nerve oneself 336.8 *strengthen*
nerve-racking 254.2 *unsafe*
nerves 612.2 *fearfulness;* 260.1 *ill health;* 461.6 *mental breakdown;* 342.7 *restlessness;* 36.12 *stress*
nerves of steel 613.1 *courage;* 228.2 *determination*

nervily 661.9 *defiantly;* 732.8 *shyly*
nerviness 327.1 *agitation;* 661.1 *defiance;* 639.13 *timidity*
nervosity 327.1 *agitation*
nervous 342.18 *active;* 327.15 *agitated;* 674.9 *blushing;* 616.4 *cautious;* 612.8 *fearful;* 625.4 *irascible;* 36.36 *psychologically disturbed;* 488.10 *sensory;* 732.1 *shy;* 337.12 *weak-willed*
nervous breakdown 461.6 *mental breakdown;* 260.17 *nervous disorder;* 36.10 *neurosis*
nervous disease 260.4 *disease*
nervous disorder 260.17; 36.9 *psychological disorder*
nervously 327.27 *agitatedly;* 328.19 *distractedly;* 612.15 *fearfully;* 625.9 *irascibly;* 639.16 *irresolutely;* 685.9 *moderately;* 732.8 *shyly;* 337.14 *weakly*
nervousness 327.1 *agitation;* 254.5 *danger;* 384.4 *defensiveness;* 612.2 *fearfulness;* 337.2 *indecisiveness;* 342.7 *restlessness;* 732.3 *shyness;* 639.13 *timidity*
nervous system 488.4 *someone or something that feels*
nervous tic 461.6 *mental breakdown;* 327.8 *spasm;* 36.12 *stress*
nervous wreck 612.6 *frightened person*
nervy 342.18 *active;* 327.15 *agitated;* 660.14 *cheeky;* 661.7 *defiant;* 612.8 *fearful;* 591.2 *oversensitive;* 639.3 *timid*
nescience 456.1 *ignorance;* 646.2 *naivety*
nescient 456.6 *ignorant*
ness 185.2 *projection*
nest 72.14; **72.24**; 565.3 *home;* 565.13 *lair;* 76.5 *larva;* 130.3 *source;* 565.18 *take up residence;* 208.4 *throng*
nestbox 72.14 *nest;* 72.19 *ornithology*
nest building 72.14 *nest*
nest egg 616.2 *insurance;* 243.10 *preparations;* 252.2 *protection;* 352.5 *reserves;* 439.1 *store;* 781.5 *wealth*
nesting 40.19 *computing terms*
nestle 490.8 *feel pleasure;* 593.27 *kiss;* 565.18 *take up residence*
nestling 130.15 *baby;* 555.4 *young animal;* 72.12 *young bird*
nest of tables 411.5 *layered thing*
Nestor 713.4 *adviser;* 296.2 *old people;* 4.12 *sage*
nest site 72.14 *nest*
net 55.7 *angle;* 49.3 *basketball equipment;* 193.2 *braid;* 74.15 *fish;* 765.15 *gainful;* 551.15 *headgear;* 633.11 *hunt;* 193.8 *interweave;* 765.5 *profit;* 440.8 *propertied;* 63.5 *real tennis;* 769.9, 788.7 *receive;* 700.13, 700.33 *snare;* 66.1 *soccer;* 645.2 *stratagem;* 215.10 *surplus;* 63.3 *tennis equipment;* 527.8 *transparent thing;* 379.2 *trap;* 165.6 *wrap;* 165.4 *wrapper*
net assets 440.5 *personal estate*
nether 155.6 *lower*
nethermost 175.3 *base*
nether regions 155.4 *low thing;* 101.1 *nonmaterial world;* 582.14 *the spiritual world*
nether world 8.12 *hell;* 101.1 *nonmaterial world;* 582.14 *the spiritual world*
netiquette 40.16 *Internet*
net player 63.6 *tennis player*
net position 63.4 *tennis terms*
net post 63.5 *real tennis*
net posts 63.11 *badminton equipment*
net profit 13.7 *corporation;* 813.5 *turnover*
net profits 788.2 *money received;* 765.5 *profit*
net receipts 765.4 *earnings;* 788.2 *money received;* 769.2 *something received*
net result 345.1 *effect;* 289.9 *sequel*
net return 765.4 *earnings*
net revenue 765.4 *earnings*
Netscape™ 40.16 *Internet*
net score 56.2 *golfing terms*
nett 203.4 *total*
netted 700.42 *trapped;* 42.10 *woven*
netting 193.2 *braid*
nettle 625.8 *make irascible;* 624.9 *offend;* 425.8 *sharp-pointed thing*
nettled 625.4 *irascible;* 624.15 *resentful*
nettle family 77.3 *seed plant*
nettle rash 260.13 *skin disease*
net weight 414.7 *weighing*
network 40.15; 373.2 *association;* 193.2 *braid;* 28.55, 39.13 *circuit;* 374.5 *combine;* 348.5 *find means;* 373.13 *intercommunicate;* 692.6 *telecommunication;* 404.4 *weave*
network architecture 40.15 *network*
network database 40.11 *application*
networked 374.7 *combined*
networking 747.3 *mutual relationship*
network television 692.24 *television broadcasting*
net worth 440.5 *personal estate*
neural computer 40.17 *artificial intelligence*
neuralgia 260.17 *nervous disorder;* 491.2 *painful condition*
neural net 40.17 *artificial intelligence*
neurasthenia 461.6 *mental breakdown*
neurilemma 260.17 *nervous disorder*
neurocomputer 40.17 *artificial intelligence*
neurohormone 33.16 *hormone*
neurohumour 33.16 *hormone*
neuroleptic 37.4 *drug type;* 37.15 *sedative*
neurological 35.22 *medical;* 488.10 *sensory*
neurological disease 260.4 *disease*
neurologist 35.13 *medical specialist*
neurology 35.3 *medical specialty;* 403.8 *science of structure*
neurone 488.4 *someone or something that feels*
neuropath 36.8 *disordered personality;* 260.19 *sick person*
neuropsychiatric 36.32 *psychological*
neuropsychiatrist 36.30 *psychiatrist*
neuropsychiatry 36.2 *psychiatry*
neuropsychology 36.1 *psychology*
neuropteran 76.10 *insectan*
neuroscience 34.1 *life science*
neurosis 36.10; 260.1 *ill health;* 461.6 *mental breakdown;* 36.9 *psychological disorder*
neurosurgeon 35.13 *medical specialist*
neurosurgery 35.9 *surgery*
neurotic 328.16 *deranged;* 36.8 *disordered personality;* 461.7 *insane person;* 461.13 *mentally ill;* 591.9 *oversensitive person;* 36.36 *psychologically disturbed*
neurotically 328.19 *distractedly;* 461.17 *insanely;* 36.39 *psychologically*
neurotic-depressive reaction 36.10 *neurosis*
neurotic disorder 36.10 *neurosis*
neuroticism 461.6 *mental breakdown;* 36.10 *neurosis*
neurotic personality 36.8 *disordered personality*
neuter 5.44 *grammatical;* 335.9 *make impotent;* 563.8 *make infertile;* 402.7 *material*
neutered 563.5 *rendered infertile;* 335.13 *unsexed*
neutering 563.2 *making infertile*
neutral 32.36 *acid;* 634.18 *avoiding;* 530.7 *colourless;* 473.4 *disinterested;* 28.52 *electric potential;* 39.36 *electronic;* 250.9 *free;* 250.7 *free person;* 533.1 *grey;* 618.9 *impartial;* 341.3 *inactive;* 618.6 *indifferent person;* 754.7 *irresolute;* 589.3 *pacifist;* 589.7 *peaceful;* 685.7 *politically moderate;* 801.7 *right;* 372.17 *unjoined*
neutral colour 529.1 *colour*
neutral-density filter 41.20 *filter*
neutral hue 530.1 *colourlessness*
neutralist 618.6 *indifferent person*
neutrality 473.1 *disinterestedness;* 250.1 *freedom;* 618.3 *impartiality;* 754.3 *irresolution;* 685.1 *moderation;* 566.11 *nation;* 589.1 *peace;* 634.12 *shyness;* 109.1 *unrelatedness*
neutralization 708.7 *cancelling out;* 32.14 *chemical reaction;* 347.1 *counteraction;* 335.1 *powerlessness;* 337.1 *weakness*
neutralize 708.16 *cancel out;* 347.3 *counteract;* 357.8 *destroy;* 110.8 *interrelate;* 343.14 *make inactive;* 685.4 *moderate;* 32.26 *react;* 394.19 *remedy;* 335.7 *remove power from*
neutralized 32.41 *analytic;* 708.20 *cancelled*
neutralizer 347.1 *counteraction*
neutralizing 708.7 *cancelling out;* 347.4 *counteracting*
neutrally 530.9 *colourlessly;* 473.8 *disinterestedly;* 250.20 *freely;* 372.22 *in isolation;* 754.9 *irresolutely*
neutral nation 85.1 *country*
neutral stick 58.3 *ice hockey*
neutral tint 530.1 *colourlessness;* 533.4 *greyness*
neutral zone 58.3 *ice hockey*
neutrino 28.77 *elementary particle;* 159.2 *little thing*
neutron 28.65 *atom;* 28.77 *elementary particle;* 159.2 *little thing;* 402.4 *matter*
neutron bomb 587.16 *bomb;* 334.8 *nuclear power*
neutron number 28.69 *isotope*
neutron star 29.11 *stellar birth*
neutrophil 431.4 *blood*
neve 62.5 *rock face*
never 709.12 *no!;* 94.15 *not ever;* 619.14 *wonderful!*
never! 708.24
never again 131.28 *conclusively;* 197.24 *once*
never a one 94.6 *absence*
never cease 279.5 *be eternal;* 202.9 *be infinite*
never despair 640.8 *hold out;* 638.11 *persist*
never die 202.9 *be infinite*
never end 620.6 *be boring;* 270.5 *be diffuse;* 202.9 *be infinite*
never-ending 132.11 *continuous;* 270.3 *diffuse;* 202.3, 279.8 *eternal*
never-failing 246.13 *successful*
never full 688.6 *gluttonous*
never give up hope 640.8 *hold out*
never ill 259.1 *healthy*
never learn 459.6 *be foolish*
never let go 360.6 *retain*
never look back 302.9 *maintain progress*
never mind 124.15 *no matter!*
never mind! 618.21
never-never land 477.8 *dreamland*
never on time 294.9 *late*
never-resting 342.20 *industrious*
never say die 610.9 *be hopeful;* 336.7 *be strong;* 134.8 *go on!;* 640.8 *hold out;* 638.11 *persist*
never say die! 610.16
never-slacking 342.20 *industrious*
never-sleeping 342.20 *industrious*
never sober 690.5 *drunken*
never solved 696.2 *unexplained*
never stop 338.2 *be full of vigour;* 342.15 *try*
never surrender 638.11 *persist*
nevertheless 317.16 *how*
never the same 227.13 *changeable;* 114.5 *diverse*
never-tiring 342.20 *industrious*
never touch 684.5 *be self-restrained*
never touch a drop 689.3 *be sober*
never vary 632.16 *have a habit*
new 295.10; **350.2**; 116.4 *dissimilar;* 130.32 *embryonic;* 211.9 *extra;* 538.4 *fresh;* 295.21 *newly;* 126.5 *novel;* 448.9 *original;* 487.1 *unaccustomed*
New Age 295.2 *trendiness*
New-Age traveller 100.5, 118.7 *nonconformist;* 227.7 *person who moves around*
New American Bible 295.7 *new thing*
new arrival 100.7; **295.8**; 289.5 *successor*
new-baked bread 502.2 *fragrant thing*
new ball 53.7 *bat*
new beginning 761.2 *restoration*
new beginnings 130.13
new birth 554.5 *life cycle;* 393.10 *revival*
new blood 289.5 *successor*
newborn 130.15 *baby;* 308.17 *beginning;* 554.15 *born;* 130.32 *embryonic;* 295.12 *immature*
newborn babe 805.4 *innocent person*
newborn baby 295.8 *new arrival*
new boy 130.14 *beginner;* 314.7 *entrant;* 100.7, 295.8 *new arrival;* 289.5 *successor*
new broom 342.10 *busy person;* 295.8 *new arrival;* 289.5 *successor*
new business 484.1 *plan*
Newcastle-upon-Tyne 87.4 *British cities*
new chapter 130.13 *new beginnings*
new city 86.10 *urban area*
New Comedy 21.12 *comedy*
newcomer 314.7 *entrant;* 805.4 *innocent person;* 100.7, 295.8 *new arrival;* 289.5 *successor*
New Consciousness 36.3 *psychiatric treatment*
new convert 295.8 *new arrival*
New Critic 17.15 *literary person*
New Criticism 719.3 *criticism*
New Deal 295.7 *new thing;* 244.11 *reformism*
New Dealer 244.12 *reformer*
New Democratic Party 12.6 *political party*
new departure 130.13 *new beginnings;* 126.1 *originality*
New Drama 21.10 *theatre movements*
new edition 244.8 *better thing;* 561.2 *print;* 112.5 *repeat*
newel 186.3 *vertical thing*
newel post 186.3 *vertical thing*
new energy 393.10 *revival*
New England clam chowder 25.43 *US dish*
New England dialect 5.26 *dialect*
New Englander 564.10 *US inhabitant*
New English Bible 7.12 *religious text*
new face 314.7 *entrant;* 100.7 *new arrival*
new-fallen snow 531.9 *white thing*
newfangled 295.11 *unfamiliar;* 5.42 *worded*
newfangled expression 5.17 *word*
newfangledness 295.1 *newness*
new-fledged 555.11 *young*
new franc 780.11 *national coins*
New General Catalogue 29.6 *star catalogue*
new generation 295.6 *avant-garde*
new girl 130.14 *beginner;* 314.7 *entrant*
new high 121.4 *summit*
new hope 393.10 *revival*
new idea 244.8 *better thing*
New Jerusalem 8.11 *heaven*
New Labour 12.6 *political party*
new-laid 554.15 *born*
new lamps for old 759.3 *something in exchange*
Newland's octaves 32.6 *chemical element*
new leaf 295.5 *fresh start;* 244.5 *improvement;* 130.13 *new beginnings*
new life 581.5 *refreshment;* 393.10 *revival*
New Look 295.2 *trendiness*
new look 553.1 *fashion;* 295.5 *fresh start;* 295.14 *renewed;* 393.8 *repair*
newly 295.21; **350.13**; 295.10 *new;* 126.8 *originally*
newly born 554.15 *born*
newly fledged 72.22 *newly hatched*
newly hatched 72.22
newly opened 130.37 *enrolled*
newly produced 295.10 *new*
newlywed 570.21 *married*
newlyweds 570.9 *married couple*
new-made 295.10 *new*
new man 760.6 *convert;* 250.7 *free person;* 567.14 *liberated man;* 295.9 *modern person;* 591.8 *sensitive person*
new mathematics 27.1 *mathematics*
new maths 295.7 *new thing*
new member 314.7 *entrant;* 295.8 *new arrival*
new money 781.6 *money*
new moon 29.17 *moon;* 295.7 *new thing*
new-mown hay 502.2 *fragrant thing*
Newness 295
newness 295.1; **350.9**; 126.1, 448.4 *originality*
New Orleans 87.2 *American cities*
new page 130.13 *new beginnings*
new penny 780.9 *British money*
new poor 782.11 *the poor*
new production 295.1 *newness;* 21.14 *production*
new recruit 295.8 *new arrival*
new resident 100.7 *new arrival*
new resolution 244.5 *improvement*
News 741
news 741.1; 713.1 *advice;* 692.25 *broadcast material;* 123.2 *important matter;* 693.1 *information;* 693.4 *mass communication;* 447.3 *matter of interest;* 711.1 *warning*
news account 741.2 *news event*
news agency 741.7 *press agency;* 693.8 *source of information*
newsagent 741.11 *news source;* 778.13 *retailer*
news analysis 741.9 *news story*
news article 741.9 *news story*
news beat 741.11 *news source*
news blackout 399.2 *censorship*
newsboy 741.11 *news source*
news brief 741.9 *news story*
news bulletin 741.9 *news story*
news bureau chief 741.4 *journalist*
news camera crew 741.4 *journalist*
news cameraman 741.4 *journalist*
newscast 693.4 *mass communication;* 741.6 *radio news*

newscaster 692.29 *broadcaster*; 693.9 *informant*; 741.4 *journalist*; 578.1 *worker*
newscasting 741.3 *reporting*
news commentator 693.9 *informant*; 741.4 *journalist*
news conference 693.4 *mass communication*; 741.2 *news event*; 740.8 *public relations*
news coverage 550.20 *fixing*; 693.4 *mass communication*
news crew 741.4 *journalist*
newsdealer 741.11 *news source*
news desk 741.8 *newsroom*
news dispatch 741.9 *news story*
news documentary 692.25 *broadcast material*
news editor 740.11 *newspaperman*
news event 741.2
news flash 741.9 *news story*
news gathering 741.3 *reporting*
newsgroup 40.16 *Internet*
news happening 741.2 *news event*
newshound 693.9 *informant*; 741.4 *journalist*
newsie 741.11 *news source*
news interpreter 719.7
news item 722.2 *article*; 550.20 *fixing*; 693.4 *mass communication*; 741.9 *news story*
newsletter 740.5 *journal*; 741.11 *news source*; 276.7 *periodical*
newsmagazine 740.5 *journal*; 741.5 *mass communication*
newsman 692.29 *broadcaster*; 741.4 *journalist*; 740.11 *newspaperman*; 744.9 *recorder*; 578.1 *worker*
news media 741.5 *mass communication*
newsmonger 693.10 *informer*
news organization 741.5 *mass communication*
news outlet 741.5 *mass communication*
newspaper 740.4; 741.5 *mass communication*
newspapering 740.3 *journalism*; 741.3 *reporting*
newspaperman 740.11; 741.4 *journalist*
newspaper proprietor 740.11 *newspaperman*
newspaperwoman 740.11 *newspaperman*
newspaper world 740.3 *journalism*
newspeak 479.5 *equivocalness*; 729.1 *faculty of speech*; 5.20 *jargon word*
news photographer 741.4 *journalist*
news pool 741.4 *journalist*
newsprint 741.11 *news source*; 435.3 *paper*
newsprint ink 532.8 *black pigment*
news programme 741.9 *news story*
newsreader 692.29 *broadcaster*; 693.9 *informant*; 741.4 *journalist*
newsreel 751.6 *radio news*
news release 693.4 *mass communication*; 741.9 *news story*
news report 692.25 *broadcast material*; 741.9 *news story*
news reporter 741.4 *journalist*; 740.11 *newspaperman*
news reporting 741.3 *reporting*
news review 741.9 *news story*
newsroom 741.8
news roundup 692.25 *broadcast material*
news service 741.7 *press agency*
newssheet 740.5 *journal*; 741.11 *news source*
news source 741.11; 719.7 *news interpreter*
news staff 741.4 *journalist*
news stall 741.11 *news source*
newsstand 741.11 *news source*; 779.9 *stall*
news story 741.9
news style 741.9 *news story*
news summary 692.25 *broadcast material*
news syndicate 693.8 *source of information*
new start 295.5 *fresh start*
news update 741.9 *news story*
new supply 393.10 *revival*
news vendor 741.11 *news source*
newswoman 692.29 *broadcaster*; 740.11 *newspaperman*
newsworthy 693.17; 741.14 *journalistic*; 123.6 *notable*
newsy 734.14 *conversational*; 741.14 *journalistic*; 693.17 *newsworthy*
new tack 130.13 *new beginnings*
new technology 356.2 *manufacture*; 352.1 *means*
new term 5.17 *word*
New Testament 7.12 *religious text*
new thing 295.7
New Thought 295.2 *trendiness*
newtlike 73.13 *amphibian*
new to 487.1 *unaccustomed*
Newtonian mechanics 28.2 *classical physics*; 402.6 *natural science*
Newtonian telescope 29.24 *telescope*
new to the job 295.12 *immature*
new town 295.7 *new thing*; 86.11 *settlement*; 87.9 *town*
New Wave 18.9 *popular music*; 295.2 *trendiness*
new way 631.7 *way*
new woman 568.11 *liberated woman*
new word 5.17 *word*
New World 86.7 *regions of the world*
New World monkeys 71.16 *primate*
new wrinkle 295.1 *newness*; 295.7 *new thing*
New Year 295.7 *new thing*
New Year Honours 813.1 *reward*
New Year's Day 298.6 *annually celebrated day*
New York 87.3; 87.2 *American cities*; 86.10 *urban area*
New York City Ballet 22.12 *ballet companies*
New Yorker 564.10 *US inhabitant*
next 147.9 *near*; 289.12 *succeeding*
next-door 86.18 *local*; 147.9, 147.12 *near*; 239.2 *nearby*
next-door neighbour 147.6 *neighbour*
next generation 295.6 *avant-garde*
next-generation 345.10 *caused*
next in line 769.6 *beneficiary*; 289.5 *successor*
next man in 289.5 *successor*
next month 283.1 *future time*; 283.14 *in the future*
next of kin 474.4 *expectant person*
next step 302.14 *development*
next to 239.8 *nearby*
next week 283.1 *future time*; 283.14 *in the future*
next world 582.14 *the spiritual world*
next year 283.1 *future time*; 283.14 *in the future*
nexus 373.2 *association*; 123.3 *chief thing*; 132.2 *consecution*; 492.6 *contiguity*; 287.3 *critical time*; 373.4 *means of connection*
NFC 46.1 *football*
NFL 46.1 *football*
NHR 32.17 *analysis*
NHS hospital 35.10 *hospital*
NHS trust hospital 35.10 *hospital*
nib 425.8 *sharp-pointed thing*
nibble 495.3 *appetizer*; 593.14 *communication of love*; 40.19 *computing terms*; 557.21 *eat*; 557.14 *mouthful*; 495.9, 557.23 *taste*
nibbler 557.18 *eater*; 495.5 *taster*
nibbles 25.10 *snack*
nibbling 557.3 *delicate eating*
Nibelung 159.4 *little person*
niblick 56.4 *golf club*
Nicaragua 88.5 *other major lakes*
nice 273.5, 698.21 *accurate*; 650.6 *benevolent*; 665.9 *careful*; 256.16 *clean*; 658.7 *courteous*; 797.3 *kind*; 235.5 *not bad*; 241.1, 490.6 *pleasant*; 255.14 *purified*
nice distinction 273.3 *accurate thing*
nice little earner 781.5 *wealth*
nicely 797.23; 658.14 *courteously*
niceness 698.8 *accuracy*; 650.1 *benevolence*; 658.1 *courtesy*; 665.4 *fastidiousness*; 797.10 *kindness*; 241.6 *pleasantness*
nice point 713.3 *precept*
nice predicament 264.5 *predicament*
nicety 273.1, 698.8 *accuracy*
niche 409.6 *category*; 183.3 *cavity*; 137.2 *class*; 410.2 *compartment*; 34.18 *ecology*; 565.2 *environment*; 736.2 *hiding place*; 62.5 *rock face*
nichts 195.2 *nothing*
nick 309.4 *closed place*; 146.2, 146.5 *crack*; 251.11 *detain*; 183.4, 183.10 *notch*; 700.33 *snare*; 774.12 *steal*; 773.10 *take away*; 773.3 *taking away*; 815.2 *the inside*
nicked 16.59 *stolen*
nickel 780.8 *American money*; 28.59 *ferromagnetism*
nickel coinage 780.13 *coinage*
nickel defence 46.10 *defence*
nickelic 32.34 *elemental*
nickeliferous 32.34 *elemental*
nickelous 32.34 *elemental*
nickel silver 700.6 *imitation*
nicker 780.9 *British money*; 515.4 *cry*
nicking 774.1 *stealing*; 773.2 *taking back*
nickles and dimes 780.4 *change*
nickname 721.8 *name*
nicknames for lovers 593.12
nicknaming 721.7 *nomenclature*
nick of time 287.3 *critical time*
nick someone for 700.30 *be fraudulent*
nicotine 496.7 *tobacco*; 394.7 *tonic*
nicotinic acid 33.13 *vitamin*
nictitation 519.2 *poor sight*
nidicolous 72.22 *newly hatched*
nidification 72.14 *nest*
nidifugous 72.22 *newly hatched*
nidify 72.24 *nest*
nidus 76.5 *larva*
niece 568.12 *woman in the family*
niello 532.11 *blacken*; 532.8 *black pigment*
Nietzschean 4.11 *follower of a doctrine*; 4.14 *of a philosophy*
Nietzscheanism 4.7 *school of thought*
NIFE cell 32.19 *electrochemistry*
niff 503.1 *stench*; 503.5 *stink*
niffy 503.3 *stinking*
Niflheim 8.12 *hell*
niftily 332.14 *swiftly*
nifty 332.1 *swift*
nifty pace 332.8 *speed*
Niger 90.5 *other major rivers*
niggard 376.36 *hoarder*; 682.5 *miser*
niggardliness 682.3 *parsimony*; 683.1 *selfishness*
niggardly 218.1 *insufficient*; 682.1 *mean*; 682.9 *meanly*; 683.4 *selfish*; 206.6 *sparse*
nigger in the woodpile 378.2 *obstacle*
nigger-rigging 238.5 *waste of effort*
niggertown 87.7 *city district*
niggle 670.18 *find fault*
niggling 670.6, 670.28 *fault-finding*; 124.4 *trivial*
niggun 10.8 *hymn*
nigh 283.11 *future*; 147.9, 147.12 *near*
night 291.2; 532.7 *blackness*; 521.6 *that which makes invisible*
night and day 132.19 *continuously*; 113.3 *opposites*; 326.1 *oscillation*
night attack 381.12 *military attack*
night-blind 519.9 *weak-sighted*
night blindness 523.1 *darkness*; 519.2 *poor sight*; 33.14 *vitamin deficiency disease*
nightcap 685.2 *moderator*; 551.22 *nightwear*; 313.9 *parting*; 343.10 *soporific*
nightclothes 551.22 *nightwear*
nightclub 291.5 *night thing*; 21.16 *theatre*
night court 16.21 *US court*
night court judge 16.24 *US judge*
night dew 429.6 *dew*
nightdress 552.4 *dishabille*; 551.22 *nightwear*
nightfall 291.1 *evening*; 305.4 *fall*
night falls 523.13 *become dark*
night fighter 586.31 *military aircraft*
night glasses 518.10 *visual aid*
nightgown 552.4 *dishabille*
nightie 552.4 *dishabille*; 551.22 *nightwear*
nightingale 516.5 *melodist*; 72.6 *songbird*
night lamping 60.2 *hunting*
nightlife 291.5 *night thing*
nightlight 522.7 *lantern*
nightly 298.12 *cyclic*; 298.16 *cyclically*; 291.6, 291.7 *evening*
night mail 321.7 *train*
nightmare 711.3 *false alarm*; 477.5 *fantasy*; 612.5 *frightener*; 96.2 *illusion*; 291.5 *night thing*
night nurse 35.16 *nurse*
night patrol 586.14 *armed forces*
nightpiece 19.10 *art subject*
nights 291.7 *evening*; 111.20 *regularly*
night safe 439.4 *storage*
night school 6.12 *educational institution*; 291.5 *night thing*
night shift 291.5 *night thing*
night-shift work 15.2 *industrial negotiations*
nightshirt 551.22 *nightwear*
night sister 35.16 *nurse*
night soil 258.4 *dirt*; 560.5 *faeces*
night sounds 254.6 *danger signal*
nightspot 21.16 *theatre*
night thing 291.5
Night-Time 291
night-time 291.6 *evening*; 294.2 *late hour*; 291.2 *night*
night vision 518.1 *vision*
night watch 586.14 *armed forces*; 384.14 *guard*; 291.3 *midnight*
night watchman 384.14 *guard*; 518.11 *observer*; 309.5 *person who closes*; 252.3 *protector*; 253.3 *security officer*; 53.4 *team*
nightwear 551.22; 552.4 *dishabille*
nigrescence 532.7 *blackness*
nigrescent 532.1 *black*
nigritude 532.7 *blackness*
nigrosine 532.8 *black pigment*
nihil 195.2 *nothing*
nihilism 588.2 *anarchism*; 408.8 *lawlessness*; 4.7 *school of thought*
nihilist 588.3 *anarchist*; 357.6 *destroyer*; 4.11 *follower of a doctrine*; 753.10 *lawbreaking*; 651.8 *malefactor*; 341.2 *nonacting person*; 4.14 *of a philosophy*; 753.5 *seditionist*; 408.11 *troublemaker*
nihilistic 588.7 *anarchistic*; 408.20 *disorderly*
nihility 98.1 *absence*; 94.2, 195.3 *nothingness*
nihil obstat 757.2 *permit*
Nihongi 7.12 *religious text*
Nikaya 7.12 *religious text*
Nikkei Dow Index 14.2 *stock exchange*
nikkyo 52.10 *aikido*
nil 94.2 *nothingness*; 195.1, 195.6 *zero*
nil desperandum 610.16 *never say die!*
Nile 90.5 *other major rivers*
Nile green 538.1 *green*
nill 27.10 *zero*
Nilometer 433.19 *measuring instrument*
Nilotic 1.13 *racial*
Nilotic type 1.6 *race*
nimble 342.18 *active*; 485.6 *skilful*; 332.1 *swift*
nimble-fingered 485.6 *skilful*
nimble-footed 332.1 *swift*
nimbleness 342.3; 332.8 *speed*
nimblewit 599.6 *humorist*
nimble-witted 599.10 *humorous*; 332.2 *mentally quick*
nimbly 342.22 *actively*; 332.14 *swiftly*
nimbostratous 31.49 *cloudy*
nimbostratus 31.18 *cloud*
nimbus 31.18 *cloud*; 522.12 *highlight*
nimiety 219.1 *excess*
Nimrod 330.16 *archer*; 60.4, 633.6 *hunter*
nincompoop 459.3 *foolish person*; 457.3 *unintelligent person*
nine 201.5; 201.16 *ninth*; 27.9 *numeral*
nine-bob note 699.16 *false thing*
nine centuries 201.9 *treble figures*
nine-day wonder 201.5 *nine*; 619.5 *person of wonder*; 149.4 *short thing*; 278.2 *transient thing*
ninefold 201.16 *ninth*
nine-hole course 56.1 *golf*
ninepins 51.4 *bowling*; 69.7 *other games*
niner 201.5 *nine*
nineteenth 196.4 *less than one*
nineteenth hole 56.2 *golfing terms*; 581.7 *refreshments*
ninetieth 196.4 *less than one*; 201.19 *twentieth*
Ninette de Valois 22.14 *famous ballet dancers*
ninety 201.8 *twenty and over*
ninety-nine per cent 205.5 *largest part*
ninety-pound weakling 337.4 *weakling*
ninny 459.3 *foolish person*; 646.3 *naive person*; 457.3 *unintelligent person*
ninth 201.16; 27.75 *equal*; 196.4 *less than one*; 18.16 *musical note*; 201.5 *nine*
ninth part 201.5 *nine*
niobic 32.34 *elemental*
niobous 32.34 *elemental*
nip 495.3 *appetizer*; 593.14 *communication of love*; 310.9 *converge*; 496.6 *cordial*; 558.13, 690.13 *drink*; 313.4 *hurry off*; 491.11 *inflict pain*; 492.3 *press*; 492.11 *touch*; 425.16 *use a sharp tool*
nip along 332.4 *be swift*
nip and tuck 119.12 *equally*; 285.14 *equal with*; 547.2 *plastic surgery*
nip-and-tuck 285.11 *equal*; 285.4 *equal race*; 119.8 *on equal terms*
nip-and-tuck race 119.2 *equilibrium*

Nipigon 88.5 *other major lakes*
nip in the air 494.7 *cold weather*
nip in the bud 481.3 *deflect;* 378.8 *hinder;* 382.16 *kill;* 293.9 *prepare;* 357.11 *ruin*
nip off 313.4 *hurry off*
nipper 555.9 *child;* 561.6 *progeny*
nippers 425.8 *sharp-pointed thing;* 438.1 *tool;* 360.3 *tools for gripping*
nippiness 494.1 *coldness;* 494.7 *cold weather*
nipping 558.1 *drinking*
nipple 182.2 *bulge;* 71.2 *mammalian characteristic*
nippy 342.18 *active;* 494.8 *cold;* 31.55 *cool;* 338.4 *vigorous*
nirvana 463.5 *death;* 8.1 *divinity;* 263.1 *ease;* 283.3 *future condition;* 8.11 *heaven;* 301.2 *repose*
nirvanic 463.9 *blank*
nishmat 10.9 *prayer*
nisi prius 16.6 *legal process*
Nisus and Euryalus 569.7 *famous friendships*
nit 258.4 *dirt;* 76.3 *pest;* 486.10 *unskilled person*
NIT Championship 49.1 *basketball*
nit-pick 678.11 *criticize;* 116.6 *differentiate;* 670.18 *find fault;* 702.13 *quibble;* 471.12 *scrutinize*
nit-picker 273.4 *accurate person;* 670.12 *critic;* 702.6 *sophist*
nit-picking 273.5 *accurate;* 471.2 *close attention;* 222.10 *detailed;* 678.1 *disparagement;* 678.15 *disparaging;* 670.6, 670.28 *fault-finding;* 576.11 *laborious;* 702.4, 702.9 *quibbling;* 124.4 *trivial;* 264.14 *troublesome*
nitrate 43.13 *fertilizer;* 32.26 *react*
nitrates 562.3 *fertilizer*
nitrile 422.4 *rubber*
nitrogen 33.15 *essential element*
nitrogenous 32.34 *elemental*
nitrogenous base 34.12 *molecular biology;* 33.10 *nucleoside*
nitroglycerine 357.7 *agent of destruction;* 587.15 *explosive*
nitrometer 26.8 *meter*
nitrometric 26.16 *micrometric*
nitrous oxide 394.5 *analgesic*
nitty-gritty 123.3 *chief thing;* 99.2 *essential content;* 93.5 *fact;* 172.5 *inner nature;* 205.5 *largest part;* 694.1 *meaning;* 139.4 *specifications*
nitwit 459.3 *foolish person;* 457.3 *unintelligent person;* 486.10 *unskilled person*
nix 708.1 *negation;* 708.23, 709.12 *no!;* 195.2 *nothing*
nixed 708.18 *rejected*
nkui 25.53 *African dish*
NMR scan 35.7 *diagnosis*
no 708.1 *negation;* 195.11 *none;* 753.1 *protest;* 399.1 *veto;* 469.10 *vote;* 195.6 *zero*
no! 704.13; 708.23; 709.12
no. 194.1 *number*
No. 8 64.4 *rugby player*
no-account 124.2 *obscure*
no Adonis 546.2 *ugly person*
no aggro 589.1 *peace*
no allegiance 250.3 *independence*
no answer 247.1 *failure*
no apologies 809.1 *impenitence*
no appeal 647.1 *severity*
Noatun 8.11 *heaven*
no authority 588.1 *anarchy*
nob 573.1 *nobleman*
no backbone 639.13 *timidity*
no-ball 53.8 *delivery;* 53.10 *score;* 274.13 *sporting error*
nobble 699.25 *be fraudulent;* 335.8 *overpower;* 774.12 *steal*
nobbling 245.11 *hurt*
no beauty 546.2 *ugly person*
Nobel Peace Prize 589.4
Nobel Prize 813.2 *prize*
no better 245.12 *deteriorated*
Nob Hill 121.4 *summit*
no bid 69.3 *card game terms*
nobility 573.2 *aristocracy;* 396.1 *authority;* 235.7 *elite;* 795.2 *good morals;* 545.1 *gorgeousness;* 566.9 *group;* 654.7 *human society;* 573.3 *nobleness;* 622.5 *stateliness;* 121.7 *the best people;* 235.6 *worth*
noble 573.4 *aristocratic;* 396.12 *authoritative;* 123.4 *bigwig;* 780.10 *former British money;* 799.4 *honourable;* 123.5 *important;* 400.12 *masterful;* 795.8 *moral;* 255.12 *morally pure;* 573.1 *nobleman;* 622.19 *stately;* 473.5 *unselfish;* 803.5 *virtuous;* 235.1 *worthy*
noble art of self-defence 52.2 *boxing*
noble family 573.3 *nobleness*
noble gas 32.6 *chemical element*
nobleman 573.1; 400.1 *master;* 566.10 *member of society*
nobleness 573.3; 799.1 *probity;* 473.2 *unselfishness;* 803.1 *virtue*
noble savage 646.3 *naive person*
noblesse oblige 658.1 *courtesy*
noblewoman 566.10 *member of society;* 573.1 *nobleman*
no bloody good 238.1 *useless*
nobly 396.23 *authoritatively;* 799.7 *honourably;* 622.36 *majestically;* 400.16 *masterfully;* 473.9 *unselfishly;* 255.18, 803.9 *virtuously;* 622.33 *with dignity;* 235.11 *worthily*
no boaster 623.16 *humble person*
nobody 98.7; 94.6 *absence;* 124.10, 195.5 *nonentity;* 195.2 *nothing;* 157.5 *shallow person*
nobody else 197.1 *one*
nobody present 98.7 *nobody*
nobody's darling 594.8 *hated person*
nobody's fool 4.12 *sage*
nobody there 98.7 *nobody*
no break 342.6 *business*
nobs 573.2 *aristocracy;* 121.7 *the best people*
no buts 698.35 *truly*
no buts about it 95.14 *certainly*
no can do 103.13 *impossible!*
no case 16.42 *acquittal*
no catch 250.12 *unconditional*
no chance 103.13 *impossible!;* 107.6 *poor chance;* 709.11 *uncooperatively*
no change 225.1 *permanence;* 111.6 *regularity*
no chicken 556.13 *middle-aged*
no choice 469.8 *choice;* 386.1 *compulsion*
nock 183.4, 183.10 *notch*
no-claims bonus 320.21 *miscellaneous motoring terms*
no common ground 372.4 *disunity;* 116.2 *unlikeness*
no comparison 116.2 *unlikeness*
no compromise 641.6 *determination;* 647.1 *severity*
no connection 109.5 *misconnection*
no-count 124.2 *obscure*
no courage 341.1 *inaction*
noctilucent cloud 31.18 *cloud*
nocturnal 523.8 *dark;* 291.6 *evening;* 70.15 *of animals*
nocturnal enuresis 560.3 *urination*
nocturnally 523.15 *darkly;* 291.7 *evening*
nocturne 19.10 *art subject*
nod 669.12 *accept;* 693.7 *advice;* 669.1 *approval;* 261.5 *be fatigued;* 367.9 *bow;* 750.28 *consent;* 367.16 *courtesy;* 658.13 *defer to;* 667.4 *mark of respect;* 326.11 *rock;* 667.19 *take off one's hat to*
nod and a wink 699.9 *falsification*
nodding 658.4 *deference;* 658.9 *deferential;* 245.12 *deteriorated;* 261.1 *fatigued;* 667.11 *in a respectful stance*
nodding donkey 437.6 *oil*
nodding off 343.4 *not awake*
noddle 442.7 *brain*
node 27.39 *angle;* 492.6 *contiguity;* 418.7 *hard substance;* 40.15 *network;* 416.4 *solid body;* 77.5 *stem;* 28.12, 326.5 *wave*
no desire for 618.1 *indifference*
no difference 111.1 *sameness*
no dilution 255.8 *simplicity*
no discipline 408.8 *lawlessness*
no distance 147.2 *short distance*
nod of approval 669.1 *approval;* 757.1 *permission*
nod off 339.4 *be inert;* 489.11 *be unfeeling;* 343.13 *sleep*
nod of the head 742.3 *gesture*
nod one's head 742.11 *gesture*
nodose 420.2 *coarse*
nodosity 418.5 *hardness;* 420.6 *roughness*
nodular 420.2 *coarse*
nodularity 418.5 *hardness*
nodule 418.7 *hard substance;* 416.4 *solid body*
nodus 264.4 *problem*
no easy task 264.3 *difficult task*
Noel 10.16 *religious festival*
no encouragement 481.6 *dissuasion*
no end 681.9 *extravagantly;* 208.13 *numerously*
no end of 202.3 *eternal;* 208.8 *numberless*
no end to 148.1 *long*
no entry 128.1 *exclusion*
noetic 442.9 *mental*
no exception 127.1 *inclusion*
no fear 103.13 *impossible!;* 709.11 *uncooperatively*
no fixed abode 733.5 *place of residence;* 109.1 *unrelatedness*
no flies on 645.4 *cunning*
no frills 95.8 *practical;* 255.16 *simple*
no fun 620.2 *boring thing*
no gentleman 659.4 *discourteous person*
noggin 442.7 *brain;* 410.13 *drinking vessel*
no gift for 486.8 *unskilfulness*
no-go 166.5 *limited;* 87.14 *urban;* 238.1 *useless*
no-go area 87.7 *city district;* 128.3 *exclusion zone;* 166.2 *limiting factor;* 103.7 *obstacle;* 251.1 *restraint;* 372.2 *setting apart;* 264.8 *snag;* 86.10 *urban area*
no going back 809.1 *impenitence*
no good 611.8 *bad;* 236.2 *inferior;* 238.1 *useless*
no-good 766.6 *loser*
no great matter 124.8 *trifle*
no great shakes 216.3, 618.10 *mediocre;* 231.8 *ordinariness;* 124.8 *trifle;* 124.4 *trivial*
no grit 639.13 *timidity*
no hangover 689.6 *sobriety*
no harm done 230.1 *perfect*
no hassle 589.1 *peace*
no holding back 636.2 *eager*
no holds barred 250.6 *liberality;* 739.3 *openness;* 585.1 *war*
no-holds-barred 250.12 *unconditional;* 52.15 *wrestling*
no-holds-barred wrestling 52.5 *wrestling*
no hope 611.1 *hopelessness*
no-hoper 303.21 *backslider;* 247.5 *failing person;* 289.8 *follower;* 611.3 *hopeless person;* 122.6 *inferior;* 766.6 *loser;* 249.5 *person in adversity;* 470.9 *rejected person*
no hurry 580.1 *leisure;* 333.8 *slowness*
no ifs or buts 93.22 *really*
no illusion 698.6 *authenticity*
no imitation 698.6 *authenticity*
no inclination for 596.1 *dislike*
noise 507.3 *audibility;* 328.5 *commotion;* 517.2 *dissonant noise;* 507.1 *loudness;* 692.19 *radio reception;* 504.8 *something heard;* 28.17 *sound;* 692.23 *television reception;* 39.14 *terminal*
noise abroad 740.13 *make public*
noiseless 506.3 *silent*
noiselessly 506.5 *silently*
noiselessness 506.4 *silence*
noisily 507.9 *loudly;* 514.20 *vociferously*
noisiness 507.2 *outcry*
noisome 236.3 *bad;* 236.5 *harmful;* 500.5 *odorous;* 236.4 *poor;* 364.8 *repulsive;* 503.3 *stinking;* 258.8 *unclean*
noisomely 364.11 *repulsively*
noisy 507.6 *loud;* 514.16 *vociferous*
no joke 123.2 *important matter;* 643.4 *solemnity*
no laughing matter 123.2 *important matter;* 643.4 *solemnity*
no less 217.7 *sufficiency*
no life 582.1 *death*
nolle prosequi 708.6 *termination*
no longer 284.23 *before now*
no longer among us 98.9 *away*
no longer law 16.57 *null*
no longer made 133.9 *discontinued*
no longer present 284.20 *former*
no longer serving 284.20 *former*
no loss of time 332.8 *speed*
no luck 249.3 *bad fortune;* 247.1 *failure*
nomad 100.5 *nonconformist*
nomadic 100.10 *foreign;* 300.16 *moving;* 118.13 *unconventional*
nomadically 100.18 *extraneously;* 300.18 *in motion*
no man 98.7 *nobody*
no manners 659.2 *bad manners*
no-man's-land 128.3 *exclusion zone*
no marksman 486.10 *unskilled person*
no marriage 571.1 *divorce*
no match 116.2 *unlikeness*
no matter 124.8 *trifle*
no matter! 124.15
no matter how 317.16 *how*
no matter what 138.14 *whatever*
no matter who 138.13 *whoever*
nombril point 743.8 *heraldic device*
nom de plume 737.8 *anonymity;* 736.7 *concealer;* 721.8 *name*
nomen 721.8 *name*
nomenclator 5.2 *linguist*
nomenclature 721.7; 220.3 *dictionary;* 5.1 *linguistics*
nominal 793.9 *cheap;* 742.14 *signifying;* 124.4 *trivial*
nominalism 160.1 *form;* 4.7 *school of thought*
nominalist 4.11 *follower of a doctrine;* 4.14 *of a philosophy*
nominally 793.15 *cheaply;* 699.41 *spuriously*
nominal price 793.1 *cheapness*
nominal scale 27.56 *nonparametric methods*
nominate 398.7 *delegate;* 7.21 *ordain;* 469.4 *pick*
nominated 65.9 *billiard;* 398.9 *delegated*
nominated ball 65.5 *snooker*
nomination 398.3 *delegation;* 7.9 *priesthood;* 469.6 *selection*
nominative 5.31 *case*
nominee 398.1 *delegate;* 469.13 *electorate*
no mixture 255.8 *simplicity*
nomological 16.45 *legislative*
nomology 16.32 *jurisprudence;* 16.31 *legislation*
no money 249.2 *economic adversity*
no morals 796.3 *sexual immorality;* 804.2 *vice*
no more 94.11; 582.19 *dead;* 3.18 *in the past*
no more work 580.3 *unemployment*
nomothetic 16.45 *legislative;* 579.17 *managerial;* 4.13 *of philosophy*
non! 708.23 *no!*
nonacceptance 670.3; 709.1 *refusal;* 470.5, 708.2 *rejection;* 113.6 *uncooperativeness*
nonaccepted 708.18 *rejected*
nonaccepting 709.8 *refused*
nonacknowledgment 672.1 *ingratitude*
nonacting person 341.2
nonaction 341.1 *inaction*
nonactive 341.3 *inactive*
nonactivist 637.16 *reluctant person*
nonaddict 689.8 *sober person*
nonadherence 657.5 *nonobservance*
nonadmission 128.1 *exclusion*
nonage 555.1 *youth*
nonagenarian 556.7 *older person;* 201.8 *twenty and over*
nonaggression 589.1 *peace*
nonaggression pact 755.3 *alliance;* 749.1 *pacification;* 589.1 *peace*
nonaggressive 589.7 *peaceful*
nonagon 201.5 *nine;* 27.44 *polygon*
nonagonal 201.16 *ninth*
nonahydrate 32.10 *salt*
nonalcoholic 689.2; 558.17 *drinkable;* 689.8 *sober person*
nonalcoholic beverage 558.6 *soft drink*
nonaligned 473.4 *disinterested;* 250.9 *free;* 85.16 *national;* 589.7 *peaceful;* 372.17 *unjoined*
nonaligned country 85.1 *country*
nonaligned nations 589.1 *peace*
nonalignment 473.1 *disinterestedness;* 250.1 *freedom;* 589.1 *peace;* 372.2 *setting apart*
no name 737.8 *anonymity;* 736.7 *concealer*
nonappearance 98.4 *absenteeism;* 526.4 *disappearance;* 521.4 *invisibility*
nonapproval 470.5 *rejection*
nonary 201.5 *nine;* 201.16 *ninth*
nonassimilated 100.11 *separate*
nonassimilation 100.3 *separateness*
nonassociation 637.13 *dissociation;* 708.2 *rejection*
nonassociative 708.17 *negative*
nonattached 372.17 *unjoined*
nonattachment 372.2 *setting apart*
nonattendance 98.4 *absenteeism*
nonattendant 98.8 *absent*
nonbearing wall 20.9 *miscellaneous architectural features*
nonbeing 98.1 *absence;* 94.1 *nonexistence;* 195.3 *nothingness*
nonbelief 451.3 *incredulity;* 708.2 *rejection*

nonbeliever 451.5 *disbeliever;* 250.8 *free-thinker;* 637.16 *reluctant person*
nonbelieving 250.10 *independent*
nonbelligerent 589.3 *pacifist*
nonbenzenoid aromatic 32.7 *chemical compound*
nonbreakable 423.1 *tough*
noncausal 107.8 *chance*
nonce word 5.17 *word*
nonchalance 265.4 *ease of manner;* 618.1 *indifference;* 666.1 *negligence*
nonchalant 618.7 *indifferent;* 666.4 *negligent*
nonchalantly 618.17 *indifferently*
nonchordate invertebrate 75.1 *invertebrate*
non-Christian 7.6
non-Christian ritual 10.7
nonclassically 28.100 *physically*
nonclastic rock 30.31 *sedimentary rock*
noncoagulation 431.5 *fluidity*
noncoercion 250.1 *freedom*
noncombatant 584.9 *enlisted;* 589.3 *pacifist;* 589.7 *peaceful*
noncommissioned 584.9 *enlisted*
noncommissioned officer 586.17 *army person;* 584.5 *military staff*
noncommittal 736.17; 355.6 *apathetic;* 634.18 *avoiding;* 618.7 *indifferent;* 754.7 *irresolute;* 685.7 *politically moderate;* 639.1 *vacillating*
noncommittally 639.16, 754.9 *irresolutely*
noncommitted 634.18 *avoiding*
noncompetitive 747.19 *associating*
noncompletion 486.9 *bungling;* 604.1 *disappointment;* 247.1 *failure;* 233.1 *incompleteness;* 218.8 *insufficiency*
noncompliance 637.14, 662.1 *disobedience;* 118.2 *dissent;* 753.1 *protest;* 709.1 *refusal*
noncompliant 662.13 *disobedient;* 753.9 *protesting;* 709.8 *refused*
noncomplying 709.8 *refused*
non compos mentis 461.11 *insane*
nonconcurrence 118.2 *dissent*
nonconductor 39.7; 334.7 *electrical power;* 28.48 *insulation*
nonconformance 118.1 *nonconformity*
nonconformer 118.7 *nonconformist*
nonconforming 118.11; 250.10 *independent;* 100.11 *separate;* 299.5 *unusual*
nonconformism 118.3; 325.13 *deviation*
Nonconformist 7.5 *Christian;* 7.16 *denominational*
nonconformist 100.5; 118.7; 118.12; 662.6; 661.4 *defiant person;* 325.20 *deviant;* 325.19 *deviant person;* 451.5 *disbeliever;* 250.8 *free-thinker;* 250.10 *independent;* 657.7 *informal;* 487.2 *not customary;* 753.4 *protester;* 753.9 *protesting*
Nonconformity 118
nonconformity 118.1; 751.3 *difference;* 662.1 *disobedience;* 114.1 *diversity;* 250.1 *freedom;* 657.1 *informality;* 100.3 *separateness;* 487.3 *unaccustomedness;* 109.1 *unrelatedness;* 299.2 *unusualness*
nonconsummation of marriage 571.1 *divorce*
noncontinuous 133.8 *discontinuous;* 27.70 *universal*
noncontributory benefit 392.4 *social assistance*
nonconvergence 188.1 *parallelism*
nonconvergent 188.3 *parallel*
nonconvertible 350.1 *unused*
nonconvulsive electric treatment 36.3 *psychiatric treatment*
noncooperation 751.1 *disagreement;* 662.1 *disobedience;* 634.15 *evasiveness;* 637.12 *opposition;* 753.1 *protest;* 709.1 *refusal;* 383.1 *resistance;* 113.6 *uncooperativeness*
noncooperative 634.18 *avoiding;* 751.9 *disagreeing;* 662.13 *disobedient;* 753.9 *protesting;* 709.8 *refused;* 383.10 *resistant;* 113.26 *uncooperative*
noncooperatively 751.11 *in disagreement;* 383.14 *resistingly*
noncooperator 751.4 *dissenter*
noncorroboration 708.1 *negation*
noncrystalline 32.33 *crystalline*
noncrystalline mineral 30.34 *mineral*
nondescript 497.5 *tasteless;* 124.1 *unimportant*
nondirective therapy 36.3 *psychiatric treatment*
nondiscriminatory 127.7 *including*
nondivergence 188.1 *parallelism*
nondivergent 188.3 *parallel*
nondrinker 634.17 *avoider;* 689.8 *sober person*
nondrinking 689.1 *sober*
nondurable 278.7 *impermanent*
nondutiable 790.15 *chargeable*
none 195.11; 94.6 *absence;* 195.2 *nothing;* 195.1 *zero*
nonelastic 423.3 *hard*
nonelastic fluid 431.1 *fluid*
nonelection 470.6 *discarding*
nonemployment 341.1 *inaction*
nonentity 124.10; 195.5; 98.1 *absence;* 122.6 *inferior;* 96.5 *insubstantial person;* 708.9 *negativist;* 94.1, 708.8 *nonexistence;* 157.5 *shallow person*
none other 111.1 *sameness*
Nones 275.11 *date*
nones 10.4 *public worship*
nonessential 109.7 *illogical;* 219.3 *superfluity;* 219.7 *superfluous;* 124.8 *trifle;* 124.1 *unimportant*
nonessential amino acid 33.8 *amino acid*
nonesuch 235.8 *exceller;* 797.16 *superior person*
nonet 374.3 *assembly;* 18.26 *musical group;* 201.5 *nine;* 747.9 *team*
nonetheless 317.16 *how*
none the worse 393.15 *cured*
none too soon 294.16 *at a late hour*
non-Euclidean geometry 27.34 *geometry*
nonexclusive 138.15 *general;* 127.7 *including*
Nonexistence 94
nonexistence 94.1; 708.8; 98.1 *absence;* 526.4 *disappearance;* 699.1 *falsehood;* 103.5 *impossibility;* 195.3 *nothingness;* 96.1 *unreality*
nonexistent 94.9; 708.21; 98.8 *absent;* 526.7 *disappeared;* 477.12 *imaginary;* 195.7 *null;* 218.4 *scarce;* 96.8 *unreal*
nonexternal 101.11 *internal*
nonexternality 101.6 *internal world*
nonexternally 101.14 *subjectively*
nonextreme 685.7 *politically moderate*
nonextremist 216.2 *medium;* 216.8 *middle classes*
nonfiction 17.4; 721.4 *factual account*
nonflammable 252.6 *safe*
nonfriction 268.1 *slipperiness*
nonfrictional 421.1 *smooth*
nonfulfilment 604.1 *disappointment;* 247.1 *failure;* 233.1 *incompleteness;* 218.8 *insufficiency*
nonfunctional 238.1 *useless*
nonfunctioning 238.1 *useless*
nonhappening 94.1 *nonexistence*
nonhuman 457.8
nonhuman existence 457.4
nonhumanly 457.12
nonillion 194.3 *large number;* 201.11 *million*
nonimitation 126.1 *originality*
nonimmunity 254.7 *vulnerability*
noninclusion 128.1 *exclusion*
nonindustrial 356.11 *productive*
noninfectious 257.4 *hygienic*
noninjurious 257.4 *hygienic*
noninterference 250.1 *freedom;* 341.1 *inaction*
nonintervention 250.1 *freedom;* 341.1 *inaction;* 589.1 *peace;* 634.12 *shyness*
noninterventional 250.9 *free*
non interventionist 341.2 *nonacting person*
nonintimidation 250.1 *freedom*
noninvolved 250.9 *free*
noninvolvement 473.1 *disinterestedness;* 250.1 *freedom;* 618.1 *indifference;* 566.11 *nation;* 100.3 *separateness;* 634.12 *shyness*
noninvolvment 589.1 *peace*
nonirritant 685.8 *moderating*
nonliability 16.42 *acquittal;* 767.1 *disposal;* 758.1 *exemption;* 250.1 *freedom;* 757.1 *permission*
nonliable 16.63 *acquitted;* 758.5 *exempt;* 250.9 *free*
nonlinear 133.11 *digressive*
nonlinear circuit 39.13 *circuit*
nonlinearity 133.7 *broken thread*
nonmalignant 257.4 *hygienic*
nonmanual 15.8 *industrial*
nonmanual worker 15.7 *employee*
nonmaterial 101.8; 11.18 *spiritual*
nonmaterial world 101.1
nonmember 128.5 *excluded person*
nonmetal 32.6 *chemical element*
non-negative 27.71 *numerical*
non-negative number 27.5 *number*
no-no 712.1 *curse;* 103.7 *obstacle*
nonobservance 657.5; 637.14, 662.1 *disobedience;* 118.2 *dissent;* 472.1 *inattention;* 708.2 *rejection*
nonobservant 662.13 *disobedient;* 487.1 *unaccustomed*
nonobserved 708.18 *rejected*
nonoccurrence 98.1 *absence;* 94.1 *nonexistence*
nonoccurrent 98.8 *absent*
no-nonsense 646.1 *naive;* 738.15 *open;* 95.8 *practical;* 4.15 *rational*
no novice 485.5 *expert*
nonparametric methods 27.56
nonparametric statistics 27.53 *statistics*
nonpareil 797.2 *best;* 116.4 *dissimilar;* 235.8 *exceller;* 121.6 *paragon;* 797.9 *the best*
nonpartisan 473.4 *disinterested;* 250.9 *free;* 250.7 *free person*
nonpayer 786.6; 784.6 *debtor;* 247.5 *failing person*
nonpaying 786.13; 784.10 *unable to pay;* 766.17 *unprofitable*
nonpaying person 247.5 *failing person*
Nonpayment 786
nonpayment 786.1; 389.1 *escape;* 753.1 *protest;* 709.1 *refusal*
nonperformance 247.1 *failure*
nonperseverance 639.11 *vacillation*
nonperson 98.6 *absentee;* 96.5 *insubstantial person;* 124.10 *nonentity*
nonphysical 101.8 *nonmaterial;* 11.18 *spiritual*
nonphysical world 101.1 *nonmaterial world*
nonplus 264.23 *cause difficulties;* 453.20 *make uncertain;* 264.4 *problem*
nonplussed 453.3, 696.6 *confused;* 264.16 *troubled*
nonpolar 32.35 *combined*
nonpolar compound 32.7 *chemical compound*
nonpolar solvent 32.3 *phase*
nonporous 309.12 *closed*
nonporously 309.16 *impermeably*
nonpreparation 262.4 *haste*
nonprescription drug 37.3 *drug*
nonpresence 98.1 *absence;* 521.4 *invisibility*
nonprevalent 487.2 *not customary*
nonprintable character 40.10 *character*
nonprofessional 486.2 *unskilled*
nonprofessional army 584.2 *the military*
non-profit-making 766.17, 776.16 *unprofitable*
nonprosecution 16.42 *acquittal*
non-radical 685.7 *politically moderate*
non-reactionary 685.7 *politically moderate*
nonrealism 718.1 *misrepresentation*
nonrealist 634.17 *avoider*
nonreality 94.5
nonrecognition 456.1 *ignorance;* 672.1 *ingratitude*
nonrecovery 766.1 *loss*
nonrecurrent 133.9 *discontinued*
nonrecyclable 766.16 *losing*
nonreflective 527.1 *transparent*
nonrenewable energy source 437.1 *fuel*
nonrepentance 809.1 *impenitence*
nonrepresentational 718.6 *misrepresented;* 717.13 *representational*
nonresident 98.10
nonresistance 663.1 *obedience;* 388.1 *submission*
nonresisting 663.7 *obedient;* 388.5 *submitting*
nonresistive 419.7 *impressionable*
nonresonance 511.3 *mutedness*
nonresonant 511.2; 513.8 *hoarse*
nonresponsibility 758.1 *exemption*
nonrestoration 766.1 *loss*
non-restriction 314.4 *right of entry*
nonresumption 247.1 *failure*
nonretention 767.1 *disposal*
nonreturnable 350.1 *unused*
nonrigid 419.1 *soft*
nonrigidity 419.8 *softness*
nonsaponifiable lipid 33.6 *lipid*
nonsatisfaction 233.1 *incompleteness;* 218.8 *insufficiency*
nonseed-bearing 77.16 *taxonomic*
nonseed-bearing plant 77.4 *lower plant*
Nonsense 697
nonsense 697.1; 699.15; 704.13 *no!;* 694.4 *type of meaning;* 696.11 *unintelligibility*
nonsense poetry 17.6 *poetry*
nonsense verse 697.1 *nonsense*
nonsensical 697.5; 459.5 *foolish;* 699.31 *hypocritical;* 694.6 *meaningful*
nonsensically 697.9; 459.8 *foolishly*
nonsequential 133.11 *digressive*
non sequitur 133.7 *broken thread;* 4.8 *philosophical term;* 702.2 *sophism;* 109.2 *unrelated thing*
nonserial 133.11 *digressive*
nonseriality 133.7 *broken thread*
nonsingle 207.6 *plural*
nonsinusoidal wave 28.16 *waveform*
nonsmoker 684.4 *self-restrained person;* 496.8 *smoking*
nonspecialist 486.2 *unskilled*
nonspecific 138.20 *generalized*
nonspecificness 138.3
nonspiritual 402.7 *material*
nonstandard 118.15 *irregular;* 5.39 *of language*
nonstandard language 5.5
nonstarter 247.5 *failing person;* 247.4 *unsuccessful thing*
nonsterile 258.8 *unclean*
nonstick 268.10 *slippery*
nonstoichiometric 32.35 *combined*
nonstoichiometric compound 32.7 *chemical compound*
nonstop 134.7 *continually;* 279.10 *continuing forever;* 132.11, 178.3 *continuous;* 132.19 *continuously;* 270.3 *diffuse;* 297.3 *frequent;* 134.6 *protracted;* 112.14 *recurrent*
nonstop talker 731.4 *talker*
nonstop talking 270.1 *diffuseness*
nonstriker 753.4 *protester;* 662.12 *reactionary*
nonsubsistence 94.1 *nonexistence*
nonsuit 16.42 *acquittal*
nonsuited 16.64 *convicted*
nonsymmetrical 408.14 *irregular*
nonsymmetry 408.2 *irregular order*
nontaxable 790.15 *chargeable*
nontoxic 252.6 *safe*
nontraditional 295.11 *unfamiliar*
nontraditionally 295.21 *newly*
nontranslucent 528.1 *opaque*
nontransparent 528.1 *opaque*
non-U 487.2 *not customary;* 574.4 *ordinary;* 675.7 *vulgar*
nonuniform 133.8 *discontinuous;* 116.4 *dissimilar;* 114.5 *diverse;* 299.4, 408.14 *irregular;* 412.12 *mixed;* 420.1 *rough*
nonuniformity 133.1 *discontinuity;* 116.1 *dissimilarity;* 114.1 *diversity;* 120.1 *inequality;* 299.1 *irregularity;* 408.2 *irregular order;* 412.1 *mixture;* 420.6 *roughness*
nonuniformly 114.10 *diversely;* 120.7 *unequally*
nonunion labour 15.1 *industrial relations*
nonuple 201.16 *ninth*
nonuplet 201.5 *nine*
Nonuse 350
nonuse 350.8; 470.6 *discarding;* 341.1 *inaction;* 355.3 *relinquishment;* 486.8 *unskilfulness*
nonuser of drugs 178.9 *straight person*
nonvenomous snake 73.3 *snake*
non-verbal glossolalia 5.5 *nonstandard language*
nonviolence 685.1 *moderation;* 749.1 *pacification;* 589.1 *peace*
nonviolent 685.6 *moderate;* 589.7 *peaceful*
nonviolent resistance 383.3 *resistance movement*
nonviscosity 431.5 *fluidity*
nonvolatile memory 40.6 *memory*
nonwage demands 15.2 *industrial negotiations*
nonwilling 709.8 *refused*
nonwillingness 709.1 *refusal*
nonworker 343.8
non-working 580.7 *leisurely*
noodle 442.7 *brain;* 459.3 *foolish person*
no oil painting 216.6 *mediocrity;* 546.2 *ugly person*

nook 183.3 *cavity;* 410.2 *compartment;* 736.2 *hiding place*
nooky 593.5 *desire*
no omission 127.1 *inclusion*
noon 290.3; 290.6
noonday 290.3 *noon*
no-one 94.6 *absence;* 98.7 *nobody;* 195.2 *nothing*
noontide 290.3 *noon*
noontime 290.3 *noon*
no orator 732.5 *shy person*
noose 179.3 *circular thing;* 814.16 *instrument of execution;* 373.9 *yoke*
noosphere 434.2 *aerosphere*
no other 197.1 *one;* 111.1 *sameness*
no pattern 408.2 *irregular order*
nope 708.23 *no!*
no picnic 264.3 *difficult task*
no place 98.21 *away*
Nō play 21.2 *play*
no preference 618.3 *impartiality*
no prejudice 618.3 *impartiality*
no priority 289.3 *subordination*
no prisoners taken 585.1 *war*
no problem 265.21 *easily*
no progress 247.1 *failure*
no quarter! 382.26
no quorum 218.8 *insufficiency*
nor' 324.4 *compass point*
Nordic 1.13 *racial;* 531.3 *white-haired*
nordic 68.12 *ski*
nordic skiing 68.1 *skiing*
Nordic type 1.6 *race*
no real alternative 469.8 *choice*
no regrets 809.1 *impenitence*
no relation 109.5 *misconnection*
no remorse 809.1 *impenitence*
no result 247.1 *failure*
no reward 672.1 *ingratitude*
Norfolk jacket 551.11 *jacket*
no rhyme or reason 408.2 *irregular order*
norimon 320.6 *litter*
norito 10.9 *prayer*
norm 216.4 *average;* 750.6 *convention;* 140.4 *guide;* 713.3 *precept;* 26.7 *standard*
normal 632.11; 216.1 *average;* 138.21, 574.3 *common;* 750.15 *conventional;* 140.10 *customary;* 117.15 *everyday;* 27.37 *line;* 27.80 *linear;* 298.14 *orderly;* 186.10 *perpendicular;* 460.4 *sane;* 27.70 *universal;* 186.3 *vertical thing*
normal behaviour 474.3 *the expected thing*
normalcy 216.4 *average*
normal distribution 27.59 *probability distribution*
normal fault 30.20 *earth movement*
normality 216.4 *average;* 298.4 *orderliness;* 460.1 *sanity*
normalize 216.10 *make average;* 298.10 *make regular;* 750.26 *make uniform;* 27.94 *order;* 409.13 *organize;* 140.14 *regulate*
normally 140.18 *as a rule;* 750.37 *conventionally;* 216.11 *on average;* 298.17 *orderly;* 138.30 *usually*
normal person 574.1 *plebeian*
normals 574.2 *the common people*
normal sight 518.1 *vision*
normal stress 38.14 *load*
normal temperature and pressure 28.38 *thermodynamics*
normal use 349.6 *use*
normal vision 518.1 *vision*
Norman 296.14 *historic*
Norman arch 20.5 *arch*
normative 216.1 *average;* 4.13 *of philosophy*
no room to spare 232.8 *full*
north 324.12; 324.4 *compass point;* 324.13 *directional*
North America 92.1 *continent*
North and South 86.7 *regions of the world*
north and south 113.3 *opposites*
northbound 324.13 *directional*
northeast 324.4 *compass point;* 324.13 *directional;* 324.12 *north*
northeast by east 324.12 *north*
northeast by north 324.12 *north*
northeaster 31.15 *wind direction*
northeasterly 324.13 *directional;* 324.12 *north;* 31.15 *wind direction;* 31.47 *windy*
northeastern 324.13 *directional*
northeast trades 31.17 *wind system*
northeastwards 324.12 *north*
northeast wind 31.15 *wind direction*
norther 31.15 *wind direction*
northerly 324.13 *directional;* 324.12 *north;* 31.15 *wind direction;* 31.47 *windy*
northern 324.13 *directional;* 86.16 *regional;* 169.6 *side*
Northerner 564.9 *British inhabitant;* 85.9 *England;* 564.10 *US inhabitant*
Northern Ireland 85.10 *Ireland*
northern lights 30.46 *aurora;* 522.4 *natural light*
northernmost 324.13 *directional*
northern pike 55.4 *American game fish*
northing 324.4 *compass point*
north light 522.10 *window*
north magnetic pole 30.45 *magnetic pole*
north-northeast 324.12 *north*
north-northwest 324.12 *north*
north of Watford 86.9 *regions of Britain*
North Pole 494.6 *Arctic*
North Sea gas 437.3 *gas*
North Sea oil 437.6 *oil*
north side 169.3 *side direction*
North-South divide 86.7 *regions of the world*
North Star 742.5 *indicator;* 522.4 *natural light*
North Wales 85.12 *Wales*
North Walian 85.12 *Wales*
northward 324.4 *compass point;* 324.13 *directional*
northwardly 324.12 *north*
northwards 324.12 *north*
northwest 324.4 *compass point;* 324.13 *directional;* 324.12 *north*
northwest by north 324.12 *north*
northwest by west 324.12 *north*
northwester 31.15 *wind direction*
northwesterly 324.13 *directional;* 324.12 *north;* 31.15 *wind direction;* 31.47 *windy*
northwestern 324.13 *directional*
North West Highlands 89.5 *British mountains*
northwestwardly 324.12 *north*
northwestwards 324.12 *north*
northwest wind 31.15 *wind direction*
North Wind 494.7 *cold weather*
north wind 31.15 *wind direction*
no score 195.1 *zero*
nose 308.4 *body orifice;* 182.2 *bulge;* 525.3 *external appearance;* 693.10 *informer;* 500.1 *odour;* 566.7 *person;* 361.5 *projecting object;* 185.3 *protuberance;* 62.5 *rock face;* 500.2 *sense of smell;* 500.7 *smell*
nose around 644.7 *be curious*
nosebag 410.8 *bag*
noseband 59.14 *horse-riding terms*
nosebleed 560.10 *bleeding*
nose candy 691.6 *drug*
no secret 455.10 *known*
nose dive 214.2 *decline;* 305.5 *dive;* 305.12 *drop;* 322.5 *flight*
nose-diving 305.18 *falling*
nosedown 305.19 *down*
nose drops 37.8 *drops*
nosegay 376.29 *bunch;* 78.1 *flower;* 502.2 *fragrant thing*
nose guard 46.3 *uniform*
nose-in-the-air 622.17 *conceited*
nose job 547.2 *plastic surgery*
noseless 501.3 *odourless*
no sense 694.4 *type of meaning*
nose out 500.7 *smell*
nose-ring 542.7 *jewellery*
nose to nose 147.14 *beside*
nose-to-nose 147.10 *juxtaposed*
nose to tail 147.14 *beside;* 132.20 *in a line*
nose-to-tail 147.10 *juxtaposed*
nosh 557.22 *eat well;* 557.7 *food;* 436.2 *provisions*
no shining knight 659.4 *discourteous person*
no-show 98.6 *absentee*
nosh-up 688.3 *act of gluttony;* 557.13 *feast*
nosily 644.9 *officiously*
no sinecure 342.6 *business*
nosiness 644.2 *prying*
nosing 500.2 *sense of smell*
no sirree 708.24 *never!*
no slouch 342.10 *busy person*
no-smoking area 501.1 *odourlessness*
no-smoking section 257.2 *salubrity*
nosologist 35.13 *medical specialist*
nosology 35.3 *medical specialty;* 260.20 *pathology*
no spring chicken 556.13 *middle-aged;* 556.7 *older person*
nostalgia 617.1 *desire;* 590.7 *emotionalism;* 3.13, 303.15 *looking back;* 462.1 *memory*
nostalgic 617.9 *desirous;* 462.7 *memorable;* 303.24 *retroactive;* 590.12 *sensitive*
nostalgically 3.25 *reportedly*
nostologist 35.13 *medical specialist*
nostology 35.3 *medical specialty*
no stomach for 596.1 *dislike;* 637.13 *dissociation*
no stone unturned 141.16 *extensively*
Nostradamus 475.8 *oracle;* 711.4 *warner*
no stranger to 455.8 *knowledgeable*
nostril 308.4 *body orifice;* 500.2 *sense of smell*
no strings attached 250.12 *unconditional*
no strong feelings 639.14 *apathy*
nostrum 484.3 *expedient plan;* 394.1 *remedy*
no success 249.3 *bad fortune*
no such thing 116.4 *dissimilar;* 94.2 *nothingness*
no surplus 217.7 *sufficiency*
no surrender 383.16 *fight on!*
no sweat 265.21 *easily;* 265.6 *easy thing*
nosy 342.21 *meddling;* 644.6 *prying*
nosy parker 342.11, 644.4 *meddler;* 518.11 *observer*
not 231.1 *imperfect*
not abide 113.17 *be against*
notability 123.4 *bigwig;* 123.1 *importance*
not a bit 94.7 *not any*
not a bit alike 116.4 *dissimilar*
notable 123.6; 123.4 *bigwig;* 139.17 *exceptional;* 738.14 *manifest;* 462.7 *memorable;* 811.2 *person of repute;* 235.1 *worthy*
not able 335.10 *powerless*
notable point 123.2 *important matter*
not a blessed one 94.6 *absence;* 195.2 *nothing*
notably 123.9 *importantly;* 235.11 *worthily*
not above temptation 804.13 *venial*
not accept 708.10 *be negative;* 350.5 *not use;* 709.5 *refuse;* 470.1 *reject*
not accepted 470.10 *rejected*
not according to law 16.55 *illegal*
not accountable 758.5 *exempt*
not acknowledge 655.13 *ignore*
not act 341.4
not activate 350.5 *not use*
not activated 350.1 *unused*
not admire 670.14 *disapprove*
not admit 708.10 *be negative*
not a fake 698.6 *authenticity*
not a few 208.6 *many*
not affordable 792.7 *dear*
not a full deck 218.8 *insufficiency*
not a full team 218.8 *insufficiency*
not a hint 94.7 *not any*
not airtight 231.1 *imperfect*
not a jot 94.7 *not any;* 195.2 *nothing*
not a lick 94.7 *not any;* 195.2 *nothing*
not a living thing 98.7 *nobody*
not allied 109.9 *misconnected*
not allow 709.6 *dissent*
not allowed 709.9 *dissenting;* 399.5 *vetoed*
not allowed visitors 260.22 *sick*
not allow to deviate 698.31 *be accurate*
not allow to forget 462.13 *remind*
not all there 233.4 *incomplete;* 457.6 *unintelligent*
not alter 418.11 *be stubborn*
not alter things 335.6 *be powerless*
not a mite 94.7 *not any;* 195.2 *nothing*
not a mouse stirring 301.2 *repose*
not amused 624.15 *resentful*
not an iota 94.7 *not any;* 195.2 *nothing*
not answerable 758.5 *exempt*
not anxious to please 659.5 *discourteous*
not any 94.7; 195.2 *nothing;* 195.6 *zero*
not any more 284.23 *before now*
not a one 94.6 *absence;* 195.2 *nothing*
not a pair 116.2 *unlikeness*
not a particle 94.7 *not any*
not a patch on 122.18 *outclassed*
not apparent 521.1 *invisible*
not appear 526.2 *depart*
not apply 100.13 *be extraneous*
not approve 670.14 *disapprove;* 470.1 *reject*
not apropos 124.1 *unimportant*
notarized statement 744.2 *certificate*
notary 744.9 *recorder*
not a sausage 195.2 *nothing*
not a scrap 94.7 *not any*
not a single person 98.7 *nobody*
not a smell 195.2 *nothing*
not a smidgen 94.7 *not any*
not a soul 98.7 *nobody;* 195.2 *nothing*
not a sound 506.4 *silence*
not a speck 94.7 *not any*
not a squeak 506.4 *silence*
not associate 708.10 *be negative*
not associated 109.9 *misconnected*
no taste 675.1 *tastelessness*
not a stitch on 552.2 *nudity*
not a suspicion 94.7 *not any*
not at all 94.14; 708.22 *negatively;* 704.13, 708.23 *no!;* 195.11 *none;* 709.11 *uncooperatively*
not at any time 94.15 *not ever*
not at home 98.10 *nonresident*
notation 18.17; 209.3 *gradation;* 194.1 *number;* 717.1 *representation;* 18.18 *written music*
not a trace 94.7 *not any*
not at risk 252.6 *safe*
not a true picture 718.1 *misrepresentation*
not attempt 634.4 *shy*
not at the moment 286.3 *another time*
not at war 589.7 *peaceful*
not at work 98.10 *nonresident*
not available 350.1 *unused*
not awake 343.4
not a whit 94.7 *not any;* 195.2 *nothing*
not bad 235.5; 259.1 *healthy;* 216.3 *mediocre;* 609.6 *satisfactory;* 413.10 *supportable*
not balance 120.5 *be unequal*
not bat an eye 341.4 *not act*
not bat an eyelid 228.8 *show determination*
not be 708.13 *be nothing*
not be absent 282.5 *be present*
not be affected by 618.12 *be indifferent*
not bear inspection 231.9 *be imperfect*
not be caught flatfooted 287.5 *take the opportunity*
not be conducive to 347.3 *counteract*
not believe 708.10 *be negative*
not believe one's eyes 619.9 *wonder*
not belong 128.9 *be excluded*
not belonging 372.17 *unjoined*
not be moved 628.6 *be pitiless*
not bend 383.7 *be obstinate;* 418.11 *be stubborn*
not bending 383.2 *obstinacy*
not be one's business 109.11 *be unconcerned*
not be tempted by 383.6 *resist*
not be thought of 470.10 *rejected*
not be willing to 709.5 *refuse*
not born yesterday 645.4 *cunning*
not bothered 473.4 *disinterested*
not breathe 301.8 *be motionless*
not breathe a word 730.13 *be voiceless;* 737.12 *keep secret*
not broken 487.1 *unaccustomed*
not budge 301.8 *be motionless;* 641.9 *be obstinate;* 640.8 *hold out;* 638.10 *insist;* 341.4 *not act;* 228.8 *show determination*
not butt in 250.15 *set free*
not buy 709.5 *refuse*
not care 618.12 *be indifferent*
not care for 666.6 *be neglectful;* 596.5 *dislike*
not cater for 470.3 *exclude*
not cause a stir 216.9 *be average*
notch 183.4; 183.10; 146.2, 146.5 *crack;* 209.3 *gradation;* 743.10 *identify;* 420.12 *make rough;* 425.15 *make sharp;* 50.4 *rowing;* 425.7 *sharp point*
not change 228.6 *be stable*
not change anything 335.6 *be powerless*
not change one's mind 641.9 *be obstinate*
not charge 768.5 *give*
not charged for 793.11 *free of charge*
not charmed 596.8 *disliking*
notched 183.7; 420.3 *barbed;* 425.4 *toothed*
notched wood 420.7 *rough thing*
not chickenfeed 123.2 *important matter*
not choose 594.14 *hate;* 215.8 *leave;* 596.6 *react against*
notch up 210.8 *calculate;* 194.10 *number;* 744.15 *register*

notchy 183.7 *notched*
not clean 258.7 *dirty*
not come 98.15 *be absent*
not come amiss 239.6 *be convenient*; 392.26 *be useful*
not come off 247.6 *fail*; 247.8 *miscarry*
not come up to 122.8 *be inferior*
not compare with 116.5 *be dissimilar*
not complete 233.5 *be incomplete*; 666.6 *be neglectful*; 486.5 *be unskilful*
not comply 753.6 *protest*; 709.5 *refuse*
not comply with 662.15 *be disobedient*; 709.6 *dissent*
not compromise 638.10 *insist*
not concentrating 472.7 *inattentive*
not concern 109.10 *be unrelated*
not confess 809.5 *be impenitent*
not confessing 809.3 *impenitent*
not conform **100.17**; **118.18**; 662.15 *be disobedient*
not connected 109.9 *misconnected*
not connect with 109.10 *be unrelated*
not consider 470.1 *reject*
not considered 128.11 *excluded*; 124.2 *obscure*
not contest 388.3 *submit*
not cooperate **637.9**; 662.15 *be disobedient*; 751.5 *disagree*; 753.6 *protest*; 709.5 *refuse*; 383.6 *resist*
not corroborate 708.10 *be negative*
not count 124.11 *be unimportant*; 470.3 *exclude*
not counted 128.11 *excluded*
not counting 128.12 *exclusively*
not covered by law 16.56 *unauthorized*
not cramp one's style 250.15 *set free*
not cramp someone's style 757.4 *be permissive*
not cricket 800.5 *dishonourable*; 465.3 *injustice*; 118.15 *irregular*; 466.3 *prejudice*; 802.11 *wrong*
not current 487.2 *not customary*
not customary **487.2**
not dangerous 252.6 *safe*
not dead 554.12 *alive*
not deep 157.1 *shallow*
not de rigueur 487.2 *not customary*
not despair 640.8 *hold out*
not deviate 178.11 *be straight*
not die 554.16 *live*
not difficult 265.9 *easy*
not dilute 255.11 *simplify*
not dirty 256.16 *clean*
not dispose of 360.7 *detain*
not dispute 707.22 *emphasize*
not do 240.5 *be inconvenient*; 335.6 *be powerless*
not doing well 249.6 *adverse*
not do justice to 468.3 *underestimate*
not done 802.13 *improper*; 118.15 *irregular*; 487.2 *not customary*
not do one's part 637.9 *not cooperate*
not drink 689.3 *be sober*
not drunk 689.1 *sober*
note 719.2 *annotation*; 471.10 *be attentive*; 515.2 *bird song*; 743.10 *identify*; 123.1 *importance*; 744.14 *inscribe*; 220.8 *list*; 18.16 *musical note*; 163.5 *outline*; 780.14 *paper money*; 744.1 *record*; 462.4 *reminder*; 575.1 *right*
not easy 378.14 *blocked*; 264.10 *difficult*
not eating 687.6 *fasting*
notebook 3.5 *chronicle*; 744.6 *record book*; 6.14 *school book*
noted 127.8 *included*; 220.11 *listed*; 744.16 *recorded*
note down 744.14 *inscribe*
not empowered 335.10 *powerless*
not enabled 335.10 *powerless*
not enclose 308.19 *open up*
not endure 596.5 *dislike*
not enough 218.8 *insufficiency*; 218.1 *insufficient*; 218.10 *insufficiently*
not enough to count 206.1 *few*
not enough work 580.1 *leisure*
not entertain 128.7 *exclude*
not entire 231.2 *incomplete*
note of explanation 719.2 *annotation*
note of hand 780.14 *paper money*
note of interrogation 705.11 *question mark*
note of warning 711.1 *warning*
notepad 744.6 *record book*
notepaper 435.3 *paper*
not equal to 27.88 *equal to*
not equate 120.5 *be unequal*
not equivocate 707.22 *emphasize*
note row 517.4 *atonality*
notes **744.3**; 3.5 *chronicle*; 163.1 *outline*
not ever **94.15**
noteworthiness 123.1 *importance*
noteworthy 139.17 *exceptional*; 462.7 *memorable*; 123.6 *notable*; 619.8 *wonderful*; 235.1 *worthy*
not excessive 685.6 *moderate*; 684.8 *self-restrained*
not exist **195.8**; 708.13 *be nothing*
not expect 630.12 *be surprised*; 486.5 *be unskilful*; 619.9 *wonder*
not extreme 685.6 *moderate*
not face 637.7 *refuse*
not fall from grace 805.8 *be innocent*
not far 147.12 *near*
not feeling like 637.1 *unwilling*
not feel well 260.24 *be unhealthy*
not find 766.9 *lose*
not finished 233.4 *incomplete*
not finish the job 486.5 *be unskilful*
not fit 100.13 *be extraneous*; 240.5 *be inconvenient*
not fit in 118.19 *be independent*
not fit in with 751.8 *be different*
not forget 360.8 *remember*
not forgetting 211.10 *additionally*; 360.5 *retentiveness*
not forgive 628.6 *be pitiless*
not for long 282.10 *for the present*
not for the world 708.23 *no!*
not free 664.6 *servile*
not fresh 236.4 *poor*
not fully 205.12 *partly*
not function 238.7 *be useless*
not functioning 245.13 *dilapidated*
not get along 751.5 *disagree*
not get it 696.9 *find unintelligible*
not get started 333.2 *hesitate*
not getting it 696.6 *confused*
not give 418.11 *be stubborn*
not give a damn 618.12 *be indifferent*
not give a fig 660.29 *ridicule*
not give a hoot 618.12 *be indifferent*
not give a monkey's 109.11 *be unconcerned*
not give an inch 638.10 *insist*
not give a toss 109.11 *be unconcerned*
not give offence 658.11 *have good manners*
not give way 383.6 *resist*
not go 238.7 *be useless*
not go amiss 239.6 *be convenient*
not go near 634.1 *avoid*
not good enough 231.1 *imperfect*; 236.2 *inferior*; 670.32 *unsatisfactory*
not go out 301.8 *be motionless*
not go well 247.8 *miscarry*
not granted 709.9 *dissenting*
not grasp it 696.9 *find unintelligible*
not grow 214.4 *decrease*
not guilty 16.63 *acquitted*; 714.12, 805.5 *innocent*; 16.7 *legal trial*
no thanks 672.1 *ingratitude*
not hard 265.9 *easy*
not have 135.7 *require*
not have a clue 456.9 *be ignorant*; 486.5 *be unskilful*
not have a penny 782.12 *be poor*
not have the skills 486.5 *be unskilful*
not have time 288.8 *be busy*
not having time 288.15 *busy*
not hear of 670.15 *withhold approval*
not heed 662.15 *be disobedient*; 666.6 *be neglectful*
not held against one 649.8 *overlooked*
not help 240.5 *be inconvenient*; 335.6 *be powerless*; 238.7 *be useless*
not here 98.21 *away*
nothing **195.2**; 98.3 *emptiness*; 124.10, 195.5 *nonentity*; 708.8 *nonexistence*; 94.2 *nothingness*; 124.8 *trifle*; 27.10, 195.1 *zero*
nothing at all 195.2 *nothing*; 94.2 *nothingness*
nothing but 255.16 *simple*
nothing daunted 353.8 *attempting*; 638.4 *undaunted*
nothing doing 708.23, 709.12 *no!*
nothing earthshattering 231.8 *ordinariness*
nothing else 197.1 *one*
nothing else but 698.37 *authentically*; 95.14 *certainly*
nothing for it but 469.8 *choice*
nothing gained 448.4 *originality*
nothing happening 341.1 *inaction*
nothing in common 116.2 *unlikeness*
nothing in excess 684.2 *moderation*
nothing in it 285.11 *equal*; 111.5, 119.1 *equality*
nothing in one's way 250.6 *liberality*
nothing in particular 124.8 *trifle*
nothing in the kitty 786.5 *insolvency*
nothing lacking 232.1 *completeness*
nothing left out 127.1 *inclusion*
nothing like 116.4 *dissimilar*
nothing like it 235.2 *best*
nothing missing 232.1 *completeness*
nothingness **94.2**; **195.3**; 98.3 *emptiness*; 141.2 *empty space*; 708.8 *nonexistence*; 124.5 *unimportance*
nothing of note 124.8 *trifle*
nothing of the kind 708.23 *no!*
nothing of the sort 116.4 *dissimilar*; 708.23 *no!*
nothing on earth 94.2 *nothingness*
nothing special 122.12 *inferior*; 216.6 *mediocrity*
nothing stirring 301.2 *repose*
nothing to add 232.1 *completeness*
nothing to boast about 216.6 *mediocrity*
nothing to boast of 124.8 *trifle*
nothing to choose between 111.5, 119.1 *equality*
nothing to confess 805.1 *innocence*
nothing to declare 805.1 *innocence*
nothing to do with 109.7 *illogical*
nothing to it 265.9 *easy*; 124.8 *trifle*
nothing to shout about 122.12 *inferior*
nothing to sneeze at 123.2 *important matter*
nothing to spare 218.9 *scarcity*
nothing to speak of 231.8 *ordinariness*; 124.8 *trifle*
nothing to worry about 124.8 *trifle*
nothing ventured 448.4 *originality*
nothing ventured, nothing gained 353.11 *here goes!*
nothing whatever 94.2 *nothingness*
not hold one's liquor 690.7 *be drunk*
not hold water 231.9 *be imperfect*
not hold with 113.17 *be against*; 606.7 *be dissatisfied*
nothosaur 73.6 *extinct reptile*
no thought for others 683.2 *egoism*
not hurt 235.10 *do good*
notice 740.9 *advertisement*; 722.2 *article*; 471.1 *attention*; 471.10 *be attentive*; 693.2 *communication*; 719.3 *criticism*; 710.2 *demand*; 449.1 *discover*; 740.3 *journalism*; 464.1 *judgment*; 475.3 *plan*; 518.12 *see*; 711.1 *warning*
noticeable 738.14 *manifest*; 488.8 *sensate*; 518.23, 520.1 *visible*
noticeably 26.17 *measurably*; 518.25, 520.11 *visibly*
notice board 740.9 *advertisement*; 738.8 *showplace*
notice of resignation 605.1 *resignation*
noticing 518.21 *seeing*
notifiable disease 260.4 *disease*
notification 713.1 *advice*; 693.2 *communication*; 740.1 *publication*; 711.1 *warning*
notificatory 740.21 *publishing*
notifier 693.9 *informant*; 740.10 *publicizer*
notify 713.5 *advise*; 6.22 *educate*; 693.11 *inform*; 475.11 *predict*; 740.14 *proclaim*; 711.5 *warn*
notifying 711.8 *warning*
not imbibe 689.3 *be sober*
no time to lose 262.4 *haste*
not immune 254.3 *vulnerable*
not impress 231.9 *be imperfect*
not improve 245.1 *deteriorate*; 245.5 *hurt*
not improved 607.4 *aggravated*; 245.12 *deteriorated*
not include 128.7 *exclude*
not included 128.11 *excluded*; 98.12 *missing*
not in contention 128.11 *excluded*
not increase 214.4 *decrease*
not in danger 252.6 *safe*
not independent 387.9 *subject*
not indulge 634.3 *abstain*; 689.3 *be sober*
not indulging 689.1 *sober*
not in error 698.15 *true*
not in good health 260.22 *sick*
not in proper condition 245.13 *dilapidated*
not in residence 98.10 *nonresident*
not insist 657.11 *not stand on ceremony*; 388.3 *submit*
not interfere 134.3 *continue*; 250.15 *set free*
not in the mood 637.1 *unwilling*
not in the pink 231.1 *imperfect*
not in time 288.13 *untimely*
not in vogue 487.2 *not customary*
not involve 109.10 *be unrelated*
not involved 634.18 *avoiding*; 618.7 *indifferent*
notion 450.1 *belief*; 484.3 *expedient plan*; 443.6, 446.1 *idea*; 477.4 *ideality*; 590.2 *impression*; 4.1 *philosophy*; 476.1 *supposition*; 642.3 *whim*
notional 477.12 *imaginary*; 4.13 *of philosophy*; 443.10 *speculative*; 476.7 *suppositional*; 446.10 *theoretical*
notionally 4.25, 446.20 *theoretically*
not just stand there 353.1 *attempt*
not just this minute 286.3 *another time*
not kept 767.12 *disposed*
not know 456.9 *be ignorant*; 486.5 *be unskilful*; 696.9 *find unintelligible*
not know how 486.5 *be unskilful*
not know oneself 760.8 *be transformed*
not lawful 335.10 *powerless*
not legal 16.55 *illegal*
not let go 640.8 *hold out*; 359.5 *preserve*; 360.6 *retain*
not liable 758.5 *exempt*
not likely 708.23, 709.12 *no!*
not like the rest 121.15 *excellent*
not liking 596.8 *disliking*
not listen 505.8 *be deaf*; 472.12 *be inattentive*; 641.9 *be obstinate*
not listen to 662.15 *be disobedient*
not long 278.8 *transiently*
not long ago 295.21 *newly*
not long to go 582.18 *dying*
not look for praise 674.14 *be modest*
not look like 116.5 *be dissimilar*
not lucky 249.8 *unlucky*
not mad 460.4 *sane*
not maintain one's position 245.1 *deteriorate*
not make a peep 506.1 *be silent*
not make a sound 506.1 *be silent*
not make ends meet 766.10 *have a financial loss*
not make out 696.9 *find unintelligible*
not make sense 696.7 *be unintelligible*
not make the grade 231.9 *be imperfect*; 122.8 *be inferior*; 335.6 *be powerless*; 247.6 *fail*
not making ends meet 766.2 *financial loss*
not many 206.1, 206.5 *few*
not match 120.5 *be unequal*
not matter 124.11 *be unimportant*
not meddle 250.15 *set free*
not meet expectations 218.5 *be insufficient*
not meet requirements 218.5 *be insufficient*
not mince one's words 646.4 *be naive*
not mind 618.12 *be indifferent*
not missed 463.11 *forgotten*
not mix 255.11 *simplify*
not move 341.4 *not act*
not much 206.5 *few*
not natural 266.2 *obscure*
not needed 238.1 *useless*
not negative 707.14 *assertive*
not nice 236.3 *bad*; 594.12 *hated*
not notice 472.12 *be inattentive*
not now 286.3 *another time*; 283.14 *in the future*
not obey 588.4 *be anarchic*; 662.15 *be disobedient*
not observe 708.10 *be negative*
not observed 487.2 *not customary*
not obstruct 308.19 *open up*
not occur 195.8 *not exist*
not offered 709.8 *refused*
not of this world 100.12 *external*; 477.12 *imaginary*
not one 98.7 *nobody*; 195.6 *zero*
not one of us 655.6 *unsocial person*
not one's best 231.6 *imperfect item*
not one's sort 596.9 *disliked*
not one's type 596.3 *disliked person*; 594.8 *hated person*; 546.2 *ugly person*
not on guard 646.1 *naive*; 254.3 *vulnerable*
not on the level 812.4 *disreputable*
not on this earth 94.16 *nowhere*
not on time 294.9 *late*
not on your life 103.13 *impossible!*; 709.11 *uncooperatively*

not on your nelly 103.13 *impossible!*; 709.11 *uncooperatively*
not open one's mouth 506.1 *be silent*
not operate 335.6 *be powerless*
Notoriety 812
notoriety 462.5 *day to remember*; 812.1 *disrespect*; 740.7 *publicity*
notorious 812.4 *disreputable*; 455.10 *known*; 738.14 *manifest*; 740.20 *well-known*
notoriously 738.16 *manifestly*
not out 134.5 *continual*
not overdoing it 684.8 *self-restrained*
not participating 343.3
not part with 360.7 *detain*
not pass 122.8 *be inferior*; 247.6 *fail*; 470.1 *reject*
not pass muster 231.9 *be imperfect*
not pass the test 122.8 *be inferior*
not pay 784.8; **786.7**
not paying 238.2 *futile*
not peanuts 123.2 *important matter*
not perfect 231.1 *imperfect*; 804.13 *venial*
not permitted 709.9 *dissenting*
not persevere 639.10 *compromise*
not plain sailing 378.2 *obstacle*
not play 637.9 *not cooperate*
not play ball 751.5 *disagree*; 637.9 *not cooperate*
not playing the ball 64.3 *rugby play*
not playing the game 800.1 *improbity*; 802.11 *wrong*
not play the ball 64.5 *play rugby*
not play the game 802.21 *do wrong*
not possible 103.1 *impossible*
not prepared 637.1 *unwilling*
not present 98.8 *absent*; 526.7 *disappeared*
not press 648.3 *be lenient*
not press charges 16.78 *acquit*
not proceed with 350.5 *not use*; 355.1 *relinquish*
not prosecute 16.78 *acquit*
not proud 623.1 *humble*
not proud of 623.3 *humbled*
not proven 16.63 *acquitted*
not pull one's weight 637.9 *not cooperate*
not push oneself forward 674.14 *be modest*; 634.4 *shy*
not put it past 104.10 *think likely*
not put up with 113.17 *be against*
not question 707.22 *emphasize*
not quite 231.11 *imperfectly*; 147.13 *nearly*
not raise a finger 341.4 *not act*
not react 341.4 *not act*
not ready 637.1 *unwilling*
not real 477.12 *imaginary*; 476.8 *supposed*
not realize one's expectations 604.4 *be disappointed*
not really 708.23 *no!*
not recommended 240.1 *inconvenient*
not redeemable 809.3 *impenitent*
not redeemed 809.3 *impenitent*
not reform 809.5 *be impenitent*
not register 696.9 *find unintelligible*
not relate 100.13 *be extraneous*
not related 109.9 *misconnected*; 124.1 *unimportant*
not relate to 109.10 *be unrelated*
not remember 463.13 *forget*
not remembered 463.11 *forgotten*
not representative 718.6 *misrepresented*
not required 350.3 *not wanted*
not resemble 116.5 *be dissimilar*
not resident 98.10 *nonresident*
not resist 663.5 *obey*; 388.3 *submit*
not respect 659.7 *be discourteous*
not respond 618.12 *be indifferent*
not responsible 758.5 *exempt*
not retain 767.9 *dispose of*
not retained 767.12 *disposed*
not right 240.1 *inconvenient*; 802.12 *incorrect*
not ring true 699.20 *be false*
no trouble 265.6 *easy thing*
not rusty 268.11 *lubricated*
not safe 254.2 *unsafe*
not satisfying 218.1 *insufficient*
not say a word 506.1 *be silent*
not secure 254.3 *vulnerable*
not see 519.14 *be blind*
not seen before 295.11 *unfamiliar*
not select 470.1 *reject*
not show up 98.15 *be absent*
not signposted 521.1 *invisible*
not singular 207.6 *plural*
not sleep 342.14 *push*
not so 708.23 *no!*
not so minded 637.1 *unwilling*
not sorry 809.3 *impenitent*
not speak 506.1 *be silent*; 730.13 *be voiceless*
not speak the truth 699.20 *be false*
not stand a chance 103.9 *be impossible*
not stand for 709.6 *dissent*
not stand on ceremony 657.11
not start 247.9 *malfunction*
not stir 339.4 *be inert*; 301.8 *be motionless*; 341.4 *not act*
not stirring 341.3 *inactive*
not stop 132.14, 134.3 *continue*
not stop at trifles 638.6 *be resolute*
not straight 800.7 *criminal*
not strong 337.8 *weak*
not subject to 758.5 *exempt*
not succeed 247.6 *fail*
not suffice 231.9 *be imperfect*; 218.5 *be insufficient*; 120.5 *be unequal*
not sufficient 218.1 *insufficient*
not support 113.17 *be against*
not take a joke 624.10 *be offended*
not take offence 658.10 *be courteous*
not take sides 618.15 *be impartial*
not tamper 250.15 *set free*
not tell apart 115.11 *make similar*
not tell the truth 798.11 *be evil*
not the done thing 802.13 *improper*
not there 98.21 *away*
not the thing 802.13 *improper*
not think much of 606.7 *be dissatisfied*
not think twice about 618.12 *be indifferent*
not to be despised 123.5 *important*
not to be drawn 645.4 *cunning*; 732.1 *shy*
not to be had 218.4 *scarce*
not to be overlooked 123.5 *important*
not to be recommended 670.32 *unsatisfactory*
not to be spared 135.4 *required*
not to be trusted 800.6 *faithless*
not today 286.3 *another time*
not tolerate 113.17 *be against*; 647.5 *be severe*; 399.3 *veto*
not tolerated 596.9 *disliked*
not tolerating 596.8 *disliking*
not to mention 211.10 *additionally*
not to mince words 799.7 *honourably*; 698.36 *truthfully*
not too little 217.1 *sufficient*
not too much 217.1 *sufficient*
not to one's taste 596.9 *disliked*
not touch 634.3 *abstain*; 383.9 *desist*; 350.5 *not use*
not touching 383.4 *desisting*
not transparent 266.2 *obscure*
not true 699.29 *false*
not true to life 116.4 *dissimilar*
not try 634.4 *shy*
not try to hide 738.4 *show oneself*
not turn a hair 618.12 *be indifferent*
not turn up 98.15 *be absent*
not understand 412.11 *be mixed up*; 696.9 *find unintelligible*
not understandable 696.1 *unintelligible*
not univocal 479.10 *equivocal*
not unlike 115.7 *similar*
not up 63.5 *real tennis*
not up to date 233.4 *incomplete*
not up to expectations 604.11 *disappointing*; 231.1 *imperfect*
not up to it 218.1 *insufficient*
not up to much 122.12 *inferior*
not up to scratch 606.5 *unsatisfactory*; 486.1 *unskilful*
not up to snuff 122.17 *defective*; 218.1 *insufficient*
not use 350.5; 441.1 *waste*
not used 350.1 *unused*
not used to 487.1 *unaccustomed*
not useful 238.1 *useless*
not using drugs 178.4 *traditional*
not utilize 350.5 *not use*
not utilized 350.1 *unused*
not utter a squeak 506.1 *be silent*
not vital 124.1 *unimportant*
not vote for 470.1 *reject*
not walk straight 690.7 *be drunk*
not want 470.3 *exclude*
not wanted 350.3
not waterproof 231.1 *imperfect*
not weaken 336.7 *be strong*
not wear 709.5 *refuse*
not weigh 124.11 *be unimportant*
not well 260.22 *sick*
not whole 205.11 *partial*
not wholly 205.12 *partly*
not with it 472.8 *absent-minded*
notwithstanding 347.5 *counter*
not work 335.6 *be powerless*; 238.7 *be useless*; 247.9 *malfunction*
not working 343.2
not working 245.13 *dilapidated*; 802.18 *gone wrong*; 335.10 *powerless*; 238.1 *useless*
not worth a bean 236.1 *worthless*
not worth a bumper 236.1 *worthless*
not worth a light 236.1 *worthless*
not worth considering 124.1 *unimportant*
not worth the effort 238.2 *futile*; 236.1 *worthless*
not worthwhile 238.2 *futile*
not worth worrying about 124.1 *unimportant*
not yield 383.7 *be obstinate*; 418.11 *be stubborn*; 638.10 *insist*
not yielding 383.2 *obstinacy*
nought 94.2 *nothingness*; 27.10, 195.1 *zero*
noumenon 446.1 *idea*; 4.8 *philosophical term*
noun 721.8 *name*; 5.35 *part of speech*
noun phrase 5.23 *phrase*
nourish 557.25 *provide food*; 554.20 *support life*; 392.20 *sustain*
nourishing 557.27 *edible*; 259.2 *healthful*; 257.4 *hygienic*
nourishment 557.7 *food*; 554.3 *life requirements*; 392.3 *sustenance*
nous 442.5 *common sense*; 442.3, 458.2 *intelligence*; 6.9 *learnedness*; 485.1 *skill*
nouveau riche 675.8 *discourteous*; 295.12 *immature*; 295.8 *new arrival*; 248.4 *prosperous person*; 781.11 *the rich*; 675.5 *vulgar person*
nouveau roman 17.2 *fiction*
nouvelle 17.2 *fiction*
nouvelle cuisine 25.1 *cookery*; 295.2 *trendiness*
Nouvelle Vague 295.2 *trendiness*
nova 522.4 *natural light*; 29.12 *variable star*
novel 126.5; 740.6 *book publishing*; 116.4 *dissimilar*; 17.2, 721.5 *fiction*; 477.4 *ideality*; 448.9 *original*; 295.11 *unfamiliar*; 356.5 *work of art*
novelette 17.2 *fiction*
novelettist 17.14 *author*
novel idea 443.6 *idea*
novelist 17.14 *author*; 721.10 *descriptive writer*; 740.12 *publisher*
novella 17.2, 721.5 *fiction*; 356.5 *work of art*
novel of ideas 17.2 *fiction*
novel of sensibility 17.2 *fiction*
novel sequence 17.2 *fiction*
novelty 124.9 *bauble*; 793.5 *cheap item*; 295.1 *newness*; 126.1, 448.4 *originality*
novelty costume 551.5 *fancy dress*
novemdecillion 194.3 *large number*; 201.11 *million*
novena 201.5 *nine*
novenary 201.16 *ninth*
novice 130.14 *beginner*; 456.5 *ignorant person*; 295.12 *immature*; 6.7 *learner*; 7.7 *monk*; 646.3 *naive person*; 295.8 *new arrival*; 486.10 *unskilled person*
novitiate 243.12 *briefing*
novocaine 489.4 *anaesthetic*
no voice 730.1 *voicelessness*
novus homo 295.8 *new arrival*
now 93.23; 282.9 *at present*; 275.27 *at what time*; 280.8 *immediately*; 285.2 *present time*
nowadays 282.9 *at present*
now and again 146.8 *apart*; 276.14 *for short periods*; 275.28, 297.2 *sometimes*
now and then 146.8 *apart*; 133.17 *discontinuously*; 276.14 *for short periods*; 299.8 *irregularly*; 275.28, 297.2 *sometimes*
no way 103.13 *impossible!*; 704.13, 708.23, 709.12 *no!*; 94.14 *not at all*; 301.11 *stop!*; 709.11 *uncooperatively*
nowhere 94.16; 98.21 *away*; 236.2 *inferior*
nowhere city 86.10 *urban area*
now here, now there 227.15 *changeably*
nowhere to be found 98.9 *away*; 766.16 *losing*
nowhere to turn 264.6 *critical situation*
no-win situation 264.5 *predicament*
no woman 98.7 *nobody*
no words wasted 269.1 *conciseness*
no work 341.1 *inaction*; 580.1 *leisure*
no worse 259.1 *healthy*
nowt 94.2 *nothingness*
now this, now that 642.6 *capriciously*; 227.15 *changeably*
noxious 236.3 *bad*; 357.14 *destructive*; 798.9 *detrimental*; 236.5 *harmful*; 500.5 *odorous*
noxiousness 798.1 *evil*; 236.11 *harmfulness*
noyade 814.13 *capital punishment*; 382.4 *slaughter*
nozzle 44.6 *garden tool*; 433.12 *sprinkler*
npn transistor 39.19 *transistor*
***n*-space** 27.35 *space*
NSU 260.14 *venereal disease*
***n*-tuple** 27.21 *set*
n-type conductivity 28.44, 39.4 *semiconductor*
n-type semiconductor 28.44, 39.4 *semiconductor*
nuance 590.2 *impression*; 209.4 *interval*
nub 173.1 *centre*; 123.3 *chief thing*; 406.1 *contents*; 99.2 *essential content*; 701.4 *gist*; 404.3 *nap*
nubbiness 420.6 *roughness*
nubbliness 420.6 *roughness*
nubby 420.2 *coarse*
nubile 570.22 *marriageable*
nubility 570.4 *marriageability*; 243.14 *preparedness*
nucleal 34.24 *nuclear*
nuclear 34.24; 173.6 *central*; 334.17, 437.10 *powered*
nuclear accident 28.75; 437.7 *nuclear power*
nuclear blast 357.5 *havoc*
nuclear bomb 587.16 *bomb*
nuclear cardiology 35.3 *medical specialty*
nuclear chemistry 32.1 *chemistry*
nuclear contamination 28.75 *nuclear accident*
nuclear deterrent 587.1 *weapon*
nuclear disarmament 589.1 *peace*
nuclear energy 28.11, 334.4 *energy*; 28.72 *nuclear fission*; 437.7 *nuclear power*
nuclear engineering 38.1 *engineering*; 28.72 *nuclear fission*
nuclear envelope 34.9 *cell nucleus*
nuclear fallout 357.7 *agent of destruction*
nuclear family 376.17 *family*
nuclear fission 28.72; 375.2 *deconstruction*; 437.7 *nuclear power*; 372.1 *separation*
nuclear-free zone 749.1 *pacification*
nuclear fuel 330.13 *fuel*; 437.7 *nuclear power*; 28.73 *nuclear reactor*; 334.6 *source of energy*
nuclear fusion 28.72 *nuclear fission*; 437.7 *nuclear power*
nuclear generating station 437.7 *nuclear power*
nuclear interaction 28.79 *fundamental interaction*
nuclear medicine 35.3 *medical specialty*
nuclear membrane 34.9 *cell nucleus*
nuclear missile 357.7 *agent of destruction*; 334.8 *nuclear power*
nuclear physics 28.3 *modern physics*; 402.6 *natural science*; 334.8 *nuclear power*
nuclear pore 34.9 *cell nucleus*
nuclear power 334.8; **437.7**; 28.11, 334.4 *energy*; 437.1 *fuel*; 28.72 *nuclear fission*; 334.6 *source of energy*
nuclear-powered 437.10 *powered*
nuclear power station 28.72 *nuclear fission*; 39.32 *power station*
nuclear reaction 28.71
nuclear reactor 28.73; 334.8, 437.7 *nuclear power*
Nuclear Regulatory Commission 334.8 *nuclear power*
nuclear reprocessing plant 767.5 *wasteyard*
nuclear sap 34.9 *cell nucleus*
nuclear submarine 587.5 *missile weapon*; 586.24 *warship*
nuclear war 585.1 *war*
nuclear warfare 585.8 *warfare*
nuclear warhead 357.7 *agent of destruction*; 334.8 *nuclear power*

nuclear waste 28.74; 437.7 *nuclear power*
nuclear weapon 357.7 *agent of destruction*; 334.8 *nuclear power*; 587.1 *weapon*
nuclear winter 357.5 *havoc*
nucleary 34.24 *nuclear*
nucleate 416.8 *be dense*; 173.6 *central*; 173.9 *centre*; 34.24 *nuclear*
nucleation 416.2 *concentration*
nucleic 34.24 *nuclear*
nucleic acid 34.9 *cell nucleus*; 34.12 *molecular biology*; 33.10 *nucleoside*
nucleic-acid structure 34.12 *molecular biology*
nucleolar 34.24 *nuclear*
nucleolate 34.24 *nuclear*
nucleolus 34.9 *cell nucleus*
nucleon 28.65 *atom*; 28.77 *elementary particle*; 402.4 *matter*
nucleonics 402.6 *natural science*; 28.72 *nuclear fission*; 334.8 *nuclear power*
nucleon number 28.69 *isotope*
nucleopeptide 34.9 *cell nucleus*
nucleophile 32.14 *chemical reaction*
nucleophilic 32.38 *reactive*
nucleophilic reaction 32.14 *chemical reaction*
nucleoplasm 34.9 *cell nucleus*
nucleoprotein 34.9 *cell nucleus*; 33.9 *protein*
nucleoside 33.10; 34.12 *molecular biology*
nucleosome 34.9 *cell nucleus*
nucleotide 34.12 *molecular biology*; 33.10 *nucleoside*
nucleus 28.65 *atom*; 34.8 *cell organ*; 173.1 *centre*; 123.3 *chief thing*; 99.2 *essential content*; 29.7 *galaxy*; 159.2 *little thing*; 402.4 *matter*; 578.4 *personnel*; 344.3 *rudiment*; 416.4 *solid body*; 130.3 *source*
nuclide 28.69 *isotope*
nuddy 552.9 *undressed*
nude 19.10 *art subject*; 552.8 *nude person*; 552.9 *undressed*
nude figure 552.8 *nude person*
nude model 552.8 *nude person*
nude painting 552.2 *nudity*
nude person 552.8
nudge 693.7 *advice*; 331.13 *blow*; 331.2 *collide*; 331.12 *collision*; 742.3, 742.11 *gesture*; 480.8 *incentive*; 327.9 *jolt*; 147.19 *meet*; 147.4 *meeting*; 492.3 *press*; 300.14 *set in motion*; 492.11 *touch*; 711.5 *warn*; 711.1 *warning*
nudie 552.2 *nudity*
nudie show 21.7 *show*
nudism 552.1 *undress*
nudist 493.5 *hot weather*; 552.8 *nude person*; 552.9 *undressed*
nudity 552.2
nugatory 124.4 *trivial*
nugget 780.16 *bullion*; 416.4 *solid body*
nuisance 607.3; 328.1 *disturbance*; 240.3 *inconvenience*; 342.11 *meddler*; 342.3 *nimbleness*; 408.11, 662.5 *troublemaker*; 242.9 *unpleasant person*
nuisance call 692.10 *telephone call*
nuke 585.13 *be at war*; 381.3 *bomb*; 94.13 *cause not to exist*; 441.2 *lay waste*
nuke 'em 382.26 *no quarter!*
null 16.57; **195.7**; 98.8 *absent*; 94.9 *nonexistent*; 238.1 *useless*
null and void 708.20 *cancelled*; 563.6 *having no effect*; 708.21 *nonexistent*; 16.57 *null*; 335.10 *powerless*; 238.1 *useless*; 399.5 *vetoed*
null hypothesis 27.54 *hypothesis testing*
nullification 708.5 *cancellation*; 347.1 *counteraction*; 357.1 *destruction*; 704.1 *refutation*; 708.4 *renunciation*
nullified 708.20 *cancelled*; 16.57 *null*; 708.18 *rejected*
nullifier 704.5 *refuter*
nullify 195.9 *annihilate*; 16.77 *annul*; 708.14 *cancel*; 347.3 *counteract*; 357.8 *destroy*; 709.6 *dissent*; 704.8 *refute*; 708.12 *renounce*
nullifying 347.4 *counteracting*
nulli secundus 121.14 *best*; 121.17 *supremely*
nullity 98.1 *absence*; 708.8 *nonexistence*; 94.2, 195.3 *nothingness*; 124.5 *unimportance*
null matrix 27.22 *matrix*
null set 27.21 *set*
numb 489.7 *anaesthetized*; 592.2 *desensitized*; 426.3 *dull*; 618.7 *indifferent*; 339.5 *inert*; 618.13 *make indifferent*; 335.8 *overpower*; 592.7 *render insensitive*; 301.5 *sedentary*
Number 194
number 27.5; **194.1**; **194.10**; **210.11**; 204.9 *be whole*; 551.1 *dress*; 27.90 *enumerate*; 743.10 *identify*; 127.4 *include*; 205.2 *particular*; 452.18 *particularity*; 733.5 *place of residence*; 203.8 *quantify*; 21.8 *scene*; 5.30 *syntax*; 203.4 *total*
number among one's possessions 763.7 *possess*
numbercruncher 210.5 *computer*
numbercrunching 210.4 *computing*
numbered 65.9 *billiard*; 743.12 *identified*; 203.6 *quantitative*
numbered ball 65.1 *billiards*
numbered with the dead 582.19 *dead*
number five 50.9 *sailor*
number four 50.9 *sailor*
numbering 210.3 *count*; 27.12 *numeration*
numberless 208.8; 202.2 *immeasurable*
numberlessness 202.5 *immeasurability*
number one 139.12 *I*; 121.6 *paragon*; 50.9 *sailor*; 246.4 *successful person*; 246.3 *successful thing*; 797.16 *superior person*
number-one 121.14, 235.2 *best*; 230.1 *perfect*
number-one driver 61.8 *driver*
number-one ranking 246.3 *successful thing*
number ones 560.6 *urine*
numberplate registration number 743.3 *means of identification*
numbers 203.5; 27.1 *mathematics*; 17.9 *metre*; 17.6 *poetry*
number six 50.9 *sailor*
number system 27.8
Number Ten 396.6 *place of authority*
number theory 27.4 *simple arithmetic*
number three 50.9 *sailor*
number two 398.4 *deputy*; 50.9 *sailor*
number-two driver 61.8 *driver*
number twos 560.5 *faeces*
number with 127.6 *subsume*
number work 210.1 *calculation*; 27.4 *simple arithmetic*
numbing 489.9 *anaesthetic*
numbly 618.17 *indifferently*; 339.7 *inertly*; 426.13 *obtusely*
numbness 592.4 *desensitization*; 426.7 *dullness*; 618.1 *indifference*; 339.1 *inertness*; 301.1 *motionlessness*; 260.17 *nervous disorder*; 260.3 *symptom*; 489.2 *unconsciousness*
numbskull 457.3 *unintelligent person*
numen 8.5 *deity*
numerable 27.73; 210.14 *calculable*
numeracy 455.3 *learning*; 27.1 *mathematics*
numeral 27.9; 194.1 *number*
numerary 194.7 *numerical*
numerate 6.18 *educated*; 455.9 *literate*; 210.11 *number*; 194.7 *numerical*
numeration 27.12; 210.1 *calculation*
numerative 210.13 *calculative*; 194.7 *numerical*
numerator 27.18 *division*; 194.5 *ratio*
numeric 194.7 *numerical*
numerical 27.71; **194.7**; 210.13 *calculative*; 407.12 *hierarchical*
numerical analysis 27.1 *mathematics*
numerical analyst 27.2 *mathematician*
numerical coefficient 27.25 *algebraic expression*
numerical forecast 31.4 *weather forecast*
numerically 194.12; 407.25 *in order*; 220.13 *inventorially*; 27.87, 210.16 *mathematically*
numerical order 407.3 *hierarchy*
numerical result 706.7
numerical taxonomy 34.17 *taxonomy*
numerologist 11.13 *diviner*
numerology 11.9 *divination*
numero uno 121.6 *paragon*; 797.16 *superior person*
numerous 297.3 *frequent*; 208.5 *multitudinous*; 207.6 *plural*
numerously 208.13; 297.1 *frequently*
numerousness 297.4 *frequency*; 207.2, 208.1 *multiplicity*
numinous 8.13 *divine*
numinously 8.19 *divinely*
numinousness 8.1 *divinity*; 11.2 *the occult*
numismatic 780.22 *monetary*
numismatically 780.28 *financially*
numismatics 780.13 *coinage*
numismatist 376.35 *collector*; 780.17 *financier*
numismatology 780.13 *coinage*
nummary 780.22 *monetary*
nummular 780.22 *monetary*
numnah 59.14 *horse-riding terms*
nun 450.5 *believer*; 572.4 *celibate person*; 797.15 *good person*; 7.7 *monk*; 255.5, 795.5 *pure person*; 803.4 *virtuous person*
Nunc Dimittis 10.9 *prayer*
nuncio 398.4 *deputy*
nuncupative 729.17 *oral*
nunnery 7.10 *priestly dwelling*; 736.6 *privacy*; 252.5 *refuge*
nunnish 572.8 *monastic*
nun's habit 551.3 *formal dress*
nuptial 755.7 *contractual*; 570.20 *matrimonial*; 10.21 *ritualistic*
nuptial benediction 570.5 *wedding*
nuptial bond 755.1 *contract*; 570.1 *marriage*
nuptial chamber 593.13 *abode of love*
nuptially 755.8 *contractually*; 570.24 *matrimonially*
nuptial Mass 10.5 *Christian rite*; 570.5 *wedding*
nuptial ode 570.6 *general terms*
nuptials 570.5 *wedding*
nuptial song 570.6 *general terms*
nuptial vows 570.5 *wedding*
nurse 35.16; 650.8 *be benevolent*; 665.11 *care for*; 665.7 *caring person*; 393.6 *cure*; 243.7 *develop*; 394.20 *doctor*; 401.6 *domestic servant*; 394.15 *healer*; 608.5 *helper*; 71.36 *lactate*; 579.1 *manage*; 579.15 *manager*; 35.17 *paramedic*; 401.4 *personal attendant*; 35.19 *practise medicine*; 359.5 *preserve*; 252.10 *protect*; 252.3 *protector*; 558.15 *provide drink*; 557.25 *provide food*; 392.19 *support*
nurse corps 584.4 *military organization*
nurse cow 43.8 *livestock*
nursed 558.16 *drinking*
nursemaid 401.6 *domestic servant*; 401.4 *personal attendant*; 252.3 *protector*
nurse practitioner 35.16 *nurse*
nurse resentment 624.8 *resent*
nursery 44.4; 562.1 *fertility*; 565.7 *room*; 344.2 *source*; 577.1 *workshop*
nursery education 6.2 *educational system*
nurseryman 44.13 *horticulturist*
nursery rhyme 17.7 *poem*
nursery school 6.12 *educational institution*
nursery slope 155.2 *lowlands*; 68.1 *skiing*
nurse's uniform 551.3 *formal dress*; 743.5 *uniform*
nurse through 393.6 *cure*
nursing 243.13 *development*; 35.25 *therapeutic*; 394.13 *therapy*; 35.8 *treatment*
nursing auxiliary 35.17 *paramedic*
nursing care 35.8 *treatment*
nursing chair 23.2 *chair*
nursing home 35.10, 394.14 *hospital*; 226.5 *resting place*
nursing home patient 260.19 *sick person*
nursing officer 35.16 *nurse*
nursling 555.9 *child*
nurture 168.8; 243.7 *develop*; 243.13 *development*; 6.22 *educate*; 6.1 *education*; 557.7 *food*; 43.18 *practise livestock farming*; 557.25 *provide food*; 392.20 *sustain*; 392.3 *sustenance*
nurtured 6.20 *refined*
nurturing 392.32 *supportive*
nusach 10.8 *hymn*
nut 80.2 *botanical fruit*; 62.4 *climbing equipment*; 118.10 *eccentric*; 373.8 *fastening*; 461.7 *insane person*; 272.3 *object of ridicule*; 438.1 *tool*; 423.7 *tough thing*
nutate 326.8 *oscillate*
nutation 326.1 *oscillation*
nutational 326.13 *oscillating*
nut bread 25.38 *bread*
nutbrown 534.1 *brown*
nutcase 118.10 *eccentric*; 461.7 *insane person*
nut college 461.8 *mental hospital*
nutcracker 554.6 *things brought to life*
nut cutlet 25.34 *vegetarian dish*
nut farm 461.8 *mental hospital*
nut hatch 461.8 *mental hospital*
nuthouse 461.8 *mental hospital*
nut key 62.4 *climbing equipment*
nutlet 80.3 *fruit structure*
nutmeg 66.2 *football play*; 496.5 *herbs*
nutmeg grater 427.13 *grater*
nut protein 25.21 *meat substitute*
Nutrasweet™ 498.2 *sweetener*
nutriment 557.7 *food*
nutrition 557.6; 557.7 *food*; 35.6 *health care*; 34.5 *physiology*
nutritional 557.27 *edible*; 394.17 *remedial*
nutritionally 25.57 *culinarily*
nutrition expert 557.19 *dietitian*
nutritionist 557.19 *dietitian*; 394.15 *healer*; 257.3 *hygienist*; 35.17 *paramedic*
nutritious 557.27 *edible*; 259.2 *healthful*; 257.4 *hygienic*
nutritiously 25.57 *culinarily*; 557.29 *edibly*; 259.8 *healthily*
nutritiousness 259.4 *healthfulness*; 257.2 *salubrity*
nutritive 557.27 *edible*; 394.17 *remedial*
nut roast 25.34 *vegetarian dish*
nuts 557.8 *animal food*; 80.1 *fruits*; 461.11 *insane*; 561.8 *organs of reproduction*; 25.10 *snack*; 79.9 *tree product*
nuts about 593.18 *in love*
nuts and bolts 123.3 *chief thing*; 99.2 *essential content*; 93.5 *fact*; 205.5 *largest part*; 438.5 *machine*; 402.4 *matter*; 694.1 *meaning*; 344.3 *rudiment*; 139.4 *specifications*; 352.2 *supplies*; 438.1 *tool*
nutshell 550.13 *casing*; 269.1 *conciseness*
nutter 461.7 *insane person*
nuttiness 461.1 *insanity*; 272.1 *ludicrousness*
nutty 459.5 *foolish*; 461.11 *insane*; 272.5 *ridiculous*; 457.6 *unintelligent*
nutty as a fruitcake 461.11 *insane*
nuzzle 593.14 *communication of love*; 492.4, 593.27 *kiss*; 492.11 *touch*
nuzzling 593.14 *communication of love*
Nyaya 4.7 *school of thought*
nyctalopia 519.2 *poor sight*
nyctalopic 519.9 *weak-sighted*
nyet! 708.23 *no!*
nylon 435.1 *materials*; 32.21 *polymer*
nylon line 55.3 *fishing tackle*
nylons 551.20 *legwear*
nylon stockings 308.6 *porous thing*
nylon webbing 62.4 *climbing equipment*
nymph 8.5 *deity*; 34.15 *developmental biology*; 76.5 *larva*; 568.6 *loose woman*; 555.4 *young animal*; 555.8 *young woman*
nymphet 568.6 *loose woman*; 555.8 *young woman*
nympho 796.9 *immoral woman*; 568.6 *loose woman*
nymphomania 36.15 *compulsion*; 461.4 *delusion*; 617.4 *sexual desire*; 796.3 *sexual immorality*
nymphomaniac 796.9 *immoral woman*; 461.7 *insane person*; 568.6 *loose woman*; 490.7 *pleased*; 490.3 *pleasure-seeker*; 796.13 *unchaste*
nystagmatic 519.9 *weak-sighted*
nystagmus 519.2 *poor sight*

oaf 457.3 *unintelligent person*; 242.9 *unpleasant person*; 486.10 *unskilled person*
oafish 457.6 *unintelligent*
oafishness 457.2 *unintelligence*
oak 418.7 *hard substance*
oak apple 79.10 *tree disease*
oaken 79.15 *woody*
oak gall 79.10 *tree disease*
oak moss 84.6 *lichen*; 82.3 *moss*
oar 330.11 *propeller*; 50.4 *rowing*
oarlock 307.4 *axle*
oarsman 323.8 *boatman*; 50.9 *sailor*
oasis 433.13 *irrigator*
oast house 43.7 *farm building*; 493.6 *fire*
oatcake 25.39 *loaf*
oaten 81.8 *grasslike*
oath 810.7 *commitment*; 712.1 *curse*; 756.1 *promise*; 707.3 *vow*
oath administrator 707.9 *affirmer*
oath of allegiance 707.3 *vow*
oath of office 707.3 *vow*
oath-taker 707.9 *affirmer*
oatmeal 25.40 *breakfast cereal*; 534.1 *brown*
oats 557.8 *animal food*; 43.12 *crop*
oat straw 43.9 *animal feedstuff*
obduracy 651.3 *callousness*; 228.2 *determination*; 809.1 *impenitence*; 418.8 *mental hardness*; 383.2, 641.5 *obstinacy*; 635.3 *wilfulness*
obdurate 651.12 *callous*; 228.11 *determined*; 809.3 *impenitent*; 418.4 *mentally*

hard; 423.5 *mentally tough*; 383.11, 641.1 *obstinate*; 628.4 *pitiless*; 264.14 *troublesome*; 641.3 *unyielding*; 635.8 *wilful*
obdurately 228.13 *determinedly*; 641.9 *obstinately*; 628.7 *pitilessly*; 423.14 *single-mindedly*
obdurateness 651.3 *callousness*; 423.9 *mental toughness*; 641.5 *obstinacy*
obeah 450.2 *religious belief*
obeah doctor 11.4 *witch*
Obedience 663
obedience 663.1; 636.8 *acquiescence*; 810.3 *allegiance*; 117.2 *compliance*; 419.12 *gentleness*; 797.11 *good behaviour*; 387.1 *subjection*; 388.1 *submission*; 623.12 *submissiveness*; 803.2 *virtues*; 9.1 *worship*
obedient 663.7; 636.3 *amenable*; 117.13 *compliant*; 407.17 *disciplined*; 803.6 *ethical*; 16.50 *law-abiding*; 810.9 *loyal*; 401.9 *serving*; 387.9 *subject*; 623.5 *submissive*; 388.5 *submitting*; 797.4 *well-behaved*
obediently 401.10; **663.10**; **797.24**; 117.16 *adaptably*; 803.10 *ethically*; 388.6 *with humility*
obedient person 663.4
obeisance 663.3; 667.2 *admiration*; 367.16 *courtesy*; 658.4 *deference*; 667.6 *greeting*; 667.4 *mark of respect*; 388.1 *submission*; 664.2 *sycophancy*
obeisant 663.9; 658.9 *deferential*; 667.9 *showing respect*; 664.7 *sycophantic*
obeisantly 658.16 *deferentially*
obelisk 744.11 *monument*; 154.6 *tall thing*
obelize 742.13 *punctuate*
obelus 742.7 *punctuation*
Oberammergau 21.2 *play*
obese 158.16 *fat*; 414.1 *heavy*; 152.1 *thick*; 181.10 *well-rounded*
obesely 158.20 *largely*
obesity 158.5 *fatness*; 414.4 *heaviness*; 219.2 *overdoing it*; 181.2 *round body*; 152.5 *thickness*
obey 663.5; 797.18 *be good*; 7.19 *be religious*; 387.8 *be subject to*; 117.8 *comply*; 810.16 *do one's duty*; 401.8 *serve*; 667.18 *show respect*; 388.3 *submit*; 9.7 *worship*; 419.16 *yield*
obey one's conscience 480.18 *be persuaded*
obey orders 140.17; 663.5 *obey*
obey regulations 117.8 *comply*
obfuscate 736.9 *disguise*; 161.4 *disorder*; 523.14 *make dark*; 524.10 *make dim*; 737.14 *make mysterious*; 266.3 *make obscure*; 528.11 *make opaque*; 702.11 *practise sophistry*
obfuscated 523.11 *benighted*; 702.8 *cunning*; 528.2 *shady*
obfuscating 264.12 *problematic*
obfuscation 702.3 *cunning*; 523.2 *darkening*; 736.5 *evasion*; 266.1 *obscurity*; 528.6 *opaqueness*
obfuscatory 266.2 *obscure*
obi 551.25 *accessories*; 9.2 *idolatry*; 450.2 *religious belief*; 11.6 *talisman*; 11.3 *witchcraft*
obiism 9.2 *idolatry*; 11.3 *witchcraft*
obit 583.2 *funeral*
obituarist 583.3 *funeral director*
obituary 582.12 *death count*; 721.4 *factual account*; 583.2, 583.11 *funeral*; 693.4 *mass communication*; 313.9 *parting*; 744.1 *record*
obituary writer 583.3 *funeral director*
object 113.18; **402.5**; 131.14 *aim*; 706.18 *answer back*; 704.10 *countercharge*; 709.6 *dissent*; 705.20 *doubt*; 483.1 *motive*; 482.6 *objective*; 5.35 *part of speech*; 694.5 *point*; 356.3 *product*; 703.19, 753.6 *protest*; 446.4 *purpose*; 344.5 *reason*; 708.11 *rebut*; 93.2 *thing*; 16.71 *try a case*
object ball 65.3 *English billiards*
object code 40.9 *programming language*
object distance 28.31 *lens element*
objectification 477.1 *imagination*
objectify 402.8 *be material*; 477.14 *imagine*
objecting 703.14 *demonstrating*; 670.26 *disagreeing*; 16.53 *litigating*; 708.19 *rebutting*; 383.10 *resistant*; 706.13 *retaliatory*
objecting to 709.9 *dissenting*
objection 113.4; 704.3 *countercharge*; 706.5 *counterstatement*; 670.4 *disagreement*; 709.2 *dissent*; 481.6 *dissuasion*; 59.7 *horseracing*; 16.5 *litigation*; 753.1 *protest*; 705.1 *question*; 708.3 *rebuttal*; 383.1 *resistance*; 637.11 *unwillingness*
objectionability 242.6
objectionable 242.2; 236.3 *bad*; 670.36 *blameworthy*; 240.1 *inconvenient*; 704.6 *refutable*; 706.13 *retaliatory*; 802.17 *unforgivable*
objection overruled 16.7 *legal trial*
objection sustained 16.7 *legal trial*
objective 482.6; 131.14 *aim*; 312.15 *destination*; 324.1 *direction*; 473.4 *disinterested*; 5.44 *grammatical*; 618.9 *impartial*; 28.30 *lens system*; 402.7 *material*; 480.11, 483.1 *motive*; 617.5 *object of desire*; 446.4 *purpose*; 4.15 *rational*; 801.7 *right*; 698.18 *truthful*; 353.6 *venture*; 458.5 *wise*
objective existence 95.1 *reality*
objective lens 29.25 *mounting*
objectively 473.8 *disinterestedly*; 5.52 *grammatically*; 618.19 *impartially*; 402.9 *materially*; 4.26 *rationally*; 698.36 *truthfully*; 458.9 *wisely*
objective psychology 36.1 *psychology*
objective reporting 741.3 *reporting*
objectivism 4.7 *school of thought*
objectivist 4.11 *follower of a doctrine*; 4.14 *of a philosophy*
objectivity 4.3 *detachment*; 473.1 *disinterestedness*; 618.3 *impartiality*; 698.5 *truthfulness*; 458.1 *wisdom*
object lesson 711.1 *warning*
object of admiration 619.4 *wonder*
object of charity 769.5 *recipient*
object of desire 617.5
object of dislike 596.2 *disliked thing*
object of one's affections 593.11 *loved one*
object of pride 622.12
object of ridicule 272.3
object of scorn 124.10 *nonentity*
object of virtu 19.6 *work of art*
object of wonder 619.4 *wonder*
object of worship 8.5 *deity*
objector 706.10 *answerer*; 670.11 *disapprover*; 751.4 *dissenter*; 16.8 *litigant*; 708.9 *negativist*; 113.11 *opposer*; 703.8, 753.4 *protester*; 637.16 *reluctant person*
object-relations theory 36.1 *psychology*
object to 113.17 *be against*; 606.7 *be dissatisfied*; 670.16, 751.5 *disagree*; 596.5 *dislike*; 594.14 *hate*; 383.6 *resist*
objet d'art 485.3 *masterpiece*; 19.6 *work of art*
objet trouvé 19.12 *sculpture*
oblast 86.5 *state*
oblate 10.18 *perform rites*; 27.83 *spherical*
oblation 807.2 *apology*; 371.22 *disgorgement*; 558.2 *drink*; 752.6, 768.3 *offering*; 10.3 *rite of worship*; 9.1 *worship*
oblational 10.21 *ritualistic*; 752.19 *sacrificial*
oblatorily 768.9 *as a gift*
oblatory 807.4 *atoning*; 768.7 *given*; 752.19 *sacrificial*
obligate 810.17 *impose a duty*
obligated 810.11 *duty-bound*; 671.4 *grateful*; 756.13 *guaranteeing*
obligation 706.9 *answerability*; 810.7 *commitment*; 386.1 *compulsion*; 136.7 *condition*; 354.3, 755.1 *contract*; 784.1 *debt*; 810.1 *duty*; 575.2 *entitlement*; 671.1 *gratitude*; 135.3 *needfulness*
obligatorily 397.16 *commandingly*; 386.11 *compellingly*
obligatory 810.12; 706.16 *answerable*; 397.14 *commanding*; 386.10 *compulsory*; 136.12 *conditional*; 99.5 *essential*; 140.9 *legal*; 135.4 *required*
oblige 706.21 *answer to*; 650.8 *be benevolent*; 658.10 *be courteous*; 648.3 *be lenient*; 386.6 *compel*; 810.17 *impose a duty*; 392.22 *improve*; 135.10 *necessitate*; 401.8 *serve*; 136.16 *specify*
obliged 706.16 *answerable*; 810.11 *duty-bound*; 671.4 *grateful*; 784.9 *in debt*; 476.9 *meant*
obliging 392.35, 650.6 *benevolent*; 747.17 *cooperative*; 658.7 *courteous*
obligingly 392.38, 650.10 *benevolently*; 658.14 *courteously*
obligingness 658.1 *courtesy*
obligor 784.6 *debtor*; 756.5 *promise-maker*; 677.7 *sycophant*
oblique 176.8; **189.4**; **325.23**; 189.6 *be oblique*; 270.4 *circumlocutory*; 324.14 *directed*; 300.17 *directional*; 27.80 *linear*; 189.2 *oblique line*; 306.9 *orbital*; 169.6 *side*
oblique angle 27.39, 176.1 *angle*; 189.2 *oblique line*
oblique-angled 176.9 *angled*
oblique light 524.1 *dimness*
oblique line 189.2
obliquely 189.8; 176.12 *askew*; 270.8, 306.12 *circuitously*; 325.28 *indirectly*; 169.10 *laterally*
oblique motion 300.5 *circuition*
obliqueness 189.1; 325.13 *deviation*
obliquity 176.2; 325.13 *deviation*; 120.1 *inequality*; 189.1 *obliqueness*
obliterate 358.1; 708.14 *cancel*; 526.3 *cause to disappear*; 256.13 *clean*; 357.8 *destroy*; 128.8 *eject*; 365.14 *erode*; 371.10 *exterminate*; 441.2 *lay waste*; 238.8 *make useless*; 212.3 *subtract*
obliterated 358.6; 94.11 *no more*; 212.5 *subtracted*
Obliteration 358
obliteration 358.3; 708.5 *cancellation*; 463.5 *death*; 357.1 *destruction*; 526.5 *disguise*; 128.2 *ejection*; 94.8 *extinction*; 212.1 *subtraction*; 365.2 *wearing away*
oblivion 463.1; 505.1 *deafness*; 94.8 *extinction*; 666.1 *negligence*; 358.3 *obliteration*; 343.9 *sleep*; 523.7 *spiritual darkness*
oblivious 463.8; 523.11 *benighted*; 519.12 *blind to*; 456.6 *ignorant*; 472.7 *inattentive*; 618.7 *indifferent*; 666.4 *negligent*; 489.6 *unfeeling*; 505.5 *unhearing*
obliviously 463.16; 472.14 *inattentively*; 618.17 *indifferently*; 489.13 *insensibly*
obliviousness 519.7 *figurative blindness*; 472.1 *inattention*; 463.1 *oblivion*
oblong 148.6; 27.84 *cubic*; 148.2 *elongated*; 27.44 *polygon*; 27.82 *polygonal*; 200.2 *quadrilateral*
O blood groups 431.4 *blood*
obloquy 678.3 *defamation*; 668.1 *disrespect*; 729.8 *speech*; 712.3 *vilification*
obnoxious 236.3 *bad*; 631.18 *badly behaved*; 798.7 *evil*; 594.12 *hated*; 242.2 *objectionable*; 364.8 *repulsive*
obnoxiously 631.20 *badly*; 798.12 *evilly*; 594.18 *hatefully*; 364.11 *repulsively*
obnoxiousness 236.9 *badness*; 812.1 *disrespect*; 798.1 *evil*; 594.4 *hatefulness*
obnoxious person 631.5 *badly behaved person*
obolus 780.12 *ancient coins*
obscene 258.9; 497.6 *coarse*; 712.8 *cursing*; 804.12 *immoral*; 539.4, 796.12 *indecent*; 5.39 *of language*; 236.4 *poor*; 364.8 *repulsive*; 675.9 *ribald*
obscene language 712.2 *offensive language*; 5.19 *swearword*
obscene literature 796.2 *indecency*
obscenely 150.7 *broadly*; 5.49 *colloquially*; 258.12 *dirtily*; 804.20 *immorally*; 364.11 *repulsively*; 712.12 *swearingly*; 497.11 *tastelessly*
obscene person 258.6 *dirty person*
obscenity 258.3; 497.4 *bad taste*; 712.1 *curse*; 796.2 *indecency*; 236.10 *poverty*
obscurantism 641.7 *opinionatedness*
obscurantist 641.8 *obstinate person*; 641.4 *set*
obscuration 532.7 *blackness*; 523.2 *darkening*; 526.5 *disguise*; 266.1 *obscurity*
obscure 124.2; **266.2**; **528.12**; 457.10 *bemuse*; 523.11 *benighted*; 519.15 *blind*; 526.3 *cause to disappear*; 696.4 *difficult*; 736.9 *disguise*; 519.13 *hidden*; 550.31 *hide*; 453.6 *indeterminate*; 523.14 *make dark*; 524.10 *make dim*; 521.8 *make invisible*; 737.14 *make mysterious*; 266.3 *make obscure*; 528.11 *make opaque*; 161.3 *make shapeless*; 453.20 *make uncertain*; 696.8 *make unintelligible*; 694.6 *meaningful*; 524.6 *murky*; 11.14, 11.20 *occult*; 521.3 *private*; 264.12 *problematic*; 528.2 *shady*; 161.5 *shapeless*; 696.1 *unintelligible*; 456.8 *unknown*; 96.8 *unreal*
obscured 736.14 *concealed*; 521.2 *difficult to see*; 524.6 *murky*; 521.3 *private*; 550.37 *protected*
obscurely 266.4; 532.12 *blackly*; 523.15 *darkly*; 524.12 *dimly*; 453.25 *indeterminately*; 11.25 *occultly*; 528.13 *opaquely*; 264.27 *problematically*; 161.6 *shapelessly*
obscureness 161.1 *shapelessness*
obscure person 124.10 *nonentity*
obscure point 696.12 *unintelligible thing*
obscuring 519.11 *blinding*; 550.1 *covering*; 523.9 *darkening*; 526.5 *disguise*
Obscurity 266
obscurity 124.6; **266.1**; **528.8**; 523.1 *darkness*; 264.1 *difficulty*; 737.7 *esotericism*; 736.5 *evasion*; 453.14 *indeterminacy*; 122.1 *inferiority*; 521.4 *invisibility*; 524.2 *murk*; 161.1 *shapelessness*; 523.7 *spiritual darkness*; 11.2 *the occult*; 696.11 *unintelligibility*
obsequial 583.11 *funeral*
obsequies 582.7 *dying day*; 583.2 *funeral*; 5.25 *inscription*; 603.2 *lament*; 729.8 *speech*
obsequious 663.7 *obedient*; 667.9 *showing respect*; 664.7, 677.16 *sycophantic*
obsequiously 677.17 *flatteringly*; 663.10 *obediently*; 5.51 *phraseologically*; 667.22 *respectfully*; 664.17 *sycophantically*
obsequiousness 663.1 *obedience*; 664.2 *sycophancy*
obsequy 667.6 *greeting*; 663.3 *obeisance*
observability 520.3 *visibility*
observable 518.23, 520.1 *visible*
observably 518.25 *visibly*
observance 601.1 *celebration*; 601.2 *commemoration*; 117.2 *compliance*; 631.1 *conduct*; 632.4 *custom*; 810.5 *discharge of duty*; 663.1 *obedience*; 7.2 *religiousness*; 10.1 *ritual*
observant 665.9 *careful*; 425.5 *mentally sharp*; 663.7 *obedient*; 518.21 *seeing*; 471.7 *watchful*; 10.22 *worshipping*
observantly 471.15 *attentively*; 663.10 *obediently*; 10.23 *ritually*; 518.26 *watchfully*
observation 518.3; 449.6 *discovery*; 446.1 *idea*; 745.1 *maxim*; 28.82 *measuring instrument*; 29.23 *observatory*; 729.7 *utterance*
observational 27.69 *theoretical*
observational astronomy 29.1 *astronomy*
observational error 28.83 *sensitivity*
observation balloon 586.31 *military aircraft*
observation car 321.6 *rolling stock*; 518.9 *viewpoint*
observation point 518.9 *viewpoint*
observation post 397.8 *vantage point*
observation tower 154.6 *tall thing*
observatory 29.23; 518.9 *viewpoint*
observe 29.37; 340.4 *act*; 745.3 *aphorize*; 97.12 *attend*; 7.19 *be religious*; 656.10 *celebrate*; 462.14, 601.16 *commemorate*; 117.8 *comply*; 449.1 *discover*; 10.18 *perform rites*; 4.20 *philosophize*; 471.11 *take note of*; 518.15 *watch*
observe a limit 684.6 *moderate*
observe a ritual 160.8 *be formal*
observe etiquette 658.11 *have good manners*
observe neutrality 589.5 *be at peace*
observe protocol 658.11 *have good manners*
observer 518.11; 322.3 *aircraft personnel*; 586.32 *airman*; 29.2 *astronomer*; 449.12 *discoverer*; 56.6 *golfer*; 97.5 *someone present*
observe routine 632.16 *have a habit*
observe the formalities 656.11 *be formal*
observe the rules 663.5 *obey*
observe tradition 632.16 *have a habit*
obsessed 11.19 *bewitched*; 471.8 *diligent*; 590.13 *passionate*; 638.1 *resolute*; 641.4 *set*
obsessed with jealousy 629.4 *jealous*
obsession 36.15, 386.1 *compulsion*; 461.4 *delusion*; 471.4 *diligence*; 590.4 *emotion*; 632.1 *habit*; 641.7 *opinionatedness*; 465.4 *prejudgment*
obsessional neurosis 36.10 *neurosis*
obsessive 632.15 *habit-forming*; 461.7 *insane person*
obsessive behaviour 461.4 *delusion*
obsessive-compulsive neurosis 36.10 *neurosis*
obsessive dieter 386.5 *compulsive person*
obsessive need 386.1 *compulsion*
obsessiveness 386.1 *compulsion*
obsidian 532.9 *black thing*; 523.4 *dark thing*; 266.2 *obscure*; 266.1 *obscurity*
obsolescence 350.10 *disuse*; 94.8 *extinction*
obsolescent 526.6 *disappearing*; 284.20 *former*
obsolescently 526.8 *fleetingly*; 350.12 *out of use*
obsolete 284.19 *antiquarian*; 526.7 *disappeared*; 350.4 *disused*; 3.18 *in the past*; 94.11 *no more*; 238.1 *useless*; 5.42 *worded*

obsolete coinage 780.15 *false money*
obsoletely 5.50 *lexically*; 350.12 *out of use*
obsoleteness 350.10 *disuse*
obstacle **103.7**; **378.2**; 604.2 *bad outcome*; 347.1 *counteraction*; 231.7 *defect*; 240.3 *inconvenience*; 59.9 *jumping*; 251.1 *restraint*; 264.8 *snag*; 416.4 *solid body*; 47.1 *track events*; 379.1 *trap*; 399.1 *veto*
obstacle course 585.6 *art of war*
obstetric 35.22, 394.18 *medical*; 561.16 *reproductive*
obstetrical 394.18 *medical*
obstetrician 35.13 *medical specialist*; 561.7 *obstetrics*
obstetrics **561.7**; 568.1 *female sex*; 35.3 *medical specialty*
Obstinacy 641
obstinacy **383.2**; **641.5**; 225.2 *conservatism*; 113.7 *contrariness*; 452.10 *conviction*; 228.2 *determination*; 662.1 *disobedience*; 809.1 *impenitence*; 418.8 *mental hardness*; 423.9 *mental toughness*; 640.1 *perseverance*; 647.1 *severity*; 267.2, 638.14 *tenacity*; 622.2 *unapproachability*; 635.3 *wilfulness*
obstinate **383.11**; **641.1**; 225.8 *conservative*; 452.2 *convinced*; 661.7 *defiant*; 661.8 *defying*; 228.11 *determined*; 662.13 *disobedient*; 809.3 *impenitent*; 418.4 *mentally hard*; 423.5 *mentally tough*; 640.10 *persevering*; 647.8 *severe*; 638.3 *strong-willed*; 267.10 *tenacious*; 264.14 *troublesome*; 622.15 *unapproachable*; 113.26 *uncooperative*; 635.8 *wilful*
obstinately **641.9**; 225.10 *conservatively*; 661.9 *defiantly*; 228.13 *determinedly*; 662.17 *disobediently*; 661.10 *in defiance*; 264.29 *perversely*; 383.14 *resistingly*; 647.11 *severely*; 423.14 *single-mindedly*; 267.12 *tenaciously*; 452.24 *with certainty*
obstinate person **641.8**; 225.3 *conservative person*
obstreperous 659.6 *bad-mannered*; 662.13 *disobedient*; 408.20 *disorderly*; 264.14 *troublesome*; 514.16 *vociferous*
obstreperously 662.17 *disobediently*; 659.10 *rudely*; 514.20 *vociferously*
obstreperousness 662.1 *disobedience*
obstruct 634.2 *avert*; 662.15 *be disobedient*; 240.5 *be inconvenient*; 264.23 *cause difficulties*; 347.3 *counteract*; 294.8 *delay*; 328.10 *disrupt*; 384.18 *fence*; 378.8 *hinder*; 238.8 *make useless*; 637.9 *not cooperate*; 708.11 *rebut*; 383.6 *resist*; 333.3 *slow down*; 384.25 *stall*; 309.8 *stop*; 399.3 *veto*; 113.20 *withstand*
obstruct a river 90.9 *stop the flow*
obstructed 333.7 *delayed*; 328.15 *disrupted*; 294.10 *held up*; 521.3 *private*; 708.18 *rejected*; 309.13 *stopped*
obstructer 378.7 *hinderer*
obstructing 294.12 *delaying*; 708.19 *rebutting*
Obstruction 378
obstruction 634.10 *avoidance*; 309.1 *closure*; 347.1 *counteraction*; 294.3 *delayed action*; 53.11 *dismissal*; 662.1 *disobedience*; 328.4 *disruption*; 56.1 *golf*; 333.12 *hesitation*; 378.1 *hindrance*; 708.3 *rebuttal*; 264.8 *snag*; 113.6 *uncooperativeness*; 399.1 *veto*
obstructionism 662.1 *disobedience*
obstructionist 378.7 *hinderer*; 113.11 *opposer*
obstructive 347.4 *counteracting*; 294.12 *delaying*; 662.13 *disobedient*; 378.13 *hindering*; 708.17 *negative*; 113.11 *opposer*; 383.10 *resistant*; 113.26 *uncooperative*; 399.5 *vetoed*
obstructively 399.7 *by veto*; 328.18 *disturbingly*; 634.22 *evasively*; 294.15 *late*; 708.22 *negatively*; 378.16 *with delay*
obstructiveness 378.1 *hindrance*; 113.6 *uncooperativeness*
obtain 632.17 *become a habit*; 316.14 *bring back*; 369.15 *draw out*; 765.9 *gain*; 138.28 *prevail*; 777.1 *purchase*; 769.9 *receive*; 773.7 *take*
obtainable 765.15 *gainful*; 778.15 *saleable*
obtain a divorce 571.7 *divorce*
obtain an extract **369.17**
obtain assistance 348.5 *find means*
obtainer 769.5 *recipient*
obtaining 369.5 *drawing out*; 632.10 *familiar*; 773.1 *taking*
obtaining an extract **369.7**
obtainment 765.1 *gain*
obtain one's objective 246.6 *be successful*
obtain under false pretenses 700.30 *be fraudulent*
obtrude 371.14 *let out*
obtrusion 371.22 *disgorgement*
obtrusive 660.15 *audacious*; 673.11 *cocky*; 738.14 *manifest*
obtrusively 660.32 *audaciously*; 673.21 *cockily*
obtrusiveness 673.3 *cockiness*
obtund 426.10 *blunt*; 685.4 *moderate*
obtundity 426.7 *dullness*
obtuse 426.3 *dull*; 592.1 *insensitive*; 524.8 *stupid*; 152.3 *thick-witted*; 457.6, 528.5 *unintelligent*
obtuse angle 27.39, 176.1 *angle*
obtuse-angled 176.9 *angled*
obtuse-angled triangle 27.43 *triangle*
obtusely **426.13**; 457.11 *unintelligently*
obtuseness 426.7 *dullness*; 524.4 *stupidity*; 457.2 *unintelligence*
obverse 167.6 *front*; 113.23 *opposite*; 113.2 *oppositeness*
obversely 113.28 *in opposition*
obviate 347.3 *counteract*; 265.18 *disentangle*; 378.8 *hinder*
obviation 378.1 *hindrance*
obvious 525.7 *appearing*; 452.1 *certain*; 725.3 *clear*; 185.7 *conspicuous*; 703.12 *demonstrable*; 703.9 *demonstrated*; 739.10 *disclosed*; 527.4 *easily seen through*; 716.9 *evident*; 93.10 *existing*; 738.14 *manifest*; 308.13 *opened up*; 695.2 *simple*; 518.23, 520.1 *visible*
obviously **308.25**; 525.15 *apparently*; 725.4 *clearly*; 716.15 *evidently*; 703.20, 738.16 *manifestly*; 449.16 *originally*; 185.10 *protuberantly*; 527.13 *transparently*; 518.25, 520.11 *visibly*
obviousness 452.9 *certainty*; 520.4, 725.1 *clarity*; 185.4 *conspicuousness*; 716.3 *evidentness*; 527.10, 738.11 *openness*; 695.10 *simplicity*
occasion 344.9 *be the cause of*; 344.1 *cause*; 601.1 *celebration*; 275.11 *date*; 107.5 *good chance*; 348.1 *instrumentality*; 135.3 *needfulness*; 222.2 *occurrence*; 308.10 *opportunity*; 280.4 *point in time*; 344.5 *reason*
occasional **275.23**; **282.7**; 206.6 *sparse*
occasional help 401.1 *servant*
occasionally 133.17 *discontinuously*; 276.14 *for short periods*; 275.28, 297.2 *sometimes*; 206.11 *sparsely*
occasional showers 31.25 *rain*
occasional verse 17.6 *poetry*
Occident 86.7 *regions of the world*
Occidental 324.13 *directional*; 86.16 *regional*
occlude 309.8 *stop*
occluded 309.13 *stopped*
occluded front 31.10 *air movement*
occlusion 31.10 *air movement*; 309.1 *closure*
occult **11.14**; **11.20**; 523.11 *benighted*; 696.4 *difficult*; 736.15 *disguised*; 523.14 *make dark*; 737.11 *mysterious*; 101.9 *parapsychological*; 696.1 *unintelligible*
occultation 736.1 *concealment*; 523.2 *darkening*; 526.5 *disguise*; 29.21 *orbit*
occulted 526.7 *disappeared*
occult influence **395.2**
occulting 522.15 *lucent*
occulting light 522.6 *electric light*
Occultism 11
occultism **11.1**; 475.2 *divination*; 737.7 *esotericism*; 738.10 *manifestation*; 696.11 *unintelligibility*
occultist **11.12**; 101.7 *believer in a nonmaterial world*; 475.8 *oracle*
occultly **11.25**; 101.13 *metaphysically*
occultness 11.2 *the occult*
occult phenomena 101.3 *spiritual world*
occult power 334.1 *power*
occupancy 763.1 *possession*; 97.3 *residence*
occupant 564.1 *inhabitant*; 763.5 *possessor*
occupation 340.1 *action*; 633.4 *activity*; 776.6 *business*; 143.4 *employment*; 482.3 *future intention*; 576.3 *job*; 703.6 *mass demonstration*; 763.1 *possession*; 381.14 *siege*; 342.2 *social activity*; 354.2 *undertaking*
occupational 340.5 *acting*; 632.9 *habitual*; 776.17 *professional*; 143.6 *situated*; 2.14 *socioeconomic*
occupational disease 260.4 *disease*
occupational-health nurse 35.16 *nurse*
occupationally 632.19 *habitually*
occupational medicine 35.1 *medicine*
occupational neurosis 36.10 *neurosis*
occupational power 12.3 *governance*
occupational prestige 2.7 *social stratification*
occupational therapist 35.17 *paramedic*
occupational therapy 36.3 *psychiatric treatment*; 394.13 *therapy*; 35.8 *treatment*
occupation troops 586.14 *armed forces*
occupied 342.19 *busy*; 564.11 *inhabited*; 349.9 *used*
occupied by 564.11 *inhabited*
occupied country 85.3 *dominion*
occupier 564.1 *inhabitant*; 763.5 *possessor*
occupy 85.18 *exert sovereignty*; 232.6 *fill*; 564.14, 565.17 *inhabit*; 763.7 *possess*; 703.19 *protest*; 97.13 *reside*
occupy 10 Downing Street 12.11 *govern*
occupy a certain standing 221.6 *be in a state of*
occupy a freehold 440.9 *own property*
occupy a post 12.11 *govern*
occupying 763.8 *possessing*; 763.1 *possession*; 97.9 *resident*
occupying force 586.14 *armed forces*
occupy oneself 340.4 *act*
occupy the White House 12.11 *govern*
occur **525.13**; 97.11 *be present*; 95.10 *be real*; 107.10 *chance*; 93.17 *exist*; 345.9 *take effect*
occur annually 298.8 *be cyclic*
occur monthly 298.8 *be cyclic*
occur periodically 297.7 *be frequent*
occur regularly 297.7 *be frequent*
occurrence **222.2**; 525.2 *being in view*; 93.1 *existence*; 27.58 *frequency distribution*; 95.1 *reality*
occurring 93.10 *existing*; 95.6 *real*
occur to one 446.14 *have an idea*
ocean **30.12**; 150.5 *broad thing*; 91.1 *sea*; 319.5 *transportable*
ocean basin 30.16 *ocean floor*
ocean blue 91.1 *sea*
ocean bottom 156.4 *deep thing*
ocean-cruising yacht 50.2 *sailing boat*
ocean current **30.13**
ocean depths 156.4 *deep thing*; 30.12 *ocean*; 91.1 *sea*
ocean floor **30.16**; 175.1 *base*; 156.4 *deep thing*; 91.1 *sea*
ocean-going 323.11 *nautical*; 91.7 *oceanic*; 319.5 *transportable*
Oceania 92.1 *continent*
oceanic **30.51**; **91.7**
oceanic bird 72.3 *water bird*
oceanic climate 31.38 *climate*
oceanic crust 30.18 *earth's crust*
oceanic ridge 30.21 *mountain building*; 30.16 *ocean floor*
oceanic rise 30.21 *mountain building*
oceanic sediment 30.27 *sediment*
oceanic trench 30.16 *ocean floor*; 30.19 *plate tectonics*
Oceanid 91.4 *sea god*
oceanographer **91.6**; 30.4 *geophysicist*; 26.9 *measurer*
oceanographic **91.8**; 156.13 *bathymetric*; 30.49 *geophysical*; 26.12 *metrical*
oceanographically **91.12**; 26.17 *measurably*
oceanography **91.5**; 156.6 *bathymetry*; 28.4 *experimental physics*; 26.1 *measurement*
ocean racing 50.1 *sailing*
ocean-racing yacht 50.2 *sailing boat*
ocean radar station ship 586.24 *warship*
ocean research vessel **30.17**
ocean shore 92.4 *coast*
ocean track 323.2 *waterway*
Oceanus 91.4 *sea god*
oceanwards 91.11 *nautically*
ocean water 30.12 *ocean*
ocean wave 30.14 *wave*
oche 69.6 *darts*
ochlocracy 588.2 *anarchism*; 12.1 *government*; 396.7 *type of rule*
ochlocrat 588.3 *anarchist*
ochlocratic 588.7 *anarchistic*
ochre 534.4 *brown pigment*; 536.2 *orangeness*
ochreous 536.1 *orange*
Ockham's razor 4.8 *philosophical term*
o'clock 281.18 *horologically*
OCR 40.13 *character recognition*
octad 201.4 *eight*
octadic 201.15 *eighth*
octagon 176.3 *angled figure*; 201.4 *eight*; 27.44 *polygon*
octagonal 176.9 *angled*; 201.15 *eighth*; 27.82 *polygonal*
octahedral 27.84 *cubic*; 201.15 *eighth*
octahedron 201.4 *eight*; 27.46 *polyhedron*
octahydrate 32.10 *salt*
octal code 40.10 *character*
octal notation 27.8 *number system*
octameter 17.9 *metre*
octane number 437.6 *oil*
octangular 201.15 *eighth*
octant 26.6 *measuring instrument*
octarchy 201.4 *eight*
octaroon 412.5 *hybrid*; 1.6 *race*; 1.13 *racial*
octastich 17.8 *part of poem*
Octateuch 201.4 *eight*
octatonic 201.15 *eighth*
octavalent 32.35 *combined*
octave 201.4 *eight*; 18.16 *musical note*; 17.8 *part of poem*
octavo 201.4 *eight*
octennial 201.15 *eighth*
octet 374.3 *assembly*; 201.4 *eight*; 18.26 *musical group*; 17.8 *part of poem*; 747.9 *team*
octillion 194.3 *large number*; 201.11 *million*
octocentenary 201.9 *treble figures*
octodecillion 194.3 *large number*; 201.11 *million*
octogenarian 556.7 *older person*; 201.8 *twenty and over*
octonary 201.4 *eight*; 201.15 *eighth*
octopod 75.19 *molluscan*
octopus 70.5 *aquatic animal*; 201.4 *eight*; 25.18 *sea fish*
octose 33.3 *carbohydrate*
octosyllabic 17.20 *metrical*
octroi 790.7 *tax*
octuple 201.4 *eight*; 201.15 *eighth*; 201.23 *quintuple*
octuplet 201.4 *eight*
ocular 518.20 *visual*
oculist 394.15 *healer*
OD 219.4 *be excessive*; 219.2 *overdoing it*
odd **194.8**; 802.14 *abnormal*; 751.10 *different*; 118.14 *eccentric*; 56.2 *golfing terms*; 461.11 *insane*; 487.2 *not customary*; 27.71 *numerical*; 696.5 *strange*; 215.10 *surplus*; 630.8 *surprising*; 120.3 *unequal*; 299.5 *unusual*; 619.8 *wonderful*
oddball 642.4 *capricious person*; 325.19 *deviant person*; 118.10, 118.14 *eccentric*; 461.7 *insane person*; 696.5 *strange*
odd bod 118.10 *eccentric*; 116.2 *unlikeness*
odd customer 118.10 *eccentric*
odd fellow 118.10 *eccentric*
odd fish 118.10 *eccentric*
odd items 211.4 *extra*
oddity 802.4 *abnormality*; 325.19 *deviant person*; 118.10 *eccentric*; 619.5 *person of wonder*; 105.5 *unexpectedness*; 655.6 *unsocial person*; 118.4 *unusualness*
odd-job man 401.1 *servant*
oddly 325.29 *erratically*; 118.21 *unconformably*; 299.9, 487.8 *unusually*
odd man out 325.19 *deviant person*; 751.4 *dissenter*; 114.1 *diversity*; 128.5 *excluded person*; 118.7 *nonconformist*; 116.2 *unlikeness*; 655.6 *unsocial person*
oddment 211.4 *extra*
oddments 205.8 *bits and pieces*; 376.32, 412.3 *miscellany*; 215.2 *residue*
odd moments 580.1 *leisure*
oddness 802.4 *abnormality*; 120.1 *inequality*; 461.1 *insanity*; 299.2 *unusualness*
odd number 120.1 *inequality*; 194.2 *kind of number*; 27.5 *number*
odds 121.3 *advantage*; 59.7 *horseracing*; 120.1 *inequality*; 102.1 *possibility*; 104.1 *probability*
odds and ends 114.2 *assortment*; 205.8 *bits and pieces*; 211.4 *extra*; 376.32, 412.3 *miscellany*; 238.6 *refuse*; 215.2 *residue*

odds and sods 205.8 *bits and pieces*; 211.4 *extra*; 412.3 *miscellany*
odds-maker 475.9 *forecaster*
odds-on 107.3 *equal chance*; 107.5 *good chance*; 102.3 *strong possibility*
odds-on bet 59.7 *horseracing*
odds-on chance 104.4 *chance*
odd stick 118.10 *eccentric*
odd-toed 71.33 *ungulate*
odd-toed ungulate 71.15 *hoofed mammal*
ode 17.7 *poem*
odeon 21.16 *theatre*
odeum 21.16 *theatre*
Odin 585.3 *gods and goddesses of war*
odious 798.7 *evil*; 594.12 *hated*; 242.1 *unpleasant*
odiously 798.12 *evilly*
odium 594.1 *hate*
odometer 742.5 *indicator*; 26.8 *meter*; 332.8 *speed*
odometry 26.2 *micrometry*
odontoid 425.4 *toothed*
odoriferous 500.5 *odorous*
odoriferously 500.10 *odorously*
odorimetry 500.1 *odour*
odorous 500.5
odorously 500.10
odorousness 500.1 *odour*
odour 500.1; 139.3 *characteristic*
odour-free 501.3 *odourless*
odourless 501.3
odourlessly 501.7
Odourlessness 501
odourlessness 501.1
odour of sanctity 500.4 *reputation*
oedema 431.3 *body fluid*; 182.2 *bulge*; 190.1 *growth*
oedematous 190.7 *bigger*; 260.23 *diseased*
Oedipus complex 36.18 *complex*; 593.2 *romantic love*
oesophagus 308.7 *passageway*
oestrogen 394.8 *drug*; 33.16 *hormone*
oestrous 298.12 *cyclic*; 292.17 *in season*
oestrous cycle 298.2 *cycle*
oeuvre 356.5 *work of art*
of academic interest 476.7 *suppositional*
of advanced years 296.11 *old*
of a fruit 80.9
of age 570.22 *marriageable*
of all sorts 114.6 *assorted*
of all work 237.1 *useful*
of a morning 290.8 *in the morning*
of animals 70.15
of another age 286.2 *occurring at a different time*
of another time 286.2 *occurring at a different time*
of another world 477.12 *imaginary*
of a philosophy 4.14
of a piece 115.7 *similar*
of a secretion 559.5
of assistance 392.30 *helping*
of authority 395.11 *influential*
of beauty 545.5 *beautiful*
of choice 121.15 *excellent*
of common occurrence 297.3 *frequent*
of concern 123.5 *important*
of consequence 123.5, 643.3 *important*
of consideration 123.5 *important*
of course 117.18 *as usual*; 452.26 *certainly!*; 345.12 *with the effect of*
of different opinions 114.7 *dissenting*
of doubtful meaning 696.4 *difficult*
of easy virtue 796.13 *unchaste*
off 98.9 *away*; 131.22 *cancelled*; 245.12 *deteriorated*; 375.5 *disintegrated*; 145.10 *distantly*; 231.1 *imperfect*; 343.2 *not working*; 236.4 *poor*; 53.14 *positioned*; 503.4 *putrid*; 218.4 *scarce*; 517.9 *unmelodious*; 242.3, 499.6 *unpalatable*
off-air 505.7 *unheard*
offal 25.31; 258.4 *dirt*; 172.4, 406.3 *insides*; 238.6 *refuse*
off and on 146.8 *apart*; 224.15, 227.15 *changeably*; 133.17 *discontinuously*; 276.14 *for short periods*; 299.4 *irregular*; 299.8 *irregularly*
off balance 120.3 *unequal*; 120.7 *unequally*
off base 802.12 *incorrect*
off beam 802.12 *incorrect*
offbeat 642.1 *capricious*; 118.14 *eccentric*; 126.5 *novel*
off beat 286.2 *occurring at a different time*
off break 53.8 *delivery*; 325.15 *deviating motion*
off-break 53.13 *bowling*
off-Broadway 21.1 *drama*; 21.5 *show business*
off-camber 61.10 *racing*
off-camber corner 61.6 *motor-racing terms*
off-centre 325.20 *deviant*; 234.6 *distorted*; 120.7 *unequally*
off chance 102.4 *remote possibility*
off-colour 231.1 *imperfect*; 260.22 *sick*
off course 766.18 *at a loss*; 328.18 *disturbingly*; 802.12 *incorrect*; 325.21 *indirect*; 189.4 *oblique*; 189.8 *obliquely*; 766.21 *out of place*
offcut 205.7 *piece*; 372.3 *separateness*
offcuts 215.2 *residue*
off cutter 53.8 *delivery*
off day 486.9 *bungling*
off drink 689.1 *sober*
off drive 53.9 *stroke*
off duty 580.7 *leisurely*; 343.2 *not working*; 580.2 *time off*
offence 46.7; **624.2**; 590.6 *bad feeling*; 16.39 *crime*; 274.8 *moral error*; 806.3 *sin*; 242.5 *unpleasantness*; 802.8 *wrongdoing*
offend 624.9; 16.73 *be illegal*; 364.4 *be repulsive*; 804.16 *be wicked*; 596.7 *cause dislike*; 242.10 *displease*; 802.21 *do wrong*; 668.23 *insult*; 242.11 *quarrel*; 802.20 *wrong*
offended 624.15 *resentful*
offended dignity 623.9 *humiliation*
offender 340.3 *doer*; 806.4 *guilty person*; 16.40 *lawbreaker*; 651.8 *malefactor*; 804.9 *wicked person*; 802.10 *wrongdoer*
offending 16.60
offensive 351.5 *abusive*; 659.6 *bad-mannered*; 585.9 *battle*; 804.15 *criminal*; 712.8 *cursing*; 661.7 *defiant*; 798.7 *evil*; 240.1 *inconvenient*; 796.12 *indecent*; 668.11 *insulting*; 802.16 *in the wrong*; 381.22 *militant*; 584.8 *military*; 381.12 *military attack*; 364.8 *repulsive*; 503.3 *stinking*; 258.8 *unclean*; 242.1 *unpleasant*; 46.19 *varsity*
offensive backfield 46.7 *offence*
offensive backs 46.7 *offence*
offensive campaign 381.12 *military attack*
offensive coordinator 46.2 *football player*
offensive drive 46.7 *offence*
offensive formation 46.7 *offence*
offensive foul 46.13 *penalty*
offensive language 712.2
offensive line 46.7 *offence*
offensive lineman 46.7 *offence*
offensively 351.6 *abusively*; 381.26 *aggresively*; 804.21 *criminally*; 661.9 *defiantly*; 258.12 *dirtily*; 798.12 *evilly*; 584.11 *militarily*; 364.11 *repulsively*; 659.10 *rudely*; 712.12 *swearingly*; 242.13 *unpleasantly*
offensiveness 659.2 *bad manners*; 798.1 *evil*; 242.5 *unpleasantness*
offensive operations 381.12 *military attack*
offensive team 46.7 *offence*
offensive terms for homosexual 567.9
offensive warfare 585.8 *warfare*
offensive weapon 587.1 *weapon*
Offer 752
offer 752.1; **752.9**; 807.6 *apologize*; 353.1 *attempt*; 776.3 *bargain*; 776.9 *bargaining*; 746.2 *basis for negotiations*; 768.5 *give*; 476.6 *propound*; 436.5 *provision*; 777.1 *purchase*; 777.7 *purchasing*; 710.1, 710.6 *request*; 813.4 *reward for service*; 476.1 *supposition*; 636.15 *volunteer*
offer a bargain 791.3 *discount*
offer a bribe 480.17 *bribe*; 813.11 *pay*
offer a defence 715.7 *be accused*
offer a discount 791.3 *discount*
offer advice 713.5 *advise*
offer a gift 752.16 *make an offering*
offer a good living 765.13 *be profitable*
offer amnesty to 708.14 *cancel*
offer an easy read 695.5 *simplify*
offer an inducement 480.17 *bribe*
offer an interpretation 719.12 *translate*
offer an oblation 807.6 *apologize*
offer an opportunity 287.4 *be timely*
offer apologies 649.13 *ask forgiveness*
offer a prayer 10.20 *pray*
offer a prize 813.9 *reward*
offer a reward 768.5 *give*; 813.9 *reward*
offer a sacrifice 752.16 *make an offering*
offer a sacrificial lamb 752.16 *make an offering*
offer a solution 746.5 *negotiate*
offer assistance 752.11 *volunteer*
offer a sweetener 480.17 *bribe*; 813.11 *pay*
offer battle 585.14 *battle*
offer collateral 253.12 *certify*
offer comfort 627.9 *sorrow*
offer consolation 627.9 *sorrow*
offer counsel 713.5 *advise*
offer criticism 719.11 *criticize*
offer easy terms 793.13 *make cheap*
offered 752.17; 436.8 *provisional*; 710.9 *requesting*; 636.5 *voluntary*
offered for arbitration 16.54 *litigated*
offerer 777.12 *purchaser*
offer factual evidence 698.30 *prove true*
offer financial assistance 752.11 *volunteer*
offer for approval 738.1 *display*
offer for sale 752.9 *offer*; 778.1 *sell*; 13.10 *trade with*
offer help 752.11 *volunteer*
offer homage 663.6 *show obeisance to*
offer hospitality 752.11 *volunteer*
offer in defence 704.10 *countercharge*
offering 752.6; **768.3**; 807.2 *apology*; 807.4 *atoning*; 768.1, 813.18 *giving*; 752.17 *offered*; 785.1 *payment*; 10.3 *rite of worship*; 636.5 *voluntary*; 9.1 *worship*
offering homage 663.9 *obeisant*
offering no advantage 238.2 *futile*
offering no benefit 238.2 *futile*
offer no apologies 809.5 *be impenitent*
offer no compromise 647.5 *be severe*
offer of a lifetime 480.10 *bribe*
offer of public service 752.5
offer one cannot refuse 480.10 *bribe*; 752.1 *offer*; 483.5 *positive stimulus*
offer one's apologies 807.6 *apologize*; 752.14 *offer reparation*
offer oneself 752.13 *be a candidate*
offer one's heart to 593.26 *court*
offer one's intercession 748.1 *mediate*
offer one's life 752.12
offer one's resignation 605.5 *resign*
offer price 790.1 *price*
offer readability 695.4 *be intelligible*
offer refuge 253.10 *secure*
offer reparation 752.14
offer resistance 383.6 *resist*
offer sacrifice 807.6 *apologize*
offer satisfaction 752.14 *offer reparation*
offer shelter 253.10 *secure*
offer sympathy to 490.10 *comfort*
offer to buy 752.10
offertory 10.6 *Eucharist*; 752.6, 768.3 *offering*; 18.5 *sacred music*
offer up 768.5 *give*; 382.20 *kill ritually*
offer value for money 793.13 *make cheap*
offer worship 10.19; **752.15**
off familiar territory 766.18 *at a loss*; 766.21 *out of place*
off food 687.6 *fasting*
off form 486.3 *clumsy*; 231.1 *imperfect*
off guard 630.6 *surprised*; 630.13 *surprisingly*
offhand 657.13 *casually*; 478.7 *extempore*; 478.1 *improvised*; 657.7 *informal*
offhanded 659.5 *discourteous*; 478.1 *improvised*; 666.5 *indifferent*
offhandedly 657.13 *casually*; 659.9 *discourteously*
offhandedness 478.4 *improvisation*; 666.2 *indifference*; 657.1 *informality*
offically 396.25 *authentically*
office 346.3 *business*; 601.3 *ceremony*; 275.3 *duration*; 143.4 *employment*; 16.2 *jurisdiction*; 10.1 *ritual*; 565.7 *room*; 810.2 *task*; 577.1 *workshop*
office assistant 401.5
office bearer 579.16 *official*
office block 356.8 *construction*; 154.6 *tall thing*
office boy 401.5 *office assistant*
office building 38.20 *building*
office-holder 579.16 *official*
office manager 579.15 *manager*
office memorandum 744.1 *record*
office of power 396.5 *position of authority*
officer 578.3 *agent*; 400.3 *leader*; 579.16 *official*; 586.8 *soldier*
officer of state 579.16 *official*
officer-training school 6.12 *educational institution*
offices 650.4 *benevolent act*; 392.2 *support*; 577.1 *workshop*
office shirt 551.8 *shirt*
office supplies 790.6 *business costs*
office worker 401.5 *office assistant*; 578.1 *worker*
official 53.3; **579.16**; 578.3 *agent*; 698.19 *authentic*; 396.12 *authoritative*; 49.2 *basketball player*; 632.12 *established*; 656.6 *formal*; 12.9, 396.14 *governmental*; 16.10 *law officer*; 400.3 *leader*; 140.9 *legal*; 579.17 *managerial*; 5.39 *of language*; 396.10 *person of authority*; 744.16 *recorded*; 10.21 *ritualistic*; 396.15 *true*; 15.10 *unionized*
official body 398.2 *representative body*
official documents 693.3 *document*
officialdom 396.4 *governance*; 400.8 *the power structure*
officialese 5.20 *jargon word*
officialism 12.3, 396.4 *governance*
official language 5.6
officially 698.37 *authentically*; 396.23 *authoritatively*; 656.12 *formally*; 15.13 *industrially*; 579.19 *managerially*; 744.17 *on the record*; 10.23 *ritually*
officialness 698.6 *authenticity*
official notice 740.1 *publication*
official oath 707.3 *vow*
official procedure 632.6 *procedure*
official publication 744.1 *record*
official punishment 814.8 *penalty*
official receiver 769.7 *collector*
official record 744.1 *record*
official reply 706.2 *acknowledgment*
official report 744.1 *record*
official representative 398.1 *delegate*
official residence 565.4
official scorer 48.2 *baseball player*
Official Secrets Act 399.2 *censorship*; 251.1 *restraint*; 737.1 *secrecy*; 736.4 *silence*; 647.2 *suppression*
official stamp 743.3 *means of identification*
officials' time-out 46.5 *game time*
official strike 15.4 *industrial dispute*
official visit 654.3 *meeting*
officiate 340.4 *act*; 748.1 *mediate*; 752.15 *offer worship*; 10.18 *perform rites*
officious 579.17 *managerial*; 342.21 *meddling*; 644.6 *prying*
officiously 644.9
officiousness 342.9 *overactivity*; 219.2 *overdoing it*; 644.2 *prying*
officious person 342.11 *meddler*
offing 145.3 *distant place*
off-key 517.9 *unmelodious*
of flesh and blood 402.7 *material*
off-limits 166.5 *limited*; 399.5 *vetoed*; 166.8 *within limits*
off-limits area 166.2 *limiting factor*; 251.1 *restraint*; 372.2 *setting apart*
off-line 40.21, 40.22 *on-line*
off-load 415.10 *lighten*; 319.4 *transport*; 371.12 *unload*
off-loaded 415.3 *lightening*
off-loading 371.20 *eviction*; 319.1 *transport*
of flowers 78.12
off-off-Broadway 21.1 *drama*; 21.5 *show business*
off one's block 461.11 *insane*
off one's chump 461.11 *insane*
off one's crust 461.11 *insane*
off one's food 260.22 *sick*
off one's guard 254.3 *vulnerable*
off one's head 328.16 *deranged*; 461.11 *insane*
off one's nuts 461.11 *insane*
off one's onion 461.11 *insane*
off one's own bat 636.18 *voluntarily*; 752.18 *voluntary*
off one's rocker 461.11 *insane*
off one's stride 486.3 *clumsy*
off one's timing 486.3 *clumsy*
off one's trolley 461.11 *insane*
off-peak 793.9 *cheap*
off-peak fare 793.4 *bargain*
off-peak supply 39.34 *power supply*
off-piste 68.12 *ski*
off-piste skiing 68.1 *skiing*
off-pitch 517.9 *unmelodious*

offprint 111.4, 111.9, 125.5 *duplicate*; 561.2 *print*; 112.5 *repeat*
offprinted 111.15 *duplicate*
off-putting 328.17 *disturbing*; 378.13 *hindering*; 364.8 *repulsive*
offscourings 258.4 *dirt*; 238.6 *refuse*; 215.2 *residue*
off-season 793.9 *cheap*
off-season fare 793.4 *bargain*
off-season traveller 793.8 *bargain hunter*
offset 708.16 *cancel out*; 113.21 *counteract*; 347.1 *counteraction*; 119.3 *equalization*; 119.11 *equalize*; 44.5 *gardening*; 212.3 *subtract*; 212.1 *subtraction*
offset lithography 561.1 *reproduction*
offsetting 347.4 *counteracting*
offshoot 205.6 *branch*; 311.5 *fork*; 356.3 *product*; 77.5 *stem*; 555.5 *young plant*
offshore 50.20; 145.8 *distant*; 91.11 *nautically*
offshore fishing 633.2 *chase*
offshore racing 50.1 *sailing*
offshore rig 437.6 *oil*
offshore rights 86.3 *regional boundary*
offshore wind 31.12 *wind*
offside 66.2 *football play*; 58.8 *hockey*; 58.5 *lacrosse*; 320.21 *miscellaneous motoring terms*; 46.13 *penalty*; 53.14 *positioned*; 64.3 *rugby play*; 64.6 *rugger*; 169.3 *side direction*; 66.5 *soccer*
off-side fielder 53.4 *team*
offside pass 58.3 *ice hockey*
offsides 58.3 *ice hockey*
off soundings 91.11 *nautically*
offspring 215.6 *person remaining*; 356.7 *produce*; 561.6 *progeny*
offstage 21.43 *on stage*
offstreet parking 318.2 *passing along*
off stride 231.1 *imperfect*
off-target 234.6 *distorted*; 802.12 *incorrect*; 325.21 *indirect*; 189.4 *oblique*; 189.8 *obliquely*
off tempo 286.2 *occurring at a different time*
off the active list 339.6 *suspended*
off the agenda 355.7 *on hold*
off the air 505.7 *unheard*
off the beam 325.21 *indirect*
off the beaten track 118.22 *out of step*; 655.11 *secluded*
off the bottle 689.1 *sober*
off the cuff 478.7 *extempore*; 478.1 *improvised*
off the fairway 325.21 *indirect*
off the hard stuff 689.1 *sober*
off the hook 758.6 *acquitted*
off-the-lip 50.13 *windsurfing*
off-the-lip turn 50.7 *windsurfing*
off the mark 325.27 *astray*; 325.21 *indirect*
off the market 218.4 *scarce*
off the menu 218.4 *scarce*
off-the-peg 280.7 *prepared for immediate use*; 160.10 *prototypical*; 243.21 *ready-made*; 551.31 *styled*
off-the-peg clothes 551.1 *dress*
off the point 109.12 *irrelevantly*; 124.1 *unimportant*; 325.25 *wandering*
off the premises 98.21 *away*
off-the-rack 160.10 *prototypical*
off the rails 408.28 *anyhow*; 328.18 *disturbingly*
off the record 734.15 *conversationally*; 738.17 *frankly*; 737.15 *in secret*
off-the-record 738.15 *open*; 737.9 *secret*
off-the-shoulder 552.10 *in dishabille*
off the side 461.11 *insane*
off the subject 109.7 *illogical*; 325.25 *wandering*
off the track 274.17 *mistaken*
off the wagon 558.16 *drinking*
off the wall 461.11 *insane*; 118.13 *unconventional*
off-track 68.12 *ski*
off-track touring 68.2 *cross-country skiing*
of fungi 83.10
off-white 522.14 *light colour*; 531.1 *white*
off-whiteness 531.7 *whiteness*
off-width 62.8 *mountaineering*
off-width crack 62.5 *rock face*
offwind 50.10 *sailing*
off with his head 814.24 *string him up!*
off with you 371.33 *go away!*
off work 343.2 *not working*
off you go 371.33 *go away!*
of good constitution 259.1 *healthy*
of good family 573.4 *aristocratic*
of good omen 475.15 *presageful*
of help 392.30 *helping*; 237.1 *useful*
of historical interest 296.14 *historic*
of humble birth 574.3 *common*
of ill omen 475.15 *presageful*
of importance 123.5 *important*
of known date 275.25
of language 5.39
of late 295.21 *newly*
of leaves 77.18
of little value 124.1 *unimportant*; 236.1 *worthless*
of many kinds 114.6 *assorted*
of many parts 485.7 *gifted*
of many words 270.3 *diffuse*
of mark 123.6 *notable*
of material 402.9 *materially*
of mature years 556.13 *middle-aged*
of mixed blood 412.12 *mixed*
of moment 694.7 *significant*
of necessity 386.9 *compelling*; 386.11 *compellingly*; 135.12 *in need*
of no account 668.17 *unrespected*
of no consequence 124.1 *unimportant*
of no effect 247.10 *failed*
of no fixed abode 227.13 *changeable*; 144.10 *replaced*
of no fixed address 144.10 *replaced*
of no great weight 124.1 *unimportant*
of no use 238.1 *useless*
of no value 668.17 *unrespected*
of old 296.19 *anciently*; 3.24 *historically*; 284.22 *in the past*
of one mind 750.31 *in accord*
of one's own accord 250.20 *freely*; 636.18 *voluntarily*
of one's own volition 250.20 *freely*
of opposite polarity 364.9 *abducent*
of philosophy 4.13
of plants 77.14
of poor quality 236.2 *inferior*
of repute 811.3 *reputable*
of roots 77.19
of second rank 124.3 *secondary*
of service 392.30 *helping*; 237.1 *useful*
of sound mind 460.4 *sane*
of stems 77.17
oft 297.1 *frequently*
often 209.9 *differentially*; 297.1 *frequently*; 112.23 *repeatedly*; 275.28 *sometimes*
often encountered 297.3 *frequent*
oftenness 297.4 *frequency*
oftentimes 297.1 *frequently*
of that ilk 111.12 *same*
of that order 158.13 *this size*
of the deepest dye 532.2 *dark*
of the essence 99.5 *essential*
of the first water 235.1 *worthy*
of the opposing party 113.28 *in opposition*
of the opposite camp 113.28 *in opposition*
of the people 574.3 *common*
of the same age 285.9 *simultaneous*
of the same generation 285.9 *simultaneous*
of the same kidney 111.12 *same*
of the same vintage 285.9 *simultaneous*
of the same year 285.9 *simultaneous*
of this date 282.6 *present*
of today 282.6 *present*
of today's date 282.6 *present*
of two minds 639.1 *vacillating*
of unsound mind 461.11 *insane*
of use 237.1 *useful*
of value 235.3 *valuable*
of weak constitution 260.21 *unhealthy*
of weight 123.5 *important*
of yore 296.19 *anciently*; 3.24 *historically*
ogee arch 20.5 *arch*
ogham 5.41 *lettered*
ogham alphabet 5.14 *alphabet*
ogle 659.7 *be discourteous*; 593.14 *communication of love*; 593.26 *court*; 593.6 *courtship*; 742.3, 742.11 *gesture*; 518.6, 518.13 *look*
ogonek 5.36 *accent*
ogre 158.10 *big person*; 804.9 *wicked person*
ogress 158.10 *big person*
oharai 10.7 *non-Christian ritual*
ohm 334.5 *unit of work*
oil 437.6; 394.9 *balm*; 25.7 *basic ingredient*; 677.9 *blarney*; 480.17 *bribe*; 557.11 *food content*; 284.10 *fossilization*; 330.13, 437.1 *fuel*; 33.6 *lipid*; 268.5 *lubricant*; 268.18 *lubricate*; 265.16 *make easy*; 435.1 *materials*; 37.7 *ointment*; 19.8 *painting*; 421.10 *polish*; 717.2 *reproduction*; 421.11 *smooth*; 419.13 *soften*; 334.6 *source of energy*; 319.5 *transportable*; 79.9 *tree product*
oil and water 113.3 *opposites*; 372.3 *separateness*
oilcan 268.8 *lubricator*; 437.6 *oil*; 421.10 *polish*
oil crisis 218.9 *scarcity*
oil drum 437.6 *oil*
oiled 268.11 *lubricated*; 421.4 *polished*
oilfield 437.6 *oil*; 439.2 *resource*
oil filter 256.10 *cleaning object*
oil-fired 493.13 *heated*; 437.10 *powered*
oil gland 559.3 *gland*
oilily 268.23
oiliness 268.3; 658.4 *deference*; 699.3 *hypocrisy*; 421.7 *smoothness*; 677.4 *unctuousness*
oiling 268.4 *anointment*
oil lamp 522.5 *incandescent light*
oilman 437.9 *power-worker*
oil of lavender 78.8 *flower product*
oil one's tongue 731.8 *talk too much*
oil on troubled waters 685.2 *moderator*; 608.3 *reliever*; 394.1 *remedy*
oil paint 19.11 *artist's materials*
oil painter 19.16 *artist*
oil painting 19.8 *painting*; 717.2 *reproduction*
oil paints 529.5 *paint*
oil pipeline 437.6 *oil*
oil platform 437.6 *oil*
oil refinery 437.6 *oil*
oil refining 32.22 *industrial chemistry*
oil reserves 437.6 *oil*
oil rig 437.6 *oil*
oils 19.11 *artist's materials*
oilseed rape 43.12 *crop*
oil shale 437.6 *oil*
oilskins 551.12 *coat*
oil slick 437.6 *oil*
oilstone 425.15 *make sharp*; 425.12 *sharpener*
oil tanker 437.6 *oil*; 586.24 *warship*
oil-tempered 418.3 *hardened*
oil the hand 480.17 *bribe*
oil the tongue 677.9 *blarney*
oil the wheels 268.20 *ease*
oil well 437.6 *oil*; 439.2 *resource*
oil-worker 437.9 *power-worker*
oily 658.9 *deferential*; 258.7 *dirty*; 599.11 *humouring*; 699.31 *hypocritical*; 421.4 *polished*; 268.13 *slippery*; 664.7 *sycophantic*; 677.15 *unctuous*
oink 515.5 *sing*
ointment 37.7; **268.6**; 394.9 *balm*
Oireachtas 12.4 *governing body*
OJ 219.4 *be excessive*; 219.2 *overdoing it*
OK 669.12 *accept*; 698.21 *accurate*; 801.12 *all right*; 669.1 *approval*; 750.28 *consent*; 56.5 *golf ball*; 235.5 *not bad*; 609.6 *satisfactory*; 235.11 *worthily*
okapi 71.15 *hoofed mammal*
okay 750.7 *consent*; 216.3 *mediocre*; 235.5 *not bad*
oke 235.5 *not bad*
okey-doke 235.5 *not bad*
Oklahoma City All-American Finals 59.12 *rodeo*
okra 43.12 *crop*
Oktoberfest 601.1 *celebration*
olam 279.2 *a long time*; 276.3 *geological period*; 30.41 *geological time*
old 296.11; 556.14 *aged*; 554.12 *alive*; 294.14 *dead*; 533.2 *grey-haired*; 3.15 *historic*; 632.11 *normal*; 284.17 *past*
old age 556.5; 556.2 *adulthood*; 245.9 *dilapidation*; 554.5 *life cycle*; 296.1 *oldness*
old-age death 582.5 *ways of dying*
old-age insurance 768.2 *gift*
old age pension 392.4 *social assistance*
old age pensioner 556.7 *older person*; 769.5 *recipient*
old-age security 253.1 *protection*
old and grey 556.14 *aged*; 296.11 *old*
old as Methuselah 556.14 *aged*
old as the hills 556.14 *aged*
old bachelor 556.8 *man*
old bag 556.9 *woman*
Old Bailey 16.20 *British court*
old ball 53.7 *bat*
old bat 556.9 *woman*
Old Bill 16.14 *police*; 253.3 *security officer*
old bone 424.3 *brittle thing*
old boy 556.8 *man*
old boy network 645.1 *cunning*
old buffer 556.8 *man*
old business 484.1 *plan*
old campaigner 586.11 *former soldier*
old chestnut 620.2 *boring thing*; 599.5 *joke*; 745.1 *maxim*
Old Clootie 8.7 *devil*
old clothes 551.1 *dress*; 238.6 *refuse*
old codger 556.8 *man*
Old Comedy 21.12 *comedy*
old country 86.4 *territorial division*
old custom 632.4 *custom*
old dog 485.5 *expert*
old duffer 556.8 *man*
old dutch 570.11 *married woman*
olden 296.12; 284.17 *past*
olden days 296.3 *antiquity*; 3.8, 284.1 *past time*
Old English 5.41 *lettered*
Old English type 5.15 *type style*
olden times 296.3 *antiquity*
older 296.11 *old*
older generation 296.2 *old people*
older man 556.8 *man*
older person 556.7
older woman 556.9 *woman*
oldest profession 796.5 *prostitution*
olde-worlde 296.12 *olden*
Old Faithful 493.8 *hot place*; 92.10 *miscellaneous*; 298.5 *regular thing*
Old Fashioned 558.8 *mixed drink*
old-fashioned 284.19 *antiquarian*; 117.14 *conformist*; 225.8 *conservative*; 658.7 *courteous*; 245.12 *deteriorated*; 350.4 *disused*; 632.11 *normal*; 487.2 *not customary*; 178.4 *traditional*; 238.1 *useless*
old-fashioned look 518.6 *look*
old-fashionedly 225.10 *conservatively*
Old Father Thames 90.4 *British rivers*
old fogy 632.8 *creature of habit*; 641.8 *obstinate person*; 556.7 *older person*; 452.11 *opinionist*
old gal 556.9 *woman*
old geezer 556.8 *man*
old girl 593.9 *lover*
old git 556.8 *man*
Old Glory 743.7 *flag*
old-gold 536.1 *orange*; 537.1 *yellow*
Old Grey Whistle Test 533.6 *figurative usage*
old guard 632.8 *creature of habit*; 640.5 *tenacious person*
old guy 556.8 *man*
old hand 396.11, 400.10, 485.5 *expert*; 136.8 *qualified person*
Old Harry 8.7 *devil*
old hat 284.19 *antiquarian*; 3.18 *in the past*; 487.2 *not customary*
Old Hornie 8.7 *devil*
old horse 59.1 *horse*
oldie 556.7 *older person*
old ivory 537.8 *yellow thing*
old joke 112.3 *repetitiveness*
old lady 593.9 *lover*; 570.11 *married woman*; 568.12 *woman in the family*
old lag 251.7 *charge*; 806.4 *guilty person*; 815.5 *prisoner*
old-line 632.11 *normal*
old maid 255.5 *pure person*; 568.5 *single girl*; 572.5 *single person*
old-maidish 572.6 *celibate*; 795.10 *moralistic*
old man 593.9 *lover*; 567.2 *male*; 567.3 *male title of address*; 556.8 *man*; 567.13 *man in the family*; 570.10 *married man*
Old Man River 90.3 *US rivers*
old master 19.16 *artist*; 396.11, 400.10 *expert*; 19.6 *work of art*
old money 781.6 *money*
Oldness 296
oldness 296.1; 556.2 *adulthood*
old newspaper 238.6 *refuse*
Old Nick 8.7 *devil*; 798.6 *evil person*
old paper 424.3 *brittle thing*
old penny 780.10 *former British money*
old people 296.2; 556.10 *the old*
old person 556.7 *older person*
old pillow 161.2 *shapeless thing*
old salt 323.7 *nautical person*
old school 641.7 *opinionatedness*; 632.6 *procedure*
old school tie 743.5 *uniform*
Old Scratchy 8.7 *devil*
old softy 648.2 *lenient person*
old soldier 485.5 *expert*; 586.11 *former soldier*; 585.11 *recruit*
old spinster 556.9 *woman*

old stager 485.5 *expert*
oldster 556.7 *older person*
old story 3.18 *in the past*
Old Testament 7.12 *religious text*
old thing **296.5**
old-time dancing 22.1 *dancing*
old-timer 556.8 *man*
old times 3.8 *past time*
old trick 645.2 *stratagem*
old trooper 586.11 *former soldier*
old witch 546.2 *ugly person*; 556.9 *woman*
old wives' medicine 35.2 *natural medicine*
old wives' tale 274.6 *fallibility*; 699.11 *half-truth*; 450.2 *religious belief*
old woman 568.2 *female*; 556.9 *woman*; 568.12 *woman in the family*
Old World 86.7 *regions of the world*
old-world 658.7 *courteous*; 632.11 *normal*; 296.12 *olden*
old-worldly 296.21 *archaically*; 658.14 *courteously*
Old World monkeys 71.16 *primate*
oleaginous 268.13 *slippery*
oleic 268.13 *slippery*
olent 500.5 *odorous*
oleum 268.5 *lubricant*
olfactible 500.5 *odorous*
olfaction 500.2 *sense of smell*
olfactive 500.6 *olfactory*
olfactologist 500.1 *odour*
olfactology 500.1 *odour*
olfactometry 500.1 *odour*
olfactorily 500.10 *odorously*
olfactory **500.6**
olfactory nerve 500.2 *sense of smell*
olfactronics 500.1 *odour*
olibanum 502.3 *incense*
olid 503.3 *stinking*
oligarch 400.5 *company leader*
oligarchic 12.9, 396.14 *governmental*; 400.12 *masterful*
oligarchy 85.1 *country*; 12.1 *government*; 396.7 *type of rule*
Oligocene period 284.3 *geological period*
Oligochaeta 75.6 *worm*
oligochaete 75.6 *worm*
oligochaetous 75.20 *wormlike*
oligoclase 30.34 *mineral*
oligomenorrhoea 560.11 *menstruation*
oligomeric protein 33.9 *protein*
oligopeptide 33.8 *amino acid*
oligophrenia 461.2 *subnormality*
oligopolist 778.12 *wholesaler*
oligopoly 778.3 *selling*
oligosaccharide 33.3 *carbohydrate*
olive branch 79.12 *figurative usage*; 749.2 *peace offering*; 589.2 *symbol of peace*
olive-drab shirt 551.8 *shirt*
olive-green 538.1 *green*
olive grove 44.2 *garden*
olive oil 25.7 *basic ingredient*
olives 25.10 *snack*
olivine 538.11 *green thing*; 30.34 *mineral*
olla podrida 25.50 *Central American dish*; 412.2 *mixed thing*
ology 455.5 *science*
olympiad 275.4 *term*
Olympian 8.14 *heavenly*; 89.7 *mountainous*; 154.12 *tall*; 655.8 *unsociable*
Olympic 52.14 *combat*; 57.11 *gymnastic*; 58.8 *hockey*; 50.10 *sailing*; 68.12 *ski*; 47.9 *track*
Olympic athlete 47.3 *athlete*
Olympic boxer 52.4 *boxer*
Olympic canoeing 50.6 *canoeing*
Olympic champion 619.5 *person of wonder*; 485.4 *skilled person*; 246.5 *victorious person*
Olympic class 50.2 *sailing boat*
Olympic Games 47.5 *competition*
Olympic Gold Medal 813.2 *prize*
Olympic gymnastics 57.1 *gymnastics*
Olympic hockey 58.1 *hockey*
Olympic ice-dancing 68.7 *ice-dancing*
Olympic lugeing 68.9 *bobsledding*
Olympic Mountains 89.4 *US mountains*
Olympic regatta 50.4 *rowing*
Olympic rowing 50.4 *rowing*
Olympic-size 67.11 *swimming*
Olympic-size pool 67.7 *swimming pool*
Olympic skating 68.6 *ice-skating*
Olympic skiing 68.1 *skiing*
Olympic wrestler 52.6 *wrestler*
Olympic wrestling 52.5 *wrestling*
Olympus 8.11 *heaven*; 154.3 *mountain*; 101.1 *nonmaterial world*
om 10.9 *prayer*
ombres chinoises 21.7 *show*
ombudsman 713.4 *adviser*; 16.23 *judge*; 748.4 *representative*
omelette 25.34 *vegetarian dish*
omelette pan 25.6 *kitchen equipment*
omen **475.5**; 474.4 *expectant person*; 738.10 *manifestation*; 129.6 *preview*; 742.1 *sign*; 711.1 *warning*; 619.4 *wonder*
omertà 737.2 *secretiveness*
ominous 249.6 *adverse*; 523.11 *benighted*; 254.1 *dangerous*; 236.5 *harmful*; 643.3 *important*; 611.6, 798.10 *inauspicious*; 475.15 *presageful*; 742.14 *signifying*; 288.13 *untimely*; 711.8 *warning*
ominously 288.19 *at the wrong time*; 254.11 *dangerously*; 523.15 *darkly*; 249.12 *in adversity*; 798.14 *inauspiciously*; 742.18 *indicatively*; 475.16 *predictively*
ominousness 798.3 *bad luck*; 475.5 *omen*; 288.2 *untimeliness*
omission **233.2**; 128.1 *exclusion*; 247.1 *failure*; 720.2 *misinterpretation*; 274.9 *trivial error*
omission mark 742.7 *punctuation*
omit 233.5 *be incomplete*; 128.7 *exclude*; 463.13 *forget*; 274.19 *make a mistake*; 720.1 *misinterpret*; 141.21 *space*; 212.3 *subtract*
omitted 128.11 *excluded*; 233.4 *incomplete*; 98.12 *missing*
omitting 128.12 *exclusively*; 233.4 *incomplete*
omnibus 320.19 *bus*
omnidirectional antenna 692.17 *antenna*
omnifarious 114.6 *assorted*
omnifariously 114.10 *diversely*
omnifariousness 114.2 *assortment*
omnipotence 8.2 *divine attribute*; 334.1 *power*
omnipotent 8.13 *divine*; 334.13 *powerful*
omnipotently 8.19 *divinely*; 334.18 *powerfully*
omnipresence **97.2**; 8.2 *divine attribute*; 138.4 *widespreadness*
omnipresent 8.13 *divine*; 97.7 *present*; 138.17 *widespread*
omniscience 8.2 *divine attribute*; 455.3 *learning*
omniscient 8.13 *divine*; 455.8 *knowledgeable*
omnisciently 8.19 *divinely*
omniscient narrator 17.3 *aspect of fiction*
omnium-gatherum 412.3 *miscellany*
omnivore 557.18 *eater*; 688.4 *glutton*; 70.4 *type of animal*
omnivorous 557.26 *eating*; 688.6 *gluttonous*; 70.15 *of animals*
omnivorously 557.28 *carnivorously*
omnivorousness 557.5 *eating habit*
omophagic 557.26 *eating*
omophagically 557.28 *carnivorously*
omophagous 557.26 *eating*
omophagously 557.28 *carnivorously*
omophagy 557.5 *eating habit*
omote 52.10 *aikido*
omphalic 173.6 *central*
omphalos 173.1 *centre*
on 97.10 *available*; 738.13 *displayed*; 302.19 *forward*; 595.7 *like*; 560.31 *menstrual*; 53.14 *positioned*; 317.17 *via*
on a back burner 355.7 *on hold*
on account **789.12**; 783.14 *on credit*
on a cliff edge 612.8 *fearful*
on a climb **62.10**
on a crash diet 687.6 *fasting*
on active duty 585.15 *warring*
on a declining scale 214.8 *decreasingly*
on a demo 703.23 *in protest*
on a diet 687.6 *fasting*
on a downer 214.6 *decreasing*
on advance 771.7 *on loan*
on a fact-finding mission 705.23 *questioningly*
on a firm basis 228.12 *stably*
on a firm footing 228.12 *stably*; 336.13 *strengthened*
on a firm foundation 336.13 *strengthened*
on a first-name basis 569.10 *familiar*
on again off again 299.8 *irregularly*
on-again-off-again 299.4 *irregular*
on a good footing 569.9 *friends with*
on a high 490.7 *pleased*
on a large scale 158.20 *largely*
on a leash 663.7 *obedient*
on a level 111.20 *regularly*
on a liquid diet 687.6 *fasting*
on all counts 232.9 *completely*
on all cylinders 342.22 *actively*; 576.12 *laboriously*
on all fours 200.14 *in fours*; 623.28 *subserviently*
on all sides 550.42 *inclusively*; 170.8 *round*; 170.5 *surrounded*
on a mission 705.23 *questioningly*
on analysis 375.7 *to pieces*
on and off 224.15, 227.15 *changeably*; 276.14 *for short periods*; 299.4 *irregular*; 299.8 *irregularly*; 275.28 *sometimes*
on and on 134.7 *continually*; 270.7 *diffusely*; 279.11 *eternally*
on an even keel 119.12 *equally*; 421.14 *smoothly*
on a par 111.16, 285.11 *equal*; 111.19 *equally*; 119.8 *on equal terms*
on a pension 605.7 *resigning*
on appro 353.9 *tentative*
on approval 469.15 *chosen*; 353.9 *tentative*
on a quest 705.23 *questioningly*
on arrival **312.22**
on a shoestring 682.9 *meanly*
on a ski run **68.17**
on a small scale 159.8 *in a small way*
on a starvation diet 687.6 *fasting*
on a string 361.13 *pendulously*
on a strong foundation 228.12 *stably*
on a tangent 270.8 *circuitously*
on a tightrope 264.16 *troubled*
on auction 752.17 *offered*
on average **216.11**; 138.31 *overall*; 104.11 *probably*
on a whim 453.27 *capriciously*
on a wild-goose chase 238.10 *uselessly*
on balance 216.11 *on average*; 138.31 *overall*
on behalf of 550.43 *alternatively*; 392.37 *in aid of*; 762.9 *instead*
on bended knee 667.11 *in a respectful stance*; 388.5 *submitting*; 623.28 *subserviently*; 664.7 *sycophantic*
on board 323.11 *nautical*; 323.12 *nautically*
on borrowed time 556.16 *maturely*
on bread and water 687.7 *abstemiously*; 687.6 *fasting*
on call 810.13 *on duty*; 97.16 *on the spot*; 243.18 *prepared*; 135.4 *required*; 392.31 *supplementary*; 237.1 *useful*
once **197.24**; 3.24 *historically*
once again 112.24 *again*
once and for all 131.28 *conclusively*; 197.24 *once*; 225.9 *permanently*; 638.17 *resolutely*
once bitten 711.9 *warned*
once bitten twice shy 616.4 *cautious*
once in a lifetime 105.10 *rarely*; 197.14 *singular*
once in a while 133.17 *discontinuously*; 299.8 *irregularly*; 275.28, 297.2 *sometimes*
once more 112.24, 295.22 *again*; 198.19 *twice*
once only 197.24 *once*
once-over 518.3 *observation*; 157.8 *shallowly*
oncer 780.9 *British money*
once removed 325.24 *diverging*
once upon a time 286.3 *another time*; 284.22 *in the past*; 275.29 *one day*
onchocerciasis 519.1 *blindness*; 75.11 *helminthic disease*; 260.7 *tropical disease*
onchosphere 75.13 *invertebrate larva*
on civvy street 589.7 *peaceful*
on cloud nine 597.4 *happy*; 174.8 *on top*
oncogenic 260.23 *diseased*
oncogenous 260.23 *diseased*
on collateral 771.6 *loaned*; 771.7 *on loan*
oncologist 35.13 *medical specialist*
oncology 35.3 *medical specialty*
oncoming 310.8 *advancing*; 312.19 *approaching*; 283.11 *future*; 302.18 *ongoing*; 113.23 *opposite*
on compassionate leave 98.10 *nonresident*
on compulsion 386.11 *compellingly*
on course 324.9 *directly*
on credit **783.14**; 784.11 *insolvently*; 771.6 *loaned*; 789.12 *on account*; 771.7 *on loan*
on dangerous ground 254.4 *endangered*
on death row 254.4 *endangered*
on deck 323.12 *nautically*
on-deck circle 48.1 *baseball*
on demand 785.21 *cash down*; 217.9 *enough*
on display 520.2 *clear*; 703.9 *demonstrated*; 738.13 *displayed*; 716.15 *evidently*
on dit 504.8 *something heard*
on double time 576.12 *laboriously*
on drive 331.14 *sporting hit*; 53.9 *stroke*
on duty **810.13**; **810.18**
One **197**
one **197.1**; **197.11**; 570.21 *married*; 27.9 *numeral*; 566.7 *person*; 111.12 *same*; 53.10 *score*; 255.16 *simple*; 204.6 *whole*
one-act play 21.2 *play*
one after another 132.18 *consecutively*; 289.14 *in succession*
one after the other 132.18 *consecutively*; 289.14 *in succession*
on eagle's wings 332.14 *swiftly*
one and all **204.12**; 204.4 *all*; 138.10 *everyone*
one and nine balls 65.6 *pool*
one and only 126.5 *novel*; 197.1 *one*; 197.14 *singular*
one and the same 197.11 *one*; 111.12 *same*; 111.1 *sameness*
one another 110.2 *interconnection*
one-arm 50.14 *punting*
one-armed 233.4 *incomplete*
one-arm punting 50.8 *punting*
on Easy Street 248.8 *prosperous*; 248.9 *prosperously*; 781.1 *wealthy*
one at a time 197.22 *one by one*; 372.20 *separately*
one behind the other 132.18 *consecutively*; 289.14 *in succession*; 148.12 *longitudinally*
one bill 780.8 *American money*
one by one **197.22**; 372.20 *separately*; 139.32 *severally*
one C 201.9 *treble figures*
one cent 780.8 *American money*
onecroid psychosis 36.11 *psychosis*
one day **275.29**
one-day event 59.11 *eventing*
one-design 50.10 *sailing*
one-design boat 50.2 *sailing boat*
one-design racing 50.7 *windsurfing*
on edge 612.8 *fearful*
one-dimensional 157.2 *superficial*
one- dimensional wave 326.5 *wave*
one-dollar bill 780.8 *American money*
one eighth 201.4 *eight*
one eye 69.3 *card game terms*
one-eyed 233.4 *incomplete*; 519.9 *weaksighted*
one-eyed jack 69.3 *card game terms*
one fifth 201.1 *five*
one fine day 283.14 *in the future*
one flesh 570.1 *marriage*; 570.9 *married couple*
one-foot upright spin 68.6 *ice-skating*
one for the book 619.4 *wonder*
one for the road 690.13 *drink*; 313.9 *parting*; 581.7 *refreshments*
one fourth 200.6 *quarter*
Onega 88.5 *other major lakes*
one-handed 486.3 *clumsy*
one-hand shot 49.4 *playing terms*
one-hit wonder 149.4 *short thing*
one-hop 178.3 *continuous*
one-horse 122.13 *insignificant*; 159.7 *little*; 124.4 *trivial*
one-horse town 122.7 *inferior thing*; 86.11 *settlement*; 87.10 *village*
one hundred 201.9 *treble figures*
one hundred and eighty 69.6 *darts*
one hundredfold 201.9 *treble figures*
one hundred per cent 204.4 *all*; 230.1 *perfect*; 230.3 *perfection*; 204.11 *wholly*
one in a hundred 107.6 *poor chance*
one in a million 325.19 *deviant person*; 235.8 *exceller*
one in a thousand 235.8 *exceller*; 619.4 *wonder*
oneirocritic 719.6 *interpreter*
oneiromancer 11.13 *diviner*
oneiromancy 11.9, 475.2 *divination*
one-legged 233.4 *incomplete*
one-liner 599.5 *joke*
one-man 197.15 *solo*
one-man band 18.26 *musical group*; 197.9 *soloist*
one-man canoe race 50.6 *canoeing*

one man one vote 12.1 *government*
one-man show 21.2 *play;* 735.1 *soliloquy;* 197.9 *soloist*
one-many 27.76 *functional*
one-metre springboard 67.6 *diving*
one-mile 47.9 *track*
one-mile race 47.1 *track events*
one mind 750.1 *accord*
one-minute suspension 58.5 *lacrosse*
on end 186.11 *vertically*
oneness **197.3**; 750.5 *conformity;* 111.1 *sameness;* 255.8 *simplicity;* 204.1 *whole*
oneness with 111.1 *sameness*
one-night stand 21.15 *engagement*
one ninth 201.5 *nine*
one of 405.8 *belonging;* 405.5 *member*
one of a kind 139.17 *exceptional;* 126.5 *novel*
one-off 114.1 *diversity;* 118.10 *eccentric;* 139.6 *exception;* 278.7 *impermanent;* 126.5 *novel;* 139.20 *personalized;* 197.14 *singular*
one of the best 235.8 *exceller*
one of the boys 285.5 *contemporary*
one of the family 654.6 *social person*
one of the gang 285.5 *contemporary*
one of the girls 285.5 *contemporary*
one of the lads 285.5 *contemporary*
one of the lasses 285.5 *contemporary*
one of these days 286.3 *another time*
one of those days 486.9 *bungling*
one of us 405.5 *member;* 127.3 *person included*
one-one 27.76 *functional*
one-on-one 58.8 *hockey*
one-on-one assignment 58.3 *ice hockey*
one or two 206.1 *few*
one over the eight 690.13 *drink;* 690.1 *drunk;* 201.4 *eight;* 219.6 *excessive*
one-parent family 654.7 *human society*
one-piece 197.12 *one-sided;* 551.31 *styled;* 67.11 *swimming*
one-piece suit 551.10 *suit*
one-piece swimsuit 551.21 *beachwear;* 67.8 *swimwear*
one-pointer 49.4 *playing terms*
on equal terms **119.8**; 111.16 *equal;* 111.19, 119.12 *equally;* 108.10 *relevantly*
onerous 236.3 *bad;* 264.10 *difficult;* 240.1 *inconvenient;* 414.3 *ponderous*
onerously 414.17 *burdensomely*
onerousness 236.9 *badness;* 414.8 *weighing down*
one's adieus 313.9 *parting*
one's age 556.1 *age*
one's all 440.4 *possessions*
one's betrothed 570.8 *spouse*
one's betters 121.7 *the best people*
one's bit 729.7 *utterance*
one's born days 554.5 *life cycle*
one's cards 371.18 *dismissal;* 144.4 *relegation;* 708.6 *termination*
one's club 654.7 *human society*
one's contemporaries 285.5 *contemporary;* 282.2 *the present day*
one's cut 791.1 *discount*
one's despair 486.10 *unskilled person*
one's duty 810.1 *duty*
one-seater toboggan 68.9 *bobsledding*
oneself 139.11 *identity*
oneself again 393.15 *cured;* 581.4 *refreshed*
oneself to 773.10 *take away*
one seventh 201.3 *seven*
one's fault 806.1 *guilt*
one's fill 217.7 *sufficiency*
one's fortune 440.5 *personal estate*
one's gang 654.7 *human society*
one's group 654.7 *human society*
one's heart's desire 617.5 *object of desire*
one's hour having come 582.18 *dying*
one-sided **197.12**; 466.10 *discriminatory;* 465.8 *unjust;* 802.11 *wrong*
one-sidedness 465.3 *injustice;* 466.3 *prejudice;* 802.1 *unfairness*
one sixth 201.2 *six*
one-size 197.12 *one-sided*
one's level best 353.5 *attempt*
one's lot 107.2 *luck*
one's marching orders 371.18 *dismissal*
one's money 440.5 *personal estate*
one's money's worth 777.6 *purchase*
one's name in lights 522.6 *electric light*
one's native ground 85.6 *native land*
one's number being up 582.18 *dying*
one's own 763.9 *possessed*
one's own boss 250.10 *independent*
one's own devices 250.6 *liberality*
one's own generation 285.5 *contemporary*
one's own hand 126.2 *original*
one's own man 250.10 *independent*
one's own master 250.10 *independent*
one's own sweet will 635.3 *wilfulness*
one's own way 250.6 *liberality*
one's peers 285.5 *contemporary*
one's piece 729.7 *utterance*
one's prime 556.4 *middle age*
one's promised 570.8 *spouse*
one's set 654.7 *human society*
one's teeth chatter 494.10 *be cold*
one-step 22.2 *dance*
one's time being up 582.18 *dying*
one's time of life 556.1 *age*
one's two cents' worth 729.7 *utterance*
one's two-pennyworth 729.7 *utterance*
one's walking papers 371.18 *dismissal*
one's word 756.1 *promise*
one's worth 440.5 *personal estate*
one-syllable word 5.17 *word*
one-tailed test 27.54 *hypothesis testing*
one tenth 201.6 *ten*
one thing after another 132.2 *consecution*
one third 199.6 *third*
one-time 296.13 *former;* 129.11 *prior;* 605.7 *resigning*
one too many 219.6 *excessive;* 219.2 *overdoing it*
one-to-one 27.76 *functional;* 119.8 *on equal terms*
one-track mind 465.3 *injustice*
one-two 66.2 *football play*
one-two-three 210.3 *count*
one-up 121.12 *superior*
one-upmanship 121.3 *advantage;* 631.9 *tactics*
one up on 329.14 *surpassing*
on everyone's lips 740.20 *well-known*
on every side 324.11 *in all directions*
one voice 750.1 *accord*
one-way 324.15 *direct;* 197.12 *one-sided*
one-way communication 692.6 *telecommunication*
one-way street 317.3 *road*
one-way system 320.3 *carriageway*
one-woman 197.15 *solo*
one-woman show 21.2 *play;* 735.1 *soliloquy;* 197.9 *soloist*
on exhibition 738.16 *manifestly*
on familiar terms 569.10 *familiar*
on file 409.24 *categorized*
on film 744.16 *recorded*
on fire **493.10**
on foot 243.17 *developing*
on form **160.12**; 259.1 *healthy;* 221.8 *in a state of*
on full volume 507.6 *loud*
on furlough 98.21 *away;* 580.7 *leisurely;* 98.10 *nonresident;* 263.6 *with ease*
ongo 302.11 *course*
ongoing **302.18**; 554.12 *alive;* 132.9 *consecutive;* 134.5 *continual;* 302.11 *course*
on good grounds 716.14 *as evidence*
on good terms with 569.9 *friends with*
on guard **54.7**; 665.9 *careful;* 384.29 *defending;* 384.32 *defensively;* 54.3 *fencing movements;* 471.7 *watchful*
on hand 97.8 *attendant;* 763.9 *possessed*
on heat 561.16 *reproductive*
on high 366.12 *exalted;* 8.14 *heavenly;* 154.19 *high;* 366.13 *highly;* 89.11 *on the mountain*
on hire 752.17 *offered*
on hold **355.7**; 226.10 *finished;* 294.10 *held up;* 339.7 *inertly;* 339.6 *suspended*
on holiday 98.21 *away;* 580.7 *leisurely;* 98.10 *nonresident;* 263.6 *with ease*
on home ground 252.6 *safe*
on hunger strike 687.6 *fasting*
on ice 494.8 *cold;* 226.10 *finished;* 294.10 *held up;* 815.8 *imprisoned;* 339.7 *inertly;* 359.7 *preserved;* 339.6 *suspended*
on impulse 642.6 *capriciously*
on information received 693.19 *reportedly*
on intimate terms 569.10 *familiar*
onion 411.5 *layered thing;* 496.2 *seasoning*
onion fly 44.12 *pests and diseases*
onion hoe 44.6 *garden tool*
onion sauce 25.15 *sauce*
onion soup 25.45 *French dish;* 25.13 *soup*
on its hindlegs 186.11 *vertically*
on its last legs 245.13, 337.9 *dilapidated*
on its own 197.21 *alone*
on its side 187.11 *horizontally*
on land 92.13 *continentally*
on leave 98.21 *away;* 580.7 *leisurely;* 98.10 *nonresident;* 263.6 *with ease*
onlie begetter 356.9 *producer*
on-line **40.21**; **40.22**; 334.15 *full of energy;* 237.1 *useful*
on loan **771.7**; **772.13**; 784.11 *insolvently;* 771.6 *loaned*
on location 98.21 *away;* 143.11 *geographically;* 98.10 *nonresident;* 97.16 *on the spot;* 142.12 *where*
onlooker 147.6 *neighbour;* 518.11 *observer;* 97.5 *someone present*
only 197.24 *once;* 197.11 *one*
only a few 206.1 *few*
only a step 147.12 *near*
only begetter 344.7 *Prime Mover*
only-begotten 197.14 *singular*
only chance 287.2 *opportunity*
only child 197.8 *loner*
only choice 469.8 *choice*
only exception 197.2 *item*
only for oneself 683.8 *selfishly*
only human 804.13 *venial*
only just 151.11 *narrowly*
only just enough 217.1 *sufficient*
only just win 246.9 *be victorious*
only passable 231.4 *ordinary*
only yesterday 284.22 *in the past;* 295.21 *newly*
on meagre rations 687.6 *fasting*
on mortgage 253.7 *guaranteed*
on my mother's life 707.26 *as God is my witness!*
on no account 94.14 *not at all;* 709.11 *uncooperatively*
on oath 756.16 *as promised;* 756.12 *promised;* 707.12 *vowed*
on occasion 276.14 *for short periods*
on-off 133.8 *discontinuous*
on offer 752.17 *offered*
onomasiological 5.38 *linguistic*
onomasiologist 5.2 *linguist*
onomastic 5.38 *linguistic*
onomastics 5.1 *linguistics;* 721.7 *nomenclature*
onomatology 721.7 *nomenclature*
onomatomania 461.4 *delusion*
onomatopoeia 125.1 *imitation;* 17.12 *poetic language*
onomatopoeic 125.12 *imitative;* 17.20 *metrical;* 5.42 *worded*
onomatopoeically 125.14 *imitatively*
onomatopoeic word 5.17 *word*
onomatopoetically 125.14 *imitatively*
on one 768.9 *as a gift*
on one's back 367.25 *courteously;* 335.12 *impotent;* 301.5 *sedentary*
on one's beam-ends 247.10 *failed;* 335.12 *impotent;* 782.2 *insolvent;* 122.18 *outclassed;* 249.7 *unprosperous*
on one's best behaviour 631.17 *well-behaved*
on one's credit account 772.13 *on loan*
on one's deathbed 294.16 *at a late hour;* 582.18 *dying;* 287.11 *in time*
on one's dignity 622.17 *conceited*
on one's doorstep 147.12 *near*
on one's feet 667.11 *in a respectful stance;* 186.11 *vertically*
on one's guard 616.4 *cautious*
on one's head 806.5 *guilty*
on one's high horse 622.17 *conceited*
on one's hind legs 366.13 *highly*
on one's Jack 197.21 *alone*
on one's knees 367.25 *courteously;* 623.3 *humbled;* 667.11 *in a respectful stance;* 623.28 *subserviently;* 664.7 *sycophantic;* 664.17 *sycophantically*
on one's last legs 249.6 *adverse;* 582.18 *dying;* 261.1 *fatigued;* 337.11 *weakened;* 337.14 *weakly*
on one's legs 259.1 *healthy*
on one's lonesome 197.21 *alone*
on one's marks 243.18 *prepared*
on one's own 197.21 *alone;* 655.10 *lonely;* 197.15 *solo*
on one's own accord 752.18 *voluntary*
on one's own account 250.20 *freely*
on one's own initiative 250.20 *freely;* 636.18 *voluntarily*
on one's own responsibility 250.20 *freely*
on one's own say-so 250.20 *freely*
on one's own volition 636.16 *voluntarily*
on one's scent 633.15 *pursuing*
on one's tail 633.15 *pursuing*
on one's tod 197.21 *alone;* 655.10 *lonely*
on one's toes 342.18 *active;* 342.22 *actively*
on one's travels 100.18 *extraneously*
on one's uppers 782.2 *insolvent;* 782.15 *poorly*
on one's way 302.19 *forward*
on one's word 756.12 *promised*
on order 135.4 *required*
on overtime 576.12 *laboriously*
on paper 744.17 *on the record;* 744.16 *recorded*
on par 111.16 *equal*
on parade 703.14 *demonstrating;* 703.23 *in protest*
on parole 391.7 *liberated*
on pins and needles 612.8 *fearful*
on probation 243.17 *developing;* 448.14 *experimentally*
on purpose 482.13 *intentionally;* 446.21 *purposively*
on Queer Street 264.16 *troubled*
on reconsideration 443.18 *thoughtfully*
on record 409.24 *categorized;* 744.16 *recorded*
on remand 251.15 *detained;* 815.8 *imprisoned*
on route to 317.17 *via*
onrush 380.3 *instance of violence;* 300.2 *momentum;* 90.6 *river flow*
on sabbatical 98.21 *away;* 580.7 *leisurely;* 98.10 *nonresident;* 263.6 *with ease*
on sale **778.18**
on schedule 293.17 *early*
on second thoughts 443.18 *thoughtfully*
on security 771.7 *on loan*
onset 525.1 *appearance;* 312.10 *arrival;* 130.1 *beginning;* 381.12 *military attack*
on several levels 411.12 *in layers*
on shaky foundations 254.2 *unsafe*
onshore wind 31.12 *wind*
on short commons 218.3 *underfed*
onshot 51.2 *grip*
on show 525.7 *appearing;* 520.2 *clear;* 703.9 *demonstrated;* 738.13 *displayed*
on sick leave 98.10 *nonresident*
onside 66.2 *football play;* 53.14 *positioned;* 66.5 *soccer*
on-side fielder 53.4 *team*
onside kick 46.12 *special team*
on sight 525.15 *apparently*
on site 143.11 *geographically;* 97.16 *on the spot;* 142.12 *where*
on-site broadcast 692.25 *broadcast material*
onslaught 670.8 *berating;* 381.12 *military attack;* 712.3 *vilification*
on slippery ground 254.4 *endangered*
on social security benefits 605.7 *resigning*
on soft drinks 689.1 *sober*
on someone's shitlist 594.12 *hated*
on spec 448.14 *experimentally*
on special offer 791.7 *at a discount;* 752.17 *offered*
on stage **21.43**; 740.22 *publicly*
on stand-by 474.5 *expecting*
on stilts 154.19 *high;* 366.13 *highly*
on-stream 334.15 *full of energy;* 237.1 *useful*
on strike 343.2 *not working*
on sure ground 252.6 *safe*
on tap 97.10 *available;* 217.9 *enough;* 97.16 *on the spot;* 436.7 *provisioning;* 778.15 *saleable;* 237.1 *useful*
on tape 744.16 *recorded*
Ontario 88.3 *US lakes*
on tenterhooks 474.12 *expectantly;* 474.5 *expecting;* 612.8 *fearful*
on terra firma 252.6 *safe*
on that ground 750.36 *accordingly*
on the active list 346.10 *operational*
on the agenda 447.8 *problematic;* 447.13 *problematically*
on the air 504.17 *aurally;* 740.19 *published*
on the alert 342.18 *active*
on the anvil 243.17 *developing*
on the assumption that 476.11 *supposing;* 4.25 *theoretically*
on the attack 381.26 *aggresively*
on the back burner 294.10 *held up*
on the back of 366.13 *highly*
on the ball 458.6 *intelligent*
on the beam 178.12 *straight*

on the beat 285.10 *synchronized;* 285.13 *synchronously*

on the beaten track 620.8 *boringly*

on the bias 176.12 *askew;* 189.8 *obliquely*

on the Bible 707.24 *truthfully*

on the bill 789.12 *on account*

on the black market 16.83 *dishonestly*

on the blind side 521.9 *invisibly*

on the blink 802.18 *gone wrong;* 350.1 *unused*

on the block 767.16 *disposably;* 778.18 *on sale*

on the boil 493.9 *hot*

on the books 744.16 *recorded*

on the border 164.11 *marginally*

on the borderline 705.24 *questionably*

on the bottle 690.5 *drunken*

on the bottom 367.24 *down*

on the bounce 706.24 *in answer*

on the brain 447.12 *topically*

on the breadline 135.5 *necessitous;* 782.1 *poor;* 782.15 *poorly*

on the bridge 579.19 *managerially;* 323.12 *nautically*

on the brink 254.11 *dangerously;* 166.6 *furthest;* 147.12 *near;* 254.2 *unsafe*

on the button 273.5, 698.21 *accurate;* 801.8 *correct*

on the cards 474.7 *expected;* 106.3 *predetermined;* 104.6 *probable*

on the cause list 16.54 *litigated*

on the cheap 793.15 *cheaply*

on the chin 52.16 *professionally*

on the coast 30.66 *geographically*

on the contrary 701.18 *arguably*

on the council 16.86 *jurisdictionally*

on the credit side 765.15 *gainful*

on the crest 89.11 *on the mountain;* 121.17 *supremely*

on the cuff 783.14 *on credit*

on the cutting edge 579.19 *managerially*

on the danger list 582.18 *dying;* 260.22 *sick*

on the decline 245.12 *deteriorated*

on the defensive 634.18 *avoiding;* 384.29 *defending;* 384.32 *defensively;* 585.15 *warring*

on the descendant 305.16 *descending*

on the diagonal 189.4 *oblique*

on the dole 341.3 *inactive;* 782.1 *poor;* 782.15 *poorly*

on the doorstep 312.22 *on arrival*

on the dot 785.21 *cash down*

on the double 332.14 *swiftly*

on the downgrade 249.6 *adverse;* 245.12 *deteriorated;* 305.17 *drooping*

on the downward path 245.12 *deteriorated*

on the drawing board 243.17 *developing;* 484.14 *planned*

on the edge 164.11 *marginally;* 254.2 *unsafe*

on the fiddle 800.5 *dishonourable;* 774.18 *fraudulent*

on the field 58.10

on the floor 367.24 *down*

on the fritz 245.13 *dilapidated;* 350.1 *unused*

on the front line 586.42 *martially*

on the game 796.13 *unchaste*

on the go 342.22 *actively;* 342.19 *busy;* 300.18 *in motion;* 576.10 *working*

on the gravy train 781.16 *wealthily*

on the ground 367.24 *down;* 97.16 *on the spot*

on the heavy side 120.7 *unequally*

on the high seas 323.11 *nautical;* 91.11, 323.12 *nautically*

on the home stretch 252.6 *safe*

on the hop 300.18 *in motion*

on the horizon 145.10 *distantly;* 283.14 *in the future*

on the house 768.9 *as a gift;* 793.15 *cheaply;* 793.11 *free of charge*

on the increase 213.6 *increasing*

on the inside 815.11 *captively*

on the instant 280.9 *in the shortest possible time*

on the international scene 764.6 *in common*

on the job 15.13 *industrially*

on-the-job 15.9 *negotiated*

on-the-job relations 15.1 *industrial relations*

on-the-job training 6.2 *educational system;* 15.2 *industrial negotiations*

on the lam 634.18 *avoiding*

on the level 799.4 *honourable;* 646.1 *naive*

on the light side 120.7 *unequally*

on the lines of 317.16 *how*

on the list 127.8 *included;* 744.16 *recorded*

on the lookout 474.5 *expecting;* 633.18 *pursuant to;* 518.21 *seeing*

on the loose 250.9 *free*

on the losing team 247.11 *defeated*

on the make 353.10 *ambitiously;* 342.19 *busy;* 765.16 *greedy;* 248.8 *prosperous;* 683.4 *selfish;* 683.8 *selfishly*

on the march 300.18 *in motion*

on the mark 273.8 *accurately;* 324.14 *directed*

on the market 752.17 *offered;* 778.18 *on sale*

on the mend 393.15 *cured;* 259.1 *healthy;* 244.14 *improved*

on the menu 436.7 *provisioning*

on the money 324.14 *directed*

on the morrow 283.14 *in the future*

on the mountain 89.11

on the move 342.19 *busy;* 300.18 *in motion;* 144.20 *out of place*

on the nail 785.21 *cash down*

on the never-never 784.11 *insolvently;* 783.14 *on credit*

on the nod 757.9 *with permission*

on the nose 698.21 *accurate;* 324.14 *directed;* 217.9 *enough;* 50.20 *offshore;* 52.16 *professionally*

on the occasion of 601.21 *in honour of*

on the off chance 102.9 *possibly*

on the offensive 381.26 *aggresively;* 381.22 *militant;* 585.15 *warring*

on the other hand 701.18 *arguably*

on the other side 329.17 *ahead;* 582.19 *dead;* 113.28 *in opposition*

on the outside 171.15 *externally;* 100.18 *extraneously*

on the payroll 401.9 *serving*

on the peak 89.11 *on the mountain*

on the pill 563.5 *rendered infertile*

on the pinnacle 89.11 *on the mountain*

on the poverty line 782.15 *poorly*

on the premises 97.17 *at home;* 97.9 *resident*

on the q.t. 737.16 *stealthily*

on the quarter 50.20 *offshore*

on the quarterdeck 323.12 *nautically*

on the quiet 737.16 *stealthily*

on the radio 504.17 *aurally*

on the rag 560.31 *menstrual*

on the rail 50.20 *offshore*

on the rampage 408.29 *riotously;* 380.6 *violent*

on the razor's edge 254.4 *endangered*

on the rebound 706.24 *in answer*

on the receiving end 769.11 *receiving*

on the record 744.17

on the right track 324.9 *directly;* 449.13 *discovering*

on the road 302.19 *forward;* 300.18 *in motion;* 316.18 *in transit;* 98.10 *nonresident;* 317.17 *via*

on the rocks 494.8 *cold;* 571.11 *divorced;* 254.4 *endangered;* 247.10 *failed;* 782.2 *insolvent*

on the run 132.18 *consecutively;* 254.4 *endangered;* 478.7 *extempore;* 300.18 *in motion;* 144.20 *out of place*

on the safe side 616.4 *cautious;* 252.6 *safe*

on the same footing 111.16 *equal;* 111.19 *equally;* 119.8 *on equal terms*

on the same level 119.8 *on equal terms*

on the same plane 119.8 *on equal terms*

on the same wavelength 374.8 *cooperative*

on the scent 60.9 *on the trail;* 633.18 *pursuant to*

on the scrap heap 355.7 *on hold*

on the sea 316.18 *in transit;* 91.11 *nautically*

on the shelf 572.6 *celibate;* 486.3 *clumsy;* 350.4 *disused;* 355.7 *on hold;* 215.10 *surplus;* 215.12 *with a remainder*

on the shelves 778.18 *on sale*

on the shoulders of 366.13 *highly*

on the sick list 260.22 *sick;* 260.25 *unhealthily*

on the side 211.10 *additionally*

on the slab 448.14 *experimentally*

on the slate 784.11 *insolvently;* 789.12 *on account;* 783.14 *on credit*

on the slide 214.6 *decreasing*

on the slippery slope 249.6 *adverse*

on the slope 189.4 *oblique*

on the sly 645.6 *cunningly;* 702.15 *hypocritically;* 737.16 *stealthily*

on the spot 97.16; 280.8 *immediately;* 147.9 *near;* 97.9 *resident;* 264.16 *troubled;* 142.12 *where*

on-the-spot 280.5 *immediate*

on-the-spot purchase 777.7 *purchasing*

on the staff 401.9 *serving*

on the stage 738.16 *manifestly*

on the stocks 243.17 *developing;* 233.4 *incomplete;* 243.22 *in preparation;* 484.14 *planned*

on the street 782.3 *beggarly*

on the streets 782.15 *poorly*

on the summit 89.11 *on the mountain*

on the surface 525.15 *apparently;* 171.15 *externally;* 738.14 *manifest;* 738.16 *manifestly;* 55.9 *on the water;* 157.8 *shallowly;* 404.15 *texturally;* 520.11 *visibly*

on the tab 784.11 *insolvently;* 789.12 *on account*

on the table 447.13 *problematically*

on the tail 50.20 *offshore*

on the threshold 164.11 *marginally*

on the throne 396.12 *authoritative;* 396.23 *authoritatively;* 12.10 *governing*

on the tilt 189.4 *oblique*

on the top 174.8 *on top*

on the track 61.11 *in a race;* 60.9 *on the trail;* 633.18 *pursuant to*

on the trail 60.9; 449.13 *discovering;* 633.18 *pursuant to;* 633.15 *pursuing*

on the treadmill 576.12 *laboriously*

on the trot 342.19 *busy;* 132.18 *consecutively;* 289.14 *in succession*

on the turn 499.6 *unpalatable*

on the up 53.20 *in*

on the up-grade 259.1 *healthy*

on the verge 147.12 *near;* 254.2 *unsafe*

on the wagon 634.19 *abstaining;* 684.8 *self-restrained;* 689.1 *sober*

on the waiting list 474.5 *expecting;* 744.16 *recorded*

on the wane 249.6 *adverse;* 556.12 *ageing;* 214.8 *decreasingly;* 337.11 *weakened*

on the warpath 381.26 *aggresively;* 381.22 *militant;* 380.6 *violent;* 585.15 *warring*

on the water 55.9

on the way 319.6 *commercially;* 316.18 *in transit*

on the way out 245.12 *deteriorated*

on the way to 760.18 *convertibly;* 302.19 *forward;* 317.17 *via*

on the whole 204.13; 140.18 *as a rule;* 150.7 *broadly;* 216.11 *on average;* 138.31 *overall*

on the wing 300.18 *in motion;* 316.18 *in transit*

on the wrong track 328.18 *disturbingly*

on thin ice 254.4 *endangered*

on this spot 142.12 *where*

on tick 784.11 *insolvently;* 783.14 *on credit*

on time 293.12, 293.17 *early;* 287.8, 287.11 *in time*

on tiptoe 154.19 *high;* 366.13 *highly*

ontogenic 34.26 *developmental*

ontogeny 93.8 *creation;* 34.15 *developmental biology*

ontological 93.11 *intrinsic*

ontologically 4.24 *philosophically*

ontological time 275.1 *time*

ontology 4.6 *branch of philosophy;* 93.3 *nature;* 97.1 *presence*

on top 174.8; 154.19 *high;* 246.15 *victorious*

on top of 211.10 *additionally*

ontotheological 7.18 *theological*

ontotheology 4.6 *branch of philosophy;* 7.13 *theology*

on tour 98.21 *away;* 98.10 *nonresident*

on trial 448.14 *experimentally;* 464.10 *judged;* 16.54 *litigated*

onus 810.1 *duty*

onus of guilt 806.2 *signs of guilt*

on vacation 98.21 *away;* 580.7 *leisurely;* 98.10 *nonresident;* 263.6 *with ease*

on velvet 248.8 *prosperous;* 248.9 *prosperously*

on view 525.7 *appearing;* 738.13 *displayed*

on visiting terms 569.10 *familiar*

onward 302.19, 330.34 *forward;* 302.18 *ongoing*

onward and upward 134.8 *go on!;* 304.26 *up*

onward course 302.11 *course;* 90.6 *river flow*

onward march 244.5 *improvement*

onwards 302.19 *forward*

on welfare 782.1 *poor;* 782.15 *poorly*

Onychophora 75.4 *arthropod;* 75.6 *worm*

onychophoran 75.4 *arthropod;* 75.6 *worm*

on your way 371.33 *go away!*

oodles 217.8 *plenty;* 208.3 *profuseness*

oogamy 84.4 *reproductive body*

oogonium 84.4 *reproductive body*

oomph 707.6 *assertiveness;* 726.1 *emphasis;* 338.1 *vigour*

Oort cloud 29.19 *comet*

oose 415.7 *light thing*

oosperm 34.15 *developmental biology*

oosphere 84.4 *reproductive body*

ooze 258.4 *dirt;* 30.63 *ebb;* 431.25 *flow;* 315.12 *leak;* 315.3 *leakage;* 371.14 *let out;* 92.3, 429.8 *marsh;* 333.1 *move slowly;* 30.27 *sediment;* 429.16, 433.32 *seep*

ooze at every pore 219.4 *be excessive*

ooze out 315.12 *leak*

oozily 431.26 *fluidly;* 429.17 *moistly;* 433.35 *wetly*

oozing 232.8 *full;* 315.3 *leakage;* 433.25 *seeping*

oozy 92.11 *continental;* 315.17 *leaky;* 429.11 *marshy*

op 35.9, 394.12 *surgery*

opacity 41.10 *graininess;* 266.1, 528.8 *obscurity;* 528.6 *opaqueness*

opal 541.5 *variegated thing*

opalescence 522.2 *quality of light;* 527.7 *semitransparency;* 541.1 *variegation*

opalescent 541.7 *iridescent;* 522.17 *lustrous;* 527.3 *semitransparent*

opal glass 527.9 *glass*

opaline 541.7 *iridescent;* 527.3 *semitransparent;* 528.2 *shady*

opaque 528.1; 24.10 *ceramic;* 524.6 *murky;* 266.2 *obscure*

opaquely 528.13; 24.12 *ornamentally*

Opaqueness 528

opaqueness 528.6; 524.2 *murk*

opaque pigment 529.4 *pigment*

opaque thing 528.7

opaque white glaze 24.3 *glaze*

open 130.24; 308.12; 308.16; 308.18; 738.15; 520.9 *appear;* 130.17, 295.19 *begin;* 190.7 *bigger;* 150.1 *broad;* 150.11 *broaden;* 150.3 *broad-minded;* 520.2 *clear;* 92.11 *continental;* 146.5 *crack;* 146.7 *cracked;* 703.10 *demonstrative;* 739.5 *disclose;* 739.10 *disclosed;* 739.11 *disclosing;* 473.4 *disinterested;* 767.9 *dispose of;* 21.38 *dramatize;* 527.4 *easily seen through;* 171.9 *externalized;* 250.9 *free;* 178.5, 799.4 *honourable;* 344.11 *inaugurate;* 250.13 *informal;* 190.5 *make bigger;* 527.12 *make transparent;* 520.10 *make visible;* 738.14 *manifest;* 646.1 *naive;* 271.3 *natural;* 171.7 *outside;* 69.10 *play;* 740.19 *published;* 370.15, 769.12 *receptive;* 372.15 *separate;* 68.12 *ski;* 698.18 *truthful;* 15.10 *unionized;* 520.1 *visible*

open a campaign 585.13 *be at war*

open a charge account 783.9 *acquire credit*

open a credit account 772.10 *buy on credit*

open air 434.5; 434.16; 171.2, 171.7 *outside;* 257.2 *salubrity*

open-air theatre 21.16 *theatre*

open an account with 776.1 *trade*

open and above-board 738.16 *manifestly*

open-and-shut 452.3 *decided;* 738.14 *manifest*

open-and-shut case 738.11 *openness;* 106.6 *premeditation;* 452.12 *something certain*

open arms 569.4 *act of friendship*

open a trade 776.1 *trade;* 13.10 *trade with*

open a way 318.10 *enter*

open a window 501.5 *deodorize*

open bidding 752.9 *offer*

open canoe 50.6 *canoeing*

open circuit 39.13 *circuit*

open-class racing 50.7 *windsurfing*

open-classroom school 6.12 *educational institution*

open cluster 29.9 *constellation*

open conflict 751.2 *argument*
open country 141.3 *geographical space*; 92.6 *lowland*; 308.8 *open space*
open court 16.19 *law court*
open cruising race 50.6 *canoeing*
open day 654.5 *party*
open door 308.13 *opened up*; 308.10 *opportunity*; 370.2 *receptivity*
open-door policy 779.4 *free market*; 314.4 *right of entry*
opened 130.37 *enrolled*; 295.13 *inaugurated*
opened up 308.13
open-ended 202.3 *eternal*
opener 308.2; 130.10 *introduction*; 129.5 *preface*; 53.4 *team*
open event 50.4 *rowing*
open exchange 713.2 *consultation*
open face 308.9 *openness*
open-face 55.8 *angling*
open-faced 308.16 *open*
open-face reel 55.3 *fishing tackle*
open fire 585.14 *battle*; 381.2, 493.6 *fire*; 330.28 *shoot*
open for bid 752.17 *offered*
open forum 734.4 *conference*
open gate 68.3 *ski racing*
open grave 583.6 *grave*
open hand 814.14 *instrument of punishment*
open-handed 650.7 *charitable*; 679.1 *generous*; 768.8, 813.18 *giving*; 217.2 *plentiful*; 473.5 *unselfish*
open-handedly 650.11 *charitably*; 473.9 *unselfishly*
open-handedness 650.2 *charity*; 679.5 *generosity*; 652.1 *philanthropy*; 473.2 *unselfishness*
open heart 308.9 *openness*
open-hearted 650.6 *benevolent*; 527.4 *easily seen through*; 308.16 *open*; 698.18 *truthful*
open-heartedness 650.1 *benevolence*; 527.10 *openness*; 698.5 *truthfulness*
open hearth 24.6 *ceramic workshop*
open-heart surgery 35.9, 394.12 *surgery*
open hostilities 585.12 *go to war*
open house 138.3 *nonspecificness*; 654.5 *party*
Opening 308
opening 308.1; 525.1 *appearance*; 130.1, 130.29, 295.4 *beginning*; 150.4 *breadth*; 69.4 *chess terms*; 146.2 *crack*; 314.5 *entrance*; 190.8 *growing*; 190.1 *growth*; 287.2, 308.10 *opportunity*; 315.7 *outlet*; 551.24 *part of garment*; 129.5 *preface*; 130.9 *premiere*; 372.3 *separateness*; 130.11 *starting point*; 102.3 *strong possibility*; 752.2 *tentative offer*
opening an umbrella indoors 475.7 *bad-luck sign*
opening batsman 53.4 *team*
opening bowler 53.4 *team*
opening ceremony 130.9 *premiere*
opening gambit 130.10 *introduction*
opening line 130.10 *introduction*
opening meet 59.8 *hunting*
opening night 525.1 *appearance*
opening one's doors 773.4 *taking in*
opening scene 21.8 *scene*
opening up 525.1 *appearance*; 308.9 *openness*
open letter 740.3 *journalism*; 138.3 *nonspecificness*
openly 308.26; **739.13**; 150.7 *broadly*; 92.13 *continentally*; 703.21 *demonstratively*; 473.8 *disinterestedly*; 799.7 *honourably*; 250.22 *informally*; 738.16 *manifestly*; 646.5 *naively*; 740.22 *publicly*; 271.8 *simply*; 178.13 *straightforwardly*; 527.13 *transparently*; 698.36 *truthfully*; 520.11 *visibly*
openly happen 738.5 *be visible*
open market 776.5 *commercial trade*; 250.1 *freedom*; 779.4 *free market*; 779.1 *market*
open mind 618.3 *impartiality*; 453.9 *uncertainty*
open-minded 150.3 *broad-minded*; 473.4 *disinterested*; 250.9 *free*; 618.9 *impartial*; 769.12 *receptive*; 801.7 *right*; 453.1 *uncertain*
open-mindedly 473.8 *disinterestedly*; 250.20 *freely*; 618.19 *impartially*
open-mindedness 150.6 *broad-mindedness*; 473.1 *disinterestedness*; 250.1 *freedom*
open mouth 711.2 *danger signal*; 619.2 *sign of wonderment*
open-mouthed 308.12 *open*; 619.7 *wide-eyed*
openness 308.9; **527.10**; **738.11**; **739.3**; 150.4 *breadth*; 150.6 *broad-mindedness*; 703.2 *demonstrativeness*; 731.2 *effusiveness*; 171.4 *externalization*; 250.4 *informality*; 646.2 *naivety*; 271.6 *naturalness*; 799.1 *probity*; 740.7 *publicity*; 370.2 *receptivity*; 698.5 *truthfulness*; 254.7 *vulnerability*
open one's doors to 773.11 *be hospitable*; 769.10 *receive someone*
open one's eyes 695.4 *be intelligible*
open one's eyes wide 619.9 *wonder*
open one's heart 308.22 *be open*; 698.29 *be truthful*
open one's heart to 739.8 *admit*
open one's mind to 473.6 *be disinterested*
open one's mouth 619.9 *wonder*
open one's pocket 787.1 *expend*
open one's purse 768.6 *give to charity*
open one's wallet 785.6 *pay*
open out 527.12 *make transparent*; 308.18 *open*
open Pandora's box 264.22 *cause trouble*
open-plan 308.13 *opened up*
open primary 469.12 *election*
open sandwich 25.11 *sandwich*
open sea 308.8 *open space*
open season 60.2 *hunting*; 292.1 *season*
open sesame 308.2 *opener*; 11.5 *spell*
open sewer 90.1 *river*
open shop 15.5 *labour law*; 15.3 *organized labour*
open space 308.8; 141.3 *geographical space*; 308.1 *opening*
open table 65.6 *pool*
open texture 527.6 *translucency*
open-textured 527.2 *translucent*
open the books 739.6 *divulge*
open the door 314.9 *enter*
open the door to 370.7 *admit*; 344.11 *inaugurate*; 265.16 *make easy*
open the floodgates 757.4 *be permissive*; 787.1 *expend*; 371.14 *let out*
open the hatches 370.7 *admit*
open the shutters 522.29 *clarify*
open the sluice gates 90.8 *cause to flow*; 371.14 *let out*
open the throttle 332.6 *accelerate*
open the windows 739.5 *disclose*
open to 254.3 *vulnerable*
open to criticism 670.36 *blameworthy*
open to debate 705.14 *questionable*
open-toed sandals 551.19 *footwear*
open to offers 752.17 *offered*
open to question 701.10 *arguable*; 705.14 *questionable*
open to suggestion 480.20 *persuadable*
open to the public 520.2 *clear*
open to view 520.2 *clear*
open universe 29.4 *cosmological model*
Open University 692.25 *broadcast material*; 6.2 *educational system*
open up 308.19; 332.6 *accelerate*; 190.6 *become bigger*; 308.22 *be open*; 698.29 *be truthful*; 739.5 *disclose*; 244.1 *improve*; 265.16 *make easy*; 308.18 *open*; 41.21 *photograph*; 130.21 *pioneer*; 738.3 *reveal*
open verdict 453.9 *uncertainty*
open vote 469.10 *vote*
open war 585.8 *warfare*
open-water 67.11 *swimming*
open-water swimming 67.1 *swimming*
open-weave 42.10 *woven*
open windows 581.1 *refresh*
opera 18.4; 21.4 *musical drama*; 21.16 *theatre*; 356.5 *work of art*
operability 102.2 *possibleness*
operable 394.18 *medical*; 102.5 *possible*; 393.14 *repairable*; 346.11 *workable*
opéra bouffe 18.4 *opera*
opera buff 21.33 *theatregoer*
opera buffa 21.4 *musical drama*; 18.4 *opera*
opéra comique 18.4 *opera*
opera glasses 28.32 *optical instrument*; 518.10 *visual aid*
operagoer 21.33 *theatregoer*
opera house 504.3 *auditorium*; 18.28 *concert hall*; 21.16 *theatre*
operand 27.13 *mathematical symbol*
operant conditioning 36.20 *conditioning*
opera semiseria 18.4 *opera*
opera seria 21.4 *musical drama*; 18.4 *opera*
opera singer 21.24 *actor*; 507.5 *loud person*; 578.1 *worker*
operate 340.4 *act*; 348.4 *be an instrument*; 631.14 *behave towards*; 407.23 *be in order*; 346.7 *be operational*; 237.9 *be useful*; 393.6 *cure*; 394.20 *doctor*; 35.20 *practise surgery*; 776.2 *speculate*; 349.1 *use*
operate a closed shop 251.9 *economize*
operate at a loss 766.10 *have a financial loss*
operate on 483.10 *manipulate*
operatic 21.39 *dramatic*; 18.32 *instrumental*
operatic music 18.3 *classical music*
operating 346.10 *operational*; 348.8 *practical*
operating at a loss 766.2 *financial loss*
operating room 394.14 *hospital*
operating system 40.8 *software*
operating table 394.14 *hospital*
operating theatre 35.10, 394.14 *hospital*
Operation 346
operation 27.14; **346.1**; 340.1 *action*; 340.2 *deed*; 348.1 *instrumentality*; 35.9, 394.12 *surgery*; 576.2 *task*; 631.8 *treatment*; 354.2 *undertaking*; 349.6 *use*; 353.6 *venture*; 585.8 *warfare*; 317.1 *way*
operational 346.10; 340.6 *effective*; 243.19 *in hand*; 585.17 *military*; 348.8 *practical*
operational command 584.4 *military organization*
operational fleet 584.4 *military organization*
operationally 346.13
operational research 579.3 *management*; 484.2 *policy*
operations 584.1 *military affairs*; 585.8 *warfare*
operations room 484.7 *planning*
operative 334.14; **346.6**; **346.12**; 340.5 *acting*; 342.18 *active*; 578.3 *agent*; 340.3 *doer*; 438.8 *machinist*; 95.8, 348.8 *practical*; 237.1 *useful*; 578.1 *worker*
operator 40.2; **346.5**; 578.3 *agent*; 755.4 *contractor*; 340.3 *doer*; 438.8 *machinist*; 27.63 *mathematical logic*; 27.13 *mathematical symbol*; 4.8 *philosophical term*; 692.13 *telephoner*; 349.8 *user*; 778.12 *wholesaler*
operator gene 34.13 *genetic material*
operculum 550.14 *animal covering*; 74.5 *fish anatomy*
operetta 21.4 *musical drama*; 18.4 *opera*
operon 34.13 *genetic material*
operoseness 576.4 *exertion*
Ophidia 73.3 *snake*
ophidian 73.11 *reptilian*; 73.3 *snake*; 73.12 *snakelike*
ophiolater 9.6 *idolater*
ophiolatrous 9.10 *idolatrous*
ophiolatry 9.2 *idolatry*
ophiological 73.14 *herpetological*
ophiologist 73.10 *herpetologist*
ophiology 73.9 *herpetology*
ophiomancer 11.13 *diviner*
ophiomancy 11.9 *divination*
ophiomorphic 73.12 *snakelike*
ophiuroid 75.3 *echinoderm*; 75.17 *echinodermal*
ophthalmia 519.2 *poor sight*
ophthalmic 518.20 *visual*
ophthalmitis 519.2 *poor sight*
ophthalmological 35.22 *medical*
ophthalmologist 519.3 *aid for poor sight*; 35.13 *medical specialist*
ophthalmology 519.3 *aid for poor sight*; 35.3 *medical specialty*
ophthalmoscope 35.7 *diagnosis*
opiate 37.4 *drug type*; 685.2 *moderator*; 608.3 *reliever*; 343.10 *soporific*
opilionid 76.2 *arachnid*
opine 590.19 *believe*; 450.8 *be of the opinion*; 4.22 *propound a philosophy*; 476.5 *suppose*; 446.17 *theorize*
opiniativeness 641.7 *opinionatedness*
opinion 713.1 *advice*; 450.1 *belief*; 631.1 *conduct*; 590.3 *feelings*; 446.5 *ideology*; 464.1 *judgment*; 701.3 *line of argument*; 4.1 *philosophy*; 476.1 *supposition*; 729.7 *utterance*
opinionated 673.14; 450.11 *believing*; 673.13 *boastful*; 452.2 *convinced*; 641.4 *set*
opinionatedness 641.7
opinion column 741.9 *news story*
opinionist 452.11
opinion poll 210.3 *count*; 469.10 *vote*
opium 489.4 *anaesthetic*; 394.8, 691.6 *drug*; 685.2 *moderator*; 343.10 *soporific*
opium den 804.8 *wicked place*
opossum shrimp 75.4 *arthropod*
oppidan 564.4 *townsman*; 87.14 *urban*; 87.11 *urbanite*
oppo 119.5 *equal*
opponent 113.13; 586.1 *combatant*; 661.4 *defiant person*; 670.11 *disapprover*; 662.6 *nonconformist*; 383.5 *resister*; 45.3 *sportsman*
opportune 222.9 *comfortable*; 239.1 *convenient*; 292.14 *seasonable*; 287.6 *timely*
opportunely 287.9; 222.18 *comfortably*; 239.7 *conveniently*
opportuneness 287.1 *timeliness*
opportunism 239.3 *convenience*; 800.1 *improbity*; 683.1 *selfishness*; 631.9 *tactics*
opportunist 354.6 *enterprising*; 479.9 *equivocator*; 683.3 *selfish person*
opportunistic 800.5 *dishonourable*; 683.4 *selfish*
opportunity 287.2; **308.10**; 239.3 *convenience*; 107.5 *good chance*; 348.1 *instrumentality*; 580.1 *leisure*; 222.2 *occurrence*; 102.1 *possibility*; 344.5 *reason*; 752.2 *tentative offer*
oppose 113.14; 701.13 *argue*; 662.15 *be disobedient*; 661.6 *be insubordinate*; 113.15 *be opposite*; 347.3 *counteract*; 381.8 *counterattack*; 586.39 *defend*; 661.5 *defy*; 704.9 *deny*; 372.12, 670.16 *disagree*; 709.6 *dissent*; 378.8 *hinder*; 703.19, 753.6 *protest*; 383.6 *resist*
oppose change 225.6 *make permanent*
opposed 249.6 *adverse*; 372.18 *disagreeable*; 670.31 *disapproved*; 113.23 *opposite*; 113.22 *oppositional*; 637.2 *refusing*; 383.10 *resistant*
opposed to 113.31; 347.4 *counteracting*
opposer 113.11; 670.11 *disapprover*; 383.5 *resister*
opposing 249.6 *adverse*; 586.33 *combative*; 347.4 *counteracting*; 381.24 *counterattacking*; 703.14 *demonstrating*; 670.26 *disagreeing*; 662.13 *disobedient*; 709.9 *dissenting*; 113.23 *opposite*; 113.22 *oppositional*; 753.9 *protesting*; 708.19 *rebutting*; 383.10 *resistant*
opposing action 347.1 *counteraction*
opposing force 347.1 *counteraction*; 113.10 *the opposition*
opposingly 113.27; 708.22 *negatively*
opposing party 113.10 *the opposition*
opposing side 113.2 *oppositeness*; 169.5 *team*
opposite 113.23; 113.25 *contrary*; 372.18 *disagreeable*; 709.9 *dissenting*; 110.5 *interconnected*; 108.5 *interrelated*; 192.1 *inversion*; 694.6 *meaningful*; 708.3 *rebuttal*; 27.43 *triangle*; 694.4 *type of meaning*
opposite angles 27.39 *angle*
opposite camp 113.10 *the opposition*
oppositely 372.23 *disagreeably*; 110.10 *reciprocally*; 108.10 *relevantly*; 709.11 *uncooperatively*
opposite meaning 694.4 *type of meaning*
oppositeness 113.2; 113.8 *contrariety*
opposite number 119.5 *equal*; 110.2 *interconnection*; 113.2 *oppositeness*
opposite pole 113.2 *oppositeness*
opposites 113.3
opposite side 113.2 *oppositeness*; 169.5 *team*
opposite tide 91.2 *tide*
Opposition 113
opposition 113.1; **637.12**; 249.1 *adversity*; 176.4 *angular measurement*; 347.1 *counteraction*; 670.4 *disagreement*; 661.2, 662.1 *disobedience*; 709.2 *dissent*; 481.6 *dissuasion*; 372.4 *disunity*; 378.1 *hindrance*; 113.2 *oppositeness*; 29.16 *planet*; 753.1 *protest*; 383.1 *resistance*
oppositional 113.22; 347.4 *counteracting*; 113.23 *opposite*
oppositionist 113.11 *opposer*
opposition party 113.10 *the opposition*
opposition rally 661.3 *act of defiance*
opposure 113.2 *oppositeness*
oppress 660.26; 396.19 *be authoritarian*; 249.11 *cause adversity*; 386.6 *compel*; 387.7 *defeat*; 466.14 *discriminate against*; 12.11 *govern*; 236.14 *ill-treat*; 414.14 *make heavy*; 400.14 *master*; 342.17 *meddle*;

351.1 *misuse*; 633.8 *pursue*; 251.8 *restrain*; 647.6 *suppress*; 651.18 *torment*; 414.13 *weigh on*; 802.20 *wrong*
oppressed 466.11 *judged*; 351.4 *misused*; 367.22 *overthrown*; 414.3 *ponderous*; 647.9 *suppressed*
oppressing 387.10 *dominating*
oppression 387.2 *domination*; 236.11 *harmfulness*; 351.2 *misuse*; 367.13 *submergence*; 647.2 *suppression*; 414.8 *weighing down*
oppressive 622.16; 16.62 *above the law*; 351.5 *abusive*; 386.9 *compelling*; 264.10 *difficult*; 387.10 *dominating*; 236.5 *harmful*; 31.52 *humid*; 651.10 *malevolent*; 400.12 *masterful*; 414.3 *ponderous*; 251.13 *restraining*; 647.8 *severe*
oppressively 351.6 *abusively*; 414.17 *burdensomely*; 386.11 *compellingly*; 367.24 *down*; 400.16 *masterfully*; 647.11 *severely*
oppressiveness 414.8 *weighing down*
oppressive person 647.4 *strict person*
oppressor 400.4 *absolute ruler*; 647.4 *strict person*
opprobrious 668.11 *insulting*; 712.9 *vituperative*
opprobriously 712.13 *vituperatively*
opprobrium 668.1 *disrespect*; 712.3 *vilification*
oppugn 113.18 *object*
oppugnancy 113.7 *contrariness*
oppugnant 113.26 *uncooperative*
opsonin 431.4 *blood*
opt 469.1 *select*
optative 5.33 *mood*
opt for 635.12 *choose*; 469.1 *select*
optic 518.2 *eye*; 522.23 *photoelectric*; 28.98 *physical*; 518.20 *visual*
optical 24.10 *ceramic*; 28.98 *physical*; 19.24 *pictorial*; 518.20 *visual*
optical aberration 28.31 *lens element*
optical activity 28.33 *photosensitivity*; 32.13 *structure*
optical astronomy 29.1 *astronomy*
optical disk 40.7 *peripheral*
optical double 29.9 *constellation*
optical element 28.29
optical fibre 28.29 *optical element*
optical glass 24.9 *industrial ceramics*
optical illusion 96.3 *delusion*; 477.5 *fantasy*; 518.5 *imagination*; 519.5 *visual distortion*
optical instrument 28.32; 520.7 *that which makes visible*; 518.10 *visual aid*
optical isomer 32.13 *structure*
optically 24.12 *ornamentally*; 28.100 *physically*; 19.30 *pictorially*; 518.24 *visually*
optical microscope 28.85 *microscope*
optical observatory 29.23 *observatory*
optical perspective 19.4 *treatment*
optical rotation 28.33 *photosensitivity*; 32.13 *structure*
optical spectrum 28.68 *emission*
optical telescope 28.85 *microscope*; 29.24 *telescope*
optic axis 28.31 *lens element*
optician 519.3 *aid for poor sight*; 394.15 *healer*
optic nerve 518.2 *eye*
optics 28.2 *classical physics*; 334.9 *electronics*; 518.10 *visual aid*
optimate 573.1 *nobleman*; 811.2 *person of repute*
optimism 598.3 *cheerfulness*; 474.1 *expectation*; 610.1 *hope*; 446.7 *idealism*
optimist 467.3; 598.4 *cheerful person*; 610.5 *hoper*; 446.9 *person of ideas*
optimistic 756.14 *auspicious*; 598.1 *cheerful*; 474.5 *expecting*; 610.11 *hopeful*; 446.13 *ideal*
optimistically 756.17 *auspiciously*; 474.12 *expectantly*; 610.15 *hopefully*; 446.22 *imaginatively*
optimum 235.2 *best*
opting out 637.2 *refusing*
option 469.8 *choice*; 250.1 *freedom*; 46.15 *play offence*; 635.1 *will*
optional 635.10 *free*; 57.11 *gymnastic*; 469.14 *selecting*
optional exercise 57.1 *gymnastics*
optionally 57.12 *competitively*; 469.17 *selectively*
option pass 46.9 *play*
option run 46.9 *play*
optoelectronics 39.1 *electronics*
optometer 26.8 *meter*
optometric 26.16 *micrometric*
optometrist 519.3 *aid for poor sight*
optometry 519.3 *aid for poor sight*; 26.2 *micrometry*
opt out 118.19 *be independent*; 637.9 *not cooperate*
opt-out 637.12 *opposition*
opt-out clause 252.1 *safety*
opulence 781.7; 490.1 *physical pleasure*
opulent 781.3; 490.6 *pleasant*; 217.2 *plentiful*; 248.8 *prosperous*
opulently 248.9 *prosperously*; 781.16 *wealthily*
opus 18.15 *composition*; 356.5 *work of art*
or 743.13 *heraldic*; 743.8 *heraldic device*; 536.1 *orange*; 537.1 *yellow*
Oracle™ 692.25 *broadcast material*
oracle 475.8; 713.4 *adviser*; 11.13 *diviner*; 479.5 *equivocalness*; 442.8 *intellectual person*; 745.1 *maxim*; 283.5 *predictor*; 458.3 *wise man*
oracular 696.4 *difficult*; 11.17 *divinatory*; 8.13 *divine*; 479.10 *equivocal*; 475.13 *predicting*; 745.2 *proverbial*; 696.1 *unintelligible*; 458.5 *wise*
oracular utterance 479.5 *equivocalness*
oral 729.17; 692.33 *communicational*; 35.23 *dental*; 1.14 *societal*
oral administration 37.13 *administration*
oral cavity 308.4 *body orifice*; 729.5 *organ of speech*
oral communication 729.1 *faculty of speech*
oral contraceptive 37.4 *drug type*; 33.16 *hormone*
oral examination 705.3 *questionnaire*
oral hygiene 256.5 *ablutions*
oral literature 17.1 *literature*
orally 729.21
oral pathologist 35.14 *dentist*
oral pathology 35.4 *dentistry*
oral surgeon 35.14 *dentist*
oral surgery 35.4 *dentistry*
oral tobacco 496.7 *tobacco*
oral tradition 1.8 *tradition*
orange 536.1; 28.28 *colour*; 691.6 *drug*; 536.3 *orange thing*
orangeade 536.3 *orange thing*; 558.6 *soft drink*; 498.5 *sweet drink*
orange blossom 536.4 *figurative usage*; 78.1 *flower*; 502.2 *fragrant thing*
Orange Bowl 46.1 *football*
orange-brown 534.1 *brown*
orange colour 536.2 *orangeness*
orange-flower water 536.4 *figurative usage*
Orange Free State 536.4 *figurative usage*
orange grove 44.2 *garden*
orange hawkweed 536.3 *orange thing*
orange juice 536.3 *orange thing*; 558.6 *soft drink*
Orangeman 536.4 *figurative usage*
Orangeman's Day 536.4 *figurative usage*
Orange March 536.4 *figurative usage*
Orangeness 536
orangeness 536.2
orange peel 238.6 *refuse*
orange pekoe 536.4 *figurative usage*; 558.3 *tea*
orange pigment 536.2 *orangeness*
orange-pink 535.1 *red*
orangery 536.4 *figurative usage*; 44.4 *nursery*; 565.7 *room*; 79.4 *trees*
orange squash 536.3 *orange thing*
orange stick 536.4 *figurative usage*
orange sunshine 691.6 *drug*; 536.3 *orange thing*
orange thing 536.3
orangewood 536.4 *figurative usage*
orate 733.7 *address*; 270.5 *be diffuse*; 722.4 *dissertate*; 729.14 *speak to*
oration 733.1 *address*; 270.1 *diffuseness*; 722.1 *dissertation*; 729.8 *speech*
orator 722.3 *dissertator*; 483.7 *motivator*; 480.12 *persuader*; 542.9 *phrasemonger*; 733.6 *public speaker*; 729.10 *speaker*; 724.5 *stylist*
oratorical 733.13; 542.10 *ornate*
oratorio 18.5 *sacred music*
oratorium 10.11 *place of worship*
oratory 729.9 *art of public speaking*; 724.4 *literary style*; 4.5 *philosophical argument*; 10.11 *place of worship*
oratrix 729.10 *speaker*
orb 179.2 *circle*; 518.2 *eye*; 743.4 *insignia*; 181.3 *round thing*; 29.10 *star*
orbicular 179.5 *circular*; 77.18 *of leaves*; 181.9 *round*
orbicularity 179.1 *circularity*; 181.1 *roundness*
orbicularly 179.8 *circularly*; 181.13 *roundly*
orbit 29.21; **306.3**; **306.6**; 298.8 *be cyclic*; 179.2, 179.6 *circle*; 298.2 *cycle*; 518.2 *eye*; 317.14 *find one's way*; 317.13 *flight path*; 86.13 *locality*; 181.12 *move round*; 29.37 *observe*; 306.1 *orbital motion*; 318.2 *passing along*; 29.35 *rocketry*; 307.8 *rotate*; 307.1 *rotation*; 181.6 *round*; 181.3 *round thing*; 317.2 *route*; 395.7 *sphere of influence*
orbital 306.9; 179.5 *circular*; 298.12 *cyclic*; 306.5 *ringroad*; 307.12 *rotary*; 32.12 *valence*
orbitally 179.8 *circularly*; 298.16 *cyclically*
Orbital Motion 306
orbital motion 306.1; 298.2 *cycle*; 307.1 *rotation*
orbital period 29.21 *orbit*
orbiter 29.33 *planetary probe*
orbiting 306.11; 306.1 *orbital motion*; 307.11 *rotating*; 307.1 *rotation*
orbiting body 306.4
orbiting observatory 29.32 *satellite*
orc 11.11 *ghost*; 70.7 *legendary beast*
orchard 44.2 *garden*; 79.4 *trees*
orchardist 44.13 *horticulturist*
Orchard Street 779.1 *market*
orchestra 374.3 *assembly*; 18.26 *musical group*; 21.17 *stage*; 376.12 *team*
orchestra conductor 578.1 *worker*
orchestra director 578.1 *worker*
orchestral music 18.3 *classical music*
orchestra pit 21.17 *stage*
orchestra stalls 21.18 *auditorium*
orchestrate 409.16 *adapt*; 631.14 *behave towards*; 18.35 *compose*; 750.24 *harmonize*; 579.1 *manage*; 516.9 *set to music*
orchestrated 18.31 *composed*; 374.8 *cooperative*; 750.13 *harmonious*
orchestration 374.2 *cooperation*; 516.4 *harmonics*; 750.4 *harmony*; 579.3 *management*; 409.9 *musical arrangement*; 18.2 *music making*; 631.8 *treatment*
orchestrator 18.24 *musician*
orchidaceous 77.16 *taxonomic*
orchids 77.3 *seed plant*
Orcus 8.12 *hell*
ORD 32.13 *structure*
ordain 7.21; 130.25 *enrol*; 635.15 *impose one's will*; 368.7 *install*; 370.10 *introduce*; 16.68 *legislate*; 407.18 *order*; 140.13 *rule*
ordained 16.46 *legislated*; 407.10 *ordered*; 106.3 *predetermined*; 7.17 *priestly*; 10.21 *ritualistic*
ordainment 7.9 *priesthood*
ordeal 491.1 *pain*
Order 407
order 27.94; **407.1**; **407.18**; 409.12 *arrange*; 409.1 *arrangement*; 409.6 *category*; 137.2 *class*; 386.2 *coercion*; 397.1, 397.9 *command*; 693.2 *communication*; 386.6 *compel*; 132.2 *consecution*; 750.6 *convention*; 710.2, 710.7 *demand*; 160.1, 160.7 *form*; 542.4 *honour*; 810.17 *impose a duty*; 635.15 *impose one's will*; 160.3 *kind*; 137.3 *kingdom*; 16.3 *law*; 16.6 *legal process*; 16.68 *legislate*; 298.10 *make regular*; 750.26 *make uniform*; 27.22 *matrix*; 745.1 *maxim*; 209.5 *measure*; 135.10 *necessitate*; 298.4 *orderliness*; 780.14 *paper money*; 589.1 *peace*; 484.9 *plan*; 484.7 *planning*; 713.3 *precept*; 293.9 *prepare*; 243.4 *prepare for action*; 777.1 *purchase*; 209.2 *rank*; 140.14 *regulate*; 108.3 *relative position*; 7.1 *religion*; 135.1 *requirement*; 253.15 *reserve*; 575.1 *right*; 10.1 *ritual*; 140.1 *rule*; 137.5 *social class*; 137.14 *sort*; 141.21 *space*; 221.1 *state*; 289.1 *succession*; 34.17 *taxonomy*; 464.2 *verdict*; 585.8 *warfare*; 317.1 *way*
order by telephone 135.10 *necessitate*; 777.1 *purchase*
ordered 407.10; 409.20 *arranged*; 137.12 *classed*; 27.75 *equal*; 16.46 *legislated*; 108.6 *ranked*; 135.4 *required*; 289.12 *succeeding*
ordered arrangement 27.21 *set*
ordered set 27.21 *set*
ordering 409.1 *arrangement*; 137.1 *classification*; 397.14 *commanding*; 121.13 *dominant*; 27.56 *nonparametric methods*
ordering relation 27.63 *mathematical logic*
orderless 408.12 *disordered*; 412.12 *mixed*
orderliness 298.4; **407.5**; 665.4 *fastidiousness*
orderly 298.14; **298.17**; **407.13**; **407.26**; 409.20 *arranged*; 665.9 *careful*; 256.16 *clean*; 750.14 *conforming*; 140.10 *customary*; 656.6 *formal*; 160.9 *formed*; 35.17 *paramedic*; 484.14 *planned*; 401.1 *servant*
order number 27.56 *nonparametric methods*
order of battle 585.9 *battle*
order of business 220.5 *list of appointments*
order of chivalry 794.1 *trophy*
order off 371.6 *send away*
order of magnitude 158.1 *size*
order of merit 794.1 *trophy*
order of service 10.6 *Eucharist*; 10.4 *public worship*; 281.2 *timetable*
order of the day 397.1 *command*; 117.5 *convention*; 484.1 *plan*; 106.6 *premeditation*; 281.2 *timetable*; 632.5 *tradition*
order of things 140.6 *custom*
order of worship 10.1 *ritual*
order one's life 243.8 *prepare oneself*
order paper 106.6 *premeditation*
order through a catalogue 777.1 *purchase*
order up 397.10 *demand*
ordinal 132.9 *consecutive*; 27.75 *equal*; 27.7 *natural number*; 194.8 *odd*; 10.10 *religious manual*
ordinal number 194.2 *kind of number*; 27.7 *natural number*
ordinal scale 27.56 *nonparametric methods*
ordinance 397.1 *command*; 16.3 *law*; 713.3 *precept*; 10.1 *ritual*; 140.1 *rule*
ordinand 7.8 *priest*
ordinarily 140.18 *as a rule*; 750.37 *conventionally*; 297.1 *frequently*; 122.20 *insignificantly*; 216.11 *on average*; 298.17 *orderly*; 138.30 *usually*
ordinariness 231.8; 216.4 *average*; 138.5 *averageness*; 122.1 *inferiority*; 618.4 *mediocrity*; 298.4 *orderliness*; 271.4 *simplicity*
ordinary 122.16; **231.4**; **574.4**; 216.1 *average*; 138.21 *common*; 750.15 *conventional*; 117.15 *everyday*; 632.10 *familiar*; 743.8 *heraldic device*; 618.10 *mediocre*; 685.6 *moderate*; 235.5 *not bad*; 298.14 *orderly*; 271.1 *simple*; 124.4 *trivial*; 349.9 *used*
ordinary bloke 574.1 *plebeian*
ordinary differential equation 27.31 *differentiation*
ordinary Joe 216.7 *average person*; 138.9 *everyman*
ordinary matter 124.8 *trifle*
ordinary person 566.7 *person*
ordinary rating 586.27 *naval man*
ordinary run 138.6 *average*
ordinary seaman 586.27 *naval man*
ordinate 27.33 *coordinates*; 26.4 *size*
ordination 10.5 *Christian rite*; 130.8 *enrolment*; 370.3 *introduction*; 7.9 *priesthood*
ordnance 587.11 *guns*
Ordnance Survey map 717.7 *map*
Ordovician period 284.3 *geological period*
ordure 258.4 *dirt*; 560.5 *faeces*
ore 32.24; 435.1 *materials*
oread 8.5 *deity*
oregano 496.5 *herbs*
ore roaster 24.6 *ceramic workshop*
organ 205.4 *component*; 348.2 *instrument*; 740.5 *journal*
organdie 527.8 *transparent thing*
organ donor 768.4 *giver*
organelle 34.8 *cell organ*
organic 403.12; 32.31 *chemical*; 32.35 *combined*; 2.13 *communal*; 34.21 *living*; 99.8 *quintessential*
organic acid 32.8 *acid*
organically 43.22 *agriculturally*; 403.18 *structurally*
organic base 32.9 *base*
organic being 34.3 *organism*
organic chemist 32.2 *chemist*
organic chemistry 32.1 *chemistry*; 402.6 *natural science*
organic compound 32.7 *chemical compound*
organic disease 260.4 *disease*
organic farm 43.6 *farm*
organic farming 43.1 *agriculture*

organic fertilizer 562.3 *fertilizer*
organic food 557.7 *food*
organic manure 43.13 *fertilizer*
organic matter 402.4 *matter*
organic pigment 529.4 *pigment*
organic psychosis 36.11 *psychosis*
organic remains 34.3 *organism*
organic sediment 30.27 *sediment*
organic solidarity 2.5 *society*
organic structure 403.1 *structure*
organism **34.3**; 554.2 *living matter*; 402.4 *matter*
organismal 403.12 *organic*
organization **409.3**; 376.15 *association*; 579.3 *management*; 407.7 *method*; 407.1 *order*; 578.4 *personnel*; 484.7 *planning*; 243.9 *preparation*; 356.1 *production*; 403.1 *structure*; 631.8 *treatment*
organizational **409.22**; 579.17 *managerial*; 403.11 *structural*
organization man 117.6 *conformist*
Organization of Petroleum-Exporting Countries 776.5 *commercial trade*; 779.4 *free market*; 13.5 *international trade*
organize **409.13**; 631.14 *behave towards*; 243.2 *do the groundwork*; 409.18 *make arrangements*; 579.1 *manage*; 407.18 *order*; 484.9 *plan*; 356.10 *produce*; 140.14 *regulate*; 2.15 *socialize*; 137.14 *sort*; 141.21 *space*; 403.14 *structure*
organize a dragnet 633.8 *pursue*
organize a search party 633.8 *pursue*
organize a vigilante committee 633.8 *pursue*
organized **409.21**; 407.10 *ordered*; 484.14 *planned*; 243.18 *prepared*; 15.10 *unionized*
organized crime 804.7 *criminality*
organized labour **15.3**
organized society 566.9 *group*
organized strike 15.4 *industrial dispute*
organizer 484.8 *planner*
organ music 18.3 *classical music*
organ notes 507.1 *loudness*
organ of speech **729.5**
organological 403.12 *organic*
organology 403.8 *science of structure*
organometallic 32.35 *combined*
organometallic compound 32.7 *chemical compound*
organs of reproduction **561.8**
organza 527.8 *transparent thing*
orgasm 490.1 *physical pleasure*; 327.8 *spasm*
orgasmic 327.19 *convulsive*
orgone theory 36.1 *psychology*
orgy 601.1 *celebration*; 686.2 *dissipation*; 557.13 *feast*; 490.4 *pleasurable things*; 217.8 *plenty*
orgy of drinking 690.14 *drinking bout*
Oriel window 20.9 *miscellaneous architectural features*
Orient 86.7 *regions of the world*
orient **324.8**; 632.18 *habituate*
Oriental 324.13 *directional*; 1.6 *race*; 1.13 *racial*; 86.16 *regional*
Orientale 59.13 *breeding*
orientalize 760.12 *naturalize*
orientalized 760.17 *naturalized*
orientate 632.18 *habituate*; 143.10 *situate*
orientated 143.6 *situated*
orientated towards 324.14 *directed*
orientation **324.3**; 632.7 *habituation*; 27.37 *line*; 143.1 *situation*; 476.1 *supposition*
orienteering 142.5 *topography*
Orient Express 321.10 *miscellaneous*
orient onself 324.8 *orient*
orifice 146.2 *crack*; 314.5 *entrance*; 308.1 *opening*; 315.7 *outlet*
oriflamme 743.7 *flag*
origin 554.4 *biological function*; 130.2 *creation*; 27.32 *graph*; 130.5 *invention*; 402.4 *matter*; 130.3 *source*
original **126.2**; **126.4**; **448.9**; 698.19 *authentic*; 344.13 *causal*; 116.4 *dissimilar*; 118.10, 118.14 *eccentric*; 68.13 *ice-skating*; 446.11 *ideational*; 477.10 *imaginative*; 130.33 *inventive*; 16.49 *judicatory*; 295.10 *new*; 487.2 *not customary*; 130.31 *prime*; 356.11 *productive*; 160.10 *prototypical*; 139.15 *special*
Originality 126
originality **126.1**; **448.4**; 698.6 *authenticity*; 443.5 *creative thought*; 57.1 *gymnastics*; 68.7 *ice-dancing*; 446.8, 477.1 *imagination*; 295.1 *newness*; 356.1 *production*; 139.1 *speciality*; 118.4 *unusualness*
originally **126.8**; **449.16**; 296.21 *archaically*; 344.14 *causally*; 160.13 *formatively*; 446.22 *imaginatively*; 130.38 *in the beginning*; 295.21 *newly*; 487.8 *unusually*
original meaning 694.4 *type of meaning*
original model 243.10 *preparations*
original sin 804.4, 806.3 *sin*
original thought 126.1 *originality*
original title 763.1 *possession*
original work 356.1 *production*
originate **126.7**; 130.17 *begin*; 344.9 *be the cause of*; 295.18 *be trendy*; 130.27 *emerge*; 443.16 *have an idea*; 446.15, 477.14 *imagine*; 130.22, 449.4 *invent*; 356.10 *produce*
originate in 345.7 *follow from*
origination 344.1 *cause*; 130.2 *creation*; 130.5, 449.9 *invention*; 356.1 *production*
originative 561.16 *reproductive*
originator **126.3**; **130.16**; 449.12 *discoverer*; 484.8 *planner*; 344.7 *Prime Mover*; 356.9 *producer*
oriole 72.6 *songbird*
Orion nebula 29.8 *interstellar medium*
orismology 721.7 *nomenclature*
orison 10.9 *prayer*
ormolu 700.6 *imitation*; 542.3 *pattern*
ornament **542.1**; **542.12**; 211.6 *add*; 545.2 *beautiful thing*; 543.4 *be elegant*; 223.4 *concomitant*; 20.19 *decorate*; 543.1 *elegance*; 244.1 *improve*; 244.5 *improvement*; 18.16 *musical note*; 266.1 *obscurity*
ornamental **44.19**; 545.5 *beautiful*; 24.10 *ceramic*; 211.9 *extra*; 266.2 *obscure*; 542.10 *ornate*; 20.17 *structured*; 79.1 *tree*; 238.1 *useless*; 541.6 *variegated*
ornamental garden **44.3**; 44.2 *garden*
ornamental grass 81.1 *grass*
ornamentally **24.12**; 20.20 *architecturally*; 44.20 *horticulturally*; 266.4 *obscurely*; 541.12 *variedly*
ornamental ware 24.1 *ceramics*
ornamentation 211.3 *additional item*; 244.5 *improvement*; 542.1 *ornament*
ornamented 543.3 *elegant*; 542.10 *ornate*; 20.17 *structured*
ornate **542.10**; 270.3 *diffuse*; 78.10 *floral*
ornately **542.13**; 724.10 *stylistically*
orneriness 662.1 *disobedience*; 625.1 *irascibility*
ornery 662.13 *disobedient*; 625.4 *irascible*
ornithischian 73.6 *extinct reptile*
ornithological **72.23**
ornithologist **72.20**; 70.11 *zoologist*
ornithology **72.19**; 70.9 *animal science*
ornithopod 73.6 *extinct reptile*
orogenesis 30.21 *mountain building*
orogenetic 154.13 *mountainous*; 89.8 *orogenic*
orogenic **89.8**; 154.13 *mountainous*; 30.54 *tectonic*
orogeny 30.21 *mountain building*
orographic 154.14 *altimetric*; 89.8 *orogenic*
orography 154.5 *height measure*
orological 89.8 *orogenic*
orologist 89.2 *orology*
orology **89.2**
orometer 89.2 *orology*
orometric 89.8 *orogenic*
orotund 510.8 *deep*; 542.10 *ornate*
orotundity 542.2 *affectation*; 729.2 *power of speech*
orphan 387.4 *dependent*; 655.7 *outsider*; 215.6 *person remaining*; 215.9 *remaining*
orphanage 252.2 *protection*
orphaned 215.9 *remaining*; 335.11 *unprotected*
orphan's home 252.2 *protection*
Orphean 516.6 *melodious*
Orphistic 19.29 *realist*
orphrey 7.11 *vestment*
orpiment 537.7 *yellow pigment*
orrery 29.23 *observatory*
orthocentre 27.43 *triangle*
orthoclase 30.34 *mineral*
orthodontic 35.23 *dental*
orthodontics 35.4 *dentistry*
orthodontist 35.14 *dentist*
Orthodox 7.16 *denominational*
orthodox 216.1 *average*; 450.11 *believing*; 117.14 *conformist*; 750.15 *conventional*; 452.2 *convinced*; 632.11 *normal*; 7.15 *religious*; 647.8 *severe*
Orthodox Jew 7.6 *non-Christian*
orthodox medicine 35.1 *medicine*
orthodoxy 750.6 *convention*; 117.4 *conventionalism*; 452.10 *conviction*; 647.1 *severity*
orthoepic 5.38 *linguistic*
orthoepist 5.2 *linguist*
orthoepy 5.1 *linguistics*; 729.6 *phonetics*
orthogonal 27.80 *linear*; 186.10 *perpendicular*
orthogonal projection 27.48 *transformation*
orthographer 5.2 *linguist*
orthographic 27.80 *linear*; 5.38 *linguistic*
orthographically 5.48 *linguistically*
orthographic convention 5.27 *spelling*
orthographic projection 717.7 *map*
orthography 5.27 *spelling*
orthologist 742.8 *signer*
orthontics 35.8 *treatment*
orthopaedic 394.18 *medical*
orthopaedics 35.3 *medical specialty*; 394.13 *therapy*
orthopaedist 35.13 *medical specialist*
orthopsychiatry 36.2 *psychiatry*
orthopteran 76.10 *insectan*
orthoptist 394.15 *healer*
orthopyroxene 30.34 *mineral*
orthorhombic 32.33 *crystalline*
orthotic 394.18 *medical*
os 154.4 *mountain range*
OS/2™ 40.8 *software*
Oscar 813.2 *prize*
Oscars 21.6 *cinema*
oscillate **326.8**; 227.11 *be changeable*; 300.13 *be in motion*; 299.6 *be irregular*; 298.7 *be regular*; 39.35 *conduct*; 510.9 *resonate*; 112.22 *resound*; 325.10 *slide*; 639.5 *vacillate*
oscillating **326.13**; 227.13 *changeable*; 300.17 *directional*; 299.4 *irregular*; 298.11 *regular*
oscillating current 28.14 *sound wave*
oscillating universe 29.4 *cosmological model*
Oscillation 326
oscillation **326.1**; 227.1 *changeableness*; 39.15 *circuit function*; 300.5 *circuition*; 334.7 *electrical power*; 299.1 *irregularity*; 298.1 *regularity*; 510.1 *resonance*; 112.6 *reverberation*; 28.12 *wave*
oscillator **326.7**; 28.55 *circuit*; 39.30 *generator*; 39.21 *rectifier*; 334.6 *source of energy*
oscillatory 299.4 *irregular*; 326.13 *oscillating*; 298.11 *regular*; 112.15 *reverberatory*
oscillograph 326.6 *measuring instrument*
oscillometer 326.6 *measuring instrument*
oscilloscope 28.90 *ammeter*; 39.23 *electrical instrument*; 326.6 *measuring instrument*
oscine 72.21 *avian*
oscitancy 343.9 *sleep*
oscitate 618.12 *be indifferent*
oscitation 618.1 *indifference*
osculate 593.27 *kiss*
osculation 593.14 *communication of love*
osculatory 10.14 *sacred object*
Oseretsky test 36.5 *psychological test*
O-shaped 306.10 *circular*
osier 373.6 *line*
osmic 32.34 *elemental*
osmidrosis 503.1 *stench*
osmious 32.34 *elemental*
osmoregulation 34.5 *physiology*
osmose 370.13 *absorb*; 318.10 *enter*
osmosis 370.5 *absorption*; 28.10 *force*; 318.3 *passage into*; 316.3 *transmission*
osmotic 370.17 *absorbent*; 318.13 *penetrating*
osmous 32.34 *elemental*
o.s.p. 563.12 *without issue*
osprey 72.5 *bird of prey*; 74.11 *fishing animal*
osseous 418.1 *hard*; 403.13 *skeletal*
ossicle 403.7 *skeleton*; 416.4 *solid body*
ossicular 403.13 *skeletal*
ossiferous 403.13 *skeletal*
ossific 418.1 *hard*
ossification 416.2 *concentration*; 403.7 *skeleton*; 418.6 *solidification*
ossified 418.3 *hardened*; 403.13 *skeletal*
ossify 416.8 *be dense*; 418.10 *solidify*
ossuary 583.4 *funeral objects*
O star 29.13 *luminosity*
osteal 403.13 *skeletal*
ostensibility 699.7 *pretence*
ostensible **525.9**; 171.8 *apparent*; 452.1 *certain*; 716.9 *evident*; 738.14 *manifest*; 699.34 *pretending*; 104.6 *probable*
ostensibly 96.19, 525.15 *apparently*; 716.15 *evidently*; 104.11 *probably*; 699.41 *spuriously*; 520.11 *visibly*
ostensorium 10.14 *sacred object*
ostentation **622.9**; 542.2 *affectation*; 673.6 *boastfulness*; 703.2 *demonstrativeness*; 727.3 *extravagance*; 699.14 *façade*; 738.10 *manifestation*; 740.8 *public relations*
ostentatious **622.21**; 673.13 *boastful*; 703.10 *demonstrative*; 727.14 *extravagant*; 699.31 *hypocritical*; 738.14 *manifest*; 542.10 *ornate*; 681.2 *unrestrained*; 675.7 *vulgar*
ostentatiously **622.35**; 673.23 *boastfully*; 703.21 *demonstratively*; 727.17 *excessively*; 542.13 *ornately*
ostentatiousness 699.3 *hypocrisy*
osteoarthritis 260.16 *rheumatism*
osteoblast 403.7 *skeleton*
osteoclast 403.7 *skeleton*
osteocyte 403.7 *skeleton*
osteography 403.8 *science of structure*
Osteolepis 74.4 *fossil fish*
osteologist 35.13 *medical specialist*
osteology 1.10 *measurement*; 35.3 *medical specialty*; 403.8 *science of structure*
osteomalacia 33.14 *vitamin deficiency disease*
osteometric 1.11 *anthropological*
osteopath 35.12, 394.15 *healer*; 393.12 *repairer*; 492.5 *toucher*
osteopathic 35.22 *medical*
osteopathy 35.2 *natural medicine*; 394.13 *therapy*; 492.2 *touching*; 35.8 *treatment*
osteotherapy 394.13 *therapy*
ostler 43.16 *farm worker*; 59.15 *horse person*
ostracism **371.19**; 128.1 *exclusion*; 670.3 *nonacceptance*; 814.7 *punishment*; 655.3 *separation*; 399.1 *veto*
ostracization 371.19 *ostracism*
ostracize **371.4**; 128.7 *exclude*; 655.13 *ignore*; 814.1 *punish*; 144.16 *replace*; 372.10 *set apart*; 399.3 *veto*; 670.15 *withhold approval*
ostracized 670.31 *disapproved*; 655.10 *lonely*; 144.10 *replaced*
ostracod 75.4 *arthropod*
ostracoderm 74.4 *fossil fish*
ostrich 634.17 *avoider*; 72.2 *flightless bird*; 332.12 *swift animal*; 477.9 *visionary*
ostrich feathers 551.1 *dress*
ostrich-like 72.21 *avian*; 341.3 *inactive*
otalgia 504.6 *otology*
otalgic 504.13 *otological*
other 115.5 *counterpart*; 100.10 *foreign*; 101.8 *nonmaterial*; 113.23 *opposite*; 109.6 *unrelated*
other cities **87.6**
other-directedness 36.7 *personality type*
other dishes **25.54**
other games **69.7**
Other Geographical Features 92
other half 115.5 *counterpart*
other major lakes **88.5**
other major rivers **90.5**
other minds 4.9 *philosophical problem*
Otherness 100
otherness 100.2 *foreignness*
other place 101.1 *nonmaterial world*
other ranks 122.6 *inferior*; 124.10 *nonentity*
others 171.5 *extraneousness*
other self 569.6 *close friend*; 139.11 *identity*; 111.3 *lookalike*
other side 113.2 *oppositeness*; 169.3 *side direction*
other things being equal 119.12 *equally*
other times 286.1 *different time*
otherwise engaged 463.8 *oblivious*
other world 101.1 *nonmaterial world*
otherworldliness 171.5 *extraneousness*; 11.2 *the occult*; 101.2 *unworldliness*
otherworldly 171.10 *extraneous*; 477.11 *fantastical*; 101.8 *nonmaterial*; 7.15 *religious*; 11.18 *spiritual*
otiose 350.3 *not wanted*; 112.12 *repetitious*; 219.7 *superfluous*; 215.10 *surplus*
otitis 504.6 *otology*
otolaryngological 504.13 *otological*
otolaryngologist 35.13 *medical specialist*; 504.6 *otology*

otolaryngology 35.3 *medical specialty;* 504.6 *otology*
otological 504.13
otologist 35.13 *medical specialist;* 504.6 *otology*
otology 504.6; 35.3 *medical specialty*
otorhinolaryngological 504.13 *otological*
otorhinolaryngologist 35.13 *medical specialist;* 504.6 *otology*
otorhinolaryngology 35.3 *medical specialty;* 504.6 *otology*
otoscope 35.7 *diagnosis*
otoscopic 504.13 *otological*
ottava rima 17.10 *verse form*
otter 74.11 *fishing animal*
otterhound 633.6 *hunter*
otter hunting 71.23 *mammal hunting*
otto 502.3 *incense*
Otto cycle 38.13 *engine cycle;* 28.38 *thermodynamics*
Ottoman 296.14 *historic*
ottoman 413.4 *rest*
Ottoman Empire 85.3 *dominion*
oubliette 309.4 *closed place;* 815.1 *prison*
ouch 514.6 *cry of pain*
ought to 810.14 *be the duty of*
Ouija ™ 11.10 *psychic phenomenon*
Ouija board™ 475.10 *cards*
Oulton Broad 88.4 *British lakes*
ounce 414.9 *avoirdupois weight*
our day 282.2 *the present day*
Our Father 10.9 *prayer*
Our Lady 8.10 *deified person*
our own day 282.2 *the present day*
ourselves 566.1 *humankind;* 139.12 *I*
our side 169.5 *team*
Ouse 90.4 *British rivers*
oust 762.4 *be a substitute;* 470.2 *discard;* 128.8 *eject;* 371.8 *evict;* 144.16 *replace;* 708.15 *terminate*
ouster 371.26 *ejector*
ousting 371.20 *eviction*
out 98.9 *away;* 53.12 *cricketing;* 69.6 *darts;* 690.3 *dead drunk;* 714.2 *defence;* 48.6 *fielding terms;* 315.18 *forth;* 103.3 *hopeless;* 53.20 *in;* 465.9 *misjudged;* 343.2 *not working;* 218.4 *scarce;* 63.4 *tennis terms;* 766.17 *unprofitable*
out-and-out 232.7 *complete*
out at elbows 782.3 *beggarly;* 552.10 *in dishabille*
outback 145.3 *distant place;* 141.3 *geographical space;* 171.2 *outside;* 86.6 *regions*
outbalance 414.12 *be heavy*
outbid 776.3 *bargain;* 329.3 *exceed;* 121.9 *outdo;* 329.14 *surpassing*
outbound 315.15 *outgoing*
outbrake 61.9 *race*
outbraking 61.6 *motor-racing terms*
outbreak 130.1 *beginning;* 315.1 *exit;* 380.3 *instance of violence*
outbreak of rain 31.25 *rain*
outbreak of war 585.4 *belligerency*
outburst 624.4 *anger;* 328.5 *commotion;* 514.1 *cry;* 371.22 *disgorgement;* 315.1 *exit;* 380.3 *instance of violence*
outcast 325.19 *deviant person;* 144.7 *displaced person;* 128.11 *excluded;* 128.5 *excluded person;* 371.27 *expellee;* 655.7 *outsider;* 144.10 *replaced;* 215.10 *surplus;* 804.9 *wicked person*
outcaste 371.27 *expellee;* 655.7 *outsider*
outclass 332.6 *accelerate;* 120.5 *be unequal;* 329.3 *exceed;* 246.11 *overmaster*
outclassed 122.18; 247.11 *defeated;* 128.11 *excluded;* 329.14 *surpassing*
outclassing 121.12 *superior*
out cold 690.3 *dead drunk;* 343.4 *not awake;* 489.8 *unconscious*
outcome 345.1 *effect;* 131.12 *end result;* 315.1 *exit;* 356.3 *product;* 289.9 *sequel;* 706.6 *solution*
outcoming 315.1 *exit*
outcrop 185.2 *projection;* 62.5 *rock face;* 520.6 *visible thing*
outcropping 62.8 *mountaineering*
outcry 507.2; 328.5 *commotion;* 514.1 *cry;* 753.1 *protest;* 670.9 *show of disapproval*
outdated 284.19 *antiquarian;* 245.12 *deteriorated;* 296.12 *olden*
out-directed 36.35 *extroverted*
outdistance 332.6 *accelerate;* 145.5 *be distant;* 121.8 *be superior;* 329.3 *exceed;* 302.9 *maintain progress;* 121.9 *outdo*
outdo 121.9; **623.26**; 332.6 *accelerate;* 645.5 *be cunning;* 120.5 *be unequal;* 254.10 *endanger;* 329.3 *exceed*
outdone 329.14 *surpassing*
outdoor 434.16 *open-air;* 171.7 *outside;* 67.11 *swimming*
outdoor game 69.1 *game*
outdoors 257.2 *salubrity*
outdoor sport 45.4 *sporting activity*
outdoor swimming pool 67.7 *swimming pool*
outdoor theatre 21.16 *theatre*
outdrive 332.6 *accelerate*
outer 525.8; 171.6 *exterior;* 100.12 *external*
outer atmosphere 434.3 *atmospheric layers*
outer block 52.9 *tae kwon do*
outer darkness 128.3 *exclusion zone*
outer ear 504.4 *ear*
outer face 171.1 *exterior*
outer layer 171.1 *exterior*
outer limit 86.3 *regional boundary*
Outer Mongolia 145.3 *distant place*
outermost 171.7 *outside*
outer product 27.50 *scalar quantity*
outer self 139.11 *identity*
outer side 171.1 *exterior*
outer skin 550.14 *animal covering*
outer space 145.3 *distant place;* 141.2 *empty space;* 29.3 *universe;* 202.6 *vastness*
outer wall 171.1 *exterior*
outface 613.15 *be courageous;* 638.8 *brace oneself;* 660.27 *dare*
outfall 315.2 *outflow;* 315.7 *outlet*
outfield 48.1 *baseball*
outfielder 48.2 *baseball player*
outfielder's glove 48.3 *baseball equipment*
outfield fence 48.1 *baseball*
outfit 21.25 *cast;* 143.2 *circumstances;* 551.1 *dress;* 243.5 *equip;* 438.7 *equipment;* 551.5 *fancy dress;* 243.11 *fitting out;* 551.35 *make clothing;* 584.4 *military organization;* 436.5 *provision;* 551.10 *suit;* 376.12 *team;* 204.5 *unit*
outfitter 551.26 *fashion designer*
outfitting 436.1 *provision*
outflank 329.3 *exceed;* 246.11 *overmaster*
outflanking 631.9 *tactics*
outflow 315.2; 767.1 *disposal;* 219.1 *excess;* 389.4 *leak;* 766.4 *lessening;* 90.6 *river flow;* 315.11 *run out;* 441.3 *waste*
outflowing 315.16; 315.2 *outflow*
outflux 315.2 *outflow*
out for 353.10 *ambitiously;* 482.11 *intending*
out for the count 489.8 *unconscious*
out front 740.22 *publicly*
outgas 32.29 *absorb*
outgassed 32.43 *absorbed*
outgassing 32.20 *surface chemistry*
outgate 315.6 *way out*
outgo 315.1 *exit;* 121.9 *outdo*
outgoer 315.8
outgoing 313.13; **315.15**; 315.1 *exit;* 36.35 *extroverted;* 605.7 *resigning;* 654.15 *sociable;* 338.4 *vigorous*
outgoingness 36.7 *personality type*
outgoings 787.5 *expense;* 315.5 *export*
outgrow 190.6 *become bigger*
outgrown 487.2 *not customary*
outgrowth 345.3 *growth*
outgunned 247.11 *defeated*
out-handle turn 68.10 *curling*
outhaul 50.3 *parts of a sailing boat*
out-Herod Herod 121.8 *be superior;* 727.10 *boast*
outhouse 211.3 *additional item;* 560.13 *lavatory;* 565.7 *room;* 565.8 *shelter;* 767.7 *toilet*
out in front 120.7 *unequally*
out in left field 128.11 *excluded*
out in the cold 128.11 *excluded*
out in the open 738.16 *manifestly;* 646.1 *naive*
outjump 121.9 *outdo*
outland 171.2 *outside*
outlander 100.6 *outsider*
outlandish 118.14 *eccentric;* 477.11 *fantastical;* 100.10 *foreign;* 619.8 *wonderful*
outlandishly 100.18 *extraneously;* 118.21 *unconformably*
outlandishness 118.4 *unusualness*
outlandish notion 642.3 *whim*
outlast 279.5 *be eternal;* 423.10 *be tough;* 277.6 *last*
outlaw 16.79 *convict;* 325.19 *deviant person;* 264.9 *difficult person;* 774.11 *dishonest person;* 118.8 *dissenter;* 128.8 *eject;* 128.5 *excluded person;* 371.27 *expellee;* 59.1 *horse;* 655.13 *ignore;* 16.75 *make illegal;* 651.8 *malefactor;* 100.5 *nonconformist;* 371.4 *ostracize;* 655.7 *outsider;* 814.1 *punish;* 399.3 *veto;* 804.9 *wicked person*
outlawed 16.64 *convicted;* 16.55 *illegal;* 655.10 *lonely*
outlawing 371.19 *ostracism;* 814.7 *punishment*
outlawry 16.43 *conviction;* 16.41 *lawlessness;* 371.19 *ostracism;* 774.5 *plundering*
outlay 790.5 *cost;* 787.5 *expense;* 315.5 *export;* 785.1 *payment;* 441.3 *waste*
outleap 121.9 *outdo*
out-Lear Lear 624.12 *become angry*
outlet 315.7; 317.11 *channel;* 92.9 *inlet*
outlie 145.5 *be distant;* 170.7 *surround*
Outline 163
outline 163.1; **163.5**; **269.2**; **484.6**; **723.2**; 269.4 *be concise;* 171.11 *be exterior;* 721.2 *brief description;* 721.14 *describe;* 243.2 *do the groundwork;* 19.20 *draw;* 19.9 *drawing;* 171.1 *exterior;* 525.3 *external appearance;* 160.1, 160.7 *form;* 701.4 *gist;* 743.1 *identification;* 717.11 *paint;* 243.10 *preparations;* 525.14 *present;* 608.6 *profile;* 476.6 *propound;* 717.1 *representation;* 149.3 *shortened version;* 723.8 *summarize;* 476.5 *suppose*
outlined 163.6; 269.3 *concise;* 19.27 *painted*
outlining 19.3 *drawing*
outlive 279.5 *be eternal;* 225.5 *be permanent;* 277.6 *last*
outlive one's spouse 571.10 *be widowed*
outlook 631.1 *conduct;* 660.27 *dare;* 474.2 *expectations;* 283.4 *looking to the future;* 4.1 *philosophy;* 104.1 *probability;* 7.1 *religion;* 518.7 *view;* 31.4 *weather forecast*
out loud 504.17 *aurally*
outlying 145.8 *distant;* 171.7 *outside;* 170.4 *surrounding*
outmanoeuvre 329.3 *exceed;* 164.7 *have an advantage;* 323.9 *navigate;* 121.9 *outdo;* 246.11 *overmaster;* 700.28 *trick*
outmanoeuvred 700.36 *deceived;* 247.11 *defeated;* 329.14 *surpassing*
outmanoeuvring 700.7 *tricking*
outmarch 332.6 *accelerate;* 121.9 *outdo*
outmatch 336.7 *be strong*
outmatched 247.11 *defeated*
outmigrant 315.8 *outgoer*
outmigrate 315.13 *emigrate*
outmigration 315.4 *emigration*
outmoded 284.19 *antiquarian;* 296.12 *olden;* 238.1 *useless*
outnumber 219.4 *be excessive;* 208.12 *overcrowd*
outnumbered 219.6 *excessive*
out of 315.19; 554.15 *born;* 345.10 *caused*
out of account 128.11 *excluded*
out of action 343.2 *not working;* 335.10 *powerless;* 238.1 *useless*
out of a job 144.11 *relegated*
out of balance 234.6 *distorted*
out-of-body experience 11.10 *psychic phenomenon*
out of bounds 145.10 *distantly;* 56.1 *golf;* 16.55 *illegal;* 329.15 *out of reach;* 399.5 *vetoed;* 166.8 *within limits*
out of breath 261.3 *panting*
out of chronological order 288.18
out of circulation 335.10 *powerless*
out of commission 350.4 *disused;* 802.18 *gone wrong;* 343.2 *not working;* 301.5 *sedentary*
out of context 234.6 *distorted*
out of control 662.13 *disobedient;* 408.20 *disorderly;* 335.12 *impotent;* 380.6 *violent*
out of countenance 623.3 *humbled*
out of danger 252.6 *safe;* 252.11 *safely*
out of date 284.19 *antiquarian;* 286.2 *occurring at a different time;* 288.18 *out of chronological order;* 288.12 *too late*
out of debt 785.16 *paid;* 781.2 *solvent*
out of doors 171.15 *externally;* 171.2 *outside*
out-of-doors 434.26; 434.5, 434.16 *open-air;* 171.7 *outside;* 257.2 *salubrity*
out of earshot 505.12 *deafly;* 145.10 *distantly;* 511.10 *faintly;* 505.7 *unheard*
out of fashion 487.2 *not customary;* 288.18 *out of chronological order;* 793.10 *shoddy*
out of favour 596.9 *disliked;* 594.12 *hated*
out of focus 521.2 *difficult to see*
out of hand 264.14 *troublesome*
out of harm's way 252.6 *safe;* 252.11 *safely*
out of harness 250.13 *informal*
out of hearing 145.10 *distantly*
out of hiding 520.11 *visibly*
out of house 98.21 *away*
out of humour 626.7 *irritable*
out of it 696.6 *confused;* 261.1 *fatigued*
out of joint 144.12 *disconnected;* 408.12 *disordered*
out of keeping 118.22 *out of step*
out of kilter 486.3 *clumsy;* 245.13 *dilapidated;* 234.6 *distorted;* 221.8 *in a state of;* 260.22 *sick*
out of kindness 650.10 *benevolently*
out of line 118.15 *irregular;* 118.22 *out of step;* 802.11 *wrong*
out of luck 249.8 *unlucky*
out of mind 766.16 *losing*
out of one's depth 766.18 *at a loss;* 696.6 *confused;* 156.16 *deep;* 766.21 *out of place;* 264.16 *troubled*
out of one's element 766.18 *at a loss;* 118.15 *irregular;* 766.21 *out of place;* 144.10 *replaced*
out of one's head 461.11 *insane*
out of one's league 335.14 *powerlessly*
out of one's mind 461.11 *insane*
out of one's misery 582.19 *dead*
out of one's skull 461.11 *insane*
out of one's tree 461.11 *insane*
out of operation 350.12 *out of use*
out of orbit 325.20 *deviant*
out of order 245.13 *dilapidated;* 408.12 *disordered;* 802.18 *gone wrong;* 221.8 *in a state of;* 412.14 *in the midst;* 412.12 *mixed;* 335.10 *powerless;* 288.13 *untimely;* 350.1 *unused;* 238.1 *useless*
out of phase 326.5 *wave*
out of place 144.20; **766.21**; 766.18 *at a loss;* 408.12 *disordered;* 240.1 *inconvenient;* 118.15 *irregular;* 655.10 *lonely;* 144.10 *replaced*
out-of-play wall 63.9 *squash terms*
out-of-pocket 787.10 *expending;* 782.2 *insolvent;* 766.17 *unprofitable*
out-of-pocket expenses 787.5 *expense*
out of practice 486.3 *clumsy*
out of print 358.6 *obliterated;* 218.4 *scarce*
out of proportion 109.8 *distorted*
out of range 505.12 *deafly;* 526.7 *disappeared;* 145.8 *distant;* 145.10 *distantly;* 389.9 *fugitively;* 521.1 *invisible;* 521.9 *invisibly;* 505.7 *unheard*
out of reach 329.15; 145.8 *distant;* 145.10 *distantly;* 126.5 *novel*
out of season 288.14 *anachronistic;* 218.4 *scarce;* 292.9 *seasonal*
out of sequence 288.18 *out of chronological order*
out of service 350.1 *unused*
out of shape 234.6 *distorted*
out of sight 98.9 *away;* 792.7 *dear;* 792.12 *dearly;* 526.7 *disappeared;* 145.8 *distant;* 145.10 *distantly;* 521.1 *invisible;* 521.9 *invisibly;* 766.16 *losing;* 766.21 *out of place;* 235.1 *worthy*
out of sorts 602.6 *depressed;* 221.8 *in a state of;* 260.22 *sick*
out of soundings 91.11 *nautically*
out of spite 651.20 *malevolently*
out of step 118.22; 114.5 *diverse;* 114.10 *diversely;* 118.15 *irregular;* 487.2 *not customary*
out of stock 218.4 *scarce*
out of sympathy 596.8 *disliking*
out of sync 486.3 *clumsy;* 286.2 *occurring at a different time*
out of temper 626.7 *irritable*
out of the Ark 296.12 *olden*
out of the black 783.15 *into the black*
out of the blue 630.13 *surprisingly;* 105.9 *unexpectedly*
out of the common 118.14 *eccentric*
out of the habit 487.1 *unaccustomed*
out of the ordinary 139.16 *characteris-*

tic; 116.4 *dissimilar;* 118.14 *eccentric;* 487.2 *not customary;* 630.8 *surprising;* 295.11 *unfamiliar*
out of the picture 526.7 *disappeared*
out of the question 103.1 *impossible;* 708.24 *never!;* 470.10 *rejected*
out of the red 783.15 *into the black;* 785.16 *paid*
out of the running 247.11 *defeated;* 335.12 *impotent;* 124.1 *unimportant*
out of the way 145.10 *distantly;* 118.22 *out of step*
out-of-the-way 145.8, 240.2 *distant;* 109.7 *illogical;* 325.21 *indirect;* 655.11 *secluded*
out of the window 766.16 *losing*
out of the wood 252.6 *safe*
out of thin air 478.7 *extempore*
out of this world 121.14 *best;* 582.19 *dead;* 597.5 *delightful;* 145.8 *distant;* 145.10 *distantly;* 118.14 *eccentric;* 241.1 *pleasant;* 121.17 *supremely;* 235.1 *worthy*
out of time 487.2 *not customary;* 286.2 *occurring at a different time*
out-of-touch 486.3 *clumsy;* 736.14 *concealed*
out of town 98.21 *away;* 98.10 *nonresident*
out of training 486.3 *clumsy*
out of true 274.22 *wrongly*
out of true alignment 234.6 *distorted*
out of tune 118.15 *irregular;* 517.9 *unmelodious*
out of turn 288.13 *untimely*
out of use 350.12; 350.4 *disused*
out of view 521.9 *invisibly;* 766.16 *losing;* 766.21 *out of place*
out of whack 245.13 *dilapidated*
out of work 341.3 *inactive;* 580.7 *leisurely;* 350.3 *not wanted;* 343.2 *not working*
out on a limb 118.14 *eccentric;* 118.22 *out of step;* 264.16 *troubled;* 254.3 *vulnerable*
out on bail 391.7 *liberated*
out on one's arse 144.11 *relegated*
out on one's ear 144.11 *relegated*
outpace 332.6 *accelerate;* 121.9 *outdo*
out-patient 35.18 *patient;* 260.19 *sick person*
out-patient clinic 35.10 *hospital*
outperform 121.9 *outdo*
outplay 121.9 *outdo;* 246.11 *overmaster*
outplayed 247.11 *defeated*
outpoint 246.11 *overmaster*
outpost 145.3 *distant place;* 166.3 *furthest point;* 86.6 *regions*
outposts 170.1 *surroundings*
outpour 371.22 *disgorgement;* 371.14 *let out;* 315.2 *outflow;* 315.11 *run out*
outpouring 270.1 *diffuseness;* 315.2 *outflow;* 315.16 *outflowing;* 217.8 *plenty*
output 40.20 *abort;* 40.19 *computing terms;* 39.35 *conduct;* 270.1 *diffuseness;* 356.10 *produce;* 356.3 *product;* 356.1 *production;* 765.6 *yield*
output signal 39.14 *terminal*
output terminal 39.14 *terminal*
outrace 121.9 *outdo*
outrage 651.7 *act of malevolence;* 659.7 *be discourteous;* 236.14 *ill-treat;* 245.10 *impairment;* 380.3 *instance of violence;* 351.2 *misuse;* 624.9 *offend;* 647.1 *severity;* 806.3 *sin;* 804.1 *wickedness*
outrageous 351.5 *abusive;* 651.11 *cruel;* 727.14 *extravagant;* 236.5 *harmful;* 804.12 *immoral;* 668.11 *insulting;* 681.2 *unrestrained;* 380.6 *violent;* 804.11 *wicked*
outrageously 351.6 *abusively;* 792.12 *dearly;* 727.17 *excessively*
outrageousness 727.3 *extravagance*
outrange 145.5 *be distant;* 121.9 *outdo*
outrank 120.5 *be unequal;* 121.9 *outdo;* 129.16 *take precedence*
outré 619.8 *wonderful*
outreach 148.9 *be long;* 121.9 *outdo;* 145.7 *reach*
outride 329.3 *exceed;* 121.9 *outdo*
outrider 223.7 *attendant*
outrigger 50.6 *canoeing;* 50.4 *rowing*
outright 232.9 *completely;* 739.13 *openly*
outright gift 768.2 *gift*
outright purchase 777.7 *purchasing*
outrival 329.3 *exceed*
outrun 332.6 *accelerate;* 329.3 *exceed;* 766.15 *lose someone;* 262.2 *make haste;* 121.9 *outdo*
outrun the constable 784.8, 786.7 *not pay*
outsail 332.6 *accelerate*
outset 130.1 *beginning;* 313.10 *place of departure;* 313.8 *start*
outshine 164.7 *have an advantage;* 121.9 *outdo*
outshone 247.11 *defeated;* 122.18 *outclassed*
Outside 171
outside 171.2; **171.7**; 128.12 *exclusively;* 100.12 *external;* 525.3 *external appearance;* 100.4 *externality;* 171.15 *externally;* 434.26 *out-of-doors;* 27.35 *space;* 520.6 *visible thing*
out side 63.12 *badminton terms*
outside agency 56.6 *golfer*
outside broadcast 692.25 *broadcast material*
outside chance 105.4 *improbability;* 102.4 *remote possibility*
outside edge 163.3 *edge;* 166.3 *furthest point*
outside home 58.6 *lacrosse player*
outside hope 102.4 *remote possibility*
outside left 66.3 *football player*
outside of 128.12 *exclusively*
outsider 100.6; **655.7**; 325.19 *deviant person;* 751.4 *dissenter;* 128.5 *excluded person;* 59.7 *horseracing;* 118.7 *nonconformist;* 655.6 *unsocial person*
outside right 66.3 *football player*
outsiders 171.5 *extraneousness*
outside run 46.9 *play*
outside ski 68.5 *ski equipment*
outside the law 16.55 *illegal*
outsize 158.15 *big;* 158.3 *large scale*
outsized 141.13 *spacious*
outskirts 145.3 *distant place;* 86.11 *settlement;* 87.8 *suburb;* 170.1 *surroundings*
outsmart 645.5 *be cunning;* 704.8 *refute;* 773.10 *take away;* 700.28 *trick*
outsmarted 700.36 *deceived*
outsmarting 700.7 *tricking*
out-speaking 729.19 *speaking*
outspoken 426.2; 707.14 *assertive;* 661.7 *defiant;* 739.11 *disclosing;* 646.1 *naive;* 738.15 *open;* 729.19 *speaking;* 698.18 *truthful*
outspokenness 426.6; 707.6 *assertiveness;* 646.2 *naivety;* 739.3 *openness;* 698.5 *truthfulness*
outspread 190.6 *become bigger;* 190.7 *bigger;* 190.5 *make bigger;* 311.11 *move apart*
outspreading 190.1 *growth*
outstanding 772.11 *borrowed;* 520.2 *clear;* 121.15 *excellent;* 123.6 *notable;* 215.10 *surplus;* 235.1 *worthy*
outstanding balance 783.1 *credit;* 772.5 *loan*
outstandingly 121.16 *superiorly;* 215.12 *with a remainder*
outstare 661.5 *defy;* 623.26 *outdo*
outstay one's welcome 620.6 *be boring;* 314.10 *invade*
outstep 121.9 *outdo*
outstretch 148.9 *be long;* 190.5 *make bigger;* 145.7 *reach*
outstretched 190.7 *bigger;* 148.1 *long*
outstretched hand 749.2 *peace offering*
outstretching 190.1 *growth*
outstrip 332.6 *accelerate;* 120.5 *be unequal;* 329.3 *exceed;* 164.7 *have an advantage;* 766.15 *lose someone;* 302.9 *maintain progress;* 262.2 *make haste;* 121.9 *outdo*
outswinger 53.8 *delivery*
out-talk 731.9
outthink 164.7 *have an advantage*
out to 482.11 *intending*
out to lunch 472.8 *absent-minded;* 328.16 *deranged;* 463.8 *oblivious;* 457.6 *unintelligent*
outtrump 121.9 *outdo*
out turn 68.16 *bobsled*
outvie 121.9 *outdo*
outvote 120.5 *be unequal*
outvoted 247.11 *defeated*
outward 167.7; 171.8 *apparent;* 100.12 *external;* 171.9 *externalized;* 315.18 *forth;* 525.8 *outer;* 171.7 *outside;* 520.1 *visible;* 520.11 *visibly*
outward appearance 171.3 *appearance;* 167.3 *show*
outward-bound 313.13, 315.15 *outgoing*
outward form 525.3 *external appearance*
outwardly 525.15 *apparently;* 171.15 *externally;* 100.18 *extraneously;* 315.18 *forth;* 520.11 *visibly*
outwardness 100.4 *externality;* 171.4 *externalization;* 171.2 *outside*
outwards 171.15 *externally;* 315.18 *forth*
outward self 139.11 *identity*
outward show 699.14 *façade;* 700.3 *hypocrisy*
outweigh 395.10 *be a prevailing influence;* 414.12 *be heavy;* 120.5 *be unequal*
out-wick 68.16 *bobsled*
outwit 645.5 *be cunning;* 164.7 *have an advantage;* 121.9 *outdo;* 704.8 *refute;* 773.10 *take away;* 700.28 *trick*
outwith the law 16.55 *illegal*
outwitted 700.36 *deceived;* 247.11 *defeated*
outwitting 700.7 *tricking*
outwork 384.11 *fortification;* 384.8 *military defences;* 576.1 *work*
outworn 284.19 *antiquarian*
ouzo 558.7 *alcoholic drink*
oval 177.2 *bend;* 27.42, 179.2 *circle;* 179.5 *circular;* 177.4 *curved;* 27.81 *curvilinear;* 61.6 *motor-racing terms;* 27.83 *spherical*
ovally 179.8 *circularly*
ovarian 559.5 *of a secretion;* 561.16 *reproductive*
ovary 78.3 *flower part;* 561.8 *organs of reproduction*
ovate 179.5 *circular;* 77.18 *of leaves*
ovately 179.8 *circularly*
ovation 669.5 *acclaim;* 601.3 *ceremony;* 600.2 *fanfare;* 601.9 *rejoicing;* 21.8 *scene*
oven 493.4 *burner;* 24.6 *ceramic workshop*
oven-fresh 295.10 *new*
oven gloves 25.6 *kitchen equipment*
ovenproof dish 25.6 *kitchen equipment*
oven-ready 25.56 *culinary;* 243.21 *ready-made*
oven-roasting 25.8 *cooking technique*
ovenware 24.1 *ceramics*
over 284.18; 232.7 *complete;* 53.8 *delivery;* 131.21 *ended;* 309.17 *finally;* 226.10 *finished;* 154.19 *high;* 103.3 *hopeless;* 550.42 *inclusively;* 3.18 *in the past;* 121.12 *superior;* 215.10 *surplus;* 317.17 *via*
overabundance 215.4 *surplus*
overabundant 215.10 *surplus*
overabundantly 215.11 *residually*
overact 21.35; 219.4 *be excessive;* 486.5 *be unskilful;* 329.4, 727.7 *exaggerate*
overacted 727.12 *exaggerated;* 219.6 *excessive*
overacting 21.22 *acting;* 727.1 *exaggeration;* 329.9 *excessiveness*
overactive 342.18 *active*
overactivity 342.9; 576.4 *exertion;* 219.2 *overdoing it*
over again 198.19 *twice*
over against 317.17 *via*
overall 138.31; 551.25 *accessories;* 138.15 *general;* 127.7 *including;* 216.11 *on average*
overall design 482.5 *final intention*
overall length 148.4 *length*
overall picture 138.7 *global view*
overall plan 484.1 *plan*
overalls 551.9 *trousers*
overambition 342.9 *overactivity*
overambitious 354.7; 329.13 *exaggerated;* 615.4 *rash*
overambitiously 354.9 *enterprisingly*
overambitiousness 622.3 *conceit*
over and above 211.10 *additionally;* 219.8 *excessively*
over and done with 131.21 *ended;* 3.18 *in the past;* 284.18 *over*
over and over 297.1 *frequently;* 112.23 *repeatedly*
over and over again 112.23, 509.19 *repeatedly*
overappreciative 669.18 *approving*
overarch 154.15 *be high;* 550.26 *overlie;* 174.7 *top*
overarching 550.1 *covering*
overarm 53.13 *bowling*
overattentive 664.7 *sycophantic*
overawe 395.10 *be a prevailing influence;* 667.21 *command respect*
overbalance 414.12 *be heavy;* 120.5 *be unequal;* 120.1 *inequality;* 305.11 *trip;* 414.8 *weighing down*
overbalanced 414.3 *ponderous;* 120.3 *unequal*
overbear 395.10 *be a prevailing influence*
overbearance 396.1 *authority*
overbearing 396.12 *authoritative;* 622.16 *oppressive;* 647.8 *severe*
overbid 776.3 *bargain;* 329.4 *exaggerate;* 329.3 *exceed*
overblouse 551.8 *shirt*
overblown 556.13 *middle-aged*
over-blunt 659.5 *discourteous*
overbridge 317.9 *bridge*
overburden 219.4 *be excessive;* 249.11 *cause adversity;* 261.6 *fatigue;* 236.14 *ill-treat;* 414.14 *make heavy*
overburdened 378.14 *blocked;* 219.6 *excessive;* 414.3 *ponderous*
overburdening 414.8 *weighing down*
overbusy 342.21 *meddling*
overcall one's hand 329.4 *exaggerate*
overcast 626.8; 31.49 *cloudy;* 523.8 *dark;* 524.5 *dim;* 533.3 *dull*
overcast sky 31.19 *cloud cover*
overcaution 616.1 *caution;* 614.1 *cowardice*
overcautious 616.4 *cautious*
overcautiously 616.7 *cautiously*
overcautiousness 616.1 *caution*
overcharge 792.10; 219.4 *be excessive;* 36.28 *cathexis;* 790.3 *fee;* 467.4 *overestimate;* 789.9 *settle accounts;* 792.2 *unfair price*
overcharged 792.7 *dear;* 219.6 *excessive*
overcharger 792.5
overcharging 792.7 *dear;* 792.2 *unfair price*
overclever 673.11 *cocky*
overclouded 31.49 *cloudy*
overcoat 551.12 *coat;* 493.3 *heater*
overcolour 727.7 *exaggerate*
overcoloured 727.12 *exaggerated*
overcolouring 727.1 *exaggeration*
overcome 381.9 *attack successfully;* 395.10 *be a prevailing influence;* 121.8 *be superior;* 586.38 *conquer;* 387.7 *defeat;* 400.14 *master;* 246.11 *overmaster;* 590.12 *sensitive*
overcome difficulties 246.7 *overcome obstacles*
overcome obstacles 246.7
overcoming 387.10 *dominating;* 387.2 *domination*
overcommend 677.8 *flatter*
overcommendation 677.1 *flattery*
overcommunicative 693.16 *informative*
overcompensate 120.5 *be unequal;* 727.7 *exaggerate*
overcompensated 727.12 *exaggerated*
overcompensation 36.19 *defence mechanism;* 727.1 *exaggeration;* 120.1 *inequality*
overcompressed 266.2 *obscure*
overcompression 266.1 *obscurity*
overconfidence 622.3 *conceit;* 452.10 *conviction;* 467.1 *overestimation;* 615.1 *rashness*
overconfident 167.9 *arrogant;* 452.2 *convinced;* 467.5 *overestimating;* 615.4 *rash*
overconfidently 467.7 *overoptimistically;* 615.6 *rashly*
overconfident person 452.11 *opinionist*
overcooked 25.56 *culinary*
overcritical 670.28 *fault-finding;* 264.14 *troublesome*
overcriticalness 670.6 *fault-finding*
overcrop 218.7 *make insufficient;* 441.1 *waste*
overcropping 351.2 *misuse*
overcrossing 317.9 *bridge;* 318.5 *crossing point*
overcrowd 208.12
overcrowded 317.15 *accessible;* 208.10 *crowded*
overdaring 254.5 *danger*
overdelicate 795.10 *moralistic*
overdevelop 190.6 *become bigger;* 190.5 *make bigger*
overdeveloped 190.7 *bigger*
overdevelopment 190.1 *growth*
overdevout 7.15 *religious*
overdiversification 342.9 *overactivity*

overdo 219.4 *be excessive*; 727.9 *be extravagant*; 232.4 *complete*; 329.4, 727.7 *exaggerate*; 699.28 *mask*; 686.11 *overindulge*
overdoing 727.1 *exaggeration*; 686.3 *overindulgence*
overdoing it 219.2; 576.4 *exertion*; 727.3 *extravagance*; 261.7 *fatigue*; 720.2 *misinterpretation*
overdo it 727.9 *be extravagant*; 261.5 *be fatigued*; 677.8 *flatter*; 217.4 *suffice*; 342.15 *try*; 576.6 *work*
overdone 243.20 *developed*; 699.39 *disguised*; 329.13, 727.12 *exaggerated*; 219.6 *excessive*; 727.14 *extravagant*; 423.3 *hard*; 231.2 *incomplete*
overdose 219.4 *be excessive*; 219.2 *overdoing it*
overdose of sleeping pills 382.7 *suicide*
overdraft 784.5 *amount owing*; 783.1 *credit*; 784.1 *debt*; 766.2 *financial loss*; 352.4 *financial resources*; 786.5 *insolvency*; 772.5 *loan*
overdramatization 718.1 *misrepresentation*
overdramatize 718.4 *misrepresent*
overdraw 783.9 *acquire credit*; 784.7 *be in debt*; 727.7 *exaggerate*; 766.10 *have a financial loss*; 718.4 *misrepresent*; 681.8 *overspend*
overdrawing 727.1 *exaggeration*
overdrawn 783.12 *charged*; 727.12 *exaggerated*; 784.9 *in debt*; 766.17 *unprofitable*
overdrawn account 786.5 *insolvency*
overdress 551.7 *frock*
overdressed 544.10 *ugly*
overdressing 551.2 *dressing*
overdrink 219.4 *be excessive*
overdrinking 219.2 *overdoing it*
overdrive 261.6 *fatigue*; 320.21 *miscellaneous motoring terms*; 334.1 *power*
overdue 294.9 *late*; 288.12 *too late*
overdue account 783.1 *credit*
overdue amount 784.5 *amount owing*
overdue payment 784.5 *amount owing*; 785.1 *payment*
overeager 636.2 *eager*
overeagerness 636.7 *eagerness*
overeat 219.4 *be excessive*; 688.5 *be greedy*; 557.22 *eat well*; 217.4 *suffice*
overeating 557.2 *appetite*; 688.6 *gluttonous*; 688.1 *gluttony*; 219.2 *overdoing it*; 686.3 *overindulgence*
overelaborate 724.8 *inelegant*; 542.12 *ornament*
overelaborated 231.2 *incomplete*
overelaboration 724.3 *inelegance*
overembellish 718.4 *misrepresent*
overemotional 590.12 *sensitive*
overemotionalism 703.2 *demonstrativeness*; 590.7 *emotionalism*
overemphasis 727.1 *exaggeration*; 718.1 *misrepresentation*
overemphasize 727.7 *exaggerate*; 718.4 *misrepresent*
overemphasized 727.12 *exaggerated*
overemphatic 727.12 *exaggerated*
overemphatically 727.16 *exaggeratedly*
overemployed 342.19 *busy*; 219.7 *superfluous*
overemployment 219.3 *superfluity*
overenlargement 213.1 *increase*
overenthuse 727.7 *exaggerate*
overenthusiasm 636.7 *eagerness*; 727.1 *exaggeration*; 615.1 *rashness*
overenthusiastic 636.2 *eager*; 727.12 *exaggerated*; 467.5 *overestimating*; 615.4 *rash*
overenthusiastically 727.16 *exaggeratedly*; 467.7 *overoptimistically*
overesteem 677.8 *flatter*
overestimate 467.2; **467.4**; 329.4, 727.7 *exaggerate*; 677.8 *flatter*; 123.8 *make important*; 720.1 *misinterpret*; 465.10 *misjudge*; 669.14 *praise*
overestimated 467.6; 727.12 *exaggerated*; 465.9 *misjudged*
overestimating 467.5
Overestimation 467
overestimation 467.1; 604.1 *disappointment*; 727.1 *exaggeration*; 329.9 *excessiveness*; 720.2 *misinterpretation*; 465.1 *misjudgment*; 219.2 *overdoing it*; 669.3 *praise*; 699.7 *pretence*
overexcited 219.6 *excessive*; 488.7 *susceptible*
overexert 261.5 *be fatigued*
overexertion 576.4 *exertion*; 261.7 *fatigue*; 342.9 *overactivity*
overexpand 219.4 *be excessive*
overexpansion 342.9 *overactivity*
overexpose 522.28 *bleach*; 727.7 *exaggerate*
overexposed 530.7 *colourless*; 727.12 *exaggerated*; 522.21 *light*
overexposed negative 530.3 *pen-and-ink sketch*
overexposed photograph 530.3 *pen-and-ink sketch*
overexposure 41.8 *composition*; 727.1 *exaggeration*; 522.3 *lightening*; 530.3 *pen-and-ink sketch*
overexpression 219.2 *overdoing it*
overextend 219.4 *be excessive*; 218.7 *make insufficient*
overextended 354.7 *overambitious*; 329.14 *surpassing*; 766.17 *unprofitable*
overextension 329.10 *expansionism*; 342.9 *overactivity*; 219.2 *overdoing it*
overfall 91.3 *wave*
overfatigued 261.1 *fatigued*
overfed 219.6 *excessive*; 158.16 *fat*
overfeed 219.4 *be excessive*
overfeeding 219.2 *overdoing it*
overfill 232.6 *fill*
overfilled 232.8 *full*
overfilling 232.2 *fullness*
overfish 218.7 *make insufficient*; 238.8 *make useless*; 351.1 *misuse*; 441.1, 563.10 *waste*
overfishing 351.2 *misuse*
overflight 322.5 *flight*
overflow 217.5 *about*; 232.5 *be complete*; 270.5 *be diffuse*; 219.4 *be excessive*; 90.2 *channel*; 208.11 *crowd*; 305.13 *drip*; 219.1 *excess*; 90.7 *flow*; 232.2 *fullness*; 315.7 *outlet*; 329.1 *overstep*; 90.6 *river flow*; 315.11 *run out*
overflowed 433.24 *flooded*
overflowing 679.3 *abundant*; 270.3 *diffuse*; 219.6 *excessive*; 217.3 *filled*; 232.8 *full*; 232.2 *fullness*; 329.11 *overrun*; 329.6 *overstepping*; 217.2 *plentiful*; 90.6 *river flow*
overfly 318.11 *cross*
over-frank 659.5 *discourteous*
overfulfil 219.4 *be excessive*; 232.4 *complete*
overfulfilment 329.9 *excessiveness*; 232.2 *fullness*; 219.3 *superfluity*
overfull 219.6 *excessive*; 232.8 *full*
overglaze 24.3 *glaze*; 24.11 *make ceramics*
overglazed 24.10 *ceramic*
overglaze decoration 24.3 *glaze*
overglazing 24.10 *ceramic*
overgo 329.1 *overstep*
overgorged 688.6 *gluttonous*
overgorging 688.6 *gluttonous*
overgraze 218.7 *make insufficient*; 351.1 *misuse*; 441.1, 563.10 *waste*
overgrazing 351.2 *misuse*
overground railway 321.1 *railway*
overgrow 190.6 *become bigger*; 329.1 *overstep*; 77.21 *vegetate*
overgrown 158.15 *big*; 190.7 *bigger*; 329.11 *overrun*; 77.13 *plantlike*
overgrowth 190.1 *growth*; 158.3 *large scale*; 329.6 *overstepping*; 420.8 *rough ground*; 215.4 *surplus*
overhang 154.15 *be high*; 283.7 *be in the future*; 550.26 *overlie*; 361.11 *project*; 185.2, 361.2 *projection*; 185.8 *protrude*; 62.5 *rock face*
overhanging 283.11 *future*; 154.9 *high*; 62.8 *mountaineering*; 361.8 *projecting*
overhaste 262.5 *hastiness*; 342.3 *nimbleness*; 615.1 *rashness*
overhastily 293.20 *prematurely*; 262.7 *rashly*
overhasty 262.3 *hasty*; 293.16 *premature*; 615.4 *rash*; 288.11 *too early*
overhaul 332.6 *accelerate*; 393.1, 393.8 *repair*; 393.3 *restore*
overhauling 393.8 *repair*
overhead 63.14 *forehand*; 154.19 *high*; 550.7 *overhead covering*
overhead beam 550.7 *overhead covering*
overhead covering 550.7
overhead locker 410.10 *cart*
overhead projector 41.12 *development*
overheads 790.6 *business costs*; 787.5 *expense*
overhead smash 63.2 *tennis strokes*
overhead wire 39.33 *power distribution*
overhear 693.15 *be informed*; 504.15 *hear*
overheat 247.9 *malfunction*
overheated 493.9 *hot*
overheating 493.1 *heat*
overhot 31.51 *hot*
overindulge 686.11; 219.4 *be excessive*; 727.9 *be extravagant*; 688.5 *be greedy*; 557.22 *eat well*; 329.4 *exaggerate*
overindulgence 686.3; 557.2 *appetite*; 329.9 *excessiveness*; 727.3 *extravagance*; 688.1 *gluttony*; 219.2 *overdoing it*
overindulgent 686.8; 329.13 *exaggerated*; 727.14 *extravagant*; 688.6 *gluttonous*; 757.8 *permitting*
overindulgently 329.16 *excessively*
overindulge oneself 219.4 *be excessive*
overindulging 688.1 *gluttony*
overjolt 219.4 *be excessive*; 219.2 *overdoing it*
overjoyed 597.4 *happy*
overjump 121.8 *be superior*; 329.1 *overstep*
overkeen 636.2 *eager*
overkill 727.7 *exaggerate*; 727.1 *exaggeration*; 120.1 *inequality*; 219.3 *superfluity*
overladen 414.2 *loaded*; 414.3 *ponderous*
overlaid 411.8 *coated*
overlap 492.12 *abut*; 219.4 *be excessive*; 492.6 *contiguity*; 184.9 *fold*; 411.1, 411.10 *layer*; 550.26 *overlie*; 219.3 *superfluity*; 184.1 *wrinkle*
overlap integral 32.12 *valence*
overlapped 411.8 *coated*
overlapping 411.8 *coated*; 550.1 *covering*; 492.9 *touching*
overlarge 158.15 *big*
overlaud 677.8 *flatter*
overlaudation 677.1 *flattery*
overlay 211.6 *add*; 411.3, 550.24 *coat*; 736.8 *conceal*; 411.10 *layer*; 542.12 *ornament*; 421.11 *smooth*
overlayer 411.1 *layer*
overlaying 411.8 *coated*; 550.1, 550.38 *covering*
overleap 121.8 *be superior*; 329.1 *overstep*
overlie 550.26; 171.11 *be exterior*; 361.11 *project*; 361.2 *projection*
overload 211.6 *add*; 219.4 *be excessive*; 378.6, 378.12 *burden*; 249.11 *cause adversity*; 414.6 *displacement*; 261.6 *fatigue*; 120.1 *inequality*; 414.14 *make heavy*; 542.12 *ornament*; 219.2 *overdoing it*; 215.4 *surplus*
overloaded 378.14 *blocked*; 219.6 *excessive*; 232.8 *full*; 414.2 *loaded*; 542.10 *ornate*; 354.7 *overambitious*; 414.3 *ponderous*; 215.10 *surplus*; 120.3 *unequal*
overloading 414.6 *displacement*
overlong 620.4 *boring*; 148.1 *long*; 329.14 *surpassing*
overlook 519.16 *be blind to*; 154.15 *be high*; 472.12 *be inattentive*; 121.8 *be superior*; 649.11 *condone*; 463.13 *forget*; 274.19 *make a mistake*; 350.5 *not use*; 388.3 *submit*; 124.12 *think unimportant*; 89.9 *tower*
overlooked 649.8; 124.2 *obscure*
overlooking 649.2 *forgivingness*; 154.9 *high*
overlord 763.6 *lord*; 400.1 *master*
overlordship 12.3 *governance*
overly 219.8 *excessively*
overlying 550.38 *covering*
overman 208.12 *overcrowd*
overmanned 208.10 *crowded*; 219.7 *superfluous*
overmanning 219.3 *superfluity*
overmaster 246.11; 381.9 *attack successfully*; 395.10 *be a prevailing influence*; 336.7 *be strong*
overmature 243.20 *developed*
overmeasure 219.2 *overdoing it*
overmighty 16.62 *above the law*
overmodest 795.10 *moralistic*
overmodesty 795.4 *self-righteousness*
overmuch 219.6 *excessive*; 219.8 *excessively*
over my dead body 708.24 *never!*; 709.12 *no!*
overnight 291.7 *evening*
overnight bag 410.8 *bag*; 410.9 *baggage*
overnight sensation 246.1 *success*
over one's head 696.4 *difficult*
overoptimism 219.2 *overdoing it*; 467.1 *overestimation*
overoptimistic 467.5 *overestimating*
overoptimistically 467.7
overorthodoxy 7.2 *religiousness*
overpaint 19.19 *paint*
overpainting 19.2 *painting*
overpass 38.21, 317.9 *bridge*; 318.5 *crossing point*; 329.1 *overstep*; 317.3 *road*
overpassing 329.6 *overstepping*
overpay 792.11
overpayment 219.2 *overdoing it*
overpiety 7.2 *religiousness*
overplay 219.4 *be excessive*; 121.8 *be superior*; 329.4 *exaggerate*; 21.35 *overact*
overplayed 219.6 *excessive*
overplaying 329.9 *excessiveness*
overplus 219.3 *superfluity*
overpolite 219.6 *excessive*
overpoliteness 219.2 *overdoing it*
overpopulate 219.4 *be excessive*; 562.6 *be fertile*; 208.12 *overcrowd*
overpopulated 208.10 *crowded*; 219.6 *excessive*
overpopulation 219.1 *excess*
overpossessive 629.4 *jealous*
overpotential 32.19 *electrochemistry*
overpower 335.8; 381.9 *attack successfully*; 336.7 *be strong*; 387.7 *defeat*; 400.14 *master*; 246.11 *overmaster*
overpowering 381.23 *attacking*; 387.10 *dominating*; 387.2 *domination*; 336.10 *potent*; 503.3 *stinking*
overpraise 219.4 *be excessive*; 727.10 *boast*; 727.4 *bombast*; 677.8 *flatter*; 677.1 *flattery*; 720.1 *misinterpret*; 219.2 *overdoing it*; 467.4 *overestimate*; 669.3, 669.14 *praise*
overpraised 727.12 *exaggerated*; 467.6 *overestimated*
overpraising 669.18 *approving*
over-preciseness 656.2 *formalism*
overprice 792.10 *overcharge*; 467.4 *overestimate*
overpriced 681.3 *costly*; 792.7 *dear*; 467.6 *overestimated*
overpricing 792.2 *unfair price*
overprint 743.10 *identify*; 358.1 *obliterate*
overprinted 736.14 *concealed*
overprinting 358.3 *obliteration*
overprize 467.4 *overestimate*
overproduce 219.4 *be excessive*
overproduction 441.3 *waste*
overproductiveness 562.2 *productiveness*
overproof 690.6 *intoxicating*
overproud 673.8 *vain*
overproudness 622.3 *conceit*; 673.1 *vanity*
overqualified 455.9 *literate*
overrate 727.10 *boast*; 329.4 *exaggerate*; 213.5 *make bigger*; 123.8 *make important*; 720.1 *misinterpret*; 465.10 *misjudge*; 467.4 *overestimate*; 740.16 *publicize*
overrated 329.13, 727.12 *exaggerated*; 465.9 *misjudged*; 467.6 *overestimated*
overrating 727.4 *bombast*; 329.9 *excessiveness*; 467.1 *overestimation*
overreach 446.18 *aim*; 645.5 *be cunning*; 329.1 *overstep*
overreaching 329.12 *excessive*
overreact 727.7 *exaggerate*; 351.1 *misuse*
overreaction 727.1 *exaggeration*
over-refinement 656.2 *formalism*
overreligious 7.15 *religious*
over-rev 61.6 *motor-racing terms*; 61.9 *race*
override 395.10 *be a prevailing influence*; 121.8 *be superior*; 483.10 *manipulate*; 246.11 *overmaster*
overriding 386.9 *compelling*; 121.13 *dominant*; 123.5 *important*
overrighteous 7.15 *religious*
overripe 419.4 *compressible*; 243.20 *developed*; 231.1 *imperfect*; 499.6 *unpalatable*
overripen 419.13 *soften*
overripeness 231.5 *imperfection*; 296.10 *staleness*
overrule 708.14 *cancel*
overruled verdict 16.4 *bad law*
overruling 396.12 *authoritative*; 121.13 *dominant*; 123.5 *important*
overrun 329.11; 381.9 *attack successfully*; 97.11 *be present*; 208.10 *crowded*; 232.6 *fill*; 90.7 *flow*; 232.8 *full*; 245.5 *hurt*; 208.12 *overcrowd*; 329.1 *overstep*; 329.6 *overstepping*; 773.7 *take*; 329.5 *transgress*; 77.21 *vegetate*

overrunning 329.6 *overstepping;* 90.6 *river flow;* 381.14 *siege;* 246.2 *victory*
oversatisfy 219.4 *be excessive*
oversea 91.11 *nautically*
overseas 145.8 *distant;* 145.10 *distantly;* 100.18 *extraneously;* 100.10 *foreign;* 91.11 *nautically*
overseas call 692.10 *telephone call*
overseas mail 692.2 *postal communication*
overseas telegram 692.8 *data transmission*
overseas territory 86.5 *state*
oversee 140.16 *direct;* 579.1 *manage;* 518.15 *watch*
overseer 579.13 *director;* 15.6 *employer;* 579.15 *manager;* 518.11 *observer*
oversell 219.4 *be excessive;* 727.10 *boast;* 792.10 *overcharge*
overselling 727.1 *exaggeration*
oversensitive 591.2; 625.4 *irascible;* 488.7 *susceptible*
oversensitively 591.13
oversensitive person 591.9
oversensitivity 591.6; 488.2 *ability to sense*
overset 367.3 *bring down;* 367.12 *downthrow;* 367.22 *overthrown*
oversexed 796.14 *lecherous*
overshadow 154.15 *be high;* 121.8 *be superior;* 523.14 *make dark;* 550.26 *overlie;* 89.9 *tower*
overshadowing 550.1 *covering;* 524.3 *dimming;* 154.9 *high*
overshift 46.10 *defence;* 46.16 *play defence*
overshoes 551.19 *footwear*
overshoot 486.7 *be clumsy;* 727.9 *be extravagant;* 120.5 *be unequal;* 322.5 *flight*
overshooting 727.3 *extravagance*
overshot 727.14 *extravagant;* 120.3 *unequal*
overshy 674.11 *shy*
oversight 472.5 *inattentive act;* 274.9 *trivial error*
oversize 158.3 *large scale*
oversized 158.15 *big;* 141.13 *spacious*
overskirt 551.6 *skirt*
oversleep 294.6 *be late*
oversman 68.11 *skier*
oversold 727.12 *exaggerated*
oversoul 8.3 *God*
overspecialization 465.3 *injustice*
overspecialized 264.12 *problematic*
overspend 681.8; 219.4 *be excessive;* 727.9 *be extravagant;* 784.7 *be in debt;* 787.1 *expend;* 766.10 *have a financial loss;* 792.11 *overpay;* 441.1 *waste*
overspender 766.6 *loser*
overspending 727.3 *extravagance;* 727.14 *extravagant;* 766.2 *financial loss;* 441.3 *waste*
overspent 766.17 *unprofitable*
overspill 219.4 *be excessive;* 219.1 *excess*
overspread 329.11 *overrun;* 329.1 *overstep*
overspreading 329.6 *overstepping*
overstaff 208.12 *overcrowd*
overstaffed 208.10 *crowded;* 219.7 *superfluous*
overstate 707.22 *emphasize;* 727.7 *exaggerate;* 699.26 *falsify;* 542.12 *ornament;* 467.4 *overestimate*
overstated 707.15 *emphasized;* 727.12 *exaggerated;* 529.12 *gaudy;* 542.10 *ornate*
overstatement 542.2 *affectation;* 707.7 *emphasis;* 727.1 *exaggeration;* 699.9 *falsification;* 467.1 *overestimation;* 699.7 *pretence*
oversteer 320.21 *miscellaneous motoring terms*
overstep 329.1; 486.7 *be clumsy;* 219.4 *be excessive;* 121.8 *be superior*
overstep oneself 446.18 *aim*
overstepped 727.14 *extravagant*
Overstepping 329
overstepping 329.6; 302.15 *improvement;* 16.38 *lawbreaking;* 381.14 *siege*
overstepping the mark 727.3 *extravagance*
overstep the mark 219.4 *be excessive;* 727.9 *be extravagant;* 329.1 *overstep*
overstock 219.4 *be excessive*
overstrain 261.6 *fatigue*
overstrained 261.1 *fatigued*
overstress 727.7 *exaggerate;* 727.1 *exaggeration*
overstressed 727.12 *exaggerated*
overstretched 219.6 *excessive*
overstretching oneself 219.2 *overdoing it*
overstrict 7.15 *religious*
overstride 329.1 *overstep*
oversubscribe 219.4 *be excessive*
oversubtlety 702.4 *quibbling*
oversupplied 793.9 *cheap*
oversupply 793.2 *declining prices;* 342.9 *overactivity;* 219.3 *superfluity;* 215.4 *surplus*
oversupply of food 557.9 *plenty*
overswarm 97.11 *be present*
overt 178.5 *honourable;* 738.14 *manifest;* 520.1 *visible*
overt act 340.2 *deed*
overtake 332.6 *accelerate;* 765.10 *augment;* 254.10 *endanger;* 329.3 *exceed;* 302.9 *maintain progress;* 262.2 *make haste;* 318.8 *pass*
overtaken 329.14 *surpassing*
overtaking 332.3 *accelerating;* 332.9 *acceleration;* 765.2 *augmentation;* 302.15 *improvement;* 320.21 *miscellaneous motoring terms;* 329.6 *overstepping;* 318.12 *passing*
overtask 261.6 *fatigue;* 351.1 *misuse*
overtax 261.6 *fatigue;* 414.14 *make heavy;* 218.7 *make insufficient;* 351.1 *misuse;* 773.8 *take back*
overtaxed 414.3 *ponderous*
overtaxing 414.3 *ponderous;* 414.8 *weighing down*
overtax one's strength 261.5 *be fatigued*
overtechnical 264.12 *problematic*
over the border 329.17 *ahead*
over the counter 767.16 *disposably*
over-the-counter drug 37.3 *drug*
over-the-counter market 779.3 *sellers' market*
over-the-counter medication 394.2 *medicine*
over the hill 296.11 *old;* 238.1 *useless*
over the horizon 521.1 *invisible*
over-the-knee socks 551.20 *legwear*
over the moon 219.6 *excessive;* 597.4 *happy*
over-the-rim shot 49.4 *playing terms*
over the top 232.10 *fully*
over-the-top 329.13 *exaggerated;* 219.6 *excessive;* 590.13 *passionate;* 615.4 *rash*
over the water 91.11 *nautically*
overthrow 588.1 *anarchy;* 588.4 *be anarchic;* 486.7 *be clumsy;* 662.16 *be subversive;* 367.3 *bring down;* 486.9 *bungling;* 340.2 *deed;* 357.9 *demolish;* 357.8 *destroy;* 357.1 *destruction;* 367.12 *downthrow;* 585.12 *go to war;* 245.4 *impair;* 246.11 *overmaster;* 704.1 *refutation;* 704.8 *refute;* 144.16 *replace;* 144.3 *replacement;* 53.10 *score;* 396.20 *take authority*
overthrowing 396.3 *acquisition of power*
overthrown 367.22; 247.11 *defeated;* 144.10 *replaced*
overtime 49.1 *basketball;* 46.5 *game time;* 15.9 *negotiated;* 276.4 *period of activity;* 576.2 *task*
overtime ban 15.4 *industrial dispute*
overtime pay 785.3 *pay;* 813.4 *reward for service*
overtime victory 246.2 *victory*
overtime work 15.2 *industrial negotiations*
overtired 245.12 *deteriorated;* 261.1 *fatigued*
overtiredness 261.7 *fatigue*
overtly 340.7 *actively;* 738.16 *manifestly*
overtness 520.3 *visibility*
overtone 170.3 *atmosphere;* 18.16, 28.20 *musical note;* 18.21 *tone*
overtop 154.15 *be high;* 121.8 *be superior;* 120.5 *be unequal;* 235.9 *be worthy;* 174.7 *top;* 89.9 *tower*
overtopping 154.9 *high;* 121.12 *superior*
overtrump 121.8 *be superior*
overture 18.4 *opera;* 129.5 *preface;* 21.8 *scene;* 752.2 *tentative offer*
overturn 367.3 *bring down;* 357.9 *demolish;* 357.8 *destroy;* 367.12 *downthrow;* 192.3 *invert;* 246.11 *overmaster;* 704.8 *refute;* 323.10 *sail;* 305.11 *trip*
overturned 367.22 *overthrown*
overturned conviction 389.1 *escape*
overturned fold 30.20 *earth movement*
overturned verdict 16.4 *bad law*
overturning 357.1 *destruction;* 367.12 *downthrow;* 305.4 *fall;* 192.1 *inversion;* 704.7 *refuting*
overuse 351.1, 351.2 *misuse*
overused 138.22 *commonplace*
overvaluation 727.1 *exaggeration;* 465.1 *misjudgment;* 467.1 *overestimation*
overvalue 727.7 *exaggerate;* 465.10 *misjudge;* 467.4 *overestimate*
overvalued 727.12 *exaggerated;* 465.9 *misjudged;* 467.6 *overestimated*
overview 397.7; 138.7 *global view;* 579.3 *management;* 723.1 *summary;* 518.7 *view;* 204.3 *whole situation*
overwarm 31.51 *hot*
overween 622.28 *disdain*
overweening 660.16 *arrogant;* 660.3 *audacity;* 622.16 *oppressive*
overweening pride 622.3 *conceit;* 467.1 *overestimation*
overweigh 414.12 *be heavy;* 414.14 *make heavy*
overweighed 414.2 *loaded*
overweight 190.7 *bigger;* 158.16 *fat;* 158.5 *fatness;* 414.1 *heavy;* 120.1 *inequality;* 219.2 *overdoing it;* 152.1 *thick;* 120.3 *unequal;* 414.7 *weighing;* 181.10 *well-rounded*
overweighted 414.2 *loaded*
overweighting 414.6 *displacement*
overwhelm 381.9 *attack successfully;* 219.4 *be excessive;* 336.7 *be strong;* 667.21 *command respect;* 357.12 *consume;* 246.10 *defeat heavily;* 232.6 *fill;* 208.12 *overcrowd*
overwhelmed 219.6 *excessive;* 232.8 *full;* 590.12 *sensitive*
overwhelming 381.23 *attacking;* 357.14 *destructive;* 590.14 *emotive;* 219.6 *excessive;* 336.10 *potent;* 380.6 *violent;* 619.8 *wonderful*
overwinter 77.22 *be dormant;* 292.6 *spend the season*
overwise 673.13 *boastful*
over with 309.17 *finally*
overwork 261.5 *be fatigued;* 576.4 *exertion;* 261.6, 261.7 *fatigue;* 218.7 *make insufficient;* 238.8 *make useless;* 351.1 *misuse;* 342.15 *try;* 349.1 *use;* 441.1, 441.3 *waste;* 576.6 *work*
overworked 342.19 *busy;* 138.22 *commonplace;* 261.1 *fatigued*
overwrite 727.7 *exaggerate;* 724.9 *style*
overwriting 727.1 *exaggeration*
overwritten 727.12 *exaggerated*
overwrought 342.18 *active;* 243.20 *developed;* 261.1 *fatigued;* 231.2 *incomplete;* 590.12 *sensitive*
overzealous 636.2 *eager;* 615.4 *rash*
overzealousness 636.7 *eagerness*
ovine 71.33 *ungulate*
oviparous 561.16 *reproductive*
ovipositor 561.8 *organs of reproduction*
ovoid 179.5 *circular;* 181.9 *round;* 27.83 *spherical*
ovule 78.3 *flower part;* 77.9 *seed*
ovum 561.8 *organs of reproduction*
ow 514.6 *cry of pain*
owe 784.7 *be in debt;* 215.8 *leave*
owe allegiance 12.13 *be governed*
owed 785.17 *payable;* 215.10 *surplus*
owe everything to 345.7 *follow from*
owe fealty 12.13 *be governed*
owe loyalty 12.13 *be governed*
owe loyalty to 387.8 *be subject to*
owe money 784.7 *be in debt*
owe nothing to 109.11 *be unconcerned*
owe obedience 12.13 *be governed*
ower 772.6 *borrower*
owing 239.1 *convenient;* 784.1 *debt;* 784.9 *in debt;* 782.2 *insolvent;* 785.17 *payable*
owing a favour 671.4 *grateful*
owing nothing 785.16 *paid*
owing nothing to 109.6 *unrelated*
owing to 345.10 *caused*
owl 475.7 *bad-luck sign;* 72.5 *bird of prey;* 291.5 *night thing*
owlet 72.12 *young bird*
owlhead 59.1 *horse*
owlish 72.21 *avian*
owl-like 72.21 *avian*
own 739.8 *admit;* 763.7 *possess*
own account 250.1 *freedom*
own assets 440.9 *own property*
own authority 250.3 *independence*
own back yard 565.2 *environment*
owned 763.9 *possessed*
owned property 763.4 *possession*
owner 59.15 *horse person;* 400.1 *master;* 763.5 *possessor;* 440.7 *property man;* 575.4 *titleholder;* 349.8 *user*
owner-occupier 564.3 *householder;* 763.5 *possessor*
ownership 763.1 *possession*
ownership papers 744.2 *certificate*
own free will 250.1 *freedom*
own goal 486.9 *bungling;* 274.13 *sporting error*
owning 763.8 *possessing;* 763.1 *possession*
own initiative 250.1 *freedom*
own personal effects 440.9 *own property*
own property 440.9
own responsibility 250.1 *freedom*
own stocks and shares 440.9 *own property*
own up 707.20, 739.8 *admit*
own volition 250.1 *freedom*
own way 250.3 *independence*
owzat 53.21 *how's that!*
ox 316.6 *beast of burden;* 567.16 *male animal*
oxblood 535.1 *red*
oxbow lake 88.1 *lake*
Oxbridge 6.13 *university*
ox cheek 25.31 *offal*
OXFAM 650.2, 652.5 *charity;* 768.3 *offering;* 710.3 *solicitation*
Oxford 87.4 *British cities*
Oxford accent 5.26 *dialect*
Oxford bags 551.9 *trousers*
Oxford blue 539.1 *blue*
Oxford-Cambridge race 50.4 *rowing*
Oxford English 5.6 *official language*
Oxford English Dictionary 5.28 *dictionary*
Oxfords 551.19 *footwear*
oxidimetric 26.16 *micrometric*
oxidimetry 26.2 *micrometry*
oxidization 245.9 *dilapidation*
oxidize 32.26 *react*
oxidoreductase 33.11 *enzyme*
oxlike 71.33 *ungulate*
oxtail 25.31 *offal*
oxtail soup 25.13 *soup*
ox tongue 25.31 *offal*
Oxus 90.5 *other major rivers*
oxyacetylene burner 493.6 *fire*
oxychromatin 34.9 *cell nucleus*
oxygen 434.1 *air;* 33.15 *essential element;* 417.5 *gas;* 554.3 *life requirements;* 581.6 *refresher*
oxygenate 432.26, 434.20 *aerate*
oxygenated 32.34 *elemental*
oxygenation 434.6 *ventilation*
oxygenic 432.24 *oxygenous*
oxygenization 434.6 *ventilation*
oxygenized 32.34 *elemental*
oxygenous 432.24
oxygen tank 62.4 *climbing equipment*
oxygen tent 394.14 *hospital;* 252.4 *safety device*
oyez 504.18 *hear hear!*
oyster 533.4 *greyness;* 25.19 *shellfish*
oystercatcher 72.3 *water bird*
oyster-like 75.19 *molluscan*
oyster loaf 25.11 *sandwich*
oysterman 633.6 *hunter*
oyster pieces 23.9 *decorative woodwork*
oyster shell 550.14 *animal covering*
oysters Rockefeller 25.43 *US dish*
oyster-white 531.1 *white*
oysterwood marquetry 23.9 *decorative woodwork*
OZ 691.6 *drug*
Oz 477.8 *dreamland*
ozone 434.1 *air;* 434.5 *open air*
ozone-friendly 538.7 *environmental;* 432.24 *oxygenous*
ozone layer 31.8 *atmosphere;* 434.3 *atmospheric layers;* 30.47 *radiation belt*
ozonic 432.24 *oxygenous*
ozonize 32.26 *react*
ozonosphere 31.8 *atmosphere;* 30.47 *radiation belt*
ozonous 432.24 *oxygenous*

PA 507.4 *sound maker*
Pablum™ 557.7 *food*
pabulum 557.7 *food*
pace 53.8 *delivery;* 300.12 *gait;* 20.9 *miscellaneous architectural features;* 333.10 *slow motion*
pace bowler 53.4 *team*

pacemaker 59.7 *horseracing;* 579.14 *leader;* 762.3 *substitute thing*
pace off 26.10 *measure*
pacer 59.2 *thoroughbred*
pacesetter 579.14 *leader*
pacey 53.13 *bowling*
pachyderm 71.14; 489.5 *unfeeling person*
pachydermatous 71.32; 152.1 *thick*
pacifiable 749.6 *pacificatory*
pacific 4.18 *detached;* 339.5 *inert;* 685.6 *moderate;* 589.7 *peaceful;* 301.6 *quiescent*
pacifically 749.7; 589.8 *peacefully*
Pacification 749
pacification 749.1; 649.3 *absolution;* 807.1 *atonement;* 748.2 *mediation;* 589.1 *peace*
pacificatory 749.6; 748.6 *mediatory;* 685.8 *moderating*
Pacific Daylight Time 275.9 *time zone*
Pacific Ocean 150.5 *broad thing*
Pacific salmon 55.4 *American game fish;* 25.17 *freshwater fish*
Pacific Standard Time 275.9 *time zone*
pacified 649.6 *forgiven;* 749.6 *pacificatory*
pacifier 748.3 *mediator;* 685.2 *moderator;* 589.3, 749.3 *pacifist*
pacifism 589.1 *peace*
pacifist 589.3; **749.3**; 4.11 *follower of a doctrine;* 4.14 *of a philosophy;* 589.7 *peaceful;* 383.5 *resister*
pacify 407.22; **749.4**; 807.5 *atone;* 609.9 *comfort;* 301.9 *make motionless;* 589.6 *make peace;* 748.1 *mediate;* 685.4 *moderate;* 752.14 *offer reparation;* 752.15 *offer worship;* 480.15 *persuade;* 608.9 *relieve;* 421.13 *smooth over*
pacifying 807.4 *atoning;* 649.4 *forgiving;* 749.1 *pacification;* 749.6 *pacificatory;* 609.5 *satisfying*
pack 320.5; 71.21 *assemblage of mammals;* 699.25 *be fraudulent;* 69.3 *card game terms;* 203.2 *certain amount;* 208.11, 376.40 *crowd;* 232.6 *fill;* 376.23 *flock;* 376.11 *group;* 633.6 *hunter;* 416.9 *make dense;* 410.5 *packet;* 243.4 *prepare for action;* 410.21 *put in a container;* 203.8 *quantify;* 439.6 *store;* 406.7 *stuff;* 208.4 *throng;* 316.10 *transferred thing;* 316.12 *transport;* 319.5 *transportable;* 204.5 *unit;* 550.25 *wrap*
package 20.18 *be an architect;* 376.27 *bundle;* 406.6 *contain;* 376.38 *group;* 127.1 *inclusion;* 410.21 *put in a container;* 40.8 *software;* 550.25 *wrap*
packaged 376.49 *grouped;* 550.37 *protected*
package deal 127.1 *inclusion*
packaged food 557.7 *food*
packager 550.17 *coverer*
packaging 410.5 *packet;* 359.1 *preservation;* 520.6 *visible thing;* 550.4 *wrapping*
pack a jury 106.2 *premeditate*
pack animal 320.9 *animal transport;* 316.6 *beast of burden;* 70.3 *domesticated animal*
pack a punch 336.7 *be strong*
pack a scrum 64.5 *play rugby*
pack away 350.6 *stop using;* 439.6 *store*
packed 410.20 *containing;* 208.10, 376.50 *crowded;* 106.4 *deliberate;* 152.2 *dense;* 232.8 *full;* 406.11 *loaded;* 203.6 *quantitative;* 309.13 *stopped;* 439.7 *stored*
packed house 21.33 *theatregoer*
packed jury 699.8 *fraud;* 465.3 *injustice;* 106.6 *premeditation*
packed like sardines 232.8 *full*
packed lunch 557.12 *meal*
packed with meaning 694.6 *meaningful*
packer 243.15 *preparer;* 578.1 *worker*
packet 410.5; 203.2 *certain amount;* 40.19 *computing terms;* 692.3 *correspondence;* 781.6 *money;* 439.1 *store;* 496.7 *tobacco*
packet of money 780.3 *fortune*
packet switching 40.14 *data transfer*
packhorse 320.9 *animal transport;* 316.6 *beast of burden;* 59.1 *horse*
pack ice 494.5 *ice;* 30.39 *iceberg*
pack in 232.6 *fill;* 314.12 *flood in;* 368.3 *impact;* 406.7 *stuff*
packing 410.20 *containing;* 359.1 *preservation;* 406.4 *stuffing*
packing box 410.6 *box*
packing case 439.4 *storage*
pack it in 133.12 *discontinue;* 226.12 *stop!*
pack-lunch 557.12 *meal*
pack mule 316.6 *beast of burden*
pack off 364.2 *eject;* 371.6 *send away*
pack of troubles 249.1 *adversity*
pack up 261.5 *be fatigued*
pact 750.3 *arrangement;* 755.1 *contract*
pad 53.6; 53.17 *bat;* 270.5 *be diffuse;* 493.14 *be hot;* 384.19 *buffer;* 152.8 *fatten;* 565.1 *habitat;* 58.3 *ice hockey;* 190.5 *make bigger;* 59.4 *saddle horse;* 419.13 *soften;* 419.11 *soft thing;* 336.8 *strengthen;* 406.7 *stuff*
padded 190.7 *bigger;* 419.4 *compressible;* 270.3 *diffuse;* 211.9 *extra;* 54.6 *fencing;* 493.13 *heated;* 406.11 *loaded;* 152.1 *thick*
padded cell 461.8 *mental hospital*
padded glove 58.3 *ice hockey*
padded gloves 54.2 *fencing equipment*
padded out 270.3 *diffuse*
padded text 219.3 *superfluity*
padding 211.3 *additional item;* 270.1 *diffuseness;* 190.4 *enlarger;* 190.1 *growth;* 112.2 *iteration;* 419.11 *soft thing;* 406.4 *stuffing;* 152.5 *thickness*
Paddington 87.5 *London*
paddle 327.22 *agitate;* 327.14 *agitator;* 50.21 *avast!;* 50.17 *canoe;* 50.6 *canoeing;* 814.3 *hit;* 50.16 *row;* 433.33 *sprinkle;* 67.1 *swimming*
paddled 50.12 *canoeing*
paddle one's own canoe 250.16 *be independent;* 197.18 *be one;* 631.11 *conduct oneself*
paddler 323.8 *boatman*
paddle wheel 330.11 *propeller;* 307.6 *rotator*
paddling 331.12 *collision;* 814.12 *corporal punishment;* 50.4, 50.11 *rowing;* 67.1, 67.11 *swimming*
paddling canoe 50.6 *canoeing*
paddock 73.7 *amphibian;* 309.4 *closed place;* 165.5 *enclose;* 165.2 *enclosed place;* 43.11 *farmland;* 59.7 *horseracing*
paddock grazing 43.3 *livestock farming*
paddy 624.4 *anger;* 43.11 *farmland*
paddy field 43.11 *farmland*
paddy wagon 320.17 *police car*
pad-lid 68.10 *curling*
padlock 373.12 *bind;* 309.7 *close;* 373.8 *fastening;* 309.3 *restrainer*
padlocked 373.16 *bound;* 309.12 *closed*
pad-nag 59.4 *saddle horse*
pad out 270.5 *be diffuse;* 213.5 *make bigger*
padre 7.8 *priest*
pads 58.1 *hockey;* 46.3 *uniform*
pad up to 53.17 *bat*
paean 669.4 *compliment;* 514.3 *cry of praise;* 10.8 *hymn;* 671.2 *thanks*
paediatric 35.22, 394.18 *medical*
paediatrician 35.13 *medical specialist*
paediatric patient 260.19 *sick person*
paediatrics 35.3 *medical specialty*
paedogenesis 34.15 *developmental biology;* 73.8 *young amphibian*
paedogenetic 34.26 *developmental*
paedophile 804.9 *wicked person*
paella 25.54 *other dishes*
paeon 17.9 *metre*
pagan 451.5 *disbeliever;* 451.6 *disbelieving;* 9.6 *idolater;* 9.10 *idolatrous*
paganism 9.2 *idolatry;* 451.4 *unbelief*
paganize 9.8 *idolatrize*
pagano-Christian 9.6 *idolater*
pagano-Christianism 9.2 *idolatry*
paganry 9.2 *idolatry*
pagans 566.3 *early human*
page 401.3 *attendant;* 570.7 *bridal party;* 692.30 *communicate;* 743.10 *identify;* 205.2 *particular;* 316.7 *transferor*
page 3 girl 796.2 *indecency*
pageant 656.3 *formal occasion;* 738.10 *manifestation;* 703.6 *mass demonstration;* 132.8 *procession;* 21.7 *show;* 518.7 *view*
pageantry 738.10 *manifestation*
pageboy 570.7 *bridal party*
Pagemaker™ 40.11 *application*
pager 504.9 *audio device;* 692.18 *radio*
paginate 743.10 *identify*
pagoda 10.11 *place of worship;* 154.6 *tall thing*
Pago Pago 145.3 *distant place*
pahoehoe 30.25 *eruption*
paid 785.16; 787.12 *expended;* 765.15 *gainful;* 788.6 *received;* 769.11 *receiving*
paid for 777.13 *bought*
paid helper 401.1 *servant*
paid in advance 785.19 *receiving pay*
paid in full 785.16 *paid*
paid out 787.12 *expended*
pail 410.11 *vessel*
pain 491.1; 249.1 *adversity;* 798.2 *affliction;* 620.6 *be boring;* 620.3 *boring person;* 236.11 *harmfulness;* 245.11 *hurt;* 240.3 *inconvenience;* 491.11 *inflict pain;* 742.1 *sign;* 602.1 *sorrow;* 260.3 *symptom;* 242.5 *unpleasantness;* 242.9 *unpleasant person*
pained 491.7 *feeling pain;* 624.15 *resentful*
painfree 265.14 *relaxed*
painful 242.4; **491.5**; 260.23 *diseased;* 602.7 *distressing;* 491.8 *inflicting pain;* 576.11 *laborious;* 814.21 *punishing;* 591.3 *sore;* 242.1 *unpleasant*
painful condition 491.2
painfully 491.13; 798.13 *destructively*
painfulness 798.2 *affliction;* 236.11 *harmfulness;* 491.1 *pain*
pain in the arse 620.3 *boring person;* 662.5 *troublemaker;* 242.9 *unpleasant person*
pain in the neck 620.3 *boring person;* 408.11, 662.5 *troublemaker;* 242.9 *unpleasant person*
painkiller 489.4 *anaesthetic;* 394.5 *analgesic;* 592.6 *desensitizing substance;* 37.4 *drug type;* 685.2 *moderator;* 608.3 *reliever*
painkilling 685.8 *moderating*
painless 265.9 *easy*
painlessly 490.11 *pleasingly*
pain relief 491.4; 394.5 *analgesic*
pain-reliever 394.5 *analgesic*
pains 576.4 *exertion*
pains and penalties 814.8 *penalty*
painstaking 342.8 *assiduity;* 665.9 *careful;* 471.8 *diligent;* 576.11 *laborious;* 576.10 *working*
paint 19.19; **529.5**; **717.11**; 211.6 *add;* 256.9 *cleaning agent;* 550.24 *coat;* 550.3 *coating;* 28.28, 529.15 *colour;* 547.4 *cosmetics;* 721.14 *describe;* 700.12, 700.32 *disguise;* 550.28 *face;* 477.14 *imagine;* 547.16 *make up;* 37.7 *ointment;* 529.4 *pigment;* 359.5 *preserve;* 359.2 *preserver;* 356.10 *produce;* 744.13 *record;* 421.11 *smooth;* 550.8 *wall covering;* 23.18 *work wood*
paintable 717.13 *representational*
paint a masterpiece 400.14 *master*
paintball 69.7 *other games*
paintbox 19.11 *artist's materials;* 547.5 *make-up box*
paintbrush 19.11 *artist's materials*
paint china 24.11 *make ceramics*
painted 19.27; 529.10 *coloured;* 550.36 *covered;* 700.41 *disguised;* 23.14 *wooden*
painted furniture 23.1 *furniture*
painted image 717.6 *image*
painter 529.6; 578.2 *artisan;* 19.16 *artist;* 125.8 *copier;* 550.17 *coverer;* 542.8 *decorator;* 373.6 *line;* 50.3 *parts of a sailing boat;* 115.4 *person who copies;* 717.4 *person who makes a representation;* 356.9 *producer;* 393.12 *repairer*
painterliness 19.4 *treatment*
painterly 19.26 *artistic;* 717.13 *representational*
painterly values 19.4 *treatment*
painting 19.2; **19.8**; 19.1 *art;* 23.1 *furniture;* 19.7 *picture;* 359.1 *preservation;* 356.1 *production;* 717.2 *reproduction;* 518.7 *view*
painting and decorating 542.5 *decorating*
Painting and Sculpture 19
painting over 358.3 *obliteration*
paint in words 477.14 *imagine*
paint majolica 24.11 *make ceramics*
paint over 211.6 *add;* 736.8 *conceal;* 358.1 *obliterate;* 760.9 *transform*
paints 19.11 *artist's materials*
paint-stripper 358.4 *eraser*
paint the town red 654.11 *be sociable;* 490.8 *feel pleasure;* 600.5 *rejoice*
paint tile 24.11 *make ceramics*
paint tube 19.11 *artist's materials*
pair 198.14; 376.24 *brace;* 69.3 *card game terms;* 115.6 *couple;* 68.13 *ice-skating;* 110.8 *interrelate;* 111.3 *lookalike;* 111.8 *make the same;* 194.8 *odd;* 53.10 *score;* 63.4 *tennis terms;* 198.1 *two*
pair bond 32.11 *chemical bond*
paired 223.19 *associated;* 750.14 *conforming;* 111.14 *lookalike;* 570.21 *married;* 108.4 *related;* 198.9 *two*
paired cable 39.27 *wire*
paired with 223.24 *with*
pairing 593.5 *desire;* 198.4 *doubling*
pair of compasses 27.49 *geometric construction*
pair off 198.14 *pair*
pair of scales 414.10 *scales*
pair of spectacles 518.10 *visual aid*
pairs 51.9 *bowls;* 68.6 *ice-skating;* 50.4 *rowing*
pair-skating 68.6 *ice-skating*
pair-skating movement 68.6 *ice-skating*
pairs match 51.1 *green bowling*
pairs sit spin 68.6 *ice-skating*
pair up 373.13 *intercommunicate;* 223.14 *keep company with*
pair up with 108.7 *relate to*
paisa 780.4 *change*
Paki-bash 466.14 *discriminate against*
Paki-basher 466.7 *bigot*
Paki-bashing 466.4 *social discrimination*
pakora 25.12 *hors d'oeuvre;* 25.49 *Indian dish*
pal 569.5 *friend;* 595.4 *likable person;* 567.3 *male title of address;* 654.6 *social person*
palace 356.8 *construction;* 565.4 *official residence;* 396.6 *place of authority*
paladin 586.1 *combatant;* 384.13 *defender*
palaeethnologist 284.11 *antiquarian*
palaeethnology 284.9 *antiquarianism*
palaeoanthropographic 1.12 *palaeoanthropological*
palaeoanthropographical 1.12 *palaeoanthropological*
palaeoanthropographically 1.17 *palaeoanthropologically*
palaeoanthropography 1.2 *palaeoanthropology*
palaeoanthropological 1.12
palaeoanthropologically 1.17
palaeoanthropologist 1.4; 284.11 *antiquarian*
palaeoanthropology 1.2; 284.9 *antiquarianism*
palaeobiogeographer 3.4 *archaeologist*
palaeobiogeographical 3.17 *archaeological*
palaeobiogeography 3.2 *archaeology*
palaeobiological 3.17 *archaeological*
palaeobiologist 3.4 *archaeologist*
palaeobiology 3.2 *archaeology*
palaeobotanical 3.17 *archaeological*
palaeobotanist 3.4 *archaeologist;* 77.12 *plant scientist*
palaeobotany 3.2 *archaeology;* 34.1 *life science;* 77.10 *plant science*
palaeoceanography 3.2 *archaeology*
Palaeocene period 284.3 *geological period*
palaeoclimatological 3.17 *archaeological*
palaeoclimatologist 284.11 *antiquarian;* 3.4 *archaeologist;* 30.3 *geologist*
palaeoclimatology 284.9 *antiquarianism;* 3.2 *archaeology;* 30.1 *earth science*
palaeocosmological 3.17 *archaeological*
palaeocosmologist 3.4 *archaeologist*
palaeocosmology 3.2 *archaeology*
palaeodendrology 3.2 *archaeology*
palaeoecological 3.17 *archaeological*
palaeoecologist 3.4 *archaeologist*
palaeoecology 3.2 *archaeology*
palaeoeremological 3.17 *archaeological*
palaeoeremology 3.2 *archaeology*
palaeoethnobotany 77.10 *plant science*
palaeoethnographer 1.4 *palaeoanthropologist*
palaeoethnographic 1.12 *palaeoanthropological*
palaeoethnographically 1.17 *palaeoanthropologically*
palaeoethnography 1.2 *palaeoanthropology*
palaeoethnological 1.12 *palaeoanthropological*
palaeoethnologically 1.17 *palaeoanthropologically*
palaeoethnologist 1.4 *palaeoanthropologist*
palaeoethnology 1.2 *palaeoanthropology*

palaeogeographer 284.11 *antiquarian;* 3.4 *archaeologist;* 30.3 *geologist*
palaeogeographical 3.17 *archaeological*
palaeogeographically 30.66 *geographically*
palaeogeography 284.9 *antiquarianism;* 3.2 *archaeology;* 30.1 *earth science*
palaeoglaciology 3.2 *archaeology*
palaeographer 284.11 *antiquarian;* 3.4 *archaeologist;* 719.6 *interpreter;* 5.2 *linguist*
palaeographical 3.17 *archaeological;* 5.38 *linguistic*
palaeography 284.9 *antiquarianism;* 3.2 *archaeology;* 5.1 *linguistics;* 719.5 *science of interpretation;* 5.12 *translation*
palaeoherpetology 3.2 *archaeology*
palaeohistological 3.17 *archaeological*
palaeohistologist 3.4 *archaeologist*
palaeohistology 3.2 *archaeology*
palaeohydrographer 3.4 *archaeologist*
palaeohydrographical 3.17 *archaeological*
palaeohydrography 3.2 *archaeology*
palaeolimnological 3.17 *archaeological*
palaeolimnologist 3.4 *archaeologist*
palaeolimnology 3.2 *archaeology*
Palaeolithic 296.15 *primal*
Palaeolithic period 284.4 *prehistoric age*
palaeolithy 3.2 *archaeology*
palaeological 3.17 *archaeological;* 5.38 *linguistic*
palaeologist 3.4 *archaeologist*
palaeology 3.2 *archaeology;* 5.1 *linguistics*
palaeomagnetic 30.49 *geophysical*
palaeomagnetism 28.58, 30.44 *geomagnetism*
palaeomammology 3.2 *archaeology*
palaeometeorological 3.17 *archaeological*
palaeometeorologist 284.11 *antiquarian;* 3.4 *archaeologist*
palaeometeorology 284.9 *antiquarianism;* 3.2 *archaeology*
palaeontographer 284.11 *antiquarian;* 3.4 *archaeologist*
palaeontographical 3.17 *archaeological*
palaeontography 284.9 *antiquarianism;* 3.2 *archaeology*
palaeontological 3.17 *archaeological;* 34.20 *biological;* 30.48 *geological*
palaeontologist 284.11 *antiquarian;* 3.4 *archaeologist;* 30.3 *geologist;* 34.19 *life scientist*
palaeontology 70.9 *animal science;* 284.9 *antiquarianism;* 3.2 *archaeology;* 30.1 *earth science;* 34.16 *evolution;* 34.1 *life science*
palaeopathological 3.17 *archaeological*
palaeopathologist 3.4 *archaeologist*
palaeopathology 3.2 *archaeology*
palaeophysiography 3.2 *archaeology*
palaeophysiological 3.17 *archaeological*
palaeophysiologist 3.4 *archaeologist*
palaeophysiology 3.2 *archaeology*
palaeophytologist 3.4 *archaeologist*
palaeophytology 3.2 *archaeology*
palaeopotamological 3.17 *archaeological*
palaeopotamologist 3.4 *archaeologist*
palaeopotamology 3.2 *archaeology*
palaeopsychological 1.12 *palaeoanthropological*
palaeopsychologically 1.17 *palaeoanthropologically*
palaeopsychologist 1.4 *palaeoanthropologist*
palaeopsychology 1.2 *palaeoanthropology*
palaeornithological 3.17 *archaeological*
palaeornithologist 3.4 *archaeologist*
palaeornithology 3.2 *archaeology*
Palaeozoic era 284.3 *geological period*
palaeozoological 3.17 *archaeological;* 70.16 *zoological*
palaeozoologist 284.11 *antiquarian;* 3.4 *archaeologist;* 70.11 *zoologist*
palaeozoology 70.9 *animal science;* 284.9 *antiquarianism;* 3.2 *archaeology*
palais de danse 22.6 *dance hall*
Palais Glide 22.2 *dance*
palanquin 320.6 *litter*
palatability 495.1 *taste;* 241.9 *tastiness*
palatable 557.27 *edible;* 490.6 *pleasant;* 241.4, 495.7 *tasty*
palatably 25.57 *culinarily;* 495.11 *tastily*
palate 466.2 *judiciousness;* 495.1 *taste*
palate-tickling 557.3 *delicate eating;* 557.27 *edible*
palatial 565.16 *manorial;* 781.3 *opulent*
palatinate 85.3 *dominion;* 396.8 *governmental organization;* 12.5 *political organization*
palaver 731.3 *talk*
palazzo pants 551.9 *trousers*
pale 531.4; 524.9 *be dim;* 522.28 *bleach;* 582.21 *deathly;* 530.6 *decolour;* 521.2 *difficult to see;* 530.8 *drained of colour;* 165.5 *enclose;* 165.3 *enclosing thing;* 128.3 *exclusion zone;* 373.8 *fastening;* 261.1 *fatigued;* 743.8 *heraldic device;* 337.10 *ill;* 522.21 *light;* 530.5 *lose colour;* 529.16 *make up;* 524.6 *murky;* 86.3 *regional boundary;* 529.13 *soft-hued;* 86.14 *sphere;* 260.21 *unhealthy;* 531.13 *whiten*
palea 81.3 *grass plant*
pale ale 558.7 *alcoholic drink*
pale as a ghost 612.7 *frightened;* 260.21 *unhealthy*
pale as ashes 530.8 *drained of colour*
pale as death 530.8 *drained of colour*
pale blue 539.1 *blue*
pale brown 534.1 *brown*
pale colour 522.14 *light colour*
pale-grey 533.1 *grey*
pale imitation 486.9 *bungling*
palely 522.30 *lightly;* 531.14 *whitely*
paleness 530.2; 529.9 *complexion;* 711.2 *danger signal;* 524.1 *dimness;* 529.3 *hue;* 521.4 *invisibility;* 522.14 *light colour;* 337.3 *poor health;* 531.7 *whiteness*
Paleo-Asiatic 5.11 *family of languages*
pale purple 540.6 *purple*
pales 384.9 *barrier*
paletot 551.12 *coat*
palette 19.11 *artist's materials*
palette knife 19.11 *artist's materials;* 426.9 *blunt instrument*
pale with anger 624.16 *angry*
pale yellow 537.1 *yellow*
palfrey 59.4 *saddle horse*
Pali Canon 7.12 *religious text*
palimony 765.4 *earnings;* 768.2 *gift;* 788.3 *income;* 440.6 *marriage settlement;* 769.2 *something received*
palimpsest 349.7 *reused product*
palindrome 192.1 *inversion;* 5.17 *word*
palindromic 5.42 *worded*
paling 384.9 *barrier;* 165.3 *enclosing thing*
palingenesis 561.1 *reproduction;* 393.10 *revival*
palinode 17.7 *poem*
palisade 384.9 *barrier;* 165.2 *enclosed place;* 384.18 *fence;* 77.6 *leaf;* 252.2 *protection;* 186.3 *vertical thing*
palisaded 384.30 *defended*
pall 620.6 *be boring;* 497.7 *be tasteless;* 596.7 *cause dislike;* 550.2 *cover;* 583.4 *funeral objects*
pallbearer 583.3 *funeral director;* 316.7 *transferor*
pallet 320.6 *litter;* 319.2 *thing transported*
palletization 319.1 *transport*
palliate 244.1 *improve;* 714.8 *justify;* 685.4 *moderate;* 136.15 *modify;* 35.19 *practise medicine;* 608.9 *relieve;* 394.19 *remedy*
palliated 136.11 *modified*
palliation 714.2 *defence;* 608.1 *ease;* 244.5 *improvement;* 136.5 *modification*
palliative 394.5 *analgesic;* 37.4 *drug type;* 685.2 *moderator;* 136.11 *modified;* 608.3 *reliever;* 608.8 *relieving;* 394.17 *remedial;* 714.11 *vindicatory*
palliatively 714.15 *in vindication*
palliator 714.5 *vindicator*
pallid 582.21 *deathly;* 530.8 *drained of colour;* 337.10 *ill;* 728.17 *insipid;* 522.21 *light;* 531.4 *pale*
pallidity 530.2 *paleness*
pallidly 728.26 *insipidly;* 531.14 *whitely*
pallidness 728.8 *insipidness*
palliness 569.1 *friendship*
pallium 551.16 *robe;* 7.11 *vestment*
pall on 596.7 *cause dislike*
pallor 529.9 *complexion;* 522.14 *light colour;* 530.2 *paleness;* 531.7 *whiteness*
pally 569.8 *friendly;* 654.15 *sociable*
palm 475.10 *cards;* 79.1 *tree;* 794.1 *trophy*
palmaceous 79.14 *treelike*
palmate 311.8 *fanlike;* 77.18 *of leaves;* 79.14 *treelike*
palmelloid 84.7 *algal*
palmer 7.7 *monk;* 7.3 *religious person*
palm frond 79.2 *tree part*
palm grease 780.2 *cash*
palmist 11.13 *diviner;* 475.9 *forecaster*
palmistry 11.9, 475.2 *divination*
palm-kernel meal 43.9 *animal feedstuff*
palm leaf 79.2 *tree part*
palm off 762.6 *give a substitute*
palm oil 780.2 *cash;* 768.2 *gift;* 79.9 *tree product*
palmreader 11.13 *diviner;* 475.9 *forecaster*
palm-reading 11.9 *divination*
palms 77.3 *seed plant*
Palm Sunday 10.15 *holy day*
palmtop 40.3 *computer*
palmy 589.7 *peaceful;* 248.8 *prosperous*
palmy days 275.5 *indefinite period;* 589.1 *peace;* 248.3 *time of plenty*
Palomar Observatory 29.23 *observatory*
palomino 59.1 *horse*
palp 492.7 *sense organ*
palpability 402.1 *material world;* 492.1 *touch*
palpable 738.14 *manifest;* 402.7 *material;* 488.8 *sensate;* 492.8 *touchable;* 520.1 *visible*
palpably 492.14; 738.16 *manifestly;* 402.9 *materially*
palpate 492.11 *touch*
palpating 492.2 *touching*
palpitant 326.14 *vibrating*
palpitate 612.12 *be fearful;* 327.24 *shake;* 326.9 *vibrate*
palpitating 326.14 *vibrating*
palpitation 327.10 *beat;* 260.10 *cardiovascular disease;* 509.1 *drumming;* 326.2 *vibration*
palpitations 261.7 *fatigue;* 612.2 *fearfulness*
palpus 492.7 *sense organ*
palsied 327.19 *convulsive;* 260.23 *diseased*
palsy 260.17 *nervous disorder*
palsy-walsy 569.8 *friendly*
palter 702.13 *quibble;* 639.5 *vacillate*
palterer 699.18 *liar*
paltering 702.4 *quibbling*
paltriness 159.1 *littleness;* 124.6 *obscurity;* 793.3 *shoddiness*
paltry 159.7 *little;* 124.2 *obscure;* 793.10 *shoddy;* 236.1 *worthless*
paltry sum 780.4 *change*
paludal 92.11 *continental*
pal up with 654.13 *fraternize*
paly 743.13 *heraldic*
palynology 77.10 *plant science*
pampas 187.3 *flat thing;* 81.2 *grassland;* 92.6 *lowland*
pamper 219.4 *be excessive;* 757.4 *be permissive;* 490.10 *comfort;* 599.15 *humour;* 392.20 *sustain*
pampered 490.7 *pleased*
pampering 599.11 *humouring*
pamper oneself 219.4 *be excessive*
pamphlet 740.9 *advertisement;* 740.5 *journal;* 356.5 *work of art*
pamphleteer 722.3 *dissertator;* 740.16 *publicize;* 740.10 *publicizer*
pamphleteering 480.5 *propaganda*
pan 670.17, 678.11, 719.11 *criticize;* 167.2 *face;* 25.6 *kitchen equipment;* 25.39 *loaf;* 41.21 *photograph;* 410.15 *pot;* 668.24 *ridicule;* 767.7 *toilet*
panacea 37.3 *drug;* 394.1 *remedy*
panacean 394.17 *remedial*
panache 726.1 *emphasis;* 724.2 *stylishness*
Pan-Africanism 566.11 *nation*
panama 551.15 *headgear*
Pan-American Games 47.5 *competition*
Pan-American Three-Day Event 59.11 *eventing*
panatella 691.6 *drug;* 496.7 *tobacco*
Panathenea 10.16 *religious festival*
pancake 187.3 *flat thing;* 59.14 *horse-riding terms;* 25.39 *loaf*
Pancake Day 10.15 *holy day*
pancake house 557.15 *eating place*
pancake landing 322.5 *flight*
pancakes and maple syrup 25.43 *US dish*
Panchen Lama 7.8 *priest*
panchromatic film 41.9 *film*
pancreatic 559.5 *of a secretion*
pancreatic juice 559.2 *secreted substance*
panda car 320.17 *police car*
panda crossing 320.3 *carriageway;* 317.5 *crossing*
Pandarus 748.3 *mediator*
pandect 16.1 *the law*
Pandects of Justinian 16.1 *the law*
pandemic 260.5 *plague;* 138.17 *widespread*
pandemonic 8.16 *devilish*
pandemonium 408.5 *confusion;* 517.2 *dissonant noise;* 412.3 *miscellany;* 507.2 *outcry*
pander 398.6 *agent;* 348.3 *assistant;* 348.4 *be an instrument;* 796.8 *immoral man;* 748.3 *mediator;* 796.18 *prostitute;* 436.3 *provider;* 436.5 *provision*
panderer 748.3 *mediator;* 436.3 *provider*
pandering 796.5 *prostitution;* 436.1 *provision*
pander to 664.11; 348.4 *be an instrument;* 392.25, 401.8 *serve;* 480.16 *tempt*
Pandora 308.3 *person who opens*
Pandora's box 798.5 *evil thing;* 379.1 *trap*
pane 527.9 *glass;* 411.4 *slice*
paned 541.9 *striped*
panegyric 669.18 *approving;* 669.4 *compliment;* 677.1 *flattery;* 467.2 *overestimate;* 729.8 *speech*
panegyrist 669.9 *praiser*
panegyrize 669.15 *compliment;* 467.4 *overestimate*
panel 23.17 *carpenter;* 376.7 *committee;* 579.7 *council;* 550.28 *face;* 464.5 *judge;* 220.6 *list of names;* 398.2 *representative body;* 411.4 *slice*
panel-back 23.14 *wooden*
panel-back chair 23.2 *chair*
panel beater 320.21 *miscellaneous motoring terms*
panelboard 23.12 *wood*
panelled 550.36 *covered;* 541.9 *striped;* 23.14 *wooden*
panelled bed 23.6 *bed*
panelling 550.8 *wall covering;* 23.12 *wood*
panel of judges 464.5 *judge;* 16.18 *tribunal*
panel saw 23.11 *woodworking tool*
panel show 21.7 *show*
panelwork 23.12 *wood*
pan fish 74.8 *food fish*
pang 236.11 *harmfulness;* 491.1 *pain;* 327.8 *spasm*
panga 425.10 *knife;* 587.8 *sharp weapon*
Pangaea 30.19 *plate tectonics*
pangolin 71.6 *insect-eating mammal*
pangs 491.1 *pain;* 808.1 *penitence*
pangs of conscience 808.1 *penitence*
pangs of jealousy 629.1 *jealousy*
panhandle 86.6 *regions;* 710.8 *solicit money*
panhandler 710.5 *beggar;* 769.5 *recipient*
panhandling 710.3 *solicitation*
panic 612.11 *be afraid;* 612.1 *fear;* 612.13 *frighten;* 262.4 *haste*
panic attack 36.12 *stress*
panic button 711.2 *danger signal*
panic buy 439.6 *store*
panicky 614.3 *cowardly;* 612.8 *fearful;* 639.3 *timid*
panicle 78.4 *flower head;* 81.3 *grass plant*
panic-stricken 612.7 *frightened*
panjandrum 727.6 *exaggerator;* 467.3 *optimist*
pan loaf 25.39 *loaf*
panned 670.33 *criticized*
pannier 410.7 *basket;* 320.11 *bicycle part;* 320.5 *pack;* 551.18 *underwear*
pannikin 410.13 *drinking vessel*
panning 670.5, 678.2, 719.3 *criticism;* 41.13 *framing*
panoplied 384.30 *defended;* 252.7 *invulnerable*
panoply 384.7 *armour;* 551.1 *dress;* 252.2 *protection*
panoply of war 585.2 *glory of war*
panorama 19.10 *art subject;* 138.7 *global view;* 518.7 *view;* 204.3 *whole situation*
panoramic 138.15 *general;* 518.20 *visual*
pan out 345.9 *take effect*
panpsychic 11.16 *psychic*
panpsychism 4.7 *school of thought*
panpsychist 4.11 *follower of a doctrine;* 11.12 *occultist*

pansy 567.9 *offensive terms for homosexual;* 540.3 *purple thing;* 337.4 *weakling*
pant 261.5 *be fatigued;* 729.13 *speak in a particular way;* 326.9 *vibrate*
Pantagruel 158.10 *big person*
pantalets 551.18 *underwear*
Pantalone 21.32 *clown*
Pantaloon 21.32 *clown;* 21.23 *role*
pantaloons 551.9 *trousers*
pant for 617.12 *desire*
pantheism 4.7 *school of thought*
pantheist 4.11 *follower of a doctrine*
pantheistic 4.14 *of a philosophy*
pantheon 583.6 *grave;* 10.11 *place of worship*
panties 551.18 *underwear*
pantile 24.9 *industrial ceramics*
panting **261.3**; 261.7 *fatigue;* 327.16 *restless*
pantisocracy 12.1 *government*
pantograph 125.5 *duplicate;* 321.5 *locomotive part*
pantomime 742.11 *gesture;* 125.3 *mockery;* 21.2 *play*
pantomime dame 21.23 *role*
pantomimic 742.15 *gestural*
pantomiming 21.22 *acting*
pantomimist 21.24 *actor*
pantothenic acid 33.13 *vitamin*
pantry 25.3 *kitchen;* 565.7 *room;* 439.4 *storage*
pants 551.9 *trousers;* 551.18 *underwear*
pantsuit 551.10 *suit*
panty girdle 551.18 *underwear*
pantyhose 551.20 *legwear*
panurgic 485.6 *skilful*
Panzer 586.21 *armoured cavalry*
panzer division 586.16 *army unit*
pap 557.7 *food;* 71.2 *mammalian characteristic;* 497.3 *tasteless items*
papa 7.8 *priest*
papacy 7.9 *priesthood*
papain 33.11 *enzyme*
papal 397.14 *commanding;* 400.12 *masterful;* 7.17 *priestly*
Papal Court 16.22 *ecclesiastical court*
papal decree 397.1 *command*
papaloi 7.8 *priest*
papal rule 12.1 *government;* 396.7 *type of rule*
papaverine 33.19 *alkaloid*
paper **435.3**; 793.6 *absence of charge;* 19.11 *artist's materials;* 722.1 *dissertation;* 693.3 *document;* 550.28 *face;* 153.11 *fineness;* 740.4 *newspaper;* 337.5 *weak thing;* 531.9 *white thing;* 18.18 *written music*
paperback 740.6 *book publishing*
paper bag 410.8 *bag*
paper-bag job 546.2 *ugly person*
paper chase 633.2 *chase*
paper chromatography 32.17 *analysis*
paperclip 360.3 *tools for gripping*
papered 550.36 *covered*
paper handkerchief 256.11 *cleaning cloth*
paperiness 153.11 *fineness*
paperless office 40.12 *electronic office*
paper mill 577.1 *workshop*
paper money **780.14**; 780.1 *money*
paper over 736.8 *conceal;* 393.1 *repair;* 760.9 *transform*
paper over the cracks 218.5 *be insufficient;* 486.5 *be unskilful;* 760.9 *transform;* 238.9 *waste effort*
papers 716.6 *documentation;* 318.6 *passport;* 744.1 *record*
paper sculpture 19.12 *sculpture*
paper tape 40.7 *peripheral*
paper tiger 96.5 *insubstantial person*
paper war 585.1 *war*
papery 424.1 *brittle;* 153.4 *fine*
Paphian 796.14 *lecherous*
papier-mâché 435.3 *paper*
papier mâché mask 551.5 *fancy dress*
papilla 182.2 *bulge;* 71.2 *mammalian characteristic*
papish 7.16 *denominational*
papist 7.5 *Christian;* 7.16 *denominational*
paprika 496.5 *herbs*
Pap test 35.7 *diagnosis*
par 216.1, 216.4 *average;* 111.16 *equal;* 111.5, 119.1 *equality;* 14.1, 780.7 *finance;* 56.2 *golfing terms;* 119.8 *on equal terms*
para 586.32 *airman*
parabaloid 27.83 *spherical*
parable 479.5 *equivocalness;* 17.2 *fiction;* 701.4 *gist;* 721.3 *narration;* 115.1 *similarity*
parablock 68.5 *ski equipment*
parabola 177.2 *bend;* 27.42 *circle*
parabolic 20.13 *arched;* 177.4 *curved;* 27.81 *curvilinear;* 20.17 *structured*
parabolically 177.7 *curvedly*
parabolic arch 20.5 *arch*
parabolic orbit 29.21 *orbit*
parabolic vault 20.7 *vault*
paraboloid 27.45 *curved surface*
paraboloid mirror 28.29 *optical element*
paracentesis 371.22 *disgorgement*
paracetamol 394.5 *analgesic;* 394.8 *drug*
parachronism 286.1 *different time;* 288.1 *wrong time*
parachronistic 288.14 *anachronistic;* 288.12 *too late*
parachronistically 288.20 *anachronistically;* 288.18 *out of chronological order*
parachute 305.12 *drop;* 252.4 *safety device*
parachute division 584.4 *military organization*
parachute troops 586.32 *airman;* 586.14 *armed forces*
parachutist 305.8 *descender*
parade 317.7 *arcade;* 525.2 *being in view;* 738.1, 738.6 *display;* 658.12 *greet;* 132.17 *line up;* 703.6 *mass demonstration;* 132.8 *procession;* 703.19 *protest*
paraded 738.13 *displayed*
parade of honour 667.5 *presenting arms*
paradigm 446.6 *ideal;* 126.2 *original;* 129.4 *precedent;* 160.2 *prototype;* 5.30 *syntax*
paradigmatic 446.13 *ideal;* 160.10 *prototypical*
paradigmatically 160.13 *formatively;* 446.24 *ideologically*
parading 703.14 *demonstrating*
paradise 21.18 *auditorium;* 597.2 *fun;* 283.3 *future condition;* 8.11 *heaven;* 554.5 *life cycle;* 279.3 *life without end;* 301.3 *resting place;* 582.14 *the spiritual world*
paradisiac 8.14 *heavenly*
paradisiacal 8.14 *heavenly;* 490.6 *pleasant*
paradisial 8.14 *heavenly*
parados 384.8 *military defences*
paradox 103.5 *impossibility;* 4.8 *philosophical term;* 27.64 *reasoning;* 702.2 *sophism;* 696.12 *unintelligible thing*
paradoxical 696.4 *difficult;* 103.1 *impossible;* 27.86 *logical;* 702.7 *sophistic*
paradoxically 103.11 *impossibly;* 702.14 *sophistically*
paradrop 322.1 *aviation*
paraffin 437.6 *oil*
paraffin lamp 522.5 *incandescent light*
paraffin stove 493.6 *fire*
paragon **121.6**; 235.8 *exceller;* 446.6 *ideal;* 230.3 *perfection;* 619.5 *person of wonder;* 622.13 *proud person;* 255.5 *pure person;* 485.4 *skilled person;* 797.16 *superior person;* 797.9 *the best;* 803.4 *virtuous person*
paragon of virtue 255.5 *pure person;* 803.4 *virtuous person*
paragraph 205.2 *particular;* 742.7 *punctuation*
paragraph bracket 68.6 *ice-skating*
paragraph double three 68.6 *ice-skating*
paragraphed 742.17 *punctuated*
paragraph loop 68.6 *ice-skating*
parakeet 72.7 *cagebird*
parallax 29.13 *luminosity*
parallel **188.3**; **188.5**; 706.21 *answer to;* 119.10 *be equal;* 108.8 *be proportionate to;* 115.10 *be similar;* 223.18 *concurrent;* 750.25 *conform;* 750.14 *conforming;* 110.9 *correlate;* 110.6 *correlative;* 706.15 *correspondent;* 324.14 *directed;* 119.5, 119.6 *equal;* 111.13 *equivalent;* 86.2 *geographical region;* 57.11 *gymnastic;* 108.5 *interrelated;* 27.80 *linear;* 111.8 *make the same;* 119.8 *on equal terms;* 188.1 *parallelism;* 108.1 *relatedness;* 115.7 *similar;* 115.1 *similarity*
parallel access 40.19 *computing terms*
parallel bars 59.11 *eventing;* 57.3 *gymnastic apparatus;* 57.5 *horizontal bar;* 59.9 *jumping;* 188.2 *parallel thing*
parallel christie 68.4 *skiing technique*
parallel computer 40.3 *computer*
parallel connection 39.16 *circuit element*
parallelepiped 188.2 *parallel thing;* 27.46 *polyhedron*
parallel evolution 34.16 *evolution*
Parallelism 188
parallelism **188.1**; 750.5 *conformity;* 110.3 *correlation;* 706.8 *correspondence;* 119.1 *equality;* 111.2 *equivalence;* 17.12 *poetic language;* 115.1 *similarity;* 162.1 *symmetry*
parallelize 110.9 *correlate*
parallel lines 27.37 *line*
parallelogram 176.3 *angled figure;* 188.2 *parallel thing;* 27.44 *polygon;* 200.2 *quadrilateral*
parallelogram of forces 27.50 *scalar quantity*
parallel sailing 323.5 *navigation*
parallel swing 68.4 *skiing technique*
parallel thing **188.2**
parallel turn 68.2 *cross-country skiing*
paralogism 702.2 *sophism*
paralogist 702.6 *sophist*
paralogistic 702.7 *sophistic*
paralyse 457.10 *bemuse;* 335.8 *overpower;* 592.7 *render insensitive*
paralysed 592.2 *desensitized;* 260.23 *diseased;* 335.12 *impotent;* 341.3 *inactive;* 339.5 *inert;* 301.4 *motionless*
paralysed with fear 612.7 *frightened*
paralysis 592.4 *desensitization;* 335.4 *disability;* 341.1 *inaction;* 339.1 *inertness;* 489.1 *lack of feeling;* 260.17 *nervous disorder;* 260.3 *symptom*
paralysis agitans 260.17 *nervous disorder*
paralytic 690.3 *dead drunk;* 260.23 *diseased;* 335.12 *impotent;* 260.19 *sick person*
paramagnet 363.3 *magnet*
paramagnetism 28.59 *ferromagnetism*
Paramatman 8.3 *God*
paramedic **35.17**; 608.5 *helper*
paramedical 35.17 *paramedic*
parameter **27.60**; 27.25 *algebraic expression;* 136.7 *condition*
parametric 136.12 *conditional;* 27.77 *given*
parametric statistics 27.53 *statistics*
paramilitary 585.17 *military*
paramount 121.14 *best;* 99.5 *essential;* 123.5 *important;* 174.5 *top*
paramountcy 123.1 *importance;* 121.1 *superiority*
paramountly 121.16 *superiorly*
paramour 593.9 *lover*
paramylum 84.3 *plant body*
parang 425.10 *knife;* 587.8 *sharp weapon*
paranoia 36.15 *compulsion;* 461.4 *delusion;* 36.16 *dissociation*
paranoiac 461.7 *insane person*
paranoid 461.13 *mentally ill;* 36.36 *psychologically disturbed*
paranoid personality 36.8 *disordered personality;* 36.16 *dissociation*
paranormal 100.12 *external;* 11.14 *occult*
paranormally 11.25 *occultly*
paransitologist 70.11 *zoologist*
parapet 378.3 *barrier;* 384.11 *fortification;* 252.5 *refuge*
paraph 743.11 *identify oneself;* 743.3 *means of identification*
paraphasia 730.3 *speech defect*
paraphasic 730.12 *inarticulate*
paraphernalia 551.25 *accessories;* 438.7 *equipment;* 412.3 *miscellany;* 440.4 *possessions*
paraphrase 694.10 *mean;* 5.24 *phrasing;* 5.46, 719.12 *translate;* 5.12, 719.4 *translation*
paraphrased 5.43 *phrasal;* 5.40 *translated*
paraphraser 719.6 *interpreter*
paraphrasing 5.43 *phrasal;* 5.40 *translated*
paraphrast 719.6 *interpreter*
paraphrastic 694.6 *meaningful;* 5.43 *phrasal;* 719.17 *translational*
paraphrenia 461.4 *delusion*
paraplegia 335.4 *disability;* 260.17 *nervous disorder*
paraplegic 335.12 *impotent;* 260.19 *sick person*
parapsychological **101.9**; 11.16 *psychic*
parapsychologically 11.25 *occultly*
parapsychologist 101.7 *believer in a nonmaterial world;* 11.12 *occultist*
parapsychology **101.4**; 11.1 *occultism;* 36.1 *psychology*
Paraquat™ 43.14 *pest control*
pararhyme 17.11 *rhyme*
parasite **75.10**; 267.4 *adherent;* 387.4 *dependent;* 34.18 *ecology;* 223.9, 267.5 *follower;* 83.5 *fungal association;* 260.6 *infection;* 77.4 *lower plant;* 343.8 *nonworker;* 76.3 *pest;* 77.2 *plant;* 654.6 *social person;* 664.3 *sponger;* 219.3 *superfluity;* 773.6 *taker;* 70.4 *type of animal*
parasite drag 322.7 *miscellaneous aviation terms*
parasitic 343.3 *not participating;* 70.15 *of animals;* 83.10 *of fungi;* 77.14 *of plants;* 664.7 *sycophantic;* 267.10 *tenacious*
parasitically **664.18**; 83.13 *saprophytically;* 267.12 *tenaciously*
parasitic flatworm 75.6 *worm*
parasitic fungus 83.5 *fungal association*
parasiticide 37.4 *drug type*
parasitic worm 75.6 *worm*
parasitism 34.18 *ecology;* 83.5 *fungal association;* 664.2 *sycophancy*
parasitize 76.16 *infest;* 664.15 *sponge*
parasitological 34.20 *biological*
parasitologist 75.15 *invertebrate zoologist;* 34.19 *life scientist;* 35.13 *medical specialist*
parasitology 70.9 *animal science;* 75.14 *invertebrate zoology;* 34.1 *life science;* 35.3 *medical specialty;* 260.20 *pathology*
parasol 550.12 *protective covering;* 523.6 *shade*
parasuicide 382.7 *suicide*
parasympatholytic 37.14 *counteracting;* 37.4 *drug type*
parasympathomimetic 37.4 *drug type;* 37.17 *stimulating*
parataxis 5.30 *syntax*
paratha 25.49 *Indian dish*
parathion 43.14 *pest control*
paratrooper 586.32 *airman;* 305.8 *descender*
paratrooper boots 551.19 *footwear*
paratroops 586.14 *armed forces*
paratyphoid 260.6 *infection*
paraxial ray 28.31 *lens element*
Parazoa 75.8 *sponge*
parazoa 554.9 *classifications of life*
parazoan 75.1 *invertebrate;* 75.8 *sponge*
parboil 493.14 *be hot;* 25.55 *cook*
parboiling 25.8 *cooking technique*
parcel 376.27 *bundle;* 203.2 *certain amount;* 406.6 *contain;* 692.3 *correspondence;* 43.11 *farmland;* 376.38 *group;* 410.5 *packet;* 205.7 *piece;* 440.1 *property;* 203.8 *quantify*
parcel bomb 700.13 *snare*
Parcel Force™ 692.2 *postal communication*
parcelled 376.49 *grouped*
parcelling out 770.1 *allocation*
parcel of land 86.12 *plot*
parcel out 770.4 *allot*
parcel post 692.2 *postal communication*
parc fermé 61.6 *motor-racing terms*
parch 493.14 *be hot;* 428.21 *dry up;* 428.18 *thirst*
parched 428.8 *baked;* 617.10 *hungry;* 428.2 *thirsty*
parchedness 428.11 *dryness*
parchment 424.3 *brittle thing;* 435.1 *materials*
parchment-like 428.3 *dried-up*
pardon 16.78, 758.10 *acquit;* 16.42, 758.2 *acquittal;* 463.6 *amnesty;* 648.3 *be lenient;* 649.9 *forgive;* 649.1 *forgiveness;* 648.1 *leniency;* 391.4 *liberate;* 627.3 *mercy;* 589.1 *peace;* 749.2 *peace offering;* 627.10 *show mercy;* 714.7 *vindicate;* 714.1 *vindication*
pardonable 649.7 *forgivable;* 714.13 *vindicable*
pardonably 16.88 *forgivingly*
pardoned 16.63, 758.6 *acquitted;* 649.6 *forgiven;* 648.5 *given consideration;* 714.12 *innocent*
pardoning 649.4 *forgiving;* 391.1 *liberation*
pare 209.6 *change gradually;* 552.15 *make nude;* 728.22 *play down;* 372.10 *set apart*
pared 728.19 *downplayed*
pared-down 728.19 *downplayed*
pare down 214.5 *make smaller;* 728.22 *play down;* 206.8 *reduce*
paregoric 37.4 *drug type;* 394.17 *remedial*
parenchymatous 84.7 *algal*
parent 449.12 *discoverer;* 395.5 *influential person;* 5.39 *of language;* 344.7 *Prime Mover;* 356.9 *producer;* 561.5 *propagator*

parentage 561.4 *development*
parental love 593.1 *love*
parent complex 36.18 *complex*
parenteral administration 37.13 *administration*
parent fixation 36.17 *fixation*
parentheses 27.25 *algebraic expression;* 742.7 *punctuation*
parenthesis 133.7 *broken thread;* 325.13 *deviation;* 368.8 *insertion;* 373.4 *means of connection*
parenthesize 742.13 *punctuate*
parenthetic 133.11 *digressive*
parenthetical 368.12 *inserted*
parenthetically 368.15 *in*
parenthood 554.4 *biological function;* 561.4 *development*
parent language 5.4
parent nuclide 28.70 *radioactivity*
parent rock 30.33 *metamorphic rock*
parent surrogate 36.25 *surrogate*
paresis 260.17 *nervous disorder*
par excellence 123.9 *importantly;* 121.17 *supremely*
parfum 502.1 *fragrance*
parfumier 502.2 *fragrant thing*
parget 550.28 *face;* 550.8 *wall covering*
parhelic circle 31.22 *sun*
parhelion 31.22 *sun*
pariah 325.19 *deviant person;* 128.5 *excluded person;* 655.7 *outsider*
pariah dog 71.9 *dog*
paring 411.4 *slice*
paring down 728.9 *downplaying*
paring knife 425.10 *knife*
parings 205.8 *bits and pieces*
pari passu 119.12 *equally;* 285.13 *synchronously*
Paris 87.6 *other cities*
Paris and Helen 593.10 *lovers*
Paris fashion 551.2 *dressing*
Paris green 538.10 *green pigment*
parish 205.1 *part;* 7.9 *priesthood;* 86.5 *state*
parish council 579.8 *British administrative council;* 16.2 *jurisdiction;* 398.2 *representative body*
parishioner 564.5 *countryman;* 87.11 *urbanite;* 10.17 *worshipper*
parish-pump 124.4 *trivial*
Paris Opera Ballet 22.12 *ballet companies*
Paris white 531.8 *whitener*
parity 40.19 *computing terms;* 750.5 *conformity;* 111.5, 119.1 *equality;* 14.1, 780.7 *finance;* 28.78 *quantum;* 115.1 *similarity*
park 165.2 *enclosed place;* 81.2 *grassland;* 538.8 *greenness;* 359.1 *preservation*
parka 62.4 *climbing equipment;* 493.3 *heater;* 551.11 *jacket*
parkin 25.36 *cake*
parking 320.21 *miscellaneous motoring terms;* 318.2 *passing along*
parking light 522.6 *electric light*
parking meter 320.21 *miscellaneous motoring terms*
parking orbit 317.13 *flight path;* 29.35 *rocketry*
parking place 318.2 *passing along*
parking space 320.21 *miscellaneous motoring terms;* 141.5 *reserved space*
parkinsonism 327.7 *shake*
Parkinson's disease 260.17 *nervous disorder*
Parkinson's law 12.3 *governance;* 342.9 *overactivity;* 140.3 *rule of nature*
park keeper 252.3, 384.15 *protector*
parkland 81.2 *grassland*
park one's carcass 565.18 *take up residence*
park oneself 367.8 *sit*
parkway 317.3 *road*
parky 494.8 *cold;* 31.55 *cool*
parlance 729.1 *faculty of speech;* 5.3 *spoken language*
parley 734.11 *confer;* 734.4, 748.5 *conference;* 713.6 *consult;* 713.2 *consultation;* 734.9 *converse*
parley with 733.9 *approach*
Parliament 579.11 *British government;* 12.4 *governing body;* 396.6 *place of authority;* 398.2 *representative body*
parliament 579.10 *legislative body*
Parliamentarian 398.1 *delegate;* 579.16 *official;* 12.8 *politician*
parliamentary 579.18; 398.9 *delegated;* 12.9, 396.14 *governmental;* 400.12 *masterful*
parliamentary committee 713.4 *adviser*
parliamentary democracy 85.1 *country*
parliamentary government 12.1 *government;* 396.7 *type of rule*
parliamentary offices 577.1 *workshop*
parliamentary reporting 741.3 *reporting*
parliamentary system 469.11 *franchise*
parlor car 321.6 *rolling stock*
parlour 565.7 *room*
parlourmaid 401.6 *domestic servant*
parlous state 254.5 *danger*
Parma violet 540.2 *purple pigment*
Parnassian 17.19 *narrative*
Parnassus 17.13 *poetic genius*
parochial 466.10 *discriminatory;* 86.18 *local;* 7.17 *priestly;* 124.4 *trivial;* 465.8 *unjust;* 87.14 *urban;* 10.22 *worshipping*
parochialism 465.3 *injustice;* 466.3 *prejudice;* 86.15 *regionalism*
parochially 16.86 *jurisdictionally;* 87.16 *municipally;* 466.17 *prejudicially;* 465.14 *unjustly*
parodic 668.14 *ridiculing*
parodied 234.8 *exaggerated;* 125.12 *imitative;* 718.6 *misrepresented*
parody 621.2 *act of derision;* 599.13 *be humorous;* 772.9 *borrow illegally;* 234.4 *distortion of the truth;* 599.4 *entertainment;* 125.9 *imitate;* 125.1 *imitation;* 274.19 *make a mistake;* 720.1 *misinterpret;* 720.2 *misinterpretation;* 718.4 *misrepresent;* 274.5, 718.1 *misrepresentation;* 125.3 *mockery;* 668.4 *ridicule*
parodying 772.3 *illegal borrowing*
parol 729.17 *oral*
parole 729.1 *faculty of speech;* 391.4 *liberate;* 391.1 *liberation;* 5.5 *nonstandard language;* 757.2 *permit;* 5.3 *spoken language*
paroled 391.7 *liberated*
parolee 391.3 *liberator*
paronomasia 479.5 *equivocalness;* 17.12 *poetic language*
paronym 5.17 *word*
paronymic 5.42 *worded*
parotid 559.5 *of a secretion*
paroxysm 624.4 *anger;* 381.20 *bout;* 380.3 *instance of violence;* 461.3 *mental deterioration;* 327.8 *spasm*
paroxysmic 327.19 *convulsive*
parquet 21.18 *auditorium;* 175.1 *base;* 550.24 *coat;* 550.9 *floor covering*
parquet circle 21.18 *auditorium*
parquet floor 550.9 *floor covering;* 541.5 *variegated thing*
parquetried 23.14 *wooden*
parquetried furniture 23.1 *furniture*
parquetry 541.2 *check;* 23.1 *furniture*
parr 74.3 *young fish*
parricide 382.3 *homicide;* 382.11 *murderer*
parried 54.6 *fencing*
parrot 72.7 *cagebird;* 117.6 *conformist;* 112.8 *creature of habit;* 125.9 *imitate;* 125.7 *imitator;* 112.16 *repeat*
parrot-fashion 125.14 *imitatively*
parrot fever 260.18 *veterinary disease*
parroting 125.12 *imitative*
parrot-like 72.21 *avian;* 125.12 *imitative;* 112.9 *repeated*
parrotry 117.1 *conformity;* 125.3 *mockery*
parry 384.24; 52.2 *boxing;* 704.10 *countercharge;* 384.1 *defence;* 364.7 *deflection;* 634.6 *evade;* 634.14 *evasion;* 54.5 *fence;* 54.3 *fencing movements;* 364.3 *fend off;* 52.11 *fight;* 66.4 *play soccer;* 385.3 *retaliate*
parrying 52.2 *boxing;* 52.14 *combat;* 54.6 *fencing;* 66.2 *football play*
parse 375.4 *deconstruct*
parsec 29.22 *astronomical unit;* 148.7 *measure of length*
parser 40.8 *software*
parsimonious 218.1 *insufficient;* 682.1 *mean;* 360.9 *retentive;* 683.4 *selfish;* 684.8 *self-restrained*
parsimoniously 218.10 *insufficiently;* 682.9 *meanly;* 683.8 *selfishly;* 360.11 *tenaciously;* 684.11 *with self-restraint*
parsimoniousness 682.3 *parsimony*
parsimony 682.3; 218.8 *insufficiency;* 683.1 *selfishness;* 684.1 *self-restraint*
parsing 375.2 *deconstruction;* 5.30 *syntax*
parsley 496.5 *herbs*
parsley family 77.3 *seed plant*
parson 7.8 *priest*
parsonage 565.4 *official residence;* 7.10 *priestly dwelling*
parson's nose 25.28 *poultry*
Part 205
part 205.1; **205.10**; **313.6**; 377.9 *be dispersed;* 203.2 *certain amount;* 405.1 *component;* 377.12 *disperse;* 372.13 *diverge;* 196.8 *divide;* 571.7 *divorce;* 196.5 *fractional;* 196.7 *fractionally;* 196.2 *fractional part;* 233.3 *incomplete thing;* 209.4 *interval;* 438.5 *machine;* 311.11 *move apart;* 205.11 *partial;* 205.2 *particular;* 405.2 *piece;* 21.23 *role;* 372.9 *separate;* 146.4 *space;* 127.2 *thing included*
partake 557.24 *have a meal*
partake of 764.4 *have joint possession*
partaker 557.18 *eater;* 764.3 *participant*
partaking 557.4 *eating meals;* 764.5 *jointly possessing;* 764.2 *participation;* 654.1 *sociability*
part and parcel 405.1 *component;* 127.8 *included*
part by part 205.12 *partly*
part company 377.9 *be dispersed;* 751.5 *disagree;* 372.13 *diverge;* 313.6 *part;* 634.8 *run away;* 311.12 *separate*
parted 146.6 *spaced*
parterre 21.18 *auditorium;* 44.2 *garden*
parterre box 21.18 *auditorium*
part for part 205.12 *partly*
part hardware 40.4 *computer*
parthenocarpic 80.9 *of a fruit*
parthenogenesis 561.3 *propagation*
parthenogenetic 561.16 *reproductive*
Parthians 284.6 *people of the past*
Parthian shot 131.10 *ending;* 645.2 *stratagem*
partiable 372.19 *separable*
partial 205.11; 466.10 *discriminatory;* 196.5 *fractional;* 231.2, 233.4 *incomplete;* 18.16, 28.20 *musical note;* 229.5 *tending to;* 120.4, 465.8 *unjust;* 802.11 *wrong*
partial deafness 505.1 *deafness*
partial derivative 27.31 *differentiation*
partial differential equation 27.31 *differentiation*
partial eclipse 524.1 *dimness*
partial excuse 714.2 *defence*
partial fraction 27.18 *division*
partiality 229.2 *attitude;* 617.1 *desire;* 569.1 *friendship;* 800.1 *improbity;* 595.2 *inclination;* 233.1 *incompleteness;* 120.2, 465.3 *injustice;* 469.7 *preference;* 802.1 *unfairness*
partial knowledge 455.2 *information*
partially 196.7 *fractionally;* 233.6 *incompletely;* 205.12 *partly;* 465.14 *unjustly*
partially deaf 505.4 *deaf*
partially ordered 27.75 *equal*
partially sighted 519.9 *weak-sighted*
partially sighted register 519.3 *aid for poor sight*
partialness 233.1 *incompleteness*
partial paralysis 260.17 *nervous disorder*
partial payment 785.1 *payment*
partial success 604.1 *disappointment*
partial to 617.9 *desirous;* 595.6 *liking*
partial truth 699.11 *half-truth*
participant 764.3; 127.3 *person included;* 97.5 *someone present*
participate 45.6; 340.4 *act;* 97.12 *attend;* 127.5 *be included;* 342.16, 654.11 *be sociable;* 631.11 *conduct oneself;* 768.6 *give to charity;* 764.4 *have joint possession;* 110.8 *interrelate;* 2.15 *socialize;* 747.13 *work together*
participate actively 342.16 *be sociable*
participate in 405.10 *compose*
participating 97.8 *attendant;* 764.5 *jointly possessing;* 342.21 *meddling*
participation 205.9; **764.2**; 127.1 *inclusion;* 747.3 *mutual relationship;* 97.2 *omnipresence;* 654.1 *sociability;* 342.2 *social activity*
participative 764.5 *jointly possessing*
participator 342.10 *busy person;* 764.3 *participant;* 578.1 *worker*
participator sport 45.4 *sporting activity*
participatory 747.17 *cooperative;* 764.5 *jointly possessing*
participatory democracy 764.1 *joint possession*
participial 5.44 *grammatical*
participle 5.35 *part of speech*
particle 205.4 *component;* 28.77 *elementary particle;* 196.3 *fragment;* 427.7 *grain;* 159.2 *little thing;* 205.1 *part;* 5.35 *part of speech;* 405.3 *unit*
particle accelerator 28.94; 334.8 *nuclear power*
particle collider 28.94 *particle accelerator*
particle counter 28.93 *radiation detector*
particle detector 28.93 *radiation detector*
particle physics 28.3 *modern physics*
particle–wave duality 28.13 *electromagnetic radiation*
parti-coloured 541.6 *variegated*
particular 205.2; **452.7**; 222.6 *aspect;* 405.8 *belonging;* 642.1 *capricious;* 665.9 *careful;* 99.9 *characteristic;* 405.1 *component;* 222.10 *detailed;* 230.2 *perfectionist;* 469.14 *selecting;* 197.14 *singular;* 139.15 *special;* 264.14 *troublesome;* 137.11 *typical*
particular instance 27.58 *frequency distribution*
particular interpretation 719.1 *interpretation*
particularity 452.18; 665.4 *fastidiousness;* 743.2 *identity;* 197.4 *singularity;* 139.1 *speciality*
particularization 698.8 *accuracy;* 452.18 *particularity;* 139.8 *specialization*
particularize 139.23; 273.7, 698.31 *be accurate;* 270.5 *be diffuse;* 222.11 *circumstantiate;* 721.16 *define;* 703.16 *explain;* 452.22 *specify*
particularized 698.21 *accurate*
particularly 222.19 *meticulously;* 139.28 *specially*
particulars 721.1 *description;* 139.4 *specifications*
particulate radiation 28.70 *radioactivity*
parting 311.2; **313.9**; 313.11 *departing;* 377.5 *divergence;* 372.1 *separation*
parting gift 671.3 *recognition*
parting of the ways 311.4 *branching;* 751.1 *disagreement*
parting shot 706.5 *counterstatement;* 131.10 *ending;* 313.9 *parting*
parting with 767.1 *disposal*
parti pris 465.4 *prejudgment;* 106.6 *premeditation*
partisan 466.7 *bigot;* 452.2 *convinced;* 466.10 *discriminatory;* 586.9 *guerrilla;* 465.5 *misjudging person;* 452.11 *opinionist;* 662.10, 753.5 *seditionist;* 587.8 *sharp weapon;* 465.8 *unjust;* 802.11 *wrong*
partisanship 452.10 *conviction;* 466.5 *favouritism;* 569.1 *friendship;* 465.3 *injustice;* 466.3 *prejudice;* 802.1 *unfairness*
partition 770.1 *allocation;* 375.4 *deconstruct;* 375.2 *deconstruction;* 372.11 *divide;* 128.3 *exclusion zone;* 205.1, 205.10 *part;* 372.3 *separateness;* 372.5 *separator;* 521.6 *that which makes invisible*
partitioned 372.15 *separate*
partition wall 166.4 *boundary marker*
partitive 205.11 *partial*
partitively 375.7 *to pieces*
partly 205.12; 196.7 *fractionally;* 233.6 *incompletely*
partly visible 521.2 *difficult to see*
part missing 233.2 *omission*
partner 223.12; **570.12**; **578.5**; 567.4 *boyfriend;* 374.6 *come together;* 223.11 *companion;* 747.10 *cooperator;* 750.22 *form an alliance;* 392.11 *helper;* 110.8 *interrelate;* 223.14 *keep company with;* 764.3 *participant;* 570.8 *spouse*
partnered 223.19 *associated;* 570.21 *married*
partnered with 223.24 *with*
partners 747.9 *team*
partnership 570.2, 750.2 *alliance;* 376.15 *association;* 223.3 *companionship;* 755.1 *contract;* 110.2 *interconnection;* 747.5 *joint control;* 764.1 *joint possession;* 108.1 *relatedness*
part of 405.8 *belonging;* 127.8 *included;* 764.5 *jointly possessing*
part of garment 551.24
part of poem 17.8
part of speech 5.35; 205.2 *particular*
part of the bargain 746.2 *basis for negotiations*
part of the furniture 225.7 *permanent*
parton 159.2 *little thing*
part ownership 764.1 *joint possession*
part payment 205.2 *particular*
part payment instalment 233.3 *incomplete thing*

partridge 60.5 *game;* 25.20 *meat;* 72.4 *table bird*
parts 406.1 *contents;* 142.1 *location*
parts of a canoe 50.6 *canoeing*
parts of a circle 179.4
parts of a punt 50.8 *punting*
parts of a sailboard 50.7 *windsurfing*
parts of a toboggan 68.9 *bobsledding*
part song 181.7 *round;* 516.2 *song*
part-time worker 15.7 *employee*
parturient 130.32 *embryonic;* 562.5 *fertile;* 561.16 *reproductive*
parturition 130.4 *conception;* 561.3 *propagation*
part with 767.9 *dispose of;* 768.5 *give*
part work 740.5 *journal*
party 376.16; 654.5; 586.14 *armed forces;* 586.16 *army unit;* 374.3, 376.1 *assembly;* 601.15 *celebrate;* 601.1 *celebration;* 557.13 *feast;* 597.2 *fun;* 376.11 *group;* 16.8 *litigant;* 764.3 *participant;* 566.7 *person;* 756.5 *promise-maker;* 600.1 *rejoicing;* 376.9, 734.3 *social gathering*
party chairman 579.15 *manager;* 12.8 *politician*
party dress 551.3 *formal dress*
party-goer 597.3 *joyful person*
party hack 117.6 *conformist*
party line 117.5 *convention;* 484.2 *policy;* 713.3 *precept;* 692.12 *public telephone system;* 631.9 *tactics*
party manager 579.15 *manager;* 12.8 *politician*
party member 764.3 *participant;* 12.6 *political party*
party-minded 654.15 *sociable*
party official 400.3 *leader;* 579.16 *official;* 396.10 *person of authority*
party-pooper 481.8 *cautionary person;* 378.7 *hinderer;* 341.2 *nonacting person*
party rule 12.1 *government*
party system 12.1 *government*
party ticket 713.3 *precept*
party to a suit 715.3 *accuser;* 16.8 *litigant*
party whip 579.15 *manager;* 396.10 *person of authority;* 12.8 *politician*
party worker 12.6 *political party*
par value 790.2 *value*
parvenu 675.8 *discourteous;* 765.7 *gainer;* 295.12 *immature;* 295.8 *new arrival;* 574.4 *ordinary;* 248.4 *prosperous person;* 622.13 *proud person;* 675.5 *vulgar person;* 781.10 *wealthy person*
paschal candle 10.14 *sacred object*
pas de chat 22.9 *ballet steps*
pas de deux 22.9 *ballet steps*
pash 593.2 *romantic love*
pasha 400.3 *leader*
paso doble 22.2 *dance;* 68.7 *ice-dancing*
pasquil 621.2 *act of derision*
pasquinade 621.2 *act of derision;* 621.6 *deride;* 678.6 *ridicule*
Pasquino 21.32 *clown*
pass 275.15; 284.14; 318.8; 793.6 *absence of charge;* 332.6 *accelerate;* 669.12 *accept;* 318.4 *access;* 797.19 *be good at;* 618.16 *be mediocre;* 246.6 *be successful;* 121.8 *be superior;* 278.4 *be transient;* 235.9 *be worthy;* 69.3 *card game terms;* 183.2 *concave land;* 560.16 *defecate;* 582.15 *die;* 526.1 *disappear;* 560.15 *excrete;* 66.2 *football play;* 277.7 *go on;* 146.3 *gulf;* 580.4 *have leisure;* 381.18 *hit;* 58.1 *hockey;* 58.3 *ice hockey;* 752.4 *illegal offer;* 330.27 *kick;* 16.68 *legislate;* 669.17 *meet with approval;* 780.24 *monetize;* 151.6 *narrow place;* 308.1 *opening;* 308.7 *passageway;* 318.6 *passport;* 750.29, 757.2 *permit;* 469.4 *pick;* 46.9, 69.10 *play;* 49.6 *play basketball;* 58.9 *play hockey;* 49.4 *playing terms;* 46.15 *play offence;* 66.4 *play soccer;* 252.2 *protection;* 136.13 *qualify;* 314.4 *right of entry;* 64.3 *rugby play;* 217.4 *suffice;* 217.7 *sufficiency;* 330.5, 330.23 *throw;* 700.8, 700.28 *trick*
pass a bad check 780.24 *monetize*
passable 669.22 *approvable;* 216.3, 618.10 *mediocre;* 685.6 *moderate;* 235.5 *not bad;* 609.6 *satisfactory;* 413.10 *supportable*
passableness 216.6, 618.4 *mediocrity*
passably 669.26 *approvably;* 618.20 *unexceptionally*
passacaglia 516.4 *harmonics*
pass a decree 397.9 *command*
passado 381.18 *hit*
Passage 318
passage 318.1; 224.1 *change;* 302.11 *course;* 59.10 *dressage;* 314.5 *entrance;* 516.4 *harmonics;* 146.1 *interval;* 300.2 *momentum;* 151.6 *narrow place;* 308.1 *opening;* 205.2 *particular;* 565.7 *room;* 317.2 *route;* 325.8 *sidestep;* 316.2 *transportation;* 323.1 *water travel*
passage into 318.3
passage of time 275.2; 277.2 *time*
passage right 10.7 *non-Christian ritual*
passageway 308.7; 318.4 *access;* 308.1 *opening*
pass and repass 326.8 *oscillate*
passant 743.13 *heraldic*
pass around the hat 710.8 *solicit money*
pass as 717.12 *stand for*
pass away 278.4 *be transient;* 94.12 *cease to exist;* 214.4 *decrease;* 582.15 *die;* 526.1 *disappear;* 131.19 *expire;* 284.14 *pass;* 313.2 *withdraw*
pass back 58.9 *play hockey*
pass-back 58.1, 58.8 *hockey*
passbook 789.5 *account book*
pass by 275.15, 318.8 *pass*
passé 284.19 *antiquarian;* 3.18 *in the past*
passed 332.3 *accelerating;* 669.23 *approved;* 582.19 *dead;* 485.8 *expert;* 58.8 *hockey;* 16.46 *legislated;* 757.7 *permitted;* 750.18 *permitting;* 66.5 *soccer*
passed away 582.19 *dead;* 94.11 *no more*
passed over 582.19 *dead;* 215.10 *surplus*
passenger 343.8 *nonworker;* 316.10 *transferred thing;* 319.5 *transportable*
passenger pigeon 72.8 *extinct bird*
passenger ship 323.3 *vessel*
passenger train 321.7 *train*
passenger transport 319.1 *transport*
passer 49.2 *basketball player;* 46.7 *offence*
passer-by 716.7 *person who gives evidence;* 97.5 *someone present;* 454.7 *verifier*
passeriform 72.21 *avian*
passerine 72.21 *avian;* 72.6 *songbird*
pas seul 22.2 *dance*
pass for 717.12 *stand for*
pass holder 793.8 *bargain hunter;* 21.33 *theatregoer*
passim 133.17 *discontinuously;* 142.12 *where*
passing 318.12; 332.3 *accelerating;* 332.9 *acceleration;* 131.3, 582.1 *death;* 526.4 *disappearance;* 526.6 *disappearing;* 66.2 *football play;* 58.1 *hockey;* 58.3 *ice hockey;* 58.5 *lacrosse;* 300.16 *moving;* 282.7 *occasional;* 318.1 *passage;* 49.4 *playing terms;* 550.41 *progressing;* 64.3 *rugby play;* 64.6 *rugger;* 278.6 *transient*
passing along 318.2
passing away 582.1 *death;* 526.4 *disappearance*
passing back 58.1 *hockey*
passing bell 582.7 *dying day;* 583.2 *funeral*
passing by 317.17 *via*
passing fancy 593.2 *romantic love;* 642.3 *whim*
passing fashion 278.2 *transient thing*
passing game 46.9 *play*
passing grade 231.5 *imperfection*
passing into law 16.31 *legislation*
passing knell 742.4 *signal*
passing the buck 758.3 *self-exemption;* 634.13 *shirking*
passing through 318.1 *passage;* 550.22 *progression*
passing up 684.1 *self-restraint*
passing word 693.7 *advice*
pass interference 46.13 *penalty*
pass into 760.7 *convert into*
pass into history 214.4 *decrease;* 284.14 *pass*
pass into oblivion 214.4 *decrease*
pass into one's hand 769.9 *receive*
passion 624.4 *anger;* 36.15 *compulsion;* 461.4 *delusion;* 593.5, 617.1 *desire;* 590.4 *emotion;* 726.1 *emphasis;* 595.1 *liking;* 491.1 *pain;* 18.5 *sacred music;* 617.4 *sexual desire;* 380.1 *violence*
passionate 590.13; 593.20 *amorous;* 617.9 *desirous;* 726.3 *emphatic;* 595.6 *liking;* 380.6 *violent;* 493.12 *warm-hearted*
passionate friendship 569.3 *familiarity*
passionately 595.11 *admiringly;* 726.7 *emphatically;* 593.30 *lovingly;* 590.20 *with feeling*
passionless 618.7 *indifferent*
passion play 21.2 *play*
passive 634.18 *avoiding;* 117.13 *compliant;* 341.3, 343.1 *inactive;* 339.5 *inert;* 663.7 *obedient;* 589.7 *peaceful;* 32.38 *reactive;* 301.5 *sedentary;* 732.1 *shy;* 5.32 *voice*
passively 117.16 *adaptably;* 343.15 *inactively;* 339.7 *inertly;* 301.10 *motionlessly;* 663.10 *obediently;* 634.23 *shyly;* 4.27 *stoically*
passiveness 618.1 *indifference;* 339.1 *inertness;* 301.1 *motionlessness;* 663.1 *obedience;* 388.1 *submission*
passive resistance 384.1 *defence;* 662.1 *disobedience;* 341.1 *inaction;* 383.3 *resistance movement*
passive resister 589.3, 749.3 *pacifist*
passive sex 388.1 *submission*
passive smoking 496.8 *smoking*
passive suspension system 61.6 *motor-racing terms*
passivity 639.14 *apathy;* 4.3 *detachment;* 341.1 *inaction;* 343.5 *inactivity;* 618.1 *indifference;* 339.1 *inertness;* 301.1 *motionlessness;* 663.1 *obedience;* 634.13 *shirking;* 388.1 *submission*
pass judgment 397.11 *have authority over;* 16.76, 464.11 *judge*
passkey 308.2 *opener*
pass laws 579.1 *manage*
pass marks 217.7 *sufficiency*
pass muster 235.9 *be worthy;* 669.17 *meet with approval;* 217.4 *suffice*
pass on 635.16 *bequeath;* 316.14 *bring back;* 131.19 *expire;* 302.1 *go forward*
pass oneself off as 699.24 *pretend*
pass one's prime 556.17 *age*
pass on the information 721.15 *recount*
pass out 690.7 *be drunk;* 335.6 *be powerless;* 489.11 *be unfeeling;* 601.20 *come out;* 315.9 *exit*
Passover 10.16 *religious festival*
pass over 649.11 *condone;* 128.7 *exclude;* 315.9 *exit;* 470.1 *reject;* 124.12 *think unimportant;* 313.2 *withdraw*
passport 318.6; 744.2 *certificate;* 716.6 *documentation;* 454.6 *evidence;* 743.3 *means of identification;* 757.2 *permit;* 253.2 *promise;* 252.2 *protection;* 314.4 *right of entry*
passport photograph 743.3 *means of identification*
pass reception 46.9 *play*
pass round 740.17 *be published;* 740.13 *make public*
pass round the hat 768.6 *give to charity*
pass rush 46.11 *defensive huddle;* 46.16 *play defence*
pass sentence 16.76 *judge*
pass the buck 800.8 *be dishonourable;* 758.12 *exempt oneself;* 341.4 *not act;* 634.5 *shirk*
pass the crisis 224.7 *be changed;* 244.2 *get better*
pass the summer aestivate 292.6 *spend the season*
pass the test 669.17 *meet with approval*
pass the winter 292.6 *spend the season*
pass through 318.8 *pass;* 550.35 *progress*
pass up 634.3 *abstain;* 684.5 *be self-restrained;* 341.4 *not act;* 709.5 *refuse;* 388.3 *submit*
pass water 433.32 *seep;* 560.17 *urinate*
pass with flying colours 246.11 *overmaster*
password 40.19 *computing terms;* 743.3 *means of identification;* 721.8 *name;* 308.2 *opener;* 757.2 *permit;* 742.1 *sign;* 585.8 *warfare*
past 284.17; 3.6 *biography;* 294.14 *dead;* 526.7 *disappeared;* 463.11 *forgotten;* 94.11 *no more;* 487.2 *not customary;* 605.7 *resigning*
pasta 25.47 *Italian dish*
past age 3.10
past and gone 526.7 *disappeared;* 284.18 *over*
past behaviour 631.1 *conduct*
paste 430.3; 267.3, 430.2 *adhesive;* 267.7 *cause to adhere;* 699.12 *fake;* 331.3 *hit;* 700.6 *imitation;* 412.2 *mixed thing;* 360.6 *retain;* 419.11 *soft thing;* 430.10 *stick;* 360.3 *tools for gripping*
pasteboard 435.3 *paper*
paste gem 699.16 *false thing*
pastel 19.11 *artist's materials;* 522.21 *light;* 19.8 *painting;* 529.13 *soft-hued;* 728.13 *subtle*
pastel colour 522.14 *light colour*
pastel drawing 19.9 *drawing*
pasteles 25.51 *West Indian dish*
pastellist 19.16 *artist*
pasteurization 256.2 *cleaning;* 257.1 *hygiene*
pasteurize 394.20 *doctor;* 257.6 *make hygienic;* 252.10 *protect;* 255.10, 256.15 *purify*
pasteurized 256.17 *cleaned;* 257.4 *hygienic*
pasteurized milk 558.5 *milk*
past historic 5.34 *tense*
past hope 611.5
pasticcio 412.2 *mixed thing;* 18.4 *opera*
pastiche 125.2 *copy;* 772.3 *illegal borrowing;* 412.2 *mixed thing*
pastille 502.2 *fragrant thing;* 394.2 *medicine;* 37.6 *pill*
pastime 69.8; 633.4 *activity;* 342.2 *social activity*
pastiness 522.14 *light colour;* 430.1 *viscosity*
past it 556.14 *aged;* 245.12 *deteriorated;* 296.11 *old;* 238.1 *useless*
past its prime 231.1 *imperfect*
past its sell-by date 284.19 *antiquarian;* 231.1 *imperfect;* 793.10 *shoddy*
past master 396.11, 400.10 *expert;* 485.4 *skilled person*
past one's best 245.12 *deteriorated;* 296.11 *old*
past one's prime 556.14 *aged;* 556.16 *maturely;* 296.11 *old*
pastor 392.14 *adviser;* 7.8 *priest*
pastorage 7.9 *priesthood*
pastoral 43.19 *agricultural;* 19.10 *art subject;* 17.19 *narrative;* 21.2 *play;* 17.7 *poem;* 7.17 *priestly*
pastoral care 7.9 *priesthood*
pastoral counselling 36.3 *psychiatric treatment*
pastoral elegy 17.7 *poem*
pastorally 43.22 *agriculturally*
pastoral poet 17.14 *author*
pastoral poetry 17.6 *poetry*
pastoral staff 743.4 *insignia*
pastorate 7.9 *priesthood*
pastoress 7.8 *priest*
pastor-ship 7.9 *priesthood*
past participle 5.35 *part of speech*
pastrami sandwich 25.11 *sandwich*
pastry 25.37; 424.3 *brittle thing;* 498.3 *dessert*
pastry bag 25.6 *kitchen equipment*
pastrycook 436.4 *caterer*
pastry cutter 25.6 *kitchen equipment*
pastry shell 550.13 *casing*
Past Time 284
past time 3.8; 284.1; 286.1 *different time*
past times 284.1 *past time*
pasturage 557.8 *animal food;* 81.2 *grassland*
pasture 557.8 *animal food;* 557.21 *eat;* 81.11 *eat grass;* 43.11 *farmland;* 538.8 *greenness;* 557.25 *provide food*
pasture grass 81.1 *grass*
pasture land 81.2 *grassland*
pastures new 130.13 *new beginnings*
pasturing 557.5 *eating habit*
pasty 530.8 *drained of colour;* 522.21 *light;* 25.32 *meat dish;* 419.2 *pliant*
PAT 46.6 *scoring*
pat 331.13 *blow;* 593.14 *communication of love;* 742.11 *gesture;* 331.6 *tap;* 492.11 *touch*
patch 40.20 *abort;* 211.3 *additional item;* 519.6 *blinder;* 541.2 *check;* 40.19 *computing terms;* 258.4 *dirt;* 258.11 *dirty;* 43.11 *farmland;* 37.12 *injection;* 86.13 *locality;* 142.1 *location;* 205.7 *piece;* 86.12 *plot;* 244.3 *rectify;* 393.1, 393.8 *repair;* 394.10 *surgical dressing;* 541.11 *variegate*
patched 782.3 *beggarly;* 541.8 *checked;* 412.12 *mixed*
patched up 393.13 *repaired*
patcher 393.12 *repairer*
patchily 412.14 *in the midst;* 541.12 *variedly*
patchiness 541.2 *check;* 231.5 *imperfection;* 120.1 *inequality;* 299.1 *irregularity;* 412.1 *mixture*
patchiness patch 541.4 *maculation*
patching 393.8 *repair*
patching up 393.8 *repair*
patchouli 502.3 *incense*
patch pocket 551.24 *part of garment*
patch test 35.7 *diagnosis*
patch together 403.17 *assemble*
patch up 244.1 *improve;* 393.1 *repair*

patch up a quarrel 749.5 *make peace*
patchwork 541.2 *check;* 374.2 *cooperation;* 412.3 *miscellany;* 542.3 *pattern*
patchwork quilt 550.10 *bed covering;* 114.3 *diverse thing;* 541.5 *variegated thing*
patchy 541.8 *checked;* 133.8 *discontinuous;* 231.1 *imperfect;* 299.4 *irregular;* 412.12 *mixed;* 122.14 *poor;* 120.3 *unequal*
patchy cloud 31.19 *cloud cover*
pâté 25.45 *French dish;* 25.12 *hors d'oeuvre;* 25.29 *sausage*
pâté de foie gras 25.29 *sausage*
patent 525.7 *appearing;* 527.4 *easily seen through;* 758.4 *licence;* 166.7 *limit;* 166.2 *limiting factor;* 738.14 *manifest;* 308.13 *opened up;* 126.7 *originate;* 750.8, 750.29, 757.2 *permit;* 757.7 *permitted;* 440.1 *property;* 518.23, 520.1 *visible*
patented 126.6 *authentic;* 166.5 *limited;* 440.8 *propertied*
patented invention 126.2 *original*
patently 308.25 *obviously;* 518.25, 520.11 *visibly*
patent medicine 394.2 *medicine;* 412.2 *mixed thing;* 394.1 *remedy*
pater 567.13 *man in the family*
paterfamilias 567.13 *man in the family*
paternal 650.6 *benevolent;* 593.17 *loving*
paternalism 12.3 *governance;* 12.1 *government*
paternal love 593.1 *love*
paternally 650.10 *benevolently*
paternity 561.4 *development;* 567.13 *man in the family*
Paternoster 10.9 *prayer;* 11.5 *spell*
paternoster 320.4 *personal transport*
path 317.6; 318.4 *access;* 324.2 *bearing;* 317.13 *flight path;* 51.2 *grip;* 318.2 *passing along;* 27.36 *point;* 373.5 *road;* 317.2 *route;* 315.6 *way out*
pathetic 611.8 *bad;* 236.2 *inferior;* 337.13 *insufficient;* 124.2 *obscure;* 627.7 *pitiful*
pathetically 337.14 *weakly*
pathetic fallacy 17.12 *poetic language*
pathfinder 322.3 *aircraft personnel;* 449.12 *discoverer;* 129.8 *precursor*
pathia 25.49 *Indian dish*
Pathian marble 19.14 *sculptor's materials*
path of least resistance 317.2 *route*
pathogen 83.5 *fungal association;* 260.6 *infection*
pathogenic 260.23 *diseased*
pathological 382.23 *deadly;* 260.23 *diseased;* 35.22, 394.18 *medical*
pathological dieting 557.3 *delicate eating*
pathological drunk 690.17 *drunkard*
pathological killer 382.11 *murderer*
pathological liar 699.18, 700.16 *liar*
pathologically 394.21 *remedially;* 260.25 *unhealthily*
pathological lying 699.6 *lying*
pathologist 35.13 *medical specialist*
pathology 260.20; 35.2 *medical specialty*
pathoneurosis 36.10 *neurosis*
pathway 318.4 *access;* 317.6 *path*
patience 4.3 *detachment;* 649.2 *forgivingness;* 648.1 *leniency;* 640.1 *perseverance;* 197.10 *single thing;* 333.8 *slowness*
patient 35.18; 251.7 *charge;* 4.18 *detached;* 448.7 *experimentee;* 648.4 *lenient;* 649.5 *merciful;* 640.10 *persevering;* 260.19 *sick person;* 333.5 *unhurried*
patiently 649.14 *forgivingly;* 648.6 *leniently;* 640.13 *persistently;* 333.16 *slowly;* 4.27 *stoically*
patina 411.3 *coat;* 245.9 *dilapidation;* 538.11 *green thing;* 529.3 *hue;* 421.10 *polish;* 522.2 *quality of light*
patinated 529.13 *soft-hued*
patio 165.2 *enclosed place;* 44.3 *ornamental garden;* 565.7 *room*
patio door 314.6 *means of entry*
patio set 44.3 *ornamental garden*
patisserie 498.3 *dessert*
patois 5.26 *dialect;* 729.1 *faculty of speech;* 139.10 *specialized language;* 5.3 *spoken language*
pat on the back 669.4, 669.15 *compliment;* 813.9 *reward*
patria 85.6 *native land*
patriarch 567.13 *man in the family;* 400.1 *master;* 7.8 *priest*
patriarchal 556.14 *aged;* 12.9, 396.14 *governmental;* 400.12 *masterful;* 296.11 *old*
patriarchally 556.16 *maturely;* 296.18 *venerably*
patriarchy 12.1 *government;* 567.1 *male sex*
patrician 573.4 *aristocratic;* 566.10 *member of society;* 573.1 *nobleman;* 396.10 *person of authority*
patricide 651.7 *act of malevolence;* 382.3 *homicide;* 382.11 *murderer*
patrimonial 440.8 *propertied;* 788.6 *received;* 215.9 *remaining*
patrimonially 788.8 *profitably;* 440.10 *proprietarily*
patrimony 215.5 *estate;* 788.4 *legacy;* 763.1 *possession;* 769.1 *receiving*
Patriot 587.5 *missile weapon*
patriot 85.14 *nationalist*
patriotic 593.17 *loving;* 86.17 *national*
patriotically 85.19, 86.20 *nationally*
patriotism 585.5 *bellicosity;* 595.1 *liking;* 593.1 *love;* 85.4 *nationalism;* 86.15 *regionalism*
patristic 7.18 *theological*
patristics 7.13 *theology*
patristic theology 7.13 *theology*
patrol 586.14 *armed forces;* 384.14 *guard;* 318.1 *passage;* 318.9 *proceed;* 252.10 *protect;* 252.3 *protector;* 251.8 *restrain;* 253.10 *secure*
patrol boat 586.24 *warship*
patrol car 320.17 *police car*
patrolman 384.14 *guard;* 518.11 *observer;* 16.17 *police officer;* 252.3 *protector*
patrol plane 586.31 *military aircraft*
patrolwoman 384.14 *guard*
patron 669.7 *advocate;* 707.9 *affirmer;* 392.15 *benefactor;* 650.5 *benevolent person;* 776.12 *custom;* 384.13 *defender;* 13.9 *economist;* 768.4 *giver;* 556.8 *man;* 21.27 *producer;* 252.3 *protector;* 777.12 *purchaser;* 97.5 *someone present;* 413.8 *supporter*
patronage 392.9; 669.1 *approval;* 396.1 *authority;* 397.4 *authorization;* 650.2 *charity;* 776.12, 777.11 *custom;* 413.7 *financial support;* 395.4 *indirect influence;* 579.3 *management;* 252.2 *protection*
patronal 413.9 *supportive*
patroness 252.3 *protector*
patronize 392.23 *advise;* 650.9 *be charitable;* 623.18 *condescend;* 622.28 *disdain;* 297.8 *frequent;* 750.30 *grant;* 396.21 *grant authority;* 599.15 *humour;* 252.10 *protect;* 413.13 *support financially*
patronized 252.6 *safe*
patronizing 396.12 *authoritative;* 297.5 *frequenting;* 622.18 *prestigious*
patron saint 392.15 *benefactor;* 8.10 *deified person;* 252.3 *protector*
patronymic 721.8 *name*
pat someone's bottom 742.11 *gesture*
pat someone's head 742.11 *gesture*
patsy 700.22 *dupe;* 247.5 *failing person;* 621.4 *laughing stock;* 335.5 *powerless person;* 762.2 *substitute person;* 337.4 *weakling*
pattens 551.19 *footwear*
patter 305.13 *drip;* 729.1 *faculty of speech;* 483.2 *inducement;* 5.20 *jargon word;* 509.11 *knock;* 5.5 *nonstandard language;* 480.1 *persuasion;* 31.62 *rain;* 5.45 *use language;* 300.15 *walk*
pattern 542.3; 409.2 *array;* 750.6 *convention;* 110.3 *correlation;* 446.19 *epitomize;* 160.1, 160.7 *form;* 36.26 *gestalt;* 632.1 *habit;* 446.6 *ideal;* 42.5 *knitting;* 407.7 *method;* 99.4 *nature;* 407.1 *order;* 126.2 *original;* 484.6 *outline;* 230.1 *perfect;* 230.3 *perfection;* 129.4, 140.5 *precedent;* 160.2 *prototype;* 298.1 *regularity;* 26.7 *standard;* 403.1, 403.14 *structure;* 541.11 *variegate;* 31.3 *weather;* 42.4 *weaving*
pattern after 125.9 *imitate*
patterned 110.6 *correlative;* 743.12 *identified;* 541.6 *variegated*
patterning 42.7 *dyeing;* 160.1 *form;* 403.5 *structuring*
pattern poetry 17.6 *poetry*
pattern settlement 15.4 *industrial dispute*
pat the bottom 593.27 *kiss*
pat the cheek 593.27 *kiss*
pat the head 593.27 *kiss*
patting 742.15 *gestural*
patulous 150.1 *broad;* 190.8 *growing*
paucity 98.2 *disappearance;* 206.3 *fewness;* 782.9 *inadequacy;* 218.9 *scarcity;* 153.12 *thinning*
Paul Jones 22.2 *dance*
Paul Pry 644.4 *meddler*
paunch 557.16 *eating utensil;* 158.8 *fat;* 172.4 *insides;* 410.18 *stomach*
paunchiness 158.5 *fatness;* 181.2 *round body*
paunchy 158.16 *fat;* 181.10 *well-rounded*
pauper 782.10 *poor person*
pauperism 782.5 *poverty*
pauperize 782.14 *impoverish*
pauperized 782.2 *insolvent*
pauropod 75.4 *arthropod*
pause 133.13; **226.3**; **226.9**; 301.8 *be motionless;* 133.5 *caesura;* 294.3 *delayed action;* 263.1 *ease;* 333.2 *hesitate;* 361.12 *interrupt;* 361.6 *interruption;* 133.3, 275.6 *interval;* 141.8 *intervening space;* 301.1 *motionlessness;* 341.4 *not act;* 18.17 *notation;* 276.1 *period;* 141.21 *space;* 312.6 *stop at;* 294.7 *wait*
pause for breath 275.6 *interval;* 226.9 *pause*
pause for thought 133.3 *interval;* 133.13 *pause*
pavane 22.4 *historic dancing*
pave 421.11 *smooth;* 550.29 *surface*
pavé 317.3 *road*
paved 317.15 *accessible*
paved road 317.3 *road*
pavement 175.1 *base;* 317.6 *path;* 550.11 *paving*
pavement artist 19.16 *artist*
pavement pizza 371.23 *vomiting*
paver 550.17 *coverer;* 243.15 *preparer*
pave the way 129.18 *forerun;* 265.16 *make easy;* 243.1 *prepare*
pavilion 53.2 *ground;* 565.9 *mobile home;* 21.16 *theatre*
paving 550.11; 175.1 *base;* 435.2 *building material;* 38.29 *construction equipment;* 550.1 *covering;* 44.3 *ornamental garden;* 421.8 *smooth thing*
paving material 435.2 *building material*
paving stone 435.2 *building material;* 317.4 *road surface*
pavior 38.26 *masonry*
paviour 243.15 *preparer*
pavis 384.7 *armour*
Pavlov 36.29 *psychologist*
pavlova 25.35 *dessert*
Pavlovian 36.33 *Freudian;* 445.8 *instinctive*
Pavlovian conditioning 36.20 *conditioning*
Pavlovian psychology 36.1 *psychology*
Pavlovian response 445.4 *instinct*
pavonine 541.7 *iridescent*
paw 492.4 *kiss;* 492.7 *sense organ;* 360.3 *tools for gripping;* 492.11 *touch*
pawkiness 599.1 *humorousness*
pawky 645.4 *cunning;* 599.10 *humorous*
pawn 348.3 *assistant;* 772.7 *borrow;* 69.4 *chess terms;* 700.22 *dupe;* 759.5 *exchange;* 122.6 *inferior;* 124.10 *nonentity*
pawnbroker 771.3, 783.5 *lender;* 759.4 *person who exchanges*
pawnbroker's 783.4 *bank*
pawnbroking 771.1 *lending*
pawned 772.11 *borrowed;* 759.7 *exchanged;* 253.7 *guaranteed*
pawner 772.6 *borrower*
pawning 772.1 *borrowing;* 759.1 *exchange*
pawn in the game 124.10 *nonentity*
pawnshop 783.4 *bank;* 759.2 *place of exchange*
pawnshop's three balls 743.3 *means of identification*
pawn ticket 756.2 *guarantee;* 253.2 *promise;* 759.3 *something in exchange*
paw the ground 624.11 *be angry;* 742.11 *gesture*
Pax 10.9 *prayer*
Pax Americana 589.1 *peace*
Pax Britannica 589.1 *peace*
Pax Romana 589.1 *peace*
pay 785.3; **785.6**; **813.11**; 780.26 *bank;* 237.10 *benefit;* 765.13 *be profitable;* 765.4 *earnings;* 787.1 *expend;* 768.5 *give;* 788.3 *income;* 483.5 *positive stimulus;* 788.7 *receive;* 813.4 *reward for service;* 769.2 *something received*
payable 785.17
payable on demand 785.17 *payable*
pay a call 560.15 *excrete*
pay a compliment 669.15 *compliment*
pay addresses to 569.14 *seek the friendship of*
pay a dividend 765.13 *be profitable*
pay an exorbitant price 785.6 *pay*
pay a pretty penny 792.11 *overpay*
pay a salary 785.11 *remunerate*
pay as you earn 790.7 *tax*
pay attention to 471.10 *be attentive;* 665.10 *be careful;* 471.14 *be solicitous;* 550.33 *fix;* 504.15 *hear*
pay a visit 654.12 *visit*
pay back 785.10; 807.5 *atone;* 775.5 *compensate;* 813.11 *pay;* 814.2 *penalize;* 393.3 *restore;* 785.13 *retaliate*
pay back taxes 775.5 *compensate*
pay by cashier's check 785.6 *pay*
pay by cheque 785.6 *pay;* 777.1 *purchase*
pay by credit card 777.1 *purchase*
pay by standing order 785.6 *pay*
pay cash 785.6 *pay*
pay cash for 777.1 *purchase*
pay cheque 765.4 *earnings;* 785.3 *pay*
pay commission 785.11 *remunerate*
pay conscious money 775.5 *compensate*
pay court to 593.26 *court;* 664.9 *fawn;* 569.14 *seek the friendship of*
pay damages 775.5 *compensate*
pay dearly 792.11 *overpay;* 785.6 *pay*
pay differential 15.2 *industrial negotiations*
pay dividends 246.8 *be effective;* 765.14 *profit*
pay double indemnity 775.5 *compensate*
payee 769.5 *recipient*
payer 785.5; 780.18 *treasurer*
pay for 777.5, 785.8 *defray;* 787.3 *donate;* 785.6 *pay;* 777.1 *purchase;* 413.13 *support financially*
pay freeze 251.2 *economic restraint*
pay homage 797.18 *be good;* 387.8 *be subject to;* 658.13 *defer to;* 663.6 *show obeisance to;* 9.7 *worship*
pay in advance 785.6 *pay;* 253.15 *reserve*
pay increase 765.2 *augmentation;* 483.5 *positive stimulus*
pay increases 13.6 *economic factors*
pay in full 785.7 *pay off*
paying 785.15; 562.5 *fertile;* 765.15 *gainful;* 785.1 *payment;* 356.11 *productive;* 237.4 *profitable;* 246.14, 813.15 *rewarding*
paying back 775.2 *compensation*
paying for 785.1 *payment*
paying guest 564.3 *householder;* 763.5 *possessor*
paying in return 785.20
paying off 783.1 *credit;* 785.1 *payment*
paying out 785.1 *payment*
pay in kind 759.5 *exchange;* 785.6 *pay;* 110.7 *reciprocate*
pay interest 784.7 *be in debt;* 765.13 *be profitable*
pay lip service 700.26 *be a hypocrite*
payload 322.1 *aviation;* 406.2 *load;* 29.35 *rocketry;* 319.2 *thing transported;* 316.10 *transferred thing*
paymaster 789.6 *accountant;* 780.17 *financier;* 785.5 *payer;* 780.18 *treasurer*
Payment 785
payment 785.1; 807.1 *atonement;* 787.4 *expenditure;* 780.6 *funds;* 768.2 *gift;* 814.8 *penalty;* 483.5 *positive stimulus;* 813.4 *reward for service*
payment in kind 110.1 *interchange;* 785.1 *payment;* 813.4 *reward for service;* 776.4 *trade*
payment-in-lieu 785.3 *pay;* 785.2 *repayment*
payment refused 784.5 *amount owing*
payments and receipts 789.1 *accounts*
Payne's grey 533.4 *greyness*
pay no attention 662.15 *be disobedient;* 472.12 *be inattentive*
pay no heed to 472.12 *be inattentive*
payoff 345.1 *effect;* 131.12 *end result;* 785.4 *grant;* 785.3 *pay;* 785.1 *payment;* 813.4 *reward for service;* 813.8 *secret money;* 289.9 *sequel*
pay off 785.7; 246.8 *be effective;* 237.10 *benefit;* 777.4 *buy off;* 323.9 *navigate;* 813.11 *pay;* 788.7 *receive;* 785.11 *remunerate;* 785.13 *retaliate;* 385.4 *serve one right;* 345.5 *show an effect;* 350.7 *stop work*
pay off a debt 391.4 *liberate*
pay off a loan 775.5 *compensate*
pay off a mortgage 391.4 *liberate*
pay off old scores 385.3, 785.13 *retaliate*

payola 785.4 *grant*
pay on call 785.6 *pay*
pay on delivery 785.6 *pay*
pay on demand 785.6 *pay*
pay one back 385.3 *retaliate*
pay one out 385.3 *retaliate*
pay one's dues 807.5 *atone*
pay one's last respects 583.8 *bury*
pay one's respects 601.16 *commemorate*; 667.18 *show respect*; 627.9 *sorrow*
pay one's share 768.6 *give to charity*; 785.9 *pay one's way*
pay one's way 785.9
pay one's whack 768.5 *give*
pay on sight 785.6 *pay*
pay on the dot 785.6 *pay*
pay on the nail 785.6 *pay*
pay on the spot 777.1 *purchase*
payout 785.3 *pay*; 785.1 *payment*
pay out 787.1 *expend*; 785.6 *pay*; 50.15 *sail*
pay packet 765.4 *earnings*; 785.3 *pay*
payphone 692.9 *telephone*
pay respect 667.18 *show respect*
pay respects 367.9 *bow*; 658.13 *defer to*; 600.6 *fête*
payroll 220.6 *list of names*; 785.3 *pay*; 578.4 *personnel*
pay slip 785.3 *pay*
pay station 692.9 *telephone*
pay taxes 768.5 *give*
pay television 692.21 *television*
pay the forfeit 807.5 *atone*
pay the freight 785.8 *defray*
pay the penalty 807.5 *atone*
pay the piper 785.8 *defray*
pay the ultimate price 814.6 *be punished*
pay through the nose 792.11 *overpay*; 785.6 *pay*
pay too much 792.11 *overpay*
pay towards 679.10 *be generous*; 768.5 *give*
pay tribute to 671.6 *be grateful*; 387.8 *be subject to*; 462.14 *commemorate*; 669.15 *compliment*; 601.17 *congratulate*; 768.5 *give*; 813.9 *reward*; 663.6 *show obeisance to*; 667.18 *show respect*
pay tribute to mammon 781.14 *seek riches*
pay under the table 480.17 *bribe*; 813.11 *pay*
pay up 785.7 *pay off*; 789.9 *settle accounts*
pay wages 785.11 *remunerate*
pay well 765.13 *be profitable*
p-block 32.6 *chemical element*
pbow 496.7 *tobacco*
PBS 692.24 *television broadcasting*
PC 40.3 *computer*; 252.3 *protector*
PCP 691.6 *drug*
p.d.q. 262.6 *hastily*; 332.14 *swiftly*
PE 576.5 *exercise*; 6.3 *subject*
pea 181.3 *round thing*
peabody 22.2 *dance*
peabrain 457.3 *unintelligent person*
Peace 589
peace 589.1; 750.1 *accord*; 263.1 *ease*; 407.8 *harmony*; 506.6 *hush!*; 301.2 *repose*; 506.4 *silence*; 580.2 *time off*
peace! 589.9
peaceable 407.17 *disciplined*; 569.8 *friendly*; 685.6 *moderate*; 589.7 *peaceful*
peaceable kingdom 589.1 *peace*
peaceableness 589.1 *peace*
peaceably 569.17 *in friendship*; 589.8 *peacefully*
peace advocate 244.12 *reformer*
peace agreement 589.1 *peace*
peace and quiet 263.1 *ease*; 407.8 *harmony*; 589.1 *peace*
peace at any price 749.1 *pacification*; 589.1 *peace*; 388.1 *submission*
peace be with you 589.9 *peace!*
peace camp 749.1 *pacification*; 589.1 *peace*
peace conference 748.5 *conference*
Peace Corps 589.2 *symbol of peace*; 752.8 *volunteer*
peaceful 589.7; 263.4 *at ease*; 407.16 *harmonious*; 339.5 *inert*; 685.6 *moderate*; 301.6 *quiescent*; 506.3 *silent*; 421.3 *soothing*; 388.5 *submitting*
peaceful approach 749.2 *peace offering*
peacefully 589.8; 339.7 *inertly*; 301.10 *motionlessly*; 749.7 *pacifically*; 506.5 *silently*; 421.15 *soothingly*; 263.6 *with ease*
peacefulness 339.1 *inertness*; 589.1 *peace*; 301.2 *repose*; 421.7 *smoothness*
peaceful protest 753.3 *gesture of protest*
peace in our time 749.1 *pacification*; 589.1 *peace*
peacekeeper 589.3 *pacifist*
peacelike 589.7 *peaceful*
peace-lover 589.3 *pacifist*
peace-loving 749.6 *pacificatory*; 589.7 *peaceful*
peacemaker 755.4 *contractor*; 748.3 *mediator*; 685.2 *moderator*; 589.3, 749.3 *pacifist*; 748.4 *representative*
peacemaking 749.1 *pacification*; 749.6 *pacificatory*; 589.1 *peace*; 589.7 *peaceful*
peacemonger 589.3 *pacifist*
peace movement 749.1 *pacification*; 589.1 *peace*; 244.11 *reformism*
peace negotiator 589.3, 749.3 *pacifist*
peacenik 589.3 *pacifist*; 244.12 *reformer*
peace offering 749.2; 807.2 *apology*; 752.6, 768.3 *offering*; 589.1 *peace*
peace of mind 4.3 *detachment*; 589.1 *peace*; 609.1 *satisfaction*
peace overture 749.2 *peace offering*
peace party 589.1 *peace*
peace pipe 589.1 *peace*; 749.2 *peace offering*; 589.2 *symbol of peace*
peace proposal 589.1 *peace*
peace protester 749.3 *pacifist*
peace sign 589.2 *symbol of peace*
peace talks 589.1 *peace*
peacetime 589.1 *peace*; 589.7 *peaceful*
peace treaty 755.3 *alliance*; 749.1 *pacification*; 589.1 *peace*
peace with honour 645.1 *cunning*
peach 739.7 *betray*; 797.17 *good thing*; 693.13 *inform on*; 536.1 *orange*; 536.3 *orange thing*; 535.7 *red thing*
peach cobbler 25.36 *cake*
peach-coloured 535.1 *red*
peacher 739.4 *discloser*
peachiness 404.2 *grain*
peachlike 421.1 *smooth*
peach melba 25.35 *dessert*
peachy 545.6 *personable*; 235.1 *worthy*
peacock 738.12 *displayer*; 72.10 *male bird*; 622.13 *proud person*; 673.7 *vain person*; 541.5 *variegated thing*
peacock blue 539.1 *blue*
peacock feather 475.7 *bad-luck sign*
peacockish 673.13 *boastful*
peacock's tail 541.5 *variegated thing*
pea crab 75.4 *arthropod*
pea family 77.3 *seed plant*
pea-green 538.1 *green*
peahen 72.11 *female bird*
pea jacket 551.12 *coat*
peak 425.14 *be sharp*; 121.8 *be superior*; 260.24 *be unhealthy*; 91.10 *billow*; 232.1 *completeness*; 154.2 *heights*; 131.7 *limit*; 530.5 *lose colour*; 89.1 *mountain*; 151.8 *narrow thing*; 230.3 *perfection*; 243.14 *preparedness*; 185.2 *projection*; 154.16 *rise*; 62.5 *rock face*; 425.8 *sharp-pointed thing*; 121.4, 174.1 *summit*; 174.7 *top*; 91.3 *wave*
Peak District 89.5 *British mountains*
peaked 530.8 *drained of colour*; 153.2 *emaciated*; 151.3 *tapered*; 260.21 *unhealthy*
peakish 530.8 *drained of colour*
peak load 39.34 *power supply*
peak of perfection 230.3 *perfection*
peaky 530.8 *drained of colour*; 260.22 *sick*; 260.21 *unhealthy*
peal 508.1, 508.5 *bang*; 507.8 *be loud*; 18.6 *campanology*; 507.1 *loudness*; 509.12, 510.10 *ring*; 510.2 *ringing*
pealing 509.18; 507.6 *loud*; 509.5, 510.7 *ringing*
pea moth 44.12 *pests and diseases*
pean 743.8 *heraldic device*
peanut butter 691.6 *drug*
peanut gallery 21.18 *auditorium*
peanuts 780.4 *change*; 43.12 *crop*; 80.5 *figurative usage*; 25.10 *snack*; 124.8 *trifle*
peanut worm 75.6 *worm*
pearl 545.3 *attractive female*; 531.9 *white thing*
pearl bulb 522.6 *electric light*
pearl-grey 533.1 *grey*
Pearl Harbor 382.15 *slaughterhouse*
pearlies 551.3 *formal dress*
pearliness 527.7 *semitransparency*; 541.1 *variegation*; 531.7 *whiteness*
pearlized 522.17 *lustrous*
pearl of price 235.8 *exceller*
pearls 425.11 *tooth*
pearls of wisdom 713.1 *advice*
pearly 533.1 *grey*; 541.7 *iridescent*; 522.17 *lustrous*; 527.3 *semitransparent*; 529.13 *soft-hued*; 531.1 *white*
pear shape 181.2 *round body*
pear-shaped 177.5, 181.10 *well-rounded*
peas 43.12 *crop*
peasant 43.19 *agricultural*; 564.5 *countryman*; 574.1 *plebeian*
peasant farmer 43.15 *agriculturist*
pease pudding 25.34 *vegetarian dish*
peashooter 330.9 *firearm*
pea soup 31.33 *fog*
peasouper 31.33 *fog*; 524.2 *murk*; 528.7 *opaque thing*; 521.6 *that which makes invisible*
peastick 44.6 *garden tool*
peat 44.7 *fertilizer*; 284.10 *fossilization*; 330.13, 437.1 *fuel*
peat bog 437.1 *fuel*; 92.3 *marsh*
peat-brown 534.1 *brown*
peat cutter 437.9 *power-worker*
peat moss 437.1 *fuel*; 82.3 *moss*
pea viner 43.10 *farm tool*
pebble 418.7 *hard substance*
pebbled 92.11 *continental*; 427.17 *grainy*
pebble-dash 550.28 *face*; 550.8 *wall covering*
pebble glasses 518.10 *visual aid*
pebble hand-axe 438.4 *prehistoric tool*
pebbles 92.4 *coast*; 30.27 *sediment*
pebbly 30.58 *earthy*; 427.17 *grainy*; 418.1 *hard*
pecan pie 25.36 *cake*
peccability 231.5 *imperfection*; 804.1 *wickedness*
peccable 231.1 *imperfect*
peccadillo 231.5 *imperfection*; 247.3 *personal fault*; 806.3 *sin*; 124.8 *trifle*; 804.3 *venial sin*
peccancy 806.1 *guilt*; 236.10 *poverty*
peccant 260.23 *diseased*; 806.5 *guilty*; 236.4 *poor*
peck 331.13 *blow*; 593.14 *communication of love*; 557.21 *eat*; 72.24 *nest*; 331.6 *tap*
peck at 557.23 *taste*
pecker 557.18 *eater*; 561.8 *organs of reproduction*
pecking 557.3 *delicate eating*
pecking order 407.3 *hierarchy*; 137.5 *social class*; 289.1 *succession*
peckings 557.7 *food*
peckish 617.10 *hungry*
peck on the cheek 569.4 *act of friendship*; 593.14 *communication of love*; 654.9 *welcome*
pecks 182.2 *bulge*
Pecksniff 699.19 *cheat*; 700.19 *hypocrite*
Pecksniffery 699.3, 700.3 *hypocrisy*
Pecksniffian 699.31, 700.37 *hypocritical*
pectic substance 33.4 *polysaccharide*
pectin 33.4 *polysaccharide*; 359.2 *preserver*
pectinate 425.4 *toothed*
pectoral 182.2 *bulge*
pectoral fin 74.5 *fish anatomy*
pectorals 336.1 *strength*
peculation 351.2 *misuse*
peculator 774.11 *dishonest person*
peculiar 99.9, 139.16 *characteristic*; 116.4 *dissimilar*; 118.14 *eccentric*; 461.11 *insane*; 630.8 *surprising*; 137.11 *typical*; 299.5 *unusual*; 619.8 *wonderful*
peculiarity 139.3 *characteristic*; 139.6 *exception*; 118.5 *idiosyncrasy*; 724.1 *style*; 118.4, 299.2 *unusualness*; 642.3 *whim*
peculiarly 139.30 *characteristically*; 116.7 *dissimilarly*; 118.21 *unconformably*; 299.9 *unusually*
peculiar trait 118.5 *idiosyncrasy*
pecuniary 13.13 *economic*; 780.22 *monetary*
pecuniary assistance 413.7 *financial support*
pecuniously 780.28 *financially*
pedagogical 6.16 *educational*
pedagogically 6.25 *educationally*
pedagogue 400.9 *educational leader*; 6.4 *educator*
pedagogy 6.1 *education*
pedal 320.11 *bicycle part*; 330.20 *propel*; 330.11 *propeller*; 438.1 *tool*
pedalfer 30.36 *soil*
pedal note 510.3 *deepness*
pedal point 18.16 *musical note*
pedal power 334.4 *energy*
pedal pushers 551.9 *trousers*
pedal wheel 24.6 *ceramic workshop*
pedant 273.4 *accurate person*; 665.6 *careful person*; 117.6 *conformist*; 466.6 *discriminating person*; 455.6 *knowledgeable person*; 641.8 *obstinate person*; 230.4 *perfectionist*; 647.4 *strict person*
pedantic 698.24; 273.5 *accurate*; 665.9 *careful*; 117.14 *conformist*; 471.8 *diligent*; 466.9 *discriminating*; 656.6 *formal*; 455.9 *literate*; 542.10 *ornate*; 230.2 *perfectionist*; 641.4 *set*; 647.8 *severe*; 264.14 *troublesome*; 465.8 *unjust*
pedantically 471.15 *attentively*; 466.16 *judiciously*; 455.15 *knowledgeably*; 698.38 *literally*; 542.13 *ornately*; 647.11 *severely*
pedantry 698.11; 273.1 *accuracy*; 471.4 *diligence*; 665.4 *fastidiousness*; 656.2 *formalism*; 647.1 *severity*
peddle 767.11 *dispose of property*; 778.1 *sell*; 776.1 *trade*
peddler 778.11 *pedlar*
peddling 778.3 *selling*; 124.4 *trivial*
pederast 796.10 *sex offender*
pederasty 796.7 *sexual assault*
pedestal 20.8 *column*; 175.2 *foot*; 413.2 *supporting part*
pedestal table 23.4 *table*
pedestrian 620.4 *boring*; 138.21 *common*; 216.3 *mediocre*
pedestrian bridge 38.21 *bridge*
pedestrian crossing 320.3 *carriageway*; 317.5 *crossing*; 318.5 *crossing point*; 252.5 *refuge*
pedestrianism 300.1 *motion*
pedestrian lights 522.6 *electric light*
pedestrian precinct 779.7 *emporium*
pedicel 77.5 *stem*
pediculicide 37.4 *drug type*
pediculosis 258.2 *uncleanness*
pediculous 258.8 *unclean*
pedicure 547.3 *beauty treatment*
pedicurist 547.13 *beautician*; 394.15 *healer*
pedigree 59.13 *breeding*; 137.8, 284.12 *genealogy*; 132.3 *line*; 573.3 *nobleness*; 255.7 *purebred*
pedigreed 255.13 *pure*
pediment 174.3 *architectural summit*
pedlar 778.11
pedocal 30.36 *soil*
pedological 30.48 *geological*
pedologist 30.3 *geologist*
pedology 30.1 *earth science*
pedometer 26.8 *meter*
Pedrolino 21.32 *clown*
peduncle 77.5 *stem*
pee 431.3 *body fluid*; 433.4 *exudate*; 608.13 *relieve oneself*; 433.32 *seep*; 560.17 *urinate*; 560.3 *urination*; 560.6 *urine*
peek 518.6, 518.13 *look*
peel 552.16; 550.13 *casing*; 411.3 *coat*; 493.16 *feel hot*; 80.3 *fruit structure*; 552.15 *make nude*; 238.6 *refuse*; 215.2 *residue*; 411.11 *scale*; 372.10 *set apart*; 212.4 *take off*
peeled 552.11 *exposed*; 552.12 *peeling*
peeler 552.8 *nude person*
peeling 552.6; **552.12**; 493.5 *hot weather*; 64.6 *rugger*
peeling off 61.6 *motor-racing terms*; 64.3 *rugby play*
peelings 205.8 *bits and pieces*; 215.2 *residue*
peel off 268.17 *liquefy*; 58.9 *play hockey*; 64.5 *play rugby*; 61.9 *race*; 411.11 *scale*; 552.14 *undress*
peel-off 58.8 *hockey*; 58.3 *ice hockey*
peen 331.15 *ram*
pee oneself 560.17 *urinate*
peep 525.12 *become visible*; 72.18 *bird song*; 518.6, 518.13 *look*; 72.26, 515.5 *sing*
pee-pee 560.17 *urinate*; 560.6 *urine*
peepers 518.2 *eye*
peephole 308.5 *hole*; 518.9 *viewpoint*
Peeping Tom 644.4 *meddler*; 518.11 *observer*
peep out 525.12 *become visible*
peepshow 21.7 *show*; 518.7 *view*
peep sight 518.10 *visual aid*
peer 119.5 *equal*; 573.1 *nobleman*; 579.16 *official*; 12.8 *politician*
peerage 573.2 *aristocracy*; 813.1 *reward*
peerer 518.11 *observer*
peer group 285.5 *contemporary*; 376.17 *family*; 376.18 *generation*; 654.7 *human society*; 2.6 *social group*
peering 518.3 *observation*
peerless 121.14, 235.2, 797.2 *best*; 116.4 *dissimilar*; 230.1 *perfect*; 99.8 *quintessential*
peerlessly 121.17 *supremely*; 797.22 *well*

peeve 607.8 *annoy;* 625.8 *make irascible*
peeved 624.15 *resentful*
peevish 701.8 *argumentative;* 659.5 *discourteous;* 625.4 *irascible;* 626.7 *irritable*
peevishly 659.9 *discourteously;* 625.9 *irascibly;* 626.14 *irritably*
peevishness 625.1 *irascibility;* 626.3 *irritableness;* 624.1 *resentment*
peewee 555.9 *child;* 159.4 *little person;* 149.5 *short person*
peg 62.4 *climbing equipment;* 373.11 *connect;* 373.8 *fastening;* 209.3 *gradation;* 361.4 *hanger;* 209.5 *measure;* 62.8 *mountaineering;* 309.2 *stopper;* 330.5, 330.23 *throw;* 438.1 *tool*
Pegasus 59.1 *horse;* 70.7 *legendary beast;* 17.13 *poetic genius*
peg away 333.1 *move slowly;* 640.6 *persevere;* 134.4 *protract;* 576.6 *work*
pegboard 738.8 *showplace*
pegged 373.15 *connected*
pegged pants 551.9 *trousers*
pegged trousers 551.9 *trousers*
peg hammer 62.4 *climbing equipment*
peg it 582.15 *die*
pegmatite 30.34 *mineral;* 24.2 *raw material*
peg out 582.15 *die;* 428.23 *drip-dry*
peg top 307.6 *rotator*
peignoir 657.6 *informal dress;* 551.16 *robe*
peine forte et dure 814.15 *instrument of torture*
pejorate 124.12 *think unimportant*
pejorative 668.13 *contemptuous;* 678.15 *disparaging;* 668.11 *insulting;* 5.17 *word;* 5.42 *worded*
pejoratively 678.18 *disparagingly;* 5.50 *lexically*
Peking duck 25.48 *Chinese dish*
Peking man 296.7 *ancient people;* 566.3 *early human;* 284.6 *people of the past*
pekoe 558.3 *tea*
pelage 71.2 *mammalian characteristic*
pelagian 91.7 *oceanic*
pelagic 30.51, 91.7 *oceanic;* 70.15 *of animals*
pelagic ooze 30.27 *sediment*
p-electron 28.65 *atom*
pelf 780.2 *cash;* 781.6 *money;* 765.5 *profit*
pelican 72.3 *water bird*
pelican crossing 320.3 *carriageway;* 317.5 *crossing;* 318.5 *crossing point;* 252.5 *refuge*
pellagra 260.4 *disease;* 557.10 *scarcity*
pellet 587.13 *ammunition;* 37.12 *injection;* 330.8 *missile;* 587.5 *missile weapon;* 181.3 *round thing*
pellicle 411.3 *coat*
pellicular 411.9 *platelike*
pell-mell 408.28 *anyhow;* 262.6 *hastily*
pellucid 725.3 *clear;* 695.2 *simple;* 527.1 *transparent*
pellucidity 725.1 *clarity;* 695.10 *simplicity;* 527.5 *transparency*
pellucidly 725.4 *clearly;* 527.13 *transparently*
pellucidness 527.5 *transparency*
pelt 550.14 *animal covering;* 331.13 *blow;* 331.3 *hit;* 31.62 *rain;* 330.29 *riddle;* 381.7 *stone;* 330.23 *throw*
peltate 77.18 *of leaves*
pelting 31.53 *rainy;* 332.1 *swift;* 330.3 *throwing*
pelt with rotten eggs 670.23 *show disapproval*
pelvic fin 74.5 *fish anatomy*
Pembroke table 23.4 *table*
pemmican 557.7 *food*
pen 71.20 *abode of mammals;* 19.11 *artist's materials;* 309.4 *closed place;* 165.5, 309.10 *enclose;* 165.2 *enclosed place;* 43.7 *farm building;* 568.14 *female animal;* 72.11 *female bird;* 655.4 *place of confinement;* 43.18 *practise livestock farming;* 815.2 *the inside*
penal 814.19 *punitive*
penal code 814.18 *penology;* 713.3 *precept;* 16.1 *the law*
penal colony 655.4 *place of confinement;* 814.7 *punishment*
penal institution 655.4 *place of confinement*
penalization 814.7 *punishment*
penalize **814.2**; 240.5 *be inconvenient*
penalizing 814.19 *punitive*
penally 814.23 *punitively*
penal servitude 814.7 *punishment*
penal settlement 655.4 *place of confinement*
penalties **49.5**
penalty **46.13**; **814.8**; 775.2 *compensation;* 66.2 *football play;* 785.4 *grant;* 59.7 *horseracing;* 790.8 *levy;* 766.1 *loss;* 251.1 *restraint;* 64.3 *rugby play;* 576.1 *work*
penalty area 66.1 *soccer*
penalty award 58.1 *hockey;* 58.3 *ice hockey;* 58.5 *lacrosse*
penalty box 58.3 *ice hockey*
penalty clause 386.3 *coercive methods*
penalty corner 58.1 *hockey*
penalty flag 46.13 *penalty*
penalty goal 64.3 *rugby play*
penalty kick 331.13 *blow;* 331.7 *kick;* 64.3 *rugby play*
penalty marker 46.13 *penalty*
penalty play 58.5 *lacrosse*
penalty plays 58.1 *hockey;* 58.3 *ice hockey*
penalty shot 58.3 *ice hockey;* 49.4 *playing terms*
penalty spot 58.1 *hockey;* 66.1 *soccer*
penalty stroke 56.3 *golf shots;* 58.1 *hockey*
penalty try 64.3 *rugby play*
penal work 576.1 *work*
penance **814.11**; 807.2 *apology;* 10.5 *Christian rite*
pen-and-ink 19.9 *drawing*
pen-and-ink sketch **530.3**
penchant 229.2 *attitude;* 617.1 *desire;* 595.2 *inclination*
pencil 19.11 *artist's materials;* 19.20 *draw*
pencil drawing 19.9 *drawing*
pencil of light 28.24 *light emission*
pencil point 425.7 *sharp point*
pencil sharpener 425.12 *sharpener*
pendant 115.5 *counterpart;* 361.3 *suspended object*
pendency 361.1 *suspension*
pendent 361.7 *suspended*
pendente lite 16.87 *in litigation*
pendentive 20.14 *roofed;* 20.17 *structured*
pendentive dome 20.6 *roof*
pendently 361.13 *pendulously*
pending 226.10 *finished;* 283.11 *future;* 361.9 *interrupted;* 275.21 *lasting through time;* 339.6 *suspended*
Pendleton Round Up 59.12 *rodeo*
pendular motion 326.1 *oscillation*
pendulate 326.8 *oscillate*
pendulation 326.1 *oscillation*
pendule 62.3 *climbing technique*
pendulous 361.7 *suspended*
pendulously **361.13**
pendulousness 361.1 *suspension*
pendulum 62.3 *climbing technique;* 28.87 *clock;* 326.7 *oscillator;* 298.5 *regular thing;* 361.3 *suspended object*
pendulum movement 298.1 *regularity*
pendulum wheel 326.7 *oscillator*
Penelope's web 238.5 *waste of effort*
penetrability 695.9 *intelligibility*
penetrable 695.1 *intelligible*
penetrate 412.10 *become mixed;* 695.4 *be intelligible;* 97.11 *be present;* 726.6 *emphasize;* 318.10 *enter;* 308.20 *hole;* 314.11 *infiltrate;* 368.2 *inject;* 46.16 *play defence;* 695.6 *understand*
penetrated 308.14 *holed*
penetrating **318.13**; 726.3 *emphatic;* 651.14 *hostile;* 314.16 *invasive;* 97.7 *present;* 513.7 *strident*
penetrating eye 518.2 *eye*
penetration 46.10 *defence;* 726.1 *emphasis;* 368.9 *injection;* 314.3 *inroad;* 412.1 *mixture;* 318.3 *passage into;* 156.3 *profundity;* 458.1 *wisdom*
pen friend 692.5 *correspondent*
penguin 72.2 *flightless bird*
penicillin 394.8 *drug;* 37.4 *drug type;* 83.6 *fungal antibiotic*
penile 561.16 *reproductive*
peninsula **92.5**; 30.11 *coast;* 151.6 *narrow place;* 185.2 *projection;* 86.1 *region*
peninsular 92.11 *continental;* 86.16 *regional*
penis 561.8 *organs of reproduction*
penitence **808.1**; 807.2 *apology;* 244.5 *improvement;* 10.3 *rite of worship;* 806.2 *signs of guilt;* 9.1 *worship*
penitent **808.6**; 807.3 *atoner;* 807.4 *atoning;* 808.3 *penitent person;* 9.9 *worshipful;* 9.5, 10.17 *worshipper*
penitential **808.7**; 807.4 *atoning;* 10.21 *ritualistic*
penitential act 807.2 *apology*
penitential exercise 807.2 *apology*
penitentially 808.8 *penitently;* 9.12 *worshipfully*
penitential rites 10.5 *Christian rite*
penitentiary 807.4 *atoning;* 808.7 *penitential;* 655.4 *place of confinement*
penitently **807.8**; **808.8**
penitent person **808.3**
penknife 425.10 *knife*
penman 17.14 *author*
pen name 737.8 *anonymity;* 736.7 *concealer;* 721.8 *name*
pennant 743.7 *flag;* 50.3 *parts of a sailing boat*
pennant winner 48.1 *baseball*
penned 165.7 *enclosed;* 360.10 *retained*
penniless 135.5 *necessitous;* 782.1 *poor;* 249.7 *unprosperous*
pennilessness 782.5 *poverty*
Pennines 89.5 *British mountains*
pennon 743.7 *flag*
penny 780.8 *American money;* 780.9 *British money;* 780.10 *former British money*
penny dreadful 17.2 *fiction*
penny-farthing 320.12 *bicycle*
penny-pincher 793.8 *bargain hunter;* 376.36 *hoarder;* 682.5 *miser*
penny-pinching 682.1 *mean*
pennyweight 414.9 *avoirdupois weight*
penny whistle 513.3 *shrillness*
penny-wise 682.1 *mean*
penological 814.19 *punitive*
penologically 814.23 *punitively*
penologist 814.18 *penology*
penology **814.18**; 16.37 *criminology*
pen pal 692.5 *correspondent*
pen pusher 721.10 *descriptive writer*
pensile 361.7 *suspended*
pensileness 361.1 *suspension*
pension 765.4 *earnings;* 413.7 *financial support;* 768.2 *gift*
pension 565.10 *hotel*
pension 788.3 *income;* 13.8 *industrial relations;* 785.3 *pay;* 14.4 *personal finance;* 813.4 *reward for service;* 392.4 *social assistance;* 769.2 *something received;* 413.13 *support financially;* 650.3 *welfare*
pensionable age 556.5 *old age*
pensionary 768.7 *given;* 769.14 *receivable*
pensioned 769.11 *receiving;* 605.7 *resigning*
pensioned-off 769.11 *receiving;* 605.7 *resigning*
pensioner 556.7 *older person;* 769.5 *recipient;* 605.3 *resigner*
pensioners 296.2 *old people*
pension fund 788.3 *income*
pension off 371.2, 767.10 *dismiss;* 350.7 *stop work*
pension programme 15.2 *industrial negotiations*
pensive 443.9 *concentrating;* 643.1 *solemn;* 4.17 *thoughtful*
pensively 4.28 *thoughtfully*
pensiveness 443.3 *thoughtfulness*
pent 151.1 *narrow*
pentachord 201.1 *five*
pentacle 201.1 *five;* 27.44 *polygon*
pentadic 201.12 *fifth*
pentagon 176.3 *angled figure;* 201.1 *five;* 27.44 *polygon*
pentagonal 176.9 *angled;* 201.12 *fifth;* 27.82 *polygonal*
Pentagonese 479.5 *equivocalness;* 5.20 *jargon word*
pentagram 201.1 *five;* 27.44 *polygon;* 11.5 *spell*
pentahedral 201.12 *fifth*
pentahedron 201.1 *five;* 27.46 *polyhedron*
pentahydrate 32.10 *salt*
pentameter 201.1 *five;* 17.9 *metre*
pentangle 27.44 *polygon*
pentangular 201.12 *fifth*
pentaprism 41.17 *lens*
pentarchy 201.1 *five*
pentastich 201.1 *five;* 17.8 *part of poem*
pentastomid 75.4 *arthropod*
Pentastomida 75.4 *arthropod*
Pentateuch 201.1 *five;* 16.1 *the law*
pentathlete 47.3 *athlete*
pentathlon 47.2 *field events;* 201.1 *five*
pentatonic 201.12 *fifth*
pentavalent 32.35 *combined*
penthouse 174.3 *architectural summit;* 154.8 *high thing;* 565.5 *house;* 440.1 *property*
pentode 39.20 *electron tube*
pentose 33.3 *carbohydrate*
pentothal interview 36.3 *psychiatric treatment*
pent-up 165.7 *enclosed;* 151.1 *narrow;* 251.14 *self-restrained*
penumbra 524.1 *dimness;* 28.24 *light emission*
pen up 165.5 *enclose*
penurious 682.1 *mean;* 782.1 *poor;* 249.7 *unprosperous*
penuriously 782.15 *poorly*
penury 782.5 *poverty*
peon 586.17 *army person;* 401.5 *office assistant;* 387.5 *subjected person;* 664.3 *sycophant*
peonage 664.1 *servility;* 387.1 *subjection*
peony 535.7 *red thing*
people 216.7 *average person;* 376.17 *family;* 566.9 *group;* 566.1 *humankind;* 565.17 *inhabit;* 564.2 *inhabitants;* 566.11 *nation;* 564.15 *settle;* 1.7 *society*
people at large 564.2 *inhabitants*
people mover 320.4 *personal transport*
people of antiquity 284.6 *people of the past*
people of the past **284.6**
people of today 285.5 *contemporary*
people's choice 12.1 *government*
peoples of the earth 566.1 *humankind*
People's Party 12.6 *political party*
people's republic 85.1 *country;* 86.4 *territorial division*
PEP 14.4 *personal finance*
pep 342.4 *energy;* 338.1 *vigour;* 334.3 *vitality*
pepe supi 25.53 *African dish*
peplum 551.24 *part of garment*
pepo 80.2 *botanical fruit*
pepper 25.7 *basic ingredient;* 381.2 *fire;* 330.29 *riddle;* 496.12 *season;* 496.2 *seasoning;* 377.18 *sprinkle;* 541.11 *variegate;* 338.1 *vigour*
pepper-and-salt 533.2 *grey-haired;* 541.10 *mottled;* 531.3 *white-haired*
peppercorn 496.2 *seasoning*
peppercorn rent 793.1 *cheapness*
peppered 541.10 *mottled;* 377.23 *sprinkled*
peppered with shot 308.14 *holed*
pepperiness 625.1 *irascibility*
peppering 377.4 *sprinkling*
pepper mill 427.11 *pulverizer*
peppermint 498.4 *confectionery;* 496.5 *herbs;* 25.41 *sweet*
peppermint tea 558.3 *tea*
pepper with shot 308.20 *hole*
peppery 625.4 *irascible;* 496.9 *piquant*
pep pill 691.6 *drug;* 394.7 *tonic*
peppy 726.3 *emphatic;* 338.4 *vigorous*
pep rally 480.4 *exhortation;* 46.14 *miscellaneous terms*
Pepsi ™ 558.6 *soft drink*
pepsin 416.5 *condenser;* 33.11 *enzyme*
pep squad 46.14 *miscellaneous terms*
pep talk 480.4 *exhortation;* 733.2 *salutation*
peptic 394.17 *remedial*
peptic ulcer 260.8 *indigestion*
peptidase 33.11 *enzyme*
peptide 33.8 *amino acid*
peptide bond 33.8 *amino acid*
peptidoglycan 33.9 *protein*
pep up 338.3 *invigorate;* 412.8 *mix*
per 348.9 *instrumentally*
peradventure 102.9 *possibly*
perambulation 300.1 *motion;* 318.1 *passage*
perambulator 320.8 *baby carriage*
per annum 298.16 *cyclically*
peraphrasis 17.12 *poetic language*
per capita 770.8 *proportionately*
perceivability 520.3 *visibility*
perceivable 518.23, 520.1 *visible*
perceive 445.9 *be intuitive;* 449.1 *discover;* 590.15 *feel;* 446.14 *have an idea;* 504.15 *hear;* 477.14 *imagine;* 6.24, 455.11 *know;* 444.11 *reason;* 695.7 *recognize;* 518.12 *see;* 488.11 *sense;* 442.12 *think;* 518.16 *visualize*
perceived 455.10 *known*
per cent 27.87 *mathematically;* 194.5 *ratio*
percentage 791.1 *discount;* 27.18 *divi-*

sion; 196.2 *fractional part;* 205.1 *part;* 765.5 *profit;* 194.5 *ratio*
percentile 27.74 *divisible;* 27.60 *parameter*
perceptibility 520.3 *visibility*
perceptible 449.15 *discoverable;* 26.14 *measurable;* 488.8 *sensate;* 492.8 *touchable;* 518.23, 520.1 *visible*
perceptibly 26.17 *measurably;* 492.16 *sensitively;* 518.25, 520.11 *visibly*
perception 449.6 *discovery;* 590.1 *feeling;* 446.1 *idea;* 446.8, 477.1 *imagination;* 445.1 *intuition;* 466.2 *judiciousness;* 455.1 *knowledge;* 442.1 *mind;* 444.1 *reason;* 6.11 *refinement;* 488.1 *sensation;* 695.12 *understanding;* 518.4 *visualization;* 458.1 *wisdom*
perceptive 466.9 *discriminating;* 590.10 *feeling;* 477.10 *imaginative;* 445.6 *intuitive;* 455.8 *knowledgeable;* 425.5 *mentally sharp;* 444.7 *reasoning;* 6.20 *refined;* 518.21 *seeing;* 591.1 *sensitive;* 488.7 *susceptible;* 458.5 *wise*
perceptively 6.27 *discerningly;* 446.22 *imaginatively;* 466.16 *judiciously;* 591.12 *sensitively*
perceptiveness 442.1 *mind;* 6.11 *refinement*
perceptual 446.10 *theoretical*
perceptual computing 40.17 *artificial intelligence*
perceptual concept 36.26 *gestalt*
perch 301.8 *be motionless;* 55.5 *British game fish;* 305.12 *drop;* 25.17 *freshwater fish;* 565.13 *lair;* 312.4 *land;* 72.14, 72.24 *nest;* 367.8 *sit;* 263.2 *take it easy;* 565.18 *take up residence*
perchance **107.14**; 102.9 *possibly*
perching 72.21 *avian*
perching bird 72.6 *songbird*
perching duck 72.3 *water bird*
perchlike 74.13 *fishlike*
percipience 442.1 *mind*
percipient 488.5 *sensible*
percoid 74.13 *fishlike*
percolate 370.13 *absorb;* 431.23 *dissolve;* 30.63 *ebb;* 318.10 *enter;* 314.11 *infiltrate;* 315.12 *leak;* 255.10, 256.15 *purify;* 429.16, 433.32 *seep;* 433.29 *water*
percolating 315.3 *leakage;* 318.13 *penetrating;* 429.12 *seeping*
percolation 370.5 *absorption;* 256.2 *cleaning;* 431.8 *fluidification;* 314.3 *inroad;* 315.3 *leakage;* 318.3 *passage into;* 429.4 *seepage;* 433.9 *soaking;* 30.10 *water cycle*
percolator 410.15 *pot*
percuss 331.2 *collide*
percussion 331.12 *collision;* 18.25 *musical instrument*
percussion cap 437.2 *lighter*
percussively 331.18 *dynamically*
per diem 298.16 *cyclically*
perdition 8.12 *hell;* 766.1 *loss;* 357.4 *ruin*
perdurability 277.4 *long-lastingness*
peremptoriness 707.6 *assertiveness;* 396.2 *authoritativeness*
peremptory 707.14 *assertive;* 396.12 *authoritative;* 810.12 *obligatory*
perennate 77.22 *be dormant*
perennial 44.17 *botanical;* 298.12 *cyclic;* 78.2 *flowering plant;* 44.9 *garden plant;* 77.14 *of plants;* 225.7, 277.9 *permanent;* 77.2 *plant;* 228.9 *stable*
perennially 275.30 *chronologically;* 298.16 *cyclically;* 277.12 *everlastingly;* 77.24 *herbaceously;* 44.20 *horticulturally;* 225.9 *permanently;* 228.12 *stably*
pererrate 325.3 *go astray*
pererration 325.16 *wandering*
perfect **230.1**; **230.5**; 273.5, 698.21 *accurate;* 698.31 *be accurate;* 543.4 *be elegant;* 121.14, 235.2, 797.2 *best;* 665.9 *careful;* 256.16 *clean;* 204.10, 232.4, 232.7 *complete;* 8.13 *divine;* 244.1 *improve;* 805.5 *innocent;* 255.12 *morally pure;* 78.12 *of flowers;* 359.7 *preserved;* 795.9 *pure;* 485.6 *skilful;* 5.34 *tense;* 204.7 *uncut;* 803.5 *virtuous;* 235.1 *worthy*
perfecta 59.7 *horseracing*
perfect cadence 516.4 *harmonics;* 18.13 *melody*
perfect candidate 136.8 *qualified person*
perfect condition 230.3 *perfection*
perfected 232.7 *complete;* 243.20 *developed;* 230.1 *perfect*
perfecter 230.4 *perfectionist*
perfect game 48.4 *pitching terms*
perfect gentleman 799.3 *honourable person*
perfectibility 231.5 *imperfection;* 302.15 *improvement*
perfectible 231.1 *imperfect;* 244.15 *improvable*
Perfection 230
perfection **230.3**; 698.8 *accuracy;* 232.1 *completeness;* 8.1 *divinity;* 665.4 *fastidiousness;* 244.5 *improvement;* 805.1 *innocence;* 400.11 *masterpiece;* 795.3 *moral purity;* 255.1 *purity;* 485.1 *skill;* 121.1 *superiority;* 797.9 *the best;* 803.1 *virtue;* 235.6 *worth*
perfectionism 342.8 *assiduity;* 665.4 *fastidiousness;* 244.5 *improvement;* 466.2 *judiciousness;* 244.11 *reformism;* 353.6 *venture*
perfectionist **230.2**; **230.4**; 353.7 *attempter;* 665.9 *careful;* 665.6 *careful person;* 466.9 *discriminating;* 466.6 *discriminating person;* 244.16 *improving;* 244.12 *reformer*
perfectly **230.7**; 698.39 *accurately;* 665.12 *carefully;* 232.9 *completely;* 8.19 *divinely;* 96.18, 446.23 *ideally;* 805.11 *innocently;* 121.17 *supremely;* 255.18, 803.9 *virtuously;* 797.22 *well*
perfectly dreadful 236.3 *bad*
perfect moment 287.1 *timeliness*
perfectness 230.3 *perfection*
perfect number 27.5 *number*
perfect participle 5.35 *part of speech*
perfect pitch 273.1 *accuracy;* 504.1 *hearing;* 18.21 *tone*
perfect sacrifice 48.5 *batting terms*
perfect silence 506.4 *silence*
perfect style 543.1 *elegance*
perfect touch 724.2 *stylishness*
perfect treasure 235.8 *exceller*
perfect vision 518.1 *vision*
perfect wreck 245.9 *dilapidation*
perfervid 342.18 *active*
perfidious 645.4, 702.8 *cunning;* 699.33 *deceitful;* 662.13 *disobedient;* 479.11 *equivocating;* 234.8 *exaggerated;* 800.6 *faithless;* 700.38 *treacherous;* 453.7 *unreliable*
perfidiously **479.13**; 662.17 *disobediently;* 234.14 *distortedly;* 702.15 *hypocritically*
perfidiousness 662.1 *disobedience;* 800.2 *faithlessness*
perfidy 479.7 *apostasy;* 662.1 *disobedience;* 234.4 *distortion of the truth;* 800.2 *faithlessness;* 700.4 *falseheartedness;* 699.6 *lying*
perflation 434.6 *ventilation*
perforate 308.20 *hole;* 425.16 *use a sharp tool*
perforated 308.14 *holed*
perforation 308.1 *opening*
perforator 425.8 *sharp-pointed thing;* 438.1 *tool*
perforce 386.11 *compellingly*
perform 21.34, 340.4, 717.10 *act;* 703.18 *appear;* 348.4 *be an instrument;* 346.7 *be operational;* 633.14 *carry on;* 601.16 *commemorate;* 232.4 *complete;* 703.15 *demonstrate;* 738.1 *display;* 663.5 *obey;* 525.13 *occur;* 18.36 *play;* 356.10 *produce*
performable 102.5 *possible*
perform a combined movement 57.10 *compete in gymnastics*
perform a function 237.9 *be useful*
perform a gymnastic routine 57.10 *compete in gymnastics*
perform a miracle 393.6 *cure*
performance **18.27**; 21.22, 717.3 *acting;* 340.1 *action;* 525.2 *being in view;* 601.1 *celebration;* 703.1 *demonstration;* 810.5 *discharge of duty;* 348.1 *instrumentality;* 520.5 *manifestation;* 18.2 *music making;* 346.1 *operation;* 356.1, 738.9 *production;* 518.7 *view;* 356.5 *work of art*
performance gain 765.2 *augmentation*
performance-oriented 348.6 *instrumental*
performance poetry 17.6 *poetry*
perform a somersault 57.10 *compete in gymnastics*
perform a stunt 340.4 *act*
perform better 765.10 *augment*
perform do 237.9 *be useful*
performed 21.39 *dramatic*
performer **717.5**; 703.7 *demonstrator;* 340.3 *doer;* 21.29 *entertainer;* 18.24 *musician;* 578.1 *worker*
performing 21.22, 340.5, 717.3 *acting*
performing area 21.17 *stage*
perform magic 224.8 *cause change*
perform one's ablutions 433.34 *hose*
perform rites 10.18
perform skilfully 797.19 *be good at*
perform the hajj 7.19 *be religious*
perform vivisection on 382.22 *kill animals*
perfrication 365.1 *friction*
perfume **502.6**; 432.26 *aerate;* 502.1 *fragrance;* 502.2 *fragrant thing;* 500.9 *impart odour to;* 433.14 *lavender water;* 371.14 *let out;* 547.16 *make up;* 500.1 *odour;* 547.6 *toiletries*
perfume bottle 502.2 *fragrant thing*
perfumed 502.4 *fragrant;* 500.5 *odorous;* 490.6 *pleasant*
perfume dynamics 502.1 *fragrance*
perfume oil 547.6 *toiletries*
perfumer 502.2 *fragrant thing*
perfumery 502.2 *fragrant thing*
perfume spray 502.2 *fragrant thing*
perfunctoriness 637.14 *disobedience;* 231.5 *imperfection;* 233.1 *incompleteness;* 618.1 *indifference*
perfunctory **472.11**; 486.4 *bungled;* 262.3 *hasty;* 231.2, 233.4 *incomplete;* 618.7 *indifferent*
perfuse 37.19 *administer;* 394.20 *doctor;* 368.2 *inject;* 35.20 *practise surgery;* 316.11 *transfer*
perfused 368.13 *injected*
perfusion 368.9 *injection;* 35.9, 394.12 *surgery;* 316.3 *transmission*
pergola 44.3 *ornamental garden*
perhaps 107.14 *perchance;* 102.9 *possibly*
per head 770.8 *proportionately*
perianth 78.3 *flower part*
periapt 11.6 *talisman*
pericarditis 260.10 *cardiovascular disease*
pericarp 80.3 *fruit structure*
peridotite 30.30 *igneous rock*
perigee 147.1 *nearness;* 29.35 *rocketry*
perigynous 78.12 *of flowers*
perihelion 147.1 *nearness;* 29.21 *orbit*
peril 254.5 *danger*
perilous 254.1 *dangerous;* 643.3 *important;* 453.7 *unreliable*
perilously 254.11 *dangerously;* 453.26 *unreliably*
perilousness 254.5 *danger*
perilous state 254.5 *danger*
perimeter 163.3 *edge;* 27.37 *line;* 66.1 *soccer;* 170.1 *surroundings*
perimetric 170.4 *surrounding*
perinatal 561.16 *reproductive*
period **276.1**; 770.3 *allotted task;* 32.6 *chemical element;* 298.2 *cycle;* 275.3, 277.1 *duration;* 30.41 *geological time;* 209.4 *interval;* 141.8 *intervening space;* 560.11 *menstruation;* 742.7 *punctuation;* 292.1 *season;* 372.5 *separator;* 28.8 *time;* 326.5 *wave;* 31.3 *weather*
periodic **275.22**; **276.9**; 27.85 *cyclic;* 132.12 *cyclical;* 300.17 *directional;* 133.8 *discontinuous;* 297.3 *frequent;* 112.14 *recurrent;* 298.11 *regular*
periodical **276.7**; **276.8**; 740.5 *journal;* 326.13 *oscillating;* 275.22 *periodic;* 298.11 *regular*
periodically **276.12**; 133.17 *discontinuously;* 297.1 *frequently;* 298.15 *regularly*
periodical publication 276.7 *periodical*
periodic function 27.29 *mathematical function;* 276.5 *recurrent period*
periodicity **276.6**; 132.6 *continuum;* 297.4 *frequency;* 326.1 *oscillation;* 298.1 *regularity*
periodic table 32.6 *chemical element*
period of activity 276.4
period of detention 815.4 *prison sentence*
period of work 576.2 *task*
periodontal 35.23 *dental*
periodontic 35.23 *dental*
periodontics 35.4 *dentistry*
periodontist 35.14 *dentist*
periodontologist 35.14 *dentist*
periodontology 35.4 *dentistry*
period pains 491.2 *painful condition*
peripatetic 4.11 *follower of a doctrine;* 300.16 *moving;* 4.14 *of a philosophy*
peripatetically 300.18 *in motion*
peripatetic philosophy 4.7 *school of thought*
peripatus 75.6 *worm*
peripeteia 17.3 *aspect of fiction*
peripheral **40.7**; 40.4 *computer;* 145.8 *distant;* 164.8 *edging;* 128.11 *excluded;* 100.12 *external;* 211.4 *extra;* 163.6 *outlined;* 124.3 *secondary;* 170.4 *surrounding*
peripherally 163.7 *essentially;* 100.18 *extraneously;* 164.11 *marginally*
peripherals 372.7 *separates*
périphérique 306.5 *ringroad*
periphery 145.3 *distant place;* 164.1 *edge;* 171.1 *exterior;* 100.4 *externality;* 170.1 *surroundings*
periphrasis 270.2 *circumlocution;* 189.3 *deviousness;* 5.24 *phrasing*
periphrastic 270.4 *circumlocutory;* 189.5 *devious;* 5.43 *phrasal*
periphrastically 270.8 *circuitously;* 189.9 *deviously;* 5.51 *phraseologically*
periscope 28.32 *optical instrument*
perish 494.10 *be cold;* 357.13 *be destroyed;* 245.1 *deteriorate;* 582.15 *die;* 526.1 *disappear;* 375.3 *disintegrate*
perishability 582.1 *death*
perishable 582.20 *deadly;* 278.6 *transient*
perishable goods 13.6 *economic factors;* 778.8 *merchandise*
perishables 13.6 *economic factors;* 778.8 *merchandise*
perishing 494.8 *cold;* 31.55 *cool*
perissodactyl 71.15 *hoofed mammal;* 71.33 *ungulate*
Perissodactyla 71.15 *hoofed mammal*
peristyle 20.8 *column*
periwig 551.15 *headgear*
perjorate 606.7 *be dissatisfied;* 668.19 *disrespect*
perjorative 606.4 *dissatisfied*
perjured 715.9 *perjurious*
perjured testimony 715.2 *false accusation*
perjure oneself 715.6 *accuse falsely;* 800.8 *be dishonourable*
perjurer 715.3 *accuser;* 699.17 *false person;* 699.18, 700.16 *liar*
perjuring 699.33 *deceitful*
perjurious **715.9**; 699.36 *falsified*
perjuriously 715.10 *accusingly*
perjury 736.5 *evasion;* 715.2 *false accusation;* 699.6 *lying*
perk 793.6 *absence of charge;* 211.4 *extra;* 768.2 *gift;* 750.9 *grant;* 483.5 *positive stimulus;* 765.5 *profit;* 366.3 *promote;* 813.4 *reward for service;* 769.2 *something received;* 219.3 *superfluity*
perked up 581.4 *refreshed*
perkily 598.9 *cheerfully;* 673.21 *cockily*
perkiness 673.3 *cockiness*
perking up 393.11 *recuperation;* 581.5 *refreshment*
perknite 30.30 *igneous rock*
perk up 581.2 *be refreshed;* 598.6 *bring cheer;* 366.3 *promote;* 366.1 *raise*
perky 598.1 *cheerful;* 673.11 *cocky*
perm 547.8 *haircut*
permafrost 494.6 *Arctic;* 31.36 *frost*
Permalloy™ 28.59 *ferromagnetism*
Permanence 225
permanence **225.1**; 640.3 *constancy;* 279.1 *eternity;* 277.4 *long-lastingness;* 359.1 *preservation;* 228.1 *stability*
permanency 277.4 *long-lastingness;* 225.1 *permanence*
permanent **225.7**; **277.9**; 279.8 *eternal;* 632.11 *normal;* 228.9 *stable*
permanently **225.9**; 277.12 *everlastingly;* 228.12 *stably*
permanent magenta 540.2 *purple pigment*
permanent magnet 28.60 *magnet*
permanent pasture 81.2 *grassland*
permanent post 252.1 *safety*
permanent secretary 579.16 *official*
permanent stoppage 226.2 *stop*
permanent tooth 425.11 *tooth*
permanent wave 547.8 *haircut*
permanent way 321.3 *rail*
per manus 316.18 *in transit*
permeability 28.61 *magnetic quantity*
permeability of vacuum 28.97 *fundamental constant*
permeable 315.17 *leaky*
permeate 370.13 *absorb;* 395.10 *be a prevailing influence;* 412.10 *become mixed;* 97.11 *be present;* 318.10 *enter;* 308.20 *hole;* 314.11 *infiltrate;* 433.29 *water*
permeated 632.13 *fixed;* 308.14 *holed*
permeating 318.13 *penetrating;* 97.7 *present*
permeation 147.8 *interaction;* 412.1

mixture; 97.2 *omnipresence*; 318.3 *passage into*; 429.4 *seepage*; 433.9 *soaking*
permeative 97.7 *present*
Permian period 284.3 *geological period*
permissible 669.22 *approvable*; 16.44 *legal*; 757.8 *permitting*
permissibly 757.9 *with permission*
Permission 757
permission 136.4; **396.9**; **757.1**; 669.1 *approval*; 538.15 *green light*; 16.29 *legalization*; 648.1 *leniency*; 758.4 *licence*; 750.8 *permit*; 314.4 *right of entry*
permissive 265.13 *easy-going*; 657.10 *free*; 648.4 *lenient*; 757.8 *permitting*; 250.12 *unconditional*
permissively 250.21 *excessively*; 648.6 *leniently*; 757.9 *with permission*
permissiveness 657.4 *freedom*; 648.1 *leniency*; 250.6 *liberality*; 757.1 *permission*
permissive parent 648.2 *lenient person*
permissive society 657.4 *freedom*; 250.6 *liberality*; 757.1 *permission*; 796.3 *sexual immorality*
permit 750.8; **750.29**; **757.2**; **757.3**; 397.4 *authorization*; 397.13 *authorize*; 648.3 *be lenient*; 716.6 *documentation*; 454.6 *evidence*; 396.21 *grant authority*; 758.4 *licence*; 265.16 *make easy*; 16.65 *make legal*; 102.7 *make possible*; 743.3 *means of identification*; 318.6 *passport*; 396.9 *permission*; 253.2 *promise*; 252.2 *protection*; 136.3 *qualifications*; 136.13 *qualify*; 314.4 *right of entry*
permit oneself 250.19 *liberalize*
permitted 757.7; 136.10, 396.16 *authorized*; 648.5 *given consideration*; 16.44 *legal*; 750.18 *permitting*
permitting 750.18; **757.8**
permittivity 28.54, 39.11 *electric field*
permittivity of vacuum 28.97 *fundamental constant*
permutable 224.14 *exchangeable*
permutation 210.1 *calculation*; 224.4, 759.1 *exchange*; 27.21 *set*
permute 224.10 *exchange*
pernicious 357.14 *destructive*; 798.9 *detrimental*; 236.5 *harmful*; 651.10 *malevolent*
pernicious anaemia 260.11 *blood disease*; 33.14 *vitamin deficiency disease*
perniciously 798.13 *destructively*; 651.20 *malevolently*
perniciousness 236.11 *harmfulness*
pernicketiness 665.4 *fastidiousness*
pernickety 665.9 *careful*; 222.10 *detailed*; 264.12 *problematic*; 264.14 *troublesome*
peroral administration 37.13 *administration*
perorate 733.7 *address*; 722.4 *dissertate*; 112.17 *iterate*; 729.14 *speak to*
peroration 722.1 *dissertation*; 112.2 *iteration*; 733.2 *salutation*; 729.8 *speech*
peroxide 522.28 *bleach*; 530.4 *colour remover*; 530.6 *decolour*; 522.3 *lightening*
peroxided 522.21 *light*
peroxisome 34.8 *cell organ*
perpendicular 186.10; 176.1 *angle*; 176.9 *angled*; 27.37 *line*; 27.80 *linear*; 178.1 *straight*; 178.7 *straight line*; 186.3 *vertical thing*
perpendicularity 178.6 *straightness*; 186.1 *verticality*
perpendicular lines 27.37 *line*
perpendicularly 186.12
perpetrate 340.4 *act*
perpetration 340.1 *action*
perpetrator 578.3 *agent*; 340.3 *doer*
perpetual 132.11 *continuous*; 202.3, 279.8 *eternal*; 632.14 *habituated*; 93.12 *lasting*; 275.21 *lasting through time*; 101.8 *nonmaterial*; 225.7, 277.9 *permanent*; 134.6 *protracted*; 228.9 *stable*
perpetual calendar 275.13 *timer*
perpetually 275.30 *chronologically*; 134.7 *continually*; 132.19 *continuously*; 202.12 *eternally*; 297.1 *frequently*; 101.13 *metaphysically*; 225.9 *permanently*; 228.12 *stably*
perpetual motion 202.7 *eternity*; 228.4 *stable thing*
perpetuate 202.9 *be infinite*; 279.6 *eternalize*; 225.6 *make permanent*; 359.5 *preserve*; 134.4 *protract*
perpetuation 279.4 *eternalization*; 359.1 *preservation*; 134.2 *protraction*
perpetuity 93.6 *continuing existence*; 202.7, 279.1 *eternity*; 101.1 *nonmaterial world*; 225.1 *permanence*; 134.2 *protraction*
perplex 457.10 *bemuse*; 696.7 *be unintelligible*; 264.23 *cause difficulties*; 453.20 *make uncertain*; 737.13 *mystify*; 528.12 *obscure*
perplexed 453.3, 696.6 *confused*; 264.16 *troubled*
perplexing 453.3 *confused*; 696.4 *difficult*; 737.11 *mysterious*; 264.12 *problematic*
perplexing question 696.12 *unintelligible thing*
perplexity 453.12 *confusion*; 451.3 *incredulity*; 264.4 *problem*; 696.11 *unintelligibility*
per pro 550.43 *alternatively*; 762.9 *instead*
perquisite 793.6 *absence of charge*; 211.4 *extra*; 768.2 *gift*; 750.9 *grant*; 765.5 *profit*; 813.4 *reward for service*; 769.2 *something received*; 219.3 *superfluity*
Perrier™ 558.6 *soft drink*
perron 304.7 *means of ascent*
perse 539.1 *blue*
per se 197.21 *alone*; 99.13 *in essence*
persecute 798.11 *be evil*; 347.3 *counteract*; 466.14 *discriminate against*; 236.14 *ill-treat*; 342.17 *meddle*; 7.20 *preach*; 814.1 *punish*; 633.8 *pursue*; 647.6 *suppress*; 651.18 *torment*; 814.4 *torture*
persecuted 466.11 *judged*; 647.9 *suppressed*
persecuting 236.5 *harmful*; 651.10 *malevolent*
persecution 347.1 *counteraction*; 236.11 *harmfulness*; 651.5 *intolerance*; 814.7 *punishment*; 633.1 *pursuit*; 7.2 *religiousness*; 647.2 *suppression*
persecution complex 36.18 *complex*
persecution mania 461.4 *delusion*
persecution to the death 814.13 *capital punishment*
persecutor 466.7 *bigot*; 641.8 *obstinate person*; 814.17 *punisher*; 7.4 *religionist*; 647.4 *strict person*
Perseverance 640
perseverance 640.1; 342.8 *assiduity*; 641.6 *determination*; 225.1 *permanence*; 134.2 *protraction*; 633.1 *pursuit*; 613.3 *steadfastness*; 267.2, 638.14 *tenacity*
persevere 640.6; 641.9 *be obstinate*; 225.5 *be permanent*; 267.8 *be tenacious*; 576.8 *exert oneself*; 633.13 *follow up*; 246.7 *overcome obstacles*; 638.11 *persist*; 134.4 *protract*; 228.8 *show determination*; 613.16 *take courage*; 342.15 *try*; 576.6 *work*
persevering 640.10; 342.20 *industrious*; 225.7 *permanent*; 613.12 *self-reliant*; 267.10, 638.2 *tenacious*; 641.3 *unyielding*; 576.10 *working*
perseveringly 225.9 *permanently*; 640.13 *persistently*
Persian 296.14 *historic*; 566.4 *modern human*
Persian carpet 550.9 *floor covering*
Persian Gulf 92.9 *inlet*
Persians 284.6 *people of the past*
Persian wheel 369.10 *excavator*; 433.13 *irrigator*
persist 638.11; 641.9 *be obstinate*; 225.5 *be permanent*; 111.11 *be regular*; 93.19 *continue to be*; 633.13 *follow up*; 554.16 *live*; 640.6 *persevere*; 134.4 *protract*; 228.8 *show determination*; 342.15 *try*
persistence 93.6 *continuing existence*; 297.4 *frequency*; 225.1 *permanence*; 640.1 *perseverance*; 134.2 *protraction*; 633.1 *pursuit*; 360.1 *retention*; 267.2, 638.14 *tenacity*
persistent 509.15 *drumming*; 297.3 *frequent*; 93.12 *lasting*; 225.7 *permanent*; 640.10 *persevering*; 134.6 *protracted*; 31.53 *rainy*; 510.6 *resonant*; 267.10, 638.2 *tenacious*; 641.3 *unyielding*
persistently 640.13; 134.7 *continually*; 297.1 *frequently*; 225.9 *permanently*; 509.19 *repeatedly*; 638.17 *resolutely*; 267.12 *tenaciously*
persistent rain 31.25 *rain*
persist in 134.4 *protract*
persisting 93.12 *lasting*; 225.7 *permanent*; 510.6 *resonant*
person 139.13; **566.7**; 554.1 *life*; 402.5 *object*; 197.1 *one*; 21.23 *role*
persona 197.1 *one*; 139.2 *personality*; 36.21 *psyche*; 167.3 *show*
personable 545.6
personage 123.4 *bigwig*; 566.7 *person*; 21.23 *role*
personal 139.19; 139.16 *characteristic*; 566.12 *human*; 101.11 *internal*; 172.12 *internalized*; 126.5 *novel*; 5.39 *of language*
personal account 721.4 *factual account*
personal aims 683.1 *selfishness*
personal alarm 384.5 *self-defence*
personal allowance 788.3 *income*; 790.7 *tax*
personal appearance 21.13 *theatrical performance*
personal assistant 401.5 *office assistant*; 578.1 *worker*
personal attack 381.16
personal attendance 97.2 *omnipresence*
personal attendant 401.4
personal bearing 631.1 *conduct*
personal belongings 316.10 *transferred thing*
personal benefit 765.1 *gain*
personal borrower 784.6 *debtor*
personal call 692.10 *telephone call*
personal CD player 504.9 *audio device*
personal column 740.3 *journalism*
personal correspondence 721.4 *factual account*
personal criticism 719.3 *criticism*
personal desires 683.1 *selfishness*
personal effects 763.4 *possession*; 440.4 *possessions*; 345.2 *visible effect*
personal error 28.83 *sensitivity*
personal estate 440.5
personal fault 247.3
personal feeling 719.1 *interpretation*
personal file 744.1 *record*
personal finance 14.4
personal foul 58.5 *lacrosse*; 46.13 *penalty*; 49.4 *playing terms*
personal freedom 635.4 *free will*
personal history 744.1 *record*
personal honour 803.1 *virtue*
personal identification number 780.21 *till*
personal identity 4.9 *philosophical problem*
personal influence 395.3
personal initiative 250.1 *freedom*
personality 139.2; 123.4 *bigwig*; 173.5 *focus*; 743.2 *identity*; 402.1 *material world*; 395.3 *personal influence*; 36.21 *psyche*
personality adjustment test 36.5 *psychological test*
personality disorder 461.4 *delusion*; 36.8 *disordered personality*
personality inventory 36.5 *psychological test*
personality research form 36.5 *psychological test*
personality tendency 36.7 *personality type*
personality test 36.5 *psychological test*
personality type 36.7
personalize 139.26
personalized 139.20
personalized numberplate 743.3 *means of identification*
personal language 5.5 *nonstandard language*
personal law 16.1 *the law*
personal liberty 250.1 *freedom*
personal loan 771.2, 772.5, 784.3 *loan*
personally 139.29; 566.15 *humanly*; 97.14 *in person*; 126.8 *originally*; 101.14 *subjectively*
personal motive 176.6 *motive*
personal note 744.4 *inscription*
personal organizer 40.3 *computer*
personal pension 392.4 *social assistance*
personal property 440.4 *possessions*
personal question 705.4 *difficult question*
personal reasons 480.11 *motive*
personal recognizance 16.6 *legal process*
personal reward 813.1 *reward*
personals 740.3 *journalism*
personal sector 13.2 *economy*
personal servant 401.4 *personal attendant*
personal stereo 504.9 *audio device*; 692.18 *radio*
personal style 724.1 *style*
personal transport 320.4; 319.1 *transport*
personalty 440.2 *legal terms*
personal violence 651.7 *act of malevolence*
persona non grata 596.3 *disliked person*; 655.6 *unsocial person*
personate 717.9 *represent*
personation 21.22 *acting*
personification 738.10 *manifestation*; 17.12 *poetic language*; 99.3 *quintessence*; 717.1 *representation*
personified 738.14 *manifest*
personify 21.34 *act*; 402.8 *be material*; 99.12 *embody*; 717.9 *represent*
person in adversity 249.5
person in authority 400.3 *leader*
person in charge 579.15 *manager*
person included 127.3
person in command 397.6
person in office 400.3 *leader*
person in responsibility 579.15 *manager*
person keeping time 281.11
person left 215.6 *person remaining*
personnel 578.4; 586.14 *armed forces*; 352.3 *human resources*; 566.7 *person*; 127.3 *person included*; 334.1 *power*; 376.13 *workforce*
personnel manager 15.6 *employer*
personnel officer 15.6 *employer*
personnel staff 584.5 *military staff*
person of active habits 342.10 *busy person*
person of authority 396.10
person of few words 732.5 *shy person*
person of ideas 446.9
person of many parts 485.4 *skilled person*
person of note 566.7 *person*
person of repute 811.2; 248.4 *prosperous person*
person of wonder 619.5
person questioned 705.10
person remaining 215.6
persons of the drama 21.25 *cast*
person-to-person call 692.10 *telephone call*
person-to-person interaction 342.2 *social activity*
person unknown 456.4 *unknown person*
person who changes costume 227.8
person who changes sex 227.9
person who closes 309.5
person who copies 115.4
person who exchanges 759.4
person who gives evidence 716.7
person who humours 599.7
person who is exchanged 227.10
person who mixes 412.7
person who moves around 227.7
person who opens 308.3
person who separates 372.8
perspective 20.1 *architecture*; 41.8 *composition*; 310.3 *convergent view*; 145.1 *distance*; 7.1 *religion*; 19.4 *treatment*; 518.9 *viewpoint*
perspective projection 27.48 *transformation*
Perspex™ 32.21 *polymer*; 527.8 *transparent thing*
perspicacious 543.3 *elegant*; 425.5 *mentally sharp*; 518.21 *seeing*; 156.11, 458.5 *wise*
perspicaciously 543.5 *elegantly*; 425.18 *sharply*; 458.9 *wisely*
perspicaciousness 425.13 *mental sharpness*
perspicacity 425.13 *mental sharpness*; 156.3 *profundity*; 518.4 *visualization*; 458.1 *wisdom*
perspicuity 725.1 *clarity*; 543.1 *elegance*; 695.10 *simplicity*; 518.4 *visualization*
perspicuous 725.3 *clear*; 703.12 *demonstrable*; 694.6 *meaningful*; 695.2 *simple*
perspicuously 725.4 *clearly*
perspicuousness 725.1 *clarity*
perspiration 431.3 *body fluid*; 433.4 *exudate*; 493.1 *heat*; 315.2 *outflow*; 559.1 *secretion*; 560.8 *sweat*
perspire 493.16 *feel hot*; 315.12 *leak*; 371.14 *let out*; 559.7 *secrete*; 429.16, 433.32 *seep*; 560.19 *sweat*
perspiring 429.12 *seeping*; 560.8 *sweat*; 560.28 *sweaty*
persuadability 480.7
persuadable 480.20; 636.3 *amenable*; 760.15 *convertible*
persuade 480.15; **760.11**; 363.11 *attract*; 609.9 *comfort*; 395.8 *influence*; 450.9 *make someone believe*; 483.9 *motivate*; 752.9 *offer*;

701.16 *plead*; 476.6 *propound*; 710.6 *request*
persuade against 481.1 *dissuade*
persuaded 452.2 *convinced*; 760.16 *influenced*; 483.12 *motivated*
persuade oneself 476.5 *suppose*
persuader 480.12; 483.7 *motivator*
persuasability 636.8 *acquiescence*
persuasible 480.20 *persuadable*
Persuasion 480
persuasion 480.1; **760.3**; 450.1 *belief*; 483.2 *inducement*; 395.1 *influence*; 334.1 *power*; 7.1 *religion*; 450.2 *religious belief*; 710.1 *request*; 137.4 *type*
persuasive 480.19; 713.7 *advising*; 450.13 *believable*; 386.9 *compelling*; 395.11 *influential*; 483.11 *motivational*; 752.17 *offered*; 104.7 *plausible*; 336.10 *potent*
persuasively 480.21; **752.20**; 336.15 *acutely*; 450.16 *believably*; 386.11 *compellingly*; 395.14, 483.14 *influentially*
persuasiveness 483.2 *inducement*; 480.1 *persuasion*
pert 673.11 *cocky*; 661.7 *defiant*; 668.10 *disrespectful*; 660.21 *impudent*
pertain 706.22 *be the answer*; 750.27 *fit*; 108.7 *relate to*
pertaining 750.16 *fitting*; 127.8 *included*
pertain to 127.5 *be included*; 810.14 *be the duty of*; 108.7 *relate to*
pertinacious 641.1 *obstinate*; 267.10 *tenacious*; 267.2 *tenacity*
pertinaciously 267.12 *tenaciously*
pertinaciousness 641.5 *obstinacy*; 640.1 *perseverance*
pertinacity 641.5 *obstinacy*; 640.1 *perseverance*
pertinence 108.1 *relatedness*
pertinent 750.16 *fitting*; 127.8 *included*; 108.4 *related*
pertinently 750.38 *fittingly*; 127.9 *inclusively*; 108.10 *relevantly*
pertly 673.21 *cockily*; 661.9 *defiantly*; 660.30 *insolently*
pertness 673.3 *cockiness*; 661.1 *defiance*; 660.11 *sauciness*
perturb 327.22 *agitate*; 264.23 *cause difficulties*; 408.22 *discompose*; 328.7 *disturb*
perturbate 327.22 *agitate*
perturbation 327.1 *agitation*; 144.1 *displacement*; 328.1 *disturbance*; 612.2 *fearfulness*
perturbed 327.15 *agitated*; 408.17 *discomposed*; 328.12 *disturbed*; 264.16 *troubled*
pertussis 260.6 *infection*; 260.9 *respiratory disease*
peruke 551.15 *headgear*
perusal 6.8 *learning*; 518.3 *observation*
peruse 518.14 *inspect*; 6.23 *learn*
Peruvian marching powder 691.6 *drug*
pervade 395.10 *be a prevailing influence*; 412.10 *become mixed*; 97.11 *be present*; 232.6 *fill*
pervading 97.7 *present*
pervasion 412.1 *mixture*; 97.2 *omnipresence*
pervasive 395.13 *dominant*; 412.12 *mixed*; 97.7 *present*; 138.17 *widespread*
pervasively 395.14 *influentially*; 412.14 *in the midst*
pervasiveness 97.2 *omnipresence*; 138.4 *widespreadness*
perverse 642.1 *capricious*; 224.11 *changeable*; 274.16 *errant*; 804.12 *immoral*; 641.2 *refractory*; 264.14 *troublesome*; 113.26 *uncooperative*
perversely 264.29; 234.14 *distortedly*; 328.18 *disturbingly*; 113.27 *opposingly*
perverseness 113.7 *contrariness*
perverse personality 36.8 *disordered personality*
perversion 245.8; 802.4 *abnormality*; 224.1 *change*; 118.6 *deviation*; 328.4 *disruption*; 234.4 *distortion of the truth*; 274.7 *errancy*; 760.2 *evolution*; 699.9 *falsification*; 720.2 *misinterpretation*; 718.1 *misrepresentation*; 351.2 *misuse*; 804.2 *vice*
perversity 113.7 *contrariness*; 641.5 *obstinacy*
pervert 245.6; 798.11 *be evil*; 236.13 *be worthless*; 224.8 *cause change*; 796.19 *corrupt*; 234.5 *defacer*; 96.16 *delude*; 325.19 *deviant person*; 328.10 *disrupt*; 234.12 *distort the truth*; 798.6 *evil person*; 699.26 *falsify*; 804.17 *make wicked*; 720.1 *misinterpret*; 465.5 *misjudging person*; 718.4 *misrepresent*; 351.1 *misuse*; 796.10 *sex offender*; 760.9 *transform*; 804.9 *wicked person*
perverted 802.14 *abnormal*; 274.16 *errant*; 234.8 *exaggerated*; 804.12 *immoral*; 718.6 *misrepresented*; 351.4 *misused*; 796.15 *unlawful*
pervertedly 351.6 *abusively*
PES 32.17 *analysis*
Pesach 10.16 *religious festival*
peseta 780.11 *national coins*
peso 780.11 *national coins*
pessary 37.9; 394.10 *surgical dressing*
pessimism 474.1 *expectation*; 611.1 *hopelessness*; 708.1 *negation*; 468.1 *underestimation*
pessimist 468.2; **670.13**; 611.3 *hopeless person*; 708.9 *negativist*; 341.2 *nonacting person*
pessimistic 474.5 *expecting*; 611.4 *hopeless*; 708.17 *negative*; 468.4 *underestimating*
pessimistically 468.6; 474.12 *expectantly*; 611.11 *hopelessly*; 708.22 *negatively*
pest 76.3; 620.3 *boring person*; 594.8 *hated person*; 260.5 *plague*; 408.11, 662.5 *troublemaker*; 242.9 *unpleasant person*
pest control 43.14
pester 264.17 *be difficult*; 240.5 *be inconvenient*; 408.22 *discompose*; 328.7 *disturb*; 670.18 *find fault*; 342.17 *meddle*; 624.9 *offend*; 710.6 *request*
pestering 670.6 *fault-finding*; 710.1 *request*
pest exterminator 382.13 *animal killer*
pesticidal 44.18 *herbicidal*
pesticide 357.7 *agent of destruction*; 382.13 *animal killer*; 43.14 *pest control*; 44.8 *weedkiller*
pestilence 357.7 *agent of destruction*; 260.5 *plague*; 236.10 *poverty*
pestle 427.22 *pulverize*; 427.11 *pulverizer*
pestle and mortar 427.11 *pulverizer*
pestled 427.18 *pulverized*
pesto 25.15 *sauce*
pests and diseases 44.12
pet 593.21 *beloved*; 469.15 *chosen*; 490.10 *comfort*; 70.3 *domesticated animal*; 490.9 *give pleasure*; 9.4 *idolized person*; 492.4, 593.27 *kiss*; 365.16 *massage*; 593.12 *nicknames for lovers*; 492.11 *touch*
petal 205.6 *branch*; 78.3 *flower part*; 77.6 *leaf*
pet animal 70.3 *domesticated animal*
petard 587.12 *historical guns*
pet aversion 596.2 *disliked thing*; 594.7 *hated thing*
pet cemetery 583.5 *cemetery*
petechia 560.10 *bleeding*
peterman 774.8 *thief*
peter out 226.6 *cease*; 94.12 *cease to exist*; 131.18 *come to an end*; 214.4 *decrease*; 526.1 *disappear*
Peter Pan collar 551.14 *neckwear*
Peter Schaufuss 22.14 *famous ballet dancers*
Peter's pence 768.3 *offering*; 790.7 *tax*
Peters' projection 163.4 *map*
pet food 557.8 *animal food*
pet hate 596.2 *disliked thing*; 612.5 *frightener*; 594.7 *hated thing*
pethidine 489.4 *anaesthetic*; 394.5 *analgesic*
pétillant 415.2 *insubstantial*
petiole 77.6 *leaf*; 77.5 *stem*
petit allegro 22.9 *ballet steps*
petite 159.7 *little*
petiteness 159.1 *littleness*
petition 733.8 *appeal to*; 757.6 *ask permission*; 16.70 *litigate*; 16.5 *litigation*; 10.20 *pray*; 10.9 *prayer*; 710.1, 710.6 *request*; 10.3 *rite of worship*; 9.1 *worship*
petitionary 10.21 *ritualistic*
petitionary prayer 10.9 *prayer*
petitioned 710.9 *requesting*
petitioner 715.3 *accuser*; 16.8 *litigant*; 744.9 *recorder*; 710.4 *requester*; 9.5, 10.17 *worshipper*
petit jury 16.26 *jury*
petit larceny 774.1 *stealing*
petit mal 461.3 *mental deterioration*; 260.17 *nervous disorder*
petits battements 22.10 *positions at the barre*
petits pois 25.45 *French dish*
petkins 593.12 *nicknames for lovers*
Pet Milk™ 558.5 *milk*
pet name 721.8 *name*
pet names 593.14 *communication of love*
pet owner 70.10 *animal welfarist*
pet peeve 596.2 *disliked thing*; 594.7 *hated thing*
Petrarchan 17.19 *narrative*
Petrarchan sonnet 17.7 *poem*
petrel 72.3 *water bird*
petrifaction 416.2 *concentration*; 418.6 *solidification*
petrifactive 418.1 *hard*
petrification 30.43 *fossil*; 284.10 *fossilization*
petrified 30.61 *fossilized*; 612.7 *frightened*; 418.3 *hardened*; 301.4 *motionless*
petrified forest 284.10 *fossilization*
petrified wood 30.43 *fossil*; 296.5 *old thing*
petrify 416.8 *be dense*; 619.10 *be wonderful*; 612.13 *frighten*; 30.62 *lithify*; 418.10 *solidify*
petrifying 612.10 *frightening*; 418.1 *hard*
petrochemical 435.1 *materials*
petrochemicals 32.22 *industrial chemistry*
petrodollar diesel 437.6 *oil*
petrogenesis 30.29
petrogenic 30.56 *petrographic*
petroglyph 19.12 *sculpture*
petrographic 30.56
petrographical 30.56 *petrographic*
petrographically 30.66 *geographically*
petrol 330.13 *fuel*; 437.6 *oil*
petrolatum 394.9 *balm*
petrol can 437.6 *oil*
petrol-driven 437.10 *powered*
petrol engine 38.11 *engine*
petroleum 284.10 *fossilization*; 435.1 *materials*; 437.6 *oil*
petroleum jelly 394.9 *balm*
petrological 30.48 *geological*; 30.56 *petrographic*
petrologically 30.66 *geographically*
petrologist 30.3 *geologist*
petrology 30.1 *earth science*
petrol-propelled 330.19 *propelled*
petrol propulsion 330.2 *method of propulsion*
petrol pump 437.6 *oil*; 439.4 *storage*
petrol station 437.6 *oil*; 226.4 *stopping place*; 439.4 *storage*
petrol tank 439.4 *storage*
petronel 587.10 *historical gun*
PET scan 35.7 *diagnosis*
pet subject 139.8 *specialization*
petticoat 551.18 *underwear*
Petticoat Lane 779.1 *market*
pettifog 702.13 *quibble*
pettifogger 700.17 *cheat*; 670.12 *critic*; 702.6 *sophist*
pettifoggery 670.6 *fault-finding*; 702.4 *quibbling*
pettifogging 670.28 *fault-finding*; 702.9 *quibbling*; 124.4 *trivial*
pettiness 159.1 *littleness*; 466.3 *prejudice*; 793.3 *shoddiness*; 124.7 *triviality*; 682.4 *unpleasantness*
petting 593.14 *communication of love*; 593.6 *courtship*; 492.2 *touching*
pettishness 642.2 *caprice*
petty 466.10 *discriminatory*; 159.7 *little*; 157.2 *superficial*; 124.4 *trivial*; 682.2 *unpleasant*
petty bureaucracy 342.9 *overactivity*
petty cash 780.2 *cash*
petty-cash book 789.5 *account book*
petty criminal 662.9 *criminal*
petty detail 124.8 *trifle*
petty officer 586.27 *naval man*
petty official 579.16 *official*
petty officialdom 12.3 *governance*; 342.9 *overactivity*; 632.6 *procedure*
petty sessions 16.19 *law court*; 464.3 *place of judgment*
petty sin 124.8 *trifle*
petty theft 774.1 *stealing*
petty thief 774.8 *thief*
petty tyrant 400.4 *absolute ruler*; 647.4 *strict person*
petulance 660.9 *discourtesy*; 625.1 *irascibility*; 626.3 *irritableness*
petulant 701.8 *argumentative*; 660.20 *discourteous*; 625.4 *irascible*; 626.7 *irritable*
petulantly 701.17 *argumentatively*; 660.36 *discourteously*; 625.9 *irascibly*; 626.14 *irritably*
petuntse 24.2 *raw material*
pew 10.12 *church*; 410.2 *compartment*
pewter 533.5 *grey thing*; 412.2 *mixed thing*; 531.9 *white thing*
peyote 691.6 *drug*
Pfannkuchen 25.46 *German dish*
pfennig 780.11 *national coins*
pH 32.19 *electrochemistry*
Phaeophyta 84.2 *algae*
phaeophyte 84.2 *algae*
phage 34.3 *organism*
phagocyte 431.4 *blood*
phalangid 76.2 *arachnid*
phalanx 586.16 *army unit*
phallic 9.10 *idolatrous*; 561.16 *reproductive*
phallicism 9.2 *idolatry*
phallicist 9.6 *idolater*
phallic symbol 562.4 *fertility cult*; 36.24 *symbolism*
phallus 562.4 *fertility cult*; 561.8 *organs of reproduction*
phanerogam 77.3 *seed plant*
phanerogamic 77.16 *taxonomic*
phansigar 586.1 *combatant*; 651.8 *malefactor*
phantasm 700.5 *falseness*; 11.11 *ghost*; 96.2 *illusion*; 518.5 *imagination*
phantasmagoria 96.2 *illusion*; 518.5 *imagination*; 412.3 *miscellany*
phantasmagorical 96.9 *illusory*; 412.12 *mixed*
phantasmagorically 412.14 *in the midst*
phantasmal 11.18 *spiritual*; 96.8 *unreal*
phantasmic 700.40 *illusory*; 11.18 *spiritual*
phantom 477.5 *fantasy*; 11.11 *ghost*; 97.6 *ghostly presence*; 96.2 *illusion*; 518.5 *imagination*; 101.9 *parapsychological*; 525.4 *something that appears*; 11.18 *spiritual*; 101.3 *spiritual world*
phantoms 582.14 *the spiritual world*
Pharaoh 400.2 *sovereign*
Pharisaic 699.31, 700.37, 702.10 *hypocritical*; 7.15 *religious*
Pharisaism 699.3, 700.3, 702.5 *hypocrisy*
Pharisee 699.19 *cheat*; 699.17 *false person*; 700.19 *hypocrite*; 7.6 *non-Christian*
pharmaceutical 37.3 *drug*; 394.2 *medicine*; 37.18 *pharmacological*
pharmaceuticals 32.22 *industrial chemistry*
pharmaceutics 37.1 *pharmacology*
pharmaceutist 37.2 *pharmacologist*
pharmacist 394.16 *druggist*; 37.2 *pharmacologist*
pharmacodynamic 37.18 *pharmacological*
pharmacodynamics 37.1 *pharmacology*
pharmacognostic 37.18 *pharmacological*
pharmacognosy 394.2 *medicine*
pharmacokinetic 37.18 *pharmacological*
pharmacokinetics 37.1 *pharmacology*
pharmacological 37.18
pharmacologist 37.2; 394.16 *druggist*
Pharmacology 37
pharmacology 37.1
pharmacopoeia 394.2 *medicine*; 37.1 *pharmacology*
pharmacy 394.16 *druggist*; 37.1 *pharmacology*
pharmocognosy 37.1 *pharmacology*
pharos 522.6 *electric light*; 323.5 *navigation*
pharyngitis 260.9 *respiratory disease*
pharynx 729.5 *organ of speech*
phase 32.3; 28.51, 39.9 *electric current*; 595.3 *likes*; 111.8 *make the same*; 29.17 *moon*; 276.4 *period of activity*; 484.10 *plan out*; 504.10 *sound quality*; 205.3 *stage*; 221.1 *state*; 28.8 *time*
phaseal 298.11 *regular*
phase angle 39.9 *electric current*
phase change 32.3 *phase*; 28.37 *temperature*
phase-contrast microscope 28.85 *microscope*
phase-contrast microscopy 34.6 *cell biology*
phased 298.11 *regular*; 285.10 *synchronized*
phase diagram 32.3 *phase*
phase difference 39.9 *electric current*
phase modulation 692.14 *radio transmission*
phases of the moon 227.3 *changeable thing*
phase speed 28.16 *waveform*
phasic 298.11 *regular*

phasing 298.1 *regularity*
phasmid 76.10 *insectan*
pheasant 25.20 *meat*; 72.4 *table bird*
pheasant season 292.1 *season*
pheasant shoot 633.2 *chase*
pheasant shooter 382.13 *animal killer*
pheasant shooting 382.9 *animal killing*; 60.2 *hunting*
phellem 79.3 *timber*
phenol 256.9 *cleaning agent*
phenolate 256.13 *clean*
phenolphthalein 32.18 *gravimetric analysis*
phenomenal 525.7 *appearing*; 93.13 *real*; 619.8 *wonderful*
phenomenalism 4.7 *school of thought*
phenomenalist 4.11 *follower of a doctrine*; 4.14 *of a philosophy*
phenomenologically 4.24 *philosophically*
phenomenological psychology 36.1 *psychology*
phenomenological theology 7.13 *theology*
phenomenology 4.6 *branch of philosophy*
phenomenon 525.2 *being in view*; 93.2 *thing*; 619.4 *wonder*
phenon formaldehyde 435.1 *materials*
phenotype 34.11 *genetics*; 34.12 *molecular biology*
pheromonal 500.5 *odorous*
pheromone 33.16 *hormone*; 500.3 *scent*; 559.2 *secreted substance*
phial 410.14 *bottle*
Philadelphia 87.2 *American cities*
Philadelphia lawyer 444.6 *arguer*
philander 796.17 *be sexually immoral*; 593.26 *court*
philanderer 227.6 *fickle person*; 796.8 *immoral man*; 567.7 *libertine*; 593.9 *lover*; 490.3 *pleasure-seeker*
philanthropic **652.6**; 392.35 *benevolent*; 650.7 *charitable*; 569.8 *friendly*; 768.8 *giving*; 636.4 *helpful*; 679.2 *magnanimous*; 803.5 *virtuous*; 752.18 *voluntary*
philanthropical 652.6 *philanthropic*
philanthropically **652.8**; 650.11 *charitably*; 752.20 *persuasively*
philanthropism 652.1 *philanthropy*
philanthropist **636.12**; **652.3**; 392.15 *benefactor*; 650.5 *benevolent person*; 679.9 *generous person*; 768.4 *giver*; 797.15 *good person*; 648.2 *lenient person*; 244.12 *reformer*; 477.9 *visionary*; 752.8 *volunteer*; 578.1 *worker*
philanthropize 652.7 *be charitable*; 768.6 *give to charity*
Philanthropy 652
philanthropy **652.1**; 650.2 *charity*; 569.1 *friendship*; 768.1 *giving*; 679.6 *magnanimity*; 803.1 *virtue*
philatelist 376.35 *collector*
Philemon and Baucis 570.9 *married couple*
philharmonic 18.29 *musical*
philippic 733.1 *address*
Philistine 117.6 *conformist*; 456.6 *ignorant*; 456.5 *ignorant person*; 592.5 *insensitive person*; 646.1 *naive*; 646.3 *naive person*; 675.5 *vulgar person*
Philistinism 592.3 *insensitiveness*; 646.2 *naivety*
philological 5.38 *linguistic*; 694.8 *semantic*
philologically 5.48 *linguistically*
philologist 5.2 *linguist*
philology 5.1 *linguistics*; 5.30 *syntax*
philoprogenitive 562.5 *fertile*
philosopher **4.10**; 713.4 *adviser*; 101.7 *believer in a nonmaterial world*; 400.9 *educational leader*; 446.9 *person of ideas*; 705.9 *questioner*; 444.5 *reasoner*; 476.4 *theorist*; 443.7 *thinker*; 458.3 *wise man*
philosopher's stone 482.6 *objective*; 394.1 *remedy*; 781.5 *wealth*
philosophical 400.13 *excellent*; 4.13 *of philosophy*; 4.15 *rational*; 443.11 *reasoning*; 705.15 *sceptical*; 446.10 *theoretical*; 443.8 *thoughtful*
philosophical argument 4.5
philosophical doctrine 4.1 *philosophy*
philosophical idealism 101.5 *idealism*
philosophical inquiry 4.4 *philosophical investigation*; 705.2 *questioning*
philosophical investigation 4.4
philosophical linguistics 5.1 *linguistics*
philosophically **4.24**; 400.16 *masterfully*; 705.23 *questioningly*; 4.26 *rationally*; 4.27 *stoically*; 446.20 *theoretically*; 443.18 *thoughtfully*
philosophical problem 4.9
philosophical speculation 4.1 *philosophy*
philosophical system 4.2
philosophical term 4.8
philosophical theology 7.13 *theology*
philosophical theory 4.1 *philosophy*
philosophism 702.1 *sophistry*
philosophist 702.6 *sophist*
philosophize **4.20**; **443.17**; 444.14 *premise*; 4.21 *rationalize*; 7.22 *theologize*
Philosophy 4
philosophy **4.1**; 446.5 *ideology*; 450.2 *religious belief*
philosophy of commonsense 4.6 *branch of philosophy*
philosophy of history 4.6 *branch of philosophy*; 3.1 *history*
philosophy of language 4.6 *branch of philosophy*
philosophy of law 4.6 *branch of philosophy*
philosophy of life 7.1 *religion*
philosophy of mind 4.6 *branch of philosophy*
philosophy of psychology 4.6 *branch of philosophy*
philosophy of religion 4.6 *branch of philosophy*
philosophy of science 4.6 *branch of philosophy*
philosophy of signs 4.6 *branch of philosophy*
philtre 490.4 *pleasurable things*; 11.5 *spell*
phiz 167.2 *face*
phlebitis 260.10 *cardiovascular disease*
phlebotomize 394.20 *doctor*
phlebotomy 371.22 *disgorgement*; 369.4 *sucking*; 394.12 *surgery*
phlegm 431.3 *body fluid*; 343.7 *idleness*; 618.1 *indifference*; 430.5 *mucus*; 560.9 *saliva*; 559.2 *secreted substance*; 605.2 *stoicism*
phlegmatic 599.12 *four humours*; 341.3 *inactive*; 618.7 *indifferent*; 343.3 *not participating*; 36.7 *personality type*; 605.8 *resigned*; 301.5 *sedentary*; 333.5 *unhurried*
phlegmatically 618.17 *indifferently*; 301.10 *motionlessly*; 605.9 *stoically*
phlegmaticalness 618.1 *indifference*
phlegmy 431.16 *rheumy*
phloem 77.5 *stem*
phobia 461.4 *delusion*; 596.1 *dislike*; 612.1 *fear*; 594.7 *hated thing*; 36.10 *neurosis*
phobic 594.9 *hater*; 594.11 *racist*
Phoenician 566.4 *modern human*
Phoenicians 284.6 *people of the past*
phoenix 72.9 *fabulous bird*; 70.7 *legendary beast*
phoenix-like 393.13 *repaired*; 561.15 *reproduced*
pholidote 71.6 *insect-eating mammal*; 71.26 *insectivorous*
phonation 729.4 *articulation*
phone 504.9 *audio device*; 693.12 *communicate*; 5.16 *spoken letter*; 692.9, 692.32 *telephone*
phone book 692.11 *dialling*; 220.3 *dictionary*; 693.5 *reference book*
phone call 692.10 *telephone call*
phonecard 772.4 *credit*; 783.2 *credit card*; 28.64 *magnetic recording*; 692.9 *telephone*
phone-in 692.25 *broadcast material*
phoneme 5.16 *spoken letter*; 729.7 *utterance*
phonemic 5.38 *linguistic*
phonemicist 5.2 *linguist*
phonemics 5.1 *linguistics*
phone number 692.11 *dialling*
phoner 692.13 *telephoner*
phonetic **729.18**; 5.38 *linguistic*
phonetically 5.48 *linguistically*; 729.21 *orally*
phonetic alphabet 5.14 *alphabet*
phonetician 5.2 *linguist*
phonetics **729.6**; 28.2 *classical physics*; 5.1 *linguistics*
phonetic spelling 5.27 *spelling*
phonetic symbol 5.14 *alphabet*
phonetist 5.2 *linguist*
phoney 699.19 *cheat*; 125.2 *copy*; 700.15 *deceiver*; 699.12, 699.37 *fake*; 700.19 *hypocrite*; 700.37, 702.10 *hypocritical*; 125.13 *imitation*; 700.39 *imitative*; 125.7 *imitator*; 699.18 *liar*; 115.8 *simulated*; 699.32 *spurious*
phoney war 585.1 *war*
phonic 729.18 *phonetic*
phoniness 699.4 *spuriousness*
phonogram 5.16 *spoken letter*
phonogramic 5.41 *lettered*
phonographic 5.41 *lettered*
phonograph record 744.7 *recording*
phonography 5.1 *linguistics*
phonological 5.38 *linguistic*
phonologist 5.2 *linguist*
phonology 5.1 *linguistics*; 729.6 *phonetics*
phonometer 26.8 *meter*
phonometric 26.16 *micrometric*
phony 96.12 *artificial*
phoronid 75.6 *worm*
Phoronida 75.6 *worm*
phosphagen 33.22 *bioenergetics*
phosphate 43.13 *fertilizer*
phosphate bond 33.22 *bioenergetics*
phosphates 562.3 *fertilizer*
phosphatide 33.6 *lipid*
phosphoglyceride 33.6 *lipid*
phospholipid 33.6 *lipid*
phosphoprotein 33.9 *protein*
phosphoresce 522.25 *light up*
phosphorescence 522.1 *light*; 28.24 *light emission*
phosphorescent 522.15 *lucent*
phosphoric 32.34 *elemental*
phosphorous 32.34 *elemental*
phosphorus 33.15 *essential element*
phosphorylation 33.22 *bioenergetics*
photic 522.23 *photoelectric*
photo 41.3, 41.21 *photograph*
photobiography 41.4 *portrait*
photo booth 41.16 *camera*
photocall 740.8 *public relations*
photocathode 39.24 *electron emission*
photocell 334.7 *electrical power*; 39.25 *photoconductivity*
photochemical 32.31 *chemical*
photochemically 32.46 *chemically*
photochemical reaction 32.14 *chemical reaction*
photochemist 32.2 *chemist*
photochemistry 32.1 *chemistry*
photochromic 529.14 *chromolithographic*
photochromic glass 24.1 *ceramics*
photochromic lenses 28.29 *optical element*
photoconduction 522.11 *photoelectricity*
photoconductive 522.23 *photoelectric*
photoconductivity **39.25**; 28.49 *electromagnetic induction*; 28.33 *photosensitivity*
photocopied 198.12 *double*; 111.15 *duplicate*; 744.16 *recorded*
photocopier **125.6**; 115.3 *copier*; 744.10 *recording instrument*
photocopy **41.7**; 115.2, 125.2, 125.10, 744.5 *copy*; 111.4, 111.9, 125.5 *duplicate*; 561.2 *print*; 744.13 *record*; 112.7 *replica*; 721.9 *representation*; 561.9 *reproduce*; 561.1, 717.2 *reproduction*; 316.16 *translate*; 198.5 *twin*
photocopying 41.2 *photoreproduction*; 561.1 *reproduction*; 316.4 *translation*
photocurrent 39.25 *photoconductivity*
photodetector 39.25 *photoconductivity*
photodiode 39.18 *diode*; 39.25 *photoconductivity*
photoelastic modelling 38.17 *civil engineering*
photoelectric **522.23**; 39.36 *electronic*
photoelectrically 39.37 *electronically*
photoelectric cell 334.7 *electrical power*; 522.11 *photoelectricity*
photoelectric effect 28.49 *electromagnetic induction*; 39.24 *electron emission*; 28.33 *photosensitivity*
photoelectric emission 39.24 *electron emission*
photoelectricity **522.11**; 334.7 *electrical power*; 28.42 *electricity*
photoelectron 39.24 *electron emission*
photoemission 522.11 *photoelectricity*
photoemissive 522.23 *photoelectric*
photo finish 312.15 *destination*; 119.2 *equilibrium*; 59.7 *horseracing*; 285.1 *same time*; 147.2 *short distance*
Photofit™ 41.4 *portrait*; 717.2 *reproduction*
photoflood 522.7 *lantern*; 41.15 *lighting*
photogenic 41.22 *photographic*; 717.13 *representational*
photogenically 41.23 *photographically*
photogrammetric 26.16 *micrometric*
photogrammetry 38.17 *civil engineering*; 26.2 *micrometry*; 41.2 *photoreproduction*
photograph **41.3**; **41.21**; 111.4, 111.9, 125.5 *duplicate*; 743.10 *identify*; 717.6 *image*; 525.5 *impression*; 743.3 *means of identification*; 744.1, 744.13 *record*; 717.9 *represent*; 717.2 *reproduction*; 518.7 *view*
photograph album 41.3 *photograph*; 462.4 *reminder*
photographed 111.15 *duplicate*; 743.12 *identified*; 744.16 *recorded*
photographer 125.8 *copier*; 115.4 *person who copies*; 717.4 *person who makes a representation*; 744.9 *recorder*
photographic **41.22**; 273.6 *correct*; 721.11 *descriptive*; 111.15 *duplicate*; 115.9 *lifelike*; 19.24 *pictorial*; 717.13 *representational*; 721.13 *representing*
photographically **41.23**; 115.14 *comparably*; 111.18 *identically*; 19.30 *pictorially*
photographic density 41.10 *graininess*
photographic likeness 717.1 *representation*
photographic memory 273.3 *accurate thing*; 462.1 *memory*; 360.5 *retentiveness*
photographic paper 41.9 *film*
photographic plate 41.9 *film*
photographic realism 698.12 *realism*
Photography 41
photography **41.1**; 19.1 *art*; 28.34 *photometry*
photogravure 41.2 *photoreproduction*; 19.7 *picture*
photointaglio 41.2 *photoreproduction*
photojournalism 41.1 *photography*
photolithography 28.34 *photometry*; 41.2 *photoreproduction*
photolysis 375.2 *deconstruction*
photolytically 375.7 *to pieces*
photomechanical transfer 115.2 *copy*
photometer 29.27 *imaging*; 28.92 *light meter*; 26.8 *meter*; 28.32 *optical instrument*; 522.11 *photoelectricity*
photometric 29.36 *astronomical*; 26.16 *micrometric*; 522.23 *photoelectric*
photometry **28.34**; 29.27 *imaging*; 26.2 *micrometry*; 28.96 *microscopy*
photomicrograph 41.7 *photocopy*
photomontage 19.7 *picture*; 41.4 *portrait*
photomultiplier 39.24 *electron emission*
photomural 41.4 *portrait*
photon 28.13 *electromagnetic radiation*; 522.1 *light*; 402.4 *matter*; 28.78 *quantum*
photo-opportunity 740.8 *public relations*
photoperiodism 276.5 *recurrent period*
photophobic 522.23 *photoelectric*
photophosphorylation 33.23 *photosynthesis*
photoprint 19.7 *picture*
photorealist 19.29 *realist*
photoreproduction **41.2**; 561.1 *reproduction*
photorespiration 33.24 *respiration*
photosensitive 24.10 *ceramic*; 522.23 *photoelectric*; 41.22 *photographic*
photosensitive glass 24.9 *industrial ceramics*
photosensitive material 28.33 *photosensitivity*
photosensitivity **28.33**; 41.10 *graininess*; 522.11 *photoelectricity*
photosensor 522.11 *photoelectricity*
photosphere 434.3 *atmospheric layers*; 29.15 *sun*
Photostat™ 115.3 *copier*; 111.4, 111.9, 125.5 *duplicate*; 115.12 *imitate*; 41.7 *photocopy*
photostated 111.15 *duplicate*
photosynthesis **33.23**; 34.5 *physiology*
photosynthesize 33.25 *metabolize*; 77.21 *vegetate*
photosynthetic 33.26 *biochemical*; 77.14 *of plants*; 34.22 *physiological*
photosynthetically 33.27 *biochemically*; 77.24 *herbaceously*
photosynthetic pigment 33.18 *pigment*

phototherapy 394.13 *therapy*
phototopography 41.1 *photography*
phototropic 522.23 *photoelectric*
photovoltaic cell 39.25 *photoconductivity*; 437.8 *renewable energy*
photovoltaic effect 28.49 *electromagnetic induction*; 39.25 *photoconductivity*; 28.33 *photosensitivity*
phrasal 5.43
phrase 5.23; **18.22**; 516.4 *harmonics*; 724.4 *literary style*; 205.2 *particular*; 724.9 *style*; 5.45 *use language*; 729.7 *utterance*
phrased 5.43 *phrasal*; 724.6 *styled*
phrasegraph 5.24 *phrasing*
phrasemaker 5.2 *linguist*
phrasemonger 542.9; 5.2 *linguist*; 724.5 *stylist*
phraseogram 5.24 *phrasing*
phraseographic 5.43 *phrasal*
phraseological 5.43 *phrasal*
phraseologically 5.51
phraseology 724.4 *literary style*; 5.24 *phrasing*; 5.3 *spoken language*
phrase-structure grammar 5.29 *grammar*
phrasing 5.24; 516.4 *harmonics*; 724.4 *literary style*; 5.43 *phrasal*
phrenic 442.9 *mental*
phrenologist 11.12 *occultist*
phrenology 11.1 *occultism*; 719.5 *science of interpretation*
Phrygian mode 18.20 *key*
phthalocyanine blue zaffre 539.5 *blueness*
phthalocyanine dye 42.6 *dye*
phthiriasis 258.2 *uncleanness*
phthisic 1.15 *physical*
phthisic build 1.9 *physical type*
phthistic 260.23 *diseased*
phycobilin 33.18 *pigment*
phycobiont 84.1 *alga*; 84.6 *lichen*
phycocyanin 84.3 *plant body*
phycoerythrin 84.3 *plant body*
phycological 84.7 *algal*
phycologist 84.2 *algae*; 77.12 *plant scientist*
phycology 84.2 *algae*; 77.10 *plant science*
phycomycetes 83.3 *fungi*
phycomycosis 83.5 *fungal association*
phylactery 10.14 *sacred object*; 11.6 *talisman*
phylloclade 77.6 *leaf*
phyllode 77.6 *leaf*
phyllosilicate 30.34 *mineral*
phylogenetic 34.27 *evolutionary*
phylogeny 34.16 *evolution*
phylum 137.3 *kingdom*; 205.1 *part*; 34.17 *taxonomy*
physic 393.6 *cure*; 394.20 *doctor*; 394.2 *medicine*
physical 1.15; **28.98**; 35.6 *health care*; 402.7 *material*
physical abuse 651.7 *act of malevolence*; 380.2 *physical violence*
physical anthropology 1.1 *anthropology*
physical attack 381.16 *personal attack*
physical being 402.1 *material world*
physical change 760.1 *conversion*
physical chemist 32.2 *chemist*
physical chemistry 32.1 *chemistry*; 28.4 *experimental physics*; 402.6 *natural science*
physical condition 402.1 *material world*; 221.5 *physical state*
physical constant 28.97 *fundamental constant*
physical contact 492.2 *touching*
physical cruelty 380.2 *physical violence*
physical disability 335.4 *disability*
physical element 402.4 *matter*
physical energy 338.1 *vigour*
physical examination 35.6 *health care*
physical existence 402.1 *material world*
physical fatigue 261.7 *fatigue*
physical fitness 336.2 *healthiness*
physical force 386.2 *coercion*; 336.1 *strength*
physical form 221.5 *physical state*
physical geography 30.1 *earth science*
physical geology 30.1 *earth science*
physical handicap 335.4 *disability*
physical improvement 244.9
physicalism 4.7 *school of thought*
physicalist 4.11 *follower of a doctrine*; 4.14 *of a philosophy*
physically 28.100; 402.9 *materially*
physically demanding 264.10 *difficult*; 261.4 *fatiguing*
physically strong 336.9
physical medicine 35.3 *medical specialty*
physical oceanography 30.2 *geophysics*
physical optics 28.2 *classical physics*
Physical Pain 491
Physical Pleasure 490
physical pleasure 490.1
physical power 423.8 *physical strength*
physical presence 402.5 *object*; 97.1 *presence*
physical punishment 491.1 *pain*
physical roughness 423.8 *physical strength*
physical science 402.6 *natural science*; 28.1 *physics*
physical state 221.5
physical strength 423.8; 336.1 *strength*
physical type 1.9; 525.3 *external appearance*
physical violence 380.2; 381.16 *personal attack*
physical weakness 335.4 *disability*
physical well-being 259.3 *health*
physical world 402.1 *material world*; 95.2 *real world*
physical wreck 245.9 *dilapidation*
physician 35.11 *doctor*; 396.11 *expert*; 394.15 *healer*
physicist 402.3 *materialist*; 28.1 *physics*
physicotheological 7.18 *theological*
physicotheology 7.13 *theology*
Physics 28
physics 28.1; 402.6 *natural science*
physiochemical 32.31 *chemical*
physiochemist 32.2 *chemist*
physiocracy 12.1 *government*
physiocratic school 13.6 *economic factors*
physiognomic 167.6 *front*
physiognomical 167.6 *front*
physiognomy 525.3 *external appearance*; 167.2 *face*; 160.6 *nature*; 719.5 *science of interpretation*
physiographer 30.3 *geologist*
physiography 30.1 *earth science*
physiological 34.22; 34.20 *biological*
physiologically 34.29 *biologically*
physiological psychology 36.1 *psychology*
physiologist 34.19 *life scientist*
physiology 34.5; 34.1 *life science*
physiotherapist 35.17 *paramedic*
physiotherapy 394.13 *therapy*; 35.8 *treatment*
physique 403.3 *form*; 160.6 *nature*; 1.9 *physical type*
physisorb 32.29 *absorb*
physisorbed 32.43 *absorbed*
physisorption 32.20 *surface chemistry*
phytobiology 34.1 *life science*
phytochemical 77.20 *botanical*
phytochemist 77.12 *plant scientist*
phytochemistry 34.1 *life science*; 77.10 *plant science*
phytochrome 33.18 *pigment*
phytoecology 34.18 *ecology*; 34.1 *life science*
phytogenesis 77.10 *plant science*
phytogenetically 77.25 *botanically*
phytogeneticist 77.12 *plant scientist*
phytogeographer 77.12 *plant scientist*
phytogeographic 77.20 *botanical*
phytogeography 77.10 *plant science*
phytographer 77.12 *plant scientist*
phytographic 77.20 *botanical*
phytography 34.1 *life science*; 77.10 *plant science*
phytohormone 33.17 *plant hormone*
phytol 33.20 *terpene*
phytological 77.20 *botanical*
phytologically 77.25 *botanically*
phytologist 77.12 *plant scientist*
phytology 34.1 *life science*; 77.10 *plant science*
phytopathological 77.20 *botanical*
phytopathologist 77.12 *plant scientist*
phytopathology 77.10 *plant science*
phytoplankton 84.1 *alga*
phytosociological 77.20 *botanical*
phytosociologically 77.25 *botanically*
phytosociologist 77.12 *plant scientist*
phytosociology 77.10 *plant science*
piacular 807.4 *atoning*
piaculum 807.2 *apology*
piaffe 59.10 *dressage*
piaffer 333.10 *slow motion*
Piaget 36.29 *psychologist*
pianissimo 511.10 *faintly*; 511.1 *faint-sounding*
piano 511.10 *faintly*; 511.1 *faint-sounding*
piastre 780.4 *change*
piazza 87.7 *city district*; 565.7 *room*
picador 382.13 *animal killer*; 586.3 *athlete*
picaresque 721.12 *narrative*
picaresque novel 17.2, 721.5 *fiction*
Piccadilly Circus 173.4 *centre of activity*
piccalilli 496.2 *seasoning*
pick 469.4; 123.3 *chief thing*; 469.9 *chosen thing*; 466.12 *discriminate*; 235.7 *elite*; 369.10 *excavator*; 622.12 *object of pride*; 308.2 *opener*; 469.6 *selection*; 425.8 *sharp-pointed thing*; 18.38 *sound*; 439.6 *store*; 212.3 *subtract*; 331.6 *tap*; 797.9 *the best*
pick a bone with 751.7 *pick a fight*
pick a fight 751.7
pick and choose 642.5 *be capricious*; 466.12 *discriminate*; 469.4 *pick*
pick a pocket 212.3 *subtract*
pick a quarrel 751.7 *pick a fight*
pick at 557.23 *taste*
pickaxe 369.10 *excavator*; 438.3 *garden tool*; 308.2 *opener*; 425.8 *sharp-pointed thing*
pick clean 256.13 *clean*
picked 469.15 *chosen*; 235.1 *worthy*
picked man 485.4 *skilled person*
picked out 520.2 *clear*; 372.17 *unjoined*
picked troops 586.14 *armed forces*
picker 256.12 *cleaner*; 557.18 *eater*
picket 586.14 *armed forces*; 378.9 *block*; 753.8 *cause mischief*; 586.39 *defend*; 384.14 *guard*; 15.4 *industrial dispute*; 703.6 *mass demonstration*; 252.3 *protector*; 703.19 *protest*; 703.8 *protester*; 814.1 *punish*; 711.4 *warner*
picketed 15.10 *unionized*
picketer 662.7, 753.4 *protester*
picket fence 360.4 *wall*
picketing 703.14 *demonstrating*; 753.3 *gesture of protest*; 15.4 *industrial dispute*; 15.10 *unionized*
picket line 128.1 *exclusion*; 15.4 *industrial dispute*; 378.2 *obstacle*
pick holes 670.18 *find fault*
pick holes in 606.7 *be dissatisfied*
picking and choosing 469.6 *selection*
picking at one's food 557.3 *delicate eating*
picking out 469.6 *selection*
pickings 469.9 *chosen thing*; 765.4 *earnings*; 774.4 *stolen goods*; 773.5 *takings*
picking up 50.8 *punting*; 366.6 *raising*
pickle 143.3, 222.4 *difficult circumstances*; 408.4 *litter*; 221.2, 264.5 *predicament*; 25.42, 359.5 *preserve*; 359.2 *preserver*; 496.12 *season*; 496.2 *seasoning*; 433.31 *steep*; 439.6 *store*
pickled 690.1 *drunk*; 496.9 *piquant*; 359.7 *preserved*; 439.7 *stored*
pickled herring 25.16 *fish dish*
pickled onion 496.2 *seasoning*
pickle-herring 21.32 *clown*
pickles 359.3 *preserved thing*
pickling 25.8 *cooking technique*; 359.1 *preservation*
picklock 314.8 *intruder*; 774.8 *thief*
pick-me-up 496.6 *cordial*; 558.2 *drink*; 581.7 *refreshments*; 394.7 *tonic*
pick off 381.2 *fire*; 382.17 *murder*; 330.31 *snipe*
pick of the bunch 235.7 *elite*; 622.12 *object of pride*; 797.16 *superior person*
pick on 466.14 *discriminate against*
pick oneself up 393.4 *be restored*
pick one's pockets 774.12 *steal*
pick one's way 264.20 *be in difficulty*; 300.13 *be in motion*
pick out 139.22 *characterize*; 466.12 *discriminate*; 369.11 *extract*; 469.4 *pick*; 518.12 *see*; 372.10 *set apart*; 197.20 *single out*; 212.3 *subtract*
pickpocket 774.12 *steal*; 774.8 *thief*
pickpocketing 774.1 *stealing*
Pick's disease 461.3 *mental deterioration*
pick someone's brains 349.4 *resort to*
pick the best 469.4 *pick*
pick the brains of 705.17 *question*
pick the lock 314.10 *invade*
pick the seam 53.18 *bowl*
pick to pieces 357.9 *demolish*; 670.18 *find fault*
pickup 504.9 *audio device*; 48.6 *fielding terms*; 332.8 *speed*; 39.22 *transformer*; 486.2 *unskilled*
pick up 393.4 *be restored*; 316.14 *bring back*; 366.4 *gather up*; 244.2 *get better*; 504.15 *hear*; 134.4 *protract*; 50.19 *punt*; 492.11 *touch*
pick up cheap 791.5 *buy at a discount*
pick up for nothing 793.14 *buy cheaply*
pick up speed 332.6 *accelerate*
pick up the bill 785.8 *defray*
pick up the pace 262.2 *make haste*
pick up the pieces 393.1 *repair*
picky 466.9 *discriminating*; 469.14 *selecting*
picky eater 557.18 *eater*
picnic 171.12 *be outside*; 601.1 *celebration*; 265.6 *easy thing*; 557.13 *feast*
picnic hamper 410.7 *basket*
picnicker 557.18 *eater*
picrite 30.30 *igneous rock*
pictogram 5.13 *letter*; 717.1 *representation*
pictograph 5.13 *letter*
pictographic 5.41 *lettered*; 19.24 *pictorial*
pictorial 19.24; **27.78**; 717.13 *representational*; 721.13 *representing*
pictorial equivalent 19.7 *picture*
pictorially 19.30; 717.14 *representationally*
Picts 284.6 *people of the past*
picture 19.7; 143.2 *circumstances*; 125.2 *copy*; 721.14 *describe*; 721.1 *description*; 477.4 *ideality*; 743.10 *identify*; 446.15, 477.14 *imagine*; 525.5 *impression*; 163.1, 163.5 *outline*; 717.11 *paint*; 41.3 *photograph*; 744.1 *record*; 721.9 *representation*; 717.2 *reproduction*; 361.3 *suspended object*; 518.7 *view*; 518.16 *visualize*
picture card 69.3 *card game terms*
picture clarity 692.23 *television reception*
pictured 743.12 *identified*
picture frame 19.11 *artist's materials*; 403.4 *framework*
picture-frame stage 21.17 *stage*
picture gallery 19.11 *artist's materials*
picture hat 551.15 *headgear*
picture hook 361.4 *hanger*
picture house 21.16 *theatre*
picture magazine 740.5 *journal*
picture marriage 570.3 *types of marriage*
picture of 111.3 *lookalike*
picture postcard 19.7 *picture*
picture quality 692.23 *television reception*
picture rail 174.3 *architectural summit*
pictures 21.3 *films*
picturesque 19.26 *artistic*; 545.5 *beautiful*; 721.11 *descriptive*
picturesquely 19.31 *artistically*
picture taking 41.1 *photography*
picture to oneself 477.14 *imagine*
picture window 518.9 *viewpoint*
picture writing 717.1 *representation*; 742.1 *sign*
piddle 608.13 *relieve oneself*; 560.17 *urinate*; 560.6 *urine*
piddling 159.7 *little*; 124.4 *trivial*
pidgin 5.10 *language type*
pidgin English 5.26 *dialect*
pi-dog 71.9 *dog*
pie 25.35, 498.3 *dessert*; 265.6 *easy thing*; 25.32 *meat dish*
piebald 541.8 *checked*; 59.1 *horse*
piece 148.5; **205.7**; **405.2**; 203.2 *certain amount*; 69.4 *chess terms*; 780.13 *coinage*; 18.15 *composition*; 43.11 *farmland*; 587.9 *firearm*; 196.2 *fractional part*; 587.11 *guns*; 197.2 *item*; 557.14 *mouthful*; 21.2 *play*; 203.8 *quantify*; 215.1 *remainder*; 21.8 *scene*; 127.2 *thing included*; 19.6, 356.5 *work of art*
pièce bien faite 21.2 *play*
piece by piece 372.20 *separately*
pièce de résistance 340.2 *deed*; 25.9 *dish*; 235.7 *elite*; 235.8 *exceller*; 485.3 *masterpiece*
piecemeal 209.10 *by degrees*; 15.8 *industrial*; 205.11 *partial*; 205.12 *partly*; 372.20 *separately*
piecemeal agreement 15.1 *industrial relations*
piece of advice 713.1 *advice*
piece of architecture 356.8 *construction*
piece of cake 705.5 *easy question*; 265.6 *easy thing*; 246.2 *victory*

piece of eight 780.12 *ancient coins;* 201.4 *eight*
piece of evidence 738.7 *showpiece*
piece of fluff 568.9 *woman considered as a sex object*
piece of good luck 248.2 *good fortune*
piece of land 205.7 *piece*
piece of luck 768.2 *gift;* 287.2 *opportunity;* 765.5 *profit*
piece of nonsense 272.4 *joke*
piece of one's mind 670.7 *blame*
piece of the action 770.2 *portion*
piece of the pie 770.2 *portion*
piece of virtu 19.6 *work of art*
piece of writing 356.5 *work of art*
piece on the board 124.10 *nonentity*
piece rate 790.3 *fee*
piece to eat 557.12 *meal*
piece together 403.17 *assemble;* 232.4 *complete;* 719.9 *decipher;* 405.13 *make;* 393.1 *repair*
piecework 576.1 *work*
pieceworker 578.1 *worker*
pie chart 409.8 *chart;* 27.32 *graph*
piecrust 424.3 *brittle thing;* 550.2 *cover*
pied 541.8 *checked;* 541.6 *variegated*
pied-à-terre 565.5 *house*
piedmont 155.7 *lowland*
pie-eyed 690.2 *slightly drunk*
pie in the sky 477.7 *idealism;* 96.4 *theorization*
pie plate 25.6 *kitchen equipment*
pier 38.21 *bridge;* 20.8 *column;* 20.9 *miscellaneous architectural features;* 361.5 *projecting object;* 185.2 *projection;* 38.27 *superstructure;* 413.2 *supporting part;* 38.24 *water system*
pierce 425.14 *be sharp;* 308.20 *hole;* 743.10 *identify;* 236.14 *ill-treat;* 314.11 *infiltrate;* 368.2 *inject;* 381.6 *stab*
pierced 308.14 *holed*
pierced ears 504.4 *ear*
piercing 505.6 *deafening;* 651.14 *hostile;* 507.6 *loud;* 308.1 *opening;* 513.9 *shrill;* 31.47 *windy*
pier glass 518.8 *reflection*
Pierian Spring 17.13 *poetic genius*
Pierrot 21.32 *clown;* 21.23 *role*
pier table 23.4 *table*
pietà 19.10 *art subject;* 10.14 *sacred object*
pietism 795.4 *self-righteousness*
pietist 7.3 *religious person*
pietistic 795.10 *moralistic*
piety 255.1 *purity;* 7.2 *religiousness;* 9.1 *worship*
piezoelectric 39.36 *electronic*
piezoelectric effect 28.49 *electromagnetic induction*
piezoelectricity 334.7 *electrical power*
piezoelectric oscillator 39.21 *rectifier*
piezometer 26.8 *meter*
piezometric 26.16 *micrometric*
piezometry 26.2 *micrometry*
piffle 697.1 *nonsense*
piffling 697.5 *nonsensical;* 124.4 *trivial*
pig 466.7 *bigot;* 258.6 *dirty person;* 659.4 *discourteous person;* 557.18 *eater;* 688.4 *glutton;* 43.8 *livestock;* 16.17 *police officer;* 253.3 *security officer*
pig ark 43.7 *farm building*
pig breeder 43.15 *agriculturist*
pigeon 700.22 *dupe;* 25.20 *meat;* 86.14 *sphere;* 72.4 *table bird*
pigeon box 692.3 *correspondence*
pigeon fancier 72.20 *ornithologist*
pigeonhole 409.15 *categorize;* 409.6 *category;* 137.2, 137.13 *class;* 692.3 *correspondence;* 294.8 *delay;* 220.8 *list;* 159.5 *little space;* 407.19 *systematize*
pigeonholed 409.24 *categorized;* 137.12 *classed;* 407.11 *grouped;* 350.1 *unused*
pigeonholing 409.5 *categorization;* 294.3 *delayed action;* 407.2 *grouping*
pigeon-like 72.21 *avian*
pigeon loft 72.19 *ornithology;* 565.12 *stall*
pig farmer 43.15 *agriculturist*
pig farming 43.3 *livestock farming*
piggery 43.7 *farm building*
piggish 688.6 *gluttonous;* 71.33 *ungulate*
piggishly 688.7 *gluttonously*
piggishness 688.1 *gluttony*
piggy 71.33 *ungulate*
piggyback 319.5 *transportable*
piggy bank 780.20 *money store*
pig-headed 641.1 *obstinate;* 635.8 *wilful*
pig-headedly 641.9 *obstinately*
pig-headedness 641.5 *obstinacy;* 635.3 *wilfulness*
pighide 435.1 *materials*
pig ignorant 456.6 *ignorant*
pig in a poke 264.5 *predicament;* 456.3 *unknown thing*
pig iron 435.1 *materials*
pig Latin 5.18 *slang*
piglet 43.8 *livestock;* 555.4 *young animal;* 71.19 *young mammal*
piglike 71.33 *ungulate*
pigman 43.16 *farm worker*
pigment **33.18**; **529.4**; 532.7 *blackness;* 28.28, 529.15 *colour*
pigmentation 532.7 *blackness;* 529.1 *colour*
pigment cell 34.7 *cell*
pigment chart 529.2 *colourfulness*
pigment deficiency 530.2 *paleness*
pigmented 529.10 *coloured;* 532.2 *dark*
pigments 19.11 *artist's materials*
pig netting 43.11 *farmland*
pigout 688.3 *act of gluttony;* 557.2 *appetite*
pig out 688.5 *be greedy;* 557.22 *eat well*
pigpen 165.2 *enclosed place;* 43.7 *farm building;* 565.8 *shelter;* 767.8 *sink*
pig's breakfast 486.9 *bungling*
pig's ear 544.6 *blunder;* 486.9 *bungling;* 408.6 *mix-up*
pig's feet 25.31 *offal*
pig's fry 25.31 *offal*
pig's head 25.31 *offal*
pigskin 550.14 *animal covering;* 46.1 *football;* 435.1 *materials*
pig's knuckles 25.31 *offal*
pigsticker 587.8 *sharp weapon*
pigsticking 633.2 *chase;* 71.23 *mammal hunting*
pigsty 309.4 *closed place;* 165.2 *enclosed place;* 43.7 *farm building;* 408.4 *litter;* 565.8 *shelter;* 767.8 *sink;* 565.12 *stall*
pigswill 557.8 *animal food;* 258.5 *swill*
pigtail 193.2 *braid;* 168.1 *rear;* 420.7 *rough thing;* 361.3 *suspended object*
pigtailed 420.3 *barbed*
pike 55.5 *British game fish;* 25.17 *freshwater fish;* 89.1, 154.3 *mountain;* 425.8 *sharp-pointed thing;* 587.8 *sharp weapon;* 67.11 *swimming*
pikelet 25.39 *loaf*
pikeman 586.13 *historical soldiery*
pike position 67.6 *diving*
Pikes Peak 89.4 *US mountains*
Pikes Peak climb 61.1 *motor racing*
pikle 43.10 *farm tool*
pilaster 20.8 *column;* 413.2 *supporting part;* 154.6 *tall thing*
pilastered 20.16 *columned*
pilau rice 25.49 *Indian dish*
pilchard 25.18 *sea fish*
pile 765.11 *acquire;* 765.3 *acquisition;* 376.37 *assemble;* 20.3 *building;* 356.8, 403.6 *construction;* 373.8 *fastening;* 743.8 *heraldic device;* 376.26 *mass;* 404.3 *nap;* 565.4 *official residence;* 439.1 *store;* 38.28 *substructure;* 413.2 *supporting part;* 154.6 *tall thing*
pile builder 88.6 *lake dweller*
pile carpet 550.9 *floor covering*
piled 376.47 *collected*
piled-on 727.14 *extravagant*
pile-drive 331.2 *collide*
pile-driver 38.29 *construction equipment;* 331.15 *ram*
piled up 439.7 *stored*
pile dweller 88.6 *lake dweller*
pile hammer 38.29 *construction equipment*
pile house 88.7 *lake dwelling*
pile in 232.6 *fill;* 304.15 *mount*
pile it on 219.4 *be excessive;* 727.9 *be extravagant;* 727.10 *boast*
pile of money 780.3 *fortune;* 781.6 *money*
pile on 211.6 *add;* 46.18 *be penalized;* 232.6 *fill*
pile Ossa upon Pelion 727.9 *be extravagant*
pile up 765.11 *acquire;* 219.4 *be excessive;* 331.2 *collide;* 439.6 *store*
pile-up 331.12 *collision;* 320.21 *miscellaneous motoring terms;* 64.3 *rugby play*
pileus 83.4 *fungal body*
pilfer 800.10 *be criminal;* 774.12 *steal;* 773.10 *take away*
pilferage 774.1 *stealing*
pilfered 774.17 *stolen*
pilferer 774.8 *thief*
pilfering 774.1 *stealing*
pilgrim 450.5 *believer;* 7.7 *monk;* 7.3 *religious person;* 9.5 *worshipper*
pilgrimage 354.2 *undertaking;* 9.1 *worship*
piling it on 727.3 *extravagance*
piling on 46.13 *penalty*
piling Ossa upon Pelion 727.3 *extravagance*
pill **37.6**; 814.10 *affliction;* 394.2 *medicine;* 181.3 *round thing*
pillage 441.4 *destruction;* 357.5 *havoc;* 357.10, 441.2 *lay waste;* 774.14 *plunder;* 774.5 *plundering;* 381.14 *siege;* 794.2 *spoils;* 774.4 *stolen goods;* 773.10 *take away*
pillager 357.6 *destroyer;* 774.9 *plunderer;* 773.6 *taker*
pillaging 774.5 *plundering;* 774.17 *stolen;* 773.3 *taking away*
pillar 20.8 *column;* 744.11 *monument;* 252.5 *refuge;* 62.5 *rock face;* 228.4 *stable thing;* 38.27 *superstructure;* 413.2 *supporting part;* 154.6 *tall thing;* 186.3 *vertical thing*
pillarbox 692.3 *correspondence;* 535.7 *red thing*
pillarbox red 535.1 *red*
pillarist 7.7 *monk*
pillar of society 123.4 *bigwig;* 228.5 *stable person*
pillar of strength 253.1 *protection*
pillar of the church 228.5 *stable person*
pillar of the community 123.4 *bigwig;* 663.4 *obedient person;* 811.2 *person of repute;* 228.5 *stable person*
Pillars of Hercules 145.3 *distant place*
pillary 621.6 *deride*
pillbox 384.12 *fort;* 551.15 *headgear*
pill bug 75.4 *arthropod*
pilliwinks 814.15 *instrument of torture*
pillock 459.3 *foolish person*
pillory 814.14 *instrument of punishment;* 251.5 *means of restraint;* 814.1 *punish*
pillow 413.4 *rest;* 301.3 *resting place;* 419.11 *soft thing*
pillowcase 550.10 *bed covering*
pillowed 263.4 *at ease;* 419.4 *compressible*
pillow lava 30.25 *eruption*
pillow sham 550.10 *bed covering*
pill-popping 691.1 *drug-taking*
pilot 322.3 *aircraft personnel;* 631.15 *conduct;* 631.10 *conductor;* 579.2 *direct;* 579.13 *director;* 223.15 *escort;* 323.7 *nautical person;* 126.2 *original;* 130.21 *pioneer;* 129.15 *precede;* 129.8 *precursor;* 252.4 *safety device;* 353.9 *tentative;* 223.8 *usher*
pilotage 322.1 *aviation;* 579.4 *directorship;* 323.5 *navigation*
pilot a ship 323.9 *navigate*
piloting 322.1 *aviation;* 324.1 *direction;* 323.5 *navigation;* 129.14 *preparatory*
pilot jack 743.7 *flag*
pilot light 493.6 *fire*
pilot officer 586.32 *airman*
pilot run 448.2 *rehearsal*
pilot scheme 484.6 *outline;* 243.10 *preparations*
pilotship 323.5 *navigation*
Piltdown Man 700.11 *hoax*
pilum 34.8 *cell organ*
pi meson 28.77 *elementary particle*
Pimms™ 558.8 *mixed drink*
pimp 398.6 *agent;* 348.3 *assistant;* 348.4 *be an instrument;* 796.8 *immoral man;* 796.18 *prostitute;* 436.3 *provider;* 436.5 *provision;* 804.9 *wicked person*
pimping 796.5 *prostitution*
pimple **548.2**; 234.3 *deformity;* 541.4 *maculation;* 260.13 *skin disease*
pimply 420.2 *coarse;* 541.10 *mottled*
PIN 40.12 *electronic office*
pin 307.4 *axle;* 69.4 *chess terms;* 373.11 *connect;* 593.26 *court;* 56.2 *golfing terms;* 542.7 *jewellery;* 593.15 *love item;* 308.2 *opener;* 425.8 *sharp-pointed thing;* 309.2 *stopper;* 124.8 *trifle;* 52.5 *wrestling*
pina colada 558.8 *mixed drink*
pinafore 551.25 *accessories*
pinafore dress 551.7 *frock*
pin back one's ears 504.15 *hear*
pince-nez 518.10 *visual aid*
pincer movement 360.2 *detention;* 381.12 *military attack*
pincers 369.10 *excavator;* 438.1 *tool;* 360.3 *tools for gripping*
pinch 412.4 *admixture;* 693.7 *advice;* 782.12 *be poor;* 593.14 *communication of love;* 191.1 *contraction;* 310.9 *converge;* 287.3 *critical time;* 46.10 *defence;* 251.11 *detain;* 222.4 *difficult circumstances;* 491.11 *inflict pain;* 782.6 *insolvency;* 159.5 *little space;* 191.5 *make smaller;* 151.10 *narrow;* 135.3 *needfulness;* 46.16 *play defence;* 264.5 *predicament;* 492.3 *press;* 50.19 *punt;* 774.12 *steal;* 773.10 *take away;* 773.3 *taking away;* 774.3 *theft;* 492.11 *touch;* 711.5 *warn;* 711.1 *warning*
pinchbeck 124.4 *trivial*
pinched 494.8 *cold;* 153.2 *emaciated;* 782.2 *insolvent;* 151.1 *narrow;* 135.5 *necessitous;* 50.14 *punting;* 191.7 *smaller;* 16.59 *stolen*
pinch hit 762.4 *be a substitute*
pinch hitter 398.5 *alternative;* 48.2 *baseball player;* 762.2 *substitute person*
pinching 191.8 *contracting;* 191.1 *contraction;* 135.6 *demanding;* 50.8 *punting;* 774.1 *stealing*
pinching out 44.5 *gardening*
pinch of snuff 496.7 *tobacco*
pinch pennies 782.12 *be poor*
pinch someone's bottom 742.11 *gesture*
pincoffin 42.6 *dye*
pin connection 38.27 *superstructure*
Pindaric 17.19 *narrative*
Pindaric ode 17.7 *poem*
pindling 159.7 *little*
pin down 386.6 *compel;* 142.11 *find;* 452.21 *make certain;* 139.24 *specify*
pine 260.24 *be unhealthy;* 602.8 *grieve*
pineal 559.5 *of a secretion*
pineapple 587.16 *bomb*
pineapple family 77.3 *seed plant*
pineapple juice 558.6 *soft drink*
pine cone 79.2 *tree part*
pine drape 582.8 *after death;* 583.4 *funeral objects*
pine for 617.12 *desire*
pine furniture 23.1 *furniture*
pine marten 79.11 *tree-related animal*
pinene 33.20 *terpene*
pine needle 425.8 *sharp-pointed thing;* 79.2 *tree part*
pinery 79.4 *trees*
pine tar 79.9 *tree product*
pinetum 79.4 *trees*
pinewood oil 79.9 *tree product*
pinfold 43.7 *farm building*
ping 509.12, 510.10 *ring;* 509.5, 510.2 *ringing*
pinging 509.5, 510.7 *ringing*
ping pong 63.1 *tennis*
pinguescent 268.13 *slippery*
pinguid 268.13 *slippery*
pinguidinous 268.13 *slippery*
pinguidity 268.3 *oiliness*
pinhead 459.3 *foolish person;* 174.2 *head;* 159.2 *little thing;* 457.3 *unintelligent person*
pinhole 308.5 *hole*
pinhole camera 41.16 *camera*
pining 617.1 *desire;* 617.9 *desirous;* 602.5 *sad;* 260.22 *sick*
pinion 38.7 *gear;* 245.5 *hurt*
pinioned 360.10 *retained*
pink 183.10 *notch;* 535.1 *red*
pink ball 65.5 *snooker*
pinked 183.7 *notched*
pink elephant 518.5 *imagination*
pink elephants 690.16 *alcoholism*
pink eye 519.2 *poor sight*
pink gin 558.8 *mixed drink*
pinkie 492.7 *sense organ*
pinking shears 425.9 *sharp-edged thing*
pinko 12.6 *political party;* 662.11 *rebel*
pink of condition 259.3 *health*
pink slip 371.18 *dismissal*
pin money 780.4 *change;* 788.3 *income;* 440.6 *marriage settlement;* 765.5 *profit;* 769.2 *something received*
pinna 82.2 *fern plant*
pinnacle 154.2 *heights;* 89.1 *mountain;* 230.3 *perfection;* 62.5 *rock face;* 121.4, 174.1 *summit*
pinnate 77.18 *of leaves*
pinned 373.15 *connected;* 360.10 *retained*
pinned down 142.7 *found;* 452.7 *particular;* 228.10 *stabilized*
pinning down 142.3 *locating;* 452.18 *particularity*
pinniped 71.29 *cetacean;* 71.11 *marine mammal*
Pinnipedia 71.11 *marine mammal*
pinnipedian 71.29 *cetacean*

pinny 551.25 *accessories*; 256.11 *cleaning cloth*
Pinocchio 159.4 *little person*; 554.6 *things brought to life*
pin one's hopes on 610.6 *hope*
pin on to 664.14 *follow*
pinpoint 273.5, 698.21 *accurate*; 698.31 *be accurate*; 173.9 *centre*; 139.22 *characterize*; 142.2 *exact location*; 142.11 *find*; 743.10 *identify*; 159.2 *little thing*; 740.16 *publicize*
pinpoint accuracy 273.1, 591.10, 698.8 *accuracy*
pinpointed 698.21 *accurate*; 173.7 *centralized*; 142.7 *found*
pinpointing 173.3 *centrality*; 173.7 *centralized*; 743.1 *identification*; 142.3 *locating*
pinprick 624.3 *cause of offence*; 624.9 *offend*; 491.1 *pain*; 157.4 *shallow thing*; 124.8 *trifle*
pins and needles 491.1 *pain*; 488.3 *stimulus*
pin someone 52.12 *wrestle*
pin someone's shoulders 52.12 *wrestle*
pin spot 51.4 *bowling*
pinstripes 551.9 *trousers*
pinstripe suit 551.10 *suit*
pint 558.2 *drink*
pinta 558.5 *milk*
pint glass 410.13 *drinking vessel*
pintle 307.4 *axle*
pinto 541.8 *checked*; 59.1 *horse*
pin to 211.6 *add*
pint of milk 558.5 *milk*
pint-size 159.7 *little*
pin-up 41.4 *portrait*
pin-up girl 545.3 *attractive female*
pinwheel 522.8 *fire*; 307.6 *rotator*
pinworm 75.10 *parasite*
piny 79.14 *treelike*
Pinyin 5.13 *letter*
pion 28.77 *elementary particle*
Pioneer 29.33 *planetary probe*
pioneer **130.21**; 586.17 *army person*; 579.2 *direct*; 449.12 *discoverer*; 129.18 *forerun*; 449.4 *invent*; 265.16 *make easy*; 126.7 *originate*; 129.8 *precursor*; 243.1 *prepare*; 243.15 *preparer*; 564.15 *settle*; 564.7 *settler*; 354.1 *undertake*; 354.4 *volunteer*
pioneering 449.13 *discovering*; 354.6 *enterprising*; 449.9 *invention*; 126.4 *original*; 129.3, 243.9 *preparation*; 129.14 *preparatory*
piononos 25.51 *West Indian dish*
pious 795.10 *moralistic*; 799.5 *pure*; 7.15 *religious*; 10.22 *worshipping*
pious fraud 700.10 *fraud*
piously 795.13 *morally*; 799.8 *purely*; 7.23 *religiously*
piousness 795.2 *good morals*; 7.2 *religiousness*
pip 80.3 *fruit structure*; 743.4 *insignia*; 626.10 *make sullen*; 509.5 *ringing*; 77.9 *seed*
pip at the post 645.5 *be cunning*; 246.9 *be victorious*
pipe 513.6 *be shrill*; 181.4 *cylinder*; 164.6 *edge*; 151.8 *narrow thing*; 308.7 *passageway*; 308.21 *provide passage for*; 439.2 *resource*; 18.39, 515.5 *sing*; 40.8 *software*; 729.13 *speak in a particular way*; 410.11 *vessel*
pipe band 18.26 *musical group*
pipeclay 24.2 *raw material*; 531.13 *whiten*; 531.8 *whitener*
pipe cleaner 256.10 *cleaning object*
piped 319.5 *transportable*
pipe down 506.1 *be silent*; 226.6 *cease*; 506.6 *hush!*; 301.11 *stop!*
pipe dream 610.3 *aspiration*; 96.2 *illusion*; 518.5 *imagination*; 446.15 *imagine*; 105.4 *improbability*; 467.2 *overestimate*; 477.6 *reverie*
pipeline 308.7 *passageway*; 436.1 *provision*; 439.3 *supply*
pipe of peace 496.7 *tobacco*
Pipe rolls 3.11 *relic*
pipe tobacco 496.7 *tobacco*
pipette 369.9 *extractor*; 369.14 *suck*
pipetting 369.4 *sucking*
pipe vein 439.2 *resource*
pipe wrench 438.1 *tool*
piping 164.2 *edging*; 589.7 *peaceful*; 513.9 *shrill*; 513.3 *shrillness*; 319.5 *transportable*
piping down 226.2 *stop*
piping hot 493.9 *hot*
piping times of peace 589.1 *peace*
pipit 72.6 *songbird*
pipkin 24.8 *ceramic object*
pipped 247.11 *defeated*
pips 542.4 *honour*; 742.4 *signal*
pipsqueak 159.4 *little person*; 124.10 *nonentity*
piquancy **496.1**; 726.1 *emphasis*
piquant **496.9**; 726.3 *emphatic*; 336.12 *strong to the senses*
piquantly **496.15**
pique 496.13 *be piquant*; 624.9 *offend*; 624.1 *resentment*
piqued 624.15 *resentful*
piquet pack 69.3 *card game terms*
piracy 772.3, 774.6 *illegal borrowing*; 774.1 *stealing*; 773.3 *taking away*
Pirani gauge 32.20 *surface chemistry*
pirate 772.6 *borrower*; 125.10 *copy*; 774.15 *infringe*; 774.10 *infringer*; 586.6 *militarist*; 323.7 *nautical person*
pirate a record 772.9 *borrow illegally*; 774.15 *infringe*
pirate a video 772.9 *borrow illegally*; 774.15 *infringe*
pirated 772.11 *borrowed*; 774.18 *fraudulent*
pirated record 115.2 *copy*
pirate flag 743.7 *flag*
piratelike 774.17 *stolen*
pirate radio 692.20 *radio broadcasting*
pirate ship 586.25 *historical naval ships*
piratess 323.7 *nautical person*
piratical 586.33 *combative*; 774.18 *fraudulent*
piratically 774.19 *thievishly*
pirating 772.3, 774.6 *illegal borrowing*
piroplasm 75.10 *parasite*
piroplasmosis 75.12 *protozoal disease*
pirouette 22.9 *ballet steps*; 57.10 *compete in gymnastics*; 59.10 *dressage*; 57.5 *horizontal bar*; 68.7 *ice-dancing*; 68.15 *ice-skate*; 307.3 *reel*; 307.8 *rotate*
pirouetting 307.2 *turning*
Pisacha 8.7 *devil*
pis aller 239.5 *convenience*; 484.3 *expedient plan*; 231.6 *imperfect item*; 762.1 *substitution*
piscary 74.7 *fishing*
piscatology 74.7 *fishing*
piscator 74.10 *fisher*; 633.6 *hunter*
piscatorial 55.8 *angling*; 74.13 *fishlike*; 633.16 *hunting*; 74.14 *ichthyological*
piscatorially 55.9 *on the water*
Pisces 74.1 *fishes*
piscicultural 74.14 *ichthyological*
pisciculturalist 74.10 *fisher*
pisciculturally 43.22 *agriculturally*
pisciculture 74.7 *fishing*; 43.3 *livestock farming*
pisciform 74.13 *fishlike*
piscine 74.13 *fishlike*
pishogue 594.2 *curse*; 450.2 *religious belief*
piskie 11.11 *ghost*
pismire 76.4 *social insect*
piss 431.3 *body fluid*; 433.4 *exudate*; 608.13 *relieve oneself*; 433.32 *seep*; 560.17 *urinate*; 560.3 *urination*; 560.6 *urine*
piss and vinegar 338.1 *vigour*
piss-ant 639.15 *indecisive person*
piss-artist 690.17 *drunkard*
piss away 441.1 *waste*
piss down 31.62 *rain*
pissed 690.1 *drunk*
pissed as a newt 690.1 *drunk*
pissed off 624.16 *angry*; 261.2 *bored*
pisshead 558.12 *drinker*; 690.17 *drunkard*
pissing down 31.53 *rainy*
piss off 313.1 *depart*; 313.15 *go!*; 371.33 *go away!*; 624.14 *make angry*; 712.15 *miscellaneous swearwords*
pisspot 560.14 *toilet*
piss-take 621.2 *act of derision*
Pista! 68.18 *danger!*
Piste! 68.18 *danger!*
piste 54.1 *fencing*; 742.1 *sign*; 68.1 *skiing*; 744.12 *vestige*
pistil 78.3 *flower part*
pistillate 78.12 *of flowers*
pistol 330.9, 587.9 *firearm*; 382.17 *murder*; 330.28 *shoot*
pistole 780.12 *ancient coins*
pistoleer 586.13 *historical soldiery*; 330.15 *shooter*
pistolet 587.10 *historical gun*
pistols 551.9 *trousers*
pistol shooting 60.1 *target shooting*
pistol-shot 508.1 *bang*
piston 38.11 *engine*; 321.5 *locomotive part*; 330.11 *propeller*; 309.2 *stopper*
piston movement 298.1 *regularity*
piston slap 320.21 *miscellaneous motoring terms*
pit 21.18 *auditorium*; 51.4 *bowling*; 437.5 *coal*; 183.2 *concave land*; 156.4 *deep thing*; 234.11 *deform*; 80.3 *fruit structure*; 320.21 *miscellaneous motoring terms*; 61.6 *motor-racing terms*; 404.3 *nap*; 252.5 *refuge*; 700.13 *snare*; 21.17 *stage*; 645.2 *stratagem*; 21.33 *theatregoer*; 379.1 *trap*; 518.9 *viewpoint*; 577.1 *workshop*
pit against 113.19 *confront*
Pitaka 7.12 *religious text*
pitapat 327.10 *beat*; 509.4 *knocking*; 326.2 *vibration*
pit bull terrier 586.4 *fighting animal*
pitch **327.25**; 227.11 *be changeable*; 189.6 *be oblique*; 532.9 *black thing*; 523.4 *dark thing*; 209.1 *degree*; 325.14 *deviating course*; 325.15 *deviating motion*; 305.12 *drop*; 56.1, 56.7 *golf*; 154.1 *height*; 142.1 *location*; 186.6 *make vertical*; 729.3 *mode of speech*; 18.16, 28.20 *musical note*; 189.1 *obliqueness*; 48.7 *play baseball*; 326.4, 326.11 *rock*; 62.5 *rock face*; 778.6 *salesmanship*; 5.16 *spoken letter*; 327.11 *stagger*; 174.1 *summit*; 330.5, 330.23, 331.4 *throw*; 367.6 *throw down*; 18.21 *tone*; 305.11 *trip*
pitch a bitch 740.14 *proclaim*
pitch and plunge 327.25 *pitch*
pitch-and-run approach 56.1 *golf*
pitch and toss 330.5 *throw*
pitch a perfect game 48.7 *play baseball*
pitch a shut-out 48.7 *play baseball*
pitch-black 532.1 *black*; 523.10 *dark-coloured*
pitch-dark 523.8 *dark*
pitch-darkness 523.1 *darkness*
pitch diameter 38.7 *gear*
pitched 189.4 *oblique*; 729.18 *phonetic*; 20.14 *roofed*
pitched battle 585.9 *battle*
pitched roof 550.7 *overhead covering*; 20.6 *roof*
pitcher 48.2 *baseball player*; 24.8 *ceramic object*; 203.3 *container*; 330.14 *thrower*; 410.11 *vessel*; 433.16 *water carrier*
pitcher plant 700.13 *snare*
pitcher's mound 48.1 *baseball*
pitcher's plate 48.1 *baseball*
pitchfork 43.10 *farm tool*; 438.3 *garden tool*; 330.24 *push*; 425.8 *sharp-pointed thing*
pitch forward 330.24 *push*
pitch in 557.22 *eat well*; 392.29 *finance*; 392.22 *improve*; 130.18 *make a beginning*; 747.13 *work together*
pitching 322.5 *flight*; 323.11 *nautical*; 326.16 *rocking*; 330.3 *throwing*; 327.3 *turbulence*; 327.17 *turbulent*
pitching coach 48.2 *baseball player*
pitching into 670.8 *berating*
pitching niblick 56.4 *golf club*
pitching terms **48.4**
pitch into 670.21 *berate*; 381.5 *strike*
pitch of perfection 243.14 *preparedness*
pitch one's tent 565.18 *take up residence*
pitchout 46.9 *play*; 46.15 *play offence*
pitchpole 50.15 *sail*
pitch roof 20.6 *roof*
pitch upon 312.2 *reach*
pitchy 532.1 *black*; 523.10 *dark-coloured*
piteous 627.7 *pitiful*
piteously 627.13 *pitifully*
pitfall 254.5 *danger*; 264.8 *snag*; 700.13 *snare*; 645.2 *stratagem*; 379.1 *trap*
pith 173.1 *centre*; 99.2 *essential content*; 80.3 *fruit structure*; 123.1 *importance*; 172.5 *inner nature*; 406.3 *insides*; 694.1 *meaning*; 694.2 *significance*; 77.5 *stem*; 447.1 *topic*
Pithecanthropus 296.7 *ancient people*; 566.3 *early human*
pith helmet 551.15 *headgear*; 550.12 *protective covering*
pithily 269.5 *concisely*; 723.11 *summarily*
pithiness 269.1 *conciseness*; 723.4 *summariness*
pithy 419.4 *compressible*; 269.3 *concise*; 726.3 *emphatic*; 745.2 *proverbial*; 694.7 *significant*; 723.6 *summary*
pithy saying 269.1 *conciseness*
pitiable 124.2 *obscure*; 627.7 *pitiful*; 236.4 *poor*
pitiably 627.13 *pitifully*
pitied 648.5 *given consideration*
pitiful **627.7**; 603.5 *lamentable*; 124.2 *obscure*; 236.4 *poor*
pitifully **627.13**
pitifulness 236.10 *poverty*
pitiless **628.4**; 651.13 *merciless*; 647.8 *severe*; 638.3 *strong-willed*; 641.3 *unyielding*
pitilessly **628.7**
pitilessness **628.1**; 809.1 *impenitence*; 647.1 *severity*; 638.14 *tenacity*
pitiless person **628.3**
pit lane 61.6 *motor-racing terms*
pit mechanic 61.8 *driver*
pit of Acheron 8.12 *hell*
pit of one's stomach 590.8 *seat of feelings*
piton 62.4 *climbing equipment*
pit pony 59.2 *thoroughbred*
pit stop 61.6 *motor-racing terms*
pitta bread 25.38 *bread*
pittance 203.2 *certain amount*; 218.8 *insufficiency*; 770.2 *portion*
pitted 420.2 *coarse*; 183.6 *concave*; 234.7 *deformed*; 548.5 *marked*
pitter-patter 327.10 *beat*; 509.4 *knocking*; 326.2 *vibration*
pittite 21.33 *theatregoer*
Pittsburgh 87.2 *American cities*
pituitary 559.5 *of a secretion*
pit wall 61.6 *motor-racing terms*
Pity **627**
pity **627.1**; **627.8**; 648.3 *be lenient*; 650.1 *benevolence*; 591.11 *be sensitive*; 473.7 *be unselfish*; 590.18 *feel for*; 648.1 *leniency*; 591.5 *sensitivity*; 473.2 *unselfishness*
pitying **627.6**; 648.4 *lenient*
pitying person **627.4**
pivot 307.4 *axle*; 22.3 *ballroom dance steps*; 173.1 *centre*; 123.3 *chief thing*; 99.2 *essential content*; 310.5 *focus*; 56.3 *golf shots*; 68.7 *ice-dancing*; 68.15 *ice-skate*; 49.6 *play basketball*; 307.8 *rotate*; 438.1 *tool*; 303.9 *turn round*
pivotal 344.13 *causal*; 173.6 *central*; 287.7 *critical*; 222.8 *difficult*; 123.5 *important*; 307.12 *rotary*
pivotally 344.14 *causally*; 287.10 *critically*
pivotal point 287.3 *critical time*; 761.3 *turning point*
pivot cartwheel 57.6 *pommel horse*
pivoting 49.4 *playing terms*; 307.11 *rotating*; 307.2 *turning*
pivot man 49.2 *basketball player*
pivot on 173.9 *centre*; 345.7 *follow from*
pixel 40.19 *computing terms*; 159.2 *little thing*
pixie 11.11 *ghost*
pixilated 690.1 *drunk*
pizza 25.47 *Italian dish*
pizza face 546.2 *ugly person*
pizzazz 338.1 *vigour*
pizzeria 557.15 *eating place*
PJs 551.22 *nightwear*
placability 649.2 *forgivingness*
placable 649.5 *merciful*
placableness 649.2 *forgivingness*
placali 25.53 *African dish*
placard 740.9 *advertisement*; 740.16 *publicize*; 738.8 *showplace*; 742.1 *sign*
placate 609.9 *comfort*; 599.15 *humour*; 749.4 *pacify*
placating 599.11 *humouring*
placatory 749.6 *pacificatory*; 589.7 *peaceful*
place 409.12 *arrange*; 409.15 *categorize*; 409.6 *category*; 143.2 *circumstances*; 137.13 *class*; 449.1 *discover*; 143.4 *employment*; 565.1 *habitat*; 59.7 *horseracing*; 209.4 *interval*; 142.9 *locate*; 142.1 *location*; 209.5 *measure*; 407.4 *position*; 209.2 *rank*; 86.1 *region*; 141.5 *reserved space*; 317.3 *road*; 143.10 *situate*; 143.1 *situation*; 221.1 *state*; 407.19 *systematize*; 810.2 *task*
place an advertisement 740.16 *publicize*
place at intervals 141.21, 146.4 *space*
placebo 37.3 *drug*; 394.2 *medicine*
place card 743.3 *means of identification*
placed 409.20 *arranged*; 409.24 *categorized*; 222.7 *circumstantial*; 137.12 *classed*; 221.8 *in a state of*; 142.6 *located*; 143.6 *situated*

placed at intervals 146.6 *spaced*
place in a situation 143.10 *situate*
place in history 462.5 *day to remember*; 3.7 *narrative*; 246.1 *success*
place in one's account 783.10 *deposit*
place in order 409.15 *categorize*
place in the foreground 123.8 *make important*; 738.3 *reveal*
place in the spotlight 738.3 *reveal*
place in the sun 248.1 *prosperity*
place kick 331.13 *blow*; 46.17, 331.7 *kick*; 64.3 *rugby play*
place kicker 46.12 *special team*
placemat 256.11 *cleaning cloth*; 550.12 *protective covering*
placement 409.1 *arrangement*; 409.5 *categorization*; 142.4 *placing*
place name 721.8 *name*
placenta 561.7 *obstetrics*; 71.5 *placental mammal*
placental 71.25 *mammalian*; 559.5 *of a secretion*
placental mammal 71.5
place of authority 396.6
place of confinement 655.4
place of contact 147.7 *interface*
place of departure 313.10
place of embarkation 313.10 *place of departure*
place of exchange 759.2
place of experimentation 448.6
place of judgment 464.3
place of pilgrimage 173.4 *centre of activity*; 482.6 *objective*
place of residence 733.5; 565.1 *habitat*
place of safety 252.5 *refuge*
place of the damned 101.1 *nonmaterial world*
place of the dead 8.12 *hell*
place of trade 759.2 *place of exchange*
place of work 577.1 *workshop*
place of worship 10.11
place on 211.6 *add*
place oneself 407.24 *line up*
placer 32.24 *ore*
place side by side 147.18 *juxtapose*
place strictures on 166.7 *limit*
place to one's credit 783.10 *deposit*
place under 127.6 *subsume*
place under an embargo 128.7 *exclude*
place under oath 707.18 *vow*
place-value notation 27.8 *number system*
place where one lives 565.1 *habitat*
placid 4.18 *detached*; 301.6 *quiescent*
placidity 4.3 *detachment*; 301.2 *repose*
placidly 301.10 *motionlessly*; 4.27 *stoically*
placidness 301.2 *repose*
placing 142.4; 409.1 *arrangement*; 409.5 *categorization*
placket 551.24 *part of garment*
placoderm 74.4 *fossil fish*
placoid 411.9 *platelike*
placoid scale 74.5 *fish anatomy*
plagiarism 125.2 *copy*; 772.3, 774.6 *illegal borrowing*; 112.2 *iteration*; 112.1 *repetition*; 773.1 *taking*; 773.3 *taking away*; 316.4 *translation*
plagiarist 772.6 *borrower*; 125.8 *copier*; 774.10 *infringer*; 115.4 *person who copies*; 773.6 *taker*
plagiarize 772.9 *borrow illegally*; 125.10 *copy*; 774.15 *infringe*; 112.16 *repeat*; 773.7 *take*; 773.10 *take away*; 316.16 *translate*
plagiarized 772.11 *borrowed*; 774.18 *fraudulent*; 125.13 *imitation*; 112.9 *repeated*
plagiarized book 699.16 *false thing*
plagiarizing 774.6 *illegal borrowing*
plagiary 774.6 *illegal borrowing*
plagioclase 30.34 *mineral*
plague 260.5; 249.1 *adversity*; 798.2 *affliction*; 357.7 *agent of destruction*; 798.11 *be evil*; 236.13 *be worthless*; 245.5 *hurt*; 76.16 *infest*; 236.10 *poverty*; 76.4 *social insect*; 329.8 *transgression*; 612.14 *worry*
plagued 798.8 *afflicted*; 329.11 *overrun*; 264.16 *troubled*; 612.9 *worried*
plagued by conscience 808.6 *penitent*
plague pit 583.6 *grave*
plague spot 260.6 *infection*
plague-stricken 260.23 *diseased*
plaguey 264.13 *inconvenient*; 236.4 *poor*
plaice 55.5 *British game fish*; 74.8 *food fish*; 25.18 *sea fish*
plaid 541.2 *check*; 541.8 *checked*; 420.12 *make rough*; 420.7 *rough thing*
Plaid Cymru 12.6 *political party*
plain 525.10 *aspectual*; 707.14 *assertive*; 620.4 *boring*; 520.2, 725.3 *clear*; 232.7 *complete*; 232.9 *completely*; 92.11 *continental*; 703.9 *demonstrated*; 527.4 *easily seen through*; 265.9 *easy*; 543.3 *elegant*; 65.3 *English billiards*; 657.9 *familiar*; 187.3 *flat thing*; 141.3 *geographical space*; 81.2 *grassland*; 178.5, 799.4 *honourable*; 187.8 *horizontal*; 724.8 *inelegant*; 122.5 *inferior state*; 250.13 *informal*; 30.7 *landform*; 92.6 *lowland*; 155.2 *lowlands*; 694.6 *meaningful*; 646.1 *naive*; 308.16, 738.15 *open*; 574.4 *ordinary*; 684.8 *self-restrained*; 271.1, 695.2, 728.14 *simple*; 421.8 *smooth thing*; 529.13 *soft-hued*; 178.2 *straightforward*; 67.11 *swimming*; 497.5 *tasteless*; 698.18 *truthful*; 544.10, 546.4 *ugly*; 647.10 *unadorned*; 518.23, 520.1 *visible*
plain as a pikestaff 520.2 *clear*
plainchant 10.8 *hymn*; 516.2 *song*
plain clothes 551.4 *informal dress*
plain-clothes officer 16.17 *police officer*
plain English 271.4, 695.10 *simplicity*
plain flour 25.7 *basic ingredient*
plain Jane 216.7 *average person*
plain jump 67.6 *diving*
plain living 684.1 *self-restraint*
plainly 647.12; 525.15 *apparently*; 426.12 *bluntly*; 620.8 *boringly*; 725.4 *clearly*; 543.5 *elegantly*; 707.25 *explicitly*; 799.7 *honourably*; 250.22 *informally*; 719.18 *in other words*; 695.13 *intelligibly*; 703.20, 738.16 *manifestly*; 694.13 *meaningfully*; 657.14 *naturally*; 308.25 *obviously*; 308.26, 739.13 *openly*; 271.8, 728.24 *simply*; 178.13 *straightforwardly*; 724.10 *stylistically*; 527.13 *transparently*; 518.25, 520.11 *visibly*; 684.11 *with self-restraint*
plainly stated 695.2 *simple*
plainly visible 185.7 *conspicuous*
plain man 646.3 *naive person*
plainness 707.6 *assertiveness*; 620.1 *boredom*; 520.4, 725.1 *clarity*; 694.3 *comprehension*; 178.8 *directness*; 543.1 *elegance*; 657.3 *familiarity*; 187.1 *horizontality*; 724.3 *inelegance*; 646.2 *naivety*; 527.10, 738.11 *openness*; 799.1 *probity*; 684.1 *self-restraint*; 265.2, 271.4, 695.10, 728.4 *simplicity*; 497.1 *tastelessness*; 698.5 *truthfulness*; 694.4 *type of meaning*; 544.3, 546.1 *ugliness*; 647.3 *unadornment*
plain prose 271.4 *simplicity*
plain reason 444.2 *reasoning*
plain sailing 265.6 *easy thing*; 323.5 *navigation*
plainsong 10.8 *hymn*
plain speaking 178.8 *directness*; 271.6 *naturalness*; 739.3 *openness*; 695.10 *simplicity*
plain-speaking 271.3 *natural*; 738.15 *open*; 729.19 *speaking*
plain speech 271.6 *naturalness*; 738.11 *openness*; 695.10 *simplicity*
plain-spoken 799.4 *honourable*; 250.13 *informal*; 693.16 *informative*; 738.15 *open*; 426.2 *outspoken*; 729.19 *speaking*
plain-spokenness 426.6 *outspokenness*
plain stitch 42.5 *knitting*
plaint 715.1 *accusation*
plaintiff 715.3 *accuser*; 444.6 *arguer*; 16.8 *litigant*; 113.11 *opposer*; 705.10 *person questioned*; 716.7 *person who gives evidence*
plaintive 603.4 *lamenting*
plaintively 603.8 *mournfully*
plain to see 520.2 *clear*
plain weave 42.4 *weaving*
plain words 308.9 *openness*; 271.4, 695.10 *simplicity*
plain wrapper 521.6 *that which makes invisible*
plait 193.2 *braid*; 373.11 *connect*; 547.8 *haircut*; 193.8 *interweave*; 373.6 *line*; 25.39 *loaf*; 412.8 *mix*; 184.3 *pleat*; 42.13 *spin*; 42.2 *spinning*
plaited 373.15 *connected*; 193.6 *interwoven*; 412.12 *mixed*; 42.9 *spun*
plaiting 193.1 *interweaving*; 42.2 *spinning*
Plan 484
plan 446.3; **475.3**; **484.1**; **484.9**; 446.18 *aim*; 585.6 *art of war*; 17.3 *aspect of fiction*; 344.10 *awaken*; 645.5 *be cunning*; 631.14 *behave towards*; 409.8 *chart*; 19.23 *design*; 243.2 *do the groundwork*; 38.30 *engineer*; 142.2 *exact location*; 474.8 *expect*; 352.6 *find means*; 482.3 *future intention*; 482.7, 635.13, 694.12 *intend*; 409.18 *make arrangements*; 30.65, 484.5 *map*; 407.7 *method*; 409.13 *organize*; 163.1, 163.5, 723.2 *outline*; 717.11 *paint*; 694.5 *point*; 106.2 *premeditate*; 106.6 *premeditation*; 243.10 *preparations*; 356.10 *produce*; 693.5 *reference book*; 717.2 *reproduction*; 706.6 *solution*; 706.20 *solve*; 403.1, 403.14 *structure*; 476.5 *suppose*; 631.9 *tactics*; 354.2 *undertaking*; 518.16 *visualize*
plan ahead 484.12
planar 187.8 *horizontal*; 27.79 *spatial*
planarian 75.6 *worm*
plan beforehand 106.2 *premeditate*
planchette 11.10 *psychic phenomenon*
Planck constant 28.97 *fundamental constant*
plane 23.17 *carpenter*; 187.4 *flattener*; 365.15 *grind*; 187.8 *horizontal*; 187.11 *horizontally*; 187.2 *horizontal surface*; 209.4 *interval*; 187.7 *make horizontal*; 586.31 *military aircraft*; 50.15 *sail*; 425.9 *sharp-edged thing*; 421.11 *smooth*; 421.9 *smoother*; 27.79 *spatial*; 27.38 *surface*; 304.19 *take off*; 438.1 *tool*; 421.2 *uniform*; 425.16 *use a sharp tool*; 50.18 *windsurf*; 23.11 *woodworking tool*
plane angle 27.39 *angle*; 28.7 *space*
plane figure 27.41 *geometric figure*
plane geometry 27.34 *geometry*
plane mirror 28.29 *optical element*
planeness 187.1 *horizontality*
plane of symmetry 27.41 *geometric figure*
plane polarization 28.15 *wave property*
plane-polarized light 28.27 *polarized light*
planer 38.9 *machine tool*; 23.11 *woodworking tool*
plane sailing 323.5 *navigation*
plane surface 187.2 *horizontal surface*; 27.38 *surface*
planet 29.16; 306.4 *orbiting body*
planetarium 29.23 *observatory*; 518.9 *viewpoint*
planetary 29.36 *astronomical*; 138.16 *universal*
planetary atmosphere 29.16 *planet*
planetary influence 344.4 *contributing factor*; 395.2 *occult influence*
planetary meteorology 31.1 *meteorology*
planetary nebula 29.8 *interstellar medium*
planetary probe 29.33
planetary system 29.14 *solar system*
planet earth 30.5 *earth*
planetesimal 306.4 *orbiting body*
planetoid 306.4 *orbiting body*; 29.16 *planet*
planetologist 30.3 *geologist*
planetology 30.1 *earth science*
plane trigonometry 27.51 *trigonometry*
plan for 482.7 *intend*
plangency 510.3 *deepness*; 603.1 *lamentation*; 507.1 *loudness*
plangent 510.8 *deep*; 603.4 *lamenting*; 507.6 *loud*
plangently 603.8 *mournfully*; 510.11 *resonantly*
planimeter 26.8 *meter*; 187.5 *planometer*
planimetric 26.16 *micrometric*
planimetry 26.2 *micrometry*
planing 50.10 *sailing*; 50.7, 50.13 *windsurfing*
planing keelboat 50.2 *sailing boat*
planish 421.11 *smooth*
planisphere 29.23 *observatory*
plank 23.17 *carpenter*; 550.28 *face*; 435.1 *materials*; 252.4 *safety device*; 411.4 *slice*; 23.12 *wood*
planking 435.1 *materials*; 550.8 *wall covering*; 23.12 *wood*
plank road 317.3 *road*
planks 59.9 *jumping*
plankton 70.5 *aquatic animal*; 159.2 *little thing*
planktonic 70.15 *of animals*
planned 484.14; 26.15, 106.4 *deliberate*; 243.17 *developing*; 482.12 *intended*; 694.9 *meant*; 409.21 *organized*; 446.12 *purposive*; 706.14 *solved*
planned event 354.2 *undertaking*
planned parenthood 563.3 *birth control*
planner 484.8; 706.10 *answerer*; 485.5 *expert*; 342.11 *meddler*; 480.14 *motivator*; 356.9 *producer*; 476.4 *theorist*
planning 484.7; **484.15**; 409.11 *arrangements*; 585.6 *art of war*; 645.4 *cunning*; 409.3 *organization*; 475.3 *plan*; 243.9 *preparation*; 356.1 *production*; 518.4 *visualization*
planning office 484.7 *planning*
planoconvex lens 28.29 *optical element*
plan of action 484.2 *policy*
plan of attack 631.9 *tactics*
plan of battle 585.6 *art of war*
plan of campaign 631.9 *tactics*
plan of the day 484.1 *plan*
planometer 187.5
plan one's family 563.9 *practise birth control*
plan out 484.10
planposition indicator 692.28 *radar*
plans 409.11 *arrangements*
plans and operations staff 584.5 *military staff*
plant 77.2; **368.6**; 77.20 *botanical*; 582.17, 583.8 *bury*; 44.15 *cultivate*; 700.18 *decoy*; 715.2 *false accusation*; 699.9 *falsification*; 699.26 *falsify*; 43.17 *farm*; 47.2 *field events*; 51.2 *grip*; 34.21 *living*; 142.9 *locate*; 562.7 *make fertile*; 356.2 *manufacture*; 34.3 *organism*; 440.5 *personal estate*; 21.33 *theatregoer*; 577.1 *workshop*
plant a car bomb 700.33 *snare*
Plantae 77.1 *plants*
planta genista 743.8 *heraldic device*
plant anatomy 77.10 *plant science*
plant and animal life 34.2 *living world*
plantation 43.6 *farm*; 763.4 *possession*; 440.1 *property*; 79.4 *trees*
plantation rubber 422.4 *rubber*
plant biochemist 33.2 *biochemist*
plant biochemistry 77.10 *plant science*
plant body 84.3; 82.2 *fern plant*; 82.4 *moss plant*
plant breeding 43.4 *arable farming*; 44.5 *gardening*
plant bug 76.3 *pest*
plant cell 34.7 *cell*
plant-covered 77.13 *plantlike*
plant cytology 77.10 *plant science*
plant disease 83.5 *fungal association*
plant ecology 34.18 *ecology*; 77.10 *plant science*
planted 368.12 *inserted*; 142.6 *located*; 715.9 *perjurious*; 77.13 *plantlike*; 79.16 *wooded*
planter 43.15 *agriculturist*; 44.4 *nursery*; 243.15 *preparer*; 356.9 *producer*; 564.7 *settler*
plant evidence 715.6 *accuse falsely*
plant geography 77.10 *plant science*
plant gland 559.3 *gland*
plant hormone 33.17
plant hunter 77.12 *plant scientist*
planting 43.5 *cultivation*; 243.13 *development*; 44.5 *gardening*; 368.8 *insertion*
plant killer 382.14
plant kingdom 77.1 *plants*
plant life 554.1 *life*; 77.1 *plants*
plantlike 77.13
plant mines 586.37 *fight*
plan to 283.8 *intend*
plant out 44.15 *cultivate*; 368.6 *plant*
plant pathology 77.10 *plant science*
plant physiology 77.10 *plant science*
plant pigment 33.18 *pigment*
plant products 356.7 *produce*
Plants 77
plants 77.1; 554.9 *classifications of life*
plant science 77.10
plant scientist 77.12
plant secretion 559.2 *secreted substance*
plantsman 44.13 *horticulturist*; 356.9 *producer*
plantswoman 356.9 *producer*
plant taxonomy 77.10 *plant science*
plan urban renewal 2.15 *socialize*
plaque 258.4 *dirt*; 462.3 *memento*; 744.11 *monument*; 411.4 *slice*
plash 90.7 *flow*; 512.1, 512.4 *hiss*; 31.62 *rain*; 90.6 *river flow*
plasher 43.10 *farm tool*
plashing 43.5 *cultivation*
plasma 431.3 *body fluid*; 28.76 *fusion reactor*; 402.4 *matter*

plasma confinement 28.76 *fusion reactor*
plasma containment 28.76 *fusion reactor*
plasmagene 34.13 *genetic material*
plasmajet propulsion 330.2 *method of propulsion*
plasmalemma 34.7 *cell*
plasma membrane 34.7 *cell*
plasma physics 28.3 *modern physics*
plasma substitute 431.4 *blood*
plasmic 34.23 *cellular*
plasmid 34.13 *genetic material*; 34.3 *organism*
plasmodesma 34.7 *cell*
Plasmodium 75.9 *protozoan*
plasmodium 83.4 *fungal body*
plasmosome 34.9 *cell nucleus*
plaster 211.6 *add*; 267.3 *adhesive*; 381.3 *bomb*; 435.2 *building material*; 550.24 *coat*; 394.20 *doctor*; 550.28 *face*; 38.26 *masonry*; 550.6 *medical covering*; 394.2 *medicine*; 393.1 *repair*; 550.27 *roof*; 19.14 *sculptor's materials*; 394.10 *surgical dressing*; 550.8 *wall covering*
plasterboard 435.4 *board*
plaster cast 550.6 *medical covering*; 19.12 *sculpture*
plaster casting 19.12 *sculpture*
plaster down 421.11 *smooth*
plastered 690.3 *dead drunk*
plasterer 578.2 *artisan*; 550.17 *coverer*
plastering 550.3 *coating*
plaster of Paris 394.10 *surgical dressing*
plaster work 550.8 *wall covering*
plastic 772.11 *borrowed*; 227.13 *changeable*; 117.11 *conformable*; 38.25 *construction material*; 772.4 *credit*; 783.25 *credit card*; 422.6 *elastic*; 160.9 *formed*; 700.39 *imitative*; 435.1 *materials*; 785.1 *payment*; 419.2 *pliant*; 32.21 *polymer*; 359.2 *preserver*; 19.25 *sculptural*
plastically 422.11 *elastically*; 160.13 *formatively*
plastic art 19.1 *art*; 19.12 *sculpture*
plastic bag 410.8 *bag*
plastic bullet 587.13 *ammunition*
plastic container 410.15 *pot*
plastic deformation 38.16 *deformation*
plastic explosive 587.15 *explosive*
plastic flow 30.26 *mass movement*
plastic furniture 23.1 *furniture*
Plasticine™ 19.14 *sculptor's materials*; 419.11 *soft thing*
plasticity 227.1 *changeableness*; 422.1 *elasticity*; 117.3 *pliancy*; 419.8 *softness*
plasticize 422.9 *make elastic*
plasticizer 32.21 *polymer*
plastic mixing 24.5 *ceramic process*
plastic money 783.2 *credit card*
plastics 32.22 *industrial chemistry*
plastic shuttle 63.11 *badminton equipment*
plastic ski 68.5 *ski equipment*
plastic spoon 700.6 *imitation*
plastic strain 38.14 *load*
plastic surgeon 547.13 *beautician*; 35.13 *medical specialist*; 393.12 *repairer*
plastic surgery **547.2**; 35.9, 394.12 *surgery*
plastic wrap 25.6 *kitchen equipment*; 527.8 *transparent thing*; 550.4 *wrapping*
plastid 34.8 *cell organ*
plastometer 26.8 *meter*
plastometric 26.16 *micrometric*
plastometry 26.2 *micrometry*
plastosome 34.8 *cell organ*
plastron 384.7 *armour*
plat du jour 25.9 *dish*
plate 24.8 *ceramic object*; 179.3 *circular thing*; 411.3, 550.24 *coat*; 550.3 *coating*; 203.3 *container*; 410.16 *crockery*; 557.16 *eating utensil*; 19.15 *engraving*; 187.3 *flat thing*; 411.10 *layer*; 743.3 *means of identification*; 19.7 *picture*; 30.19 *plate tectonics*; 794.1 *trophy*; 587.1 *weapon*
plateau 187.3 *flat thing*; 154.2 *heights*; 209.4 *interval*; 30.7 *landform*; 92.7 *upland*
plate boundary 30.19 *plate tectonics*
plate camera 41.16 *camera*
plated 411.8 *coated*
plate engraving 19.15 *engraving*
plate girder 38.27 *superstructure*
plate-girder bridge 38.21 *bridge*
plate glass 527.9 *glass*; 24.9 *industrial ceramics*
plate-layer 321.9 *railway worker*; 578.1 *worker*
platelike **411.9**
plate margin 30.19 *plate tectonics*
plate steel 38.25 *construction material*
plate tectonics **30.19**; 30.2 *geophysics*; 403.8 *science of structure*
platform 67.6 *diving*; 187.3 *flat thing*; 484.2 *policy*; 740.7 *publicity*; 317.10 *railway*; 321.8 *railway station*; 67.11 *swimming*
platform diving 67.6 *diving*
platform heels 551.19 *footwear*
platform scale 414.10 *scales*
platform soles 154.8 *high thing*
plating 411.3 *coat*
platinic 32.34 *elemental*
platiniferous 32.34 *elemental*
platinized 32.34 *elemental*
platinoid 32.34 *elemental*
platinous 32.34 *elemental*
platinum 235.2 *best*; 780.16 *bullion*; 531.9 *white thing*
platinum black 32.15 *catalysis*
platinum-blond 531.3 *white-haired*; 537.3 *yellow-haired*
platinum metal 32.6 *chemical element*
platinum resistance thermometer 28.89 *thermometer*
platitude 138.8 *generalization*; 745.1 *maxim*; 698.4 *truism*
platitudinous 138.22 *commonplace*; 745.2 *proverbial*; 698.17 *truistic*
platitudinously 745.4 *proverbially*
Platonic 160.9 *formed*; 101.10 *idealistic*; 593.17 *loving*; 4.14 *of a philosophy*; 795.9 *pure*
Platonically 160.13 *formatively*; 101.14 *subjectively*
Platonic form 160.1 *form*
Platonic Idea 446.1 *idea*
Platonic love 593.1 *love*
Platonic solid 27.46 *polyhedron*
Platonism 160.1 *form*; 101.5 *idealism*; 4.7 *school of thought*
Platonist 101.7 *believer in a nonmaterial world*; 4.11 *follower of a doctrine*
platoon 586.16 *army unit*; 376.14 *force*; 584.4 *military organization*
platoon commander 584.5 *military staff*
platter 410.16 *crockery*; 187.3 *flat thing*
platyhelminth 75.6 *worm*
Platyhelminthes 75.6 *worm*
platyhelminthic 75.20 *wormlike*
plaudit 669.5 *acclaim*
plausibility **104.3**; 450.4 *believability*; 102.1 *possibility*
plausible **104.7**; 450.13 *believable*; 4.15 *rational*; 95.9 *realizable*
plausibly 701.18 *arguably*; 450.16 *believably*; 102.11 *potentially*; 4.26 *rationally*; 699.41 *spuriously*
play **18.36**; **21.2**; **46.9**; **53.15**; **69.10**; 21.34, 717.10 *act*; 340.1 *action*; 141.6 *available space*; 53.17 *bat*; 346.7 *be operational*; 340.2 *deed*; 526.2 *depart*; 395.1 *influence*; 525.13 *occur*; 346.1 *operation*; 45.6 *participate*; 699.24 *pretend*; 738.9 *production*; 250.5 *scope*; 304.17 *spring up*; 356.5 *work of art*
playa 92.3 *marsh*
play about 340.4 *act*
play above par 120.5 *be unequal*
play a character 717.10 *act*
play a confidence trick 700.28 *trick*
play-act 21.34 *act*; 676.4 *be affected*; 699.24 *pretend*
play-acting 21.22 *acting*; 699.7 *pretence*; 699.34 *pretending*
play-action 46.9 *play*
play-actor 21.24 *actor*
play a dangerous game 645.5 *be cunning*
play a double role 699.21 *double-deal*
play a frame 51.8 *bowl*
play a joke on 599.13 *be humorous*; 700.31 *hoax*
play along with 388.3 *submit*
play a part 699.24 *pretend*
play a part in 340.4 *act*
play a role 221.6 *be in a state of*
play a role in 395.8 *influence*
play around 639.9 *change sides*; 593.26 *court*
play a trick 604.8 *be dishonest*
play a trick on 700.28 *trick*
play back 46.16 *play defence*; 112.20 *renew*
play ball 747.11 *cooperate*
play baseball **48.7**
play basketball **49.6**
play below par 120.5 *be unequal*
play billiards **65.8**
Playboy 796.2 *indecency*
playboy 796.8 *immoral man*; 490.3 *pleasure-seeker*; 654.6 *social person*
playbroker 21.27 *producer*
play by ear 18.36 *play*
play by the rules 799.6 *be honourable*
play cat and mouse 633.11 *hunt*
play construction 21.9 *dramaturgy*
play defence **46.16**
play dirty pool 800.8 *be dishonourable*
play doctor 21.26 *dramatist*
play dough 419.11 *soft thing*
play down **728.22**; 678.10 *disparage*; 214.5 *make smaller*; 685.4 *moderate*; 506.2 *silence*; 468.3 *underestimate*
played-down 728.19 *downplayed*; 271.1 *simple*
played out 131.22 *cancelled*
player 21.24 *actor*; 113.12 *competitor*; 340.3 *doer*; 18.24 *musician*; 717.5 *performer*; 45.3 *sportsman*; 53.4 *team*; 578.1 *worker*
play fake 46.9 *play*
play false 604.8 *be dishonest*
play fast and loose 227.12 *be irresolute*
play field hockey 58.9 *play hockey*
play fixer 21.26 *dramatist*
play flat 517.10 *lack harmony*
play follow-my-leader 125.11 *emulate*
play follow-the-leader 125.11 *emulate*
play footsie 742.11 *gesture*; 593.27 *kiss*
play for a draw 384.26 *act on the defensive*
play for time 645.5 *be cunning*; 378.9 *block*; 294.8 *delay*
playful 642.1 *capricious*; 805.5 *innocent*
playfully 805.11 *innocently*
playfulness 642.2 *caprice*; 805.1 *innocence*
play god 396.19 *be authoritarian*
playgoer 21.33 *theatregoer*
play golf 56.7 *golf*
playground 6.15 *schoolroom*
playgroup 6.12 *educational institution*
play havoc with 245.4 *impair*
play hell 264.22 *cause trouble*
play hell with 357.11 *ruin*
play hide-and-seek 521.7 *become invisible*; 736.11 *conceal oneself*; 634.6 *evade*
play hob 264.22 *cause trouble*
play hockey **58.9**
play hooky 98.18 *abscond*; 526.2 *depart*; 389.5 *escape*; 634.9 *play truant*; 355.2 *withdraw*
playhouse 21.16 *theatre*
playing 21.22, 717.3 *acting*; 18.2 *music making*
playing a character 717.3 *acting*
playing area 21.17 *stage*
playing card 69.3 *card game terms*
playing court 49.1 *basketball*
playing dead 125.4 *camouflage*
playing down 728.9 *downplaying*
playing down the table 65.3 *English billiards*
playing engagement 21.15 *engagement*
playing field 6.15 *schoolroom*
playing for time 631.9 *tactics*
playing from hand 65.3 *English billiards*
playing possum 125.4 *camouflage*
playing short-handed 58.3 *ice hockey*
playing terms **49.4**
playing the part of 717.3 *acting*
playing the stock market 776.8 *speculation*
playing up 631.18 *badly behaved*
playing up the table 65.3 *English billiards*
playing with fire 615.1 *rashness*
playing with one's food 557.3 *delicate eating*
play it by ear 616.5 *be cautious*
play it cool 589.5 *be at peace*
play it low-key 388.3 *submit*
playland 21.1 *drama*
playlet 21.2 *play*
playmaker 66.3 *football player*
play match point 222.12 *come to a juncture*
playmate 569.5 *friend*
play merry hell with 357.11 *ruin*
play no part in 634.1 *avoid*
play of colour 541.1 *variegation*
play off 349.3 *exploit*
play off against 349.3 *exploit*
play of fancy 477.4 *ideality*
play offence **46.15**
playoff game 46.1 *football*
play on 349.3 *exploit*; 483.10 *manipulate*
play one's cards right 797.19 *be good at*
play one's cards well 485.10 *be skilful*
play one's part 631.11 *conduct oneself*
play on words 479.1 *be equivocal*; 697.2 *solecism*; 697.6 *talk nonsense*
play politics 754.4 *compromise*
play possum 699.24 *pretend*
play producer 356.9 *producer*
playroom 565.7 *room*
play rugby **64.5**
play Russian roulette 254.9 *face danger*
play safe 616.5 *be cautious*; 252.9 *be safe*
play school 6.12 *educational institution*
play second fiddle 216.9 *be average*; 623.19 *be humble*; 674.14 *be modest*; 122.10 *follow*
play sharp 517.10 *lack harmony*
play silly buggers 459.7 *play the fool*
play soccer **66.4**
playsuit 551.23 *children's clothes*
play the ball 64.5 *play rugby*
play the devil's advocate 661.6 *be insubordinate*
play the devil with 357.11 *ruin*
play the fool **459.7**; 599.13 *be humorous*; 272.6 *be ridiculous*; 697.8 *fool*; 457.9 *lack intellect*; 21.35 *overact*
play the fop 673.17 *be affected*
play the fox 645.5 *be cunning*
play the futures market 14.5 *invest*; 776.2 *speculate*
play the game 801.14 *be fair*; 631.12 *behave well*; 117.8 *comply*
play the lead 21.34 *act*; 121.10 *lead*
play the market 780.27 *invest*
play the part of 717.10 *act*
play therapy 36.3 *psychiatric treatment*
play the stock exchange 14.5 *invest*
play the stock market 776.2 *speculate*
play the waiting game 294.8 *delay*
plaything 124.9 *bauble*; 793.5 *cheap item*; 700.22 *dupe*
plaything of the gods 249.5 *person in adversity*
play to the gallery 703.18 *appear*; 676.4 *be affected*; 21.35 *overact*
play tricks with 645.5 *be cunning*
play truant **634.9**; 98.18 *abscond*; 526.2 *depart*; 389.5 *escape*; 634.8 *run away*; 355.2 *withdraw*
play up 631.13 *behave badly*
play upon 346.9 *take action*
play upon words 479.5 *equivocalness*; 720.1 *misinterpret*
play up to 664.9 *fawn*; 569.14 *seek the friendship of*
play with 485.11 *be expert*; 492.11 *touch*
play with dynamite 254.8 *be in danger*
play with fire 459.6 *be foolish*; 254.8 *be in danger*; 615.5 *be rash*
play with one's food 557.23 *taste*
play with one's thoughts 477.14 *imagine*
playwright 17.14 *author*; 721.10 *descriptive writer*; 21.26 *dramatist*; 356.9 *producer*
play writer 21.26 *dramatist*
play writing 21.9 *dramaturgy*
plaza 87.7 *city district*
plea **701.5**; 706.5 *counterstatement*; 714.2 *defence*; 16.5 *litigation*; 705.1 *question*
plea-bargaining 16.7 *legal trial*
pleach 193.8 *interweave*
pleached 193.6 *interwoven*
pleaching 43.5 *cultivation*; 193.1 *interweaving*
plead **701.16**; 706.18 *answer back*; 714.8 *justify*; 16.70 *litigate*; 705.17 *question*
plead a case 476.6 *propound*
pleader 701.6 *arguer*; 480.12 *persuader*; 748.4 *representative*; 714.5 *vindicator*
plead for **384.22**
plead for forgiveness 649.13 *ask forgiveness*; 627.12 *ask for mercy*
plead for mercy 627.12 *ask for mercy*
plead for one's life 627.12 *ask for mercy*
plead guilty 739.8 *admit*; 806.8 *be guilty*; 16.80 *convict oneself*; 16.72 *stand trial*
pleading 701.12 *apologetic*; 480.2 *flattery*; 483.2 *inducement*; 16.5 *litigation*; 701.5 *plea*; 705.12 *questioning*; 706.13 *retaliatory*

pleadings 16.7 *legal trial*
plead nolo contendere 16.72 *stand trial*
plead not guilty 16.72 *stand trial*
plead one's own cause 714.8 *justify*
plead to the charge 16.72 *stand trial*
plead with 627.12 *ask for mercy*
plea for peace 749.2 *peace offering*
pleasant **241.1**; **490.6**; **498.7**; 617.8 *desirable*; 569.8 *friendly*; 428.5 *rainless*; 31.50 *warm*
pleasantly **241.15**; 617.17 *desirably*; 569.17 *in friendship*; 498.9 *sweetly*
Pleasantness 241
pleasantness **241.6**; 490.1 *physical pleasure*; 498.1 *sweetness*
pleasant person 241.11
pleasant remark 241.10 *pleasant thing*
pleasantries 658.3 *courtesies*
pleasantry 599.5 *joke*; 241.10 *pleasant thing*
pleasant sensation 490.1 *physical pleasure*
pleasant taste 495.1 *taste*
pleasant thing 241.10
please 597.8 *cause joy*; 241.13, 490.9 *give pleasure*; 599.15 *humour*; 609.8 *satisfy*
pleased **490.7**; 671.4 *grateful*; 597.4 *happy*; 609.4 *satisfied*
pleased as Punch 671.4 *grateful*; 597.4 *happy*; 622.14 *proud*
pleased with oneself 622.17 *conceited*
please oneself 588.4 *be anarchic*; 250.16 *be independent*; 16.74 *be lawless*; 683.6 *be selfish*; 490.8 *feel pleasure*; 635.14 *follow one's own will*
pleasing 599.11 *humouring*; 595.5 *likable*; 593.22 *lovable*; 241.1, 490.6 *pleasant*; 609.5 *satisfying*
pleasingly **490.11**; 595.10 *with great liking*
pleasing qualities 593.4 *lovability*
pleasurable 617.8 *desirable*; 241.1, 490.6 *pleasant*
pleasurableness 241.6 *pleasantness*
pleasurable things 490.4
pleasure **241.7**; 597.1 *happiness*; 595.3 *likes*; 241.11 *pleasant person*; 609.1 *satisfaction*; 635.1 *will*
pleasure boat 323.3 *vessel*
pleasure-bound 686.6 *self-indulgent*
pleasure garden 44.2 *garden*
pleasure-giving 490.6 *pleasant*
pleasure-loving 241.5
pleasure-loving person 241.12
pleasure principle 36.22 *libido*; 490.1 *physical pleasure*
pleasure punt 50.8 *punting*
pleasure punting 50.8 *punting*
pleasure-seeker **490.3**; 686.5 *self-indulgent person*
pleasure-seeking 490.7 *pleased*; 241.5 *pleasure-loving*; 686.1 *self-indulgence*; 686.6 *self-indulgent*
pleat **184.3**; **184.10**; 411.1 *layer*; 551.35 *make clothing*; 551.24 *part of garment*
pleated 184.7 *folded*; 551.31 *styled*
pleated dress 184.4 *wrinkled thing*
pleated skirt 551.6 *skirt*
pleb 574.1 *plebeian*; 675.5 *vulgar person*
plebby 574.3 *common*; 675.7 *vulgar*
plebeian **574.1**; 138.21, 574.3 *common*; 623.2 *lowly*; 122.16, 574.4 *ordinary*; 675.7 *vulgar*
plebiscite 464.1 *judgment*; 469.10 *vote*
plebs 566.9 *group*
plecopteran 76.10 *insectan*
pledge 750.23 *arrange*; 750.3 *arrangement*; 450.3 *believing*; 654.11 *be sociable*; 772.7 *borrow*; 253.12 *certify*; 810.7 *commitment*; 354.3, 755.1 *contract*; 558.14 *drink to*; 452.14 *guarantee*; 810.17 *impose a duty*; 452.21 *make certain*; 253.2, 253.11, 756.1, 756.7 *promise*; 316.10 *transferred thing*; 354.1 *undertake*; 707.3, 707.18 *vow*
pledged 750.12 *arranged*; 810.11 *duty-bound*; 253.7, 452.4 *guaranteed*; 756.13 *guaranteeing*; 784.9 *in debt*; 756.12 *promised*; 707.12 *vowed*
pledgee 783.5 *lender*
pledge oneself 810.15 *be liable*; 756.7 *promise*
pledge one's honour 756.7 *promise*
pledge one's word 756.7 *promise*
pledger 707.9 *affirmer*; 772.6 *borrower*; 452.15 *guarantor*
pledget 394.10 *surgical dressing*
pledging 772.1 *borrowing*; 756.13 *guaranteeing*
pledgor 784.6 *debtor*
plenary 232.7 *complete*
plenipotentiary 334.13 *powerful*
plenitude 219.1 *excess*; 562.1 *fertility*; 232.2 *fullness*; 217.8 *plenty*; 436.1 *provision*
plenteous 208.9 *ample*; 416.6 *dense*; 562.5 *fertile*; 781.4 *lush*; 217.2 *plentiful*
plenteously 416.10 *densely*; 217.9 *enough*
plenteousness 679.8 *abundance*; 217.8 *plenty*
plentiful **217.2**; 679.3 *abundant*; 208.9 *ample*; 219.6 *excessive*; 562.5 *fertile*; 781.4 *lush*; 439.7 *stored*
plentifully 217.9 *enough*; 679.12 *generously*
plentifulness 217.8 *plenty*
plenty **217.8**; **557.9**; 679.8 *abundance*; 97.4 *availability*; 97.10 *available*; 793.2 *declining prices*; 219.1 *excess*; 562.1 *fertility*; 781.7 *opulence*; 208.3 *profuseness*; 248.1 *prosperity*; 246.1 *success*; 439.3 *supply*
plenty of rope 250.6 *liberality*
plenty to do 342.6 *business*
pleonasm 270.1 *diffuseness*; 100.1 *extraneousness*; 5.22 *many words*, 219.3 *superfluity*; 215.4 *surplus*
pleonastic 270.3 *diffuse*; 100.8 *extraneous*; 112.12 *repetitious*; 219.7 *superfluous*; 215.10 *surplus*; 5.42 *worded*
pleonastically 5.50 *lexically*; 215.11 *residually*
plesiosaur 73.6 *extinct reptile*
plethora 219.1 *excess*
plethoric 219.6 *excessive*
pleurisy 260.9 *respiratory disease*
Plexiglass™ 32.21 *polymer*; 527.8 *transparent thing*
pliability 636.8 *acquiescence*; 6.10 *educability*; 422.1 *elasticity*; 480.7 *persuadability*; 419.8 *softness*; 265.3 *wieldiness*
pliable 636.3 *amenable*; 6.17 *educable*; 422.6 *elastic*; 419.2 *pliant*; 265.12 *wieldy*
pliableness 419.8 *softness*
pliably 6.26 *studiously*
pliance 663.1 *obedience*
pliancy **117.3**; 636.8 *acquiescence*; 639.14 *apathy*; 227.1 *changeableness*; 422.1 *elasticity*; 480.7 *persuadability*; 664.1 *servility*; 419.8 *softness*; 265.3 *wieldiness*
pliant **419.2**; 636.3 *amenable*; 227.13 *changeable*; 117.11 *conformable*; 422.6 *elastic*; 663.7 *obedient*; 664.6 *servile*; 388.5 *submitting*; 639.4 *unsteady*; 265.12 *wieldy*
pliantly 117.16 *adaptably*; 227.15 *changeably*; 422.11 *elastically*; 663.10 *obediently*; 419.17 *softly*
plica 184.1 *wrinkle*
plical 184.7 *folded*
plicate 184.7 *folded*
plicately 184.12 *doubly*
plication 184.1 *wrinkle*
plicature 184.1 *wrinkle*
plié 22.10 *positions at the barre*
pliers 369.10 *excavator*; 438.1 *tool*; 360.3 *tools for gripping*
plight 249.1 *adversity*; 143.3, 222.4 *difficult circumstances*; 221.2, 264.5 *predicament*
plighted 570.22 *marriageable*
plight one's troth 570.15 *marry*; 705.22 *pop the question*; 756.7 *promise*; 593.28 *win the love of*
Plimsoll line 742.5 *indicator*; 26.6 *measuring instrument*
plimsolls 551.19 *footwear*
plinth 175.2 *foot*
Pliocene period 284.3 *geological period*
Plistocene period 284.3 *geological period*
PLO 586.14 *armed forces*
plod 333.1 *move slowly*; 640.6 *persevere*; 333.10 *slow motion*; 576.6 *work*
plod along 333.1 *move slowly*
plodder 333.15 *slow person*
plodding 342.20 *industrious*; 640.1 *perseverance*; 640.10 *persevering*; 333.4 *slow*; 576.10 *working*
ploddy 253.3 *security officer*
plod on 134.4 *protract*
PLO member 586.9 *guerrilla*
plonk 690.12 *alcohol*; 511.9 *be nonresonant*; 508.6 *crack*; 511.5 *dull sound*; 558.9 *wine*
plonker 456.5 *ignorant person*; 457.3 *unintelligent person*
plop 511.9 *be nonresonant*; 508.2, 508.6 *crack*; 324.9 *directly*; 305.10 *droop*; 511.5 *dull sound*
plop down 305.10 *droop*
plot **86.12**; **484.4**; **484.13**; 446.18 *aim*; 17.3 *aspect of fiction*; 645.5 *be cunning*; 662.16 *be subversive*; 583.5 *cemetery*; 374.6 *come together*; 374.2 *cooperation*; 645.1 *cunning*; 243.2 *do the groundwork*; 21.9 *dramaturgy*; 43.11 *farmland*; 701.4 *gist*; 27.32 *graph*; 721.3 *narration*; 323.9 *navigate*; 342.9 *overactivity*; 717.11 *paint*; 770.2 *portion*; 106.6 *premeditation*; 440.1 *property*; 27.96 *represent*; 737.2 *secretiveness*; 645.2 *stratagem*; 662.3 *subversion*; 447.1 *topic*
plot horoscopes 11.23 *divine*
plot of land 43.11 *farmland*; 86.12 *plot*
plot-spinner 484.8 *planner*
plotted 26.13 *measured*
plotter **700.20**; 645.3 *cunning person*; 699.17 *false person*; 40.7 *peripheral*; 484.8 *planner*
plotting 645.4 *cunning*; 323.5 *navigation*; 484.15 *planning*
plotzed 690.3 *dead drunk*
plough 247.6 *fail*; 43.17 *farm*; 43.10 *farm tool*; 425.16 *use a sharp tool*; 184.8 *wrinkle*
ploughable 43.20 *farmable*
plough a lonely furrow 197.18 *be one*
ploughed 247.10 *failed*; 43.20 *farmable*; 184.6 *wrinkly*
ploughed field 184.4 *wrinkled thing*
ploughed land 43.11 *farmland*
plough horse 59.2 *thoroughbred*
ploughing 43.5 *cultivation*
ploughman 43.16 *farm worker*; 243.15 *preparer*
ploughman's lunch 25.44 *British dish*; 557.12 *meal*
ploughshare 425.9 *sharp-edged thing*
plover 25.20 *meat*; 72.3 *water bird*
plowed under 690.3 *dead drunk*
ploy 484.3 *expedient plan*; 645.2 *stratagem*; 700.8 *trick*
pluck 613.1 *courage*; 638.16 *fortitude*; 362.3 *jerk*; 552.15 *make nude*; 362.13 *pull at*; 372.10 *set apart*; 18.38 *sound*; 640.4 *stamina*; 336.1 *strength*; 212.4 *take off*; 492.11 *touch*; 338.1 *vigour*
pluck at one's heartstrings 363.11 *attract*
plucked 552.12 *peeling*; 144.9 *removed*
plucking 552.7 *depilation*
plucking out 144.2 *removal*
pluck out 369.11 *extract*; 144.15 *remove*
pluck up 366.4 *gather up*
pluck up courage 613.16 *take courage*
plucky 613.9 *courageous*; 640.12 *indomitable*; 336.11 *strong in spirit*
plug **39.28**; 740.9 *advertisement*; 55.2 *artificial fly*; 550.2, 550.23 *cover*; 360.7 *detain*; 360.2 *detention*; 726.6 *emphasize*; 112.18 *harp*; 59.1 *horse*; 740.16 *publicize*; 215.1 *remainder*; 393.1 *repair*; 330.28 *shoot*; 700.13 *snare*; 309.8 *stop*; 309.2 *stopper*; 496.7 *tobacco*
plug a hole 393.1 *repair*
plug along 333.1 *move slowly*
plug away 640.6 *persevere*; 342.15 *try*
plugged 309.13 *stopped*
plugged nickel 124.8 *trifle*
plug hat 551.15 *headgear*
plug in 346.8 *activate*; 39.35 *conduct*; 437.11 *fuel*; 334.11 *give power*
plug the gap 384.21 *entrench*
plug ugly 546.4 *ugly*
plug up 393.1 *repair*
plum 235.7 *elite*; 797.17 *good thing*; 765.5 *profit*; 540.6 *purple*; 540.3 *purple thing*; 535.7 *red thing*; 773.5 *takings*; 235.1 *worthy*
plumage **72.17**; 550.14 *animal covering*
plumb 273.8, 698.39 *accurately*; 232.7 *complete*; 232.9 *completely*; 156.14 *deepen*; 156.4 *deep thing*; 324.9 *directly*; 186.6 *make vertical*; 26.10 *measure*; 186.12 *perpendicularly*; 186.4 *plumb line*; 178.1 *straight*; 186.8 *vertical*; 186.3 *vertical thing*; 414.11 *weight*
plumbago 268.5 *lubricant*
plumb bob 361.3 *suspended object*; 414.11 *weight*
plumber 578.2 *artisan*; 308.3 *person who opens*; 393.12 *repairer*
plumbic 32.34 *elemental*
plumbiferous 32.34 *elemental*
plumbing 256.2 *cleaning*
plumb line **186.4**; 156.4 *deep thing*; 26.6 *measuring instrument*; 178.7 *straight line*
plumb on 273.8 *accurately*
plumb the depths 122.11 *become inferior*; 156.14 *deepen*
plumb the ocean depths 91.9 *sail the high seas*
plumb wicket 421.8 *smooth thing*
plum-coloured 540.6 *purple*
plume 551.5 *fancy dress*; 72.17 *plumage*
plumed 622.21 *ostentatious*
plumes 551.15 *headgear*
plummet 793.12 *be cheap*; 305.12 *drop*; 186.7 *fall vertically*; 414.11 *weight*
plummeting 305.4 *fall*; 305.18 *falling*
plummet lead 55.3 *fishing tackle*
plummy 235.1 *worthy*
plump 190.6 *become bigger*; 511.9 *be nonresonant*; 324.9 *directly*; 305.10 *droop*; 511.5 *dull sound*; 158.16 *fat*; 190.5 *make bigger*; 419.13 *soften*; 152.1 *thick*; 181.10 *well-rounded*
plump as a dumpling 158.16 *fat*
plump as a partridge 158.16 *fat*
plump down 305.10 *droop*
plump for 392.23 *advise*; 635.12 *choose*; 469.1 *select*
plumpishness 158.5 *fatness*
plumply 158.20 *largely*
plumpness 158.5 *fatness*; 181.2 *round body*; 152.5 *thickness*
plump out 190.6 *become bigger*
plum pudding 25.35 *dessert*
plump up 190.5 *make bigger*; 419.13 *soften*
plum sawfly 44.12 *pests and diseases*
plumulae 72.17 *plumage*
plumule 77.9 *seed*; 77.5 *stem*
plunder **774.14**; 586.38 *conquer*; 245.4 *impair*; 357.10, 441.2 *lay waste*; 774.5 *plundering*; 765.5, 765.14 *profit*; 794.2 *spoils*; 774.4 *stolen goods*; 773.10 *take away*; 773.5 *takings*
plundered 773.12 *taking*
plunderer **774.9**; 765.7 *gainer*; 586.6 *militarist*
plundering **774.5**; 765.16 *greedy*; 774.17 *stolen*; 773.12 *taking*; 773.3 *taking away*
plunderous 774.17 *stolen*
plunge 256.5 *ablutions*; 793.12 *be cheap*; 122.11 *become inferior*; 357.13 *be destroyed*; 300.13 *be in motion*; 332.4 *be swift*; 367.3 *bring down*; 214.2 *decline*; 793.2 *declining prices*; 214.4 *decrease*; 156.14 *deepen*; 67.10, 305.5 *dive*; 305.12 *drop*; 186.7 *fall vertically*; 368.4 *immerse*; 368.10 *immersion*; 327.25 *pitch*; 323.10 *sail*; 327.11 *stagger*; 186.1 *verticality*
plunge bath 256.6 *bath*
plunge in 368.3 *impact*
plunge into 314.13 *fall into*; 130.18 *make a beginning*; 354.1 *undertake*
plunging 156.8 *deep*; 300.6 *descending motion*; 300.17 *directional*; 305.4 *fall*; 305.18 *falling*; 367.13 *submergence*; 186.8 *vertical*
plunging fire 381.15 *firing*
plunging neckline 552.4 *dishabille*
plunk 511.9 *be nonresonant*; 331.13 *blow*; 508.2, 508.6 *crack*; 324.9 *directly*; 511.5 *dull sound*; 331.3 *hit*
pluperfect 5.34 *tense*
plural **207.6**; 5.44 *grammatical*; 203.6 *quantitative*
pluralism 12.1 *government*; 207.2 *multiplicity*; 4.7 *school of thought*; 396.7 *type of rule*
pluralist **207.5**; 4.11 *follower of a doctrine*; 4.14 *of a philosophy*
Plurality 207
plurality **207.1**; 203.5 *numbers*
pluralize 207.9
plurally **207.10**; 5.52 *grammatically*
pluralness 207.1 *plurality*
plural number 207.1 *plurality*
plurify 207.9 *pluralize*
plus 211.10 *additionally*; 27.88 *equal to*; 211.4 *extra*
plus fours 551.9 *trousers*
plush 781.3 *opulent*; 419.3 *smooth*; 419.11 *soft thing*
plushiness 419.9 *smoothness*
plushness 781.7 *opulence*
plushy 781.3 *opulent*; 419.3 *smooth*

plus sign 27.13 *mathematical symbol*; 742.1 *sign*
Pluto 29.16 *planet*
plutocracy **781.9**; 12.1 *government*; 396.7 *type of rule*
plutocrat 400.5 *company leader*; 248.4 *prosperous person*; 14.3 *stockbroker*; 781.10 *wealthy person*
plutocratic 12.9, 396.14 *governmental*; 400.12 *masterful*
pluton 30.30 *igneous rock*
Plutonian 29.36 *astronomical*; 8.16 *devilish*
plutonic 30.56 *petrographic*
plutonic intrusion 30.30 *igneous rock*
plutonic rock 30.30 *igneous rock*
plutonium 437.7 *nuclear power*; 28.73 *nuclear reactor*
Plutus 781.10 *wealthy person*
pluvial **31.54**
pluviometer 433.19 *measuring instrument*; 31.7 *weather instruments*
pluviometric 31.42 *barometric*
pluviosity 429.2 *mistiness*; 31.26 *raininess*
pluvious 31.54 *pluvial*
ply 340.4 *act*; 298.7 *be regular*; 411.1 *layer*; 349.1 *use*
plying 323.11 *nautical*
Plymouth 87.4 *British cities*
Plymouth Sound 92.9 *inlet*
ply one's trade 340.4 *act*
ply the oar 576.6 *work*
plywood 38.25 *construction material*; 411.5 *layered thing*; 435.1 *materials*; 550.8 *wall covering*; 23.12 *wood*
p.m. 290.4 *afternoon*; 291.1 *evening*; 281.18 *horologically*
PMT 111.4 *duplicate*; 41.7 *photocopy*; 561.1 *reproduction*
pneuma 36.21 *psyche*; 11.7 *spirit*
pneumatic 434.14 *aerial*; 432.22 *aerostatic*; 419.4 *compressible*
pneumatically 432.29 *aerostatically*; 434.25 *airily*; 419.17 *softly*
pneumatics 432.12 *aerostatics*
pneumatometer 26.8 *meter*; 432.15 *vaporimeter*
pneumatometry 26.2 *micrometry*
pneumatostatics 432.12 *aerostatics*
pneumoconiosis 260.9 *respiratory disease*
pneumodynamically 432.29 *aerostatically*
pneumodynamics 432.12 *aerostatics*
pneumonia 494.3 *chill*; 260.6 *infection*; 260.9 *respiratory disease*
pneumonic 434.19 *respiratory*
pneumonic plague 260.5 *plague*
p–n junction 28.44, 39.4 *semiconductor*
p–n junction diode 39.18 *diode*
pnp transistor 39.19 *transistor*
Po 90.5 *other major rivers*
po 560.14 *toilet*
Poaceae 81.1 *grass*
poaceous 81.8 *grasslike*
poach 25.55 *cook*; 633.11 *hunt*; 60.7 *shoot*; 774.12 *steal*; 329.5 *transgress*
poached 92.11 *continental*; 25.56 *culinary*
poached fish 25.16 *fish dish*
poacher 60.4, 633.6 *hunter*; 25.6 *kitchen equipment*; 774.8 *thief*
poaching 25.8 *cooking technique*; 774.1 *stealing*; 774.17 *stolen*
po-boy 25.11 *sandwich*
pock 404.3 *nap*
pocked 420.2 *coarse*; 183.6 *concave*; 541.10 *mottled*
pocket 585.10 *battleground*; 65.1 *billiards*; 137.2 *class*; 65.3 *English billiards*; 159.7 *little*; 780.20 *money store*; 551.24 *part of garment*; 46.9 *play*; 769.9 *receive*
pocket billiard table 65.5 *snooker*
pocketbook 780.20 *money store*
pocket borough 469.12 *election*
pocket calculator 210.5 *computer*
pocket comb 256.10 *cleaning object*
pocketed 65.9 *billiard*
pocket edition 159.2 *little thing*
pocketful 203.3 *container*
pocket hold 62.5 *rock face*
pocketing the ball 65.2 *billiards play*
pocketknife 425.10 *knife*
pocketless table 65.4 *carom*
pocket money 780.4 *change*; 768.2 *gift*; 788.3 *income*; 765.5 *profit*; 769.2 *something received*
pocket rot 79.10 *tree disease*
pocket-size 159.7 *little*
pocket the affront 649.12 *show mercy*
pocket the ball 65.8 *play billiards*
pocket the insult 388.4 *succumb*
pocket torch 522.7 *lantern*
pocket veto 399.1 *veto*
pocket watch 281.7 *watch*
pockmark 183.3 *cavity*; 234.11 *deform*; 234.3 *deformity*; 183.9 *make concave*; 260.13 *skin disease*; 548.1 *spot*
pockmarked 420.2 *coarse*; 183.6 *concave*; 234.7 *deformed*; 548.5 *marked*; 541.10 *mottled*
pocky 420.2 *coarse*
pococurante 618.7 *indifferent*; 618.6 *indifferent person*
pod 80.2 *botanical fruit*; 550.13 *casing*; 171.1 *exterior*
PO'd 624.16 *angry*
podded 171.6 *exterior*
podetium 84.6 *lichen*
podginess 158.5 *fatness*; 152.5 *thickness*
podgy 419.4 *compressible*; 158.16 *fat*; 152.1 *thick*; 181.10 *well-rounded*
podiatrist 394.15 *healer*
podiatry 35.6 *health care*; 394.12 *surgery*
podium 20.9 *miscellaneous architectural features*; 21.17 *stage*
Podunk 655.5 *solitary place*
podzol 30.36 *soil*
poem **17.7**; 356.5 *work of art*
poesy 17.13 *poetic genius*; 17.6 *poetry*
poet 17.14 *author*; 721.10 *descriptive writer*; 5.2 *linguist*; 356.9 *producer*; 477.9 *visionary*
poetaster 17.14 *author*
poetess 17.14 *author*
poetic 477.10 *imaginative*; 17.19 *narrative*
poetical 17.19 *narrative*
poetically **17.22**
poetic diction 17.12 *poetic language*
poetic drama 21.2 *play*
poetic frenzy 477.2 *inspiration*
poetic genius **17.13**
poetic imagination 477.1 *imagination*
poeticism 17.12 *poetic language*
poeticize 477.15 *fantasize*
poetic justice 814.9 *retribution*; 714.4 *revenge*
poetic language **17.12**
poetic licence 250.1 *freedom*; 477.4 *ideality*; 17.12 *poetic language*; 699.7 *pretence*
poetic prose 17.5 *prose*
poetics 17.6 *poetry*
poetic truth 234.4 *distortion of the truth*
poetize 17.21 *write*
poet laureate 17.14 *author*; 121.6 *paragon*
poetry **17.6**; 477.4 *ideality*; 17.21 *write*
Pogonophora 75.6 *worm*
pogonophoran 75.6 *worm*
pogo stick 422.3 *elastic thing*
pogrom 382.4 *slaughter*; 466.4 *social discrimination*
poignancy 726.1 *emphasis*; 496.1 *piquancy*; 496.4 *stimulation*
poignant 721.11 *descriptive*; 726.3 *emphatic*; 488.9 *exciting*; 496.10 *stimulating*
poignantly 496.16 *stimulatingly*
poikilotherm 73.1 *reptile*
poikilothermic 74.13 *fishlike*; 73.11 *reptilian*
poilu 586.8 *soldier*
point **27.36**; **694.5**; 222.6 *aspect*; 275.11 *date*; 324.6, 579.2 *direct*; 19.15 *engraving*; 142.2 *exact location*; 55.3 *fishing tackle*; 742.3, 742.11 *gesture*; 701.4 *gist*; 58.3 *ice hockey*; 209.4 *interval*; 447.2 *issue*; 58.6 *lacrosse player*; 131.7 *limit*; 701.3 *line of argument*; 159.2 *little thing*; 425.15 *make sharp*; 795.7 *moral*; 151.8 *narrow thing*; 222.2 *occurrence*; 197.1 *one*; 92.5 *peninsula*; 280.4 *point in time*; 185.2 *projection*; 742.7 *punctuation*; 446.4 *purpose*; 705.1 *question*; 19.14 *sculptor's materials*; 425.7 *sharp point*; 60.7 *shoot*; 143.1 *situation*; 174.1 *summit*; 324.7 *take a direction*; 53.4 *team*; 447.1 *topic*; 349.6 *use*; 237.5 *usefulness*
point a moral 795.12 *moralize*
point at 482.10 *aim*; 742.11 *gesture*
point at infinity 27.36 *point*
point at issue 447.2 *issue*
point-blank 273.5 *accurate*; 698.39 *accurately*; 324.9 *directly*; 271.8 *simply*
point-blank refusal 709.1 *refusal*
pointed 176.7 *angular*; 707.14 *assertive*; 269.3 *concise*; 310.7 *convergent*; 707.15 *emphasized*; 726.3 *emphatic*; 447.7 *focused*; 27.80 *linear*; 694.6 *meaningful*; 425.1 *sharp*; 143.6 *situated*; 723.6 *summary*; 151.3 *tapered*
pointed for 324.14 *directed*
pointedly 269.5 *concisely*; 707.25 *explicitly*; 482.13 *intentionally*; 425.18 *sharply*; 723.11 *summarily*; 447.14 *thematically*
pointedness 707.6 *assertiveness*; 269.1 *conciseness*; 425.6 *sharpness*; 723.4 *summariness*
pointed out 726.4 *emphasized*
pointed shoes 551.19 *footwear*
pointed up 726.4 *emphasized*
pointer 693.7 *advice*; 716.4 *indication*; 742.5 *indicator*; 28.82 *measuring instrument*; 60.6 *sporting dog*; 520.7 *that which makes visible*
pointillism 541.4 *maculation*
pointillist 19.29 *realist*
point in common 115.1 *similarity*
pointing 324.5 *directions*; 716.8 *evidential*; 742.3 *gesture*; 19.12 *sculpture*; 742.14 *signifying*
pointing machine 19.14 *sculptor's materials*
pointing out 743.1 *identification*; 520.5 *manifestation*; 742.1 *sign*
pointing to 715.8 *accusatory*; 229.5 *tending to*
point in time **280.4**
pointless 426.1 *blunt*; 270.4 *circumlocutory*; 100.8 *extraneous*; 459.5 *foolish*; 238.2, 617.1 *futile*
pointlessly 100.18 *extraneously*; 426.11 *smoothly*
pointlessness 270.2 *circumlocution*; 100.1 *extraneousness*; 459.1 *folly*; 238.4 *futility*; 109.1 *unrelatedness*
point of action 164.3 *cutting edge*
point of Aries 292.2 *spring*
point of arrival 312.15 *destination*
point of departure 130.11 *starting point*
point of etiquette 656.5 *etiquette*
point of inflection 27.36 *point*
point of land 92.5 *peninsula*
point of Libra 292.4 *autumn*
point of no return 222.3 *critical moment*; 287.3 *critical time*
point of view 17.3 *aspect of fiction*; 450.1 *belief*; 525.3 *external appearance*; 443.6 *idea*; 4.1 *philosophy*; 7.1 *religion*; 476.1 *supposition*; 518.9 *viewpoint*
point one's finger 742.11 *gesture*
point out 139.22 *characterize*; 703.15 *demonstrate*; 324.6 *direct*; 738.1 *display*; 726.6 *emphasize*; 743.10 *identify*; 693.11 *inform*; 518.18, 520.10 *make visible*; 525.14 *present*; 447.11 *raise the point*; 738.3 *reveal*; 742.9 *use signs*
points 121.3 *advantage*; 321.3 *rail*; 317.10 *railway*
points game 68.10 *curling*
pointsman 321.9 *railway worker*
points table 61.1 *motor racing*
point system 52.2 *boxing*
point the finger at 715.5 *accuse*
point the way 324.6 *direct*; 129.15 *precede*; 742.9 *use signs*
point to 446.18 *aim*; 324.6, 579.2 *direct*; 447.10 *focus on*; 694.10 *mean*; 475.11 *predict*; 139.24 *specify*; 229.4 *tend*; 742.9 *use signs*
point-to-point racing 59.6 *horsemanship*; 59.7 *horseracing*
point up 726.6 *emphasize*; 525.14 *present*; 738.3 *reveal*
pointy 425.1 *sharp*
poise 265.4 *ease of manner*; 119.11 *equalize*; 119.2 *equilibrium*; 631.2 *good conduct*; 304.20 *hover*; 301.1 *motionlessness*
poised 301.4 *motionless*
poison 357.7 *agent of destruction*; 558.7 *alcoholic drink*; 382.13 *animal killer*; 798.11 *be evil*; 814.13 *capital punishment*; 32.15 *catalysis*; 32.39 *catalytic*; 594.16 *cause hate*; 258.11 *dirty*; 798.5 *evil thing*; 260.6 *infection*; 814.16 *instrument of execution*; 382.22 *kill animals*; 624.14 *make angry*; 245.3 *make worse*; 382.17 *murder*; 236.10 *poverty*; 394.3 *prophylactic*; 32.26 *react*
poisoned 236.4 *poor*
poisoned apple 700.14 *fatal gift*
poisoned arrow 587.6 *historical missile weapon*
poisoner 798.6 *evil person*; 382.11 *murderer*
poisoning 260.2 *illness*; 245.10 *impairment*; 260.6 *infection*; 582.6 *killing*; 382.2 *murder*
poisonous 254.1 *dangerous*; 382.23 *deadly*; 260.23 *diseased*; 236.5 *harmful*; 594.10 *hating*; 651.14 *hostile*; 258.8 *unclean*; 499.6 *unpalatable*
poisonous gas 432.3 *miasma*
poisonously 594.18 *hatefully*
poisonousness 236.11 *harmfulness*; 260.6 *infection*
poisonous snake 382.10 *killer*
poison-pen letter 678.4 *aspersion*
Poisson distribution 27.59 *probability distribution*
poke 410.8 *bag*; 331.13 *blow*; 593.14 *communication of love*; 742.11 *gesture*; 331.3 *hit*; 331.1 *impel*; 492.3 *press*; 381.5 *strike*; 492.11 *touch*
poke along 333.1 *move slowly*
poke bonnet 551.15 *headgear*
pokecheck 58.3 *ice hockey*; 58.9 *play hockey*
pokechecking 58.3 *ice hockey*
poke fun at 599.13 *be humorous*; 621.6 *deride*; 668.24, 678.14 *ridicule*
poke in 368.2 *inject*
poke one's nose in 644.7 *be curious*; 342.17 *meddle*
poke out 185.8 *protrude*
poker dice 69.5 *dice*
poker face 696.11 *unintelligibility*
poker-faced 736.17 *noncommittal*; 643.1 *solemn*; 696.1 *unintelligible*
pokerlike 418.2 *tough*
pokerwork 542.3 *pattern*
pokily 333.17 *in slow motion*
pokiness 159.1 *littleness*; 793.3 *shoddiness*
poking 333.4 *slow*
pokingly 333.17 *in slow motion*
poking out 185.5 *protuberant*
pokunt 8.5 *deity*
poky 159.7 *little*; 793.10 *shoddy*; 333.4 *slow*; 815.2 *the inside*
pol 579.15 *manager*; 12.8 *politician*
polar 494.8 *cold*; 32.35 *combined*; 131.24 *limiting*; 174.5 *top*
polar air 31.10 *air movement*
polar bear 74.11 *fishing animal*
polar bond 32.11 *chemical bond*
polar climate 31.38 *climate*
polar compound 32.7 *chemical compound*
polar coordinates 27.33 *coordinates*
polar front 31.10 *air movement*
polarimeter 28.92 *light meter*; 26.8 *meter*
polarimetric 26.16 *micrometric*
polarimetry 26.2 *micrometry*; 32.13 *structure*
Polaris 742.5 *indicator*; 587.5 *missile weapon*; 522.4 *natural light*
polarity 113.8 *contrariety*; 347.1 *counteraction*; 334.4 *energy*; 113.2 *oppositeness*
polarity reversal 30.44 *geomagnetism*
polarization 347.1 *counteraction*; 751.1 *disagreement*; 32.19 *electrochemistry*; 113.2 *oppositeness*; 364.5 *repulsion*; 28.15 *wave property*
polarize 113.15 *be opposite*; 347.3 *counteract*; 751.5 *disagree*
polarized 334.16 *charged*; 113.25 *contrary*; 347.4 *counteracting*; 113.23 *opposite*
polarized light **28.27**
polarizing 751.9 *disagreeing*
polarizing filter 41.20 *filter*
polarizing microscope 28.85 *microscope*
polar lights 30.46 *aurora*
polarogram 32.17 *analysis*
polarographic 32.41 *analytic*
polarography 32.17 *analysis*
Polaroid™ 41.16 *camera*; 28.27 *polarized light*
Polaroid™ film 41.9 *film*
polaroid glasses 518.10 *visual aid*
polar opposition 113.2 *oppositeness*
polar solvent 32.3 *phase*
polar wandering 30.45 *magnetic pole*
polar zone 31.39 *climatic zone*
polder 92.6 *lowland*
pole 307.4 *axle*; 145.3 *distant place*; 47.2 *field events*; 131.7 *limit*; 330.20 *propel*; 174.1 *summit*; 154.6 *tall thing*; 79.3 *timber*; 438.1 *tool*; 186.3 *vertical thing*; 23.12 *wood*
pole a canoe 50.19 *punt*

poleaxe 382.17 *murder*; 587.8 *sharp weapon*; 382.18 *slaughter*
pole-body-foot movement 50.8, 50.14 *punting*
polecat 804.10 *bad person*; 503.2 *something that makes an unpleasant smell*
pole-jump 304.5 *jump*
polemic 751.2 *argument*; 444.9 *argumentative*; 701.2 *logical argument*; 17.4 *nonfiction*; 4.5 *philosophical argument*; 585.1 *war*
polemical 751.9 *disagreeing*; 701.9 *hostile*
polemically 701.17 *argumentatively*; 4.24 *philosophically*
polemicist 444.6, 701.6 *arguer*
polemicize 701.13 *argue*; 4.23 *discuss philosophically*
polemics 734.4 *conference*; 444.3 *debate*
polemist 701.6 *arguer*
polenta 25.40 *breakfast cereal*
pole plant 68.4 *skiing technique*
pole position 121.3 *advantage*; 61.6 *motor-racing terms*; 129.2 *priority*
poles apart 116.4 *dissimilar*; 372.4 *disunity*; 113.2 *oppositeness*
Pole Star 579.5 *guide*; 742.5 *indicator*; 363.3 *magnet*; 522.4 *natural light*
pole-vault 47.2 *field events*; 304.5 *jump*
pole-vaulter 47.3, 336.5 *athlete*
pole-vaulting 47.2 *field events*
police 16.14; 586.39 *defend*; 12.11 *govern*; 396.18 *have authority*; 579.1 *manage*; 407.22 *pacify*; 582.9 *person dealing with the dead*; 252.10 *protect*; 252.3 *protector*; 251.8 *restrain*; 253.10 *secure*
police barrier 252.4 *safety device*
police car 320.17
police commissioner 16.17 *police officer*
police constable 252.3 *protector*; 253.3 *security officer*
police court 16.19 *law court*; 464.3 *place of judgment*
police dog 71.9 *dog*; 252.3 *protector*
police force 16.14 *police*; 253.4 *security forces*
police inspector 16.17 *police officer*
police lieutenant 16.17 *police officer*
police magistrate 16.23 *judge*
policeman 586.2 *defender*; 251.6 *lawmaker*; 397.6 *person in command*; 396.10 *person of authority*; 16.17 *police officer*; 252.3 *protector*; 253.3 *security officer*; 742.8 *signer*
policeman's uniform 551.3 *formal dress*
police officer 16.17; 252.3 *protector*; 253.3 *security officer*
police rank 396.5 *position of authority*
police record 744.1 *record*
police report 693.3 *document*
police sergeant 16.17 *police officer*; 252.3 *protector*
police siren 742.4 *signal*
police state 396.7 *type of rule*
police station 87.13 *municipal building*; 396.6 *place of authority*
police superintendent 16.17 *police officer*
police van 320.17 *police car*
police whistle 711.2 *danger signal*; 742.4 *signal*
policewoman 396.10 *person of authority*; 252.3 *protector*; 253.3 *security officer*
Polichinelle 21.32 *clown*
policy 484.2; 340.1 *action*; 631.1 *conduct*; 117.5 *convention*; 645.1 *cunning*; 140.6 *custom*; 340.2 *deed*; 579.3 *management*; 632.6 *procedure*; 631.9 *tactics*
polio 260.6 *infection*; 260.17 *nervous disorder*
poliomyelitis 260.6 *infection*; 260.17 *nervous disorder*
polis 12.5 *political organization*
polish 421.10; 543.4 *be elegant*; 53.18 *bowl*; 256.13 *clean*; 256.9 *cleaning agent*; 256.1 *cleanness*; 550.24 *coat*; 265.4 *ease of manner*; 543.1, 549.1 *elegance*; 522.27 *glaze*; 658.2 *good manners*; 244.1 *improve*; 244.5 *improvement*; 230.5 *perfect*; 230.3 *perfection*; 35.21 *practise dentistry*; 522.2 *quality of light*; 365.12 *rub*; 421.11 *smooth*
polished 421.4; 256.17 *cleaned*; 543.3 *elegant*; 400.13 *excellent*; 658.8 *good-mannered*; 17.16 *literary*; 522.17 *lustrous*; 62.8 *mountaineering*; 230.1 *perfect*; 255.14 *purified*; 6.20, 549.5 *refined*
polished hold 62.5 *rock face*
polishing 365.5; 256.2 *cleaning*; 35.4 *dentistry*
polish off 131.16 *cease*; 204.10 *complete*; 557.22 *eat well*; 342.15 *try*
polish the apple 664.9 *fawn*
polish up 6.23 *learn*
polite 658.7 *courteous*; 543.3 *elegant*; 241.2 *likable*; 667.9 *showing respect*; 631.17 *well-behaved*
polite listener 631.3 *well-behaved person*
polite literature 17.1 *literature*
politely 658.14 *courteously*; 658.15 *genteelly*; 241.15 *pleasantly*; 667.22 *respectfully*; 631.19 *well*
politeness 241.8 *amiability*; 658.1 *courtesy*; 543.1 *elegance*; 549.3, 656.5 *etiquette*; 631.2 *good conduct*
polite regard 667.3 *respectfulness*
politesse 656.5 *etiquette*
politic 713.8 *advisable*; 616.4 *cautious*; 239.1 *convenient*; 485.6 *skilful*; 458.5 *wise*
political 631.16 *behaving*; 12.9, 396.14 *governmental*; 579.17 *managerial*; 2.12 *sociological*
political action 15.4 *industrial dispute*
political activism 342.5 *activism*
political activist 340.3 *doer*; 703.8 *protester*
political administration 12.1 *government*
political animal 566.4 *modern human*
political association 480.14 *motivator*
political authority 12.1 *government*
political behaviour 2.1 *sociology*
political border 147.7 *interface*
political campaign 469.12 *election*
political cartoonist 19.16 *artist*
political economist 579.13 *director*
political economy 579.3 *management*
political entity 566.11 *nation*; 86.4 *territorial division*
political favours 483.5 *positive stimulus*
political history 3.1 *history*
political institution 2.8 *human institution*
political line 484.2 *policy*
politically 12.14; 579.19 *managerially*; 396.24 *ministerially*; 86.20 *nationally*; 2.16 *sociologically*
politically correct 5.39 *of language*
politically moderate 685.7
political map 163.4 *map*
political movement 342.5 *activism*
political organization 12.5; 12.1 *government*; 2.4 *social organization*
political party 12.6; 2.8 *human institution*
political party platform 484.2 *policy*
political party ticket 484.2 *policy*
political persecution 466.4 *social discrimination*
political philosophy 4.6 *branch of philosophy*
political plank 484.2 *policy*
political possession 440.1 *property*
political prisoner 815.5 *prisoner*
political refugee 100.7 *new arrival*
political reporting 741.3 *reporting*
political representative 398.1 *delegate*
political rule 12.1 *government*
political science 12.2 *politics*; 631.9 *tactics*
political sociology 2.1 *sociology*
political symbol 742.1 *sign*
political system 12.1 *government*
political trick 645.2 *stratagem*
politician 12.8; 579.15 *manager*; 483.7 *motivator*; 542.9 *phrasemonger*; 484.8 *planner*; 401.2 *public servant*
politicking 12.1 *government*
politico 12.8 *politician*
politics 12.2; 396.4 *governance*; 631.9 *tactics*
polity 12.1 *government*; 566.11 *nation*
polka 22.2 *dance*; 22.4 *historic dancing*
polka dot 541.4 *maculation*
poll 210.3 *count*; 220.6 *list of names*; 210.11 *number*; 705.17 *question*; 705.2 *questioning*; 705.3 *questionnaire*; 149.10 *shorten*; 469.5, 469.10 *vote*
pollack 55.5 *British game fish*
pollard 79.18 *manage trees*; 79.1 *tree*
pollarding 79.6 *tree management*
polled 705.16 *questioned*; 149.8 *shortened*
pollen 78.3 *flower part*; 561.8 *organs of reproduction*; 427.10 *spore*
pollen analysis 77.10 *plant science*
pollen grain 78.3 *flower part*; 427.10 *spore*
pollen tube 78.3 *flower part*
pollinate 44.15 *cultivate*; 562.7 *make fertile*; 561.13 *propagate*
pollination 78.6; 562.2 *productiveness*; 561.3 *propagation*
pollinator 561.5 *propagator*
polling 469.12 *election*
polling booth 469.12 *election*
polling day 469.12 *election*
polling district 469.12 *election*
polling place 469.12 *election*
polling station 469.12 *election*
polliwog 73.8 *young amphibian*; 555.4 *young animal*
polls 469.12 *election*
pollster 210.6 *calculator*; 210.7 *mathematician*; 705.9 *questioner*
poll tax 790.7 *tax*
pollutant 31.8 *atmosphere*; 798.5 *evil thing*
pollute 412.10 *become mixed*; 798.11 *be evil*; 236.13 *be worthless*; 258.11 *dirty*; 238.8 *make useless*; 245.3 *make worse*; 351.1 *misuse*; 441.1 *waste*
polluted 548.4 *blemished*; 258.7 *dirty*; 351.4 *misused*
polluted area 577.1 *workshop*
polluted river 90.1 *river*
polluter 351.3 *abuser*; 441.7 *destroyer*; 766.6 *loser*
polluting 236.5 *harmful*
pollution 31.8 *atmosphere*; 258.1 *dirtiness*; 34.18 *ecology*; 798.5 *evil thing*; 236.11 *harmfulness*; 245.10 *impairment*; 260.6 *infection*; 351.2 *misuse*; 412.1 *mixture*
poll watcher 469.13 *electorate*
Pollyanna 610.5 *hoper*
polo 59.6 *horsemanship*
polonaise 22.4 *historic dancing*
polo-neck 551.13 *sweater*
polony 25.29 *sausage*
polo pony 59.5 *pony*
polo shirt 551.8 *shirt*
poltergeist 11.11 *ghost*; 236.11 *harmfulness*; 378.7 *hinderer*
poltergeistism 11.1 *occultism*
poltroon 614.2 *coward*
poltroonery 614.1 *cowardice*
polyadic 4.16 *dialectical*
polyamide 435.1 *materials*
polyandrous 570.23 *monogamous*
polyandry 207.2 *multiplicity*; 570.3 *types of marriage*
polyatomic 32.35 *combined*
polycarbonate 32.21 *polymer*
polycarpellary 80.9 *of a fruit*
Polychaeta 75.6 *worm*
polychaete 75.6 *worm*
polychaetous 75.20 *wormlike*
polychromatic 529.10 *coloured*; 541.6 *variegated*
polychromatically 529.18 *colourfully*; 541.12 *variedly*
polychromatism 529.2 *colourfulness*; 541.1 *variegation*
polychrome 529.10 *coloured*; 529.2 *colourfulness*; 19.8 *painting*; 28.98 *physical*; 541.6 *variegated*
polychromy 541.1 *variegation*
polyclinic 35.10 *hospital*
polyester 435.1 *materials*; 32.21 *polymer*
polyethylene 435.1 *materials*
polygamist 570.10 *married man*; 207.5 *pluralist*
polygamous 570.23 *monogamous*
polygamously 570.24 *matrimonially*
polygamy 207.2 *multiplicity*; 570.3 *types of marriage*
polyglot 5.2 *linguist*; 5.38 *linguistic*; 207.5 *pluralist*; 729.19 *speaking*; 719.17 *translational*; 207.7 *various*
polyglot dictionary 5.28 *dictionary*
polyglot medley 5.5 *nonstandard language*
polyglottism 5.1 *linguistics*
polygon 27.44; 207.2 *multiplicity*
polygonal 27.82; 176.9 *angled*; 207.7 *various*
polygraph 36.4 *psychometrics*
polygynist 570.10 *married man*
polygynous 570.23 *monogamous*
polygyny 207.2 *multiplicity*; 570.3 *types of marriage*
polyhedral 176.9 *angled*; 27.84 *cubic*
polyhedron 27.46; 176.3 *angled figure*; 207.2 *multiplicity*
polyline 27.44 *polygon*
polymath 485.5 *expert*; 442.8 *intellectual person*; 207.5 *pluralist*
polymathic 6.18 *educated*; 455.8 *knowledgeable*
polymathy 6.9 *learnedness*; 455.3 *learning*
polymer 32.21
polymer chemist 32.2 *chemist*
polymer chemistry 32.1 *chemistry*
polymeric 32.44; 32.38 *reactive*
polymerization 32.14 *chemical reaction*; 32.21 *polymer*
polymerize 32.26 *react*
polymers 435.1 *materials*
polymethylmethacrylate 32.21 *polymer*
polymorphous 114.6 *assorted*; 207.7 *various*
Polynesian 1.6 *race*; 1.13 *racial*
polynomial 27.25 *algebraic expression*; 27.76 *functional*
polynomial expression 27.25 *algebraic expression*
polynucleotide 34.12 *molecular biology*
polyp 75.7 *coelenterate*
polypeptide 33.8 *amino acid*
polypeptide chain 34.12 *molecular biology*
polyphagia 688.1 *gluttony*
polyphagous 688.6 *gluttonous*
Polyphemus 158.10 *big person*
polyphone 5.16 *spoken letter*
polyphonic 516.7 *harmonious*; 5.41 *lettered*
polyphonically 5.48 *linguistically*
polyphonic prose 17.5 *prose*
polyphonous 5.41 *lettered*
polyphonously 5.48 *linguistically*
polyphony 516.4 *harmonics*
polyploid 44.5 *gardening*; 34.25 *genetic*
polyploidy 34.14 *chromosome*
polypoid 75.21 *coelenterate*
polypoid invertebrate 75.7 *coelenterate*
polypropylene 435.1 *materials*; 32.21 *polymer*
polyrhythm 275.12 *musical time*
polysaccharide 33.4
polysemous 694.6 *meaningful*
polysemy 694.3 *comprehension*; 479.5 *equivocalness*
polysome 34.8 *cell organ*
polystyrene 493.3 *heater*; 435.1 *materials*; 32.21 *polymer*
polysyllabic 270.3 *diffuse*; 148.1 *long*; 5.39 *of language*
polysyllabically 5.48 *linguistically*
polysyllabic language 5.10 *language type*
polysyllable 5.17 *word*
polysynthetic 5.39 *of language*
polysynthetic language 5.10 *language type*
polytechnic 6.13 *university*
polytheism 207.2 *multiplicity*
polytheist 207.5 *pluralist*
polythene 435.1 *materials*; 32.21 *polymer*; 550.4 *wrapping*
polythene bag 410.8 *bag*
polytonic 5.39 *of language*
polytonic language 5.10 *language type*
polytunnel 44.4 *nursery*
polyunsaturated fat 33.7 *fat*
polyunsaturates 557.11 *food content*
polyurethane 435.1 *materials*; 32.21 *polymer*
polyurethane rubber 422.4 *rubber*
Pom 564.9 *British inhabitant*
poma 68.1 *skiing*
pomade 268.7; 268.19 *anoint*; 502.2 *fragrant thing*
pomander 502.2 *fragrant thing*
pomatum 268.7 *pomade*
pome 80.2 *botanical fruit*
pomiculture 44.1 *horticulture*
pomiferous 80.6 *fruiting*
pomme 743.13 *heraldic*
pommel 57.6 *pommel horse*
pommel horse 57.6
pomological 44.16 *horticultural*
pomologically 44.20 *horticulturally*
pomologist 44.13 *horticulturist*; 77.12 *plant scientist*
pomology 34.1 *life science*; 77.10 *plant science*
pomp 656.1 *formality*; 622.6 *majesty*; 738.10 *manifestation*
pomp and circumstance 622.6 *majesty*

pom-pom 587.11 *guns;* 587.12 *historical guns*
pomposity 542.2 *affectation;* 727.4 *bombast;* 544.4 *inelegance of speech;* 622.6 *majesty;* 673.1 *vanity*
pompous 673.13 *boastful;* 727.15 *bombastic;* 656.8 *ceremonious;* 673.11 *cocky;* 622.17 *conceited;* 656.6 *formal;* 544.9 *inelegant;* 542.10 *ornate;* 622.19 *stately*
pompously 673.24; 727.16 *exaggeratedly;* 542.13 *ornately*
pompousness 673.3 *cockiness*
pompous twit 673.7 *vain person*
poncho 551.25 *accessories*
pond 44.3 *ornamental garden;* 88.2 *small lake;* 67.7 *swimming pool*
ponder 482.7 *intend;* 4.20 *philosophize;* 443.12 *think;* 443.15 *think about;* 619.12 *wonder whether*
ponderable 402.7 *material*
pondered 443.10 *speculative*
pondering 443.4 *deliberation;* 4.4 *philosophical investigation;* 443.10 *speculative*
ponderosity 414.8 *weighing down*
ponderous 414.3; 620.4 *boring;* 264.15, 486.3 *clumsy;* 542.10 *ornate*
ponderously 264.28 *awkwardly;* 620.8 *boringly;* 414.17 *burdensomely;* 542.13 *ornately*
ponderousness 620.1 *boredom;* 544.4 *inelegance of speech;* 414.8 *weighing down*
ponder over 464.12 *estimate*
pondlike 88.9 *lakelike*
pond scum 84.1 *alga*
pong 245.2 *decay;* 500.8 *have odour;* 503.1 *stench;* 503.5 *stink*
pongid 71.34 *primate*
Pongidae 71.16 *primate*
pongids 71.16 *primate*
ponging 258.8 *unclean*
pongy 503.3 *stinking;* 258.8 *unclean*
poniard 587.8 *sharp weapon*
pons asinorum 379.1 *trap*
pontif 7.8 *priest*
pontifex maximus 7.8 *priest*
pontiff 400.6 *religious leader*
pontifical 707.14 *assertive;* 397.14 *commanding;* 400.12 *masterful;* 7.17 *priestly;* 10.10 *religious manual*
pontificalia 7.11 *vestment*
pontificals 7.11 *vestment*
pontificate 733.7 *address;* 452.20 *be certain;* 397.9 *command;* 722.4 *dissertate;* 795.12 *moralize;* 7.9 *priesthood*
pontificator 733.6 *public speaker*
pontoon 318.5 *crossing point*
pontoon bridge 38.21, 317.9 *bridge*
pony 59.5; 780.9 *British money;* 125.2 *copy;* 410.13 *drinking vessel;* 59.1 *horse;* 719.4 *translation;* 201.8 *twenty and over*
Pony Express 320.9 *animal transport;* 316.8 *messenger;* 692.2 *postal communication;* 332.11 *swift thing*
ponytail 547.8 *haircut;* 420.7 *rough thing;* 361.3 *suspended object*
ponytailed 420.3 *barbed*
pony trekking 59.6 *horsemanship*
poo 560.16 *defecate;* 560.5 *faeces*
pooch 71.9 *dog*
poodle 664.3 *sycophant*
poodle-faking 593.6 *courtship*
pooh-pooh 468.3 *underestimate*
pooh-pooh theory 5.37 *linguistic theory*
pool 65.6; 765.11 *acquire;* 765.3 *acquisition;* 65.1 *billiards;* 374.5 *combine;* 764.1 *joint possession;* 157.4 *shallow thing;* 88.2 *small lake;* 439.1, 439.6 *store*
pool ball 65.1 *billiards*
pooled 747.18 *joint*
pool hall 65.1 *billiards*
pooling of resources 747.4 *joint operation*
pool interests 747.14 *join with*
pool of labour 352.3 *human resources*
pool player 65.7 *billiards player*
pool resources 747.14 *join with*
pool table 65.6 *pool*
pool together 765.11 *acquire*
Poona 63.10 *badminton*
poonghie 7.8 *priest*
poop 560.5 *faeces;* 247.6 *fail*
poop deck 168.1 *rear*
pooped 261.1 *fatigued*
poo-poo 560.5 *faeces*
poop-scoop 256.10 *cleaning object*
poor 122.14; **236.4**; **782.1**; 611.8 *bad;* 670.27 *critical;* 245.12 *deteriorated;* 604.11 *disappointing;* 231.1 *imperfect;* 233.4 *incomplete;* 563.3 *infertile;* 218.1, 337.13 *insufficient;* 623.2 *lowly;* 685.6 *moderate;* 135.5 *necessitous;* 786.13 *nonpaying;* 124.2 *obscure;* 793.10 *shoddy;* 124.4 *trivial;* 766.17 *unprofitable;* 249.7 *unprosperous;* 218.2 *unprovided*
poor as dirt 782.1 *poor*
poor as Job 782.1 *poor*
poor as Lazarus 782.1 *poor*
poor as Mother Hubbard 782.1 *poor*
poor-boy 25.11 *sandwich*
poor chance 107.6
Poor Clare 782.10 *poor person*
poor dab 337.4 *weakling*
poor definition 521.4 *invisibility*
poor diction 544.5 *mispronunciation*
poor dress 552.4 *dishabille*
poor ear 504.1 *hearing*
poor effort 231.6 *imperfect item*
poor hand 486.10 *unskilled person*
poor health 337.3; 249.1 *adversity;* 260.1 *ill health*
poor hearing 505.1 *deafness*
poorhouse 782.7 *beggary*
poor imitation 116.3 *disguise*
poor judgment 465.1 *misjudgment*
poor light 523.1 *darkness;* 524.1 *dimness;* 522.10 *window*
poor likeness 718.1 *misrepresentation*
poorly 782.15; 122.21 *badly;* 337.10 *ill;* 249.12 *in adversity;* 233.6 *incompletely;* 218.10 *insufficiently;* 260.22 *sick;* 337.14 *weakly;* 245.14 *worse*
poorly defined 696.3 *unrecognizable*
poorly disciplined 662.13 *disobedient*
poorly dressed 552.10 *in dishabille*
poorly fed 687.6 *fasting*
poorly off 782.1 *poor*
poorly timed 240.1 *inconvenient*
poor memory 463.3
poorness 623.8 *lowliness;* 782.5 *poverty;* 793.3 *shoddiness*
poor opinion 670.2 *disrespect*
poor performance 486.9 *bungling*
poor person 782.10; 249.5 *person in adversity*
poor prospect 105.4 *improbability;* 102.4 *remote possibility*
poor quality 122.4; 236.8 *inferiority*
poor-quality 122.14 *poor;* 124.4 *trivial*
poor reception 505.3 *inaudibility*
poor relation 289.8 *follower;* 231.6 *imperfect item;* 122.6 *inferior;* 124.10 *nonentity;* 782.10 *poor person*
poor relief 608.4 *charity;* 2.10 *social services;* 652.4 *welfare state*
poor representation 717.1 *representation*
poor return 766.2 *financial loss;* 563.1 *infertility*
poor risk 249.5 *person in adversity*
poor second 122.6 *inferior*
poor shot 486.10 *unskilled person*
poor show 486.9 *bungling*
poor sight 519.2; 524.2 *murk*
poor table 557.10 *scarcity*
poor third 122.6 *inferior*
poor timing 240.3 *inconvenience;* 288.2 *untimeliness*
poor turnout 206.1 *few*
poor visibility 521.4 *invisibility;* 524.2 *murk;* 31.35 *visibility*
poor vision 519.2 *poor sight*
poor white 782.11 *the poor*
poor White trash 124.10 *nonentity;* 655.7 *outsider*
poor wretch 249.5 *person in adversity;* 602.3 *sad person*
Pooter 216.8 *middle classes*
pop 772.7 *borrow;* 508.2, 508.6 *crack;* 18.33 *jazz;* 567.3 *male title of address;* 567.13 *man in the family;* 18.9 *popular music;* 558.6 *soft drink*
pop at 381.2 *fire*
pope 396.10 *person of authority;* 7.8 *priest;* 400.6 *religious leader;* 121.5 *superior*
popedom 7.9 *priesthood*
popeyed 518.21 *seeing;* 619.7 *wide-eyed*
pop fan 593.9 *lover*
pop group 374.3 *assembly;* 18.26 *musical group;* 376.12 *team*
pop gun 508.3 *banger;* 330.9 *firearm*
pop in 314.9 *enter;* 368.2 *inject*
pop into one's head 446.14 *have an idea*
popish 7.16 *denominational*
poplin 193.4 *textile*
pop music 18.9 *popular music*
pop off 582.15 *die*
pop one's clogs 582.15 *die*
pop out 520.9 *appear;* 315.9 *exit*
pop-out 50.13 *windsurfing*
pop-out board 50.7 *windsurfing*
popover 25.39 *loaf*
poppadom 25.38 *bread;* 25.49 *Indian dish*
popper 55.2 *artificial fly;* 373.8 *fastening*
poppet 555.9 *child;* 593.12 *nicknames for lovers*
popping 772.1 *borrowing;* 508.9 *crackling;* 771.1 *lending*
popping crease 53.5 *wicket*
popping eyes 619.2 *sign of wonderment*
popple 91.10 *billow*
poppy 780.2 *cash;* 535.7 *red thing;* 343.10 *soporific*
poppycock 697.1 *nonsense*
Poppy Day 298.6 *annually celebrated day;* 78.9 *figurative usage*
poppy day 601.5 *anniversary*
pop shop 771.4 *lending institution*
pop single 48.5 *batting terms*
pop song 18.9 *popular music*
pop star 235.8 *exceller;* 593.11 *loved one;* 121.6 *paragon*
popster 18.24 *musician*
pop the question 705.22; 710.6 *request;* 593.28 *win the love of*
populace 138.11 *general public;* 566.9 *group;* 564.2 *inhabitants*
popular 654.16; 669.24 *admired;* 216.1 *average;* 617.7 *desired;* 12.9, 396.14 *governmental;* 595.5 *likable;* 593.22 *lovable;* 138.19 *prevailing;* 811.3 *reputable;* 695.2 *simple;* 778.16 *sold;* 740.20 *well-known*
popular belief 450.1 *belief*
Popular Coalition 12.6 *political party*
popular front 12.6 *political party*
popularity 669.2 *admiration;* 216.4 *average;* 593.1 *love;* 654.2 *social ambition*
popularization 695.10 *simplicity*
popularize 138.26; 719.8 *interpret;* 265.16 *make easy;* 695.5 *simplify*
popularized 695.2 *simple*
popularizer 719.6 *interpreter*
popular literature 17.1 *literature*
popularly 595.10 *with great liking*
popular melody 516.1 *melody*
popular misconception 274.6 *fallibility*
popular movement 342.5 *activism*
popular music 18.9
popular newspaper 741.5 *mass communication*
popular press 740.3 *journalism;* 741.5 *mass communication*
popular price 793.1 *cheapness*
popular psychology 36.1 *psychology*
popular regard 593.1 *love*
popular song 18.9 *popular music;* 516.2 *song*
popular will 12.1 *government*
populate 562.6 *be fertile;* 565.17 *inhabit;* 564.15 *settle*
populated 564.11 *inhabited*
population 27.57; 34.18 *ecology;* 564.2 *inhabitants;* 1.7 *society*
population drift 377.7 *sprawl*
population explosion 562.2 *productiveness*
population genetics 34.11 *genetics*
population growth 13.4 *economic development*
population inversion 28.26 *laser*
population study 2.2 *sociological research*
populist 12.6 *political party*
pop up 520.9 *appear;* 312.1 *arrive;* 48.5 *batting terms;* 525.12 *become visible;* 112.21 *be repeated;* 107.10 *chance;* 48.7 *play baseball;* 304.17 *spring up*
porcelain 424.3 *brittle thing;* 24.1 *ceramics;* 356.7 *produce*
porcelain clay 24.2 *raw material*
porcelain enamel 24.1 *ceramics*
porcelain insulation 24.9 *industrial ceramics*
porcelain mark 24.4
porch 314.6 *means of entry;* 308.7 *passageway;* 565.7 *room;* 317.2 *route*
porcine 71.33 *ungulate*
porcupine 425.8 *sharp-pointed thing*
pore 308.4 *body orifice;* 315.7 *outlet*
pore fungi 83.3 *fungi*
pore over 518.14 *inspect*
Porifera 75.8 *sponge*
poriferan 75.8 *sponge;* 75.22 *spongelike*
poriferous 75.22 *spongelike*
pork 25.24; **25.25**; 25.20 *meat*
pork barrel 480.10 *bribe;* 483.5 *positive stimulus*
porker 688.4 *glutton;* 43.8 *livestock*
pork pie 234.4 *distortion of the truth*
pork-pie hat 551.15 *headgear*
pork sausage 25.29 *sausage*
porky 234.4 *distortion of the truth;* 105.6 *implausibility*
porn 796.2 *indecency;* 258.3 *obscenity*
pornographer 798.6 *evil person;* 796.10 *sex offender*
pornographic 552.11 *exposed;* 796.12 *indecent;* 258.9 *obscene;* 236.4 *poor*
pornographically 552.17 *nakedly*
pornographic magazine 552.2 *nudity*
pornographic novel 17.2 *fiction*
pornography 798.5 *evil thing;* 796.2 *indecency;* 258.3 *obscenity;* 236.10 *poverty*
porous 183.6 *concave;* 308.14 *holed;* 315.17 *leaky*
porously 308.27 *cavernously*
porous pottery 24.1 *ceramics*
porous thing 308.6
porphyritic texture 30.28 *rock*
porridge 25.40 *breakfast cereal;* 25.44 *British dish;* 251.4 *detention;* 815.7 *imprisonment;* 815.4 *prison sentence;* 68.1 *skiing*
porringer 410.16 *crockery*
port 631.1 *conduct;* 312.15 *destination;* 92.9 *inlet;* 40.7 *peripheral;* 313.10 *place of departure;* 535.7 *red thing;* 169.1 *side;* 226.4 *stopping place;* 38.24 *water system;* 315.6 *way out;* 558.9 *wine*
portability 415.5 *lightness;* 159.1 *littleness*
portable 415.1 *light;* 159.7 *little;* 316.17 *transferable;* 319.5 *transportable*
portable radio 62.4 *climbing equipment;* 692.18 *radio*
portable stereo player 507.4 *sound maker*
portable television 692.22 *television set*
portable toilet 767.7 *toilet*
portage 319.1, 319.4 *transport;* 316.2 *transportation*
portal 314.6 *means of entry;* 308.7 *passageway*
portative 316.17 *transferable*
portcullis 378.3 *barrier;* 384.12 *fort;* 743.8 *heraldic device*
porte-cochere 314.6 *means of entry*
portend 694.12 *intend;* 475.11 *predict*
portent 474.4 *expectant person;* 475.5 *omen;* 711.1 *warning;* 619.4 *wonder*
portentous 475.15 *presageful*
portentously 475.16 *predictively*
portentousness 475.5 *omen*
porter 401.3 *attendant;* 62.7 *mountaineer;* 309.5 *person who closes;* 321.9 *railway worker;* 316.7 *transferor;* 578.1 *worker*
porterage 316.2 *transportation*
Porterhouse steak 25.23 *beef;* 25.43 *US dish*
porterwhisky 558.7 *alcoholic drink*
portfolio 410.9 *baggage;* 439.5 *collection;* 16.2 *jurisdiction;* 440.5 *personal estate;* 744.1 *record*
porthole 308.5 *hole*
portico 317.7 *arcade;* 314.6 *means of entry;* 20.9 *miscellaneous architectural features;* 565.7 *room*
port in a storm 312.16 *stopover*
portion 770.2; 203.2 *certain amount;* 196.2 *fractional part;* 209.4 *interval;* 440.6 *marriage settlement;* 557.14 *mouthful;* 205.1 *part;* 148.5, 205.7, 405.2 *piece;* 436.1 *provision;* 203.8 *quantify*
portioned 209.7 *gradational*
portionless 782.2 *insolvent*
portion out 770.4 *allot*
Portland Bill 92.5 *peninsula*
Portland cement 435.2 *building material;* 24.9 *industrial ceramics;* 38.26 *masonry;* 550.11 *paving*
portliness 158.5 *fatness;* 181.2 *round body;* 152.5 *thickness*
portly 158.16 *fat;* 152.1 *thick;* 181.10 *well-rounded*
portmanteau 410.9 *baggage;* 269.3 *concise;* 439.4 *storage;* 5.42 *worded*
portmanteau word 5.21 *catchword;* 374.4 *compound;* 269.1 *conciseness*
Portobello Road 779.1 *market*
port of call 226.4 *stopping place*

portrait 41.4; 19.10 *art subject*; 125.2 *copy*; 721.1 *description*; 111.3 *lookalike*; 744.1 *record*; 721.9 *representation*; 717.2 *reproduction*
portraitist 19.16 *artist*
portrait painter 19.16 *artist*
portrait sculpture 19.12 *sculpture*
portraiture 41.1 *photography*; 717.2 *reproduction*
portray 717.10 *act*; 99.11 *characterize*; 721.14 *describe*; 19.20 *draw*; 115.12 *imitate*; 163.5 *outline*; 717.9 *represent*; 17.21 *write*
portrayal 21.22, 717.3 *acting*; 721.1 *description*; 163.1 *outline*; 717.1 *representation*; 115.1 *similarity*
portraying 717.3 *acting*; 717.13 *representational*
Portsmouth 87.4 *British cities*
port tack 50.15 *sail*
port tacking 50.1 *sailing*
Portuguese GP at Estoril 61.2 *Formula 1 race*
pose 676.1 *affectedness*; 676.4 *be affected*; 631.1 *conduct*; 631.11 *conduct oneself*; 705.21 *confuse*; 699.7 *pretence*; 699.24 *pretend*; 4.22 *propound a philosophy*; 525.4 *something that appears*
pose as 717.10 *act*; 699.24 *pretend*
Poseidon 323.7 *nautical person*; 91.4 *sea god*
pose problems 264.17 *be difficult*
poser 699.19 *cheat*; 700.15 *deceiver*; 703.7 *demonstrator*; 705.4 *difficult question*; 551.27 *model*; 737.3 *mystification*; 676.2 *pretender*; 264.4 *problem*
poset 27.23 *algebra*
poseur 699.19 *cheat*; 700.15 *deceiver*; 125.7 *imitator*; 676.2 *pretender*
posh 553.7 *fashionable*
posing 717.3 *acting*; 125.12 *imitative*; 699.7 *pretence*; 699.34 *pretending*
posing pouch 552.4 *dishabille*
posit 4.22 *propound a philosophy*; 476.5 *suppose*
position 407.4; 409.12 *arrange*; 450.1 *belief*; 346.3 *business*; 409.6 *category*; 143.2, 222.1 *circumstances*; 324.1 *direction*; 143.4 *employment*; 446.5 *ideology*; 701.3 *line of argument*; 142.9 *locate*; 142.1 *location*; 209.5 *measure*; 308.10 *opportunity*; 4.2 *philosophical system*; 27.36 *point*; 185.1 *prominence*; 143.5, 209.2 *rank*; 143.10 *situate*; 143.1 *situation*; 137.5 *social class*; 28.7 *space*; 221.1 *state*; 707.2 *statement*; 476.1 *supposition*; 407.19 *systematize*
positional 142.8 *locational*
positional notation 27.8 *number system*
positioned 53.14; 142.6 *located*; 143.6 *situated*
position in society 143.5 *rank*
position of authority 396.5
position of power 334.1 *power*
position of strength 334.1 *power*
position paper 707.2 *statement*
positions at the barre 22.10
position vector 27.50 *scalar quantity*
positive 707.14 *assertive*; 450.11 *believing*; 452.2 *convinced*; 703.12 *demonstrable*; 111.4, 111.15 *duplicate*; 334.7 *electrical power*; 39.36 *electronic*; 726.3 *emphatic*; 392.33 *helpful*; 610.11 *hopeful*; 695.1 *intelligible*; 27.71 *numerical*; 194.8 *odd*; 93.13 *real*; 396.15 *true*
positive charge 28.50 *electric charge*
positive correlation 27.61 *correlation*
positive declaration 707.2 *statement*
positive discrimination 119.3 *equalization*; 466.5 *favouritism*
positive electrode 334.7 *electrical power*
positive feedback 39.15 *circuit function*
positive ion 28.66 *ion*
positively 707.23 *affirmatively*; 396.25 *authentically*; 450.15 *believingly*; 452.23 *certainly*; 39.37 *electronically*; 726.7 *emphatically*; 392.36 *helpfully*; 610.15 *hopefully*; 27.87 *mathematically*; 93.22 *really*
positiveness 707.6 *assertiveness*; 452.10 *conviction*; 695.9 *intelligibility*
positive number 27.5 *number*
positive outlook 726.1 *emphasis*
positive reinforcement 36.20 *conditioning*
positive stimulus 483.5
positive thinking 610.1 *hope*
positive vetting 252.2 *protection*
positive vote 469.10 *vote*
positivism 452.10 *conviction*; 402.2 *materialization*; 4.7 *school of thought*
positivist 4.11 *follower of a doctrine*; 402.3 *materialist*; 4.14 *of a philosophy*; 452.11 *opinionist*
positron 28.77 *elementary particle*
posologist 394.16 *druggist*; 35.13 *medical specialist*
posology 35.3 *medical specialty*; 37.1 *pharmacology*
posse 750.2 *alliance*; 376.11 *group*; 16.17 *police officer*
posse comitatus 16.17 *police officer*
possess 763.7; 683.6 *be selfish*; 11.21 *bewitch*; 8.18 *devilize*; 349.5 *dispose of*; 440.9 *own property*; 773.7 *take*
possess an even temper 658.10 *be courteous*
possessed 763.9; 11.19 *bewitched*; 440.8 *propertied*
possessed of 763.8 *possessing*
possessing 763.8; 763.1 *possession*; 440.8 *propertied*
possessing narcotics 691.2 *drug pushing*
Possession 763
possession 763.1; **763.4**; 46.7 *offence*; 49.4 *playing terms*; 440.1 *property*; 64.3 *rugby play*; 773.1 *taking*; 86.4 *territorial division*; 349.6 *use*; 11.3 *witchcraft*
possession ball 49.4 *playing terms*
possession in common 764.1 *joint possession*
Possessions 440
possessions 440.4; 781.5 *wealth*
possessive 593.20 *amorous*; 617.9 *desirous*; 629.4 *jealous*; 683.4 *selfish*; 773.12 *taking*
possessive love 593.2 *romantic love*
possessively 763.10; 773.13 *avariciously*; 629.9 *jealously*; 683.8 *selfishly*
possessiveness 629.2 *distrust*; 128.4 *exclusiveness*; 629.1 *jealousy*; 593.2 *romantic love*; 683.1 *selfishness*
possess magical power 334.10 *be powerful*
possess narcotics 691.10 *drug oneself*
possessor 763.5; 575.4 *titleholder*
possessorship 763.1 *possession*
possessory 763.8 *possessing*
possess power 396.18 *have authority*
possess special power 334.10 *be powerful*
possess spirit 334.10 *be powerful*
possess strength 336.7 *be strong*
possess with 440.9 *own property*
posset 558.7 *alcoholic drink*
possibilities 756.3 *potential*
Possibility 102
possibility 102.1; 476.2 *basis of supposition*; 474.1 *expectation*; 474.2 *expectations*; 308.10 *opportunity*; 104.3 *plausibility*; 265.3 *wieldiness*
possibility of perfection 231.5 *imperfection*
possible 102.5; 756.14 *auspicious*; 450.13 *believable*; 265.10 *feasible*; 756.15 *future*; 104.7 *plausible*; 102.6 *potential*; 334.13 *powerful*; 283.12 *predictable*; 95.9 *realizable*
possible choice 469.8 *choice*
possible need 436.1 *provision*
possibleness 102.2
possible outcome 27.62 *probability*
possible worlds 4.9 *philosophical problem*
possibly 102.9; 756.17 *auspiciously*; 107.14 *perchance*; 756.18 *potentially*; 334.18 *powerfully*; 283.16 *predictably*; 476.10 *supposedly*
possum 634.17 *avoider*
possuming 633.2 *chase*
post 316.13; 789.7 *account*; 346.3 *business*; 23.17 *carpenter*; 20.8 *column*; 693.12 *communicate*; 692.31 *correspond*; 692.3 *correspondence*; 143.4 *employment*; 43.11 *farmland*; 373.8 *fastening*; 59.7 *horseracing*; 220.8 *list*; 142.9 *locate*; 142.1 *location*; 733.10 *send*; 143.10 *situate*; 413.11 *support*; 413.2 *supporting part*; 154.6 *tall thing*; 316.10 *transferred thing*; 186.3 *vertical thing*; 23.12 *wood*
postage 790.6 *business costs*
postage meter 692.3 *correspondence*
postage stamp 692.3 *correspondence*
postal 692.33 *communicational*
postal address 142.2 *exact location*
postal card 692.3 *correspondence*
postal communication 692.2
postal district 142.2 *exact location*
post a letter bomb 700.33 *snare*
postal order 692.3 *correspondence*; 780.14 *paper money*
postal service 692.2 *postal communication*
Postal Union 692.2 *postal communication*
postal vote 469.10 *vote*
postal worker 692.4
post and rail 165.3 *enclosing thing*
post and rails 59.9 *jumping*
post a parcel bomb 700.33 *snare*
postbag 692.3 *correspondence*
postbellum 589.7 *peaceful*
post bills 740.16 *publicize*
postbox 692.3 *correspondence*
postboy 59.15 *horse person*
postbus 316.5 *means of transport*
postcard 692.3 *correspondence*; 316.10 *transferred thing*
postcode 692.3 *correspondence*; 142.2 *exact location*; 733.5 *place of residence*
postdate 288.5 *mistime*
postdated 288.12 *too late*
posted 692.34 *communicated*; 693.18 *informed*; 142.6 *located*; 143.6 *situated*
poster 740.9 *advertisement*; 19.7 *picture*; 738.8 *showplace*; 742.1 *sign*
poster artist 19.16 *artist*
poste restante 692.2 *postal communication*
posterior 168.4 *rear*; 168.2 *rear end*
posterity 289.6; 283.2 *future generation*
postern 384.12 *fort*; 314.6 *means of entry*; 308.7 *passageway*; 168.1, 168.4 *rear*
poster paint 529.5 *paint*
post-existence 283.3 *future condition*
post-free 793.11 *free of charge*; 758.8 *tax-free*
postglacial 31.40 *climatic change*; 30.60 *glaciated*
postglaciation 31.40 *climatic change*
postgraduate 6.21 *curricular*; 6.7 *learner*; 136.8 *qualified person*
posthaste 262.6 *hastily*; 280.9 *in the shortest possible time*; 332.14 *swiftly*
post horse 59.2 *thoroughbred*
posthumous 294.14 *dead*; 582.22 *postmortem*
posthumously 582.23 *fatally*; 294.18 *formerly*; 301.10 *motionlessly*
post-hypnotic suggestion 36.3 *psychiatric treatment*
postilion 59.15 *horse person*
postimpressionist 19.29 *realist*
postindustrial 356.11 *productive*
posting 142.4 *placing*; 316.2 *transportation*
postlude 289.9 *sequel*
postman 316.8 *messenger*; 692.4 *postal worker*
postmark 692.3 *correspondence*
postmaster 692.4 *postal worker*
postmaster general 692.4 *postal worker*
postmeridian 290.7 *afternoon*; 291.6 *evening*
post meridiem 291.7 *evening*
postmistress 692.4 *postal worker*
postmodern 17.16 *literary*; 295.10 *new*
postmodernism 295.2 *trendiness*
postmodernist 295.9 *modern person*; 19.29 *realist*
postmortem 582.22; 582.8 *after death*; 35.7 *diagnosis*; 582.23 *fatally*; 583.12 *funereally*; 583.7 *inquest*; 289.9 *sequel*
postmortem examination 582.8 *after death*
post-mortem examination 583.7 *inquest*
postnatal 561.16 *reproductive*
post-obit 582.22 *postmortem*
post-obitum 583.12 *funereally*
Post Office 692.2 *postal communication*
post office 692.2 *postal communication*
post-office box 692.3 *correspondence*
Post Office savings bank 780.19 *treasury*
post-paid 692.34 *communicated*; 793.11 *free of charge*; 785.19 *receiving pay*
post pattern 46.9 *play*
postpone 634.7 *be evasive*; 294.8 *delay*; 637.8 *hold back*; 361.12 *interrupt*; 355.2 *withdraw*
postponed 294.10 *held up*; 361.9 *interrupted*
postponement 637.15 *delay*; 294.3 *delayed action*; 361.6 *interruption*
postponing 637.4 *procrastinating*
postprandial 263.4 *at ease*; 25.56 *culinary*
posts 63.3 *tennis equipment*
postscript 211.3 *additional item*; 134.1 *continuity*; 131.10 *ending*; 168.1 *rear*; 289.9 *sequel*
post-structuralism 403.9 *artistic structure*; 4.7 *school of thought*
post-structuralist 4.11 *follower of a doctrine*; 17.15 *literary person*
post the banns 756.1 *promise*
post-traumatic stress disorder 36.12 *stress*
postulant 7.7 *monk*
postulate 701.3 *line of argument*; 4.8 *philosophical term*; 4.20 *philosophize*; 4.1 *philosophy*; 444.14 *premise*; 4.22 *propound a philosophy*; 701.15 *state*; 476.5 *suppose*; 476.1 *supposition*; 27.89 *theorize*; 27.65 *theory*
postulated 701.11 *logical*; 476.8 *supposed*
postulation 476.1 *supposition*
postulatory 476.7 *suppositional*
posture 676.1 *affectedness*; 676.4 *be affected*; 222.1 *circumstances*; 631.1 *conduct*; 631.11 *conduct oneself*; 340.2 *deed*; 525.3 *external appearance*; 160.6 *nature*; 699.7 *pretence*; 699.24 *pretend*; 221.1 *state*
posturing 699.34 *pretending*
postwar 589.7 *peaceful*
postwoman 692.4 *postal worker*
posy 376.29 *bunch*; 78.1 *flower*; 502.2 *fragrant thing*
pot 410.15; 69.3 *card game terms*; 24.8 *ceramic object*; 203.3 *container*; 44.15 *cultivate*; 691.6 *drug*; 368.1 *insert*; 24.11 *make ceramics*; 359.5 *preserve*; 359.2 *preserver*; 492.3 *press*; 813.2 *prize*; 410.21 *put in a container*; 330.31 *snipe*; 723.8 *summarize*; 794.1 *trophy*
pot a ball 65.8 *play billiards*
potable 558.17 *drinkable*; 252.6 *safe*; 495.7 *tasty*
potage 25.13 *soup*
potash 43.13, 562.3 *fertilizer*
potassium 33.15 *essential element*
potassium–argon dating 30.42 *dating*; 28.70 *radioactivity*
potate 558.13 *drink*
potation 558.2, 690.13 *drink*; 558.1 *drinking*
potations 690.12 *alcohol*
potato blight 357.7 *agent of destruction*
potato bread 25.38 *bread*
potato chips 25.10 *snack*
potatoes 43.12 *crop*
potato field 43.11 *farmland*
potato harvester 43.10 *farm tool*
potato picker 43.16 *farm worker*
potato planter 43.10 *farm tool*
potato salad 25.14 *salad*
potbellied 158.16 *fat*; 152.1 *thick*; 181.10 *well-rounded*
potbelly 158.8 *fat*; 181.2 *round body*; 410.18 *stomach*; 152.5 *thickness*
potboiler 721.5 *fiction*
potboiling 124.4 *trivial*
potboy 401.3 *attendant*
poteen 558.7 *alcoholic drink*
potence 396.1 *authority*
potency 396.1 *authority*; 395.1 *influence*; 237.7 *instrumentality*; 334.1 *power*; 336.1 *strength*
potent 336.10; 396.12 *authoritative*; 743.8 *heraldic device*; 395.11 *influential*; 690.6 *intoxicating*; 334.13 *powerful*
potentate 400.3 *leader*
potential 102.6; **756.3**; 334.2 *ability*; 756.14 *auspicious*; 28.52, 39.10 *electric potential*; 334.4 *energy*; 756.15 *future*; 102.1 *possibility*; 102.5 *possible*; 334.13 *powerful*; 283.12 *predictable*
potential difference 28.52, 39.10 *electric potential*; 334.4 *energy*
potential energy 28.11, 334.4 *energy*
potentiality 334.2 *ability*; 395.1 *influence*; 102.1 *possibility*; 136.1 *qualification*
potentially 102.11; **756.18**; 756.17 *auspiciously*; 334.18 *powerfully*; 283.16 *predictably*
potentiometer 28.90 *ammeter*; 39.23 *electrical instrument*; 26.8 *meter*; 39.17 *resistor*
potentiometry 26.2 *micrometry*

potently 336.15 *acutely*; 396.23 *authoritatively*; 395.14 *influentially*; 334.18 *powerfully*
pother 408.9 *disorder*; 727.7 *exaggerate*; 727.1 *exaggeration*
potherb 77.2 *plant*; 44.11 *vegetable*
pothole 183.2 *concave land*; 156.4 *deep thing*; 172.1 *interior*; 420.12 *make rough*
potholed 420.2 *coarse*
potholed road 420.8 *rough ground*
potholer 156.5 *submariner*
potholing 156.1 *depth*; 305.7 *tunnelling*
potion 558.2 *drink*; 37.3 *drug*; 394.2 *medicine*; 412.2 *mixed thing*
potlatch 10.7 *non-Christian ritual*; 10.3 *rite of worship*
potluck 107.2 *luck*; 557.12 *meal*
potluck dinner 654.5 *party*
pot magnet 28.60 *magnet*
pot of gold 756.4 *promised land*; 781.5 *wealth*
Potomac 90.3 *US rivers*
pot on 44.15 *cultivate*
pot plant 78.1 *flower*; 77.2 *plant*
potpourri 502.2 *fragrant thing*; 376.32, 412.3 *miscellany*; 412.2 *mixed thing*
pot roast 25.32 *meat dish*
pot-roast 25.55 *cook*
pot-roasting 25.8 *cooking technique*
pots and pans 410.15 *pot*
potsherd 205.7 *piece*
potshoot 330.31 *snipe*
potshot 330.7 *shot*; 330.31 *snipe*
pots of money 781.6 *money*
potted 410.20 *containing*; 690.1 *drunk*; 359.7 *preserved*; 723.7 *shortened*
potted version 723.2 *outline*
potter **24.7**; 578.2 *artisan*; 300.15 *walk*
pottering 342.19 *busy*; 300.17 *directional*; 342.7 *restlessness*; 300.9 *slow motion*
potter's clay 435.1 *materials*; 24.2 *raw material*
potter's earth 24.2 *raw material*
potter's wheel 24.6 *ceramic workshop*; 760.4 *medium of conversion*; 307.6 *rotator*
potter's workplace 24.6 *ceramic workshop*
pottery 424.3 *brittle thing*; 24.1 *ceramics*; 24.6 *ceramic workshop*; 410.16 *crockery*; 356.7 *produce*
pottery factory 24.6 *ceramic workshop*
potting 410.20 *containing*
potting a ball 65.5 *snooker*
potting compost 44.7 *fertilizer*
potting on 44.5 *gardening*
potting shed 44.4 *nursery*
potty 459.5 *foolish*; 410.15 *pot*; 560.14, 767.7 *toilet*
potty-trained 560.26 *urinary*
pot-valiant 690.1 *drunk*
pouch 410.8 *bag*; 71.4 *pouched mammal*
pouched mammal **71.4**
Poujadism 12.1 *government*
poult 43.8 *livestock*; 72.12 *young bird*
poulterer 436.3 *provider*
poultice 394.20 *doctor*; 493.3 *heater*; 37.7 *ointment*; 394.10 *surgical dressing*
poulticing 394.13 *therapy*
poultry **25.28**; 43.8 *livestock*; 25.20 *meat*
poultry farm 43.6 *farm*
poultry farmer 43.15 *agriculturist*
poultry farming 43.3 *livestock farming*
pounce 332.9 *acceleration*; 332.4 *be swift*; 305.5 *dive*; 305.12 *drop*; 427.5 *powder*
pounce on 630.10 *ambush*
pounce upon 381.5 *strike*
pound 71.20 *abode of mammals*; 381.1 *attack*; 414.9 *avoirdupois weight*; 331.5, 427.26 *beat*; 491.10 *be painful*; 331.13 *blow*; 509.8 *drum*; 165.2 *enclosed place*; 331.3 *hit*; 412.8 *mix*; 815.1 *prison*; 112.22 *resound*; 18.38 *sound*; 565.12 *stall*
poundage 791.1 *discount*; 414.4 *heaviness*
poundal 334.5 *unit of work*
pound coin 780.9 *British money*
pounder 427.11 *pulverizer*
pound-foolish 727.14 *extravagant*
pound-foolishness 727.3 *extravagance*
pound for pound 204.11 *wholly*
pound in 368.3 *impact*
pounding 509.1, 509.15 *drumming*; 491.5 *painful*; 427.4 *pulverization*
pound net 700.13 *snare*
pound note 780.9 *British money*
pound of flesh 784.4 *interest*; 628.1 *pitilessness*; 647.1 *severity*
pound sterling 780.1 *money*
pour 217.5 *about*; 208.11, 376.40 *crowd*; 305.3 *downflow*; 305.13 *drip*; 90.7, 431.25 *flow*; 31.62 *rain*; 315.11 *run out*; 367.6 *throw down*
pour a broadside into 381.2 *fire*
pourboire 813.7 *bounty*; 768.2 *gift*
pour cold water on 602.10 *depress*
pour down 305.13 *drip*
pour down the drain 766.11 *be wasteful*; 441.1, 681.7 *waste*
pour in 310.10 *come together*; 314.12 *flood in*; 368.2 *inject*; 410.21 *put in a container*; 406.7 *stuff*
pouring 305.16 *descending*; 562.5 *fertile*; 31.53 *rainy*
pour it on 332.5 *run like a shot*
pour oil upon 268.19 *anoint*
pour on 433.29 *water*
pour out 270.5 *be diffuse*; 768.5 *give*; 371.14 *let out*; 315.11 *run out*; 367.6 *throw down*
pour vitriol 670.22 *vituperate*
pour vitriol upon 712.6 *vilify*
pour wrath onto 624.13 *vent one's anger*
pout 626.9 *be sullen*; 234.2 *facial distortion*; 625.7 *frown*; 742.3, 742.11 *gesture*; 659.8 *get angry*; 234.10 *make faces*; 626.2 *sign of sullenness*
pouting 625.5 *showing irascibility*; 626.6 *sullen*
Poverty 782
poverty **236.10**; **782.5**; 122.2 *deficiency*; 245.7 *deterioration*; 249.2 *economic adversity*; 233.1 *incompleteness*; 135.3 *needfulness*; 218.9 *scarcity*
poverty level 218.8 *insufficiency*; 135.3 *needfulness*
poverty line 782.5 *poverty*
poverty of intellect 457.1 *lack of intellect*
poverty-stricken 782.1 *poor*; 249.7 *unprosperous*
poverty trap 135.3 *needfulness*; 782.5 *poverty*
POW 655.7 *outsider*; 815.5 *prisoner*; 387.5 *subjected person*
POW camp 655.4 *place of confinement*
powder **427.5**; **427.21**; 547.4 *cosmetics*; 587.15 *explosive*; 551.5 *fancy dress*; 551.35 *make clothing*; 529.16 *make up*; 394.2 *medicine*; 37.6 *pill*; 427.22 *pulverize*; 215.2 *residue*; 377.18 *sprinkle*; 541.11 *variegate*
powder and shot 587.13 *ammunition*
powder barrel 587.4 *arsenal*
powder blue 539.1 *blue*
powder box 410.6 *box*
powder boy 586.27 *naval man*
powdered 541.10 *mottled*; 427.18 *pulverized*; 377.23 *sprinkled*
powdered milk 558.5 *milk*
powdered sugar 498.2 *sweetener*
powdered wig 551.15 *headgear*
powder flask 587.4 *arsenal*
powder-grey 533.1 *grey*
powder horn 587.4 *arsenal*
Powderiness 427
powderiness **427.1**
powdering 427.4 *pulverization*; 377.4 *sprinkling*
powder keg 587.4 *arsenal*; 379.1 *trap*
powder magazine 587.4 *arsenal*
powder monkey 586.27 *naval man*
powder room 560.13 *lavatory*; 767.7 *toilet*
powder snow 494.5 *ice*; 68.1 *skiing*
powdery **427.15**; 424.1 *brittle*; 428.6 *desert*
powdery mildew 44.12 *pests and diseases*
powdery snow 31.30 *snow*
Power 334
power **194.6**; **334.1**; 340.1 *action*; 140.8, 396.1, 397.3 *authority*; 85.1 *country*; 8.2 *divine attribute*; 726.1 *emphasis*; 28.11 *energy*; 576.4 *exertion*; 437.11 *fuel*; 334.12 *generate power*; 334.11 *give power*; 396.21 *grant authority*; 331.1 *impel*; 123.1 *importance*; 331.11 *impulsion*; 395.1 *influence*; 237.7, 348.1 *instrumentality*; 121.2 *leadership*; 579.3 *management*; 352.1 *means*; 27.17 *multiplication*; 346.1 *operation*; 647.1 *severity*; 336.1 *strength*; 346.9 *take action*; 86.4 *territorial division*; 349.6 *use*; 338.1 *vigour*; 380.1 *violence*
power abuse 351.2 *misuse*
power amplifier 39.21 *rectifier*
powerband 61.6 *motor-racing terms*
power behind the throne 396.1 *authority*; 736.7 *concealer*; 344.8 *contributor*; 398.4 *deputy*; 395.4 *indirect influence*
power broker 395.4 *indirect influence*
power cable 437.4 *electricity*
power conversion 39.34 *power supply*
power cord 334.7 *electrical power*
power cut 523.2 *darkening*; 437.4 *electricity*; 39.34 *power supply*; 218.9 *scarcity*
power distribution 39.33
power dive 332.9 *acceleration*; 305.5 *dive*; 305.12 *drop*
power down 335.8 *overpower*
power-driven 438.9 *mechanical*
power-driven saw 23.11 *woodworking tool*
powered **334.17**; **437.10**; 438.9 *mechanical*
powered up 334.15 *full of energy*
power factor 39.26 *electrical energy*
power failure 335.1 *powerlessness*
powerful **334.13**; **423.4**; 164.10 *advantaged*; 396.12 *authoritative*; 348.7 *causal*; 340.6 *effective*; 726.3 *emphatic*; 395.11 *influential*; 237.3 *instrumental*; 507.6 *loud*; 123.6 *notable*; 336.9 *physically strong*; 336.10 *potent*; 140.12 *ruling*; 397.15 *self-assured*; 338.4 *vigorous*; 380.6 *violent*
powerful build 423.8 *physical strength*
powerful influence 395.1 *influence*
powerfully **334.18**; **423.13**; **437.12**; 164.12 *at an advantage*; 396.23 *authoritatively*; 397.16 *commandingly*; 340.8 *effectively*; 330.34 *forward*; 395.14 *influentially*; 348.9 *instrumentally*; 336.14 *strongly*; 349.11 *usefully*; 380.10 *violently*
powerfulness 396.2 *authoritativeness*; 334.1 *power*
powerful person 123.4 *bigwig*
power generation 39.32 *power station*
power harrow 43.10 *farm tool*
powerhead 50.7 *windsurfing*
power hitter 48.2 *baseball player*
powerhouse 342.10 *busy person*; 39.32 *power station*; 334.6 *source of energy*; 577.1 *workshop*
powerless **335.10**; 341.3 *inactive*; 124.2 *obscure*; 339.6 *suspended*; 238.1 *useless*; 337.8 *weak*
powerlessly **335.14**; 341.5 *without action*
Powerlessness 335
powerlessness **335.1**; 588.1 *anarchy*; 124.6 *obscurity*; 238.3 *uselessness*
powerless person **335.5**
power line 334.7 *electrical power*; 39.33 *power distribution*
power mower 44.6 *garden tool*
power of attorney 762.1 *substitution*
power of conception 444.1 *reason*
power of imagination 477.1 *imagination*
power of reason 444.1 *reason*
power of seeing 518.1 *vision*
power of speech **729.2**
power of the purse 14.1, 780.7 *finance*
power of three 199.1 *three*
power of two 198.1 *two*
power pack 334.7 *electrical power*; 437.4 *electricity*; 39.34 *power supply*
power plant 39.32 *power station*; 334.6 *source of energy*; 577.1 *workshop*
power-plant worker 578.2 *artisan*
power play 58.3 *ice hockey*
power point 437.4 *electricity*; 39.28 *plug*
power production 39.32 *power station*
power regulation 39.34 *power supply*
powers 8.6 *angel*
power-saw 79.7 *timber production*
power series 27.20 *sequence*
power shovel 38.29 *construction equipment*
powers of darkness 8.7 *devil*
power source **39.29**
power station **39.32**; 28.56 *electrical energy*; 437.4 *electricity*; 28.11 *energy*; 334.6 *source of energy*; 577.1 *workshop*
power structure 209.2 *rank*
power supply **39.34**; 28.56 *electrical energy*
power sweep 46.9 *play*
power transistor 39.19 *transistor*
power up 334.11 *give power*
power vacuum 588.1 *anarchy*; 335.1 *powerlessness*
power wheel 24.6 *ceramic workshop*
power-worker **437.9**
powwow 734.11 *confer*; 734.4 *conference*; 713.2 *consultation*; 746.3 *discussion*; 746.5 *negotiate*
PPS 211.3 *additional item*
practicability 239.3 *convenience*; 102.2 *possibleness*
practicable 239.1 *convenient*; 265.10 *feasible*; 746.8 *negotiated*; 102.5 *possible*; 95.9 *realizable*; 237.1 *useful*; 346.11 *workable*
practicableness 239.3 *convenience*; 265.3 *wieldiness*
practical **95.8**; **348.8**; 713.8 *advisable*; 239.1 *convenient*; 265.10 *feasible*; 392.33 *helpful*; 746.8 *negotiated*; 102.5 *possible*; 4.15 *rational*; 349.9 *used*; 237.1 *useful*; 265.12 *wieldy*; 346.11 *workable*
practical ability 485.1 *skill*
practical compromise 754.1 *compromise*
practical criticism 719.3 *criticism*
practical experience 455.3 *learning*
practicality 239.3 *convenience*; 348.1 *instrumentality*; 102.2 *possibleness*; 95.1 *reality*; 349.6 *use*; 237.5 *usefulness*; 265.3 *wieldiness*
practical joke 700.11 *hoax*; 599.5 *joke*; 697.3 *tomfoolery*; 124.8 *trifle*
practical joker 697.4 *buffoon*; 700.15 *deceiver*
practical knowledge 485.1 *skill*
practically **102.10**; 32.46 *chemically*; 239.7 *conveniently*; 392.36 *helpfully*; 147.13 *nearly*; 204.13 *on the whole*; 346.13 *operationally*; 4.26 *rationally*; 237.12, 349.11 *usefully*
practical person 340.3 *doer*
practice 340.1 *action*; 243.12 *briefing*; 117.5 *convention*; 140.6 *custom*; 576.5 *exercise*; 448.8 *experimental*; 160.5 *formality*; 656.3 *formal occasion*; 455.3 *learning*; 394.11 *medical art*; 35.1 *medicine*; 713.3 *precept*; 243.10 *preparations*; 632.6 *procedure*; 448.2 *rehearsal*; 112.1 *repetition*; 694.4 *type of meaning*; 349.6 *use*; 317.1, 631.7 *way*
practice run 448.2 *rehearsal*
practise 340.4 *act*; 633.14 *carry on*; 394.20 *doctor*; 576.9 *exercise*; 632.18 *habituate*; 243.8 *prepare oneself*; 448.12 *rehearse*; 112.16 *repeat*; 349.1 *use*
practise abstinence 795.11 *be moral*
practise at 400.15 *learn*
practise atheism 708.10 *be negative*
practise birth control 563.9
practise celibacy 572.9 *be celibate*
practise creative accounting 789.7 *account*
practised 632.12 *established*; 485.8 *expert*; 632.14 *habituated*; 6.19, 455.8 *knowledgeable*; 243.18 *prepared*; 136.9 *qualified*
practise dentistry 35.21
practised eye 485.5 *expert*
practised hand 485.5 *expert*
practise etiquette 160.8 *be formal*
practise forestry 79.18 *manage trees*
practise horticulture 44.14
practise hygiene 257.5 *by hygienic*
practise judo 52.13
practise livestock farming 43.18
practise magic 700.29 *juggle*
practise medicine 35.19; 394.20 *doctor*
practise nudism 552.14 *undress*
practise one's religion 101.12 *enter a nonmaterial world*
practise philanthropy 650.9 *be charitable*
practise self-defence 52.11 *fight*
practise sophistry 702.11
practise sorcery 700.28 *trick*
practise spiritualism 11.22 *conjure*
practise subversion 588.4 *be anarchic*
practise surgery 35.20
practise tae kwon do 52.13 *practise judo*
practise tax evasion 786.7 *not pay*
practise the golden rule 650.8 *be benevolent*
practise usury 771.5 *lend*
practise virtue 803.8 *be virtuous*
practise witchcraft 395.10 *be a prevailing influence*; 334.10 *be powerful*; 11.21 *bewitch*; 700.28 *trick*
practising 645.4 *cunning*; 7.15 *religious*; 112.1 *repetition*; 576.10 *working*
practising Christian 450.5 *believer*; 7.5 *Christian*
practitioner 578.3 *agent*; 340.3 *doer*; 396.11, 400.10, 485.5 *expert*

prado 317.7 *arcade*
praedial 43.19 *agricultural*; 440.8 *propertied*
praedium 440.1 *property*
praenomen 721.8 *name*
praetor 579.16 *official*
Praetorian Guard 586.12 *ceremonial troops*
pragmatic 239.1 *convenient*; 4.18 *detached*; 448.8 *experimental*; 746.8 *negotiated*; 95.8 *practical*; 4.15 *rational*; 349.9 *used*; 237.1 *useful*
pragmatically 746.9 *feasibly*; 4.26 *rationally*; 2.16 *sociologically*; 349.11 *usefully*
pragmatic sociology 2.1 *sociology*
pragmatism 239.3 *convenience*; 448.3 *experimentation*; 95.3 *realism*; 4.7 *school of thought*
pragmatist 95.4 *realist*
Prague 87.6 *other cities*
prairie 187.3 *flat thing*; 141.3 *geographical space*; 81.2 *grassland*; 92.6 *lowland*
praise **667.17**; **669.3**; **669.14**; 671.6 *be grateful*; 669.4, 669.15 *compliment*; 601.17 *congratulate*; 600.2 *fanfare*; 600.6 *fête*; 677.8 *flatter*; 677.1 *flattery*; 413.14 *give moral support*; 10.19 *offer worship*; 241.10 *pleasant thing*; 671.3 *recognition*; 813.1, 813.9 *reward*; 10.3 *rite of worship*; 671.2 *thanks*; 9.1, 9.7 *worship*
praised 813.16 *rewarded*; 9.11 *worshipped*
praise heaven 671.7 *give thanks*
praise oneself 683.7 *be egoistic*
praiser **669.9**
praise-singer 9.5 *worshipper*
praise to the skies 669.15 *compliment*
praiseworthiness 797.8 *good*; 235.6 *worth*
praiseworthy **669.21**; 617.8 *desirable*; 797.1 *good*; 667.13 *respectable*; 235.1, 803.7 *worthy*
praising 677.12 *flattering*; 671.5 *thanking*; 9.9 *worshipful*
praline 25.41 *sweet*
pram 320.8 *baby carriage*
prance 22.15 *dance*
prancing 304.24 *leaping*
prandial 25.56 *culinary*
prang 381.3 *bomb*; 305.12 *drop*
prank 599.5 *joke*; 697.3 *tomfoolery*; 642.3 *whim*
prankish 642.1 *capricious*
prankster 697.4 *buffoon*; 642.4 *capricious person*
prat 459.3 *foolish person*; 457.3 *unintelligent person*
prate 731.7 *be talkative*; 734.10 *chat*
pratfall 305.4 *fall*
prating 731.6 *effusive*; 731.3 *talk*
prattle 734.2, 734.10 *chat*; 731.3 *talk*
prattle on 731.7 *be talkative*
prattler 729.10 *speaker*
prattling 731.6 *effusive*
prawn 75.4 *arthropod*; 25.19 *shellfish*
prawn cocktail 25.12 *hors d'oeuvre*
praxis 340.1 *action*; 750.6 *convention*; 140.6 *custom*; 632.1 *habit*; 10.1 *ritual*; 1.8 *tradition*; 631.6 *way of life*
pray **10.20**; 807.6 *apologize*; 710.6 *request*; 9.7 *worship*
prayer **10.9**; 710.1 *request*; 10.3 *rite of worship*; 392.2 *support*; 671.2 *thanks*
prayer book 10.10 *religious manual*
prayer cap 7.11 *vestment*
prayer for the dead 10.9 *prayer*
prayerful 7.15 *religious*; 9.9 *worshipful*; 10.22 *worshipping*
prayerfully 10.23 *ritually*
prayerfulness 7.2 *religiousness*
prayermat 10.14 *sacred object*
prayer meeting 10.4 *public worship*
prayer of thanks 671.2 *thanks*
prayers 10.4 *public worship*
prayer shawl 10.14 *sacred object*
prayerwheel 307.6 *rotator*; 10.14 *sacred object*
pray for 617.12 *desire*; 710.6 *request*
praying 10.3 *rite of worship*; 9.1 *worship*
praying gesture 742.3 *gesture*
pray to 733.8 *appeal to*
preach **7.20**; 722.4 *dissertate*; 795.12 *moralize*; 760.11 *persuade*; 4.22 *propound a philosophy*
preach at 733.7 *address*
preacher 760.5 *converter*; 722.3 *dissertator*; 6.4 *educator*; 395.5 *influential person*; 483.7 *motivator*; 733.6 *public speaker*; 7.4 *religionist*; 729.10 *speaker*
preachify 7.20 *preach*
preachiness 7.2 *religiousness*
preach to 729.14 *speak to*
preach to the converted 238.9 *waste effort*
preachy 6.16 *educational*; 7.15 *religious*
Preakness 59.7 *horseracing*
preamble 130.10 *introduction*; 729.8 *speech*
prearrange 243.2 *do the groundwork*; 409.18 *make arrangements*; 484.12 *plan ahead*; 106.2 *premeditate*
prearranged 106.4 *deliberate*; 409.21 *organized*
prearrangement 106.6 *premeditation*; 243.9 *preparation*
Precambrian era 284.3 *geological period*
Precambrian Palaeozoic 296.15 *primal*
precarious 227.13 *changeable*; 453.7 *unreliable*; 254.2 *unsafe*
precariously 227.15 *changeably*; 254.11 *dangerously*; 453.26 *unreliably*
precariousness 254.5 *danger*; 453.15 *unreliability*
precast 38.32 *structural*
precast concrete 38.25 *construction material*
precaution 616.2 *insurance*; 252.2 *protection*; 436.1 *provision*
precautionary 243.16 *preparatory*
precautionary steps 252.4 *safety device*
precautions 252.4 *safety device*
precede **129.15**; **293.8**; 123.7 *be important*; 579.2 *direct*; 209.5 *measure*
precede in time 293.8 *precede*
Precedence 129
precedence **129.1**; 123.1 *importance*; 126.1 *originality*; 209.2 *rank*; 121.1 *superiority*
precedent **129.4**; **140.5**; 16.7 *legal trial*; 126.2 *original*; 129.10 *preceding*; 713.3 *precept*
preceding **129.10**; 284.19 *antiquarian*; 167.6 *front*; 129.1 *precedence*; 293.15 *precursory*; 209.8 *ranked*
precentor 579.14 *leader*; 7.8 *priest*
precept **713.3**; 713.1 *advice*; 397.1 *command*; 810.6 *ethics*; 140.4 *guide*; 443.6 *idea*; 16.3 *law*; 745.1 *maxim*; 795.7 *moral*; 4.1 *philosophy*; 698.4 *truism*
preceptive 745.2 *proverbial*; 698.17 *truistic*
preceptor 6.4 *educator*
preceptress 6.4 *educator*
precession 29.13 *luminosity*; 29.21 *orbit*; 129.1 *precedence*; 300.10 *regular movement*
precessional 129.10 *preceding*
pre-Christian 3.15 *historic*
precinct 87.7 *city district*; 469.12 *election*; 165.2 *enclosed place*; 147.5 *near place*; 86.5 *state*; 86.10 *urban area*
precincts 170.1 *surroundings*
precinct station 87.13 *municipal building*
preciosity 656.2 *formalism*; 542.1 *ornament*
precious 676.3 *affected*; 656.6 *formal*; 593.12 *nicknames for lovers*; 542.10 *ornate*; 235.3, 792.8 *valuable*
precious few 206.5 *few*
precious heart 593.12 *nicknames for lovers*
precious little 206.5 *few*
preciously 542.13 *ornately*; 792.13 *valuably*
precious metal 780.16 *bullion*; 780.1 *money*
preciousness 656.2 *formalism*; 542.1 *ornament*; 792.6 *value*
precipice 305.3 *downflow*; 89.1, 154.3 *mountain*; 305.6 *slide*; 379.1 *trap*; 186.3 *vertical thing*
precipitance 262.5 *hastiness*; 472.2 *impetuosity*; 293.5 *prematurity*; 615.1 *rashness*
precipitancy 615.1 *rashness*
precipitant 262.3 *hasty*; 615.4 *rash*
precipitantly 262.6 *hastily*
precipitate 344.10 *awaken*; 416.8 *be dense*; 332.4 *be swift*; 357.8 *destroy*; 258.4 *dirt*; 305.13 *drip*; 30.63 *ebb*; 345.1 *effect*; 262.1 *hasten*; 262.3 *hasty*; 32.3 *phase*; 293.16 *premature*; 293.9 *prepare*; 31.62 *rain*; 615.4 *rash*; 215.2 *residue*; 345.5 *show an effect*; 416.4 *solid body*; 32.25 *solidify*; 212.3 *subtract*; 332.1 *swift*; 371.13 *throw away*; 288.11 *too early*
precipitated 215.9 *remaining*; 32.32 *solid*
precipitately 262.6 *hastily*; 293.20 *prematurely*; 380.10 *violently*
precipitateness 262.5 *hastiness*; 615.1 *rashness*
precipitation **31.24**; 416.2 *concentration*; 357.1 *destruction*; 367.12 *downthrow*; 371.20 *eviction*; 32.3 *phase*; 32.5 *process*; 332.8 *speed*; 212.1 *subtraction*; 330.3 *throwing*; 30.10 *water cycle*
precipitative 293.16 *premature*
precipitous 472.10 *careless*; 367.20 *falling*; 293.16 *premature*; 332.1 *swift*; 186.8 *vertical*
precipitously 293.20 *prematurely*
precipitousness 186.1 *verticality*
precis 269.4 *be concise*; 214.1 *decrease*; 214.5 *make smaller*; 163.1, 163.5, 269.2 *outline*; 149.3 *shortened version*; 723.8 *summarize*; 723.1 *summary*
precise 273.5, 591.4, 698.21 *accurate*; 665.9 *careful*; 801.8 *correct*; 222.10 *detailed*; 656.6 *formal*; 695.1 *intelligible*; 230.1 *perfect*; 230.2 *perfectionist*; 139.15 *special*
precisely 273.8, 698.39 *accurately*; 665.12 *carefully*; 801.20 *correctly*; 324.9 *directly*; 656.12 *formally*; 222.19 *meticulously*; 230.7 *perfectly*; 139.28 *specially*
precise measurement 273.3 *accurate thing*
preciseness 273.1, 698.8 *accuracy*; 801.2 *correctness*; 656.2 *formalism*; 656.1 *formality*; 695.9 *intelligibility*; 230.3 *perfection*; 265.2 *simplicity*
precisian 117.6 *conformist*; 7.4 *religionist*
precision 273.1, 591.10, 698.8 *accuracy*; 665.1 *carefulness*; 801.2 *correctness*; 695.9 *intelligibility*; 27.8 *number system*; 28.83 *sensitivity*; 265.2 *simplicity*
precision bombing 381.13 *air attack*
precision instrument 273.3 *accurate thing*
precisionism 656.2 *formalism*
precisionist 19.29 *realist*
precision tool 438.1 *tool*
precis writer 723.5 *summarizer*
pre-classical 3.15 *historic*
preclude 128.7 *exclude*; 378.8 *hinder*
precluded 128.11 *excluded*
preclusion 128.1 *exclusion*; 378.1 *hindrance*
preclusive 128.10 *excluding*; 378.13 *hindering*
preclusively 378.16 *with delay*
precocial 72.22 *newly hatched*
precocious 660.15 *audacious*; 293.16 *premature*
precociously 660.32 *audaciously*; 660.30 *insolently*; 293.20 *prematurely*
precociousness 293.5 *prematurity*
precocity 293.5 *prematurity*
precognition **445.2**; 11.9 *divination*; 101.4 *parapsychology*; 11.8 *psychic power*
precognitive **445.7**; 11.17 *divinatory*; 101.9 *parapsychological*
preconceive 465.11 *be unjust*; 106.2 *premeditate*
preconceived 465.8 *unjust*
preconceived idea 465.4 *prejudgment*
preconceived opinion 106.6 *premeditation*
preconception 465.4 *prejudgment*
preconcert 106.2 *premeditate*
precondemn 466.13 *prejudge*
precondition 135.1 *requirement*
preconscious 36.21 *psyche*
preconsultation 243.9 *preparation*
precooked 280.7 *prepared for immediate use*; 243.21 *ready-made*
precursive 293.15 *precursory*
precursor **129.8**; 579.13 *director*; 293.4 *early comer*; 475.5 *omen*; 564.7 *settler*
precursors 582.13 *the dead*
precursory **129.13**; **293.15**; 130.36 *introductory*; 475.13 *predicting*
predacious 70.15 *of animals*; 774.17 *stolen*
predate 129.15, 293.8 *precede*
predator 382.13 *animal killer*; 651.8 *malefactor*; 773.6 *taker*; 70.4 *type of animal*
predatorily 773.13 *avariciously*; 774.19 *thievishly*
predatory 72.21 *avian*; 774.17 *stolen*; 773.12 *taking*
predecease 582.15 *die*
predecessor **129.9**; 293.4 *early comer*
pre-decimal coinage 780.10 *former British money*
predeliberation 106.6 *premeditation*
predestinate 106.1 *predetermine*
predestination 452.16 *inevitability*; 4.9 *philosophical problem*; 106.5 *predetermination*
predestine 694.12 *intend*; 482.9 *intend for*; 106.1 *predetermine*
predestined 452.5 *inevitable*; 694.9 *meant*; 106.3 *predetermined*
Predetermination 106
predetermination **106.5**; 452.16 *inevitability*; 482.2 *intentionality*; 465.4 *prejudgment*; 243.9 *preparation*
predetermine **106.1**; 243.2 *do the groundwork*; 483.10 *manipulate*; 484.12 *plan ahead*; 482.8 *resolve*
predetermined **106.3**; 452.5 *inevitable*; 482.12 *intended*
predicament **221.2**; **264.5**; 249.1 *adversity*; 453.12 *confusion*; 254.5 *danger*; 143.3, 222.4 *difficult circumstances*; 611.2 *hopeless situation*; 135.3 *needfulness*
predicate 707.17 *affirm*; 5.44 *grammatical*; 5.35 *part of speech*; 476.5 *suppose*
predicate calculus 27.63 *mathematical logic*
predication 707.2 *statement*
predicational 707.10 *affirmative*
predicative 707.10 *affirmative*
predict **474.9**; **475.11**; 11.23 *divine*; 31.57, 129.19 *forecast*; 283.9 *look ahead*; 484.12 *plan ahead*; 104.10 *think likely*; 711.5 *warn*
predictability 452.17 *infallibility*; 104.1 *probability*
predictable **283.12**; 11.17 *divinatory*; 474.7 *expected*; 756.15 *future*; 632.9 *habitual*; 452.6 *infallible*; 475.14 *predicted*; 104.6 *probable*; 228.9 *stable*
predictably **283.16**; 474.13 *expectedly*; 756.18 *potentially*; 475.16 *predictively*; 104.11 *probably*; 228.12 *stably*
predicted **475.14**; 11.17 *divinatory*; 474.7 *expected*; 283.13 *foreseen*; 756.15 *future*
predicting **475.13**; 711.8 *warning*
Prediction 475
prediction **475.1**; 11.9 *divination*; 474.2 *expectations*; 283.4 *looking to the future*; 484.2 *policy*; 104.1 *probability*; 711.1 *warning*
predictive 11.17 *divinatory*; 475.13 *predicting*; 104.6 *probable*
predictively **475.16**
predictor **283.5**; 11.13 *diviner*
predigest 695.5 *simplify*
predigested 557.27 *edible*; 243.21 *ready-made*
predilection 229.2 *attitude*; 593.7 *choice*; 617.1 *desire*; 595.2 *inclination*; 465.3 *injustice*; 469.7 *preference*; 495.2 *taste of life*
predispose 465.12 *bias*; 243.2 *do the groundwork*; 395.8 *influence*; 483.10 *manipulate*
predisposed 595.6 *liking*; 465.8 *unjust*
predispose oneself 595.8 *prefer*
predisposition 229.2 *attitude*; 595.2 *inclination*; 465.3 *injustice*
predominance 396.1 *authority*; 216.4 *average*; 395.1 *influence*; 334.1 *power*; 121.1 *superiority*
predominant 396.12 *authoritative*; 216.1 *average*; 121.14 *best*; 395.13 *dominant*; 334.13 *powerful*; 138.19 *prevailing*
predominantly 395.14 *influentially*; 216.11 *on average*; 204.13 *on the whole*; 334.18 *powerfully*; 121.16 *superiorly*; 138.32 *universally*
predominate 395.10 *be a prevailing influence*; 216.9 *be average*; 123.7 *be important*; 334.10 *be powerful*; 121.8 *be superior*; 140.15 *be the rule*; 396.18 *have authority*; 138.28 *prevail*
predominating 138.19 *prevailing*
predomination 121.1 *superiority*
pre-eminence 123.1 *importance*; 129.2 *priority*; 121.1 *superiority*; 235.6 *worth*
pre-eminent 396.12 *authoritative*; 121.14 *best*; 123.5 *important*; 129.12 *primary*
pre-eminently 123.9 *importantly*; 129.23 *primarily*
pre-empt 776.3 *bargain*; 293.7 *be early*; 128.7 *exclude*; 288.5 *mistime*; 69.10 *play*;

293.9 *prepare*; 777.1 *purchase*; 129.16 *take precedence*
pre-empted 128.11 *excluded*
pre-emption 128.1 *exclusion*; 763.2 *legal terms*; 129.1 *precedence*; 293.5 *prematurity*; 777.7 *purchasing*; 288.2 *untimeliness*
pre-emptive 777.14 *buying*; 128.10 *excluding*; 584.8 *military*; 129.10 *preceding*; 293.16 *premature*; 288.11 *too early*
pre-emptive bid 69.3 *card game terms*
pre-emptively 777.17 *acquisitively*; 584.11 *militarily*; 288.18 *out of chronological order*; 129.23 *primarily*
pre-emptive strike 381.12 *military attack*
pre-emptor 777.12 *purchaser*
preen 72.24 *nest*
preen oneself 622.29 *feel pride*; 673.16 *show off*
pre-established 106.4 *deliberate*
prefab 403.6 *construction*
prefabricate 20.18 *be an architect*; 356.10 *produce*
prefabricated 243.21 *ready-made*
prefabrication 403.6 *construction*
preface 129.5; 211.6 *add*; 167.10 *be in front*; 167.1 *front*; 130.10 *introduction*
prefatorial 129.13 *precursory*
prefatory 130.36 *introductory*; 129.13 *precursory*
prefect 579.16 *official*
prefecture 396.5 *position of authority*
prefer 469.2; **595.8**; 617.12 *desire*; 466.12 *discriminate*; 392.28 *further*
preferability 469.7 *preference*
preferable 469.15 *chosen*; 235.1 *worthy*
preferably 469.17 *selectively*
prefer charges 16.70 *litigate*
preference 469.7; 593.7 *choice*; 617.1 *desire*; 595.2 *inclination*; 593.11 *loved one*; 129.2 *priority*; 495.2 *taste of life*; 635.1 *will*
preferential 466.10 *discriminatory*; 469.14 *selecting*; 413.9 *supportive*; 465.8 *unjust*
preferentially 466.17 *prejudicially*; 469.17 *selectively*; 465.14 *unjustly*
preferential treatment 466.5 *favouritism*; 465.3 *injustice*; 413.6 *moral support*
preferment 302.12 *advance*; 392.8 *furtherance*; 7.9 *priesthood*
prefer not to 596.5 *dislike*
preferred 593.21 *beloved*; 469.15 *chosen*; 121.12 *superior*
preferrring 595.6 *liking*
prefer soft drinks 689.3 *be sober*
prefiguration 475.1 *prediction*
prefigure 475.11 *predict*
prefigurement 475.5 *omen*; 475.1 *prediction*
prefiguring 475.13 *predicting*
prefix 129.7; 211.6 *add*; 211.3 *additional item*; 167.10 *be in front*; 167.1 *front*; 5.35 *part of speech*
prefixation 129.7 *prefix*
prefixed 211.8 *additional*; 130.36 *introductory*
prefixion 211.1 *addition*; 129.7 *prefix*
prefrontal leucotomy 36.3 *psychiatric treatment*
preggers 561.16 *reproductive*
preglacial 296.15 *primal*
pregnability 254.7 *vulnerability*
pregnable 335.11 *unprotected*; 254.3 *vulnerable*
pregnancy 554.4 *biological function*; 182.2 *bulge*; 130.4 *conception*; 232.2 *fullness*; 561.3 *propagation*
pregnancy test 35.7 *diagnosis*
pregnant 130.32 *embryonic*; 474.6 *expectant*; 562.5 *fertile*; 123.5 *important*; 561.16 *reproductive*
pregnant moment 287.3 *critical time*
pregnant with doom 475.15 *presageful*
pregnant with meaning 694.6 *meaningful*
pregnant woman 561.7 *obstetrics*
preheated 493.13 *heated*
prehensile 360.9 *retentive*
prehensility 360.1 *retention*
prehension 360.1 *retention*
prehistoric 3.15 *historic*; 284.17 *past*; 296.15 *primal*
prehistoric age 284.4
prehistorical 3.16 *historical*; 284.17 *past*
prehistorically 3.24 *historically*
prehistoric animal 296.8
prehistoric anthropologist 284.11 *antiquarian*
prehistoric anthropology 284.9 *antiquarianism*; 1.2 *palaeoanthropology*
prehistoric archaeologist 284.11 *antiquarian*
prehistoric archaeology 284.9 *antiquarianism*; 3.2 *archaeology*
prehistoric man 296.7 *ancient people*
prehistoric people 284.6 *people of the past*
prehistoric tool 438.4
prehistory 3.10 *past age*; 284.1 *past time*
prejudge 466.13; 465.11 *be unjust*
prejudged 465.8 *unjust*
prejudgment 465.4; 466.3 *prejudice*
prejudice 466.3; **622.11**; 229.2 *attitude*; 465.12 *bias*; 596.1 *dislike*; 274.6 *fallibility*; 519.7 *figurative blindness*; 569.1 *friendship*; 800.1 *improbity*; 595.2 *inclination*; 395.8 *influence*; 120.2, 465.3 *injustice*; 483.10 *manipulate*; 641.7 *opinionatedness*; 469.7 *preference*; 466.13 *prejudge*; 594.3 *race hatred*; 802.1 *unfairness*
prejudiced 622.23; 466.10 *discriminatory*; 800.5 *dishonourable*; 595.6 *liking*; 274.17 *mistaken*; 594.11 *racist*; 229.5 *tending to*; 120.4, 465.8 *unjust*; 802.11 *wrong*
prejudiced against 596.8 *disliking*
prejudices 446.5 *ideology*
prejudicial 466.10 *discriminatory*; 798.7 *evil*; 236.5 *harmful*; 229.5 *tending to*; 465.8 *unjust*
prejudicially 466.17; 798.12 *evilly*; 229.6 *probably*; 120.8 *unjustly*
prejudicial treatment 465.3 *injustice*
prelapsarian 805.5 *innocent*; 805.7 *naive*; 296.15 *primal*
prelapsarian innocence 805.3 *naivety*
prelate 7.8 *priest*
prelatic 7.17 *priestly*
prelature 7.9 *priesthood*
preliminaries 167.1 *front*; 130.10 *introduction*; 129.5 *preface*; 243.10 *preparations*
preliminarily 420.15 *incompletely*; 243.23 *preparatorily*
preliminary 130.36 *introductory*; 129.13 *precursory*; 243.16 *preparatory*; 420.5 *unfinished*
preliminary course 243.10 *preparations*
preliminary race 47.1 *track events*
preliminary sketch 420.10 *rough idea*
preliminary step 243.10 *preparations*
preliminary swing 47.2 *field events*
preliminary warning 475.3 *plan*
prelims 167.1 *front*; 130.10 *introduction*; 129.5 *preface*
prelude 167.10 *be in front*; 130.10 *introduction*; 18.4 *opera*; 129.5 *preface*
preludial 130.36 *introductory*
premarital 570.20 *matrimonial*
premature 293.16
premature baby 293.4 *early comer*
premature baldness 552.5 *baldness*
prematurely 293.20
prematureness 293.5 *prematurity*
prematurity 293.5; 288.2 *untimeliness*
premed 35.9 *surgery*
premedication 37.3 *drug*; 35.9 *surgery*
premeditate 106.2; 482.8 *resolve*
premeditated 106.4 *deliberate*; 482.12 *intended*; 484.14 *planned*
premeditated murder 382.2 *murder*
premeditation 106.6; 482.2 *intentionality*; 243.9 *preparation*
pre-menstrual syndrome 36.12 *stress*
premier 579.13 *director*; 12.7 *governor*; 395.5 *influential person*; 400.3 *leader*; 397.6 *person in command*; 396.10 *person of authority*; 121.5 *superior*
premier danseur 230.4 *perfectionist*
premiere 130.9; 525.1 *appearance*; 295.19 *begin*; 295.4 *beginning*; 21.38 *dramatize*; 295.13 *inaugurated*; 21.13 *theatrical performance*
premiered 130.37 *enrolled*; 295.13 *inaugurated*
première partie 23.9 *decorative woodwork*
premiere performance 21.13 *theatrical performance*
premiership 579.4 *directorship*; 121.2 *leadership*; 396.5 *position of authority*
premise 444.14; 450.1 *belief*; 444.4 *explanation*; 443.16 *have an idea*; 443.6 *idea*; 28.6 *law*; 701.3 *line of argument*; 27.63 *mathematical logic*; 4.1 *philosophy*; 4.22 *propound a philosophy*; 27.64 *reasoning*; 476.5 *suppose*; 476.1 *supposition*; 27.65 *theory*; 176.5 *viewpoint*
premised 476.8 *supposed*
premises 716.1 *evidence*; 352.4 *financial resources*
premium 813.7 *bounty*; 43.2 *Common Agricultural Policy*; 784.4 *interest*; 788.2 *money received*; 785.1 *payment*; 790.2 *value*
premium bond 107.3 *equal chance*; 780.14 *paper money*
Premium Savings Bond 780.14 *paper money*
premolar 425.11 *tooth*
premonition 11.9 *divination*; 283.4 *looking to the future*; 475.1 *prediction*; 129.6 *preview*; 11.10 *psychic phenomenon*; 11.8 *psychic power*; 711.1 *warning*
premonition of disaster 711.1 *warning*
premonitory 11.17 *divinatory*; 475.13 *predicting*; 711.8 *warning*
prenatal clinic 35.10 *hospital*
prenatal diagnosis 35.7 *diagnosis*
preoccupation 386.1 *compulsion*; 36.13 *depression*; 471.4 *diligence*; 482.3 *future intention*
preoccupied 471.8 *diligent*; 463.8 *oblivious*; 4.17 *thoughtful*
preordain 106.1 *predetermine*
preordained 106.3 *predetermined*
preordination 106.5 *predetermination*
pre-owned 349.9 *used*
prep 35.20 *practise surgery*
prepaid 785.19 *receiving pay*
Preparation 243
preparation 129.3; **243.9**; 517.4 *atonality*; 665.3 *circumspection*; 37.3 *drug*; 6.1 *education*; 576.5 *exercise*; 283.4 *looking to the future*; 394.2 *medicine*; 293.5 *prematurity*; 106.6 *premeditation*; 356.1 *production*; 436.1 *provision*; 130.7 *rudiments*
preparations 243.10; 409.11 *arrangements*
preparative 243.16 *preparatory*
preparatively 243.23 *preparatorily*
preparatorily 243.23; 129.22 *in anticipation*; 293.20 *prematurely*
preparatory 129.14; **243.16**; 130.36 *introductory*; 293.16 *premature*
preparatory school 6.12 *educational institution*
preparatory work 243.10 *preparations*
prepare 243.1; **293.9**; 665.10 *be careful*; 6.22 *educate*; 576.9 *exercise*; 352.6 *find means*; 409.18 *make arrangements*; 484.12 *plan ahead*; 436.5 *provision*; 403.14 *structure*; 229.4 *tend*; 711.5 *warn*
prepare a balance sheet 789.7 *account*
prepare a brief 16.70 *litigate*
prepare a budget 789.7 *account*
prepare a case 16.70 *litigate*
prepare a cash-flow forecast 789.7 *account*
prepare a meal 25.55 *cook*
prepare a statement 789.9 *settle accounts*
prepared 243.18; 556.11 *adult*; 665.9 *careful*; 25.56 *culinary*; 384.30 *defended*; 474.5 *expecting*; 484.14 *planned*; 436.8 *provisional*; 136.9 *qualified*; 229.5 *tending to*; 711.9 *warned*; 636.1 *willing*
prepared for immediate use 280.7
preparedly 556.16 *maturely*
preparedness 243.14; 229.2 *attitude*; 556.3 *maturity*; 136.1 *qualification*
prepared speech 733.1 *address*
prepared text 707.2 *statement*
prepare for 243.3 *be prepared*; 283.10 *expect*; 482.7 *intend*
prepare for action 243.4
prepare for blastoff 243.4 *prepare for action*
prepare for burial 583.8 *bury*
prepare for publication 740.15 *publish*
prepare for surgery 35.20 *practise surgery*
prepare for takeoff 243.4 *prepare for action*
prepare for use 349.1 *use*
prepare for war 585.12 *go to war*
prepare oneself 243.8; 439.6 *store*; 354.1 *undertake*
preparer 243.15
prepare the ground 243.2 *do the groundwork*
prepare the way 265.16 *make easy*
prepare to dive 243.4 *prepare for action*
preparing 409.11 *arrangements*; 243.9 *preparation*; 243.16 *preparatory*
prepatella bursitis 260.16 *rheumatism*
prep book 6.14 *school book*
prepense 106.4 *deliberate*
preplanned 106.4 *deliberate*
preponderance 120.1 *inequality*; 207.3 *majority*; 121.1 *superiority*
preponderant 121.14 *best*
preponderantly 121.16 *superiorly*
preponderate 120.5 *be unequal*
preposition 5.35 *part of speech*
prepositional 5.44 *grammatical*
prepositionally 5.52 *grammatically*
prepositional phrase 5.23 *phrase*
prepositive 130.36 *introductory*
preposterous 477.11 *fantastical*; 459.5 *foolish*; 103.1 *impossible*; 697.5 *nonsensical*; 272.5 *ridiculous*; 681.2 *unrestrained*
preposterously 697.9 *nonsensically*; 272.8 *ridiculously*
prepotence 121.1 *superiority*
prepotency 121.1 *superiority*
pre-prandial 25.56 *culinary*
prep school 6.12 *educational institution*
prepublication 475.3 *plan*
prerequisite 386.1 *compulsion*; 386.10 *compulsory*; 136.7 *condition*; 99.5 *essential*; 135.4 *required*; 135.1 *requirement*
prerogative 396.1 *authority*; 250.1 *freedom*; 129.2 *priority*; 801.6 *right*; 121.1 *superiority*
presage 129.19 *forecast*; 694.12 *intend*; 283.9 *look ahead*; 475.5 *omen*; 475.11 *predict*; 475.1 *prediction*
presageful 475.15; 742.14 *signifying*; 711.8 *warning*
presbyopia 519.2 *poor sight*
presbyopic 519.9 *weak-sighted*
presbyteral 7.17 *priestly*
Presbyterian 7.5 *Christian*
presbytery 10.12 *church*; 7.10 *priestly dwelling*
pre-school 555.11 *young*
pre-school education 6.2 *educational system*
pre-school playgroup 6.12 *educational institution*
prescience 283.4 *looking to the future*
prescient 8.13 *divine*; 475.13 *predicting*
prescribe 713.5 *advise*; 397.9 *command*; 394.20 *doctor*; 579.1 *manage*; 35.19 *practise medicine*; 140.13 *rule*; 136.16 *specify*
prescribed 136.12 *conditional*; 57.11 *gymnastic*
prescribed diet 687.1 *fasting*
prescribed exercise 57.1 *gymnastics*
prescribed form 656.5 *etiquette*; 10.1 *ritual*
prescribed punishment 814.8 *penalty*
prescribed remedy 394.1 *remedy*
prescribe medication 393.6 *cure*
prescriber 713.4 *adviser*
prescript 397.1 *command*; 713.3 *precept*
prescription 37.5; 713.1 *advice*; 397.1 *command*; 140.4 *guide*; 763.2 *legal terms*; 394.2 *medicine*; 713.3 *precept*; 394.1 *remedy*; 140.1 *rule*; 136.6 *specification*; 632.5 *tradition*; 35.8 *treatment*
prescription drug 37.3 *drug*
prescriptive 713.7 *advising*; 216.1 *average*; 397.14 *commanding*; 136.12 *conditional*; 140.9 *legal*; 4.13 *of philosophy*
prescriptively 397.16 *commandingly*; 136.18 *with qualification*
prescriptive right 228.4 *stable thing*
preselect 469.4 *pick*
Presence 97
presence 97.1; 312.10 *arrival*; 525.2 *being in view*; 137.9 *distinction*; 93.1 *existence*; 11.11 *ghost*; 97.6 *ghostly presence*; 631.2 *good conduct*; 127.1 *inclusion*; 95.1 *reality*; 397.5 *self-assurance*; 520.3 *visibility*
presenile dementia 461.3 *mental deterioration*
present 97.7; **282.6**; **525.14**; 717.10 *act*; 525.7 *appearing*; 569.15 *be hospitable*; 324.6 *direct*; 738.1 *display*; 21.38 *dramatize*; 93.10 *existing*; 768.2 *gift*; 768.5 *give*; 750.9, 750.30 *grant*; 130.23 *inaugurate*; 601.19 *install*; 752.6 *offering*; 356.10 *produce*; 436.5 *provision*; 717.9 *represent*; 813.9 *reward*; 724.9 *style*; 5.34 *tense*; 447.6 *topical*; 520.1 *visible*; 752.11 *volunteer*
present a bold front 661.5 *defy*
present a brave face 661.5 *defy*
present a false air 699.28 *mask*
present age 285.2 *present time*

present an account 789.9 *settle accounts*
present and correct 282.8 *available*
present a puzzle 696.7 *be unintelligible*
present arms 658.12 *greet;* 667.20 *salute*
presentation 733.1 *address;* 525.1 *appearance;* 658.3 *courtesies;* 703.1 *demonstration;* 738.6 *display;* 768.2 *gift;* 768.1 *giving;* 137.7 *lecture;* 654.5 *party;* 130.9 *premiere;* 738.9 *production;* 717.1 *representation;* 752.2 *tentative offer*
present day 285.2 *present time*
present difficulties 264.17 *be difficult*
presented 738.13 *displayed;* 130.37 *enrolled;* 750.19 *granted*
presenter 21.24 *actor;* 692.29 *broadcaster;* 703.7 *demonstrator;* 738.12 *displayer;* 21.29 *entertainer;* 768.4 *giver;* 729.10 *speaker;* 578.1 *worker*
presentient 445.7 *precognitive;* 475.13 *predicting*
presentiment 590.2 *impression;* 445.2 *precognition;* 475.1 *prediction*
presenting arms 667.5
present itself 525.12 *become visible*
presently 282.9 *at present;* 93.23 *now;* 293.18 *soon*
presentment 703.1 *demonstration;* 768.1 *giving;* 750.9 *grant;* 717.1 *representation;* 21.13 *theatrical performance*
present moment 285.2 *present time*
present no difficulties 265.15 *be easy*
present oneself 97.12 *attend*
present participle 5.35 *part of speech*
present problems 264.17 *be difficult*
present tense 282.3 *actuality*
present the facts 698.30 *prove true*
present the main points 163.5 *outline*
present throughout 97.7 *present*
Present Time 282
present time 282.1; 285.2
present with an ultimatum 397.10 *demand*
Preservation 359
preservation 359.1; 134.1 *continuity;* 384.1 *defence;* 360.2 *detention;* 225.1 *permanence;* 372.2 *setting apart;* 439.4 *storage*
preservationism 538.16 *green politics*
preservationist 359.4
preservation order 359.2 *preserver*
preservative 557.11 *food content;* 359.2 *preserver;* 359.6 *preserving*
preservatively 359.8
preserve 25.42; 359.5; 134.3 *continue;* 360.7 *detain;* 428.21 *dry up;* 279.6 *eternalize;* 257.6 *make hygienic;* 225.6 *make permanent;* 252.10 *protect;* 372.10 *set apart;* 439.6 *store;* 498.2 *sweetener*
preserved 359.7; 225.7 *permanent;* 360.10 *retained;* 252.6 *safe;* 439.7 *stored;* 350.1 *unused*
preserved fish 74.8 *food fish*
preserved thing 359.3
preserve for posterity 744.13 *record*
preserve one's dignity 622.31 *save face*
preserve one's honour 799.6 *be honourable;* 622.31 *save face*
preserve one's reputation 622.31 *save face*
preserver 359.2; 252.3 *protector;* 252.4 *safety device*
preserves 359.3 *preserved thing*
preserving 359.6; 384.1 *defence;* 252.8 *tutelary*
preserving pan 25.6 *kitchen equipment*
preset 106.4 *deliberate;* 106.2 *premeditate*
preset tuning 692.18 *radio;* 692.22 *television set*
preshrink 191.5 *make smaller;* 42.15 *treat*
preshrinkage 191.1 *contraction*
preshrinking 191.1 *contraction;* 42.8 *fabric treatment*
preshrunk 191.7 *smaller;* 42.11 *treated*
preside 654.11 *be sociable;* 579.2 *direct;* 16.76 *judge;* 685.4 *moderate*
presidency 12.3 *governance;* 121.2 *leadership;* 396.5 *position of authority*
president 579.13 *director;* 12.7 *governor;* 395.5 *influential person;* 400.3 *leader;* 397.6 *person in command;* 396.10 *person of authority;* 121.5 *superior*
president-elect 469.13 *electorate*
presidential 12.9, 396.14 *governmental;* 579.17 *managerial;* 565.16 *manorial*
presidentially 396.24 *ministerially;* 12.14 *politically*
presidential palace 565.4 *official residence*
preside over 140.16 *direct;* 396.18 *have authority*
presidium 579.7 *council*
pre-Socratic philosophy 4.7 *school of thought*
press 492.3; 713.5 *advise;* 367.5 *bear down on;* 331.13 *blow;* 342.6 *business;* 23.5 *cabinet;* 386.6 *compel;* 191.4 *contractor;* 115.3 *copier;* 208.11 *crowd;* 369.9 *extractor;* 187.4 *flattener;* 262.1 *hasten;* 331.1 *impel;* 638.10 *insist;* 183.9 *make concave;* 117.9 *make conform;* 187.7 *make horizontal;* 191.5 *make smaller;* 153.16 *make thin;* 483.10 *manipulate;* 741.5 *mass communication;* 369.17 *obtain an extract;* 49.6 *play basketball;* 376.21 *scrum;* 404.13, 421.11 *smooth;* 421.9 *smoother;* 208.4 *throng;* 814.4 *torture;* 492.11 *touch*
press a claim 710.7 *demand*
press agency 741.7
press agent 738.12 *displayer;* 693.9 *informant;* 741.4 *journalist;* 483.7 *motivator;* 719.7 *news interpreter;* 21.27 *producer;* 740.10 *publicizer;* 748.4 *representative*
press announcement 740.8 *public relations;* 707.2 *statement*
Press Association 741.7 *press agency;* 693.8 *source of information*
press baron 740.11 *newspaperman*
press box 46.4 *stadium*
press charges 16.70 *litigate*
press conference 738.10 *manifestation;* 693.4 *mass communication;* 741.2 *news event;* 740.8 *public relations*
press cutting 744.1 *record*
press drill 38.9 *machine tool*
pressed 208.10 *crowded;* 187.9 *flattened;* 782.2 *insolvent;* 191.7 *smaller;* 153.5 *thinned*
pressed duck 25.45 *French dish*
pressed flower 78.1 *flower*
pressed for time 262.3 *hasty*
pressed man 586.27 *naval man;* 586.8 *soldier*
press forward 302.3 *press on*
pressgang 386.3 *coercive methods;* 386.7 *force*
press home 726.6 *emphasize*
press in 314.12 *flood in;* 368.3 *impact*
pressing 331.13 *blow;* 386.9 *compelling;* 191.1 *contraction;* 135.6 *demanding;* 369.7 *obtaining an extract;* 414.3 *ponderous;* 336.10 *potent;* 744.7 *recording;* 638.2 *tenacious*
pressing defence 49.4 *playing terms*
pressing one's suit 593.6 *courtship*
press into service 349.4 *resort to*
press inwards 183.9 *make concave*
press laws 251.1 *restraint*
press notice 741.9 *news story*
press of business 342.6 *business*
press office 741.8 *newsroom;* 740.8 *public relations;* 693.8 *source of information*
press officer 741.4 *journalist;* 719.7 *news interpreter;* 21.27 *producer*
press of sail 332.8 *speed*
press on 302.3; 367.5 *bear down on;* 633.13 *follow up;* 331.1 *impel*
press one's suit 593.26 *court*
pressor 37.4 *drug type*
press photographer 740.11 *newspaperman;* 744.9 *recorder*
press release 693.4 *mass communication;* 741.9 *news story;* 740.8 *public relations*
press room 741.8 *newsroom*
press secretary 741.4 *journalist*
press service 693.8 *source of information*
press stud 373.8 *fastening*
press the button 346.8 *activate;* 585.13 *be at war*
press the emergency button 711.7 *raise the alarm*
press to one's bosom 593.27 *kiss*
press upon 414.13 *weigh on*
pressure 340.1 *action;* 249.1 *adversity;* 396.1 *authority;* 348.4 *be an instrument;* 331.13 *blow;* 386.2 *coercion;* 386.6 *compel;* 191.4 *contraction;* 334.4 *energy;* 576.4 *exertion;* 28.10 *force;* 432.7 *gaseousness;* 262.4 *haste;* 396.18 *have authority;* 483.2 *inducement;* 395.1 *influence;* 348.1 *instrumentality;* 336.3 *intensity;* 480.15 *persuade;* 480.1 *persuasion;* 710.1, 710.6 *request;* 251.8 *restrain;* 251.1 *restraint;* 638.14 *tenacity;* 28.38 *thermodynamics;* 414.8 *weighing down*
pressure-cook 25.55 *cook*
pressure cooker 25.6 *kitchen equipment*
pressure cooking 25.1 *cookery*
pressured 483.12 *motivated;* 480.20 *persuadable*
pressure gauge 28.88 *barometer;* 26.8 *meter;* 432.15 *vapormeter*
pressure gradient 31.6 *weather data*
pressure group 374.3 *assembly;* 395.6 *group influence;* 480.14, 483.7 *motivator*
pressure of deadlines 342.6 *business*
pressure of work 342.6 *business*
pressure system 31.11 *weather system*
pressure tendency 31.6 *weather data*
pressure turn 68.4 *skiing technique*
pressuring 348.7 *causal*
pressurize 395.8 *influence*
pressurized 414.3 *ponderous;* 251.13 *restraining*
pressurized-water reactor 334.8, 437.7 *nuclear power;* 28.73 *nuclear reactor*
Prestel™ 692.25 *broadcast material*
prestidigitation 700.9 *sleight of hand*
prestidigitator 21.29 *entertainer*
prestige 622.4; 669.2 *admiration;* 137.9 *distinction;* 811.1 *estimation;* 123.1 *importance;* 395.3 *personal influence;* 185.1 *prominence;* 248.1 *prosperity;* 783.7 *repute;* 667.1 *respect;* 2.7 *social stratification;* 121.1 *superiority*
prestigious 622.18; 121.15 *excellent;* 395.11 *influential;* 123.6 *notable;* 667.12 *respected*
prestigiously 811.7 *eminently;* 395.14 *influentially;* 121.16 *superiorly*
prestissimo 332.14 *swiftly*
presto 262.3 *hasty;* 332.14 *swiftly*
prestressed 38.32 *structural*
prestressed concrete 20.4, 435.2 *building material;* 38.25 *construction material*
presumable 104.6 *probable;* 476.8 *supposed*
presumably 104.11 *probably*
presume 450.8 *be of the opinion;* 660.23 *be proud;* 660.22 *be rude;* 660.27 *dare;* 661.5 *defy;* 660.28 *get above oneself;* 610.6 *hope;* 250.19 *liberalize;* 474.9 *predict;* 4.22 *propound a philosophy;* 476.5 *suppose;* 446.17 *theorize;* 104.10 *think likely*
presumed 222.7 *circumstantial;* 104.6 *probable;* 476.8 *supposed;* 446.10 *theoretical*
presume on 349.4 *resort to*
presumingly 4.25 *theoretically*
presumption 660.5 *bravado;* 661.1 *defiance;* 474.1, 610.2 *expectation;* 446.1 *idea;* 104.1 *probability;* 615.1 *rashness;* 476.1 *supposition*
presumptiousness 660.3 *audacity*
presumptive 104.6 *probable;* 476.7 *suppositional*
presumptively 4.25 *theoretically*
presumptuous 660.16 *arrogant;* 661.7 *defiant*
presumptuously 660.33 *arrogantly;* 661.9 *defiantly*
presuppose 476.5 *suppose;* 27.89 *theorize*
presupposition 4.1 *philosophy;* 465.4 *prejudgment;* 476.1 *supposition;* 27.65 *theory*
presurmise 476.5 *suppose*
pre-tax profit 813.5 *turnover*
preteens 555.1 *youth*
pretence 699.7; 676.1 *affectedness;* 340.2 *deed;* 700.3, 702.5 *hypocrisy;* 525.4 *something that appears;* 476.1 *supposition*
pretend 699.24; 340.4 *act;* 96.12 *artificial;* 676.4 *be affected;* 700.26 *be a hypocrite;* 702.12 *deceive;* 477.12 *imaginary;* 477.14 *imagine;* 476.5 *suppose*
pretended 96.12 *artificial;* 702.10 *hypocritical;* 476.8 *supposed*
pretender 676.2; 699.19 *cheat;* 700.15 *deceiver;* 699.17 *false person*
pretending 699.34; 700.37 *hypocritical;* 699.7 *pretence;* 476.1 *supposition*
pretend it never happened 749.5 *make peace*
pretend not to see 341.4 *not act*
pretend to be 717.9 *represent*
pretension 542.2 *affectation;* 676.1 *affectedness;* 622.3 *conceit;* 699.7 *pretence;* 486.8 *unskilfulness*
pretentious 676.3 *affected;* 673.13 *boastful;* 673.11 *cocky;* 270.3 *diffuse;* 329.13 *exaggerated;* 542.10 *ornate;* 699.34 *pretending;* 486.2 *unskilled;* 5.42 *worded*
pretentiously 676.5 *affectedly;* 673.21 *cockily;* 5.50 *lexically;* 542.13 *ornately*
pretentiousness 542.2 *affectation;* 676.1 *affectedness*
preternatural 11.14 *occult*
preternaturalism 11.1 *occultism*
pretext 444.4 *explanation;* 701.3 *line of argument;* 483.1 *motive;* 699.7 *pretence;* 344.5 *reason;* 645.2 *stratagem*
Pretoria 87.6 *other cities*
prettify 545.8 *beautify;* 525.14 *present*
prettily 547.15 *beautify*
prettiness 545.1 *gorgeousness*
pretty 545.3 *attractive female;* 545.5 *beautiful;* 685.9 *moderately;* 209.11 *to a degree*
pretty boy 567.9 *offensive terms for homosexual*
pretty good 259.1 *healthy;* 235.5 *not bad*
pretty much the same 115.7 *similar*
pretty names 593.14 *communication of love*
pretty pass 222.4 *difficult circumstances;* 264.5 *predicament*
pretty penny 792.1 *high price*
pretty pickle 264.5 *predicament*
pretty printing 40.7 *peripheral*
pretzels 25.10 *snack*
prevail 138.28; 395.10 *be a prevailing influence;* 216.9 *be average;* 632.17 *become a habit;* 297.7 *be frequent;* 334.10 *be powerful;* 121.8 *be superior;* 140.15 *be the rule;* 246.9 *be victorious;* 93.19 *continue to be;* 246.7 *overcome obstacles*
prevailing 138.19; 216.1 *average;* 121.14 *best;* 395.13 *dominant;* 334.13 *powerful;* 31.47 *windy*
prevailingly 216.11 *on average;* 334.18 *powerfully*
prevailing wind 31.15 *wind direction*
prevail over 387.7 *defeat*
prevail upon 483.10 *manipulate;* 483.9 *motivate;* 480.15 *persuade;* 701.16 *plead*
prevalence 216.4 *average;* 297.4 *frequency;* 395.1 *influence;* 334.1 *power*
prevalent 216.1 *average;* 395.13 *dominant;* 93.10 *existing;* 632.10 *familiar;* 297.3 *frequent;* 334.13 *powerful;* 138.19 *prevailing*
prevalently 297.1 *frequently;* 334.18 *powerfully*
prevaricate 800.8 *be dishonourable;* 479.1 *be equivocal;* 634.7 *be evasive;* 189.7 *deviate;* 736.13 *equivocate;* 453.19 *hesitate;* 702.13 *quibble*
prevaricating 699.33 *deceitful;* 479.10 *equivocal;* 702.9 *quibbling*
prevarication 189.3 *deviousness;* 479.5 *equivocalness;* 736.5 *evasion;* 634.15 *evasiveness;* 702.4 *quibbling*
prevaricator 699.18, 700.16 *liar;* 702.6 *sophist*
prevenience 293.5 *prematurity*
prevenient 293.16 *premature*
preveniently 293.20 *prematurely*
prevent 634.2 *avert;* 113.21, 347.3 *counteract;* 481.3 *deflect;* 294.8 *delay;* 128.7 *exclude;* 378.8 *hinder;* 293.9 *prepare;* 251.8 *restrain;* 399.3 *veto*
preventable 634.20 *avoidable*
preventably 634.22 *evasively*
preventative 347.4 *counteracting;* 347.1 *counteraction;* 359.6 *preserving;* 394.3 *prophylactic;* 394.17 *remedial;* 399.5 *vetoed*
prevent defence 46.10 *defence*
prevent disease 257.5 *by hygienic*
prevented 128.11 *excluded*
prevent from falling 366.1 *raise*
prevention 634.10 *avoidance;* 347.1 *counteraction;* 294.3 *delayed action;* 128.1 *exclusion;* 378.1 *hindrance;* 251.1 *restraint;* 113.6 *uncooperativeness;* 399.1 *veto*
preventive 634.18 *avoiding;* 347.4 *counteracting;* 347.1 *counteraction;* 128.10 *excluding;* 378.13 *hindering;* 359.6 *preserving;* 394.3 *prophylactic;* 394.17 *remedial;* 251.13 *restraining;* 35.25 *therapeutic;* 399.5 *vetoed*
preventive action 484.2 *policy*
preventively 399.7 *by veto;* 347.5 *counter;* 634.22 *evasively;* 359.8 *preservatively;* 251.16 *under restraints;* 378.16 *with delay*
preventive measure 252.2 *protection*
preventive medicine 35.6 *health care;* 257.1 *hygiene;* 394.11 *medical art;* 35.1 *medicine;* 359.1 *preservation*
preview 129.6; 525.1 *appearance;* 21.38 *dramatize;* 205.2 *particular;* 475.3 *plan;*

738.9 *production;* 21.13 *theatrical performance*
previous 294.14 *dead;* 296.13 *former;* 129.11 *prior;* 288.11 *too early*
previously 286.3 *another time;* 129.20 *before;* 296.20 *formerly*
previously owned 349.9 *used*
prevision 518.4 *visualization*
prewar 296.12 *olden;* 589.7 *peaceful*
prey 60.5 *game;* 766.6 *loser;* 465.6 *misjudged person;* 482.6 *objective;* 249.5 *person in adversity;* 633.7 *the hunted;* 70.4 *type of animal;* 466.8 *victim of discrimination*
prey on 557.22 *eat well*
prey upon 236.14 *ill-treat;* 774.14 *plunder*
prial 69.3 *card game terms*
priapic 796.14 *lecherous*
priapism 796.3 *sexual immorality*
Price 790
price 790.1; **790.11**; 787.5 *expense;* 59.7 *horseracing;* 235.6 *worth*
price charged 790.1 *price*
price control 251.2 *economic restraint;* 790.1 *price*
price controls 13.2 *economy*
price cut 793.1 *cheapness;* 790.1 *price;* 212.2 *subtracted item*
price cutting 212.1 *subtraction*
priced 790.14
price fall 793.2 *declining prices*
price-fixing 251.2 *economic restraint;* 790.3 *fee*
price freeze 251.2 *economic restraint;* 166.2 *limiting factor*
price increase 765.2 *augmentation*
price index 13.3 *economic statistics*
priceless 237.4 *profitable;* 272.5 *ridiculous;* 235.3, 792.8 *valuable*
pricelessly 792.13 *valuably*
pricelessness 792.6 *value;* 235.6 *worth*
price list 220.4 *bill;* 790.1 *price*
price on one's head 16.43 *conviction*
price range 790.1 *price*
price reduction 791.1 *discount*
prices 13.3 *economic statistics*
price support 13.6 *economic factors;* 768.2 *gift*
price-wage spiral 13.6 *economic factors*
price war 790.1 *price*
pricey 681.3 *costly;* 792.7 *dear*
pricing 13.6 *economic factors*
prick 425.14 *be sharp;* 308.20 *hole;* 491.11 *inflict pain;* 567.2 *male;* 483.9 *motivate;* 561.8 *organs of reproduction;* 491.1 *pain;* 425.8 *sharp-pointed thing;* 488.3 *stimulus*
prick a punt 50.19 *punt*
pricked 308.14 *holed*
pricked by conscience 808.6 *penitent*
pricked up 186.9 *unbowed*
pricking 308.1 *opening;* 425.2 *spiked*
pricking of conscience 808.1 *penitence*
prickle 420.11 *be rough;* 425.14 *be sharp;* 420.7 *rough thing;* 488.11 *sense;* 425.8 *sharp-pointed thing;* 488.3 *stimulus*
prickliness 488.2 *ability to sense;* 751.1 *disagreement;* 625.1 *irascibility;* 365.9 *irritation;* 425.6 *sharpness*
prickly 420.3 *barbed;* 751.9 *disagreeing;* 488.9 *exciting;* 625.4 *irascible;* 425.2 *spiked;* 622.15 *unapproachable*
prickly heat 260.13 *skin disease*
prick out 44.15 *cultivate*
prick up 186.6 *make vertical*
prick up one's ears 644.7 *be curious;* 504.15 *hear;* 471.11 *take note of*
pricky 425.2 *spiked*
Pride 622
pride 622.1; 660.4 *arrogance;* 71.21 *assemblage of mammals;* 673.6 *boastfulness;* 656.1 *formality;* 797.17 *good thing;* 804.5 *seven deadly sins;* 738.7 *showpiece*
pride and joy 797.17 *good thing;* 622.12 *object of pride*
prideful 673.13 *boastful;* 622.14 *proud*
pridefully 622.32 *proudly*
pridefulness 622.1 *pride*
pride of place 622.12 *object of pride;* 129.2 *priority;* 121.1 *superiority*
prier 644.4 *meddler;* 518.11 *observer*
priest 7.8; 713.4 *adviser;* 572.4 *celibate person;* 760.5 *converter;* 583.3 *funeral director;* 797.15 *good person;* 395.5 *influential person;* 400.6 *religious leader;* 803.4 *virtuous person*
priestcraft 9.2 *idolatry*
priestess 7.8 *priest*
priest hole 252.5 *refuge*
priesthood 7.9
priestly 7.17; 572.8 *monastic*
priestly dwelling 7.10
priestly government 12.1 *government*
priest-ridden 7.15 *religious*
priest's cap 7.11 *vestment*
priestship 7.9 *priesthood*
prig 795.6 *moralist;* 255.6 *prude*
priggish 795.10 *moralistic;* 255.12 *morally pure*
priggishly 255.18 *virtuously*
priggishness 255.1 *purity;* 795.4 *self-righteousness*
prill 43.13 *fertilizer*
prim 117.14 *conformist;* 656.6 *formal;* 795.10 *moralistic;* 255.12 *morally pure*
prima ballerina 22.13 *ballet dancer;* 21.30 *dancer;* 230.4 *perfectionist;* 485.4 *skilled person*
primacy 123.1 *importance;* 7.9 *priesthood;* 129.2 *priority;* 185.1 *prominence;* 121.1 *superiority*
prima donna 21.24 *actor;* 123.4 *bigwig;* 18.24 *musician;* 121.6 *paragon;* 622.13 *proud person;* 485.4 *skilled person*
prima facie 716.8 *evidential;* 100.18 *extraneously;* 454.9 *verificatory;* 518.24 *visually*
prima-facie evidence 716.5 *legal evidence*
primal 296.15; 344.13 *causal;* 3.15 *historic;* 284.17 *past;* 130.31 *prime*
primal therapy 36.3 *psychiatric treatment;* 394.13 *therapy*
primarily 129.23; 296.21 *archaically;* 344.14 *causally;* 130.40 *first;* 123.9 *importantly;* 99.13 *in essence;* 130.42 *principally;* 121.16 *superiorly*
primary 129.12; 130.29 *beginning;* 121.14 *best;* 344.13 *causal;* 469.12 *election;* 185.6 *eminent;* 173.8 *focal;* 123.5 *important;* 99.6 *intrinsic;* 197.11 *one;* 72.17 *plumage;* 698.17 *truistic*
primary cell 28.43 *electrical conduction;* 39.5 *electrolytic conduction;* 39.29 *power source*
primary character 30.33 *metamorphic rock*
primary chord 18.16 *musical note*
primary clay 24.2 *raw material*
primary coil 39.22 *transformer*
primary colour 529.1 *colour*
primary colours 28.28 *colour*
primary consumer 34.18 *ecology*
primary education 6.2 *educational system*
primary election 469.12 *election*
primary evidence 716.5 *legal evidence*
primary group 2.6 *social group*
primary growth 260.12 *cancer*
primary health care 35.1 *medicine*
primary memory 40.6 *memory*
primary mirror 29.25 *mounting*
primary premise 698.4 *truism*
primary producer 34.18 *ecology*
primary quality 4.9 *philosophical problem*
primary radar 692.28 *radar*
primary rainbow 31.27 *rainbow*
primary school 6.12 *educational institution*
primary source 173.5 *focus*
primary structure 33.9 *protein*
primary triads 529.1 *colour*
primary wave 30.23 *seismic wave*
primate 71.16; **71.34**; 396.10 *person of authority;* 7.8 *priest*
Primates 71.16 *primate*
primatial 71.34 *primate*
primatologist 71.22 *mammologist*
primatology 71.16 *primate*
prime 130.31; 121.14 *best;* 455.14 *cause to know;* 27.74 *divisible;* 6.22 *educate;* 235.7 *elite;* 123.5 *important;* 330.32 *load;* 290.1 *morning;* 194.8 *odd;* 243.4 *prepare for action;* 10.4 *public worship;* 248.3 *time of plenty;* 235.1 *worthy*
prime a witness 106.2 *premeditate*
prime beef 567.4 *boyfriend*
prime condition 243.14 *preparedness*
prime cut 235.7 *elite*
primed 106.4 *deliberate;* 6.19, 455.8 *knowledgeable;* 243.18 *prepared*
primed witness 106.6 *premeditation*
prime factor 27.17 *multiplication*
prime lending rate 780.7 *finance*
prime matter 402.4 *matter*
prime meridian 86.2 *geographical region*
prime minister 579.13 *director;* 12.7 *governor;* 395.5 *influential person;* 400.3 *leader;* 397.6 *person in command;* 396.10 *person of authority;* 121.5 *superior*
prime ministership 121.2 *leadership*
Prime Mover 344.7; 8.3 *God*
prime mover 38.11 *engine;* 480.14, 483.7 *motivator;* 130.16 *originator;* 356.9 *producer*
prime number 194.2 *kind of number;* 27.5 *number*
prime of life 556.2 *adulthood*
primer 529.5 *paint;* 6.14 *school book*
prime rate 784.3 *loan*
prime-time programme 692.25 *broadcast material*
primeval 293.14; 284.17 *past;* 296.15 *primal;* 130.31 *prime*
primeval forest 79.4 *trees*
primeval humanity 566.3 *early human*
primevally 293.19; 296.21 *archaically*
primeval man 566.3 *early human*
primeval stage 293.3 *early stage*
primicarb 44.8 *weedkiller*
primigravida 561.7 *obstetrics*
priming 587.15 *explosive;* 243.9 *preparation*
primitive 344.13 *causal;* 293.4 *early comer;* 646.1 *naive;* 574.4 *ordinary;* 284.17 *past;* 296.15 *primal;* 130.31 *prime;* 293.14 *primeval;* 19.29 *realist;* 721.13 *representing*
primitive human 566.3 *early human*
primitive humanity 566.3 *early human*
primitively 296.21 *archaically;* 344.14 *causally;* 19.30 *pictorially;* 293.19 *primevally*
primitive man 296.7 *ancient people*
primitiveness 296.3 *antiquity;* 293.3 *early stage;* 646.2 *naivety*
primitive self 36.21 *psyche*
primitive society 566.9 *group*
primitive stage 293.3 *early stage*
primly 656.12 *formally;* 255.18 *virtuously*
primness 117.4 *conventionalism;* 656.1 *formality;* 255.1 *purity;* 795.4 *self-righteousness*
primogenitary 769.14 *receivable*
primogeniture 769.1 *receiving*
primordial 344.13 *causal;* 34.26 *developmental;* 3.15 *historic;* 296.15 *primal;* 130.31 *prime*
primordial fireball 29.4 *cosmological model*
primordially 296.21 *archaically;* 344.14 *causally;* 3.24 *historically*
primordial soup 130.3 *source*
primordium 34.15 *developmental biology*
primp 545.8, 547.15 *beautify;* 551.33 *dress up;* 244.1 *improve*
primrose 537.8 *yellow thing*
primrose path 245.7 *deterioration;* 78.9 *figurative usage;* 317.2 *route*
primrose-yellow 537.1 *yellow*
primum mobile 8.3 *God;* 344.7 *Prime Mover*
primus inter pares 121.5 *superior*
prince 400.2 *sovereign*
Prince Albert 551.12 *coat*
princeliness 622.6 *majesty*
princely 573.4 *aristocratic;* 679.1 *generous;* 12.10 *governing;* 396.14 *governmental;* 622.19 *stately;* 575.6 *worshipful*
Prince of Darkness 8.7 *devil*
Prince of Peace 8.4 *God the Son*
Prince of Wales 400.2 *sovereign*
Prince of Wales chequer 541.2 *check*
Prince Philip Cup 50.5 *Henley trophies*
prince regent 400.2 *sovereign*
princess 400.2 *sovereign*
Princess Elizabeth Cup 50.5 *Henley trophies*
princess-line 551.31 *styled*
principal 121.14, 235.2 *best;* 579.13 *director;* 400.9 *educational leader;* 6.4 *educator;* 173.8 *focal;* 173.5 *focus;* 400.12 *masterful;* 396.10 *person of authority;* 121.5 *superior*
principal boy 21.23 *role*
principal character 21.23 *role*
principal girl 21.23 *role*
principalities and powers 400.8 *the power structure*
principality 8.6 *angel;* 85.3 *dominion;* 396.8 *governmental organization;* 12.5 *political organization;* 86.4 *territorial division*
principally 130.42; 121.16 *superiorly*
principal nursing officer 35.16 *nurse*
principal part 205.5 *largest part*
principate 85.3 *dominion*
principle 450.1 *belief;* 99.2 *essential content;* 140.4 *guide;* 443.6 *idea;* 28.6 *law;* 402.4 *matter;* 745.1 *maxim;* 4.1 *philosophy;* 713.3 *precept;* 450.2 *religious belief;* 344.3 *rudiment;* 27.65 *theory;* 698.4 *truism;* 344.6 *undertaking*
principle component analysis 27.55 *statistical methods*
principled 810.8 *dutiful;* 803.6 *ethical;* 799.4 *honourable;* 795.8 *moral;* 698.17 *truistic*
principles 446.5 *ideology;* 795.1 *morality;* 4.2 *philosophical system;* 799.1 *probity;* 130.7 *rudiments;* 803.2 *virtues;* 631.6 *way of life*
prink 547.15 *beautify;* 551.33 *dress up;* 244.1 *improve*
print 561.2; 41.12 *development;* 111.4, 111.9, 125.5 *duplicate;* 19.22 *engrave;* 42.3 *fabric;* 345.6 *have a visible effect;* 5.13 *letter;* 228.7 *make stable;* 780.24 *monetize;* 717.11 *paint;* 41.21 *photograph;* 19.7 *picture;* 740.15 *publish;* 744.13 *record;* 112.7 *replica;* 717.9 *represent;* 561.9 *reproduce;* 717.2 *reproduction;* 744.12 *vestige;* 345.2 *visible effect*
printable 795.10 *moralistic;* 757.8 *permitting*
printable character 40.10 *character*
printed 111.15 *duplicate;* 5.41 *lettered;* 740.19 *published;* 744.16 *recorded;* 561.15 *reproduced*
printed circuit 39.13 *circuit*
printed circuit board 39.13 *circuit*
printer 115.3, 125.8 *copier;* 19.18 *engraver;* 40.7 *peripheral;* 115.4 *person who copies;* 740.12 *publisher*
printer's ink 532.8 *black pigment*
printing 41.12 *development;* 42.7 *dyeing;* 744.8 *registration;* 561.1 *reproduction*
printing error 274.12 *typing error*
printing mark 742.7 *punctuation*
printing over 358.3 *obliteration*
print journalism 741.1 *news*
printmaker 717.4 *person who makes a representation*
print media 741.5 *mass communication*
print off 561.9 *reproduce*
printout 40.7 *peripheral*
print over 358.1 *obliterate*
prion 33.9 *protein*
prior 129.11; 296.13 *former;* 3.15 *historic;* 7.7 *monk*
prior conditions 135.1 *requirement*
prior consideration 475.1 *prediction*
prioress 7.7 *monk*
prioritization 407.1 *order*
prioritize 129.17 *give priority;* 407.19 *systematize*
priority 129.2; 123.3 *chief thing;* 726.1 *emphasis;* 123.1 *importance;* 121.1 *superiority*
priority mail 692.2 *postal communication*
prior to 129.20 *before*
priory 7.10 *priestly dwelling*
prism 176.3 *angled figure;* 529.2 *colourfulness;* 41.17 *lens;* 28.29 *optical element;* 27.46 *polyhedron;* 541.5 *variegated thing;* 519.5 *visual distortion*
prismatic 176.9 *angled;* 529.10 *coloured;* 27.84 *cubic;* 541.6 *variegated*
prismatoid 27.46 *polyhedron*
prismoid 27.46 *polyhedron*
Prison 815
prison 815.1; 38.20 *building;* 309.4 *closed place;* 165.2 *enclosed place;* 172.2 *inside;* 814.14 *instrument of punishment;* 396.6 *place of authority;* 655.4 *place of confinement;* 226.5 *resting place;* 372.2 *setting apart*
prison camp 655.4 *place of confinement;* 815.1 *prison*
prison cell 815.3; 226.5 *resting place*
prison clothes 743.5 *uniform*
prison colony 815.1 *prison*
prisoner 815.5; 715.4 *accused person;* 251.7 *charge;* 309.6 *closed-in person;* 806.4 *guilty person;* 655.7 *outsider;* 387.5 *subjected person*
prisoner at the bar 16.8 *litigant*
prisoner before the court 16.8 *litigant*
prisoner behind bars 815.5 *prisoner*
prisoner of conscience 815.5 *prisoner*

prisoner's broad arrow 743.3 *means of identification*
prison fare 687.2 *short rations*
prison farm 815.1 *prison*
prison governor 815.6 *prison officer*
prison guard 251.6 *lawmaker;* 815.6 *prison officer*
prison house 814.14 *instrument of punishment*
prison inmate 806.4 *guilty person*
prison officer 815.6
prison sentence 815.4; 16.43 *conviction;* 814.7 *punishment*
prison term 16.7 *legal trial*
pristine 805.5 *innocent;* 130.31 *prime*
privacy 736.6; 197.5 *aloneness;* 172.6 *internalization;* 521.4 *invisibility;* 252.5 *refuge;* 737.1 *secrecy;* 736.4 *silence;* 696.11 *unintelligibility;* 655.1 *unsociability*
private 521.3; 586.17 *army person;* 736.14 *concealed;* 776.19 *corporate;* 128.10 *excluding;* 122.6 *inferior;* 172.12 *internalized;* 139.19 *personal;* 655.11 *secluded;* 737.9 *secret;* 586.8 *soldier;* 319.5 *transportable;* 696.1 *unintelligible;* 655.8 *unsociable*
private automatic branch exchange 692.12 *public telephone system*
private box 692.3 *correspondence*
private branch exchange 692.12 *public telephone system*
private car 320.16 *car*
private caterer 436.4 *caterer*
private club 128.4 *exclusiveness;* 736.6 *privacy*
private company 776.7 *company*
private detective 449.12 *discoverer;* 16.17 *police officer;* 252.3 *protector*
private enterprise 776.5 *commercial trade;* 13.6 *economic factors;* 13.1 *economics*
private enterprise economy 13.1 *economics*
privateer 586.25 *historical naval ships;* 586.6 *militarist;* 323.7 *nautical person;* 774.9 *plunderer*
privateering 774.5 *plundering;* 774.17 *stolen*
private exchange 692.12 *public telephone system*
private eye 449.12 *discoverer;* 16.17 *police officer;* 252.3 *protector*
private garden 736.6 *privacy*
private hospital 35.10 hospital
private income 765.4 *earnings;* 788.3 *income*
private insurance 392.4 *social assistance*
private investigator 252.3 *protector*
private language 729.1 *faculty of speech*
private law 16.1 *the law*
privately 736.18; 737.15 *in secret;* 674.17 *modestly;* 139.29 *personally;* 655.14 *unsocially*
private manual branch exchange 692.12 *public telephone system*
private means 250.3 *independence*
private medicine 35.1 *medicine*
private meeting 737.1 *secrecy*
private nurse 35.16 *nurse*
private parts 205.4 *component;* 561.8 *organs of reproduction*
private police 16.17 *police officer*
private quarters 655.5 *solitary place*
private road 317.3 *road*
privates 205.4 *component;* 561.8 *organs of reproduction*
private sale 778.3 *selling*
private school 6.12 *educational institution*
private sector 776.5 *commercial trade;* 13.1 *economics;* 13.2 *economy*
private security company 253.4 *security forces*
private soldier 586.8 *soldier*
private space 252.5 *refuge*
private tuition 6.1 *education*
private tutor 6.4 *educator*
private world 655.1 *unsociability*
privation 766.1 *loss;* 782.5 *poverty*
privatization 776.5 *commercial trade;* 13.1 *economics*
privatize 776.1 *trade;* 13.10 *trade with*
privatized 776.19 *corporate;* 13.13 *economic*
privilege 758.9 *exempt;* 758.1 *exemption;* 250.1 *freedom;* 750.9, 750.30 *grant;* 758.4 *licence;* 129.2 *priority;* 121.1 *superiority*
privileged 758.5 *exempt;* 250.9 *free;* 750.19 *granted;* 2.14 *socioeconomic*
privileged class 2.7 *social stratification;* 781.11 *the rich*
privileged will 635.5 *will*
privvy member 561.8 *organs of reproduction*
privy 560.13 *lavatory;* 737.9 *secret;* 767.7 *toilet*
Privy Council 579.7 *council*
Privy Councillor's oath 736.4 *silence*
privy purse 765.4 *earnings;* 788.3 *income*
privy seal 743.3 *means of identification*
Prix des Nations 59.9 *jumping*
prix fixe 790.1 *price*
Prize 794
prize 813.2; 669.11 *approve;* 235.7 *elite;* 768.2 *gift;* 797.17 *good thing;* 575.3 *honours;* 595.7 *like;* 593.23 *love;* 744.11 *monument;* 482.6 *objective;* 617.5 *object of desire;* 765.5 *profit;* 667.15 *respect;* 769.2 *something received;* 774.4 *stolen goods;* 773.5 *takings;* 794.1 *trophy;* 790.2 *value;* 788.5 *winnings*
prized 593.21 *beloved;* 667.12 *respected;* 235.3 *valuable*
prizefight 52.2 *boxing;* 52.11 *fight*
prizefighter 586.3 *athlete;* 52.4 *boxer*
prizefighting 52.2 *boxing*
prize-giver 768.4 *giver*
prize-giving 768.1 *giving*
prize money 813.2 *prize*
prizewinner 235.8 *exceller;* 121.6 *paragon;* 769.5 *recipient;* 485.4 *skilled person;* 246.5 *victorious person*
prizewinning 246.15 *victorious*
PR man 480.12 *persuader;* 740.10 *publicizer*
pro 396.11, 400.10, 485.5 *expert;* 669.19 *supporting*
pro-active 334.15 *full of energy*
probabilism 104.5 *probability theory*
Probability 104
probability 27.62; **104.1**; 229.2 *attitude;* 476.2 *basis of supposition;* 107.7 *calculation of chance;* 28.81 *causality;* 703.5 *demonstrability;* 474.1 *expectation;* 107.5 *good chance;* 4.8 *philosophical term;* 104.3 *plausibility*
probability curve 104.5 *probability theory*
probability density function 27.59 *probability distribution;* 104.5 *probability theory*
probability distribution 27.59; 104.5 *probability theory*
probability function 104.5 *probability theory*
probability theory 104.5; 27.53 *statistics*
probable 104.6; 450.13 *believable;* 474.7 *expected;* 756.15 *future;* 104.7 *plausible;* 283.12 *predictable;* 95.9 *realizable;* 229.5 *tending to*
probable error 27.60 *parameter;* 28.83 *sensitivity*
probably 104.11; **229.6**; 703.22 *demonstrably;* 756.18 *potentially;* 283.16 *predictably*
probate court 16.19 *law court*
probation 448.1 *experiment*
probational 448.8 *experimental*
probationary 243.17 *developing;* 448.8 *experimental;* 15.9 *negotiated;* 353.9 *tentative*
probationary period 243.12 *briefing;* 15.2 *industrial negotiations*
probationer 130.14 *beginner;* 35.16 *nurse;* 486.10 *unskilled person*
probative 716.8 *evidential;* 703.13 *proven;* 454.9 *verificatory*
probatory 703.13 *proven*
probe 156.14 *deepen;* 156.4 *deep thing;* 449.11 *detector;* 448.1, 448.11 *experiment;* 308.20 *hole;* 26.10 *measure;* 308.2 *opener;* 705.17 *question;* 705.2 *questioning*
probed 308.14 *holed;* 705.16 *questioned*
prober 705.9 *questioner*
probing 156.13 *bathymetric;* 156.6 *bathymetry;* 705.8 *curiosity;* 705.12 *questioning*
probingly 705.23 *questioningly*
probity 799.1; 795.2 *good morals;* 805.1 *innocence;* 646.2 *naivety;* 801.3 *properness;* 783.7 *repute;* 801.4 *righteousness;* 698.5 *truthfulness;* 803.1 *virtue*
problem 264.4; 447.2 *issue;* 737.3 *mystification;* 103.7 *obstacle;* 221.2 *predicament;* 705.1 *question;* 696.12 *unintelligible thing*
problematic 264.12; **447.8**; **705.13**; 701.10 *arguable;* 453.3 *confused;* 737.11 *mysterious*
problematically 264.27; **447.13**; 453.24 *confusingly;* 705.24 *questionably*
problem child 264.9 *difficult person*
problem drinker 690.17 *drunkard*
problem novel 17.2 *fiction*
problem play 21.2 *play*
pro bono publico 652.8 *philanthropically;* 237.12 *usefully*
Proboscidea 71.14 *pachyderm*
proboscidean 71.14 *pachyderm;* 71.32 *pachydermatous*
proboscis 185.3 *protuberance;* 500.2 *sense of smell;* 492.7 *sense organ;* 488.4 *someone or something that feels*
Pro Bowl 46.1 *football*
procacity 660.1 *insolence*
procedural 340.6 *effective;* 160.11, 656.6 *formal;* 140.9 *legal*
procedurally 160.14 *conventionally;* 656.12 *formally*
procedure 632.6; 340.1 *action;* 140.6 *custom;* 160.5 *formality;* 656.3 *formal occasion;* 16.34 *legal formality;* 346.1 *operation;* 484.2 *policy;* 27.66 *proof;* 10.1 *ritual;* 317.1, 631.7 *way*
proceed 318.9; 340.4 *act;* 300.13 *be in motion;* 134.3 *continue;* 345.7 *follow from;* 302.1 *go forward;* 277.7 *go on;* 354.1 *undertake*
proceeding 340.1 *action;* 340.2 *deed;* 302.18 *ongoing;* 318.12 *passing;* 317.1 *way*
proceedings 16.6 *legal process;* 447.3 *matter of interest*
proceeds 765.4 *earnings;* 788.2 *money received;* 769.2 *something received;* 773.5 *takings;* 765.6 *yield*
proceed with caution 616.5 *be cautious*
process 32.5; 340.1 *action;* 409.15 *categorize;* 224.8 *cause change;* 224.1 *change;* 32.14 *chemical reaction;* 277.3 *continuity;* 760.7 *convert into;* 397.2 *demand;* 356.2 *manufacture;* 352.1 *means;* 346.1 *operation;* 41.21 *photograph;* 359.5 *preserve;* 356.10 *produce;* 717.9 *represent;* 289.1 *succession;* 346.9 *take action;* 760.9 *transform;* 317.1, 631.7 *way*
process data 409.15 *categorize*
processed 409.24 *categorized;* 356.12 *produced;* 243.21 *ready-made*
processed food 557.7 *food;* 359.3 *preserved thing*
processing 760.1 *conversion;* 760.14 *converting;* 41.12 *development;* 356.2 *manufacture;* 359.1 *preservation*
procession 132.8; 132.1 *consecutiveness;* 289.1 *succession*
processionally 10.23 *ritually*
process of death 582.1 *death*
processor 40.5; 40.4 *computer*
process-server 16.10 *law officer;* 397.6 *person in command*
prochronism 286.1 *different time;* 288.1 *wrong time*
prochronistic 288.14 *anachronistic;* 288.11 *too early*
prochronistically 288.20 *anachronistically;* 288.18 *out of chronological order*
proclaim 740.14; 707.17 *affirm;* 397.9 *command;* 123.8 *make important;* 4.22 *propound a philosophy;* 738.3 *reveal;* 742.12 *signal;* 729.11 *speak*
proclaimed 740.19 *published;* 707.11 *stated*
proclaimer 707.9 *affirmer;* 740.10 *publicizer;* 742.8 *signer*
proclaiming 742.16 *signalling*
proclamation 397.1 *command;* 738.10 *manifestation;* 740.1 *publication;* 707.2 *statement;* 742.6 *word*
proclamatory 707.10 *affirmative*
proclivity 229.2 *attitude;* 595.2 *inclination;* 445.4 *instinct;* 632.2 *tendency*
proconsul 398.4 *deputy;* 400.3 *leader;* 579.16 *official;* 396.10 *person of authority*
proconsulate 396.5 *position of authority*
procrastinate 634.7 *be evasive;* 343.12 *be inactive;* 639.7 *be irresolute;* 666.6 *be neglectful;* 294.8 *delay;* 637.8 *hold back;* 361.12 *interrupt;* 341.4 *not act*
procrastinating 637.4; 294.12 *delaying;* 333.6 *hesitant;* 341.3 *inactive;* 666.5 *indifferent;* 343.3 *not participating*
procrastination 637.15 *delay;* 294.3 *delayed action;* 634.15 *evasiveness;* 333.12 *hesitation;* 343.7 *idleness;* 341.1 *inaction;* 666.2 *indifference;* 361.6 *interruption;* 227.2 *irresolution*
procrastinator 294.5 *delayer;* 666.3 *negligent person;* 637.16 *reluctant person;* 333.15 *slow person*
procreant 562.5 *fertile;* 561.16 *reproductive*
procreate 190.6 *become bigger;* 554.19 *give birth to;* 562.7 *make fertile;* 561.13 *propagate*
procreation 554.4 *biological function;* 190.1 *growth;* 562.2 *productiveness;* 561.3 *propagation*
procreative 562.5 *fertile;* 561.16 *reproductive*
procreatively 190.10 *largely*
procreator 561.5 *propagator*
Procrustean law 140.3 *rule of nature*
proctor 579.1 *manage;* 579.15 *manager*
proctorship 579.3 *management*
procumbent 187.10 *lying*
procurable 765.15 *gainful*
procural 765.1 *gain*
procurance 765.1 *gain*
procuration 765.1 *gain*
procurator 579.15 *manager*
procurator fiscal 464.6 *justice;* 16.10 *law officer*
procure 344.10 *awaken;* 348.4 *be an instrument;* 316.14 *bring back;* 369.15 *draw out;* 765.9 *gain;* 483.9 *motivate;* 480.15 *persuade;* 796.18 *prostitute;* 436.5 *provision;* 777.1 *purchase;* 346.9 *take action*
procurement 765.1 *gain*
procurer 348.3 *assistant;* 765.7 *gainer;* 796.8 *immoral man;* 436.3 *provider;* 769.5 *recipient;* 778.12 *wholesaler*
procuring 796.5 *prostitution;* 436.1 *provision*
procyonid 71.8 *flesh-eating mammal*
Procyonidae 71.8 *flesh-eating mammal*
prod 331.13 *blow;* 742.11 *gesture;* 331.1 *impel;* 480.8 *incentive;* 483.10 *manipulate;* 492.3 *press;* 425.8 *sharp-pointed thing;* 483.3 *stimulus;* 492.11 *touch;* 425.16 *use a sharp tool*
prodded 483.12 *motivated*
prodder 62.4 *climbing equipment*
prodigal 681.1 *extravagant;* 459.5 *foolish;* 686.8 *overindulgent;* 217.2 *plentiful;* 681.6, 787.11 *spendthrift;* 766.17 *unprofitable;* 441.8 *wasteful;* 441.6 *waster*
prodigality 727.1 *exaggeration;* 681.4, 787.6 *extravagance;* 686.3 *overindulgence;* 217.8 *plenty;* 441.3 *waste*
prodigally 766.20 *at a loss;* 787.14 *generously;* 441.10 *wastefully*
prodigal returned 808.3 *penitent person*
prodigal son 808.3 *penitent person;* 681.6 *spendthrift;* 804.9 *wicked person*
prodigal's return 312.13 *return*
prodigious 158.15 *big;* 727.12 *exaggerated;* 235.1 *worthy*
prodigiously 727.17 *excessively*
prodigiousness 158.2 *bigness*
prodigous 619.8 *wonderful*
prodigy 235.8 *exceller;* 121.6 *paragon;* 619.5 *person of wonder;* 485.4 *skilled person;* 525.4 *something that appears;* 797.16 *superior person;* 105.5 *unexpectedness*
produce 130.26; **356.7**; **356.10**; 27.97 *align;* 765.13 *be profitable;* 344.9 *be the cause of;* 703.15 *demonstrate;* 243.7 *develop;* 21.38 *dramatize;* 553.9 *fashion;* 160.7 *form;* 80.1 *fruits;* 345.8 *grow;* 345.3 *growth;* 477.14 *imagine;* 148.10 *lengthen;* 562.7 *make fertile;* 561.13 *propagate;* 436.1, 436.5 *provision;* 738.3 *reveal;* 559.7 *secrete;* 345.5 *show an effect;* 2.15 *socialize;* 765.6 *yield*
produced 356.12; 554.15 *born;* 738.13 *displayed;* 160.9 *formed*
produce market 779.1 *market*
produce offspring 561.13 *propagate*
produce power 334.12 *generate power*
producer 21.27; **356.9**; 578.3 *agent;* 703.7 *demonstrator;* 449.12 *discoverer;* 34.18 *ecology;* 344.7 *Prime Mover*
produce results 239.6 *be convenient;* 392.26 *be useful*
producer gas 437.3 *gas*
producer goods 13.2 *economy*
produce secretion 559.7 *secrete*
produce seeds 562.6 *be fertile*
producible 738.13 *displayed*

producing 356.1 *production*
product 356.3; 32.14 *chemical reaction;* 345.1 *effect;* 194.4 *mathematical result;* 778.8 *merchandise;* 27.17, 207.4 *multiplication;* 706.7 *numerical result;* 436.1 *provision;* 765.6 *yield*
product dumping 219.3 *superfluity*
production 21.14; **356.1**; **738.9**; 340.1 *action;* 346.3 *business;* 344.1 *cause;* 243.13 *development;* 13.6 *economic factors;* 160.4 *forming;* 403.5 *structuring;* 21.13 *theatrical performance;* 356.5 *work of art;* 765.6 *yield*
production budget 789.2 *budgeting*
production car racing 61.1 *motor racing*
production cost budget 789.2 *budgeting*
production costs 13.6 *economic factors*
production efficiency 13.6 *economic factors*
production engineering 38.1 *engineering*
production line 620.2 *boring thing;* 356.2 *manufacture;* 376.33 *putting together;* 577.1 *workshop*
production manager 15.6 *employer*
production metallurgy 32.23 *metallurgy*
productive 356.11; 344.13 *causal;* 340.6 *effective;* 43.20 *farmable;* 562.5 *fertile;* 80.6 *fruiting;* 477.10 *imaginative;* 781.4 *lush;* 237.4 *profitable;* 2.14 *socioeconomic;* 765.19 *yielding*
productive capacity 562.2 *productiveness*
productively 356.13; 43.22 *agriculturally;* 344.14 *causally;* 340.8 *effectively;* 160.13 *formatively;* 80.11 *fructiferously;* 562.8 *fruitfully;* 765.20 *gainfully;* 2.16 *sociologically*
productiveness 562.2; 237.8 *benefit;* 270.1 *diffuseness;* 217.8 *plenty;* 356.1 *production*
productivity 237.8 *benefit;* 270.1 *diffuseness;* 13.6 *economic factors;* 217.8 *plenty;* 356.1 *production;* 562.2 *productiveness*
product testing 778.7 *market*
proem 129.5 *preface;* 729.8 *speech*
proemial 130.36 *introductory;* 129.13 *precursory*
profanation 712.1 *curse;* 351.2 *misuse*
profane 351.5 *abusive;* 594.13 *angry;* 712.8 *cursing;* 668.27 *desecrate;* 258.11 *dirty;* 804.14 *impious;* 245.3 *make worse;* 351.1 *misuse;* 258.8 *unclean*
profane language 712.2 *offensive language*
profanely 351.6 *abusively;* 804.20 *immorally;* 712.12 *swearingly*
profaneness 804.6 *religious sin*
profaner 804.9 *wicked person*
profanity 712.1 *curse;* 594.6 *swearing;* 258.2 *uncleanness*
profess 707.17 *affirm;* 450.7 *believe;* 4.22 *propound a philosophy*
professed 756.12 *promised;* 707.11 *stated*
professedly 96.19 *apparently*
profession 776.6 *business;* 576.3 *job;* 756.1 *promise;* 707.2 *statement;* 810.2 *task*
professional 776.17; 52.14 *combat;* 340.3 *doer;* 340.6 *effective;* 400.13 *excellent;* 396.11, 396.17, 400.10, 485.5, 485.8 *expert;* 632.9 *habitual;* 15.8 *industrial;* 342.20 *industrious;* 694.6 *meaningful;* 216.8 *middle classes;* 136.9 *qualified;* 136.8 *qualified person;* 139.14 *specialist;* 139.21 *specialized;* 46.19 *varsity;* 485.9 *well-made*
professional army 586.15 *army;* 584.2 *the military*
professional athlete 336.5 *athlete*
professional baseball 48.1 *baseball*
professional basketball 49.1 *basketball*
professional bowler 51.6 *bowler*
professional boxer 52.4 *boxer*
professional boxing 52.1 *combat sports*
professional code 810.6 *ethics*
professional consultant 713.4 *adviser*
professional football 46.1 *football;* 66.1 *soccer*
professional footballer 66.3 *football player*
Professional Golfers Association 56.1 *golf*
professional ice hockey 58.3 *ice hockey*
professionalism 556.3 *maturity;* 485.1 *skill*
professional journal 740.5 *journal*
professional killer 382.11 *murderer*
professionally 52.16; 136.17 *capably;* 396.26 *expertly;* 632.19 *habitually;* 400.16 *masterfully;* 485.12 *skilfully*
professional murderer 382.11 *murderer*
professional person 578.1 *worker*
Professional Punting Championship 50.8 *punting*
professional skill 485.1 *skill*
professional soldier 586.6 *militarist;* 586.8 *soldier*
professional team 58.3 *ice hockey*
professional wrestler 52.6 *wrestler*
professional wrestling 52.1 *combat sports;* 52.5 *wrestling*
professor 713.4 *adviser;* 707.9 *affirmer;* 579.13 *director;* 400.9 *educational leader;* 6.4 *educator;* 396.11, 485.5 *expert;* 136.8 *qualified person;* 443.7 *thinker;* 578.1 *worker*
professorate 6.6 *instructorship*
professor emeritus 6.4 *educator*
professorhood 6.6 *instructorship*
professorial 443.11 *reasoning*
professorship 6.6 *instructorship*
proffer 752.1, 752.9 *offer;* 756.7 *promise*
proffer aid 392.17 *help*
proffer one's good offices 748.1 *mediate*
proficiency 797.12; 334.2 *ability;* 265.1 *easiness;* 455.3 *learning;* 230.3 *perfection;* 136.1 *qualification;* 485.1 *skill*
proficient 797.5; 400.13 *excellent;* 485.8 *expert;* 455.8 *knowledgeable;* 230.1 *perfect;* 334.13 *powerful;* 136.9 *qualified;* 485.6 *skilful*
proficiently 136.17 *capably;* 455.15 *knowledgeably;* 400.16 *masterfully;* 334.18 *powerfully;* 485.12 *skilfully*
proficient person 578.2 *artisan;* 619.5 *person of wonder;* 485.4 *skilled person*
profile 608.6; 19.10 *art subject;* 721.1 *description;* 525.3 *external appearance;* 167.2 *face;* 160.1 *form;* 17.4 *nonfiction;* 163.1, 163.5 *outline;* 163.2 *shadow;* 169.1 *side*
profil perdu 19.10 *art subject*
Profit 765
profit 765.5; **765.14**; 239.6 *be convenient;* 569.16 *be favourable;* 392.21 *be helpful;* 237.8, 237.10, 797.13 *benefit;* 248.5 *be prosperous;* 239.3 *convenience;* 13.7 *corporation;* 215.3 *difference;* 797.20 *do good;* 13.6 *economic factors;* 765.9 *gain;* 345.8 *grow;* 345.3 *growth;* 213.4 *increase;* 483.5 *positive stimulus;* 356.7 *produce;* 776.1 *trade;* 813.5 *turnover;* 349.6 *use;* 781.5 *wealth*
profitability 237.8, 797.13 *benefit;* 765.1 *gain;* 392.10 *helpfulness;* 213.1 *increase*
profitable 237.4; **776.15**; **785.18**; 392.34, 797.6 *beneficial;* 239.1 *convenient;* 617.8 *desirable;* 13.13 *economic;* 569.12 *favourable;* 562.5 *fertile;* 765.15 *gainful;* 797.1 *good;* 356.11 *productive;* 788.6 *received;* 246.14, 813.15 *rewarding;* 349.10 *usable;* 235.4 *worthwhile*
profitableness 765.1 *gain*
profitable return 813.5 *turnover*
profitable transaction 765.1 *gain*
profitably 788.8; **813.20**; 777.17 *acquisitively;* 13.14 *economically;* 569.20 *favourably;* 562.8 *fruitfully;* 765.20 *gainfully;* 392.36 *helpfully;* 778.17 *marketably;* 356.13 *productively;* 246.16 *successfully;* 237.12, 349.11, 797.26 *usefully;* 235.11 *worthily*
profit after tax 813.5 *turnover*
profit-and-loss account 789.1 *accounts;* 13.7 *corporation*
profit by 485.10 *be skilful;* 349.3 *exploit;* 237.11 *find useful;* 244.2 *get better;* 342.14 *push;* 287.5 *take the opportunity*
profit by example 711.6 *be warned*
profit by one's mistakes 711.6 *be warned*
profiteer 13.9 *economist;* 765.9 *gain;* 765.7 *gainer;* 792.10 *overcharge;* 776.1 *trade;* 776.10 *trader*
profiteering 792.7 *dear;* 792.4 *extortion;* 765.1 *gain;* 248.8 *prosperous;* 776.4 *trade*
profit from 244.1 *improve*
profitless 247.10 *failed;* 238.2 *futile;* 766.17 *unprofitable*
profitlessness 238.4 *futility*
profitmaking 765.1 *gain;* 765.15 *gainful;* 776.15 *profitable;* 776.4 *trade*
profit margin 13.6 *economic factors;* 813.5 *turnover*
profit motive 13.6 *economic factors*
profits 788.2 *money received;* 765.5 *profit;* 769.2 *something received;* 781.5 *wealth*
profit-sharing 15.2 *industrial negotiations;* 764.5 *jointly possessing;* 764.1 *joint possession;* 15.9 *negotiated*
profit-taking 765.1 *gain;* 765.15 *gainful;* 773.1 *taking*
profligacy 686.2 *dissipation;* 681.4 *extravagance;* 490.1 *physical pleasure;* 796.3 *sexual immorality;* 804.2 *vice*
profligate 686.7 *dissipated;* 681.1 *extravagant;* 804.12 *immoral;* 796.14 *lecherous;* 490.7 *pleased;* 681.6, 787.11 *spendthrift;* 804.9 *wicked person*
profligately 787.14 *generously*
profluence 90.6 *river flow*
profluent 90.10 *fluvial;* 302.18 *ongoing*
pro forma 656.12 *formally*
profound 156.9 *deep-seated;* 4.19 *learned;* 266.2 *obscure;* 443.10 *speculative;* 442.11 *thoughtful;* 696.1 *unintelligible;* 156.11, 458.5 *wise*
profoundly 156.17; 442.15 *intelligently;* 266.4 *obscurely;* 510.11 *resonantly;* 4.29 *wisely*
profoundness 156.3 *profundity;* 442.6 *thoughtfulness;* 696.11 *unintelligibility*
profound thought 443.2 *intellectual exercise*
profundity 156.3; 510.3 *deepness;* 156.7 *deep thinking;* 443.4 *deliberation;* 266.1 *obscurity;* 442.6 *thoughtfulness;* 458.1 *wisdom*
profuse 679.3 *abundant;* 208.9 *ample;* 270.3 *diffuse;* 219.6 *excessive;* 727.14 *extravagant;* 562.5 *fertile;* 217.2 *plentiful;* 681.2 *unrestrained*
profusely 270.7 *diffusely;* 217.9 *enough;* 727.17 *excessively*
profuseness 208.3; 270.1 *diffuseness;* 727.3 *extravagance*
profusion 679.8 *abundance;* 219.1 *excess;* 727.3 *extravagance;* 562.1 *fertility;* 781.7 *opulence;* 217.8 *plenty;* 208.3 *profuseness;* 681.5 *unrestrainedness*
progenitor 344.7 *Prime Mover*
progeny 561.6
progesterone 394.8 *drug*
prognosis 35.7 *diagnosis;* 474.2 *expectations;* 35.6 *health care;* 260.20 *pathology;* 475.1 *prediction;* 104.1 *probability*
prognostic 35.24 *diagnostic;* 474.5 *expecting;* 475.5 *omen;* 711.8 *warning*
prognosticate 35.19 *practise medicine;* 475.11 *predict;* 104.10 *think likely*
prognostication 475.5 *omen;* 475.1 *prediction*
prognosticator 475.9 *forecaster*
program 409.15 *categorize;* 40.8 *software*
programmable calculator 40.3 *computer*
programme 340.1 *action;* 631.14 *behave towards;* 692.25 *broadcast material;* 409.8 *chart;* 406.9 *itemize;* 220.5 *list of appointments;* 475.3, 484.1, 484.9 *plan;* 484.10 *plan out;* 631.9 *tactics;* 281.2 *timetable;* 447.1 *topic;* 354.2 *undertaking*
programmed 447.7 *focused;* 406.12 *itemized;* 220.11 *listed*
programme-maker 356.9 *producer*
programmer 40.2 *operator*
programme-seller 21.28 *stagehand*
programming 40.1 *computing*
programming language 40.9; 40.8 *software*
progress 550.35; 342.13 *be busy;* 132.13 *be consecutive;* 300.13 *be in motion;* 248.5 *be prosperous;* 246.6 *be successful;* 760.8 *be transformed;* 134.3 *continue;* 134.1, 277.3 *continuity;* 6.1 *education;* 318.10 *enter;* 760.2 *evolution;* 633.13 *follow up;* 302.10 *forward motion;* 244.2 *get better;* 302.1 *go forward;* 277.7 *go on;* 244.5 *improvement;* 213.1, 213.4 *increase;* 300.3 *motion towards;* 318.2 *passing along;* 289.1 *succession;* 317.1 *way*
progressing 550.41; 760.14 *converting;* 300.17 *directional;* 302.17 *forward;* 213.6 *increasing*
progression 550.22; 132.1 *consecutiveness;* 134.1, 277.3 *continuity;* 302.10 *forward motion;* 407.3 *hierarchy;* 244.5 *improvement;* 300.3 *motion towards;* 27.20 *sequence;* 289.1 *succession;* 317.1 *way*
progressionist 244.12 *reformer*
progressive 132.9 *consecutive;* 134.5 *continual;* 300.17 *directional;* 6.16 *educational;* 354.6 *enterprising;* 302.17 *forward;* 209.7 *gradational;* 407.12 *hierarchical;* 244.16 *improving;* 213.6 *increasing;* 302.16 *progressive person;* 244.12 *reformer*
Progressive Conservative Party 12.6 *political party*
Progressive Democrats 12.6 *political party*
progressive jazz 18.8 *jazz*
progressively 244.17 *better;* 209.10 *by degrees;* 132.18 *consecutively;* 134.7 *continually;* 6.25 *educationally;* 354.9 *enterprisingly;* 330.34 *forward;* 213.8 *increasingly;* 300.18 *in motion;* 407.25 *in order;* 302.20 *in progress*
progressiveness 302.10 *forward motion*
progressive person 302.16
progressive tax 790.7 *tax*
progressive taxation 13.6 *economic factors*
progressivism 244.11 *reformism*
progressivist 244.12 *reformer*
progress report 693.3 *document*
prog rock 18.9 *popular music*
prohibit 708.10 *be negative;* 399.4 *censor;* 397.9 *command;* 347.3 *counteract;* 709.6 *dissent;* 128.7 *exclude;* 378.8 *hinder;* 655.13 *ignore;* 166.7 *limit;* 16.75 *make illegal;* 103.8 *make impossible;* 301.9 *make motionless;* 371.4 *ostracize;* 251.8 *restrain;* 399.3 *veto;* 670.15 *withhold approval*
prohibit drinking 684.5 *be self-restrained*
prohibited 709.9 *dissenting;* 128.11 *excluded;* 103.4 *forbidden;* 16.55 *illegal;* 655.10 *lonely;* 708.18 *rejected;* 251.13 *restraining;* 684.8 *self-restrained;* 399.5 *vetoed*
prohibiting 709.9 *dissenting;* 378.13 *hindering;* 708.19 *rebutting;* 399.5 *vetoed*
Prohibition 3.10 *past age;* 689.7 *prohibition;* 244.11 *reformism;* 795.4 *self-righteousness;* 399.1 *veto*
prohibition 689.7; 397.1 *command;* 709.2 *dissent;* 128.1 *exclusion;* 378.1 *hindrance;* 16.35 *illegality;* 166.2 *limiting factor;* 103.7 *obstacle;* 708.2 *rejection;* 251.1 *restraint;* 684.1 *self-restraint;* 399.1 *veto*
prohibitionary 709.9 *dissenting*
prohibitionism 244.11 *reformism*
prohibitionist 795.6 *moralist;* 244.12 *reformer;* 684.4 *self-restrained person;* 689.1 *sober;* 689.8 *sober person*
prohibitive 397.14 *commanding;* 681.3 *costly;* 792.7 *dear;* 128.10 *excluding;* 378.13 *hindering;* 166.5 *limited;* 251.13 *restraining;* 399.5 *vetoed*
prohibitively 399.7 *by veto;* 397.16 *commandingly;* 792.12 *dearly;* 708.22 *negatively;* 251.16 *under restraints;* 378.16 *with delay*
prohibitory 399.5 *vetoed*
project 361.11; 21.34 *act;* 100.16 *be external;* 447.5 *educational topic;* 315.10 *emerge;* 171.14 *externalize;* 482.3 *future intention;* 331.1 *impel;* 163.5 *outline;* 41.21 *photograph;* 446.3, 484.1, 484.9 *plan;* 106.6 *premeditation;* 356.1 *production;* 330.20 *propel;* 185.8 *protrude;* 27.96, 717.9 *represent;* 482.8 *resolve;* 576.2 *task;* 354.2 *undertaking*
projected 100.12 *external;* 171.9 *externalized;* 167.7 *outward*
projected image 167.3 *show*
projectile 330.18; 587.13 *ammunition;* 330.8 *missile*
projecting 361.8; 100.12 *external*
projecting object 361.5
projecting part 361.2 *projection*
projection 185.2; **361.2**; 21.22 *acting;* 36.19 *defence mechanism;* 100.4 *externality;* 171.4 *externalization;* 477.4 *ideality;* 717.6 *image;* 738.10 *manifestation;* 717.7 *map;* 163.1 *outline;* 92.5 *peninsula;* 608.6 *profile;* 185.2 *projection;* 425.8 *sharp-pointed thing;* 330.3 *throwing;* 27.48 *transformation*
projectional 163.6 *outlined*
projection circulaire 68.4 *skiing technique*
projection map 163.4 *map*
projective geometry 27.34 *geometry*
projective test 36.5 *psychological test*
projector 41.14 *cine film;* 484.8 *planner;* 518.8 *reflection;* 21.20 *stage lighting*
prokaryote 34.3 *organism*
prokaryotic 34.23 *cellular*
prokaryotic cell 34.7 *cell*
prolapse 305.10 *droop*
prolate 27.83 *spherical*

prole 574.1 *plebeian*; 675.5 *vulgar person*
prolegomenon 722.1 *dissertation*
prolepsis 288.1 *wrong time*
proleptic 288.11 *too early*
proletarian 574.3 *common*; 574.1 *plebeian*
proletarianism 12.1 *government*
proletariat 216.7 *average person*; 578.4 *personnel*; 574.2 *the common people*
proliferate 217.5 *about*; 765.10 *augment*; 562.6 *be fertile*; 213.4 *increase*; 561.12 *multiply*; 83.12 *mushroom*; 207.9 *pluralize*
proliferated 207.8 *multiplicative*
proliferating 207.8 *multiplicative*
proliferation 213.1 *increase*; 207.4 *multiplication*; 217.8 *plenty*; 561.1 *reproduction*
proliferative 207.8 *multiplicative*
prolific 270.3 *diffuse*; 562.5 *fertile*; 213.6 *increasing*; 781.4 *lush*; 217.2 *plentiful*; 356.11 *productive*; 765.19 *yielding*
prolificacy 217.8 *plenty*
prolifically 270.7 *diffusely*; 217.9 *enough*; 562.8 *fruitfully*; 765.20 *gainfully*; 213.8 *increasingly*; 356.13 *productively*
prolificness 217.8 *plenty*
prolix 620.4 *boring*; 270.3 *diffuse*; 112.12 *repetitious*; 731.5 *talkative*
prolixity 620.1 *boredom*; 270.1 *diffuseness*; 729.2 *power of speech*; 731.1 *talkativeness*
prologue 21.24 *actor*; 167.1 *front*; 129.5 *preface*; 21.8 *scene*; 729.8 *speech*
prolong 294.8 *delay*; 148.10 *lengthen*; 213.5 *make bigger*; 359.5 *preserve*; 134.4 *protract*
prolongation 211.1 *addition*; 294.3 *delayed action*; 213.1 *increase*; 148.4 *length*; 359.1 *preservation*; 134.2 *protraction*
prolonged 294.10 *held up*; 148.1 *long*; 134.6 *protracted*
prolonged noise 507.1 *loudness*
prolonged note 18.19 *tempo*
prom 376.10 *dance*; 22.1 *dancing*; 18.27 *performance*
promenade 317.7 *arcade*; 22.1 *dancing*; 167.1 *front*; 132.17 *line up*; 132.8 *procession*
promenade concert 18.27 *performance*
promenader 21.33 *theatregoer*
Promethean 554.12 *alive*
prominence **185.1**; 520.4 *clarity*; 182.1 *convexity*; 716.3 *evidentness*; 154.1, 366.8 *height*; 123.1 *importance*; 726.2 *seriousness*; 29.15 *sun*; 121.1 *superiority*
prominent 525.7 *appearing*; 520.2 *clear*; 182.4 *convex*; 185.6 *eminent*; 716.9 *evident*; 154.11, 366.12 *exalted*; 121.15 *excellent*; 123.5 *important*; 738.14 *manifest*; 123.6 *notable*
prominent feature 185.3 *protuberance*
prominently 182.6 *convexly*; 185.11 *eminently*; 716.15 *evidently*; 123.9 *importantly*; 121.16 *superiorly*
promiscuity 757.1 *permission*; 247.3 *personal fault*; 245.8 *perversion*; 796.3 *sexual immorality*
promiscuous 618.8 *careless*; 796.13 *unchaste*
promiscuously 618.18 *carelessly*
promiscuousness 618.2 *carelessness*
Promise 756
promise **253.2**; **253.11**; **756.1**; **756.7**; 750.23 *arrange*; 750.3 *arrangement*; 569.16 *be favourable*; 104.8 *be probable*; 253.12 *certify*; 610.4 *comfort*; 810.7 *commitment*; 354.3, 755.1 *contract*; 482.4 *formulated intention*; 452.14 *guarantee*; 610.10 *inspire hope*; 452.21 *make certain*; 102.1 *possibility*; 475.11 *predict*; 252.10 *protect*; 482.8 *resolve*; 354.1 *undertake*; 707.3, 707.18 *vow*
promised **756.12**; 750.12 *arranged*; 755.7 *contractual*; 474.7 *expected*; 283.13 *foreseen*; 253.7, 452.4 *guaranteed*; 570.22 *marriageable*; 354.5 *undertaken*; 707.12 *vowed*
promised land **756.4**; 610.3 *aspiration*; 477.8 *dreamland*; 482.6 *objective*
promise-maker **756.5**
promise-making 756.1 *promise*
promise oneself **756.11**
promiser 452.15 *guarantor*; 756.5 *promise-maker*
promises 483.2 *inducement*
promise to pay 784.1 *debt*; 756.8 *guarantee*
promise well 248.7, 756.9 *be auspicious*
promising 756.14 *auspicious*; 610.14 *cheering*; 569.12 *favourable*; 102.6 *potential*; 475.15 *presageful*; 248.8 *prosperous*
promisingly 756.17 *auspiciously*; 569.20 *favourably*; 610.15 *hopefully*; 475.16 *predictively*; 248.9 *prosperously*
promissory 756.13 *guaranteeing*
promissory note 756.2 *guarantee*; 780.14 *paper money*; 755.2 *purchase contract*
promitosis 34.10 *cell division*
promo 740.8 *public relations*
promontory 92.11 *continental*; 92.5 *peninsula*; 185.2 *projection*
promorphology 403.8 *science of structure*
promote **366.3**; 348.4 *be an instrument*; 239.6 *be convenient*; 237.9 *be useful*; 15.11 *conduct industrial relations*; 344.12 *determine*; 352.6 *find means*; 302.8, 392.28 *further*; 244.1 *improve*; 395.8 *influence*; 265.16 *make easy*; 123.8 *make important*; 740.16 *publicize*; 32.26 *react*; 738.3 *reveal*; 778.1 *sell*; 776.1 *trade*
promoted 738.13 *displayed*; 366.12 *exalted*; 15.9 *negotiated*
promoter 707.9 *affirmer*; 392.15 *benefactor*; 693.9 *informant*; 467.3 *optimist*; 480.12 *persuader*; 484.8 *planner*; 21.27 *producer*; 740.10 *publicizer*
promoting 392.33 *helpful*; 392.30 *helping*; 348.6 *instrumental*
promotion 289.4 *accession*; 302.12 *advance*; 392.8 *furtherance*; 244.5 *improvement*; 15.2 *industrial negotiations*; 348.1 *instrumentality*; 366.7 *lift*; 738.10 *manifestation*; 243.9 *preparation*; 480.5 *propaganda*; 778.3 *selling*
promotional 348.6 *instrumental*; 15.9 *negotiated*
promotional literature 480.6 *advertising*
promotional manager 738.12 *displayer*
promotion tour 740.6 *book publishing*
promotive 348.6 *instrumental*
prompt 130.20 *activate*; 342.18 *active*; 693.7 *advice*; 713.5 *advise*; 21.38 *dramatize*; 636.2 *eager*; 293.12 *early*; 262.3 *hasty*; 280.5 *immediate*; 483.9 *motivate*; 480.15 *persuade*; 462.13 *remind*; 462.4 *reminder*; 332.1 *swift*
prompt book 21.2 *play*
prompted 21.39 *dramatic*; 483.12 *motivated*
prompter 713.4 *adviser*; 480.14, 483.7 *motivator*; 462.4 *reminder*; 21.28 *stagehand*
prompter's box 21.17 *stage*
prompting 480.1 *persuasion*
promptitude 293.1 *earliness*; 280.1 *immediacy*; 342.3 *nimbleness*; 332.8 *speed*
promptly 342.22 *actively*; 293.17 *early*; 262.6 *hastily*; 280.8 *immediately*; 332.14 *swiftly*
promptness 636.7 *eagerness*; 293.1 *earliness*; 262.4 *haste*; 280.1 *immediacy*; 332.8 *speed*
promulgate 397.9 *command*; 740.13 *make public*
promulgation 740.1 *publication*
pronate 54.5 *fence*
pronated 54.6 *fencing*
pronation 54.3 *fencing movements*
prone 155.5 *low*; 187.10 *lying*; 104.6 *probable*; 367.8 *sit*; 636.1 *willing*
proneness 229.2 *attitude*; 187.1 *horizontality*; 155.1 *lowness*; 104.1 *probability*
prone to 229.5 *tending to*
prone to sickness 260.21 *unhealthy*
prong 311.5 *fork*; 198.8 *half*; 425.7 *sharp point*
pronged 311.9 *branched*
pronominal 5.44 *grammatical*
pronoun 5.35 *part of speech*
pronounce 707.17 *affirm*; 745.3 *aphorize*; 397.9 *command*; 16.76 *judge*; 740.14 *proclaim*; 4.22 *propound a philosophy*; 140.13 *rule*; 5.45 *use language*
pronounced 726.4 *emphasized*; 5.38 *linguistic*; 738.14 *manifest*; 729.16 *speech*; 707.11 *stated*
pronounce guilty 16.79 *convict*
pronounce man and wife 570.16 *join in marriage*
pronouncement 397.1 *command*; 740.1 *publication*; 707.2 *statement*; 729.7 *utterance*; 464.2 *verdict*
pronounce sentence 464.11 *judge*; 16.71 *try a case*
pronto 262.6 *hastily*; 332.14 *swiftly*
Pronuba 570.14 *gods and goddesses of marriage*
pronunciamento 740.1 *publication*
pronunciation 5.1 *linguistics*; 729.3 *mode of speech*; 729.6 *phonetics*
proof **27.66**; **454.5**; **703.4**; **716.2**; 452.9 *certainty*; 452.13, 698.7, 707.4 *confirmation*; 690.6 *intoxicating*; 252.7 *invulnerable*; 16.7 *legal trial*; 738.10 *manifestation*; 484.6 *outline*; 428.10 *waterproof*
proof against 592.1 *insensitive*
proof copy 484.6 *outline*
proofed 418.3 *hardened*
proof of purchase 253.2 *promise*; 788.1 *receipt*
proof of regard 813.1 *reward*
proofread 244.3 *rectify*
proofreader 740.12 *publisher*; 393.12 *repairer*; 244.13 *reviser*
proofreading 244.6 *rectification*
prop 330.11 *propeller*; 252.5 *refuge*; 307.6 *rotator*; 64.4 *rugby player*; 228.3 *stabilizer*; 21.21 *stage requisite*; 392.19, 413.11 *support*; 392.13 *supporter*; 413.2 *supporting part*; 438.1 *tool*
propaganda **480.5**; 234.4 *distortion of the truth*; 699.11 *half-truth*; 483.2 *inducement*; 740.8 *public relations*; 702.2 *sophism*; 585.7 *war measures*
propaganda machine 699.11 *half-truth*
propagandist 234.5 *defacer*; 722.3 *dissertator*; 699.18 *liar*; 483.7 *motivator*; 480.12 *persuader*; 740.10 *publicizer*; 702.6 *sophist*
propagandize 234.12 *distort the truth*; 450.9 *make someone believe*; 245.6 *pervert*; 702.11 *practise sophistry*; 740.16 *publicize*
propagate **561.13**; 344.9 *be the cause of*; 692.30 *communicate*; 44.15 *cultivate*; 377.16 *distribute*; 213.5 *make bigger*; 562.7 *make fertile*; 740.13 *make public*; 207.9 *pluralize*; 356.10 *produce*
propagated 692.34 *communicated*; 377.22 *distributed*
propagation **561.3**; 554.4 *biological function*; 344.1 *cause*; 377.1 *dispersion*; 44.5 *gardening*; 213.1 *increase*; 84.6 *lichen*; 82.4 *moss plant*; 562.2 *productiveness*; 692.6 *telecommunication*
propagator **561.5**; 562.1 *fertility*; 44.4 *nursery*; 344.7 *Prime Mover*; 344.2 *source*
propagatory 562.5 *fertile*
propagule 84.4 *reproductive body*
propane 437.3 *gas*
propel **330.20**; 262.1 *hasten*; 331.1 *impel*; 366.2 *send up*; 300.14 *set in motion*; 331.4 *throw*; 316.12 *transport*
propellant **330.12**; **371.28**; 587.15 *explosive*; 300.16 *moving*; 330.11 *propeller*; 330.17 *propulsive*; 29.35 *rocketry*; 432.11 *vaporizer*
propelled **330.19**
propeller **330.11**; 307.6 *rotator*
propelling 300.16 *moving*; 330.1 *propulsion*; 330.17 *propulsive*
propelment 330.1 *propulsion*
propensity 485.2 *aptitude*; 229.2 *attitude*; 595.2 *inclination*; 104.2, 632.2 *tendency*
proper 117.14 *conformist*; 239.1 *convenient*; 617.8 *desirable*; 16.44 *legal*; 795.8 *moral*; 803.5 *virtuous*
proper eating 557.6 *nutrition*
proper fraction 27.18 *division*; 196.1 *fraction*; 194.5 *ratio*
proper gentleman 658.6 *courteous person*
properly **801.18**; 698.39 *accurately*; 801.17 *by rights*; 136.17 *capably*; 16.81 *legally*; 803.9 *virtuously*; 631.19 *well*
proper match 570.4 *marriageability*
proper motion 29.13 *luminosity*
properness **801.3**; 803.1 *virtue*
proper noun 721.8 *name*; 5.35 *part of speech*
pro persona 398.12 *by proxy*
propertied **440.8**; 763.8 *possessing*; 781.1 *wealthy*
propertied class 781.11 *the rich*
proper time 239.3 *convenience*; 287.1 *timeliness*
proper treatment 349.6 *use*
property **440.1**; 334.2 *ability*; 139.3 *characteristic*; 438.7 *equipment*; 352.4 *financial resources*; 99.4 *nature*; 763.4 *possession*; 21.21 *stage requisite*; 439.1 *store*; 345.2 *visible effect*; 781.5 *wealth*
property man **440.7**
property owner 400.1 *master*; 763.5 *possessor*; 440.7 *property man*
property-owning 763.8 *possessing*
property rights 763.1 *possession*
property roll 220.6 *list of names*
property tax 788.2 *money received*; 790.7 *tax*
prop forward 64.4 *rugby player*
prophase 34.10 *cell division*
prophecy 11.9 *divination*; 283.4 *looking to the future*; 11.1 *occultism*; 475.1 *prediction*; 719.5 *science of interpretation*
prophesy 11.23 *divine*; 283.9 *look ahead*; 475.11 *predict*
prophet 713.4 *adviser*; 11.13 *diviner*; 293.4 *early comer*; 445.5 *intuitive person*; 475.8 *oracle*; 283.5 *predictor*; 121.5 *superior*; 711.4 *warner*; 458.3 *wise man*
prophetess 475.8 *oracle*; 283.5 *predictor*
prophetic 11.17 *divinatory*; 475.13 *predicting*; 293.16 *premature*; 742.14 *signifying*
prophetically 742.18 *indicatively*; 11.25 *occultly*; 475.16 *predictively*; 293.20 *prematurely*
prophet of doom 611.3 *hopeless person*; 475.8 *oracle*
prophylactic **394.3**; 563.3 *birth control*; 347.2 *counteracting thing*; 37.4 *drug type*; 378.13 *hindering*; 257.1 *hygiene*; 257.4 *hygienic*; 359.6 *preserving*; 394.17 *remedial*; 35.25 *therapeutic*; 252.8 *tutelary*
prophylactically 359.8 *preservatively*
prophylactic psychiatry 36.2 *psychiatry*
prophylaxis 378.3 *barrier*; 35.6 *health care*; 257.1 *hygiene*; 394.3 *prophylactic*; 252.2 *protection*
propinquity 97.4 *availability*; 147.1 *nearness*; 108.1 *relatedness*
propitiate 807.5 *atone*; 748.1 *mediate*; 752.14 *offer reparation*; 10.19, 752.15 *offer worship*; 749.4 *pacify*; 609.11 *recompense*; 9.7 *worship*
propitiation 807.1 *atonement*; 10.5 *Christian rite*; 748.2 *mediation*; 752.6 *offering*; 749.1 *pacification*; 609.2 *reparation*; 9.1 *worship*
propitiator 748.3 *mediator*; 748.4 *representative*
propitiatory 807.4 *atoning*; 748.6 *mediatory*; 749.6 *pacificatory*; 752.19 *sacrificial*
propitious 756.14 *auspicious*; 392.34 *beneficial*; 610.14 *cheering*; 569.12 *favourable*; 797.1 *good*; 475.15 *presageful*; 248.8 *prosperous*; 287.6 *timely*; 235.4 *worthwhile*
propitiously 756.17 *auspiciously*; 569.20 *favourably*; 610.15 *hopefully*; 287.9 *opportunely*; 248.9 *prosperously*
propitiousness 610.4 *comfort*; 797.8 *good*; 287.1 *timeliness*
proponent 444.6 *arguer*; 714.5 *vindicator*
proportion 27.91 *add*; 108.8 *be proportionate to*; 110.9 *correlate*; 110.3 *correlation*; 27.18 *division*; 543.1 *elegance*; 119.11 *equalize*; 119.2 *equilibrium*; 196.2 *fractional part*; 209.3 *gradation*; 233.3 *incomplete thing*; 108.2 *interrelatedness*; 216.10 *make average*; 158.18 *measure*; 407.7 *method*; 205.1 *part*; 770.2 *portion*; 194.5 *ratio*; 158.1 *size*; 141.21 *space*; 162.6 *symmetrize*; 162.1 *symmetry*
proportionable 209.7 *gradational*
proportional 110.6 *correlative*; 27.74 *divisible*; 543.3 *elegant*; 196.5 *fractional*; 209.7 *gradational*; 108.5 *interrelated*; 205.11 *partial*; 141.11 *spatial*; 162.4 *symmetrical*
proportionality 110.3 *correlation*; 108.2 *interrelatedness*; 115.1 *similarity*; 162.1 *symmetry*
proportionally 110.11 *correlatively*; 209.9 *differentially*; 205.12 *partly*; 110.10 *reciprocally*; 108.10 *relevantly*; 162.7 *symmetrically*
proportional notation 18.18 *written music*
proportional representation 469.11 *franchise*; 12.1 *government*; 396.7 *type of rule*
proportional tax 790.7 *tax*
proportional taxation 13.6 *economic factors*

proportional to 27.88 *equal to*
proportionate 110.6 *correlative;* 119.6 *equal;* 205.11 *partial;* 162.4 *symmetrical*
proportionately **770.8**; 110.11 *correlatively;* 205.12 *partly;* 110.10 *reciprocally;* 108.10 *relevantly;* 162.7 *symmetrically*
proportioned 110.6 *correlative;* 162.4 *symmetrical*
proportionment 110.3 *correlation*
proportions 203.1 *quantity;* 141.1 *space*
proposable 710.9 *requesting*
proposal 713.1 *advice;* 593.6 *courtship;* 482.3 *future intention;* 752.1 *offer;* 446.3, 484.1 *plan;* 710.1 *request;* 476.1 *supposition*
propose 392.23, 713.5 *advise;* 707.17 *affirm;* 446.18 *aim;* 745.3 *aphorize;* 705.20 *doubt;* 447.10 *focus on;* 302.8 *further;* 413.14 *give moral support;* 482.7 *intend;* 752.9 *offer;* 469.4 *pick;* 484.9 *plan;* 705.22 *pop the question;* 476.6 *propound;* 4.22 *propound a philosophy;* 710.6 *request;* 701.15 *state;* 593.28 *win the love of*
propose a merger 776.3 *bargain*
propose a motion 476.6 *propound*
propose conditions 136.16 *specify*
proposed 447.7 *focused;* 701.11 *logical;* 446.12 *purposive;* 710.9 *requesting;* 476.8 *supposed*
proposed action 484.1 *plan*
proposed conduct 631.1 *conduct*
proposed line of action 484.1 *plan*
proposer 484.8 *planner;* 413.8 *supporter*
proposing 593.6 *courtship*
proposition 713.1 *advice;* 450.1 *belief;* 28.6 *law;* 701.3 *line of argument;* 27.63 *mathematical logic;* 752.1 *offer;* 4.1 *philosophy;* 484.1 *plan;* 705.1 *question;* 710.1, 710.6 *request;* 707.2 *statement;* 476.1 *supposition;* 27.65 *theory;* 447.1 *topic*
propositional 707.10 *affirmative;* 701.11 *logical;* 752.17 *offered;* 710.9 *requesting;* 476.7 *suppositional;* 27.69, 446.10 *theoretical*
propositional calculus 4.6 *branch of philosophy;* 27.63 *mathematical logic*
propound **476.6**; 713.5 *advise*
propound a philosophy **4.22**
propping up 413.1 *support*
propraetor 398.4 *deputy*
proprietarily **440.10**
proprietary 440.8 *propertied*
proprietary drug 394.2 *medicine*
proprietary name 37.3 *drug*
proprietary rights 763.1 *possession*
proprieties 656.5 *etiquette*
proprietor 400.1 *master;* 763.5 *possessor*
proprietorial 763.8 *possessing*
proprietorship 763.1 *possession*
propriety 239.3 *convenience;* 543.1, 549.1 *elegance;* 656.1 *formality;* 795.2 *good morals;* 801.3 *properness;* 255.1 *purity;* 136.1 *qualification*
prop root 77.7 *root*
Propulsion 330
propulsion **330.1**; 371.17 *expulsion;* 331.11 *impulsion;* 300.2 *momentum*
propulsive **330.17**; 334.15 *full of energy*
propulsor 330.11 *propeller*
propulsory 330.17 *propulsive*
prop up 359.5 *preserve;* 366.1 *raise;* 336.8 *strengthen;* 392.19, 413.11 *support*
propylaeum 314.6 *means of entry;* 20.9 *miscellaneous architectural features*
pro rata 205.12 *partly;* 770.8 *proportionately*
prorate 770.4 *allot*
prorogation 294.3 *delayed action*
prorogue 294.8 *delay*
prorogued 294.10 *held up*
proruption 315.1 *exit*
prosaic 620.4 *boring;* 216.3 *mediocre;* 646.1 *naive;* 271.1 *simple*
prosaically 620.8 *boringly;* 271.8 *simply*
prosaicness 620.1 *boredom*
proscenium 167.1 *front;* 21.17 *stage*
proscenium arch 21.17 *stage*
proscenium box 21.18 *auditorium*
proscenium stage 21.17 *stage*
proscribe 399.4 *censor;* 397.9 *command;* 16.79 *convict;* 128.7 *exclude;* 166.7 *limit;* 16.75 *make illegal;* 371.4 *ostracize;* 814.1 *punish;* 136.16 *specify;* 712.7 *wish ill*
proscribed 399.6 *censored;* 136.12 *conditional;* 16.64 *convicted;* 16.55 *illegal;* 712.10 *maledictive*
proscripted 166.5 *limited*
proscription 399.2 *censorship;* 397.1 *command;* 16.43 *conviction;* 128.1 *exclusion;* 16.35 *illegality;* 166.1 *limitation;* 712.4 *malediction;* 371.19 *ostracism;* 814.7 *punishment;* 136.6 *specification*
proscriptive 399.6 *censored;* 397.14 *commanding;* 136.12 *conditional*
proscriptively 397.16 *commandingly;* 399.8 *under censorship;* 136.18 *with qualification*
prose **17.5**; 271.4 *simplicity;* 17.21 *write*
prosecute 715.5 *accuse;* 340.4 *act;* 633.14 *carry on;* 16.70 *litigate*
prosecuted 715.8 *accusatory*
prosecution 715.1 *accusation;* 16.7 *legal trial;* 16.5 *litigation;* 633.1 *pursuit*
prosecutor 715.3 *accuser;* 16.8 *litigant*
prose fiction 17.2 *fiction;* 17.5 *prose*
proselyte 760.6 *convert;* 722.3 *dissertator;* 479.9 *equivocator*
proselyter 760.5 *converter*
proselytization 760.3 *persuasion*
proselytize 722.4 *dissertate;* 450.9 *make someone believe;* 760.11 *persuade;* 7.20 *preach*
proselytized 760.13 *converted;* 760.16 *influenced*
proselytizer 760.5 *converter;* 722.3 *dissertator*
proselytizing 760.3 *persuasion*
prose poetry 17.5 *prose*
prose rhythm 17.5 *prose*
prose style 17.5 *prose*
prosify 17.21 *write*
prosimian 71.34 *primate*
prosimians 71.16 *primate*
prosiness 620.1 *boredom*
prosit 558.18 *cheers!*
prosodics 729.6 *phonetics*
prosody 17.9 *metre;* 729.6 *phonetics;* 18.19 *tempo*
prosopopoeia 17.12 *poetic language*
prospect 19.10 *art subject;* 474.1 *expectation;* 448.11 *experiment;* 482.3 *future intention;* 283.4 *looking to the future;* 102.1 *possibility;* 475.1 *prediction;* 104.1 *probability;* 518.7 *view*
prospective 474.7 *expected;* 756.15 *future;* 482.11 *intending;* 102.6 *potential;* 104.6 *probable*
prospectively 102.11, 756.18 *potentially*
prospective parents 474.4 *expectant person*
prospector 449.12 *discoverer;* 356.9 *producer*
prospects 610.4 *comfort;* 474.2 *expectations;* 283.4 *looking to the future*
prospectus 220.5 *list of appointments;* 723.2 *outline;* 475.3 *plan;* 484.2 *policy*
prosper 312.9 *achieve;* 342.13 *be busy;* 222.14 *be comfortable;* 562.6 *be fertile;* 248.5 *be prosperous;* 246.6 *be successful;* 302.5 *develop;* 797.21 *do well;* 244.2 *get better;* 781.13 *get rich;* 213.4 *increase;* 765.14 *profit*
prospering 248.8 *prosperous*
Prosperity 248
prosperity **248.1**; 302.12 *advance;* 797.13 *benefit;* 222.5 *comfortable circumstances;* 244.5 *improvement;* 213.1 *increase;* 562.2 *productiveness;* 765.5 *profit;* 393.10 *revival;* 246.1 *success;* 781.5 *wealth*
prosperous **248.8**; 222.9 *comfortable;* 562.5 *fertile;* 475.15 *presageful;* 246.13 *successful;* 781.1 *wealthy;* 765.17 *well-off*
prosperously **248.9**; 222.18 *comfortably;* 765.20 *gainfully;* 246.16 *successfully;* 781.16 *wealthily*
prosperousness 248.1 *prosperity*
prosperous person **248.4**
prostaglandin 33.16 *hormone*
prostate 561.8 *organs of reproduction*
prostate cancer 260.12 *cancer*
prostate gland 561.8 *organs of reproduction*
prostatic 559.5 *of a secretion*
prosthesis 762.3 *substitute thing;* 394.12 *surgery*
prosthetic dentistry 35.4 *dentistry*
prosthetic group 33.11 *enzyme;* 33.9 *protein*
prosthetics 394.12 *surgery*
prosthodontic 35.23 *dental*
prosthodontics 35.4 *dentistry*
prosthodontist 35.14 *dentist*
prostitute **568.7**; **796.18**; 796.9 *immoral woman;* 351.1 *misuse;* 245.6 *pervert*
prostituted 796.13 *unchaste*
prostitution **796.5**; 351.2 *misuse;* 245.8 *perversion;* 776.4 *trade*
prostrate 261.6 *fatigue;* 261.1 *fatigued;* 335.12 *impotent;* 667.11 *in a respectful stance;* 155.5 *low;* 187.10 *lying;* 187.7 *make horizontal;* 77.14 *of plants;* 335.8 *overpower;* 7.15 *religious;* 367.23 *sedentary;* 260.22 *sick;* 367.8 *sit;* 388.5 *submitting;* 664.7 *sycophantic;* 9.9 *worshipful*
prostrate oneself 187.6 *be horizontal;* 155.8 *be low;* 7.19 *be religious;* 367.9 *bow;* 658.13 *defer to;* 808.5 *do penance;* 664.10 *knuckle under;* 663.6 *show obeisance to;* 667.19 *take off one's hat to;* 9.7 *worship*
prostration 367.16 *courtesy;* 357.1 *destruction;* 335.4 *disability;* 261.7 *fatigue;* 187.1 *horizontality;* 155.1 *lowness;* 667.4 *mark of respect;* 663.3 *obeisance;* 7.2 *religiousness;* 388.1 *submission;* 664.2 *sycophancy;* 260.3 *symptom;* 808.2 *type of penance;* 9.1 *worship*
prostyle 20.9 *miscellaneous architectural features*
prosy 620.4 *boring;* 270.3 *diffuse*
protagonist 21.23 *role*
protagonistic 21.39 *dramatic*
protagonistically 21.44 *dramatically*
Protagorean 4.11 *follower of a doctrine;* 4.14 *of a philosophy*
protanopia 519.2 *poor sight*
protanopic 519.9 *weak-sighted*
protasis 5.23 *phrase*
protean 227.13 *changeable*
protease 33.11 *enzyme*
protect **252.10**; **550.30**; 384.17, 586.39 *defend;* 251.11 *detain;* 251.9 *economize;* 223.15 *escort;* 46.15 *play offence;* 359.5 *preserve;* 253.10 *secure;* 336.8 *strengthen;* 392.20 *sustain;* 370.9 *welcome*
protected **550.37**; 223.20 *accompanied;* 384.30 *defended;* 758.5 *exempt;* 257.4 *hygienic;* 359.7 *preserved;* 252.6 *safe;* 253.6 *secure*
protected area 359.1 *preservation*
protected building 359.3 *preserved thing*
protected from wet 428.10 *waterproof*
protected species 359.3 *preserved thing*
protecting 359.6 *preserving;* 336.4 *strengthening;* 252.8 *tutelary*
protection **252.2**; **253.1**; 616.1 *caution;* 776.5 *commercial trade;* 347.2 *counteracting thing;* 257.1 *hygiene;* 579.3 *management;* 413.6 *moral support;* 46.9 *play;* 359.1 *preservation;* 370.2 *receptivity;* 384.2 *safeguard;* 252.1 *safety;* 252.4 *safety device;* 550.15 *shelter;* 392.4 *social assistance;* 471.5 *solicitude;* 439.4 *storage;* 336.1 *strength*
protectionism 776.5 *commercial trade;* 13.6 *economic factors;* 251.2 *economic restraint;* 85.4 *nationalism*
protectionist 251.6 *lawmaker;* 85.14 *nationalist*
protection money 790.8 *levy;* 813.8 *secret money*
protection quota 13.6 *economic factors*
protection racket 774.7 *dishonesty;* 251.2 *economic restraint;* 773.3 *taking away*
protective 384.29 *defending;* 257.4 *hygienic;* 359.6 *preserving;* 251.13 *restraining;* 253.6 *secure;* 471.9 *solicitous;* 336.13 *strengthened;* 252.8 *tutelary*
protective belt 384.6 *protective clothing*
protective clothing **384.6**; 252.4 *safety device*
protective coloration 526.5, 700.12 *disguise*
protective colouration 125.4 *camouflage*
protective colouring 384.4 *defensiveness;* 550.16 *disguise;* 521.6 *that which makes invisible*
protective covering **550.12**
protective custody 251.4 *detention;* 252.2 *protection*
protective duty 776.5 *commercial trade*
protective glasses 518.10 *visual aid*
protectively 384.32 *defensively;* 359.8 *preservatively;* 252.11 *safely;* 253.16 *surely;* 251.16 *under restraints*
protective quota 776.5 *commercial trade*
protective shoulder 58.3 *ice hockey*
protective tariff 776.5 *commercial trade;* 251.2 *economic restraint*
protect oneself 252.9 *be safe*
protector **252.3**; **384.15**; 586.14 *armed forces;* 223.7 *attendant;* 586.12 *ceremonial troops;* 586.2 *defender;* 400.3 *leader;* 579.15 *manager;* 253.3 *security officer;* 413.8 *supporter;* 711.4 *warner*
protectorate 85.3 *dominion;* 396.8 *governmental organization;* 12.5 *political organization;* 763.4 *possession;* 252.2 *protection;* 86.4 *territorial division*
protectress 252.3 *protector*
protect the ball 64.5 *play rugby*
protect the interests of 384.22 *plead for*
protégé 387.4 *dependent*
protein **33.9**; 557.11 *food content;* 34.12 *molecular biology*
protein diet 557.6 *nutrition*
protein-rich 557.27 *edible*
protein sequencing 34.12 *molecular biology*
protein structure 34.12 *molecular biology;* 33.9 *protein*
protein synthesis 34.13 *genetic material*
pro tem 282.7 *occasional*
proteoglycan 33.9 *protein*
proteolysis 33.11 *enzyme*
proteolytic enzyme 33.11 *enzyme*
Protest 753
protest **703.19**; **753.1**; **753.6**; 637.6 *be unwilling;* 586.39 *defend;* 661.5 *defy;* 118.2 *dissent;* 481.6 *dissuasion;* 703.6 *mass demonstration;* 786.1 *nonpayment;* 118.18 *not conform;* 113.18 *object;* 113.4 *objection;* 342.14 *push;* 708.11 *rebut;* 708.3 *rebuttal;* 383.6 *resist;* 383.1 *resistance;* 670.9 *show of disapproval;* 637.11 *unwillingness;* 711.5 *warn;* 711.1 *warning*
protest a bill 786.8 *stop payment*
protest against 481.1 *dissuade;* 113.14 *oppose*
Protestant 7.5 *Christian;* 7.16 *denominational*
protestant 708.17 *negative;* 708.9 *negativist;* 662.6 *nonconformist;* 753.4 *protester;* 753.9 *protesting*
protestation 753.1 *protest*
protested bill 786.3 *bad payment*
protester **662.7**; **703.8**; **753.4**; 118.8, 751.4 *dissenter;* 708.9 *negativist;* 113.11 *opposer;* 637.16 *reluctant person*
protesting **753.9**; 703.14 *demonstrating;* 670.26 *disagreeing;* 709.9 *dissenting;* 637.5 *reluctant;* 383.10 *resistant;* 711.8 *warning*
protestingly 383.14 *resistingly*
protest march 753.3 *gesture of protest;* 703.6 *mass demonstration*
protest meeting 753.3 *gesture of protest;* 376.4 *rally*
protestor 661.4 *defiant person*
protest sign 742.1 *sign*
protest song 753.3 *gesture of protest*
Proteus 114.2 *assortment;* 227.3 *changeable thing*
prothalamion 17.7 *poem*
prothalamium 570.6 *general terms*
prothallus 82.2 *fern plant*
prothesis 129.7 *prefix*
protist 75.1 *invertebrate;* 34.3 *organism;* 70.4 *type of animal*
protochordate **75.2**; 75.1, 75.16 *invertebrate*
protocol 40.19 *computing terms;* 40.14 *data transfer;* 553.4 *design;* 549.3, 656.5 *etiquette;* 160.11 *formal;* 160.5, 656.1 *formality;* 631.2 *good conduct;* 658.2 *good manners;* 632.5 *tradition*
protohistoric 3.15 *historic;* 284.17 *past*
protohistorical 3.16 *historical*
protohistorically 3.24 *historically*
protohistory 3.10 *past age;* 284.1 *past time*
protohuman 296.7 *ancient people*
Proto-Indo-European 5.11 *family of languages*
proto-martyr 752.7 *martyr*
protomer 33.9 *protein*
proton 28.65 *atom;* 28.50 *electric charge;* 28.77 *elementary particle;* 159.2 *little thing;* 402.4 *matter*
protonema 84.3 *plant body*
protonic 32.36 *acid*
protonic acid 32.8 *acid*
proton mass 28.97 *fundamental constant*
proton number 28.69 *isotope*
proton synchrotron 28.94 *particle accelerator*
protoplasm 34.7 *cell;* 554.2 *living matter;* 402.4 *matter;* 130.3 *source*
protoplasmatic 554.14 *biotic*

protoplasmic 554.14 *biotic;* 34.23 *cellular*
protoplast 34.7 *cell*
protoplastic 554.14 *biotic*
protostar 29.11 *stellar birth*
Prototheria 71.3 *egg-laying mammal*
prototherian 71.3 *egg-laying mammal;* 71.25 *mammalian*
prototypal 126.4 *original*
prototype **160.2**; 446.6 *ideal;* 475.4 *model;* 126.2 *original;* 484.6 *outline;* 129.4, 140.5 *precedent;* 243.10 *preparations;* 26.7 *standard*
prototypical **160.10**; 446.13 *ideal*
prototypically 160.13 *formatively*
Protozoa 554.9 *classifications of life;* 75.9 *protozoan*
protozoal disease **75.12**
protozoan **75.9**; **75.23**; 75.1, 75.16 *invertebrate;* 159.7 *little;* 159.2 *little thing;* 75.10 *parasite;* 70.4 *type of animal*
protozoic 75.23 *protozoan*
protozoological 75.23 *protozoan*
protozoologist 75.15 *invertebrate zoologist;* 70.11 *zoologist*
protozoology 70.9 *animal science;* 75.14 *invertebrate zoology*
protract **134.4**; 270.5 *be diffuse;* 378.9 *block;* 294.8 *delay;* 148.10 *lengthen*
protracted **134.6**; 270.3 *diffuse;* 294.10 *held up;* 148.1 *long*
protractedly 134.7 *continually;* 294.15 *late*
protraction **134.2**; 294.3 *delayed action;* 270.1 *diffuseness;* 213.1 *increase;* 148.4 *length*
protractor 176.4 *angular measurement;* 27.49 *geometric construction;* 26.6 *measuring instrument*
protreptic 480.19 *persuasive*
protruberance 361.2 *projection*
protrude **185.8**; 182.5 *be convex;* 315.10 *emerge*
protrudent 185.5 *protuberant*
protruding 182.4 *convex*
protrusion 182.1 *convexity;* 185.3 *protuberance*
protuberance **185.3**; 182.1 *convexity;* 404.3 *nap*
protuberant **185.5**
protuberantly **185.10**; 182.6 *convexly*
proturan 76.10 *insectan*
proud **622.14**; 660.16 *arrogant;* 673.13 *boastful;* 656.6 *formal;* 185.5 *protuberant*
proud as a peacock 622.14 *proud*
proud bearing 622.5 *stateliness*
proud-looking 622.14 *proud*
proudly **622.32**; 660.33 *arrogantly;* 673.23 *boastfully;* 185.11 *eminently*
proudness 622.1 *pride*
proud person **622.13**
proudspirited 622.14 *proud*
provability 703.5 *demonstrability*
provable 703.12 *demonstrable;* 93.13 *real*
prove **454.2**; **703.17**; **716.12**; 707.19 *confirm;* 95.12 *establish reality;* 448.11 *experiment;* 714.8 *justify;* 452.21 *make certain;* 701.15 *state;* 27.89 *theorize*
prove acceptable 217.4 *suffice*
prove adequate 217.4 *suffice*
prove a fiasco 247.8 *miscarry*
proved **698.20**; 452.1 *certain;* 716.8 *evidential;* 455.10 *known;* 454.8 *verifiable*
proved guilty 806.5 *guilty*
prove false **800.9**
prove fruitful 756.10 *show potential*
prove guilty 16.79 *convict*
prove helpful 237.9 *be useful*
prove infertile 563.7 *be infertile*
prove innocent 16.78 *acquit*
prove itself 239.6 *be convenient*
proven **703.13**; 698.20 *proved*
provenance 130.3 *source*
provender 557.8 *animal food;* 557.7 *food;* 436.2 *provisions*
proven fact 273.3 *accurate thing*
proven way 631.7 *way*
prove one's point 95.12 *establish reality;* 703.17 *prove*
proverb 745.3 *aphorize;* 5.21 *catchword;* 745.1 *maxim;* 795.7 *moral;* 698.4 *truism*
proverbial **745.2**; 698.17 *truistic;* 5.42 *worded*
proverbialist 5.2 *linguist*
proverbially **745.4**; 5.51 *phraseologically;* 4.25 *theoretically*
prove real 698.30 *prove true*
prove the contrary 704.8 *refute*
prove the truth of 714.8 *justify*
prove too much for 121.8 *be superior*
prove true **698.30**
provide 243.5 *equip;* 352.6 *find means;* 768.5 *give;* 750.30 *grant;* 359.5 *preserve;* 356.10 *produce;* 436.5 *provision;* 439.6 *store;* 752.11 *volunteer*
provide a background 108.7 *relate to*
provide a benefit 569.16 *be favourable*
provide a chance 287.4 *be timely*
provide aid 650.9 *be charitable*
provide a living for 554.20 *support life*
provide an alibi for 252.10 *protect*
provide an opportunity 752.9 *offer*
provide a role model 631.11 *conduct oneself*
provide a sweetener 785.11 *remunerate*
provide collateral 772.7 *borrow*
provided 436.8 *provisional*
provide drink **558.15**
provided that 222.15 *under the circumstances*
provide firepower 243.5 *equip*
provide food **557.25**
provide for 768.5 *give;* 436.5 *provision;* 217.4 *suffice;* 413.13 *support financially;* 554.20 *support life;* 392.20 *sustain*
provide for oneself 436.5 *provision*
provide money 781.15 *make rich*
provide more oxygen 581.1 *refresh*
Providence 8.3 *God*
providence 616.1 *caution;* 107.2 *luck;* 287.1 *timeliness*
provide needed funds 650.9 *be charitable*
provide no enjoyment 620.6 *be boring*
provident 616.4 *cautious*
providential 8.13 *divine;* 292.14 *seasonable;* 287.6 *timely*
providentiality 287.1 *timeliness*
providentially 8.19 *divinely;* 287.9 *opportunely*
providently 616.7 *cautiously*
provide on-the-job training 15.11 *conduct industrial relations*
provide passage for **308.21**
provider **436.3**; 768.4 *giver;* 243.15 *preparer*
provide shade 79.19 *grow*
provide the basis 243.2 *do the groundwork*
provide the means 392.29 *finance*
provide the wherewithal 352.6 *find means*
provide with arms 243.5 *equip*
provide with teeth 243.5 *equip*
providing 436.1 *provision;* 436.7 *provisioning*
providing passage **308.15**
province 85.3 *dominion;* 396.8 *governmental organization;* 12.5 *political organization;* 7.9 *priesthood;* 86.14 *sphere;* 86.5 *state;* 6.3 *subject*
provinces 86.6 *regions*
provincial 574.3 *common;* 117.14 *conformist;* 564.5 *countryman;* 86.18 *local;* 646.3 *naive person;* 86.17 *national;* 564.12 *native;* 465.8 *unjust*
provincialism 5.26 *dialect;* 465.3 *injustice;* 86.15 *regionalism*
provincially 86.20 *nationally*
provincial newspaper 741.5 *mass communication*
provincial paper 740.4 *newspaper*
proving 454.5 *proof*
proving ground 448.6 *place of experimentation*
provirus 34.3 *organism*
provision **436.1**; **436.5**; 746.2 *basis for negotiations;* 136.7 *condition;* 413.7 *financial support;* 243.11 *fitting out;* 780.6 *funds;* 768.1 *giving;* 750.9 *grant;* 359.1 *preservation;* 359.5 *preserve;* 252.2 *protection;* 557.25 *provide food;* 135.1 *requirement;* 393.9 *restoration;* 439.1, 439.6 *store;* 392.3 *sustenance*
Provisional 662.10 *seditionist*
provisional **436.8**; 222.7 *circumstantial;* 136.12 *conditional;* 448.8 *experimental;* 478.1 *improvised;* 231.2 *incomplete;* 746.8 *negotiated;* 282.7 *occasional;* 243.16 *preparatory;* 762.7 *substitute;* 217.1 *sufficient;* 453.1 *uncertain;* 349.9 *used*
provisionally 221.9 *conditionally;* 448.14 *experimentally;* 746.9 *feasibly;* 282.10 *for the present;* 762.9 *instead;* 243.23 *preparatorily;* 222.16 *relatively;* 136.18 *with qualification*
provisioner 243.15 *preparer;* 778.13 *retailer*
provisioning **436.7**; 25.1 *cookery;* 243.11 *fitting out;* 436.1 *provision*
provision merchant 436.3 *provider;* 778.13 *retailer*
provision oneself 436.5 *provision*
Provisions **436**
provisions **436.2**; 211.4 *extra;* 557.7 *food;* 352.2 *supplies*
proviso 746.2 *basis for negotiations;* 136.7 *condition;* 135.1 *requirement*
provisory 136.12 *conditional;* 746.8 *negotiated*
Provo 662.10 *seditionist*
provocation 607.2 *annoyance;* 344.1 *cause;* 624.3 *cause of offence;* 483.2 *inducement*
provocative 381.21 *aggressive;* 661.8 *defying;* 751.9 *disagreeing;* 701.9 *hostile;* 796.12 *indecent;* 617.11 *lustful;* 483.11 *motivational;* 480.19 *persuasive;* 675.9 *ribald;* 496.10 *stimulating*
provocatively 701.17 *argumentatively;* 707.25 *explicitly;* 661.10 *in defiance;* 751.11 *in disagreement;* 483.14 *influentially;* 617.20 *lustfully;* 480.21 *persuasively;* 496.16 *stimulatingly*
provocativeness 661.1 *defiance;* 751.1 *disagreement*
provoke 130.20 *activate;* 607.8 *annoy;* 660.25, 706.18 *answer back;* 344.10 *awaken;* 496.13 *be piquant;* 661.5 *defy;* 751.5 *disagree;* 483.9 *motivate;* 624.9 *offend;* 751.7 *pick a fight*
provoke action 711.5 *warn*
provoke an engagement 585.14 *battle*
provoked 483.12 *motivated;* 624.15 *resentful*
provoke thought 726.6 *emphasize*
provoking 607.5 *aggravating;* 483.11 *motivational*
provost 400.9 *educational leader;* 396.10 *person of authority;* 400.6 *religious leader*
provost general 16.10 *law officer*
provost marshal 16.17 *police officer*
prow 167.1 *front;* 50.3 *parts of a sailing boat;* 62.5 *rock face*
prowess 613.8 *courageous act;* 613.2 *heroism;* 485.1 *skill*
prowl after 633.9 *follow*
prowl car 320.17 *police car*
prowler 774.8 *thief*
proximal 147.9 *near*
proximate 147.9 *near;* 289.12 *succeeding*
proximity 97.4 *availability;* 280.2 *closeness;* 147.1, 239.4 *nearness*
proxy 746.7 *act as a go-between;* 578.3 *agent;* 398.5 *alternative;* 717.8 *representative;* 762.7 *substitute;* 762.2 *substitute person;* 550.21 *substitution*
Prozac™ 394.8 *drug*
PR person 740.10 *publicizer*
PR representative 719.7 *news interpreter*
prude **255.6**; 117.6 *conformist;* 670.11 *disapprover;* 795.6 *moralist*
prudence 616.1 *caution;* 665.3 *circumspection;* 239.3 *convenience;* 684.2 *moderation;* 680.1 *thrift;* 803.2 *virtues;* 458.1 *wisdom*
prudent 713.8 *advisable;* 665.9 *careful;* 616.4 *cautious;* 239.1 *convenient;* 803.6 *ethical;* 684.9 *moderate;* 680.4 *thrifty;* 458.5 *wise*
prudently 713.9 *advisably;* 616.7 *cautiously;* 680.7 *economically;* 803.10 *ethically;* 684.12 *moderately;* 458.9 *wisely*
prudery 117.4 *conventionalism;* 255.1 *purity;* 795.4 *self-righteousness;* 647.3 *unadornment*
prudish 674.10 *bashful;* 117.14 *conformist;* 795.10 *moralistic;* 255.12 *morally pure;* 647.10 *unadorned*
prudishly 647.12 *plainly;* 255.18 *virtuously*
prudishness 674.3 *bashfulness;* 255.1 *purity;* 795.4 *self-righteousness*
prune 44.15 *cultivate;* 369.12 *displace;* 191.5, 214.5 *make smaller;* 79.18 *manage trees;* 25.42 *preserve;* 206.8 *reduce;* 372.10 *set apart;* 149.10 *shorten;* 212.4 *take off;* 425.16 *use a sharp tool*
pruned 44.19 *ornamental;* 149.8, 723.7 *shortened;* 191.7 *smaller*
pruner 44.6 *garden tool;* 425.9 *sharp-edged thing*
pruning 191.1 *contraction;* 369.2 *displacement;* 44.5 *gardening;* 723.2 *outline;* 149.2 *shortening;* 79.6 *tree management*
pruning saw 438.3 *garden tool*
pruning shears 425.9 *sharp-edged thing*
prurience 593.5 *desire;* 796.2 *indecency;* 258.3 *obscenity;* 644.2 *prying*
prurient 796.12 *indecent;* 258.9 *obscene;* 644.6 *prying*
pruriently 258.12 *dirtily;* 644.9 *officiously*
prurigo 260.13 *skin disease*
pruritis 260.13 *skin disease*
pruritus 327.5 *restlessness*
prusik 62.9 *mountaineer*
prusiking 62.3 *climbing technique;* 62.8 *mountaineering*
Prussian blue 539.5 *blueness*
PR woman 740.10 *publicizer*
pry 644.7 *be curious;* 342.17 *meddle;* 644.4 *meddler;* 705.17 *question*
prying **644.2**; **644.6**; 705.8 *curiosity;* 342.21 *meddling;* 518.3 *observation;* 705.12 *questioning*
prying person 342.11 *meddler*
PS 211.3 *additional item*
psalm 10.8 *hymn;* 17.7 *poem;* 18.5 *sacred music;* 516.2 *song*
psalmic 18.32 *instrumental*
psalmist 516.5 *melodist;* 18.24 *musician*
psalmodic 18.32 *instrumental*
psalmody 10.8 *hymn;* 18.5 *sacred music*
psalm-singing 10.8 *hymn;* 10.3 *rite of worship;* 9.1 *worship*
psalter 10.8 *hymn*
psephological 210.13 *calculative;* 469.16 *elective*
psephologist 469.13 *electorate;* 210.7 *mathematician*
psephology 469.12 *election;* 210.2 *statistics*
psephomancer 11.13 *diviner*
psephomancy 11.9 *divination*
pseud 700.15 *deceiver;* 699.12 *fake;* 699.17 *false person*
pseudo 96.12 *artificial;* 699.12 *fake;* 702.10 *hypocritical;* 125.13 *imitation;* 115.8 *simulated*
pseudoaromatic 32.7 *chemical compound;* 32.35 *combined*
pseudocoelomate 75.16 *invertebrate*
pseudolanguage 40.9 *programming language*
pseudologist 699.18 *liar*
pseudologue 700.16 *liar*
pseudology 699.6 *lying*
pseudonym 737.8 *anonymity;* 736.7 *concealer;* 721.8 *name*
pseudonymity 721.7 *nomenclature*
pseudoparenchymatous 84.7 *algal*
pseudopsychological 11.16 *psychic*
pseudopsychology 11.1 *occultism*
pseudo-scorpion 76.2 *arachnid*
pseudostatement 17.12 *poetic language*
pseudosyllogism 702.2 *sophism*
pseudosyllogistic 702.7 *sophistic*
psi faculty 11.8 *psychic power*
psittaciform 72.21 *avian*
psittacine 72.21 *avian*
psittacosis 260.18 *veterinary disease*
psocopteran 76.10 *insectan*
psychalgia 36.12 *stress*
psyche **36.21**; 139.11 *identity;* 101.6 *internal world;* 139.2 *personality;* 11.7 *spirit*
psychedelic 691.9 *addictive;* 37.17 *stimulating*
psychedelically 691.11 *in a trance*
psychedelic drug 37.4 *drug type*
psyched up 243.18 *prepared*
psychiatric 36.32 *psychological*
psychiatrically 36.39 *psychologically*
psychiatric care 36.3 *psychiatric treatment;* 461.9 *treatment*
psychiatric hospital **36.31**; 461.8 *mental hospital*
psychiatric social worker 36.30 *psychiatrist*
psychiatric treatment **36.3**
psychiatric unit 461.8 *mental hospital;* 36.31 *psychiatric hospital*
psychiatric ward 461.8 *mental hospital;* 36.31 *psychiatric hospital*
psychiatrist **36.30**; **461.10**; 713.4 *adviser;* 35.11 *doctor;* 394.15 *healer;* 36.29 *psychologist;* 393.12 *repairer*

psychiatry 36.2; 35.3 *medical specialty*; 394.13 *therapy*
psychic 11.16; 101.7 *believer in a nonmaterial world*; 11.13 *diviner*; 101.8 *nonmaterial*; 11.12 *occultist*; 101.9 *parapsychological*
psychical 101.8 *nonmaterial*; 11.16 *psychic*
psychically 101.13 *metaphysically*; 11.25 *occultly*
psychic apparatus 36.21 *psyche*
psychic determinism 36.1 *psychology*
psychic energy 36.22 *libido*
psychicist 11.12 *occultist*
psychic phenomena 101.4 *parapsychology*
psychic phenomenon 11.10
psychic power 11.8
psychic research 11.1 *occultism*; 101.4 *parapsychology*
psychics 11.1 *occultism*
psychism 11.1 *occultism*
psychist 11.12 *occultist*
psycho 36.8 *disordered personality*; 461.7 *insane person*; 382.11 *murderer*
psychoacoustics 36.1 *psychology*
psychoanalyse 101.12 *enter a nonmaterial world*; 36.38 *psychologize*
psychoanalysis 101.6 *internal world*; 36.3 *psychiatric treatment*; 36.1 *psychology*; 394.13 *therapy*; 461.9 *treatment*
psychoanalyst 713.4 *adviser*; 101.7 *believer in a nonmaterial world*; 394.15 *healer*; 461.10 *psychiatrist*; 36.29 *psychologist*; 393.12 *repairer*
psychoanalytic 101.11 *internal*
psychoanalytical 36.32 *psychological*
psychoanalytically 101.14 *subjectively*
psychoanalytic method 36.3 *psychiatric treatment*
psychoanalytic theory 36.1 *psychology*
psychobabble 729.1 *faculty of speech*; 5.20 *jargon word*; 5.5 *nonstandard language*; 139.10 *specialized language*
psychobiochemistry 36.1 *psychology*
psychobiological 36.32 *psychological*
psychobiologist 36.29 *psychologist*
psychobiology 36.1 *psychology*
psychocatharsis 36.3 *psychiatric treatment*
psychochemist 36.29 *psychologist*
psychodiagnosis 36.2 *psychiatry*
psychodiagnostic 36.32 *psychological*
psychodiagnostics 36.2 *psychiatry*
psychodrama 21.2 *play*; 36.3 *psychiatric treatment*
psychodynamics 36.1 *psychology*
psychogalvanic response 36.4 *psychometrics*
psychogalvanic skin response 36.4 *psychometrics*
psychogalvanometer 36.4 *psychometrics*
psychogenesis 36.1 *psychology*
psychogenetic 36.32 *psychological*
psychogenetics 36.1 *psychology*
psychogenic 36.32 *psychological*
psychogenic disorder 36.9 *psychological disorder*
psychogeriatric 36.32 *psychological*
psychogeriatrician 36.30 *psychiatrist*
psychogeriatrics 36.2 *psychiatry*
psychognosis 36.1 *psychology*
psychogogy 36.20 *conditioning*
psychogram 36.4 *psychometrics*
psychographer 36.29 *psychologist*
psychographist 11.12 *occultist*
psychography 11.1 *occultism*; 36.1 *psychology*; 36.4 *psychometrics*
psychokinesis 11.1 *occultism*; 101.4 *parapsychology*; 36.1 *psychology*
psychokinetic 101.9 *parapsychological*; 11.16 *psychic*
psycholinguist 5.2 *linguist*
psycholinguistics 5.1 *linguistics*; 36.1 *psychology*
psycholingustic 5.38 *linguistic*
psychological 36.32; 1.11 *anthropological*; 442.9 *mental*
psychological counselling 36.3 *psychiatric treatment*
psychological cure 393.11 *recuperation*
psychological disorder 36.9
psychological drama 21.2 *play*
psychologically 36.39
psychologically disturbed 36.36
psychological me 36.21 *psyche*
psychological medicine 36.2 *psychiatry*
psychological novel 17.2 *fiction*
psychological screening 36.4 *psychometrics*
psychological stress 36.12 *stress*
psychological test 36.5
psychological thriller 17.2 *fiction*
psychological time 275.1 *time*
psychological warfare 612.4 *intimidation*; 36.1 *psychology*; 585.1 *war*; 585.8 *warfare*
psychologism 36.1 *psychology*
psychologist 36.29
psychologize 36.38
psychologue 36.29 *psychologist*
psychology 36.1; 631.1 *conduct*; 394.13 *therapy*
Psychology and Psychiatry 36
psychomancer 11.13 *diviner*
psychomancy 11.9 *divination*
psychometer 11.12 *occultist*; 36.4 *psychometrics*
psychometric 26.16 *micrometric*; 36.32 *psychological*
psychometrics 36.4; 36.1 *psychology*
psychometrist 11.12 *occultist*
psychometry 26.2 *micrometry*; 11.8 *psychic power*; 36.1 *psychology*; 36.4 *psychometrics*
psych oneself up 243.8 *prepare oneself*
psychoneurological 36.32 *psychological*
psychoneurosis 461.6 *mental breakdown*; 36.10 *neurosis*; 36.1 *psychology*
psychoneurotic 36.8 *disordered personality*
psychopath 36.8 *disordered personality*; 461.7 *insane person*; 382.11 *murderer*; 380.4 *violent creature*
psychopathia martialis 36.10 *neurosis*
psychopathic 461.13 *mentally ill*; 382.24 *murderous*; 36.36 *psychologically disturbed*
psychopathic killer 382.11 *murderer*
psychopathic personality 36.8 *disordered personality*
psychopathological 36.32 *psychological*
psychopathologist 36.29 *psychologist*
psychopathology 36.1 *psychology*
psychopathy 36.11, 461.5 *psychosis*
psychopharmacological 36.32 *psychological*
psychopharmacology 36.1 *psychology*
psychophysical 36.32 *psychological*
psychophysicist 36.29 *psychologist*
psychophysics 36.1 *psychology*
psychophysiologist 36.29 *psychologist*
psychophysiology 36.1 *psychology*
psychorrhagy 11.1 *occultism*
psychosensory 11.16 *psychic*
psychosexual 36.32 *psychological*
psychosexual development 36.1 *psychology*
psychosexuality 36.1 *psychology*
psychosis 36.11; **461.5**; 36.9 *psychological disorder*
psychosocial 36.32 *psychological*
psychosocial medicine 36.2 *psychiatry*
psychosociologist 36.29 *psychologist*
psychosociology 36.1 *psychology*
psychosomatic 260.23 *diseased*; 36.32 *psychological*
psychosomatic medicine 36.2 *psychiatry*
psychosomatics 36.1 *psychology*
psychosophical 11.16 *psychic*
psychosophy 11.1 *occultism*
psychosurgery 36.3 *psychiatric treatment*; 35.9 *surgery*
psychotechnical 36.32 *psychological*
psychotechnics 36.1 *psychology*
psychotechnologist 36.29 *psychologist*
psychotechnology 36.1 *psychology*
psychotherapeutic 36.32 *psychological*
psychotherapeutics 36.3 *psychiatric treatment*
psychotherapeutist 36.30 *psychiatrist*
psychotherapist 713.4 *adviser*; 394.15 *healer*; 36.30, 461.10 *psychiatrist*; 36.29 *psychologist*; 393.12 *repairer*
psychotherapy 36.3 *psychiatric treatment*; 393.11 *recuperation*; 394.13 *therapy*; 461.9 *treatment*
psychotic 328.16 *deranged*; 36.8 *disordered personality*; 461.7 *insane person*; 461.13 *mentally ill*; 36.36 *psychologically disturbed*
psychotically 328.19 *distractedly*; 461.17 *insanely*
psychotic personality 36.8 *disordered personality*
psychotropic drug 36.3 *psychiatric treatment*
psychrometer 433.19 *measuring instrument*; 31.7 *weather instruments*
psychrometric 31.42 *barometric*
psych up 338.3 *invigorate*
PT 576.5 *exercise*; 6.3 *subject*
P. T. Barnum 740.8 *public relations*
PT boat 586.24 *warship*
Pteraspis 74.4 *fossil fish*
pteridological 82.5 *fernlike*
pteridologist 82.2 *fern plant*; 77.12 *plant scientist*
pteridology 82.2 *fern plant*; 77.10 *plant science*
Pteridophyta 77.4 *lower plant*
pteridophyte 82.1 *fern*; 82.5 *fernlike*; 77.4 *lower plant*
pteridophytes 554.9 *classifications of life*
pteridophytic 82.5 *fernlike*
pteridophytous 82.5 *fernlike*
pteridosperm 82.1 *fern*
pterodactyl 296.8 *prehistoric animal*
pterosaur 73.6 *extinct reptile*
pteryla 72.17 *plumage*
PTFE 435.1 *materials*; 32.21 *polymer*
Ptolemaic universe 29.4 *cosmological model*
ptomaine poisoning 260.8 *indigestion*; 260.6 *infection*
ptyalism 560.9 *saliva*
p-type conductivity 28.44, 39.4 *semiconductor*
p-type semiconductor 28.44, 39.4 *semiconductor*
pub 565.10 *hotel*; 654.4 *meeting place*
pub circuit 21.15 *engagement*
pub-crawl 690.14 *drinking bout*; 690.8 *get drunk*
pub-crawler 690.17 *drunkard*
pub-crawling 690.5 *drunken*
puberty 561.4 *development*; 243.14 *preparedness*; 555.1 *youth*
pubescence 555.1 *youth*
pubescent 555.11 *young*
public 776.19 *corporate*; 12.9 *governmental*; 566.9 *group*; 654.7 *human society*; 564.2 *inhabitants*; 764.5 *jointly possessing*; 455.10 *known*; 738.14 *manifest*; 566.13 *national*; 308.13 *opened up*; 138.19 *prevailing*; 740.19 *published*; 654.15 *sociable*; 87.14 *urban*; 520.1 *visible*
public-address system 504.9 *audio device*; 740.1 *publication*; 507.4 *sound maker*; 28.18 *source of sound*
public affairs 12.2 *politics*
publican 436.4 *caterer*
public assistance 392.4 *social assistance*
Publication 740
publication 740.1; 525.1 *appearance*; 693.2 *communication*; 703.1 *demonstration*; 377.1 *dispersion*; 739.2 *divulgence*; 738.10 *manifestation*; 475.3 *plan*; 6.14 *school book*; 711.1 *warning*; 742.6 *word*
public baths 256.6 *bath*
public benefit 237.8 *benefit*
public broadcasting 692.24 *television broadcasting*
public building 38.20 *building*
public comment 740.3 *journalism*
public company 776.7 *company*; 764.1 *joint possession*
public convenience 560.13 *lavatory*; 767.7 *toilet*
public corporation 764.1 *joint possession*
public debt 13.4 *economic development*
public discussion 740.7 *publicity*
public domain 764.1 *joint possession*
public enemy 594.8 *hated person*
public enterprise 13.1 *economics*
public entertainer 21.29 *entertainer*
public expenditure 13.6 *economic factors*
public eye 740.7 *publicity*
public file 744.1 *record*
public forum 740.7 *publicity*
public garden 44.2 *garden*
public good 237.8 *benefit*
public hall 654.4 *meeting place*
public-health inspector 257.3 *hygienist*
public-health medicine 35.6 *health care*; 35.1 *medicine*
public-health physician 35.11 *doctor*
public house 558.11 *drink provider*
public image 525.5 *impression*
public information officer 719.7 *news interpreter*
public inquiry 713.4 *adviser*
publicist 738.12 *displayer*; 722.3 *dissertator*; 550.18 *fixer*; 693.9 *informant*; 483.7 *motivator*; 480.12 *persuader*; 740.10 *publicizer*; 748.4 *representative*
publicity 740.7; 480.6 *advertising*; 520.4 *clarity*; 550.20 *fixing*; 738.10 *manifestation*; 693.4 *mass communication*; 480.5 *propaganda*
publicity agent 693.9 *informant*; 480.12 *persuader*; 740.10 *publicizer*
publicity man 21.27 *producer*
publicity manager 21.27 *producer*
publicity woman 21.27 *producer*
publicize 740.16; 693.12 *communicate*; 739.6 *divulge*; 550.33 *fix*; 123.8 *make important*; 741.13 *report*; 738.3 *reveal*
publicized 703.9 *demonstrated*; 738.13 *displayed*
publicizer 740.10; 739.4 *discloser*; 738.12 *displayer*; 722.3 *dissertator*; 693.9 *informant*; 719.7 *news interpreter*; 480.12 *persuader*
public-key cryptography 737.4 *brainteaser*
public knowledge 740.7 *publicity*
public land 764.1 *joint possession*
Public Lending Right 740.6 *book publishing*
public limited company 776.7 *company*; 13.7 *corporation*
publicly 740.22; 703.20, 738.16 *manifestly*; 87.16 *municipally*; 308.25 *obviously*
public money 780.19 *treasury*
publicness 740.7 *publicity*
public notice 740.1 *publication*
public nuisance 594.8 *hated person*
public office holder 401.2 *public servant*
public official 401.2 *public servant*
public opinion 12.1 *government*; 395.6 *group influence*; 464.1 *judgment*; 16.18 *tribunal*
public opinion poll 469.10 *vote*
public ownership 13.1 *economics*; 764.1 *joint possession*
public persona 171.3 *appearance*; 525.5 *impression*
public property 440.1 *property*
public prosecutor 715.3 *accuser*; 464.6 *justice*; 16.10 *law officer*
public provision 392.4 *social assistance*
public purse 780.19 *treasury*
public recognition 740.7 *publicity*; 813.1 *reward*
public record 3.5 *chronicle*; 744.1 *record*
public relations 740.8; 480.6 *advertising*; 579.3 *management*; 741.1 *news*
public relations man 707.9 *affirmer*; 398.4 *deputy*; 738.12 *displayer*; 550.18 *fixer*; 719.7 *news interpreter*
public relations officer 693.9 *informant*; 480.12 *persuader*; 740.10 *publicizer*; 748.4 *representative*
public relations person 483.7 *motivator*
public relations practitioner 741.4 *journalist*
public relations release 707.2 *statement*
public sale 778.4 *sale*
public school 6.12 *educational institution*
public sector 776.5 *commercial trade*; 13.1 *economics*; 13.2 *economy*; 15.10 *unionized*
public sector borrowing 784.2 *national debt*
public sector borrowing requirement 784.2 *national debt*
public sector union 15.3 *organized labour*
public servant 401.2; 579.16 *official*; 752.8 *volunteer*
public service announcement 692.25 *broadcast material*
public speaker 733.6; 729.10 *speaker*
public speech 733.1 *address*
public spirit 652.2 *public spiritedness*
public spirited 652.6 *philanthropic*
public spiritedness 652.2
public telephone 692.12 *public telephone system*; 692.9 *telephone*
public telephone system 692.12

public transport 316.5 *means of transport*
public utilities 13.1 *economics*
public utility 237.8 *benefit*
public warning 711.1 *warning*
public weal 797.13 *benefit*
public welfare 768.2 *gift*; 650.3 *welfare*
public worship 10.4
publish 740.15; 693.12 *communicate*; 703.15 *demonstrate*; 738.1 *display*; 377.16 *distribute*; 739.6 *divulge*; 525.14 *present*; 740.14 *proclaim*; 741.13 *report*; 738.3 *reveal*; 742.12 *signal*
publishable 795.10 *moralistic*
published 740.19; 703.9 *demonstrated*; 738.13 *displayed*; 377.22 *distributed*
publisher 740.12; 693.9 *informant*; 742.8 *signer*
publisher's catalogue 220.2 *table*
publish freely 250.14 *be free*
publishing 740.21; 740.6 *book publishing*; 740.1 *publication*; 561.1 *reproduction*; 742.16 *signalling*
publishing contract 755.2 *purchase contract*
publish the banns 570.15 *marry*; 593.28 *win the love of*
pub sign 743.3 *means of identification*
pub theatre 21.1 *drama*
puce 534.1 *brown*; 540.6 *purple*
Puck 700.15 *deceiver*; 11.11 *ghost*
puck 330.10 *ball*; 58.3 *ice hockey*
puck-carrier 58.4 *ice hockey player*
pucker 191.6 *become smaller*; 191.5 *make smaller*; 184.3, 184.10 *pleat*; 184.1, 184.8 *wrinkle*
puckered 191.7 *smaller*; 184.6 *wrinkly*
puckered up 191.7 *smaller*
puckering 191.8 *contracting*; 191.1 *contraction*
puckering up 191.1 *contraction*
pucker up 191.6 *become smaller*; 191.5 *make smaller*
puckish 236.5 *harmful*
puck possession 58.3 *ice hockey*
pud 25.9 *dish*
pudding 25.35, 498.3 *dessert*; 25.9 *dish*; 557.14 *mouthful*
pudding basin 25.6 *kitchen equipment*
puddle 157.4 *shallow thing*
puddle in 44.15 *cultivate*
pudency 795.3 *moral purity*; 255.1 *purity*
pudenda 561.8 *organs of reproduction*
pudgy 419.4 *compressible*
puerile 459.5 *foolish*; 124.4 *trivial*; 457.6 *unintelligent*
puerilely 457.11 *unintelligently*
puerility 459.1 *folly*; 457.2 *unintelligence*; 555.1 *youth*
puerperal 561.16 *reproductive*
puerperal psychosis 36.11 *psychosis*
puff 722.2 *article*; 261.5 *be fatigued*; 434.22 *blow*; 669.15 *compliment*; 719.3 *criticism*; 719.11 *criticize*; 677.8 *flatter*; 371.14 *let out*; 740.16 *publicize*; 740.8 *public relations*; 496.14 *smoke*; 496.8 *smoking*; 419.11 *soft thing*
puff away 330.28 *shoot*
puffball mushroom 25.33 *vegetable*
puffed 727.12 *exaggerated*
puffed-out chest 622.10 *boastfulness*
puffed up 676.3 *affected*; 190.7 *bigger*; 622.22, 673.13 *boastful*; 727.13 *enlarged*
puffer 321.4 *locomotive*
puffery 676.1 *affectedness*; 727.1 *exaggeration*
puffily 190.10 *largely*
puffin 72.3 *water bird*
puffiness 158.5 *fatness*; 190.1 *growth*
puffing 261.3 *panting*
puffing and blowing 261.3 *panting*
Puffing Billy 321.10 *miscellaneous*
puffing up 727.2 *enlargement*
puff job 740.9 *advertisement*
puff of wind 31.14 *windiness*
puff pastry 25.37 *pastry*
puff piece 740.9 *advertisement*
puff puff 321.4 *locomotive*
puff sleeve 551.24 *part of garment*
puff up 190.6 *become bigger*; 669.15 *compliment*; 727.8 *enlarge*; 190.5 *make bigger*; 366.2 *send up*
puff up with pride 673.18 *make conceited*
puffy 676.3 *affected*; 190.7 *bigger*; 158.16 *fat*
pug 586.3 *athlete*; 52.4 *boxer*; 24.6 *ceramic workshop*; 24.11 *make ceramics*
pugging 24.10 *ceramic*; 24.5 *ceramic process*
pugilism 52.2 *boxing*
pugilist 586.3 *athlete*; 52.4 *boxer*
pugilistic 52.14 *combat*; 586.35 *martial*; 585.16 *warlike*
pugilistically 586.42 *martially*
pug mill 24.6 *ceramic workshop*
pugnacious 381.21 *aggressive*; 586.33 *combative*; 701.9 *hostile*; 584.8 *military*; 585.16 *warlike*
pugnaciously 586.41 *aggressively*
pugnaciousness 585.5 *bellicosity*
pugnacity 381.11 *attack*; 585.5 *bellicosity*
pug-nosed 149.7 *short*
puissance 396.1 *authority*; 334.1 *power*
puissant 396.12 *authoritative*; 336.10 *potent*; 334.13 *powerful*
puja 7.2 *religiousness*; 10.3 *rite of worship*; 9.1 *worship*
puke 371.15 *vomit*; 371.23 *vomiting*
pukey 236.4 *poor*; 371.30 *vomiting*
puking 371.23 *vomiting*
pukish 236.4 *poor*
pukka 698.19 *authentic*
pulchritude 545.1 *gorgeousness*
pulchritudinous 545.5 *beautiful*
Pulcinella 21.32 *clown*
pule 514.13 *cry*; 515.5 *sing*
pulicide 37.4 *drug type*
Pulitzer Prize 740.6 *book publishing*; 813.2 *prize*
pull 362.2; **362.11**; 363.4 *allurement*; 363.11 *attract*; 363.1 *attraction*; 330.26, 331.10 *bat*; 395.10 *be a prevailing influence*; 486.7 *be clumsy*; 325.2 *divert*; 394.20 *doctor*; 576.4 *exertion*; 369.1 *extraction*; 56.7 *golf*; 56.3 *golf shots*; 395.4 *indirect influence*; 395.1 *influence*; 483.9 *motivate*; 35.21 *practise dentistry*; 492.3 *press*; 300.14 *set in motion*; 331.14 *sporting hit*; 121.1 *superiority*; 330.5 *throw*; 492.11 *touch*; 325.5 *twist*; 380.8 *use violence*; 576.6 *work*
pull a bonehead play 245.4 *impair*
pull a boner 245.4 *impair*
pull a fast one 645.5 *be cunning*; 700.23 *deceive*
pull a long face 643.8 *be serious*
pull apart 375.4 *deconstruct*; 357.9 *demolish*; 268.17 *liquefy*
pull aside 325.2 *divert*
pull at 362.13
pullback 303.11 *retreat*
pull back 362.14 *draw in*; 251.8 *restrain*; 303.2 *retreat*
pull down 367.3 *bring down*; 375.4 *deconstruct*; 357.9 *demolish*; 367.2 *flatten*; 765.9 *gain*
pull down the blind 523.14 *make dark*
pulled 144.9 *removed*
pulled muscle 245.11 *hurt*; 260.16 *rheumatism*
pulled open 308.12 *open*
puller 362.6 *towline*
pullet 43.8 *livestock*; 72.12 *young bird*
pulley 38.8 *machine element*; 38.6 *simple machine*; 438.1 *tool*
pull faces 742.11 *gesture*
pull for 514.12 *cheer*
pull hair 52.12 *wrestle*
pull hard 353.2 *try hard*
pull in 362.14 *draw in*; 320.21 *miscellaneous motoring terms*; 312.6 *stop at*
pull-in 557.15 *eating place*
pulling 363.8 *attracting*; 558.1 *drinking*; 41.13 *framing*; 334.15 *full of energy*; 362.1 *traction*; 362.8 *tractional*
pulling back 303.11 *retreat*; 362.1 *traction*; 362.8 *tractional*
pulling down 765.1 *gain*
pulling no punches 726.3 *emphatic*
pulling one's leg 700.11 *hoax*
pulling out 313.7 *departure*; 369.1 *extraction*
pulling power 363.2; 334.4 *energy*; 362.1 *traction*
pulling the goalie 58.3 *ice hockey*
pulling together 747.4 *joint operation*
pulling towards 362.5 *magnetism*
pulling up 144.2 *removal*
pull it off 246.6 *be successful*; 253.13 *secure one's objective*
Pullman 316.5 *means of transport*; 321.6 *rolling stock*
pull no punches 269.4 *be concise*; 726.6 *emphasize*; 647.6 *suppress*
pull off 246.6 *be successful*; 268.17 *liquefy*
pull off someone's clothes 552.15 *make nude*
pull on 551.34 *wear*
pull-on 551.31 *styled*
pull oneself up 366.5 *arise*
pull one's finger out 130.18 *make a beginning*
pull one's leg 700.31 *hoax*; 668.24 *ridicule*
pull one's punches 634.3 *abstain*; 648.3 *be lenient*
pull open 308.18 *open*
pullout 303.11 *retreat*
pull out 369.11 *extract*; 362.13 *pull at*; 144.15 *remove*; 303.2 *retreat*; 388.3 *submit*; 212.3 *subtract*; 313.2 *withdraw*
pullover 551.13 *sweater*
pullover shirt 551.8 *shirt*
pull rank 622.28 *disdain*
pull someone's leg 599.13 *be humorous*
pull strings 348.4 *be an instrument*; 396.18 *have authority*; 395.8 *influence*; 484.13 *plot*
pull the emergency handle 711.7 *raise the alarm*
pull the goalie out 58.9 *play hockey*
pull the plug on 131.16 *cease*
pull the strings 579.1 *manage*
pull the trigger 586.37 *fight*; 381.2 *fire*; 60.7, 330.28 *shoot*
pull through 393.4 *be restored*; 256.10 *cleaning object*
pull together 750.22 *form an alliance*; 747.13 *work together*
pull to pieces 678.11 *criticize*; 375.4 *deconstruct*; 357.9 *demolish*
pull towards 362.15; 363.11 *attract*
pullulate 190.6 *become bigger*; 562.6 *be fertile*; 208.11 *crowd*; 555.18 *grow*; 130.26 *produce*
pullulating 190.8 *growing*; 555.13 *maturing*
pullulation 130.4 *conception*; 190.1 *growth*
pull up 301.8 *be motionless*; 226.6 *cease*; 144.15 *remove*
pull up stakes 313.3 *quit*
pull wires 396.18 *have authority*; 395.8 *influence*; 484.13 *plot*
pulmonary 434.19 *respiratory*; 172.10 *visceral*
pulmonary phthisis 260.9 *respiratory disease*
pulp 357.9 *demolish*; 80.3 *fruit structure*; 435.3 *paper*; 419.13 *soften*; 419.11 *soft thing*; 497.3 *tasteless items*; 124.4 *trivial*
pulped 357.15 *destroyed*
pulp fiction 740.6 *book publishing*; 17.2, 721.5 *fiction*
pulpiness 419.10 *compressibility*; 431.5 *fluidity*
pulping 433.10 *steeping*
pulpit 10.12 *church*; 50.3 *parts of a sailing boat*; 740.7 *publicity*
pulpiteer 733.6 *public speaker*; 7.4 *religionist*
pulp magazine 740.5 *journal*
pulpwood 79.3 *timber*
pulpy 419.4 *compressible*
pulsar 29.11 *stellar birth*
pulsate 298.7 *be regular*; 509.8 *drum*; 112.22 *resound*; 327.24 *shake*; 326.9 *vibrate*
pulsatile 298.11 *regular*; 326.14 *vibrating*
pulsating 298.11 *regular*; 510.6 *resonant*; 112.15 *reverberatory*; 327.18 *shaky*; 326.14 *vibrating*
pulsatingly 298.15 *regularly*
pulsating variable 29.12 *variable star*
pulsation 509.1 *drumming*; 298.1 *regularity*; 112.6 *reverberation*; 326.2 *vibration*
pulsative 326.14 *vibrating*
pulsatory 298.11 *regular*; 326.14 *vibrating*
pulse 298.7 *be regular*; 509.8 *drum*; 509.1 *drumming*; 334.7 *electrical power*; 28.51 *electric current*; 297.4 *frequency*; 275.12 *musical time*; 298.5 *regular thing*; 112.22 *resound*; 112.6 *reverberation*; 327.24 *shake*; 18.19 *tempo*; 25.33, 44.11 *vegetable*; 326.9 *vibrate*; 326.2 *vibration*; 28.16 *waveform*
pulsebeat 298.5 *regular thing*
pulse code modulation 692.14 *radio transmission*
pulsed signal 692.14 *radio transmission*
pulsejet propulsion 330.2 *method of propulsion*
pulse radar 692.28 *radar*
pulses 80.1 *fruits*
pulse train 39.14 *terminal*; 28.16 *waveform*
pulsimeter 26.8 *meter*
pulsing 112.15 *reverberatory*; 326.14 *vibrating*
pulsion 330.1 *propulsion*
pulsive 331.17 *impelling*; 330.17 *propulsive*
pulverable 427.20 *pulverizable*
pulverableness 427.2 *crumbliness*
pulverizable 427.20
pulverization 427.4; 357.2 *destroying*
pulverize 427.22; 331.5 *beat*; 357.9 *demolish*; 245.4 *impair*; 365.16 *massage*; 412.8 *mix*; 372.9 *separate*; 419.13 *soften*
pulverized 427.18; 357.15 *destroyed*
pulverizer 427.11
pulverous 427.15 *powdery*
pulverulence 427.1 *powderiness*
pulverulent 427.15 *powdery*; 427.20 *pulverizable*
pumice 256.9 *cleaning agent*; 365.7 *eraser*; 30.25 *eruption*
pumice stone 256.9 *cleaning agent*
pummel 331.5 *beat*; 52.11 *fight*
pummelling 52.2 *boxing*; 331.12 *collision*
pump 190.4 *enlarger*; 369.9 *extractor*; 334.12 *generate power*; 705.18 *interrogate*; 433.13 *irrigator*; 190.5 *make bigger*; 369.14 *suck*; 50.18 *windsurf*
pump a fish 55.7 *angle*
pump bilge 560.17 *urinate*
pumped 705.16 *questioned*; 319.5 *transportable*
pumped storage scheme 334.6 *source of energy*
pumped-up 190.7 *bigger*
pumpernickel 25.38 *bread*
pump full of lead 330.29 *riddle*
pump in 436.5 *provision*
pumping 705.2 *questioning*; 369.4 *sucking*; 319.5 *transportable*; 50.7, 50.13 *windsurfing*
pumping iron 576.5 *exercise*
pumpkin 536.3 *orange thing*
pumpkin bread 25.38 *bread*
pumpkin lantern 522.7 *lantern*
pumpkin pie 25.36 *cake*
pump oil 437.11 *fuel*
pump one's hand 658.12 *greet*
pump out 417.6 *make sparse*; 369.14 *suck*; 371.11 *void*
pump petrol 437.11 *fuel*
pump room 394.14 *hospital*
pumps 551.19 *footwear*
pump up 190.5 *make bigger*
pun 479.1 *be equivocal*; 599.13 *be humorous*; 479.5 *equivocalness*; 599.5 *joke*; 17.12 *poetic language*; 697.2 *solecism*; 697.6 *talk nonsense*
Punch 21.32 *clown*
punch 558.7 *alcoholic drink*; 331.13 *blow*; 726.1 *emphasis*; 586.37 *fight*; 331.3, 381.18 *hit*; 743.10 *identify*; 412.2 *mixed thing*; 308.2 *opener*; 492.3 *press*; 160.2 *prototype*; 331.15 *ram*; 19.14 *sculptor's materials*; 331.14 *sporting hit*; 381.5 *strike*; 498.5 *sweet drink*; 59.2 *thoroughbred*; 438.1 *tool*; 492.11 *touch*; 438.10 *use tools*; 338.1 *vigour*
Punch-and-Judy show 21.7 *show*
punch bowl 410.16 *crockery*
punch cattle 43.18 *practise livestock farming*
punched card 40.7 *peripheral*
punched full of holes 308.14 *holed*
punched open 308.12 *open*
puncheon 410.11 *vessel*; 23.12 *wood*
puncher 586.3 *athlete*; 52.4 *boxer*; 43.16 *farm worker*; 331.15 *ram*
punch full of holes 308.20 *hole*
punch in 312.5 *get in*; 183.9 *make concave*; 576.6 *work*
Punchinello 21.32 *clown*
punching 381.23 *attacking*; 52.15 *wrestling*
punch line 131.10 *ending*
punch open 308.18 *open*

punch out 160.7 *form*; 313.2 *withdraw*; 576.6 *work*
punch-up 408.9 *disorder*; 380.3 *instance of violence*
punchy 726.3 *emphatic*; 338.4 *vigorous*
punctilio 656.5 *etiquette*
punctilious 698.21 *accurate*; 810.8 *dutiful*; 656.6 *formal*; 230.2 *perfectionist*; 407.14 *well-ordered*
punctiliousness 698.8 *accuracy*; 656.2 *formalism*; 407.6 *methodicalness*
punctual 293.12 *early*; 287.8 *in time*
punctuality 293.1 *earliness*; 342.3 *nimbleness*
punctually 293.17 *early*; 287.11 *in time*
punctualness 293.1 *earliness*
punctuate 742.13
punctuated 742.17
punctuation 742.7; 5.30 *syntax*
punctuation mark 373.4 *means of connection*; 742.7 *punctuation*
puncture 728.21 *detract from*; 35.7 *diagnosis*; 308.20 *hole*; 314.11 *infiltrate*; 491.11 *inflict pain*; 491.3 *injury*; 378.2 *obstacle*; 308.1 *opening*
punctured 728.18 *deflated*; 308.14 *holed*; 491.6 *injured*
punctured tyre 214.3 *decreasing thing*
puncturing 728.10 *deflation*
pundit 6.4 *educator*; 485.5 *expert*; 442.8 *intellectual person*; 7.8 *priest*; 4.12 *sage*
pung 320.10 *sled*
pungency 726.1 *emphasis*; 500.1 *odour*; 496.1 *piquancy*
pungent 499.5 *acid*; 164.10 *advantaged*; 726.3 *emphatic*; 502.4 *fragrant*; 500.5 *odorous*; 496.9 *piquant*; 336.12 *strong to the senses*; 495.7 *tasty*
pungently 336.15 *acutely*; 164.12 *at an advantage*; 502.7 *fragrantly*; 496.15 *piquantly*; 499.10 *sourly*; 495.11 *tastily*
pungent taste 495.1 *taste*
punily 159.8 *in a small way*
puniness 159.1 *littleness*; 153.7 *thinness*; 337.1 *weakness*
punish 814.1; 714.10 *avenge*; 647.5 *be severe*; 491.11 *inflict pain*; 16.75 *make illegal*; 251.8 *restrain*; 385.3 *retaliate*
punishable 814.22; 16.58 *unjust*
punishable offence 16.39 *crime*
punishably 814.23 *punitively*
punished 814.20; 251.13 *restraining*
punisher 814.17; 714.6 *avenger*; 382.10 *killer*
punishing 814.21; 264.10 *difficult*; 261.4 *fatiguing*; 576.11 *laborious*; 814.19 *punitive*; 714.14 *vindictive*
punishing experience 814.10 *affliction*
punishingly 264.26 *arduously*; 814.23 *punitively*; 714.16 *vindictively*
punishing work 576.1 *work*
Punishment 814
punishment 814.7; 16.43 *conviction*; 16.33 *litigation*; 491.1 *pain*; 251.1 *restraint*; 385.1 *retaliation*; 714.4 *revenge*
punish oneself 806.9 *appear guilty*; 808.5 *do penance*
punish with death 814.5 *execute*
punitive 814.19; 385.5 *retaliatory*; 714.14 *vindictive*
punitively 814.23; 714.16 *vindictively*
punitive tax 790.7 *tax*
punitory 814.19 *punitive*
punk 118.8 *dissenter*; 236.2 *inferior*; 18.33 *jazz*; 437.2 *lighter*; 651.8 *malefactor*
punkah 494.4 *cooler*
punk band 18.26 *musical group*
punk rock 18.9 *popular music*
punnet 410.7 *basket*; 410.6 *box*
punt 50.19; 331.13 *blow*; 330.27, 331.7 *kick*; 50.8 *punting*; 46.12 *special team*; 330.5 *throw*
punter 323.8 *boatman*; 59.15 *horse person*; 50.9 *sailor*
punter 50.8 *punting*
punting 50.8; **50.14**
punting techniques 50.8 *punting*
punt pole 50.8 *punting*
punt-race 50.19 *punt*
punt-racing 50.8 *punting*
puny 159.7 *little*; 124.2 *obscure*; 153.1 *thin*; 337.8 *weak*
pup 71.9 *dog*; 71.35 *give birth*; 561.11 *have young*; 555.4 *young animal*; 71.19 *young mammal*; 555.7 *young man*
pupa 34.15 *developmental biology*; 76.5 *larva*; 344.3 *rudiment*; 555.4 *young animal*
pupal 34.26 *developmental*; 76.13 *immature*
pupate 76.17 *develop*
pupil 130.14 *beginner*; 173.2 *central thing*; 518.2 *eye*; 6.7 *learner*
pupilage 555.1 *youth*
pupils 137.6 *students*
puppet 348.3 *assistant*; 700.22 *dupe*; 717.6 *image*; 96.5 *insubstantial person*; 159.2 *little thing*; 85.16 *national*; 124.10 *nonentity*; 387.5 *subjected person*; 664.3 *sycophant*
puppet government 12.1 *government*; 396.7 *type of rule*
puppet regime 85.3 *dominion*
puppetry 21.7 *show*
puppet show 21.7 *show*
puppy 71.9 *dog*; 555.4 *young animal*
puppy-dog 71.9 *dog*
puppyish 71.28 *carnivorous*
puppy love 593.2 *romantic love*
Purana 7.12 *religious text*
purblind 519.9 *weak-sighted*
purblindness 519.2 *poor sight*
purchasable 777.13 *bought*
Purchase 777
purchase 777.1; **777.6**; 390.1 *deliver*; 390.2 *deliverance*; 787.1 *expend*; 787.4 *expenditure*; 362.4 *friction*; 366.9 *lifter*; 50.3 *parts of a sailing boat*
purchase by mail order 777.1 *purchase*
purchase contract 755.2
purchased 777.13 *bought*
purchase of premises 790.6 *business costs*
purchase on account 777.7 *purchasing*
purchase on credit 777.7 *purchasing*
purchase price 790.5 *cost*
purchaser 777.12; 13.9 *economist*; 763.5 *possessor*; 769.5 *recipient*; 787.8 *spender*; 776.10 *trader*
purchases 777.6 *purchase*
purchase tax 790.7 *tax*
purchasing 777.7; 777.14 *buying*
purchasing power 13.2 *economy*
purdah 736.3 *covering up*; 655.3 *separation*; 521.6 *that which makes invisible*; 568.13 *womenfolk*
pure 255.13; **531.5**; **795.9**; **799.5**; 698.19 *authentic*; 674.10 *bashful*; 256.16 *clean*; 725.3 *clear*; 232.7 *complete*; 543.3 *elegant*; 803.6 *ethical*; 257.4 *hygienic*; 805.5 *innocent*; 801.10 *moral*; 255.12 *morally pure*; 350.2 *new*; 5.39 *of language*; 230.1 *perfect*; 7.15 *religious*; 684.8 *self-restrained*; 271.1 *simple*; 32.32 *solid*; 336.12 *strong to the senses*; 28.99 *theoretical*; 527.1 *transparent*; 204.7 *uncut*; 572.7 *virginal*; 235.1 *worthy*
pure and simple 255.16 *simple*
pure as driven snow 803.5 *virtuous*
purebred 255.7; 59.13 *breeding*; 43.21 *domesticated*; 59.17 *equine*; 255.13 *pure*; 59.2 *thoroughbred*
pure colour 28.28 *colour*
purée 25.13 *soup*
pure gold 235.8 *exceller*
pure heart 646.3 *naive person*; 799.2 *purity*
purely 255.19; **799.8**; 698.37 *authentically*; 572.12 *celibately*; 725.4 *clearly*; 230.8 *completely*; 803.10 *ethically*; 805.11 *innocently*; 795.13 *morally*; 350.13 *newly*; 197.24 *once*; 271.8 *simply*; 684.11 *with self-restraint*
pure mathematics 27.1 *mathematics*
pure motives 805.1 *innocence*
pureness 255.1 *purity*
pure of heart 805.5 *innocent*
pure person 255.5; **795.5**
pure physics 28.4 *experimental physics*
pure speculation 476.3 *conjecture*
pure-white 531.1 *white*
purgation 807.2 *apology*; 560.2 *defecation*; 255.2 *purification*; 256.3 *religious cleansing*; 371.21 *removal*; 808.2 *type of penance*; 714.1 *vindication*
purgative 255.4; **394.6**; 807.4 *atoning*; 256.2 *cleaning*; 256.18 *cleansing*; 37.4 *drug type*; 371.29 *expulsive*; 560.25 *faecal*; 371.28 *propellant*; 255.15 *purifying*; 37.17 *stimulating*
purgative agent 255.4 *purgative*
purgatively 807.8 *penitently*; 255.19 *purely*
purgatorial 807.4 *atoning*; 8.16 *devilish*; 491.5 *painful*
purgatorially 807.8 *penitently*
purgatory 807.2 *apology*; 256.18 *cleansing*; 8.12 *hell*; 491.1 *pain*; 255.15 *purifying*; 256.3 *religious cleansing*
purge 814.13 *capital punishment*; 560.16 *defecate*; 560.2 *defecation*; 394.20 *doctor*; 814.5 *execute*; 371.10 *exterminate*; 358.1 *obliterate*; 358.3 *obliteration*; 255.4, 394.6 *purgative*; 255.10, 256.15 *purify*; 382.4, 382.18 *slaughter*; 714.7 *vindicate*; 371.11 *void*
purged 256.17 *cleaned*
purging 256.2 *cleaning*; 255.2 *purification*; 255.15 *purifying*; 394.17 *remedial*; 371.21 *removal*; 37.17 *stimulating*; 714.1 *vindication*
puri 25.38 *bread*; 25.49 *Indian dish*
Purification 10.15 *holy day*
purification 255.2; 807.2 *apology*; 10.5 *Christian rite*; 256.2 *cleaning*; 257.1 *hygiene*; 244.5 *improvement*; 369.7 *obtaining an extract*; 256.3 *religious cleansing*; 808.2 *type of penance*
purificatory 256.18 *cleansing*; 255.15 *purifying*
purified 255.14; 256.17 *cleaned*; 255.13, 795.9 *pure*
purifier 255.3; 256.9 *cleaning agent*
purify 255.10; **256.15**; 32.30 *extract*; 244.1 *improve*; 257.6 *make hygienic*; 527.12 *make transparent*; 369.17 *obtain an extract*; 549.6 *refine*
purifying 255.15; 807.4 *atoning*
purify oneself 807.6 *apologize*; 255.10, 256.15 *purify*
Purim 10.16 *religious festival*
purine base 33.10 *nucleoside*
purism 471.4 *diligence*; 656.2 *formalism*
purist 471.8 *diligent*; 466.6 *discriminating person*; 230.2, 230.4 *perfectionist*; 19.29 *realist*; 647.4 *strict person*; 543.2 *stylist*; 647.10 *unadorned*
puristic 656.6 *formal*
puritan 7.5 *Christian*; 670.11 *disapprover*; 795.6 *moralist*; 795.10 *moralistic*; 255.5 *pure person*; 684.4 *self-restrained person*; 647.4 *strict person*
puritanical 255.12 *morally pure*; 684.8 *self-restrained*; 647.10 *unadorned*
puritanically 647.12 *plainly*; 255.18 *virtuously*; 684.11 *with self-restraint*
puritanism 255.1 *purity*; 684.1 *self-restraint*; 795.4 *self-righteousness*; 647.3 *unadornment*
Purity 255
purity 255.1; **531.11**; **799.2**; 698.6 *authenticity*; 725.1 *clarity*; 256.1 *cleanness*; 543.1 *elegance*; 529.3 *hue*; 805.1 *innocence*; 795.3 *moral purity*; 350.9 *newness*; 230.3 *perfection*; 684.1 *self-restraint*; 271.4 *simplicity*; 527.5 *transparency*; 572.2 *virginity*; 803.2 *virtues*
purity of heart 805.1 *innocence*
purl 90.7 *flow*
purlieus 147.5 *near place*
purling 90.10 *fluvial*
purloin 774.12 *steal*; 773.10 *take away*
purloined 774.17 *stolen*
purloiner 774.8 *thief*
purloining 774.1 *stealing*; 773.3 *taking away*
purl stitch 42.5 *knitting*
purohita 7.8 *priest*
purple 540.6; 540.9 *empurple*; 266.2 *obscure*
purple-blue 540.6 *purple*
purple-brown 534.1 *brown*
purple colour 540.1 *purpleness*
purpled 540.6 *purple*
purple dye 529.4 *pigment*; 540.2 *purple pigment*
purple emperor 540.3 *purple thing*
purple-fringed orchid 540.3 *purple thing*
purple gallinule 540.3 *purple thing*
purple grackle 540.3 *purple thing*
purple haze 691.6 *drug*; 540.3 *purple thing*
purple heart 691.6 *drug*; 540.3 *purple thing*
purple martin 540.3 *purple thing*
Purpleness 540
purpleness 540.1
purple passage 540.4 *figurative usage*; 729.2 *power of speech*
purple passages 542.1 *ornament*
purple patch 727.12 *exaggerated*; 727.1 *exaggeration*; 540.4 *figurative usage*
purple pigment 540.2
purple prose 727.4 *bombast*; 540.4 *figurative usage*; 266.1 *obscurity*
purple-red 540.6 *purple*; 535.1 *red*
purple thing 540.3
purple with rage 540.8 *furious*
purplish 540.6 *purple*
purplish-blue 539.1 *blue*
purplishness 540.1 *purpleness*
purply 540.6 *purple*
purpore 743.8 *heraldic device*
purport 694.10 *mean*; 694.1 *meaning*; 345.4 *significance*
purportedly 96.19 *apparently*; 4.25 *theoretically*
purporting 694.6 *meaningful*
purpose 446.4; 131.14 *aim*; 482.7, 635.13, 694.12 *intend*; 482.1 *intention*; 176.6, 483.1 *motive*; 694.5 *point*; 344.5 *reason*; 638.12 *resolution*; 638.7 *resolve*; 344.6 *undertaking*; 349.6 *use*; 237.5 *usefulness*; 635.1 *will*
purposed 482.12 *intended*
purposeful 643.2 *earnest*; 482.12 *intended*; 635.7 *iron-willed*; 484.15 *planning*; 638.1 *resolute*
purposefully 484.16 *as planned*; 638.17 *resolutely*
purposefulness 638.12 *resolution*
purposeless 642.1 *capricious*; 238.2 *futile*
purposelessness 642.2 *caprice*; 238.4 *futility*
purposely 482.13 *intentionally*
purposive 446.12; 482.11 *intending*; 638.1 *resolute*
purposively 446.21
purpure 743.13 *heraldic*; 540.6 *purple*
purr 515.1 *animal cry*; 609.7 *be satisfied*; 515.4 *cry*; 490.8 *feel pleasure*; 509.9 *hum*; 509.2 *humming*; 597.7 *show joy*; 511.8 *sound faint*
purring 511.4 *faint sound*
purse 410.8 *bag*; 780.6 *funds*; 191.5 *make smaller*; 780.20 *money store*
pursed 191.7 *smaller*
pursed lips 742.3 *gesture*
purse of Fortunatus 781.5 *wealth*
purse one's lips 742.11 *gesture*
purse-pride 622.3 *conceit*
purse-proud 622.17 *conceited*
purser 789.6 *accountant*; 322.3 *aircraft personnel*; 780.17 *financier*; 785.5 *payer*; 436.3 *provider*; 780.18 *treasurer*
purse seine 700.13 *snare*
purse-snatching 774.1 *stealing*
purse strings 396.1 *authority*; 14.1, 780.7 *finance*
pursing 191.8 *contracting*; 191.1 *contraction*
pursuance 633.1 *pursuit*
pursuant 633.15 *pursuing*; 289.12 *succeeding*
pursuant to 633.18; 482.14 *for*
pursue 633.8; 340.4 *act*; 631.11 *conduct oneself*; 593.26 *court*; 617.13 *like*; 134.4 *protract*; 705.17 *question*; 139.27 *specialize*; 638.9 *undertake*
pursued 633.17
pursue one's course 134.4 *protract*
pursue one's ends 633.12 *aim at*
pursue one's goals 633.12 *aim at*
pursue one's interest 633.12 *aim at*
pursue one's interests 683.6 *be selfish*
pursuer 633.5; 16.8 *litigant*; 593.9 *lover*
pursuing 633.15; 633.1 *pursuit*
Pursuit 633
pursuit 633.1; 633.2 *chase*; 449.7 *detection*; 482.3 *future intention*; 134.2 *protraction*; 300.10 *regular movement*; 342.2 *social activity*; 139.8 *specialization*
pursuit of love 593.6 *courtship*
pursuivant 743.9 *herald*
purulence 431.3 *body fluid*; 260.6 *infection*; 560.7 *pus*; 260.15 *ulcer*
purulent 560.27; 260.23 *diseased*; 431.16 *rheumy*
purulently 431.26 *fluidly*
purvey 557.25 *provide food*; 436.5 *provision*
purveyance 436.1 *provision*
purveying 436.1 *provision*
purveyor 436.4 *caterer*
purveyor of filth 258.6 *dirty person*
purview 482.3 *future intention*
pus 560.7; 431.3 *body fluid*; 258.4 *dirt*; 430.5 *mucus*; 260.15 *ulcer*
push 330.24; **342.14**; 707.6 *assertiveness*; 381.1 *attack*; 707.21 *be assertive*; 338.2 *be*

full of vigour; 331.13 *blow;* 767.11 *dispose of property;* 342.4 *energy;* 576.4 *exertion;* 302.8 *further;* 742.3, 742.11 *gesture;* 262.4 *haste;* 262.1 *hasten;* 331.1 *impel;* 395.1 *influence;* 483.10 *manipulate;* 381.12 *military attack;* 58.9 *play hockey;* 66.4 *play soccer;* 492.3 *press;* 302.3 *press on;* 330.20 *propel;* 330.1 *propulsion;* 740.16 *publicize;* 778.1 *sell;* 300.14 *set in motion;* 213.2 *spread;* 381.5 *strike;* 776.1 *trade;* 316.12 *transport;* 576.6 *work*
push around 331.1 *impel*
push-bike 320.12 *bicycle*
pushbutton 348.8 *practical*
pushbutton telephone 692.9 *telephone*
pushbutton war 585.1 *war*
push car 320.7 *handcart*
pushcart 410.10 *cart;* 320.7 *handcart*
pushchair 320.8 *baby carriage*
push down 367.5 *bear down on*
pushed 58.8 *hockey;* 782.2 *insolvent*
pushed open 308.12 *open*
pushed through 262.3 *hasty*
pusher 707.9 *affirmer;* 342.10 *busy person;* 691.5 *drug pusher;* 331.15 *ram*
push forward 262.1 *hasten*
push hard 353.2 *try hard*
pushily 660.33 *arrogantly;* 330.34 *forward*
push in 368.3 *impact;* 58.9 *play hockey*
push-in 58.1, 58.8 *hockey*
pushiness 660.4 *arrogance;* 707.6 *assertiveness*
pushing 342.18 *active;* 66.2 *football play;* 41.13 *framing;* 742.15 *gestural;* 262.3 *hasty;* 58.1 *hockey;* 58.5 *lacrosse;* 330.17 *propulsive*
pushing down 367.13 *submergence*
pushing power 334.4 *energy*
pushing under 367.13 *submergence*
pushing up daisies 583.10 *buried*
push into 480.15 *persuade*
push off 313.1 *depart;* 313.15 *go!;* 371.33 *go away!;* 323.9 *navigate;* 313.5 *set out*
push on 302.3 *press on*
push oneself forward 673.16 *show off*
push one's way 633.13 *follow up*
push on with 340.4 *act*
push open 308.18 *open*
push out 371.7 *drive out*
pushover 388.2 *appeaser;* 50.12 *canoeing;* 700.22 *dupe;* 705.5 *easy question;* 265.6 *easy thing;* 335.5 *powerless person;* 246.2 *victory;* 337.4 *weakling*
pushover stroke 50.6 *canoeing*
pushpin 373.8 *fastening;* 425.8 *sharp-pointed thing*
pushpit 50.3 *parts of a sailing boat*
push shot 65.4 *carom*
push stroke 65.3 *English billiards;* 58.1 *hockey*
push to extremes 638.6 *be resolute*
push too far 624.14 *make angry*
push up 776.3 *bargain;* 304.18 *jump*
push up daisies 582.15 *die*
pushy 660.16 *arrogant;* 707.14 *assertive;* 342.21 *meddling;* 338.4 *vigorous*
pusillanimity 614.1 *cowardice;* 337.2 *indecisiveness;* 639.13 *timidity*
pusillanimous 614.3 *cowardly;* 732.1 *shy;* 639.3 *timid;* 337.12 *weak-willed*
pusillanimously 614.5 *cravenly;* 639.16 *irresolutely;* 732.8 *shyly*
puss 71.10 *cat;* 167.2 *face*
pussies 427.5 *powder*
pussiness 560.7 *pus*
pussy 561.8 *organs of reproduction;* 560.27 *purulent;* 431.16 *rheumy*
pussyfoot 616.5 *be cautious;* 479.1 *be equivocal;* 634.7 *be evasive;* 702.13 *quibble;* 388.3 *submit*
pussyfooter 702.6 *sophist*
pussyfooting 634.15 *evasiveness;* 702.4, 702.9 *quibbling*
pustulate 548.7 *blemish*
pustule 548.2 *pimple;* 560.7 *pus;* 260.13 *skin disease*
put 719.8 *interpret;* 142.9 *locate;* 143.10 *situate;* 724.9 *style;* 724.6 *styled;* 330.5, 330.23 *throw*
put a bomb under 332.7 *hurry someone up*
put about 740.13 *make public;* 323.9 *navigate*
put a case 476.6 *propound*
put a construction on 719.8 *interpret*
put a crimp in 378.8 *hinder*
put across one's knee 814.3 *hit*
put a curse on 712.7 *wish ill*
put a damper on 685.4 *moderate;* 251.8 *restrain*
put a D-notice on 737.12 *keep secret*
put a face on 547.16 *make up*
put ahead 302.8 *further*
put a hex on 712.7 *wish ill*
put a jinx on 712.7 *wish ill*
put a lid on 367.5 *bear down on;* 550.23 *cover;* 521.8 *make invisible*
put a mark on 743.10 *identify*
put a match to 493.15 *burn;* 437.11 *fuel*
put among 127.6 *subsume*
Putana 8.7 *devil*
put an edge on 425.15 *make sharp*
put an embargo on 128.7 *exclude*
put an end to 195.9 *annihilate;* 131.16 *cease;* 357.8 *destroy;* 133.12 *discontinue;* 278.5 *make transient*
put another way 694.10 *mean*
put a plaster on 393.6 *cure;* 394.20 *doctor*
put a point on 425.15 *make sharp*
put aside 128.7 *exclude;* 482.9 *intend for;* 372.10 *set apart;* 350.6 *stop using;* 439.6 *store;* 439.7 *stored*
put a spell on 712.7 *wish ill*
put a stop to 684.5 *be self-restrained;* 647.5 *be severe;* 226.8 *cause to cease;* 131.16 *cease;* 166.7 *limit;* 301.9 *make motionless;* 251.8 *restrain*
put asunder 372.14 *come between;* 571.7 *divorce*
put a tax on 790.12 *charge*
putative 450.14 *believed;* 476.8 *supposed;* 476.7 *suppositional;* 96.10, 446.10 *theoretical*
putatively 96.19 *apparently;* 446.20 *theoretically*
put at rest 228.7 *make stable*
put at risk 254.10 *endanger*
put away 461.16 *certify;* 357.8 *destroy;* 571.7 *divorce;* 558.13 *drink;* 557.22 *eat well;* 815.9 *imprison;* 814.1 *punish;* 439.6 *store*
put back 393.3 *restore;* 303.5 *turn back*
put back into operation 393.1 *repair*
put back together 376.45 *reassemble;* 393.1 *repair*
put between 368.1 *insert;* 133.16 *interrupt*
put body into 336.8 *strengthen*
put by 439.6 *store;* 439.7 *stored*
putdown 623.10 *abasement;* 621.2 *act of derision;* 668.5 *insult*
put down 623.23 *abase;* 246.9 *be victorious;* 678.11 *criticize;* 367.4 *debase;* 621.6 *deride;* 357.8 *destroy;* 678.10 *disparage;* 623.3 *humbled;* 744.14 *inscribe;* 668.23 *insult;* 382.16 *kill;* 382.22 *kill animals;* 220.8 *list;* 367.1 *lower;* 124.13 *make unimportant;* 785.6 *pay;* 251.8 *restrain*
put down for hearing 16.71 *try a case*
put down one's gun 749.5 *make peace*
put dynamite under 330.30 *blow up;* 332.7 *hurry someone up*
put first 129.17 *give priority*
put for 324.7 *take a direction*
put forth 476.6 *propound;* 313.5 *set out*
put forward 707.17 *affirm;* 703.15 *demonstrate;* 302.8 *further;* 525.14 *present;* 476.6 *propound;* 4.22 *propound a philosophy;* 447.11 *raise the point;* 636.15 *volunteer*
put forward a counterargument 4.23 *discuss philosophically*
put forward a notion 476.6 *propound*
put heads together 374.6 *come together;* 713.6 *consult;* 746.5 *negotiate;* 747.13 *work together*
put heart into 338.3 *invigorate*
put in 44.15 *cultivate;* 314.9 *enter;* 368.1 *insert;* 312.6 *stop at;* 127.6 *subsume*
put-in 64.3 *rugby play*
put in a claim 710.7 *demand*
put in advance 167.10 *be in front*
put in an appearance 520.9 *appear;* 97.12 *attend*
put in a nutshell 269.4 *be concise*
put in bold relief 738.1 *display*
put in bondage 251.11 *detain*
put in bright lights 123.8 *make important*
put in capital letters 123.8 *make important*
put in check 246.9 *be victorious*
put in clauses 746.6 *make conditions*
put in cold storage 294.8 *delay*
put in commission 243.4 *prepare for action*
put in context 222.11 *circumstantiate*
put in danger 254.10 *endanger*
put in detention 814.1 *punish*
put in double jeopardy 254.10 *endanger*
put in front 302.8 *further*
put in headlines 740.16 *publicize*
put in inverted order 192.3 *invert*
put in italics 726.6 *emphasize*
put in its context 108.7 *relate to*
put in jeopardy 254.10 *endanger*
put in limbo 350.6 *stop using*
put in mothballs 350.6 *stop using;* 439.6 *store*
put in one's debt 235.10 *do good*
put in one's defence 16.72 *stand trial*
put in order 409.12 *arrange;* 409.15 *categorize;* 407.18 *order;* 393.1 *repair*
put in place 142.9 *locate*
put in place of 762.6 *give a substitute*
put in plain words 695.5 *simplify*
put in possession 440.9 *own property*
put in quarantine 257.6 *make hygienic*
put in quotes 742.13 *punctuate*
put in readiness 243.4 *prepare for action*
put in reserve 350.6 *stop using*
put in solitary 815.9 *imprison*
put in solitary confinement 815.9 *imprison*
put in splints 394.20 *doctor*
put in the clear 714.7 *vindicate*
put in the corner 814.1 *punish*
put in the dock 715.5 *accuse*
put in the kitty 439.6 *store*
put in the microwave 25.55 *cook*
put in the minutes 744.13 *record*
put in the oven 25.55 *cook*
put in the picture 693.11 *inform*
put in the shade 523.14 *make dark;* 623.22 *shame*
put in the slot 368.1 *insert*
put in the stocks 814.1 *punish*
put into 719.12 *translate*
put into circulation 377.16 *distribute*
put into code 719.12 *translate*
put into disorder 161.4 *disorder*
put into effect 631.14 *behave towards*
put into legal effect 16.46 *legislated*
put into one's hands 752.11 *volunteer*
put into operation 349.1 *use*
put into port 312.4 *land*
put into practice 340.4 *act;* 631.14 *behave towards;* 349.1 *use*
put into quarantine 251.11 *detain*
put into shape 409.12 *arrange;* 160.7 *form*
put into use 340.4 *act*
put into verse 17.21 *write*
put into words 160.7 *form;* 729.11 *speak;* 5.47 *word*
put into working order 393.1 *repair*
put in trim 409.19 *tidy*
put in working order 243.4 *prepare for action*
put it bluntly 707.21 *be assertive;* 269.4 *be concise*
put itself right 393.6 *cure*
put life into 338.3 *invigorate;* 336.8 *strengthen*
put money up front 785.6 *pay*
put new life into 554.21 *invigorate*
put off 481.4; 639.7 *be irresolute;* 596.7 *cause dislike;* 395.9 *change;* 294.8 *delay;* 596.8 *disliking;* 242.10 *displease;* 328.10 *disrupt;* 481.1 *dissuade;* 364.3 *fend off;* 637.8 *hold back;* 361.12 *interrupt;* 361.9 *interrupted;* 341.4 *not act;* 552.14 *undress;* 355.2 *withdraw*
put off a decision 639.7 *be irresolute*
put off the scent 501.5 *deodorize;* 325.7 *misdirect*
put off until tomorrow 666.6 *be neglectful*
put out of commission 238.8 *make useless*
put on 699.25 *be fraudulent;* 738.1 *display;* 21.38 *dramatize;* 522.24 *light;* 699.24 *pretend;* 366.1 *raise;* 551.34 *wear*
put-on 96.12 *artificial;* 699.8 *fraud;* 699.35 *fraudulent;* 699.34 *pretending;* 700.8 *trick*
put on a front 699.24 *pretend*
put on airs 676.4 *be affected;* 660.23 *be proud;* 673.16 *show off*
put on alert 243.4 *prepare for action*
put on an act 702.12 *deceive*
put on a pedestal 9.8 *idolatrize;* 366.3 *promote;* 667.16 *revere*
put on a spurt 338.2 *be full of vigour*
put on a uniform 585.12 *go to war*
put on blinkers 466.13 *prejudge*
put on display 738.1 *display;* 520.10 *make visible*
put one in mind 711.5 *warn*
put one over 645.5 *be cunning*
put one's back into 336.8 *strengthen*
put one's back up 596.7 *cause dislike*
put one's bristles up 624.9 *offend*
put one's case 701.16 *plead*
put one's cross on 743.11 *identify oneself*
put oneself between 748.1 *mediate*
put oneself first 683.6 *be selfish;* 686.10 *indulge oneself*
put oneself last 473.7 *be unselfish*
put oneself out 576.8 *exert oneself*
put oneself through hell 807.6 *apologize*
put one's faith in 450.7 *believe*
put one's feet up 666.6 *be neglectful;* 263.2, 265.20 *take it easy*
put one's finger on 139.22 *characterize*
put one's foot down 332.6 *accelerate;* 647.5 *be severe;* 397.10 *demand;* 638.10 *insist;* 228.8 *show determination*
put one's fur up 624.9 *offend*
put one's hand to 743.11 *identify oneself*
put one's heart into 638.9 *undertake*
put one's mark on 743.11 *identify oneself;* 139.26 *personalize*
put one's mind to 342.15 *try*
put one's oar in 133.16 *interrupt;* 342.17 *meddle*
put one's signature to 742.9 *use signs*
put one's tongue out 660.29 *ridicule*
put one's trust in 610.6 *hope*
put on half rations 218.7 *make insufficient*
put on hold 294.8 *delay;* 361.12 *interrupt*
put on ice 294.8 *delay*
put on layaway 783.9 *acquire credit;* 482.9 *intend for*
put on one's calendar 631.14 *behave towards*
put on one's guard 711.5 *warn*
put on one side 325.9 *shove aside;* 212.3 *subtract*
put on paper 744.14 *inscribe*
put on parole 391.4 *liberate*
put on radio 738.2 *display something*
put on record 744.13 *record*
put on sale 778.1 *sell*
put on short commons 218.7 *make insufficient*
put on show 738.1 *display*
put on side 673.16 *show off*
put on speed 332.6 *accelerate*
put on television 738.2 *display something*
put on the agenda 476.6 *propound;* 447.11 *raise the point*
put on the block 767.11 *dispose of property*
put on the brake 226.6 *cease*
put on the drag 333.3 *slow down*
put on the feedbag 557.22 *eat well*
put on the Index 399.4 *censor*
put on the list 744.15 *register*
put on the map 123.8 *make important;* 740.16 *publicize*
put on the market 767.11 *dispose of property*
put on the rack 814.4 *torture*
put on the scales 414.15 *weigh*
put on the shelf 350.6 *stop using*
put onto paper 19.23 *design*
put on trial 715.5 *accuse;* 448.11 *experiment;* 16.70 *litigate*
put on view 738.1 *display;* 520.10 *make visible*
put on weight 765.10 *augment;* 190.6 *become bigger;* 414.12 *be heavy;* 152.8 *fatten;* 213.4 *increase*
put on widow's weeds 571.10 *be widowed*
put others first 623.19 *be humble*

put out 240.5 *be inconvenient*; 264.23 *cause difficulties*; 357.8 *destroy*; 328.10 *disrupt*; 371.8 *evict*; 371.1 *expel*; 623.17 *humiliate*; 624.14 *make angry*; 740.13 *make public*; 740.15 *publish*; 264.16 *troubled*
put-out 48.6 *fielding terms*; 626.7 *irritable*; 624.15 *resentful*
put out a feeler 752.9 *offer*; 353.4 *test*
put out of action 245.4 *impair*; 335.8 *overpower*
put out of bounds 399.3 *veto*
put out of commission 335.8 *overpower*; 350.6 *stop using*
put out of countenance 623.17 *humiliate*
put out of gear 328.8 *disarrange*
put out of joint 144.18 *disconnect*
put out of kilter 234.9 *distort*
put out of mind 472.12 *be inattentive*
put out of reach 103.8 *make impossible*
put out of sight 521.8 *make invisible*
put outside the law 399.3 *veto*
put out the bunting 667.20 *salute*
put out the fire 749.4 *pacify*
put out to grass 767.10 *dismiss*; 81.11 *eat grass*; 557.25 *provide food*; 350.7 *stop work*
put out to pasture 767.10 *dismiss*
put over 695.5 *simplify*
put paid to 131.16 *cease*
put pressure on 386.6 *compel*; 395.8 *influence*
put put 320.16 *car*
putrefaction 582.1 *death*; 245.9 *dilapidation*; 375.1 *disintegration*; 236.10 *poverty*; 503.2 *something that makes an unpleasant smell*; 258.2 *uncleanness*
putrefy 258.10 *be dirty*; 245.2 *decay*; 375.3 *disintegrate*; 83.11 *moulder*
putrefying 236.4 *poor*
putrescence 503.2 *something that makes an unpleasant smell*; 258.2 *uncleanness*
putrescent 503.4 *putrid*
putrid **503.4**; 375.5 *disintegrated*; 236.4 *poor*
putridly 375.8 *destructively*
putridness 236.10 *poverty*
put right **801.15**; 324.6 *direct*; 693.11 *inform*; 244.3 *rectify*; 394.19 *remedy*; 393.1 *repair*; 393.13 *repaired*
put rudder on 325.2 *divert*
putsch 753.2 *disorder*; 662.4 *revolution*
put screw on 325.2 *divert*
put someone's eyes out 519.15 *blind*
put something aside 243.3 *be prepared*
put store by 123.8 *make important*
putt 56.7 *golf*; 56.3 *golf shots*
puttees 551.20 *legwear*
putter 56.4 *golf club*
puttering 342.19 *busy*; 342.7 *restlessness*
put the brakes on 251.8 *restrain*
put the clock back 281.14 *keep time*; 284.15 *look back*; 3.23 *turn back time*
put the clock forward 281.14 *keep time*
put the clocks back 275.18 *adjust the clock*
put the clocks forward 275.18 *adjust the clock*
put the finger on 715.5 *accuse*; 742.9 *use signs*
put the flags out 370.9 *welcome*
put the frighteners on 612.13 *frighten*; 647.6 *suppress*; 651.18 *torment*
put the hammer down 332.4 *be swift*; 334.11 *give power*
put the helm down 323.9 *navigate*
put the helm up 323.9 *navigate*
put the horns on 796.17 *be sexually immoral*
put the jinx on 249.11 *cause adversity*
put the kibosh on 335.8 *overpower*; 357.11 *ruin*
put the lid on 131.16 *cease*; 309.7 *close*; 737.12 *keep secret*; 251.8 *restrain*; 506.2 *silence*
put the phone down 226.6 *cease*
put the screws on 386.7 *force*; 480.15 *persuade*; 647.6 *suppress*
put the shot 330.23 *throw*
put the skids under 249.11 *cause adversity*; 245.5 *hurt*; 357.11 *ruin*
put the squeeze on 710.8 *solicit money*
put the stoppers on 131.16 *cease*
put the touch on 710.8 *solicit money*
put the whammy on 798.11 *be evil*; 249.11 *cause adversity*
put the wind up 612.13 *frighten*; 651.18 *torment*
put through the hoop 705.18 *interrogate*
put through the shredder 355.1 *relinquish*
putting 56.3 *golf shots*
putting aside 372.2 *setting apart*
putting back 393.9 *restoration*
putting down 678.1 *disparagement*; 251.1 *restraint*
putting green 56.1 *golf*
putting in cold storage 294.3 *delayed action*
putting in mint condition 393.8 *repair*
putting in order 409.1 *arrangement*; 407.1 *order*
putting into effect 340.1 *action*
putting off 637.15 *delay*; 294.3 *delayed action*; 361.6 *interruption*
putting off till tomorrow 341.1 *inaction*
putting on 21.14 *production*; 700.7 *tricking*
putting on airs 542.2 *affectation*; 673.13 *boastful*
putting one's heads together 734.4 *conference*
putting on hold 294.3 *delayed action*
putting on ice 294.3 *delayed action*
putting on the market 767.2 *disposal of property*
putting out of joint 144.5 *disconnection*
putting right 244.6 *rectification*; 393.8 *repair*
putting the boot in 631.8 *treatment*
putting together **376.33**
putto 8.6 *angel*
put to 713.5 *advise*
put to auction 778.1 *sell*
put to bad use 351.1 *misuse*
put to bed 394.20 *doctor*; 740.15 *publish*
put to death 382.19, 814.5 *execute*
put to flight 247.11 *defeated*; 246.10 *defeat heavily*; 377.13 *dismiss*; 330.21 *move forward*
put together **376.44**; 403.17 *assemble*; 376.47 *collected*; 374.5 *combine*; 406.8 *embody*; 405.13 *make*; 243.4 *prepare for action*; 356.10 *produce*
put to good use 349.3 *exploit*
put to inconvenience 240.5 *be inconvenient*
put to it 264.23 *cause difficulties*
put to one's shifts 782.2 *insolvent*
put to rights 407.21, 409.19 *tidy*
put to sea 323.9 *navigate*; 313.5 *set out*
put to shame 121.8 *be superior*; 812.4 *bring into disrepute*; 668.21 *disregard*; 623.22 *shame*
put to silence 506.2 *silence*
put to sleep 489.12 *anaesthetize*; 261.6 *fatigue*; 382.16 *kill*; 382.22 *kill animals*
put to the block 778.1 *sell*
put to the sword 585.13 *be at war*; 357.10 *lay waste*; 382.17 *murder*; 382.18 *slaughter*; 647.6 *suppress*
put to the test 448.11 *experiment*
put to the vote 469.5 *vote*
put to torture 814.4 *torture*
put to trouble 240.5 *be inconvenient*
put to use 349.1 *use*; 349.9 *used*
put to work 576.7 *work for*
putty 267.3 *adhesive*; 419.11 *soft thing*
putty in one's hands 639.14 *apathy*; 480.7 *persuadability*; 483.6 *suggestibility*
putty-like 419.2 *pliant*; 664.6 *servile*; 639.4 *unsteady*
putu 25.53 *African dish*
put under 489.12 *anaesthetize*
put under an obligation 810.17 *impose a duty*
put under arrest 251.11 *detain*
put under duress 386.6 *compel*
put under the hammer 767.11 *dispose of property*
put under wraps 521.8 *make invisible*
put up 403.16 *construct*; 154.18 *erect*; 469.4 *pick*; 436.5 *provision*; 366.1 *raise*; 361.10 *suspend*
put-up 106.4 *deliberate*; 715.2 *false accusation*; 699.35 *fraudulent*; 715.9 *perjurious*; 484.4 *plot*
put up a front 702.12 *deceive*; 699.28 *mask*
put up at 565.18 *take up residence*
put up collateral 440.9 *own property*
put up for sale 767.11 *dispose of property*; 752.9 *offer*; 778.1 *sell*
put up front 167.10 *be in front*
put-up job 715.2 *false accusation*; 699.8 *fraud*; 484.4 *plot*; 106.6 *premeditation*
put up money 785.8 *defray*
put upon 211.6 *add*; 236.14 *ill-treat*
put up one's sword 749.5 *make peace*
put up prices 792.10 *overcharge*
put up the banns 756.7 *promise*
put up the shutters 226.7 *stop working*
put up to 483.10 *manipulate*
put up with 413.12 *bear*; 649.12 *show mercy*; 388.4 *succumb*; 762.5 *take a substitute*
put wise 693.11 *inform*
put zest into 554.21 *invigorate*
puzzle 696.7 *be unintelligible*; 619.10 *be wonderful*; 264.23 *cause difficulties*; 705.21 *confuse*; 696.9 *find unintelligible*; 453.20 *make uncertain*; 412.9 *mix up*; 737.3 *mystification*; 737.13 *mystify*; 528.12 *obscure*; 619.5 *person of wonder*; 264.4 *problem*; 705.1 *question*; 696.12 *unintelligible thing*
puzzled 453.3, 696.6 *confused*; 412.13 *mixed-up*; 264.16 *troubled*; 619.6 *wondering*
puzzlement 453.12 *confusion*; 705.8 *curiosity*; 619.1 *wonder*
puzzle out 719.9 *decipher*
puzzle over 412.11 *be mixed up*
puzzler 696.12 *unintelligible thing*
puzzling 453.3 *confused*; 696.4 *difficult*; 737.11 *mysterious*; 264.12, 705.13 *problematic*; 619.8 *wonderful*
puzzlingly 453.24 *confusingly*; 705.24 *questionably*
PVC 32.21 *polymer*
PVS 435.1 *materials*; 93.9 *mere existence*
pyaemia 260.6 *infection*
pycnogonid 75.4 *arthropod*
Pycnogonida 75.4 *arthropod*
pyelogram 35.7 *diagnosis*
pyelography 35.7 *diagnosis*
Pygmalion's statue 554.6 *things brought to life*
pygmy 159.7 *little*; 159.4 *little person*; 149.5 *short person*
pyjamas 552.4 *dishabille*; 551.22 *nightwear*
pylon 334.7 *electrical power*; 437.4 *electricity*; 39.33 *power distribution*; 38.19 *structure*; 154.6 *tall thing*; 186.3 *vertical thing*
pyloric 559.5 *of a secretion*
pyramid 176.3 *angled figure*; 356.8, 403.6 *construction*; 583.6 *grave*; 744.11 *monument*; 27.46 *polyhedron*; 425.8 *sharp-pointed thing*; 228.4 *stable thing*; 284.7 *thing of the past*
pyramidal 176.9 *angled*; 310.7 *convergent*; 27.84 *cubic*; 425.1 *sharp*
pyramidologist 11.12 *occultist*
pyramidology 11.1 *occultism*
pyramid spot 65.3 *English billiards*; 65.5 *snooker*
Pyramus and Thisbe 593.10 *lovers*
pyranometer 26.8 *meter*
pyranose 33.3 *carbohydrate*
pyre 583.1 *burial*; 493.6 *fire*
Pyrenees 89.6 *other major mountains and ranges*
pyrenoid 84.3 *plant body*
pyrethrum 44.8 *weedkiller*
pyretic 260.23 *diseased*
pyrexia 493.1 *heat*; 260.3 *symptom*
pyrexial 493.12 *warm-hearted*
pyridoxal phosphate 33.12 *coenzyme*
pyrimidine base 33.10 *nucleoside*
pyroclastic 30.56 *petrographic*; 30.55 *volcanic*
pyroclastic material 30.25 *eruption*
pyroclastic rock 30.30 *igneous rock*
pyrogen 37.4 *drug type*
pyrogenic 493.10 *on fire*
pyroglaze 24.11 *make ceramics*
pyroglazer 24.7 *potter*
pyrographer 23.13 *carpenter*; 542.8 *decorator*
pyrographic 23.15 *woodcrafted*
pyrography 542.3 *pattern*; 23.8 *woodwork*
pyrogravure 23.8 *woodwork*
pyrolater 9.6 *idolater*
pyrolatrous 9.10 *idolatrous*
pyrolatry 9.2 *idolatry*
pyrolyse 32.26 *react*
pyrolysis 32.14 *chemical reaction*
pyromancer 11.13 *diviner*
pyromancy 11.9, 475.2 *divination*
pyromania 461.4 *delusion*; 493.6 *fire*
pyromaniac 357.6 *destroyer*; 493.7 *fireman*; 380.4 *violent creature*
pyrometer 24.6 *ceramic workshop*; 26.8 *meter*; 28.89 *thermometer*
pyrometric 24.10 *ceramic*; 26.16 *micrometric*
pyrometrically 24.12 *ornamentally*
pyrometric cone 24.6 *ceramic workshop*
pyrometry 26.2 *micrometry*; 28.96 *microscopy*; 28.41 *thermometry*
pyrophoric alloy 522.8 *fire*
pyrophosphate 33.12 *coenzyme*
pyrosis 260.8 *indigestion*; 491.2 *painful condition*
pyrotechnics 522.8 *fire*
pyroxene 30.34 *mineral*
pyrrhic 22.4 *historic dancing*; 17.9 *metre*
Pyrrhic victory 240.3 *inconvenience*; 246.2 *victory*
Pyrrhonism 705.6 *uncertainty*
Pyrrhonist 4.11 *follower of a doctrine*; 4.14 *of a philosophy*; 705.15 *sceptical*
Pythagorean 4.11 *follower of a doctrine*; 4.14 *of a philosophy*
Pythagoreanism 4.7 *school of thought*
Pythia 475.8 *oracle*
Pythian oracle 475.8 *oracle*
python 73.3 *snake*
Pythonesque 599.10 *humorous*; 272.5 *ridiculous*
pythoness 11.13 *diviner*; 475.8 *oracle*
pythonism 11.9 *divination*
pythonist 11.13 *diviner*
pyx 10.14 *sacred object*
pyxidium 80.2 *botanical fruit*

qadi 7.8 *priest*
qasisha 7.8 *priest*
qawwali 18.10 *world music*
QED 27.66 *proof*
Q-ship 586.24 *warship*
quack 515.2 *bird song*; 699.19 *cheat*; 700.15 *deceiver*; 35.11 *doctor*; 394.15 *healer*; 456.5 *ignorant person*; 700.39 *imitative*; 456.7 *semiskilled*; 515.5 *sing*; 702.6 *sophist*; 486.2 *unskilled*; 486.10 *unskilled person*
quacker 731.4 *talker*
quackery 456.2 *half-knowledge*; 702.5 *hypocrisy*; 699.4 *spuriousness*; 700.7 *tricking*; 486.8 *unskilfulness*
quacking 68.10 *curling*
quackish 699.32 *spurious*; 486.2 *unskilled*
quackishness 699.4 *spuriousness*
quackism 699.4 *spuriousness*
quack remedy 394.1 *remedy*
quacksalver 700.15 *deceiver*
quackster 699.19 *cheat*; 700.15 *deceiver*
quad 165.2 *enclosed place*; 200.1 *four*
quadragenarian 201.8 *twenty and over*
Quadragesima 10.15 *holy day*
Quadragesimal 687.6 *fasting*
Quadragesimal fare 687.1 *fasting*
quadrangle 176.3 *angled figure*; 309.4 *closed place*; 165.2 *enclosed place*; 27.44 *polygon*; 200.2 *quadrilateral*
quadrangular 176.9 *angled*
quadrant 176.4 *angular measurement*; 27.42 *circle*; 26.6 *measuring instrument*; 323.5 *navigation*; 179.4 *parts of a circle*; 200.6 *quarter*
quadrantal 27.81 *curvilinear*
quadraphonic 200.9 *tetramerous*
quadraphonic sound 504.10 *sound quality*
quadrate 200.8 *quadrilateral*; 200.11 *quadruple*
quadratic 200.7 *four*; 27.76 *functional*
quadratic equation 27.27 *equation*
quadrennial 200.3 *foursome*; 200.9 *tetramerous*
quadrennially 200.13 *four times*
quadrennium 200.3 *foursome*
quadricycle 320.12 *bicycle*
quadrifid 200.10 *quartered*
quadrihydrate 32.10 *salt*
quadrilateral **200.2**; **200.8**; 176.9 *angled*; 176.3 *angled figure*; 27.44 *polygon*; 27.82 *polygonal*; 169.6 *side*
quadrille 59.10 *dressage*; 200.3 *foursome*; 22.4 *historic dancing*
quadrillion 194.3 *large number*; 201.11 *million*
quadripartite 200.10 *quartered*
quadripartite vault 20.7 *vault*
quadripartition 200.5 *quadrisection*

quadriplegia 335.4 *disability*; 260.17 *nervous disorder*
quadriplegic 335.12 *impotent*; 260.19 *sick person*
quadrisect 200.12
quadrisected 200.10 *quartered*
quadrisection 200.5
quadrivalent 32.35 *combined*; 200.9 *tetramerous*
quadroon 412.5 *hybrid*; 1.6 *race*; 1.13 *racial*
quadruped 200.3 *foursome*; 59.1 *horse*; 200.9 *tetramerous*; 70.4 *type of animal*
quadrupedal 70.15 *of animals*
quadruple 200.11; 200.1, 200.7 *four*; 213.5 *make bigger*; 50.11 *rowing*
quadruple sculling 50.4 *rowing*
quadruple sculls 50.4 *rowing*
quadruplet 200.1 *four*
quadruplex 200.7 *four*
quadruplicate 200.7 *four*; 200.11 *quadruple*
quadruplicating 200.4 *quadruplication*
quadruplication 200.4; 213.1 *increase*
quadruplicature 200.4 *quadruplication*
quadruplicity 200.4 *quadruplication*
quadrupling 200.4 *quadruplication*
quadruply 200.13 *four times*
quadrupole 28.50 *electric charge*
quaestor 780.17 *financier*; 579.16 *official*; 780.18 *treasurer*
quaff 558.13 *drink*; 690.8 *get drunk*
quaffer 558.12 *drinker*
quaffing 558.1 *drinking*
quag 92.3 *marsh*
quaggy 92.11 *continental*
quagmire 264.6 *critical situation*; 258.4 *dirt*; 92.3, 429.8 *marsh*; 379.1 *trap*
quail 614.4 *be a coward*; 612.11 *be afraid*; 60.5 *game*; 25.20 *meat*; 72.4 *table bird*
quaint 696.5 *strange*
quake 30.64 *fold*; 380.3 *instance of violence*; 30.22 *seismic activity*; 327.24 *shake*
quake in one's boots 612.11 *be afraid*
Quaker 7.5 *Christian*; 589.3 *pacifist*; 255.5 *pure person*
quakily 327.28 *shakily*
quaking 612.8 *fearful*; 612.2 *fearfulness*; 327.6 *shaking*; 327.18 *shaky*
quaky 327.18 *shaky*
Qualification 136
qualification 136.1; 334.2 *ability*; 485.2 *aptitude*; 746.2 *basis for negotiations*; 224.1 *change*; 136.7 *condition*; 239.3 *convenience*; 714.2 *defence*; 412.1 *mixture*; 136.5 *modification*; 251.1 *restraint*; 136.6 *specification*; 217.7 *sufficiency*
qualifications 136.3; 139.4 *specifications*
qualificatory 136.12 *conditional*
qualified 136.9; 224.12 *changed*; 239.1 *convenient*; 400.13 *excellent*; 485.8 *expert*; 6.19, 455.8 *knowledgeable*; 412.12 *mixed*; 334.13 *powerful*; 243.18 *prepared*
qualified for 750.16 *fitting*
qualifiedness 136.1 *qualification*
qualified person 136.8
qualify 136.13; 334.10 *be powerful*; 246.6 *be successful*; 235.9 *be worthy*; 224.8 *cause change*; 714.8 *justify*; 412.8 *mix*; 685.4 *moderate*; 136.15 *modify*; 136.16 *specify*; 217.4 *suffice*
qualify for 239.6 *be convenient*; 797.19 *be good at*; 750.27 *fit*
qualifying 714.11 *vindicatory*
qualitative analysis 32.17 *analysis*
qualities 803.2 *virtues*
quality 136.2 *ability*; 229.2 *attitude*; 139.3 *characteristic*; 549.1 *elegance*; 797.8 *good*; 99.4 *nature*; 573.3 *nobleness*; 724.1 *style*; 121.1 *superiority*; 235.6 *worth*; 622.8 *worthiness*; 235.1 *worthy*
quality daily 740.4 *newspaper*
quality of light 522.2
quality press 741.5 *mass communication*
qualm 451.1 *disbelief*; 637.13 *dissociation*
qualms 612.2 *fearfulness*; 808.1 *penitence*; 806.2 *signs of guilt*
quandary 453.12 *confusion*; 222.4 *difficult circumstances*; 611.2 *hopeless situation*; 264.4 *problem*
quango 579.6 *governing body*; 376.16 *party*
quangocracy 12.1 *government*
quantifiability 26.3 *measurability*
quantifiable 210.14 *calculable*; 26.14 *measurable*; 27.73 *numerable*
quantifiably 210.16 *mathematically*
quantification 26.1 *measurement*; 27.12 *numeration*
quantified 26.13 *measured*; 203.6 *quantitative*
quantifier 26.9 *measurer*; 4.8 *philosophical term*
quantify 203.8; 27.90 *enumerate*; 26.10, 209.5 *measure*; 210.11 *number*; 139.24, 452.22 *specify*
quantifying 210.13 *calculative*; 27.12 *numeration*
quantitation 26.1 *measurement*
quantitative 203.6; 32.41 *analytic*; 26.12 *metrical*
quantitative analysis 32.17 *analysis*
quantitatively 203.7; 26.17 *measurably*
quantitative metre 17.9 *metre*
Quantity 203
quantity 203.1; 209.1 *degree*; 194.4 *mathematical result*; 17.9 *metre*; 452.18 *particularity*; 26.4 *size*; 439.1 *store*
quantity of electricity 28.50 *electric charge*
quantity of heat 28.35 *heat*
quantity surveyor 38.18 *civil engineer*
quantize 210.11 *number*; 203.8 *quantify*
quantized 28.98 *physical*; 203.6 *quantitative*
quantized property 28.78 *quantum*
quantum 28.78; 203.2 *certain amount*; 402.4 *matter*; 28.98 *physical*
quantum chemistry 32.1 *chemistry*
quantum chromodynamics 28.80 *quantum theory*
quantum electrodynamics 28.80 *quantum theory*
quantum electrothermodynamics 28.3 *modern physics*
quantum field theory 28.5 *theory*
quantum gravity 28.3 *modern physics*
quantum jump 28.67 *excited atom*; 28.80 *quantum theory*
quantum leap 443.6 *idea*; 304.5 *jump*; 28.80 *quantum theory*; 442.2 *ways of thinking*
quantum mathematics 4.6 *branch of philosophy*
quantum mechanical 28.98 *physical*
quantum mechanically 28.100 *physically*
quantum mechanics 32.1 *chemistry*; 28.3 *modern physics*; 402.6 *natural science*; 28.80 *quantum theory*
quantum number 28.78 *quantum*
quantum of radiation 28.78 *quantum*
quantum physics 4.6 *branch of philosophy*
quantum statistics 28.3 *modern physics*
quantum theory 28.80; 28.3 *modern physics*; 28.5 *theory*
quantum uncertainty 28.80 *quantum theory*
quarantine 251.11 *detain*; 251.4 *detention*; 372.11 *divide*; 128.7 *exclude*; 128.3 *exclusion zone*; 257.1 *hygiene*; 655.13 *ignore*; 257.6 *make hygienic*; 359.1 *preservation*; 394.3 *prophylactic*; 252.2 *protection*; 655.3 *separation*; 372.2 *setting apart*; 767.8 *sink*
quarantined 251.15 *detained*; 260.22 *sick*
quarantined house 767.8 *sink*
quarantine flag 743.7 *flag*; 767.8 *sink*
quark 28.77 *elementary particle*; 159.2 *little thing*; 402.4 *matter*
quark colour 28.77 *elementary particle*
quark flavour 28.77 *elementary particle*
QuarkXPress™ 40.11 *application*
quarrel 242.8; **242.11**; **624.5**; 342.1 *activity*; 586.40, 701.13, 751.6 *argue*; 701.1, 751.2 *argument*; 330.10 *ball*; 624.11 *be angry*; 625.6 *be irascible*; 517.11, 751.5 *disagree*; 517.6 *disagreement*; 587.6 *historical missile weapon*; 16.5 *litigation*; 425.8 *sharp-pointed thing*; 585.1 *war*
quarreller 586.5, 701.6 *arguer*; 751.4 *dissenter*; 242.9 *unpleasant person*
quarrelling 701.7 *arguing*; 751.9 *disagreeing*; 16.53 *litigating*; 242.2 *objectionable*
quarrelsome 381.21 *aggressive*; 586.34, 701.8 *argumentative*; 751.9 *disagreeing*; 625.4 *irascible*; 626.7 *irritable*; 16.53 *litigating*; 242.2 *objectionable*
quarrelsomeness 751.1 *disagreement*; 625.1 *irascibility*; 16.5 *litigation*
quarrier 369.10 *excavator*
quarry 183.2 *concave land*; 369.13 *dig out*; 60.5 *game*; 30.65 *map*; 482.6 *objective*; 356.10 *produce*; 439.2 *resource*; 344.2 *source*; 633.7 *the hunted*; 577.1 *workshop*
quarrying 369.3 *digging out*
quarryman 183.5 *digger*
quarry tile 24.9 *industrial ceramics*
quarte and tierce 381.18 *hit*
quarter 200.6; 780.8 *American money*; 49.1 *basketball*; 87.7 *city district*; 324.1 *direction*; 372.11 *divide*; 196.5 *fractional*; 46.5 *game time*; 743.8 *heraldic device*; 743.10 *identify*; 648.1 *leniency*; 196.4 *less than one*; 142.9 *locate*; 627.3 *mercy*; 205.1 *part*; 50.3 *parts of a sailing boat*; 200.12 *quadrisect*; 50.15 *sail*; 565.18 *take up residence*; 275.4 *term*; 276.2 *time period*
quarterback 579.14 *leader*; 46.7 *offence*; 46.15 *play offence*
quarterback sneak 46.9 *play*
quartered 200.10; 372.15 *separate*
quarter horse 59.1 *horse*
quartering 743.8 *heraldic device*; 200.5 *quadrisection*; 50.10 *sailing*
quarter ladder 304.9 *ladder*
quarterly 276.13 *for specified periods*; 200.13 *four times*; 740.5 *journal*; 200.10 *quartered*
quarterly period 292.1 *season*
quartermaster 323.7 *nautical person*; 436.3 *provider*
quartermaster corps 584.4 *military organization*
quarter note 18.17 *notation*
quarter-pounder 25.11 *sandwich*
quarters 565.1 *habitat*; 301.3 *resting place*; 693.8 *source of information*
quarter sessions 16.19 *law court*; 464.3 *place of judgment*
quarterstaff 587.7 *blunt weapon*; 54.1 *fencing*
quartet 374.3 *assembly*; 200.1 *four*; 18.26 *musical group*; 747.9 *team*
quart of milk 558.5 *milk*
quartz 418.7 *hard substance*
quartz clock 28.87, 281.6 *clock*
quartz glass 527.9 *glass*
quartz–iodine lamp 28.25 *light source*
quartz–iodine light 522.6 *electric light*
quartz oscillator 39.21 *rectifier*
quartz watch 281.7 *watch*
quasar 29.7 *galaxy*
quash 16.78 *acquit*; 708.14 *cancel*; 357.8 *destroy*; 704.8 *refute*; 251.8 *restrain*
quashing 16.42 *acquittal*; 251.1 *restraint*
quashing of the charge 714.1 *vindication*
quash the conviction 16.78 *acquit*
quasi 96.12 *artificial*; 125.14 *imitatively*; 205.12 *partly*; 115.7 *similar*; 476.8 *supposed*
quasi-realism 4.7 *school of thought*
quasi-realist 4.11 *follower of a doctrine*; 4.14 *of a philosophy*
quatercentenary 462.5 *day to remember*; 201.9 *treble figures*
quaternary 200.7 *four*
quaternary base 32.9 *base*
Quaternary period 284.3 *geological period*
quaternary structure 33.9 *protein*
quaternity 200.1 *four*
quatrain 200.3 *foursome*; 17.8 *part of poem*
quatre 200.1 *four*
quatrefoil 200.3 *foursome*
quattuordecillion 194.3 *large number*; 201.11 *million*
quaver 18.17 *notation*; 327.24 *shake*; 18.39 *sing*; 509.13 *trill*
quavering 327.6 *shaking*; 327.18 *shaky*
quavery 327.18 *shaky*
quay 779.7 *emporium*; 38.24 *water system*
queasiness 596.4 *sign of dislike*; 260.3 *symptom*
queasy 596.8 *disliking*; 260.22 *sick*
queasy stomach 260.3 *symptom*
Quebec 87.6 *other cities*
queeb 236.8 *inferiority*
queen 71.10 *cat*; 69.4 *chess terms*; 71.18 *female mammal*; 567.9 *offensive terms for homosexual*; 396.10 *person of authority*; 69.10 *play*; 76.4 *social insect*; 400.2 *sovereign*
Queen-Anne 23.7 *furniture style*
Queen-Anne chair 23.2 *chair*
queen bee 395.5 *influential person*; 76.4 *social insect*
queen it 660.27 *dare*
queen it over 622.28 *disdain*
queenlike 12.10 *governing*
queenly 12.10 *governing*; 396.14 *governmental*; 622.19 *stately*
queen mother 400.2 *sovereign*; 571.6 *surviving spouse*
Queen of Angels 8.10 *deified person*
Queen of Heaven 8.10 *deified person*
queen of night 29.17 *moon*
queen-post truss 23.10 *carpenter's term*
queen regent 400.2 *sovereign*
Queens 87.3 *New York*
Queen's 5.39 *of language*
Queen's Bench 464.3 *place of judgment*
Queen's counsel 16.13 *lawyer*
Queen's English 729.1 *faculty of speech*; 5.6 *official language*
queen's evidence 739.2 *divulgence*
Queen's highway 320.2 *road*
queen-size 158.15 *big*; 158.3 *large scale*
queen-size bed 23.6 *bed*
Queen's Messenger 692.4 *postal worker*
queer 802.14 *abnormal*; 118.14 *eccentric*; 378.8 *hinder*; 567.17 *male*; 567.9 *offensive terms for homosexual*; 260.22 *sick*
queer-bash 466.14 *discriminate against*
queer-basher 466.7 *bigot*
queer-bashing 466.4 *social discrimination*
queer fish 325.19 *deviant person*
queer in the head 461.11 *insane*
queerly 118.21 *unconformably*
queerness 802.4 *abnormality*; 118.4 *unusualness*
queer one's pitch 236.13 *be worthless*
queer specimen 118.10 *eccentric*
Queer Street 135.3 *needfulness*
queer street 782.6 *insolvency*
quell 246.9 *be victorious*; 586.38 *conquer*; 357.8 *destroy*; 400.14 *master*; 749.4 *pacify*; 251.8 *restrain*; 506.2 *silence*
quelling 251.1 *restraint*; 246.15 *victorious*
quench 357.8 *destroy*; 481.5 *discourage*; 523.14 *make dark*; 609.8 *satisfy*; 217.4 *suffice*
quench one's thirst 685.5 *moderate one's hunger*
quenelle 25.16 *fish dish*
quern 427.11 *pulverizer*
quernstone 427.11 *pulverizer*
querulous 701.8 *argumentative*; 625.4 *irascible*
querulously 625.9 *irascibly*
querulousness 625.1 *irascibility*
query 4.20 *philosophize*; 742.7 *punctuation*; 705.1, 705.17 *question*; 705.11 *question mark*; 619.12 *wonder whether*
querying 705.2 *questioning*
query language 40.9 *programming language*
quest 633.1 *pursuit*; 705.17 *question*; 705.2 *questioning*; 354.2 *undertaking*; 353.6 *venture*
quest after 633.8 *pursue*
quester 353.7 *attempter*; 448.5 *experimenter*; 633.5 *pursuer*
questing 633.15 *pursuing*; 705.12 *questioning*
Question 705
question 705.1; **705.17**; 644.7 *be curious*; 453.18 *be uncertain*; 704.9 *deny*; 451.8 *disbelieve*; 701.14 *discuss*; 705.20 *doubt*; 705.18 *interrogate*; 447.2 *issue*; 4.20 *philosophize*; 447.11 *raise the point*; 708.11 *rebut*; 729.7 *utterance*; 619.12 *wonder whether*
questionable 105.2; **705.14**; 701.10 *arguable*; 451.7 *disbelieved*; 812.4 *disreputable*; 800.6 *faithless*; 453.1 *uncertain*
questionableness 705.7; 105.6 *implausibility*; 453.9 *uncertainty*
questionably 705.24; 105.8 *improbably*; 708.22 *negatively*; 447.13 *problematically*; 451.11 *unbelievably*; 453.23 *uncertainly*
question and answer 706.3
question and answer session 734.6 *interview*; 705.3 *questionnaire*
questioned 705.16; 447.8 *problematic*; 708.18 *rejected*
questioner 705.9; 644.3 *curious person*; 710.4 *requester*; 453.17 *uncertain person*
questioning 705.2; **705.12**; 644.1 *curiosity*; 644.5 *curious*; 16.6 *legal process*; 701.2 *logical argument*; 4.4 *philosophical investigation*; 708.3 *rebuttal*; 708.19 *rebutting*; 705.6 *uncertainty*
questioningly 705.23; 644.8 *curiously*

questioning of potential jurors 16.7 *legal trial*
question mark 705.11; 742.7 *punctuation*; 453.9 *uncertainty*
question master 692.29 *broadcaster*
questionnaire 705.3; 2.2 *sociological research*
question paper 705.3 *questionnaire*
question potential jurors 16.71 *try a case*
question-time 705.3 *questionnaire*
queue 40.19 *computing terms*; 132.2 *consecution*; 132.1 *consecutiveness*; 132.17 *line up*; 148.5 *piece*; 132.8 *procession*; 289.1 *succession*
queue up 132.17, 407.24 *line up*
queue up for 474.10 *wait*
quibble 702.13; 273.3 *accurate thing*; 701.13 *argue*; 479.1 *be equivocal*; 466.12 *discriminate*; 479.5 *equivocalness*; 670.18 *find fault*; 702.2 *sophism*; 384.25 *stall*; 639.5 *vacillate*
quibbler 273.4 *accurate person*; 670.12 *critic*; 466.6 *discriminating person*; 702.6 *sophist*
quibbling 702.4; **702.9**; 701.7 *arguing*; 466.9 *discriminating*; 479.5 *equivocalness*; 670.6, 670.28 *fault-finding*; 466.2 *judiciousness*; 16.52 *legalistic*
quiche 25.45 *French dish*
quiche Lorraine 25.45 *French dish*
quick 342.18 *active*; 554.12 *alive*; 293.12 *early*; 6.17 *educable*; 43.11 *farmland*; 262.3 *hasty*; 262.8 *hurry up!*; 280.5 *immediate*; 280.8 *immediately*; 458.6 *intelligent*; 485.6 *skilful*; 332.1 *swift*; 278.6 *transient*
quick as a flash 332.1 *swift*
quick as a wink 332.1 *swift*
quick as lightning 332.1 *swift*
quick as the wind 332.1 *swift*
quick-change artist 21.29 *entertainer*; 227.8 *person who changes costume*
quick count 46.8 *huddle*
quicken 332.6 *accelerate*; 488.13 *arouse sensation*; 392.28 *further*; 262.1 *hasten*; 554.16 *live*; 336.8 *strengthen*
quickening 332.3 *accelerating*; 332.9 *acceleration*; 265.7 *easing*
quicken one's speed 332.6 *accelerate*
quick-firing gun 587.11 *guns*
quick-footed 332.1 *swift*
quick-frozen 494.9 *heat-resistant*
quick kick 46.17 *kick*; 46.12 *special team*
quick-kicker 46.12 *special team*
quicklime 43.13 *fertilizer*
quickly 293.17 *early*; 262.6 *hastily*; 6.26 *studiously*; 332.14 *swiftly*; 278.8 *transiently*
quick march 300.12 *gait*; 332.11 *swift thing*
quickness 442.4 *cleverness*; 293.1 *earliness*; 6.10 *educability*; 262.4 *haste*; 342.3 *nimbleness*; 332.8 *speed*; 278.1 *transience*
quickness of mind 332.10
quick one 558.2 *drink*; 581.7 *refreshments*
quick on the draw 332.1 *swift*
quick on the trigger 332.1 *swift*
quick pace 332.8 *speed*
quick passions 625.1 *irascibility*
quick retreat 332.11 *swift thing*
quicksand 264.6 *critical situation*; 92.3, 429.8 *marsh*; 379.1 *trap*
quickset 43.11 *farmland*
quicksilver 227.3 *changeable thing*; 332.2 *mentally quick*
quickstep 22.2, 22.15 *dance*; 68.7 *ice-dancing*
quick temper 625.1 *irascibility*
quick-tempered 625.4 *irascible*
quick-thinking 332.2 *mentally quick*
quick-witted 599.10 *humorous*; 442.10, 458.6 *intelligent*; 332.2 *mentally quick*; 425.5 *mentally sharp*; 485.6 *skilful*
quick-wittedly 332.14 *swiftly*
quick-wittedness 442.4 *cleverness*; 458.2 *intelligence*; 425.13 *mental sharpness*; 332.10 *quickness of mind*
quid 780.9 *British money*; 99.1 *essence*; 496.7 *tobacco*
quiddity 99.1 *essence*; 93.3 *nature*
quidnunc 644.4 *meddler*
quid pro quo 813.6 *compensation*; 759.1 *exchange*; 110.1 *interchange*; 385.1 *retaliation*; 762.1 *substitution*
quids in 781.1 *wealthy*
quiescence 592.4 *desensitization*; 263.1 *ease*; 341.1 *inaction*; 343.5 *inactivity*; 339.1 *inertness*; 589.1 *peace*; 301.2 *repose*; 506.4 *silence*; 421.7 *smoothness*
quiescency 301.2 *repose*
quiescent 301.6; 263.4 *at ease*; 592.2 *desensitized*; 341.3, 343.1 *inactive*; 339.5 *inert*; 589.7 *peaceful*; 506.3 *silent*; 421.3 *soothing*
quiescently 421.15 *soothingly*
quiet 263.4 *at ease*; 481.5 *discourage*; 263.1 *ease*; 511.1 *faint-sounding*; 407.16 *harmonious*; 407.8 *harmony*; 506.6 *hush!*; 341.1 *inaction*; 341.3, 343.1 *inactive*; 343.5 *inactivity*; 339.5 *inert*; 337.13 *insufficient*; 685.4, 685.6 *moderate*; 511.7 *mute*; 589.7 *peaceful*; 301.6 *quiescent*; 608.9 *relieve*; 301.2 *repose*; 674.13, 728.15 *reserved*; 655.11 *secluded*; 251.14 *self-restrained*; 732.1 *shy*; 506.2, 506.4 *silence*; 506.3 *silent*; 529.13 *soft-hued*; 421.3 *soothing*; 228.1 *stability*; 228.9 *stable*; 388.5 *submitting*; 580.2 *time off*
quiet as a lamb 589.7 *peaceful*; 506.3 *silent*
quiet as a mouse 301.4 *motionless*; 506.3 *silent*
quiet as death 301.6 *quiescent*
quieten 214.5 *make smaller*; 228.7 *make stable*; 685.4 *moderate*; 511.7 *mute*; 506.2 *silence*
quiet end 582.5 *ways of dying*
quieten down 228.6 *be stable*; 226.8 *cause to cease*; 228.7 *make stable*
quietening 685.1 *moderation*
quietism 301.2 *repose*
quiet life 589.1 *peace*
quietly 511.10 *faintly*; 339.7 *inertly*; 674.17 *modestly*; 301.10 *motionlessly*; 589.8 *peacefully*; 728.25 *reservedly*; 732.8 *shyly*; 506.5 *silently*; 421.15 *soothingly*; 228.12 *stably*; 4.27 *stoically*; 655.14 *unsocially*; 337.14 *weakly*; 263.6 *with ease*; 341.5 *without action*
quietly spoken 729.19 *speaking*
quietness 407.8 *harmony*; 341.1 *inaction*; 343.5 *inactivity*; 685.1 *moderation*; 301.2 *repose*; 728.5 *reserve*; 251.3 *self-restraint*; 732.3 *shyness*; 506.4 *silence*
quiet person 728.11 *modest person*
quiet sun 29.15 *sun*
quietude 582.1 *death*; 4.3 *detachment*; 407.8 *harmony*; 301.2 *repose*; 506.4 *silence*; 228.1 *stability*
quietus 16.42 *acquittal*; 131.3 *death*; 582.4 *death sentence*; 382.5 *execution*
quiet wedding 570.5 *wedding*
quiff 547.8 *haircut*
quill 691.1 *drug-taking*; 72.17 *plumage*; 425.8 *sharp-pointed thing*
quillwort 82.1 *fern*
quilt 550.10 *bed covering*; 493.3 *heater*
quilted 68.12 *ski*
quilted clothing 68.5 *ski equipment*
quilter 550.17 *coverer*
quim 561.8 *organs of reproduction*
quin 201.1 *five*
quinary 201.12 *fifth*
quincentenary 462.5 *day to remember*; 201.9 *treble figures*
quincunx 176.4 *angular measurement*; 201.1 *five*
quindecagon 201.7 *double figures*
quindecagonal 201.18 *eleventh*
quindecaplet 201.7 *double figures*
quindecennial 201.7 *double figures*; 201.18 *eleventh*
quindecillion 194.3 *large number*; 201.11 *million*
quinine 33.19 *alkaloid*; 394.4 *antidote*; 394.3 *prophylactic*
quinquagenarian 201.8 *twenty and over*
quinquennial 201.12 *fifth*; 201.1 *five*; 276.8 *periodical*
quinquennially 201.24 *fivefold*; 276.13 *for specified periods*
quinquennium 201.1 *five*; 276.2 *time period*
quinquepartite 201.12 *fifth*
quinquereme 201.1 *five*; 586.25 *historical naval ships*
quinquevalent 32.35 *combined*
quint 201.1 *five*
quintain 482.6 *objective*
quintessence 99.3; 406.1 *contents*; 369.8 *extract*; 446.6 *ideal*; 230.3 *perfection*; 717.1 *representation*; 797.9 *the best*; 235.6 *worth*
quintessential 99.8; 797.2 *best*; 406.10 *containing*; 750.15 *conventional*; 446.13 *ideal*; 717.13 *representational*; 139.15 *special*
quintessentially 406.13 *structurally*
quintet 374.3 *assembly*; 201.1 *five*; 18.26 *musical group*; 747.9 *team*
quintic 201.12 *fifth*
quintile 176.4 *angular measurement*
quintillion 194.3 *large number*; 201.11 *million*
quintuple 201.23; 201.12 *fifth*; 201.1 *five*
quintuplet 201.1 *five*
quintuplicate 201.12 *fifth*; 201.1 *five*; 201.23 *quintuple*
quip 599.13 *be humorous*; 599.5 *joke*; 697.2 *solecism*; 702.2 *sophism*; 697.6 *talk nonsense*
quipping 599.3 *wit*
quire 435.3 *paper*
quirk 139.3 *characteristic*; 231.7 *defect*; 118.5 *idiosyncrasy*; 702.2 *sophism*; 642.3 *whim*
quirkiness 642.2 *caprice*; 118.4 *unusualness*
quirky 642.1 *capricious*; 139.16 *characteristic*; 118.14 *eccentric*; 599.10 *humorous*
quirt 814.14 *instrument of punishment*
quisling 747.10 *cooperator*; 479.9 *equivocator*; 662.10 *seditionist*; 700.21 *traitor*; 804.9 *wicked person*
quit 313.3; 226.6 *cease*; 133.12 *discontinue*; 372.13 *diverge*; 355.9 *forget it!*; 341.4 *not act*; 605.5 *resign*; 634.8 *run away*; 355.2 *withdraw*
quitclaim 391.1 *liberation*
quite 256.20 *clean*; 230.8, 232.9 *completely*; 685.9 *moderately*; 204.13 *on the whole*; 209.11 *to a degree*
quite a few 208.2 *multitude*
quite another thing 116.4 *dissimilar*
quite some 208.6 *many*
quite something 619.4 *wonder*
quite the contrary 708.23 *no!*
quit it 582.15 *die*; 226.12 *stop!*
quit one's hold 355.1 *relinquish*
quit one's post 355.2 *withdraw*
quitrent 790.3 *fee*
quits 807.1 *atonement*; 111.16 *equal*; 111.5, 119.1 *equality*
quittance 807.1 *atonement*; 391.1 *liberation*; 785.1 *payment*; 253.2 *promise*
quitter 388.2 *appeaser*; 634.17 *avoider*; 479.9 *equivocator*; 605.3 *resigner*
quit the saddle 312.4 *land*
quit the scene 582.15 *die*; 634.9 *play truant*; 313.3 *quit*
quit the single state 570.15 *marry*
quitting 605.1 *resignation*
quitting work 605.1 *resignation*
quit work 605.5 *resign*; 350.7 *stop work*; 576.6 *work*
quiver 587.4 *arsenal*; 612.11 *be afraid*; 494.10 *be cold*; 376.27 *bundle*; 327.12 *flicker*; 327.7, 327.24 *shake*; 439.4 *storage*; 326.9 *vibrate*
quivering 327.6 *shaking*; 327.18 *shaky*; 326.14 *vibrating*; 326.2 *vibration*
quiveringly 327.28 *shakily*
quiver with rage 624.11 *be angry*
quivery 327.18 *shaky*
quixotic 477.11 *fantastical*
quixotry 477.4 *ideality*
quiz 644.7 *be curious*; 705.17 *question*; 705.3 *questionnaire*
quiz master 705.9 *questioner*
quiz show 692.25 *broadcast material*; 21.7 *show*
quiz-show host 21.29 *entertainer*
quizzed 705.16 *questioned*
quizzical 621.5 *derisive*; 705.13 *problematic*
quizzically 705.23 *questioningly*
quizzing glass 518.10 *visual aid*
quod 815.2 *the inside*
quod erat demonstrandum 703.4 *proof*
quodlibet 181.7 *round*
quoin 174.3 *architectural summit*
quoit 330.10 *ball*
quondam 284.20, 296.13 *former*
quorate 232.7 *complete*
Quorn™ 25.21 *meat substitute*
quorum 203.2 *certain amount*; 232.2 *fullness*; 579.10 *legislative body*; 398.2 *representative body*; 217.7 *sufficiency*
quota 203.2 *certain amount*; 43.2 *Common Agricultural Policy*; 27.18 *division*; 232.2 *fullness*; 166.2 *limiting factor*; 205.1 *part*; 770.2 *portion*
quotable 795.10 *moralistic*
quotation 5.21 *catchword*; 112.2 *iteration*; 205.2 *particular*; 790.1 *price*
quotation mark 742.7 *punctuation*
quote 111.7 *be the same*; 5.21 *catchword*; 703.16 *explain*; 112.17 *iterate*; 205.2 *particular*; 738.3 *reveal*; 729.11 *speak*; 139.24 *specify*
quote a price 790.11 *price*
quote chapter and verse 222.11 *circumstantiate*
quoted 738.13 *displayed*; 112.10 *iterated*; 742.17 *punctuated*
quoted price 790.1 *price*
quote oneself 112.17 *iterate*
quotes 742.7 *punctuation*
quotidian 298.12 *cyclic*; 117.15 *everyday*; 632.9 *habitual*; 271.1 *simple*
quotient 27.18 *division*; 205.1 *part*
Quran 7.12 *religious text*

R18 certificate 399.2 *censorship*
RA 19.16 *artist*
rabato 551.14 *neckwear*
rabbi 396.10 *person of authority*; 7.8 *priest*; 400.6 *religious leader*; 121.5 *superior*
rabbic 400.12 *masterful*
rabbinate 7.9 *priesthood*
rabbinic 7.17 *priestly*
rabbinical 400.12 *masterful*
rabbinically 7.23 *religiously*
rabbit 614.2 *coward*; 729.1 *faculty of speech*; 612.6 *frightened person*; 60.5 *game*; 71.12 *gnawing mammal*; 25.20 *meat*
rabbit farming 43.3 *livestock farming*
rabbit food 557.8 *animal food*
rabbit guard 44.6 *garden tool*
rabbithole 308.7 *passageway*
rabbit hunter 382.13 *animal killer*
rabbit hunting 382.9 *animal killing*; 60.2 *hunting*
rabbiting 633.2 *chase*; 71.23 *mammal hunting*
rabbit-like 71.31
rabbit on 270.5 *be diffuse*; 731.7 *be talkative*; 735.4 *monopolize the conversation*
rabbit punch 52.2 *boxing*
rabbit's foot 475.6 *good-luck sign*; 11.6 *talisman*
rabbity 71.31 *rabbit-like*
rabble 376.20 *crowd*; 138.11 *general public*; 122.6 *inferior*; 675.6 *vulgar herd*
rabble-rouse 733.7 *address*; 586.36 *combat*
rabble-rouser 662.8 *agitator*; 586.5 *arguer*; 579.14 *leader*; 480.14, 483.7 *motivator*; 753.4 *protester*; 733.6 *public speaker*
rabble-rousing 586.34 *argumentative*
Rabelaisian 712.8 *cursing*; 796.12 *indecent*; 675.9 *ribald*
rabid 624.16 *angry*; 461.12 *manic*; 380.6 *violent*
rabid animal 382.10 *killer*
rabidly 624.18 *angrily*
rabies 260.6 *infection*; 461.3 *mental deterioration*; 260.18 *veterinary disease*
race 1.6; **47.7**; **61.9**; 342.12 *be active*; 332.4 *be swift*; 633.2 *chase*; 631.1 *conduct*; 289.2 *descent*; 576.5 *exercise*; 329.3 *exceed*; 43.10 *farm tool*; 90.7 *flow*; 137.8 *genealogy*; 566.9 *group*; 262.2 *make haste*; 61.1 *motor racing*; 323.9 *navigate*; 342.3 *nimbleness*; 59.16 *ride*; 90.6 *river flow*; 50.16 *row*; 68.3 *ski racing*; 1.7 *society*; 332.11 *swift thing*; 34.17 *taxonomy*; 47.1 *track events*
race against a deadline 262.4 *haste*
race against time 262.4 *haste*
race a punt 50.19 *punt*
race card 59.7 *horseracing*
race consciousness 566.11 *nation*
racecourse 179.2 *circle*; 59.7 *horseracing*; 317.6 *path*
race hatred 594.3; 466.4 *social discrimination*
racehorse 332.12 *swift animal*; 59.2 *thoroughbred*
racemate 32.13 *structure*
raceme 78.4 *flower head*
race meeting 59.7 *horseracing*
race memory 462.1 *memory*
racemic mixture 32.13 *structure*
racemization 32.13 *structure*
racemize 32.26 *react*
racemized 32.37 *structural*
racemose 78.12 *of flowers*
racemose inflorescence 78.4 *flower head*
race neck-and-neck 111.10 *be equal*

Race of the Year 61.5 *motorcycle racing*
race psychology 36.1 *psychology*
racer 47.3 *athlete;* 61.8 *driver;* 332.12 *swift animal;* 332.13 *swift person;* 59.2 *thoroughbred*
racetrack 61.1 *motor racing*
racewalker 47.3 *athlete*
racewalking 47.1 *track events*
raceway 61.1 *motor racing*
rachial 77.17 *of stems*
rachilla 81.3 *grass plant;* 77.5 *stem*
rachis 82.2 *fern plant;* 72.17 *plumage;* 77.5 *stem*
Rachmanism 647.2 *suppression*
racial 1.13; 566.12 *human;* 1.14 *societal;* 2.14 *socioeconomic*
racial discrimination 128.4 *exclusiveness;* 466.4 *social discrimination*
racial group 566.9 *group;* 2.6 *social group*
racial harassment 651.5 *intolerance*
racial hatred 651.5 *intolerance*
racial intolerance 465.3 *injustice*
racialism 465.3 *injustice;* 651.5 *intolerance;* 466.4 *social discrimination*
racialist 466.7 *bigot;* 466.10 *discriminatory;* 465.5 *misjudging person;* 594.11 *racist*
racially 566.15 *humanly;* 466.17 *prejudicially;* 1.18 *societally;* 2.16 *sociologically*
racially prejudiced 622.23 *prejudiced;* 802.11 *wrong*
racial memory 1.8 *tradition*
racial phobia 594.3 *race hatred*
racial prejudice 465.3 *injustice;* 622.11 *prejudice*
racial unconscious 36.21 *psyche*
racily 497.11 *tastelessly*
raciness 497.4 *bad taste;* 726.1 *emphasis;* 496.1 *piquancy*
racing 61.10; 633.2 *chase;* 90.10 *fluvial;* 262.3 *hasty;* 59.6 *horsemanship;* 59.7 *horseracing;* 50.4 *rowing;* 68.3 *ski racing;* 332.8 *speed;* 332.1 *swift;* 47.9 *track;* 47.1 *track events*
racing bicycle 320.12 *bicycle*
racing boat 50.4 *rowing*
racing canoe 50.6 *canoeing*
racing car 332.11 *swift thing*
racing circuit 61.1 *motor racing*
racing driver 332.13 *swift person*
racing forecaster 475.9 *forecaster*
racing governing body 61.7
racing handlebars 320.11 *bicycle part*
racing oar 50.4 *rowing*
racing pole 50.8 *punting*
racing punt 50.8 *punting*
racing river 90.1 *river*
racing saddle 59.14 *horse-riding terms*
racing ski 68.2 *cross-country skiing*
racing-step turn 68.4 *skiing technique*
racing steward 59.15 *horse person*
racing suit 68.5 *ski equipment*
racing track 59.7 *horseracing;* 317.6 *path*
racing tyre 61.1 *motor racing*
racism 465.3 *injustice;* 651.5 *intolerance;* 85.4 *nationalism;* 594.3 *race hatred;* 466.4 *social discrimination*
racist 594.11; 466.7 *bigot;* 466.10 *discriminatory;* 128.10 *excluding;* 594.9 *hater;* 651.8 *malefactor;* 651.10 *malevolent;* 465.5 *misjudging person;* 85.14 *nationalist;* 465.8 *unjust*
rack 410.4; 65.1 *billiards;* 403.4 *framework;* 236.14 *ill-treat;* 491.11 *inflict pain;* 814.15 *instrument of torture;* 255.10, 256.15 *purify;* 333.10 *slow motion;* 814.4 *torture*
rack and pinion 38.7 *gear;* 320.21 *miscellaneous motoring terms*
rack-and-pinion railway 317.10 *railway*
rack and ruin 245.9 *dilapidation;* 357.4 *ruin*
racket 342.1 *activity;* 63.11 *badminton equipment;* 328.5 *commotion;* 408.5 *confusion;* 800.3 *criminality;* 517.2 *dissonant noise;* 422.3 *elastic thing;* 700.10 *fraud;* 576.3 *job;* 507.2 *outcry;* 484.4 *plot;* 509.3 *rattle;* 327.2 *tumult*
racketeer 800.10 *be criminal;* 774.11 *dishonest person;* 800.4 *dishonourable person;* 773.6 *taker;* 776.1 *trade;* 776.10 *trader;* 804.9 *wicked person*
racketeering 800.3 *criminality;* 776.4 *trade*
rackety 507.6 *loud*
racking 814.12 *corporal punishment;* 491.5 *painful*
rack of equipment 62.4 *climbing equipment*
rack one's brains 696.9 *find unintelligible;* 443.12 *think*
rack railway 317.10, 321.1 *railway*
rack-rent 792.4 *extortion;* 792.10 *overcharge*
rack-renter 792.5 *overcharger*
raconteur 721.10 *descriptive writer*
Racquet Sports 63
racy 497.6 *coarse;* 726.3 *emphatic;* 796.12 *indecent;* 496.9 *piquant*
rad 797.1 *good;* 797.27 *great!;* 235.1 *worthy*
radar 692.28; 504.9 *audio device;* 449.11 *detector;* 28.13 *electromagnetic radiation;* 579.5 *guide;* 742.5 *indicator;* 323.5 *navigation*
radar astronomy 29.1 *astronomy;* 692.28 *radar*
radar beacon 322.6 *flight control*
radar beam 692.28 *radar*
radar guidance 692.28 *radar*
radar indicator 692.28 *radar*
radar navigation 692.28 *radar*
radar receiver 769.8 *receiver*
radarscope 692.28 *radar*
radar screen 692.28 *radar*
radar surveillance 692.28 *radar*
radar tracking 692.28 *radar*
radar trap 332.8 *speed*
raddle 535.9 *redden*
radiaesthesia 11.9 *divination*
radiaesthetic 11.16 *psychic*
radial 310.7 *convergent;* 27.81 *curvilinear;* 300.17 *directional;* 311.7 *radiating;* 141.11 *spatial*
radial-arm saw 23.11 *woodworking tool*
radially 311.16 *divergently*
radial motion 300.5 *circuition*
radial velocity 29.13 *luminosity*
radiance 545.1 *gorgeousness;* 522.1 *light;* 311.3 *radiation*
radiant 307.4 *axle;* 598.1 *cheerful;* 522.15 *lucent;* 29.20 *meteor;* 311.7 *radiating*
radiant energy 334.4 *energy*
radiant heat 493.1 *heat*
radiantly 598.9 *cheerfully;* 311.16 *divergently;* 522.30 *lightly*
radiate 311.13; 377.10 *diverge;* 334.12 *generate power;* 371.14 *let out;* 522.25 *light up;* 29.37 *observe;* 311.7 *radiating;* 31.61 *shine;* 316.11 *transfer*
radiate light 522.25 *light up*
radiating 311.7; 372.16 *apart;* 310.7 *convergent;* 377.24 *divergent;* 371.29 *expulsive*
radiation 311.3; 357.7 *agent of destruction;* 31.9 *atmospheric process;* 587.16 *bomb;* 377.5 *divergence;* 371.25 *emission;* 28.36 *heat flow;* 522.1 *light;* 28.12, 326.5 *wave;* 587.1 *weapon*
radiation balance 31.9 *atmospheric process*
radiation belt 30.47; 29.16 *planet*
radiation detector 28.93
radiation exposure 28.75 *nuclear accident*
radiation fog 31.33 *fog*
radiation frost 31.36 *frost*
radiation physics 28.3 *modern physics*
radiative 31.43 *atmospheric*
radiator 692.17 *antenna;* 493.3 *heater;* 371.28 *propellant*
radical 175.3 *base;* 344.13 *causal;* 118.8 *dissenter;* 727.6 *exaggerator;* 194.9 *fractional;* 797.1 *good;* 123.5 *important;* 244.16 *improving;* 172.11 *intrinsic;* 118.12, 662.6 *nonconformist;* 77.19 *of roots;* 113.11 *opposer;* 244.12 *reformer;* 344.3 *rudiment;* 235.1 *worthy*
radicalism 244.11 *reformism*
radically 99.14 *at heart;* 244.17 *better;* 344.14 *causally*
radical mastectomy 394.12 *surgery*
radical reform 244.5 *improvement*
Radicals 12.6 *political party*
radical sign 27.13 *mathematical symbol*
radical therapy 36.3 *psychiatric treatment*
radical treatment 35.8 *treatment*
radicle 77.7 *root;* 77.9 *seed*
radicular 77.19 *of roots*
radio 692.18; 504.9 *audio device;* 504.11 *aural;* 692.30 *communicate;* 692.1 *communications;* 28.13 *electromagnetic radiation;* 334.9 *electronics;* 740.13 *make public;* 693.4 *mass communication;* 740.2 *mass media*
Radio 1 692.20 *radio broadcasting*
Radio 2 692.20 *radio broadcasting*
Radio 3 692.20 *radio broadcasting*
Radio 4 692.20 *radio broadcasting*
Radio 5 692.20 *radio broadcasting*
radioactive 254.1 *dangerous;* 236.5 *harmful*
radioactive cloud 587.16 *bomb;* 587.1 *weapon*
radioactive dating 30.42 *dating*
radioactive decay 28.70 *radioactivity*
radioactive series 28.70 *radioactivity*
radioactive substance 28.70 *radioactivity*
radioactive waste 334.8 *nuclear power;* 28.74 *nuclear waste*
radioactivity 28.70; 587.16 *bomb;* 371.25 *emission;* 334.8 *nuclear power;* 587.1 *weapon*
radio amplifier 39.21 *rectifier*
radio astronomy 29.1 *astronomy;* 692.27 *signalling*
radio audience measurement 740.2 *mass media*
radiobeacon 692.27 *signalling*
radio-beacon station 323.5 *navigation*
radio beam 692.14 *radio transmission*
radio bearing 692.27 *signalling*
radiobiology 34.1 *life science*
radio broadcaster 692.29 *broadcaster*
radio broadcasting 692.20
radio car 692.20 *radio broadcasting*
radiocarbon dating 281.3 *chronology;* 30.42 *dating;* 28.70 *radioactivity*
radio channel 692.14 *radio transmission*
radiochemical 32.31 *chemical*
radiochemical reaction 32.14 *chemical reaction*
radiochemist 32.2 *chemist*
radiochemistry 32.1 *chemistry*
Radio City Rockettes 22.5 *dancer*
radio communication 692.1 *communications*
radio compass 692.27 *signalling*
radio control 692.27 *signalling*
radio direction-finding 692.27 *signalling*
radio dish 29.26 *radio telescope*
radio drama 21.2 *play*
radio dramatist 21.26 *dramatist*
radioed 692.34 *communicated*
radio engineer 578.2 *artisan*
radio engineering 692.6 *telecommunication*
radio frequency 297.6; 692.14 *radio transmission*
radio-frequency band 297.6 *radio frequency*
radio galaxy 29.7 *galaxy*
radiogoniometer 692.27 *signalling*
radiograph 35.7 *diagnosis;* 41.3 *photograph*
radiographer 35.17 *paramedic*
radiography 35.7 *diagnosis;* 41.1 *photography;* 28.70 *radioactivity*
radio ham 692.29 *broadcaster*
radio interferometer 28.85 *microscope;* 29.26 *radio telescope*
radioisotope 28.70 *radioactivity*
radiolarian 75.9 *protozoan*
radio link 692.14 *radio transmission*
radiological 35.22 *medical*
radiologist 35.13 *medical specialist*
radiology 35.3 *medical specialty;* 28.70 *radioactivity*
radioluminescence 28.24 *light emission*
radio marker 692.27 *signalling*
radio mast 692.20 *radio broadcasting;* 154.6 *tall thing*
radiometer 29.27 *imaging;* 28.92 *light meter;* 26.8 *meter*
radiometric 26.16 *micrometric*
radiometric dating 30.42, 275.8 *dating;* 28.70 *radioactivity*
radiometry 26.2 *micrometry*
radio microphone 692.16 *transmitter*
radiomobile 692.20 *radio broadcasting*
radio navigation 692.27 *signalling*
radio news 741.6
radionuclide 28.70 *radioactivity*
radio observatory 29.23 *observatory*
radio operator 692.29 *broadcaster*
radio oscillator 39.21 *rectifier*
radiopager 504.9 *audio device;* 692.18 *radio*
radiopaging 504.9 *audio device*
radio personality 21.29 *entertainer*
radiophone 504.9 *audio device;* 692.9 *telephone;* 692.16 *transmitter*
radiophonic 504.11 *aural*
radiophonics 504.1 *hearing*
radio play 21.2 *play*
radio producer 356.9 *producer*
radio programme 738.9 *production*
radio receiver 504.9 *audio device;* 692.18 *radio;* 769.8 *receiver*
radio reception 692.19
radio set 692.18 *radio*
radio signal 692.14 *radio transmission*
radio signalling 692.27 *signalling*
radiosonde 31.5 *weather station*
radio spectrum 28.13 *electromagnetic radiation;* 692.14 *radio transmission*
radio station 692.20 *radio broadcasting*
radiotelegraph 692.8 *data transmission*
radiotelegraphy 692.6 *telecommunication*
radiotelephone 504.9 *audio device;* 692.9 *telephone*
radiotelephony 504.9 *audio device;* 692.6 *telecommunication*
radio telescope 29.26; 28.85 *microscope*
radiotherapist 35.13 *medical specialist*
radiotherapy 28.70 *radioactivity;* 394.13 *therapy;* 35.8 *treatment*
radio tower 692.20 *radio broadcasting*
radio transmission 692.14
radio transmitter 692.16 *transmitter*
radio wave 692.14 *radio transmission;* 326.5 *wave*
radio waves 28.13 *electromagnetic radiation*
radius 150.4 *breadth;* 27.42 *circle;* 119.7 *dividing line;* 310.5 *focus;* 27.37 *line;* 179.4 *parts of a circle;* 311.3 *radiation;* 141.7 *range;* 158.1 *size;* 28.7 *space*
radius vector 27.50 *scalar quantity*
radix 77.7 *root;* 344.3 *rudiment*
radix point 27.8 *number system*
RAF 50.7 *windsurfing*
raffia 373.6 *line*
raffle 107.3 *equal chance;* 788.5 *winnings*
raffle ticket 743.3 *means of identification*
raft 38.28 *substructure;* 316.12 *transport*
rafter 435.1 *materials;* 413.2 *supporting part;* 23.12 *wood*
rafters 550.7 *overhead covering*
rag 599.13 *be humorous;* 551.1 *dress;* 42.3 *fabric;* 700.11, 700.31 *hoax;* 740.4 *newspaper;* 205.7 *piece;* 668.24 *ridicule;* 21.19 *stage set*
raga 18.20 *key*
ragamuffin 258.6 *dirty person;* 18.9 *popular music*
rag-and-bone man 778.11 *pedlar;* 767.6 *rubbish collector*
ragbag 114.3 *diverse thing;* 412.3 *miscellany*
rag doll 717.6 *image*
rage 594.5, 594.17, 624.4 *anger;* 590.6 *bad feeling;* 342.12 *be active;* 624.11 *be angry;* 395.10 *be a prevailing influence;* 380.7 *be violent;* 553.1 *fashion*
ragga 18.9 *popular music*
ragged 782.3 *beggarly;* 700.36 *deceived;* 552.10 *in dishabille;* 420.1 *rough;* 408.15 *untidy*
ragged edge 164.1 *edge*
raggedness 782.7 *beggary;* 114.1 *diversity;* 420.6 *roughness*
ragger 700.15 *deceiver*
raging 624.4 *anger;* 624.16 *angry;* 381.23 *attacking;* 357.14 *destructive;* 590.13 *passionate;* 31.48 *stormy;* 380.6 *violent*
raging fury 594.5 *anger*
raglan 551.12 *coat*
raglan sleeve 551.24 *part of garment*
ragout 412.2 *mixed thing*
rag paper 435.3 *paper*
rag-picker 782.10 *poor person*
rags 782.7 *beggary;* 205.8 *bits and pieces;* 552.4 *dishabille;* 551.1 *dress*
rags and bones 238.6 *refuse*
ragtime 18.8 *jazz*
ragtime band 18.26 *musical group*
rai 18.10 *world music*
raid 381.1 *attack;* 585.13 *be at war;* 586.38 *conquer;* 357.5 *havoc;* 314.3 *inroad;* 314.10 *invade;* 357.10 *lay waste;* 381.12 *military attack;* 774.14 *plunder;* 774.5 *plundering;* 773.10 *take away;* 773.3 *taking away;* 585.8 *warfare*
raider 381.19 *attacker;* 357.6 *destroyer;* 586.9 *guerrilla;* 586.25 *historical naval*

ships; 314.8 *intruder*; 586.6 *militarist*; 774.9 *plunderer*; 773.6 *taker*
raiding 357.5 *havoc*; 774.5 *plundering*; 774.17 *stolen*; 773.3 *taking away*
raiding party 586.14 *armed forces*
rail 321.3; 670.21 *berate*; 165.5 *enclose*; 43.11 *farmland*; 729.14 *speak to*; 319.1 *transport*; 319.5 *transportable*; 72.3 *water bird*; 50.18 *windsurf*; 50.7 *windsurfing*
rail against 670.21 *berate*; 712.6 *vilify*
rail at 668.25 *taunt*
railcar 321.6 *rolling stock*
railcard 793.4 *bargain*
railhead 321.8 *railway station*
railing 670.8 *berating*; 165.3 *enclosing thing*; 252.4 *safety device*; 50.7 *windsurfing*
raillery 659.1, 660.9 *discourtesy*
railroad 386.7 *force*; 262.1 *hasten*; 317.10, 321.1 *railway*; 387.6 *subject*
railroaded 262.3 *hasty*
railroad yard 317.10 *railway*
rails 321.3 *rail*; 317.10 *railway*
rail station 321.8 *railway station*
Rail Transport 321
rail transport 316.5 *means of transport*
railway 317.10; **321.1**; 38.19 *structure*; 319.5 *transportable*
railway bridge 38.21, 317.9 *bridge*
railway engineering 38.17 *civil engineering*
railway express 316.2 *transportation*
railway halt 226.4 *stopping place*
railway line 317.10 *railway*
railwayman 321.9 *railway worker*
railway signal 742.4 *signal*
railway signals 692.27 *signalling*
railway station 321.8; 312.15 *destination*; 313.10 *place of departure*; 226.4 *stopping place*
railway system 321.1 *railway*
railway tracks 188.2 *parallel thing*
railway tunnel 38.22, 317.8 *tunnel*
railway worker 321.9
rain 31.25; **31.62**; 217.5 *about*; 305.3 *downflow*; 305.13 *drip*; 429.2 *mistiness*; 31.24 *precipitation*; 433.1 *water*
rain-bearing cloud 31.18 *cloud*
rain blows down on 331.5 *beat*
rainbow 31.27; 28.28 *colour*; 529.2 *colourfulness*; 132.2 *consecution*; 177.3 *curved things*; 114.3 *diverse thing*; 522.12 *highlight*; 541.5 *variegated thing*
rainbow-coloured 541.6 *variegated*
rainbow effect 541.1 *variegation*
rainbow's end 31.27 *rainbow*
rainbow trout 55.4 *American game fish*; 25.17 *freshwater fish*
rain cats and dogs 217.5 *about*; 305.13 *drip*; 31.62 *rain*
rain cloud 31.18 *cloud*
raincoat 551.12 *coat*
rain damage 31.26 *raininess*
rain dance 22.4 *historic dancing*; 10.7 *non-Christian ritual*; 31.26 *raininess*
rain day 31.24 *precipitation*
rain dew 429.6 *dew*
raindrop 31.24 *precipitation*
rain erosion 30.35 *weathering*
rainfall 367.11 *lowering*; 429.2 *mistiness*; 31.24 *precipitation*; 31.25 *rain*; 433.3 *wateriness*
rainforest 493.8 *hot place*; 79.4 *trees*
rainforest climate 31.38 *climate*
rain gauge 433.19 *measuring instrument*; 31.7 *weather instruments*
rain god 8.5 *deity*
rain hat 551.15 *headgear*
rainier 31.53 *rainy*
rainily 31.65 *meteorologically*
raininess 31.26; 429.2 *mistiness*; 433.3 *wateriness*
raining 331.12 *collision*
raining cats and dogs 31.53 *rainy*
rainless 428.5; 31.45 *fine*
rainmaking 31.26 *raininess*
rainproof 428.10 *waterproof*
rain stopped play 53.1 *cricket match*
rainstorm 31.25 *rain*; 380.5 *violent weather*
rainwater 31.25 *rain*; 433.1 *water*
rainy 31.53; 429.10 *misty*
rainy day 249.4 *time of adversity*
rainy day policy 616.2 *insurance*
rainy season 31.26 *raininess*; 292.1 *season*
raise 154.17; **366.1**; 27.91 *add*; 302.12 *advance*; 765.2 *augmentation*; 69.3 *card game terms*; 243.7 *develop*; 6.22 *educate*; 141.20 *extend*; 302.8 *further*; 244.1 *improve*; 415.10 *lighten*; 190.5, 213.5 *make bigger*; 186.6 *make vertical*; 168.8 *nurture*; 69.10 *play*; 483.5 *positive stimulus*; 43.18 *practise livestock farming*; 356.10 *produce*; 561.13 *propagate*; 813.4 *reward for service*; 403.15 *shape*
raise a cry 514.10 *cry out*
raise a finger 340.4 *act*
raise all hell 507.8 *be loud*
raise an embargo 767.9 *dispose of*
raise an objection 753.6 *protest*
raise a rafter 23.17 *carpenter*
raise a rumpus 408.26 *be disorderly*
raise a storm 380.7 *be violent*
raise Cain 624.11 *be angry*; 507.8 *be loud*; 264.22 *cause trouble*
raise children 168.8 *nurture*
raised 366.11; 190.7 *bigger*; 43.21 *domesticated*; 356.12 *produced*; 6.20 *refined*; 186.9 *unbowed*
raised expectations 604.1 *disappointment*
raised eyebrow 670.10 *disapproving look*
raised eyebrows 742.3 *gesture*; 753.3 *gesture of protest*
raised fist 753.3 *gesture of protest*
raise difficulties 264.23 *cause difficulties*; 264.24 *create difficulties*
raise doubts about 704.9 *deny*
raised seam 53.7 *bat*
raised temperature 493.1 *heat*
raise expectations 475.11 *predict*
raise from cuttings 213.5 *make bigger*
raise from seed 213.5 *make bigger*; 561.13 *propagate*
raise from the dead 554.19 *give birth to*
raise funds 765.9 *gain*; 710.8 *solicit money*
raise ghosts 11.22 *conjure*
raise hell 624.11 *be angry*; 408.26 *be disorderly*; 264.22 *cause trouble*; 740.14 *proclaim*
raise hob 264.22 *cause trouble*
raise money 772.7 *borrow*; 352.6 *find means*
raise money for 650.9 *be charitable*
raise objections 113.18 *object*
raise one's banner 585.12 *go to war*
raise one's consciousness 488.13 *arouse sensation*
raise one's expectations 604.6 *disappoint*
raise one's eyebrows 742.11 *gesture*; 670.23 *show disapproval*
raise one's fist 753.6 *protest*
raise one's glass 601.17 *congratulate*; 558.14 *drink to*
raise one's hackles 624.12 *become angry*
raise one's hand 742.11 *gesture*; 469.5 *vote*
raise one's hand against 381.5 *strike*
raise one's hat 658.12 *greet*
raise one's hopes 610.10 *inspire hope*
raise one's sights 213.5 *make bigger*; 302.7 *make one's way*
raise one's voice 703.18 *appear*; 507.8 *be loud*; 514.10 *cry out*; 726.6 *emphasize*; 738.4 *show oneself*
raise one's voice against 753.6 *protest*
raiser 43.15 *agriculturist*; 366.10 *elevator*
raise someone's hackles 624.9 *offend*
raise steam 323.9 *navigate*; 243.4 *prepare for action*
raise suspicions 451.9 *cause disbelief*
raise taxes 773.8 *take back*
raise the alarm 711.7; 742.12 *signal*
raise the bid 13.11 *deal*; 792.11 *overpay*
raise the curtain 739.5 *disclose*; 21.38 *dramatize*
raise the curtain on 520.10 *make visible*
raise the devil 624.11 *be angry*; 408.26 *be disorderly*; 264.22 *cause trouble*
raise the dust 342.12 *be active*
raise the flag 667.20 *salute*
raise the hunt 633.10 *chase*
raise the issue 705.20 *doubt*; 447.11 *raise the point*
raise the point 447.11
raise the pressure 338.2 *be full of vigour*
raise the price 792.10 *overcharge*
raise the rafters 507.8 *be loud*
raise the roof 669.16 *acclaim*; 624.11 *be angry*; 507.8 *be loud*; 264.22 *cause trouble*; 740.14 *proclaim*
raise the roof over 753.6 *protest*
raise the stakes 213.5 *make bigger*
raise the tempo 332.6 *accelerate*
raise to the peerage 573.5 *make noble*
raise trade barriers 776.1 *trade*
raise up 554.19 *give birth to*; 186.6 *make vertical*; 366.1 *raise*
raisin 25.42 *preserve*
raisin bread 25.38 *bread*
Raising 366
raising 366.6; 6.1 *education*; 190.1 *growth*; 415.4 *leavening*; 186.2 *making vertical*; 186.9 *unbowed*
raising agent 434.11 *aeration*; 366.10 *elevator*; 415.8 *leavening*
raison d'être 482.5 *final intention*; 344.5 *reason*
raitha 25.12 *hors d'oeuvre*; 25.49 *Indian dish*
Raj 8.11 *heaven*
raj 12.3 *governance*
rajah 400.3 *leader*; 400.2 *sovereign*
Rajput 586.6 *militarist*
rake 256.10 *cleaning object*; 44.15 *cultivate*; 362.12 *drag*; 369.10 *excavator*; 43.17 *farm*; 381.2 *fire*; 44.6, 438.3 *garden tool*; 796.8 *immoral man*; 567.7 *libertine*; 322.7 *miscellaneous aviation terms*; 490.3 *pleasure-seeker*; 425.8 *sharp-pointed thing*; 421.11 *smooth*; 421.9 *smoother*; 480.13 *tempter*; 321.7 *train*; 425.16 *use a sharp tool*; 438.10 *use tools*; 804.9 *wicked person*
raked 44.19 *ornamental*
rakehell 796.8 *immoral man*
rake in 362.12 *drag*
rake in the cash 781.13 *get rich*
rake it in 781.12 *be rich*; 781.13 *get rich*; 765.14 *profit*
rake off 752.9 *offer*; 765.14 *profit*; 791.4 *take a discount*
rake-off 791.1 *discount*; 790.3 *fee*; 768.2 *gift*; 752.4 *illegal offer*; 765.5 *profit*; 813.8 *secret money*; 212.2 *subtracted item*; 788.5 *winnings*
rake out 256.13 *clean*; 362.12 *drag*; 369.11 *extract*
rake up the past 462.12 *remember*
raki 558.7 *alcoholic drink*
raking arch 20.5 *arch*
raking fire 381.15 *firing*
raking it in 765.1 *gain*; 781.1 *wealthy*
rakish 796.14 *lecherous*
rakish angle 189.2 *oblique line*
raku firing 24.5 *ceramic process*
raku kiln 24.6 *ceramic workshop*
rale 512.1 *hiss*
rallentando 18.19 *tempo*
rally 376.4; 376.1 *assembly*; 585.14 *battle*; 393.4 *be restored*; 336.7 *be strong*; 376.42 *call together*; 374.5 *combine*; 244.2 *get better*; 585.12 *go to war*; 703.6 *mass demonstration*; 483.9 *motivate*; 703.19 *protest*; 393.11 *recuperation*; 393.3 *restore*; 393.10 *revival*; 392.19 *support*; 63.4 *tennis terms*; 330.5 *throw*; 585.7 *war measures*; 742.6 *word*
rally cross 61.5 *motorcycle racing*
rallying 703.14 *demonstrating*; 14.1 *finance*; 61.1 *motor racing*; 393.11 *recuperation*
rallying cry 514.1 *cry*; 711.2 *danger signal*; 480.4 *exhortation*; 585.2 *glory of war*; 742.6 *word*
rallying symbol 742.1 *sign*
rally round 376.39 *come together*; 747.13 *work together*
rally round the flag 585.12 *go to war*
RAM 462.6 *artificial memory*; 40.6 *memory*
ram 331.15; 381.1 *attack*; 587.7 *blunt weapon*; 331.2 *collide*; 357.9 *demolish*; 43.8 *livestock*; 567.16 *male animal*; 71.17 *male mammal*; 438.1 *tool*; 438.10 *use tools*
Ramadan 687.3 *fast day*; 10.16 *religious festival*
Ramapithecus 566.3 *early human*
ramble 270.6 *be circuitous*; 461.14 *become insane*; 100.13 *be extraneous*; 100.14 *be foreign*; 696.7 *be unintelligible*; 109.10 *be unrelated*; 325.3 *go astray*; 133.15 *lose one's train of thought*
ramble on 270.5 *be diffuse*; 731.7 *be talkative*
rambler 44.9 *garden plant*
rambling 227.13 *changeable*; 270.2 *circumlocution*; 270.4 *circumlocutory*; 100.10 *foreign*; 5.22 *many words*; 219.7 *superfluous*; 696.1 *unintelligible*; 325.16, 325.25 *wandering*
rambling speech 219.3 *superfluity*
rambling wreck 245.9 *dilapidation*
Rambo 336.6 *muscleman*
Ramboesque 585.16 *warlike*
Ramboism 585.5 *bellicosity*
rambunctious 507.6 *loud*
ram down 331.2 *collide*; 232.6 *fill*; 416.9 *make dense*
ram down one's throat 386.7 *force*
ramekin 410.16 *crockery*
ramification 205.6 *branch*; 311.4 *branching*; 377.5 *divergence*; 190.1 *growth*; 198.7 *halving*; 373.4 *means of connection*
ramified 198.13 *half*
ramiform 377.24 *divergent*
ramify 190.6 *become bigger*; 311.14 *branch*; 377.10 *diverge*; 198.16 *halve*; 190.5 *make bigger*
ram in 232.6 *fill*; 368.3 *impact*
ramjet propulsion 330.2 *method of propulsion*
rammer 331.15 *ram*
ramming 331.12 *collision*; 331.17 *impelling*
ramose 311.9 *branched*
ramosely 311.16 *divergently*
ramous 311.9 *branched*
ramously 311.16 *divergently*
ramp 304.14 *climb*; 700.10 *fraud*; 189.1 *obliqueness*; 176.2 *obliquity*; 62.5 *rock face*; 304.16 *stand up*; 304.2 *upturn*
rampage 342.12 *be active*; 327.21 *be agitated*; 624.11 *be angry*; 408.26 *be disorderly*; 507.8 *be loud*; 380.7 *be violent*; 408.9 *disorder*
rampageous 408.20 *disorderly*
rampaging 624.16 *angry*; 357.14 *destructive*
rampant 588.6 *anarchic*; 743.13 *heraldic*; 796.14 *lecherous*; 304.23 *rising*; 186.9 *unbowed*; 380.6 *violent*; 138.17 *widespread*
rampant arch 20.5 *arch*
rampantness 138.4 *widespreadness*
rampart 378.3 *barrier*; 128.3 *exclusion zone*; 384.12 *fort*; 384.11 *fortification*; 252.5 *refuge*; 384.2 *safeguard*; 413.11 *support*; 413.2 *supporting part*
ramped 62.8 *mountaineering*
ram-raid 774.12 *steal*; 774.3 *theft*
ram-raiding 774.1 *stealing*
ramrod 587.9 *firearm*; 331.15 *ram*
ramshackle 245.13 *dilapidated*; 254.2 *unsafe*
ranch 43.6 *farm*; 43.18 *practise livestock farming*; 440.1 *property*
rancher 43.15 *agriculturist*; 557.20 *food provider*; 356.9 *producer*
ranchero 43.15 *agriculturist*
ranch foreman 579.14 *leader*
ranch house 20.3 *building*; 565.5 *house*
ranch-house cook 25.2 *cook*
ranching 43.3 *livestock farming*
ranchman 43.15 *agriculturist*
rancho 43.6 *farm*
rancid 375.5 *disintegrated*; 503.4 *putrid*; 242.3, 499.6 *unpalatable*
rancidity 503.2 *something that makes an unpleasant smell*
rancidness 499.2 *unpalatability*
rancorous 594.10 *hating*; 651.14 *hostile*; 499.7 *splenetic*
rancorously 594.18 *hatefully*; 499.11 *splenetically*
rancour 651.4 *bitterness*; 236.11 *harmfulness*; 594.1 *hate*; 624.1 *resentment*; 499.4 *spleen*
rand 780.11 *national coins*
R and D worker 448.5 *experimenter*
randiness 593.5 *desire*; 617.4 *sexual desire*
random 453.8 *capricious*; 107.8 *chance*; 300.17 *directional*; 133.8 *discontinuous*; 109.7 *illogical*; 299.4, 408.14 *irregular*; 412.12 *mixed*; 163.6 *outlined*; 325.22 *undirected*
random access 40.19 *computing terms*
random chance 107.1 *chance*
randomly 107.13 *by chance*; 453.27 *capriciously*; 408.27 *in disorder*; 412.14 *in the midst*; 299.8 *irregularly*
random motion 300.5 *circuition*
randomness 453.16 *capriciousness*; 107.1 *chance*; 274.2 *inaccuracy*; 299.1 *irregularity*; 408.2 *irregular order*; 412.1 *mixture*; 342.7 *restlessness*; 109.1 *unrelatedness*
randomness of recurrence 299.1 *irregularity*
random number 227.3 *changeable thing*; 27.7 *natural number*

random sample 107.3 *equal chance;* 163.1 *outline;* 27.57 *population*
random sampling 27.57 *population*
random variable 27.57 *population*
R and R 581.5 *refreshment*
randy 593.20 *amorous;* 796.14 *lecherous;* 617.11 *lustful*
Raney nickel 32.15 *catalysis*
range **141.7**; 334.2 *ability;* 409.12 *arrange;* 132.16 *arrange consecutively;* 150.4 *breadth;* 209.1 *degree;* 565.2 *environment;* 141.20 *extend;* 81.2 *grassland;* 250.18 *have scope;* 504.1 *hearing;* 92.6 *lowland;* 27.29 *mathematical function;* 778.8 *merchandise;* 89.1 *mountain;* 27.60 *parameter;* 469.6 *selection;* 26.4, 158.1 *size;* 137.14 *sort;* 504.10 *sound quality;* 439.3 *supply;* 518.9 *viewpoint;* 520.3 *visibility*
ranged 409.20 *arranged*
rangefinder 51.4 *bowling;* 41.18 *exposure time;* 324.3 *orientation;* 520.7 *that which makes visible*
range horse 59.1 *horse*
range of choice 469.6 *selection*
range of colour 529.2 *colourfulness*
ranger 79.8 *forester*
range with 747.14 *join with*
ranginess 154.1 *height;* 153.7 *thinness*
ranging 250.11
ranging freely 250.11 *ranging*
rangy 154.12 *tall;* 153.1 *thin*
rani 400.2 *sovereign*
rank **143.5**; **209.2**; 586.16 *army unit;* 132.16 *arrange consecutively;* 409.15 *categorize;* 409.6 *category;* 108.9 *have a relative position;* 123.1 *importance;* 796.12 *indecent;* 121.10 *lead;* 158.18, 209.5 *measure;* 584.1 *military affairs;* 584.4 *military organization;* 27.56 *nonparametric methods;* 27.94 *order;* 77.13 *plantlike;* 217.2 *plentiful;* 236.4 *poor;* 407.4 *position;* 108.3 *relative position;* 137.5 *social class;* 137.14 *sort;* 141.21 *space;* 221.1 *state;* 503.3 *stinking;* 407.19 *systematize*
rank air fume 432.3 *miasma*
rank and file 586.17 *army person;* 216.7 *average person;* 138.11 *general public;* 574.2 *the common people;* 675.6 *vulgar herd*
ranked **108.6**; **209.8**; 409.24 *categorized;* 137.12 *classed;* 27.75 *equal;* 407.12 *hierarchical;* 221.8 *in a state of*
rank first 121.10 *lead*
rank high 667.21 *command respect;* 667.15 *respect*
Rankine cycle 38.13 *engine cycle*
ranking 409.5 *categorization;* 137.1 *classification;* 209.3 *gradation;* 221.8 *in a state of;* 27.56 *nonparametric methods;* 123.6 *notable;* 407.4 *position;* 221.1 *state*
rankle 245.2 *decay;* 560.18 *fester;* 624.9 *offend*
rankling 560.7 *pus;* 624.1 *resentment*
rank low 668.19 *disrespect*
rankly 503.6 *stinkingly*
rankness 236.10 *poverty;* 296.10 *staleness;* 499.2 *unpalatability*
ransack 357.10 *lay waste;* 774.14 *plunder*
ransacker 774.9 *plunderer;* 773.6 *taker*
ransacking 774.5 *plundering*
ransom 777.3 *buy back;* 390.1 *deliver;* 390.2 *deliverance;* 759.1 *exchange;* 775.4 *give back;* 775.1 *giving back;* 785.4 *grant;* 790.8 *levy;* 814.8 *penalty;* 777.9 *repurchase;* 393.9 *restoration;* 393.3 *restore*
ransomed 777.13 *bought;* 759.7 *exchanged*
ransomer 777.12 *purchaser*
rant 733.1, 733.7 *address;* 542.2 *affectation;* 729.9 *art of public speaking;* 624.11 *be angry;* 270.5 *be diffuse;* 727.10 *boast;* 753.7 *complain;* 659.8 *get angry;* 542.12 *ornament;* 21.35 *overact;* 729.14 *speak to;* 697.6 *talk nonsense*
rant and rave 624.11 *be angry;* 270.5 *be diffuse*
ranter 753.4 *protester;* 733.6 *public speaker;* 729.10 *speaker;* 731.4 *talker*
ranting 729.9 *art of public speaking;* 727.4 *bombast;* 729.20 *eloquent;* 461.12 *manic;* 542.10 *ornate*
ranunculaceous 77.16 *taxonomic*
rap 331.13 *blow;* 814.12 *corporal punishment;* 508.2, 508.6 *crack;* 670.5 *criticism;* 670.17 *criticize;* 729.1 *faculty of speech;* 780.15 *false money;* 331.3 *hit;* 18.9 *popular music;* 731.3 *talk;* 331.6 *tap*
rapacious 688.6 *gluttonous;* 773.12 *taking*
rapaciously 773.13 *avariciously*
rapacity 688.1 *gluttony;* 773.1 *taking*
rap across the knuckles 814.1 *punish;* 814.7 *punishment*
rape 651.7 *act of malevolence;* 381.9 *attack successfully;* 585.13 *be at war;* 16.39 *crime;* 804.7 *criminality;* 43.12 *crop;* 357.5 *havoc;* 236.14 *ill-treat;* 245.4 *impair;* 357.10 *lay waste;* 381.16 *personal attack;* 380.2 *physical violence;* 774.14 *plunder;* 774.5 *plundering;* 796.20 *seduce;* 796.7 *sexual assault;* 381.14 *siege;* 773.7 *take;* 773.1 *taking;* 651.18 *torment;* 380.8 *use violence*
rape alarm 384.5 *self-defence*
raped 773.12 *taking*
rapeseed 77.9 *seed*
Raphael 8.6 *angel*
rapid 300.17 *directional;* 262.3 *hasty;* 280.5 *immediate;* 332.1 *swift;* 497.5 *tasteless*
rapid-fire 381.15 *firing;* 332.1 *swift*
rapidity 262.4 *haste;* 300.8 *rapid motion;* 332.8 *speed*
rapidly 262.6 *hastily;* 280.8 *immediately;* 300.18 *in motion;* 332.14 *swiftly*
rapid motion 300.8
rapids 90.2 *channel;* 305.3 *downflow;* 90.6 *river flow;* 379.1 *trap*
rapid slalom pole 68.3 *ski racing*
rapid tempo 332.8 *speed*
rapid-transit system 321.1 *railway*
rapier 425.8 *sharp-pointed thing;* 587.8 *sharp weapon*
rapine 357.5 *havoc*
raping 774.5 *plundering*
rapist 381.19 *attacker;* 662.9 *criminal;* 798.6 *evil person;* 16.40 *lawbreaker;* 651.8 *malefactor;* 774.9 *plunderer;* 796.10 *sex offender;* 773.6 *taker;* 380.4 *violent creature;* 804.9 *wicked person*
rap on the knuckles 624.5 *quarrel*
rap over the knuckles 670.7 *blame;* 670.20 *censure;* 814.12 *corporal punishment;* 814.3 *hit*
rapparee 586.9 *guerrilla*
rappel 62.3 *climbing technique;* 305.9 *descend;* 62.9 *mountaineer*
rapper 22.4 *historic dancing*
rapping 331.12 *collision*
rap poet 17.14 *author*
rap poetry 17.6 *poetry*
rapport 750.1 *accord;* 569.2 *friendly relations;* 108.1 *relatedness*
rapportage 740.3 *journalism*
rapprochement 749.1 *pacification*
rapscallion 804.9 *wicked person*
rapt 471.8 *diligent;* 619.6 *wondering*
raptness 619.1 *wonder*
raptor 72.5 *bird of prey*
raptorial 72.21 *avian*
rapture 590.4 *emotion;* 597.1 *happiness;* 463.1 *oblivion*
rapturous 593.19 *enamoured;* 463.8 *oblivious;* 590.13 *passionate*
rapturously 590.20 *with feeling*
rara avis 619.5 *person of wonder*
rare 434.12 *airy;* 25.56 *culinary;* 118.14 *eccentric;* 121.15 *excellent;* 415.2 *insubstantial;* 218.4 *scarce;* 206.6, 417.1 *sparse;* 153.5 *thinned;* 105.3 *unexpected;* 235.3, 792.8 *valuable;* 619.8 *wonderful;* 235.1 *worthy*
rare chance 107.6 *poor chance*
rare-earth element 32.6 *chemical element*
raree show 21.7 *show*
rarefaction **417.4**; 153.12 *thinning*
rarefactional 417.2 *rarefied*
rarefied **417.2**; 153.5 *thinned*
rarefy 417.6 *make sparse;* 153.16 *make thin;* 206.8 *reduce*
rare gas 32.6 *chemical element;* 432.1 *gas*
rarely **105.10**; 218.10 *insufficiently;* 206.11 *sparsely;* 121.16 *superiorly;* 792.13 *valuably*
rareness 206.4 *rarity;* 417.3 *sparseness;* 118.4 *unusualness;* 792.6 *value*
rarified 434.12 *airy*
raring to go 636.2 *eager;* 243.18 *prepared*
rarity **206.4**; 434.1 *air;* 415.5 *lightness;* 417.3 *sparseness;* 105.5 *unexpectedness;* 118.4 *unusualness;* 792.6 *value;* 235.6 *worth*
rascal 800.4 *dishonourable person;* 812.2 *disreputable character;* 662.5 *troublemaker;* 804.9 *wicked person*
rascally 645.4 *cunning;* 804.11 *wicked*
rase 367.2 *flatten*
rash **615.4**; 613.13 *adventurous;* 588.6 *anarchic;* 472.10, 618.8 *careless;* 459.5 *foolish;* 262.3 *hasty;* 332.2 *mentally quick;* 354.7 *overambitious;* 467.5 *overestimating;* 260.13 *skin disease;* 478.2 *spontaneous;* 260.3 *symptom*
rasher 25.30 *bacon;* 205.7 *piece;* 411.4 *slice*
rashly **262.7**; **615.6**; 588.8 *anarchically;* 618.18 *carelessly;* 613.18 *courageously;* 254.11 *dangerously;* 354.9 *enterprisingly;* 459.8 *foolishly;* 472.14 *inattentively;* 467.7 *overoptimistically*
rash move 615.2
Rashness 615
rashness **615.1**; 613.4 *adventurousness;* 618.2 *carelessness;* 254.5 *danger;* 661.1 *defiance;* 459.1 *folly;* 262.5 *hastiness;* 472.2 *impetuosity;* 472.1 *inattention;* 336.3 *intensity;* 467.1 *overestimation;* 332.8 *speed*
Rashnu 8.6 *angel*
rash person **459.4**; **615.3**
rashy 260.23 *diseased*
rasorial 72.21 *avian*
rasp 513.4 *be strident;* 515.6 *buzz;* 365.7 *eraser;* 427.25 *grate;* 365.15 *grind;* 512.4 *hiss;* 517.10 *lack harmony;* 513.5 *sound hoarse*
raspberry 512.2 *catcall;* 514.7 *cry of disapproval;* 80.5 *figurative usage;* 742.3 *gesture;* 753.3 *gesture of protest;* 535.7 *red thing;* 670.9 *show of disapproval;* 668.6 *taunt*
raspberry beetle 44.12 *pests and diseases*
raspberry midge 44.12 *pests and diseases*
rasping 517.7 *dissonant;* 365.3 *grinding;* 513.8 *hoarse;* 365.11 *rough*
raspingly 365.17 *abrasively;* 517.12 *dissonantly;* 513.10 *stridently*
raspings 427.6 *crumb*
rasping sound 513.2 *hoarseness*
Rasputin 483.7 *motivator*
Rasta 7.6 *non-Christian*
Rastafarian 7.6 *non-Christian*
raster 40.19 *computing terms*
rat 479.3 *apostatize;* 804.10 *bad person;* 739.7 *betray;* 614.2 *coward;* 355.4 *deserter;* 479.9 *equivocator;* 693.10 *informer;* 693.13 *inform on;* 716.7 *person who gives evidence;* 454.3 *testify;* 700.21 *traitor;* 716.13 *turn queen's evidence;* 454.7 *verifier;* 711.4 *warner;* 355.2 *withdraw*
rataplan 326.2 *vibration*
rat-arsed 690.1 *drunk*
rat-a-tat 509.4 *knocking;* 326.2 *vibration*
ratatouille 25.45 *French dish*
rat-catcher 382.13 *animal killer;* 71.24, 633.6 *hunter*
ratchet 425.8 *sharp-pointed thing*
ratchet wheel 307.6 *rotator*
rate 409.15 *categorize;* 209.1 *degree;* 27.18 *division;* 464.12 *estimate;* 787.5 *expense;* 790.3 *fee;* 108.9 *have a relative position;* 26.10, 209.5 *measure;* 790.11 *price;* 203.8 *quantify;* 137.14 *sort*
rateable 790.15 *chargeable*
rateable value 790.7 *tax*
rate a movie 399.4 *censor*
rate-capped 251.13 *restraining*
rate-capping 251.2 *economic restraint*
rate constant 32.14 *chemical reaction*
rated 409.24 *categorized;* 137.12 *classed;* 209.7 *gradational;* 26.13 *measured;* 790.14 *priced;* 108.6 *ranked*
rate-determining step 32.14 *chemical reaction*
rate for the job 790.3 *fee*
rate of change 27.31 *differentiation*
rate of interest 784.4 *interest*
rate of speed 332.8 *speed*
rate of striking 50.4 *rowing*
ratepayer 790.10 *taxpayer*
rates 788.2 *money received;* 790.7 *tax*
rat-faced 690.1 *drunk*
rat flea 76.3 *pest*
rather 685.9 *moderately;* 469.17 *selectively;* 209.11 *to a degree*
ratification 707.4 *confirmation;* 750.7 *consent;* 755.1 *contract;* 16.31 *legislation;* 757.1 *permission;* 703.4 *proof;* 454.4 *verification*
ratificatory 750.17 *consenting;* 454.9 *verificatory*
ratified 750.17 *consenting;* 755.7 *contractual;* 16.46 *legislated;* 703.13 *proven;* 707.13 *supported;* 454.10 *verified*
ratifier 707.9 *affirmer;* 755.4 *contractor*
ratify 669.12 *accept;* 707.19 *confirm;* 750.28 *consent;* 755.5 *contract;* 95.12 *establish reality;* 743.11 *identify oneself;* 16.68 *legislate;* 228.7 *make stable;* 757.3 *permit;* 703.17 *prove;* 454.1 *verify*
ratifying 750.17 *consenting*
rat-infested 245.13 *dilapidated*
rating 409.5 *categorization;* 209.3 *gradation;* 123.1 *importance;* 464.1 *judgment;* 26.1 *measurement;* 586.27 *naval man;* 108.3 *relative position;* 137.5 *social class;* 790.7 *tax*
ratings 740.2 *mass media*
ratio **194.5**; 27.18 *division;* 209.3 *gradation;* 108.2 *interrelatedness;* 770.2 *portion*
ratiocinate 460.6 *be sane;* 701.14 *discuss;* 4.20 *philosophize;* 444.11 *reason;* 442.12, 443.12 *think*
ratiocination 701.2 *logical argument;* 442.1 *mind;* 4.4 *philosophical investigation;* 444.2 *reasoning;* 443.1 *thought;* 442.2 *ways of thinking*
ratiocinative 4.15, 444.8 *rational*
ration 770.4 *allot;* 43.9 *animal feedstuff;* 203.2 *certain amount;* 251.2 *economic restraint;* 251.9 *economize;* 196.2 *fractional part;* 209.3 *gradation;* 166.7 *limit;* 218.7 *make insufficient;* 770.2 *portion;* 436.1 *provision;* 203.8 *quantify*
rational **4.15**; **444.8**; **460.5**; 701.12 *apologetic;* 27.72 *complex;* 27.6 *complex number;* 27.74 *divisible;* 442.9 *mental;* 685.6 *moderate;* 194.8 *odd;* 409.22 *organizational;* 484.14 *planned;* 443.11, 444.7 *reasoning;* 458.5 *wise*
rationale 701.3 *line of argument;* 480.11, 483.1 *motive;* 344.5 *reason;* 442.2 *ways of thinking*
rational-emotive therapy 36.3 *psychiatric treatment*
rationalism 444.2 *reasoning;* 4.7 *school of thought;* 7.13 *theology*
rationalist 451.5 *disbeliever;* 4.11 *follower of a doctrine;* 250.8 *free-thinker;* 250.10 *independent;* 4.14 *of a philosophy;* 444.5 *reasoner*
rationalistic 250.10 *independent;* 444.8 *rational*
rationalistically 250.20 *freely*
rationality **460.2**; 4.3 *detachment;* 442.1 *mind;* 444.1 *reason;* 444.2 *reasoning*
rationalization 760.1 *conversion;* 214.1 *decrease;* 36.19 *defence mechanism;* 13.6 *economic factors;* 244.5 *improvement;* 409.3 *organization;* 4.1 *philosophy;* 484.7 *planning;* 701.5 *plea;* 444.2 *reasoning*
rationalize **4.21**; 244.1 *improve;* 298.10 *make regular;* 214.5 *make smaller;* 409.13 *organize;* 484.9 *plan;* 701.16 *plead;* 444.11 *reason;* 244.3 *rectify;* 206.8 *reduce;* 407.19 *systematize;* 442.12 *think;* 760.9 *transform*
rationalized 409.21 *organized*
rationalizing 444.2 *reasoning*
rationally **4.26**; 701.20 *apologetically;* 409.28 *in place;* 442.15 *intelligently;* 444.15 *reasonably;* 460.7 *sanely;* 443.18 *thoughtfully;* 458.9 *wisely*
rational number 27.6 *complex number;* 194.2 *kind of number*
rational person 443.7 *thinker*
rational psychology 36.1 *psychology*
rationed 203.6 *quantitative;* 251.13 *restraining;* 218.2 *unprovided*
rationing 251.2 *economic restraint;* 166.2 *limiting factor;* 585.7 *war measures*
ration oneself 674.14 *be modest;* 684.5 *be self-restrained*
rations 557.7 *food;* 436.1 *provision*
ratio scale 27.56 *nonparametric methods*
ratite 72.21 *avian;* 72.2 *flightless bird*
ratlike 71.30 *rodent-like*
ratlin 304.9 *ladder*
ratline 304.9 *ladder;* 50.3 *parts of a sailing boat;* 373.7 *tackle*
rat poison 43.14 *pest control*
rat race 342.3 *nimbleness;* 307.3 *reel*
rat run 320.2 *road*
ratsbane 382.13 *animal killer*
rat's nest 408.4 *litter*
rattan 814.14 *instrument of punishment*
rat-tat-tat 508.2 *crack;* 509.4 *knocking*
ratted 690.1 *drunk*
ratter 71.10 *cat;* 479.9 *equivocator*
ratting 479.7 *apostasy;* 633.2 *chase;* 71.23 *mammal hunting*
rattish 71.30 *rodent-like*
rattle **509.3**; **509.10**; 124.9 *bauble;* 507.8 *be loud;* 508.6 *crack;* 481.2 *deter;* 328.7

disturb; 381.2 *fire*; 507.1 *loudness*; 507.4 *sound maker*; 326.9 *vibrate*; 337.7 *weaken*
rattle along 332.4 *be swift*
rattled 614.3 *cowardly*; 328.12 *disturbed*; 639.3 *timid*
rattle on 731.7 *be talkative*
rattler 73.3 *snake*
rattlesnake 73.3 *snake*
rattle the windows 507.8 *be loud*
rattletrap 320.16 *car*
rattling 509.17; 508.9 *crackling*; 507.6 *loud*; 332.1 *swift*
rattling pace 332.8 *speed*
rattling thunder 507.1 *loudness*
rat trap 782.7 *beggary*; 320.11 *bicycle part*; 245.9 *dilapidation*; 43.14 *pest control*; 700.13 *snare*
ratty 624.16 *angry*; 71.30 *rodent-like*
raucous 517.7 *dissonant*; 513.7 *strident*
raucously 517.12 *dissonantly*
raucousness 730.2 *inarticulation*; 513.1 *stridency*
ravage 381.9 *attack successfully*; 585.13 *be at war*; 245.4 *impair*; 357.10, 441.2 *lay waste*; 774.14 *plunder*
ravager 357.6 *destroyer*; 774.9 *plunderer*
ravages of time 245.9 *dilapidation*; 275.2 *passage of time*
ravaging 774.5 *plundering*; 774.17 *stolen*
Ravana 8.7 *devil*
rave 624.11 *be angry*; 461.14 *become insane*; 727.10 *boast*; 376.10 *dance*; 22.1 *dancing*; 542.12 *ornament*; 654.5 *party*; 600.5 *rejoice*; 600.1 *rejoicing*; 697.6 *talk nonsense*
rave about 669.15 *compliment*; 740.16 *publicize*
ravelin 384.11 *fortification*
raven 475.7 *bad-luck sign*; 617.14 *be hungry*; 532.1 *black*; 532.9 *black thing*; 523.4 *dark thing*; 557.22 *eat well*; 72.6 *songbird*
raven-haired 532.4 *black-haired*
ravening 218.3 *underfed*; 380.6 *violent*
ravenous 557.26 *eating*; 687.6 *fasting*; 688.6 *gluttonous*; 617.10 *hungry*; 218.3 *underfed*
ravenously 687.7 *abstemiously*; 557.28 *carnivorously*; 688.7 *gluttonously*; 617.19 *hungrily*
ravenousness 688.1 *gluttony*
Ravensburger waltz 68.7 *ice-dancing*
rave on 735.4 *monopolize the conversation*
raver 597.3 *joyful person*; 600.4 *rejoicer*; 654.6 *social person*
rave review 669.4 *compliment*; 719.3 *criticism*; 246.3 *successful thing*
ravine 183.2 *concave land*; 156.4 *deep thing*; 146.3 *gulf*; 30.7 *landform*; 151.6 *narrow place*; 92.8 *valley*
raving 727.4 *bombast*; 727.15 *bombastic*; 461.12 *manic*; 590.13 *passionate*; 735.5 *soliloquizing*
raving beauty 545.3 *attractive female*
raving mad 461.11 *insane*
ravings 461.4 *delusion*; 735.1 *soliloquy*
ravish 774.14 *plunder*; 796.20 *seduce*; 773.7 *take*; 380.8 *use violence*
ravisher 774.9 *plunderer*
ravishment 774.5 *plundering*; 796.7 *sexual assault*; 773.1 *taking*
raw 538.3; 494.8 *cold*; 31.55 *cool*; 25.56 *culinary*; 712.8 *cursing*; 130.32 *embryonic*; 491.7 *feeling pain*; 529.12 *gaudy*; 295.12, 555.12 *immature*; 231.2, 233.4 *incomplete*; 491.5 *painful*; 437.10 *powered*; 161.5 *shapeless*; 591.3 *sore*; 487.1 *unaccustomed*; 552.9 *undressed*; 420.5 *unfinished*; 486.2 *unskilled*; 31.47 *windy*
rawboned 153.1 *thin*
raw deal 249.1 *adversity*; 802.7 *sense of wrong*
raw feelings 591.6 *oversensitivity*
raw glaze 24.3 *glaze*
rawhide 550.14 *animal covering*; 435.1 *materials*
rawly 295.24, 555.15 *immaturely*
raw material 24.2; 402.4 *matter*; 344.3 *rudiment*; 352.2 *supplies*
raw materials 435.1 *materials*
raw nerve 624.3 *cause of offence*; 488.4 *someone or something that feels*
rawness 295.3, 555.3 *immaturity*; 231.5 *imperfection*; 233.1 *incompleteness*; 161.1 *shapelessness*; 591.7 *soreness*; 486.8 *unskilfulness*
raw recruit 130.14 *beginner*; 295.8 *new arrival*; 486.10 *unskilled person*
raw sienna 534.4 *brown pigment*; 536.2 *orangeness*
raw umber 534.4 *brown pigment*
ray 522.1 *light*; 27.37 *line*; 311.13 *radiate*; 311.3 *radiation*; 326.5 *wave*
rayed 311.7 *radiating*
ray-finned fish 74.2 *fish*
ray floret 78.4 *flower head*
ray of hope 610.1 *hope*
ray of light 28.24 *light emission*
ray of sunshine 598.4 *cheerful person*; 608.3 *reliever*
rayon 435.1 *materials*; 42.12 *natural*
rayonist 19.29 *realist*
rays of the sun 522.1 *light*; 522.4 *natural light*
raze 365.13 *abrade*; 357.9 *demolish*; 367.2 *flatten*; 441.2 *lay waste*; 187.7 *make horizontal*; 358.1 *obliterate*
razed to the ground 187.10 *lying*; 358.6 *obliterated*
raze to the ground 357.9 *demolish*; 367.2 *flatten*; 187.7 *make horizontal*
razing 357.2 *destroying*
razor 552.7 *depilation*; 425.9 *sharp-edged thing*; 425.16 *use a sharp tool*
razor blade 425.9 *sharp-edged thing*
razor edge 425.7 *sharp point*
razor-edged 425.3 *sharp-edged*
razor's edge 164.3 *cutting edge*; 254.5 *danger*; 151.8 *narrow thing*
razor-sharp 425.5 *mentally sharp*; 425.3 *sharp-edged*
razor wire 384.9 *barrier*
RBI leader 48.2 *baseball player*
RC 7.16 *denominational*
RE 6.3 *subject*
reabsorb 370.13 *absorb*
reach 145.7; **312.2**; 334.2 *ability*; 492.12 *abut*; 765.10 *augment*; 504.16 *be heard*; 209.1 *degree*; 627.11 *excite pity*; 141.20 *extend*; 141.3 *geographical space*; 12.3 *governance*; 148.4 *length*; 50.19 *punt*; 141.7 *range*; 50.15 *sail*; 158.1 *size*; 217.4 *suffice*
reach a better world 582.15 *die*
reachable 504.14 *hearable*; 102.5 *possible*; 492.8 *touchable*
reach a compromise 754.4 *compromise*
reach a crescendo 765.10 *augment*
reach a crisis 222.13 *get into difficulties*
reach a lower level 305.9 *descend*
reach a mass audience 695.5 *simplify*
reach a milestone 222.12 *come to a juncture*
reach an all-time low 195.10 *hit rock bottom*
reach a new high 121.8 *be superior*
reach an impasse 378.9 *block*
reach a stage 760.8 *be transformed*; 222.12 *come to a juncture*
reach a stalemate 378.9 *block*
reach boiling point 624.12 *become angry*
reach full growth 232.5 *be complete*
reaching 312.17 *achievement*; 51.9 *bowls*; 209.7 *gradational*; 50.8, 50.14 *punting*; 50.1 *sailing*
reaching a mass audience 695.2 *simple*
reaching shot 51.2 *grip*
reach manhood 556.18 *mature*
reach maturity 232.5 *be complete*
reach-me-down 551.1 *dress*
reach new heights 121.8 *be superior*
reach one's destination 317.14 *find one's way*; 312.2 *reach*
reach one's goal 204.10 *complete*; 253.13 *secure one's objective*
reach one's majority 556.18 *mature*
reach one's nadir 122.11 *become inferior*; 305.10 *droop*
reach one's threshold 166.7 *limit*
reach out 148.9 *be long*; 302.7 *make one's way*; 145.7 *reach*
reach perfection 232.5 *be complete*
reach safety 252.9 *be safe*
reach the bottom 156.14 *deepen*
reach the depths 305.10 *droop*
reach the other side 318.11 *cross*
reach there 312.2 *reach*
reach the top 312.9 *achieve*; 304.13 *ascend*; 400.14 *master*
reach the turning point 222.12 *come to a juncture*
reach the zenith 304.13 *ascend*
reach to 145.7 *reach*
reach towards 302.7 *make one's way*
react 32.26; **706.19**; 347.3 *counteract*; 342.14 *push*; 110.7 *reciprocate*; 385.3 *retaliate*; 761.6 *reverse*; 488.11 *sense*; 345.5 *show an effect*
react against 596.6; 347.3 *counteract*
reactance 28.53, 39.12 *resistance*
reactant 32.14 *chemical reaction*
react automatically 445.10 *be instinctive*
reacted 761.11 *reversed*
reacting 345.10 *caused*; 110.4 *reciprocal*
reacting to 345.10 *caused*
reaction 706.4; 113.7 *contrariness*; 347.1 *counteraction*; 345.1 *effect*; 590.1 *feeling*; 446.1 *idea*; 110.1 *interchange*; 393.9 *restoration*; 761.1 *reversion*; 488.1 *sensation*
reactionarily 225.10 *conservatively*
reactionary 662.12; 225.8 *conservative*; 225.3 *conservative person*; 347.4 *counteracting*; 641.8 *obstinate person*; 113.11 *opposer*; 12.6 *political party*; 761.10 *regressive*; 383.5 *resister*; 383.12 *resisting*; 303.24 *retroactive*; 641.4 *set*; 113.26 *uncooperative*
reaction formation 36.19 *defence mechanism*
reactionist 113.26 *uncooperative*
reaction order 32.14 *chemical reaction*
reaction propulsion 330.2 *method of propulsion*
reactions 484.2 *policy*
reaction turbine 38.12 *turbine*
reaction wood 79.3 *timber*
reactivate 393.1 *repair*
reactivation 393.8 *repair*; 393.10 *revival*
reactive 32.38; **706.12**; 347.4 *counteracting*; 761.10 *regressive*
reactive depression 36.13 *depression*
reactively 347.5 *counter*; 706.24 *in answer*; 761.13 *reversibly*
reactive neurosis 36.10 *neurosis*
reactive power 39.26 *electrical energy*
reactology 36.1 *psychology*
reactor 28.73 *nuclear reactor*
reactor core 28.73 *nuclear reactor*
react sharply 342.14 *push*
read 40.20 *abort*; 631.14 *behave towards*; 692.34 *communicated*; 719.9 *decipher*; 46.8 *huddle*; 518.14 *inspect*; 719.8 *interpret*; 6.23 *learn*; 550.35 *progress*; 4.21 *rationalize*; 769.13 *received*; 707.11 *stated*; 5.46 *translate*
readability 543.1 *elegance*; 695.10 *simplicity*
readable 543.3 *elegant*; 695.2 *simple*
readably 543.5 *elegantly*
read between the lines 719.8 *interpret*
readdress 316.13 *post*; 733.10 *send*
read easily 695.4 *be intelligible*
reader 400.9 *educational leader*; 6.4 *educator*; 40.7 *peripheral*; 550.22 *progression*; 733.6 *public speaker*; 769.5 *recipient*; 6.14 *school book*
readership 6.6 *instructorship*; 740.2 *mass media*
read hieroglyphics 719.9 *decipher*
readied 243.18 *prepared*
readies 780.2 *cash*; 352.4 *financial resources*
readily 595.11 *admiringly*; 136.17 *capably*; 293.17 *early*; 265.21 *easily*; 243.22 *in preparation*; 663.10 *obediently*; 346.13 *operationally*; 229.6 *probably*; 636.16 *willingly*
read in 7.21 *ordain*
readiness 229.2 *attitude*; 97.4 *availability*; 665.3 *circumspection*; 293.1 *earliness*; 265.1 *easiness*; 6.10 *educability*; 595.2 *inclination*; 556.3 *maturity*; 342.3 *nimbleness*; 663.1 *obedience*; 230.3 *perfection*; 243.14 *preparedness*; 136.1 *qualification*; 287.1 *timeliness*; 237.5 *usefulness*; 636.6 *willingness*
readiness to take offence 625.1 *irascibility*
reading 733.1 *address*; 719.1 *interpretation*; 6.8 *learning*; 26.1 *measurement*; 28.82 *measuring instrument*; 729.8 *speech*
reading cards 475.2 *divination*
reading desk 23.4 *table*
reading glass 518.10 *visual aid*
reading glasses 518.10 *visual aid*
reading in 7.9 *priesthood*
reading lamp 522.6 *electric light*
reading list 220.2 *table*
reading of the verdict 16.7 *legal trial*
read into 719.8 *interpret*; 720.1 *misinterpret*
readjust 754.4 *compromise*; 119.11 *equalize*
readjustment 119.3 *equalization*; 393.9 *restoration*
read lips 719.12 *translate*
read minds 11.24 *experience psychic phenomena*
readmission 370.1 *admittance*
readmit 370.7 *admit*
read one's hand 475.12 *divine*
read one's palm 475.12 *divine*
read-only 40.21 *on-line*
readout 26.1 *measurement*; 28.82 *measuring instrument*
read palms 11.23 *divine*
read sign language 719.12 *translate*
read signs 11.23 *divine*
read something into it 234.12 *distort the truth*
read tea leaves 11.23 *divine*; 283.9 *look ahead*
read the banns 756.1 *promise*
read the cards 475.12 *divine*
read the chart 323.9 *navigate*
read the defence 46.15 *play offence*
read the entrails 475.12 *divine*
read the future 475.12 *divine*
read the riot act 670.21 *berate*
read the runes 475.12 *divine*
read the signs 475.12 *divine*
read the stars 475.12 *divine*
read the Tarot 11.23 *divine*
read the wedding service 570.16 *join in marriage*
read the wedding vows 570.16 *join in marriage*
readthrough 21.14 *production*
read through 21.37 *rehearse*
read up on 6.23 *learn*
ready 342.18 *active*; 97.10, 282.8 *available*; 665.9 *careful*; 293.12 *early*; 6.17 *educable*; 474.5 *expecting*; 595.6 *liking*; 239.2 *nearby*; 663.7 *obedient*; 230.1 *perfect*; 243.18 *prepared*; 243.4 *prepare for action*; 436.8 *provisional*; 136.9 *qualified*; 485.6 *skilful*; 229.5 *tending to*; 237.1 *useful*; 636.1 *willing*
ready and willing 636.2 *eager*
ready cash 785.1 *payment*
ready for another round 581.4 *refreshed*
ready for anything 243.19 *in hand*; 485.6 *skilful*
ready for bed 261.1 *fatigued*
ready for hearing 16.54 *litigated*
ready-formed 243.21 *ready-made*
ready for more 581.4 *refreshed*
ready for sleep 261.1 *fatigued*
ready for use 243.19 *in hand*; 237.1 *useful*
ready-furnished 243.21 *ready-made*
ready-made 243.21; 356.12 *produced*; 160.10 *prototypical*; 19.12 *sculpture*; 551.31 *styled*
ready-made verdict 106.6 *premeditation*
ready-mixed 243.21 *ready-made*
ready money 780.2 *cash*; 780.6 *funds*
ready oneself 243.8 *prepare oneself*
ready reckoner 210.5 *computer*
ready to 229.5 *tending to*
ready to break 424.1 *brittle*
ready to burst 424.1 *brittle*; 219.6 *excessive*; 217.3 *filled*
ready-to-cook 25.56 *culinary*; 243.21 *ready-made*
ready to crack 424.1 *brittle*
ready to die for 473.5 *unselfish*
ready-to-eat 280.7 *prepared for immediate use*
ready to go 243.18 *prepared*
ready to hand 282.8 *available*; 243.19 *in hand*
ready to rest 261.1 *fatigued*
ready-to-serve 25.56 *culinary*; 243.21 *ready-made*
ready to split 424.1 *brittle*
ready to use 243.21 *ready-made*
ready-to-wear 280.7 *prepared for immediate use*; 243.21 *ready-made*; 551.31 *styled*
ready-to-wear clothes 551.1 *dress*
ready wit 599.3 *wit*
reaffirm 726.6 *emphasize*
reafforest 393.3 *restore*
reafforestation 393.9 *restoration*
reafforested 79.16 *wooded*
reagent 32.14 *chemical reaction*
real 93.13; **95.6**; 126.6, 698.19 *authentic*;

452.1 *certain*; 3.19 *chronicled*; 27.72 *complex*; 27.6 *complex number*; 698.16 *existing*; 16.51 *legitimate*; 402.7 *material*; 194.8 *odd*; 97.7 *present*; 440.8 *propertied*; 492.8 *touchable*
real ale 558.7 *alcoholic drink*
real analysis 27.30 *calculus*
real bargain 777.6 *purchase*
real bastard 264.3 *difficult task*
real bitch 264.3 *difficult task*
real bore 620.2 *boring thing*
real bugger 264.3 *difficult task*
real estate 440.1 *property*
real-estate agent 440.7 *property man*
real George 235.1 *worthy*
realign 409.14 *rearrange*
realigned 409.23 *rearranged*
realignment 409.4 *rearrangement*
real image 28.31 *lens element*
realism 95.3; **698.12**; 273.2 *correctness*; 717.1 *representation*; 4.7 *school of thought*; 21.10 *theatre movements*
realist 19.29; **95.4**; 21.42 *activist*; 340.3 *doer*; 4.11 *follower of a doctrine*; 402.3 *materialist*; 4.14 *of a philosophy*
realistic 95.7; 450.13 *believable*; 452.1 *certain*; 273.6 *correct*; 721.11 *descriptive*; 115.9, 698.25 *lifelike*; 17.16 *literary*; 95.8 *practical*; 4.15 *rational*; 717.13 *representational*; 721.13 *representing*
realistically 115.14 *comparably*; 721.18 *descriptively*; 21.44 *dramatically*; 19.30 *pictorially*; 4.26 *rationally*; 717.14 *representationally*
realistic representation 698.12 *realism*
realities 95.5
Reality 95
reality 95.1; **698.2**; 452.9 *certainty*; 123.3 *chief thing*; 93.4 *demonstrable existence*; 3.14 *historicalness*; 97.1 *presence*; 492.1 *touch*
reality therapy 36.3 *psychiatric treatment*
realizable 95.9; 695.1 *intelligible*; 102.5 *possible*
realization 525.1 *appearance*; 232.3 *completion*; 590.1 *feeling*; 449.8 *finding out*; 765.1 *gain*; 455.1 *knowledge*; 402.2 *materialization*; 717.1 *representation*; 695.12 *understanding*
realize 780.26 *bank*; 693.15 *be informed*; 402.8 *be material*; 93.20 *bring into being*; 232.4 *complete*; 590.15 *feel*; 449.3 *find out*; 765.9 *gain*; 446.14 *have an idea*; 477.14 *imagine*; 455.11 *know*; 95.11 *make real*; 230.5 *perfect*; 525.14 *present*; 4.21 *rationalize*; 717.9 *represent*; 778.1 *sell*; 488.11 *sense*; 695.6 *understand*
realized 525.7 *appearing*; 402.7 *material*
realize one's capital 13.10 *trade with*
realize one's potential 232.5 *be complete*
realizing 590.10 *feeling*
real life 95.3 *realism*
real-life 721.11 *descriptive*; 95.7 *realistic*
real-life story 721.4 *factual account*
really 93.22; **95.13**; 454.12 *assuredly*; 698.37 *authentically*; 452.23 *certainly*; 643.11 *earnestly*; 643.12 *indeed*; 97.14 *in person*; 3.25 *reportedly*; 698.35 *truly*; 619.14 *wonderful!*
really! 454.13
really mean 694.10 *mean*; 482.8 *resolve*
really move 332.4 *be swift*
really-truly 95.14 *certainly*; 698.35 *truly*
realm 85.3 *dominion*; 396.8 *governmental organization*; 566.11 *nation*; 12.5 *political organization*; 86.14 *sphere*; 6.3 *subject*; 86.4 *territorial division*; 137.4 *type*
realm of light 8.11 *heaven*
realm of Pluto 8.12 *hell*
realness 698.6 *authenticity*; 3.14 *historicalness*
real number 27.6 *complex number*; 194.2 *kind of number*
real part 27.6 *complex number*
real person 402.5 *object*
realpolitik 645.1 *cunning*; 631.9 *tactics*
real presence 10.6 *Eucharist*
real property 440.1 *property*
real saint 7.3 *religious person*
real self 139.11 *identity*
real sod 264.3 *difficult task*
real tennis 63.5; 63.1 *tennis*
real time 40.19 *computing terms*; 275.7 *time measurement*
realtor 440.7 *property man*
realty 440.1 *property*
real wages 13.6 *economic factors*
real war 585.1 *war*
real world 95.2; 402.1 *material world*
ream 308.20 *hole*; 435.3 *paper*
reamed 308.14 *holed*
reamer 256.10 *cleaning object*; 308.2 *opener*
reanimate 554.21 *invigorate*; 581.1 *refresh*; 393.5 *revive*
reanimation 554.5 *life cycle*; 581.5 *refreshment*; 561.1 *reproduction*; 393.10 *revival*
reap 43.17 *farm*; 813.14 *gain*; 149.10 *shorten*; 439.6 *store*
reap a profit 813.14 *gain*; 765.14 *profit*
reaper 376.35 *collector*
reaping hook 43.10 *farm tool*
reappear 276.10 *be periodical*; 112.21 *be repeated*; 393.4 *be restored*; 525.13 *occur*
reappearance 525.6; 112.4 *return*; 393.10 *revival*
reappearing 112.14 *recurrent*; 561.15 *reproduced*
reappoint 775.4 *give back*; 393.3 *restore*
reappointment 775.1 *giving back*
reap the benefit of 237.11 *find useful*
reap the fruits 246.6 *be successful*; 813.14 *gain*
reap the harvest 246.6 *be successful*
reap the profit from 237.11 *find useful*
rear 168.1; **168.4**; 366.5 *arise*; 586.14 *armed forces*; 186.5 *be vertical*; 6.22 *educate*; 131.25 *hindmost*; 213.5 *make bigger*; 168.8 *nurture*; 113.2 *oppositeness*; 43.18 *practise livestock farming*; 356.10 *produce*; 561.13 *propagate*; 154.16 *rise*; 304.16 *stand up*
rear-admiral 586.27 *naval man*
rear cushion 51.4 *bowling*
rear-dump truck 38.29 *construction equipment*
reared 43.21 *domesticated*; 356.12 *produced*; 6.20 *refined*; 186.9 *unbowed*
rear end 168.2
rear entrance 168.1 *rear*
rearguard 586.14 *armed forces*; 384.14 *guard*; 711.4 *warner*
rearing 6.1 *education*; 186.2 *making vertical*; 366.6 *raising*; 304.23 *rising*; 186.9 *unbowed*
rearing up 168.3
rear its head 525.12 *become visible*
rear light 522.6 *electric light*
rear mast 168.1 *rear*
rear one's head 738.4 *show oneself*
rear part 168.1 *rear*
rearrange 409.14; 224.8 *cause change*; 32.26 *react*; 409.19 *tidy*
rearranged 409.23; 224.12 *changed*
rearrangement 409.4; 224.1 *change*; 32.14 *chemical reaction*
rear sentry 711.4 *warner*
rear up 168.7; 186.5 *be vertical*; 154.16 *rise*; 304.16 *stand up*
rear-view mirror 28.29 *optical element*; 518.8 *reflection*
rearward 303.28 *backwards*; 168.9 *in the rear*; 168.4 *rear*
Reason 444
reason 344.5; **444.1**; **444.11**; 131.14 *aim*; 714.2 *defence*; 701.14 *discuss*; 342.4 *energy*; 464.12 *estimate*; 442.3 *intelligence*; 719.8 *interpret*; 480.11, 483.1 *motive*; 446.4 *purpose*; 460.2 *rationality*; 4.21 *rationalize*; 706.6 *solution*; 706.20 *solve*; 476.5 *suppose*; 27.89 *theorize*; 442.12, 443.12 *think*; 443.1 *thought*; 458.1 *wisdom*
reasonability 104.3 *plausibility*
reasonable 450.13 *believable*; 793.9 *cheap*; 648.4 *lenient*; 684.9, 685.6 *moderate*; 104.7 *plausible*; 102.5 *possible*; 446.12 *purposive*; 4.15, 460.5 *rational*; 444.7 *reasoning*; 442.11 *thoughtful*; 714.13 *vindicable*
reasonable charge 793.1 *cheapness*
reasonableness 793.1 *cheapness*; 4.3 *detachment*; 648.1 *leniency*; 684.2, 685.1 *moderation*; 460.2 *rationality*
reasonable person 460.3 *sane person*
reasonably 444.15; 701.20 *apologetically*; 450.16 *believably*; 793.15 *cheaply*; 706.26 *correspondingly*; 442.15 *intelligently*; 648.6 *leniently*; 684.12, 685.9 *moderately*; 102.10 *practically*; 446.21 *purposively*; 4.26 *rationally*; 460.7 *sanely*
reason behind 344.5 *reason*
reasoned 446.12 *purposive*; 4.15 *rational*; 706.14 *solved*
reasoner 444.5; 586.5 *arguer*
reasoning 27.64; **443.11**; **444.2**; **444.7**; 464.1 *judgment*; 16.7 *legal trial*; 701.3 *line of argument*; 701.2 *logical argument*; 442.9 *mental*; 480.11 *motive*; 4.4 *philosophical investigation*; 443.1 *thought*; 443.8 *thoughtful*; 442.2 *ways of thinking*; 458.5 *wise*
reasons 716.1 *evidence*
reason why 344.5 *reason*
reassemble 376.45; 393.1 *repair*; 393.3 *restore*
reassembling 393.8 *repair*
reassert 726.6 *emphasize*
reassurance 610.4 *comfort*; 608.1 *ease*; 613.6 *encouragement*
reassure 609.9 *comfort*; 613.17 *give courage*; 610.10 *inspire hope*; 608.9 *relieve*
reassured 608.7 *relieved*
reassuring 610.14 *cheering*; 613.14 *encouraging*; 608.8 *relieving*; 392.32, 413.9 *supportive*
reassuringly 608.15 *comfortingly*
Réaumur scale 493.2 *heat measurement*
reawaken 393.4 *be restored*; 393.5 *revive*
reawakening 393.10 *revival*
rebarbative 596.9 *disliked*; 242.1 *unpleasant*
rebarbatively 596.11 *disgustingly*
rebate 791.1, 791.3 *discount*; 212.2 *subtracted item*
rebated 791.6 *discounted*
rebel 662.11; 588.3 *anarchist*; 588.4 *be anarchic*; 661.6 *be insubordinate*; 662.16 *be subversive*; 380.7 *be violent*; 753.8 *cause mischief*; 381.8 *counterattack*; 661.4 *defiant person*; 325.19 *deviant person*; 118.8 *dissenter*; 585.12 *go to war*; 100.5 *nonconformist*; 118.18 *not conform*; 113.11 *opposer*; 753.4 *protester*
rebel angel 8.7 *devil*
rebellion 588.1 *anarchy*; 661.2 *disobedience*; 753.2 *disorder*; 118.2 *dissent*; 800.2 *faithlessness*; 16.41 *lawlessness*; 662.4 *revolution*; 381.14 *siege*
rebellious 588.6 *anarchic*; 381.24 *counterattacking*; 661.8 *defying*; 408.20 *disorderly*; 800.6 *faithless*; 753.10 *lawbreaking*; 16.61 *lawless*; 118.12 *nonconformist*; 383.12 *resisting*; 100.11 *separate*; 662.14 *subversive*
rebelliously 588.8 *anarchically*; 753.11 *disapprovingly*; 800.11 *dishonourably*; 661.10 *in defiance*; 16.84 *lawlessly*; 383.14 *resistingly*; 408.29 *riotously*; 662.18 *subversively*; 118.21 *unconformably*
rebelliousness 661.2 *disobedience*; 408.8 *lawlessness*; 662.4 *revolution*
rebel yell 661.3 *act of defiance*; 585.2 *glory of war*; 742.6 *word*
rebirth 760.2 *evolution*; 561.1 *reproduction*; 112.4 *return*; 393.10 *revival*
rebirthing 394.13 *therapy*
reboant 510.6 *resonant*
reborn 554.12 *alive*; 708.20 *cancelled*; 760.16 *influenced*; 393.13 *repaired*; 112.11 *reprinted*; 561.15 *reproduced*
rebound 422.8 *be elastic*; 57.10 *compete in gymnastics*; 422.1 *elasticity*; 49.6 *play basketball*; 49.4 *playing terms*; 57.6 *pommel horse*; 510.9 *resonate*; 761.8 *return*; 64.3 *rugby play*
rebounder 49.2 *basketball player*
rebounding 422.6 *elastic*; 49.4 *playing terms*; 510.1 *resonance*; 510.6 *resonant*
rebuff 659.3 *act of discourtesy*; 249.1 *adversity*; 709.2, 709.6 *dissent*; 655.13 *ignore*; 668.5, 668.23 *insult*; 637.12 *opposition*; 706.19 *react*; 706.4 *reaction*; 470.1 *reject*; 470.5 *rejection*; 364.1 *repel*; 364.6 *repulse*; 383.6 *resist*; 383.1 *resistance*; 399.1, 399.3 *veto*
rebuffed 709.9 *dissenting*; 706.12 *reactive*
rebuffing 668.11 *insulting*; 383.10 *resistant*
rebuild 295.20 *make new*; 393.3 *restore*
rebuildable 295.15 *renewable*
rebuilder 393.12 *repairer*
rebuilding 295.5 *fresh start*; 393.9 *restoration*; 547.1 *transfiguration*
rebuilt 295.14 *renewed*; 393.13 *repaired*
rebuke 623.14; 606.7 *be dissatisfied*; 670.7 *blame*; 670.20 *censure*; 606.2 *expression of dissatisfaction*; 814.1 *punish*; 814.7 *punishment*; 712.6 *vilify*
rebuked 670.34 *censured*; 623.3 *humbled*
rebuking 670.30 *censuring*
rebus 737.4 *brain-teaser*; 743.8 *heraldic device*
rebut 708.11; 706.18 *answer back*; 704.10 *countercharge*; 709.6 *dissent*; 714.8 *justify*; 113.18 *object*
rebuttable 714.13 *vindicable*
rebuttal 708.3; 704.3 *countercharge*; 706.5 *counterstatement*; 714.2 *defence*; 704.2 *denial*; 709.2 *dissent*; 16.7 *legal trial*; 113.4 *objection*
rebutted 708.18 *rejected*; 706.13 *retaliatory*
rebutter 16.7 *legal trial*; 708.9 *negativist*
rebut the charge 714.8 *justify*
rebutting 708.19; 704.7 *refuting*; 714.11 *vindicatory*
recalcitrance 113.7 *contrariness*; 347.1 *counteraction*; 662.1 *disobedience*; 118.2 *dissent*; 383.2 *obstinacy*; 637.12 *opposition*; 753.1 *protest*; 709.1 *refusal*
recalcitrant 347.4 *counteracting*; 661.8 *defying*; 662.13 *disobedient*; 118.12 *nonconformist*; 383.11 *obstinate*; 662.7 *protester*; 753.9 *protesting*; 706.12 *reactive*; 641.2 *refractory*; 709.8 *refused*; 113.26 *uncooperative*
recalcitrantly 706.24 *in answer*
recalcitrate 706.19 *react*
recalcitration 706.4 *reaction*
recall 708.14 *cancel*; 708.5 *cancellation*; 36.23, 462.1 *memory*; 479.4 *recant*; 479.8 *recantation*; 3.22, 360.8, 462.12 *remember*; 393.9 *restoration*; 393.3 *restore*; 360.5 *retentiveness*; 112.19 *return to*; 708.6 *termination*
recalled 708.20 *cancelled*; 3.19 *chronicled*
recall from the grave 393.10 *revival*
recalling 3.13 *looking back*; 360.5 *retentiveness*
recall of ambassadors 751.1 *disagreement*
recall one's words 479.4 *recant*
recall to life 393.5 *revive*
recant 479.4; 808.4 *be penitent*; 7.19 *be religious*; 708.14 *cancel*; 704.9 *deny*; 767.9 *dispose of*; 355.1 *relinquish*; 708.12 *renounce*; 761.9 *reply*; 761.6 *reverse*; 470.4 *revoke*; 773.9 *withdraw a statement*
recantation 479.8; 470.7 *abrogation*; 708.5 *cancellation*; 704.2 *denial*; 808.1 *penitence*; 355.3 *relinquishment*; 708.4 *renunciation*; 761.1 *reversion*
recanted 708.18 *rejected*; 761.11 *reversed*
recanter 355.4 *deserter*; 479.9 *equivocator*; 708.9 *negativist*; 704.5 *refuter*
recanting 479.11 *equivocating*; 773.2 *taking back*
recant one's errors 808.4 *be penitent*
recap 112.17 *iterate*; 112.2 *iteration*; 723.8 *summarize*; 723.1 *summary*
recapitulate 112.17 *iterate*; 721.15 *recount*; 462.13 *remind*; 695.5 *simplify*; 723.8 *summarize*
recapitulation 34.16 *evolution*; 112.2 *iteration*; 723.1 *summary*; 464.2 *verdict*
recapitulative 112.12 *repetitious*
recapture 477.14 *imagine*; 462.12 *remember*; 773.8 *take back*; 773.2 *taking back*
recapturing 773.2 *taking back*
recast 484.10 *plan out*; 244.3 *rectify*
recce 518.3 *observation*
recede 526.1 *disappear*; 761.6 *reverse*
recede into the distance 303.2 *retreat*
receding 303.23
Receipt 788
receipt 788.1; 706.2 *acknowledgment*; 370.1 *admittance*; 716.6 *documentation*; 785.1 *payment*; 713.3 *precept*; 253.2 *promise*; 440.1 *property*; 769.9, 788.7 *receive*; 744.1 *record*
receipted 788.6 *received*
receipted payment 785.1 *payment*
receipt for payment 785.1 *payment*
receipt in full 785.1 *payment*
receipt of custom 769.3 *acknowledgment of payment*
receipts 52.2 *boxing*; 783.3 *deposit*; 765.4 *earnings*; 352.4 *financial resources*; 788.2 *money received*; 769.2 *something received*; 773.5 *takings*
receipts and expenditures 789.1 *accounts*
receivable 769.14; 370.14 *admissive*
receivables 784.5 *amount owing*; 785.1 *payment*
receive 769.9; **788.7**; 370.7 *admit*; 53.17 *bat*; 658.10 *be courteous*; 692.30 *communicate*; 127.4 *include*; 63.13 *serve*
receive a benefit 765.9 *gain*

receive a bequest 765.14 profit; 769.9 receive
receive a bonus 765.14 profit
receive absolution 807.7 be punished; 10.18 perform rites
receive a death sentence 582.16 meet one's fate
receive a final notice 710.7 demand
receive a free gift 765.14 profit
receive a fringe benefit 765.14 profit
receive a golden handshake 765.14 profit; 313.2 withdraw
receive a good omen 756.10 show potential
receive a legacy 765.14 profit
receive alimony 765.12 earn
receive an advance 765.12 earn
receive an honorary degree 813.12 be rewarded
receive an injunction 710.7 demand
receive a pawn ticket 756.8 guarantee
receive a pay increase 765.10 augment
receive a pension 765.12 earn
receive a raise 765.10 augment
receive a rise 765.10 augment
receive a stipend 765.12 earn
receive a summons 715.7 be accused
receive a sweetener 813.13 get paid
receive a tip 765.14 profit
receive a title 813.12 be rewarded
receive a voucher 756.8 guarantee
receive a windfall profit 765.14 profit
receive Christ 7.19 be religious
receive communion 7.19 be religious
received 769.13; 788.6; 789.11 accounted; 450.14 believed; 692.34 communicated; 632.12 established; 1.14 societal
received idea 117.5 convention
received into the church 769.13 received
received meaning 694.4 type of meaning
Received Pronunciation 5.6 official language
Received Standard 5.6 official language
receive forgiveness 807.7 be punished
receive guests 769.10 receive someone
receive help 392.18
receive immunity 389.5 escape
receive into the church 7.20 preach; 769.10 receive someone
receive maintenance 765.12 earn
receive no proposals 572.9 be celibate
receive notice 711.6 be warned
receive one's death warrant 582.16 meet one's fate
receive one's due 813.12 be rewarded
receive one's marriage lines 570.15 marry
receive palimony 765.12 earn
receive permission 757.5 be permitted
receiver 769.8; 63.12 badminton terms; 769.7 collector; 46.7 offence; 692.18 radio; 29.26 radio telescope; 769.5 recipient; 773.6 taker; 692.9 telephone; 692.22 television set; 63.6 tennis player
receiver of honours 769.5 recipient
receiver of stolen property 774.11 dishonest person; 769.5 recipient
receive royalties 765.12 earn
receivership 13.7 corporation; 769.1 receiving
receive social security 769.9 receive
receive social security payments 765.12 earn
receive someone 769.10
receive the sacrament 10.18 perform rites
receive welfare payments 392.18 receive help
receive with grateful thanks 671.6 be grateful
receive with open arms 671.6 be grateful
Receiving 769
receiving 769.1; 769.11; 370.1 admittance; 765.1 gain
receiving antenna 692.17 antenna
receiving family friends 583.2 funeral
receiving pay 785.19
receiving team 46.12 special team
recency 295.1 newness
recension 244.6 rectification
recent 295.10 new
recently 284.22 in the past; 295.21 newly
recentness 295.1 newness
recent occurrence 295.1 newness
recent past 284.1 past time
receptacle 410.1 container; 78.3 flower part; 439.4 storage
receptible 370.14 admissive
reception 312.12; 601.4; 769.4; 370.1 admittance; 658.3 courtesies; 314.1 entry; 557.13 feast; 127.1 inclusion; 654.3 meeting; 692.19 radio reception; 769.1 receiving; 769.4 reception; 376.9 social gathering; 504.10 sound quality; 692.23 television reception
reception committee 601.4 reception
receptionist 744.9 recorder
reception room 769.4 reception; 565.7 room
receptive 370.15; 769.12; 6.17 educable; 569.8 friendly; 480.20 persuadable; 769.11 receiving; 591.1 sensitive; 483.13 suggestible; 636.1 willing
receptively 370.18; 769.15; 483.14 influentially; 569.17 in friendship; 6.26 studiously
receptiveness 370.2 receptivity; 488.1 sensation; 636.6 willingness
receptivity 370.2; 6.10 educability; 488.1 sensation; 591.5 sensitivity; 483.6 suggestibility
recess 183.3 cavity; 410.2 compartment; 263.1 ease; 226.9 pause; 581.6 refresher; 303.11 retreat; 580.2 time off
recesses 172.2 inside
recession 300.4, 303.10 backward motion; 793.2 declining prices; 214.3 decreasing thing; 245.7 deterioration; 249.2 economic adversity; 13.2 economy; 563.1 infertility; 782.6 insolvency; 761.1 reversion; 778.5 sales; 343.6 unemployment
recessional 10.5 Christian rite; 18.5 sacred music
recessionary 563.3 infertile
recessive 34.25 genetic; 303.23 receding; 761.10 regressive
recessiveness 34.11 genetics
Rechabite 684.4 self-restrained person; 689.8 sober person
Rechabitism 684.1 self-restraint
rechargable battery 39.29 power source
recharge 437.11 fuel
rechargeable 39.36 electronic
recheck 454.1 verify
recherché 469.15 chosen; 235.1 worthy
recidivate 303.1 go backwards; 761.6 reverse
recidivation 303.19 backsliding
recidivism 303.19 backsliding; 245.7 deterioration; 761.1 reversion; 804.1 wickedness
recidivist 303.21 backslider; 245.12 deteriorated; 479.11 equivocating; 479.9 equivocator; 806.4 guilty person; 16.40 lawbreaker; 761.10 regressive
recidivistic 761.10 regressive
recidivous 761.10 regressive; 804.11 wicked
recipe 25.1 cookery; 484.3 expedient plan; 713.3 precept; 394.1 remedy
recipience 769.1 receiving; 370.2 receptivity
recipiency 370.2 receptivity
recipient 392.12; 769.5; 474.4 expectant person; 769.11 receiving; 370.15 receptive
reciprocal 110.4; 750.14 conforming; 706.15 correspondent; 115.5 counterpart; 27.74 divisible; 27.18 division; 111.13 equivalent; 759.6 in exchange; 108.5 interrelated; 747.18 joint; 326.13 oscillating; 298.11 regular; 385.5 retaliatory; 162.4 symmetrical
reciprocally 110.10; 162.8 equally; 706.24 in answer; 759.8 in exchange; 298.15 regularly; 108.10 relevantly
reciprocal manners 631.1 conduct
reciprocate 110.7; 747.12; 706.21 answer to; 298.7 be regular; 111.7 be the same; 750.25 conform; 759.5 exchange; 326.8 oscillate; 385.3, 785.13 retaliate
reciprocated 759.7 exchanged
reciprocating 110.4 reciprocal
reciprocating engine 38.11 engine
reciprocation 750.5 conformity; 119.3 equalization; 111.2 equivalence; 759.1 exchange; 110.1 interchange; 108.2 interrelatedness; 326.1 oscillation; 385.1 retaliation; 162.1 symmetry
reciprocative 759.6 in exchange; 326.13 oscillating; 110.4 reciprocal
reciprocatory 110.4 reciprocal
Reciprocity 110
reciprocity 759.1 exchange; 108.2 interrelatedness; 747.3 mutual relationship; 298.1 regularity; 162.1 symmetry
reciprocity failure 41.10 graininess
recital 733.1 address; 18.27 performance; 112.1 repetition; 729.8 speech
recitation 733.1 address
recitation of rights 16.6 legal process
recitative 18.4 opera
recite 112.17 iterate; 744.13 record; 721.15 recount; 21.37 rehearse; 729.11 speak
reciter 21.29 entertainer
recite the creed 7.19 be religious
recite the rosary 10.20 pray
reckless 618.8 careless; 661.7 defiant; 459.5 foolish; 262.3 hasty; 332.2 mentally quick; 448.9 original; 615.4 rash
recklessly 618.18 carelessly; 254.11 dangerously; 661.9 defiantly; 459.8 foolishly; 472.14 inattentively; 448.15 inventively; 262.7, 615.6 rashly
recklessness 618.2 carelessness; 459.1 folly; 262.5 hastiness; 472.2 impetuosity; 448.4 originality; 615.1 rashness
reckless speed 332.8 speed
reckon 210.8 calculate; 464.12 estimate; 26.10 measure; 194.10 number; 474.9 predict; 446.17 theorize; 104.10 think likely
reckonable 210.14 calculable
reckon among 127.6 subsume
reckoned 26.13 measured
reckoner 210.6 calculator
reckoning 789.3, 789.10 accounting; 790.4 bill; 210.1 calculation; 210.3 count; 194.4 mathematical result; 27.1 mathematics; 26.1 measurement; 27.12 numeration; 814.9 retribution
reckon on 482.7 intend
reckon up 27.90 enumerate
reckon without one's host 486.5 be unskilful
reclaim 349.3 exploit; 244.1 improve; 393.3 restore; 773.8 take back
reclaimed 808.6 penitent; 393.13 repaired; 349.9 used
reclaimed land 349.7 reused product
reclaimed rubber 422.4 rubber
reclaiming 773.2 taking back
reclamation 393.9 restoration; 349.6 use
reclination 187.1 horizontality
recline 187.6 be horizontal; 155.8 be low; 367.8 sit; 263.2 take it easy
recliner 23.2 chair
reclining 187.1 horizontality; 155.5 low; 155.1 lowness; 187.10 lying; 23.14 wooden
reclining chair 23.2 chair
recluse 572.4 celibate person; 736.7 concealer; 118.9 hermit; 197.8 loner; 109.3 unconnected person; 655.6 unsocial person
reclusion 355.3 relinquishment
reclusive 197.16 alone; 736.14 concealed; 118.16 solitary; 372.17 unjoined; 109.6 unrelated; 655.8 unsociable
reclusive life 572.3 monasticism
reclusiveness 655.1 unsociability
recognition 671.3; 669.2 admiration; 17.3 aspect of fiction; 750.7 consent; 658.3 courtesies; 449.6 discovery; 743.1 identification; 36.23, 462.1 memory; 667.1 respect; 813.1 reward; 695.12 understanding
recognition of one's services 671.3 recognition
recognition scene 21.8 scene
recognizability 695.11; 520.3 visibility
recognizable 695.3; 449.15 discoverable; 743.12 identified; 738.14 manifest; 518.23, 520.1 visible
recognizably 449.16 originally; 518.25 visibly
recognizance 16.6 legal process; 253.2 promise
recognize 695.7; 783.11; 658.10 be courteous; 671.6 be grateful; 750.28 consent; 449.1 discover; 743.10 identify; 127.4 include; 455.11 know; 462.12 remember; 813.9 reward; 518.12 see
recognized 750.17 consenting; 632.12 established; 743.12 identified; 455.10 known; 813.16 rewarded
recognized procedure 632.6 procedure
recoil 303.7; 614.4 be a coward; 612.11 be afraid; 422.8 be elastic; 347.3 counteract; 347.1 counteraction; 637.13 dissociation; 422.1 elasticity; 110.1 interchange; 304.5 jump; 706.19 react; 596.6 react against; 706.4 reaction; 110.7 reciprocate; 637.7 refuse; 364.5 repulsion; 303.17 resilience; 385.3 retaliate; 761.8 return; 761.6 reverse; 761.1 reversion; 634.12 shyness
recoil at 594.14 hate
recoiled 761.11 reversed
recoiling 422.6 elastic; 706.12 reactive; 110.4 reciprocal; 303.25 reversed
recollect 3.20 chronicle; 360.8, 462.12 remember
recollected 3.19 chronicled
recollection 3.5 chronicle; 36.23, 462.1 memory; 360.5 retentiveness
recombinant DNA technology 34.12 molecular biology
recommence 130.28 begin again; 134.4 protract; 761.7 restore
recommencement 134.2 protraction; 761.2 restoration
recommend 713.5 advise; 413.14 give moral support; 483.9 motivate; 469.4 pick; 669.13 support
recommendable 713.8 advisable
recommendation 669.6; 713.1 advice; 669.1 approval; 716.6 documentation; 454.6 evidence; 757.2 permit
recommendatory 713.7 advising
recommended 713.8 advisable; 669.23 approved
recommended diet 557.6 nutrition
recommended for leniency 16.63 acquitted
recommended for mercy 16.63 acquitted
recommender 713.4 adviser; 669.7 advocate
recommend for leniency 16.78 acquit
recommend for mercy 16.78 acquit
recommending 669.19 supporting
recompense 609.11; 807.1 atonement; 775.5 compensate; 775.2 compensation; 759.1, 759.5 exchange; 785.10 pay back; 609.2 reparation; 785.2 repayment; 813.1, 813.9 reward
recompensing 807.4 atoning
reconcilable 750.10 in accord
reconcile 807.5 atone; 649.9 forgive; 748.1 mediate; 136.15 modify; 749.4 pacify; 609.11 recompense; 108.7 relate to
reconciled 649.6 forgiven; 136.11 modified
reconcilement 749.1 pacification
reconciliation 649.3 absolution; 750.1 accord; 807.1 atonement; 748.2 mediation; 136.5 modification; 749.1 pacification; 609.2 reparation; 605.4 resignedness
reconciliatory 807.4 atoning
reconciling 649.4 forgiving; 750.10 in accord
recondite 736.14 concealed; 696.4 difficult; 528.4 inscrutable; 266.2 obscure; 521.3 private; 264.12 problematic
reconditeness 736.1 concealment; 264.1 difficulty
recondition 244.1 improve; 393.2 refurbish
reconditioned 393.13 repaired
reconditioning 244.5 improvement; 393.8 repair
reconnaissance 518.3 observation
reconnaissance battalion 584.4 military organization
reconnaissance party 586.14 armed forces; 129.8 precursor
reconnoitre 129.18 forerun; 518.14 inspect
reconnoitring 129.14 preparatory
reconsider 244.4; 443.14 have second thoughts
reconsideration 244.7
reconstitute 393.3 restore
reconstituted 393.13 repaired
reconstitution 393.9 restoration
reconstruct 295.20 make new; 393.3 restore; 3.23 turn back time
reconstructed 295.14 renewed; 393.13 repaired
reconstructible 295.15 renewable
Reconstruction 3.10 past age
reconstruction 476.3 conjecture; 295.5 fresh start; 561.1 reproduction; 393.9 restoration
reconvene 393.3 restore
reconversion 393.9, 761.2 restoration
reconvert 761.7 restore
Record 744
record 744.1; 744.13; 789.7 account; 504.9 audio device; 121.14, 235.2 best; 409.7 catalogue; 409.15 categorize; 3.5, 3.20 chronicle; 281.15 chronologize; 439.5

collection; 692.30 *communicate*; 47.5 *competition*; 40.19 *computing terms*; 631.1 *conduct*; 721.1 *description*; 693.3 *document*; 716.6 *documentation*; 716.1 *evidence*; 743.10 *identify*; 16.7 *legal trial*; 220.8 *list*; 721.3 *narration*; 17.4 *nonfiction*; 136.3 *qualifications*; 744.7 *recording*; 721.15 *recount*; 215.1 *remainder*; 462.4 *reminder*; 717.9 *represent*; 275.16 *time*; 454.1 *verify*
record book 744.6
record-breaker 235.8 *exceller*; 797.17 *good thing*; 121.6 *paragon*; 246.4 *successful person*
record-breaking 121.14, 235.2, 797.2 *best*; 47.9 *track*; 619.8 *wonderful*
record collection 439.5 *collection*
recorded 744.16; 789.11 *accounted*; 3.19 *chronicled*; 692.34 *communicated*; 716.8 *evidential*; 127.8 *included*; 220.11 *listed*; 454.8 *verifiable*
recorded delivery 692.2 *postal communication*
recorded material 744.1 *record*
recorded proceedings 744.1 *record*
recorded sunshine 31.22 *sun*
recorder 744.9; 281.13 *chronicler*; 721.10 *descriptive writer*; 3.3 *historian*; 16.23 *judge*; 52.7 *judo*; 464.6 *justice*; 16.13 *lawyer*; 744.10 *recording instrument*
record high 121.4 *summit*
record-holder 121.6 *paragon*
record-holding 121.14 *best*
recording 692.26; **744.7**; 692.25 *broadcast material*; 3.5 *chronicle*; 28.82 *measuring instrument*; 744.1 *record*; 744.8 *registration*
Recording Angel 16.23 *judge*
recording device 28.82 *measuring instrument*
recording instrument 744.10; 28.82 *measuring instrument*
recording of evidence 16.7 *legal trial*
recording system 29.27 *imaging*
record-keeper 744.9 *recorder*
record-keeping 744.8 *registration*
record low 122.5 *inferior state*
record piracy 774.6 *illegal borrowing*
record pirate 125.8 *copier*; 774.10 *infringer*; 115.4 *person who copies*
records 789.5 *account book*
record size 158.3 *large scale*
record-size 158.15 *big*
recount 721.15; 693.12 *communicate*; 112.17 *iterate*; 744.13 *record*
recounted 112.10 *iterated*
recounter 312.14 *meeting*
recounting 112.2 *iteration*
recoup 302.4 *make good time*; 385.3 *retaliate*; 773.8 *take back*
recoupment 775.2 *compensation*; 773.2 *taking back*
recourse 352.1 *means*; 252.5 *refuge*; 349.6 *use*
recover 581.2 *be refreshed*; 393.4 *be restored*; 336.7 *be strong*; 347.3 *counteract*; 390.1 *deliver*; 54.5 *fence*; 244.2 *get better*; 259.6 *get healthy*; 56.7 *golf*; 50.19 *punt*; 393.1 *repair*; 761.7 *restore*; 50.16 *row*; 773.8 *take back*
recoverable 393.14 *repairable*; 761.12 *reversible*
recoverably 393.17 *repairably*
recovered 581.4 *refreshed*; 393.13 *repaired*; 761.11 *reversed*; 204.8 *sound*
recover from the lunge 54.5 *fence*
recovering 244.14 *improved*; 50.11 *rowing*
recover lost ground 765.10 *augment*; 302.4 *make good time*
recover one's costs 773.8 *take back*
recover one's health 259.6 *get healthy*
recover one's losses 773.8 *take back*
recovery 390.2 *deliverance*; 244.5 *improvement*; 50.8 *punting*; 393.11 *recuperation*; 581.5 *refreshment*; 394.1 *remedy*; 393.9, 761.2 *restoration*; 393.10 *revival*; 50.4 *rowing*; 67.11 *swimming*; 773.2 *taking back*
recovery shot 56.3 *golf shots*
recovery stroke 67.2 *swimming technique*
recreancy 479.7 *apostasy*
recreant 614.3 *cowardly*; 479.9 *equivocator*; 804.9 *wicked person*
recreate 561.12 *multiply*; 244.3 *rectify*; 581.1 *refresh*
re-created 561.15 *reproduced*
re-creating 561.15 *reproduced*
recreation 633.4 *activity*; 69.8 *pastime*; 581.5 *refreshment*; 580.2 *time off*
recreational 69.9; 580.6 *leisure*; 581.3 *refreshing*; 67.11 *swimming*; 52.15 *wrestling*
recreational architecture 20.1 *architecture*
recreational canoeing 50.6 *canoeing*
recreational diving 67.6 *diving*
recreational education 6.2 *educational system*
recreational karate 52.8 *karate*
recreationally 69.11
recreational swimming 67.1 *swimming*
recreational therapy 36.3 *psychiatric treatment*
recreation room 565.7 *room*
recreative 581.3 *refreshing*
recriminate 715.5 *accuse*; 670.19 *blame*; 714.8 *justify*
recriminated 715.8 *accusatory*
recrimination 715.1 *accusation*; 670.7 *blame*; 714.2 *defence*
recriminative 670.29 *blaming*
recriminatory 715.8 *accusatory*; 385.5 *retaliatory*
recruit 585.11; 130.14 *beginner*; 584.10 *enlist*; 585.12 *go to war*; 244.1 *improve*; 6.7 *learner*; 213.5 *make bigger*; 483.9 *motivate*; 581.1 *refresh*; 393.5 *revive*; 586.8 *soldier*; 211.7 *support*
recruited 586.35 *martial*
recruiting 584.1 *military affairs*
recruitment 244.5 *improvement*; 581.5 *refreshment*; 393.9 *restoration*; 393.10 *revival*; 585.7 *war measures*
recruits 586.14 *armed forces*
recrystallization 30.29 *petrogenesis*
recrystallize 30.62 *lithify*
rectal 172.10 *visceral*
rectal administration 37.13 *administration*
rectangle 176.3 *angled figure*; 148.6 *oblong*; 27.44 *polygon*; 200.2 *quadrilateral*
rectangular 176.9 *angled*; 148.2 *elongated*; 186.10 *perpendicular*; 27.82 *polygonal*; 200.8 *quadrilateral*
rectangular backboard 49.3 *basketball equipment*
rectangular coordinates 27.33 *coordinates*
rectangular pulse 28.16 *waveform*
rectifiable 393.14 *repairable*
rectification 244.6; 807.1 *atonement*; 39.15 *circuit function*; 244.5 *improvement*; 393.8 *repair*; 801.5 *righting wrong*
rectified 393.13 *repaired*
rectifier 39.21; 28.55 *circuit*; 39.34 *power supply*; 393.12 *repairer*
rectify 244.3; 807.5 *atone*; 244.1 *improve*; 230.5 *perfect*; 801.15 *put right*; 393.1 *repair*
rectifying 807.4 *atoning*
rectilinear 27.80 *linear*; 178.1 *straight*
rectilinearity 178.6 *straightness*
rectitude 795.2 *good morals*; 797.10 *kindness*; 799.2 *purity*; 801.4 *righteousness*; 803.1 *virtue*
rector 579.13 *director*; 7.8 *priest*
rectorate 7.9 *priesthood*
rectorship 7.9 *priesthood*
rectory 565.4 *official residence*; 7.10 *priestly dwelling*
rectrix 72.17 *plumage*
rectum 172.4 *insides*
reculade 303.11 *retreat*
recumbency 187.1 *horizontality*; 155.1 *lowness*
recumbent 155.5 *low*; 187.10 *lying*
recumbent fold 30.20 *earth movement*
recuperate 581.2 *be refreshed*; 393.4 *be restored*; 244.2 *get better*; 259.6 *get healthy*
recuperating 244.14 *improved*
recuperation 393.11; 259.3 *health*; 244.5 *improvement*; 394.11 *medical art*; 581.5 *refreshment*; 394.1 *remedy*
recuperative 393.16 *restorative*
recur 297.7 *be frequent*; 202.9 *be infinite*; 276.10 *be periodical*; 298.7 *be regular*; 462.15 *be remembered*; 112.21 *be repeated*; 134.3 *continue*; 525.13 *occur*; 510.9 *resonate*
recurrence 134.1 *continuity*; 132.6 *continuum*; 297.4 *frequency*; 276.6 *periodicity*; 525.6 *reappearance*; 298.1 *regularity*; 112.1 *repetition*; 510.1 *resonance*; 112.4 *return*; 393.10 *revival*
recurrent 112.14; 134.5 *continual*; 132.12 *cyclical*; 297.3 *frequent*; 632.14 *habituated*; 276.8 *periodical*; 298.11 *regular*
recurrently 134.7 *continually*; 297.1 *frequently*; 276.12 *periodically*; 112.23 *repeatedly*; 510.11 *resonantly*
recurrent nova 29.12 *variable star*
recurrent pattern 276.5 *recurrent period*
recurrent period 276.5
recurring 525.7 *appearing*; 300.17 *directional*; 297.3 *frequent*; 202.1 *infinite*; 112.14 *recurrent*; 298.11 *regular*
recurring decimal 27.18 *division*
recurring movement 300.10 *regular movement*
recursion 27.28 *algorithm*; 312.13 *return*
recursive procedure 27.28 *algorithm*
recusance 704.2 *denial*; 118.2 *dissent*; 753.1 *protest*; 708.2 *rejection*
recusancy 708.2 *rejection*
recusant 662.13 *disobedient*; 118.8 *dissenter*; 708.17 *negative*; 118.12 *nonconformist*; 662.7 *protester*; 753.9 *protesting*; 704.5 *refuter*
recyclable 375.5 *disintegrated*; 761.12 *reversible*; 237.2 *usable*
recyclale 349.10 *usable*
recycle 349.3 *exploit*; 775.4 *give back*; 112.20 *renew*; 393.3, 761.7 *restore*
recycled 112.11 *reprinted*; 761.11 *reversed*; 349.9 *used*
recycled paper 775.1 *giving back*
recycled substance 349.7 *reused product*
recycler 775.3 *returner*
recycling 775.1 *giving back*; 393.9, 761.2 *restoration*; 112.4 *return*; 349.6 *use*
Red 535.8 *figurative usage*; 12.6 *political party*; 662.11 *rebel*; 244.12 *reformer*; 90.3 *US rivers*
red 535.1; 674.9 *blushing*; 28.28 *colour*; 25.56 *culinary*
redact 244.3 *rectify*; 5.46 *translate*
redacted 5.40 *translated*
redaction 244.6 *rectification*; 5.12 *translation*
red admiral 535.7 *red thing*
red alert 711.2 *danger signal*; 535.8 *figurative usage*
red algae 84.2 *algae*
redan 384.8 *military defences*
red-and-white 52.15 *wrestling*
red ant 76.4 *social insect*
red as a beetroot 535.2 *red-faced*
red as a lobster 535.2 *red-faced*
red-bait 466.14 *discriminate against*
red-baiter 466.7 *bigot*
redbaiting 466.4 *social discrimination*
red ball 65.4 *carom*; 65.3 *English billiards*; 65.5 *snooker*
red beans with rice 25.43 *US dish*
red bird 535.7 *red thing*
red-blind 519.9 *weak-sighted*
red-blindness 519.2 *poor sight*
red blood cell 431.4 *blood*; 535.7 *red thing*
red-blooded 336.9 *physically strong*; 338.4 *vigorous*
redbrick university 6.13 *university*
red bug 76.3 *pest*; 535.7 *red thing*
redcap 401.3 *attendant*; 316.7 *transferor*
red card 535.7 *red thing*
red carpet 535.8 *figurative usage*; 656.1 *formality*; 667.5 *presenting arms*
red-carpet treatment 601.4 *reception*
red caviar 25.16 *fish dish*
red-cheeked 535.2 *red-faced*
red cheeks 535.7 *red thing*
red clover 43.12 *crop*; 535.7 *red thing*
redcoat 535.8 *figurative usage*; 586.8 *soldier*
red coats 585.2 *glory of war*
red colour 535.5 *redness*
red complexion 535.5 *redness*
red cosmetic 535.6 *red pigment*
Red Crescent 535.8 *figurative usage*
Red Cross 650.2, 652.5 *charity*; 535.8 *figurative usage*; 768.3 *offering*
redcurrant 535.7 *red thing*
red deal 23.12 *wood*
red deer 60.5 *game*; 535.7 *red thing*
red demand 397.2 *demand*
redden 535.9; 624.12 *become angry*; 529.15 *colour*; 529.16 *make up*
reddened 535.2 *red-faced*
reddening 674.2, 674.9 *blushing*; 29.21 *orbit*; 535.5 *redness*
red devils 592.6 *desensitizing substance*
reddish-brown 534.1 *brown*
reddish-yellow 536.1 *orange*
red-dog 46.16 *play defence*
red duster 743.7 *flag*
red dwarf 535.7 *red thing*
red dye 529.4 *pigment*; 535.6 *red pigment*
rede 713.1 *advice*
redecorate 224.8 *cause change*; 393.2 *refurbish*; 760.9 *transform*
redecorated 224.12 *changed*; 393.13 *repaired*
redecoration 224.1 *change*
redeem 807.5 *atone*; 777.3 *buy back*; 390.1 *deliver*; 649.9 *forgive*; 775.4 *give back*; 244.1 *improve*; 391.4 *liberate*; 785.7 *pay off*; 393.3 *restore*
redeemable 390.4 *deliverable*; 785.17 *payable*; 393.14 *repairable*
redeemably 390.6 *extricably*; 393.17 *repairably*
redeemed 777.13 *bought*; 8.15 *deified*; 649.6 *forgiven*; 393.13 *repaired*; 775.6 *restoring*
redeemed soul 8.10 *deified person*
redeemer 390.3 *deliverer*; 391.3 *liberator*; 777.12 *purchaser*; 775.3 *returner*
redeeming 649.4 *forgiving*; 775.6 *restoring*
redeeming feature 235.6 *worth*
redemption 649.3 *absolution*; 807.1 *atonement*; 390.2 *deliverance*; 759.1 *exchange*; 775.1 *giving back*; 244.5 *improvement*; 391.1 *liberation*; 359.1 *preservation*; 777.9 *repurchase*; 393.9 *restoration*
redemptional 775.6 *restoring*
redemptive 777.14 *buying*; 391.7 *liberated*; 785.20 *paying in return*; 359.6 *preserving*; 393.16 *restorative*; 775.6 *restoring*
redemptively 775.7; 777.17 *acquisitively*
Red Ensign 743.7 *flag*
redesign 295.5 *fresh start*; 295.20 *make new*
redesignable 295.15 *renewable*
redesigned 295.14 *renewed*
red-eye 41.8 *composition*; 558.8 *mixed drink*
red-eyed 603.4 *lamenting*; 519.9 *weak-sighted*
red-eye flight 535.8 *figurative usage*
red eyes 519.2 *poor sight*
red face 674.2 *blushing*
red-faced 535.2
red face-off spot 58.3 *ice hockey*
red flag 711.2 *danger signal*; 743.7 *flag*; 742.4 *signal*
red fox 535.7 *red thing*
red giant 535.7 *red thing*; 29.11 *stellar birth*
red glow 522.8 *fire*
red goal line 58.3 *ice hockey*
red grouse 535.7 *red thing*
red hair 535.7 *red thing*
red-haired 535.3
red-handed 340.5 *acting*; 340.7 *actively*; 806.6 *appearing guilty*; 806.11 *guiltily*; 382.24 *murderous*
red-handedly 806.11 *guiltily*
red-handedness 806.1 *guilt*
red hands 806.2 *signs of guilt*
redhead 535.7 *red thing*
red heat 522.8 *fire*
red herring 700.12 *disguise*; 634.14 *evasion*; 535.8 *figurative usage*; 702.2 *sophism*; 645.2 *stratagem*; 124.8 *trifle*; 109.2 *unrelated thing*; 238.5 *waste of effort*
red-hot 493.9 *hot*; 535.2 *red-faced*; 380.6 *violent*
red-hot mama 535.8 *figurative usage*
redia 75.13 *invertebrate larva*
redingote 551.12 *coat*
red ink 535.7 *red thing*
redintegrate 393.3 *restore*
redintegration 393.8 *repair*
redirect 733.10 *send*
rediscover 449.4 *invent*
rediscovery 449.9 *invention*
redivivus 393.13 *repaired*
red lead 535.6 *red pigment*
red-letter day 275.11 *date*; 535.8 *figurative usage*; 656.3 *formal occasion*; 123.2 *important matter*
red light 711.2 *danger signal*; 481.6 *dissuasion*; 522.6 *electric light*; 670.3 *nonacceptance*; 535.7 *red thing*; 709.1 *refusal*; 742.4 *signal*; 399.1 *veto*
red-light district 796.6 *brothel*; 87.7 *city district*; 535.8 *figurative usage*
red meat 25.20 *meat*; 535.7 *red thing*
redneck 466.7 *bigot*; 564.5 *countryman*;

535.8 *figurative usage*; 592.5 *insensitive person*
Redness 535
redness 535.5; 493.5 *hot weather*
red nose 690.16 *alcoholism*
red-nosed 690.5 *drunken*
redo 484.10 *plan out*; 244.4 *reconsider*; 112.16 *repeat*; 393.3 *restore*
red ochre 535.6 *red pigment*
redolence 500.1 *odour*
redolent 500.5 *odorous*
redone 393.13 *repaired*
redouble 338.3 *invigorate*; 213.5 *make bigger*; 112.16 *repeat*
redoubled 112.9 *repeated*
redoublement 54.3 *fencing movements*
redoubling 213.1 *increase*; 112.1 *repetition*; 112.12 *repetitious*
redoubt 384.8 *military defences*
redoubtable 336.10 *potent*
redound 229.4 *tend*
red pepper 535.7 *red thing*
red pigment 535.6
red planet 535.7 *red thing*
redraft 244.3 *rectify*
red rash 535.5 *redness*
redress 807.5 *atone*; 807.1 *atonement*; 801.15 *put right*; 394.1 *remedy*; 393.9 *restoration*; 385.3 *retaliate*; 385.1 *retaliation*
redressing 807.4 *atoning*
redress the balance 119.11 *equalize*; 385.3 *retaliate*
reds 592.6 *desensitizing substance*
red salmon 535.7 *red thing*
Red Sea 535.8 *figurative usage*
redshift 29.21 *orbit*
redshirt 398.5 *alternative*; 46.2 *football player*
red snapper 535.7 *red thing*
red spider mite 44.12 *pests and diseases*
red squirrel 535.7 *red thing*
Red Star delivery 692.2 *postal communication*
reds under the bed 535.8 *figurative usage*
red tape 294.3 *delayed action*; 535.8 *figurative usage*; 12.3, 396.4 *governance*; 378.2 *obstacle*; 342.9 *overactivity*; 219.2 *overdoing it*; 632.6 *procedure*
red thing 535.7
red tide 84.1 *alga*
reduce 206.8; 623.23 *abase*; 191.6 *become smaller*; 153.14 *become thin*; 760.7 *convert into*; 375.4 *deconstruct*; 791.3 *discount*; 263.3 *ease*; 687.5 *fast*; 245.5 *hurt*; 367.1 *lower*; 191.5, 214.5 *make smaller*; 685.4 *moderate*; 163.5 *outline*; 41.21 *photograph*; 728.22 *play down*; 203.8 *quantify*; 32.26 *react*; 778.1 *sell*; 149.10 *shorten*; 723.8 *summarize*; 557.23 *taste*; 152.7 *thicken*; 760.9 *transform*; 337.7 *weaken*
reduced 212.7; 793.9 *cheap*; 152.2 *dense*; 728.19 *downplayed*; 206.7 *fewer*; 623.3 *humbled*; 367.17 *lowered*; 752.17 *offered*; 191.7 *smaller*
reduced circumstances 122.5 *inferior state*; 782.5 *poverty*
reduced payment 786.2 *stoppage*
reduced pressure 417.3 *sparseness*
reduced price 793.1 *cheapness*
reduced price rate 790.1 *price*
reduced rate 793.1 *cheapness*
reduced to a jelly 612.7 *frightened*
reduced to clear 793.9 *cheap*
reduced to poverty 782.2 *insolvent*
reduced to slavery 387.9 *subject*
reduce in number 337.7 *weaken*
reduce one's importance 124.13 *make unimportant*
reduce pressure 417.6 *make sparse*
reduce speed 214.5 *make smaller*; 333.3 *slow down*
reduce the fine 16.78 *acquit*
reduce the price 793.13 *make cheap*
reduce the price of 791.3 *discount*
reduce the temperature 685.4 *moderate*
reduce to 760.9 *transform*
reduce to ashes 493.15 *burn*
reduce to chaos 588.5 *misgovern*
reduce to its elements 255.11 *simplify*
reduce to order 409.12 *arrange*
reduce to poverty 782.14 *impoverish*
reduce to powder 427.22 *pulverize*
reduce to rags 245.5 *hurt*
reduce to servitude 387.6 *subject*
reduce to silence 730.15 *strike dumb*
reduce to the ranks 367.4 *debase*; 814.1 *punish*
reduce weight 415.10 *lighten*
reducible 760.15 *convertible*
reducing 191.8 *contracting*; 687.1, 687.6 *fasting*; 557.6 *nutrition*; 153.3 *slimming*
reducing to dust 427.4 *pulverization*
reductio ad absurdum 701.2 *logical argument*; 4.8 *philosophical term*; 704.1 *refutation*
reduction 210.1 *calculation*; 191.1 *contraction*; 760.1 *conversion*; 375.2 *deconstruction*; 214.1 *decrease*; 791.1 *discount*; 27.24 *evaluation*; 367.11 *lowering*; 685.1 *moderation*; 163.1 *outline*; 149.2 *shortening*
reduction division 34.10 *cell division*
reductionism 4.7 *school of thought*
reductionist 4.11 *follower of a doctrine*; 4.14 *of a philosophy*
reduction of nuclear stockpiles 749.1 *pacification*
reductive 214.7 *decrescent*; 212.6 *subtractive*
reductively 375.8 *destructively*; 367.24 *down*
redundance 793.2 *declining prices*; 270.1 *diffuseness*; 219.1 *excess*; 329.9 *excessiveness*
redundancy 270.1 *diffuseness*; 470.6 *discarding*; 371.18 *dismissal*; 128.2 *ejection*; 219.1 *excess*; 100.1 *extraneousness*; 341.1 *inaction*; 15.2 *industrial negotiations*; 112.2 *iteration*; 350.8 *nonuse*; 342.9 *overactivity*; 144.4 *relegation*; 111.1 *sameness*; 219.3 *superfluity*; 215.4 *surplus*; 708.6 *termination*; 343.6, 580.3 *unemployment*; 238.3 *uselessness*
redundancy money 813.4 *reward for service*
redundancy pay 785.3 *pay*
redundant 793.9 *cheap*; 270.3 *diffuse*; 219.6 *excessive*; 100.8 *extraneous*; 226.10 *finished*; 341.3 *inactive*; 580.7 *leisurely*; 15.9 *negotiated*; 350.3 *not wanted*; 343.2 *not working*; 217.2 *plentiful*; 470.10 *rejected*; 112.12 *repetitious*; 111.12 *same*; 219.7 *superfluous*; 215.10 *surplus*; 238.1 *useless*; 5.42 *worded*
redundantly 219.8 *excessively*; 350.12 *out of use*; 215.11 *residually*; 215.12 *with a remainder*
redundant worker 470.9 *rejected person*
reduplicate 112.16 *repeat*
reduplicated 112.9 *repeated*
reduplication 112.1 *repetition*; 561.1 *reproduction*
redware 24.1 *ceramics*
red wine 535.7 *red thing*; 558.9 *wine*
redwing 535.7 *red thing*
red with anger 624.16 *angry*
red with rage 624.16 *angry*
redwood 535.7 *red thing*; 154.6 *tall thing*
redwood tree 158.9 *big thing*
re-echo 509.8 *drum*; 112.1 *repetition*; 510.1 *resonance*; 510.9 *resonate*; 112.22 *resound*; 112.6 *reverberation*
re-echoed 112.9 *repeated*
re-echoing 112.12 *repetitious*; 510.6 *resonant*
reed 81.3 *grass plant*; 337.5 *weak thing*
reed basket 410.7 *basket*
reed cutter 81.5 *grass cutter*
reeds 77.3 *seed plant*
re-educate 117.10 *assimilate*; 760.9 *transform*
re-education 36.20 *conditioning*; 760.2 *evolution*
reedy 81.9 *grassy*; 513.9 *shrill*
reef 92.2 *island*; 157.4 *shallow thing*; 333.3 *slow down*; 379.1 *trap*
reef a sail 50.15 *sail*
reefer 691.6 *drug*; 551.11 *jacket*; 323.7 *nautical person*
reefer man 691.5 *drug pusher*
reefing 50.1 *sailing*
reef point 50.3 *parts of a sailing boat*
reefy 157.1 *shallow*
reek 432.27 *give off*; 500.8 *have odour*; 371.14 *let out*; 432.3 *miasma*; 503.1 *stench*; 503.5 *stink*
reeking 432.18 *miasmic*; 503.3 *stinking*
reel 307.3; 227.11 *be changeable*; 690.7 *be drunk*; 41.9 *film*; 55.3 *fishing tackle*; 22.4 *historic dancing*; 327.25 *pitch*; 326.4, 326.11 *rock*; 307.9 *roll*
re-elect 469.5 *vote*
reel in 55.7 *angle*; 362.12 *drag*; 633.11 *hunt*
reeling 690.10 *drunkenness*; 326.16 *rocking*; 307.11 *rotating*; 690.2 *slightly drunk*; 307.2 *turning*
reemphasize 112.17 *iterate*
re-enthrone 775.4 *give back*
re-enthronement 775.1 *giving back*
re-entrance 314.1 *entry*; 312.13 *return*; 303.12 *reversal*
re-entrant 20.17 *structured*
re-entrant angle 27.39 *angle*
re-entrant corner 20.9 *miscellaneous architectural features*
re-entry 314.1 *entry*; 317.13 *flight path*; 312.13 *return*; 303.12 *reversal*; 29.35 *rocketry*
re-equipped 393.13 *repaired*
re-erect 393.3 *restore*
re-erection 393.9 *restoration*
re-establish 775.4 *give back*; 393.3 *restore*
re-establishment 775.1 *giving back*; 393.9 *restoration*
reeve 579.15 *manager*
re-examination 16.7 *legal trial*; 244.7 *reconsideration*
re-examine 244.3 *rectify*
reface 393.1 *repair*
refashion 244.3 *rectify*; 393.2 *refurbish*
refashioning 393.9 *restoration*
refection 557.12 *meal*; 581.7 *refreshments*
refectory 557.15 *eating place*
refer 35.19 *practise medicine*
referee 713.4 *adviser*; 49.2 *basketball player*; 65.7 *billiards player*; 52.4 *boxer*; 46.2 *football player*; 56.6 *golfer*; 473.3 *impartial person*; 16.23, 464.5, 464.11 *judge*; 58.6 *lacrosse player*; 748.1 *mediate*; 748.3 *mediator*; 685.4 *moderate*; 685.2 *moderator*; 281.11 *person keeping time*; 742.8 *signer*; 52.9 *tae kwon do*; 52.6 *wrestler*
referee's whistle 742.4 *signal*
reference 713.2 *consultation*; 716.6 *documentation*; 811.1 *estimation*; 454.6, 716.1 *evidence*; 743.10 *identify*; 108.2 *interrelatedness*; 396.9 *permission*; 757.2 *permit*; 4.8 *philosophical term*; 669.6 *recommendation*; 108.1 *relatedness*; 694.4 *type of meaning*
reference book 693.5; 740.6 *book publishing*; 220.3 *dictionary*
referenced 743.12 *identified*; 742.17 *punctuated*
reference editor 740.12 *publisher*
reference list 220.2 *table*
reference mark 742.7 *punctuation*
reference point 27.36 *point*
references 136.3 *qualifications*
referendum 464.1 *judgment*; 469.10 *vote*
referential failure 4.9 *philosophical problem*
referment 713.2 *consultation*
referral 35.6 *health care*
refer to 734.11 *confer*; 713.6 *consult*; 694.10 *mean*; 108.7 *relate to*; 729.11 *speak*
refer to arbitration 713.6 *consult*
refill 232.6 *fill*; 232.2 *fullness*; 436.1 *provision*; 436.6 *replenish*; 439.6 *store*; 217.4 *suffice*
refilled 232.8 *full*
refilling 232.2 *fullness*
refine 549.6; 273.7, 698.31 *be accurate*; 543.4 *be elegant*; 6.22 *educate*; 32.30 *extract*; 244.1 *improve*; 527.12 *make transparent*; 369.17 *obtain an extract*; 230.5 *perfect*; 255.10, 256.15 *purify*; 32.25 *solidify*
refined 6.20; **549.5**; 698.21 *accurate*; 256.17 *cleaned*; 466.9 *discriminating*; 543.3 *elegant*; 656.6 *formal*; 658.8 *good-mannered*; 437.10 *powered*; 255.13, 795.9 *pure*; 549.5 *refined*; 404.9 *smooth*; 529.13 *soft-hued*; 32.32 *solid*; 728.13 *subtle*; 495.8 *tasteful*
refined gold 235.8 *exceller*
refined palate 557.3 *delicate eating*; 466.2 *judiciousness*
refined person 549.4
refined sugar 498.2 *sweetener*
Refinement 549
refinement 6.11; 273.1, 698.8 *accuracy*; 543.1 *elegance*; 658.2 *good manners*; 545.1 *gorgeousness*; 404.2 *grain*; 244.5 *improvement*; 466.2 *judiciousness*; 369.7 *obtaining an extract*; 654.2 *social ambition*; 728.3 *subtlety*; 495.2 *taste of life*
refine oil 437.11 *fuel*
refinery 32.22 *industrial chemistry*; 577.1 *workshop*
refining 256.2 *cleaning*; 32.22 *industrial chemistry*; 32.23 *metallurgy*; 437.6 *oil*
refit 393.2 *refurbish*; 393.8 *repair*
refitted 393.13 *repaired*
reflation 14.1, 780.7 *finance*; 190.1 *growth*
reflationary 14.6 *financial*
reflect 525.11 *appear*; 115.10 *be similar*; 111.7 *be the same*; 443.13 *concentrate*; 750.25 *conform*; 701.14 *discuss*; 522.27 *glaze*; 446.15 *imagine*; 125.9 *imitate*; 518.18 *make visible*; 4.20 *philosophize*; 462.12 *remember*; 27.96, 717.9 *represent*
reflected 325.26 *diffractive*; 525.8 *outer*
reflected image 717.6 *image*
reflected sound 504.8 *something heard*
reflecting 750.14 *conforming*; 528.3 *mirror-like*; 525.8 *outer*; 717.13 *representational*; 518.20 *visual*; 458.5 *wise*
reflection 518.8; 31.9 *atmospheric process*; 115.5 *counterpart*; 325.18 *diffraction*; 111.2 *equivalence*; 522.12 *highlight*; 446.1 *idea*; 717.6 *image*; 125.1 *imitation*; 525.5 *impression*; 701.2 *logical argument*; 111.3 *lookalike*; 462.1 *memory*; 528.6 *opaqueness*; 28.29 *optical element*; 4.4 *philosophical investigation*; 717.1 *representation*; 510.1 *resonance*; 162.2 *symmetry operation*; 442.6, 443.3 *thoughtfulness*; 27.48 *transformation*; 729.7 *utterance*; 519.5 *visual distortion*; 28.15 *wave property*
reflection grating 28.29 *optical element*
reflection hologram 41.5 *stereoscopic image*
reflection nebula 29.8 *interstellar medium*
reflective 443.9 *concentrating*; 111.13 *equivalent*; 446.11 *ideational*; 528.3 *mirror-like*; 421.4 *polished*; 4.17, 442.11 *thoughtful*
reflectively 111.18 *identically*; 442.15 *intelligently*; 701.19 *logically*; 510.11 *resonantly*; 446.20 *theoretically*; 4.28, 443.18 *thoughtfully*
reflectiveness 442.6 *thoughtfulness*
reflector 692.17 *antenna*; 41.15 *lighting*; 518.8 *reflection*; 29.24 *telescope*; 520.7 *that which makes visible*
reflect upon 443.13 *concentrate*
reflex 36.20 *conditioning*; 632.7 *habituation*; 590.2 *impression*; 445.8 *instinctive*; 706.4 *reaction*; 303.17 *resilience*; 303.25 *reversed*; 478.5 *spontaneity*
reflex angle 27.39 *angle*
reflexive 5.44 *grammatical*; 706.12 *reactive*; 761.10 *regressive*; 303.26 *resilient*
reflexively 303.28 *backwards*; 706.24 *in answer*; 761.13 *reversibly*
reflexive relation 27.63 *mathematical logic*
reflexive verb 5.35 *part of speech*
reflex lens 41.17 *lens*
reflexologist 35.12 *healer*
reflexology 35.2 *natural medicine*; 36.1 *psychology*
reflowing 300.4 *backward motion*; 300.17 *directional*
refluence 300.4 *backward motion*; 303.12 *reversal*; 90.6 *river flow*; 91.2 *tide*
refluent 300.17 *directional*; 90.10 *fluvial*; 706.12 *reactive*; 303.23 *receding*
reflux 300.4 *backward motion*; 706.4 *reaction*; 303.12 *reversal*; 90.6 *river flow*; 91.2 *tide*
refluxing 32.5 *process*
reforest 393.3 *restore*
reforestation 79.5 *forestry*; 393.9 *restoration*
Reform 7.16 *denominational*
reform 650.8 *be benevolent*; 224.7 *be changed*; 295.17 *become new*; 808.4 *be penitent*; 760.8 *be transformed*; 224.8 *cause change*; 487.5 *disaccustom*; 244.2 *get better*; 244.1 *improve*; 244.5, 302.15 *improvement*; 801.15 *put right*; 244.3 *rectify*; 393.2 *refurbish*; 393.3 *restore*; 801.5 *righting wrong*; 2.15 *socialize*; 760.9 *transform*
reformable 244.15 *improvable*
reformation 224.1 *change*; 760.2 *evolution*; 244.5 *improvement*; 808.1 *penitence*; 393.9 *restoration*; 801.5 *righting wrong*
reformational 224.11 *changeable*
reformative 708.20 *cancelled*; 224.11 *changeable*; 244.16 *improving*
reformatory 244.10; 309.4 *closed place*; 244.16 *improving*; 655.4 *place of confinement*; 815.1 *prison*

reformed 708.20 *cancelled*; 244.14 *improved*; 808.6 *penitent*
reformed character 808.3 *penitent person*
reformed prostitute 808.3 *penitent person*
reformer 244.12; 353.7 *attempter*; 650.5 *benevolent person*; 224.6, 227.4 *editor*; 302.16 *progressive person*; 393.12 *repairer*
reforming 244.16 *improving*; 652.6 *philanthropic*
reformism 244.11; 652.2 *public spiritedness*
reformist 302.17 *forward*; 244.16 *improving*; 244.12 *reformer*; 393.12 *repairer*
reform school 815.1 *prison*; 244.10 *reformatory*
reformulate 393.3 *restore*
reformulation 393.9 *restoration*
refound 393.3 *restore*
refract 325.12 *deflect*; 522.27 *glaze*
refracted 325.26 *diffractive*
refracted colour 529.2 *colourfulness*
refractile 325.26 *diffractive*
refraction 325.18 *diffraction*; 28.29 *optical element*; 519.5 *visual distortion*; 28.15 *wave property*
refractive 325.26 *diffractive*; 527.1 *transparent*
refractive index 28.29 *optical element*
refractivity 28.29 *optical element*
refractometer 26.8 *meter*
refractometric 26.16 *micrometric*
refractometry 26.2 *micrometry*
refractor 29.24 *telescope*
refractorily 24.12 *ornamentally*
refractoriness 113.7 *contrariness*; 637.14, 662.1 *disobedience*; 383.2 *obstinacy*; 753.1 *protest*
refractory 641.2; 642.1 *capricious*; 24.10 *ceramic*; 32.7 *chemical compound*; 661.8 *defying*; 383.11 *obstinate*; 753.9 *protesting*; 264.14 *troublesome*; 113.26 *uncooperative*
refractory brick 24.9 *industrial ceramics*
refractory clay 24.2 *raw material*
refractory ware 24.1 *ceramics*
refrain 634.3 *abstain*; 684.5 *be self-restrained*; 516.1 *melody*; 509.6 *musical repetition*; 341.4 *not act*; 17.8 *part of poem*
refrainer 383.5 *resister*
refrain from 226.6 *cease*; 383.9 *desist*; 133.12 *discontinue*
refraining 634.11 *abstinence*; 383.4, 383.13 *desisting*; 341.1 *inaction*; 341.3 *inactive*; 684.8 *self-restrained*
refrainment 684.1 *self-restraint*
refrangible 325.26 *diffractive*
refresh 581.1; 490.10 *comfort*; 244.1 *improve*; 338.3 *invigorate*; 295.20 *make new*; 436.6 *replenish*; 393.5 *revive*; 336.8 *strengthen*
refreshed 581.4; 608.7 *relieved*; 295.14 *renewed*
refresher 581.6; 790.3 *fee*; 394.7 *tonic*
refreshing 581.3; 257.4 *hygienic*; 338.5 *invigorating*; 490.6 *pleasant*; 608.8 *relieving*; 336.4 *strengthening*; 235.4 *worthwhile*
refreshingly 581.8; 608.15 *comfortingly*
Refreshment 581
refreshment 581.5; 263.1 *ease*; 244.5 *improvement*; 557.12 *meal*; 393.10 *revival*; 336.4 *strengthening*; 434.6 *ventilation*; 338.1 *vigour*
refreshment room 557.15 *eating place*
refreshments 581.7
refresh oneself 581.2 *be refreshed*
refresh one's memory 462.13 *remind*
refrigerant 494.4 *cooler*; 494.9 *heat-resistant*
refrigerate 418.9 *harden*; 494.12 *make cold*; 359.5 *preserve*; 581.1 *refresh*
refrigerated 494.9 *heat-resistant*
refrigeration 28.35 *heat*; 359.1 *preservation*; 581.5 *refreshment*; 434.6 *ventilation*
refrigerator 410.3 *cabinet*; 494.4 *cooler*; 28.35 *heat*; 25.4 *kitchen container*; 359.2 *preserver*; 439.4 *storage*
refuel 437.11 *fuel*; 436.6 *replenish*; 439.6 *store*
refuge 252.5; 384.12 *fort*; 736.2 *hiding place*; 252.2, 253.1 *protection*; 370.2 *receptivity*; 301.3 *resting place*; 565.11 *retreat*; 550.15 *shelter*
refugee 634.17 *avoider*; 144.7 *displaced person*; 389.3 *escaper*; 371.27 *expellee*; 100.7 *new arrival*; 655.7 *outsider*; 144.10 *replaced*; 109.3 *unconnected person*
refulgence 522.1 *light*
refulgent 522.15 *lucent*
refund 775.5 *compensate*; 775.2 *compensation*; 791.1, 791.3 *discount*; 785.10 *pay back*; 785.2 *repayment*; 212.2 *subtracted item*
refundable 785.17 *payable*
refunded 775.6 *restoring*
refunder 775.3 *returner*
refunding 775.6 *restoring*
refurbish 393.2; 244.1 *improve*; 295.20 *make new*
refurbished 295.14 *renewed*; 393.13 *repaired*
refurbisher 393.12 *repairer*
refurbishment 295.5 *fresh start*; 244.5 *improvement*; 547.1 *transfiguration*
Refusal 709
refusal 709.1; 383.4 *desisting*; 661.2 *disobedience*; 128.1 *exclusion*; 378.1 *hindrance*; 59.9 *jumping*; 94.3 *negativeness*; 670.3 *nonacceptance*; 113.4 *objection*; 637.12 *opposition*; 470.5, 708.2 *rejection*; 364.6 *repulse*; 383.1 *resistance*; 634.12 *shyness*; 399.1 *veto*
refusal of bail 251.4 *detention*
refusal of belief 708.2 *rejection*
refusal of consent 709.1 *refusal*; 708.2 *rejection*
refusal to act 341.1 *inaction*
refusal to mix 655.1 *unsociability*
refusal to obey orders 662.1 *disobedience*; 753.1 *protest*
refusal to pay 786.1 *nonpayment*; 753.1 *protest*; 709.1 *refusal*
refusal to recant 809.1 *impenitence*
refusal to work 709.1 *refusal*; 383.1 *resistance*
refuse 238.6; **637.7**; **709.5**; 661.6 *be insubordinate*; 708.10 *be negative*; 360.7 *detain*; 258.4 *dirt*; 128.7 *exclude*; 594.14 *hate*; 378.8 *hinder*; 350.5 *not use*; 470.1 *reject*; 364.1 *repel*; 215.2 *residue*; 383.6 *resist*; 634.4 *shy*; 604.7 *thwart*; 399.3 *veto*; 441.5 *waste product*; 670.15 *withhold approval*; 113.20 *withstand*
refuse bail 251.11 *detain*
refuse collector 256.12 *cleaner*
refuse consent 708.10 *be negative*
refuse credence 708.11 *rebut*
refused 709.8; 604.9 *disappointed*; 670.31 *disapproved*; 708.18 *rejected*; 360.10 *retained*; 399.5 *vetoed*
refuse dump 238.6 *refuse*; 767.8 *sink*; 439.4 *storage*
refuse flatly 709.5 *refuse*
refuse food 687.5 *fast*; 766.9 *lose*
refuse heap 767.5 *wasteyard*
refusenik 709.4 *refuser*; 383.5 *resister*
refuse oneself 709.7; 383.9 *desist*
refuse payment 786.8 *stop payment*
refuse permission 709.5 *refuse*; 399.3 *veto*
refuse point-blank 709.5 *refuse*
refuser 709.4; 708.9 *negativist*; 383.5 *resister*
refuse to accept 708.10 *be negative*
refuse to act 341.4 *not act*
refuse to believe 451.8 *disbelieve*
refuse to bow down 383.6 *resist*
refuse to bow to 661.5 *defy*
refuse to budge 383.7 *be obstinate*; 225.5 *be permanent*; 113.20 *withstand*
refuse to comment 732.7 *keep quiet*
refuse to cooperate 662.15 *be disobedient*
refuse to obey orders 662.15 *be disobedient*; 753.6 *protest*
refuse to pay 786.7 *not pay*; 709.5 *refuse*
refuse to recant 809.5 *be impenitent*
refuse to say sorry 659.7 *be discourteous*
refuse to stoop 622.24 *be proud*
refuse to work 709.5 *refuse*
refuse to yield 423.10 *be tough*
refusing 637.2; 708.19 *rebutting*; 709.8 *refused*; 383.10 *resistant*
refusing oneself 709.3 *abnegation*; 383.4 *desisting*
refusing to eat 260.22 *sick*
refutability 704.4
refutable 704.6; 701.10 *arguable*; 761.12 *reversible*; 714.13 *vindicable*
refutably 704.12; 761.13 *reversibly*
Refutation 704
refutation 704.1; 708.7 *cancelling out*; 704.3 *countercharge*; 706.5 *counterstatement*; 714.2 *defence*; 704.2 *denial*; 709.2 *dissent*; 113.4 *objection*; 753.1 *protest*; 708.3 *rebuttal*; 761.5 *reply*
refutative 704.7 *refuting*; 706.13 *retaliatory*
refutatory 704.7 *refuting*; 706.13 *retaliatory*
refute 704.8; 706.18 *answer back*; 708.16 *cancel out*; 704.9 *deny*; 4.23 *discuss philosophically*; 709.6 *dissent*; 705.20 *doubt*; 714.8 *justify*; 113.18 *object*; 708.11 *rebut*; 479.4 *recant*; 761.9 *reply*
refuted 708.18 *rejected*; 761.11 *reversed*
refuter 704.5
refuting 704.7; 709.9 *dissenting*; 708.19 *rebutting*; 714.11 *vindicatory*
regain 773.8 *take back*
regain consciousness 488.12 *awake*; 554.16 *live*
regained safety 252.1 *safety*
regaining 773.2 *taking back*
regaining one's figure 557.6 *nutrition*
regain one's breath 581.2 *be refreshed*
regain one's freedom 571.7 *divorce*
regain one's strength 393.4 *be restored*
regal 396.12 *authoritative*; 12.10 *governing*; 396.14 *governmental*; 622.19 *stately*
regale 599.13 *be humorous*; 557.13 *feast*; 490.9 *give pleasure*; 557.24 *have a meal*; 557.25 *provide food*
regalement 557.4 *eating meals*
regalia 551.1 *dress*; 656.4 *formal dress*; 743.4 *insignia*; 7.11 *vestment*
regality 396.1 *authority*
regally 622.36 *majestically*
regard 669.2 *admiration*; 471.1 *attention*; 471.10 *be attentive*; 450.8 *be of the opinion*; 464.12 *estimate*; 811.1 *estimation*; 569.1 *friendship*; 518.13 *look*; 593.1 *love*; 123.8 *make important*; 500.4 *reputation*; 667.1, 667.15 *respect*
regardant 743.13 *heraldic*
regard as 762.5 *take a substitute*
regarded 593.21 *beloved*
regarded highly by 569.9 *friends with*
regardful 667.8 *respectful*
regard highly 669.11 *approve*; 667.15 *respect*
regarding 108.10 *relevantly*
regardless 317.16 *how*; 615.4 *rash*
regardlessness 615.1 *rashness*
regards 658.3 *courtesies*; 667.7 *respects*
regatta 50.4 *rowing*; 50.1 *sailing*
Regency 23.7 *furniture style*
regency 12.3 *governance*; 12.1 *government*; 396.7 *type of rule*
regeneracy 393.10 *revival*
regenerate 760.8 *be transformed*; 244.1 *improve*; 295.20 *make new*; 808.6 *penitent*; 393.5 *revive*
regenerated 760.13 *converted*; 295.14 *renewed*
regenerating 760.14 *converting*
regeneration 760.2 *evolution*; 295.5 *fresh start*; 244.5 *improvement*; 561.1 *reproduction*; 393.10 *revival*
regenerative 562.5 *fertile*
regent 400.9 *educational leader*
Regent's Park 87.5 *London*
reggae 18.9 *popular music*; 18.10 *world music*
regicidal 753.10 *lawbreaking*
regicide 753.2 *disorder*; 382.3 *homicide*; 382.11 *murderer*; 662.2 *violation of the law*
regime 12.3 *governance*; 396.8 *governmental organization*; 579.3 *management*; 557.6 *nutrition*
regimen 12.3 *governance*; 579.3 *management*; 557.6 *nutrition*; 394.13 *therapy*
regiment 586.16 *army unit*; 374.3 *assembly*; 647.5 *be severe*; 386.6 *compel*; 376.14 *force*; 12.3 *governance*; 584.4 *military organization*; 387.6 *subject*
regimental colours 743.7 *flag*
regimental commander 584.5 *military staff*
regimentals 551.3, 656.4 *formal dress*; 743.5 *uniform*
regimentation 111.6 *regularity*; 647.1 *severity*
regimented 663.7 *obedient*; 111.17 *regular*; 647.8 *severe*
Regina 400.2 *sovereign*
region 86.1; 141.3 *geographical space*; 205.1 *part*; 12.5 *political organization*; 86.5 *state*
regional 86.16; 141.12 *extensive*; 16.48 *jurisdictional*; 5.39 *of language*
regional accent 729.3 *mode of speech*
regional boundary 86.3
regional climate 31.38 *climate*
regional council 579.8 *British administrative council*; 16.2 *jurisdiction*; 86.5 *state*
regional enteritis 260.8 *indigestion*
regional forecast 31.4 *weather forecast*
regionalism 86.15
regionalist 19.29 *realist*
regionalization 377.6 *decentralization*; 375.2 *deconstruction*
regionalize 377.15 *decentralize*; 375.4 *deconstruct*
regionalized 377.26 *decentralized*
regional language 5.4 *parent language*
regionally 86.19 *geographically*; 16.86 *jurisdictionally*
regional metamorphism 30.32 *metamorphism*
regional novel 17.2 *fiction*
regional official 579.16 *official*
regional pronunciation 5.26 *dialect*
regionism 5.26 *dialect*
Regions 86
regions 86.6
regions of Britain 86.9
regions of the US 86.8
regions of the world 86.7
regisseur 21.27 *producer*
register 744.15; 789.7 *account*; 789.5 *account book*; 695.4 *be intelligible*; 409.7 *catalogue*; 409.15 *categorize*; 3.20 *chronicle*; 209.1 *degree*; 406.5 *divisions*; 743.10 *identify*; 370.10 *introduce*; 406.9 *itemize*; 220.1, 220.8 *list*; 220.6 *list of names*; 40.6 *memory*; 744.13 *record*; 744.6 *record book*; 717.9 *represent*; 471.11 *take note of*; 18.21 *tone*
registered 789.11 *accounted*; 3.19 *chronicled*; 692.34 *communicated*; 406.12 *itemized*; 220.11 *listed*; 744.16 *recorded*
registered blind 519.8 *blind*
Registered General Nurse 35.16 *nurse*
registered historic building 359.3 *preserved thing*
registered letter 692.3 *correspondence*
registered mail 692.2 *postal communication*
Registered Nurse 35.16 *nurse*
registered voter 469.13 *electorate*
register one's vote 469.5 *vote*
registrar 35.11 *doctor*; 744.9 *recorder*
registration 744.8; 370.3 *introduction*; 220.7 *listing*; 320.21 *miscellaneous motoring terms*
registration document 744.2 *certificate*; 320.21 *miscellaneous motoring terms*
registration number 320.21 *miscellaneous motoring terms*
registry 220.1 *list*; 744.6 *record book*; 744.8 *registration*
registry office wedding 570.5 *wedding*
regma 80.2 *botanical fruit*
regnal 12.10 *governing*
regnancy 12.3 *governance*; 396.7 *type of rule*
regnant 12.10 *governing*; 395.11 *influential*
regolith 30.36 *soil*
regrater 778.13 *retailer*
regress 303.10 *backward motion*; 300.13 *be in motion*; 245.1 *deteriorate*; 303.1 *go backwards*; 284.15 *look back*; 323.9 *navigate*; 112.19 *return to*; 761.6 *reverse*; 333.3 *slow down*
regressed 761.11 *reversed*
regression 300.4, 303.10 *backward motion*; 214.1 *decrease*; 36.19 *defence mechanism*; 245.7 *deterioration*; 761.1 *reversion*
regression analysis 13.3 *economic statistics*; 27.55 *statistical methods*
regression neurosis 36.10 *neurosis*
regression therapy 36.3 *psychiatric treatment*
regressive 761.10; 214.7 *decrescent*; 245.12 *deteriorated*; 300.17 *directional*; 303.23 *receding*
regressively 300.18 *in motion*; 761.13 *reversibly*
regressive tax 790.7 *tax*
regressive taxation 13.6 *economic factors*
regret 604.4 *be disappointed*; 249.9 *be in trouble*; 808.4 *be penitent*; 582.17 *bury*; 627.2 *condolence*; 604.1 *disappointment*; 603.6 *lament*; 627.5 *misfortune*; 808.1 *penitence*; 806.2 *signs of guilt*; 602.1 *sorrow*
regretful 806.6 *appearing guilty*; 808.6 *penitent*

regretfully 806.11 *guiltily*; 808.8 *penitently*; 637.17 *unwillingly*
regretfulness 808.1 *penitence*
regret it 814.6 *be punished*
regretless 809.3 *impenitent*
regrets 807.2 *apology*; 604.1 *disappointment*; 808.1 *penitence*
regrettable 603.5 *lamentable*
regretted 582.19 *dead*
regretting 807.4 *atoning*; 808.1 *penitence*; 808.6 *penitent*
regroup 374.5 *combine*
regrouping 409.4 *rearrangement*
regular 111.17; **298.11**; 97.8 *attendant*; 216.1 *average*; 138.21 *common*; 750.15 *conventional*; 632.8 *creature of habit*; 300.17 *directional*; 584.9 *enlisted*; 119.6 *equal*; 162.5 *even*; 297.3 *frequent*; 209.7 *gradational*; 5.44 *grammatical*; 407.15, 632.9 *habitual*; 750.13 *harmonious*; 452.6 *infallible*; 158.14 *medium*; 78.12 *of flowers*; 298.14 *orderly*; 276.8 *periodical*; 112.14 *recurrent*; 586.8 *soldier*; 97.5 *someone present*; 27.79 *spatial*; 140.11, 421.2, 698.22 *uniform*; 407.14 *well-ordered*
regular army 586.15 *army*
regular customer 632.8 *creature of habit*; 777.12 *purchaser*; 97.5 *someone present*
regular feature 693.4 *mass communication*
regular features 162.3 *evenness*
regular forces 584.2 *the military*
regular guy 574.1 *plebeian*
regular income 788.3 *income*
Regularity 298
regularity 111.6; **298.1**; 216.4 *average*; 162.3 *evenness*; 297.4 *frequency*; 632.1 *habit*; 750.4 *harmony*; 452.17 *infallibility*; 407.7 *method*; 298.4 *orderliness*; 276.6 *periodicity*; 112.3 *repetitiveness*; 421.7 *smoothness*; 140.7, 698.9 *uniformity*
regularize 698.31 *be accurate*; 407.20 *harmonize*; 216.10 *make average*; 276.11 *make periodical*; 298.10 *make regular*; 111.8 *make the same*; 750.26 *make uniform*; 244.3 *rectify*; 162.6 *symmetrize*
regularly 111.20; **298.15**; 750.35 *consistently*; 209.9 *differentially*; 119.13 *equitably*; 297.1 *frequently*; 5.52 *grammatically*; 632.19 *habitually*; 407.27 *methodically*; 298.17 *orderly*; 276.12 *periodically*; 421.14 *smoothly*
regular motion 560.2 *defecation*
regular movement 300.10
regular occurrence 297.4 *frequency*; 298.1 *regularity*
regular polygon 27.44 *polygon*
regular polyhedron 27.46 *polyhedron*
regular practice 576.5 *exercise*
regular recurrence 134.1 *continuity*; 298.1 *regularity*
regular return 298.2 *cycle*
regular thing 298.5
regulate 140.14; 397.9 *command*; 140.16 *direct*; 407.20, 750.24 *harmonize*; 276.11 *make periodical*; 298.10 *make regular*; 111.8 *make the same*; 579.1 *manage*; 685.4 *moderate*; 136.15 *modify*; 251.8 *restrain*
regulated 216.1 *average*; 750.15 *conventional*; 140.10 *customary*; 750.13 *harmonious*; 136.11 *modified*
regulated diet 557.6 *nutrition*
regulation 216.1 *average*; 397.1 *command*; 140.10 *customary*; 16.31 *legislation*; 579.3 *management*; 685.1 *moderation*; 136.5 *modification*; 298.4 *orderliness*; 713.3 *precept*; 140.1 *rule*; 631.8 *treatment*
regulation by law 16.31 *legislation*
regulation by statute 16.31 *legislation*
regulations 810.6 *ethics*; 378.2 *obstacle*
regulator gene 34.13 *genetic material*
regulatory 378.14 *blocked*; 397.14 *commanding*; 15.8 *industrial*; 140.9 *legal*
regurgitate 303.3 *reverse*; 371.15 *vomit*
regurgitation 303.12 *reversal*; 371.23 *vomiting*
rehabilitate 117.10 *assimilate*; 775.4 *give back*; 244.1 *improve*; 35.19 *practise medicine*; 393.3 *restore*; 760.9 *transform*; 714.7 *vindicate*
rehabilitated 649.6 *forgiven*; 714.12 *innocent*
rehabilitating 649.4 *forgiving*
rehabilitation 649.3 *absolution*; 760.2 *evolution*; 775.1 *giving back*; 244.5 *improvement*; 117.3 *pliancy*; 393.9 *restoration*; 35.8 *treatment*; 714.1 *vindication*
rehash 224.8 *cause change*; 112.20 *renew*; 112.5 *repeat*; 719.12 *translate*
rehashed 112.11 *reprinted*
rehearsal 448.2; 243.10 *preparations*; 21.14 *production*; 112.1 *repetition*
rehearse 21.37; **448.12**; 243.6 *brief*; 243.8 *prepare oneself*; 721.15 *recount*; 112.16 *repeat*
reheat 493.14 *be hot*; 25.55 *cook*; 112.20 *renew*
reheated 493.13 *heated*; 112.11 *reprinted*
reheating 322.7 *miscellaneous aviation terms*
rehoboam 410.14 *bottle*
Rehschnitzel 25.46 *German dish*
Reich 36.29 *psychologist*
Reichian 36.33 *Freudian*
Reichian psychology 36.1 *psychology*
reify 402.8 *be material*; 93.20 *bring into being*; 95.11 *make real*
reign 140.8 *authority*; 140.16 *direct*; 275.3 *duration*; 12.11 *govern*; 12.3, 396.4 *governance*; 396.18 *have authority*; 395.3 *personal influence*; 138.28 *prevail*
reigning 396.12 *authoritative*; 12.10 *governing*; 395.11 *influential*; 140.12 *ruling*
reigning champion 246.5 *victorious person*
reign of terror 651.7 *act of malevolence*; 588.1 *anarchy*; 612.4 *intimidation*
reign supreme 395.10 *be a prevailing influence*; 12.11 *govern*; 396.18 *have authority*
reimburse 807.5 *atone*; 775.5 *compensate*; 785.10 *pay back*
reimbursement 807.1 *atonement*; 775.2 *compensation*; 785.2 *repayment*
rein 378.10 *restrain*; 378.4 *restraint*
reincarnate 402.8 *be material*
reincarnated 402.7 *material*; 112.11 *reprinted*
reincarnation 554.5 *life cycle*; 402.2 *materialization*; 561.1 *reproduction*; 112.4 *return*; 554.8 *theories of life*
reincarnationism 11.1 *occultism*
reindeer 316.6 *beast of burden*
reindeer moss 84.6 *lichen*; 82.3 *moss*
reinforce 384.20; 707.19 *confirm*; 95.12 *establish reality*; 418.9 *harden*; 213.5 *make bigger*; 436.6 *replenish*; 393.3 *restore*; 336.8 *strengthen*; 211.7, 392.19, 413.11 *support*
reinforced 211.8 *additional*; 418.3 *hardened*; 393.13 *repaired*; 336.13 *strengthened*; 707.13 *supported*
reinforced concrete 20.4, 435.2 *building material*; 38.25 *construction material*; 418.7 *hard substance*; 323.4 *shipbuilding*
reinforced glass 527.9 *glass*
reinforced plastic 38.25 *construction material*
reinforcement 211.1 *addition*; 211.3 *additional item*; 36.27 *association of ideas*; 36.20 *conditioning*; 707.4 *confirmation*; 211.5 *extra person*; 213.1 *increase*; 436.1 *provision*; 393.8 *repair*; 393.9 *restoration*; 336.4 *strengthening*; 413.1 *support*; 326.5 *wave*
reinforcements 586.14 *armed forces*; 211.4 *extra*; 392.11 *helper*
reinforcing 336.4 *strengthening*
rein in 684.5 *be self-restrained*; 251.12 *gag*; 333.3 *slow down*
reins 579.5 *guide*; 59.14 *horse-riding terms*; 579.3 *management*; 251.5 *means of restraint*; 252.4 *safety device*; 373.9 *yoke*
reins of government 12.3, 396.4 *governance*; 579.3 *management*
reinstall 393.3 *restore*
reinstallation 393.9 *restoration*
reinstalment 393.9 *restoration*
reinstate 775.4 *give back*; 761.7 *restore*; 714.7 *vindicate*
reinstated 649.6 *forgiven*; 761.11 *reversed*
reinstatement 775.1 *giving back*; 761.2 *restoration*; 714.1 *vindication*
reinstator 775.3 *returner*
reinstitute 393.3 *restore*
reinstitution 393.9 *restoration*
reintegrate 393.3 *restore*
reintegration 393.8 *repair*
reinterpret 760.9 *transform*
reintroduce 393.3 *restore*
reintroduction 393.9 *restoration*
reinvest 775.4 *give back*
reinvestment 775.1 *giving back*; 393.9 *restoration*
reinvigorate 338.3 *invigorate*; 555.17 *make young*; 581.1 *refresh*; 393.5 *revive*; 336.8 *strengthen*
reinvigorating 338.5 *invigorating*
reinvigoration 581.5 *refreshment*
reissue 525.6 *reappearance*; 112.20 *renew*; 112.5 *repeat*
reissued 112.11 *reprinted*
reiterant 112.12 *repetitious*
reiterate 270.5 *be diffuse*; 276.10 *be periodical*; 726.6 *emphasize*; 112.17 *iterate*; 640.6 *persevere*; 509.14 *repeat*
reiterated 112.10 *iterated*; 640.11 *steady*
reiteration 640.3 *constancy*; 270.1 *diffuseness*; 726.1 *emphasis*; 112.2 *iteration*; 509.7 *repeated word*
reiterative 270.3 *diffuse*; 726.3 *emphatic*; 112.12 *repetitious*
reiteratively 112.23 *repeatedly*
reiterativeness 270.1 *diffuseness*
reject 470.1; 113.17 *be against*; 606.7 *be dissatisfied*; 708.10 *be negative*; 637.6 *be unwilling*; 708.14 *cancel*; 16.79 *convict*; 704.9 *deny*; 596.5 *dislike*; 709.6 *dissent*; 128.7 *exclude*; 371.10 *exterminate*; 247.5 *failing person*; 594.14 *hate*; 655.13 *ignore*; 231.6 *imperfect item*; 122.6 *inferior*; 215.8 *leave*; 766.6 *loser*; 350.5 *not use*; 655.7 *outsider*; 238.6, 709.5 *refuse*; 470.8 *rejected thing*; 364.1 *repel*; 128.6 *thing excluded*; 604.7 *thwart*; 350.11 *unused thing*; 399.3 *veto*; 469.5 *vote*; 670.15 *withhold approval*
reject an offer 218.6 *be unsatisfied*
reject authority 588.4 *be anarchic*
rejected 470.10; **708.18**; 604.9 *disappointed*; 670.31 *disapproved*; 596.9 *disliked*; 709.9 *dissenting*; 128.11 *excluded*; 655.10 *lonely*; 215.9 *remaining*; 372.17 *unjoined*; 606.5 *unsatisfactory*; 399.5 *vetoed*
rejected person 470.9
rejected thing 470.8
rejecting 709.9 *dissenting*; 708.19 *rebutting*
Rejection 470
rejection 470.5; **708.2**; 708.5 *cancellation*; 36.19 *defence mechanism*; 704.2 *denial*; 596.1 *dislike*; 606.1 *dissatisfaction*; 350.10 *disuse*; 128.1 *exclusion*; 371.17 *expulsion*; 451.3 *incredulity*; 670.3 *nonacceptance*; 113.4 *objection*; 637.12 *opposition*; 709.1 *refusal*; 364.6 *repulse*; 655.3 *separation*; 372.2 *setting apart*; 453.10 *suspicion*; 399.1 *veto*
reject one's appeal 16.79 *convict*
reject one's defence 16.79 *convict*
rejects 793.4 *bargain*; 122.7 *inferior thing*; 215.2 *residue*
reject someone's advances 364.1 *repel*
rejoice 600.5; 601.15 *celebrate*; 597.7 *show joy*
rejoicer 600.4
Rejoicing 600
rejoicing 600.1; **600.9**; **601.9**; 601.1 *celebration*
rejoicingly 600.11
rejoin 706.17 *answer*; 704.10 *countercharge*; 714.8 *justify*; 312.8 *meet*; 376.45 *reassemble*; 708.11 *rebut*
rejoinder 706.1 *answer*; 704.3 *countercharge*; 714.2 *defence*; 660.9 *discourtesy*; 16.7 *legal trial*; 708.3 *rebuttal*; 385.1 *retaliation*
rejoining 312.14 *meeting*; 708.19 *rebutting*; 714.11 *vindicatory*
rejuvenate 554.21 *invigorate*; 295.20 *make new*; 555.17 *make young*; 581.1 *refresh*; 393.5 *revive*
rejuvenated 295.14 *renewed*
rejuvenating 338.5 *invigorating*
rejuvenation 295.5 *fresh start*; 581.5 *refreshment*; 393.10 *revival*
rejuvenescence 393.10 *revival*
rekindle 393.5 *revive*
relapse 303.19 *backsliding*; 804.16 *be wicked*; 245.1 *deteriorate*; 245.7 *deterioration*; 303.1 *go backwards*; 112.19 *return to*; 761.6 *reverse*; 761.1 *reversion*
relapsed 245.12 *deteriorated*; 479.11 *equivocating*
relapse into silence 506.1 *be silent*
relapsing 303.23 *receding*
relate 3.20 *chronicle*; 373.13 *intercommunicate*; 112.17 *iterate*; 744.13 *record*; 721.15 *recount*; 108.7 *relate to*; 729.11 *speak*
related 108.4; 3.19 *chronicled*; 373.14 *connective*; 127.8 *included*; 112.10 *iterated*; 115.7 *similar*
Relatedness 108
relatedness 108.1
relate to 108.7; 127.5 *be included*; 590.18 *feel for*
relating 112.2 *iteration*
relation 373.3 *associate*; 373.2 *association*; 112.2 *iteration*; 27.63 *mathematical logic*; 3.7 *narrative*; 27.14 *operation*; 108.1 *relatedness*
relational 27.76 *functional*; 108.5 *interrelated*
relational database 40.11 *application*
relational operator 27.63 *mathematical logic*; 27.13 *mathematical symbol*
relationship 373.2 *association*; 593.8 *love affair*; 27.63 *mathematical logic*; 27.14 *operation*; 108.1 *relatedness*
relative 373.3 *associate*; 222.7 *circumstantial*; 209.7 *gradational*; 108.5 *interrelated*
relative age 30.41 *geological time*
relative aperture 28.31 *lens element*
relative atomic mass 28.69 *isotope*
relative bearing 324.2 *bearing*
relative condition 222.1 *circumstances*
relative course 324.2 *bearing*
relative density 416.3; 28.9 *mass*
relative frequency 27.58 *frequency distribution*
relative humidity 429.3 *humidity*; 31.6 *weather data*
relatively 222.16; 209.9 *differentially*
relativeness 209.3 *gradation*; 108.2 *interrelatedness*
relative permeability 28.61 *magnetic quantity*
relative permittivity 28.54, 39.11 *electric field*
relative pitch 18.21 *tone*
relative position 108.3
relative quantity 209.3 *gradation*
relatives 376.17 *family*
relative velocity 28.8 *time*
relativism 4.7 *school of thought*
relativist 4.11 *follower of a doctrine*; 4.14 *of a philosophy*
relativistic 28.98 *physical*
relativistically 28.100 *physically*
relativistic quantum mechanics 28.3 *modern physics*
relativity 141.9 *fourth dimension*; 108.2 *interrelatedness*
relativity theory 28.3 *modern physics*
relaunch 393.3 *restore*
relaunching 393.9 *restoration*
relax 685.3 *be moderate*; 301.8 *be motionless*; 419.14 *ease*; 685.4 *moderate*; 341.4 *not act*; 657.11 *not stand on ceremony*; 226.9 *pause*; 608.9 *relieve*; 372.9 *separate*; 627.10 *show mercy*; 333.3 *slow down*; 419.13 *soften*; 263.2 *take it easy*; 654.12 *visit*; 337.7 *weaken*
relaxant 37.4 *drug type*
relaxation 263.1, 608.1 *ease*; 657.4 *freedom*; 341.1 *inaction*; 250.4 *informality*; 580.1 *leisure*; 391.1 *liberation*; 685.1 *moderation*
relaxation therapy 36.3 *psychiatric treatment*
relaxed 265.14; 263.4 *at ease*; 265.13 *easy-going*; 341.3 *inactive*; 250.13 *informal*; 580.7 *leisurely*; 490.7 *pleased*; 608.7 *relieved*; 268.10 *slippery*; 657.8 *sociable*; 419.1 *soft*; 419.6 *soft-hearted*; 333.5 *unhurried*; 337.8 *weak*
relaxedly 657.13 *casually*
relaxedness 657.2 *sociability*
relaxing 263.4 *at ease*; 241.3 *comfortable*; 341.1 *inaction*; 490.6 *pleasant*; 608.8 *relieving*
relax one's efforts 341.4 *not act*
relax one's grip 767.9 *dispose of*
relax restrictions 391.4 *liberate*
relay 692.25 *broadcast material*; 692.30 *communicate*; 298.2 *cycle*; 740.13 *make public*; 67.11 *swimming*; 47.9 *track*
relay box 47.1 *track events*
relayed 692.34 *communicated*
relay event 67.1 *swimming*
relay race 47.1 *track events*
relay racing 47.1 *track events*
relay station 692.20 *radio broadcasting*; 29.32 *satellite*; 692.24 *television broadcasting*
release 649.3 *absolution*; 649.10 *absolve*; 16.78, 758.10 *acquit*; 16.42, 758.2 *acquittal*; 608.2 *aid*; 525.1 *appearance*; 131.3 *death*; 390.1 *deliver*; 390.2 *deliverance*;

371.2 *dismiss*; 738.1 *display*; 767.1 *disposal*; 767.9 *dispose of*; 21.38 *dramatize*; 389.1 *escape*; 47.2 *field events*; 250.1 *freedom*; 391.4 *liberate*; 391.1 *liberation*; 740.13 *make public*; 785.1 *payment*; 757.2 *permit*; 525.14 *present*; 355.1 *relinquish*; 393.3 *restore*; 608.10 *save*; 559.7 *secrete*; 559.1 *secretion*; 372.9 *separate*; 250.15 *set free*; 714.7 *vindicate*; 714.1 *vindication*; 582.5 *ways of dying*
release a paper 707.17 *affirm*
released 16.63, 758.6 *acquitted*; 582.19 *dead*; 767.12 *disposed*; 649.6 *forgiven*; 250.9 *free*; 714.12 *innocent*; 391.7 *liberated*; 372.15 *separate*; 707.11 *stated*
released prisoner 389.3 *escaper*; 250.7 *free person*
release one's hold 767.9 *dispose of*
release seeds 80.10 *fruit*
release the ball 51.8 *bowl*
release therapy 36.3 *psychiatric treatment*
releasing 767.1 *disposal*
releasing hormone 33.16 *hormone*
relecommunicational 692.33 *communicational*
relegate 144.17; 371.3 *disbar*; 128.7 *exclude*; 124.13 *make unimportant*; 316.15 *take away*
relegated 144.11
relegation 144.4; 371.18 *dismissal*; 128.1 *exclusion*; 316.1 *transfer*
relent 685.3 *be moderate*; 627.10, 649.12 *show mercy*; 388.3 *submit*; 419.16 *yield*
relentless 452.5 *inevitable*; 628.5 *inflexible*; 638.3 *strong-willed*
relentless attack 381.12 *military attack*
relentlessly 452.25 *inevitably*; 628.7 *pitilessly*; 647.11 *severely*
relentlessness 452.16 *inevitability*; 628.2 *inflexibility*; 638.14 *tenacity*
relevance 706.8 *correspondence*; 694.1 *meaning*; 136.1 *qualification*; 108.1 *relatedness*
relevant 706.15 *correspondent*; 716.8 *evidential*; 750.16 *fitting*; 123.5 *important*; 346.12 *operative*; 703.13 *proven*; 108.4 *related*
relevant facts 716.1 *evidence*
relevantly 108.10; 716.14 *as evidence*; 706.26 *correspondingly*; 750.38 *fittingly*; 346.13 *operationally*
reliability 450.4 *believability*; 452.17 *infallibility*; 225.1 *permanence*; 799.1 *probity*; 783.7 *repute*; 228.1 *stability*; 638.15 *will*
reliability trial 61.1 *motor racing*
reliable 450.13 *believable*; 799.4 *honourable*; 452.6 *infallible*; 225.7 *permanent*; 252.6 *safe*; 228.9 *stable*; 638.5 *steady*; 396.15 *true*
reliably 396.25 *authentically*; 799.7 *honourably*; 225.9 *permanently*; 228.12 *stably*; 253.16 *surely*
reliance 450.3 *believing*; 474.1 *expectation*; 253.1 *protection*
reliant 253.7 *guaranteed*
relic 3.11; 462.3, 794.3 *memento*; 296.5 *old thing*; 215.1 *remainder*; 10.14 *sacred object*; 571.6 *surviving spouse*; 11.6 *talisman*; 284.7 *thing of the past*; 744.12 *vestige*
relic of the past 296.5 *old thing*
relics 582.11 *dead person*
relict 215.1 *remainder*; 284.7 *thing of the past*
Relief 608
relief 650.4 *benevolent act*; 608.4, 652.5 *charity*; 30.6 *continent*; 390.2 *deliverance*; 389.1 *escape*; 525.3 *external appearance*; 211.5 *extra person*; 160.1 *form*; 768.2 *gift*; 154.5 *height measure*; 391.1 *liberation*; 415.6 *lightening*; 627.3 *mercy*; 685.1 *moderation*; 393.11 *recuperation*; 581.5 *refreshment*; 19.13 *relief-carving*; 394.1 *remedy*; 163.2 *shadow*; 392.4 *social assistance*; 762.2 *substitute person*; 550.21 *substitution*; 550.40 *substitutive*; 212.1 *subtraction*; 392.2 *support*; 580.2 *time off*
relief-carving 19.13
relief map 163.4, 717.7 *map*
relief pitcher 48.2 *baseball player*
relief printing 23.8 *woodwork*
relief worker 398.4 *deputy*
relieve 608.9; 762.4 *be a substitute*; 650.8 *be benevolent*; 490.10 *comfort*; 550.34 *cover for*; 390.1 *deliver*; 263.3 *ease*; 391.4 *liberate*; 415.10 *lighten*; 685.4 *moderate*; 35.19 *practise medicine*; 581.1 *refresh*; 394.19 *remedy*; 212.3 *subtract*; 392.19 *support*
relieved 608.7; 389.8 *escaping*
relieve from duty 608.12
relieve one of 774.12 *steal*
relieve oneself 608.13; 560.15 *excrete*
reliever 608.3
relieving 608.8; 415.3 *lightening*; 581.3 *refreshing*; 37.16 *soothing*
relievo 608.6 *profile*; 19.13 *relief-carving*
Religion 7
religion 7.1; 632.4 *custom*; 137.8 *genealogy*; 450.2 *religious belief*; 101.2 *unworldliness*
religionist 7.4
religiose 699.31 *hypocritical*
religiosity 699.3 *hypocrisy*; 7.2 *religiousness*
religious 7.15; 7.7 *monk*; 101.8 *nonmaterial*; 799.5 *pure*; 7.3 *religious person*; 2.12 *sociological*; 7.18 *theological*; 10.22 *worshipping*
religious architecture 20.1 *architecture*
religious belief 450.2
religious believer 101.7 *believer in a nonmaterial world*
religious broadcasting 692.25 *broadcast material*
religious celibate 572.4 *celibate person*; 255.5, 795.5 *pure person*
religious ceremony 656.3 *formal occasion*
religious cleansing 256.3
religious conversion 760.3 *persuasion*
religious disobedience 662.1 *disobedience*
religious ecstasy 36.14 *trance*
religious education 7.13 *theology*
religious fasting 687.1 *fasting*
religious feeling 450.2 *religious belief*
religious festival 10.16
religious group 7.1 *religion*
religious history 3.1 *history*
religious institution 2.8 *human institution*
religious instruction 7.13 *theology*
religious leader 400.6
religiously 7.23; 101.13 *metaphysically*; 799.8 *purely*; 2.16 *sociologically*
religious mania 461.4 *delusion*
religious manual 10.10
religious movement 7.1 *religion*
religiousness 7.2
religious observance 632.4 *custom*; 10.1 *ritual*
religious organization 2.4 *social organization*
religious painter 19.16 *artist*
religious persecution 466.4 *social discrimination*
religious person 7.3
religious practice 10.1 *ritual*
religious rite 433.15 *holy water*
religious sacrifice 382.6 *ritual killing*
religious sin 804.6
religious studies 7.13 *theology*
religious symbol 742.1 *sign*
religious teacher 719.6 *interpreter*
religious text 7.12
religious war 585.1 *war*
reline 393.1 *repair*
relinquish 355.1; 684.5 *be self-restrained*; 226.6 *cease*; 767.9 *dispose of*; 372.13 *diverge*; 766.9 *lose*; 708.12 *renounce*; 605.5 *resign*; 350.6 *stop using*; 388.3 *submit*; 313.2 *withdraw*
relinquish authority 757.4 *be permissive*
relinquish control 350.7 *stop work*
relinquished 355.5; 709.10 *abnegating*; 767.12 *disposed*; 708.18 *rejected*; 684.8 *self-restrained*
relinquisher 605.3 *resigner*
relinquishing 709.10 *abnegating*
Relinquishment 355
relinquishment 355.3; 709.3 *abnegation*; 226.1 *cessation*; 767.1 *disposal*; 708.4 *renunciation*; 605.1 *resignation*; 684.1 *self-restraint*; 388.1 *submission*
relinquish one's life 582.16 *meet one's fate*
reliquary 10.13 *shrine*
relish 597.6 *enjoy*; 490.8 *feel pleasure*; 495.4 *flavour*; 241.14, 595.7 *like*; 595.3 *likes*; 593.23 *love*; 496.2 *seasoning*; 495.9, 557.23 *taste*
relishable 495.7 *tasty*
relishing 557.3 *delicate eating*
relive 284.15 *look back*
reload 436.6 *replenish*
relocate 224.7 *be changed*; 144.14 *displace*; 313.3 *quit*; 142.10 *settle*; 316.15 *take away*
relocated 144.8 *displaced*; 144.10 *replaced*
relocation 224.1 *change*; 144.1 *displacement*; 144.3 *replacement*; 316.1 *transfer*
reluctance 616.1 *caution*; 596.1 *dislike*; 333.12 *hesitation*; 674.6 *reserve*; 383.1 *resistance*; 634.12 *shyness*; 637.11 *unwillingness*
reluctant 637.5; 634.18 *avoiding*; 616.4 *cautious*; 596.8 *disliking*; 481.10 *dissuaded*; 333.6 *hesitant*; 674.13 *reserved*; 383.10 *resistant*; 637.1 *unwilling*
reluctantly 616.7 *cautiously*; 596.10 *discontentedly*; 383.14 *resistingly*; 634.23 *shyly*; 333.16 *slowly*; 637.17 *unwillingly*
reluctant person 637.16
rely on 452.20 *be certain*; 450.7 *believe*; 610.6 *hope*; 349.4 *resort to*
rely on supposition 476.5 *suppose*
remade 295.14 *renewed*; 393.13 *repaired*; 112.11 *reprinted*
remain 215.7 *be left*; 301.8 *be motionless*; 93.19 *continue to be*; 640.9 *endure*; 277.6 *last*; 134.4 *protract*
remain at a distance 145.6 *keep away*
remain at anchor 301.8 *be motionless*
remain at rest 225.5 *be permanent*
remain a virgin 572.10 *be continent*; 795.11 *be moral*
remain celibate 795.11 *be moral*
Remainder 215
remainder 215.1; 27.18 *division*; 345.1 *effect*; 440.2 *legal terms*; 194.4 *mathematical result*; 706.7 *numerical result*; 205.1 *part*; 3.11 *relic*; 778.1 *sell*; 219.3 *superfluity*; 284.7 *thing of the past*; 350.11 *unused thing*
remaindered 350.3 *not wanted*
remain fixed 228.6 *be stable*
remain forever 279.5 *be eternal*
remain good-humoured 658.10 *be courteous*
remaining 215.9; 3.15 *historic*; 350.3 *not wanted*; 219.7 *superfluous*; 767.15 *unclaimed*
remain ***in situ*** 301.8 *be motionless*
remain intransigent 418.11 *be stubborn*
remain neutral 250.16 *be independent*
remain neutral about 618.15 *be impartial*
remain obstinate 809.5 *be impenitent*
remain on one's hands 219.5 *be superfluous*
remain pure 795.11 *be moral*
remain raw 161.3 *make shapeless*
remains 582.11 *dead person*; 716.4 *indication*; 122.7 *inferior thing*; 3.11 *relic*; 215.1 *remainder*; 284.7 *thing of the past*; 350.11 *unused thing*; 744.12 *vestige*
remain seated 301.8 *be motionless*; 668.22 *show disrespect*
remain the same 225.5 *be permanent*
remain unchanged 225.5 *be permanent*
remain unmarried 572.9 *be celibate*
remain unmoved 618.12 *be indifferent*
remain unrepentant 809.5 *be impenitent*
remain unsolved 696.10 *be unexplained*
remake 295.5 *fresh start*; 295.20 *make new*; 112.20 *renew*; 112.5 *repeat*; 393.3, 761.7 *restore*
remand 294.8 *delay*; 294.3 *delayed action*; 251.11 *detain*; 251.4 *detention*
remanded 294.10 *held up*
remanence 28.63 *magnetic phenomenon*
remark 745.3 *aphorize*; 464.1 *judgment*; 729.7 *utterance*
remarkable 520.2 *clear*; 139.17 *exceptional*; 123.6 *notable*; 619.8 *wonderful*
remarkably 139.30 *characteristically*; 123.9 *importantly*; 619.13 *wonderfully*
remarriage 570.3 *types of marriage*
remarried 570.21 *married*
remarry 570.15 *marry*
remedial 394.17; 392.34 *beneficial*; 347.4 *counteracting*; 6.16 *educational*; 257.4 *hygienic*; 244.16 *improving*; 608.8 *relieving*; 393.16 *restorative*; 706.14 *solved*; 35.25 *therapeutic*
remedial education 6.2 *educational system*
remedially 394.21; 244.17 *better*; 706.26 *correspondingly*; 347.5 *counter*; 6.25 *educationally*; 393.17 *repairably*
remedial measure 394.1 *remedy*
Remedy 394
remedy 394.1; **394.19**; 347.2 *counteracting thing*; 347.1 *counteraction*; 484.3 *expedient plan*; 244.5 *improvement*; 352.1 *means*; 392.5 *medical assistance*; 394.2 *medicine*; 713.3 *precept*; 244.3 *rectify*; 393.11 *recuperation*; 608.3 *reliever*; 393.1, 393.8 *repair*; 706.6 *solution*; 706.20 *solve*; 392.2, 392.19 *support*
remember 3.22; **360.8**; **462.12**; 650.8 *be benevolent*; 462.14, 601.16 *commemorate*; 446.14 *have an idea*; 400.15 *learn*; 284.15 *look back*; 462.11 *memorize*; 112.19 *return to*; 695.6 *understand*
remembered 462.7 *memorable*
remember forever 279.6 *eternalize*
remembering 462.8; 3.13 *looking back*; 462.1 *memory*; 284.21 *retrospective*
remember wrongly 463.14 *be forgetful*
remembrance 601.2 *commemoration*; 279.4 *eternalization*; 3.13 *looking back*; 462.1 *memory*; 215.1 *remainder*; 360.5 *retentiveness*; 284.2 *retrospection*
remembrancer 713.4 *adviser*
remembrance service 601.2 *commemoration*
Remembrance Sunday 601.5 *anniversary*; 298.6 *annually celebrated day*
remex 72.17 *plumage*
remigrate 303.5 *turn back*
remigrating 303.27 *returning*
remigration 313.7 *departure*
remind 462.13; 711.5 *warn*
reminder 462.4; 693.7 *advice*; 713.4 *adviser*; 123.2 *important matter*; 744.1 *record*; 215.1 *remainder*
reminding 462.7 *memorable*
remind oneself 462.13 *remind*
reminisce 284.15, 303.8 *look back*; 721.15 *recount*; 3.22, 462.12 *remember*
reminiscence 3.13, 303.15 *looking back*; 462.1 *memory*; 721.3 *narration*; 284.2 *retrospection*
reminiscence therapy 36.3 *psychiatric treatment*
reminiscent 462.7 *memorable*
reminiscently 462.16 *memorably*; 3.25 *reportedly*
reminiscing 303.15 *looking back*; 284.21 *retrospective*
remise 54.3 *fencing movements*
remiss 472.10 *careless*; 666.4 *negligent*; 637.4 *procrastinating*
remissible 714.13 *vindicable*
remission 608.1 *ease*; 649.1 *forgiveness*; 685.1 *moderation*; 212.2 *subtracted item*; 714.1 *vindication*
remission of sin 649.1 *forgiveness*
remissive 714.11 *vindicatory*
remissively 714.15 *in vindication*
remissness 637.15 *delay*; 666.1 *negligence*
remit 649.10 *absolve*; 685.3 *be moderate*; 785.6 *pay*; 316.12 *transport*; 714.7 *vindicate*
remittable 785.17 *payable*
remittal 714.1 *vindication*
remittance 780.6 *funds*; 785.1 *payment*
remittance man 315.8 *outgoer*
remitted 649.6 *forgiven*
remit the penalty 16.78 *acquit*
remnant 215.1 *remainder*
remnants 215.2 *residue*
remodel 224.8 *cause change*; 244.3 *rectify*; 393.2 *refurbish*; 760.9 *transform*
remodelled 224.12 *changed*
remodelling 224.1 *change*; 393.9 *restoration*
remonstrance 481.6 *dissuasion*
remonstrate 701.13 *argue*; 670.16 *disagree*; 481.1 *dissuade*; 113.18 *object*; 711.5 *warn*
remonstration 606.2 *expression of dissatisfaction*; 113.4 *objection*
remora 267.4 *adherent*
Remorse 808
remorse 807.2 *apology*; 627.2 *condolence*; 808.1 *penitence*; 806.2 *signs of guilt*
remorseful 806.6 *appearing guilty*; 808.6 *penitent*
remorsefully 806.11 *guiltily*; 808.8 *penitently*
remorsefulness 808.1 *penitence*
remorseless 809.3 *impenitent*; 628.4 *pitiless*

remorselessly 809.6 *impenitently*; 628.7 *pitilessly*
remorselessness 809.1 *impenitence*; 628.1 *pitilessness*
remorsing 808.6 *penitent*
remortgage 783.1 *credit*; 784.3 *loan*
remote 521.2 *difficult to see*; 145.8, 240.2 *distant*; 109.7 *illogical*; 105.1 *improbable*; 524.6 *murky*; 655.11 *secluded*; 655.8 *unsociable*
remote age 3.9 *distant past*
remote ages 284.1 *past time*
remote control 579.5 *guide*; 692.22 *television set*
remotely 145.10 *distantly*; 655.14 *unsocially*
remoteness 145.1, 240.4 *distance*; 524.2 *murk*; 521.6 *that which makes invisible*; 655.1 *unsociability*
remote possibility 102.4; 105.4 *improbability*
remote sensing 28.95 *mensuration*
remould 224.8 *cause change*; 244.3 *rectify*
remoulded 224.12 *changed*
remoulding 224.1 *change*
remount 762.3 *substitute thing*; 59.3 *warhorse*
removable 369.18 *extractive*; 212.6 *subtractive*; 316.17 *transferable*
removably 369.21 *away*; 212.9 *decreasingly*
removal 144.2; **371.21**; 708.5 *cancellation*; 144.1 *displacement*; 767.1 *disposal*; 145.1 *distance*; 128.2 *ejection*; 371.20 *eviction*; 369.1 *extraction*; 358.3 *obliteration*; 144.3 *replacement*; 372.2 *setting apart*; 212.1 *subtraction*; 773.3 *taking away*; 708.6 *termination*; 316.1 *transfer*
removal of the body 583.7 *inquest*
removal van 410.10 *cart*
remove 144.15; 708.14 *cancel*; 526.3 *cause to disappear*; 25.9 *dish*; 128.8 *eject*; 371.8 *evict*; 369.11 *extract*; 209.3 *gradation*; 141.8 *intervening space*; 557.14 *mouthful*; 358.1 *obliterate*; 313.3 *quit*; 100.15 *separate*; 372.10 *set apart*; 212.3 *subtract*; 316.15, 773.10 *take away*; 708.15 *terminate*; 319.4 *transport*; 552.14 *undress*; 371.11 *void*; 300.15 *walk*
remove all doubt 703.17 *prove*
remove all obstacles 757.3 *permit*
remove all signs of 708.14 *cancel*
remove any trace 358.1 *obliterate*
remove authority from 335.7 *remove power from*
removed 144.9; 144.8 *displaced*; 144.10 *replaced*; 100.11 *separate*; 146.6 *spaced*; 212.5 *subtracted*; 109.6 *unrelated*; 655.8 *unsociable*
removed from the record 649.8 *overlooked*
remove doubt 454.1 *verify*
remove errors 244.3 *rectify*
remove friction 421.11 *smooth*
removement 316.1 *transfer*
remove one's name from 355.2 *withdraw*
remove power from 335.7
remover 773.6 *taker*
remove the dirt 256.13 *clean*
remunerate 785.11; 813.11 *pay*; 813.9 *reward*
remuneration 765.4 *earnings*; 788.3 *income*; 785.3 *pay*; 813.1 *reward*; 813.4 *reward for service*
remunerative 562.5 *fertile*; 765.15 *gainful*; 356.11 *productive*; 237.4, 785.18 *profitable*; 246.14, 813.15 *rewarding*
remuneratively 765.20 *gainfully*; 356.13 *productively*; 788.8, 813.20 *profitably*
remunerativeness 765.1 *gain*
Renaissance 3.15 *historic*; 284.5 *historical period*; 3.10 *past age*; 19.29 *realist*
renaissance 554.5 *life cycle*; 112.4 *return*; 393.10 *revival*
Renaissance man 207.5 *pluralist*; 485.4 *skilled person*
Renaissance perspective 19.4 *treatment*
Renaissance tragedy 21.11 *tragedy*
renal 172.10 *visceral*
renal graft 394.12 *surgery*
renascent 393.13 *repaired*; 561.15 *reproduced*
rend 146.5 *crack*; 557.21 *eat*; 750.30 *grant*; 372.9 *separate*
rend asunder 357.9 *demolish*
render 698.34; 550.28 *face*; 768.5 *give*; 750.30 *grant*; 719.8 *interpret*; 431.24 *melt*; 369.17 *obtain an extract*; 18.36 *play*; 717.9 *represent*; 760.9 *transform*; 719.12 *translate*
render assistance 652.7 *be charitable*
render averse 481.4 *put off*
rendered 750.19 *granted*; 719.15 *interpreted*
rendered infertile 563.5
render faithfully 698.34 *render*
render good 775.5 *compensate*
render hard 418.9 *harden*
render harmless 238.8 *make useless*
render incorrectly 720.1 *misinterpret*
rendering 20.1 *architecture*; 719.1 *interpretation*; 369.7 *obtaining an extract*; 717.1 *representation*; 5.40 *translated*; 5.12, 719.4 *translation*; 550.8 *wall covering*
render insensible 489.12 *anaesthetize*
render insensitive 592.7
render lip service 699.22 *be hypocritical*
render necessary 135.10 *necessitate*
render soft 419.13 *soften*
render thanks 671.6 *be grateful*
render unconscious 489.12 *anaesthetize*
render unfit 238.8 *make useless*
rendezvous 376.8; 376.39 *come together*; 312.8 *meet*; 312.14, 654.3 *meeting*; 29.35 *rocketry*
rendition 719.1 *interpretation*; 369.7 *obtaining an extract*
rend the eardrums 507.8 *be loud*
rend the skies 507.8 *be loud*
renegade 634.17 *avoider*; 760.6 *convert*; 325.19 *deviant person*; 118.8 *dissenter*; 479.11 *equivocating*; 479.9 *equivocator*; 118.12 *nonconformist*; 804.9 *wicked person*
renege 760.10 *be converted*; 708.14 *cancel*; 479.4 *recant*; 761.6 *reverse*
reneger 479.9 *equivocator*
reneging 708.5 *cancellation*
renew 112.20; 224.8 *cause change*; 244.1 *improve*; 295.20 *make new*; 581.1 *refresh*; 393.2 *refurbish*; 393.5 *revive*
renewable 295.15; 437.10 *powered*
renewable energy 437.8; 28.11 *energy*
renewable energy source 437.1 *fuel*; 334.6 *source of energy*
renewal 224.1 *change*; 295.5 *fresh start*; 244.5 *improvement*; 581.5 *refreshment*; 393.8 *repair*; 561.1 *reproduction*; 112.4 *return*; 393.10 *revival*
renewed 295.14; 224.12 *changed*; 393.13 *repaired*; 112.11 *reprinted*; 561.15 *reproduced*; 640.11 *steady*
renewing 561.15 *reproduced*
renew one's efforts 640.6 *persevere*
renew oneself 295.17 *become new*; 581.2 *be refreshed*
renitency 637.12 *opposition*; 383.1 *resistance*
renitent 383.10 *resistant*
rennet 416.5 *condenser*
rennin 33.11 *enzyme*
renounce 708.12; 684.5 *be self-restrained*; 708.14 *cancel*; 704.9 *deny*; 470.2 *discard*; 767.9 *dispose of*; 753.6 *protest*; 479.4 *recant*; 709.7 *refuse oneself*; 355.1 *relinquish*
renounce authority 388.3 *submit*
renounced 708.18 *rejected*
renounce drinking 684.5 *be self-restrained*
renouncement 605.1 *resignation*
renouncer 605.3 *resigner*
renounce the throne 605.5 *resign*
renouncing 704.7 *refuting*
renovate 244.1 *improve*; 295.20 *make new*; 581.1 *refresh*; 393.2 *refurbish*
renovated 244.14 *improved*; 295.14 *renewed*; 393.13 *repaired*
renovation 295.5 *fresh start*; 244.5 *improvement*; 581.5 *refreshment*; 393.8 *repair*; 561.1 *reproduction*
renovator 393.12 *repairer*
renown 740.7 *publicity*; 575.1 *right*; 246.13 *successful*
renowned 575.5 *entitled*; 455.10 *known*; 811.3 *reputable*; 740.20 *well-known*
rent 372.16 *apart*; 146.2 *crack*; 146.7 *cracked*; 790.3 *fee*; 564.14 *inhabit*; 788.2 *money received*; 763.7 *possess*; 372.3 *separateness*
rental 790.3 *fee*
rental contract 755.2 *purchase contract*
rent arrears 249.2 *economic adversity*
rent boy 796.8 *immoral man*; 567.7 *libertine*
rent collector 376.35, 769.7 *collector*
rented 564.11 *inhabited*
renter 564.3 *householder*
rent-free 793.11 *free of charge*
rentier 769.7 *collector*; 343.8 *nonworker*
rent-payer 763.5 *possessor*
rent-roll 788.2 *money received*; 440.1 *property*
renunciate 708.10 *be negative*; 709.6 *dissent*; 605.5 *resign*
renunciation 708.4; 704.2 *denial*; 767.1 *disposal*; 709.2 *dissent*; 753.1 *protest*; 479.8 *recantation*; 708.2 *rejection*; 355.3 *relinquishment*; 605.1 *resignation*; 684.1 *self-restraint*
renunciation of wealth 782.8
renunciative 709.9 *dissenting*; 708.17 *negative*; 684.8 *self-restrained*
renunciatory 709.9 *dissenting*; 708.17 *negative*; 605.7 *resigning*
renvers 59.10 *dressage*
reoccur 297.7 *be frequent*; 298.7 *be regular*; 112.21 *be repeated*
reoccur constantly 298.7 *be regular*
reoccurring 112.14 *recurrent*
reorder 224.8 *cause change*; 409.14 *rearrange*
reordered 224.12 *changed*; 409.23 *rearranged*
reordering 224.1 *change*; 409.4 *rearrangement*
reorganization 224.1 *change*; 760.1 *conversion*; 295.5 *fresh start*; 409.4 *rearrangement*; 244.6 *rectification*; 393.9 *restoration*
reorganize 224.7 *be changed*; 224.8 *cause change*; 295.20 *make new*; 409.14 *rearrange*; 244.3 *rectify*; 393.3 *restore*; 760.9 *transform*
reorganized 224.12 *changed*; 409.23 *rearranged*; 295.14 *renewed*
reorient 393.3 *restore*
reorientation 36.20 *conditioning*; 393.9 *restoration*
rep 578.3 *agent*; 21.1 *drama*; 21.15 *engagement*; 59.15 *horse person*; 748.4 *representative*; 778.10 *salesman*; 729.10 *speaker*
repaint 295.20 *make new*; 393.2 *refurbish*
repainted 295.14 *renewed*
repainting 295.5 *fresh start*
Repair 393
repair 393.1; **393.8**; 807.5 *atone*; 224.8 *cause change*; 224.1 *change*; 244.1 *improve*; 244.5 *improvement*; 801.15 *put right*; 244.6 *rectification*; 244.3 *rectify*; 581.1 *refresh*; 581.5 *refreshment*; 221.1 *state*
repairable 393.14
repairably 393.17
repaired 393.13; 224.12 *changed*; 244.14 *improved*
repairer 393.12; 244.13 *reviser*
repairing 224.1 *change*
repairman 578.2 *artisan*; 393.12 *repairer*
repairs 393.8 *repair*
repair ship 586.24 *warship*
repaper 393.2 *refurbish*
reparable 393.14 *repairable*
reparably 393.17 *repairably*
reparation 609.2; 807.1 *atonement*; 775.2, 813.6 *compensation*; 749.2 *peace offering*; 393.8 *repair*; 393.9 *restoration*; 385.1 *retaliation*; 808.2 *type of penance*
reparations 393.9 *restoration*
reparative 807.4 *atoning*; 393.16 *restorative*; 775.6 *restoring*
reparatory 807.4 *atoning*; 813.17 *compensatory*; 775.6 *restoring*
repartee 706.1 *answer*; 734.2 *chat*; 759.1 *exchange*; 599.3 *wit*
repast 557.12 *meal*
repatriate 775.4 *give back*; 371.4 *ostracize*; 393.3 *restore*
repatriation 775.1 *giving back*; 371.19 *ostracism*; 393.9 *restoration*
repay 807.5 *atone*; 775.5 *compensate*; 813.11 *pay*; 785.10 *pay back*; 747.12 *reciprocate*; 385.3 *retaliate*
repayable 772.11 *borrowed*
repayable amount 772.5 *loan*
repaying 807.4 *atoning*
repayment 785.2; 807.1 *atonement*; 775.2 *compensation*; 385.1 *retaliation*; 814.9 *retribution*
repayment plan 772.1 *borrowing*
repay with interest 213.5 *make bigger*
repeal 708.14 *cancel*; 708.5 *cancellation*; 708.12 *renounce*; 708.4 *renunciation*; 399.3 *veto*
repealed 708.20 *cancelled*; 708.18 *rejected*
repealer 708.9 *negativist*
repealing 708.5 *cancellation*; 399.1 *veto*
repeat 112.5; **112.16**; **509.14**; 620.6 *be boring*; 270.5 *be diffuse*; 276.10 *be periodical*; 111.11, 298.7 *be regular*; 111.7 *be the same*; 692.25 *broadcast material*; 692.30 *communicate*; 134.3 *continue*; 198.12, 198.15 *double*; 726.6 *emphasize*; 125.9 *imitate*; 112.17 *iterate*; 694.10 *mean*; 640.6 *persevere*; 525.6 *reappearance*; 721.15 *recount*; 561.9 *reproduce*; 695.5 *simplify*
repeatable 795.10 *moralistic*
repeated 112.9; 525.7 *appearing*; 620.4 *boring*; 692.34 *communicated*; 270.3 *diffuse*; 198.12 *double*; 509.15 *drumming*; 297.3 *frequent*; 694.6 *meaningful*; 561.15 *reproduced*; 111.12 *same*; 640.11 *steady*
repeated decimal 27.18 *division*
repeated efforts 640.2 *commitment*
repeatedly 112.23; **509.19**; **561.17**; 620.8 *boringly*; 134.7, 640.14 *continually*; 297.1 *frequently*; 276.12 *periodically*; 298.15 *regularly*
Repeated Sound 509
repeated word 509.7
repeater 587.9 *firearm*; 281.7 *watch*
repeating 112.2 *iteration*; 509.18 *pealing*; 298.11 *regular*; 112.1 *repetition*; 112.12 *repetitious*
repeating rifle 587.9 *firearm*
repeat itself 297.7 *be frequent*
repeat oneself 620.6 *be boring*; 270.5 *be diffuse*; 297.7 *be frequent*; 112.17 *iterate*
repeat order 112.5 *repeat*
repeat performance 112.5 *repeat*
repeat wrongly 720.1 *misinterpret*
repel 364.1; 364.4 *be repulsive*; 596.7 *cause dislike*; 594.16 *cause hate*; 395.9 *change*; 242.10 *displease*; 655.13 *ignore*; 481.4 *put off*; 709.5 *refuse*; 470.1 *reject*; 383.6 *resist*; 384.26 *retaliate*
repelled 596.8 *disliking*
repellence 364.5 *repulsion*; 383.1 *resistance*
repellency 364.5 *repulsion*
repellent 364.8 *repulsive*; 383.10 *resistant*
repellently 364.11 *repulsively*; 383.14 *resistingly*
repellent quality 364.5 *repulsion*
repeller 383.5 *resister*
repelling 364.9 *abducent*; 594.12 *hated*; 364.5 *repulsion*; 383.10 *resistant*
repent 807.6 *apologize*; 808.4 *be penitent*; 7.19 *be religious*; 761.9 *reply*
repentance 807.2 *apology*; 808.1 *penitence*; 761.1 *reversion*
repentant 807.4 *atoning*; 808.6 *penitent*
repentantly 807.8, 808.8 *penitently*
repenter 807.3 *atoner*
repenting 808.6 *penitent*
repercussion 132.4; 347.1 *counteraction*; 345.1 *effect*; 706.4 *reaction*
repercussive 132.10; 706.12 *reactive*
repertoire 439.5 *collection*; 778.8 *merchandise*; 439.3 *supply*
repertory 439.5 *collection*; 21.1 *drama*; 220.1 *list*
repertory circuit 21.15 *engagement*
repertory company 21.25 *cast*
repertory player 21.24 *actor*
repertory show 21.7 *show*
repetiteur 223.6 *accompanier*; 18.24 *musician*
Repetition 112
repetition 112.1; 620.1 *boredom*; 640.3 *constancy*; 134.1 *continuity*; 270.1 *diffuseness*; 198.4 *doubling*; 726.1 *emphasis*; 297.4 *frequency*; 125.1 *imitation*; 5.22 *many words*; 276.6 *periodicity*; 17.12 *poetic language*; 111.6, 298.1 *regularity*; 112.5 *repeat*; 112.3 *repetitiveness*; 561.1 *reproduction*; 111.1 *sameness*
repetitional 112.12 *repetitious*
repetitious 112.12; 620.4 *boring*; 297.3 *frequent*; 276.8 *periodical*; 111.17 *regular*; 111.12 *same*
repetitiously 620.8 *boringly*; 111.18 *identically*; 276.12 *periodically*; 298.15 *regularly*; 112.23 *repeatedly*
repetitiousness 620.1 *boredom*; 112.3 *repetitiveness*
repetitive 620.4 *boring*; 134.5 *continual*; 132.12 *cyclical*; 270.3 *diffuse*; 726.3 *em-*

phatic; 297.3 *frequent*; 509.16 *humming*; 275.22 *periodic*; 276.8 *periodical*; 111.17, 298.11 *regular*; 112.12 *repetitious*; 111.12 *same*
repetitive job 632.3 *way*
repetitively 620.8 *boringly*; 134.7 *continually*; 270.7 *diffusely*; 297.1 *frequently*; 111.18 *identically*; 276.12 *periodically*; 111.20 *regularly*; 112.23, 509.19 *repeatedly*
repetitiveness 112.3; 620.1 *boredom*; 270.1 *diffuseness*; 276.6 *periodicity*; 729.2 *power of speech*; 298.1 *regularity*
rephrase 694.10 *mean*; 719.12 *translate*; 5.47 *word*
replace 144.16; 746.7 *act as a go-between*; 706.23 *answer for*; 608.11 *assist*; 762.4 *be a substitute*; 550.34 *cover for*; 767.9 *dispose of*; 224.10 *exchange*; 289.11 *follow in office*; 775.4 *give back*; 393.3 *restore*; 717.12 *stand for*; 350.6 *stop using*; 371.5 *take the place of*
replaceable 224.14 *exchangeable*
replaced 144.10; 762.8 *substituted*
replacement 144.3; 398.5 *alternative*; 224.4 *exchange*; 775.1 *giving back*; 608.5 *helper*; 717.8 *representative*; 393.9 *restoration*; 762.7 *substitute*; 762.2 *substitute person*; 550.21, 762.1 *substitution*; 289.5 *successor*
replacements 586.14 *armed forces*
replacer 227.4 *editor*
replant 393.3 *restore*
replanting 393.9 *restoration*
replay 112.20 *renew*; 112.5 *repeat*
replayed 112.11 *reprinted*
replaying 112.5 *repeat*
replenish 436.6; 232.6 *fill*; 393.3 *restore*; 439.6 *store*; 217.4 *suffice*
replenished 232.8 *full*
replenishment 232.2 *fullness*; 436.1 *provision*; 393.9 *restoration*
replete 219.6 *excessive*; 217.3 *filled*; 232.8 *full*
replete with meaning 694.6 *meaningful*
repletion 232.2 *fullness*; 217.7 *sufficiency*
replica 112.7; 125.2 *copy*; 111.4, 125.5 *duplicate*; 717.6 *image*; 525.5 *impression*; 561.2 *print*; 717.1 *representation*
replicate 125.10 *copy*; 198.15 *double*; 111.9 *duplicate*; 115.12 *imitate*; 207.9 *pluralize*; 112.16 *repeat*; 561.9 *reproduce*
replicated 111.15 *duplicate*; 112.9 *repeated*; 115.8 *simulated*
replication 706.1 *answer*; 111.4 *duplicate*; 112.1 *repetition*; 561.1 *reproduction*
replied 761.11 *reversed*
replier 706.10 *answerer*
reply 761.5; **761.9**; 706.1, 706.17 *answer*; 692.31 *correspond*; 704.3, 704.10 *countercharge*; 729.11 *speak*; 729.7 *utterance*
reply for the defence 714.2 *defence*
replying 706.11 *answering*
report 741.13; 97.12 *attend*; 508.1 *bang*; 3.5, 3.20 *chronicle*; 693.12 *communicate*; 693.2 *communication*; 721.1 *description*; 693.3 *document*; 6.22 *educate*; 811.1 *estimation*; 716.1 *evidence*; 721.4 *factual account*; 550.33 *fix*; 719.13 *interpret news*; 740.3 *journalism*; 464.1 *judgment*; 507.1 *loudness*; 740.1 *publication*; 740.15 *publish*; 744.1 *record*; 721.15 *recount*; 504.8 *something heard*; 31.4 *weather forecast*
reportable 741.14 *journalistic*
reportage 3.5 *chronicle*; 721.3 *narration*; 741.3 *reporting*
report card 744.1 *record*
reported 3.19 *chronicled*; 716.8 *evidential*; 741.14 *journalistic*
reportedly 3.25; **693.19**; 716.14 *as evidence*; 741.15 *journalistically*
reported speech 5.23 *phrase*
reporter 721.10 *descriptive writer*; 739.4 *discloser*; 693.9 *informant*; 741.4 *journalist*; 464.5 *judge*; 719.7 *news interpreter*; 740.11 *newspaperman*; 744.9 *recorder*
report for duty 97.12 *attend*
reporting 741.3; 740.3 *journalism*
reportorial 741.14 *journalistic*
reportorially 741.15 *journalistically*
repose 301.2; 301.8 *be motionless*; 581.2 *be refreshed*; 263.1 *ease*; 580.4 *have leisure*; 341.1 *inaction*; 580.1 *leisure*; 341.4 *not act*; 581.6 *refresher*; 581.5 *refreshment*; 343.9 *sleep*; 263.2 *take it easy*
reposeful 263.4 *at ease*; 263.5 *labour-saving*; 580.7 *leisurely*; 301.6 *quiescent*
reposefully 263.6 *with ease*
reposing 301.6 *quiescent*
repository 439.5 *collection*; 410.1 *container*
repossess 371.8 *evict*; 773.8 *take back*
repossessed 784.10 *unable to pay*
repossession 784.5 *amount owing*; 371.20 *eviction*; 773.2 *taking back*
repot a ball 65.8 *play billiards*
repotting 44.5 *gardening*
repoussé 19.28 *sculpted*
reprehend 670.20 *censure*
reprehensibility 806.1 *guilt*
reprehensible 670.36 *blameworthy*; 798.7 *evil*; 806.5 *guilty*; 236.4 *poor*; 802.17 *unforgivable*; 804.11 *wicked*
reprehensibly 798.12 *evilly*; 806.11 *guiltily*
reprehension 670.7 *blame*
reprehensive 806.5 *guilty*
reprehensively 806.11 *guiltily*
represent 27.96; **398.8**; **717.9**; 21.34 *act*; 706.23 *answer for*; 762.4 *be a substitute*; 123.7 *be important*; 99.11 *characterize*; 721.14 *describe*; 19.20 *draw*; 446.19 *epitomize*; 477.14 *imagine*; 716.10 *make evident*; 694.10 *mean*; 163.5 *outline*; 475.11 *predict*; 699.24 *pretend*; 744.13 *record*; 698.34 *render*; 742.10 *signify*; 17.21 *write*
Representation 717
representation 717.1; **721.9**; 21.22 *acting*; 111.4 *duplicate*; 111.2 *equivalence*; 125.1 *imitation*; 525.5 *impression*; 738.10 *manifestation*; 163.1 *outline*; 19.7 *picture*; 699.7 *pretence*; 744.1 *record*; 518.8 *reflection*; 742.1 *sign*; 762.3 *substitute thing*; 762.1 *substitution*
representational 717.13; 721.11 *descriptive*; 721.13 *representing*
representationalism 698.12 *realism*
representationally 717.14
Representative 398.1 *delegate*; 579.16 *official*; 12.8 *politician*
representative 717.8; **748.4**; 398.6, 578.3 *agent*; 216.1 *average*; 398.1 *delegate*; 398.9 *delegated*; 111.13 *equivalent*; 703.11 *explanatory*; 400.3 *leader*; 698.25 *lifelike*; 738.14 *manifest*; 579.16 *official*; 163.6 *outlined*; 396.10 *person of authority*; 717.13 *representational*; 721.13 *representing*; 778.10 *salesman*; 742.14 *signifying*; 729.10 *speaker*; 762.2 *substitute person*; 137.11 *typical*
representative body 398.2
representative government 12.1 *government*; 396.7 *type of rule*
representatively 398.11; 706.27 *answerably*; 742.18 *indicatively*; 717.14 *representationally*
representative sample 163.1 *outline*
representing 721.13; 717.13 *representational*; 742.14 *signifying*
represent the interests of 398.8 *represent*
represent to oneself 477.14 *imagine*
represent unfairly 718.4 *misrepresent*
repress 634.7 *be evasive*; 684.5 *be self-restrained*; 399.4 *censor*; 347.3 *counteract*; 387.7 *defeat*; 357.8 *destroy*; 360.7 *detain*; 358.2 *forget*; 378.8 *hinder*; 166.7 *limit*; 685.4 *moderate*; 251.8 *restrain*; 647.6 *suppress*
repress a smile 643.8 *be serious*
repressed 684.8 *self-restrained*; 36.37 *subconscious*; 647.9 *suppressed*
repressing 387.10 *dominating*
repression 347.1 *counteraction*; 36.19 *defence mechanism*; 357.1 *destruction*; 360.2 *detention*; 387.2 *domination*; 634.15 *evasiveness*; 358.5 *forgetfulness*; 378.1 *hindrance*; 166.2 *limiting factor*; 251.1 *restraint*; 684.1 *self-restraint*; 647.2 *suppression*; 399.1 *veto*
repressive 634.18 *avoiding*; 347.4 *counteracting*; 387.10 *dominating*; 378.13 *hindering*; 166.5 *limited*; 684.8 *self-restrained*; 647.8 *severe*; 399.5 *vetoed*
repressively 399.7 *by veto*; 347.5 *counter*; 647.11 *severely*; 378.16 *with delay*; 684.11 *with self-restraint*
repressive regime 399.1 *veto*
repress one's desires 684.5 *be self-restrained*
reprieval 390.2 *deliverance*
reprieve 16.78 *acquit*; 16.42 *acquittal*; 708.14 *cancel*; 708.5 *cancellation*; 294.8 *delay*; 294.3 *delayed action*; 390.1 *deliver*; 390.2 *deliverance*; 389.1 *escape*; 649.9 *forgive*; 649.1 *forgiveness*; 391.4 *liberate*; 391.1 *liberation*; 627.3 *mercy*; 608.10 *save*; 627.10 *show mercy*
reprieved 16.63 *acquitted*; 708.20 *cancelled*; 389.8 *escaping*; 649.6 *forgiven*
reprieved prisoner 389.3 *escaper*
reprieving 649.4 *forgiving*
reprimand 670.7 *blame*; 670.20 *censure*; 606.2 *expression of dissatisfaction*; 814.1 *punish*; 814.7 *punishment*; 623.14 *rebuke*; 711.1 *warning*
reprimanded 670.34 *censured*
reprimanding 670.30 *censuring*
reprint 41.12 *development*; 111.4, 111.9 *duplicate*; 561.2 *print*; 112.20 *renew*; 112.5 *repeat*; 561.9 *reproduce*
reprinted 112.11; 111.15 *duplicate*
reprisal 761.2 *restoration*; 385.1 *retaliation*; 814.9 *retribution*; 714.4 *revenge*
reprise 284.15 *look back*; 516.1 *melody*; 284.2 *retrospection*; 112.4 *return*
reproach 715.1 *accusation*; 715.5 *accuse*; 670.7 *blame*; 670.20 *censure*; 806.1 *guilt*; 712.3 *vilification*; 712.6 *vilify*
reproachable 806.5 *guilty*
reproached 670.34 *censured*
reproachful 670.30 *censuring*; 806.5 *guilty*; 624.15 *resentful*; 712.9 *vituperative*
reproachfully 670.37 *disapprovingly*; 806.11 *guiltily*; 624.17 *resentfully*; 712.13 *vituperatively*
reproachfulness 806.1 *guilt*
reproaching 670.30 *censuring*
reproachless 805.5 *innocent*
reproach oneself 808.4 *be penitent*
reprobate 670.19 *blame*; 806.4 *guilty person*; 804.14 *impious*; 804.9 *wicked person*
reprobation 670.7 *blame*; 606.1 *dissatisfaction*
reprocess 112.20 *renew*; 393.3 *restore*
reprocessed 112.11 *reprinted*
reprocessing 393.9 *restoration*
reproduce 561.9; 190.6 *become bigger*; 125.10 *copy*; 111.9 *duplicate*; 554.19 *give birth to*; 115.12 *imitate*; 213.5 *make bigger*; 356.10 *produce*; 112.16 *repeat*; 717.9 *represent*
reproduced 561.15; 111.15 *duplicate*; 112.9 *repeated*
reproduce oneself 561.10
Reproduction 561
reproduction 561.1; **717.2**; 554.4 *biological function*; 115.2, 125.2 *copy*; 198.4 *doubling*; 111.4 *duplicate*; 190.1 *growth*; 213.1 *increase*; 36.23 *memory*; 34.5 *physiology*; 19.7 *picture*; 562.2 *productiveness*; 112.1 *repetition*
reproductive 561.16; 34.22 *physiological*; 112.12 *repetitious*; 76.4 *social insect*
reproductive body 84.4; 83.4 *fungal body*
reproductive cell 34.7 *cell*
reproductively 561.18; 190.10 *largely*
reproductive organ 82.2 *fern plant*; 82.4 *moss plant*
reproductive organs 561.8 *organs of reproduction*
reprogramme 393.3 *restore*
reprogramming 393.9 *restoration*
reproof 670.7 *blame*; 481.6 *dissuasion*; 606.2 *expression of dissatisfaction*; 814.7 *punishment*
reprovable 806.5 *guilty*
reprove 606.7 *be dissatisfied*; 670.20 *censure*; 481.1 *dissuade*; 814.1 *punish*; 711.5 *warn*
reprove oneself 808.4 *be penitent*
reprover 606.3 *dissatisfied person*
reproving look 670.10 *disapproving look*
rep show 21.7 *show*
reptant 73.11 *reptilian*
reptilarium 73.9 *herpetology*
reptile 73.1; 70.4 *type of animal*
reptile house 73.9 *herpetology*
reptilelike 73.11 *reptilian*
Reptiles and Amphibians 73
Reptilia 73.1 *reptile*
reptilian 73.11; 73.1 *reptile*
reptiliary 73.9 *herpetology*
reptiliform 73.11 *reptilian*
reptiloid 73.11 *reptilian*
republic 85.1 *country*; 396.8 *governmental organization*; 566.11 *nation*; 12.5 *political organization*; 86.4 *territorial division*
Republican 225.3 *conservative person*
republican 12.9, 396.14 *governmental*; 85.16, 86.17, 566.13 *national*
republicanism 12.1 *government*; 396.7 *type of rule*
Republican Party 12.6 *political party*
republican state 566.11 *nation*
Republican whip 400.3 *leader*; 396.10 *person of authority*
republication 525.6 *reappearance*
Republic Day 601.5 *anniversary*
republic of letters 17.1 *literature*
repudiate 708.10 *be negative*; 708.14 *cancel*; 704.9 *deny*; 709.6 *dissent*; 753.6 *protest*; 479.4 *recant*; 355.1 *relinquish*; 708.12 *renounce*; 470.4 *revoke*; 786.8 *stop payment*
repudiated 753.9 *protesting*; 708.18 *rejected*
repudiating 709.9 *dissenting*; 704.7 *refuting*
repudiation 470.7 *abrogation*; 708.5 *cancellation*; 704.2 *denial*; 709.2 *dissent*; 753.1 *protest*; 479.8 *recantation*; 708.2 *rejection*; 708.4 *renunciation*
repudiation of debts 786.1 *nonpayment*
repudiative 708.17 *negative*
repudiator 704.5 *refuter*
repugn 704.9 *deny*
repugnance 596.1 *dislike*; 637.13 *dissociation*; 594.1 *hate*; 113.1 *opposition*
repugnancy 113.1 *opposition*
repugnant 113.25 *contrary*; 596.9 *disliked*; 594.12 *hated*; 113.22 *oppositional*; 364.8 *repulsive*
repugnantly 596.11 *disgustingly*; 364.11 *repulsively*
repulse 364.6; 395.9 *change*; 668.5, 668.23 *insult*; 384.24 *parry*; 709.1 *refusal*; 709.5 *refuse*; 470.1 *reject*; 470.5 *rejection*; 364.1 *repel*; 383.6 *resist*; 383.1 *resistance*; 384.26 *retaliate*
repulsing 668.11 *insulting*; 383.10 *resistant*
Repulsion 364
repulsion 364.5; 596.1 *dislike*; 334.4 *energy*; 594.1 *hate*; 395.1 *influence*; 709.1 *refusal*; 383.1 *resistance*
repulsive 364.8; 596.9 *disliked*; 594.12 *hated*; 546.4 *ugly*; 258.8 *unclean*; 242.1 *unpleasant*
repulsive force 364.5 *repulsion*
repulsively 364.11; 596.11 *disgustingly*; 546.6 *hideously*; 242.13 *unpleasantly*
repulsiveness 364.5 *repulsion*; 546.1 *ugliness*; 242.5 *unpleasantness*
repurchase 777.9; 777.3 *buy back*
reputable 811.3; 185.6 *eminent*; 799.4 *honourable*; 667.13 *respectable*
reputably 799.7 *honourably*
Reputation 811
reputation 500.4; 811.1 *estimation*; 123.1 *importance*; 395.3 *personal influence*; 622.4 *prestige*; 783.7 *repute*
repute 783.7; 123.1 *importance*; 395.3 *personal influence*; 799.1 *probity*; 185.1 *prominence*; 500.4 *reputation*; 667.1 *respect*
reputed 811.4; 476.8 *supposed*
reputedly 811.6; 476.10 *supposedly*; 4.25 *theoretically*
Request 710
request 710.1; **710.6**; 757.6 *ask permission*; 617.12 *desire*; 16.70 *litigate*; 16.5 *litigation*; 135.10 *necessitate*; 617.5 *object of desire*; 701.5 *plea*; 701.16 *plead*; 10.20 *pray*; 10.9 *prayer*; 476.6 *propound*; 740.16 *publicize*; 705.1, 705.17 *question*; 135.1 *requirement*
request credit 772.7 *borrow*
requested 617.7 *desired*; 752.17 *offered*; 710.9 *requesting*; 135.4 *required*
requester 710.4
request euthanasia 382.21 *commit suicide*
request for credit 772.1 *borrowing*
request for money 772.1 *borrowing*
request for support 752.5 *offer of public service*
requesting 710.9; 705.12 *questioning*
request money 772.7 *borrow*
request stop 226.4 *stopping place*
request support 752.13 *be a candidate*
requiem 583.2 *funeral*; 603.2 *lament*; 18.5 *sacred music*
Requiem Mass 10.5 *Christian rite*; 18.5 *sacred music*
require 135.7; 706.21 *answer to*; 218.5 *be insufficient*; 218.6 *be unsatisfied*; 386.6 *compel*; 397.10, 474.11 *demand*; 617.12 *desire*;

810.17 *impose a duty*; 710.6 *request*; 777.2 *shop*; 136.16 *specify*
required 135.4; 706.16 *answerable*; 386.10 *compulsory*; 617.7 *desired*; 123.5 *important*; 476.9 *meant*; 710.9 *requesting*; 251.13 *restraining*
required giving 768.2 *gift*
required number 217.7 *sufficiency*
require explanation 696.10 *be unexplained*
Requirement 135
requirement 135.1; 706.9 *answerability*; 746.2 *basis for negotiations*; 123.3 *chief thing*; 386.1 *compulsion*; 617.1 *desire*; 231.5 *imperfection*; 617.5 *object of desire*; 710.1 *request*; 251.1 *restraint*; 777.8 *shopping*; 217.7 *sufficiency*
require no explanation 738.5 *be visible*
require qualifications 251.8 *restrain*
require some effort 264.17 *be difficult*
requiring 233.4 *incomplete*
requiring effort 264.10 *difficult*
requiring great effort 576.11 *laborious*
requisite 386.10 *compulsory*; 136.7 *condition*; 99.5 *essential*; 135.4 *required*; 135.1 *requirement*
requisite number 232.2 *fullness*
requisition 397.2, 397.10, 710.2, 710.7 *demand*; 349.5 *dispose of*; 386.7 *force*; 135.10 *necessitate*; 135.1 *requirement*; 773.7 *take*; 773.1 *taking*
requisitional 136.12 *conditional*
requisitionary 710.10 *demanding*; 773.12 *taking*
requitable 110.4 *reciprocal*
requital 807.1 *atonement*; 813.6 *compensation*; 775.1 *giving back*; 110.1 *interchange*; 814.9 *retribution*; 714.4 *revenge*
requite 807.5 *atone*; 714.10 *avenge*; 759.5 *exchange*; 775.4 *give back*; 813.11 *pay*; 110.7, 747.12 *reciprocate*; 385.3, 785.13 *retaliate*
requited 759.7 *exchanged*; 110.4 *reciprocal*
requiting 714.14 *vindictive*
reredos 19.8 *painting*
rerun 692.25 *broadcast material*; 692.30 *communicate*; 112.20 *renew*; 112.5 *repeat*
reschedule one's debts 784.8 *not pay*
rescind 708.14 *cancel*; 479.4 *recant*; 708.12 *renounce*
rescindable 708.20 *cancelled*
rescinded 708.20 *cancelled*; 708.18 *rejected*
rescinding 708.5 *cancellation*
rescindment 708.5 *cancellation*; 708.4 *renunciation*
rescript 706.2 *acknowledgment*; 16.3 *law*; 713.3 *precept*
rescuable 390.4 *deliverable*
rescue 384.23; 608.2 *aid*; 650.4 *benevolent act*; 390.1 *deliver*; 390.2 *deliverance*; 389.1 *escape*; 775.4 *give back*; 775.1 *giving back*; 392.17 *help*; 391.4 *liberate*; 391.1 *liberation*; 359.5 *preserve*; 252.10 *protect*; 393.9 *restoration*; 393.3 *restore*; 252.1 *safety*; 608.10 *save*; 250.15 *set free*; 392.2 *support*
rescued 390.4 *deliverable*; 391.7 *liberated*
rescue device 359.2 *preserver*
rescuer 384.15; 390.3 *deliverer*; 797.15 *good person*; 391.3 *liberator*; 595.4 *likable person*; 359.4 *preservationist*
rescue team 390.3 *deliverer*
research 631.14 *behave towards*; 243.2 *do the groundwork*; 448.11 *experiment*; 448.3 *experimentation*; 6.23 *learn*; 4.4 *philosophical investigation*; 4.20 *philosophize*; 705.17 *question*; 705.2 *questioning*
research and development 13.6 *economic factors*; 448.3 *experimentation*
research data 476.2 *basis of supposition*
researched 705.16 *questioned*; 448.10 *tested*
researcher 353.7 *attempter*; 739.4 *discloser*; 448.5 *experimenter*; 396.11 *expert*; 6.7 *learner*; 26.9 *measurer*; 4.10 *philosopher*; 633.5 *pursuer*; 705.9 *questioner*; 476.4 *theorist*
research establishment 448.6 *place of experimentation*
research fellowship 6.6 *instructorship*
researching 448.8 *experimental*; 705.12 *questioning*
research into 400.15 *learn*
research laboratory 577.1 *workshop*
research satellite 29.32 *satellite*
research scientist 448.5 *experimenter*
research worker 448.5 *experimenter*; 476.4 *theorist*
resection 372.3 *separateness*; 35.9 *surgery*
reseda 538.1 *green*
resell 778.1 *sell*
resemblance 115.1 *similarity*
resemble 525.11 *appear*; 115.10 *be similar*; 750.25 *conform*; 110.9 *correlate*; 717.9 *represent*
resembling 750.14 *conforming*; 115.7 *similar*
resent 624.8; 606.7 *be dissatisfied*; 625.6 *be irascible*; 629.6 *be jealous*; 596.5 *dislike*; 682.8 *grudge*; 594.14 *hate*
resent competition 629.6 *be jealous*
resentful 624.15; 596.8 *disliking*; 538.5 *green-eyed*; 594.10 *hating*; 651.14 *hostile*; 625.4 *irascible*; 626.7 *irritable*; 629.4 *jealous*
resentfully 624.17; 596.10 *discontentedly*; 594.18 *hatefully*; 625.9 *irascibly*; 626.14 *irritably*; 629.9 *jealously*
resentfulness 625.1 *irascibility*; 624.1 *resentment*
resentment 624.1; 590.6 *bad feeling*; 651.4 *bitterness*; 596.1 *dislike*; 594.1 *hate*; 629.1 *jealousy*
reservation 746.2 *basis for negotiations*; 136.7 *condition*; 451.1 *disbelief*; 655.4 *place of confinement*; 359.1 *preservation*; 705.1 *question*; 744.8 *registration*; 372.2 *setting apart*
reserve 145.4; **253.15**; **674.6**; **728.5**; 398.5 *alternative*; 309.4 *closed place*; 294.8 *delay*; 165.5 *enclose*; 165.2 *enclosed place*; 584.9 *enlisted*; 66.3 *football player*; 608.5 *helper*; 135.10 *necessitate*; 350.8 *nonuse*; 350.5 *not use*; 469.4 *pick*; 655.4 *place of confinement*; 293.9 *prepare*; 359.5 *preserve*; 410.21 *put in a container*; 744.15 *register*; 352.5 *reserves*; 251.3 *self-restraint*; 372.10 *set apart*; 732.3 *shyness*; 736.4 *silence*; 136.16 *specify*; 439.6 *store*; 762.7 *substitute*; 762.2 *substitute person*; 550.21 *substitution*; 550.40 *substitutive*; 655.1 *unsociability*
reserved 145.9; **674.13**; **728.15**; 136.12 *conditional*; 410.20 *containing*; 645.4 *cunning*; 135.4 *required*; 251.14 *self-restrained*; 732.1 *shy*; 736.16 *silent*; 350.1 *unused*
reservedly 145.11; **728.25**; 732.8 *shyly*
reserved nature 251.3 *self-restraint*
reserved section 165.2 *enclosed place*
reserved space 141.5
reserve equipment 211.4 *extra*
reserve fleet 584.4 *military organization*
reserve for 482.9 *intend for*
reserve forces 584.2 *the military*
reserve fund 439.1 *store*
reserve liability 780.6 *funds*
reserves 352.5; 586.14 *armed forces*; 211.4 *extra*; 780.6 *funds*; 392.11 *helper*; 243.10 *preparations*; 436.1 *provision*; 439.1 *store*; 584.2 *the military*; 780.19 *treasury*
reservist 586.8 *soldier*; 762.2 *substitute person*
reservoir 410.1 *container*; 38.23 *dam*; 88.1 *lake*; 439.4 *storage*; 439.1 *store*; 433.16 *water carrier*
reset 224.8 *cause change*
reshape 224.8 *cause change*; 234.12 *distort the truth*; 760.9 *transform*
reshaped 224.12 *changed*
reshaping 224.1 *change*
reship 319.4 *transport*
reshowing 112.5 *repeat*
reshown 112.11 *reprinted*
reside 97.13; 564.14 *inhabit*
reside at 554.17 *dwell*
reside in 405.12 *be one of*; 565.17 *inhabit*; 142.10 *settle*
residence 97.3; 565.1 *habitat*; 733.5 *place of residence*
resident 97.9; **564.13**; 35.11 *doctor*; 564.1 *inhabitant*; 565.14 *inhabiting*; 763.5 *possessor*
residential 564.11 *inhabited*; 565.14 *inhabiting*; 97.9 *resident*; 87.14 *urban*
residential area 87.7 *city district*
residential building 38.20 *building*
residential zone 87.7 *city district*
residentiary 564.1 *inhabitant*; 565.14 *inhabiting*
residents 564.2 *inhabitants*
resider 564.1 *inhabitant*
residing 565.14 *inhabiting*; 564.13 *resident*
residual 194.4 *mathematical result*; 215.9 *remaining*; 215.2 *residue*
residual insecticide 43.14 *pest control*
residually 215.11
residual magnetization 28.63 *magnetic phenomenon*
residuary 215.9 *remaining*
residue 215.2; 258.4 *dirt*; 27.18 *division*; 345.1 *effect*
residuum 258.4 *dirt*; 215.2 *residue*
resign 605.5; 315.14 *be dismissed*; 479.2 *equivocate*; 580.4 *have leisure*; 355.1 *relinquish*; 303.2 *retreat*; 350.7 *stop work*; 226.7 *stop working*; 388.3 *submit*; 708.15 *terminate*; 313.2, 355.2 *withdraw*
Resignation 605
resignation 605.1; 4.3 *detachment*; 350.10 *disuse*; 355.3 *relinquishment*; 303.11 *retreat*; 372.2 *setting apart*; 226.2 *stop*; 388.1 *submission*; 623.12 *submissiveness*; 708.6 *termination*; 580.3 *unemployment*
resigned 605.8; 355.6 *apathetic*; 4.18 *detached*; 663.7 *obedient*; 605.7 *resigning*; 623.5 *submissive*; 388.5 *submitting*
resignedly 355.8 *apathetically*; 4.27 *stoically*
resignedness 605.4
resigned to one's fate 605.4 *resignedness*
resigner 605.3
resigning 605.7; 303.11 *retreat*
resign oneself 605.6; 623.21 *humble oneself*; 388.3 *submit*
resign oneself to 757.4 *be permissive*
resign under pressure 605.5 *resign*
resilience 303.17; 422.2 *adaptability*; 422.1 *elasticity*; 423.8 *physical strength*; 336.1 *strength*
resilient 303.26; 422.7 *adaptive*; 422.6 *elastic*; 423.4 *powerful*; 336.11 *strong in spirit*
resiliently 422.12 *adaptably*; 423.13 *powerfully*
resin 430.2 *adhesive*; 502.3 *incense*; 32.21 *polymer*; 559.2 *secreted substance*; 79.9 *tree product*
resinous 79.14 *treelike*
resist 383.6; 585.14 *battle*; 661.6 *be insubordinate*; 423.10 *be tough*; 637.6 *be unwilling*; 347.3 *counteract*; 381.8 *counterattack*; 586.39 *defend*; 383.16 *fight on!*; 378.8 *hinder*; 113.14 *oppose*; 753.6 *protest*; 709.5 *refuse*; 384.26, 385.3 *retaliate*; 113.20 *withstand*
Resistance 383
resistance 28.53; **39.12**; **383.1**; 586.14 *armed forces*; 347.1 *counteraction*; 384.1 *defence*; 36.19 *defence mechanism*; 364.7 *deflection*; 661.2, 662.1 *disobedience*; 481.6 *dissuasion*; 334.7 *electrical power*; 334.4 *energy*; 365.1 *friction*; 418.5 *hardness*; 378.1 *hindrance*; 641.5 *obstinacy*; 113.1, 637.12 *opposition*; 709.1 *refusal*; 662.4 *revolution*; 336.1 *strength*; 423.6 *toughness*
resistance fighter 586.9 *guerrilla*; 753.5 *seditionist*
resistance movement 383.3; 662.4 *revolution*
resistance to compaction 38.15 *strength of materials*
resistance to sliding 38.15 *strength of materials*
resistant 383.10; 347.4 *counteracting*; 364.10 *defensive*; 709.8 *refused*; 637.5 *reluctant*; 336.13 *strengthened*; 418.2, 423.1 *tough*; 113.26 *uncooperative*
resistantly 347.5 *counter*; 364.12 *defensively*; 383.14 *resistingly*; 418.12, 423.12 *toughly*; 709.11 *uncooperatively*
resist authority 588.4 *be anarchic*
resist breaking 423.10 *be tough*
resist change 225.5 *be permanent*
resist control 588.4 *be anarchic*
resister 383.5; 113.11 *opposer*; 637.16 *reluctant person*
resist incursions 585.13 *be at war*
resisting 383.12; 347.4 *counteracting*; 381.24 *counterattacking*; 384.29 *defending*; 709.8 *refused*; 383.10 *resistant*; 423.1 *tough*
resistingly 383.14; 347.5 *counter*; 423.12 *toughly*; 709.11 *uncooperatively*
resistive 39.36 *electronic*
resistivity 28.53, 39.12 *resistance*
resistor 39.17; 28.55 *circuit*
resist temptation 255.9 *be pure*; 803.8 *be virtuous*
resojet propulsion 330.2 *method of propulsion*
resole 393.1 *repair*
resoling 393.8 *repair*
resolute 638.1; 342.18 *active*; 228.11 *determined*; 643.2 *earnest*; 482.11 *intending*; 635.7 *iron-willed*; 640.10 *persevering*; 613.12 *self-reliant*; 336.11 *strong in spirit*; 641.3 *unyielding*
resolutely 638.17; 336.15 *acutely*; 228.13 *determinedly*; 640.13 *persistently*
resoluteness 638.12 *resolution*; 613.3 *steadfastness*; 635.2 *willpower*
Resolution 638
resolution 29.28; **638.12**; 342.8 *assiduity*; 309.1 *closure*; 760.1 *conversion*; 375.2 *deconstruction*; 228.2, 641.6 *determination*; 739.1 *disclosure*; 643.5 *earnestness*; 516.4 *harmonics*; 750.4 *harmony*; 482.2 *intentionality*; 719.1 *interpretation*; 18.13 *melody*; 28.32 *optical instrument*; 640.1 *perseverance*; 484.1 *plan*; 21.8 *scene*; 372.1 *separation*; 706.6 *solution*; 336.1 *strength*; 32.13 *structure*; 635.2 *willpower*
resolutive 431.9 *solvent*
resolvable 760.15 *convertible*; 372.19 *separable*
resolve 482.8; **638.7**; 309.9 *close down*; 760.7 *convert into*; 719.9 *decipher*; 375.4 *deconstruct*; 228.2 *determination*; 431.23 *dissolve*; 131.15 *end*; 27.90 *enumerate*; 750.24 *harmonize*; 482.2 *intentionality*; 423.9 *mental toughness*; 484.9 *plan*; 106.6 *premeditation*; 4.21 *rationalize*; 638.12 *resolution*; 140.13 *rule*; 372.10 *set apart*; 706.20 *solve*; 635.2 *willpower*
resolve beforehand 106.2 *premeditate*
resolved 309.14 *closed down*; 228.11 *determined*; 423.5 *mentally tough*; 638.1 *resolute*; 706.14 *solved*
resolve into 760.9 *transform*
resolvent 431.9 *solvent*
resolve problems 749.4 *pacify*
resolving 706.6 *solution*
resolving power 28.32 *optical instrument*; 29.28 *resolution*; 372.1 *separation*
Resonance 510
resonance 510.1; 750.4 *harmony*; 507.1 *loudness*; 112.6 *reverberation*; 28.14 *sound wave*; 18.21 *tone*; 326.2 *vibration*; 326.5 *wave*
resonant 510.6; 509.15 *drumming*; 750.13 *harmonious*; 504.14 *hearable*; 507.6 *loud*; 516.6 *melodious*; 542.10 *ornate*; 112.15 *reverberatory*; 326.14 *vibrating*
resonant circuit 39.13 *circuit*
resonant frequency 39.13 *circuit*; 28.14 *sound wave*; 326.5 *wave*
resonantly 510.11; 750.33 *harmoniously*; 516.11 *melodiously*; 509.19 *repeatedly*
resonate 510.9; 509.8 *drum*; 750.24 *harmonize*; 326.9 *vibrate*
resonating 750.13 *harmonious*; 510.6 *resonant*
resonating chamber 510.5 *resonator*
resonation 510.1 *resonance*
resonator 510.5
resorb 370.13 *absorb*
resorbence 370.5 *absorption*
resorption 370.5 *absorption*
resort 393.7; 484.3 *expedient plan*; 352.1 *means*; 252.5 *refuge*; 645.2 *stratagem*; 349.6 *use*
resort to 349.4
resort to arms 585.4 *belligerency*
resort to fisticuffs 380.7 *be violent*
resort to greenmail 776.3 *bargain*
resort to violence 380.7 *be violent*
resort to war 585.12 *go to war*
resound 112.22; 508.5 *bang*; 504.16 *be heard*; 507.8 *be loud*; 509.8 *drum*; 750.24 *harmonize*; 510.9 *resonate*
resounding 750.13 *harmonious*; 507.6 *loud*; 510.1 *resonance*; 510.6 *resonant*
resoundingly 750.33 *harmoniously*; 510.11 *resonantly*
resource 439.2; 484.3 *expedient plan*; 706.6 *solution*; 645.2 *stratagem*
resourceful 645.4 *cunning*; 354.6 *enterprising*; 562.5 *fertile*; 477.10 *imaginative*; 484.15 *planning*; 485.6 *skilful*; 336.11 *strong in spirit*
resourcefully 484.17 *conspiratorially*; 562.8 *fruitfully*; 477.17 *imaginatively*; 485.12 *skilfully*
resourcefulness 645.1 *cunning*; 477.1

imagination; 562.2 *productiveness*; 485.1 *skill*; 336.1 *strength*
resource management 436.1 *provision*
resources 222.1 *circumstances*; 435.1 *materials*; 440.5 *personal estate*; 352.2 *supplies*; 781.5 *wealth*
Respect 667
respect 667.1; **667.15**; 669.2 *admiration*; 810.3 *allegiance*; 669.11 *approve*; 650.8 *be benevolent*; 117.2 *compliance*; 117.8 *comply*; 658.3 *courtesies*; 367.16 *courtesy*; 593.1 *love*; 123.8 *make important*; 663.3 *obeisance*; 9.7 *worship*; 235.6 *worth*
respectability 216.8 *middle classes*; 799.1 *probity*
respectable 667.13; 799.4 *honourable*; 235.5 *not bad*; 811.3 *reputable*
respectably 799.7 *honourably*
respected 667.12; 669.24 *admired*; 593.21 *beloved*; 811.3 *reputable*; 235.1 *worthy*
respect for legal principles 16.28 *legality*
respect for the law 16.28 *legality*
respectful 667.8; 669.18 *approving*; 658.8 *good-mannered*; 810.9 *loyal*; 663.9 *obeisant*
respectfully 667.22; 658.15 *genteelly*; 663.10 *obediently*; 810.18 *on duty*
respectfulness 667.3; 658.3 *courtesies*
respective 139.15 *special*
respectively 770.8 *proportionately*; 108.10 *relevantly*; 139.32 *severally*
respects 667.7
respect the law 16.67 *follow the law*
respiration 33.24; **434.8**; 554.4 *biological function*; 370.4 *intake*; 34.5 *physiology*; 581.5 *refreshment*
respirator 394.14 *hospital*; 359.2 *preserver*; 252.4 *safety device*
respiratory 434.19; 34.22 *physiological*
respiratory chain 33.24 *respiration*
respiratory disease 260.9; 260.4 *disease*
respiratory organ 434.8 *respiration*
respiratory pigment 33.18 *pigment*
respire 434.21; 581.2 *be refreshed*; 370.12 *draw in*; 371.14 *let out*; 554.16 *live*
respiring 434.19 *respiratory*
respite 16.78 *acquit*; 294.3 *delayed action*; 390.2 *deliverance*; 263.1, 608.1 *ease*; 275.6 *interval*; 226.3 *pause*; 580.2 *time off*
resplendence 522.1 *light*
resplendent 522.16 *bright*
respond 706.17 *answer*; 704.10 *countercharge*; 4.23 *discuss philosophically*; 20.9 *miscellaneous architectural features*; 342.14 *push*; 747.12 *reciprocate*; 761.9 *reply*; 488.11 *sense*; 729.11 *speak*
responded 761.11 *reversed*
respondence 706.1 *answer*
respondent 715.4 *accused person*; 706.10 *answerer*; 706.11 *answering*; 734.7 *conversationalist*; 16.8 *litigant*
responder 704.5 *refuter*
responding 422.7 *adaptive*; 706.11 *answering*; 704.7 *refuting*
respond quickly 422.10 *be adaptable*
respond to treatment 393.4 *be restored*; 259.6 *get healthy*
response 706.1 *answer*; 704.3 *countercharge*; 10.8 *hymn*; 706.4 *reaction*; 761.5 *reply*; 488.1 *sensation*; 28.83 *sensitivity*; 729.7 *utterance*
response to therapy 393.11 *recuperation*
response to treatment 393.11 *recuperation*
responsibility 706.9 *answerability*; 784.1 *debt*; 579.4 *directorship*; 810.1 *duty*; 474.2 *expectations*; 806.1 *guilt*; 348.1 *instrumentality*; 346.4 *management*; 205.9 *participation*
responsible 706.16 *answerable*; 670.36 *blameworthy*; 344.13, 348.7 *causal*; 384.29 *defending*; 354.6 *enterprising*; 806.5 *guilty*; 799.4 *honourable*; 784.9 *in debt*; 810.10 *liable*
responsibleness 810.1 *duty*
responsible person 579.15 *manager*
responsibly 354.8; 706.27 *answerably*; 344.14 *causally*; 799.7 *honourably*; 810.18 *on duty*
responsion 706.1 *answer*
responsive 422.7 *adaptive*; 706.11 *answering*; 590.10 *feeling*; 591.1 *sensitive*; 488.7 *susceptible*
responsively 422.12 *adaptably*; 706.24 *in answer*
responsiveness 422.2 *adaptability*; 590.5 *good feeling*; 591.5 *sensitivity*
responsory 706.4 *reaction*
respotting a ball 65.5 *snooker*
rest 413.4; 77.22 *be dormant*; 215.7 *be left*; 301.8 *be motionless*; 581.2 *be refreshed*; 143.9 *be situated*; 228.6 *be stable*; 133.5 *caesura*; 582.1 *death*; 263.1 *ease*; 65.3 *English billiards*; 580.4 *have leisure*; 341.1 *inaction*; 133.3 *interval*; 580.1 *leisure*; 341.4 *not act*; 18.17 *notation*; 133.13, 226.3, 226.9 *pause*; 589.1 *peace*; 581.6 *refresher*; 581.5 *refreshment*; 215.1 *remainder*; 301.2 *repose*; 506.4 *silence*; 343.9, 343.13 *sleep*; 228.1 *stability*; 304.10 *step*; 263.2 *take it easy*
rest and be thankful 301.8 *be motionless*; 263.2 *take it easy*
rest and recreation 294.3 *delayed action*
restart 61.6 *motor-racing terms*; 134.4 *protract*; 61.9 *race*; 112.20 *renew*; 761.7 *restore*
rest assured 450.7 *believe*; 610.6 *hope*
restate 112.17 *iterate*; 509.14 *repeat*; 5.46, 719.12 *translate*
restated 112.10 *iterated*; 5.40 *translated*
restatement 112.2 *iteration*; 509.7 *repeated word*; 5.12 *translation*
restating 5.40 *translated*
restaurant 557.15 *eating place*; 654.4 *meeting place*; 565.7 *room*
restaurant car 321.6 *rolling stock*
restaurateur 436.4 *caterer*; 557.20 *food provider*
rested 581.4 *refreshed*
rest energy 334.4 *energy*
rest from one's labours 263.1 *ease*; 263.2 *take it easy*
restful 263.4 *at ease*; 241.3 *comfortable*; 263.5 *labour-saving*; 490.6 *pleasant*; 301.6 *quiescent*; 228.9 *stable*
restfully 301.10 *motionlessly*; 581.8 *refreshingly*; 228.12 *stably*; 263.6 *with ease*
restfulness 263.1 *ease*; 301.2 *repose*
rest home 35.10, 394.14 *hospital*
resting 263.4 *at ease*; 580.7 *leisurely*; 343.4 *not awake*; 350.3 *not wanted*; 343.2 *not working*; 301.6 *quiescent*; 215.9 *remaining*
resting bud 77.8 *bud*
resting place 226.5; **301.3**
Rest in Peace 583.4 *funeral objects*
restitute 813.11 *pay*; 785.10 *pay back*; 393.3 *restore*; 385.4 *serve one right*
restitution 807.1 *atonement*; 813.6 *compensation*; 775.1 *giving back*; 749.2 *peace offering*; 814.8 *penalty*; 394.1 *remedy*; 785.2 *repayment*; 393.9, 761.2 *restoration*; 714.1 *vindication*
restitutional 807.4 *atoning*
restitutive 807.4 *atoning*; 761.10 *regressive*; 775.6 *restoring*
restitutory 807.4 *atoning*; 761.10 *regressive*; 775.6 *restoring*
restive 662.13 *disobedient*; 641.2 *refractory*
restively 662.17 *disobediently*
restiveness 662.1 *disobedience*
restless 327.16; 342.18 *active*; 639.2 *changeable*; 662.13 *disobedient*; 299.4 *irregular*; 227.14 *irresolute*; 300.16 *moving*
restlessly 342.22 *actively*; 327.27 *agitatedly*; 662.17 *disobediently*; 300.18 *in motion*; 299.8 *irregularly*
restlessness 327.5; **342.7**; 662.1 *disobedience*; 299.1 *irregularity*; 227.2 *irresolution*; 300.2 *momentum*
restock 436.6 *replenish*; 393.3 *restore*
rest on one's laurels 341.4 *not act*; 226.9 *pause*; 263.2 *take it easy*
rest on one's oars 301.8 *be motionless*; 341.4 *not act*; 226.9 *pause*; 263.2 *take it easy*
restorable 295.15 *renewable*; 393.14 *repairable*; 775.6 *restoring*; 761.12 *reversible*
Restoration 21.42 *activist*
restoration 393.9; **761.2**; 224.1 *change*; 390.2 *deliverance*; 295.5 *fresh start*; 775.1 *giving back*; 244.5 *improvement*; 814.8 *penalty*; 581.5 *refreshment*; 393.8 *repair*; 561.1 *reproduction*; 112.4 *return*; 336.4 *strengthening*; 547.1 *transfiguration*; 714.1 *vindication*
Restoration comedy 21.12 *comedy*
restoration to health 393.11 *recuperation*
restorative 393.16; 496.6 *cordial*; 257.4 *hygienic*; 244.16 *improving*; 581.6 *refresher*; 581.3 *refreshing*; 608.8 *relieving*; 394.17 *remedial*; 496.10 *stimulating*; 394.7 *tonic*
restoratively 244.17 *better*
restore 393.3; **761.7**; 496.13 *be piquant*; 224.8 *cause change*; 390.1 *deliver*; 775.4 *give back*; 244.1 *improve*; 338.3, 554.21 *invigorate*; 259.7 *make healthy*; 295.20 *make new*; 749.4 *pacify*; 35.19 *practise medicine*; 581.1 *refresh*; 393.2 *refurbish*; 394.19 *remedy*; 112.20 *renew*; 392.19 *support*; 714.7 *vindicate*
restored 554.12 *alive*; 224.12 *changed*; 649.6 *forgiven*; 244.14 *improved*; 714.12 *innocent*; 581.4 *refreshed*; 608.7 *relieved*; 295.14 *renewed*; 393.13 *repaired*; 112.11 *reprinted*; 775.6 *restoring*; 761.11 *reversed*; 336.13 *strengthened*
restored to health 259.1 *healthy*
restore harmony 749.4 *pacify*
restore one to favour 775.4 *give back*
restore order 407.22 *pacify*
restore peace 749.4 *pacify*
restorer 224.6 *editor*; 393.12 *repairer*; 775.3 *returner*; 244.13 *reviser*
restore the status quo 761.7 *restore*
restore to consciousness 554.19 *give birth to*
restore to health 393.6 *cure*; 259.7 *make healthy*
restore to sanity 460.6 *be sane*
restore vitality 393.5 *revive*
restoring 775.6; 775.1 *giving back*; 338.5 *invigorating*; 336.4 *strengthening*
restrain 251.8; **309.11**; **378.10**; 218.5 *be insufficient*; 647.5 *be severe*; 226.8 *cause to cease*; 399.4 *censor*; 386.6 *compel*; 347.3 *counteract*; 387.7 *defeat*; 481.3 *deflect*; 294.8 *delay*; 360.7 *detain*; 378.8 *hinder*; 166.7 *limit*; 685.4 *moderate*; 728.22 *play down*; 136.16 *specify*
restrained 378.14 *blocked*; 333.7 *delayed*; 4.18 *detached*; 407.17 *disciplined*; 728.19 *downplayed*; 543.3 *elegant*; 294.10 *held up*; 685.6 *moderate*; 674.13, 728.15 *reserved*; 251.13 *restraining*; 684.8 *self-restrained*; 271.1 *simple*; 36.37 *subconscious*; 728.13 *subtle*; 647.10 *unadorned*; 333.5 *unhurried*
restrainedly 4.27 *stoically*
restrainedness 728.3 *subtlety*
restrainer 309.3
restrain from 383.9 *desist*
restraining 251.13; 378.14 *blocked*; 386.9 *compelling*; 347.4 *counteracting*; 294.12 *delaying*; 360.9 *retentive*
restraining hand 251.5 *means of restraint*; 685.2 *moderator*
restraining line 46.4 *stadium*
restrain oneself 251.10; 684.5 *be self-restrained*; 647.7 *be unadorned*
Restraint 251
restraint 251.1; **378.4**; 386.2 *coercion*; 347.1 *counteraction*; 333.9 *deceleration*; 294.3 *delayed action*; 481.7 *deterrence*; 387.2 *domination*; 728.9 *downplaying*; 543.1 *elegance*; 378.1 *hindrance*; 16.6 *legal process*; 166.1 *limitation*; 685.1 *moderation*; 685.2 *moderator*; 674.6, 728.5 *reserve*; 251.1 *restraint*; 684.1 *self-restraint*; 647.1 *severity*; 271.4 *simplicity*; 333.8 *slowness*; 728.3 *subtlety*; 647.3 *unadornment*; 399.1 *veto*
restraint of trade 251.2 *economic restraint*; 13.5 *international trade*
restrain trade 251.9 *economize*
restrict 218.5 *be insufficient*; 399.4 *censor*; 378.8 *hinder*; 737.12 *keep secret*; 166.7 *limit*; 191.5, 214.5 *make smaller*; 685.4 *moderate*; 151.10 *narrow*; 251.8 *restrain*; 136.16 *specify*; 399.3 *veto*
restrict consumption 251.9 *economize*
restricted 399.6 *censored*; 136.12 *conditional*; 128.10 *excluding*; 815.8 *imprisoned*; 166.5 *limited*; 159.7 *little*; 685.6 *moderate*; 151.1 *narrow*; 251.13 *restraining*; 737.9 *secret*; 684.8 *self-restrained*; 191.7 *smaller*; 235.1 *worthy*
restricted area 166.2 *limiting factor*; 251.1 *restraint*
restricted information 399.2 *censorship*
restrict imports 251.9 *economize*
restricting 191.8 *contracting*; 251.13 *restraining*
restriction 191.1 *contraction*; 214.1 *decrease*; 378.1 *hindrance*; 166.1 *limitation*; 151.5 *narrowness*; 27.64 *reasoning*; 251.1 *restraint*; 684.1 *self-restraint*; 136.6 *specification*; 212.2 *subtracted item*; 399.1 *veto*
restriction endonuclease 33.11 *enzyme*
restriction enzyme 33.11 *enzyme*; 34.12 *molecular biology*
restrictionist 251.6 *lawmaker*
restriction on movement 251.4 *detention*
restrictive 399.6 *censored*; 136.12 *conditional*; 191.8 *contracting*; 128.10 *excluding*; 378.13 *hindering*; 166.5 *limited*; 251.13 *restraining*; 684.8 *self-restrained*; 399.5 *vetoed*
restrictively 399.8 *under censorship*; 251.16 *under restraints*; 378.16 *with delay*; 136.18 *with qualification*; 684.11 *with self-restraint*
restrictiveness 128.4 *exclusiveness*
restrictive practice 251.2 *economic restraint*; 166.2 *limiting factor*
restrictive trade agreement 13.5 *international trade*
restrict oneself 684.5 *be self-restrained*
restrict one's movement 251.11 *detain*
restrict supplies 251.9 *economize*
rest room 560.13 *lavatory*; 767.7 *toilet*
restructure 224.8 *cause change*; 295.5 *fresh start*; 295.20 *make new*; 409.14 *rearrange*; 760.9 *transform*
restructured 224.12 *changed*; 409.23 *rearranged*; 295.14 *renewed*
restructuring 224.1 *change*; 409.4 *rearrangement*
restructuring of industry 13.4 *economic development*
rest with 810.14 *be the duty of*
restyle 224.8 *cause change*
restyled 224.12 *changed*
restyling 224.1 *change*
result 215.7 *be left*; 345.1 *effect*; 131.12 *end result*; 345.7 *follow from*; 348.1 *instrumentality*; 27.14 *operation*; 356.3 *product*; 215.1 *remainder*; 132.4 *repercussion*; 289.9 *sequel*; 706.6 *solution*; 289.10 *succeed*
resultant 345.10 *caused*; 215.9 *remaining*; 132.10 *repercussive*; 27.50 *scalar quantity*; 706.14 *solved*
result from 345.7 *follow from*; 289.10 *succeed*
result in 344.9 *be the cause of*; 694.12 *intend*; 345.5 *show an effect*
resulting 345.10 *caused*
resulting from 345.10 *caused*
results 27.14 *operation*
resume 393.4 *be restored*; 112.17 *iterate*; 134.4 *protract*; 112.20 *renew*; 761.7 *restore*; 723.8 *summarize*
résumé 3.6 *biography*; 716.6 *documentation*; 721.4 *factual account*; 112.2 *iteration*; 269.2 *outline*; 744.1 *record*; 149.3 *shortened version*; 723.1 *summary*
resumed 761.11 *reversed*
resumption 134.2 *protraction*; 393.9, 761.2 *restoration*
resupply 436.6 *replenish*
resurface 393.1 *repair*
resurfacing 393.8 *repair*
resurgence 561.1 *reproduction*; 393.10 *revival*
resurgent 393.13 *repaired*; 561.15 *reproduced*
resurrect 554.21 *invigorate*; 295.20 *make new*; 393.5 *revive*
resurrected 295.14 *renewed*
resurrection 295.5 *fresh start*; 554.5 *life cycle*; 561.1 *reproduction*; 393.10 *revival*
resurrectional 561.15 *reproduced*
resurrectionary 561.15 *reproduced*
resurrection day 464.4 *judgment day*; 393.10 *revival*
resuscitate 554.19 *give birth to*; 581.1 *refresh*; 393.5 *revive*
resuscitated 393.13 *repaired*
resuscitation 581.5 *refreshment*; 561.1 *reproduction*; 393.10 *revival*; 67.3 *survival swimming*
retable 19.8 *painting*
retail 13.13 *economic*; 740.13 *make public*; 776.13 *mercantile*; 778.1 *sell*; 778.3 *selling*
retailer 778.13; 436.3 *provider*; 776.10 *trader*

retailer's 779.8 *store*
retailing 13.2 *economy*
retail outlet 779.8 *store*
retail price 790.1 *price*
retail price index 13.3 *economic statistics*
retain 360.6; 316.14 *bring back*; 360.7 *detain*; 455.11 *know*; 400.15 *learn*; 462.11 *memorize*; 359.5 *preserve*; 709.5 *refuse*; 439.6 *store*; 695.6 *understand*
retained 360.10; 709.8 *refused*
retainer 664.5 *adherent*; 122.6 *inferior*; 813.4 *reward for service*; 401.1 *servant*; 316.7 *transferor*
retainers 223.10 *attendance*
retaining 360.9 *retentive*; 413.9 *supportive*
retaining wall 38.19 *structure*; 413.2 *supporting part*; 360.4 *wall*
retainment 360.1 *retention*
retaliate 384.26; **385.3**; **785.13**; 381.8 *counterattack*; 704.10 *countercharge*; 113.18 *object*; 813.11 *pay*; 814.2 *penalize*; 110.7 *reciprocate*; 761.7 *restore*
Retaliation 385
retaliation 385.1; 813.6 *compensation*; 704.3 *countercharge*; 706.5 *counterstatement*; 759.1 *exchange*; 110.1 *interchange*; 761.2 *restoration*; 814.9 *retribution*; 381.14 *siege*
retaliative 385.5 *retaliatory*
retaliator 714.6 *avenger*; 814.17 *punisher*
retaliatory 385.5; **706.13**; 813.17 *compensatory*; 381.24 *counterattacking*; 759.6 *in exchange*; 814.19 *punitive*; 110.4 *reciprocal*; 704.7 *refuting*
retard 684.5 *be self-restrained*; 294.8 *delay*; 378.8 *hinder*; 214.5 *make smaller*; 251.8 *restrain*; 333.3 *slow down*
retardation 333.9 *deceleration*; 214.1 *decrease*; 378.1 *hindrance*; 294.1 *lateness*; 251.1 *restraint*
retarded 333.7 *delayed*; 457.7 *intellectually subnormal*
retarding 294.12 *delaying*
retardment 333.9 *deceleration*
retch 371.15 *vomit*
retching 260.8 *indigestion*; 371.23 *vomiting*
retell 112.17 *iterate*; 721.15 *recount*; 244.3 *rectify*
retelling 112.2 *iteration*
Retention 360
retention 360.1; 36.23, 462.1 *memory*; 763.1 *possession*; 359.1 *preservation*; 709.1 *refusal*; 360.5 *retentiveness*
retentive 360.9
retentiveness 360.5; 462.1 *memory*
rethink 443.14 *have second thoughts*
retiarius 586.3 *athlete*
reticence 616.1 *caution*; 730.5 *mutism*; 674.6, 728.5 *reserve*; 732.3 *shyness*; 736.4 *silence*; 655.1 *unsociability*
reticent 616.4 *cautious*; 645.4 *cunning*; 674.13, 728.15 *reserved*; 737.10 *secretive*; 732.1 *shy*; 736.16 *silent*; 730.11 *speechless*; 655.8 *unsociable*
reticently 728.25 *reservedly*; 732.8 *shyly*; 655.14 *unsocially*
reticular 34.23 *cellular*
reticulate 193.8 *interweave*; 193.6 *interwoven*; 83.10 *of fungi*; 541.9 *striped*
reticulately 541.12 *variedly*
reticulation 193.1 *interweaving*; 541.3 *striping*
reticulum 34.7 *cell*
retina 518.2 *eye*
retinopathy 519.2 *poor sight*
retinue 223.10 *attendance*; 289.1 *succession*
retiral 605.1 *resignation*
retire 98.16 *absent oneself*; 315.14 *be dismissed*; 301.8 *be motionless*; 655.12 *be unsocial*; 526.2 *depart*; 371.2 *dismiss*; 674.15 *escape notice*; 580.4 *have leisure*; 605.5 *resign*; 303.2 *retreat*; 761.6 *reverse*; 634.8 *run away*; 350.7 *stop work*; 226.7 *stop working*; 388.3 *submit*; 384.28 *survive*; 313.2, 355.2 *withdraw*
retired 355.6 *apathetic*; 350.4 *disused*; 284.20, 296.13 *former*; 250.13 *informal*; 580.7 *leisurely*; 15.9 *negotiated*; 350.3 *not wanted*; 605.7 *resigning*; 761.11 *reversed*
retired list 220.6 *list of names*
retired person 556.7 *older person*
retiree 355.4 *deserter*; 556.7 *older person*; 605.3 *resigner*
retire from the world 655.12 *be unsocial*
retirement 313.7 *departure*; 350.10 *disuse*; 15.2 *industrial negotiations*; 296.1 *oldness*; 355.3 *relinquishment*; 605.1 *resignation*; 303.11 *retreat*; 761.1 *reversion*; 372.2 *setting apart*; 634.12 *shyness*; 226.2 *stop*; 580.3 *unemployment*; 655.1 *unsociability*
retirement age 556.5 *old age*
retirement benefit 768.2 *gift*; 788.3 *income*; 13.8 *industrial relations*; 253.1 *protection*; 650.3 *welfare*
retirement gift 671.3 *recognition*
retirement home 226.5 *resting place*
retirement pay 765.4 *earnings*
retirement pension 785.3 *pay*; 813.4 *reward for service*; 392.4 *social assistance*
retiring 15.9 *negotiated*; 674.13, 728.15 *reserved*; 605.7 *resigning*; 674.11 *shy*; 674.4 *shyness*; 655.8 *unsociable*
retiring disposition 674.6, 728.5 *reserve*
retold 112.10 *iterated*
retort 706.1, 706.17 *answer*; 660.25 *answer back*; 704.3, 704.10 *countercharge*; 714.2 *defence*; 759.5 *exchange*; 110.1 *interchange*; 714.8 *justify*; 507.1 *loudness*; 760.4 *medium of conversion*; 623.14 *rebuke*; 708.11 *rebut*; 708.3 *rebuttal*; 110.7 *reciprocate*; 761.5, 761.9 *reply*; 385.3 *retaliate*; 385.1 *retaliation*; 432.11 *vaporizer*
retorted 706.11 *answering*; 761.11 *reversed*
retorting 708.19 *rebutting*; 714.11 *vindicatory*
retortion 708.3 *rebuttal*; 761.5 *reply*
retouch 699.26 *falsify*; 393.2 *refurbish*
retouching 699.9 *falsification*
retrace 462.12 *remember*
retrace one's steps 112.19 *return to*; 303.3 *reverse*; 303.5 *turn back*
retract 708.14 *cancel*; 362.14 *draw in*; 479.4 *recant*; 708.12 *renounce*; 761.6 *reverse*; 773.9 *withdraw a statement*
retractability 362.1 *traction*
retractable 362.9 *retractive*
retractably 362.16 *magnetically*
retractation 708.5 *cancellation*; 479.8 *recantation*; 708.4 *renunciation*
retracted 708.18 *rejected*; 761.11 *reversed*
retractile 303.23 *receding*; 362.9 *retractive*
retractility 362.1 *traction*
retracting 773.2 *taking back*
retraction 708.5 *cancellation*; 479.8 *recantation*; 708.4 *renunciation*; 761.1 *reversion*; 362.1 *traction*
retractive 362.9
retractiveness 362.1 *traction*
retractor 708.9 *negativist*
retrain 15.11 *conduct industrial relations*
retrained 15.9 *negotiated*
retraining 15.2 *industrial negotiations*; 15.9 *negotiated*
retrally 303.28 *backwards*
retread 393.1 *repair*
retreat 303.2; **303.11**; **565.11**; 98.16 *absent oneself*; 249.1 *adversity*; 300.4 *backward motion*; 614.4 *be a coward*; 521.7 *become invisible*; 247.7 *be defeated*; 197.18 *be one*; 247.2 *defeat*; 526.2 *depart*; 313.7 *departure*; 526.4 *disappearance*; 389.1, 389.5 *escape*; 300.19 *go!*; 172.2 *inside*; 7.10 *priestly dwelling*; 736.6 *privacy*; 550.30 *protect*; 252.5 *refuge*; 761.6 *reverse*; 761.1 *reversion*; 634.8 *run away*; 655.3 *separation*; 550.15 *shelter*; 634.4 *shy*; 634.12 *shyness*; 655.5 *solitary place*; 388.3 *submit*; 313.2 *withdraw*; 742.6 *word*
retreated 761.11 *reversed*
retreater 389.3 *escaper*
retreating 303.23 *receding*
retreat into 172.14 *go inside*
retreat into one's shell 736.11 *conceal oneself*
retrench 214.5 *make smaller*; 251.8 *restrain*; 680.6 *save*; 149.10 *shorten*
retrenchment 680.2 *act of thrift*; 214.1 *decrease*; 251.1 *restraint*; 372.3 *separateness*; 149.2 *shortening*; 212.1 *subtraction*
retrial 16.7 *legal trial*
retribution 814.9; 385.1 *retaliation*; 714.4 *revenge*
retributive 813.17 *compensatory*; 785.20 *paying in return*; 814.19 *punitive*; 385.5 *retaliatory*; 714.14 *vindictive*
retributive justice 814.9 *retribution*
retributively 814.23 *punitively*; 714.16 *vindictively*
retrievable 393.14 *repairable*; 761.12 *reversible*; 773.12 *taking*
retrievably 773.13 *avariciously*; 761.13 *reversibly*
retrieval 390.2 *deliverance*; 393.9, 761.2 *restoration*; 773.2 *taking back*
retrieve 316.14 *bring back*; 347.3 *counteract*; 390.1 *deliver*; 761.7 *restore*; 60.7 *shoot*; 773.8 *take back*
retrieved 761.11 *reversed*
retriever 60.6 *sporting dog*
retro 286.2 *occurring at a different time*; 284.21 *retrospective*
retroact 706.19 *react*
retroaction 303.10 *backward motion*; 347.1 *counteraction*; 706.4 *reaction*; 761.1 *reversion*
retroactive 303.24; 347.4 *counteracting*; 3.18 *in the past*; 706.12 *reactive*; 761.10 *regressive*; 284.21 *retrospective*
retroactively 347.5 *counter*; 3.24 *historically*; 706.24 *in answer*; 761.13 *reversibly*
retroactive pay 785.3 *pay*
retrocede 775.4 *give back*; 303.1 *go backwards*; 393.3 *restore*
retrocession 303.10 *backward motion*; 775.1 *giving back*; 393.9 *restoration*
retrocessive 303.22 *backward*
retroflex 303.1 *go backwards*
retroflexion 303.10 *backward motion*; 761.1 *reversion*
retrogradation 303.10 *backward motion*; 245.7 *deterioration*
retrograde 303.22 *backward*; 245.1 *deteriorate*; 245.12 *deteriorated*; 303.1 *go backwards*; 761.10 *regressive*
retrograde metamorphism 30.32 *metamorphism*
retrograde state 761.1 *reversion*
retrogress 300.13 *be in motion*; 245.1 *deteriorate*; 303.1 *go backwards*; 761.6 *reverse*
retrogression 303.10 *backward motion*; 245.7 *deterioration*; 761.1 *reversion*
retrogressive 303.22 *backward*; 245.12 *deteriorated*; 300.17 *directional*; 286.2 *occurring at a different time*
retrorocket 29.35 *rocketry*
retrospect 462.2
retrospection 284.2; 462.1 *memory*; 761.1 *reversion*; 443.3 *thoughtfulness*
retrospective 284.21; 738.6 *display*; 761.10 *regressive*; 462.8 *remembering*; 303.24 *retroactive*; 462.2 *retrospect*; 284.2 *retrospection*
retrospective action 761.1 *reversion*
retrospectively 284.24; 3.24 *historically*; 462.16 *memorably*; 761.13 *reversibly*
retroussé 304.22 *ascending*; 149.7 *short*
retroverse 761.10 *regressive*
retroversion 192.1 *inversion*; 761.1 *reversion*
retrovert 192.3 *invert*
retrovirus 260.6 *infection*; 34.3 *organism*
retrovirus disease 260.4 *disease*
retsina 558.9 *wine*
return 112.4; **303.20**; **312.13**; **761.4**; **761.8**; 706.17 *answer*; 298.8 *be cyclic*; 237.8 *benefit*; 276.10 *be periodical*; 112.21 *be repeated*; 298.2 *cycle*; 313.7 *departure*; 693.3 *document*; 765.4 *earnings*; 775.4 *give back*; 775.1 *giving back*; 303.1 *go backwards*; 110.1 *interchange*; 46.17 *kick*; 312.4 *land*; 276.6 *periodicity*; 356.7 *produce*; 134.2 *protraction*; 436.1 *provision*; 706.19 *react*; 706.4 *reaction*; 525.6 *reappearance*; 110.7 *reciprocate*; 744.1 *record*; 298.1 *regularity*; 470.1 *reject*; 393.3 *restore*; 385.3 *retaliate*; 761.6 *reverse*; 761.1 *reversion*; 46.12 *special team*; 330.5, 330.23 *throw*; 303.5 *turn back*; 813.5 *turnover*; 325.11 *turn round*; 469.5 *vote*
returnable 761.12 *reversible*
return action 347.1 *counteraction*
return a favour 671.6 *be grateful*
return a soft answer 749.4 *pacify*
return a verdict 16.76 *judge*
return blow for blow 381.8 *counterattack*
return correspondence 706.2 *acknowledgment*
returned 706.11 *answering*; 469.15 *chosen*; 470.10 *rejected*; 761.11 *reversed*
returned-letter office 692.2 *postal communication*
returned to health 393.15 *cured*
return empty-handed 247.6 *fail*
returner 775.3
return from the grave 393.4 *be restored*
return good for evil 650.8 *be benevolent*; 385.3 *retaliate*; 649.12 *show mercy*
return home 761.8 *return*
returning 303.27; 775.1 *giving back*; 276.8 *periodical*; 706.12 *reactive*; 112.14 *recurrent*; 298.11 *regular*; 393.9 *restoration*
returning good for evil 385.1 *retaliation*
returning home 761.4 *return*
return like for like 385.3 *retaliate*
return match 112.5 *repeat*
return once again 298.8 *be cyclic*
return receipt 692.2 *postal communication*
returns 765.4 *earnings*; 469.12 *election*; 788.2 *money received*; 769.2 *something received*
return signal 692.28 *radar*
return thanks 671.6 *be grateful*
return the compliment 759.5 *exchange*; 747.12 *reciprocate*; 385.3 *retaliate*
return ticket 761.4 *return*
return to 112.19; 134.4 *protract*
return to base 303.17 *resilience*
return to fashion 393.10 *revival*
return to go 130.28 *begin again*
return to health 259.6 *get healthy*; 393.11 *recuperation*
return to mint condition 393.3 *restore*
return to normal 393.4 *be restored*; 393.11 *recuperation*; 393.9 *restoration*
return to the past 284.15 *look back*
Reuben sandwich 25.11 *sandwich*
reunion 376.9 *social gathering*
reupholster 393.1 *repair*
reusable 237.2, 349.10 *usable*
reusably 349.11 *usefully*
reuse 349.3 *exploit*; 349.6 *use*
reused 349.9 *used*
reused product 349.7
Reuters 741.7 *press agency*; 693.8 *source of information*
revalidate 393.3 *restore*
revamp 224.8 *cause change*; 393.2 *refurbish*
rev counter 26.8 *meter*
reveal 738.3; 527.11 *be transparent*; 703.15 *demonstrate*; 449.2 *detect*; 739.5 *disclose*; 6.22 *educate*; 171.14 *externalize*; 740.13 *make public*; 518.18, 520.10 *make visible*; 20.9 *miscellaneous architectural features*; 308.18 *open*; 475.11 *predict*; 525.14 *present*; 356.10 *produce*; 742.10 *signify*; 552.14 *undress*
revealed 525.7 *appearing*; 703.9 *demonstrated*; 739.10 *disclosed*; 449.14 *discovered*; 738.14 *manifest*; 740.19 *published*; 698.15 *true*
revealer 739.4 *discloser*
revealing 739.11 *disclosing*; 449.13 *discovering*; 6.16 *educational*; 693.16 *informative*; 742.14 *signifying*; 527.2 *translucent*; 552.1 *undress*
revealing dress 552.4 *dishabille*
revealingly 6.25 *educationally*; 742.18 *indicatively*; 552.17 *nakedly*; 449.16 *originally*
reveal itself 525.12 *become visible*
reveal oneself 738.4 *show oneself*
reveal one's mind 738.4 *show oneself*
reveal one's opinions 738.4 *show oneself*
reveal one's thoughts 738.4 *show oneself*
reveal to the public 738.1 *display*
reveille 742.6 *word*
revel 601.15 *celebrate*; 601.1 *celebration*; 690.14 *drinking bout*; 557.24 *have a meal*; 600.5 *rejoice*; 600.1 *rejoicing*
revelation 525.1 *appearance*; 703.1 *demonstration*; 449.7 *detection*; 739.1 *disclosure*; 738.10 *manifestation*; 475.1 *prediction*; 525.4 *something that appears*; 630.4 *surprising thing*; 698.3 *the truth*; 520.3 *visibility*
revelatory 739.12; 703.9 *demonstrated*; 449.13 *discovering*; 6.16 *educational*
revel in 490.8 *feel pleasure*
reveller 690.17 *drunkard*; 597.3 *joyful person*; 600.4 *rejoicer*
revelling 600.9 *rejoicing*
revelry 601.1 *celebration*; 597.2 *fun*; 490.4 *pleasurable things*; 654.1 *sociability*
revels 601.1 *celebration*

revenge **714.4**; 714.10 *avenge*; 385.3 *retaliate*; 385.1 *retaliation*; 814.9 *retribution*
revenge! 385.7
revengeful 798.7 *evil*; 651.13 *merciless*; 628.4 *pitiless*; 814.19 *punitive*; 385.5 *retaliatory*; 714.14 *vindictive*
revengefully 798.12 *evilly*; 714.16 *vindictively*
revengefulness 798.1 *evil*; 628.1 *pitilessness*
revenge killing 382.1 *killing*
revenge oneself 814.2 *penalize*; 785.13 *retaliate*
revenger **385.2**; 814.17 *punisher*
revenge tragedy 21.11 *tragedy*
revenue 765.4 *earnings*; 13.6 *economic factors*; 352.4 *financial resources*; 788.2 *money received*; 440.5 *personal estate*; 356.7 *produce*; 769.2 *something received*; 773.5 *takings*
reverb 504.10 *sound quality*
reverberant 509.15 *drumming*
reverberantly 706.24 *in answer*; 510.11 *resonantly*
reverberate 504.16 *be heard*; 507.8 *be loud*; 509.8 *drum*; 706.19 *react*; 510.9 *resonate*; 112.22 *resound*
reverberating 510.6 *resonant*
reverberation **112.6**, 28.21 *architectural acoustics*; 509.1 *drumming*; 507.1 *loudness*; 706.4 *reaction*; 132.4 *repercussion*; 510.1 *resonance*; 504.8 *something heard*
reverberation chamber 28.21 *architectural acoustics*
reverberation time 28.21 *architectural acoustics*
reverberative 509.15 *drumming*; 510.6 *resonant*
reverberatory **112.15**; 24.10 *ceramic*; 24.6 *ceramic workshop*; 706.12 *reactive*; 132.10 *repercussive*
reverberatory kiln 24.6 *ceramic workshop*
reverdie 17.7 *poem*
revere **667.16**; 7.19 *be religious*; 367.9 *bow*; 593.23 *love*; 10.19 *offer worship*; 9.7 *worship*
revered 593.21 *beloved*; 667.12 *respected*; 9.11 *worshipped*
reverence 667.2 *admiration*; 810.3 *allegiance*; 367.16 *courtesy*; 663.3 *obeisance*; 10.19 *offer worship*; 7.2 *religiousness*; 667.16 *revere*; 10.3 *rite of worship*; 9.1, 9.7 *worship*
reverenced 667.12 *respected*
reverend father 7.7 *monk*
reverend mother 7.7 *monk*
reverent **667.10**; 7.15 *religious*; 9.9, 575.6 *worshipful*; 10.22 *worshipping*
reverential 810.9 *loyal*; 663.9 *obeisant*; 7.15 *religious*; 667.10 *reverent*; 9.9 *worshipful*
reverentially 663.10 *obediently*; 7.23 *religiously*; 667.22 *respectfully*; 9.12 *worshipfully*
reverently 667.22 *respectfully*
reverie **477.6**; 443.3 *thoughtfulness*; 36.14 *trance*
reversal **303.12**; 708.5 *cancellation*; 224.1 *change*; 247.2 *defeat*; 704.2 *denial*; 479.6 *equivocation*; 192.1 *inversion*; 766.1 *loss*; 113.2 *oppositeness*; 704.1 *refutation*; 761.1 *reversion*; 630.4 *surprising thing*
reverse **303.3**; **761.6**; 224.7 *be changed*; 113.15 *be opposite*; 708.14 *cancel*; 224.11 *changeable*; 62.3 *climbing technique*; 113.25 *contrary*; 704.9 *deny*; 192.1 *inversion*; 192.3 *invert*; 766.1 *loss*; 62.9 *mountaineer*; 113.23 *opposite*; 113.2 *oppositeness*; 46.9 *play*; 708.11 *rebut*; 708.3 *rebuttal*; 303.12 *reversal*; 303.25 *reversed*; 333.3 *slow down*; 67.11 *swimming*; 325.11 *turn round*
reverse-charge call 692.10 *telephone call*
reverse curve 48.4 *pitching terms*
reversed **303.25**; **761.11**; 192.2 *inverted*; 113.23 *opposite*; 708.18 *rejected*
reverse direction 303.10 *backward motion*; 325.11 *turn round*
reverse dive 67.6 *diving*
reversed-phase 32.41 *analytic*
reverse fault 30.20 *earth movement*
reverse killian hold 68.7 *ice-dancing*
reverse one's field 303.3 *reverse*
reverse order 407.3 *hierarchy*
reverse punch 52.9 *tae kwon do*
reverse snowplough 68.4 *skiing technique*
reverse sweep 53.9 *stroke*
reverse twist 63.2 *tennis strokes*
reverse word dictionary 5.28 *dictionary*
reversible **761.12**; 32.38 *reactive*; 303.25 *reversed*
reversible reaction 32.14 *chemical reaction*
reversibly **761.13**
reversing 303.12 *reversal*
reversing light 522.6 *electric light*
Reversion 761
reversion **761.1**; 708.5 *cancellation*; 303.16 *countermotion*; 36.19 *defence mechanism*; 122.2 *deficiency*; 775.1 *giving back*; 192.1 *inversion*; 440.2 *legal terms*; 303.12 *reversal*
reversional 761.10 *regressive*
reversionary 761.10 *regressive*
reversion to type 245.7 *deterioration*
revert 224.7 *be changed*; 245.1 *deteriorate*; 303.1 *go backwards*; 112.19 *return to*; 761.6 *reverse*; 325.11 *turn round*
reverted 761.11 *reversed*
revert to bachelorhood 571.7 *divorce*
revet 550.28 *face*
revetment 550.8 *wall covering*
revictual 436.6 *replenish*
review 722.2 *article*; 693.2 *communication*; 719.3 *criticism*; 719.11 *criticize*; 693.3 *document*; 464.12 *estimate*; 656.3 *formal occasion*; 734.6 *interview*; 112.17 *iterate*; 112.2 *iteration*; 740.5 *journal*; 464.1 *judgment*; 6.8 *learning*; 284.15 *look back*; 17.4 *nonfiction*; 705.17 *question*; 705.2 *questioning*; 244.7 *reconsideration*; 721.15 *recount*; 244.3 *rectify*; 3.22, 462.12 *remember*; 462.13 *remind*; 462.2 *retrospect*; 284.2 *retrospection*; 21.7 *show*; 723.1 *summary*
reviewed 705.16 *questioned*
reviewer 722.3 *dissertator*; 719.6 *interpreter*; 464.5 *judge*; 705.9 *questioner*; 21.33 *theatregoer*
reviewing 3.13 *looking back*
revile 606.7 *be dissatisfied*; 381.10 *criticize*; 678.13, 712.6 *vilify*; 670.22 *vituperate*
revilement 670.8 *berating*; 381.16 *personal attack*; 678.5 *scorn*; 712.3 *vilification*
reviling 712.9 *vituperative*
revisable 295.15 *renewable*
revisal 295.5 *fresh start*; 244.6 *rectification*
revise 224.8 *cause change*; 295.20 *make new*; 484.6 *outline*; 484.10 *plan out*; 244.6 *rectification*; 244.3 *rectify*
revised 224.12 *changed*; 244.14 *improved*; 295.14 *renewed*
revised copy 484.6 *outline*
revised edition 244.8 *better thing*; 561.2 *print*
Revised Version 7.12 *religious text*
reviser **244.13**; 224.6 *editor*
revision 224.1 *change*; 484.6 *outline*; 244.6 *rectification*
revisionism 118.3 *nonconformism*
revisionist 227.4 *editor*
revisionist history 3.1 *history*
revitalization 581.5 *refreshment*; 393.10 *revival*; 338.1 *vigour*
revitalize 338.3, 554.21 *invigorate*; 581.1 *refresh*; 436.6 *replenish*; 393.5 *revive*
revitalized 581.4 *refreshed*
revitalizing 338.5 *invigorating*; 581.3 *refreshing*
revival **393.10**; 224.1 *change*; 295.5 *fresh start*; 244.5 *improvement*; 554.5 *life cycle*; 760.3 *persuasion*; 21.14 *production*; 581.5 *refreshment*; 561.1 *reproduction*; 761.2 *restoration*; 112.4 *return*; 336.4 *strengthening*
revivalism 760.3 *persuasion*; 393.10 *revival*
revivalist 7.5 *Christian*
revive **393.5**; 496.13 *be piquant*; 581.2 *be refreshed*; 393.4 *be restored*; 336.7 *be strong*; 598.6 *bring cheer*; 224.8 *cause change*; 394.20 *doctor*; 244.2 *get better*; 554.19 *give birth to*; 244.1 *improve*; 338.3 *invigorate*; 554.16 *live*; 259.7 *make healthy*; 295.20 *make new*; 760.11 *persuade*; 581.1 *refresh*; 112.20 *renew*; 393.3, 761.7 *restore*; 336.8 *strengthen*; 392.19 *support*
revived 554.12 *alive*; 224.12 *changed*; 760.16 *influenced*; 581.4 *refreshed*; 295.14 *renewed*; 393.13 *repaired*; 112.11 *reprinted*; 761.11 *reversed*; 336.13 *strengthened*
reviver 496.6 *cordial*; 581.6 *refresher*; 394.7 *tonic*
revivescence 393.10 *revival*
revive the spirit 554.21 *invigorate*
revivification 295.5 *fresh start*; 554.5 *life cycle*; 393.10 *revival*; 336.4 *strengthening*
revivified 295.14 *renewed*
revivify 295.20 *make new*; 393.5 *revive*; 336.8 *strengthen*
revivifying 338.5 *invigorating*; 336.4 *strengthening*
reviving 598.2 *cheering*; 338.5 *invigorating*; 581.3 *refreshing*; 393.16 *restorative*; 336.4 *strengthening*
rev limiter 61.6 *motor-racing terms*
revocation 708.5 *cancellation*; 479.8 *recantation*; 708.4 *renunciation*
revocatory 709.9 *dissenting*; 708.17 *negative*
revoke **470.4**; 708.14 *cancel*; 357.8 *destroy*; 767.9 *dispose of*; 479.4 *recant*; 708.12 *renounce*; 399.3 *veto*
revoked 708.20 *cancelled*
revoking 709.9 *dissenting*; 479.8 *recantation*
revolt **383.8**; 588.4 *be anarchic*; 224.7 *be changed*; 364.4 *be repulsive*; 662.16 *be subversive*; 760.8 *be transformed*; 224.8 *cause change*; 596.7 *cause dislike*; 753.8 *cause mischief*; 224.1 *change*; 753.2 *disorder*; 242.10 *displease*; 606.6 *dissatisfy*; 118.2 *dissent*; 585.12 *go to war*; 16.41 *lawlessness*; 118.18 *not conform*; 383.3 *resistance movement*; 662.4 *revolution*; 585.1 *war*
revolter 12.6 *political party*; 662.11 *rebel*; 753.5 *seditionist*
revolting 596.9 *disliked*; 594.12 *hated*; 236.4 *poor*; 242.1 *unpleasant*
revolution **662.4**; 396.3 *acquisition of power*; 661.3 *act of defiance*; 588.1 *anarchy*; 224.1 *change*; 298.2 *cycle*; 367.12 *downthrow*; 760.2 *evolution*; 408.8 *lawlessness*; 29.21 *orbit*; 306.1 *orbital motion*; 244.11 *reformism*; 383.3 *resistance movement*; 307.1 *rotation*; 585.1 *war*
revolutionarily 295.21 *newly*
revolutionary 588.6 *anarchic*; 588.3 *anarchist*; 224.11 *changeable*; 357.6 *destroyer*; 357.14 *destructive*; 118.8 *dissenter*; 224.6, 227.4 *editor*; 753.10 *lawbreaking*; 295.10 *new*; 118.12 *nonconformist*; 126.5 *novel*; 113.11 *opposer*; 306.9 *orbital*; 367.22 *overthrown*; 662.11 *rebel*; 244.12 *reformer*; 383.5 *resister*; 383.12 *resisting*; 753.5 *seditionist*; 662.14 *subversive*; 380.4 *violent creature*
revolutionist 357.6 *destroyer*; 662.11 *rebel*
revolutionize 224.8 *cause change*; 126.7 *originate*
revolutions 307.1 *rotation*
revolutions per minute 307.1 *rotation*
revolve 298.8 *be cyclic*; 179.6 *circle*; 29.37 *observe*; 306.6 *orbit*; 307.8 *rotate*
revolver 330.9, 587.9 *firearm*
revolving 298.12 *cyclic*; 298.11 *regular*; 307.11 *rotating*; 307.1 *rotation*
revolving door 307.6 *rotator*
revolving fund 14.1, 780.7 *finance*
revolving stage 21.17 *stage*
revs 307.1 *rotation*
revue 21.7 *show*
revulsion 594.1 *hate*; 634.12 *shyness*
rev up 346.8 *activate*; 243.4 *prepare for action*; 509.10 *rattle*
Reward 813
reward **813.1**; **813.9**; 671.6 *be grateful*; 480.17 *bribe*; 601.17 *congratulate*; 768.2 *gift*; 768.5 *give*; 785.3 *pay*; 765.5 *profit*; 671.3 *recognition*; 785.11 *remunerate*; 794.1 *trophy*; 790.2 *value*
reward card 791.1 *discount*
rewarded **813.16**; 769.11 *receiving*
rewarder 768.4 *giver*
reward for service **813.4**
rewarding **246.14**; **813.15**; 765.15 *gainful*; 785.18 *profitable*
rewardingly **813.19**; 246.16 *successfully*
reward of conduct 631.1 *conduct*
rewed 570.15 *marry*
reword 5.46, 719.12 *translate*; 5.47 *word*
reworded 5.40 *translated*
rewording 5.40 *translated*; 5.12, 719.4 *translation*
rewritable 40.21 *on-line*
rewrite 543.4 *be elegant*; 244.3 *rectify*; 5.47 *word*
rewriter 244.13 *reviser*
rewritten 244.14 *improved*
Rex 400.2 *sovereign*
Reynard 645.3 *cunning person*
RFC 64.1 *rugger*
R-form 32.13 *structure*
RFU 64.1 *rugger*
RGA 32.20 *surface chemistry*
Rhadamanthine 16.49 *judicatory*
Rhadamanthus 16.23 *judge*
rhapsodic 477.10 *imaginative*; 17.19 *narrative*
rhapsodist 17.14 *author*; 477.9 *visionary*
rhapsodize 477.15 *fantasize*; 697.6 *talk nonsense*
rhapsody 477.4 *ideality*
rhea 72.2 *flightless bird*
rheometer 26.8 *meter*
rheometric 26.16 *micrometric*
rheometry 26.2 *micrometry*
rheostat 39.17 *resistor*
Rhesus factor 431.4 *blood*
rhetoric 542.2 *affectation*; 729.9 *art of public speaking*; 270.1 *diffuseness*; 724.4 *literary style*; 542.1 *ornament*; 4.5 *philosophical argument*
rhetorical 270.3 *diffuse*; 729.20 *eloquent*; 544.9 *inelegant*; 733.13 *oratorical*; 542.10 *ornate*; 702.7 *sophistic*
rhetorically 729.21 *orally*; 4.24 *philosophically*; 702.14 *sophistically*; 724.10 *stylistically*
rhetorical question 705.5 *easy question*
rhetorician 483.7 *motivator*; 480.12 *persuader*; 542.9 *phrasemonger*; 733.6 *public speaker*; 729.10 *speaker*; 724.5 *stylist*
rheum 431.3 *body fluid*; 560.9 *saliva*; 559.2 *secreted substance*
rheumatic 260.23 *diseased*
rheumatic fever 260.16 *rheumatism*
rheumatic heart disease 260.10 *cardiovascular disease*
rheumaticky 260.23 *diseased*
rheumatics 260.16 *rheumatism*
rheumatism **260.16**; 491.2 *painful condition*
rheumatoid 260.23 *diseased*
rheumatoid arthritis 260.16 *rheumatism*
rheumatologist 35.13 *medical specialist*
rheumatology 35.3 *medical specialty*
rheuminess 431.5 *fluidity*
rheumy **431.16**; 560.29 *salivating*
Rh factor 431.4 *blood*
Rhine 90.5 *other major rivers*
Rhine wine 558.9 *wine*
rhinitis 260.9 *respiratory disease*
rhino 780.2 *cash*
rhinoceros 71.15 *hoofed mammal*; 71.14 *pachyderm*
rhinocerotic 71.32 *pachydermatous*
rhino-hided 592.1 *insensitive*
rhinological 500.6 *olfactory*
rhinoplastic 394.18 *medical*
rhinoplasty 394.12 *surgery*
rhinorrhoea 260.9 *respiratory disease*
rhizine 84.6 *lichen*
rhizoid 83.4 *fungal body*; 82.4 *moss plant*; 77.19 *of roots*; 84.3 *plant body*; 77.7 *root*
rhizome 44.9 *garden plant*; 77.5 *stem*
rhizomorph 83.4 *fungal body*; 77.7 *root*
Rh negative 431.4 *blood*
rhodamine dye 42.6 *dye*
rhodic 32.34 *elemental*
rhododendron 540.3 *purple thing*
Rhodophyta 84.2 *algae*
rhodophyte 84.2 *algae*
rhodous 32.34 *elemental*
rhomb 27.44 *polygon*
rhombic 32.33 *crystalline*; 27.82 *polygonal*
rhombic crystal 32.4 *crystal*
rhombohedron 27.46 *polyhedron*
rhomboid 176.3 *angled figure*; 189.2 *oblique line*; 27.44 *polygon*
rhomboidal 176.9 *angled*; 27.82 *polygonal*
rhombus 176.3 *angled figure*; 27.44 *polygon*; 200.2 *quadrilateral*
rhonchus 512.1 *hiss*
Rhône 90.5 *other major rivers*
Rh-positive 431.4 *blood*
rhubarb 751.2 *argument*; 5.5 *nonstandard language*
rhubarb! rhubarb! 731.12
rhumb line 324.3 *orientation*
rhyme **17.11**; 516.8, 750.24 *harmonize*; 750.4 *harmony*; 115.12 *imitate*; 17.7 *poem*; 17.6 *poetry*; 509.7 *repeated word*; 112.22

resound; 112.6 *reverberation;* 162.1 *symmetry;* 5.45 *use language;* 17.21 *write*
rhymed 112.15 *reverberatory*
rhymer 17.14 *author*
rhyme royal 17.10 *verse form*
rhyme scheme 17.11 *rhyme*
rhymester 17.14 *author*
rhyming 516.7, 750.13 *harmonious;* 17.20 *metrical;* 112.15 *reverberatory;* 115.7 *similar;* 5.42 *worded*
rhyming couplet 17.8 *part of poem*
rhyming dictionary 5.28 *dictionary*
rhyming slang 5.26 *dialect;* 5.18 *slang*
rhyming word 5.17 *word*
Rhynocephalia 73.1 *reptile*
rhynocephalian 73.2 *lizard*
rhythm 403.9 *artistic structure;* 543.1 *elegance;* 57.8 *floor exercises;* 516.4 *harmonics;* 17.9 *metre;* 509.6 *musical repetition;* 275.12 *musical time;* 298.1 *regularity;* 300.10 *regular movement;* 298.5 *regular thing;* 112.6 *reverberation;* 18.19 *tempo;* 326.2 *vibration*
rhythmic 132.12 *cyclical;* 300.17 *directional;* 543.3 *elegant;* 57.11 *gymnastic;* 298.11 *regular;* 112.15 *reverberatory;* 326.14 *vibrating*
rhythmical 17.20 *metrical;* 298.11 *regular;* 112.15 *reverberatory;* 326.14 *vibrating*
rhythmically 543.5 *elegantly;* 47.10 *fast;* 18.42 *musically;* 17.22 *poetically;* 298.15 *regularly;* 509.19 *repeatedly*
rhythmic gymnastics 57.1 *gymnastics*
rhythmic pattern 729.6 *phonetics*
rhythmics 18.14 *harmonics*
rhythm method 563.3 *birth control*
rhythm 'n' blues 18.9 *popular music*
rhythm section 223.6 *accompanier*
RI 6.3 *subject*
Rialto 779.5 *stock market*
rialto 759.2 *place of exchange*
rib 25.23 *beef;* 599.13 *be humorous;* 20.19 *decorate;* 25.27 *lamb;* 20.9 *miscellaneous architectural features;* 62.5 *rock face;* 38.27 *superstructure*
ribald 675.9; 712.8 *cursing;* 796.12 *indecent;* 258.9 *obscene*
ribaldly 712.12 *swearingly*
ribaldry 712.1 *curse;* 796.2 *indecency;* 258.3 *obscenity*
ribband 373.6 *line*
ribbed 404.8 *rough;* 20.17 *structured;* 20.15 *vaulted*
ribbon 373.10 *band;* 542.6 *decorative articles;* 551.15 *headgear;* 575.3 *honours;* 743.4 *insignia;* 593.15 *love item;* 744.11 *monument;* 794.1 *trophy*
ribbon development 329.10 *expansionism;* 377.7 *sprawl*
ribbons 373.9 *yoke*
ribbonworm 75.6 *worm*
riblets 25.27 *lamb*
ribonucleotide 33.10 *nucleoside*
ribosomal 34.23 *cellular*
ribosomal RNA 34.13 *genetic material*
ribosome 34.8 *cell organ*
ribs 24.6 *ceramic workshop;* 169.1 *side;* 413.2 *supporting part*
rib-tickling 272.5 *ridiculous*
rib vault 20.7 *vault*
rice 43.12 *crop*
rice paddy 43.11 *farmland*
rice pancake 25.49 *Indian dish*
rice paper 424.3 *brittle thing;* 435.3 *paper*
rice pudding 25.35 *dessert*
rich 529.11 *colourful;* 510.8 *deep;* 270.3 *diffuse;* 557.27 *edible;* 562.5 *fertile;* 516.6 *melodious;* 542.10 *ornate;* 217.2 *plentiful;* 356.11 *productive;* 248.8 *prosperous;* 268.13 *slippery;* 780.23 *solvent;* 235.3 *valuable;* 781.1 *wealthy;* 765.17 *well-off*
rich and poor 113.3 *opposites*
Richard's paradox 4.9 *philosophical problem*
rich as Croesus 781.1 *wealthy;* 765.17 *well-off*
rich as King Midas 765.17 *well-off*
rich as Rockefeller 781.1 *wealthy*
rich as Solomon 781.1 *wealthy*
rich earth 562.1 *fertility*
riches 780.3 *fortune;* 781.6 *money;* 217.8 *plenty;* 246.1 *success*
riches of Solomon 781.6 *money*
rich food 557.7 *food*
rich harvest 562.1 *fertility;* 217.8 *plenty*
rich in 217.3 *filled*
richly 765.20 *gainfully;* 248.9 *prosperously;* 510.11 *resonantly;* 781.16 *wealthily*
richly decorated 542.10 *ornate*
richly furnished 781.3 *opulent*
Richmond 87.3 *New York*
richness 510.3 *deepness;* 270.1 *diffuseness;* 219.1 *excess;* 562.1 *fertility;* 495.4 *flavour;* 217.8 *plenty;* 781.5 *wealth*
rich person 765.7 *gainer;* 248.4 *prosperous person;* 781.10 *wealthy person*
rich pickings 774.4 *stolen goods;* 773.5 *takings*
rich soil 562.1 *fertility*
Richter scale 30.22 *seismic activity*
rich uncle 768.4 *giver*
rich vein 217.8 *plenty;* 439.2 *resource*
rich vocabulary 270.1 *diffuseness;* 729.2 *power of speech*
rick 376.27 *bundle;* 43.10 *farm tool*
rickets 260.4 *disease;* 557.10 *scarcity;* 33.14 *vitamin deficiency disease*
rickettsia 34.3 *organism*
rickettsial 34.21 *living*
rickety 245.13 *dilapidated;* 260.23 *diseased;* 231.1 *imperfect;* 254.2 *unsafe;* 337.8 *weak*
ricky-tick 124.4 *trivial*
ricochet 761.6 *reverse;* 761.1 *reversion*
rictus 234.2 *facial distortion;* 327.8 *spasm*
rid 608.10 *save*
riddance 390.2 *deliverance;* 767.1 *disposal;* 128.2 *ejection;* 389.1 *escape;* 766.1 *loss;* 255.2 *purification*
riddle 330.29; 737.4 *brain-teaser;* 256.10 *cleaning object;* 705.4 *difficult question;* 479.5 *equivocalness;* 438.3 *garden tool;* 697.2 *solecism;* 696.12 *unintelligible thing;* 438.10 *use tools*
riddled with holes 308.14 *holed*
riddle-me-ree 737.4 *brain-teaser*
riddle of the sphinx 737.5 *difficult problem*
riddle with holes 308.20 *hole*
riddling 705.13 *problematic*
ride 59.16; 323.10 *sail;* 319.4 *transport*
ride a broomstick 11.21 *bewitch*
ride against 381.1 *attack*
ride and tie 326.8 *oscillate;* 326.18 *to and fro*
ride a thermal 322.10 *fly*
ride a tiger 254.8 *be in danger*
ride a wave 50.18 *windsurf*
ride bareback 59.16 *ride*
ride down 381.9 *attack successfully;* 633.10 *chase*
ride full tilt at 381.1 *attack;* 633.10 *chase*
ride hard 332.4 *be swift*
ride height 61.6 *motor-racing terms*
ride it out 252.9 *be safe*
ride on a rail 371.7 *drive out*
ride out a storm 50.15 *sail*
ride out the storm 323.10 *sail*
rider 211.3 *additional item;* 586.20 *cavalryman;* 59.15 *horse person*
ride roughshod over 396.19 *be authoritarian;* 331.7 *kick;* 660.26 *oppress;* 668.22 *show disrespect;* 647.6 *suppress*
ride shotgun 252.10 *protect*
ride side-saddle 59.16 *ride*
ride the tiger 615.5 *be rash*
ride to hounds 633.11 *hunt*
ridge 43.11 *farmland;* 373.4 *means of connection;* 89.1 *mountain;* 154.4 *mountain range;* 151.6 *narrow place;* 62.5 *rock face;* 68.1 *skiing;* 174.1 *summit;* 31.11 *weather system*
ridged 420.2 *coarse;* 62.8 *mountaineering;* 68.12 *ski*
ridgepole 174.3 *architectural summit*
ridger 43.10 *farm tool*
ridgetree 79.12 *figurative usage*
ridicule 660.29; 668.4; 668.24; 678.6; 678.14; 451.8 *disbelieve;* 659.1 *discourtesy;* 470.3 *exclude;* 720.1 *misinterpret;* 660.8 *rudeness;* 670.23 *show disapproval;* 670.9 *show of disapproval;* 700.28 *trick*
ridiculed 700.36 *deceived;* 670.35 *hissed*
ridiculer 678.9
ridiculing 668.14; 621.5 *derisive;* 720.2 *misinterpretation;* 678.17 *scornful*
ridiculous 272.5; 459.5 *foolish;* 103.1 *impossible;* 697.5 *nonsensical*
ridiculously 272.8; 459.8 *foolishly;* 103.11 *impossibly;* 697.9 *nonsensically*
Ridiculousness 272
ridiculousness 459.1 *folly*
riding 320.9 *animal transport;* 59.6 *horsemanship;* 300.2 *momentum;* 300.16 *moving;* 318.2 *passing along;* 86.5 *state*
riding at anchor 228.9 *stable*
riding boots 551.19 *footwear*
riding breeches 551.9 *trousers*
riding habit 551.3 *formal dress;* 551.6 *skirt*
riding horse 59.4 *saddle horse*
riding jacket 551.11 *jacket*
riding lights 522.6 *electric light*
riding pants 551.9 *trousers*
riding pony 59.5 *pony*
riding school 6.12 *educational institution;* 59.14 *horse-riding terms*
rid of 390.1 *deliver*
rid oneself of 389.6 *elude;* 214.5 *make smaller;* 371.13 *throw away*
riesling 558.9 *wine*
rife 208.9 *ample;* 562.5 *fertile;* 138.17 *widespread*
rifeness 208.3 *profuseness;* 138.4 *widespreadness*
riff 18.13 *melody;* 18.37 *syncopate*
riffle 91.10 *billow;* 90.7 *flow;* 90.6 *river flow;* 91.3 *wave*
riff-raff 675.6 *vulgar herd*
rifle 508.3 *banger;* 330.9, 587.9 *firearm;* 587.11 *guns;* 633.3 *hunting and fishing equipment*
rifle brigade 586.16 *army unit*
rifled bore 587.9 *firearm*
rifle fire 381.15 *firing*
rifleman 586.13 *historical soldiery;* 330.15 *shooter*
rifle practice 585.6 *art of war*
rifle shooting 60.1 *target shooting*
rifle sling 60.3 *hunting equipment*
rift 751.2 *argument;* 146.2 *crack;* 231.7 *defect;* 372.3 *separateness*
rift valley 30.7 *landform*
rig 234.12 *distort the truth;* 551.1 *dress;* 699.26 *falsify;* 551.5 *fancy dress;* 50.3 *parts of a sailing boat;* 702.11 *practise sophistry;* 50.15 *sail;* 373.7 *tackle*
rigadoon 22.4 *historic dancing*
rigged 551.29 *dressed;* 243.18 *prepared*
rigged out 243.18 *prepared*
rigging 699.9 *falsification;* 50.3 *parts of a sailing boat;* 373.7 *tackle*
Right 801
right 575.1; 801.6; 801.7; 801.16; 698.21 *accurate;* 273.8 *accurately;* 396.1 *authority;* 52.14 *combat;* 239.1 *convenient;* 324.9 *directly;* 797.1 *good;* 795.2 *good morals;* 231.1 *imperfect;* 464.9 *judicious;* 16.44 *legal;* 16.28 *legality;* 795.8 *moral;* 12.6 *political party;* 440.1 *property;* 28.78 *quantum;* 393.1 *repair;* 393.13 *repaired;* 169.6 *side;* 178.1 *straight;* 121.1 *superiority;* 698.15 *true*
right! 698.40
right-about 303.13 *about-turn*
right-about-face 303.13 *about-turn;* 303.9 *turn round*
right about-turn 761.1 *reversion*
right amount 217.7 *sufficiency*
right and left 170.8 *round*
right angle 27.39, 176.1 *angle;* 186.3 *vertical thing*
right-angled 176.9 *angled;* 186.10 *perpendicular*
right-angled triangle 176.3 *angled figure;* 27.43 *triangle*
right arm 334.1 *power*
right as a trivet 230.1 *perfect*
right ascension 29.5 *celestial sphere;* 26.4 *size*
right as rain 230.1 *perfect*
right away 293.17 *early;* 262.6 *hastily;* 280.8 *immediately*
right a wrong 801.15 *put right*
right centre three-quarter 64.4 *rugby player*
right Charlie 459.3 *foolish person*
right cross 52.2 *boxing*
right defence 58.4 *ice hockey player*
righteous 797.3 *kind;* 795.8, 801.10 *moral;* 255.12 *morally pure;* 799.5 *pure;* 803.5 *virtuous*
righteously 799.8 *purely;* 255.18, 803.9 *virtuously*
righteousness 801.4; 795.2 *good morals;* 797.10 *kindness;* 799.2 *purity;* 803.1 *virtue*
right field 48.1 *baseball*
right fielder 48.2 *baseball player*
right form 656.5 *etiquette*
rightful 698.19 *authentic;* 396.12 *authoritative;* 801.9 *in the right;* 16.51 *legitimate*
rightful authority 396.1 *authority*
rightfully 698.37 *authentically;* 396.23 *authoritatively;* 801.16 *right*
rightfulness 698.6 *authenticity;* 16.30 *legitimacy*
rightful possession 763.1 *possession*
right half 66.3 *football player*
right hand 334.1 *power;* 169.1 *side*
right-hand 61.10 *racing*
right-handed 492.10 *handed;* 492.5 *toucher*
right-handed hitter 48.2 *baseball player*
right-handedness 492.7 *sense organ*
right-hand entry 783.3 *deposit*
right-hander 61.6 *motor-racing terms*
right-hand kink 61.6 *motor-racing terms*
right-hand man 398.4 *deputy;* 392.11, 608.5 *helper;* 401.5 *office assistant;* 289.7, 387.3 *subordinate*
right-hand side 169.3 *side direction*
right honourable 575.6 *worshipful*
right hook 52.2 *boxing*
right idea 484.3 *expedient plan*
righting 807.4 *atoning*
righting wrong 801.5
right in the head 460.4 *sane*
rightism 225.2 *conservatism*
rightist 225.8 *conservative;* 12.6 *political party*
right itself 393.6 *cure*
rightly 698.39 *accurately;* 16.81 *legally;* 801.16 *right*
rightly served 385.5 *retaliatory*
right-minded 801.11; 795.8 *moral*
right moment 275.11 *date;* 287.1 *timeliness*
right mood 636.9 *goodwill*
rightness 698.8 *accuracy;* 801.1 *fairness;* 797.8 *good;* 698.1 *truth*
right now 282.9 *at present;* 262.8 *hurry up!;* 280.8 *immediately*
righto 698.40 *right!*
right of choice 469.6 *selection*
right of entry 314.4
right of possession 763.1 *possession*
right of purchase 777.7 *purchasing*
right of representation 469.11 *franchise*
right of way 318.4 *access;* 317.2 *route*
right-on 656.7 *dressed-up*
right oneself 119.11 *equalize*
right qualities 217.7 *sufficiency*
rights 250.2 *free speech*
right side 169.3 *side direction*
right stick 58.3 *ice hockey*
rights under law 228.4 *stable thing*
right time 239.3 *convenience;* 275.11 *date;* 222.2 *occurrence;* 287.1 *timeliness;* 275.7 *time measurement*
right time and place 239.3 *convenience*
right to a hair 698.39 *accurately*
right to an inch 698.39 *accurately*
right to a T 698.39 *accurately*
right to a turn 698.39 *accurately*
right to bear arms 250.2 *free speech*
right to left 326.18 *to and fro*
right-to-work law 15.5 *labour law*
right triangle 27.43 *triangle*
right up one's alley 239.1 *convenient*
right up one's street 239.1 *convenient*
right uppercut 52.2 *boxing;* 331.14 *sporting hit*
rightward 324.10 *clockwise*
right wing 58.4 *ice hockey player;* 58.6 *lacrosse player*
right-wing 225.8 *conservative*
right-winger 225.3 *conservative person;* 12.6 *political party*
right-wing politics 225.2 *conservatism*
right wing three-quarter 64.4 *rugby player*
right you are 698.40 *right!*
rigid 424.1 *brittle;* 416.6 *dense;* 656.6 *formal;* 423.3 *hard;* 383.11 *obstinate;* 698.24 *pedantic;* 225.7 *permanent;* 647.8 *severe;* 178.1 *straight;* 418.2 *tough;* 641.3 *unyielding*
rigid control 36.19 *defence mechanism*
rigidity 273.1 *accuracy;* 418.5 *hardness;* 301.1 *motionlessness;* 383.2 *obstinacy;* 698.11 *pedantry;* 225.1 *permanence;* 647.1 *severity*
rigidly 416.10 *densely;* 656.12 *formally;* 424.5 *fragilely;* 225.9 *permanently;* 383.14 *resistingly;* 647.11 *severely;* 418.12, 423.12 *toughly*

rigidness 424.2 *brittleness*; 656.1 *formality*; 418.5 *hardness*; 423.6 *toughness*
rigid with fear 612.7 *frightened*
rigmarole 270.1 *diffuseness*
Rigoberta Menchu 589.4 *Nobel Peace Prize*
rigor 327.7 *shake*
rigorism 641.7 *opinionatedness*
rigorist 641.8 *obstinate person*
rigor mortis 582.8 *after death*
rigorous 273.5, 698.21 *accurate*; 698.24 *pedantic*; 647.8 *severe*
rigorously 698.38 *literally*; 647.11 *severely*
rigorousness 273.1, 698.8 *accuracy*; 698.11 *pedantry*; 647.1 *severity*
rigorous proof 27.66 *proof*
rigour 273.1, 698.8 *accuracy*; 418.5 *hardness*; 698.11 *pedantry*; 27.64 *reasoning*; 647.1 *severity*
rigout 551.1 *dress*
rig out 551.33 *dress up*; 243.5 *equip*; 551.35 *make clothing*
rig the market 776.2 *speculate*
Rigveda 10.8 *hymn*; 7.12 *religious text*
rile 327.22 *agitate*; 258.11 *dirty*; 625.8 *make irascible*; 624.9 *offend*
riled 625.4 *irascible*; 624.15 *resentful*
rill 90.1 *river*
rille 29.17 *moon*
rillet 90.1 *river*
rillettes 25.45 *French dish*
rim 49.3 *basketball equipment*; 164.5 *border*; 163.3, 164.1 *edge*; 131.7 *limit*
rimaye 62.5 *rock face*
rime 31.36 *frost*; 494.5 *ice*
rimose 146.7 *cracked*; 184.6 *wrinkly*
rimosely 184.12 *doubly*
rind 550.13 *casing*; 171.1 *exterior*; 80.3 *fruit structure*
rinderpest 260.18 *veterinary disease*
rind, pips, and all 232.9 *completely*; 204.5 *unit*; 204.11 *wholly*
ring **306.7**; **509.12**; **510.10**; 27.23 *algebra*; 507.8 *be loud*; 27.42, 179.2 *circle*; 179.3 *circular thing*; 711.2 *danger signal*; 373.8 *fastening*; 570.6 *general terms*; 376.11 *group*; 542.7 *jewellery*; 40.15 *network*; 542.12 *ornament*; 27.21 *set*; 18.38 *sound*; 45.2 *sportsground*; 692.32 *telephone*
ring a bell 462.13 *remind*
ring closure 32.14 *chemical reaction*
ring down the curtain 131.16 *cease*; 582.15 *die*; 226.7 *stop working*
ringer 699.19 *cheat*; 700.15 *deceiver*; 59.7 *horseracing*; 525.5 *impression*; 72.20 *ornithologist*; 762.2 *substitute person*; 198.5 *twin*
ring false 699.20 *be false*
ring finger 492.7 *sense organ*
ring in 129.19 *forecast*; 312.5 *get in*
ringing **509.5**; **510.2**; **510.7**; 507.6 *loud*; 542.10 *ornate*; 72.19 *ornithology*; 742.16 *signalling*
ringing gold 780.1 *money*
ringing in the ears 504.8 *something heard*
ringing off 226.2 *stop*
ringing round 165.1 *enclosure*
ringing tones 507.1 *loudness*
ringing true 698.25 *lifelike*
ringing-up 211.2 *mathematical addition*
ring in the ear 507.8 *be loud*; 510.10 *ring*
ringleader 662.8 *agitator*; 579.14 *leader*; 480.14, 483.7 *motivator*
ringlet 180.2 *coil*
ringlike 27.81 *curvilinear*
ring main 39.34 *power supply*
ringmaster 21.31 *circus performer*; 579.14 *leader*; 21.27 *producer*
ring nebula 29.8 *interstellar medium*
ring-necked pheasant 60.5 *game*
ring off 226.6 *cease*; 692.32 *telephone*
ring of invisibility 11.6 *talisman*
ring of truth 698.12 *realism*
ring opening 32.14 *chemical reaction*
ring-ring 509.5 *ringing*
ringroad **306.5**; 317.3 *road*
rings 57.3 *gymnastic apparatus*
ring-shaped 179.5 *circular*; 27.81 *curvilinear*
ringside seat 147.5 *near place*; 518.9 *viewpoint*
ring spot 44.12 *pests and diseases*; 79.10 *tree disease*
ring the bell 246.8 *be effective*; 246.6 *be successful*; 711.7 *raise the alarm*
ring the changes 227.11 *be changeable*; 114.8 *be diverse*; 224.8 *cause change*
ring the church bells 742.12 *signal*
ring tone 692.11 *dialling*
ring true 698.33 *seem lifelike*
ringworm 83.5 *fungal association*; 260.13 *skin disease*
rink 51.1 *green bowling*; 58.3 *ice hockey*
rinky-dink 124.4 *trivial*
rinse 256.14 *bathe*; 433.34 *hose*; 433.11 *wash*
rinsing 256.5 *ablutions*; 433.11 *wash*
Rio de Janeiro 87.6 *other cities*
Rio Grande 90.3 *US rivers*
rioja 558.9 *wine*
riot 217.5 *about*; 662.15 *be disobedient*; 408.26 *be disorderly*; 219.4 *be excessive*; 380.7 *be violent*; 753.8 *cause mischief*; 328.5 *commotion*; 408.9, 753.2 *disorder*; 219.1 *excess*; 562.1 *fertility*; 380.3 *instance of violence*; 16.41 *lawlessness*; 217.8 *plenty*; 662.2 *violation of the law*
rioter 662.10 *seditionist*; 408.11 *troublemaker*
rioting 753.2 *disorder*; 16.41 *lawlessness*; 662.2 *violation of the law*
riot of colour 529.2 *colourfulness*; 541.1 *variegation*
riotous 588.6 *anarchic*; 662.13 *disobedient*; 408.20 *disorderly*; 686.7 *dissipated*; 219.6 *excessive*; 753.10 *lawbreaking*; 16.61 *lawless*; 217.2 *plentiful*; 380.6 *violent*
riotous living 686.2 *dissipation*
riotously **408.29**; 662.17 *disobediently*; 16.84 *lawlessly*
riot policeman 252.3 *protector*
rip 23.17 *carpenter*; 372.9 *separate*; 372.3 *separateness*
rip along 332.4 *be swift*
ripcord 373.6 *line*
ripe 556.11 *adult*; 243.20 *developed*; 80.9 *of a fruit*; 296.11 *old*; 230.1 *perfect*
ripe for marriage 570.22 *marriageable*
ripely 556.16 *maturely*; 296.18 *venerably*
ripen 556.17 *age*; 760.8 *be transformed*; 243.7 *develop*; 80.10 *fruit*; 244.2 *get better*; 556.18 *mature*; 230.5 *perfect*; 419.13 *soften*
ripened 243.20 *developed*; 230.1 *perfect*
ripeness 556.2 *adulthood*; 570.4 *marriageability*; 556.4 *middle age*; 230.3 *perfection*; 243.14 *preparedness*; 287.1 *timeliness*
ripening 243.13 *development*
ripen into 760.7 *convert into*
ripe old age 259.3 *health*; 556.5 *old age*; 296.1 *oldness*
rip off 699.25, 700.30 *be fraudulent*; 526.3 *cause to disappear*; 13.12 *cheat*; 792.10 *overcharge*; 773.10 *take away*; 700.28 *trick*
rip-off 125.2 *copy*; 774.7 *dishonesty*; 792.4 *extortion*; 790.3 *fee*; 699.8, 700.10 *fraud*; 699.35 *fraudulent*; 777.6 *purchase*; 774.17 *stolen*; 774.4 *stolen goods*; 773.12 *taking*; 773.3 *taking away*; 700.8 *trick*
rip-off artist 792.5 *overcharger*
riposte 706.1, 706.17 *answer*; 704.3 *countercharge*; 54.5 *fence*; 54.3 *fencing movements*; 384.24 *parry*; 385.3 *retaliate*; 385.1 *retaliation*
rip out 369.16 *extort*; 369.11 *extract*; 144.15 *remove*; 212.3 *subtract*
ripped 144.9 *removed*
ripping 369.6 *extorsion*; 235.1 *worthy*
ripping out 369.1 *extraction*; 144.2 *removal*
ripple 327.21 *be agitated*; 420.11 *be rough*; 91.10 *billow*; 420.9 *broken water*; 90.7 *flow*; 61.6 *motor-racing terms*; 184.3, 184.10 *pleat*; 90.6 *river flow*; 28.14 *sound wave*; 91.3 *wave*
ripple bed 394.14 *hospital*
rippled 420.1 *rough*
rippled lake 184.4 *wrinkled thing*
rippling 90.10 *fluvial*; 420.1 *rough*
ripplingly 184.12 *doubly*
ripply 90.10 *fluvial*; 420.1 *rough*
rip saw 23.11 *woodworking tool*
riptide 91.2 *tide*
Rip van Winkle 343.11 *sleeper*
rise **154.16**; 302.12 *advance*; 525.1 *appearance*; 366.5 *arise*; 304.13 *ascend*; 304.1 *ascent*; 765.2 *augmentation*; 342.12 *be active*; 190.6 *become bigger*; 525.12 *become visible*; 300.13 *be in motion*; 415.9 *be light*; 186.5 *be vertical*; 91.10 *billow*; 244.2 *get better*; 585.12 *go to war*; 154.1 *height*; 244.5 *improvement*; 213.4 *increase*; 483.5 *positive stimulus*; 302.3 *press on*; 213.2 *spread*; 667.19 *take off one's hat to*; 89.9 *tower*; 91.3 *wave*
rise above 121.8 *be superior*; 329.3 *exceed*; 89.9 *tower*
rise above oneself 473.7 *be unselfish*
rise above one's station 660.28 *get above oneself*
rise above temptation 803.8 *be virtuous*
rise and fall 91.10 *billow*
rise and shine 342.12 *be active*
rise and shine! **342.23**
rise early 342.13 *be busy*
rise from the dead 393.4 *be restored*
rise higher 302.3 *press on*
rise in arms 662.16 *be subversive*
rise in price 765.10 *augment*; 792.9 *be dear*; 213.4 *increase*
rise in the world 248.5 *be prosperous*; 246.6 *be successful*; 244.2 *get better*
riser 304.10 *step*
rise to a maximum 213.4 *increase*
rise to a peak 121.8 *be superior*; 213.4 *increase*
rise to fame 248.5 *be prosperous*
rise to one's feet 186.5 *be vertical*; 304.16 *stand up*; 667.19 *take off one's hat to*
rise to the occasion 706.22 *be the answer*; 638.8 *brace oneself*; 478.3 *improvise*; 246.7 *overcome obstacles*; 217.4 *suffice*; 342.15 *try*
rise up 366.5 *arise*; 304.13 *ascend*; 186.5 *be vertical*; 383.16 *fight on!*; 168.7 *rear up*; 383.8 *revolt*; 154.16 *rise*
rishi 7.8 *priest*
risible 599.9 *funny*; 272.5 *ridiculous*
rising **304.23**; 300.7 *ascending motion*; 304.1 *ascent*; 792.7 *dear*; 300.17 *directional*; 14.6 *financial*; 190.8 *growing*; 190.1 *growth*; 154.9 *high*; 244.14 *improved*; 667.11 *in a respectful stance*; 395.11 *influential*; 186.2 *making vertical*; 248.8 *prosperous*; 246.13 *successful*
rising air 304.2 *upturn*
rising current 304.2 *upturn*
rising damp 429.4 *seepage*
rising exchange rate 14.1, 780.7 *finance*
rising from the dead 393.10 *revival*
rising ground 154.2 *heights*; 304.2 *upturn*
rising of the curtain 21.8 *scene*
rising pressure 31.6 *weather data*
rising price 213.3 *increasing thing*; 792.3 *inflationary price*
rising river 254.6 *danger signal*; 711.1 *warning*
rising star 246.4 *successful person*
rising tide 213.3 *increasing thing*; 91.2 *tide*
rising up 168.3 *rearing up*
rising water 379.1 *trap*
risk **453.22**; 107.1 *chance*; 254.5 *danger*; 705.20 *doubt*; 254.10 *endanger*; 448.1 *experiment*; 254.9 *face danger*; 236.11 *harmfulness*; 448.13 *invent*; 14.5 *invest*; 448.4 *originality*; 705.7 *questionableness*; 615.2 *rash move*; 776.2 *speculate*; 107.12 *take a chance*; 104.10 *think likely*; 453.15 *unreliability*
risked 448.10 *tested*
risk-free 252.6 *safe*
riskily 254.11 *dangerously*; 448.15 *inventively*; 705.24 *questionably*; 453.26 *unreliably*
riskiness 254.5 *danger*; 705.7 *questionableness*
risk it 107.12 *take a chance*
risk-taking 107.7 *calculation of chance*; 615.4 *rash*
risky 107.8 *chance*; 254.1 *dangerous*; 236.5 *harmful*; 448.9 *original*; 776.15 *profitable*; 705.14 *questionable*; 453.7 *unreliable*; 254.2 *unsafe*
risky venture 254.5 *danger*
Risorgimento 3.10 *past age*
risotto 25.47 *Italian dish*
risqué 712.8 *cursing*; 539.4, 796.12 *indecent*; 258.9 *obscene*
rissole 25.32 *meat dish*
rissoles 25.20 *meat*
ritardando 333.17 *in slow motion*
rite 601.3 *ceremony*; 632.4 *custom*; 656.3 *formal occasion*; 16.34 *legal formality*; 10.1 *ritual*; 1.8 *tradition*
ritenuto 333.17 *in slow motion*
rite of passage 601.3 *ceremony*; 656.3 *formal occasion*; 370.3 *introduction*
rite of spring 10.7 *non-Christian ritual*
rite of worship **10.3**
rites 658.3 *courtesies*
Ritual 10
ritual **10.1**; 601.12 *ceremonial*; 656.8 *ceremonious*; 601.3 *ceremony*; 632.4 *custom*; 160.11, 656.6 *formal*; 160.5 *formality*; 656.3 *formal occasion*; 632.11 *normal*; 1.8 *tradition*
ritual act 10.5 *Christian rite*
ritual dance 22.4 *historic dancing*
ritual drama 21.10 *theatre movements*
ritualism **10.2**; 656.2 *formalism*; 7.2 *religiousness*
ritualistic **10.21**; 656.8 *ceremonious*; 160.11 *formal*; 7.15 *religious*
ritualistically 10.23 *ritually*
rituality 10.2 *ritualism*
ritualization 10.2 *ritualism*
ritualize 656.9 *formalize*; 10.18 *perform rites*
ritual killing **382.6**; 382.1 *killing*
ritually **10.23**; 160.14 *conventionally*; 656.12 *formally*; 1.18 *societally*
ritually clean 256.16 *clean*; 255.14 *purified*
ritually prepared 256.16 *clean*
ritual mutilation 10.7 *non-Christian ritual*
ritual observance 601.3 *ceremony*
ritual practice 10.1 *ritual*
ritual prostitution 10.7 *non-Christian ritual*
rituals 658.3 *courtesies*
ritzy 792.7 *dear*; 656.7 *dressed-up*; 781.3 *opulent*
ritzy price 792.1 *high price*
rival **629.3**; 235.9 *be worthy*; 113.12 *competitor*; 113.19 *confront*; 113.24 *discordant*; 629.4 *jealous*
rival in love 629.3 *rival*
rivalry 113.5 *conflict*; 629.1 *jealousy*
rive 146.5 *crack*; 372.9 *separate*
riven 372.16 *apart*; 146.7 *cracked*
river **90.1**; 166.4 *boundary marker*; 317.11 *channel*; 67.7 *swimming pool*; 319.5 *transportable*; 323.2 *waterway*
river bed 175.1 *base*
river blindness 519.1 *blindness*; 75.11 *helminthic disease*; 260.7 *tropical disease*
river crossing 90.2 *channel*
river engineering 38.17 *civil engineering*
river erosion 30.35 *weathering*
river flow **90.6**
river fog 31.33 *fog*
River Ganges 10.13 *shrine*
River Godavari 10.13 *shrine*
riverhead 90.2 *channel*
river horse 71.14 *pachyderm*
riverine 30.52 *coastal*
river island 92.2 *island*
River Kistna 10.13 *shrine*
River Narbada 10.13 *shrine*
river network 30.8 *drainage*
river of time 277.2 *time*
Rivers 90
riverscape 19.10 *art subject*
river's end 90.2 *channel*
riverside 90.2 *channel*; 164.1 *edge*; 164.8 *edging*
river's mouth 90.2 *channel*
river system 90.1 *river*
river travel 323.1 *water travel*
rivet 373.11 *connect*; 373.8 *fastening*; 38.27 *superstructure*
riveted 373.15 *connected*
rivulet 90.1 *river*
riyal 780.11 *national coins*
RNA 34.9 *cell nucleus*; 34.13 *genetic material*; 33.10 *nucleoside*
roach 55.5 *British game fish*; 691.6 *drug*; 76.1 *insect*; 215.1 *remainder*
road **317.3**; **320.2**; **373.5**; 318.4 *access*; 318.2 *passing along*; 317.2 *route*; 38.19 *structure*; 319.1 *transport*; 319.5 *transportable*
roadbed 321.3 *rail*; 317.10 *railway*
roadblock 384.9 *barrier*; 309.4 *closed place*; 481.6 *dissuasion*; 378.2 *obstacle*
roadbook 693.5 *reference book*
road bridge 38.21 *bridge*
road circuit 61.6 *motor-racing terms*
road fatality 582.5 *ways of dying*
road-fund licence 320.21 *miscellaneous motoring terms*
road haulage 320.15 *motor transport*

road hog 683.3 *selfish person*
roadholding 320.21 *miscellaneous motoring terms*
road junction 193.5 *crossroads*
roadman 578.1 *worker*
road map 163.4, 484.5, 717.7 *map*; 693.5 *reference book*
road metal 317.4 *road surface*
road name 733.5 *place of residence*
road patrol 318.7 *traffic controller*
road race 61.1 *motor racing*
road-race 61.9 *race*
road racing 61.1 *motor racing*
road rage 320.21 *miscellaneous motoring terms*
road report 31.4 *weather forecast*
roadrunner 332.12 *swift animal*
road show 21.7 *show*
roadside 164.1 *edge*; 164.8 *edging*; 147.9 *near*
roadside café 557.15 *eating place*
roadsign 742.5 *indicator*; 742.1 *sign*
roadster 320.12 *bicycle*; 320.16 *car*; 59.4 *saddle horse*
road surface 317.4; 550.11 *paving*
roadsweeper 256.10 *cleaning object*
road system 320.2 *road*
road tax 320.21 *miscellaneous motoring terms*
road test 320.21 *miscellaneous motoring terms*; 448.2 *rehearsal*
road-test 448.12 *rehearse*
road to hell 804.8 *wicked place*
road to ruin 254.5 *danger*; 357.4 *ruin*
Road Transport 320
road transport 320.1; 316.5 *means of transport*; 320.15 *motor transport*
road transportation 320.1 *road transport*
road tunnel 38.22 *tunnel*
roadway 317.3 *road*
road worker 578.1 *worker*
roadworthy 316.17 *transferable*; 319.5 *transportable*
roam 100.14 *be foreign*; 250.16 *be independent*; 300.15 *walk*
roaming 100.10 *foreign*
roan 534.1 *brown*; 59.1 *horse*; 541.10 *mottled*
roar 342.12 *be active*; 507.8 *be loud*; 380.7 *be violent*; 31.58 *blow*; 514.1, 515.4 *cry*; 514.10 *cry out*; 726.6 *emphasize*; 599.14 *laugh*; 507.2 *outcry*; 21.35 *overact*; 729.12 *speak loudly*
roaring 624.4 *anger*; 624.16 *angry*; 515.1 *animal cry*; 507.2 *outcry*; 380.6 *violent*; 514.16 *vociferous*
roaring drunk 690.1 *drunk*
roaring forties 86.2 *geographical region*; 31.17 *wind system*
roaring success 246.1 *success*
roaring trade 248.1 *prosperity*
roar one's approval 669.16 *acclaim*
roast 428.19 *bake*; 493.14 *be hot*; 25.55 *cook*; 25.32 *meat dish*; 668.24 *ridicule*
roast alive 382.17 *murder*
roast beef 25.44 *British dish*
roast-beef sandwich 25.11 *sandwich*
roasted 25.56 *culinary*; 493.13 *heated*
roaster 43.8 *livestock*; 410.15 *pot*
roasting 670.8 *berating*; 25.8 *cooking technique*; 493.9 *hot*
roasting pan 25.6 *kitchen equipment*
roasting tin 410.15 *pot*
rob 800.10 *be criminal*; 662.15 *be disobedient*; 586.38 *conquer*; 782.14 *impoverish*; 766.9 *lose*; 806.10 *sin*; 774.12 *steal*; 608.14 *take away*; 337.7 *weaken*
rob a bank 774.12 *steal*
rob a grave 774.14 *plunder*
rob a train 774.12 *steal*
robbed 782.2 *insolvent*
robber 386.4 *coercive person*; 662.9 *criminal*; 798.6 *evil person*; 765.7 *gainer*; 16.40 *lawbreaker*; 586.6 *militarist*; 773.6 *taker*; 774.8 *thief*; 804.9 *wicked person*
robber crab 75.4 *arthropod*
robbers' lair 804.8 *wicked place*
robbery 16.39 *crime*; 804.7 *criminality*; 766.1 *loss*; 774.1 *stealing*; 774.3 *theft*; 662.2 *violation of the law*
robbery with violence 774.1 *stealing*
robbing 774.1 *stealing*
robbing the till 774.1 *stealing*
robe 551.16; 550.5 *body covering*; 551.32 *dress*; 657.6 *informal dress*
robed 263.4 *at ease*; 551.29 *dressed*; 550.37 *protected*
robe-de-chambre 551.16 *robe*
Robert Helpmann 22.14 *famous ballet dancers*
robes 656.4 *formal dress*; 7.11 *vestment*
robes of office 743.4 *insignia*
Robin Hood 774.8 *thief*
robin redbreast 535.7 *red thing*
robin's-egg blue 539.1 *blue*
Robinson Crusoe 655.6 *unsocial person*
Robinson Crusoe and Friday 569.7 *famous friendships*
rob of freedom 387.6 *subject*
rob of life 382.16 *kill*
roborant 394.7 *tonic*
robot 112.8 *creature of habit*; 566.8 *humanlike machine*; 717.6 *image*; 438.5 *machine*; 489.5 *unfeeling person*
robot dancing 22.1 *dancing*
robotic 438.9 *mechanical*; 40.21 *on-line*; 356.11 *productive*
robotically 40.22 *on-line*
robotics 40.17 *artificial intelligence*; 40.1 *computing*; 22.1 *dancing*; 356.2 *manufacture*; 438.6 *mechanics*
rob the till 774.12 *steal*
robust 259.1 *healthy*; 336.9 *physically strong*; 423.4 *powerful*; 338.4 *vigorous*
robust health 259.3 *health*
robustly 423.13 *powerfully*; 336.14 *strongly*
robustness 259.3 *health*; 423.8 *physical strength*; 338.1 *vigour*
roc 72.9 *fabulous bird*; 70.7 *legendary beast*
roche moutonnée 154.3 *mountain*
rock 30.28; **326.4**; **326.11**; 49.3 *basketball equipment*; 227.11 *be changeable*; 120.5 *be unequal*; 22.15 *dance*; 691.6 *drug*; 638.16 *fortitude*; 418.1 *hard*; 418.7 *hard substance*; 685.4 *moderate*; 327.25 *pitch*; 18.9 *popular music*; 252.5 *refuge*; 460.3 *sane person*; 30.27 *sediment*; 416.4 *solid body*; 228.4 *stable thing*; 327.11 *stagger*; 18.37 *syncopate*; 379.1 *trap*
rock and roll 22.2, 22.15 *dance*
rockback 47.2 *field events*
rock band 18.26 *musical group*
rock bottom 175.1 *base*; 122.5 *inferior state*; 195.4 *zero level*
rock-bottom 175.3 *base*; 793.9 *cheap*; 156.10 *deeper*
rock-bottom price 793.1 *cheapness*
rockbound 420.2 *coarse*
rock-carving 19.12 *sculpture*
rock-climb 62.9 *mountaineer*
rock climber 304.11 *ascender*; 62.7, 89.3 *mountaineer*
rock climbing 89.1 *mountain*; 62.1 *mountaineering*
rock crusher 815.5 *prisoner*; 427.11 *pulverizer*
rock crystal 527.9 *glass*
rock division 30.41 *geological time*
Rockefeller 781.10 *wealthy person*
rocker 320.14 *cyclist*; 68.6 *ice-skating*; 326.7 *oscillator*; 50.7 *windsurfing*
rockery 44.3 *ornamental garden*
rocket 304.11 *ascender*; 792.9 *be dear*; 670.7 *blame*; 606.2 *expression of dissatisfaction*; 522.8 *fire*; 213.4 *increase*; 330.8 *missile*; 587.5 *missile weapon*; 742.4 *signal*; 332.11 *swift thing*; 304.19 *take off*
rocket bomb 587.16 *bomb*
rocket engine 38.11 *engine*
rocket fuel 330.13 *fuel*; 437.3 *gas*
rocketing 792.7 *dear*; 304.23 *rising*
rocketing up 304.4 *taking off*
rocket-launcher 587.5 *missile weapon*
rocket man 141.10 *spaceman*
rocket pilot 141.10 *spaceman*
rocket propulsion 330.2 *method of propulsion*; 29.35 *rocketry*
rocketry 29.35; 587.2 *arms*
rocket site 587.5 *missile weapon*
rock face 62.5
rock fall 30.26 *mass movement*
rock formation 30.28 *rock*
rock-forming mineral 30.34 *mineral*; 30.28 *rock*
rock garden 44.2 *garden*
rock group 374.3 *assembly*; 376.12 *team*
rock-hard 418.1, 423.3 *hard*; 638.3 *strong-willed*
Rockies 154.4 *mountain range*
rockily 92.13 *continentally*
rockiness 227.1 *changeableness*; 418.5 *hardness*
rocking 326.16; 120.3 *unequal*; 23.14 *wooden*
rocking chair 23.2 *chair*; 326.7 *oscillator*
rocking stone 326.7 *oscillator*
rocklike 418.1 *hard*; 225.7 *permanent*; 228.9 *stable*
rock mechanics 38.17 *civil engineering*
rock 'n' roll 18.9 *popular music*
Rock of Ages 252.5 *refuge*
Rock of Gibraltar 252.5 *refuge*; 228.5 *stable person*
rock opera 21.4 *musical drama*
rock painting 19.8 *painting*
rock plant 44.9 *garden plant*
rocks 182.2 *bulge*; 561.8 *organs of reproduction*
rocks ahead 254.6 *danger signal*
rock salmon 25.18 *sea fish*
rock-solid 418.2 *tough*
rock-steady 225.7 *permanent*
rock the boat 118.18 *not conform*
rock to sleep 685.4 *moderate*
rock tripe 84.6 *lichen*
rockumentary 21.2 *play*
rocky 227.13 *changeable*; 420.2 *coarse*; 92.11 *continental*; 30.58 *earthy*; 418.1 *hard*
rocky coast 92.4 *coast*
Rocky Mountains 89.4 *US mountains*
rococo 23.7 *furniture style*; 19.29 *realist*
rod 181.4 *cylinder*; 518.2 *eye*; 587.9 *firearm*; 480.8 *incentive*; 814.14 *instrument of punishment*; 38.8 *machine element*; 151.8 *narrow thing*
rod and line 633.3 *hunting and fishing equipment*
rod and reel 633.3 *hunting and fishing equipment*
rod and tackle 633.3 *hunting and fishing equipment*
rod brake 320.11 *bicycle part*
rodent 71.12 *gnawing mammal*
Rodentia 71.12 *gnawing mammal*
rodentian 71.30 *rodent-like*
rodenticide 382.13 *animal killer*; 43.14 *pest control*
rodent-like 71.30
rodent operative 71.24 *hunter*
rodeo 59.12; 376.2 *herding*; 21.7 *show*
Rodeo Drive 551.2 *dressing*
rodeo rider 59.15 *horse person*
Rod Laver 63.7 *famous tennis players*
rod of empire 12.3 *governance*
rodomontade 733.1 *address*; 542.2 *affectation*
rod-shaped 27.83 *spherical*
roe 74.5 *fish anatomy*
roebuck 71.17 *male mammal*
rogallo 322.8 *aircraft*
rogan josh 25.49 *Indian dish*
rogate 10.20 *pray*
rogation 10.9 *prayer*
roger 561.14 *have sex*
Rogerian therapy 36.3 *psychiatric treatment*
rogering 593.5 *desire*
Rogers' process scale 36.5 *psychological test*
Roget's Thesaurus 5.28 *dictionary*
rogue 700.15 *deceiver*; 800.4 *dishonourable person*; 812.2 *disreputable character*; 651.8 *malefactor*; 804.9 *wicked person*
roguery 804.1 *wickedness*
rogues' gallery 41.4 *portrait*
rogue wave 91.3 *wave*
roguish 804.11 *wicked*
roil 327.22 *agitate*; 258.11 *dirty*; 328.8 *disarrange*; 307.10 *swirl*; 327.3 *turbulence*
roiled 328.13 *disarranged*
roister 408.26 *be disorderly*; 600.5 *rejoice*
roisterer 600.4 *rejoicer*
roistering 600.1 *rejoicing*
role 21.23; 205.9 *participation*; 221.1 *state*
role model 631.1 *conduct*
role-play 717.10 *act*
role-playing 21.22, 717.3 *acting*; 631.1 *conduct*; 36.3 *psychiatric treatment*
role theory 2.2 *sociological research*
roll 307.9; **330.22**; 227.11 *be changeable*; 91.10 *billow*; 376.27 *bundle*; 31.60 *cloud*; 180.6 *convolute*; 325.15 *deviating motion*; 305.12 *drop*; 509.8 *drum*; 509.1 *drumming*; 43.10 *farm tool*; 322.5 *flight*; 184.9 *fold*; 302.10 *forward motion*; 265.19 *go easily*; 302.1 *go forward*; 421.12 *go smoothly*; 220.6 *list of names*; 25.39 *loaf*; 507.1 *loudness*; 187.7 *make horizontal*; 181.11 *make round*; 81.12 *manage grassland*; 148.5, 205.7 *piece*; 327.25 *pitch*; 744.6 *record book*; 307.3 *reel*; 326.4, 326.11 *rock*; 421.11 *smooth*; 327.11 *stagger*; 394.10 *surgical dressing*; 307.10 *swirl*; 300.15 *walk*; 91.3 *wave*; 184.1 *wrinkle*
roll about in 307.10 *swirl*
roll along 307.9 *roll*
roll a sail 50.15 *sail*
roll a slab 24.11 *make ceramics*
rollback 214.1 *decrease*; 303.18 *setback*
roll back 214.5 *make smaller*
rollbook 744.6 *record book*
roll by 275.15 *pass*
roll call 220.6 *list of names*; 721.7 *nomenclature*
roll-caller 5.2 *linguist*
rolled 187.9 *flattened*; 184.7 *folded*; 421.2 *uniform*
rolled into one 197.13 *whole*
rolled out 153.5 *thinned*
rolled ribs 25.22 *beef*
rolled steel 38.25 *construction material*
rolled-up 191.7 *smaller*
roller 181.4 *cylinder*; 187.4 *flattener*; 44.6, 438.3 *garden tool*; 427.11 *pulverizer*; 421.9 *smoother*; 30.14, 91.3 *wave*
roller bandage 373.6 *line*
roller bearing 307.4 *axle*; 38.8 *machine element*
rollerblades 316.5 *means of transport*
roller blind 523.6 *shade*
roller-reefed 50.10 *sailing*
rollers 373.8 *fastening*
roller-skate 421.12 *go smoothly*
roller skates 316.5 *means of transport*
roll film 41.9 *film*
rollick 600.7 *dance*
roll in 217.5 *about*; 219.4 *be excessive*; 765.13 *be profitable*; 310.10 *come together*
rolling 92.11 *continental*; 509.15 *drumming*; 322.5 *flight*; 89.7, 154.13 *mountainous*; 323.11 *nautical*; 91.7 *oceanic*; 326.16 *rocking*; 307.11 *rotating*; 327.3 *turbulence*; 327.17 *turbulent*; 307.2 *turning*; 781.1 *wealthy*
rolling friction 28.10 *force*; 365.1 *friction*
rolling in 232.8 *full*
rolling in it 248.8 *prosperous*; 781.1 *wealthy*; 765.17 *well-off*
rolling in money 781.1 *wealthy*
rolling on 302.10 *forward motion*
rolling pin 181.4 *cylinder*; 187.4 *flattener*; 25.6 *kitchen equipment*; 307.6 *rotator*; 421.9 *smoother*
rolling stock 321.6
rolling the jack 51.1 *green bowling*
rolling tobacco 496.7 *tobacco*
roll in money 781.12 *be rich*
roll in the aisles 599.14, 600.8 *laugh*
roll in the dirt 258.10 *be dirty*
rollmop 25.16 *fish dish*; 74.8 *food fish*
Roll of Arms 743.9 *herald*
roll of cloud 31.20 *cloud appearance*
roll on 302.1 *go forward*; 302.6 *march on*; 275.15 *pass*; 134.4 *protract*
roll-on 501.2 *deodorant*; 551.18 *underwear*
roll one's own 197.18 *be one*
roll one's sleeves up 638.9 *undertake*
rollout 46.9 *play*; 46.15 *play offence*
roll out 703.15 *demonstrate*; 187.7 *make horizontal*; 153.16 *make thin*
roll over 367.7 *lean*
roll the jack 51.7 *bowl*
roll-top 23.14 *wooden*
roll-top desk 23.4 *table*
roll up 312.1 *arrive*; 191.6 *become smaller*; 310.10 *come together*; 184.9 *fold*; 181.11 *make round*; 191.5 *make smaller*; 307.9 *roll*; 439.6 *store*
roll up in 551.32 *dress*
roll up one's sleeves 243.8 *prepare oneself*; 576.6 *work*
roll up the blind 522.29 *clarify*
roll-your-own 496.7, 496.11 *tobacco*
roly-poly 25.35 *dessert*; 158.16 *fat*; 158.12 *fat person*
ROM 462.6 *artificial memory*; 40.6 *memory*
Roman 296.14 *historic*; 5.41 *lettered*; 566.4 *modern human*
roman 17.2 *fiction*
roman à clef 17.2, 721.5 *fiction*
Roman alphabet 5.14 *alphabet*
roman à thèse 17.2 *fiction*
Roman balance 414.10 *scales*
Roman candle 522.8 *fire*
Roman Catholic 7.5 *Christian*; 7.16 *denominational*
Romance 5.11 *family of languages*

romance 17.2, 721.5 *fiction*; 477.4 *ideality*; 593.8 *love affair*; 477.6 *reverie*; 697.6 *talk nonsense*
romancer 17.14 *author*; 699.18 *liar*; 477.9 *visionary*
romancing 477.10 *imaginative*
Roman comedy 21.12 *comedy*
Roman eagle 743.6 *national emblem*
Roman Empire 85.3 *dominion*; 3.10 *past age*
Romanesque 296.14 *historic*
roman fleuve 17.2 *fiction*
Roman holiday 382.4 *slaughter*
Roman numeral 194.1 *number*; 27.9 *numeral*
Roman orgy 557.13 *feast*
Roman Republic 3.10 *past age*
romantic 593.20 *amorous*; 17.17 *fictional*; 446.13 *ideal*; 477.10 *imaginative*; 18.32 *instrumental*; 17.16 *literary*; 721.12 *narrative*; 446.9 *person of ideas*; 699.34 *pretending*; 19.29 *realist*; 590.12 *sensitive*; 21.40 *tragic*; 96.11 *unrealistic*; 96.6 *unrealistic person*; 477.9 *visionary*
romantically 21.44 *dramatically*; 446.22, 477.17 *imaginatively*; 593.30 *lovingly*
romantic ballet 22.8 *ballet*
romantic comedy 21.12 *comedy*
romanticism 590.7 *emotionalism*; 446.7 *idealism*; 593.3 *lovingness*; 477.6 *reverie*
romanticist 477.9 *visionary*
romanticization 699.7 *pretence*
romanticize 477.15 *fantasize*; 96.15 *idealize*; 446.15 *imagine*; 721.15 *recount*
romanticized 699.34 *pretending*
romantic lighting 524.1 *dimness*
romantic love **593.2**
romantic music 18.3 *classical music*
romantic novel 740.6 *book publishing*
romantic poet 17.14 *author*
romantic tie 593.8 *love affair*
romantic tragedy 21.11 *tragedy*
romany 11.13 *diviner*
Rome 87.6 *other cities*; 12.5 *political organization*
Romeo 593.9 *lover*; 480.13 *tempter*
Romeo and Juliet 593.10 *lovers*
rompers 551.23 *children's clothes*
romp home 332.6 *accelerate*; 246.10 *defeat heavily*
rondeau 17.7 *poem*; 17.10 *verse form*
rondel 17.7 *poem*
rondure 177.2 *bend*
rood 10.14 *sacred object*
rood screen 10.12 *church*
roof **20.6**; **550.27**; 174.3 *architectural summit*; 154.8 *high thing*; 550.7 *overhead covering*; 62.5 *rock face*; 174.7 *top*
roofed **20.14**; 550.36 *covered*; 565.14 *inhabiting*; 174.6 *topped*
roofed in 550.36 *covered*
roofer 550.17 *coverer*
roof garden 44.2 *garden*
roof in 550.27 *roof*
roofing 550.7 *overhead covering*
roofing material 435.2 *building material*
roofing tile 24.9 *industrial ceramics*
roof ladder 304.9 *ladder*
roof over one's head 565.1 *habitat*
rooftop 174.3 *architectural summit*; 550.7 *overhead covering*
rooftree 79.12 *figurative usage*
rook 69.4 *chess terms*; 654.10 *social animal*; 72.6 *songbird*
rookery 72.14 *nest*
rookie 49.2 *basketball player*; 130.14 *beginner*; 46.2 *football player*; 295.12 *immature*; 6.7 *learner*; 295.8 *new arrival*; 586.8 *soldier*; 486.10 *unskilled person*
Rookie of the Year 48.2 *baseball player*
room **565.7**; 141.6 *available space*; 127.1 *inclusion*; 172.2 *inside*; 146.1 *interval*; 141.5 *reserved space*; 250.5 *scope*; 158.1 *size*; 439.4 *storage*; 565.18 *take up residence*
roomer 564.3 *householder*
roomette 321.6 *rolling stock*
room for improvement 231.5 *imperfection*
room freshener 256.9 *cleaning agent*
roomful 203.3 *container*
roominess 158.2 *bigness*; 150.4 *breadth*; 141.4 *spaciousness*
roommate 569.5 *friend*; 564.3 *householder*; 764.3 *participant*
room overhead 141.6 *available space*
rooms 565.1 *habitat*
room temperature 493.1 *heat*
room to manoeuvre 141.6 *available space*
room to spare 141.6 *available space*
roomy 434.12 *airy*; 158.15, 679.4 *big*; 150.1 *broad*; 141.13 *spacious*
roost 565.13 *lair*; 72.14 *nest*; 263.2 *take it easy*; 565.18 *take up residence*
rooster 43.8 *livestock*; 567.16 *male animal*; 72.10 *male bird*
root **77.7**; 175.1, 175.4 *base*; 27.27 *equation*; 84.6 *lichen*; 228.7 *make stable*; 82.4 *moss plant*; 5.35 *part of speech*; 194.6 *power*; 344.3 *rudiment*; 130.3 *source*; 44.11 *vegetable*; 77.21 *vegetate*; 5.17 *word*; 5.42 *worded*
root and branch 232.9 *completely*; 357.16 *destructively*; 204.11 *wholly*
root aphid 44.12 *pests and diseases*
root beer 558.6 *soft drink*
root canal work 35.4 *dentistry*
root cap 77.7 *root*
root crop 43.12 *crop*
rooted 632.13 *fixed*; 77.19 *of roots*; 296.12 *olden*; 228.10 *stabilized*
rootedness 228.1 *stability*
rooted to the spot 612.7 *frightened*; 301.4 *motionless*; 228.10 *stabilized*; 619.7 *wide-eyed*
rooter 669.8 *admirer*; 514.9 *crier*
root for 669.16 *acclaim*; 514.12 *cheer*; 338.3 *invigorate*; 483.9 *motivate*
root hair 77.7 *root*
rooting out 369.1 *extraction*
rootless 227.13 *changeable*; 144.10 *replaced*; 109.6 *unrelated*
rootlessness 109.1 *unrelatedness*
rootlet 77.7 *root*
rootlike 77.19 *of roots*
rootlike part 77.7 *root*
root mean square 27.17 *multiplication*
root nodule 77.7 *root*
root of all evil 780.2 *cash*
root out 371.10 *exterminate*; 369.11 *extract*; 144.15 *remove*; 212.3 *subtract*
root rot 44.12 *pests and diseases*
roots 80.1 *fruits*
root sign 27.25 *algebraic expression*
rootstock 44.5 *gardening*; 77.7 *root*; 344.3 *rudiment*; 77.5 *stem*
root tuber 77.7 *root*
root up 357.8 *destroy*
root vegetable 80.1 *fruits*; 25.33, 44.11 *vegetable*
rope 62.4 *climbing equipment*; 691.6 *drug*; 382.5 *execution*; 814.16 *instrument of execution*; 373.6 *line*; 435.1 *materials*; 382.2 *murder*; 50.3 *parts of a sailing boat*; 309.11 *restrain*; 309.3 *restrainer*; 252.4 *safety device*; 373.7 *tackle*; 438.1 *tool*; 52.5 *wrestling*
rope and pulley 366.9 *lifter*
rope bridge 38.21, 317.9 *bridge*
rope horse 59.12 *rodeo*
rope ladder 304.9 *ladder*
rope off 62.9 *mountaineer*
rope out 251.8 *restrain*
ropes 52.2 *boxing*
rope's end 814.14 *instrument of punishment*
ropewalker 21.31 *circus performer*
ropiness 430.1 *viscosity*
roping off 62.3 *climbing technique*
ropy 416.7 *condensed*; 236.2 *inferior*; 430.8 *viscous*
roric 429.10 *misty*
Rorschach test 36.5 *psychological test*
rosaceous 77.16 *taxonomic*
rosaniline 535.6 *red pigment*
rosarian 44.13 *horticulturist*
rosarium 44.3 *ornamental garden*
rosary 5.22 *many words*; 10.9 *prayer*
rosary beads 10.14 *sacred object*
Roscius 21.24 *actor*
rose 502.2 *fragrant thing*; 44.6 *garden tool*; 535.7 *red thing*; 433.12 *sprinkler*
rosé 558.9 *wine*
roseate 535.1 *red*
rose bed 44.3 *ornamental garden*
Rose Bowl 46.1 *football*
rose bowl 410.16 *crockery*
rose-coloured 610.14 *cheering*; 535.1 *red*
rose-coloured glasses 610.1 *hope*
rose family 77.3 *seed plant*
rose garden 502.2 *fragrant thing*; 44.2 *garden*
rose grower 44.13 *horticulturist*
rose growing 44.1 *horticulture*
rose madder 535.6 *red pigment*
rosemary 496.5 *herbs*
rose oil 78.8 *flower product*
roseola 260.6 *infection*
rose-pink 535.1 *red*
rose-red 535.1 *red*
rosery 44.3 *ornamental garden*
rose-tinted 610.14 *cheering*
rose-tinted view 610.1 *hope*
rosette 78.9 *figurative usage*; 743.4 *insignia*
rose water 78.8 *flower product*; 502.2 *fragrant thing*; 433.14 *lavender water*; 685.2 *moderator*
rose window 78.9 *figurative usage*; 522.10 *window*
Rosh Chodesh 10.15 *holy day*
Rosh Hashanah 10.15 *holy day*
Rosicrucian 11.14 *occult*; 11.12 *occultist*
Rosicrucianism 11.1 *occultism*
rosily 756.17 *auspiciously*; 535.10 *ruddily*
Rosinante 59.1 *horse*
rosiness 259.3 *health*; 535.5 *redness*
roster 220.6 *list of names*
rostrum 740.7 *publicity*; 21.17 *stage*
rosy 756.14 *auspicious*; 610.14 *cheering*; 259.1 *healthy*; 545.6 *personable*; 248.8 *prosperous*; 535.1 *red*; 535.2 *red-faced*
rosy-cheeked 259.1 *healthy*; 535.2 *red-faced*
rosy cheeks 529.9 *complexion*; 259.3 *health*; 535.7 *red thing*
rosy-fingered dawn 290.1 *morning*
rot 258.10 *be dirty*; 563.7 *be infertile*; 278.4 *be transient*; 236.13 *be worthless*; 245.2 *decay*; 245.9 *dilapidation*; 258.4 *dirt*; 375.3 *disintegrate*; 375.1 *disintegration*; 83.1 *fungus*; 296.17 *grow old*; 245.5 *hurt*; 83.11 *moulder*; 697.1 *nonsense*; 260.15 *ulcer*; 258.2 *uncleanness*
rota 298.2 *cycle*; 220.6 *list of names*; 289.1 *succession*
rotary **307.12**; 300.17 *directional*; 306.9 *orbital*
rotary beater 25.6 *kitchen equipment*
rotary drill 307.6 *rotator*
rotary engine 438.5 *machine*
rotary mower 43.10 *farm tool*; 44.6 *garden tool*
rotary pump 32.20 *surface chemistry*
rotate **307.8**; 298.8 *be cyclic*; 300.13 *be in motion*; 179.6 *circle*; 22.15 *dance*; 90.7 *flow*; 29.37 *observe*; 27.96 *represent*
rotating **307.11**; 298.12 *cyclic*
rotating air mass 31.16 *wind vortex*
Rotation 307
rotation **307.1**; 300.5 *circuition*; 132.6 *continuum*; 298.2 *cycle*; 47.2 *field events*; 29.21 *orbit*; 306.1 *orbital motion*; 162.2 *symmetry operation*; 27.48 *transformation*
rotational 298.12 *cyclic*; 300.17 *directional*; 307.12 *rotary*; 50.13 *windsurfing*
rotational axis 29.21 *orbit*
rotational motion 307.1 *rotation*
rotational period 29.21 *orbit*
rotational sail 50.7 *windsurfing*
rotational symmetry 27.41 *geometric figure*; 162.2 *symmetry operation*
rotation turn 68.4 *skiing technique*
rotative 298.12 *cyclic*; 307.12 *rotary*
rotator **307.6**
rotatory 300.17 *directional*; 306.9 *orbital*; 307.12 *rotary*
rotavate 44.15 *cultivate*; 43.17 *farm*
Rotavator™ 43.10 *farm tool*; 44.6, 438.3 *garden tool*
rot down 375.3 *disintegrate*
rote 632.7 *habituation*
rotgut 690.12 *alcohol*; 558.7 *alcoholic drink*
rotifer 75.6 *worm*
Rotifera 75.6 *worm*
rotisserie 557.15 *eating place*
Rotkohl 25.46 *German dish*
rotor 39.31 *electric motor*; 330.11 *propeller*; 307.6 *rotator*
rotted 375.5 *disintegrated*; 258.8 *unclean*
rotten 44.17 *botanical*; 245.12 *deteriorated*; 337.9 *dilapidated*; 260.23 *diseased*; 800.5 *dishonourable*; 375.5 *disintegrated*; 798.7 *evil*; 83.9 *fungal*; 236.4 *poor*; 503.4 *putrid*; 499.6 *unpalatable*; 804.11 *wicked*
rotten apple 804.10 *bad person*
rotten borough 469.12 *election*
rotten egg 503.2 *something that makes an unpleasant smell*
rotten luck 249.3 *bad fortune*; 107.2 *luck*
rottenness 245.9 *dilapidation*; 798.1 *evil*; 236.10 *poverty*; 296.10 *staleness*; 499.2 *unpalatability*
rotten to the core 809.3 *impenitent*; 236.4 *poor*; 804.11 *wicked*
rotter 804.10 *bad person*
Rotter incomplete sentences blank 36.5 *psychological test*
rotting 260.23 *diseased*; 375.6 *disintegrating*; 375.1 *disintegration*; 503.4 *putrid*; 258.8 *unclean*
rotting vegetables 503.2 *something that makes an unpleasant smell*
rotund 179.5 *circular*; 158.16 *fat*; 181.9 *round*; 152.1 *thick*
rotunda 20.9 *miscellaneous architectural features*
rotundity 179.1 *circularity*; 158.5 *fatness*; 181.1 *roundness*; 152.5 *thickness*
rotundly 179.8 *circularly*; 181.13 *roundly*
rouble 780.11 *national coins*
roué 796.8 *immoral man*; 490.3 *pleasure-seeker*
rouge 529.15 *colour*; 529.9 *complexion*; 547.4 *cosmetics*; 529.16 *make up*; 535.9 *redden*; 535.6 *red pigment*
Rouge Croix 743.9 *herald*
rouged 535.2 *red-faced*
Rouge Dragon 743.9 *herald*
rough **264.11**; **365.11**; **404.8**; **420.1**; 233.5 *be incomplete*; 651.12 *callous*; 586.1 *combatant*; 586.33 *combative*; 133.8 *discontinuous*; 659.5 *discourteous*; 448.8 *experimental*; 56.1 *golf*; 236.5 *harmful*; 513.8 *hoarse*; 233.4 *incomplete*; 233.3 *incomplete thing*; 299.4 *irregular*; 420.12 *make rough*; 651.8 *malefactor*; 484.6 *outline*; 58.9 *play hockey*; 423.4 *powerful*; 243.10 *preparations*; 63.5 *real tennis*; 420.10 *rough idea*; 420.14 *roughly*; 31.48 *stormy*; 425.4 *toothed*; 327.17 *turbulent*; 544.10 *ugly*; 499.6 *unpalatable*; 380.6 *violent*; 380.4 *violent creature*
roughage 43.9 *animal feedstuff*; 557.11 *food content*
rough air 420.6 *roughness*
rough and ready 486.4 *bungled*; 262.3 *hasty*; 231.2 *incomplete*; 420.5 *unfinished*; 237.1 *useful*
rough and tumble 408.9 *disorder*; 262.3 *hasty*
rough approximation 420.10 *rough idea*
rough book 6.14 *school book*
roughcast 420.12 *make rough*; 484.6 *outline*; 420.1 *rough*; 420.7 *rough thing*
rough copy 19.9 *drawing*; 420.10 *rough idea*
rough diamond 646.3 *naive person*
rough draft 19.9 *drawing*; 448.2 *rehearsal*; 717.2 *reproduction*
roughed 58.8 *hockey*
rough edge 420.6 *roughness*
rough-edged 420.2 *coarse*
roughen 404.12 *coarsen*; 420.12 *make rough*
rough endoplasmic reticulum 34.8 *cell organ*
roughened 420.1 *rough*
roughen up 420.12 *make rough*
rough fibre 420.6 *roughness*
rough going 264.3 *difficult task*; 420.6 *roughness*
rough-going 264.11 *rough*
rough-grained 420.2 *coarse*
rough grazing 43.11 *farmland*
rough ground **420.8**; 264.3 *difficult task*; 420.6 *roughness*
rough guess 476.3 *conjecture*
rough hair 420.6 *roughness*
rough handling 631.8 *treatment*; 380.1 *violence*
rough-hew 243.2 *do the groundwork*; 160.7 *form*; 420.12 *make rough*
rough-hewn 233.4 *incomplete*; 420.1 *rough*
roughhouse 380.7 *be violent*; 408.9 *disorder*; 380.3 *instance of violence*
rough idea **420.10**
roughing 58.8 *hockey*; 58.3 *ice hockey*
roughing the kicker 46.13 *penalty*
roughing the passer 46.13 *penalty*
roughly **420.14**; 365.17 *abrasively*; 659.9 *discourteously*; 233.6 *incompletely*; 299.8 *irregularly*; 147.13 *nearly*; 216.11 *on average*; 58.10 *on the field*; 423.13 *powerfully*; 404.15 *texturally*
roughly speaking 216.11 *on average*

rough measure 26.1 measurement
roughneck 651.8 malefactor
Roughness 420
roughness 420.6; 651.3 callousness; 133.1 discontinuity; 659.1 discourtesy; 365.1 friction; 404.2 grain; 513.2 hoarseness; 544.2 impropriety; 233.1 incompleteness; 120.1 inequality; 299.1 irregularity; 496.4 stimulation; 380.1 violence
rough out 420.13 be unfinished; 721.14 describe; 160.7 form; 163.5 outline; 717.11 paint
rough outline 19.9 drawing
rough patch 249.4 time of adversity
rough puff pastry 25.37 pastry
roughride 61.9 race
rough-rider 586.20 cavalryman; 59.15 horse person
roughriding 61.6 motor-racing terms
rough road 420.8 rough ground
rough sea 91.3 wave
rough shooting 60.2 hunting
rough sketch 243.10 preparations
rough skin 420.6 roughness
rough surface 420.6 roughness
rough terrain 264.3 difficult task
rough texture 420.6 roughness
rough the kicker 46.18 be penalized
rough the passer 46.18 be penalized
rough thing 420.7
rough up 404.12 coarsen; 420.12 make rough
rough water 420.6 roughness; 91.3 wave
rough weather 380.5 violent weather
rough working 420.10 rough idea
roulette 69.7 other games
roulette wheel 307.6 rotator
round 170.8; **181.6**; **181.7**; **181.8**; **181.9**; **307.13**; 587.13 ammunition; 508.1 bang; 25.23 beef; 426.10 blunt; 381.20 bout; 52.2 boxing; 179.5, 306.10 circular; 69.2 contest; 132.6 continuum; 177.4 curved; 27.81 curvilinear; 298.2 cycle; 690.13 drink; 543.3 elegant; 119.6 equal; 119.11 equalize; 553.9 fashion; 158.16 fat; 160.7 form; 86.13 locality; 179.7 make circular; 509.6 musical repetition; 194.8 odd; 318.1 passage; 307.3 reel; 112.4 return; 516.2 song; 45.1 sport; 205.3 stage; 304.10 step; 332.1 swift; 152.1 thick; 632.3 way; 181.10 well-rounded; 204.3 whole situation; 52.5 wrestling
roundabout 320.3 carriageway; 179.2 circle; 306.12 circuitously; 270.4 circumlocutory; 318.5 crossing point; 189.5 devious; 479.10 equivocal; 325.21 indirect; 306.9 orbital; 5.43 phrasal; 317.3 road; 170.5 surrounded
round about 325.27 astray; 143.11 geographically; 216.11 on average; 170.8 round; 317.17 via
roundaboutness 306.2 circuitousness
roundabout phrase 270.2 circumlocution; 5.24 phrasing
roundabout way 179.2 circle; 306.5 ringroad; 317.2 route
round a cape 92.12 be marooned
round and about 324.11 in all directions; 170.5 surrounded
round and round 227.15 changeably; 298.16 cyclically; 307.13 round; 326.18 to and fro
round angle 27.39 angle
round-arm blow 331.14 sporting hit
round as a ball 181.9 round
round ball 49.3 basketball equipment
roundboard 50.7 windsurfing
round body 181.2
round down 27.91 add
rounded 20.13 arched; 426.1 blunt; 179.5 circular; 27.81 curvilinear; 510.8 deep; 119.6 equal; 160.9 formed; 5.43 phrasal; 421.2 uniform; 177.5 well-rounded
rounded arch 20.5 arch
rounded out 181.10 well-rounded
rounded phrase 5.24 phrasing
rounded up 376.46 assembled
roundel 17.7 poem
roundelay 17.7 poem; 516.2 song
rounders bat 331.15 ram
round-eyed 619.7 wide-eyed
round-faced 158.16 fat
round here 143.11 geographically
round house 331.14 sporting hit
rounding 306.1 orbital motion
rounding down 27.18 division
rounding out 555.13 maturing
rounding up 27.18 division; 119.3 equalization
roundly 181.13; 179.8 circularly; 177.7 curvedly; 119.13 equitably; 158.20 largely; 426.11 smoothly; 332.14 swiftly
Roundness 181
roundness 181.1; 177.2 bend; 426.5 bluntness; 179.1 circularity; 158.5 fatness; 152.5 thickness
round of ammunition 587.13 ammunition
round of applause 669.5 acclaim; 671.3 recognition
round of drinks 690.13 drink
round off 204.10, 232.4 complete; 131.15 end; 181.11 make round
round-off 57.10 compete in gymnastics; 57.8 floor exercises
round of visits 654.3 meeting
round on 385.3 retaliate; 381.5 strike
round out 182.5 be convex; 555.18 grow; 181.11 make round
round pace 332.8 speed
round-robin 710.1 request; 710.9 requesting
rounds 306.3 orbit; 50.8 punting
round shot 587.14 historical ammunition
roundsman 778.12 wholesaler
round steak 25.23 beef
round sum 780.5 sum
round table 713.2 consultation; 579.7 council; 398.2 representative body
round-table conference 734.4 conference
round-table discussion 746.3 discussion
round the bend 328.16 deranged
round the clock 132.19 continuously; 69.6 darts
round thing 181.3
round trip 179.2 circle; 306.3 orbit; 761.4 return; 181.6 round
roundup 376.30 compilation; 376.2 herding
round up 765.11 acquire; 27.91 add; 119.11 equalize; 376.43 herd; 43.18 practise livestock farming
round upon 712.6 vilify
roundworm 75.6 worm
roup 778.4 sale
rouse 593.25 be loved; 369.15 draw out; 338.3 invigorate; 625.8 make irascible; 483.9 motivate
roused 483.12 motivated
rouse easily 625.6 be irascible
rouse oneself 342.12 be active
rousing 514.17 cheering; 338.5 invigorating; 483.11 motivational; 480.19 persuasive
rousingly 483.14 influentially
rout 247.2 defeat; 246.10 defeat heavily; 377.13 dismiss; 208.4 throng; 327.2 tumult; 246.2 victory
route 317.2; 324.2 bearing; 579.2 direct; 62.1 mountaineering; 318.2 passing along; 320.2 road
routed 247.11 defeated
route map 693.5 reference book
router 23.11 woodworking tool
routine 340.1 action; 216.1 average; 138.5 averageness; 138.21 common; 750.6 convention; 140.6 custom; 140.10 customary; 298.2 cycle; 298.12 cyclic; 160.11 formal; 160.5 formality; 656.3 formal occasion; 407.15, 632.9 habitual; 407.7 method; 112.13 monotonous; 298.4 orderliness; 298.14 orderly; 632.6 procedure; 111.17 regular; 111.6 regularity; 112.3 repetitiveness; 10.1 ritual; 21.8 scene; 132.7 stability; 317.1, 631.7, 632.3 way
routinely 160.14, 750.37 conventionally; 298.16 cyclically; 209.9 differentially; 297.1 frequently; 407.27 methodically; 216.11 on average; 298.17 orderly; 111.20 regularly; 138.30 usually
routineness 138.5 averageness
routine procedure 631.7 way
routine work 632.3 way
routinization 409.3 organization
rout out 371.7 drive out
roux 25.15 sauce
rove 325.3 go astray
roving 227.13 changeable
roving eye 518.6 look; 796.3 sexual immorality
row 50.16; 342.1 activity; 751.6 argue; 701.1, 751.2 argument; 408.9 disorder; 517.2 dissonant noise; 43.11 farmland; 327.4 fuss; 380.3 instance of violence; 411.2 level; 27.22 matrix; 507.2 outcry; 330.20 propel; 242.8 quarrel; 317.3 road; 178.7 straight line
rowboat 50.4 rowing; 323.3 vessel
rowdily 586.41 aggressively
rowdiness 408.8 lawlessness
rowdy 586.1 combatant; 586.33 combative; 662.9 criminal; 408.20 disorderly; 507.6 loud
rowel 425.8 sharp-pointed thing
rower 323.8 boatman; 50.9 sailor
row house 20.3 building; 565.5 house
rowing 50.4; **50.11**; 701.7 arguing; 576.5 exercise; 362.2 pull; 323.1 water travel
rowing association 50.4 rowing
rowing boat 323.3 vessel
rowing race 50.4 rowing
rowing technique 50.4 rowing
rowlack arch 20.5 arch
rowlock 307.4 axle; 50.4 rowing
rows of nodding plumes 585.2 glory of war
royal 396.12 authoritative; 121.13 dominant; 656.6 formal; 12.10 governing; 396.14 governmental; 400.12 masterful; 622.19 stately
Royal Air Force 586.29 air force
Royal Air Force Academy 584.3 military training
Royal Automobile Club 61.7 racing governing body
Royal Ballet 22.12 ballet companies
royal blue 539.1 blue
royal box 21.18 auditorium
Royal Caledonian Curling Club 68.10 curling
Royal Canadian Henley 50.4 rowing
Royal Canadian Mounted Police 16.14 police
Royal Canoe Club 50.6 canoeing
royal command 397.1 command
Royal Commission 579.7 council
Royal Danish Ballet 22.12 ballet companies
royal enclosure 165.2 enclosed place
Royal Festival Ballet 22.12 ballet companies
royal flush 69.3 card game terms
Royal Greenwich Observatory 29.23 observatory
royal jelly 394.7 tonic
royally 396.23 authoritatively; 656.12 formally; 622.36 majestically; 400.16 masterfully; 121.16 superiorly
Royal Mail 316.8 messenger; 692.2 postal communication
Royal Marine Commandos 586.28 marines
Royal Marines 586.28 marines
Royal Military Academy 585.6 art of war
Royal Military College 584.3 military training
Royal Military Police 584.6 military law
Royal Naval College 584.3 military training
Royal Naval Reserve 586.22 navy
Royal Naval Reservist 586.27 naval man
Royal Naval Volunteer Reserve 586.22 navy
Royal Navy 586.22 navy
Royal Observatory Edinburgh 29.23 observatory
royal prerogative 396.1 authority
royal road 265.6 easy thing; 317.3 road
royal tennis 63.5 real tennis; 63.1 tennis
royalties 788.2 money received
royalty 396.1 authority; 765.4 earnings; 788.2 money received; 785.3 pay
royal we 656.1 formality
Royal Yachting Association 50.1 sailing
rozzer 16.17 police officer; 253.3 security officer
rpm 332.8 speed
RR Lyrae star 29.12 variable star
RSI 260.16 rheumatism
RSJ 38.27 superstructure
RS-ski 68.5 ski equipment
RSVP 706.2 acknowledgment
rub 365.12; 428.20 absorb; 493.14 be hot; 526.3 cause to disappear; 256.13 clean; 287.3 critical time; 394.20 doctor; 576.4 exertion; 365.1 friction; 492.4 kiss; 147.19 meet; 378.2 obstacle; 421.11 smooth; 492.11 touch; 576.6 work
rub-a-dub 509.4 knocking
rub against 365.13 abrade
rubbed out 358.6 obliterated; 212.5 subtracted
rubbed the wrong way 624.16 angry
rubber 422.4; 563.3 birth control; 69.3 card game terms; 256.10 cleaning object; 357.6 destroyer; 422.6 elastic; 358.4, 365.7 eraser; 422.9 make elastic; 521.6 that which makes invisible; 79.9 tree product
rubber ball 422.3 elastic thing
rubber band 422.3 elastic thing
rubber bullet 587.13 ammunition
rubber cheque 786.3 bad payment; 780.15 false money
rubber-chicken circuit 21.15 engagement
rubber dinghy 252.4 safety device
rubber hose 814.14 instrument of punishment
rubberiness 422.1 elasticity; 419.8 softness; 423.6 toughness
rubberize 422.9 make elastic; 42.15 treat
rubberized 422.6 elastic; 42.11 treated
rubber-legged 486.3 clumsy
rubberlike 422.6 elastic
rubber mask 551.5 fancy dress
rubberneck 644.7 be curious; 518.12 see
rubbernecker 644.4 meddler; 518.11 observer
rubbernecking 644.2 prying
rubber plant 422.4 rubber
rubber plantation 422.4 rubber
rubber ring 67.3 survival swimming
rubbers 551.19 footwear
rubber-soled shoes 551.19 footwear
rubber stamp 669.12 accept; 669.1 approval; 750.28 consent; 757.2 permit
rubberstamped 750.17 consenting
rubber tapping 79.6 tree management
rubber tree 422.4 rubber
rubbery 422.6 elastic; 423.3 hard; 419.1 soft
rubbing 68.10 curling; 125.5 duplicate; 365.1 friction; 365.10 frictional; 147.11 meeting; 365.5 polishing; 492.2 touching
rubbing against 365.2 wearing away
rubbing noses 569.4 act of friendship
rubbing out 382.2 murder; 358.3 obliteration; 212.1 subtraction; 773.3 taking away; 365.2 wearing away
rubbing together 365.2 wearing away
rubbish 258.4 dirt; 767.3 disposable things; 699.12 fake; 700.6 imitation; 236.8 inferiority; 408.4 litter; 697.1 nonsense; 238.6 refuse; 215.2 residue; 441.5 waste product
rubbish bin 256.10 cleaning object; 410.11 vessel; 767.4 wastebin
rubbish collector 767.6
rubbish dump 238.6 refuse; 767.8 sink; 439.4 storage
rubbish heap 238.6 refuse; 767.8 sink; 767.5 wasteyard
rubbish pile 238.6 refuse; 767.8 sink
rubbish scow 767.4 wastebin
rubbish truck 767.4 wastebin
rubbishy 699.37 fake; 700.39 imitative; 236.2 inferior; 124.4 trivial; 238.1 useless
rubble 205.8 bits and pieces
rubby-dubby 55.1 angling
rubdown 365.6 massage
rub down 427.25 grate; 365.16 massage; 43.18 practise livestock farming; 421.11 smooth
rube 646.3 naive person; 87.12 rural dweller; 486.10 unskilled person
rubefacient 37.4 drug type; 535.5 redness; 37.17 stimulating
rubefaction 535.5 redness
rubefy 535.9 redden
Rube Goldberg 477.11 fantastical
rubella 260.6 infection
rubeola 260.6 infection
rubescence 535.5 redness
rubescent 535.2 red-faced
rube town 87.10 village
rub gently 365.16 massage
Rubicon 222.3 critical moment
rubicund 535.2 red-faced
rubicundity 535.5 redness
rubidium–strontium dating 30.42 dating
rubiginous 534.1 brown

Rubik Cube™ 737.4 *brain-teaser*
rub in 726.6 *emphasize*
rub it in 607.6 *aggravate*
rub noses 492.11 *touch*
rub off 552.15 *make nude*; 358.1 *obliterate*
rub of the green 56.1 *golf*
rub on 302.6 *march on*
rub one's eyes 619.9 *wonder*
rub out 526.3 *cause to disappear*; 256.13 *clean*; 357.8 *destroy*; 128.8 *eject*; 365.14 *erode*; 371.10 *exterminate*; 521.8 *make invisible*; 382.17 *murder*; 358.1 *obliterate*; 212.3 *subtract*; 773.10 *take away*
rubric 713.3 *precept*; 10.10 *religious manual*; 447.1 *topic*
rubricate 535.9 *redden*
rub shoulders with 654.11 *be sociable*; 147.19 *meet*
rub the wrong way 596.7 *cause dislike*; 404.14 *go against the grain*; 626.12 *make irritable*; 751.7 *pick a fight*
rub up 522.27 *glaze*; 6.23 *learn*; 365.12 *rub*
ruby 235.8 *exceller*; 535.1 *red*; 535.7 *red thing*
ruby laser 28.26 *laser*
ruby port 558.9 *wine*
ruby wedding 601.5 *anniversary*
ruby wedding anniversary 298.6 *annually celebrated day*
ruche 184.3 *pleat*
ruched 184.7 *folded*; 551.31 *styled*
ruck 138.6 *average*; 216.7 *average person*; 376.20 *crowd*; 64.5 *play rugby*; 184.10 *pleat*; 64.3 *rugby play*; 208.4 *throng*; 184.1 *wrinkle*
rucked 551.31 *styled*
rucked up 184.7 *folded*
rucksack 410.9 *baggage*; 62.4 *climbing equipment*; 316.10 *transferred thing*
ruckus 751.2 *argument*; 408.9 *disorder*; 380.3 *instance of violence*
ructation 371.24, 432.5 *belch*
ruction 751.2 *argument*; 328.5 *commotion*; 408.9 *disorder*
rudd 55.5 *British game fish*
rudder 119.4 *equilizer*; 579.5 *guide*; 323.5 *navigation*; 50.3 *parts of a sailing boat*; 438.1 *tool*
rudderless 335.12 *impotent*
rudderpost 50.3 *parts of a sailing boat*
ruddily 535.10
ruddiness 529.9 *complexion*; 535.5 *redness*
ruddle 535.9 *redden*; 535.6 *red pigment*
ruddy 674.9 *blushing*; 259.1 *healthy*; 712.11 *miscellaneous euphemisms*; 535.2 *red-faced*
ruddy complexion 259.3 *health*
rude 660.19; 149.9 *abrupt*; 5.36 *accent*; 631.18 *badly behaved*; 659.6 *bad-mannered*; 486.3 *clumsy*; 668.10 *disrespectful*; 233.4 *incomplete*; 544.8 *indecorous*; 242.2 *objectionable*; 258.9 *obscene*; 5.39 *of language*; 672.3 *ungrateful*; 655.8 *unsociable*; 380.6 *violent*
rude gesture 659.3 *act of discourtesy*; 668.7 *sign of disrespect*
rude health 259.3 *health*
rudely 659.10; **660.35**; 631.20 *badly*; 258.12 *dirtily*; 668.28 *disrespectfully*; 672.7 *ungratefully*; 655.14 *unsocially*; 380.10 *violently*
rudeness 660.8; 149.6 *abruptness*; 631.4 *bad conduct*; 659.2 *bad manners*; 668.1 *disrespect*; 544.2 *impropriety*; 672.1 *ingratitude*; 660.1 *insolence*; 242.6 *objectionability*; 258.3 *obscenity*
rude person 631.5 *badly behaved person*; 659.4 *discourteous person*; 596.3 *disliked person*
rude remark 661.3 *act of defiance*
rude word 5.19 *swearword*
rude words 659.3 *act of discourtesy*
rudiment 344.3; 34.15 *developmental biology*; 420.10 *rough idea*
rudimental 159.7 *little*; 130.35 *rudimentary*
rudimentary 130.35; 175.3 *base*; 344.13 *causal*; 34.26 *developmental*; 159.7 *little*; 420.15 *unfinished*
rudiments 130.7
Rudolf Nureyev 22.14 *famous ballet dancers*
rue 496.5 *herbs*; 603.6 *lament*
rueful 808.6 *penitent*
ruefully 808.8 *penitently*
rue the day 808.4 *be penitent*
rufescence 535.5 *redness*
rufescent 535.1 *red*
ruff 551.14 *neckwear*; 69.10 *play*; 72.17 *plumage*
ruffian 586.1 *combatant*; 662.9 *criminal*; 651.8 *malefactor*; 382.11 *murderer*; 380.4 *violent creature*
ruffianism 16.41 *lawlessness*
ruffle 327.22 *agitate*; 542.6 *decorative articles*; 328.7 *disturb*; 408.24 *make disordered*; 420.12 *make rough*; 624.9 *offend*; 184.3, 184.10 *pleat*
ruffled 327.15 *agitated*; 328.12 *disturbed*; 420.1 *rough*; 408.15 *untidy*
ruffle feelings 659.7 *be discourteous*
ruffle one's feathers 624.9 *offend*
ruffle someone's temper 624.14 *make angry*
ruffle the dignity 624.9 *offend*
rufous 535.1 *red*
rug 175.1 *base*; 550.5 *body covering*; 550.9 *floor covering*; 551.15 *headgear*; 46.4 *stadium*; 547.10 *wig*
rugby 64.1 *rugger*
rugby ball 330.10 *ball*; 64.1 *rugger*
rugby boots 551.19 *footwear*
rugby coach 64.4 *rugby player*
Rugby Football 64
rugby football 64.1 *rugger*
rugby ground 64.1 *rugger*
Rugby League 64.1 *rugger*
rugby match 64.1 *rugger*
rugby pack 64.1 *rugger*
rugby pitch 64.1 *rugger*
rugby play 64.3
rugby player 64.4
rugby referee 64.4 *rugby player*
rugby side 64.1 *rugger*
rugby stadium 64.1 *rugger*
Rugby Union 64.1 *rugger*
Rugby World Cup 64.2 *championship*
rugged 651.12 *callous*; 659.5 *discourteous*; 264.11, 420.1 *rough*; 647.8 *severe*; 423.1 *tough*
rugged individualist 250.7 *free person*
ruggedly 420.14 *roughly*; 336.14 *strongly*; 423.12 *toughly*
ruggedness 264.1 *difficulty*; 420.6 *roughness*; 647.1 *severity*; 423.6 *toughness*
rugger 64.1; **64.6**
rugose 420.1 *rough*
rugosely 420.14 *roughly*
rugosity 420.6 *roughness*
rugrat 130.15 *baby*; 555.9 *child*
ruin 357.4; **357.11**; 249.1 *adversity*; 798.2 *affliction*; 131.4 *annihilation*; 236.13 *be worthless*; 395.9 *change*; 796.19 *corrupt*; 766.13 *destroy*; 441.4, 766.5 *destruction*; 245.9 *dilapidation*; 247.1 *failure*; 305.4 *fall*; 236.11 *harmfulness*; 236.14 *ill-treat*; 245.4 *impair*; 782.14 *impoverish*; 782.6, 786.5 *insolvency*; 441.2 *lay waste*; 245.8 *perversion*; 245.6 *pervert*; 3.11 *relic*; 284.7 *thing of the past*
ruination 245.9 *dilapidation*; 245.10 *impairment*; 357.4 *ruin*
ruined 131.23 *annihilated*; 357.15 *destroyed*; 245.12 *deteriorated*; 245.13 *dilapidated*; 375.5 *disintegrated*; 804.12 *immoral*; 236.2 *inferior*; 782.2 *insolvent*; 766.16 *losing*; 786.13 *nonpaying*; 122.18 *outclassed*; 766.17 *unprofitable*
ruin oneself 245.1 *deteriorate*; 792.11 *overpay*
ruin one's name 804.16 *be wicked*
ruin one's plans 481.3 *deflect*; 604.6 *disappoint*
ruinous 249.6 *adverse*; 357.14 *destructive*; 245.13 *dilapidated*; 236.5 *harmful*; 766.17 *unprofitable*; 380.6 *violent*
ruinously 357.16 *destructively*
ruins 215.1 *remainder*; 357.4 *ruin*
Rule 140
rule 140.1; **140.13**; 397.3 *authority*; 216.4 *average*; 138.5 *averageness*; 395.10 *be a prevailing influence*; 397.1, 397.9 *command*; 210.5 *computer*; 631.1 *conduct*; 117.5 *convention*; 140.16 *direct*; 85.18 *exert sovereignty*; 27.49 *geometric construction*; 12.11 *govern*; 12.3, 396.4 *governance*; 396.18 *have authority*; 397.11 *have authority over*; 464.11 *judge*; 16.3, 28.6 *law*; 121.2 *leadership*; 298.10 *make regular*; 579.1 *manage*; 400.14 *master*; 745.1 *maxim*; 26.6 *measuring instrument*; 407.7 *method*; 298.4 *orderliness*; 187.5 *planometer*; 484.2 *policy*; 713.3 *precept*; 138.28 *prevail*; 27.65 *theory*; 16.71 *try a case*
rule absolutely 12.11 *govern*; 396.18 *have authority*
rule a territory 440.9 *own property*
rulebook 140.2 *canon*
ruled out 103.4 *forbidden*
rule of conduct 810.6 *ethics*
rule of custom 713.3 *precept*
rule of expediency 239.3 *convenience*
rule of law 407.9 *discipline*; 12.1 *government*; 396.7 *type of rule*
rule of nature 140.3
rule of terror 396.7 *type of rule*
rule of thumb 448.3 *experimentation*; 140.3 *rule of nature*; 26.7 *standard*
rule of wealth 12.1 *government*
rule out 128.7 *exclude*; 103.8 *make impossible*; 358.1 *obliterate*
rule over 140.16 *direct*; 397.11 *have authority over*
ruler 210.5 *computer*; 27.49 *geometric construction*; 814.14 *instrument of punishment*; 400.3 *leader*; 26.6 *measuring instrument*; 396.10 *person of authority*; 187.5 *planometer*; 121.5 *superior*
rules 631.1 *conduct*; 810.6 *ethics*; 632.5 *tradition*
rules and regulations 632.5 *tradition*
rules of business 631.1 *conduct*; 632.5 *tradition*
rules of conduct 656.5 *etiquette*
rules of inference 27.64 *reasoning*
rules of life 631.1 *conduct*
rules of the game 631.9 *tactics*
rules of the road 631.1 *conduct*
rules of the sea 323.5 *navigation*
rule the roost 396.19 *be authoritarian*; 140.16 *direct*; 396.18 *have authority*
ruling 140.12; 396.12 *authoritative*; 397.1 *command*; 397.14 *commanding*; 121.13 *dominant*; 12.10 *governing*; 395.11 *influential*; 16.7 *legal trial*; 140.1 *rule*; 2.14 *socioeconomic*; 464.2 *verdict*
ruling class 573.2 *aristocracy*; 2.7 *social stratification*
ruling party 400.8 *the power structure*
ruling passion 641.7 *opinionatedness*
rum 558.7 *alcoholic drink*; 118.14 *eccentric*; 272.5 *ridiculous*
rum and black 558.8 *mixed drink*
rum and Coke 558.8 *mixed drink*
rum and pep 558.8 *mixed drink*
rumba 22.2, 22.15 *dance*; 68.7 *ice-dancing*
rumble 751.2 *argument*; 508.5 *bang*; 509.8 *drum*; 509.1 *drumming*; 507.1 *loudness*; 695.6 *understand*
rumbling 509.1 *drumming*
rumbling thunder 507.1 *loudness*
rumbustious 507.6 *loud*
Rum Collins 558.8 *mixed drink*
ruminant 71.15 *hoofed mammal*; 4.17 *thoughtful*; 71.33 *ungulate*
Ruminantia 71.15 *hoofed mammal*
ruminate 557.21 *eat*; 81.11 *eat grass*; 71.37 *graze*; 4.20 *philosophize*; 443.12 *think*
rumination 557.5 *eating habit*; 443.1 *thought*
ruminative 4.17, 443.8 *thoughtful*
ruminatively 4.28 *thoughtfully*
rummage sale 791.2 *bargain*; 779.10 *bazaar*; 793.7 *discounter*; 767.2 *disposal of property*; 778.4 *sale*
rummer 558.10 *drink container*; 410.13 *drinking vessel*
rum one 118.10 *eccentric*
rumour 693.7 *advice*; 740.13 *make public*; 447.3 *matter of interest*; 740.1 *publication*; 504.8 *something heard*
rump 25.22 *beef*; 168.2 *rear end*; 215.1 *remainder*
rumple 327.22 *agitate*; 404.14 *go against the grain*; 408.24 *make disordered*; 420.12 *make rough*; 184.1, 184.8 *wrinkle*
rumpled 184.6 *wrinkly*
rum punch 558.7 *alcoholic drink*
rumpus 751.2 *argument*; 328.5 *commotion*; 408.9 *disorder*; 380.3 *instance of violence*; 507.2 *outcry*
rumpus room 565.7 *room*
rumpy-pumpy 593.5 *desire*
run 71.20 *abode of mammals*; 332.6 *accelerate*; 332.9 *acceleration*; 355.3 *attempt*; 138.6, 216.4 *average*; 342.12 *be active*; 395.10 *be a prevailing influence*; 324.2 *bearing*; 631.14 *behave towards*; 346.7 *be operational*; 332.4 *be swift*; 68.9 *bobsledding*; 69.3 *card game terms*; 633.2 *chase*; 132.2 *consecution*; 132.14 *continue*; 134.1 *continuity*; 526.2 *depart*; 140.16 *direct*; 21.15 *engagement*; 576.9 *exercise*; 560.18 *fester*; 90.7, 431.25 *flow*; 300.12 *gait*; 277.7 *go on*; 331.1 *impel*; 121.10 *lead*; 268.17 *liquefy*; 530.5 *lose colour*; 262.2 *make haste*; 579.1 *manage*; 431.24 *melt*; 381.12 *military attack*; 300.2 *momentum*; 148.5 *piece*; 46.9 *play*; 57.6 *pommel horse*; 43.18 *practise livestock farming*; 47.7 *race*; 90.1 *river*; 90.6 *river flow*; 317.2 *route*; 64.3 *rugby play*; 634.8 *run away*; 50.15 *sail*; 53.10 *score*; 372.9 *separate*; 372.3 *separateness*; 68.1 *skiing*; 565.12 *stall*; 289.1 *succession*; 47.1 *track events*; 469.5 *vote*; 300.15 *walk*; 632.3 *way*
runabout 320.16 *car*
run abreast 119.10 *be equal*; 188.5 *parallel*
run across 107.11 *chance upon*
run a dead heat 285.8 *run equally*
run a deficit 766.10 *have a financial loss*
run after 316.14 *bring back*; 633.10 *chase*; 617.13 *like*; 664.11 *pander to*; 569.14 *seek the friendship of*
run aground 249.9 *be in trouble*; 312.4 *land*; 323.10 *sail*
run a lap 298.8 *be cyclic*
run along 371.33 *go away!*
run amok 461.14 *become insane*; 408.26 *be disorderly*; 380.7 *be violent*; 590.17 *feel deeply*; 357.10 *lay waste*; 381.5 *strike*
run-and-bump 61.10 *racing*
run-and-bump tactic 61.6 *motor-racing terms*
run and run 132.14 *continue*
run-and-shoot offence 46.7 *offence*
run a pattern 46.15 *play offence*
run a protection racket 773.10 *take away*
run a punt 50.19 *punt*
run around 593.26 *court*
run as a candidate 752.13 *be a candidate*
run a second edition 111.9 *duplicate*
run a stone 68.16 *bobsled*
run at 381.1 *attack*
run at a loss 766.10 *have a financial loss*
run a temperature 493.16 *feel hot*
run a tight ship 647.5 *be severe*
runaway 98.6 *absentee*; 634.17 *avoider*; 634.18 *avoiding*; 355.4 *deserter*; 526.4 *disappearance*; 479.9 *equivocator*; 389.3 *escaper*; 389.8 *escaping*; 300.16 *moving*; 332.1 *swift*
run away 634.8; 98.18 *abscond*; 332.6 *accelerate*; 614.4 *be a coward*; 247.7 *be defeated*; 252.9 *be safe*; 526.2 *depart*; 389.5 *escape*; 313.4 *hurry off*; 570.15 *marry*; 303.2 *retreat*
runaway success 246.1 *success*
runaway tongue 731.1 *talkativeness*
runaway victory 246.2 *victory*
runaway wedding 389.1 *escape*
run away with 608.14, 773.10 *take away*
run back 46.17 *kick*; 303.2 *retreat*; 303.3 *reverse*; 46.12 *special team*
run bases 48.7 *play baseball*
run before a gale 323.9 *navigate*
run before the wind 323.9 *navigate*
run counter 113.15 *be opposite*
run counter to 113.16 *be contrary*; 347.3 *counteract*
rundle 304.10 *step*
run down 381.9 *attack successfully*; 606.7 *be dissatisfied*; 226.6 *cease*; 633.10 *chase*; 670.17 *criticize*; 670.33 *criticized*; 214.4 *decrease*; 449.2 *detect*; 678.10 *disparage*; 350.4 *disused*; 218.7 *make insufficient*; 214.5 *make smaller*; 668.20 *scorn*; 260.21 *unhealthy*; 337.8 *weak*
run-down 245.12 *deteriorated*; 245.13 *dilapidated*; 48.6 *fielding terms*; 723.1 *summary*
run down one's account 787.1 *expend*
rune 5.13 *letter*; 742.1 *sign*; 11.5 *spell*
run equally 285.8
runes 475.10 *cards*; 717.1 *representation*
run faster 765.10 *augment*
run for 324.7 *take a direction*

run for it 634.24 *hands off!*; 634.8 *run away*
run for office 752.13 *be a candidate*
run for one's life 313.4 *hurry off*; 634.8 *run away*
run for port 252.9 *be safe*; 323.10 *sail*
run for your life 634.24 *hands off!*
run foul of 331.2 *collide*
run full stride 47.7 *race*
rung 181.4 *cylinder*; 209.4 *interval*; 304.10 *step*
run helter-skelter 262.2 *make haste*
runic 5.41 *lettered*; 11.14 *occult*
runic alphabet 5.14 *alphabet*
runic letter 5.14 *alphabet*
runic verse 17.6 *poetry*
run in 53.18 *bowl*; 251.11 *detain*; 368.3 *impact*; 773.10 *take away*
run-in 751.2 *argument*
run interference for 392.24 *back*
run into 492.12 *abut*; 107.11 *chance upon*; 312.8 *meet*
run into danger 254.8 *be in danger*
run into debt 784.7 *be in debt*
run into money 792.9 *be dear*
run into the ground 349.3 *exploit*
run into trouble 221.7 *be in a predicament*; 264.20 *be in difficulty*
run its course 277.7 *go on*; 284.14 *pass*
run level 119.10 *be equal*; 50.16 *row*
run like a blue-streak 332.5 *run like a shot*
run like a flash 332.5 *run like a shot*
run like a hare 332.5 *run like a shot*
run like a shot 332.5
run like a streak 332.5 *run like a shot*
run like crazy 332.5 *run like a shot*
run like greased lightning 332.5 *run like a shot*
run like hell 262.2 *make haste*
run like lightning 332.5 *run like a shot*
run like mad 332.5 *run like a shot*
run like sin 332.5 *run like a shot*
run like sixty 332.5 *run like a shot*
run like the clappers 332.5 *run like a shot*
run like the devil 262.2 *make haste*; 332.5 *run like a shot*
run like the wind 332.5 *run like a shot*
run like wildfire 332.5 *run like a shot*
run low 214.4 *decrease*; 441.1 *waste*
run messages for 748.1 *mediate*
run neck and neck 119.10 *be equal*; 285.8 *run equally*
runnel 90.1 *river*
runner 47.3, 336.5 *athlete*; 48.2 *baseball player*; 68.9 *bobsledding*; 62.4 *climbing equipment*; 550.9 *floor covering*; 44.5 *gardening*; 59.7 *horseracing*; 46.7 *offence*; 401.5 *office assistant*; 77.5 *stem*; 332.13 *swift person*; 53.4 *team*
runner-up 336.5 *athlete*
runner-up prize 813.2 *prize*
runnily 431.26 *fluidly*; 268.22 *slimily*; 433.35 *wetly*
runniness 268.2; 431.5 *fluidity*; 153.12 *thinning*; 433.3 *wateriness*
running 342.18 *active*; 51.9 *bowls*; 132.9 *consecutive*; 134.5 *continual*; 576.5 *exercise*; 54.6 *fencing*; 431.8 *fluidification*; 90.10 *fluvial*; 262.3 *hasty*; 257.1 *hygiene*; 289.14 *in succession*; 579.3 *management*; 300.1 *motion*; 300.16 *moving*; 346.10 *operational*; 57.6 *pommel horse*; 50.8, 50.14 *punting*; 560.27 *purulent*; 560.7 *pus*; 64.3 *rugby play*; 64.6 *rugger*; 268.10 *slippery*; 21.41 *stagestruck*; 332.1 *swift*; 47.1 *track events*
running account 789.1 *accounts*
running around 796.3 *sexual immorality*
running a stone 68.10 *curling*
running at a loss 766.2 *financial loss*
running attack 54.3 *fencing movements*
running away 526.4 *disappearance*
running back 46.7 *offence*
running belay 62.3 *climbing technique*
running changes 18.20 *key*
running costs 790.6 *business costs*
running dog 117.6 *conformist*
running down 678.1 *disparagement*
running flush 69.3 *card game terms*
running game 46.9 *play*
running hop 47.2 *field events*
running lights 522.6 *electric light*
running offence 49.4 *playing terms*
running on 731.5 *talkative*
running out 59.9 *jumping*
running over 219.6 *excessive*; 232.8 *full*
running repairs 393.8 *repair*
running rigging 50.3 *parts of a sailing boat*
running riot 727.3 *extravagance*
running shoes 551.19 *footwear*; 47.4 *sports equipment*
running shorts 47.4 *sports equipment*
running shot 51.2 *grip*
running sore 798.2 *affliction*; 315.2 *outflow*
running start 121.3 *advantage*
running steps 22.3 *ballroom dance steps*
running story 741.9 *news story*
running the gauntlet 814.12 *corporal punishment*
running to earth 142.3 *locating*
running to seed 556.12 *ageing*
running total 194.4 *mathematical result*
running vest 47.4 *sports equipment*
running water 431.2 *juice*; 90.1 *river*; 433.1 *water*
running with the ball 49.5 *penalties*
run nip and tuck 119.10 *be equal*; 285.8 *run equally*
runny 431.15 *flowing*; 337.13 *insufficient*; 315.17 *leaky*; 268.10 *slippery*; 153.5 *thinned*
runny nose 315.2 *outflow*; 260.9 *respiratory disease*
run of bad luck 107.2 *luck*
runoff 30.10 *water cycle*
run off 30.63 *ebb*; 313.4 *hurry off*; 634.8 *run away*
run off with 773.10 *take away*
run of good luck 107.2 *luck*
run of luck 248.2 *good fortune*; 246.1 *success*
run-of-the-mill 138.6 *average*; 138.21 *common*; 297.3 *frequent*; 216.3 *mediocre*
run on 132.13 *be consecutive*; 134.3 *continue*; 135.2 *need*
run one hard 254.10 *endanger*
run one's head against 331.2 *collide*
run one's mouth 219.4 *be excessive*
run on in order 298.7 *be regular*
run on rails 421.12 *go smoothly*
run on savings 787.6 *extravagance*
run on the rocks 254.10 *endanger*
run out 315.11; 218.5 *be insufficient*; 226.6 *cease*; 131.18 *come to an end*; 53.19 *dismiss*; 53.11 *dismissal*; 315.9 *exit*; 331.1 *impel*; 284.14 *pass*; 441.1 *waste*
run out of gas 226.6 *cease*
run out of luck 249.9 *be in trouble*
run out of steam 333.2 *hesitate*
run out of time 131.18 *come to an end*
run out of town 371.7 *drive out*
run out on 355.2 *withdraw*
run over 232.5 *be complete*
run parallel 188.5 *parallel*
run pell-mell 262.2 *make haste*
run rings around 121.8 *be superior*
run riot 342.12 *be active*; 408.26 *be disorderly*; 219.4 *be excessive*; 727.9 *be extravagant*; 380.7 *be violent*
run round in circles 342.13 *be busy*
runs batted in 48.5 *batting terms*
runs-batted-in leader 48.2 *baseball player*
run smoothly 265.19 *go easily*
runt 159.4 *little person*; 149.5 *short person*; 153.9 *thin person*
run the gauntlet 661.5 *defy*; 254.9 *face danger*
run the hurry-up offence 46.15 *play offence*
run the offence 46.15 *play offence*
run the power sweep 46.15 *play offence*
run the quarterback sneak 46.15 *play offence*
run the risk of 254.8 *be in danger*
run through 395.10 *be a prevailing influence*; 412.10 *become mixed*; 97.11 *be present*; 357.12, 787.2 *consume*; 308.20 *hole*; 491.11 *inflict pain*; 382.17 *murder*; 21.37 *rehearse*; 381.6 *stab*; 441.1 *waste*
run-through 65.2 *billiards play*; 51.9 *bowls*; 21.14 *production*
run-through shot 51.2 *grip*
runtiness 159.1 *littleness*
run to 145.7 *reach*; 349.4 *resort to*
run to earth 449.2 *detect*; 142.11 *find*
run together 374.5 *combine*; 310.10 *come together*
run to ground 633.9 *follow*
run to seed 563.7 *be infertile*; 556.13 *middle-aged*; 77.21 *vegetate*; 441.1 *waste*
run to waste 441.1 *waste*
run true to form 117.7 *conform*
runty 159.7 *little*
run up 356.10 *produce*
run-up 47.2 *field events*
run up a bill 783.9 *acquire credit*; 784.7 *be in debt*
run up a debt 772.10 *buy on credit*
run up an account 783.9 *acquire credit*; 784.7 *be in debt*; 772.10 *buy on credit*
run up an overdraft 766.10 *have a financial loss*
runway 322.4 *airport*; 317.13 *flight path*; 38.19 *structure*
runway lights 522.6 *electric light*
run wild 408.26 *be disorderly*; 380.7 *be violent*; 250.19 *liberalize*
run with 223.14 *keep company with*
run with the pack 117.8 *comply*
rupee 780.11 *national coins*
rupture 751.6 *argue*; 751.2 *argument*; 146.2, 146.5 *crack*; 38.16 *deformation*; 38.31 *load*; 308.18 *open*; 308.1 *opening*; 491.2 *painful condition*; 372.9 *separate*; 372.3 *separateness*
ruptured 146.7 *cracked*; 308.12 *open*; 372.15 *separate*
rural 43.19 *agricultural*; 2.13 *communal*; 86.17 *national*; 319.5 *transportable*; 87.14 *urban*; 538.2 *verdant*
rural area 86.6 *regions*
rural dweller 87.12
rural economics 43.1 *agriculture*
rural economist 43.15 *agriculturist*
ruralism 2.5 *society*
ruralist 564.5 *countryman*
rurally 43.22 *agriculturally*; 87.16 *municipally*
rural road 320.2 *road*
rural sector 2.5 *society*
rural society 2.5 *society*
rural sociology 2.5 *society*; 2.1 *sociology*
rural-urban 2.13 *communal*
rural-urban migration 2.5 *society*
rural village 87.10 *village*
Ruritania 477.8 *dreamland*
RURP 62.4 *climbing equipment*
ruse 484.3 *expedient plan*; 702.2 *sophism*; 645.2 *stratagem*; 379.1 *trap*; 700.8 *trick*
rush 332.9 *acceleration*; 381.1 *attack*; 342.12 *be active*; 327.21 *be agitated*; 332.4 *be swift*; 376.40 *crowd*; 46.11 *defensive huddle*; 90.7 *flow*; 81.1 *grass*; 262.4 *haste*; 262.1 *hasten*; 262.3 *hasty*; 380.3 *instance of violence*; 262.2 *make haste*; 381.12 *military attack*; 300.2 *momentum*; 46.16 *play defence*; 90.6 *river flow*; 124.8 *trifle*; 327.2 *tumult*; 300.15 *walk*
rush about 380.7 *be violent*
rush along 262.1 *hasten*
rush around 338.2 *be full of vigour*
rush at 381.1 *attack*; 633.10 *chase*
rush basket 410.7 *basket*
rushed 262.3 *hasty*
rushed into 262.3 *hasty*
rushed off one's feet 342.19 *busy*
rush family 77.3 *seed plant*
rush headlong 380.7 *be violent*; 262.2 *make haste*
rush hour 291.4 *evening thing*; 290.2 *morning thing*
rush in 314.12 *flood in*; 314.10 *invade*
rushing 90.10 *fluvial*; 262.3 *hasty*; 300.1 *motion*; 300.16 *moving*
rushing the puck 58.3 *ice hockey*
rushing to and fro 342.19 *busy*
rush into 615.5 *be rash*
rush job 262.4 *haste*
rush light 522.5 *incandescent light*
rush off 313.4 *hurry off*; 262.2 *make haste*
rush one's fences 615.5 *be rash*; 262.2 *make haste*
rush the passer 46.16 *play defence*
rush the puck 58.9 *play hockey*
rush through 262.2 *make haste*
rush to and fro 342.12 *be active*; 262.2 *make haste*
rushy 81.9 *grassy*
rusk 25.38 *bread*
Russell's paradox 4.9 *philosophical problem*
russet 534.1 *brown*; 535.1 *red*
Russian ballet 22.8 *ballet*
Russian bear 743.6 *national emblem*
Russian dance 22.4 *historic dancing*
Russian doll 411.5 *layered thing*
Russian salad 25.14 *salad*
Russian tea 558.3 *tea*
Russify 760.12 *naturalize*
rust 357.7 *agent of destruction*; 296.3 *antiquity*; 258.10 *be dirty*; 563.7 *be infertile*; 245.2 *decay*; 245.9 *dilapidation*; 258.4 *dirt*; 375.3 *disintegrate*; 375.1 *disintegration*; 296.17 *grow old*; 245.5 *hurt*; 341.4 *not act*; 44.12 *pests and diseases*; 535.7 *red thing*; 524.11 *tarnish*; 79.10 *tree disease*; 337.1 *weakness*; 427.28 *weather*
Rust Belt 577.1 *workshop*
rust-coloured 534.1 *brown*; 535.1 *red*
rusted 337.9 *dilapidated*
rustic 43.19 *agricultural*; 564.5 *countryman*; 646.3 *naive person*; 564.12 *native*; 574.4 *ordinary*; 574.1 *plebeian*; 87.12 *rural dweller*
rustically 43.22 *agriculturally*
rusticate 20.19 *decorate*; 371.3 *disbar*; 371.4 *ostracize*
rusticated 20.17 *structured*
rustication 20.9 *miscellaneous architectural features*; 371.19 *ostracism*
rustic brick 20.4 *building material*
rustic fence 44.3 *ornamental garden*
rustiness 245.9 *dilapidation*; 513.2 *hoarseness*; 487.3 *unaccustomedness*; 486.8 *unskilfulness*
rusting 350.4 *disused*; 32.19 *electrochemistry*
rustle 511.4 *faint sound*; 512.1, 512.4 *hiss*; 511.8 *sound faint*
rustle cattle 774.12 *steal*
rustle of spring 292.2 *spring*
rustler 774.8 *thief*
rustle up 243.2 *do the groundwork*
rustling 511.4 *faint sound*; 512.1 *hiss*; 512.6 *hissing*
rustproof 252.7 *invulnerable*
rustre 743.8 *heraldic device*
rusts 83.3 *fungi*
rusty 534.1 *brown*; 486.3 *clumsy*; 245.13 *dilapidated*; 524.7 *dimmed*; 375.5 *disintegrated*; 375.6 *disintegrating*; 513.8 *hoarse*; 487.1 *unaccustomed*
rusty-dusty 168.2 *rear end*
rusty hinge 513.3 *shrillness*
rut 620.2 *boring thing*; 140.6 *custom*; 184.2 *furrow*; 317.6 *path*; 112.3 *repetitiveness*; 420.8 *rough ground*; 181.6 *round*; 68.1 *skiing*; 132.7 *stability*; 632.3 *way*; 184.8 *wrinkle*
ruth 627.2 *condolence*
ruthful 627.7 *pitiful*
ruthless 651.13 *merciless*; 628.4 *pitiless*; 638.3 *strong-willed*
ruthlessly 482.13 *intentionally*
ruthlessness 651.3 *callousness*; 628.1 *pitilessness*; 638.14 *tenacity*
Rutland Water 88.4 *British lakes*
rutted 420.2 *coarse*; 68.12 *ski*; 184.6 *wrinkly*
ruttily 184.12 *doubly*
rutting 292.17 *in season*; 796.14 *lecherous*
ruttish 796.14 *lecherous*
rutty 420.2 *coarse*; 184.6 *wrinkly*
Rydal Water 88.4 *British lakes*
Rydberg constant 28.97 *fundamental constant*
rye 558.7 *alcoholic drink*; 43.12 *crop*
rye bread 25.38 *bread*
ryegrass 43.12 *crop*
rye whiskey 558.7 *alcoholic drink*

sab 378.9 *block*
Sabaic 9.10 *idolatrous*
Sabaism 9.2 *idolatry*
Sabaist 9.6 *idolater*
Sabbatarian 7.4 *religionist*
Sabbatarianism 10.2 *ritualism*
Sabbath 263.1 *ease*; 10.15 *holy day*
sabbatical 263.4 *at ease*; 263.1 *ease*; 98.5 *leave of absence*; 757.2 *permit*; 580.2 *time off*
sabbatical leave 98.5 *leave of absence*
Sabbatism 10.2 *ritualism*
sabbing 378.2 *obstacle*
Sabellian 5.11 *family of languages*
Sabine women 749.3 *pacifist*
sable 550.14 *animal covering*; 532.1 *black*; 532.9 *black thing*; 523.10 *dark-coloured*; 743.13 *heraldic*; 743.8 *heraldic device*
sabotage 662.16 *be subversive*; 378.9

block; 766.13 *destroy;* 441.4, 766.5 *destruction;* 357.3 *destructiveness;* 328.10 *disrupt;* 328.4 *disruption;* 245.10 *impairment;* 441.2 *lay waste;* 238.8 *make useless;* 378.2 *obstacle;* 662.3 *subversion*
sabotaged 328.15 *disrupted*
saboteur 357.6 *destroyer;* 699.17 *false person;* 378.7 *hinderer;* 700.20 *plotter;* 385.2 *revenger;* 662.10 *seditionist*
sabots 551.19 *footwear*
sabre 54.6 *fencing;* 54.2 *fencing equipment;* 382.17 *murder;* 587.8 *sharp weapon*
sabre-fence 54.5 *fence*
sabre-fencing 54.1 *fencing*
sabre leg 23.3 *chair leg*
sabre-rattling 585.5 *bellicosity;* 381.22 *militant;* 585.1 *war*
sabres 586.19 *cavalry*
sabre-toothed tiger 296.8 *prehistoric animal*
sabreur 586.1 *combatant*
sabulosity 427.3 *graininess*
sabulous 427.17 *grainy*
sac 410.19 *inflatable*
saccharic acid 33.3 *carbohydrate*
saccharide 33.3 *carbohydrate*
saccharimeter 26.8 *meter*
saccharimetry 26.2 *micrometry*
saccharine 677.13 *honeyed;* 498.6 *sweet;* 498.2 *sweetener*
saccharine sweet 677.13 *honeyed*
saccharinity 498.1 *sweetness*
saccharometer 26.8 *meter*
sacerdotal 7.17 *priestly*
sacerdotalism 7.9 *priesthood*
sac fungi 83.3 *fungi*
sack 410.8 *bag;* 226.8 *cause to cease;* 15.11 *conduct industrial relations;* 203.3 *container;* 46.11 *defensive huddle;* 371.2, 580.5, 767.10 *dismiss;* 128.8, 364.2 *eject;* 551.7 *frock;* 357.10, 441.2 *lay waste;* 343.14 *make inactive;* 46.16 *play defence;* 774.14 *plunder;* 774.5 *plundering;* 144.17 *relegate;* 608.12 *relieve from duty;* 350.7 *stop work;* 773.10 *take away;* 773.3 *taking away;* 708.15 *terminate;* 558.9 *wine*
sackcloth 420.7 *rough thing;* 193.4 *textile*
sackcloth and ashes 807.2 *apology;* 603.1 *lamentation;* 808.2 *type of penance*
sack coat 551.11 *jacket*
sack dress 161.2 *shapeless thing*
sacked 708.20 *cancelled;* 767.13 *dismissed;* 226.10 *finished;* 580.7 *leisurely;* 15.9 *negotiated;* 350.3 *not wanted;* 144.11 *relegated*
sacked out 261.1 *fatigued*
sacker 774.9 *plunderer;* 773.6 *taker*
sacking 371.18 *dismissal;* 767.1 *disposal;* 128.2 *ejection;* 15.2 *industrial negotiations;* 774.5 *plundering;* 226.2 *stop;* 773.3 *taking away;* 193.4 *textile*
sack out 581.2 *be refreshed*
sacral 10.21 *ritualistic*
sacrament 10.5 *Christian rite;* 10.1 *ritual*
sacramental 10.21 *ritualistic*
sacramentalism 10.2 *ritualism*
sacramentally 10.23 *ritually*
sacramentarianism 10.2 *ritualism*
sacrament of marriage 570.1 *marriage*
sacrarium 10.13 *shrine*
sacred 8.13 *divine*
sacred dance 22.4 *historic dancing*
sacredly 8.19 *divinely*
sacred music 18.5
sacredness 8.1 *divinity*
sacred object 10.14
sacred place 10.13 *shrine*
sacred symbol 742.1 *sign*
sacred text 7.12 *religious text*
sacred writings 7.12 *religious text*
sacrifice 807.2 *apology;* 48.5 *batting terms;* 473.7 *be unselfish;* 357.8 *destroy;* 768.5 *give;* 382.20 *kill ritually;* 766.9 *lose;* 766.1 *loss;* 793.13 *make cheap;* 752.6, 768.3 *offering;* 10.19 *offer worship;* 48.7 *play baseball;* 10.3 *rite of worship;* 382.6 *ritual killing;* 762.3 *substitute thing;* 212.2 *subtracted item;* 9.1, 9.7 *worship*
sacrificed 582.19 *dead;* 752.19 *sacrificial*
sacrifice fly 48.5 *batting terms*
sacrifice oneself 473.7 *be unselfish;* 752.12 *offer one's life;* 636.15 *volunteer*
sacrifice one's life 752.12 *offer one's life*
sacrificer 768.4 *giver*
sacrifice to 807.6 *apologize*
sacrifice to Bacchus 690.8 *get drunk*
sacrificial 752.19; 807.4 *atoning;* 793.9 *cheap;* 357.14 *destructive;* 768.7 *given;* 10.21 *ritualistic*
sacrificial anode 32.19 *electrochemistry*
sacrificial knife 10.14 *sacred object*
sacrificial lamb 752.7 *martyr;* 752.6 *offering*
sacrificially 768.9 *as a gift;* 807.8 *penitently;* 752.20 *persuasively;* 9.12 *worshipfully*
sacrificial offering 752.6 *offering*
sacrilege 712.1 *curse;* 804.6 *religious sin*
sacrilegious 712.8 *cursing;* 802.15 *immoral;* 804.14 *impious*
sacrilegiously 804.20 *immorally;* 712.12 *swearingly*
sacring bell 10.14 *sacred object;* 742.4 *signal*
sacristy 10.12 *church*
sacrosanct 8.13 *divine;* 252.7 *invulnerable*
sacrosanctity 8.1 *divinity*
sad 532.6; 602.5; 798.8 *afflicted;* 539.3 *depressed;* 604.9 *disappointed;* 583.11 *funeral;* 240.1 *inconvenient;* 603.4 *lamenting;* 627.7 *pitiful;* 236.4 *poor*
sadden 604.6 *disappoint;* 602.8 *grieve*
saddened 602.5 *sad*
sadder but wiser man 808.3 *penitent person*
saddle 320.11 *bicycle part;* 59.14 *horse-riding terms;* 414.14 *make heavy;* 89.1 *mountain;* 154.4 *mountain range;* 57.6 *pommel horse;* 413.4 *rest;* 59.16 *ride*
saddleback 154.4 *mountain range*
saddlebag 410.8 *bag;* 320.11 *bicycle part;* 320.5 *pack*
saddle-bronc-riding 59.12 *rodeo*
saddlecloth 550.14 *animal covering*
saddled 810.11 *duty-bound;* 414.3 *ponderous;* 243.18 *prepared*
saddled with 378.14 *blocked*
saddle horse 59.4
saddler 59.15 *horse person*
saddle tank 321.5 *locomotive part*
saddletree 79.12 *figurative usage*
saddle with 211.6 *add;* 378.12 *burden;* 810.17 *impose a duty*
saddling 414.8 *weighing down*
Sadducee 7.6 *non-Christian*
sad ending 798.2 *affliction*
sadhearted 602.5 *sad*
sadheartedness 602.1 *sorrow*
sadhu 7.3 *religious person*
sadism 651.2 *cruelness;* 796.7 *sexual assault*
sadist 651.8 *malefactor;* 796.10 *sex offender;* 804.9 *wicked person*
sadistic 651.11 *cruel;* 491.8 *inflicting pain;* 628.4 *pitiless;* 796.15 *unlawful*
sadistically 651.20 *malevolently;* 628.7 *pitilessly*
sadistic cruelty 651.2 *cruelness*
sadistic tyrant 628.3 *pitiless person*
Sadler's Wells Ballet 22.12 *ballet companies*
sadly 602.11; 798.13 *destructively;* 249.12 *in adversity;* 603.8 *mournfully*
sadness 249.1 *adversity;* 603.1 *lamentation;* 236.10 *poverty;* 602.1 *sorrow*
sado-masochism 796.7 *sexual assault*
sado-masochistic 796.15 *unlawful*
sad person 602.3
sad sack 249.5 *person in adversity*
SAD syndrome 36.13 *depression*
safari hunt 633.2 *chase*
safari hunter 633.6 *hunter*
safari park 70.8 *animal welfare*
safe 252.6; 253.5; 410.6 *box;* 452.1 *certain;* 736.2 *hiding place;* 805.5 *innocent;* 780.20 *money store;* 359.7 *preserved;* 609.4 *satisfied;* 253.6 *secure;* 439.4 *storage*
safe and sound 259.1 *healthy;* 230.1 *perfect;* 252.6 *safe;* 253.6 *secure;* 253.16 *surely*
safe as houses 252.6 *safe;* 253.6 *secure*
safe bet 107.5 *good chance;* 452.12 *something certain*
safe-blower 774.8 *thief*
safe-blowing 774.1 *stealing*
safe-breaker 774.8 *thief*
safe-breaking 774.1 *stealing*
safe conduct 318.6 *passport;* 252.2 *protection*
safe-conduct pass 757.2 *permit*
safe-cracker 774.8 *thief*
safe-cracking 774.1 *stealing*
safe-deposit 736.2 *hiding place;* 780.20 *money store;* 439.4 *storage*
safe-deposit box 780.20 *money store*
safe distance 634.10 *avoidance;* 252.1 *safety*
safeguard 384.2; 665.11 *care for;* 392.7 *convenience;* 384.17 *defend;* 223.15 *escort;* 616.2 *insurance;* 359.5 *preserve;* 253.11 *promise;* 252.10 *protect;* 252.2, 253.1 *protection;* 352.5 *reserves;* 252.4 *safety device;* 253.10 *secure;* 370.9 *welcome*
safeguarded 253.6 *secure*
safeguarding 384.1 *defence*
safeguard oneself 616.5 *be cautious*
safe hands 252.2 *protection*
safe house 736.2 *hiding place;* 252.2 *protection;* 550.15 *shelter*
safe job 252.1 *safety*
safekeep 253.10 *secure*
safekeeping 384.1 *defence;* 359.1 *preservation;* 252.2, 253.1 *protection*
safelight 41.12 *development*
safely 252.11; 222.18 *comfortably;* 589.8 *peacefully;* 253.16 *surely*
safeness 253.1 *protection;* 252.1 *safety*
safe place 252.5 *refuge;* 252.1 *safety*
safe retreat 252.5 *refuge*
Safety 252
safety 252.1; 65.2 *billiards play;* 65.4 *carom;* 46.10 *defence;* 62.8 *mountaineering;* 253.1 *protection;* 46.6 *scoring*
safety and health 15.2 *industrial negotiations*
safety barrier 61.6 *motor-racing terms*
safety belt 359.2 *preserver;* 252.4 *safety device*
safety bicycle 320.12 *bicycle*
safety catch 373.8 *fastening;* 309.3 *restrainer;* 252.4 *safety device*
safety chain 252.4 *safety device*
safety curtain 21.19 *stage set*
safety deposit box 253.5 *safe*
safety device 252.4; 359.2 *preserver*
safety first 616.2 *insurance*
safety glass 527.9 *glass;* 24.9 *industrial ceramics;* 411.5 *layered thing*
safety goggles 252.4 *safety device*
safety harness 252.4 *safety device*
safety hat 551.15 *headgear*
safety helmet 252.4 *safety device*
safety in numbers 252.1 *safety*
safety lamp 522.7 *lantern*
safety lock 252.4 *safety device*
safety match 522.8 *fire;* 437.2 *lighter;* 252.4 *safety device*
safety net 252.4 *safety device*
safety pin 373.8 *fastening;* 252.4 *safety device*
safety razor 252.4 *safety device*
safety rope 62.4 *climbing equipment*
safety ski stick 68.5 *ski equipment*
safety strap 68.5 *ski equipment*
safety valve 389.2 *means of escape;* 252.1 *safety;* 252.4 *safety device*
safety zone 252.5 *refuge*
saffron 496.5 *herbs;* 536.1 *orange;* 536.3 *orange thing*
saffron robe 570.6 *general terms*
saffron veil 570.6 *general terms*
sag 793.12 *be cheap;* 337.6 *be weak;* 305.10 *droop;* 305.2 *sinkage;* 419.13 *soften;* 388.4 *succumb;* 361.1 *suspension*
saga 692.25 *broadcast material;* 721.3 *narration;* 17.7 *poem*
sagacious 6.18 *educated;* 442.10 *intelligent;* 455.8 *knowledgeable;* 4.19 *learned;* 485.6 *skilful;* 458.5 *wise*
sagaciously 6.25 *educationally;* 442.15 *intelligently;* 458.9 *wisely*
sagaciousness 458.1 *wisdom*
sagacity 442.4 *cleverness;* 455.3 *learning;* 156.3 *profundity;* 485.1 *skill;* 458.1 *wisdom*
sage 4.12; 713.4 *adviser;* 667.14 *awe-inspiring;* 123.4 *bigwig;* 156.7 *deep thinking;* 400.9 *educational leader;* 496.5 *herbs;* 442.8 *intellectual person;* 442.10 *intelligent;* 455.6 *knowledgeable person;* 475.8 *oracle;* 396.10 *person of authority;* 485.4 *skilled person;* 458.3 *wise man*
sage-green 538.1 *green*
sagging 305.17 *drooping;* 305.2 *sinkage;* 361.7 *suspended;* 337.8 *weak*
sagittal 425.1 *sharp*
Sagittarius 330.16 *archer*
sagittate 77.18 *of leaves;* 425.1 *sharp*
Sahara 150.5 *broad thing;* 428.14 *desert;* 493.8 *hot place*
Saharan 428.6 *desert*
sahib 567.3 *male title of address;* 400.1 *master*
said 729.16 *speech*
said again 112.10 *iterated*
said before 112.10 *iterated*
sail 50.15; 323.10; 265.19 *go easily;* 323.9 *navigate;* 586.22 *navy;* 50.3 *parts of a sailing boat;* 50.18 *windsurf;* 50.7 *windsurfing*
sail against 381.1 *attack*
sailboard 50.18 *windsurf;* 50.7 *windsurfing*
Sailboard class 50.2 *sailing boat*
sailboat 323.3 *vessel*
sailboat on calm waters 339.3 *inert thing*
sail by the lee 50.15 *sail*
sail close-hauled 50.15 *sail*
sailcloth jacket 54.2 *fencing equipment*
sail downwind 50.15 *sail*
sailfish 55.4 *American game fish*
sail for 324.7 *take a direction*
sail home 265.17 *do easily*
sailing 50.1; 50.10; 323.11 *nautical;* 318.2 *passing along;* 323.1 *water travel;* 50.7 *windsurfing*
sailing aid 323.5 *navigation*
sailing boat 50.2; 323.3 *vessel*
sailing boat designer 50.9 *sailor*
sailing canoe 50.6 *canoeing*
sailing master 400.10 *expert;* 323.7 *nautical person*
sailing techniques 50.1 *sailing*
sailing trophy 50.1 *sailing*
sailing wind 50.1 *sailing*
sail into 381.5 *strike*
sail on a run 50.15 *sail*
sailor 50.9; 323.7 *nautical person;* 586.27 *naval man*
sailorly 323.11 *nautical*
sailorman 323.7 *nautical person*
sailor's dance 22.4 *historic dancing*
sail the high seas 91.9
sail the ocean 91.9 *sail the high seas*
sail under false colours 699.24 *pretend*
sainfoin 43.12 *crop*
saint 8.10 *deified person;* 768.4 *giver;* 797.15 *good person;* 805.4 *innocent person;* 255.5, 795.5 *pure person;* 7.3 *religious person;* 803.4 *virtuous person;* 631.3 *well-behaved person*
Saint Christopher's medal 475.6 *good-luck sign*
sainted 582.19 *dead*
sainthood 795.3 *moral purity*
sainting 8.9 *deification*
saintlike 803.5 *virtuous*
saintliness 795.2 *good morals;* 805.1 *innocence;* 803.1 *virtue*
saintly 8.14 *heavenly;* 805.5 *innocent;* 795.8 *moral;* 230.1 *perfect;* 799.5 *pure;* 7.15 *religious;* 803.5 *virtuous*
saints 582.14 *the spiritual world*
saints and sinners 113.3 *opposites*
saint's day 601.5 *anniversary;* 298.6 *annually celebrated day;* 275.11 *date*
salaam 367.9 *bow;* 367.16 *courtesy;* 658.13 *defer to;* 667.4 *mark of respect;* 663.3 *obeisance;* 733.2 *salutation;* 663.6 *show obeisance to;* 667.19 *take off one's hat to*
salaaming 658.4 *deference*
salable commodity 778.8 *merchandise*
salacious 796.12 *indecent;* 258.9 *obscene*
salaciously 258.12 *dirtily;* 796.21 *immorally*
salaciousness 796.2 *indecency;* 258.3 *obscenity;* 796.3 *sexual immorality*
salad 25.14; 25.9 *dish;* 223.5 *side-dish*
salad bowl 410.16 *crockery*
salad cream 25.15 *sauce*
salad days 275.5 *indefinite period;* 805.3 *naivety;* 248.3 *time of plenty;* 555.1 *youth*
salad dressing 25.15 *sauce;* 496.2 *seasoning*
salad fork 557.16 *eating utensil*
salad niçoise 25.14 *salad*
salad vegetable 25.33, 44.11 *vegetable*
salad vegetables 80.1 *fruits*
salamandrian 73.13 *amphibian*
salami 25.29 *sausage*
salaried 788.6 *received;* 769.11 *receiving;* 785.19 *receiving pay*
salary 765.4 *earnings;* 788.3 *income;* 785.3 *pay;* 483.5 *positive stimulus;* 813.4 *reward for service;* 769.2 *something received*
salary bill 790.6 *business costs*

salary earner 578.1 *worker*
salary negotiations 15.1 *industrial relations*
salchow jump 68.6 *ice-skating*
Sale 778
sale 778.4; 791.2 *bargain*; 752.3 *business offer*; 793.9 *cheap*; 767.2 *disposal of property*; 778.3 *selling*
saleability 767.2 *disposal of property*; 778.7 *market*
saleable 778.15; 767.14 *for sale*; 768.7 *given*; 776.13 *mercantile*
saleableness 767.2 *disposal of property*
saleably 778.17 *marketably*
sale and lease back 767.2 *disposal of property*
sale by auction 778.4 *sale*
sale goods 793.4 *bargain*
sale merchandise 793.4 *bargain*
sale of office 778.3 *selling*
sale of the century 791.2 *bargain*; 480.9 *enticement*; 778.4 *sale*
sale of work 779.10 *bazaar*; 778.4 *sale*
sale price 793.1 *cheapness*; 790.1 *price*
sale-price 752.17 *offered*
sale-priced 793.9 *cheap*
saleroom 779.1 *market*
sales 778.5
salesclerk 401.3 *attendant*
sales conference 778.6 *salesmanship*
sales coverage 778.3 *selling*
sales force 778.10 *salesman*
sales forecasting 778.6 *salesmanship*
salesgirl 778.10 *salesman*
salesman 778.10; 483.7 *motivator*; 480.12 *persuader*; 729.10 *speaker*
salesman of the month 485.5 *expert*
salesmanship 778.6; 480.1 *persuasion*
sales patter 778.6 *salesmanship*
salesperson 778.10 *salesman*; 729.10 *speaker*
sales pitch 480.1 *persuasion*
sales promotion 480.6 *advertising*
sales representative 778.10 *salesman*
sales revenue 13.6 *economic factors*; 788.2 *money received*
sales talk 483.2 *inducement*; 480.1 *persuasion*; 778.6 *salesmanship*
sales tax 13.6 *economic factors*; 788.2 *money received*; 790.7 *tax*
sales volume 788.2 *money received*
saleswoman 778.10 *salesman*; 729.10 *speaker*
salience 185.1 *prominence*
salient 525.7 *appearing*; 585.10 *battleground*; 520.2 *clear*; 185.6 *eminent*; 738.14 *manifest*
salient angle 27.39 *angle*
Salienta 73.7 *amphibian*
salientian 73.7, 73.13 *amphibian*
salient point 123.3 *chief thing*
salimeter 26.8 *meter*
salimetric 26.16 *micrometric*
salimetry 26.2 *micrometry*
salina 88.1 *lake*; 92.3 *marsh*
saline 32.36 *acid*
salinity 30.12 *ocean*
salinometer 26.8 *meter*
salinometric 26.16 *micrometric*
salinometry 26.2 *micrometry*
saliva 560.9; 431.3 *body fluid*; 433.4 *exudate*; 268.5 *lubricant*; 559.2 *secreted substance*
salivant 371.29 *expulsive*
salivary 371.29 *expulsive*; 559.5 *of a secretion*
salivary gland 560.9 *saliva*
salivate 560.20; 617.14 *be hungry*; 557.22 *eat well*; 315.12 *leak*; 559.7 *secrete*; 429.16, 433.32 *seep*
salivating 560.29; 559.4 *secretory*
salivation 560.9 *saliva*; 559.1 *secretion*
sallet 384.7 *armour*
sallow 530.8 *drained of colour*; 531.4 *pale*; 260.21 *unhealthy*; 537.4 *yellow-faced*
sallowness 531.7 *whiteness*
sally 381.8 *counterattack*; 315.10 *emerge*; 381.14 *siege*
sally forth 315.10 *emerge*; 313.5 *set out*; 130.19 *start off*
sally port 384.12 *fort*
salmagundi 412.2 *mixed thing*
salmon 55.4 *American game fish*; 55.5 *British game fish*; 74.8 *food fish*; 25.17 *freshwater fish*
salmon fishing 633.2 *chase*
salmon-pink 535.1 *red*
salmon sandwich 25.11 *sandwich*
salmon trout 25.17 *freshwater fish*
Salomonic column 20.8 *column*
salon 19.11 *artist's materials*; 18.28 *concert hall*; 654.4 *meeting place*; 565.7 *room*
saloon 320.16 *car*; 50.8 *punting*
salp 75.2 *protochordate*
salsa 18.10 *world music*
SALT 755.3 *alliance*
salt 32.10; 25.7 *basic ingredient*; 699.25 *be fraudulent*; 243.7 *develop*; 557.11 *food content*; 323.7 *nautical person*; 359.5 *preserve*; 359.2 *preserver*; 496.12 *season*; 496.2 *seasoning*
salt a mine 699.25 *be fraudulent*
saltant 304.24 *leaping*
saltation 304.5 *jump*
saltatorial 304.24 *leaping*
saltatorily 327.29 *jerkily*
saltatory 327.19 *convulsive*; 304.24 *leaping*
salt away 439.6 *store*
salted 359.7 *preserved*
salted mine 699.8 *fraud*
salted nuts 25.10 *snack*
salt flat 428.14 *desert*; 92.3 *marsh*
salt-free diet 557.6 *nutrition*
salt gland 559.3 *gland*
salt-glaze 24.3 *glaze*
salt-glazed 24.10 *ceramic*
salt-glazed porcelain 24.1 *ceramics*
saltimbanco 699.19 *cheat*; 21.31 *circus performer*; 700.15 *deceiver*
saltiness 495.4 *flavour*
saltire 743.8 *heraldic device*
SALT I Treaty 749.1 *pacification*
salt lake 88.1 *lake*
saltlick 557.8 *animal food*
salt marsh 92.3, 429.8 *marsh*
salt of the earth 123.4 *bigwig*; 235.7 *elite*; 799.3 *honourable person*
saltpan 92.3 *marsh*
saltpetre 587.15 *explosive*
salt pork 25.30 *bacon*; 557.7 *food*
salt sea 91.1 *sea*
salt tax 790.9 *historical taxes*
salt water 91.1 *sea*; 433.1 *water*
saltwater bait fishing 55.1 *angling*
saltwater fish 74.1 *fishes*; 25.18 *sea fish*
saltwater fisherman 55.6 *angler*
saltwater fishing 55.1 *angling*
saltwater trolling 55.1 *angling*
salty 323.11 *nautical*; 91.7 *oceanic*; 496.9 *piquant*; 495.7 *tasty*
salty taste 495.1 *taste*
salubrious 256.16 *clean*; 797.1 *good*; 259.2 *healthful*; 257.4 *hygienic*; 160.12 *on form*; 359.6 *preserving*; 394.17 *remedial*; 252.6 *safe*; 235.4 *worthwhile*
salubriously 259.8 *healthily*; 257.7 *hygienically*
salubriousness 259.4 *healthfulness*; 257.2 *salubrity*
salubrity 257.2; 259.4 *healthfulness*
salut! 312.23 *hello!*
salutary 392.34 *beneficial*; 797.1 *good*; 259.2 *healthful*; 257.4 *hygienic*; 237.4 *profitable*; 235.4 *worthwhile*
salutation 733.2; 514.4 *cry of greeting*; 667.6 *greeting*; 658.5 *sign of courtesy*
salutations 667.7 *respects*
salutatory 733.14 *vocative*
salutatory address 733.2 *salutation*
salute 601.8; **601.18**; **667.20**; 733.9 *approach*; 558.14 *drink to*; 600.2 *fanfare*; 600.6 *fête*; 742.11 *gesture*; 658.12 *greet*; 667.6 *greeting*; 667.4 *mark of respect*; 658.5 *sign of courtesy*
salutiferous 394.17 *remedial*
saluting 667.11 *in a respectful stance*
salvable 390.4 *deliverable*
salvably 390.6 *extricably*
salvage 608.2 *aid*; 790.6 *business costs*; 390.1 *deliver*; 390.2 *deliverance*; 393.9 *restoration*; 393.3 *restore*; 3.23 *turn back time*
salvageable 390.4 *deliverable*
salvage company 390.3 *deliverer*
salvaged 393.13 *repaired*
salvager 393.12 *repairer*
salvation 608.2 *aid*; 708.5 *cancellation*; 390.2 *deliverance*; 391.1 *liberation*; 359.1 *preservation*; 393.9 *restoration*
Salvation Army 650.2 *charity*
Salvation Army bonnet 7.11 *vestment*
salvationism 7.2 *religiousness*
salvationist 7.4 *religionist*
salva veritate 4.8 *philosophical term*
salve 394.5 *analgesic*; 268.19 *anoint*; 394.9 *balm*; 677.2 *blarney*; 490.10 *comfort*; 37.7, 268.6 *ointment*
salve one's conscience 805.8 *be innocent*; 808.5 *do penance*
salver 410.16 *crockery*
salvo 508.1 *bang*; 381.15 *firing*; 601.8 *salute*; 330.7 *shot*
sal volatile 496.6 *cordial*; 394.7 *tonic*
salvor 393.12 *repairer*
Salyut 29.30 *spacecraft*
samadhi 11.10 *psychic phenomenon*
samara 80.2 *botanical fruit*
Samaritan 652.3 *philanthropist*
Samaveda 10.8 *hymn*; 7.12 *religious text*
samba 22.2 *dance*
Sam Brown belt 373.10 *band*
same 111.12; 750.14 *conforming*; 119.6 *equal*; 115.7 *similar*
same damn thing 620.2 *boring thing*
same date 285.1 *same time*
same day 285.1 *same time*
same degree 119.1 *equality*
same meaning 694.4 *type of meaning*
Sameness 111
sameness 111.1; 620.1 *boredom*; 750.5 *conformity*; 132.5 *continuity*; 119.1 *equality*; 122.5 *inferior state*; 115.1 *similarity*
same old round 112.3 *repetitiveness*
same old story 620.2 *boring thing*; 111.6 *regularity*; 112.3 *repetitiveness*
same old thing 620.2 *boring thing*; 111.6 *regularity*
same quantity 119.1 *equality*
Same Time 285
same time 285.1
Samhain 10.16 *religious festival*
Sammael 8.7 *devil*
samosa 25.12 *hors d'oeuvre*; 25.49 *Indian dish*
samphire 25.33 *vegetable*
sample 495.3 *appetizer*; 772.9 *borrow illegally*; 35.7 *diagnosis*; 27.93 *equate*; 448.11 *experiment*; 703.3 *explanation*; 163.1, 163.5 *outline*; 163.6 *outlined*; 205.2 *particular*; 27.57 *population*; 448.2 *rehearsal*; 717.8 *representative*; 738.7 *showpiece*; 495.9, 557.23 *taste*
sample freedom 250.14 *be free*
sampler 495.3 *appetizer*; 18.25 *musical instrument*; 495.5 *taster*
sample size 27.57 *population*
sample statistic 27.57 *population*
sampling 495.3 *appetizer*; 27.57 *population*
samsara 554.8 *theories of life*
Samson 336.6 *muscleman*
samurai 586.6 *militarist*
San Andreas fault 30.20 *earth movement*; 92.10 *miscellaneous*
sanative 257.4 *hygienic*; 393.16 *restorative*
sanatorium 35.10, 394.14 *hospital*; 257.1 *hygiene*; 6.15 *schoolroom*
sanctification 575.1 *right*
sanctified 8.15 *deified*; 799.5 *pure*; 803.5 *virtuous*
sanctify 601.16 *commemorate*; 8.17 *deify*
sanctimonious 676.3 *affected*; 699.31, 700.37 *hypocritical*; 795.10 *moralistic*; 255.12 *morally pure*; 7.15 *religious*
sanctimonious fraud 700.19 *hypocrite*
sanctimoniously 795.13 *morally*; 255.18 *virtuously*
sanctimoniousness 676.1 *affectedness*; 699.3 *hypocrisy*; 255.1 *purity*; 7.2 *religiousness*; 795.4 *self-righteousness*
sanctimony 676.1 *affectedness*; 699.3 *hypocrisy*; 255.1 *purity*; 7.2 *religiousness*; 795.4 *self-righteousness*
sanction 669.12 *accept*; 392.23 *advise*; 669.1 *approval*; 13.6 *economic factors*; 396.21 *grant authority*; 16.29 *legalization*; 16.65 *make legal*; 396.9, 757.1 *permission*; 750.8, 750.29, 757.3 *permit*
sanctioned 396.16 *authorized*; 16.44 *legal*; 757.7 *permitted*; 750.18 *permitting*
sanctions 386.3 *coercive methods*; 585.8 *warfare*
sanctitude 8.1 *divinity*
sanctity 8.1 *divinity*; 799.2 *purity*; 803.1 *virtue*
sanctuary 10.12 *church*; 309.4 *closed place*; 736.2 *hiding place*; 172.2 *inside*; 252.2, 253.1 *protection*; 370.2 *receptivity*; 252.5 *refuge*; 565.11 *retreat*; 10.13 *shrine*; 655.5 *solitary place*; 773.4 *taking in*
sanctum 736.6 *privacy*; 252.5 *refuge*; 10.13 *shrine*; 655.5 *solitary place*
sanctum sanctorum 165.2 *enclosed place*; 252.5 *refuge*; 10.13 *shrine*
Sanctus 10.8 *hymn*
sanctus bell 10.14 *sacred object*
sand 23.17 *carpenter*; 92.4 *coast*; 427.9 *grit*; 38.26 *masonry*; 435.1 *materials*; 536.3 *orange thing*; 427.21 *powder*; 365.12 *rub*; 30.27 *sediment*; 421.11 *smooth*; 30.36 *soil*
sandals 551.19 *footwear*
sandalwood 502.3 *incense*
sandbag 587.7 *blunt weapon*; 331.8 *club*; 814.14 *instrument of punishment*; 384.8 *military defences*; 382.17 *murder*
sandbank 90.2 *channel*; 30.11 *coast*; 92.2 *island*; 376.26 *mass*; 157.4 *shallow thing*; 379.1 *trap*
sand bar 30.11 *coast*; 92.2 *island*; 157.4 *shallow thing*; 379.1 *trap*
sandblast 256.13 *clean*; 365.12 *rub*
sandblasting 365.2 *wearing away*
sand-blind 519.9 *weak-sighted*
sand-blindness 519.2 *poor sight*
sandbox 321.5 *locomotive part*
sand casting 19.12 *sculpture*
sand castle 424.3 *brittle thing*; 337.5 *weak thing*
sand column 31.16 *wind vortex*
sand dance 22.2 *dance*
sand dollar 75.3 *echinoderm*
sand dune 30.11 *coast*; 428.14 *desert*; 30.37 *dune*; 154.3 *mountain*
sand dunes 563.1 *infertility*
sander 365.7 *eraser*; 421.9 *smoother*; 438.1 *tool*; 23.11 *woodworking tool*
sand flea 76.3 *pest*
sandglass 281.9 *hourglass*
sand hopper 75.4 *arthropod*; 75.10 *parasite*
Sandhurst 585.6 *art of war*
sandiness 427.3 *graininess*
sanding 365.5 *polishing*
sanding disc 365.7 *eraser*
sandman 343.9 *sleep*
sandpaper 427.12 *abrasive*; 365.7 *eraser*; 420.12 *make rough*; 425.15 *make sharp*; 420.7 *rough thing*; 365.12 *rub*; 425.12 *sharpener*; 421.11 *smooth*; 421.9 *smoother*; 23.11 *woodworking tool*
sandpiper 72.3 *water bird*
sand pit 47.2 *field events*
sands 92.10 *miscellaneous*
sand shot 56.3 *golf shots*
sandspit 92.5 *peninsula*
sandstone 20.4 *building material*; 38.26 *masonry*
sandstorm 524.2 *murk*; 528.7 *opaque thing*; 380.5 *violent weather*; 31.12 *wind*
sand trap 56.1 *golf*
sand wave 30.11 *coast*
sandwich 25.11; 411.10 *layer*; 411.5 *layered thing*
sandwich bar 557.15 *eating place*
sandwich board 740.9 *advertisement*
sandwich boards 738.8 *showplace*
sandwich compound 32.7 *chemical compound*
sandwich course 6.2 *educational system*
sandwich-maker 493.4 *burner*; 25.5 *cooker*
sandwichman 740.10 *publicizer*
sandy 92.11 *continental*; 428.6 *desert*; 30.58 *earthy*; 427.17 *grainy*; 535.3 *red-haired*
sane 460.4; 695.1 *intelligible*; 444.7 *reasoning*
sanely 460.7; 444.15 *reasonably*
saneness 444.1 *reason*; 460.1 *sanity*
sane person 460.3
Sanforize™ 191.5 *make smaller*; 42.15 *treat*
Sanforized™ 191.7 *smaller*; 42.11 *treated*
Sanforizing™ 42.8 *fabric treatment*
San Francisco 87.2 *American cities*
sang-froid 684.3 *calmness*; 4.3 *detachment*; 265.4 *ease of manner*; 685.1 *moderation*
sangha 10.17 *worshipper*
Sangreal 756.4 *promised land*; 10.14 *sacred object*
sangria 558.8 *mixed drink*
sanguinarily 431.26 *fluidly*; 535.10 *ruddily*

sanguinary 535.4 *bloody*; 382.24 *murderous*
sanguine 474.5 *expecting*; 599.12 *four humours*; 610.11 *hopeful*; 36.7 *personality type*; 535.2 *red-faced*; 605.8 *resigned*
sanguinely 431.26 *fluidly*; 605.9 *stoically*
sanguineous 431.18, 535.4 *bloody*
sanguineously 535.10 *ruddily*
sanguinity 605.2 *stoicism*
Sanhedrin 579.7 *council*
Sanhedrist 579.16 *official*
sanies 431.3 *body fluid*; 560.7 *pus*
sanious 431.16 *rheumy*
sanitarian 257.3 *hygienist*
sanitarily 257.7 *hygienically*
sanitary 256.16 *clean*; 256.18 *cleansing*; 259.2 *healthful*; 257.4 *hygienic*; 255.15 *purifying*; 394.17 *remedial*
sanitary engineer 256.12 *cleaner*; 257.3 *hygienist*
sanitary inspector 257.3 *hygienist*
sanitary precaution 394.3 *prophylactic*; 252.2 *protection*
sanitate 394.20 *doctor*; 257.6 *make hygienic*; 252.10 *protect*; 255.10 *purify*
sanitation 256.2 *cleaning*; 257.1 *hygiene*; 394.3 *prophylactic*; 255.2 *purification*
sanitize 257.6 *make hygienic*; 252.10 *protect*; 255.10, 256.15 *purify*
Sanity 460
sanity 460.1; 444.1 *reason*
Sankhya 4.7 *school of thought*
sankyo 52.10 *aikido*
sannyasi 7.3 *religious person*; 655.6 *unsocial person*
sans-culotte 662.11 *rebel*
sans-culottism 662.4 *revolution*
sans pareil 121.14 *best*
sans serif 5.41 *lettered*
sans serif type 5.15 *type style*
Santa Claus 679.9 *generous person*; 768.4 *giver*
santification 8.9 *deification*
santon 655.6 *unsocial person*
sanyasin 450.5 *believer*
sap 183.2 *concave land*; 700.22 *dupe*; 99.2 *essential content*; 245.5 *hurt*; 431.2 *juice*; 335.7 *remove power from*; 305.15 *tunnel*; 337.7 *weaken*
sapid 495.7 *tasty*
sapidity 495.1 *taste*
sapience 442.4 *cleverness*; 458.1 *wisdom*
sapient 442.11 *thoughtful*; 458.5 *wise*
Sapir-Whorf hypothesis 5.37 *linguistic theory*
sapless 428.3 *dried-up*
sapling 77.2 *plant*; 79.1 *tree*; 555.5 *young plant*
saponaceous 268.13 *slippery*
saponacity 268.3 *oiliness*
saponifiable lipid 33.6 *lipid*
saponification 33.7 *fat*; 32.5 *process*
saponify 32.26 *react*
sapped 245.12 *deteriorated*; 337.11 *weakened*
sapper 586.17 *army person*; 183.5 *digger*
Sapphic 568.10 *homosexual*; 17.19 *narrative*
Sapphic ode 17.7 *poem*
Sapphics 17.10 *verse form*
sapphire 539.1 *blue*; 539.6 *blue thing*
sappiness 431.5 *fluidity*; 431.7 *juiciness*; 555.2 *youthfulness*
sapping 305.7 *tunnelling*
sappy 431.15 *flowing*; 538.4 *fresh*; 292.10 *spring*
saprophyte 83.5 *fungal association*; 77.4 *lower plant*
saprophytic 83.10 *of fungi*; 77.14 *of plants*
saprophytically 83.13; 77.24 *herbaceously*
sap the foundations of 357.9 *demolish*
sapwood 79.3 *timber*; 23.12 *wood*
saraband 22.4 *historic dancing*
sarasparilla 558.6 *soft drink*
sarcasm 621.1 *mockery*; 668.4 *ridicule*; 599.3 *wit*
sarcastic 621.5 *derisive*; 651.14 *hostile*; 599.10 *humorous*; 668.14 *ridiculing*; 678.17 *scornful*; 499.7 *splenetic*
sarcastically 599.16 *humorously*; 668.29 *mockingly*; 499.11 *splenetically*
sarcoma 260.12 *cancer*
sarcophagus 410.6 *box*; 583.1 *burial*
sardine 74.8 *food fish*; 25.18 *sea fish*
sardonic 621.5 *derisive*
sari 551.16 *robe*
sark 551.8 *shirt*
Sarnath 10.13 *shrine*
sarnie 25.11 *sandwich*
sarong 551.6 *skirt*
sartor 551.26 *fashion designer*
sartorial 551.31 *styled*
Sartrism 4.7 *school of thought*
Sartrist 4.11 *follower of a doctrine*
SAS 586.14 *armed forces*; 235.7 *elite*
sash 551.25 *accessories*; 373.10 *band*; 179.3 *circular thing*; 743.4 *insignia*
sash weight 708.7 *cancelling out*
Sasquatch 70.7 *legendary beast*; 89.3 *mountaineer*
sass 661.3 *act of defiance*; 660.25 *answer back*; 167.5 *boldness*; 660.2 *cheek*; 661.5 *defy*
sassily 660.31 *cheekily*; 668.28 *disrespectfully*
sassiness 660.11 *sauciness*
sassy 167.9 *arrogant*; 659.6 *bad-mannered*; 660.14 *cheeky*; 661.7 *defiant*; 668.10 *disrespectful*
Satan 236.12 *bad person*; 8.7 *devil*; 798.6 *evil person*; 699.18, 700.16 *liar*; 804.6 *religious sin*; 480.13 *tempter*
satanic 651.11 *cruel*; 8.16 *devilish*; 9.10 *idolatrous*; 804.14 *impious*; 11.15 *witchlike*
satanically 8.20 *devilishly*; 804.20 *immorally*
Satanism 9.2 *idolatry*; 804.6 *religious sin*
Satanist 9.6 *idolater*; 804.9 *wicked person*
satchel 410.8 *bag*
sate 620.6 *be boring*; 219.4 *be excessive*; 596.7 *cause dislike*; 557.22 *eat well*; 232.6 *fill*; 490.9 *give pleasure*; 609.8 *satisfy*; 217.4 *suffice*
sated 261.2, 620.5 *bored*; 596.8 *disliking*; 557.26 *eating*; 219.6 *excessive*; 217.3 *filled*; 232.8 *full*
satellite 29.18; **29.32**; 664.5 *adherent*; 387.4 *dependent*; 223.9, 267.5 *follower*; 122.6 *inferior*; 85.16 *national*; 306.4 *orbiting body*
satellite communication 692.7
satellite link 373.2 *association*
satellite nation 85.3 *dominion*
satellite radio 692.20 *radio broadcasting*
satellite status 387.1 *subjection*
satellite television 692.21 *television*; 692.24 *television broadcasting*
satellite tracking 29.32 *satellite*
satiate 620.6 *be boring*; 219.4 *be excessive*; 490.9 *give pleasure*; 609.8 *satisfy*; 217.4 *suffice*
satiated 261.2, 620.5 *bored*; 219.6 *excessive*; 217.3 *filled*; 232.8 *full*; 609.4 *satisfied*
satiating 620.4 *boring*; 219.6 *excessive*; 609.5 *satisfying*
satiation 609.1 *satisfaction*
satiety 620.1 *boredom*; 232.2 *fullness*; 219.2 *overdoing it*; 609.1 *satisfaction*; 217.7 *sufficiency*; 219.3 *superfluity*
satin 404.2 *grain*; 404.9 *smooth*; 421.8 *smooth thing*; 419.11 *soft thing*; 193.4 *textile*
satininess 404.2 *grain*; 419.9, 421.7 *smoothness*
satinlike 419.3 *smooth*
satin-smooth 421.5 *smooth as a peach*
satiny 404.9, 419.3, 421.1 *smooth*
satire 621.2 *act of derision*; 21.12 *comedy*; 599.4 *entertainment*; 125.3 *mockery*; 17.7 *poem*; 668.4, 678.6 *ridicule*
satirical 621.5 *derisive*; 599.10 *humorous*; 668.14 *ridiculing*
satirical comedy 21.12 *comedy*
satirically 599.16 *humorously*; 621.7, 668.29 *mockingly*
satirical poetry 17.6 *poetry*
satirist 17.14 *author*; 621.3 *derider*; 599.6 *humorist*; 678.9 *ridiculer*
satirize 599.13 *be humorous*; 621.6 *deride*; 125.9 *imitate*; 668.24, 678.14 *ridicule*
Satisfaction 609
satisfaction 609.1; **622.7**; 669.1 *approval*; 807.1 *atonement*; 813.6 *compensation*; 785.1 *payment*; 490.1 *physical pleasure*; 241.7 *pleasure*; 813.1 *reward*; 217.7 *sufficiency*
satisfactorily 609.12; 669.26 *approvably*; 217.9 *enough*; 801.18 *properly*
satisfactoriness 609.3
satisfactory 609.6; 669.22 *approvable*; 235.5 *not bad*; 217.1 *sufficient*
satisfactory amount 217.7 *sufficiency*
satisfied 609.4; 669.18 *approving*; 452.2 *convinced*; 217.3 *filled*; 622.20 *fulfilled*; 232.8 *full*; 749.6 *pacificatory*; 490.7 *pleased*
satisfy 609.8; 807.5 *atone*; 232.6 *fill*; 241.13, 490.9 *give pleasure*; 669.17 *meet with approval*; 749.4 *pacify*; 785.7 *pay off*; 813.9 *reward*; 217.4 *suffice*; 27.89 *theorize*
satisfying 609.5; 807.4 *atoning*; 749.6 *pacificatory*; 241.1, 490.6 *pleasant*; 813.15 *rewarding*; 217.1 *sufficient*
satisfyingly 490.11 *pleasingly*; 813.19 *rewardingly*
satisfy one's appetite 685.5 *moderate one's hunger*
satori 8.11 *heaven*; 301.2 *repose*
satrap 400.4 *absolute ruler*
satsuma 536.3 *orange thing*
Sattyaloka 8.11 *heaven*
saturate 219.4 *be excessive*; 97.11 *be present*; 232.6 *fill*; 32.25 *solidify*; 433.29 *water*
saturated 31.43 *atmospheric*; 32.35 *combined*; 433.22 *diluted*; 219.6 *excessive*; 232.8 *full*; 32.32 *solid*; 433.23 *wet*
saturated compound 32.7 *chemical compound*
saturated fat 33.7 *fat*
saturated fats 557.11 *food content*
saturated solution 32.3 *phase*
saturation 31.9 *atmospheric process*; 433.5 *dilution*; 219.1 *excess*; 232.2 *fullness*; 529.3 *hue*; 429.3 *humidity*; 412.1 *mixture*; 433.9 *soaking*
saturation bombing 381.13 *air attack*; 585.8 *warfare*
saturation level 41.10 *graininess*
saturation point 219.1 *excess*; 232.2 *fullness*; 429.3 *humidity*
Saturday 10.15 *holy day*
Saturday night special 587.9 *firearm*
Saturn 29.16 *planet*
Saturnalia 10.16 *religious festival*
saturnalia 601.1 *celebration*; 686.2 *dissipation*
Saturnian 29.36 *astronomical*
Saturnia regna 248.3 *time of plenty*
saturnine 626.6 *sullen*
saturninely 626.13 *sullenly*
Saturn V 29.35 *rocketry*
satyagraha 749.1 *pacification*; 4.7 *school of thought*
satyr 8.5 *deity*; 796.8 *immoral man*
satyriasis 36.15 *compulsion*; 461.4 *delusion*; 617.4 *sexual desire*; 796.3 *sexual immorality*
satyr play 21.12 *comedy*
sauce 25.15; 211.3 *additional item*; 659.2 *bad manners*; 167.5 *boldness*; 25.55 *cook*; 661.1 *defiance*; 431.2 *juice*; 495.10 *make taste*; 496.2 *seasoning*; 223.5 *side-dish*
saucebox 660.12 *impudent person*
sauce espagnole 25.15 *sauce*
saucepan 25.6 *kitchen equipment*; 410.15 *pot*
saucer 24.8 *ceramic object*; 179.3 *circular thing*; 410.16 *crockery*; 187.3 *flat thing*
saucer dome 20.6 *roof*
sauce suprême 25.15 *sauce*
saucily 660.31 *cheekily*; 661.9 *defiantly*; 659.10 *rudely*
sauciness 660.11; 661.1 *defiance*
saucy 659.6 *bad-mannered*; 660.14 *cheeky*; 661.7 *defiant*; 668.10 *disrespectful*
Sauerbraten 25.46 *German dish*
Sauerkraut 25.46 *German dish*
sault 90.2 *channel*
sauna 256.6 *bath*; 493.8 *hot place*
saunter 300.12 *gait*; 333.1 *move slowly*; 333.10 *slow motion*; 300.15 *walk*
sauntering 333.4 *slow*
Sauria 73.2 *lizard*
saurian 73.2 *lizard*; 73.11 *reptilian*
saurischian 73.6 *extinct reptile*
sauropod 73.6 *extinct reptile*
sauropterygian 73.6 *extinct reptile*
sausage 25.29
sausagemeat 25.29 *sausage*
sauté 25.55 *cook*
sautéed 25.56 *culinary*
sautéeing 25.8 *cooking technique*
Sauternes 498.5 *sweet drink*; 558.9 *wine*
savage 624.16 *angry*; 381.23 *attacking*; 659.6 *bad-mannered*; 651.11 *cruel*; 659.4 *discourteous person*; 236.14 *ill-treat*; 491.11 *inflict pain*; 651.17 *kill*; 382.24 *murderous*; 646.1 *naive*; 646.3 *naive person*; 381.5 *strike*; 380.6 *violent*; 380.4 *violent creature*; 675.5 *vulgar person*; 804.9 *wicked person*
savage beast 380.4 *violent creature*
savagely 651.20 *malevolently*; 659.10 *rudely*
savageness 651.2 *cruelness*
savagery 651.2 *cruelness*; 646.2 *naivety*; 380.2 *physical violence*
savages 566.3 *early human*
savaging 491.3 *injury*
savanna 81.2 *grassland*; 92.6 *lowland*; 77.1 *plants*
savant 485.5 *expert*; 442.8 *intellectual person*; 455.6 *knowledgeable person*; 4.12 *sage*
save 608.10; **680.6**; 765.11 *acquire*; 616.5 *be cautious*; 243.3 *be prepared*; 212.8 *by subtraction*; 390.1 *deliver*; 360.7 *detain*; 128.12 *exclusively*; 66.2 *football play*; 392.17 *help*; 682.7 *hoard*; 780.27 *invest*; 391.4 *liberate*; 350.5 *not use*; 760.11 *persuade*; 48.4 *pitching terms*; 66.4 *play soccer*; 359.5 *preserve*; 765.14 *profit*; 252.10 *protect*; 384.23 *rescue*; 393.3 *restore*; 439.6 *store*
saveable 390.4 *deliverable*
save and except 212.8 *by subtraction*
save by the bell 390.1 *deliver*; 52.11 *fight*
saved 789.11 *accounted*; 8.15 *deified*; 390.4 *deliverable*; 760.16 *influenced*; 391.7 *liberated*; 359.7 *preserved*; 393.13 *repaired*; 360.10 *retained*; 439.7 *stored*; 350.1 *unused*
saved by the bell 390.4 *deliverable*
save face 622.31
save from 390.1 *deliver*
saveloy 25.29 *sausage*
save one's ass 252.9 *be safe*
save one's bacon 252.9 *be safe*; 389.5 *escape*
save oneself 389.5 *escape*
save oneself the trouble 265.20 *take it easy*
save one's face 622.31 *save face*
save one's own skin 716.13 *turn queen's evidence*
save one's skin 252.9 *be safe*; 389.5 *escape*
saver 680.3; 783.6 *depositor*; 765.7 *gainer*
save someone's bacon 348.4 *be an instrument*
Save the Children 652.5 *charity*
save the life of 554.20 *support life*
save up 765.11 *acquire*; 682.7 *hoard*; 359.5 *preserve*; 439.6 *store*
Savile Row 551.2 *dressing*
saving 390.4 *deliverable*; 390.2 *deliverance*; 360.2 *detention*; 359.1 *preservation*; 680.4 *thrifty*
saving clause 136.7 *condition*
saving grace 803.2 *virtues*
saving qualities 803.2 *virtues*
savings 616.2 *insurance*; 14.4 *personal finance*; 243.10 *preparations*; 765.5 *profit*; 252.2 *protection*; 439.1 *store*; 773.5 *takings*; 350.11 *unused thing*; 781.5 *wealth*
savings account 789.1 *accounts*; 780.6 *funds*; 252.2 *protection*; 439.1 *store*; 781.5 *wealth*
savings account deposit 783.3 *deposit*
savings and loan association 771.4 *lending institution*; 780.19 *treasury*
savings bank 783.4 *bank*; 780.19 *treasury*
saving up 359.1 *preservation*
saving your grace 667.23
saving your reverence 667.23 *saving your grace*
saviour 390.3 *deliverer*; 768.4 *giver*; 391.3 *liberator*; 595.4 *likable person*; 359.4 *preservationist*; 384.15 *rescuer*
savoir-faire 631.2 *good conduct*; 658.2 *good manners*; 455.1 *knowledge*; 6.11 *refinement*; 485.1 *skill*; 654.2 *social ambition*
savoir-vivre 658.2 *good manners*; 654.2 *social ambition*
savorous 500.5 *odorous*; 495.7 *tasty*
savory 496.5 *herbs*
savour 139.3 *characteristic*; 495.4 *flavour*; 241.14, 595.7 *like*; 500.1 *odour*; 500.4 *reputation*; 495.9, 557.23 *taste*
savouries 25.9 *dish*
savouring 557.3 *delicate eating*
savour of 115.10 *be similar*; 694.10 *mean*
savoury 557.27 *edible*; 496.9 *piquant*; 241.4, 495.7 *tasty*
savoury food 557.7 *food*
savvy 442.5 *common sense*; 455.11 *know*; 455.1 *knowledge*; 6.9 *learnedness*; 695.6 *understand*
saw 23.17 *carpenter*; 517.10 *lack har-*

mony; 38.9 *machine tool;* 745.1 *maxim;* 795.7 *moral;* 308.18 *open;* 308.2 *opener;* 372.9 *separate;* 425.9 *sharp-edged thing;* 513.5 *sound hoarse;* 79.7 *timber production;* 438.1 *tool;* 425.16 *use a sharp tool;* 438.10 *use tools;* 23.11 *woodworking tool*
sawbench 79.7 *timber production*
sawbones 35.11 *doctor;* 394.15 *healer*
sawbuck 780.8 *American money*
sawdust 427.5 *powder;* 215.2 *residue*
sawed 308.12 *open*
saw-edge 420.6 *roughness;* 425.7 *sharp point*
saw-edged 425.3 *sharp-edged*
sawlike 183.7 *notched*
sawmill 79.7 *timber production;* 577.1 *workshop*
sawn-off 149.8 *shortened*
sawn-off shotgun 587.9 *firearm*
saw-toothed 183.7 *notched*
saw-tooth wave 326.5 *wave*
sawyer 578.2 *artisan;* 23.13 *carpenter*
saxe blue 539.1 *blue*
saxicolous 84.8 *lichenoid*
Saxon 296.14 *historic*
Saxon blue 539.5 *blueness*
Saxons 284.6 *people of the past*
say 707.17 *affirm;* 147.13 *nearly;* 729.11 *speak;* 701.15 *state;* 707.2 *statement;* 121.1 *superiority;* 729.7 *utterance*
sayable 757.8 *permitting*
say again 112.17 *iterate*
say aye 750.28 *consent*
say clearly 694.10 *mean*
say directly 694.10 *mean*
sayer 729.10 *speaker*
say farewell 313.6 *part*
say goodbye to 766.9 *lose*
say good morning to 733.9 *approach*
say grace 671.7 *give thanks;* 10.20 *pray*
say hear hear 750.28 *consent*
say hello 658.12 *greet*
say "I do" 570.15 *marry;* 756.7 *promise*
saying 745.1 *maxim;* 795.7 *moral;* 707.2 *statement*
saying again 112.2 *iteration*
saying little 732.2 *sparing with words*
say in other words 694.10 *mean*
say it again 509.14 *repeat*
say it all 232.5 *be complete*
say magic words 11.21 *bewitch*
say no 708.10 *be negative;* 753.6 *protest;* 709.5 *refuse*
say nothing 251.10 *restrain oneself*
say no to 470.1 *reject;* 364.1 *repel;* 399.3 *veto;* 670.15 *withhold approval*
say one is sorry 807.6 *apologize;* 808.4 *be penitent*
say one's prayers 10.20 *pray*
say one will 756.7 *promise*
say 'Our Father' 10.20 *pray*
say outright 271.7 *be simple*
say over again 112.17 *iterate*
say over and over 112.18 *harp*
say plainly 694.10 *mean*
say prayers 10.19 *offer worship;* 9.7 *worship*
say so 707.21 *be assertive;* 397.9 *command*
say-so 250.1 *freedom;* 396.9 *permission;* 707.2 *statement*
say thank you 671.6 *be grateful*
say the Lord's Prayer 10.20 *pray*
say the magic word 757.3 *permit*
say the prayers 752.15 *offer worship*
say the word 750.28 *consent*
say together 285.7 *synchronize*
say to oneself 735.3 *soliloquize*
say yes to 757.3 *permit;* 756.7 *promise*
SBA 322.6 *flight control*
sc 139.31 *namely*
scab 550.14 *animal covering;* 325.19 *deviant person;* 751.4 *dissenter;* 15.7 *employee;* 479.9 *equivocator;* 594.8 *hated person;* 44.12 *pests and diseases;* 753.4 *protester;* 662.12 *reactionary;* 709.4 *refuser;* 420.7 *rough thing*
scabbard 587.4 *arsenal*
scabbing over 393.11 *recuperation*
scabby 420.2 *coarse;* 258.8 *unclean*
scab formation 393.11 *recuperation*
scabicide 37.4 *drug type*
scabies 260.13 *skin disease*
scab over 393.6 *cure*
scabrid 548.5 *marked*
scabrous 420.2 *coarse;* 796.12 *indecent;* 548.5 *marked;* 258.9 *obscene*
scabrousness 420.6 *roughness*
scads 208.2 *multitude*
scads of money 780.3 *fortune;* 781.6 *money*
scaffold 382.5 *execution;* 403.4 *framework;* 814.16 *instrument of execution;* 243.10 *preparations;* 413.11 *support*
scaffolding 243.10 *preparations;* 413.2 *supporting part*
scag 691.6 *drug*
scag jones 691.4 *drug taker*
scalable 304.25 *ladder-like*
scalar 304.25 *ladder-like;* 27.50 *scalar quantity*
scalariform 304.25 *ladder-like*
scalar product 27.50 *scalar quantity*
scalar quantity **27.50**
scald 493.14 *be hot;* 25.55 *cook;* 491.11 *inflict pain;* 491.3 *injury;* 44.12 *pests and diseases*
scalding 493.9 *hot;* 491.5 *painful*
scale **411.11**; 550.14 *animal covering;* 420.11 *be rough;* 304.14 *climb;* 89.10 *climb a mountain;* 132.2 *consecution;* 209.1 *degree;* 74.5 *fish anatomy;* 108.2 *interrelatedness;* 18.20 *key;* 304.9 *ladder;* 209.5 *measure;* 26.6, 28.82 *measuring instrument;* 18.16 *musical note;* 552.16 *peel;* 76.3 *pest;* 205.7 *piece;* 57.6 *pommel horse;* 420.7 *rough thing;* 414.10 *scales;* 158.1 *size;* 411.4 *slice;* 304.10 *step*
scale a peak 62.9 *mountaineer*
scale armour 384.7 *armour*
scaled 209.7 *gradational*
scaled-down 191.7 *smaller*
scale down 191.5, 214.5 *make smaller;* 206.8 *reduce*
scale drawing 484.5 *map*
scale insect 76.3 *pest;* 44.12 *pests and diseases*
scale leaf 77.6 *leaf*
scalene 176.9 *angled;* 120.3 *unequal*
scalene triangle 176.3 *angled figure;* 27.43 *triangle*
scale off 552.16 *peel*
scales **414.10**; 258.4 *dirt;* 25.6 *kitchen equipment;* 26.7 *standard;* 28.86 *weighing instrument*
scale the heights 304.14 *climb*
scaliness 411.6 *layering;* 420.6 *roughness*
scaling 35.4 *dentistry;* 304.6 *mounting*
scaling-down 191.1 *contraction*
scaling the heights 304.6 *mounting*
scallop 550.14 *animal covering;* 180.6 *convolute;* 25.19 *shellfish*
scalloped 183.7 *notched*
scalloped edge 420.6 *roughness*
scallop shell 180.3 *convoluted thing*
scallywag 812.2 *disreputable character;* 662.5 *troublemaker*
scalp 550.14 *animal covering;* 552.15 *make nude;* 794.2 *spoils*
scalpel 425.10 *knife*
scaly 420.2 *coarse;* 427.19 *crumbly;* 74.14 *ichthyological;* 411.9 *platelike;* 73.11 *reptilian*
scaly anteater 71.6 *insect-eating mammal*
scam 800.10 *be criminal;* 700.30 *be fraudulent;* 800.3 *criminality;* 774.7 *dishonesty;* 812.3 *disreputable action;* 700.10 *fraud;* 786.1 *nonpayment;* 702.2 *sophism;* 645.2 *stratagem*
scamp 662.5 *troublemaker;* 804.9 *wicked person*
scamper 332.6 *accelerate;* 332.9 *acceleration;* 332.4 *be swift;* 300.12 *gait;* 262.2 *make haste*
scamper away 313.4 *hurry off*
scampering 262.3 *hasty*
scampi-and-chips circuit 21.15 *engagement*
scan 35.7 *diagnosis;* 464.12 *estimate;* 518.14 *inspect;* 518.3 *observation;* 35.19 *practise medicine;* 705.17 *question;* 692.28 *radar;* 717.9 *represent*
scandal 678.3 *defamation;* 802.9 *dishonour;* 812.1 *disrespect;* 715.2 *false accusation;* 236.10 *poverty*
scandalize 619.10 *be wonderful;* 596.7 *cause dislike*
scandalized 619.6 *wondering*
scandalizing 804.13 *venial;* 619.8 *wonderful*
scandalmonger 678.8 *defamer;* 741.4 *journalist;* 644.4 *meddler*
scandalous 678.16 *defamatory;* 812.4 *disreputable;* 802.15 *immoral;* 236.4 *poor;* 804.13 *venial*
scandalously 804.18 *wickedly*
scandal sheet 741.5 *mass communication*
scandent 304.22 *ascending*
scandic 32.34 *elemental*
Scandinavian 5.11 *family of languages;* 23.7 *furniture style*
scanned 17.20 *metrical*
scanner 40.13 *character recognition;* 40.19 *computing terms;* 449.11 *detector;* 394.14 *hospital;* 518.11 *observer;* 40.7 *peripheral*
scanning 35.7 *diagnosis;* 17.20 *metrical;* 518.3 *observation*
scanning electron microscope 28.85 *microscope*
scanning transmission electron microscope 28.85 *microscope*
scansion 17.9 *metre*
scansorial 304.22 *ascending*
scant **153.6**; 782.4 *inadequate;* 233.4 *incomplete;* 218.1 *insufficient;* 159.7 *little;* 206.6 *sparse*
scant courtesy 659.2 *bad manners*
scanties 551.18 *underwear*
scantily 782.17 *inadequately;* 233.6 *incompletely;* 218.10 *insufficiently;* 206.11 *sparsely;* 153.17 *thin*
scantiness 98.2 *disappearance;* 206.3 *fewness;* 782.9 *inadequacy;* 233.1 *incompleteness;* 218.8 *insufficiency;* 159.1 *littleness;* 149.1 *shortness;* 153.12 *thinning*
scantling 158.1 *size*
scantly 782.17 *inadequately;* 218.10 *insufficiently*
scantness 782.9 *inadequacy;* 233.1 *incompleteness;* 218.8 *insufficiency;* 159.1 *littleness*
scanty 151.2 *fine;* 782.4 *inadequate;* 233.4 *incomplete;* 218.1 *insufficient;* 159.7 *little;* 153.6 *scant;* 149.7 *short;* 206.6 *sparse*
scapegoat 807.3 *atoner;* 766.6 *loser;* 465.6 *misjudged person;* 249.5 *person in adversity;* 769.5 *recipient;* 762.2 *substitute person;* 466.8 *victim of discrimination*
scaphopod 75.5 *mollusc*
Scaphopoda 75.5 *mollusc*
scapular 7.11 *vestment*
scar 550.14 *animal covering;* 234.3 *deformity;* 245.5 *hurt;* 743.10 *identify;* 546.5 *make ugly;* 743.3 *means of identification;* 154.3 *mountain;* 548.1 *spot;* 186.3 *vertical thing*
scarab 11.6 *talisman*
Scaramouch 21.32 *clown;* 21.23 *role*
scarce **218.4**; 782.4 *inadequate;* 206.6, 417.1 *sparse;* 792.8 *valuable*
scarce as hen's teeth 218.4 *scarce*
scarcely 231.11 *imperfectly;* 218.10 *insufficiently;* 206.11 *sparsely;* 209.11 *to a degree;* 792.13 *valuably*
scarcely any 206.5 *few*
scarcely like 116.4 *dissimilar*
scarcely to be expected 105.1 *improbable*
scarceness 206.3 *fewness;* 218.9 *scarcity;* 417.3 *sparseness*
scarcity **218.9**; **557.10**; 214.1 *decrease;* 98.2 *disappearance;* 206.3 *fewness;* 782.9 *inadequacy;* 417.3 *sparseness;* 439.3 *supply;* 792.6 *value*
scarcity value 790.2, 792.6 *value*
scare 711.3 *false alarm;* 612.13 *frighten;* 711.7 *raise the alarm;* 651.18 *torment*
scarebaby 612.6 *frightened person*
scarecrow 717.6 *image;* 43.14 *pest control;* 153.9 *thin person;* 546.2 *ugly person*
scared 614.3 *cowardly;* 612.7 *frightened;* 337.12 *weak-willed*
scared rabbit 332.12 *swift animal*
scared shitless 612.7 *frightened*
scared stiff 612.7 *frightened*
scaredy-cat 614.2 *coward;* 612.6 *frightened person*
scaremonger 612.5 *frightener;* 711.4 *warner*
scarer 612.5 *frightener*
scare shitless 612.13 *frighten*
scare the pants off 612.13 *frighten*
scare up 765.11 *acquire*
scarf 550.5 *body covering;* 551.15 *headgear;* 551.14 *neckwear;* 165.4 *wrapper*
scarf joint 23.10 *carpenter's term*
scarf up 557.22 *eat well*
scaring 612.10 *frightening*
scarlatina 260.6 *infection*
scarlet 804.12 *immoral;* 535.1 *red;* 796.13 *unchaste*
scarlet fever 260.6 *infection;* 535.5 *redness*
Scarlett and Rhett 593.10 *lovers*
scarlet woman 796.9 *immoral woman*
scarp 384.11 *fortification;* 30.7 *landform;* 176.2 *obliquity;* 186.3 *vertical thing*
scarper 526.2 *depart;* 313.4 *hurry off*
scarred 234.7 *deformed;* 743.12 *identified;* 548.5 *marked*
scary 612.10 *frightening*
scat 262.2 *make haste;* 634.9 *play truant*
scathe 236.13 *be worthless;* 245.5 *hurt*
scatheless 230.1 *perfect*
scatologic 560.25 *faecal*
scatological 712.8 *cursing;* 560.25 *faecal;* 796.12 *indecent;* 258.9 *obscene;* 5.39 *of language;* 675.9 *ribald*
scatologically **560.33**; 5.49 *colloquially*
scatologize 712.5 *curse*
scatology 712.1 *curse;* 258.3 *obscenity;* 5.19 *swearword*
scatter **206.9**; 377.9 *be dispersed;* 316.14 *bring back;* 526.3 *cause to disappear;* 375.4 *deconstruct;* 246.10 *defeat heavily;* 325.12 *deflect;* 357.8 *destroy;* 325.18 *diffraction;* 408.21 *disorder;* 377.12 *disperse;* 372.13 *diverge;* 427.21 *powder;* 311.13 *radiate;* 372.9 *separate;* 300.14 *set in motion;* 433.33 *sprinkle;* 367.6 *throw down;* 441.1 *waste*
scatter around 377.17 *sow*
scatterbrain 463.7 *forgetful person;* 472.6 *inattentive person;* 457.3 *unintelligent person*
scatterbrained 408.16 *confused;* 227.14 *irresolute;* 486.1 *unskilful*
scatter diagram 409.8 *chart;* 27.32 *graph*
scattered 372.16 *apart;* 325.26 *diffractive;* 377.19 *dispersed;* 206.6 *sparse*
scattered showers 31.25 *rain*
scattergram 27.32 *graph*
scattering 31.9 *atmospheric process;* 375.2 *deconstruction;* 526.4 *disappearance;* 377.1 *dispersion;* 377.28 *dispersive;* 367.20 *falling;* 206.1 *few;* 28.71 *nuclear reaction;* 311.3 *radiation;* 372.1 *separation;* 28.15 *wave property*
scattering of the ashes 583.1 *burial*
scatterment 377.1 *dispersion*
scatter seed 43.17 *farm*
scatter to the winds 766.14 *go to waste;* 377.17 *sow*
scatty 227.14 *irresolute*
scavenger 256.12 *cleaner;* 258.6 *dirty person;* 70.4 *type of animal*
scavenger bird 256.12 *cleaner*
Scavenger's Daughter 814.15 *instrument of torture*
scenario 17.3 *aspect of fiction;* 143.2 *circumstances;* 701.4 *gist;* 721.3 *narration;* 21.2 *play;* 484.2 *policy*
scenarioist 21.26 *dramatist*
scenario writer 21.26 *dramatist*
scenarist 21.26 *dramatist*
scend 91.10 *billow*
scene **21.8**; 624.4 *anger;* 19.10 *art subject;* 143.2 *circumstances;* 340.2 *deed;* 656.3 *formal occasion;* 738.8 *showplace;* 143.1 *situation;* 139.8 *specialization;* 21.19 *stage set;* 170.1 *surroundings;* 518.7 *view*
scene bay 21.17 *stage*
scene dock 21.17 *stage*
scene of desolation 357.5 *havoc*
scene of destruction 441.4 *destruction;* 357.5 *havoc*
scene painter 19.16 *artist;* 21.28 *stagehand*
scene painting 19.2 *painting*
scenery 143.1 *situation;* 21.19 *stage set;* 170.1 *surroundings;* 518.7 *view*
scene shifter 21.28 *stagehand*
scenic 19.26 *artistic;* 545.5 *beautiful;* 518.20 *visual*
scenically 19.31 *artistically*
scenic railway 321.1 *railway*
scenic route 306.5 *ringroad*
scent **500.3**; 693.15 *be informed;* 370.12 *draw in;* 502.1 *fragrance;* 502.2 *fragrant thing;* 59.8 *hunting;* 500.9 *impart odour to;* 716.4 *indication;* 433.14 *lavender water;* 371.14 *let out;* 500.1 *odour;* 502.6 *perfume;* 742.1 *sign;* 547.6 *toiletries;* 744.12 *vestige*
scent bottle 502.2 *fragrant thing*
scented 502.4 *fragrant;* 500.5 *odorous*
scented soap 256.9 *cleaning agent;* 502.2 *fragrant thing*
scent game 60.7 *shoot*
scent gland 559.3 *gland;* 71.2 *mammalian characteristic;* 500.3 *scent*

scentless 501.3 *odourless*
scentlessness 501.1 *odourlessness*
scent out 370.12 *draw in;* 633.9 *follow;* 60.7 *shoot*
sceptic 616.4 *cautious;* 451.5 *disbeliever;* 4.11 *follower of a doctrine;* 705.9 *questioner;* 637.16 *reluctant person;* 453.17 *uncertain person*
sceptical **705.15**; 451.6 *disbelieving;* 611.4 *hopeless;* 4.14 *of a philosophy;* 637.5 *reluctant;* 453.1 *uncertain*
sceptically 616.7 *cautiously;* 451.10 *disbelievingly;* 705.23 *questioningly;* 453.23 *uncertainly*
scepticism 616.1 *caution;* 451.1 *disbelief;* 611.1 *hopelessness;* 4.7 *school of thought;* 453.10 *suspicion;* 705.6 *uncertainty*
sceptre 743.4 *insignia*
Schadenfreude 651.3 *callousness*
schedule 409.8 *chart;* 406.5 *divisions;* 406.9 *itemize;* 281.14 *keep time;* 220.8 *list;* 220.5 *list of appointments;* 409.18 *make arrangements;* 407.1 *order;* 475.3, 484.1 *plan;* 484.10 *plan out;* 275.16 *time;* 281.2 *timetable*
scheduled 406.12 *itemized;* 220.11 *listed*
scheduled event 283.6 *future event*
scheduled flight 322.1 *aviation*
schedule of events 484.1 *plan*
scheduling 281.1 *timekeeping*
Schellingian 4.11 *follower of a doctrine;* 4.14 *of a philosophy*
schema 409.8 *chart*
schematic 409.26 *diagrammatic;* 406.12 *itemized;* 407.10 *ordered;* 409.22 *organizational;* 484.14 *planned;* 446.12 *purposive*
schematically 484.16 *as planned;* 409.28 *in place;* 446.21 *purposively;* 406.15 *thematically*
schematize 406.9 *itemize;* 409.13 *organize*
scheme 446.18 *aim;* 17.3 *aspect of fiction;* 645.5 *be cunning;* 409.8 *chart;* 406.5 *divisions;* 407.7 *method;* 407.1 *order;* 446.3, 484.1, 484.9 *plan;* 484.4, 484.13 *plot;* 702.11 *practise sophistry;* 702.2 *sophism;* 700.8, 700.28 *trick*
schemer 645.3 *cunning person;* 699.17 *false person;* 484.8 *planner;* 700.20 *plotter;* 702.6 *sophist*
scheming 645.4 *cunning;* 700.34 *deceiving;* 800.5 *dishonourable;* 484.7, 484.15 *planning*
scherma 54.1 *fencing*
scherzo 22.4 *historic dancing*
Schiff's reagent 33.5 *sugar test*
schilling 780.11 *national coins*
schism 751.2 *argument;* 118.3 *nonconformism;* 355.3 *relinquishment;* 662.4 *revolution;* 372.1 *separation*
schismatic 751.9 *disagreeing;* 118.8 *dissenter;* 118.12 *nonconformist;* 662.14 *subversive*
schismatical 118.12 *nonconformist*
schismatically 751.11 *in disagreement;* 662.18 *subversively*
schismatize 355.2 *withdraw*
schistose 30.57 *chalky*
schistosity 30.33 *metamorphic rock*
schistosomiasis 75.11 *helminthic disease;* 260.7 *tropical disease*
schizo 36.8 *disordered personality;* 461.13 *mentally ill*
schizoaffective psychosis 36.11 *psychosis*
schizocarp 80.2 *botanical fruit*
schizocarpic 80.9 *of a fruit*
schizocarpic fruit 80.2 *botanical fruit*
schizoid 372.16 *apart;* 36.8 *disordered personality;* 461.7 *insane person;* 461.13 *mentally ill;* 36.36 *psychologically disturbed*
schizoidism 36.16 *dissociation*
schizoid personality 36.8 *disordered personality;* 36.16 *dissociation;* 461.5 *psychosis*
schizophrenia 36.16 *dissociation;* 36.11, 461.5 *psychosis*
schizophrenic 227.5 *changeable person;* 461.7 *insane person;* 461.13 *mentally ill*
schizothyme 36.8 *disordered personality*
schizothymia 36.16 *dissociation*
schizothymic personality 36.8 *disordered personality*
Schläger-Mensur 54.1 *fencing*
schlemiel 700.22 *dupe*
schlep 316.12 *transport*
schlock 236.8 *inferiority*
schlocky 236.2 *inferior*
schmear 768.2 *gift*
Schmidt telescope 29.24 *telescope*
schmuck 700.22 *dupe*
schmutter business 553.3 *fashion business*
schnook 700.22 *dupe;* 335.5 *powerless person*
schnozzle 185.3 *protuberance;* 500.2 *sense of smell*
schola cantorum 6.12 *educational institution*
scholar 471.6 *attentive person;* 400.9 *educational leader;* 396.11, 485.5 *expert;* 458.4 *intellectual;* 442.8 *intellectual person;* 455.6 *knowledgeable person;* 6.7 *learner;* 769.5 *recipient;* 139.14 *specialist;* 443.7 *thinker*
scholarliness 6.9 *learnedness*
scholarly 6.18 *educated;* 400.13 *excellent;* 4.19 *learned;* 17.16 *literary;* 455.9 *literate;* 443.11 *reasoning;* 139.21 *specialized*
scholarship 392.6 *financial assistance;* 768.2 *gift;* 813.3 *grant;* 788.3 *income;* 6.9 *learnedness;* 6.8, 455.3 *learning;* 765.5 *profit;* 769.2 *something received*
scholarship winner 769.5 *recipient*
Scholastic 4.11 *follower of a doctrine*
scholastic 6.18 *educated;* 6.16 *educational;* 7.14 *theologian*
scholastically 6.26 *studiously*
scholasticism 4.7 *school of thought*
scholastic theology 7.13 *theology*
scholiast 719.6 *interpreter*
scholiastic 719.16 *annotative*
scholium 719.2 *annotation*
school 71.21 *assemblage of mammals;* 117.10 *assimilate;* 38.20 *building;* 455.14 *cause to know;* 356.8 *construction;* 6.22 *educate;* 6.12 *educational institution;* 74.1 *fishes;* 376.23 *flock;* 2.8 *human institution;* 760.4 *medium of conversion;* 7.1 *religion;* 450.2 *religious belief;* 139.8 *specialization*
schoolable 6.17 *educable*
school age 555.1 *youth*
school-age 555.11 *young*
School Attendance Officer 6.5 *educationalist*
school bag 410.8 *bag*
school board 6.5 *educationalist*
school book **6.14**
schoolboy 6.7 *learner;* 555.7 *young man*
schoolchildren 555.10 *the young*
schooldays 555.1 *youth*
school dictionary 5.28 *dictionary*
schooled 455.9 *literate*
schoolfellow 569.5 *friend*
schoolgirl 6.7 *learner;* 555.8 *young woman*
school grammar 5.29 *grammar*
schoolhouse 6.15 *schoolroom*
schooling 6.1 *education;* 455.3 *learning*
school letter 743.4 *insignia*
schoolman 6.4 *educator*
schoolmarm 400.9 *educational leader*
schoolmarmish 6.16 *educational*
schoolmaster 400.9 *educational leader;* 6.4 *educator*
schoolmastery 6.6 *instructorship*
schoolmate 569.5 *friend;* 595.4 *likable person*
schoolmistress 400.9 *educational leader;* 6.4 *educator*
school notes 744.3 *notes*
school nurse 35.16 *nurse*
school of thought **4.7**; 4.2 *philosophical system*
school prefect 579.16 *official*
school report 744.1 *record*
school ring 743.5 *uniform*
schoolroom **6.15**
school teacher 6.4 *educator*
school term 276.4 *period of activity*
school uniform 551.3, 656.4 *formal dress;* 743.5 *uniform*
school work 576.1 *work*
schoolyard 6.15 *schoolroom*
schooner 410.13 *drinking vessel;* 50.2 *sailing boat*
Schottky diode 39.18 *diode*
Schrödinger equation 326.5 *wave*
Schrödinger's cat 4.9 *philosophical problem;* 28.80 *quantum theory*
Schule 6.12 *educational institution*
Schuss 68.1 *skiing*
schuss 68.14 *ski*
schussing 68.12 *ski*
schussing position 68.4 *skiing technique*
schyzothymia 36.8 *disordered personality*
sciamachy 477.4 *ideality*
sciatica 260.17 *nervous disorder;* 491.2 *painful condition*
science **455.5**; 402.6 *natural science*
science fiction 721.5 *fiction;* 477.4 *ideality*
science-fiction novel 17.2 *fiction*
science of colour 529.8 *chromatics*
science of forces 331.11 *impulsion*
science of interpretation **719.5**; 5.12 *translation*
science of language 5.1 *linguistics*
science of law 16.32 *jurisprudence*
science of man 1.1 *anthropology*
science of matter 402.6 *natural science*
science of physical properties 402.6 *natural science*
science of rotation **307.7**
science of rotatory motion 307.7 *science of rotation*
science of structure **403.8**
science of the mind 36.1 *psychology*
science park 577.1 *workshop*
science subject 6.3 *subject*
science topic 447.5 *educational topic*
scientific 698.21 *accurate;* 448.8 *experimental;* 705.15 *sceptical;* 407.14 *well-ordered*
scientifically 448.14 *experimentally;* 705.23 *questioningly;* 485.12 *skilfully*
scientific aptitude test 36.5 *psychological test*
scientific exactness 698.8 *accuracy*
scientific investigation 705.2 *questioning*
scientific man 566.4 *modern human*
scientific perspective 19.4 *treatment*
scientific researcher 476.4 *theorist*
scientism 402.2 *materialization*
scientist 448.5 *experimenter;* 396.11, 485.5 *expert;* 455.6 *knowledgeable person;* 402.3 *materialist;* 26.9 *measurer;* 705.9 *questioner;* 476.4 *theorist;* 578.1 *worker*
scientological 11.16 *psychic*
scientology 11.1 *occultism*
sci-fi 17.2, 721.5 *fiction*
scil. 139.31 *namely*
scilicet 139.31 *namely*
scimitar 425.10 *knife;* 587.8 *sharp weapon*
scintilla 522.8 *fire;* 437.2 *lighter*
scintillate 458.8 *be intelligent;* 522.25 *light up*
scintillating 522.16 *bright*
scintillatingly 522.30 *lightly*
scintillation 29.21 *orbit;* 522.2 *quality of light*
scintillation counter 28.93 *radiation detector*
sciolism 456.2 *half-knowledge*
scion 205.6 *branch;* 44.5 *gardening;* 77.5 *stem;* 555.5 *young plant*
sciopticon 21.20 *stage lighting*
scissile 424.1 *brittle;* 372.19 *separable*
scission 424.2 *brittleness;* 372.3 *separateness*
scissor 50.10 *sailing;* 425.16 *use a sharp tool*
scissor gybe 50.15 *sail;* 50.1 *sailing*
scissors 57.6 *pommel horse;* 425.9 *sharp-edged thing*
scissors block 46.9 *play*
scissors kick 67.2 *swimming technique*
scissors style 47.2 *field events*
scissors turn 68.4 *skiing technique*
scissure 146.2 *crack*
sciurine 71.30 *rodent-like*
sciuromorphs 71.12 *gnawing mammal*
sclaff 56.7 *golf;* 56.3 *golf shots*
sclera 518.2 *eye*
scleroprotein 33.9 *protein*
sclerosis 418.6 *solidification*
sclerotic 418.1 *hard*
sclerotization 33.9 *protein*
scobicula 427.15 *powdery*
scobiform 427.15 *powdery*
scoff 599.13 *be humorous;* 557.22 *eat well;* 557.7 *food;* 660.29, 678.14 *ridicule;* 668.6, 668.25 *taunt*
scoff at 621.6 *deride;* 451.8 *disbelieve*
scoff at virtue 804.16 *be wicked*
scoffing 659.1 *discourtesy;* 621.1 *mockery;* 678.17 *scornful;* 668.15 *taunting*
scoffingly 659.10 *rudely*
scold 670.20 *censure;* 625.3 *irascible person;* 814.1 *punish;* 712.6 *vilify*
scolded 670.34 *censured*
scolding 670.7 *blame;* 670.30 *censuring;* 814.7 *punishment*
sconce 522.6 *electric light*
scone 25.39 *loaf*
scoop 369.10 *excavator;* 740.3 *journalism;* 410.17 *ladle;* 693.4 *mass communication;* 741.9 *news story;* 58.9 *play hockey;* 740.15 *publish;* 741.13 *report;* 741.3 *reporting;* 62.5 *rock face;* 316.15 *take away*
scooped 410.20 *containing;* 58.8 *hockey*
scooping 58.1 *hockey*
scoop out 183.9 *make concave*
scoop stroke 58.1 *hockey*
scoot 332.4 *be swift;* 634.8 *run away;* 320.10 *sled*
scooter 320.13 *motorcycle*
scop 17.14 *author*
scope **250.5**; 334.2 *ability;* 141.6 *available space;* 150.4 *breadth;* 209.1 *degree;* 694.1 *meaning;* 287.2 *opportunity;* 141.7 *range;* 26.4, 158.1 *size;* 86.14 *sphere;* 518.9 *viewpoint*
scope sight 60.3 *hunting equipment*
scorch 381.9 *attack successfully;* 428.19 *bake;* 585.13 *be at war;* 332.4 *be swift;* 493.15 *burn;* 245.4 *impair*
scorched 428.8 *baked;* 493.13 *heated*
scorched earth 357.5 *havoc*
scorched earth policy 563.1 *infertility;* 585.8 *warfare*
scorcher 31.23 *heat;* 493.5 *hot weather;* 332.13 *swift person*
scorching 493.9 *hot;* 332.8 *speed;* 332.1 *swift;* 380.6 *violent;* 493.11 *warm*
score **53.10**; **220.10**; 789.3 *accounting;* 409.16 *adapt;* 784.5 *amount owing;* 53.17 *bat;* 300; 51.8 *bowl;* 210.8 *calculate;* 18.35 *compose;* 783.1 *credit;* 66.2 *football play;* 184.2 *furrow;* 209.3 *gradation;* 194.4 *mathematical result;* 209.5 *measure;* 409.9 *musical arrangement;* 183.4, 183.10 *notch;* 27.12 *numeration;* 706.7 *numerical result;* 48.7 *play baseball;* 46.15 *play offence;* 64.5 *play rugby;* 66.4 *play soccer;* 744.15 *register;* 516.9 *set to music;* 706.20 *solve;* 246.3 *successful thing;* 201.8 *twenty and over;* 184.8 *wrinkle;* 18.18 *written music*
score a bull's-eye 273.7, 698.31 *be accurate*
score an own goal 486.7 *be clumsy*
score a perfect game 51.8 *bowl*
score a point 246.11 *overmaster*
score a run 48.7 *play baseball*
score a spare 51.8 *bowl*
score a strike 51.8 *bowl*
score a success 246.6 *be successful*
score a try 64.5 *play rugby*
scoreboard 53.2 *ground;* 744.1 *record;* 66.1 *soccer;* 46.4 *stadium*
scoreboard clock 46.4 *stadium*
score card 27.67 *calculator;* 56.2 *golfing terms*
scored 18.31 *composed;* 66.5 *soccer;* 184.6 *wrinkly*
scorekeeper 52.8 *karate;* 744.9 *recorder*
score out 358.1 *obliterate*
score points against 704.8 *refute*
scorer 49.2 *basketball player;* 18.24 *musician;* 53.3 *official*
scores 208.2 *multitude*
scoresheet 744.1 *record*
score through 358.1 *obliterate*
scoria 258.4 *dirt;* 238.6 *refuse;* 215.2 *residue*
scoring **46.6**; 66.2 *football play*
scoring a bull's-eye 698.8 *accuracy*
scoring desk 49.3 *basketball equipment*
scorn **668.20**; **678.5**; 606.7 *be dissatisfied;* 661.6 *be insubordinate;* 668.3 *contempt;* 451.1 *disbelief;* 451.8 *disbelieve;* 606.1 *dissatisfaction;* 470.3 *exclude;* 124.13 *make unimportant;* 621.1 *mockery;* 660.29, 678.14 *ridicule;* 468.3 *underestimate*
scorned 594.12 *hated;* 623.3 *humbled*
scorned person 124.10 *nonentity*
scornful **678.17**; 512.7 *catcalling;* 668.13 *contemptuous;* 621.5 *derisive;* 451.6 *disbelieving;* 606.4 *dissatisfied;* 468.4 *underestimating*
scornfully 668.30 *contemptuously;* 606.8 *discontentedly;* 678.18 *disparagingly;* 621.7 *mockingly;* 468.6 *pessimistically*
Scornfulness 678

scornfulness 668.3 *contempt*
scorning 668.15 *taunting*
scorpion 76.2 *arachnid*
Scot 564.9 *British inhabitant*; 85.11 *Scotland*
scot and lot 790.9 *historical taxes*
Scotch 558.7 *alcoholic drink*
scotch 131.16 *cease*; 378.8 *hinder*; 245.5 *hurt*
Scotch broth 25.44 *British dish*; 25.13 *soup*
Scotch mist 31.34 *mist*; 429.2 *mistiness*
Scotch tape 267.3 *adhesive*
Scotch whisky 558.7 *alcoholic drink*
scot-free 389.8 *escaping*; 250.9, 391.8 *free*; 793.11 *free of charge*; 391.7 *liberated*
Scotland 85.11
Scotland Yard 16.15 *British police*
scotopia 518.1 *vision*
Scots Guard 586.12 *ceremonial troops*
Scotsman 85.11 *Scotland*
Scotticism 5.26 *dialect*
Scottish accent 5.26 *dialect*
Scottish country dancing 22.1 *dancing*
Scottish Grand Committee 12.4 *governing body*
Scottish hockey 58.7 *hurling*
Scottish Mountaineering Club 62.6 *mountaineering association*
Scottish mountains 89.5 *British mountains*
Scottish National Party 12.6 *political party*
Scottishness 85.11 *Scotland*
Scottish reel 22.4 *historic dancing*
Scottish Six-Days trial 61.1 *motor racing*
Scottish thistle 743.6 *national emblem*
scoundrel 800.4 *dishonourable person*; 812.2 *disreputable character*; 798.6 *evil person*; 651.8 *malefactor*; 804.9 *wicked person*
scour 332.4 *be swift*; 256.13 *clean*; 365.12 *rub*
scoured 256.17 *cleaned*; 30.59 *weathered*
scourer 256.10 *cleaning object*
scourge 249.1 *adversity*; 441.7 *destroyer*; 814.3 *hit*; 814.14 *instrument of punishment*; 260.5 *plague*; 236.10 *poverty*
scourge oneself 808.5 *do penance*
scourger 814.17 *punisher*
scourging 814.12 *corporal punishment*
scouring 365.4 *scraping*
scouring out 371.21 *removal*
scouring pad 256.9 *cleaning agent*
scouring powder 256.9 *cleaning agent*
scourings 258.4 *dirt*; 238.6 *refuse*; 215.2 *residue*
Scouse 564.9 *British inhabitant*
scout 449.12 *discoverer*; 293.4 *early comer*; 470.3 *exclude*; 518.14 *inspect*; 586.31 *military aircraft*; 518.11 *observer*; 129.8 *precursor*; 711.4 *warner*
scout ahead 293.8 *precede*
scout's honour 707.26 *as God is my witness!*
scout signs 742.1 *sign*
scout the territory 243.1 *prepare*
scowl 659.3 *act of discourtesy*; 624.11 *be angry*; 626.11 *be irritable*; 670.10 *disapproving look*; 234.2 *facial distortion*; 625.7 *frown*; 742.3, 742.11 *gesture*; 659.8 *get angry*; 518.6, 518.13 *look*; 234.10 *make faces*; 670.23 *show disapproval*; 624.6 *sign of anger*; 596.4 *sign of dislike*; 625.2 *sign of irascibility*; 626.4 *sign of irritableness*
scowling 626.7 *irritable*; 625.5 *showing irascibility*
scrabble up 304.14 *climb*
scrag end 25.26 *lamb*; 215.1 *remainder*; 131.8 *tail*
scragginess 159.1 *littleness*; 153.7 *thinness*
scraggliness 420.6 *roughness*
scraggly 420.2 *coarse*
scraggy 420.2 *coarse*; 159.7 *little*; 153.1 *thin*; 218.3 *underfed*
scram 313.15 *go!*; 371.33 *go away!*; 634.24 *hands off!*; 313.4 *hurry off*; 634.9 *play truant*
scramble 342.12 *be active*; 114.8 *be diverse*; 304.14 *climb*; 25.55 *cook*; 408.21 *disorder*; 300.12 *gait*; 262.4 *haste*; 696.8 *make unintelligible*; 412.1 *mixture*; 412.9 *mix up*; 62.9 *mountaineer*; 342.3 *nimbleness*; 61.9 *race*
scrambled 25.56 *culinary*; 719.15 *interpreted*; 412.12 *mixed*; 412.13 *mixed-up*; 408.18 *muddled*; 264.12 *problematic*; 696.1 *unintelligible*
scrambled pork brains 25.43 *US dish*
scrambler 412.6 *mixer*
scrambling 62.3 *climbing technique*; 25.8 *cooking technique*; 61.5 *motorcycle racing*; 61.6 *motor-racing terms*; 62.8 *mountaineering*
scrap 751.6 *argue*; 701.1, 751.2 *argument*; 585.9 *battle*; 131.16 *cease*; 470.2 *discard*; 767.9 *dispose of*; 196.3 *fragment*; 159.3 *little piece*; 205.7 *piece*; 242.8, 242.11 *quarrel*; 238.6 *refuse*; 355.1 *relinquish*; 350.6 *stop using*; 371.13 *throw away*
scrapbook 723.3 *compendium*; 744.6 *record book*; 462.4 *reminder*
scrape 365.13 *abrade*; 157.6 *be shallow*; 256.13 *clean*; 331.12 *collision*; 19.22 *engrave*; 427.25 *grate*; 513.2 *hoarseness*; 623.21 *humble oneself*; 491.11 *inflict pain*; 491.3 *injury*; 517.10 *lack harmony*; 214.5 *make smaller*; 667.4 *mark of respect*; 147.19 *meet*; 264.5 *predicament*; 680.6 *save*; 365.4 *scraping*; 663.6 *show obeisance to*; 513.5 *sound hoarse*; 697.3 *tomfoolery*; 425.16 *use a sharp tool*
scrape and save 786.11 *be parsimonious*
scraped 491.6 *injured*
scrape home 246.9 *be victorious*
scrape off 552.15 *make nude*
scrape one's feet 742.11 *gesture*
scraper 38.29 *construction equipment*; 365.7 *eraser*; 425.9 *sharp-edged thing*
scrape through 231.9 *be imperfect*; 246.9 *be victorious*; 389.5 *escape*; 384.28 *survive*
scrape together 765.11 *acquire*
scrapie 260.18 *veterinary disease*
scraping 365.4; 517.7 *dissonant*; 513.8 *hoarse*; 664.7 *sycophantic*
scraping by 218.2 *unprovided*
scrapings 215.2 *residue*
scrapped 131.22 *cancelled*; 350.4 *disused*; 355.5 *relinquished*
scrappily 233.6 *incompletely*; 205.12 *partly*
scrappiness 233.1 *incompleteness*
scrapping 701.7 *arguing*; 767.1 *disposal*; 350.10 *disuse*
scrappy 133.8 *discontinuous*; 233.4 *incomplete*; 205.11 *partial*
scraps 238.6 *refuse*; 215.2 *residue*; 441.5 *waste product*
scrapyard 767.5 *wasteyard*
scratch 365.13 *abrade*; 65.2 *billiards play*; 131.16 *cease*; 231.7 *defect*; 184.2 *furrow*; 513.2 *hoarseness*; 59.7 *horseracing*; 236.14 *ill-treat*; 231.2 *incomplete*; 491.11 *inflict pain*; 491.3 *injury*; 65.6 *pool*; 122.14 *poor*; 365.4 *scraping*; 157.4 *shallow thing*; 513.5 *sound hoarse*; 124.8 *trifle*; 486.2 *unskilled*; 425.16 *use a sharp tool*; 355.2 *withdraw*; 184.8 *wrinkle*
scratch a living 782.12 *be poor*
scratch each other's back 759.5 *exchange*
scratched 231.1 *imperfect*; 184.6 *wrinkly*
scratchiness 420.6 *roughness*
scratching 365.4 *scraping*
scratch line 47.2 *field events*
scratch out 357.8 *destroy*; 358.1 *obliterate*
scratchpad 19.11 *artist's materials*; 40.6 *memory*; 744.6 *record book*; 6.14 *school book*
scratch player 56.6 *golfer*
scratch the surface 157.6 *be shallow*
scratch through 358.1 *obliterate*
scratchy 420.3 *barbed*; 513.8 *hoarse*
scrawl 696.7 *be unintelligible*; 696.8 *make unintelligible*; 696.12 *unintelligible thing*
scrawly 696.1 *unintelligible*
scrawniness 159.1 *littleness*; 153.7 *thinness*
scrawny 159.7 *little*; 153.1 *thin*
scream 507.8 *be loud*; 513.6 *be shrill*; 31.58 *blow*; 514.1 *cry*; 514.6 *cry of pain*; 514.10 *cry out*; 254.6 *danger signal*; 491.12 *express pain*; 507.2 *outcry*; 740.14 *proclaim*; 711.7 *raise the alarm*; 513.3 *shrillness*; 697.2 *solecism*; 729.12 *speak loudly*
screamer 274.10 *blunder*; 740.3 *journalism*
screaming 529.12 *gaudy*; 507.6 *loud*; 507.2 *outcry*; 514.16 *vociferous*
scream therapy 36.3 *psychiatric treatment*
scree 316.10 *transferred thing*
screech 513.6 *be shrill*; 515.2 *bird song*; 31.58 *blow*; 514.1 *cry*; 491.12 *express pain*; 513.3 *shrillness*; 515.5 *sing*; 729.12 *speak loudly*
screech owl 72.5 *bird of prey*
screed 733.1 *address*; 722.1 *dissertation*
screen 519.15 *blind*; 519.6 *blinder*; 372.6 *boundary*; 384.19 *buffer*; 409.15 *categorize*; 41.14 *cine film*; 256.10 *cleaning object*; 736.8 *conceal*; 736.3 *covering up*; 41.12 *development*; 738.2 *display something*; 128.3 *exclusion zone*; 24.11 *make ceramics*; 521.8 *make invisible*; 528.11 *make opaque*; 528.7 *opaque thing*; 49.6 *play basketball*; 58.9 *play hockey*; 49.4 *playing terms*; 308.6 *porous thing*; 35.19 *practise medicine*; 525.14 *present*; 252.10, 550.30 *protect*; 252.2 *protection*; 550.12 *protective covering*; 308.21 *provide passage for*; 384.2 *safeguard*; 550.15 *shelter*; 692.22 *television set*; 521.6 *that which makes invisible*
screened 409.24 *categorized*; 24.10 *ceramic*; 736.14 *concealed*; 58.8 *hockey*; 521.3 *private*; 550.37 *protected*; 252.6 *safe*; 655.11 *secluded*
screen idol 363.6 *charmer*
screening 409.5 *categorization*; 24.10 *ceramic*; 24.5 *ceramic process*; 550.1 *covering*; 736.3 *covering up*; 523.9 *darkening*; 35.7 *diagnosis*; 58.8 *hockey*; 58.3 *ice hockey*; 49.4 *playing terms*
screening test 35.7 *diagnosis*
screen off 372.11 *divide*; 128.7 *exclude*
screen pass 46.9 *play*
screenplay 21.2 *play*
screen print 42.3 *fabric*
screen printing 19.1 *art*; 42.7 *dyeing*
screenwriter 17.14 *author*; 21.26 *dramatist*
screenwriting 21.6 *cinema*
screw 700.30 *be fraudulent*; 65.2 *billiards play*; 23.17 *carpenter*; 373.11 *connect*; 325.6 *distort*; 373.8 *fastening*; 561.14 *have sex*; 59.1 *horse*; 251.6 *lawmaker*; 593.29 *make love*; 792.10 *overcharge*; 309.5 *person who closes*; 815.6 *prison officer*; 330.11 *propeller*; 307.9 *roll*; 307.6 *rotator*; 38.6 *simple machine*; 438.1 *tool*; 438.10 *use tools*
screw around 796.17 *be sexually immoral*
screw around with 245.4 *impair*
screwball 118.10 *eccentric*; 461.7 *insane person*; 48.4 *pitching terms*
screw down 253.14 *make fast*
screwdriver 369.10 *excavator*; 558.8 *mixed drink*; 438.1 *tool*
screwed 373.15 *connected*
screwed-up 486.4 *bungled*; 408.19 *mixed-up*; 238.1 *useless*; 184.6 *wrinkly*
screw factory 461.8 *mental hospital*
screwgate 62.4 *climbing equipment*
screwing 593.5 *desire*
screwing around 796.3 *sexual immorality*
screw loose 328.6 *derangement*; 461.1 *insanity*; 233.2 *omission*
screw propeller 330.11 *propeller*
screwthread 180.2 *coil*
screw up 486.7 *be clumsy*; 408.23 *confuse*; 245.4 *impair*; 274.19 *make a mistake*; 351.1 *misuse*; 243.4 *prepare for action*; 184.8 *wrinkle*
screw-up 274.10 *blunder*; 408.6 *mix-up*; 378.2 *obstacle*
screw up one's courage 336.8 *strengthen*; 613.16 *take courage*
screw up one's eyes 519.14 *be blind*
screwworm 76.5 *larva*; 76.3 *pest*
screwy 461.11 *insane*
scribble 696.7 *be unintelligible*; 721.14 *describe*; 19.9 *drawing*; 696.8 *make unintelligible*; 696.12 *unintelligible thing*
scribbled 696.1 *unintelligible*
scribbled out 358.6 *obliterated*
scribble out 708.14 *cancel*; 358.1 *obliterate*
scribbler 721.10 *descriptive writer*; 486.10 *unskilled person*
scribe 17.14 *author*; 281.13 *chronicler*; 7.8 *priest*; 744.9 *recorder*
scrim 21.19 *stage set*; 527.8 *transparent thing*
scrimmage 701.1, 751.2 *argument*
scrimp 786.11 *be parsimonious*; 682.7 *hoard*; 680.6 *save*
scrimper 680.3 *saver*
scrimping 682.1 *mean*
scrimpy 680.4 *thrifty*
scrimshank 634.5 *shirk*
scrimshanker 634.17 *avoider*
scrimshaw 19.12 *sculpture*
scrip 780.14 *paper money*
scrip certificate 780.14 *paper money*
script 21.38 *dramatize*; 21.2 *play*
scripted 21.39 *dramatic*
scriptural 7.18 *theological*
scripture 7.12 *religious text*; 7.13 *theology*
script writer 721.10 *descriptive writer*; 21.26 *dramatist*
script writing 21.9 *dramaturgy*
scrobis 10.14 *sacred object*
scrofulous 796.12 *indecent*
scroll 40.20 *abort*; 220.6 *list of names*; 3.11 *relic*; 307.9 *roll*
scrolled 20.17 *structured*
scroll leg 23.3 *chair leg*
scrollwork 542.3 *pattern*
scroll worker 542.8 *decorator*
scrooch down 367.8 *sit*
Scrooge 793.8 *bargain hunter*; 665.6 *careful person*; 376.36 *hoarder*; 682.5 *miser*
scrotal 561.16 *reproductive*
scrotum 561.8 *organs of reproduction*
scrounge 772.7 *borrow*; 710.8 *solicit money*; 774.12 *steal*; 773.7 *take*
scrounger 710.5 *beggar*; 343.8 *nonworker*; 774.8 *thief*
scrounging 710.11 *begging*; 774.18 *fraudulent*; 710.3 *solicitation*; 774.1 *stealing*; 773.1 *taking*
scrub 398.5 *alternative*; 526.3 *cause to disappear*; 256.13 *clean*; 576.4 *exertion*; 358.1 *obliterate*; 77.1 *plants*; 365.12 *rub*; 365.4 *scraping*; 576.6 *work*
scrubbed 256.17 *cleaned*; 255.14 *purified*
scrubber 256.12 *cleaner*
scrubbiness 159.1 *littleness*
scrubbing 256.2 *cleaning*; 365.4 *scraping*
scrubbing brush 256.10 *cleaning object*; 420.7 *rough thing*
scrubby 44.17 *botanical*; 159.7 *little*
scrub out 708.14 *cancel*
scruffily 782.16 *meanly*
scruffiness 782.7 *beggary*; 236.10 *poverty*; 793.3 *shoddiness*; 258.2 *uncleanness*; 408.3 *untidiness*
scruffy 782.3 *beggarly*; 124.2 *obscure*; 236.4 *poor*; 793.10 *shoddy*; 258.8 *unclean*; 408.15 *untidy*
scrum 376.21; 64.3 *rugby play*
scrum half 64.4 *rugby player*
scrummage 376.21 *scrum*
scrumping 774.1 *stealing*
scrumple 184.8 *wrinkle*
scrumpled 184.6 *wrinkly*
scrumptious 557.27 *edible*; 490.6 *pleasant*; 495.7 *tasty*; 235.1 *worthy*
scrumptiously 495.11 *tastily*
scrunch 427.26 *beat*; 557.21 *eat*; 513.5 *sound hoarse*; 184.8 *wrinkle*
scrunched 184.6 *wrinkly*
scrunchie 184.4 *wrinkled thing*
scrungy 236.4 *poor*
scruple 414.9 *avoirdupois weight*; 451.1 *disbelief*; 637.13 *dissociation*
scruples 665.3 *circumspection*; 795.1 *morality*; 808.1 *penitence*; 799.1 *probity*
scrupulous 273.5 *accurate*; 665.9 *careful*; 810.8 *dutiful*; 656.6 *formal*; 799.4 *honourable*; 795.8 *moral*; 230.2 *perfectionist*
scrupulously 799.7 *honourably*
scrupulousness 273.1 *accuracy*; 665.3 *circumspection*; 178.8 *directness*; 656.2 *formalism*; 799.1 *probity*
scrutability 695.9 *intelligibility*
scrutable 695.1 *intelligible*
scrutator 518.11 *observer*
scrutineer 518.11 *observer*; 705.9 *questioner*
scrutinize 471.12; 518.14 *inspect*; 4.20 *philosophize*; 705.17 *question*
scrutinized 705.16 *questioned*
scrutinizer 518.11 *observer*
scrutinizing 471.7 *watchful*
scrutiny 471.3 *carefulness*; 518.3 *observation*; 4.4 *philosophical investigation*; 705.2 *questioning*
scry 518.17 *imagine*
scrying 518.5 *imagination*
scuba-dive 67.10 *dive*
scuba-diver 67.4 *swimmer*
scuba-diving 67.1 *swimming*
scubbin 43.10 *farm tool*

Scud 330.8 *missile;* 587.5 *missile weapon*
scud 31.18, 31.60 *cloud;* 323.9 *navigate;* 31.12 *wind*
scuff 365.13 *abrade;* 333.1 *move slowly;* 365.4 *scraping*
scuffing 365.4 *scraping*
scuffle 701.13 *argue;* 701.1 *argument;* 328.5 *commotion;* 242.8 *quarrel*
scuffling 701.7 *arguing*
scuffs 551.19 *footwear*
scull 50.16 *row;* 50.4 *rowing*
sculler 323.8 *boatman;* 50.9 *sailor*
scullery 565.7 *room*
sculling 50.4 *rowing*
scullion 256.12 *cleaner*
scull racing 50.4 *rowing*
sculls 50.4 *rowing*
sculpt **19.21**; 553.9 *fashion;* 160.7 *form;* 717.11 *paint;* 356.10 *produce*
sculpted **19.28**
sculptor **19.17**; 717.4 *person who makes a representation;* 356.9 *producer*
sculptor's materials **19.14**
sculptor's tools 760.4 *medium of conversion*
sculptor's wax 19.14 *sculptor's materials*
sculptress 717.4 *person who makes a representation*
sculptural **19.25**
sculpturally 19.30 *pictorially*
sculpture **19.12**; 19.1 *art;* 717.6 *image;* 356.1 *production*
sculptured 160.9 *formed;* 19.28 *sculpted*
sculpturing 19.12 *sculpture*
sculpt wood 23.18 *work wood*
scum 411.3 *coat;* 258.4 *dirt;* 122.6 *inferior;* 124.10 *nonentity;* 255.10, 256.15 *purify;* 238.6 *refuse;* 215.2 *residue;* 675.6 *vulgar herd*
scumble 19.19 *paint*
scumbling 19.4 *treatment*
scummy 258.7 *dirty;* 411.9 *platelike;* 793.10 *shoddy*
scum of the earth 124.10 *nonentity;* 804.9 *wicked person*
scuola 6.12 *educational institution*
scupper 103.8 *make impossible;* 357.11 *ruin*
scurf 427.6 *crumb;* 258.4 *dirt;* 215.2 *residue;* 411.4 *slice*
scurfy 427.19 *crumbly;* 411.9 *platelike;* 258.8 *unclean*
scurrility 712.1 *curse;* 668.1 *disrespect;* 678.5 *scorn;* 712.3 *vilification*
scurrilous 712.8 *cursing;* 678.16 *defamatory;* 668.10 *disrespectful*
scurrilously 712.12 *swearingly*
scurry 342.12 *be active;* 332.4 *be swift;* 262.4 *haste;* 262.2 *make haste*
scurrying 300.16 *moving*
scurvy 260.4 *disease;* 557.10 *scarcity;* 218.3 *underfed;* 33.14 *vitamin deficiency disease*
scutage 790.9 *historical taxes*
scute 550.14 *animal covering*
scuttle 614.4 *be a coward;* 332.4 *be swift;* 367.3 *bring down;* 262.2 *make haste;* 314.6 *means of entry;* 410.11 *vessel*
scuttlebutt 693.7 *advice*
scutum 384.7 *armour*
Scyphozoa 75.7 *coelenterate*
scyphozoan 75.7, 75.21 *coelenterate*
scythe 43.10 *farm tool;* 438.3 *garden tool;* 81.5 *grass cutter;* 81.12 *manage grassland;* 425.9 *sharp-edged thing;* 425.16 *use a sharp tool*
sea **91.1**; 539.6 *blue thing;* 29.17 *moon;* 91.7 *oceanic*
sea air 502.2 *fragrant thing;* 434.5 *open air;* 257.2 *salubrity*
sea angler 55.6 *angler*
sea area 31.4 *weather forecast*
sea attack 381.12 *military attack*
sea battles 585.8 *warfare*
sea bed 175.1 *base;* 156.4 *deep thing;* 91.1 *sea*
Seabee 586.27 *naval man*
seabird 72.3 *water bird*
sea biscuit 75.3 *echinoderm*
seaboard 92.4 *coast*
sea bombardment 585.8 *warfare*
seaborne 323.11 *nautical*
sea bottom 156.4 *deep thing;* 91.1 *sea*
sea breeze 50.1 *sailing;* 31.12 *wind*
sea cadet 323.7 *nautical person*
sea change 224.1 *change;* 244.5 *improvement*
sea cliff 92.4 *coast*
sea cucumber 75.3 *echinoderm*
sea dog 485.5 *expert;* 323.7 *nautical person*
sea duck 72.3 *water bird*
seafarer 323.7 *nautical person*
seafaring 323.11 *nautical;* 91.7 *oceanic;* 323.1 *water travel*
seafaring man 323.7 *nautical person*
sea fight 585.9 *battle*
sea fish **25.18**; 74.1 *fishes*
sea fishing 633.2 *chase;* 74.7 *fishing*
sea floor 175.1 *base;* 156.4 *deep thing;* 30.16 *ocean floor*
seafloor spreading 30.19 *plate tectonics*
sea fog 31.33 *fog*
seafood 75.4 *arthropod;* 25.19 *shellfish*
seafront 317.7 *arcade;* 167.1 *front*
sea god **91.4**; 323.7 *nautical person*
sea-going 323.11 *nautical;* 91.7 *oceanic*
sea-green 538.1 *green*
seagull 72.3 *water bird*
sea ice 30.39 *iceberg*
sea king 323.7 *nautical person*
seal 70.5 *aquatic animal;* 139.3 *characteristic;* 309.7 *close;* 750.28 *consent;* 755.1, 755.5 *contract;* 111.4 *duplicate;* 454.6 *evidence;* 743.10 *identify;* 737.12 *keep secret;* 24.11 *make ceramics;* 743.3 *means of identification;* 757.2 *permit;* 24.4 *porcelain mark;* 253.2, 253.11 *promise;* 393.1 *repair;* 638.7 *resolve;* 733.10 *send;* 309.2 *stopper*
sea lane 318.2 *passing along;* 317.6 *path;* 317.2 *route;* 91.1 *sea;* 323.2 *waterway*
sealed 309.12 *closed;* 750.17 *consenting;* 737.9 *secret*
sealed book 11.2 *the occult*
sealed orders 737.1 *secrecy*
sea level 175.1 *base;* 187.2 *horizontal surface;* 155.2 *lowlands;* 30.12 *ocean*
sea lily 75.3 *echinoderm*
sealing off 309.1 *closure*
sealing wax 267.3 *adhesive*
seal-like 71.29 *cetacean*
sea loch 88.1 *lake*
seal of approval 669.1 *approval*
seal off 309.7 *close*
seal of the confessional 737.1 *secrecy*
Sea Lord 323.7 *nautical person*
seal-point 534.5 *brown thing*
seal up 736.8 *conceal*
seam 53.7 *bat;* 53.18 *bowl;* 492.6 *contiguity;* 184.2 *furrow;* 411.1 *layer;* 551.35 *make clothing;* 439.2 *resource;* 184.8 *wrinkle*
sea mail 692.2 *postal communication*
seaman 323.7 *nautical person;* 586.27 *naval man;* 585.11 *recruit*
seaman-like 323.11 *nautical*
seamanship 585.6 *art of war;* 323.5 *navigation;* 631.9 *tactics*
sea mark 742.5 *indicator;* 323.5 *navigation*
seam bowler 53.4 *team*
seamed 184.6 *wrinkly*
seamed stockings 551.20 *legwear*
seamer 53.8 *delivery;* 53.4 *team*
sea mist 524.2 *murk*
seamless 132.11 *continuous*
seamless stockings 551.20 *legwear*
seamount 30.16 *ocean floor*
seamstress 551.26 *fashion designer;* 393.12 *repairer*
Seanad Éireann 12.4 *governing body;* 579.10 *legislative body*
seance 738.10 *manifestation;* 11.10 *psychic phenomenon*
sea nymph 8.5 *deity;* 91.4 *sea god*
sea of 208.4 *throng*
sea of flames 493.6 *fire*
sea operations 585.8 *warfare*
sea otter 74.11 *fishing animal*
sea path 317.6 *path;* 317.2 *route*
sea power 586.22 *navy*
sear 491.10 *be painful;* 493.15 *burn;* 191.5 *make smaller;* 191.7 *smaller*
sea raiding 585.8 *warfare*
search 449.7 *detection;* 4.4 *philosophical investigation;* 4.20 *philosophize;* 633.1 *pursuit;* 705.17 *question;* 705.2 *questioning;* 354.2 *undertaking*
search engine 40.16 *Internet*
searcher 353.7 *attempter;* 4.10 *philosopher;* 633.5 *pursuer*
search for 647.6 *be curious;* 633.8 *pursue*
searching 633.15 *pursuing;* 705.12 *questioning;* 353.9 *tentative*
searchingly 705.23 *questioningly*
searchlight 522.6 *electric light*
search me 456.13 *who knows?*
search one's soul 808.4 *be penitent*
search out 705.17 *question*
search party member 633.5 *pursuer*
search warrant 397.2 *demand;* 16.6 *legal process*
seared 191.7 *smaller*
seared conscience 809.1 *impenitence*
searing 191.8 *contracting;* 191.1 *contraction;* 428.13 *drying;* 493.9 *hot;* 491.5 *painful*
sea room 141.6 *available space*
sea rover 323.7 *nautical person*
Seas 91
sea salt 25.7 *basic ingredient;* 496.2 *seasoning*
seascape 19.10 *art subject;* 518.7 *view*
sea scout 323.7 *nautical person*
sea serpent 91.4 *sea god*
seashore 92.4 *coast*
seasick 371.30 *vomiting*
seaside 30.11, 92.4 *coast;* 164.1 *edge;* 164.8 *edging*
Season 292
season **292.1**; **292.7**; **496.12**; 211.6 *add;* 25.55 *cook;* 243.7 *develop;* 632.18 *habituate;* 412.8 *mix;* 359.5 *preserve;* 276.5 *recurrent period;* 275.4 *term*
seasonable **292.14**; 239.1 *convenient;* 287.6 *timely*
seasonably 287.9 *opportunely*
seasonal **31.46**; **292.9**; 298.12 *cyclic;* 740.5 *journal;* 276.8 *periodical*
seasonally **292.18**; 298.16 *cyclically*
seasoned **292.15**; 243.20 *developed;* 485.8 *expert;* 632.14 *habituated;* 496.9 *piquant*
seasoning **496.2**; 211.3 *additional item;* 412.4 *admixture;* 25.7 *basic ingredient;* 243.13 *development;* 495.4 *flavour;* 632.7 *habituation*
season of the year 292.1 *season*
season skiing ticket 68.1 *skiing*
seasons of the year 298.5 *regular thing*
season ticket 793.4 *bargain*
sea squirt 75.2 *protochordate*
sea star 75.3 *echinoderm*
sea survey 91.5 *oceanography*
sea swivel 55.1 *angling*
seat 50.6 *canoeing;* 142.1 *location;* 141.5 *reserved space;* 50.4 *rowing;* 143.1 *situation*
seat belt 359.2 *preserver;* 252.4 *safety device*
seat connection 38.27 *superstructure*
seated 143.6 *situated*
seating 21.18 *auditorium;* 141.5 *reserved space*
seating capacity 141.5 *reserved space*
SEATO 755.3 *alliance*
seat of feelings **590.8**
seat of government 87.1 *city;* 396.5 *position of authority*
seat of justice 464.3 *place of judgment;* 16.18 *tribunal*
seat of life 554.1 *life*
seat of thought 442.7 *brain*
seat oneself 367.8 *sit*
sea transport 316.5 *means of transport*
sea travel 323.1 *water travel*
sea trip 323.1 *water travel*
sea trout 55.4 *American game fish;* 55.5 *British game fish;* 25.17 *freshwater fish*
Seattle 87.2 *American cities*
sea urchin 75.3 *echinoderm*
sea wall 378.3 *barrier;* 92.4 *coast;* 252.4 *safety device;* 38.24 *water system*
seaward 324.10 *clockwise*
seawards 91.11 *nautically*
sea water 30.12 *ocean;* 91.1 *sea;* 433.1 *water*
seawave 30.14 *wave*
seaway 141.6 *available space;* 323.2 *waterway*
seaweed 84.1 *alga;* 77.4 *lower plant;* 25.33 *vegetable*
seaweed marquetry 23.9 *decorative woodwork*
seaweed meal 43.13 *fertilizer*
seaworthy 252.7 *invulnerable;* 323.11 *nautical;* 91.7 *oceanic;* 230.1 *perfect;* 316.17 *transferable;* 319.5 *transportable*
sea zoo 565.12 *stall*
sebaceous 559.5 *of a secretion;* 559.4 *secretory;* 268.13 *slippery*
sebaceous gland 71.2 *mammalian characteristic*
Sebastian 752.7 *martyr*
sebiferous 559.4 *secretory*
Sebring 12-hour race 61.3 *sports-car race*
sebum 559.2 *secreted substance*
secant 27.52 *trigonometric function*
secateurs 44.6, 438.3 *garden tool;* 425.9 *sharp-edged thing*
secede 662.16 *be subversive;* 355.2 *withdraw*
seceder 479.9 *equivocator;* 662.11 *rebel*
secern 559.7 *secrete*
secernment 559.1 *secretion*
secession 355.3 *relinquishment;* 662.4 *revolution*
secessionist 479.9 *equivocator;* 662.11 *rebel*
seclude 736.8 *conceal;* 372.11 *divide;* 128.7 *exclude;* 655.13 *ignore;* 371.4 *ostracize*
secluded **655.11**; 736.14 *concealed;* 250.9 *free;* 655.10 *lonely;* 329.15 *out of reach;* 737.9 *secret;* 372.17 *unjoined*
seclude oneself 655.12 *be unsocial;* 172.14 *go inside*
seclusion 197.5 *aloneness;* 128.1 *exclusion;* 250.1 *freedom;* 172.2 *inside;* 371.19 *ostracism;* 736.6 *privacy;* 252.2 *protection;* 355.3 *relinquishment;* 655.3 *separation;* 372.2 *setting apart*
seclusionist 118.9 *hermit;* 197.8 *loner*
seclusive 655.8 *unsociable*
seclusiveness 655.1 *unsociability*
second **198.21**; 392.23 *advise;* 51.3 *bowls player;* 52.4 *boxer;* 707.19 *confirm;* 707.4 *confirmation;* 750.28 *consent;* 198.12 *double;* 27.75 *equal;* 413.14 *give moral support;* 392.11 *helper;* 231.6 *imperfect item;* 122.6 *inferior;* 280.3 *instant;* 148.8 *measure of time;* 18.16 *musical note;* 469.4 *pick;* 762.7 *substitute;* 289.12 *succeeding;* 275.4 *term;* 276.2 *time period;* 198.9 *two;* 454.1 *verify*
secondarily 100.18 *extraneously;* 198.21 *second;* 124.14 *unimportantly;* 345.12 *with the effect of*
secondariness 100.1 *extraneousness;* 122.1 *inferiority;* 124.5 *unimportance*
secondary **124.3**; 345.10 *caused;* 46.10 *defence;* 100.8 *extraneous;* 122.12 *inferior;* 72.17 *plumage;* 198.9 *two*
secondary battery 39.29 *power source*
secondary cell 28.43 *electrical conduction;* 39.5 *electrolytic conduction;* 39.29 *power source*
secondary character 30.33 *metamorphic rock*
secondary chord 18.16 *musical note*
secondary clay 24.2 *raw material*
secondary coil 39.22 *transformer*
secondary colour 529.1 *colour*
secondary colours 28.28 *colour*
secondary consumer 34.18 *ecology*
secondary education 6.2 *educational system*
secondary electron 39.24 *electron emission*
secondary emission 39.24 *electron emission*
secondary evidence 716.5 *legal evidence*
secondary growth 260.12 *cancer*
secondary matter 124.8 *trifle*
secondary picketing 15.4 *industrial dispute*
secondary quality 4.9 *philosophical problem*
secondary radar 692.28 *radar*
secondary rainbow 31.27 *rainbow*
secondary road 317.3 *road*
secondary school 6.12 *educational institution*
secondary structure 33.9 *protein*
secondary triads 529.1 *colour*
secondary wave 30.23 *seismic wave*
second banana 599.6 *humorist*
second base 48.1 *baseball*
second-baseman 48.2 *baseball player*
second best 754.2 *half-measure;* 231.6 *imperfect item;* 122.1 *inferiority;* 216.6 *mediocrity;* 762.1 *substitution*
second-best 754.6 *compromising;* 604.11 *disappointing;* 231.1 *imperfect;* 122.12 *inferior;* 216.3 *mediocre*
second birth 393.10 *revival*
second chance 627.3 *mercy;* 393.10 *revival*
second childhood 556.5 *old age;* 393.10 *revival*

second class 231.5 *imperfection*; 122.1 *inferiority*; 289.3 *subordination*
second-class 793.9 *cheap*; 574.3 *common*; 231.1 *imperfect*; 122.12, 236.2 *inferior*; 216.3 *mediocre*; 289.13 *subordinate*
second-class fare 793.4 *bargain*
second-class mail 692.2 *postal communication*
second-class stamp 692.3 *correspondence*
second coming 525.6 *reappearance*
second crop 562.1 *fertility*; 765.6 *yield*
second-degree burn 493.1 *heat*
second-degree murder 382.2 *murder*
second derivative 27.31 *differentiation*
second division 216.6 *mediocrity*; 289.3 *subordination*
second-division 216.3 *mediocre*; 289.13 *subordinate*
second early 43.12 *crop*
second echelon 586.14 *armed forces*
seconded 750.17 *consenting*; 454.8 *verifiable*
second edition 111.4 *duplicate*
second eleven 122.1 *inferiority*; 289.3 *subordination*
seconder 707.9 *affirmer*; 413.8 *supporter*
second fiddle 122.1 *inferiority*; 124.10 *nonentity*; 289.7 *subordinate*
second finger 492.7 *sense organ*
second gallery 63.5 *real tennis*
second-generation 345.10 *caused*
second guard 54.3 *fencing movements*
second hand 742.5 *indicator*
second-hand 349.9 *used*
second-hand clothes 552.4 *dishabille*; 551.1 *dress*; 349.7 *reused product*
second-hand sale 778.4 *sale*
second-hand shop 793.7 *discounter*
second helping 557.14 *mouthful*; 112.5 *repeat*
second honeymoon 393.10 *revival*
second house 21.13 *theatrical performance*
second husband 570.10 *married man*
second-in-command 398.4 *deputy*
seconding 392.9 *patronage*
second law 28.38 *thermodynamics*
second lieutenant 586.17 *army person*
second line 392.11 *helper*
secondly 289.15 *as follows*; 198.21 *second*
second marriage 570.3 *types of marriage*
second mortgage 783.1 *credit*; 784.3 *loan*
second name 721.8 *name*
second nature 632.1 *habit*
second opinion 35.6 *health care*; 464.1 *judgment*
second-order 32.38 *reactive*
second place 289.3 *subordination*
second printing 111.4 *duplicate*
second prize 813.2 *prize*
second rank 122.1 *inferiority*
second-rate 604.11 *disappointing*; 231.1 *imperfect*; 122.12, 236.2 *inferior*; 216.3 *mediocre*; 793.10 *shoddy*; 124.4 *trivial*
second-ratedness 793.3 *shoddiness*
second-rater 216.7 *average person*; 247.5 *failing person*; 122.6 *inferior*
second row 64.4 *rugby player*
second-row forward 64.4 *rugby player*
seconds 793.4 *bargain*; 551.1 *dress*; 122.7 *inferior thing*; 557.14 *mouthful*
second self 115.5 *counterpart*
second sex 568.1 *female sex*
second showing 525.6 *reappearance*
second sight 518.5 *imagination*; 283.4 *looking to the future*; 445.2 *precognition*; 11.8 *psychic power*; 488.1 *sensation*
second-sighted 445.7 *precognitive*
second slip 53.4 *team*
second spring 393.10 *revival*
second string 122.1 *inferiority*
second-stringer 122.6 *inferior*
second thought 244.8 *better thing*
second thoughts 616.1 *caution*; 479.6 *equivocation*
second to none 235.2 *best*; 121.17 *supremely*
second wife 570.11 *married woman*
second wind 121.3 *advantage*
Second World War 585.1 *war*
second youth 393.10 *revival*
Secrecy 737
secrecy 737.1; 737.7 *esotericism*; 172.6 *internalization*; 521.4 *invisibility*; 484.4 *plot*; 550.15 *shelter*; 732.3 *shyness*; 11.2 *the occult*; 696.11 *unintelligibility*
secret 737.9; 523.11 *benighted*; 399.6 *censored*; 645.4 *cunning*; 736.15 *disguised*; 123.5 *important*; 172.12 *internalized*; 11.14 *occult*; 10.9 *prayer*; 521.3 *private*; 550.37 *protected*; 737.1 *secrecy*; 696.12 *unintelligible thing*; 456.8 *unknown*; 456.3 *unknown thing*
secret agent 737.2 *secretiveness*
secretaire 410.3 *cabinet*; 23.4 *table*
secretarial college 6.12 *educational institution*
secretariat 16.2 *jurisdiction*; 579.3 *management*; 396.5 *position of authority*; 577.1 *workshop*
secret art 737.7 *esotericism*
secretary 398.4 *deputy*; 400.3 *leader*; 401.5 *office assistant*; 579.16 *official*; 12.8 *politician*; 744.9 *recorder*; 387.3 *subordinate*; 578.1 *worker*
secretary-general 579.16 *official*
secretary of state 400.3 *leader*
Secretary of the Treasury 780.18 *treasurer*
secret ballot 469.10 *vote*
secret book 696.12 *unintelligible thing*
secret compartment 736.2 *hiding place*
secret document 399.2 *censorship*
secret drawer 700.12 *disguise*; 550.15 *shelter*
secret drinker 690.17 *drunkard*
secrete 559.7; 736.8 *conceal*; 560.15 *excrete*; 315.12 *leak*; 371.14 *let out*; 439.6 *store*
secreted substance 559.2
secret formula 737.7 *esotericism*
secret garden 655.5 *solitary place*
secret influence 645.1 *cunning*; 395.4 *indirect influence*; 484.4 *plot*
secreting 559.4 *secretory*
Secretion 559
secretion 559.1; 736.1 *concealment*; 371.22 *disgorgement*; 560.1 *excretion*; 431.6 *flow*; 315.2 *outflow*; 34.5 *physiology*; 559.2 *secreted substance*
secretionary 559.4 *secretory*
secretive 737.10; 616.4 *cautious*; 399.6 *censored*; 172.12 *internalized*; 736.17 *noncommittal*; 559.4 *secretory*; 732.2 *sparing with words*
secretively 172.16 *inwardly*; 11.25 *occultly*; 399.8 *under censorship*
secretiveness 737.2; 172.6 *internalization*
secret language 696.12 *unintelligible thing*
secret lore 737.7 *esotericism*
secretly 645.6 *cunningly*; 737.15 *in secret*; 521.9 *invisibly*; 11.25 *occultly*; 736.18 *privately*
secret meeting 737.1 *secrecy*
secret money 813.8
secretory 559.4; 560.24 *excretory*; 371.29 *expulsive*; 34.22 *physiological*
secretory mechanism 559.1 *secretion*
secret panel 736.2 *hiding place*
secret passage 700.12 *disguise*; 736.2 *hiding place*; 389.2 *means of escape*
secret passageway 550.15 *shelter*
secret place 172.2 *inside*; 252.5 *refuge*
secret places 590.8 *seat of feelings*
secret plan 484.4 *plot*
secret plot 342.9 *overactivity*
Secret Service 252.3 *protector*; 737.2 *secretiveness*
Secret Service member 586.2 *defender*
secret sign 742.1 *sign*
secret signal 743.3 *means of identification*
secret society 737.7 *esotericism*; 662.3 *subversion*
secret surveillance system 521.5 *invisible thing*
secret symbol 742.1 *sign*
secret weapon 123.3 *chief thing*; 587.1 *weapon*
secret word 743.3 *means of identification*
sect 137.8 *genealogy*; 7.1 *religion*
sectarian 7.16 *denominational*; 753.4 *protester*; 465.8 *unjust*
sectarianism 465.3 *injustice*
section 586.16 *army unit*; 409.6 *category*; 461.16 *certify*; 137.2 *class*; 525.3 *external appearance*; 196.2 *fractional part*; 27.41 *geometric figure*; 406.9 *itemize*; 584.4 *military organization*; 205.2 *particular*; 148.5, 205.7, 405.2 *piece*; 86.12 *plot*; 86.1 *region*; 372.3 *separateness*; 35.9 *surgery*; 34.17 *taxonomy*; 321.2 *track*
sectional 196.5 *fractional*; 86.17 *national*; 205.11 *partial*
sectionalize 372.11 *divide*; 205.10 *part*
sectionalized 205.11 *partial*
sectionally 406.15 *thematically*
sectioned 406.12 *itemized*
sectioning 34.6 *cell biology*
sections 406.5 *divisions*
sector 585.10 *battleground*; 27.42 *circle*; 40.19 *computing terms*; 27.41 *geometric figure*; 205.1 *part*; 179.4 *parts of a circle*; 405.2 *piece*; 86.1 *region*
secular 298.13 *anniversary*
secularism 7.13 *theology*
secularist 451.5 *disbeliever*
secularly 298.16 *cyclically*
secure 253.6; **253.10**; 373.12 *bind*; 316.14 *bring back*; 452.1 *certain*; 309.7 *close*; 222.9 *comfortable*; 384.17 *defend*; 369.15 *draw out*; 765.9 *gain*; 756.8 *guarantee*; 452.6 *infallible*; 452.21 *make certain*; 228.7 *make stable*; 252.10 *protect*; 769.9 *receive*; 252.6 *safe*; 609.4 *satisfied*; 228.9 *stable*
secure a fall 52.12 *wrestle*
secure a loan 772.7 *borrow*
secure an acquittal 389.5 *escape*
secure a personal loan 772.7 *borrow*
secured 772.11 *borrowed*; 373.16 *bound*; 309.12 *closed*; 384.30 *defended*; 756.13 *guaranteeing*; 771.6 *loaned*; 440.8 *propertied*; 769.13 *received*
secured debt 784.1 *debt*
secured loan 771.2, 772.5, 784.3 *loan*
secure exemption 389.5 *escape*
securely 222.18 *comfortably*; 373.17 *in connection with*; 252.11 *safely*; 228.12 *stably*
securement 765.1 *gain*
secureness 228.1 *stability*
secure one's object 246.6 *be successful*
secure one's objective 253.13
secure position 253.1 *protection*; 252.1 *safety*
secure the basics 352.6 *find means*
secure to 253.14 *make fast*
Securicor™ 253.4 *security forces*
securing 772.11 *borrowed*; 756.13 *guaranteeing*
securities 440.5 *personal estate*
securities market 779.5 *stock market*
Security 253
security 610.4 *comfort*; 222.5 *comfortable circumstances*; 755.1 *contract*; 756.2 *guarantee*; 452.17 *infallibility*; 16.6 *legal process*; 248.1 *prosperity*; 252.1 *safety*; 384.5 *self-defence*; 316.10 *transferred thing*
security alarm 711.2 *danger signal*
security blanket 413.6 *moral support*
security camera 41.16 *camera*
security check 252.2 *protection*
security clearance 757.1 *permission*
Security Council 579.7 *council*
security forces 253.4; 252.3 *protector*
security guard 384.14 *guard*; 252.3 *protector*; 711.4 *warner*
security man 518.11 *observer*; 252.3 *protector*; 711.4 *warner*
security officer 253.3; 16.17 *police officer*
security pass 716.6 *documentation*
security risk 700.20 *plotter*
security system 252.2, 253.1 *protection*
sedan 320.6 *litter*
sedate 656.6 *formal*; 343.14 *make inactive*; 685.4 *moderate*; 35.20 *practise surgery*; 608.9 *relieve*; 643.1 *solemn*; 622.19 *stately*
sedated 343.4 *not awake*; 608.7 *relieved*
sedately 622.33 *with dignity*
sedateness 656.1 *formality*; 622.6 *majesty*; 685.1 *moderation*
sedation 608.1 *ease*; 685.1 *moderation*; 35.9 *surgery*
sedative 37.15; 394.4 *antidote*; 394.8 *drug*; 37.4 *drug type*; 685.8 *moderating*; 685.2 *moderator*; 608.3 *reliever*; 608.8 *relieving*; 343.10 *soporific*
sedentary 301.5; **367.23**; 343.1 *inactive*; 301.4 *motionless*
sedentary person 301.7
sedge 81.1 *grass*
sedge family 77.3 *seed plant*
sedgy 81.9 *grassy*
sediment 30.27; 258.4 *dirt*; 376.26 *mass*; 215.2 *residue*; 416.4 *solid body*; 316.10 *transferred thing*
sedimentary 30.56 *petrographic*; 215.9 *remaining*
sedimentary rock 30.31; 30.28 *rock*
sedimentation 416.2 *concentration*; 258.4 *dirt*; 30.29 *petrogenesis*; 212.1 *subtraction*; 30.35 *weathering*
sedition 342.5 *activism*; 588.1 *anarchy*; 753.2 *disorder*; 800.2 *faithlessness*; 16.41 *lawlessness*; 662.4 *revolution*; 662.3 *subversion*
seditionary 588.3 *anarchist*; 662.10 *seditionist*
seditionist 662.10; **753.5**; 480.14 *motivator*
seditious 588.6 *anarchic*; 800.6 *faithless*; 753.10 *lawbreaking*; 16.61 *lawless*; 662.14 *subversive*
seditiously 588.8 *anarchically*; 753.11 *disapprovingly*; 800.11 *dishonourably*; 662.18 *subversively*
seditiousness 662.3 *subversion*
seduce 796.20; 363.12 *lure*; 804.17 *make wicked*; 483.10 *manipulate*; 480.16 *tempt*
seduced 483.12 *motivated*; 796.13 *unchaste*
seducer 363.6 *charmer*; 700.15 *deceiver*; 699.17 *false person*; 593.9 *lover*; 483.7 *motivator*; 490.3 *pleasure-seeker*; 480.13 *tempter*
seduction 363.4 *allurement*; 480.3 *incentive*; 483.2 *inducement*; 593.8 *love affair*; 796.3 *sexual immorality*
seductive 593.20 *amorous*; 395.12 *appealing*; 363.9 *attractive*; 593.22 *lovable*; 617.11 *lustful*; 490.6 *pleasant*
seductively 363.14 *attractively*; 395.14, 483.14 *influentially*; 593.30 *lovingly*; 617.20 *lustfully*
seductiveness 363.4 *allurement*; 480.3 *incentive*; 483.2 *inducement*
seductress 363.6 *charmer*; 483.7 *motivator*; 490.3 *pleasure-seeker*; 480.13 *tempter*
sedulity 342.8 *assiduity*; 640.2 *commitment*
sedulous 471.8 *diligent*; 342.20 *industrious*; 640.10 *persevering*
sedulously 471.15 *attentively*; 799.7 *honourably*; 222.19 *meticulously*
sedulousness 471.3 *carefulness*; 640.2 *commitment*
see 518.12; 97.12 *attend*; 449.1 *discover*; 446.14 *have an idea*; 477.14 *imagine*; 455.11 *know*; 7.9 *priesthood*; 695.7 *recognize*; 488.11 *sense*; 654.12 *visit*
seeable 520.1 *visible*
see again 312.8 *meet*
see another woman 796.17 *be sexually immoral*
see at a glance 695.7 *recognize*
see auras 11.24 *experience psychic phenomena*
see badly 519.14 *be blind*
see coming 474.8 *expect*
seed 77.9; 409.15 *categorize*; 44.15 *cultivate*; 562.3 *fertilizer*; 80.3 *fruit structure*; 159.2 *little thing*; 81.12 *manage grassland*; 561.8 *organs of reproduction*; 356.7 *produce*; 344.3 *rudiment*; 485.4 *skilled person*; 130.3 *source*; 377.17 *sow*
seed bank 77.11 *herbarium*
seed-bearing 77.16 *taxonomic*
seedbed 43.11 *farmland*; 562.1 *fertility*; 130.3, 344.2 *source*
seed cake 25.36 *cake*
seed capsule 80.3 *fruit structure*; 77.9 *seed*
seedcase 77.9 *seed*
seed coat 550.13 *casing*; 77.9 *seed*
seed drill 43.10 *farm tool*; 44.6 *garden tool*
seeded 409.24 *categorized*; 469.15 *chosen*
seeded player 485.4 *skilled person*
seeded position 121.3 *advantage*
seed fern 82.1 *fern*
seedily 782.16 *meanly*
seediness 782.7 *beggary*; 260.1 *ill health*
seeding 409.5 *categorization*; 377.1 *dispersion*
seed itself 562.6 *be fertile*
seed leaf 77.6 *leaf*; 77.9 *seed*
seedling 44.9 *garden plant*; 77.2 *plant*; 77.9 *seed*; 555.5 *young plant*
seed oneself 561.11 *have young*
see double 519.14 *be blind*; 690.7 *be drunk*
seed plant 77.3
seed pod 80.3 *fruit structure*; 77.9 *seed*
seeds 80.1 *fruits*; 238.6 *refuse*
seed shrimp 75.4 *arthropod*

seedsman 44.13 *horticulturist*
seed stalk 77.9 *seed;* 77.5 *stem*
seedtime 292.2 *spring*
seed tray 44.4 *nursery*
seedy **548.6**; 782.3 *beggarly;* 245.13 *dilapidated;* 260.22 *sick;* 544.10 *ugly;* 337.8 *weak*
see eye to eye 750.21 *be in accord*
see fair play 801.14 *be fair*
see fit 635.12 *choose;* 469.2 *prefer*
see how it feels 385.7 *revenge!*
see how it goes 222.11 *circumstantiate*
seeing **518.21**; 29.23 *observatory;* 518.1 *vision*
seeing a bride 475.6 *good-luck sign*
seeing a chimney sweep 475.6 *good-luck sign*
seeing double 690.10 *drunkenness;* 519.2 *poor sight;* 690.2 *slightly drunk;* 519.9 *weak-sighted*
seeing one's family 654.3 *meeting*
seeing red 624.16 *angry*
seeing to 607.3 *nuisance*
see it all 695.6 *understand*
see it coming 283.10 *expect*
see it through 252.9 *be safe;* 640.9 *endure*
see justice done 801.14 *be fair*
seek 353.1 *attempt;* 449.2 *detect;* 4.20 *philosophize;* 633.8 *pursue;* 705.17 *question*
seek acquaintance 654.13 *fraternize*
seek advice 713.6 *consult*
seek a favour 757.6 *ask permission*
seek a second opinion 35.19 *practise medicine*
seek a verdict 16.70 *litigate*
seeker 4.10 *philosopher;* 633.5 *pursuer;* 705.9 *questioner;* 710.4 *requester*
seek help 757.6 *ask permission*
seeking 353.8 *attempting;* 482.11 *intending;* 633.15 *pursuing;* 633.1 *pursuit;* 353.6 *venture*
seeking advice 713.2 *consultation*
seeking a verdict 16.5 *litigation*
seeking justice 16.5 *litigation*
seeking legal protection 16.5 *litigation*
seek justice 16.70 *litigate*
seek legal protection 16.70 *litigate*
seek opinion 713.6 *consult*
seek out 644.7 *be curious*
seek payment 783.8 *credit*
seek riches **781.14**
seek safety 252.9 *be safe*
seek seclusion 355.2 *withdraw*
seek the company of 569.14 *seek the friendship of*
seek the friendship of **569.14**
seek to 353.1 *attempt*
seem 525.11 *appear;* 171.13 *appear outwardly;* 699.28 *mask*
seem guilty 806.9 *appear guilty*
seeming 171.8 *apparent;* 699.39 *disguised;* 699.14 *façade;* 525.9 *ostensible;* 699.34 *pretending;* 115.1 *similarity;* 525.4 *something that appears*
seemingly 96.19, 525.15 *apparently;* 171.15 *externally;* 699.41 *spuriously;* 476.10 *supposedly;* 4.25 *theoretically;* 520.11 *visibly*
seemingness 171.3 *appearance*
seeming real 698.25 *lifelike*
seem lifelike **698.33**
seem like 525.11 *appear;* 115.10 *be similar*
seem likely 104.8 *be probable*
seemliness 549.1 *elegance;* 801.3 *properness*
seemly 239.1 *convenient*
seem propitious 569.16 *be favourable*
seem real 698.33 *seem lifelike*
seem to be 525.11 *appear*
seem true to life 698.33 *seem lifelike*
seem true to nature 698.33 *seem lifelike*
seen 692.34 *communicated;* 449.14 *discovered;* 455.10 *known;* 769.13 *received*
see no difference 115.11 *make similar*
see no one 655.12 *be unsocial*
see no way out 221.7 *be in a predicament*
see off 226.8 *cause to cease;* 371.6 *send away*
see oneself in print 740.17 *be published*
see one's summer 556.17 *age*
seep **429.16**; **433.32**; 305.9 *descend;* 431.25 *flow;* 314.11 *infiltrate;* 315.12 *leak;* 315.3 *leakage*
seepage **429.4**; 314.3 *inroad;* 389.4 *leak;* 315.3 *leakage*
seep away 766.12 *lessen*
seep down 305.9 *descend*
seep in 370.13 *absorb*
seeping **429.12**; **433.25**; 370.5 *absorption;* 315.3 *leakage*
seeping away 766.4 *lessening*
see pink elephants 690.7 *be drunk*
seep out 315.12, 389.7 *leak*
seer 11.13 *diviner;* 445.5 *intuitive person;* 518.11 *observer;* 475.8 *oracle;* 283.5 *predictor;* 477.9 *visionary;* 458.3 *wise man*
see red 624.12 *become angry;* 380.7 *be violent;* 590.17 *feel deeply*
seeress 518.11 *observer*
see round corners 527.12 *make transparent;* 518.12 *see*
seersucker 193.4 *textile*
seesaw 227.12 *be irresolute;* 108.2 *interrelatedness;* 326.8 *oscillate;* 326.13 *oscillating;* 326.7 *oscillator;* 110.4 *reciprocal;* 110.7 *reciprocate;* 326.18 *to and fro;* 639.5 *vacillate*
seesawing 227.14 *irresolute*
see signs 11.24 *experience psychic phenomena*
seethe 327.21 *be agitated;* 624.11 *be angry;* 25.55 *cook;* 208.11, 376.40 *crowd;* 433.31 *steep;* 307.10 *swirl;* 327.3 *turbulence*
see the catch 645.5 *be cunning*
see the end of 134.4 *protract*
see the last of 226.8 *cause to cease*
see the light 525.12 *become visible;* 808.4 *be penitent;* 449.3 *find out;* 695.6 *understand*
see the little people 11.24 *experience psychic phenomena*
see the sights 518.12 *see*
see the whole picture 222.11 *circumstantiate*
seething 376.50 *crowded;* 433.10 *steeping;* 327.3 *turbulence;* 327.17 *turbulent;* 493.12 *warm-hearted*
seething mob 342.6 *business*
see things 96.13, 518.17 *imagine*
seething with 232.8 *full*
see through 638.6 *be resolute;* 458.7 *be wise;* 392.29 *finance;* 527.12 *make transparent;* 695.6 *understand*
see-through 527.2 *translucent*
see through rose-coloured glasses 477.15 *fantasize;* 96.15 *idealize;* 446.15 *imagine*
see to 631.14 *behave towards*
see visions 477.15 *fantasize*
see you 313.14 *goodbye!*
see you later 313.14 *goodbye!*
Seger cone 24.6 *ceramic workshop*
segment 372.11 *divide;* 196.2 *fractional part;* 27.41 *geometric figure;* 205.1, 205.10 *part;* 179.4 *parts of a circle;* 205.7, 405.2 *piece*
segmental 20.13 *arched;* 405.6 *component;* 196.5 *fractional;* 205.11 *partial;* 20.17 *structured*
segmental arch 20.5 *arch*
segmental vault 20.7 *vault*
segmentation 372.3 *separateness*
segmented 75.20 *wormlike*
segmented worm 75.6 *worm*
segment stage 21.17 *stage*
segregate 466.12 *discriminate;* 372.11 *divide;* 128.7 *exclude;* 655.13 *ignore;* 100.15 *separate*
segregated 466.11 *judged;* 100.11 *separate;* 109.6 *unrelated*
segregation 466.1 *discrimination;* 128.1 *exclusion;* 252.2 *protection;* 594.3 *race hatred;* 100.3 *separateness;* 655.3 *separation;* 372.2 *setting apart;* 466.4 *social discrimination*
segregationist 372.8 *person who separates*
seiche 30.14 *wave*
seif 30.37 *dune*
seigneur 400.1 *master*
seigneury 440.3 *historic property terms*
seignorial 440.8 *propertied*
Seine 90.5 *other major rivers*
seine 74.15 *fish;* 74.7 *fishing;* 700.13, 700.33 *snare*
seisin 763.2 *legal terms*
seism 30.22 *seismic activity*
seismatical 326.17 *waving*
seismic 123.6 *notable;* 380.6 *violent;* 30.55 *volcanic;* 326.17 *waving*
seismic activity **30.22**
seismic event 30.22 *seismic activity*
seismicity 30.22 *seismic activity;* 326.5 *wave*
seismic seawave 30.14 *wave*
seismic wave **30.23**; 28.14 *sound wave;* 326.5 *wave*
seismograph 326.6 *measuring instrument;* 744.10 *recording instrument;* 30.23 *seismic wave*
seismographic 30.49 *geophysical;* 326.17 *waving*
seismography 30.2 *geophysics*
seismological 30.49 *geophysical;* 326.17 *waving*
seismologically 30.66 *geographically*
seismologist 30.4 *geophysicist*
seismology 30.2 *geophysics*
seismometer 326.6 *measuring instrument;* 26.8 *meter*
seismometric 30.49 *geophysical;* 326.17 *waving*
seismoscope 326.6 *measuring instrument*
seize 251.11 *detain;* 360.6 *retain;* 773.7 *take;* 773.8 *take back;* 492.11 *touch;* 695.6 *understand*
seized 260.22 *sick*
seize on 123.8 *make important*
seize one's chance 293.11 *get ahead;* 287.5 *take the opportunity*
seize one's opportunity 287.5 *take the opportunity*
seize power 773.7 *take;* 12.12, 396.20 *take authority*
seizer 773.6 *taker*
seize the crown 588.4 *be anarchic*
seize the day 287.5 *take the opportunity*
seize the moment 293.11 *get ahead*
seize the occasion 293.11 *get ahead*
seize the opportunity 342.14 *push*
seize up 247.9 *malfunction*
seizing one's chance 293.6 *getting ahead*
seizing the moment 293.6 *getting ahead*
seizing the occasion 293.6 *getting ahead*
seizure 381.20 *bout;* 260.2 *illness;* 461.3 *mental deterioration;* 260.17 *nervous disorder;* 360.1 *retention;* 327.8 *spasm;* 773.1 *taking;* 773.2 *taking back*
seizure of power 396.3 *acquisition of power;* 773.1 *taking*
sejant 743.13 *heraldic*
selachian 74.2 *fish;* 74.13 *fishlike*
seldom 206.11 *sparsely*
seldom if ever 105.10 *rarely*
seldom met with 206.6 *sparse*
seldom seen 206.6 *sparse*
select **469.1**; 409.15 *categorize;* 139.22 *characterize;* 635.12 *choose;* 469.15 *chosen;* 723.9 *compile;* 466.12 *discriminate;* 128.10 *excluding;* 396.21 *grant authority;* 595.8 *prefer;* 372.10 *set apart;* 235.1 *worthy*
select building materials 20.18 *be an architect*
select committee 713.4 *adviser;* 579.6 *governing body*
selected 409.24 *categorized;* 469.15 *chosen;* 396.13 *elected;* 68.13 *ice-skating;* 466.11 *judged;* 235.1 *worthy*
select few 121.7 *the best people*
selecting **469.14**; 464.8 *judging*
Selection 469
selection **469.6**; 396.3 *acquisition of power;* 409.5 *categorization;* 469.9 *chosen thing;* 723.3 *compendium;* 466.1 *discrimination;* 595.2 *inclination;* 464.1 *judgment;* 595.3 *likes;* 372.2 *setting apart*
selection of music 68.7 *ice-dancing*
selective 466.9 *discriminating;* 464.8 *judging;* 469.14 *selecting;* 372.17 *unjoined*
selective facts 234.4 *distortion of the truth*
selective killing 382.9 *animal killing*
selectively **469.17**; 466.15 *discriminatingly;* 372.22 *in isolation;* 464.13 *judicially*
selectiveness 466.1 *discrimination*
selectivity 466.1 *discrimination*
selector 466.6 *discriminating person;* 372.8 *person who separates*
Selene 29.17 *moon*
selenic 32.34 *elemental*
selenious 32.34 *elemental*
selenium 33.15 *essential element*
selenium meter 41.18 *exposure time*
selenous 32.34 *elemental*
self 139.11, 743.2 *identity;* 101.6 *internal world;* 36.21 *psyche*
self-abasement **623.11**
self-abasing **623.4**
self-abnegating 623.4 *self-abasing;* 473.5 *unselfish*
self-abnegation 623.11 *self-abasement;* 684.1 *self-restraint;* 473.2 *unselfishness*
self-absorbed **686.9**; 683.5 *egoistic;* 172.12 *internalized*
self-absorption **686.4**; 683.2 *egoism;* 172.6 *internalization;* 463.1 *oblivion*
self-accusation 808.1 *penitence;* 806.2 *signs of guilt*
self-accusing 808.6 *penitent*
self-accusingly 808.8 *penitently*
self-adhesive film 25.6 *kitchen equipment*
self-admiration **673.4**; 622.3 *conceit*
self-admirer 673.7 *vain person*
self-admiring **673.10**; 622.17 *conceited*
self-applause 673.4 *self-admiration*
self-appointed 636.5 *voluntary*
self-appointed task 636.10 *voluntary work*
self-approbation 673.2 *self-satisfaction*
self-approving 673.10 *self-admiring*
self-assertion 707.6 *assertiveness;* 396.2 *authoritativeness;* 661.1 *defiance*
self-assertive 707.14 *assertive;* 396.12 *authoritative;* 673.11 *cocky;* 336.11 *strong in spirit*
self-assertively 673.21 *cockily*
self-assertiveness 673.3 *cockiness*
self-assurance **397.5**; 167.4 *assurance;* 452.10 *conviction;* 661.1 *defiance;* 673.2 *self-satisfaction*
self-assured **397.15**; 167.8 *assured;* 452.2 *convinced;* 661.7 *defiant;* 673.9 *self-satisfied*
self-assuredly 397.16 *commandingly;* 661.9 *defiantly;* 673.20 *smugly*
self-centred 683.5 *egoistic;* 686.9 *self-absorbed;* 673.12 *self-interested;* 139.18 *subjective*
self-centredness 683.2 *egoism;* 686.4 *self-absorption;* 673.5 *self-interest*
self-certification 758.3 *self-exemption*
self-command 638.15 *will*
self-commiseration 627.1 *pity*
self-compassion 627.1 *pity*
self-conceit 673.6 *boastfulness*
self-conceited 673.13 *boastful*
self-concern 683.1 *selfishness*
self-concerned 683.4 *selfish*
self-condemnation 808.1 *penitence*
self-condemning 808.6 *penitent*
self-confidence 167.4 *assurance;* 673.3 *cockiness;* 452.10 *conviction;* 622.1 *pride;* 397.5 *self-assurance*
self-confident 167.8 *assured;* 673.11 *cocky;* 452.2 *convinced;* 622.14 *proud;* 397.15 *self-assured*
self-confidently 673.21 *cockily;* 397.16 *commandingly;* 622.32 *proudly*
self-congratulation 673.2 *self-satisfaction*
self-congratulatory 673.9 *self-satisfied;* 673.20 *smugly*
self-conscious 676.3 *affected;* 674.11, 732.1 *shy*
self-consciously 676.5 *affectedly;* 732.8 *shyly*
self-consciousness 674.4, 732.3 *shyness*
self-consideration 683.1 *selfishness*
self-contained 232.7 *complete;* 250.10 *independent;* 732.1 *shy;* 655.8 *unsociable*
self-containment 655.1 *unsociability*
self-content 673.2 *self-satisfaction*
self-contented 673.9 *self-satisfied*
self-contentedly 673.20 *smugly*
self-contradicting 274.17 *mistaken*
self-contradiction 274.4 *faulty reasoning;* 103.5 *impossibility*
self-contradictory 274.15 *erroneous;* 103.1 *impossible*
self-control 4.3 *detachment;* 473.1 *disinterestedness;* 166.2 *limiting factor;* 685.1 *moderation;* 251.3, 684.1 *self-restraint;* 803.2 *virtues;* 638.15 *will;* 635.2 *willpower*
self-controlled 4.18 *detached;* 473.4 *disinterested;* 803.6 *ethical;* 635.7 *iron-willed;* 685.6 *moderate;* 251.14, 684.8 *self-restrained;* 638.5 *steady*
self-convicted 16.64 *convicted*
self-deceived 700.36 *deceived*
self-deception **700.2**; 96.3 *delusion;* 274.6 *fallibility;* 465.1 *misjudgment*
self-defeating 103.1 *impossible*
self-defence **384.5**; 52.1 *combat sports;* 383.3 *resistance movement*

self-defensive 52.14 *combat;* 383.12 *resisting*
self-defensively 384.32 *defensively*
self-denial 709.3 *abnegation;* 634.11 *abstinence;* 383.4 *desisting;* 684.1 *self-restraint;* 647.3 *unadornment;* 473.2 *unselfishness;* 572.2 *virginity*
self-denying 709.10 *abnegating;* 383.13 *desisting;* 684.8 *self-restrained;* 473.5 *unselfish*
self-deprecating **674.12**; 623.4 *self-abasing*
self-deprecation **674.5**; 468.1 *underestimation*
self-depreciation 468.1 *underestimation*
self-destruct 357.13 *be destroyed;* 245.1 *deteriorate*
self-destruction 382.7 *suicide*
self-destructive 382.24 *murderous*
self-determination 85.1 *country;* 635.4 *free will;* 250.3 *independence*
self-determined 635.10 *free*
self-determining 250.9 *free;* 85.16 *national*
self-devoted 686.9 *self-absorbed*
self-devotion 638.13 *concentration;* 683.2 *egoism;* 686.4 *self-absorption*
self-discipline 814.11 *penance;* 251.3, 684.1 *self-restraint*
self-disciplined 251.14, 684.8 *self-restrained*
self-display 673.6 *boastfulness*
self-distrustful 674.12 *self-deprecating*
self-doubt 611.1 *hopelessness;* 674.5 *self-deprecation*
self-doubting 623.4 *self-abasing;* 674.12 *self-deprecating*
self-education 6.2 *educational system;* 455.3 *learning*
self-effacement 623.11 *self-abasement;* 674.5 *self-deprecation;* 468.1 *underestimation;* 473.2 *unselfishness*
self-effacing 623.4 *self-abasing;* 674.12 *self-deprecating;* 732.1 *shy;* 473.5 *unselfish*
self-employed 250.10 *independent*
self-employed person 578.1 *worker*
self-endearing 673.10 *self-admiring*
self-endearment 673.4 *self-admiration*
self-esteem 622.1 *pride;* 673.4 *self-admiration*
self-esteeming 622.14 *proud*
self-evidence 716.3 *evidentness;* 695.10 *simplicity*
self-evident 452.1 *certain;* 703.12 *demonstrable;* 716.9 *evident;* 738.14 *manifest;* 695.2 *simple;* 27.69 *theoretical*
self-evidently 716.15 *evidently*
self-examination 4.4 *philosophical investigation*
self-exemption **758.3**
self-existence **93.7**
self-existent **93.14**
self-existing 93.14 *self-existent*
self-explanatory 695.2 *simple*
self-expression 250.3 *independence*
self-expressive 250.13 *informal*
self-flagellation 808.2 *type of penance*
self-flattery 673.4 *self-admiration*
self-fulfilling prophecy 106.5 *predetermination*
self-glorification 622.10 *boastfulness;* 727.4 *bombast*
self-glorify 727.10 *boast*
self-glorifying 622.22 *boastful;* 727.15 *bombastic;* 673.10 *self-admiring*
self-governing 250.9 *free;* 12.9, 396.14 *governmental;* 85.16 *national*
self-governing state 85.1 *country*
self-government 12.1 *government;* 250.3 *independence;* 396.7 *type of rule*
self-gratification 490.1 *physical pleasure;* 686.1 *self-indulgence*
self-gratifying 686.6 *self-indulgent*
self-help group 395.6 *group influence*
selfhood 101.6 *internal world*
self-humiliation 808.2 *type of penance*
self-hypnosis 36.3 *psychiatric treatment*
self-immolation 752.6 *offering;* 382.7 *suicide*
self-importance 622.1 *pride;* 673.1 *vanity*
self-important 622.14 *proud;* 673.8 *vain*
self-importantly 673.19 *vainly*
self-imposed 354.5 *undertaken*
self-imposed task 354.2 *undertaking*
self-improvement 244.5 *improvement*
self-inductance 28.53, 39.12 *resistance*
self-induction 28.63 *magnetic phenomenon*
self-indulge 688.5 *be greedy*
Self-Indulgence 686
self-indulgence **686.1**; 688.1 *gluttony;* 490.1 *physical pleasure;* 241.7 *pleasure;* 683.1 *selfishness*
self-indulgent **686.6**; 688.6 *gluttonous;* 490.7 *pleased;* 241.5 *pleasure-loving;* 683.4 *selfish*
self-indulgently **686.12**; 688.7 *gluttonously;* 683.8 *selfishly*
self-indulgent person **686.5**
self-infatuated 673.10 *self-admiring*
self-infatuation 673.4 *self-admiration*
selfing 78.6 *pollination*
self-instruction 455.3 *learning*
self-interest **673.5**; 683.1 *selfishness*
self-interested **673.12**; 683.4 *selfish*
selfish **683.4**; 631.18 *badly behaved;* 653.3 *misanthropic;* 686.9 *self-absorbed;* 673.12 *self-interested;* 139.18 *subjective;* 472.9 *thoughtless;* 672.3 *ungrateful;* 463.10 *unthinking*
selfishly **673.22**; **683.8**; 631.20 *badly;* 472.14 *inattentively;* 653.5 *misanthropically;* 672.7 *ungratefully*
selfish motive 483.1 *motive*
Selfishness 683
selfishness **683.1**; 631.4 *bad conduct;* 672.1 *ingratitude;* 653.1 *misanthropy;* 359.1 *preservation;* 686.4 *self-absorption;* 673.5 *self-interest;* 472.4 *thoughtlessness;* 463.4 *unthinkingness*
selfish person **683.3**
selfless 473.5 *unselfish*
selflessly 473.9 *unselfishly*
selflessness 650.2 *charity;* 473.2 *unselfishness*
self-loss 463.1 *oblivion*
self-love 683.2 *egoism;* 593.1 *love;* 686.4 *self-absorption;* 673.4 *self-admiration*
self-loving 683.5 *egoistic;* 686.9 *self-absorbed;* 673.10 *self-admiring*
self-lovingly 683.9 *egoistically*
self-made 646.1 *naive;* 486.2 *unskilled*
self-made man 248.4 *prosperous person;* 246.4 *successful person;* 781.10 *wealthy person*
self-mastered 638.5 *steady*
self-mastery 684.1 *self-restraint;* 638.15 *will*
self-mortification 814.11 *penance;* 647.3 *unadornment*
self-motivated 250.10 *independent;* 483.12 *motivated*
self-obsessed 686.9 *self-absorbed*
self-obsession 686.4 *self-absorption*
self-opinion 641.7 *opinionatedness*
self-opinionated 673.13 *boastful*
self-pity 627.1 *pity;* 683.1 *selfishness*
self-pitying 627.7 *pitiful*
self-pleaser 683.3 *selfish person*
self-pleasing 683.1 *selfishness*
self-pollination 78.6 *pollination*
self-possessed 4.18 *detached;* 638.5 *steady*
self-possession 4.3 *detachment;* 685.1 *moderation;* 638.15 *will*
self-praise 622.3 *conceit;* 683.2 *egoism;* 673.4 *self-admiration*
self-praising 622.17 *conceited*
self-preservation 616.1 *caution;* 359.1 *preservation;* 683.1 *selfishness*
self-promotion 480.5 *propaganda*
self-propelled 300.16 *moving;* 330.19 *propelled*
self-protection 616.1 *caution*
self psychology 36.1 *psychology*
self-punishing 808.7 *penitential*
self-punishment 814.11 *penance;* 808.2 *type of penance*
self-raising 415.4 *leavening*
self-raising flour 25.7 *basic ingredient;* 415.8 *leavening*
self-regard 622.1 *pride*
self-regarding 622.14 *proud*
self-regulating 119.6 *equal;* 250.9 *free*
self-regulating market 250.1 *freedom*
self-regulatory 250.9 *free*
self-reliance 250.3 *independence;* 613.3 *steadfastness*
self-reliant **613.12**; 250.10 *independent*
self-reliantly 622.32 *proudly*
self-remorse 808.1 *penitence*
self-renunciation 709.3 *abnegation*
self-renunciatory 709.10 *abnegating*
self-reproach 808.1 *penitence;* 806.2 *signs of guilt*
self-reproachful 808.6 *penitent*
self-reproaching 808.6 *penitent*
self-respect 622.1 *pride*
self-respecting 673.10 *self-admiring*
self-restrained **251.14**; **684.8**; 4.18 *detached;* 638.5 *steady;* 647.10 *unadorned*
self-restrained person **684.4**
Self-Restraint 684
self-restraint **251.3**; **684.1**; 709.3 *abnegation;* 383.4 *desisting;* 4.3 *detachment;* 473.1 *disinterestedness;* 166.2 *limiting factor;* 647.3 *unadornment;* 638.15 *will*
self-righteous 795.10 *moralistic;* 7.15 *religious*
self-righteousness **795.4**
self-rule 12.3 *governance;* 12.1 *government;* 250.3 *independence*
self-ruling 250.9 *free;* 12.9 *governmental*
self-sacrifice 709.3 *abnegation;* 768.3 *offering;* 7.2 *religiousness;* 473.2 *unselfishness*
self-sacrificing 709.10 *abnegating;* 7.15 *religious;* 473.5 *unselfish*
selfsame 111.12 *same*
selfsameness 111.1 *sameness*
self-satisfaction **673.2**; 609.1 *satisfaction*
self-satisfied **673.9**; 609.4 *satisfied*
self-scourging 808.2 *type of penance*
self-seeker 683.3 *selfish person*
self-seeking 683.4 *selfish;* 683.1 *selfishness*
self-server 683.3 *selfish person*
self-service 436.1 *provision;* 436.7 *provisioning*
self-service restaurant 557.15 *eating place*
self-serving 683.1 *selfishness*
self-serving politician 645.3 *cunning person*
self-slaughter 382.7 *suicide*
self-starter 340.3 *doer*
self-styled 451.7 *disbelieved;* 673.12 *self-interested*
self-submission 623.11 *self-abasement*
self-submitting 623.4 *self-abasing*
self-sufficiency 232.1 *completeness;* 250.3 *independence;* 684.1 *self-restraint;* 673.2 *self-satisfaction;* 781.8 *solvency;* 217.7 *sufficiency;* 622.2 *unapproachability*
self-sufficient 232.7 *complete;* 250.10 *independent;* 684.8 *self-restrained;* 673.9 *self-satisfied;* 217.1 *sufficient;* 622.15 *unapproachable;* 372.17 *unjoined;* 655.8 *unsociable*
self-sufficiently 372.22 *in isolation;* 673.20 *smugly;* 655.14 *unsocially;* 684.11 *with self-restraint*
self-supporting 250.10 *independent*
self-surrender 7.2 *religiousness*
self-surrendering 7.15 *religious*
self-taught 6.17 *educable;* 646.1 *naive;* 486.2 *unskilled*
self-timer 41.18 *exposure time*
self-will 641.5 *obstinacy;* 635.3 *wilfulness*
self-willed 588.6 *anarchic;* 641.1 *obstinate;* 635.8 *wilful*
self-worship 686.4 *self-absorption;* 673.4 *self-admiration*
self-worshipping 686.9 *self-absorbed;* 673.10 *self-admiring*
Seliwanoff's test 33.5 *sugar test*
sell **778.1**; 700.30 *be fraudulent;* 778.2 *be sold;* 767.11 *dispose of property;* 700.10 *fraud;* 436.5 *provision;* 740.16 *publicize;* 776.1 *trade*
Sellafield 437.7 *nuclear power*
sell again 778.1 *sell*
sell a gold brick 700.28 *trick*
sell at a loss 766.10 *have a financial loss;* 778.1 *sell*
sell at a profit 765.14 *profit;* 778.1 *sell;* 13.10 *trade with*
sell at a sacrifice 778.1 *sell*
sell badly 778.2 *be sold*
sell by auction 778.1 *sell*
sell dear 792.10 *overcharge*
sell down the river 693.13 *inform on;* 800.9 *prove false*
seller **778.9**; 13.9 *economist;* 778.11 *pedlar;* 776.10 *trader;* 578.1 *worker*
sellers' market **779.3**; 13.6 *economic factors;* 792.3 *inflationary price;* 135.2 *need;* 218.9 *scarcity*
sell for 790.13 *cost*
sell forward 778.1 *sell*
selling **778.3**; 767.2 *disposal of property;* 13.2 *economy*
selling line 778.8 *merchandise*
selling off 767.2 *disposal of property*
selling price 790.1 *price*
sell like hot cakes 740.18 *become famous;* 778.2 *be sold*
sell off 767.11 *dispose of property;* 778.1 *sell*
sell on credit 783.8 *credit*
Sellotape™ 267.3 *adhesive*
sell out 778.2 *be sold;* 639.9 *change sides;* 800.9 *prove false;* 778.1 *sell;* 388.3 *submit;* 355.2 *withdraw*
sell-out 800.2 *faithlessness;* 778.4 *sale;* 388.1 *submission;* 246.3 *successful thing;* 21.13 *theatrical performance*
sell over the counter 767.11 *dispose of property;* 778.1 *sell*
sell property 767.11 *dispose of property*
sell short 678.10 *disparage;* 778.1 *sell;* 728.20 *understate*
sell the family silver 782.13 *lose one's money*
sell to 776.1 *trade*
sell under the counter 767.11 *dispose of property;* 778.1 *sell*
sell up 778.1 *sell*
sell well 740.18 *become famous;* 778.2 *be sold*
selvage 164.2 *edging;* 42.4 *weaving*
semanteme 5.35 *part of speech*
semantic **694.8**; 5.38 *linguistic*
semantically 5.48 *linguistically;* 4.24 *philosophically*
semantic content 694.1 *meaning*
semantic field 694.4 *type of meaning*
semantic flow 694.1 *meaning*
semanticist 5.2 *linguist*
semantic net 40.17 *artificial intelligence*
semantics 4.6 *branch of philosophy;* 5.1 *linguistics;* 694.1 *meaning;* 40.9 *programming language*
semantic shift 694.4 *type of meaning*
semaphore 5.8 *artificial language;* 505.1 *deafness;* 742.4, 742.12 *signal;* 692.27 *signalling;* 730.6 *silent speech;* 321.2 *track*
semaphoric 742.16 *signalling*
semaphorically 742.18 *indicatively*
semasiological 5.38 *linguistic;* 694.8 *semantic*
semasiologist 5.2 *linguist*
semasiology 5.1 *linguistics;* 694.1 *meaning*
sematology 694.1 *meaning*
semblance 699.14 *façade;* 518.5 *imagination;* 717.1 *representation;* 115.1 *similarity;* 525.4 *something that appears*
seme 743.13 *heraldic*
semeiology 35.3 *medical specialty*
sememe 5.17 *word*
semen 431.3 *body fluid;* 562.3 *fertilizer;* 561.8 *organs of reproduction;* 559.2 *secreted substance*
semen sample 35.7 *diagnosis*
semester 276.4 *period of activity;* 275.4 *term*
semi 565.5 *house*
semiannual 298.12 *cyclic*
semiannually 298.16 *cyclically*
semiarid climate 31.38 *climate*
semiautomatic 587.9 *firearm*
semibreve 18.17 *notation*
semicircle 177.2 *bend;* 27.42, 179.2 *circle;* 54.3 *fencing movements;* 198.8 *half;* 205.1 *part*
semicircular 179.5 *circular;* 177.4 *curved;* 27.81 *curvilinear*
semicircular apse 20.10 *church architecture*
semicircular arch 20.5 *arch*
semicircular canals 504.5 *internal ear*
semicolon 742.7 *punctuation*
semiconductor **28.44**; **39.4**; 28.43 *electrical conduction;* 334.7 *electrical power*
semiconductor device 39.16 *circuit element;* 28.44 *semiconductor*
semiconductor laser 28.26 *laser*
semiconductor memory 40.6 *memory*
semidark 524.5 *dim*
semidarkness 524.1 *dimness*
semidetached 565.16 *manorial;* 20.12 *structural*
semidetached house 20.3 *building;* 565.5 *house;* 216.8 *middle classes*
semi-final race 47.1 *track events*
semihumid climate 31.38 *climate*

semiliquid 152.2 *dense*
semiliquidity 419.10 *compressibility*; 431.5 *fluidity*
semi-literacy 456.2 *half-knowledge*
semi-literate 456.7 *semiskilled*
semimajor axis 29.21 *orbit*
semimatt finish 41.12 *development*
semimetal 32.6 *chemical element*
semimonthly 298.12 *cyclic*; 298.16 *cyclically*; 740.5 *journal*
seminal 344.13 *causal*; 559.5 *of a secretion*; 126.4 *original*; 561.16 *reproductive*
seminal fluid 561.8 *organs of reproduction*; 559.2 *secreted substance*
seminally 126.8 *originally*
seminar 734.4 *conference*; 137.7 *lecture*
seminary 6.12 *educational institution*
semiological 719.14 *interpretive*; 694.8 *semantic*; 742.14 *signifying*
semiologically 742.18 *indicatively*
semiologist 742.8 *signer*
semiology 694.1 *meaning*; 719.5 *science of interpretation*; 742.2 *symbolism*
semiopaque 24.10 *ceramic*; 527.3 *semitransparent*; 528.2 *shady*
semiopaque glaze 24.3 *glaze*
semiopaquely 24.12 *ornamentally*
semiotic 694.8 *semantic*; 742.14 *signifying*
semiotician 742.8 *signer*
semiotics 4.6 *branch of philosophy*; 694.1 *meaning*; 742.2 *symbolism*
semipolar bond 32.11 *chemical bond*
semiprofessional 216.8 *middle classes*
semiquaver 18.17 *notation*
semi-schooled 456.7 *semiskilled*
semi-sextile 176.4 *angular measurement*
semiskilled 456.7; 15.8 *industrial*; 486.2 *unskilled*
semiskilled worker 578.2 *artisan*; 216.7 *average person*; 15.7 *employee*; 346.6 *operative*
semiskimmed milk 558.5 *milk*
Semitic 5.11 *family of languages*
semitone 18.16 *musical note*
semitransparency 527.7; 524.2 *murk*; 531.7 *whiteness*
semitransparent 527.3; 541.7 *iridescent*; 531.2 *whitened*
semitransparently 531.14 *whitely*
semitransparent pigment 529.4 *pigment*
semiweekly 298.12 *cyclic*; 298.16 *cyclically*
semmit 551.18 *underwear*
semolina 25.35 *dessert*
sempiternal 279.8 *eternal*; 225.7 *permanent*
sempiternally 225.9 *permanently*
sempiternity 279.1 *eternity*
Semtex™ 357.7 *agent of destruction*; 587.15 *explosive*
Senate 12.4 *governing body*; 398.2 *representative body*; 579.12 *US government*
senate 579.10 *legislative body*
Senate majority leader 579.14 *leader*; 12.8 *politician*
Senate minority leader 579.14 *leader*; 12.8 *politician*
Senator 398.1 *delegate*; 400.3 *leader*; 579.16 *official*; 396.10 *person of authority*; 12.8 *politician*
senatorial 398.9 *delegated*; 12.9 *governmental*; 400.12 *masterful*; 579.18 *parliamentary*
senatorial government 12.1 *government*
Senatorially 398.11 *representatively*
senatus 579.10 *legislative body*
Senatus Populusque Romanus 12.1 *government*
send 733.10; 316.14 *bring back*; 597.8 *cause joy*; 692.31 *correspond*; 768.5 *give*; 300.14 *set in motion*; 316.12, 319.4 *transport*
send about one's business 371.6 *send away*
send abroad 315.13 *emigrate*
send after 633.8 *pursue*
send a letter to 692.31 *correspond*
send a message 742.12 *signal*
send an order for 135.10 *necessitate*
send an SOS 742.12 *signal*
send a signal 742.12 *signal*
send a telegram 692.31 *correspond*
send away 371.6; 526.3 *cause to disappear*; 377.13 *dismiss*; 371.4 *ostracize*
send back 775.4 *give back*; 470.1 *reject*
send before the beak 715.5 *accuse*
send before the judge 715.5 *accuse*
send by hand 316.13 *post*
send down 371.3 *disbar*; 309.10 *enclose*; 815.9 *imprison*; 814.1 *punish*
send flying 330.24 *push*; 316.12 *transport*
send for 633.8 *pursue*
send forth 371.14 *let out*; 316.12 *transport*
send headlong 367.3 *bring down*; 330.24 *push*
send home 377.13 *dismiss*; 391.4 *liberate*
send in 370.8 *show in*
sending 319.1 *transport*; 316.2 *transportation*
sending back 775.1 *giving back*
sending home 377.2 *disbandment*
sending to Coventry 670.3 *nonacceptance*; 371.19 *ostracism*; 814.7 *punishment*; 655.3 *separation*; 655.1 *unsociability*
send in one's papers 605.5 *resign*
sendoff 313.9 *parting*
send off 377.13 *dismiss*; 330.32 *load*; 371.6 *send away*; 330.28 *shoot*; 316.12 *transport*
send on 692.31 *correspond*; 733.10 *send*
send one's apologies 709.5 *refuse*
send one's condolences 627.9 *sorrow*
send one's regrets 658.10 *be courteous*
send one's respects 658.10 *be courteous*
send one to sleep 620.6 *be boring*
send out 432.27 *give off*; 371.14 *let out*
send over the edge 461.15 *make insane*
send packing 128.8, 364.2 *eject*; 371.6 *send away*
send Season's greetings 292.6 *spend the season*
send smoke signals 742.12 *signal*
send the marines 586.36 *combat*
send to blazes 660.29 *ridicule*; 712.6 *vilify*
send to Coventry 128.7 *exclude*; 655.13 *ignore*; 371.4 *ostracize*; 814.1 *punish*; 372.10 *set apart*; 399.3 *veto*; 670.15 *withhold approval*
send to one's account 382.16 *kill*
send to one's Maker 382.16 *kill*
send to prison 251.11 *detain*
send to the block 814.5 *execute*
send to the bottom 367.3 *bring down*
send to the chair 814.5 *execute*
send to the devil 712.6 *vilify*
send to the gallows 814.5 *execute*
send to the scaffold 382.19, 814.5 *execute*
send to the showers 371.6 *send away*
send to the stake 382.19, 814.5 *execute*
send up 366.2; 599.13 *be humorous*; 621.6 *deride*; 125.9 *imitate*; 815.9 *imprison*; 21.35 *overact*; 668.24, 678.14 *ridicule*
send-up 621.2 *act of derision*; 599.4 *entertainment*; 125.3 *mockery*; 668.4, 678.6 *ridicule*
send up the river 251.11 *detain*; 815.9 *imprison*
Senecan 4.11 *follower of a doctrine*; 4.14 *of a philosophy*
Senecan tragedy 21.11 *tragedy*
senescence 556.5 *old age*
senescent 556.12 *ageing*; 245.12 *deteriorated*; 296.11 *old*
seneschal 396.10 *person of authority*
senhor 567.3 *male title of address*
senile 556.14 *aged*; 245.12 *deteriorated*; 459.5 *foolish*; 335.12 *impotent*; 457.7 *intellectually subnormal*; 457.5 *lacking intellect*; 296.11 *old*
senile dementia 335.4 *disability*; 461.3 *mental deterioration*
senilely 556.16 *maturely*; 457.11 *unintelligently*; 296.18 *venerably*
senility 245.9 *dilapidation*; 335.4 *disability*; 459.1 *folly*; 457.1 *lack of intellect*; 556.5 *old age*; 296.1 *oldness*; 337.3 *poor health*
senior 556.11 *adult*; 396.12 *authoritative*; 400.5 *company leader*; 121.15 *excellent*; 296.11 *old*; 556.7 *older person*; 129.9 *predecessor*; 129.12 *primary*; 121.5 *superior*
senior aircraftman 586.32 *airman*
senior citizen 556.7 *older person*
senior citizens 296.2 *old people*
senior commander 584.5 *military staff*
senior high 6.12 *educational institution*
senior house officer 35.11 *doctor*
seniority 556.2 *adulthood*; 396.1 *authority*; 15.2 *industrial negotiations*; 556.5 *old age*; 296.1 *oldness*; 129.2 *priority*; 121.1 *superiority*
senior nursing officer 579.15 *manager*; 35.16 *nurse*
senior officer 584.5 *military staff*
senior registrar 35.11 *doctor*
senior service 586.22 *navy*; 584.2 *the military*
senmurv 72.9 *fabulous bird*
senna pods 394.6 *purgative*
sennet 18.22 *phrase*; 742.6 *word*
señor 567.3 *male title of address*
señora 568.3 *female title of address*
señorita 568.3 *female title of address*
sensate 488.8
Sensation 488
sensation 488.1; 727.1 *exaggeration*; 590.1 *feeling*; 554.1 *life*; 34.5 *physiology*; 246.1 *success*; 404.1 *texture*; 492.1 *touch*; 619.4 *wonder*
sensational 488.9 *exciting*; 21.40 *tragic*; 740.20 *well-known*; 619.8 *wonderful*; 235.1 *worthy*
sensationalism 673.6 *boastfulness*; 21.9 *dramaturgy*; 727.1 *exaggeration*; 740.8 *public relations*; 4.7 *school of thought*
sensationalist 727.6 *exaggerator*
sensationalize 727.7 *exaggerate*
sensationalized 727.12 *exaggerated*
sensationally 488.14; 727.16 *exaggeratedly*
sense 488.11; 442.5 *common sense*; 590.15 *feel*; 590.1 *feeling*; 590.16 *feel in one's bones*; 442.3, 458.2 *intelligence*; 695.9 *intelligibility*; 464.1 *judgment*; 6.24 *know*; 694.1 *meaning*; 4.8 *philosophical term*; 444.1 *reason*; 345.4 *significance*
sense data 4.8 *philosophical term*
sense datum 488.1 *sensation*
senseless 459.5 *foolish*; 457.5 *lacking intellect*; 697.5 *nonsensical*; 463.8 *oblivious*; 489.6 *unfeeling*
senseless killing 382.1 *killing*
senselessly 459.8 *foolishly*; 463.16 *obliviously*; 457.11 *unintelligently*
senselessness 459.1 *folly*; 457.1 *lack of intellect*; 272.1 *ludicrousness*; 697.1 *nonsense*; 463.1 *oblivion*
sense of community 2.5 *society*
sense of danger 254.5 *danger*
sense of duty 810.4; 799.1 *probity*
sense of hearing 504.1 *hearing*
sense of indebtedness 671.1 *gratitude*
sense of language 724.4 *literary style*
sense of mystery 619.1 *wonder*
sense of obligation 671.1 *gratitude*
sense of responsibility 799.1 *probity*
sense of security 253.1 *protection*; 252.1 *safety*
sense of sight 518.1 *vision*
sense of smell 500.2
sense of taste 495.1 *taste*
sense of time 275.1 *time*
sense of touch 492.1 *touch*
sense of wonder 619.1 *wonder*
sense of wrong 802.7
sense organ 492.7; 488.4 *someone or something that feels*
sense perception 488.1 *sensation*; 492.1 *touch*
sense vibrations 11.24 *experience psychic phenomena*
sensibilia 4.8 *philosophical term*
sensibilities 590.3 *feelings*
sensibility 464.1 *judgment*; 466.2 *judiciousness*; 554.1 *life*; 6.11 *refinement*; 591.5 *sensitivity*
sensible 488.5; 713.8 *advisable*; 793.9 *cheap*; 590.10 *feeling*; 402.7 *material*; 685.6 *moderate*; 95.8 *practical*; 4.15, 460.5 *rational*; 444.7 *reasoning*; 6.20 *refined*; 442.11 *thoughtful*; 237.1 *useful*; 458.5 *wise*
sensibleness 442.5 *common sense*
sensible price 793.1 *cheapness*
sensibly 442.15 *intelligently*; 402.9 *materially*; 4.26 *rationally*; 444.15 *reasonably*; 458.9 *wisely*
sensing 590.10 *feeling*; 445.6 *intuitive*
sensitive 590.12; **591.1**; 466.9 *discriminating*; 543.3 *elegant*; 590.10 *feeling*; 419.7 *impressionable*; 445.6 *intuitive*; 464.9 *judicious*; 6.20, 549.5 *refined*; 488.5 *sensible*; 492.8 *touchable*
sensitively 492.16; **591.12**; 6.27 *discerningly*; 466.16 *judiciously*; 419.18 *softheartedly*
sensitive man 567.14 *liberated man*
sensitiveness 419.12 *gentleness*; 591.5 *sensitivity*
sensitive payment 768.2 *gift*
sensitive person 591.8; 590.9 *feeling person*
sensitive plant 591.9 *oversensitive person*; 488.4 *someone or something that feels*
sensitive to touch 492.8 *touchable*
Sensitivity 591
sensitivity 28.83; **591.5**; 488.2 *ability to sense*; 41.10 *graininess*; 477.3 *insight*; 466.2 *judiciousness*; 480.7 *persuadability*; 6.11 *refinement*; 492.1 *touch*
sensitivity training 36.3 *psychiatric treatment*
sensitivity training group 36.3 *psychiatric treatment*
sensitized 591.3 *sore*
sensitometer 26.8 *meter*
sensitometry 26.2 *micrometry*
sensor 449.11 *detector*
sensorial 488.10 *sensory*
sensorium 488.4 *someone or something that feels*
sensory 488.10; 492.8 *touchable*
sensory awareness training 36.3 *psychiatric treatment*
sensory pattern 36.26 *gestalt*
sensual 402.7 *material*; 490.6 *pleasant*; 490.7 *pleased*; 686.6 *self-indulgent*
sensualism 402.2 *materialization*; 490.1 *physical pleasure*
sensualist 490.3 *pleasure-seeker*; 686.5 *self-indulgent person*
sensuality 488.2 *ability to sense*; 402.2 *materialization*; 686.1 *self-indulgence*
sensually 402.9 *materially*
sensual pleasure 490.1 *physical pleasure*
sensum 488.1 *sensation*
sensuous 488.7 *susceptible*; 492.8 *touchable*
sensuousness 488.2 *ability to sense*; 490.1 *physical pleasure*
sent 692.34 *communicated*
sent after 633.15 *pursuing*
sent back 470.10 *rejected*
sentence 16.79 *convict*; 16.43 *conviction*; 251.11 *detain*; 251.4 *detention*; 16.7 *legal trial*; 16.33 *litigation*; 205.2 *particular*; 814.2 *penalize*; 814.8 *penalty*; 276.4 *period of activity*; 5.23 *phrase*; 729.7 *utterance*; 464.2 *verdict*
sentenced 16.64 *convicted*; 251.15 *detained*
sentenced to death 16.64 *convicted*; 582.18 *dying*
sentencer 814.17 *punisher*
sentence structure 724.4 *literary style*
sentence to death 16.79 *convict*; 814.5 *execute*
sentencing 814.8 *penalty*
sentential 5.43 *phrasal*
sententious 269.3 *concise*; 726.3 *emphatic*; 464.8 *judging*; 745.2 *proverbial*
sententiously 269.5 *concisely*
sententiousness 269.1 *conciseness*
sentience 554.1 *life*; 488.1 *sensation*
sentient 590.10 *feeling*; 488.5 *sensible*; 591.1 *sensitive*
sentiment 450.1 *belief*; 446.1 *idea*; 593.1 *love*; 593.3 *lovingness*; 4.1 *philosophy*; 488.1 *sensation*
sentimental 593.20 *amorous*; 446.13 *ideal*; 593.17 *loving*; 590.12, 591.1 *sensitive*
sentimental attachment 595.1 *liking*; 593.3 *lovingness*
sentimental comedy 21.12 *comedy*
sentimentality 590.7 *emotionalism*; 593.3 *lovingness*; 591.5 *sensitivity*
sentimentally 590.21 *emotionally*; 446.22 *imaginatively*; 593.30 *lovingly*
sentiments 590.3 *feelings*
sentinel 586.14 *armed forces*; 384.14 *guard*; 518.11 *observer*; 309.5 *person who closes*; 252.3 *protector*; 253.3 *security officer*; 711.4 *warner*; 665.8 *watchful person*
sentry 586.14 *armed forces*; 384.14 *guard*; 518.11 *observer*; 309.5 *person who closes*; 252.3 *protector*; 253.3 *security officer*; 711.4 *warner*; 665.8 *watchful person*
sent to Coventry 655.10 *lonely*
sepal 205.6 *branch*; 78.3 *flower part*; 77.6 *leaf*

separability 372.3 *separateness*; 372.1 *separation*
separable 372.19
separate 100.11; **100.15**; **311.12**; **372.9**; **372.15**; 197.16 *alone*; 377.9 *be dispersed*; 375.4 *deconstruct*; 133.14, 144.18 *disconnect*; 466.12 *discriminate*; 377.12 *disperse*; 311.6 *divergent*; 571.7 *divorce*; 111.4 *duplicate*; 466.11 *judged*; 145.6 *keep away*; 268.17 *liquefy*; 369.17 *obtain an extract*; 205.10, 313.6 *part*; 469.4 *pick*; 377.20 *separated*; 197.20 *single out*; 32.25 *solidify*; 146.4 *space*; 146.6 *spaced*; 109.6 *unrelated*
separated 377.20; 197.16 *alone*; 144.12 *disconnected*; 375.5 *disintegrated*; 145.8 *distant*; 311.6 *divergent*; 571.11 *divorced*; 655.10 *lonely*; 100.11, 372.15 *separate*; 197.17 *single*; 146.6 *spaced*; 109.6 *unrelated*
separately 372.20; 146.8 *apart*; 375.8 *destructively*; 144.21 *disconnectedly*; 466.15 *discriminatingly*; 311.16 *divergently*; 100.18 *extraneously*; 109.12 *irrelevantly*; 197.22 *one by one*
separateness 100.3; **372.3**; 197.5 *aloneness*; 109.1 *unrelatedness*
separate out 375.4 *deconstruct*
separates 372.7; 551.10 *suit*
separating 466.9 *discriminating*; 372.1 *separation*
Separation 372
separation 372.1; **571.2**; **655.3**; 375.2 *deconstruction*; 144.5 *disconnection*; 466.1 *discrimination*; 145.1 *distance*; 377.5 *divergence*; 146.1 *interval*; 369.7 *obtaining an extract*; 311.2, 313.9 *parting*; 32.5 *process*; 197.6 *singleness*
separatism 197.5 *aloneness*; 372.3 *separateness*
separatist 197.16 *alone*; 372.8 *person who separates*; 753.4 *protester*
separative 32.40 *synthetic*; 372.17 *unjoined*
separatively 372.22 *in isolation*
separator 372.5; 369.9 *extractor*
separatrix 189.2 *oblique line*
Sephardic 7.16 *denominational*
sepia 534.4 *brown pigment*; 41.12 *development*
sepoy 586.6 *militarist*
seppuku 814.11 *penance*; 382.7 *suicide*
sepsis 260.6 *infection*; 258.2 *uncleanness*
septenary 201.3 *seven*; 201.14 *seventh*
septendecillion 194.3 *large number*; 201.11 *million*
septennial 201.14 *seventh*
septennially 201.24 *fivefold*
septet 374.3 *assembly*; 18.26 *musical group*; 17.8 *part of poem*; 201.3 *seven*; 747.9 *team*
septic 236.4 *poor*; 767.8 *sink*; 258.8 *unclean*
septicaemia 260.6 *infection*
septic tank 238.6 *refuse*; 767.8 *sink*; 439.4 *storage*; 767.5 *wasteyard*
septillion 194.3 *large number*; 201.11 *million*
septivalent 32.35 *combined*
septuagenarian 556.7 *older person*; 201.8 *twenty and over*
Septuagesima 10.15 *holy day*
Septuagint 7.12 *religious text*
septuple 201.23 *quintuple*; 201.3 *seven*; 201.14 *seventh*
septuplet 201.3 *seven*
septuplicate 201.3 *seven*; 201.14 *seventh*
sepulchral 510.8 *deep*; 583.11 *funeral*
sepulchrally 583.12 *funereally*
sepulchral monument 583.4 *funeral objects*
sepulchre 309.4 *closed place*; 583.6 *grave*
sepulture 583.1 *burial*
sequel 289.9; 244.8 *better thing*; 134.1 *continuity*; 345.1 *effect*
sequence 27.20; 132.2 *consecution*; 134.1 *continuity*; 516.4 *harmonics*; 407.3 *hierarchy*; 289.1 *succession*
sequence dancing 22.1 *dancing*
sequencer 18.25 *musical instrument*
sequent 134.5 *continual*
sequential 345.10 *caused*; 132.9 *consecutive*; 134.5 *continual*; 407.12 *hierarchical*; 289.12 *succeeding*
sequential access 40.19 *computing terms*
sequentially 132.18 *consecutively*; 134.7 *continually*; 407.25 *in order*
sequential scanning 692.21 *television*
sequester 372.11 *divide*; 128.7 *exclude*; 655.13 *ignore*; 786.7 *not pay*; 773.8 *take back*
sequestered 736.14 *concealed*; 301.6 *quiescent*; 655.11 *secluded*
sequestered nook 655.5 *solitary place*
sequestering of the jury 16.7 *legal trial*
sequester the jury 16.71 *try a case*
sequestrate 814.1 *punish*; 608.14 *take away*
sequestration 128.1 *exclusion*; 814.7 *punishment*; 773.2 *taking back*
sequestrator 769.7 *collector*; 773.6 *taker*
sequin 522.2 *quality of light*; 541.5 *variegated thing*
sequined 522.16 *bright*
sequoia 154.6 *tall thing*
sérac 30.38 *glacier*; 62.5 *rock face*
seraglio 593.13 *abode of love*; 568.13 *womenfolk*
seraph 8.6 *angel*
seraphic 8.14 *heavenly*; 593.22 *lovable*; 7.15 *religious*; 803.5 *virtuous*
seraphically 8.19 *divinely*
sere 245.12 *deteriorated*; 428.3 *dried-up*; 34.18 *ecology*
serenade 593.26 *court*; 593.15 *love item*; 516.2 *song*
serenader 516.5 *melodist*
serendipitous 107.8 *chance*; 630.8 *surprising*
serendipitously 107.13 *by chance*
serendipity 449.6 *discovery*; 211.4 *extra*; 107.2 *luck*; 630.4 *surprising thing*
serene 4.18 *detached*; 265.13 *easy-going*; 589.7 *peaceful*; 301.6 *quiescent*; 609.4 *satisfied*
serenely 589.8 *peacefully*; 4.27 *stoically*; 609.13 *with satisfaction*
serenity 4.3 *detachment*; 263.1 *ease*; 301.2 *repose*; 609.1 *satisfaction*; 421.7 *smoothness*
serf 574.1 *plebeian*; 401.7 *slave*; 387.5 *subjected person*; 664.3 *sycophant*
serfdom 664.1 *servility*; 387.1 *subjection*
sergeant 586.17 *army person*
sergeant aircrew 586.32 *airman*
sergeant major 647.4 *strict person*
serial 692.25 *broadcast material*; 132.9 *consecutive*; 407.12 *hierarchical*; 740.5 *journal*; 721.3 *narration*; 21.2 *play*; 298.11 *regular*; 298.5 *regular thing*; 517.9 *unmelodious*
serialism 517.4 *atonality*
serialization 298.1 *regularity*
serialize 298.10 *make regular*; 740.15 *publish*
serialized 298.11 *regular*
serial killer 798.6 *evil person*; 651.8 *malefactor*; 382.11 *murderer*; 380.4 *violent creature*
serial killing 651.7 *act of malevolence*
serially 132.18 *consecutively*; 298.15 *regularly*
serial order 407.3 *hierarchy*
serial printer 40.7 *peripheral*
seriate 132.9 *consecutive*
sericultural 76.14 *entomological*
sericulturalist 76.8 *entomologist*
sericulture 76.7 *study*
series 517.4 *atonality*; 692.25 *broadcast material*; 132.2 *consecution*; 30.41 *geological time*; 407.3 *hierarchy*; 740.5 *journal*; 18.20 *key*; 220.1 *list*; 276.5 *recurrent period*; 27.20 *sequence*; 289.1 *succession*; 34.17 *taxonomy*; 204.5 *unit*
series connection 39.16 *circuit element*
serious 726.5; 254.1 *dangerous*; 156.9 *deep-seated*; 123.5, 643.3 *important*; 482.11 *intending*; 795.10 *moralistic*; 260.22 *sick*; 694.7 *significant*; 271.1 *simple*; 643.1 *solemn*; 626.6 *sullen*; 638.2 *tenacious*
serious climbing 62.1 *mountaineering*
Serious Crime Squad 16.15 *British police*
serious literature 17.1 *literature*
seriously 123.9 *importantly*; 643.12 *indeed*; 638.17 *resolutely*; 643.10 *solemnly*; 626.13 *sullenly*; 707.24 *truthfully*
serious-minded 482.11 *intending*
seriousness 726.2; 638.13 *concentration*; 123.1 *importance*; 795.4 *self-righteousness*; 694.2 *significance*; 271.4 *simplicity*
serious person 643.7
serious press 740.3 *journalism*; 693.4 *mass communication*
sermon 733.1 *address*; 670.7 *blame*; 270.1 *diffuseness*; 722.1 *dissertation*; 740.1 *publication*; 729.8 *speech*
sermoner 733.6 *public speaker*
sermonist 733.6 *public speaker*
sermonize 733.7 *address*; 722.4 *dissertate*; 795.12 *moralize*; 7.20 *preach*; 4.22 *propound a philosophy*; 729.14 *speak to*
sermonizer 733.6 *public speaker*; 7.4 *religionist*; 729.10 *speaker*
serologist 35.13 *medical specialist*
serology 35.3 *medical specialty*
seropus 560.7 *pus*
serosity 431.7 *juiciness*
serotest 35.7 *diagnosis*
serous 431.16 *rheumy*
serous fluid 431.3 *body fluid*
serpent 645.3 *cunning person*; 512.3 *hisser*; 122.6 *inferior*; 73.3 *snake*; 700.21 *traitor*
Serpentes 73.3 *snake*
serpentiform 73.12 *snakelike*
serpentine 180.4 *convolutional*; 645.4 *cunning*; 90.10 *fluvial*; 325.21 *indirect*; 73.12 *snakelike*; 541.5 *variegated thing*
serpenting 59.10 *dressage*
serpigo 260.13 *skin disease*
serrate 420.12 *make rough*; 425.15 *make sharp*; 183.10 *notch*; 77.18 *of leaves*
serrated 420.2 *coarse*; 183.7 *notched*; 425.4 *toothed*
serration 183.4 *notch*; 420.6 *roughness*; 425.6 *sharpness*
serried 132.11 *continuous*; 376.50 *crowded*; 416.6 *dense*
serriform 183.7 *notched*
serrulation 183.4 *notch*
serum 431.3 *body fluid*
Servant 401
servant 401.1; 664.5 *adherent*; 388.2 *appeaser*; 348.3 *assistant*; 392.16 *home help*; 122.6 *inferior*; 124.10 *nonentity*; 663.4 *obedient person*; 579.16 *official*; 387.3 *subordinate*; 578.1 *worker*
servant girl 401.6 *domestic servant*
servant's uniform 551.3 *formal dress*
serve 63.13; **392.25**; **401.8**; 348.4 *be an instrument*; 239.6 *be convenient*; 617.16 *be desirable*; 392.21 *be helpful*; 569.15 *be hospitable*; 346.7 *be operational*; 387.8 *be subject to*; 237.9 *be useful*; 797.20 *do good*; 750.27 *fit*; 663.5 *obey*; 664.11 *pander to*; 436.5 *provision*; 217.4, 609.10 *suffice*; 63.2 *tennis strokes*; 330.23 *throw*; 576.7 *work for*
serve a citation 715.5 *accuse*
serve an apprenticeship 6.23 *learn*; 243.8 *prepare oneself*
serve as a makeshift 217.4 *suffice*
serve as a model 395.8 *influence*
serve as an example 108.7 *relate to*
serve as a representative 398.8 *represent*
serve a sentence 815.10 *be in prison*
serve as host 569.15 *be hospitable*
serve as proxy 762.4 *be a substitute*
serve a stretch 815.10 *be in prison*; 251.11 *detain*
serve a summons 715.5 *accuse*
serve a use 569.16 *be favourable*
serve badly 604.6 *disappoint*
serve involuntarily 387.8 *be subject to*
serve notice on 16.70 *litigate*
serve one right 385.4
serve one's country 585.12 *go to war*
serve one's king 585.12 *go to war*
serve one's turn 237.9 *be useful*
serve one well 237.10 *benefit*
server 401.3 *attendant*; 63.12 *badminton terms*; 40.15 *network*; 63.5 *real tennis*; 63.6 *tennis player*; 330.14 *thrower*
serve the time 239.6 *be convenient*
serve the times 664.13 *conform*
serve time 251.11 *detain*
serve up 436.5 *provision*
serve with a writ 715.5 *accuse*
service 650.4 *benevolent act*; 601.3 *ceremony*; 143.4 *employment*; 656.3 *formal occasion*; 768.1 *giving*; 348.1 *instrumentality*; 663.2 *loyalty*; 346.4 *management*; 584.8 *military*; 359.1 *preservation*; 359.5 *preserve*; 436.1, 436.5 *provision*; 393.1, 393.8 *repair*; 393.3 *restore*; 10.1 *ritual*; 778.6 *salesmanship*; 387.1 *subjection*; 392.2 *support*; 346.9 *take action*; 810.2 *task*; 63.2 *tennis strokes*; 330.5 *throw*; 349.6 *use*; 237.5 *usefulness*
serviceability 348.1 *instrumentality*; 237.6 *usability*; 349.6 *use*
serviceable 392.33 *helpful*; 95.8, 348.8 *practical*; 237.2 *usable*
serviceably 392.36 *helpfully*; 237.12 *usefully*
service an order 436.5 *provision*
service box 63.9 *squash terms*
service ceiling 322.5 *flight*
service charge 790.3 *fee*
service contract 755.2 *purchase contract*
service court line 63.8 *squash*
service fee 790.3 *fee*
service line 63.5 *real tennis*; 63.8 *squash*; 63.4 *tennis terms*
serviceman 586.8 *soldier*
service penthouse 63.5 *real tennis*
service road 373.5 *road*
services 586.14 *armed forces*; 13.6 *economic factors*
service side 63.5 *real tennis*
services no longer required 708.6 *termination*
service station 226.4 *stopping place*
servicewoman 586.8 *soldier*; 586.10 *woman soldier*
servicing 348.8 *practical*; 359.1 *preservation*; 393.8 *repair*
serviette 256.11 *cleaning cloth*
servile 664.6; 599.11 *humouring*; 663.7 *obedient*; 401.9 *serving*; 667.9 *showing respect*; 387.9 *subject*; 388.5 *submitting*; 677.16 *sycophantic*
servilely 401.10, 663.10 *obediently*; 387.11 *under subjection*
Servility 664
servility 664.1; 663.1 *obedience*; 387.1 *subjection*; 677.5 *sycophancy*
serving 401.9; 392.30 *helping*; 557.14 *mouthful*; 387.9 *subject*
serving a sentence 251.15 *detained*; 815.8 *imprisoned*
serving girl 401.6 *domestic servant*
serving maid 401.6 *domestic servant*
serving man 401.6 *domestic servant*
serving one's country 585.8 *warfare*
serving the purpose 750.16 *fitting*
servitor 401.1 *servant*
servitude 639.14 *apathy*; 251.4 *detention*; 387.1 *subjection*; 388.1 *submission*
servomechanism 38.5 *dynamic structure*; 438.5 *machine*
servomotor 438.5 *machine*
sesame seeds 496.5 *herbs*
sesquicentenary 601.5 *anniversary*
sesquicentennial 298.3, 298.13 *anniversary*; 601.14 *centennial*
sesquicentennially 298.16 *cyclically*
sesquihydrate 32.10 *salt*
sesquipedal 148.1 *long*
sesquipedalian 270.3 *diffuse*; 148.1 *long*; 542.10 *ornate*; 5.17 *word*; 5.42 *worded*
sesquipedalianism 544.4 *inelegance of speech*; 148.4 *length*
sesquiterpene 33.20 *terpene*
Sesselbahn 68.1 *skiing*
sessile 267.9 *adhesive*; 84.7 *algal*; 83.10 *of fungi*; 77.18 *of leaves*
session 69.2 *contest*; 579.7 *council*; 276.4 *period of activity*; 376.6 *sitting*
sessions 16.19 *law court*; 16.7 *legal trial*
sessions judge 16.23 *judge*; 464.6 *justice*
sestet 17.8 *part of poem*
sestina 17.7 *poem*; 17.10 *verse form*
Set 8.7 *devil*
set 27.21; **641.4**; 698.21 *accurate*; 27.23 *algebra*; 409.12 *arrange*; 376.25 *assemblage*; 374.3, 376.1 *assembly*; 353.5 *attempt*; 216.1 *average*; 698.31 *be accurate*; 324.2 *bearing*; 416.8 *be dense*; 409.6 *category*; 137.2 *class*; 376.19 *clique*; 439.5 *collection*; 416.7 *condensed*; 44.15 *cultivate*; 393.6 *cure*; 106.4 *deliberate*; 305.9 *descend*; 553.4 *design*; 324.6 *direct*; 324.14 *directed*; 324.1 *direction*; 394.20 *doctor*; 553.1 *fashion*; 632.13 *fixed*; 376.23 *flock*; 566.9 *group*; 418.3 *hardened*; 46.8 *huddle*; 127.1 *inclusion*; 452.5 *inevitable*; 142.6 *located*; 298.10 *make regular*; 228.7 *make stable*; 300.2 *momentum*; 160.6 *nature*; 5.43 *phrasal*; 243.18 *prepared*; 740.15 *publish*; 64.6 *rugger*; 143.10 *situate*; 143.6 *situated*; 137.5 *social class*; 418.10 *solidify*; 139.24 *specify*; 45.1 *sport*; 21.19 *stage set*; 324.7 *take a direction*; 63.4 *tennis terms*; 152.7 *thicken*; 275.16 *time*; 204.5 *unit*; 555.5 *young plant*
seta 82.4 *moss plant*; 77.5 *stem*

set a bad example 631.13 *behave badly;* 804.17 *make wicked*
set a booby trap 700.33 *snare*
set about 354.1 *undertake;* 576.6 *work*
set a ceiling 203.8 *quantify*
set a course 323.9 *navigate*
set a curfew 166.7 *limit*
set a date for 281.14 *keep time;* 275.16 *time*
set adrift 372.13 *diverge*
set afloat 344.11 *inaugurate;* 330.33 *start*
set a floor 203.8 *quantify*
set against 113.15 *be opposite;* 596.7 *cause dislike;* 113.19 *confront;* 372.11 *divide;* 594.10 *hating;* 481.4 *put off*
set a good example 631.12 *behave well;* 803.8 *be virtuous*
set a gun 700.33 *snare*
set algebra 27.23 *algebra*
set alight 493.15 *burn;* 522.24 *light*
set a lower limit 203.8 *quantify*
set a new record 121.8 *be superior*
set an example 631.11 *conduct oneself;* 446.19 *epitomize*
set an upper limit 203.8 *quantify*
set apart **372.10**; 139.22 *characterize;* 758.9 *exempt;* 136.15 *modify;* 469.4 *pick;* 146.4 *space;* 146.6 *spaced;* 372.17 *unjoined*
set a precedent 130.21 *pioneer*
set a price 790.11 *price*
set a quota 166.7 *limit;* 203.8 *quantify*
set a record 121.8 *be superior;* 47.6 *compete in track and field*
set a riddle 705.21 *confuse*
set a sail 50.15 *sail*
set aside 708.14 *cancel;* 708.20 *cancelled;* 470.2 *discard;* 135.10 *necessitate;* 469.4 *pick;* 372.10 *set apart;* 350.6 *stop using;* 439.6 *store;* 439.7 *stored;* 316.15 *take away*
set-aside 43.2 *Common Agricultural Policy*
set aside the sentence 16.78 *acquit*
set at ease 609.9 *comfort*
set a time for 281.14 *keep time;* 275.16 *time*
set at large 390.1 *deliver;* 391.4 *liberate*
set at liberty 758.10 *acquit;* 391.4 *liberate*
set at loggerheads 624.14 *make angry*
set at odds 596.7 *cause dislike;* 751.7 *pick a fight*
set a trap for 449.2 *detect;* 484.13 *plot*
set a trend 295.18 *be trendy;* 129.18 *forerun;* 483.9 *motivate*
set at rest 95.12 *establish reality*
setback **303.18**; 249.1 *adversity;* 604.2 *bad outcome;* 245.7 *deterioration;* 481.6 *dissuasion;* 247.1 *failure;* 333.12 *hesitation;* 766.1 *loss*
set back 294.8 *delay;* 333.7 *delayed;* 333.3 *slow down*
set before someone's eyes 738.1 *display*
set by the ears 594.16 *cause hate;* 624.14 *make angry*
set dance 22.4 *historic dancing*
set designer 21.27 *producer*
set difference 27.21 *set*
set down 623.23 *abase;* 707.17 *affirm;* 670.20 *censure;* 623.3 *humbled;* 220.8 *list;* 367.1 *lower*
set-down 623.10 *abasement;* 670.7 *blame*
set eyes on 449.1 *discover*
set fair 428.5 *rainless*
set fire to 493.15 *burn;* 522.24 *light*
set foot in 314.9 *enter;* 312.5 *get in*
set form 656.5 *etiquette*
set forth 4.22 *propound a philosophy;* 313.5 *set out*
set forward 354.1 *undertake*
set free **250.15**; 649.10 *absolve;* 758.10 *acquit;* 390.1 *deliver;* 391.4 *liberate;* 608.10 *save;* 372.9 *separate;* 714.7 *vindicate*
set going 346.8 *activate;* 349.5 *dispose of;* 331.1 *impel;* 344.11 *inaugurate;* 330.33 *start;* 354.1 *undertake*
set gun 700.13 *snare*
SETI 29.34
setiform 420.3 *barbed*
set in 225.5 *be permanent;* 228.6 *be stable;* 368.5 *inset;* 31.59 *storm*
set in action 349.5 *dispose of*
set in concrete 228.7 *make stable*
set in granite 228.7 *make stable*
set in motion **300.14**; 130.20 *activate;* 349.5 *dispose of;* 331.1 *impel;* 344.11 *inaugurate;* 483.9 *motivate;* 356.10 *produce;* 330.33 *start*
set in one's ways 632.13 *fixed;* 641.4 *set*
set in opposition 113.21 *counteract*
set in order 407.18 *order;* 243.4 *prepare for action*
set in stone 228.7 *make stable*
set in towards 324.7 *take a direction*
set no store by 728.22 *play down;* 468.3 *underestimate*
set of beliefs 4.2 *philosophical system;* 7.1 *religion*
set off 344.10 *awaken;* 119.11 *equalize;* 437.11 *fuel;* 130.19 *start off;* 212.3 *subtract*
set off against 113.21 *counteract*
set off an alarm 742.12 *signal*
set of four 200.1 *four*
set of points 27.36 *point*
set of rules 713.3 *precept*
set of teeth 425.11 *tooth*
set of terms 746.2 *basis for negotiations*
set of three 199.1 *three*
set of two 198.1 *two*
set on 593.18 *in love;* 381.5 *strike*
set one a problem 264.17 *be difficult*
set one back 790.13 *cost*
set on edge 420.12 *make rough*
set one off 272.7 *make one laugh*
set one's cap at 593.26 *court*
set one's cap for 633.12 *aim at*
set one's compass for 324.7 *take a direction*
set one's course 633.12 *aim at*
set one's course for 324.7 *take a direction*
set one's dignity aside 623.21 *humble oneself*
set oneself against 670.16 *disagree*
set one's face 638.8 *brace oneself*
set one's face against 113.17 *be against;* 670.16 *disagree*
set one's heart on 617.12 *desire;* 595.7 *like;* 756.11 *promise oneself;* 638.9 *undertake*
set one's sights higher 213.5 *make bigger*
set one's sights on 446.18, 482.10 *aim;* 617.12 *desire;* 324.7 *take a direction*
set on fire 493.15 *burn*
set on foot 344.11 *inaugurate*
set on its feet 228.7 *make stable*
set on one's feet 392.29 *finance*
setose 420.3 *barbed*
set out **313.5**; 409.12 *arrange;* 738.1 *display;* 141.21 *space;* 724.9 *style*
set out for 324.7 *take a direction*
set out on foot 330.33 *start*
set parameters 166.7 *limit*
set pattern dancing 68.7 *ice-dancing*
set phrase 5.24 *phrasing*
set piece 656.3 *formal occasion;* 21.8 *scene*
set position 47.1 *track events*
set purpose 482.1 *intention*
set requirements 135.10 *necessitate*
set right 801.15 *put right;* 244.3 *rectify;* 714.7 *vindicate*
set rolling 307.9 *roll*
set sail 323.9 *navigate;* 323.10 *sail;* 313.5 *set out;* 130.19 *start off*
set scrum 64.3 *rugby play*
set shot 49.4 *playing terms*
set snares 633.11 *hunt*
set someone up properly 336.8 *strengthen*
set speech 733.1 *address*
set square 176.4 *angular measurement;* 27.49 *geometric construction;* 26.6 *measuring instrument;* 186.4 *plumb line*
set store by 667.15 *respect*
set straight 324.6 *direct;* 739.6 *divulge*
sett 71.20 *abode of mammals;* 565.13 *lair*
settee 23.2 *chair*
set terms 5.24 *phrasing*
set the alarm 275.18 *adjust the clock;* 281.14 *keep time;* 243.4 *prepare for action*
set the ball rolling 130.20 *activate*
set the example 129.18 *forerun*
set the fashion 129.18 *forerun;* 395.8 *influence;* 483.9 *motivate*
set the pace 483.9 *motivate*
set the record straight 739.6 *divulge*
set the stage 243.2 *do the groundwork*
set the trend 395.8 *influence*
setting 698.8 *accuracy;* 143.2, 222.1 *circumstances;* 18.15 *composition;* 416.7 *condensed;* 701.4 *gist;* 142.1 *location;* 143.1 *situation;* 418.6 *solidification;* 21.19 *stage set;* 170.1 *surroundings*
setting apart 372.2
setting aside 770.1 *allocation;* 708.5 *cancellation;* 372.2 *setting apart*
setting circle 29.25 *mounting*
setting free 389.1 *escape;* 391.1 *liberation*
setting in motion 130.6 *inauguration*
setting lotion 268.7 *pomade*
setting of court date 16.7 *legal trial*
setting of the sun 291.1 *evening*
setting up 130.6 *inauguration;* 356.2 *manufacture*
settle **142.10**; **564.15**; 409.12, 750.23 *arrange;* 632.17 *become a habit;* 183.8 *be concave;* 414.12 *be heavy;* 685.3 *be moderate;* 301.8 *be motionless;* 23.2 *chair;* 409.17 *come to an arrangement;* 755.5 *contract;* 305.9 *descend;* 30.63 *ebb;* 131.15 *end;* 314.14 *enrol;* 85.18 *exert sovereignty;* 392.29 *finance;* 565.17 *inhabit;* 464.11 *judge;* 452.21 *make certain;* 785.7 *pay off;* 814.2 *penalize;* 293.8 *precede;* 703.17 *prove;* 638.7 *resolve;* 140.13 *rule;* 609.10 *suffice*
settle accounts 789.9
settle an account 785.7 *pay off*
settle a score 785.13 *retaliate*
settle a strike 15.12 *have an industrial dispute*
settled 789.11 *accounted;* 750.12 *arranged;* 754.6 *compromising;* 452.3 *decided;* 131.21 *ended;* 31.45 *fine;* 142.6 *located;* 785.16 *paid;* 703.13 *proven;* 564.13 *resident;* 228.10 *stabilized*
settle differences 748.1 *mediate;* 749.4 *pacify*
settle down 685.3 *be moderate;* 301.8 *be motionless;* 228.6 *be stable*
settled purpose 482.1 *intention*
settle for 776.3 *bargain*
settle in 228.6 *be stable;* 314.14 *enrol*
settlement **86.11**; 409.10 *agreement;* 750.3 *arrangement;* 754.1 *compromise;* 755.1 *contract;* 85.3 *dominion;* 392.6 *financial assistance;* 768.1 *giving;* 785.1 *payment;* 703.4 *proof*
settlement on account 785.1 *payment*
settlement out of court 16.7 *legal trial*
settle on 305.12 *drop;* 469.1 *select*
settle on a date 275.16 *time*
settle on a time 275.16 *time*
settle one's differences 589.6 *make peace*
settler **564.7**; 131.13 *ender;* 314.7 *entrant;* 100.7 *new arrival;* 315.8 *outgoer*
settle the matter 95.12 *establish reality;* 464.11 *judge*
settle up 813.11 *pay*
settle with 814.2 *penalize*
settling 142.4 *placing*
settlor 768.4 *giver*
set to 688.5 *be greedy;* 557.22 *eat well;* 130.18 *make a beginning;* 354.1, 638.9 *undertake;* 576.6 *work*
set-to 701.1, 751.2 *argument;* 408.9 *disorder;* 242.8 *quarrel*
set to music **516.9**; 18.35 *compose*
set to rights 801.15 *put right;* 393.1 *repair*
set to work 130.18 *make a beginning*
set to work on 243.2 *do the groundwork*
set two 63.9 *squash terms*
setup 143.2, 222.1 *circumstances;* 106.4 *deliberate;* 265.6 *easy thing;* 403.3 *form;* 160.9 *formed;* 160.4 *forming;* 61.6 *motor-racing terms;* 407.1 *order*
set up 403.16 *construct;* 393.6 *cure;* 392.29 *finance;* 130.23, 344.11 *inaugurate;* 142.9 *locate;* 405.13 *make;* 279.7 *make permanent;* 228.7 *make stable;* 186.6 *make vertical;* 407.18 *order;* 106.2 *premeditate;* 356.10 *produce;* 61.9 *race;* 366.1 *raise;* 366.11 *raised;* 143.10 *situate*
set up house 564.15 *settle*
set up house together 570.15 *marry*
set upon 638.1 *resolute*
set up one's standard 585.12 *go to war*
set up shop 354.1 *undertake*
seven **201.3**; 27.9 *numeral;* 201.14 *seventh*
seven ages of man 554.5 *life cycle*
seven centuries 201.9 *treble figures*
seven days 201.3 *seven*
seven deadly sins **804.5**; 201.3 *seven*
sevener 201.3 *seven*
sevenfold 201.24 *fivefold;* 201.14 *seventh*
seven-footer 154.7 *tall person*
seven-league boots 332.11 *swift thing;* 11.6 *talisman*
seven lean years 218.9 *scarcity*
seven sacraments 10.5 *Christian rite*
seven seas 91.1 *sea*
seven-sided 27.82 *polygonal*
seven-stone weakling 337.4 *weakling*
seventeenth 196.4 *less than one*
seventeen-year locust 76.3 *pest*
seventh **201.14**; 27.75 *equal;* 201.24 *fivefold;* 196.4 *less than one;* 18.16 *musical note;* 201.3 *seven*
Seventh-Day Adventist 7.5 *Christian*
seventh guard 54.3 *fencing movements*
seventh heaven 174.1 *summit*
seventhly 201.24 *fivefold*
seventh part 201.3 *seven*
seventieth 196.4 *less than one;* 201.19 *twentieth*
seventy 201.8 *twenty and over*
seventy-four 587.12 *historical guns*
seven years of plenty 217.8 *plenty*
sever 133.14 *disconnect;* 571.7 *divorce;* 205.10 *part;* 372.9 *separate;* 212.4 *take off*
severable 372.19 *separable*
several 207.6 *plural;* 207.1 *plurality;* 452.8 *unspecified*
severally **139.32**; 207.10 *plurally;* 372.20 *separately*
severalty 372.3 *separateness*
severance 372.1 *separation;* 372.2 *setting apart;* 212.1 *subtraction*
severance of cordial relations 751.1 *disagreement*
severance pay 785.3 *pay;* 813.4 *reward for service*
severe **647.8**; 651.12 *callous;* 494.8 *cold;* 264.10 *difficult;* 659.5 *discourteous;* 795.10 *moralistic;* 698.24 *pedantic;* 628.4 *pitiless;* 336.10 *potent;* 251.13 *restraining;* 271.1 *simple;* 643.1 *solemn;* 380.6 *violent*
severed 212.7 *reduced;* 372.15 *separate*
severe frost 31.36 *frost*
severely **647.11**; 659.9 *discourteously;* 651.20 *malevolently;* 628.7 *pitilessly;* 643.10 *solemnly;* 251.16 *under restraints;* 380.10 *violently*
severe weather 494.7 *cold weather*
Severity 647
severity **647.1**; 651.3 *callousness;* 117.4 *conventionalism;* 264.1 *difficulty;* 659.1 *discourtesy;* 236.11 *harmfulness;* 643.6 *importance;* 336.3 *intensity;* 698.11 *pedantry;* 628.1 *pitilessness;* 251.1 *restraint;* 271.4 *simplicity;* 643.4 *solemnity;* 631.8 *treatment;* 380.1 *violence*
Severn 90.4 *British rivers*
sever relations 751.5 *disagree*
sever ties 372.9 *separate*
Sèvres' royal monogram 24.4 *porcelain mark*
sew 373.11 *connect;* 193.8 *interweave;* 551.35 *make clothing;* 356.10 *produce*
sewage 560.4 *excrement;* 43.13 *fertilizer;* 215.2 *residue;* 503.2 *something that makes an unpleasant smell;* 258.5 *swill*
sewage farm 767.5 *wasteyard*
sewage system 38.24 *water system*
sewage works 238.6 *refuse;* 439.4 *storage*
sewer 317.11 *channel;* 256.10 *cleaning object;* 551.26 *fashion designer;* 308.7 *passageway;* 236.10 *poverty;* 767.8 *sink;* 503.2 *something that makes an unpleasant smell;* 38.22 *tunnel;* 767.4 *wastebin*
sewerage 256.2 *cleaning;* 560.4 *excrement;* 258.5 *swill*
sewer gas 503.2 *something that makes an unpleasant smell*
sewing machine 193.3 *weaving*
sewing room 577.1 *workshop*
sewn 373.15 *connected*
sewn up 253.8 *accomplished*
sew up 253.13 *secure one's objective*
sex 554.4 *biological function;* 593.5 *desire;* 137.3 *kingdom;* 561.3 *propagation*
sex act 593.5 *desire*
sexagenarian 556.7 *older person;* 201.8 *twenty and over*
sexagenary 201.8 *twenty and over*
sex appeal 363.4 *allurement;* 480.3 *incentive;* 593.4 *lovability*
sexcentenary 462.5 *day to remember;* 201.9 *treble figures*
sex chromosome 34.14 *chromosome*
sex comedy 21.12 *comedy*
sex-crazy 796.14 *lecherous*
sex criminal 796.10 *sex offender*

sexdecillion 194.3 *large number*; 201.11 *million*
sex drive 36.22 *libido*
sex education 6.3 *subject*
sexennial 201.13 *sixth*
sexennially 201.24 *fivefold*
sex fiend 796.10 *sex offender*
sex hormone 33.16 *hormone*
sexily 363.14 *attractively*; 593.30 *lovingly*; 617.20 *lustfully*
sexiness 593.5 *desire*; 593.4 *lovability*; 796.3 *sexual immorality*
sex instinct 36.22 *libido*
sexism 465.3 *injustice*; 466.4 *social discrimination*
sexist 466.7 *bigot*; 466.10 *discriminatory*; 128.10 *excluding*; 653.3 *misanthropic*; 465.5 *misjudging person*; 622.23 *prejudiced*; 465.8 *unjust*
sexist loner 653.2 *misanthrope*
sexivalent 32.35 *combined*
sexless 795.9 *pure*; 335.13 *unsexed*
sex-mad 796.14 *lecherous*; 796.13 *unchaste*
sex maniac 461.7 *insane person*
sex murderer 380.4 *violent creature*
sex offender 796.10
sexpartite 201.13 *sixth*
sexpartite vault 20.7 *vault*
sexploitation 796.2 *indecency*
sexpot 483.7 *motivator*; 490.3 *pleasure-seeker*
sex role 2.3 *social environment*
sex scene 21.8 *scene*
sex show 21.7 *show*
sex symbol 363.6 *charmer*
sext 10.4 *public worship*
sextant 28.84 *altimeter*; 176.4 *angular measurement*; 26.6 *measuring instrument*; 323.5 *navigation*; 28.32 *optical instrument*; 179.4 *parts of a circle*
sex test 47.5 *competition*
sextet 374.3 *assembly*; 18.26 *musical group*; 201.2 *six*; 747.9 *team*
sex therapy 36.3 *psychiatric treatment*
sextile 176.4 *angular measurement*; 201.2 *six*
sextillion 194.3 *large number*; 201.11 *million*
sexton 583.3 *funeral director*; 7.8 *priest*
sextuple 201.23 *quintuple*; 201.2 *six*; 201.13 *sixth*
sextuplet 201.2 *six*
sextuplicate 201.23 *quintuple*; 201.2 *six*; 201.13 *sixth*
sexual 593.20 *amorous*; 561.16 *reproductive*
sexual abstinence 684.1 *self-restraint*
sexual abuse 651.7 *act of malevolence*; 236.11 *harmfulness*; 796.7 *sexual assault*
sexual abuser 662.9 *criminal*
sexual activity 554.4 *biological function*
sexual appetite 617.4 *sexual desire*
sexual assault 796.7; 651.7 *act of malevolence*; 380.2 *physical violence*; 773.1 *taking*
sexual awakening 561.4 *development*
sexual delinquency 796.3 *sexual immorality*
sexual desire 617.4
sexual deviancy 796.7 *sexual assault*
sexual deviant 325.19 *deviant person*
sexual discrimination 128.4 *exclusiveness*; 466.4 *social discrimination*
sexual disease 260.14 *venereal disease*
sexual harassment 236.11 *harmfulness*; 651.5 *intolerance*
sexual immorality 796.3
sexual impotence 335.4 *disability*
sexual indulgence 796.3 *sexual immorality*
sexual intercourse 554.4 *biological function*; 593.5 *desire*; 490.1 *physical pleasure*; 561.3 *propagation*
sexuality 617.4 *sexual desire*; 796.3 *sexual immorality*
sexual jealousy 629.1 *jealousy*
sexual licence 796.3 *sexual immorality*
sexual love 593.5 *desire*; 593.2 *romantic love*
sexually 561.18 *reproductively*
sexually abstinent 684.8 *self-restrained*
sexually abuse 796.20 *seduce*; 651.18 *torment*
sexually assault 796.20 *seduce*
sexually attractive 363.9 *attractive*
sexually desirable 617.11 *lustful*
sexually enslaving 593.20 *amorous*
sexually explicit literature 796.2 *indecency*
sexually transmitted disease 260.4 *disease*; 260.14 *venereal disease*
sexual offence 796.7 *sexual assault*
sexual perversion 796.7 *sexual assault*
sexual pleasure 490.1 *physical pleasure*
sexual possession 773.1 *taking*
sexual relations 593.5 *desire*
sexual reproduction 554.4 *biological function*; 84.4 *reproductive body*
sexual submission 388.1 *submission*
sexual union 593.5 *desire*
sexual urge 593.5 *desire*; 617.4 *sexual desire*
sex-worker 568.7 *prostitute*
sexy 593.20 *amorous*; 363.9 *attractive*; 796.14 *lecherous*; 617.11 *lustful*; 480.19 *persuasive*; 490.6 *pleasant*
Seyfert galaxy 29.7 *galaxy*
sfumato 19.4 *treatment*
sgian-dhu 587.8 *sharp weapon*
sgraffito 24.1 *ceramics*
sh 506.6 *hush!*
sh! 512.9
shabbily 544.11 *inelegantly*; 782.16 *meanly*
shabbiness 782.7 *beggary*; 245.9 *dilapidation*; 122.4 *poor quality*; 236.10 *poverty*; 793.3 *shoddiness*; 544.3 *ugliness*; 258.2 *uncleanness*; 682.4 *unpleasantness*; 408.3 *untidiness*
shabby 782.3 *beggarly*; 245.13 *dilapidated*; 124.2 *obscure*; 236.4 *poor*; 548.6 *seedy*; 793.10 *shoddy*; 544.10 *ugly*; 258.8 *unclean*; 682.2 *unpleasant*; 408.15 *untidy*; 349.9 *used*
Shabuoth 10.15 *holy day*
shack 565.8 *shelter*
shacking up 570.1 *marriage*
shackle 373.12 *bind*; 251.12 *gag*; 373.4 *means of connection*; 309.11, 378.10 *restrain*
shackled 378.14 *blocked*, 373.16 *bound*
shackles 251.5 *means of restraint*; 378.4 *restraint*
shack up with 570.18 *live together*
shadchan 570.13 *matchmaker*
shade 523.6; 28.28, 529.15 *colour*; 523.1 *darkness*; 524.1 *dimness*; 11.11 *ghost*; 529.3 *hue*; 96.2 *illusion*; 209.4 *interval*; 523.14 *make dark*; 524.10 *make dim*; 209.5 *measure*; 19.19 *paint*; 252.10, 550.30 *protect*; 550.12 *protective covering*; 581.1 *refresh*; 581.5 *refreshment*; 728.6 *suggestion*; 521.6 *that which makes invisible*
shaded 529.10 *coloured*; 523.8 *dark*; 19.27 *painted*; 79.16 *wooded*
shade in 523.14 *make dark*
shade off 209.6 *change gradually*
shade of feeling 590.2 *impression*
shades 551.25 *accessories*; 551.21 *beachwear*; 550.12 *protective covering*; 523.6 *shade*; 518.10 *visual aid*
shades of death 582.1 *death*
shade tree 79.1 *tree*
shadily 523.15 *darkly*; 800.11 *dishonourably*
shadiness 800.3 *criminality*; 189.3 *deviousness*; 524.1 *dimness*; 16.38 *lawbreaking*
shading 523.2, 523.9 *darkening*; 524.3 *dimming*; 209.3 *gradation*; 19.4 *treatment*
shading-in 523.2 *darkening*
shading off 209.7 *gradational*
shadoof 369.10 *excavator*; 433.13 *irrigator*
shadow 163.2; 664.5 *adherent*; 96.7 *artificiality*; 223.16 *attend*; 111.7 *be the same*; 532.9 *black thing*; 569.6 *close friend*; 115.5 *counterpart*; 523.1 *darkness*; 523.4 *dark thing*; 524.1 *dimness*; 119.5 *equal*; 111.2 *equivalence*; 477.5 *fantasy*; 633.9 *follow*; 223.9 *follower*; 96.2 *illusion*; 209.4 *interval*; 28.24 *light emission*; 523.14 *make dark*; 524.10 *make dim*; 633.5 *pursuer*; 523.7 *spiritual darkness*; 147.17 *stay near*; 153.9 *thin person*; 19.4 *treatment*
shadow box 52.11 *fight*
shadow boxing 52.2 *boxing*; 477.4 *ideality*
shadowed 161.5 *shapeless*
shadow figure 717.6 *image*
shadow forth 475.11 *predict*
shadowgraph 41.3 *photograph*
shadowiness 728.7 *imperceptibility*; 101.2 *unworldliness*
shadowing 523.9 *darkening*; 524.3 *dimming*; 111.13 *equivalent*; 633.1 *pursuit*
shadow of death 254.5 *danger*; 582.1 *death*
shadow play 21.7 *show*
shadows 523.1 *darkness*
shadow show 21.7 *show*
shadow-skate 68.15 *ice-skate*
shadow skating 68.6 *ice-skating*
shadowy 523.11 *benighted*; 696.4 *difficult*; 521.2 *difficult to see*; 524.5 *dim*; 477.12 *imaginary*; 728.16 *imperceptible*; 524.6 *murky*; 101.8 *nonmaterial*; 11.18 *spiritual*; 96.8 *unreal*
shady 528.2; 523.11 *benighted*; 800.7 *criminal*; 523.8 *dark*; 189.5 *devious*; 524.5 *dim*; 800.5 *dishonourable*; 812.4 *disreputable*; 16.60 *offending*; 705.14 *questionable*; 79.16 *wooded*
shady business 774.7 *dishonesty*
shady character 800.4 *dishonourable person*
shady past 812.1 *disrespect*
shaft 307.4 *axle*; 20.8 *column*; 156.4 *deep thing*; 56.4 *golf club*; 561.14 *have sex*; 587.6 *historical missile weapon*; 308.5 *hole*; 38.8 *machine element*; 330.8 *missile*; 439.2 *resource*; 413.2 *supporting part*; 154.6 *tall thing*; 438.1 *tool*
shaft horse 59.2 *thoroughbred*
shafting 20.9 *miscellaneous architectural features*
shaft tomb 583.6 *grave*
shag 561.14 *have sex*; 404.3 *nap*; 420.7 *rough thing*; 496.7 *tobacco*; 72.3 *water bird*
shag ass 332.4 *be swift*
shagged 420.3 *barbed*
shagginess 420.6 *roughness*
shaggy 420.3 *barbed*
shaggy dog story 599.5 *joke*; 699.10 *lie*; 727.5 *tall story*
shagwit 456.5 *ignorant person*
shah 400.2 *sovereign*
Shaitan 8.7 *devil*
shake 327.7; **327.24**; 327.22 *agitate*; 612.11 *be afraid*; 227.11 *be changeable*; 299.6 *be irregular*; 391.5 *be liberated*; 337.6 *be weak*; 453.21 *change*; 481.2 *deter*; 328.7 *disturb*; 30.64 *fold*; 612.13 *frighten*; 245.5 *hurt*; 299.1 *irregularity*; 412.8 *mix*; 18.16 *musical note*; 326.4, 326.11 *rock*; 50.15 *sail*; 380.8 *use violence*; 326.9 *vibrate*; 326.12 *wave*; 337.7 *weaken*; 23.12 *wood*
shake a leg 342.23 *rise and shine!*
shakedown 773.3 *taking away*
shake down 773.10 *take away*
shakedown artist 773.6 *taker*
shake free 391.5 *be liberated*
shake hands 492.12 *abut*; 569.15 *be hospitable*; 649.9 *forgive*; 658.12 *greet*; 749.5 *make peace*
shake hands on 750.23 *arrange*; 776.3 *bargain*
shake hands with 769.10 *receive someone*; 654.14 *welcome*
shake in one's shoes 327.24 *shake*
shake like a leaf 612.11 *be afraid*; 327.24 *shake*
shaken 327.15 *agitated*; 245.12 *deteriorated*; 328.12 *disturbed*; 412.12 *mixed*; 639.3 *timid*
shaken up 327.15 *agitated*
shake off 332.6 *accelerate*; 391.5 *be liberated*; 389.6 *elude*; 371.10 *exterminate*; 766.15 *lose someone*; 371.6 *send away*
shake of the head 742.3 *gesture*
shake on 776.3 *bargain*
shake on a deal 755.5 *contract*
shake one's head 708.10 *be negative*; 742.11 *gesture*; 709.5 *refuse*
shake on it 649.9 *forgive*; 749.5 *make peace*; 756.7 *promise*
shake out 50.17 *canoe*
Shaker 23.7 *furniture style*
shaker 327.14 *agitator*; 412.6 *mixer*
Shaker chair 23.2 *chair*
shakes 260.3 *symptom*
Shakespearean 17.19 *narrative*
Shakespearean actor 507.5 *loud person*
Shakespearean comedy 21.12 *comedy*
Shakespearean sonnet 17.7 *poem*
Shakespearean tragedy 21.11 *tragedy*
shake to pieces 357.9 *demolish*
shake up 114.8 *be diverse*; 409.14 *rearrange*; 419.13 *soften*; 337.7 *weaken*
shake-up 409.4 *rearrangement*; 244.6 *rectification*
shake with passion 624.11 *be angry*
shakily 327.28; 227.15 *changeably*; 800.11 *dishonourably*; 299.8 *irregularly*; 453.26 *unreliably*
shakiness 227.1 *changeableness*; 254.5 *danger*; 299.1 *irregularity*; 337.3 *poor health*; 453.15 *unreliability*
shaking 327.6; 612.8 *fearful*; 612.2 *fearfulness*; 299.4 *irregular*; 412.1 *mixture*; 326.4 *rock*; 326.16 *rocking*; 327.18 *shaky*; 326.14 *vibrating*; 326.2 *vibration*; 326.17 *waving*
shaking like a leaf 612.8 *fearful*
shaking out 50.6 *canoeing*
shaking palsy 327.7 *shake*
shako 384.7 *armour*; 551.15 *headgear*
shaky 327.18; 227.13 *changeable*; 245.13 *dilapidated*; 800.6 *faithless*; 612.8 *fearful*; 337.10 *ill*; 231.1 *imperfect*; 299.4 *irregular*; 453.7 *unreliable*; 254.2 *unsafe*
shale 424.3 *brittle thing*
shall 283.8 *intend*
shallow 157.1; 171.8 *apparent*; 666.5 *indifferent*; 563.3 *infertile*; 337.13 *insufficient*; 155.5 *low*; 157.7 *make shallow*; 456.7 *semiskilled*; 157.4 *shallow thing*; 124.4 *trivial*
shallow-bottomed 157.1 *shallow*
shallow-bottomed boat 157.4 *shallow thing*
shallow cut 157.4 *shallow thing*
shallow depression 31.11 *weather system*
shallow-fry 25.55 *cook*
shallow groove 62.5 *rock face*
shallowly 157.8
Shallowness 157
shallowness 157.3; 171.3 *appearance*; 666.2 *indifference*; 155.1 *lowness*; 218.9 *scarcity*; 124.7 *triviality*
shallow person 157.5
shallow-rooted 157.1 *shallow*
shallows 157.4 *shallow thing*; 379.1 *trap*
shallow structure 5.29 *grammar*
shallow thing 157.4
shallow water 157.4 *shallow thing*; 379.1 *trap*
shaly 30.57 *chalky*
sham 96.12 *artificial*; 96.7 *artificiality*; 699.19 *cheat*; 125.2 *copy*; 700.15 *deceiver*; 699.39 *disguised*; 699.14 *façade*; 699.12, 699.37 *fake*; 700.11 *hoax*; 700.3 *hypocrisy*; 700.19 *hypocrite*; 702.10 *hypocritical*; 125.13 *imitation*; 700.39 *imitative*; 645.2 *stratagem*; 700.28 *trick*
shaman 711.4 *warner*; 458.3 *wise man*; 11.4 *witch*
shamaness 11.4 *witch*
shamanic 11.15 *witchlike*
shamanism 11.1 *occultism*; 11.3 *witchcraft*
shamanist 11.4 *witch*
shamanize 11.21 *bewitch*
shamble 333.1 *move slowly*; 333.10 *slow motion*
shambles 486.9 *bungling*; 357.5 *havoc*; 408.4 *litter*; 767.8 *sink*; 382.15 *slaughterhouse*
shambling 486.3 *clumsy*; 333.4 *slow*
shambolic 408.15 *untidy*
shame 623.22; 812.4 *bring into disrepute*; 796.19 *corrupt*; 802.9 *dishonour*; 668.21 *disregard*; 623.13 *disrepute*; 812.1 *disrespect*; 107.15 *hard luck!*; 800.1 *improbity*; 754.3 *irresolution*; 804.17 *make wicked*; 795.3 *moral purity*; 808.1 *penitence*; 236.10 *poverty*; 814.1 *punish*; 814.7 *punishment*; 806.2 *signs of guilt*
shamed 623.3 *humbled*
shamefaced 806.6 *appearing guilty*; 674.10 *bashful*; 674.9 *blushing*; 623.3 *humbled*; 802.15 *immoral*; 808.6 *penitent*
shamefaced look 623.13 *disrepute*
shamefacedly 806.11 *guiltily*; 808.8 *penitently*; 674.18 *shyly*
shamefacedness 674.3 *bashfulness*; 623.13 *disrepute*
shamefastly 674.18 *shyly*
shamefastness 674.3 *bashfulness*; 623.13 *disrepute*
shameful 806.6 *appearing guilty*; 800.5 *dishonourable*; 668.12 *disregardful*; 802.15 *immoral*; 808.6 *penitent*; 236.4 *poor*
shamefully 800.11 *dishonourably*; 806.11 *guiltily*; 808.8 *penitently*; 236.15 *worthlessly*
shamefulness 808.1 *penitence*
shameless 660.16 *arrogant*; 661.7 *defiant*; 812.4 *disreputable*; 802.15 *immoral*;

809.3 *impenitent*; 660.21 *impudent*; 738.15 *open*; 796.13 *unchaste*; 804.11 *wicked*
shameless hussy 809.2 *impenitent person*
shameless lie 699.10 *lie*
shamelessly 660.33 *arrogantly*; 661.9 *defiantly*; 809.6 *impenitently*
shameless lying 699.6 *lying*
Shamelessness 809
shamelessness 660.4 *arrogance*; 673.3 *cockiness*; 661.1 *defiance*; 809.1 *impenitence*; 796.3 *sexual immorality*; 804.1 *wickedness*
shame oneself 804.16 *be wicked*
shame the devil 803.8 *be virtuous*
shammer 699.19 *cheat*; 645.3 *cunning person*; 700.15 *deceiver*
shamming 700.7 *tricking*
shammy 256.11 *cleaning cloth*
shampoo 256.5 *ablutions*; 256.14 *bathe*; 256.9 *cleaning agent*; 365.6, 365.16 *massage*; 255.3 *purifier*
shampooer 365.8 *masseur*
shamrock 11.6 *talisman*; 199.2 *trident*
shanghai 69.6 *darts*; 774.13 *kidnap*; 700.33 *snare*; 773.10 *take away*
shanghaier 774.8 *thief*
shanghaiing 774.2 *kidnapping*; 700.13 *snare*
Shangri-la 477.8 *dreamland*; 482.6 *objective*; 756.4 *promised land*
shank 330.26 *bat*; 55.3 *fishing tackle*
shanks's pony 320.4 *personal transport*
Shannon 90.5 *other major rivers*
shantung 193.4 *textile*
shanty 565.8 *shelter*; 516.2 *song*
shanty town 86.11 *settlement*
shapable 419.2 *pliant*
SHAPE 584.5 *military staff*
shape 403.15; 23.17 *carpenter*; 139.3 *characteristic*; 721.14 *describe*; 6.22 *educate*; 525.3 *external appearance*; 553.9 *fashion*; 160.1, 160.7, 403.3 *form*; 750.24 *harmonize*; 259.3 *health*; 743.1 *identification*; 24.11 *make ceramics*; 117.9 *make conform*; 160.6 *nature*; 717.11 *paint*; 221.5 *physical state*; 484.10 *plan out*; 356.10 *produce*; 19.21 *sculpt*; 163.2 *shadow*; 419.13 *soften*; 221.1 *state*; 760.9 *transform*; 137.4 *type*
shape a course 484.10 *plan out*
shaped 160.9 *formed*; 750.13 *harmonious*
shapeless 161.5; 408.14 *irregular*; 266.2 *obscure*; 420.5 *unfinished*
shapelessly 161.6; 420.15 *incompletely*
Shapelessness 161
shapelessness 161.1; 408.2 *irregular order*; 266.1 *obscurity*; 420.10 *rough idea*
shapeless thing 161.2
shapeliness 162.3 *evenness*; 545.1 *gorgeousness*; 181.2 *round body*
shapely 545.5 *beautiful*; 162.5 *even*; 181.10 *well-rounded*
shape one's career 631.11 *conduct oneself*
shaper 38.9 *machine tool*; 23.11 *woodworking tool*
shape up 221.6 *be in a state of*; 244.1 *improve*
shaping 160.1 *form*; 160.4 *forming*; 356.1 *production*; 403.5 *structuring*
shard 196.3 *fragment*; 205.7 *piece*; 427.22 *pulverize*; 215.1 *remainder*
sharded 427.18 *pulverized*
sharding 427.4 *pulverization*
share 770.4 *allot*; 127.5 *be included*; 654.11 *be sociable*; 203.2 *certain amount*; 196.8 *divide*; 196.2 *fractional part*; 768.5 *give*; 198.17 *go halves*; 764.4 *have joint possession*; 110.8 *interrelate*; 764.1 *joint possession*; 26.11 *measure out*; 205.1, 205.10 *part*; 770.2 *portion*; 253.2 *promise*; 436.1 *provision*; 203.8 *quantify*; 425.9 *sharp-edged thing*; 439.6 *store*; 747.13 *work together*
share a common hatred 596.5 *dislike*
share and share alike 764.4 *have joint possession*; 764.5 *jointly possessing*
share-buyer 777.12 *purchaser*
sharecrop 43.17 *farm*
sharecropper 43.15 *agriculturist*; 764.3 *participant*
sharecropping 43.1 *agriculture*; 764.1 *joint possession*
shared 398.10 *decentralized*; 747.18 *joint*
shared delusions 461.4 *delusion*
shared feelings 764.2 *participation*
shared frontier 147.7 *interface*
shared grief 627.2 *condolence*
shared out 770.7 *allocated*
shared ownership 764.1 *joint possession*
shared responsibility 398.3 *delegation*
shared sorrow 627.2 *condolence*
shared suffering 627.2 *condolence*
share expenses 764.4 *have joint possession*; 785.9 *pay one's way*
share farmer 764.3 *participant*
share farming 43.1 *agriculture*
share grief 627.9 *sorrow*
shareholder 764.3 *participant*; 440.7 *property man*
share one's sorrow 627.9 *sorrow*
share out 770.4 *allot*; 372.11 *divide*; 768.5 *give*; 216.10 *make average*; 26.11 *measure out*
share-pusher 778.12 *wholesaler*
share-pushing 776.4 *trade*
sharer 764.3 *participant*
share-seller 778.9 *seller*
share shop 779.5 *stock market*
share the work 398.7 *delegate*
shareware 40.8 *software*
share with 768.5 *give*
Sharing 764
sharing 770.1 *allocation*; 754.1 *compromise*; 119.6 *equal*; 119.1 *equality*; 110.2 *interconnection*; 747.3 *mutual relationship*; 764.2 *participation*; 654.1 *sociability*
sharing out 770.1 *allocation*
shark 55.4 *American game fish*; 699.19, 700.17 *cheat*; 774.11 *dishonest person*; 382.10 *killer*; 792.5 *overcharger*; 773.6 *taker*
shark fishing 74.7 *fishing*
sharkish 74.13 *fishlike*
sharklike 74.13 *fishlike*
shark net 74.7 *fishing*
Sharons 574.2 *the common people*
sharp 425.1; 499.5 *acid*; 164.10 *advantaged*; 520.2 *clear*; 420.2 *coarse*; 494.8 *cold*; 645.4 *cunning*; 645.3 *cunning person*; 700.34 *deceiving*; 659.5 *discourteous*; 726.3 *emphatic*; 485.5 *expert*; 594.10 *hating*; 651.14 *hostile*; 442.10, 458.6 *intelligent*; 625.4 *irascible*; 18.16 *musical note*; 496.9 *piquant*; 6.20 *refined*; 624.15 *resentful*; 513.9 *shrill*; 336.12 *strong to the senses*; 495.7 *tasty*; 517.9 *unmelodious*; 380.6 *violent*; 31.47 *windy*
sharp as a needle 425.1 *sharp*
sharp as a razor 425.3 *sharp-edged*
sharp as a tack 425.5 *mentally sharp*
sharp as broken glass 425.2 *spiked*
sharp corner 176.1 *angle*
sharp-cornered 176.7 *angular*
sharp ear 504.1 *hearing*
sharp edge 164.3 *cutting edge*; 420.6 *roughness*; 425.7 *sharp point*
sharp-edged 425.3
sharp-edged thing 425.9
sharpen 338.3 *invigorate*; 494.12 *make cold*; 425.15 *make sharp*; 380.9 *make violent*; 499.8 *sour*
sharpened 425.1 *sharp*
sharpener 425.12
sharper 645.3 *cunning person*; 774.11 *dishonest person*
sharp eye 518.2 *eye*
sharp-eyed 425.5 *mentally sharp*; 518.21 *seeing*; 471.7 *watchful*
sharp fellow 342.10 *busy person*
sharp flavouring 499.1 *sourness*
sharp frost 31.36 *frost*
sharpie 342.10 *busy person*
sharply 425.18; 336.15 *acutely*; 164.12 *at an advantage*; 659.9 *discourteously*; 594.18 *hatefully*; 625.9 *irascibly*; 496.15 *piquantly*; 624.17 *resentfully*; 420.14 *roughly*; 499.10 *sourly*; 425.19 *suddenly*
Sharpness 425
sharpness 425.6; 651.4 *bitterness*; 520.4 *clarity*; 442.4 *cleverness*; 41.8 *composition*; 645.1 *cunning*; 164.3 *cutting edge*; 659.1 *discourtesy*; 726.1 *emphasis*; 625.1 *irascibility*; 517.3 *musical dissonance*; 485.1 *skill*; 499.1 *sourness*
sharp-nosed 500.5 *odorous*
sharp note 513.3 *shrillness*
sharp point 425.7
sharp-pointed 425.1 *sharp*
sharp-pointed thing 425.8
sharp practice 800.3 *criminality*; 645.1 *cunning*; 812.3 *disreputable action*; 699.9 *falsification*; 699.8 *fraud*; 700.7 *tricking*
sharp-set 425.3 *sharp-edged*
sharpshooter 381.19 *attacker*; 586.8 *soldier*
sharpshooting 381.15 *firing*
sharp taste 495.1 *taste*
sharp temper 625.1 *irascibility*
sharp tongue 651.4 *bitterness*
sharp-tongued 659.5 *discourteous*; 625.4 *irascible*; 425.5 *mentally sharp*
sharp weapon 587.8
sharp-witted 458.6 *intelligent*; 425.5 *mentally sharp*
sharp-wittedness 425.13 *mental sharpness*
shastra 7.12 *religious text*
shatter 424.4 *be brittle*; 278.4 *be transient*; 357.9 *demolish*; 375.3 *disintegrate*; 372.9 *separate*
shatterable 424.1 *brittle*
shattered 372.16 *apart*; 424.1 *brittle*; 420.2 *coarse*; 357.15 *destroyed*; 375.5 *disintegrated*
shattered silence 507.1 *loudness*
shattered surface 420.6 *roughness*
shattering 424.1 *brittle*; 357.2 *destroying*; 123.6 *notable*; 372.1 *separation*; 619.8 *wonderful*
shatter one's hopes 611.10 *disappoint*
shatterproof 252.7 *invulnerable*; 423.11 *make tough*; 418.2, 423.1 *tough*
shatterproof glass 252.4 *safety device*
shatter the dreams of 278.5 *make transient*
shatter the eardrums 507.8 *be loud*
shatter the peace 507.8 *be loud*; 586.36 *combat*
shave 256.13 *clean*; 552.7 *depilation*; 547.9 *hair removal*; 552.15 *make nude*; 191.5, 214.5 *make smaller*; 147.19 *meet*; 411.11 *scale*; 149.10 *shorten*; 421.11 *smooth*; 492.11 *touch*
shaved 552.13 *hairless*; 149.8 *shortened*
shaven 256.17 *cleaned*; 552.13 *hairless*; 149.8 *shortened*
shaving 552.7 *depilation*; 153.11 *fineness*; 547.9 *hair removal*; 159.3 *little piece*; 149.2 *shortening*; 411.4 *slice*
shaving mirror 28.29 *optical element*; 518.8 *reflection*
shavings 205.8 *bits and pieces*; 258.4 *dirt*; 238.6 *refuse*; 215.2 *residue*
shawl 551.25 *accessories*; 551.14 *neckwear*
shawl collar 551.14 *neckwear*
she 568.2 *female*
sheading 86.5 *state*
sheaf 376.27 *bundle*
shear 552.7 *depilation*; 38.31 *load*; 552.15 *make nude*; 191.5 *make smaller*; 372.10 *set apart*; 149.10 *shorten*; 27.48 *transformation*; 425.16 *use a sharp tool*
sheared 149.8 *shortened*
shearing 552.7 *depilation*; 149.2 *shortening*
shearing shaving 191.1 *contraction*
shears 44.6, 438.3 *garden tool*; 425.9 *sharp-edged thing*
shear strain 38.14 *load*
shear stress 38.14 *load*
shearwater 72.3 *water bird*
sheath 587.4 *arsenal*; 563.3 *birth control*; 81.3 *grass plant*; 410.5 *packet*; 410.21 *put in a container*; 165.6 *wrap*; 165.4 *wrapper*; 550.4 *wrapping*
sheath dress 551.7 *frock*
sheathe 411.3 *coat*; 362.14 *draw in*; 551.32 *dress*; 368.5 *inset*; 550.25 *wrap*
sheathed 411.8 *coated*; 410.20 *containing*; 550.37 *protected*
sheathe the sword 749.5 *make peace*
sheathing 23.12 *wood*; 550.4 *wrapping*
sheathing board 23.12 *wood*
sheath knife 425.10 *knife*
sheave 50.3 *parts of a sailing boat*; 438.1 *tool*
shed 211.3 *additional item*; 560.32 *cast-off*; 214.4 *decrease*; 487.5 *disaccustom*; 371.10 *exterminate*; 552.16 *peel*; 552.12 *peeling*; 321.8 *railway station*; 355.1 *relinquish*; 565.8 *shelter*; 439.4 *storage*; 367.6 *throw down*
shed blessings on 248.7 *be auspicious*
shed blood 585.13 *be at war*; 382.16 *kill*; 647.6 *suppress*
shed crocodile tears 800.8 *be dishonourable*; 699.22 *be hypocritical*
shedding 371.22 *disgorgement*; 552.6, 552.12 *peeling*
shedding light 522.3 *lightening*
shedding light on 522.15 *lucent*
shedding of daylight on 738.10 *manifestation*
she-devil 625.3 *irascible person*; 651.9 *vixen*
shed leaves 77.22 *be dormant*
shed light on 522.29 *clarify*
shed one's skin 560.23 *cast*
shed seeds 77.21 *vegetate*
shed tears 429.16 *seep*; 603.7 *weep*
shedu 8.7 *devil*
sheen 522.2 *quality of light*
sheep 117.6 *conformist*; 125.7 *imitator*; 43.8 *livestock*; 10.17 *worshipper*
sheep and goats 113.3 *opposites*
sheep breeder 43.15 *agriculturist*
sheep-dip 43.14 *pest control*
sheepdog 376.34 *assembler*; 71.9 *dog*
sheep farm 43.6 *farm*
sheep farmer 43.15 *agriculturist*; 356.9 *producer*
sheep farming 43.3 *livestock farming*
sheepfold 43.7 *farm building*
sheephide 435.1 *materials*
sheepish 806.6 *appearing guilty*; 674.9 *blushing*; 623.3 *humbled*; 337.12 *weak-willed*
sheepishly 806.11 *guiltily*; 674.18 *shyly*; 337.14 *weakly*
sheepishness 337.2 *indecisiveness*
sheep-like 117.13 *compliant*; 663.7 *obedient*; 71.33 *ungulate*
sheep netting 43.11 *farmland*
sheep ranch 43.6 *farm*
sheeprot 260.18 *veterinary disease*
sheep's currants 560.5 *faeces*
sheep's eyes 593.14 *communication of love*; 593.6 *courtship*; 518.6 *look*
sheepskin 435.1 *materials*
sheep tick 76.3 *pest*
sheeptrack 420.8 *rough ground*
sheer 325.1 *deviate*; 325.14 *deviating course*; 153.4 *fine*; 186.12 *perpendicularly*; 50.8 *punting*; 255.16 *simple*; 527.2 *translucent*; 186.8 *vertical*; 42.10 *woven*
sheer drop 305.6 *slide*
sheer fabric 524.2 *murk*; 527.8 *transparent thing*
sheerness 153.11 *fineness*; 527.6 *translucency*; 186.1 *verticality*
sheer perfection 230.3 *perfection*
sheer stockings 551.20 *legwear*
sheet 550.10 *bed covering*; 23.17 *carpenter*; 411.3 *coat*; 740.4 *newspaper*; 435.3 *paper*; 205.2 *particular*; 50.3 *parts of a sailing boat*
sheet anchor 252.2 *protection*; 252.4 *safety device*; 373.9 *yoke*
sheet glass 527.9 *glass*
sheet in 50.15 *sail*
sheeting 23.12 *wood*
sheeting in 50.1 *sailing*
sheeting out 50.1 *sailing*
sheet lightning 522.4 *natural light*; 31.21 *thunderstorm*
sheet music 18.18 *written music*
sheet of cloud 31.20 *cloud appearance*
sheet of fire 493.6 *fire*
sheet of rain 31.25 *rain*
sheet out 50.15 *sail*
sheets 373.7 *tackle*
sheet steel 38.25 *construction material*
sheet winch 50.3 *parts of a sailing boat*
she-goat 568.14 *female animal*
sheik 400.3 *leader*; 593.9 *lover*; 121.5 *superior*
sheikh 7.8 *priest*
sheila 568.2 *female*
shekel 780.12 *ancient coins*
shekels 780.2 *cash*
Shekinah 8.2 *divine attribute*
Sheldon scale 1.10 *measurement*
shelf 410.3 *cabinet*; 411.2 *level*; 185.2 *projection*; 410.4 *rack*; 157.4 *shallow thing*; 439.4 *storage*; 413.2 *supporting part*
shelf room 439.4 *storage*
shelf space 439.4 *storage*
shell 587.13 *ammunition*; 550.14 *animal covering*; 587.16 *bomb*; 550.13 *casing*; 72.15 *eggs*; 171.1 *exterior*; 381.2 *fire*; 403.4 *framework*; 80.3 *fruit structure*; 583.4 *funeral objects*; 418.7 *hard substance*; 330.8 *missile*; 587.5 *missile weapon*; 215.1 *remainder*; 369.14 *suck*; 38.27 *superstructure*
shellback 485.5 *expert*
shell burst 507.1 *loudness*
shellfish 25.19; 70.5 *aquatic animal*; 75.4 *arthropod*

shelling 369.4 *sucking*
shell jacket 551.11 *jacket*
shell-like 504.4 *ear*
shell money 780.1 *money*
shell on brass 23.9 *decorative woodwork*
shell out 787.1 *expend;* 768.5 *give;* 785.6 *pay*
shell-pink 535.1 *red*
shell shock 461.6 *mental breakdown;* 36.10 *neurosis*
shell-shocked 335.12 *impotent;* 585.17 *military*
shell suit 551.4 *informal dress;* 47.4 *sports equipment;* 551.10 *suit*
shell suits 657.6 *informal dress*
shelly 171.6 *exterior*
shelter 384.10; 550.15; 565.8; 773.11 *be hospitable;* 736.2 *hiding place;* 359.5 *preserve;* 252.10 *protect;* 252.2, 253.1 *protection;* 410.21 *put in a container;* 370.2 *receptivity;* 301.3 *resting place;* 312.16 *stopover;* 773.4 *taking in;* 370.9 *welcome*
shelter belt 79.4 *trees*
sheltered 410.20 *containing;* 565.14 *inhabiting;* 252.6 *safe;* 253.6 *secure*
sheltered housing 565.11 *retreat*
sheltering 410.20 *containing*
shelterless 782.3 *beggarly;* 254.3 *vulnerable*
sheltie 59.5 *pony*
shelve 634.7 *be evasive;* 294.8 *delay;* 637.8 *hold back;* 361.12 *interrupt;* 355.2 *withdraw*
shelved 410.20 *containing;* 361.9 *interrupted*
shelves 23.5 *cabinet*
shelving 637.15 *delay;* 361.6 *interruption;* 410.4 *rack*
shemozzle 328.5 *commotion;* 507.2 *outcry*
shenanigan 700.7 *tricking*
shenanigans 697.3 *tomfoolery*
Sheol 8.12 *hell;* 582.14 *the spiritual world*
shepherd 376.34 *assembler;* 579.2 *direct;* 223.15 *escort;* 43.16 *farm worker;* 376.43 *herd;* 579.14 *leader;* 43.18 *practise livestock farming;* 252.10 *protect;* 252.3 *protector;* 223.8 *usher*
shepherded 223.20 *accompanied;* 376.46 *assembled*
shepherdess 43.16 *farm worker*
shepherding 376.2 *herding*
shepherdlike 252.8 *tutelary*
shepherd's pie 25.44 *British dish*
Sheraton 23.7 *furniture style*
Sheraton chair 23.2 *chair*
sherbet 558.6 *soft drink;* 498.5 *sweet drink*
sherd 196.3 *fragment;* 205.7 *piece*
sheriff 16.25 *British judge;* 16.10 *law officer;* 400.3 *leader;* 396.10 *person of authority;* 252.3 *protector*
sheriff court 16.20 *British court;* 16.19 *law court*
Sherpa guide 62.7 *mountaineer*
sherry 558.9 *wine*
sherry glass 558.10 *drink container;* 410.13 *drinking vessel*
sherry party 654.5 *party*
she-wolf 380.4 *violent creature*
SHF transmitter 692.16 *transmitter*
shiatsu 35.2 *natural medicine*
shibboleth 743.3 *means of identification;* 742.1 *sign;* 742.6 *word*
shield 384.7 *armour;* 384.19 *buffer;* 743.8 *heraldic device;* 30.7 *landform;* 28.73 *nuclear reactor;* 813.2 *prize;* 252.10, 550.30 *protect;* 252.2, 253.1 *protection;* 550.12 *protective covering;* 253.10 *secure*
shield-bearer 316.7 *transferor*
shielded 758.5 *exempt;* 550.37 *protected;* 252.6 *safe;* 253.6 *secure*
shielding 550.1 *covering*
shield volcano 30.24 *volcanic activity*
shift 770.3 *allotted task;* 224.7 *be changed;* 645.5 *be cunning;* 300.13 *be in motion;* 332.4 *be swift;* 224.8 *cause change;* 224.1, 453.21 *change;* 760.1 *conversion;* 760.7 *convert into;* 298.2 *cycle;* 325.15 *deviating motion;* 144.14 *displace;* 144.1 *displacement;* 275.3 *duration;* 484.3 *expedient plan;* 46.8 *huddle;* 209.4 *interval;* 276.4 *period of activity;* 645.2 *stratagem;* 212.3 *subtract;* 631.9 *tactics;* 316.15 *take away;* 576.2, 810.2 *task;* 316.1 *transfer;* 700.8, 700.28 *trick;* 551.18 *underwear;* 300.15 *walk;* 576.6 *work*
shifted 144.8 *displaced*
shift for oneself 250.16 *be independent;* 631.11 *conduct oneself*
shift gears 479.2 *equivocate*
shiftily 224.15, 227.15 *changeably;* 453.26 *unreliably*
shiftiness 645.1, 702.3 *cunning;* 700.1 *deception;* 699.13 *evasion;* 227.2 *irresolution;* 453.15 *unreliability*
shifting 224.11, 227.13 *changeable;* 144.8 *displaced;* 325.21 *indirect;* 300.16 *moving;* 316.1 *transfer;* 316.17 *transferable*
shifting one's ground 479.6 *equivocation*
shifting sands 227.3 *changeable thing*
shift into 760.7 *convert into*
shift lens 41.17 *lens*
shift one's ground 639.9 *change sides;* 479.2 *equivocate*
shift the blame 800.8 *be dishonourable;* 758.12 *exempt oneself*
shift the responsibility 758.12 *exempt oneself*
shifty 224.11 *changeable;* 645.4, 702.8 *cunning;* 700.34 *deceiving;* 699.38 *evasive;* 227.14 *irresolute;* 453.7 *unreliable;* 639.1 *vacillating*
shiho nage 52.10 *aikido*
Shiite 7.6 *non-Christian*
shill 700.18 *decoy;* 740.16 *publicize;* 740.10 *publicizer*
shillelagh 587.7 *blunt weapon*
shilling 780.10 *former British money*
shillyshally 479.1 *be equivocal;* 227.12 *be irresolute;* 333.2 *hesitate;* 639.5 *vacillate*
shillyshallying 333.7 *delayed;* 333.11 *lingering*
shime-waza 52.7 *judo*
shimmer 522.2 *quality of light;* 31.61 *shine*
shimmering 522.17 *lustrous;* 522.2 *quality of light*
shimmery 522.17 *lustrous*
shimmy 180.2 *coil;* 180.6 *convolute;* 22.2 *dance;* 320.21 *miscellaneous motoring terms*
shin 25.22 *beef*
shindig 22.1 *dancing;* 408.9 *disorder;* 654.5 *party;* 376.9 *social gathering*
shindy 751.2 *argument;* 654.5 *party;* 376.9 *social gathering*
shine 31.61; 53.7 *bat;* 545.7 *be beautiful;* 137.15 *be in a class of one's own;* 458.8 *be intelligent;* 485.10 *be skilful;* 53.18 *bowl;* 256.13 *clean;* 256.1 *cleanness;* 139.25 *excel;* 522.25 *light up;* 595.3 *likes;* 29.37 *observe;* 522.2 *quality of light;* 593.2 *romantic love;* 421.11 *smooth;* 421.7 *smoothness*
shine brightly 31.61 *shine*
shine on 248.7 *be auspicious*
shiner 491.3 *injury*
shine some light on 739.5 *disclose*
shine through 520.9 *appear;* 527.11 *be transparent*
shine up to 569.14 *seek the friendship of*
shingle 435.2 *building material;* 23.17 *carpenter;* 30.11, 92.4 *coast;* 427.9 *grit;* 411.10 *layer;* 550.26 *overlie;* 30.27 *sediment;* 23.12 *wood*
shingled 92.11 *continental;* 427.17 *grainy*
shingled roof 411.5 *layered thing*
shingles 550.7 *overhead covering;* 260.13 *skin disease*
shingly 427.17 *grainy*
shin guard 58.1 *hockey;* 58.3 *ice hockey*
shin guards 48.3 *baseball equipment*
shininess 522.2 *quality of light;* 421.7 *smoothness*
shining 522.16 *bright;* 256.16 *clean;* 522.15 *lucent;* 365.5 *polishing;* 255.14 *purified;* 522.2 *quality of light*
shining armour 585.2 *glory of war*
shining light 522.13 *enlightenment*
shinny up 304.14 *climb*
shin pad 384.6 *protective clothing*
shinpads 66.1 *soccer*
shinplaster 780.14 *paper money*
Shinto text 7.12 *religious text*
shinty 58.7 *hurling*
shinty stick 58.7 *hurling*
shin up 304.14 *climb*
shiny 522.17 *lustrous;* 528.3 *mirror-like;* 421.4 *polished;* 255.14 *purified*
ship 316.12, 319.4 *transport;* 323.3 *vessel*
shipbuilder 578.2 *artisan;* 323.7 *nautical person*
shipbuilding 323.4
shipbuilding contract 323.4 *shipbuilding*
shipbuilding skill 323.4 *shipbuilding*
shipbuilding yard 323.4 *shipbuilding*
ship chandler 436.3 *provider*
ship design 323.4 *shipbuilding*
ship designer 323.7 *nautical person*
ship halfpenny 780.10 *former British money*
shipmate 569.5 *friend;* 323.7 *nautical person*
ship materials 323.4 *shipbuilding*
shipment 406.2 *load;* 319.2 *thing transported;* 316.10 *transferred thing;* 319.1 *transport;* 316.2 *transportation*
ship of the line 586.24 *warship*
ship out 585.13 *be at war;* 323.9 *navigate*
shipped 319.5 *transportable*
shipper 319.3 *transporter*
shipping 319.5 *transportable;* 316.2 *transportation;* 323.1 *water travel*
shipping forecast 31.4 *weather forecast*
shipping lane 317.6 *path;* 91.1 *sea*
ship's chronometer 323.5 *navigation*
ship's colours 743.7 *flag*
ship's compass 323.5 *navigation*
shipshape 407.13 *orderly;* 485.9 *well-made*
shipshape condition 243.14 *preparedness*
ship's log 323.5 *navigation*
ship's master 323.7 *nautical person*
ship specifications 323.4 *shipbuilding*
ship's speed 323.6 *nautical speed*
ship's steering 323.5 *navigation*
ship's steward 323.7 *nautical person*
ship's timekeeper 323.5 *navigation*
ship-to-shore telephone 692.9 *telephone*
shipwreck 357.4, 357.11 *ruin*
shipwright 578.2 *artisan*
shipyard 577.1 *workshop*
shire 86.5 *state*
shire town 87.4 *British cities*
shirk 634.5; 639.6 *hesitate;* 637.7 *refuse*
shirker 634.17 *avoider;* 666.3 *negligent person;* 341.2 *nonacting person;* 343.8 *nonworker;* 637.16 *reluctant person*
shirking 634.13; 637.3 *cautious*
shirr 184.3, 184.10 *pleat*
shirt 551.8
shirtdress 551.7 *frock*
shirt-front 551.24 *part of garment*
shirtsleeves 657.6 *informal dress*
shirtwaist 551.7 *frock*
shirtwaister 551.7 *frock*
shirty 626.7 *irritable;* 624.15 *resentful*
shish kebab 25.54 *other dishes*
shit 431.3 *body fluid;* 534.5 *brown thing;* 560.16 *defecate;* 258.4 *dirt;* 812.2 *disreputable character;* 560.5 *faeces;* 712.15 *miscellaneous swearwords;* 697.1 *nonsense;* 242.9 *unpleasant person*
shitbag 242.9 *unpleasant person*
shitfaced 690.3 *dead drunk*
shithouse 659.4 *discourteous person;* 560.13 *lavatory*
shitlist 594.4 *hatefulness*
shit oneself 612.11 *be afraid;* 560.16 *defecate*
shit scared 612.7 *frightened*
shittily 560.33 *scatologically*
shitty 560.25 *faecal;* 260.22 *sick;* 238.1 *useless*
shitwork 576.1 *work*
shiver 612.11 *be afraid;* 424.4 *be brittle;* 494.10 *be cold;* 357.9 *demolish;* 372.9 *separate;* 327.24 *shake;* 326.9 *vibrate*
shivering 260.23 *diseased;* 327.6 *shaking;* 327.18 *shaky;* 326.14 *vibrating;* 326.2 *vibration*
shivers 612.2 *fearfulness;* 327.7 *shake;* 260.3 *symptom*
shivery 494.8 *cold;* 327.18 *shaky*
shoal 74.1 *fishes;* 376.23 *flock;* 157.7 *make shallow;* 157.1 *shallow;* 157.4 *shallow thing;* 208.4 *throng;* 379.1 *trap*
shoaliness 157.3 *shallowness*
shoals 157.4 *shallow thing*
shoal water 379.1 *trap*
shoaly 157.1 *shallow*
shock 630.3; 630.11 *amaze;* 604.2 *bad outcome;* 804.16 *be wicked;* 619.10 *be wonderful;* 596.7 *cause dislike;* 331.12 *collision;* 612.13 *frighten;* 260.2 *illness;* 380.3 *instance of violence;* 327.9, 327.23 *jolt;* 381.12 *military attack;* 30.22 *seismic activity;* 36.12 *stress;* 380.8 *use violence;* 619.1 *wonder*
shockability 795.4 *self-righteousness*
shockable 674.10 *bashful;* 795.10 *moralistic*
shock absorber 685.2 *moderator;* 422.5 *spring*
shock cord 50.3 *parts of a sailing boat*
shocked 327.15 *agitated;* 630.7 *amazed;* 619.6 *wondering*
shocked silence 619.2 *sign of wonderment*
shockheaded 420.3 *barbed*
shocking 612.10 *frightening;* 804.12 *immoral;* 796.12 *indecent;* 236.4 *poor;* 630.8 *surprising;* 619.8 *wonderful*
shockingly 331.18 *dynamically*
shocking manners 659.2 *bad manners*
shocking pink 535.1 *red*
shocking temper 626.3 *irritableness*
shockproof 423.1 *tough*
shock reaction 36.12 *stress*
shock stall 322.5 *flight*
shock tactics 381.12 *military attack*
shock therapy 36.3 *psychiatric treatment;* 461.9 *treatment*
shock treatment 36.3 *psychiatric treatment;* 394.13 *therapy*
shock trooper 586.1 *combatant*
shock troops 586.14 *armed forces*
shock wave 28.14 *sound wave;* 326.5 *wave*
shod 551.29 *dressed*
shoddily 122.21 *badly;* 424.5 *fragilely*
shoddiness 793.3; 666.2 *indifference;* 236.8 *inferiority;* 122.4 *poor quality;* 675.2 *tawdriness;* 408.3 *untidiness*
shoddy 793.10; 424.1 *brittle;* 700.39 *imitative;* 666.5 *indifferent;* 236.2 *inferior;* 122.14 *poor;* 124.4 *trivial;* 254.2 *unsafe;* 408.15 *untidy;* 337.8 *weak*
shoe 69.3 *card game terms;* 551.32 *dress;* 50.8 *punting;* 38.27 *superstructure*
shoeblack 401.3 *attendant;* 256.12 *cleaner*
shoe box 410.6 *box*
shoe brush 256.10 *cleaning object*
shoed 551.29 *dressed*
shoelace 373.6 *line*
shoemaker 551.26 *fashion designer*
shoemaking 551.2 *dressing*
shoe polish 256.9 *cleaning agent;* 421.10 *polish*
shoe-repairer 393.12 *repairer*
shoes 551.19 *footwear*
shoe seller 778.13 *retailer*
shoeshine boy 401.3 *attendant;* 256.12 *cleaner*
shoeshiner 256.12 *cleaner*
shoetree 79.12 *figurative usage*
shogun 400.4 *absolute ruler*
shonin 7.7 *monk*
shoo 313.15 *go!*
shoo-in 246.5 *victorious person*
shoo off 371.6 *send away*
shooping 514.17 *cheering*
shoot 60.7; 330.28; 633.19 *after him!;* 585.14 *battle;* 190.6 *become bigger;* 491.10 *be painful;* 205.6 *branch;* 90.2 *channel;* 111.9 *duplicate;* 382.19, 814.5 *execute;* 586.37 *fight;* 381.2 *fire;* 66.2 *football play;* 308.20 *hole;* 633.11 *hunt;* 60.2 *hunting;* 491.11 *inflict pain;* 368.2 *inject;* 382.22 *kill animals;* 382.17 *murder;* 41.21 *photograph;* 49.6 *play basketball;* 66.4 *play soccer;* 717.9 *represent;* 77.9 *seed;* 77.5 *stem;* 77.21 *vegetate;* 42.4 *weaving;* 555.5 *young plant*
shoot a cat 371.15 *vomit*
shoot ahead 329.3 *exceed*
shoot ahead of 121.8 *be superior*
shoot an air ball 49.6 *play basketball*
shoot an arrow 425.16 *use a sharp tool*
shoot-and-run offence 49.4 *playing terms*
shoot an eagle 56.7 *golf*
shoot a picture 717.9 *represent*
shoot at 381.2 *fire;* 330.28 *shoot*
shoot back 385.3 *retaliate*
shoot down 367.3 *bring down;* 381.2 *fire;* 131.17 *kill;* 382.17 *murder;* 330.28 *shoot;* 382.18 *slaughter*
shoot down in flames 367.3 *bring down;* 131.17 *kill;* 357.11 *ruin*
shooter 330.15; 49.2 *basketball player;* 53.8 *delivery;* 330.9 *firearm;* 60.4 *hunter;* 586.8 *soldier*
shoot gravy 691.10 *drug oneself*
shooting 60.8; 330.6; 382.9 *animal killing;* 814.13 *capital punishment;* 633.2 *chase;* 382.5 *execution;* 381.15 *firing;* 66.2

football play; 190.8 *growing;* 190.1 *growth;* 633.16 *hunting;* 582.6 *killing;* 382.2 *murder;* 491.5 *painful;* 49.4 *playing terms;* 330.7 *shot*
shooting association 60.2 *hunting*
shooting box 60.2 *hunting*
shooting brake 320.16 *car*
shooting circle 58.1 *hockey*
shooting gallery 691.1 *drug-taking*
shooting in the dark 274.2 *inaccuracy*
shooting iron 587.9 *firearm*
shooting jacket 551.11 *jacket*
shooting kit 60.3 *hunting equipment*
shooting oneself 382.7 *suicide*
shooting party 60.2 *hunting*
shooting script 21.2 *play*
shooting season 292.1 *season*
shooting star 475.6 *good-luck sign;* 29.20 *meteor;* 522.4 *natural light;* 278.2 *transient thing*
shooting stick 60.3 *hunting equipment;* 413.4 *rest*
shooting the rapids 50.6 *canoeing*
shooting up 691.1 *drug-taking;* 304.4 *taking off*
shoot off one's mouth 739.7 *betray*
shoot one's cookies 371.15 *vomit*
shoot oneself 382.21 *commit suicide*
shoot one's mouth off 731.8 *talk too much*
shoot-out 585.9 *battle*
shoot par 56.7 *golf*
shoot straight 799.6 *be honourable*
shoot the rapids 50.17 *canoe*
shoot through 318.8 *pass;* 634.8 *run away*
shoot to kill 382.26 *no quarter!*
shoot up 190.6 *become bigger;* 691.10 *drug oneself;* 213.4 *increase;* 154.16 *rise;* 366.2 *send up;* 304.17 *spring up;* 77.21 *vegetate*
shoot with an arrow 425.16 *use a sharp tool*
shop **777.2**; 38.20 *building;* 787.1 *expend;* 693.13 *inform on;* 779.8 *store;* 577.1 *workshop*
shopaholic 787.9 *spendthrift*
shop around 793.14 *buy cheaply*
shop assistant 401.3 *attendant;* 778.10 *salesman;* 578.1 *worker*
shop at 349.2 *frequent*
shop floor 376.13 *workforce;* 577.1 *workshop*
shop for 777.2 *shop*
shop girl 778.10 *salesman*
shop goods 778.8 *merchandise*
shopkeeper 436.3 *provider;* 778.13 *retailer*
shoplift 800.10 *be criminal;* 774.12 *steal;* 773.10 *take away*
shoplifter 386.5 *compulsive person;* 774.8 *thief*
shoplifting 804.7 *criminality;* 774.1 *stealing*
shop manager 579.15 *manager*
shop owner 578.3 *agent;* 778.13 *retailer*
shopper 777.12 *purchaser;* 787.8 *spender;* 349.8 *user*
shopping **777.8**; 777.14 *buying;* 787.4 *expenditure;* 777.6 *purchase*
shopping and fucking novel 17.2 *fiction*
shopping arcade 87.7 *city district*
shopping area 87.7 *city district*
shopping bag 410.8 *bag;* 316.10 *transferred thing*
shopping basket 410.7 *basket*
shopping by mail order 777.8 *shopping*
shopping centre 173.4 *centre of activity;* 87.7 *city district;* 779.7 *emporium*
shopping list 220.4 *bill;* 135.1 *requirement;* 777.8 *shopping*
shopping mall 173.4 *centre of activity;* 87.7 *city district;* 779.7 *emporium*
shopping precinct 87.7 *city district*
shopping spree 777.8 *shopping*
shopping trolley 410.10 *cart;* 320.7 *handcart*
Shops Act 15.5 *labour law*
shopsoiled 548.4 *blemished;* 122.17 *defective;* 245.13 *dilapidated;* 791.6 *discounted;* 231.1 *imperfect;* 793.10 *shoddy;* 349.9 *used*
shopsoiled item 231.6 *imperfect item*
shop steward 776.11 *chamber of commerce member;* 15.7 *employee;* 579.16 *official*
shop till one drops 787.1 *expend;* 777.2 *shop*
shopwalker 778.10 *salesman*
shop window 779.2 *fair;* 738.8 *showplace;* 779.9 *stall;* 520.7 *that which makes visible;* 527.8 *transparent thing;* 518.9 *viewpoint*
shopworn 122.17 *defective;* 791.6 *discounted;* 793.10 *shoddy*
shore 30.11, 92.4 *coast;* 164.1 *edge;* 167.1 *front;* 418.9 *harden;* 86.3 *regional boundary;* 392.19 *support*
shore bird 72.3 *water bird*
shore direction-finding station 323.5 *navigation*
shoreline 30.11, 92.4 *coast;* 164.1 *edge*
shore patrol 16.14 *police*
shore up 418.9 *harden;* 359.5 *preserve;* 392.19, 413.11 *support*
shorn 149.8 *shortened;* 191.7 *smaller*
shorn of 766.16 *losing*
short **149.7**; **149.12**; 424.1 *brittle;* 269.3 *concise;* 659.5 *discourteous;* 558.2 *drink;* 233.4 *incomplete;* 782.2 *insolvent;* 625.4 *irascible;* 159.7 *little;* 155.5 *low;* 98.12 *missing;* 212.7 *reduced;* 218.4 *scarce;* 732.2 *sparing with words;* 723.6 *summary;* 278.6 *transient;* 356.5 *work of art*
shortage 214.1 *decrease;* 98.2 *disappearance;* 247.1 *failure;* 206.3 *fewness;* 782.9 *inadequacy;* 120.1 *inequality;* 135.2 *need;* 218.9 *scarcity*
shortage of cash 782.6 *insolvency*
shortage of funds 782.6 *insolvency*
short allowance 218.8 *insufficiency*
shortan 322.6 *flight control*
short and sweet 269.3 *concise;* 149.7 *short;* 723.6 *summary*
short answer 659.3 *act of discourtesy;* 706.1 *answer*
short-arm blow 331.14 *sporting hit*
short-back-and-sides 547.8 *haircut*
shortbread 25.39 *loaf*
short-change 700.30 *be fraudulent*
short-changer 700.17 *cheat*
short circuit 39.13 *circuit;* 334.7 *electrical power;* 61.6 *motor-racing terms*
shortcoming 231.7 *defect;* 804.3 *venial sin*
short commons 218.8 *insufficiency;* 687.2 *short rations*
short-course 67.11 *swimming*
short-course pool 67.7 *swimming pool*
shortcrust pastry 25.37 *pastry*
short cut 324.2 *bearing;* 317.2 *route;* 147.2 *short distance;* 149.4 *short thing*
short distance **147.2**
short-distance 68.13 *ice-skating*
short-distance racing 68.8 *speed-skating*
short division 27.18 *division*
short drink 558.2 *drink*
short duration **278.3**
shorten **149.10**; 191.6 *become smaller;* 269.4 *be concise;* 245.5 *hurt;* 191.5, 214.5 *make smaller;* 421.11 *smooth;* 723.8 *summarize;* 212.4 *take off*
shortened **149.8**; **723.7**; 269.3 *concise;* 233.4 *incomplete;* 212.7 *reduced;* 191.7 *smaller*
shortened version **149.3**
shortener 723.5 *summarizer*
shortening **149.2**; 25.7 *basic ingredient;* 269.1 *conciseness;* 191.8 *contracting;* 191.1 *contraction;* 214.1 *decrease;* 723.2 *outline;* 212.1 *subtraction*
shorten sail 252.9 *be safe;* 333.3 *slow down*
shorten someone's life 382.16 *kill*
shorten the life of 278.5 *make transient*
shortfall 231.7 *defect;* 122.2 *deficiency;* 247.1 *failure;* 766.2 *financial loss;* 231.5 *imperfection;* 120.1 *inequality;* 218.8 *insufficiency;* 135.2 *need;* 233.2 *omission;* 212.2 *subtracted item*
short fuse 625.1 *irascibility;* 626.4 *sign of irritableness*
shorthand 149.4 *short thing*
short-handed 58.8 *hockey;* 231.2 *incomplete;* 218.2 *unprovided*
short legs 149.4 *short thing*
shortlist 220.8 *list;* 220.6 *list of names;* 469.6 *selection*
shortlived 278.6 *transient*
short loin 25.23 *beef*
shortly 149.12 *short;* 293.18 *soon;* 723.11 *summarily;* 278.8 *transiently*
Shortness 149
shortness **149.1**; 269.1 *conciseness;* 659.1 *discourtesy;* 159.1 *littleness;* 155.1 *lowness;* 732.3 *shyness;* 723.4 *summariness*
shortness of breath 261.7 *fatigue*
short note 18.19 *tempo*
short novel 356.5 *work of art*
short of 212.8 *by subtraction;* 128.12 *exclusively;* 233.4 *incomplete;* 122.19 *inferiorly*
short of breath 261.3 *panting*
short of cash 782.2 *insolvent*
short of funds 782.2 *insolvent*
short one 558.2 *drink*
short-order cook 25.2 *cook*
short-order food 557.7 *food*
short pants 551.9 *trousers*
short period 32.6 *chemical element*
short person **149.5**
short plate 25.23 *beef*
short-range 319.5 *transportable*
short rations **687.2**
short run 21.13 *theatrical performance*
shorts 49.3 *basketball equipment;* 552.4 *dishabille;* 149.4 *short thing;* 66.1 *soccer;* 551.9 *trousers;* 551.18 *underwear*
short service line 63.12 *badminton terms*
short shorts 551.9 *trousers*
short shrift 628.1 *pitilessness*
short sight 519.2 *poor sight;* 518.1 *vision*
short-sighted 518.22 *bespectacled;* 519.9 *weak-sighted*
short-sightedness 519.2 *poor sight*
short ski 68.5 *ski equipment*
short sleeve 551.24 *part of garment*
short-sleeved 551.31 *styled*
short-sleeved shirt 551.8 *shirt*
short space of time 278.3 *short duration*
short-staffed 231.2 *incomplete*
short stop 48.2 *baseball player*
short story 17.2, 721.5 *fiction;* 356.5 *work of art*
short-story writer 17.14 *author*
short stuff 149.5 *short person*
short supply 218.9 *scarcity*
short sword 587.8 *sharp weapon*
short temper 625.1 *irascibility*
short-tempered 149.9 *abrupt;* 625.4 *irascible*
short-term 278.6 *transient*
short-term debt 784.1 *debt*
short-term forecast 31.4 *weather forecast*
short-term loan 771.2 *loan*
short thing **149.4**
short time 278.3 *short duration*
short-track 68.13 *ice-skating*
short-track racing 68.8 *speed-skating*
short wave 297.6 *radio frequency;* 692.14 *radio transmission*
short-wave radio 692.16 *transmitter*
short way 147.2 *short distance*
short word 5.17 *word*
short words 695.10 *simplicity*
shorty 149.5 *short person*
short zoom 41.17 *lens*
shot **330.7**; 587.13 *ammunition;* 353.5 *attempt;* 63.12 *badminton terms;* 330.10 *ball;* 508.1 *bang;* 476.3 *conjecture;* 68.10 *curling;* 690.3 *dead drunk;* 691.6 *drug;* 448.1 *experiment;* 47.2 *field events;* 55.3 *fishing tackle;* 51.2 *grip;* 587.6 *historical missile weapon;* 308.14 *holed;* 633.6 *hunter;* 368.9 *injection;* 541.7 *iridescent;* 394.2 *medicine;* 330.8 *missile;* 412.12 *mixed;* 41.3 *photograph;* 49.4 *playing terms;* 181.8 *round;* 330.15 *shooter*
shot across the bows 711.2 *danger signal;* 381.15 *firing*
shot bowl 51.2 *grip*
shot-clock 49.3 *basketball equipment*
shotgun 508.3 *banger;* 330.9, 587.9 *firearm;* 633.3 *hunting and fishing equipment;* 60.3 *hunting equipment*
shotgun formation 46.7 *offence*
shotgun patrol 16.16 *US police*
shotgun wedding 570.5 *wedding*
shot in the dark 476.3 *conjecture;* 107.6 *poor chance*
Shotokai 52.8 *karate*
Shotokan 52.8 *karate*
shot put 47.2 *field events*
shot-put 330.5 *throw*
shot-putter 47.3 *athlete;* 330.14 *thrower*
shot-putting 47.2 *field events*
shots down 51.2 *grip*
shot silk 541.5 *variegated thing*
shots up 51.2 *grip*
shot through with 541.7 *iridescent;* 412.12 *mixed*
shot to pieces 372.16 *apart*
shot up 366.11 *raised*
shot velocity 47.2 *field events*
should 386.8 *be compelled;* 810.14 *be the duty of*
shoulder 340.4 *act;* 331.2 *collide;* 331.1 *impel;* 25.26, 25.27 *lamb;* 25.25 *pork;* 366.3 *promote;* 330.24 *push;* 366.1 *raise;* 482.8 *resolve;* 354.1 *undertake*
shoulder a musket 585.13 *be at war*
shoulder arms 243.8 *prepare oneself*
shoulder bag 410.8 *bag*
shoulder belt 373.10 *band*
shoulder clasping 742.3 *gesture*
shouldered arch 20.5 *arch*
shoulder-guard 58.3 *ice hockey*
shoulder harness 252.4 *safety device*
shoulder-high 154.12 *tall*
shouldering 331.12 *collision*
shouldering responsibility 354.6 *enterprising*
shoulder-length 148.1 *long*
shoulder one's responsibilities 810.16 *do one's duty*
shoulder pad 551.25 *accessories;* 58.5 *lacrosse;* 384.6 *protective clothing*
shoulder responsibility 762.4 *be a substitute*
shoulder sling 62.4 *climbing equipment*
shoulder to shoulder 267.11 *cohesively;* 747.20 *cooperatively;* 750.32 *in alliance*
shoulder-to-shoulder 267.9 *adhesive;* 147.9 *near*
should it be that 222.15 *under the circumstances*
should it so happen 222.15 *under the circumstances*
shout 507.8 *be loud;* 598.5, 598.8 *cheer;* 514.1 *cry;* 514.10 *cry out;* 600.7 *dance;* 711.2 *danger signal;* 726.6 *emphasize;* 600.2 *fanfare;* 507.2 *outcry;* 740.14 *proclaim;* 742.12 *signal;* 729.12 *speak loudly;* 742.6 *word*
shout bravo 669.16 *acclaim*
shout down 660.25 *answer back;* 251.12 *gag;* 659.8 *get angry;* 514.14 *hiss;* 731.9 *out-talk;* 704.8 *refute;* 670.23 *show disapproval;* 730.15 *strike dumb*
shouter 514.9 *crier;* 742.8 *signer*
shout for 514.12 *cheer*
shout for more 669.16 *acclaim*
shout from the rooftops 740.14 *proclaim*
shouting 624.4 *anger;* 507.6 *loud;* 507.2 *outcry;* 742.16 *signalling;* 594.6 *swearing;* 514.16 *vociferous*
shouting from the rooftops 738.14 *manifest*
shout oneself hoarse 514.10 *cry out*
shout out 514.10 *cry out*
shove 331.13 *blow;* 742.3, 742.11 *gesture;* 331.1 *impel;* 64.5 *play rugby;* 330.20 *propel;* 330.1 *propulsion;* 50.19 *punt;* 50.8 *punting;* 330.24, 342.14 *push;* 64.3 *rugby play;* 300.14 *set in motion;* 576.6 *work*
shove around 647.5 *be severe*
shove aside **325.9**; 668.22 *show disrespect*
shovel 203.3 *container;* 369.10 *excavator;* 43.10 *farm tool;* 438.3 *garden tool;* 410.17 *ladle;* 425.9 *sharp-edged thing;* 316.15 *take away;* 425.16 *use a sharp tool;* 438.10 *use tools*
shovel hat 551.15 *headgear*
shovel in 557.22 *eat well*
shovelled 410.20 *containing*
shove off 313.15 *go!;* 371.33 *go away!*
shover 331.15 *ram*
shove shot 65.4 *carom*
shoving 262.3 *hasty;* 330.17 *propulsive*
show **21.7**; **167.3**; 525.11 *appear;* 700.26 *be a hypocrite;* 525.12 *become visible;* 525.2 *being in view;* 518.19, 520.8 *be visible;* 703.15 *demonstrate;* 703.1 *demonstration;* 579.2 *direct;* 739.5 *disclose;* 738.1, 738.6 *display;* 376.31 *exhibition;* 699.14 *façade;* 779.2 *fair;* 656.3 *formal occasion;* 59.7 *horseracing;* 700.3 *hypocrisy;* 743.10 *identify;* 719.8 *interpret;* 716.10 *make evident;* 518.18, 520.10 *make visible;* 520.5 *manifestation;* 699.28 *mask;* 21.4 *musical drama;* 308.18 *open;* 622.9 *ostentation;* 18.27 *performance;* 21.2 *play;* 525.14 *present;* 356.10 *produce;* 738.9 *production;* 4.22 *propound a philosophy;* 454.2 *prove;* 4.21 *rationalize;* 738.3 *reveal;* 717.12 *stand for;*

701.15 *state;* 21.13 *theatrical performance;* 518.7 *view*
showable 738.13 *displayed*
show acuteness 425.17 *be mentally sharp*
show a false face 700.26 *be a hypocrite*
show a false front 700.26 *be a hypocrite;* 699.28 *mask*
show an affinity 229.4 *tend*
show an effect 345.5
show anger 742.11 *gesture*
show apathy for 388.3 *submit*
show appreciation 671.6 *be grateful*
show approval for 595.8 *prefer*
show a profit 765.13 *be profitable*
show aptitude 485.10 *be skilful;* 595.8 *prefer*
show arena 59.9 *jumping*
show a talent for 485.10 *be skilful*
show a tendency 104.8 *be probable;* 229.4 *tend*
show a trend 229.4 *tend*
show authority 397.11 *have authority over*
show a weakness for 595.7 *like*
show bad faith 699.20 *be false*
show benevolence 652.7 *be charitable;* 569.13 *befriend*
show bias 120.6 *be unjust*
showbiz 21.5 *show business*
showboat 21.16 *theatre*
show business 21.5
show candour 250.17 *be informal*
showcase 738.8 *showplace;* 520.7 *that which makes visible;* 527.8 *transparent thing*
show caution 333.2 *hesitate*
show compassion 473.7 *be unselfish;* 649.12 *show mercy*
show compunction 808.4 *be penitent*
show concern 650.8 *be benevolent*
show consideration 650.8 *be benevolent;* 648.3 *be lenient;* 471.14 *be solicitous*
show contempt 661.6 *be insubordinate*
show courage 661.5 *defy*
show courtesies 658.10 *be courteous*
show courtesy 663.6 *show obeisance to*
show determination 228.8
show devotion to 663.5 *obey*
show disapproval 670.23; 753.6 *protest*
show discontent 753.6 *protest*
show displeasure 594.14 *hate*
show disrespect 668.22
show dissatisfaction 753.6 *protest*
show dog 71.9 *dog*
showdown 449.7 *detection;* 739.1 *disclosure*
show empathy 595.7 *like*
show enterprise 354.1 *undertake*
shower 217.5 *about;* 256.6 *bath;* 256.14 *bathe;* 305.3 *downflow;* 305.13 *drip;* 376.22 *flood;* 367.11 *lowering;* 217.8 *plenty;* 31.25, 31.62 *rain;* 581.6 *refresher;* 377.18, 433.33 *sprinkle;* 330.23 *throw;* 367.6 *throw down;* 433.11 *wash*
shower attention on 471.14 *be solicitous*
shower bath 433.11 *wash*
shower gel 256.9 *cleaning agent;* 502.2 *fragrant thing*
shower head 433.11 *wash*
showeriness 429.2 *mistiness;* 31.26 *raininess*
showering 367.20 *falling;* 433.11 *wash*
showerproof 252.7 *invulnerable;* 42.15 *treat;* 42.11 *treated;* 428.10 *waterproof*
shower room 565.7 *room*
shower upon 768.5 *give*
shower with arrows 330.28 *shoot*
showery 429.10 *misty;* 31.53 *rainy*
show false colours 700.32 *disguise*
show favour 768.5 *give*
show favouritism 802.22 *discriminate*
show fear 612.11 *be afraid*
show feelings 591.11 *be sensitive*
show fickleness 642.5 *be capricious*
show fight 342.14 *push;* 384.26 *retaliate*
show fortitude 491.9 *feel pain*
show genius 443.17 *philosophize*
show gentleness 419.15 *be kind*
show girl 21.30 *dancer;* 21.29 *entertainer*
show good faith 663.5 *obey*
show good grounds 714.8 *justify*
show gratitude 671.6 *be grateful*
show greed 773.7 *take*
show hostility 372.12, 670.16, 751.5 *disagree*
show how 703.16 *explain*
show humility 663.6 *show obeisance to*
show ignorance 457.9 *lack intellect*
show ill will 651.16 *be malevolent*
showily 622.35 *ostentatiously*
show impatience 625.6 *be irascible*
show in 370.8
show inconsideration for 472.13 *be thoughtless*
show indifference 473.6 *be disinterested;* 497.7 *be tasteless*
showiness 542.2 *affectation;* 673.6 *boastfulness;* 520.4 *clarity;* 703.2 *demonstrativeness;* 675.1 *tastelessness*
showing 525.7 *appearing;* 525.2 *being in view;* 703.1 *demonstration;* 739.10 *disclosed;* 738.6 *display;* 21.41 *stagestruck;* 518.7 *view;* 520.1 *visible*
showing irascibility 625.5
showing leniency 419.7 *impressionable*
showing off 673.6 *boastfulness;* 703.2 *demonstrativeness;* 738.10 *manifestation;* 467.1 *overestimation*
showing preference 469.14 *selecting*
showing respect 667.9
showing signs of 260.22 *sick*
showing symptoms of 260.22 *sick*
show insolence 661.5 *defy*
show insubordination 662.15 *be disobedient*
show intelligence 425.17 *be mentally sharp*
show interest 644.7 *be curious;* 342.16 *be sociable*
show ire 594.17 *anger*
show its face 739.9 *be disclosed*
show its true colours 739.9 *be disclosed*
show joy 597.7
showjumper 59.15 *horse person*
showjumping 59.11 *eventing;* 59.6 *horsemanship;* 59.9 *jumping*
show kindness 658.10 *be courteous*
show leniency 419.15 *be kind;* 648.3 *be lenient*
show love 658.10 *be courteous*
show loyalty to 267.8 *be tenacious*
showman 703.7 *demonstrator;* 738.12 *displayer;* 21.27 *producer*
showmanship 21.22 *acting;* 676.1 *affectedness;* 21.9 *dramaturgy;* 740.8 *public relations*
show mercy 627.10; 649.12; 758.10 *acquit;* 650.8 *be benevolent;* 648.3 *be lenient;* 749.4 *pacify;* 252.10 *protect*
show moderation 674.14 *be modest*
shown 739.10 *disclosed;* 738.13 *displayed;* 743.12 *identified;* 703.13 *proven*
show no concern for 618.12 *be indifferent*
shown off 738.13 *displayed*
show no fight 388.4 *succumb*
show no flexibility 383.7 *be obstinate;* 628.6 *be pitiless*
show no interest in 473.6 *be disinterested*
show no leniency 628.6 *be pitiless*
show no mercy 628.6 *be pitiless;* 647.5 *be severe*
show no pity 628.6 *be pitiless;* 647.5 *be severe*
show no respect 668.22 *show disrespect*
show no respect for 657.11 *not stand on ceremony*
show no sympathy 628.6 *be pitiless*
shown up 743.12 *identified*
show obeisance to 663.6
show of disapproval 670.9
show off 673.16; 340.4 *act;* 703.18 *appear;* 676.4 *be affected;* 485.11 *be expert;* 622.27 *be ostentatious;* 738.1 *display;* 738.3 *reveal*
show-off 703.7 *demonstrator;* 452.11 *opinionist;* 676.2 *pretender;* 673.7 *vain person;* 675.5 *vulgar person*
show of force 647.2 *suppression*
show of hands 469.10 *vote*
show of respect 667.4 *mark of respect*
show one's Achilles' heel 231.9 *be imperfect*
show one's cards 739.6 *divulge*
show one's colours 638.8 *brace oneself;* 585.12 *go to war*
show one's distaste 637.10 *grudge*
show oneself 738.4; 525.12 *become visible*
show oneself up 812.4 *bring into disrepute*
show one's face 97.12 *attend;* 738.4 *show oneself*
show one's fangs 626.11 *be irritable*
show one's gratitude 813.9 *reward*
show one's hand 739.6 *divulge*
show one's heels 262.2 *make haste*
show one's ignorance 486.5 *be unskilful*
show one's mettle 613.15 *be courageous;* 384.26 *retaliate*
show one's paces 673.16 *show off*
show one's true colours 738.4 *show oneself*
show one's years 556.17 *age*
show partiality 120.6 *be unjust;* 802.22 *discriminate*
show phases 227.11 *be changeable*
show photographs 738.2 *display something*
showpiece 738.7
show pity 627.8 *pity*
showplace 738.8
show poor attention 618.14 *be careless*
show potential 756.10; 334.10 *be powerful*
show prejudice 120.6 *be unjust;* 229.4 *tend*
show promise 302.5 *develop;* 756.10 *show potential*
show readiness 293.7 *be early*
show refinement 658.11 *have good manners*
show reluctance 383.6 *resist*
show resentment 596.5 *dislike*
show resilience 422.8 *be elastic*
show respect 667.18; 797.18 *be good;* 799.6 *be honourable;* 123.8 *make important;* 663.6 *show obeisance to*
show results 246.8 *be effective;* 246.6 *be successful*
showroom 738.8 *showplace*
show round 738.1 *display*
show self-restraint 647.7 *be unadorned;* 251.10 *restrain oneself*
show signs of 104.8 *be probable;* 716.10 *make evident;* 742.10 *signify*
show signs of emotion 590.17 *feel deeply*
show sincerity 698.29 *be truthful*
show skill for 797.19 *be good at*
show someone the door 371.1 *expel;* 364.1 *repel*
show stamina 423.10 *be tough*
show strength 423.10 *be tough*
show stubbornness 228.8 *show determination*
show style 543.4 *be elegant;* 724.9 *style*
show sufficient grounds for 4.21 *rationalize*
show talent 334.10 *be powerful;* 229.4 *tend*
show taste 543.4 *be elegant*
show tenaciousness 360.6 *retain*
show tenderness 419.15 *be kind*
show the door 659.7 *be discourteous;* 144.17 *relegate*
show the flag 585.12 *go to war;* 738.4 *show oneself*
show them what's what 704.8 *refute*
show the ropes 370.10 *introduce*
show the way 579.2 *direct;* 129.15 *precede;* 243.1 *prepare;* 742.9 *use signs*
show the white feather 614.4 *be a coward*
show the white flag 388.3 *submit*
show through 520.9 *appear;* 739.9 *be disclosed;* 527.11 *be transparent;* 518.19 *be visible*
show tolerance 649.12 *show mercy*
show treachery 699.23 *be deceitful*
show unconcern 472.12 *be inattentive*
show understanding 627.8 *pity*
show up 520.9, 525.11 *appear;* 312.1 *arrive;* 97.12 *attend;* 525.12 *become visible;* 449.5 *be discovered;* 738.5 *be visible;* 449.2 *detect;* 739.5 *disclose;* 525.14 *present;* 704.8 *refute;* 738.4 *show oneself*
show up again 112.21 *be repeated*
show up well 738.5 *be visible*
show variety 227.11 *be changeable*
show willing 636.13 *be willing;* 747.13 *work together*
show willingness 342.14 *push*
show wisdom 444.12 *be reasonable*
showy 676.3 *affected;* 520.2 *clear;* 703.10 *demonstrative;* 529.12 *gaudy;* 738.14 *manifest;* 542.10 *ornate;* 622.21 *ostentatious;* 681.2 *unrestrained;* 675.4 *vulgar*
show zeal 342.14 *push*
shrapnel 587.13 *ammunition;* 587.5 *missile weapon*
shred 25.55 *cook;* 357.9 *demolish;* 196.3 *fragment;* 427.25 *grate;* 205.7 *piece;* 355.1 *relinquish;* 372.9 *separate*
shredded 357.15 *destroyed;* 205.11 *partial;* 427.18 *pulverized*
shredder 427.13 *grater*
shredding 357.2 *destroying;* 427.4 *pulverization*
shrew 590.9 *feeling person;* 594.8 *hated person;* 625.3 *irascible person;* 568.8 *nasty woman;* 242.9 *unpleasant person;* 380.4 *violent creature;* 651.9 *vixen*
shrewd 645.4 *cunning;* 442.10, 458.6 *intelligent;* 464.9 *judicious;* 455.8 *knowledgeable;* 425.5 *mentally sharp;* 6.20 *refined;* 485.6 *skilful*
shrewd businessman 665.6 *careful person*
shrewd idea 476.3 *conjecture*
shrewdly 645.6 *cunningly;* 442.15, 458.10 *intelligently;* 425.18 *sharply;* 485.12 *skilfully*
shrewdness 442.4 *cleverness;* 645.1 *cunning;* 425.13 *mental sharpness;* 458.1 *wisdom*
shrewish 625.4 *irascible;* 626.7 *irritable*
shrewishness 625.1 *irascibility*
shriek 507.8 *be loud;* 513.6 *be shrill;* 31.58 *blow;* 514.1 *cry;* 514.6 *cry of pain;* 514.10 *cry out;* 491.12 *express pain;* 507.2 *outcry;* 513.3 *shrillness;* 729.12 *speak loudly*
shrieking 529.12 *gaudy*
shrievalty 16.2 *jurisdiction*
shrift 807.2 *apology;* 649.1 *forgiveness*
shrike 72.6 *songbird*
shrill 513.9; 507.8 *be loud;* 517.7 *dissonant;* 507.6 *loud*
shrillness 513.3; 507.1 *loudness*
shrilly 513.10 *stridently*
shrimp 75.4 *arthropod;* 74.15 *fish;* 633.11 *hunt;* 159.4 *little person;* 25.19 *shellfish;* 149.5 *short person*
shrimp balls 25.48 *Chinese dish*
shrimper 74.7 *fishing;* 633.6 *hunter*
shrimplike 75.18 *arthropodous*
shrimp loaf 25.11 *sandwich*
shrine 10.13; 583.6 *grave;* 744.11 *monument;* 10.11 *place of worship*
shrink 614.4 *be a coward;* 612.11 *be afraid;* 191.6 *become smaller;* 612.12 *be fearful;* 732.6 *be shy;* 214.4 *decrease;* 245.1 *deteriorate;* 394.15 *healer;* 766.12 *lessen;* 191.5 *make smaller;* 36.30, 461.10 *psychiatrist;* 303.6 *shrink back;* 634.4 *shy*
shrinkability 191.2 *contractibility*
shrinkable 191.9 *contractible*
shrinkage 191.1 *contraction;* 214.1 *decrease;* 766.4 *lessening;* 212.1 *subtraction*
shrink back 303.6; 674.15 *escape notice*
shrinker 634.17 *avoider*
shrink from 594.14 *hate;* 596.6 *react against;* 637.7, 709.5 *refuse*
shrink from public gaze 674.15 *escape notice*
shrinking 634.18 *avoiding;* 637.3 *cautious;* 191.8 *contracting;* 191.1 *contraction;* 214.1 *decrease;* 637.13 *dissociation;* 151.9 *narrowing;* 674.11, 732.1 *shy;* 634.12 *shyness*
shrinking violet 78.9 *figurative usage;* 623.16 *humble person;* 674.7, 728.11 *modest person;* 591.9 *oversensitive person;* 488.4 *someone or something that feels*
shrink-wrapped 252.7 *invulnerable*
shrive 649.9 *forgive;* 10.18 *perform rites*
shrivel 556.17 *age;* 191.6 *become smaller;* 493.14 *be hot;* 214.4 *decrease;* 245.1 *deteriorate;* 428.21 *dry up;* 191.5 *make smaller;* 441.1 *waste*
shrivelled 556.14 *aged;* 428.3 *dried-up;* 153.2 *emaciated;* 563.3 *infertile;* 159.7 *little;* 191.7 *smaller*
shrivelled-up 191.7 *smaller*
shrivelling 191.8 *contracting;* 191.1 *contraction*
shrivel up 191.6 *become smaller*
shriven 649.6 *forgiven*
shrive oneself 807.6 *apologize*
shriving 649.4 *forgiving*
Shropshire Hills 89.5 *British mountains*
shroud 550.5 *body covering;* 736.8 *conceal;* 550.2 *cover;* 551.32 *dress;* 583.4 *funeral objects;* 551.17 *grave clothes;* 550.31 *hide;* 523.14 *make dark;* 524.10 *make dim;* 50.3 *parts of a sailing boat;* 252.10 *protect;* 523.6 *shade;* 373.7 *tackle;* 521.6 *that which*

makes invisible; 550.25 *wrap;* 550.4 *wrapping*
shrouded 550.37 *protected*
shrouded in mystery 696.2 *unexplained;* 696.1 *unintelligible*
shroud in mystery 696.8 *make unintelligible*
Shrove Tuesday 10.15 *holy day*
shrub 44.9 *garden plant;* 77.2 *plant;* 79.1 *tree*
shrubbery 44.3 *ornamental garden*
shrubby 44.17 *botanical;* 79.14 *treelike*
shrug 742.11 *gesture*
shrugged-off 728.19 *downplayed*
shrugging off 728.9 *downplaying*
shrug off 618.12 *be indifferent;* 758.12 *exempt oneself;* 728.22 *play down;* 124.12 *think unimportant;* 468.3 *underestimate*
shrug one's shoulders 456.9 *be ignorant;* 388.3 *submit*
shrunk 159.7 *little;* 191.7 *smaller*
shrunken 159.7 *little;* 191.7 *smaller*
shrunken head 794.2 *spoils*
shrunkenness 191.1 *contraction;* 159.1 *littleness*
shruti 7.12 *religious text*
shtook 264.7 *awkward situation*
shtoom 732.1 *shy;* 730.11 *speechless*
shuck 550.13 *casing;* 80.3 *fruit structure*
shudder 612.11 *be afraid;* 494.10 *be cold;* 327.23 *jolt;* 596.6 *react against;* 327.7, 327.24 *shake*
shudder at 594.14 *hate*
shuddering 327.6 *shaking;* 327.18 *shaky;* 596.4 *sign of dislike*
shuffle 114.8 *be diverse;* 69.3 *card game terms;* 22.2, 22.15 *dance;* 408.21 *disorder;* 479.2 *equivocate;* 699.27 *evade;* 759.1, 759.5 *exchange;* 300.12 *gait;* 742.11 *gesture;* 762.6 *give a substitute;* 412.9 *mix up;* 69.10 *play;* 702.13 *quibble;* 325.9 *shove aside;* 333.10 *slow motion;* 702.2 *sophism;* 762.1 *substitution;* 316.11 *transfer;* 639.5 *vacillate;* 300.15 *walk*
shuffle along 333.1 *move slowly*
shuffled 408.12 *disordered;* 412.12 *mixed*
shuffle off 634.8 *run away*
shuffler 22.5 *dancer*
shuffle the cards 224.10 *exchange;* 243.4 *prepare for action*
shuffling 479.11 *equivocating;* 699.13 *evasion;* 699.38 *evasive;* 759.1 *exchange;* 702.4, 702.9 *quibbling;* 333.4 *slow*
shufty 518.6 *look*
Shukokai 52.8 *karate*
shul 10.11 *place of worship*
shun 634.1 *avoid;* 736.11 *conceal oneself;* 128.7 *exclude;* 655.13 *ignore;* 596.6 *react against*
shun alcohol 684.5 *be self-restrained*
shun company 655.12 *be unsocial*
shunned 128.11 *excluded;* 655.10 *lonely;* 350.3 *not wanted*
shunning 634.19 *abstaining;* 634.10 *avoidance;* 128.1 *exclusion*
shunt 144.14 *displace;* 144.1 *displacement;* 320.21 *miscellaneous motoring terms;* 330.21 *move forward;* 330.1 *propulsion;* 325.9 *shove aside;* 316.15 *take away*
shunted 144.8 *displaced*
shunter 321.4 *locomotive*
shun the limelight 674.15 *escape notice*
shunting engine 321.4 *locomotive*
shunting yard 317.10 *railway*
shush 512.4 *hiss*
shushing 512.1 *hiss*
shut 309.7 *close;* 309.12 *closed;* 165.5 *enclose*
shutdown 309.1 *closure;* 247.10 *failed;* 247.1 *failure;* 226.2 *stop;* 343.6 *unemployment*
shut down 226.8 *cause to cease;* 131.16 *cease;* 309.14 *closed down;* 309.9 *close down;* 247.6 *fail;* 343.14 *make inactive;* 226.7 *stop working*
shut-eye 263.1 *ease;* 343.9 *sleep*
shut in 165.5 *enclose;* 260.22 *sick*
shut-in 251.7 *charge;* 309.6 *closed-in person;* 251.15 *detained;* 165.7 *enclosed;* 335.5 *powerless person;* 301.5 *sedentary;* 301.7 *sedentary person;* 260.19 *sick person*
shut-in personality 36.8 *disordered personality*
shut off 489.11 *be unfeeling*
shut oneself off 489.11 *be unfeeling*
shut oneself up 655.12 *be unsocial*
shut one's eyes to 519.16 *be blind to*
shut one's trap 736.12 *be silent*
shut out 128.7 *exclude;* 128.11 *excluded;* 655.13 *ignore*
shut-out 48.4 *pitching terms*
shutter 550.2 *cover;* 41.18 *exposure time;* 523.14 *make dark;* 528.7 *opaque thing;* 521.6 *that which makes invisible*
shutter priority 41.18 *exposure time*
shutter release 41.18 *exposure time*
shutters 523.6 *shade*
shutter speed 41.18 *exposure time*
shut the door on 128.7 *exclude;* 655.13 *ignore;* 399.3 *veto*
shutting down 226.2 *stop*
shutting up 226.2 *stop*
shuttle 63.11 *badminton equipment;* 227.11 *be changeable;* 298.7 *be regular;* 759.5 *exchange;* 193.8 *interweave;* 326.8 *oscillate;* 326.7 *oscillator;* 761.4, 761.8 *return;* 29.30 *spacecraft;* 42.4, 193.3 *weaving*
shuttlecock 63.10 *badminton;* 63.11 *badminton equipment;* 326.8 *oscillate;* 326.7 *oscillator*
shuttle movement 298.1 *regularity*
shuttle service 326.1 *oscillation;* 298.5 *regular thing*
shuttlewise 326.18 *to and fro*
shuttling 761.4 *return*
shut up 736.12 *be silent;* 226.8 *cause to cease;* 226.6 *cease;* 309.7 *close;* 309.12 *closed;* 309.10 *enclose;* 309.15 *enclosed;* 506.6 *hush!;* 655.13 *ignore;* 226.12 *stop!*
shut up shop 131.16 *cease;* 226.7 *stop working*
shut your face 226.12 *stop!*
shut your trap 226.12 *stop!*
Shwe Dagon 10.13 *shrine*
shy **634.4**; **655.9**; **674.11**; **732.1**; 634.18 *avoiding;* 378.11 *be inhibited;* 630.12 *be surprised;* 637.3 *cautious;* 453.3 *confused;* 614.3 *cowardly;* 596.8 *disliking;* 639.6 *hesitate;* 378.15 *inhibitive;* 646.1 *naive;* 795.9 *pure;* 145.9 *reserved;* 251.14 *self-restrained;* 303.6 *shrink back;* 325.8 *sidestep;* 381.7 *stone;* 330.5, 330.23 *throw*
shy away 252.9 *be safe;* 637.7 *refuse;* 303.6 *shrink back*
shy away from 709.5 *refuse*
shying 59.9 *jumping*
Shylock 771.3 *lender;* 786.6 *nonpayer;* 792.5 *overcharger*
shyly **634.23**; **674.18**; **732.8**; 596.10 *discontentedly;* 378.18 *inhibitively;* 145.11 *reservedly;* 655.14 *unsocially;* 251.17 *with self-restraint*
Shyness 732
shyness **634.12**; **655.2**; **674.4**; **732.3**; 453.12 *confusion;* 384.4 *defensiveness;* 637.13 *dissociation;* 378.5 *inhibition;* 145.4 *reserve;* 251.3 *self-restraint;* 596.4 *sign of dislike*
shy of 233.4 *incomplete*
shy off 325.8 *sidestep*
shy person **732.5**; 728.11 *modest person*
shyster 700.17 *cheat;* 800.4 *dishonourable person;* 702.6 *sophist*
SI 26.12 *metrical*
sial 30.18 *earth's crust*
sialagogue 371.29 *expulsive*
sialic 30.53 *solid-earth*
sialogogic 559.6 *inducing secretion*
sialoid 559.5 *of a secretion*
sialorrhoea 560.9 *saliva*
Siamese twin 111.3 *lookalike*
Siamese twins 198.6 *twins*
Siberia 494.6 *Arctic;* 145.3 *distant place;* 655.4 *place of confinement*
Siberian 494.8 *cold;* 31.55 *cool*
sibilance 512.1 *hiss*
sibilant 512.3 *hisser;* 512.6 *hissing;* 730.12 *inarticulate;* 5.41 *lettered;* 5.16 *spoken letter*
sibilantly 512.8
sibilate 512.4 *hiss;* 729.13 *speak in a particular way*
sibilation 512.1 *hiss;* 507.1 *loudness;* 730.3 *speech defect*
sibyl 11.13 *diviner;* 445.5 *intuitive person;* 475.8 *oracle;* 458.3 *wise man*
sibyllic 475.13 *predicting*
sibylline 11.17 *divinatory;* 475.13 *predicting*
Sibylline books 475.8 *oracle*
Sibyl of Cumae 296.2 *old people*
sic 698.38 *literally*
siccant 428.9 *drying*
siccative 19.11 *artist's materials;* 428.15 *dryer;* 428.9 *drying*
siccity 428.11 *dryness*
Sicilian Vespers 382.4 *slaughter*
sick **260.22**; **538.6**; 798.8 *afflicted;* 497.6 *coarse;* 690.4 *crapulous;* 461.13 *mentally ill;* 371.23, 371.30 *vomiting*
sick and tired of 261.2, 620.5 *bored;* 596.8 *disliking*
sick bay 394.14 *hospital*
sickbed 394.14 *hospital;* 260.2 *illness*
sicken 219.4 *be excessive;* 364.4 *be repulsive;* 260.24 *be unhealthy;* 337.6 *be weak;* 596.7 *cause dislike;* 245.1 *deteriorate;* 499.9 *disgust;* 242.10 *displease;* 606.6 *dissatisfy*
sicken at 596.5 *dislike*
sickened 596.8 *disliking;* 371.30 *vomiting*
sickened with 232.8 *full*
sickening 596.9 *disliked;* 219.6 *excessive;* 371.29 *expulsive;* 236.4 *poor;* 364.8 *repulsive;* 241.2 *unpleasant*
sick headache 491.2 *painful condition*
sick humour 599.3 *wit*
sickie 98.5 *leave of absence*
sickiness 260.1 *ill health*
sickle 43.10 *farm tool;* 438.3 *garden tool;* 425.9 *sharp-edged thing;* 425.16 *use a sharp tool*
sick leave 15.2 *industrial negotiations;* 98.5 *leave of absence;* 757.2 *permit*
sickle-cell anaemia 260.11 *blood disease*
sickle-cell disease 260.11 *blood disease*
sickliness 337.3 *poor health;* 498.1 *sweetness*
sick list 220.6 *list of names*
sickly 530.8 *drained of colour;* 337.10 *ill;* 498.6 *sweet;* 260.21 *unhealthy*
sickly hue 529.9 *complexion*
sickly-sweet 498.6 *sweet*
sick mind 461.1 *insanity*
sickness 798.2 *affliction;* 690.15 *crapulence;* 260.1 *ill health;* 260.2 *illness;* 236.10 *poverty;* 371.23 *vomiting*
sickness benefit 392.4 *social assistance*
sicko 461.7 *insane person*
sick of 261.2, 620.5 *bored;* 596.8 *disliking*
sick person **260.19**; 316.9 *disease carrier;* 35.18 *patient;* 335.5 *powerless person;* 337.4 *weakling*
sickroom 394.14 *hospital;* 6.15 *schoolroom*
sick unto death 582.18 *dying*
sick up 371.15 *vomit*
sick with disappointment 604.9 *disappointed*
sic transit gloria mundi 278.2 *transient thing*
siddur 10.10 *religious manual*
Side 169
side **169.1**; **169.6**; 169.7 *be alongside;* 65.2 *billiards play;* 622.10, 673.6 *boastfulness;* 525.3 *external appearance;* 27.37 *line;* 25.25 *pork;* 325.8 *sidestep;* 169.9 *side with;* 143.1 *situation;* 27.38 *surface;* 316.15 *take away;* 53.4 *team*
side arms 587.2 *arms*
sideband 692.14 *radio transmission*
sideboard 23.5, 410.3 *cabinet*
sideboards 58.3 *ice hockey;* 169.1 *side*
side boundary line 63.12 *badminton terms*
side by side 147.14 *beside;* 267.11 *cohesively;* 223.22 *hand in hand;* 188.7 *in parallel*
side-by-side 267.9 *adhesive;* 147.10 *juxtaposed;* 169.10 *laterally;* 147.9 *near*
sidecar class 61.5 *motorcycle racing*
side chair 23.2 *chair*
sidecut 68.4 *skiing technique*
sidecutting 68.12 *ski;* 68.4 *skiing technique*
side direction 169.3
side-dish **223.5**; 25.9 *dish;* 557.14 *mouthful*
side door 314.6 *means of entry;* 317.2 *route;* 169.1 *side*
side effect 211.3 *additional item;* 37.3 *drug;* 345.1 *effect;* 345.2 *visible effect*
side elevation 169.1 *side*
side entrance 317.2 *route;* 169.1 *side*
side-glance 593.14 *communication of love;* 593.6 *courtship*
side horse 57.6 *pommel horse*
side-impact bar 320.21 *miscellaneous motoring terms*
side issue 211.3 *additional item*
side judge 46.2 *football player*
sidekick 569.5 *friend;* 392.11 *helper;* 122.6 *inferior;* 595.4 *likable person;* 387.3 *subordinate;* 413.8 *supporter*
side kick 52.9 *tae kwon do*
side ladder 304.9 *ladder*
sidelight 522.6 *electric light;* 50.3 *parts of a sailing boat*
sidelights 524.1 *dimness*
sideline 164.1 *edge;* 164.8 *edging;* 64.1 *rugger;* 46.4 *stadium*
side-line crew 46.2 *football player*
sidelong 189.5 *devious;* 189.9 *deviously;* 189.4 *oblique;* 169.6 *side;* 518.26 *watchfully*
sidelong look 518.6 *look*
side of a coin 169.2 *surface*
side of bacon 25.30 *bacon*
side of the face 169.1 *side*
side-path 317.6 *path*
side penthouse 63.5 *real tennis*
side pressure 480.2 *flattery*
side rail 65.4 *carom*
side reaction 32.14 *chemical reaction*
sidereal 29.36 *astronomical*
sidereally 29.39 *astronomically*
sidereal time 281.3 *chronology;* 275.9 *time zone*
siderite 363.3 *magnet;* 29.20 *meteor*
side road 320.2 *road*
siderolite 29.20 *meteor*
sideromancer 11.13 *diviner*
sideromancy 11.9 *divination*
side saddle 59.14 *horse-riding terms*
side salad 25.14 *salad*
side scene 21.19 *stage set*
sideshow 21.7 *show;* 124.8 *trifle*
sideslip 325.15 *deviating motion;* 322.5 *flight;* 320.21 *miscellaneous motoring terms;* 68.14 *ski;* 68.4 *skiing technique;* 305.14, 325.10 *slide*
sideslipping 68.12 *ski;* 68.4 *skiing technique*
sidespin 56.3 *golf shots*
side-splitting 599.9 *funny;* 600.10 *laughing;* 272.5 *ridiculous*
sidestep **325.8**; 479.1 *be equivocal;* 634.7 *be evasive;* 68.2 *cross-country skiing;* 325.15 *deviating motion;* 634.15 *evasiveness;* 169.8 *move sideways;* 68.14 *ski;* 68.4 *skiing technique*
sidestepper 634.17 *avoider*
sidestepping 68.12 *ski;* 68.4 *skiing technique*
side street 317.3 *road*
sidestroke 67.1 *swimming*
side table 23.4 *table*
side tank 321.5 *locomotive part*
side to side 326.18 *to and fro*
sidetrack 270.2 *circumlocution;* 317.10 *railway;* 325.9 *shove aside;* 325.8 *sidestep;* 321.2 *track*
sidetracked 270.4 *circumlocutory*
side up to 169.7 *be alongside*
side view 169.1 *side*
sidewalk 317.6 *path;* 550.11 *paving*
sideward 300.17 *directional*
sideward motion 300.5 *circuition*
sidewards 169.10 *laterally*
sideways 150.8 *breadthwise;* 325.28 *indirectly;* 169.10 *laterally;* 189.4 *oblique;* 189.8 *obliquely;* 518.26 *watchfully*
sideways look 518.6 *look*
side whiskers 169.1 *side*
sidewinder 331.14 *sporting hit*
sidewise 169.10 *laterally*
side with **169.9**; **469.3**; 392.24 *back;* 750.22 *form an alliance*
siding 317.10 *railway;* 169.1 *side;* 321.2 *track;* 23.12 *wood*
sidle 169.8 *move sideways;* 325.8 *sidestep*
siege **381.14**; 251.11 *detain;* 251.4 *detention*
siege cap 384.7 *armour*
siegecraft 585.6 *art of war;* 584.1 *military affairs*
siege gun 587.11 *guns*
sieges 585.8 *warfare*
Siegfried Line 384.9 *barrier;* 147.7 *interface*
sierra 89.1 *mountain;* 154.4 *mountain range;* 420.8 *rough ground*
Sierra Nevada Mountains 89.4 *US mountains*
siesta 290.4 *afternoon;* 343.9 *sleep*
sieve 409.15 *categorize;* 256.10 *cleaning object;* 308.6 *porous thing;* 308.21 *provide passage for;* 255.10, 256.15 *purify*
sievelike 308.14 *holed*

sift 409.15 *categorize*; 469.4 *pick*; 255.10, 256.15 *purify*; 407.19 *systematize*
sifted 409.24 *categorized*; 427.18 *pulverized*
sifting 409.5 *categorization*
sift out 409.15 *categorize*
sigh 31.58 *blow*; 593.26 *court*; 514.13 *cry*; 514.6 *cry of pain*; 742.3, 742.11 *gesture*; 602.8 *grieve*; 603.2 *lament*; 626.2 *sign of sullenness*; 511.8 *sound faint*; 730.16 *speak in a low voice*; 729.13 *speak in a particular way*; 603.7 *weep*; 730.4 *whispering*
sighing 593.6 *courtship*; 514.18 *crying*; 511.4 *faint sound*; 742.15 *gestural*; 730.12 *inarticulate*
sight 312.3 *approach*; 554.4 *biological function*; 449.1 *discover*; 449.6 *discovery*; 587.9 *firearm*; 518.12 *see*; 488.1 *sensation*; 525.4 *something that appears*; 518.7 *view*; 520.6 *visible thing*; 518.1 *vision*; 619.4 *wonder*
sight a coastline 92.12 *be marooned*
sighted 518.21 *seeing*
sight for sore eyes 518.7 *view*
sight hole 518.9 *viewpoint*
sight in 60.7 *shoot*
sighting 449.6 *discovery*
sighting-in 60.2 *hunting*
sight land 323.10 *sail*
sightless 519.8 *blind*
sightlessness 519.1 *blindness*
sightline 520.3 *visibility*
sightly 525.10 *aspectual*
sight on 324.7 *take a direction*
sight quarry 60.7 *shoot*
sight screen 53.2 *ground*; 518.10 *visual aid*
sightsee 644.7 *be curious*; 518.12 *see*
sightseeing 644.5 *curious*
sightseer 644.3 *curious person*; 518.11 *observer*
sight unseen 521.9 *invisibly*
sigil 743.3 *means of identification*
sigillary 743.12 *identified*
sigla 742.1 *sign*
sigma 512.3 *hisser*
Sign 742
sign 742.1; 505.8 *be deaf*; 397.1 *command*; 223.4 *concomitant*; 750.28 *consent*; 755.5 *contract*; 742.11 *gesture*; 730.14 *have difficulty speaking*; 743.11 *identify oneself*; 5.13 *letter*; 520.10 *make visible*; 738.10 *manifestation*; 743.3 *means of identification*; 194.1 *number*; 475.5 *omen*; 757.3 *permit*; 738.8 *showplace*; 260.3 *symptom*; 520.7 *that which makes visible*; 719.12 *translate*; 742.9 *use signs*; 454.1 *verify*; 520.6 *visible thing*; 711.1 *warning*; 619.4 *wonder*; 5.47 *word*
sign a confession 16.80 *convict oneself*
sign a decree 397.9 *command*
signal 281.10; **742.4**; **742.12**; 693.7 *advice*; 397.1, 397.9 *command*; 692.30 *communicate*; 520.10 *make visible*; 738.14 *manifest*; 738.10 *manifestation*; 5.5 *nonstandard language*; 123.6 *notable*; 317.10 *railway*; 742.1 *sign*; 692.27 *signalling*; 39.14 *terminal*; 693.14 *tip*; 321.2 *track*; 742.9 *use signs*; 520.6 *visible thing*; 711.1 *warning*
signal battalion 584.4 *military organization*
signal box 317.10 *railway*; 321.2 *track*
signal-caller 46.7 *offence*
signal fire 522.8 *fire*
signalize 601.16 *commemorate*; 742.10 *signify*
signalizing 742.14 *signifying*
signal lamp 742.4 *signal*
signalled 317.15 *accessible*; 692.34 *communicated*
signaller 742.8 *signer*; 711.4 *warner*
signalling 692.27; **742.16**; 692.1 *communications*; 742.4 *signal*; 742.14 *signifying*; 730.6 *silent speech*
signalman 321.9 *railway worker*
sign a loan agreement 772.7 *borrow*
signal rocket 742.4 *signal*
signals 46.8 *huddle*
signal-to-noise ratio 39.14 *terminal*
sign an affidavit 707.18 *vow*
sign a pact 755.5 *contract*
sign a petition 710.6 *request*
sign a promissory note 756.8 *guarantee*
sign a round robin 710.6 *request*
signatory 755.4 *contractor*; 743.12 *identified*; 756.5 *promise-maker*; 742.8 *signer*; 454.7 *verifier*
sign a treaty 755.5 *contract*
sign a truce 749.5 *make peace*
signature 755.1 *contract*; 454.6 *evidence*; 744.4 *inscription*; 18.20 *key*; 743.3 *means of identification*; 721.8 *name*; 18.17 *notation*; 126.2 *original*; 757.2 *permit*; 253.2 *promise*; 742.1 *sign*
signature tune 516.1 *melody*
signboard 743.3 *means of identification*; 520.6 *visible thing*
signed 520.2 *clear*; 750.17 *consenting*; 755.7 *contractual*; 756.13 *guaranteeing*; 743.12 *identified*; 27.71 *numerical*
signed agreement 354.3 *contract*
signed number 27.5 *number*
signed sealed and delivered 755.7 *contractual*
signed up 586.35 *martial*
signer 742.8; 755.4 *contractor*; 756.5 *promise-maker*
signet 755.1 *contract*; 743.3 *means of identification*
signet ring 743.5 *uniform*
signficantly 742.18 *indicatively*
significance 345.4; **694.2**; 27.61 *correlation*; 123.1, 643.6 *importance*; 395.1 *influence*; 348.1 *instrumentality*; 446.4 *purpose*; 726.2 *seriousness*
significance level 27.54 *hypothesis testing*
significance test 27.54 *hypothesis testing*
significant 694.7; 344.13, 348.7 *causal*; 716.8 *evidential*; 123.5, 643.3 *important*; 395.11 *influential*; 346.12 *operative*; 475.15 *presageful*; 446.12 *purposive*; 726.5 *serious*
significant digits 27.8 *number system*
significant figures 27.8 *number system*
significant form 160.1 *form*; 19.4 *treatment*
significantly 716.14 *as evidence*; 344.14 *causally*; 123.9 *importantly*; 395.14 *influentially*; 348.9 *instrumentally*; 694.13 *meaningfully*; 346.13 *operationally*; 475.16 *predictively*; 446.21 *purposively*
signification 694.1 *meaning*; 742.1 *sign*
significative 694.6 *meaningful*; 742.14 *signifying*
signify 742.10; 123.7 *be important*; 446.19 *epitomize*; 694.10 *mean*; 475.11 *predict*; 139.24 *specify*; 701.15 *state*
signifying 742.14; 475.13 *predicting*
signify little 124.11 *be unimportant*
sign in 312.5 *get in*
signing 505.1 *deafness*; 742.15 *gestural*; 742.3 *gesture*; 730.6 *silent speech*
signing on 341.3 *inactive*; 343.2 *not working*
sign language 729.4 *articulation*; 5.8 *artificial language*; 505.1 *deafness*; 742.3 *gesture*; 730.6 *silent speech*
sign-language reader 719.6 *interpreter*
sign-language reading 719.4 *translation*
sign-maker 742.8 *signer*
sign of alarm 711.2 *danger signal*
sign of anger 624.6
sign of courtesy 658.5
sign of dislike 596.4
sign of disrespect 668.7
sign off 313.2 *withdraw*
sign of illness 742.1 *sign*; 260.3 *symptom*
sign of irascibility 625.2
sign of irritableness 626.4
sign of politeness 658.5 *sign of courtesy*
sign of sullenness 626.2
sign of the Cross 10.5 *Christian rite*
sign of the times 742.1 *sign*; 229.1 *tendency*
sign of wonderment 619.2
sign on 782.12 *be poor*; 314.14 *enrol*; 368.7 *install*
sign one's death warrant 16.79 *convict*
sign one's name 742.9 *use signs*
sign one's score card 56.7 *golf*
signor 567.3 *male title of address*
signora 568.3 *female title of address*
signorina 568.3 *female title of address*
sign out 313.2 *withdraw*
sign painter 19.16 *artist*
sign painting 19.2 *painting*
signpost 324.6 *direct*; 742.5 *indicator*; 520.10 *make visible*; 324.3 *orientation*; 742.1 *sign*; 520.7 *that which makes visible*; 742.9 *use signs*; 520.6 *visible thing*
signposted 317.15 *accessible*; 520.2 *clear*; 324.14 *directed*
signs 452.13 *confirmation*; 742.1 *sign*
signs of guilt 806.2
signs of the times 475.5 *omen*; 711.1 *warning*
sign the death warrant 382.19 *execute*
sign the pledge 689.4 *give up alcohol*
sign up 220.9 *enlist*; 368.7 *install*; 354.1 *undertake*
sike 90.1 *river*
Sikh 7.6 *non-Christian*
silage 43.9 *animal feedstuff*; 557.8 *animal food*; 439.4 *storage*
silage clamp 43.10 *farm tool*
silaging 43.5 *cultivation*
sild 25.18 *sea fish*
Silence 506
silence 506.2; **506.4**; **736.4**; 357.8 *destroy*; 251.12 *gag*; 732.4 *guarded speech*; 506.6 *hush!*; 343.5 *inactivity*; 505.10 *muffle*; 511.7 *mute*; 730.5 *mutism*; 358.1 *obliterate*; 335.8 *overpower*; 704.8 *refute*; 301.2 *repose*; 737.1 *secrecy*; 619.2 *sign of wonderment*; 730.15 *strike dumb*
silenced 511.2 *nonresonant*; 730.11 *speechless*; 619.7 *wide-eyed*
silencer 511.6; 505.3 *inaudibility*; 730.8 *mute*
silencing 357.1 *destruction*
silent 506.3; **736.16**; 268.11 *lubricated*; 301.6 *quiescent*; 737.10 *secretive*; 655.9 *shy*; 732.2 *sparing with words*; 730.11 *speechless*; 655.8 *unsociable*; 730.9 *voiceless*; 619.7 *wide-eyed*
silent about 128.10 *excluding*
silent as the grave 506.3 *silent*
silent as the tomb 506.3 *silent*
silent discharge 39.6 *electric discharge*
silently 506.5; 732.8 *shyly*; 655.14 *unsocially*; 730.17 *voicelessly*
silent reproach 670.10 *disapproving look*
silent service 586.22 *navy*
silent speech 730.6
Silenus 690.17 *drunkard*
silhouette 532.9 *black thing*; 523.4 *dark thing*; 19.20 *draw*; 19.9 *drawing*; 525.3 *external appearance*; 160.1, 160.7 *form*; 717.6 *image*; 523.14 *make dark*; 41.4 *portrait*; 525.14 *present*; 608.6 *profile*; 163.2 *shadow*
silica 418.7 *hard substance*; 24.2 *raw material*
silicate 30.34 *mineral*
silicic 32.34 *elemental*
silicon 33.15 *essential element*; 39.4 *semiconductor*
silicon chip 39.13 *circuit*; 159.2 *little thing*
silicone 268.5 *lubricant*
silicone rubber 422.4 *rubber*
Silicon Valley 86.8 *regions of the US*
silicosis 260.9 *respiratory disease*
silicula 80.2 *botanical fruit*
siliqua 80.2 *botanical fruit*
silk 404.2 *grain*; 435.1 *materials*; 42.12 *natural*; 421.8 *smooth thing*; 419.11 *soft thing*; 76.6 *spinner*; 193.4 *textile*
silken 42.12 *natural*; 490.6 *pleasant*; 419.3, 421.1 *smooth*
silken repose 301.2 *repose*
silk gland 76.6 *spinner*
silk hat 551.15 *headgear*
silkily 419.17 *softly*; 404.15 *texturally*
silkiness 404.2 *grain*; 419.9, 421.7 *smoothness*
silks 551.5 *fancy dress*; 59.7 *horseracing*
silk-screen printing 19.1 *art*
silk stockings 551.20 *legwear*
silkworm 76.5 *larva*; 76.6 *spinner*; 75.6 *worm*
silky 42.12 *natural*; 404.9, 419.3, 421.1 *smooth*
sill 175.2 *foot*; 30.30 *igneous rock*
siller 780.1 *money*
silliness 459.1 *folly*; 697.3 *tomfoolery*
silly 459.5 *foolish*; 697.5 *nonsensical*; 53.14 *positioned*; 157.2 *superficial*; 457.6 *unintelligent*; 486.1 *unskilful*
silly idiot 457.3 *unintelligent person*
silly mid on 53.4 *team*
silly point 53.4 *team*
silly question 705.5 *easy question*
silly season 292.1 *season*; 697.3 *tomfoolery*
silo 43.7 *farm building*; 587.5 *missile weapon*; 359.2 *preserver*; 439.4 *storage*; 410.11 *vessel*
silt 215.2 *residue*; 30.27 *sediment*; 30.36 *soil*; 316.10 *transferred thing*
silt up 157.7 *make shallow*
silty 30.58 *earthy*
Silurian period 284.3 *geological period*
Silver 59.1 *horse*
silver 780.16 *bullion*; 780.4 *change*; 550.24 *coat*; 529.15 *colour*; 533.1, 533.8 *grey*; 533.5 *grey thing*; 780.1 *money*; 47.9 *track*; 531.1 *white*; 531.13 *whiten*; 531.9 *white thing*
silver bullet 11.6 *talisman*
silver coating 28.29 *optical element*
silver coinage 780.13 *coinage*
silver cup 743.4 *insignia*; 482.6 *objective*; 794.1 *trophy*
silver dollar 780.8 *American money*
silvered 533.1 *grey*; 531.1 *white*
silver frost 31.29 *hail*
Silver Goblets 50.5 *Henley trophies*
silver-grey 533.1 *grey*
silver halide 41.11 *emulsion*
silveriness 531.7 *whiteness*
silver inlay 23.9 *decorative woodwork*
silver jubilee 601.5 *anniversary*; 298.6 *annually celebrated day*; 201.8 *twenty and over*
silver leaf 44.12 *pests and diseases*
silver lining 610.1 *hope*
silver medal 47.5 *competition*; 57.1 *gymnastics*; 743.4 *insignia*; 794.1 *trophy*
silver-medal 123.6 *notable*
silver medallist 47.3, 336.5 *athlete*; 485.4 *skilled person*
silver plate 550.3 *coating*; 743.4 *insignia*; 482.6 *objective*
silverpoint drawing 19.9 *drawing*
silver polish 421.10 *polish*
silver print 41.12 *development*
silver salmon 55.4 *American game fish*
silverside 25.22 *beef*
silversmith 578.2 *artisan*
silver-toned 516.6 *melodious*
silver-tongued 729.20 *eloquent*
silver-tongued orator 733.6 *public speaker*
silver vault 439.4 *storage*
silver wedding 601.5 *anniversary*
silver wedding anniversary 298.6 *annually celebrated day*
silvery 533.1 *grey*; 516.6 *melodious*; 531.1 *white*
silvical 79.17 *arboricultural*
silvicultural 79.17 *arboricultural*; 44.16 *horticultural*
silviculturally 79.20 *arboriculturally*
silviculture 79.5 *forestry*; 44.1 *horticulture*; 77.10 *plant science*
silviculturist 79.8 *forester*
sima 30.18 *earth's crust*
simian 71.34 *primate*
similar 115.7; 750.14 *conforming*; 110.6 *correlative*; 119.6 *equal*; 111.13 *equivalent*; 108.5 *interrelated*; 694.6 *meaningful*; 717.13 *representational*
Similarity 115
similarity 115.1; 750.1 *accord*; 117.1, 750.5 *conformity*; 110.3 *correlation*; 111.2 *equivalence*; 525.5 *impression*; 108.2 *interrelatedness*; 108.1 *relatedness*; 717.1 *representation*
similar look 115.1 *similarity*
similarly 115.13; 110.11 *correlatively*; 119.12 *equally*; 108.10 *relevantly*; 222.15 *under the circumstances*; 750.34 *uniformly*
similar relation 108.2 *interrelatedness*
similar triangles 27.43 *triangle*
similation 115.1 *similarity*
simile 111.2 *equivalence*; 721.3 *narration*; 542.1 *ornament*; 17.12 *poetic language*; 115.1 *similarity*
similitude 115.1 *similarity*; 27.48 *transformation*
simious 71.34 *primate*
simmer 327.21 *be agitated*; 624.11 *be angry*; 493.14 *be hot*; 434.24 *bubble*; 25.55 *cook*
simmer down 419.14 *ease*
simmering 25.8 *cooking technique*; 493.9 *hot*
Simon Legree 236.12 *bad person*
simony 778.3 *selling*
simpatico 569.8 *friendly*
simple 255.16; **271.1**; **695.2**; **728.14**; 725.3 *clear*; 265.9 *easy*; 543.3 *elegant*; 657.9 *familiar*; 459.5 *foolish*; 456.6 *ignorant*; 457.7 *intellectually subnormal*; 457.5 *lacking intellect*; 394.2 *medicine*; 646.1,

805.7 *naive*; 77.18 *of leaves*; 574.4 *ordinary*; 529.13 *soft-hued*; 178.2 *straightforward*; 698.18 *truthful*; 647.10 *unadorned*; 27.70 *universal*
simple arithmetic 27.4
simple as ABC 265.9 *easy*
simple eloquence 695.10 *simplicity*
simple fraction 27.18 *division*; 196.1 *fraction*; 194.5 *ratio*
simple fruit 80.2 *botanical fruit*
simple glyceride 33.7 *fat*
simple harmonic motion 298.1 *regularity*; 28.8 *time*
simple-hearted 271.3 *natural*
simple interest 213.3 *increasing thing*; 784.4 *interest*; 765.5 *profit*
simple language 695.10 *simplicity*
simple life 684.1 *self-restraint*
simple lipid 33.6 *lipid*
simple machine 38.6
simple melody 516.1 *melody*
simple microscope 28.85 *microscope*
simple-minded 457.7 *intellectually subnormal*; 457.5 *lacking intellect*; 646.1 *naive*
simple-mindedly 457.11 *unintelligently*
simple-mindedness 457.1 *lack of intellect*; 646.2 *naivety*
simpleness 255.8, 265.2, 271.4, 728.4 *simplicity*; 698.5 *truthfulness*
simple picture 163.1 *outline*
simple reflex 36.20 *conditioning*
Simple Simon 457.3 *unintelligent person*
simple soul 646.3 *naive person*
simple sugar 33.3 *carbohydrate*
simpleton 459.3 *foolish person*; 456.5 *ignorant person*; 646.3 *naive person*; 457.3 *unintelligent person*
simple truth 738.11 *openness*
simplex 27.41 *geometric figure*
Simplicity 271
simplicity 255.8; **265.2**; **271.4**; **695.10**; **728.4**; 725.1 *clarity*; 178.8 *directness*; 543.1 *elegance*; 657.3 *familiarity*; 623.7 *humility*; 646.2, 805.3 *naivety*; 255.1 *purity*; 647.3 *unadornment*
simplification 375.2 *deconstruction*; 265.7 *easing*; 27.24 *evaluation*; 719.1 *interpretation*; 409.4 *rearrangement*; 695.10 *simplicity*; 719.4 *translation*
simplified 719.15 *interpreted*; 265.11 *made easy*; 409.23 *rearranged*; 255.16, 695.2 *simple*
simplifier 719.6 *interpreter*
simplify 255.11; **695.5**; 271.7 *be simple*; 375.4 *deconstruct*; 719.8 *interpret*; 265.16 *make easy*; 27.92 *manipulate*; 409.14 *rearrange*; 719.12 *translate*
simplifying 265.7 *easing*
simplistic 255.17 *direct*
simplistically 265.21 *easily*; 255.20 *homogenously*
simply 271.8; **728.24**; 725.4 *clearly*; 265.21 *easily*; 543.5 *elegantly*; 695.13 *intelligibly*; 805.12 *naively*; 657.14 *naturally*; 197.24 *once*; 647.12 *plainly*; 698.36 *truthfully*
simulacrum 699.14 *façade*; 96.2 *illusion*
simulate 96.17 *fabricate*; 115.12 *imitate*; 699.28 *mask*; 448.12 *rehearse*
simulated 115.8; 96.12 *artificial*; 699.39 *disguised*; 448.8 *experimental*; 477.12 *imaginary*; 700.39 *imitative*
simulated wood 699.16 *false thing*; 700.6 *imitation*
simulation 96.7 *artificiality*; 125.4 *camouflage*; 125.2 *copy*; 699.14 *façade*; 125.1 *imitation*; 27.65 *theory*
simulcast 692.25 *broadcast material*
simultaneity 285.1 *same time*; 223.2 *synchronism*
simultaneous 285.9; 223.18 *concurrent*
simultaneous equations 27.27 *equation*
simultaneously 285.12; 223.23 *concurrently*
simurg 72.9 *fabulous bird*
sin 802.23; **804.4**; **806.3**; **806.10**; 236.9 *badness*; 662.15 *be disobedient*; 804.16 *be wicked*; 662.1 *disobedience*; 796.16 *do wrong*; 798.1 *evil*; 16.38 *lawbreaking*; 274.8 *moral error*; 247.3 *personal fault*; 274.20 *transgress*; 804.1 *wickedness*; 802.8 *wrongdoing*
Sinai 428.14 *desert*
Sinbad the Sailor 323.7 *nautical person*
sin-bin 58.3 *ice hockey*
since before the Flood 296.19 *anciently*
since days of yore 296.19 *anciently*
since God knows when 296.19 *anciently*
since long ago 296.19 *anciently*
sincere 126.6 *authentic*; 156.9 *deep-seated*; 255.17 *direct*; 643.2 *earnest*; 799.4 *honourable*; 646.1 *naive*; 308.16 *open*; 698.18 *truthful*
sincerely 643.11 *earnestly*; 255.20 *homogenously*; 799.7 *honourably*; 646.5 *naively*; 308.26 *openly*; 126.8 *originally*; 698.36 *truthfully*
sincere thanks 671.2 *thanks*
sincerity 643.5 *earnestness*; 646.2 *naivety*; 308.9 *openness*; 799.1 *probity*; 698.5 *truthfulness*
since the big bang 296.19 *anciently*
since the year one 296.19 *anciently*
sine 27.52 *trigonometric function*
sinecure 265.6 *easy thing*; 341.1 *inaction*; 580.1 *leisure*
sinecurist 343.8 *nonworker*
sine curve 27.40 *curve*
sine qua non 746.2 *basis for negotiations*; 123.3 *chief thing*; 136.7 *condition*; 135.12 *in need*; 135.1 *requirement*; 476.1 *supposition*
sine rule 27.51 *trigonometry*
sine wave 177.3 *curved things*; 326.5 *wave*; 28.16 *waveform*
sinews 423.8 *physical strength*; 336.1 *strength*
sinewy 336.9 *physically strong*; 423.4 *powerful*
sinfonia 18.4 *opera*
sinfonietta 18.26 *musical group*
sinful 806.7; 236.3 *bad*; 274.16 *errant*; 798.7 *evil*; 802.16 *in the wrong*; 804.11 *wicked*
sinfully 798.12 *evilly*; 802.28 *immorally*; 804.18 *wickedly*
sinfulness 236.9 *badness*; 662.1 *disobedience*; 806.3 *sin*; 802.5 *unrighteousness*; 804.1 *wickedness*
sing 18.39; **72.26**; **515.5**; **516.10**; 715.5 *accuse*; 739.7 *betray*; 693.13 *inform on*; 542.12 *ornament*; 597.7 *show joy*; 454.3 *testify*; 716.13 *turn queen's evidence*
singable 18.30 *harmonic*; 516.6 *melodious*
sing a different tune 224.7 *be changed*
Singapore sling 558.8 *mixed drink*
sing a requiem 583.8 *bury*
singe 532.11 *blacken*; 534.7 *brown*; 493.15 *burn*
singed 532.3 *blackened*; 534.2 *browned*; 493.13 *heated*
singer 18.23; 516.5 *melodist*; 18.24 *musician*; 578.1 *worker*
sing for one's supper 782.12 *be poor*
sing Happy Birthday 601.17 *congratulate*
sing hymns 10.19 *offer worship*; 9.7 *worship*
sing in a round 509.13 *trill*
singing 515.8; 72.21 *avian*; 542.10 *ornate*
single 197.17; 48.5 *batting terms*; 572.6 *celibate*; 69.6 *darts*; 56.1 *golf*; 655.10 *lonely*; 197.1, 197.11 *one*; 452.7 *particular*; 744.7 *recording*; 50.11 *rowing*; 255.16 *simple*; 197.7, 572.5 *single person*; 139.15 *special*; 204.6 *whole*
single-action 55.8 *angling*
single-action reel 55.3 *fishing tackle*
single aspect 163.1 *outline*
single-barrelled gun 587.9 *firearm*
single bed 23.6 *bed*
single-bladed 50.12 *canoeing*
single-bladed paddle 50.6 *canoeing*
single-blade race 50.6 *canoeing*
single blessedness 572.1 *celibacy*
single-blind trial 448.2 *rehearsal*
single-breasted 551.31 *styled*
single-celled 34.23 *cellular*
single-celled invertebrate 75.1 *invertebrate*
single coverage 46.10 *defence*
single cream 197.10 *single thing*
single crystal 32.4 *crystal*
single decker 320.19 *bus*; 197.10 *single thing*
single entry 789.1 *accounts*
single European market 779.4 *free market*
single file 148.5 *piece*; 197.10 *single thing*
single-foot 333.10 *slow motion*
single girl 568.5; 572.5 *single person*
single-handed 55.8 *angling*; 50.10 *sailing*; 197.15 *solo*
single-handed dinghy 50.2 *sailing boat*
single-handedly 197.21 *alone*
single-handed racing 50.1 *sailing*
single-handed rod 55.3 *fishing tackle*
Single-handed Transatlantic Race 50.1 *sailing*
single-hearted 646.1 *naive*
single instance 197.2 *item*
single kayak race 50.6 *canoeing*
single lane 320.3 *carriageway*
single-leg 57.11 *gymnastic*
single-leg circle 57.6 *pommel horse*
single-lens reflex 41.16 *camera*
single-loop goniometer 323.5 *navigation*
single man 567.5; 572.5 *single person*
single market 779.4 *free market*
single-masted boat 50.2 *sailing boat*
single meaning 694.3 *comprehension*
single-minded 471.8 *diligent*; 255.17 *direct*; 635.7 *iron-willed*; 423.5 *mentally tough*; 638.1 *resolute*
single-mindedly 423.14; 255.20 *homogenously*; 638.17 *resolutely*
single-mindedness 640.2 *commitment*; 638.13 *concentration*; 641.6 *determination*; 471.4 *diligence*; 423.9 *mental toughness*; 635.2 *willpower*
singleness 197.6; 572.1 *celibacy*; 197.3 *oneness*; 655.1 *unsociability*
singleness of purpose 640.2 *commitment*
single-oar 50.11 *rowing*
single-oar rowing 50.4 *rowing*
single out 197.20; 139.22 *characterize*; 469.4 *pick*; 372.10 *set apart*
single overarm 67.2 *swimming technique*
single paddle 50.17 *canoe*
single-paddle canoeing 50.6 *canoeing*
single parent 197.7 *single person*
single person 197.7; **572.5**
single-phase supply 39.34 *power supply*
single-point tool 38.9 *machine tool*
single quotes 742.7 *punctuation*
single rhyme 17.11 *rhyme*
single-rhythm crawl 67.2 *swimming technique*
singles 51.9 *bowls*; 63.14 *forehand*; 63.4 *tennis terms*
singles court 63.3 *tennis equipment*
single sculling 50.4 *rowing*
single sculls 50.4 *rowing*
single-sex school 6.12 *educational institution*
single-shot 60.8 *shooting*
single-shot rifle 60.3 *hunting equipment*
single sideband transmission 692.14 *radio transmission*
single-sided 68.12 *ski*
single-sided skating 68.3 *ski racing*
singles match 51.1 *green bowling*
single space 146.1 *interval*
single span 38.21 *bridge*
singles player 63.6 *tennis player*
single state 572.1 *celibacy*
singlestick 54.1 *fencing*
single-storey 155.5 *low*; 565.16 *manorial*; 20.12 *structural*
single-storey building 20.3 *building*
single-support phase 47.2 *field events*
singlet 551.18 *underwear*
single tenoner 23.11 *woodworking tool*
single thing 197.10
single ticket 197.10 *single thing*
singleton 197.1 *one*; 197.10 *single thing*
single track 151.8 *narrow thing*; 320.2 *road*; 197.10 *single thing*
single-track 151.4 *narrow-leaved*
single-use 278.7 *impermanent*
single-wing formation 46.7 *offence*
single woman 568.5 *single girl*
sing like a bird 515.5 *sing*
sing like a canary 739.7 *betray*
singly 572.12 *celibately*; 197.22 *one by one*; 372.20 *separately*; 139.32 *severally*
sing out 514.15; 729.13 *speak in a particular way*
sing praises 9.7 *worship*
Sing Sing 815.1 *prison*
sing small 623.20 *submit*
singsong 112.13 *monotonous*; 517.9 *unmelodious*
Singspiel 21.4 *musical drama*; 18.4 *opera*
sing the praises of 514.12 *cheer*; 669.15 *compliment*; 601.17 *congratulate*; 600.6 *fête*; 667.17 *praise*
sing together 18.39 *sing*; 285.7 *synchronize*
singular 197.14; 116.4 *dissimilar*; 118.14 *eccentric*; 121.15 *excellent*; 5.44 *grammatical*; 452.7 *particular*; 99.8 *quintessential*; 139.15 *special*; 109.6 *unrelated*
singularity 197.4; 139.3 *characteristic*; 452.18 *particularity*; 29.11 *stellar birth*; 109.1 *unrelatedness*; 118.4 *unusualness*
singularly 139.30 *characteristically*; 116.7 *dissimilarly*; 5.52 *grammatically*; 109.12 *irrelevantly*; 121.17 *supremely*; 118.21 *unconformably*
sinister 249.6 *adverse*; 523.11 *benighted*; 798.7 *evil*; 236.5 *harmful*; 743.13 *heraldic*; 475.15 *presageful*
sinisterly 798.12 *evilly*; 249.12 *in adversity*
sinister side 169.1 *side*
sinistral 492.10 *handed*
sinistrality 492.7 *sense organ*
sink 767.8; 556.17 *age*; 410.12 *bath*; 122.11 *become inferior*; 183.8 *be concave*; 357.13 *be destroyed*; 261.5 *be fatigued*; 414.12 *be heavy*; 300.13 *be in motion*; 249.9 *be in trouble*; 786.9 *be unable to pay*; 260.24 *be unhealthy*; 367.3 *bring down*; 249.11 *cause adversity*; 214.4 *decrease*; 156.14 *deepen*; 305.9 *descend*; 245.1 *deteriorate*; 796.16 *do wrong*; 247.6 *fail*; 357.11 *ruin*
sinkable 305.16 *descending*
sinkage 305.2; 156.1 *depth*; 414.6 *displacement*
sink a mineshaft 308.20 *hole*
sink a shaft 183.9 *make concave*
sink below the horizon 526.1 *disappear*
sink down 305.9 *descend*
sinker 25.36 *cake*; 55.3 *fishing tackle*; 330.5 *throw*; 414.11 *weight*; 50.7 *windsurfing*
sinkhole 367.14 *depression*
sink in 695.4 *be intelligible*
sinking 556.12 *ageing*; 55.8 *angling*; 183.1 *concavity*; 214.2 *decline*; 214.6 *decreasing*; 156.1 *depth*; 305.16 *descending*; 300.6 *descending motion*; 300.17 *directional*; 582.18 *dying*; 367.11 *lowering*; 357.4 *ruin*; 367.13 *submergence*
sinking fast 357.15 *destroyed*; 582.18 *dying*
sinking fund 14.1, 780.7 *finance*
sinking plug 55.2 *artificial fly*
sinking stomach 612.2 *fearfulness*
sink into 760.7 *convert into*; 314.13 *fall into*
sink into oblivion 463.12 *be forgotten*
sink into obscurity 122.10 *follow*
sink into the earth 305.15 *tunnel*
sink low 122.11 *become inferior*
sink money 787.1 *expend*
sink one's capital in 14.5 *invest*; 776.2 *speculate*
sink one's money in 777.1 *purchase*
sink one's teeth into 557.22 *eat well*
sink or swim 107.8 *chance*; 640.8 *hold out*
sink or swim together 747.13 *work together*
sink through the floor 623.24 *be humiliated*
sink to the bottom 156.14 *deepen*; 305.10 *droop*
sink without trace 122.11 *become inferior*; 521.7 *become invisible*; 357.13 *be destroyed*; 463.12 *be forgotten*; 94.12 *cease to exist*; 526.1 *disappear*; 358.1 *obliterate*
sinless 805.5 *innocent*; 255.12 *morally pure*; 230.1 *perfect*; 795.9 *pure*; 803.5 *virtuous*
sinlessly 803.9 *virtuously*
sinlessness 805.1 *innocence*; 795.3 *moral purity*; 255.1 *purity*; 803.1 *virtue*
sinner 766.6 *loser*; 651.8 *malefactor*; 804.9 *wicked person*; 802.10 *wrongdoer*
Sinn Féin 12.6 *political party*
sinning 662.13 *disobedient*; 16.60 *offending*; 806.3 *sin*; 804.11 *wicked*
sin of omission 806.3 *sin*
Sino-Tibetan 5.11 *family of languages*
sinter 32.30 *extract*; 316.10 *transferred thing*
sinuous 180.4 *convolutional*; 73.12 *snakelike*; 326.17 *waving*; 177.5 *well-rounded*
sinuousity 177.1 *curvature*
sinuously 180.8 *circularly*; 177.7 *curvedly*
sinuousness 180.1 *convolution*

sinusitis 260.9 *respiratory disease*
sinusoid 27.40 *curve*
sinusoidal 177.4 *curved;* 27.85 *cyclic;* 326.17 *waving*
sinusoidally 177.7 *curvedly*
sinusoidal wave 28.16 *waveform*
sip 558.2, 558.13 *drink*
siphon 369.9 *extractor;* 369.14 *suck;* 316.11 *transfer*
siphonaceous 84.7 *algal*
siphonapteran 76.10 *insectan*
siphoning 369.4 *sucking*
siphon off 369.14 *suck;* 371.11 *void*
siphon the python 560.17 *urinate*
sipper 558.12 *drinker*
sipping 558.1 *drinking*
sipunculid 75.6 *worm*
Sipunculida 75.6 *worm*
sir 567.3 *male title of address;* 400.1 *master*
sire 59.13 *breeding;* 59.1 *horse;* 344.7 *Prime Mover;* 130.26 *produce;* 561.13 *propagate;* 561.5 *propagator*
sired 554.15 *born*
siren 363.6 *charmer;* 711.2 *danger signal;* 70.7 *legendary beast;* 507.1 *loudness;* 363.5 *lure;* 483.7 *motivator;* 91.4 *sea god;* 281.10, 742.4 *signal;* 507.4 *sound maker;* 480.13 *tempter;* 651.9 *vixen;* 11.4 *witch*
Sirenia 71.11 *marine mammal*
sirenian 71.29 *cetacean;* 71.11 *marine mammal*
siren song 480.3 *incentive;* 363.5 *lure*
Sir Galahad 795.5 *pure person*
Sir John Mandeville 699.18, 700.16 *liar*
sirloin 25.22, 25.23 *beef*
sirocco 493.8 *hot place;* 380.5 *violent weather*
Sir Roger de Coverley 22.4 *historic dancing*
sis 568.12 *woman in the family*
sissy 614.2 *coward;* 614.3 *cowardly;* 567.9 *offensive terms for homosexual;* 337.4 *weakling;* 337.12 *weak-willed*
sister 569.6 *close friend;* 750.5 *conformity;* 285.5 *contemporary;* 119.5 *equal;* 568.3 *female title of address;* 568.11 *liberated woman;* 579.15 *manager;* 7.7 *monk;* 35.16 *nurse;* 127.3 *person included;* 568.12 *woman in the family*
sister city 87.1 *city*
sisterhood 376.15 *association;* 569.1 *friendship;* 747.9 *team*
sisterly 650.6 *benevolent;* 569.8 *friendly*
sisterly interest 569.1 *friendship*
Sister Moon 29.17 *moon*
Sisyphean 238.2 *futile*
Sisyphean task 103.7 *obstacle*
sit 367.8; 221.6 *be in a state of;* 301.8 *be motionless;* 143.9 *be situated;* 57.10 *compete in gymnastics*
sit an examination 705.19 *be questioned*
sit back 637.8 *hold back;* 341.4 *not act;* 263.2 *take it easy*
sit cheek by jowl 267.6 *adhere*
sitcom 692.25 *broadcast material;* 21.12 *comedy;* 599.4 *entertainment*
sit down 301.8 *be motionless;* 305.10 *droop;* 15.12 *have an industrial dispute;* 367.8 *sit;* 263.2 *take it easy*
sit-down 709.8 *refused;* 15.10 *unionized*
sit-down meal 557.12 *meal*
sit-down strike 753.3 *gesture of protest;* 15.4 *industrial dispute;* 709.1 *refusal*
sit down together 734.11 *confer*
site 142.9 *locate;* 142.1 *location;* 143.10 *situate;* 143.1 *situation*
sited 142.6 *located;* 143.6 *situated*
sit-harness 62.4 *climbing equipment*
sit in 753.8 *cause mischief;* 15.12 *have an industrial dispute;* 703.19 *protest*
sit-in 661.3 *act of defiance;* 753.3 *gesture of protest;* 15.4 *industrial dispute;* 703.6 *mass demonstration;* 376.4 *rally;* 709.8 *refused;* 15.10 *unionized*
sit in committee 734.11 *confer*
sit in conclave 713.6 *consult*
sit in council 734.11 *confer;* 713.6 *consult*
siting 142.4 *placing*
sit in judgment 16.69 *have jurisdiction over;* 16.76, 464.11 *judge;* 16.71 *try a case*
sit in on 97.12 *attend*
sit it out 134.4 *protract*
sit on 357.8 *destroy;* 623.17 *humiliate;* 251.8 *restrain;* 387.6 *subject*
sit on a goldmine 781.12 *be rich*
sit on one's hands 341.4 *not act*
sit on one's tail 633.9 *follow*
sit on the bench 16.69 *have jurisdiction over;* 16.76 *judge*
sit on the board 400.14 *master*
sit on the fence 216.9 *be average;* 479.1 *be equivocal;* 618.15 *be impartial;* 639.7 *be irresolute;* 754.4 *compromise;* 453.19 *hesitate;* 341.4 *not act*
sit on the shelf 572.9 *be celibate*
sit on the throne 140.16 *direct;* 12.11 *govern;* 396.18 *have authority*
sit round a table 713.6 *consult*
sit-sling 62.4 *climbing equipment*
sit spin 68.6 *ice-skating*
sitter 19.11 *artist's materials;* 252.3 *protector;* 168.2 *rear end;* 50.9 *sailor*
sit tight 301.8 *be motionless;* 641.9 *be obstinate;* 637.8 *hold back;* 341.4 *not act*
sitting 376.6; 579.7 *council;* 60.2 *hunting;* 57.6 *pommel horse;* 11.10 *psychic phenomenon;* 367.23 *sedentary*
sitting duck 700.22 *dupe;* 265.6 *easy thing;* 254.7 *vulnerability*
sitting on the fence 800.2 *faithlessness;* 216.2 *medium*
sitting pretty 246.13 *successful*
sitting room 769.4 *reception;* 565.7 *room*
sitting target 254.7 *vulnerability*
sitting tenant 564.3 *householder;* 763.5 *possessor;* 440.7 *property man*
situate 143.10; 142.9 *locate*
situated 143.6; 222.7 *circumstantial;* 221.8 *in a state of;* 142.6 *located;* 142.8 *locational*
situating 142.4 *placing*
Situation 143
situation 143.1; 170.3 *atmosphere;* 222.1 *circumstances;* 324.1 *direction;* 142.1 *location;* 264.5 *predicament;* 221.1 *state*
situational 143.7; 170.6 *atmospheric;* 222.7 *circumstantial*
situational neurosis 36.10 *neurosis*
situation comedy 692.25 *broadcast material;* 21.12 *comedy*
situations vacant 143.4 *employment*
sit up 186.5 *be vertical*
sit-up-and-beg 320.12 *bicycle*
sit up late 294.6 *be late*
sit-upon 168.2 *rear end*
sitvac column 143.4 *employment*
sitzbath 410.12 *bath*
six 201.2; 582.8 *after death;* 583.6 *grave;* 27.9 *numeral;* 53.10 *score;* 201.13 *sixth;* 246.3 *successful thing*
sixain 201.2 *six*
six and two threes 111.5 *equality*
six-beat crawl 67.2 *swimming technique*
six centuries 201.9 *treble figures*
sixer 201.2 *six*
six feet deep 583.12 *funereally*
six feet under 583.10 *buried;* 582.19 *dead*
six-figure 201.21 *thousandth*
sixfold 201.24 *fivefold;* 201.13 *sixth*
six-footer 201.2 *six;* 154.7, 158.11 *tall person*
six-gear 61.10 *racing*
six-gear straight 61.6 *motor-racing terms*
sixpence 780.10 *former British money*
six-pocket table 65.3 *English billiards*
six-shooter 330.9, 587.9 *firearm;* 201.2 *six*
six-sided 27.82 *polygonal*
sixteen 201.7 *double figures*
sixteenth 201.18 *eleventh;* 196.4 *less than one*
sixteenth note 18.17 *notation*
sixth 201.13; 27.75 *equal;* 201.24 *fivefold;* 196.4 *less than one;* 18.16 *musical note;* 201.2 *six*
sixth-form 6.21 *curricular;* 201.2 *six*
sixth-form college 6.12 *educational institution*
sixth-former 6.7 *learner*
sixth guard 54.3 *fencing movements*
sixthly 201.24 *fivefold*
sixth part 201.2 *six*
sixth sense 590.2 *impression;* 445.2 *precognition;* 11.8 *psychic power;* 488.1 *sensation;* 201.2 *six;* 101.3 *spiritual world;* 442.2 *ways of thinking*
sixtieth 196.4 *less than one;* 201.19 *twentieth*
sixty 201.8 *twenty and over*
sixty-four dollar question 705.4 *difficult question*
sixty-fourth note 18.17 *notation*
six ways from Sunday 141.16 *extensively*
six-wheeler 61.5 *motorcycle racing*
six-yard 66.5 *soccer*
six-yard box 66.1 *soccer*
sizable 158.15 *big*
sizableness 158.2 *bigness*
Size 158
size 26.4; **158.1**; 267.3, 430.2 *adhesive;* 19.11 *artist's materials;* 209.1 *degree;* 550.28 *face;* 743.1 *identification;* 123.1 *importance;* 158.18 *measure;* 430.3 *paste;* 203.8 *quantify;* 203.1 *quantity;* 27.35, 141.1 *space;* 550.8 *wall covering*
sizeable 141.13 *spacious*
sizeably 141.15 *spaciously*
sized 209.7 *gradational;* 203.6 *quantitative*
size up 464.12 *estimate;* 26.10 *measure*
sizzle 624.11 *be angry;* 508.6 *crack;* 512.1, 512.4 *hiss*
sizzler 31.23 *heat;* 493.5 *hot weather*
sizzling 624.16 *angry;* 508.2 *crack;* 508.9 *crackling;* 512.1 *hiss;* 512.6 *hissing;* 31.51, 493.9 *hot;* 493.11 *warm*
sjambok 814.14 *instrument of punishment*
ska 18.9 *popular music;* 18.10 *world music*
skald 17.14 *author*
skate 55.5 *British game fish;* 421.12 *go smoothly;* 59.1 *horse;* 68.6 *ice-skating;* 25.18 *sea fish;* 268.16 *slip*
skateboard 316.5 *means of transport*
skate on thin ice 254.8 *be in danger*
skating association 68.6 *ice-skating*
skating boot 68.6 *ice-skating*
skating equipment 68.6 *ice-skating*
skean 587.8 *sharp weapon*
skedaddle 252.9 *be safe;* 332.4 *be swift;* 371.33 *go away!;* 262.4 *haste;* 313.4 *hurry off;* 262.2 *make haste;* 634.9 *play truant*
skeet 330.6 *shooting*
skeeter 76.1 *insect*
skeet shooting 330.6 *shooting;* 60.1 *target shooting*
skeg 50.7 *windsurfing*
skein 72.13 *assemblage of birds;* 193.2 *braid;* 376.27 *bundle*
skeletal 403.13; 582.21 *deathly;* 582.18 *dying;* 153.2 *emaciated;* 337.10 *ill;* 163.6 *outlined;* 38.32 *structural*
skeletal frame 38.27 *superstructure*
skeletally 163.7 *essentially;* 403.18 *structurally*
skeleton 403.7; 68.9 *bobsledding;* 582.11 *dead person;* 403.4 *framework;* 163.1, 484.6, 723.2 *outline;* 215.1 *remainder;* 413.2 *supporting part;* 153.9 *thin person*
skeleton in the cupboard 812.1 *disrespect;* 798.5 *evil thing;* 737.1 *secrecy*
skeleton key 308.2 *opener*
skeleton shrimp 75.4 *arthropod*
skeleton staff 206.3 *fewness*
skep 410.7 *basket*
skepping out 59.14 *horse-riding terms*
skerry 92.2 *island*
sketch 269.4 *be concise;* 233.5 *be incomplete;* 420.13 *be unfinished;* 721.14 *describe;* 243.2 *do the groundwork;* 19.20 *draw;* 19.9 *drawing;* 17.2 *fiction;* 160.7 *form;* 233.3 *incomplete thing;* 163.1, 163.5, 484.6 *outline;* 717.11 *paint;* 484.10 *plan out;* 21.2 *play;* 243.10 *preparations;* 744.1 *record;* 448.2 *rehearsal;* 448.12 *rehearse;* 721.9 *representation;* 717.2 *reproduction;* 21.8 *scene;* 723.8 *summarize;* 723.1 *summary;* 476.5 *suppose;* 356.5 *work of art*
sketchbook 19.11 *artist's materials*
sketched 19.27 *painted*
sketcher 19.16 *artist;* 125.8 *copier;* 115.4 *person who copies;* 717.4 *person who makes a representation*
sketchily 233.6, 420.15 *incompletely;* 218.10 *insufficiently*
sketch in 108.7 *relate to*
sketchiness 233.1 *incompleteness;* 420.10 *rough idea*
sketching 19.3 *drawing*
sketch map 163.4, 717.7 *map*
sketch out 721.14 *describe;* 163.5 *outline;* 717.11 *paint;* 484.10 *plan out;* 723.8 *summarize*
sketchpad 19.11 *artist's materials*
sketchy 233.4 *incomplete;* 218.1 *insufficient;* 420.5 *unfinished*
skew 189.6 *be oblique;* 120.5 *be unequal;* 325.13 *deviation;* 325.6 *distort;* 27.80 *linear;* 176.8 *oblique*
skew arch 20.5 *arch*
skewbald 541.8 *checked;* 59.1 *horse*
skew distribution 27.59 *probability distribution*
skewed 176.8, 189.4, 325.23 *oblique*
skewed bridge 38.21 *bridge*
skewer 373.11 *connect;* 373.8 *fastening;* 425.8 *sharp-pointed thing;* 425.16 *use a sharp tool*
skew gear 38.7 *gear*
skew lines 27.37 *line*
skewness 234.1 *distortion;* 120.1 *inequality;* 189.1 *obliqueness;* 176.2 *obliquity;* 27.59 *probability distribution*
skewwhiff 234.6 *distorted;* 176.8, 189.4 *oblique;* 120.3 *unequal*
ski 68.12; **68.14**; 421.12 *go smoothly;* 68.5 *ski equipment*
skiagraphy 20.1 *architecture*
ski boots 551.19 *footwear*
ski championship 68.3 *ski racing*
ski clothes 68.5 *ski equipment*
skid 325.15 *deviating motion;* 421.12 *go smoothly;* 320.21 *miscellaneous motoring terms;* 305.14, 325.10 *slide;* 268.16 *slip*
skidder 268.16 *slip;* 79.7 *timber production*
skidding 305.18 *falling;* 322.5 *flight*
skiddy 421.4 *polished;* 268.10 *slippery*
skid lid 551.15 *headgear*
skidoo 371.33 *go away!*
skidpan 320.21 *miscellaneous motoring terms;* 61.6 *motor-racing terms*
skid-proof 317.15 *accessible*
skid row 87.7 *city district;* 86.10 *urban area*
skid-row 87.14 *urban*
ski du Fond 68.1 *skiing*
ski equipment 68.5
skier 68.11
skiff 50.4 *rowing*
skiffle 18.11 *folk music*
skiffle group 18.26 *musical group*
skiff-race 50.16 *row*
skiff racing 50.4 *rowing*
skiing 68.1; 68.12 *ski*
skiing association 68.1 *skiing*
skiing on ice 68.1 *skiing*
skiing posture 68.4 *skiing technique*
skiing snow 68.1 *skiing*
skiing technique 68.4
ski jacket 68.5 *ski equipment*
ski jump 189.2 *oblique line;* 68.1 *skiing*
ski-jump 304.5 *jump;* 68.14 *ski*
ski-jumping 68.1 *skiing*
skilful 485.6; 645.4 *cunning;* 400.13 *excellent;* 492.10 *handed;* 477.10 *imaginative;* 458.6 *intelligent;* 6.19 *knowledgeable;* 230.1 *perfect;* 797.5 *proficient;* 136.9 *qualified*
skilfully 485.12; **797.25**; 136.17 *capably;* 396.26 *expertly;* 400.16 *masterfully;* 6.26 *studiously*
skilfulness 265.1 *easiness;* 797.12 *proficiency;* 485.1 *skill*
skilful person 485.4 *skilled person*
skilful use 485.1 *skill*
ski lift 317.12 *cableway;* 366.10 *elevator;* 304.8 *lift;* 68.1 *skiing*
Skill 485
skill 485.1; **733.3**; 136.2, 334.2 *ability;* 645.1 *cunning;* 340.2 *deed;* 265.1 *easiness;* 477.1 *imagination;* 455.2 *information;* 579.3 *management;* 352.1 *means;* 230.3 *perfection;* 356.1 *production;* 139.7 *special skill;* 631.9 *tactics;* 317.1 *way;* 235.6 *worth*
skilled 400.13 *excellent;* 396.17, 485.8 *expert;* 15.8 *industrial;* 458.6 *intelligent;* 6.19, 455.8 *knowledgeable;* 4.19 *learned;* 230.1 *perfect;* 264.12 *problematic;* 797.5 *proficient;* 136.9 *qualified;* 485.6 *skilful*
skilled person 485.4
skilled worker 578.2 *artisan;* 15.7 *employee;* 400.10, 485.5 *expert;* 438.8 *machinist;* 216.8 *middle classes;* 346.5 *operator;* 136.8 *qualified person*
skillet 25.6 *kitchen equipment;* 410.15 *pot*
skills 136.3 *qualifications*
skilly 25.40 *breakfast cereal;* 497.3 *tasteless items*
skim 492.12 *abut;* 157.6 *be shallow;* 245.5 *hurt;* 147.19 *meet;* 469.4 *pick;* 492.3 *press;* 255.10, 256.15 *purify;* 305.14 *slide;* 492.11 *touch*
skimmed milk 558.5 *milk*
skimmer 25.6 *kitchen equipment*
skimmings 215.2 *residue*
Skimobile 320.10 *sled*
skim off 469.4 *pick*

skim off the cream 469.4 *pick*
ski-mountaineering 68.1 *skiing*
ski move 68.4 *skiing technique*
skim over 157.6 *be shallow*
skimp 682.7 *hoard*; 218.7 *make insufficient*; 149.10 *shorten*
skimped 218.2 *unprovided*
skimpily 782.17 *inadequately*; 218.10 *insufficiently*
skimpiness 206.3 *fewness*; 782.9 *inadequacy*; 218.8 *insufficiency*; 159.1 *littleness*; 149.1 *shortness*
skimp on 233.5 *be incomplete*
skimpy 782.4 *inadequate*; 233.4 *incomplete*; 218.1 *insufficient*; 159.7 *little*; 149.7 *short*
skin 550.14 *animal covering*; 550.13 *casing*; 411.3 *coat*; 365.14 *erode*; 171.1 *exterior*; 525.3 *external appearance*; 80.3 *fruit structure*; 435.1 *materials*; 792.10 *overcharge*; 356.7 *produce*; 215.2 *residue*; 372.10 *set apart*; 157.4 *shallow thing*; 212.4 *take off*; 520.6 *visible thing*
skin alive 670.21 *berate*
skin-and-bone 153.2 *emaciated*; 337.10 *ill*; 218.3 *underfed*
skin cancer 260.12 *cancer*; 260.4 *disease*; 260.13 *skin disease*
skin colour 525.3 *external appearance*
skin-deep 157.2 *superficial*
skin disease 260.13
skin-dive 67.10 *dive*
skin-diver 67.4 *swimmer*
skin diving 67.1 *swimming*
skin flick 796.2 *indecency*
skinflint 793.8 *bargain hunter*; 682.5 *miser*; 786.6 *nonpayer*; 786.13 *nonpaying*
skinfold 1.10 *measurement*
skin friction 365.1 *friction*
skinful 232.2 *fullness*
skin fungi 83.3 *fungi*
skin game 774.7 *dishonesty*
skin graft 394.12 *surgery*
skinhead 552.5 *baldness*; 586.1 *combatant*; 547.8 *haircut*; 651.8 *malefactor*
skink 73.2 *lizard*
skin lesion 260.13 *skin disease*
skinned alive 670.34 *censured*
Skinner 36.29 *psychologist*
Skinnerian 36.33 *Freudian*
Skinnerian psychology 36.1 *psychology*
skinniness 153.7 *thinness*
skinning alive 670.8 *berating*
skinny 337.10 *ill*; 153.1 *thin*; 218.3 *underfed*
skinny-dip 552.14 *undress*
skinny-dipper 552.8 *nude person*
skinny-dipping 552.11 *exposed*; 552.1 *undress*
skin over 171.11 *be exterior*
skin-popping 691.1 *drug-taking*
skint 782.2 *insolvent*; 135.5 *necessitous*; 249.7 *unprosperous*
skin test 35.7 *diagnosis*
skintight 267.9 *adhesive*; 551.31 *styled*
ski orienteering 68.3 *ski racing*
skip 98.18 *abscond*; 51.3 *bowls player*; 22.15, 600.7 *dance*; 389.5 *escape*; 300.12 *gait*; 313.4 *hurry off*; 327.29 *jerkily*; 304.5, 304.18 *jump*; 68.11 *skier*; 767.4 *wastebin*
ski pants 68.5 *ski equipment*; 551.9 *trousers*
skip off 313.4 *hurry off*
ski pole 68.5 *ski equipment*
skipper 579.2 *direct*; 579.13 *director*; 323.7 *nautical person*; 50.15 *sail*; 50.9 *sailor*
skipping 304.24 *leaping*
skip town 736.11 *conceal oneself*
ski race 68.3 *ski racing*
ski racer 68.11 *skier*
ski racing 68.3
ski rambling 68.2 *cross-country skiing*
skirl 507.8 *be loud*; 513.4 *be strident*; 513.1 *stridency*
skirmish 585.9, 585.14 *battle*
skirmisher 586.8 *soldier*
skirmishes 585.8 *warfare*
skirr 332.4 *be swift*
skirt 551.6; 169.7 *be alongside*; 164.5 *border*; 164.1 *edge*; 318.8 *pass*; 306.7 *ring*; 147.17 *stay near*; 568.9 *woman considered as a sex object*
skirt around 179.6 *circle*
skirt-chaser 593.9 *lover*
skirted 164.9 *skirting*
skirting 164.9; 169.6 *side*
skirting board 175.2 *foot*
skirt round 634.7 *be evasive*
ski run 68.1 *skiing*
skis 62.4 *climbing equipment*
skish 55.1 *angling*
ski slope 68.1 *skiing*
ski socks 551.20 *legwear*
ski stick 68.5 *ski equipment*
ski stopper 68.5 *ski equipment*
skisuit 68.5 *ski equipment*
ski sweater 551.13 *sweater*
skit 21.2 *play*; 678.6 *ridicule*
ski teaching method 68.1 *skiing*
ski touring 68.2 *cross-country skiing*
ski-tow 68.1 *skiing*
ski trail 68.1 *skiing*
skittish 453.8, 642.1 *capricious*
skittishness 674.3 *bashfulness*
skittles 51.4 *bowling*; 69.7 *other games*
ski turn 68.4 *skiing technique*
skive 343.12 *be inactive*; 634.9 *play truant*; 634.5 *shirk*; 425.16 *use a sharp tool*
skive off 98.18 *abscond*; 389.5 *escape*
skiver 98.6 *absentee*; 634.17 *avoider*; 425.10 *knife*; 343.8 *nonworker*
skiving 634.13 *shirking*
skivvies 551.18 *underwear*
skivvy 401.6 *domestic servant*
skivvy shirt 551.18 *underwear*
ski wax 68.5 *ski equipment*
skol 558.18 *cheers!*
skua 72.3 *water bird*
skulduggery 800.3 *criminality*; 700.7 *tricking*
skulk 614.4 *be a coward*; 645.5 *be cunning*; 634.6 *evade*
skulker 634.17 *avoider*
skulking 634.18 *avoiding*; 634.14 *evasion*
skull 384.7 *armour*; 582.3 *symbol of death*; 323.3 *vessel*
skull and crossbones 743.7 *flag*; 582.3 *symbol of death*
skullcap 551.15 *headgear*; 7.11 *vestment*
skullduggery 812.3 *disreputable action*
skunk 804.10 *bad person*; 503.2 *something that makes an unpleasant smell*; 246.2 *victory*
Sky 692.24 *television broadcasting*
sky 539.6 *blue thing*; 141.2 *empty space*; 8.11 *heaven*; 154.8 *high thing*; 366.2 *send up*; 174.1 *summit*; 29.3 *universe*
sky blue 539.1 *blue*
skycap 401.3 *attendant*; 316.7 *transferor*
skydive 305.12 *drop*
sky-diver 305.8 *descender*
sky-high 681.3 *costly*; 792.7 *dear*; 154.9 *high*
skyhook 62.4 *climbing equipment*
skyjack 322.1 *aviation*; 774.12 *steal*; 773.10 *take away*
skyjacker 773.6 *taker*; 774.8 *thief*
skyjacking 774.1 *stealing*; 774.17 *stolen*; 773.3 *taking away*
Skylab 29.30 *spacecraft*
skylark 340.4 *act*; 304.11 *ascender*; 304.14 *climb*; 697.8 *fool*
skylarking 601.1 *celebration*; 304.6 *mounting*; 697.3 *tomfoolery*
skylight 308.7 *passageway*; 522.10 *window*
skylight filter 41.20 *filter*
skyline 145.3 *distant place*; 163.3 *edge*; 187.3 *flat thing*; 520.3 *visibility*
Sky Pilot 7.8 *priest*
skyrocket 304.11 *ascender*; 213.4 *increase*; 304.19 *take off*
skyrocketing 792.7 *dear*; 304.24 *leaping*
skyrocketing price 792.3 *inflationary price*
skyscape 19.10 *art subject*
skyscraper 20.3, 38.20 *building*; 356.8, 403.6 *construction*; 154.6 *tall thing*; 186.3 *vertical thing*
skyscraping 154.9 *high*
sky survey 29.6 *star catalogue*
Skytext™ 692.25 *broadcast material*
skyward 154.20 *higher*; 304.26 *up*
sky wave 692.15 *transmitted wave*; 326.5 *wave*
skyway 317.13 *flight path*
skywriting 322.1 *aviation*
slab 187.3 *flat thing*; 744.11 *monument*; 205.7 *piece*; 62.5 *rock face*; 411.4 *slice*; 38.28 *substructure*; 152.5 *thickness*; 23.12 *wood*
slabber 560.9 *saliva*; 560.20 *salivate*
slabbinness 430.1 *viscosity*
slabby 430.8 *viscous*
slab method 24.5 *ceramic process*
slack 472.10 *careless*; 437.5 *coal*; 333.7 *delayed*; 666.5 *indifferent*; 339.5 *inert*; 343.3 *not participating*; 301.5 *sedentary*; 268.10 *slippery*; 419.1 *soft*; 333.5 *unhurried*; 408.15 *untidy*; 337.8 *weak*
slacken 214.4 *decrease*; 263.3 *ease*; 685.4 *moderate*; 372.9 *separate*; 419.13 *soften*; 337.7 *weaken*
slackening 333.9 *deceleration*; 214.1 *decrease*
slacken off 226.6 *cease*; 333.3 *slow down*
slacker 634.17 *avoider*; 618.6 *indifferent person*; 343.8 *nonworker*; 333.15 *slow person*
slackly 419.17 *softly*
slackness 666.2 *indifference*; 339.1 *inertness*; 333.8 *slowness*; 419.8 *softness*; 337.1 *weakness*
slack off 263.2 *take it easy*
slack-rope artist 21.31 *circus performer*
slacks 551.4, 657.6 *informal dress*; 551.9 *trousers*
slack suit 551.4 *informal dress*; 551.10 *suit*
slag 258.4 *dirt*; 567.7 *libertine*; 568.6 *loose woman*; 356.3 *product*; 238.6 *refuse*; 215.2 *residue*; 408.10 *slattern*
slag heap 238.6 *refuse*
slag off 606.7 *be dissatisfied*; 678.11 *criticize*
slàinte 558.18 *cheers!*
slake 490.10 *comfort*; 609.8 *satisfy*
slaked lime 43.13 *fertilizer*
slake one's thirst 558.13 *drink*; 685.5 *moderate one's hunger*
slalom course 325.14 *deviating course*; 50.7 *windsurfing*
slalomer 68.11 *skier*
slalom pole 68.3 *ski racing*
slalom race 68.3 *ski racing*
slalom racer 68.11 *skier*
slalom racing 50.6 *canoeing*; 68.3 *ski racing*; 50.7 *windsurfing*
slalom ski 68.5 *ski equipment*
slam 508.1, 508.5 *bang*; 330.26 *bat*; 507.8 *be loud*; 331.13 *blow*; 69.3 *card game terms*; 670.5, 678.2 *criticism*; 670.17, 678.11 *criticize*; 331.3 *hit*; 507.1 *loudness*; 50.10 *sailing*
slam dunk 49.6 *play basketball*
slam gybe 50.15 *sail*; 50.1 *sailing*
slam into 331.2 *collide*
slammer 309.4 *closed place*; 815.2 *the inside*
slamming 508.8 *banging*; 507.2 *outcry*
slammock 258.6 *dirty person*
slander 715.6 *accuse falsely*; 381.10 *criticize*; 678.3 *defamation*; 678.12 *defame*; 715.2 *false accusation*; 236.11 *harmfulness*; 236.14 *ill-treat*; 699.6 *lying*; 720.1 *misinterpret*; 720.2 *misinterpretation*; 381.16 *personal attack*; 712.3 *vilification*; 712.6 *vilify*
slandered 715.9 *perjurious*
slanderer 678.8 *defamer*
slandering 699.33 *deceitful*
slanderous 381.25 *critical*; 678.16 *defamatory*; 699.36 *falsified*; 720.3 *misinterpreted*; 715.9 *perjurious*; 712.9 *vituperative*
slanderously 715.10 *accusingly*; 678.18 *disparagingly*; 720.5 *misrepresentedly*; 712.13 *vituperatively*
slang 5.18; 729.1 *faculty of speech*; 5.39 *of language*; 5.3 *spoken language*; 712.6 *vilify*
slanging match 701.1, 751.2 *argument*; 712.3 *vilification*
slang term 5.18 *slang*
slang word 5.18 *slang*
slangy 5.39 *of language*
slant 189.6 *be oblique*; 46.10 *defence*; 325.14 *deviating course*; 325.13 *deviation*; 699.9 *falsification*; 699.26 *falsify*; 719.13 *interpret news*; 718.4 *misrepresent*; 189.1 *obliqueness*; 176.2 *obliquity*; 46.16 *play defence*; 702.11 *practise sophistry*; 176.5 *viewpoint*
slanted 176.10 *biased*; 27.80 *linear*; 718.6 *misrepresented*; 189.4, 325.23 *oblique*
Slantedness 189
slanting 699.9 *falsification*; 176.8, 189.4 *oblique*
slant-in pass 46.9 *play*
slant-top 23.14 *wooden*
slant-top desk 23.4 *table*
slap 331.13 *blow*; 814.12 *corporal punishment*; 547.4 *cosmetics*; 508.2, 508.6 *crack*; 742.3, 742.11 *gesture*; 814.3 *hit*; 236.14 *ill-treat*; 480.8 *incentive*; 492.3 *press*; 492.11 *touch*
slapdash 486.4 *bungled*; 472.10 *careless*; 486.3 *clumsy*; 262.3 *hasty*; 666.5 *indifferent*; 615.4 *rash*
slaphead 552.5 *baldness*
slap in the face 623.10 *abasement*; 668.5, 668.23 *insult*; 624.5 *quarrel*
slap one's thighs 599.14 *laugh*
slap on the wrist 814.12 *corporal punishment*; 814.3 *hit*
slapped down 623.3 *humbled*
slapped in the face 623.3 *humbled*
slapping 814.12 *corporal punishment*; 742.15 *gestural*
slapstick 21.32 *clown*; 21.12 *comedy*; 599.4 *entertainment*; 599.10 *humorous*; 272.5 *ridiculous*; 21.40 *tragic*
slapstick comedian 21.32 *clown*
slapstick comedy 272.2
slap-up 781.3 *opulent*
slash 791.3 *discount*; 308.20 *hole*; 491.11 *inflict pain*; 491.3 *injury*; 793.13 *make cheap*; 214.5 *make smaller*; 373.4 *means of connection*; 189.2 *oblique line*; 58.9 *play hockey*; 372.9 *separate*; 372.5 *separator*; 149.10 *shorten*; 381.6 *stab*; 560.3 *urination*
slash-and-burn 43.4 *arable farming*
slashed 793.9 *cheap*; 58.8 *hockey*; 308.14 *holed*
slashed price 793.1 *cheapness*
slashing 381.23 *attacking*; 726.3 *emphatic*; 58.8 *hockey*; 58.3 *ice hockey*; 58.5 *lacrosse*
slashing one's wrists 382.7 *suicide*
slash one's wrists 382.21 *commit suicide*
slat 23.17 *carpenter*; 153.11 *fineness*; 411.4 *slice*; 23.12 *wood*
slate 606.7 *be dissatisfied*; 424.3 *brittle thing*; 20.4, 435.2 *building material*; 670.17, 678.11, 719.11 *criticize*; 533.5 *grey thing*; 281.14 *keep time*; 38.26 *masonry*; 484.2 *policy*; 411.4 *slice*
slate blue 539.1 *blue*
slate-coloured 533.1 *grey*
slated 670.33 *criticized*
slate-grey 523.3 *dark colour*; 533.1 *grey*
slate loose 461.1 *insanity*
slater 75.4 *arthropod*
slates 550.7 *overhead covering*
slating 670.5, 678.2 *criticism*
slatted 23.16 *joined*
slattern 408.10; 258.6 *dirty person*
slatternliness 408.3 *untidiness*
slatternly 486.3 *clumsy*; 258.7 *dirty*; 408.15 *untidy*
slaty 30.57 *chalky*
slaty cleavage 30.28 *rock*
slaughter 382.4; **382.18**; 651.7 *act of malevolence*; 381.9 *attack successfully*; 585.13 *be at war*; 814.13 *capital punishment*; 357.9 *demolish*; 357.8 *destroy*; 357.2 *destroying*; 814.5 *execute*; 651.17 *kill*; 380.2 *physical violence*; 381.14 *siege*
slaughtered 582.19 *dead*
slaughterer 382.10 *killer*; 380.4 *violent creature*
slaughterhouse 382.15; 357.5 *havoc*; 767.8 *sink*
slaughtering 382.9 *animal killing*
slaughterman 382.13 *animal killer*
slaughterous 382.24 *murderous*
slave 401.7; 388.2 *appeaser*; 348.3 *assistant*; 342.10 *busy person*; 122.6 *inferior*; 663.4 *obedient person*; 387.5 *subjected person*; 664.3 *sycophant*; 342.15 *try*; 466.8 *victim of discrimination*; 576.6 *work*; 578.1 *worker*
slave away 576.6 *work*
slave-driver 647.4 *strict person*
slave-girl 401.7 *slave*
slave of the lamp 348.3 *assistant*
slaver 258.11 *dirty*; 315.12 *leak*; 371.14 *let out*; 560.9 *saliva*; 560.20 *salivate*
slave-raider 774.9 *plunderer*
slavering 560.29 *salivating*
slavery 386.3 *coercive methods*; 251.4 *detention*; 664.1 *servility*; 387.1 *subjection*; 773.3 *taking away*; 576.1 *work*
slave to drink 690.17 *drunkard*
slave to fashion 125.7 *imitator*
slave trade 776.4 *trade*
slave unit 41.19 *flash*
slavey 401.6 *domestic servant*

slavish 125.1 *imitation;* 663.7 *obedient;* 664.6 *servile;* 388.5 *submitting*
slavishly 663.10 *obediently;* 664.16 *with servility*
slavishness 125.1 *imitation;* 663.1 *obedience;* 664.1 *servility;* 388.1 *submission*
Slavonic 5.11 *family of languages*
slay 585.13 *be at war;* 94.13 *cause not to exist;* 382.16 *kill*
slay en masse 382.18 *slaughter*
slayer 382.10 *killer*
slaying 382.1 *killing*
sleaze 800.3 *criminality;* 700.1 *deception;* 258.1 *dirtiness;* 699.1 *falsehood;* 236.10 *poverty*
sleaziness 258.1 *dirtiness;* 236.10 *poverty*
sleazo 236.4 *poor*
sleazoid 236.4 *poor*
sleazy 258.7 *dirty;* 800.5 *dishonourable;* 236.4 *poor*
sled 320.10; 316.5 *means of transport;* 316.12 *transport*
sledge 316.5 *means of transport;* 331.15 *ram;* 320.10 *sled;* 316.12 *transport*
sledge dog 316.6 *beast of burden*
sledgehammer 331.2 *collide;* 331.15 *ram*
sledgehammering 331.12 *collision*
sleek 407.13 *orderly;* 268.10 *slippery;* 421.1 *smooth;* 421.6 *smooth-mannered*
sleekly 421.14 *smoothly;* 421.16 *suavely*
sleekness 268.1 *slipperiness;* 421.7 *smoothness*
sleep 343.9; **343.13**; 261.5 *be fatigued;* 339.4 *be inert;* 301.8 *be motionless;* 489.11 *be unfeeling;* 263.1 *ease;* 291.5 *night thing;* 226.3, 226.9 *pause;* 301.2 *repose;* 263.2 *take it easy;* 489.2 *unconsciousness*
sleep around 796.17 *be sexually immoral;* 593.29 *make love*
sleeper 343.11; 59.7 *horseracing;* 341.2 *nonacting person;* 321.3 *rail;* 317.10 *railway;* 321.6 *rolling stock*
sleepily 343.17; 339.7 *inertly;* 489.13 *insensibly;* 261.8 *tiredly*
sleep-in 703.6 *mass demonstration*
sleep-inducing 620.4 *boring*
sleepiness 261.7 *fatigue;* 339.1 *inertness;* 343.9 *sleep;* 489.2 *unconsciousness*
sleeping 343.4 *not awake;* 301.5 *sedentary*
sleeping around 593.5 *desire;* 796.3 *sexual immorality*
sleeping bag 62.4 *climbing equipment*
Sleeping Beauty 343.11 *sleeper*
sleeping car 321.6 *rolling stock*
sleeping dog 379.1 *trap*
sleeping draught 489.4 *anaesthetic;* 592.6 *desensitizing substance;* 608.3 *reliever*
sleeping partner 124.10 *nonentity;* 343.8 *nonworker*
sleeping pill 489.4 *anaesthetic;* 592.6 *desensitizing substance;* 394.8 *drug;* 37.4 *drug type;* 685.2 *moderator;* 608.3 *reliever;* 343.10 *soporific*
sleeping place 565.1 *habitat*
sleeping room 565.7 *room*
sleeping sickness 260.6 *infection;* 75.12 *protozoal disease*
sleeping together 593.5 *desire*
sleeping with 593.5 *desire*
sleep it off 581.2 *be refreshed;* 689.5 *sober up*
sleepless 342.18 *active;* 488.6 *conscious;* 640.11 *steady*
sleeplessness 342.7 *restlessness*
sleep like a log 343.13 *sleep*
sleep off 393.4 *be restored*
sleep on a volcano 254.8 *be in danger*
sleep one's last sleep 582.15 *die*
sleep on it 294.8 *delay;* 443.14 *have second thoughts*
sleepsuit 551.23 *children's clothes*
sleep therapy 36.3 *psychiatric treatment*
sleep through 393.4 *be restored*
sleep together 593.29 *make love*
sleep treatment 36.3 *psychiatric treatment*
sleepwalk 489.11 *be unfeeling*
sleepwalker 489.5 *unfeeling person*
sleepwalking 477.6 *reverie;* 36.14 *trance*
sleepwear 551.22 *nightwear*
sleep with 593.29 *make love*
sleepy 489.10; 261.1 *fatigued;* 339.5 *inert;* 343.4 *not awake;* 301.6 *quiescent*
sleepyhead 343.11 *sleeper;* 333.15 *slow person*
sleepy sickness 260.7 *tropical disease*
sleet 31.29 *hail;* 494.5 *ice;* 31.24 *precipitation;* 31.63 *snow*
sleety 494.8 *cold;* 31.55 *cool*
sleeve 743.7 *flag;* 551.24 *part of garment*
sleigh 316.5 *means of transport;* 320.10 *sled*
sleight 645.1 *cunning;* 702.1 *sophistry;* 700.8 *trick;* 700.7 *tricking*
sleight of hand 700.9; 96.3 *delusion*
sleight-of-hand 700.40 *illusory*
sleight-of-hand artist 21.29 *entertainer*
slender 218.1 *insufficient;* 151.1 *narrow;* 153.1 *thin;* 79.14 *treelike*
slenderize 153.14 *become thin*
slenderizing 153.3 *slimming*
slender means 782.5 *poverty*
slenderness 151.5 *narrowness;* 153.7 *thinness*
sleuth 633.9 *follow;* 633.5 *pursuer*
slew 50.15 *sail*
slice 411.4; 330.26, 331.10 *bat;* 486.7 *be clumsy;* 486.9 *bungling;* 325.2 *divert;* 56.7 *golf;* 56.3 *golf shots;* 557.14 *mouthful;* 205.7 *piece;* 770.2 *portion;* 372.9 *separate;* 331.14 *sporting hit;* 330.5, 330.23 *throw;* 425.16 *use a sharp tool*
sliced 205.11 *partial*
sliced bread 25.38 *bread*
slice of life 21.2 *play;* 95.3 *realism*
slice of the cake 770.2 *portion*
slicer 425.10 *knife*
slice service 63.2 *tennis strokes*
slick 645.4 *cunning;* 700.34 *deceiving;* 407.13 *orderly;* 421.4 *polished;* 485.6 *skilful;* 268.10 *slippery;* 421.1, 421.11 *smooth;* 421.6 *smooth-mannered*
slick down 421.11 *smooth*
slicked up 551.30 *dressed-up*
slicker 551.12 *coat;* 564.4 *townsman*
slickly 268.23 *oilily;* 421.14 *smoothly*
slickness 268.1 *slipperiness;* 421.7 *smoothness*
slid 305.6 *slide*
slidder 305.14 *slide*
slide 305.6; **305.14**; **325.10**; 254.8 *be in danger;* 245.1 *deteriorate;* 41.12 *development;* 90.7 *flow;* 265.19 *go easily;* 421.12 *go smoothly;* 38.31 *load;* 30.26 *mass movement;* 341.4 *not act;* 189.2 *oblique line;* 189.1 *obliqueness;* 41.3 *photograph;* 518.8 *reflection;* 50.16 *row;* 268.16 *slip;* 421.8 *smooth thing;* 527.8 *transparent thing*
slide back 761.6 *reverse*
slide carrier 41.12 *development*
slide down 305.14 *slide*
slide home 48.7 *play baseball*
slide in 368.5 *inset*
slide into 760.7 *convert into*
slide off 61.9 *race*
slide projector 41.12 *development*
slider 48.4 *pitching terms;* 330.5 *throw*
slide rule 210.5 *computer*
slide show 21.7 *show*
sliding 38.16 *deformation;* 245.12 *deteriorated;* 305.18 *falling;* 305.6 *slide;* 268.13 *slippery;* 804.11 *wicked*
sliding friction 365.1 *friction*
sliding off 61.6 *motor-racing terms*
sliding outrigger seat 50.6 *canoeing*
sliding pads 48.3 *baseball equipment*
sliding panel 700.12 *disguise*
sliding-scale 15.9 *negotiated*
sliding-scale rates 15.2 *industrial negotiations*
sliding seat 50.4 *rowing*
slidy 268.10 *slippery*
slight 661.6 *be insubordinate;* 472.13 *be thoughtless;* 122.17 *defective;* 678.10 *disparage;* 470.3 *exclude;* 623.17 *humiliate;* 728.16 *imperceptible;* 337.13 *insufficient;* 668.5, 668.23 *insult;* 159.7 *little;* 470.5 *rejection;* 364.1 *repel;* 417.1 *sparse;* 157.2 *superficial;* 153.1 *thin;* 124.1 *unimportant*
slight build 153.7 *thinness*
slighting 678.1 *disparagement;* 678.15 *disparaging;* 668.11 *insulting*
slightingly 678.18 *disparagingly*
slighting remark 678.4 *aspersion*
slightly 122.21 *badly;* 196.7 *fractionally;* 159.8 *in a small way;* 685.9 *moderately;* 205.12 *partly;* 203.7 *quantitatively;* 209.11 *to a degree;* 337.14 *weakly*
slightly built 153.1 *thin*
slightly drunk 690.2
slightness 159.1 *littleness;* 157.3 *shallowness;* 417.3 *sparseness;* 153.7 *thinness*
slight smell 500.1 *odour*
slight transgression 804.3 *venial sin*
slim 191.6 *become smaller;* 153.14 *become thin;* 687.5 *fast;* 766.9 *lose;* 191.5 *make smaller;* 251.10 *restrain oneself;* 191.7 *smaller;* 153.1 *thin*
slim chance 105.4 *improbability;* 102.4 *remote possibility*
slim down 153.14 *become thin*
slime 430.7; 258.4 *dirt;* 429.8 *marsh*
slime moulds 83.3 *fungi*
slimily 268.22
sliminess 258.1 *dirtiness;* 268.2 *runniness;* 677.4 *unctuousness*
slimmer 766.7 *dieter;* 557.18 *eater;* 153.9 *thin person*
slimming 153.3; 191.8 *contracting;* 191.1 *contraction;* 153.10 *diet;* 557.27 *edible;* 687.1, 687.6 *fasting;* 766.1 *loss;* 557.6 *nutrition*
slimming diet 687.1 *fasting;* 557.6 *nutrition*
slimming pills 153.10 *diet*
slimness 153.7 *thinness*
slimy 658.9 *deferential;* 258.7 *dirty;* 599.11 *humouring;* 268.10 *slippery;* 664.7 *sycophantic;* 677.15 *unctuous*
sling 413.3 *body support;* 330.9 *firearm;* 587.6 *historical missile weapon;* 558.8 *mixed drink;* 381.7 *stone;* 394.10 *surgical dressing;* 330.5, 330.23 *throw*
slinger 330.14 *thrower*
slinging 330.3 *throwing*
sling mud 678.12 *defame*
sling one's hook 313.3 *quit*
sling out 470.2 *discard*
sling psychrometer 433.19 *measuring instrument*
slings and arrows 798.3 *bad luck*
sling shoes 551.19 *footwear*
slingshot 357.7 *agent of destruction;* 422.3 *elastic thing;* 330.8 *missile*
slingstone 330.8 *missile*
slink 736.11 *conceal oneself*
slink in 314.11 *infiltrate*
slink off 313.1 *depart;* 634.8 *run away*
slinky 551.31 *styled*
sliotar 58.7 *hurling*
slip 268.16; 254.8 *be in danger;* 249.9 *be in trouble;* 487.4 *be unaccustomed;* 804.16 *be wicked;* 205.6 *branch;* 453.21 *change;* 245.1 *deteriorate;* 24.3 *glaze;* 421.12 *go smoothly;* 472.5 *inattentive act;* 159.4 *little person;* 274.19 *make a mistake;* 320.21 *miscellaneous motoring terms;* 465.10 *misjudge;* 151.6 *narrow place;* 24.2 *raw material;* 806.3 *sin;* 305.6, 305.14, 325.10 *slide;* 53.4 *team;* 153.9 *thin person;* 305.11 *trip;* 274.9 *trivial error;* 551.18 *underwear*
slip anchor 50.15 *sail*
slip away 98.16 *absent oneself;* 313.3 *quit*
slip back 303.4; 245.1 *deteriorate;* 303.1 *go backwards;* 761.6 *reverse*
slip by 736.11 *conceal oneself*
slip casting 24.5 *ceramic process*
slipcover 550.12 *protective covering*
slip friction 365.1 *friction*
slip in 314.11 *infiltrate;* 368.5 *inset*
slip into 551.34 *wear*
slipknot 373.6 *line*
slip money to 768.5 *give*
slip of a girl 555.8 *young woman*
slip off 552.14 *undress*
slip of the pen 274.9 *trivial error*
slip of the tongue 274.9 *trivial error*
slip on 551.34 *wear*
slip one's collar 389.5 *escape*
slip one's lead 389.5 *escape*
slip one's mind 463.12 *be forgotten*
slip-ons 551.19 *footwear*
slip out 98.16 *absent oneself*
slip out of 552.14 *undress*
slipover 551.13 *sweater*
slippage 218.8 *insufficiency;* 135.2 *need;* 233.2 *omission;* 305.6 *slide*
slipped disc 260.16 *rheumatism*
slipper 814.3 *hit*
slippered 263.4 *at ease*
Slipperiness 268
slipperiness 268.1; 645.1, 702.3 *cunning;* 254.5 *danger;* 227.2 *irresolution;* 421.7 *smoothness*
slipper pad 68.5 *ski equipment*
slippers 551.19 *footwear;* 551.4, 657.6 *informal dress*
slippery 268.10; **268.13**; 634.18 *avoiding;* 645.4 *cunning;* 700.34 *deceiving;* 800.5 *dishonourable;* 479.11 *equivocating;* 421.4 *polished;* 453.7 *unreliable;* 254.2 *unsafe*
slippery as an eel 421.5 *smooth as a peach*
slippery customer 800.4 *dishonourable person;* 479.9 *equivocator*
slippery slope 264.6 *critical situation;* 254.5 *danger;* 357.4 *ruin*
slipping 486.3 *clumsy;* 245.12 *deteriorated;* 582.18 *dying;* 254.4 *endangered;* 305.18 *falling;* 804.11 *wicked*
slipping away 582.18 *dying*
slipping back 245.7 *deterioration*
slippy 268.10 *slippery*
slip-ring rotor 39.31 *electric motor*
slip road 320.3 *carriageway;* 373.5 *road*
slips 577.1 *workshop*
slipshod 472.10 *careless;* 666.5 *indifferent;* 408.15 *untidy*
slipshodness 408.3 *untidiness*
slip stage 21.17 *stage*
slipstream 322.7 *miscellaneous aviation terms;* 61.9 *race*
slipstreaming 61.6 *motor-racing terms*
slip-strike fault 30.20 *earth movement*
slip the cable 634.8 *run away*
slip the collar 391.5 *be liberated*
slip through 389.5 *escape*
slip through one's fingers 367.6 *throw down*
slip through someone's fingers 389.5 *escape*
slip up 802.19 *be wrong;* 247.6 *fail;* 274.19 *make a mistake;* 305.11 *trip*
slip-up 472.5 *inattentive act;* 274.9 *trivial error;* 247.4 *unsuccessful thing*
slipware 24.1 *ceramics*
slipway 421.8 *smooth thing*
slit 146.2, 146.5 *crack;* 146.7 *cracked;* 184.2 *furrow;* 183.4, 183.10 *notch;* 183.7 *notched;* 561.8 *organs of reproduction;* 372.9 *separate;* 372.3 *separateness;* 184.8 *wrinkle*
slither 305.6, 305.14 *slide;* 268.16 *slip*
slitheriness 268.1 *slipperiness;* 421.7 *smoothness*
slithering 305.18 *falling;* 73.11 *reptilian*
slithery 421.4 *polished;* 268.10, 268.13 *slippery*
slit skirt 551.6 *skirt*
sliver 196.3 *fragment;* 159.3 *little piece;* 557.14 *mouthful;* 205.7 *piece;* 411.4 *slice*
Sloane Ranger 235.7 *elite;* 553.6 *fashionable élite;* 573.1 *nobleman;* 248.4 *prosperous person*
Sloanes 765.8 *wealthy people*
slob 666.3 *negligent person;* 408.10 *slattern;* 486.10 *unskilled person;* 675.5 *vulgar person*
slobber 258.11 *dirty;* 315.12 *leak;* 371.14 *let out;* 560.9 *saliva;* 560.20 *salivate;* 429.16 *seep;* 433.33 *sprinkle*
slobbering 560.29 *salivating*
slobber over 593.27 *kiss*
slobbish 408.15 *untidy*
slobbishness 408.3 *untidiness*
sloe 532.9 *black thing;* 499.3 *sour thing*
sloe-black 532.1 *black*
sloe-eyed 532.4 *black-haired*
sloe gin 499.3 *sour thing*
slog 53.17, 330.26 *bat;* 331.13 *blow;* 331.3 *hit;* 640.6 *persevere;* 342.15 *try;* 576.6 *work*
slogan 5.21 *catchword;* 745.1 *maxim;* 509.7 *repeated word;* 742.6 *word*
slog at 576.8 *exert oneself*
slog away 640.6 *persevere*
slogger 586.3 *athlete;* 342.10 *busy person*
slogging 342.19 *busy;* 342.20 *industrious;* 576.10 *working*
slogging away 640.10 *persevering*
sloop 50.2 *sailing boat;* 586.24 *warship*
slop 486.7 *be clumsy;* 315.11 *run out;* 433.33 *sprinkle;* 497.3 *tasteless items;* 367.6 *throw down;* 441.1 *waste*
slope 27.97 *align;* 176.11 *angle;* 189.6 *be oblique;* 325.14 *deviating course;* 27.37 *line;* 189.1 *obliqueness;* 176.2 *obliquity;* 68.1 *skiing;* 305.6, 305.14 *slide;* 304.2 *upturn*
sloped 177.4 *curved;* 176.8, 189.4 *oblique*
slope off 313.1 *depart;* 634.9 *play truant*
slope up 304.21 *upturn*
sloping 177.4 *curved;* 27.80 *linear;* 176.8, 189.4 *oblique*
slop over 232.5 *be complete;* 315.11 *run out*
sloppily 666.7 *negligently*
sloppiness 274.2 *inaccuracy;* 666.2 *indifference;* 408.3 *untidiness*

slopping over 232.8 *full*
sloppy 472.10 *careless;* 666.5 *indifferent;* 590.12 *sensitive;* 551.31 *styled*
sloppy joe 551.13 *sweater*
sloppy sweater 161.2 *shapeless thing*
sloppy thinking 274.4 *faulty reasoning*
slops 551.1 *dress;* 258.5 *swill;* 337.5 *weak thing*
slosh 90.7 *flow;* 90.6 *river flow;* 429.14 *sprinkle;* 258.5 *swill*
sloshed 690.3 *dead drunk*
slot 409.6 *category;* 137.2 *class;* 146.2, 146.5 *crack;* 184.2 *furrow;* 308.20 *hole;* 58.3 *ice hockey;* 308.1 *opening;* 372.3 *separateness;* 184.8 *wrinkle*
slot formation 46.7 *offence*
sloth 343.7 *idleness;* 339.1 *inertness;* 93.9 *mere existence;* 804.5 *seven deadly sins;* 333.14 *slow creature;* 333.8 *slowness;* 333.15 *slow person*
slothful 339.5 *inert;* 343.3 *not participating;* 333.5 *unhurried;* 93.16 *vegetating*
slothfully 343.16 *impassively*
slothfulness 343.7 *idleness*
slot machine 780.21 *till*
slotted 184.6 *wrinkly*
slouch 343.12 *be inactive;* 155.8 *be low;* 305.10 *droop;* 333.10 *slow motion*
sloucher 333.15 *slow person*
slouch hat 551.15 *headgear*
slouching 333.4 *slow*
slough 560.23 *cast;* 560.12 *dead tissue;* 258.4 *dirt;* 92.3 *marsh;* 552.16 *peel;* 355.1 *relinquish;* 215.2 *residue;* 767.8 *sink;* 350.6 *stop using;* 258.5 *swill*
Slough of Despond 602.2 *depression*
slough off 487.5 *disaccustom;* 355.1 *relinquish*
sloughy 552.12 *peeling*
sloven 258.6 *dirty person;* 666.3 *negligent person;* 408.10 *slattern*
slovenliness 258.1 *dirtiness;* 666.2 *indifference;* 408.3 *untidiness*
slovenly 486.3 *clumsy;* 258.7 *dirty;* 666.5 *indifferent;* 408.15 *untidy*
slow 333.4; 263.4 *at ease;* 620.4 *boring;* 53.13 *bowling;* 51.9 *bowls;* 616.4 *cautious;* 26.15 *deliberate;* 300.17 *directional;* 426.3 *dull;* 459.5 *foolish;* 456.6 *ignorant;* 337.10 *ill;* 339.5 *inert;* 457.5 *lacking intellect;* 294.9 *late;* 580.7 *leisurely;* 343.3 *not participating;* 32.38 *reactive;* 251.8 *restrain;* 251.13 *restraining;* 333.3 *slow down;* 333.16 *slowly*
slow as death 333.4 *slow*
slow-as-slow 333.4 *slow*
slow bowler 53.4 *team*
slow burn 624.1 *resentment*
slow-changing 209.7 *gradational*
slow clock 333.13 *slow thing*
slowcoach 294.4 *latecomer;* 333.15 *slow person*
slow creature 333.14
slow delivery 53.8 *delivery*
slow development 294.1 *lateness*
slow down 333.3; 301.8 *be motionless;* 214.4 *decrease;* 245.1 *deteriorate;* 15.12 *have an industrial dispute;* 214.5 *make smaller;* 263.2 *take it easy*
slow-down 214.1 *decrease;* 333.12 *hesitation;* 15.4 *industrial dispute;* 15.10 *unionized*
slowed down 333.7 *delayed*
slow film 41.10 *graininess*
slow-footed 333.4 *slow*
slow foxtrot 22.2 *dance*
slow-goer 333.15 *slow person*
slow green 51.1 *green bowling*
slow handclap 753.3 *gesture of protest;* 670.9 *show of disapproval*
slowing 294.12 *delaying*
slowing down 333.9 *deceleration;* 245.7 *deterioration;* 251.1 *restraint*
slow lane 320.3 *carriageway*
slow learner 247.5 *failing person;* 294.4 *latecomer*
slowly 333.16; 620.8 *boringly;* 209.10 *by degrees;* 339.7 *inertly;* 300.18 *in motion;* 294.15 *late;* 251.16 *under restraints*
slowly but surely 209.10 *by degrees*
slow motion 300.9; **333.10**
slow-moving 333.4 *slow*
Slowness 333
slowness 333.8; 620.1 *boredom;* 616.1 *caution;* 209.1 *degree;* 637.13 *dissociation;* 343.7 *idleness;* 337.2 *indecisiveness;* 339.1 *inertness;* 457.1 *lack of intellect;* 294.1 *lateness;* 251.1 *restraint;* 300.9 *slow motion;* 486.8 *unskilfulness*
slow off the mark 333.6 *hesitant*
slow-paced 333.4 *slow*
slow person 333.15
slowpoke 294.4 *latecomer;* 333.15 *slow person*
slow progress 343.7 *idleness*
slow-ranging 209.7 *gradational*
slow reaction 32.14 *chemical reaction*
slow-running 333.4 *slow*
slow start 333.12 *hesitation*
slow starter 616.3 *cautious person;* 294.4 *latecomer;* 333.15 *slow person*
slow thing 333.13
slow train 333.13 *slow thing;* 321.7 *train*
slow up 333.3 *slow down*
slow wheel 24.6 *ceramic workshop*
slow wicket 53.5 *wicket*
slow-witted 456.6 *ignorant;* 152.3 *thick-witted*
slow-worm 73.2 *lizard*
slubbed 420.2 *coarse*
sludge 258.4 *dirt;* 43.13 *fertilizer;* 429.8 *marsh;* 215.2 *residue*
sludgy 31.55 *cool;* 429.11 *marshy*
slug 587.13 *ammunition;* 331.13 *blow;* 52.11 *fight;* 331.3 *hit;* 330.8 *missile;* 44.12 *pests and diseases;* 333.14 *slow creature;* 333.15 *slow person*
slugabed 294.4 *latecomer*
sluggard 294.4 *latecomer;* 343.8 *nonworker;* 301.7 *sedentary person;* 333.15 *slow person*
sluggardly 333.5 *unhurried*
slugged 52.14 *combat*
slugger 52.4 *boxer*
slugging 52.2 *boxing;* 52.14 *combat*
sluggish 263.4 *at ease;* 592.2 *desensitized;* 90.10 *fluvial;* 341.3 *inactive;* 618.7 *indifferent;* 339.5 *inert;* 294.9 *late;* 343.3 *not participating;* 637.4 *procrastinating;* 301.5 *sedentary;* 333.5 *unhurried*
sluggishly 90.13 *fluently;* 343.16 *impassively;* 618.17 *indifferently;* 339.7 *inertly;* 294.15 *late;* 301.10 *motionlessly;* 333.16 *slowly*
sluggish market 793.2 *declining prices*
sluggishness 637.15 *delay;* 592.4 *desensitization;* 343.7 *idleness;* 618.1 *indifference;* 339.1 *inertness;* 333.8 *slowness*
sluglike 75.19 *molluscan*
slug pellet 43.14 *pest control;* 44.8 *weedkiller*
sluice 256.14 *bathe;* 315.7 *outlet;* 433.29 *water*
sluicegate 38.24 *water system*
sluiceway 90.2 *channel*
slum 782.7 *beggary;* 87.7 *city district;* 245.9 *dilapidation;* 408.4 *litter;* 565.8 *shelter;* 767.8 *sink;* 546.3 *ugly place*
slumber 339.4 *be inert;* 301.8 *be motionless;* 301.2 *repose;* 343.9, 343.13 *sleep*
slumberer 343.11 *sleeper*
slumbering 301.5 *sedentary*
slumberous 339.5 *inert;* 343.4 *not awake*
slum-dweller 782.10 *poor person;* 87.11 *urbanite*
slum hustler 124.10 *nonentity*
slumminess 258.1 *dirtiness*
slummy 782.3 *beggarly;* 245.13 *dilapidated;* 258.7 *dirty;* 86.18 *local*
slump 793.12 *be cheap;* 214.2, 303.14 *decline;* 793.2 *declining prices;* 214.4 *decrease;* 214.3 *decreasing thing;* 245.1 *deteriorate;* 245.7 *deterioration;* 305.10 *droop;* 249.2 *economic adversity;* 13.2 *economy;* 563.1 *infertility;* 782.6 *insolvency;* 30.26 *mass movement;* 305.2 *sinkage;* 343.6 *unemployment*
slump down 305.10 *droop*
slumping 793.9 *cheap;* 305.16 *descending*
slumping market 249.2 *economic adversity*
slums 86.10 *urban area*
slur 678.4 *aspersion;* 381.10 *criticize;* 802.9 *dishonour;* 812.1 *disrespect;* 381.16 *personal attack;* 236.10 *poverty;* 678.13 *vilify*
slur one's words 690.7 *be drunk*
slurp 557.21 *eat;* 370.11 *ingest;* 370.4 *intake*
slurping 557.1 *eating;* 370.4 *intake*
slurred speech 690.10 *drunkenness*
slurry 43.13, 562.3 *fertilizer*
slurry pit 43.10 *farm tool*
slurry scraper 43.10 *farm tool*
slurry tank 43.10 *farm tool*
slurry tanker 43.10 *farm tool*
slush 494.5 *ice;* 68.1 *skiing;* 31.30 *snow*
slush fund 480.10 *bribe;* 768.2 *gift;* 752.4 *illegal offer;* 483.5 *positive stimulus;* 813.8 *secret money*
slushy 31.55 *cool;* 429.11 *marshy*
slut 258.6 *dirty person;* 796.9 *immoral woman;* 666.3 *negligent person;* 408.10 *slattern*
slut's wool 427.5 *powder*
sluttish 258.7 *dirty;* 666.5 *indifferent;* 408.15 *untidy*
sluttishly 258.12 *dirtily*
sluttishness 258.1 *dirtiness;* 666.2 *indifference;* 408.3 *untidiness*
sly 268.15 *crafty;* 645.4, 702.8 *cunning;* 737.10 *secretive*
slyboots 645.3 *cunning person;* 485.5 *expert*
sly looks 593.6 *courtship*
slyly 645.6 *cunningly;* 268.24 *duplicitously;* 702.15 *hypocritically*
slyness 645.1, 702.3 *cunning;* 268.9 *duplicity*
St Andrews' 56.1 *golf*
St Andrew's cross 743.7 *flag*
St Anthony's fire 260.13 *skin disease*
St Bartholomew's Day Massacre 382.4 *slaughter*
St Bernard 22.2 *dance*
St Christopher 11.6 *talisman*
St Elmo's fire 522.9 *firefly*
St George's cross 743.7 *flag*
St Lawrence 90.5 *other major rivers*
St Louis 87.2 *American cities*
St Luke's summer 493.5 *hot weather*
St Martin's summer 493.5 *hot weather;* 292.3 *summer*
St Patrick's cross 743.7 *flag*
St Swithin's day 31.3 *weather*
St Valentine's Day murder 382.2 *murder*
St Vitus's dance 260.17 *nervous disorder;* 327.7 *shake*
SM 21.27 *producer*
smack 412.4 *admixture;* 331.13 *blow;* 593.14 *communication of love;* 814.12 *corporal punishment;* 508.2, 508.6 *crack;* 324.9 *directly;* 691.6 *drug;* 331.3, 814.3 *hit;* 593.27 *kiss;* 728.6 *suggestion;* 495.9 *taste*
smack-dab 324.9 *directly*
smacker 780.8 *American money;* 780.9 *British money;* 593.14 *communication of love*
smacking 814.12 *corporal punishment*
smack of 115.10 *be similar;* 742.10 *signify*
smack on the lips 593.14 *communication of love*
smack on the wrist 814.1 *punish;* 814.7 *punishment*
small 196.6; 122.13 *insignificant;* 337.13 *insufficient;* 159.7 *little;* 623.2 *lowly;* 203.6 *quantitative;* 124.4 *trivial;* 124.1 *unimportant;* 682.2 *unpleasant;* 337.8 *weak*
small ad 740.9 *advertisement;* 693.4 *mass communication*
small ads 793.7 *discounter*
small amount 203.2 *certain amount;* 206.1 *few;* 218.8 *insufficiency*
small-animal practice 35.5 *veterinary medicine*
small arms 587.2 *arms*
small beer 122.6 *inferior;* 216.6 *mediocrity;* 124.10 *nonentity;* 124.8 *trifle*
small chance 105.4 *improbability;* 107.6 *poor chance;* 102.4 *remote possibility*
small change 780.4 *change;* 216.6 *mediocrity;* 124.10 *nonentity;* 759.3 *something in exchange;* 124.8 *trifle*
small circle 27.42 *circle*
small claims court 16.19 *law court*
small consideration 759.1 *exchange*
small eater 557.18 *eater*
smaller 191.7; 122.13 *insignificant;* 203.6 *quantitative*
smallest 27.75 *equal;* 122.13 *insignificant*
smallest room 565.7 *room;* 767.7 *toilet*
small fault 804.3 *venial sin*
small fragment 205.1 *part*
small frame 153.7 *thinness*
small-framed 153.1 *thin*
small fry 122.6 *inferior;* 159.4 *little person;* 216.6 *mediocrity;* 124.10 *nonentity;* 149.5 *short person;* 337.4 *weakling*
small game 70.1 *animals;* 60.5 *game;* 124.10 *nonentity*
small-game hunting 60.2 *hunting*
small gap 151.6 *narrow place*
small group 2.6 *social group*
smallholder 43.15 *agriculturist;* 564.5 *countryman*
smallholding 43.6 *farm;* 440.1 *property*
small hours 294.2 *late hour;* 291.3 *midnight*
smallish 159.7 *little*
smallishness 159.1 *littleness*
small lake 88.2
small letter 5.15 *type style*
small-lettered 5.41 *lettered*
small-minded 466.10 *discriminatory;* 682.2 *unpleasant*
small-mindedly 466.17 *prejudicially*
small-mindedness 466.3 *prejudice*
smallmouth black bass 55.4 *American game fish*
Smallness 159
smallness 122.3 *inferior numbers;* 159.1 *littleness;* 623.8 *lowliness;* 124.7 *triviality;* 337.1 *weakness*
small number 206.1 *few*
small office 577.1 *workshop*
small potatoes 122.6 *inferior;* 216.6 *mediocrity;* 124.10 *nonentity;* 124.8 *trifle*
smallpox 260.6 *infection;* 260.13 *skin disease*
small print 746.2 *basis for negotiations;* 136.7 *condition*
small quantity 203.2 *certain amount;* 206.1 *few;* 218.8 *insufficiency*
small risk 107.5 *good chance*
smalls 551.18 *underwear*
small scale 159.1 *littleness*
small-scale 159.7 *little*
small screen 692.21 *television;* 692.22 *television set*
small shot 587.13 *ammunition;* 330.8 *missile*
small slam 69.3 *card game terms*
small stream 90.1 *river*
small talk 734.2 *chat;* 731.3 *talk*
small-time 122.13 *insignificant;* 216.3 *mediocre;* 124.4 *trivial*
small town 216.8 *middle classes;* 86.11 *settlement*
small-town 122.13 *insignificant;* 86.18 *local*
small toy 124.9 *bauble*
smalt 539.5 *blueness*
smarm 677.9 *blarney;* 599.15 *humour;* 677.4 *unctuousness*
smarmily 677.17 *flatteringly;* 421.16 *suavely*
smarminess 677.4 *unctuousness*
smarmy 599.11 *humouring;* 421.6 *smooth-mannered;* 664.7 *sycophantic;* 677.15 *unctuous*
smart 342.18 *active;* 242.12, 491.10 *be painful;* 645.4 *cunning;* 551.30 *dressed-up;* 543.3 *elegant;* 553.7 *fashionable;* 491.9 *feel pain;* 656.6 *formal;* 599.10 *humorous;* 442.10, 458.6 *intelligent;* 455.8 *knowledgeable;* 425.5 *mentally sharp;* 407.13 *orderly;* 485.6 *skilful;* 551.31 *styled;* 332.1 *swift*
smart alec 458.4 *intellectual;* 455.6 *knowledgeable person*
smart alec answer 706.1 *answer*
smart aleck 660.12 *impudent person;* 442.8 *intellectual person;* 673.7 *vain person*
smart-alecky 673.13 *boastful;* 660.14 *cheeky*
smartarse 660.12 *impudent person;* 458.4 *intellectual;* 442.8 *intellectual person;* 458.6 *intelligent;* 455.6 *knowledgeable person;* 673.7 *vain person*
smart-arsed 673.13 *boastful;* 660.14 *cheeky*
smart card 40.3 *computer;* 40.12 *electronic office;* 28.64 *magnetic recording;* 308.2 *opener*
smart cookie 485.5 *expert*
smart customer 485.5 *expert*
smarten up 547.15 *beautify;* 244.1 *improve;* 393.2 *refurbish;* 407.21 *tidy*
smart for it 814.6 *be punished*
smart guy 485.5 *expert*
smarting 491.1 *pain;* 242.4, 491.5 *painful;* 624.15 *resentful*
smartly 551.36 *dressily;* 543.5 *elegantly;* 656.12 *formally;* 442.15 *intelligently;* 425.18 *sharply;* 332.14 *swiftly*
smart money 813.8 *secret money*

smartness 645.1 *cunning;* 656.1 *formality;* 458.2 *intelligence;* 425.13 *mental sharpness*
smart pace 332.8 *speed*
smarts 455.4 *intellect*
smart under 624.8 *resent*
smarty pants 660.12 *impudent person;* 442.8 *intellectual person;* 455.6 *knowledgeable person;* 673.7 *vain person*
smash 63.12 *badminton terms;* 331.10 *bat;* 427.26 *beat;* 331.2 *collide;* 331.12 *collision;* 375.4 *deconstruct;* 357.9 *demolish;* 797.17 *good thing;* 491.11 *inflict pain;* 492.3 *press;* 251.8 *restrain;* 357.4 *ruin;* 372.9 *separate;* 63.13 *serve;* 246.1 *success;* 63.2 *tennis strokes;* 330.5, 330.23 *throw;* 492.11 *touch;* 380.8 *use violence*
smash and grab raid 774.3 *theft*
smashed 690.3 *dead drunk;* 375.5 *disintegrated*
smasher 545.3 *attractive female;* 235.8 *exceller*
smash hit 235.8 *exceller;* 797.17 *good thing;* 485.3 *masterpiece;* 246.1 *success;* 21.13 *theatrical performance*
smashing 331.12 *collision;* 797.1 *good;* 331.17 *impelling;* 427.4 *pulverization;* 251.1 *restraint;* 619.14 *wonderful!;* 235.1 *worthy*
smash to matchwood 357.9 *demolish*
smash to pieces 375.3 *disintegrate*
smash to smithereens 357.9 *demolish*
smash up 331.2 *collide;* 357.9 *demolish*
smash-up 331.12 *collision;* 357.4 *ruin*
smatter 377.18 *sprinkle*
smattered 377.23 *sprinkled*
smatterer 124.10 *nonentity*
smattering 455.2 *information;* 377.4 *sprinkling;* 728.6 *suggestion*
smattering of knowledge 456.2 *half-knowledge*
smear 268.19 *anoint;* 678.4 *aspersion;* 548.7 *blemish;* 381.10 *criticize;* 678.12 *defame;* 258.4 *dirt;* 258.11 *dirty;* 524.10 *make dim;* 62.9 *mountaineer;* 381.16 *personal attack;* 548.1 *spot*
smear campaign 678.3 *defamation*
smearer 678.8 *defamer*
smear glaze 24.3 *glaze*
smearing 62.3 *climbing technique;* 678.16 *defamatory*
smear test 34.6 *cell biology;* 35.7 *diagnosis*
smeghead 456.5 *ignorant person*
Smell 500
smell 500.7; 258.10 *be dirty;* 554.4 *biological function;* 139.3 *characteristic;* 245.2 *decay;* 370.12 *draw in;* 500.8 *have odour;* 500.1 *odour;* 488.1 *sensation;* 488.11 *sense;* 503.5 *stink*
smell a rat 451.8 *disbelieve*
smell at 500.7 *smell*
smell bad 503.5 *stink*
smeller 500.2 *sense of smell*
smell fishy 800.8 *be dishonourable*
smell foul 503.5 *stink*
smellies 547.6 *toiletries*
smellily 503.6 *stinkingly*
smelliness 500.1 *odour;* 503.1 *stench*
smelling 500.5 *odorous;* 500.2 *sense of smell*
smelling bottle 500.2 *sense of smell*
smelling of drink 690.5 *drunken*
smelling salts 496.6 *cordial;* 500.2 *sense of smell;* 394.7 *tonic*
smell-less 501.3 *odourless*
smell like a drain 503.5 *stink*
smell like a midden 503.5 *stink*
smell of 500.8 *have odour;* 742.10 *signify*
smell of drains 503.2 *something that makes an unpleasant smell*
smell of rotten eggs 503.5 *stink*
smell of success 500.4 *reputation*
smell out 449.2 *detect;* 500.7 *smell*
smell powder 585.13 *be at war*
smell sweet 502.5 *be fragrant*
smell trap 501.2 *deodorant*
smelly 500.5 *odorous;* 503.3 *stinking*
smelly feet 503.2 *something that makes an unpleasant smell*
smelt 493.14 *be hot;* 431.24 *melt*
smelter 24.6 *ceramic workshop;* 493.6 *fire;* 577.1 *workshop*
smidgen 412.4 *admixture;* 206.1 *few;* 205.7 *piece;* 728.6 *suggestion*
smile 598.7 *be cheerful;* 742.3, 742.11 *gesture;* 658.12 *greet;* 597.7 *show joy;* 658.5 *sign of courtesy*
smile on 248.7 *be auspicious*
smiler 598.4 *cheerful person*
smiles of fortune 248.2 *good fortune*
smiling 598.1 *cheerful;* 742.15 *gestural;* 654.15 *sociable*
smiling reception 654.9 *welcome*
smir 31.25 *rain*
smirch 532.11 *blacken;* 796.19 *corrupt;* 678.12 *defame;* 258.11 *dirty*
smircher 678.8 *defamer*
smite 382.17 *murder*
smite hip and thigh 382.18 *slaughter*
smith 578.2 *artisan;* 160.7 *form*
smithereens 427.6 *crumb*
Smithfield 43.1 *agriculture;* 779.1 *market*
smithy 577.1 *workshop*
smitten 593.19 *enamoured;* 593.18 *in love*
smock 191.5 *make smaller;* 551.8 *shirt;* 551.18 *underwear*
smocked 191.7 *smaller*
smocker 542.8 *decorator*
smocking 542.3 *pattern*
smog 31.33 *fog;* 432.3 *miasma;* 524.2 *murk;* 427.5 *powder*
smoggy 31.56 *foggy;* 524.6 *murky;* 432.19 *smoky*
smog-laden 524.6 *murky*
smoke 496.14; 624.11 *be angry;* 519.6 *blinder;* 493.15 *burn;* 243.7 *develop;* 258.4 *dirt;* 691.10 *drug oneself;* 428.17 *dry;* 493.6 *fire;* 432.27 *give off;* 371.14 *let out;* 528.11 *make opaque;* 432.3 *miasma;* 524.2 *murk;* 500.1 *odour;* 528.7 *opaque thing;* 32.3 *phase;* 359.5 *preserve;* 496.12 *season;* 521.6 *that which makes invisible;* 527.8 *transparent thing*
smoke alarm 252.4 *safety device*
smoke a pipe 496.14 *smoke*
smoke blue 539.1 *blue*
smoke cigarettes 496.14 *smoke*
smoke cigars 496.14 *smoke*
smoked 524.6 *murky;* 496.9 *piquant;* 359.7 *preserved;* 527.3 *semitransparent;* 528.2 *shady*
smoked bacon 25.30 *bacon*
smoked fish 25.16 *fish dish;* 74.8 *food fish*
smoked glass 524.2 *murk;* 523.6 *shade*
smoked haddock 25.16 *fish dish;* 74.8 *food fish*
smoked mackerel 25.16 *fish dish*
smoke-dry 428.17 *dry*
smoked salmon 25.44 *British dish;* 25.16 *fish dish*
smoked trout 25.16 *fish dish*
smoke-filled 524.6 *murky*
smoke-free 501.3 *odourless;* 496.11 *tobacco*
smoke-free area 496.8 *smoking*
smoke-free zone 501.1 *odourlessness*
smokehole 308.7 *passageway*
smokehouse 43.7 *farm building*
smoke-laden 524.6 *murky*
smokeless 501.3 *odourless*
smokeless area 257.2 *salubrity*
smokeless zone 501.1 *odourlessness*
smoke out 369.12 *displace;* 371.7 *drive out*
smoker 386.5 *compulsive person;* 654.5 *party;* 496.8 *smoking*
smoker's cough 260.9 *respiratory disease;* 496.8 *smoking*
smoker's requisites 496.8 *smoking*
smokescreen 519.6 *blinder;* 550.2 *cover;* 736.3 *covering up;* 700.12 *disguise;* 528.7 *opaque thing;* 384.10 *shelter;* 645.2 *stratagem;* 521.6 *that which makes invisible*
smoke signal 742.4 *signal*
smoke signals 505.1 *deafness;* 692.27 *signalling*
smokestack 308.7 *passageway;* 154.6 *tall thing*
smoke the peace pipe 589.5 *be at peace;* 649.9 *forgive;* 749.5 *make peace*
Smokey 396.10 *person of authority;* 253.3 *security officer*
Smokey Bear 16.17 *police officer*
smokily 432.30; 533.9 *greyly;* 527.13 *transparently*
smokiness 496.1 *piquancy;* 527.7 *semitransparency*
smoking 496.8; 24.5 *ceramic process;* 25.8 *cooking technique;* 496.3 *curing;* 691.1 *drug-taking;* 493.9 *hot;* 359.1 *preservation;* 432.19 *smoky;* 496.11 *tobacco;* 432.10 *vaporization*
smoking area 496.8 *smoking*
smoking compartment 496.8 *smoking*
smoking jacket 551.4, 657.6 *informal dress*
smoking-related 496.11 *tobacco*
smoking-room story 796.2 *indecency*
smoky 432.19; 416.7 *condensed;* 532.2 *dark;* 258.7 *dirty;* 25.16 *fish dish;* 533.1 *grey;* 524.6 *murky;* 496.9 *piquant;* 527.3 *semitransparent;* 528.2 *shady*
Smoky Mountains 89.4 *US mountains*
smolt 74.3 *young fish*
smooch 593.27 *kiss*
smooching 593.14 *communication of love;* 593.6 *courtship*
smoodge 593.27 *kiss*
smoodging 593.14 *communication of love;* 593.6 *courtship*
smooth 404.9; **404.13**; **419.3**; **421.1**; **421.11**; 317.15 *accessible;* 426.1, 426.10 *blunt;* 51.9 *bowls;* 132.11 *continuous;* 700.34 *deceiving;* 265.9 *easy;* 543.3 *elegant;* 119.11 *equalize;* 658.8 *good-mannered;* 552.13 *hairless;* 187.8 *horizontal;* 265.16 *make easy;* 187.7 *make horizontal;* 181.11 *make round;* 111.8 *make the same;* 365.16 *massage;* 516.6 *melodious;* 685.8 *moderating;* 407.13 *orderly;* 490.6, 498.7 *pleasant;* 301.6 *quiescent;* 63.5 *real tennis;* 111.17 *regular;* 365.12 *rub;* 268.10 *slippery;* 407.21, 409.19 *tidy*
smooth as a peach 421.5
smooth as glass 421.5 *smooth as a peach*
smooth as marble 421.5 *smooth as a peach*
smooth as satin 421.5 *smooth as a peach*
smooth as velvet 421.5 *smooth as a peach*
smoothbore 587.9 *firearm*
smooth delivery 51.2 *grip*
smooth down 187.7 *make horizontal;* 421.11 *smooth*
smoothed 426.1 *blunt;* 187.9 *flattened;* 421.1 *smooth*
smoothen 187.7 *make horizontal;* 421.11 *smooth*
smooth endoplasmic reticulum 34.8 *cell organ*
smoothened 187.9 *flattened*
smoother 421.9
smooth-faced 552.13 *hairless*
smooth-haired 421.1 *smooth*
smoothie 645.3 *cunning person;* 664.3 *sycophant*
smoothing 265.7 *easing;* 365.5 *polishing;* 421.1 *smooth*
smoothing iron 421.9 *smoother*
smoothing plane 23.11 *woodworking tool*
smoothly 421.14; **426.11**; 265.21 *easily;* 543.5 *elegantly;* 658.15 *genteelly;* 187.11 *horizontally;* 301.10 *motionlessly;* 111.20 *regularly;* 419.17 *softly;* 498.9 *sweetly;* 404.15 *texturally*
smooth-mannered 421.6
Smoothness 421
smoothness 265.5; **419.9**; **421.7**; 426.5 *bluntness;* 658.1 *courtesy;* 645.1 *cunning;* 543.1 *elegance;* 404.2 *grain;* 187.1 *horizontality;* 407.5 *orderliness;* 490.1 *physical pleasure;* 111.6 *regularity;* 268.1 *slipperiness;* 498.1 *sweetness*
smooth one's ruffled feathers 749.4 *pacify*
smooth out 216.10 *make average;* 187.7 *make horizontal;* 404.13, 421.11 *smooth;* 419.13 *soften;* 178.10 *straighten*
smooth over 421.13; 268.20 *ease;* 685.4 *moderate;* 749.4 *pacify*
smooth road 265.6 *easy thing*
smooth-running 268.11 *lubricated;* 265.12 *wieldy*
smooth-shaven 552.13 *hairless*
smooth-skinned 421.1 *smooth*
smooth-spoken 677.13 *honeyed;* 421.6 *smooth-mannered*
smooth surface 421.7 *smoothness*
smooth-surfaced 421.1 *smooth*
smooth talk 268.21 *cheat*
smooth talker 645.3 *cunning person;* 677.6 *flatterer;* 729.10 *speaker*
smooth-talking 729.20 *eloquent*
smooth texture 421.7 *smoothness*
smooth-textured 421.1 *smooth*
smooth the way 268.20 *ease;* 265.16 *make easy*
smooth the way for 104.9 *make probable*
smooth thing 421.8
smooth-tongued 677.13 *honeyed*
smooth water 421.8 *smooth thing*
smorgasbord 25.12 *hors d'oeuvre;* 376.32 *miscellany*
smother 736.8 *conceal;* 357.8 *destroy;* 382.17 *murder;* 335.8 *overpower;* 66.4 *play soccer;* 251.8 *restrain;* 506.2 *silence*
smothered 736.14 *concealed;* 511.2 *nonresonant*
smothering 357.1 *destruction;* 251.1 *restraint*
smoulder 624.11 *be angry;* 339.4 *be inert;* 626.11 *be irritable;* 493.15 *burn*
smouldering 624.16 *angry;* 493.9 *hot;* 339.5 *inert;* 626.7 *irritable;* 301.5 *sedentary*
smriti 7.12 *religious text*
smudge 532.11 *blacken;* 548.7 *blemish;* 231.7 *defect;* 258.4 *dirt;* 258.11 *dirty;* 548.1 *spot*
smudged 258.7 *dirty*
smudgy 532.2 *dark*
smug 622.17 *conceited;* 658.9 *deferential;* 795.10 *moralistic;* 609.4 *satisfied;* 673.10 *self-admiring;* 673.9 *self-satisfied*
smuggle 800.10 *be criminal;* 776.1 *trade*
smuggled 16.59 *stolen*
smuggler 776.10 *trader*
smuggling 776.4 *trade*
smugly 673.20
smugness 609.1 *satisfaction;* 795.4 *self-righteousness;* 673.2 *self-satisfaction*
smur 548.3 *blot on the landscape*
smut 532.9 *black thing;* 523.4 *dark thing;* 258.4 *dirt;* 796.2 *indecency*
smuts 83.3 *fungi;* 427.5 *powder*
smuttiness 258.3 *obscenity*
smutty 539.4, 796.12 *indecent;* 258.9 *obscene;* 675.9 *ribald*
snack 25.10; 557.24 *have a meal;* 557.12 *meal;* 581.7 *refreshments*
snack bar 557.15 *eating place*
snacking 557.4 *eating meals*
snacks 557.7 *food*
snaffle 774.12 *steal*
snafu 378.8 *hinder;* 408.19 *mixed-up;* 408.6 *mix-up;* 264.5 *predicament*
snag 264.8; 378.9 *block;* 254.5 *danger;* 231.7 *defect;* 378.2 *obstacle;* 379.1 *trap;* 79.2 *tree part*
snagged 420.2 *coarse;* 425.4 *toothed*
snaggled 420.2 *coarse*
snaggletooth 425.11 *tooth*
snaggle-toothed 425.4 *toothed*
snaggy 420.2 *coarse;* 254.1 *dangerous;* 425.4 *toothed*
snail 44.12 *pests and diseases;* 25.19 *shellfish;* 333.14 *slow creature;* 333.15 *slow person*
snail-like 75.19 *molluscan;* 333.4 *slow*
snail-paced 333.4 *slow*
snail shell 550.14 *animal covering;* 180.3 *convoluted thing*
snail's pace 333.10 *slow motion*
snake 73.3; 180.6 *convolute;* 180.3 *convoluted thing;* 645.3 *cunning person;* 362.12 *drag;* 14.1 *finance;* 512.3 *hisser;* 651.8 *malefactor;* 700.21 *traitor;* 325.5 *twist;* 804.9 *wicked person*
snake and mongoose 586.4 *fighting animal*
snakebite 558.8 *mixed drink*
snake charmer 21.31 *circus performer;* 73.10 *herpetologist*
snake eyes 69.5 *dice*
snake in the grass 236.12 *bad person;* 645.3 *cunning person;* 800.4 *dishonourable person;* 798.6 *evil person;* 378.7 *hinderer;* 651.8 *malefactor;* 700.21 *traitor;* 804.9 *wicked person*
snakelike 73.12; 73.11 *reptilian*
snake worship 9.2 *idolatry*
snake worshipper 9.6 *idolater*
snake-worshipping 9.10 *idolatrous*
snakily 268.22 *slimily*
snaking 90.10 *fluvial;* 325.21 *indirect*
snaky 73.12 *snakelike*
snap 515.1 *animal cry;* 624.11 *be angry;* 424.4 *be brittle;* 422.8 *be elastic;* 626.11 *be irritable;* 373.11 *connect;* 508.2, 508.6 *crack;* 515.4 *cry;* 265.6 *easy thing;* 422.1 *elasticity;* 742.11 *gesture;* 46.8 *huddle;* 41.3, 41.21 *photograph;* 717.9 *represent;* 372.9 *separate;* 624.6 *sign of anger;* 625.2 *sign of irascibility;* 626.4 *sign of irritableness;*

729.13 *speak in a particular way*; 478.2 *spontaneous*; 330.23 *throw*; 338.1 *vigour*
snap at 625.6 *be irascible*; 624.13 *vent one's anger*
snapback 422.1 *elasticity*
snap back 422.8 *be elastic*
snap count 46.8 *huddle*
snap decision 478.5 *spontaneity*
snaplink 62.4 *climbing equipment*
snap off 424.4 *be brittle*
snap of the fingers 124.7 *triviality*
snap one's fingers at 662.15 *be disobedient*; 661.6 *be insubordinate*; 660.29 *ridicule*; 124.12 *think unimportant*
snap one's head off 625.6 *be irascible*
snap out of it 581.2 *be refreshed*; 393.4 *be restored*
snapper 55.4 *American game fish*
snappily 332.14 *swiftly*
snapping 624.16 *angry*; 422.6 *elastic*; 626.7 *irritable*
snappish 625.4 *irascible*; 626.7 *irritable*
snappishness 624.4 *anger*
snappy 659.5 *discourteous*; 625.4 *irascible*; 332.1 *swift*; 338.4 *vigorous*
snappy dresser 553.5 *fashion model*; 551.27 *model*
snappy pace 332.8 *speed*
snap ring 62.4 *climbing equipment*
snap roll 322.5 *flight*
snaps 373.8 *fastening*
snapshot 41.3 *photograph*; 744.1 *record*
snap up 688.5 *be greedy*; 557.22 *eat well*; 777.1 *purchase*
snare 700.13; **700.33**; 363.5 *lure*; 43.14 *pest control*; 379.1, 379.2 *trap*
snared 700.42 *trapped*
snark 70.7 *legendary beast*
snarl 515.1 *animal cry*; 624.11 *be angry*; 626.11 *be irritable*; 515.4 *cry*; 234.2 *facial distortion*; 625.7 *frown*; 408.24 *make disordered*; 234.10 *make faces*; 264.5 *predicament*; 624.6 *sign of anger*; 625.2 *sign of irascibility*; 626.4 *sign of irritableness*; 729.13 *speak in a particular way*; 408.7 *tangle*
snarled-up 408.19 *mixed-up*
snarling 626.7 *irritable*; 625.5 *showing irascibility*
snarling dog 254.6 *danger signal*
snarl up 408.23 *confuse*
snarl-up 408.6 *mix-up*; 264.5 *predicament*
snatch 362.3 *jerk*; 362.13 *pull at*; 774.12 *steal*; 773.7 *take*; 608.14 *take away*; 774.3 *theft*; 492.11 *touch*
snatch a bag 774.12 *steal*
snatch a purse 774.12 *steal*
snatch at 633.10 *chase*; 362.13 *pull at*
snatch block 50.3 *parts of a sailing boat*
snatcher 773.6 *taker*
snatch from the grave 393.6 *cure*
snatching 774.1 *stealing*; 773.1 *taking*
snatchy 133.8 *discontinuous*
snazzily 551.36 *dressily*
snazzy 553.7 *fashionable*; 551.31 *styled*
sneak 614.4 *be a coward*; 699.23 *be deceitful*; 700.23 *deceive*; 46.15 *play offence*
sneak after 633.9 *follow*
sneakers 49.3 *basketball equipment*; 551.19 *footwear*; 57.2 *gymnastic clothing*
sneakily 702.15 *hypocritically*
sneak in 314.11 *infiltrate*
sneakiness 702.3 *cunning*; 699.5 *deceitfulness*; 700.1 *deception*
sneaking 664.7 *sycophantic*
sneaking suspicion 476.2 *basis of supposition*
sneak off 389.5 *escape*; 634.8 *run away*
sneak off with 774.12 *steal*
sneak out 98.16 *absent oneself*; 389.5 *escape*
sneak thief 774.8 *thief*
sneaky 702.8 *cunning*; 699.33 *deceitful*; 700.34 *deceiving*
sneer 660.6 *contempt*; 234.2 *facial distortion*; 234.10 *make faces*; 660.29, 678.14 *ridicule*; 670.9 *show of disapproval*; 668.6, 668.25 *taunt*
sneer at 596.6 *react against*
sneered at 670.35 *hissed*
sneering 660.6 *contempt*; 660.17 *contemptuous*; 678.17 *scornful*; 668.15 *taunting*
sneeringly 660.34 *contemptuously*; 621.7 *mockingly*
sneeze 512.1, 512.4 *hiss*
sneeze at 470.3 *exclude*
sneezer 815.2 *the inside*
sneezing 512.1 *hiss*; 512.6 *hissing*
snick 53.17 *bat*; 53.9 *stroke*
snicker 599.14 *laugh*
snickersnee 587.8 *sharp weapon*
snide 678.16 *defamatory*; 780.15 *false money*; 236.5 *harmful*; 651.14 *hostile*
snideness 651.4 *bitterness*
sniff 370.12 *draw in*; 370.4 *intake*; 500.2 *sense of smell*; 500.7 *smell*; 668.6, 668.25 *taunt*
sniff at 470.3 *exclude*; 596.6 *react against*; 500.7 *smell*; 557.23 *taste*
sniffer dog 449.12 *discoverer*; 71.9 *dog*; 252.3 *protector*; 500.2 *sense of smell*
sniffing 691.1 *drug-taking*; 370.4 *intake*; 500.2 *sense of smell*
sniffle 370.12 *draw in*; 370.4 *intake*; 500.2 *sense of smell*; 500.7 *smell*
sniffly 260.23 *diseased*
sniff out 644.7 *be curious*; 449.2 *detect*; 633.9 *follow*; 500.7 *smell*
snifter 558.2, 690.13 *drink*
snigger 514.2 *cry of joy*; 514.11, 599.14 *laugh*; 600.3 *laughter*
snigger about 621.6 *deride*
sniggle 700.13, 700.33 *snare*
snip 793.4 *bargain*; 159.4 *little person*; 205.7 *piece*
snipe 330.31; 25.20 *meat*; 72.4 *table bird*; 72.3 *water bird*
snipe at 670.17 *criticize*; 381.2 *fire*
sniper 381.19 *attacker*; 330.15 *shooter*; 586.8 *soldier*
sniping 381.15 *firing*; 381.16 *terrorist attack*; 585.8 *warfare*
snippet 159.3 *little piece*; 205.7 *piece*
snippets 412.3 *miscellany*
snitch 715.5 *accuse*; 715.3 *accuser*; 693.10 *informer*; 693.13 *inform on*; 774.12 *steal*
snitcher 715.3 *accuser*
snitching 774.1 *stealing*
snivel 603.7 *weep*
sniveller 603.3 *lamenter*
snivelling 664.7 *sycophantic*
snob 622.13 *proud person*
snobbery 622.3 *conceit*; 549.3 *etiquette*; 622.11 *prejudice*
snobbish 622.17 *conceited*; 668.13 *contemptuous*; 465.8 *unjust*
Sno-Cat 320.10 *sled*
snood 551.15 *headgear*
snook 55.4 *American game fish*; 660.7 *insult*; 668.7 *sign of disrespect*
snooker 65.5; 264.23 *cause difficulties*; 378.8 *hinder*
snookered 65.9 *billiard*; 264.16 *troubled*
snooker player 65.7 *billiards player*
Snooker, Pool, and Billiards 65
snooker table 65.5 *snooker*
snookums 593.12 *nicknames for lovers*
snoop 644.7 *be curious*; 644.4 *meddler*
snooping 644.2, 644.6 *prying*
snoopy 644.6 *prying*
snoot 185.3 *protuberance*; 500.2 *sense of smell*
snooty 622.17 *conceited*; 668.13 *contemptuous*; 673.8 *vain*
snooze 339.4 *be inert*; 263.1 *ease*; 343.9, 343.13 *sleep*; 263.2 *take it easy*; 489.2 *unconsciousness*
snore 507.8 *be loud*; 620.2 *boring thing*; 513.2 *hoarseness*; 513.5 *sound hoarse*
snoring 513.8 *hoarse*; 507.1 *loudness*
snorkel 67.9 *swim*; 67.1 *swimming*
snorkeler 67.4 *swimmer*
snorkeling 67.1 *swimming*
snort 515.4 *cry*; 690.13 *drink*; 691.6 *drug*; 691.10 *drug oneself*; 513.2 *hoarseness*; 660.29 *ridicule*; 626.4 *sign of irritableness*; 513.5 *sound hoarse*; 668.6, 668.25 *taunt*
snorting 691.1 *drug-taking*; 513.8 *hoarse*; 261.3 *panting*
snot 431.3 *body fluid*; 258.4 *dirt*; 430.5 *mucus*; 560.9 *saliva*
snotty 668.13 *contemptuous*
snout 30.38 *glacier*; 716.7 *person who gives evidence*; 185.3 *protuberance*; 500.2 *sense of smell*; 454.7 *verifier*
snow 31.30; **31.63**; 217.5 *about*; 305.13 *drip*; 691.6 *drug*; 494.5 *ice*; 31.24 *precipitation*; 419.11 *soft thing*; 692.23 *television reception*; 521.6 *that which makes invisible*; 700.28 *trick*; 531.9 *white thing*
snow and ice climbing 62.1 *mountaineering*
snowball 765.10 *augment*; 330.10 *ball*; 190.6 *become bigger*; 22.2 *dance*; 494.5 *ice*; 213.4 *increase*; 213.3 *increasing thing*; 558.8 *mixed drink*; 330.23 *throw*
snowball effect 132.4 *repercussion*
snowballer 330.14 *thrower*
snowballing 190.8 *growing*; 213.6 *increasing*
snowballing effect 213.1 *increase*
snowball's chance in hell 107.6 *poor chance*
snow bed 31.30 *snow*
snow-blind 519.8 *blind*; 519.10 *blinded*
snow-blinded 519.10 *blinded*
snow blindness 519.1 *blindness*
snowboard 320.10 *sled*
snow bollard belay 62.3 *climbing technique*
snowbound 494.8 *cold*; 251.15 *detained*
snow-capped 89.7 *mountainous*; 531.2 *whitened*
snow-capped mountain 89.1 *mountain*
snow-clad 31.55 *cool*; 89.7 *mountainous*
snow-clad peak 89.1 *mountain*
snow cover 31.30 *snow*
snow-covered 31.55 *cool*; 531.2 *whitened*
snow crystal 494.5 *ice*
Snowdon 89.5 *British mountains*
Snowdonia 89.5 *British mountains*; 154.4 *mountain range*
snowdrift 494.5 *ice*; 376.26 *mass*; 31.30 *snow*
snowed in 494.8 *cold*
snowed under 354.7 *overambitious*
snowfall 494.5 *ice*; 31.24 *precipitation*; 31.30 *snow*
snowflake 427.6 *crumb*; 494.5 *ice*; 415.7 *light thing*; 31.24 *precipitation*; 419.11 *soft thing*
snow flurry 494.5 *ice*
snow-forest climate 31.38 *climate*
snowglasses 62.4 *climbing equipment*
snow house 494.6 *Arctic*
snowily 31.65 *meteorologically*
snowiness 531.7 *whiteness*
snow job 700.7 *tricking*
snowline 494.6 *Arctic*
snowman 424.3 *brittle thing*; 494.5 *ice*; 717.6 *image*
snowmobile 320.10 *sled*
snowplough 256.10 *cleaning object*; 68.12, 68.14 *ski*; 68.4 *skiing technique*
snowplough brake 68.2 *cross-country skiing*
snowplough glide 68.2 *cross-country skiing*
snowploughing 68.12 *ski*; 68.4 *skiing technique*
snowplough turn 68.2 *cross-country skiing*; 68.4 *skiing technique*
snowplough wedeln 68.4 *skiing technique*
Snow Queen 494.5 *ice*
snow season 292.1 *season*
snow shed 321.8 *railway station*
snowshoes 551.19 *footwear*
snow shower 31.30 *snow*
snow ski 68.14 *ski*
snow-skiing 68.1 *skiing*
snowslide 305.3 *downflow*
snowslip 305.3 *downflow*
snowstorm 494.5 *ice*; 31.30 *snow*; 380.5 *violent weather*
snow under 208.12 *overcrowd*
snow-white 255.14 *purified*; 531.1 *white*
snowy 256.16 *clean*; 494.8 *cold*; 31.55 *cool*; 795.9 *pure*; 255.14 *purified*; 531.1 *white*
snowy picture 692.23 *television reception*
snub 659.3 *act of discourtesy*; 634.1 *avoid*; 634.10 *avoidance*; 659.7 *be discourteous*; 426.1 *blunt*; 367.4 *debase*; 709.6 *dissent*; 470.3 *exclude*; 606.2 *expression of dissatisfaction*; 623.17 *humiliate*; 655.13 *ignore*; 668.5, 668.23 *insult*; 371.4 *ostracize*; 470.5 *rejection*; 364.1 *repel*; 364.6 *repulse*; 149.7 *short*
snubbed 470.10 *rejected*
snubbing 668.11 *insulting*
snubness 149.1 *shortness*
snub-nosed 149.7 *short*
snuff 370.12 *draw in*; 370.4 *intake*; 382.16 *kill*; 523.14 *make dark*; 500.7 *smell*; 496.7 *tobacco*
snuffbox 410.6 *box*; 496.7 *tobacco*
snuff-coloured 534.1 *brown*
snuff it 94.12 *cease to exist*; 582.15 *die*
snuffle 370.12 *draw in*; 512.4 *hiss*; 370.4 *intake*; 500.7 *smell*
snuffler 700.19 *hypocrite*; 500.2 *sense of smell*
snuffly 260.23 *diseased*
snuff movie 796.2 *indecency*
snuff out 94.13 *cause not to exist*; 357.8 *destroy*; 523.14 *make dark*
snug 263.4 *at ease*; 241.3 *comfortable*; 493.9 *hot*; 252.7 *invulnerable*; 159.7 *little*; 490.6 *pleasant*; 490.7 *pleased*; 565.7 *room*; 252.6 *safe*; 428.10 *waterproof*
snuggery 410.2 *compartment*; 565.5 *house*; 490.4 *pleasurable things*; 565.7 *room*
snuggle 490.8 *feel pleasure*; 593.27 *kiss*
snuggling 593.14 *communication of love*
snugness 159.1 *littleness*
so 750.36 *accordingly*; 317.16 *how*; 115.13 *similarly*; 222.15 *under the circumstances*
soak 370.13 *absorb*; 256.14 *bathe*; 219.4 *be excessive*; 97.11 *be present*; 232.6 *fill*; 690.8 *get drunk*; 369.17 *obtain an extract*; 792.10 *overcharge*; 433.9 *soaking*; 433.29 *water*
soakage 433.9 *soaking*
soakaway 767.8 *sink*
soaked 690.3 *dead drunk*; 219.6 *excessive*; 632.13 *fixed*; 433.23 *wet*
soaked to the skin 433.23 *wet*
soaker 690.17 *drunkard*
soak in 370.13 *absorb*; 305.9 *descend*; 314.11 *infiltrate*
soaking 433.9; 256.5 *ablutions*; 370.17 *absorbent*; 24.5 *ceramic process*; 558.1, 690.11 *drinking*; 369.7 *obtaining an extract*
soaking wet 433.23 *wet*
soak through 318.10 *enter*
soak up 370.13, 428.20 *absorb*; 374.5 *combine*; 558.13 *drink*
so and so 566.7 *person*
soap 256.14 *bathe*; 692.25 *broadcast material*; 256.9 *cleaning agent*; 268.5 *lubricant*; 268.18 *lubricate*; 721.3 *narration*; 21.2 *play*; 255.3 *purifier*; 419.11 *soft thing*
soap and water 256.9 *cleaning agent*; 255.3 *purifier*; 433.11 *wash*
soapbox 740.7 *publicity*; 21.17 *stage*
soapbox orator 662.8 *agitator*; 733.6 *public speaker*; 729.10 *speaker*
soapbox oratory 729.9 *art of public speaking*
soapflakes 256.9 *cleaning agent*; 255.3 *purifier*
soapily 268.23 *oilily*
soapiness 268.3 *oiliness*
soaping 256.5 *ablutions*
soap opera 692.25 *broadcast material*; 721.3 *narration*; 21.2 *play*
soap pad 256.9 *cleaning agent*
soap powder 256.9 *cleaning agent*
soap the ways 268.20 *ease*; 265.16 *make easy*
soapy 658.9 *deferential*; 421.4 *polished*; 268.13 *slippery*; 664.7 *sycophantic*; 531.2 *whitened*
soar 304.13 *ascend*; 158.19 *be big*; 792.9 *be dear*; 154.15 *be high*; 300.13 *be in motion*; 415.9 *be light*; 72.25, 322.10 *fly*; 213.4 *increase*; 304.19 *take off*; 89.9 *tower*
soarer 304.11 *ascender*
soaring 300.7 *ascending motion*; 792.7 *dear*; 300.17 *directional*; 322.5 *flight*; 154.9 *high*; 89.7 *mountainous*; 304.23 *rising*; 304.4 *taking off*
soaring prices 792.3 *inflationary price*
sob 514.13 *cry*; 514.6 *cry of pain*; 602.8 *grieve*; 729.13 *speak in a particular way*; 603.7 *weep*
sobbing 514.18 *crying*; 603.1 *lamentation*
sober 689.1; 4.18 *detached*; 803.6 *ethical*; 685.4, 685.6 *moderate*; 460.4 *sane*; 684.8 *self-restrained*; 271.1 *simple*; 529.13 *soft-hued*; 643.1 *solemn*
sober as a judge 689.1 *sober*; 643.1 *solemn*
sober down 460.6 *be sane*; 685.4 *moderate*
sobered up 689.1 *sober*
soberly 689.9; 803.10 *ethically*; 460.7 *sanely*; 643.10 *solemnly*; 4.27 *stoically*; 622.33 *with dignity*
soberness 684.1 *self-restraint*; 271.4 *simplicity*; 689.6 *sobriety*; 803.2 *virtues*

sober person 689.8; 684.4 *self-restrained person*
sobersides 684.4 *self-restrained person*; 643.7 *serious person*
sober up 689.5; 685.3 *be moderate*; 460.6 *be sane*
so big 158.13 *this size*
Sobriety 689
sobriety 689.6; 4.3 *detachment*; 685.1 *moderation*; 460.1 *sanity*; 684.1 *self-restraint*
sobriquet 721.8 *name*
sob story 603.2 *lament*
soca 18.10 *world music*
socage 440.3 *historic property terms*; 763.3 *medieval ownership*
so-called 96.12 *artificial*; 451.7 *disbelieved*; 702.10 *hypocritical*; 125.13 *imitation*; 699.34 *pretending*; 476.8 *supposed*
Soccer 66
soccer 66.1; **66.5**
soccer football 66.1 *soccer*
Sociability 654
sociability 654.1; **657.2**; 650.1 *benevolence*; 598.3 *cheerfulness*; 658.1 *courtesy*; 731.2 *effusiveness*; 569.1 *friendship*; 342.2 *social activity*
sociable 654.15; **657.8**; 342.18 *active*; 97.8 *attendant*; 650.6 *benevolent*; 598.1 *cheerful*; 658.7 *courteous*; 731.6 *effusive*; 569.8 *friendly*
sociableness 654.1 *sociability*
sociably 654.18; 650.10 *benevolently*; 658.14 *courteously*; 731.11 *effusively*; 569.17 *in friendship*
social 654.3 *meeting*; 566.13 *national*; 70.15 *of animals*; 654.15 *sociable*; 376.9, 734.3 *social gathering*; 2.12 *sociological*
social ability 654.1 *sociability*
social action 2.9 *social change*
social activity 342.2; 654.1 *sociability*
social affair 654.3 *meeting*
social ambition 654.2
social animal 654.10
social anthropologist 566.6 *studier of mankind*
social anthropology 1.1 *anthropology*; 2.1 *sociology*; 566.5 *study of mankind*
social assistance 392.4
social benefit 2.9 *social change*
social butterfly 654.6 *social person*
social call 654.3 *meeting*
social change 2.9; 244.11 *reformism*
Social Chapter 15.5 *labour law*
social charter 15.1 *industrial relations*
social circle 654.7 *human society*
social class 137.5; 654.7 *human society*; 2.7 *social stratification*
social classes 566.9 *group*
social class system 2.7 *social stratification*
social climbing 654.2 *social ambition*
social code 656.5 *etiquette*
social conduct 656.5 *etiquette*
social conscience 652.2 *public spiritedness*
social consciousness 652.2 *public spiritedness*
social contact 2.3 *social environment*
social control 2.9 *social change*
social convention 656.5 *etiquette*
social courtesies 658.3 *courtesies*
social custom 632.4 *custom*
social dance 22.4 *historic dancing*
social demand 654.2 *social ambition*
Social Democratic Party 12.6 *political party*
social differences 2.3 *social environment*
social discrimination 466.4; 128.4 *exclusiveness*; 622.11 *prejudice*
social disease 260.14 *venereal disease*
social diversity 2.7 *social stratification*
social drinker 558.12 *drinker*; 690.17 *drunkard*; 689.8 *sober person*
social engineering 2.9 *social change*
social environment 2.3
social gathering 376.9; **734.3**; 654.3 *meeting*
social graces 656.5 *etiquette*; 654.2 *social ambition*
social group 2.6; 376.17 *family*; 566.9 *group*; 654.7 *human society*
social heterogeneity 2.5 *society*
social history 3.1 *history*
social image 656.5 *etiquette*
social insect 76.4
social institution 2.8 *human institution*
social interaction 2.3 *social environment*
social intercourse 734.1 *conversation*; 654.1 *sociability*
socialism 12.1 *government*; 764.1 *joint possession*; 747.6 *movement*; 566.11 *nation*; 652.2 *public spiritedness*; 244.11 *reformism*; 4.7 *school of thought*; 396.7 *type of rule*; 650.3 *welfare*
socialist 4.11 *follower of a doctrine*; 12.9 *governmental*; 747.18 *joint*; 85.16 *national*; 4.14 *of a philosophy*; 764.3 *participant*; 244.12 *reformer*
socialist country 85.1 *country*
socialistic 12.9, 396.14 *governmental*; 764.5 *jointly possessing*; 85.16, 566.13 *national*; 652.6 *philanthropic*
socialistically 764.6 *in common*; 396.24 *ministerially*; 85.19 *nationally*; 652.8 *philanthropically*
socialist realist 19.29 *realist*
Socialists 12.6 *political party*
socialist state 566.11 *nation*
socialite 342.10 *busy person*; 412.7 *person who mixes*; 654.6 *social person*
sociality 654.1 *sociability*
socialization 244.5 *improvement*; 764.1 *joint possession*; 2.3 *social environment*
socialize 2.15; 85.17 *become a nation*; 764.4 *have joint possession*; 244.1 *improve*; 223.14 *keep company with*
social lion 654.6 *social person*
socially 566.15 *humanly*; 654.18 *sociably*; 2.16 *sociologically*
socially accepted 632.12 *established*; 654.16 *popular*
socially active person 342.10 *busy person*
socially disposed 654.15 *sociable*
socially successful 654.16 *popular*
social manners 632.5 *tradition*
social-minded 654.15 *sociable*
social-mindedness 654.1 *sociability*
social mobility 2.7 *social stratification*
social morphology 2.1 *sociology*
social movement 2.9 *social change*; 2.7 *social stratification*
socialness 654.1 *sociability*
social novel 17.2 *fiction*
social obligation 2.9 *social change*
social order 2.3 *social environment*
social organization 2.4
social outcast 766.6 *loser*
social person 654.6
social planning 2.9 *social change*
social policy 2.9 *social change*
social position 221.1 *state*
social prestige 2.7 *social stratification*
social procedures 656.5 *etiquette*
social progress 2.9 *social change*
social psychologist 2.11 *sociologist*
social psychology 36.1 *psychology*; 2.1 *sociology*
social pyramid 2.7 *social stratification*
social rank 209.2 *rank*
social realist 19.29 *realist*
social reformer 627.4 *pitying person*; 2.11 *sociologist*
social relations 654.1 *sociability*; 2.3 *social environment*
social role 2.3 *social environment*
social round 654.3 *meeting*
social science 2.1 *sociology*; 566.5 *study of mankind*
social scientist 2.11 *sociologist*
social season 292.1 *season*
social security 253.1 *protection*; 252.1 *safety*; 392.4 *social assistance*; 2.10 *social services*; 413.8 *supporter*; 650.3 *welfare*; 652.4 *welfare state*
social security benefit 768.2 *gift*
social security number 743.3 *means of identification*
social security payments 765.4 *earnings*
social services 2.10; 392.4 *social assistance*; 413.8 *supporter*; 650.3 *welfare*; 652.4 *welfare state*
social set 654.7 *human society*
social skill 485.1 *skill*
social skills 654.1 *sociability*
social state 12.5 *political organization*
social status 137.5 *social class*; 2.7 *social stratification*
social stratification 2.7
social structure 2.7 *social stratification*
social success 654.2 *social ambition*
social survey 2.2 *sociological research*
social system 2.4 *social organization*
social tact 658.1 *courtesy*
social trait 2.3 *social environment*
social transformation 2.9 *social change*
social usage 632.4 *custom*
social welfare 650.3 *welfare*; 652.4 *welfare state*
social whirl 654.3 *meeting*
social work 2.10 *social services*; 650.3 *welfare*
social worker 713.4 *adviser*; 650.5 *benevolent person*; 665.7 *caring person*; 652.3 *philanthropist*; 244.12 *reformer*; 2.11 *sociologist*; 752.8 *volunteer*; 578.1 *worker*
societal 1.14; 566.13 *national*; 2.12 *sociological*
societally 1.18
society 1.7; **2.5**; 750.2 *alliance*; 374.3 *assembly*; 376.15 *association*; 223.3 *companionship*; 566.9 *group*; 97.2 *omnipresence*; 2.4 *social organization*
sociobiological 34.20 *biological*; 2.12 *sociological*
sociobiologically 2.16 *sociologically*
sociobiologist 34.19 *life scientist*; 2.11 *sociologist*
sociobiology 70.9 *animal science*; 34.1 *life science*; 2.1 *sociology*
sociodrama 21.2 *play*
socioeconomic 2.14
socioeconomically 2.16 *sociologically*
sociolinguist 5.2 *linguist*
sociolinguistic 5.38 *linguistic*
sociolinguistics 5.1 *linguistics*
sociologese 2.2 *sociological research*
sociological 2.12; 1.11 *anthropological*
sociological analysis 2.2 *sociological research*
sociological jargon 2.2 *sociological research*
sociologically 2.16
sociological method 2.2 *sociological research*
sociological model 2.2 *sociological research*
sociological perspective 2.2 *sociological research*
sociological research 2.2
sociological theory 2.2 *sociological research*
sociological tool 2.2 *sociological research*
sociologist 2.11; 566.6 *studier of mankind*
Sociology 2
sociology 2.1; 554.7 *studies of life*; 566.5 *study of mankind*
sociology of knowledge 2.1 *sociology*
sociometric technique 2.2 *sociological research*
sociopath 36.8 *disordered personality*
sociopathic 36.36 *psychologically disturbed*
socio-political group 566.9 *group*
sock 21.12 *comedy*; 52.11 *fight*; 331.3 *hit*
sock and buskin 551.5 *fancy dress*
sock away 350.6 *stop using*; 439.6 *store*
socket 183.3 *cavity*; 437.4 *electricity*; 39.28 *plug*
socking 52.2 *boxing*
socks 551.20 *legwear*
Socrates 4.12 *sage*
Socrates and the fool 113.3 *opposites*
Socratic 348.7 *causal*; 4.14 *of a philosophy*
Socratic elenchus 705.2 *questioning*
Socraticism 4.7 *school of thought*
Socratist 4.11 *follower of a doctrine*
sod 264.3 *difficult task*; 81.2 *grassland*; 81.12 *manage grassland*; 566.7 *person*; 205.7 *piece*
soda 256.9 *cleaning agent*; 558.8 *mixed drink*; 255.3 *purifier*; 558.6 *soft drink*
soda biscuit 25.39 *loaf*
soda bread 25.38 *bread*
soda cracker 25.39 *loaf*
soda fountain 557.15 *eating place*; 558.6 *soft drink*
soda jerk 401.3 *attendant*
sodality 747.2 *fellowship*; 569.1 *friendship*
sod all 195.2 *nothing*
soda water 433.2 *drinking water*; 558.6 *soft drink*
sodden 690.5 *drunken*; 429.11 *marshy*; 429.9 *moist*; 433.23 *wet*
soddenness 429.1 *moisture*
sodium 33.15 *essential element*
sodium lamp 522.6 *electric light*
sod off 313.1 *depart*; 313.15 *go!*
sodomy 796.7 *sexual assault*
sod's law 140.3 *rule of nature*
sofa 23.2 *chair*; 413.4 *rest*; 419.11 *soft thing*
sofa bed 23.6 *bed*
soft 419.1; 593.20 *amorous*; 24.10 *ceramic*; 227.13 *changeable*; 117.11 *conformable*; 614.3 *cowardly*; 558.17 *drinkable*; 511.1 *faint-sounding*; 504.14 *hearable*; 506.6 *hush!*; 415.2 *insubstantial*; 337.13 *insufficient*; 648.4 *lenient*; 516.6 *melodious*; 685.8 *moderating*; 689.2 *nonalcoholic*; 663.7 *obedient*; 627.6 *pitying*; 490.6 *pleasant*; 506.3 *silent*; 421.1 *smooth*; 529.13 *soft-hued*; 417.1 *sparse*; 388.5 *submitting*; 457.6 *unintelligent*; 337.8 *weak*
soft as a kiss 419.5 *soft as butter*
soft as a sigh 419.5 *soft as butter*
soft as a whisper 419.5 *soft as butter*
soft as butter 419.5
soft as dough 419.5 *soft as butter*
soft as down 419.5 *soft as butter*
soft as putty 419.5 *soft as butter*
soft as silk 419.5 *soft as butter*
soft as soap 419.5 *soft as butter*
soft as velvet 419.5 *soft as butter*
soft as wax 419.5 *soft as butter*
soft coal 435.1 *materials*
soft-core pornography 796.2 *indecency*
soft corn 260.15 *ulcer*
soft currency 780.1 *money*
soft damp snow 68.1 *skiing*
soft drink 558.6; 498.5 *sweet drink*
soft drug 691.6 *drug*
soften 419.13; 490.60 *comfort*; 627.11 *excite pity*; 244.1 *improve*; 714.8 *justify*; 685.4 *moderate*; 136.15 *modify*; 511.7 *mute*; 608.9 *relieve*; 649.12 *show mercy*; 337.7 *weaken*
softened 136.11 *modified*; 419.1 *soft*
softening 214.6 *decreasing*; 136.5 *modification*; 419.1 *soft*; 419.8 *softness*
softening of the brain 335.4 *disability*; 461.3 *mental deterioration*
softening-up 419.8 *softness*
soften the blow 634.3 *abstain*
soften the tone 419.14 *ease*
soften up 677.9 *blarney*; 243.2 *do the groundwork*; 419.13 *soften*; 337.7 *weaken*
soft-fire 24.11 *make ceramics*
soft firing 24.5 *ceramic process*
soft focus 524.2 *murk*
soft-focus 524.6 *murky*
soft focusing 41.13 *framing*
soft fruit 80.1 *fruits*; 44.10 *fruit tree*
soft-fruit growing 44.1 *horticulture*
soft furnishing 42.3 *fabric*
soft furnishings 23.1 *furniture*; 550.8 *wall covering*
soft glaze 24.3 *glaze*
soft-grained 79.15 *woody*
soft hail 31.29 *hail*
soft heart 231.7 *defect*; 627.1 *pity*
soft-hearted 419.6; 650.6 *benevolent*; 627.6 *pitying*; 590.12, 591.1 *sensitive*
soft-heartedly 419.18; 650.10 *benevolently*
soft-heartedness 650.1 *benevolence*; 627.1 *pity*
soft-hued 529.13
soft in the head 457.6 *unintelligent*
soft landing 29.35 *rocketry*
soft light 41.15 *lighting*; 522.2 *quality of light*
softly 419.17; 227.15 *changeably*; 511.10 *faintly*; 648.6 *leniently*; 415.11 *lightly*; 663.10 *obediently*; 589.8 *peacefully*; 506.5 *silently*; 421.15 *soothingly*; 337.14 *weakly*
softly-softly 333.6 *hesitant*; 333.17 *in slow motion*
soft metal 18.9 *popular music*
Softness 419
softness 419.8; 227.1 *changeableness*; 404.2 *grain*; 335.3 *helplessness*; 529.3 *hue*; 648.1 *leniency*; 415.5 *lightness*; 511.3 *mutedness*; 663.1 *obedience*; 480.7 *persuadability*; 490.1 *physical pleasure*; 117.3 *pliancy*; 506.4 *silence*; 421.7 *smoothness*; 417.3 *sparseness*; 337.1 *weakness*
soft-nosed bullet 587.13 *ammunition*
soft option 265.6 *easy thing*
soft palate 729.5 *organ of speech*
soft-paste 24.10 *ceramic*
soft-paste porcelain 24.1 *ceramics*
soft pedal 505.3 *inaudibility*; 730.8 *mute*; 511.6 *silencer*
soft-pedal 685.4 *moderate*; 511.7 *mute*; 506.2 *silence*; 468.3 *underestimate*
soft pitch 48.4 *pitching terms*
soft porn 796.2 *indecency*

soft return 40.19 *computing terms*
soft rock 18.9 *popular music*
soft roe 74.5 *fish anatomy*; 25.16 *fish dish*
soft rot 44.12 *pests and diseases*; 79.10 *tree disease*
soft sector 40.19 *computing terms*
soft sell 480.6 *advertising*; 483.2 *inducement*; 778.6 *salesmanship*
soft-shoe shuffle 22.2 *dance*
soft shoulder 320.3 *carriageway*; 164.1 *edge*
soft ski 68.5 *ski equipment*
soft soap 677.2 *blarney*; 658.1 *courtesy*; 480.2 *flattery*; 699.3, 700.3 *hypocrisy*
soft-soap 700.26 *be a hypocrite*; 658.10 *be courteous*; 699.22 *be hypocritical*; 677.9 *blarney*; 664.9 *fawn*; 599.15 *humour*
soft-soaping 677.13 *honeyed*; 699.31 *hypocritical*; 664.2 *sycophancy*; 664.7 *sycophantic*
soft sound 511.4 *faint sound*
soft-speaking 729.19 *speaking*
soft-spoken 729.19 *speaking*
soft spot 231.7 *defect*; 595.3 *likes*; 254.7 *vulnerability*
soft thing 419.11
soft tick 76.2 *arachnid*
soft tongue 658.1 *courtesy*
soft-tongued 658.8 *good-mannered*
soft touch 700.22 *dupe*; 265.6 *easy thing*
soft toy 717.6 *image*
soft underbelly 488.2 *ability to sense*; 231.7 *defect*; 254.7 *vulnerability*
soft vacuum 32.20 *surface chemistry*
software 40.8; 40.4 *computer*
soft water 433.1 *water*
softwood 79.1 *tree*; 23.12 *wood*; 79.15 *woody*
softwood paddle 50.6 *canoeing*
soft words 593.14 *communication of love*; 658.1 *courtesy*
softy 337.4 *weakling*
soggily 92.13 *continentally*; 429.17 *moistly*; 419.17 *softly*
sogginess 419.10 *compressibility*; 429.1 *moisture*
soggy 419.4 *compressible*; 92.11 *continental*; 429.11 *marshy*; 429.9 *moist*; 433.23 *wet*
so happen 107.10 *chance*
Soho 87.5 *London*
soigné 551.30 *dressed-up*; 543.3 *elegant*; 6.20 *refined*
soignée 656.7 *dressed-up*
soil 30.36; 548.7 *blemish*; 796.19 *corrupt*; 678.12 *defame*; 560.16 *defecate*; 258.4 *dirt*; 258.11 *dirty*; 245.5 *hurt*; 435.1 *materials*
soiled 548.4 *blemished*; 258.7 *dirty*; 231.1 *imperfect*
soil erosion 563.1 *infertility*; 30.36 *soil*
soil horizon 30.36 *soil*
soiling 258.1 *dirtiness*
soil mechanics 38.17 *civil engineering*
soil one's hands 576.6 *work*
soil profile 30.36 *soil*
soil structure 30.36 *soil*
soil texture 30.36 *soil*
so inclined 482.11 *intending*
soirée 291.4 *evening thing*; 654.3 *meeting*; 376.9, 734.3 *social gathering*
so it seems 446.24 *ideologically*
sojourn 564.14, 565.17 *inhabit*; 654.12 *visit*
soke 86.5 *state*
Sol 29.15 *sun*
sol 32.3 *phase*
solace 608.1 *ease*; 608.9 *relieve*
solar 29.36 *astronomical*; 91.7 *oceanic*; 334.17, 437.10 *powered*
solar activity 29.15 *sun*
solar battery 39.29 *power source*; 437.8 *renewable energy*; 334.6 *source of energy*
solar cell 39.25 *photoconductivity*; 39.29 *power source*; 29.32 *satellite*; 334.6 *source of energy*
solar cycle 29.15 *sun*
solar eclipse 523.1 *darkness*; 29.15 *sun*
solar energy 28.11 *energy*; 522.11 *photoelectricity*; 39.29 *power source*; 437.8 *renewable energy*; 334.6 *source of energy*
solar flare 29.15 *sun*
solar heating 493.3 *heater*
solarimeter 26.8 *meter*
solarium 394.14 *hospital*; 493.5 *hot weather*; 565.7 *room*
solarization 41.13 *framing*
solar mass 29.22 *astronomical unit*
solar panel 493.3 *heater*; 39.29 *power source*; 29.32 *satellite*; 334.6 *source of energy*
solar power 437.8 *renewable energy*; 334.6 *source of energy*; 31.22 *sun*
solar-powered 437.10 *powered*
solar radiation 31.22 *sun*
solar spectrum 29.15 *sun*
solar system 29.14
solar telescope 29.24 *telescope*
solar tide 91.2 *tide*
solar time 281.3 *chronology*; 275.9 *time zone*
solar wind 29.14 *solar system*
solatium 813.6 *compensation*
sold 778.16
sold a pup 700.36 *deceived*
solder 267.3 *adhesive*; 493.14 *be hot*; 267.7 *cause to adhere*; 19.14 *sculptor's materials*
soldering 267.1 *adhesion*
soldering iron 493.3 *heater*; 19.14 *sculptor's materials*
soldier 586.8; 585.13 *be at war*; 586.1 *combatant*; 382.10 *killer*; 663.4 *obedient person*; 585.11 *recruit*; 76.4 *social insect*
soldier ant 76.4 *social insect*
soldiering 585.8 *warfare*
soldierlike 586.35 *martial*; 585.17 *military*
soldierly 613.10 *chivalrous*; 586.35 *martial*; 584.8, 585.17 *military*
soldier of fortune 586.6 *militarist*
soldier on 638.11 *persist*
soldiership 585.6 *art of war*
sold into slavery 387.9 *subject*
soldo 780.12 *ancient coins*
sold off 767.14 *for sale*
sold on 593.18 *in love*
sold out 232.8 *full*; 218.4 *scarce*; 778.16 *sold*
sole 572.6 *celibate*; 128.10 *excluding*; 74.8 *food fish*; 175.2 *foot*; 56.4 *golf club*; 197.11 *one*; 393.1 *repair*
solecism 697.2; 5.29 *grammar*; 274.11 *grammatical error*; 675.4 *inelegance*; 544.4 *inelegance of speech*; 720.2 *misinterpretation*; 351.2 *misuse*; 702.2 *sophism*; 702.1 *sophistry*
solecist 702.6 *sophist*
solecistic 351.5 *abusive*; 544.9 *inelegant*; 720.3 *misinterpreted*; 702.7 *sophistic*
solecistically 351.6 *abusively*; 702.14 *sophistically*
solely 197.24 *once*
solemn 643.1; 601.12 *ceremonial*; 656.8 *ceremonious*; 601.11 *commemorative*; 160.11, 656.6 *formal*; 123.5 *important*; 7.15 *religious*; 726.5 *serious*; 506.3 *silent*; 622.19 *stately*; 10.22 *worshipping*
solemn affirmation 707.3 *vow*
solemn entreaty 710.1 *request*
solemness 656.1 *formality*
Solemnity 643
solemnity 643.4; 160.5, 656.1 *formality*; 123.1 *importance*; 622.6 *majesty*; 10.1 *ritual*; 726.2 *seriousness*; 506.4 *silence*
solemnization 601.2 *commemoration*; 10.2 *ritualism*
solemnize 340.4 *act*; 160.8 *be formal*; 601.16 *commemorate*; 656.9 *formalize*; 10.18 *perform rites*
solemnly 643.10; 160.14 *conventionally*; 726.7 *emphatically*; 656.12 *formally*; 7.23 *religiously*; 10.23 *ritually*; 622.33 *with dignity*
solemnly promise 756.7 *promise*
solemnness 506.4 *silence*
solemn oath 707.3 *vow*
solemn observance 601.3 *ceremony*; 10.1 *ritual*
solemn promise 756.1 *promise*
solemn silence 506.4 *silence*
solemn wedding 570.5 *wedding*
solemn word 707.3 *vow*
solenoid 28.60, 363.3 *magnet*
sole possession 763.1 *possession*
sole rights 128.4 *exclusiveness*
sole survivor 215.6 *person remaining*
solfege 18.17 *notation*
solfeggio 18.17 *notation*
solferino 535.6 *red pigment*
solicit 796.18 *prostitute*; 710.6 *request*; 778.1 *sell*
solicitation 710.3; 480.2 *flattery*; 483.2 *inducement*; 710.1 *request*
solicitation of votes 752.5 *offer of public service*
solicit business 776.1 *trade*
soliciting 796.5 *prostitution*; 710.1 *request*; 778.3 *selling*
soliciting money 710.3 *solicitation*
solicit money 710.8
solicitor 713.4 *adviser*; 398.6 *agent*; 16.13 *lawyer*; 746.4 *negotiator*; 710.4 *requester*
Solicitor General 16.11 *British law officer*; 16.12 *US law officer*
solicitous 471.9; 650.6 *benevolent*; 658.7 *courteous*; 629.5 *distrustful*; 612.9 *worried*
solicitously 650.10 *benevolently*; 658.14 *courteously*; 658.15 *genteelly*; 629.9 *jealously*
solicitousness 658.1 *courtesy*; 629.2 *distrust*
solicitude 471.5; 665.2 *consideration*; 658.1 *courtesy*; 612.3 *worry*
solicit votes 752.13 *be a candidate*
solid 32.32; 267.9 *adhesive*; 698.19 *authentic*; 132.11 *continuous*; 416.6 *dense*; 160.9 *formed*; 232.8 *full*; 27.41 *geometric figure*; 414.1 *heavy*; 452.6 *infallible*; 402.7 *material*; 528.1 *opaque*; 225.7 *permanent*; 32.3 *phase*; 97.7 *present*; 95.6 *real*; 111.12 *same*; 726.5 *serious*; 416.4 *solid body*; 781.2 *solvent*; 27.79 *spatial*; 228.9 *stable*; 638.5 *steady*; 152.1 *thick*; 492.8 *touchable*; 418.2, 423.1 *tough*; 235.3 *valuable*; 197.13 *whole*; 79.15 *woody*
solid angle 27.39 *angle*; 28.7 *space*
solidarity 750.1 *accord*; 232.1 *completeness*; 747.2 *fellowship*; 569.1 *friendship*; 197.3 *oneness*; 111.1 *sameness*
solid body 416.4; 414.4 *heaviness*
solid-coloured ball 65.6 *pool*
solid-earth 30.53
solid-earth geophysics 30.2 *geophysics*
solid figure 27.41 *geometric figure*
solid footing 228.4 *stable thing*
solid foundations 228.4 *stable thing*
solid fuel 330.13, 437.1 *fuel*; 29.35 *rocketry*
solid geometry 27.34 *geometry*
solid gold 780.16 *bullion*
solidification 418.6; 416.2 *concentration*
solidified 416.7 *condensed*; 418.3 *hardened*
solidify 32.25; **418.10**; 267.6 *adhere*; 416.8 *be dense*; 97.11 *be present*; 452.21 *make certain*; 152.7 *thicken*
solidifying 416.7 *condensed*
solidity 698.6 *authenticity*; 232.1 *completeness*; 416.1 *density*; 418.5 *hardness*; 452.17 *infallibility*; 402.1 *material world*; 197.3 *oneness*; 528.6 *opaqueness*; 225.1 *permanence*; 97.1 *presence*; 95.1 *reality*; 781.8 *solvency*; 228.1 *stability*; 152.5 *thickness*; 492.1 *touch*
solidly 267.11 *cohesively*; 232.9 *completely*; 416.10 *densely*; 160.13 *formatively*; 750.31 *in accord*; 97.14 *in person*; 402.9 *materially*; 528.13 *opaquely*; 492.14 *palpably*; 225.9 *permanently*; 228.12 *stably*; 423.12 *toughly*
solid mass 416.4 *solid body*
solidness 416.1 *density*; 423.6 *toughness*
solid of revolution 27.45 *curved surface*
solid rocket booster 29.35 *rocketry*
solid silver 780.16 *bullion*
solid-state 39.36 *electronic*; 28.98 *physical*
solid-state device 39.16 *circuit element*
solid-state memory 40.6 *memory*
solid-state physics 28.3 *modern physics*
solid substance 402.4 *matter*
solid surface 27.38 *surface*
solidus 373.4 *means of connection*; 189.2 *oblique line*; 742.7 *punctuation*; 372.5 *separator*
soliloquist 735.2; 197.9 *soloist*; 729.10 *speaker*
soliloquize 735.3; 729.15 *talk to oneself*
soliloquizer 735.2 *soliloquist*; 729.10 *speaker*
soliloquizing 735.5
Soliloquy 735
soliloquy 735.1; 21.8 *scene*; 197.9 *soloist*; 729.8 *speech*
soling 393.8 *repair*
Soling class 50.2 *sailing boat*
solipsism 101.6 *internal world*; 4.7 *school of thought*; 673.2 *self-satisfaction*
solipsist 101.7 *believer in a nonmaterial world*; 4.11 *follower of a doctrine*; 101.11 *internal*; 341.2 *nonacting person*; 4.14 *of a philosophy*
solipsistic 101.11 *internal*; 673.12 *self-interested*; 139.18 *subjective*
solipsistically 673.22 *selfishly*
solitaire 118.9 *hermit*; 197.10 *single thing*
solitarily 572.12 *celibately*
solitariness 197.5 *aloneness*; 655.3 *separation*
solitary 118.16; 197.16 *alone*; 325.19 *deviant person*; 118.9 *hermit*; 815.7 *imprisonment*; 655.10 *lonely*; 197.8 *loner*; 653.2 *misanthrope*; 70.15 *of animals*; 197.11 *one*; 815.3 *prison cell*
solitary confinement 251.4 *detention*; 815.7 *imprisonment*; 172.2 *inside*; 815.3 *prison cell*
solitary person 655.6 *unsocial person*
solitary place 655.5
solitary state 572.3 *monasticism*
solitude 197.5 *aloneness*; 655.3 *separation*
solitudinarian 118.9 *hermit*
solmization 18.17 *notation*
solo 197.15; 197.21 *alone*; 22.8 *ballet*; 516.1 *melody*; 62.9 *mountaineer*; 514.8 *musical cry*; 197.11 *one*; 197.9 *soloist*
solo dance 22.2 *dance*
solo effort 197.9 *soloist*
soloing 62.3 *climbing technique*; 62.8 *mountaineering*
soloist 197.9; 516.5 *melodist*; 18.24 *musician*
soloistic 735.5 *soliloquizing*
Solomon 16.23 *judge*; 570.10 *married man*; 372.8 *person who separates*; 4.12 *sage*; 458.3 *wise man*
Solon 4.12 *sage*
so long 313.14 *goodbye!*
so long as 275.26 *all the time*
solstice 29.5 *celestial sphere*
solstitial 292.9 *seasonal*
solubility 431.8 *fluidification*; 412.1 *mixture*
solubilization 431.8 *fluidification*
solubilize 431.23 *dissolve*
soluble 431.21 *liquefiable*; 412.12 *mixed*; 27.73 *numerable*; 706.14 *solved*
soluble dye 42.6 *dye*
solubleness 431.5 *fluidity*
solubly 706.25 *conclusively*
solute 32.3 *phase*
solution 431.10; **706.6**; 374.4 *compound*; 433.5 *dilution*; 27.27 *equation*; 431.8 *fluidification*; 719.1 *interpretation*; 412.2 *mixed thing*; 706.7 *numerical result*; 27.14 *operation*; 32.3 *phase*; 394.1 *remedy*
solution set 27.27 *equation*
solvable 27.73 *numerable*
solvate 32.26 *react*
solve 706.20; 210.8 *calculate*; 719.9 *decipher*; 431.23 *dissolve*; 27.90 *enumerate*; 4.21 *rationalize*; 738.3 *reveal*
solved 706.14
solvency 781.8
solvent 431.9; **780.23**; **781.2**; 19.11 *artist's materials*; 431.19 *liquefied*; 32.3 *phase*; 153.13 *thinner*; 765.17 *well-off*
solvent front 32.17 *analysis*
solvently 780.28 *financially*
solver 706.10 *answerer*
so many 203.6 *quantitative*
somatic 402.7 *material*
somatic cell 34.7 *cell*
somatology 566.5 *study of mankind*
somatype 1.9 *physical type*
sombre 523.11 *benighted*; 524.5 *dim*; 533.3 *dull*; 583.11 *funeral*; 532.6 *sad*; 529.13 *soft-hued*; 643.1 *solemn*; 622.19 *stately*; 626.6 *sullen*
sombrely 523.15 *darkly*; 583.12 *funereally*; 533.9 *greyly*; 626.13 *sullenly*
sombreness 523.1 *darkness*; 523.7 *spiritual darkness*
sombrero 551.15 *headgear*
some 203.2 *certain amount*; 206.1, 206.5 *few*; 207.6 *plural*; 207.1 *plurality*; 203.6 *quantitative*; 203.7 *quantitatively*
somebody 123.4 *bigwig*; 566.7 *person*; 811.2 *person of repute*
someday 286.3 *another time*; 275.27 *at what time*; 283.14 *in the future*
somehow 352.7 *by means of*; 317.16 *how*; 102.11 *potentially*
somehow or other 317.16 *how*
someone 566.7 *person*
someone in a hurry 342.10 *busy person*
someone present 97.5
someone promised 756.6
someone's undoing 357.4 *ruin*

some other time 286.3 *another time*; 286.1 *different time*; 283.14 *in the future*
somersault 57.10 *compete in gymnastics*; 67.6 *diving*; 57.8 *floor exercises*; 192.1 *inversion*; 192.3 *invert*; 68.14 *ski*
somersaulting 68.12 *ski*; 68.1 *skiing*
something 402.5 *object*; 93.2 *thing*
something between them 593.8 *love affair*
something certain 452.12
something else 116.4 *dissimilar*; 109.7 *illogical*
something extra 121.3 *advantage*; 768.2 *gift*; 219.3 *superfluity*
something for nothing 793.6 *absence of charge*; 765.5 *profit*
something heard 504.8
something in common 108.1 *relatedness*
something incredible 619.4 *wonder*
something in exchange 759.3
something in hand 121.3 *advantage*; 439.1 *store*
something in reserve 121.3 *advantage*; 352.5 *reserves*; 439.1 *store*
something like 115.7 *similar*
something new 126.1 *originality*
something off 791.1 *discount*
something over 219.3 *superfluity*
something owing 784.1 *debt*
something received 769.2
something that appears 525.4
sometime 286.3 *another time*; 275.27 *at what time*; 294.14 *dead*; 284.20, 296.13 *former*; 605.7 *resigning*
some time 275.5 *indefinite period*
some time ago 3.24 *historically*; 284.22 *in the past*
sometimes 275.28; **297.2**
somewhat 203.2 *certain amount*; 685.9 *moderately*; 205.12 *partly*; 209.11 *to a degree*
somewhere 97.15 *here*
somewhere else 98.21 *away*
some while back 284.22 *in the past*
so minded 482.11 *intending*
sommelier 401.3 *attendant*
somnabulate 489.11 *be unfeeling*
somnambulism 477.6 *reverie*; 36.14 *trance*
somnambulist 489.5 *unfeeling person*; 477.9 *visionary*
somnifacient 37.4 *drug type*; 343.10 *soporific*
somnifer 489.4 *anaesthetic*
somniferous 489.9 *anaesthetic*
somnific 489.9 *anaesthetic*
somnolence 343.9 *sleep*; 489.2 *unconsciousness*
somnolent 343.4 *not awake*; 489.10 *sleepy*
somnolently 489.13 *insensibly*; 343.17 *sleepily*
so much 203.6 *quantitative*
so much nonsense 696.1 *unintelligible*
son 567.3 *male title of address*; 567.13 *man in the family*; 18.10 *world music*
Son and Holy Ghost 8.3 *God*
sonant 5.41 *lettered*; 5.16 *spoken letter*
sonar 504.9 *audio device*; 156.6 *bathymetry*; 449.11 *detector*; 323.5 *navigation*; 28.22 *sounding*
sonata 18.3 *classical music*; 356.5 *work of art*
sonata form 160.3 *kind*
son et lumière 656.3 *formal occasion*; 522.12 *highlight*; 21.7 *show*
song 516.2; 18.13, 516.1 *melody*; 514.8 *musical cry*; 17.7 *poem*; 17.6 *poetry*
song and dance 327.4 *fuss*; 507.2 *outcry*; 342.9 *overactivity*; 21.7 *show*; 21.5 *show business*
song and dance man 21.29 *entertainer*
songbird 72.6; 516.5 *melodist*
songster 72.7 *cagebird*; 516.5 *melodist*; 18.24 *musician*; 18.23 *singer*
songwriter 516.5 *melodist*; 18.24 *musician*
sonic boom 508.1 *bang*; 507.1 *loudness*; 28.19 *sound propagation*
sonic depth finder 504.9 *audio device*
sonic speed 332.8 *speed*
sonnet 17.7 *poem*; 17.10 *verse form*
sonneteer 17.14 *author*
sonnet sequence 17.7 *poem*
sonny 567.3 *male title of address*
sonobuoy 504.9 *audio device*
son of a bitch 804.10 *bad person*
Son of God 8.4 *God the Son*
Son of Man 8.4 *God the Son*
sonority 510.3 *deepness*; 507.1 *loudness*
sonorous 510.8 *deep*; 504.14 *hearable*; 507.6 *loud*; 542.10 *ornate*
sonorously 507.9 *loudly*; 510.11 *resonantly*
sonorousness 510.3 *deepness*; 507.1 *loudness*
soon 293.18; 286.3 *another time*; 293.17 *early*; 283.14 *in the future*
soon counted 206.5 *few*
sooner 469.17 *selectively*
sooner or later 286.3 *another time*
sooping 68.10 *curling*
soot 532.9 *black thing*; 523.4 *dark thing*; 258.4 *dirt*; 427.5 *powder*
soothe 490.10 *comfort*; 419.14 *ease*; 241.13 *give pleasure*; 301.9 *make motionless*; 685.4 *moderate*; 749.4 *pacify*; 608.9 *relieve*; 394.19 *remedy*; 421.13 *smooth over*; 627.9 *sorrow*
soothed 608.7 *relieved*
soothing 37.16; **421.3**; 241.3 *comfortable*; 268.12 *lubricant*; 685.8 *moderating*; 749.6 *pacificatory*; 490.6 *pleasant*; 608.8 *relieving*; 394.17 *remedial*
soothing influence 685.2 *moderator*
soothingly 421.15; 608.15 *comfortingly*; 749.7 *pacifically*
soothing syrup 394.9 *balm*; 268.6 *ointment*
soothsay 11.23, 475.12 *divine*
soothsayer 11.13 *diviner*; 475.8 *oracle*; 283.5 *predictor*
soothsaying 11.9, 475.2 *divination*
sooty 532.1 *black*; 258.7 *dirty*; 427.15 *powdery*
sooty mould 44.12 *pests and diseases*
sop 480.8 *incentive*; 648.1 *leniency*; 483.3 *stimulus*
sophism 702.2
sophist 702.6; 701.6 *arguer*; 645.3 *cunning person*; 4.11 *follower of a doctrine*; 4.10 *philosopher*
sophister 702.6 *sophist*
sophistic 702.7; 701.11 *logical*; 699.32 *spurious*
sophistical 645.4 *cunning*; 4.14 *of a philosophy*; 702.7 *sophistic*
sophistically 702.14; 4.24 *philosophically*
sophisticate 485.5 *expert*; 245.3 *make worse*; 412.8 *mix*
sophisticated 645.4, 702.8 *cunning*; 543.3 *elegant*; 455.9 *literate*; 412.12 *mixed*; 6.20, 549.5 *refined*; 421.6 *smooth-mannered*; 724.7 *stylish*; 485.9 *well-made*
sophisticatedly 6.27 *discerningly*; 421.16 *suavely*
sophistication 645.1, 702.3 *cunning*; 543.1, 549.1 *elegance*; 658.2 *good manners*; 245.10 *impairment*; 412.1 *mixture*; 6.11 *refinement*; 485.1 *skill*
sophisticator 702.6 *sophist*
Sophistry 702
sophistry 702.1; 645.1 *cunning*; 479.5 *equivocalness*; 274.4 *faulty reasoning*; 701.2 *logical argument*; 477.6 *reverie*; 699.4 *spuriousness*
Sophoclean tragedy 21.11 *tragedy*
sophomore 6.7 *learner*
soporific 343.10; 489.9 *anaesthetic*; 620.4 *boring*; 592.6 *desensitizing substance*; 394.8 *drug*; 37.4 *drug type*; 685.8 *moderating*; 685.2 *moderator*; 343.4 *not awake*; 608.3 *reliever*; 37.15 *sedative*
soporifically 620.8 *boringly*; 343.17 *sleepily*
soppiness 429.1 *moisture*
sopping 433.23 *wet*
sopping wet 433.23 *wet*
soprano 18.32 *instrumental*; 516.5 *melodist*
sorb 32.29, 370.13 *absorb*
sorbed 32.43 *absorbed*
sorbent 370.17 *absorbent*
sorbet 25.35 *dessert*
sorbitol 33.3 *carbohydrate*
sorcerer 224.6 *editor*; 394.15 *healer*; 475.8 *oracle*; 619.5 *person of wonder*; 11.4 *witch*
sorceress 11.4 *witch*
sorcerize 11.21 *bewitch*
sorcerous 700.35 *deceptive*; 11.15 *witchlike*
sorcery 236.11 *harmfulness*; 395.2 *occult influence*; 334.1 *power*; 804.6 *religious sin*; 700.7 *tricking*; 11.3 *witchcraft*; 619.3 *wonder-working*
sordid 236.4 *poor*; 258.8 *unclean*; 682.2 *unpleasant*; 408.15 *untidy*
sordidly 258.12 *dirtily*
sordidness 236.10 *poverty*; 408.3 *untidiness*
sordino 505.3 *inaudibility*; 511.6 *silencer*
sore 591.3; 798.8 *afflicted*; 798.2 *affliction*; 260.23 *diseased*; 261.1 *fatigued*; 491.7 *feeling pain*; 625.4 *irascible*; 242.4, 491.5 *painful*; 236.4 *poor*; 624.15 *resentful*; 260.3 *symptom*; 260.15 *ulcer*
soredium 84.6 *lichen*
sorehead 625.3 *irascible person*; 626.5 *sullen person*
soreness 591.7; 491.1 *pain*; 624.1 *resentment*
sore point 624.3 *cause of offence*; 751.1 *disagreement*; 591.6 *oversensitivity*
sore spot 491.1 *pain*; 488.3 *stimulus*
sore throat 491.2 *painful condition*; 260.9 *respiratory disease*; 260.3 *symptom*
sorghum 43.12 *crop*
sororicide 382.3 *homicide*; 382.11 *murderer*
sorority 376.15 *association*; 747.2 *fellowship*; 569.1 *friendship*; 566.9 *group*; 747.9 *team*
sorority house 6.15 *schoolroom*
sorosilicate 30.34 *mineral*
sorosis 80.2 *botanical fruit*
sorption 370.5 *absorption*; 32.20 *surface chemistry*
sorrel 534.1 *brown*; 496.5 *herbs*; 59.1 *horse*
sorrily 806.11 *guiltily*
sorriness 808.1 *penitence*
Sorrow 602
sorrow 602.1; **627.9**; 249.1 *adversity*; 798.2 *affliction*; 249.9 *be in trouble*; 627.2 *condolence*; 602.8 *grieve*; 603.6 *lament*; 603.1 *lamentation*
sorrowful 798.8 *afflicted*; 603.4 *lamenting*; 808.6 *penitent*; 602.5 *sad*
sorrowfully 798.13 *destructively*; 808.8 *penitently*; 602.11 *sadly*
sorrowfulness 603.1 *lamentation*; 602.1 *sorrow*
sorry 806.6 *appearing guilty*; 807.4 *atoning*; 602.7 *distressing*; 124.2 *obscure*; 808.6 *penitent*
sorry! 808.9
sorry for 627.6 *pitying*
sorry for oneself 627.7 *pitiful*
sorry plight 264.5 *predicament*
sort 137.14; **721.6**; 409.15 *categorize*; 692.31 *correspond*; 466.12 *discriminate*; 160.3 *kind*; 158.18, 209.5 *measure*; 372.10 *set apart*; 407.19 *systematize*; 137.4 *type*
sorted 409.24 *categorized*; 469.15 *chosen*; 137.12 *classed*; 209.7 *gradational*; 466.11 *judged*
sorted out 409.24 *categorized*; 706.14 *solved*
sorter 692.4 *postal worker*
sortes Biblicae 475.10 *cards*
sortes Homericae 475.10 *cards*
sortes Virgilianae 475.10 *cards*
sortie 322.1 *aviation*; 380.3 *instance of violence*; 381.14 *siege*
sortilege 11.9, 475.2 *divination*; 11.3 *witchcraft*
sorting 409.5 *categorization*; 466.1 *discrimination*
sorting office 692.2 *postal communication*
sorting out 409.5 *categorization*; 706.6 *solution*
sortkey 40.19 *computing terms*
sort of 209.11 *to a degree*
sort out 409.15 *categorize*; 719.9 *decipher*; 256.15 *purify*; 801.15 *put right*; 255.11 *simplify*; 706.20 *solve*; 407.19 *systematize*
sorus 82.2 *fern plant*
SOS 711.2 *danger signal*; 742.4 *signal*; 742.6 *word*
SOSENET 40.15 *network*
so-so 216.3, 618.10 *mediocre*; 685.6 *moderate*; 235.5 *not bad*; 231.4 *ordinary*; 609.6 *satisfactory*; 413.10 *supportable*; 618.20 *unexceptionally*
sot 690.17 *drunkard*
soteriological 7.18 *theological*
soteriology 7.13 *theology*
Sotheby's 779.1 *market*
so they say 811.6 *reputedly*
so to speak 694.13 *meaningfully*; 115.13 *similarly*
soto-ude-uke 52.8 *karate*
sottish 690.5 *drunken*
sottishness 690.11 *drinking*
sotto voce 511.10 *faintly*; 737.15 *in secret*; 730.17 *voicelessly*
sou 780.12 *ancient coins*; 780.4 *change*
soubresauté 22.9 *ballet steps*
soubrette 21.23 *role*
soufflé 434.10 *air bubble*; 25.35 *dessert*; 25.45 *French dish*; 415.7 *light thing*
soufflé dish 25.6 *kitchen equipment*
sough 31.58 *blow*
sought 633.17 *pursued*; 705.16 *questioned*
sought-after 617.7 *desired*; 654.16 *popular*; 778.16 *sold*
soul 139.11 *identity*; 172.5 *inner nature*; 101.6 *internal world*; 18.33 *jazz*; 554.1 *life*; 197.1 *one*; 566.7 *person*; 18.9 *popular music*; 36.21 *psyche*; 99.3 *quintessence*; 590.8 *seat of feelings*; 11.7 *spirit*; 18.10 *world music*
soul body 11.7 *spirit*
soul food 557.7 *food*; 25.43 *US dish*
soul in bliss 8.10 *deified person*
soul in glory 8.10 *deified person*
soulless 628.4 *pitiless*
soul mate 115.5 *counterpart*; 593.11 *loved one*; 570.8 *spouse*
soul mates 593.10 *lovers*
soul of wit 269.1 *conciseness*
souls 582.14 *the spiritual world*
soul-search 4.20 *philosophize*; 705.17 *question*
soul-searching 705.8 *curiosity*; 808.1 *penitence*
sound 18.38; **28.17**; **204.8**; 507.3 *audibility*; 698.19 *authentic*; 504.16 *be heard*; 507.8 *be loud*; 317.11 *channel*; 28.2 *classical physics*; 156.14 *deepen*; 156.4 *deep thing*; 448.1 *experiment*; 253.9 *fast*; 797.1 *good*; 750.24 *harmonize*; 259.1 *healthy*; 504.15 *hear*; 799.4 *honourable*; 452.6 *infallible*; 92.9 *inlet*; 27.86 *logical*; 26.10 *measure*; 235.5 *not bad*; 230.1 *perfect*; 336.9 *physically strong*; 95.8 *practical*; 4.15, 460.5 *rational*; 510.10 *ring*; 252.6 *safe*; 485.6 *skilful*; 780.23, 781.2 *solvent*; 504.8 *something heard*; 228.9 *stable*; 442.11 *thoughtful*; 235.3 *valuable*; 235.4 *worthwhile*
soundalike 762.7 *substitute*; 762.2 *substitute person*
sound a retreat 303.2 *retreat*
sound argument 27.64 *reasoning*
sound as a bell 259.1 *healthy*; 230.1 *perfect*; 336.9 *physically strong*
sound a siren 711.7 *raise the alarm*
sound asleep 343.4 *not awake*
sound a warning 711.7 *raise the alarm*
sound barrier 28.19 *sound propagation*; 332.8 *speed*
sound bite 205.2 *particular*
sound box 510.5 *resonator*
sound currency 780.1 *money*
sound dead 511.9 *be nonresonant*
sounddesk 21.17 *stage*
sounder 156.4 *deep thing*; 448.1 *experiment*
sound faint 511.8; 730.16 *speak in a low voice*
sound generator 28.18 *source of sound*
sound hoarse 513.5
sounding 28.22; 156.13 *bathymetric*; 156.6 *bathymetry*; 750.13 *harmonious*; 504.1 *hearing*; 510.7 *ringing*
sounding board 510.5 *resonator*
sounding brass 510.2 *ringing*
sounding line 156.4 *deep thing*
soundingly 750.33 *harmoniously*
sounding out 448.1 *experiment*
sounding true 698.25 *lifelike*
sound insulation 28.21 *architectural acoustics*; 505.3 *inaudibility*
sound judgment 442.5 *common sense*
soundless 156.8 *deep*; 301.6 *quiescent*; 506.3 *silent*
soundlessly 506.5 *silently*
soundlessness 156.1 *depth*; 506.4 *silence*
sound level 28.19 *sound propagation*
sound like 750.25 *conform*
soundly 253.17 *fastly*; 4.26 *rationally*; 228.12 *stably*; 336.14 *strongly*
sound maker 507.4
sound man 21.28 *stagehand*
sound mind 460.1 *sanity*

soundness 698.6 *authenticity;* 797.8 *good;* 259.3 *health;* 336.2 *healthiness;* 452.17 *infallibility;* 160.6 *nature;* 230.3 *perfection;* 799.1 *probity;* 27.64 *reasoning;* 781.8 *solvency;* 228.1 *stability;* 235.6 *worth*
soundness of mind 460.1 *sanity;* 458.1 *wisdom*
sound one's horn 711.7 *raise the alarm*
sound out 448.11 *experiment;* 705.17 *question*
sound-power level 28.19 *sound propagation*
sound-pressure level 28.19 *sound propagation*
soundproof 505.10 *muffle;* 511.2 *nonresonant;* 506.3 *silent;* 505.7 *unheard*
soundproofing 28.21 *architectural acoustics;* 505.3 *inaudibility*
sound propagation 28.19
sound proposition 783.1 *credit*
sound quality 504.10; 692.23 *television reception*
sound receiver 504.9 *audio device*
sound recordist 21.28 *stagehand*
sound the alarm 711.7 *raise the alarm*
sound the charge 381.1 *attack;* 585.14 *battle*
sound the depth 50.15 *sail*
sound the fire alarm 711.7 *raise the alarm*
sound the last post 583.8 *bury*
sound the praises of 669.15 *compliment*
sound the trumpet 483.9 *motivate*
sound the trumpets 742.12 *signal*
sound true 698.33 *seem lifelike*
sound wave 28.14; 326.5 *wave*
soup 25.13; 25.9 *dish;* 431.2 *juice;* 412.2 *mixed thing;* 557.14 *mouthful*
soup and fish 551.3 *formal dress*
soup bowl 410.16 *crockery*
soupçon 412.4 *admixture;* 495.3 *appetizer;* 206.1 *few;* 728.6 *suggestion*
souped-up 334.16 *charged;* 332.1 *swift*
soup of the day 25.9 *dish*
soup's on 25.58 *grub's on!*
soup spoon 557.16 *eating utensil;* 410.17 *ladle*
soup up 334.11 *give power;* 338.3 *invigorate;* 336.8 *strengthen*
sour 499.8; 499.5 *acid;* 594.16 *cause hate;* 375.5 *disintegrated;* 594.10 *hating;* 651.14 *hostile;* 625.4 *irascible;* 629.4 *jealous;* 626.10 *make sullen;* 496.9 *piquant;* 503.4 *putrid;* 626.6 *sullen;* 495.7 *tasty;* 604.7 *thwart;* 242.3 *unpalatable*
source 130.3; 344.2; 739.4 *discloser;* 693.10 *informer;* 126.2 *original;* 126.3 *originator;* 436.1 *provision;* 439.2 *resource;* 693.8 *source of information;* 39.19 *transistor*
source code 40.9 *programming language*
source electrode 39.19 *transistor*
source of a river 90.2 *channel*
source of energy 334.6
source of information 693.8
source of pride 622.12 *object of pride*
source of sound 28.18
source of trouble 379.1 *trap*
sources of resonance 510.4
sour cream 499.3 *sour thing*
sourdine 505.3 *inaudibility*
sourdough biscuit 25.39 *loaf*
sourdough bread 25.38 *bread*
soured 604.9 *disappointed*
soured cream 499.3 *sour thing*
sour grapes 629.1 *jealousy;* 499.4 *spleen*
sour look 659.3 *act of discourtesy*
sourly 499.10; 594.18 *hatefully;* 625.9 *irascibly;* 503.6 *stinkingly;* 626.13 *sullenly*
sour milk 503.2 *something that makes an unpleasant smell;* 499.3 *sour thing*
Sourness 499
sourness 499.1; 651.4 *bitterness;* 596.1 *dislike;* 495.4 *flavour;* 625.1 *irascibility;* 496.1 *piquancy;* 296.10 *staleness;* 626.1 *sullenness*
sourpuss 602.4 *depressing person;* 670.13 *pessimist;* 499.4 *spleen*
sour taste 499.1 *sourness;* 495.1 *taste;* 495.2 *taste of life*
sour thing 499.3
sour wine 499.3 *sour thing*
sous chef 25.2 *cook*
souse 367.3 *bring down;* 690.17 *drunkard;* 690.8 *get drunk;* 368.4 *immerse;* 359.5 *preserve;* 496.12 *season;* 433.9 *soaking;* 433.29 *water*
soused 690.3 *dead drunk;* 367.19 *fallen;* 496.9 *piquant;* 359.7 *preserved;* 433.23 *wet*
sousing 433.9 *soaking;* 367.13 *submergence*
soutane 7.11 *vestment*
souter 551.26 *fashion designer*
south 324.4 *compass point;* 324.13 *directional;* 324.12 *north*
South America 92.1 *continent*
southbound 324.13 *directional*
southeast 324.4 *compass point;* 324.13 *directional;* 324.12 *north*
southeast by east 324.12 *north*
southeast by south 324.12 *north*
southeaster 31.15 *wind direction*
southeasterly 324.13 *directional;* 324.12 *north;* 31.15 *wind direction;* 31.47 *windy*
southeastern 324.13 *directional*
southeast trades 31.17 *wind system*
southeastwardly 324.12 *north*
southeastwards 324.12 *north*
southeast wind 31.15 *wind direction*
southerly 324.13 *directional;* 324.12 *north;* 31.15 *wind direction;* 31.47 *windy*
southern 324.13 *directional;* 86.16 *regional;* 169.6 *side*
Southern accent 5.26 *dialect*
Southern Cross 742.5 *indicator*
Southerner 564.9 *British inhabitant;* 85.9 *England*
Southern fried chicken 25.43 *US dish*
southern lights 30.46 *aurora;* 522.4 *natural light*
southernmost 324.13 *directional*
southing 324.4 *compass point*
South Kensington 87.5 *London*
south magnetic pole 30.45 *magnetic pole*
South Pacific 493.8 *hot place*
southpaw 52.4 *boxer*
South Pole 494.6 *Arctic*
South Seas hurricane 31.16 *wind vortex*
south side 169.3 *side direction*
south-southeast 324.12 *north*
south-southwest 324.12 *north*
South Wales 85.12 *Wales*
South Walian 85.12 *Wales*
southward 324.4 *compass point;* 324.13 *directional*
southwardly 324.12 *north*
southwards 324.12 *north*
Southwark 87.5 *London*
southwest 324.4 *compass point;* 324.13 *directional;* 324.12 *north*
southwest by south 324.12 *north*
southwest by west 324.12 *north*
southwester 551.12 *coat;* 551.15 *headgear;* 31.15 *wind direction*
southwesterly 324.13 *directional;* 324.12 *north;* 31.15 *wind direction;* 31.47 *windy*
southwestern 324.13 *directional*
southwestwardly 324.12 *north*
southwestwards 324.12 *north*
southwest wind 31.15 *wind direction*
south wind 493.8 *hot place;* 31.15 *wind direction*
souvenir 768.2 *gift;* 462.3, 794.3 *memento;* 744.11 *monument;* 3.11 *relic;* 215.1 *remainder*
souvlaki 25.52 *Greek dish*
sov 780.9 *British money*
sovereign 400.2; 8.13 *divine;* 121.13 *dominant;* 780.10 *former British money;* 12.10 *governing;* 396.14 *governmental;* 400.12 *masterful;* 85.16 *national;* 396.10 *person of authority;* 334.13 *powerful;* 394.17 *remedial;* 140.12 *ruling*
Sovereign of the Seas 586.25 *historical naval ships*
sovereign remedy 394.1 *remedy*
sovereign state 85.1 *country;* 86.4 *territorial division*
sovereignty 140.8, 397.3 *authority;* 85.1 *country;* 8.2 *divine attribute;* 12.3, 396.4 *governance;* 121.2 *leadership;* 763.1 *possession;* 334.1 *power*
soviet 579.7 *council*
Soviet bloc 85.2 *union of nations*
Soviet hammer and sickle 743.6 *national emblem*
sovietism 12.1 *government*
sow 377.17; 138.25 *broadcast;* 44.15 *cultivate;* 43.17 *farm;* 568.14 *female animal;* 71.18 *female mammal;* 43.8 *livestock;* 356.10 *produce;* 367.6 *throw down*
sow above 329.3 *exceed*
sowar 586.20 *cavalryman;* 59.15 *horse person;* 586.6 *militarist*
sowbelly 25.30 *bacon*
sow bug 75.4 *arthropod*
sow dissension 594.16 *cause hate;* 751.7 *pick a fight*
sower 243.15 *preparer*
so what? 618.21 *never mind!;* 124.15 *no matter!*
sowing 43.5 *cultivation;* 243.13 *development;* 377.1 *dispersion*
sown 377.22 *distributed;* 356.12 *produced*
sow one's oats 804.16 *be wicked*
sow one's wild oats 250.19 *liberalize;* 686.11 *overindulge*
sow seed 81.12 *manage grassland*
sow the seed 243.2 *do the groundwork*
sow the seeds 344.11 *inaugurate;* 130.22 *invent*
soya 25.21 *meat substitute*
soyabean meal 43.9 *animal feedstuff*
soyabeans 43.12 *crop*
soy sauce 25.15 *sauce;* 496.2 *seasoning*
Soyuz 29.31 *space travel*
sozzled 690.3 *dead drunk*
spa 394.14 *hospital;* 257.1 *hygiene*
Space 141
space 27.35; 28.7; 141.1; 141.21; 146.4; 409.12 *arrange;* 275.3 *duration;* 94.4 *emptiness;* 127.1 *inclusion;* 146.1, 209.4 *interval;* 18.17 *notation;* 308.1 *opening;* 276.1 *period;* 203.1 *quantity;* 86.1 *region;* 158.1 *size;* 141.11 *spatial;* 439.4 *storage;* 29.3 *universe;* 202.6 *vastness*
space age 29.31 *space travel*
space between 146.1 *interval*
space biologist 34.19 *life scientist*
space biology 34.1 *life science*
space cadet 461.7 *insane person*
space capsule 29.30 *spacecraft*
space-case 461.7 *insane person*
space coordinates 28.7 *space*
spacecraft 29.30
spaced 146.6
spaced-out 691.7 *drugged;* 459.5 *foolish;* 463.8 *oblivious;* 146.6 *spaced*
space engineering 29.29 *astronautics*
space exploration 29.29 *astronautics*
spaceflight 29.31 *space travel*
space frame 403.4 *framework;* 38.27 *superstructure*
space heater 493.3 *heater*
space heating 493.3 *heater*
space helmet 29.31 *space travel*
space invader 100.6 *outsider*
spacelab 29.30 *spacecraft*
space laboratory 29.30 *spacecraft*
spaceman 141.10; 29.31 *space travel*
space medicine 29.29 *astronautics;* 35.3 *medical specialty*
space navigation 29.29 *astronautics*
space observatory 29.32 *satellite*
space out 409.12 *arrange;* 145.6 *keep away;* 206.9 *scatter;* 141.21, 146.4 *space*
space platform 29.30 *spacecraft*
space port 29.31 *space travel*
space probe 29.30 *spacecraft*
space research 29.29 *astronautics*
space science 29.29 *astronautics*
spaceship 306.4 *orbiting body;* 29.30 *spacecraft*
space shuttle 29.30 *spacecraft*
space station 29.30 *spacecraft*
spacesuit 29.31 *space travel;* 551.10 *suit*
space technology 29.29 *astronautics*
space the final frontier 141.2 *empty space*
space-time 141.9 *fourth dimension;* 28.7 *space;* 141.11 *spatial;* 275.1 *time*
space-time continuum 141.9 *fourth dimension;* 28.7 *space;* 275.1 *time*
space travel 29.31
space traveller 141.10 *spaceman*
spacewalk 29.31 *space travel*
space wave 692.15 *transmitted wave*
spacewoman 141.10 *spaceman;* 29.31 *space travel*
spacial 308.14 *holed;* 141.11 *spatial*
spacing 146.1 *interval*
spacious 141.13; 158.15, 679.4 *big*
spaciously 141.15; 158.20 *largely*
spaciousness 141.4; 158.2 *bigness;* 150.4 *breadth*
spade 69.3 *card game terms;* 44.15 *cultivate;* 43.17 *farm;* 44.6, 438.3 *garden tool;* 56.4 *golf club;* 410.17 *ladle;* 183.9 *make concave;* 425.9 *sharp-edged thing;* 316.15 *take away;* 425.16 *use a sharp tool;* 576.6 *work*
spade mashie 56.4 *golf club*
spade oar 50.4 *rowing*
spadework 243.10 *preparations;* 344.3 *rudiment;* 130.7 *rudiments;* 576.1 *work*
spadix 78.4 *flower head*
spaghetti house 557.15 *eating place*
spaghetti junction 320.3 *carriageway;* 318.5 *crossing point;* 193.5 *crossroads;* 317.3, 373.5 *road*
spahi 586.20 *cavalryman*
span 150.10; 150.4 *breadth;* 38.21, 317.9 *bridge;* 318.11 *cross;* 275.3 *duration;* 141.20 *extend;* 141.8 *intervening space;* 148.4 *length;* 550.26 *overlie;* 198.14 *pair;* 276.1 *period;* 373.5 *road;* 198.1 *two*
spandex 422.3 *elastic thing*
spandrel 20.9 *miscellaneous architectural features*
spang 324.9 *directly*
spangle 522.25 *light up;* 522.2 *quality of light;* 541.11 *variegate;* 541.5 *variegated thing*
spangles 542.6 *decorative articles*
spangly 522.16 *bright*
spaniel 664.9 *fawn;* 664.3 *sycophant*
Spanish bayonet 425.8 *sharp-pointed thing*
Spanish GP at Jerez 61.2 *Formula 1 race*
Spanish mackerel 55.4 *American game fish*
Spanish moss 84.6 *lichen;* 82.3 *moss*
Spanish Riding School 59.10 *dressage*
spank 331.5 *beat;* 331.13 *blow;* 814.12 *corporal punishment*
spanker 158.9 *big thing*
spanking 158.15 *big;* 331.12 *collision;* 814.12 *corporal punishment;* 332.1 *swift*
spanking rate 332.8 *speed*
spanking wind 31.14 *windiness*
spanned 317.15 *accessible*
spanner 438.1 *tool;* 360.3 *tools for gripping*
spanner in the works 378.2 *obstacle*
spanning 550.1, 550.38 *covering*
spar 701.13 *argue;* 52.11, 586.37 *fight;* 50.3 *parts of a sailing boat;* 38.27 *superstructure*
spare 634.3 *abstain;* 758.10 *acquit;* 648.3 *be lenient;* 51.5 *bowling delivery;* 390.1 *deliver;* 349.5, 767.9 *dispose of;* 211.9 *extra;* 649.9 *forgive;* 580.6 *leisure;* 350.5 *not use;* 359.5 *preserve;* 252.10 *protect;* 252.4 *safety device;* 627.10 *show mercy;* 271.1 *simple;* 439.7 *stored;* 219.3 *superfluity;* 219.7 *superfluous;* 215.10 *surplus;* 153.1 *thin;* 218.3 *underfed;* 350.1 *unused;* 350.11 *unused thing*
spare cash 219.3 *superfluity*
spare copy 744.5 *copy*
spared 758.6 *acquitted;* 649.6 *forgiven;* 252.6 *safe*
spare hours 263.1 *ease;* 580.1 *leisure*
sparely 215.12 *with a remainder*
spareness 271.4 *simplicity;* 153.7 *thinness*
spare no effort 576.8 *exert oneself*
spare no expense 679.10 *be generous;* 787.1 *expend;* 768.5 *give*
spare none 382.18 *slaughter*
spare one's blushes 728.22 *play down*
spare one's words 732.7 *keep quiet*
spare part 252.4 *safety device;* 405.3 *unit*
spare parts 211.4 *extra*
spare rib 25.24, 25.25 *pork*
spares 211.4 *extra;* 215.4 *surplus*
spare the rod 648.3 *be lenient*
spare time 263.1 *ease;* 580.1 *leisure*
spare tyre 158.8 *fat;* 410.18 *stomach;* 219.3 *superfluity*
spare wheel 219.3 *superfluity*
sparge 429.5, 433.33 *sprinkle;* 433.12 *sprinkler*
spargefaction 433.8 *watering*
sparger 433.12 *sprinkler*
sparging 433.8 *watering*
sparing 649.1 *forgiveness;* 649.4 *forgiving;* 684.8 *self-restrained;* 680.4 *thrifty*
sparingly 684.11 *with self-restraint*
sparing of words 269.3 *concise*
sparing with words 732.2
spark 344.1 *cause;* 28.46, 39.6 *electric discharge;* 522.8 *fire;* 437.2 *lighter;* 522.25 *light up;* 522.2 *quality of light*
spark discharge 28.46, 39.6 *electric discharge*

sparking 522.16 *bright*
sparking plug 437.2 *lighter*
sparkle 545.7 *be beautiful*; 598.7 *be cheerful*; 434.24 *bubble*; 726.1 *emphasis*; 726.6 *emphasize*; 522.25 *light up*; 522.2 *quality of light*; 338.1 *vigour*
sparkler 522.8 *fire*
sparklers 542.6 *decorative articles*; 518.2 *eye*
sparkling 522.16 *bright*; 598.1 *cheerful*; 558.17 *drinkable*; 726.3 *emphatic*; 432.21 *gassy*; 415.2 *insubstantial*; 415.5 *lightness*
sparkling burgundy 558.9 *wine*
sparkling water 558.6 *soft drink*
sparkling wine 558.9 *wine*
spark off 130.20 *activate*; 344.10 *awaken*
sparky 522.22 *enlightened*
sparring 52.2 *boxing*; 52.14 *combat*
sparring helmet 52.2 *boxing*
sparring partner 586.3 *athlete*; 52.4 *boxer*
sparrow 72.6 *songbird*
sparse **206.6**; **417.1**; 377.19 *dispersed*; 563.3 *infertile*; 203.6 *quantitative*; 153.6 *scant*; 218.4 *scarce*
sparsely **206.11**; **417.7**; 377.30 *diffusely*; 218.10 *insufficiently*; 203.7 *quantitatively*; 153.17 *thin*
Sparseness 417
sparseness **417.3**; 206.3 *fewness*; 153.12 *thinning*
sparsity 206.3 *fewness*
Sparta 12.5 *political organization*
Spartan 687.6 *fasting*; 251.6 *lawmaker*; 251.14, 684.8, *self-restrained*; 684.4 *self-restrained person*; 271.1 *simple*; 647.4 *strict person*; 680.4 *thrifty*; 647.10 *unadorned*
Spartan fare 218.8 *insufficiency*; 687.2 *short rations*
Spartanism 4.3 *detachment*; 251.3, 684.1 *self-restraint*; 647.3 *unadornment*
Spartan race 586.7 *militarist nation*
Spartan simplicity 728.4 *simplicity*
spasm **327.8**; 381.20 *bout*; 260.2 *illness*; 380.3 *instance of violence*; 260.17 *nervous disorder*; 342.3 *nimbleness*; 491.1 *pain*; 260.3 *symptom*
spasmodic 227.13 *changeable*; 327.19 *convulsive*; 133.8 *discontinuous*; 114.5 *diverse*; 299.4, 408.14 *irregular*; 380.6 *violent*
spasmodically 227.15 *changeably*; 133.17 *discontinuously*; 408.27 *in disorder*; 114.11, 299.8 *irregularly*; 327.29 *jerkily*
spasmodicalness 133.1 *discontinuity*
spasmolytic 37.14 *counteracting*; 37.4 *drug type*
spastic 327.19 *convulsive*; 260.23 *diseased*; 260.19 *sick person*
spat 751.6 *argue*; 701.1, 751.2 *argument*
spatchcock 25.55 *cook*
spate 219.1 *excess*; 376.22 *flood*; 217.8 *plenty*; 31.25 *rain*; 90.6 *river flow*
spathe 78.3 *flower part*
spatial **27.79**; **141.11**; 86.16 *regional*
spatial extension 27.35, 141.1 *space*
spatially **141.14**; 86.19 *geographically*; 27.87 *mathematically*; 141.15 *spaciously*
spatiotemporal 402.7 *material*; 141.11 *spatial*
spatiotemporally 141.15 *spaciously*; 141.14 *spatially*
spats 551.20 *legwear*
spatter 258.11 *dirty*; 327.26 *flicker*; 31.62 *rain*; 377.18, 429.5, 429.14, 433.33 *sprinkle*
spatterdashes 551.20 *legwear*
spattered 429.12 *seeping*; 377.23 *sprinkled*
spattering 377.4 *sprinkling*; 433.8 *watering*
spatula 19.11 *artist's materials*; 426.9 *blunt instrument*; 25.6 *kitchen equipment*; 410.17 *ladle*; 19.14 *sculptor's materials*
spavin 260.18 *veterinary disease*
spavined 260.23 *diseased*
spa water 433.2 *drinking water*
spawn 554.19 *give birth to*; 561.11 *have young*; 213.4 *increase*; 356.7, 356.10 *produce*; 561.13 *propagate*; 555.4 *young animal*
spawned 554.15 *born*
spawning 561.3 *propagation*
spay 335.9 *make impotent*; 563.8 *make infertile*; 212.4 *take off*
spayed 563.5 *rendered infertile*; 335.13 *unsexed*
spaying 563.2 *making infertile*
speak **729.11**; 707.17 *affirm*; 507.8 *be loud*; 692.30 *communicate*; 734.9 *converse*; 739.6 *divulge*; 5.45 *use language*
speak about 722.4 *dissertate*
speak badly 696.7 *be unintelligible*
speak clearly 695.5 *simplify*
speak directly 150.12 *be broad-minded*
speaker **729.10**; 21.24 *actor*; 504.9 *audio device*; 579.13 *director*; 722.3 *dissertator*; 542.9 *phrasemonger*; 692.18 *radio*; 507.4 *sound maker*; 28.18 *source of sound*; 731.4 *talker*
speak ex cathedra 707.21 *be assertive*
speak for 706.23 *answer for*; 398.8 *represent*
speak for itself 695.4 *be intelligible*; 738.5 *be visible*; 716.10 *make evident*
speak freely 250.14 *be free*
speak gobbledegook 696.7 *be unintelligible*
speak highly of 669.13 *support*
speak ill of 678.13 *vilify*
speaking **729.19**; 729.1 *faculty of speech*; 115.9 *lifelike*
speaking clock 281.6 *clock*
speaking in tongues 729.2 *power of speech*; 7.2 *religiousness*
speaking likeness 717.1 *representation*
speaking part 21.23 *role*
speaking voice 729.1 *faculty of speech*
speak in muted tones 730.16 *speak in a low voice*
speak in tongues 696.7 *be unintelligible*; 7.20 *preach*
speak loudly 729.12
speak of 694.10 *mean*
speak one's mind 703.18 *appear*; 646.4 *be naive*; 178.11 *be straight*
speak oracles 479.1 *be equivocal*
speak out 703.18 *appear*; 707.21 *be assertive*; 739.6 *divulge*; 113.18 *object*; 738.4 *show oneself*
speak out against 753.6 *protest*
speak plainly 799.6 *be honourable*; 646.4 *be naive*; 271.7 *be simple*; 738.4 *show oneself*
speak simply 271.7 *be simple*
speak slowly 333.2 *hesitate*
speak softly 730.16 *speak in a low voice*
speak *sotto voce* 730.16 *speak in a low voice*
speak the truth 799.6 *be honourable*; 178.11 *be straight*; 698.29 *be truthful*
speak to **729.14**; 733.7 *address*
speak to one's understanding 695.4 *be intelligible*
speak truthfully 799.6 *be honourable*
speak under one's breath 730.16 *speak in a low voice*
speak up 507.8 *be loud*; 738.4 *show oneself*; 729.12 *speak loudly*
speak up for 714.8 *justify*; 669.13 *support*
speak volumes 695.4 *be intelligible*; 694.10 *mean*
speak well of 669.13 *support*
speak with forked tongue 479.1 *be equivocal*; 234.12 *distort the truth*
speak with two voices 479.1 *be equivocal*
spear 586.37 *fight*; 81.3 *grass plant*; 382.17 *murder*; 58.9 *play hockey*; 425.8 *sharp-pointed thing*; 381.6 *stab*; 425.16 *use a sharp tool*
spear-carrier 21.24 *actor*; 413.8 *supporter*
speared 58.8 *hockey*
spearhead 586.14 *armed forces*; 381.19 *attacker*; 167.10 *be in front*; 123.3 *chief thing*; 167.1 *front*; 121.10 *lead*; 579.14 *leader*; 130.21 *pioneer*; 129.15 *precede*; 425.8 *sharp-pointed thing*
spearing 58.8 *hockey*; 58.3 *ice hockey*
spearlike 425.1 *sharp*
spearman 586.13 *historical soldiery*
spear side 567.15 *menfolk*
special **139.9**; **139.15**; 469.15 *chosen*; 222.10 *detailed*; 25.9 *dish*; 139.17 *exceptional*; 56.5 *golf ball*; 694.6 *meaningful*; 742.14 *signifying*; 197.14 *singular*; 137.11 *typical*
special affinity 569.3 *familiarity*
Special Air Service 584.2 *the military*
special area 165.2 *enclosed place*
Special Boat Service 584.2 *the military*
Special Branch 16.15 *British police*
special case 118.6 *deviation*; 114.1 *diversity*; 139.6 *exception*; 128.1 *exclusion*
special constable 16.17 *police officer*; 253.3 *security officer*
special correspondent 721.10 *descriptive writer*; 693.9 *informant*; 740.11 *newspaperman*
special court martial 584.6 *military law*
special day 601.5 *anniversary*; 123.2 *important matter*; 600.1 *rejoicing*
special delivery 692.2 *postal communication*
special-delivery messenger 692.4 *postal worker*
special diet 557.6 *nutrition*
special dispensation 128.1 *exclusion*
special edition 741.5 *mass communication*; 740.4 *newspaper*
special effects man 21.28 *stagehand*
special effort 340.2 *deed*
special envoy 579.16 *official*
special faculty 485.1 *skill*
Special Forces 586.14 *armed forces*; 235.7 *elite*; 584.2 *the military*
special gift 334.1 *power*
special handling 692.2 *postal communication*
special hospital 461.8 *mental hospital*; 36.31 *psychiatric hospital*
special interest 342.2 *social activity*; 139.8 *specialization*
special-interest group 480.14, 483.7 *motivator*
specialism 485.1 *skill*
special issue 741.5 *mass communication*
specialist **139.14**; 400.13 *excellent*; 396.11, 400.10, 485.5 *expert*; 35.13 *medical specialist*; 121.6 *paragon*; 136.8 *qualified person*; 139.21 *specialized*; 46.19 *varsity*
specialist publication 740.5 *journal*
specialist source 719.7 *news interpreter*
spécialité de la maison 25.9 *dish*; 139.9 *special*
Speciality 139
speciality **139.1**; 25.9 *dish*; 197.4 *singularity*; 485.1 *skill*; 724.1 *style*; 6.3 *subject*
speciality of the house 25.9 *dish*; 139.9 *special*
specialization 139.8
specialize **139.27**; 400.14 *master*
specialized **139.21**; 6.21 *curricular*; 485.8 *expert*; 694.6 *meaningful*; 264.12 *problematic*
specialized company 13.7 *corporation*
specialized language 139.10
specialized meaning 694.4 *type of meaning*
specialize in 396.22 *be an authority on*; 400.15 *learn*; 139.27 *specialize*
special jury 16.26, 464.7 *jury*
specially **139.28**; 742.18 *indicatively*; 222.19 *meticulously*
special meaning 694.4 *type of meaning*
specialness 197.4 *singularity*; 139.1 *speciality*
special nurse 35.16 *nurse*
special offer 791.2, 793.4 *bargain*; 752.3 *business offer*; 480.9 *enticement*; 483.5 *positive stimulus*
special patrol 16.16 *US police*
special patrol group 16.15 *British police*
special power 334.1 *power*
special prayer 10.9 *prayer*
special price 791.2 *bargain*
special request 710.1 *request*
special sale 752.3 *business offer*
special school 6.12 *educational institution*; 461.8 *mental hospital*
special skill 139.7
special study 139.8 *specialization*
special subject 139.8 *specialization*
special team 46.12
special theory of relativity 28.5 *theory*
special topic 447.5 *educational topic*
special treat 630.4 *surprising thing*
special treatment 758.1 *exemption*; 392.8 *furtherance*
special-treatment steel 323.4 *shipbuilding*
specialty 485.1 *skill*
specialty team 46.12 *special team*
speciarness 676.1 *affectedness*
speciation 34.16 *evolution*
specie 780.13 *coinage*; 780.1 *money*
species 137.3 *kingdom*; 205.1 *part*; 721.6 *sort*; 34.17 *taxonomy*; 137.4 *type*
speciesism 128.4 *exclusiveness*
specific 99.9 *characteristic*; 222.10 *detailed*; 452.7 *particular*; 394.17 *remedial*; 394.1 *remedy*; 139.15 *special*; 34.28 *taxonomic*; 137.11 *typical*
specifically 34.29 *biologically*; 222.19 *meticulously*; 139.28 *specially*; 137.16 *taxonomically*
specification **136.6**; 721.1 *description*; 693.3 *document*; 407.2 *grouping*; 166.2 *limiting factor*; 452.18 *particularity*; 135.1 *requirement*
specifications 139.4
specific gravity 414.5 *gravity*; 28.9 *mass*; 416.3 *relative density*
specific heat 493.2 *heat measurement*
specific heat capacity 28.36 *heat flow*
specificity 139.1 *speciality*
specific latent heat 28.38 *thermodynamics*
specificness 452.18 *particularity*
specific quality 139.1 *speciality*
specific remedy 394.1 *remedy*
specified 136.12 *conditional*; 407.11 *grouped*; 452.7 *particular*
specified value 28.83 *sensitivity*
specify **136.16**; **139.24**; **452.22**; 222.11 *circumstantiate*; 721.16 *define*; 743.10 *identify*; 166.7 *limit*
specimen 703.3 *explanation*; 717.8 *representative*; 738.7 *showpiece*
specimen shrub 44.9 *garden plant*
specimen tree 44.9 *garden plant*; 79.1 *tree*
speciosity 676.1 *affectedness*
specious 676.3 *affected*; 96.12 *artificial*; 525.9 *ostensible*; 702.7 *sophistic*; 699.32 *spurious*; 486.2 *unskilled*
speciously 702.14 *sophistically*; 699.41 *spuriously*
speciousness 702.1 *sophistry*; 699.4 *spuriousness*
specious reasoning 702.1 *sophistry*
speck 196.3 *fragment*; 427.7 *grain*; 159.3 *little piece*; 541.4 *maculation*; 205.7 *piece*; 548.1 *spot*; 377.18 *sprinkle*
speckle 541.4 *maculation*; 412.8 *mix*; 377.18 *sprinkle*; 541.11 *variegate*
speckled 412.12 *mixed*; 541.10 *mottled*; 377.23 *sprinkled*
speckled effect 412.3 *miscellany*
speckledy 541.10 *mottled*
speckling 412.3 *miscellany*; 377.4 *sprinkling*
specs 139.4 *specifications*; 518.10 *visual aid*
spectacle 738.6 *display*; 21.9 *dramaturgy*; 656.3 *formal occasion*; 703.6 *mass demonstration*; 738.9 *production*; 21.7 *show*; 525.4 *something that appears*; 518.7 *view*; 619.4 *wonder*
spectacles 519.3 *aid for poor sight*; 28.29 *optical element*; 520.7 *that which makes visible*; 527.8 *transparent thing*; 518.10 *visual aid*
spectacle theatre 21.16 *theatre*
spectacular 525.7 *appearing*; 520.2 *clear*; 21.39 *dramatic*; 529.12 *gaudy*; 518.23 *visible*
spectate 97.12 *attend*; 518.12 *see*
spectator 644.3 *curious person*; 518.11 *observer*; 716.7 *person who gives evidence*; 769.5 *recipient*; 97.5 *someone present*; 21.33 *theatregoer*; 454.7 *verifier*
spectator sport 45.4 *sporting activity*; 518.7 *view*
spectometer 32.17 *analysis*
spectral 522.23 *photoelectric*; 97.7 *present*; 11.18 *spiritual*; 96.8 *unreal*; 541.6 *variegated*
spectral colour 28.28, 529.1 *colour*
spectral type 29.13 *luminosity*
spectre 477.5 *fantasy*; 612.5 *frightener*; 11.11 *ghost*; 97.6 *ghostly presence*; 96.2 *illusion*; 518.5 *imagination*; 525.4 *something that appears*
spectrograph 32.17 *analysis*; 529.8 *chromatics*; 29.27 *imaging*; 28.91 *spectrometer*
spectrographic 32.41 *analytic*; 529.14 *chromolithographic*
spectrographic analysis 32.17 *analysis*
spectrography 529.8 *chromatics*
spectrometer **28.91**; 529.8 *chromatics*; 29.27 *imaging*; 26.8 *meter*; 28.32 *optical instrument*
spectrometric 29.36 *astronomical*; 26.16 *micrometric*; 28.98 *physical*
spectrometrically 28.100 *physically*
spectrometry 32.17 *analysis*; 29.27 *imaging*; 26.2 *micrometry*; 28.96 *microscopy*
spectrophotometer 529.8 *chromatics*;

26.8 *meter*; 28.32 *optical instrument*; 28.91 *spectrometer*
spectrophotometric 529.14 *chromolithographic*; 26.16 *micrometric*
spectrophotometry 529.8 *chromatics*; 26.2 *micrometry*
spectroscope 529.8 *chromatics*; 28.91 *spectrometer*
spectroscopic 32.41 *analytic*; 529.10 *coloured*; 28.98 *physical*
spectroscopically 28.100 *physically*
spectroscopic binary 29.9 *constellation*
spectroscopy 28.96 *microscopy*; 28.3 *modern physics*; 518.10 *visual aid*
spectrum 32.17 *analysis*; 529.2 *colourfulness*; 132.2 *consecution*; 522.12 *highlight*; 141.7 *range*; 541.5 *variegated thing*; 541.1 *variegation*
spectrum analysis 529.8 *chromatics*
speculate 776.2; 453.18 *be uncertain*; 448.11 *experiment*; 443.16 *have an idea*; 14.5 *invest*; 4.20 *philosophize*; 475.11 *predict*; 777.1 *purchase*; 453.22 *risk*; 476.5 *suppose*; 353.3 *tackle*; 107.12 *take a chance*; 443.12 *think*; 619.12 *wonder whether*
speculation 776.8; 450.1 *belief*; 107.7 *calculation of chance*; 476.3 *conjecture*; 475.2 *divination*; 448.3 *experimentation*; 444.4 *explanation*; 274.2 *inaccuracy*; 464.1 *judgment*; 4.4 *philosophical investigation*; 4.1 *philosophy*; 96.4 *theorization*; 446.2 *theory*; 443.3 *thoughtfulness*; 354.2 *undertaking*; 353.6 *venture*
speculative 443.10; 777.14 *buying*; 254.1 *dangerous*; 354.6 *enterprising*; 448.8 *experimental*; 4.13 *of philosophy*; 776.15 *profitable*; 476.7 *suppositional*; 96.10, 446.10 *theoretical*; 4.17 *thoughtful*; 453.1 *uncertain*; 453.5 *uncertified*
speculatively 353.10 *ambitiously*; 448.14 *experimentally*; 778.17 *marketably*; 476.10 *supposedly*; 4.25 *theoretically*; 453.23 *uncertainly*
speculator 448.5 *experimenter*; 475.9 *forecaster*; 346.5 *operator*; 4.10 *philosopher*; 440.7 *property man*; 777.12 *purchaser*; 14.3 *stockbroker*; 476.4 *theorist*; 776.10 *trader*; 96.6 *unrealistic person*; 354.4 *volunteer*; 778.12 *wholesaler*
speculum 518.8 *reflection*
Speech 729
speech 729.8; **729.16**; 733.1 *address*; 692.1 *communications*; 740.1 *publication*; 21.8 *scene*; 504.8 *something heard*; 5.3 *spoken language*
speech-act theory 4.9 *philosophical problem*
speech community 5.26 *dialect*; 376.17 *family*
speech defect 730.3; 544.5 *mispronunciation*; 729.3 *mode of speech*
speechifier 729.10 *speaker*
speechify 733.7 *address*; 729.14 *speak to*
speechifying 729.9 *art of public speaking*; 5.22 *many words*
speech impediment 544.5 *mispronunciation*; 729.3 *mode of speech*; 730.3 *speech defect*
speechless 730.11; 630.7 *amazed*; 506.3 *silent*; 732.2 *sparing with words*; 619.7 *wide-eyed*
speechlessness 732.4 *guarded speech*; 730.5 *mutism*; 506.4 *silence*
speechless with rage 624.16 *angry*
speech-maker 733.6 *public speaker*; 729.10 *speaker*
speech-making 729.9 *art of public speaking*
speech sound 5.16 *spoken letter*; 729.7 *utterance*
speech therapist 35.17 *paramedic*
speech therapy 35.8 *treatment*
speed 332.8; 332.4 *be swift*; 209.1 *degree*; 691.6 *drug*; 265.1 *easiness*; 297.4 *frequency*; 392.28 *further*; 262.4 *haste*; 38.9 *machine tool*; 265.16 *make easy*; 262.2 *make haste*; 342.3 *nimbleness*; 300.8 *rapid motion*; 28.8 *time*
speed and endurance 59.11 *eventing*
speedball 691.6 *drug*
speedboat 332.11 *swift thing*
speed demon 332.13 *swift person*
speeder 332.13 *swift person*; 59.2 *thoroughbred*
speed freak 332.13 *swift person*
speedily 262.6 *hastily*; 280.8 *immediately*; 332.14 *swiftly*
speediness 332.8 *speed*
speeding 300.17 *directional*; 265.7 *easing*; 262.3 *hasty*; 213.1 *increase*; 332.8 *speed*; 332.1 *swift*
speeding-up 332.3 *accelerating*
speed limit 166.2 *limiting factor*; 320.21 *miscellaneous motoring terms*; 251.1 *restraint*
speed maniac 332.13 *swift person*
speed measurement 332.8 *speed*
speed of light 332.8 *speed*; 28.16 *waveform*
speed of sound 28.19 *sound propagation*; 332.8 *speed*; 28.16 *waveform*
speed of thought 332.10 *quickness of mind*
speedometer 742.5 *indicator*; 26.8 *meter*; 744.10 *recording instrument*; 332.8 *speed*
speed-skate 68.15 *ice-skate*
speed-skater 68.11 *skier*
speed-skating 68.8
speed-skating circuit 68.8 *speed-skating*
speed-skating race 68.8 *speed-skating*
speed-skating track 68.8 *speed-skating*
speed-skiing 68.1 *skiing*
speed sprayer 433.12 *sprinkler*
speed the parting guest 313.6 *part*
speed trap 320.21 *miscellaneous motoring terms*; 332.8 *speed*
speed up 332.6 *accelerate*; 332.9 *acceleration*; 262.1 *hasten*; 262.8 *hurry up!*; 213.5 *make bigger*; 262.2 *make haste*
speedway 61.10 *racing*
speedway race 61.1 *motor racing*
speedway racing 61.1 *motor racing*
speedy 342.18 *active*; 300.17 *directional*; 262.3 *hasty*; 280.5 *immediate*; 332.1 *swift*
speleology 305.7 *tunnelling*
spell 11.5; 381.20 *bout*; 594.2 *curse*; 275.3 *duration*; 236.11 *harmfulness*; 141.8 *intervening space*; 712.4 *malediction*; 694.10 *mean*; 276.1 *period*; 276.4 *period of activity*; 483.5 *positive stimulus*; 292.1 *season*; 31.3 *weather*; 5.47 *word*
spellbind 11.21 *bewitch*; 619.10 *be wonderful*; 362.15 *pull towards*
spellbinder 11.4 *witch*
spellbinding 483.11 *motivational*; 11.3 *witchcraft*; 11.15 *witchlike*; 619.3 *wonder-working*
spellbound 11.19 *bewitched*; 301.4 *motionless*; 483.12 *motivated*; 480.20 *persuadable*; 619.6 *wondering*
spellcasting 11.3 *witchcraft*
spellcraft 11.3 *witchcraft*
spell danger 711.5 *warn*
spell disaster 711.5 *warn*
spelling 5.27
spelling bee 5.27 *spelling*
spelling checker 40.11 *application*
spelling game 5.27 *spelling*
spelling mistake 274.11 *grammatical error*
spelling pronunciation 5.27 *spelling*
spell of duty 576.1 *work*
spell of work 770.3 *allotted task*; 576.2 *task*
spell out 222.11 *circumstantiate*; 719.9 *decipher*; 719.8 *interpret*; 694.10 *mean*; 139.23 *particularize*; 4.21 *rationalize*; 695.5 *simplify*; 5.47 *word*
spelunker 156.5 *submariner*
spelunking 156.1 *depth*
spencer 551.11 *jacket*
spend 787.1 *expend*; 580.4 *have leisure*; 785.6 *pay*; 777.2 *shop*; 349.1 *use*; 441.1 *waste*
spend a penny 560.17 *urinate*
spender 787.8; 13.9 *economist*; 777.12 *purchaser*; 681.6 *spendthrift*
spending 787.10 *expending*; 787.4 *expenditure*; 315.5 *export*; 785.15 *paying*; 777.8 *shopping*; 441.3 *waste*
spending money 780.4 *change*; 788.3 *income*; 765.5 *profit*
spending money like water 787.11 *spendthrift*
spending plan 680.2 *act of thrift*
spending spree 681.4, 787.6 *extravagance*
spend lavishly 787.1 *expend*; 777.2 *shop*
spend money like water 787.1 *expend*; 681.8 *overspend*; 441.1 *waste*
spend on 349.1 *use*
spend, spend, spend 681.8 *overspend*
spend the season 292.6
spend the summer 292.6 *spend the season*
spend the winter 292.6 *spend the season*
spendthrift 681.6; **787.9**; **787.11**; 681.1 *extravagant*; 441.8 *wasteful*; 441.6 *waster*
Spenserian 17.19 *narrative*
Spenserian stanza 17.10 *verse form*
spent 789.11 *accounted*; 337.9 *dilapidated*; 787.12 *expended*; 261.1 *fatigued*; 766.16 *losing*; 315.16 *outflowing*; 284.18 *over*; 349.9 *used*; 238.1 *useless*
spent cartridge 587.13 *ammunition*
sperm 562.3 *fertilizer*; 561.8 *organs of reproduction*; 344.3 *rudiment*
spermatangium 84.4 *reproductive body*
spermatic 561.16 *reproductive*
spermatium 84.4 *reproductive body*
Spermatophyta 77.3 *seed plant*
spermatophyte 77.3 *seed plant*
spermatophytes 554.9 *classifications of life*
spermatozoa 561.8 *organs of reproduction*
spermatozoid 84.4 *reproductive body*
sperm bank 439.4 *storage*
sperm duct 308.7 *passageway*
spermicidal 37.14 *counteracting*
spermicide 563.3 *birth control*; 37.4 *drug type*
spew 371.14 *let out*; 315.11 *run out*; 371.15 *vomit*
spew out 431.25 *flow*; 315.11 *run out*
Spey 90.4 *British rivers*
sphagnum 82.3 *moss*
sphenopsid 82.1 *fern*
sphere 86.14; **447.4**; 179.2 *circle*; 27.45 *curved surface*; 141.7 *range*; 143.5 *rank*; 181.3 *round thing*; 137.5 *social class*; 139.8 *specialization*; 29.10 *star*; 6.3 *subject*; 137.4 *type*
spherelike 179.5 *circular*; 181.9 *round*
sphere of influence 395.7; 85.3 *dominion*; 12.1 *government*
spheric 179.5 *circular*; 181.9 *round*
spherical 27.83; 179.5 *circular*; 181.9 *round*
spherical aberration 28.31 *lens element*; 29.25 *mounting*
spherical coordinates 27.33 *coordinates*
spherical geometry 27.34 *geometry*
spherical lens 28.29 *optical element*
spherically 179.8 *circularly*; 27.87 *mathematically*; 181.13 *roundly*
sphericalness 179.1 *circularity*; 181.1 *roundness*
spherical sailing 323.5 *navigation*
spherical triangle 27.43 *triangle*
spherical trigonometry 27.51 *trigonometry*
sphericity 181.1 *roundness*; 27.38 *surface*
spheroid 27.45 *curved surface*; 181.3 *round thing*
spheroidal 179.5 *circular*; 27.83 *spherical*
spheroidally 179.8 *circularly*
spherosome 34.8 *cell organ*
sphingolipid 33.6 *lipid*
sphingomyelin 33.6 *lipid*
sphinxlike 696.4 *difficult*; 696.1 *unintelligible*
sphragistics 743.5 *uniform*
spice 211.6 *add*; 412.4 *admixture*; 25.7 *basic ingredient*; 25.55 *cook*; 502.1 *fragrance*; 495.10 *make taste*; 412.8 *mix*; 359.2 *preserver*
spice cake 25.36 *cake*
spiced 496.9 *piquant*
spiced green bananas 25.49 *Indian dish*
spiced wine 558.7 *alcoholic drink*; 498.5 *sweet drink*
spices 583.1 *burial*; 502.2 *fragrant thing*; 496.5 *herbs*; 500.2 *sense of smell*
spicily 502.7 *fragrantly*
spiciness 502.1 *fragrance*; 496.1 *piquancy*
spick-and-span 256.16 *clean*; 295.12 *immature*; 407.13 *orderly*; 255.14 *purified*
spiculate 425.14 *be sharp*
spicule 425.8 *sharp-pointed thing*
spicy 502.4 *fragrant*; 500.5 *odorous*; 496.9 *piquant*; 336.12 *strong to the senses*; 495.7 *tasty*
spicy taste 495.1 *taste*
spider 76.2 *arachnid*; 76.6 *spinner*; 193.3 *weaving*
spider crab 75.4 *arthropod*
spideriness 151.7 *fineness*
spider-like 76.11 *arachnidan*; 75.18 *arthropodous*
spiderling 76.5 *larva*
spider's web 193.2 *braid*; 76.6 *spinner*
spidery 76.11 *arachnidan*; 75.18 *arthropodous*; 151.2 *fine*
spiel 68.10 *curling*; 729.1 *faculty of speech*; 778.6 *salesmanship*; 731.1 *talkativeness*
spieler 740.10 *publicizer*
spiel man 21.31 *circus performer*
spiffed up 551.30, 656.7 *dressed-up*
spiffing 235.1 *worthy*
spifflicate 357.11 *ruin*
spiff up 551.33 *dress up*
spiffy 797.1 *good*; 235.1 *worthy*
spigot 309.2 *stopper*
spike 384.9 *barrier*; 78.4 *flower head*; 81.3 *grass plant*; 378.8 *hinder*; 46.14 *miscellaneous terms*; 412.8 *mix*; 62.5 *rock face*; 425.16 *use a sharp tool*
spiked 425.2
spiked device 814.15 *instrument of torture*
spiked shoes 47.4 *sports equipment*
spike heels 551.19 *footwear*
spikelet 78.4 *flower head*; 81.3 *grass plant*
spikenard 502.3 *incense*; 268.6 *ointment*
spikes 551.19 *footwear*; 47.4 *sports equipment*
spike someone's guns 378.8 *hinder*; 335.8 *overpower*
spiky 425.2 *spiked*
spill 486.7 *be clumsy*; 305.4 *fall*; 522.8 *fire*; 90.7 *flow*; 192.1 *inversion*; 192.3 *invert*; 437.2 *lighter*; 315.2 *outflow*; 315.11 *run out*; 367.6 *throw down*; 441.1 *waste*
spillage 367.11 *lowering*; 90.6 *river flow*; 441.3 *waste*
spill blood 560.21 *bleed*
spilling 371.22 *disgorgement*; 305.18, 367.20 *falling*
spill one's guts 693.13 *inform on*
spillover 90.6 *river flow*
spill over 329.1 *overstep*; 315.11 *run out*
spill the beans 739.7 *betray*; 449.2 *detect*; 693.13 *inform on*
spill the brains of 382.17 *murder*
spillway 90.2 *channel*
spilt milk 766.3 *waste*
spilt salt 475.7 *bad-luck sign*
spin 42.13; 298.8 *be cyclic*; 300.13 *be in motion*; 53.18 *bowl*; 53.8 *delivery*; 322.5 *flight*; 322.10 *fly*; 68.15 *ice-skate*; 68.6 *ice-skating*; 719.13 *interpret news*; 193.8 *interweave*; 356.10 *produce*; 28.78 *quantum*; 307.3 *reel*; 307.9 *roll*; 307.8 *rotate*; 307.1 *rotation*
spina bifida 260.17 *nervous disorder*
spinakoturikopita 25.52 *Greek dish*
spin a long tale 270.5 *be diffuse*
spin a web 645.5 *be cunning*
spin a yarn 105.7 *be improbable*; 96.16 *delude*; 721.15 *recount*; 727.11 *tell a tall story*
spin bowler 53.4 *team*
spin-cast 55.7 *angle*
spin-casting 55.1 *angling*
spindle 307.4 *axle*; 34.10 *cell division*; 151.8 *narrow thing*; 307.6 *rotator*
spindle fibres 34.10 *cell division*
spindle-legged 153.1 *thin*
spindlelegs 153.9 *thin person*
spindle sander 23.11 *woodworking tool*
spindle-shaped 151.2 *fine*; 425.1 *sharp*
spindling 151.2 *fine*
spindly 151.2 *fine*
spin doctor 234.5 *defacer*; 550.18 *fixer*; 719.7 *news interpreter*; 480.12 *persuader*; 740.10 *publicizer*
spindrift 434.10 *air bubble*; 31.30 *snow*
spin-dry 428.23 *drip-dry*
spin-dryer 428.15 *dryer*; 307.6 *rotator*
spine 418.7 *hard substance*; 77.6 *leaf*; 71.2 *mammalian characteristic*; 154.4 *mountain range*; 425.8 *sharp-pointed thing*; 413.2 *supporting part*
spinel 30.34 *mineral*
spineless 537.5, 614.3 *cowardly*; 335.12 *impotent*; 639.3 *timid*; 337.12 *weak-willed*
spinelessly 614.5 *cravenly*
spinelessness 337.2 *indecisiveness*; 639.13 *timidity*
spinerette 42.2 *spinning*
sping lobster 25.19 *shellfish*
spininess 420.6 *roughness*; 425.6 *sharpness*
spin like a teetotum 307.8 *rotate*
spin money 781.13 *get rich*
spinnaker 50.3 *parts of a sailing boat*
spinner 76.6; 55.2 *artificial fly*; 578.2 *ar-*

tisan; 700.13 *snare;* 42.2 *spinning;* 53.4 *team;* 193.3 *weaving*
spinneret 76.6 *spinner*
spinney 79.4 *trees*
spinning 42.2; 55.1, 55.8 *angling;* 306.11 *orbiting;* 307.11 *rotating;* 307.2 *turning*
spinning jenny 307.6 *rotator;* 42.2 *spinning*
spinning motion 307.1 *rotation*
spinning mule 42.2 *spinning*
spinning out 148.4 *length;* 61.6 *motor-racing terms;* 50.7 *windsurfing*
spinning rod 55.3 *fishing tackle*
spinning top 181.5 *cone;* 307.6 *rotator*
spinning wheel 307.6 *rotator;* 42.2 *spinning;* 193.3 *weaving*
spin off 345.5 *show an effect*
spin-off 345.1 *effect;* 356.3 *product*
spin off from 345.7 *follow from*
spin of the wheel 254.5 *danger;* 107.3 *equal chance*
spin one's wheels 238.9 *waste effort*
spinose 425.2 *spiked*
spinosity 425.6 *sharpness*
spinous 425.2 *spiked*
spin out 270.5 *be diffuse;* 294.8 *delay;* 148.10 *lengthen;* 134.4 *protract;* 61.9 *race;* 731.8 *talk too much;* 50.18 *windsurf*
spin-out 61.6 *motor-racing terms;* 50.7 *windsurfing*
spin round 307.8 *rotate*
spinster 255.5 *pure person;* 568.5 *single girl;* 197.7, 572.5 *single person*
spinsterhood 572.1 *celibacy*
spinsterish 572.6 *celibate*
spinsterlike 572.6 *celibate*
spinsterly 572.6 *celibate*
spin words 724.9 *style*
spiny 420.2 *coarse;* 425.2 *spiked*
spiny anteater 71.6 *insect-eating mammal*
spin yarn 307.9 *roll*
spiny-headed worm 75.6 *worm*
spiny lobster 75.4 *arthropod*
spiracle 74.5 *fish anatomy;* 315.7 *outlet*
spiral 304.13 *ascend;* 177.2 *bend;* 306.10 *circular;* 180.2 *coil;* 180.6 *convolute;* 180.4 *convolutional;* 27.40, 177.6 *curve;* 27.81 *curvilinear;* 214.4 *decrease;* 305.12 *drop;* 322.5 *flight;* 322.10 *fly;* 213.4 *increase;* 306.6 *orbit;* 306.1 *orbital motion;* 213.2 *spread;* 307.2 *turning;* 304.2 *upturn*
spiral balance 414.10 *scales*
spiral down 305.12 *drop*
spiraled 177.4 *curved*
spiral galaxy 29.7 *galaxy*
spiralling 792.7 *dear;* 304.24 *leaping;* 306.1 *orbital motion;* 306.11 *orbiting;* 307.2 *turning*
spiralling prices 792.3 *inflationary price*
spiralling up 304.4 *taking off*
spirally 180.8 *circularly*
spiral spring 422.5 *spring*
spiral staircase 304.7 *means of ascent*
spirant 5.41 *lettered;* 5.16 *spoken letter*
spire 304.13 *ascend;* 154.15 *be high;* 81.3 *grass plant;* 174.2 *head;* 151.8 *narrow thing;* 425.8 *sharp-pointed thing;* 304.19 *take off;* 154.6 *tall thing;* 89.9 *tower*
spirelet 20.10 *church architecture*
spirillum 34.3 *organism*
spirit 11.7; 406.1 *contents;* 613.1 *courage;* 8.5 *deity;* 726.1 *emphasis;* 342.4 *energy;* 369.8 *extract;* 638.16 *fortitude;* 11.11 *ghost;* 139.11 *identity;* 96.2 *illusion;* 101.6 *internal world;* 554.1 *life;* 694.1 *meaning;* 622.1 *pride;* 99.3 *quintessence;* 590.8 *seat of feelings;* 101.3 *spiritual world;* 496.4 *stimulation;* 338.1 *vigour;* 334.3 *vitality*
spirit away 526.3 *cause to disappear;* 774.13 *kidnap*
spirited 342.18 *active;* 613.9 *courageous;* 726.3 *emphatic;* 334.15 *full of energy;* 554.13 *lively;* 622.14 *proud;* 496.10 *stimulating;* 338.4 *vigorous*
spiritedly 496.16 *stimulatingly*
spirit gum 21.21 *stage requisite*
spiritism 11.1 *occultism*
spiritist 11.12 *occultist*
spirit lamp 522.5 *incandescent light*
spiritless 618.7 *indifferent*
spiritlessly 618.17 *indifferently*
spiritlessness 618.1 *indifference*
spirit level 187.5 *planometer*
Spirit of God 8.3 *God*
spirit of the age 229.1 *tendency*
spiritous 558.17 *drinkable;* 690.6 *intoxicating*
spirit-raising 11.10 *psychic phenomenon*
spirit rapper 11.12 *occultist*
spirit rapping 11.1 *occultism*
spirits 690.12 *alcohol;* 221.4 *state of mind;* 582.14 *the spiritual world*
spiritual 11.18; 101.8 *nonmaterial;* 101.9 *parapsychological;* 7.15 *religious;* 18.5 *sacred music;* 516.2 *song;* 803.5 *virtuous*
spiritual body 11.7 *spirit*
spiritual darkness 523.7
spiritualism 11.1 *occultism;* 101.3 *spiritual world*
spiritualist 101.7 *believer in a nonmaterial world;* 719.6 *interpreter;* 11.12 *occultist;* 101.9 *parapsychological*
spiritualistic 101.9 *parapsychological;* 11.16 *psychic*
spirituality 795.2 *good morals;* 7.2 *religiousness;* 11.2 *the occult;* 101.2 *unworldliness;* 803.1 *virtue*
spiritualization 101.2 *unworldliness*
spiritualize 101.12 *enter a nonmaterial world;* 11.20 *occult*
spiritual loss 766.1 *loss*
spiritual love 593.1 *love*
spiritually 8.19 *divinely;* 101.13 *metaphysically;* 11.25 *occultly;* 7.23 *religiously;* 803.9 *virtuously*
spiritual marriage 572.3 *monasticism;* 570.3 *types of marriage*
spiritualness 101.2 *unworldliness*
spiritual rebirth 760.3 *persuasion*
spiritual world 101.3
spirit world 521.5 *invisible thing;* 101.3 *spiritual world;* 11.2 *the occult*
spirit writing 11.1 *occultism*
spirometer 26.8 *meter;* 432.15 *vaporimeter*
spirometric 26.16 *micrometric*
spirometry 26.2 *micrometry*
spissitude 430.1 *viscosity*
spit 626.11 *be irritable;* 493.4 *burner;* 30.11 *coast;* 25.5 *cooker;* 115.5 *counterpart;* 508.6 *crack;* 373.8 *fastening;* 327.26 *flicker;* 111.3 *lookalike;* 268.5 *lubricant;* 151.6 *narrow place;* 92.5 *peninsula;* 185.2 *projection;* 31.62 *rain;* 307.6 *rotator;* 560.9 *saliva;* 560.20 *salivate;* 433.32 *seep;* 425.8 *sharp-pointed thing;* 371.15 *vomit*
spit and polish 256.1 *cleanness;* 656.1 *formality;* 632.5 *tradition*
spit at 668.26 *cock a snook*
spitball 48.4 *pitching terms;* 330.5 *throw*
spite 590.6 *bad feeling;* 651.16 *be malevolent;* 236.13 *be worthless;* 651.4 *bitterness;* 236.11 *harmfulness;* 594.1 *hate;* 236.14 *ill-treat;* 682.4 *unpleasantness*
spiteful 236.5 *harmful;* 594.10 *hating;* 651.14 *hostile;* 624.15 *resentful;* 682.2 *unpleasant;* 714.14 *vindictive*
spitefully 594.18 *hatefully;* 651.20 *malevolently;* 624.17 *resentfully;* 714.16 *vindictively;* 236.15 *worthlessly*
spitefulness 651.4 *bitterness;* 236.11 *harmfulness;* 594.1 *hate;* 626.3 *irritableness*
spitfire 590.9 *feeling person;* 625.3 *irascible person;* 380.4 *violent creature*
spit on one's palms 576.6 *work*
spit out 371.15 *vomit*
spit-roast 25.55 *cook*
spit-roasting 25.8 *cooking technique*
spit tacks 594.17 *anger;* 327.21 *be agitated*
spitter 330.5 *throw*
spitting 508.2 *crack;* 508.9 *crackling;* 560.9 *saliva;* 560.29 *salivating*
spitting distance 147.2 *short distance*
spitting image 750.5 *conformity;* 115.5 *counterpart;* 717.6 *image;* 111.3 *lookalike;* 717.1, 721.9 *representation;* 198.5 *twin*
spittle 431.3 *body fluid;* 433.4 *exudate;* 268.5 *lubricant;* 560.9 *saliva*
spittoon 767.8 *sink*
spit upon 594.14 *hate*
spiv 700.17 *cheat;* 800.4 *dishonourable person*
splanchnic 172.10 *visceral*
splanchnography 403.8 *science of structure*
splanchnology 403.8 *science of structure*
splash 258.11 *dirty;* 90.7 *flow;* 512.1, 512.4 *hiss;* 541.4 *maculation;* 123.8 *make important;* 738.10 *manifestation;* 740.16 *publicize;* 90.6 *river flow;* 377.18, 429.5, 429.14, 433.33 *sprinkle;* 433.11 *wash*
splashdown 317.13 *flight path;* 29.35 *rocketry*
splash down 317.14 *find one's way*
splashed 429.12 *seeping*
splashing 433.8 *watering*
splash of colour 529.2 *colourfulness*
splash out 679.10 *be generous;* 787.1 *expend*
splash out on 681.8 *overspend*
splashy 429.11 *marshy*
splat 23.12 *wood*
splatter 31.62 *rain;* 377.18, 429.5, 433.33 *sprinkle*
splattered 377.23 *sprinkled*
splattering 377.4 *sprinkling*
splatterpunk novel 17.2 *fiction*
splay 150.9 *be broad;* 190.6 *become bigger;* 150.4 *breadth;* 150.1 *broad;* 377.10 *diverge;* 190.1 *growth;* 190.5 *make bigger;* 311.12 *separate*
splay apart 311.12 *separate*
splayed 190.7 *bigger;* 150.1 *broad;* 311.8 *fanlike*
splaying 377.5 *divergence;* 190.8 *growing;* 190.1 *growth;* 311.2 *parting*
spleen 499.4; 651.4 *bitterness;* 594.1 *hate;* 172.4 *insides;* 626.3 *irritableness;* 624.1 *resentment*
spleenful 594.10 *hating*
spleenfully 594.18 *hatefully*
splendid 522.16 *bright;* 797.1 *good;* 781.3 *opulent;* 235.1 *worthy*
splendid isolation 655.3 *separation*
splendidly 797.22 *well;* 619.13 *wonderfully;* 235.11 *worthily*
splendidness 797.8 *good*
splendiferous 235.1 *worthy*
splendour 545.1 *gorgeousness;* 522.1 *light*
splenetic 499.7; 651.14 *hostile;* 624.15 *resentful*
splenetically 499.11
splice 492.12 *abut;* 393.1 *repair*
spliced 570.21 *married;* 108.4 *related*
splice ropes 50.15 *sail*
splicing 393.8 *repair*
spliff 691.6 *drug*
spline 53.7 *bat*
splint 413.3 *body support;* 394.10 *surgical dressing*
splint armour 384.7 *armour*
splinter 424.4 *be brittle;* 375.3 *disintegrate;* 196.3 *fragment;* 151.8 *narrow thing;* 205.7 *piece;* 420.7 *rough thing;* 372.9 *separate*
splintering 424.1 *brittle;* 424.2 *brittleness*
splintery 424.1 *brittle*
split 770.4 *allot;* 372.16 *apart;* 751.6 *argue;* 751.2 *argument;* 424.4 *be brittle;* 357.13 *be destroyed;* 739.7 *betray;* 337.6 *be weak;* 51.8 *bowl;* 51.10 *bowling;* 51.5 *bowling delivery;* 424.1 *brittle;* 424.2 *brittleness;* 146.2, 146.5 *crack;* 146.7 *cracked;* 375.4 *deconstruct;* 196.8 *divide;* 571.1, 571.7 *divorce;* 571.11 *divorced;* 313.4 *hurry off;* 693.13 *inform on;* 133.4 *interruption;* 183.4, 183.10 *notch;* 183.7 *notched;* 308.12, 308.18 *open;* 308.1 *opening;* 205.10 *part;* 311.12, 372.9 *separate;* 372.3 *separateness;* 372.1 *separation*
split apart 146.5 *crack*
split down the middle 770.4 *allot;* 198.17 *go halves;* 216.10 *make average*
split four ways 200.12 *quadrisect*
split hairs 273.7 *be accurate;* 116.6 *differentiate;* 466.12 *discriminate;* 670.18 *find fault;* 136.15 *modify;* 702.13 *quibble*
split half-and-half 111.10 *be equal*
split hat trick 53.8 *delivery*
split image 41.4 *portrait*
split infinitive 274.11 *grammatical error*
split in half 198.13 *half;* 198.16 *halve*
split in three 199.11 *trisect*
split in two 198.16 *halve*
split jump 68.6 *ice-skating*
split-level 565.16 *manorial*
split-level house 565.5 *house*
split lutz lift 68.6 *ice-skating*
split off 311.12 *separate*
split one's ears 513.4 *be strident*
split one's sides 514.11, 599.14, 600.8 *laugh*
split personality 36.8 *disordered personality;* 36.16 *dissociation;* 198.3 *duality;* 461.5 *psychosis*
splits 57.8 *floor exercises*
split second 280.3 *instant*
split-second 280.5 *immediate*
split-shot 55.3 *fishing tackle*
splitter 79.7 *timber production*
split the difference 754.4 *compromise;* 764.4 *have joint possession;* 216.10 *make average*
split the ears 507.8 *be loud*
split the uprights 46.17 *kick*
split three ways 199.11 *trisect*
split tin 25.39 *loaf*
splitting 424.1 *brittle;* 424.2 *brittleness;* 36.19 *defence mechanism;* 491.5 *painful;* 372.1 *separation*
splitting headache 491.2 *painful condition;* 260.3 *symptom*
splitting in four 200.5 *quadrisection*
splitting in half 198.7 *halving*
splitting in three 199.5 *trisection*
splitting in two 198.7 *halving*
splitting the atom 28.72 *nuclear fission*
splitting the difference 754.1 *compromise*
split two ways 198.17 *go halves;* 198.13 *half*
split up 377.9 *be dispersed;* 571.7 *divorce;* 372.9 *separate*
split-up 377.5 *divergence;* 571.1 *divorce;* 377.20 *separated*
split up with 751.5 *disagree*
splodge 541.4 *maculation*
splotch 541.4 *maculation*
splurge 787.1 *expend;* 787.6 *extravagance;* 490.8 *feel pleasure;* 490.4 *pleasurable things;* 441.1, 441.3 *waste*
splutter 327.26 *flicker;* 512.1, 512.4 *hiss;* 371.14 *let out;* 560.20 *salivate*
spluttering 327.20 *flickering;* 560.29 *salivating*
spoil 486.7 *be clumsy;* 219.4 *be excessive;* 757.4 *be permissive;* 471.14 *be solicitous;* 236.13 *be worthless;* 548.7 *blemish;* 224.8 *cause change;* 395.9 *change;* 490.10 *comfort;* 245.2 *decay;* 766.13 *destroy;* 296.17 *grow old;* 599.15 *humour;* 245.4 *impair;* 546.5 *make ugly;* 351.1 *misuse;* 412.8 *mix;* 61.9 *race;* 357.11 *ruin;* 499.8 *sour;* 337.7 *weaken*
spoilage 245.10 *impairment;* 238.6 *refuse;* 296.10 *staleness*
spoiled 548.4 *blemished;* 648.5 *given consideration;* 233.4 *incomplete;* 236.2 *inferior;* 490.7 *pleased*
spoiled child 593.11 *loved one*
spoiled rotten 648.5 *given consideration*
spoiler 234.5 *defacer;* 357.6 *destroyer;* 119.4 *equilizer;* 651.8 *malefactor;* 774.9 *plunderer;* 741.3 *reporting;* 228.3 *stabilizer;* 773.6 *taker*
spoil for a fight 751.7 *pick a fight*
spoiling 766.5 *destruction;* 599.11 *humouring;* 245.10 *impairment;* 648.1 *leniency;* 648.4 *lenient;* 61.6 *motor-racing terms;* 471.5 *solicitude*
spoiling for 636.2 *eager;* 243.18 *prepared*
spoiling for a fight 381.22 *militant*
spoil one's chances 288.7 *lose one's chance*
spoil oneself 683.6 *be selfish*
spoil one's pleasure 604.6 *disappoint*
spoil one's reputation 247.6 *fail*
spoils 794.2; 765.5 *profit;* 774.4 *stolen goods;* 773.5 *takings*
spoils of office 774.4 *stolen goods*
spoils of war 765.5 *profit;* 794.2 *spoils;* 774.4 *stolen goods;* 773.5 *takings*
spoilsport 481.8 *cautionary person;* 602.4 *depressing person;* 606.3 *dissatisfied person;* 378.7 *hinderer;* 342.11 *meddler;* 670.13 *pessimist*
spoils system 483.5 *positive stimulus*
spoilt 548.4 *blemished;* 122.17 *defective;* 245.12 *deteriorated;* 351.4 *misused*
spoke 320.11 *bicycle part;* 311.3 *radiation;* 304.10 *step*
spoked 311.7 *radiating*
spoken 692.34 *communicated;* 5.39 *of language;* 729.16 *speech*
spoken for 570.22 *marriageable;* 756.12 *promised*
spoken language 5.3; 729.1 *faculty of speech*
spoken letter 5.16
spoken radio 504.9 *audio device*
spoken unit 5.17 *word*
spoken word 729.7 *utterance*
spokes 310.5 *focus*
spokeshave 425.9 *sharp-edged thing;* 421.9 *smoother;* 23.11 *woodworking tool*

spokesman 578.3 *agent*; 398.4 *deputy*; 693.9 *informant*; 741.4 *journalist*; 719.7 *news interpreter*; 733.6 *public speaker*; 717.8, 748.4 *representative*; 729.10 *speaker*
spokesperson 578.3 *agent*; 398.4 *deputy*; 693.9 *informant*; 733.6 *public speaker*; 717.8, 748.4 *representative*; 729.10 *speaker*
spokeswoman 578.3 *agent*; 398.4 *deputy*; 733.6 *public speaker*; 748.4 *representative*; 729.10 *speaker*
spoliate 766.13 *destroy*; 774.14 *plunder*
spoliation 766.5 *destruction*; 357.5 *havoc*; 774.5 *plundering*; 773.3 *taking away*
spolitory 774.17 *stolen*
spondaic 17.20 *metrical*
spondee 17.9 *metre*
spondulix 780.2 *cash*
sponge **75.8**; **370.6**; **664.15**; 370.13, 428.20 *absorb*; 434.10 *air bubble*; 70.5 *aquatic animal*; 343.12 *be inactive*; 772.7 *borrow*; 793.14 *buy cheaply*; 256.13 *clean*; 256.10 *cleaning object*; 690.17 *drunkard*; 428.15 *dryer*; 358.4 *eraser*; 433.34 *hose*; 415.7 *light thing*; 308.6 *porous thing*; 710.8 *solicit money*; 664.3 *sponger*
sponge bag 410.8 *bag*
sponge bath 256.6 *bath*
sponge cake 25.36 *cake*; 498.3 *dessert*
spongelike **75.22**
sponge off 256.13 *clean*; 358.1 *obliterate*
sponge on 664.15 *sponge*
spongeous 370.17 *absorbent*
sponge out 358.1 *obliterate*
sponger **664.3**; 793.8 *bargain hunter*; 710.5 *beggar*; 772.6 *borrower*; 267.5 *follower*; 343.8 *nonworker*
sponge rubber 422.4 *rubber*
sponge up 558.13 *drink*
spongeware 24.1 *ceramics*
spongiform encephalopathy 461.3 *mental deterioration*
sponginess 419.10 *compressibility*; 417.3 *sparseness*
sponging 370.5 *absorption*; 710.11 *begging*; 710.3 *solicitation*; 664.2 *sycophancy*; 664.7 *sycophantic*
spongy 370.17 *absorbent*; 419.4 *compressible*; 183.6 *concave*; 92.11 *continental*; 308.14 *holed*; 417.1 *sparse*; 75.22 *spongelike*
sponsor 392.23 *advise*; 669.7 *advocate*; 707.9 *affirmer*; 392.15 *benefactor*; 392.29 *finance*; 352.6 *find means*; 413.8 *supporter*; 413.13 *support financially*
sponsorship 392.6 *financial assistance*; 352.4 *financial resources*; 413.7 *financial support*; 392.9 *patronage*; 252.2 *protection*
spontaneity **478.5**
spontaneous **478.2**; 250.13 *informal*; 445.8 *instinctive*; 646.1 *naive*; 15.10 *unionized*; 636.5 *voluntary*
spontaneous abortion 563.1 *infertility*
spontaneous combustion 493.6 *fire*
spontaneous generation 561.3 *propagation*
spontaneously **636.17**; 478.7 *extempore*; 15.13 *industrially*; 250.22 *informally*; 445.11 *intuitively*
spontaneous person 478.6 *improviser*
spontaneous strike 15.4 *industrial dispute*
spoof 621.2 *act of derision*; 700.11, 700.31 *hoax*; 125.9 *imitate*; 125.3 *mockery*; 700.28 *trick*
spoofed 700.36 *deceived*
spoofer 700.15 *deceiver*
spook 328.7 *disturb*; 11.11 *ghost*; 97.6 *ghostly presence*; 96.2 *illusion*
spooked 11.19 *bewitched*
spookily 11.26 *magically*
spooky 612.10 *frightening*; 11.18 *spiritual*
spool 40.20 *abort*; 41.9 *film*; 307.6 *rotator*
spoon 55.2 *artificial fly*; 203.3 *container*; 593.26 *court*; 557.16 *eating utensil*; 369.10 *excavator*; 56.4 *golf club*; 593.27 *kiss*; 410.17 *ladle*; 412.6 *mixer*; 316.15 *take away*
spoonbill 72.3 *water bird*
spoon bread 25.38 *bread*
spooned 410.20 *containing*
spoonerism 5.29 *grammar*; 274.11 *grammatical error*; 272.4 *joke*; 697.2 *solecism*
spoon in 557.22 *eat well*
spooning 593.14 *communication of love*; 593.6 *courtship*
spoon oar 50.4 *rowing*
spoor 633.9 *follow*; 716.4 *indication*; 744.12 *vestige*
spooring 633.1 *pursuit*
sporadic 133.8 *discontinuous*; 377.19 *dispersed*; 114.5 *diverse*; 299.4, 408.14 *irregular*; 275.23 *occasional*; 276.9 *periodic*; 206.6 *sparse*
sporadically 377.30 *diffusely*; 133.17 *discontinuously*; 408.27 *in disorder*; 114.11, 299.8 *irregularly*; 275.28 *sometimes*
sporadicalness 133.1 *discontinuity*; 299.1 *irregularity*
sporadicness 206.4 *rarity*
sporangium 82.2 *fern plant*
spore **427.10**; 34.7 *cell*; 82.2 *fern plant*; 83.4 *fungal body*; 344.3 *rudiment*
spore capsule 82.4 *moss plant*
spore case 82.2 *fern plant*
spore-producing protozoan 75.9 *protozoan*
sporicide 37.4 *drug type*
sporophore 83.4 *fungal body*
sporophyte 82.2 *fern plant*
sporozoan 75.9 *protozoan*; 75.23 *protozoan*
Sport 45
sport **45.1**; 738.1 *display*; 576.5 *exercise*; 700.11 *hoax*; 257.1 *hygiene*; 567.3 *male title of address*
sported 738.13 *displayed*
sportily 551.36 *dressily*
sporting **45.5**; 799.4 *honourable*; 801.11 *right-minded*
sporting activity **45.4**
sporting chance 104.4 *chance*; 107.4 *fair chance*; 102.3 *strong possibility*
sporting dog **60.6**
sporting error **274.13**
sporting feat 485.3 *masterpiece*
sporting gun 587.9 *firearm*
sporting hit **331.14**
sporting jacket 551.11 *jacket*
sportingly **45.7**; 799.7 *honourably*
sporting rifle 60.3 *hunting equipment*
sportive 45.5 *sporting*
sport karate 52.8 *karate*
sport of kings 59.7 *horseracing*
sports 576.5 *exercise*
sports and recreation 15.2 *industrial negotiations*
sports bag 410.8 *bag*
sports book 740.6 *book publishing*
sports car 320.16 *car*; 332.11 *swift thing*
sports-car race **61.3**; 61.1 *motor racing*
sports-car racing 61.1 *motor racing*
sportscast 741.6 *radio news*
sportscaster 741.4 *journalist*
sportscasting 741.3 *reporting*
sports coat 551.11 *jacket*
sports correspondent 721.10 *descriptive writer*
sports desk 741.8 *newsroom*
sports edition 740.4 *newspaper*
sports editor 741.4 *journalist*; 740.11 *newspaperman*
sports equipment **47.4**
sports field 6.15 *schoolroom*
sports forecaster 475.9 *forecaster*
sportsground **45.2**
sports jacket 551.4 *informal dress*; 551.11 *jacket*
sportsman **45.3**; 336.5, 586.3 *athlete*; 799.3 *honourable person*; 60.4, 633.6 *hunter*
sportsmanlike 799.4 *honourable*; 801.11 *right-minded*
sports outfit 743.5 *uniform*
sportsperson 60.4 *hunter*
sports reporter 741.4 *journalist*
sports shirt 551.8 *shirt*
sports skirt 551.6 *skirt*
sports trophy 794.1 *trophy*
sports uniform 743.5 *uniform*
sportswear 551.1 *dress*; 551.4 *informal dress*
sportswoman 586.3 *athlete*; 799.3 *honourable person*; 60.4, 633.6 *hunter*; 45.3 *sportsman*
sporty 45.5 *sporting*; 551.31 *styled*
sporty person 336.5 *athlete*
sporty type 45.3 *sportsman*
sporule 427.10 *spore*
spot **548.1**; 548.7 *blemish*; 231.7 *defect*; 234.11 *deform*; 234.3 *deformity*; 258.4 *dirt*; 258.11 *dirty*; 449.1 *discover*; 142.2 *exact location*; 245.5 *hurt*; 121.2 *leadership*; 142.9 *locate*; 142.1 *location*; 541.4 *maculation*; 548.2 *pimple*; 264.5 *predicament*; 695.7 *recognize*; 518.12 *see*; 143.1 *situation*; 260.13 *skin disease*; 377.18 *sprinkle*; 21.20 *stage lighting*; 541.11 *variegate*
spot cash 780.2 *cash*
spotless 256.16 *clean*; 805.5 *innocent*; 255.12 *morally pure*; 230.1 *perfect*; 255.13, 531.5, 795.9 *pure*; 803.5 *virtuous*
spotlessly 256.19 *cleanly*; 805.11 *innocently*; 230.7 *perfectly*; 255.19 *purely*
spotlessness 256.1 *cleanness*; 805.1 *innocence*; 230.3 *perfection*; 255.1, 531.11 *purity*
spotlight 738.1 *display*; 522.6 *electric light*; 726.6 *emphasize*; 522.24 *light*; 41.15 *lighting*; 520.10 *make visible*; 738.10 *manifestation*; 740.7 *publicity*; 740.16 *publicize*; 738.3 *reveal*; 21.20 *stage lighting*; 520.7 *that which makes visible*
spotlighted 520.2 *clear*
spotlit 522.18 *lit*
spot meter 41.18 *exposure time*
spot of bother 264.7 *awkward situation*; 328.5 *commotion*; 408.9 *disorder*; 607.3 *nuisance*; 378.2 *obstacle*; 242.8 *quarrel*
spot of enforcement 46.13 *penalty*
spot of trouble 264.7 *awkward situation*
spot on 273.5, 698.21 *accurate*; 698.39 *accurately*; 801.8 *correct*; 230.1 *perfect*
spot pass 46.9 *play*
spot putt 56.7 *golf*; 56.3 *golf shots*
spots 69.5 *dice*; 260.3 *symptom*
spot stroke 65.2 *billiards play*
spotted 65.9 *billiard*; 258.7 *dirty*; 449.14 *discovered*; 231.1 *imperfect*; 548.5 *marked*; 541.10 *mottled*; 377.23 *sprinkled*
spotted dick 25.35 *dessert*
spotted wilt 44.12 *pests and diseases*
spotter 449.12 *discoverer*; 518.11 *observer*
spot the ball 65.8 *play billiards*
spottiness 299.1 *irregularity*; 541.4 *maculation*
spotting 449.6 *discovery*; 377.4 *sprinkling*
spotty 234.7 *deformed*; 133.8 *discontinuous*; 260.23 *diseased*; 299.4 *irregular*; 541.10 *mottled*
spot white ball 65.3 *English billiards*
spousal 570.20 *matrimonial*; 570.5 *wedding*
spouse **570.8**; 567.13 *man in the family*; 223.12 *partner*; 568.12 *woman in the family*
spousehood 570.1 *marriage*
spouseless 572.6 *celibate*
spout 371.22 *disgorgement*; 431.25 *flow*; 371.14 *let out*; 315.7 *outlet*; 315.11 *run out*; 304.17 *spring up*; 731.8 *talk too much*; 304.2 *upturn*
spouter 304.12 *geyser*
spout out 315.11 *run out*
sprachgefühl 5.1 *linguistics*
sprain 245.11 *hurt*; 491.11 *inflict pain*; 491.3 *injury*; 380.3 *instance of violence*; 380.8 *use violence*; 337.7 *weaken*
sprained 491.6 *injured*
sprat 74.8 *food fish*; 25.18 *sea fish*
sprawl **377.7**; 190.6 *become bigger*; 377.9 *be dispersed*; 187.6 *be horizontal*; 305.4 *fall*; 190.1 *growth*; 187.1 *horizontality*; 190.5 *make bigger*; 263.2 *take it easy*; 305.11 *trip*
sprawled **377.25**; 187.10 *lying*
sprawling 305.18 *falling*; 190.8 *growing*; 190.1 *growth*; 187.1 *horizontality*; 187.10 *lying*; 377.25 *sprawled*
sprawly 190.8 *growing*
spray 432.26 *aerate*; 434.10 *air bubble*; 205.6 *branch*; 376.29 *bunch*; 44.15 *cultivate*; 43.17 *farm*; 381.15 *firing*; 78.1 *flower*; 37.10 *inhalant*; 81.12 *manage grassland*; 502.6 *perfume*; 43.14 *pest control*; 330.7 *shot*; 377.18, 429.14, 433.33 *sprinkle*; 433.12 *sprinkler*; 77.5 *stem*; 432.11 *vaporizer*; 44.8 *weedkiller*
spray can 433.12 *sprinkler*
spray-can painting 19.8 *painting*
spray deodorant 501.2 *deodorant*
sprayed 377.23 *sprinkled*
sprayer 43.10 *farm tool*; 44.6 *garden tool*; 433.12 *sprinkler*
spraygun 19.11 *artist's materials*
spraying 429.5 *sprinkle*; 377.4 *sprinkling*; 433.8 *watering*
spread **213.2**; 688.3 *act of gluttony*; 765.10 *augment*; 765.2 *augmentation*; 395.10 *be a prevailing influence*; 190.6 *become bigger*; 550.10 *bed covering*; 377.9 *be dispersed*; 740.17 *be published*; 190.7 *bigger*; 138.24, 150.11 *broaden*; 550.24 *coat*; 377.1 *dispersion*; 377.16 *distribute*; 377.22 *distributed*; 141.20 *extend*; 43.6 *farm*; 557.13 *feast*; 187.9 *flattened*; 79.19 *grow*; 190.1 *growth*; 213.4 *increase*; 411.10 *layer*; 190.5 *make bigger*; 187.7 *make horizontal*; 740.13 *make public*; 322.7 *miscellaneous aviation terms*; 311.11 *move apart*; 308.19 *open up*; 27.60 *parameter*; 311.2 *parting*; 490.4 *pleasurable things*; 372.1 *separation*; 158.1 *size*; 316.11 *transfer*; 316.3 *transmission*
spreadability 190.2 *enlargeability*
spreadable 190.9 *enlargeable*
spread abroad 740.17 *be published*; 740.13 *make public*
spread around 770.4 *allot*; 740.19 *published*
spread a rumour 740.13 *make public*
spread canvas 323.9 *navigate*; 313.5 *set out*
spread eagle 743.8 *heraldic device*; 743.4 *insignia*
spread-eagle 187.6 *be horizontal*; 148.9 *be long*; 311.14 *branch*; 367.3 *bring down*; 814.1 *punish*; 367.8 *sit*; 305.11 *trip*
spreadeagled 311.8 *fanlike*; 187.10 *lying*
spreader 190.4 *enlarger*; 44.6 *garden tool*
spread far and wide 219.4 *be excessive*
spread fence 59.9 *jumping*
spread formation 46.7 *offence*
spread foundation 38.28 *substructure*
spreading 765.2 *augmentation*; 377.28 *dispersive*; 190.8 *growing*; 190.1 *growth*; 213.6 *increasing*; 372.1 *separation*; 316.3 *transmission*
spreading abroad 740.1 *publication*
spreading like wildfire 213.6 *increasing*
spreading out 190.1 *growth*; 311.2 *parting*
spreading the word 740.1 *publication*
spread like wildfire 395.10 *be a prevailing influence*; 190.6 *become bigger*; 740.17 *be published*
spread on 550.24 *coat*
spread oneself thin 342.13 *be busy*
spread one's wings 114.8 *be diverse*
spread out 190.6 *become bigger*; 377.9 *be dispersed*; 141.20 *extend*; 190.5 *make bigger*; 311.11 *move apart*; 738.3 *reveal*; 206.9 *scatter*; 141.21 *space*
spread-out 190.7 *bigger*; 150.1 *broad*; 206.6 *sparse*
spread over 550.24 *coat*; 232.6 *fill*
spread sail 313.5 *set out*
spreadsheet 40.11 *application*; 409.8 *chart*; 220.2 *table*
spread the good news 7.20 *preach*
spread the load 398.7 *delegate*
spread the word 740.13 *make public*; 450.9 *make someone believe*
spread the Word 7.20 *preach*
Sprechgesang 18.4 *opera*
spree 690.14 *drinking bout*; 787.6 *extravagance*; 490.4 *pleasurable things*; 441.3 *waste*
sprig 205.6 *branch*; 555.5 *young plant*
sprightliness 554.1 *life*
sprightly 342.18 *active*; 554.13 *lively*
spring **292.2**; **292.10**; **422.5**; 332.6 *accelerate*; 332.9 *acceleration*; 422.8 *be elastic*; 332.4 *be swift*; 180.2 *coil*; 422.1 *elasticity*; 422.3 *elastic thing*; 366.10 *elevator*; 130.27 *emerge*; 334.4 *energy*; 47.8, 304.5, 304.18 *jump*; 438.5 *machine*; 315.2 *outflow*; 50.3 *parts of a sailing boat*; 298.5 *regular thing*; 439.2 *resource*; 419.13 *soften*; 344.2 *source*; 433.1 *water*
spring apart 372.9 *separate*
spring balance 414.10 *scales*; 28.86 *weighing instrument*
spring barley 43.12 *crop*
springboard 67.6 *diving*; 422.3 *elastic thing*; 366.10 *elevator*; 57.3 *gymnastic apparatus*; 392.1 *help*; 304.8 *lift*; 313.10 *place of departure*; 57.6 *pommel horse*; 67.11 *swimming*
springboard diving 67.6 *diving*
spring catch 373.8 *fastening*
spring-clean 256.13 *clean*
spring-cleaning 256.2 *cleaning*
springe 379.1 *trap*
springer 20.9 *miscellaneous architectural features*
spring forward 332.6 *accelerate*
spring from 345.7 *follow from*

spring greens 538.9 *greenstuff*; 25.33 *vegetable*
spring gun 700.13 *snare*
springily 422.11 *elastically*
springiness 422.1 *elasticity*; 334.4 *energy*; 419.8 *softness*
springing 422.6 *elastic*; 304.24 *leaping*; 419.8 *softness*
springlike 538.4 *fresh*; 31.46 *seasonal*; 292.10 *spring*; 493.11 *warm*
spring oats 43.12 *crop*
spring on 630.9 *surprise*
spring roll 25.48 *Chinese dish*
spring rounds 10.7 *non-Christian ritual*
springs 413.4 *rest*
spring sale 778.4 *sale*
spring scale 414.10 *scales*
spring tide 154.8 *high thing*; 213.3 *increasing thing*; 298.5 *regular thing*; 292.2 *spring*; 30.15, 91.2 *tide*
springtime 292.2 *spring*
springtime of life 555.1 *youth*
spring-tine harrows 43.10 *farm tool*
spring up 304.17; 190.6 *become bigger*; 30.63 *ebb*; 130.27 *emerge*; 213.4 *increase*; 83.12 *mushroom*
spring up like mushrooms 562.6 *be fertile*; 561.12 *multiply*
spring upon 630.10 *ambush*
spring water 558.6 *soft drink*; 433.1 *water*
spring wheat 43.12 *crop*
spring wood 79.3 *timber*
springy 422.6 *elastic*; 419.2 *pliant*
sprinkle 377.18; **429.5**; **429.14**; **433.33**; 44.15 *cultivate*; 412.8 *mix*; 10.18 *perform rites*; 427.21 *powder*; 206.9 *scatter*; 367.6 *throw down*; 541.11 *variegate*; 433.29 *water*
sprinkled 377.23; 541.10 *mottled*; 206.6 *sparse*
sprinkler 433.12; 256.10 *cleaning object*; 44.6 *garden tool*
sprinkler head 433.12 *sprinkler*
sprinkler system 252.4 *safety device*
sprinkling 377.4; 412.4 *admixture*; 10.5 *Christian rite*; 367.20 *falling*; 206.1 *few*; 157.3 *shallowness*; 429.5 *sprinkle*; 728.6 *suggestion*; 433.8 *watering*
sprinkling of water 256.3 *religious cleansing*
sprinkling system 433.12 *sprinkler*
sprint 332.6 *accelerate*; 332.9 *acceleration*; 262.2 *make haste*; 61.1 *motor racing*; 47.7 *race*; 47.1 *track events*
sprinter 47.3, 336.5 *athlete*; 59.7 *horseracing*; 332.13 *swift person*; 59.2 *thoroughbred*
sprinting 68.12 *ski*; 47.9 *track*; 47.1 *track events*
sprinting race 68.2 *cross-country skiing*
sprint race 50.4 *rowing*; 47.1 *track events*
sprint racing 47.1 *track events*
sprint-skate 68.15 *ice-skate*
sprint-skating 68.8 *speed-skating*
sprit 50.3 *parts of a sailing boat*; 50.8 *punting*
sprite 40.19 *computing terms*; 11.11 *ghost*; 159.4 *little person*
spritzer 558.8 *mixed drink*
sprocket 425.8 *sharp-pointed thing*
sprocket wheel 307.6 *rotator*
sprog 130.15 *baby*; 561.6 *progeny*
sprout 190.6 *become bigger*; 130.27 *emerge*; 345.8 *grow*; 561.11 *have young*; 213.4 *increase*; 77.5 *stem*; 77.21 *vegetate*; 555.5 *young plant*
sprouting 190.8 *growing*; 190.1 *growth*
sprout up 190.6 *become bigger*; 77.21 *vegetate*
spruce 256.13, 256.16 *clean*; 551.30 *dressed-up*; 407.13 *orderly*
spruced up 551.30 *dressed-up*
spruce up 547.15 *beautify*; 256.13 *clean*; 551.33 *dress up*; 244.1 *improve*; 581.1 *refresh*; 407.21 *tidy*
sprung 422.6 *elastic*; 419.1 *soft*
sprung rhythm 17.9 *metre*
spry 342.18 *active*; 338.4 *vigorous*
spumante 558.9 *wine*
spume 434.10 *air bubble*; 415.7 *light thing*; 30.14, 91.3 *wave*
spumy 531.2 *whitened*
spun 42.9
spunk 613.1 *courage*; 638.16 *fortitude*; 437.2 *lighter*; 336.1 *strength*; 338.1 *vigour*; 334.3 *vitality*
spunky 613.9 *courageous*; 338.4 *vigorous*
spun out 270.3 *diffuse*; 148.1 *long*
spun-out 61.10 *racing*
spur 205.6 *branch*; 598.8 *cheer*; 262.4 *haste*; 262.1 *hasten*; 332.7 *hurry someone up*; 331.1 *impel*; 480.8 *incentive*; 213.1 *increase*; 425.15 *make sharp*; 483.9 *motivate*; 89.1 *mountain*; 154.4 *mountain range*; 752.9 *offer*; 92.5 *peninsula*; 483.3 *stimulus*; 321.2 *track*; 79.2 *tree part*
spur gear 38.7 *gear*; 438.5 *machine*
spurious 699.32; 96.12 *artificial*; 189.5 *devious*; 234.8 *exaggerated*; 699.29 *false*; 705.14 *questionable*; 115.8 *simulated*; 702.7 *sophistic*
spuriously 699.41; 115.14 *comparably*; 189.9 *deviously*; 234.14 *distortedly*; 702.14 *sophistically*
spuriousness 699.4; 189.3 *deviousness*; 234.4 *distortion of the truth*; 699.1 *falsehood*
spurious signal 39.14 *terminal*
spurn 661.6 *be insubordinate*; 709.6 *dissent*; 128.7 *exclude*; 594.14 *hate*; 668.5, 668.23 *insult*; 371.4 *ostracize*; 470.1 *reject*; 470.5 *rejection*; 364.1 *repel*
spurned 596.9 *disliked*; 594.12 *hated*
spurned lover 470.9 *rejected person*
spurning 668.5 *insult*; 668.11 *insulting*; 364.6 *repulse*
spur-of-the-moment 480.11 *motive*; 478.2 *spontaneous*
spur on 598.8 *cheer*; 213.5 *make bigger*; 483.9 *motivate*
spurred on 483.12 *motivated*; 480.20 *persuadable*
spurs 542.4 *honour*; 794.1 *trophy*
spurt 332.6 *accelerate*; 332.9 *acceleration*; 342.12 *be active*; 371.22 *disgorgement*; 262.4 *haste*; 389.7 *leak*; 371.14 *let out*; 262.2 *make haste*; 342.3 *nimbleness*; 315.11 *run out*; 304.17 *spring up*; 302.13 *step*; 304.2 *upturn*
spurt of activity 478.5 *spontaneity*
spurt out 315.11 *run out*
spur wheel 438.5 *machine*; 307.6 *rotator*
Sputnik 306.4 *orbiting body*; 29.32 *satellite*
sputter 32.29 *absorb*; 327.12, 327.26 *flicker*; 512.1, 512.4 *hiss*; 371.14 *let out*; 509.10 *rattle*
sputtering 327.20 *flickering*; 509.17 *rattling*; 32.20 *surface chemistry*
sputter-ion pump 32.20 *surface chemistry*
sputtery 327.20 *flickering*
sputum 559.2 *secreted substance*
sputum test 35.7 *diagnosis*
spy 662.16 *be subversive*; 449.1 *discover*; 449.12 *discoverer*; 342.17 *meddle*; 644.4 *meddler*; 716.7 *person who gives evidence*; 737.2 *secretiveness*; 753.5 *seditionist*; 518.12 *see*; 711.4 *warner*
spyglass 518.10 *visual aid*
spyhole 518.9 *viewpoint*
spying 518.3 *observation*; 662.3 *subversion*
spy on 518.15 *watch*
spy plane 586.31 *military aircraft*
spy satellite 29.32 *satellite*
spy story 17.2, 721.5 *fiction*
squab 158.16 *fat*; 25.20 *meat*; 72.12 *young bird*
squabble 342.1 *activity*; 701.13, 751.6 *argue*; 701.1, 751.2 *argument*; 342.12 *be active*; 242.8, 242.11 *quarrel*
squabbling 701.7 *arguing*; 751.9 *disagreeing*; 242.7 *dissension*
squad 586.16 *army unit*; 376.14 *force*; 584.4 *military organization*; 578.4 *personnel*; 376.12 *team*
squad car 320.17 *police car*
squadron 586.30 *air force unit*; 586.16 *army unit*; 374.3 *assembly*; 376.14 *force*; 584.4 *military organization*; 586.23 *naval unit*
squadron leader 586.32 *airman*
squalene 33.20 *terpene*
squalid 782.3 *beggarly*; 258.7 *dirty*; 236.4 *poor*; 544.10 *ugly*; 258.8 *unclean*; 682.2 *unpleasant*; 408.15 *untidy*
squalidity 258.1 *dirtiness*
squalidness 258.1 *dirtiness*; 236.10 *poverty*; 408.3 *untidiness*
squall 514.10 *cry out*; 327.13 *tempest*; 379.1 *trap*; 327.3 *turbulence*; 380.5 *violent weather*; 31.12 *wind*
squally 31.47 *windy*
squalor 782.7 *beggary*; 258.1 *dirtiness*; 236.10 *poverty*; 682.4 *unpleasantness*
squama 411.4 *slice*
Squamata 73.1 *reptile*
squamation 411.6 *layering*
squamose 411.9 *platelike*
squamosely 411.12 *in layers*
squamous 74.14 *ichthyological*; 411.9 *platelike*; 73.11 *reptilian*
squamously 411.12 *in layers*
squamulose 411.9 *platelike*
squander 766.11 *be wasteful*; 357.12 *consume*; 787.1 *expend*; 218.7 *make insufficient*; 351.1 *misuse*; 686.11 *overindulge*; 349.1 *use*; 441.1, 681.7 *waste*
squandered 238.2 *futile*; 766.16 *losing*
squanderer 766.6 *loser*; 681.6, 787.9 *spendthrift*; 441.6 *waster*
squandering 681.4 *extravagance*; 766.17 *unprofitable*; 441.3, 766.3 *waste*
square 698.39 *accurately*; 27.91, 210.9 *add*; 176.9 *angled*; 176.3 *angled figure*; 176.4 *angular measurement*; 586.16 *army unit*; 698.31 *be accurate*; 426.1 *blunt*; 480.17 *bribe*; 777.4 *buy off*; 69.4 *chess terms*; 87.7 *city district*; 775.5 *compensate*; 117.6, 117.14 *conformist*; 324.9 *directly*; 198.15 *double*; 119.6 *equal*; 119.11 *equalize*; 160.7 *form*; 53.2 *ground*; 799.4 *honourable*; 213.5 *make bigger*; 186.6 *make vertical*; 27.17 *multiplication*; 323.9 *navigate*; 186.10 *perpendicular*; 186.4 *plumb line*; 27.44 *polygon*; 27.82 *polygonal*; 53.14 *positioned*; 200.2, 200.8 *quadrilateral*; 801.7 *right*; 50.16 *row*; 228.5 *stable person*; 158.17 *stocky*; 53.4 *team*; 178.4 *traditional*; 198.1 *two*
square accounts 789.9 *settle accounts*
square bracket 373.4 *means of connection*
square brackets 27.25 *algebraic expression*; 742.7 *punctuation*
square bridge 38.21 *bridge*
square cut 53.17 *bat*; 53.9 *stroke*
squared 698.21 *accurate*; 119.6 *equal*; 160.9 *formed*; 50.11 *rowing*; 198.1, 198.9 *two*
square dance 22.1 *dancing*; 200.3 *foursome*; 22.4 *historic dancing*; 654.5 *party*
square deal 801.1 *fairness*
square-in pass 46.9 *play*
square it 807.5 *atone*
square John 117.6 *conformist*
square leg 53.4 *team*
square-leg umpire 53.3 *official*
squarely 273.8, 698.39 *accurately*; 801.20 *correctly*; 324.9 *directly*; 119.13 *equitably*; 200.13 *four times*; 799.7 *honourably*; 52.16 *professionally*
square match 56.2 *golfing terms*
square matrix 27.22 *matrix*
square meal 557.12 *meal*
squareness 158.6 *squatness*; 186.1 *verticality*
square one 130.1 *beginning*; 130.11 *starting point*
square-out pass 46.9 *play*
square peg 655.6 *unsocial person*
square-rigged 50.10 *sailing*
square-rigger 50.2 *sailing boat*
square root 27.17 *multiplication*; 194.6 *power*
square root sign 27.13 *mathematical symbol*
square shooter 799.3 *honourable person*
square the account 385.3 *retaliate*
square things 807.5 *atone*
square-toed shoes 551.19 *footwear*
square wave 326.5 *wave*; 28.16 *waveform*
square with 117.7, 750.25 *conform*
square with facts 698.27 *be true*
square with the evidence 698.27 *be true*
square with the facts 698.29 *be truthful*
squaring 698.8 *accuracy*; 807.1 *atonement*; 807.4 *atoning*; 775.2 *compensation*; 50.4, 50.11 *rowing*
squaring the circle 737.5 *difficult problem*; 27.49 *geometric construction*
squash 63.8; 367.5 *bear down on*; 427.26 *beat*; 357.8 *destroy*; 512.1, 512.4 *hiss*; 623.17 *humiliate*; 236.14 *ill-treat*; 704.8 *refute*; 558.6 *soft drink*; 419.13 *soften*; 63.8 *squash*
squash ball 63.9 *squash terms*
squash court 63.8 *squash*
squashed 623.3 *humbled*
squashed flat 187.9 *flattened*
squash equipment 63.9 *squash terms*
squash flat 155.9 *lower*; 187.7 *make horizontal*
squashily 512.8 *sibilantly*
squashiness 419.10 *compressibility*
squash racket 63.9 *squash terms*
squash rackets 63.8 *squash*
squash terms 63.9
squashy 419.4 *compressible*; 92.11 *continental*; 431.15 *flowing*; 429.11 *marshy*
squat 100.16 *be external*; 155.8 *be low*; 367.16 *courtesy*; 565.1 *habitat*; 565.17 *inhabit*; 159.7 *little*; 155.5 *low*; 763.7 *possess*; 564.15 *settle*; 565.8 *shelter*; 149.7 *short*; 367.8 *sit*; 158.17 *stocky*; 773.7 *take*; 329.5 *transgress*
squatness 158.6; 159.1 *littleness*; 155.1 *lowness*; 149.1 *shortness*
squat on 763.7 *possess*
squatted 564.11 *inhabited*
squatter 564.6 *illegal occupant*; 100.8 *intruder*; 782.10 *poor person*; 763.5 *possessor*
squatterism 763.1 *possession*
squatters' rights 763.1 *possession*
squatting 57.11 *gymnastic*; 763.8 *possessing*; 763.1 *possession*; 367.23 *sedentary*
squatting vault 57.6 *pommel horse*
squaw 570.11 *married woman*; 568.12 *woman in the family*
squawk 507.8 *be loud*; 513.4 *be strident*; 515.2 *bird song*; 753.7 *complain*; 491.12 *express pain*; 753.3 *gesture of protest*; 515.5 *sing*; 513.1 *stridency*
squawking 513.7 *strident*
squawky 513.7 *strident*
squeak 513.6 *be shrill*; 515.2 *bird song*; 515.4 *cry*; 513.3 *shrillness*; 729.13 *speak in a particular way*
squeaker 693.10 *informer*
squeakiness 513.3 *shrillness*
squeaking 513.9 *shrill*
squeaky 513.9 *shrill*
squeaky clean 801.11 *right-minded*
squeal 715.5 *accuse*; 513.6 *be shrill*; 739.7 *betray*; 515.4 *cry*; 514.6 *cry of pain*; 491.12 *express pain*; 693.13 *inform on*; 513.3 *shrillness*; 454.3 *testify*; 716.13 *turn queen's evidence*
squealer 715.3 *accuser*; 739.4 *discloser*; 479.9 *equivocator*; 693.10 *informer*; 716.7 *person who gives evidence*; 454.7 *verifier*; 711.4 *warner*
squeamish 596.8 *disliking*; 795.10 *moralistic*; 260.22 *sick*; 639.3 *timid*
squeamishness 795.4 *self-righteousness*; 639.13 *timidity*
squeegee 256.10 *cleaning object*
squeezable 419.4 *compressible*
squeeze 267.6 *adhere*; 647.5 *be severe*; 593.14 *communication of love*; 386.6 *compel*; 191.1 *contraction*; 214.1 *decrease*; 576.4 *exertion*; 658.12 *greet*; 593.27 *kiss*; 416.9 *make dense*; 191.5, 214.5 *make smaller*; 369.17 *obtain an extract*; 48.7 *play baseball*; 264.5 *predicament*; 251.8 *restrain*; 251.1 *restraint*; 360.6 *retain*; 360.1 *retention*; 376.21 *scrum*
squeeze credit 251.9 *economize*
squeezed 406.11 *loaded*; 191.7 *smaller*
squeezed dry 428.4 *dried-out*
squeeze in 232.6 *fill*; 314.12 *flood in*; 368.3 *impact*; 416.9 *make dense*; 406.7 *stuff*
squeeze one's hand 658.12 *greet*
squeeze out 369.12 *displace*
squeeze play 48.5 *batting terms*
squeezer 191.4 *contractor*
squeeze someone's hand 742.11 *gesture*
squeeze the trigger 60.7 *shoot*
squeeze together 416.9 *make dense*
squeezing 593.14 *communication of love*; 191.1 *contraction*; 135.6 *demanding*; 369.7 *obtaining an extract*
squeezing out 369.2 *displacement*
squelch 429.15 *be moist*; 481.5 *discourage*; 512.1, 512.4 *hiss*; 429.8 *marsh*; 251.8 *restrain*
squelchiness 419.10 *compressibility*
squelching 251.1 *restraint*
squelchy 419.4 *compressible*; 429.11 *marshy*
squib 508.3 *banger*; 678.6 *ridicule*
squib kick 46.12 *special team*
squid 25.18 *sea fish*; 700.13 *snare*
squiffy 690.2 *slightly drunk*
squiggle 180.2 *coil*; 180.6 *convolute*

squiggly 180.4 *convolutional*
squilgee 256.10 *cleaning object*
squillion 194.3 *large number;* 201.11 *million*
squinch 20.9 *miscellaneous architectural features*
squint 519.14 *be blind;* 234.2 *facial distortion;* 518.6, 518.13 *look;* 20.9 *miscellaneous architectural features;* 519.2 *poor sight;* 518.9 *viewpoint*
squinting 519.9 *weak-sighted*
squire 223.7 *attendant;* 593.26 *court;* 223.15 *escort;* 763.6 *lord;* 593.9 *lover;* 567.3 *male title of address;* 400.1 *master;* 664.11 *pander to*
squirearchy 12.1 *government*
squirm 327.21 *be agitated;* 674.16 *be self-conscious;* 180.2 *coil;* 180.6 *convolute;* 491.9 *feel pain;* 327.7, 327.24 *shake*
squirming 180.4 *convolutional;* 327.18 *shaky*
squirmy 327.18 *shaky*
squirrel 376.36 *hoarder*
squirrel away 350.6 *stop using;* 439.6 *store*
squirrel hunting 60.2 *hunting*
squirrel-like 71.30 *rodent-like*
squirrel tank 461.8 *mental hospital*
squirt 371.22 *disgorgement;* 433.34 *hose;* 371.14 *let out;* 159.4 *little person;* 124.10 *nonentity;* 149.5 *short person*
squirt gun 433.12 *sprinkler*
squirt in 368.2 *inject*
squirting 433.8 *watering*
squish 512.1, 512.4 *hiss*
squishy 419.4 *compressible;* 92.11 *continental*
squit 159.4 *little person;* 124.10 *nonentity*
Sraosha 8.6 *angel*
Sri 567.3 *male title of address*
stab 381.6; 353.5 *attempt;* 491.10 *be painful;* 448.1 *experiment;* 381.18 *hit;* 308.20 *hole;* 236.14 *ill-treat;* 491.11 *inflict pain;* 491.3 *injury;* 382.17 *murder;* 491.1 *pain;* 66.4 *play soccer;* 372.9 *separate*
stabbed 308.14 *holed*
stabbing 381.18 *hit;* 651.14 *hostile;* 582.6 *killing;* 491.5 *painful*
stabile 19.12 *sculpture*
Stability 228
stability 132.7; **228.1**; 407.9 *discipline;* 119.2 *equilibrium;* 407.8 *harmony;* 452.17 *infallibility;* 38.14 *load;* 277.4 *long-lastingness;* 301.1 *motionlessness;* 225.1 *permanence;* 460.1 *sanity;* 336.1 *strength;* 638.15 *will*
stabilization 228.1 *stability*
stabilize 228.6 *be stable;* 119.11 *equalize;* 407.20 *harmonize;* 452.21 *make certain;* 253.14 *make fast;* 225.6 *make permanent;* 228.7 *make stable;* 32.25 *solidify*
stabilized 228.10; 32.32 *solid*
stabilizer 228.3; 32.15 *catalysis;* 119.4 *equilizer;* 32.3 *phase;* 32.21 *polymer*
stab in the back 678.12 *defame;* 800.2 *faithlessness;* 381.16 *personal attack;* 800.9 *prove false*
stabismic 519.9 *weak-sighted*
stable 228.9; 71.20 *abode of mammals;* 119.6 *equal;* 43.7 *farm building;* 253.9 *fast;* 376.23 *flock;* 407.16 *harmonious;* 452.6 *infallible;* 225.7 *permanent;* 43.18 *practise livestock farming;* 410.21 *put in a container;* 460.5 *rational;* 298.11 *regular;* 565.12 *stall;* 312.16 *stopover;* 439.4 *storage;* 439.6 *store;* 565.18 *take up residence;* 577.1 *workshop*
stableboy 401.6 *domestic servant;* 43.16 *farm worker;* 59.15 *horse person*
stable colours 743.5 *uniform*
stable companion 569.6 *close friend*
stabled 410.20 *containing*
stable equilibrium 28.10 *force;* 228.1 *stability*
stable horse 59.1 *horse*
stable lad 59.15 *horse person*
stableman 401.6 *domestic servant;* 43.16 *farm worker*
stable management 59.14 *horse-riding terms*
stable person 228.5
stable state 119.2 *equilibrium*
stable thing 228.4
stabling 410.20 *containing;* 439.4 *storage*
stably 228.12; 119.13 *equitably*
stab to death 382.17 *murder*
staccato 508.9 *crackling;* 508.10 *explosively;* 326.14 *vibrating;* 326.2 *vibration*
stack 765.11 *acquire;* 765.3 *acquisition;* 376.37 *assemble;* 699.25 *be fraudulent;* 69.3 *card game terms;* 30.11 *coast;* 322.6 *flight control;* 376.26 *mass;* 69.10 *play;* 439.1, 439.6 *store;* 186.3 *vertical thing*
stacked 376.47 *collected;* 106.4 *deliberate;* 439.7 *stored*
stacked deck 699.8 *fraud*
stacking 322.6 *flight control*
stacks of money 780.3 *fortune*
stack the cards 106.2 *premeditate*
stack the deck 700.30 *be fraudulent*
stack up 221.6 *be in a state of*
stack up with 119.10 *be equal*
stadial 30.40 *glaciation*
stadium 46.4; 38.20 *building;* 654.4 *meeting place;* 45.2 *sportsground;* 21.16 *theatre;* 518.9 *viewpoint*
staff 586.14 *armed forces;* 587.7 *blunt weapon;* 413.3 *body support;* 352.6 *find means;* 579.6 *governing body;* 392.11 *helper;* 352.3 *human resources;* 15.8 *industrial;* 743.4 *insignia;* 6.6 *instructorship;* 18.17 *notation;* 127.3 *person included;* 578.4 *personnel;* 334.1 *power;* 436.5 *provision;* 7.11 *vestment;* 376.13 *workforce*
staff college 585.6 *art of war;* 584.3 *military training*
staffed 436.8 *provisional*
staff member 15.7 *employee;* 401.5 *office assistant;* 127.3 *person included;* 387.3 *subordinate*
staff nurse 35.16 *nurse*
staff officers 584.5 *military staff*
staff of life 557.7 *food;* 554.3 *life requirements*
staff representative 15.7 *employee*
staffroom 6.15 *schoolroom*
staff work 585.6 *art of war;* 579.3 *management*
stag 14.5 *invest;* 567.16 *male animal;* 71.17 *male mammal;* 777.1 *purchase;* 777.12 *purchaser;* 776.2 *speculate*
stage 21.17; **205.3**; 738.1 *display;* 30.41 *geological time;* 209.4 *interval;* 411.2 *level;* 222.2 *occurrence;* 308.8 *open space;* 356.10 *produce;* 312.16 *stopover;* 170.1 *surroundings*
stage a comeback 112.20 *renew*
stage a coup 144.16 *replace;* 12.12 *take authority*
stage a demo 703.19 *protest*
stage a play 738.2 *display something*
stage appearance 525.2 *being in view*
stage a revolt 662.16 *be subversive*
stage a shoot-out 585.14 *battle*
stage a sit-down 753.8 *cause mischief*
stage a sit-in 661.6 *be insubordinate;* 703.19 *protest*
stage a strike 226.7 *stop working*
stage box 21.18 *auditorium*
stage business 21.22 *acting*
stage carpenter 21.28 *stagehand*
stagecraft 21.9 *dramaturgy*
staged 21.39 *dramatic*
staged event 740.8 *public relations*
stage director 356.9 *producer*
stagedom 21.1 *drama*
stage door 21.17 *stage*
stage-door Johnny 21.33 *theatregoer*
stage drunk 21.23 *role*
stage fever 21.22 *acting*
stage fright 21.22 *acting;* 612.2 *fearfulness;* 674.4 *shyness*
stagehand 21.28
stage Irishman 21.23 *role*
stage L 21.17 *stage*
stage left 21.43 *on stage;* 21.17 *stage*
stage lighting 21.20
stage-manage 21.38 *dramatize*
stage management 21.14 *production*
stage manager 738.12 *displayer;* 21.27 *producer*
stage name 737.8 *anonymity;* 736.7 *concealer;* 721.8 *name*
stage performer 21.24 *actor*
stage play 21.2 *play*
stage player 21.24 *actor*
stage presence 21.22 *acting*
stage presentation 21.13 *theatrical performance*
stage property 21.21 *stage requisite*
stage R 21.17 *stage*
stage requisite 21.21
stage right 21.43 *on stage;* 21.17 *stage*
stage screw 21.19 *stage set*
stage set 21.19
stage setting 21.19 *stage set*
stage show 21.7 *show*
stagestruck 21.41
stage technician 21.28 *stagehand*
stage villain 21.23 *role*
stage whisper 21.22 *acting;* 512.1 *hiss;* 730.16 *speak in a low voice;* 730.4 *whispering*
stagey 676.3 *affected*
stagflation 13.2 *economy;* 14.1, 780.7 *finance*
stagger 327.11; 630.11 *amaze;* 227.11 *be changeable;* 690.7 *be drunk;* 261.5 *be fatigued;* 299.6 *be irregular;* 337.6 *be weak;* 619.10 *be wonderful;* 451.9 *cause disbelief;* 481.2 *deter;* 612.13 *frighten;* 299.1 *irregularity;* 327.25 *pitch;* 326.11 *rock;* 305.11 *trip;* 300.15 *walk*
stagger along 313.1 *depart;* 333.1 *move slowly*
stagger belief 619.10 *be wonderful*
staggered 630.7 *amazed*
staggering 690.10 *drunkenness;* 299.4 *irregular;* 299.1 *irregularity;* 326.16 *rocking;* 690.2 *slightly drunk;* 333.4 *slow;* 630.8 *surprising*
staggers 327.8 *spasm;* 260.18 *veterinary disease*
stag hunt 633.2 *chase;* 60.2 *hunting*
stag hunting 59.8, 60.2 *hunting;* 71.23 *mammal hunting*
staginess 703.2 *demonstrativeness*
staging 21.9 *dramaturgy;* 21.14 *production*
stagnancy 301.1 *motionlessness*
stagnant 341.3, 343.1 *inactive;* 339.5 *inert;* 563.3 *infertile;* 88.9 *lakelike;* 301.4 *motionless;* 93.16 *vegetating*
stagnantly 88.10 *limnologically;* 301.10 *motionlessly*
stagnant water 88.2 *small lake;* 258.5 *swill*
stagnate 343.12 *be inactive;* 339.4 *be inert;* 563.7 *be infertile;* 301.8 *be motionless;* 93.21 *merely exist;* 341.4 *not act*
stagnating 339.5 *inert;* 563.3 *infertile;* 93.16 *vegetating*
stagnation 592.4 *desensitization;* 13.2 *economy;* 780.7 *finance;* 341.1 *inaction;* 339.1 *inertness;* 563.1 *infertility;* 93.9 *mere existence;* 301.1 *motionlessness*
stag party 567.15 *menfolk;* 654.5 *party;* 376.9 *social gathering*
stagy 703.10 *demonstrative;* 21.39 *dramatic*
staid 117.14 *conformist;* 656.6 *formal;* 643.1 *solemn*
staidness 656.1 *formality;* 643.4 *solemnity*
stain 412.4 *admixture;* 412.10 *become mixed;* 548.7 *blemish;* 550.24 *coat;* 550.3 *coating;* 529.15 *colour;* 523.3 *dark colour;* 231.7 *defect;* 122.2 *deficiency;* 234.11 *deform;* 234.3 *deformity;* 258.4 *dirt;* 258.11 *dirty;* 802.9 *dishonour;* 245.5 *hurt;* 529.4 *pigment;* 548.1 *spot;* 541.11 *variegate;* 744.12 *vestige*
stained 529.10 *coloured;* 550.36 *covered;* 523.10 *dark-coloured;* 258.7 *dirty;* 231.1 *imperfect;* 233.4 *incomplete;* 527.3 *semitransparent*
stained glass 19.1 *art;* 527.9 *glass;* 541.5 *variegated thing;* 522.10 *window*
stained-glass window 114.3 *diverse thing;* 19.7 *picture*
staining 34.6 *cell biology;* 42.7 *dyeing*
staining pigment 529.4 *pigment*
stainless 256.16 *clean;* 805.5 *innocent;* 255.13 *pure;* 803.5 *virtuous*
stainlessly 803.9 *virtuously*
stainlessness 805.1 *innocence;* 255.1 *purity;* 803.1 *virtue*
stainless steel 38.25 *construction material*
stain removal 42.8 *fabric treatment*
stair 209.4 *interval;* 304.10 *step*
stair carpet 550.9 *floor covering*
staircase 132.2 *consecution;* 304.7 *means of ascent;* 317.2 *route*
stairhead 174.3 *architectural summit*
stairs 132.2 *consecution;* 304.7 *means of ascent;* 373.4 *means of connection*
stairway 304.7 *means of ascent;* 373.4 *means of connection*
stake 44.15 *cultivate;* 254.10 *endanger;* 43.11 *farmland;* 373.8 *fastening;* 44.6 *garden tool;* 814.16 *instrument of execution;* 186.3 *vertical thing*
stakeholder 780.18 *treasurer*
stake one's claim to 773.7 *take*
stake-out 665.5 *watchfulness*
stakes 384.9 *barrier*
Stakhanovite 342.10 *busy person;* 578.1 *worker*
stalactite 186.3 *vertical thing*
stalagmite 186.3 *vertical thing*
stale 284.19 *antiquarian;* 620.4 *boring;* 245.2 *decay;* 245.12 *deteriorated;* 261.1 *fatigued;* 231.1 *imperfect;* 112.13 *monotonous;* 487.2 *not customary;* 296.12 *olden;* 236.4 *poor;* 503.3 *stinking;* 497.5 *tasteless;* 499.6 *unpalatable;* 560.17 *urinate;* 349.9 *used*
stale line 59.8 *hunting*
stalely 620.8 *boringly;* 296.18 *venerably*
stalemate 384.26 *act on the defensive;* 111.10 *be equal;* 226.8 *cause to cease;* 309.1 *closure;* 111.5 *equality;* 119.2 *equilibrium;* 341.1 *inaction;* 301.9 *make motionless;* 301.1 *motionlessness;* 378.2 *obstacle;* 264.8 *snag;* 226.2 *stop*
stalemated 111.16 *equal;* 341.3 *inactive*
staleness 296.10; 620.1 *boredom;* 497.1 *dilution;* 261.7 *fatigue;* 231.5 *imperfection;* 236.10 *poverty;* 503.1 *stench;* 487.3 *unaccustomedness;* 499.2 *unpalatability*
stale repetition 112.3 *repetitiveness*
Stalin 236.12 *bad person;* 798.6 *evil person;* 594.8 *hated person*
Stalingrad 382.15 *slaughterhouse*
Stalinism 647.2 *suppression*
stalk 205.6 *branch;* 181.4 *cylinder;* 633.9 *follow;* 83.4 *fungal body;* 300.12 *gait;* 633.11 *hunt;* 82.4 *moss plant;* 356.7 *produce;* 60.7 *shoot;* 77.5 *stem;* 300.15 *walk*
stalked 77.18 *of leaves*
stalked barnacle 75.4 *arthropod*
stalker 60.4, 633.6 *hunter*
stalking 633.2 *chase;* 60.2 *hunting;* 633.1 *pursuit;* 60.8 *shooting*
stalking-horse 645.2 *stratagem*
stalking stick 60.3 *hunting equipment*
stall 384.25; **565.12**; **779.9**; 71.20 *abode of mammals;* 378.9 *block;* 226.6 *cease;* 23.2 *chair;* 10.12 *church;* 410.2 *compartment;* 294.8 *delay;* 247.1 *failure;* 43.7 *farm building;* 322.5 *flight;* 378.8 *hinder;* 247.9 *malfunction;* 320.21 *miscellaneous motoring terms;* 639.5 *vacillate*
stalled 294.10 *held up*
staller 378.7 *hinderer;* 639.15 *indecisive person*
stall-holder 778.14 *street trader*
stalling 247.1 *failure;* 322.5 *flight;* 639.1 *vacillating*
stalling for time 631.9 *tactics*
stallion 59.1 *horse;* 567.7 *libertine;* 567.16 *male animal;* 71.17 *male mammal*
stall-keeper 778.11 *pedlar;* 778.14 *street trader*
stalls 21.18 *auditorium;* 21.33 *theatregoer;* 518.9 *viewpoint*
stalwart 259.1 *healthy;* 336.9 *physically strong;* 423.4 *powerful*
stalwartly 423.13 *powerfully*
stalwartness 423.8 *physical strength*
stamen 205.6 *branch;* 78.3 *flower part;* 561.8 *organs of reproduction*
stamina 640.4; 342.8 *assiduity;* 613.1 *courage;* 423.8 *physical strength;* 334.1 *power;* 336.1 *strength*
staminate 78.12 *of flowers*
stammer 806.9 *appear guilty;* 486.7 *be clumsy;* 690.7 *be drunk;* 674.16 *be self-conscious;* 730.14 *have difficulty speaking;* 732.7 *keep quiet;* 729.3 *mode of speech;* 806.2 *signs of guilt;* 730.3 *speech defect*
stammerer 674.7 *modest person*
stammering 806.6 *appearing guilty;* 486.3 *clumsy;* 690.10 *drunkenness;* 732.4 *guarded speech;* 730.12 *inarticulate;* 674.11 *shy;* 730.3 *speech defect;* 696.11 *unintelligibility*
stamp 669.16 *acclaim;* 267.4 *adherent;* 507.8 *be loud;* 331.13 *blow;* 139.3 *characteristic;* 99.11 *characterize;* 750.28 *consent;* 692.31 *correspond;* 692.3 *correspondence;* 111.4, 111.9 *duplicate;* 160.7 *form;* 300.12 *gait;* 742.11 *gesture;* 743.10 *identify;* 331.7 *kick;* 183.9 *make concave;* 228.7 *make stable;* 780.24 *monetize;* 99.4 *nature;* 757.2 *permit;* 253.2, 253.11 *promise;* 160.2 *prototype;* 733.10 *send;* 221.1 *state;* 137.4 *type*
stamp collection 439.5 *collection*

stamp collector 376.35 *collector*
stamped 750.17 *consenting*; 111.15 *duplicate*; 780.22 *monetary*
stamped coinage 780.13 *coinage*
stampede 332.4 *be swift*; 380.7 *be violent*; 386.7 *force*; 262.4 *haste*; 262.1 *hasten*
stampeded 262.3 *hasty*
stamped on one's memory 462.7 *memorable*
stamping 669.5 *acclaim*; 742.15 *gestural*; 507.2 *outcry*
stamping foot 742.3 *gesture*
stamping ground 565.2 *environment*; 86.13 *locality*; 142.1 *location*
stamping the foot 624.4 *anger*
stamp of approval 669.1 *approval*
stamp off 313.1 *depart*
stamp on 331.7 *kick*; 647.6 *suppress*
stamp one's feet 494.10 *be cold*; 493.14 *be hot*; 335.6 *be powerless*
stamp one's foot 624.11 *be angry*
stamp out 94.13 *cause not to exist*; 357.8 *destroy*
stamp tax 790.9 *historical taxes*
stamp with impatience 342.12 *be active*
stance 450.1 *belief*; 52.2 *boxing*; 56.3 *golf shots*; 446.5 *ideology*; 701.3 *line of argument*; 160.6 *nature*; 4.2 *philosophical system*; 62.5 *rock face*; 707.2 *statement*
stanchion 66.1 *soccer*
stand 585.9, 585.14 *battle*; 413.12 *bear*; 221.6 *be in a state of*; 450.1 *belief*; 301.8 *be motionless*; 143.9 *be situated*; 228.6 *be stable*; 186.5 *be vertical*; 143.2 *circumstances*; 93.19 *continue to be*; 785.8 *defray*; 787.3 *donate*; 21.15 *engagement*; 175.2 *foot*; 768.5 *give*; 446.5 *ideology*; 277.6 *last*; 301.1 *motionlessness*; 383.1 *resistance*; 143.10 *situate*; 779.9 *stall*; 707.2 *statement*; 217.4 *suffice*; 413.2 *supporting part*; 476.1 *supposition*; 667.19 *take off one's hat to*; 79.4 *trees*; 176.5, 518.9 *viewpoint*; 469.5 *vote*
stand above suspicion 805.8 *be innocent*
stand above the law 16.74 *be lawless*
stand accused 715.7 *be accused*
stand a chance 102.8 *be possible*
stand a fair chance 104.8 *be probable*
stand against 381.8 *counterattack*; 113.14 *oppose*; 383.6 *resist*
stand against a wall 814.5 *execute*
stand aghast 612.11 *be afraid*
stand a good chance 102.8 *be possible*; 104.8 *be probable*
stand alone 250.16 *be independent*; 197.18 *be one*
stand aloof 634.1 *avoid*; 197.18 *be one*; 655.12 *be unsocial*; 145.6 *keep away*
stand apart 634.1 *avoid*; 197.18 *be one*
standard **26.7**; 216.1, 216.4 *average*; 138.21 *common*; 750.6 *convention*; 750.15 *conventional*; 140.10 *customary*; 117.15 *everyday*; 743.7 *flag*; 44.10 *fruit tree*; 209.3 *gradation*; 209.7 *gradational*; 140.4 *guide*; 446.6 *ideal*; 158.14 *medium*; 235.5 *not bad*; 5.39 *of language*; 230.1 *perfect*; 230.3 *perfection*; 129.4 *precedent*; 79.1 *tree*; 27.70 *universal*
standard atmosphere 28.38 *thermodynamics*
standard-bearer 586.8 *soldier*
standard deviation 27.60 *parameter*; 28.83 *sensitivity*
Standard English 5.29 *grammar*
standard error 27.60 *parameter*; 28.83 *sensitivity*
standard event 59.12 *rodeo*
standard gauge 321.3 *rail*; 317.10 *railway*
standardization 32.18 *gravimetric analysis*; 409.3 *organization*; 111.6 *regularity*
standardize 216.10 *make average*; 117.9 *make conform*; 111.8 *make the same*; 750.26 *make uniform*; 27.94 *order*; 409.13 *organize*; 140.14 *regulate*; 407.19 *systematize*
standardized 32.41 *analytic*; 750.15 *conventional*; 111.17 *regular*
standard lamp 522.6 *electric light*
standard language 5.6 *official language*
standard lens 41.17 *lens*
standardly 446.24 *ideologically*
standardness 216.4 *average*; 138.5 *averageness*
standard of living 13.6 *economic factors*
standard palette 529.5 *paint*
standard practice 632.6 *procedure*
standard price 790.1 *price*
standard procedure 632.6 *procedure*
standard rate of taxation 13.6 *economic factors*
standards 446.5 *ideology*; 795.1 *morality*; 4.2 *philosophical system*; 135.1 *requirement*
standard solution 32.18 *gravimetric analysis*
standard temperature and pressure 28.38 *thermodynamics*
standard usage 632.4 *custom*; 5.6 *official language*
stand a round 785.9 *pay one's way*
stand as a candidate 752.13 *be a candidate*
stand aside 605.5 *resign*
stand at the door 312.3 *approach*
stand at the head 129.15 *precede*
stand away 145.6 *keep away*
stand back 634.1 *avoid*; 145.6 *keep away*; 303.2 *retreat*
stand back of 392.24 *back*
stand bail 253.11 *promise*
stand bail for 756.8 *guarantee*
stand before the judge 715.7 *be accused*
stand behind 392.24 *back*; 413.14 *give moral support*
standby 21.24 *actor*; 392.11 *helper*; 352.5 *reserves*
stand by 97.12 *attend*; 392.24 *back*; 335.6 *be powerless*; 294.8 *delay*; 384.21 *entrench*; 413.14 *give moral support*; 341.4 *not act*; 243.8 *prepare oneself*; 474.10 *wait*
stand-by fare 793.4 *bargain*
stand by oneself 197.18 *be one*
stand clear 634.1 *avoid*
stand clear of 145.6 *keep away*
stand close to 147.15 *be near*
stand condemned 806.8 *be guilty*
stand defenceless 335.6 *be powerless*
stand down 605.5 *resign*; 226.7 *stop working*; 388.3 *submit*; 355.2 *withdraw*
standee 21.33 *theatregoer*
stand erect 622.24 *be proud*; 186.5 *be vertical*
stand far away 145.5 *be distant*
stand fast 301.8 *be motionless*; 225.5 *be permanent*; 638.10 *insist*
stand firm 585.13 *be at war*; 301.8 *be motionless*; 383.7, 641.9 *be obstinate*; 225.5 *be permanent*; 228.6 *be stable*; 384.21 *entrench*; 640.8 *hold out*; 638.10 *insist*; 228.8 *show determination*; 113.20 *withstand*
stand for **717.12**; 694.10 *mean*; 398.8 *represent*; 742.10 *signify*
stand for office 752.13 *be a candidate*
stand guard 665.11 *care for*
stand high 667.21 *command respect*
stand in 762.4 *be a substitute*; 550.34 *cover for*; 398.8 *represent*
stand-in 21.24 *actor*; 398.5 *alternative*; 211.5 *extra person*; 608.5 *helper*; 717.8 *representative*; 762.2 *substitute person*; 550.21 *substitution*; 550.40 *substitutive*
stand in amazement 619.9 *wonder*
stand in for 746.7 *act as a go-between*; 706.23 *answer for*; 608.11 *assist*; 717.12 *stand for*
stand in front 167.10 *be in front*; 384.21 *entrench*
stand in full view 738.4 *show oneself*
standing 143.2, 222.1 *circumstances*; 123.1 *importance*; 667.11 *in a respectful stance*; 88.9 *lakelike*; 301.4 *motionless*; 225.7 *permanent*; 143.5, 209.2 *rank*; 783.7 *repute*; 137.5 *social class*; 221.1 *state*; 186.8 *vertical*
standing army 586.15 *army*; 584.2 *the military*
standing at attention 667.5 *presenting arms*
standing by 282.8 *available*; 243.18 *prepared*
standing committee 579.6 *governing body*
standing custom 632.4 *custom*
standing firm 383.11 *obstinate*
standing jump 304.5 *jump*
standing on ceremony 656.6 *formal*
standing order 16.3 *law*; 785.1 *payment*; 140.1 *rule*
standing out 185.5 *protuberant*; 695.3 *recognizable*
standing ovation 669.5 *acclaim*; 601.9 *rejoicing*; 21.8 *scene*
standing rigging 50.3 *parts of a sailing boat*
standing room 21.18 *auditorium*; 141.5 *reserved space*
standing room only 232.8 *full*
standing start 333.12 *hesitation*
standing stone 284.7 *thing of the past*
standing the test 698.15 *true*
standing up 186.2 *making vertical*; 698.15 *true*; 186.8 *vertical*
standing water 88.2 *small lake*; 433.1 *water*
standing wave 28.12 *wave*
stand in need of 218.6 *be unsatisfied*; 135.7 *require*
stand in relation to 108.7 *relate to*
stand in the breach 254.9 *face danger*
stand in the dock 715.7 *be accused*; 16.72 *stand trial*
stand in the light 486.7 *be clumsy*
stand in the open 738.4 *show oneself*
stand in with 747.14 *join with*
stand like a post 301.8 *be motionless*
stand no nonsense 638.10 *insist*
standoff 226.2 *stop*
stand off 145.6 *keep away*
stand-off half 64.4 *rugby player*
standoffish 145.9 *reserved*; 118.16 *solitary*; 622.15 *unapproachable*; 655.8 *unsociable*
standoffishly 145.11 *reservedly*
standoffishness 145.4 *reserve*; 655.1 *unsociability*
stand on 50.15 *sail*
stand on ceremony 160.8, 656.11 *be formal*
stand on end 186.6 *make vertical*
stand one's ground 225.5 *be permanent*; 228.8 *show determination*; 113.20 *withstand*
stand on one's dignity 622.24 *be proud*
stand on one's head 192.3 *invert*
stand on tiptoe 366.5 *arise*; 148.9 *be long*; 154.16 *rise*
stand or fall together 747.13 *work together*
stand out 116.5 *be dissimilar*; 137.15 *be in a class of one's own*; 695.8 *be recognizable*; 518.19, 520.8, 738.5 *be visible*; 139.25 *excel*; 743.11 *identify oneself*; 185.8 *protrude*
stand out a mile 738.5 *be visible*
stand outside the law 16.74 *be lawless*
stand pat 225.5 *be permanent*; 228.8 *show determination*
standpipe 433.13 *irrigator*
standpoint 450.1 *belief*; 143.2 *circumstances*; 476.1 *supposition*; 176.5 *viewpoint*
stand poles apart 372.12 *disagree*
stand ready 384.21 *entrench*; 243.8 *prepare oneself*
stand responsible for 810.15 *be liable*
stand revealed 739.9 *be disclosed*
stand rigid 383.7 *be obstinate*
stands 48.1 *baseball*
stand shoulder to shoulder 267.6 *adhere*; 747.13 *work together*
stand side by side 267.6 *adhere*; 169.7 *be alongside*
standstill 309.1 *closure*; 390.2 *deliverance*; 119.2 *equilibrium*; 341.1 *inaction*; 301.1 *motionlessness*; 264.8 *snag*; 226.2 *stop*
stand still 301.8 *be motionless*
stand surety 253.11 *promise*; 252.10 *protect*
stand the cost 785.8 *defray*
stand the racket 814.6 *be punished*
stand the test 698.27 *be true*; 235.9 *be worthy*
stand to attention 186.5 *be vertical*
stand together 747.13 *work together*
stand to reason 738.5 *be visible*
stand trial **16.72**
stand up **304.16**; 366.5 *arise*; 698.27 *be true*; 186.5 *be vertical*; 738.4 *show oneself*; 604.7 *thwart*
stand-up collar 551.14 *neckwear*
stand-up comedy 21.12 *comedy*; 599.4 *entertainment*
stand-up comic 21.29 *entertainer*; 599.6 *humorist*
stand up for 413.14 *give moral support*; 714.8 *justify*; 252.10 *protect*
stand up in law 16.66 *be legal*
stand-up meal 557.12 *meal*
stand upright 186.5 *be vertical*
stand up straight 622.24 *be proud*; 186.5 *be vertical*
stand up to 613.15 *be courageous*; 661.5 *defy*; 708.11 *rebut*; 217.4 *suffice*; 113.20 *withstand*
stand up well 228.6 *be stable*
Stanford-Binet Intelligence Scale 36.6 *intelligence test*
Stanford-Binet test 36.6 *intelligence test*
Stanford revision 36.6 *intelligence test*
Stanley Cup 58.3 *ice hockey*
Stanley knife™ 438.1 *tool*
stannary 577.1 *workshop*
stannic 32.34 *elemental*
stanniferous 24.10 *ceramic*; 32.34 *elemental*
stanniferous ware 24.1 *ceramics*
stannous 32.34 *elemental*
stanza 17.8 *part of poem*
Stanzione™ 68.6 *ice-skating*
stapes 504.5 *internal ear*
staple 373.11 *connect*; 373.8 *fastening*; 123.5 *important*; 435.1 *materials*; 778.8 *merchandise*; 360.6 *retain*; 425.8 *sharp-pointed thing*; 404.5 *textile*; 360.3 *tools for gripping*
stapled 373.15 *connected*; 360.10 *retained*
staple food 557.7 *food*
stapler 360.3 *tools for gripping*
staple to 211.6 *add*
star **29.10**; 21.24 *actor*; 123.4 *bigwig*; 21.38 *dramatize*; 522.13 *enlightenment*; 121.15 *excellent*; 235.8 *exceller*; 173.5 *focus*; 542.4 *honour*; 742.5 *indicator*; 743.4 *insignia*; 121.10 *lead*; 522.4 *natural light*; 40.15 *network*; 306.4 *orbiting body*; 121.6 *paragon*; 566.7 *person*; 811.2 *person of repute*; 619.5 *person of wonder*; 742.7 *punctuation*; 485.4 *skilled person*; 246.4 *successful person*; 797.16 *superior person*
star atlas 29.6 *star catalogue*
starboard 169.1 *side*
starboard tack 50.15 *sail*
starboard tacking 50.1 *sailing*
starbright 522.20 *starry*
starburst galaxy 29.7 *galaxy*
star catalogue **29.6**
starch 256.13 *clean*; 557.11 *food content*; 418.9 *harden*; 84.3 *plant body*; 33.4 *polysaccharide*; 421.11 *smooth*
Star Chamber 16.20 *British court*; 579.7 *council*; 464.3 *place of judgment*
star chart 11.9 *divination*
starched 256.17 *cleaned*; 418.2 *tough*
starched collar 551.14 *neckwear*
starchily 656.12 *formally*
starchiness 656.1 *formality*; 418.5 *hardness*; 383.2 *obstinacy*
starching 418.5 *hardness*
starchy 656.6 *formal*; 383.11 *obstinate*; 418.2 *tough*; 622.15 *unapproachable*
Star class 50.2 *sailing boat*
star-crossed 249.8 *unlucky*
star-crossed lover 766.6 *loser*
star-crossed lovers 593.10 *lovers*
stardom 246.1 *success*
stardust 477.6 *reverie*
stare 659.7 *be discourteous*; 518.6, 518.13 *look*; 619.9 *wonder*
stare down 638.8 *brace oneself*
starer 518.11 *observer*
starfish 70.5 *aquatic animal*; 75.3 *echinoderm*
stargaze 472.12 *be inattentive*; 518.17 *imagine*
stargazer 29.2 *astronomer*; 518.11 *observer*
stargazing 472.8 *absent-minded*; 472.3 *absent-mindedness*; 29.1 *astronomy*; 518.5 *imagination*
star in 525.13 *occur*
staring 518.21 *seeing*
star in the firmament 246.4 *successful person*
stark 520.2, 725.3 *clear*; 232.9 *completely*; 529.12 *gaudy*; 563.3 *infertile*; 271.1, 728.14 *simple*; 336.12 *strong to the senses*; 418.2 *tough*
starkers 552.9 *undressed*
starkly 271.8, 728.24 *simply*; 418.12 *toughly*
stark-naked 552.9 *undressed*
starkness 520.4, 725.1 *clarity*; 271.4, 728.4 *simplicity*
stark raving mad 461.11 *insane*
stark-staring 738.14 *manifest*
stark staring mad 461.11 *insane*
starless 523.8 *dark*

starlet 21.24 *actor*; 246.4 *successful person*
starlight 522.4 *natural light*
starlight waltz 68.7 *ice-dancing*
starlike 425.2 *spiked*
starling 72.6 *songbird*
starlit 522.18 *lit*
star map 717.7 *map*
Star of Bethlehem 522.4 *natural light*
star player 485.4 *skilled person*
star-pointed 425.2 *spiked*
star quality 21.22 *acting*
starring 21.41 *stagestruck*
starring role 21.23 *role*
star-rise 304.3 *sunrise*
starry **522.20**; 29.36 *astronomical*
starry-eyed 477.11 *fantastical*; 597.4 *happy*; 610.11 *hopeful*
stars 344.4 *contributing factor*; 395.2 *occult influence*
Stars and Bars 743.7 *flag*
Stars and Stripes 743.7 *flag*; 85.7 *United States*
star-shaped 425.2 *spiked*
star-shaped figure 27.44 *polygon*
star shell 587.5 *missile weapon*
starshine 522.4 *natural light*
star-spangled 522.20 *starry*
Star-Spangled Banner 743.7 *flag*
starstruck 21.41 *stagestruck*
star-studded 29.36 *astronomical*; 522.20 *starry*
star system 376.28 *cluster*
start **302.2**; **313.8**; **330.33**; 121.3 *advantage*; 612.12 *be fearful*; 130.17, 308.24 *begin*; 130.1, 295.4, 308.11 *beginning*; 630.12 *be surprised*; 711.2 *danger signal*; 59.7 *horseracing*; 331.1 *impel*; 344.11 *inaugurate*; 362.3 *jerk*; 327.9 *jolt*; 483.9 *motivate*; 61.6 *motor-racing terms*; 126.7 *originate*; 47.7, 61.9 *race*; 313.5 *set out*; 630.3 *shock*; 130.11 *starting point*; 47.1 *track events*; 354.1 *undertake*
START 2 749.1 *pacification*
start a fight 381.1 *attack*
start afresh 649.10 *absolve*; 295.17 *become new*; 130.28 *begin again*; 112.20 *renew*; 761.7 *restore*
start again 393.4 *be restored*; 112.20 *renew*; 761.7 *restore*
start an action 16.70 *litigate*
start anew 295.17 *become new*; 130.28 *begin again*; 761.7 *restore*
start a prairie fire 92.12 *be marooned*
start a row 342.12 *be active*
start aside 634.4 *shy*
start climbing the wall 461.14 *become insane*
start early 293.7 *be early*
starter 495.3 *appetizer*; 47.3 *athlete*; 48.2 *baseball player*; 130.14 *beginner*; 25.9 *dish*; 130.12 *first move*; 25.12 *hors d'oeuvre*; 557.14 *mouthful*
starter's gun 711.2 *danger signal*; 742.4 *signal*
starter's orders 59.7 *horseracing*
start from the beginning 295.17 *become new*
start game 633.11 *hunt*
start going 130.20 *activate*; 330.33 *start*
starting 130.29, 308.17 *beginning*
starting afresh 112.4 *return*
starting again 112.4 *return*
starting block 130.11 *starting point*
starting blocks 47.4 *sports equipment*
starting grid 61.6 *motor-racing terms*
starting gun 281.10 *signal*
starting pistol 47.4 *sports equipment*; 130.11 *starting point*
starting point **130.11**; 313.10 *place of departure*
starting position 47.1 *track events*
starting post 130.11 *starting point*
startle 619.10 *be wonderful*; 612.13 *frighten*; 711.7 *raise the alarm*; 630.9 *surprise*
startled 630.6 *surprised*
startling 612.10 *frightening*
start off **130.19**; 330.33 *start*
start out 313.5 *set out*; 130.19 *start off*
start the ball rolling 330.33 *start*
start too soon 293.7 *be early*
start up 130.20, 346.8 *activate*; 633.11 *hunt*; 130.23 *inaugurate*; 304.17 *spring up*
start-up capital 352.4 *financial resources*
start-up costs 790.6 *business costs*
star turn 68.2 *cross-country skiing*; 68.4 *skiing technique*
starvation 617.3 *appetite*; 153.8 *emaciation*; 218.9, 557.10 *scarcity*; 687.2 *short rations*; 582.5 *ways of dying*
starvation diet 687.1 *fasting*; 218.8 *insufficiency*
starvation rations 218.8 *insufficiency*; 436.1 *provision*
starve 153.15 *be emaciated*; 617.14 *be hungry*; 782.12 *be poor*; 684.5 *be self-restrained*; 557.22 *eat well*; 687.5 *fast*; 682.7 *hoard*; 337.7 *weaken*
starved 153.2 *emaciated*; 687.6 *fasting*; 617.10 *hungry*; 218.3 *underfed*
starved of 218.2 *unprovided*
starveling 218.3 *underfed*
starve oneself 766.9 *lose*
starve out 585.13 *be at war*; 381.4 *besiege*; 251.11 *detain*
starve to death 582.16 *meet one's fate*; 382.17 *murder*
starving 782.3 *beggarly*; 557.3 *delicate eating*; 153.2 *emaciated*; 687.6 *fasting*; 617.10 *hungry*; 135.5 *necessitous*; 218.3 *underfed*
starving out 251.4 *detention*
Star Wars 587.5 *missile weapon*; 252.4 *safety device*; 585.8 *warfare*
star watching 29.1 *astronomy*
star worship 9.2 *idolatry*
star worshipper 9.6 *idolater*
star-worshipping 9.10 *idolatrous*
stash 736.8 *conceal*; 736.2 *hiding place*
stash away 439.6 *store*
stasis 119.2 *equilibrium*; 301.1 *motionlessness*; 228.1 *stability*
statant 743.13 *heraldic*
State 221
state **86.5**; **221.1**; **701.15**; 707.17 *affirm*; 143.2, 222.1 *circumstances*; 85.1 *country*; 447.10 *focus on*; 656.1 *formality*; 716.11 *give evidence*; 12.9 *governmental*; 396.8 *governmental organization*; 259.3 *health*; 566.11 *nation*; 85.16, 86.17, 566.13 *national*; 440.5 *personal estate*; 12.5 *political organization*; 4.22 *propound a philosophy*; 729.11 *speak*; 724.9 *style*; 86.4 *territorial division*; 454.3 *testify*; 5.45 *use language*
state attorney general 16.12 *US law officer*
state banquet 557.13 *feast*
state capital 87.2 *American cities*
state control 12.3 *governance*; 396.7 *type of rule*
statecraft 579.3 *management*; 12.2 *politics*
state crew 21.28 *stagehand*
stated **707.11**; 701.11 *logical*
state election 469.12 *election*
State Enrolled Nurse 35.16 *nurse*
state enterprise 776.5 *commercial trade*
state farm 43.6 *farm*
state highway 317.3 *road*
state highway patrol 16.16 *US police*
statehood 85.1 *country*; 250.3 *independence*; 566.11 *nation*
state in plain English 695.5 *simplify*
state insurance 392.4 *social assistance*
stateless 100.10 *foreign*; 144.10 *replaced*
stateless person 144.7 *displaced person*; 100.7 *new arrival*; 655.7 *outsider*
statelet 85.3 *dominion*
stateliness **622.5**; 656.1 *formality*
state lottery 107.3 *equal chance*
stately **622.19**; 656.8 *ceremonious*; 543.3 *elegant*; 656.6 *formal*; 542.10 *ornate*
stately home 356.8 *construction*; 565.4 *official residence*
statement **707.2**; **789.4**; 220.4, 790.4 *bill*; 397.1 *command*; 693.2 *communication*; 721.1 *description*; 693.3 *document*; 454.6 *evidence*; 28.6 *law*; 716.5 *legal evidence*; 701.3 *line of argument*; 27.63 *mathematical logic*; 4.1 *philosophy*; 740.1 *publication*; 744.1 *record*; 447.1 *topic*; 729.7 *utterance*
statement of account 693.3 *document*; 789.4 *statement*
statement of belief 450.2 *religious belief*
statement of defence 704.3 *countercharge*
statement of facts 721.1 *description*
statement under oath 756.1 *promise*; 707.3 *vow*
state occasion 656.1 *formality*
state of affairs **221.3**; 143.2, 222.1 *circumstances*
state of grace 8.1 *divinity*; 805.1 *innocence*
state of health 221.5 *physical state*; 257.2 *salubrity*
state of indebtedness 784.1 *debt*
state of matrimony 570.1 *marriage*
state of mind **221.4**; 590.4 *emotion*
state of nature 552.2 *nudity*
state of order 407.5 *orderliness*
state of peace 589.1 *peace*
state of play 222.1 *circumstances*
state of siege 585.4 *belligerency*
state of sobriety 689.6 *sobriety*
state of the art 295.1 *newness*
state-of-the-art 295.10 *new*
state of war 585.4 *belligerency*
state of wonder 619.1 *wonder*
state one's terms 776.3 *bargain*
state-owned industry 13.1 *economics*
state ownership 764.1 *joint possession*
state pension 392.4 *social assistance*
state plainly 695.5 *simplify*
state prison 815.1 *prison*
state prosecuting attorney 16.12 *US law officer*
state prosecutor 16.12 *US law officer*
state provision 392.4 *social assistance*
State Registered Nurse 35.16 *nurse*
state school 6.12 *educational institution*
state secret 737.1 *secrecy*
state's evidence 739.2 *divulgence*
States General 579.10 *legislative body*
Stateside 85.7 *United States*
statesman 12.7 *governor*; 579.15 *manager*; 748.3 *mediator*; 484.8 *planner*
statesmanlike 631.16 *behaving*; 485.6 *skilful*; 458.5 *wise*
statesmanship 579.3 *management*; 748.2 *mediation*; 484.2 *policy*; 12.2 *politics*; 631.9 *tactics*
states' righter 250.7 *free person*
states' rights 250.3 *independence*
state supreme court 16.21 *US court*
state Supreme Court Justice 16.24 *US judge*
stateswoman 12.7 *governor*
state system 12.1 *government*
state tax 790.7 *tax*
state terms 136.16 *specify*
state under oath 707.18 *vow*
static 517.5 *atmospheric dissonance*; 119.6 *equal*; 343.1 *inactive*; 339.5 *inert*; 301.4 *motionless*; 62.8 *mountaineering*; 225.7 *permanent*; 28.98 *physical*; 692.19 *radio reception*
statically 343.15 *inactively*; 301.10 *motionlessly*; 28.100 *physically*
static electrical conduction 39.3 *electricity*
static electricity 334.7 *electrical power*; 28.42, 39.3 *electricity*
static friction 28.10 *force*; 365.1 *friction*
static load 38.14 *load*
static rope 62.4 *climbing equipment*
statics 28.2 *classical physics*
static warfare 585.8 *warfare*
station 143.4 *employment*; 43.6 *farm*; 142.9 *locate*; 142.1 *location*; 313.10 *place of departure*; 317.10 *railway*; 321.8 *railway station*; 143.5, 209.2 *rank*; 575.1 *right*; 143.10 *situate*; 137.5 *social class*; 226.4 *stopping place*; 810.2 *task*
stationarily 301.10 *motionlessly*
stationary 32.41 *analytic*; 57.11 *gymnastic*; 341.3, 343.1 *inactive*; 301.4 *motionless*; 225.7 *permanent*
stationary depression 31.11 *weather system*
stationary high 31.11 *weather system*
stationary phase 32.17 *analysis*
stationary point 27.36 *point*
stationary rings **57.7**
stationary target 482.6 *objective*
station break 692.25 *broadcast material*
stationed 142.6 *located*; 143.6 *situated*
stationery 435.3 *paper*
station identification 692.20 *radio broadcasting*
stationing 142.4 *placing*
station in life 221.1 *state*
station manager 321.9 *railway worker*
stationmaster 321.9 *railway worker*
station wagon 320.16 *car*
statism 12.3 *governance*; 12.1 *government*
statistic 27.57 *population*
statistical 789.10 *accounting*; 210.13 *calculative*; 27.68 *mathematical*; 28.98 *physical*
statistical analysis 27.53 *statistics*
statistical inference 27.53 *statistics*
statistically 789.13 *financially*; 28.100 *physically*
statistically proven 698.20 *proved*
statistical mechanic 32.2 *chemist*
statistical mechanics 32.1 *chemistry*; 28.3 *modern physics*
statistical methods **27.55**
statistical physics 28.3 *modern physics*
statistical probability 104.5 *probability theory*
statistician 789.6 *accountant*; 27.2, 210.7 *mathematician*
statistico-mechanical 32.31 *chemical*
statistics **27.53**; **210.2**; 107.7 *calculation of chance*; 698.7 *confirmation*; 693.6 *information technology*; 717.7 *map*; 27.1 *mathematics*
stator 39.31 *electric motor*
statuary 19.17 *sculptor*; 19.12 *sculpture*
statue 717.6 *image*; 462.3 *memento*; 744.11 *monument*; 19.12 *sculpture*
Statue of Liberty 250.3 *independence*
statuesque 19.26 *artistic*; 545.5 *beautiful*; 622.19 *stately*; 154.12 *tall*
statuette 717.6 *image*; 19.12 *sculpture*; 794.1 *trophy*
stature 154.1 *height*
status 409.6 *category*; 222.1 *circumstances*; 123.1 *importance*; 407.4 *position*; 143.5, 209.2 *rank*; 108.3 *relative position*; 221.1 *state*
status group 2.6 *social group*
status quo 143.2, 222.1 *circumstances*; 119.2 *equilibrium*
status-seeking 654.2 *social ambition*
statute 16.3 *law*; 713.3 *precept*; 140.1 *rule*
statute book 140.2 *canon*; 16.1 *the law*
statute law 16.1 *the law*
statutory 140.9 *legal*; 16.46 *legislated*
staunch 569.11 *devoted*; 394.20 *doctor*; 632.13 *fixed*; 452.6 *infallible*; 663.8 *loyal*; 640.10 *persevering*; 336.10 *potent*; 638.5 *steady*; 309.8 *stop*; 90.9 *stop the flow*
staunched 309.13 *stopped*
staunchly 569.19 *devotedly*; 663.10 *obediently*
staunchness 640.3 *constancy*; 569.3 *familiarity*; 452.17 *infallibility*; 663.2 *loyalty*; 638.15 *will*
stave 587.7 *blunt weapon*; 435.1 *materials*; 18.17 *notation*; 17.8 *part of poem*; 304.10 *step*; 23.12 *wood*
stave in 367.2 *flatten*; 183.9 *make concave*
stave off 384.24 *parry*
stay 215.7 *be left*; 301.8 *be motionless*; 225.5 *be permanent*; 228.6 *be stable*; 226.8 *cause to cease*; 93.19 *continue to be*; 294.8 *delay*; 294.3 *delayed action*; 554.17 *dwell*; 564.14, 565.17 *inhabit*; 361.12 *interrupt*; 361.6 *interruption*; 277.6 *last*; 16.6 *legal process*; 373.4 *means of connection*; 654.3 *meeting*; 378.2 *obstacle*; 226.9 *pause*; 134.4 *protract*; 333.3 *slow down*; 226.2 *stop*; 301.11 *stop!*; 309.8 *stop*; 373.7 *tackle*; 654.12 *visit*; 294.7 *wait*
stay alert 425.17 *be mentally sharp*; 471.11 *take note of*
stay at 142.10 *settle*
stay at home 301.8 *be motionless*; 252.9 *be safe*; 655.12 *be unsocial*
stay-at-home 655.10 *lonely*; 301.5 *sedentary*; 655.6 *unsocial person*
stay at one's post 810.16 *do one's duty*
stay at peace 589.5 *be at peace*; 749.4 *pacify*
stay away 98.15 *be absent*; 526.2 *depart*
stay away from 634.1 *avoid*
stay away in droves 98.15 *be absent*
stay cool 251.10 *restrain oneself*
stay devoted to 595.7 *like*
stayed 361.9 *interrupted*
stayer 59.7 *horseracing*; 641.8 *obstinate person*; 640.5 *tenacious person*; 59.2 *thoroughbred*
stay flexible 422.10 *be adaptable*
stay-in 15.10 *unionized*
stay in a rut 641.9 *be obstinate*; 620.7 *suffer boredom*
stay in control 250.16 *be independent*
stay indoors 301.8 *be motionless*
staying 565.14 *inhabiting*
staying away 526.4 *disappearance*
staying power 277.4 *long-lastingness*; 334.1 *power*; 640.4 *stamina*; 336.1 *strength*
stay in line 117.8 *comply*; 663.5 *obey*
stay innocent 255.9 *be pure*
stay in one place 228.6 *be stable*

stay in one's lane 47.7 *race*
stay in one's shell 618.12 *be indifferent*; 655.12 *be unsocial*
stay-in strike 15.4 *industrial dispute*
stay in the background 216.9 *be average*
stay in the black 783.10 *deposit*
stay in the shadows 736.11 *conceal oneself*
stay in time 285.7 *synchronize*
stay near 147.17
stay neutral 341.4 *not act*
stay of execution 294.3 *delayed action*
stay on 134.4 *protract*
stay one's hand 226.9 *pause*
stay on good terms 569.13 *befriend*
stay on the beam 324.7 *take a direction*
stay on the shelf 778.2 *be sold*; 341.4 *not act*
stay out 128.9 *be excluded*
stay out late 294.6 *be late*
stay outside 128.9 *be excluded*
stay packed away 341.4 *not act*
stay pure 572.10 *be continent*
stay put 301.8 *be motionless*; 641.9 *be obstinate*; 228.6 *be stable*; 638.10 *insist*
stays 551.18 *underwear*
staysail 50.3 *parts of a sailing boat*
stay single 572.9 *be celibate*
stay sober 689.3 *be sober*
stay still 341.4 *not act*
stay the course 423.10 *be tough*; 277.6 *last*
stay too long 620.6 *be boring*
stay underground 389.6 *elude*
stay unmarried 250.16 *be independent*
stay up late 294.6 *be late*
stay virtuous 255.9 *be pure*
stay within bounds 685.3 *be moderate*
stay within one's limits 251.10 *restrain oneself*
stay with it 228.8 *show determination*
stay young 555.16 *be young*
steadfast 569.11 *devoted*; 253.9 *fast*; 799.4 *honourable*; 452.6 *infallible*; 635.7 *iron-willed*; 663.8 *loyal*; 225.7 *permanent*; 613.12 *self-reliant*; 228.9 *stable*; 336.11 *strong in spirit*; 638.4 *undaunted*
steadfastly 613.18 *courageously*; 569.19 *devotedly*; 253.17 *fastly*; 799.7 *honourably*; 663.10 *obediently*; 225.9 *permanently*; 228.12 *stably*
steadfastness 613.3; 640.3 *constancy*; 569.3 *familiarity*; 452.17 *infallibility*; 663.2 *loyalty*; 225.1 *permanence*; 799.1 *probity*; 228.1 *stability*; 336.1 *strength*; 638.15 *will*; 635.2 *willpower*
steadily 750.35 *consistently*; 134.7 *continually*; 119.13 *equitably*; 297.1 *frequently*; 298.17 *orderly*; 225.9 *permanently*; 111.20, 298.15 *regularly*; 228.12 *stably*
steadiness 119.2 *equilibrium*; 297.4 *frequency*; 452.17 *infallibility*; 685.1 *moderation*; 301.1 *motionlessness*; 298.4 *orderliness*; 225.1 *permanence*; 132.7, 228.1 *stability*; 638.15 *will*
steading 43.6 *farm*
steady 638.5; **640.11**; 750.14 *conforming*; 134.5 *continual*; 4.18 *detached*; 360.7 *detain*; 119.6 *equal*; 253.9 *fast*; 297.3 *frequent*; 407.16 *harmonious*; 452.6 *infallible*; 593.9 *lover*; 452.21 *make certain*; 253.14 *make fast*; 298.10 *make regular*; 228.7 *make stable*; 685.6 *moderate*; 301.4 *motionless*; 298.14 *orderly*; 225.7 *permanent*; 31.53 *rainy*; 460.5 *rational*; 111.17, 298.11 *regular*; 228.9 *stable*
steady as a rock 228.9 *stable*
steady drizzle 31.25 *rain*
steady flow 28.8 *time*
steady progress 302.10 *forward motion*
steady state 29.4 *cosmological model*; 119.2 *equilibrium*; 132.7, 228.1 *stability*
steady stream 132.8 *procession*
steak 205.7 *piece*
steak and kidney 25.31 *offal*
steak au poivre 25.45 *French dish*
steakhouse 557.15 *eating place*
steak knife 557.16 *eating utensil*
steak tartare 25.45 *French dish*
steal 774.12; 793.4 *bargain*; 800.10 *be criminal*; 772.9 *borrow illegally*; 526.3 *cause to disappear*; 765.14 *profit*; 806.10 *sin*; 774.4 *stolen goods*; 608.14, 773.10 *take away*; 774.3 *theft*
steal a car 774.12 *steal*
steal a glance 518.13 *look*
steal a march on 645.5 *be cunning*; 121.8 *be superior*; 329.3 *exceed*; 293.9 *prepare*
steal away 736.11 *conceal oneself*; 389.5 *escape*; 634.8 *run away*
stealer 774.8 *thief*
steal every heart 593.25 *be loved*
Stealing 774
stealing 774.1; 772.3 *illegal borrowing*; 765.5 *profit*; 773.3 *taking away*
stealings 774.4 *stolen goods*
stealing the puck 58.3 *ice hockey*
steal one's stuff 772.9 *borrow illegally*
steal someone's thunder 121.8 *be superior*; 378.8 *hinder*
stealth 645.1 *cunning*; 737.2 *secretiveness*
steal the puck 58.9 *play hockey*
steal the show 121.8 *be superior*; 21.35 *overact*
stealthily 737.16; 645.6 *cunningly*
stealthiness 645.1 *cunning*; 737.2 *secretiveness*
stealthy 645.4 *cunning*; 737.10 *secretive*; 333.5 *unhurried*
steam 493.14 *be hot*; 25.55 *cook*; 432.27 *give off*; 493.1 *heat*; 371.14 *let out*; 524.2 *murk*; 528.7 *opaque thing*; 330.12 *propellant*; 560.19 *sweat*; 433.3 *wateriness*; 432.4 *water vapour*
steam away 338.2 *be full of vigour*
steam bath 256.6 *bath*
steamboat 323.3 *vessel*
steam-distil 32.25 *solidify*
steamed 25.56 *culinary*
steamed pudding 25.35 *dessert*
steamed up 524.6 *murky*; 528.2 *shady*
steam engine 38.11 *engine*; 438.5 *machine*
steamer 25.6 *kitchen equipment*; 321.4 *locomotive*; 410.15 *pot*
steamer route 323.2 *waterway*
steamily 432.30 *smokily*
steaminess 493.1 *heat*
steaming 24.5 *ceramic process*; 25.8 *cooking technique*; 493.9 *hot*; 323.11 *nautical*; 432.19 *smoky*; 432.10 *vaporization*
steam iron 187.4 *flattener*; 493.3 *heater*
steam locomotive 321.4 *locomotive*
steam-operated 334.17, 437.10 *powered*
steam power 334.4 *energy*
steam-powered 334.17 *powered*
steam pressure 334.4 *energy*
steam-propelled 330.19 *propelled*
steam propulsion 330.2 *method of propulsion*
steam radio 504.9 *audio device*
steam reforming 32.22 *industrial chemistry*
steamrolled 421.2 *uniform*
steamroller 386.4 *coercive person*; 386.9 *compelling*; 357.9 *demolish*; 187.4 *flattener*; 386.7 *force*; 427.11 *pulverizer*; 421.9 *smoother*
steamrolling 386.9 *compelling*
steamship 323.3 *vessel*
steam turbine 38.12 *turbine*
steam up 524.9 *be dim*; 528.10 *be opaque*
steamy 524.6 *murky*; 432.19 *smoky*; 493.11 *warm*
steatopygic 158.16 *fat*
steatopygous 158.16 *fat*
steed 59.1 *horse*; 59.3 *warhorse*
steel 20.4 *building material*; 38.25 *construction material*; 164.3 *cutting edge*; 638.16 *fortitude*; 533.5 *grey thing*; 418.1 *hard*; 418.9 *harden*; 418.7 *hard substance*; 412.2 *mixed thing*; 425.12 *sharpener*; 323.4 *shipbuilding*
steel band 18.26 *musical group*
steel blue 539.1 *blue*
steel-clad 252.7 *invulnerable*
steeled 418.3 *hardened*; 638.4 *undaunted*
steel engraving 19.15 *engraving*
steel-grey 533.1 *grey*
steel helmet 384.7 *armour*
steeliness 228.2 *determination*; 418.5 *hardness*; 638.14 *tenacity*
steeling 418.6 *solidification*
steel oneself 809.5 *be impenitent*; 638.8 *brace oneself*; 336.8 *strengthen*; 613.16 *take courage*
steel plate 19.15 *engraving*
steel-plate armour 384.7 *armour*; 587.1 *weapon*
steel poles 57.5 *horizontal bar*
steel-rimmed glasses 518.10 *visual aid*
steel rule 26.6 *measuring instrument*
steel wool 420.7 *rough thing*
steelworker 578.2 *artisan*
steelworks 577.1 *workshop*
steely 651.12 *callous*; 228.11 *determined*; 533.1 *grey*; 418.1 *hard*; 638.3 *strong-willed*
steelyard 414.10 *scales*; 28.86 *weighing instrument*; 577.1 *workshop*
steely-eyed 651.12 *callous*
steep 433.31; 304.22 *ascending*; 256.14 *bathe*; 681.3 *costly*; 792.7 *dear*; 264.10 *difficult*; 368.4 *immerse*; 176.8 *oblique*; 369.17 *obtain an extract*; 419.13 *soften*; 379.1 *trap*
steeped 433.23 *wet*
steeped in vice 804.12 *immoral*
steepen 304.21 *upturn*
steeping 433.10; 369.7 *obtaining an extract*
steeple 425.8 *sharp-pointed thing*; 154.6 *tall thing*
steeplechase 633.2 *chase*; 59.7 *horseracing*; 304.5 *jump*; 59.16 *ride*; 47.1 *track events*
steeplechaser 47.3 *athlete*; 59.15 *horse person*; 59.2 *thoroughbred*
steeplechasing 59.6 *horsemanship*; 59.7 *horseracing*; 304.5 *jump*
steeplejack 304.11 *ascender*
steeply 792.12 *dearly*
steepness 89.1 *mountain*; 176.2 *obliquity*; 186.1 *verticality*
steep price 792.1 *high price*
steer 68.16 *bobsled*; 631.15 *conduct*; 140.16, 324.6, 579.2 *direct*; 43.8 *livestock*; 567.16 *male animal*; 323.9 *navigate*; 50.16 *row*; 50.15 *sail*
steerable 324.14 *directed*
steerage 324.1 *direction*; 579.4 *directorship*
steer a middle course 754.4 *compromise*
steer a straight course 324.7 *take a direction*
steer clear 634.1 *avoid*; 145.6 *keep away*; 325.8 *sidestep*
steer for 633.12 *aim at*; 631.11 *conduct oneself*; 323.9 *navigate*; 324.7 *take a direction*
steering 68.9 *bobsledding*; 324.16 *directing*; 324.1 *direction*; 579.4 *directorship*; 68.13 *ice-skating*; 579.17 *managerial*; 323.5 *navigation*
steering committee 579.6 *governing body*
steering oar 323.5 *navigation*
steering wheel 307.6 *rotator*
steer one away from 481.3 *deflect*
steer one's career 631.11 *conduct oneself*
steersman 579.13 *director*; 323.7 *nautical person*
steersmanship 579.4 *directorship*
steer towards 324.6 *direct*
steer with the foot 50.18 *windsurf*
steer-wrestling 59.12 *rodeo*
Stefan–Boltzmann constant 28.97 *fundamental constant*
Steffi Graf 63.7 *famous tennis players*
stegophilist 304.11 *ascender*
Steilhang 68.1 *skiing*
Stein 558.10 *drink container*; 410.13 *drinking vessel*
stellar 29.36 *astronomical*
stellar association 29.9 *constellation*
stellar birth 29.11
stellar cluster 29.9 *constellation*
stellar evolution 29.11 *stellar birth*
stellar group 29.9 *constellation*
stellar population 29.9 *constellation*
stellar statistics 29.1 *astronomy*
stellate 425.2 *spiked*
stellular 425.2 *spiked*
stem 77.5; 205.6, 311.14 *branch*; 226.8 *cause to cease*; 113.19 *confront*; 82.2 *fern plant*; 311.5 *fork*; 81.3 *grass plant*; 5.35 *part of speech*; 50.3 *parts of a sailing boat*; 84.3 *plant body*; 344.3 *rudiment*; 68.14 *ski*; 413.2 *supporting part*; 496.7 *tobacco*; 5.17 *word*
stem christie 68.4 *skiing technique*
stem cutting 44.5 *gardening*
stemming 68.4 *skiing technique*
stem rot 44.12 *pests and diseases*
stem the flow 90.9 *stop the flow*
stem the tide 246.7 *overcome obstacles*; 113.20 *withstand*
stem tissue 77.5 *stem*
stem to stern 148.11 *lengthily*
stem tuber 77.5 *stem*
stem turn 68.2 *cross-country skiing*; 68.4 *skiing technique*
Stench 503
stench 503.1; 500.1 *odour*; 258.2 *uncleanness*
stench trap 501.2 *deodorant*
stencil 115.2, 125.10 *copy*; 19.20 *draw*; 125.5 *duplicate*; 160.2 *prototype*
stenciller 115.3 *copier*; 125.6 *photocopier*
Sten gun 587.11 *guns*
stenographer 744.9 *recorder*
stenopetalous 151.4 *narrow-leaved*
stenophyllous 151.4 *narrow-leaved*
stenosis 191.1 *contraction*; 151.9 *narrowing*
Stentor 507.5 *loud person*
stentorian 507.6 *loud*; 510.6 *resonant*; 514.16 *vociferous*
stentorian tones 507.1 *loudness*
stentorian voice 507.4 *sound maker*
step 302.13; **304.10**; 353.5 *attempt*; 32.14 *chemical reaction*; 340.2 *deed*; 300.12 *gait*; 145.2 *great distance*; 209.4 *interval*; 411.2 *level*; 436.1 *provision*; 317.2 *route*; 147.2 *short distance*
step ashore 312.4 *land*
step aside 169.8 *move sideways*; 388.3 *submit*
step between 372.14 *come between*
step by step 209.10 *by degrees*; 407.25 *in order*; 333.16 *slowly*
step-by-step procedure 27.28 *algorithm*
step-cut 62.9 *mountaineer*
step-cutting 62.3 *climbing technique*; 62.8 *mountaineering*
step dad 762.2 *substitute person*
step dance 22.2 *dance*
step-down transformer 39.22 *transformer*
step family 762.2 *substitute person*
stepfather 550.21 *substitution*
step father 762.2 *substitute person*
step forward 302.1 *go forward*
step function 27.29 *mathematical function*
stephanotis 502.2 *fragrant thing*
Stephen 752.7 *martyr*
Stephenson's Rocket 321.10 *miscellaneous*
step in 748.1 *mediate*; 551.34 *wear*
step-in 551.31 *styled*
step-ins 551.18 *underwear*
stepladder 304.9 *ladder*; 373.4 *means of connection*; 317.2 *route*
stepmother 762.2 *substitute person*; 550.21 *substitution*
step on it 332.6 *accelerate*; 332.4 *be swift*; 334.11 *give power*; 300.19 *go!*; 262.8 *hurry up!*
step on someone's lines 293.9 *prepare*
step on someone's toes 624.9 *offend*
step on the gas 332.6 *accelerate*; 437.11 *fuel*; 334.11 *give power*; 338.3 *invigorate*
step on the ladder 302.13 *step*
step out of 552.14 *undress*
step out of line 660.28 *get above oneself*
step over 318.11 *cross*
steppe 187.3 *flat thing*; 141.3 *geographical space*; 81.2 *grassland*; 92.6 *lowland*; 77.1 *plants*
stepped 304.25 *ladder-like*
stepper 59.2 *thoroughbred*
stepping a curve 68.2 *cross-country skiing*
stepping-in 748.2 *mediation*
stepping on a crack 475.7 *bad-luck sign*
stepping stone 209.4 *interval*; 373.4 *means of connection*; 222.2 *occurrence*; 287.2 *opportunity*; 550.11 *paving*; 304.10 *step*
stepping stones 318.4 *access*; 38.21, 317.9 *bridge*
stepping up 213.1 *increase*
steps 340.1 *action*; 132.2 *consecution*; 154.8 *high thing*; 352.1 *means*; 304.7 *means of ascent*; 373.4 *means of connection*; 484.2 *policy*; 57.6 *pommel horse*; 243.10 *preparations*
stepstool 304.10 *step*
step turn 68.4 *skiing technique*
step up 302.8 *further*; 338.3 *invigorate*; 213.5 *make bigger*
step up the pace 332.6 *accelerate*
step-up transformer 39.22 *transformer*
step wide 311.14 *branch*

stercoraceous 560.25 *faecal;* 258.8 *unclean*
stercoral 560.25 *faecal*
stercorous 560.25 *faecal*
stereochemistry 32.13 *structure*
stereoisomer 32.13 *structure*
stereoisomeric 32.37 *structural*
stereometric 26.16 *micrometric*
stereometry 26.2 *micrometry*
stereomicroscope 28.85 *microscope*
stereophonic sound 504.10 *sound quality*
stereophotography 41.1 *photography*
stereoregular 32.44 *polymeric*
stereoregular polymer 32.21 *polymer*
stereoscopic 141.11 *spatial;* 518.20 *visual*
stereoscopic image 41.5
stereoscopy 518.10 *visual aid*
stereospecific 32.44 *polymeric*
stereospecific polymerization 32.21 *polymer*
stereotaxy 36.3 *psychiatric treatment*
stereotype 750.6 *convention;* 117.9 *make conform;* 228.7 *make stable;* 111.8 *make the same;* 750.26 *make uniform;* 21.23 *role*
stereotyped 138.22 *commonplace;* 117.15 *everyday;* 632.11 *normal;* 745.2 *proverbial;* 228.10 *stabilized*
stereotypical 138.22 *commonplace;* 750.15 *conventional;* 21.40 *tragic;* 137.11 *typical*
stereotypically 21.44 *dramatically*
steric 32.37 *structural*
steric effect 32.13 *structure*
steric hindrance 32.13 *structure*
sterigma 83.4 *fungal body*
sterile 256.16 *clean;* 257.4 *hygienic;* 563.3 *infertile;* 255.14 *purified;* 335.13 *unsexed*
sterilely 255.19 *purely*
sterility 335.4 *disability;* 238.4 *futility;* 563.1 *infertility;* 335.1 *powerlessness*
sterilization 256.2 *cleaning;* 257.1 *hygiene;* 563.2 *making infertile;* 335.1 *powerlessness;* 359.1 *preservation;* 394.3 *prophylactic;* 255.2 *purification*
sterilize 394.20 *doctor;* 257.6 *make hygienic;* 335.9 *make impotent;* 563.8 *make infertile;* 238.8 *make useless;* 255.10, 256.15 *purify*
sterilized 256.17 *cleaned;* 257.4 *hygienic;* 255.14 *purified;* 563.5 *rendered infertile;* 335.13 *unsexed*
sterilizing 255.15 *purifying*
sterling 698.19 *authentic;* 780.1 *money;* 123.6 *notable;* 235.3 *valuable*
sterling balances 780.6 *funds*
sterling-based 780.22 *monetary*
sterling silver 698.6 *authenticity*
stern 651.12 *callous;* 50.6 *canoeing;* 670.30 *censuring;* 423.5 *mentally tough;* 795.10 *moralistic;* 50.3 *parts of a sailing boat;* 168.1 *rear;* 168.2 *rear end;* 647.8 *severe;* 643.1 *solemn;* 638.3 *strong-willed;* 626.6 *sullen*
stern ladder 304.9 *ladder*
stern light 522.6 *electric light*
sternly 647.11 *severely;* 423.14 *single-mindedly;* 643.10 *solemnly;* 626.13 *sullenly*
sternmost 168.9 *in the rear*
sternness 651.3 *callousness;* 423.9 *mental toughness;* 795.4 *self-righteousness;* 647.1 *severity;* 643.4 *solemnity;* 626.1 *sullenness;* 638.14 *tenacity*
sternutator 37.4 *drug type*
sternway 300.4 *backward motion*
steroid 394.8 *drug;* 37.4 *drug type;* 33.6 *lipid*
steroid hormone 33.16 *hormone*
sterol 33.6 *lipid*
stertor 513.2 *hoarseness*
stertorous 513.8 *hoarse*
stertorousness 507.1 *loudness*
stethoscope 504.9 *audio device;* 35.7 *diagnosis*
stetson 551.15 *headgear;* 743.5 *uniform*
stevedore 243.15 *preparer;* 316.7 *transferor;* 319.3 *transporter;* 578.1 *worker*
Stevenson screen 31.7 *weather instruments*
stew 624.4 *anger;* 624.11 *be angry;* 493.14 *be hot;* 25.55 *cook;* 243.7 *develop;* 25.32 *meat dish;* 412.2 *mixed thing*
steward 322.3 *aircraft personnel;* 401.3 *attendant;* 401.6 *domestic servant;* 579.15 *manager;* 579.16 *official;* 436.3 *provider;* 780.18 *treasurer*
stewardess 322.3 *aircraft personnel;* 401.3 *attendant*
Stewards' Cup 50.5 *Henley trophies*
stewardship 579.3 *management*
stewed 25.56 *culinary;* 690.1 *drunk*
stewed fruit 25.35 *dessert*
stewing 243.17 *developing*
stew pan 25.6 *kitchen equipment*
Stheno 11.4 *witch*
stiacciato 19.13 *relief-carving*
stichomythia 21.9 *dramaturgy*
sticht plate 62.4 *climbing equipment*
stick 430.10; 267.6 *adhere;* 413.12 *bear;* 632.17 *become a habit;* 425.14 *be sharp;* 637.6 *be unwilling;* 587.7 *blunt weapon;* 413.3 *body support;* 267.7 *cause to adhere;* 226.6 *cease;* 373.11 *connect;* 501.2 *deodorant;* 691.6 *drug;* 365.15 *grind;* 308.20 *hole;* 814.14 *instrument of punishment;* 142.9 *locate;* 301.9 *make motionless;* 435.1 *materials;* 646.3 *naive person;* 151.8 *narrow thing;* 242.8 *quarrel;* 492.11 *touch;* 486.10 *unskilled person;* 425.16 *use a sharp tool;* 23.12 *wood*
stickability 342.8 *assiduity*
stick at it 134.4 *protract*
stick at nothing 638.6 *be resolute*
stick by 392.24 *back*
stickcheck 58.3 *ice hockey;* 58.9 *play hockey*
stickchecking 58.3 *ice hockey*
stick close 267.6 *adhere*
sticker 743.3 *means of identification;* 425.8 *sharp-pointed thing*
stick fast 301.8 *be motionless;* 228.6 *be stable;* 423.10 *be tough;* 638.10 *insist;* 228.8 *show determination*
stick figure 163.1 *outline*
stick glove 58.3 *ice hockey*
stickily 267.11 *cohesively;* 429.17 *moistly;* 560.33 *scatologically;* 360.11 *tenaciously;* 430.12 *viscously*
stick in 211.6 *add;* 368.1 *insert*
Stickiness 267
stickiness 267.1 *adhesion;* 429.3 *humidity;* 360.1 *retention;* 430.1 *viscosity*
sticking 267.1 *adhesion*
sticking one's nose in 342.9 *overactivity*
sticking out 361.8 *projecting;* 185.5 *protuberant*
sticking out one's tongue 659.3 *act of discourtesy*
sticking plaster 267.3 *adhesive;* 762.3 *substitute thing;* 394.10 *surgical dressing*
stick in one's craw 624.9 *offend*
stick in one's throat 596.7 *cause dislike;* 242.10 *displease*
stick insect 76.1 *insect*
stick in the mind 462.15 *be remembered*
stick-in-the-mud 620.3 *boring person;* 117.6 *conformist;* 225.8 *conservative;* 225.3 *conservative person;* 632.8 *creature of habit;* 641.8 *obstinate person;* 452.11 *opinionist;* 383.5 *resister;* 301.5 *sedentary;* 301.7 *sedentary person;* 333.15 *slow person*
stick it out 640.9 *endure;* 638.11 *persist;* 228.8 *show determination*
stickle 776.3 *bargain;* 637.6 *be unwilling*
stickler 641.8 *obstinate person;* 230.4 *perfectionist;* 647.4 *strict person*
stick like a leech 267.6 *adhere;* 360.6 *retain*
stick like a limpet 267.6 *adhere*
stick like glue 267.6 *adhere;* 633.9 *follow;* 640.8 *hold out*
stick one's neck out 459.6 *be foolish;* 615.5 *be rash;* 254.9 *face danger*
stick one's nose in 748.1 *mediate*
stick on some slap 547.16 *make up*
stick onto 211.6 *add;* 267.6 *adhere*
stick out 182.5 *be convex;* 520.8 *be visible;* 743.11 *identify oneself;* 185.8 *protrude*
stick out for 776.3 *bargain*
stick out one's tongue 742.11 *gesture*
stick out over 361.11 *project*
sticks 59.7 *horseracing*
sticks and stones 457.4 *nonhuman existence*
stick someone up 774.12 *steal*
stick to 211.6 *add;* 267.8 *be tenacious;* 267.7 *cause to adhere;* 134.4 *protract;* 360.6 *retain;* 147.17 *stay near*
stick together 267.6 *adhere;* 267.7 *cause to adhere;* 373.13 *intercommunicate*
stick-to-itive 342.20 *industrious;* 267.10 *tenacious*
stick-to-itiveness 342.8 *assiduity;* 267.2 *tenacity*
stick to one's fingers 769.9 *receive*
stick to one's guns 452.20 *be certain;* 383.7, 641.9 *be obstinate;* 707.19 *confirm;* 640.8 *hold out;* 228.8 *show determination*
stick to the facts 273.7 *be accurate;* 698.29 *be truthful*
stick to the letter 273.7 *be accurate*
stick to the point 108.7 *relate to*
stick to the rules 160.8 *be formal;* 799.6 *be honourable;* 117.8 *comply;* 140.17 *obey orders*
stick to the truth 799.6 *be honourable;* 178.11 *be straight*
stick up 186.6 *make vertical;* 366.1 *raise*
stick-up 774.3 *theft*
stick up for 392.24 *back;* 413.14 *give moral support;* 714.8 *justify*
stick-up job 774.3 *theft*
stick-up man 774.11 *dishonest person*
stick with it 134.8 *go on!;* 228.8 *show determination*
sticky 267.9 *adhesive;* 373.14 *connective;* 254.1 *dangerous;* 31.52 *humid;* 429.9 *moist;* 264.12, 705.13 *problematic;* 360.9 *retentive;* 560.28 *sweaty;* 430.8 *viscous;* 493.11 *warm*
sticky boots 62.4 *climbing equipment*
sticky-fingered 774.17 *stolen*
sticky fingers 774.1 *stealing*
sticky label 267.4 *adherent*
sticky moment 705.4 *difficult question*
sticky tape 267.3 *adhesive*
sticky wicket 264.7 *awkward situation;* 53.5 *wicket*
stiff 486.3 *clumsy;* 582.19 *dead;* 690.3 *dead drunk;* 582.11 *dead person;* 792.7 *dear;* 264.10 *difficult;* 261.1 *fatigued;* 656.6 *formal;* 423.3 *hard;* 544.9 *inelegant;* 301.4 *motionless;* 266.2 *obscure;* 383.11 *obstinate;* 542.10 *ornate;* 50.10 *sailing;* 251.14 *self-restrained;* 228.9 *stable;* 418.2 *tough;* 622.15 *unapproachable;* 641.3 *unyielding*
stiff as a board 418.2 *tough*
stiff as a poker 418.2 *tough*
stiff as a ramrod 418.2 *tough*
stiff as buckram 418.2 *tough*
stiff boat 50.2 *sailing boat*
stiff collar 551.14 *neckwear*
stiffen 228.6 *be stable;* 423.10 *be tough;* 418.9 *harden;* 228.8 *show determination;* 418.10 *solidify;* 336.8 *strengthen*
stiffened 418.3 *hardened*
stiffening 418.5 *hardness;* 228.1 *stability;* 336.4 *strengthening*
stiffen one's resolve 336.8 *strengthen*
stiffen the sinews 336.8 *strengthen*
stiffly 792.12 *dearly;* 656.12 *formally;* 266.4 *obscurely;* 383.14 *resistingly;* 228.12 *stably;* 418.12, 423.12 *toughly;* 251.17 *with self-restraint*
stiff neck 641.5 *obstinacy*
stiff-necked 661.7 *defiant;* 641.2 *refractory;* 622.15 *unapproachable*
stiff-neckedly 622.32 *proudly*
stiff-neckedness 656.1 *formality;* 622.2 *unapproachability*
stiff-necked pride 622.2 *unapproachability*
stiffness 656.1 *formality;* 418.5 *hardness;* 544.4 *inelegance of speech;* 301.1 *motionlessness;* 266.1 *obscurity;* 383.2 *obstinacy;* 251.3 *self-restraint;* 228.1 *stability;* 38.15 *strength of materials;* 260.3 *symptom;* 423.6 *toughness*
stiff one 558.2 *drink*
stiff opposition 113.1 *opposition*
stiff price 792.1 *high price*
stiff ski 68.5 *ski equipment*
stiff upper lip 638.16 *fortitude;* 613.2 *heroism*
stiff wind 31.14 *windiness*
stiff with 232.8 *full*
stiff with cold 494.8 *cold*
stifle 399.4 *censor;* 736.8 *conceal;* 357.8 *destroy;* 128.7 *exclude;* 378.8 *hinder;* 382.17 *murder;* 511.7 *mute;* 335.8 *overpower;* 251.8 *restrain;* 506.2 *silence*
stifled 736.14 *concealed;* 511.1 *faint-sounding;* 511.2 *nonresonant*
stifling 382.23 *deadly;* 357.1 *destruction;* 251.13 *restraining;* 251.1 *restraint;* 493.11 *warm*
stigma 802.9 *dishonour;* 78.3 *flower part;* 743.3 *means of identification;* 564.1 *organs of reproduction;* 84.3 *plant body;* 548.1 *spot*
stigmatized 743.12 *identified*
stile 314.6 *means of entry*
stiletto 425.8 *sharp-pointed thing;* 587.8 *sharp weapon*
still 263.4 *at ease;* 582.19 *dead;* 558.17 *drinkable;* 341.3, 343.1 *inactive;* 339.5 *inert;* 88.9 *lakelike;* 685.4, 685.6 *moderate;* 301.4 *motionless;* 301.10 *motionlessly;* 511.7 *mute;* 589.7 *peaceful;* 301.6 *quiescent;* 301.2 *repose;* 506.2 *silence;* 506.3 *silent;* 421.3 *soothing;* 432.11 *vaporizer*
still as a statue 301.4 *motionless*
still as death 301.4 *motionless*
stillbirth 582.11 *dead person;* 582.1 *death*
stillborn 582.19 *dead;* 247.10 *failed*
still breathing 554.12 *alive*
still feel hungry 218.6 *be unsatisfied*
still fishing 55.1 *angling*
still hunting 60.2 *hunting*
still-life 19.10 *art subject;* 402.5 *object;* 41.4 *portrait*
still-life painter 19.16 *artist*
still more 121.17 *supremely*
stillness 263.1 *ease;* 407.8 *harmony;* 341.1 *inaction;* 343.5 *inactivity;* 339.1 *inertness;* 301.1 *motionlessness;* 589.1 *peace;* 301.2 *repose;* 506.4 *silence;* 421.7 *smoothness*
still remaining 215.10 *surplus*
still room 25.3 *kitchen;* 565.7 *room;* 439.4 *storage*
still small voice 810.4 *sense of duty*
Stillson™ 438.1 *tool*
still standing 225.7 *permanent*
still the same 225.9 *permanently*
still tired 261.1 *fatigued*
still water 88.2 *small lake*
still wine 558.9 *wine*
stilly 301.10 *motionlessly;* 506.3 *silent;* 421.15 *soothingly*
stilted 676.3 *affected;* 656.6 *formal;* 544.9 *inelegant;* 542.10 *ornate*
stilted arch 20.5 *arch*
stiltedly 656.12 *formally*
stiltedness 544.4 *inelegance of speech*
stilt house 88.7 *lake dwelling*
Stilton 539.6 *blue thing*
stilt root 77.7 *root*
stilts 154.8 *high thing*
stilt village 88.7 *lake dwelling*
stimulant 496.6 *cordial;* 394.8, 691.6 *drug;* 690.6 *intoxicating;* 581.6 *refresher;* 483.3, 488.3 *stimulus;* 394.7 *tonic*
stimulate 346.8 *activate;* 488.13 *arouse sensation;* 344.10 *awaken;* 690.9 *be intoxicating;* 496.13 *be piquant;* 617.15 *cause desire;* 369.15 *draw out;* 490.9 *give pleasure;* 338.3 *invigorate;* 213.5 *make bigger;* 483.9 *motivate;* 581.1 *refresh*
stimulated 483.12 *motivated;* 581.4 *refreshed*
stimulated emission 28.26 *laser*
stimulating 37.17; 496.10; 488.9 *exciting;* 369.18 *extractive;* 338.5 *invigorating;* 483.11 *motivational;* 480.19 *persuasive;* 581.3 *refreshing;* 476.7 *suppositional*
stimulatingly 496.16; 369.22 *expressively;* 483.14 *influentially*
stimulation 496.4; 342.1 *activity;* 344.1 *cause;* 369.5 *drawing out;* 690.10 *drunkenness;* 213.1 *increase;* 483.1 *motive;* 581.5 *refreshment;* 488.3 *stimulus;* 338.1 *vigour*
stimulative 394.17 *remedial*
stimulus 483.3; 488.3; 344.4 *contributing factor;* 480.8 *incentive;* 213.1 *increase*
stimulus-response psychology 36.1 *psychology*
sting 604.8 *be dishonest;* 699.25 *be fraudulent;* 242.12, 491.10 *be painful;* 496.13 *be piquant;* 425.14 *be sharp;* 774.7 *dishonesty;* 484.3 *expedient plan;* 699.8 *fraud;* 236.11 *harmfulness;* 76.16 *infest;* 491.11 *inflict pain;* 624.9 *offend;* 792.10 *overcharge;* 496.1 *piquancy;* 425.7 *sharp point;* 425.8 *sharp-pointed thing;* 700.8 *trick*
stingily 218.10 *insufficiently;* 683.8 *selfishly*
stinginess 218.8 *insufficiency;* 682.3 *parsimony;* 683.1 *selfishness*
stinging 651.14 *hostile;* 242.4, 491.5 *painful;* 496.9 *piquant;* 425.2 *spiked*
sting in the tail 131.10 *ending*
stingy 218.1 *insufficient;* 682.1 *mean;* 683.4 *selfish;* 425.2 *spiked*
stink 503.5; 258.10 *be dirty;* 245.2 *decay;* 500.8 *have odour;* 500.1 *odour;* 236.10 *poverty;* 503.1 *stench;* 258.2 *uncleanness*
stinkard 503.2 *something that makes an unpleasant smell*

stink-bomb 503.2 *something that makes an unpleasant smell*
stinker 804.10 *bad person;* 503.2 *something that makes an unpleasant smell*
stinkhorn 503.2 *something that makes an unpleasant smell*
stinking 503.3; 596.9 *disliked;* 796.12 *indecent;* 500.5 *odorous;* 236.4 *poor;* 258.8 *unclean*
stinking drunk 690.3 *dead drunk*
stinkingly 503.6
stinking of liquor 690.5 *drunken*
stinking rich 781.1 *wealthy*
stinko 690.3 *dead drunk*
stink of 217.5 *about;* 219.4 *be excessive*
stink of money 781.12 *be rich*
stink out 503.5 *stink*
stink to high heaven 503.5 *stink*
stink trap 501.2 *deodorant*
stinky 236.4 *poor;* 258.8 *unclean*
stint 770.3 *allotted task;* 203.2 *certain amount;* 209.1 *degree;* 275.3 *duration;* 682.7 *hoard;* 209.4 *interval;* 218.7 *make insufficient;* 276.4 *period of activity;* 576.2 *task*
stinted 218.2 *unprovided*
stinting 684.8 *self-restrained*
stintingly 684.11 *with self-restraint*
stipe 83.4 *fungal body;* 84.3 *plant body;* 77.5 *stem*
stipend 765.4 *earnings;* 392.6 *financial assistance;* 413.7 *financial support;* 768.2 *gift;* 813.3 *grant;* 785.3 *pay;* 769.2 *something received*
stipendiary 768.7 *given;* 413.9 *supportive*
stipendiary magistrate 464.6 *justice*
stipple 541.11 *variegate*
stippling 541.4 *maculation*
stipulate 746.6 *make conditions;* 135.10 *necessitate;* 251.8 *restrain;* 136.16, 139.24, 452.22 *specify*
stipulated 136.12 *conditional;* 27.77 *given;* 452.7 *particular*
stipulation 746.2 *basis for negotiations;* 136.7 *condition;* 452.18 *particularity;* 135.1 *requirement;* 251.1 *restraint;* 476.1 *supposition*
stipulatory 136.12 *conditional;* 746.8 *negotiated*
stipule 77.6 *leaf*
stir 342.1 *activity;* 327.22 *agitate;* 488.13 *arouse sensation;* 342.12 *be active;* 114.8 *be diverse;* 300.13 *be in motion;* 593.25 *be loved;* 496.13 *be piquant;* 31.58 *blow;* 25.55 *cook;* 408.9 *disorder;* 328.7 *disturb;* 412.8 *mix;* 300.2 *momentum;* 307.10 *swirl;* 815.2 *the inside;* 327.2 *tumult;* 327.3 *turbulence*
stir-fried 25.56 *culinary*
stir-fry 25.48 *Chinese dish;* 25.55 *cook*
stir-frying 25.8 *cooking technique*
stirk 43.8 *livestock*
Stirling engine 38.11 *engine*
stir one's stumps 342.12 *be active*
stirred 412.12 *mixed;* 488.7 *susceptible*
stirred up 327.15 *agitated*
stirrer 342.11, 644.4 *meddler;* 412.6 *mixer;* 412.7 *person who mixes;* 408.11 *troublemaker*
stirring 342.18 *active;* 342.1 *activity;* 342.19 *busy;* 488.9 *exciting;* 412.1 *mixture;* 300.2 *momentum;* 300.16 *moving;* 123.6 *notable*
stirrup 62.4 *climbing equipment*
stirrup bone 504.5 *internal ear*
stirrup cup 558.10 *drink container;* 313.9 *parting*
stir the blood 624.9 *offend*
stir the possum 638.9 *undertake*
stir up 327.22 *agitate;* 528.11 *make opaque;* 380.9 *make violent;* 624.9 *offend*
stir up trouble 751.7 *pick a fight*
stitch 373.11 *connect;* 373.8 *fastening;* 42.5 *knitting;* 373.6 *line;* 551.35 *make clothing;* 491.1 *pain*
stitched 373.15 *connected*
stitcher 551.26 *fashion designer*
stitching 53.7 *bat*
stithy 577.1 *workshop*
St. Moritz Tobogganing Club 68.9 *bobsledding*
stoba 25.51 *West Indian dish*
stochastic 107.8 *chance*
stochastic process 27.57 *population*
stochastics 107.7 *calculation of chance*
stochastic variable 27.57 *population*
Stocherkahn 50.8 *punting*
stock 765.3 *acquisition;* 216.1 *average;* 750.15 *conventional;* 70.3 *domesticated animal;* 117.15 *everyday;* 632.10 *familiar;* 232.6 *fill;* 44.5 *gardening;* 137.8 *genealogy;* 59.8 *hunting;* 431.2 *juice;* 373.6 *line;* 220.1 *list;* 43.8 *livestock;* 435.1 *materials;* 778.8 *merchandise;* 551.14 *neckwear;* 168.8 *nurture;* 440.5 *personal estate;* 745.2 *proverbial;* 436.1, 436.5 *provision;* 344.3 *rudiment;* 778.1 *sell;* 1.7 *society;* 25.13 *soup;* 77.5 *stem;* 439.1, 439.6 *store;* 352.2 *supplies*
stockade 384.9 *barrier;* 165.2 *enclosed place;* 384.12 *fort;* 815.1 *prison;* 252.2 *protection*
stockbreeder 43.15 *agriculturist;* 356.9 *producer*
stockbreeding 356.2 *manufacture*
stockbroker 14.3; 746.4 *negotiator;* 759.4 *person who exchanges;* 776.10 *trader;* 778.12 *wholesaler*
stockbroker belt 86.11 *settlement;* 87.8 *suburb*
stock-car race 61.1 *motor racing*
stock-car racing 61.1 *motor racing*
stock character 21.23 *role*
stock company 21.25 *cast*
stocked 436.8 *provisional*
stock exchange 14.2; 780.7 *finance;* 299.3 *irregular thing;* 759.2 *place of exchange;* 779.5 *stock market*
stock farm 43.6 *farm;* 577.1 *workshop*
stock farmer 43.15 *agriculturist*
stockfish 74.8 *food fish*
stockholder 440.7 *property man*
stockhorse 59.4 *saddle horse*
stockiness 149.1 *shortness;* 158.6 *squatness*
stocking 780.20 *money store*
stocking cap 551.15 *headgear*
stockings 48.3 *baseball equipment;* 551.20 *legwear*
stocking stitch 42.5 *knitting*
stock-in-trade 438.7 *equipment;* 352.4 *financial resources;* 778.8 *merchandise;* 440.5 *personal estate;* 439.1 *store*
stock-jobber 14.3 *stockbroker;* 776.10 *trader;* 778.12 *wholesaler*
stock-jobbing 776.4 *trade*
stockkeeper 43.15 *agriculturist*
stockman 43.16 *farm worker*
stock market 779.5; 780.7 *finance;* 14.2 *stock exchange*
stock market decline 249.2 *economic adversity*
stock of words 5.22 *many words*
stock part 21.23 *role*
stockperson 43.16 *farm worker*
stock phrase 745.1 *maxim*
stockpile 765.11 *acquire;* 765.3 *acquisition;* 376.25 *assemblage;* 376.37 *assemble;* 436.5 *provision;* 350.6 *stop using;* 439.1, 439.6 *store;* 350.11 *unused thing*
stockpiled 376.47 *collected*
stock raiser 43.15 *agriculturist*
stock rearing 43.3 *livestock farming*
stockroom 439.4 *storage*
stock rustling 774.1 *stealing*
stocks 814.14 *instrument of punishment;* 251.5 *means of restraint*
stock saddle 59.14 *horse-riding terms*
stocks and bonds 352.4 *financial resources;* 440.5 *personal estate*
stocks and shares 352.4 *financial resources;* 440.5 *personal estate*
stock-still 301.4 *motionless*
stock-taking 210.3 *count*
stock-taking sale 778.4 *sale*
stock up 765.11 *acquire;* 436.5 *provision;* 439.6 *store*
stock up one's cupboards 439.6 *store*
stock up one's freezer 439.6 *store*
stock up one's larder 439.6 *store*
stocky 158.17; 1.15 *physical;* 149.7 *short;* 152.1 *thick*
stocky build 1.9 *physical type*
stodge 557.7 *food*
stodgily 620.8 *boringly*
stodginess 620.1 *boredom;* 271.4 *simplicity*
stodgy 620.4 *boring;* 117.14 *conformist;* 271.1 *simple;* 430.8 *viscous*
stogies 551.19 *footwear*
stoic 684.10 *calm;* 4.11 *follower of a doctrine;* 592.5 *insensitive person;* 649.5 *merciful;* 4.14 *of a philosophy;* 301.6 *quiescent*
stoical 4.18 *detached;* 473.4 *disinterested;* 452.6 *infallible;* 605.8 *resigned*
stoically 4.27; **605.9**; 684.13 *calmly;* 473.8 *disinterestedly;* 301.10 *motionlessly*
stoichiometric 26.16 *micrometric*
stoichiometric compound 32.7 *chemical compound*
stoichiometric synthesis 32.16 *synthesis*
stoichiometry 26.2 *micrometry*
stoicism 605.2; 684.3 *calmness;* 4.3 *detachment;* 473.1 *disinterestedness;* 649.2 *forgivingness;* 452.17 *infallibility;* 4.7 *school of thought*
stoke 437.11 *fuel;* 213.5 *make bigger*
stoker 437.9 *power-worker*
stoke up 243.4 *prepare for action*
STOL 322.7 *miscellaneous aviation terms*
stole 551.14 *neckwear;* 7.11 *vestment*
stolen 16.59; **774.17**; 772.11 *borrowed*
stolen base 48.6 *fielding terms*
stolen goods 774.4
stolen property 16.36
stolid 339.5 *inert;* 301.6 *quiescent;* 489.6 *unfeeling;* 457.6, 528.5 *unintelligent*
stolidity 339.1 *inertness;* 528.9 *stupidity;* 457.2 *unintelligence*
stolidly 301.10 *motionlessly;* 528.13 *opaquely;* 457.11 *unintelligently*
stolon 77.5 *stem*
stoma 77.6 *leaf;* 308.7 *passageway*
stomach 410.18; 413.12 *bear;* 557.16 *eating utensil;* 172.4 *insides;* 388.4 *succumb*
stomachache 260.8 *indigestion;* 491.2 *painful condition*
stomach cancer 260.12 *cancer;* 260.8 *indigestion*
stomacher 551.24 *part of garment*
stomach flu 260.8 *indigestion*
stomach sweetbread 25.31 *offal*
stomach traverse 62.3 *climbing technique*
stomach ulcer 260.8 *indigestion*
stomp 331.13 *blow;* 22.2, 22.15 *dance;* 742.11 *gesture;* 331.7 *kick*
stone 381.7; 414.9 *avoirdupois weight;* 20.4, 435.2 *building material;* 38.25 *construction material;* 19.15 *engraving;* 814.5 *execute;* 80.3 *fruit structure;* 418.1 *hard;* 418.7 *hard substance;* 587.6 *historical missile weapon;* 38.26 *masonry;* 330.8 *missile;* 317.4 *road surface;* 30.28 *rock;* 30.27 *sediment;* 416.4 *solid body;* 330.23 *throw;* 414.8 *weighing down*
Stone Age 3.10 *past age;* 284.4 *prehistoric age*
Stone-Age 296.15 *primal*
Stone-Age man 296.7 *ancient people;* 566.3 *early human*
stone-blind 519.8 *blind*
stone-blindness 519.1 *blindness*
stone-broke 782.2 *insolvent;* 249.7 *unprosperous*
stone-carver 19.17 *sculptor*
stone-carving 19.12 *sculpture*
stone-cold sober 689.1 *sober*
stonecutting 19.12 *sculpture*
stoned 690.3 *dead drunk;* 691.7 *drugged*
stone dead 582.19 *dead*
stone deaf 505.4 *deaf*
stone fruit 80.1 *fruits;* 44.10 *fruit tree*
Stonehenge 737.6 *natural mystery;* 296.5 *old thing;* 10.13 *shrine;* 284.7 *thing of the past*
stone mason 20.2 *architect*
stone sculpture 19.12 *sculpture*
stoneshot 330.7 *shot*
stone-slinger 330.14 *thrower*
stone's throw 147.2 *short distance*
stone-throwing 330.3 *throwing*
stone to death 382.19, 814.5 *execute*
stonewall 53.17 *bat;* 294.8 *delay;* 736.13 *equivocate;* 637.9 *not cooperate;* 731.9 *outtalk;* 384.25 *stall;* 604.7 *thwart*
stone wall 378.3 *barrier;* 166.4 *boundary marker;* 418.7 *hard substance;* 360.4 *wall*
stonewalled 604.9 *disappointed;* 294.10 *held up*
stonewaller 294.5 *delayer*
stonewalling 294.3 *delayed action;* 53.9 *stroke*
stoneware 24.1 *ceramics;* 418.7 *hard substance;* 356.7 *produce*
stonework 356.8 *construction;* 38.26 *masonry*
stonily 420.14 *roughly;* 418.12 *toughly*
stoniness 418.5 *hardness*
stoning 814.13 *capital punishment;* 382.5 *execution;* 381.18 *hit*
stony 651.12 *callous;* 420.2 *coarse;* 30.58 *earthy;* 418.1 *hard;* 563.3 *infertile;* 135.5 *necessitous;* 638.3 *strong-willed;* 249.7 *unprosperous*
stony-broke 782.2 *insolvent;* 249.7 *unprosperous*
stony-faced 643.1 *solemn*
stony-hearted 651.12 *callous;* 418.4 *mentally hard;* 628.4 *pitiless*
stony-heartedness 651.3 *callousness*
stony meteorite 29.20 *meteor*
stooge 668.9 *butt;* 700.22 *dupe;* 21.29 *entertainer;* 621.4 *laughing stock;* 124.10 *nonentity;* 272.3 *object of ridicule;* 387.3 *subordinate;* 664.3 *sycophant;* 486.10 *unskilled person*
stooge for 664.11 *pander to*
stook 43.10 *farm tool*
stool 715.5 *accuse;* 479.3 *apostatize;* 23.2 *chair;* 258.4 *dirt;* 560.5 *faeces;* 693.13 *inform on;* 560.14, 767.7 *visit;* 79.1 *tree*
stoolie 715.3 *accuser;* 700.18 *decoy*
stooling 44.5 *gardening*
stool of repentance 814.14 *instrument of punishment*
stool pigeon 715.3 *accuser;* 700.18 *decoy;* 479.9 *equivocator;* 693.10 *informer;* 716.7 *person who gives evidence*
stool sample 35.7 *diagnosis*
stoop 155.8 *be low;* 664.8 *be servile;* 623.18 *condescend;* 367.16 *courtesy;* 245.1 *deteriorate;* 305.5 *dive;* 664.10 *knuckle under;* 10.19 *offer worship;* 663.6 *show obeisance to;* 367.8 *sit;* 388.4 *succumb;* 667.19 *take off one's hat to*
stooped 177.4 *curved;* 155.5 *low*
stooping 623.15 *condescension;* 305.18 *falling;* 57.11 *gymnastic;* 667.11 *in a respectful stance;* 155.5 *low;* 667.4 *mark of respect;* 367.23 *sedentary;* 664.7 *sycophantic*
stooping vault 57.6 *pommel horse*
stop 226.2; **309.8**; 301.8 *be motionless;* 131.16, 226.6 *cease;* 399.4 *censor;* 131.2, 133.2 *cessation;* 309.1 *closure;* 550.23 *cover;* 481.3 *deflect;* 312.15 *destination;* 360.7 *detain;* 360.2 *detention;* 133.12 *discontinue;* 394.20 *doctor;* 119.2 *equilibrium;* 378.8 *hinder;* 341.1 *inaction;* 361.12 *interrupt;* 247.9 *malfunction;* 301.1 *motionlessness;* 341.4 *not act;* 35.21 *practise dentistry;* 742.7 *punctuation;* 317.10 *railway;* 393.1 *repair;* 251.8 *restrain;* 50.10 *sailing;* 506.2 *silence;* 264.8 *snag;* 309.2 *stopper;* 226.4 *stopping place;* 350.6 *stop using;* 708.15 *terminate;* 294.7 *wait;* 355.2 *withdraw*
stop! 226.12; **301.11**
stop abruptly 226.6 *cease*
stop a gap 393.1 *repair*
stop and go 299.4 *irregular;* 299.8 *irregularly*
stop and think 244.4 *reconsider*
stop at 312.6
stop at nothing 628.6 *be pitiless;* 638.6 *be resolute*
stop bath 41.12 *development*
stop breathing 226.6 *cease;* 582.15 *die*
stopcock 309.2 *stopper;* 438.1 *tool*
stop dead 226.6 *cease*
stop down 41.21 *photograph*
stop fighting 749.5 *make peace;* 388.3 *submit*
stop from spreading 251.8 *restrain*
stopgap 754.6 *compromising;* 119.4 *equilizer;* 484.3 *expedient plan;* 608.5 *helper;* 231.6 *imperfect item;* 243.16 *preparatory;* 762.7 *substitute;* 762.1 *substitution*
stopgap measure 754.2 *half-measure*
stopgap measures 218.8 *insufficiency*
stop-go 133.8 *discontinuous;* 299.4 *irregular*
stop gybe 50.15 *sail;* 50.1 *sailing*
stop in one's tracks 301.8 *be motionless;* 226.6 *cease;* 330.28 *shoot*
stop in time 244.4 *reconsider*
stop it 226.12 *stop!*
stop light 522.6 *electric light;* 742.4 *signal*
stop negotiations 355.2 *withdraw*
stop off 312.6 *stop at;* 654.12 *visit*
stopover 312.16; 133.3 *interval*
stop over 133.13 *pause;* 312.6 *stop at;* 654.12 *visit*
stoppage 786.2; 131.2 *cessation;* 309.1 *closure;* 247.1 *failure;* 301.1 *motionlessness;*

378.2 *obstacle*; 264.8 *snag*; 226.2 *stop*; 708.6 *termination*
stop payment 786.8
stopped 309.13; 708.20 *cancelled*; 133.9 *discontinued*; 226.10 *finished*; 103.4 *forbidden*; 361.9 *interrupted*
stopped up 309.13 *stopped*
stopper 309.2; 550.2, 550.23 *cover*; 360.2 *detention*; 131.13 *ender*; 685.2 *moderator*; 252.4 *safety device*; 309.8 *stop*
Stopping 226
stopping 50.12 *canoeing*; 226.1 *cessation*; 378.1 *hindrance*; 361.6 *interruption*; 251.1 *restraint*; 394.12 *surgery*
stopping at nothing 638.2 *tenacious*
stopping place 226.4; 312.15 *destination*
stopping stroke 50.6 *canoeing*
stopping train 333.13 *slow thing*; 321.7 *train*
stopping work 15.4 *industrial dispute*
stop-press edition 740.4 *newspaper*
stop running 247.9 *malfunction*
stop short 301.8 *be motionless*; 226.6 *cease*
stop someone's mouth 506.2 *silence*
stop talking 506.1 *be silent*; 226.6 *cease*
stop tap 131.11 *finality*
stop the bleeding 394.20 *doctor*
stop the flow 90.9
stop the gap 384.21 *entrench*
stop thief 633.19 *after him!*; 226.12 *stop!*
stop thrust 54.3 *fencing movements*
stop up 50.19 *punt*; 309.8 *stop*
stop-up 50.8 *punting*
stop using 350.6; 767.9 *dispose of*; 355.1 *relinquish*
stopwatch 742.5 *indicator*; 744.10 *recording instrument*; 281.10 *signal*
stop work 350.7; 15.12 *have an industrial dispute*; 226.7 *stop working*
stop working 226.7
storage 439.4; 410.20 *containing*; 40.6 *memory*; 350.8 *nonuse*; 359.1 *preservation*; 141.5 *reserved space*
storage battery 334.7 *electrical power*; 39.29 *power source*; 439.4 *storage*
storage building 38.20 *building*
storage jar 410.15 *pot*
storage pol·;saccharide 33.4 *polysaccharide*
storage space 141.5 *reserved space*; 439.4 *storage*
Store 439
store 439.1; **439.6**; **779.8**; 765.3 *acquisition*; 376.25 *assemblage*; 376.37 *assemble*; 38.20 *building*; 374.5 *combine*; 736.8 *conceal*; 410.1 *container*; 360.7 *detain*; 780.6 *funds*; 764.1 *joint possession*; 43.8 *livestock*; 40.6 *memory*; 778.8 *merchandise*; 350.8 *nonuse*; 350.5 *not use*; 243.10 *preparations*; 243.4 *prepare for action*; 359.5 *preserve*; 252.10 *protect*; 252.2 *protection*; 436.5 *provision*; 410.21 *put in a container*; 352.5 *reserves*; 372.10 *set apart*; 780.19 *treasury*; 350.11 *unused thing*; 577.1 *workshop*
store away 765.11 *acquire*; 350.6 *stop using*
store-bought 551.31 *styled*
store-bought clothes 551.1 *dress*
store cattle 43.8 *livestock*
store coal 439.6 *store*
stored 439.7; 410.20 *containing*; 359.7 *preserved*; 350.1 *unused*
store energy 334.12 *generate power*
store fuel 439.6 *store*
storehouse 439.4 *storage*
storehouse of words 5.28 *dictionary*
store in a database 744.13 *record*
store information 3.20 *chronicle*
store in one's heart 462.11 *memorize*
store in the archives 744.13 *record*
store in the barn 439.6 *store*
store in the garage 439.6 *store*
storekeeper 789.6 *accountant*; 436.3 *provider*; 778.13 *retailer*
store manager 579.15 *manager*
store of memories 439.4 *storage*
store owner 578.3 *agent*; 778.13 *retailer*
storeroom 565.7 *room*; 439.4 *storage*
stores 557.7 *food*; 436.1 *provision*
storeship 439.4 *storage*; 586.24 *warship*
store the mind 6.23 *learn*
store window 738.8 *showplace*; 779.9 *stall*
storey 411.2 *level*; 410.4 *rack*
storified 17.19 *narrative*
storing 410.20 *containing*
storing the mind 6.8 *learning*
stork 561.7 *obstetrics*; 72.3 *water bird*
storm 31.59; 357.7 *agent of destruction*; 624.4 *anger*; 381.9 *attack successfully*; 624.11 *be angry*; 408.26 *be disorderly*; 507.8 *be loud*; 246.9 *be victorious*; 380.7 *be violent*; 586.36 *combat*; 586.38 *conquer*; 376.22 *flood*; 314.10 *invade*; 507.1 *loudness*; 381.14 *siege*; 327.13 *tempest*; 379.1 *trap*; 380.5 *violent weather*; 31.13 *wind strength*
storm along 332.4 *be swift*
storm blown over 252.1 *safety*
storm brewing 254.6 *danger signal*
storm cloud 31.18 *cloud*
storm clouds 249.1 *adversity*
storm cone 711.2 *danger signal*
storm door 314.6 *means of entry*
stormer 381.19 *attacker*; 586.1 *combatant*
storm-force 31.47 *windy*
storm force ten 31.14 *windiness*
storm glass 31.7 *weather instruments*
storm home 246.10 *defeat heavily*
stormily 31.65 *meteorologically*
storm in 314.10 *invade*
storm in a teacup 751.2 *argument*; 727.1 *exaggeration*; 467.2 *overestimate*
storminess 380.1 *violence*
storming 381.23 *attacking*
storm out 313.1 *depart*
storm petrel 711.1 *warning*
stormproof 428.10 *waterproof*
storm signal 711.2 *danger signal*
storm-tossed 420.4 *bumpy*; 245.13 *dilapidated*
storm trooper 381.19 *attacker*; 586.1 *combatant*
storm troops 586.14 *armed forces*
storm warning 711.1 *warning*
storm wave 30.14 *wave*
stormy 31.48; 523.8 *dark*; 524.5 *dim*; 327.17 *turbulent*; 380.6 *violent*
stormy sea 299.3 *irregular thing*
Storting 579.10 *legislative body*
story 17.3 *aspect of fiction*; 3.6 *biography*; 21.9 *dramaturgy*; 17.2 *fiction*; 701.4 *gist*; 477.4 *ideality*; 699.10 *lie*; 447.3 *matter of interest*; 721.3 *narration*; 356.5 *work of art*
storybook 477.12 *imaginary*
storyline 17.3 *aspect of fiction*; 721.3 *narration*
story so far 222.1 *circumstances*
storyteller 17.14 *author*; 721.10 *descriptive writer*; 699.18, 700.16 *liar*
stoup 410.13 *drinking vessel*
stout 558.7 *alcoholic drink*; 158.16 *fat*; 414.1 *heavy*; 336.9 *physically strong*; 158.17 *stocky*; 336.13 *strengthened*; 152.1 *thick*; 181.10 *well-rounded*
stout-hearted 613.9 *courageous*; 336.11 *strong in spirit*
stout-heartedness 613.1 *courage*; 336.1 *strength*
stoutly 414.16 *heavily*; 158.20 *largely*; 336.14 *strongly*
stoutness 158.5 *fatness*; 181.2 *round body*; 152.5 *thickness*
stout try 353.5 *attempt*
stove 493.4 *burner*; 24.6 *ceramic workshop*; 25.5 *cooker*
stovepipe hat 551.15 *headgear*
stow 232.6 *fill*; 243.4 *prepare for action*; 439.6 *store*
stowage 406.2 *load*; 141.5 *reserved space*; 158.1 *size*; 439.4 *storage*
stowaway 100.16 *be external*; 100.8 *intruder*; 109.3 *unconnected person*
stow away 736.8 *conceal*; 243.4 *prepare for action*; 439.6 *store*
stowed 439.7 *stored*
stow it 506.6 *hush!*; 226.12 *stop!*
STP 691.6 *drug*
strabismus 519.2 *poor sight*
straddle 311.14 *branch*; 318.11 *cross*; 141.20 *extend*; 381.2 *fire*; 57.5 *horizontal bar*; 150.10 *span*
straddled-leg 57.11 *gymnastic*
straddled-leg vault 57.6 *pommel horse*
straddle style 47.2 *field events*
strafe 381.13 *air attack*; 381.2 *fire*; 381.15 *firing*; 814.1 *punish*
straggle 377.9 *be dispersed*; 325.3 *go astray*
straggling 148.1 *long*; 377.25 *sprawled*
straggly 377.25 *sprawled*
straight 178.1; **178.12**; 698.21 *accurate*; 698.39 *accurately*; 69.3 *card game terms*; 52.14 *combat*; 750.14 *conforming*; 255.17, 324.15 *direct*; 324.9 *directly*; 117.15 *everyday*; 799.4 *honourable*; 690.6 *intoxicating*; 27.80 *linear*; 801.10 *moral*; 61.6 *motor-racing terms*; 407.13 *orderly*; 228.5 *stable person*; 698.22 *uniform*; 186.8 *vertical*; 186.11 *vertically*; 407.14 *well-ordered*; 23.14 *wooden*
straight across 324.9 *directly*
straight ahead 324.9 *directly*
straight angle 27.39 *angle*
straight as a dye 324.9 *directly*
straight as an arrow 324.9 *directly*; 178.1 *straight*
straight away 324.15 *direct*; 262.6 *hastily*; 280.8 *immediately*
straight chair 23.2 *chair*
straight down 186.8 *vertical*
straight down the line 178.5 *honourable*
straight drama 21.1 *drama*
straight drive 331.14 *sporting hit*
straightedge 27.49 *geometric construction*
straight-edged 27.80 *linear*
straighten 178.10; 698.31 *be accurate*; 244.1 *improve*; 117.9 *make conform*; 186.6 *make vertical*; 244.3 *rectify*; 407.21, 409.19 *tidy*
straightened 178.1 *straight*; 409.27 *tidied*
straightened out 178.1 *straight*; 409.27 *tidied*
straightening 186.2 *making vertical*
straightening out 244.6 *rectification*
straighten out 244.1 *improve*; 244.3 *rectify*; 393.1 *repair*; 178.10 *straighten*
straighten the record 739.6 *divulge*
straighten up 186.5 *be vertical*; 407.21, 409.19 *tidy*
straight face 643.4 *solemnity*
straight-faced 643.1 *solemn*
straight fence 59.11 *eventing*; 59.9 *jumping*
straight fertilizer 43.13 *fertilizer*
straightforward 178.2; 725.3 *clear*; 324.15 *direct*; 324.9 *directly*; 527.4 *easily seen through*; 265.9 *easy*; 178.5, 799.4 *honourable*; 801.10 *moral*; 646.1 *naive*; 271.3 *natural*; 738.15 *open*; 426.2 *outspoken*; 695.2 *simple*; 698.18 *truthful*
straightforwardly 178.13; 426.12 *bluntly*; 725.4 *clearly*; 646.5 *naively*
straightforwardness 725.1 *clarity*; 178.8 *directness*; 646.2 *naivety*; 271.6 *naturalness*; 527.10 *openness*; 426.6 *outspokenness*; 799.1 *probity*; 695.10 *simplicity*; 698.5 *truthfulness*
straight from the shoulder 707.14 *assertive*; 255.17 *direct*; 799.7 *honourably*; 308.26 *openly*; 698.18 *truthful*; 338.6 *with vigour*
straight glass 410.13 *drinking vessel*
straight handlebars 320.11 *bicycle part*
straight hang 57.7 *stationary rings*
straight left 52.2 *boxing*; 331.14 *sporting hit*
straight line 178.7; 27.37 *line*
straight-line 51.10 *bowling*; 61.9 *race*
straight-lined 27.80 *linear*; 178.1 *straight*
straight-line delivery 51.5 *bowling delivery*
straight-lining 61.6 *motor-racing terms*
straightly 324.9 *directly*; 178.12 *straight*
straight man 21.29 *entertainer*; 599.6 *humorist*; 621.4 *laughing stock*; 272.3 *object of ridicule*; 21.23 *role*
Straightness 178
straightness 178.6; 407.6 *methodicalness*; 407.5 *orderliness*; 698.9 *uniformity*; 186.1 *verticality*
straight news 741.1 *news*; 741.9 *news story*
straight part 21.23 *role*
straight person 178.9
straight pin 373.8 *fastening*
straight position 67.6 *diving*
straight punch 52.2 *boxing*
straight-rail 65.9 *billiard*
straight-rail billiards 65.4 *carom*
straight run 68.1 *skiing*
straight-shooter 178.9 *straight person*
straight skirt 551.6 *skirt*
straight talking 178.8 *directness*
straight through 178.3 *continuous*
straight thrust 54.3 *fencing movements*
straight up 698.21 *accurate*; 154.20 *higher*; 178.5, 799.4 *honourable*; 799.7 *honourably*; 89.11 *on the mountain*; 186.8 *vertical*
straight up and down 186.12 *perpendicularly*
straight-up-and-down 186.8 *vertical*
strain 412.4 *admixture*; 353.5 *attempt*; 229.2 *attitude*; 625.6 *be irascible*; 334.10 *be powerful*; 109.10 *be unrelated*; 264.1 *difficulty*; 234.9 *distort*; 234.1 *distortion*; 30.20 *earth movement*; 422.1 *elasticity*; 329.4, 727.7 *exaggerate*; 576.4 *exertion*; 576.8 *exert oneself*; 699.26 *falsify*; 261.6, 261.7 *fatigue*; 30.64 *fold*; 28.10 *force*; 44.5 *gardening*; 137.8 *genealogy*; 245.11 *hurt*; 315.12 *leak*; 38.14, 38.31 *load*; 18.13, 516.1 *melody*; 351.1 *misuse*; 99.4 *nature*; 346.1 *operation*; 17.8 *part of poem*; 334.1 *power*; 702.11 *practise sophistry*; 362.2 *pull*; 255.10, 256.15 *purify*; 1.7 *society*; 724.1 *style*; 316.11 *transfer*; 353.2 *try hard*; 137.4 *type*; 380.8 *use violence*; 337.7 *weaken*; 576.1 *work*
strained 329.13, 727.12 *exaggerated*; 261.1 *fatigued*; 612.8 *fearful*; 109.7 *illogical*; 625.4 *irascible*
strained sense 720.2 *misinterpretation*
strainer 256.10 *cleaning object*; 255.3 *purifier*
strainer arch 20.5 *arch*
strain every nerve 576.8 *exert oneself*
strain gauge 28.88 *barometer*
straining 727.1 *exaggeration*; 576.4 *exertion*; 699.9 *falsification*; 315.3 *leakage*
straining the sense 720.2 *misinterpretation*
strain one's credulity 105.7 *be improbable*
strain oneself 342.15 *try*
strain one's lungs 514.10 *cry out*
strain one's voice 507.8 *be loud*
strain the sense 720.1 *misinterpret*
strain to the utmost 576.8 *exert oneself*
strait 317.11 *channel*; 151.1 *narrow*; 151.6 *narrow place*
straiten 151.10 *narrow*
straitened 151.1 *narrow*; 782.1 *poor*
straitened circumstance 782.5 *poverty*
straitened circumstances 122.5 *inferior state*
straitjacket 191.4 *contractor*; 251.12 *gag*; 251.5 *means of restraint*; 309.11 *restrain*; 309.3 *restrainer*
strait-laced 117.14 *conformist*; 795.10 *moralistic*; 684.8 *self-restrained*; 647.10 *unadorned*
strait-lacedness 656.1 *formality*
straitness 151.5 *narrowness*
Strait of Messina 92.9 *inlet*
straits 92.9 *inlet*; 151.6 *narrow place*
stramash 507.2 *outcry*
strand 92.4 *coast*; 164.1 *edge*; 167.1 *front*; 151.8 *narrow thing*
stranded 355.5 *relinquished*; 228.10 *stabilized*; 254.3 *vulnerable*
strange 696.5; 116.4 *dissimilar*; 118.14 *eccentric*; 171.10 *extraneous*; 100.10 *foreign*; 594.12 *hated*; 487.2 *not customary*; 448.9 *original*; 11.18 *spiritual*; 456.8 *unknown*; 109.6 *unrelated*; 619.8 *wonderful*
strangely 116.7 *dissimilarly*; 325.29 *erratically*; 100.18 *extraneously*; 448.15 *inventively*; 109.12 *irrelevantly*; 118.21 *unconformably*; 487.8 *unusually*
strangeness 171.5 *extraneousness*; 100.2 *foreignness*; 448.4 *originality*; 28.78 *quantum*; 118.4 *unusualness*
strange noise 254.6 *danger signal*
stranger 100.6 *outsider*; 109.3 *unconnected person*
strangers 171.5 *extraneousness*
strange to say 619.13 *wonderfully*
Strangford Lough 88.4 *British lakes*
strangle 357.8 *destroy*; 814.5 *execute*; 191.5 *make smaller*; 382.17 *murder*; 335.8 *overpower*; 360.6 *retain*; 309.8 *stop*; 52.12 *wrestle*
strangled 360.10 *retained*; 191.7 *smaller*
stranglehold 360.1 *retention*; 52.5 *wrestling*
strangler 382.11 *murderer*
strangles 260.18 *veterinary disease*
strangling 191.8 *contracting*; 191.1 *contraction*; 360.9 *retentive*; 52.5 *wrestling*
strangulate 191.5 *make smaller*
strangulated 191.7 *smaller*
strangulation 814.13 *capital punishment*; 309.1 *closure*; 191.1 *contraction*; 382.2 *murder*

strap 373.10 *band*; 814.3 *hit*; 814.14 *instrument of punishment*; 425.15 *make sharp*; 425.12 *sharpener*; 57.7 *stationary rings*; 63.3 *tennis equipment*
strapless 552.10 *in dishabille*
strapless dress 551.7 *frock*
strappado 814.12 *corporal punishment*
strapped 782.2 *insolvent*
strapping 259.1 *healthy*; 336.9 *physically strong*; 423.4 *powerful*; 158.17 *stocky*; 338.4 *vigorous*
stratagem 645.2; 484.3 *expedient plan*; 485.1 *skill*; 702.2 *sophism*; 631.9 *tactics*; 379.1 *trap*; 700.8 *trick*
strategic 584.8 *military*; 484.14 *planned*
strategical 631.16 *behaving*; 645.4 *cunning*; 585.17 *military*
strategically 484.16 *as planned*; 645.6 *cunningly*; 702.15 *hypocritically*; 584.11 *militarily*
Strategic Arms Control Treaty 749.1 *pacification*
Strategic Arms Limitation Talks 749.1 *pacification*; 589.1 *peace*
Strategic Arms Reduction Talks 589.1 *peace*
strategic bombing 381.13 *air attack*; 585.8 *warfare*
Strategic Defense Initiative 587.5 *missile weapon*; 252.4 *safety device*; 585.8 *warfare*
strategic importance 123.1 *importance*
strategic objectives 584.1 *military affairs*
strategist 645.3 *cunning person*; 485.5 *expert*; 480.14, 483.7 *motivator*; 484.8 *planner*
strategy 585.6 *art of war*; 484.2 *policy*; 631.9 *tactics*
strath 92.6 *lowland*
Strathspey 22.4 *historic dancing*
straticulate 411.7 *layered*
stratification 409.5 *categorization*; 550.1 *covering*; 411.6 *layering*
stratified 409.24 *categorized*; 411.7 *layered*; 30.56 *petrographic*
stratified rock 30.31 *sedimentary rock*
stratified society 566.9 *group*
stratiform 31.49 *cloudy*; 411.7 *layered*
stratify 411.10 *layer*
stratigrapher 30.3 *geologist*
stratigraphical 30.48 *geological*
stratigraphy 30.1 *earth science*
stratocracy 12.1 *government*
stratocumulus 31.18 *cloud*
strato-isothermal region 434.3 *atmospheric layers*
stratopause 31.8 *atmosphere*
stratosphere 31.8 *atmosphere*; 434.3 *atmospheric layers*; 154.8 *high thing*
stratospheric 31.43, 434.13 *atmospheric*
stratous 31.49 *cloudy*
stratum 434.3 *atmospheric layers*; 187.3 *flat thing*; 411.1 *layer*; 30.31 *sedimentary rock*; 137.5 *social class*
stratus 31.18 *cloud*
straw 43.9 *animal feedstuff*; 81.4 *cereal grass*; 44.15 *cultivate*; 81.3 *grass plant*; 415.7 *light thing*; 124.8 *trifle*
strawberry 535.7 *red thing*
strawberry-blond 537.3 *yellow-haired*
strawberry mark 80.5 *figurative usage*; 541.4 *maculation*; 743.3 *means of identification*; 535.7 *red thing*
strawberry roan 59.1 *horse*
strawboard 435.4 *board*
straw-burning 43.5 *cultivation*
straw-coloured 537.1 *yellow*
straw hat 551.15 *headgear*; 21.5 *show business*
straw-hat circuit 21.15 *engagement*
straw man 96.5 *insubstantial person*; 337.4 *weakling*
straw poll 469.10 *vote*
stray 377.9 *be dispersed*; 254.8 *be in danger*; 250.16 *be independent*; 804.16 *be wicked*; 144.7 *displaced person*; 796.16 *do wrong*; 325.3 *go astray*; 325.21 *indirect*; 118.15 *irregular*; 133.15 *lose one's train of thought*; 655.7 *outsider*; 377.25 *sprawled*; 300.15 *walk*
stray capacitance 39.12 *resistance*
stray from the topic 109.10 *be unrelated*
straying 325.16, 325.25 *wandering*
streak 412.4 *admixture*; 332.4 *be swift*; 258.11 *dirty*; 151.8 *narrow thing*; 522.4 *natural light*; 148.5 *piece*; 541.3 *striping*; 552.14 *undress*; 541.11 *variegate*
streaked 541.9 *striped*
streaker 552.8 *nude person*
streakiness 541.3 *striping*
streaking 552.1 *undress*
streak of lightning 332.11 *swift thing*
streak of luck 248.2 *good fortune*
streaky bacon 25.30 *bacon*
stream 217.5 *about*; 219.4 *be excessive*; 300.13 *be in motion*; 317.11 *channel*; 208.11, 376.40 *crowd*; 376.22 *flood*; 90.7, 431.25 *flow*; 314.2 *influx*; 371.14 *let out*; 300.2 *momentum*; 315.2 *outflow*; 217.8 *plenty*; 132.8 *procession*; 31.62 *rain*; 90.1 *river*; 90.6 *river flow*; 137.6 *students*; 439.3 *supply*; 229.1 *tendency*; 300.15 *walk*
stream course 30.8 *drainage*
streamer 55.2 *artificial fly*; 743.7 *flag*; 740.3 *journalism*
streamers 522.4 *natural light*; 601.8 *salute*
streaming 219.6 *excessive*; 562.5 *fertile*; 90.10 *fluvial*; 300.16 *moving*; 315.2 *outflow*; 31.53 *rainy*; 268.10 *slippery*; 433.23 *wet*
streaming eyes 315.2 *outflow*
streamlet 90.1 *river*
streamline 409.14 *rearrange*; 244.3 *rectify*; 421.11 *smooth*
streamlined 409.23 *rearranged*; 421.1 *smooth*; 332.1 *swift*
streamlining 265.7 *easing*; 409.4 *rearrangement*
stream of consciousness 17.3 *aspect of fiction*; 36.27 *association of ideas*; 443.5 *creative thought*; 721.3 *narration*; 36.21 *psyche*; 735.1 *soliloquy*
stream-of-consciousness novel 17.2 *fiction*
stream of rain 31.25 *rain*
stream past 132.17 *line up*
streams of sweat 560.8 *sweat*
street 317.3, 373.5 *road*
street Arab 258.6 *dirty person*
streetcar 317.10 *railway*
streetcar line 317.10 *railway*
street cleaner 256.12 *cleaner*
street cred 811.1 *estimation*
street credibility 811.1 *estimation*; 221.1 *state*
street fight 662.2 *violation of the law*
street-fighter 340.3 *doer*
streetlamp 522.6 *electric light*
streetlight 522.6 *electric light*; 154.6 *tall thing*
street map 484.5 *map*
street market 779.1 *market*
street musician 18.24 *musician*
street name 733.5 *place of residence*
Street of Shame 740.3 *journalism*
street party 600.1 *rejoicing*
street performer 21.29 *entertainer*
street railway 317.10 *railway*
street riot 662.2 *violation of the law*
streets ahead 121.12 *superior*
street seller 778.11 *pedlar*; 778.14 *street trader*
street smarts 334.2 *ability*; 442.5 *common sense*; 455.4 *intellect*
street sweeper 767.6 *rubbish collector*
street theatre 21.1 *drama*
street trader 778.14; 514.9 *crier*; 793.7 *discounter*
street urchin 258.6 *dirty person*; 555.7 *young man*
street vendor 778.11 *pedlar*; 778.14 *street trader*
streetwalk 796.18 *prostitute*
streetwalker 796.9 *immoral woman*; 804.9 *wicked person*
streetwalking 796.5 *prostitution*
streetwise 458.6 *intelligent*; 6.19, 455.8 *knowledgeable*
Strength 336
strength 336.1; 396.1 *authority*; 726.1 *emphasis*; 418.5 *hardness*; 259.3 *health*; 395.1 *influence*; 156.2 *intensity*; 334.1 *power*; 485.1 *skill*; 228.1 *stability*; 640.4 *stamina*; 423.6 *toughness*; 338.1 *vigour*; 380.1 *violence*
strengthen 336.8; 413.14 *give moral support*; 334.11 *give power*; 418.9 *harden*; 253.14 *make fast*; 423.11 *make tough*; 252.10 *protect*; 581.1 *refresh*; 384.20 *reinforce*; 393.3 *restore*; 392.19, 413.11 *support*
strengthened 336.13; 418.3 *hardened*; 393.13 *repaired*; 423.2 *toughened*
strengthening 336.4; 338.5 *invigorating*; 393.9 *restoration*; 413.1 *support*
strengthen oneself 336.8 *strengthen*
strength exercises 57.1 *gymnastics*
strength of character 638.15 *will*
strength of materials 38.15
strength of purpose 635.2 *willpower*
strength of will 635.2 *willpower*
strenuous 342.18 *active*; 264.10 *difficult*; 726.3 *emphatic*; 576.11 *laborious*; 640.10 *persevering*; 814.21 *punishing*; 338.4 *vigorous*
strenuous climbing 62.1 *mountaineering*
strenuously 264.26 *arduously*; 726.7 *emphatically*; 576.12 *laboriously*
strenuousness 264.1 *difficulty*
strepsipteran 76.10 *insectan*
streptomycin 394.8 *drug*; 83.6 *fungal antibiotic*
stress 36.12; 334.10 *be powerful*; 331.13 *blow*; 234.9 *distort*; 234.1 *distortion*; 707.7, 726.1 *emphasis*; 707.22, 726.6 *emphasize*; 576.4 *exertion*; 28.10 *force*; 331.1 *impel*; 123.1 *importance*; 336.3 *intensity*; 38.14, 38.31 *load*; 123.8 *make important*; 17.9 *metre*; 729.3 *mode of speech*; 346.1 *operation*; 334.1 *power*; 742.13 *punctuate*; 5.16 *spoken letter*; 336.8 *strengthen*
stress a point 707.22 *emphasize*
stressed 707.15, 726.4 *emphasized*; 729.18 *phonetic*
stressed point 707.7 *emphasis*
stress reaction 36.12 *stress*
stretch 770.3 *allotted task*; 190.6 *become bigger*; 422.8 *be elastic*; 148.9 *be long*; 251.4 *detention*; 275.3 *duration*; 422.6 *elastic*; 422.1 *elasticity*; 190.2 *enlargeability*; 329.4, 727.7 *exaggerate*; 576.4 *exertion*; 141.20 *extend*; 141.3 *geographical space*; 190.1 *growth*; 141.8 *intervening space*; 148.4 *length*; 148.10 *lengthen*; 190.5, 213.5 *make bigger*; 151.10 *narrow*; 276.1 *period*; 815.4 *prison sentence*; 141.7 *range*; 145.7 *reach*; 576.2 *task*
stretchability 422.1 *elasticity*; 190.2 *enlargeability*
stretchable 422.6 *elastic*; 190.9 *enlargeable*; 419.2 *pliant*
stretch a point 648.3 *be lenient*; 754.4 *compromise*; 329.4 *exaggerate*
stretched 190.7 *bigger*; 422.6 *elastic*; 727.12 *exaggerated*; 699.36 *falsified*; 213.7 *increased*; 148.1 *long*
stretched out 190.7 *bigger*; 148.1 *long*
stretcher 19.11 *artist's materials*; 190.4 *enlarger*; 394.14 *hospital*; 320.6 *litter*; 38.26 *masonry*; 373.4 *means of connection*; 316.5 *means of transport*; 50.4 *rowing*
stretcher-bearer 35.17 *paramedic*; 316.7 *transferor*
stretcher bond 38.26 *masonry*
stretcher case 260.19 *sick person*
stretch fabric 422.3 *elastic thing*
stretchiness 422.1 *elasticity*
stretching 422.6 *elastic*; 422.1 *elasticity*; 727.1 *exaggeration*; 190.8 *growing*; 190.1 *growth*; 27.47 *topology*
stretching out 190.1 *growth*; 148.4 *length*
stretching the meaning 720.2 *misinterpretation*
stretch jeans 422.3 *elastic thing*
stretch limo 320.16 *car*
stretch of the imagination 477.1 *imagination*; 727.5 *tall story*
stretch oneself 148.9 *be long*
stretch one's legs 581.2 *be refreshed*
stretch one's neck 814.5 *execute*
stretch out 190.6 *become bigger*; 148.9 *be long*; 190.5 *make bigger*; 145.7 *reach*
stretch the imagination 727.11 *tell a tall story*
stretch the meaning 720.1 *misinterpret*
stretch the point 757.4 *be permissive*
stretch the truth 234.12 *distort the truth*
stretch to 145.7 *reach*
stretchy 422.6 *elastic*; 190.9 *enlargeable*
strew 377.17 *sow*
strewing 377.1 *dispersion*
strewn 377.22 *distributed*
stria 541.3 *striping*
striate 541.9 *striped*; 541.11 *variegate*
striated 30.59 *weathered*
striation 541.3 *striping*; 30.35 *weathering*
stricken 260.23 *diseased*
stricken in years 556.14 *aged*; 556.16 *maturely*
strict 750.15 *conventional*; 698.24 *pedantic*; 7.15 *religious*; 251.13 *restraining*; 684.8 *self-restrained*; 647.8 *severe*
strict control 251.1 *restraint*
strict discipline 647.1 *severity*
strictly 7.23 *religiously*; 647.11 *severely*; 251.16 *under restraints*; 684.11 *with self-restraint*
strictly controlled 251.13 *restraining*
strictly speaking 698.38 *literally*
strictly teetotal 689.1 *sober*
strictness 273.1 *accuracy*; 117.4 *conventionalism*; 698.11 *pedantry*; 7.2 *religiousness*; 251.1 *restraint*; 647.1 *severity*
strict observance 7.2 *religiousness*; 10.1 *ritual*
strict person 647.4
strict teetotaller 689.8 *sober person*
stricture 670.7 *blame*; 166.2 *limiting factor*; 151.9 *narrowing*
stride 300.12 *gait*; 302.13 *step*; 300.15 *walk*
stridency 513.1; 517.1 *dissonance*; 507.1 *loudness*
strident 513.7; 517.7 *dissonant*; 507.6 *loud*
stridently 513.10; 517.12 *dissonantly*; 507.9 *loudly*
striders 551.9 *trousers*
stridor 507.1 *loudness*; 729.3 *mode of speech*; 513.1 *stridency*; 18.21 *tone*
stridulantly 515.10 *howlingly*
stridulate 515.6 *buzz*
stridulation 515.3 *insect noise*
stridulous 515.9 *humming*; 513.7 *strident*
stridulously 515.10 *howlingly*
strife 701.1 *argument*; 113.5 *conflict*; 751.1 *disagreement*; 242.8 *quarrel*
strigiform 72.21 *avian*
strigil 256.10 *cleaning object*
strigose 420.3 *barbed*
strike 381.5; 365.13 *abrade*; 55.1 *angling*; 381.1 *attack*; 330.26 *bat*; 662.15 *be disobedient*; 378.9 *block*; 331.13 *blow*; 51.5 *bowling delivery*; 753.8 *cause mischief*; 662.1 *disobedience*; 586.37 *fight*; 449.10 *find*; 437.11 *fuel*; 753.3 *gesture of protest*; 15.12 *have an industrial dispute*; 331.3, 814.3 *hit*; 58.1 *hockey*; 236.14 *ill-treat*; 13.8 *industrial relations*; 522.24 *light*; 367.10 *lower the flag*; 703.6 *mass demonstration*; 381.12 *military attack*; 301.1 *motionlessness*; 382.17 *murder*; 378.2 *obstacle*; 48.4 *pitching terms*; 58.9 *play hockey*; 66.4 *play soccer*; 492.3 *press*; 703.19 *protest*; 709.1 *refusal*; 709.5 *refuse*; 355.3 *relinquishment*; 383.6 *resist*; 383.1 *resistance*; 439.2 *resource*; 50.16 *row*; 330.28 *shoot*; 226.2 *stop*; 226.7 *stop working*; 492.11 *touch*; 380.8 *use violence*; 355.2 *withdraw*
strike a bad patch 264.20 *be in difficulty*
strike a balance 754.4 *compromise*; 119.11 *equalize*; 216.10 *make average*; 414.15 *weigh*
strike a ball 331.10 *bat*
strike a bargain 755.5 *contract*
strike a blow for 340.4 *act*
strike a light 522.24 *light*
strike an average 754.4 *compromise*
strike a rich vein 248.6 *be fortunate*
strike at 331.3 *hit*; 48.7 *play baseball*; 381.5 *strike*
strike back at 381.8 *counterattack*
strike blind 519.15 *blind*
strike-bound 709.8 *refused*
strike-breaker 15.7 *employee*; 479.9 *equivocator*; 662.12 *reactionary*
strike-breaking 15.4 *industrial dispute*; 15.10 *unionized*
strike camp 313.3 *quit*
strike colours 388.3 *submit*
strike dumb 730.15; 630.11 *amaze*; 619.10 *be wonderful*
strike first 381.1 *attack*
strike force 381.19 *attacker*
strike hard 338.2 *be full of vigour*
strike it lucky 248.6 *be fortunate*; 248.5 *be prosperous*
strike it rich 248.6 *be fortunate*; 248.5 *be prosperous*; 781.13 *get rich*
strike notice 15.4 *industrial dispute*
strike off 371.3 *disbar*; 128.8 *eject*
strike off the register 708.15 *terminate*
strike off the roll 371.3 *disbar*
strike oil 248.6 *be fortunate*; 437.11 *fuel*
strike one 446.14 *have an idea*
strike out 708.14 *cancel*; 357.8 *destroy*;

128.8 *eject*; 358.1 *obliterate*; 48.7 *play baseball*; 313.5 *set out*
strike-out 48.4 *pitching terms*
strike out for 324.7 *take a direction*
striker 65.7 *billiards player*; 355.4 *deserter*; 15.7 *employee*; 66.3 *football player*; 58.2 *hockey player*; 662.7, 703.8, 753.4 *protester*; 709.4 *refuser*; 53.4 *team*; 330.14 *thrower*
strike root 228.6 *be stable*
strike root in 395.8 *influence*
striker-out 63.5 *real tennis*
strike settlement 15.4 *industrial dispute*
strike the first blow 381.1 *attack*
strike through 358.1 *obliterate*
strike up 18.36 *play*
strike up a friendship 569.13 *befriend*
strike up an acquaintance 569.13 *befriend*
strike upon 312.2 *reach*
strike with admiration 619.10 *be wonderful*
strike zone 48.4 *pitching terms*
striking 381.23 *attacking*; 520.2 *clear*; 814.12 *corporal punishment*; 703.14 *demonstrating*; 721.11 *descriptive*; 488.9 *exciting*; 66.2 *football play*; 58.1 *hockey*; 15.4 *industrial dispute*; 695.1 *intelligible*; 738.14 *manifest*; 709.8 *refused*; 383.10 *resistant*; 50.4, 50.11 *rowing*; 336.12 *strong to the senses*; 15.10 *unionized*; 619.8 *wonderful*
striking circle 58.1 *hockey*
striking distance 147.2 *short distance*
striking force 586.14 *armed forces*
striking likeness 717.1, 721.9 *representation*
striking off 371.18 *dismissal*
striking out 212.1 *subtraction*
striking the cushion 65.4 *carom*
strim 44.15 *cultivate*
Strimmer™ 44.6, 438.3 *garden tool*
Strine 5.26 *dialect*
string 132.15 *concatenate*; 132.2 *consecution*; 65.3 *English billiards*; 404.6 *fibre*; 376.23 *flock*; 28.79 *fundamental interaction*; 373.6 *line*; 20.9 *miscellaneous architectural features*; 148.5 *piece*; 304.10 *step*
string along 700.27 *be false*
string along with 747.14 *join with*
string bag 410.8 *bag*
string band 18.26 *musical group*
stringed instrument 510.4 *sources of resonance*
stringency 647.1 *severity*
stringent 647.8 *severe*
stringently 647.11 *severely*
stringer 693.9 *informant*; 20.9 *miscellaneous architectural features*; 740.11 *newspaperman*; 439.2 *resource*; 38.27 *superstructure*
string him up 382.26 *no quarter!*
string him up! 814.24
stringiness 423.8 *physical strength*; 423.6 *toughness*; 430.1 *viscosity*
stringing 65.5 *snooker*
stringing out 148.4 *length*
string of invectives 712.1 *curse*
string out 132.16 *arrange consecutively*; 148.10 *lengthen*; 206.9 *scatter*
stringpuller 396.10 *person of authority*
string pulling 396.1 *authority*; 484.4 *plot*
string quartet 374.3 *assembly*; 18.26 *musical group*
strings 746.2 *basis for negotiations*; 395.4 *indirect influence*; 18.25 *musical instrument*
string section 223.6 *accompanier*
string tie 551.14 *neckwear*
string together 132.15 *concatenate*
string up 382.19, 814.5 *execute*
stringy 423.4 *powerful*; 430.8 *viscous*
strip 256.13 *clean*; 371.3 *disbar*; 43.11 *farmland*; 782.14 *impoverish*; 411.1 *layer*; 357.10 *lay waste*; 766.9 *lose*; 552.14 *make nude*; 151.8 *narrow thing*; 148.5 *piece*; 411.11 *scale*; 372.10 *set apart*; 212.4 *take off*; 552.14 *undress*; 337.7 *weaken*
strip bare 739.5 *disclose*; 357.10 *lay waste*; 372.10 *set apart*; 552.14 *undress*; 337.7 *weaken*
strip-casting 55.1 *angling*
strip clean 256.13 *clean*
strip club 552.2 *nudity*
stripe 331.5 *beat*; 331.13 *blow*; 814.12 *corporal punishment*; 743.4 *insignia*; 151.8 *narrow thing*; 99.4 *nature*; 148.5 *piece*; 541.3 *striping*; 137.4 *type*; 541.11 *variegate*
striped 541.9
striped ball 65.6 *pool*
striped bass 55.4 *American game fish*
stripes 542.4 *honour*
strip grazing 43.3 *livestock farming*
striping 541.3
strip joint 552.2 *nudity*
strip light 522.6 *electric light*; 28.25 *light source*
stripling 555.7 *young man*
strip off 212.4 *take off*; 552.14 *undress*
strip of land 770.2 *portion*
strip-o-gram 552.8 *nude person*; 552.2 *nudity*
stripped 552.11 *exposed*; 782.2 *insolvent*; 552.9 *undressed*
stripped-down 271.1 *simple*
stripped naked 552.9 *undressed*
stripped of 766.16 *losing*
stripped to the buff 552.9 *undressed*
stripper 21.30 *dancer*; 738.12 *displayer*; 21.29 *entertainer*; 552.8 *nude person*
stripping 371.18 *dismissal*; 766.1 *loss*; 552.1 *undress*
stripping bare 552.1 *undress*
strip poker 552.1 *undress*
strip-search 552.15 *make nude*; 552.1 *undress*
strip-searched 552.9 *undressed*
strip show 21.7 *show*
striptease 21.7 *show*; 21.5 *show business*; 552.1 *undress*
striptease artist 21.30 *dancer*; 21.29 *entertainer*
striptease artiste 738.12 *displayer*; 552.8 *nude person*
striptease dancer 552.8 *nude person*
stripteaser 738.12 *displayer*; 552.8 *nude person*
strip the assets of 773.10 *take away*
Strip the Willow 22.4 *historic dancing*
strip to the buff 552.14 *undress*
stripy 541.8 *checked*; 541.9 *striped*
strive 576.8 *exert oneself*; 353.2 *try hard*
strive after 482.10 *aim*
strive against 113.14 *oppose*
strive for 633.12 *aim at*
strive in vain 335.6 *be powerless*
striver 353.7 *attempter*; 448.5 *experimenter*
striving 353.8 *attempting*
strobe 21.20 *stage lighting*
strobe lighting 522.6 *electric light*
stroboscope 28.90 *ammeter*; 522.6 *electric light*; 21.20 *stage lighting*
stroboscopic 522.15 *lucent*
stroke 53.9; 50.21 *avast!*; 331.13 *blow*; 50.6 *canoeing*; 260.10 *cardiovascular disease*; 593.14 *communication of love*; 814.12 *corporal punishment*; 340.2 *deed*; 579.2 *direct*; 579.13 *director*; 335.4 *disability*; 65.3 *English billiards*; 742.11 *gesture*; 56.3 *golf shots*; 331.3 *hit*; 58.1 *hockey*; 260.2 *illness*; 492.4, 593.27 *kiss*; 365.16 *massage*; 461.3 *mental deterioration*; 189.2 *oblique line*; 58.9 *play hockey*; 742.7 *punctuation*; 50.16 *row*; 50.4 *rowing*; 50.9 *sailor*; 327.8 *spasm*; 67.1 *swimming*; 330.5 *throw*; 492.11 *touch*
stroked 65.9 *billiard*
stroke of genius 340.2 *deed*; 485.3 *masterpiece*; 619.3 *wonder-working*
stroke of luck 287.2 *opportunity*
stroke of policy 484.2 *policy*
stroke of work 576.2 *task*
stroke play 56.1 *golf*; 56.2 *golfing terms*
stroke side 50.4 *rowing*
stroking 365.6 *massage*; 492.2 *touching*
stroll 300.12 *gait*; 333.1 *move slowly*; 333.10 *slow motion*; 300.15 *walk*
stroller 320.8 *baby carriage*
strolling 333.4 *slow*
strolling player 21.24 *actor*
stromatolite 84.5 *algal product*
strong 32.36 *acid*; 342.18 *active*; 396.12 *authoritative*; 529.11 *colourful*; 416.6 *dense*; 558.17 *drinkable*; 726.3 *emphatic*; 259.1 *healthy*; 796.12 *indecent*; 395.11 *influential*; 690.6 *intoxicating*; 252.7 *invulnerable*; 336.9 *physically strong*; 496.9 *piquant*; 334.13 *powerful*; 204.8 *sound*; 228.9 *stable*; 418.2, 423.1 *tough*; 338.4 *vigorous*; 380.6 *violent*; 31.47 *windy*
strong acid 32.8 *acid*
strong ale 558.7 *alcoholic drink*
strong alkali 32.9 *base*
strong-arm 386.9 *compelling*; 386.7 *force*
strong-arm man 586.1 *combatant*; 336.6 *muscleman*; 252.3 *protector*
strong-arm tactics 386.3 *coercive methods*; 380.2 *physical violence*
strong as a bull 336.9 *physically strong*
strong as a horse 259.1 *healthy*; 336.9 *physically strong*
strong as a lion 336.9 *physically strong*
strong as an ox 259.1 *healthy*; 336.9 *physically strong*
strongbox 780.20 *money store*; 439.4 *storage*
strong breeze 31.13 *wind strength*
strong card 485.1 *skill*
strong cheese 503.2 *something that makes an unpleasant smell*
strong currency 14.1 *finance*
strong drink 690.12 *alcohol*
strong feeling 590.4 *emotion*; 342.4 *energy*
strong flavour 495.4 *flavour*; 496.1 *piquancy*
strong foundation 228.4 *stable thing*
strong gale 31.13 *wind strength*
strong hand 352.1 *means*; 647.1 *severity*
stronghold 384.12 *fort*; 252.5 *refuge*
strong in 6.19 *knowledgeable*
strong in spirit 336.11
strong interaction 28.79 *fundamental interaction*
strong language 726.1 *emphasis*; 712.2 *offensive language*
strongly 336.14; 396.23 *authoritatively*; 416.10 *densely*; 726.7 *emphatically*; 395.14 *influentially*; 334.18 *powerfully*; 228.12 *stably*; 418.12, 423.12 *toughly*
strongly worded 707.14 *assertive*; 707.15 *emphasized*; 726.3 *emphatic*
strongman 336.5 *athlete*; 21.31 *circus performer*
strong-minded 638.3 *strong-willed*
strong nuclear interaction 28.79 *fundamental interaction*
strong point 384.12 *fort*; 485.1 *skill*; 139.7 *special skill*; 235.6 *worth*
strong position 334.1 *power*
strong possibility 102.3; 104.4 *chance*
strong pulse 554.1 *life*
strongroom 780.20 *money store*; 439.4 *storage*
strong safety 46.10 *defence*
strong side 46.7 *offence*
strong silent type 732.5 *shy person*
strong smell 500.1 *odour*
strong-smelling 336.12 *strong to the senses*
strong suit 235.6 *worth*
strong sun 31.22 *sun*
strong-tasting 336.12 *strong to the senses*
strong to the senses 336.12
strong vocational interest test 36.5 *psychological test*
strong-willed 638.3
strong wind 420.6 *roughness*; 380.5 *violent weather*; 31.14 *windiness*
strong woman 336.6 *muscleman*
strong words 707.6 *assertiveness*
strop 425.15 *make sharp*; 425.12 *sharpener*
strophe 17.8 *part of poem*
stroppiness 662.1 *disobedience*
stroppy 408.20 *disorderly*; 624.15 *resentful*; 264.14 *troublesome*
struck 58.8 *hockey*
struck dumb 630.7 *amazed*; 730.11 *speechless*; 619.7 *wide-eyed*
struck off 708.20 *cancelled*; 128.11 *excluded*
struck out 708.20 *cancelled*
structural 20.12; **32.37**; **38.32**; **403.11**; 32.33 *crystalline*; 5.44 *grammatical*; 5.38 *linguistic*; 356.11 *productive*; 99.8 *quintessential*
structural connection 38.27 *superstructure*
structural design 323.4 *shipbuilding*
structural engineer 38.18 *civil engineer*
structural engineering 38.17 *civil engineering*
structural formula 32.13 *structure*
structural framework 38.27 *superstructure*
structural-functional 2.14 *socioeconomic*
structural-functionalism 2.2 *sociological research*
structural gene 34.13 *genetic material*
structural geology 30.1 *earth science*
structural glass 24.9 *industrial ceramics*
structural grammar 5.29 *grammar*
structuralism 1.5 *anthropological concept*; 403.9 *artistic structure*; 5.1 *linguistics*; 36.1 *psychology*; 4.7 *school of thought*
structural isomer 32.13 *structure*
structuralist 1.11 *anthropological*; 4.11 *follower of a doctrine*; 5.2 *linguist*; 17.15 *literary person*
structural linguistics 5.29 *grammar*; 5.1 *linguistics*
structural loading 38.14 *load*
structurally 38.33; **403.18**; **406.13**; 20.20 *architecturally*; 5.48 *linguistically*; 404.15 *texturally*
structural material 38.25 *construction material*
structural member 38.27 *superstructure*
structural model 323.4 *shipbuilding*
structural polysaccharide 33.4 *polysaccharide*
structural psychology 36.1 *psychology*
structural test 323.4 *shipbuilding*
Structure 403
structure 32.13; **38.19**; **403.1**; **403.14**; 34.4 *anatomy*; 409.12 *arrange*; 409.2 *array*; 17.3 *aspect of fiction*; 20.18 *be an architect*; 20.3 *building*; 356.8 *construction*; 406.1 *contents*; 32.4 *crystal*; 553.4 *design*; 406.8 *embody*; 99.1 *essence*; 160.1, 160.7 *form*; 405.13 *make*; 402.4 *matter*; 407.7 *method*; 407.1, 407.18 *order*; 356.10 *produce*; 356.1 *production*; 221.1 *state*; 404.1 *texture*
structured 20.17; 409.20 *arranged*; 406.10 *containing*; 407.10 *ordered*
structuring 403.5; 409.1 *arrangement*; 409.3 *organization*
struggle 249.1 *adversity*; 751.6 *argue*; 751.2 *argument*; 353.5 *attempt*; 264.3 *difficult task*; 576.4 *exertion*; 576.8 *exert oneself*; 264.19 *have difficulty*; 327.25 *pitch*; 353.2 *try hard*; 354.2 *undertaking*
struggler 353.7 *attempter*; 586.1 *combatant*
struggle up 304.14 *climb*
struggle with 264.18 *find difficult*
struggling 380.6 *violent*
struggling for breath 582.18 *dying*
strum 18.38 *sound*
strumpet 796.9 *immoral woman*; 593.9 *lover*; 568.7 *prostitute*
strung out 148.1 *long*; 206.6 *sparse*
strut 622.22 *be ostentatious*; 23.17 *carpenter*; 23.10 *carpenter's term*; 300.12 *gait*; 373.4 *means of connection*; 673.16 *show off*; 38.27 *superstructure*; 413.2 *supporting part*; 300.15 *walk*
struthioniform 72.21 *avian*
struthious 72.21 *avian*
strutting 622.22 *boastful*; 23.10 *carpenter's term*; 622.17 *conceited*
strychnine 33.19 *alkaloid*
stub 769.3 *acknowledgment of payment*; 426.1 *blunt*; 253.2 *promise*; 788.1 *receipt*; 744.1 *record*; 215.1 *remainder*; 496.7 *tobacco*
stubbily 426.11 *smoothly*
stubbiness 426.5 *bluntness*; 149.1 *shortness*
stubble 81.4 *cereal grass*; 43.11 *farmland*; 238.6 *refuse*; 215.2 *residue*; 420.7 *rough thing*
stubbled 420.3 *barbed*
stubbly 420.3 *barbed*
stubborn 225.8 *conservative*; 452.2 *convinced*; 661.7 *defiant*; 228.11 *determined*; 662.13 *disobedient*; 418.4 *mentally hard*; 423.5 *mentally tough*; 383.11, 641.1 *obstinate*; 640.10 *persevering*; 647.8 *severe*; 638.3 *strong-willed*; 267.10 *tenacious*; 264.14 *troublesome*; 113.26 *uncooperative*; 635.8 *wilful*
stubborn as a mule 641.1 *obstinate*
stubbornly 225.10 *conservatively*; 661.9 *defiantly*; 228.13 *determinedly*; 662.17 *disobediently*; 418.13 *inflexibly*; 641.9 *obstinately*; 113.27 *opposingly*; 264.29 *perversely*; 647.11 *severely*; 423.14 *single-mindedly*; 267.12 *tenaciously*; 452.24 *with certainty*
stubbornness 225.2 *conservatism*; 113.7 *contrariness*; 452.10 *conviction*; 228.2 *determination*; 662.1 *disobedience*; 809.1 *impenitence*; 418.8 *mental hardness*; 423.9 *mental toughness*; 383.2, 641.5 *obstinacy*; 640.1 *perseverance*; 647.1 *severity*; 267.2, 638.14 *tenacity*; 635.3 *wilfulness*
stubborn persistence 641.6 *determination*

stubby 426.1 *blunt;* 149.7 *short*
stucco 20.19 *decorate;* 550.28 *face;* 19.14 *sculptor's materials;* 550.8 *wall covering*
stuck 373.15 *connected;* 423.3 *hard;* 308.14 *holed;* 301.4 *motionless;* 264.16 *troubled*
stuck fast 228.9 *stable*
stuck firm 360.10 *retained*
stuck-in-a-groove 112.12 *repetitious*
stuck on 593.18 *in love*
stuck on oneself 683.5 *egoistic;* 673.10 *self-admiring*
stuck-out tongue 742.3 *gesture*
stuck-up 673.13 *boastful;* 622.17 *conceited;* 673.8 *vain*
stud 59.13 *breeding;* 363.6 *charmer;* 373.8 *fastening;* 59.1 *horse;* 542.7 *jewellery;* 567.7 *libertine;* 420.12 *make rough;* 567.16 *male animal;* 377.18 *sprinkle;* 541.11 *variegate*
studbook 59.13 *breeding*
studded 420.2 *coarse;* 541.10 *mottled;* 377.23 *sprinkled*
studding 377.4 *sprinkling*
student 130.14 *beginner;* 6.7 *learner;* 550.22 *progression;* 705.9 *questioner;* 387.3 *subordinate;* 443.7 *thinker;* 486.10 *unskilled person*
student council 713.4 *adviser*
student days 555.1 *youth*
student loan 771.2 *loan*
student number 743.3 *means of identification*
student nurse 35.16 *nurse*
student of literature 17.15 *literary person*
students 137.6
student teacher 6.4 *educator*
stud groom 59.15 *horse person*
studhorse 59.1 *horse;* 567.16 *male animal*
studied 26.15, 106.4 *deliberate;* 482.12 *intended;* 705.16 *questioned*
studier of mankind 566.6
studies of life 554.7
studio 19.11 *artist's materials;* 565.5 *house;* 448.6 *place of experimentation;* 565.7 *room;* 577.1 *workshop*
studio couch 23.2 *chair*
studio flash 41.15 *lighting*
studio lighting 41.15 *lighting*
studio photograph 41.4 *portrait*
studious 471.8 *diligent;* 6.18 *educated;* 342.20 *industrious;* 550.41 *progressing;* 4.17 *thoughtful*
studiously 6.26; 471.15 *attentively;* 4.28 *thoughtfully*
studiousness 342.8 *assiduity;* 471.4 *diligence;* 6.9 *learnedness*
studs 23.10 *carpenter's term*
studwork 23.10 *carpenter's term*
study 76.7; 631.14 *behave towards;* 443.13 *concentrate;* 722.1 *dissertation;* 19.9 *drawing;* 482.3 *future intention;* 244.2 *get better;* 455.13 *get to know;* 518.14 *inspect;* 6.23 *learn;* 6.8 *learning;* 27.1 *mathematics;* 17.4 *nonfiction;* 518.3 *observation;* 4.4 *philosophical investigation;* 4.20 *philosophize;* 243.10 *preparations;* 243.8 *prepare oneself;* 736.6 *privacy;* 550.35 *progress;* 705.17 *question;* 705.2 *questioning;* 447.11 *raise the point;* 565.7 *room;* 471.12 *scrutinize;* 655.5 *solitary place;* 139.27 *specialize;* 19.6 *work of art;* 577.1 *workshop*
studying 4.17 *thoughtful*
study of algae 84.2 *algae*
study of conduct 631.1 *conduct*
study of ferns 82.2 *fern plant*
study of fish 74.6
study of fungi 83.8
study of lichens 84.6 *lichen*
study of mammals 71.1 *mammal*
study of mankind 566.5
study of mosses 82.4 *moss plant*
study of names 721.7 *nomenclature*
study of place names 721.7 *nomenclature*
study of primates 71.16 *primate*
study on a scholarship 765.14 *profit*
study plants 77.23
study the Bible 7.22 *theologize*
study theology 7.22 *theologize*
study up on 6.23 *learn*
stuff 406.7; 219.4 *be excessive;* 688.5 *be greedy;* 406.1 *contents;* 25.55 *cook;* 99.1 *essence;* 232.6 *fill;* 190.5 *make bigger;* 435.1 *materials;* 402.4 *matter;* 763.4 *possession;* 440.4 *possessions;* 359.5 *preserve;* 238.6 *refuse;* 336.8 *strengthen;* 404.5 *textile*
stuff and nonsense 697.1 *nonsense*
stuffed 190.7 *bigger;* 25.56 *culinary;* 557.26 *eating;* 219.6 *excessive;* 211.9 *extra;* 217.3 *filled;* 232.8 *full;* 688.6 *gluttonous;* 406.11 *loaded;* 359.7 *preserved;* 309.13 *stopped*
stuffed animal 359.3 *preserved thing*
stuffed Idaho potato 25.43 *US dish*
stuffed marrow 25.34 *vegetarian dish*
stuffed shirt 673.7 *vain person*
stuffed up 309.13 *stopped*
stuffed vine leaves 25.52 *Greek dish*
stuffily 620.8 *boringly*
stuff in 368.3 *impact*
stuffiness 620.1 *boredom;* 656.1 *formality;* 493.1 *heat*
stuffing 406.4; 211.3 *additional item;* 190.4 *enlarger;* 688.6 *gluttonous;* 190.1 *growth;* 309.2 *stopper;* 368.11 *thing inserted*
stuffing oneself 557.2 *appetite*
stuff oneself 688.5 *be greedy;* 557.22 *eat well;* 217.4 *suffice*
stuffy 620.4 *boring;* 416.7 *condensed;* 117.14 *conformist;* 493.9 *hot*
stumble 486.7 *be clumsy;* 804.16 *be wicked;* 305.4 *fall;* 465.10 *misjudge;* 327.25 *pitch;* 327.11 *stagger;* 305.11 *trip*
stumble on 449.1 *discover*
stumble upon 107.11 *chance upon;* 312.2 *reach*
stumbling 486.3 *clumsy;* 305.4 *fall;* 305.18 *falling*
stumbling block 378.2 *obstacle;* 251.1 *restraint;* 379.1 *trap*
stump 457.10 *bemuse;* 696.7 *be unintelligible;* 205.6 *branch;* 264.23 *cause difficulties;* 705.21 *confuse;* 53.19 *dismiss;* 453.20 *make uncertain;* 737.13 *mystify;* 215.1 *remainder;* 79.2 *tree part;* 53.5 *wicket*
stump along 333.1 *move slowly*
stumped 696.6 *confused;* 264.16 *troubled*
stumper 705.4 *difficult question;* 53.4 *team*
stumpie 53.4 *team*
stumpiness 155.1 *lowness;* 149.1 *shortness*
stumping 53.11 *dismissal;* 469.12 *election*
stump orator 733.6 *public speaker*
stump oratory 729.9 *art of public speaking*
stump up 785.6 *pay*
stumpy 155.5 *low;* 149.7 *short*
stun 630.11 *amaze;* 489.12 *anaesthetize;* 507.8 *be loud;* 457.10 *bemuse;* 619.10 *be wonderful;* 505.9 *deafen;* 52.11 *fight*
stun and stab 65.2 *billiards play*
stung 624.15 *resentful*
stunned 630.7 *amazed;* 505.4 *deaf;* 489.8 *unconscious*
stunned into silence 630.7 *amazed*
stunner 619.5 *person of wonder*
stunning 519.11 *blinding;* 235.1 *worthy*
stunt 340.4 *act;* 485.11 *be expert;* 340.2 *deed;* 46.10 *defence;* 484.3 *expedient plan;* 191.5 *make smaller;* 485.3 *masterpiece;* 46.16 *play defence;* 149.10 *shorten;* 68.12 *ski*
stunted 159.7 *little;* 155.5 *low;* 149.7 *short;* 191.7 *smaller;* 218.3 *underfed*
stuntedness 159.1 *littleness;* 155.1 *lowness;* 149.1 *shortness*
stunting 191.8 *contracting*
stunt man 398.5 *alternative;* 21.31 *circus performer;* 115.5 *counterpart;* 613.7 *courageous person;* 340.3 *doer;* 762.2 *substitute person;* 550.21 *substitution*
stunt-skiing 68.1 *skiing*
stupa 10.13 *shrine*
stupefaction 630.2 *amazement;* 592.4 *desensitization;* 619.1 *wonder*
stupefied 630.7 *amazed;* 690.3 *dead drunk;* 592.2 *desensitized;* 619.6 *wondering*
stupefy 630.11 *amaze;* 489.12 *anaesthetize;* 690.9 *be intoxicating;* 619.10 *be wonderful;* 592.7 *render insensitive*
stupendous 158.15 *big;* 619.8 *wonderful*
stupendously 619.13 *wonderfully*
stupid 524.8; 459.5 *foolish;* 456.6 *ignorant;* 152.3 *thick-witted;* 457.6, 528.5 *unintelligent;* 486.1 *unskilful*
Stupidity 457
stupidity 524.4; **528.9**; 459.1 *folly;* 456.1 *ignorance;* 457.2 *unintelligence*
stupidly 459.8 *foolishly;* 456.12 *ignorantly;* 528.13 *opaquely;* 457.11 *unintelligently*
stupid question 705.5 *easy question*
stupid with fatigue 261.1 *fatigued*
stupor 36.13 *depression;* 592.4 *desensitization;* 463.1 *oblivion;* 343.9 *sleep;* 36.14 *trance;* 489.2 *unconsciousness;* 619.1 *wonder*
sturdily 336.14 *strongly;* 423.12 *toughly*
sturdiness 423.6 *toughness*
sturdy 259.1 *healthy;* 336.9 *physically strong;* 152.1 *thick;* 423.1 *tough*
Sturm und Drang 21.9 *dramaturgy;* 21.10 *theatre movements*
stutter 486.7 *be clumsy;* 690.7 *be drunk;* 730.14 *have difficulty speaking;* 732.7 *keep quiet;* 729.3 *mode of speech;* 730.3 *speech defect*
stutterer 674.7 *modest person*
stuttering 624.16 *angry;* 486.3 *clumsy;* 690.10 *drunkenness;* 732.4 *guarded speech;* 730.12 *inarticulate;* 730.3 *speech defect;* 696.11 *unintelligibility*
St. Valentine's Day 298.6 *annually celebrated day*
sty 71.20 *abode of mammals;* 43.7 *farm building;* 565.12 *stall*
Stygian 523.8 *dark*
Stygian darkness 582.14 *the spiritual world*
Stygian gloom 523.1 *darkness*
Stygian shore 582.14 *the spiritual world*
Style 724
style 724.1; **724.9**; 409.2 *array;* 631.1 *conduct;* 117.5 *convention;* 115.2 *copy;* 553.4 *design;* 137.9 *distinction;* 543.1, 549.1 *elegance;* 19.15 *engraving;* 525.3 *external appearance;* 553.1, 553.9 *fashion;* 78.3 *flower part;* 160.5 *formality;* 547.8 *haircut;* 551.35 *make clothing;* 694.1 *meaning;* 561.8 *organs of reproduction;* 729.2 *power of speech;* 622.4 *prestige;* 485.1 *skill;* 221.1 *state;* 733.11 *title;* 137.4 *type;* 317.1 *way*
styled 551.31; **724.6**; 160.9 *formed*
style of cooking 25.1 *cookery*
stylet 587.8 *sharp weapon*
styling gel 268.7 *pomade*
styling mousse 268.7 *pomade*
stylish 724.7; 551.30, 656.7 *dressed-up;* 543.3 *elegant;* 553.7 *fashionable;* 160.11 *formal;* 160.9 *formed;* 221.8 *in a state of;* 622.18 *prestigious;* 551.31 *styled;* 485.9 *well-made*
stylishly 221.9 *conditionally;* 160.14 *conventionally;* 551.36 *dressily;* 543.5 *elegantly;* 553.10 *fashionably;* 160.13 *formatively;* 485.12 *skilfully;* 724.10 *stylistically*
stylishness 724.2; 543.1 *elegance;* 553.2 *fashionableness*
stylish writer 543.2, 724.5 *stylist*
stylist 543.2; **724.5**; 542.9 *phrasemonger*
stylistically 724.10
stylistics 5.1 *linguistics*
stylite 118.9 *hermit;* 197.8 *loner;* 7.7 *monk*
stylization 656.1 *formality*
stylize 656.9 *formalize*
stylized 19.26 *artistic;* 656.6 *formal;* 160.9 *formed*
stylobate 20.8 *column*
stylus 425.8 *sharp-pointed thing*
stymie 378.8 *hinder*
styptic 191.8 *contracting;* 191.4 *contractor;* 416.6 *dense*
Styrofoam™ cup 558.10 *drink container*
Styx 90.5 *other major rivers;* 582.14 *the spiritual world*
suable 16.54 *litigated*
suan pan 210.5 *computer*
suave 543.3 *elegant;* 658.8 *good-mannered;* 6.20 *refined;* 421.6 *smooth-mannered*
suavely 421.16; 6.27 *discerningly;* 543.5 *elegantly;* 658.15 *genteelly*
suaveness 658.1 *courtesy;* 543.1 *elegance*
suavity 658.1 *courtesy;* 543.1 *elegance;* 6.11 *refinement*
sub 398.5 *alternative;* 49.2 *basketball player;* 46.2 *football player;* 740.15 *publish;* 741.13 *report;* 762.2 *substitute person*
subabdominal 155.6 *lower*
subacid 499.5 *acid*
subacidity 499.1 *sourness*
subalpine 155.7 *lowland;* 89.7, 154.13 *mountainous*
subaltern 122.6 *inferior;* 4.8 *philosophical term;* 401.1 *servant;* 289.7 *subordinate*
subaqua 91.7 *oceanic;* 67.11 *swimming;* 156.12 *under*
subaqua swimmer 67.4 *swimmer*
subaqua swimming 67.1 *swimming*
subaquatic 91.7 *oceanic;* 156.12 *under*
subaqueous 91.7 *oceanic;* 156.12 *under*
subatomic 159.7 *little*
subatomically 159.9 *microscopically*
subatomic particle 28.77 *elementary particle;* 159.2 *little thing*
subaudition 719.1 *interpretation*
subauricular 155.6 *lower*
subaxillary 155.6 *lower*
subbase 155.4 *low thing*
subbasement 565.7 *room*
subbed copy 741.10 *copy*
sub-bottom profiling 30.17 *ocean research vessel*
subbranch 205.6 *branch;* 137.3 *kingdom*
subcartilaginous 155.6 *lower*
subcategory 409.6 *category;* 137.2 *class;* 205.1 *part*
subclass 409.6 *category;* 137.2 *class;* 137.3 *kingdom;* 205.1 *part;* 34.17 *taxonomy*
subclavian 155.6 *lower*
subconscious 36.37; 445.4 *instinct;* 101.11 *internal;* 101.6 *internal world;* 36.21 *psyche;* 11.16 *psychic*
subconsciously 11.25 *occultly;* 36.39 *psychologically*
subconscious self 139.11 *identity*
subcontinent 30.6, 92.1 *continent*
subcontinental 92.11 *continental*
subcontinentally 92.13 *continentally*
subcontrary 113.23 *opposite*
subcortex 172.1 *interior;* 155.4 *low thing*
subcortical 172.7 *interior;* 155.6 *lower*
subcranial 155.6 *lower*
subcutaneous 172.7 *interior;* 155.6 *lower*
subcutaneous injection 37.12 *injection*
subdivide 27.91 *add;* 770.4 *allot;* 196.8, 372.11 *divide;* 406.9 *itemize;* 205.10 *part;* 137.14 *sort*
subdivided 406.12 *itemized;* 372.15 *separate*
subdivision 770.1 *allocation;* 409.6 *category;* 137.2 *class;* 196.2 *fractional part;* 205.1 *part;* 405.2 *piece;* 372.3 *separateness;* 34.17 *taxonomy*
subdivisional 196.5 *fractional*
subdivisions 406.5 *divisions*
subdominant 18.16 *musical note*
subdorsal 155.6 *lower*
subdual 251.1 *restraint*
subduction zone 30.19 *plate tectonics*
subdue 395.10 *be a prevailing influence;* 246.9 *be victorious;* 586.38 *conquer;* 419.14 *ease;* 400.14 *master;* 685.4 *moderate;* 511.7 *mute;* 749.4 *pacify;* 251.8 *restrain;* 506.2 *silence;* 387.6 *subject;* 773.7 *take*
subdued 511.1 *faint-sounding;* 685.6 *moderate;* 728.15 *reserved;* 388.5 *submitting*
subduedness 728.5 *reserve*
subdue oneself 388.3 *submit*
subduer 246.5 *victorious person*
subduing 773.1 *taking*
subedit 740.15 *publish;* 244.3 *rectify;* 741.13 *report*
subediting 244.6 *rectification*
subeditor 741.4 *journalist;* 740.11 *newspaperman;* 393.12 *repairer;* 244.13 *reviser*
subfamily 137.3 *kingdom;* 205.1 *part;* 34.17 *taxonomy*
subfloor 155.4 *low thing*
subfusc 523.10 *dark-coloured;* 551.3, 656.4 *formal dress*
subgenus 137.3 *kingdom;* 205.1 *part*
subgiant 29.13 *luminosity*
subglottal 155.6 *lower*
subgrade 155.4 *low thing*
subgroup 409.6 *category;* 137.2 *class;* 205.1 *part*
subgun 587.11 *guns*
subhuman 70.14 *animalian;* 651.11 *cruel;* 566.12 *human*
subjacency 155.4 *low thing*
subjacent 155.6 *lower*
subject 6.3; **387.6**; **387.9**; 403.9 *artistic structure;* 19.11 *artist's materials;* 17.3 *aspect of fiction;* 246.9 *be victorious;* 447.5 *educational topic;* 99.1 *essence;* 448.7 *experimentee;* 701.4 *gist;* 768.4 *giver;* 122.6 *inferior;* 18.13, 516.1 *melody;* 564.8 *national;*

5.35 *part of speech*; 401.9 *serving*; 139.8 *specialization*; 122.15 *subordinate*; 647.6 *suppress*; 773.7 *take*; 447.1 *topic*; 344.6 *undertaking*; 335.11 *unprotected*
subject and predicate 5.23 *phrase*
subjected 387.9 *subject*; 647.9 *suppressed*
subjected person 387.5
subject-group 137.6 *students*
subjecting 387.9 *subject*
Subjection 387
subjection 387.1; 12.3 *governance*; 236.11 *harmfulness*; 381.14 *siege*; 647.2 *suppression*; 773.1 *taking*
subjective 139.18; 447.7 *focused*; 5.44 *grammatical*; 96.9 *illusory*; 477.12 *imaginary*; 101.11 *internal*; 465.8 *unjust*
subjective existence 96.1 *unreality*
subjectively 101.14; 5.52 *grammatically*; 465.14 *unjustly*
subjective probability 104.5 *probability theory*
subjectivism 477.6 *reverie*; 4.7 *school of thought*
subjectivist 4.11 *follower of a doctrine*
subjectivistic 4.14 *of a philosophy*
subjectivity 274.6 *fallibility*; 101.6 *internal world*; 96.1 *unreality*
subject matter 406.5 *divisions*; 99.2 *essential content*; 694.1 *meaning*; 447.1 *topic*
subject of investigation 447.4 *sphere*
subject to 345.10 *caused*
subject to jurisdiction 16.48 *jurisdictional*
subject to terms 746.8 *negotiated*
subjoin 211.6 *add*
subjoined 211.8 *additional*
sub judice 16.87 *in litigation*; 464.10 *judged*; 16.54 *litigated*
subjugate 395.10 *be a prevailing influence*; 396.19 *be authoritarian*; 246.9 *be victorious*; 400.14 *master*; 387.6 *subject*; 647.6 *suppress*; 773.7 *take*
subjugated 387.9 *subject*; 647.9 *suppressed*
subjugation 247.2 *defeat*; 387.1 *subjection*; 647.2 *suppression*; 773.1 *taking*
subjugator 246.5 *victorious person*
subjunctive 5.33 *mood*
subjunctively 5.52 *grammatically*
subkingdom 137.3 *kingdom*; 34.17 *taxonomy*
sublease 763.1 *possession*
subletly 549.2
sublevation 366.6 *raising*
sub-lieutenant 586.27 *naval man*
sublimate 8.17 *deify*; 369.8 *extract*; 432.25 *gasify*; 244.1 *improve*; 366.3 *promote*; 255.10, 256.15 *purify*
sublimated 31.43 *atmospheric*; 795.9 *pure*
sublimation 31.9 *atmospheric process*; 36.19 *defence mechanism*; 244.5 *improvement*; 369.7 *obtaining an extract*; 32.3 *phase*; 28.37 *temperature*; 432.10 *vaporization*
sublimation point 28.37 *temperature*
sublime 8.13 *divine*; 154.11, 366.12 *exalted*; 432.25 *gasify*; 415.2 *insubstantial*; 230.1 *perfect*; 241.1 *pleasant*; 726.5 *serious*; 473.5 *unselfish*
sublimely 8.19 *divinely*; 154.19 *high*; 366.13 *highly*; 415.11 *lightly*; 473.9 *unselfishly*
subliminal 521.2 *difficult to see*; 36.21 *psyche*; 36.37 *subconscious*
subliminally 36.39 *psychologically*
subliminal self 139.11 *identity*; 36.21 *psyche*
sublimity 8.1 *divinity*; 154.1, 366.8 *height*; 726.2 *seriousness*; 121.1 *superiority*; 473.2 *unselfishness*
sublittoral 91.7 *oceanic*
submachine gun 587.11 *guns*
submarine 156.4 *deep thing*; 305.8 *descender*; 587.5 *missile weapon*; 30.51, 91.7 *oceanic*; 156.12 *under*; 586.24 *warship*
submarine canyon 30.16 *ocean floor*
submarine chaser 586.24 *warship*
submarine division 584.4 *military organization*
submariner 156.5; 309.6 *closed-in person*; 305.8 *descender*; 586.27 *naval man*
submarine tender 586.24 *warship*
submarine warfare 585.8 *warfare*
submediant 18.16 *musical note*
submental 155.6 *lower*
submerge 367.3 *bring down*; 156.14 *deepen*; 305.9 *descend*; 357.8 *destroy*; 90.7 *flow*; 368.4 *immerse*; 358.1 *obliterate*; 433.29 *water*
submerged 92.11 *continental*; 367.19 *fallen*; 433.24 *flooded*; 368.14 *immersed*; 521.1 *invisible*; 155.7 *lowland*; 156.12 *under*
submerged coast 92.4 *coast*
submerged log 323.5 *navigation*
submergence 367.13; 368.10 *immersion*; 305.2 *sinkage*
submerse 433.29 *water*
submersed 433.24 *flooded*; 368.14 *immersed*
submersible 156.4 *deep thing*; 305.16 *descending*; 30.17 *ocean research vessel*
submersion 156.1 *depth*; 368.10 *immersion*; 90.6 *river flow*; 433.9 *soaking*
subminiature 159.7 *little*
Submission 388
submission 388.1; 713.1 *advice*; 810.3 *allegiance*; 639.14 *apathy*; 117.2 *compliance*; 247.2 *defeat*; 663.1 *obedience*; 664.1 *servility*; 707.2 *statement*; 476.1 *supposition*; 752.2 *tentative offer*
submissive 623.5; 117.13 *compliant*; 265.13 *easy-going*; 810.9 *loyal*; 663.7 *obedient*; 589.7 *peaceful*; 664.6 *servile*; 667.9 *showing respect*; 388.5 *submitting*
submissively 117.16 *adaptably*; 663.10 *obediently*; 419.18 *soft-heartedly*; 623.28 *subserviently*; 664.16 *with servility*
submissiveness 623.12; 639.14 *apathy*; 663.1 *obedience*; 664.1 *servility*; 388.1 *submission*
submit 388.3; **623.20**; 713.5 *advise*; 707.17 *affirm*; 483.8 *be motivated*; 480.18 *be persuaded*; 117.8 *comply*; 663.5 *obey*; 752.9 *offer*; 476.6 *propound*; 388.4 *succumb*; 355.2 *withdraw*; 419.16 *yield*; 122.9 *yield to*
submit a report 721.15 *recount*
submitted 707.11 *stated*
submitted for judgment 464.10 *judged*; 16.54 *litigated*
submitter 707.9 *affirmer*
submitting 388.5; 663.7 *obedient*; 589.7 *peaceful*; 623.4 *self-abasing*; 667.9 *showing respect*; 388.1 *submission*
submit to 413.12 *bear*
submit to a whim 642.5 *be capricious*
submit to judgment 16.72 *stand trial*
submontane 155.7 *lowland*
submucosa 155.4 *low thing*
submultiple 27.17 *multiplication*
subnormal 457.7 *intellectually subnormal*; 122.14 *poor*
subnormality 461.2
subnormally 122.21 *badly*
suboceanic 30.51 *oceanic*; 156.12 *under*
suborbital 155.6 *lower*
suborder 409.6 *category*; 137.3 *kingdom*; 34.17 *taxonomy*
subordinacy 387.1 *subjection*
subordinate 122.15; **289.7**; **289.13**; **387.3**; 392.11 *helper*; 122.6 *inferior*; 348.6 *instrumental*; 124.10 *nonentity*; 401.1 *servant*; 387.6, 387.9 *subject*
subordinate clause 205.2 *particular*
subordinate judge 16.23 *judge*
subordinately 122.22 *basely*
subordinate position 122.1 *inferiority*; 387.1 *subjection*
subordinate role 387.1 *subjection*
subordinating 5.44 *grammatical*
subordinating conjunction 5.35 *part of speech*
subordination 289.3; 117.2 *compliance*; 122.1 *inferiority*; 348.1 *instrumentality*; 155.1 *lowness*; 407.4 *position*; 387.1 *subjection*
suborn 480.17 *bribe*; 777.4 *buy off*
subornment 777.10 *bribery*
subpanation 10.6 *Eucharist*
subperiod 30.41 *geological time*
subphylum 137.3 *kingdom*; 34.17 *taxonomy*
sub-plane 50.18 *windsurf*
sub-planing 50.13 *windsurfing*
subplot 17.3 *aspect of fiction*; 21.9 *dramaturgy*; 701.4 *gist*; 721.3 *narration*
subpoena 397.2, 397.10 *demand*; 16.6 *legal process*
subpolar zone 31.39 *climatic zone*
sub rosa 737.15 *in secret*
subscapular 155.6 *lower*
subscribe 679.11 *give*; 743.11 *identify oneself*; 752.16 *make an offering*; 785.6 *pay*
subscriber 679.9 *generous person*; 768.4 *giver*; 692.13 *telephoner*
subscriber line 692.12 *public telephone system*
subscriber trunk dialling 692.11 *dialling*
subscribe to 392.23 *advise*; 755.5 *contract*; 768.5 *give*; 4.22 *propound a philosophy*
subscript 155.6 *lower*; 155.4 *low thing*
subscription 790.3 *fee*; 679.7 *gift*; 768.1 *giving*; 785.4 *grant*; 752.6, 768.3 *offering*; 785.1 *payment*
subscription list 693.4 *mass communication*
subsection 137.2 *class*; 205.2 *particular*
subsequence 289.1 *succession*
subsequent 345.10 *caused*; 289.12 *succeeding*
subsequently 345.12 *with the effect of*
subserve 237.9 *be useful*; 392.28 *further*
subservience 122.1 *inferiority*; 348.1 *instrumentality*; 663.1 *obedience*; 664.1 *servility*; 387.1 *subjection*; 388.1 *submission*; 623.12 *submissiveness*
subservient 237.3, 348.6 *instrumental*; 663.7 *obedient*; 664.6 *servile*; 387.9 *subject*; 623.5 *submissive*; 388.5 *submitting*; 122.15 *subordinate*; 392.31 *supplementary*; 349.9 *used*
subserviently 623.28; 122.22 *basely*; 348.9 *instrumentally*; 663.10 *obediently*; 387.11 *under subjection*; 664.16 *with servility*
subset 137.2 *class*; 27.21 *set*
subshell 28.65 *atom*
subside 300.13 *be in motion*; 301.8 *be motionless*; 214.4 *decrease*; 305.9 *descend*; 30.64 *fold*
subsidence 214.1 *decrease*; 305.3 *downflow*; 30.20 *earth movement*; 305.2 *sinkage*
subsidiarity 377.6 *decentralization*
subsidiary 211.8 *additional*; 122.6 *inferior*; 237.3 *instrumental*; 124.3 *secondary*; 122.15 *subordinate*; 392.31 *supplementary*; 413.9 *supportive*
subsidiary office 577.1 *workshop*
subsiding 214.6 *decreasing*; 305.16 *descending*; 300.17 *directional*
subsiding motion 300.6 *descending motion*
subsidization 768.1 *giving*; 392.9 *patronage*
subsidize 392.29 *finance*; 352.6 *find means*; 768.5 *give*; 813.10 *grant*; 413.13 *support financially*
subsidized 768.7 *given*
subsidy 43.2 *Common Agricultural Policy*; 13.6 *economic factors*; 392.6 *financial assistance*; 352.4 *financial resources*; 413.7 *financial support*; 768.2 *gift*; 785.4, 813.3 *grant*; 765.5 *profit*; 436.1 *provision*
subsist 215.7 *be left*; 225.5 *be permanent*; 557.21 *eat*; 93.17 *exist*; 554.16 *live*
subsistence 93.1 *existence*; 413.7 *financial support*; 554.1 *life*; 554.3 *life requirements*; 225.1 *permanence*; 392.3 *sustenance*
subsistence farming 43.1 *agriculture*; 217.7 *sufficiency*
subsistence level 218.8 *insufficiency*; 135.3 *needfulness*; 782.5 *poverty*
subsistent 93.10 *existing*
subsisting 225.7 *permanent*
subsoil 172.1 *interior*; 155.4 *low thing*; 30.36 *soil*
subsoiler 43.10 *farm tool*
subsonic 28.98 *physical*
subsonically 28.100 *physically*
subsonic speed 28.19 *sound propagation*
subspecies 137.3 *kingdom*; 205.1 *part*; 34.17 *taxonomy*
subspecific 34.28 *taxonomic*
substance 123.3 *chief thing*; 406.1 *contents*; 99.1 *essence*; 403.2 *fabric*; 352.4 *financial resources*; 160.1 *form*; 123.1 *importance*; 435.1 *materials*; 402.4 *matter*; 694.1 *meaning*; 440.5 *personal estate*; 203.1 *quantity*; 95.1, 698.2 *reality*; 694.2 *significance*; 781.8 *solvency*; 93.2 *thing*
substandard 236.2 *inferior*; 337.13 *insufficient*; 5.39 *of language*; 122.14 *poor*; 606.5 *unsatisfactory*
substandard housing 782.7 *beggary*
substandard language 5.5 *nonstandard language*
substandard usage 5.5 *nonstandard language*
substantial 698.19 *authentic*; 158.15 *big*; 406.10 *containing*; 698.16 *existing*; 93.11 *intrinsic*; 797.7 *large*; 402.7 *material*; 95.6 *real*; 694.7 *significant*; 336.13 *strengthened*; 152.1 *thick*; 492.8 *touchable*; 454.9 *verificatory*
substantial capital 781.5 *wealth*
substantiality 698.7 *confirmation*; 123.1 *importance*; 797.14 *largeness*; 402.1 *material world*; 93.3 *nature*; 95.1, 698.2 *reality*
substantialize 402.8 *be material*
substantially 99.13 *in essence*; 158.20 *largely*; 402.9 *materially*; 204.13 *on the whole*; 492.14 *palpably*; 406.13 *structurally*
substantial resources 781.5 *wealth*
substantiate 402.8 *be material*; 222.11 *circumstantiate*; 707.19 *confirm*; 95.12 *establish reality*; 448.11 *experiment*; 743.10 *identify*; 714.8 *justify*; 452.21 *make certain*; 454.2, 703.17 *prove*; 698.30 *prove true*
substantiated 743.12 *identified*; 698.20 *proved*; 703.13 *proven*; 707.13 *supported*
substantiation 698.7, 707.4 *confirmation*; 743.1 *identification*; 454.5, 703.4, 716.2 *proof*
substantive 5.44 *grammatical*; 93.11 *intrinsic*; 5.35 *part of speech*; 95.6 *real*
substantivity 95.1 *reality*
substation 39.33 *power distribution*
substitutable 224.14 *exchangeable*; 759.6 *in exchange*; 550.40 *substitutive*
substitute 762.7; 21.24 *actor*; 578.3 *agent*; 398.5 *alternative*; 48.2 *baseball player*; 49.2 *basketball player*; 767.9 *dispose of*; 371.26 *ejector*; 224.10, 759.5 *exchange*; 211.5 *extra person*; 46.2, 66.3 *football player*; 608.5 *helper*; 231.6 *imperfect item*; 27.92 *manipulate*; 352.1 *means*; 759.4 *person who exchanges*; 32.26 *react*; 144.16 *replace*; 144.10 *replaced*; 717.8 *representative*; 350.6 *stop using*; 387.9 *subject*; 387.3 *subordinate*; 550.21 *substitution*; 550.40 *substitutive*; 289.5 *successor*; 413.8 *supporter*; 413.9 *supportive*; 36.25 *surrogate*; 371.5 *take the place of*
substituted 762.8; 759.7 *exchanged*; 700.39 *imitative*
substitute for 608.11 *assist*; 550.34 *cover for*; 413.14 *give moral support*; 398.8 *represent*; 717.12 *stand for*
substitute person 762.2
substitute thing 762.3
Substitution 762
substitution 550.21; **762.1**; 32.14 *chemical reaction*; 36.19 *defence mechanism*; 767.1 *disposal*; 27.24 *evaluation*; 224.4, 759.1 *exchange*; 785.2 *repayment*; 144.3 *replacement*
substitutional 32.38 *reactive*; 762.7 *substitute*
substitutive 550.40; 759.6 *in exchange*; 762.7 *substitute*
substrate 32.15 *catalysis*; 33.11 *enzyme*
substrative 172.7 *interior*
substratosphere 434.3 *atmospheric layers*
substratum 175.1 *base*; 172.1 *interior*; 411.1 *layer*; 155.4 *low thing*
substructural 38.32, 403.11 *structural*
substructurally 403.18 *structurally*
substructure 38.28; 403.6 *construction*; 175.2 *foot*; 413.2 *supporting part*
subsume 127.6; 405.11 *consist of*; 406.8 *embody*
subsuming 406.10 *containing*
subsurface 30.50 *terrestrial*
subsurface water 30.9 *groundwater*
subtend 27.97 *align*; 113.15 *be opposite*
subterfuge 700.1 *deception*; 736.5 *evasion*; 700.9 *sleight of hand*; 702.2 *sophism*; 702.1 *sophistry*; 645.2 *stratagem*; 379.1 *trap*
subterranean 8.16 *devilish*; 30.50 *terrestrial*; 156.12 *under*
subterranean water 30.9 *groundwater*
subterraneity 156.1 *depth*
subterraneous 156.12 *under*
subterrestrial 156.12 *under*
subtitle 721.2 *brief description*
subtle 728.13; 273.5, 698.21 *accurate*; 645.4 *cunning*; 404.10 *delicate*
subtle body 11.7 *spirit*
subtleness 698.8 *accuracy*
subtlety 728.3; 273.1, 698.8 *accuracy*; 442.4 *cleverness*; 645.1 *cunning*; 702.4 *quibbling*
subtle word 693.7 *advice*
subtly 702.14 *sophistically*; 404.15 *textually*

subtonic 18.16 *musical note*
subtopia 87.8 *suburb*
subtopian 87.14 *urban*
subtract 212.3; 27.91, 210.9 *add*; 791.3 *discount*; 766.9 *lose*; 720.1 *misinterpret*; 203.8 *quantify*; 372.10 *set apart*; 773.10 *take away*
subtracted 212.5; 98.12 *missing*
subtracted item 212.2
Subtraction 212
subtraction 27.16; **212.1**; 210.1 *calculation*; 203.2 *certain amount*; 214.1 *decrease*; 120.1 *inequality*; 766.1 *loss*; 720.2 *misinterpretation*; 773.3 *taking away*
subtractive 212.6
subtractive colour 529.4 *pigment*
subtractive process 28.28 *colour*
subtrahend 212.2 *subtracted item*; 27.16 *subtraction*
subtribe 34.17 *taxonomy*
subtropical 44.19 *ornamental*; 86.16 *regional*
subtropical climate 31.38 *climate*
subtropical dry zone 31.39 *climatic zone*
subtropically 86.19 *geographically*; 44.20 *horticulturally*
subtropical winter rainy zone 31.39 *climatic zone*
subtropics 31.39 *climatic zone*; 86.2 *geographical region*; 493.8 *hot place*
subungulate 71.14 *pachyderm*; 71.32 *pachydermatous*
suburb 87.8; 216.8 *middle classes*; 170.1 *surroundings*
suburban 620.4 *boring*; 565.15 *environmental*; 86.17 *national*; 564.12 *native*; 170.4 *surrounding*; 87.14 *urban*
suburban dweller 87.11 *urbanite*
suburbanite 216.8 *middle classes*; 564.4 *townsman*; 87.11 *urbanite*
suburbanites 574.2 *the common people*
suburbanization 87.1 *city*; 2.5 *society*
suburbanize 87.15 *urbanize*
suburbanized 87.14 *urban*
suburban whine 729.3 *mode of speech*
suburbia 216.8 *middle classes*; 86.11 *settlement*; 87.8 *suburb*
suburbs 86.11 *settlement*
subvariety 137.3 *kingdom*
subvene 392.28 *further*
subvention 392.6 *financial assistance*; 768.2 *gift*; 768.1 *giving*; 785.4, 813.3 *grant*; 436.1 *provision*
subventionary 768.7 *given*
subventionize 392.29 *finance*
subversion 662.3; 588.1 *anarchy*; 224.1 *change*; 357.1 *destruction*; 367.12 *downthrow*; 245.8 *perversion*; 704.1 *refutation*
subversive 662.14; 588.3 *anarchist*; 224.11 *changeable*; 357.14 *destructive*; 367.22 *overthrown*; 700.20 *plotter*; 662.10 *seditionist*
subversively 662.18; 224.15 *changeably*; 367.24 *down*
subversiveness 662.3 *subversion*
subvert 588.4 *be anarchic*; 662.16 *be subversive*; 367.3 *bring down*; 224.8 *cause change*; 357.9 *demolish*; 357.8 *destroy*; 245.6 *pervert*
subverted 367.22 *overthrown*
subway 156.4 *deep thing*; 317.10, 321.1 *railway*; 38.22, 317.8 *tunnel*
sub-zero temperature 494.2 *freezing*
succedaneum 762.3 *substitute thing*
succeed 289.10; 312.9 *achieve*; 608.11 *assist*; 762.4 *be a substitute*; 222.14 *be comfortable*; 132.13 *be consecutive*; 248.5 *be prosperous*; 298.7 *be regular*; 246.6 *be successful*; 204.10 *complete*; 134.3 *continue*; 797.21 *do well*; 289.11 *follow in office*; 244.2 *get better*; 253.13 *secure one's objective*; 246.12 *succeed to*; 396.20 *take authority*
succeed achieve one's aim 239.6 *be convenient*
succeeding 289.12; 132.9 *consecutive*; 246.13 *successful*
succeed to 246.12; 289.11 *follow in office*; 765.14 *profit*; 769.9 *receive*
succeed to the throne 12.12 *take authority*
succentor 7.8 *priest*
Success 246
success 246.1; 302.12 *advance*; 222.5 *comfortable circumstances*; 27.58 *frequency distribution*; 244.5 *improvement*; 248.1 *prosperity*; 248.4 *prosperous person*; 622.7 *satisfaction*; 246.4 *successful person*; 121.1 *superiority*; 495.2 *taste of life*; 21.13 *theatrical performance*
successful 246.13; 248.8 *prosperous*
successful attack 246.2 *victory*
successful battle 246.2 *victory*
successful defence 16.42 *acquittal*; 714.2 *defence*
successfully 246.16; 248.9 *prosperously*
successful person 246.4; 248.4 *prosperous person*
successful production 21.13 *theatrical performance*
successful prosecution 16.43 *conviction*
successful speculation 765.1 *gain*
successful thing 246.3
Succession 289
succession 289.1; 396.3 *acquisition of power*; 132.1 *consecutiveness*; 134.1 *continuity*; 34.18 *ecology*; 769.1 *receiving*
successional 396.13 *elected*; 289.12 *succeeding*
successive 132.9 *consecutive*; 289.12 *succeeding*
successively 132.18 *consecutively*; 289.14 *in succession*
successiveness 132.1 *consecutiveness*; 289.1 *succession*
successor 289.5; 769.6 *beneficiary*; 474.4 *expectant person*; 215.6 *person remaining*; 762.2 *substitute person*
successors 283.2 *future generation*
success story 246.1 *success*
succinct 269.3 *concise*; 149.7 *short*; 723.6 *summary*
succinctly 269.5 *concisely*; 149.12 *short*
succinctness 269.1 *conciseness*; 732.4 *guarded speech*; 149.1 *shortness*; 723.4 *summariness*
succintly 723.11 *summarily*
succotash 25.43 *US dish*
succour 608.2 *aid*; 413.14 *give moral support*; 413.6 *moral support*; 394.1, 394.19 *remedy*; 392.2, 392.19 *support*
succourer 652.3 *philanthropist*; 392.13 *supporter*
succouring 392.32 *supportive*
succubus 8.7 *devil*
succulence 431.7 *juiciness*
succulent 44.17 *botanical*; 557.27 *edible*; 431.15 *flowing*; 44.9 *garden plant*; 80.9 *of a fruit*; 77.14 *of plants*; 77.2 *plant*; 490.6 *pleasant*; 241.4, 495.7 *tasty*
succulent fruit 80.2 *botanical fruit*
succulently 25.57 *culinarily*; 557.29 *edibly*; 431.26 *fluidly*; 80.11 *fructiferously*; 77.24 *herbaceously*; 44.20 *horticulturally*; 429.17 *moistly*; 495.11 *tastily*
succumb 388.4; 690.7 *be drunk*; 261.5 *be fatigued*; 483.8 *be motivated*; 480.18 *be persuaded*; 582.15 *die*
succumbing 388.1 *submission*
succus entericus 559.2 *secreted substance*
succussatory 327.18 *shaky*; 326.17 *waving*
succussion 327.6 *shaking*
succussive 327.18 *shaky*; 326.17 *waving*
such a one 566.7 *person*
such being the case 221.9 *conditionally*
suchlike 115.1 *similarity*
suchness 99.4 *nature*
suck 369.14; 370.12 *draw in*; 558.13 *drink*; 557.21 *eat*; 370.4 *intake*; 664.3 *sycophant*
suck dry 441.1 *waste*
sucker 205.6 *branch*; 700.22 *dupe*; 267.5 *follower*; 459.3 *foolish person*; 44.5 *gardening*; 646.3 *naive person*; 77.5 *stem*; 450.6 *trusting person*; 555.5 *young plant*
suck in 370.12 *draw in*
sucking 369.4; 558.1 *drinking*; 370.4 *intake*
sucking out 369.4 *sucking*
suckle 370.12 *draw in*; 71.36 *lactate*; 43.18 *practise livestock farming*; 558.15 *provide drink*; 557.25 *provide food*
suckled 558.16 *drinking*
suckler beef 43.8 *livestock*
suckler cow 43.8 *livestock*
suck out 369.14 *suck*
suck up to 471.14 *be solicitous*; 677.10 *cajole*; 664.9 *fawn*; 599.15 *humour*; 569.14 *seek the friendship of*; 421.13 *smooth over*
sucrose 557.11 *food content*; 498.2 *sweetener*
suction 334.4 *energy*; 370.4 *intake*; 369.4 *sucking*
sudation 560.8 *sweat*
sudatorium 256.6 *bath*
sudatory 371.29 *expulsive*; 559.6 *inducing secretion*; 559.4 *secretory*; 560.28 *sweaty*
sudd 92.3 *marsh*
sudden 478.2 *spontaneous*; 630.8 *surprising*; 332.1 *swift*; 278.6 *transient*
sudden action 340.2 *deed*
sudden change 224.1 *change*
sudden death 49.1 *basketball*; 211.4 *extra*; 46.5 *game time*; 63.9 *squash terms*; 582.5 *ways of dying*
sudden-death victory 246.2 *victory*
suddenly 425.19; 508.10 *explosively*; 478.7 *extempore*; 149.12 *short*; 293.18 *soon*; 630.13 *surprisingly*; 332.14 *swiftly*; 278.8 *transiently*
sudden motion 327.9 *jolt*
suddenness 278.1 *transience*
sudden pain 254.6 *danger signal*
sudden progress 302.13 *step*
sudden pull 362.3 *jerk*
Sudden Sound 508
sudden thought 478.5 *spontaneity*
sudor 560.8 *sweat*
sudoral 559.5 *of a secretion*
sudoresis 560.8 *sweat*
sudoric 560.28 *sweaty*
sudorific 371.29 *expulsive*; 559.6 *inducing secretion*; 37.17 *stimulating*; 560.28 *sweaty*
suds 434.10 *air bubble*
sue 715.5 *accuse*; 593.26 *court*; 16.70 *litigate*
suede 550.14 *animal covering*
suede gloves 551.25 *accessories*
suedehead 547.8 *haircut*
sue for divorce 571.7 *divorce*
sue for peace 589.6, 749.5 *make peace*; 388.3 *submit*
suer claimant 16.8 *litigant*
suet 25.7 *basic ingredient*
suet crust pastry 25.37 *pastry*
suet pudding 25.35 *dessert*
suety 268.13 *slippery*
suffer 785.14 *atone*; 413.12 *bear*; 249.9 *be in trouble*; 260.24 *be unhealthy*; 491.9 *feel pain*; 624.8 *resent*; 388.4 *succumb*
sufferable 413.10 *supportable*
suffer a financial disaster 249.10 *need money*
suffer a sea change 760.8 *be transformed*
suffer a setback 766.10 *have a financial loss*
suffer boredom 620.7
suffer defeat 247.7 *be defeated*
sufferer 249.5 *person in adversity*; 769.5 *recipient*; 602.3 *sad person*; 260.19 *sick person*; 466.8 *victim of discrimination*
suffer execution 582.16 *meet one's fate*
suffer from anorexia 687.5 *fast*
suffer from inertia 341.4 *not act*
suffer from poor health 249.9 *be in trouble*
suffer humiliation 249.9 *be in trouble*
suffering 249.1 *adversity*; 798.2, 814.10 *affliction*; 491.7 *feeling pain*; 236.11 *harmfulness*; 491.1 *pain*; 602.1 *sorrow*
suffer in patience 388.4 *succumb*
suffer loss 766.9 *lose*; 441.1 *waste*
suffer misfortune 249.9 *be in trouble*
suffer pangs of jealousy 629.6 *be jealous*
suffer punishment 814.6 *be punished*
suffer purgatory 807.6 *apologize*
suffice 217.4; **609.10**; 216.9 *be average*; 136.14 *be qualified*; 237.9 *be useful*; 235.9 *be worthy*
Sufficiency 217
sufficiency 217.7; 97.4 *availability*; 232.1 *completeness*; 237.7 *instrumentality*; 219.2 *overdoing it*; 136.1 *qualification*; 27.64 *reasoning*; 609.3 *satisfactoriness*
sufficient 217.1; 97.10 *available*; 232.7 *complete*; 237.3 *instrumental*; 27.86 *logical*; 235.5 *not bad*; 436.7 *provisioning*; 609.6 *satisfactory*
sufficiently 217.9 *enough*
sufficient size 797.14 *largeness*
sufficient-size 797.7 *large*
sufficing 436.7 *provisioning*; 609.6 *satisfactory*; 217.1 *sufficient*
suffix 211.6 *add*; 211.3 *additional item*; 131.10 *ending*; 5.35 *part of speech*; 168.1 *rear*
suffixion 211.1 *addition*
suffocate 219.4 *be excessive*; 357.8 *destroy*; 382.17 *murder*; 335.8 *overpower*
suffocating 382.23 *deadly*; 493.9 *hot*
suffocation 357.1 *destruction*; 382.2 *murder*
suffragan 7.8 *priest*
suffrage 469.11 *franchise*; 10.9 *prayer*
suffragette 469.13 *electorate*; 568.11 *liberated woman*; 662.7, 753.4 *protester*; 244.12 *reformer*
suffragettism 469.11 *franchise*; 244.11 *reformism*
suffragism 244.11 *reformism*
suffragist 469.13 *electorate*; 662.7, 753.4 *protester*; 244.12 *reformer*
suffuse 97.11 *be present*; 232.6 *fill*; 412.8 *mix*
suffusing 97.7 *present*
suffusion 412.1 *mixture*
suffusive 97.7 *present*
Sufi 4.11 *follower of a doctrine*; 7.6 *non-Christian*
Sufic 4.14 *of a philosophy*
Sufism 4.7 *school of thought*
sugar 25.7 *basic ingredient*; 677.9 *blarney*; 33.3 *carbohydrate*; 780.2 *cash*; 557.11 *food content*; 593.12 *nicknames for lovers*; 498.8 *sweeten*; 498.2 *sweetener*
sugar acid 33.3 *carbohydrate*
sugar alcohol 33.3 *carbohydrate*
sugar beet 43.12 *crop*
sugar-beet pulp 43.9 *animal feedstuff*
Sugar Bowl 46.1 *football*
sugar bowl 410.16 *crockery*
sugar-coat 498.8 *sweeten*
sugar-coated 498.6 *sweet*
sugar daddy 567.4 *boyfriend*; 768.4 *giver*; 593.9 *lover*
sugar derivative 33.3 *carbohydrate*
sugared 498.6 *sweet*
sugar-free diet 557.6 *nutrition*
sugariness 498.1 *sweetness*
sugaring 547.9 *hair removal*
sugar loaf 498.2 *sweetener*
sugar lump 498.2 *sweetener*
sugar spoon 410.17 *ladle*
sugar test 33.5
sugar the pill 490.9 *give pleasure*; 483.9 *motivate*; 498.8 *sweeten*; 480.16 *tempt*
sugar tongs 360.3 *tools for gripping*
sugary 677.13 *honeyed*; 498.6 *sweet*
suggest 713.5 *advise*; 115.10 *be similar*; 395.8 *influence*; 716.10 *make evident*; 694.10 *mean*; 483.9 *motivate*; 752.9 *offer*; 484.9 *plan*; 475.11 *predict*; 476.6 *propound*; 710.6 *request*; 742.10 *signify*; 701.15 *state*; 446.17 *theorize*; 693.14 *tip*
suggested 476.8 *supposed*
suggester 480.14 *motivator*
suggestibility 483.6; 639.14 *apathy*; 480.7 *persuadability*; 591.5 *sensitivity*
suggestible 483.13; 591.1 *sensitive*; 639.4 *unsteady*
suggesting 693.16 *informative*; 742.14 *signifying*
suggestion 728.6; 693.7, 713.1 *advice*; 36.20 *conditioning*; 590.2 *impression*; 500.1 *odour*; 475.3, 484.1 *plan*; 710.1 *request*; 476.1 *supposition*; 752.2 *tentative offer*; 446.2 *theory*
suggestionism 36.3 *psychiatric treatment*
suggestion therapy 36.3 *psychiatric treatment*
suggest itself 446.14 *have an idea*
suggestive 395.12 *appealing*; 344.13 *causal*; 721.11 *descriptive*; 796.12 *indecent*; 694.6 *meaningful*; 483.11 *motivational*; 742.14 *signifying*; 476.7 *suppositional*; 446.10 *theoretical*
suggestively 344.14 *causally*; 796.21 *immorally*; 742.18 *indicatively*; 395.14, 483.14 *influentially*
suggestiveness 476.1 *supposition*
suicidal 602.6 *depressed*; 357.14 *destructive*; 611.4 *hopeless*; 382.24 *murderous*
suicidally 382.25 *lethally*
suicide 382.7; 10.7 *non-Christian ritual*; 814.11 *penance*; 582.5 *ways of dying*
suicide bombing 381.13 *air attack*
suicide pact 755.1 *contract*; 382.7 *suicide*
suicide squeeze 48.5 *batting terms*
suid 71.15 *hoofed mammal*
Suidae 71.15 *hoofed mammal*
sui generis 139.17 *exceptional*; 126.5 *novel*
suing 593.6 *courtship*; 16.53 *litigating*
suit 551.10; 715.1 *accusation*; 239.6 *be convenient*; 617.16 *be desirable*; 136.14 *be*

qualified; 706.22 *be the answer*; 117.7 *conform*; 593.6 *courtship*; 750.27 *fit*; 16.5 *litigation*; 111.3 *lookalike*; 566.7 *person*; 701.5 *plea*; 710.1 *request*; 733.2 *salutation*
suitability 239.3 *convenience*; 706.8 *correspondence*; 617.2 *desirability*; 136.1 *qualification*; 287.1 *timeliness*; 237.5 *usefulness*
suitable 119.9 *adequate*; 370.14 *admissive*; 222.9 *comfortable*; 239.1 *convenient*; 706.15 *correspondent*; 617.8 *desirable*; 750.16 *fitting*; 797.1 *good*; 570.22 *marriageable*; 136.9 *qualified*; 292.14 *seasonable*; 217.1 *sufficient*; 287.6 *timely*; 237.1 *useful*
suitable match 570.4 *marriageability*
suitableness 797.8 *good*; 136.1 *qualification*
suitable party 570.4 *marriageability*
suitably 222.18 *comfortably*; 706.26 *correspondingly*; 617.17 *desirably*; 750.38 *fittingly*; 287.9 *opportunely*; 801.18 *properly*
suit at law 16.5 *litigation*
suitcase 410.9 *baggage*; 439.4 *storage*
suite 223.10 *attendance*; 132.2 *consecution*; 289.1 *succession*
suited 136.9 *qualified*; 287.6 *timely*
suited for 485.7 *gifted*
suitedness 136.1 *qualification*
suited to the weather 292.14 *seasonable*
suite of programs 40.19 *computing terms*
suiting 193.4 *textile*
suit of cards 132.2 *consecution*
suit of clothes 551.1 *dress*
suit oneself 250.16 *be independent*
suit one's purpose 237.9 *be useful*
suitor 471.6 *attentive person*; 267.5 *follower*; 16.8 *litigant*; 593.9 *lover*; 710.4 *requester*
suit the occasion 239.6 *be convenient*; 287.4 *be timely*
Sukhavati 8.11 *heaven*
Sukkoth 10.16 *religious festival*
sulk 606.7 *be dissatisfied*; 626.9 *be sullen*; 602.9 *despair*; 637.10 *grudge*
sulker 659.4 *discourteous person*; 606.3 *dissatisfied person*; 637.16 *reluctant person*; 626.5 *sullen person*
sulkily 659.9 *discourteously*; 626.13 *sullenly*
sulkiness 637.14 *disobedience*; 626.1 *sullenness*
sulking 606.4 *dissatisfied*
sulky 606.4 *dissatisfied*; 637.5 *reluctant*; 626.6 *sullen*
sullen 626.6; 620.5 *bored*; 659.5 *discourteous*; 594.10 *hating*; 651.15 *inconsiderate*; 625.4 *irascible*; 732.1 *shy*; 643.1 *solemn*; 499.7 *splenetic*; 655.8 *unsociable*
sullen look 626.2 *sign of sullenness*
sullenly 626.13; 659.9 *discourteously*; 594.18 *hatefully*; 625.9 *irascibly*; 643.10 *solemnly*; 499.11 *splenetically*; 655.14 *unsociably*
Sullenness 626
sullenness 626.1; 624.4 *anger*; 620.1 *boredom*; 659.1 *discourtesy*; 637.14 *disobedience*; 594.1 *hate*; 625.1 *irascibility*; 732.3 *shyness*; 643.4 *solemnity*; 499.4 *spleen*; 655.1 *unsociability*
sullen person 626.5
sully 532.11 *blacken*; 796.19 *corrupt*; 678.12 *defame*; 258.11 *dirty*; 524.11 *tarnish*
sulpha drug 394.8 *drug*; 37.4 *drug type*
sulphates 562.3 *fertilizer*
sulphonamide 394.8 *drug*; 37.4 *drug type*
sulphonate 32.26 *react*
sulphone 37.4 *drug type*
sulphonic 32.34 *elemental*
sulphonous 32.34 *elemental*
sulphur 33.15 *essential element*; 537.8 *yellow thing*
sulphur dioxide 503.2 *something that makes an unpleasant smell*
sulphuretted 32.34 *elemental*
sulphuric 32.34 *elemental*
sulphurize 32.26 *react*
sulphurous 624.16 *angry*; 8.16 *devilish*; 32.34 *elemental*; 503.3 *stinking*; 537.2 *yellowish*
sulphurously 624.18 *angrily*
sulphuryl 32.34 *elemental*
sultan 400.2 *sovereign*; 121.5 *superior*
sultana 25.42 *preserve*
sultanate 85.3 *dominion*; 86.4 *territorial division*
sultriness 493.5 *hot weather*
sultry subtropical 493.11 *warm*
sum 780.5; 27.91, 210.9, 211.6 *add*; 27.15 *addition*; 194.4 *mathematical result*; 694.1 *meaning*; 706.7 *numerical result*; 706.20 *solve*; 203.4 *total*; 204.2 *whole thing*
sum and substance 123.3 *chief thing*; 694.1 *meaning*
sum asked for 790.1 *price*
sum entrusted 784.3 *loan*
Sumerian 566.4 *modern human*
Sumerians 284.6 *people of the past*
Sumerological 3.17 *archaeological*
Sumerologist 3.4 *archaeologist*; 1.4 *palaeoanthropologist*
Sumerology 3.2 *archaeology*; 1.2 *palaeoanthropology*
summarily 16.85; **723.11**; 269.5 *concisely*; 293.17 *early*; 3.25 *reportedly*
summariness 723.4
summarize 723.8; 269.4 *be concise*; 3.20 *chronicle*; 112.17 *iterate*; 163.5 *outline*; 149.10 *shorten*
summarized 269.3 *concise*; 163.6 *outlined*; 723.7 *shortened*
summarizer 723.5
Summary 723
summary 723.1; **723.6**; 721.2 *brief description*; 3.5 *chronicle*; 269.3 *concise*; 722.1 *dissertation*; 293.12 *early*; 701.4 *gist*; 112.2 *iteration*; 205.5 *largest part*; 163.1, 269.2, 484.6 *outline*; 397.7 *overview*; 149.7 *short*; 149.3 *shortened version*
summary court 16.19 *law court*
summary court martial 16.19 *law court*; 584.6 *military law*
summation 27.15 *addition*; 211.2 *mathematical addition*; 194.4 *mathematical result*; 204.2 *whole thing*
summer 292.3; **292.11**; 493.5 *hot weather*; 298.5 *regular thing*; 292.6 *spend the season*; 248.3 *time of plenty*; 654.12 *visit*
summer drought 493.5 *hot weather*
summer holiday 298.5 *regular thing*
summer house 44.3 *ornamental garden*; 565.7 *room*
summer lightning 522.4 *natural light*; 31.21 *thunderstorm*
summerlike 292.11 *summer*
summerly 292.18 *seasonally*
summer monsoon 31.17 *wind system*
summer pudding 25.35 *dessert*
summer sale 778.4 *sale*
summer school 6.12 *educational institution*
summer soldier 699.19 *cheat*; 700.19 *hypocrite*
summer solstice 10.15 *holy day*; 292.3 *summer*
summertide 292.3 *summer*
summertime 281.3 *chronology*; 493.5 *hot weather*; 292.3 *summer*
summer tree 79.12 *figurative usage*
summer wood 79.3 *timber*
summery 31.46 *seasonal*; 292.11 *summer*; 493.11 *warm*
summing up 112.2 *iteration*; 16.7 *legal trial*; 464.2 *verdict*
summit 121.4; **174.1**; 232.1 *completeness*; 579.7 *council*; 746.3 *discussion*; 154.2 *heights*; 123.5 *important*; 131.7 *limit*; 89.1 *mountain*; 230.3 *perfection*; 62.5 *rock face*; 425.8 *sharp-pointed thing*; 734.5 *talks*
summital 174.5 *top*
summit conference 746.3 *discussion*
summit meeting 746.3 *discussion*; 734.5 *talks*
summit talks 734.5 *talks*
summon 715.5 *accuse*; 376.42 *call together*; 710.7 *demand*; 617.12 *desire*; 16.70 *litigate*; 742.12 *signal*
summoned 715.8 *accusatory*; 376.46 *assembled*
summoner 16.10 *law officer*; 397.6 *person in command*; 742.8 *signer*
summoning 742.16 *signalling*
summoning sound 742.4 *signal*
summons 715.1 *accusation*; 397.2, 710.2 *demand*; 16.6 *legal process*; 16.33 *litigation*; 742.6 *word*
summon spirits 11.22 *conjure*
summon up 369.15 *draw out*; 477.14 *imagine*; 462.12 *remember*
sum of money 780.5 *sum*
sumo wrestler 336.5, 586.3 *athlete*
sump 183.3 *cavity*; 175.2 *foot*; 238.6 *refuse*; 767.8 *sink*; 439.4 *storage*
sumpter 316.6 *beast of burden*
sumptuary 787.10 *expending*; 780.22 *monetary*
sumptuous 781.3 *opulent*; 490.6 *pleasant*
sumptuousness 781.7 *opulence*
sums 210.1 *calculation*; 27.1 *mathematics*; 27.4 *simple arithmetic*
sum total 204.2 *whole thing*
sum up 210.9, 211.6 *add*; 269.4 *be concise*; 204.9 *be whole*; 112.17 *iterate*; 464.11 *judge*; 194.10 *number*; 149.10 *shorten*; 723.8 *summarize*; 16.71 *try a case*
sun 29.15; **31.22**; 428.19 *bake*; 173.2 *central thing*; 428.14 *desert*; 522.4 *natural light*; 306.4 *orbiting body*; 742.1 *sign*
sunbaked 428.8 *baked*; 418.3 *hardened*; 493.11 *warm*
sunbath 493.5 *hot weather*
sunbathe 493.16 *feel hot*
sunbather 493.5 *hot weather*
sunbathing 493.5 *hot weather*; 31.22 *sun*
sunbeam 522.1 *light*; 522.4 *natural light*
sun bed 394.14 *hospital*; 493.5 *hot weather*
Sunbelt 493.8 *hot place*; 86.8 *regions of the US*
sun-block cream 62.4 *climbing equipment*
sunbonnet 550.5 *body covering*; 551.15 *headgear*
sunburn 534.7 *brown*; 534.3 *brownness*; 493.5 *hot weather*; 31.22 *sun*
sunburnt 532.3 *blackened*; 534.2 *browned*; 535.2 *red-faced*
sundae 25.35 *dessert*
sun dance 10.7 *non-Christian ritual*
Sunday 10.15 *holy day*
Sunday best 551.1 *dress*; 656.4 *formal dress*
Sunday go-to-meeting clothes 551.1 *dress*
Sunday lunch 557.12 *meal*
Sunday newspaper 741.5 *mass communication*
Sunday-opening laws 795.4 *self-righteousness*
Sunday painter 19.16 *artist*
Sunday paper 740.4 *newspaper*
Sunday school 6.12 *educational institution*
sun deck 493.8 *hot place*
sunder 372.14 *come between*; 377.12 *disperse*; 198.16 *halve*; 372.9 *separate*
sundered 372.16 *apart*
sundial 176.4 *angular measurement*; 281.9 *hourglass*
sundown 291.1 *evening*
sundowner 558.2 *drink*
sundress 551.21 *beachwear*; 551.7 *frock*
sun-dried 428.8 *baked*; 24.10 *ceramic*; 359.7 *preserved*
sun-dried brick 24.9 *industrial ceramics*
sundries 211.4 *extra*; 778.8 *merchandise*; 376.32 *miscellany*
sundry 114.6 *assorted*; 207.7 *various*
sun-dry 428.19 *bake*; 359.5 *preserve*
sun-drying 359.1 *preservation*
sunflower 536.3 *orange thing*
sunflower oil 25.7 *basic ingredient*
sunflower-seed meal 43.9 *animal feedstuff*
Sunflower State 78.9 *figurative usage*
sung 575.5 *entitled*
sunglasses 551.25 *accessories*; 551.21 *beachwear*; 62.4 *climbing equipment*; 28.29 *optical element*; 550.12 *protective covering*; 523.6 *shade*; 68.5 *ski equipment*; 518.10 *visual aid*
sun hat 551.15 *headgear*; 550.12 *protective covering*; 523.6 *shade*
sunk 602.6 *depressed*; 357.15 *destroyed*; 367.19 *fallen*; 308.14 *holed*; 766.16 *losing*; 156.12 *under*
sunken 183.6 *concave*; 156.8 *deep*; 367.19 *fallen*; 155.7 *lowland*
sunken-eyed 153.2 *emaciated*
sunken eyes 153.8 *emaciation*
sunken garden 44.2 *garden*
sunken reef 379.1 *trap*
sunk line 55.3 *fishing tackle*
sun lamp 522.6 *electric light*; 394.14 *hospital*; 493.5 *hot weather*
sunless 523.8 *dark*; 524.5 *dim*
sunlessness 523.1 *darkness*
sunlight 28.23, 522.1 *light*; 522.4 *natural light*; 29.15, 31.22 *sun*
sunlit 522.18 *lit*
sun lounge 493.8 *hot place*; 565.7 *room*
sun lounger 44.3 *ornamental garden*
Sunna 7.12 *religious text*; 1.8 *tradition*
sunned 428.8 *baked*
sunnier 31.45 *fine*
sunniness 598.3 *cheerfulness*; 428.14 *desert*
sunning 428.13 *drying*
Sunnite 7.6 *non-Christian*
sunny 522.19; 598.1 *cheerful*; 610.14 *cheering*; 31.45 *fine*; 241.2 *likable*; 428.5 *rainless*; 493.11 *warm*
sunny period 31.23 *heat*
sunny South 428.14 *desert*
sunny spell 31.23 *heat*
sunny weather 31.23 *heat*
sun oneself 493.16 *feel hot*
sun porch 565.7 *room*
sun print 41.12 *development*
sunray lamp 522.6 *electric light*
sunrise 304.3; 324.4 *compass point*; 293.2 *early hour*; 290.1 *morning*
sunrise and sunset 298.5 *regular thing*
sunrise industry 356.2 *manufacture*
sunscreen 550.12 *protective covering*
sunset 324.4 *compass point*; 291.1 *evening*; 291.4 *evening thing*; 305.4 *fall*; 294.2 *late hour*; 535.7 *red thing*
sunshade 550.12 *protective covering*; 523.6 *shade*
sunshine 522.4 *natural light*; 29.15, 31.22 *sun*
sunshine recorder 31.7 *weather instruments*
sunshine-yellow 537.1 *yellow*
sunshiny 522.19 *sunny*
sunspot 541.4 *maculation*; 29.15 *sun*
sunspot cycle 29.15 *sun*
sunstroke 493.5 *hot weather*; 31.22 *sun*
sunsuit 551.23 *children's clothes*
suntan 532.11 *blacken*; 534.7 *brown*; 534.3 *brownness*; 493.16 *feel hot*; 493.5 *hot weather*; 31.22 *sun*
suntan lotion 550.12 *protective covering*; 31.22 *sun*
suntanned 532.3 *blackened*; 534.2 *browned*
suntanning 31.22 *sun*
sunup 293.2 *early hour*; 290.1 *morning*; 304.3 *sunrise*
sun visor 523.6 *shade*
sun worship 9.2 *idolatry*
sun worshipper 493.5 *hot weather*; 9.6 *idolater*; 31.22 *sun*
sun-worshipping 9.10 *idolatrous*
sup 558.2, 558.13 *drink*; 557.24 *have a meal*
super 21.24 *actor*; 797.1 *good*; 797.27 *great!*; 121.12 *superior*; 235.1 *worthy*
Super-8 41.14 *cine film*
superabound 217.5 *about*; 219.4 *be excessive*; 329.4 *exaggerate*
superabundance 679.8 *abundance*; 270.1 *diffuseness*; 219.1 *excess*; 217.8 *plenty*; 562.2 *productiveness*; 215.4 *surplus*
superabundant 679.3 *abundant*; 208.9 *ample*; 270.3 *diffuse*; 219.6 *excessive*; 217.2 *plentiful*; 215.10 *surplus*
superabundantly 215.11 *residually*
superadd 211.6 *add*
superaddition 211.1 *addition*; 211.4 *extra*
superannuate 371.2 *dismiss*
superannuated 350.4 *disused*; 284.20 *former*; 350.3 *not wanted*
superannuation 350.10 *disuse*
superb 121.15 *excellent*; 797.1 *good*; 230.1 *perfect*; 485.6 *skilful*; 235.1 *worthy*
superbike 320.13 *motorcycle*; 61.5 *motorcycle racing*
superbly 121.16 *superiorly*; 797.22 *well*
superbness 797.8 *good*
Super Bowl 46.1 *football*
Supercalc™ 40.11 *application*
supercharged 334.16 *charged*
supercilious 668.13 *contemptuous*; 622.14 *proud*; 673.10 *self-admiring*
superciliously 673.21 *cockily*; 668.30 *contemptuously*
superciliousness 668.3 *contempt*
superclass 34.17 *taxonomy*
supercluster 29.7 *galaxy*
supercollider 334.8 *nuclear power*
supercomputer 40.3 *computer*

superconducting magnet 28.60 magnet; 28.45 superconductivity
superconductivity **28.45**; 334.7 electrical power
superconductor 334.7 electrical power; 334.8 nuclear power; 28.45 superconductivity
supercooled 31.43 atmospheric
supercooling 31.9 atmospheric process
super-duper 235.1 worthy
superego 101.6 internal world; 36.21 psyche; 11.7 spirit
supereminence 235.6 worth
supereminent 121.14 best
supererogation 219.3 superfluity
supererogatory 211.9 extra; 219.7 superfluous
superfamily 34.17 taxonomy
superficial **157.2**; 171.8 apparent; 486.4 bungled; 639.2 changeable; 265.9 easy; 100.12 external; 100.8 extraneous; 262.3 hasty; 233.4 incomplete; 666.5 indifferent; 525.8 outer; 167.7 outward; 472.11 perfunctory; 456.7 semiskilled; 702.7 sophistic; 27.79, 141.11 spatial; 124.4 trivial; 520.1 visible
superficial area 27.38 surface
superficiality 171.3 appearance; 100.1 extraneousness; 456.2 half-knowledge; 472.1 inattention; 233.1 incompleteness; 666.2 indifference; 157.3 shallowness; 265.2 simplicity; 124.7 triviality
superficially 96.19, 525.15 apparently; 265.21 easily; 171.15 externally; 100.18 extraneously; 233.6 incompletely; 738.16 manifestly; 157.8 shallowly; 124.14 unimportantly; 520.11 visibly
superficial wound 157.4 shallow thing
superficies 171.1 exterior; 525.3 external appearance; 157.3 shallowness
superfine 797.1 good; 235.1 worthy
superfluity **219.3**; 793.2 declining prices; 270.1 diffuseness; 211.4 extra; 100.1 extraneousness; 350.8 nonuse; 781.7 opulence; 217.8 plenty; 562.2 productiveness; 215.4 surplus; 681.5 unrestrainedness; 238.3 uselessness; 441.3 waste
superfluous **219.7**; 793.9 cheap; 270.3 diffuse; 211.9 extra; 100.8 extraneous; 350.3 not wanted; 217.2 plentiful; 215.10 surplus; 238.1 useless; 441.9 waste
superfluously 211.10 additionally; 219.8 excessively; 100.18 extraneously; 350.12 out of use; 215.11 residually; 441.10 wastefully; 215.12 with a remainder
superfluousness 219.3 superfluity; 238.3 uselessness
superfly 235.1 worthy
supergiant 29.13 luminosity
supergiant elliptical 29.7 galaxy
super giant slalom race 68.3 ski racing
super giant slalom racing 68.3 ski racing
Supergirl 336.6 muscleman
superglue 267.3 adhesive; 267.7 cause to adhere
super G race 68.3 ski racing
supergrass 715.3 accuser; 739.4 discloser; 693.10 informer; 716.7 person who gives evidence
superheavy 32.34 elemental
superheavy element 32.6 chemical element
superhero 235.8 exceller; 336.6 muscleman
superhet receiver 692.18 radio
superhighway 317.3, 320.2 road
superhuman 264.10 difficult
superhumanity 11.2 the occult
superhuman task 264.3 difficult task
superimpose 211.6 add; 550.23 cover
superimposed 550.38 covering
superimposition 211.1 addition; 550.1 covering
superintend 140.16 direct; 579.1 manage
superintendence 579.3 management
superintendency 396.5 position of authority
superintendent 579.13 director; 579.15 manager; 121.5 superior
Superior 88.3 US lakes
superior **121.5**; **121.12**; 396.12 authoritative; 123.4 bigwig; 400.5 company leader; 579.13 director; 116.4 dissimilar; 797.1 good; 154.10 higher; 123.5 important; 244.14 improved; 395.11 influential; 123.6 notable; 396.10 person of authority; 336.10 potent; 334.13 powerful; 129.12 primary; 397.15 self-assured; 235.1 worthy
superioress 7.7 monk
Superiority 121
superiority **121.1**; 396.1 authority; 668.3 contempt; 579.4 directorship; 797.8 good; 12.3 governance; 123.1 importance; 120.1 inequality; 230.3 perfection; 334.1 power; 129.2 priority; 336.1 strength; 235.6 worth
superiority complex 36.18 complex; 622.11 prejudice
superiorly **121.16**; 397.16 commandingly
superior person **797.16**; 123.4 bigwig
superior planet 29.16 planet
superior power 395.1 influence
superjock 235.8 exceller
superlative 121.14, 797.2 best; 727.12 exaggerated; 727.1 exaggeration; 154.11 exalted; 5.44 grammatical; 797.9 the best; 235.1 worthy
superlatively 727.16 exaggeratedly; 5.52 grammatically; 121.16 superiorly; 121.17 supremely
Superman 336.6 muscleman
superman 123.4 bigwig; 613.7 courageous person; 235.8 exceller; 121.6 paragon; 619.5 person of wonder; 246.4 successful person; 797.16 superior person; 630.5 surpriser
supermarket 557.17 food shop; 779.8 store
supermodel 553.5 fashion model
supermom 235.8 exceller
supernal 8.14 heavenly; 154.9 high; 101.8 nonmaterial
supernatant 32.33 crystalline
supernatant liquid 32.4 crystal
supernatural 8.13 divine; 100.12 external; 11.14 occult; 101.9 parapsychological
supernatural being 8.5 deity
supernaturalism 11.1 occultism; 101.3 spiritual world
supernaturalist 101.7 believer in a nonmaterial world; 11.12 occultist
supernaturality 11.2 the occult
supernaturally 8.19 divinely; 100.18 extraneously; 101.13 metaphysically; 11.25 occultly
supernaturalness 11.2 the occult
supernatural tale 17.2 fiction
supernature 11.2 the occult
supernormal 121.14 best; 11.14 occult
supernormalness 11.2 the occult
supernova 522.4 natural light; 29.11 stellar birth
supernova remnant 29.11 stellar birth
supernumerary 21.24 actor; 211.4, 211.9 extra; 21.23 role; 439.7 stored
superpatriot 466.7 bigot
superpatriotic 466.10 discriminatory
superpatriotically 466.17 prejudicially
superpatriotism 466.4 social discrimination
superphysical 11.14 occult
superphysicalness 11.2 the occult
superposition 211.1 addition
superpower 85.1 country; 395.6 group influence; 12.5 political organization; 86.4 territorial division
superpower diplomacy 585.1 war
supersaturate 32.25 solidify
supersaturated 219.6 excessive; 32.32 solid
supersaturated solution 32.3 phase
supersaturation 219.1 excess
superscription 743.3 means of identification
supersede 762.4 be a substitute; 470.2 discard; 767.9 dispose of; 350.6 stop using; 371.5 take the place of
superseded 350.4 disused; 16.57 null; 762.8 substituted
superseder 371.26 ejector
supersensible 11.14 occult; 101.9 parapsychological
supersensitiveness 11.2 the occult
supersession 762.1 substitution
supersonic 332.1 swift; 319.5 transportable
supersonically 319.6 commercially; 332.14 swiftly
supersonic flight 332.11 swift thing
supersonic speed 28.19 sound propagation; 332.8 speed
superstar 21.24 actor; 9.4 idolized person; 121.6 paragon; 797.16 superior person
superstition 274.6 fallibility; 9.2 idolatry; 7.1 religion; 450.2 religious belief
superstitious 9.10 idolatrous
superstitiously 11.26 magically
superstore 779.8 store
superstratum 171.1 exterior; 411.1 layer; 174.4 top layer
superstring 28.79 fundamental interaction
superstructural 38.32, 403.11 structural
superstructurally 403.18 structurally
superstructure **38.27**; 403.6 construction
supertax 790.7 tax
supertonic 18.16 musical note
supervene 345.7 follow from; 289.10 succeed
supervention 211.1 addition
supervise 140.16 direct; 579.1 manage; 518.15 watch
supervised 15.8 industrial
supervise staff 579.1 manage
supervising 324.5 directions; 15.8 industrial
supervision 579.3 management; 518.3 observation; 631.8 treatment
supervisor 15.6 employer; 579.15 manager; 518.11 observer
supervisory 579.17 managerial
supervisory body 579.6 governing body
superwoman 613.7 courageous person; 568.11 liberated woman; 121.6 paragon; 619.5 person of wonder; 246.4 successful person; 797.16 superior person; 630.5 surpriser
supinate 54.5 fence; 367.8 sit
supinated 54.6 fencing
supination 367.16 courtesy; 54.3 fencing movements
supine 335.12 impotent; 155.5 low; 187.10 lying; 301.5, 367.23 sedentary; 388.5 submitting
supine floating 67.1 swimming
supineness 187.1 horizontality; 155.1 lowness; 388.1 submission
supper 557.12 meal
supper party 654.5 party
supping 558.1 drinking; 557.4 eating meals
supplant 762.4 be a substitute; 289.11 follow in office; 144.16 replace; 371.5 take the place of
supplantation 144.3 replacement
supplanted 350.4 disused; 144.10 replaced; 762.8 substituted
supplanter 371.26 ejector; 762.2 substitute person
supplanting 762.1 substitution
supple 227.13 changeable; 422.6 elastic; 479.11 equivocating; 419.2 pliant; 664.6 servile
supplely 422.11 elastically
supplement 211.6 add; 211.1 addition; 392.26 be useful; 232.4 complete; 134.3 continue; 134.1 continuity; 790.3 fee; 295.5 fresh start; 232.2 fullness; 213.1 increase; 213.5 make bigger; 295.20 make new; 740.4 newspaper; 168.1 rear; 368.11 thing inserted
supplemental 211.8 additional; 134.5 continual; 168.4 rear
supplementally 134.7 continually
supplementarily 211.10 additionally; 213.8 increasingly
supplementary **392.31**; 232.7 complete; 213.6 increasing; 295.14 renewed
supplementary angles 27.39 angle
supplementary medicine 35.2 natural medicine
supplementation 211.1 addition
supplemented 213.7 increased
supplementing 392.30 helping
suppleness 227.1 changeableness; 645.1 cunning; 422.1 elasticity; 485.1 skill; 419.8 softness
suppliant 710.4 requester
supplicant 710.4 requester; 9.9 worshipful; 9.5, 10.17 worshipper
supplicate 10.20 pray; 710.6 request
supplicating 9.9 worshipful
supplication 10.9 prayer; 710.1 request; 10.3 rite of worship; 9.1 worship
supplicatory 10.21 ritualistic; 9.9 worshipful
supplied 436.8 provisional
supplier 13.9 economist; 436.3 provider
supplies **352.2**; 557.7 food; 778.8 merchandise; 436.1 provision
supply **439.3**; 243.5 equip; 232.6 fill; 352.6 find means; 243.11 fitting out; 768.5 give; 359.5 preserve; 356.10 produce; 436.1, 436.5 provision; 439.6 store; 762.2 substitute person
supply and demand 13.6 economic factors
supply base 439.4 storage
supplying 768.1 giving; 436.1 provision; 436.7 provisioning
supply line 436.1 provision
supply service 584.4 military organization
supply ship 586.24 warship
supply-side economics 13.3 economic statistics
supply staff 584.5 military staff
supply teacher 6.4 educator; 762.2 substitute person
Support 413
support **211.7**; **392.2**; **392.19**; **413.1**; **413.11**; **669.13**; 21.34 act; 21.24 actor; 392.23 advise; 608.2 aid; 669.1 approval; 175.1, 175.4 base; 348.4 be an instrument; 650.8 be benevolent; 20.8 column; 610.4 comfort; 707.19 confirm; 707.4 confirmation; 750.7, 750.28 consent; 134.3 continue; 134.1 continuity; 747.11 cooperate; 747.1 cooperation; 360.7 detain; 787.3 donate; 787.7 donation; 392.29 finance; 352.4 financial resources; 569.1 friendship; 768.2 gift; 679.11 give; 392.11 helper; 348.1 instrumentality; 228.7 make stable; 346.4 management; 392.9 patronage; 627.8 pity; 384.22 plead for; 35.19 practise medicine; 359.1 preservation; 359.5 preserve; 454.5 proof; 4.22 propound a philosophy; 252.10 protect; 252.2, 253.1 protection; 454.2, 703.17, 716.12 prove; 436.1, 436.5 provision; 366.1 raise; 252.5 refuge; 253.10 secure; 169.9, 469.3 side with; 228.3 stabilizer; 336.8 strengthen; 217.4 suffice; 413.2 supporting part; 554.20 support life; 392.20 sustain; 392.3 sustenance; 346.9 take action; 438.1 tool; 454.1 verify
supportable **413.10**
support an analogy 108.7 relate to
support civil rights 250.14 be free
supported **707.13**; 669.23 approved; 20.16 columned; 750.17 consenting; 134.5 continual; 707.13 supported
support equal rights 250.14 be free
supporter **392.13**; **413.8**; 669.8 admirer; 669.7 advocate; 707.9 affirmer; 384.13 defender; 267.5 follower; 768.4 giver; 608.5 helper; 122.6 inferior; 551.18 underwear
supporters 743.8 heraldic device
supporters' club 669.8 admirer
support financially **413.13**
support fleet 584.4 military organization
support free love 250.19 liberalize
support human rights 250.14 be free
supporting **669.19**; 175.3 base; 392.30 helping; 413.9 supportive
supporting actor 21.24 actor
supporting cast 21.25 cast
supporting character 21.23 role
supporting garment **413.5**
supporting member 38.27 superstructure
supporting part **413.2**; 21.23 role
supporting role 122.1 inferiority; 21.23 role
supportive **392.32**; **413.9**; 707.10 affirmative; 747.17 cooperative; 569.11 devoted; 348.6 instrumental; 366.11 raised; 669.19 supporting; 267.10 tenacious; 454.9 verificatory; 714.11 vindicatory
supportive evidence 714.2 defence
supportively 569.19 devotedly; 392.36 helpfully; 348.9 instrumentally; 714.15 in vindication; 788.8 profitably; 454.11 verifiably
supportive statement 707.4 confirmation
supportive theory 36.3 psychiatric treatment
support life **554.20**
support player 64.4 rugby player
support the church 7.19 be religious
support unit 584.4 military organization
support women's liberation 250.14 be free; 391.6 treat equally
supposability 476.2 basis of supposition
supposable 476.8 supposed
suppose **476.5**; 450.8 be of the opinion; 447.10 focus on; 443.16 have an idea;

477.14 *imagine*; 4.20 *philosophize*; 4.22 *propound a philosophy*; 446.17 *theorize*; 104.10 *think likely*
supposed 476.8; 450.14 *believed*; 447.7 *focused*; 811.4 *reputed*
supposedly 476.10; 450.16 *believably*; 811.6 *reputedly*; 447.14 *thematically*; 4.25 *theoretically*
supposer 476.4 *theorist*
suppose so 476.5 *suppose*
supposing 476.11; 476.7 *suppositional*; 222.15 *under the circumstances*
Supposition 476
supposition 476.1; 713.1 *advice*; 450.1 *belief*; 443.6 *idea*; 4.1 *philosophy*; 707.2 *statement*; 27.65, 446.2 *theory*; 447.1 *topic*
suppositional 476.7; 707.10 *affirmative*; 477.12 *imaginary*; 443.10 *speculative*; 446.10 *theoretical*
suppositious 476.7 *suppositional*
suppositive 476.8 *supposed*; 476.7 *suppositional*
suppository 37.9 *pessary*; 394.10 *surgical dressing*; 368.11 *thing inserted*
suppress 647.6; 367.5 *bear down on*; 634.7 *be evasive*; 246.9 *be victorious*; 399.4 *censor*; 736.8 *conceal*; 347.3 *counteract*; 387.7 *defeat*; 357.8 *destroy*; 360.7 *detain*; 128.7 *exclude*; 358.2 *forget*; 737.12 *keep secret*; 720.1 *misinterpret*; 251.8 *restrain*; 730.15 *strike dumb*
suppressant 251.1 *restraint*
suppressed 647.9; 736.14 *concealed*; 367.22 *overthrown*; 251.13 *restraining*; 737.9 *secret*; 36.37 *subconscious*
suppressed desire 36.19 *defence mechanism*
suppressing 37.14 *counteracting*; 387.10 *dominating*; 251.13 *restraining*
suppression 647.2; 347.1 *counteraction*; 36.19 *defence mechanism*; 357.1 *destruction*; 360.2 *detention*; 387.2 *domination*; 634.15 *evasiveness*; 128.1 *exclusion*; 358.5 *forgetfulness*; 720.2 *misinterpretation*; 251.1 *restraint*; 737.1 *secrecy*; 736.4 *silence*; 367.13 *submergence*; 399.1 *veto*
suppressive 634.18 *avoiding*; 347.4 *counteracting*; 387.10 *dominating*; 251.13 *restraining*; 399.5 *vetoed*
suppressively 399.7 *by veto*
suppurate 245.2 *decay*; 560.18 *fester*; 371.14 *let out*
suppurated 431.16 *rheumy*
suppurating 431.16 *rheumy*
suppuration 431.3 *body fluid*; 431.6 *flow*; 260.6 *infection*; 560.7 *pus*
suppurative 560.27 *purulent*; 431.16 *rheumy*
supramundane 8.13 *divine*; 11.18 *spiritual*
supranatural 11.14 *occult*
supranaturalism 11.1 *occultism*
supranature 11.2 *the occult*
supremacy 140.8, 396.1 *authority*; 8.2 *divine attribute*; 12.3 *governance*; 123.1 *importance*; 129.2 *priority*; 121.1 *superiority*; 797.9 *the best*
suprematist 19.29 *realist*
supreme 396.12 *authoritative*; 121.14, 235.2, 797.2 *best*; 8.13 *divine*; 154.11 *exalted*; 400.13 *excellent*; 123.5 *important*; 230.1 *perfect*; 129.12 *primary*; 140.12 *ruling*; 174.5 *top*
Supreme Being 344.7 *Prime Mover*
supreme control 579.4 *directorship*; 12.3 *governance*
Supreme Court judge 400.3 *leader*
Supreme Court Justice 16.9 *lawmaker*
Supreme Court of Judicature 16.20 *British court*
supreme issue 123.3 *chief thing*
supremely 121.17; 396.23 *authoritatively*; 8.19 *divinely*; 123.9 *importantly*; 400.16 *masterfully*; 129.23 *primarily*
Supreme Soviet 579.10 *legislative body*
surcharge 219.4 *be excessive*; 414.6 *displacement*; 790.3 *fee*; 792.10 *overcharge*; 789.9 *settle accounts*; 792.2 *unfair price*
surcoat 551.12 *coat*
surd 194.9 *fractional*; 27.17 *multiplication*; 194.6 *power*; 730.9 *voiceless*; 730.4 *whispering*
sure 450.11 *believing*; 452.1 *certain*; 452.2 *convinced*; 228.11 *determined*; 726.3 *emphatic*; 474.7 *expected*; 474.5 *expecting*; 756.15 *future*; 799.4 *honourable*; 283.12 *predictable*; 252.6 *safe*; 253.6 *secure*; 396.15 *true*; 454.10 *verified*
sure bet 102.3 *strong possibility*
sure defence 252.2 *protection*
sure enough 454.12 *assuredly*; 698.19 *authentic*
surefire 246.13 *successful*
surefire winner 246.4 *successful person*
sure-footed 485.6 *skilful*; 246.13 *successful*
surely 253.16; 454.12 *assuredly*; 396.25 *authentically*; 452.23 *certainly*; 452.25 *inevitably*; 756.18 *potentially*
sureness 452.10 *conviction*
sure sign 742.1 *sign*
sure thing 265.6 *easy thing*; 107.5 *good chance*; 59.7 *horseracing*; 452.12 *something certain*; 102.3 *strong possibility*
surety 452.9 *certainty*; 452.10 *conviction*; 16.6 *legal process*; 756.5 *promise-maker*; 252.2 *protection*; 454.4 *verification*
sure winner 246.5 *victorious person*
surf 30.14, 91.3 *wave*
surface 27.38; **169.2**; **550.29**; 171.8 *apparent*; 525.12 *become visible*; 171.11 *be exterior*; 415.9 *be light*; 30.5 *earth*; 315.10 *emerge*; 171.1, 171.6 *exterior*; 525.3 *external appearance*; 100.4 *externality*; 525.8 *outer*; 167.7 *outward*; 5.43 *phrasal*; 317.4 *road surface*; 323.10 *sail*; 157.3 *shallowness*; 141.1 *space*; 141.11 *spatial*; 304.17 *spring up*; 157.2 *superficial*; 404.1 *texture*; 174.4 *top layer*; 520.1 *visible*; 520.6 *visible thing*
surface appearance 171.3 *appearance*
surface area 27.38 *surface*
surface chemistry 32.20
surface current 30.13 *ocean current*
surface feature 30.7 *landform*
surface integral 27.31 *differentiation*
surface mail 692.2 *postal communication*
surface measurement 27.38 *surface*
surface of revolution 27.45 *curved surface*
surface plug 55.2 *artificial fly*
surface show 167.3 *show*
surface structure 5.29 *grammar*; 5.24 *phrasing*
surface tension 28.10 *force*
surface texture 404.1 *texture*
surface-to-air missile 587.5 *missile weapon*
surface wave 30.23 *seismic wave*; 326.5 *wave*
surface wind 31.12 *wind*
surfacing 304.1 *ascent*; 315.15 *outgoing*; 550.11 *paving*
surfeit 219.3 *superfluity*; 215.4 *surplus*
surf fishing 55.1 *angling*
surficial 30.50 *terrestrial*
surfing 40.16 *Internet*
surge 304.13 *ascend*; 342.12 *be active*; 91.10 *billow*; 376.40 *crowd*; 376.22 *flood*; 90.7 *flow*; 213.4 *increase*; 507.1 *loudness*; 90.6 *river flow*; 315.11 *run out*; 213.2 *spread*; 307.10 *swirl*; 304.2 *upturn*; 307.4 *vortex*; 91.3 *wave*
surge back 91.10 *billow*
surge forward 380.7 *be violent*
surgeon 35.11 *doctor*; 394.15 *healer*; 35.13 *medical specialist*; 308.3 *person who opens*; 372.8 *person who separates*; 393.12 *repairer*
surgery 35.9; **394.12**; 35.10, 394.14 *hospital*; 392.5 *medical assistance*; 35.3 *medical specialty*; 35.8 *treatment*
surgical 35.22, 394.18 *medical*
surgical air strike 381.13 *air attack*
surgical assistant 35.17 *paramedic*
surgical dressing 394.10; 550.6 *medical covering*
surgical intervention 35.9 *surgery*
surgical knife 425.10 *knife*
surgically 35.26 *medically*; 394.21 *remedially*
surgical mask 550.6 *medical covering*
surgical operation 35.9, 394.12 *surgery*
surgical registrar 35.11 *doctor*
surgical treatment 35.9 *surgery*; 35.8 *treatment*
surging 90.10 *fluvial*; 507.1 *loudness*; 91.7 *oceanic*
surliness 659.1 *discourtesy*; 626.1 *sullenness*
surly 486.3 *clumsy*; 659.5 *discourteous*; 626.7 *irritable*; 626.6 *sullen*
surmisable 476.8 *supposed*
surmise 450.1 *belief*; 450.8 *be of the opinion*; 476.3 *conjecture*; 464.12 *estimate*; 443.16 *have an idea*; 443.6 *idea*; 464.1 *judgment*; 4.20 *philosophize*; 476.5 *suppose*
surmised 476.8 *supposed*
surmiser 4.10 *philosopher*; 476.4 *theorist*
surmount 154.15 *be high*; 304.14 *climb*; 329.3 *exceed*; 246.7 *overcome obstacles*; 174.7 *top*; 89.9 *tower*
surmounted 329.14 *surpassing*
surname 721.8 *name*
surpass 121.8 *be superior*; 120.5 *be unequal*; 235.9 *be worthy*; 329.3 *exceed*
surpass belief 619.10 *be wonderful*
surpassing 329.14; 121.12 *superior*
surpassingly 121.16 *superiorly*
surplice 7.11 *vestment*
surplus 215.4; **215.10**; 215.3 *difference*; 329.12 *excessive*; 329.9 *excessiveness*; 211.4, 211.9 *extra*; 205.1 *part*; 217.8 *plenty*; 219.3 *superfluity*; 219.7 *superfluous*
surplusage 219.3 *superfluity*
surprisal 630.3 *shock*
Surprise 630
surprise 630.1; **630.9**; 381.1 *attack*; 619.10 *be wonderful*; 604.6 *disappoint*; 379.1, 379.2 *trap*; 105.5 *unexpectedness*; 619.1 *wonder*
surprise attack 254.5 *danger*; 381.12 *military attack*
surprise blow 381.12 *military attack*
surprised 630.6; 619.6 *wondering*
surprise offensive 381.12 *military attack*
surprise party 654.5 *party*
surpriser 630.5
surprising 630.8; 619.8 *wonderful*
surprisingly 630.13; 619.13 *wonderfully*
surprising thing 630.4
surreal 717.13 *representational*; 721.13 *representing*
surrealistic 17.16 *literary*; 717.13 *representational*; 721.13 *representing*
surrender 247.7 *be defeated*; 767.9 *dispose of*; 768.1 *giving*; 589.6 *make peace*; 589.1 *peace*; 355.1 *relinquish*; 355.3 *relinquishment*; 605.5 *resign*; 605.1 *resignation*; 388.1 *submission*; 388.3 *submit*
surrendered 355.5 *relinquished*
surrenderer 387.5 *subjected person*
surrendering 768.1 *giving*; 388.5 *submitting*
surrender oneself 7.19 *be religious*
surrender one's life 582.16 *meet one's fate*
surrender one's ticket 312.4 *land*
surreptitious 700.34 *deceiving*; 737.10 *secretive*
surreptitiousness 700.1 *deception*
surrogacy 252.2 *protection*; 762.1 *substitution*
surrogate 36.25; 398.5 *alternative*; 550.34 *cover for*; 762.7 *substitute*; 762.2 *substitute person*; 550.21 *substitution*; 550.40 *substitutive*; 252.8 *tutelary*
surrogate mother 762.2 *substitute person*; 550.21 *substitution*
surrogation 762.1 *substitution*
surround 170.7; 585.13 *be at war*; 171.11 *be exterior*; 381.4 *besiege*; 179.6 *circle*; 163.3 *edge*; 165.5 *enclose*; 141.20 *extend*; 410.21 *put in a container*; 306.7 *ring*; 170.7 *surround*; 550.25 *wrap*
surrounded 170.5; 410.20 *containing*; 254.4 *endangered*
surrounding 170.4; 143.8, 222.7 *circumstantial*; 565.15 *environmental*
Surroundings 170
surroundings 170.1; 222.1 *circumstances*; 565.2 *environment*; 171.1 *exterior*; 147.5 *near place*
Sursum Corda 366.7 *lift*; 10.9 *prayer*
surtax 790.7 *tax*
surtax bracket 781.5 *wealth*
surtitle 18.4 *opera*
surtout 551.12 *coat*
surveillance 471.3 *carefulness*; 579.3 *management*; 518.3 *observation*; 252.2 *protection*; 384.5 *self-defence*; 665.5 *watchfulness*
surveillant 252.3 *protector*
survey 665.11 *care for*; 722.4 *dissertate*; 722.1 *dissertation*; 38.30 *engineer*; 464.12 *estimate*; 142.11 *find*; 518.14 *inspect*; 464.1 *judgment*; 30.65 *map*; 26.10 *measure*; 26.1 *measurement*; 518.3 *observation*; 163.1, 163.5 *outline*; 397.7 *overview*; 717.11 *paint*; 4.4 *philosophical investigation*; 4.20 *philosophize*; 705.17 *question*; 705.2 *questioning*; 471.12 *scrutinize*; 2.2 *sociological research*; 723.1 *summary*; 204.3 *whole situation*
surveyed 142.8 *locational*; 26.13 *measured*; 705.16 *questioned*
surveying 38.17 *civil engineering*; 26.1 *measurement*; 142.5 *topography*; 471.7 *watchful*
survey map 717.7 *map*
surveyor 38.18 *civil engineer*; 464.5 *judge*; 210.7 *mathematician*; 26.9 *measurer*; 705.9 *questioner*
survivability 554.5 *life cycle*; 336.1 *strength*; 423.6 *toughness*
survival 93.6 *continuing existence*; 554.5 *life cycle*; 277.4 *long-lastingness*; 225.1 *permanence*; 134.2 *protraction*; 215.1 *remainder*; 67.11 *swimming*; 284.7 *thing of the past*
survival device 67.3 *survival swimming*
survival of the fittest 34.16 *evolution*
survival swimming 67.3
survive 384.28; 77.22 *be dormant*; 215.7 *be left*; 225.5 *be permanent*; 393.4 *be restored*; 252.9 *be safe*; 423.10 *be tough*; 93.19 *continue to be*; 640.9 *endure*; 389.5 *escape*; 277.6 *last*; 554.16 *live*; 134.4 *protract*
survive from the past 296.16 *be old*
survive one's spouse 571.10 *be widowed*
surviving 554.12 *alive*; 93.12 *lasting*; 225.7 *permanent*; 640.10 *persevering*; 215.9 *remaining*
surviving spouse 571.6
survivor 389.3 *escaper*; 554.1 *life*; 215.6 *person remaining*; 571.6 *surviving spouse*
Susan B. Anthony dollar 780.8 *American money*
susceptibilities 590.3 *feelings*
susceptibility 488.2 *ability to sense*; 229.2 *attitude*; 6.10 *educability*; 593.3 *lovingness*; 480.7 *persuadability*; 591.5 *sensitivity*; 483.6 *suggestibility*; 254.7 *vulnerability*
susceptible 488.7; 6.17 *educable*; 590.10 *feeling*; 419.7 *impressionable*; 591.1 *sensitive*; 483.13 *suggestible*; 254.3 *vulnerable*
susceptibly 483.14 *influentially*; 419.18 *soft-heartedly*; 6.26 *studiously*
susceptivity 480.7 *persuadability*
sushi 25.54 *other dishes*
suspect 715.4 *accused person*; 616.5 *be cautious*; 450.8 *be of the opinion*; 453.18 *be uncertain*; 451.8 *disbelieve*; 451.7 *disbelieved*; 705.20 *doubt*; 705.10 *person questioned*; 476.5 *suppose*; 446.17 *theorize*; 619.12 *wonder whether*
suspected 451.7 *disbelieved*; 446.10 *theoretical*
suspect on the lam 634.17 *avoider*; 633.7 *the hunted*
suspend 361.10; 16.77 *annul*; 708.14 *cancel*; 294.8 *delay*; 371.3 *disbar*; 133.12 *discontinue*; 371.2 *dismiss*; 128.8 *eject*; 361.12 *interrupt*; 343.14 *make inactive*; 301.9 *make motionless*; 226.9 *pause*; 814.1 *punish*; 350.6 *stop using*; 708.15 *terminate*; 399.3 *veto*
suspended 339.6; **361.7**; 708.20 *cancelled*; 294.10 *held up*; 341.3 *inactive*; 133.10, 361.9 *interrupted*; 16.57 *null*; 335.10 *powerless*; 301.5 *sedentary*; 350.1 *unused*; 399.5 *vetoed*
suspended animation 489.2 *unconsciousness*
suspended cymbal 361.3 *suspended object*
suspended note 18.19 *tempo*
suspended object 361.3
suspender 373.8 *fastening*; 361.4 *hanger*; 551.20 *legwear*
suspender belt 361.4 *hanger*; 551.18 *underwear*
suspenders 373.8 *fastening*
suspend growth 77.22 *be dormant*
suspend hostilities 749.5 *make peace*; 226.9 *pause*
suspendibility 361.1 *suspension*
suspendible 361.7 *suspended*
suspense 474.1 *expectation*; 301.1 *motionlessness*
suspense account 789.1 *accounts*
Suspension 361
suspension 361.1; 708.5 *cancellation*; 374.4 *compound*; 294.3 *delayed action*; 371.18 *dismissal*; 128.2 *ejection*; 341.1 *inaction*; 343.5 *inactivity*; 133.4, 361.6 *interruption*; 412.2 *mixed thing*; 301.1 *mo-*

tionlessness; 350.8 *nonuse;* 226.3 *pause;* 814.7 *punishment;* 431.10 *solution;* 18.19 *tempo;* 708.6 *termination;* 399.1 *veto*
suspension bridge 38.21, 317.9 *bridge;* 361.3 *suspended object*
suspension of disbelief 450.3 *believing*
suspension of hostilities 749.1 *pacification;* 226.3 *pause*
suspension system 422.5 *spring*
suspensive 361.7 *suspended*
suspensively 361.13 *pendulously*
suspensiveness 361.1 *suspension*
suspicion **453.10**; 412.4 *admixture;* 476.2 *basis of supposition;* 616.1 *caution;* 476.3 *conjecture;* 451.1 *disbelief;* 629.2 *distrust;* 206.1 *few;* 455.2 *information;* 728.6 *suggestion;* 446.2 *theory*
suspicious 616.4 *cautious;* 451.7 *disbelieved;* 451.6 *disbelieving;* 812.4 *disreputable;* 629.5 *distrustful;* 705.14 *questionable;* 453.1 *uncertain*
suspiciously 451.10 *disbelievingly;* 629.9 *jealously;* 705.24 *questionably;* 453.23 *uncertainly*
suspiciousness 451.1 *disbelief;* 629.2 *distrust;* 453.10 *suspicion*
suss 455.13 *get to know;* 446.14 *have an idea;* 455.4 *intellect*
sussed 6.19, 455.8 *knowledgeable*
sussultatory 326.17 *waving*
sustain **392.20**; 134.3 *continue;* 95.12 *establish reality;* 413.14 *give moral support;* 640.7 *maintain;* 225.6 *make permanent;* 359.5 *preserve;* 454.2, 716.12 *prove;* 557.25 *provide food;* 336.8 *strengthen;* 346.9 *take action*
sustained 134.5 *continual;* 297.3 *frequent;* 148.1 *long;* 225.7 *permanent*
sustained climbing 62.1 *mountaineering*
sustained note 18.21 *tone*
sustainer 413.8 *supporter*
sustaining 557.27 *edible;* 392.32, 413.9 *supportive*
sustainingly 297.1 *frequently*
sustaining pedal 510.5 *resonator*
sustainment 413.7 *financial support;* 297.4 *frequency;* 392.3 *sustenance*
sustenance **392.3**; 134.1 *continuity;* 413.7 *financial support;* 557.7 *food;* 554.3 *life requirements;* 436.2 *provisions;* 581.7 *refreshments*
sustentation 392.3 *sustenance*
sustention 392.3 *sustenance*
susurrate 512.4 *hiss;* 511.8 *sound faint*
susurration 511.4 *faint sound;* 512.1 *hiss*
sutemi-waza 52.7 *judo*
sutler 778.11 *pedlar;* 436.3 *provider;* 778.14 *street trader*
sutra 7.12 *religious text*
suttee 752.7 *martyr;* 382.7 *suicide*
suture 35.20 *practise surgery;* 35.9 *surgery*
suzerain 396.14 *governmental;* 400.3 *leader*
suzerainty 397.3 *authority;* 12.3, 396.4 *governance*
Svarog 8.11 *heaven*
svelte 153.1 *thin*
Svengali 483.7 *motivator*
swab 428.20 *absorb;* 256.13 *clean;* 256.10 *cleaning object;* 428.15 *dryer;* 586.27 *naval man;* 394.10 *surgical dressing;* 486.10 *unskilled person*
swabber 256.12 *cleaner;* 428.15 *dryer*
swabbie 323.7 *nautical person;* 586.27 *naval man*
swabby 585.11 *recruit*
swaddle 551.32 *dress*
swaddling clothes 551.23 *children's clothes*
swag 410.8 *bag;* 780.2 *cash;* 305.10 *droop;* 327.25 *pitch;* 765.5 *profit;* 326.4, 326.11 *rock;* 794.2 *spoils;* 774.4 *stolen goods;* 16.36 *stolen property;* 773.5 *takings*
swagger 622.27 *be ostentatious;* 660.24 *be vain;* 300.12 *gait*
swaggerer 586.1 *combatant;* 660.12 *impudent person;* 622.13 *proud person*
swaggering 622.22, 673.13 *boastful*
swaggeringly 622.35 *ostentatiously*
swain 593.9 *lover;* 567.2 *male*
swallow 37.19 *administer;* 450.7 *believe;* 558.2, 558.13 *drink;* 557.21 *eat;* 370.11 *ingest;* 370.4 *intake;* 332.12 *swift animal;* 67.11 *swimming;* 441.1 *waste*
swallow dive 67.6 *diving*
swallowing 558.1 *drinking;* 557.1 *eating;* 370.4 *intake*
swallow insults 664.8 *be servile*
swallow-like 72.21 *avian*
swallow one's medicine 807.7 *be punished*
swallow one's pride 623.20 *submit*
swallowtail 743.7 *flag;* 198.8 *half*
swallow the pill 388.4 *succumb*
swallow up 357.12 *consume*
swami 400.9 *educational leader;* 396.10 *person of authority*
swamp 357.12 *consume;* 264.6 *critical situation;* 232.6 *fill;* 90.7 *flow;* 92.3, 429.8 *marsh;* 208.12 *overcrowd;* 157.4 *shallow thing;* 433.29 *water*
swamped 90.11, 433.24 *flooded;* 232.8 *full;* 335.12 *impotent*
swamp-forest 92.3 *marsh*
swampiness 429.7 *bogginess*
swampland 92.3 *marsh*
swampy 92.11 *continental;* 429.11 *marshy*
swan 72.3 *water bird;* 531.9 *white thing*
swanherd 43.16 *farm worker*
swank 676.4 *be affected;* 622.27 *be ostentatious;* 660.24 *be vain;* 622.10 *boastfulness;* 673.3 *cockiness;* 676.2 *pretender;* 622.13 *proud person;* 673.16 *show off;* 673.7 *vain person*
swankily 673.21 *cockily;* 622.35 *ostentatiously*
swankpot 622.13 *proud person*
swanky 676.3 *affected;* 622.22 *boastful;* 673.11 *cocky*
Swan Lake 22.11 *classical ballets*
swannery 72.19 *ornithology*
swan's-down 72.17 *plumage;* 421.8 *smooth thing;* 419.11 *soft thing*
Swansea 87.4 *British cities*
swan song 353.5 *attempt;* 131.3 *death;* 582.7 *dying day;* 603.2 *lament*
swap 224.4, 224.10, 759.1, 759.5 *exchange;* 762.6 *give a substitute;* 110.1 *interchange;* 110.7 *reciprocate;* 762.1 *substitution;* 776.1, 776.4 *trade;* 316.1, 316.11 *transfer*
swap ideas 713.6 *consult*
swapped 759.7 *exchanged;* 110.4 *reciprocal;* 762.8 *substituted*
swapper 227.4 *editor*
swapping 759.1 *exchange;* 776.13 *mercantile*
sward 81.2 *grassland;* 538.8 *greenness*
swardy 81.9 *grassy*
swarf 205.8 *bits and pieces*
Swarga 8.11 *heaven*
swarm 217.5 *about;* 562.6 *be fertile;* 208.11, 376.20, 376.40 *crowd;* 376.23 *flock;* 213.4 *increase;* 76.16 *infest;* 76.4 *social insect;* 152.7 *thicken;* 208.4 *throng*
swarm in 314.12 *flood in*
swarming 376.50 *crowded;* 152.2 *dense;* 219.6 *excessive;* 329.11 *overrun*
swarm like ants 208.11 *crowd*
swarm like flies 208.11 *crowd*
swarm over 633.12 *aim at;* 773.7 *take*
swarm up 304.13 *ascend*
swarm with 219.4 *be excessive;* 76.16 *infest*
swart 532.2 *dark*
swarthily 532.12 *blackly*
swarthiness 532.7 *blackness;* 523.3 *dark colour*
swarthy 532.2 *dark;* 523.10 *dark-coloured*
swartness 532.7 *blackness*
swash 90.7 *flow*
swashbuckler 586.1 *combatant*
swashing 433.8 *watering*
swastika 742.1 *sign;* 11.6 *talisman*
swat 331.13 *blow;* 331.3 *hit*
swatch 205.7 *piece*
swathe 394.20 *doctor;* 551.32 *dress;* 184.11 *enfold;* 43.17 *farm;* 43.11 *farmland;* 550.25 *wrap*
swathed 550.37 *protected*
swather 43.10 *farm tool*
swathing 184.5 *enfoldment*
sway 340.4 *act;* 340.1 *action;* 140.8, 397.3 *authority;* 227.11 *be changeable;* 298.7 *be regular;* 120.5 *be unequal;* 12.3, 396.4 *governance;* 121.2 *leadership;* 579.1 *manage;* 326.8 *oscillate;* 395.3 *personal influence;* 327.25 *pitch;* 334.1 *power;* 326.4, 326.11 *rock;* 327.11 *stagger;* 639.5 *vacillate*
swaying 227.13 *changeable;* 326.16 *rocking;* 120.3 *unequal*
sway the crowd 702.11 *practise sophistry*
swear 707.17 *affirm;* 594.17 *anger;* 712.5 *curse;* 659.8 *get angry;* 716.11 *give evidence;* 756.7 *promise;* 5.45 *use language;* 707.18 *vow*
swear an indictment 715.5 *accuse*
swear an oath 707.18 *vow*
swear by 450.7 *believe*
swearer 707.9 *affirmer;* 756.5 *promise-maker;* 454.7 *verifier*
swear in 707.18 *vow*
swearing **594.6**; 707.1 *affirmation;* 594.13 *angry;* 659.6 *bad-mannered;* 712.1 *curse;* 712.8 *cursing;* 756.1 *promise*
swearing in 707.3 *vow*
swearingly **712.12**
swearing off 767.1 *disposal;* 708.4 *renunciation*
swearing on the Bible 756.1 *promise;* 707.3 *vow*
swear like a trooper 712.5 *curse*
swear off 684.5 *be self-restrained;* 767.9 *dispose of;* 479.4 *recant;* 355.1 *relinquish;* 708.12 *renounce*
swear on oath 756.7 *promise;* 707.18 *vow*
swear on the Bible 707.18 *vow*
swear to 716.11 *give evidence*
swear to God 707.18 *vow*
swearword **5.19**; 712.1 *curse*
sweat **560.8**; **560.19**; 340.4 *act;* 593.24 *be in love;* 431.3 *body fluid;* 711.2 *danger signal;* 433.4 *exudate;* 493.16 *feel hot;* 431.25 *flow;* 493.1 *heat;* 315.12 *leak;* 371.14 *let out;* 315.2 *outflow;* 559.7 *secrete;* 559.2 *secreted substance;* 429.16, 433.32 *seep;* 503.2 *something that makes an unpleasant smell;* 353.2 *try hard;* 576.1, 576.6 *work*
sweatband 551.15 *headgear*
sweat blood 576.8 *exert oneself;* 576.6 *work;* 612.14 *worry*
sweater **551.13**; 550.5 *body covering*
sweat for nothing 238.9 *waste effort*
sweat gland 308.4 *body orifice;* 559.3 *gland;* 71.2 *mammalian characteristic*
sweatily 431.26 *fluidly;* 559.8 *glandularly;* 560.33 *scatologically*
sweatiness 493.1 *heat;* 503.1 *stench*
sweating 315.2 *outflow;* 559.1 *secretion;* 559.4 *secretory;* 429.12 *seeping;* 560.8 *sweat;* 560.28 *sweaty;* 576.10 *working*
sweating sickness 260.4 *disease;* 260.7 *tropical disease*
sweat like a trooper 560.19 *sweat*
sweat of one's brow 576.4 *exertion;* 576.1 *work*
sweat of one's brows 560.8 *sweat*
sweat scraper 59.14 *horse-riding terms*
sweat shirt 551.4 *informal dress;* 551.8 *shirt*
sweatshop 577.1 *workshop*
sweat socks 551.20 *legwear*
sweaty **560.28**; 371.29 *expulsive;* 31.52 *humid;* 559.4 *secretory;* 503.3 *stinking*
sweaty socks 503.2 *something that makes an unpleasant smell*
swedes 43.12 *crop*
Swedish 57.11 *gymnastic*
Swedish gymnastics 57.1 *gymnastics*
sweeny 260.18 *veterinary disease*
sweep 53.17 *bat;* 68.16 *bobsled;* 50.12 *canoeing;* 256.13 *clean;* 376.40 *crowd;* 246.10 *defeat heavily;* 325.14 *deviating course;* 107.3 *equal chance;* 141.20 *extend;* 265.19 *go easily;* 330.21 *move forward;* 46.9 *play;* 46.15 *play offence;* 61.9 *race;* 141.7 *range;* 50.4, 50.11 *rowing;* 53.9 *stroke*
sweep along 332.4 *be swift*
sweepback 322.7 *miscellaneous aviation terms*
sweep before one 330.21 *move forward*
sweep clean 649.10 *absolve*
sweeper 256.12 *cleaner;* 66.3 *football player;* 61.6 *motor-racing terms*
sweeping 216.1 *average;* 256.2 *cleaning;* 232.7 *complete;* 68.10 *curling;* 138.15 *general;* 138.20 *generalized;* 127.7 *including;* 61.6 *motor-racing terms*
sweepingness 138.3 *nonspecificness*
sweepings 258.4 *dirt;* 122.7 *inferior thing;* 238.6 *refuse;* 215.2 *residue*
sweeping statement 138.8 *generalization*
sweep off one's feet 593.28 *win the love of*
sweep out 371.11 *void*
sweep rowing 50.4 *rowing*
sweepstake 107.3 *equal chance*
sweep stroke 50.6 *canoeing*
sweep the board 235.9 *be worthy;* 246.10 *defeat heavily*
sweep the boards 246.9 *be victorious*
sweep under the carpet 736.8 *conceal;* 521.8 *make invisible*
sweep up 304.13 *ascend;* 256.13 *clean*
sweet **25.41**; **498.6**; 545.5 *beautiful;* 658.7 *courteous;* 25.35, 498.3 *dessert;* 25.9 *dish;* 558.17 *drinkable;* 557.27 *edible;* 593.22 *lovable;* 516.6 *melodious;* 557.14 *mouthful;* 241.1, 490.6 *pleasant;* 495.7 *tasty*
sweet and sour 113.3 *opposites*
sweet-and-sour 498.6 *sweet*
sweet and sour pork 25.48 *Chinese dish*
sweet and twenty 555.11 *young*
sweet as a nut 498.6 *sweet*
sweetbread 25.31 *offal*
sweet by-and-by 283.1 *future time*
sweet cicely 502.2 *fragrant thing*
sweet dreams 263.1 *ease*
sweet drink **498.5**
sweeten **498.8**; 558.13 *drink;* 685.4 *moderate;* 558.15 *provide drink*
sweetened 498.6 *sweet*
sweetener **498.2**; 768.2 *gift;* 785.4 *grant;* 813.8 *secret money*
sweetening 498.2 *sweetener*
sweeten the kitty 768.5 *give*
sweeten the pot 785.11 *remunerate;* 480.16 *tempt*
sweet FA 195.2 *nothing*
sweet Fanny Adams 195.2 *nothing;* 94.2 *nothingness*
sweet fuck all 195.2 *nothing*
sweetheart 567.4 *boyfriend;* 568.4 *girlfriend;* 593.9 *lover;* 593.12 *nicknames for lovers*
sweetheart name 721.8 *name*
sweet herb 44.11 *vegetable*
sweetie 593.12 *nicknames for lovers;* 25.41 *sweet*
sweeties 498.4 *confectionery*
sweetish 498.6 *sweet*
sweetkins 593.12 *nicknames for lovers*
sweetly **498.9**; 658.14 *courteously;* 516.11 *melodiously;* 495.11 *tastily*
sweetmeat 25.41 *sweet*
sweetmeats 490.4 *pleasurable things;* 498.2 *sweetener*
Sweetness 498
sweetness **498.1**; 658.1 *courtesy;* 495.4 *flavour;* 593.4 *lovability;* 490.1 *physical pleasure;* 498.1 *sweetness*
sweet nothings 593.14 *communication of love*
sweet on 593.18 *in love*
sweet pea 502.2 *fragrant thing*
sweet potato 593.9 *lover*
sweet potato pie 25.36 *cake*
sweet roll 25.36 *cake*
sweets 498.4 *confectionery;* 593.12 *nicknames for lovers*
sweet-scented 502.4 *fragrant*
sweet sherry 558.9 *wine*
sweet shop 498.4 *confectionery;* 557.17 *food shop*
sweet sixteen 555.11 *young*
sweet sleep 263.1 *ease*
sweet smell 502.1 *fragrance;* 500.1 *odour*
sweet-smelling 502.4 *fragrant;* 490.6 *pleasant*
sweet smell of success 246.1 *success*
sweet-sounding 516.6 *melodious*
sweet-talk 645.5 *be cunning;* 699.22 *be hypocritical;* 677.2, 677.9 *blarney;* 593.14 *communication of love;* 593.26 *court;* 702.12 *deceive;* 699.3, 700.3 *hypocrisy;* 483.9 *motivate;* 480.15 *persuade;* 483.5 *positive stimulus*
sweet-talker 702.6 *sophist*
sweet-talking 658.1 *courtesy;* 658.8 *good-mannered;* 677.13 *honeyed;* 699.31, 702.10 *hypocritical*
sweet taste 495.1 *taste;* 495.2 *taste of life*
sweet tongue 658.1 *courtesy*
sweet-tongued 658.8 *good-mannered*
sweet tooth 498.1 *sweetness*
sweet wine 498.5 *sweet drink;* 558.9 *wine*
swell 211.6 *add;* 190.6 *become bigger;* 232.5 *be complete;* 182.5 *be convex;* 507.8 *be loud;* 660.24 *be vain;* 91.10 *billow;* 209.6 *change gradually;* 797.1 *good;* 345.8 *grow;* 190.1 *growth;* 213.4 *increase;* 507.1 *loudness;* 190.5 *make bigger;* 185.8 *pro-*

trude; 366.2 *send up*; 213.2 *spread*; 327.13 *tempest*; 327.3 *turbulence*; 30.14, 91.3 *wave*; 235.1 *worthy*
swelled 190.7 *bigger*
swelled head 622.13 *proud person*
swellelegant 235.1 *worthy*
swelling 182.2 *bulge*; 182.4 *convex*; 182.1 *convexity*; 190.3 *enlarged thing*; 190.8, 345.11 *growing*; 190.1, 345.3 *growth*; 213.1 *increase*; 507.6 *loud*; 91.7 *oceanic*; 548.2 *pimple*; 185.3 *protuberance*; 185.5 *protuberant*; 260.13 *skin disease*; 213.2 *spread*; 260.3 *symptom*; 260.15 *ulcer*
swell out 182.5 *be convex*
swell the ranks 376.41 *band together*; 211.7 *support*
swell with pride 622.29 *feel pride*
swelter 493.16 *feel hot*; 560.19 *sweat*
sweltering 31.51 *hot*; 493.11 *warm*
swelteringly 31.65 *meteorologically*
sweltry 31.51 *hot*
swept 256.17 *cleaned*
swept clean 649.8 *overlooked*
swerve 189.6 *be oblique*; 325.1 *deviate*; 325.15 *deviating motion*; 144.14 *displace*; 144.1 *displacement*; 479.2 *equivocate*; 189.1 *obliqueness*
swerved 144.8 *displaced*
swerving 325.15 *deviating motion*; 144.8 *displaced*; 325.21 *indirect*
swift 332.1; 262.3 *hasty*; 332.12 *swift animal*
Swiftair 692.2 *postal communication*
swift animal 332.12
swiftly 332.14; 262.6 *hastily*; 280.8 *immediately*
swift-moving 332.1 *swift*
Swiftness 332
swiftness 262.4 *haste*; 332.8 *speed*
swift person 332.13
swift thing 332.11
swifty 280.5 *immediate*
swig 558.13 *drink*; 690.8 *get drunk*
swigging 558.1 *drinking*; 690.5 *drunken*
swill 258.5; 256.14 *bathe*; 558.13 *drink*; 690.8 *get drunk*
swiller 558.12 *drinker*; 690.17 *drunkard*
swilling 558.1, 558.16, 690.11 *drinking*; 690.5 *drunken*
swim 67.9; 415.9 *be light*; 576.9 *exercise*; 50.8 *punting*; 67.11 *swimming*
swim against the current 264.19 *have difficulty*
swim against the tide 118.19 *be independent*
swim-and-tow 67.3 *survival swimming*
swim bladder 74.5 *fish anatomy*
swim in 217.5 *about*; 219.4 *be excessive*
swimmer 67.4
Swimming 67
swimming 67.1; **67.11**; 576.5 *exercise*; 257.1 *hygiene*; 323.11 *nautical*
swimming area 67.7 *swimming pool*
swimming association 67.5
swimming bath 256.6 *bath*; 88.2 *small lake*; 67.7 *swimming pool*
swimming beach 67.7 *swimming pool*
swimming costume 551.21 *beachwear*; 67.8 *swimwear*
swimming equipment 67.1 *swimming*
swimming hole 88.2 *small lake*; 67.7 *swimming pool*
swimming in clothes 67.3 *survival swimming*
swimming lake 67.7 *swimming pool*
swimmingly 248.9 *prosperously*; 485.12 *skilfully*; 246.16 *successfully*
swimming movements 67.2 *swimming technique*
swimming pool 67.7; 256.6 *bath*; 88.2 *small lake*
swimming rescue 67.3 *survival swimming*
swimming stroke 67.1 *swimming*
swimming team 67.1 *swimming*
swimming technique 67.2
swimming the English Channel 67.1 *swimming*
swimming trunks 67.8 *swimwear*
swimming under water 67.1 *swimming*
swimsuit 551.21 *beachwear*; 67.8 *swimwear*
swimsuited 552.10 *in dishabille*
swim under water 67.9 *swim*
swim upstream 264.19 *have difficulty*
swimwear 67.8; 552.4 *dishabille*
swim with the stream 117.8 *comply*; 265.20 *take it easy*
swim with the tide 664.14 *follow*
swindle 774.16 *act dishonestly*; 800.10 *be criminal*; 645.5 *be cunning*; 604.8 *be dishonest*; 699.25, 700.30 *be fraudulent*; 13.12 *cheat*; 800.3 *criminality*; 774.7 *dishonesty*; 484.3 *expedient plan*; 699.8, 700.10 *fraud*; 786.7 *not pay*; 792.10 *overcharge*; 645.2 *stratagem*; 773.10 *take away*; 773.3 *taking away*; 700.28 *trick*
swindled 604.10 *deceived*; 774.18 *fraudulent*
swindler 699.19, 700.17 *cheat*; 645.3 *cunning person*; 700.15, 718.3 *deceiver*; 774.11 *dishonest person*; 699.17 *false person*; 804.9 *wicked person*
swindling 800.7 *criminal*; 699.35 *fraudulent*; 786.1 *nonpayment*
swine 43.8 *livestock*; 804.9 *wicked person*
swine fever 260.18 *veterinary disease*
swineherd 43.16 *farm worker*
swinepox 260.18 *veterinary disease*
swing 340.1 *action*; 141.6 *available space*; 227.11 *be changeable*; 814.6 *be punished*; 298.7 *be regular*; 120.5 *be unequal*; 331.13 *blow*; 53.18 *bowl*; 53.13 *bowling*; 52.2 *boxing*; 68.2 *cross-country skiing*; 53.8 *delivery*; 325.15 *deviating motion*; 52.11 *fight*; 331.3 *hit*; 57.5 *horizontal bar*; 18.8 *jazz*; 62.9 *mountaineer*; 346.1 *operation*; 326.8 *oscillate*; 326.1 *oscillation*; 326.7 *oscillator*; 327.25 *pitch*; 48.7 *play baseball*; 298.1 *regularity*; 761.4, 761.8 *return*; 326.4, 326.11 *rock*; 307.8 *rotate*; 50.16 *row*; 68.14 *ski*; 325.10 *slide*; 331.14 *sporting hit*; 327.11 *stagger*; 57.7 *stationary rings*; 361.10 *suspend*; 361.3 *suspended object*; 361.1 *suspension*; 18.37 *syncopate*; 104.2 *tendency*; 63.2 *tennis strokes*
swing and sway 298.7 *be regular*
swing around 303.13 *about-turn*; 761.8 *return*
swingback 47.2 *field events*
swing back 761.8 *return*
swing bowler 53.4 *team*
swing bridge 38.21 *bridge*
swinger 18.24 *musician*; 490.3 *pleasure-seeker*
swing from 361.10 *suspend*
swinging 62.3 *climbing technique*; 57.5 *horizontal bar*; 18.33 *jazz*; 326.13 *oscillating*; 298.11 *regular*; 326.4 *rock*; 57.7 *stationary rings*; 361.7 *suspended*; 120.3 *unequal*
swingingly 265.21 *easily*
swing in with 747.14 *join with*
swingletree 79.12 *figurative usage*
swing of the pendulum 326.1 *oscillation*; 761.4 *return*
swing round 307.8 *rotate*; 303.9 *turn round*
swing to the hill 68.2 *cross-country skiing*; 68.14 *ski*
swingy ice 68.10 *curling*
swinish 71.33 *ungulate*
swink 576.1 *work*
swipe 331.13 *blow*; 331.3, 381.18 *hit*; 774.12 *steal*; 381.5 *strike*; 330.5 *throw*
swiping 774.1 *stealing*
swirl 307.10; 327.22 *agitate*; 90.7 *flow*; 307.3 *reel*; 90.6 *river flow*; 327.3 *turbulence*; 307.4 *vortex*
swirling 307.11 *rotating*; 307.2 *turning*
swish 553.7 *fashionable*; 512.1, 512.4 *hiss*
swishingly 512.8 *sibilantly*
Swiss cross 743.6 *national emblem*
Swiss Guard 586.12 *ceremonial troops*
Swiss neutrality 566.11 *nation*
Swiss roll 25.36 *cake*
switch 479.3 *apostatize*; 587.7 *blunt weapon*; 205.6 *branch*; 311.15 *change direction*; 144.14 *displace*; 144.1 *displacement*; 759.1, 759.5 *exchange*; 762.6 *give a substitute*; 814.3 *hit*; 814.14 *instrument of punishment*; 39.28 *plug*; 321.3 *rail*; 317.10 *railway*; 325.9 *shove aside*; 762.1 *substitution*; 438.1 *tool*; 321.2 *track*; 316.11 *transfer*
switchback 317.10 *railway*
switchblade 425.10 *knife*
switchboard 692.12 *public telephone system*; 21.17 *stage*
switchboard operator 692.13 *telephoner*
Switch card™ 785.1 *payment*; 777.7 *purchasing*
switched 144.8 *displaced*; 759.7 *exchanged*; 762.8 *substituted*
switched off 335.10 *powerless*; 339.6 *suspended*; 505.7 *unheard*
switched on 334.14 *operative*; 488.5 *sensible*
switching 39.15 *circuit function*; 759.1 *exchange*
switching circuit 39.13 *circuit*
switch off 489.11 *be unfeeling*; 335.8 *overpower*
switch on 130.20, 346.8 *activate*; 39.35 *conduct*; 437.11 *fuel*; 334.11 *give power*; 522.24 *light*
switch on a light 522.24 *light*
switch over 479.3 *apostatize*
switch yard 321.8 *railway station*
swivel 307.4 *axle*; 587.12 *historical guns*; 307.8 *rotate*; 50.4 *rowing*; 303.9 *turn round*
swivel chair 23.2 *chair*
swivelling 307.11 *rotating*
swiz 700.10 *fraud*
swizzle 700.30 *be fraudulent*; 700.10 *fraud*
swizzled 700.36 *deceived*
swollen 190.7 *bigger*; 622.22 *boastful*; 182.4 *convex*; 260.23 *diseased*; 158.16 *fat*; 213.7 *increased*; 542.10 *ornate*; 366.11 *raised*; 152.1 *thick*
swollen adenoids 260.9 *respiratory disease*
swollen head 622.13 *proud person*; 673.7 *vain person*
swollen-headed 622.22 *boastful*; 673.8 *vain*
swollen-headedness 673.1 *vanity*
swollenness 190.1 *growth*
swoon 261.5 *be fatigued*; 335.4 *disability*; 261.7 *fatigue*; 489.2 *unconsciousness*
swooning 261.1 *fatigued*
swoop 332.9 *acceleration*; 332.4 *be swift*; 305.5 *dive*; 305.12 *drop*
swooping 305.4 *fall*; 305.18 *falling*
swoosh 332.9 *acceleration*; 512.1, 512.4 *hiss*
sword 357.7 *agent of destruction*; 586.1 *combatant*; 425.10 *knife*; 425.8 *sharp-pointed thing*; 587.8 *sharp weapon*
sword and sorcery novel 17.2 *fiction*
sword dance 22.4 *historic dancing*
swordfish 55.4 *American game fish*; 25.18 *sea fish*
sword in hand 585.15 *warring*
swordlike 425.3 *sharp-edged*
Sword of Damocles 254.5 *danger*; 612.4 *intimidation*
sword of state 743.4 *insignia*
swordplay 54.5 *fence*; 54.1 *fencing*; 21.2 *play*
sword point 425.7 *sharp point*
swordsman 586.1 *combatant*
swordstick 587.8 *sharp weapon*
swordthrust 381.18 *hit*
sworn 755.7 *contractual*; 810.11 *duty-bound*; 756.12 *promised*; 707.12 *vowed*
sworn enemy 596.3 *disliked person*; 594.8 *hated person*
sworn off 684.8 *self-restrained*
sworn statement 744.2 *certificate*; 707.3 *vow*
sworn testimony 707.3 *vow*
sworn to 663.8 *loyal*; 707.12 *vowed*
swot 442.8 *intellectual person*; 6.23 *learn*; 6.7 *learner*
swotting 6.8 *learning*
swotty 6.18 *educated*
swung dash 742.7 *punctuation*
sybarite 490.3 *pleasure-seeker*; 686.5 *self-indulgent person*
sybaritic 490.7 *pleased*; 686.6 *self-indulgent*
sybaritism 686.1 *self-indulgence*
syconus 80.2 *botanical fruit*
sycophancy 664.2; **677.5**; 658.4 *deference*
sycophant 664.3; **677.7**; 388.2 *appeaser*; 658.6 *courteous person*; 223.9, 267.5, 289.8 *follower*; 623.16 *humble person*; 599.7 *person who humours*; 387.3 *subordinate*
sycophantic 664.7; **677.16**; 658.9 *deferential*; 599.11 *humouring*; 663.8 *loyal*; 421.6 *smooth-mannered*; 388.5 *submitting*; 267.10 *tenacious*
sycophantically 664.17; 658.16 *deferentially*; 677.17 *flatteringly*; 421.16 *suavely*; 267.12 *tenaciously*
Sydney 87.6 *other cities*
Sydney to Hobart Race 50.1 *sailing*
syllabary 5.14 *alphabet*
syllabic 5.41 *lettered*
syllabic metre 17.9 *metre*
syllabic script 5.13 *letter*
syllabification 375.2 *deconstruction*
syllabify 375.4 *deconstruct*; 5.47 *word*
syllable 5.16 *spoken letter*; 729.7 *utterance*; 5.47 *word*
syllabus 220.5 *list of appointments*; 723.2 *outline*; 6.3 *subject*; 220.2 *table*
syllogism 4.5 *philosophical argument*; 4.8 *philosophical term*; 444.2 *reasoning*
syllogist 4.10 *philosopher*; 444.5 *reasoner*
syllogize 4.21 *rationalize*
sylph 11.11 *ghost*; 153.9 *thin person*
sylphic 153.1 *thin*
sylphlike 153.1 *thin*
sylvan 44.16 *horticultural*; 79.16 *wooded*
sylvatic 79.16 *wooded*
sylvestral 79.16 *wooded*
symbiont 34.18 *ecology*; 70.4 *type of animal*
symbiosis 223.1 *accompaniment*; 374.1 *combination*; 34.18 *ecology*; 83.5 *fungal association*; 110.2 *interconnection*; 84.6 *lichen*; 554.1 *life*; 747.3 *mutual relationship*; 387.1 *subjection*
symbiote 34.18 *ecology*
symbiotic 84.7 *algal*; 554.14 *biotic*; 223.18 *concurrent*; 374.8, 747.17 *cooperative*; 110.5 *interconnected*; 70.15 *of animals*; 387.9 *subject*
symbiotic alga 84.1 *alga*
symbiotically 84.9 *algologically*; 223.23 *concurrently*; 374.10 *in combination*; 110.10 *reciprocally*; 83.13 *saprophytically*
symbiotic fungus 83.5 *fungal association*
symbol 9.3 *idol*; 717.6 *image*; 5.13 *letter*; 194.1 *number*; 742.1 *sign*; 762.3 *substitute thing*; 36.24 *symbolism*; 11.6 *talisman*; 1.8 *tradition*
symbolic 738.14 *manifest*; 694.6 *meaningful*; 11.14 *occult*; 5.39 *of language*; 717.13 *representational*; 721.13 *representing*; 10.21 *ritualistic*; 742.14 *signifying*; 2.12 *sociological*; 124.4 *trivial*
symbolical 743.12 *identified*; 5.41 *lettered*; 742.14 *signifying*
symbolically 743.14 *identifiably*; 742.18 *indicatively*; 5.48 *linguistically*; 694.13 *meaningfully*; 19.30 *pictorially*; 717.14 *representationally*; 10.23 *ritually*; 2.16 *sociologically*
symbolic anthropology 1.1 *anthropology*
symbolic costume 551.5 *fancy dress*
symbolic interaction 2.3 *social environment*
symbolic language 5.10 *language type*
symbolic logic 27.63 *mathematical logic*
symbolics 11.1 *occultism*; 10.2 *ritualism*
symbolism 36.24; **742.2**; 17.3 *aspect of fiction*; 11.1 *occultism*; 10.2 *ritualism*
symbolist 17.14 *author*; 19.29 *realist*; 742.8 *signer*
symbolistic 742.14 *signifying*
symbolistically 742.18 *indicatively*
symbolization 738.10 *manifestation*; 717.1 *representation*; 36.24, 742.2 *symbolism*
symbolize 762.6 *give a substitute*; 694.10 *mean*; 11.20 *occult*; 717.9 *represent*; 742.10 *signify*
symbolizer 742.8 *signer*
symbol list 742.1 *sign*
symbol of death 582.3
symbol of peace 589.2
symbological 742.14 *signifying*
symbologist 742.8 *signer*
symbology 742.2 *symbolism*
symmetric 298.11 *regular*; 162.4 *symmetrical*
symmetrical 162.4; 110.6 *correlative*; 706.15 *correspondent*; 543.3 *elegant*; 111.16, 119.6 *equal*; 750.13 *harmonious*; 407.10 *ordered*; 298.11 *regular*; 115.7 *similar*; 27.79 *spatial*
symmetrically 162.7; 115.14 *comparably*; 110.11 *correlatively*; 706.26 *correspondingly*; 543.5 *elegantly*; 119.13 *equitably*; 407.27 *methodically*; 298.15 *regularly*
symmetricalness 162.1 *symmetry*
symmetric figure 27.41 *geometric figure*

symmetric relation 27.63 *mathematical logic*

symmetrize 162.6; 108.8 *be proportionate to;* 750.24 *harmonize;* 216.10 *make average;* 111.8 *make the same*

Symmetry 162

symmetry 162.1; 110.3 *correlation;* 706.8 *correspondence;* 543.1 *elegance;* 111.5 *equality;* 119.2 *equilibrium;* 27.41 *geometric figure;* 545.1 *gorgeousness;* 750.4 *harmony;* 407.7 *method;* 298.1 *regularity*

symmetry element 162.2 *symmetry operation*

symmetry operation 162.2

sympathetic 392.35, 650.6 *benevolent;* 569.8 *friendly;* 750.10 *in accord;* 764.5 *jointly possessing;* 595.6 *liking;* 593.17 *loving;* 627.6 *pitying;* 590.12, 591.1 *sensitive;* 419.6 *soft-hearted;* 413.9 *supportive;* 473.5 *unselfish*

sympathetically 595.11 *admiringly;* 363.14 *attractively;* 392.38, 650.10 *benevolently;* 750.31 *in accord;* 764.6 *in common;* 569.17 *in friendship;* 593.30 *lovingly;* 627.13 *pitifully;* 591.12 *sensitively;* 473.9 *unselfishly*

sympathetic magic 11.3 *witchcraft*

sympathetic resonance 510.1 *resonance*

sympathies 590.3 *feelings*

sympathize 650.8 *be benevolent;* 591.11 *be sensitive;* 590.18 *feel for;* 477.16 *have insight;* 627.8 *pity;* 392.20 *sustain*

sympathizer 650.5 *benevolent person;* 590.9 *feeling person;* 764.3 *participant;* 627.4 *pitying person;* 591.8 *sensitive person;* 413.8 *supporter*

sympathize with 473.7 *be unselfish;* 490.10 *comfort;* 595.7 *like;* 593.23 *love;* 627.8 *pity*

sympathizing 627.6 *pitying*

sympatholytic 37.14 *counteracting;* 37.4 *drug type*

sympathomimetic 37.4 *drug type;* 37.17 *stimulating*

sympathy 750.1 *accord;* 363.1 *attraction;* 593.7 *choice;* 627.2 *condolence;* 747.2 *fellowship;* 569.2 *friendly relations;* 590.5 *good feeling;* 477.3 *insight;* 595.1 *liking;* 413.6 *moral support;* 764.2 *participation;* 627.1 *pity;* 591.5 *sensitivity;* 392.3 *sustenance;* 473.2 *unselfishness*

sympathy in grief 627.2 *condolence*

sympathy lock-out 15.4 *industrial dispute*

sympathy strike 15.4 *industrial dispute;* 764.2 *participation*

symphonic 750.13 *harmonious*

symphonically 750.33 *harmoniously*

symphonic music 18.3 *classical music*

symphonious 18.30 *harmonic;* 750.13 *harmonious*

symphonize 750.24 *harmonize;* 516.9 *set to music*

symphony 750.4 *harmony;* 356.5 *work of art*

symphony orchestra 374.3 *assembly;* 18.26 *musical group*

symphylan 75.4 *arthropod*

symphysis 374.1 *combination*

symphystic 374.7 *combined*

symposiarch 579.14 *leader*

symposium 376.5, 734.4 *conference;* 722.1 *dissertation;* 4.5 *philosophical argument*

symptom 260.3; 223.4 *concomitant;* 716.4 *indication;* 738.10 *manifestation;* 475.5 *omen;* 742.1 *sign;* 711.1 *warning*

symptomatic 35.24 *diagnostic;* 475.13 *predicting;* 742.14 *signifying;* 711.8 *warning*

symptomatically 742.18 *indicatively*

symptomatological 35.24 *diagnostic;* 742.14 *signifying*

symptomatology 35.3 *medical specialty;* 719.5 *science of interpretation;* 742.2 *symbolism*

symptomize 742.10 *signify*

synaesthesia 36.27 *association of ideas;* 17.12 *poetic language*

synagogue 10.11 *place of worship*

synandrous 78.12 *of flowers*

syn–anti isomer 32.13 *structure*

sync 285.3 *synchronism;* 285.7 *synchronize*

syncarpous 80.9 *of a fruit*

synchromesh 438.5 *machine*

synchronic 5.38 *linguistic;* 19.29 *realist*

synchronicity 374.1 *combination;* 111.2 *equivalence;* 11.10 *psychic phenomenon*

synchronic linguistics 5.1 *linguistics*

synchronism 223.2; **285.3**; 750.4 *harmony*

synchronization 374.2 *cooperation;* 750.4 *harmony;* 18.13 *melody;* 285.3 *synchronism*

synchronize 285.7; 223.13 *accompany;* 275.18 *adjust the clock;* 374.6 *come together;* 119.11 *equalize;* 407.20, 516.8, 750.24 *harmonize;* 111.8 *make the same*

synchronized 285.10; 374.8 *cooperative;* 516.7, 750.13 *harmonious;* 67.11 *swimming*

synchronized flash 41.19 *flash*

synchronized swimming 67.1 *swimming*

synchronize watches 275.18 *adjust the clock;* 281.14 *keep time*

synchronous 374.8 *cooperative;* 111.13 *equivalent;* 18.30 *harmonic;* 516.7, 750.13 *harmonious;* 285.10 *synchronized*

synchronous-induction motor 39.31 *electric motor*

synchronously 285.13; 516.12, 750.33 *harmoniously;* 111.18 *identically;* 374.10 *in combination*

synchronous motor 39.31 *electric motor*

synchrotron 334.8 *nuclear power;* 28.94 *particle accelerator*

synclastic surface 27.38 *surface*

syncline 30.20 *earth movement;* 184.1 *wrinkle*

syncopal 269.3 *concise*

syncopate 18.37; 516.9 *set to music*

syncopated 516.7 *harmonious;* 18.33 *jazz*

syncopated steps 22.3 *ballroom dance steps*

syncopation 516.4 *harmonics;* 18.8 *jazz;* 275.12 *musical time;* 18.19 *tempo*

syncopator 18.24 *musician*

syncope 269.1 *conciseness;* 723.2 *outline;* 149.2 *shortening*

syncretic 374.7 *combined;* 412.12 *mixed*

syncretically 374.10 *in combination*

syncretism 374.1 *combination;* 412.1 *mixture*

syncretize 374.5 *combine*

syncytial 34.23 *cellular*

syncytium 34.7 *cell*

syndeton 5.30 *syntax*

syndicalism 588.2 *anarchism;* 12.1 *government;* 4.7 *school of thought;* 396.7 *type of rule*

syndicalist 588.3 *anarchist;* 4.11 *follower of a doctrine;* 4.14 *of a philosophy;* 12.6 *political party*

syndicalistic 588.7 *anarchistic*

syndicate 374.3 *assembly;* 376.15 *association;* 741.7 *press agency;* 740.15 *publish;* 741.13 *report*

syndicated programme 692.25 *broadcast material*

syndiotactic 32.44 *polymeric*

syndiotactic polymer 32.21 *polymer*

syndrome 223.4 *concomitant;* 738.10 *manifestation;* 475.5 *omen;* 742.1 *sign;* 260.3 *symptom*

synecdoche 17.12 *poetic language*

synecology 34.18 *ecology*

syneresis 191.1 *contraction*

synergetic 747.17 *cooperative*

synergetically 747.20 *cooperatively*

synergic 750.11 *allied;* 747.17 *cooperative*

synergism 747.1 *cooperation*

synergistic 747.17 *cooperative*

synergistically 747.20 *cooperatively*

synergize 750.22 *form an alliance*

synergy 750.2 *alliance;* 747.1 *cooperation;* 747.3 *mutual relationship*

syngamy 412.1 *mixture*

synizesis 191.1 *contraction*

synod 376.5 *conference;* 579.7 *council*

synodal 579.18 *parliamentary*

synodic 29.36 *astronomical*

synonym 119.3 *equalization;* 762.3 *substitute thing;* 694.4 *type of meaning;* 5.17 *word*

synonym dictionary 5.28 *dictionary*

synonymic 5.42 *worded*

synonymity 750.5 *conformity;* 119.3 *equalization;* 111.2 *equivalence;* 694.4 *type of meaning*

synonymous 750.14 *conforming;* 111.13 *equivalent;* 694.6 *meaningful;* 115.7 *similar;* 719.17 *translational*

synonymously 115.14 *comparably;* 111.18 *identically*

synonymousness 111.2 *equivalence;* 694.4 *type of meaning*

synonymy 750.5 *conformity;* 111.2 *equivalence;* 115.1 *similarity;* 694.4 *type of meaning*

synopsis 220.5 *list of appointments;* 163.1, 269.2 *outline;* 149.3 *shortened version;* 723.1 *summary;* 204.3 *whole situation*

synopsize 269.4 *be concise;* 163.5 *outline;* 149.10 *shorten;* 723.8 *summarize*

synopsized 163.6 *outlined;* 723.7 *shortened*

synoptic 138.15 *general;* 31.41 *meteorologic;* 149.7 *short*

synoptically 31.65 *meteorologically*

Synoptic Gospels 7.12 *religious text*

synoptic map 31.4 *weather forecast*

synoptic meteorology 31.1 *meteorology*

synovia 268.5 *lubricant*

synpetalous 78.12 *of flowers*

synsepalous 78.12 *of flowers*

syntactic 5.44 *grammatical;* 5.38 *linguistic*

syntactically 5.52 *grammatically;* 5.48 *linguistically*

syntactic analysis 5.30 *syntax*

syntactic meaning 5.30 *syntax*

syntactics 5.1 *linguistics*

syntactic structure 5.30 *syntax*

syntax 5.30; 40.9 *programming language*

synthesis 32.16; 32.1 *chemistry;* 374.1 *combination;* 412.2 *mixed thing;* 4.5 *philosophical argument;* 4.8 *philosophical term*

synthesize 32.27; 374.5 *combine;* 111.8 *make the same;* 33.25 *metabolize;* 356.10 *produce;* 444.11 *reason*

synthesized 32.40 *synthetic*

synthesizer 18.25 *musical instrument*

synthetic 32.40; 96.12 *artificial;* 32.31 *chemical;* 4.16 *dialectical;* 42.3 *fabric;* 125.13 *imitation;* 700.39 *imitative;* 356.12 *produced;* 19.29 *realist;* 115.8 *simulated;* 32.16 *synthesis*

synthetically 32.46 *chemically;* 115.14 *comparably;* 125.14 *imitatively;* 699.41 *spuriously*

synthetic chemist 32.2 *chemist*

synthetic compound 32.16 *synthesis*

synthetic drug 394.8 *drug*

synthetic dye 42.6 *dye;* 529.4 *pigment*

synthetic fabric 42.3 *fabric*

synthetic fibre 42.1 *fibre*

synthetic plasma 431.4 *blood*

synthetic resin 435.1 *materials*

synthetic rubber 700.6 *imitation;* 422.4 *rubber*

syntone 36.7 *personality type*

syntony 36.7 *personality type*

syphilis 260.4 *disease;* 260.14 *venereal disease*

syphilitic 260.23 *diseased*

syphilitic sore 260.14 *venereal disease*

syringe 369.9 *extractor;* 433.34 *hose;* 368.11 *thing inserted;* 433.11 *wash*

syrinx 72.16 *avian anatomy*

syrup 430.6 *gelatin;* 498.2 *sweetener*

syrupiness 498.1 *sweetness;* 430.1 *viscosity*

syrupy 430.9 *gelatinous;* 498.6 *sweet*

Sysop 40.16 *Internet*

system 750.6 *convention;* 140.6 *custom;* 160.1 *form;* 30.41 *geological time;* 407.7 *method;* 407.1 *order;* 409.3 *organization;* 484.2 *policy;* 632.6 *procedure;* 317.1 *way;* 204.2 *whole thing*

systematic 34.20 *biological;* 140.10 *customary;* 160.9 *formed;* 15.9 *negotiated;* 407.10 *ordered;* 409.22 *organizational;* 484.14 *planned;* 34.28 *taxonomic;* 407.14 *well-ordered*

systematically 484.16 *as planned;* 34.29 *biologically;* 160.13 *formatively;* 632.19 *habitually;* 409.28 *in place;* 407.27 *methodically;* 140.19 *to rule*

systematic error 28.83 *sensitivity*

systematics 34.1 *life science;* 407.6 *methodicalness;* 34.17 *taxonomy*

systematic sampling 27.57 *population*

systematic theology 7.13 *theology*

systematic wage structure 15.2 *industrial negotiations*

systematic zoologist 70.11 *zoologist*

systematic zoology 70.9 *animal science*

systematism 407.6 *methodicalness*

systematization 407.6 *methodicalness;* 409.3 *organization;* 484.7 *planning*

systematize 407.19; 160.7 *form;* 298.10 *make regular;* 750.26 *make uniform;* 409.13 *organize;* 484.9 *plan;* 140.14 *regulate*

systematized 409.21 *organized*

systematizer 484.8 *planner*

systematology 407.6 *methodicalness*

Système International d'Unités 26.5 *measuring system*

systemic 5.44 *grammatical*

systemic fungicide 44.8 *weedkiller*

systemic grammar 5.29 *grammar*

systemic herbicide 43.14 *pest control*

systems analysis 40.1 *computing;* 27.1 *mathematics*

systems analyst 210.6 *calculator;* 27.2 *mathematician;* 40.2 *operator;* 484.8 *planner*

systole 191.1 *contraction*

systole and diastole 326.1 *oscillation*

syzygy 147.1 *nearness;* 29.16 *planet*

Szondi test 36.5 *psychological test*

ta 671.9 *thank you!*

taanit 10.16 *religious festival*

tab 211.3 *additional item;* 743.10 *identify*

tabard 551.11 *jacket*

Tabasco™ 558.8 *mixed drink;* 496.2 *seasoning*

Tabasco sauce 25.15 *sauce*

tabby 541.10 *mottled*

tabby cat 541.5 *variegated thing*

tabernacle 10.11 *place of worship;* 10.14 *sacred object;* 10.13 *shrine*

tabes 153.8 *emaciation*

tabescence 191.1 *contraction;* 153.8 *emaciation*

tabescent 191.8 *contracting;* 153.2 *emaciated*

tabetic 153.2 *emaciated*

table 23.4; **220.2**; 634.7 *be evasive;* 409.8 *chart;* 210.5 *computer;* 294.8 *delay;* 406.5 *divisions;* 187.3 *flat thing;* 361.12 *interrupt;* 411.1 *layer;* 220.1 *list;* 20.9 *miscellaneous architectural features;* 744.6 *record book;* 413.2 *supporting part;* 355.2 *withdraw*

tableau 656.3 *formal occasion;* 19.7 *picture;* 21.7 *show;* 518.7 *view*

tableau vivant 21.7 *show*

table bird 72.4

tablecloth 256.11 *cleaning cloth;* 550.12 *protective covering*

tabled 294.10 *held up;* 361.9 *interrupted;* 406.12 *itemized*

table d'hôte 25.56 *culinary*

table lamp 522.6 *electric light*

tableland 187.3 *flat thing;* 154.2 *heights;* 92.7 *upland*

table manners 557.4 *eating meals;* 632.5 *tradition*

tablemat 256.11 *cleaning cloth*

table of contents 220.2 *table*

tables 210.2 *statistics*

table salt 25.7 *basic ingredient*

table setting 542.1 *ornament*

tablespoon 203.3 *container;* 557.16 *eating utensil;* 410.17 *ladle*

tablet 187.3 *flat thing;* 394.2 *medicine;* 744.11 *monument;* 37.6 *pill;* 744.6 *record book;* 411.4 *slice*

table talk 734.2 *chat*

table tapper 11.12 *occultist*

table tapping 11.1 *occultism*

table tennis 63.1 *tennis*

table wine 558.9 *wine*

tabling 294.3 *delayed action;* 361.6 *interruption*

tabloid 394.2 *medicine;* 740.4 *newspaper*

tabloid press 740.3 *journalism;* 693.4, 741.5 *mass communication*

taboo 1.5 *anthropological concept;* 128.7 *exclude;* 128.11 *excluded;* 128.1 *exclusion;* 1.8 *tradition;* 399.1 *veto;* 399.5 *vetoed*

taboo word 5.19 *swearword*

tabs 21.19 *stage set*

tabular 137.10 *classificatory;* 409.26 *diagrammatic;* 187.8 *horizontal;* 406.12 *itemized;* 27.78 *pictorial*

tabula rasa 98.3 *emptiness;* 358.4 *eraser;* 295.5 *fresh start*

tabularly 220.13 *inventorially*

tabulate 409.15 *categorize;* 406.9 *itemize;* 220.8 *list;* 744.13 *record;* 744.15 *register;* 137.14 *sort;* 407.19 *systematize*

tabulated 409.24 *categorized*; 406.12 *itemized*; 220.11 *listed*
tabulation 409.5 *categorization*; 220.7 *listing*
tabulation of ballots 469.12 *election*
tabulator 210.5 *computer*
tacheometer 26.8 *meter*
tacheometric 26.16 *micrometric*
tacheometry 26.2 *micrometry*
tachi dori 52.10 *aikido*
tachi-waza 52.7 *judo*
tachometer 26.8 *meter*; 332.8 *speed*
tachometric 26.16 *micrometric*
tachometry 26.2 *micrometry*
tachycardia 260.10 *cardiovascular disease*
tachymeter 26.8 *meter*
tachymetric 26.16 *micrometric*
tachymetry 26.2 *micrometry*
tachyon 275.1 *time*
tacit 694.6 *meaningful*; 506.3 *silent*
taciturn 634.18 *avoiding*; 269.3 *concise*; 655.9, 732.1 *shy*; 506.3, 736.16 *silent*; 730.11 *speechless*
taciturnity 269.1 *conciseness*; 730.5 *mutism*; 732.3 *shyness*; 506.4, 736.4 *silence*; 655.1 *unsociability*
taciturnly 655.14 *unsocially*
tack 324.2 *bearing*; 227.11 *be changeable*; 373.11 *connect*; 325.1 *deviate*; 325.14 *deviating course*; 479.2 *equivocate*; 373.8 *fastening*; 557.7 *food*; 59.14 *horse-riding terms*; 323.9 *navigate*; 50.15 *sail*; 50.1 *sailing*; 425.8 *sharp-pointed thing*; 68.14 *ski*; 438.1 *tool*; 438.10 *use tools*; 300.15 *walk*; 317.1 *way*
tacked 373.15 *connected*
tackily 497.11 *tastelessly*; 430.12 *viscously*
tackiness 497.4 *bad taste*; 236.8 *inferiority*; 675.2 *tawdriness*; 544.3 *ugliness*; 430.1 *viscosity*
tacking 68.2 *cross-country skiing*; 50.1, 50.10 *sailing*
tackle **353.3**; **373.7**; 340.4 *act*; 353.5 *attempt*; 438.7 *equipment*; 66.2 *football play*; 366.9 *lifter*; 130.18 *make a beginning*; 46.7 *offence*; 50.3 *parts of a sailing boat*; 64.5 *play rugby*; 66.4 *play soccer*; 64.3 *rugby play*; 354.1, 638.9 *undertake*
tackled 64.6 *rugger*; 66.5 *soccer*
tackler 353.7 *attempter*
tackling 66.2 *football play*; 64.3 *rugby play*
tack on 211.6 *add*
tacky 267.9 *adhesive*; 497.6 *coarse*; 236.2 *inferior*; 429.9 *moist*; 548.6 *seedy*; 793.10 *shoddy*; 544.10 *ugly*; 430.8 *viscous*
taco 25.50 *Central American dish*
tact 658.1 *courtesy*; 579.3 *management*; 485.1, 733.3 *skill*; 631.8 *treatment*; 458.1 *wisdom*
tactful 658.7 *courteous*; 458.5 *wise*
tactfully 658.14 *courteously*; 658.15 *genteelly*
tactfulness 658.1 *courtesy*
tactic 32.44 *polymeric*; 645.2 *stratagem*; 631.9 *tactics*
tactical 631.16 *behaving*; 645.4 *cunning*; 340.6 *effective*; 584.8, 585.17 *military*; 484.14 *planned*
tactical advantage 631.9 *tactics*
tactical bombing 381.13 *air attack*; 585.8 *warfare*
tactically 484.16 *as planned*; 645.6 *cunningly*; 584.11 *militarily*
tactical nuclear warfare 585.8 *warfare*
tactical nuclear weapon 587.1 *weapon*
tactical unit 584.4 *military organization*
tactical vom 371.23 *vomiting*
tactician 645.3 *cunning person*; 485.5 *expert*; 480.14, 483.7 *motivator*; 484.8 *planner*
tactics **631.9**; 585.6 *art of war*; 645.1 *cunning*; 340.2 *deed*; 484.2 *policy*; 485.1 *skill*; 645.2 *stratagem*; 317.1 *way*
tactics of war 585.6 *art of war*
tactile 19.25 *sculptural*; 488.8 *sensate*; 492.1 *touch*; 492.8 *touchable*
tactile values 19.4 *treatment*
tactility 492.1 *touch*
tactless 486.3 *clumsy*; 659.5 *discourteous*; 592.1 *insensitive*; 487.2 *not customary*
tactlessly 659.9 *discourteously*; 592.8 *unfeelingly*
tactlessness 486.9 *bungling*; 659.1 *discourtesy*; 592.3 *insensitiveness*
tactual 492.8 *touchable*
tadpole 73.8 *young amphibian*; 555.4 *young animal*
tadpole shrimp 75.4 *arthropod*
taedium vitae 620.1 *boredom*
tae kwon do **52.9**; 52.1 *combat sports*
tae kwon do combinations 52.9 *tae kwon do*
tae kwon do grade 52.9 *tae kwon do*
tae kwon do patterns 52.9 *tae kwon do*
tae kwon do technique 52.9 *tae kwon do*
taenia 174.3 *architectural summit*
taeniacide 37.4 *drug type*
Taff 90.4 *British rivers*
taffeta 193.4 *textile*
Taffy 564.9 *British inhabitant*
taffy 267.4 *adherent*; 25.41 *sweet*
tag 211.6 *add*; 211.3 *additional item*; 770.4 *allot*; 743.10 *identify*; 373.6 *line*; 745.1 *maxim*; 743.3 *means of identification*; 721.8 *name*
tag along 223.16 *attend*; 168.6 *be in the rear*
tag day 768.3 *offering*
tag football 46.1 *football*
tagged 743.12 *identified*
tagging 770.1 *allocation*
tag on 211.6 *add*
tag-out 48.6 *fielding terms*
tag-team 52.15 *wrestling*
tag-team wrestling 52.5 *wrestling*
Tagula 5.11 *family of languages*
Tahoe 88.3 *US lakes*
taiga 79.4 *trees*
tail **131.8**; 211.3 *additional item*; 223.16 *attend*; 29.19 *comet*; 633.9 *follow*; 223.9 *follower*; 131.25 *hindmost*; 633.5 *pursuer*; 168.4 *rear*; 168.2 *rear end*; 147.17 *stay near*
tailback 132.8 *procession*; 289.1 *succession*
tail beam 20.9 *miscellaneous architectural features*
tail between the legs 623.9 *humiliation*
tail coat 551.3 *formal dress*
tailed amphibian 73.7 *amphibian*
tail end 168.1 *rear*; 131.8 *tail*
tail feather 72.17 *plumage*
tail fin 74.5 *fish anatomy*
tailgate 147.17 *stay near*
tailgate picnic 557.13 *feast*
tail guard 59.14 *horse-riding terms*
tail in a gate 264.7 *awkward situation*
tailing 633.1 *pursuit*
tailless 212.7 *reduced*
tailless amphibian 73.7 *amphibian*
tailless mouse 40.7 *peripheral*
tail light 522.6 *electric light*
tail off 226.6 *cease*; 131.18 *come to an end*; 214.4 *decrease*
tailor 578.2 *artisan*; 550.17 *coverer*; 224.6 *editor*; 553.9 *fashion*; 551.26 *fashion designer*; 551.35 *make clothing*; 393.12 *repairer*; 778.13 *retailer*
tailored 160.9 *formed*; 551.31 *styled*
tailoring 551.2 *dressing*; 160.4 *forming*
tailor-made 356.12 *produced*; 160.10 *prototypical*; 551.31 *styled*
tailor-made clothes 551.1 *dress*
tailor-make 551.35 *make clothing*
tailor's dummy 717.6 *image*
tailor's goose 421.9 *smoother*
tailpiece 211.3 *additional item*; 20.9 *miscellaneous architectural features*; 168.1 *rear*
tail rhyme 17.11 *rhyme*
tails 551.3, 656.4 *formal dress*; 551.11 *jacket*
tailskid 320.21 *miscellaneous motoring terms*
tailspin 214.2 *decline*; 320.21 *miscellaneous motoring terms*
tailwind 434.4 *air flow*; 322.5 *flight*; 392.1 *help*; 330.12 *propellant*; 31.15 *wind direction*
taint 231.7 *defect*; 258.11 *dirty*; 260.6 *infection*; 245.3 *make worse*; 236.10 *poverty*; 728.6 *suggestion*; 258.2 *uncleanness*
tainted 260.23 *diseased*; 231.1 *imperfect*; 236.4 *poor*; 503.4 *putrid*; 258.8 *unclean*
tajine 25.6 *kitchen equipment*
takable 769.14 *receivable*
takahe 72.2 *flightless bird*
take **773.7**; 55.1 *angling*; 776.3 *bargain*; 246.9 *be victorious*; 741.10 *copy*; 765.4 *earnings*; 135.9 *find necessary*; 386.7 *force*; 788.2 *money received*; 41.3 *photograph*; 769.9, 788.7 *receive*; 774.4 *stolen goods*; 476.5 *suppose*; 773.5 *takings*; 316.12 *transport*; 441.1 *waste*
take aback 630.9 *surprise*
take a back seat 216.9 *be average*; 623.19 *be humble*; 473.7 *be unselfish*; 674.15 *escape notice*; 122.10 *follow*
take a bath 256.14 *bathe*
take a beating 247.7 *be defeated*
take a bow 21.34 *act*
take a break 581.2 *be refreshed*; 580.4 *have leisure*; 226.9 *pause*
take a breather 301.8 *be motionless*; 581.2 *be refreshed*; 226.9 *pause*; 263.2 *take it easy*
take a bribe 813.13 *get paid*
take account of 127.4 *include*
take a chance **107.12**; 254.9 *face danger*; 102.7 *make possible*; 353.3 *tackle*; 104.10 *think likely*
take a chill 494.10 *be cold*
take a cold bath 251.10 *restrain oneself*
take a commission 585.12 *go to war*
take a corner 66.4 *play soccer*
take a crack at 448.13 *invent*; 354.1 *undertake*
take action **346.9**; 340.4 *act*; 576.8 *exert oneself*; 15.12 *have an industrial dispute*
take a day off 226.9 *pause*; 98.17 *take leave of absence*
take a deep breath 581.2 *be refreshed*
take a dip 67.9 *swim*
take a direction **324.7**
take a discount **791.4**
take a dislike to 596.5 *dislike*
take a dive 700.30 *be fraudulent*
take a dose 203.8 *quantify*
take a drubbing 247.7 *be defeated*
take advantage of 340.4 *act*; 485.10 *be skilful*; 631.11 *conduct oneself*; 349.3 *exploit*; 237.11 *find useful*; 244.2 *get better*; 244.1 *improve*; 351.1 *misuse*; 796.20 *seduce*; 700.28 *trick*
take advice 713.6 *consult*
take a fall 305.11 *trip*
take a fancy to 593.24 *be in love*; 595.7 *like*
take a firm grip 395.10 *be a prevailing influence*
take a flier 254.9 *face danger*
take after 115.10 *be similar*; 125.9 *imitate*
take a gander 518.14 *inspect*
take ages 294.6 *be late*
take a guess at 619.12 *wonder whether*
take a header 305.11 *trip*
take a high tone 660.27 *dare*
take a holiday 580.4 *have leisure*; 226.9 *pause*; 263.2 *take it easy*
take a hostage 773.10 *take away*
take a husband 570.15 *marry*
take aim 482.10 *aim*
take a kickback 752.9 *offer*
take a leak 560.17 *urinate*
take a liking to 593.24 *be in love*
take a maiden voyage 295.19 *begin*
take amiss 624.10 *be offended*; 624.8 *resent*
take an airing 434.20 *aerate*
take a nap 263.2 *take it easy*
take an aversion to 594.14 *hate*
take an ego trip 683.7 *be egoistic*
take an interest in 593.23 *love*
take an opinion poll 469.5 *vote*
take a nosedive 214.4 *decrease*; 305.11 *trip*
take an overdose 382.21 *commit suicide*
take an upturn 304.21 *upturn*
take apart 375.4 *deconstruct*; 357.9 *demolish*; 372.9 *separate*; 350.6 *stop using*
take a pee 608.13 *relieve oneself*
take a penalty kick 64.5 *play rugby*
take a percentage 765.14 *profit*
take a photo 717.9 *represent*
take a photograph 41.21 *photograph*
take a picture 744.13 *record*; 717.9 *represent*
take a plane 317.14 *find one's way*
take a poll 469.5 *vote*
take a position 585.14 *battle*
take a pot shot 381.2 *fire*; 330.31 *snipe*
take a powder 371.33 *go away!*; 313.4 *hurry off*
take a profit 765.14 *profit*
take a rain check 762.5 *take a substitute*
take a recess 581.2 *be refreshed*
take a resolution 638.7 *resolve*
take a rest 263.2 *take it easy*
take a risk 107.12 *take a chance*
take a running jump 371.33 *go away!*; 305.11 *trip*
take a sabbatical 580.4 *have leisure*; 133.13 *pause*
take a salary advance 772.7 *borrow*
take as a model 125.9 *imitate*
take a second helping 218.6 *be unsatisfied*
take a share 770.5 *get one's allotment*; 764.4 *have joint possession*
take a shine 522.27 *glaze*
take a shine to 593.24 *be in love*
take a short cut 149.11 *cut short*; 317.14 *find one's way*
take a shot at 354.1 *undertake*
take a shower 256.14 *bathe*
take a shufty 518.14 *inspect*
take a stand 703.18 *appear*; 738.4 *show oneself*
take a stand against 381.8 *counterattack*
take a strong line 397.10 *demand*
take a substitute **762.5**
take a summer holiday 298.7 *be regular*
take a supporting role 122.10 *follow*
take a trip 691.10 *drug oneself*
take a tumble 305.11 *trip*
take a turn 179.6 *circle*
take authority **12.12**; **396.20**
take a vacation 580.4 *have leisure*; 226.9 *pause*
take a walk 371.33 *go away!*
takeaway 557.15 *eating place*; 436.1 *provision*; 436.7 *provisioning*; 349.10 *usable*
take away **316.15**; **608.14**; **773.10**; 27.91, 210.9 *add*; 526.3 *cause to disappear*; 766.9 *lose*; 814.1 *punish*; 372.10 *set apart*; 212.3 *subtract*
take away one's freedom 387.6 *subject*
take-away window 557.15 *eating place*
take a whack at 354.1 *undertake*
take a wife 570.15 *marry*
take a wrong turn 325.3 *go astray*
take back **773.8**; 479.4 *recant*; 462.13 *remind*; 708.12 *renounce*; 761.7 *restore*
take by force 386.7 *force*
take by storm 381.9 *attack successfully*; 246.9 *be victorious*; 480.15 *persuade*
take by surprise 630.9 *surprise*; 379.2 *trap*
take by the hand 392.23 *advise*
take captive 773.10 *take away*
take care 616.5 *be cautious*; 711.10 *look out!*
take care of 340.4 *act*; 665.11 *care for*; 550.33 *fix*; 579.1 *manage*; 557.25 *provide food*; 401.8 *serve*
take care of oneself 259.5 *be healthy*
take chances 448.13 *invent*
take charge of 665.11 *care for*; 252.10 *protect*; 354.1 *undertake*
take charity 392.18 *receive help*
take cognizance 16.69 *have jurisdiction over*; 16.71 *try a case*
take cognizance of 127.4 *include*
take command 121.8 *be superior*; 12.12, 396.20 *take authority*
take communion 9.7 *worship*
take compassionate leave 758.12 *exempt oneself*
take control 12.12 *take authority*
take courage **613.16**
take cover 736.11 *conceal oneself*
take custody of 251.11 *detain*
take cuttings 44.15 *cultivate*; 561.13 *propagate*
take disciplinary action 814.1 *punish*
take down 623.23 *abase*; 367.3 *bring down*; 557.21 *eat*; 744.14 *inscribe*; 367.1 *lower*
take down a peg 623.23 *abase*
take Draconian measures 647.5 *be severe*
take drugs 691.10 *drug oneself*
take early retirement 580.4 *have leisure*; 605.5 *resign*
take effect **345.9**; 340.4 *act*; 346.7 *be operational*
take evasive action 384.26 *act on the defensive*; 634.6 *evade*
take every course 557.22 *eat well*
take exception 113.18 *object*
take exception to 624.8 *resent*
take fire 624.12 *become angry*
take five 581.2 *be refreshed*; 133.13, 226.9 *pause*; 263.2 *take it easy*
take flight 389.5 *escape*; 313.4 *hurry off*; 634.8 *run away*

take for a ride 382.17 *murder;* 773.10 *take away;* 700.28 *trick*
take for granted 450.7 *believe;* 672.6 *be ungrateful;* 474.9 *predict;* 476.5 *suppose;* 104.10 *think likely*
take for oneself 773.7 *take*
take French leave 98.18 *abscond;* 250.14 *be free;* 526.2 *depart;* 389.5 *escape;* 634.8 *run away*
take fright 612.11 *be afraid*
take guard 53.17 *bat*
take half measures 218.5 *be insufficient;* 639.10 *compromise*
take heart 610.9 *be hopeful;* 613.16 *take courage*
take heed 711.6 *be warned*
take hold 395.10 *be a prevailing influence*
take hold of 267.6 *adhere;* 360.6 *retain;* 773.7 *take*
take hold of one 632.17 *become a habit*
take holy orders 572.11 *be monastic;* 7.21 *ordain*
take home 769.9 *receive*
take-home pay 785.3 *pay;* 813.4 *reward for service;* 769.2 *something received*
take-home work 576.1 *work*
take hostage 251.11 *detain*
take ill 624.10 *be offended*
take in 211.6 *add;* 37.19 *administer;* 370.7 *admit;* 773.11 *be hospitable;* 314.14 *enrol;* 455.13 *get to know;* 127.4 *include;* 191.5 *make smaller;* 450.9 *make someone believe;* 252.10 *protect;* 769.9 *receive;* 439.6 *store;* 773.7 *take;* 695.6 *understand*
take-in 765.4 *earnings*
take in bad part 624.10 *be offended*
take industrial action 662.15 *be disobedient;* 753.8 *cause mischief;* 15.12 *have an industrial dispute*
take in exchange 762.5 *take a substitute*
take in food 557.21 *eat*
take in good part 658.10 *be courteous;* 649.12 *show mercy*
take in hand 392.23 *advise;* 407.22 *pacify;* 773.7 *take;* 354.1 *undertake*
take in one's stride 485.11 *be expert;* 265.17 *do easily*
take in oxygen 581.2 *be refreshed*
take in sail 333.3 *slow down*
take in supplies 436.5 *provision*
take into account 127.4 *include*
take into consideration 127.4 *include*
take into custody 251.11 *detain;* 773.10 *take away*
take into one's arms 593.27 *kiss*
take into one's head 476.5 *suppose*
take in tow 392.23 *advise;* 362.11 *pull*
take in vain 351.1 *misuse*
take issue 113.18 *object*
take issue with 585.14 *battle;* 708.11 *rebut*
take it 388.4 *succumb;* 476.5 *suppose*
take it easy **263.2**; **265.20**; 616.5 *be cautious;* 250.17 *be informal;* 666.6 *be neglectful;* 245.1 *deteriorate;* 333.1 *move slowly*
take it from one 388.4 *succumb*
take it lying down 388.4 *succumb*
take it out of 623.25 *deflate;* 261.6 *fatigue*
take it out on 624.13 *vent one's anger*
take it slowly 616.5 *be cautious*
take it that 4.21 *rationalize*
take judicial notice 16.69 *have jurisdiction over*
take leave 98.16 *absent oneself;* 580.4 *have leisure*
take leave of absence **98.17**
take lessons 6.23 *learn*
take liberties 659.7 *be discourteous;* 757.5 *be permitted;* 660.22 *be rude;* 660.27 *dare;* 250.19 *liberalize*
take liberties with 242.11 *quarrel*
take life 382.16 *kill*
take measures 340.4 *act;* 243.1 *prepare*
take minutes 744.14 *inscribe*
take money away 773.10 *take away*
take more grass 51.7 *bowl*
taken 769.13, 788.6 *received;* 476.8 *supposed*
taken aback 630.6 *surprised*
taken as read 476.8 *supposed*
taken away 98.12 *missing;* 212.5 *subtracted*
taken back 649.6 *forgiven*
taken bad 260.22 *sick*
taken by God 582.19 *dead*
taken care of 781.2 *solvent*
take neither side 618.15 *be impartial*
taken for a ride 700.36 *deceived*
taken for granted 476.8 *supposed*
taken ill 260.22 *sick*
taken in 700.36 *deceived;* 769.13 *received*
take no advice 641.9 *be obstinate*
take no chances 252.9 *be safe*
take no interest 618.12 *be indifferent*
take no notice of 519.16 *be blind to;* 472.12 *be inattentive;* 666.6 *be neglectful*
take no offence 649.12 *show mercy*
take no part in 98.15 *be absent*
take no prisoners 382.26 *no quarter!;* 382.18 *slaughter*
take no risks 616.5 *be cautious*
take note of **471.11**
take nourishment 557.21 *eat*
taken over 769.13 *received*
taken prisoner 387.9 *subject*
taken to the cleaners 604.10 *deceived*
taken with 593.18 *in love*
takeoff 67.6 *diving;* 599.4 *entertainment;* 47.2 *field events;* 322.5 *flight;* 125.3 *mockery;* 668.4, 678.6 *ridicule;* 213.2 *spread;* 313.8 *start;* 304.4 *taking off;* 47.9 *track*
take off **212.4**; **304.19**; 21.34, 717.10 *act;* 621.2 *act of derision;* 599.13 *be humorous;* 791.3 *discount;* 322.10 *fly;* 313.4 *hurry off;* 125.9 *imitate;* 213.4 *increase;* 668.24, 678.14 *ridicule;* 313.5 *set out;* 130.19 *start off;* 350.6 *stop using;* 773.10 *take away;* 552.14 *undress*
take offence 624.10 *be offended*
take offence at 596.5 *dislike*
take off for 324.7 *take a direction*
take office 12.12, 396.20 *take authority*
takeoff point 47.2 *field events*
take off someone's hands 769.9 *receive*
takeoff strip 317.13 *flight path*
take off the gloves 647.6 *suppress*
take off weight 687.5 *fast*
take on 340.4 *act;* 772.8 *adopt;* 624.11 *be angry;* 113.19 *confront;* 381.8 *counterattack;* 756.8 *guarantee;* 370.10 *introduce;* 439.6 *store;* 353.3 *tackle;* 773.7 *take;* 354.1, 638.9 *undertake;* 752.11 *volunteer*
take on all comers 638.8 *brace oneself*
take on a pilot 323.9 *navigate*
take on board 773.11 *be hospitable;* 406.6 *contain*
take on depth 695.4 *be intelligible*
take one's bearings 324.8 *orient*
take one's breath away 619.10 *be wonderful;* 730.15 *strike dumb*
take one's chance 342.14 *push;* 287.5 *take the opportunity*
take one's coat off 576.6 *work*
take one's commission 791.4 *take a discount*
take one's cue from 713.6 *consult*
take one's cut 770.5 *get one's allotment*
take one's departure 313.1 *depart*
take one's ease 580.4 *have leisure;* 263.2 *take it easy*
take oneself off 313.6 *part*
take one's fancy 490.9 *give pleasure*
take one's gruel 814.6 *be punished*
take one's heritage 246.12 *succeed to*
take one's leave 98.16 *absent oneself;* 313.1 *depart;* 313.6 *part*
take one's lumps 388.4 *succumb*
take one's medicine 814.6 *be punished*
take one's own life 382.21 *commit suicide*
take one's percentage 791.4 *take a discount*
take one's pick 469.4 *pick*
take one's place 750.25 *conform;* 407.24 *line up*
take one's pleasure with 796.20 *seduce*
take one's punishment 807.7 *be punished*
take one's revenge 651.19 *be pitiless*
take one's time 616.5 *be cautious;* 294.6 *be late;* 580.4 *have leisure;* 333.2 *hesitate*
take one's turn 298.7 *be regular*
take one up on 661.5 *defy*
take on oneself 482.8 *resolve*
take on one's shoulders 354.1 *undertake*
take on responsibility 762.4 *be a substitute*
take on supplies 436.5 *provision*
take on the responsibility 810.15 *be liable*
take on too much 354.1 *undertake*
take on trust 450.7 *believe*
take on water 436.5 *provision*
take orders 663.5 *obey*
take out 51.7 *bowl;* 128.8 *eject;* 369.11 *extract;* 358.1 *obliterate;* 356.10 *produce;* 569.14 *seek the friendship of;* 212.3 *subtract;* 773.10 *take away*
take-out 68.10 *curling*
take out a loan 783.9 *acquire credit;* 772.7 *borrow*
take out a mortgage 772.7 *borrow;* 763.7 *possess*
take out a tackler 64.5 *play rugby*
take out a tenancy 763.7 *possess*
take out credit 783.9 *acquire credit*
take out insurance 616.5 *be cautious*
take out of context 234.12 *distort the truth;* 720.1 *misinterpret*
take out of print 358.1 *obliterate*
takeover 289.4 *accession;* 776.9 *bargaining;* 13.7 *corporation;* 346.2 *joint operation;* 703.6 *mass demonstration;* 777.7 *purchasing;* 144.3 *replacement;* 773.1, 773.12 *taking*
take over 381.9 *attack successfully;* 395.10 *be a prevailing influence;* 762.4 *be a substitute;* 586.38 *conquer;* 13.11 *deal;* 289.11 *follow in office;* 703.19 *protest;* 769.9 *receive;* 144.16 *replace;* 773.7 *take;* 12.12, 396.20 *take authority*
takeover bid 752.3 *business offer;* 13.7 *corporation;* 777.7 *purchasing;* 773.1 *taking*
take over from 608.11 *assist*
take over the mantle 289.11 *follow in office*
take over the reins 289.11 *follow in office;* 12.12, 396.20 *take authority*
takeover zone 47.1 *track events*
take pains 616.5 *be cautious;* 342.15 *try*
take part 97.12 *attend;* 127.5 *be included;* 47.6 *compete in track and field;* 45.6 *participate*
take part in 340.4 *act;* 764.4 *have joint possession*
take pity 627.14 *have pity!*
take pity on 627.8 *pity;* 627.10 *show mercy*
take place 345.9 *take effect*
take pleasure in 597.6 *enjoy;* 490.8 *feel pleasure;* 593.23 *love*
take poison 382.21 *commit suicide*
take possession of 773.7 *take*
take potluck 654.11 *be sociable*
take precautions 616.5 *be cautious;* 243.3 *be prepared;* 252.9 *be safe;* 563.9 *practise birth control*
take precedence **129.16**; 123.7 *be important;* 121.10 *lead*
take pride in 622.25 *be proud of;* 622.29 *feel pride*
take priority 129.16 *take precedence*
take prisoner 387.7 *defeat;* 251.11 *detain;* 815.9 *imprison*
take profits 773.7 *take*
taker **773.6**; 371.26 *ejector;* 763.5 *possessor;* 777.12 *purchaser;* 769.5 *recipient;* 774.8 *thief*
take refuge 252.9 *be safe;* 172.14 *go inside*
take reprisals 385.3 *retaliate*
take responsibility 762.4 *be a substitute*
take responsibility for 756.7 *promise*
take risks 615.5 *be rash*
take rooms 564.14 *inhabit*
take root 632.17 *become a habit;* 225.5 *be permanent;* 228.6 *be stable;* 395.8 *influence;* 77.21 *vegetate*
take second best 762.5 *take a substitute*
take seriously **643.9**; 123.8 *make important*
take sexual possession of 773.7 *take*
take shame 623.24 *be humiliated*
take shape 93.18 *come to be*
take short steps 333.1 *move slowly*
take sides 465.11 *be unjust;* 169.9, 469.3 *side with*
take some doing 264.17 *be difficult*
take someone's word for 450.7 *believe*
take something off 791.3 *discount*
take soundings 156.14 *deepen;* 323.9 *navigate*
take stance 53.17 *bat*
take statements 16.71 *try a case*
take steps 340.4 *act;* 243.1 *prepare*
take stock 789.8 *audit;* 210.11 *number*
take stock of 443.15 *think about;* 518.16 *visualize*
take sword in hand 243.8 *prepare oneself*
take tentative steps 616.5 *be cautious*
take that 385.7 *revenge!*
take the airline 324.7 *take a direction*
take the attitude 4.22 *propound a philosophy*
take the auspices 475.12 *divine*
take the backtrack 303.3 *reverse*
take the blame 762.4 *be a substitute;* 670.24 *be open to criticism*
take the chair 579.2 *direct;* 685.4 *moderate*
take the championship 246.9 *be victorious*
take the chill off 493.14 *be hot*
take the consequences 814.6 *be punished*
take the cup 246.9 *be victorious*
take the edge off 426.10 *blunt;* 481.5 *discourage;* 685.4 *moderate*
take the fancy of 593.28 *win the love of*
take the field 585.13 *be at war;* 53.15 *play;* 48.7 *play baseball*
take the first step 130.21 *pioneer*
take the floor 733.7 *address;* 729.14 *speak to*
take the gloves off 386.7 *force*
take the guise of 525.11 *appear*
take the heat 388.4 *succumb*
take the heat off 388.3 *submit*
take the helm 167.10 *be in front;* 579.2 *direct;* 289.11 *follow in office;* 396.20 *take authority*
take the high road 317.14 *find one's way*
take the initiative 130.21 *pioneer*
take the lead 123.7 *be important;* 167.10 *be in front;* 121.10 *lead*
take the lid off 739.5 *disclose;* 520.10 *make visible*
take the limelight 123.7 *be important*
take the long-term view 283.10 *expect*
take the long view 283.10 *expect*
take the mean 216.10 *make average*
take the measurements of 26.10 *measure*
take the mick 621.6 *deride*
take the mickey 621.6 *deride*
take the middle way 685.3 *be moderate*
take the oath 716.11 *give evidence*
take the offensive 381.1 *attack;* 585.13 *be at war*
take the omens 475.12 *divine*
take the opportunity **287.5**; 293.11 *get ahead*
take the opposing side 113.15 *be opposite*
take the part of 392.24 *back*
take the piss 621.6 *deride*
take the place of **371.5**; 762.4 *be a substitute*
take the pledge 684.5 *be self-restrained;* 251.10 *restrain oneself*
take the plunge 613.15 *be courageous;* 638.8 *brace oneself;* 130.18 *make a beginning;* 570.15 *marry;* 469.3 *side with*
take the prize 246.9 *be victorious;* 235.9 *be worthy*
take the Queen's shilling 584.10 *enlist*
take the rap 762.4 *be a substitute;* 670.24 *be open to criticism;* 814.6 *be punished*
take the reciprocal course 303.3 *reverse*
take the shape of 525.11 *appear;* 760.8 *be transformed*
take the square root 27.91 *add*
take the stage 21.34 *act*
take the stand 16.70 *litigate*
take the strain 217.4 *suffice*
take the sun 324.8 *orient*
take the train 317.14 *find one's way*
take the veil 572.11 *be monastic;* 655.12 *be unsocial;* 7.21 *ordain*
take the weight of 414.15 *weigh*
take the wraps off 739.5 *disclose*
take things easy 388.3 *submit*
take things slowly 666.6 *be neglectful*
take thought for tomorrow 283.10 *expect*
take time off 263.2 *take it easy;* 98.17 *take leave of absence*
take time out 580.4 *have leisure;* 133.13 *pause*
take to 593.24 *be in love;* 632.18 *habituate;* 595.7 *like*

take to arms 380.7 *be violent*; 585.12 *go to war*
take to bits 357.9 *demolish*
take to court 16.70 *litigate*
take to heart 624.10 *be offended*; 591.11 *be sensitive*; 590.17 *feel deeply*
take to mean 719.8 *interpret*; 4.21 *rationalize*
take too much time 46.18 *be penalized*
take to one's bed 260.24 *be unhealthy*
take to one's bosom 360.7 *detain*
take to oneself 211.6 *add*
take to one's heels 389.5 *escape*; 313.4 *hurry off*; 634.8 *run away*
take to pieces 375.4 *deconstruct*; 357.9 *demolish*; 238.8 *make useless*; 372.9 *separate*
take to task 670.20 *censure*; 814.1 *punish*
take to the cleaners 604.8 *be dishonest*; 782.14 *impoverish*; 773.10 *take away*
take to the hills 736.11 *conceal oneself*
take to the limit 204.10 *complete*
take to the masses 138.26 *popularize*
take to the road 171.12 *be outside*; 317.14 *find one's way*
take turns 110.7 *reciprocate*
take umbrage 624.10 *be offended*; 242.11 *quarrel*
take unawares 630.9 *surprise*
take under one's wing 392.23 *advise*; 252.10 *protect*
take untimely action 288.6
take up 370.13 *absorb*; 733.12 *address oneself to*; 392.23 *advise*; 289.11 *follow in office*; 366.4 *gather up*; 632.16 *have a habit*; 769.9 *receive*; 50.15 *sail*; 469.1 *select*; 149.10 *shorten*; 354.1, 638.9 *undertake*; 349.1 *use*
take up again 134.4 *protract*
take up an option 469.1 *select*
take up a position 143.9 *be situated*
take up arms 380.7 *be violent*
take up arms for 384.22 *plead for*
take up no room 159.6 *be little*
take upon oneself 354.1 *undertake*
take upon one's shoulders 810.15 *be liable*
take up residence 565.18; 142.10 *settle*
take up residence in 763.7 *possess*
take-up spool 41.18 *exposure time*
take up the cause 585.12 *go to war*
take up the cudgels 585.12 *go to war*
take up time 148.10 *lengthen*
take up with 569.13 *befriend*
take vows 7.21 *ordain*
take what's on offer 754.4 *compromise*
take wing 72.25 *fly*; 313.3 *quit*
take wrong 720.1 *misinterpret*
Taking 773
taking 773.1; **773.12**; 765.1 *gain*; 763.1 *possession*; 769.1, 769.11 *receiving*; 774.1 *stealing*
taking advantage of 700.7 *tricking*
taking all things together 216.11 *on average*
taking an overdose 382.7 *suicide*
taking apart 375.2 *deconstruction*
taking a part 21.22 *acting*
taking a role 21.22 *acting*
taking away 773.3; 766.1 *loss*; 144.2 *removal*; 372.2 *setting apart*; 212.1 *subtraction*
taking back 773.2; 761.2 *restoration*
taking back one's words 479.8 *recantation*
taking by storm 381.14 *siege*; 773.6 *taker*; 246.2 *victory*
taking counsel 713.2 *consultation*
taking everything into consideration 204.13 *on the whole*
taking food 557.1 *eating*
taking for granted 672.1 *ingratitude*
taking hold 773.1 *taking*
taking in 773.4; 370.1 *admittance*; 191.1 *contraction*; 773.1 *taking*
taking in hand 773.1 *taking*
taking into account 464.14 *considering*
taking issue with 708.3 *rebuttal*
taking it easy 260.22 *sick*
taking it that 222.15 *under the circumstances*
taking liberties 329.8 *transgression*
taking life 382.1 *killing*
taking measures 243.9 *preparation*
taking money away 773.3 *taking away*
taking of evidence 16.7 *legal trial*
taking off 304.4
taking on 773.1 *taking*
taking one's time 333.5 *unhurried*
taking on responsibility 354.6 *enterprising*
taking out 593.6 *courtship*; 773.3 *taking away*
taking out a loan 772.1 *borrowing*
taking over 289.4 *accession*; 396.3 *acquisition of power*; 773.1 *taking*
taking pains 576.4 *exertion*
taking part 342.21 *meddling*
taking possession 763.1 *possession*; 773.1 *taking*
taking precedence 123.5 *important*; 129.1 *precedence*
takings 773.5; 765.4 *earnings*; 788.2 *money received*; 769.2 *something received*
taking steps 243.9 *preparation*
taking the auspices 475.2 *divination*
taking the opportunity 293.6 *getting ahead*
taking the plunge 570.1 *marriage*
taking the waters 433.7 *hydrotherapeutics*
taking to task 670.7 *blame*
taking up 50.1 *sailing*
taking without owner's consent 774.3 *theft*
talapoin 7.7 *monk*
talc 427.5 *powder*
talcum powder 502.2 *fragrant thing*
tale 721.3 *narration*
talebearer 693.10 *informer*
talent 136.2, 334.2 *ability*; 780.12 *ancient coins*; 229.3, 485.2 *aptitude*; 19.5 *artistry*; 265.1 *easiness*; 458.2 *intelligence*; 797.12 *proficiency*; 139.7 *special skill*
talented 485.7 *gifted*; 458.6 *intelligent*; 455.8 *knowledgeable*; 334.13 *powerful*; 797.5 *proficient*; 136.9 *qualified*; 485.6 *skilful*
talentless 486.1 *unskilful*
talent spotter 21.33 *theatregoer*
tale of woe 603.2 *lament*
talion 385.1 *retaliation*
talisman 11.6; 475.6 *good-luck sign*; 359.2 *preserver*; 10.14 *sacred object*; 742.1 *sign*
talismanic 11.15 *witchlike*
talk 731.3; 733.1 *address*; 731.7 *be talkative*; 692.30 *communicate*; 734.1 *conversation*; 734.9 *converse*; 739.6 *divulge*; 703.3 *explanation*; 729.1 *faculty of speech*; 504.8 *something heard*; 729.11 *speak*; 5.3 *spoken language*; 5.45 *use language*
talk about 740.13 *make public*; 678.13 *vilify*
talkative 731.5; 734.12 *conversing*; 270.3 *diffuse*; 739.11 *disclosing*; 693.16 *informative*; 729.19 *speaking*
talkatively 731.10
Talkativeness 731
talkativeness 731.1; 270.1 *diffuseness*; 729.2 *power of speech*
talk at length 731.7 *be talkative*
talk back 660.25, 706.18 *answer back*
talk big 660.24 *be vain*; 673.16 *show off*
talk dirty 712.5 *curse*
talk double Dutch 696.7 *be unintelligible*
talk down 322.6 *flight control*
talker 731.4; 706.10 *answerer*; 734.7 *conversationalist*; 729.10 *speaker*
talk filthy 712.5 *curse*
talk for effect 673.16 *show off*
talk-in 734.4 *conference*
talk in clichés 509.14 *repeat*
talking 692.1 *communications*; 734.12 *conversing*; 729.1 *faculty of speech*; 729.19 *speaking*
talking big 542.2 *affectation*
talking bird 72.7 *cagebird*
talking book 519.3 *aid for poor sight*
talking dirty 712.1 *curse*
talking head 692.29 *broadcaster*
talking in superlatives 727.4 *bombast*
talking-to 670.7 *blame*
talking to oneself 735.5 *soliloquizing*
talk in riddles 696.7 *be unintelligible*
talk in superlatives 727.10 *boast*
talk into 483.9 *motivate*; 480.15 *persuade*
talk like an idiot 696.7 *be unintelligible*
talk nonsense 697.6; 696.7 *be unintelligible*
talk off the subject 100.13 *be extraneous*
talk of the town 812.2 *disreputable character*; 246.4 *successful person*
talk one's head off 731.8 *talk too much*
talk out of 481.1 *dissuade*
talk out of turn 739.7 *betray*
talk over 734.11 *confer*
talk plainly 178.11 *be straight*
talk privately 734.10 *chat*
talk radio 504.9 *audio device*
talk round 634.7 *be evasive*; 685.4 *moderate*; 480.15 *persuade*
talks 734.5; 748.5 *conference*
talk shit 702.12 *deceive*
talk show 692.25 *broadcast material*
talk straight 178.11 *be straight*; 739.6 *divulge*
talk sweetly 700.26 *be a hypocrite*
talk tête-à-tête 734.10 *chat*
talk through one's hat 697.6 *talk nonsense*
talk to 733.7 *address*; 729.14 *speak to*
talk together 734.9 *converse*
talk too long 620.6 *be boring*
talk too much 731.8; 219.4 *be excessive*
talk to oneself 729.15; 735.3 *soliloquize*
talk to the wall 735.3 *soliloquize*
talk turkey 269.4 *be concise*; 271.7 *be simple*; 739.6 *divulge*; 694.10 *mean*
tall 154.12; 154.9 *high*; 148.1 *long*
tallboy 23.5, 410.3 *cabinet*
tall drink 690.12 *alcohol*; 558.2 *drink*
taller 154.10 *higher*
tallest 154.10 *higher*
tallied 789.11 *accounted*
tallith 551.14 *neckwear*; 10.14 *sacred object*; 7.11 *vestment*
tall money 781.6 *money*
tallness 158.2 *bigness*; 154.1 *height*; 148.4 *length*
tall order 264.3 *difficult task*; 354.2 *undertaking*
tallow 268.5 *lubricant*
tallow candle 522.5 *incandescent light*
tallow-faced 530.8 *drained of colour*
tallowy 268.13 *slippery*
tall person 154.7; **158.11**
tall-ship racing 50.1 *sailing*
tall story 727.5; 234.4 *distortion of the truth*; 105.6 *implausibility*; 599.5 *joke*; 699.10 *lie*; 721.3 *narration*
tall tale 699.10 *lie*
tall thing 154.6
tally 789.3 *accounting*; 784.5 *amount owing*; 706.21 *answer to*; 108.8 *be proportionate to*; 115.10 *be similar*; 111.7 *be the same*; 210.8 *calculate*; 117.7, 750.25 *conform*; 110.9 *correlate*; 110.3 *correlation*; 706.8 *correspondence*; 210.3 *count*; 783.1 *credit*; 406.5 *divisions*; 119.11 *equalize*; 406.9 *itemize*; 220.1 *list*; 211.2 *mathematical addition*; 194.4 *mathematical result*; 743.3 *means of identification*; 194.10, 210.11 *number*; 27.12 *numeration*; 706.7 *numerical result*; 744.1 *record*; 744.15 *register*; 220.10 *score*
tally-ho 633.19 *after him!*; 633.2 *chase*; 514.5 *hunting cry*
tallying 706.15 *correspondent*; 210.3 *count*
tally stick 27.67 *calculator*
Talmud 7.12 *religious text*; 1.8 *tradition*
Talmud Torah 6.12 *educational institution*
talon 425.8 *sharp-pointed thing*; 360.3 *tools for gripping*
talons 72.16 *avian anatomy*
tamale 25.50 *Central American dish*
tamanoas 8.5 *deity*
tambour 20.9 *miscellaneous architectural features*; 63.5 *real tennis*
tame 632.18 *habituate*; 685.4 *moderate*; 663.7 *obedient*; 252.6 *safe*; 301.5 *sedentary*; 387.6 *subject*; 388.5 *submitting*; 497.5 *tasteless*
tame animal 70.3 *domesticated animal*
tamed 632.14 *habituated*; 70.15 *of animals*
tamely 663.10 *obediently*
tameness 663.1 *obedience*; 388.1 *submission*; 497.1 *tastelessness*
tam-o'shanter 551.15 *headgear*
tamoxifen 394.8 *drug*
tamp 331.2 *collide*; 416.9 *make dense*; 331.15 *ram*
tamper 245.4 *impair*; 342.17 *meddle*; 331.15 *ram*
tamperer 342.11 *meddler*
tampering 342.9 *overactivity*
tampering with 699.9 *falsification*
tamper with 224.8 *cause change*; 328.10 *disrupt*; 699.26 *falsify*; 412.8 *mix*; 492.11 *touch*
tamping iron 331.15 *ram*
tampion 309.2 *stopper*; 368.11 *thing inserted*
tampon 309.8 *stop*; 309.2 *stopper*; 394.10 *surgical dressing*; 368.11 *thing inserted*
tan 532.11 *blacken*; 534.1, 534.7 *brown*; 550.24 *coat*; 529.15 *colour*; 493.16 *feel hot*; 814.3 *hit*; 493.5 *hot weather*; 423.11 *make tough*; 536.1 *orange*
tandem 320.12 *bicycle*; 198.2 *double*; 50.7, 50.13 *windsurfing*
tandem exchange 692.12 *public telephone system*
tandem race 50.6 *canoeing*
tandoori 25.49 *Indian dish*
tang 496.1 *piquancy*
tanga 551.21 *beachwear*
Tanganyika 88.5 *other major lakes*
tangency 147.3 *juxtaposition*
tangent 310.7 *convergent*; 325.13 *deviation*; 310.5 *focus*; 147.10 *juxtaposed*; 27.37 *line*; 189.4 *oblique*; 189.1 *obliqueness*; 176.2 *obliquity*; 27.52 *trigonometric function*
tangential 310.7 *convergent*; 147.10 *juxtaposed*; 27.80 *linear*; 176.8 *oblique*
tangentially 147.14 *beside*
tangent rule 27.51 *trigonometry*
tangerine 536.3 *orange thing*
tangibility 402.1 *material world*; 95.1, 698.2 *reality*; 492.1 *touch*; 520.3 *visibility*
tangible 698.16 *existing*; 402.7 *material*; 440.8 *propertied*; 95.6 *real*; 488.8 *sensate*; 492.8 *touchable*; 520.1 *visible*
tangible assets 440.5 *personal estate*
tangible object 402.5 *object*
tangibles 440.5 *personal estate*
tangibly 402.9 *materially*; 492.14 *palpably*
tanginess 496.1 *piquancy*
tangle 408.7; 114.8 *be diverse*; 408.24 *make disordered*; 420.12 *make rough*; 412.3 *miscellany*; 264.5 *predicament*; 700.33 *snare*
tangled 416.7 *condensed*; 412.12 *mixed*; 408.18 *muddled*
tango 22.2, 22.15 *dance*
tango romantica 68.7 *ice-dancing*
tangram 737.4 *brain-teaser*
tangy 499.5 *acid*; 496.9 *piquant*
tank 586.21 *armoured cavalry*; 321.5 *locomotive part*; 439.4 *storage*; 815.2 *the inside*; 410.11 *vessel*
tanka 17.7 *poem*
tankage 158.1 *size*
tankard 558.10 *drink container*; 410.13 *drinking vessel*
tank assault 381.12 *military attack*
tank-buster 586.31 *military aircraft*
tanked up 690.1 *drunk*
tank engine 321.4 *locomotive*
tanker 321.4 *locomotive*; 323.3 *vessel*
tank farmer 43.15 *agriculturist*
tank farming 43.4 *arable farming*
tank top 551.8 *shirt*
tanktown 87.10 *village*
tank transporter 586.21 *armoured cavalry*
tank trap 379.1 *trap*
tank up 690.8 *get drunk*
tank wagon 321.6 *rolling stock*
tanned 532.3 *blackened*; 534.2 *browned*; 423.2 *toughened*
tanner 550.17 *coverer*; 780.10 *former British money*
tannin 559.2 *secreted substance*
tanning 493.5 *hot weather*
Tannoy™ 504.9 *audio device*; 740.1 *publication*
tan one's hide 814.3 *hit*
tantalic 32.34 *elemental*
tantalization 604.1 *disappointment*; 480.3 *incentive*
tantalize 617.15 *cause desire*; 593.26 *court*; 604.6 *disappoint*; 363.12 *lure*; 483.9 *motivate*; 480.16 *tempt*
tantalizer 480.13 *tempter*
tantalizing 483.11 *motivational*; 480.19 *persuasive*
tantalizingly 604.13 *disappointingly*; 483.14 *influentially*; 593.30 *lovingly*
tantalous 32.34 *elemental*
tantamount 119.6 *equal*; 694.6 *meaningful*
tantara 513.1 *stridency*
tantivy 332.9 *acceleration*

tant pis 124.15 *no matter!*
tantrum 624.4 *anger*
Taoism 4.7 *school of thought*
Taoist 7.16 *denominational*; 4.11 *follower of a doctrine*; 4.14 *of a philosophy*
tap **331.6**; 331.13 *blow*; 508.2, 508.6 *crack*; 504.15 *hear*; 433.13 *irrigator*; 509.11 *knock*; 79.18 *manage trees*; 315.7 *outlet*; 436.5 *provision*; 710.8 *solicit money*; 309.2 *stopper*; 369.14 *suck*; 439.3 *supply*; 773.10 *take away*; 492.11 *touch*; 316.11 *transfer*
tapas 25.54 *other dishes*
tap dance 22.2 *dance*
tap-dance 22.15 *dance*
tap dancer 21.30, 22.5 *dancer*
tap dancing 22.1 *dancing*
tape 504.9 *audio device*; 62.4 *climbing equipment*; 692.30 *communicate*; 373.11 *connect*; 504.15 *hear*; 373.6 *line*; 744.13 *record*; 744.6 *record book*; 692.26, 744.7 *recording*
tape collection 439.5 *collection*
taped 692.34 *communicated*; 744.16 *recorded*
tapedeck cassette 692.26 *recording*
tape machine 744.10 *recording instrument*
tape measure 210.5 *computer*; 26.6 *measuring instrument*
tape punch 40.7 *peripheral*
taper 310.9 *converge*; 522.8 *fire*; 310.11 *focus*; 437.2 *lighter*; 425.15 *make sharp*; 151.10 *narrow*; 151.9, 310.6 *narrowing*; 151.8 *narrow thing*
tape-record 692.30 *communicate*; 744.13 *record*
tape recorder 504.9 *audio device*; 115.3 *copier*; 125.6 *photocopier*; 692.26 *recording*; 744.10 *recording instrument*
tape recording 125.5 *duplicate*; 692.26 *recording*
tapered **151.3**; 425.1 *sharp*
tapering 310.7 *convergent*; 209.7 *gradational*; 151.9, 310.6 *narrowing*; 425.1 *sharp*; 151.3 *tapered*
taper off 209.6 *change gradually*; 214.4 *decrease*
taper to a point 425.14 *be sharp*
tape streamer 40.7 *peripheral*
tapestry 19.1 *art*; 542.3 *pattern*; 19.7 *picture*; 550.8 *wall covering*
tapeworm 75.10 *parasite*; 75.6 *worm*
tapioca 25.35 *dessert*
tapirs 71.15 *hoofed mammal*
tap one's foot 742.11 *gesture*
tap out a message 742.12 *signal*
tapper 79.8 *forester*; 331.15 *ram*
tapping 331.12 *collision*; 371.22 *disgorgement*; 369.4 *sucking*; 79.6 *tree management*
tapping foot 742.3 *gesture*
taproot 77.7 *root*; 344.3 *rudiment*
taps 583.2 *funeral*; 742.6 *word*
tapster 79.8 *forester*
tap water 433.2 *drinking water*
tar 430.2 *adhesive*; 532.9 *black thing*; 323.7 *nautical person*; 550.11 *paving*; 585.11 *recruit*; 550.29 *surface*; 496.7 *tobacco*
taradiddle 699.10 *lie*
taramasalata 25.16 *fish dish*; 25.52 *Greek dish*; 25.12 *hors d'oeuvre*
tar and feather 814.1 *punish*
tarantella 22.4 *historic dancing*
tarantism 327.8 *spasm*
tarantula 76.2 *arachnid*
Tarapon 5.11 *family of languages*
Tardigrada 75.4 *arthropod*
tardigrade 75.4 *arthropod*; 333.7 *delayed*
tardily 294.15 *late*
tardiness 333.12 *hesitation*; 294.1 *lateness*; 288.2 *untimeliness*
tardy 333.7 *delayed*; 294.9 *late*; 343.3 *not participating*; 288.12 *too late*
tare 791.1, 791.3 *discount*
tare and tret 791.1 *discount*
tares 238.6 *refuse*
Targa Florio 61.3 *sports-car race*
target 311.14, 446.18 *aim*; 384.7 *armour*; 668.9 *butt*; 324.1 *direction*; 482.6 *objective*; 446.4 *purpose*; 692.28 *radar*
target area 482.6 *objective*
targeted 446.12 *purposive*
targeting 446.12 *purposive*
target shooter 330.15 *shooter*
target shooting **60.1**
Targum 7.12 *religious text*
tariff 220.4 *bill*; 13.6 *economic factors*; 790.8 *levy*; 166.2 *limiting factor*; 788.2 *money received*; 790.1 *price*
tariff barrier 776.5 *commercial trade*; 13.6 *economic factors*
tariff duty 13.6 *economic factors*
tariff wall 251.2 *economic restraint*; 128.3 *exclusion zone*
Tarmac™ 175.1 *base*; 435.2 *building material*; 38.25 *construction material*; 550.11 *paving*; 317.4 *road surface*; 421.11 *smooth*; 421.8 *smooth thing*; 550.29 *surface*
Tarmacadam™ 317.4 *road surface*
tarn 88.1 *lake*
tarnish **524.11**; 530.6 *decolour*; 678.12 *defame*; 258.11 *dirty*; 524.2 *murk*; 548.1 *spot*
tarnished 524.7 *dimmed*; 258.7 *dirty*
tarnishing 678.16 *defamatory*; 678.5 *scorn*
Tarot cards 475.10 *cards*; 11.9 *divination*
Tarot reader 11.13 *diviner*
Tarot-reading 11.9 *divination*
tarp 550.7 *overhead covering*
tarpaulin 550.7 *overhead covering*
tarpon 55.4 *American game fish*
tarragon 496.5 *herbs*
tarring and feathering 814.7 *punishment*
tarry 301.8 *be motionless*; 333.2 *hesitate*; 294.7 *wait*
tart 499.5 *acid*; 25.36 *cake*; 659.5 *discourteous*; 651.14 *hostile*; 796.9 *immoral woman*; 625.4 *irascible*; 626.7 *irritable*; 496.9 *piquant*; 568.7 *prostitute*; 495.7 *tasty*; 568.9 *woman considered as a sex object*
tartan 541.2 *check*; 541.8 *checked*; 743.5 *uniform*; 541.5 *variegated thing*
tartar 258.4 *dirt*; 625.3 *irascible person*
Tartarean 8.16 *devilish*
tartare sauce 25.15 *sauce*
tartaric acid 499.3 *sour thing*
Tartarus 8.12 *hell*
tarted up 547.14 *beautified*; 551.30 *dressed-up*
tartly 659.9 *discourteously*; 626.14 *irritably*; 496.15 *piquantly*; 499.10 *sourly*
tartness 651.4 *bitterness*; 659.1 *discourtesy*; 625.1 *irascibility*; 496.1 *piquancy*; 499.1 *sourness*
tart taste 495.1 *taste*
Tartuffe 699.19 *cheat*; 718.3 *deceiver*; 700.19 *hypocrite*; 125.7 *imitator*; 676.2 *pretender*
Tartuffery 699.3, 700.3, 702.5 *hypocrisy*
Tartuffian 700.37 *hypocritical*
Tartuffism 700.3 *hypocrisy*
tart up 545.8 *beautify*; 551.33, 553.8 *dress up*; 547.16 *make up*; 525.14 *present*
tarty 551.30 *dressed-up*; 544.10 *ugly*; 796.13 *unchaste*
Tarzan 336.6 *muscleman*
Tashi Lumpo 10.13 *shrine*
tasimeter 26.8 *meter*
tasimetric 26.16 *micrometric*
tasimetry 26.2 *micrometry*
task **576.2**; **810.2**; 814.10 *affliction*; 346.3 *business*; 340.2 *deed*; 261.6 *fatigue*; 354.2 *undertaking*; 349.1 *use*; 576.7 *work for*
task force 586.14 *armed forces*; 584.4 *military organization*
task force commander 584.5 *military staff*
task group 584.4 *military organization*
taskmaster 647.4 *strict person*
taskmistress 647.4 *strict person*
taskwork 576.1 *work*
taslich 10.7 *non-Christian ritual*
Tasmanian shrimp 75.4 *arthropod*
tassel 81.3 *grass plant*; 361.3 *suspended object*
tastable 495.7 *tasty*
Taste 495
taste **495.1**; **495.9**; **557.23**; 554.4 *biological function*; 139.3 *characteristic*; 617.1 *desire*; 558.13 *drink*; 543.1, 549.1 *elegance*; 464.1 *judgment*; 466.2 *judiciousness*; 595.3 *likes*; 469.7 *preference*; 6.11 *refinement*; 488.1 *sensation*; 488.11 *sense*; 728.6 *suggestion*; 229.1 *tendency*
taste bad 499.8 *sour*
taste battle 585.13 *be at war*
taste bud **495.5**
taste flat 497.7 *be tasteless*
taste foul 499.8 *sour*
tasteful **495.8**; 545.5 *beautiful*; 466.9 *discriminating*; 543.3 *elegant*; 553.7 *fashionable*; 545.6 *personable*; 241.1 *pleasant*; 6.20, 549.5 *refined*; 728.13 *subtle*; 495.7 *tasty*
tastefully 6.27 *discerningly*; 543.5 *elegantly*; 553.10 *fashionably*; 466.16 *judiciously*; 495.11 *tastily*
tastefulness 543.1, 549.1 *elegance*
tasteless **497.5**; 620.4 *boring*; 497.6 *coarse*; 245.12 *deteriorated*; 675.8 *discourteous*; 802.13 *improper*; 544.8 *indecorous*; 728.17 *insipid*; 337.13 *insufficient*; 544.10 *ugly*
tasteless items 497.3
tastelessly **497.11**; 620.8 *boringly*; 544.11 *inelegantly*; 728.26 *insipidly*; 495.11 *tastily*; 337.14 *weakly*
tastelessness **497.1**; **675.1**; 497.4 *bad taste*; 620.1 *boredom*; 544.2 *impropriety*; 728.8 *insipidness*
taste of life 495.2
taster **495.5**; 557.18 *eater*; 129.6 *preview*
taste stale 497.7 *be tasteless*
taste test 495.5 *taste bud*
taste treat 495.5 *taste bud*
tastily **495.11**; 557.29 *edibly*
tastiness **241.9**; 490.1 *physical pleasure*; 495.1 *taste*
tasting 495.3 *appetizer*; 557.3 *delicate eating*; 558.1 *drinking*
tasting cup 495.5 *taste bud*
tasty **241.4**; **495.7**; 557.27 *edible*
tat 793.5 *cheap item*; 193.8 *interweave*
tattered 782.3 *beggarly*; 552.10 *in dishabille*
tatters 782.7 *beggary*; 205.8 *bits and pieces*; 552.4 *dishabille*; 551.1 *dress*
tatting 193.2 *braid*
tattle 734.2 *chat*; 504.8 *something heard*
tattler 479.9 *equivocator*; 693.10 *informer*; 731.4 *talker*
tattling 731.6 *effusive*
tattoo 711.2 *danger signal*; 509.8 *drum*; 509.1 *drumming*; 656.3 *formal occasion*; 743.10 *identify*; 743.3 *means of identification*; 601.8 *salute*; 330.7 *shot*; 742.6 *word*
tattooed 743.12 *identified*
tattooing 542.3 *pattern*
tatty 782.3 *beggarly*; 245.13 *dilapidated*; 122.14 *poor*; 548.6 *seedy*; 793.10 *shoddy*
taught a lesson 711.9 *warned*
taunt **668.6**; **668.25**; 661.3 *act of defiance*; 706.18 *answer back*; 661.6 *be insubordinate*; 660.7 *insult*; 624.9 *offend*; 660.29 *ridicule*; 670.9 *show of disapproval*
taunted 670.35 *hissed*
taunting **668.15**; 660.18 *insulting*
tauon 28.77 *elementary particle*
taupe 533.1 *grey*; 533.4 *greyness*
taurine 71.33 *ungulate*
taut 418.2 *tough*
tauten 418.9 *harden*
tautly 418.12 *toughly*
tautness 418.5 *hardness*
tautological 270.3 *diffuse*; 27.86 *logical*; 694.6 *meaningful*; 112.12 *repetitious*; 111.12 *same*; 219.7 *superfluous*
tautologically 270.7 *diffusely*; 111.18 *identically*
tautologize 270.5 *be diffuse*; 694.10 *mean*
tautologous 270.3 *diffuse*; 219.7 *superfluous*
tautologously 270.7 *diffusely*
tautology 270.1 *diffuseness*; 274.11 *grammatical error*; 112.2 *iteration*; 5.22 *many words*; 4.8 *philosophical term*; 27.64 *reasoning*; 111.1 *sameness*; 219.3 *superfluity*
tautonym 721.8 *name*; 5.17 *word*
tautonymic 5.42 *worded*
tavern 565.10 *hotel*
tavern's bush 743.3 *means of identification*
tawdriness **675.2**; 497.4 *bad taste*; 236.8 *inferiority*; 544.3 *ugliness*
tawdry 497.6 *coarse*; 236.2 *inferior*; 793.10 *shoddy*; 124.4 *trivial*; 544.10 *ugly*; 675.7 *vulgar*
tawny 534.1 *brown*; 537.1 *yellow*
tawny port 558.9 *wine*
tawse 814.14 *instrument of punishment*
tax **790.7**; 790.12 *charge*; 710.7 *demand*; 787.5 *expense*; 261.6 *fatigue*; 768.2 *gift*; 785.4 *grant*; 414.14 *make heavy*; 788.2 *money received*; 773.8 *take back*; 773.5 *takings*; 349.1 *use*; 414.8 *weighing down*; 576.7 *work for*
taxable 790.15 *chargeable*; 13.13 *economic*; 768.7 *given*; 773.12 *taking*
taxable income 13.6 *economic factors*; 790.7 *tax*
tax assessor 790.10 *taxpayer*
taxation 13.6 *economic factors*; 790.7 *tax*
tax avoidance 13.6 *economic factors*; 389.1 *escape*; 786.1 *nonpayment*
tax benefit 768.2 *gift*
tax collector 376.35, 769.7 *collector*; 790.10 *taxpayer*
tax computation 790.7 *tax*
tax consultant 790.10 *taxpayer*
tax declaration 790.7 *tax*
tax-deductible 790.15 *chargeable*
tax demand 397.2 *demand*; 790.7 *tax*
tax disc 320.21 *miscellaneous motoring terms*
tax dodger 389.3 *escaper*; 786.6 *nonpayer*
tax-dodging 389.1 *escape*
taxed 414.3 *ponderous*
taxes 788.2 *money received*; 790.7 *tax*
tax evader 634.17 *avoider*; 774.11 *dishonest person*; 389.3 *escaper*; 786.6 *nonpayer*; 709.4 *refuser*
tax evasion 800.3 *criminality*; 774.7 *dishonesty*; 13.6 *economic factors*; 389.1 *escape*; 786.1 *nonpayment*; 709.1 *refusal*
tax-exempt 790.15 *chargeable*
tax exile 786.6 *nonpayer*
tax form 790.7 *tax*
tax-free **758.8**; 790.15 *chargeable*; 793.11 *free of charge*; 758.13 *with impunity*
tax haven 389.1 *escape*; 786.1 *nonpayment*
taxi 320.18 *cab*; 316.5 *means of transport*; 300.15 *walk*
taxicab 320.18 *cab*
taxidermy 359.1 *preservation*
taxi driver 316.7 *transferor*
taxing 414.3 *ponderous*; 814.21 *punishing*; 773.2 *taking back*; 414.8 *weighing down*
taxi rank 226.4 *stopping place*
taxiway 322.4 *airport*; 317.13 *flight path*
tax office 790.7 *tax*
taxon 34.17 *taxonomy*
taxonomic **34.28**; **77.16**; 34.20 *biological*; 409.25 *categorical*; 137.10 *classificatory*; 407.12 *hierarchical*; 220.11 *listed*
taxonomically **137.16**; 34.29 *biologically*; 407.25 *in order*; 409.28 *in place*; 220.13 *inventorially*
taxonomic group 34.17 *taxonomy*
taxonomist 34.19 *life scientist*
taxonomy **34.17**; 409.5 *categorization*; 137.1 *classification*; 554.9 *classifications of life*; 407.2 *grouping*; 34.1 *life science*; 220.7 *listing*; 721.7 *nomenclature*
tax owed 790.7 *tax*
taxpayer **790.10**; 15.7 *employee*
tax payment 790.7 *tax*
tax-raising 773.12 *taking*; 773.2 *taking back*
tax rate 790.7 *tax*
tax refund 790.7 *tax*
tax return 693.3 *document*; 790.7 *tax*
tax roll 220.6 *list of names*
tax shelter 389.1 *escape*; 786.1 *nonpayment*
tax system 790.7 *tax*
tax table 790.7 *tax*
tax write-off 768.2 *gift*
tayberry 412.5 *hybrid*
T-bar 68.12 *ski*
T-bar lift 68.1 *skiing*
T-beam 38.27 *superstructure*
T-bone 25.22 *beef*; 61.9 *race*
T-boned 61.10 *racing*
T-boning 61.6 *motor-racing terms*; 61.10 *racing*
TCA cycle 33.24 *respiration*
t-distribution 27.59 *probability distribution*
tea **558.3**; 691.6 *drug*; 557.12 *meal*; 654.3 *meeting*
teabag 308.6 *porous thing*
tea break 263.1 *ease*; 275.6 *interval*
tea caddy 410.11 *vessel*
teacake 25.39 *loaf*
teach 713.5 *advise*; 117.10 *assimilate*; 243.6 *brief*; 455.14 *cause to know*; 738.1 *display*; 6.22 *educate*; 632.18 *habituate*; 693.11 *inform*; 400.14 *master*
teachability 6.10 *educability*; 695.9 *intelligibility*
teachable 6.17 *educable*; 695.1 *intelligible*
teachableness 480.7 *persuadability*

teacher 713.4 *adviser;* 760.5 *converter;* 644.3 *curious person;* 579.13 *director;* 722.3 *dissertator;* 400.9 *educational leader;* 6.4 *educator;* 485.5 *expert;* 719.6 *interpreter;* 455.6 *knowledgeable person;* 396.10 *person of authority;* 243.15 *preparer;* 4.12 *sage;* 578.1 *worker*
teacher's pet 593.11 *loved one;* 663.4 *obedient person;* 337.4 *weakling*
teacher training 6.2 *educational system*
tea chest 410.6 *box*
teach freely 250.14 *be free*
teach-in 734.4 *conference*
teaching 6.1 *education;* 455.3 *learning;* 795.7 *moral;* 4.2 *philosophical system*
teaching contract 755.2 *purchase contract*
teaching hospital 35.10 *hospital*
teachings 446.5 *ideology*
teach manners 244.1 *improve*
teach one his place 623.17 *humiliate*
teach wickedness 804.17 *make wicked*
teacup 558.10 *drink container;* 410.13 *drinking vessel*
tea dance 22.1 *dancing*
tea-drinker 689.8 *sober person*
tea-drinking 689.1 *sober;* 689.6 *sobriety*
tea estate 43.6 *farm*
tea for two 557.12 *meal*
tea garden 44.2 *garden*
tea gown 551.7 *frock*
teahouse 557.15 *eating place*
teak 418.7 *hard substance*
tea lady 401.5 *office assistant*
tea leaf 804.10 *bad person*
tea-leaf reader 11.13 *diviner*
tea-leaf reading 11.9 *divination*
tea leaves 475.10 *cards*
team **53.4**; **169.5**; **376.12**; **747.9**; 750.2 *alliance;* 71.21 *assemblage of mammals;* 374.3 *assembly;* 198.14 *pair;* 127.3 *person included;* 578.4 *personnel;* 198.1 *two*
team captain 579.14 *leader*
team dinghy racing 50.1 *sailing*
team mates 747.9 *team*
team member 405.5 *member;* 45.3 *sportsman*
team spirit 750.1 *accord;* 747.2 *fellowship*
teamster 579.14 *leader*
team up 376.41 *band together;* 750.22 *form an alliance;* 223.14 *keep company with*
team up with 374.6 *come together;* 747.14 *join with*
teamwork 747.4 *joint operation*
tea party 557.13 *feast;* 654.5 *party*
tea plantation 43.6 *farm*
tea planter 43.15 *agriculturist*
teapot 410.15 *pot*
tear 431.3 *body fluid;* 146.2, 146.5 *crack;* 231.7 *defect;* 557.21 *eat;* 236.14 *ill-treat;* 491.11 *inflict pain;* 491.3 *injury;* 308.18 *open;* 308.1 *opening;* 372.9 *separate;* 372.3 *separateness*
tearable 424.1 *brittle;* 372.19 *separable*
tear along 332.4 *be swift*
tear apart 670.17 *criticize;* 357.9 *demolish;* 372.9 *separate*
tear dew 429.6 *dew*
tear down 357.9 *demolish;* 367.2 *flatten*
teardrop 431.3 *body fluid*
tearful 603.4 *lamenting;* 602.5 *sad;* 429.12 *seeping;* 590.12 *sensitive;* 690.2 *slightly drunk*
tearfully 431.26 *fluidly;* 559.8 *glandularly;* 603.8 *mournfully*
tearfulness 603.1 *lamentation*
tearing 424.1 *brittle;* 369.6 *extorsion*
tearing apart 372.3 *separateness*
tearing hurry 262.4 *haste*
tearing one's hair 742.3 *gesture*
tearing out 369.1 *extraction;* 144.2 *removal*
tearing rage 624.4 *anger*
tear into 381.5 *strike*
tear-jerking 603.5 *lamentable;* 627.7 *pitiful*
tearlike 431.16 *rheumy*
tear limb from limb 357.9 *demolish;* 814.5 *execute*
tear loose 391.5 *be liberated*
tear off 332.6 *accelerate;* 313.4 *hurry off;* 262.2 *make haste;* 552.15 *make nude*
tear off the mask 739.5 *disclose;* 738.4 *show oneself*
tear oneself away 313.6 *part*
tear oneself away from 605.5 *resign*
tear one's hair 742.11 *gesture*
tearoom 557.15 *eating place*
tear out 369.16 *extort;* 369.11 *extract;* 144.15 *remove*
tears 431.3 *body fluid;* 433.4 *exudate;* 559.2 *secreted substance*
tears for oneself 627.1 *pity*
tears of rage 594.5, 624.4 *anger*
tears of self-pity 627.1 *pity*
tears of sympathy 627.2 *condolence*
tear-stained 429.12 *seeping*
tear to bits 357.9 *demolish;* 372.9 *separate*
tear to pieces 357.9 *demolish*
tear to rags 357.9 *demolish*
tear to shreds 678.11 *criticize;* 357.9 *demolish*
tear up 357.8 *destroy;* 355.1 *relinquish*
tear up the road 332.4 *be swift*
tease 607.8 *annoy;* 642.5 *be capricious;* 599.13 *be humorous;* 697.4 *buffoon;* 642.4 *capricious person;* 593.26 *court;* 604.6 *disappoint;* 604.1 *disappointment;* 599.6 *humorist;* 624.9 *offend;* 668.24 *ridicule;* 480.16 *tempt*
teaser 740.9 *advertisement;* 737.4 *brainteaser;* 697.4 *buffoon;* 599.6 *humorist;* 264.4 *problem;* 21.19 *stage set*
teaset 410.16 *crockery*
teashop 558.11 *drink provider;* 557.15 *eating place*
teasing 480.2 *flattery;* 599.10 *humorous;* 483.2 *inducement;* 483.11 *motivational;* 480.19 *persuasive;* 668.6 *taunt;* 668.15 *taunting;* 599.3 *wit*
teasingly 483.14 *influentially*
teaspoon 203.3 *container;* 557.16 *eating utensil;* 410.17 *ladle*
teat 71.2 *mammalian characteristic*
tea table 23.4 *table*
tea towel 256.11 *cleaning cloth*
tea trolley 320.7 *handcart*
tea urn 410.15 *pot*
technical 6.21 *curricular;* 694.6 *meaningful;* 264.12 *problematic;* 139.21 *specialized;* 124.4 *trivial*
technical drawing 19.3 *drawing;* 721.9 *representation;* 717.2 *reproduction*
technical error **274.14**
technical foul 58.5 *lacrosse;* 49.5 *penalties;* 49.4 *playing terms*
technical hitch 378.2 *obstacle;* 226.2 *stop*
technicality 264.1 *difficulty;* 484.3 *expedient plan;* 389.2 *means of escape;* 713.3 *precept;* 124.8 *trifle*
technical journal 740.5 *journal*
technical knockout 52.2 *boxing*
technical knowledge 485.1 *skill*
technical language 139.10 *specialized language*
technically 6.26 *studiously*
technical meaning 694.4 *type of meaning*
technical problems 378.2 *obstacle*
technical rehearsal 21.14 *production*
technical skill 485.1 *skill*
technical subject 6.3 *subject*
technical term 5.20 *jargon word;* 721.8 *name*
technical word 5.20 *jargon word*
technician 578.2 *artisan;* 485.5 *expert;* 438.8 *machinist;* 38.4 *mechanical engineer;* 346.5 *operator;* 136.8 *qualified person*
Technicolor™ 529.7 *colour painting*
technicoloured 529.10 *coloured*
technics 438.6 *mechanics*
technique 455.2 *information;* 352.1 *means;* 485.1 *skill;* 724.1 *style;* 19.4 *treatment;* 317.1 *way*
techniques of the bokken 52.10 *aikido*
techno 18.9 *popular music*
technobabble 729.1 *faculty of speech;* 5.20 *jargon word;* 139.10 *specialized language*
technocracy 12.1 *government*
technocratic 12.9 *governmental*
technological 438.9 *mechanical*
technologically 438.11 *instrumentally*
technology 13.6 *economic factors;* 356.2 *manufacture;* 352.1 *means;* 438.6 *mechanics;* 402.6 *natural science;* 356.1 *production;* 455.5 *science*
technospeak 5.20 *jargon word*
tectology 403.8 *science of structure*
tectonic **30.54**; 20.11 *architectural;* 403.11 *structural*
tectonically 20.20 *architecturally;* 403.18 *structurally*
tectonic forces 30.20 *earth movement*
tectonics 20.1 *architecture;* 30.1 *earth science;* 356.2 *manufacture;* 403.1 *structure*
tectosilicate 30.34 *mineral*
tectrix 72.17 *plumage*
tedder 43.10 *farm tool*
teddy 551.18 *underwear*
teddy bear 717.6 *image*
Te Deum 10.8 *hymn;* 671.2 *thanks;* 601.7 *thanksgiving*
tedious 236.3 *bad;* 620.4 *boring;* 270.3 *diffuse;* 261.4 *fatiguing;* 240.1, 264.13 *inconvenient;* 112.13 *monotonous;* 271.1 *simple*
tediously 264.28 *awkwardly;* 620.8 *boringly;* 240.6 *inconveniently;* 261.9 *tiringly*
tediousness 236.9 *badness;* 620.1 *boredom;* 271.4 *simplicity*
tedium 620.1 *boredom;* 270.1 *diffuseness;* 112.3 *repetitiveness*
tee 56.2 *golfing terms*
teed 690.3 *dead drunk*
teed up 243.18 *prepared*
teeing ground 56.1 *golf*
teeing off 56.3 *golf shots*
tee line 68.10 *curling*
teem 217.5 *about;* 562.6 *be fertile;* 208.11, 376.40 *crowd;* 130.26 *produce;* 31.62 *rain*
teeming 376.50 *crowded;* 152.2 *dense;* 219.6 *excessive;* 562.5 *fertile;* 217.3 *filled;* 329.11 *overrun*
teeming with 232.8 *full*
teem with 219.4 *be excessive;* 76.16 *infest*
teenage 555.11 *young*
teenaged 555.11 *young*
teenager 201.7 *double figures;* 566.7 *person;* 555.6 *young person*
teenage runaway 634.17 *avoider*
teen idol 363.6 *charmer*
teens 201.7 *double figures;* 555.1 *youth*
teensy-weensy 124.4 *trivial*
teeny 159.7 *little;* 124.4 *trivial*
teenybopper 593.9 *lover;* 555.6 *young person*
teeny-weeny 159.7 *little;* 124.4 *trivial*
tee off 56.7 *golf;* 130.18 *make a beginning*
Tees 90.4 *British rivers*
teeter 227.11 *be changeable;* 337.6 *be weak;* 326.8 *oscillate;* 326.7 *oscillator;* 327.25 *pitch;* 639.5 *vacillate*
teeterboard 326.7 *oscillator*
teetering 227.13 *changeable;* 639.4 *unsteady;* 337.8 *weak*
teetering on the edge 254.2 *unsafe*
teeter on the edge 254.8 *be in danger*
teeter-totter 326.8 *oscillate;* 326.7 *oscillator*
teetery-bender 326.7 *oscillator*
teeth 557.16 *eating utensil;* 729.5 *organ of speech;* 360.3 *tools for gripping;* 587.1 *weapon;* 531.9 *white thing*
teething troubles 378.2 *obstacle;* 264.8 *snag*
teethless 426.4 *toothless*
teetotal 684.8 *self-restrained;* 689.1 *sober*
teetotalism 684.1 *self-restraint;* 689.6 *sobriety*
teetotaller 634.17 *avoider;* 795.6 *moralist;* 709.4 *refuser;* 684.4 *self-restrained person;* 689.8 *sober person*
teetotally 684.11 *with self-restraint*
tee up 243.4 *prepare for action*
tefillin 10.14 *sacred object*
Teflon™ 435.1 *materials;* 32.21 *polymer*
teg 43.8 *livestock*
tegumen 550.13 *casing*
tektite 29.20 *meteor*
telaesthesia 11.1 *occultism*
telaesthetic 11.12 *occultist;* 11.16 *psychic*
telebanking 14.1 *finance*
telecamera 692.21 *television*
telecast 692.25 *broadcast material;* 692.30 *communicate;* 740.13 *make public*
telecasting 740.2 *mass media*
telecommunication **692.6**; 740.2 *mass media*
telecommunications 692.1 *communications;* 40.14 *data transfer;* 39.1, 334.9 *electronics*
telecommunicator 742.8 *signer*
telecommuting 40.15 *network*
teleconference 746.3 *discussion*
teleconferencing 747.8 *conferring;* 40.12 *electronic office*
telecottage 692.6 *telecommunication*
telegram 693.2 *communication;* 692.8 *data transmission;* 316.10 *transferred thing*
telegraph 693.12 *communicate;* 692.31 *correspond;* 692.8 *data transmission;* 334.9 *electronics;* 332.11 *swift thing;* 316.10 *transferred thing*
telegrapher 692.29 *broadcaster;* 742.8 *signer*
telegraphese 269.1 *conciseness;* 5.20 *jargon word*
telegraphic 692.33 *communicational;* 269.3 *concise;* 742.16 *signalling*
telegraphically 269.5 *concisely;* 742.18 *indicatively*
telegraphist 692.29 *broadcaster;* 742.8 *signer*
telegraph messenger 742.8 *signer*
telegraph operator 742.8 *signer*
telegraph pole 692.12 *public telephone system;* 154.6 *tall thing*
telegraph signal 742.4 *signal*
telegraphy 692.6 *telecommunication*
Teleia 570.14 *gods and goddesses of marriage*
teleinformatics 692.6 *telecommunication*
telekinesis 11.1 *occultism;* 11.8 *psychic power*
telekinetic 11.12 *occultist;* 11.16 *psychic*
telemark 68.2 *cross-country skiing;* 68.14 *ski;* 68.4 *skiing technique*
telemarking 68.4 *skiing technique*
Telemessage™ 693.2 *communication;* 692.8 *data transmission*
telemeter 26.8 *meter*
telemetric 26.16 *micrometric*
telemetry 28.95 *mensuration;* 26.2 *micrometry;* 29.32 *satellite*
telemon 19.12 *sculpture*
Telenet 40.15 *network*
teleological 482.11 *intending;* 446.12 *purposive*
teleology 4.6 *branch of philosophy;* 482.5 *final intention;* 283.4 *looking to the future*
teleost fish 74.2 *fish*
telepathic 101.9 *parapsychological;* 445.7 *precognitive;* 11.16 *psychic*
telepathically 101.13 *metaphysically;* 11.25 *occultly*
telepathic dream 11.10 *psychic phenomenon*
telepathic hallucination 11.10 *psychic phenomenon*
telepathic transmission 11.1 *occultism*
telepathist 101.7 *believer in a nonmaterial world;* 11.12 *occultist;* 475.8 *oracle*
telepathy 11.1 *occultism;* 101.4 *parapsychology;* 445.2 *precognition;* 11.8 *psychic power;* 488.1 *sensation*
téléphérique 68.1 *skiing*
telephone **692.9**; **692.32**; 504.9 *audio device;* 504.11 *aural;* 693.12 *communicate;* 334.9 *electronics;* 332.11 *swift thing*
telephone answering machine 504.9 *audio device*
telephone bell 510.4 *sources of resonance*
telephone book 692.11 *dialling*
telephone booth 692.9 *telephone*
telephone box 692.9 *telephone*
telephone call **692.10**
telephone directory 692.11 *dialling;* 220.3 *dictionary;* 693.5 *reference book*
telephone engineer 692.13 *telephoner*
telephone engineering 692.6 *telecommunication*
telephone exchange 692.12 *public telephone system*
telephone kiosk 692.9 *telephone*
telephoneline 692.12 *public telephone system*
telephone mechanic 692.13 *telephoner*
telephone number 692.11 *dialling;* 743.3 *means of identification*
telephone numbers 208.2 *multitude;* 759.3 *something in exchange*
telephone operator 346.5 *operator;* 692.13 *telephoner*
telephone pole 692.12 *public telephone system*
telephoner **692.13**
telephone receiver 769.8 *receiver*
telephone ring 742.4 *signal*
telephone set 692.9 *telephone*
telephone tap 504.9 *audio device*
telephone tapper 504.2 *hearer*
telephone wire 692.12 *public telephone system*
telephonic 504.11 *aural;* 692.33 *communicational*

telephonically 504.17 *aurally*
telephonist 346.5 *operator*; 692.13 *telephoner*
telephony 692.6 *telecommunication*
telephotography 41.1 *photography*
telephoto lens 41.17 *lens*; 518.8 *reflection*
telephoto zoom 41.17 *lens*
teleplay 21.2 *play*
teleport 11.24 *experience psychic phenomena*
teleportation 11.1 *occultism*
teleprinter 692.8 *data transmission*
Teleran™ 322.6 *flight control*
telergic 11.16 *psychic*
telergy 11.1 *occultism*
telescope **29.24**; 191.6 *become smaller*; 269.4 *be concise*; 191.5 *make smaller*; 28.85 *microscope*; 28.32 *optical instrument*; 149.10 *shorten*; 520.7 *that which makes visible*; 518.10 *visual aid*
telescoped 191.7 *smaller*
telescopic 29.36 *astronomical*; 191.9 *contractible*; 518.20 *visual*
telescopic loader 43.10 *farm tool*
telescopic rod 55.3 *fishing tackle*
telescopic sight 60.3 *hunting equipment*; 518.10 *visual aid*
telescopy 518.10 *visual aid*
teleshop 777.1 *purchase*
teleshopper 777.12 *purchaser*
teleshopping 777.14 *buying*; 777.8 *shopping*
télésiège 68.1 *skiing*
telestial kingdom 8.11 *heaven*
Teletex™ 692.8 *data transmission*
Teletext™ 692.25 *broadcast material*
telethon 692.25 *broadcast material*; 652.5 *charity*; 710.3 *solicitation*
teletypewriter 692.8 *data transmission*
televangelist 692.29 *broadcaster*; 7.5 *Christian*; 760.5 *converter*
televise 692.30, 693.12 *communicate*; 738.2 *display something*; 740.13 *make public*
televised 692.34 *communicated*; 740.19 *published*
television **692.21**; 692.1 *communications*; 21.1 *drama*; 28.13 *electromagnetic radiation*; 334.9 *electronics*; 693.4 *mass communication*; 740.2 *mass media*
television broadcaster 692.29 *broadcaster*
television broadcasting **692.24**
television camera 692.21 *television*
television channel 692.24 *television broadcasting*
television director 356.9 *producer*
television drama 21.2 *play*
television dramatist 21.26 *dramatist*
television engineer 578.2 *artisan*
television evangelist 760.5 *converter*
television mast 692.24 *television broadcasting*
television news 741.6 *radio news*
television personality 21.29 *entertainer*
television play 21.2 *play*
television producer 356.9 *producer*
television programme 738.9 *production*
television ratings 740.2 *mass media*
television receiver 39.20 *electron tube*
television reception **692.23**
television review 719.3 *criticism*
television set **692.22**
television station 692.24 *television broadcasting*
television time out 46.5 *game time*
television tower 692.24 *television broadcasting*
television trial 16.7 *legal trial*
television tube 24.9 *industrial ceramics*; 692.21 *television*
teleworking 40.15 *network*
telex 693.12 *communicate*; 693.2 *communication*; 692.31 *correspond*; 692.8 *data transmission*; 316.13 *post*
telex machine 692.8 *data transmission*; 125.6 *photocopier*
tell 713.5 *advise*; 123.7 *be important*; 455.14 *cause to know*; 739.6 *divulge*; 6.22 *educate*; 693.11 *inform*; 693.13 *inform on*; 694.10 *mean*; 194.10, 210.11 *number*; 721.15 *recount*; 729.11 *speak*
tell a cock-and-bull story 234.12 *distort the truth*
tell all 739.6 *divulge*
tell a story 721.15 *recount*
tell a tale 721.15 *recount*
tell a tall story **727.11**
tell dirty jokes 712.5 *curse*
teller 210.6 *calculator*; 693.9 *informant*; 780.18 *treasurer*
teller of dirty jokes 258.6 *dirty person*
teller of tales 721.10 *descriptive writer*
tell fortunes 11.23, 475.12 *divine*
telling 348.7 *causal*; 210.3 *count*; 123.5 *important*; 395.11 *influential*; 695.1 *intelligible*; 694.6 *meaningful*; 480.19 *persuasive*; 336.10 *potent*
telling off 670.7 *blame*; 606.2 *expression of dissatisfaction*; 814.7 *punishment*
tell its own story 738.5 *be visible*
tell its own tale 695.4 *be intelligible*
tell lies 800.8 *be dishonourable*
tell of 694.10 *mean*
tell off 670.20 *censure*; 514.14 *hiss*; 814.1 *punish*
tell on 739.7 *betray*; 693.13 *inform on*
tell oneself 735.3 *soliloquize*
tell porkies 234.12 *distort the truth*
telltale 739.4 *discloser*; 479.9 *equivocator*; 716.8 *evidential*; 693.10 *informer*; 447.9 *local*; 694.6 *meaningful*; 716.7 *person who gives evidence*; 742.14 *signifying*; 63.8 *squash*
tell tales 105.7 *be improbable*; 716.13 *turn queen's evidence*
telltale sign 739.2 *divulgence*; 716.4 *indication*; 742.1 *sign*
tell the same story 111.7 *be the same*
tell the truth 698.29 *be truthful*
tell the world 740.13 *make public*
tell to one's face 738.4 *show oneself*
tell upon 338.2 *be full of vigour*; 395.8 *influence*
tellurian 29.36 *astronomical*; 566.12 *human*; 566.7 *person*
telluric 29.36 *astronomical*; 32.34 *elemental*
tellurometer 26.8 *meter*
tellurous 32.34 *elemental*
telly 692.22 *television set*
telophase 34.10 *cell division*
telpher 317.12 *cableway*; 321.1 *railway*
telpherage 316.2 *transportation*
telpher line 317.12 *cableway*
telpher way 317.12 *cableway*
Telstar™ 29.32 *satellite*; 692.7 *satellite communication*
temazepam 394.8 *drug*
temblor 30.22 *seismic activity*
temerity 661.1 *defiance*; 615.1 *rashness*
temp 398.4 *deputy*
temper 634.3 *abstain*; 594.5 *anger*; 684.5 *be self-restrained*; 243.7 *develop*; 419.14 *ease*; 32.30 *extract*; 418.9 *harden*; 418.5 *hardness*; 423.11 *make tough*; 292.8 *mitigate*; 412.8 *mix*; 685.4 *moderate*; 136.15 *modify*; 608.9 *relieve*; 221.4 *state of mind*; 336.8 *strengthen*
tempera 19.11 *artist's materials*; 19.8 *painting*
temperament **599.8**; 479.6 *equivocation*; 626.3 *irritableness*; 99.4 *nature*; 139.2 *personality*; 221.4 *state of mind*; 642.3 *whim*
temperamental 642.1 *capricious*; 639.2 *changeable*; 221.8 *in a state of*; 625.4 *irascible*; 626.7 *irritable*; 591.2 *oversensitive*; 590.13 *passionate*; 488.7 *susceptible*
temperamentally 221.9 *conditionally*; 625.9 *irascibly*; 626.14 *irritably*; 591.13 *oversensitively*
temperamentalness 625.1 *irascibility*
temperamental person 227.5 *changeable person*
temperance 634.11 *abstinence*; 4.3 *detachment*; 685.1 *moderation*; 795.3 *moral purity*; 251.3, 684.1 *self-restraint*; 689.6 *sobriety*; 399.1 *veto*; 803.2 *virtues*
temperance society 689.8 *sober person*
temperate 634.19 *abstaining*; 4.18 *detached*; 803.6 *ethical*; 685.6 *moderate*; 795.9 *pure*; 251.14, 684.8 *self-restrained*; 689.1 *sober*; 31.50, 493.11 *warm*
temperate climate 31.38 *climate*
temperately 634.21 *away*; 803.10 *ethically*; 685.9 *moderately*; 689.9 *soberly*; 4.27 *stoically*; 251.17, 684.11 *with self-restraint*
temperateness 684.1 *self-restraint*
temperate zone 31.39 *climatic zone*
temperature **28.37**; 493.1 *heat*; 493.2 *heat measurement*; 260.3 *symptom*
temperature scale 28.37 *temperature*
tempered 418.3 *hardened*; 292.16 *mitigated*; 412.12 *mixed*; 685.6 *moderate*; 684.8 *self-restrained*; 423.2 *toughened*
tempering 418.6 *solidification*; 336.4 *strengthening*; 728.6 *suggestion*
temper oneself 336.8 *strengthen*
temper tantrum 624.4 *anger*
tempest **327.13**; 332.11 *swift thing*; 380.5 *violent weather*; 31.14 *windiness*
tempest in a teapot 751.2 *argument*
tempestuous 420.4 *bumpy*; 31.48 *stormy*; 332.1 *swift*; 327.17 *turbulent*; 380.6 *violent*
template 160.2 *prototype*
temple 356.8 *construction*; 10.11 *place of worship*; 252.5 *refuge*; 169.1 *side*
temple state 12.5 *political organization*
tempo **18.19**; 516.4 *harmonics*; 275.12 *musical time*; 298.1 *regularity*; 298.5 *regular thing*; 326.2 *vibration*
temporal **275.20**; 281.17 *timekeeping*
temporalities 440.4 *possessions*
temporally 275.30 *chronologically*
temporarily 282.10 *for the present*; 762.9 *instead*; 278.8 *transiently*
temporary 754.6 *compromising*; 278.7 *impermanent*; 282.7 *occasional*; 762.7 *substitute*; 275.20 *temporal*
temporary measure 762.1 *substitution*
temporary stoppage 226.2 *stop*
temporary substitute 754.2 *half-measure*; 218.8 *insufficiency*
temporary truce 749.1 *pacification*; 589.1 *peace*
temporary worker 398.4 *deputy*
temporize 645.5 *be cunning*; 294.8 *delay*
temporizing 645.1, 645.4 *cunning*
tempo rubato 18.19 *tempo*
temps de poisson 22.9 *ballet steps*
tempt **480.16**; 344.10 *awaken*; 617.15 *cause desire*; 593.26 *court*; 395.8 *influence*; 363.12 *lure*; 804.17 *make wicked*; 483.10 *manipulate*
temptation 363.4 *allurement*; 344.1 *cause*; 480.2 *flattery*; 595.1 *liking*
tempter **480.13**; 483.7 *motivator*
tempt fate 459.6 *be foolish*; 254.9 *face danger*; 353.3 *tackle*
tempting 395.12 *appealing*; 363.9 *attractive*; 617.8 *desirable*; 595.5 *likable*; 593.22 *lovable*; 483.11 *motivational*; 480.19 *persuasive*; 241.4 *tasty*
temptingly 617.17 *desirably*; 483.14 *influentially*; 593.30 *lovingly*; 480.21 *persuasively*; 595.10 *with great liking*
tempting offer 483.5 *positive stimulus*; 813.4 *reward for service*
tempt providence 615.5 *be rash*; 254.9 *face danger*; 353.3 *tackle*
temptress 363.6 *charmer*; 593.9 *lover*; 483.7 *motivator*; 480.13 *tempter*
tempus fugit 277.2 *time*
temulent 690.6 *intoxicating*
ten **201.6**; 201.17 *tenth*
tenable 450.13 *believable*; 252.7 *invulnerable*; 102.5 *possible*
tenably 102.10 *practically*
tenacious **267.10**; **638.2**; 635.7 *iron-willed*; 640.10 *persevering*; 423.4 *powerful*; 360.9 *retentive*; 613.12 *self-reliant*; 336.11 *strong in spirit*; 641.3 *unyielding*
tenaciously **267.12**; **360.11**; 613.18 *courageously*; 641.9 *obstinately*; 640.13 *persistently*; 423.13 *powerfully*; 336.14 *strongly*; 430.12 *viscously*
tenaciousness 360.1 *retention*; 267.2 *tenacity*; 430.1 *viscosity*
tenacious of life 554.12 *alive*
tenacious person **640.5**
tenacity **267.2**; **638.14**; 641.6 *determination*; 640.1 *perseverance*; 423.8 *physical strength*; 360.1 *retention*; 613.3 *steadfastness*; 336.1 *strength*; 430.1 *viscosity*; 635.2 *willpower*
tenancy 275.3 *duration*; 763.1 *possession*
tenancy in common 764.1 *joint possession*
tenant 564.3 *householder*; 763.5 *possessor*; 440.7 *property man*
tenanted 564.11 *inhabited*
tenant farmer 43.15 *agriculturist*
tenantry 763.1 *possession*
ten-beat crawl 67.2 *swimming technique*
ten cents 780.8 *American money*
ten centuries 201.9 *treble figures*
tench 55.5 *British game fish*
tenchi nage 52.10 *aikido*
Ten Commandments 810.6 *ethics*; 228.4 *stable thing*; 201.6 *ten*; 16.1 *the law*
tend **229.4**; 394.20 *doctor*; 43.18 *practise livestock farming*; 35.19 *practise medicine*; 469.2 *prefer*; 359.5 *preserve*; 252.10 *protect*; 392.25, 401.8 *serve*; 392.19 *support*; 324.7 *take a direction*
Tendency 229
tendency **104.2**; **229.1**; **632.2**; 136.2 *ability*; 485.2 *aptitude*; 324.2 *bearing*; 593.7 *choice*; 553.4 *design*; 482.5 *final intention*; 595.2 *inclination*; 469.7 *preference*; 345.4 *significance*
tendentious 229.5 *tending to*
tendentiously 229.6 *probably*
tendentiousness 482.5 *final intention*
tender 593.20 *amorous*; 776.3 *bargain*; 776.9 *bargaining*; 260.23 *diseased*; 768.5 *give*; 415.2 *insubstantial*; 648.4 *lenient*; 321.5 *locomotive part*; 242.4, 491.5 *painful*; 627.6 *pitying*; 50.10 *sailing*; 590.12, 591.1 *sensitive*; 419.6 *soft-hearted*; 591.3 *sore*; 488.7 *susceptible*; 492.8 *touchable*; 586.24 *warship*
tender age 555.1 *youth*
tender boat 50.2 *sailing boat*
tendered 776.18 *contractual*
tender feeling 590.5 *good feeling*; 595.1 *liking*; 593.3 *lovingness*
tenderfoot 130.14 *beginner*; 805.4 *innocent person*; 100.7 *new arrival*; 109.3 *unconnected person*
tender heart 627.1 *pity*
tender-hearted 627.6 *pitying*; 591.1 *sensitive*; 419.6 *soft-hearted*
tender-heartedly 627.13 *pitifully*
tender-heartedness 627.1 *pity*
tenderize 419.13 *soften*
Tenderloin 87.7 *city district*
tenderloin 25.23 *beef*; 25.25 *pork*
tender loving care 665.2 *consideration*; 392.3 *sustenance*
tenderly 650.10 *benevolently*; 665.13 *caringly*; 648.6 *leniently*; 415.11 *lightly*; 593.30 *lovingly*; 627.13 *pitifully*; 591.12 *sensitively*; 419.18 *soft-heartedly*
tenderness 488.2 *ability to sense*; 419.12 *gentleness*; 648.1 *leniency*; 415.5 *lightness*; 595.1 *liking*; 593.3 *lovingness*; 491.1 *pain*; 627.1 *pity*; 591.5 *sensitivity*; 591.7 *soreness*
tender spot 624.3 *cause of offence*; 254.7 *vulnerability*
tending 237.3 *instrumental*; 595.6 *liking*; 104.6 *probable*; 392.32 *supportive*; 104.2 *tendency*; 35.25 *therapeutic*
tending to **229.5**
ten-dollar bill 780.8 *American money*
tendon 373.6 *line*; 403.7 *skeleton*
tendril 205.6 *branch*; 77.6 *leaf*; 360.3 *tools for gripping*
tend to 27.94 *order*; 4.22 *propound a philosophy*
tend to go 324.7 *take a direction*
tendus 22.10 *positions at the barre*
tenebrous 523.8 *dark*; 524.5 *dim*
tenement 565.6 *apartment block*; 440.2 *legal terms*; 440.1 *property*; 767.8 *sink*
tenement building 767.8 *sink*
tenement district 87.7 *city district*
tenet 140.4 *guide*; 4.1 *philosophy*; 713.3 *precept*; 450.2 *religious belief*
tenets 446.5 *ideology*
tenfold 201.24 *fivefold*; 201.17 *tenth*
ten-gallon hat 551.15 *headgear*
ten-metre platform 67.6 *diving*
ten million 201.11 *million*
ten-minute penalty 58.3 *ice hockey*
tenne 743.13 *heraldic*; 743.8 *heraldic device*
tenner 780.8 *American money*; 780.9 *British money*; 201.6 *ten*
Tennessee 90.3 *US rivers*
tennis **63.1**; 63.5 *real tennis*
tennis ball 330.10 *ball*; 422.3 *elastic thing*; 63.3 *tennis equipment*
tennis court 421.8 *smooth thing*; 63.3 *tennis equipment*
tennis elbow 260.16 *rheumatism*
tennis equipment **63.3**
tennis player **63.6**
tennis racket 331.15 *ram*; 63.3 *tennis equipment*
tennis shoes 551.19 *footwear*
tennis skirt 551.6 *skirt*
tennis strokes **63.2**
tennis terms **63.4**
tenon 23.17 *carpenter*; 23.10 *carpenter's term*
tenoner 23.11 *woodworking tool*

tenon saw 23.11 *woodworking tool*
tenor 324.2 *bearing*; 209.1 *degree*; 18.32 *instrumental*; 694.1 *meaning*; 516.5 *melodist*; 724.1 *style*; 104.2, 229.1 *tendency*
tenor clef 18.17 *notation*
ten out of ten 230.3 *perfection*
ten pence 780.9 *British money*
ten-per-center 21.27 *producer*
ten-per-cent man 21.27 *producer*
tenpin 51.10 *bowling*
tenpin bowler 51.6 *bowler*
tenpin bowling 51.4 *bowling*
ten-pound note 780.9 *British money*
tense 5.34; 342.18 *active*; 612.8 *fearful*; 418.9 *harden*; 5.30 *syntax*; 418.2 *tough*
ten-second backcourt violation 49.5 *penalties*
ten-second line 49.1 *basketball*
tensely 418.12 *toughly*
tenseness 418.5 *hardness*
tensibility 422.1 *elasticity*
tensible 422.6 *elastic*
tensile 422.6 *elastic*
tensileness 419.8 *softness*
tensile strength 336.1 *strength*
tensimeter 26.8 *meter*
tensiometer 26.8 *meter*
tension 422.1 *elasticity*; 334.4 *energy*; 612.2 *fearfulness*; 418.5 *hardness*; 365.9 *irritation*; 38.14 *load*
tension traverse 62.3 *climbing technique*
tension wood 79.3 *timber*
tensity 418.5 *hardness*
tens of thousands 208.2 *multitude*
tensor 27.50 *scalar quantity*
tens place 27.8 *number system*
tent 62.4 *climbing equipment*; 394.14 *hospital*; 565.9 *mobile home*; 550.7 *overhead covering*; 394.10 *surgical dressing*
tentacle 492.7 *sense organ*; 488.4 *someone or something that feels*; 360.3 *tools for gripping*
tentation 448.1 *experiment*
tentative 353.9; 616.4 *cautious*; 486.3 *clumsy*; 448.8 *experimental*; 333.6 *hesitant*
tentative explanation 476.1 *supposition*
tentatively 353.10 *ambitiously*; 616.7 *cautiously*; 333.16 *slowly*
tentativeness 616.1 *caution*; 333.12 *hesitation*
tentative offer 752.2
tented 550.36 *covered*
tenth 201.17; 27.75 *equal*; 201.24 *fivefold*; 196.4 *less than one*; 205.1 *part*; 201.6 *ten*
tenthly 201.24 *fivefold*
ten thousand 201.10 *thousand*
tenth part 201.6 *ten*
tenths 790.7 *tax*
ten to one 104.11 *probably*
tenuity 151.7 *fineness*; 417.3 *sparseness*
tenuous 151.2 *fine*; 159.7 *little*; 417.1 *sparse*; 96.8 *unreal*
tenuously 159.8 *in a small way*; 417.7 *sparsely*
tenuousness 159.1 *littleness*; 417.3 *sparseness*
tenure 275.3 *duration*; 440.2 *legal terms*; 276.4 *period of activity*; 763.1 *possession*
tenzone 17.7 *poem*
tepee 565.9 *mobile home*; 550.7 *overhead covering*
tephra 30.25 *eruption*
tepid 493.9 *hot*
tepidity 493.1 *heat*
tepidness 493.1 *heat*
tequila sunrise 558.8 *mixed drink*; 536.3 *orange thing*
teratologic 727.12 *exaggerated*
teratological 727.12 *exaggerated*
teratologist 727.6 *exaggerator*; 35.13 *medical specialist*
teratology 35.3 *medical specialty*; 727.5 *tall story*; 619.3 *wonder-working*
terce 290.1 *morning*; 10.4 *public worship*
tercentenary 462.5 *day to remember*; 201.9 *treble figures*
tercentennial 201.9 *treble figures*
tercentennially 298.16 *cyclically*
tercet 17.8 *part of poem*
tergiversate 224.7 *be changed*; 662.15 *be disobedient*; 227.12 *be irresolute*; 739.7 *betray*; 245.1 *deteriorate*; 479.2 *equivocate*; 693.13 *inform on*; 355.1 *relinquish*; 708.12 *renounce*; 639.5 *vacillate*
tergiversating 245.12 *deteriorated*; 479.11 *equivocating*; 639.1 *vacillating*
tergiversation 224.2 *change of mind*; 245.7 *deterioration*; 662.1 *disobedience*; 739.2 *divulgence*; 479.6 *equivocation*; 800.2 *faithlessness*; 227.2 *irresolution*; 639.11 *vacillation*
tergiversator 303.21 *backslider*; 760.6 *convert*; 325.19 *deviant person*; 479.9 *equivocator*; 639.15 *indecisive person*; 662.10 *seditionist*
tergiversatory 662.13 *disobedient*
term 275.4; 27.25 *algebraic expression*; 277.1 *duration*; 721.8 *name*; 276.1 *period*; 276.4 *period of activity*; 292.1 *season*; 733.11 *title*; 5.17 *word*
termagant 625.3 *irascible person*; 380.4 *violent creature*
terminal 39.14; 322.4 *airport*; 312.19 *approaching*; 382.23, 582.20 *deadly*; 312.15 *destination*; 145.8 *distant*; 131.20 *ending*; 131.6 *end point*; 611.5 *past hope*; 40.7 *peripheral*; 260.22 *sick*; 226.4 *stopping place*
terminal bud 77.8 *bud*
terminal case 35.18 *patient*
terminal disease 260.2 *illness*
terminal illness 249.1 *adversity*; 260.2 *illness*; 582.5 *ways of dying*
terminally 582.23 *fatally*; 382.25 *lethally*
terminally ill 582.18 *dying*
terminal patient 582.10 *dying person*
terminal point 312.15 *destination*
terminal velocity 322.5 *flight*
terminate 708.15; 232.5 *be complete*; 131.16, 226.6 *cease*; 309.9 *close down*; 232.4 *complete*; 357.8 *destroy*; 133.12 *discontinue*; 638.7 *resolve*; 345.5 *show an effect*
terminated 708.20 *cancelled*; 232.7 *complete*; 133.9 *discontinued*; 131.21 *ended*
termination 708.6; 131.2, 133.2, 226.1 *cessation*; 309.1 *closure*; 232.3 *completion*; 345.1 *effect*; 39.28 *plug*
terminator 29.17 *moon*
terminological inexactitude 234.4 *distortion of the truth*; 699.10 *lie*
terminologically 220.13 *inventorially*
terminologist 5.2 *linguist*
terminology 220.3 *dictionary*; 721.7 *nomenclature*
terminus 312.15 *destination*; 131.6 *end point*; 317.10 *railway*; 321.8 *railway station*; 226.4 *stopping place*
termitarium 76.4 *social insect*
termite 654.10 *social animal*; 76.4 *social insect*
termite colony 76.4 *social insect*
term of imprisonment 276.4 *period of activity*
term of office 276.4 *period of activity*
term report 693.3 *document*
terms 409.10 *agreement*; 746.2 *basis for negotiations*; 222.1 *circumstances*
terms and conditions 15.1 *industrial relations*
terms of endearment 593.12 *nicknames for lovers*
terms of reference 136.6 *specification*
tern 72.3 *water bird*
ternary 32.35 *combined*; 27.71 *numerical*; 199.7 *three*
ternary compound 32.7 *chemical compound*
terotechnology 438.6 *mechanics*
terpene 33.20; 33.6 *lipid*
Terpsichore 22.1 *dancing*
Terpsichorean 21.30 *dancer*; 21.39 *dramatic*
terrace 43.11 *farmland*; 187.3 *flat thing*; 411.2 *level*; 44.3 *ornamental garden*; 317.3 *road*; 62.5 *rock face*; 518.9 *viewpoint*
terraced 411.7 *layered*; 565.16 *manorial*; 62.8 *mountaineering*; 20.12 *structural*
terraced house 20.3 *building*; 565.5 *house*
terracotta 24.1 *ceramics*; 24.9 *industrial ceramics*; 38.26 *masonry*; 19.14 *sculptor's materials*; 19.12 *sculpture*
terra firma 312.15 *destination*
terrain 30.6 *continent*; 565.2 *environment*; 86.1 *region*
terra incognita 737.8 *anonymity*; 456.3 *unknown thing*
terrapin 73.4 *chelonian*
terrestrial 30.50; 29.36 *astronomical*; 70.15 *of animals*; 77.14 *of plants*
terrestrially 29.39 *astronomically*
terrestrial magnetism 28.58, 30.44 *geomagnetism*
terrestrial planet 29.16 *planet*
terrestrial reptile 73.6 *extinct reptile*
terre verte 538.10 *green pigment*
terrible 236.3, 611.8 *bad*; 798.15 *bad luck!*; 798.7 *evil*; 612.10 *frightening*; 249.13 *too bad!*
terribleness 798.1 *evil*
terribly 798.12 *evilly*
terrific 797.1 *good*; 235.1 *worthy*
terrified 612.7 *frightened*
terrify 612.13 *frighten*
terrifying 612.10 *frightening*
terrigenous 30.51, 91.7 *oceanic*
terrine 410.16 *crockery*
Territorial 252.3 *protector*; 586.8 *soldier*
territorial 565.15 *environmental*; 396.14 *governmental*; 440.8 *propertied*; 86.16 *regional*; 2.14 *socioeconomic*
Territorial Army 586.15 *army*; 252.3 *protector*; 584.2 *the military*
territorial division 86.4
territorial limits 86.3 *regional boundary*
territorially 565.20 *environmentally*; 86.19 *geographically*; 440.10 *proprietarily*; 2.16 *sociologically*
territorial waters 86.3 *regional boundary*
territory 85.3 *dominion*; 565.2 *environment*; 396.8 *governmental organization*; 142.1 *location*; 12.5 *political organization*; 440.1 *property*; 86.1 *region*; 86.14 *sphere*; 395.7 *sphere of influence*; 86.5 *state*; 86.4 *territorial division*
terror 612.1 *fear*; 651.8 *malefactor*; 380.4 *violent creature*
terrorful 651.11 *cruel*
terrorism 651.2 *cruelness*; 481.7 *deterrence*; 753.2 *disorder*; 245.10 *impairment*; 612.4 *intimidation*; 380.2 *physical violence*; 383.3 *resistance movement*; 662.4 *revolution*; 662.3 *subversion*
terrorist 588.3 *anarchist*; 381.19 *attacker*; 386.4 *coercive person*; 798.6 *evil person*; 612.5 *frightener*; 586.9 *guerrilla*; 382.10 *killer*; 753.10 *lawbreaking*; 651.8 *malefactor*; 382.11 *murderer*; 383.5 *resister*; 383.12 *resisting*; 662.10, 753.5 *seditionist*; 774.8 *thief*; 380.4 *violent creature*; 804.9 *wicked person*
terrorist attack 381.16
terrorist bomb 379.1 *trap*
terroristic 651.11 *cruel*
terrorist killing 382.2 *murder*
terrorization 612.4 *intimidation*
terrorize 381.9 *attack successfully*; 662.16 *be subversive*; 753.8 *cause mischief*; 586.38 *conquer*; 481.2 *deter*; 612.13 *frighten*; 647.6 *suppress*; 651.18 *torment*
terrorized 612.7 *frightened*
terror-struck 612.7 *frightened*
terror tactics 381.16 *terrorist attack*
terse 269.3 *concise*; 149.7 *short*; 732.2 *sparing with words*; 723.6 *summary*
tersely 269.5 *concisely*; 149.12 *short*; 723.11 *summarily*
terseness 269.1 *conciseness*; 732.4 *guarded speech*; 149.1 *shortness*; 723.4 *summariness*
tertian 298.12 *cyclic*
tertiary 199.7 *three*
tertiary chord 18.16 *musical note*
tertiary education 6.2 *educational system*
Tertiary period 284.3 *geological period*
tertiary structure 33.9 *protein*
tertium quid 199.6 *third*
tervalent 32.35 *combined*
terza rima 17.10 *verse form*
Tesla coil 32.20 *surface chemistry*
TESSA 14.4 *personal finance*
tessellate 541.11 *variegate*
tessellated 541.8 *checked*; 368.12 *inserted*
tessellation 541.2 *check*; 374.2 *cooperation*; 368.8 *insertion*
tessera 24.8 *ceramic object*; 541.2 *check*; 743.3 *means of identification*
test 353.4; 35.7 *diagnosis*; 448.1, 448.11 *experiment*; 448.8 *experimental*; 27.66 *proof*; 705.17 *question*; 705.3 *questionnaire*; 26.7 *standard*; 495.9 *taste*; 707.3 *vow*
testa 550.13 *casing*; 77.9 *seed*
testament 768.1 *giving*; 635.5 *will*
testamental 768.7 *given*
testamentary 768.7 *given*; 440.8 *propertied*
testate 768.7 *given*
testator 768.4 *giver*; 316.7 *transferor*
test ban 749.1 *pacification*
test card 692.23 *television reception*
test case 16.5 *litigation*; 126.2 *original*
test design 475.4 *model*
test drive 320.21 *miscellaneous motoring terms*
test-driver 448.5 *experimenter*
tested 448.10; 669.23 *approved*; 569.11 *devoted*; 235.1 *worthy*
testee 448.7 *experimentee*
tester 353.7 *attempter*; 448.5 *experimenter*; 464.5 *judge*; 705.9 *questioner*; 495.5 *taste bud*
testes 561.8 *organs of reproduction*
test flight 448.2 *rehearsal*
test for 35.19 *practise medicine*
testicles 182.2 *bulge*; 561.8 *organs of reproduction*
testicular 559.5 *of a secretion*
testificatory 454.9 *verificatory*
testifier 707.9 *affirmer*; 693.9 *informant*; 454.7 *verifier*
testify 454.3; 716.11 *give evidence*; 693.11 *inform*; 756.7 *promise*; 721.15 *recount*; 707.18 *vow*
testily 626.14 *irritably*
testimonial 744.2 *certificate*; 716.6 *documentation*; 454.6 *evidence*; 744.11 *monument*; 396.9 *permission*; 757.2 *permit*; 756.12 *promised*; 703.4 *proof*; 136.3 *qualifications*; 671.3 *recognition*; 669.6 *recommendation*; 601.6 *tribute*
testimonial banquet 601.6 *tribute*
testimonial evidence 716.5 *legal evidence*
testimony 716.5 *legal evidence*; 16.7 *legal trial*; 701.3 *line of argument*; 396.9 *permission*; 756.1 *promise*; 703.4 *proof*
testiness 625.1 *irascibility*
testing 448.8 *experimental*; 448.3 *experimentation*; 353.9 *tentative*
test match 53.1 *cricket match*
test model 475.4 *model*
test pilot 322.3 *aircraft personnel*; 448.5 *experimenter*
test someone's patience 625.8 *make irascible*
test statistic 27.54 *hypothesis testing*
test the alarm system 711.7 *raise the alarm*
test the depth 448.11 *experiment*
test the ground 746.5 *negotiate*
test the water 448.11 *experiment*
test tube 760.4 *medium of conversion*
test-tube baby 561.3 *propagation*
testudo 384.7 *armour*
testy 701.8 *argumentative*; 659.5 *discourteous*; 625.4 *irascible*; 626.7 *irritable*
tetanus 260.6 *infection*
tetchily 625.9 *irascibly*
tetchiness 625.1 *irascibility*
tetchy 625.4 *irascible*; 626.7 *irritable*; 488.7 *susceptible*
tête-à-tête 734.2 *chat*; 713.2 *consultation*; 734.15 *conversationally*; 654.3 *meeting*
tether 373.12 *bind*; 251.12 *gag*; 251.5 *means of restraint*; 378.10 *restrain*; 378.4 *restraint*; 373.9 *yoke*
tethered 378.14 *blocked*; 373.16 *bound*; 228.10 *stabilized*
tetrachord 18.16 *musical note*
tetracycline 37.4 *drug type*
tetrad 200.1 *four*
tetradactyl 200.3 *foursome*
tetragon 176.3 *angled figure*; 27.44 *polygon*; 200.2 *quadrilateral*
tetragonal 32.33 *crystalline*; 27.82 *polygonal*
tetragonal crystal 32.4 *crystal*
tetragram 200.3 *foursome*
tetragrammation 200.3 *foursome*
tetrahedral 200.8 *quadrilateral*
tetrahedron 27.46 *polyhedron*; 200.2 *quadrilateral*
tetralogy 200.3 *foursome*; 21.2 *play*
tetramerous 200.9
tetrameter 200.3 *foursome*; 17.9 *metre*
tetraplegia 335.4 *disability*; 260.17 *nervous disorder*
tetrapod 200.3 *foursome*
tetrasaccharide 33.3 *carbohydrate*
tetrastich 17.8 *part of poem*
tetraterpene 33.20 *terpene*
tetravalent 32.35 *combined*; 200.9 *tetramerous*
tetrode 39.20 *electron tube*
tetrose 33.3 *carbohydrate*
tetter 260.13 *skin disease*

Teukl 8.7 *devil*
Teutonic 5.11 *family of languages*
Teutonism 5.26 *dialect*
te-waza 52.7 *judo*
TEX 40.11 *application*
Texas accent 5.26 *dialect*
Texas Leaguer 48.5 *batting terms*
Texas League single 48.5 *batting terms*
text 694.1 *meaning;* 205.2 *particular;* 21.2 *play;* 713.3 *precept;* 447.1 *topic*
textbook 740.6 *book publishing;* 6.14 *school book*
text editor 40.11 *application*
textile **193.4**; **404.5**; 42.3 *fabric;* 435.1 *materials;* 356.7 *produce*
texts 475.10 *cards*
text transmission 692.8 *data transmission*
textual 698.23 *literal*
textual critic 719.6 *interpreter*
textual criticism 719.3 *criticism*
textualism 698.10 *literalness*
textual note 719.2 *annotation*
textural **404.7**; 403.11 *structural*
texturally **404.15**
Texture **404**
texture **404.1**; 403.2 *fabric;* 30.28 *rock;* 492.1 *touch;* 42.4 *weaving*
textured 420.1 *rough;* 404.7 *textural*
textured lighting 41.15 *lighting*
T-formation 46.7 *offence*
TGV 321.10 *miscellaneous*
thalassaemia 260.11 *blood disease;* 260.4 *disease*
thalassic 30.51, 91.7 *oceanic*
thalassographer 91.6 *oceanographer*
thalassographic 91.8 *oceanographic*
thalassography 91.5 *oceanography*
thalassometer 91.2 *tide*
thalassotherapy 394.13 *therapy*
Thalia 21.12 *comedy*
thallic 32.34 *elemental*
thallium scan 35.7 *diagnosis*
thalloid 84.7 *algal*
Thallophyta 77.4 *lower plant*
thallophyte 84.1 *alga;* 77.4 *lower plant*
thallophytic 77.16 *taxonomic*
thallose liverwort 82.3 *moss*
thallous 32.34 *elemental*
thallus 83.4 *fungal body;* 84.3 *plant body*
Thalo purple 540.2 *purple pigment*
Thalo red 535.6 *red pigment*
Thalo yellow green 538.10 *green pigment*
Thames 90.4 *British rivers*
Thames Cup 50.5 *Henley trophies*
Thames punt 50.8 *punting*
thanatopsis 603.2 *lament*
Thanatos 582.2 *death personified;* 36.22 *libido*
thane 763.6 *lord*
thank 671.6 *be grateful;* 813.9 *reward*
thankful 671.4 *grateful;* 609.4 *satisfied*
thankfully 671.8 *gratefully;* 609.13 *with satisfaction*
thankfulness 671.1 *gratitude;* 609.1 *satisfaction*
thank God 671.7 *give thanks;* 671.9 *thank you!*
thank goodness 671.9 *thank you!*
thank heaven 671.9 *thank you!*
thanking **671.5**
thankless **672.5**; 238.2 *futile*
thanklessly 672.7 *ungratefully*
thanklessness 238.4 *futility;* 672.1 *ingratitude*
thankless person **672.2**
thankless task 672.1 *ingratitude;* 576.1 *work*
thank offering 768.3 *offering;* 671.3 *recognition*
thank one's lucky stars 671.7 *give thanks*
thanks **671.2**; 813.1 *reward;* 601.7 *thanksgiving;* 671.9 *thank you!*
thanks a lot 671.9 *thank you!*
Thanksgiving 601.5 *anniversary*
thanksgiving **601.7**; 10.6 *Eucharist;* 600.2 *fanfare;* 10.3 *rite of worship;* 671.2 *thanks;* 9.1 *worship*
Thanksgiving Day 298.6 *annually celebrated day*
thanks to 392.37 *in aid of;* 348.9 *instrumentally*
thanks to Mother Nature 562.8 *fruitfully*
thank you 671.2 *thanks*
thank you! **671.9**
thank-you card 671.3 *recognition*
thank-you gift 671.3 *recognition*
thank-you letter 671.3 *recognition*
thank you very much 671.9 *thank you!*
that being so 750.36 *accordingly;* 222.15 *under the circumstances*
that being the case 750.36 *accordingly;* 222.15 *under the circumstances*
thatch 435.2 *building material;* 550.7 *overhead covering;* 393.1 *repair;* 550.27 *roof*
thatched 550.36 *covered*
thatched cottage 20.3 *building*
thatcher 578.2 *artisan;* 550.17 *coverer;* 81.5 *grass cutter*
Thatcher's children 673.5 *self-interest*
that is 703.22 *demonstrably;* 719.18 *in other words*
that is to say 703.22 *demonstrably;* 719.18 *in other words;* 139.31 *namely*
that's awful 798.15 *bad luck!*
that's enough 506.6 *hush!;* 226.12 *stop!*
that's for sure 698.40 *right!*
that's it 446.25 *got it!;* 698.40 *right!;* 226.12 *stop!*
that's the idea 446.25 *got it!*
that's the one 454.13 *really!*
that which makes invisible **521.6**
that which makes visible **520.7**
thaumatology 619.3 *wonder-working*
thaumaturge 619.5 *person of wonder;* 630.5 *surpriser;* 11.4 *witch*
thaumaturgia 11.3 *witchcraft*
thaumaturgic 619.8 *wonderful*
thaumaturgically 11.26 *magically*
thaumaturgics 11.3 *witchcraft*
thaumaturgist 11.4 *witch*
thaumaturgize 11.21 *bewitch*
thaumaturgy 11.3 *witchcraft;* 619.3 *wonder-working*
thaw 493.14 *be hot;* 627.11 *excite pity;* 431.8 *fluidification;* 493.5 *hot weather;* 268.17 *liquefy;* 431.24 *melt;* 31.63 *snow;* 419.13 *soften*
thawable 431.21 *liquefiable*
thawed 431.19 *liquefied*
thawing 431.8 *fluidification;* 431.20 *liquefying*
the 1,000 Guineas 59.7 *horseracing*
the 18th Amendment 689.7 *prohibition*
the 2,000 Guineas 59.7 *horseracing*
the Absolute Idea 446.1 *idea*
the absolute truth 698.3 *the truth*
the accused 715.4 *accused person*
the Acropolis 61.4 *motor rally*
the actual truth 698.3 *the truth*
the administration 396.4 *governance*
the afterlife 279.3 *life without end*
the age of amphibians 284.3 *geological period*
the age of reptiles 284.3 *geological period*
the aggregate 204.4 *all*
the Alamo 382.15 *slaughterhouse*
the all clear 757.1 *permission*
the Almighty 8.3 *God*
the Alpine 61.4 *motor rally*
the altogether 552.2 *nudity*
the Americans 85.7 *United States*
the America's Cup 50.1 *sailing*
the ancients 566.4 *modern human;* 284.6 *people of the past*
the ancient world 284.1 *past time*
the angel of death 357.6 *destroyer*
the animal kingdom 554.1 *life*
thearchy 12.1 *government*
the arts 19.1 *art;* 17.1 *literature;* 455.5 *science*
theatre **21.16**; 38.20 *building;* 356.8 *construction;* 86.14 *sphere;* 518.9 *viewpoint*
theatre craft 21.9 *dramaturgy*
théâtre du quotidien 21.10 *theatre movements*
theatregoer **21.33**; 97.5 *someone present*
theatre-in-the-round 21.16 *theatre*
theatre movements **21.10**
theatre nuclear warfare 585.8 *warfare*
theatre nuclear weapon 587.1 *weapon*
theatre of cruelty 21.10 *theatre movements*
theatre of fact 21.10 *theatre movements*
theatre of operations 584.1 *military affairs*
theatre of silence 21.10 *theatre movements*
theatre of the absurd 21.10 *theatre movements*
theatre of war 585.10 *battleground;* 751.1 *disagreement;* 167.1 *front*
theatre review 719.3 *criticism*
theatre sister 35.16 *nurse*
theatre ticket 743.3 *means of identification*
théâtre total 21.10 *theatre movements*
theatrical 676.3 *affected;* 703.10 *demonstrative;* 21.39 *dramatic*
theatrical agent 21.27 *producer*
theatrical convention 21.9 *dramaturgy*
theatrical cosmetics 21.21 *stage requisite*
theatrical costume 551.5 *fancy dress;* 21.21 *stage requisite*
theatrical engagement 21.15 *engagement*
theatricality 676.1 *affectedness;* 673.6 *boastfulness;* 21.9 *dramaturgy*
theatricalize 21.38 *dramatize*
theatrically 676.5 *affectedly;* 703.21 *demonstratively;* 21.44 *dramatically;* 673.24 *pompously*
theatrical make-up 21.21 *stage requisite*
theatrical performance **21.13**
theatrical production 356.5 *work of art*
theatricals 21.1 *drama*
theatrical technique 21.22 *acting*
theatrics 703.2 *demonstrativeness;* 21.1 *drama;* 21.9 *dramaturgy*
the authorities 396.4 *governance;* 400.8 *the power structure*
the average punter 566.7 *person*
the axe 371.18 *dismissal;* 708.6 *termination*
the back of beyond 145.3 *distant place*
the bad 804.9 *wicked person*
the Band of Hope 689.8 *sober person*
the bar 576.5 *exercise*
the basic fact 93.5 *fact*
the basics 93.5 *fact;* 435.1 *materials;* 352.1 *means*
the battery 48.2 *baseball player*
the beak 16.23 *judge;* 464.6 *justice*
the bench 464.6 *justice;* 464.3 *place of judgment*
the best **797.9**; 469.9 *chosen thing;* 121.7 *the best people;* 246.15 *victorious*
the best ever 797.9 *the best*
the best people **121.7**
the Betty Ford Clinic 689.8 *sober person*
the beyond 582.1 *death*
the Big Apple 87.3 *New York*
the big apple 22.2 *dance*
the big C 260.12 *cancer*
the big cheese 121.5 *superior*
the big E 128.2 *ejection;* 144.4 *relegation;* 364.6 *repulse;* 708.6 *termination*
the big enchilada 121.5 *superior*
the big house 309.4 *closed place;* 815.2 *the inside*
the big lie 699.10 *lie*
the big picture 482.5 *final intention*
the big sleep 582.1 *death*
the big time 246.1 *success*
the Big Top 21.7 *show;* 21.5 *show business*
the Bill of Rights 250.2 *free speech;* 228.4 *stable thing*
the billow 91.1 *sea*
the bird 753.3 *gesture of protest;* 668.6 *taunt*
the biz 121.6 *paragon*
the black 783.3 *deposit*
the Black Death 357.7 *agent of destruction*
the blahs 618.1 *indifference*
the Blessed One 8.3 *God*
the Blessed Virgin 8.10 *deified person*
the blind 519.4 *blind people*
the blue 91.1 *sea*
the blues 602.2 *depression;* 68.7 *ice-dancing;* 626.2 *sign of sullenness*
the board 396.4 *governance;* 400.8 *the power structure*
the boards 21.1 *drama;* 21.5 *show business;* 21.17 *stage*
the boat race 50.4 *rowing*
the Book 7.12 *religious text*
the book 815.4 *prison sentence*
the boondocks 145.3 *distant place*
the boonies 145.3 *distant place*
the boot 371.18 *dismissal;* 767.1 *disposal;* 128.2 *ejection;* 371.17 *expulsion;* 144.4 *relegation;* 708.6 *termination*
the bounce 371.17 *expulsion;* 144.4 *relegation;* 708.6 *termination*
the Bowery 87.3 *New York*
the bowler hat 708.6 *termination*
the Bowry 87.3 *New York*
the box 692.22 *television set*
the boys 567.15 *menfolk*
the boys in blue 16.14 *police*
the brass 121.7 *the best people*
the brass ring 617.5 *object of desire*
the breaks 248.2 *good fortune*
the brightest and best 121.7 *the best people*
the briny 91.1 *sea;* 433.1 *water*
the briny deep 91.1 *sea*
the British 85.8 *Great Britain*
the British Isles 85.8 *Great Britain*
the Broads 88.4 *British lakes*
the Bronx 87.3 *New York*
the brush 19.2 *painting*
the brushoff 371.19 *ostracism*
the bucket 50.8 *punting*
the buff 552.2 *nudity*
the bullet 708.6 *termination*
the bum's rush 371.17 *expulsion*
the burden of years 296.1 *oldness*
theca 84.3 *plant body*
the Capitol 396.6 *place of authority;* 400.8 *the power structure*
the case 93.5 *fact;* 698.3 *the truth*
the case in point 452.18 *particularity*
the cat's pyjamas 797.16 *superior person*
the chair 814.16 *instrument of execution*
the channels 327.1 *agitation*
the chop 767.1 *disposal;* 708.6 *termination*
the chosen 469.9 *chosen thing*
the chuck 371.17 *expulsion*
the Church 7.9 *priesthood*
the City 87.5 *London;* 779.5 *stock market*
the civilized world 566.4 *modern human*
the classics 17.1 *literature*
the claw 51.2 *grip*
the clergy 7.9 *priesthood*
the clerisy 17.15 *literary person*
the cloak of night 291.2 *night*
the cloth 7.9 *priesthood*
the clothing business 551.2 *dressing*
the Coast 86.8 *regions of the US*
the Code of Hammurabi 228.4 *stable thing*
the cold shoulder 371.19 *ostracism*
the collywobbles 612.2 *fearfulness*
the Common Enemy 8.7 *devil*
the common lot 216.4 *average*
the common people **574.2**
the common rule 15.1 *industrial relations*
the commons 574.2 *the common people*
the common touch 658.1 *courtesy;* 657.3 *familiarity*
the Commonwealth 566.11 *nation*
the Commonwealth of Nations 764.1 *joint possession*
the condemned 582.10 *dying person*
the conscious 101.6 *internal world*
the Conservative Party 225.2 *conservatism*
the contemporary world 282.2 *the present day*
the corridors of power 400.8 *the power structure*
the couch 36.3 *psychiatric treatment*
the country club set 781.11 *the rich*
the county set 781.11 *the rich*
the cover of ***Time*** 740.7 *publicity*
the covers 53.4 *team*
the crack of doom 283.3 *future condition*
the cream 469.9 *chosen thing*
the cream of society 781.11 *the rich*
the Creation 130.2 *creation*
the Creator 8.3 *God;* 130.16 *originator;* 344.7 *Prime Mover*
the creeps 488.3 *stimulus*
the crowd 654.7 *human society*
the crud 260.4 *disease*
the crunch 264.6 *critical situation;* 123.2 *important matter*
the current situation 282.2 *the present day*
the curse 560.11 *menstruation*
the Curse of Eve 560.11 *menstruation*
the D 65.3 *English billiards*
thé dansant 22.1 *dancing*
the dark of night 291.2 *night*

the day after tomorrow 283.1 *future time*
the day before yesterday 284.22 *in the past*; 284.1 *past time*
the dead 582.13; 582.12 *death count*
the dead and dying 582.12 *death count*
the dead of night 291.3 *midnight*
the Dead Sea 88.1 *lake*
the deaf 505.2 *deaf people*
the deceased 582.11 *dead person*
the deep 91.1 *sea*
the deeps 156.4 *deep thing*
the defensive 384.1 *defence*
the defunct 582.11 *dead person*
the Deity 344.7 *Prime Mover*
the Deluge 90.6 *river flow*
the deprived 782.11 *the poor*
the depths 156.4 *deep thing*
the Derby 59.7 *horseracing*
the Devil 8.7 *devil*
the devil take it 712.16 *euphemisms*
the directorship 396.4 *governance*; 400.8 *the power structure*
the dirt 93.5 *fact*
the disadvantaged 782.11 *the poor*
the distant future 283.1 *future time*
the doldrums 602.2 *depression*
the dole 13.8 *industrial relations*; 253.1 *protection*; 650.3 *welfare*; 652.4 *welfare state*
the done thing 549.3 *etiquette*; 474.3 *the expected thing*; 632.5 *tradition*
the dope 93.5 *fact*
the Dow 14.2 *stock exchange*
the draft 584.1 *military affairs*; 585.7 *war measures*
the dregs of society 782.11 *the poor*
the drill 317.1 *way*
the drink 91.1 *sea*
the dumps 602.2 *depression*; 626.2 *sign of sullenness*
the elbow 128.2 *ejection*; 144.4 *relegation*; 708.6 *termination*
the elderly 296.2 *old people*; 556.10 *the old*
the elect 235.7 *elite*
the elements 31.3 *weather*
the elite 121.7 *the best people*
the Emerald Isle 85.10 *Ireland*
the end 232.1 *completeness*; 131.13 *ender*
the end of time 283.3 *future condition*
the Enemy 8.7 *devil*
the enemy 113.10 *the opposition*
the English 85.9 *England*
the English season 292.1 *season*
the environmental movement 244.11 *reformism*
the Erinys 624.7 *gods and goddesses of anger*
the essentials 93.5 *fact*; 205.5 *largest part*; 435.1 *materials*
the Establishment 396.4 *governance*; 395.6 *group influence*; 228.4 *stable thing*; 121.7 *the best people*; 400.8 *the power structure*
the Eternal 8.3 *God*
the eternal feminine 568.1 *female sex*
the Eumenides 624.7 *gods and goddesses of anger*
the Everglades 92.3 *marsh*
the evil eye 798.4 *evil power*; 236.11 *harmfulness*; 712.4 *malediction*
the Evil One 8.7 *devil*; 798.6 *evil person*
the exact same 111.1 *sameness*
the exact time 281.3 *chronology*
the exact truth 698.3 *the truth*
the expected thing 474.3
the exploited 466.8 *victim of discrimination*
the external 100.4 *externality*
the facts 698.3 *the truth*
the faithful 7.3 *religious person*
the fallen 582.12 *death count*
the far future 283.1 *future time*
the far past 284.1 *past time*
the fashion world 551.2 *dressing*
the Father 8.3 *God*
the father of medicine 394.15 *healer*
the Fearsome Foursome 46.10 *defence*
the fidgets 327.5, 342.7 *restlessness*
the field 59.7 *horseracing*; 113.10 *the opposition*
the filth 16.14 *police*
the final blow 131.13 *ender*
the final thrill 582.1 *death*
the finger 753.3 *gesture of protest*
the flesh 796.3 *sexual immorality*
the Flood 90.6 *river flow*
the footlights 21.1 *drama*
the force 16.14 *police*
the four elements 402.4 *matter*
the Four Freedoms 250.2 *free speech*
the four last things 482.5 *final intention*
the fourth dimension 521.5 *invisible thing*; 275.1 *time*
the Franciscan order 782.8 *renunciation of wealth*
the French disease 260.14 *venereal disease*
the Fringe 21.1 *drama*
the front four 46.10 *defence*
theft 774.3; 16.39 *crime*; 765.5 *profit*; 774.1 *stealing*; 773.3 *taking away*
the fundamentals 93.5 *fact*
the Furies 624.7 *gods and goddesses of anger*
the future 286.1 *different time*; 283.1 *future time*
the fuzz 16.14 *police*; 253.3 *security officer*
the f-word 5.19 *swearword*
the gate 371.18 *dismissal*; 769.2 *something received*
the gen 93.5 *fact*
the genuine article 698.6 *authenticity*; 126.2 *original*
the giggles 600.3 *laughter*
the girls 568.13 *womenfolk*
the glitterati 781.11 *the rich*
the globe 30.5 *earth*
the Glorious Koran 7.12 *religious text*
the go-ahead 397.4 *authorization*; 757.1 *permission*
the go-by 668.5 *insult*
the gods 21.18 *auditorium*; 8.5 *deity*
the God squad 7.5 *Christian*
the golden rule 631.1 *conduct*
the Good Book 7.12 *religious text*
the good life 222.5 *comfortable circumstances*; 781.7 *opulence*; 490.1 *physical pleasure*; 248.1 *prosperity*
the goods 235.8 *exceller*
the Good Shepherd 8.4 *God the Son*
the gospel truth 698.3 *the truth*
the Government 400.8 *the power structure*
the government 396.4 *governance*
the Grand Challenge Cup 50.5 *Henley trophies*
the grand scheme 482.5 *final intention*
the Grand Slam 56.1 *golf*
the grand style 17.12 *poetic language*
the grape 558.9 *wine*
the great adventure 582.1 *death*
the great American game 48.1 *baseball*
the Great Divide 145.3 *distant place*
the great divide 582.1 *death*
the greatest 123.4 *bigwig*; 235.8 *exceller*; 121.6 *paragon*
the Great Lakes 88.3 *US lakes*
the Great Leveller 582.2 *death personified*
the great outdoors 434.5 *open air*; 171.2 *outside*
the Great Salt Lake 88.1 *lake*
the Great Spirit 8.3 *God*
The Great Train Robbery 774.3 *theft*
the great unwashed 216.7 *average person*; 376.20 *crowd*; 138.11 *general public*; 503.2 *something that makes an unpleasant smell*; 675.6 *vulgar herd*
The Great War 585.1 *war*
the Great Wen 87.5 *London*
the green-eyed monster 594.1 *hate*
the green light 757.1 *permission*; 714.1 *vindication*
the green stuff 538.12 *figurative usage*
the Grim Reaper 582.2 *death personified*; 357.6 *destroyer*
the gross amount 204.4 *all*
the grumps 626.2 *sign of sullenness*
the hand of God 348.3 *assistant*
the hand of time 357.6 *destroyer*
the happy couple 570.9 *married couple*
the happy hunting ground 756.4 *promised land*
the happy land 8.11 *heaven*
the hard of hearing 505.2 *deaf people*
the hard right 225.2 *conservatism*
the hard way 264.25 *difficultly*; 264.3 *difficult task*; 576.4 *exertion*; 378.17 *in the way*; 576.12 *laboriously*
the have-nots 782.11 *the poor*
the haves 248.4 *prosperous person*; 781.11 *the rich*; 765.8 *wealthy people*
the heave-ho 128.2 *ejection*; 144.4 *relegation*
the heavens 434.1 *air*
the heavies 740.4 *newspaper*
the heebie-jeebies 612.2 *fearfulness*
the height of fashion 282.4 *up-to-dateness*
the heights 121.4 *summit*
the Henley Royal Regatta 50.4 *rowing*
the hereafter 283.3 *future condition*; 554.5 *life cycle*; 279.3 *life without end*
the here and now 282.1 *present time*; 95.1 *reality*
the high command 396.4 *governance*; 400.8 *the power structure*
the Highlands 86.9 *regions of Britain*; 85.11 *Scotland*
the high road 265.6 *easy thing*
the Hill 396.6 *place of authority*; 400.8 *the power structure*
the hoi polloi 376.20 *crowd*
the hole 815.3 *prison cell*
the Holocaust 814.13 *capital punishment*; 382.4 *slaughter*
the Holy Ghost 8.3 *God*
the Holy Spirit 8.3 *God*
the honest-to-God truth 698.3 *the truth*
the honest-to-goodness truth 698.3 *the truth*
the honest truth 698.3 *the truth*
the horrors 690.16 *alcoholism*
the hots 617.4 *sexual desire*
the hot seat 814.16 *instrument of execution*
the how 317.1 *way*
the HP 777.7 *purchasing*
the human family 566.9 *group*
the humanities 17.1 *literature*; 455.5 *science*
the hundred days 201.9 *treble figures*
the hunted 633.7
the ideal 230.3 *perfection*
the idea of 476.1 *supposition*
theileriosis 75.12 *protozoal disease*
the immortals 8.5 *deity*
the Index 399.2 *censorship*
the individual 139.5 *the special*
the in-group 400.8 *the power structure*
the inner circle 396.4 *governance*; 400.8 *the power structure*
the Inquisition 814.15 *instrument of torture*
the inside 815.2
the instalment plan 777.7 *purchasing*
the intended 756.6 *someone promised*
the interior 172.3 *inland*
the in thing 632.4 *custom*; 295.2 *trendiness*
the invisible man 521.5 *invisible thing*
the Irish 85.10 *Ireland*
the Isle of Dogs 87.5 *London*
theism 7.2 *religiousness*; 4.7 *school of thought*
theist 450.5 *believer*; 4.11 *follower of a doctrine*
theistic 8.13 *divine*; 4.14 *of a philosophy*
theistically 8.19 *divinely*
the jerks 327.8 *spasm*
the jet set 781.11 *the rich*; 765.8 *wealthy people*
the jimjams 612.2 *fearfulness*
the jitters 612.2 *fearfulness*
the Jockey Club 59.7 *horseracing*
the joint 691.6 *drug*
the judiciary 464.6 *justice*
the jump 164.4 *advantage*
the jumps 612.2 *fearfulness*
the King of Light 8.3 *God*
the kiss off 708.6 *termination*
the know 693.1 *information*
the Kremlin 400.8 *the power structure*
the Ladies' World Championship 68.10 *curling*
the lads 567.15 *menfolk*
the Lake District 88.4 *British lakes*
the Last Day 464.4 *judgment day*
the last debt 582.1 *death*
the last straw 131.13 *ender*
the Last Summoner 582.2 *death personified*
the last word 295.2 *trendiness*
the last word in 121.14 *best*
the late lamented 582.11 *dead person*
the latest 553.1 *fashion*
the latest craze 295.2 *trendiness*
the latest fashion 551.2 *dressing*; 295.2 *trendiness*
the latest style 551.2 *dressing*
the latest thing 295.2 *trendiness*
the laugh's on you 385.7 *revenge!*
the law 16.1
the lead 129.2 *priority*
the length and breadth 204.4 *all*
the letter 273.2 *correctness*
the life of Riley 490.2 *good time*
the light fails 523.13 *become dark*
the like of 115.1 *similarity*; 137.4 *type*
the limit 232.1 *completeness*; 131.13 *ender*
the Line 86.2 *geographical region*
the literal truth 273.2 *correctness*
the living 566.1 *humankind*; 554.1 *life*
the long run 283.1 *future time*
the long sleep 582.1 *death*
the long term 283.1 *future time*
the Lord 8.3 *God*
the Lord of Wisdom 8.3 *God*
the Lord's Prayer 10.9 *prayer*
the lost 582.12 *death count*
the lot 204.4 *all*
the low-down 716.1 *evidence*; 698.3 *the truth*
the lower classes 782.11 *the poor*
the lower regions 582.14 *the spiritual world*
the Lowlands 85.11 *Scotland*
the McCoy 698.6 *authenticity*
the Mafia 804.7 *criminality*
the magic word 757.1 *permission*
the magistracy 464.6 *justice*
the Magna Carta 250.3 *independence*
the main 205.5 *largest part*
the main man 121.5 *superior*
the Maker 8.3 *God*
the making of 244.5 *improvement*
the man 123.4 *bigwig*; 566.7 *person*; 815.6 *prison officer*
them and us 376.19 *clique*
the man in black 523.4 *dark thing*
the masses 376.20 *crowd*; 566.9 *group*; 122.6 *inferior*; 574.2 *the common people*
the Masters 56.1 *golf*
thematic 447.7 *focused*; 406.12 *itemized*
thematically 406.15; **447.14**
thematic apperception test 36.5 *psychological test*
theme 403.9 *artistic structure*; 17.3 *aspect of fiction*; 722.1 *dissertation*; 701.4 *gist*; 18.13, 516.1 *melody*; 447.1 *topic*
the media 693.4 *mass communication*; 740.2 *mass media*
the Melting Pot 85.7 *United States*
theme park 619.4 *wonder*
themes 406.5 *divisions*
theme song 516.1 *melody*
the Method 21.22 *acting*
the middle of nowhere 145.3 *distant place*
the Midlands 172.3 *inland*
the Midwest 172.3 *inland*
the military 584.2
the millennium 283.3 *future condition*; 756.4 *promised land*
the mind's eye 477.1 *imagination*
the ministry 7.9 *priesthood*
the minority 206.2 *least*
the mob 804.7 *criminality*; 122.6 *inferior*
the modern day 282.2 *the present day*
the modern world 282.2 *the present day*
the month of Maying 292.2 *spring*
the moon 145.3 *distant place*
the mopes 626.2 *sign of sullenness*
the morrow 283.1 *future time*
the most 121.6 *paragon*; 121.17 *supremely*
the Mother 8.3 *God*
themselves 139.12 *I*
the mulligrubs 626.2 *sign of sullenness*
the mumps 626.2 *sign of sullenness*
the Muses 8.5 *deity*; 17.13 *poetic genius*
then 286.3 *another time*; 275.27 *at what time*
the naked ape 566.7 *person*
the naked truth 698.3 *the truth*
The National Rifle Association 60.2 *hunting*
the nature of things 221.3 *state of affairs*
the near future 283.1 *future time*
the needy 782.11 *the poor*
the Net 40.16 *Internet*
the Netherlands' Tulip Rally 61.4 *motor rally*
the never-never 772.4, 783.1 *credit*; 777.7 *purchasing*

the new generation 555.10 *the young*
the new rich 781.11 *the rich*
the New York season 292.1 *season*
the next world 283.3 *future condition;* 279.3 *life without end*
the nine-to-five 632.3 *way*
the nitty-gritty 402.4 *matter;* 344.3 *rudiment*
the noble animal 566.7 *person*
the noble experiment 689.7 *prohibition*
the nod 757.1 *permission*
the nonce 282.2 *the present day*
the normal 474.3 *the expected thing*
the North 85.10 *Ireland;* 86.9 *regions of Britain*
the Northern Irish 85.10 *Ireland*
the North Pole 145.3 *distant place*
the nouveaux riches 765.8 *wealthy people*
the nude 552.2 *nudity*
The Nutcracker 22.11 *classical ballets*
the Oaks 59.7 *horseracing*
the objective truth 698.3 *the truth*
the Occident 324.4 *compass point*
the occult 11.2; 101.3 *spiritual world*
theocracy 8.2 *divine attribute;* 12.1 *government;* 396.7 *type of rule*
theocratic 8.13 *divine;* 12.9 *governmental*
theocratically 8.19 *divinely*
theodolite 28.84 *altimeter;* 176.4 *angular measurement;* 38.17 *civil engineering;* 26.8 *meter;* 28.32 *optical instrument*
the OK 757.1 *permission;* 714.1 *vindication*
the old 556.10
the Old Adam 804.6 *religious sin*
the old country 85.6 *native land*
the older generation 556.10 *the old*
the old folks 556.7 *older person*
the old heave-ho 371.17 *expulsion;* 708.6 *termination*
the Old Man 400.7 *military leader;* 396.10 *person of authority*
the old, old story 593.8 *love affair*
the old way 632.4 *custom*
theologer 7.14 *theologian*
theologian 7.14
theological 7.18
theological hermeneutics 7.13 *theology*
theologically 7.23 *religiously*
theological metaphysics 7.13 *theology*
theological virtues 803.2 *virtues*
theologician 7.14 *theologian*
theologist 7.14 *theologian*
theologize 7.22
theologizer 7.14 *theologian*
theologue 7.14 *theologian*
theology 7.13; 4.6 *branch of philosophy*
the Olympians 8.5 *deity*
theomancer 11.13 *diviner*
theomancy 11.9 *divination*
theomania 461.4 *delusion*
theomorphic 8.13 *divine*
the one and only 126.1 *originality*
theopathic 7.15 *religious*
theopathy 7.2 *religiousness*
the Open 56.1 *golf*
the open 171.2 *outside*
the Open Sesame 757.1 *permission*
theophanic 525.7 *appearing*
theophany 8.8 *divine manifestation;* 738.10 *manifestation;* 525.4 *something that appears*
the opposition 113.10
the oppressed 466.8 *victim of discrimination*
the ordinary 216.4 *average*
theorem 28.6 *law;* 745.1 *maxim;* 476.1 *supposition;* 27.65 *theory;* 447.1 *topic*
theorematic 27.69 *theoretical*
theoremic 27.69 *theoretical*
theorem proving 40.17 *artificial intelligence*
theoretical 27.69; **28.99**; **96.10**; **446.10**; 444.10 *causal;* 32.31 *chemical;* 4.13 *of philosophy;* 443.10 *speculative;* 476.7 *suppositional*
theoretical chemist 32.2 *chemist*
theoretical chemistry 32.1 *chemistry*
theoretical framework 27.65 *theory*
theoretical linguistics 5.1 *linguistics*
theoretically 4.25; **446.20**; 32.46 *chemically;* 96.18 *ideally;* 27.87 *mathematically;* 476.10 *supposedly*
theoretical physics 28.4 *experimental physics*
theoretician 446.9 *person of ideas;* 4.10 *philosopher;* 476.4 *theorist*
the Orient 324.4 *compass point*
theories of life 554.8
theorist 476.4; 4.10 *philosopher*
theorization 96.4
theorize 27.89; **96.14**; **446.17**; 745.3 *aphorize;* 443.16 *have an idea;* 444.14 *premise;* 476.5 *suppose*
theorizer 446.9 *person of ideas;* 4.10 *philosopher;* 476.4 *theorist;* 96.6 *unrealistic person*
theory 27.65; **28.5**; **446.2**; 450.1 *belief;* 444.4 *explanation;* 443.6 *idea;* 27.1 *mathematics;* 476.1 *supposition;* 96.4 *theorization;* 176.5 *viewpoint*
theory builder 476.4 *theorist*
theory of everything 28.79 *fundamental interaction*
theory of knowledge 4.1 *philosophy*
theory of probabilities 107.7 *calculation of chance*
theory of relativity 402.6 *natural science*
theory of social systems 2.2 *sociological research*
theosophical 11.16 *psychic*
theosophist 11.12 *occultist*
theosophy 11.1 *occultism*
the other day 284.22 *in the past*
the other man 211.5 *extra person;* 629.3 *rival*
the other side 582.1 *death;* 171.5 *extraneousness;* 101.3 *spiritual world;* 113.10 *the opposition*
the other way around 192.4 *inversely*
the other woman 593.9 *lover;* 629.3 *rival*
the outside 128.3 *exclusion zone*
the Oval 53.2 *ground*
the over-the-hill gang 556.10 *the old*
the palm 51.2 *grip*
the paranormal 100.4 *externality;* 11.2 *the occult*
the partially sighted 519.4 *blind people*
the particular 452.18 *particularity;* 139.5 *the special*
the past 286.1 *different time;* 3.8, 284.1 *past time*
the peace process 749.1 *pacification*
the Pearly Gates 8.11 *heaven*
the pencil 19.2 *painting*
the Pentagon 400.8 *the power structure*
the people 574.2 *the common people;* 675.6 *vulgar herd*
the people's 764.5 *jointly possessing*
the persecuted 466.8 *victim of discrimination*
the picture 222.1 *circumstances;* 93.5 *fact*
the pigs 16.14 *police*
the pill 563.3 *birth control*
the pits 249.1 *adversity;* 247.1 *failure*
the plains 92.6 *lowland*
the plain truth 698.3 *the truth*
the play 21.1 *drama*
the plural 207.1 *plurality*
the political right 225.2 *conservatism*
the poor 782.11
the possible 217.7 *sufficiency*
the pouts 626.2 *sign of sullenness*
the powers that be 396.4 *governance;* 395.6 *group influence;* 400.8 *the power structure*
the power structure 400.8; 396.4 *governance;* 121.7 *the best people*
the present 282.1 *present time*
the present day 282.2
the present generation 282.2 *the present day*
the present moment 282.1 *present time*
the present situation 282.2 *the present day*
the present time 282.2 *the present day*
the Preserver 8.3 *God*
the press 692.1 *communications;* 740.3 *journalism;* 693.4 *mass communication;* 49.4 *playing terms*
the pretty way 306.5 *ringroad*
the prime of life 556.4 *middle age;* 555.1 *youth*
the Principality 85.12 *Wales*
the privileged 781.11 *the rich*
the probabilities 107.7 *calculation of chance*
the proles 675.6 *vulgar herd*
the proper thing 810.1 *duty*
the push 128.2 *ejection;* 371.17 *expulsion;* 708.6 *termination*
the quick 566.1 *humankind*
the rackets 804.7 *criminality*
the rage 295.2 *trendiness*
the rag trade 551.2 *dressing;* 553.3 *fashion business*
the rains 31.26 *raininess*
the ranks 586.17 *army person*
therapeutic 35.25; 713.7 *advising;* 392.34 *beneficial;* 37.18 *pharmacological;* 394.17 *remedial*
therapeutically 394.21 *remedially*
therapeutic radiology 35.8 *treatment*
therapeutics 394.11 *medical art;* 37.1 *pharmacology;* 394.13 *therapy;* 35.8 *treatment*
therapeutist 394.15 *healer*
therapist 713.4 *adviser;* 35.12, 394.15 *healer;* 36.29 *psychologist*
therapsid 73.6 *extinct reptile*
therapy 394.13; 713.1 *advice;* 392.5 *medical assistance;* 260.20 *pathology;* 35.8 *treatment*
Theravada 7.12 *religious text*
the raw 552.2 *nudity*
there 525.7 *appearing;* 282.8 *available;* 97.15 *here;* 142.12 *where*
thereabouts 147.12 *near;* 142.12 *where*
the ready 780.2 *cash*
the real article 126.2 *original*
the realities 93.5 *fact*
the real McCoy 126.2 *original*
the realms of possibility 102.2 *possibleness*
the real Simon Pure 698.6 *authenticity*
the real stuff 334.2 *ability*
the real thing 698.6 *authenticity;* 93.4 *demonstrable existence;* 126.2 *original;* 593.2 *romantic love*
the real world 698.2 *reality*
thereat 142.12 *where*
the red 783.1 *credit;* 784.1 *debt*
The Redeemer 8.4 *God the Son;* 391.3 *liberator;* 775.3 *returner*
therefore 750.36 *accordingly*
the remote future 283.1 *future time*
the remote past 284.1 *past time*
the Republic 85.10 *Ireland*
the Republic of Ireland 85.10 *Ireland*
there she blows 633.19 *after him!*
the Resurrection 393.10 *revival*
the revealed truth 698.3 *the truth*
theriac 394.4 *antidote*
theriacal 394.17 *remedial*
therianthropic 70.14 *animalian*
therianthropism 70.7 *legendary beast*
the rich 781.11
the rich and famous 765.8 *wealthy people*
the right stuff 334.2 *ability*
the right thing 810.1 *duty*
the right wing 225.2 *conservatism*
the ring 21.7 *show*
theriolater 9.6 *idolater*
theriolatrous 9.10 *idolatrous*
theriolatry 9.2 *idolatry*
theriomorphic 70.14 *animalian*
the riper years 556.4 *middle age*
the rising generation 555.10 *the young*
the rising young 555.10 *the young*
the Riviera 92.4 *coast*
therm 493.2 *heat measurement*
thermae 256.6 *bath;* 394.14 *hospital;* 493.8 *hot place;* 257.1 *hygiene;* 92.10 *miscellaneous*
thermal 31.10 *air movement;* 31.43 *atmospheric;* 92.11 *continental;* 493.9 *hot;* 493.8 *hot place;* 28.98 *physical;* 437.10 *powered*
thermal conductivity 28.36 *heat flow*
thermal efficiency 38.13 *engine cycle*
thermal equilibrium 28.36 *heat flow*
thermal imaging 28.41 *thermometry*
thermal ink jet printer 40.7 *peripheral*
thermally 92.13 *continentally;* 28.100 *physically;* 437.12 *powerfully*
thermal metamorphism 30.32 *metamorphism*
thermal power station 39.32 *power station*
thermal radiation 28.40 *heating effect*
thermal reactor 437.7 *nuclear power;* 28.73 *nuclear reactor*
thermal spring 30.25 *eruption;* 92.10 *miscellaneous*
thermal underwear 62.4 *climbing equipment;* 551.18 *underwear*
thermal wear 493.3 *heater*
thermic 493.9 *hot*
thermionic cathode 39.24 *electron emission*
thermionic emission 39.24 *electron emission;* 28.40 *heating effect*
thermionic valve 39.20 *electron tube*
thermobarometer 26.8 *meter*
thermochemistry 32.1 *chemistry*
thermocouple 28.89 *thermometer*
thermodynamic 32.31 *chemical;* 28.98 *physical*
thermodynamically 32.46 *chemically;* 28.100 *physically*
thermodynamics 28.38; 32.1 *chemistry;* 28.2 *classical physics;* 402.6 *natural science*
thermodynamic temperature 28.38 *thermodynamics*
thermoelectric 39.36 *electronic*
thermoelectrically 39.37 *electronically*
thermoelectric effect 28.49 *electromagnetic induction;* 28.40 *heating effect*
thermoelectric generator 39.30 *generator*
thermoelectricity 334.7 *electrical power;* 28.42 *electricity;* 28.40 *heating effect*
thermograph 493.2 *heat measurement;* 31.7 *weather instruments*
thermographic 31.42 *barometric*
thermography 35.7 *diagnosis*
thermoluminescence 281.3 *chronology;* 28.24 *light emission*
thermoluminescent dating 275.8 *dating*
thermometer 28.89; 493.2 *heat measurement;* 742.5 *indicator;* 26.8 *meter;* 31.7 *weather instruments*
thermometric 31.42 *barometric;* 26.16 *micrometric*
thermometry 28.41; 26.2 *micrometry;* 28.96 *microscopy*
thermonuclear 493.10 *on fire;* 334.17, 437.10 *powered*
thermonuclear fusion 28.72 *nuclear fission*
thermonuclear reaction 334.8 *nuclear power*
thermonuclear reactor 28.76 *fusion reactor*
thermopile 26.8 *meter;* 28.89 *thermometer*
thermoplastic 435.1 *materials*
thermoplastic material 32.21 *polymer*
Thermos™ 410.14 *bottle;* 558.10 *drink container;* 493.3 *heater;* 359.2 *preserver*
thermoset 435.1 *materials*
thermosetting plastic 32.21 *polymer*
thermosphere 154.8 *high thing*
thermostat 493.3 *heater*
the road to hell 245.7 *deterioration*
the roaring game 68.10 *curling*
the Roaring Twenties 3.10 *past age*
the ruling class 396.4 *governance;* 121.7 *the best people;* 400.8 *the power structure*
the run of 250.6 *liberality*
the runs 560.2 *defecation;* 260.8 *indigestion*
the sack 371.18 *dismissal;* 128.2 *ejection;* 144.4 *relegation;* 708.6 *termination;* 580.3 *unemployment*
the St Leger 59.7 *horseracing*
the saints 235.7 *elite*
the same 119.2 *equilibrium;* 111.1 *sameness*
the sands of time 275.2 *passage of time*
thesaurus 40.11 *application;* 740.6 *book publishing;* 439.5 *collection;* 5.28, 220.3 *dictionary;* 412.3 *miscellany;* 693.5 *reference book;* 6.14 *school book*
The Saviour 768.4 *giver;* 8.4 *God the Son;* 391.3 *liberator*
the scenes 21.1 *drama*
the scoop 93.5 *fact*
the score 222.1 *circumstances;* 93.5 *fact*
the Scottish 85.11 *Scotland*
the scythe of time 357.6 *destroyer*
the Season 292.1 *season;* 292.5 *winter*
the second sex 568.13 *womenfolk*
the secret 719.1 *interpretation*
these days 282.9 *at present*
the senses 488.1 *sensation*
The Serpentine 88.4 *British lakes*
the services 584.2 *the military*
the shades 582.14 *the spiritual world*
the shakes 327.7 *shake*

the shape of things 221.3 *state of affairs*
the shits 560.2 *defecation*
the shivers 488.3 *stimulus*
the shove 128.2 *ejection*; 708.6 *termination*
the sight 518.5 *imagination*
the sightless 519.4 *blind people*
the Silver Broom 68.10 *curling*
the silver screen 21.3 *films*
the simple truth 698.3 *the truth*
thesis 722.1 *dissertation*; 28.6 *law*; 701.3 *line of argument*; 17.4 *nonfiction*; 4.5 *philosophical argument*; 4.8 *philosophical term*; 4.1 *philosophy*; 707.2 *statement*; 476.1 *supposition*; 447.1 *topic*
thesis novel 17.2 *fiction*
the sisterhood 568.13 *womenfolk*
the Six Counties 85.10 *Ireland*
the sixties 757.1 *permission*
the size of it 143.2 *circumstances*; 221.3 *state of affairs*
the skids 245.7 *deterioration*
the sky 434.1 *air*
The Sleeping Beauty 22.11 *classical ballets*
the slips 53.4 *team*
the small hours 293.2 *early hour*
the Smoke 87.5 *London*; 86.10 *urban area*
Thesmophoria 10.16 *religious festival*
the sober truth 698.3 *the truth*
the Somme 382.15 *slaughterhouse*
the South 85.10 *Ireland*; 86.9 *regions of Britain*
the South Pole 145.3 *distant place*
the special 139.5
the specific 452.18 *particularity*; 139.5 *the special*
the specifics 93.5 *fact*
Thespian 21.24 *actor*; 21.39 *dramatic*
Thespian art 21.1 *drama*
the spiritual world 582.14
Thespis 21.1 *drama*
the spot 65.3 *English billiards*; 65.5 *snooker*
the Square Mile 87.5 *London*
the stage 21.1 *drama*; 21.5 *show business*
the staggers 120.1 *inequality*
the stake 382.5 *execution*; 493.6 *fire*
the Star Chamber 814.15 *instrument of torture*
the States 85.7 *United States*
the status quo 225.1 *permanence*
the sticks 145.3 *distant place*; 86.6 *regions*
the straight and narrow 803.1 *virtue*
the straight truth 698.3 *the truth*
the subconscious 11.7 *spirit*
the sulks 637.14 *disobedience*; 626.2 *sign of sullenness*
the sullens 626.2 *sign of sullenness*
the sum and substance 204.4 *all*
the sun sets 523.13 *become dark*
the supernatural 100.4 *externality*; 11.2 *the occult*
the supersensible 11.2 *the occult*
the Supreme Being 8.3 *God*
the Supreme Soul 8.3 *God*
the Swedish Midnight Sun 61.4 *motor rally*
the Swinging Sixties 3.10 *past age*
the sword 585.1 *war*
the syndicate 804.7 *criminality*
the system 396.4 *governance*
the tartan 551.3 *formal dress*
the Teacher 8.3 *God*
The Tempter 8.7 *devil*
the Ten Commandments 713.3 *precept*
the theatre 21.1 *drama*
the thing 123.3 *chief thing*
the thing to do 656.1 *formality*
the third degree 705.2 *questioning*
the Three Musketeers 569.7 *famous friendships*
the thumbs-up 757.1 *permission*
the time ahead 283.1 *future time*
the time being 282.2 *the present day*
the time now 281.3 *chronology*
the times 222.1 *circumstances*
Thetis 91.4 *sea god*
the top 396.4 *governance*; 400.8 *the power structure*
the top brass 400.8 *the power structure*
the tops 235.8 *exceller*; 246.4 *successful person*
the total 204.4 *all*
the touch 710.3 *solicitation*
the train 796.7 *sexual assault*
the Trinity 8.3 *God*
the trots 560.2 *defecation*; 260.8 *indigestion*
the truth 698.3
the Turf 59.7 *horseracing*
the Twelve Tables 713.3 *precept*
the two 198.9 *two*
the ultimate truth 698.3 *the truth*
the unalloyed truth 698.3 *the truth*
the unattainable 617.5 *object of desire*
the unborn 289.6 *posterity*
the unconscious 101.6 *internal world*; 11.7 *spirit*
the underground 588.1 *anarchy*
the underprivileged 782.11 *the poor*
the underprivileged class 782.11 *the poor*
the undersigned 755.4 *contractor*
the underworld 283.3 *future condition*
the unexpected 630.4 *surprising thing*
the unforeseen 630.4 *surprising thing*; 105.5 *unexpectedness*
the unique 139.5 *the special*
the unities 21.9 *dramaturgy*
the Universal Self 8.3 *God*
the unknown 100.2 *foreignness*; 696.11 *unintelligibility*; 456.3 *unknown thing*
the unpredictable 630.4 *surprising thing*
the unqualified truth 698.3 *the truth*
the unseen 521.5 *invisible thing*
the unvarnished truth 698.3 *the truth*
the upper class 765.8 *wealthy people*
the upper classes 781.11 *the rich*
the upper crust 781.11 *the rich*; 765.8 *wealthy people*
the upper hand 396.1 *authority*
the upwardly mobile 248.4 *prosperous person*
theurgically 11.26 *magically*
theurgist 11.4 *witch*
theurgize 11.21 *bewitch*
theurgy 11.3 *witchcraft*
the US Open 56.1 *golf*
the US PGA 56.1 *golf*
the usual 216.4 *average*; 474.3 *the expected thing*
the utmost 232.1 *completeness*
the veil 572.3 *monasticism*
the very best 797.9 *the best*
the very same 111.1 *sameness*
the very thing 698.6 *authenticity*; 797.17 *good thing*
the very truth 698.3 *the truth*
the very words 698.10 *literalness*; 111.1 *sameness*
the Virgin 572.4 *celibate person*; 8.10 *deified person*
the Virgin Mary 8.10 *deified person*; 795.5 *pure person*
the Virgin Mother 8.10 *deified person*
the visual arts 19.1 *art*
the visually handicapped 519.4 *blind people*
the visually impaired 519.4 *blind people*
the vitals 172.4 *insides*
the Volstead Prohibition Act 689.7 *prohibition*
the Wandering Jew 100.7 *new arrival*
the war years 585.4 *belligerency*
the Water Carrier 316.7 *transferor*
the way it is 222.1 *circumstances*
the way it looks 104.2 *tendency*
the way of 317.1 *way*
the way of gentleness 52.7 *judo*
the way things are 216.4 *average*; 221.3 *state of affairs*
the Web 40.16 *Internet*
the weed 496.7 *tobacco*
the wee small hours 293.2 *early hour*
the welfare 392.4 *social assistance*
the well-heeled 781.11 *the rich*; 765.8 *wealthy people*
the well-off 781.11 *the rich*
the well-to-do 781.11 *the rich*; 765.8 *wealthy people*
the Welsh 85.12 *Wales*
the West 13.4 *economic development*
the West End 21.1 *drama*
the wet 31.26 *raininess*
the wherewithal 352.1 *means*
the whim-whams 642.3 *whim*
the whip hand 396.1 *authority*
the white flag 388.1 *submission*
the White House 396.6 *place of authority*; 400.8 *the power structure*
the whites 431.3 *body fluid*
the whole 204.4 *all*
the whole bang shoot 204.5 *unit*
the whole caboodle 203.4 *total*; 204.5 *unit*
the whole hog 232.1 *completeness*
the whole lot 204.4 *all*
the whole picture 222.1 *circumstances*
the whole shebang 138.10 *everyone*; 204.5 *unit*
the whole shooting match 138.10 *everyone*; 204.5 *unit*
the whole story 93.5 *fact*
the whole thing 203.4 *total*
the whole time 275.26 *all the time*
the whole world 204.4 *all*; 138.10 *everyone*
the why 344.5 *reason*
the why and wherefore 344.5 *reason*
the wicked 804.9 *wicked person*
the willies 612.2 *fearfulness*
the Wise One 8.3 *God*
the witching hour 291.3 *midnight*
the womb of time 283.1 *future time*
the Woolsack 464.3 *place of judgment*
the Word 8.8 *divine manifestation*; 7.12 *religious text*
the Word made Flesh 8.8 *divine manifestation*
the works 211.3 *additional item*
the world 204.4 *all*; 30.5 *earth*; 566.1 *humankind*
the World Championship 68.3 *ski racing*
the World Championships 50.4 *rowing*
the World Cup 68.3 *ski racing*
the World Curling Championship 68.10 *curling*
the world of today 282.2 *the present day*
the world over 141.16 *extensively*; 138.32 *universally*
the world population 566.1 *humankind*
the worse for 245.12 *deteriorated*
the worse for liquor 690.1 *drunk*
the worse for wear 245.13, 337.9 *dilapidated*; 766.16 *losing*
the worst 249.1 *adversity*
the wrong way 420.14 *roughly*
thews 336.1 *strength*
the year dot 3.9 *distant past*
the years ahead 283.1 *future time*
the young 555.10
the younger generation 555.10 *the young*
thiamin 33.12 *coenzyme*
thick 152.1; **152.9**; 416.6 *dense*; 258.7 *dirty*; 569.10 *familiar*; 31.56 *foggy*; 456.6 *ignorant*; 592.1 *insensitive*; 524.6 *murky*; 528.1 *opaque*; 203.6 *quantitative*; 524.8 *stupid*; 152.3 *thick-witted*; 457.6, 528.5 *unintelligent*; 430.8 *viscous*
thick and fast 297.1 *frequently*; 208.14 *in crowds*
thick-ankled 152.1 *thick*
thick as a plank 528.5 *unintelligent*
thick as flies 376.50 *crowded*
thick as thieves 223.19 *associated*; 569.10 *familiar*
thick-barked 152.1 *thick*
thick-bodied 152.1 *thick*
thick cloud 31.19 *cloud cover*; 524.1 *dimness*
thick-coated 152.1 *thick*
thicken 152.7; **430.11**; 416.8 *be dense*; 528.10 *be opaque*; 152.8 *fatten*; 213.4 *increase*; 213.5 *make bigger*; 528.11 *make opaque*; 418.10 *solidify*
thickened 152.2 *dense*
thickener 416.5 *condenser*
thickening 416.5 *condenser*; 152.6 *denseness*; 416.1 *density*; 213.1 *increase*; 430.1 *viscosity*
thicket 416.4 *solid body*; 79.4 *trees*
thick-fingered 152.1 *thick*
thick fog 254.6 *danger signal*; 31.33 *fog*
thick-growing 416.6 *dense*
thick head 690.15 *crapulence*
thickheaded 456.6 *ignorant*; 152.1 *thick*; 457.6, 528.5 *unintelligent*
thickheadedness 528.9 *stupidity*; 457.2 *unintelligence*
thickie 457.3 *unintelligent person*
thick-jawed 152.1 *thick*
thick-leaved 152.1 *thick*
thick-legged 152.1 *thick*
thick-lipped 152.1 *thick*
thickly 416.10 *densely*; 203.7 *quantitatively*; 152.9 *thick*; 430.12 *viscously*
thick mist 31.34 *mist*
thick-necked 152.1 *thick*
Thickness 152
thickness 152.5; 416.1 *density*; 411.1 *layer*; 528.6 *opaqueness*; 203.1 *quantity*; 28.7 *space*; 524.4 *stupidity*
thickness of voice 730.2 *inarticulation*
thicko 456.5 *ignorant person*
thick of the action 342.1 *activity*
thick of things 342.1 *activity*
thick on the ground 208.9 *ample*; 376.50 *crowded*; 416.6 *dense*
thick rib 25.22 *beef*
thick-ribbed 152.1 *thick*
thick seam 25.31 *offal*
thickset 416.6 *dense*; 149.7 *short*; 158.17 *stocky*; 152.1 *thick*
thick skin 489.313 *heedlessness*
thick-skinned 152.4; 618.7 *indifferent*; 592.1 *insensitive*; 418.4 *mentally hard*; 423.5 *mentally tough*; 152.1 *thick*
thick slice 152.5 *thickness*
thick speech 690.10 *drunkenness*
thick-stalked 152.1 *thick*
thick-stemmed 152.1 *thick*
thick-walled 152.1 *thick*
thick with 152.2 *dense*
thick-witted 152.3
thick-wristed 152.1 *thick*
thief 774.8; 662.9 *criminal*; 765.7 *gainer*; 314.8 *intruder*; 16.40 *lawbreaker*; 804.9 *wicked person*
thieve 800.10 *be criminal*; 774.12 *steal*; 773.10 *take away*
thievery 774.1 *stealing*
thieving 800.7 *criminal*; 800.3 *criminality*; 774.1 *stealing*; 774.17 *stolen*; 773.12 *taking*; 773.3 *taking away*
thievish 774.17 *stolen*
thievishly 774.19
thievishness 800.3 *criminality*; 774.1 *stealing*
thigh boots 551.19 *footwear*
thigh-high 154.12 *tall*
thimblerig 700.29 *juggle*; 700.9 *sleight of hand*
thimblerigger 700.17 *cheat*
thimblewit 456.5 *ignorant person*
thin 153.1; **153.17**; 434.12 *airy*; 191.6 *become smaller*; 31.60 *cloud*; 44.15 *cultivate*; 214.4 *decrease*; 377.14, 433.30, 497.8 *dilute*; 369.12 *displace*; 431.23 *dissolve*; 687.6 *fasting*; 552.13 *hairless*; 337.10 *ill*; 233.4 *incomplete*; 218.1, 337.13 *insufficient*; 159.7 *little*; 191.5 *make smaller*; 417.6 *make sparse*; 153.16 *make thin*; 79.18 *manage trees*; 151.1 *narrow*; 203.6 *quantitative*; 206.8 *reduce*; 191.7 *smaller*; 206.6, 417.1 *sparse*; 212.3 *subtract*; 157.2 *superficial*; 497.5 *tasteless*; 527.2 *translucent*; 218.3 *underfed*; 337.7 *weaken*
thin air 434.1 *air*
thin as a lath 153.2 *emaciated*
thin as a rail 218.3 *underfed*
thin climbing 62.1 *mountaineering*
thin cloud 31.19 *cloud cover*
thin down 153.16 *make thin*
thin-faced 153.1 *thin*
thing 93.2; 222.6 *aspect*; 402.5 *object*; 356.3 *product*; 95.1 *reality*; 139.8 *specialization*
thing deducted 212.2 *subtracted item*
thing excluded 128.6
thing included 127.2
thing inserted 368.11
thing of beauty 545.2 *beautiful thing*
thing of the past 284.7; 296.5 *old thing*
thin gruel 337.5 *weak thing*
things 763.4 *possession*; 440.4 *possessions*
things as they are 698.2 *reality*
things brought to life 554.6
things contained 406.1 *contents*
thing transported 319.2
thingumabob 402.5 *object*; 438.1 *tool*
thingumajig 402.5 *object*
thingummy 402.5 *object*; 438.1 *tool*
thin house 21.33 *theatregoer*
thin ice 424.3 *brittle thing*; 62.2 *climbing dangers*; 379.1 *trap*
think 442.12; **443.12**; 590.19 *believe*; 450.8 *be of the opinion*; 464.12 *estimate*; 446.15, 477.14 *imagine*; 474.9 *predict*;

444.11 *reason*; 476.5 *suppose*; 619.12 *wonder whether*
thinkable 477.13 *imaginable*; 102.5 *possible*
think about 443.15; 4.20 *philosophize*
think again 808.4 *be penitent*; 479.2 *equivocate*; 443.14 *have second thoughts*; 244.4 *reconsider*
think ahead 484.12 *plan ahead*
think aloud 735.3 *soliloquize*
think back 462.12 *remember*
think best 713.5 *advise*; 635.12 *choose*
think better of 808.4 *be penitent*; 244.4 *reconsider*
think better of it 479.2 *equivocate*
think deeply 443.12 *think*
thinker 443.7; 400.9 *educational leader*; 442.8 *intellectual person*; 446.9 *person of ideas*; 4.10 *philosopher*; 444.5 *reasoner*; 476.4 *theorist*; 458.3 *wise man*
think everything of 123.8 *make important*
think fit 469.2 *prefer*
think freely 250.14 *be free*
think hard 443.12 *think*
think highly of 669.11 *approve*; 667.15 *respect*
think ill of 670.14 *disapprove*
thinking 476.2 *basis of supposition*; 446.1 *idea*; 442.9 *mental*; 444.7 *reasoning*; 443.1 *thought*; 4.17, 443.8 *thoughtful*; 458.5 *wise*
thinking aloud 735.5 *soliloquizing*
thinking cap 443.5 *creative thought*
thinking on one's feet 478.4 *improvisation*
think it beneath one 622.28 *disdain*
think it best to 469.2 *prefer*
think laterally 352.6 *find means*
think likely 104.10
think little of 670.14 *disapprove*
think logically 444.11 *reason*
think negatively 611.9 *be hopeless*
think no more of 463.13 *forget*; 649.9 *forgive*
think nothing of 265.17 *do easily*
think of 477.14 *imagine*; 482.7 *intend*; 130.22 *invent*; 356.10 *produce*; 756.11 *promise oneself*; 462.12 *remember*
think of others first 473.7 *be unselfish*
think of the future 283.9 *look ahead*
think one is it 673.15 *be vain*
think oneself God Almighty 673.15 *be vain*
think only of oneself 683.6 *be selfish*
think on one's feet 478.3 *improvise*; 262.2 *make haste*
think out 4.21 *rationalize*
think over 443.14 *have second thoughts*
think positively 610.8 *be optimistic*
think profoundly 443.12 *think*
think tank 579.7 *council*; 448.6 *place of experimentation*
think the best of 669.11 *approve*
think the world of 595.7 *like*; 593.23 *love*; 667.16 *revere*
think the worst of 611.9 *be hopeless*
think through 631.14 *behave towards*; 4.21 *rationalize*
think twice 616.5 *be cautious*; 612.12 *be fearful*
think unimportant 124.12
think up 446.15, 477.14 *imagine*; 478.3 *improvise*; 484.11 *invent*; 356.10 *produce*
think well of 669.11 *approve*; 667.15 *respect*
think well of oneself 673.15 *be vain*
thin-legged 153.1 *thin*
thinly 203.7 *quantitatively*; 206.11, 417.7 *sparsely*; 153.17 *thin*; 337.14 *weakly*
thinned 153.5; 433.22 *diluted*; 417.2 *rarefied*
thinned-out 417.2 *rarefied*
thinner 153.13; 19.11 *artist's materials*; 431.9 *solvent*
Thinness 153
thinness 153.7; 415.5 *lightness*; 159.1 *littleness*; 151.5 *narrowness*; 337.3 *poor health*; 203.1 *quantity*; 417.3 *sparseness*; 497.1 *tastelessness*; 527.6 *translucency*
thinning 153.12; 191.8 *contracting*; 191.1 *contraction*; 369.2 *displacement*; 417.4 *rarefaction*; 417.2 *rarefied*; 79.6 *tree management*
thinning out 369.2 *displacement*
thin on the ground 153.6 *scant*; 218.4 *scarce*; 206.6 *sparse*
thin on top 552.13 *hairless*
thin out 44.15 *cultivate*; 214.4 *decrease*; 377.14 *dilute*; 369.12 *displace*; 214.5 *make smaller*; 417.6 *make sparse*; 153.16 *make thin*; 206.8 *reduce*; 212.3 *subtract*; 337.7 *weaken*
thin person 153.9
thin red line 586.14 *armed forces*
thin rib 25.22 *beef*
thin skin 488.2 *ability to sense*; 625.1 *irascibility*
thin-skinned 625.4 *irascible*; 591.2 *oversensitive*; 488.7 *susceptible*
thin space 146.1 *interval*
thin-spun 404.10 *delicate*
Thiokol™ 422.4 *rubber*
Thio violet 540.2 *purple pigment*
third 199.6; **199.14**; 51.3 *bowls player*; 27.75 *equal*; 196.4 *less than one*; 18.16 *musical note*; 205.1 *part*; 199.7 *three*
third age 556.5 *old age*; 199.6 *third*
third base 48.1 *baseball*
third-baseman 48.2 *baseball player*
third-base umpire 48.2 *baseball player*
third class 231.5 *imperfection*
third-class 793.9 *cheap*; 231.1 *imperfect*; 122.12, 236.2 *inferior*
third-class mail 692.2 *postal communication*
third degree 814.12 *corporal punishment*; 199.6 *third*
third-degree burn 493.1 *heat*
third eye 11.8 *psychic power*; 11.7 *spirit*; 199.6 *third*
third finger 492.7 *sense organ*
third guard 54.3 *fencing movements*
third law 28.38 *thermodynamics*
thirdly 199.14 *third*
third man 53.4 *team*
Third Market 779.5 *stock market*
third-order 32.38 *reactive*
third part 199.6 *third*
third party 618.6 *indifferent person*; 748.3 *mediator*; 199.6 *third*
third person 199.6 *third*
third-person narrative 17.3 *aspect of fiction*
third power 199.6 *third*
third-rate 231.1 *imperfect*; 122.12, 236.2 *inferior*; 124.4 *trivial*
third-rater 122.6 *inferior*
third slip 53.4 *team*
third-stream jazz 18.8 *jazz*
Third World 13.4 *economic development*; 231.5 *imperfection*; 12.5 *political organization*; 86.7 *regions of the world*; 782.11 *the poor*; 199.6 *third*
third-world country 85.1 *country*
Thirlmere 88.4 *British lakes*
thirst 428.12; **428.18**; 617.3 *appetite*; 617.14 *be hungry*; 617.1 *desire*
thirst for 617.12 *desire*; 428.18 *thirst*
thirst for blood 651.17 *kill*
thirst for knowledge 644.7 *be curious*
thirstily 428.24 *drily*; 617.19 *hungrily*
thirstiness 617.3 *appetite*; 428.12 *thirst*
thirsting 428.2 *thirsty*
thirsting for blood 382.24 *murderous*
thirst-quencher 558.2 *drink*; 558.6 *soft drink*
thirst-quenching 263.5 *labour-saving*
thirsty 428.2; 690.5 *drunken*; 617.10 *hungry*
thirsty soul 690.17 *drunkard*
thirteen 201.7 *double figures*
thirteenth 201.18 *eleventh*; 196.4 *less than one*
thirtieth 196.4 *less than one*; 201.19 *twentieth*
thirty-second note 18.17 *notation*
thirty-second suspension 58.5 *lacrosse*
thirtysomething 556.13 *middle-aged*
this afternoon 275.27 *at what time*; 282.1 *present time*
this big 158.13 *this size*
this day 282.1 *the present day*
this day and age 282.2 *the present day*
this evening 275.27 *at what time*; 282.1 *present time*
this hour 282.1 *present time*
this instant 282.1 *present time*
this is it 582.24 *I'm dying!*
this moment 282.1 *present time*
this moment in time 282.1 *present time*
this morning 275.27 *at what time*; 282.1 *present time*
this second 282.1 *present time*
this size 158.13
this time 282.2 *the present day*
thistle 420.7 *rough thing*; 425.8 *sharp-pointed thing*
thistledown 415.7 *light thing*; 419.11 *soft thing*
thistly 425.2 *spiked*
this very day 282.1 *present time*
this very minute 282.1 *present time*
thither 142.12 *where*
thixotropic 32.32 *solid*
thixotropy 32.3 *phase*
tholepin 50.4 *rowing*
tholos 284.7 *thing of the past*
Thomas Cup 63.10 *badminton*
Thomism 4.7 *school of thought*
Thomist 4.11 *follower of a doctrine*; 4.14 *of a philosophy*
Thompson submachine gun™ 587.11 *guns*
thong 551.21 *beachwear*; 552.4 *dishabille*; 814.14 *instrument of punishment*; 373.6 *line*
thongs 551.19 *footwear*
thorn 420.7 *rough thing*; 425.8 *sharp-pointed thing*
thorn forest 79.4 *trees*
thorniness 425.6 *sharpness*
thorn in one's flesh 264.9 *difficult person*
thorny 264.12 *problematic*; 425.2 *spiked*
thorny problem 264.4 *problem*
thorough 665.9 *careful*; 232.7 *complete*; 576.11 *laborious*; 638.2 *tenacious*; 576.10 *working*
thorough bass 516.4 *harmonics*
thoroughbred 59.2; 573.4 *aristocratic*; 59.13 *breeding*; 43.21 *domesticated*; 59.17 *equine*; 255.13 *pure*; 255.7 *purebred*; 332.12 *swift animal*
thoroughfare 318.2 *passing along*; 317.3 *road*
thoroughgoing 232.7 *complete*; 336.10 *potent*
thoroughly 665.12 *carefully*; 230.8, 232.9 *completely*; 156.17 *profoundly*
thoroughness 665.1 *carefulness*
thou 196.4 *less than one*
though 476.11 *supposing*
Thought 443
thought 443.1; 476.2 *basis of supposition*; 450.1 *belief*; 443.6, 446.1 *idea*; 477.4 *ideality*; 717.6 *image*; 701.2 *logical argument*; 4.1 *philosophy*; 728.6 *suggestion*; 729.7 *utterance*
thought for others 473.2 *unselfishness*
thoughtful 4.17; **442.11**; **443.8**; 650.6 *benevolent*; 658.7 *courteous*; 797.3 *kind*; 643.1 *solemn*; 458.5 *wise*
thoughtfully 4.28; **443.18**; 650.10 *benevolently*; 658.14 *courteously*; 658.15 *genteelly*; 442.15 *intelligently*; 701.19 *logically*; 643.10 *solemnly*; 6.26 *studiously*; 446.20 *theoretically*; 458.9 *wisely*
thoughtfulness 442.6; **443.3**; 650.1 *benevolence*; 658.1 *courtesy*; 4.3 *detachment*; 797.10 *kindness*; 643.4 *solemnity*
thoughtless 472.9; 519.12 *blind to*; 659.5 *discourteous*; 262.3 *hasty*; 472.7 *inattentive*; 651.15 *inconsiderate*; 666.4 *negligent*; 615.4 *rash*; 672.3 *ungrateful*; 457.6 *unintelligent*; 486.1 *unskilful*; 463.10 *unthinking*
thoughtlessly 659.9 *discourteously*; 472.14 *inattentively*; 463.16 *obliviously*; 262.7 *rashly*; 672.7 *ungratefully*
thoughtlessness 472.4; 486.9 *bungling*; 659.1 *discourtesy*; 519.7 *figurative blindness*; 459.1 *folly*; 262.5 *hastiness*; 472.1 *inattention*; 651.6 *inconsiderateness*; 672.1 *ingratitude*; 666.1 *negligence*; 457.2 *unintelligence*; 463.4 *unthinkingness*
thought of 356.12 *produced*
thought process 443.1 *thought*
thought-provoking 726.3 *emphatic*; 447.8 *problematic*; 496.10 *stimulating*; 476.7 *suppositional*
thought reader 11.12 *occultist*
thought transference 11.1 *occultism*
thought-up 477.12 *imaginary*
thousand 201.10; 208.7 *myriad*
thousandfold 201.21 *thousandth*
Thousand Island dressing 25.15 *sauce*
thousand-leggers 75.4 *arthropod*
thousand million 201.11 *million*
thousands 208.2 *multitude*
thousandth 201.21; 196.4 *less than one*
thraldom 387.1 *subjection*
thrall 401.7 *slave*; 387.5 *subjected person*
thrash 331.5 *beat*; 121.8 *be superior*; 246.10 *defeat heavily*; 557.13 *feast*; 814.3 *hit*; 491.11 *inflict pain*; 376.9 *social gathering*
thrash about 327.21 *be agitated*; 327.25 *pitch*
thrashed 247.11 *defeated*
thrashing 331.12 *collision*; 814.12 *corporal punishment*; 247.2 *defeat*; 331.17 *impelling*; 246.2 *victory*; 380.6 *violent*
thrashing of a lifetime 814.12 *corporal punishment*
thrash metal 18.9 *popular music*
thrash out 734.11 *confer*
thrash punk 18.9 *popular music*
thread 132.15 *concatenate*; 132.2 *consecution*; 42.1, 404.6 *fibre*; 373.6 *line*; 151.8 *narrow thing*; 84.3 *plant body*; 337.5 *weak thing*
threadbare 782.3 *beggarly*; 552.10 *in dishabille*; 349.9 *used*
threadlike 151.2 *fine*
threads 551.1 *dress*
threat 661.3 *act of defiance*; 651.7 *act of malevolence*; 249.1 *adversity*; 386.2 *coercion*; 254.5 *danger*; 397.2, 710.2 *demand*; 482.4 *formulated intention*; 480.8 *incentive*; 483.4 *negative stimulus*; 712.3 *vilification*; 711.1 *warning*
threaten 798.11 *be evil*; 661.6 *be insubordinate*; 283.7 *be in the future*; 397.10, 710.7 *demand*; 481.2 *deter*; 254.10 *endanger*; 386.7 *force*; 475.11 *predict*; 482.8 *resolve*; 651.18 *torment*; 712.6 *vilify*; 711.5 *warn*
threaten danger 254.10 *endanger*
threatened 710.10 *demanding*
threatening 381.21 *aggressive*; 523.11 *benighted*; 254.1 *dangerous*; 710.10 *demanding*; 357.1 *destruction*; 357.14 *destructive*; 283.11 *future*; 612.4 *intimidation*; 380.6 *violent*; 712.9 *vituperative*; 711.8 *warning*
threateningly 254.11 *dangerously*
threaten one's life 254.10 *endanger*
threat of dismissal 483.4 *negative stimulus*
Three 199
three 199.1; **199.7**; 68.6 *ice-skating*; 27.9 *numeral*; 53.10 *score*
three abreast 199.13 *in threes*
three-ball match 56.1 *golf*
three by three 199.13 *in threes*
three-card trick 700.9 *sleight of hand*
three cheers 669.5 *acclaim*; 600.2 *fanfare*
three-cornered 199.8 *three-sided*
three-course meal 557.12 *meal*
three-cushion billiards 65.4 *carom*
three-day event 59.11 *eventing*
three-decker 586.25 *historical naval ships*; 199.2 *trident*
three-dimensional 27.79, 141.11 *spatial*; 199.8 *three-sided*; 518.20 *visual*
three-dimensionally 141.15 *spaciously*
three-dimensionally 141.14 *spatially*
three-dimensional space 27.35 *space*
threefold 199.7 *three*; 199.12 *thrice*
threefoldness 199.3 *threeness*
three-footed 199.8 *three-sided*
three-hander 199.2 *trident*
three hundred 201.9 *treble figures*
three hundred and one 69.6 *darts*
three-leaved 199.8 *three-sided*
three-legged 199.8 *three-sided*
three-man 50.10 *sailing*
three-man combination attack 58.3 *ice hockey*
three-man keelboat 50.2 *sailing boat*
three-metre springboard 67.6 *diving*
Three Mile Island 28.75 *nuclear accident*; 437.7 *nuclear power*
three-mile limit 166.3 *furthest point*
three-minute suspension 58.5 *lacrosse*
threeness 199.3
three of a kind 69.3 *card game terms*
three-on-a-side 51.9 *bowls*
three-on-a-side match 51.1 *green bowling*
three-part 199.9 *trisected*
three-parted 199.9 *trisected*
threepenny bit 780.10 *former British money*
three-phase supply 39.34 *power supply*
three-piece suit 551.10 *suit*
three-ply 411.7 *layered*; 199.8 *three-sided*
three-pointed 199.8 *three-sided*
three-pointer 49.4 *playing terms*
three-point landing 322.5 *flight*

three-point turn 320.21 *miscellaneous motoring terms*
three-pronged 199.8 *three-sided*
three-quarter 196.5 *fractional*
three-quarter back 64.4 *rugby player*
three-quarter-length portrait 19.10 *art subject*
three-quarters 196.7 *fractionally;* 196.4 *less than one*
three-ring circus 740.8 *public relations*
threescore 201.8 *twenty and over*
threescore and ten 201.8 *twenty and over*
threescore years and ten 275.3 *duration;* 554.5 *life cycle;* 556.5 *old age*
three-second lane violation 49.5 *penalties*
three-sided 199.8; 27.82 *polygonal*
threesome 56.1 *golf;* 199.1 *three*
three-storeyed 411.7 *layered*
three-tiered 411.7 *layered*
three times 199.12 *thrice*
three times as much 199.7 *three*
three turn 68.7 *ice-dancing*
three-way 199.8 *three-sided*
three-wheeler 199.2 *trident*
thremmatologist 70.10 *animal welfarist*
thremmatology 70.8 *animal welfare;* 43.3 *livestock farming*
threnodic 603.4 *lamenting*
threnodist 603.3 *lamenter*
threnodize 603.6 *lament*
threnody 603.2 *lament;* 17.7 *poem*
thresh 327.21 *be agitated*
threshold 175.2 *foot;* 147.7 *interface;* 166.2 *limiting factor;* 314.6 *means of entry*
threshold of hearing 505.3 *inaudibility*
threshold of pain 488.2 *ability to sense*
thrice 199.12
Thrift 680
thrift 680.1; 359.1 *preservation*
thriftily 680.7 *economically*
thriftiness 680.1 *thrift*
thriftless 681.1 *extravagant;* 441.8 *wasteful*
thriftlessly 441.10 *wastefully*
thriftlessness 441.3 *waste*
thrift shop 793.7 *discounter*
thrifty 680.4; 616.4 *cautious*
thrill 488.13 *arouse sensation;* 327.10 *beat;* 597.8 *cause joy;* 597.2 *fun;* 490.9 *give pleasure;* 488.1 *sensation;* 327.24 *shake;* 488.3 *stimulus*
thrilled 597.4 *happy;* 488.7 *susceptible*
thriller 740.6 *book publishing;* 17.2, 721.5 *fiction*
thrilling 721.11 *descriptive;* 488.9 *exciting*
thrips 44.12 *pests and diseases*
thrive 342.13 *be busy;* 190.6 *become bigger;* 562.6 *be fertile;* 338.2 *be full of vigour;* 259.5 *be healthy;* 248.5 *be prosperous;* 246.6 *be successful;* 797.21 *do well;* 213.4 *increase*
thriving 562.5 *fertile;* 190.8 *growing;* 190.1 *growth;* 259.1 *healthy;* 248.1 *prosperity;* 248.8 *prosperous;* 246.1 *success;* 246.13 *successful*
throat 557.16 *eating utensil;* 729.5 *organ of speech;* 308.7 *passageway*
throat cancer 260.12 *cancer*
throatiness 513.2 *hoarseness*
throaty 260.23 *diseased;* 513.8 *hoarse;* 729.18 *phonetic*
throb 327.10 *beat;* 242.12, 491.10 *be painful;* 298.7 *be regular;* 509.8 *drum;* 327.9 *jolt;* 491.1 *pain;* 298.1 *regularity;* 112.22 *resound;* 112.6 *reverberation;* 327.7, 327.24 *shake;* 488.3 *stimulus;* 326.9 *vibrate;* 326.2 *vibration*
throbbing 327.10 *beat;* 509.1, 509.15 *drumming;* 491.1 *pain;* 491.5 *painful;* 298.11 *regular;* 112.6 *reverberation;* 112.15 *reverberatory;* 327.6 *shaking;* 327.18 *shaky;* 326.14 *vibrating;* 326.2 *vibration*
throbbingly 491.13 *painfully*
throe 380.3 *instance of violence*
throes 491.1 *pain;* 327.8 *spasm*
thrombosis 431.4 *blood;* 260.10 *cardiovascular disease;* 416.2 *concentration;* 416.4 *solid body*
thrombus 416.4 *solid body;* 309.2 *stopper*
throne 743.4 *insignia;* 560.14 *toilet;* 16.18 *tribunal*
throne of God 8.11 *heaven*
thrones 8.6 *angel*
throng 208.4; 208.11, 376.20, 376.40 *crowd*
thronged 208.10 *crowded*
throng in 314.12 *flood in*
throttle 335.8 *overpower;* 251.8 *restrain;* 360.6 *retain;* 309.8 *stop*
throttle down 333.3 *slow down*
throttling 251.1 *restraint;* 360.9 *retentive*
through 317.15 *accessible;* 150.8 *breadthwise;* 352.7 *by means of:* 318.14 *by the way;* 131.21 *ended;* 348.9 *instrumentally;* 317.17 *via*
through a glass darkly 524.12 *dimly*
through and through 232.10 *fully*
through arbitration 15.13 *industrially*
through bridge 38.21 *bridge*
through charity 650.11 *charitably*
through fire and water 640.13 *persistently*
through nature's bounty 562.8 *fruitfully*
through negotiations 15.13 *industrially*
throughout 232.9 *completely;* 275.21 *lasting through time*
throughout eternity 279.11 *eternally*
throughout the world 141.16 *extensively;* 764.6 *in common*
throughput 356.1 *production;* 316.3 *transmission*
through rose-coloured glasses 446.22 *imaginatively*
through self-denial 383.15 *abstemiously*
through street 317.3 *road*
through the courts 16.81 *legally*
through the green 56.1 *golf*
through the instrumentality of 348.9 *instrumentally*
through the legislative process 16.81 *legally*
through the night 291.7 *evening*
through thick and thin 279.11 *eternally;* 232.10 *fully;* 640.13 *persistently*
throughway 317.3 *road*
throw 330.5; **330.23**; **331.4**; 69.6 *darts;* 69.5 *dice;* 576.4 *exertion;* 160.7 *form;* 24.11 *make ceramics;* 69.10 *play;* 50.19 *punt;* 50.8 *punting;* 372.9 *separate;* 300.14 *set in motion;* 367.6 *throw down*
throw a cat-fit 624.11 *be angry*
throw a completion 46.15 *play offence*
throw a conniption fit 624.11 *be angry*
throw a crackback block 46.18 *be penalized*
throw a curve 48.7 *play baseball*
throw a fast ball 48.7 *play baseball*
throw a fight 700.30 *be fraudulent;* 52.11 *fight*
throw a fit 327.21 *be agitated;* 624.11 *be angry;* 590.17 *feel deeply*
throw a lifeline to 390.1 *deliver;* 608.10 *save*
throw a party 654.11 *be sociable;* 600.5 *rejoice;* 601.18 *salute*
throw a pass 46.15 *play offence*
throw a pot 24.11 *make ceramics*
throw around 377.17 *sow*
throw aside 470.2 *discard*
throw a slider 48.7 *play baseball*
throw a stone 381.7 *stone*
throw at 381.7 *stone*
throw a tantrum 624.12 *become angry;* 590.17 *feel deeply*
throwaway 278.7 *impermanent;* 238.6 *refuse;* 349.10 *usable;* 237.1 *useful;* 238.1 *useless;* 441.9 *waste*
throw away 371.13; 766.11 *be wasteful;* 357.12 *consume;* 470.2 *discard;* 767.9 *dispose of;* 787.1 *expend;* 355.1 *relinquish;* 350.6 *stop using;* 21.36 *underact;* 441.1 *waste*
throw away an opportunity 288.7 *lose one's chance*
throwaway manner 660.7 *insult*
throw away the scabbard 585.12 *go to war*
throw a whammy on 712.7 *wish ill*
throw a wild pitch 48.7 *play baseball*
throw a wobbler 624.11 *be angry*
throw a wobbly 614.4 *be a coward;* 590.17 *feel deeply*
throw axel 68.6 *ice-skating*
throwback 245.7 *deterioration;* 303.18 *setback*
throw back 384.24 *parry*
throw bombs 381.3 *bomb*
throw cold water on 481.5 *discourage;* 378.8 *hinder;* 685.4 *moderate*
throw down 367.6; 357.9 *demolish*
throw down the gauntlet 661.6 *be insubordinate;* 638.8 *brace oneself*
thrower 330.14; 47.3 *athlete*
throw flowers 669.16 *acclaim*
throw-forward 64.3 *rugby play*
throw further 765.10 *augment*
throw in 69.10 *play;* 64.5 *play rugby;* 66.4 *play soccer*
throw-in 66.2 *football play;* 330.5 *throw*
throwing 330.3; 24.5 *ceramic process*
throwing a fight 52.2 *boxing*
throwing in the towel 605.1 *resignation*
throwing out 371.17 *expulsion*
throwing out time 131.11 *finality*
throwing overboard 371.20 *eviction*
throwing the crosse 58.5 *lacrosse*
throw in irons 251.12 *gag*
throw in one's hand 355.2 *withdraw*
throw in prison 251.11 *detain*
throw in the air 366.2 *send up*
throw in the cooler 815.9 *imprison*
throw in the slammer 309.10 *enclose*
throw in the sponge 355.2 *withdraw*
throw in the tank 815.9 *imprison*
throw in the towel 605.5 *resign;* 388.3 *submit*
throw into a tizzy 328.7 *disturb*
throw into confusion 328.7 *disturb*
throw into disarray 408.21 *disorder*
throw into disorder 328.8 *disarrange*
throw in together 747.13 *work together*
throw into relief 738.3 *reveal*
throw into the shade 121.8 *be superior*
throw in with 747.14 *join with*
throw it all away 288.7 *lose one's chance*
throw light on 522.29 *clarify;* 719.8 *interpret;* 738.3 *reveal*
throw money at 787.1 *expend*
throw money away 681.8 *overspend*
throw mud 678.12 *defame;* 670.23 *show disapproval*
thrown 24.10 *ceramic;* 160.9 *formed;* 366.11 *raised*
thrown away 470.10 *rejected*
thrown out 709.8 *refused;* 144.10 *replaced*
thrown-out case 16.42 *acquittal*
thrown over 596.9 *disliked*
thrown together 486.4 *bungled*
thrown to the lions 254.4 *endangered*
throw off 391.5 *be liberated;* 487.5 *disaccustom;* 371.10 *exterminate;* 552.16 *peel*
throw off balance 120.5 *be unequal*
throw off discipline 408.26 *be disorderly*
throw off the scent 700.27 *be false;* 389.6 *elude;* 634.6 *evade*
throw off the trail 389.6 *elude*
throw off the yoke 391.5 *be liberated*
throw of the dice 254.5 *danger;* 107.3 *equal chance*
throw one's arms around 593.27 *kiss*
throw oneself at 633.12 *aim at*
throw one's weight around 395.10 *be a prevailing influence;* 396.19 *be authoritarian;* 622.28 *disdain;* 660.28 *get above oneself;* 660.26 *oppress*
throw open 738.3 *reveal*
throw out 357.8 *destroy;* 470.2 *discard;* 128.8, 364.2 *eject;* 371.1 *expel;* 331.1 *impel;* 48.7 *play baseball;* 212.3 *subtract;* 371.13 *throw away*
throw-out 48.6 *fielding terms*
throw out an idea 476.6 *propound*
throwout level 55.1 *angling*
throw out of gear 144.14 *displace;* 372.9 *separate*
throw over 355.2 *withdraw*
throw overboard 415.10 *lighten;* 350.6 *stop using;* 371.13 *throw away;* 367.6 *throw down*
throw rug 550.9 *floor covering*
throw salchow 68.6 *ice-skating*
throw someone a curve 700.29 *juggle*
throw someone a curveball 700.29 *juggle*
throw something together 25.55 *cook*
throwstick 587.6 *historical missile weapon*
throw stones 670.23 *show disapproval*
throw stones at 331.4 *throw*
throw the book at 715.5 *accuse;* 670.21 *berate;* 814.2 *penalize*
throw the casting vote 120.5 *be unequal*
throw the crosse 58.9 *play hockey*
throw the javelin 330.23 *throw*
throw the whammy on 594.15 *curse*
throw together 478.3 *improvise*
throw to the dogs 357.12 *consume*
throw up 371.15 *vomit*
throw up a roadblock 378.9 *block*
throw up one's hands 696.9 *find unintelligible*
throw up the game 355.2 *withdraw*
thrum 509.8 *drum;* 517.10 *lack harmony;* 112.22 *resound;* 18.38 *sound*
thrumming 509.1, 509.15 *drumming*
thrupenny bit 780.10 *former British money*
thrush 83.5 *fungal association;* 72.6 *songbird*
thrushlike 72.21 *avian*
thrust 332.9 *acceleration;* 707.6 *assertiveness;* 381.1 *attack;* 324.2 *bearing;* 707.21 *be assertive;* 331.13 *blow;* 334.4 *energy;* 54.5 *fence;* 381.18 *hit;* 331.1 *impel;* 395.1 *influence;* 381.12 *military attack;* 330.20 *propel;* 330.12 *propellant;* 330.1 *propulsion;* 342.14 *push;* 29.35 *rocketry;* 381.6 *stab;* 260.18 *veterinary disease*
thrust ahead 332.6 *accelerate*
thrust at 381.6 *stab*
thrust bearing 307.4 *axle*
thrust down 367.5 *bear down on*
thruster 342.10 *busy person;* 330.11 *propeller*
thrust fault 30.20 *earth movement*
thrustful 342.18 *active;* 707.14 *assertive;* 331.17 *impelling*
thrust in 368.3 *impact*
thrusting 342.18 *active;* 331.12 *collision;* 331.17 *impelling;* 338.4 *vigorous*
thrustingly 330.34 *forward*
thrusting under 367.13 *submergence*
thrust oneself forward 342.14 *push*
thrust out 128.8 *eject*
thrust stage 21.17 *stage*
thud 508.1 *bang;* 511.9 *be nonresonant;* 511.5 *dull sound*
thug 351.3 *abuser;* 586.1 *combatant;* 234.5 *defacer;* 774.11 *dishonest person;* 651.8 *malefactor;* 382.11 *murderer;* 380.4 *violent creature;* 804.9 *wicked person*
thuggery 382.2 *murder;* 380.2 *physical violence*
thuggish 586.33 *combative*
Thule 145.3 *distant place*
thumb 492.7 *sense organ*
Thumbelina 159.4 *little person;* 149.5 *short person*
thumbing 742.15 *gestural*
thumbnail 163.6 *outlined*
thumbnail sketch 721.2 *brief description;* 19.9 *drawing;* 159.2 *little thing;* 163.1 *outline;* 723.1 *summary*
thumb one's nose at 668.26 *cock a snook*
thumbprint 743.3 *means of identification*
thumbscrew 814.15 *instrument of torture;* 814.4 *torture*
thumbs down 16.43 *conviction;* 670.3 *nonacceptance;* 709.1 *refusal;* 399.1 *veto*
thumbs up 16.42 *acquittal;* 669.1 *approval;* 300.11 *bodily movement*
thumbtack 373.8 *fastening;* 425.8 *sharp-pointed thing*
thumb-twiddling 620.1 *boredom;* 620.4 *boring*
thump 508.1 *bang;* 511.9 *be nonresonant;* 331.13 *blow;* 511.5 *dull sound;* 331.3 *hit*
thumping 158.15 *big*
thunder 508.5 *bang;* 507.8 *be loud;* 726.6 *emphasize;* 507.1 *loudness;* 740.14 *proclaim;* 729.12 *speak loudly;* 31.59 *storm;* 31.21 *thunderstorm;* 712.6 *vilify;* 380.5 *violent weather*
thunder along 332.4 *be swift*
thunder and lightning 742.1 *sign;* 380.5 *violent weather*
thunderbolt 522.4 *natural light;* 630.3 *shock;* 31.21 *thunderstorm*
thunderbolts of Thor 507.1 *loudness*
thunderbowl 767.7 *toilet*
thunderbox 560.14, 767.7 *toilet*
thunderclap 508.1 *bang;* 507.1 *loudness;* 31.21 *thunderstorm*
thundercloud 31.18 *cloud;* 523.4 *dark thing*
thunderer 380.4 *violent creature*
thundering 508.8 *banging;* 158.15 *big;* 510.8 *deep;* 510.3 *deepness;* 507.6 *loud;* 712.3 *vilification;* 514.16 *vociferous*
thundering storm 507.1 *loudness*

thunderous 507.6 *loud*; 514.16 *vociferous*
thunderous applause 669.5 *acclaim*
thunderously 514.20 *vociferously*
thunder out 514.10 *cry out*
thunderstorm 31.21; 28.47 *electric storm*
thunderstruck 630.7 *amazed*; 619.6 *wondering*
thundery 523.8 *dark*; 31.48 *stormy*
thundery shower 31.25 *rain*
thundrous 508.8 *banging*
thurible 502.3 *incense*; 10.14 *sacred object*
thurifer 502.3 *incense*
thurification 10.5 *Christian rite*
thurifier 7.8 *priest*
thurify 502.6 *perfume*
thus 750.36 *accordingly*; 317.16 *how*; 222.15 *under the circumstances*; 750.34 *uniformly*
thusness 99.4 *nature*; 97.1 *presence*
thwack 331.13 *blow*; 331.3, 814.3 *hit*; 331.1 *impel*
thwart 604.7; 236.13 *be worthless*; 50.6 *canoeing*; 226.8 *cause to cease*; 113.21, 347.3 *counteract*; 378.8 *hinder*; 176.8 *oblique*; 50.4 *rowing*
thwarted 604.9 *disappointed*
thwarting 378.13 *hindering*
thyme 496.5 *herbs*
thymine 34.12 *molecular biology*; 33.10 *nucleoside*
thyroidal 559.5 *of a secretion*
thyrse 78.4 *flower head*
thysanopteran 76.10 *insectan*
thysanuran 76.10 *insectan*
Tia Maria™ 558.7 *alcoholic drink*
tiara 551.15 *headgear*; 542.7 *jewellery*; 7.11 *vestment*
Tiber 90.5 *other major rivers*
tic 234.2 *facial distortion*; 742.3 *gesture*; 260.17 *nervous disorder*; 519.2 *poor sight*; 327.8 *spasm*
tic douloureux 260.17 *nervous disorder*
tick 76.2 *arachnid*; 298.7 *be regular*; 750.7, 750.28 *consent*; 772.4, 783.1 *credit*; 743.10 *identify*; 280.3 *instant*; 509.11 *knock*; 509.4 *knocking*; 76.3 *pest*; 777.7 *purchasing*; 298.1 *regularity*; 326.9 *vibrate*
ticked 750.17 *consenting*
ticker tape 601.8 *salute*
ticker-tape parade 667.5 *presenting arms*
ticker-tape welcome 601.4 *reception*
ticket 769.3 *acknowledgment of payment*; 211.3 *additional item*; 744.2 *certificate*; 716.6 *documentation*; 469.12 *election*; 454.6 *evidence*; 743.10 *identify*; 743.3 *means of identification*; 757.2 *permit*; 484.2 *policy*; 253.2 *promise*; 314.4 *right of entry*
ticket agent 21.27 *producer*; 778.12 *wholesaler*
ticket collector 21.28 *stagehand*
ticket counterfoil 743.3 *means of identification*
ticketholder 314.7 *entrant*
ticket stub 743.3 *means of identification*; 253.2 *promise*
ticking 509.17 *rattling*; 298.11 *regular*
ticking-off 670.7 *blame*
ticking parcel 254.6 *danger signal*
tickle 593.14 *communication of love*; 490.9 *give pleasure*; 492.3 *press*; 488.11 *sense*; 488.3 *stimulus*; 492.11 *touch*
tickled pink 597.4 *happy*; 490.7 *pleased*
tickled to death 597.4 *happy*; 490.7 *pleased*
tickle one's fancy 272.7 *make one laugh*; 495.9 *taste*
tickle one's palate 495.9 *taste*
tickle one's palm 785.11 *remunerate*
tickle pink 490.9 *give pleasure*
ticklike 76.11 *arachnidan*
tickling 593.14 *communication of love*
ticklish 264.12 *problematic*; 591.3 *sore*; 254.2 *unsafe*
ticklish business 254.5 *danger*
ticklish issue 751.1 *disagreement*
ticklishness 488.2 *ability to sense*; 254.5 *danger*; 591.7 *soreness*
ticklish spot 264.5 *predicament*
tickly 488.9 *exciting*
tick off 670.20 *censure*; 743.10 *identify*; 194.10 *number*; 372.10 *set apart*
tick off names 744.15 *register*
tick over 346.7 *be operational*
ticktack 742.3 *gesture*
ticktock 509.11 *knock*; 509.4 *knocking*; 326.9 *vibrate*
tidal 227.13 *changeable*; 30.52 *coastal*; 88.9 *lakelike*; 91.7 *oceanic*; 298.11 *regular*
tidal barrage 334.6 *source of energy*
tidal bore 90.2 *channel*
tidal current 30.13 *ocean current*; 91.2 *tide*
tidal energy 437.8 *renewable energy*
tidal flats 157.4 *shallow thing*
tidal flood 91.2 *tide*
tidal flow 298.1 *regularity*; 91.2 *tide*
tidally 30.66 *geographically*; 91.11 *nautically*
tidal pool 88.2 *small lake*
tidal power 28.11 *energy*; 437.8 *renewable energy*; 334.6 *source of energy*; 91.2 *tide*
tidal range 30.15, 91.2 *tide*
tidal rise and fall 91.2 *tide*
tidal stream 91.2 *tide*
tidal table 91.2 *tide*
tidal wave 420.9 *broken water*; 154.8 *high thing*; 380.3 *instance of violence*; 379.1 *trap*; 30.14, 91.3, 326.5 *wave*
tiddler 159.4 *little person*; 149.5 *short person*
tiddly 159.7 *little*; 690.2 *slightly drunk*
tide 30.15; **91.2**; 302.11 *course*; 298.5 *regular thing*; 91.1 *sea*
tide chart 91.2 *tide*
tide gate 91.2 *tide*
tide gauge 91.2 *tide*
tideland 91.2 *tide*
tideline 164.1 *edge*
tidemark 742.5 *indicator*; 26.6 *measuring instrument*; 744.12 *vestige*
tide of time 277.2 *time*
tide over 392.29 *finance*
tide race 91.2 *tide*
tide-rode 50.10 *sailing*
tide-rode boat 50.2 *sailing boat*
tidewater 91.2 *tide*
tideway 91.2 *tide*
tidied 409.27
tidily 256.19 *cleanly*; 409.28 *in place*; 407.26 *orderly*
tidiness 665.4 *fastidiousness*; 407.5 *orderliness*; 581.5 *refreshment*
tidings 693.1 *information*
tidy 407.21; **409.19**; 158.15 *big*; 665.9 *careful*; 256.13, 256.16 *clean*; 244.1 *improve*; 407.13 *orderly*; 545.6 *personable*; 581.1 *refresh*; 409.27 *tidied*
tidying 256.2 *cleaning*; 244.5 *improvement*
tidying up 581.5 *refreshment*
tidy step 145.2 *great distance*
tidy sum 781.6 *money*; 208.2 *multitude*
tidy up 244.1 *improve*; 581.1 *refresh*; 178.10 *straighten*; 407.21, 409.19 *tidy*
tie 119.10 *be equal*; 373.12 *bind*; 810.7 *commitment*; 373.11 *connect*; 111.5 *equality*; 285.4 *equal race*; 119.2 *equilibrium*; 251.12 *gag*; 44.6 *garden tool*; 810.17 *impose a duty*; 373.6 *line*; 228.7 *make stable*; 373.4 *means of connection*; 551.14 *neckwear*; 321.3 *rail*; 317.10 *railway*; 108.1 *relatedness*; 108.7 *relate to*; 393.1 *repair*; 309.11, 378.10 *restrain*; 378.4 *restraint*; 285.8 *run equally*; 38.27 *superstructure*; 743.5 *uniform*; 551.34 *wear*
tie a fly 55.7 *angle*
tie a game 111.10 *be equal*
tie beam 373.4 *means of connection*
tie clasp 373.8 *fastening*; 360.3 *tools for gripping*
tied 55.8 *angling*; 373.16 *bound*; 373.15 *connected*; 810.11 *duty-bound*; 111.16, 285.11 *equal*; 119.8 *on equal terms*; 108.4 *related*; 228.10 *stabilized*
tied down 251.13 *restraining*
tied fly 55.2 *artificial fly*
tied game 111.5 *equality*; 119.2 *equilibrium*
tie down 386.6 *compel*
tied score 119.2 *equilibrium*
tied up with 108.4 *related*
tie-dye 529.15 *colour*; 42.15 *treat*
tie-dyed 42.11 *treated*
tie-dyeing 42.7 *dyeing*
tie hand and foot 251.12 *gag*; 335.8 *overpower*
tie in 44.15 *cultivate*; 747.16 *join*
tie-in 747.7 *association*
tie in knots 408.22 *discompose*
tie into 108.7 *relate to*
tie in with 750.25 *conform*; 108.7 *relate to*
Tien 8.11 *heaven*
tie one's hands 378.10 *restrain*
tie-on label 743.3 *means of identification*
tiepin 373.8 *fastening*; 542.7 *jewellery*
tier 411.10 *layer*; 411.2 *level*; 137.5 *social class*
tierce 199.6 *third*
tierceron ridge rib 20.7 *vault*
tie the knot 755.5 *contract*; 570.15 *marry*
tie the nuptial knot 570.16 *join in marriage*
tie the wedding knot 570.16 *join in marriage*
tie to 211.6 *add*
tie together 108.7 *relate to*
tie up 251.12 *gag*; 747.16 *join*; 312.4 *land*; 335.8 *overpower*; 763.7 *possess*; 108.7 *relate to*; 393.1 *repair*; 323.10 *sail*
tie-up 570.2 *alliance*; 747.7 *association*; 108.1 *relatedness*
tie up with 570.19 *merge*
tiff 751.6 *argue*; 701.1, 751.2 *argument*; 242.8, 624.5 *quarrel*
tiffany 527.8 *transparent thing*
Tiffany glass 24.1 *ceramics*
tiffin 557.12 *meal*
tiger 613.7 *courageous person*; 567.16 *male animal*; 541.5 *variegated thing*; 380.4 *violent creature*
tiger hunt 633.2 *chase*
tiger hunter 633.6 *hunter*
tigerish 71.28 *carnivorous*; 380.6 *violent*
tiger-like 71.28 *carnivorous*
tiger's-eye 541.5 *variegated thing*
tight 267.9 *adhesive*; 690.1 *drunk*; 232.8 *full*; 252.7 *invulnerable*; 166.5 *limited*; 682.1 *mean*; 151.1 *narrow*; 230.1 *perfect*; 64.6 *rugger*; 191.7 *smaller*; 418.2 *tough*
tight-arse 682.5 *miser*; 684.4 *self-restrained person*
tight-arsed 682.1 *mean*; 684.8 *self-restrained*
tight corner 264.6 *critical situation*
tighten 191.6 *become smaller*; 418.9 *harden*; 191.5 *make smaller*; 151.10 *narrow*; 50.15 *sail*
tightened 191.7 *smaller*
tightened headband 814.15 *instrument of torture*
tightening 191.8 *contracting*; 191.1 *contraction*
tighten one's belt 782.12 *be poor*; 684.5 *be self-restrained*; 687.5 *fast*; 680.6 *save*
tighten one's grip 360.6 *retain*
tighten up on 407.22 *pacify*
tightfisted 682.1 *mean*; 360.9 *retentive*
tightfistedness 682.3 *parsimony*
tight grip 360.1 *retention*
tight-knit 269.3 *concise*
tight-lipped 736.17 *noncommittal*; 732.1 *shy*; 506.3 *silent*
tightly 267.11 *cohesively*; 151.11 *narrowly*; 418.12 *toughly*
tightness 191.1 *contraction*; 418.5 *hardness*; 151.5 *narrowness*; 682.3 *parsimony*
tight rein 647.1 *severity*
tightrope walker 336.5 *athlete*; 21.31 *circus performer*
tights 551.20 *legwear*
tight scrum 64.3 *rugby play*
tight ship 647.1 *severity*
tight skirt 551.6 *skirt*
tight spot 264.6 *critical situation*; 159.5 *little space*
tight squeeze 264.6 *critical situation*; 159.5 *little space*; 151.6 *narrow place*
tight-wad 682.5 *miser*
tigon 412.5 *hybrid*
tigress 568.14 *female animal*; 71.18 *female mammal*; 625.3 *irascible person*; 380.4 *violent creature*; 651.9 *vixen*
Tigris 90.5 *other major rivers*
tiki 11.6 *talisman*
tikka 25.49 *Indian dish*
tilde 5.36 *accent*; 742.7 *punctuation*
tile 175.1 *base*; 435.2 *building material*; 24.8 *ceramic object*; 550.24 *coat*; 551.15 *headgear*; 24.11 *make ceramics*; 38.26 *masonry*; 317.4 *road surface*; 550.27 *roof*; 411.4 *slice*
tiled 550.36 *covered*
tile painter 24.7 *potter*
tiler 578.2 *artisan*; 550.17 *coverer*
tiles 550.9 *floor covering*; 550.7 *overhead covering*
tiling 24.8 *ceramic object*; 550.9 *floor covering*
till 780.21; 275.26 *all the time*; 210.5 *computer*; 43.17 *farm*; 30.38 *glacier*; 244.1 *improve*; 50.8 *punting*; 439.4 *storage*
tillable 43.20 *farmable*
tillage 43.5 *cultivation*; 243.13 *development*
till doomsday 279.11 *eternally*
tilled 43.20 *farmable*
tiller 43.15 *agriculturist*; 579.5 *guide*; 323.5 *navigation*; 50.3 *parts of a sailing boat*; 438.1 *tool*
tiller of the soil 43.15 *agriculturist*
till hell freezes over 202.12 *eternally*; 131.27 *to the end*
till now 284.23 *before now*; 3.24 *historically*
till the soil 43.17 *farm*
tilt 176.11 *angle*; 189.6 *be oblique*; 120.5 *be unequal*; 586.37 *fight*; 51.2 *grip*; 120.1 *inequality*; 367.7 *lean*; 189.1 *obliqueness*; 176.2 *obliquity*; 305.6, 305.14 *slide*; 330.23 *throw*
tilt at 381.1 *attack*; 633.10 *chase*
tilt at windmills 238.9 *waste effort*
tilted 176.8 *oblique*
tilter 586.3 *athlete*
tilth 43.5 *cultivation*
tilting 189.4 *oblique*
tilting at windmills 477.4 *ideality*
tilting of the scales 120.1 *inequality*
tilt the bowl 51.7 *bowl*
Tim 281.6 *clock*
timber 79.3; 23.17 *carpenter*; 38.25 *construction material*; 435.1 *materials*; 23.12 *wood*
timbered 23.16 *joined*; 79.16 *wooded*
timbering 356.8 *construction*; 23.12 *wood*
timber joint 23.10 *carpenter's term*
timberland 79.4 *trees*
timber line 79.4 *trees*
timberman 79.8 *forester*
timber production 79.7
timber tree 79.1 *tree*
timberwork 23.12 *wood*; 23.8 *woodwork*
timber yard 79.7 *timber production*
timbre 729.3 *mode of speech*
Timbuktu 145.3 *distant place*
Time 275
time 28.8; **275.1**; **275.16**; **277.2**; 357.6 *destroyer*; 251.4 *detention*; 209.4 *interval*; 281.14 *keep time*; 298.10 *make regular*; 26.10 *measure*; 276.1 *period*; 815.4 *prison sentence*; 292.1 *season*; 141.21 *space*; 18.19 *tempo*
time after time 297.1 *frequently*; 112.23 *repeatedly*
time allowed 59.9 *jumping*
time and again 297.1 *frequently*; 112.23 *repeatedly*
time and motion study 579.3 *management*
time and tide 275.2 *passage of time*
time badly 465.10 *misjudge*; 288.6 *take untimely action*
time-based 275.20 *temporal*
time beater 281.11 *person keeping time*
time bomb 587.16 *bomb*; 281.10 *signal*; 379.1 *trap*
time clock 275.13 *timer*
time-consuming 441.8 *wasteful*
time copy 741.10 *copy*
timed 68.13 *ice-skating*; 298.11 *regular*; 285.10 *synchronized*
timedivision multiplex 692.14 *radio transmission*
time flies 277.2 *time*
time for oneself 580.1 *leisure*
time-fuse 437.2 *lighter*; 281.10 *signal*
time-honoured 275.21 *lasting through time*; 632.11 *normal*; 296.12 *olden*; 667.12 *respected*; 1.14 *societal*
time immemorial 296.3 *antiquity*; 3.9 *distant past*; 277.5 *long duration*; 284.1 *past time*
time indicator 742.5 *indicator*
time interval 146.1 *interval*
time it right 275.16 *time*
timekeeper 275.14; **281.5**; 47.3 *athlete*; 742.5 *indicator*; 52.7 *judo*; 52.8 *karate*; 26.9 *measurer*; 281.11 *person keeping time*; 744.9 *recorder*; 742.8 *signer*
Timekeeping 281
timekeeping 281.1; **281.17**; 275.10 *chronometry*
time-killing 620.4 *boring*
time lag 133.3 *interval*; 294.1 *lateness*
time lapse 141.8 *intervening space*
time-lapse photography 41.1 *photography*

timeless 279.8 *eternal*
timelessness 279.1 *eternity*
time limit 59.9 *jumping*
Timeliness 287
timeliness 287.1; 239.3 *convenience*; 293.1 *earliness*
timely 287.6; 239.1 *convenient*; 293.12 *early*; 292.14 *seasonable*; 447.6 *topical*
time machine 275.1 *time*
time measurement 275.7
time of adversity 249.4
time of day 281.3 *chronology*
time off 580.2; 263.1 *ease*; 98.5 *leave of absence*; 226.3 *pause*
time of night 281.3 *chronology*
time of plenty 248.3
time of sorrow 249.4 *time of adversity*
time of the month 560.11 *menstruation*
Time of Troubles 3.10 *past age*
time of war 585.4 *belligerency*
time of year 292.1 *season*
time on one's hands 620.2 *boring thing*; 341.1 *inaction*; 580.1 *leisure*
time-out 46.5 *game time*; 133.3, 275.6 *interval*; 226.3 *pause*; 580.2 *time off*
time out of mind 296.3 *antiquity*; 3.24 *historically*; 284.22 *in the past*
time period 276.2
timepiece 281.5 *timekeeper*; 275.13 *timer*
timer 275.13; 49.2 *basketball player*; 281.10 *signal*
time-related 275.20 *temporal*
time-rock unit 30.41 *geological time*
timer's desk 49.3 *basketball equipment*
times 27.91 *add*; 27.88 *equal to*
time-saving 263.5 *labour-saving*; 680.4 *thrifty*
time-saving device 392.7 *convenience*
Timese 741.9 *news story*
timeserver 117.6 *conformist*; 645.3 *cunning person*; 479.9 *equivocator*; 664.3 *sycophant*; 700.21 *traitor*
timeserving 239.3 *convenience*; 645.4 *cunning*; 479.11 *equivocating*; 664.2 *sycophancy*; 664.7 *sycophantic*
times gone by 284.1 *past time*
time-share apartment 764.1 *joint possession*
time-share owner 764.3 *participant*
time sharing 40.19 *computing terms*; 764.5 *jointly possessing*; 764.1 *joint possession*
time shift 286.1 *different time*
time signal 281.10, 742.4 *signal*
time signature 275.12 *musical time*; 18.17 *notation*
timeslip 275.1 *time*
time-space 141.9 *fourth dimension*
Time Span 276
time span 556.1 *age*; 275.3 *duration*; 276.1 *period*
times past 284.1 *past time*
time's scythe 357.6 *destroyer*
Times Square 173.4 *centre of activity*; 87.3 *New York*
time's winged chariot 275.2 *passage of time*
time switch 281.10 *signal*
times without number 297.1 *frequently*
timetable 281.2; 281.14 *keep time*; 220.8 *list*; 220.5 *list of appointments*; 484.1 *plan*; 484.10 *plan out*; 693.5 *reference book*; 6.3 *subject*; 275.16 *time*
timetabled 220.11 *listed*
timetabling 281.1 *timekeeping*
time the enemy 275.2 *passage of time*
time the great healer 275.2 *passage of time*
time thrust 54.3 *fencing movements*
time to come 283.1 *future time*
time to kill 620.2 *boring thing*; 341.1 *inaction*; 580.1 *leisure*
time to oneself 580.1 *leisure*
time to spare 293.1 *earliness*; 580.1 *leisure*; 333.8 *slowness*
time travel 275.1 *time*
time traveller 286.1 *different time*
time-travel paradox 4.9 *philosophical problem*
time up 131.11 *finality*
time warp 286.1 *different time*; 133.3 *interval*; 275.1 *time*
time-wasting 238.2 *futile*
time without end 279.1 *eternity*
timeworn 296.12 *olden*
time zone 275.9; 166.4 *boundary marker*; 281.3 *chronology*
timid 639.3; 453.3 *confused*; 614.3 *cowardly*; 612.8 *fearful*; 655.9, 674.11, 732.1 *shy*; 337.12 *weak-willed*
timidity 639.13; 453.12 *confusion*; 614.1 *cowardice*; 655.2, 674.4, 732.3 *shyness*
timidly 614.5 *cravenly*; 612.15 *fearfully*; 674.18, 732.8 *shyly*; 655.14 *unsocially*; 337.14 *weakly*
timidness 674.4, 732.3 *shyness*
timing 516.4 *harmonics*; 68.7 *ice-dancing*; 298.1 *regularity*; 18.19 *tempo*; 281.1 *timekeeping*
timing device 281.10 *signal*; 275.13 *timer*
timocracy 781.9 *plutocracy*
timorous 614.3 *cowardly*; 612.8 *fearful*; 674.11, 732.1 *shy*; 337.12 *weak-willed*
timorously 614.5 *cravenly*; 612.15 *fearfully*; 674.18 *shyly*
timorousness 614.1 *cowardice*; 612.2 *fearfulness*; 337.2 *indecisiveness*; 674.4 *shyness*
timothy 43.12 *crop*
timpani 18.25 *musical instrument*
tin 410.6 *box*; 25.39 *loaf*; 359.5 *preserve*; 359.2 *preserver*; 410.21 *put in a container*; 238.6 *refuse*
tin bath 410.12 *bath*
tin can 410.6 *box*
tinct 529.10 *coloured*
tinctorial 529.10 *coloured*
tincture 412.4 *admixture*; 229.2 *attitude*; 529.15 *colour*; 529.3 *hue*
tinder 437.2 *lighter*
tinderbox 410.6 *box*; 437.2 *lighter*
tine 425.7 *sharp point*
tinea 83.5 *fungal association*
tin-enamel 24.11 *make ceramics*
tin-enamelled 24.10 *ceramic*
tin-enamelled ware 24.1 *ceramics*
tin fish 587.16 *bomb*
ting-a-ling 510.2 *ringing*
tinge 412.4 *admixture*; 529.15 *colour*; 529.3 *hue*; 412.8 *mix*; 728.6 *suggestion*
tinged 529.10 *coloured*; 412.12 *mixed*
tin-glaze 24.11 *make ceramics*
tin-glazed 24.10 *ceramic*
tin-glazed earthenware 24.1 *ceramics*
tingle 491.10 *be painful*; 492.13 *be touched by*; 488.11 *sense*; 488.3 *stimulus*
tingling 491.5 *painful*; 591.3 *sore*; 591.7 *soreness*
tingly 488.9 *exciting*
tin god 400.4 *absolute ruler*; 660.12 *impudent person*; 579.16 *official*
tin hat 384.7 *armour*; 551.15 *headgear*
tinily 159.8 *in a small way*
tininess 159.1 *littleness*
tinker 578.2 *artisan*; 645.5 *be cunning*; 218.5 *be insufficient*; 486.5 *be unskilful*; 245.4 *impair*; 342.17 *meddle*; 778.11 *pedlar*; 393.12 *repairer*; 492.11 *touch*; 486.10 *unskilled person*; 238.9 *waste effort*
tinkering 486.9 *bungling*; 218.8 *insufficiency*; 238.5 *waste of effort*
tinker's damn 712.1 *curse*; 124.8 *trifle*
tinker with 224.8 *cause change*; 492.11 *touch*
tinkle 608.13 *relieve oneself*; 510.10 *ring*; 510.2 *ringing*; 692.10 *telephone call*
tinkling 510.7 *ringing*
tin lizzie 320.16 *car*
tin mine 577.1 *workshop*
tinned 410.20 *containing*; 359.7 *preserved*
tinned food 557.7 *food*; 359.3 *preserved thing*
tinner 359.4 *preservationist*
tinning 410.20 *containing*; 359.1 *preservation*
tinnitus 504.8 *something heard*
tinny 513.9 *shrill*
tin-opener 308.2 *opener*
Tin Pan Alley 18.12
tinpot 793.10 *shoddy*
tinsel 124.9 *bauble*; 699.12 *fake*; 700.6 *imitation*; 522.2 *quality of light*
tinselled 699.37 *fake*
tinselly 522.16 *bright*
tinsmith 578.2 *artisan*
tint 28.28, 529.15 *colour*; 529.3 *hue*; 19.19 *paint*; 529.4 *pigment*
tinted 529.10 *coloured*; 19.27 *painted*; 527.3 *semitransparent*
tinted glasses 518.10 *visual aid*
tinting 19.2 *painting*
tintinnabular 510.7 *ringing*
tintinnabulate 510.10 *ring*
tintinnabulation 510.2 *ringing*
tintometer 529.8 *chromatics*; 26.8 *meter*
tint tool 23.11 *woodworking tool*
tin whistle 513.3 *shrillness*
tiny 159.7 *little*; 196.6 *small*; 124.4 *trivial*
tiny tot 555.9 *child*
tip 693.14; 693.7, 713.1 *advice*; 176.11 *angle*; 671.6 *be grateful*; 189.6 *be oblique*; 331.13 *blow*; 813.7 *bounty*; 480.17 *bribe*; 211.4 *extra*; 679.7, 768.2 *gift*; 768.5 *give*; 367.7 *lean*; 131.7 *limit*; 408.4 *litter*; 189.1 *obliqueness*; 785.3, 813.11 *pay*; 483.5 *positive stimulus*; 765.5 *profit*; 671.3 *recognition*; 238.6 *refuse*; 785.11 *remunerate*; 767.8 *sink*; 439.4 *storage*; 174.1 *summit*; 331.6 *tap*; 711.5 *warn*; 711.1 *warning*
tip in 49.6 *play basketball*
tip-in 49.4 *playing terms*
tip off 6.22 *educate*; 693.14 *tip*; 711.5 *warn*
tip-off 693.7 *advice*; 711.1 *warning*
tipped 174.6 *topped*
tipper 768.4 *giver*; 693.10 *informer*
tippet 551.14 *neckwear*; 7.11 *vestment*
Tippex™ 521.8 *make invisible*; 521.6 *that which makes invisible*
tipple 558.13, 690.13 *drink*; 690.8 *get drunk*
tippler 690.17 *drunkard*
tippling 558.16, 690.11 *drinking*; 690.5 *drunken*
tipsily 690.18 *drunkenly*
tipsiness 690.10 *drunkenness*
tipstaff 16.11 *British law officer*
tipster 475.9 *forecaster*; 59.15 *horse person*; 693.10 *informer*
tipsy 690.2 *slightly drunk*
tip the balance 414.12 *be heavy*
tip the board 50.18 *windsurf*
tip the scales 414.12 *be heavy*; 120.5 *be unequal*; 395.9 *change*
tip the wink 669.12 *accept*; 750.28 *consent*
tiptoe 736.11 *conceal oneself*
tip to one side 189.6 *be oblique*
tiptop 121.14, 235.2 *best*; 174.8 *on top*; 174.1 *summit*; 174.5 *top*
tip top 55.3 *fishing tackle*
tip-top condition 259.3 *health*
tip well 679.10 *be generous*; 813.11 *pay*
tirade 733.1 *address*; 670.8 *berating*; 270.1 *diffuseness*; 722.1 *dissertation*; 729.8 *speech*
tiramisu 25.47 *Italian dish*
tire 620.6 *be boring*; 261.5 *be fatigued*; 247.6 *fail*; 261.6 *fatigue*; 388.4 *succumb*
tired 261.2, 620.5 *bored*; 245.12 *deteriorated*; 261.1 *fatigued*; 335.12 *impotent*; 260.21 *unhealthy*; 337.11 *weakened*
tired and emotional 690.2 *slightly drunk*
tired bones 245.9 *dilapidation*
tired brain 261.7 *fatigue*
tired-eyed 261.1 *fatigued*
tired-looking 261.1 *fatigued*
tiredly 261.8
Tiredness 261
tiredness 335.4 *disability*; 261.7 *fatigue*; 337.3 *poor health*
tired of 620.5 *bored*
tired of living 620.5 *bored*
tired out 261.1 *fatigued*; 335.12 *impotent*
tired to death 620.5 *bored*; 261.1 *fatigued*
tireless 342.20 *industrious*; 638.2 *tenacious*; 576.10 *working*
tirelessness 342.8 *assiduity*; 640.2 *commitment*
tireless worker 342.10 *busy person*
tire oneself out 261.5 *be fatigued*
tire out 261.6 *fatigue*
tiresome 620.4 *boring*; 261.4 *fatiguing*; 240.1, 264.13 *inconvenient*
tiresomely 240.6 *inconveniently*
tiresomeness 620.1 *boredom*
tire to death 261.6 *fatigue*
tiring 620.4 *boring*; 261.4 *fatiguing*; 576.11 *laborious*
tiringly 261.9; 620.8 *boringly*
tiro 6.7 *learner*
tisane 558.3 *tea*; 394.7 *tonic*
Tishah b'Av 687.3 *fast day*
Tisiphone 624.7 *gods and goddesses of anger*
tissue 256.11 *cleaning cloth*; 403.2 *fabric*; 153.11 *fineness*; 554.2 *living matter*; 404.5 *textile*
tissue culture 34.6 *cell biology*
tissue paper 435.3 *paper*; 337.5 *weak thing*; 550.4 *wrapping*
tissue sample 35.7 *diagnosis*
tissue structure 34.4 *anatomy*
tit 72.6 *songbird*
Titan 158.10 *big person*; 336.6 *muscleman*
Titaness 158.10 *big person*
Titania 11.11 *ghost*
titanic 158.15 *big*; 32.34 *elemental*
titanium white 531.8 *whitener*
titanous 32.34 *elemental*
titbit 495.3 *appetizer*; 235.7 *elite*; 557.14 *mouthful*
titbits 557.7 *food*
titch 159.4 *little person*; 149.5 *short person*
titchy 159.7 *little*
titfer 551.15 *headgear*
tit for tat 759.1 *exchange*; 110.1 *interchange*; 108.2 *interrelatedness*; 385.1 *retaliation*; 385.6 *with vengeance*
tit-for-tat 759.6 *in exchange*; 110.4 *reciprocal*
tithe 790.12 *charge*; 768.6 *give to charity*; 768.3 *offering*; 205.1 *part*; 790.7 *tax*; 201.6 *ten*; 124.8 *trifle*
tithing 768.1 *giving*; 86.5 *state*
Tithonus 296.2 *old people*
Titian 536.1 *orange*; 535.3 *red-haired*
Titicaca 88.5 *other major lakes*
titillate 488.13 *arouse sensation*; 496.13 *be piquant*; 617.15 *cause desire*; 490.9 *give pleasure*
titillated 595.6 *liking*; 490.7 *pleased*
titillating 488.9 *exciting*; 796.12 *indecent*; 595.5 *likable*; 617.11 *lustful*; 490.6 *pleasant*; 496.10 *stimulating*
titillatingly 595.10 *with great liking*
titillation 595.1 *liking*; 490.1 *physical pleasure*; 496.4 *stimulation*; 488.3 *stimulus*
tit in the wringer 264.7 *awkward situation*
titivate 545.8, 547.15 *beautify*; 551.33 *dress up*; 244.1 *improve*
titivation 244.5 *improvement*
Title 575
title 733.11; 744.2 *certificate*; 47.5 *competition*; 542.4 *honour*; 743.3 *means of identification*; 721.8 *name*; 763.1 *possession*; 440.1 *property*; 813.1 *reward*
titled 743.12 *identified*
title deed 744.2 *certificate*; 253.2 *promise*
titled person 573.1 *nobleman*
titleholder 575.4; 52.4 *boxer*; 235.8 *exceller*; 485.4 *skilled person*; 246.5 *victorious person*
titleless 574.3 *common*
title page 130.10 *introduction*
title part 21.23 *role*
title role 21.23 *role*
title to fame 235.6 *worth*
Titoism 12.1 *government*
titration 32.18 *gravimetric analysis*
titre 32.18 *gravimetric analysis*
tits 182.2 *bulge*
titter 514.2 *cry of joy*; 514.11, 599.14, 600.8 *laugh*; 600.3 *laughter*
titterer 600.4 *rejoicer*
tittering 600.10 *laughing*; 600.3 *laughter*
tittle 196.3 *fragment*; 159.3 *little piece*; 124.8 *trifle*
tittle-tattle 644.7 *be curious*; 734.2 *chat*; 644.2 *prying*; 504.8 *something heard*; 731.3 *talk*
tittle-tattler 734.8 *chatterer*; 644.4 *meddler*; 731.4 *talker*
titubant 305.18 *falling*
titubate 305.12 *drop*
titubation 305.4 *fall*
titular 12.10 *governing*; 476.8 *supposed*
titular head 335.5 *powerless person*
tiz-woz 327.4 *fuss*
tizz 327.4 *fuss*
tizzy 624.4 *anger*; 327.4 *fuss*
T-junction 320.3 *carriageway*
TLC 32.17 *analysis*
TNT 357.7 *agent of destruction*; 587.15 *explosive*
to 314.18 *into*; 317.17 *via*
to a certain extent 205.12 *partly*; 166.8 *within limits*
to a cinder 493.17 *warmly*
toad 664.3 *sycophant*
toadeater 664.3 *sycophant*

to a degree 209.11; 685.9 *moderately*; 205.12 *partly*
toad-in-the-hole 25.44 *British dish*
toadish 73.13 *amphibian*
toadlet 73.8 *young amphibian*
toadlike 73.13 *amphibian*
toadstool 83.2 *mushroom*
to advantage 392.36 *helpfully*
toady 388.2 *appeaser*; 471.14 *be solicitous*; 677.11 *be sycophantic*; 479.9 *equivocator*; 664.9 *fawn*; 599.7 *person who humours*; 421.13 *smooth over*; 388.4 *succumb*; 664.3, 677.7 *sycophant*
toadying 599.11 *humouring*; 388.5 *submitting*; 664.2 *sycophancy*; 664.7 *sycophantic*
toadyish 677.16 *sycophantic*
toadyism 677.5 *sycophancy*
toady to 658.13 *defer to*; 599.15 *humour*
to a great degree 209.11 *to a degree*
to a hair 273.8 *accurately*
to a limited extent 231.11 *imperfectly*
to all appearances 96.19, 525.15 *apparently*; 171.15 *externally*; 520.11 *visibly*
to all places 141.19
to and fro 326.18; 227.15 *changeably*; 759.8 *in exchange*; 110.10 *reciprocally*; 298.15 *regularly*
to-and-fro 300.17 *directional*; 326.13 *oscillating*; 298.11 *regular*
to-and-fro movement 300.5 *circuition*; 298.1 *regularity*
to a nicety 273.8 *accurately*
to an increasing extent 213.8 *increasingly*
to apologize 808.8 *penitently*
to approval 669.26 *approvably*
to a small degree 209.11 *to a degree*
toast 569.4 *act of friendship*; 428.19 *bake*; 658.10 *be courteous*; 493.14 *be hot*; 654.11 *be sociable*; 25.38 *bread*; 534.7 *brown*; 462.14 *commemorate*; 601.17 *congratulate*; 25.55 *cook*; 658.3 *courtesies*; 558.2 *drink*; 558.14 *drink to*; 601.6 *tribute*
toasted 534.2 *browned*; 25.56 *culinary*; 493.13 *heated*
toasted sandwich 25.11 *sandwich*
toaster 493.4 *burner*; 25.5 *cooker*
toastie 25.38 *bread*
toasting 25.8 *cooking technique*
toastmaster 579.14 *leader*
toast of the town 235.8 *exceller*
to a T 273.8 *accurately*
to atone for 775.7 *redemptively*
to a turn 230.7 *perfectly*
tobacco 496.7; **496.11**; 43.12 *crop*
tobacco auctioneer 507.5 *loud person*
tobacco belt 43.11 *farmland*
tobacco leaf 534.5 *brown thing*
tobacconist 778.13 *retailer*; 496.8 *smoking*
tobacco pouch 496.7 *tobacco*
tobacco sachet 496.7 *tobacco*
to be 283.11 *future*
to be blamed 802.16 *in the wrong*
to be clear 719.18 *in other words*
to be disposed of 767.14 *for sale*
to be exact 698.39 *accurately*
to be expected 216.11 *on average*; 104.11 *probably*
to be jumped at 469.15 *chosen*
to be specific 139.28 *specially*
to be sure 454.12 *assuredly*
to be taken seriously 123.5 *important*
to bits 372.21 *apart*; 375.7 *to pieces*
to blame 670.36 *blameworthy*; 806.5 *guilty*
toboggan 68.16 *bobsled*; 320.10 *sled*; 305.14 *slide*
toboggan chute 68.9 *bobsledding*
tobogganist 68.11 *skier*
toboggan race 68.9 *bobsledding*
toboggan racing 68.9 *bobsledding*
toboggan run 68.9 *bobsledding*
to boot 211.10 *additionally*
toby jug 24.8 *ceramic object*; 410.13 *drinking vessel*
to capacity 232.10 *fully*
Tocharian 5.11 *family of languages*
to coin a phrase 745.4 *proverbially*
to come 283.11, 756.15 *future*
to convince 483.14 *influentially*
to crown all 123.9 *importantly*; 121.17 *supremely*
tocsin 711.2 *danger signal*
today 282.9 *at present*; 275.27 *at what time*; 282.1, 285.2 *present time*
toddle 300.15 *walk*
toddle along 313.1 *depart*; 333.1 *move slowly*
toddler 555.9 *child*
toddling 300.17 *directional*
toddy 558.7 *alcoholic drink*; 496.6 *cordial*
to death 620.8 *boringly*
to design 482.15 *according to plan*
to-do 342.1 *activity*; 701.1 *argument*; 328.5 *commotion*; 408.9 *disorder*; 727.1 *exaggeration*; 327.4 *fuss*
toe 175.2 *foot*; 56.4 *golf club*; 492.7 *sense organ*
toeclip 320.11 *bicycle part*
toe dance 22.8 *ballet*; 22.2 *dance*
toehold 308.10 *opportunity*; 360.1 *retention*
toe in the door 308.10 *opportunity*
toe in the water 752.2 *tentative offer*
toe jump 68.6 *ice-skating*
toenail 418.7 *hard substance*
toe piece 68.5 *ski equipment*
toe the line 160.8 *be formal*; 111.11 *be regular*; 117.8 *comply*; 750.25 *conform*; 663.5 *obey*; 140.17 *obey orders*
toe traverse 62.3 *climbing technique*
to excess 219.8 *excessively*
to explain 719.18 *in other words*
to express appreciation 671.8 *gratefully*
toff 573.1 *nobleman*
toffee 267.4 *adherent*; 534.5 *brown thing*; 498.4 *confectionery*; 25.41 *sweet*
toffee apple 25.41 *sweet*
toffeenose 622.13 *proud person*; 673.7 *vain person*
toffee-nosed 622.17 *conceited*
to fill the bill 239.7 *conveniently*
toft 43.6 *farm*; 440.3 *historic property terms*
tofu 25.21 *meat substitute*
toga 551.16 *robe*
toga virilis 551.16 *robe*
together 223.21; **376.51**; 310.12 *convergently*; 747.20 *cooperatively*; 750.31 *in accord*; 374.10 *in combination*; 764.6 *in common*; 15.13 *industrially*; 749.7 *pacifically*; 460.4 *sane*; 285.12 *simultaneously*
togetherness 223.3 *companionship*; 747.2 *fellowship*; 569.1 *friendship*; 654.8 *good company*
together with 211.10 *additionally*; 223.24, 747.22 *with*
togged 551.30 *dressed-up*
toggery 551.1 *dress*
toggle 373.8 *fastening*
toggle pin 373.8 *fastening*
to good effect 395.14 *influentially*
to good purpose 246.16 *successfully*
togs 551.1 *dress*
to hand 97.10, 282.8 *available*; 147.9 *near*; 97.16 *on the spot*
to hell and back 141.19 *to all places*
toil 264.3 *difficult task*; 576.1, 576.6 *work*
toil and trouble 576.4 *exertion*
toiler 342.10 *busy person*; 578.1 *worker*
toilet 560.14; **767.7**; 256.5 *ablutions*; 547.3 *beauty treatment*; 551.2 *dressing*; 560.13 *lavatory*; 736.6 *privacy*; 565.7 *room*
toilet bag 547.5 *make-up box*
toilet bowl 767.7 *toilet*
toilet paper 256.11 *cleaning cloth*; 435.3 *paper*
toiletries 547.6; 502.2 *fragrant thing*
toilet roll 256.11 *cleaning cloth*
toilet soap 256.9 *cleaning agent*
toilette 547.3 *beauty treatment*; 551.2 *dressing*
toilet tissue 256.11 *cleaning cloth*
toilet-trained 560.26 *urinary*
toilet water 502.2 *fragrant thing*; 547.6 *toiletries*
toilsome 264.10 *difficult*; 576.11 *laborious*
to infinity 279.11 *eternally*; 202.10 *infinitely*
toing and froing 326.1 *oscillation*
tokamak 28.76 *fusion reactor*
Tokay 558.9 *wine*
to keep 360.11 *tenaciously*
token 139.3 *characteristic*; 768.2 *gift*; 716.4 *indication*; 738.14 *manifest*; 738.10 *manifestation*; 743.3 *means of identification*; 462.3, 794.3 *memento*; 742.1 *sign*; 769.2 *something received*; 124.4 *trivial*
token economy 36.3 *psychiatric treatment*
tokenism 699.3, 700.3 *hypocrisy*
tokenistic 700.37 *hypocritical*
token of esteem 768.2 *gift*
token of one's gratitude 671.3 *recognition*
token of remembrance 794.3 *memento*
Tokyo 87.6 *other cities*
told 3.19 *chronicled*
Toledo 587.8 *sharp weapon*
to leeward 50.20 *offshore*
to leg 53.20 *in*
tolerability 618.4 *mediocrity*; 609.3 *satisfactoriness*
tolerable 216.3, 618.10 *mediocre*; 235.5 *not bad*; 231.4 *ordinary*; 609.6 *satisfactory*; 413.10 *supportable*
tolerableness 216.6 *mediocrity*
tolerably 217.9 *enough*; 618.20 *unexceptionally*
tolerance 650.1 *benevolence*; 4.3 *detachment*; 37.3 *drug*; 649.2 *forgivingness*; 250.1 *freedom*; 648.1 *leniency*; 757.1 *permission*
tolerant 650.6 *benevolent*; 4.18 *detached*; 265.13 *easy-going*; 250.9, 657.10 *free*; 341.3 *inactive*; 648.4 *lenient*; 649.5 *merciful*; 589.7 *peaceful*; 757.8 *permitting*; 685.7 *politically moderate*
tolerantly 650.10 *benevolently*; 649.14 *forgivingly*; 250.20 *freely*; 648.6 *leniently*; 757.9 *with permission*
tolerate 413.12 *bear*; 650.8 *be benevolent*; 250.14 *be free*; 648.3 *be lenient*; 341.4 *not act*; 757.3 *permit*; 649.12 *show mercy*
toleration 650.1 *benevolence*; 250.1, 657.4 *freedom*; 648.1 *leniency*; 757.1 *permission*
to let 752.17 *offered*
to little purpose 247.12 *unsuccessfully*
toll 790.8 *levy*; 211.2 *mathematical addition*; 711.7 *raise the alarm*; 509.12, 510.10 *ring*; 510.2 *ringing*
toll bridge 38.21, 317.9 *bridge*; 373.5 *road*
toll call 692.10 *telephone call*
Tollen's reagent 33.5 *sugar test*
tollgate 314.6 *means of entry*; 378.2 *obstacle*
tolling 510.7 *ringing*
toll road 317.3, 320.2, 373.5 *road*
toll the knell 583.8 *bury*
Toltecs 284.6 *people of the past*
tom 71.10 *cat*; 71.17 *male mammal*; 568.7 *prostitute*
tomahawk 587.8 *sharp weapon*
to make amends 807.8 *penitently*
Tom and Jerry 113.3 *opposites*
to matchwood 372.21 *apart*
tomato 535.7 *red thing*
tomato juice 558.6 *soft drink*
tomato ketchup 25.15 *sauce*
tomato sauce 25.15 *sauce*
tomato soup 25.13 *soup*
tomb 582.8 *after death*; 309.4 *closed place*; 356.8 *construction*; 583.6 *grave*; 744.11 *monument*; 301.3 *resting place*
tombola 107.3 *equal chance*; 412.3 *miscellany*
tomboy 555.8 *young woman*
tombstone 583.4 *funeral objects*; 744.11 *monument*
tom cat 567.16 *male animal*
Tom Collins 558.8 *mixed drink*
Tom, Dick, and Harry 574.2 *the common people*; 675.6 *vulgar herd*
Tom, Dick, or Harry 216.7 *average person*
tomfoolery 697.3; 459.2 *act of folly*
tommy 585.11 *recruit*; 586.8 *soldier*
Tommy Atkins 586.8 *soldier*
Tommy gun™ 587.11 *guns*
tomogram 35.7 *diagnosis*
tomography 35.7 *diagnosis*
tomorrow 286.3 *another time*; 275.27 *at what time*; 283.1 *future time*; 283.14 *in the future*
tomorrow afternoon 283.1 *future time*
tomorrow evening 283.1 *future time*
tomorrow morning 283.1 *future time*
tomorrow night 283.1 *future time*
Tom Thumb 159.4 *little person*; 149.5 *short person*
tom-tom 509.1 *drumming*
tom turkey 72.10 *male bird*
ton 414.9 *avoirdupois weight*; 780.3 *fortune*; 201.9 *treble figures*
tonal 18.30 *harmonic*; 5.39 *of language*; 729.18 *phonetic*
tonality 516.4 *harmonics*; 18.21 *tone*
tonal language 5.10 *language type*
tonally 5.48 *linguistically*
tonal range 41.8 *composition*
tonal sequence 516.4 *harmonics*
tone 18.21; 17.3 *aspect of fiction*; 170.3 *atmosphere*; 229.2 *attitude*; 529.15 *colour*; 631.1 *conduct*; 692.11 *dialling*; 422.1 *elasticity*; 259.3 *health*; 529.3 *hue*; 729.3 *mode of speech*; 18.16, 28.20 *musical note*; 19.19 *paint*; 500.4 *reputation*; 221.1 *state*; 724.1 *style*; 104.2 *tendency*; 19.4 *treatment*; 317.1 *way*
to near starvation 687.7 *abstemiously*
tone control 692.18 *radio*; 504.10 *sound quality*
toned 529.10 *coloured*
toned-down 728.19 *downplayed*
tone-deaf 505.4 *deaf*; 646.1 *naive*
tone deafness 505.1 *deafness*
tone down 529.15 *colour*; 530.6 *decolour*; 419.14 *ease*; 685.4 *moderate*; 136.15 *modify*; 728.22 *play down*; 524.11 *tarnish*
toneless 530.7 *colourless*; 505.7 *unheard*; 517.9 *unmelodious*
tonelessly 530.9 *colourlessly*; 505.12 *deafly*
tone of voice 631.1 *conduct*; 729.3 *mode of speech*
tonepad 40.7 *peripheral*
tone row 18.20 *key*
tone up 244.1 *improve*
Tonga Trench 30.16 *ocean floor*
tongs 360.3 *tools for gripping*
tongue 557.16 *eating utensil*; 729.1 *faculty of speech*; 59.8 *hunting*; 25.31 *offal*; 729.5 *organ of speech*; 92.5 *peninsula*; 18.38 *sound*; 5.3 *spoken language*
tongue-in-cheek 676.3 *affected*; 700.1 *deception*; 700.35 *deceptive*; 677.12 *flattering*; 699.3 *hypocrisy*; 699.31, 702.10 *hypocritical*
tongue-lash 670.21 *berate*; 712.6 *vilify*
tongue-lashing 670.8 *berating*
tongueless 506.3 *silent*
tongue-tied 730.11 *speechless*
tonic 394.7; 496.6 *cordial*; 37.3 *drug*; 37.4 *drug type*; 422.6 *elastic*; 259.2 *healthful*; 558.8 *mixed drink*; 18.16 *musical note*; 480.19 *persuasive*; 729.18 *phonetic*; 581.6 *refresher*; 581.3 *refreshing*; 394.17 *remedial*; 37.17 *stimulating*; 483.3 *stimulus*; 336.4 *strengthening*
tonic-clonic fit 461.3 *mental deterioration*
tonicity 422.1 *elasticity*
tonic sol-fa 18.17 *notation*
tonic water 558.6 *soft drink*; 394.7 *tonic*
tonight 282.9 *at present*; 275.27 *at what time*; 282.1 *present time*
toning 529.11 *colourful*
tonjon 320.6 *litter*
tonnage 414.4 *heaviness*; 406.2 *load*; 158.1 *size*
tonnage and poundage 790.8 *levy*
tonnara 74.7 *fishing*
to no avail 238.10 *uselessly*
to no extent 94.14 *not at all*
ton of bricks 414.11 *weight*
tonometer 26.8 *meter*
tonometric 26.16 *micrometric*
tonometry 26.2 *micrometry*
tonoplast 34.8 *cell organ*
to no purpose 247.12 *unsuccessfully*; 238.10 *uselessly*
tons 208.3 *profuseness*
tonsillectomy 394.12 *surgery*
tonsillitis 260.9 *respiratory disease*
tonsure 552.7 *depilation*
tonsured 552.13 *hairless*
tontine 765.4 *earnings*; 788.3 *income*; 764.1 *joint possession*; 769.2 *something received*
ton-up 332.1 *swift*
tonus 422.1 *elasticity*
too 211.10 *additionally*
too bad 236.3 *bad*; 124.15 *no matter!*
too bad! 249.13
too big 158.15 *big*
too clever by half 673.11 *cocky*; 645.4 *cunning*; 458.6 *intelligent*
too clever for 645.4 *cunning*
too early 288.11; 288.18 *out of chronological order*; 293.16 *premature*; 293.20 *prematurely*
too far 145.10 *distantly*
too few 206.5 *few*; 206.7 *fewer*; 218.8 *insufficiency*; 218.1 *insufficient*
too few to mention 206.1 *few*

to off 53.20 in
too hot to handle 16.59 stolen
too human 804.13 venial
Tool 438
tool 438.1; 578.3 agent; 392.7 convenience; 700.22 dupe; 38.5 dynamic structure; 122.6 inferior; 348.2 instrument; 352.1 means; 561.8 organs of reproduction; 387.3 subordinate; 664.3 sycophant
too late 288.12; 294.16 at a late hour; 288.18 out of chronological order
toolbox 40.19 computing terms
toolhouse 438.2 toolroom
too little 218.8 insufficiency; 218.1 insufficient
tool-kit 438.2 toolroom
toolroom 438.2
tools 438.7 equipment; 352.1 means
tools for gripping 360.3
tool shed 438.2 toolroom
tools of the trade 352.1 means
tool-user 438.8 machinist
tool-using 438.9 mechanical
too many 219.1 excess; 219.6 excessive
too many cooks 486.9 bungling
too much 620.4 boring; 219.1 excess; 219.6 excessive; 219.8, 727.17 excessively; 217.8 plenty
too much for 335.14 powerlessly
to one's advantage 239.1 convenient; 237.4 profitable
to one's amazement 619.13 wonderfully
to one's chagrin 251.17 with self-restraint
to one's credit 811.7 eminently
to one's discredit 804.18 wickedly
to one's embarrassment 251.17 with self-restraint
to one's face 661.9 defiantly; 738.17 frankly; 703.20 manifestly
to one's fancy 593.22 lovable
to one's heart's content 217.9 enough
to one side 169.10 laterally
to one's liking 490.6 pleasant
to one's mind 593.22 lovable
to one's own design 482.15 according to plan
to one's own specifications 482.15 according to plan
to one's sorrow 798.13 destructively
to one's surprise 619.13 wonderfully
to one's taste 593.22 lovable; 490.6 pleasant
to one's utmost 576.12 laboriously
too precious for words 792.8 valuable
to order 397.16 commandingly; 663.10 obediently
too small 218.1 insufficient
too soon 288.18 out of chronological order; 293.16 premature; 293.20 prematurely
toot 711.2 danger signal; 507.1 loudness; 711.7 raise the alarm; 510.10 ring; 18.38 sound
tooth 425.11; 183.4 notch; 360.3 tools for gripping
toothache 491.2 painful condition
tooth and nail 576.12 laboriously; 380.10 violently
toothbrush 256.10 cleaning object
toothed 425.4; 183.7 notched; 77.18 of leaves
tooth for a tooth 759.1 exchange
tooth fungi 83.3 fungi
toothless 426.4; 71.26 insectivorous
toothlessly 426.11 smoothly
toothless mammal 71.13
toothlessness 426.8
toothless tiger 426.8 toothlessness
toothlike 425.4 toothed
toothpaste 256.9 cleaning agent; 394.3 prophylactic; 255.3 purifier
toothpick 256.10 cleaning object; 369.10 excavator; 425.8 sharp-pointed thing
tooth powder 394.3 prophylactic
toothsome 495.7 tasty
toothy 425.4 toothed
tootle 510.10 ring
toot one's own horn 673.17 be affected
tootsie roll 691.6 drug
Top 174
top 174.5; 174.7; 154.15 be high; 121.14, 797.2 best; 121.8 be superior; 304.14 climb; 550.24 coat; 181.5 cone; 550.2, 550.23 cover; 44.15 cultivate; 69.6 darts; 154.2 heights; 123.5 important; 121.2 leadership; 131.7 limit; 81.12 manage grassland; 79.18 manage trees; 551.24 part of garment; 230.1 perfect; 230.3 perfection; 492.3 press; 307.6 rotator; 551.8 shirt; 309.8 stop; 309.2 stopper; 121.4, 174.1 summit; 169.2 surface; 89.9 tower
toparchy 85.3 dominion
topaz 537.8 yellow thing
top banana 235.8 exceller; 599.6 humorist
top billing 740.8 public relations
top boots 551.19 footwear
top brass 123.4 bigwig; 235.8 exceller; 579.6 governing body; 395.5 influential person; 121.7 the best people
topcoat 551.12 coat; 411.1 layer
top condition 243.14 preparedness
top cushion 65.1 billiards
top dog 400.5 company leader; 235.8 exceller; 566.7 person; 396.10 person of authority; 121.5 superior
top drawer 235.7 elite; 121.7 the best people
top-drawer 573.4 aristocratic; 121.12 superior
top-dress 44.15 cultivate; 43.17 farm; 562.7 make fertile; 81.12 manage grassland
top dressing 562.3 fertilizer; 174.4 top layer
tope 558.13 drink; 690.8 get drunk; 10.13 shrine
topee 550.12 protective covering
toper 558.12 drinker; 690.17 drunkard; 686.5 self-indulgent person
to perfection 805.11 innocently; 230.7 perfectly
top-flight 121.15 excellent; 123.6 notable; 485.6 skilful; 235.1 worthy
top floor 174.3 architectural summit; 154.8 high thing
topgallant 174.2 head
topgallant mast 174.2 head; 154.8 high thing
topgallant sail 174.2 head
top gun 381.19 attacker
top hat 551.15 headgear
top-heaviness 120.1 inequality
top-heavy 486.3 clumsy; 158.16 fat; 414.3 ponderous; 120.3 unequal; 254.2 unsafe
Tophet 8.12 hell
top-hole 235.2 best; 797.1 good
topiarist 44.13 horticulturist
topiary 44.3 ornamental garden
Topic 447
topic 447.1; 701.4 gist; 447.2 issue; 701.3 line of argument; 694.1 meaning; 447.4 sphere; 476.1 supposition; 344.6 undertaking
topical 447.6; 701.10 arguable; 406.12 itemized; 295.10 new; 282.6 present; 476.8 supposed
topical administration 37.13 administration
topicality 295.1 newness; 282.4 up-to-dateness
topically 447.12; 701.18 arguably; 295.21 newly; 406.15 thematically
topic for discussion 447.3 matter of interest
topics 406.5 divisions
to pieces 375.7
toping 558.1 drinking; 690.5 drunken
topknot 174.2 head
top layer 174.4
to please oneself 588.8 anarchically
topless 552.11 exposed; 552.10 in dishabille
topless dancer 552.8 nude person
topless dress 551.7 frock
toplessness 552.1 undress
topless waitress 552.8 nude person
top-level 123.5 important; 579.17 managerial; 485.6 skilful
top-level meeting 579.7 council
top man 396.10 person of authority
top marks 797.9 the best
topmast 174.2 head; 154.8 high thing
topmost 121.14 best; 154.10 higher; 123.5 important; 89.7 mountainous; 174.5 top
topnotch 121.14, 235.2 best; 797.1 good; 485.6 skilful; 235.1 worthy
topnotcher 235.8 exceller; 797.16 superior person
top off 232.6 fill; 174.7 top
top of the bill 21.8 scene; 21.41 stagestruck
top of the class 246.4 successful person
top of the division 246.15 victorious
top of the inning 48.1 baseball
top of the league 246.15 victorious
top of the milk 558.5 milk
top of the pops 235.8 exceller
top of the pyramid 121.4 summit
top of the tree 129.2 priority
top of the world 174.1 summit
topographer 26.9 measurer
topographic 154.14 altimetric; 26.12 metrical; 86.16 regional
topographical 142.8 locational; 143.7 situational; 30.50 terrestrial
topographically 142.13; 30.66, 143.11 geographically; 26.17 measurably
topographical poetry 17.6 poetry
topographic surveying 38.17 civil engineering
topography 142.5; 30.6 continent; 154.5 height measure; 26.1 measurement; 143.1 situation
topological 27.68 mathematical
topology 27.47
top oneself 382.21 commit suicide
toponym 721.8 name
toponymy 721.7 nomenclature
top out 174.7 top
topped 174.6; 550.36 covered
topped off 232.8 full
topped up 232.8 full; 406.11 loaded
top people 235.7 elite; 121.7 the best people
topper 43.10 farm tool; 551.15 headgear; 551.11 jacket
top person 123.4 bigwig
topping 550.3 coating; 550.1 covering; 154.9 high; 89.7 mountainous; 174.4 top layer; 79.6 tree management; 235.1 worthy
topping lift 50.3 parts of a sailing boat
topping-out ceremony 232.3 completion
topping-up 436.1 provision
topple 367.3 bring down; 357.9 demolish; 367.7 lean; 305.11 trip
topple a government 588.4 be anarchic
toppled 367.22 overthrown
topple over 305.11 trip
toppling 367.12 downthrow; 367.20 falling; 120.3 unequal
top pocket 65.3 English billiards; 65.5 snooker
top priority 129.2 priority
top-rank 123.6 notable
top-ranked 121.14 best
top-ranking 121.14 best
top rope 62.9 mountaineer
top roping 62.3 climbing technique
tops 235.2 best; 797.9 the best
topsail 174.2 head
top-secret 399.6 censored; 123.5 important; 737.9 secret
top-secret clearance 757.1 permission
top-secret document 399.2 censorship
top-secret file 737.1 secrecy
top seed 235.8 exceller; 485.4 skilled person
top selection 485.4 skilled person
top set 573.2 aristocracy
topside 25.22 beef; 174.4 top layer
topsoil 550.2 cover; 411.1 layer; 30.36 soil; 174.4 top layer
top speed 332.8 speed
top storey 174.3 architectural summit
top surface 174.4 top layer
topsy-turviness 408.4 litter
topsy-turvy 408.28 anyhow; 192.4 inversely; 192.2 inverted; 114.11 irregularly; 408.4 litter; 412.12 mixed; 408.18 muddled
topsy-turvydom 412.3 miscellany
top-ten 123.6 notable
top the charts 246.6 be successful
top twenty 18.9 popular music
top up 232.6 fill; 436.6 replenish; 439.6 store; 406.7 stuff; 217.4 suffice
to put it succinctly 269.5 concisely
toque 551.15 headgear
tor 89.1, 154.3 mountain
Torah 7.12 religious text
Torah scrolls 10.14 sacred object
torch 493.15 burn; 62.4 climbing equipment; 493.6 fire; 522.7 lantern; 437.2 lighter
torchbearer 243.15 preparer
torchlight 522.7 lantern
torchlit 522.18 lit
torch singer 18.23 singer
torch song 18.9 popular music; 516.2 song
toreador 382.13 animal killer; 586.3 athlete
toreador pants 551.9 trousers
toreutic 19.25 sculptural
tori 52.10 aikido; 52.7 judo
toric 27.83 spherical
toric lens 28.29 optical element
Tories 12.6 political party
torment 651.18; 798.11 be evil; 236.13 be worthless; 596.7 cause dislike; 236.14 ill-treat; 491.11 inflict pain; 624.9 offend; 491.1 pain; 602.1 sorrow; 647.6 suppress; 814.4 torture; 612.14 worry
tormented 491.7 feeling pain; 602.5 sad; 612.9 worried
tormenting 491.8 inflicting pain
tormentor 21.19 stage set
torn 424.1 brittle; 146.7 cracked; 491.6 injured; 308.12 open; 144.9 removed; 372.15 separate
tornadic 307.12 rotary
tornado 420.9 broken water; 180.3 convoluted thing; 379.1 trap; 380.5 violent weather; 307.4 vortex; 31.16 wind vortex
Tornado class 50.2 sailing boat
tornado watch 31.4 weather forecast
tornaria 75.13 invertebrate larva
toroid 27.45 curved surface
toroidal 27.83 spherical
Toronto 87.6 other cities
torpedo 587.16 bomb; 367.3 bring down; 381.2 fire; 330.8 missile; 587.5 missile weapon; 586.26 naval mine; 357.11 ruin; 330.31 snipe; 321.2 track
torpedo boat 587.5 missile weapon; 586.24 warship
torpedoed 357.15 destroyed
torpid 592.2 desensitized; 339.5 inert; 343.4 not awake; 343.3 not participating; 93.16 vegetating
torpidity 339.1 inertness
torpor 592.4 desensitization; 343.7 idleness; 339.1 inertness; 93.9 mere existence; 301.1 motionlessness; 489.2 unconsciousness
torque 28.10 force; 542.7 jewellery; 325.17 torsion; 307.2 turning
torque wrench 438.1 tool
torrefy 428.19 bake
torrent 90.6 river flow; 332.11 swift thing
torrential 90.10 fluvial; 31.53 rainy
torrentially 90.13 fluently
torrential rain 31.25 rain
torrid 31.51 hot; 493.12 warm-hearted
torse 743.8 heraldic device
torsion 325.17; 38.16 deformation; 234.1 distortion; 28.10 force; 307.2 turning
torsional 307.12 rotary
torsional strength 336.1 strength
torsional wave 28.12 wave
torsion balance 28.86 weighing instrument
torsion scale 414.10 scales
torso 205.6 branch; 717.6 image; 215.1 remainder; 19.12 sculpture
tort 16.39 crime; 802.7 sense of wrong; 806.3 sin
torte 25.36 cake
tortilla 25.50 Central American dish
tortious 16.58 unjust
tortoise 73.4 chelonian; 333.14 slow creature; 333.15 slow person
tortoiseshell 541.8 checked; 541.5 variegated thing
tortoiseshell butterfly 541.5 variegated thing
tortoiseshell cat 541.5 variegated thing
tortoiseshell inlay 23.9 decorative woodwork
tortoise's pace 333.10 slow motion
tortuous 180.4 convolutional; 544.9 inelegant; 266.2 obscure; 542.10 ornate; 702.7 sophistic
tortuously 180.8 circularly; 266.4 obscurely
tortuousness 542.2 affectation; 266.1 obscurity
torture 814.4; 651.7 act of malevolence; 381.9 attack successfully; 386.3 coercive methods; 814.12 corporal punishment; 236.14 ill-treat; 491.11 inflict pain; 705.18 interrogate; 491.1 pain; 380.2 physical violence; 647.6 suppress; 647.2 suppression; 651.18 torment; 380.8 use violence
torture chamber 814.15 instrument of torture
tortured 491.7 feeling pain; 814.20 punished; 647.9 suppressed

torture oneself 806.9 *appear guilty*
torturer 386.4 *coercive person;* 651.8 *malefactor;* 814.17 *punisher*
torture the law 16.73 *be illegal*
torturing 491.8 *inflicting pain*
torturous 651.11 *cruel;* 814.21 *punishing*
to rule 140.19
torus 27.45 *curved surface;* 27.47 *topology*
Tory 225.3 *conservative person;* 12.6 *political party*
to satisfaction 669.26 *approvably*
to scale 108.10 *relevantly*
tosh 697.1 *nonsense*
to shreds 372.21 *apart*
to smithereens 372.21 *apart;* 375.7 *to pieces*
to some degree 209.11 *to a degree*
to some extent 685.9 *moderately;* 205.12 *partly;* 108.10 *relevantly;* 209.11 *to a degree*
to some purpose 246.16 *successfully*
to spare 215.10 *surplus*
toss 91.10 *billow;* 305.12 *drop;* 327.11 *stagger;* 330.5, 330.23, 331.4 *throw*
toss and tumble 327.25 *pitch*
toss and turn 327.21 *be agitated;* 327.25 *pitch*
tossed salad 25.14 *salad*
tosser 330.14 *thrower*
toss in a blanket 814.1 *punish*
tossing 342.18 *active;* 323.11 *nautical;* 326.16 *rocking*
tossing and turning 227.14 *irresolute;* 327.5 *restlessness*
tossing in a blanket 814.7 *punishment*
toss off one's glass 558.13 *drink*
toss out 371.1 *expel*
tosspot 690.17 *drunkard*
toss-up 107.3 *equal chance*
tostada 25.50 *Central American dish*
to such an extent 203.7 *quantitatively*
to summarize 149.12 *short*
to sum up 269.5 *concisely*
tot 159.4 *little person*
total 194.11; **203.4**; **210.10**; 211.6 *add;* 27.15 *addition;* 204.9 *be whole;* 232.7 *complete;* 211.2 *mathematical addition;* 194.4 *mathematical result;* 706.7 *numerical result;* 230.1 *perfect;* 203.6 *quantitative;* 706.20 *solve;* 204.6 *whole;* 204.2 *whole thing*
total abstinence 684.1 *self-restraint*
total blank 463.2 *blankness*
total commitment 640.2 *commitment;* 638.13 *concentration*
total deafness 505.1 *deafness*
total defeat 247.2 *defeat*
total destruction 585.1 *war*
total eclipse 523.1 *darkness*
total exhaustion 261.7 *fatigue*
total immersion 10.5 *Christian rite*
total internal reflection 28.29 *optical element*
totalitarian 12.9, 396.14 *governmental;* 566.13 *national;* 647.8 *severe*
totalitarian dictatorship 12.1 *government*
totalitarianism 12.1 *government;* 566.11 *nation;* 647.2 *suppression;* 396.7 *type of rule*
totalitarian state 566.11 *nation*
totality 232.1 *completeness;* 203.4 *total;* 29.3 *universe;* 204.1 *whole;* 204.2 *whole thing*
totalizator 59.7 *horseracing*
totalize 210.9 *add*
totalizer 210.5 *computer*
totalling 210.3 *count;* 211.2 *mathematical addition*
total loss 766.1 *loss;* 357.4 *ruin*
totally 256.20 *clean;* 230.8, 232.9 *completely;* 203.7 *quantitatively;* 204.11 *wholly*
totally deaf 505.4 *deaf*
total recall 462.1 *memory*
total serialism 517.4 *atonality*
total silence 506.4 *silence*
total situation 222.1 *circumstances*
total sum 204.2 *whole thing*
total theatre 21.10 *theatre movements*
total up 211.6 *add*
total war 585.1 *war*
to tatters 372.21 *apart*
tote 59.7 *horseracing;* 316.12 *transport*
tote bag 410.8 *bag*
to tell the truth 799.7 *honourably;* 698.35 *truly*
totem 8.5 *deity;* 10.14 *sacred object;* 11.6 *talisman*
totem dance 22.4 *historic dancing*
totemic 9.10 *idolatrous;* 11.15 *witchlike*
totemism 9.2 *idolatry;* 11.3 *witchcraft*
totemist 9.6 *idolater*
totemistic 9.10 *idolatrous;* 10.21 *ritualistic;* 11.15 *witchlike*
totemize 9.8 *idolatrize*
totem pole 10.14 *sacred object*
tote up 211.6 *add;* 194.10 *number*
to that place 142.12 *where*
to the amount of 790.16 *at a price*
to the bitter end 277.10 *for the duration;* 232.10 *fully;* 640.13 *persistently;* 131.27 *to the end*
to the boiling point 493.17 *warmly*
to the brim 232.10 *fully;* 406.14 *internally*
to the contrary 708.23 *no!*
to the core 232.10 *fully;* 406.14 *internally*
to the effect that 694.13 *meaningfully*
to the end 131.27; 277.10 *for the duration;* 232.10 *fully*
to the fore 167.11 *in front*
to the four winds 377.31 *everywhere;* 141.19 *to all places*
to the full 217.9 *enough;* 681.9 *extravagantly;* 232.10 *fully*
to the good 392.36 *helpfully*
to the ground 367.24 *down*
to the heart 232.10 *fully*
to the highest degree 121.17 *supremely*
to the last breath 232.10 *fully*
to the last gasp 131.27 *to the end*
to the last man 232.10 *fully;* 640.13 *persistently*
to the letter 125.14 *imitatively;* 698.38 *literally;* 230.7 *perfectly*
to the life 125.14 *imitatively*
to the marrow 232.10 *fully*
to the maximum 232.10 *fully*
to the minute 293.17 *early*
to the nth degree 273.8 *accurately*
to the point 426.12 *bluntly;* 269.3 *concise;* 269.5 *concisely;* 123.5 *important;* 446.21 *purposively;* 447.14 *thematically*
to the purpose 239.1 *convenient*
to the quick 491.13 *painfully*
to the rear 168.9 *in the rear*
to the rescue! 390.5
to the same degree 119.12 *equally*
to the second 293.17 *early*
to the side 169.10 *laterally*
to the top 232.10 *fully;* 406.14 *internally*
to the touch 404.15 *texturally*
to the tune of 790.16 *at a price;* 203.7 *quantitatively*
to the utmost 232.10 *fully*
totter 227.11 *be changeable;* 254.8 *be in danger;* 337.6 *be weak;* 245.1 *deteriorate;* 327.25 *pitch;* 326.11 *rock;* 327.11 *stagger;* 305.11 *trip*
totter along 333.1 *move slowly*
tottering 227.13 *changeable;* 305.16 *descending;* 245.12 *deteriorated;* 333.4 *slow;* 254.2 *unsafe;* 639.4 *unsteady;* 337.8 *weak*
tottery 245.13 *dilapidated;* 337.8 *weak*
tot up 210.9, 211.6 *add;* 194.10 *number*
tot up to 210.10 *total*
Touch 492
touch 492.1; **492.11**; 492.12 *abut;* 412.4 *admixture;* 157.6 *be shallow;* 554.4 *biological function;* 331.13 *blow;* 139.3 *characteristic;* 627.11 *excite pity;* 54.5 *fence;* 54.3 *fencing movements;* 742.3 *gesture;* 245.4 *impair;* 455.2 *information;* 147.18 *juxtapose;* 147.3 *juxtaposition;* 342.17 *meddle;* 147.4 *meeting;* 108.7 *relate to;* 64.1 *rugger;* 488.1 *sensation;* 488.11 *sense;* 485.1 *skill;* 728.6 *suggestion;* 331.6 *tap;* 404.1 *texture;* 349.1 *use*
touchable 492.8
touch and go 227.13 *changeable;* 119.2 *equilibrium;* 254.2 *unsafe*
touch a raw nerve 488.13 *arouse sensation;* 491.11 *inflict pain*
touch a sore point 492.12 *abut*
touchback 46.12 *special team*
touch bottom 156.14 *deepen;* 305.10 *droop*
touch depth 305.10 *droop*
touchdown 305.5 *dive;* 322.5 *flight;* 312.11 *landing;* 46.6 *scoring;* 246.3 *successful thing*
touch down 305.12 *drop;* 312.4 *land;* 64.3 *rugby play*
touched 461.11 *insane*
touched up 547.14 *beautified;* 699.39 *disguised;* 727.12 *exaggerated;* 244.14 *improved;* 295.14 *renewed*
toucher 492.5; 51.2 *grip;* 492.7 *sense organ*
touch football 46.1 *football*
touchily 625.9 *irascibly;* 626.14 *irritably*
touchiness 488.2 *ability to sense;* 625.1 *irascibility;* 626.3 *irritableness;* 591.6 *oversensitivity;* 622.2 *unapproachability*
touching 492.2; **492.9**; 772.1 *borrowing;* 590.14 *emotive;* 147.10 *juxtaposed;* 147.3 *juxtaposition;* 239.2 *nearby;* 627.7 *pitiful;* 108.10 *relevantly;* 773.1 *taking*
touching a sailor 475.6 *good-luck sign*
touching ball 65.2 *billiards play*
touchingly 590.20 *with feeling*
touch-in-goal line 64.1 *rugger*
touching one's cap 658.4 *deference*
touching up 727.1 *exaggeration;* 699.14 *façade;* 19.2 *painting*
touchline 64.1 *rugger;* 66.1 *soccer*
touch off 344.10 *awaken;* 437.11 *fuel*
touch of frost 31.36 *frost*
touch one's cap 658.13 *defer to*
touch one's forelock 658.13 *defer to*
touch-operated 492.10 *handed*
touchpaper 437.2 *lighter*
touch rock bottom 122.11 *become inferior*
touch-sensitive 492.8 *touchable*
touch someone 772.7 *borrow*
touchstone 26.7 *standard*
touch the surface 157.6 *be shallow*
touch up 727.7 *exaggerate;* 699.14 *façade;* 244.1 *improve;* 295.20 *make new;* 699.28 *mask;* 19.19 *paint;* 393.2 *refurbish;* 773.7 *take;* 492.11 *touch*
touch upon 108.7 *relate to*
touch wood 610.9 *be hopeful*
touchy 625.4 *irascible;* 626.7 *irritable;* 591.2 *oversensitive;* 590.13 *passionate;* 488.7 *susceptible;* 622.15 *unapproachable*
tough 418.2; **423.1**; 651.12 *callous;* 586.1 *combatant;* 586.33 *combative;* 613.9 *courageous;* 228.11 *determined;* 264.10 *difficult;* 261.4 *fatiguing;* 592.1 *insensitive;* 651.8 *malefactor;* 418.4 *mentally hard;* 383.11 *obstinate;* 336.9 *physically strong;* 628.4 *pitiless;* 264.12, 705.13 *problematic;* 647.8 *severe;* 336.13 *strengthened;* 336.11 *strong in spirit;* 380.4 *violent creature;* 430.8 *viscous;* 585.16 *warlike*
tough as leather 423.3 *hard*
tough as nails 423.3 *hard*
tough as old boots 423.3 *hard;* 418.4 *mentally hard*
tough assignment 264.3 *difficult task*
tough as steel 638.3 *strong-willed*
tough decision 469.8 *choice*
toughen 423.10 *be tough;* 418.9 *harden;* 292.7 *season;* 336.8 *strengthen*
toughened 423.2; 418.3 *hardened;* 292.15 *seasoned;* 336.13 *strengthened*
toughened glass 527.9 *glass;* 252.4 *safety device*
toughening 418.5 *hardness;* 336.4 *strengthening*
tough guy 336.6 *muscleman;* 380.4 *violent creature*
tough lineup to buck 264.3 *difficult task*
tough luck 107.2 *luck*
toughly 418.12; **423.12**; 228.13 *determinedly;* 628.7 *pitilessly;* 383.14 *resistingly;* 647.11 *severely*
Toughness 423
toughness 423.6; 613.1 *courage;* 416.1 *density;* 228.2, 641.6 *determination;* 264.1 *difficulty;* 418.5 *hardness;* 418.8 *mental hardness;* 383.2 *obstinacy;* 647.1 *severity;* 336.1 *strength;* 430.1 *viscosity*
tough nut to crack 705.4 *difficult question*
tough proposition 264.3 *difficult task*
tough something out 423.10 *be tough*
tough thing 423.7
tough time 249.4 *time of adversity*
toupé 547.10 *wig*
toupee 551.15 *headgear*
tour 21.15 *engagement;* 306.3 *orbit;* 276.4 *period of activity*
tour de force 340.2 *deed;* 484.3 *expedient plan;* 797.17 *good thing;* 400.11, 485.3 *masterpiece*
tourer 320.16 *car*
touring 68.2 *cross-country skiing;* 68.12 *ski;* 68.1 *skiing*
touring company 21.25 *cast*
touring ski 68.2 *cross-country skiing;* 68.5 *ski equipment*
tourist 644.3 *curious person;* 518.11 *observer;* 227.7 *person who moves around;* 550.22 *progression*
tourist-class 793.9 *cheap*
tourist fare 793.4 *bargain*
tourist route 306.5 *ringroad*
tourist season 292.1 *season*
tournament 656.3 *formal occasion;* 45.1 *sport*
tournament casting 55.1 *angling*
tourniquet 191.4 *contractor;* 373.6 *line;* 309.2 *stopper;* 394.10 *surgical dressing*
tour of duty 275.3 *duration;* 276.4 *period of activity*
tours en l'air 22.9 *ballet steps*
to us 558.18 *cheers!*
tousle 408.24 *make disordered;* 420.12 *make rough*
tousled 408.15 *untidy*
tout 740.16 *publicize;* 740.10 *publicizer;* 710.6 *request;* 778.1 *sell;* 778.12 *wholesaler*
tout à fait 698.39 *accurately*
tout le monde 138.10 *everyone*
tovarisch 567.3 *male title of address;* 12.6 *political party*
tow 404.6 *fibre;* 320.21 *miscellaneous motoring terms;* 362.2, 362.11 *pull*
towage 362.1 *traction*
to war 585.18
towards 317.17 *via*
towed 319.5 *transportable*
towed log 323.5 *navigation*
towel 428.20 *absorb;* 256.11 *cleaning cloth;* 428.15 *dryer*
towelling 428.15 *dryer;* 193.4 *textile*
tower 89.9; 158.19 *be big;* 154.15 *be high;* 20.3 *building;* 356.8, 403.6 *construction;* 384.12 *fort;* 304.20 *hover;* 252.5 *refuge;* 228.4 *stable thing;* 38.27 *superstructure;* 154.6 *tall thing;* 362.6 *towline*
tower above 154.15 *be high;* 121.8 *be superior;* 89.9 *tower*
tower block 565.6 *apartment block;* 38.20 *building;* 154.6 *tall thing*
tower crane 38.29 *construction equipment*
towering 158.15 *big;* 154.9 *high;* 89.7 *mountainous*
towering inferno 493.6 *fire*
toweringly 154.19 *high*
Tower of Babel 412.3 *miscellany*
Tower of Pisa 189.2 *oblique line*
Tower of Silence 583.6 *grave*
tower of strength 707.9 *affirmer;* 336.6 *muscleman;* 252.2 *protection;* 252.5 *refuge;* 228.5 *stable person;* 392.13, 413.8 *supporter*
tower over 395.10 *be a prevailing influence*
tow-haired 537.3 *yellow-haired*
towhead 537.6 *yellowness*
tow-headed 522.21 *light;* 531.3 *white-haired*
to whose advantage? 237.12 *usefully*
towing 362.1 *traction;* 362.8 *tractional;* 319.5 *transportable*
to wit 719.18 *in other words;* 139.31 *namely*
towline 362.6; 373.6 *line*
town 87.9; 87.1 *city;* 86.11 *settlement;* 87.14 *urban*
town centre 173.4 *centre of activity*
town council 579.8 *British administrative council;* 16.2 *jurisdiction;* 398.2 *representative body;* 579.9 *US administrative council*
town crier 514.9 *crier;* 507.5 *loud person*
town dump 767.5 *wasteyard*
towndweller 564.4 *townsman*
townee 564.4 *townsman;* 87.11 *urbanite*
town gas 437.3 *gas*
town hall 87.13 *municipal building*
town-hall meeting 740.7 *publicity*
town house 20.3 *building;* 565.5 *house*
town meeting 764.1 *joint possession;* 398.2 *representative body*
town plan 163.4, 484.5, 717.7 *map*
town-planner 484.8 *planner*
townscape 19.10 *art subject;* 518.7 *view*
townsfolk 564.4 *townsman*
township 86.11 *settlement;* 87.9 *town*
township jazz 18.10 *world music*
township jive 18.10 *world music*
townsman 564.4; 87.11 *urbanite*

townspeople 564.4 *townsman*
townsperson 564.4 *townsman*
townswoman 564.4 *townsman*
town wall 384.11 *fortification*
towny 565.15 *environmental*
to wonder at 619.8 *wonderful*
towpath 317.6 *path*
towrope 373.6 *line*; 362.6 *towline*
toxaemia 260.6 *infection*
toxic 254.1 *dangerous*; 382.23 *deadly*; 798.9 *detrimental*; 260.23 *diseased*; 236.5 *harmful*; 258.8 *unclean*; 499.6 *unpalatable*
toxicity 236.11 *harmfulness*; 260.6 *infection*
toxicologist 35.13 *medical specialist*
toxicology 35.3 *medical specialty*
toxin 260.6 *infection*
toxocariasis 75.11 *helminthic disease*; 260.6 *infection*
toxophilite 330.16 *archer*
toxophily 330.6 *shooting*
toxoplasma 75.10 *parasite*
toxoplasmosis 75.12 *protozoal disease*
toy 124.9 *bauble*; 793.5 *cheap item*; 593.26 *court*; 700.22 *dupe*; 159.2 *little thing*; 124.4 *trivial*
toy boy 567.4 *boyfriend*; 664.3 *sponger*
toy dog 71.9 *dog*
toy gun 330.9 *firearm*
toying 593.6 *courtship*
toying with one's food 557.3 *delicate eating*
toy theatre 21.16 *theatre*
toy with 492.11 *touch*
toy with one's food 557.23 *taste*
trace 721.17 *describe a circle*; 19.20 *draw*; 163.5 *outline*; 717.11 *paint*; 215.1 *remainder*; 728.6 *suggestion*; 744.12 *vestige*; 345.2 *visible effect*
trace back 3.21 *antiquarianize*; 284.15 *look back*; 761.8 *return*
traced 19.27 *painted*
trace element 33.15 *essential element*
trace horse 59.2 *thoroughbred*
trace program 40.9 *programming language*
tracer flare 381.13 *air attack*
tracery 193.2 *braid*
traces 742.1 *sign*; 373.9 *yoke*
trachea 434.8 *respiration*
tracheitis 260.9 *respiratory disease*
trachoma 519.1 *blindness*; 260.7 *tropical disease*
tracing 19.3, 19.9 *drawing*; 125.5 *duplicate*; 163.1 *outline*; 721.9 *representation*; 717.2 *reproduction*
tracing paper 435.3 *paper*
track **47.9**; **321.2**; 223.16 *attend*; 324.2 *bearing*; 633.9 *follow*; 716.4 *indication*; 61.6 *motor-racing terms*; 318.2 *passing along*; 317.6 *path*; 317.10 *railway*; 215.1 *remainder*; 373.5 *road*; 317.2 *route*; 60.7 *shoot*; 742.1 *sign*; 45.2 *sportsground*; 137.6 *students*; 31.21 *thunderstorm*; 744.12 *vestige*; 184.8 *wrinkle*
track and field 47.9 *track*
track down 449.2 *detect*; 142.11 *find*
tracked down 142.7 *found*
tracker 60.4, 633.6 *hunter*
tracker dog 71.9 *dog*
track events **47.1**
tracking 60.2 *hunting*; 633.1 *pursuit*; 60.8 *shooting*
tracking device 324.3 *orientation*
tracking down 449.7 *detection*; 142.3 *locating*
tracking station 29.32 *satellite*
trackman 321.9 *railway worker*
trackmarks 691.1 *drug-taking*
track record 3.5 *chronicle*; 631.1 *conduct*
tracks 691.1 *drug-taking*; 317.10 *railway*
tracksuit 57.2 *gymnastic clothing*; 551.4 *informal dress*; 47.4 *sports equipment*; 551.10 *suit*
tracksuits 657.6 *informal dress*
tract 722.1 *dissertation*; 447.5 *educational topic*; 141.3 *geographical space*; 86.12 *plot*; 440.1 *property*; 141.1 *space*
tractability 636.8 *acquiescence*; 663.1 *obedience*; 480.7 *persuadability*; 419.8 *softness*; 483.6 *suggestibility*
tractable 636.3 *amenable*; 117.13 *compliant*; 265.13 *easy-going*; 810.9 *loyal*; 663.7 *obedient*; 480.20 *persuadable*; 419.2 *pliant*; 388.5 *submitting*; 483.13 *suggestible*; 265.12 *wieldy*
tractably 483.14 *influentially*; 663.10 *obediently*
tractate 722.1 *dissertation*
tractile 419.2 *pliant*
Traction 362
traction **362.1**; 334.4 *energy*; 320.21 *miscellaneous motoring terms*
tractional **362.8**
traction engine 362.6 *towline*
traction unit 321.5 *locomotive part*
tractive 362.8 *tractional*
tractor 43.10 *farm tool*; 362.6 *towline*; 320.20 *truck*
tractor driver 43.16 *farm worker*
tractor shed 43.7 *farm building*
trad 18.8, 18.33 *jazz*
Trade 776
trade **776.1**; **776.4**; 224.4, 224.10, 759.1, 759.5 *exchange*; 576.3 *job*; 785.6 *pay*; 436.5 *provision*; 110.7 *reciprocate*; 314.4 *right of entry*; 778.1 *sell*; 778.3 *selling*; 139.8 *specialization*; 316.1 *transfer*
tradeable 224.14 *exchangeable*
trade agreement 755.3 *alliance*; 776.9 *bargaining*; 13.5 *international trade*
trade barrier 776.5 *commercial trade*; 13.6 *economic factors*
trade book 740.6 *book publishing*
traded 759.7 *exchanged*
trade delegation 398.2 *representative body*
trade fair 779.2 *fair*
trade gap 784.2 *national debt*
trade in 776.1 *trade*
trade integration 13.5 *international trade*
trade journal 740.5 *journal*
trade language 5.7 *international language*
trademark 139.3 *characteristic*; 743.3 *means of identification*; 721.8 *name*; 126.7 *originate*; 24.4 *porcelain mark*; 742.1 *sign*
trademarked 126.6 *authentic*; 743.12 *identified*
trademarked product 126.2 *original*
tradename 743.3 *means of identification*; 721.8 *name*
trade off 759.5 *exchange*; 110.7 *reciprocate*; 776.1 *trade*
trade-off 754.1 *compromise*; 119.3 *equalization*; 759.1 *exchange*; 110.1 *interchange*; 685.1 *moderation*; 746.8 *negotiated*; 746.1 *negotiation*; 110.4 *reciprocal*; 776.4 *trade*
trade on 349.3 *exploit*
trade organ 740.5 *journal*
trade paper 740.5 *journal*
trade plate 320.21 *miscellaneous motoring terms*
trader **776.10**; 13.9 *economist*; 227.4 *editor*; 346.5 *operator*; 778.13 *retailer*
trade restriction 776.5 *commercial trade*
trade show 779.2 *fair*
trade sign 743.3 *means of identification*
tradesman 578.2 *artisan*; 778.13 *retailer*
tradesman's entrance 168.1 *rear*; 317.2 *route*
Trades Union Congress 13.8 *industrial relations*
trade supplement 740.4 *newspaper*
trade tariff 252.2 *protection*
trade union 376.15 *association*; 776.5 *commercial trade*; 13.8 *industrial relations*; 15.3 *organized labour*
trade unionist 776.11 *chamber of commerce member*; 13.9 *economist*; 578.1 *worker*
trade union official 15.7 *employee*
trade war 585.1 *war*
trade winds 31.17 *wind system*
trade with **13.10**; 776.1 *trade*
trading 13.2 *economy*; 776.13 *mercantile*; 778.3 *selling*; 776.4 *trade*
trading centre 779.7 *emporium*
trading company 779.8 *store*
trading deficit 784.2 *national debt*
trading house 779.8 *store*
trading post 779.7 *emporium*
trading ring 166.2 *limiting factor*
tradition **1.8**; **296.6**; **632.5**; 117.5, 750.6 *convention*; 140.6, 632.4 *custom*; 160.5 *formality*; 3.7 *narrative*; 298.4 *orderliness*; 474.3 *the expected thing*
traditional **178.4**; 216.1 *average*; 3.19 *chronicled*; 117.14 *conformist*; 225.8 *conservative*; 750.15 *conventional*; 140.10 *customary*; 160.11 *formal*; 18.33 *jazz*; 632.11 *normal*; 383.11 *obstinate*; 296.12 *olden*; 298.14 *orderly*; 1.14 *societal*
traditional belief 450.2 *religious belief*
traditional grammar 5.29 *grammar*
traditionalism 117.4 *conventionalism*; 632.6 *procedure*
traditionalist 450.5 *believer*; 117.6, 117.14 *conformist*; 225.8 *conservative*; 225.3 *conservative person*; 632.8 *creature of habit*; 663.4 *obedient person*; 383.5 *resister*
traditionalistic 117.14 *conformist*
traditional jazz 18.8 *jazz*
traditionally 117.19 *according to rule*; 225.10 *conservatively*; 160.14, 750.37 *conventionally*; 632.19 *habitually*, 298.17 *orderly*; 3.25 *reportedly*; 383.14 *resistingly*; 1.18 *societally*
traditional medicine 35.2 *natural medicine*
traditionary 632.11 *normal*
traditions 631.6 *way of life*
traditive 632.11 *normal*
traduce 678.12 *defame*; 720.1 *misinterpret*
traducement 678.3 *defamation*; 720.2 *misinterpretation*
traffic 759.5 *exchange*; 320.21 *miscellaneous motoring terms*; 300.2 *momentum*; 318.2 *passing along*; 778.3 *selling*; 776.1, 776.4 *trade*
traffic accident 582.5 *ways of dying*
trafficator 522.6 *electric light*
traffic calming 320.21 *miscellaneous motoring terms*
traffic circle 320.3 *carriageway*; 317.3 *road*
traffic controller **318.7**
traffic cop 16.17 *police officer*; 318.7 *traffic controller*
traffic death 382.8 *accidental killing*
traffic engineer 318.7 *traffic controller*
traffic engineering 38.17 *civil engineering*
traffic flow 318.2 *passing along*
traffic in 778.1 *sell*; 776.1 *trade*; 13.10 *trade with*
traffic in drugs 691.10 *drug oneself*
traffic island 252.5 *refuge*
traffic jam 320.21 *miscellaneous motoring terms*; 378.2 *obstacle*; 318.2 *passing along*; 132.8 *procession*
trafficker 778.12 *wholesaler*
trafficking 778.3 *selling*; 776.4 *trade*
traffic lane 317.2 *route*
traffic light 538.15 *green light*; 742.4 *signal*
traffic lights 320.3 *carriageway*; 318.5 *crossing point*; 522.6 *electric light*
traffic load 318.2 *passing along*
traffic of the state 21.1 *drama*
traffic pattern 322.6 *flight control*; 318.2 *passing along*
traffic police 318.7 *traffic controller*
traffic signals 522.6 *electric light*
traffic warden 318.7 *traffic controller*
tragedian 21.24 *actor*; 21.26 *dramatist*
tragedienne 21.24 *actor*
tragedy **21.11**; 798.2 *affliction*; 245.7 *deterioration*
tragic **21.40**; 249.6 *adverse*; 798.8 *afflicted*; 602.7 *distressing*; 17.19 *narrative*
tragically 798.13 *destructively*; 21.44 *dramatically*; 249.12 *in adversity*
tragic drama 21.11 *tragedy*
tragic flaw 231.7 *defect*; 21.11 *tragedy*; 254.7 *vulnerability*
tragic loves 593.10 *lovers*
tragic muse 21.11 *tragedy*
tragicomedy 21.12 *comedy*; 21.11 *tragedy*
tragicomic 21.40 *tragic*
tragic poet 17.14 *author*; 21.26 *dramatist*
trail 122.8 *be inferior*; 168.6 *be in the rear*; 633.9 *follow*; 333.2 *hesitate*; 716.4 *indication*; 317.6 *path*; 362.11 *pull*; 50.19 *punt*; 215.1 *remainder*; 317.2 *route*; 500.3 *scent*; 60.7 *shoot*; 742.1 *sign*; 361.10 *suspend*; 744.12 *vestige*
trailbike 320.12 *bicycle*
trailblaze 130.21 *pioneer*
trailblazer 129.8 *precursor*; 243.15 *preparer*
trailblazing 129.14 *preparatory*
trailer 740.9 *advertisement*; 43.10 *farm tool*; 633.6 *hunter*; 316.5 *means of transport*; 565.9 *mobile home*; 129.6 *preview*; 320.20 *truck*
trail horse 59.1 *horse*
trailing 50.8, 50.14 *punting*; 633.1 *pursuit*
trail shot 51.2 *grip*
train **321.7**; 71.21 *assemblage of mammals*; 117.10 *assimilate*; 243.6 *brief*; 455.14 *cause to know*; 15.11 *conduct industrial relations*; 132.2 *consecution*; 44.15 *cultivate*; 579.2 *direct*; 6.22 *educate*; 576.9 *exercise*; 632.8 *habituate*; 6.23 *learn*; 316.5 *means of transport*; 551.24 *part of garment*; 243.8 *prepare oneself*; 132.8 *procession*; 356.10 *produce*; 362.11 *pull*; 168.1 *rear*; 59.16 *ride*; 289.1 *succession*
trainable 6.17 *educable*
train-bearer 570.7 *bridal party*
trained 485.8 *expert*; 632.14 *habituated*; 6.19, 455.8 *knowledgeable*; 663.7 *obedient*; 41.19 *ornamental*; 243.18 *prepared*
trainee 130.14 *beginner*; 6.7 *learner*; 486.10 *unskilled person*
trainee nurse 35.16 *nurse*
trainer 52.4 *boxer*; 579.13 *director*; 6.4 *educator*; 59.15 *horse person*; 586.31 *military aircraft*; 243.15 *preparer*
trainers 551.19 *footwear*
training 243.12 *briefing*; 6.1 *education*; 576.5 *exercise*; 57.11 *gymnastic*; 632.7 *habituation*
training and education 15.2 *industrial negotiations*
training camp 46.14 *miscellaneous terms*
training drill 585.6 *art of war*
training officer 15.6 *employer*
training shoes 57.2 *gymnastic clothing*
training staff 584.5 *military staff*
training tracks 59.7 *horseracing*
trainload 406.2 *load*
train of thoughts 443.5 *creative thought*
train robber 774.8 *thief*
train robbery 774.1 *stealing*; 774.3 *theft*
trainspotter 620.3 *boring person*
train spotter 321.10 *miscellaneous*; 518.11 *observer*
train spotting 321.10 *miscellaneous*
train station 173.4 *centre of activity*; 226.4 *stopping place*
train ticket 743.3 *means of identification*
train upon 324.7 *take a direction*
traipse 333.1 *move slowly*
trait 139.3 *characteristic*; 525.3 *external appearance*; 743.1 *identification*; 99.4 *nature*; 632.2 *tendency*
traitor **700.21**; 760.6 *convert*; 800.4 *dishonourable person*; 479.9 *equivocator*; 798.6 *evil person*; 699.17 *false person*; 227.6 *fickle person*; 651.8 *malefactor*; 662.10 *seditionist*; 804.9 *wicked person*
traitorous 479.11 *equivocating*; 227.14 *irresolute*
traitorously 227.15 *changeably*; 479.13 *perfidiously*
traitor's death 814.13 *capital punishment*
traject 318.11 *cross*; 331.1 *impel*; 330.20 *propel*
trajectile 330.8 *missile*; 330.18 *projectile*
trajection 330.3 *throwing*
trajectory 27.40 *curve*; 317.13 *flight path*; 29.21 *orbit*; 29.35 *rocketry*; 317.2 *route*
trajinera 50.8 *punting*
tralineate 325.1 *deviate*
tram 316.5 *means of transport*; 317.10, 321.1 *railway*
tramcar 321.1 *railway*
tram driver 316.7 *transferor*
tramline 43.11 *farmland*; 317.10 *railway*; 68.1 *skiing*
tramlines 63.12 *badminton terms*; 63.4 *tennis terms*; 632.3 *way*
trammels 251.5 *means of restraint*
tramontane 145.8 *distant*; 100.10 *foreign*; 100.6 *outsider*
tramp 710.5 *beggar*; 258.6 *dirty person*; 300.12 *gait*; 118.7 *nonconformist*; 343.8 *nonworker*; 249.5 *person in adversity*; 227.7 *person who moves around*; 782.10 *poor person*; 300.15 *walk*
trample 381.9 *attack successfully*; 236.14 *ill-treat*; 331.7 *kick*
trampled down 187.9 *flattened*
trample down 187.7 *make horizontal*
trample in the dust 367.2 *flatten*
trample on 660.26 *oppress*; 387.6 *subject*
trample over 635.15 *impose one's will*
trample underfoot 246.10 *defeat heavily*; 357.9 *demolish*; 236.14 *ill-treat*
trampoline 422.3 *elastic thing*; 366.10 *elevator*; 304.8 *lift*
tramp steamer 316.5 *means of transport*

tramway 321.1 *railway*
trance 36.14; 592.4 *desensitization*; 301.1 *motionlessness*; 463.1 *oblivion*; 18.9 *popular music*; 11.10 *psychic phenomenon*; 477.6 *reverie*; 343.9 *sleep*; 489.2 *unconsciousness*
trance dance 22.4 *historic dancing*
trance-like 463.8 *oblivious*
trance speaking 11.1 *occultism*
trance state 36.14 *trance*
tranche 205.2 *particular*; 205.7 *piece*
trannie 692.18 *radio*
tranquil 263.4 *at ease*; 4.18 *detached*; 407.16 *harmonious*; 341.3 *inactive*; 685.6 *moderate*; 589.7 *peaceful*; 301.6 *quiescent*
tranquillity 4.3 *detachment*; 263.1 *ease*; 407.8 *harmony*; 341.1 *inaction*; 301.2 *repose*
tranquillization 608.1 *ease*; 685.1 *moderation*
tranquillize 301.9 *make motionless*; 685.4 *moderate*; 749.4 *pacify*; 608.9 *relieve*
tranquillizer 489.4 *anaesthetic*; 592.6 *desensitizing substance*; 394.8 *drug*; 37.4 ***drug** type*; 685.2 *moderator*; 608.3 *reliever*
tranquillizing 685.8 *moderating*; 37.15 *sedative*
tranquilly 301.10 *motionlessly*; 589.8 *peacefully*; 341.5 *without action*
transact 340.4 *act*; 750.23 *arrange*; 631.14 *behave towards*; 759.5 *exchange*; 776.1 *trade*
transact business 746.5 *negotiate*
transaction 340.1 *action*; 750.3 *arrangement*; 340.2 *deed*; 759.1 *exchange*; 778.3 *selling*; 776.4 *trade*
transactional analysis 36.3 *psychiatric treatment*
transactionalism 1.5 *anthropological concept*
transactionalist 1.11 *anthropological*
transactions 744.1 *record*; 631.8 *treatment*
transalpine 145.8 *distant*
transaminase 33.11 *enzyme*
transatlantic 145.8 *distant*; 100.10 *foreign*; 50.10 *sailing*
transatlantic racing 50.1 *sailing*
transceiver 504.9 *audio device*
transcend 797.19 *be good at*; 121.8 *be superior*; 235.9 *be worthy*; 8.17 *deify*; 329.3 *exceed*
transcended 329.14 *surpassing*
transcendence 329.7 *crossing*; 8.1 *divinity*; 230.3 *perfection*; 121.1 *superiority*
transcendency 121.1 *superiority*
transcendent 121.14 *best*; 8.13 *divine*; 202.2 *immeasurable*; 101.8 *nonmaterial*; 126.5 *novel*; 230.1 *perfect*; 7.15 *religious*
transcendental 121.14 *best*; 27.72 *complex*; 8.13 *divine*; 11.16 *psychic*; 696.1 *unintelligible*
transcendental argument 4.9 *philosophical problem*
transcendental idealism 101.5 *idealism*
transcendentalism 101.5 *idealism*; 11.1 *occultism*; 4.7 *school of thought*; 696.11 *unintelligibility*
transcendentalist 4.11 *follower of a doctrine*; 11.12 *occultist*; 4.14 *of a philosophy*
transcendentally 8.19 *divinely*; 11.25 *occultly*; 121.16 *superiorly*
transcendental meditation 36.3 *psychiatric treatment*
transcendental number 27.6 *complex number*; 194.2 *kind of number*
transcendently 8.19 *divinely*; 101.13 *metaphysically*; 121.16 *superiorly*
transcending 121.14 *best*
transcontinental 145.8 *distant*
transcribe 18.35 *compose*; 744.14 *inscribe*; 5.46, 316.16, 719.12 *translate*
transcribed 692.34 *communicated*; 125.12 *imitative*
transcriber 115.4 *person who copies*
transcript 125.5 *duplicate*
transcription 692.25 *broadcast material*; 224.1 *change*; 18.15 *composition*; 316.4, 719.4 *translation*
transcursion 329.7 *crossing*; 318.1 *passage*
transdermal injection 37.12 *injection*
transducer 28.55 *circuit*; 39.22 *transformer*
transducing 318.12 *passing*
transduction 318.1 *passage*; 316.3 *transmission*
transect 189.6 *be oblique*; 198.16 *halve*
transept 10.12 *church*; 20.10 ***church** architecture*
transeunt 315.15 *outgoing*
Transfer 316
transfer 316.1; **316.11**; 289.4 *accession*; 635.16 *bequeath*; 224.8 *cause change*; 755.5 *contract*; 760.1 *conversion*; 760.7 *convert into*; 318.11 *cross*; 398.7 *delegate*; 144.14 *displace*; 767.1 *disposal*; 125.5 *duplicate*; 768.2 *gift*; 768.5 *give*; 768.1 *giving*; 46.14 *miscellaneous terms*; 32.26 *react*; 355.1 *relinquish*; 355.3 *relinquishment*; 144.3 *replacement*; 761.2 *restoration*; 778.1 *sell*; 778.3 *selling*; 300.14 *set in motion*
transferable 316.17; 760.15 *convertible*; 767.14 *for sale*; 768.7 *given*; 746.8 *negotiated*
transferable vote 469.10 *vote*
transfer a decal 24.11 *make ceramics*
transferase 33.11 *enzyme*
transferee 777.12 *purchaser*
transference 36.27 *association of ideas*; 224.1 *change*; 760.1 *conversion*; 144.1 *displacement*; 315.5 *export*; 318.1 *passage*; 316.1 *transfer*
transference neurosis 36.10 *neurosis*
transferor 316.7; 778.9 *seller*
transfer orbit 29.35 *rocketry*
transfer printing 24.3 *glaze*
transferral 316.1 *transfer*
transferred 144.8 *displaced*; 694.6 *meaningful*; 144.10 *replaced*
transferred epithet 17.12 *poetic language*
transferred thing 316.10
transferring 760.14 *converting*; 768.8 *giving*; 318.12 *passing*
transfer RNA 34.13 *genetic material*
transfers 15.2 *industrial negotiations*
transfer thoughts 11.24 *experience psychic phenomena*
transfiguration 547.1; 760.1 *conversion*; 244.5 *improvement*; 224.3 *transformation*
transfigure 545.8 *beautify*; 760.7 *convert into*; 244.1 *improve*; 224.9, 760.9 *transform*
transfigured 760.13 *converted*
transfiguring 760.14 *converting*
transfinite number 27.11 *infinity*; 27.7 *natural number*
transfix 228.7 *make stable*
transfixed 301.4 *motionless*; 228.10 *stabilized*; 619.7 *wide-eyed*
transform 224.9; **760.9**; 545.8 *beautify*; 760.7 *convert into*; 244.1 *improve*; 27.96 *represent*
transformable 760.15 *convertible*
transformation 27.48; **224.3**; 210.1 *calculation*; 760.1 *conversion*; 244.5 *improvement*; 27.29 *mathematical function*; 547.1 *transfiguration*; 619.3 *wonder-working*
transformational 5.44 *grammatical*
transformational-generative 5.44 *grammatical*
transformational grammar 5.29 *grammar*
transformation-generative grammar 5.29 *grammar*
transformation scene 21.8 *scene*; 21.19 *stage set*
transformative 224.13
transformed 760.13 *converted*; 244.14 *improved*
transform energy 334.12 *generate power*
transformer 39.22; 224.5 *changer*; 28.55 *circuit*; 334.7 *electrical power*; 39.34 *power supply*
transform fault 30.19 *plate tectonics*
transforming 760.14 *converting*
transfusable 316.17 *transferable*
transfuse 394.20 *doctor*; 368.2 *inject*; 35.20 *practise surgery*; 316.11 *transfer*
transfusion 368.9 *injection*; 412.1 *mixture*; 318.1 *passage*; 35.9, 394.12 *surgery*; 316.3 *transmission*
transgress 274.20; **329.5**; 662.15 *be disobedient*; 804.16 *be wicked*; 802.21 *do wrong*; 118.20 *infringe a law*; 806.10 *sin*
transgressing 662.13 *disobedient*; 16.60 *offending*; 806.7 *sinful*; 804.11 *wicked*
transgression 329.8; 16.38 *lawbreaking*; 274.8 *moral error*; 806.3 *sin*; 662.2 *violation of the law*; 804.1 *wickedness*; 802.8 *wrongdoing*
transgressive 802.16 *in the wrong*
transgressor 804.9 *wicked person*; 802.10 *wrongdoer*
Transience 278
transience 278.1; 227.1 *changeableness*; **582.1** *death*; 149.1 *shortness*; 453.15 *unreliability*
transiency 582.1 *death*
transient 278.6; 224.11, 227.13 *changeable*; 222.7 *circumstantial*; 32.35 *combined*; 582.20 *deadly*; 526.6 *disappearing*; 315.15 *outgoing*; 149.7 *short*; 453.7 *unreliable*
transient current 28.51 *electric current*
transient discharge 28.46, 39.6 *electric discharge*
transient disturbance 28.12 *wave*
transiently 278.8; 526.8 *fleetingly*; 453.26 *unreliably*
transient thing 278.2
transilience 329.7 *crossing*
transilient 318.12 *passing*
transistor 39.19; 28.55 *circuit*; 334.7 *electrical power*; 28.44 *semiconductor*
transistor amplifier 39.19 *transistor*
transistorize 334.11 *give power*
transistor radio 504.9 *audio device*; 692.18 *radio*
transistor switch 39.19 *transistor*
transit 318.11 *cross*; 300.2 *momentum*; 29.37 *observe*; 29.21 *orbit*; 318.1 *passage*; 316.2 *transportation*
transition 224.1 *change*; 760.1 *conversion*; 28.67 *excited atom*; 47.2 *field events*; 28.37 *temperature*; 316.1 *transfer*; 316.2 *transportation*
transitional 224.11 *changeable*; 300.16 *moving*; 318.12 *passing*
transitionally 318.14 *by the way*; 224.15 *changeably*; 300.18 *in motion*
transition element 32.6 *chemical element*
transition state 32.14 *chemical reaction*
transition temperature 28.45 *superconductivity*; 28.37 *temperature*
transitive 5.44 *grammatical*
transitively 5.52 *grammatically*
transitive relation 27.63 *mathematical logic*
transitive verb 5.35 *part of speech*
transitorily 278.8 *transiently*
transitoriness 278.1 *transience*
transitory 224.11 *changeable*; 278.6 *transient*
Transit system 323.5 *navigation*
transit van 410.10 *cart*
translatable 760.15 *convertible*; 5.43 *phrasal*
translate 5.46; **316.16**; **719.12**; 224.8 *cause change*; 760.7 *convert into*; 318.11 *cross*; 265.16 *make easy*; 27.96 *represent*; 760.9 *transform*
translated 5.40; 760.13 *converted*; 719.15 *interpreted*; 5.43 *phrasal*
translate the truth 234.12 *distort the truth*
translating 5.43 *phrasal*; 5.40 *translated*
translation 5.12; **316.4**; **719.4**; 224.1 *change*; 760.1 *conversion*; 5.24 *phrasing*; 162.2 *symmetry operation*; 27.48 *transformation*
translational 719.17
translator 719.6 *interpreter*; 5.2 *linguist*
translator's error 720.2 *misinterpretation*
transliterate 5.46, 316.16, 719.12 *translate*
transliterated 5.40 *translated*
transliteration 5.12, 316.4, 719.4 *translation*
translocate 144.14 *displace*; 316.11 *transfer*
translocation 144.1 *displacement*; 316.1 *transfer*
translucence 527.6 *translucency*
translucency 527.6; 527.7 *semitransparency*
translucent 527.2; 24.10 *ceramic*; 527.3 *semitransparent*
translucent ceramics 24.1 *ceramics*
translucently 24.12 *ornamentally*; 527.13 *transparently*
translumbar injection 37.12 *injection*
transmarine 145.8 *distant*
transmigration 316.1 *transfer*
transmigration of souls 224.3 *transformation*
transmissible 692.35 *communicable*; 316.17 *transferable*
transmission 316.3; 692.25 *broadcast material*; 693.2 *communication*; 331.11 *impulsion*; 318.1 *passage*; 692.6 *telecommunication*; 28.15 *wave property*
transmissional 692.33 *communicational*
transmission density 41.10 *graininess*
transmission line 39.33 *power distribution*; 692.6 *telecommunication*
transmission of disease 316.3 *transmission*
transmissive 316.17 *transferable*
transmit 504.16 *be heard*; 692.30, 693.12 *communicate*; 39.35, 631.15 *conduct*; 318.11 *cross*; 768.5 *give*; 740.13 *make public*; 741.13 *report*; 733.10 *send*; 316.11 *transfer*; 316.12 *transport*
transmit colour 529.17 *colourcast*
transmit light 527.11 *be transparent*
transmittable 692.35 *communicable*; 316.17 *transferable*
transmittal 316.1 *transfer*
transmittance 316.1 *transfer*
transmitted 504.11 *aural*; 692.34 *communicated*
transmitted wave 692.15
transmitter 692.16; 316.9 *disease carrier*
transmit thoughts 11.24 *experience psychic phenomena*
transmitting antenna 692.17 *antenna*
transmogrification 224.3 *transformation*
transmogrify 224.9 *transform*
transmontane 145.8 *distant*
transmundane 145.8 *distant*; 101.8 *nonmaterial*; 11.18 *spiritual*
transmutable 760.15 *convertible*
transmutation 760.1 *conversion*; 28.71 *nuclear reaction*; 224.3 *transformation*
transmutative 224.13 *transformative*
transmute 760.7 *convert into*; 224.9, 760.9 *transform*
transmuted 760.13 *converted*
transmuting 760.14 *converting*
transoceanic 145.8 *distant*
transom 50.3 *parts of a sailing boat*; 413.2 *supporting part*
transpacific 145.8 *distant*
Transparency 527
transparency 527.5; 725.1 *clarity*; 41.12 *development*; 521.4 *invisibility*; 41.3 *photograph*; 695.10 *simplicity*; 21.19 *stage set*; 527.8 *transparent thing*
transparent 527.1; 24.10 *ceramic*; 725.3 *clear*; 739.10 *disclosed*; 521.1 *invisible*; 646.1 *naive*; 695.2 *simple*
transparent glaze 24.3 *glaze*
transparently 527.13; 725.4 *clearly*; 24.12 *ornamentally*
transparent pigment 529.4 *pigment*
transparent thing 527.8
transpersonal theory 36.3 *psychiatric treatment*
transphysical 11.16 *psychic*
transphysical science 11.1 *occultism*
transpicuous 527.1 *transparent*
transpiration 34.5 *physiology*; 316.3 *transmission*; 30.10 *water cycle*
transpire 739.9 *be disclosed*; 738.5 *be visible*; 30.63 *ebb*; 345.9 *take effect*; 316.11 *transfer*
transplacement 316.1 *transfer*
transplant 44.15 *cultivate*; 368.8 *insertion*; 368.6 *plant*; 35.20 *practise surgery*; 762.3 *substitute thing*; 394.12 *surgery*; 316.11 *transfer*
transplantation 368.8 *insertion*; 35.9 *surgery*; 316.1 *transfer*
transplanted 368.12 *inserted*
transplant surgery 394.12 *surgery*
transpolar 145.8 *distant*
transpontine 145.8 *distant*
Transport 319
transport 316.12; **319.1**; **319.4**; 318.11 *cross*; 144.14 *displace*; 597.1 *happiness*; 300.2 *momentum*; 371.4 *ostracize*; 814.1 *punish*; 593.2 *romantic love*; 300.14 *set in motion*; 319.5 *transportable*; 316.2 *transportation*
transportable 319.5; 316.17 *transferable*
transportation 316.2; 300.2 *momentum*; 371.19 *ostracism*; 814.7 *punishment*; 319.1 *transport*; 319.5 *transportable*
transportation corps 584.4 *military organization*
transportation engineering 38.17 *civil engineering*
transportative 316.17 *transferable*
transport box 43.10 *farm tool*
transport café 557.15 *eating place*
transport charges 790.6 *business costs*

transport door-to-door 319.4 *transport*
transported 597.4 *happy*; 319.5 *transportable*
transporter **319.3**; 316.7 *transferor*; 320.20 *truck*
transporter bridge 38.21 *bridge*
transport goods 319.4 *transport*
transporting 319.5 *transportable*
transportive 316.17 *transferable*
transport of love 593.2 *romantic love*
transport plane 586.31 *military aircraft*
transport ship 586.24 *warship*
transport system 319.1 *transport*
transposable 760.15 *convertible*; 316.17 *transferable*
transposal 316.1 *transfer*
transpose 18.35 *compose*; 760.7 *convert into*; 224.10, 759.5 *exchange*; 192.3 *invert*; 27.22 *matrix*; 300.14 *set in motion*; 316.11 *transfer*
transposed 760.13 *converted*; 759.7 *exchanged*
transposition 760.1 *conversion*; 224.4, 759.1 *exchange*; 192.1 *inversion*; 18.20 *key*; 316.1 *transfer*
transpositional 224.14 *exchangeable*; 192.2 *inverted*
transposon 34.13 *genetic material*
transsexual **567.11**; 568.10 *homosexual*; 227.9 *person who changes sex*
transship 144.14 *displace*; 319.4 *transport*
transshipment 144.1 *displacement*; 319.1 *transport*; 316.2 *transportation*
Trans-Siberian Railway 321.10 *miscellaneous*
transubstantial 10.21 *ritualistic*; 224.13 *transformative*
transubstantiate 224.9 *transform*
transubstantiation 10.6 *Eucharist*; 224.3 *transformation*
transudate 560.4 *excrement*
transudating 318.13 *penetrating*
transudation 560.4 *excrement*; 560.1 *excretion*; 315.2 *outflow*; 318.3 *passage into*; 559.1 *secretion*
transudative 560.24 *excretory*; 315.17 *leaky*
transudatory 559.4 *secretory*
transude 560.15 *excrete*; 559.7 *secrete*
transumption 316.4 *translation*
transuranic 32.34 *elemental*
transuranic element 32.6 *chemical element*
transversal 27.37 *line*
transverse 150.1 *broad*; 176.8, 189.4 *oblique*
transverse dune 30.37 *dune*
transverse load 38.14 *load*
transversely 150.8 *breadthwise*; 189.8 *obliquely*
transverseness 189.1 *obliqueness*
transverse ridge rib 20.7 *vault*
transverse wave 28.12, 326.5 *wave*
transvestite 567.11 *transsexual*
Trap 379
trap **379.1**; **379.2**; 630.10 *ambush*; 308.4 *body orifice*; 264.23 *cause difficulties*; 309.4 *closed place*; 736.3 *covering up*; 254.5 *danger*; 480.9 *enticement*; 633.11 *hunt*; 633.3 *hunting and fishing equipment*; 382.22 *kill animals*; 384.8 *military defences*; 46.9 *play*; 46.15 *play offence*; 66.4 *play soccer*; 484.13 *plot*; 700.13, 700.33 *snare*; 21.17 *stage*; 645.2 *stratagem*; 773.10 *take away*
trapa 7.7 *monk*
trap door 700.12 *disguise*; 314.6 *means of entry*; 389.2 *means of escape*; 700.13 *snare*; 379.1 *trap*
trapeze 361.3 *suspended object*
trapeze artist 336.5 *athlete*; 21.31 *circus performer*
trapezium 27.44 *polygon*; 200.2 *quadrilateral*
trapezoid 27.44 *polygon*; 200.2 *quadrilateral*
trap for the unwary 379.1 *trap*
trapped **700.42**; 254.4 *endangered*; 66.5 *soccer*; 630.6 *surprised*
trapper 382.13 *animal killer*; 71.24, 633.6 *hunter*
trapping 382.9 *animal killing*; 633.2 *chase*; 66.2 *football play*; 71.23 *mammal hunting*
trappings 211.3 *additional item*; 438.7 *equipment*; 440.4 *possessions*
Trappist 732.5 *shy person*
trapshooter 330.15 *shooter*
trapshooting 330.6 *shooting*; 60.1 *target shooting*
trash 124.9 *bauble*; 205.8 *bits and pieces*; 258.4 *dirt*; 767.3 *disposable things*; 236.8 *inferiority*; 441.2 *lay waste*; 408.4 *litter*; 124.10 *nonentity*; 697.1 *nonsense*; 655.7 *outsider*; 238.6 *refuse*; 215.2 *residue*; 441.5 *waste product*
trash can 410.11 *vessel*
trash dump 238.6 *refuse*; 767.8 *sink*; 439.4 *storage*
trashiness 236.8 *inferiority*
trashing 247.2 *defeat*
trashy 236.2 *inferior*; 793.10 *shoddy*; 124.4 *trivial*; 238.1 *useless*
trattoria 557.15 *eating place*
trauma 260.4 *disease*; 491.3 *injury*; 36.12 *stress*
traumatic 394.18 *medical*; 491.5 *painful*; 394.10 *surgical dressing*
traumatic disease 260.4 *disease*
traumatic neurosis 36.10 *neurosis*
traumatism 36.12 *stress*
traumatize 491.11 *inflict pain*
traumatized 491.7 *feeling pain*; 36.36 *psychologically disturbed*
travail 249.1 *adversity*; 576.8 *exert oneself*; 561.7 *obstetrics*; 576.1 *work*
travel 100.14 *be foreign*; 302.10 *forward motion*; 302.1 *go forward*; 300.2 *momentum*; 49.6 *play basketball*; 318.9 *proceed*; 300.15 *walk*
travel at maximum speed 332.4 *be swift*
travel bag 410.9 *baggage*
travel by water 323.9 *navigate*
travelcard 793.4 *bargain*
travel in a circle 179.6 *circle*
travel in space 29.38 *launch*
travelled out 261.1 *fatigued*
traveller 644.3 *curious person*; 449.12 *discoverer*; 118.7 *nonconformist*; 778.11 *pedlar*; 227.7 *person who moves around*; 550.22 *progression*; 778.10 *salesman*
traveller's cheque 780.14 *paper money*
traveller's tale 699.10 *lie*; 727.5 *tall story*
travelling 100.10 *foreign*; 300.16 *moving*; 49.5 *penalties*; 550.41 *progressing*; 250.11 *ranging*; 118.13 *unconventional*
travelling circus 21.7 *show*
travelling clock 281.6 *clock*
travelling companion 223.11 *companion*
travelling salesman 778.10 *salesman*
travelling through 550.22 *progression*
travelling wave 28.12 *wave*
travel off season 793.14 *buy cheaply*
travelogue 721.3 *narration*; 17.4 *nonfiction*; 693.5 *reference book*; 356.5 *work of art*
travel report 31.4 *weather forecast*
travel second-class 793.14 *buy cheaply*
travel-sick 371.30 *vomiting*
travel through 550.35 *progress*
travel tourist-class 793.14 *buy cheaply*
travel-weary 261.1 *fatigued*
travel with 223.14 *keep company with*
travel writing 17.4 *nonfiction*
travers 59.10 *dressage*
traversal 550.22 *progression*
traverse 113.15 *be opposite*; 347.3 *counteract*; 318.11 *cross*; 62.9 *mountaineer*; 113.14 *oppose*; 318.1 *passage*; 550.35 *progress*; 68.12, 68.14 *ski*
traverse downhill 68.2 *cross-country skiing*
traverser 550.22 *progression*
traverse table 323.5 *navigation*
traversing 318.1 *passage*; 318.12 *passing*; 550.22 *progression*; 68.4 *skiing technique*
travesty 621.2 *act of derision*; 486.9 *bungling*; 234.4 *distortion of the truth*; 727.7 *exaggerate*; 727.1 *exaggeration*; 125.9 *imitate*; 720.1 *misinterpret*; 720.2 *misinterpretation*; 718.4 *misrepresent*; 274.5, 718.1 *misrepresentation*; 125.3 *mockery*
travolator 316.5 *means of transport*; 320.4 *personal transport*
trawl 362.12 *drag*; 74.15 *fish*; 74.7 *fishing*; 633.11 *hunt*; 362.2 *pull*; 700.13, 700.33 *snare*
trawled 700.42 *trapped*
trawler 74.7 *fishing*; 633.6 *hunter*; 323.7 *nautical person*; 323.3 *vessel*
trawlerman 55.6 *angler*; 74.10 *fisher*; 633.6 *hunter*
tray 410.16 *crockery*; 187.3 *flat thing*
treacherous **700.38**; 254.1 *dangerous*; 699.33 *deceitful*; 479.11 *equivocating*; 800.6 *faithless*; 453.7 *unreliable*; 254.2 *unsafe*
treacherously 254.11 *dangerously*; 800.11 *dishonourably*; 479.13 *perfidiously*; 453.26 *unreliably*
treacherousness 254.5 *danger*; 700.4 *falseheartedness*; 227.2 *irresolution*; 453.15 *unreliability*
treachery 479.7 *apostasy*; 254.5 *danger*; 699.5 *deceitfulness*; 800.2 *faithlessness*; 700.4 *falseheartedness*
treacle 267.4 *adherent*; 430.6 *gelatin*; 498.2 *sweetener*
treacliness 430.1 *viscosity*
treacly 430.9 *gelatinous*; 498.6 *sweet*
tread 300.12 *gait*; 209.4 *interval*; 50.8 *punting*; 317.2 *route*; 304.10 *step*; 349.1 *use*; 300.15 *walk*
tread a measure 22.15 *dance*
tread carefully 665.10 *be careful*; 264.20 *be in difficulty*
tread downward 305.9 *descend*
tread flat 187.7 *make horizontal*
treading water 67.1 *swimming*
treadle 330.20 *propel*
treadmill 620.2 *boring thing*; 132.6 *continuum*; 814.15 *instrument of torture*; 111.6 *regularity*; 307.6 *rotator*; 632.3 *way*; 576.1 *work*
tread on 236.14 *ill-treat*; 331.7 *kick*; 387.6 *subject*; 647.6 *suppress*
tread on dangerous ground 254.8 *be in danger*
tread on eggs 264.20 *be in difficulty*
tread on someone's toes 668.22 *show disrespect*
treads and risers 304.7 *means of ascent*
tread the beaten path 632.16 *have a habit*
tread the boards 21.34 *act*
tread the primrose path 245.1 *deteriorate*
tread under foot 647.6 *suppress*
tread warily 665.10 *be careful*; 616.5 *be cautious*; 637.8 *hold back*
tread water 301.8 *be motionless*; 341.4 *not act*; 67.9 *swim*
treason 661.3 *act of defiance*; 699.5 *deceitfulness*; 753.2 *disorder*; 800.2 *faithlessness*; 700.4 *falseheartedness*; 662.3 *subversion*
treasonable 662.14 *subversive*
treasonable activities 662.3 *subversion*
treasonist 700.21 *traitor*
treasonous 699.33 *deceitful*; 800.6 *faithless*; 753.10 *lawbreaking*; 700.38 *treacherous*
treasure 545.3 *attractive female*; 235.8 *exceller*; 780.6 *funds*; 797.17 *good thing*; 595.4 *likable person*; 595.7 *like*; 593.23 *love*; 400.11 *masterpiece*; 359.5 *preserve*; 252.10 *protect*; 667.15 *respect*; 439.1, 439.6 *store*
treasure chest 780.20 *money store*
treasured 593.21 *beloved*; 359.7 *preserved*; 235.3 *valuable*
treasure house 439.4 *storage*; 780.19 *treasury*
treasure map 163.4 *map*
treasurer **780.18**; 789.6 *accountant*; 780.17 *financier*; 785.5 *payer*; 436.3 *provider*
treasure-trove 449.10 *find*; 765.5 *profit*
treasury **780.19**; 723.3 *compendium*; 439.4 *storage*
treasury note 780.14 *paper money*
treasury of words 5.28 *dictionary*
treat **42.15**; 631.14 *behave towards*; 393.6 *cure*; 785.8 *defray*; 394.20 *doctor*; 787.3 *donate*; 597.2 *fun*; 768.5 *give*; 490.9 *give pleasure*; 259.7 *make healthy*; 241.10 *pleasant thing*; 490.4 *pleasurable things*; 35.19 *practise medicine*; 394.19 *remedy*; 392.19 *support*; 630.4 *surprising thing*; 346.9 *take action*; 349.1 *use*
treatable 393.14 *repairable*
treat as 762.5 *take a substitute*
treat as a leper 655.13 *ignore*
treat as an outsider 655.13 *ignore*
treat cruelly 245.6 *pervert*
treated **42.11**
treated like dirt 387.9 *subject*
treated like shit 387.9 *subject*
treat equally **391.6**
treat in detail 139.23 *particularize*
treatise 722.1 *dissertation*; 447.5 *educational topic*; 17.4 *nonfiction*
treat kindly 648.3 *be lenient*
treat lightly 648.3 *be lenient*
treat like dirt 668.27 *desecrate*; 387.6 *subject*
treat like shit 668.27 *desecrate*; 387.6 *subject*
treatment **19.4**; **35.8**; **461.9**; **631.8**; 356.2 *manufacture*; 392.5 *medical assistance*; 346.1 *operation*; 394.13 *therapy*; 349.6 *use*
treat rough 647.6 *suppress*
treat rudely 659.7 *be discourteous*
treat teeth 35.21 *practise dentistry*
treat unfairly 465.11 *be unjust*; 466.14 *discriminate against*
treat well 650.8 *be benevolent*
treat with deference 658.13 *defer to*
treat with politeness 658.11 *have good manners*
treaty 755.3 *alliance*; 750.3 *arrangement*; 749.1 *pacification*
treaty-maker 755.4 *contractor*
treaty-making 755.7 *contractual*; 746.8 *negotiated*; 746.1 *negotiation*; 734.5 *talks*
Treaty of Paris 755.3 *alliance*
Treaty of Rome 755.3 *alliance*
Treaty of Versailles 755.3 *alliance*
treble 69.6 *darts*; 18.32 *instrumental*; 59.9 *jumping*; 504.10 *sound quality*; 199.1, 199.7 *three*; 199.10 *triple*
treble clef 18.20 *key*; 18.17 *notation*
treble figures **201.9**
treble hook 55.3 *fishing tackle*
trebleness 199.3 *threeness*
treble top 69.6 *darts*
trebling 213.1 *increase*; 199.4 *triplication*
trebly 199.12 *thrice*
trebuchet 587.6 *historical missile weapon*
tredecillion 194.3 *large number*; 201.11 *million*
tree **79.1**; 264.23 *cause difficulties*; 44.9 *garden plant*; 77.2 *plant*
tree-covered 79.16 *wooded*
tree creeper 79.11 *tree-related animal*
tree disease **79.10**
tree farm 43.6 *farm*; 79.4 *trees*; 577.1 *workshop*
tree farmer 79.8 *forester*
tree farming 43.4 *arable farming*; 79.5 *forestry*
tree felling 79.6 *tree management*
tree fern 82.1 *fern*; 79.1 *tree*
tree frog 79.11 *tree-related animal*
treehopper 79.11 *tree-related animal*
tree kangaroo 79.11 *tree-related animal*
treeless 563.3 *infertile*
treelike **79.14**; 311.9 *branched*
treelikeness 311.4 *branching*
tree line 79.4 *trees*
tree litter 79.4 *trees*
tree mallow 79.1 *tree*
tree management **79.6**
tree moss 82.3 *moss*
tree mythology **79.13**
treen 79.5 *forestry*; 23.8 *woodwork*; 79.15 *woody*
treenail 373.8 *fastening*
tree nursery 79.4 *trees*
treenware 79.5 *forestry*
tree nymph 8.5 *deity*; 79.13 *tree mythology*
tree of Jesse 79.13 *tree mythology*
tree of knowledge 79.13 *tree mythology*
tree of life 79.13 *tree mythology*
tree part **79.2**
tree planting 79.5 *forestry*
tree product **79.9**
tree-related animal **79.11**
tree ring 79.3 *timber*
tree-ring dating 275.8 *dating*; 79.3 *timber*
Trees 79
trees **79.4**
tree-shaped 311.9 *branched*
tree shrew 79.11 *tree-related animal*
tree snake 79.11 *tree-related animal*
tree sparrow 79.11 *tree-related animal*
tree stump 79.2 *tree part*
tree surgeon 79.8 *forester*
tree surgery 79.6 *tree management*
treetop 174.2 *head*
tree worship 9.2 *idolatry*
tree worshipper 9.6 *idolater*
tree-worshipping 9.10 *idolatrous*

trefoil 743.8 *heraldic device*; 199.2 *trident*
Tregean 4.11 *follower of a doctrine*
trellis 193.2 *braid*; 44.3 *ornamental garden*
Trematoda 75.6 *worm*
trematode 75.6 *worm*
tremble 612.11 *be afraid*; 227.11 *be changeable*; 494.10 *be cold*; 337.6 *be weak*; 30.64 *fold*; 327.24 *shake*; 326.9 *vibrate*
tremble in the balance 254.8 *be in danger*
trembling 612.8 *fearful*; 612.2 *fearfulness*; 327.6 *shaking*; 327.18 *shaky*
trembling in the balance 254.2 *unsafe*
tremblingly 327.28 *shakily*
trembling palsy 327.7 *shake*
tremelloid 430.9 *gelatinous*
tremendous 158.15 *big*
tremolo 18.16 *musical note*; 509.6 *musical repetition*
tremor 711.2 *danger signal*; 380.3 *instance of violence*; 327.9 *jolt*; 260.17 *nervous disorder*; 327.7 *shake*; 326.2 *vibration*; 326.5 *wave*
tremors 690.16 *alcoholism*
tremulous 612.8 *fearful*; 327.18 *shaky*; 639.3 *timid*; 326.17 *waving*
tremulously 612.15 *fearfully*; 327.28 *shakily*
tremulousness 327.6 *shaking*; 639.13 *timidity*
trench 183.2 *concave land*; 146.2, 146.5 *crack*; 44.15 *cultivate*; 165.3 *enclosing thing*; 184.2 *furrow*; 384.8 *military defences*; 252.5 *refuge*; 184.8 *wrinkle*
trenchancy 726.1 *emphasis*
trenchant 269.3 *concise*; 726.3 *emphatic*; 123.5 *important*; 336.10 *potent*
trenchantly 269.5 *concisely*
trench coat 551.12 *coat*
trencher 38.29 *construction equipment*
trencherman 557.18 *eater*; 688.4 *glutton*
trencherwoman 688.4 *glutton*
trench fever 260.6 *infection*
trench gun 587.11 *guns*
trenching machine 38.29 *construction equipment*
trench-mortar 587.11 *guns*
trench warfare 585.8 *warfare*
trend 324.2 *bearing*; 117.5 *convention*; 115.2 *copy*; 632.4 *custom*; 325.1 *deviate*; 553.1 *fashion*; 482.5 *final intention*; 160.5 *formality*; 595.3 *likes*; 300.2 *momentum*; 295.7 *new thing*; 345.4 *significance*; 132.7 *stability*; 221.1 *state*; 324.7 *take a direction*; 104.2, 229.1 *tendency*
trendify 295.20 *make new*; 393.2 *refurbish*
trendily **295.23**; 221.9 *conditionally*; 553.10 *fashionably*
trendiness **295.2**
trending 229.5 *tending to*
trendsetter 551.27 *model*; 295.9 *modern person*; 129.8 *precursor*
trendsetting 295.16 *avant-garde*; 553.7 *fashionable*
trendsetting group 295.6 *avant-garde*
trend upwards 304.21 *upturn*
trendy 295.16 *avant-garde*; 553.7 *fashionable*; 160.11 *formal*; 221.8 *in a state of*; 295.10 *new*
Trent 90.4 *British rivers*
trepan 394.20 *doctor*; 308.20 *hole*; 308.2 *opener*
trepang 75.3 *echinoderm*
trephination 394.12 *surgery*
trephine 394.20 *doctor*; 308.20 *hole*; 308.2 *opener*
trepidation 612.2 *fearfulness*
trespass 662.15 *be disobedient*; 100.16 *be external*; 804.16 *be wicked*; 16.39 *crime*; 802.21 *do wrong*; 314.10 *invade*; 16.38 *lawbreaking*; 564.15 *settle*; 806.3, 806.10 *sin*; 329.5 *transgress*; 329.8 *transgression*; 662.2 *violation of the law*; 804.1 *wickedness*; 802.8 *wrongdoing*
trespasser 128.5 *excluded person*; 564.6 *illegal occupant*; 100.8, 314.8 *intruder*; 802.10 *wrongdoer*
trespassing 100.12 *external*; 100.4 *externality*; 314.3 *inroad*; 314.16 *invasive*; 16.60 *offending*; 329.11 *overrun*; 806.7 *sinful*; 804.11 *wicked*
trestle 317.10 *railway*
trestle bridge 38.21 *bridge*
trestletree 79.12 *figurative usage*
tresure 743.8 *heraldic device*
trews 551.9 *trousers*
trey 69.3 *card game terms*; 199.1 *three*
triable 16.47 *liable to law*; 16.58 *unjust*
triacidic 32.36 *acid*
triacidic base 32.9 *base*
triad 18.16 *musical note*; 199.1 *three*
triadic 199.7 *three*
trial 814.10 *affliction*; 264.3 *difficult task*; 448.1 *experiment*; 448.8 *experimental*; 16.7 *legal trial*; 16.33 *litigation*; 243.10 *preparations*; 705.3 *questionnaire*; 448.2 *rehearsal*; 353.9 *tentative*; 353.6 *venture*
trial and error 448.1 *experiment*
trial at the bar 16.7 *legal trial*
trial balloon 740.1 *publication*; 448.2 *rehearsal*; 645.2 *stratagem*
trial by jury 16.7 *legal trial*
trial by law 16.7 *legal trial*
trial by one's peers 16.7 *legal trial*
trial in court 16.7 *legal trial*
triality 199.3 *threeness*
trial judge 464.6 *justice*
trial jury 16.26, 464.7 *jury*; 16.13 *lawyer*
trial marriage 570.3 *types of marriage*
trial run 243.10 *preparations*; 448.2 *rehearsal*
trials 249.1 *adversity*
trials and tribulations 249.1 *adversity*
triangle **27.43**; 176.3 *angled figure*; 65.1 *billiards*; 814.15 *instrument of torture*; 27.44 *polygon*; 510.4 *sources of resonance*; 199.2 *trident*
triangle fortification 384.11 *fortification*
triangular 176.9 *angled*; 27.82 *polygonal*; 199.8 *three-sided*
triangular offence 58.3 *ice hockey*
triangulate 142.11 *find*; 26.10 *measure*; 199.8 *three-sided*
triangulated 26.13 *measured*
triangulation 26.1 *measurement*; 142.5 *topography*; 27.51 *trigonometry*
triangulation point 742.5 *indicator*
triangulation station 154.8 *high thing*
Triassic period 284.3 *geological period*
triatomic 32.35 *combined*
tribade 568.10 *homosexual*
tribal 566.13 *national*; 564.12 *native*; 1.14 *societal*
tribalism 12.1 *government*; 566.9 *group*; 396.7 *type of rule*
tribal killer 382.10 *killer*
tribally 1.18 *societally*
tribal memory 215.1 *remainder*; 1.8 *tradition*
tribal system 12.1 *government*
tribal warrior 586.8 *soldier*
tribasic 32.36 *acid*
tribasic acid 32.8 *acid*
tribe 373.3 *associate*; 289.2 *descent*; 376.17 *family*; 137.8 *genealogy*; 566.9 *group*; 564.2 *inhabitants*; 1.7 *society*; 34.17 *taxonomy*
tribrach 17.9 *metre*
tribulation 264.3 *difficult task*
tribunal **16.18**; 579.7 *council*; 16.49 *judicatory*; 16.2 *jurisdiction*; 464.3 *place of judgment*
tribunal of penance 16.18 *tribunal*
tribune gallery 10.12 *church*; 20.10 *church architecture*
tributary 768.7 *given*; 768.4 *giver*; 122.6 *inferior*; 90.1 *river*; 122.15 *subordinate*
tribute **601.6**; 669.4 *compliment*; 768.2 *gift*; 785.4 *grant*; 790.8 *levy*; 462.3 *memento*; 785.1 *payment*; 241.10 *pleasant thing*; 671.3 *recognition*; 813.1 *reward*; 769.2 *something received*
tribute-payer 768.4 *giver*
trice 362.11 *pull*
tricentenary 298.3, 298.13 *anniversary*
tricentennial 601.14 *centennial*
tricentennially 298.16 *cyclically*
triceps 336.1 *strength*
trichoic 541.6 *variegated*
trichologist 547.13 *beautician*
trichology 547.7 *hairdressing*
trichomatic 541.6 *variegated*
trichomonad 75.9 *protozoan*
trichomoniasis 75.12 *protozoal disease*
trichopteran 76.10 *insectan*
trichotomize 199.11 *trisect*
trichotomous 199.9 *trisected*
trichotomy 199.5 *trisection*
trichroism 541.1 *variegation*
trichromatism 541.1 *variegation*
trick **700.8**; **700.28**; 645.5 *be cunning*; 604.8 *be dishonest*; 700.27 *be false*; 699.25 *be fraudulent*; 139.3 *characteristic*; 705.21 *confuse*; 702.12 *deceive*; 96.3 *delusion*; 484.3 *expedient plan*; 800.1 *improbity*; 141.8 *intervening space*; 599.5 *joke*; 700.29 *juggle*; 389.2 *means of escape*; 485.1 *skill*; 702.2 *sophism*; 645.2 *stratagem*; 631.9 *tactics*; 576.2 *task*; 632.2 *tendency*; 697.3 *tomfoolery*; 379.1, 379.2 *trap*
trick cycle 320.12 *bicycle*
trick cyclist 35.11 *doctor*; 36.30, 461.10 *psychiatrist*
tricked 604.10, 700.36 *deceived*
tricked out 547.14 *beautified*; 551.30 *dressed-up*
trickery 645.1 *cunning*; 736.5 *evasion*; 699.8 *fraud*; 800.1 *improbity*; 700.9 *sleight of hand*; 700.7 *tricking*
trickily 705.24 *questionably*
trickiness 702.3 *cunning*; 268.9 *duplicity*; 700.5 *falseness*
tricking **700.7**
trickle 206.1 *few*; 90.7 *flow*; 315.12 *leak*; 315.3 *leakage*; 333.1 *move slowly*; 429.16 *seep*; 124.8 *trifle*
trickling 315.3 *leakage*
trick of fortune 604.2 *bad outcome*
trick of the light 96.3 *delusion*; 604.3 *mirage*
trick play 46.9 *play*
trick question 705.4 *difficult question*
tricks of the trade 352.1 *means*; 645.2 *stratagem*; 700.7 *tricking*
trickster 700.17 *cheat*; 645.3 *cunning person*; 700.15, 718.3 *deceiver*; 774.11 *dishonest person*; 485.5 *expert*; 702.6 *sophist*
tricksy 645.4 *cunning*
tricky 645.4, 702.8 *cunning*; 254.1 *dangerous*; 700.34 *deceiving*; 800.5 *dishonourable*; 699.35 *fraudulent*; 700.40 *illusory*; 264.12, 705.13 *problematic*
tricky business 774.7 *dishonesty*
tricky situation 143.3 *difficult circumstances*; 264.5 *predicament*
tricky spot 264.5 *predicament*
triclinic 32.33 *crystalline*
triclinic crystal 32.4 *crystal*
Tricolour 743.7 *flag*
tricolour 541.5 *variegated thing*
tricorn 551.15 *headgear*; 199.8 *three-sided*; 199.2 *trident*
tricornered 199.8 *three-sided*
tricycle 320.12 *bicycle*; 199.2 *trident*
tridem 50.7, 50.13 *windsurfing*
Trident 587.5 *missile weapon*
trident **199.2**; 311.5 *fork*; 199.8 *three-sided*
tridentate 199.8 *three-sided*
trident-like 311.9 *branched*
tridimensional 199.8 *three-sided*
tried 485.8 *expert*; 448.10 *tested*
tried and tested 452.1 *certain*; 136.9 *qualified*
tried-and-true 569.11 *devoted*
tried-and-true method 631.7 *way*
triedness 569.3 *familiarity*
triennial 199.8 *three-sided*; 199.2 *trident*
triennium 199.2 *trident*
trier 353.7 *attempter*; 448.5 *experimenter*; 640.5 *tenacious person*
trifid 199.9 *trisected*
trifle **124.8**; 793.5 *cheap item*; 593.26 *court*; 25.35 *dessert*
trifler 642.4 *capricious person*; 124.10 *nonentity*
trifles 124.8 *trifle*
trifle with 642.5 *be capricious*; 245.4 *impair*
trifling 159.7 *little*; 157.2 *superficial*; 124.4 *trivial*
trifling fault 124.8 *trifle*
trifold 199.7 *three*
trifoliate 77.18 *of leaves*; 199.8 *three-sided*
triforium 317.7 *arcade*; 10.12 *church*; 20.10 *church architecture*
triforking 311.4 *branching*
triform 199.7 *three*
trifurcate 311.14 *branch*; 199.11 *trisect*
trifurcated 311.9 *branched*; 199.9 *trisected*
trifurcation 311.4 *branching*; 199.5 *trisection*
trig 27.51 *trigonometry*
trigamy 570.3 *types of marriage*
trigeminal neuralgia 260.17 *nervous disorder*
Trigger 59.1 *horse*
trigger 587.9 *firearm*; 437.11 *fuel*; 438.1 *tool*
trigger-happy 586.33 *combative*; 382.24 *murderous*; 615.4 *rash*
trigger off 130.20 *activate*; 344.10 *awaken*
triglyceride 33.7 *fat*
triglyphic 20.17 *structured*
trigon 27.43 *triangle*
trigonal 32.33 *crystalline*; 199.8 *three-sided*
trigonal crystal 32.4 *crystal*
trigonometrical 27.68, 210.15 *mathematical*
trigonometrically 27.87, 210.16 *mathematically*
trigonometric function **27.52**; 27.29 *mathematical function*
trigonometrician 210.7 *mathematician*
trigonometry **27.51**; 176.4 *angular measurement*; 210.1 *calculation*; 27.1 *mathematics*
trig point 154.8 *high thing*
trihebdomadary 199.2 *trident*
trihedral 199.8 *three-sided*
trihedron 199.2 *trident*
trihydrate 32.10 *salt*
trike 320.12 *bicycle*
trilateral 176.9 *angled*; 169.6 *side*; 199.8 *three-sided*
trilby 551.15 *headgear*
trilingual 729.19 *speaking*; 199.8 *three-sided*
trill **509.13**; 90.7 *flow*; 729.3 *mode of speech*; 18.16 *musical note*; 509.6 *musical repetition*; 307.9 *roll*; 18.39, 516.10 *sing*
trillion 194.3 *large number*; 201.11 *million*; 208.7 *myriad*
trillions 208.2 *multitude*
trillionth 201.22 *millionth*
trilobite 75.4 *arthropod*; 30.43 *fossil*; 284.10 *fossilization*; 296.8 *prehistoric animal*
trilogy 21.2 *play*; 199.2 *trident*
trim 698.31 *be accurate*; 479.1 *be equivocal*; 23.17 *carpenter*; 209.6 *change gradually*; 256.13 *clean*; 164.6 *edge*; 547.8 *haircut*; 259.3 *health*; 793.13 *make cheap*; 117.9 *make conform*; 191.5, 214.5 *make smaller*; 322.7 *miscellaneous aviation terms*; 160.6 *nature*; 407.13 *orderly*; 542.12 *ornament*; 551.24 *part of garment*; 545.6 *personable*; 221.5 *physical state*; 206.8 *reduce*; 149.10 *shorten*
trimaran 199.2 *trident*
trim back 245.5 *hurt*
trim down to size 124.13 *make unimportant*
trimester 199.2 *trident*
trimestrial 199.8 *three-sided*
trimeter 17.9 *metre*; 199.2 *trident*
trimetric 199.8 *three-sided*
trimmed 698.21 *accurate*; 547.14 *beautified*; 256.17 *cleaned*; 23.16 *joined*; 542.10 *ornate*; 149.8 *shortened*; 191.7 *smaller*; 551.31 *styled*
trimmed joist 23.10 *carpenter's term*
trimmer 117.6 *conformist*; 191.4 *contractor*; 479.1 *equivocator*; 700.21 *traitor*
trimming 698.8 *accuracy*; 23.10 *carpenter's term*; 191.1 *contraction*; 164.2 *edging*; 23.16 *joined*; 542.1 *ornament*; 149.2 *shortening*
trimmings 211.3 *additional item*; 215.2 *residue*
trimorphic 199.7 *three*
trimorphism 199.3 *threeness*
trim the sails 323.9 *navigate*
Trimurti 8.3 *God*
trinal 199.7 *three*
trinary 199.7 *three*
trine 176.4 *angular measurement*; 199.1, 199.7 *three*
trinely 199.12 *thrice*
Trinitarian 7.5 *Christian*
trinity 199.1 *three*
trinket 124.9 *bauble*; 793.5 *cheap item*
trinkets 542.6 *decorative articles*
trinkgeld 813.7 *bounty*; 768.2 *gift*
trinomial 27.76 *functional*; 199.2 *trident*
trio 374.3 *assembly*; 18.26 *musical group*; 747.9 *team*; 199.1 *three*
triode 39.20 *electron tube*
triolet 17.7 *poem*; 17.10 *verse form*
triose 33.3 *carbohydrate*
trip **305.11**; 486.7 *be clumsy*; 804.16 *be wicked*; 378.9 *block*; 22.15 *dance*; 691.1 *drug-taking*; 305.4 *fall*; 66.2 *football play*; 366.4 *gather up*; 367.7 *lean*; 367.11 *lowering*; 465.10 *misjudge*; 318.1 *passage*; 49.6

play basketball; 58.9 *play hockey;* 64.5 *play rugby;* 66.4 *play soccer;* 700.33 *snare;* 300.15 *walk*
triparted 199.9 *trisected*
tripartite 199.9 *trisected*
tripartition 199.5 *trisection*
tripe 172.4 *insides;* 697.1 *nonsense;* 25.31 *offal*
tripedal 199.8 *three-sided*
tripeptide 33.8 *amino acid*
triphibious war 585.1 *war*
trip-hop 18.9 *popular music*
Tripitaka 7.12 *religious text*
triple 199.10; 48.5 *batting terms;* 51.5 *bowling delivery;* 213.5 *make bigger;* 199.1, 199.7 *three;* 47.9 *track*
triple-A 381.13 *air attack*
Triple-A league 48.1 *baseball*
triple bar 59.9 *jumping*
triple crown 64.2 *championship;* 246.3 *successful thing;* 7.11 *vestment*
Triple Entente 755.3 *alliance*
triple jump 47.2 *field events*
triple jumper 47.3 *athlete*
triple jumping 47.2 *field events*
triple metre 17.9 *metre*
tripleness 199.3 *threeness*
triple play 48.6 *fielding terms*
triple point 28.37 *temperature*
triple point of water 28.38 *thermodynamics*
triples 51.9 *bowls*
triples match 51.1 *green bowling*
triplet 17.8 *part of poem;* 199.2 *trident*
triple-tongue 18.38 *sound*
triple vaccine 394.3 *prophylactic*
triplex 199.7 *three*
triplicate 111.4, 111.9, 111.15 *duplicate;* 199.7 *three;* 199.10 *triple*
triplicating 199.4 *triplication*
triplication 199.4; 213.1 *increase*
triplicity 199.3 *threeness*
tripling 199.4 *triplication*
triploid 44.5 *gardening*
triply 199.12 *thrice*
tripod 475.10 *cards;* 41.18 *exposure time;* 413.2 *supporting part;* 199.2 *trident*
tripodic 199.8 *three-sided*
trip out 691.10 *drug oneself*
trip over 486.7 *be clumsy*
tripped 58.8 *hockey;* 66.5 *soccer*
tripping 342.18 *active;* 543.3 *elegant;* 305.18, 367.20 *falling;* 58.1, 58.8 *hockey;* 58.3 *ice hockey;* 58.5 *lacrosse;* 516.6 *melodious;* 49.5 *penalties;* 64.3 *rugby play*
trip switch 39.28 *plug;* 309.2 *stopper*
trip the light fantastic 22.15 *dance*
trip to the moon 29.31 *space travel*
triptych 19.8 *painting;* 199.2 *trident*
triptyque 320.21 *miscellaneous motoring terms*
trip up 623.23 *abase;* 378.9 *block;* 700.33 *snare*
tripwire 384.8 *military defences;* 700.13, 700.33 *snare*
trireme 586.25 *historical naval ships*
trisaccharide 33.3 *carbohydrate*
trisect 199.11
trisected 199.9
trisection 199.5
trishaw 320.12 *bicycle*
Tristan and Isolde 593.10 *lovers*
tristich 17.8 *part of poem;* 199.2 *trident*
tritanopia 519.2 *poor sight*
tritanopic 519.9 *weak-sighted*
trite 620.4 *boring;* 138.22 *commonplace;* 632.10 *familiar;* 112.13 *monotonous;* 745.2 *proverbial;* 497.5 *tasteless*
trite expression 138.8 *generalization*
tritely 620.8 *boringly*
triteness 620.1 *boredom;* 497.1 *dilution*
triterpene 33.20 *terpene*
tritiate 32.26 *react*
triticale 43.12 *crop*
Triton 91.4 *sea god*
Triton among the minnows 121.5 *superior*
triturable 427.20 *pulverizable*
triturate 427.22 *pulverize*
triturated 427.18 *pulverized*
trituration 427.4 *pulverization*
triturator 427.11 *pulverizer*
triumph 121.8 *be superior;* 246.9 *be victorious;* 601.3 *ceremony;* 600.5 *rejoice;* 600.1 *rejoicing;* 601.8 *salute;* 246.2 *victory*
triumphal 601.12 *ceremonial;* 246.15 *victorious*
triumphal arch 601.4 *reception*
triumphal procession 585.2 *glory of war*
triumphant 121.14 *best;* 600.9 *rejoicing;* 246.15 *victorious*
triumphantly 600.11 *rejoicingly;* 246.16 *successfully;* 121.16 *superiorly*
triumphant success 246.1 *success*
triumph of justice 714.1 *vindication*
triumph over 623.26 *outdo*
triumvirate 12.1 *government;* 747.9 *team;* 199.2 *trident*
triune 199.1, 199.7 *three*
trivalent 32.35 *combined*
trivet 199.2 *trident*
trivia 124.8 *trifle*
trivial 124.4; 100.8 *extraneous;* 618.11 *insignificant;* 159.7 *little;* 157.2 *superficial*
trivial error 274.9
triviality 124.7; 100.1 *extraneousness;* 618.5 *insignificance;* 157.3 *shallowness;* 124.8 *trifle*
trivialize 124.13 *make unimportant;* 668.20 *scorn*
trivialized 668.17 *unrespected*
trivially 100.18 *extraneously;* 618.20 *unexceptionally;* 124.14 *unimportantly*
trivia quiz 705.5 *easy question*
tRNA 33.10 *nucleoside*
troat 515.4 *cry*
trochaic 17.20 *metrical*
troche 37.6 *pill*
trochee 17.9 *metre*
trochilic 307.12 *rotary*
trochilics 307.7 *science of rotation*
trochoid 27.40 *curve*
trochophore 75.13 *invertebrate larva*
trodden 317.15 *accessible;* 632.10 *familiar*
trodden flat 187.9 *flattened*
troglodyte 655.6 *unsocial person*
troglodytes 566.3 *early human*
troika 320.10 *sled;* 747.9 *team;* 199.2 *trident*
Troilus and Cressida 593.10 *lovers*
Trojan 342.10 *busy person*
Trojan horse 40.19 *computing terms;* 699.16 *false thing;* 700.14 *fatal gift;* 645.2 *stratagem*
troll 55.7 *angle;* 362.12 *drag;* 11.11 *ghost;* 70.7 *legendary beast;* 307.9, 330.22 *roll*
trolled 55.8 *angling*
trolley 410.10 *cart;* 320.7 *handcart;* 316.5 *means of transport*
trolleybus 320.19 *bus*
trolley line 317.10 *railway*
trolling 55.1, 55.8 *angling;* 307.11 *rotating;* 307.2 *turning*
trollop 796.9 *immoral woman*
trompe l'oeil 96.3 *delusion;* 477.5 *fantasy;* 23.1 *furniture;* 19.4 *treatment*
troop 586.16 *army unit;* 71.21 *assemblage of mammals;* 208.11, 376.40 *crowd;* 376.23 *flock;* 376.14 *force;* 584.4 *military organization;* 208.4 *throng*
troop carrier 586.31 *military aircraft*
trooper 586.20 *cavalryman;* 59.15 *horse person;* 586.8 *soldier*
trooping the Colour 656.3 *formal occasion*
troops 586.14 *armed forces*
troopship 586.24 *warship*
trope 542.1 *ornament;* 5.24 *phrasing;* 17.12 *poetic language;* 694.4 *type of meaning*
trophoplasm 34.7 *cell*
trophy 794.1; 235.7 *elite;* 768.2 *gift;* 743.4 *insignia;* 462.3 *memento;* 744.11 *monument;* 482.6 *objective;* 617.5 *object of desire;* 813.2 *prize;* 765.5 *profit;* 769.2 *something received*
tropic 86.2 *geographical region*
tropical 44.19 *ornamental;* 86.16 *regional;* 493.11 *warm*
tropical air 31.10 *air movement*
tropical climate 31.38 *climate*
tropical disease 260.7; 260.4 *disease*
tropical fern 82.1 *fern*
tropical fish 74.2 *fish*
tropical forest 79.4 *trees*
tropical hardwood 79.1 *tree*
tropical heat 493.5 *hot weather*
tropically 86.19 *geographically;* 44.20 *horticulturally*
tropical meaning 694.4 *type of meaning*
tropical medicine 35.1 *medicine*
tropical revolving storm 31.16 *wind vortex*
tropical storm 31.16 *wind vortex*
tropical summer rainy zone 31.39 *climatic zone*
Tropic of Cancer 493.8 *hot place*
Tropic of Capricorn 493.8 *hot place*
tropics 31.39 *climatic zone;* 86.2 *geographical region;* 493.8 *hot place*
tropology 719.5 *science of interpretation*
tropopause 31.8 *atmosphere;* 434.3 *atmospheric layers*
troposphere 31.8 *atmosphere;* 434.3 *atmospheric layers*
tropospheric 31.43, 434.13 *atmospheric*
Trot 12.6 *political party*
trot 332.4 *be swift;* 300.12 *gait;* 59.16 *ride;* 333.10 *slow motion;* 719.4 *translation*
trot along 313.1 *depart*
trot out 112.18 *harp;* 738.3 *reveal*
trot out clichés 509.14 *repeat*
Trotskyist 662.11 *rebel*
Trotskyists 12.6 *political party*
trotter 25.24 *pork;* 59.2 *thoroughbred*
trotters 25.31 *offal*
trotting 55.1 *angling*
troubadour 17.14 *author;* 21.29 *entertainer;* 516.5 *melodist;* 18.24 *musician*
troubadour poem 17.7 *poem*
trouble 798.2 *affliction;* 327.22 *agitate;* 798.11 *be evil;* 240.5 *be inconvenient;* 236.13 *be worthless;* 249.11 *cause adversity;* 264.23 *cause difficulties;* 328.5 *commotion;* 143.3, 222.4 *difficult circumstances;* 408.9 *disorder;* 328.7 *disturb;* 576.4 *exertion;* 261.6 *fatigue;* 240.3 *inconvenience;* 342.17 *meddle;* 607.3 *nuisance;* 378.2 *obstacle;* 221.2 *predicament;* 612.14 *worry*
trouble ahead 249.1 *adversity*
trouble and strife 570.11 *married woman;* 223.12 *partner;* 568.12 *woman in the family*
troubled 264.16; 798.8 *afflicted;* 327.15 *agitated;* 328.12 *disturbed;* 612.9 *worried*
troublefree 265.14 *relaxed*
troublemaker 408.11; **662.5**; 586.5, 701.6 *arguer;* 236.12 *bad person;* 645.3 *cunning person;* 264.9 *difficult person;* 751.4 *dissenter;* 798.6 *evil person;* 378.7 *hinderer;* 342.11 *meddler;* 483.7 *motivator;* 753.4 *protester;* 242.9 *unpleasant person;* 804.9 *wicked person*
troublemaking 586.34 *argumentative*
trouble oneself 576.8 *exert oneself*
troubles 249.1 *adversity;* 798.2 *affliction*
troubleshooter 392.14, 713.4 *adviser;* 748.3 *mediator*
troubleshooting 748.2 *mediation*
troublesome 264.14; 249.6 *adverse;* 143.8 *circumstantial;* 222.8 *difficult;* 240.1, 264.13 *inconvenient;* 576.11 *laborious;* 342.21 *meddling*
troublesomeness 240.3 *inconvenience*
trouble spot 260.6 *infection;* 379.1 *trap*
troubling 264.13 *inconvenient;* 264.12 *problematic*
troublous 327.15 *agitated;* 798.9 *detrimental*
troublously 327.27 *agitatedly*
trough 410.12 *bath;* 183.3 *cavity;* 183.2 *concave land;* 43.10 *farm tool;* 184.2 *furrow;* 122.5 *inferior state;* 91.3, 326.5 *wave;* 31.11 *weather system;* 184.8 *wrinkle*
trounce 331.5 *beat;* 121.8 *be superior;* 246.10 *defeat heavily;* 814.3 *hit;* 357.11 *ruin*
trounced 122.18 *outclassed*
trouncing 331.12 *collision;* 814.12 *corporal punishment;* 247.2 *defeat;* 246.2 *victory*
troupe 21.25 *cast;* 376.12 *team*
trouper 21.24 *actor*
trouser press 187.4 *flattener;* 421.9 *smoother*
trousers 551.9
trouser suit 551.10 *suit*
trousseau 551.1 *dress;* 439.1 *store*
trout 55.4 *American game fish;* 55.5 *British game fish;* 74.8 *food fish;* 25.17 *freshwater fish*
trout farm 43.6 *farm*
trout fishing 633.2 *chase*
trouvaille 449.10 *find*
trouvère 17.14 *author;* 516.5 *melodist*
trove 765.5 *profit*
trow 11.11 *ghost*
trowel 44.6, 438.3 *garden tool;* 410.17 *ladle;* 425.9 *sharp-edged thing;* 421.9 *smoother;* 425.16 *use a sharp tool*
troy weight 414.9 *avoirdupois weight;* 26.5 *measuring system*
truancy 98.4 *absenteeism;* 634.16 *desertion;* 526.4 *disappearance;* 389.1 *escape;* 355.3 *relinquishment*
truancy officer 6.5 *educationalist*
truant 98.11; 98.6 *absentee;* 634.17 *avoider;* 355.4 *deserter;* 526.4 *disappearance;* 389.3 *escaper;* 389.8 *escaping;* 634.9 *play truant;* 709.4 *refuser*
truantism 98.4 *absenteeism*
truce 294.3 *delayed action;* 390.2 *deliverance;* 301.1 *motionlessness;* 749.1 *pacification;* 226.3 *pause;* 589.1 *peace*
truceless war 585.1 *war*
truck 320.20; 410.10 *cart;* 759.1, 759.5 *exchange;* 743.7 *flag;* 316.5 *means of transport;* 321.6 *rolling stock;* 776.1, 776.4 *trade;* 316.12 *transport;* 319.5 *transportable*
truckage 316.2 *transportation*
truck driver 316.7 *transferor*
trucker 316.7 *transferor*
truck farm 43.6 *farm*
truck farmer 43.15 *agriculturist*
truck farming 43.4 *arable farming;* 80.4 *fruit eating;* 44.1 *horticulture*
truck garden 44.2 *garden;* 44.14 *practise horticulture*
truck gardener 44.13 *horticulturist*
truck in 436.5 *provision*
trucking 320.1 *road transport*
truckle 664.9 *fawn*
truckle bed 23.6 *bed*
truckling 664.2 *sycophancy;* 664.7 *sycophantic*
truckload 203.3 *container;* 406.2 *load*
truculence 659.2 *bad manners;* 651.1 *malevolence*
truculency 651.1 *malevolence*
truculent 381.21 *aggressive;* 659.6 *bad-mannered;* 651.14 *hostile*
truculently 651.20 *malevolently*
trudge 333.1 *move slowly;* 333.10 *slow motion*
trudgen 67.11 *swimming*
trudgen stroke 67.2 *swimming technique*
true 396.15; **698.15**; 126.6 *authentic;* 698.31 *be accurate;* 452.1 *certain;* 3.19 *chronicled;* 801.8 *correct;* 569.11 *devoted;* 698.26 *faithful;* 799.4 *honourable;* 455.10 *known;* 16.51 *legitimate;* 27.86 *logical;* 663.8 *loyal;* 516.6 *melodious;* 93.13, 95.6 *real;* 178.1 *straight;* 707.12 *vowed*
true bearing 324.2 *bearing*
true believer 450.5 *believer*
true bill 715.1 *accusation*
true blue 225.3 *conservative person;* 113.11 *opposer*
true-blue 225.8 *conservative;* 698.26 *faithful;* 632.13 *fixed;* 799.4 *honourable;* 663.8 *loyal;* 113.26 *uncooperative*
trued 698.21 *accurate*
true fern 82.1 *fern*
true fruit 80.2 *botanical fruit*
true fungi 83.3 *fungi*
true gentleman 622.13 *proud person*
true grass 81.1 *grass*
true grit 640.4 *stamina*
true inlay 23.9 *decorative woodwork*
true lady 799.3 *honourable person*
true look 698.12 *realism*
true love 593.11 *loved one;* 593.2 *romantic love*
true moss 82.3 *moss*
trueness 452.9 *certainty;* 801.2 *correctness;* 698.13 *faithfulness;* 569.3 *familiarity;* 799.1 *probity;* 698.1 *truth*
true picture 717.1, 721.9 *representation*
true report 698.8 *accuracy*
true representation 698.8 *accuracy*
true self 139.11 *identity*
true sound 698.12 *realism*
true-speaking 729.19 *speaking*
true to form 139.16 *characteristic*
true-to-life 273.6 *correct;* 721.11 *descriptive;* 115.9, 698.25 *lifelike;* 95.7 *realistic;* 717.13 *representational;* 721.13 *representing*
true-to-nature 115.9, 698.25 *lifelike*
true to scale 698.25 *lifelike*
true to the core 799.4 *honourable*
true to the facts 698.21 *accurate*
true to the letter 698.10 *literalness*

true-to-the-letter 273.6 *correct;* 698.23 *literal*
true to the spirit 698.25 *lifelike*
true-to-type 115.9 *lifelike*
true wind 50.1 *sailing*
truffle 25.33 *vegetable*
truffle hunter 83.8 *study of fungi*
trug 410.7 *basket;* 44.6 *garden tool*
truing 698.8 *accuracy*
truism 698.4; 745.1 *maxim;* 509.7 *repeated word*
truistic 698.17
truly 698.35; 396.25, 698.37 *authentically;* 95.14, 452.23 *certainly;* 801.20 *correctly;* 569.19 *devotedly;* 643.11 *earnestly;* 799.7 *honourably;* 125.14 *imitatively;* 126.8 *originally;* 93.22 *really;* 707.24 *truthfully*
trumeau 20.9 *miscellaneous architectural features*
trump 121.8 *be superior;* 69.3 *card game terms;* 485.3 *masterpiece;* 352.1 *means;* 246.11 *overmaster*
trump card 123.3 *chief thing;* 484.3 *expedient plan;* 352.1 *means*
trumped-up 699.36 *falsified;* 715.9 *perjurious*
trumped-up charge 715.2 *false accusation*
trumpery 124.9 *bauble;* 124.4 *trivial*
trumpet 507.8 *be loud;* 669.15 *compliment;* 181.5 *cone;* 515.4 *cry;* 585.2 *glory of war;* 740.14 *proclaim;* 510.10 *ring;* 18.38 *sound;* 507.4 *sound maker;* 510.4 *sources of resonance;* 729.12 *speak loudly*
trumpet blast 507.1 *loudness*
trumpet call 711.2 *danger signal;* 480.4 *exhortation;* 742.6 *word*
trumpeter 742.8 *signer*
trumpet-tongued 507.6 *loud*
trump hand 121.3 *advantage*
trumping up 699.9 *falsification*
trumps 352.1 *means*
Trump Tower 779.7 *emporium*
trump up 699.26 *falsify*
trump up a charge 715.6 *accuse falsely*
truncate 27.91 *add;* 269.4 *be concise;* 245.5 *hurt;* 149.10 *shorten;* 723.8 *summarize*
truncated 269.3 *concise;* 233.4 *incomplete;* 149.8, 723.7 *shortened*
truncated cone 27.45 *curved surface*
truncated decimal 27.18 *division*
truncated pyramid 27.46 *polyhedron*
truncation 269.1 *conciseness;* 27.18 *division;* 723.2 *outline;* 149.2 *shortening*
truncheon 587.7 *blunt weapon;* 331.16 *weapons*
trundle 307.9, 330.22 *roll;* 300.15 *walk*
trundling 307.2 *turning*
trunk 317.15 *accessible;* 410.9 *baggage;* 205.6 *branch;* 181.4 *cylinder;* 185.3 *protuberance;* 215.1 *remainder;* 77.5 *stem;* 439.4 *storage;* 79.2 *tree part*
trunk exchange 692.12 *public telephone system*
trunk line 692.12 *public telephone system;* 317.10 *railway*
trunk road 317.3, 320.2 *road*
trunks 67.8 *swimwear;* 551.18 *underwear*
trunkwood 79.3 *timber*
trunnion 307.4 *axle*
truss 376.27 *bundle;* 23.17 *carpenter;* 23.10 *carpenter's term;* 376.38 *group;* 20.9 *miscellaneous architectural features;* 38.27 *superstructure*
truss bridge 38.21 *bridge*
trussed 376.49 *grouped*
trussing needle 25.6 *kitchen equipment*
trust 755.3 *alliance;* 450.7 *believe;* 450.3 *believing;* 646.4 *be naive;* 452.10 *conviction;* 474.1, 610.2 *expectation;* 610.6 *hope;* 166.2 *limiting factor;* 783.7 *repute;* 316.10 *transferred thing*
trustee 398.6 *agent;* 400.9 *educational leader;* 769.5 *recipient;* 780.18 *treasurer*
trustful 450.11 *believing;* 569.11 *devoted*
trustfully 450.15 *believingly;* 569.19 *devotedly*
trust fund 780.6 *funds*
trustiness 799.1 *probity*
trusting 450.11 *believing;* 452.2 *convinced;* 646.1 *naive*
trust in God 7.19 *be religious;* 7.2 *religiousness*
trusting person 450.6
trusting soul 700.22 *dupe*
trustworthily 569.19 *devotedly*
trustworthiness 450.4 *believability;* 452.17 *infallibility;* 799.1 *probity*
trustworthy 450.13 *believable;* 569.11 *devoted;* 698.26 *faithful;* 178.5, 799.4 *honourable;* 452.6 *infallible;* 252.6 *safe*
trusty 799.4 *honourable*
trusty blade 587.8 *sharp weapon*
trusty steed 59.1 *horse*
Truth 698
truth 698.1; 450.1 *belief;* 452.9 *certainty;* 273.2, 801.2 *correctness;* 714.2 *defence;* 93.4 *demonstrable existence;* 178.8 *directness;* 8.2 *divine attribute;* 3.14 *historicalness;* 27.63 *mathematical logic;* 745.1 *maxim;* 646.2 *naivety;* 739.3 *openness;* 334.1 *power;* 799.1 *probity;* 27.64 *reasoning*
truth condition 4.8 *philosophical term*
truthful 698.18; 273.6 *correct;* 178.5, 799.4 *honourable;* 801.10 *moral;* 646.1 *naive;* 738.15 *open;* 95.7 *realistic*
truthfully 698.36; **707.24**; 799.7 *honourably;* 178.13 *straightforwardly*
truthfulness 698.5; 178.8 *directness;* 799.1 *probity*
truthful person 698.14
truth function 4.8 *philosophical term*
truthless 699.29 *false*
truthlessly 699.40 *falsely*
truthlessness 699.1 *falsehood*
truth table 27.63 *mathematical logic;* 4.8 *philosophical term*
truth value 27.63 *mathematical logic;* 4.8 *philosophical term*
try 342.15; 715.5 *accuse;* 340.4 *act;* 353.1, 353.5 *attempt;* 476.3 *conjecture;* 576.8 *exert oneself;* 448.1, 448.11 *experiment;* 448.13 *invent;* 16.76, 464.11 *judge;* 16.70 *litigate;* 356.1 *production;* 705.17 *question;* 64.3 *rugby play;* 246.3 *successful thing;* 495.9 *taste;* 354.1 *undertake;* 354.2 *undertaking;* 349.1 *use*
try a case 16.71; 16.69 *have jurisdiction over*
try and try again 640.6 *persevere;* 353.2 *try hard*
try for 482.10 *aim*
try for a miracle 103.10 *attempt the impossible*
try hard 353.2; 342.15 *try*
trying 353.8 *attempting;* 448.8 *experimental;* 448.3 *experimentation;* 261.4 *fatiguing;* 264.13 *inconvenient;* 242.1 *unpleasant*
trying hard 640.10 *persevering*
try in vain 604.4 *be disappointed*
try it on 631.13 *behave badly*
try on 551.34 *wear*
try one's best 576.8 *exert oneself*
try one's hand 448.13 *invent*
try one's hand at 353.1 *attempt*
try one's luck 448.13 *invent;* 353.3 *tackle;* 107.12 *take a chance*
try one's patience 264.22 *cause trouble*
try one's strength 448.13 *invent*
tryout 448.2 *rehearsal*
try out 448.11 *experiment;* 448.12 *rehearse*
trypanosome 75.10 *parasite;* 75.9 *protozoan*
trypanosomiasis 75.12 *protozoal disease;* 260.7 *tropical disease*
trypsin 33.11 *enzyme*
trysail 50.3 *parts of a sailing boat*
try scorer 64.4 *rugby player*
try something new 295.18 *be trendy*
try square 26.6 *measuring instrument;* 186.4 *plumb line*
tryst 654.3 *meeting;* 376.8 *rendezvous*
try the latest craze 295.18 *be trendy*
try to say 694.10 *mean*
tsar 400.2 *sovereign*
tsarina 400.2 *sovereign*
T-shape 176.1 *angle*
T-shirt 551.4 *informal dress;* 551.8 *shirt;* 551.18 *underwear*
tsk 512.9 *sh!*
T-square 176.4 *angular measurement;* 27.49 *geometric construction;* 26.6 *measuring instrument;* 186.4 *plumb line*
tsunami 420.9 *broken water;* 154.8 *high thing;* 28.14 *sound wave;* 30.14, 91.3, 325.6 *wave*
t tale 699.10 *lie*
TTL meter 41.18 *exposure time*
TT race 61.5 *motorcycle racing*
tuatara 73.2 *lizard*
tub 256.6, 410.12 *bath*
tubbiness 158.5 *fatness;* 181.2 *round body;* 152.5 *thickness*
tubby 158.16 *fat;* 152.1 *thick;* 181.10 *well-rounded*
tube 183.2 *concave land;* 181.4 *cylinder;* 334.7 *electrical power;* 151.8 *narrow thing;* 308.7 *passageway;* 317.10, 321.1 *railway;* 510.4 *sources of resonance;* 692.21 *television;* 317.8 *tunnel*
tube dress 551.7 *frock*
tuber 44.9 *garden plant;* 77.7 *root;* 344.3 *rudiment;* 77.5 *stem;* 25.33, 44.11 *vegetable*
tubercular 260.23 *diseased*
tuberculosis 260.6 *infection;* 260.9 *respiratory disease*
tuberculous 260.23 *diseased*
tuberose 502.2 *fragrant thing*
tuberous 77.14 *of plants*
tuberous root 77.7 *root*
tuberous-rooted 77.19 *of roots*
tubers 80.1 *fruits*
tube station 226.4 *stopping place*
tub of lard 158.12 *fat person*
tub-thump 733.7 *address;* 729.14 *speak to*
tub-thumper 753.4 *protester;* 733.6 *public speaker;* 729.10 *speaker*
tub-thumping 729.9 *art of public speaking;* 729.20 *eloquent*
tub to a whale 700.12 *disguise*
tubular 181.9 *round*
tubular furniture 23.1 *furniture*
tubulidentate 71.6 *insect-eating mammal;* 71.26 *insectivorous*
TUC 15.3 *organized labour*
tuck 557.7 *food;* 191.5 *make smaller;* 184.3, 184.10 *pleat;* 587.8 *sharp weapon;* 68.4 *skiing technique;* 67.11 *swimming*
tuck dive 67.6 *diving*
tucked 68.12 *ski;* 191.7 *smaller;* 551.31 *styled*
tucker 557.7 *food;* 551.14 *neckwear*
tucker bag 410.8 *bag*
tuckered out 261.1 *fatigued*
tucket 510.2 *ringing*
tuck in 61.9 *race*
tucking 68.12 *ski*
tucking in 61.6 *motor-racing terms*
tuck in to 688.5 *be greedy;* 557.22 *eat well*
tuck jump 67.6 *diving*
tuck one's tail 623.20 *submit*
tuck position 67.6 *diving*
tuck shop 557.17 *food shop*
tuck up 184.10 *pleat*
Tudor 23.7 *furniture style;* 296.14 *historic*
Tudor arch 20.5 *arch*
Tudor rose 743.8 *heraldic device*
Tudor times 3.10 *past age*
tuft 81.2 *grassland*
tug 363.11 *attract;* 363.1 *attraction;* 362.12 *drag;* 576.4 *exertion;* 369.1 *extraction;* 331.1 *impel;* 492.3 *press;* 362.2, 362.11 *pull;* 362.13 *pull at;* 300.14 *set in motion;* 492.11 *touch;* 576.6 *work*
tugboat 362.6 *towline*
tugging 363.8 *attracting;* 362.1 *traction;* 362.8 *tractional*
tugging out 369.1 *extraction*
tug of war 362.2 *pull*
tug one's forelock 664.10 *knuckle under;* 667.19 *take off one's hat to*
tug out 369.11 *extract*
tuition 6.1 *education*
tumble 424.4 *be brittle;* 357.13 *be destroyed;* 254.8 *be in danger;* 57.10 *compete in gymnastics;* 305.4 *fall;* 367.7 *lean;* 367.11 *lowering;* 326.11 *rock;* 327.11 *stagger;* 307.10 *swirl;* 305.11 *trip*
tumbledown 424.1 *brittle;* 305.16 *descending;* 357.15 *destroyed;* 245.13, 337.9 *dilapidated;* 375.6 *disintegrating;* 254.2 *unsafe*
tumble down 357.13 *be destroyed*
tumbledown shack 565.8 *shelter*
tumble-dry 256.13 *clean;* 428.23 *drip-dry*
tumble-dryer 428.15 *dryer*
tumbler 336.5 *athlete;* 21.31 *circus performer;* 558.10 *drink container;* 410.13 *drinking vessel*
tumble to 695.6 *understand*
tumbling 305.16 *descending;* 305.18, 367.20 *falling;* 57.8 *floor exercises*
tumefaction 190.1 *growth*
tumescence 182.1 *convexity;* 190.1 *growth*
tumescent 182.4 *convex;* 190.8 *growing*
tumid 190.7 *bigger;* 542.10 *ornate*
tumidity 190.1 *growth*
tumidly 190.10 *largely*
tumidness 190.1 *growth*
tumify 190.6 *become bigger*
tummy 172.4 *insides;* 410.18 *stomach*
tummyache 491.2 *painful condition*
tumour 182.2 *bulge;* 260.12 *cancer;* 190.3 *enlarged thing;* 260.3 *symptom*
tump 154.3 *mountain;* 205.7 *piece*
tumult 327.2; 342.1 *activity;* 328.5 *commotion;* 408.5 *confusion;* 517.2 *dissonant noise;* 380.3 *instance of violence;* 507.2 *outcry;* 662.2 *violation of the law*
tumultation 327.2 *tumult*
tumultuous 662.13 *disobedient;* 380.6 *violent*
tumultuously 662.17 *disobediently*
tumulus 583.6 *grave;* 154.3 *mountain*
tun 410.11 *vessel*
tuna 55.4 *American game fish;* 25.18 *sea fish*
tunable laser 28.26 *laser*
tuna sandwich 25.11 *sandwich*
tundra 31.39 *climatic zone*
tundra climate 31.38 *climate*
tune 18.34, 516.8 *harmonize;* 18.13, 516.1 *melody;* 18.22 *phrase;* 243.4 *prepare for action;* 393.1 *repair*
tuned 243.18 *prepared*
tuned circuit 39.13 *circuit*
tuned radio-frequency receiver 692.18 *radio*
tuneful 18.30 *harmonic;* 516.6 *melodious*
tunefully 516.11 *melodiously;* 18.42 *musically*
Tunefulness 516
tunefulness 18.1 *music*
tune in 692.30 *communicate;* 750.24 *harmonize;* 504.15 *hear*
tuneless 517.9 *unmelodious*
tunelessly 517.12 *dissonantly*
tunelessness 517.3 *musical dissonance*
tuneless voice 730.2 *inarticulation*
tune out 505.8 *be deaf*
tuner 692.18 *radio*
tune up 18.34, 516.8 *harmonize;* 243.4 *prepare for action;* 336.8 *strengthen*
tune-up 393.8 *repair*
tungsten lamp 28.25 *light source*
tungsten light 41.15 *lighting*
tungstic 32.34 *elemental*
tungstous 32.34 *elemental*
tunic 551.5 *fancy dress;* 551.11 *jacket;* 551.16 *robe*
tunicate 75.2 *protochordate*
tunicle 7.11 *vestment*
tuning 243.9 *preparation;* 692.18 *radio;* 393.8 *repair*
tunnel 38.22; **305.15**; **317.8**; 183.2 *concave land;* 318.5 *crossing point;* 156.14 *deepen;* 156.4 *deep thing;* 38.30 *engineer;* 308.20 *hole;* 565.13 *lair;* 183.9 *make concave;* 151.6 *narrow place;* 308.7 *passageway;* 510.4 *sources of resonance;* 38.19 *structure*
tunnel kiln 24.6 *ceramic workshop*
tunnelled 308.14 *holed*
tunneller 183.5 *digger;* 308.3 *person who opens*
tunnelling 305.7; 156.1 *depth;* 38.19 *structure*
tunnel out 391.5 *be liberated*
tunnel vision 471.4 *diligence;* 465.3 *injustice;* 519.2 *poor sight*
tup 43.8 *livestock;* 567.16 *male animal*
Tupperware™ 410.16 *crockery*
tu quoque 714.2 *defence;* 110.1 *interchange*
Turanian 5.11 *family of languages*
turban 551.15 *headgear;* 7.11 *vestment*
Turbellaria 75.6 *worm*
turbellarian 75.6 *worm*
turbid 258.7 *dirty;* 528.2 *shady*
turbidity 258.1 *dirtiness;* 528.6 *opaqueness;* 327.3 *turbulence*
turbinate 180.4 *convolutional*
turbinated 307.12 *rotary*
turbination 180.2 *coil;* 307.1 *rotation*
turbine 38.12; 437.4 *electricity;* 438.5 *machine;* 39.32 *power station;* 330.11 *propeller;* 307.6 *rotator;* 334.6 *source of energy*
turbo 330.11 *propeller*
turbocharger 334.6 *source of energy*
turbojet propulsion 330.2 *method of propulsion*

Turbo language™ 40.9 *programming language*
turboprop propulsion 330.2 *method of propulsion*
turbosupercharger 334.6 *source of energy*
turbot 74.8 *food fish;* 25.18 *sea fish*
turbulence 327.3; 408.5 *confusion;* 322.7 *miscellaneous aviation terms;* 420.6 *roughness;* 28.8 *time;* 380.1 *violence*
turbulent 327.17; 420.4 *bumpy;* 408.20 *disorderly;* 91.7 *oceanic;* 380.6 *violent*
turbulently 420.14 *roughly*
turbulent sea 91.3 *wave*
turd 560.5 *faeces*
turdine 72.21 *avian*
tureen 410.16 *crockery*
turf 44.9 *garden plant;* 81.2 *grassland;* 538.8 *greenness;* 59.7 *horseracing;* 437.2 *lighter;* 86.13 *locality;* 142.1 *location;* 81.12 *manage grassland;* 205.7 *piece;* 395.7 *sphere of influence*
turf accountant 59.15 *horse person*
turf out 371.1 *expel*
turfy 419.4 *compressible;* 81.9 *grassy*
turgescence 542.2 *affectation;* 190.1 *growth*
turgescent 190.8 *growing*
turgid 190.7 *bigger;* 270.3 *diffuse;* 544.9 *inelegant;* 542.10 *ornate*
turgidity 542.2 *affectation;* 190.1 *growth;* 544.4 *inelegance of speech*
turgidly 270.7 *diffusely;* 190.10 *largely;* 542.13 *ornately*
turgidness 190.1 *growth*
Turing machine 40.3 *computer*
turistas 560.2 *defecation*
turkey 51.5 *bowling delivery;* 60.5 *game;* 25.20 *meat;* 72.4 *table bird;* 21.13 *theatrical performance;* 247.4 *unsuccessful thing*
turkey buzzard 256.12 *cleaner*
turkey cock 72.10 *male bird;* 673.7 *vain person*
Turkey red 535.1 *red*
turkey sandwich 25.11 *sandwich*
turkey shoot 633.2 *chase*
turkey trot 22.2 *dance*
Turkic 5.11 *family of languages*
Turkish bath 256.6 *bath;* 493.8 *hot place*
Turkish baths 256.6 *bath*
Turkish carpet 550.9 *floor covering*
Turkish crescent and star 743.6 *national emblem*
Turkish tobacco 496.7 *tobacco*
turmoil 342.1 *activity;* 588.1 *anarchy;* 328.5 *commotion;* 408.5 *confusion;* 517.2 *dissonant noise;* 357.5 *havoc;* 507.2 *outcry;* 327.2 *tumult;* 662.2 *violation of the law*
turn 340.4 *act;* 485.2 *aptitude;* 227.11 *be changeable;* 224.7 *be changed;* 645.5 *be cunning;* 298.8 *be cyclic;* 177.2 *bend;* 189.6 *be oblique;* 7.19 *be religious;* 426.10 *blunt;* 53.18 *bowl;* 224.1 *change;* 306.2 *circuitousness;* 180.2 *coil;* 57.10 *compete in gymnastics;* 631.11 *conduct oneself;* 132.2 *consecution;* 180.6 *convolute;* 303.16 *countermotion;* 177.6 *curve;* 298.2 *cycle;* 245.2 *decay;* 325.14 *deviating course;* 43.17 *farm;* 553.9 *fashion;* 47.2 *field events;* 322.5 *flight;* 160.7 *form;* 57.5 *horizontal bar;* 68.7 *ice-dancing;* 595.2 *inclination;* 719.8 *interpret;* 719.1 *interpretation;* 141.8 *intervening space;* 24.11 *make ceramics;* 179.7 *make circular;* 181.11 *make round;* 720.2 *misinterpretation;* 18.16 *musical note;* 160.6 *nature;* 189.1 *obliqueness;* 306.3, 306.6 *orbit;* 384.24 *parry;* 276.4 *period of activity;* 57.6 *pommel horse;* 595.8 *prefer;* 307.3 *reel;* 303.3, 761.6 *reverse;* 307.8 *rotate;* 181.6 *round;* 21.8 *scene;* 630.3 *shock;* 68.14 *ski;* 499.8 *sour;* 289.1 *succession;* 67.1 *swimming;* 324.7 *take a direction;* 229.1 *tendency;* 303.5 *turn back;* 325.5 *twist;* 184.1 *wrinkle*
turn a blind eye 634.1 *avoid;* 519.16 *be blind to;* 341.4 *not act*
turnabout 303.13 *about-turn;* 393.10 *revival*
turn about 759.8 *in exchange;* 761.6 *reverse;* 325.11 *turn round*
turn a corner 306.8 *detour;* 325.1 *deviate*
turn a deaf ear 505.8 *be deaf;* 641.9 *be obstinate;* 628.6 *be pitiless;* 341.4 *not act*
turn against 760.10 *be converted;* 625.6 *be irascible;* 479.2 *equivocate;* 800.9 *prove false;* 481.4 *put off*
turn all to gold 781.12 *be rich*
turn and turn about 132.18 *consecutively;* 759.8 *in exchange;* 110.1 *interchange;* 110.10 *reciprocally;* 298.15 *regularly*
turn an honest penny 765.12 *earn*
turn a phrase 543.4 *be elegant*
turn a pot 24.11 *make ceramics*
turnaround 303.13 *about-turn*
turn around 303.9 *turn round*
turn a sentence 5.45 *use language*
turn aside 634.1 *avoid;* 325.8 *sidestep*
turn at the table 65.8 *play billiards*
turn away 634.1 *avoid;* 596.6 *react against;* 637.7, 709.5 *refuse;* 371.6 *send away;* 325.8 *sidestep;* 604.7 *thwart*
turn away from 594.14 *hate*
turn back 303.5; 224.7 *be changed;* 224.8 *cause change;* 364.1 *repel;* 761.6 *reverse;* 388.3 *submit;* 384.28 *survive;* 325.11 *turn round;* 313.2 *withdraw*
turn back the clock 284.15 *look back;* 761.6 *reverse*
turn back the tide 103.10 *attempt the impossible*
turn back time 3.23; 103.10 *attempt the impossible;* 284.15 *look back*
turn back to front 192.3 *invert*
turn backwards 192.3 *invert;* 761.6 *reverse*
turn blue 539.9 *blue*
turncoat 760.6 *convert;* 355.4 *deserter;* 479.9 *equivocator;* 227.6 *fickle person;* 639.15 *indecisive person;* 700.21 *traitor*
turndown 637.12 *opposition;* 399.1 *veto*
turn down 419.14 *ease;* 524.10 *make dim;* 214.5 *make smaller;* 709.5 *refuse;* 470.1 *reject;* 399.3 *veto;* 670.15 *withhold approval*
turned 160.9 *formed;* 242.3, 499.6 *unpalatable*
turned around 192.4 *inversely;* 303.25 *reversed*
turned away 604.9 *disappointed;* 709.8 *refused*
turned comma 742.7 *punctuation*
turned down 709.8 *refused;* 470.10 *rejected*
turned into 760.13 *converted*
turned off 505.7 *unheard*
turned on 691.7 *drugged;* 796.14 *lecherous;* 490.7 *pleased*
turned out 551.29 *dressed*
turned over 184.7 *folded*
turned-up 304.22 *ascending;* 149.7 *short*
turner 578.2 *artisan;* 23.13 *carpenter;* 24.7 *potter*
turn every stone 576.8 *exert oneself*
turn for the better 244.5 *improvement;* 393.11 *recuperation*
turn for the worse 245.7 *deterioration*
turn from sin 808.4 *be penitent*
turn grey 533.8 *grey*
turn head 622.30 *make proud*
turn heads 593.25 *be loved*
turn head-to-wind 50.15 *sail*
turn ideas into profits 776.1 *trade*
turn indicator 742.5 *indicator*
turning 307.2; 224.11 *changeable;* 227.1 *changeableness;* 306.2 *circuitousness;* 43.5 *cultivation;* 177.4 *curved;* 57.11 *gymnastic;* 325.21 *indirect;* 595.6 *liking;* 189.4 *oblique;* 306.9 *orbital;* 306.1 *orbital motion;* 306.11 *orbiting;* 57.6 *pommel horse;* 307.11 *rotating*
turning back 761.1 *reversion*
turning back to front 192.1 *inversion*
turning backwards 192.1 *inversion;* 761.1 *reversion*
turning circle 320.21 *miscellaneous motoring terms*
turning down 709.1 *refusal*
turning inside out 192.1 *inversion*
turning kick 52.9 *tae kwon do*
turning point 761.3; 17.3 *aspect of fiction;* 303.16 *countermotion;* 222.3 *critical moment;* 287.3 *critical time;* 123.2 *important matter;* 209.4 *interval*
turning renegade 479.7 *apostasy*
turning space 141.6 *available space*
turning stroke 50.6 *canoeing*
turning the lights down 523.2 *darkening*
turning traitor 479.7 *apostasy*
turning up 142.3 *locating*
turning upside down 192.1 *inversion*
turn inside out 224.8 *cause change;* 192.3 *invert*
turn into 760.7 *convert into;* 314.9 *enter;* 760.9 *transform;* 719.12 *translate*
turn into money 765.12 *earn*
turnip 281.7 *watch*
turnip lantern 522.7 *lantern*
turnips 43.12 *crop*
turnkey 309.5 *person who closes;* 815.6 *prison officer*
turnkey operation 40.19 *computing terms*
turn of a card 254.5 *danger*
turn of expression 5.24 *phrasing*
turn off 618.13 *make indifferent;* 350.6 *stop using*
turn of mind 229.2 *attitude*
turn of phrase 5.24 *phrasing*
turn of the card 107.3 *equal chance*
turn of the tide 303.12 *reversal;* 761.3 *turning point*
turn on 130.20, 346.8 *activate;* 593.25 *be loved;* 617.15 *cause desire;* 593.26 *court;* 691.10 *drug oneself;* 345.7 *follow from;* 334.11 *give power;* 522.24 *light;* 483.9 *motivate*
turn-on 480.2 *flattery;* 483.5 *positive stimulus*
turn on a dime 303.9 *turn round*
turn one against 596.7 *cause dislike*
turn one aside 481.3 *deflect*
turn one's back 637.9 *not cooperate;* 634.8 *run away;* 303.9 *turn round*
turn one's back on 659.7 *be discourteous;* 472.13 *be thoughtless;* 767.9 *dispose of;* 479.2 *equivocate;* 470.3 *exclude;* 655.13 *ignore;* 709.5 *refuse;* 668.22 *show disrespect;* 313.2 *withdraw*
turn one's coat 479.3 *apostatize*
turn one's hand to 354.1 *undertake*
turn one's head 619.10 *be wonderful;* 673.18 *make conceited;* 593.28 *win the love of*
turn one's stomach 364.4 *be repulsive;* 499.9 *disgust*
turn on one's heel 303.9 *turn round*
turn on the forehand 59.10 *dressage*
turn on the gas 432.27 *give off*
turn on the tap 371.14 *let out*
turnout 551.2 *dressing;* 656.3 *formal occasion;* 15.4 *industrial dispute;* 376.3 *meeting;* 356.3 *product;* 356.1 *production;* 317.10 *railway*
turn out 221.6 *be in a state of;* 551.33 *dress up;* 371.8 *evict;* 371.1 *expel;* 658.12 *greet;* 655.13 *ignore;* 356.10 *produce;* 144.16 *replace;* 561.9 *reproduce;* 345.9 *take effect*
turn out of doors 371.8 *evict*
turn out the guard 711.7 *raise the alarm;* 667.20 *salute*
turn out well 246.8 *be effective;* 246.7 *overcome obstacles*
turnover 813.5; 25.36 *cake;* 765.4 *earnings;* 788.2 *money received;* 46.9 *play;* 773.5 *takings*
turn over 184.9 *fold;* 768.5 *give;* 776.1 *trade;* 316.11 *transfer*
turn over one's stock 778.1 *sell;* 776.1 *trade*
turn over to 398.7 *delegate*
turn pale 612.11 *be afraid;* 530.5 *lose colour*
turnpike 314.6 *means of entry;* 317.3, 320.2, 373.5 *road*
turn professional 485.11 *be expert*
turn prohibitionist 689.4 *give up alcohol*
turn queen's evidence 716.13; 739.7 *betray;* 693.13 *inform on;* 454.3 *testify*
turn red 674.16 *be self-conscious*
turn renegade 479.3 *apostatize*
turn right round 307.8 *rotate*
turnround 393.10 *revival*
turn round 303.9; **325.11**; 323.9 *navigate*
turn someone's head 480.15 *persuade*
turn sour 625.6 *be irascible;* 604.6 *disappoint;* 499.8 *sour*
turnspit 307.6 *rotator*
turn state's evidence 739.7 *betray*
turnstile 314.6 *means of entry;* 378.2 *obstacle*
turntable 321.3 *rail;* 317.10 *railway;* 307.6 *rotator*
turntable chair 55.1 *angling*
turn tail 614.4 *be a coward;* 634.9 *play truant;* 634.4 *shy;* 303.9 *turn round*
turn the corner 224.7 *be changed;* 393.4 *be restored;* 244.2 *get better*
turn the edge 426.10 *blunt*
turn the heat on 386.7 *force*
turn the lights out 523.14 *make dark*
turn the other cheek 623.21 *humble oneself;* 749.4 *pacify;* 649.12 *show mercy*
turn the scale 344.12 *determine*
turn the scales 414.12 *be heavy*
turn the sound down 505.10 *muffle*
turn the tables 192.3 *invert*
turn the tables on 708.16 *cancel out*
turn the thumbs down 399.3 *veto*
turn thumbs down on 670.15 *withhold approval*
turn to 130.18 *make a beginning;* 349.4 *resort to;* 229.4 *tend*
turn to account 349.3 *exploit*
turn to ashes 278.4 *be transient*
turn to dust 357.13 *be destroyed*
turn to God 760.10 *be converted*
turn to good account 797.21 *do well;* 237.11 *find useful;* 287.5 *take the opportunity*
turn to nothing 94.12 *cease to exist*
turn to profit 765.14 *profit*
turn to sin 760.10 *be converted*
turn traitor 479.3 *apostatize;* 760.10 *be converted*
turn turtle 323.10 *sail*
turn up 520.9 *appear;* 312.1 *arrive;* 97.12 *attend;* 525.12 *become visible;* 449.5 *be discovered;* 107.10 *chance;* 142.11 *find;* 184.9 *fold;* 149.10 *shorten;* 304.21 *upturn*
turn-up 551.24 *part of garment*
turn up missing 98.15 *be absent*
turn up one's nose 637.10 *grudge*
turn up one's toes 582.15 *die*
turn upside down 224.8 *cause change;* 357.9 *demolish;* 192.3 *invert;* 408.24 *make disordered*
turn up the juice 338.3 *invigorate*
turn up the nose 596.6 *react against*
turn up trumps 706.22 *be the answer;* 246.7 *overcome obstacles*
turn white 556.17 *age*
turn wood 23.18 *work wood*
turpentine 19.11 *artist's materials*
turpitude 800.1 *improbity;* 804.2 *vice*
turquoise 539.1 *blue;* 539.6 *blue thing*
turret 384.12 *fort;* 154.6 *tall thing*
turret lathe 38.9 *machine tool*
turret ship 586.25 *historical naval ships*
turtle 73.4 *chelonian*
turtledoves 593.10 *lovers*
turtlelike 73.11 *reptilian*
turtleneck 551.13 *sweater*
turtle shell 550.14 *animal covering*
turtle's neck 184.4 *wrinkled thing*
Tuscan 20.16 *columned*
Tuscan order 20.8 *column*
tush 168.2 *rear end;* 512.9 *sh!*
Tushita 8.11 *heaven*
tusk 425.11 *tooth*
tusked 425.4 *toothed*
tusklike 425.4 *toothed*
tusk tenon joint 23.10 *carpenter's term*
tussle 751.6 *argue;* 751.2 *argument*
tussock 376.27 *bundle;* 81.2 *grassland*
tussore 193.4 *textile*
tutelage 6.1 *education;* 6.6 *instructorship;* 392.9 *patronage;* 252.2 *protection;* 387.1 *subjection*
tutelary 252.8; 392.15 *benefactor;* 384.29 *defending*
tutelary god 252.3 *protector*
Tutivillus 8.7 *devil*
tutor 713.4 *adviser;* 579.13 *director;* 6.22 *educate;* 400.9 *educational leader;* 6.4 *educator;* 400.14 *master;* 401.4 *personal attendant;* 243.15 *preparer;* 252.3 *protector;* 4.12 *sage;* 387.6 *subject*
tutorage 6.6 *instructorship*
tutored 243.18 *prepared*
tutorial 387.9 *subject*
tutorial partner 6.7 *learner*
tutoring 6.1 *education*
tutorship 6.6 *instructorship*
tutti 507.9 *loudly;* 507.1 *loudness*
tut-tut 753.7 *complain;* 670.23 *show disapproval*

tut-tut at 606.7 *be dissatisfied*
tutu 551.6 *skirt*
tu-whit tu-whoo 515.2 *bird song*
tux 551.3, 656.4 *formal dress*
tuxedo 551.3, 656.4 *formal dress*
TV 692.22 *television set*
TV camera 41.16 *camera*
TV dinner 557.12 *meal*
TV evangelist 7.5 *Christian*
TV game 692.26 *recording*
TV mobile 692.24 *television broadcasting*
TVP 25.21 *meat substitute*
TV programme 738.9 *production*
twaddle 697.1 *nonsense*
twain 198.1 *two*
twang 513.2 *hoarseness*; 729.3 *mode of speech*; 510.10 *ring*; 18.38 *sound*; 513.5 *sound hoarse*
twangy 729.18 *phonetic*; 513.7 *strident*
twat 561.8 *organs of reproduction*
tweak 491.11 *inflict pain*; 362.3 *jerk*; 492.3 *press*; 362.13 *pull at*; 492.11 *touch*
tweed 420.2 *coarse*; 420.7 *rough thing*; 193.4 *textile*
tweed coat 551.11 *jacket*
Tweedledum and Tweedledee 115.6 *couple*; 111.3 *lookalike*; 198.6 *twins*
tweeds 551.10 *suit*
tweed suit 551.10 *suit*
tweedy 420.2 *coarse*; 193.6 *interwoven*; 404.8 *rough*
tweet 72.18 *bird song*; 72.26, 515.5 *sing*
tweeting 515.8 *singing*
tweet-tweet 515.2 *bird song*
tweezers 369.10 *excavator*; 438.1 *tool*; 360.3 *tools for gripping*
twelfth 201.18 *eleventh*; 196.4 *less than one*
Twelfth Day 201.7 *double figures*
twelfth man 398.5 *alternative*; 201.7 *double figures*; 608.5 *helper*; 762.2 *substitute person*
Twelfth Night 201.7 *double figures*; 10.15 *holy day*
twelve 201.7 *double figures*
twelve just men 16.26 *jury*
twelvemo 159.7 *little*; 159.2 *little thing*
twelvemonth 201.7 *double figures*
twelve-note composition 517.4 *atonality*
twelve-note scale 517.4 *atonality*
Twelve Tables 228.4 *stable thing*; 16.1 *the law*
twelve-tone 18.32 *instrumental*
twelve-tone music 18.3 *classical music*
twelve-tone scale 18.20 *key*
twentieth 201.19; 196.4 *less than one*
twentieth man 398.5 *alternative*
twenty and over 201.8
twenty-dollar bill 780.8 *American money*
twenty-five 69.6 *darts*; 201.8 *twenty and over*
twenty-five cents 780.8 *American money*
twenty-five percent 200.6 *quarter*
twenty-four 201.8 *twenty and over*
twenty-four carat 698.19 *authentic*
twenty-four-carat gold 698.6 *authenticity*
twenty pence 780.9 *British money*
twenty-pound note 780.9 *British money*
twerp 124.10 *nonentity*
twice 198.19
twice a month 298.16 *cyclically*
twice as much 198.19 *twice*
twice a week 298.16 *cyclically*
twice a year 298.16 *cyclically*
twice over 112.24 *again*; 198.19 *twice*
twice-told 112.10 *iterated*
twice-told tale 620.2 *boring thing*
twice-told tales 270.1 *diffuseness*
Twickenham 64.1 *rugger*
twiddle one's thumbs 341.4 *not act*; 620.7 *suffer boredom*
twiddling one's thumbs 620.5 *bored*; 341.1 *inaction*
twig 205.6 *branch*; 455.11 *know*; 77.5 *stem*; 79.2 *tree part*; 695.6 *understand*; 555.5 *young plant*
twigginess 153.7 *thinness*
twiggy 153.1 *thin*
twiglets™ 25.10 *snack*
twilight 131.9 *close*; 523.1 *darkness*; 245.7 *deterioration*; 524.1 *dimness*; 291.1, 291.6 *evening*
twilight of the gods 131.5 *fate*
twilit 524.5 *dim*
twill 193.4 *textile*; 42.10 *woven*
twilled 404.8 *rough*
twill weave 42.4 *weaving*
twin 198.5; 706.21 *answer to*; 750.14 *conforming*; 750.5 *conformity*; 115.2 *copy*; 706.8 *correspondence*; 706.15 *correspondent*; 115.5 *counterpart*; 198.12, 198.15 *double*; 119.5 *equal*; 110.8 *interrelate*; 111.3, 111.14 *lookalike*; 111.8 *make the same*; 198.14 *pair*
twin bed 23.6 *bed*
twin bill 321.7 *train*
twin cable 39.27 *wire*
twine 180.6 *convolute*; 177.6 *curve*; 193.8 *interweave*; 373.6 *line*; 325.5 *twist*
twine around 267.6 *adhere*
twined 193.6 *interwoven*; 42.9 *spun*
twiner 77.2 *plant*
twinge 491.1 *pain*
twinge of conscience 808.1 *penitence*; 806.2 *signs of guilt*
twining 193.1 *interweaving*; 77.14 *of plants*; 42.2 *spinning*
twinkle 227.11 *be changeable*; 327.12, 327.26 *flicker*; 742.3, 742.11 *gesture*; 522.25 *light up*; 29.37 *observe*; 522.2 *quality of light*
twinkling 522.16 *bright*; 280.3 *instant*; 29.21 *orbit*; 522.2 *quality of light*
twinklingly 522.30 *lightly*
twinkling of an eye 280.3 *instant*
twin-lens reflex 41.16 *camera*
twinned 750.14 *conforming*; 108.4 *related*; 285.9 *simultaneous*; 198.9 *two*
twinned city 87.1 *city*
twinning 198.4 *doubling*
twins 198.6; 115.6 *couple*
twin screws 330.11 *propeller*
twinset 551.13 *sweater*
Twin Stars 198.6 *twins*
twin-tub 256.7 *washer*
twirl 180.2 *coil*; 180.6 *convolute*; 90.7 *flow*; 307.3 *reel*; 90.6 *river flow*; 307.8 *rotate*
twirled 180.4 *convolutional*
twirling 307.11 *rotating*; 307.2 *turning*
twist 325.5; 340.4 *act*; 176.11 *angle*; 645.5 *be cunning*; 189.6 *be oblique*; 465.12 *bias*; 180.2 *coil*; 631.11 *conduct oneself*; 180.6 *convolute*; 22.2, 22.15 *dance*; 96.16 *delude*; 234.9, 325.6 *distort*; 234.1 *distortion*; 699.9 *falsification*; 699.26 *falsify*; 68.13 *ice-skating*; 380.3 *instance of violence*; 719.8 *interpret*; 719.1 *interpretation*; 193.8 *interweave*; 73.15 *live as a reptile*; 161.3 *make shapeless*; 720.1 *misinterpret*; 720.2 *misinterpretation*; 465.10 *misjudge*; 718.4 *misrepresent*; 718.1 *misrepresentation*; 189.1 *obliqueness*; 245.6 *pervert*; 702.11 *practise sophistry*; 307.9 *roll*; 42.13 *spin*; 630.4 *surprising thing*; 760.9 *transform*; 380.8 *use violence*
twist and turn 180.6 *convolute*; 327.24 *shake*; 325.5 *twist*
twisted 180.4 *convolutional*; 690.3 *dead drunk*; 231.3 *deformed*; 699.36 *falsified*; 718.6 *misrepresented*; 189.4, 325.23 *oblique*; 42.9 *spun*; 465.8 *unjust*
twistedness 180.1 *convolution*; 234.1 *distortion*
twisted pair 39.27 *wire*
twister 420.9 *broken water*; 180.3 *convoluted thing*; 379.1 *trap*; 307.4 *vortex*; 31.16 *wind vortex*
twisting 699.9 *falsification*; 325.21 *indirect*; 720.2 *misinterpretation*; 73.12 *snake-like*; 67.11 *swimming*; 325.17 *torsion*; 307.2 *turning*
twisting dive 67.6 *diving*
twist lift 68.6 *ice-skating*
twist one's arm 386.6 *compel*; 480.15 *persuade*
twist someone's arm 483.10 *manipulate*
twist the law 16.73 *be illegal*
twist the words 720.1 *misinterpret*
twist together 180.6 *convolute*
twist-turned leg 23.3 *chair leg*
twist words 234.12 *distort the truth*
twit 599.13 *be humorous*; 459.3 *foolish person*; 272.3 *object of ridicule*; 668.25 *taunt*; 457.3 *unintelligent person*; 337.4 *weakling*
twitch 612.12 *be fearful*; 491.9 *feel pain*; 742.3 *gesture*; 362.3 *jerk*; 327.23 *jolt*; 260.17 *nervous disorder*; 492.3 *press*; 362.13 *pull at*; 327.24 *shake*; 327.8 *spasm*; 492.11 *touch*
twitcher 72.20 *ornithologist*
twitchety 327.19 *convulsive*
twitchiness 327.5 *restlessness*
twitchy 327.19 *convulsive*; 612.8 *fearful*; 327.16 *restless*
twitter 327.1 *agitation*; 327.21 *be agitated*; 72.18, 515.2 *bird song*; 327.24 *shake*; 72.26, 515.5 *sing*
twittering 515.2 *bird song*; 515.8 *singing*
twittery 515.8 *singing*
Two 198
two 198.1; **198.9**; 27.9 *numeral*; 53.10 *score*
two abreast 198.9 *two*; 198.20 *two by two*
two and six 780.10 *former British money*
two-bit 793.10 *shoddy*; 124.4 *trivial*
two bits 780.8 *American money*
two-by-four 23.16 *joined*; 159.7 *little*; 23.12 *wood*
two by two 198.20; 198.9 *two*
two centred arch 20.5 *arch*
two cheers 728.2 *detraction*
two-dimensional 187.8 *horizontal*; 27.79, 141.11 *spatial*; 198.10 *two-sided*; 518.20 *visual*
two-dimensional figure 27.38 *surface*
two-dollar piece 780.8 *American money*
two dozen 201.8 *twenty and over*
two-edged 479.10 *equivocal*
two-edged sword 240.3 *inconvenience*; 587.8 *sharp weapon*
two-faced 198.11 *double-edged*; 699.30 *duplicitous*; 479.11 *equivocating*; 800.6 *faithless*
two-facedness 198.3 *duality*; 699.2 *duplicity*
two-faced person 479.9 *equivocator*
twofer 793.4 *bargain*
two-fingered salute 668.7 *sign of disrespect*
two-finger gesture 742.3 *gesture*
two fingers 558.2 *drink*
twofold 198.19 *twice*; 198.9 *two*
two-foot punt 50.8 *punting*
two-handed sword 587.8 *sharp weapon*
two-hander 734.1 *conversation*; 198.2 *double*; 21.2 *play*
two-hand shot 49.4 *playing terms*
two-horse race 59.7 *horseracing*
two-hundred 201.9 *treble figures*
two-level 198.10 *two-sided*
two-man 50.10 *sailing*
two-man bobsled 68.9 *bobsledding*
two-man canoe race 50.6 *canoeing*
two-man dinghy 50.2 *sailing boat*
two-man keelboat 50.2 *sailing boat*
two-man trapeze boat 50.2 *sailing boat*
two-masted 50.10 *sailing*
two-masted boat 50.2 *sailing boat*
two-minute drill 46.7 *offence*
two-minute offence 46.7 *offence*
two-minute warning 49.1 *basketball*; 46.5 *game time*
two of a kind 115.6 *couple*; 111.3 *lookalike*
two-one-two 58.8 *hockey*
two-one-two system 58.3 *ice hockey*
two or three 206.1 *few*; 207.1 *plurality*
two-part harmony 18.13 *melody*
twopence 780.9 *British money*; 124.8 *trifle*
twopenny 793.10 *shoddy*; 124.4 *trivial*
twopenny-halfpenny 793.9 *cheap*; 124.4 *trivial*
two-phase 68.12 *ski*
two-phase glide 68.2 *cross-country skiing*
two-phase supply 39.34 *power supply*
two-phase uphill 68.2 *cross-country skiing*
two-phase walk 68.2 *cross-country skiing*
two-piece 198.2 *double*; 551.31 *styled*; 67.11 *swimming*
two-piece suit 551.10 *suit*
two-piece swimsuit 551.21 *beachwear*; 67.8 *swimwear*
two-ply 411.7 *layered*; 198.10 *two-sided*
two-point conversion 46.6 *scoring*
two-pointer 49.4 *playing terms*
twoscore 201.8 *twenty and over*
two-seater 198.2 *double*
two-seater toboggan 68.9 *bobsledding*
two-shilling piece 780.10 *former British money*
two-sided 198.10; 169.6 *side*
twosome 198.1 *two*
two-step 22.2 *dance*
two-storey 198.10 *two-sided*
two-storeyed 411.7 *layered*
two-stroke 198.10 *two-sided*
two-stroke cycle 38.13 *engine cycle*
two-tailed test 27.54 *hypothesis testing*
two-thirds 196.7 *fractionally*; 196.4 *less than one*
two-tiered 411.7 *layered*
two-time 700.23, 702.12 *deceive*; 699.21 *double-deal*; 800.9 *prove false*
two-timer 700.17 *cheat*; 800.4 *dishonourable person*; 227.6 *fickle person*
two times 198.19 *twice*
two-timing 198.11 *double-edged*; 702.10 *hypocritical*
two track 59.10 *dressage*
two-up-two-down 565.5 *house*
two voices 479.5 *equivocalness*
two-way 759.6 *in exchange*; 110.5 *interconnected*; 198.10 *two-sided*
two-way communication 692.6 *telecommunication*
two-way mirror 527.9 *glass*
two-way traffic 759.1 *exchange*
two weeks 201.7 *double figures*
two-wheeler 198.2 *double*
Tyburn tree 814.16 *instrument of execution*
tycoon 123.4 *bigwig*; 400.5 *company leader*; 780.17 *financier*; 765.7 *gainer*; 248.4 *prosperous person*; 781.10 *wealthy person*
tying the knot 570.1 *marriage*; 570.5 *wedding*
tying the tubes 563.2 *making infertile*
tying up 312.11 *landing*
tyke 71.9 *dog*
tympanic cavity 504.5 *internal ear*
tympanic membrane 504.5 *internal ear*
tympanum 174.3 *architectural summit*; 504.5 *internal ear*
type 137.4; 216.4 *average*; 137.13 *class*; 750.6 *convention*; 160.3 *kind*; 5.13 *letter*; 99.4 *nature*; 475.5 *omen*; 566.7 *person*; 717.1 *representation*; 721.6 *sort*; 26.7 *standard*
typecast 21.38 *dramatize*; 21.40 *tragic*
type-cutter 19.18 *engraver*
typed 5.41 *lettered*
type of animal 70.4
type of meaning 694.4
type of penance 808.2
type of rule 396.7
typeset 740.15 *publish*
typesetter 740.12 *publisher*
types of marriage 570.3
type style 5.15
Typhan 8.7 *devil*
typhoid 260.6 *infection*
typhoid fever 260.4 *disease*
Typhon 158.10 *big person*
typhoon 380.5 *violent weather*; 31.16 *wind vortex*
typhus 260.6 *infection*
typical 137.11; 216.1 *average*; 99.9, 139.16 *characteristic*; 750.15 *conventional*; 140.10 *customary*; 117.15 *everyday*; 738.14 *manifest*; 632.11 *normal*; 298.14 *orderly*; 717.13 *representational*; 742.14 *signifying*
typically 750.37 *conventionally*; 742.18 *indicatively*; 216.11 *on average*; 717.14 *representationally*; 137.16 *taxonomically*; 138.30 *usually*
typical value 27.60 *parameter*
typification 738.10 *manifestation*; 717.1 *representation*
typify 111.11 *be regular*; 475.11 *predict*; 717.9 *represent*; 742.10 *signify*
typifying 750.15 *conventional*
typing error 274.12
typing paper 435.3 *paper*
typist 744.9 *recorder*
typo 274.12 *typing error*
typographer 19.18 *engraver*
typographical error 274.12 *typing error*
Tyr 585.3 *gods and goddesses of war*
tyrannical 16.62 *above the law*; 660.16 *arrogant*; 387.10 *dominating*; 396.14 *governmental*; 395.11 *influential*; 651.10 *malevolent*; 579.17 *managerial*; 342.21 *meddling*; 647.8 *severe*; 380.6 *violent*
tyrannically 395.14 *influentially*; 651.20 *malevolently*; 647.11 *severely*; 16.85 *summarily*; 380.10 *violently*
tyrannicide 753.2 *disorder*; 382.3 *homi-*

cide; 382.11 *murderer*; 662.2 *violation of the law*
tyrannization 651.5 *intolerance*
tyrannize 395.10 *be a prevailing influence*; 396.19 *be authoritarian*; 387.7 *defeat*; 12.11 *govern*; 236.14 *ill-treat*; 342.17 *meddle*; 647.6 *suppress*; 651.18 *torment*
tyrannized 647.9 *suppressed*
tyrannosaurus 296.8 *prehistoric animal*
tyrannously 380.10 *violently*
tyranny 660.4 *arrogance*; 387.2 *domination*; 236.11 *harmfulness*; 395.3 *personal influence*; 647.2 *suppression*; 396.7 *type of rule*
tyrant 400.4 *absolute ruler*; 594.8 *hated person*; 251.6 *lawmaker*; 651.8 *malefactor*; 396.10 *person of authority*; 814.17 *punisher*; 7.4 *religionist*; 804.9 *wicked person*
tyre 179.3 *circular thing*
tyremark 744.12 *vestige*
tyre stagger 61.6 *motor-racing terms*
Tyrian purple 42.6 *dye*; 540.2 *purple pigment*
tyro 130.14 *beginner*; 295.8 *new arrival*
Tyrolean 62.8 *mountaineering*
Tyrolean hat 551.15 *headgear*
Tyrolean traverse 62.3 *climbing technique*
tzatziki 25.52 *Greek dish*

U 573.4 *aristocratic*; 549.5 *refined*
Uber Cup 63.10 *badminton*
übermensch 797.16 *superior person*
ubiquitous 8.13 *divine*; 395.13 *dominant*; 97.7 *present*; 112.14 *recurrent*; 138.17 *widespread*
ubiquitously 8.19 *divinely*; 395.14 *influentially*
ubiquitousness 97.2 *omnipresence*
ubiquity 97.2 *omnipresence*; 138.4 *widespreadness*
U-boat 586.24 *warship*
uchi-ude-uke 52.8 *karate*
udder 71.2 *mammalian characteristic*
udometer 433.19 *measuring instrument*; 31.7 *weather instruments*
udometric 31.42 *barometric*
UFO 29.34 *SETI*; 456.3 *unknown thing*; 619.4 *wonder*
ufological 11.18 *spiritual*
ufologist 11.12 *occultist*
ufology 11.1 *occultism*
UFOs 737.6 *natural mystery*
UFO sighting 11.10 *psychic phenomenon*
uglify 245.5 *hurt*
Ugliness 546
ugliness 544.3; **546.1**; 234.3 *deformity*; 525.3 *external appearance*; 364.5 *repulsion*
ugly 544.10; **546.4**; 525.10 *aspectual*; 254.1 *dangerous*; 234.7 *deformed*; 364.8 *repulsive*; 31.48 *stormy*
ugly customer 804.10 *bad person*; 812.2 *disreputable character*; 625.3 *irascible person*; 651.8 *malefactor*
ugly duckling 325.19 *deviant person*
ugly person 546.2
ugly place 546.3
UHF transmitter 692.16 *transmitter*
uhlan 586.20 *cavalryman*
UHT milk 558.5 *milk*
uhv 32.20 *surface chemistry*
uka 52.7 *judo*
ukase 397.1 *command*; 740.1 *publication*; 140.1 *rule*
uke 52.10 *aikido*
ulcer 260.15; 491.2 *painful condition*
ulcerate 624.14 *make angry*; 245.3 *make worse*
ulcerated 260.23 *diseased*
ulceration 245.10 *impairment*; 260.15 *ulcer*
ulcerous 260.23 *diseased*
ullage 233.2 *omission*
Ullswater 88.4 *British lakes*
Ulster 85.10 *Ireland*
ulster 551.12 *coat*
Ulster Democratic Unionist Party 12.6 *political party*
Ulster Unionist Party 12.6 *political party*
ulterior 145.8 *distant*; 100.12 *external*
ulterior motive 482.1 *intention*; 480.11, 483.1 *motive*
ultima ratio regum 585.1 *war*
ultimate 121.14 *best*; 344.13 *causal*; 145.8 *distant*; 131.20 *ending*; 230.3 *perfection*; 174.5 *top*
ultimate aim 482.5 *final intention*
ultimately 344.14 *causally*; 131.26 *finally*; 283.14 *in the future*
ultimate purpose 482.5 *final intention*
ultimate tensile strength 38.15 *strength of materials*
ultima Thule 145.3 *distant place*
ultimatum 752.3 *business offer*; 397.2, 710.2 *demand*; 482.4 *formulated intention*; 135.1 *requirement*; 711.1 *warning*
ultrabasic rock 30.30 *igneous rock*
ultracentrifuge 307.6 *rotator*
ultraconservative 641.4 *set*
ultracool 251.14 *self-restrained*
ultracritical 670.28 *fault-finding*
ultra heat treatment 359.1 *preservation*
ultrahigh frequency 297.6 *radio frequency*
ultramafite 30.30 *igneous rock*
ultramarine 539.1 *blue*; 539.5 *blueness*; 145.8 *distant*
ultrametamorphic rock 30.33 *metamorphic rock*
ultramicroscope 28.85 *microscope*
ultramicroscopic 159.7 *little*
ultramodern 295.10 *new*
ultramodernist 295.9 *modern person*
ultramontane 145.8 *distant*; 100.10 *foreign*; 100.6 *outsider*
ultramundane 145.8 *distant*
ultranational 85.16 *national*
ultranationalism 566.11 *nation*; 85.4 *nationalism*; 466.4 *social discrimination*
ultranationalist 466.7 *bigot*; 85.14 *nationalist*
ultranationalistic 466.10 *discriminatory*; 85.16 *national*
ultranationalistically 466.17 *prejudicially*
ultrasonic 28.98 *physical*; 332.1 *swift*; 505.7 *unheard*
ultrasonically 28.100 *physically*; 332.14 *swiftly*
ultrasonic cleaning 28.22 *sounding*
ultrasonic frequency 28.19 *sound propagation*
ultrasonic imaging 28.22 *sounding*
ultrasonics 28.2 *classical physics*
ultrasonic speed 332.8 *speed*
ultrasonic wave 28.14 *sound wave*
ultrasonic welding 28.22 *sounding*
ultrasound 505.3 *inaudibility*; 28.17 *sound*
ultrasound scan 35.7 *diagnosis*
ultrasound scanner 504.9 *audio device*
ultrastructure 34.6 *cell biology*
ultraviolet astronomy 29.1 *astronomy*
ultraviolet light 522.1 *light*
ultraviolet radiation 28.13 *electromagnetic radiation*; 31.22 *sun*
ultraviolet spectrometry 32.17 *analysis*
ultraviolet spectrum 28.68 *emission*
ultrawide lens 41.17 *lens*
ululant 515.7; 514.18 *crying*; 602.5 *sad*; 513.7 *strident*
ululate 507.8 *be loud*; 513.4 *be strident*; 514.13, 515.4 *cry*; 602.8 *grieve*; 603.7 *weep*
ululation 515.1 *animal cry*; 514.6 *cry of pain*; 603.2 *lament*; 507.2 *outcry*; 513.1 *stridency*
umbel 78.4 *flower head*
umbelliferous 78.12 *of flowers*; 77.16 *taxonomic*
umbilical 173.6 *central*
umbilical cord 173.2 *central thing*; 373.6 *line*; 561.7 *obstetrics*
umbra 28.24 *light emission*
umbrage 624.2 *offence*; 242.5 *unpleasantness*
umbrageous 523.8 *dark*
umbrella 127.7 *including*; 252.2 *protection*; 550.12 *protective covering*
umlaut 5.36 *accent*; 742.7 *punctuation*; 372.5 *separator*
umpirage 464.1 *judgment*; 748.2 *mediation*
umpire 713.4 *adviser*; 49.2 *basketball player*; 51.3 *bowls player*; 15.6 *employer*; 46.2 *football player*; 473.3 *impartial person*; 16.23, 464.5, 464.11 *judge*; 748.1 *mediate*; 748.3 *mediator*; 685.4 *moderate*; 685.2 *moderator*; 53.3 *official*; 63.6 *tennis player*
umpire's chair 63.3 *tennis equipment*
umpire's mask 48.3 *baseball equipment*
umpteen 194.3 *large number*; 208.6 *many*; 208.2 *multitude*
umpteenth 201.18 *eleventh*
UN 85.2 *union of nations*
unabashed 660.15 *audacious*; 622.17 *conceited*; 661.7 *defiant*
unabashedly 661.9 *defiantly*
unabbreviated 232.7 *complete*
unabetted 197.15 *solo*
unable 335.10 *powerless*; 486.1 *unskilful*; 238.1 *useless*
unable to act 341.3 *inactive*
unable to be seen 521.1 *invisible*
unable to forget 462.8 *remembering*
unable to get by 782.1 *poor*
unable to hack it 218.1 *insufficient*
unable to pay 784.10; 786.13 *nonpaying*
unable to understand 696.6 *confused*
unable to wait 262.3 *hasty*
unabridged 232.7 *complete*; 148.1 *long*; 204.7 *uncut*
unabridged dictionary 5.28 *dictionary*
unaccented 729.18 *phonetic*
unacceptable 231.1 *imperfect*; 218.1 *insufficient*; 470.10 *rejected*; 242.1 *unpleasant*; 670.32 *unsatisfactory*
unacceptably 218.10 *insufficiently*
unaccepted 670.31 *disapproved*; 470.10 *rejected*
unaccessibility 103.6 *hopelessness*
unaccessible 103.3 *hopeless*
unacclaimed 486.1 *unskilful*
unaccommodated 218.2 *unprovided*
unaccommodating 651.15 *inconsiderate*
unaccompanied 197.15 *solo*
unaccomplished 486.1 *unskilful*
unaccountability 107.1 *chance*; 696.11 *unintelligibility*
unaccountable 588.6 *anarchic*; 107.9 *causeless*; 758.5 *exempt*; 696.1 *unintelligible*; 619.8 *wonderful*
unaccountably 107.13 *by chance*; 696.13 *unintelligibly*; 758.13 *with impunity*
unaccused 252.6 *safe*
unaccustomed 487.1; 486.3 *clumsy*
unaccustomedly 487.6
Unaccustomedness 487
unaccustomedness 487.3
unachievable 103.3 *hopeless*
unacknowledged 672.4 *unthanked*
unactuality 156.1 *unreality*
unadaptable 418.4 *mentally hard*; 486.1 *unskilful*
unadapted 486.1 *unskilful*
unadjusted 486.3 *clumsy*
unadorned 271.2; **647.10**; 725.3 *clear*; 646.1 *naive*; 695.2, 728.14 *simple*
unadorned simplicity 271.4 *simplicity*
unadorned style 695.10 *simplicity*
unadornment 271.5; **647.3**; 695.10 *simplicity*
unadulterated 126.6, 698.19 *authentic*; 256.16 *clean*; 232.7 *complete*; 255.13 *pure*; 255.16, 271.1 *simple*; 204.7 *uncut*
unadulterated truth 738.11 *openness*
unadulteration 698.6 *authenticity*
unadventurous 616.4 *cautious*; 486.1 *unskilful*
unadvisable 240.1 *inconvenient*
unaesthetic 544.10, 546.4 *ugly*
unaffected 4.18 *detached*; 255.17 *direct*; 657.9 *familiar*; 618.7 *indifferent*; 657.7 *informal*; 592.1 *insensitive*; 646.1 *naive*; 271.3 *natural*; 271.1, 728.14 *simple*; 698.18 *truthful*
unaffectedly 657.15
unaffectedness 657.3 *familiarity*; 646.2 *naivety*; 271.6 *naturalness*; 728.4 *simplicity*; 698.5 *truthfulness*
unaffectionate 618.7 *indifferent*
unaffiliated 100.11 *separate*; 109.6 *unrelated*
unaffordable 681.3 *costly*
unafraid 613.12 *self-reliant*
unaggressive 339.5 *inert*; 589.7 *peaceful*
unagitated 301.6 *quiescent*
unaided 197.15 *solo*
unalienable 99.5 *essential*
unalike 116.4 *dissimilar*
unallied 109.6 *unrelated*
unalloyed 230.1 *perfect*; 255.16 *simple*
unalterable 418.4 *mentally hard*; 225.7 *permanent*
unalterably 418.13 *inflexibly*; 225.9 *permanently*; 228.12 *stably*
unaltered 111.17 *regular*; 228.10 *stabilized*
unambiguity 694.3 *comprehension*; 695.9 *intelligibility*
unambiguous 725.3 *clear*; 452.3 *decided*; 527.4 *easily seen through*; 178.5 *honourable*; 695.1 *intelligible*; 694.6 *meaningful*
unambiguously 725.4 *clearly*; 230.8 *completely*; 695.13 *intelligibly*; 694.13 *meaningfully*
unambiguousness 725.1 *clarity*; 694.3 *comprehension*; 265.2 *simplicity*
unambiguous passage 694.3 *comprehension*
unambitious 674.12 *self-deprecating*
unambivalence 695.9 *intelligibility*
unambivalent 695.1 *intelligible*
unamiable 651.15 *inconsiderate*
unanimity 750.1 *accord*
unanimous 516.7 *harmonious*; 750.10 *in accord*; 197.13 *whole*
unanimously 747.20 *cooperatively*; 516.12 *harmoniously*; 750.31 *in accord*; 197.23 *wholly*
unanimousness 750.1 *accord*
unanimous verdict 16.7 *legal trial*
unannounced 630.8 *surprising*
unanswerable 758.5 *exempt*
unanswerably 758.13 *with impunity*
unanswered 453.2 *irresolute*
unanticipated 630.8 *surprising*; 105.3 *unexpected*
unapologetic 809.3 *impenitent*
unapologized for 809.4 *unatoned*
unapparent 521.1 *invisible*
unappeasable 641.3 *unyielding*
unappetizing 497.5 *tasteless*; 242.3, 499.6 *unpalatable*
unapplied 4.13 *of philosophy*; 350.1 *unused*
unappreciated 596.9 *disliked*
unappreciation 672.1 *ingratitude*
unappreciative 672.3 *ungrateful*
unappreciatively 672.7 *ungratefully*
unappreciativeness 672.1 *ingratitude*
unappreciative person 672.2 *thankless person*
unapproachability 622.2; 240.4 *distance*; 655.1 *unsociability*
unapproachable 622.15; 121.14 *best*; 240.2 *distant*; 103.3 *hopeless*; 145.9 *reserved*; 655.8 *unsociable*
unapproachably 103.12 *hopelessly*
unappropriated 767.15 *unclaimed*
unapproved 670.31 *disapproved*; 606.5 *unsatisfactory*
unapproving 670.25 *disapproving*; 606.4 *dissatisfied*
unapt 240.1 *inconvenient*; 486.1 *unskilful*; 238.1 *useless*
unaptness 486.8 *unskilfulness*; 238.3 *uselessness*
unarm 238.8 *make useless*
unarmed 589.7 *peaceful*; 335.11 *unprotected*; 254.3 *vulnerable*
unarmoured 254.3 *vulnerable*
unaroused 301.5 *sedentary*
unarranged 408.13 *unordered*
unartificial 646.1 *naive*
unascertained 453.5 *uncertified*
unashamed 809.3 *impenitent*
unashamedly 809.6 *impenitently*
unasked 572.6 *celibate*
unaspiring 618.10 *mediocre*; 674.8 *modest*
unassailability 336.1 *strength*
unassailable 252.7 *invulnerable*
unassembled 377.21 *disbanded*
unassertive 757.8 *permitting*; 732.1 *shy*
unassertively 757.9 *with permission*
unassimilable 372.17 *unjoined*
unassimilated 372.17 *unjoined*
unassisted 197.15 *solo*
unassuming 623.1 *humble*; 657.7 *informal*; 674.8 *modest*; 646.1 *naive*; 271.3 *natural*; 728.15 *reserved*; 271.1 *simple*; 698.18 *truthful*
unassumingly 728.25 *reservedly*; 657.15 *unaffectedly*
unassuming nature 674.1 *modesty*
unassumingness 674.1 *modesty*
unatonable 804.11 *wicked*
unatoned 809.4
unattached 572.6 *celibate*; 227.13 *changeable*; 250.10 *independent*; 372.17 *unjoined*
unattached female 568.5 *single girl*
unattached male 567.5 *single man*
unattached man 572.5 *single person*
unattackable 252.7 *invulnerable*
unattainability 103.6 *hopelessness*

unattainable 103.3 *hopeless*
unattainably 103.12 *hopelessly*
unattempted 634.20 *avoidable*
unattended 254.3 *vulnerable*
unattired 552.9 *undressed*
unattractive 525.10 *aspectual*; 242.2 *objectionable*; 544.10, 546.4 *ugly*
unattractiveness 242.6 *objectionability*
unauthentic 699.32 *spurious*
unauthenticated 453.5 *uncertified*
unauthenticity 699.4 *spuriousness*
unauthorization 16.35 *illegality*
unauthorized **16.56**; 774.18 *fraudulent*; 335.10 *powerless*; 399.5 *vetoed*
unauthorized absence 98.4 *absenteeism*
unauthorized borrowing 772.3, 774.6 *illegal borrowing*
unauthorized person 335.5 *powerless person*
unavailability 240.4 *distance*; 103.6 *hopelessness*
unavailable 98.8 *absent*; 240.2 *distant*; 103.3 *hopeless*; 218.4 *scarce*
unavailing 238.2 *futile*
unavoidability 452.16 *inevitability*
unavoidable 386.9 *compelling*; 386.10 *compulsory*; 452.5 *inevitable*; 810.12 *obligatory*
unavoidably 386.11 *compellingly*; 452.25 *inevitably*
unaware 519.12 *blind to*; 456.6 *ignorant*; 618.7 *indifferent*; 592.1 *insensitive*; 463.8 *oblivious*; 630.6 *surprised*; 505.5 *unhearing*; 254.3 *vulnerable*
unawareness 519.7 *figurative blindness*; 456.1 *ignorance*; 592.3 *insensitiveness*
unawares 254.11 *dangerously*; 805.11 *innocently*; 630.13 *surprisingly*
unbalance 120.5 *be unequal*; 328.11 *derange*; 120.1 *inequality*; 461.15 *make insane*
unbalanced 486.3 *clumsy*; 328.16 *deranged*; 234.6 *distorted*; 461.11 *insane*; 120.3 *unequal*; 254.2 *unsafe*, 802.11 *wrong*
unbalanced line 46.7 *offence*
unbalanced mind 461.1 *insanity*
unballast 415.10 *lighten*
unballasted 120.3 *unequal*
unbar 390.1 *deliver*; 265.16 *make easy*; 308.19 *open up*
unbarred 308.13 *opened up*
unbearable 491.5 *painful*
unbearable pressure 576.4 *exertion*
unbeatable 121.14, 235.2 *best*; 383.12 *resisting*; 246.15 *victorious*
unbeaten 235.2 *best*; 640.12 *indomitable*; 350.2 *new*; 638.4 *undaunted*; 295.11 *unfamiliar*; 246.15 *victorious*
unbecoming 802.13 *improper*; 546.4 *ugly*
unbefitting 802.13 *improper*; 288.13 *untimely*
unbefittingly 288.19 *at the wrong time*
unbeing 98.1 *absence*; 94.1 *nonexistence*
unbeknown 456.8 *unknown*
unbelief **451.4**; 708.2 *rejection*
unbelievability **451.2**; 105.6 *implausibility*
unbelievable **103.2**; 451.7 *disbelieved*; 105.2 *questionable*; 619.8 *wonderful*
unbelievably **451.11**; 105.8 *improbably*
unbelieved 451.7 *disbelieved*
unbeliever 451.5 *disbeliever*
unbelieving 451.6 *disbelieving*; 453.1 *uncertain*
unbelievingly 451.10 *disbelievingly*
unbend 623.18 *condescend*; 627.10, 649.12 *show mercy*; 419.13 *soften*; 178.10 *straighten*; 263.2 *take it easy*; 654.12 *visit*
unbending 628.5 *inflexible*; 418.4 *mentally hard*; 383.11 *obstinate*; 647.8 *severe*; 638.3 *strong-willed*; 622.15 *unapproachable*; 641.3 *unyielding*
unbendingly 383.14 *resistingly*
unbendingness 418.8 *mental hardness*
unbenevolent 651.15 *inconsiderate*
unbent 178.1 *straight*
unbiased 150.3 *broad-minded*; 473.4 *disinterested*; 250.9 *free*; 618.9 *impartial*; 464.9 *judicious*; 4.15 *rational*; 801.7 *right*; 698.18 *truthful*
unbiased attitude 618.3 *impartiality*
unbidden 636.5 *voluntary*
unbigoted 150.3 *broad-minded*
unbind 390.1 *deliver*; 767.9 *dispose of*; 391.4 *liberate*; 372.9 *separate*; 250.15 *set free*
unbinding 391.1 *liberation*
unblamable 805.5 *innocent*
unblameworthiness 805.1 *innocence*
unblameworthy 805.5 *innocent*
unbleached 533.1 *grey*; 531.1 *white*
unblemished 805.5 *innocent*; 230.1 *perfect*; 255.13 *pure*
unblended 255.16 *simple*
unblessed 249.8 *unlucky*
unblest 712.10 *maledictive*
unblock 265.16 *make easy*; 308.19 *open up*
unblocked 308.13 *opened up*
unblunted 425.1 *sharp*
unblurred 185.7 *conspicuous*; 695.1 *intelligible*
unblushing 622.17 *conceited*; 809.3 *impenitent*; 660.21 *impudent*; 796.13 *unchaste*
unblushingly 809.6 *impenitently*
unboastful 674.8 *modest*
unboastfulness 674.1 *modesty*
unboat 312.4 *land*
unbolt 391.4 *liberate*; 308.19 *open up*
unbolted 308.13 *opened up*
unbosom oneself 739.8 *admit*
unbought 350.3 *not wanted*; 793.10 *shoddy*
unbound 389.8 *escaping*; 250.9 *free*; 758.7 *independent*
unbowed **186.9**; 613.9 *courageous*; 383.12 *resisting*; 246.15 *victorious*
unbreakability 423.6 *toughness*
unbreakable 416.6 *dense*; 252.7 *invulnerable*; 225.7 *permanent*; 418.2, 423.1 *tough*
unbreakable glass 550.12 *protective covering*
unbreakableness 423.6 *toughness*
unbridgeable 696.1 *unintelligible*
unbridle 391.4 *liberate*
unbridled 588.6 *anarchic*; 250.9 *free*; 250.12 *unconditional*; 380.6 *violent*
unbridling 391.1 *liberation*
unbroken 232.7 *complete*; 750.14 *conforming*; 134.5 *continual*; 132.11 *continuous*; 324.15 *direct*; 302.18 *ongoing*; 230.1 *perfect*; 487.1 *unaccustomed*; 204.7 *uncut*; 421.2 *uniform*
unbroken line 178.7 *straight line*
unbrokenness 132.5 *continuity*
unbuild 357.9 *demolish*
unburden 390.1 *deliver*; 265.18 *disentangle*; 391.4 *liberate*; 415.10 *lighten*; 371.12 *unload*
unburdening 265.8 *disentanglement*; 391.1 *liberation*; 415.3, 415.6 *lightening*
unburden oneself 739.8 *admit*
unburdensome 265.9 *easy*
unburnished 258.7 *dirty*
unbury 583.9 *exhume*
unbusinesslike 486.1 *unskilful*
unbutton 372.9 *separate*; 552.14 *undress*
unbuttoned 263.4 *at ease*; 250.13 *informal*
unbuttoning 372.1 *separation*
uncage 391.4 *liberate*
uncalculated 478.1 *improvised*
uncalled-for 329.12 *excessive*; 660.18 *insulting*
uncamouflaged 738.14 *manifest*
uncandid 800.5 *dishonourable*; 699.31 *hypocritical*
uncandidly 800.11 *dishonourably*; 699.42 *hypocritically*
uncandidness 699.3 *hypocrisy*
uncandour 699.3 *hypocrisy*
uncanny 11.18 *spiritual*
uncanny silence 506.4 *silence*
uncared for 596.9 *disliked*
uncaring 651.15 *inconsiderate*; 618.7 *indifferent*; 592.1 *insensitive*; 666.4 *negligent*; 628.4 *pitiless*; 472.9 *thoughtless*
uncaringly 618.17 *indifferently*
uncaused 107.9 *causeless*
unceasing 342.18 *active*; 279.10 *continuing forever*; 277.9 *permanent*; 134.6 *protracted*; 640.11 *steady*
unceasingly 134.7 *continually*
uncensored 796.12 *indecent*
unceremonious 657.7 *informal*
unceremoniously 657.12 *informally*
unceremoniousness 657.1 *informality*
uncertain **453.1**; 642.1 *capricious*; 107.8 *chance*; 227.13 *changeable*; 486.3 *clumsy*; 254.1 *dangerous*; 451.6 *disbelieving*; 105.1 *improbable*; 266.2 *obscure*; 705.14 *questionable*; 696.2 *unexplained*; 639.1 *vacillating*
uncertain future 283.3 *future condition*
uncertainly **453.23**; 227.15 *changeably*; 451.10 *disbelievingly*; 105.8 *improbably*; 639.16 *irresolutely*
uncertainness 453.9 *uncertainty*
uncertain person **453.17**
Uncertainty 453
uncertainty **453.9**; **705.6**; 642.2 *caprice*; 107.1 *chance*; 227.1 *changeableness*; 254.5 *danger*; 451.1 *disbelief*; 479.5 *equivocalness*; 474.1 *expectation*; 456.1 *ignorance*; 105.4 *improbability*; 227.2 *irresolution*; 266.1 *obscurity*; 705.1 *question*; 705.7 *questionableness*; 696.11 *unintelligibility*; 639.11 *vacillation*; 619.1 *wonder*
uncertainty principle 28.81 *causality*; 28.6 *law*; 104.5 *probability theory*
uncertified **453.5**
unchain 390.1 *deliver*; 391.4 *liberate*; 372.9 *separate*; 250.15 *set free*
unchained 389.8 *escaping*; 250.9 *free*; 372.15 *separate*
unchaining 391.1 *liberation*
unchallengeable 452.3 *decided*; 801.9 *in the right*; 252.7 *invulnerable*
unchangeability 228.1 *stability*
unchangeable 225.7 *permanent*; 111.17 *regular*; 228.9 *stable*; 638.5 *steady*
unchangeableness 228.1 *stability*; 698.9 *uniformity*
unchanged 111.17 *regular*; 228.10 *stabilized*
unchanging 279.8 *eternal*; 452.6 *infallible*; 225.7 *permanent*; 111.17 *regular*; 228.9 *stable*; 698.22 *uniform*
unchaperoned 197.15 *solo*
unchargeable 793.11 *free of charge*
uncharged 793.11 *free of charge*; 768.7 *given*
uncharitable 651.15 *inconsiderate*; 683.4 *selfish*; 647.8 *severe*
uncharitableness 651.6 *inconsiderateness*; 647.1 *severity*
uncharitably 683.8 *selfishly*; 647.11 *severely*
uncharted 456.8 *unknown*
unchartered 16.56 *unauthorized*
unchaste **796.13**; 804.12 *immoral*
unchastened 809.3 *impenitent*
unchastised 16.63 *acquitted*
unchastity 796.3 *sexual immorality*
unchecked 250.9 *free*; 453.5 *uncertified*
unchivalrous 659.6 *bad-mannered*; 242.2 *objectionable*
unchivalrously 659.9 *discourteously*
unchosen 596.9 *disliked*; 594.12 *hated*; 470.10 *rejected*
unchristian 651.15 *inconsiderate*
uncial 5.41 *lettered*; 5.15 *type style*
uncircumscribed 141.12 *extensive*
uncircumspect 459.5 *foolish*; 615.4 *rash*
uncivil 659.5 *discourteous*; 668.10 *disrespectful*; 242.2 *objectionable*; 655.8 *unsociable*
uncivilized 646.1 *naive*
uncivilized state 646.2 *naivety*
uncivilly 659.9 *discourteously*; 655.14 *unsocially*
unclad 552.9 *undressed*
unclaimed **767.15**
unclasp 372.9 *separate*
unclassified 412.12 *mixed*; 408.13 *unordered*
uncle 388.7 *I/we surrender!*; 771.3 *lender*; 567.13 *man in the family*; 226.12 *stop!*
unclean **258.8**; 258.7 *dirty*; 796.12 *indecent*; 351.4 *misused*; 408.15 *untidy*
uncleaned 258.7 *dirty*
uncleanly 258.12 *dirtily*; 258.8 *unclean*
uncleanness **258.2**; 258.1 *dirtiness*; 245.10 *impairment*; 796.2 *indecency*; 408.3 *untidiness*
unclear 696.4 *difficult*; 521.2 *difficult to see*; 511.1 *faint-sounding*; 453.6 *indeterminate*; 528.4 *inscrutable*; 694.6 *meaningful*; 524.6 *murky*; 266.2 *obscure*; 264.12 *problematic*; 161.5 *shapeless*; 696.1 *unintelligible*
unclearly 161.6 *shapelessly*
unclearness 453.14 *indeterminacy*; 528.8 *obscurity*; 161.1 *shapelessness*; 696.11 *unintelligibility*
unclench 767.9 *dispose of*; 355.1 *relinquish*
uncle's 771.4 *lending institution*
Uncle Sam 85.7 *United States*; 564.10 *US inhabitant*
Uncle Sugar 85.7 *United States*
Uncle Tom 388.2 *appeaser*
unclinch 767.9 *dispose of*
uncloak 739.5 *disclose*; 552.14 *undress*
unclog 265.16 *make easy*; 371.11 *void*
unclose 739.5 *disclose*; 308.18 *open*
unclosed 308.12 *open*
unclot 431.23 *dissolve*
unclothe 552.14 *undress*
unclothed 552.9 *undressed*
unclothing 552.1 *undress*
unclotted 431.14 *fluid*
unclotting 431.8 *fluidification*
uncloud 527.12 *make transparent*
unclouded 522.19 *sunny*; 527.1 *transparent*
unclubability 655.1 *unsociability*
unclutter 265.18 *disentangle*
uncluttered 271.1 *simple*
uncluttering 265.8 *disentanglement*
uncoded 695.2 *simple*
uncoil 148.10 *lengthen*; 178.10 *straighten*
uncoloured 530.7 *colourless*; 255.13 *pure*; 271.2 *unadorned*
uncombed 408.15 *untidy*
uncombined 375.5 *disintegrated*; 32.34 *elemental*; 255.16 *simple*
uncomfortable 328.12 *disturbed*; 491.5 *painful*; 242.1 *unpleasant*
uncomfortable with 487.1 *unaccustomed*
uncomfortably 487.6 *unaccustomedly*
uncomforting 596.9 *disliked*
uncommendable 240.1 *inconvenient*; 670.32 *unsatisfactory*
uncommended 670.33 *criticized*
uncommitted 634.18 *avoiding*; 639.1 *vacillating*
uncommitted vote 639.11 *vacillation*
uncommitted voter 639.15 *indecisive person*
uncommon 139.16 *characteristic*; 487.2 *not customary*; 206.6 *sparse*; 299.5 *unusual*
uncommonly 105.10 *rarely*; 118.21 *unconformably*; 299.9, 487.8 *unusually*
uncommonness 118.4, 299.2 *unusualness*
uncommunicative 736.17 *noncommittal*; 732.1 *shy*; 655.8 *unsociable*
uncommunicatively 732.8 *shyly*
uncommunicativeness 732.3 *shyness*; 655.1 *unsociability*
uncompact 417.1 *sparse*
uncompanionable 655.8 *unsociable*
uncompassionateness 628.1 *pitilessness*
uncompelled 250.10 *independent*
uncompensated 120.3 *unequal*; 786.14 *unpaid*
uncompetitive 747.19 *associating*; 589.7 *peaceful*
uncomplaining 609.4 *satisfied*
uncompleted 486.4 *bungled*; 233.4 *incomplete*
uncompliant 118.12 *nonconformist*; 709.8 *refused*
uncomplicated 265.9 *easy*; 646.1 *naive*; 271.1, 695.2 *simple*; 178.2 *straightforward*
uncomplicatedness 265.2 *simplicity*
uncomplimentary 670.27 *critical*; 659.5 *discourteous*
uncomplying 662.13 *disobedient*
uncompounded 255.16 *simple*
uncompressed 415.2 *insubstantial*; 417.1 *sparse*
uncompromising 726.3 *emphatic*; 647.8 *severe*; 638.3 *strong-willed*; 641.3 *unyielding*
uncompromisingly 647.11 *severely*
unconcealed 738.14 *manifest*; 520.1 *visible*
unconcern 519.7 *figurative blindness*; 472.1 *inattention*; 618.1 *indifference*; 666.1 *negligence*
unconcerned 519.12 *blind to*; 4.18 *detached*; 472.7 *inattentive*; 651.15 *inconsiderate*; 618.7 *indifferent*; 666.4 *negligent*; 388.5 *submitting*; 505.5 *unhearing*
uncondemned 16.63 *acquitted*
uncondensed state 268.2 *runniness*
unconditional **250.12**; 810.12 *obligatory*; 757.7 *permitted*
unconditionally 232.9 *completely*; 250.21 *excessively*; 757.9 *with permission*
unconditional surrender 388.1 *submission*
unconditioned 250.12 *unconditional*

unconditioned reflex 36.20 *conditioning*
unconfined 232.7 *complete;* 141.12 *extensive;* 250.9, 391.8 *free;* 250.11 *ranging*
unconfirmability 453.13 *indemonstrability*
unconfirmable 453.4 *indemonstrable*
unconfirmed report 740.1 *publication*
unconformable 118.11 *nonconforming*
unconformably **118.21**
unconformist 325.19 *deviant person*
unconformity 118.1 *nonconformity*
unconfutability 698.6 *authenticity*
unconfuted 698.19 *authentic*
uncongealed 431.14 *fluid*
uncongenial 655.8 *unsociable*
uncongeniality 655.1 *unsociability*
unconnected 133.8 *discontinuous;* 100.8 *extraneous;* 372.17 *unjoined;* 109.6 *unrelated*
unconnectedness 100.2 *foreignness;* 109.1 *unrelatedness*
unconnected person **109.3**
unconquerable 384.31 *entrenched;* 640.12 *indomitable;* 246.15 *victorious*
unconquered 640.12 *indomitable;* 638.4 *undaunted*
unconscious **489.8**; 519.12 *blind to;* 592.2 *desensitized;* 456.6 *ignorant;* 335.12 *impotent;* 618.7 *indifferent;* 592.1 *insensitive;* 445.4 *instinct;* 101.11 *internal;* 343.4 *not awake;* 463.8 *oblivious;* 36.21 *psyche;* 11.16 *psychic;* 36.37 *subconscious*
unconsciously 456.12 *ignorantly;* 618.17 *indifferently;* 805.11 *innocently;* 489.13 *insensibly;* 463.16 *obliviously;* 36.39 *psychologically;* 343.17 *sleepily;* 101.14 *subjectively*
unconscious memory 36.23 *memory*
unconscious mind 36.21 *psyche*
unconsciousness **489.2**; 592.4 *desensitization;* 335.4 *disability;* 519.7 *figurative blindness;* 456.1 *ignorance;* 101.6 *internal world;* 463.1 *oblivion;* 343.9 *sleep;* 260.3 *symptom*
unconsenting 753.9 *protesting;* 709.8 *refused;* 637.2 *refusing*
unconsolidated 30.56 *petrographic;* 268.10 *slippery*
unconsoling 596.9 *disliked*
unconstitutional 16.56 *unauthorized*
unconstrained 657.10 *free;* 758.7 *independent;* 250.13 *informal;* 646.1 *naive*
unconstrainedly 657.15 *unaffectedly*
unconstraint 657.4 *freedom;* 250.4 *informality;* 757.1 *permission*
unconsumed 215.10 *surplus;* 350.1 *unused*
unconsummated 572.6 *celibate*
uncontaminated 256.16 *clean;* 230.1 *perfect;* 255.13 *pure;* 204.7 *uncut*
uncontentious 589.7 *peaceful*
uncontestable 452.3 *decided*
uncontested 750.20 *agreeable*
uncontradicted 750.20 *agreeable*
uncontrite 809.3 *impenitent*
uncontrived 646.1 *naive*
uncontrol 686.3 *overindulgence*
uncontrollable 381.23 *attacking;* 641.2 *refractory;* 380.6 *violent*
uncontrollable tremor 327.7 *shake*
uncontrolled 588.6 *anarchic;* 408.20 *disorderly;* 262.3 *hasty;* 250.10, 758.7 *independent;* 686.8 *overindulgent*
uncontrolled imagination 477.4 *ideality*
unconventional **118.13**; 250.10 *independent;* 657.7 *informal;* 657.1 *informality;* 487.2 *not customary;* 299.5 *unusual*
unconventional behaviour 118.3 *nonconformism*
unconventionalist 118.7 *nonconformist*
unconventionality 118.3 *nonconformism;* 487.3 *unaccustomedness;* 299.2 *unusualness*
unconventionally 118.21 *unconformably;* 299.9, 487.8 *unusually*
unconventional medicine 35.2 *natural medicine*
unconversant 486.2 *unskilled*
unconverted 350.1 *unused*
unconvinced 637.2 *refusing*
unconvincing 337.13 *insufficient*
uncooperative **113.26**; 637.3 *cautious;* 662.13 *disobedient;* 378.13 *hindering;* 709.8 *refused;* 383.10 *resistant*
uncooperatively **709.11**; 113.27 *opposingly;* 378.16 *with delay*
uncooperativeness **113.6**; 662.1 *disobedience;* 383.1 *resistance*
uncopied 126.6 *authentic*
uncordial 651.15 *inconsiderate*
uncork 308.19 *open up*
uncorked 308.13 *opened up*
uncorroborated 453.5 *uncertified*
uncorrupt 805.5 *innocent;* 255.12 *morally pure;* 803.5 *virtuous*
uncorrupted 805.5 *innocent;* 255.12 *morally pure;* 803.5 *virtuous*
uncorruptible 805.5 *innocent*
uncorruptibly 255.18 *virtuously*
uncorruptness 803.1 *virtue*
uncostly 793.9 *cheap*
uncountable 202.2 *immeasurable;* 208.8 *numberless*
uncounted 208.8 *numberless*
uncouple 372.9 *separate*
uncoupling 372.1 *separation*
uncourtliness 659.1 *discourtesy*
uncourtly 659.5 *discourteous;* 659.9 *discourteously*
uncouth 659.6 *bad-mannered;* 486.3 *clumsy;* 675.8 *discourteous;* 544.8 *indecorous;* 646.1 *naive;* 242.2 *objectionable;* 546.4 *ugly*
uncouthly 659.10 *rudely*
uncouthness 544.2 *impropriety;* 675.4 *inelegance;* 646.2 *naivety*
uncover 449.2 *detect;* 739.5 *disclose;* 518.18, 520.10 *make visible;* 308.18 *open;* 308.19 *open up;* 356.10 *produce;* 738.3 *reveal;* 212.4 *take off;* 552.14 *undress*
uncovered 520.2 *clear;* 739.10 *disclosed;* 449.14 *discovered;* 738.14 *manifest;* 308.12, 738.15 *open;* 308.13 *opened up;* 552.9 *undressed;* 254.3 *vulnerable*
uncovering 449.7 *detection;* 739.1 *disclosure;* 738.10 *manifestation;* 552.1 *undress*
uncover one's head 667.19 *take off one's hat to*
uncracked 230.1 *perfect*
uncrease 421.11 *smooth*
uncreated 93.14 *self-existent*
uncreated being 93.7 *self-existence*
uncredited 672.4 *unthanked*
uncritical 669.18 *approving*
uncrown 588.4 *be anarchic*
uncrowned king 123.4 *bigwig;* 395.5 *influential person*
uncrumpled 421.2 *uniform*
unction 268.4 *anointment;* 10.5 *Christian rite;* 37.7, 268.6 *ointment;* 7.2 *religiousness*
unctional 268.13 *slippery*
unctuosity 268.3 *oiliness;* 677.4 *unctuousness*
unctuous **677.15**; 658.9 *deferential;* 599.11 *humouring;* 699.31 *hypocritical;* 7.15 *religious;* 268.13 *slippery;* 421.6 *smooth-mannered;* 664.7 *sycophantic*
unctuously 658.16 *deferentially;* 677.17 *flatteringly;* 699.42 *hypocritically;* 268.23 *oilily;* 421.16 *suavely*
unctuousness **677.4**; 658.4 *deference;* 699.3 *hypocrisy;* 268.3 *oiliness;* 7.2 *religiousness;* 421.7 *smoothness*
uncultivated 563.3 *infertile*
uncultured 659.6 *bad-mannered;* 675.8 *discourteous;* 646.1 *naive;* 574.4 *ordinary*
uncurbed 250.9 *free*
uncurl 178.10 *straighten*
uncurled 178.1 *straight*
uncurtain 739.5 *disclose*
uncut **204.7**; 232.7 *complete;* 161.5 *shapeless;* 42.10 *woven*
undamaged 230.1 *perfect;* 252.6 *safe;* 204.7 *uncut*
undamped 428.1 *dry*
undated 288.10 *mistimed*
undaunted **638.4**; 613.9 *courageous;* 640.12 *indomitable*
undauntedness 613.1 *courage*
undead 11.11 *ghost;* 11.15 *witchlike*
undecagon 201.7 *double figures*
undecahydrate 32.10 *salt*
undecayed 359.7 *preserved*
undeceitful 799.4 *honourable*
undeceive 693.11 *inform*
undecennial 201.18 *eleventh*
undeceptive 799.4 *honourable*
undecidable 27.73 *numerable*
undecided 701.10 *arguable;* 250.9 *free;* 250.7 *free person;* 453.2 *irresolute;* 447.8 *problematic;* 639.1 *vacillating*
undecided voter 250.7 *free person*
undecillion 194.3 *large number;* 201.11 *million*
undecipherable 696.1 *unintelligible*
undeclared war 585.1 *war*
undecorated 271.2 *unadorned*
undefeated 640.12 *indomitable;* 383.12 *resisting;* 246.15 *victorious*
undefended 335.11 *unprotected;* 254.3 *vulnerable*
undefended part 254.7 *vulnerability*
undefiled 256.16 *clean;* 805.5 *innocent;* 795.9, 799.5 *pure;* 255.16 *simple*
undefined 521.2 *difficult to see;* 453.6 *indeterminate;* 161.5 *shapeless;* 96.8 *unreal;* 696.3 *unrecognizable*
undemanding 265.9 *easy;* 265.13 *easygoing;* 609.4 *satisfied*
undemocratic 622.23 *prejudiced;* 647.8 *severe;* 120.4 *unjust*
undemocratically 120.8 *unjustly*
undeniable 452.3 *decided;* 703.12 *demonstrable;* 93.13 *real*
undeniableness 698.6 *authenticity*
undeniably 698.37 *authentically;* 643.12 *indeed*
undenied 698.19 *authentic*
undependability 637.14 *disobedience;* 800.2 *faithlessness*
undependable 800.6 *faithless;* 453.7 *unreliable;* 486.1 *unskilful*
under **156.12**; 550.42 *inclusively;* 122.19 *inferiorly;* 155.10 *low*
under a ban 712.10 *maledictive*
under a black cloud 626.13 *sullenly*
under a burden 414.17 *burdensomely*
under a charter 757.9 *with permission*
underachievement 231.5 *imperfection*
underachiever 247.5 *failing person*
under a cloud 249.8 *unlucky*
underact **21.36**; 486.5 *be unskilful*
underage 555.11 *young*
underaged 555.11 *young*
under an agreement 754.8 *compromisingly*
under an arrangement 754.8 *compromisingly*
under an emotional strain 593.30 *lovingly*
under an injunction 399.7 *by veto*
under a patent 757.9 *with permission*
underarm 53.13 *bowling*
under arrest 251.15 *detained;* 815.8 *imprisoned*
under a spell 712.10 *maledictive*
under authorization 757.9 *with permission*
under bad weather 62.10 *on a climb*
underbelly 155.4 *low thing*
underbid 776.3 *bargain;* 69.3 *card game terms*
underbody 155.4 *low thing*
underbuilding 403.6 *construction*
under canvas 323.12 *nautically*
undercapitalized 218.2 *unprovided*
undercarriage 175.2 *foot;* 155.4 *low thing;* 413.2 *supporting part*
under censorship **399.8**
under certain conditions 746.9 *feasibly;* 222.16 *relatively*
undercharge 793.13 *make cheap;* 789.9 *settle accounts*
under cloak of darkness 737.16 *stealthily*
underclothed 552.10 *in dishabille*
underclothes 551.18 *underwear*
undercoat 411.1 *layer;* 529.5 *paint*
undercoated 411.8 *coated*
under consideration 243.17 *developing;* 243.22 *in preparation;* 464.10 *judged;* 484.14 *planned;* 447.13 *problematically*
under construction 243.22 *in preparation;* 403.19 *in production*
under contract 15.13 *industrially*
under control 407.17 *disciplined;* 166.5 *limited;* 684.9 *moderate;* 684.12 *moderately;* 663.7 *obedient;* 251.13 *restraining;* 166.8 *within limits*
under controls 251.16 *under restraints*
undercooked 25.56 *culinary;* 233.4 *incomplete*
undercover 737.10 *secretive*
under cover 521.9 *invisibly;* 252.11 *safely*
undercover agent 736.7 *concealer;* 737.2 *secretiveness*
undercrossing 318.5 *crossing point*
under curfew 166.5 *limited*
undercurrent 113.5 *conflict;* 590.2 *impression;* 90.6 *river flow;* 91.3 *wave*
undercut 793.13 *make cheap;* 778.1 *sell*
undercut steak 25.22 *beef*
underdeveloped 233.4 *incomplete;* 356.11 *productive;* 161.5 *shapeless*
underdeveloped countries 13.4 *economic development*
underdeveloped world 86.7 *regions of the world*
underdevelopment 231.5 *imperfection;* 233.1 *incompleteness;* 486.8 *unskilfulness*
under discussion 484.14 *planned;* 447.13 *problematically;* 705.14 *questionable;* 705.24 *questionably*
under doctor's orders 260.25 *unhealthily*
underdog 247.5 *failing person;* 766.6 *loser;* 249.5 *person in adversity;* 466.8 *victim of discrimination*
underdone 25.56 *culinary;* 233.4 *incomplete*
underdressed 552.10 *in dishabille*
underdressing 551.2 *dressing*
under duress 386.11 *compellingly;* 596.10 *discontentedly;* 637.17 *unwillingly*
undereat 153.15 *be emaciated*
underemphasis 728.1 *understatement*
underemphasize 728.20 *understate*
underemphasized 728.12 *understated*
underemployed 341.3 *inactive*
underemployment 341.1 *inaction*
underestimate **468.3**; 678.10 *disparage;* 668.19 *disrespect;* 214.5 *make smaller;* 720.1 *misinterpret;* 465.10 *misjudge;* 124.12 *think unimportant;* 468.1 *underestimation;* 728.20 *understate*
underestimated **468.5**; 465.9 *misjudged;* 728.12 *understated;* 668.18 *undervalued*
underestimating **468.4**
Underestimation **468**
underestimation **468.1**; 214.1 *decrease;* 668.2 *disesteem;* 678.1 *disparagement;* 720.2 *misinterpretation;* 465.1 *misjudgment;* 728.1 *understatement*
under examination 448.14 *experimentally*
underexpose 523.14 *make dark*
underexposed 530.7 *colourless;* 523.8 *dark*
underexposed negative 530.3 *pen-and-ink sketch*
underexposed photograph 530.3 *pen-and-ink sketch*
underexposure 41.8 *composition;* 523.2 *darkening;* 530.3 *pen-and-ink sketch*
under false pretences 699.40 *falsely*
underfed **218.3**; 782.3 *beggarly;* 153.2 *emaciated;* 687.6 *fasting;* 218.1 *insufficient;* 260.21 *unhealthy*
underfelt 155.4 *low thing*
underfinanced 218.2 *unprovided*
under fire 254.4 *endangered;* 586.42 *martially*
underfloor heating 493.3 *heater*
underfoot 155.10 *low*
underframe 413.11 *support;* 413.2 *supporting part*
under full steam 332.14 *swiftly*
underfunded 218.2 *unprovided*
under-gardener 44.13 *horticulturist*
undergarments 551.18 *underwear*
undergird 392.19 *support*
underglaze 24.3 *glaze;* 24.11 *make ceramics*
underglazed 24.10 *ceramic*
underglaze decoration 24.3 *glaze*
underglazing 24.10 *ceramic*
undergo 413.12 *bear;* 590.15 *feel*
undergo a change 224.7 *be changed*
undergo a personality change 760.8 *be transformed*
undergo privation 766.12 *lessen*
undergo repairs 393.4 *be restored*
undergo treatment for 260.24 *be unhealthy*
undergrad 6.7 *learner*
undergraduate 6.7 *learner*
underground 586.14 *armed forces;* 156.4 *deep thing;* 8.20 *devilishly;* 526.8 *fleetingly;* 155.10 *low;* 317.10, 321.1 *railway;* 30.50 *terrestrial;* 317.8 *tunnel;* 156.12 *under*
underground activities 662.3 *subversion*
underground cable 437.4 *electricity;* 39.33 *power distribution*

underground economy 779.3 *sellers' market*
underground fighter 586.9 *guerrilla*
underground literature 17.1 *literature*
underground press 740.3 *journalism*
underground railway 321.1 *railway*
underground river 90.1 *river*
underground shelter 252.5 *refuge;* 384.10 *shelter*
underground stem 77.5 *stem*
underground water 30.9 *groundwater*
undergrowth 420.8 *rough ground;* 79.4 *trees*
under guard 252.6 *safe*
underhand 645.4, 702.8 *cunning;* 700.35 *deceptive;* 812.4 *disreputable;* 737.10 *secretive*
under hand and seal 756.16 *as promised;* 756.12 *promised*
underhand dealing 737.2 *secretiveness*
underhand dealings 800.3 *criminality*
underhanded 800.7 *criminal;* 699.35 *fraudulent*
underhanded deal 645.1 *cunning;* 699.8, 700.10 *fraud*
underhandedly 800.11 *dishonourably*
underhandedness 700.1 *deception*
under hatches 582.19 *dead*
under house arrest 251.15 *detained;* 814.20 *punished*
under investigation 701.18 *arguably*
underlaid 155.6 *lower*
underlay 155.8 *be low;* 411.1 *layer;* 155.4 *low thing;* 413.2 *supporting part*
underlayer 175.1 *base;* 411.1 *layer*
under licence 757.9 *with permission*
underlie 175.4 *base;* 172.13 *be interior;* 155.8 *be low*
underline 726.6 *emphasize;* 743.10 *identify;* 123.8 *make important;* 520.10 *make visible;* 742.13 *punctuate;* 336.8 *strengthen*
underlined 707.15, 726.4 *emphasized;* 742.17 *punctuated*
underling 247.5 *failing person;* 122.6 *inferior;* 124.10 *nonentity;* 574.1 *plebeian;* 401.1 *servant;* 387.3 *subordinate*
underlining 726.1 *emphasis;* 742.7 *punctuation;* 520.7 *that which makes visible*
underloaded 120.3 *unequal*
under lock and key 815.11 *captively;* 815.8 *imprisoned;* 252.6 *safe;* 252.11 *safely*
underlying 175.3 *base;* 155.6 *lower*
underlying cause 344.1 *cause*
underlying structure 5.29 *grammar*
underman 206.8 *reduce*
undermanned 231.2 *incomplete;* 206.6 *sparse;* 218.2 *unprovided*
undermine 588.4 *be anarchic;* 645.5 *be cunning;* 378.8 *hinder;* 245.5 *hurt;* 192.3 *invert;* 484.13 *plot;* 704.8 *refute;* 335.7 *remove power from;* 305.15 *tunnel;* 337.7 *weaken*
undermined 245.12 *deteriorated*
undermining 192.1 *inversion;* 704.1 *refutation;* 305.7 *tunnelling*
undermost 175.3 *base;* 155.6 *lower*
underneath 175.2 *foot;* 521.9 *invisibly;* 155.10 *low;* 155.4 *low thing*
under no circumstances 94.14 *not at all*
under notice to quit 767.13 *dismissed*
undernourished 153.2 *emaciated;* 218.1 *insufficient;* 218.3 *underfed;* 260.21 *unhealthy*
under oath 707.24 *truthfully*
under obligation 706.16 *answerable;* 671.4 *grateful;* 354.8 *responsibly*
under one's belt 253.8 *accomplished*
under one's breath 730.17 *voicelessly*
under one's command 387.9 *subject*
under one's nose 97.10 *available;* 520.2 *clear;* 703.20 *manifestly;* 147.12 *near;* 97.16 *on the spot*
under one's own steam 197.21 *alone*
under one's thumb 663.7 *obedient;* 387.9 *subject*
under orders 663.10 *obediently;* 387.11 *under subjection*
underpaid 782.1 *poor;* 218.2 *unprovided*
underpaint 19.19 *paint*
underpainting 19.2 *painting*
under par 122.19 *inferiorly*
underpart 155.4 *low thing*
underpass 318.5 *crossing point;* 156.4 *deep thing;* 308.7 *passageway;* 317.3, 373.5 *road;* 38.22, 317.8 *tunnel*
underpin 175.4 *base;* 413.11 *support*
underpinning 38.28 *substructure;* 413.1 *support;* 413.2 *supporting part*
under plain cover 521.9 *invisibly*
underplay 728.22 *play down;* 728.20 *understate*
underplayed 728.19 *downplayed*
underplaying 728.9 *downplaying*
under pleasant circumstances 569.17 *in friendship*
underpopulated 206.6 *sparse*
underpopulation 206.3 *fewness*
underpraise 728.21 *detract from;* 720.1 *misinterpret;* 468.3 *underestimate*
under press of sail 332.14 *swiftly*
under pressure 386.11 *compellingly;* 262.6 *hastily;* 637.17 *unwillingly*
under pressure to 386.11 *compellingly*
underprice 468.3 *underestimate*
underpriced 793.9 *cheap;* 468.5 *underestimated*
underprivileged 782.1 *poor*
under protest 383.14 *resistingly;* 637.17 *unwillingly*
underrate 678.10 *disparage;* 668.19 *disrespect;* 720.1 *misinterpret;* 465.10 *misjudge;* 124.12 *think unimportant;* 468.3 *underestimate;* 728.20 *understate*
underrated 465.9 *misjudged;* 468.5 *underestimated;* 728.12 *understated;* 668.18 *undervalued*
underrating 468.1 *underestimation*
underreckon 728.20 *understate*
underreckoned 728.12 *understated*
underreckoning 728.1 *understatement*
under remission 251.13 *restraining*
under restraint 166.5 *limited;* 251.13 *restraining*
under restraints 251.16
under restrictions 251.16 *under restraints;* 166.8 *within limits*
under sail 300.18 *in motion;* 323.12 *nautically*
underscore 726.6 *emphasize;* 743.10 *identify;* 742.13 *punctuate;* 336.8 *strengthen*
underscored 707.15 *emphasized*
underscoring 726.1 *emphasis*
undersea 30.51, 91.7 *oceanic;* 156.12 *under*
underseal 320.21 *miscellaneous motoring terms*
undersea warfare 585.8 *warfare*
undersecretary 579.16 *official;* 12.8 *politician*
undersell 793.13 *make cheap*
under sentence 254.4 *endangered*
under sentence of death 582.18 *dying*
under shelter 252.6 *safe*
undershift 46.10 *defence;* 46.16 *play defence*
undershirt 551.18 *underwear*
undershoot 120.5 *be unequal;* 322.5 *flight*
undershot 120.3 *unequal*
underside 175.2 *foot;* 155.4 *low thing*
under siege 254.4 *endangered;* 586.42 *martially*
undersign 743.11 *identify oneself*
undersize 159.7 *little;* 159.1 *littleness*
underskirt 551.18 *underwear*
undersoil 155.4 *low thing*
under someone's influence 395.14 *influentially*
undersown 43.20 *farmable*
understaff 206.8 *reduce*
understaffed 206.6 *sparse;* 218.2 *unprovided*
understand 695.6; 650.8 *be benevolent;* 693.15 *be informed;* 450.8 *be of the opinion;* 156.15 *be profound;* 458.7 *be wise;* 590.15 *feel;* 449.3 *find out;* 446.14 *have an idea;* 477.16 *have insight;* 694.11 *infer;* 719.8 *interpret;* 6.24, 455.11 *know;* 400.15 *learn;* 627.8 *pity;* 4.21 *rationalize;* 444.11 *reason;* 476.5 *suppose;* 518.16 *visualize*
understandability 695.9 *intelligibility;* 265.2 *simplicity*
understandable 695.1 *intelligible*
understandably 695.13 *intelligibly*
understand by 694.11 *infer*
understanding 695.12; 409.10 *agreement;* 810.7 *commitment;* 754.1 *compromise;* 755.1 *contract;* 522.13 *enlightenment;* 590.1, 590.10 *feeling;* 449.8 *finding out;* 569.8 *friendly;* 569.2 *friendly relations;* 446.1 *idea;* 750.10 *in accord;* 477.3 *insight;* 442.3, 458.2 *intelligence;* 442.10 *intelligent;* 719.1 *interpretation;* 455.1 *knowledge;* 593.1 *love;* 749.1 *pacification;* 627.1 *pity;* 627.6 *pitying;* 156.3 *profundity;* 444.1 *reason;* 444.7 *reasoning;* 413.9 *supportive;* 518.4 *visualization;* 458.1 *wisdom;* 156.11 *wise*
understandingly 750.31 *in accord*
understate 728.20; 678.10 *disparage;* 699.26 *falsify;* 468.3 *underestimate*
understated 728.12; 529.13 *soft-hued*
Understatement 728
understatement 728.1; 678.1 *disparagement;* 699.9 *falsification;* 468.1 *underestimation*
under steam 323.12 *nautically*
understeer 320.21 *miscellaneous motoring terms*
understood 632.12 *established;* 476.8 *supposed*
understrapper 124.10 *nonentity*
under strength 337.13 *insufficient;* 218.2 *unprovided*
under strict regulations 647.11 *severely*
understructure 403.6 *construction*
understudy 21.34 *act;* 21.24 *actor;* 398.5 *alternative;* 706.23 *answer for;* 762.4 *be a substitute;* 115.5 *counterpart;* 550.34 *cover for;* 608.5 *helper;* 398.8 *represent;* 762.2 *substitute person;* 550.21 *substitution*
understudy for 608.11 *assist*
under subjection 387.11
under supervision 15.13 *industrially*
undersupply 206.3 *fewness*
undersurface 175.2 *foot;* 172.1 *interior;* 155.4 *low thing*
undersurfaced 172.7 *interior*
under suspicion 715.8 *accusatory*
undertake 354.1; **638.9**; 340.4 *act;* 733.12 *address oneself to;* 633.14 *carry on;* 448.13 *invent;* 482.8 *resolve;* 353.3 *tackle*
undertaken 354.5
undertaker 353.7 *attempter;* 340.3 *doer;* 583.3 *funeral director;* 582.9 *person dealing with the dead*
undertake to 756.7 *promise*
Undertaking 354
undertaking 344.6; **354.2**; 346.3, 776.6 *business;* 755.1 *contract;* 340.2 *deed;* 482.3 *future intention;* 356.1 *production;* 342.2 *social activity;* 353.6 *venture*
under the aegis of 252.11 *safely*
under the auspices of 392.37 *in aid of*
under the best circumstances 446.23 *ideally*
under the circumstances 222.15; 750.36 *accordingly;* 143.12 *circumstantially*
under the counter 16.83 *dishonestly;* 767.16 *disposably;* 776.20 *in trade;* 737.16 *stealthily*
under-the-counter 645.4 *cunning*
under-the-counter purchase 645.1 *cunning*
under the doctor 260.25 *unhealthily*
under the ground 30.66 *geographically*
under the hammer 767.16 *disposably;* 778.18 *on sale*
under the influence 690.1 *drunk;* 690.18 *drunkenly*
under the open sky 434.26 *out-of-doors*
under the protection of 252.6 *safe*
under the sun 141.16 *extensively*
under the sway of 387.9 *subject*
under the table 690.3 *dead drunk*
under-the-table 645.4 *cunning*
under-the-table deal 645.1 *cunning*
under the thumb 251.13 *restraining;* 664.6 *servile*
under the weather 337.10 *ill;* 260.22 *sick*
under the wing of 252.6 *safe*
underthings 551.18 *underwear*
undertone 170.3 *atmosphere;* 511.4 *faint sound;* 18.21 *tone;* 730.4 *whispering*
undertow 90.6 *river flow;* 379.1 *trap;* 91.3 *wave*
under training 243.17 *developing*
under treatment 260.25 *unhealthily*
undertrick 69.3 *card game terms*
underuse 350.8 *nonuse;* 350.5 *not use*
underused 350.3 *not wanted*
underutilization 350.8 *nonuse*
underutilize 350.5 *not use*
undervaluation 214.1 *decrease;* 668.2 *disesteem;* 465.1 *misjudgment;* 468.1 *underestimation;* 728.1 *understatement*
undervalue 678.10 *disparage;* 668.19 *disrespect;* 214.5 *make smaller;* 465.10 *misjudge;* 468.3 *underestimate;* 728.20 *understate*
undervalued 668.18; 465.9 *misjudged;* 468.5 *underestimated;* 728.12 *understated*
undervaluing the self 674.5 *self-deprecation*
under warrant 252.6 *safe;* 757.9 *with permission*
under warranty 253.7 *guaranteed*
underwater 67.12 *by swimming;* 91.7 *oceanic;* 55.9 *on the water;* 67.11 *swimming;* 156.12 *under*
underwater breathing tube 67.1 *swimming*
underwater explorer 91.6 *oceanographer*
underwater mask 67.1 *swimming*
underwater photography 41.1 *photography*
underwater plug 55.2 *artificial fly*
underwater swimmer 305.8 *descender;* 67.4 *swimmer*
underwater swimming 67.1 *swimming*
under way 300.18 *in motion;* 243.22 *in preparation;* 302.20 *in progress;* 323.12 *nautically*
underwear 551.18; 552.4 *dishabille*
underweight 122.17 *defective;* 120.1 *inequality;* 415.1 *light;* 153.1 *thin;* 120.3 *unequal;* 414.7 *weighing*
underwhelming 728.16 *imperceptible*
underwood 79.4 *trees*
underworld 804.7 *criminality;* 156.4 *deep thing;* 8.12 *hell;* 101.1 *nonmaterial world;* 582.14 *the spiritual world*
under wraps 736.14 *concealed;* 521.3 *private*
underwrite 750.28 *consent;* 755.5 *contract;* 13.11 *deal;* 756.8 *guarantee;* 253.11 *promise;* 413.13 *support financially*
underwriter 413.8 *supporter*
underwriting 107.7 *calculation of chance;* 253.2 *promise*
underwritten 750.17 *consenting;* 756.13 *guaranteeing*
undeserving 236.4 *poor*
undesigned 107.9 *causeless*
undesigning 646.1 *naive*
undesirability 240.3 *inconvenience*
undesirable 596.9 *disliked;* 812.2 *disreputable character;* 802.13 *improper;* 240.1 *inconvenient;* 804.9 *wicked person*
undesired 596.9 *disliked*
undesirous 596.8 *disliking;* 618.7 *indifferent*
undetectability 521.4 *invisibility*
undetectable 521.1 *invisible*
undetermined 138.20 *generalized;* 452.8 *unspecified;* 639.1 *vacillating*
undeterred 640.12 *indomitable*
undeveloped 245.12 *deteriorated;* 555.12 *immature;* 231.2, 233.4 *incomplete;* 350.2 *new;* 102.6 *potential;* 161.5 *shapeless;* 486.2 *unskilled;* 555.11 *young*
undeveloped world 86.7 *regions of the world*
undevelopment 555.3 *immaturity;* 231.5 *imperfection;* 161.1 *shapelessness*
undeviating 750.14 *conforming;* 452.2 *convinced;* 324.15 *direct;* 452.6 *infallible;* 111.17 *regular;* 698.22 *uniform*
undeviatingly 698.39 *accurately;* 324.9 *directly*
undies 551.18 *underwear*
undifferentiated 750.14 *conforming;* 132.11 *continuous;* 111.12 *same;* 255.16 *simple*
undifferentiation 132.5 *continuity*
undignified 544.7 *graceless*
undiluted 558.17 *drinkable;* 690.6 *intoxicating;* 255.13 *pure;* 336.12 *strong to the senses*
undiminished 230.1 *perfect;* 204.7 *uncut*
undine 8.5 *deity;* 37.11 *linctus;* 91.4 *sea god*
undiplomatic 486.1 *unskilful*
undiplomatically 486.11 *unskilfully*
undirected 325.22
undiscernible 696.1 *unintelligible*
undiscerning 519.12 *blind to;* 486.1 *unskilful*
undischarged bankrupt 786.6 *nonpayer*
undisciplined 588.6 *anarchic;* 642.1 *capricious;* 662.13 *disobedient;* 408.20 *disorderly;* 686.8 *overindulgent*
undisclosed 737.9 *secret*
undiscouraged 640.12 *indomitable*
undiscoverable 696.1 *unintelligible*

undiscriminating 669.18 *approving;* 497.6 *coarse*
undisguised 255.17 *direct;* 527.4 *easily seen through;* 738.14 *manifest;* 646.1 *naive;* 698.18 *truthful;* 520.1 *visible*
undisguisedly 738.16 *manifestly*
undismayed 613.9 *courageous*
undisposed of 350.1 *unused*
undisputed 450.14 *believed;* 452.3 *decided;* 707.16 *definite*
undisputedness 707.8 *definiteness*
undissembling 646.1 *naive*
undissolved 416.7 *condensed*
undistinguished 623.1 *humble;* 623.7 *humility;* 216.3 *mediocre*
undistracted 471.8 *diligent*
undistributed middle 4.9 *philosophical problem*
undisturbed 4.18 *detached;* 301.6 *quiescent*
undiversified 111.17 *regular*
undivided 232.7 *complete;* 134.5 *continual;* 204.7 *uncut;* 197.13 *whole*
undivided attention 471.2 *close attention*
undividedness 197.3 *oneness*
undivulged 737.9 *secret*
undo 347.3 *counteract;* 357.8 *destroy;* 268.17 *liquefy;* 238.8 *make useless,* 761.7 *restore;* 372.9 *separate;* 552.14 *undress*
undocumented 453.5 *uncertified*
undoing 357.1 *destruction;* 372.1 *separation*
undomesticated 487.1 *unaccustomed*
undone 357.15 *destroyed;* 372.15 *separate;* 268.10 *slippery*
undoubted 698.19 *authentic;* 104.6 *probable*
undoubtedly 707.23 *affirmatively;* 698.37 *authentically;* 95.14, 452.23 *certainly*
undoubting 450.11 *believing;* 452.2 *convinced*
undrained 92.11 *continental*
undramatic 271.1 *simple*
undramatically 271.8 *simply*
undrape 552.14 *undress*
undraped 552.9 *undressed*
Undress 552
undress 552.1; **552.14**; 657.6 *informal dress*
undressed 552.9
undressing 552.1 *undress*
undrinkable 499.6 *unpalatable*
undrooping 640.11 *steady*
undue 329.12 *excessive;* 240.1 *inconvenient*
undueness 240.3 *inconvenience*
undulancy 326.4 *rock*
undulant 326.17 *waving*
undulate 298.7 *be regular;* 91.10 *billow;* 180.6 *convolute;* 326.12 *wave*
undulating 154.13 *mountainous;* 298.11 *regular;* 326.17 *waving*
undulating land 92.7 *upland*
undulatingly 298.15 *regularly*
undulating motion 298.1 *regularity*
undulation 177.2 *bend;* 180.1 *convolution;* 298.1 *regularity;* 326.4 *rock;* 28.12, 91.3 *wave*
undulatory 180.4 *convolutional;* 420.1 *rough;* 326.17 *waving;* 177.5 *well-rounded*
unduplicated 126.6 *authentic*
undutiful 662.13 *disobedient*
undutifulness 662.1 *disobedience*
undyed 533.1 *grey;* 255.13 *pure;* 531.1 *white*
undying 202.3, 279.8 *eternal;* 225.7, 277.9 *permanent;* 134.6 *protracted*
undyingly 225.9 *permanently*
unearned income 765.4 *earnings*
unearth 449.2 *detect;* 369.13 *dig out;* 284.16 *excavate;* 583.9 *exhume;* 142.11 *find;* 738.3 *reveal*
unearthed 739.10 *disclosed;* 449.14 *discovered;* 142.7 *found*
unearthing 369.3 *digging out;* 142.3 *locating*
unearthliness 11.2 *the occult;* 101.2 *unworldliness*
unearthly 8.13 *divine;* 101.8 *nonmaterial;* 11.18 *spiritual*
unearthly hour 293.2 *early hour*
unearth the past 284.16 *excavate*
unease 798.2 *affliction;* 327.1 *agitation;* 612.2 *fearfulness;* 342.7 *restlessness*
uneasily 327.27 *agitatedly;* 328.19 *distractedly;* 612.15 *fearfully*
uneasiness 612.2 *fearfulness;* 612.3 *worry*
uneasy 327.15 *agitated;* 486.3 *clumsy;* 328.12 *disturbed;* 612.8 *fearful*
uneasy conscience 808.1 *penitence*
uneasy peace 585.1 *war*
uneasy truce 589.1 *peace*
uneatable 242.3, 499.6 *unpalatable*
uneconomic 681.1 *extravagant;* 238.2 *futile;* 441.8 *wasteful*
uneconomical 441.8 *wasteful*
uneconomically 681.9 *extravagantly;* 441.10 *wastefully*
unedged 426.1 *blunt*
uneducable 486.2 *unskilled*
uneducated 456.6 *ignorant;* 646.1 *naive;* 5.39 *of language;* 487.1 *unaccustomed;* 486.2 *unskilled*
uneducated speech 5.5 *nonstandard language*
unelaborate 728.14 *simple*
unelaborately 728.24 *simply*
unelaborateness 728.4 *simplicity*
unembellished 271.2 *unadorned*
unembellishment 271.5 *unadornment*
unembodied 101.8 *nonmaterial;* 11.18 *spiritual*
unemotional 4.18 *detached;* 618.7 *indifferent;* 592.1 *insensitive;* 489.6 *unfeeling*
unemotionally 618.17 *indifferently;* 4.27 *stoically;* 592.8 *unfeelingly*
unemphatic 271.1 *simple*
unemployability 238.3 *uselessness*
unemployable 350.1 *unused;* 238.1 *useless*
unemployed 341.3 *inactive;* 580.7 *leisurely;* 350.3 *not wanted;* 343.2 *not working;* 335.10 *powerless;* 301.5 *sedentary*
unemployment 343.6; **580.3**; 470.6 *discarding;* 249.2 *economic adversity;* 13.6 *economic factors;* 341.1 *inaction;* 350.8 *nonuse*
unemployment benefit 392.4 *social assistance;* 652.4 *welfare state*
unemployment benefits 253.1 *protection;* 650.3 *welfare*
unemployment compensation 392.4 *social assistance*
unemployment insurance 13.8 *industrial relations;* 392.4 *social assistance*
unenclosed 308.13 *opened up*
unending 279.10 *continuing forever;* 132.11 *continuous;* 202.3, 279.8 *eternal;* 134.6 *protracted*
unendingly 134.7, 640.14 *continually*
unendowed 486.1 *unskilful*
unendurable 236.3 *bad*
unengaged 343.2 *not working*
unenjoyable 620.4 *boring*
unenlightened 523.11 *benighted;* 519.12 *blind to;* 456.6 *ignorant;* 486.1 *unskilful*
unenlightenment 519.7 *figurative blindness;* 456.1 *ignorance*
unenthusiasm 637.13 *dissociation*
unenthusiastic 637.3 *cautious*
unenthusiastically 637.17 *unwillingly*
unequable 120.3 *unequal*
unequal 120.3; 486.3 *clumsy;* 751.10 *different;* 116.4 *dissimilar;* 109.8, 234.6 *distorted;* 27.75 *equal;* 299.4 *irregular;* 2.14 *socioeconomic*
unequalize 120.5 *be unequal*
unequalled 121.14, 235.2, 797.2 *best;* 230.1 *perfect;* 120.3 *unequal*
unequally 120.7; 751.12 *differently;* 109.13 *disproportionately;* 116.7 *dissimilarly;* 114.10 *diversely;* 299.8 *irregularly;* 27.87 *mathematically*
unequalness 299.1 *irregularity*
unequal to 218.1 *insufficient*
unequipped 231.2 *incomplete;* 486.1 *unskilful*
unequivocal 452.3 *decided;* 707.16 *definite;* 726.3 *emphatic;* 695.1 *intelligible*
unequivocally 707.23 *affirmatively;* 230.8, 232.9 *completely;* 799.7 *honourably*
unequivocalness 707.8 *definiteness*
unerring 273.6, 801.8 *correct;* 805.5 *innocent;* 255.12 *morally pure;* 698.22 *uniform;* 803.5 *virtuous*
unerringly 698.39 *accurately;* 805.11 *innocently;* 255.18 *virtuously*
unerringness 698.9 *uniformity*
unerroneousness 698.1 *truth*
unescorted 197.15 *solo;* 254.3 *vulnerable*
unessayed 350.1 *unused*
unessential 100.8 *extraneous*
unethical 800.5 *dishonourable;* 796.11, 802.15 *immoral*
unethically 800.11 *dishonourably*
unethicalness 796.1 *immorality*
uneuphonious 544.9 *inelegant*
unevasive 695.2 *simple*
uneven 133.8 *discontinuous;* 114.5 *diverse;* 231.1 *imperfect;* 299.4 *irregular;* 183.7 *notched;* 420.1 *rough;* 120.3 *unequal;* 802.11 *wrong*
unevenly 114.10 *diversely;* 231.11 *imperfectly;* 299.8 *irregularly;* 183.12 *jaggedly;* 420.14 *roughly;* 120.7 *unequally*
unevenness 133.1 *discontinuity;* 114.1 *diversity;* 231.5 *imperfection;* 120.1 *inequality;* 299.1 *irregularity;* 420.6 *roughness;* 802.1 *unfairness*
uneven parallel bars 57.7 *stationary rings*
uneventful 124.4 *trivial*
unexaggerated 698.18 *truthful*
unexcelled 121.14 *best*
unexceptionable 235.5 *not bad*
unexceptional 138.21 *common;* 117.15 *everyday;* 632.10 *familiar;* 216.3, 618.10 *mediocre;* 685.6 *moderate*
unexceptionally 618.20
unexcitable 339.5 *inert*
unexciting 497.5 *tasteless*
unexcusable 804.11 *wicked*
unexercised 350.1 *unused*
unexisting 708.21 *nonexistent*
unexpected 105.3; 642.1 *capricious;* 107.8 *chance;* 105.1 *improbable;* 696.5 *strange;* 630.8 *surprising;* 619.8 *wonderful*
unexpected attack 379.1 *trap*
unexpected event 379.1 *trap*
unexpected gift 630.4 *surprising thing*
unexpected loss of life 582.5 *ways of dying*
unexpectedly 105.9; 107.13 *by chance;* 630.13 *surprisingly*
unexpectedness 105.5; 630.1 *surprise*
unexpected occurrence 630.4 *surprising thing*
unexpended 439.7 *stored*
unexpended balance 439.1 *store*
unexpensive 793.9 *cheap*
unexpensively 793.15 *cheaply*
unexpired 215.10 *surplus*
unexplainable 107.9 *causeless;* 696.1 *unintelligible*
unexplained 696.2
unexploded bomb 339.3 *inert thing*
unexploited 350.2 *new*
unexplored 655.11 *secluded;* 295.11 *unfamiliar;* 456.8 *unknown*
unexposed 252.6 *safe*
unexpurgated 232.7 *complete;* 796.12 *indecent;* 204.7 *uncut*
unfading 529.10 *coloured;* 225.7 *permanent*
unfailing 225.7 *permanent;* 134.6 *protracted;* 640.11 *steady*
unfailingly 225.9 *permanently*
unfair 466.10 *discriminatory;* 800.5 *dishonourable;* 718.6 *misrepresented;* 120.4, 465.8 *unjust;* 802.11 *wrong*
unfair advantage 765.1 *gain*
unfair labour practices 15.1 *industrial relations*
unfairly 800.11 *dishonourably;* 466.17 *prejudicially;* 120.8, 465.14 *unjustly;* 718.8 *unrepresentatively;* 802.25 *wrongly*
unfairly treated 465.9 *misjudged*
unfairness 802.1; 800.1 *improbity;* 465.3 *injustice;* 466.3 *prejudice*
unfair opponent 596.3 *disliked person*
unfair price 792.2
unfair representation 718.1 *misrepresentation*
unfaithful 639.2 *changeable;* 451.6 *disbelieving;* 479.11 *equivocating;* 800.6 *faithless;* 227.14 *irresolute;* 796.14 *lecherous;* 700.38 *treacherous*
unfaithfully 227.15 *changeably;* 800.11 *dishonourably;* 479.13 *perfidiously*
unfaithfulness 662.1 *disobedience;* 800.2 *faithlessness;* 796.4 *illicit love;* 593.8 *love affair;* 247.3 *personal fault*
unfallaciousness 698.1 *truth*
unfallen 795.9 *pure*
unfalseness 698.1 *truth*
unfaltering 640.11 *steady*
unfamiliar 295.11; 448.9 *original;* 487.1 *unaccustomed;* 456.8 *unknown*
unfamiliarity 456.1 *ignorance;* 295.1 *newness;* 448.4 *originality;* 487.3 *unaccustomedness*
unfamiliar word 5.17 *word*
unfanciness 728.4 *simplicity*
unfancy 728.14 *simple*
unfashionable 525.10 *aspectual;* 675.8 *discourteous;* 487.2 *not customary;* 544.10 *ugly*
unfashionably 544.11 *inelegantly*
unfasten 390.1 *deliver;* 308.19 *open up;* 372.9 *separate*
unfastened 308.13 *opened up;* 372.17 *unjoined*
unfastening 372.1 *separation*
unfastidious 258.8 *unclean*
unfathomable 156.8 *deep;* 202.2 *immeasurable;* 528.4 *inscrutable;* 696.1 *unintelligible*
unfathomableness 156.1 *depth*
unfathomably 696.13 *unintelligibly*
unfathomed 156.8 *deep*
unfavourable 249.6 *adverse;* 670.27 *critical;* 357.14 *destructive;* 798.10 *inauspicious;* 113.22 *oppositional;* 475.15 *presageful;* 288.13 *untimely*
unfavourableness 798.3 *bad luck;* 288.2 *untimeliness*
unfavourable review 670.5 *criticism*
unfavourable verdict 16.43 *conviction;* 16.7 *legal trial*
unfavourably 288.19 *at the wrong time;* 249.12 *in adversity;* 798.14 *inauspiciously*
unfearing 613.12 *self-reliant;* 638.4 *undaunted*
unfeasibility 103.6 *hopelessness*
unfeasible 103.3 *hopeless*
unfeathered 552.12 *peeling*
unfed 687.6 *fasting;* 218.3 *underfed*
unfeeling 489.6; 651.12 *callous;* 592.2 *desensitized;* 426.3 *dull;* 651.15 *inconsiderate;* 618.7 *indifferent;* 592.1 *insensitive;* 423.5 *mentally tough;* 628.4 *pitiless;* 638.3 *strong-willed*
unfeelingly 592.8; 618.17 *indifferently;* 489.13 *insensibly;* 628.7 *pitilessly;* 423.14 *single-mindedly*
unfeelingness 651.3 *callousness;* 423.9 *mental toughness;* 628.1 *pitilessness*
unfeeling person 489.5
unfeigning 271.3 *natural*
unfeminine 659.5 *discourteous;* 675.7 *vulgar*
unfenced 308.13 *opened up*
unfermented 689.2 *nonalcoholic*
unfertilized 563.5 *rendered infertile*
unfetter 390.1 *deliver;* 391.4 *liberate;* 372.9 *separate;* 250.15 *set free*
unfettered 250.9 *free;* 391.7 *liberated;* 250.11 *ranging;* 372.15 *separate*
unfettering 391.1 *liberation*
unfictitious 698.15 *true*
unfictitiousness 698.1 *truth*
unfilled 231.2 *incomplete;* 98.14 *unoccupied;* 218.2 *unprovided*
unfinished 420.5; 231.2, 233.4 *incomplete;* 205.11 *partial;* 161.5 *shapeless;* 486.2 *unskilled*
unfinished piece 420.10 *rough idea*
unfinished state 233.1 *incompleteness*
unfit 231.1 *imperfect;* 802.13 *improper;* 240.1 *inconvenient;* 238.8 *make useless;* 335.10 *powerless;* 260.21 *unhealthy;* 486.1 *unskilful;* 238.1 *useless*
unfit for consideration 470.10 *rejected*
unfit for human consumption 470.10 *rejected*
unfitness 231.5 *imperfection;* 240.3 *inconvenience;* 335.1 *powerlessness;* 486.8 *unskilfulness;* 238.3 *uselessness*
unfitting 802.13 *improper;* 240.1 *inconvenient*
unfittingness 240.3 *inconvenience*
unfixed 372.17 *unjoined*
unflagging 342.20 *industrious;* 423.4 *powerful;* 640.11 *steady*
unflagging efforts 640.2 *commitment*
unflanked 254.3 *vulnerable*
unflattering 659.5 *discourteous;* 698.18 *truthful*
unflavoured 255.13 *pure;* 497.5 *tasteless*
unflawed 230.1 *perfect*
unfledged 130.32 *embryonic;* 72.22 *newly hatched;* 552.12 *peeling;* 555.11 *young*
unfleshly 101.8 *nonmaterial*
unflinching 613.9 *courageous;* 638.4 *undaunted*
unfluent 544.9 *inelegant*

unfocused 521.2 *difficult to see*
unfold 190.6 *become bigger;* 209.6 *change gradually;* 93.18 *come to be;* 739.5 *disclose;* 703.16 *explain;* 345.7 *follow from;* 148.10 *lengthen;* 308.18 *open;* 356.10 *produce;* 4.21 *rationalize;* 738.3 *reveal;* 178.10 *straighten;* 77.21 *vegetate*
unfolded 190.7 *bigger;* 308.12 *open*
unfolding 525.1 *appearance;* 525.7 *appearing;* 78.5 *flowering;* 190.8 *growing;* 190.1 *growth;* 738.10 *manifestation*
unforced 478.2 *spontaneous;* 636.5, 752.18 *voluntary*
unforeseeable 107.8 *chance;* 105.3 *unexpected*
unforeseeableness 105.5 *unexpectedness*
unforeseeably 105.9 *unexpectedly*
unforeseen 107.8 *chance;* 630.8 *surprising;* 105.3 *unexpected*
unforeseen result 630.4 *surprising thing*
unforgettable 462.7 *memorable;* 123.6 *notable*
unforgettably 462.16 *memorably*
unforgivable **802.17**; 806.5 *guilty;* 804.11 *wicked*
unforgivably 806.11 *guiltily;* 714.16 *vindictively*
unforgiving 628.4 *pitiless;* 647.8 *severe;* 714.14 *vindictive*
unforgivingly 628.7 *pitilessly*
unforgivingness 628.1 *pitilessness*
unforgotten 462.7 *memorable*
unform 161.3 *make shapeless*
unformed 161.5 *shapeless*
unforthcoming 634.18 *avoiding;* 732.1 *shy;* 655.8 *unsociable*
unfortified 255.13 *pure;* 335.11 *unprotected;* 254.3 *vulnerable;* 337.8 *weak*
unfortunate 288.17 *accidental;* 107.8 *chance;* 247.10 *failed;* 247.5 *failing person;* 798.10 *inauspicious;* 240.1 *inconvenient;* 249.5 *person in adversity;* 249.8 *unlucky;* 466.8 *victim of discrimination*
unfortunately 107.13 *by chance;* 249.12 *in adversity;* 798.14 *inauspiciously;* 288.21 *mistakenly;* 247.12 *unsuccessfully*
unfoul 371.11 *void*
unfouling 371.21 *removal*
unfounded 704.6 *refutable;* 702.7 *sophistic*
unfragranced 255.13 *pure*
unfrank 699.31 *hypocritical*
unfrankness 699.3 *hypocrisy*
unfree 401.9 *serving;* 387.9 *subject*
unfreeze 431.24 *melt*
unfreezing 767.1 *disposal;* 431.8 *fluidification*
unfriendliness 659.1 *discourtesy;* 651.6 *inconsiderateness;* 113.1 *opposition;* 655.1 *unsociability*
unfriendly 381.21 *aggressive;* 659.5 *discourteous;* 596.8 *disliking;* 651.15 *inconsiderate;* 113.22 *oppositional;* 655.8 *unsociable*
unfrock 371.3 *disbar;* 128.8 *eject;* 814.1 *punish;* 708.15 *terminate*
unfrocking 371.18 *dismissal;* 814.7 *punishment*
unfruitful 563.3 *infertile*
unfuddled 689.1 *sober*
unfuddled brain 689.6 *sobriety*
unfulfilled 218.2 *unprovided*
unfulfilled expectations 604.1 *disappointment*
unfulfilling 604.11 *disappointing*
unfunny 620.4 *boring*
unfunny joke 620.2 *boring thing*
unfurl 739.5 *disclose;* 148.10 *lengthen;* 738.3 *reveal;* 178.10 *straighten*
unfurled 738.13 *displayed*
unfurnished 218.2 *unprovided*
unfussily 728.24 *simply*
unfussiness 728.4 *simplicity*
unfussy 728.14 *simple*
ungainly 264.15, 486.3 *clumsy;* 544.7 *graceless;* 546.4 *ugly*
ungallant 659.5 *discourteous*
ungallantly 659.9 *discourteously*
ungallantness 659.1 *discourtesy*
ungarbed 552.9 *undressed*
ungarnished 271.2 *unadorned*
ungathered 350.2 *new*
ungenerosity 682.3 *parsimony*
ungenerous 651.15 *inconsiderate;* 682.1 *mean;* 683.4 *selfish*
ungenerously 682.9 *meanly;* 683.8 *selfishly*
ungenerousness 651.6 *inconsiderateness;* 682.3 *parsimony*
ungenial 651.15 *inconsiderate*
ungent 37.7 *ointment*
ungentle 651.12 *callous;* 659.5 *discourteous*
ungentlemanlike 659.5 *discourteous*
ungentlemanliness 659.1 *discourtesy*
ungentlemanly 659.5 *discourteous;* 659.9 *discourteously;* 800.5 *dishonourable;* 675.7 *vulgar*
ungentleness 659.1 *discourtesy*
ungently 659.9 *discourteously*
ungenuine 699.29 *false;* 699.32 *spurious*
ungenuinely 699.40 *falsely;* 699.41 *spuriously*
ungenuineness 699.1 *falsehood;* 699.4 *spuriousness*
unget-at-able 145.8 *distant*
ungettable 252.7 *invulnerable*
ungifted 486.1 *unskilful*
ungiving 418.4 *mentally hard*
unglazed 24.10 *ceramic*
unglazed earthenware 24.1 *ceramics*
unglue 268.17 *liquefy*
ungodliness 804.6 *religious sin*
ungodly 798.7 *evil;* 804.14 *impious*
ungovernable 250.10 *independent;* 16.61 *lawless;* 641.2 *refractory;* 380.6 *violent*
ungoverned 588.6 *anarchic;* 250.9 *free;* 250.10 *independent*
ungraceful 486.3 *clumsy;* 544.7 *graceless*
ungracious 631.18 *badly behaved;* 622.22 *boastful;* 659.5 *discourteous;* 651.15 *inconsiderate;* 242.2 *objectionable;* 672.3 *ungrateful;* 655.8 *unsociable*
ungraciously 631.20 *badly;* 659.9 *discourteously;* 651.20 *malevolently;* 672.7 *ungratefully;* 655.14 *unsocially*
ungraciousness 631.4 *bad conduct;* 659.1 *discourtesy;* 651.6 *inconsiderateness;* 672.1 *ingratitude;* 242.6 *objectionability;* 655.1 *unsociability*
ungraded 408.13 *unordered*
ungrateful **672.3**; 463.10 *unthinking*
ungratefully **672.7**
ungratefulness 672.1 *ingratitude*
ungrateful wretch 672.2 *thankless person*
ungrateful yob 672.2 *thankless person*
ungregarious 655.8 *unsociable*
ungregariousness 655.1 *unsociability*
ungrudging 679.1 *generous*
ungrudgingly 679.12 *generously*
unguarded 478.2 *spontaneous;* 335.11 *unprotected;* 254.3 *vulnerable;* 337.8 *weak*
unguent **268.14**; 268.19 *anoint;* 37.7, 268.6 *ointment*
unguentary 268.14 *unguent*
unguentous 268.14 *unguent*
unguentum 268.6 *ointment*
unguessed 105.3 *unexpected*
unguiculate 71.28 *carnivorous*
unguided 646.1 *naive;* 325.22 *undirected*
unguinous 268.13 *slippery*
ungulant 71.15 *hoofed mammal*
ungulate **71.33**; 71.15 *hoofed mammal*
unguligrade 71.33 *ungulate*
unhabituated 486.3 *clumsy;* 487.1 *unaccustomed*
unhackneyed 487.2 *not customary*
unhallow 258.11 *dirty*
unhallowed 258.8 *unclean*
unhampered 308.13 *opened up*
unhand 767.9 *dispose of;* 391.4 *liberate*
unhandiness 486.8 *unskilfulness*
unhanding 391.1 *liberation*
unhandled 350.2 *new*
unhandy 486.3 *clumsy*
unhappily 249.12 *in adversity;* 602.11 *sadly*
unhappiness 670.1 *disapproval;* 602.1 *sorrow;* 655.1 *unsociability*
unhappy 486.4 *bungled;* 539.3 *depressed;* 670.25 *disapproving;* 240.1 *inconvenient;* 603.4 *lamenting;* 602.5 *sad*
unharboured 144.10 *replaced*
unhardened 337.8 *weak*
unharmed 259.1 *healthy;* 252.6 *safe;* 204.7 *uncut*
unharmonious 372.18 *disagreeable;* 751.9 *disagreeing;* 242.1 *unpleasant*
unharmoniously 372.23 *disagreeably*
unharmoniousness 751.1 *disagreement*
unharmonized 517.9 *unmelodious*
unharness 312.4 *land*
unharvested 350.2 *new*
unhazardous 252.6 *safe*
unhealthily **260.25**
unhealthiness 798.2 *affliction;* 236.1 *harmfulness;* 260.1 *ill health*
unhealthy **260.21**; 798.8 *afflicted;* 254.1 *dangerous;* 382.23 *deadly;* 530.8 *drained of colour;* 236.5 *harmful;* 231.1 *imperfect;* 258.8 *unclean*
unhealthy situation 254.5 *danger*
unheard **505.7**; 674.13 *reserved*
unheard of 126.5 *novel;* 295.11 *unfamiliar;* 505.7 *unheard;* 456.8 *unknown;* 619.8 *wonderful*
unhearing **505.5**; 505.4 *deaf;* 341.3 *inactive*
unheated 494.8 *cold*
unheaviness 415.5 *lightness*
unheavy 415.1 *light*
unheedful 651.15 *inconsiderate*
unheeding 472.7 *inattentive;* 505.5 *unhearing*
unhelpful 637.3 *cautious;* 378.13 *hindering;* 651.15 *inconsiderate;* 240.1 *inconvenient;* 113.26 *uncooperative;* 238.1 *useless*
unhelpfully 240.6 *inconveniently;* 113.27 *opposingly;* 238.10 *uselessly;* 378.16 *with delay*
unhelpfulness 651.6 *inconsiderateness;* 637.12 *opposition;* 113.6 *uncooperativeness;* 238.3 *uselessness*
unheroic 614.3 *cowardly;* 231.4 *ordinary;* 639.3 *timid*
unhesitant 638.4 *undaunted*
unhesitating 450.11 *believing;* 452.2 *convinced*
unhesitatingly 450.15 *believingly*
unhewn 161.5 *shapeless*
unhidden 520.1 *visible*
unhindered 250.9 *free;* 308.13 *opened up*
unhinge 328.11 *derange;* 144.18 *disconnect;* 461.15 *make insane*
unhinged 802.14 *abnormal;* 328.16 *deranged;* 144.12 *disconnected;* 461.11 *insane*
unhinging 144.5 *disconnection*
unhistorical 477.12 *imaginary*
unhitch 312.4 *land;* 372.9 *separate*
unholiness 258.2 *uncleanness*
unholy 258.8 *unclean*
unholy joy 651.3 *callousness*
unholy mess 408.4 *litter;* 264.5 *predicament*
unholy terror 612.1 *fear;* 651.8 *malefactor*
unhook 372.9 *separate;* 552.14 *undress*
unhorse 372.9 *separate*
unhostile 569.8 *friendly*
unhouse 371.8 *evict*
unhoused 144.10 *replaced*
unhurried **333.5**; 263.4 *at ease;* 26.15 *deliberate;* 580.7 *leisurely;* 301.6 *quiescent;* 265.14 *relaxed*
unhurriedly 580.8 *leisurely;* 333.16 *slowly*
unhurriedness 333.8 *slowness*
unhurt 230.1 *perfect;* 252.6 *safe;* 204.7 *uncut*
unhygienic 254.1 *dangerous;* 260.23 *diseased;* 258.8 *unclean*
unicameral 197.12 *one-sided;* 579.18 *parliamentary*
unicell 34.7 *cell*
unicellular 84.7 *algal;* 34.23 *cellular;* 197.12 *one-sided*
unicellular organism 34.7 *cell;* 554.2 *living matter*
unicorn 743.8 *heraldic device;* 70.7 *legendary beast*
unicycle 320.12 *bicycle;* 197.10 *single thing*
unidentical 116.4 *dissimilar*
unidentifiable 521.1 *invisible;* 696.3 *unrecognizable*
unidentifiably 521.9 *invisibly*
unidentified 521.1 *invisible;* 456.8 *unknown*
unidirectional 324.15 *direct;* 197.12 *one-sided*
unification 747.7 *association;* 374.1 *combination*
unified 374.7 *combined;* 255.16 *simple;* 197.13, 204.6 *whole*
unified field theory 28.79 *fundamental interaction*
uniflagellate 84.7 *algal*
uniflorous 44.16 *horticultural*
uniform **46.3**; **140.11**; **421.2**; **698.22**; **743.5**; 49.3 *basketball equipment;* 620.4 *boring;* 529.11 *colourful;* 750.14 *conforming;* 132.11 *continuous;* 188.4 *correlated;* 300.17 *directional;* 551.32 *dress;* 119.6 *equal;* 162.5 *even;* 551.3, 656.4 *formal dress;* 551.35 *make clothing;* 112.13 *monotonous;* 298.14 *orderly;* 111.17 *regular;* 255.16 *simple;* 162.4 *symmetrical;* 27.70 *universal;* 407.14 *well-ordered*
uniformed 551.29 *dressed;* 656.7 *dressed-up;* 585.15 *warring*
uniformitarian 34.27 *evolutionary*
uniformitarianism 34.16 *evolution;* 30.41 *geological time*
uniformity **140.7**; **698.9**; 620.1 *boredom;* 117.1, 750.5 *conformity;* 132.5 *continuity;* 162.3 *evenness;* 407.7 *method;* 298.4 *orderliness;* 188.1 *parallelism;* 111.6 *regularity;* 112.3 *repetitiveness;* 111.1 *sameness;* 115.1 *similarity;* 255.8 *simplicity;* 421.7 *smoothness;* 162.1 *symmetry*
uniform labour law policy 15.5 *labour law*
uniformly **750.34**; 620.8 *boringly;* 119.13 *equitably;* 27.87 *mathematically;* 407.27 *methodically;* 298.17 *orderly;* 111.20 *regularly;* 421.14 *smoothly;* 162.7 *symmetrically*
uniform movement 300.10 *regular movement*
uniformness 750.5 *conformity*
uniform slops 551.3 *formal dress*
uniform with 115.7 *similar*
unify 197.19 *become one;* 204.9 *be whole;* 374.5 *combine;* 373.11 *connect;* 111.8 *make the same;* 403.15 *shape;* 255.11 *simplify*
unigravida 561.7 *obstetrics*
unilateral 250.9 *free;* 197.12 *one-sided;* 109.6 *unrelated*
unilateral disarmament 749.1 *pacification*
unilateralism 197.5 *aloneness;* 109.1 *unrelatedness*
unilateralist 197.16 *alone*
unilaterality 250.3 *independence*
unilingual 729.19 *speaking*
unilluminated 523.8 *dark*
unimaginability 103.5 *impossibility*
unimaginable 103.1 *impossible;* 619.8 *wonderful*
unimaginably 103.11 *impossibly*
unimaginative 138.22 *commonplace;* 592.1 *insensitive;* 271.1 *simple;* 457.6 *unintelligent;* 465.8 *unjust*
unimaginatively 457.11 *unintelligently*
unimaginativeness 457.2 *unintelligence*
unimitated 126.6, 698.19 *authentic;* 126.4 *original*
unimolecular reaction 32.14 *chemical reaction*
unimpaired 232.7 *complete;* 204.7 *uncut*
unimpassioned 4.18 *detached*
unimpeachable 452.3 *decided;* 801.9 *in the right;* 669.21 *praiseworthy*
unimpeded 250.9 *free;* 308.13 *opened up*
Unimportance 124
unimportance **124.5**; 623.7 *humility;* 122.1 *inferiority;* 618.5 *insignificance;* 236.7 *worthlessness*
unimportant **124.1**; 623.1 *humble;* 109.7 *illogical;* 122.13, 618.11 *insignificant;* 159.7 *little;* 674.11 *shy;* 157.2 *superficial;* 236.1 *worthless*
unimportantly **124.14**; 159.8 *in a small way;* 122.20 *insignificantly;* 618.20 *unexceptionally*
unimportant person 124.10 *nonentity*
unimposing 674.8 *modest*
unimpressed 606.4 *dissatisfied;* 618.7 *indifferent*
unimpressible 592.1 *insensitive*
unimpressionable 592.1 *insensitive*
unimpressive 728.16 *imperceptible;* 231.1 *imperfect;* 674.8 *modest;* 486.1 *unskilful*
unimpressively 728.27 *imperceptibly*
unimpressiveness 728.7 *imperceptibility*
unimproved 245.12 *deteriorated*
uninfectious 257.4 *hygienic*
uninflated 271.1 *simple*
uninfluenceable 250.9 *free*
uninfluenced 250.9 *free;* 250.10 *independent;* 641.3 *unyielding*
uninfluential 339.6 *suspended;* 124.1 *unimportant*
uninformative 736.17 *noncommittal;* 732.2 *sparing with words*

uninformed 456.6 *ignorant*; 486.1 *unskilful*
uninfringeable 99.5 *essential*
uninhabited 655.11 *secluded*; 98.14 *unoccupied*
uninhibited 250.13 *informal*; 646.1 *naive*; 250.12 *unconditional*
uninhibitedness 250.6 *liberality*
uninitiated 456.6 *ignorant*; 646.1 *naive*; 486.2 *unskilled*
uninjured 252.6 *safe*; 204.7 *uncut*
uninquisitive 618.7 *indifferent*
uninspired 138.22 *commonplace*; 271.1 *simple*; 497.5 *tasteless*
uninstructed 456.6 *ignorant*; 487.1 *unaccustomed*; 486.1 *unskilful*; 486.2 *unskilled*
unintelligence **457.2**; 459.1 *folly*; 456.1 *ignorance*; 486.8 *unskilfulness*
unintelligent **457.6**; **528.5**; 459.5 *foolish*; 524.8 *stupid*
unintelligently **457.11**; 459.8 *foolishly*
unintelligent person **457.3**
Unintelligibility **696**
unintelligibility **696.11**; 264.1 *difficulty*; 408.1 *disorder*; 266.1, 528.8 *obscurity*
unintelligible **696.1**; 736.15 *disguised*; 730.12 *inarticulate*; 528.4 *inscrutable*; 737.11 *mysterious*; 266.2 *obscure*; 264.12 *problematic*
unintelligible speech 730.3 *speech defect*
unintelligible thing **696.12**
unintelligibly **696.13**; 266.4 *obscurely*; 528.13 *opaquely*; 264.27 *problematically*
unintended 107.9 *causeless*
unintentional 107.9 *causeless*
unintentionally 107.13 *by chance*
uninterested 618.7 *indifferent*; 343.3 *not participating*
uninteresting 620.4 *boring*
uninterestingly 620.8 *boringly*
uninterrupted 134.5 *continual*; 132.11, 178.3 *continuous*; 324.15 *direct*
uninterrupted course 134.1 *continuity*
uninterruption 132.5 *continuity*
unintoxicated 689.1 *sober*
unintoxicated state 689.6 *sobriety*
uninucleate 34.24 *nuclear*
uninventive 457.6 *unintelligent*
uninventively 457.11 *unintelligently*
uninventiveness 457.2 *unintelligence*
uninvited 655.10 *lonely*
uninvited guest 564.6 *illegal occupant*; 100.8 *intruder*; 109.3 *unconnected person*
uninviting 497.5 *tasteless*; 499.6 *unpalatable*; 242.1 *unpleasant*
uninvolved 725.3 *clear*; 473.4 *disinterested*; 265.9 *easy*; 618.7 *indifferent*; 271.1, 695.2 *simple*; 372.17 *unjoined*; 109.6 *unrelated*
uninvolvement 695.10 *simplicity*
union 223.1 *accompaniment*; 570.2, 750.2 *alliance*; 376.15, 747.7 *association*; 373.1 *connection*; 755.1 *contract*; 374.2 *cooperation*; 764.1 *joint possession*; 147.3 *juxtaposition*; 570.1 *marriage*; 310.4 *meeting place*; 412.1 *mixture*; 197.3 *oneness*; 27.21 *set*; 15.10 *unionized*
union branch 15.3 *organized labour*
union demands 15.3 *organized labour*
union dues 15.3 *organized labour*
Union flag 743.7 *flag*
unionism 15.1 *industrial relations*
unionized **15.10**
Union Jack 743.7 *flag*
union labour 15.1 *industrial relations*
union-management relations 15.1 *industrial relations*
union member 15.7 *employee*; 764.3 *participant*
union of nations **85.2**; 86.4 *territorial division*
union recognition 15.2 *industrial negotiations*
union shop 15.3 *organized labour*
union strike 15.4 *industrial dispute*
union subscriptions 15.3 *organized labour*
union suit 551.18 *underwear*
uniped 197.10 *single thing*
uniplanar 197.12 *one-sided*
unipolar 197.12 *one-sided*
unique 698.19 *authentic*; 121.14 *best*; 116.4 *dissimilar*; 114.5 *diverse*; 118.14 *eccentric*; 139.17 *exceptional*; 128.10 *excluding*; 126.5 *novel*; 99.8 *quintessential*; 197.14 *singular*; 139.15 *special*; 120.3 *unequal*; 27.70 *universal*; 299.5 *unusual*; 235.3 *valuable*
uniquely 197.21 *alone*; 698.37 *authentically*; 139.30 *characteristically*; 114.10 *diversely*; 126.8 *originally*; 105.10 *rarely*; 121.17 *supremely*; 120.7 *unequally*
uniqueness 698.6 *authenticity*; 114.1 *diversity*; 743.2 *identity*; 126.1 *originality*; 197.4 *singularity*; 139.1 *speciality*; 118.4 *unusualness*
unirrigated 428.1 *dry*
unisex 197.12 *one-sided*; 551.31 *styled*
unisex clothes 551.1 *dress*
unisexual 197.12 *one-sided*; 561.16 *reproductive*
unison 516.4 *harmonics*; 750.4 *harmony*; 18.13 *melody*
unisonous 750.13 *harmonious*
unit **204.5**; **405.3**; 586.16 *army unit*; 410.3 *cabinet*; 376.14 *force*; 197.1 *one*; 376.16 *party*; 566.7 *person*; 405.2 *piece*; 204.2 *whole thing*
Unitarian 7.5 *Christian*
unite 376.41 *band together*; 197.19 *become one*; 204.9 *be whole*; 267.7 *cause to adhere*; 374.5 *combine*; 310.10 *come together*; 232.4 *complete*; 373.11 *connect*; 750.22 *form an alliance*; 747.16 *join*; 570.16 *join in marriage*; 111.8 *make the same*; 570.19 *merge*; 376.44 *put together*
united 374.7 *combined*; 232.7 *complete*; 373.15 *connected*; 755.7 *contractual*; 376.48 *cumulate*; 750.10 *in accord*; 747.18 *joint*; 764.5 *jointly possessing*; 570.21 *married*; 111.12 *same*; 197.13 *whole*
united action 747.4 *joint operation*
united front 747.4 *joint operation*
United Kingdom 85.8 *Great Britain*
unitedly 267.11 *cohesively*; 750.31 *in accord*; 764.6 *in common*; 223.21, 376.51 *together*
United Nations 579.7 *council*; 566.9 *group*; 764.1 *joint possession*; 589.2 *symbol of peace*
United Nations Organization 764.1 *joint possession*
United Nations peacekeeping force 589.3 *pacifist*
United Nations secretary-general 579.16 *official*
United Press International 741.7 *press agency*; 693.8 *source of information*
United States **85.7**
United States Automobile Club 61.7 *racing governing body*
United States Curling Association 68.10 *curling*
United States Military Academy 584.3 *military training*
United States Naval Academy 584.3 *military training*
United States of America 85.7 *United States*
United Way 652.5 *charity*; 768.3 *offering*; 710.3 *solicitation*
unite efforts 747.13 *work together*
unite in holy wedlock 570.16 *join in marriage*
unite to 211.6 *add*
unit furniture 23.1 *furniture*
uniting 374.1 *combination*; 310.7 *convergent*
unit of being 402.4 *matter*
unit of electrical power 334.5 *unit of work*
unit of work **334.5**
units place 27.8 *number system*
unit vector 27.50 *scalar quantity*
unity 750.1 *accord*; 267.1 *adhesion*; 403.9 *artistic structure*; 232.1 *completeness*; 374.2 *cooperation*; 197.1 *one*; 197.3 *oneness*; 111.1 *sameness*; 204.1 *whole*
UNIVAC 40.3 *computer*
univalent 32.35 *combined*
univalent chromosome 34.14 *chromosome*
univalve 75.19 *molluscan*
universal **27.70**; **138.16**; 29.36 *astronomical*; 216.1 *average*; 141.12 *extensive*; 632.10 *familiar*; 138.15 *general*; 127.7 *including*; 204.6 *whole*; 50.13 *windsurfing*
universal benevolence 652.2 *public spiritedness*
universal constant 28.97 *fundamental constant*
universal indicator 32.18 *gravimetric analysis*
universalism 85.5 *internationalism*
universalist 85.15 *internationalist*
universality 216.4 *average*; 232.1 *completeness*; 138.1 *generality*; 127.1 *inclusion*; 85.5 *internationalism*; 204.1 *whole*
universalize 138.23 *generalize*
universal joint 50.7 *windsurfing*
universally **138.32**; 29.39 *astronomically*; 141.16 *extensively*; 127.9, 550.42 *inclusively*; 204.11 *wholly*
universal motor 39.31 *electric motor*
universal peace 589.1 *peace*
universal quantifier 27.63 *mathematical logic*
universal set 27.21 *set*
universal solvent 431.9 *solvent*
universal suffrage 469.11 *franchise*
universal symbol 36.24 *symbolism*
Universal Time 281.3 *chronology*
universe **29.3**; 95.2 *real world*; 204.2 *whole thing*
university **6.13**
university hospital 35.10 *hospital*
university president 400.9 *educational leader*
university press 740.12 *publisher*
univocal 694.3 *comprehension*; 695.1 *intelligible*; 694.6 *meaningful*
UNIX™ 40.8 *software*
unjam 265.16 *make easy*
unjoined **372.17**; 133.8 *discontinuous*
unjust **16.58**; **120.4**; **465.8**; 236.3 *bad*; 800.5 *dishonourable*; 718.6 *misrepresented*; 802.11 *wrong*
unjustifiable 806.5 *guilty*; 802.17 *unforgivable*
unjustifiably 806.11 *guiltily*
unjustly **120.8**; **465.14**; 718.8 *unrepresentatively*; 802.25 *wrongly*
unkempt 420.3 *barbed*; 245.13 *dilapidated*; 258.7 *dirty*; 408.15 *untidy*
unkemptness 408.3 *untidiness*
unkennel 739.5 *disclose*; 371.8 *evict*
unkind 659.5 *discourteous*; 798.7 *evil*; 651.15 *inconsiderate*; 242.2 *objectionable*; 682.2 *unpleasant*
unkindest cut of all 668.5 *insult*
unkindliness 651.6 *inconsiderateness*
unkindly 659.9 *discourteously*; 798.12 *evilly*; 651.15 *inconsiderate*; 651.20 *malevolently*
unkindness 798.1 *evil*; 236.11 *harmfulness*; 651.6 *inconsiderateness*; 242.6 *objectionability*
unknot 391.4 *liberate*
unknotting 391.1 *liberation*
unknowable 528.4 *inscrutable*; 737.11 *mysterious*; 696.1 *unintelligible*; 456.8 *unknown*; 696.3 *unrecognizable*
unknowing 456.6 *ignorant*
unknowingly 456.12 *ignorantly*; 805.11 *innocently*
unknown **456.8**; 27.25 *algebraic expression*; 254.1 *dangerous*; 100.10 *foreign*; 737.11 *mysterious*; 124.10, 195.5 *nonentity*; 655.11 *secluded*; 453.1 *uncertain*; 295.11 *unfamiliar*; 696.1 *unintelligible*
unknown country 737.8 *anonymity*
unknown disease 260.4 *disease*
unknownness 295.1 *newness*
unknown person **456.4**; 737.8 *anonymity*
unknown quantity 27.25 *algebraic expression*; 737.8 *anonymity*; 456.3 *unknown thing*
unknown territory 456.3 *unknown thing*
unknown thing **456.3**
unknown to law 16.56 *unauthorized*
Unknown Warrior 737.8 *anonymity*
unlaboured 543.3 *elegant*
unlace 372.9 *separate*; 552.14 *undress*
unlade 415.10 *lighten*; 371.12 *unload*
unlading 415.6 *lightening*
unladylike 659.5 *discourteous*; 675.7 *vulgar*
unlamented 594.12 *hated*
unlatch 308.19 *open up*; 372.9 *separate*
unlatched 308.13 *opened up*
unlavish 680.4 *thrifty*
unlawful **796.15**; 804.15 *criminal*; 16.55 *illegal*; 802.16 *in the wrong*; 399.5 *vetoed*
unlawful act 804.7 *criminality*
unlawful carnal knowledge 796.4 *illicit love*
unlawful desires 796.4 *illicit love*
unlawful entry 774.1 *stealing*
unlawful killing 382.2 *murder*
unlawfully 399.7 *by veto*; 804.21 *criminally*; 16.89 *guiltily*; 16.82 *illegally*; 802.28 *immorally*
unlawfulness **802.6**; 16.35 *illegality*; 465.3 *injustice*
unleaded 437.10 *powered*
unleaded petrol 437.6 *oil*
unlearn 463.13 *forget*
unlearned 646.1 *naive*
unleash 739.5 *disclose*; 391.4 *liberate*
unleashing 391.1 *liberation*
unleash the war dogs 585.12 *go to war*
unlegislated 16.56 *unauthorized*
unless 222.15 *under the circumstances*
unlettered 456.6 *ignorant*
unlicensed 16.56 *unauthorized*
unlicked 161.5 *shapeless*
unlighted 523.8 *dark*
unlikable 236.3 *bad*; 596.9 *disliked*
unlike 116.4 *dissimilar*; 718.6 *misrepresented*; 120.3 *unequal*
unlike a gentleman 659.9 *discourteously*
unlikelihood 105.4 *improbability*; 453.13 *indemonstrability*; 705.7 *questionableness*
unlikeliness 105.4 *improbability*; 453.13 *indemonstrability*
unlikely 105.1 *improbable*; 453.4 *indemonstrable*; 705.14 *questionable*
unlikeness **116.2**; 120.1 *inequality*
unlimited 232.7 *complete*; 202.1 *infinite*; 61.10 *racing*; 250.12 *unconditional*
unlimited class 61.5 *motorcycle racing*
unlimited space 141.2 *empty space*
unlisted securities market 779.5 *stock market*
unlit 254.1 *dangerous*; 523.8 *dark*
unlived-in 98.14 *unoccupied*
unload **371.12**; 265.18 *disentangle*; 312.4 *land*; 415.10 *lighten*; 793.13 *make cheap*; 778.1 *sell*; 212.3 *subtract*; 316.15 *take away*; 319.4 *transport*
unloaded 415.3 *lightening*; 319.5 *transportable*
unloader 319.3 *transporter*
unloading 371.20 *eviction*; 415.3, 415.6 *lightening*; 318.2 *passing along*; 319.1 *transport*; 319.5 *transportable*
unload on the market 778.1 *sell*
unlock 390.1 *deliver*; 767.9 *dispose of*; 391.4 *liberate*; 308.19 *open up*; 372.9 *separate*
unlock a code 719.9 *decipher*
unlocked 719.15 *interpreted*; 308.13 *opened up*
unloose 390.1 *deliver*; 391.4 *liberate*
unloosed 372.15 *separate*
unloosen 391.4 *liberate*
unloose the purse strings 785.6 *pay*
unloosing 391.1 *liberation*
unlovable 596.9 *disliked*; 594.12 *hated*
unloved 596.9 *disliked*; 594.12 *hated*
unlovely 546.4 *ugly*
unluckily 107.13 *by chance*; 249.12 *in adversity*; 798.14 *inauspiciously*; 288.21 *mistakenly*; 247.12 *unsuccessfully*
unlucky **249.8**; 288.17 *accidental*; 107.8 *chance*; 247.10 *failed*; 798.10 *inauspicious*
unlucky choice 469.8 *choice*
unlucky person 249.5 *person in adversity*; 466.8 *victim of discrimination*
unmake 357.8 *destroy*; 161.3 *make shapeless*; 761.7 *restore*; 372.9 *separate*
unmaking 357.1 *destruction*
unmalleability 418.8 *mental hardness*
unmalleable 418.4 *mentally hard*; 383.11 *obstinate*
unman 245.5 *hurt*; 335.9 *make impotent*; 563.8 *make infertile*; 238.8 *make useless*; 212.4 *take off*
unmanageable 486.3 *clumsy*; 662.13 *disobedient*; 408.20 *disorderly*; 641.2 *refractory*; 264.14 *troublesome*
unmanageably 264.28 *awkwardly*
unmanly 567.17 *male*
unmanned 98.14 *unoccupied*; 335.13 *unsexed*
unmanned crossing 321.2 *track*
unmanned satellite 29.32 *satellite*
unmannered 668.10 *disrespectful*
unmannerliness 659.2 *bad manners*; 668.1 *disrespect*
unmannerly 659.6 *bad-mannered*; 655.8 *unsociable*
unmarked 521.1 *invisible*; 230.1 *perfect*
unmarked car 320.17 *police car*
unmarketable 793.10 *shoddy*
unmarred 230.1 *perfect*

unmarried 572.6 *celibate*; 250.10 *independent*; 655.10 *lonely*; 197.17 *single*
unmarried condition 572.1 *celibacy*
unmarried man 567.5 *single man*; 197.7, 572.5 *single person*
unmarried mother 568.5 *single girl*
unmarried state 250.3 *independence*
unmarried woman 568.5 *single girl*; 197.7 *single person*
unmarry 571.7 *divorce*
unmask 449.2 *detect*; 739.5 *disclose*; 518.18, 520.10 *make visible*; 738.3 *reveal*
unmasked 739.10 *disclosed*; 449.14 *discovered*
unmasking 449.7 *detection*
unmask oneself 738.4 *show oneself*
unmatchable 121.14 *best*
unmatchably 121.17 *supremely*
unmatched 121.14, 235.2 *best*; 126.5 *novel*; 230.1 *perfect*
unmated 572.6 *celibate*
unmeant 107.9 *causeless*
unmeasured 217.2 *plentiful*
unmediated 445.7 *precognitive*
unmedicated 255.13 *pure*
unmeditated 478.1 *improvised*
unmelodious 517.9; 513.7 *strident*
unmelodiously 517.12 *dissonantly*
unmelodiousness 517.3 *musical dissonance*
unmelted 416.7 *condensed*; 494.9 *heat-resistant*
unmemorable 463.11 *forgotten*
unmentionable 399.6 *censored*; 796.12 *indecent*; 675.9 *ribald*
unmentionables 551.18 *underwear*
unmentioned 452.8 *unspecified*
unmercifully 628.7 *pitilessly*
unmercifulness 628.1 *pitilessness*
unmethodical 408.16 *confused*
unmethodically 408.27 *in disorder*; 299.4 *irregular*; 299.8 *irregularly*
unmethodicalness 299.1 *irregularity*
unmilitant 589.7 *peaceful*
unmilitary 589.7 *peaceful*
unmindful 519.12 *blind to*; 472.7 *inattentive*; 651.15 *inconsiderate*; 666.4 *negligent*; 489.6 *unfeeling*; 672.3 *ungrateful*; 463.10 *unthinking*
unmindfully 472.14 *inattentively*
unmindfulness 472.1 *inattention*; 651.6 *inconsiderateness*; 666.1 *negligence*; 463.4 *unthinkingness*
unmingled 255.16 *simple*
unmissable 520.2 *clear*
unmissed 594.12 *hated*
unmistakable 452.1 *certain*; 738.14 *manifest*; 336.10 *potent*; 695.3 *recognizable*; 520.1 *visible*
unmistakably 336.15 *acutely*; 695.13 *intelligibly*
unmistaken 452.1 *certain*; 698.25 *lifelike*; 698.15 *true*
unmistakenness 698.1 *truth*
unmitigated 232.7 *complete*; 255.17 *direct*; 380.6 *violent*
unmitigating 232.7 *complete*
unmixed 256.16 *clean*; 690.6 *intoxicating*; 230.1 *perfect*; 255.16, 271.1 *simple*; 372.17 *unjoined*; 235.1 *worthy*
unmodern 286.2 *occurring at a different time*
unmoistened 428.1 *dry*
unmolested 252.6 *safe*
unmoor 323.9 *navigate*; 313.5 *set out*
unmotivated 107.9 *causeless*; 478.2 *spontaneous*
unmount 238.8 *make useless*
unmourned 594.12 *hated*
unmovable 301.4 *motionless*
unmoved 809.3 *impenitent*; 618.7 *indifferent*; 301.4 *motionless*; 628.4 *pitiless*; 301.6 *quiescent*; 641.3 *unyielding*
unmoving 339.5 *inert*; 301.4 *motionless*
unmuddied 256.16 *clean*; 255.13 *pure*
unmusical 505.4 *deaf*; 646.1 *naive*; 513.7 *strident*; 517.9 *unmelodious*
unmusicality 730.2 *inarticulation*
unmusicalness 505.1 *deafness*
unmuzzled 250.9 *free*
unnamed 456.8 *unknown*; 452.8 *unspecified*
unnatural 118.17 *abnormal*; 676.3 *affected*; 651.12 *callous*; 700.39 *imitative*; 544.9 *inelegant*
unnaturally 699.41 *spuriously*; 118.21 *unconformably*
unnaturalness 651.3 *callousness*; 118.6 *deviation*
unnavigable 264.11 *rough*; 157.1 *shallow*
unnecessarily 219.8 *excessively*; 124.14 *unimportantly*; 441.10 *wastefully*
unnecessary 487.2 *not customary*; 350.3 *not wanted*; 219.7 *superfluous*; 124.1 *unimportant*; 238.1 *useless*; 441.8 *wasteful*
unnecessary expenditure 441.3 *waste*
unnecessary roughness 58.5 *lacrosse*
unneeded 350.3 *not wanted*; 238.1 *useless*
unneighbourly 659.5 *discourteous*; 655.8 *unsociable*
unnerve 481.2 *deter*; 612.13 *frighten*; 335.9 *make impotent*; 337.7 *weaken*
unnerved 335.12 *impotent*; 337.12 *weak-willed*
unnerving 612.10 *frightening*
unnoteworthy 216.3 *mediocre*
unnoticeable 521.1 *invisible*
unnoticeably 521.9 *invisibly*; 728.23 *unobtrusively*
unnoticed 521.1 *invisible*
unnumbered 202.2 *immeasurable*; 208.8 *numberless*
unobjectionable 750.20 *agreeable*; 235.5 *not bad*
unobliging 651.15 *inconsiderate*
unobligingness 651.6 *inconsiderateness*
unobservant 519.12 *blind to*; 472.7 *inattentive*
unobserved 521.1 *invisible*
unobstructed 308.13 *opened up*; 527.1 *transparent*
unobstructed view 527.5 *transparency*
unobtainability 103.6 *hopelessness*
unobtainable 103.3 *hopeless*; 218.4 *scarce*
unobtrusive 674.8 *modest*; 728.12 *understated*
unobtrusively 728.23; 674.17 *modestly*
unobtrusiveness 674.1 *modesty*; 728.1 *understatement*
unoccupied 98.14; 341.3 *inactive*; 580.6 *leisure*; 580.7 *leisurely*; 343.2 *not working*
unofficial 588.6 *anarchic*; 657.7 *informal*; 657.1 *informality*; 16.56 *unauthorized*; 453.5 *uncertified*; 15.10 *unionized*
unofficial action 15.4 *industrial dispute*
unofficially 588.8 *anarchically*; 15.13 *industrially*; 657.15 *unaffectedly*
unofficial strike 15.4 *industrial dispute*
unoiled 513.8 *hoarse*
unopened 309.12 *closed*; 350.2 *new*
unopposed 750.20 *agreeable*
unordered 408.13; 412.12 *mixed*
unordered arrangement 27.21 *set*
unorganized 408.13 *unordered*
unoriginal 345.10 *caused*; 632.10 *familiar*; 125.12, 700.39 *imitative*; 457.6 *unintelligent*
unoriginality 457.2 *unintelligence*
unoriginally 125.14 *imitatively*; 345.12 *with the effect of*
unornamented 271.2 *unadorned*
unorthodox 274.16 *errant*; 118.12 *nonconformist*; 299.5 *unusual*
unorthodox medicine 35.2 *natural medicine*
unorthodoxy 274.7 *errancy*; 118.3 *nonconformism*; 299.2 *unusualness*
unostentatious 674.8 *modest*; 674.1 *modesty*; 728.14 *simple*
unostentatiously 728.24 *simply*
unostentatiousness 728.4 *simplicity*
unowned 767.15 *unclaimed*
unpacific 585.16 *warlike*
unpack 739.5 *disclose*; 371.12 *unload*
unpaid 786.14; 793.11 *free of charge*; 784.9 *in debt*; 752.18 *voluntary*
unpaid amount 784.5 *amount owing*
unpaid bill 783.1 *credit*
unpaid work 636.10 *voluntary work*
unpaid worker 752.8 *volunteer*; 636.11 *willing worker*
unpainted 271.2 *unadorned*
unpalatability 499.2; 495.1 *taste*; 242.5 *unpleasantness*
unpalatable 242.3; **499.6**; 495.7 *tasty*; 242.1 *unpleasant*
unparalleled 121.14, 235.2 *best*; 126.5 *novel*
unpardonable 806.5 *guilty*; 802.17 *unforgivable*; 804.11 *wicked*
unpardonably 806.11 *guiltily*; 804.18 *wickedly*
unparliamentary language 712.2 *offensive language*
unpartnered 572.6 *celibate*
unpaved road 299.3 *irregular thing*
unpayable 786.14 *unpaid*
unpayable debt 786.5 *insolvency*
unpeaceful 327.16 *restless*
unpeacefully 327.27 *agitatedly*
unpeel 268.17 *liquefy*
unpeople 371.9 *depopulate*
unpeopled 98.14 *unoccupied*
unperceivable 521.1 *invisible*
unperceived 521.1 *invisible*; 456.8 *unknown*
unperceptive 426.3 *dull*; 457.6 *unintelligent*
unperceptiveness 457.2 *unintelligence*
unperfumed 501.3 *odourless*
unpermissibility 399.1 *veto*
unpersevering 639.2 *changeable*
unperson 96.5 *insubstantial person*; 195.5 *nonentity*
unpersuadable 641.2 *refractory*
unperturbed 4.18 *detached*; 301.6 *quiescent*
unperturbedly 301.10 *motionlessly*
unphilanthropic 651.15 *inconsiderate*
unphysical 101.8 *nonmaterial*; 11.18 *spiritual*
unpick 372.9 *separate*
unpigmented 530.7 *colourless*
unpitiful 628.4 *pitiless*
unpitying 628.4 *pitiless*
unplanned 486.4 *bungled*; 107.9 *causeless*
unpleasant 242.1; **682.2**; 236.3 *bad*; 751.9 *disagreeing*; 659.5 *discourteous*; 495.7 *tasty*; 499.6 *unpalatable*
unpleasant job 576.2 *task*
unpleasantly 242.13; 659.9 *discourteously*; 751.11 *in disagreement*; 499.10 *sourly*; 236.15 *worthlessly*
Unpleasantness 242
unpleasantness 242.5; **682.4**; 236.9 *badness*; 751.1 *disagreement*; 659.1 *discourtesy*
unpleasant person 242.9
unpleasant smell 500.1 *odour*; 503.1 *stench*
unpleasant taste 495.1 *taste*
unpleasing 242.1 *unpleasant*
unpliability 418.8 *mental hardness*
unpliable 418.4 *mentally hard*
unpliant 418.4 *mentally hard*
unplucked 350.2 *new*
unplug 372.9 *separate*
unplugged 372.15 *separate*
unplumbed 156.8 *deep*
unpoetical 646.1 *naive*; 271.1 *simple*
unpointed 426.1 *blunt*
unpolished 486.4 *bungled*; 524.7 *dimmed*; 258.7 *dirty*; 675.8 *discourteous*; 231.2 *incomplete*; 544.8 *indecorous*; 646.1 *naive*; 420.5 *unfinished*
unpoliteness 659.1 *discourtesy*
unpolluted 256.16 *clean*; 255.13 *pure*; 252.6 *safe*
unpopular 596.9 *disliked*; 594.12 *hated*; 655.10 *lonely*; 606.5 *unsatisfactory*
unpopular cause 470.8 *rejected thing*
unpopularity 670.1 *disapproval*; 594.4 *hatefulness*
unpossessed 767.15 *unclaimed*
unpowered 335.10 *powerless*
unpractical 486.1 *unskilful*; 238.1 *useless*
unpractised 486.3 *clumsy*; 487.2 *not customary*
unpraiseworthy 670.32 *unsatisfactory*
unprecedented 116.4 *dissimilar*; 487.2 *not customary*; 126.5 *novel*; 630.8 *surprising*; 295.11 *unfamiliar*; 619.8 *wonderful*
unpredictability 642.2 *caprice*; 28.81 *causality*; 107.1 *chance*; 227.1 *changeableness*; 114.1 *diversity*; 299.1 *irregularity*; 630.1 *surprise*; 105.5 *unexpectedness*; 453.15 *unreliability*
unpredictable 642.1 *capricious*; 107.8 *chance*; 227.13 *changeable*; 114.5 *diverse*; 453.4 *indemonstrable*; 299.4 *irregular*; 630.8 *surprising*; 105.3 *unexpected*; 453.7 *unreliable*
unpredictably 107.13 *by chance*; 227.15 *changeably*; 114.10 *diversely*; 299.8 *irregularly*; 105.9 *unexpectedly*; 453.26 *unreliably*
unpredicted 105.3 *unexpected*
unprejudiced 150.3 *broad-minded*; 473.4 *disinterested*; 250.9 *free*; 618.9 *impartial*; 4.15 *rational*; 801.7 *right*; 458.5 *wise*
unpremeditated 107.9 *causeless*; 478.1 *improvised*
unpremeditation 478.4 *improvisation*
unprepared 486.4 *bungled*; 262.3 *hasty*; 555.12 *immature*; 478.1 *improvised*; 233.4 *incomplete*; 294.9 *late*; 630.6 *surprised*; 486.2 *unskilled*; 254.3 *vulnerable*
unpreparedly 555.15 *immaturely*; 294.15 *late*
unpreparedness 555.3 *immaturity*; 233.1 *incompleteness*; 294.1 *lateness*; 630.1 *surprise*
unprepossessing 596.9 *disliked*; 546.4 *ugly*
unpretending 674.8 *modest*; 646.1 *naive*; 698.18 *truthful*
unpretentious 255.17 *direct*; 623.1 *humble*; 674.8 *modest*; 646.1 *naive*; 271.3 *natural*; 271.1, 728.14 *simple*; 698.18 *truthful*
unpretentiously 255.20 *homogenously*; 674.17 *modestly*; 271.8, 728.24 *simply*
unpretentiousness 623.7 *humility*; 674.1 *modesty*; 646.2 *naivety*; 271.6 *naturalness*; 271.4, 728.4 *simplicity*
unpreventability 452.16 *inevitability*
unpreventable 452.5 *inevitable*
unprincipled 800.5 *dishonourable*; 796.11, 802.15 *immoral*; 804.11 *wicked*
unprintable 399.6 *censored*; 796.12 *indecent*; 675.9 *ribald*
unprocurable 218.4 *scarce*
unproductive 247.10 *failed*; 238.2 *futile*; 563.3 *infertile*
unproductively 563.11; 247.12 *unsuccessfully*
unproductiveness 247.1 *failure*; 238.4 *futility*; 563.1 *infertility*; 218.9 *scarcity*; 766.3 *waste*
unproductivity 563.1 *infertility*
unprofessional 240.1 *inconvenient*; 486.1 *unskilful*
unprofessional conduct 806.3 *sin*
unprofessionally 486.11 *unskilfully*
unprofitability 238.4 *futility*; 563.1 *infertility*
unprofitable 766.17; **776.16**; 238.2 *futile*; 240.1 *inconvenient*; 563.3 *infertile*; 672.5 *thankless*
unprofitableness 563.1 *infertility*
unprofitably 778.17 *marketably*; 672.7 *ungratefully*; 563.11 *unproductively*; 238.10 *uselessly*
unprogressive 225.8 *conservative*; 245.12 *deteriorated*; 341.3 *inactive*; 646.1 *naive*
unprogressively 225.10 *conservatively*
unprohibitive 757.8 *permitting*
unprolific 563.3 *infertile*
unpromising 105.1 *improbable*; 486.1 *unskilful*
unprompted 478.2 *spontaneous*; 636.5, 752.18 *voluntary*
unpronounceable 696.1 *unintelligible*
unpropitious 249.6 *adverse*; 611.6 *inauspicious*; 113.22 *oppositional*; 288.13 *untimely*
unpropitiously 288.19 *at the wrong time*; 249.12 *in adversity*
unpropitiousness 288.2 *untimeliness*
unprosperous 249.7
unprotected 335.11; 308.13 *opened up*; 254.3 *vulnerable*; 337.8 *weak*
unprovability 453.13 *indemonstrability*
unprovable 453.4 *indemonstrable*
unproved 453.5 *uncertified*
unprovided 218.2
unprovided for 782.1 *poor*; 218.2 *unprovided*
unprovoked 478.2 *spontaneous*
unpunctual 294.9 *late*; 288.12 *too late*; 288.13 *untimely*
unpunctuality 294.1 *lateness*; 288.2 *untimeliness*
unpunctually 294.15 *late*; 288.18 *out of chronological order*
unpunishable 758.5 *exempt*
unpunished 16.63 *acquitted*
unpurified 258.8 *unclean*
unqualified 698.19 *authentic*; 232.7 *complete*; 255.17 *direct*; 240.1 *inconvenient*; 335.10 *powerless*; 470.10 *rejected*; 456.7 *semiskilled*; 486.2 *unskilled*; 238.1 *useless*
unqualifiedness 698.6 *authenticity*
unquelled 383.12 *resisting*

unquestionability 698.6 *authenticity;* 707.8 *definiteness*
unquestionable 698.19 *authentic;* 707.16 *definite;* 703.12 *demonstrable;* 99.5 *essential;* 103.1 *impossible;* 104.6 *probable*
unquestionableness 698.6 *authenticity;* 707.8 *definiteness*
unquestionably 707.23 *affirmatively;* 452.23 *certainly;* 103.11 *impossibly;* 643.12 *indeed;* 104.11 *probably*
unquestioned 698.19 *authentic;* 450.14 *believed*
unquestioning 450.11 *believing;* 452.2 *convinced*
unquiet 327.16 *restless;* 342.7 *restlessness*
unquietly 327.27 *agitatedly*
unquietness 342.7 *restlessness*
unquotable 796.12 *indecent;* 675.9 *ribald*
unratified 453.5 *uncertified*
unravel 719.9 *decipher;* 390.1 *deliver;* 265.18 *disentangle;* 372.9 *separate;* 255.11 *simplify;* 421.11 *smooth;* 178.10 *straighten;* 409.19 *tidy*
unravelled 255.16 *simple;* 409.27 *tidied*
unravelling 390.2 *deliverance;* 372.1 *separation*
unreachable 103.3 *hopeless;* 329.15 *out of reach*
unreactive 339.5 *inert;* 32.38 *reactive*
unreadability 696.11 *unintelligibility*
unreadable 620.4 *boring;* 696.1 *unintelligible*
unreadably 696.13 *unintelligibly*
unreadily 555.15 *immaturely;* 294.15 *late*
unreadiness 555.3 *immaturity;* 233.1 *incompleteness;* 294.1 *lateness;* 630.1 *surprise*
unready 555.12 *immature;* 233.4 *incomplete;* 294.9 *late;* 254.3 *vulnerable*
unreal **94.10**; **96.8**; 98.8 *absent;* 477.11 *fantastical;* 700.40 *illusory;* 477.12 *imaginary;* 101.8 *nonmaterial;* 699.32 *spurious;* 476.8 *supposed*
unrealistic **96.11**; 116.4 *dissimilar;* 105.1 *improbable*
unrealistically 116.7 *dissimilarly*
unrealistic person 96.6
Unreality 96
unreality **96.1**; 98.1 *absence;* 699.1 *falsehood;* 477.4 *ideality;* 103.5 *impossibility;* 94.5 *nonreality;* 101.2 *unworldliness*
unrealized 456.8 *unknown*
unrealness 699.4 *spuriousness*
unreaped 350.2 *new*
unreason 457.1 *lack of intellect;* 457.4 *nonhuman existence*
unreasonable 642.1 *capricious;* 792.7 *dear;* 103.1 *impossible;* 702.7 *sophistic*
unreasoningly 457.12 *nonhumanly*
unrecanting 809.3 *impenitent*
unreceptiveness 655.1 *unsociability*
unrecognizable **696.3**; 760.13 *converted;* 736.15 *disguised;* 521.1 *invisible*
unrecognizably 521.9 *invisibly*
unrecognized 736.15 *disguised;* 521.1 *invisible;* 456.8 *unknown;* 672.4 *unthanked*
unrecompensed 786.14 *unpaid*
unreconciled 809.3 *impenitent;* 637.2 *refusing*
unrecorded 358.6 *obliterated*
unrecounted 128.11 *excluded*
unredeemed 809.3 *impenitent;* 804.11 *wicked*
unreduced 230.1 *perfect*
unrefined 659.6 *bad-mannered;* 486.3 *clumsy;* 675.8 *discourteous;* 231.2 *incomplete;* 544.8 *indecorous;* 646.1 *naive;* 258.8 *unclean;* 420.5 *unfinished*
unrefined sugar 498.2 *sweetener*
unrefinement 544.2 *impropriety*
unreformed 809.3 *impenitent*
unrefreshed 261.1 *fatigued*
unrefutability 698.6 *authenticity*
unrefuted 698.19 *authentic;* 452.3 *decided*
unregarded 668.18 *undervalued*
unregenerated 809.3 *impenitent*
unregistered 358.6 *obliterated*
unregretful 809.3 *impenitent*
unregretfully 809.6 *impenitently*
unregretted 809.4 *unatoned*
unregretting 809.3 *impenitent*
unregular 299.4 *irregular*
unregularity 299.1 *irregularity*
unregularly 299.8 *irregularly*
unregulated 250.9 *free*
unrehearsed 478.1 *improvised*
unreined 588.6 *anarchic*
unrelated **109.6**; 116.4 *dissimilar;* 100.8 *extraneous;* 100.10 *foreign;* 109.9 *misconnected;* 372.17 *unjoined*
Unrelatedness 109
unrelatedness **109.1**; 100.2 *foreignness;* 124.5 *unimportance;* 116.2 *unlikeness*
unrelated thing 109.2
unrelaxed 418.2 *tough*
unrelenting 628.5 *inflexible;* 134.6 *protracted;* 641.3 *unyielding*
unrelentingly 134.7 *continually;* 628.7 *pitilessly;* 647.11 *severely*
unreliability **453.15**; 642.2 *caprice;* 227.1 *changeableness;* 637.14 *disobedience;* 800.2 *faithlessness;* 705.7 *questionableness*
unreliable **453.7**; 642.1 *capricious;* 227.13 *changeable;* 451.7 *disbelieved;* 800.6 *faithless;* 702.10 *hypocritical;* 705.14 *questionable;* 254.2 *unsafe;* 639.4 *unsteady*
unreliable narrator 17.3 *aspect of fiction*
unreliableness 479.7 *apostasy*
unreliably **453.26**; 227.15 *changeably;* 800.11 *dishonourably;* 702.15 *hypocritically;* 705.24 *questionably;* 451.11 *unbelievably*
unrelieved 132.11 *continuous*
unrelished 596.9 *disliked*
unremarkable 216.3 *mediocre;* 685.6 *moderate;* 486.1 *unskilful*
unremarkableness 216.6 *mediocrity*
unremitting 132.11 *continuous;* 202.3 *eternal;* 576.11 *laborious;* 134.6 *protracted;* 112.14 *recurrent;* 640.11 *steady*
unremittingly 134.7 *continually*
unremorseful 809.3 *impenitent;* 628.4 *pitiless*
unremorsefully 809.6 *impenitently*
unremorsefulness 628.1 *pitilessness*
unremunerated 786.14 *unpaid*
unremunerative 776.16 *unprofitable*
unrepeatable expression 712.1 *curse*
unrepeated 133.9 *discontinued;* 197.14 *singular*
unrepentant 809.3 *impenitent*
unrepented 809.4 *unatoned*
unrepenting 809.3 *impenitent*
unreplenished 218.2 *unprovided*
unreported 128.11 *excluded*
unrepresentative 718.6 *misrepresented*
unrepresentatively 718.8
unreproachful 649.5 *merciful*
unrequired 350.3 *not wanted*
unrequite 672.6 *be ungrateful*
unrequited 470.10 *rejected;* 672.4 *unthanked*
unrequited love 249.1 *adversity*
unresembling 116.4 *dissimilar*
unresentful 649.5 *merciful*
unresentfulness 649.2 *forgivingness*
unreserved 734.12 *conversing;* 739.11 *disclosing;* 646.1 *naive;* 308.16, 738.15 *open*
unreservedly 734.15 *conversationally;* 250.21 *excessively;* 739.13 *openly*
unreservedness 739.3 *openness*
unresisting 663.7 *obedient;* 589.7 *peaceful;* 388.5 *submitting*
unresistingly 663.10 *obediently*
unresolved 517.8 *disagreeing;* 453.2 *irresolute;* 737.11 *mysterious;* 696.2 *unexplained;* 639.1 *vacillating*
unrespected 668.17
unresponsive 651.15 *inconsiderate;* 618.7 *indifferent;* 339.5 *inert;* 592.1 *insensitive;* 628.4 *pitiless;* 489.6 *unfeeling*
unresponsively 618.17 *indifferently;* 628.7 *pitilessly*
unresponsiveness 36.13 *depression;* 592.3 *insensitiveness*
unrest 300.2 *momentum;* 327.5, 342.7 *restlessness*
unrested 261.1 *fatigued*
unrestrained **681.2**; 588.6 *anarchic;* 703.10 *demonstrative;* 250.9 *free;* 686.8 *overindulgent;* 380.6 *violent*
unrestrainedly 758.13 *with impunity*
unrestrainedness 681.5
unrestraint 588.1 *anarchy;* 250.1 *freedom;* 686.3 *overindulgence*
unrestricted 232.7 *complete;* 141.12 *extensive;* 391.8 *free;* 758.7 *independent;* 308.13 *opened up;* 138.19 *prevailing;* 250.12 *unconditional*
unretractable 707.13 *supported*
unretracted 707.13 *supported*
unrevealed 737.9 *secret*
unrevengeful 649.5 *merciful*
unrevengefulness 649.2 *forgivingness*
unrevered 668.17 *unrespected*
unreverenced 668.17 *unrespected*
unrewarded 238.2 *futile;* 786.14 *unpaid;* 672.4 *unthanked*
unrewarding 238.2 *futile;* 672.5 *thankless*
unrhymed poetry 17.11 *rhyme*
unrhythmic 299.4 *irregular*
unrhythmical 299.4 *irregular*
unrhythmically 299.8 *irregularly*
unriddle 719.9 *decipher*
unrig 238.8 *make useless*
unrighteous 802.16 *in the wrong;* 804.11 *wicked*
unrighteousness **802.5**; 804.1 *wickedness*
unrinsed 258.7 *dirty*
unripe 499.5 *acid;* 233.4 *incomplete;* 80.9 *of a fruit;* 538.3 *raw;* 487.1 *unaccustomed;* 486.2 *unskilled;* 288.13 *untimely*
unripeness 231.5 *imperfection;* 233.1 *incompleteness;* 499.1 *sourness;* 486.8 *unskilfulness;* 288.2 *untimeliness*
unrivalled 121.14 *best;* 230.1 *perfect*
unrobe 552.14 *undress*
unrobed 552.9 *undressed*
unroll 739.5 *disclose;* 148.10 *lengthen;* 738.3 *reveal;* 178.10 *straighten*
unrolling 738.10 *manifestation*
unrough 421.1 *smooth*
unroughly 421.14 *smoothly*
unruffled 4.18 *detached;* 618.7 *indifferent;* 301.6 *quiescent;* 421.2 *uniform*
unruffled surface 421.7 *smoothness*
unruliness 588.1 *anarchy;* 662.1 *disobedience;* 408.8 *lawlessness;* 250.6 *liberality*
unruly 588.6 *anarchic;* 662.13 *disobedient;* 408.20 *disorderly;* 641.2 *refractory;* 250.12 *unconditional;* 380.6 *violent*
unsaddle 415.10 *lighten*
unsaddling 415.6 *lightening*
unsafe **254.2**; 236.5 *harmful;* 337.8 *weak*
unsafely 337.14 *weakly*
unsaid 128.11 *excluded*
unsalable 793.10 *shoddy*
unsalaried 793.11 *free of charge*
unsaleability 238.3 *uselessness*
unsaleable 793.10 *shoddy;* 238.1 *useless*
unsalted 497.5 *tasteless*
unsalvageable 766.16 *losing*
unsanctified by custom 487.2 *not customary*
unsated 218.2 *unprovided*
unsatisfactorily 218.10 *insufficiently;* 337.14 *weakly*
unsatisfactory **606.5**; **670.32**; 604.11 *disappointing;* 231.1 *imperfect;* 233.4 *incomplete;* 236.2 *inferior;* 218.1, 337.13 *insufficient*
unsatisfactory work 486.9 *bungling*
unsatisfied 218.2 *unprovided*
unsatisfied hopes 604.1 *disappointment*
unsatisfying 604.11 *disappointing;* 497.5 *tasteless*
unsaturated 32.35 *combined;* 32.32 *solid*
unsaturated compound 32.7 *chemical compound*
unsaturated fat 33.7 *fat*
unsaturated solution 32.3 *phase*
unsavouriness 497.1 *tastelessness*
unsavoury 596.9 *disliked;* 499.6 *unpalatable;* 242.1 *unpleasant*
unsay 479.4 *recant*
unsayable 399.6 *censored*
unscarred 230.1 *perfect*
unscathed 230.1 *perfect;* 252.6 *safe;* 204.7 *uncut*
unscented 501.3 *odourless*
unscholarly 456.6 *ignorant*
unschooled 456.6 *ignorant*
unscientific 646.1 *naive;* 486.2 *unskilled*
unscoured 258.7 *dirty*
unscramble 719.9 *decipher;* 375.4 *deconstruct;* 265.18 *disentangle;* 4.21 *rationalize;* 255.11 *simplify;* 706.20 *solve;* 178.10 *straighten*
unscrambled 719.15 *interpreted;* 706.14 *solved*
unscrambling 265.8 *disentanglement;* 706.6 *solution;* 719.4 *translation*
unscratched 230.1 *perfect*
unscreen 739.5 *disclose*
unscrubbed 258.7 *dirty*
unscrupulous 800.5 *dishonourable;* 796.11 *immoral;* 666.5 *indifferent;* 804.11 *wicked*
unscrupulously 800.11 *dishonourably;* 804.18 *wickedly*
unscrupulousness 796.1 *immorality;* 800.1 *improbity;* 666.2 *indifference*
unseal 739.5 *disclose;* 308.19 *open up*
unsealed 308.13 *opened up*
unsearchable 696.1 *unintelligible*
unseasonable 240.1 *inconvenient;* 288.13 *untimely*
unseasonableness 288.2 *untimeliness*
unseasonably 288.19 *at the wrong time*
unseasonal 31.46 *seasonal*
unseasoned 255.13 *pure;* 538.3 *raw;* 497.5 *tasteless;* 487.1 *unaccustomed;* 486.2 *unskilled*
unseat 588.4 *be anarchic;* 144.14 *displace;* 144.16 *replace;* 372.9 *separate*
unseating 144.3 *replacement*
unsecure 254.2 *unsafe*
unsecured 771.6 *loaned*
unsecured debt 784.1 *debt*
unsecured loan 771.2, 784.3 *loan*
unseeable 521.1 *invisible*
unseeing 519.8 *blind;* 341.3 *inactive*
unseemliness 812.1 *disrespect;* 675.3 *grossness;* 802.3 *impropriety;* 240.3 *inconvenience;* 804.3 *venial sin*
unseemly 675.8 *discourteous;* 802.13 *improper;* 240.1 *inconvenient;* 544.8 *indecorous;* 546.4 *ugly;* 804.13 *venial*
unseen 736.14 *concealed;* 519.13 *hidden;* 521.1 *invisible;* 674.13 *reserved;* 696.1 *unintelligible;* 456.8 *unknown*
unseen world 582.14 *the spiritual world*
unsegregated 127.8 *included*
unselected 470.10 *rejected*
unselfish **473.5**; 650.7 *charitable;* 803.5 *virtuous*
unselfishly **473.9**; 650.11 *charitably;* 803.9 *virtuously*
unselfishness **473.2**; 650.2 *charity;* 652.1 *philanthropy;* 803.1 *virtue*
unsensational 271.1 *simple*
unseparated 127.8 *included*
unserious 699.31 *hypocritical*
unseriously 699.42 *hypocritically*
unseriousness 699.3 *hypocrisy*
unserviceable 238.1 *useless*
unserviceableness 238.3 *uselessness*
unsettle 375.4 *deconstruct;* 408.22 *discompose;* 328.7 *disturb*
unsettled 701.10 *arguable;* 227.13 *changeable;* 408.17 *discomposed;* 328.12 *disturbed;* 453.2 *irresolute;* 31.46 *seasonal;* 98.14 *unoccupied*
unsettledness 453.11 *irresoluteness*
unsettling 328.17 *disturbing;* 240.1 *inconvenient*
unsex 335.9 *make impotent*
unsexed 335.13
unshackle 391.4 *liberate*
unshackled 250.9, 391.8 *free;* 391.7 *liberated*
unshackling 391.1 *liberation*
unshakable 613.9 *courageous;* 452.6 *infallible;* 228.9 *stable;* 638.4 *undaunted*
unshakably 228.12 *stably*
unshaken 4.18 *detached;* 253.7 *guaranteed;* 638.4 *undaunted*
unshape 161.3 *make shapeless*
unshaped 161.5 *shapeless*
unshapely 546.4 *ugly*
unshared 763.9 *possessed;* 763.8 *possessing*
unsharp 426.1 *blunt*
unsharpened 426.1 *blunt;* 421.2 *uniform*
unsharpness 426.5 *bluntness*
unshatterable 423.1 *tough*
unshaven 420.3 *barbed*
unsheathe the sword 585.12 *go to war*
unshepherded 254.3 *vulnerable*
unshielded 308.13 *opened up;* 254.3 *vulnerable*
unship 371.12 *unload*
unshorn 420.3 *barbed*
unshrinking 613.9 *courageous;* 638.4 *undaunted*
unshriven 809.3 *impenitent*
unshroud 739.5 *disclose*
unsifted 420.1 *rough;* 408.13 *unordered*
unsighted 519.8 *blind;* 521.1 *invisible*
unsightliness 546.1 *ugliness*
unsightly 525.10 *aspectual;* 546.4 *ugly;* 408.15 *untidy*
unsigned 27.71 *numerical;* 453.5 *uncertified*
unsimilarity 116.1 *dissimilarity*

unsinkable 415.2 *insubstantial*
unskilful **486.1**; 487.1 *unaccustomed*; 238.1 *useless*
unskilfully **486.11**; **487.7**
Unskilfulness 486
unskilfulness **486.8**; 456.1 *ignorance*; 236.8 *inferiority*; 487.3 *unaccustomedness*; 238.3 *uselessness*
unskilled **486.2**; 456.6 *ignorant*; 15.8 *industrial*; 236.2 *inferior*; 646.1 *naive*; 538.3 *raw*; 238.1 *useless*
unskilled labourer 578.1 *worker*
unskilled person **486.10**
unskilled worker 216.7 *average person*; 15.7 *employee*; 346.6 *operative*
unsleeping 342.20 *industrious*; 640.11 *steady*
unsmiling 659.5 *discourteous*; 626.7 *irritable*; 643.1 *solemn*
unsmoked bacon 25.30 *bacon*
unsmooth 420.1 *rough*
unsmoothly 420.14 *roughly*
unsmoothness 420.6 *roughness*
unsnarl 265.18 *disentangle*; 409.19 *tidy*
unsnarled 409.27 *tidied*
unsnarling 265.8 *disentanglement*
Unsociability 655
unsociability **655.1**; 653.1 *misanthropy*; 626.1 *sullenness*
unsociable **655.8**; 659.5 *discourteous*; 653.3 *misanthropic*; 732.1 *shy*; 736.16 *silent*; 118.16 *solitary*
unsociableness 653.1 *misanthropy*; 655.1 *unsociability*
unsociably 659.9 *discourteously*
unsocial habits 655.1 *unsociability*
unsocially **655.14**
unsocial person **655.6**; 653.2 *misanthrope*
unsoiled 256.16 *clean*; 805.5 *innocent*
unsold 350.3 *not wanted*
unsolicitous 659.5 *discourteous*
unsolicitousness 659.1 *discourtesy*
unsolvable 27.73 *numerable*; 696.2 *unexplained*
unsolved 696.2 *unexplained*
unsophisticated 255.17 *direct*; 646.1, 805.7 *naive*; 271.3 *natural*; 574.4 *ordinary*; 538.3 *raw*
unsophisticated person 646.3 *naive person*
unsophistication 646.2, 805.3 *naivety*
unsorrowful 809.3 *impenitent*
unsorry 809.3 *impenitent*
unsorted 412.12 *mixed*; 408.13 *unordered*
unsought 634.20 *avoidable*
unsound 802.14 *abnormal*; 122.17 *defective*; 337.10 *ill*; 231.1 *imperfect*; 802.12 *incorrect*; 27.86 *logical*; 236.4 *poor*; 704.6 *refutable*; 702.7 *sophistic*; 260.21 *unhealthy*; 453.7 *unreliable*; 254.2 *unsafe*; 486.2 *unskilled*
unsoundable 156.8 *deep*
unsound argument 27.64 *reasoning*
unsounded 156.8 *deep*; 506.3 *silent*
unsound horse 59.1 *horse*
unsoundly 122.21 *badly*; 704.12 *refutably*; 702.14 *sophistically*; 337.14 *weakly*
unsound mind 461.1 *insanity*
unsoundness 254.5 *danger*; 231.5 *imperfection*; 802.2 *incorrectness*; 782.6 *insolvency*; 236.10 *poverty*; 704.4 *refutability*; 702.1 *sophistry*; 453.15 *unreliability*; 254.7 *vulnerability*
unsparing 217.2 *plentiful*; 647.8 *severe*
unsparingly 647.11 *severely*
unspeakable 236.3 *bad*; 696.1 *unintelligible*; 619.8 *wonderful*
unspeakableness 696.11 *unintelligibility*
unspeakably 619.13 *wonderfully*
unspecific 138.20 *generalized*
unspecified **452.8**; 138.20 *generalized*
unspeciousness 698.1 *truth*
unspectacular 216.3 *mediocre*
unspeller 11.12 *occultist*
unspent 439.7 *stored*; 215.10 *surplus*; 350.1 *unused*
unspiced 255.13 *pure*
unspiritual 402.7 *material*
unspirituality 402.2 *materialization*
unspoiled 235.5 *not bad*; 230.1 *perfect*; 204.7 *uncut*
unspoilt 255.13 *pure*
unspoken 737.9 *secret*; 506.3 *silent*; 456.8 *unknown*
unsportsmanlike 800.5 *dishonourable*; 802.11 *wrong*
unsportsmanlike conduct 46.13 *penalty*
unspotted 805.5 *innocent*; 230.1 *perfect*
unsprung 423.3 *hard*; 418.2 *tough*
unspuriousness 698.1 *truth*
unstable 642.1 *capricious*; 227.13, 639.2 *changeable*; 328.16 *deranged*; 114.5 *diverse*; 299.4 *irregular*; 590.13 *passionate*; 278.6 *transient*; 120.3 *unequal*; 453.7 *unreliable*; 254.2 *unsafe*
unstable equilibrium 28.10 *force*
unstableness 453.15 *unreliability*
unstable person 36.8 *disordered personality*
unstaffed 98.14 *unoccupied*
unstained 256.16 *clean*; 230.1 *perfect*
unstalked 77.18 *of leaves*
unstarched 419.1 *soft*
unstatesmanlike 486.1 *unskilful*
unstatutory 16.56 *unauthorized*
unstaunch 614.3 *cowardly*; 639.4 *unsteady*
unsteadfast 614.3 *cowardly*; 639.4 *unsteady*
unsteadily 227.15 *changeably*; 114.10 *diversely*; 424.5 *fragilely*; 299.8 *irregularly*; 327.28 *shakily*; 453.26 *unreliably*; 337.14 *weakly*
unsteadiness 327.1 *agitation*; 227.1 *changeableness*; 254.5 *danger*; 299.1 *irregularity*; 453.15 *unreliability*
unsteady **639.4**; 327.15 *agitated*; 424.1 *brittle*; 227.13 *changeable*; 486.3 *clumsy*; 245.13 *dilapidated*; 337.10 *ill*; 231.1 *imperfect*; 299.4 *irregular*; 327.18 *shaky*; 453.7 *unreliable*; 254.2 *unsafe*
unsteerable 486.3 *clumsy*
unsterilized 258.8 *unclean*
unstick 268.17 *liquefy*; 372.9 *separate*
unstiffen 419.13 *soften*
unstiffened 419.1 *soft*
unstinting 679.1 *generous*
unstirring 301.6 *quiescent*
unstitch 372.9 *separate*
unstocked 218.2 *unprovided*
unstop 308.19 *open up*
unstoppable 452.5 *inevitable*; 134.6 *protracted*
unstopped 308.13 *opened up*
unstressed 729.18 *phonetic*
unstring 372.9 *separate*; 419.13 *soften*
unstrung 419.1 *soft*; 337.8 *weak*
unstuck 372.15 *separate*
unstudied 646.1 *naive*
unstuffy 657.7 *informal*
unsturdiness 424.2 *brittleness*
unsturdy 424.1 *brittle*
unsubdued 383.12 *resisting*
unsubjected 250.10 *independent*
unsubmissive 118.12 *nonconformist*; 383.12 *resisting*
unsubmissively 383.14 *resistingly*
unsubstantial 477.12 *imaginary*; 521.1 *invisible*; 728.12 *understated*; 96.8 *unreal*
unsubstantiality 728.1 *understatement*; 96.1 *unreality*
unsubstantialness 101.2 *unworldliness*
unsuccessful 249.6 *adverse*; 604.11 *disappointing*; 247.10 *failed*; 238.2 *futile*; 563.6 *having no effect*; 766.17 *unprofitable*; 218.2 *unprovided*; 486.1 *unskilful*
unsuccessful applicant 247.5 *failing person*; 470.9 *rejected person*
unsuccessful candidate 247.5 *failing person*; 766.6 *loser*
unsuccessful challenger 247.5 *failing person*
unsuccessful competitor 247.5 *failing person*
unsuccessful defence 16.43 *conviction*
unsuccessfully **247.12**; 766.20 *at a loss*; 249.12 *in adversity*; 486.11 *unskilfully*; 238.10 *uselessly*
unsuccessful thing **247.4**
unsuccessive 133.8 *discontinuous*
unsuitability 240.3 *inconvenience*; 238.3 *uselessness*
unsuitable 751.10 *different*; 802.13 *improper*; 240.1 *inconvenient*; 470.10 *rejected*; 288.13 *untimely*; 238.1 *useless*
unsuitableness 288.2 *untimeliness*
unsuitable time 288.2 *untimeliness*
unsuitably 288.19 *at the wrong time*; 751.12 *differently*; 802.27 *improperly*
unsuited 288.13 *untimely*
unsullied 256.16 *clean*; 805.5 *innocent*; 255.13 *pure*
unsupplied 218.2 *unprovided*
unsupported 197.15 *solo*; 254.3 *vulnerable*
unsure 453.1 *uncertain*; 639.1 *vacillating*
unsureness 453.9 *uncertainty*
unsure of oneself 674.11 *shy*
unsurpassable 121.14, 235.2 *best*; 230.1 *perfect*
unsurpassably 121.17 *supremely*
unsurpassed 121.14, 235.2 *best*
unsurpassedly 121.17 *supremely*
unsurprised 474.5 *expecting*; 618.7 *indifferent*
unsurprising 474.7 *expected*
unsurprisingly 474.13 *expectedly*
unsusceptibility 592.3 *insensitiveness*
unsusceptible 592.1 *insensitive*
unsuspecting 450.11 *believing*; 646.1 *naive*; 630.6 *surprised*
unsuspectingly 450.15 *believingly*
unsuspicious 646.1 *naive*
unsweetened 499.5 *acid*
unswept 258.7 *dirty*
unswerving 452.2 *convinced*; 324.15 *direct*
unswervingly 324.9 *directly*; 178.12 *straight*
unsymmetrical 234.6 *distorted*; 299.4, 408.14 *irregular*
unsymmetrically 234.13 *asymmetrically*
unsymmetry 408.2 *irregular order*
unsympathetic 637.3 *cautious*; 596.8 *disliking*; 651.15 *inconsiderate*; 113.22 *oppositional*; 628.4 *pitiless*
unsympathetically 596.10 *discontentedly*; 628.7 *pitilessly*
unsympatheticness 628.1 *pitilessness*
unsympathizing 628.4 *pitiless*
unsynchronized 286.2 *occurring at a different time*
unsystematic 408.16 *confused*; 299.4 *irregular*
unsystematical 299.4 *irregular*
unsystematically 408.27 *in disorder*; 299.8 *irregularly*
untainted 256.16 *clean*; 805.5 *innocent*; 230.1 *perfect*
untalented 486.1 *unskilful*
untamed 634.18 *avoiding*; 487.1 *unaccustomed*; 380.6 *violent*
untamed horse 59.1 *horse*
untangle 390.1 *deliver*; 265.18 *disentangle*; 178.10 *straighten*; 409.19 *tidy*
untangled 409.27 *tidied*
untangling 390.2 *deliverance*
untapped 350.2 *new*
untarnished 256.16 *clean*; 255.13 *pure*
untaught 456.6 *ignorant*; 646.1 *naive*; 478.2 *spontaneous*; 487.1 *unaccustomed*; 486.2 *unskilled*
untax 415.10 *lighten*
untaxed 793.11 *free of charge*
untaxing 415.6 *lightening*
unteachable 641.4 *set*; 486.2 *unskilled*
untearable 423.1 *tough*
untempered 337.8 *weak*
untenability 451.2 *unbelievability*
untenable 451.7 *disbelieved*; 103.3 *hopeless*; 702.7 *sophistic*; 335.11 *unprotected*; 337.8 *weak*
untenableness 702.1 *sophistry*
untenanted 98.14 *unoccupied*
untested 538.3 *raw*; 453.5 *uncertified*; 295.11 *unfamiliar*
untethered 250.11 *ranging*
unthanked **672.4**
unthankful 672.3 *ungrateful*
unthankfulness 672.1 *ingratitude*
unthawed 416.7 *condensed*
unthinkability 103.5 *impossibility*
unthinkable 103.1 *impossible*
unthinkably 103.11 *impossibly*
unthinking **463.10**; 262.3 *hasty*; 472.7 *inattentive*; 472.9 *thoughtless*; 457.6 *unintelligent*
unthinkingly 463.16 *obliviously*; 457.11 *unintelligently*
unthinkingness **463.4**
unthorough 231.2 *incomplete*
unthoughtful 651.15 *inconsiderate*
unthreading 372.1 *separation*
unthreatened 252.6 *safe*
unthreatening 252.6 *safe*
unthriftiness 681.4 *extravagance*
unthrifty 681.1 *extravagant*
unthrone 588.4 *be anarchic*
untidily 258.12 *dirtily*; 114.10 *diversely*
untidiness **408.3**; 258.1 *dirtiness*; 666.2 *indifference*
untidy **408.15**; 327.22 *agitate*; 258.7, 258.11 *dirty*; 245.4 *impair*; 666.5 *indifferent*; 408.24 *make disordered*
untie 390.1 *deliver*; 265.18 *disentangle*; 767.9 *dispose of*; 372.9 *separate*; 250.15 *set free*; 552.14 *undress*
untied 389.8 *escaping*; 372.15 *separate*
untie one's hands 391.4 *liberate*
untie the knot 571.7 *divorce*
untie the purse-strings 787.1 *expend*
until 275.26 *all the time*
until hell freezes over 279.11 *eternally*
untilled 350.2 *new*
until now 284.23 *before now*; 3.24 *historically*
until the Greek Calends 279.11 *eternally*
untimeliness **288.2**; 486.9 *bungling*; 328.4 *disruption*; 240.3 *inconvenience*; 288.1 *wrong time*
untimely **288.13**; 240.1 *inconvenient*; 465.9 *misjudged*; 288.10 *mistimed*
untimely action 288.2 *untimeliness*
untimely end 582.5 *ways of dying*
untimely occurrence 288.2 *untimeliness*
untinged 255.13 *pure*
untiring 423.4 *powerful*; 640.11 *steady*
untiringly 423.13 *powerfully*
untold 128.11 *excluded*; 202.2 *immeasurable*; 208.8 *numberless*; 737.9 *secret*; 456.8 *unknown*
untouchable 655.7 *outsider*; 145.9 *reserved*; 122.15 *subordinate*
untouched 256.16 *clean*; 809.3 *impenitent*; 618.7 *indifferent*; 350.2 *new*; 795.9 *pure*; 204.7 *uncut*
untouched by evil 805.5 *innocent*
untouched by human hand 356.12 *produced*
untoward 240.1 *inconvenient*
untraditional 487.2 *not customary*
untrainable horse 59.1 *horse*
untrained 231.2 *incomplete*; 538.3 *raw*; 487.1 *unaccustomed*; 486.1 *unskilful*; 486.2 *unskilled*
untranslatable 696.1 *unintelligible*
untravelled 301.5 *sedentary*
untried 538.3 *raw*; 453.5 *uncertified*; 295.11 *unfamiliar*; 350.1 *unused*
untrimmed 271.2 *unadorned*; 120.3 *unequal*
untrodden 350.2 *new*; 295.11 *unfamiliar*
untroubled 685.6 *moderate*; 301.6 *quiescent*
untroublesome 265.12 *wieldy*
untrue 274.15 *erroneous*; 699.29 *false*; 477.12 *imaginary*; 802.12 *incorrect*; 718.6 *misrepresented*; 476.8 *supposed*
untrueness 274.3 *erroneousness*; 699.1 *falsehood*
untrustworthiness 479.7 *apostasy*; 800.2 *faithlessness*; 705.7 *questionableness*; 453.15 *unreliability*
untrustworthy 268.15 *crafty*; 604.12 *deceptive*; 800.6 *faithless*; 705.14 *questionable*; 453.7 *unreliable*; 254.2 *unsafe*
untruth 479.5 *equivocalness*; 274.3 *erroneousness*; 736.5 *evasion*; 711.3 *false alarm*; 699.1 *falsehood*
untruthful 800.5 *dishonourable*; 798.7 *evil*; 234.8 *exaggerated*; 699.29 *false*; 802.12 *incorrect*
untruthfully 800.11 *dishonourably*; 234.14 *distortedly*; 798.12 *evilly*; 699.40 *falsely*; 802.26 *wrong*
untruthfulness 234.4 *distortion of the truth*; 798.1 *evil*; 699.1 *falsehood*; 800.1 *improbity*; 802.2 *incorrectness*
untuned 517.9 *unmelodious*
untuneful 517.9 *unmelodious*
untutored 456.6 *ignorant*; 646.1 *naive*; 486.2 *unskilled*
untwist 178.10 *straighten*
untying 372.1 *separation*
untypical 116.4 *dissimilar*
unusable 470.10 *rejected*; 350.1 *unused*; 238.1 *useless*
unusably 350.12 *out of use*
unused **350.1**; 486.3 *clumsy*; 343.2 *not working*; 439.7 *stored*; 215.10 *surplus*; 295.11 *unfamiliar*; 441.9 *waste*
unused thing **350.11**
unusual **299.5**; 139.16 *characteristic*;

116.4 *dissimilar*; 114.5 *diverse*; 118.14 *eccentric*; 487.2 *not customary*; 630.8 *surprising*; 619.8 *wonderful*
unusually 299.9; **487.8**; 116.7 *dissimilarly*; 114.10 *diversely*; 295.21 *newly*; 118.21 *unconformably*
unusualness 118.4; **299.2**
unutterable 696.1 *unintelligible*; 619.8 *wonderful*
unuttered 506.3 *silent*
unvalued 594.12 *hated*
unvanquished 246.15 *victorious*
unvariable 111.17 *regular*
unvariableness 111.6 *regularity*
unvariably 111.20 *regularly*
unvaried 509.16 *humming*; 111.17 *regular*
unvarnished 646.1 *naive*; 271.2 *unadorned*
unvarying 620.4 *boring*; 750.14 *conforming*; 119.6 *equal*; 134.6 *protracted*; 111.17 *regular*; 111.12 *same*; 228.9 *stable*
unveering 324.15 *direct*
unveeringly 324.9 *directly*
unveil 295.19 *begin*; 449.2 *detect*; 739.5 *disclose*; 130.24 *open*; 738.3 *reveal*; 552.14 *undress*
unveiled 130.37 *enrolled*; 552.11 *exposed*; 295.13 *inaugurated*
unveiling 295.4 *beginning*; 449.7 *detection*; 739.1 *disclosure*; 130.9 *premiere*
unveil oneself 738.4 *show oneself*
unvenerated 668.17 *unrespected*
unventilated 503.3 *stinking*
unveraciously 699.40 *falsely*
unverifiability 453.13 *indemonstrability*
unverifiable 453.4 *indemonstrable*; 705.14 *questionable*
unverified 476.7 *suppositional*; 453.5 *uncertified*
unverified supposition 476.3 *conjecture*
unverity 699.1 *falsehood*
unversatile 486.1 *unskilful*
unversed 646.1 *naive*; 486.2 *unskilled*
unviable 103.3 *hopeless*
unvirtuous 804.12 *immoral*; 796.13 *unchaste*
unvirtuousness 804.2 *vice*
unvisited 655.11 *secluded*
unvoiced 730.9 *voiceless*
unwanted 596.9 *disliked*; 594.12 *hated*; 350.3 *not wanted*; 470.10 *rejected*; 793.10 *shoddy*; 215.10 *surplus*; 238.1 *useless*; 441.9 *waste*
unwariness 615.1 *rashness*
unwarlike 339.5 *inert*; 589.7 *peaceful*
unwarned 254.3 *vulnerable*
unwarrantable 16.58 *unjust*
unwarranted 329.12 *excessive*; 16.56 *unauthorized*
unwary 615.4 *rash*; 489.6 *unfeeling*
unwashed 258.7 *dirty*; 503.3 *stinking*
unwasteful 680.4 *thrifty*
unwatered 428.1 *dry*
unwavering 228.11 *determined*; 452.6 *infallible*; 640.11 *steady*; 638.4 *undaunted*
unwaveringly 228.13 *determinedly*
unwearied 342.20 *industrious*; 640.11 *steady*
unwed 572.6 *celibate*
unwed condition 572.1 *celibacy*
unwedded 572.6 *celibate*; 250.10 *independent*; 655.10 *lonely*; 795.9 *pure*; 197.17 *single*
unwed man 572.5 *single person*
unweeded 77.13 *plantlike*
unweighable 415.1 *light*
unweighableness 415.5 *lightness*
unweighting 68.12 *ski*; 68.4 *skiing technique*
unwelcome 596.9 *disliked*; 594.12 *hated*; 242.1 *unpleasant*
unwelcome guest 314.8 *intruder*; 654.6 *social person*
unwelcome necessity 594.7 *hated thing*
unwelcoming 655.8 *unsociable*
unwell 249.6 *adverse*; 260.22 *sick*
unwhetted 426.1 *blunt*
unwholesome 236.5 *harmful*; 796.12 *indecent*; 503.3 *stinking*; 499.6 *unpalatable*
unwholesomeness 499.2 *unpalatability*
unwieldily 264.28 *awkwardly*
unwieldiness 264.2 *awkwardness*; 158.2 *bigness*; 240.3 *inconvenience*; 414.8 *weighing down*
unwieldy 264.15, 486.3 *clumsy*; 240.1 *inconvenient*; 414.3 *ponderous*; 120.3 *unequal*
unwilling 637.1; 634.18 *avoiding*; 596.8 *disliking*; 662.13 *disobedient*; 481.10 *dissuaded*; 333.6 *hesitant*; 378.13 *hindering*; 709.8 *refused*; 383.10 *resistant*; 113.26 *uncooperative*
unwillingly 637.17; 596.10 *discontentedly*; 662.17 *disobediently*; 383.14 *resistingly*; 634.23 *shyly*; 709.11 *uncooperatively*; 378.16 *with delay*
Unwillingness 637
unwillingness 637.11; 596.1 *dislike*; 662.1 *disobedience*; 333.12 *hesitation*; 378.1 *hindrance*; 709.1 *refusal*; 383.1 *resistance*; 634.12 *shyness*; 113.6 *uncooperativeness*
unwind 419.14 *ease*; 341.4 *not act*; 263.2 *take it easy*
unwiped 258.7 *dirty*
unwise 459.5 *foolish*; 240.1 *inconvenient*; 457.6 *unintelligent*; 486.1 *unskilful*
unwisely 459.8 *foolishly*; 457.11 *unintelligently*
unwitnessed 521.1 *invisible*
unwitting 456.6 *ignorant*
unwittingly 456.12 *ignorantly*
unwonted 487.2 *not customary*; 487.1 *unaccustomed*
unwooed 572.6 *celibate*
unworkability 103.6 *hopelessness*; 238.3 *uselessness*
unworkable 103.3 *hopeless*; 335.10 *powerless*; 238.1 *useless*
unworkably 103.12 *hopelessly*
Unworldliness 101
unworldliness 101.2; 646.2, 805.3 *naivety*; 11.2 *the occult*
unworldly 646.1, 805.7 *naive*; 101.8 *nonmaterial*; 11.18 *spiritual*
unworthily 122.22 *basely*
unworthiness 236.10 *poverty*
unworthy 122.12 *inferior*; 236.4 *poor*
unwrap 739.5 *disclose*; 552.15 *make nude*; 520.10 *make visible*; 308.18 *open*
unwrapped 308.12 *open*
unwrinkled 187.8 *horizontal*; 421.2 *uniform*
unwritten 358.6 *obliterated*; 729.17 *oral*; 1.14 *societal*
unwritten agreement 756.1 *promise*
unwritten code 810.6 *ethics*
unwritten constitution 16.1 *the law*
unwritten law 713.3 *precept*; 16.1 *the law*; 632.5 *tradition*
unyielding 641.3; 452.5 *inevitable*; 628.5 *inflexible*; 635.7 *iron-willed*; 418.4 *mentally hard*; 423.5 *mentally tough*; 383.11 *obstinate*; 336.11 *strong in spirit*; 638.3 *strong-willed*
unyieldingly 628.7 *pitilessly*; 647.11 *severely*; 336.14 *strongly*
unyieldingness 628.2 *inflexibility*; 418.8 *mental hardness*; 423.9 *mental toughness*
unzealous 637.3 *cautious*
unzip 372.9 *separate*; 552.14 *undress*
unzipped 372.15 *separate*
up 304.26; 598.1 *cheerful*; 154.20 *higher*; 610.11 *hopeful*; 190.5 *make bigger*; 186.12 *perpendicularly*; 28.78 *quantum*; 366.1 *raise*; 237.1 *useful*; 186.11 *vertically*; 317.17 *via*
up against it 249.6 *adverse*; 782.2 *insolvent*; 120.7 *unequally*
upalong 304.26 *up*
up and about 259.1 *healthy*; 300.18 *in motion*
up and away 322.11 *aeronautically*
up-and-coming 342.18 *active*; 248.8 *prosperous*
up-and-coming star 246.4 *successful person*
up and doing 340.5 *acting*; 342.19 *busy*; 346.10 *operational*
up and down 186.12 *perpendicularly*; 298.15 *regularly*; 326.18 *to and fro*
up-and-down 326.13 *oscillating*; 186.8 *vertical*
up and go 313.1 *depart*
up and going 346.10 *operational*
Upanishad 7.12 *religious text*
uparching 304.22 *ascending*
upasaka 7.7 *monk*
upasika 7.7 *monk*
up a tree 264.16 *troubled*
up back 46.7 *offence*
upbeat 610.11 *hopeful*; 18.19 *tempo*
up before the beak 464.10 *judged*; 16.54 *litigated*
upbend 304.2, 304.21 *upturn*
upbraid 670.20 *censure*
upbraided 670.34 *censured*
upbraiding 670.7 *blame*; 670.30 *censuring*
upbringing 6.1 *education*
upbuoy 366.1 *raise*
upbuoyed 366.11 *raised*
upbuoying 366.6 *raising*
upcast 304.22 *ascending*; 366.1 *raise*; 366.11 *raised*; 366.6 *raising*; 304.2, 304.21 *upturn*
upchuck 371.15 *vomit*
upclimb 304.14 *climb*; 62.9 *mountaineer*; 62.1 *mountaineering*; 304.6 *mounting*
upclimber 304.11 *ascender*; 62.7 *mountaineer*
upcoming 304.1 *ascent*; 283.11 *future*; 294.13 *later*; 304.23 *rising*
upcountry 172.3, 172.9 *inland*; 86.17 *national*
upcurve 330.5 *throw*; 304.2, 304.21 *upturn*
update 295.20 *make new*
updateable 295.15 *renewable*
updated 295.14 *renewed*
updated model 244.8 *better thing*
updated version 244.8 *better thing*
updating 295.5 *fresh start*
updraught 434.4 *air flow*; 31.10 *air movement*; 304.2 *upturn*
upend 186.6 *make vertical*
upended 186.8 *vertical*
upending 186.2 *making vertical*
up for auction 752.17 *offered*
up for grabs 778.18 *on sale*
up for sale 752.17 *offered*; 778.18 *on sale*
up for trial 464.10 *judged*; 16.54 *litigated*
upfront 178.5 *honourable*
up front 167.11 *in front*
upgang 304.1 *ascent*
upgo 304.13 *ascend*; 304.1 *ascent*
upgoing 304.1 *ascent*; 304.23 *rising*
upgrade 40.20 *abort*; 304.22 *ascending*; 302.8 *further*; 244.1 *improve*; 295.20 *make new*; 393.2 *refurbish*; 304.2 *upturn*
upgradeable 295.15 *renewable*
upgraded 366.12 *exalted*; 295.14 *renewed*
upgrading 295.5 *fresh start*; 244.5 *improvement*; 366.7 *lift*
upgrow 304.13 *ascend*
upgrowth 304.2 *upturn*
uphaul 50.3 *parts of a sailing boat*
upheaval 408.5 *confusion*; 328.1 *disturbance*; 408.8 *lawlessness*; 366.6 *raising*; 357.4 *ruin*
upheave 304.13 *ascend*; 304.18 *jump*; 366.1 *raise*
uphill 304.22 *ascending*; 304.1 *ascent*; 264.10 *difficult*; 264.25 *difficultly*; 576.11 *laborious*; 304.26 *up*
uphill christie 68.4 *skiing technique*
uphill ski 68.5 *ski equipment*
uphill struggle 264.3 *difficult task*
uphill task 264.3 *difficult task*
uphillward 304.22 *ascending*; 304.26 *up*
uphill work 576.1 *work*
uphoist 366.1 *raise*
uphold 392.23 *advise*; 134.3 *continue*; 95.12 *establish reality*; 413.14 *give moral support*; 714.8 *justify*; 359.5 *preserve*; 366.1 *raise*; 669.13 *support*
upholder 413.8 *supporter*
upholding 413.9 *supportive*
upholster 550.24 *coat*; 152.8 *fatten*; 23.18 *work wood*
upholstered 23.14 *wooden*
upholstered chair 23.2 *chair*
upholsterer 550.17 *coverer*
upholstery 438.7 *equipment*; 23.1 *furniture*; 550.12 *protective covering*; 419.11 *soft thing*; 152.5 *thickness*
up in arms 342.18 *active*; 113.29 *at odds*; 751.9 *disagreeing*; 586.42 *martially*; 381.22 *militant*; 624.15 *resentful*; 383.12 *resisting*; 585.15 *warring*
up in the world 248.8 *prosperous*
upkeep 413.7 *financial support*; 359.1 *preservation*; 392.3 *sustenance*
upkick 67.2 *swimming technique*
upland 92.7; 92.11 *continental*; 141.3 *geographical space*; 154.2 *heights*; 89.7 *mountainous*
upleap 304.17 *spring up*; 304.2 *upturn*
uplift 598.6 *bring cheer*; 30.20 *earth movement*; 154.1 *height*; 244.1 *improve*; 244.5 *improvement*; 415.10 *lighten*; 154.17, 366.1 *raise*; 366.6 *raising*; 304.2 *upturn*
uplifted 304.22 *ascending*; 154.9 *high*; 366.11 *raised*
uplifting 598.2 *cheering*; 366.6 *raising*
uplighter 522.12 *highlight*
uplighting 522.12 *highlight*
up line 321.2 *track*
uplong 304.26 *up*
up-market 792.7 *dear*
up-market price 792.1 *high price*
upmost 121.14 *best*; 154.10 *higher*; 174.5 *top*
up north 304.26 *up*
up on 485.8 *expert*
up on a charge 715.8 *accusatory*
upon one's honour 707.24 *truthfully*
upon one's word 756.16 *as promised*; 707.24 *truthfully*
upper 691.6 *drug*; 27.75 *equal*; 121.15 *excellent*; 154.10 *higher*; 2.14 *socioeconomic*
upper atmosphere 31.8 *atmosphere*; 434.3 *atmospheric layers*
upper bound 27.21 *set*
upper-case 5.41 *lettered*
upper-case letter 5.15 *type style*
Upper Chamber 579.11 *British government*; 12.4 *governing body*; 579.12 *US government*
upper circle 21.18 *auditorium*
upper class 235.7 *elite*; 566.9 *group*; 654.7 *human society*; 2.7 *social stratification*; 121.7 *the best people*
upper-class 573.4 *aristocratic*
upper classe 573.2 *aristocracy*
upper-class twit 573.1 *nobleman*
upper crust 235.7 *elite*; 121.7 *the best people*
upper edge 163.3 *edge*
upper extremity 174.1 *summit*
upper hand 121.3, 164.4 *advantage*; 395.1 *influence*
Upper House 579.11 *British government*; 12.4 *governing body*; 579.12 *US government*
upper limit 203.2 *certain amount*; 27.31 *differentiation*; 166.2 *limiting factor*
Upper Lough Erne 88.4 *British lakes*
upper middle class 566.9 *group*
uppermost 121.14 *best*; 154.10 *higher*; 123.5 *important*; 174.5 *top*
upper partial 18.21 *tone*
upper regions 174.1 *summit*
uppers and lowers 425.11 *tooth*
upper side 174.4 *top layer*
upper storey 442.7 *brain*
upper surface 174.4 *top layer*
upper wind 31.12 *wind*
upping 304.1 *ascent*
uppish 660.16 *arrogant*
uppishness 660.4 *arrogance*
uppitiness 660.4 *arrogance*; 622.3 *conceit*
uppity 660.16 *arrogant*; 622.17 *conceited*
upraise 415.10 *lighten*; 186.6 *make vertical*; 366.1 *raise*
upraised 154.9 *high*; 366.11 *raised*; 186.9 *unbowed*
upraising 186.2 *making vertical*
uprear 366.5 *arise*; 186.5 *be vertical*; 154.16 *rise*
upreared 154.9 *high*; 366.11 *raised*; 186.9 *unbowed*
uprearing 186.2 *making vertical*; 366.6 *raising*
upright 810.8 *dutiful*; 799.4 *honourable*; 805.5 *innocent*; 16.50 *law-abiding*; 27.80 *linear*; 795.8, 801.10 *moral*; 667.13 *respectable*; 186.8 *vertical*; 186.11 *vertically*; 186.3 *vertical thing*; 803.5 *virtuous*
upright fold 30.20 *earth movement*
uprightly 805.11 *innocently*; 186.11 *vertically*; 803.9 *virtuously*
uprightness 795.2 *good morals*; 805.1 *innocence*; 799.1 *probity*; 801.4 *righteousness*; 186.1 *verticality*; 803.1 *virtue*
uprights 46.4 *stadium*
uprisal 304.1 *ascent*
uprise 304.13 *ascend*; 304.1 *ascent*; 662.16 *be subversive*; 186.5 *be vertical*; 154.1 *height*; 154.16 *rise*; 57.7 *stationary rings*

uprising 342.5 *activism*; 304.1 *ascent*; 753.2 *disorder*; 154.9 *high*; 408.8 *lawlessness*; 186.2 *making vertical*; 383.3 *resistance movement*; 662.4 *revolution*; 304.23 *rising*
uproar 328.5 *commotion*; 408.5 *confusion*; 514.1 *cry*; 517.2 *dissonant noise*; 380.3 *instance of violence*; 507.2 *outcry*
uproarious 599.9 *funny*; 507.6 *loud*; 380.6 *violent*; 514.16 *vociferous*
uproariously 507.9 *loudly*; 514.20 *vociferously*
uproot 357.8 *destroy*; 128.8 *eject*; 371.8 *evict*; 369.11 *extract*; 144.15 *remove*; 212.3 *subtract*
uprooted 369.19 *dislodged*; 144.9 *removed*
uprooting 357.2 *destroying*; 369.1 *extraction*; 369.18 *extractive*; 144.2 *removal*
uprush 219.1 *excess*; 213.2 *spread*; 304.2 *upturn*
UPS 32.17 *analysis*
ups and downs 326.1 *oscillation*
upset 327.22 *agitate*; 327.15 *agitated*; 327.1 *agitation*; 240.5 *be inconvenient*; 364.4 *be repulsive*; 120.5 *be unequal*; 367.3 *bring down*; 596.7 *cause dislike*; 357.9 *demolish*; 604.6 *disappoint*; 604.9 *disappointed*; 408.22 *discompose*; 408.17 *discomposed*; 408.1 *disorder*; 144.14 *displace*; 328.7 *disturb*; 328.1 *disturbance*; 328.12 *disturbed*; 367.12 *downthrow*; 378.8 *hinder*; 240.3 *inconvenience*; 192.1 *inversion*; 192.3 *invert*; 367.22 *overthrown*
upset one's applecart 378.8 *hinder*
upset stomach 260.8 *indigestion*; 491.2 *painful condition*
upsetting 328.17 *disturbing*
up shit creek 222.8 *difficult*
upshoot 304.17 *spring up*; 304.2 *upturn*
upshot 345.1 *effect*; 131.12 *end result*; 51.2 *grip*; 289.9 *sequel*; 706.6 *solution*
upside 174.4 *top layer*
up side 56.2 *golfing terms*
upside-down 408.28 *anyhow*; 192.4 *inversely*; 192.2 *inverted*; 408.18 *muddled*
upside-down cake 25.36 *cake*
upslope 304.1 *ascent*
upspin 304.13 *ascend*
upspring 190.6 *become bigger*; 304.17 *spring up*
upstage 21.43 *on stage*; 21.35 *overact*; 21.17 *stage*
upstairs 154.19 *high*; 446.20 *theoretically*; 304.26 *up*
upstairs and downstairs 141.16 *extensively*
upstairs maid 401.6 *domestic servant*
upstanding 799.4 *honourable*; 667.11 *in a respectful stance*; 801.10 *moral*; 366.11 *raised*; 186.8 *vertical*
upstart 289.8 *follower*; 295.12 *immature*; 660.12 *impudent person*; 295.8 *new arrival*; 302.16 *progressive person*; 304.17 *spring up*; 57.7 *stationary rings*
upstarts 57.5 *horizontal bar*
upstate 172.3, 172.9 *inland*
up sticks 313.3 *quit*
upstream 304.13 *ascend*; 324.11 *in all directions*; 304.26 *up*
upstreamward 304.26 *up*
upsurge 304.13 *ascend*; 219.1 *excess*; 213.2 *spread*; 304.2 *upturn*
upsurgence 304.2 *upturn*
upswarm 304.13 *ascend*
upsweep 304.2, 304.21 *upturn*
upsweep method 47.1 *track events*
upswing 56.3 *golf shots*; 244.5 *improvement*; 213.2 *spread*; 304.2 *upturn*
upswinging 366.7 *lift*
upsy-daisy 304.27 *alley-oop!*
up the ante 69.10 *play*
up the chute 357.15 *destroyed*
up-the-middle hit 48.5 *batting terms*
up the pole 461.11 *insane*; 561.16 *reproductive*
up the river 251.15 *detained*; 815.8 *imprisoned*
up the spout 561.16 *reproductive*
up the stick 561.16 *reproductive*
upthrow 366.1 *raise*; 366.6 *raising*; 304.2 *upturn*
upthrust 366.6 *raising*
uptight 117.14 *conformist*; 612.8 *fearful*; 625.4 *irascible*; 251.14, 684.8 *self-restrained*
uptightness 751.1 *disagreement*
up to 119.9 *adequate*; 334.13 *powerful*
up to date 447.12 *topically*
up-to-date 302.17 *forward*; 693.18 *informed*; 6.19 *knowledgeable*; 295.10 *new*; 282.6 *present*; 447.6 *topical*
up-to-dateness 282.4; 295.1 *newness*
up to everything 645.4 *cunning*
up to here with 232.8 *full*
up to no good 800.5 *dishonourable*
up to now 284.23 *before now*
up to one's ass 342.19 *busy*
up to one's ears 342.19 *busy*
up to one's eyes 342.19 *busy*; 156.16 *deep*
up to one's neck 342.19 *busy*
up to par 801.12 *all right*
up to snuff 235.5 *not bad*; 217.1 *sufficient*
up to something 800.5 *dishonourable*; 484.15 *planning*
up to the ears 232.10 *fully*
up to the eyes 232.10 *fully*
up to the knees 154.19 *high*
up to the mark 119.9 *adequate*; 235.5 *not bad*; 217.1 *sufficient*
up to the minute 447.12 *topically*
up-to-the-minute 447.6 *topical*
up to the neck 232.10 *fully*
up to the shoulders 154.19 *high*
up to the waist 154.19 *high*
up to this moment 284.23 *before now*
up to this time 284.23 *before now*
uptown 87.7 *city district*; 324.14 *directed*; 324.11 *in all directions*; 86.18 *local*; 304.26 *up*; 87.14 *urban*; 86.10 *urban area*
uptowner 87.11 *urbanite*
uptrend 304.2 *upturn*
uptrending 366.6 *raising*
upturn 304.2; **304.21**; 244.5 *improvement*; 393.11 *recuperation*; 213.2 *spread*
upturned 304.22 *ascending*
up-unweighting 68.4 *skiing technique*
uPVC 32.21 *polymer*
upward 304.22 *ascending*; 300.17 *directional*; 2.14 *socioeconomic*
upward curve 213.2 *spread*
upwardly mobile 248.8 *prosperous*
upward mobility 244.5 *improvement*; 654.2 *social ambition*; 2.7 *social stratification*
upward motion 300.7 *ascending motion*; 304.1 *ascent*
upwards 154.20 *higher*; 304.26 *up*
upwards of 207.6 *plural*
upward trend 213.2 *spread*
up-welling 30.13 *ocean current*
upwind 304.13 *ascend*; 324.14 *directed*; 324.11 *in all directions*; 501.7 *odourlessly*
upwind of 501.3 *odourless*
upwith 304.22 *ascending*; 304.26 *up*
up you get 342.23 *rise and shine!*
ura 52.10 *aikido*
uracil 34.12 *molecular biology*; 33.10 *nucleoside*
Ural-Altaic 5.11 *family of languages*
Uralian ndi 5.11 *family of languages*
Urals 154.4 *mountain range*
Uranian 29.36 *astronomical*
uranic 32.34 *elemental*
uranium 435.1 *materials*; 437.7 *nuclear power*; 28.73 *nuclear reactor*
uranium–lead dating 30.42 *dating*
uranographer 29.2 *astronomer*
uranographic 29.36 *astronomical*
uranography 29.1 *astronomy*
uranous 32.34 *elemental*
Uranus 29.16 *planet*
uranyl 32.34 *elemental*
urban 87.14; 2.13 *communal*; 565.15 *environmental*; 86.17 *national*; 564.12 *native*; 319.5 *transportable*
urban area 86.10
urban blight 245.9 *dilapidation*
urban clearway 320.2 *road*
urban complex 87.1 *city*
urban culture 2.5 *society*
urban dweller 87.11 *urbanite*
urbane 658.7 *courteous*; 645.4 *cunning*; 658.8 *good-mannered*; 6.20, 549.5 *refined*; 421.6 *smooth-mannered*; 654.15 *sociable*
urbanely 6.27 *discerningly*; 658.15 *genteelly*; 421.16 *suavely*
urban environment 2.5 *society*
urban guerrilla 382.10 *killer*; 662.10, 753.5 *seditionist*
urbanism 2.5 *society*
urbanite 87.11; 564.4 *townsman*
urbanities 658.3 *courtesies*
urbanity 549.1 *elegance*; 658.2 *good manners*; 6.11 *refinement*
urbanization 87.1 *city*; 2.5 *society*
urbanize 87.15; 2.15 *socialize*
urbanized 2.13 *communal*
urbanizing 2.13 *communal*
urban myth 17.2 *fiction*
urban planning 38.17 *civil engineering*; 2.5 *society*
urban renewal 2.5 *society*
urban sector 2.5 *society*
urban society 2.5 *society*
urban sociology 2.1 *sociology*
urban sprawl 377.7 *sprawl*; 86.10 *urban area*
urban spread 87.1 *city*
urceole 10.14 *sacred object*
urchin 258.6 *dirty person*; 555.7 *young man*
urea 560.6 *urine*
urea-formaldehyde 435.1 *materials*
ureter 308.7 *passageway*
ureteroscope 35.7 *diagnosis*
ureteroscopy 35.7 *diagnosis*
urethra 308.4 *body orifice*
urge 713.5 *advise*; 386.6 *compel*; 36.15, 386.1 *compulsion*; 461.4 *delusion*; 617.1 *desire*; 726.6 *emphasize*; 262.4 *haste*; 262.1 *hasten*; 331.1 *impel*; 638.10 *insist*; 480.15 *persuade*; 476.6 *propound*; 710.6 *request*
urged 483.12 *motivated*
urge forward 332.7 *hurry someone up*
urgency 254.5 *danger*; 726.1 *emphasis*; 262.4 *haste*; 280.1 *immediacy*; 123.1 *importance*; 336.3 *intensity*; 135.3 *needfulness*; 129.2 *priority*; 710.1 *request*
urgent 280.6 *allowing no delay*; 386.9 *compelling*; 135.6 *demanding*; 726.3 *emphatic*; 262.3 *hasty*; 280.5 *immediate*; 123.5 *important*; 336.10 *potent*; 710.9 *requesting*; 638.2 *tenacious*
urgently 336.15 *acutely*; 710.12 *by request*; 386.11 *compellingly*; 726.7 *emphatically*; 262.6 *hastily*; 123.9 *importantly*; 135.12 *in need*
urge on 332.7 *hurry someone up*
urging 480.2 *flattery*; 710.1 *request*
Uriah Heep 388.2 *appeaser*; 367.15 *debasement*; 623.16 *humble person*; 664.3, 677.7 *sycophant*
uric acid 560.6 *urine*
uricosumic 37.17 *stimulating*
Uriel 8.6 *angel*
urinal 560.13 *lavatory*; 767.7 *toilet*
urinalysis 560.3 *urination*
urinary 560.26
urinate 560.17; 371.14 *let out*; 608.13 *relieve oneself*; 433.32 *seep*
urination 560.3; 433.4 *exudate*
urinative 560.26 *urinary*
urine 560.6; 431.3 *body fluid*; 433.4 *exudate*; 503.2 *something that makes an unpleasant smell*
urine sample 35.7 *diagnosis*
urinometer 560.3 *urination*
URL 40.16 *Internet*
Urmia 88.5 *other major lakes*
urn 583.8 *bury*; 24.8 *ceramic object*; 583.4 *funeral objects*; 410.11 *vessel*
urn burial 583.1 *burial*
urned 583.10 *buried*
Urochordata 75.2 *protochordate*
urochordate 75.16 *invertebrate*; 75.2 *protochordate*
Urodela 73.7 *amphibian*
urodele 73.7 *amphibian*
urogenital disease 260.4 *disease*
urological 35.22 *medical*
urologist 35.13 *medical specialist*
urology 35.3 *medical specialty*
uronic acid 33.3 *carbohydrate*
ursid 71.8 *flesh-eating mammal*
Ursidae 71.8 *flesh-eating mammal*
ursine 71.28 *carnivorous*
urticaria 260.13 *skin disease*
us 566.1 *humankind*; 139.12 *I*
usability 237.6; 239.3 *convenience*
usable 237.2; **349.10**; 239.1 *convenient*; 346.10 *operational*; 95.8 *practical*
usably 237.12, 349.11 *usefully*
US administrative council 579.9
usage 632.4 *custom*; 553.4 *design*; 632.1 *habit*; 10.1 *ritual*; 694.4 *type of meaning*; 349.6 *use*; 237.5 *usefulness*
US Air Force 586.29 *air force*
US Army 586.15 *army*
US Constitution 228.4 *stable thing*
US court 16.21
US dish 25.43
Use 349
use 349.1; **349.6**; 340.4 *act*; 340.1 *action*; 797.13 *benefit*; 631.11 *conduct oneself*; 787.2 *consume*; 135.9 *find necessary*; 237.11 *find useful*; 632.1 *habit*; 392.1 *help*; 123.1 *importance*; 244.1 *improve*; 348.1 *instrumentality*; 694.5 *point*; 485.1 *skill*; 664.15 *sponge*; 346.9 *take action*; 237.5 *usefulness*
use a compass 323.9 *navigate*
use a condom 378.9 *block*; 563.9 *practise birth control*
use a credit card 772.10 *buy on credit*
use a crib 719.12 *translate*
use a footpath 317.14 *find one's way*
use aikido techniques 52.13 *practise judo*
use a light hand 648.3 *be lenient*
use a pedestrian crossing 317.14 *find one's way*
use a pony 719.12 *translate*
use as a doormat 387.6 *subject*
use a sextant 323.9 *navigate*
use as one's own 772.8 *adopt*
use a trot 719.12 *translate*
use backspin 56.7 *golf*
use bad language 712.5 *curse*
use bait 55.7 *angle*
use billingsgate 712.5 *curse*
use body language 742.11 *gesture*
use brute force 334.10 *be powerful*; 423.10 *be tough*; 647.6 *suppress*
use bully-boy tactics 651.18 *torment*
use common speech 271.7 *be simple*
used 349.9; **787.13**; 632.14 *habituated*; 351.4 *misused*
used car 349.7 *reused product*
use dead reckoning 323.9 *navigate*
use diplomacy 658.11 *have good manners*
used up 337.9 *dilapidated*; 350.4 *disused*; 335.12 *impotent*; 349.9, 787.13 *used*
use earplugs 505.10 *muffle*
use every muscle 576.8 *exert oneself*
use expletives 712.5 *curse*
use few words 732.7 *keep quiet*
use footwork 54.5 *fence*
use force 334.10 *be powerful*; 336.8 *strengthen*; 380.8 *use violence*
use force against 386.7 *force*
useful 237.1; 797.6 *beneficial*; 239.1 *convenient*; 706.15 *correspondent*; 340.6 *effective*; 569.12 *favourable*; 265.10 *feasible*; 765.15 *gainful*; 392.33 *helpful*; 123.5 *important*; 348.6 *instrumental*; 349.10 *usable*; 346.11 *workable*; 235.4 *worthwhile*
usefully 237.12; **349.11**; **797.26**; 706.26 *correspondingly*; 340.8 *effectively*; 569.20 *favourably*; 392.36 *helpfully*; 348.9 *instrumentally*; 346.13 *operationally*
Usefulness 237
usefulness 237.5; 797.13 *benefit*; 239.3 *convenience*; 706.8 *correspondence*; 392.10 *helpfulness*; 123.1 *importance*; 348.1 *instrumentality*; 349.6 *use*
useful work 38.10 *work*
use gobbledegook 266.3 *make obscure*
use language 5.45
use lateral thinking 443.15 *think about*
useless 238.1; 245.12 *deteriorated*; 247.10 *failed*; 611.7 *futile*; 240.1 *inconvenient*; 335.10 *powerless*; 793.10 *shoddy*; 672.5 *thankless*; 124.4 *trivial*; 350.1 *unused*; 441.9 *waste*; 236.1 *worthless*
useless exercise 342.9 *overactivity*
useless expenditure 441.3 *waste*
useless gesture 340.2 *deed*
uselessly 238.10; 240.6 *inconveniently*; 350.12 *out of use*; 335.14 *powerlessly*; 672.7 *ungratefully*; 247.12 *unsuccessfully*; 441.10 *wastefully*
Uselessness 238
uselessness 238.3; 247.1 *failure*; 335.1 *powerlessness*; 219.3 *superfluity*; 124.7 *triviality*; 236.7 *worthlessness*
useless work 342.9 *overactivity*
use long words 270.5 *be diffuse*; 542.12 *ornament*
use Morse code 742.12 *signal*
use muscle 336.8 *strengthen*
Usenet 40.16 *Internet*
use obscene language 712.5 *curse*
use of machinery 348.1 *instrumentality*
use one's authority 12.11 *govern*
use one's best endeavours 576.8 *exert oneself*
use one's brain 443.12 *think*

use one's brute strength 334.10 *be powerful*
use one's connections 348.5 *find means*
use one's eyes 518.12 *see*
use one's good offices 348.4 *be an instrument*
use one's head 442.13 *be intelligent*; 458.7 *be wise*; 443.12 *think*
use one's imagination 477.14 *imagine*
use one's influence 348.4 *be an instrument*
use one's intelligence 458.7 *be wise*
use one's own initiative 250.16 *be independent*
use people 349.3 *exploit*
use physical force 386.7 *force*
use plain English 271.7 *be simple*
use plain words 308.22 *be open*; 694.10 *mean*
use profanity 712.5 *curse*
user 349.8
user-friendly 265.11 *made easy*; 40.21 *on-line*
use short words 695.5 *simplify*
use sign language 505.8 *be deaf*; 742.11 *gesture*; 730.14 *have difficulty speaking*; 719.12 *translate*
use signs 742.9
use simple language 695.5 *simplify*
use skilfully 485.10 *be skilful*
use soft words 658.10 *be courteous*
use strong words 707.21 *be assertive*
use symbols 742.9 *use signs*
use tact 658.10 *be courteous*
use tactics 340.4 *act*
use terrorist tactics 753.8 *cause mischief*
use the bathroom 608.13 *relieve oneself*
use the knife 394.20 *doctor*
use therapy 393.6 *cure*
use the services of 349.2 *frequent*
use the side entrance 317.14 *find one's way*
use the tradesman's entrance 317.14 *find one's way*
use the vernacular 724.9 *style*
use to advantage 349.3 *exploit*
use tools 438.10
use to the full 349.3 *exploit*
use up 226.8 *cause to cease*; 787.2 *consume*; 349.5 *dispose of*; 135.9 *find necessary*; 245.5 *hurt*; 238.8 *make useless*; 335.7 *remove power from*; 349.1 *use*; 441.1, 681.7 *waste*
use up one's credit 787.1 *expend*
use violence 380.8; 386.7 *force*
use wrongly 351.1 *misuse*
US government 579.12; 12.4 *governing body*
U-shape 176.1 *angle*
U-shaped valley 30.7 *landform*
usher 223.8; 401.3 *attendant*; 570.7 *bridal party*; 631.15 *conduct*; 631.10 *conductor*; 223.15 *escort*; 370.8 *show in*; 21.28 *stagehand*
ushered 223.20 *accompanied*
usherette 21.28 *stagehand*
usher in 129.19 *forecast*; 475.11 *predict*; 769.10 *receive someone*; 370.8 *show in*
using 352.7 *by means of*
using as one's own 772.2 *adoption*
using force 710.12 *by request*
using short words 695.2 *simple*
using simple language 695.2 *simple*
using strength 423.12 *toughly*
using up 441.3 *waste*
US inhabitant 564.10
US judge 16.24
US lakes 88.3
US law officer 16.12
US mountains 89.4
US National Guard 584.2 *the military*
US National War College 584.3 *military training*
US of A 85.7 *United States*
US Open 63.1 *tennis*
US police 16.16
US Postal Service 692.2 *postal communication*
usquebaugh 558.7 *alcoholic drink*
US rivers 90.3
US Savings Bond 780.14 *paper money*
US Soccer Football Association 66.1 *soccer*
US Supreme Court 16.21 *US court*
usual 216.1 *average*; 138.21, 574.3 *common*; 750.15 *conventional*; 140.10 *customary*; 117.15 *everyday*; 407.15, 632.9 *habitual*; 271.1 *simple*; 124.4 *trivial*
usually 138.30; 140.18 *as a rule*; 750.37 *conventionally*; 297.1 *frequently*; 632.19 *habitually*; 216.11 *on average*
usualness 138.5 *averageness*; 295.1 *newness*; 271.4 *simplicity*
usual policy 632.6 *procedure*
usual text 719.1 *interpretation*
usual way 317.1 *way*
usufruct 349.6 *use*
usurer 780.17 *financier*; 765.7 *gainer*; 771.3, 783.5 *lender*; 792.5 *overcharger*
usurious 792.7 *dear*; 771.6 *loaned*
usuriously 792.12 *dearly*
usurp 588.4 *be anarchic*; 661.6 *be insubordinate*; 144.16 *replace*; 773.7 *take*; 12.12 *take authority*; 371.5 *take the place of*; 329.5 *transgress*
usurpation 396.3 *acquisition of power*; 588.1 *anarchy*; 16.41 *lawlessness*; 773.1 *taking*; 329.8 *transgression*
usurp authority 588.4 *be anarchic*
usurper 661.4 *defiant person*; 773.6 *taker*
usurp power 396.20 *take authority*
usurp the throne 12.12 *take authority*
usury 792.4 *extortion*; 765.1 *gain*; 784.4 *interest*; 771.1 *lending*
US Weather Bureau 31.4 *weather forecast*
utensil 438.1 *tool*
utensils 410.16 *crockery*; 438.7 *equipment*
uterine 172.10 *visceral*
uterus 172.4 *insides*; 561.8 *organs of reproduction*; 71.5 *placental mammal*
utilitarian 4.11 *follower of a doctrine*; 392.33 *helpful*; 4.14 *of a philosophy*; 652.6 *philanthropic*; 652.3 *philanthropist*; 95.8 *practical*; 349.9 *used*; 237.1 *useful*
utilitarianism 239.3 *convenience*; 652.2 *public spiritedness*; 4.7 *school of thought*; 237.5 *usefulness*
utilities 790.6 *business costs*
utility 239.3 *convenience*; 392.10 *helpfulness*; 123.1 *importance*; 348.1 *instrumentality*; 349.6 *use*; 237.5 *usefulness*
utility principle 4.8 *philosophical term*
utility room 565.7 *room*
utilizable 348.6 *instrumental*; 349.10 *usable*
utilization 349.6 *use*; 237.5 *usefulness*
utilize 237.11 *find useful*; 349.1 *use*
utilized 349.9 *used*
uti possidetis 763.2 *legal terms*
utmost 121.14 *best*
utmost height 174.1 *summit*
utmost speed 332.8 *speed*
Utopia 610.3 *aspiration*; 477.8 *dreamland*; 17.2 *fiction*; 446.6 *ideal*; 467.2 *overestimate*; 756.4 *promised land*; 619.4 *wonder*
Utopian 4.11 *follower of a doctrine*; 610.5 *hoper*; 446.13 *ideal*; 477.10 *imaginative*; 244.16 *improving*; 4.14 *of a philosophy*; 446.9 *person of ideas*; 652.3 *philanthropist*; 244.12 *reformer*; 96.11 *unrealistic*; 477.9 *visionary*
Utopianism 446.7, 477.7 *idealism*; 244.11 *reformism*; 4.7 *school of thought*; 96.4 *theorization*
utter 707.17 *affirm*; 745.3 *aphorize*; 232.7 *complete*; 739.6 *divulge*; 780.24 *monetize*; 230.1 *perfect*; 255.16 *simple*; 729.11 *speak*; 5.45 *use language*
utterance 729.7; 729.4 *articulation*; 707.2 *statement*
utter bore 620.3 *boring person*; 620.2 *boring thing*
utter defeat 247.2 *defeat*
utter devotion 638.13 *concentration*
uttered 729.16 *speech*; 707.11 *stated*
utterer 729.10 *speaker*
utter failure 357.4 *ruin*
utter loss 766.1 *loss*
utterly 256.20 *clean*; 230.8, 232.9 *completely*; 204.11 *wholly*
utterly bad 236.3 *bad*
utterly detest 594.14 *hate*
utter profanities 594.17 *anger*
U-turn 303.13 *about-turn*; 177.2 *bend*; 224.1 *change*; 306.2 *circuitousness*; 479.6 *equivocation*; 800.2 *faithlessness*; 320.21 *miscellaneous motoring terms*; 306.6 *orbit*; 761.1 *reversion*; 773.2 *taking back*
UVA 28.13 *electromagnetic radiation*; 31.22 *sun*
UVB 28.13 *electromagnetic radiation*; 31.22 *sun*
UV filter 41.20 *filter*
uvula 729.5 *organ of speech*
uxoricide 382.3 *homicide*; 382.11 *murderer*
uxorious 593.17 *loving*
uxoriousness 593.2 *romantic love*
uzi 587.11 *guns*

V-1 587.16 *bomb*; 587.5 *missile weapon*
V-2 587.16 *bomb*; 587.5 *missile weapon*
V-8 juice™ 558.6 *soft drink*
vacancy 463.2 *blankness*; 94.4, 98.3 *emptiness*; 457.1 *lack of intellect*; 308.10 *opportunity*; 124.5 *unimportance*
vacant 98.13; 463.9 *blank*; 457.5 *lacking intellect*; 94.9, 708.21 *nonexistent*; 350.3 *not wanted*; 343.2 *not working*; 308.13 *opened up*; 98.14 *unoccupied*; 218.2 *unprovided*
vacantly 98.20 *absently*; 463.16 *obliviously*; 308.26 *openly*; 457.11 *unintelligently*
vacant moments 580.1 *leisure*
vacate 98.16 *absent oneself*; 98.19 *leave empty*; 605.5 *resign*; 313.2, 355.2 *withdraw*
vacate one's seat 304.16 *stand up*
vacation 263.4 *at ease*; 298.7 *be regular*; 263.1 *ease*; 98.5 *leave of absence*; 226.3, 226.9 *pause*; 757.2 *permit*; 815.4 *prison sentence*; 581.6 *refresher*; 298.5 *regular thing*; 580.2 *time off*
vacation time 15.2 *industrial negotiations*
vaccinate 394.20 *doctor*; 368.2 *inject*; 257.6 *make hygienic*; 35.19 *practise medicine*; 252.10 *protect*
vaccinated 257.4 *hygienic*; 368.13 *injected*; 252.6 *safe*
vaccination 35.6 *health care*; 257.1 *hygiene*; 368.9 *injection*; 394.3 *prophylactic*; 252.2 *protection*
vaccine 394.3 *prophylactic*
vacillate 326.10; **639.5**; 642.5 *be capricious*; 224.7 *be changed*; 227.12 *be irresolute*; 479.2 *equivocate*; 453.19 *hesitate*; 384.25 *stall*
vacillating 326.15; **639.1**; 224.11 *changeable*; 479.11 *equivocating*; 227.14, 453.2 *irresolute*; 337.12 *weak-willed*
vacillatingly 224.15 *changeably*
Vacillation 639
vacillation 326.3; **639.11**; 224.2 *change of mind*; 479.6 *equivocation*; 453.11 *irresoluteness*; 227.2 *irresolution*
vacillatory 326.15 *vacillating*
vacuity 463.2 *blankness*; 94.4, 98.3 *emptiness*; 457.1 *lack of intellect*; 708.8 *nonexistence*; 417.3 *sparseness*
vacuole 34.8 *cell organ*
vacuous 463.9 *blank*; 457.5 *lacking intellect*; 708.21 *nonexistent*; 417.1 *sparse*; 98.13 *vacant*
vacuously 98.20 *absently*; 463.16 *obliviously*; 417.7 *sparsely*; 457.11 *unintelligently*
vacuousness 417.3 *sparseness*
vacuum 256.13 *clean*; 94.4, 98.3 *emptiness*; 417.5 *gas*; 708.8 *nonexistence*; 28.7 *space*; 417.1 *sparse*; 369.14 *suck*; 32.20 *surface chemistry*
vacuum cleaner 256.10 *cleaning object*
vacuum-distil 32.25 *solidify*
vacuum filtration 32.5 *process*
vacuum flask 558.10 *drink container*; 359.2 *preserver*
vacuum gauge 28.88 *barometer*; 32.20 *surface chemistry*
vacuuming 256.2 *cleaning*; 369.4 *sucking*
vacuum-packed 309.12 *closed*; 252.7 *invulnerable*; 230.1 *perfect*
vacuum-packed food 557.7 *food*; 359.3 *preserved thing*
vacuum pump 369.9 *extractor*; 32.20 *surface chemistry*
vacuum-sealed 252.7 *invulnerable*
vacuum tube 334.7 *electrical power*
vade mecum 693.5 *reference book*
va-et-vien 326.1 *oscillation*
vagabond 655.7 *outsider*
vagary 118.6 *deviation*; 477.4 *ideality*; 697.3 *tomfoolery*; 642.3 *whim*
vagina 308.4 *body orifice*; 561.8 *organs of reproduction*
vaginal 561.16 *reproductive*
vagrancy 325.16 *wandering*
vagrant 710.5 *beggar*; 227.13 *changeable*; 258.6 *dirty person*; 118.7 *nonconformist*; 343.8 *nonworker*; 227.7 *person who moves around*; 782.10 *poor person*; 325.25 *wandering*
vague 696.4 *difficult*; 479.10 *equivocal*; 138.20 *generalized*; 728.16 *imperceptible*; 453.6 *indeterminate*; 524.6 *murky*; 736.17 *noncommittal*; 266.2 *obscure*; 528.2 *shady*; 161.5 *shapeless*; 732.2 *sparing with words*; 420.5 *unfinished*; 96.8 *unreal*
vaguely 524.12 *dimly*; 728.27 *imperceptibly*; 420.15 *incompletely*; 453.25 *indeterminately*; 266.4 *obscurely*
Vagueness 270
vagueness 479.5 *equivocalness*; 736.5 *evasion*; 728.7 *imperceptibility*; 452.19, 453.14 *indeterminacy*; 524.2 *murk*; 266.1 *obscurity*; 420.10 *rough idea*; 161.1 *shapelessness*
vague suspicion 476.3 *conjecture*
Vaikuntha 8.11 *heaven*
vain 673.8; 622.17 *conceited*; 683.5 *egoistic*; 238.2, 611.7 *futile*; 686.9 *self-absorbed*
vain attempt 247.1 *failure*
vain expectation 604.1 *disappointment*
vainglorious 622.17 *conceited*; 673.10 *self-admiring*
vaingloriously 673.19 *vainly*
vaingloriousness 673.4 *self-admiration*
vainglory 622.3 *conceit*
vain labour 766.3 *waste*
vainly 673.19; 683.9 *egoistically*; 467.7 *overoptimistically*
vainness 673.1 *vanity*
vain person 673.7; 738.12 *displayer*; 622.13 *proud person*
vain pride 673.1 *vanity*
vair 743.8 *heraldic device*
Vaisesika 4.7 *school of thought*
valance 550.10 *bed covering*; 164.2 *edging*
valanced 164.9 *skirting*
Valaskjalf 8.11 *heaven*
vale 183.2 *concave land*; 92.6 *lowland*; 92.8 *valley*
valediction 658.3 *courtesies*; 313.9 *parting*; 733.2 *salutation*
valedictorian 769.5 *recipient*; 246.4 *successful person*
valedictory 313.11 *departing*; 313.9 *parting*; 733.2 *salutation*; 729.8 *speech*; 733.14 *vocative*
valedictory address 313.9 *parting*; 733.2 *salutation*
valence 32.12
valence band 28.44 *semiconductor*
valence bond 32.11 *chemical bond*
valence-bond theory 32.12 *valence*
valency 32.12 *valence*
valentine 593.11 *loved one*; 593.15 *love item*
valentines 759.3 *something in exchange*
vale of tears 798.2 *affliction*
valet 551.28; 401.3 *attendant*; 256.13 *clean*; 393.3 *restore*
valeta 22.2 *dance*
valeting 359.1 *preservation*
valetudinarian 260.19 *sick person*; 260.21 *unhealthy*
valetudinarianism 260.1 *ill health*
Valhalla 8.11 *heaven*; 101.1 *nonmaterial world*; 756.4 *promised land*
valiance 613.1 *courage*
valiant 613.9 *courageous*
valiant effort 353.5 *attempt*
valiantly 353.10 *ambitiously*; 613.18 *courageously*
valid 698.19 *authentic*; 444.10 *causal*; 3.19 *chronicled*; 801.8 *correct*; 16.44 *legal*; 27.86 *logical*; 334.14 *operative*; 750.18 *permitting*; 95.6 *real*; 237.2 *usable*
valid argument 27.64 *reasoning*
validate 707.19 *confirm*; 750.28 *consent*; 95.12 *establish reality*; 16.65 *make legal*; 228.7 *make stable*; 757.3 *permit*; 703.17, 716.12 *prove*; 698.30 *prove true*; 27.89 *theorize*; 454.1 *verify*
validated 750.18 *permitting*; 698.20 *proved*; 707.13 *supported*; 454.10 *verified*
validating 454.9 *verificatory*
validation 698.7, 707.4 *confirmation*; 16.31 *legislation*; 757.1 *permission*; 27.64 *reasoning*; 454.4 *verification*
validatory 707.10 *affirmative*
validity 698.6 *authenticity*; 452.9 *certainty*; 801.2 *correctness*; 3.14 *historicalness*; 16.28 *legality*; 334.1 *power*; 95.1 *reality*; 27.64 *reasoning*
validly 16.81 *legally*; 3.25 *reportedly*

valid point 444.4 *explanation*
valise 410.9 *baggage*
Valium™ 394.8 *drug*
Valkyrie 586.10 *woman soldier*
valley 92.8; 183.2 *concave land*; 156.4 *deep thing*; 146.3 *gulf*; 30.7 *landform*; 155.2 *lowlands*
valley floor 30.7 *landform*
Valley Girl 235.7 *elite*
valley glacier 30.38 *glacier*
valley wind 31.12 *wind*
vallum 384.11 *fortification*
valorization 790.7 *tax*
valorous 613.9 *courageous*
valour 613.1 *courage*
valse 22.2 *dance*
valuable 235.3; **792.8**; 392.34 *beneficial*; 797.1 *good*; 123.5 *important*; 237.4 *profitable*
valuableness 792.6 *value*
valuables 440.5 *personal estate*
valuably 792.13
valuate 790.11 *price*
valuation 209.3 *gradation*; 464.1 *judgment*; 26.1 *measurement*; 790.2 *value*
valuator 26.9 *measurer*
value 790.2; **792.6**; 789.7 *account*; 669.11 *approve*; 209.1 *degree*; 119.3 *equalization*; 464.12 *estimate*; 797.8 *good*; 529.3 *hue*; 123.1 *importance*; 593.23 *love*; 123.8 *make important*; 694.1 *meaning*; 26.10 *measure*; 27.14 *operation*; 694.5 *point*; 790.11 *price*; 667.15 *respect*; 26.4 *size*; 237.6 *usability*; 235.6 *worth*; 622.8 *worthiness*
value-added tax 13.6 *economic factors*; 788.2 *money received*
valued 209.7 *gradational*; 26.13 *measured*; 790.14 *priced*; 667.12 *respected*; 235.3 *valuable*; 235.1 *worthy*
valued at 790.14 *priced*
value for money 793.1 *cheapness*
value judgment 464.1 *judgment*; 4.2 *philosophical system*; 4.8 *philosophical term*
valueless 793.10 *shoddy*; 124.4 *trivial*; 238.1 *useless*; 236.1 *worthless*
valuer 464.5 *judge*; 26.9 *measurer*
values 2.3 *social environment*; 19.4 *treatment*
value system 4.2 *philosophical system*; 2.3 *social environment*
valuta 14.1, 780.7 *finance*
valve 334.7 *electrical power*; 39.20 *electron tube*; 309.2 *stopper*
valvular lesion 260.10 *cardiovascular disease*
vambrace 384.7 *armour*
vamoose 98.18 *abscond*; 526.2 *depart*; 389.5 *escape*; 313.15 *go!*; 371.33 *go away!*; 313.4 *hurry off*
vamoosed 98.9 *away*
vamp 363.6 *charmer*; 593.26 *court*; 478.3 *improvise*; 593.9 *lover*; 483.7 *motivator*; 480.13 *tempter*
vampire 11.11 *ghost*; 773.6 *taker*
vampiric 11.15 *witchlike*
vampirish 11.15 *witchlike*
vampirism 11.3 *witchcraft*
vamp up 244.1 *improve*
van 586.14 *armed forces*; 295.6 *avant-garde*; 410.10 *cart*; 316.5 *means of transport*; 321.6 *rolling stock*; 63.4 *tennis terms*; 320.20 *truck*
vanadic 32.34 *elemental*
vanadous 32.34 *elemental*
Van Allen belt 434.3 *atmospheric layers*
Van Allen belts 29.16 *planet*; 30.47 *radiation belt*
vandal 234.5 *defacer*; 357.6, 441.7 *destroyer*; 651.8 *malefactor*; 408.11 *troublemaker*; 380.4 *violent creature*
vandalism 651.2 *cruelness*; 441.4 *destruction*; 357.3 *destructiveness*; 408.8 *lawlessness*; 380.2 *physical violence*; 662.2 *violation of the law*
vandalize 662.15 *be disobedient*; 245.4 *impair*; 357.10, 441.2 *lay waste*
Vandals 284.6 *people of the past*
Van de Graaff accelerator 28.94 *particle accelerator*
Van de Graaff generator 39.30 *generator*
van der Waals equation 28.38 *thermodynamics*
van der Waals force 32.11 *chemical bond*
Vandyke brown 534.4 *brown pigment*
Vandyke collar 551.14 *neckwear*
vane 72.17 *plumage*
vang 50.3 *parts of a sailing boat*
vanguard 586.14 *armed forces*; 295.6 *avant-garde*; 167.1 *front*; 384.14 *guard*; 129.8 *precursor*; 129.2 *priority*; 252.3 *protector*; 711.4 *warner*
vanilla 502.2 *fragrant thing*; 496.5 *herbs*
vanish 98.18 *abscond*; 521.7 *become invisible*; 278.4 *be transient*; 94.12 *cease to exist*; 736.11 *conceal oneself*; 526.1 *disappear*; 389.5 *escape*; 377.11 *explode*; 195.8 *not exist*; 27.94 *order*; 313.3 *quit*
vanished 98.9 *away*; 526.7 *disappeared*; 94.11 *no more*; 195.7 *null*
vanisher 521.5 *invisible thing*
vanishing 526.4 *disappearance*; 526.6 *disappearing*; 389.1 *escape*; 521.4 *invisibility*
vanishing cream 521.5 *invisible thing*; 255.3 *purifier*
vanishing into thin air 389.1 *escape*
vanishing point 310.3 *convergent view*; 526.4 *disappearance*; 145.3 *distant place*; 41.18 *exposure time*; 521.6 *that which makes invisible*; 19.4 *treatment*
vanishing trick 526.4 *disappearance*
vanish into thin air 278.4 *be transient*; 736.11 *conceal oneself*; 389.5 *escape*
vanishment 98.2 *disappearance*
vanitas 19.10 *art subject*
Vanity 673
vanity 673.1; 622.3 *conceit*; 683.2 *egoism*; 238.4 *futility*; 467.1 *overestimation*; 686.4 *self-absorption*
vanity of vanities 238.4 *futility*
vanquish 246.9 *be victorious*; 387.7 *defeat*; 400.14 *master*
vanquisher 246.5 *victorious person*
vantage 121.3 *advantage*
vantage ground 121.3 *advantage*; 334.1 *power*; 631.9 *tactics*
vantage point 397.8; 121.3 *advantage*; 154.8 *high thing*
vapid 728.17 *insipid*
vapidity 728.8 *insipidness*; 497.1 *tastelessness*
vapidly 728.26 *insipidly*
vapidness 497.1 *tastelessness*
vaporescent 432.23 *volatile*
vaporific 432.23 *volatile*
vaporimeter 432.15; 26.8 *meter*
vaporing 432.19 *smoky*
vaporizable 432.23 *volatile*
vaporization 432.10; 377.3 *dilution*; 526.4 *disappearance*; 415.5 *lightness*; 369.7 *obtaining an extract*; 28.37 *temperature*; 441.3 *waste*
vaporize 527.11 *be transparent*; 493.15 *burn*; 94.13 *cause not to exist*; 526.3 *cause to disappear*; 357.8 *destroy*; 377.14 *dilute*; 428.17 *dry*; 432.25 *gasify*; 371.14 *let out*; 415.10 *lighten*; 417.6 *make sparse*; 358.1 *obliterate*; 369.17 *obtain an extract*; 32.25 *solidify*; 441.1 *waste*
vaporized 377.27 *dilute*; 358.6 *obliterated*
vaporizer 432.11; 433.12 *sprinkler*
vaporosity 432.7 *gaseousness*
vaporous 432.16 *gaseous*; 477.12 *imaginary*; 417.1 *sparse*; 527.2 *translucent*
vaporously 432.28 *aerily*
vaporousness 432.7 *gaseousness*; 527.6 *translucency*
vapour 477.5 *fantasy*; 432.1 *gas*; 432.7 *gaseousness*; 500.1 *odour*; 527.8 *transparent thing*; 433.3 *wateriness*
vapourability 432.8 *volatility*
vapourable 432.23 *volatile*
vapour bath 256.6 *bath*
vapouriness 432.7 *gaseousness*
vapourish 432.16 *gaseous*
vapourizability 432.8 *volatility*
vapour-like 432.16 *gaseous*
vapourous 32.32 *solid*
vapour pressure 28.10 *force*
vapour trail 716.4 *indication*
vapoury 432.16 *gaseous*
variability 642.2 *caprice*; 453.16 *capriciousness*; 227.1 *changeableness*; 114.1 *diversity*; 639.12 *inconstancy*; 120.1 *inequality*; 299.1 *irregularity*
variable 27.25 *algebraic expression*; 453.8, 642.1 *capricious*; 224.11, 227.13, 639.2 *changeable*; 227.3 *changeable thing*; 222.7 *circumstantial*; 114.5 *diverse*; 27.77 *given*; 299.4 *irregular*; 194.1 *number*; 203.5 *numbers*; 203.6 *quantitative*; 120.3 *unequal*
variableness 299.1 *irregularity*
variable point 27.36 *point*
variable resistor 39.17 *resistor*
variable star 29.12; 29.10 *star*
variable wind 31.13 *wind strength*
variably 453.27 *capriciously*; 224.15, 227.15 *changeably*; 114.10 *diversely*; 299.8 *irregularly*; 203.7 *quantitatively*; 222.16 *relatively*; 120.7 *unequally*
variance 751.3 *difference*; 116.1 *dissimilarity*
variant 118.17 *abnormal*; 227.13 *changeable*; 118.6 *deviation*; 751.10 *different*
variant reading 719.1 *interpretation*
variate 27.77 *given*
variation 224.1 *change*; 325.13 *deviation*; 116.1 *dissimilarity*; 114.1 *diversity*; 136.5 *modification*; 27.60 *parameter*
variational 136.11 *modified*
variational calculus 27.30 *calculus*
varicoloured 541.6 *variegated*
varicose veins 260.10 *cardiovascular disease*
varied 227.13 *changeable*; 224.12 *changed*; 114.5 *diverse*; 68.13 *ice-skating*; 136.11 *modified*
variedly 541.12
variegate 541.11; 114.8 *be diverse*; 224.8 *cause change*; 529.15 *colour*; 412.8 *mix*
variegated 541.6; 227.13 *changeable*; 529.10 *coloured*; 114.5 *diverse*; 412.12 *mixed*; 120.3 *unequal*
variegated thing 541.5
Variegation 541
variegation 541.1; 114.2 *assortment*; 224.1 *change*; 227.1 *changeableness*; 529.2 *colourfulness*; 114.1 *diversity*; 412.3 *miscellany*
variety 224.1 *change*; 227.1 *changeableness*; 116.1 *dissimilarity*; 114.1 *diversity*; 44.5 *gardening*; 68.7 *ice-dancing*; 299.1 *irregularity*; 160.3 *kind*; 137.3 *kingdom*; 412.3 *miscellany*; 207.2 *multiplicity*; 469.6 *selection*; 21.5 *show business*; 721.6 *sort*; 67.11 *swimming*; 34.17 *taxonomy*; 137.4 *type*; 541.1 *variegation*
variety artist 21.29 *entertainer*
variety circuit 21.15 *engagement*
variety diving 67.6 *diving*
variety meat 25.31 *offal*
variety show 692.25 *broadcast material*; 412.3 *miscellany*; 21.7 *show*
variety theatre 21.16 *theatre*
Varilite™ 21.20 *stage lighting*
variola 260.6 *infection*; 260.13 *skin disease*
variola porcina 260.18 *veterinary disease*
variometer 26.8 *meter*
variorum 719.2 *annotation*
various 207.7; 114.6 *assorted*; 116.4 *dissimilar*
variously 116.7 *dissimilarly*; 114.10 *diversely*; 207.10 *plurally*; 120.7 *unequally*
variousness 114.1 *diversity*
various opinions 114.4 *dissension*
varmint 70.2 *animal*
varnish 19.11 *artist's materials*; 256.9 *cleaning agent*; 550.24 *coat*; 550.3 *coating*; 736.8 *conceal*; 96.16 *delude*; 700.12, 700.32 *disguise*; 727.7 *exaggerate*; 727.1 *exaggeration*; 699.14 *façade*; 699.28 *mask*; 529.4 *pigment*; 421.10 *polish*; 359.5 *preserve*; 359.2 *preserver*; 421.11 *smooth*
varnished 550.36 *covered*; 699.39, 700.41 *disguised*; 727.12 *exaggerated*; 421.4 *polished*
varnishing 359.1 *preservation*
varsity 46.19; 6.21 *curricular*
varsity player 49.2 *basketball player*; 46.2 *football player*; 485.4 *skilled person*
Varuna 91.4 *sea god*
vary 642.5 *be capricious*; 227.11 *be changeable*; 224.7 *be changed*; 751.8 *be different*; 114.8 *be diverse*; 299.6 *be irregular*; 120.5 *be unequal*; 453.21 *change*; 325.1 *deviate*; 116.6 *differentiate*; 136.15 *modify*; 27.94 *order*; 326.8 *oscillate*; 639.5 *vacillate*
varying 299.4 *irregular*
vascular 77.16 *taxonomic*
vascular bundle 77.5 *stem*
vascular disease 260.10 *cardiovascular disease*
vascular plant 77.2 *plant*
vas deferens 561.8 *organs of reproduction*
vase 24.8 *ceramic object*; 410.11 *vessel*
vasectomize 335.9 *make impotent*; 563.8 *make infertile*
vasectomized 563.5 *rendered infertile*; 335.13 *unsexed*
vasectomy 563.2 *making infertile*; 335.1 *powerlessness*; 394.12 *surgery*
Vaseline™ 394.9 *balm*
Vaslav Nijinsky 22.14 *famous ballet dancers*
vasoconstrictor 37.4 *drug type*
vasodilator 37.4 *drug type*
vasopressor 37.4 *drug type*
vassal 122.6 *inferior*; 401.7 *slave*
vassalage 387.1 *subjection*
vast 158.15 *big*; 202.2 *immeasurable*; 141.13 *spacious*
vastly 202.11 *immeasurably*; 141.15 *spaciously*
vast majority 205.5 *largest part*
vastness 202.6; 158.2 *bigness*; 141.4 *spaciousness*
VAT 790.7 *tax*
vat 410.12 *bath*; 410.11 *vessel*
vat dye 42.6 *dye*
Vaterland 85.6 *native land*
vates 11.13 *diviner*
vatic 475.13 *predicting*
Vatican 7.10 *priestly dwelling*
vaticinate 475.12 *divine*; 475.11 *predict*
vaticination 475.2 *divination*
vaticinator 475.8 *oracle*
vaudeville 21.5 *show business*
vaudeville artist 21.29 *entertainer*
vaudeville circuit 21.15 *engagement*
vaudeville house 21.16 *theatre*
vaudeville show 21.7 *show*
vaudeville theatre 21.16 *theatre*
vaudevillian 21.29 *entertainer*; 21.40 *tragic*
vault 20.7; 57.10 *compete in gymnastics*; 20.19 *decorate*; 156.4 *deep thing*; 182.3 *dome*; 583.6 *grave*; 154.8 *high thing*; 57.5 *horizontal bar*; 304.5, 304.18 *jump*; 304.8 *lift*; 57.6 *pommel horse*; 253.5 *safe*; 439.4 *storage*; 38.27 *superstructure*
vaulted 20.15; 182.4 *convex*; 177.4 *curved*
vaulter 47.3 *athlete*; 57.9 *gymnasts*
vaulting 57.11 *gymnastic*; 57.5 *horizontal bar*; 304.24 *leaping*; 57.6 *pommel horse*; 20.7 *vault*
vaulting horse 57.6 *pommel horse*
vaulting pit 47.2 *field events*
vault of heaven 29.3 *universe*
vault up 304.17 *spring up*
vaunt 738.1 *display*
V-bottom 50.6, 50.12 *canoeing*
VD 260.14 *venereal disease*
VDU 39.20 *electron tube*; 40.7 *peripheral*
veal 25.20 *meat*
veal calf 43.8 *livestock*
vection 316.2 *transportation*
vectitation 316.2 *transportation*
vector 324.2 *bearing*; 316.9 *disease carrier*; 260.6 *infection*; 27.50 *scalar quantity*; 70.4 *type of animal*
vectoring 322.5 *flight*
vector product 27.50 *scalar quantity*
vector quantity 27.50 *scalar quantity*
vector sum 27.50 *scalar quantity*
vecture 316.2 *transportation*
Veda 7.12 *religious text*
V-E Day 601.5 *anniversary*; 298.6 *annually celebrated day*
vedette 586.14 *armed forces*
Vedic hymn 10.8 *hymn*
veer 227.11 *be changeable*; 299.6 *be irregular*; 189.6 *be oblique*; 31.58 *blow*; 325.1 *deviate*; 144.14 *displace*; 144.1 *displacement*; 299.1 *irregularity*; 323.9 *navigate*; 189.1 *obliqueness*; 303.9 *turn round*
veer around 303.9 *turn round*
veered 144.8 *displaced*
veering 227.1 *changeableness*; 325.15 *deviating motion*; 144.8 *displaced*; 325.21 *indirect*; 299.4 *irregular*; 299.1 *irregularity*; 31.15 *wind direction*
vegan 557.18 *eater*; 557.26 *eating*; 80.4 *fruit eating*; 684.8 *self-restrained*; 684.4 *self-restrained person*
veganism 557.5 *eating habit*; 684.1 *self-restraint*
vegetable 25.33; **44.11**; 44.16 *horticultural*; 339.2 *inert person*; 457.8 *nonhuman*; 77.2 *plant*; 77.13 *plantlike*; 457.3 *unintelligent person*
vegetable casserole 25.34 *vegetarian dish*
vegetable chilli 25.34 *vegetarian dish*
vegetable curry 25.34 *vegetarian dish*

vegetable dye 42.6 *dye;* 529.4 *pigment*
vegetable existence 93.9 *mere existence*
vegetable flan 25.34 *vegetarian dish*
vegetable garden 44.2 *garden*
vegetable grower 44.13 *horticulturist*
vegetable growing 44.1 *horticulture*
vegetable juice 558.6 *soft drink*
vegetable kingdom 77.1 *plants*
vegetable life 554.1 *life;* 457.4 *nonhuman existence;* 77.1 *plants*
vegetable market 779.1 *market*
vegetable mill 25.6 *kitchen equipment*
vegetable oil 25.7 *basic ingredient*
vegetable pathology 34.1 *life science*
vegetable peeler 25.6 *kitchen equipment*
vegetable physiology 34.1 *life science*
vegetable remedy 394.2 *medicine*
vegetables 80.1 *fruits;* 223.5 *side-dish*
vegetable soup 25.13 *soup*
vegetal 44.16 *horticultural;* 77.13 *plantlike*
vegetarian 557.18 *eater;* 557.26 *eating;* 80.4 *fruit eating;* 80.8 *fruit-eating;* 684.8 *self-restrained;* 684.4 *self-restrained person*
vegetarian diet 557.6 *nutrition*
vegetarian dish 25.34
vegetarianism 557.5 *eating habit;* 80.4 *fruit eating;* 684.1 *self-restraint*
vegetate 77.21; 190.6 *become bigger;* 77.22 *be dormant;* 343.12 *be inactive;* 339.4 *be inert;* 301.8 *be motionless;* 93.21 *merely exist;* 341.4 *not act*
vegetating 93.16; 339.5 *inert;* 301.5 *sedentary*
vegetation 190.1 *growth;* 341.1 *inaction;* 339.1 *inertness;* 93.9 *mere existence;* 301.1 *motionlessness;* 457.4 *nonhuman existence;* 77.1 *plants*
vegetation spirit 8.5 *deity*
vegetative 44.16 *horticultural;* 457.8 *nonhuman;* 77.13 *plantlike*
veggie 557.18 *eater*
vehemence 624.4 *anger;* 707.6 *assertiveness;* 590.4 *emotion;* 726.1 *emphasis;* 342.4 *energy;* 336.2 *healthiness;* 380.1 *violence*
vehement 707.14 *assertive;* 726.3 *emphatic;* 590.13 *passionate;* 336.10 *potent;* 338.4 *vigorous;* 380.6 *violent;* 493.12 *warm-hearted*
vehemently 726.7 *emphatically;* 707.25 *explicitly;* 380.10 *violently;* 590.20 *with feeling*
vehicle 348.2 *instrument;* 352.1 *means;* 316.5 *means of transport;* 21.2 *play;* 37.5 *prescription*
veil 550.5 *body covering;* 736.8 *conceal;* 550.16, 700.12, 700.32 *disguise;* 83.4 *fungal body;* 551.15 *headgear;* 550.31 *hide;* 523.14 *make dark;* 524.10 *make dim;* 521.8 *make invisible;* 524.2 *murk;* 11.20 *occult;* 521.6 *that which makes invisible;* 7.11 *vestment*
veiled 736.14 *concealed;* 700.41 *disguised;* 172.12 *internalized;* 524.6 *murky;* 521.3 *private;* 550.37 *protected*
veiling 736.3 *covering up*
veil of cloud 31.20 *cloud appearance*
vein 412.4 *admixture;* 229.2 *attitude;* 270.1 *diffuseness;* 411.1 *layer;* 77.6 *leaf;* 32.24 *ore;* 308.7 *passageway;* 439.2 *resource;* 221.4 *state of mind;* 724.1 *style;* 541.11 *variegate*
veined 541.9 *striped*
Velcro 373.8 *fastening*
Velcro™ 551.24 *part of garment*
veld 141.3 *geographical space;* 81.2 *grassland;* 92.6 *lowland*
veliger 75.13 *invertebrate larva*
velites 586.8 *soldier*
vellicate 327.24 *shake*
vellication 327.8 *spasm*
vellicative 327.19 *convulsive*
vellum 435.1 *materials*
velo 23.11 *woodworking tool*
velocipede 320.12 *bicycle*
velocity 262.4 *haste;* 342.3 *nimbleness;* 300.8 *rapid motion;* 332.8 *speed;* 28.8 *time*
velocity ratio 38.10 *work*
velour 421.8 *smooth thing*
velouté 25.15 *sauce*
velutinous 404.11 *fluffy*
Velvet 59.1 *horse*
velvet 265.6 *easy thing;* 419.3 *smooth;* 421.8 *smooth thing;* 419.11 *soft thing;* 193.4 *textile*
velveteen 421.8 *smooth thing;* 419.11 *soft thing;* 193.4 *textile*
velvet glove 648.1 *leniency;* 631.8 *treatment*
velvetiness 419.9, 421.7 *smoothness*
velvetlike 419.3 *smooth*
velvety 404.11 *fluffy;* 516.6 *melodious;* 419.3, 421.1 *smooth*
venal 800.5 *dishonourable*
venality 800.1 *improbity*
vend 767.11 *dispose of property;* 778.1 *sell*
vendee 777.12 *purchaser*
vendetta 242.8 *quarrel*
vendibility 778.7 *market*
vendible 778.8 *merchandise;* 778.15 *saleable*
vending 778.3 *selling*
vending machine 557.15 *eating place;* 779.9 *stall*
vendition 778.3 *selling*
vendor 778.9 *seller;* 776.10 *trader*
vendue 778.4 *sale*
veneer 411.3, 550.24 *coat;* 550.3 *coating;* 525.3 *external appearance;* 700.3 *hypocrisy;* 411.10 *layer;* 157.4 *shallow thing;* 23.18 *work wood*
veneered 411.8 *coated*
veneer furniture 23.1 *furniture*
veneering 23.1 *furniture*
Venera 29.33 *planetary probe*
venerability 622.6 *majesty*
venerable 556.14 *aged;* 296.11 *old;* 296.12 *olden;* 667.13 *respectable;* 622.19 *stately*
venerableness 296.1 *oldness*
venerably 296.18; 296.21 *archaically;* 622.36 *majestically;* 556.16 *maturely*
venerate 7.19 *be religious;* 10.19 *offer worship;* 667.16 *revere;* 9.7 *worship*
venerated 9.11 *worshipped*
veneration 667.2 *admiration;* 7.2 *religiousness;* 10.3 *rite of worship;* 9.1 *worship*
venerational 667.10 *reverent;* 9.9 *worshipful*
venerative 667.10 *reverent*
venerator 9.5, 10.17 *worshipper*
venereal 260.23 *diseased*
venereal disease 260.14; 260.4 *disease*
venereal ulcer 260.14 *venereal disease*
venereologist 35.13 *medical specialist*
venereology 35.3 *medical specialty*
venery 593.5 *desire;* 71.23 *mammal hunting;* 796.3 *sexual immorality*
venesection 371.22 *disgorgement;* 369.4 *sucking;* 394.12 *surgery*
Venetian blind 550.12 *protective covering;* 523.6 *shade*
Venetian red 535.6 *red pigment*
vengeance 385.1 *retaliation;* 714.4 *revenge*
vengeful 651.13 *merciless;* 628.4 *pitiless;* 385.5 *retaliatory;* 714.14 *vindictive*
vengefully 628.7 *pitilessly;* 714.16 *vindictively*
vengefulness 651.4 *bitterness*
venial 804.13; 649.7 *forgivable;* 124.1 *unimportant;* 714.13 *vindicable*
venially 649.14 *forgivingly;* 714.15 *in vindication*
venial sin 804.3; 806.3 *sin;* 124.8 *trifle*
venison 25.20 *meat*
Venn diagram 409.8 *chart*
venoclysis 37.12 *injection*
venogram 35.7 *diagnosis*
venography 35.7 *diagnosis*
venom 651.4 *bitterness;* 594.1 *hate;* 236.10 *poverty*
venomous 678.16 *defamatory;* 236.5 *harmful;* 594.10 *hating;* 651.14 *hostile;* 714.14 *vindictive*
venomously 594.18 *hatefully;* 714.16 *vindictively*
venomousness 651.4 *bitterness;* 236.11 *harmfulness*
venomous snake 73.3 *snake*
venous 308.15 *providing passage*
venous blood 431.4 *blood*
venously 308.27 *cavernously*
vent 739.6 *divulge;* 389.2 *means of escape;* 315.7 *outlet;* 308.7 *passageway;* 308.21 *provide passage for;* 371.11 *void;* 30.24 *volcanic activity*
ventage 315.7 *outlet*
venter 82.4 *moss plant*
venthole 315.7 *outlet*
ventilate 434.20 *aerate;* 501.5 *deodorize;* 739.6 *divulge;* 494.12 *make cold;* 257.6 *make hygienic;* 740.13 *make public;* 255.10, 256.15 *purify;* 581.1 *refresh*
ventilated 434.17; 257.4 *hygienic;* 501.3 *odourless;* 740.19 *published*
ventilating system 434.7 *ventilator*
ventilation 434.6; 256.2 *cleaning;* 501.1 *odourlessness;* 740.1 *publication;* 255.2 *purification;* 581.5 *refreshment;* 257.2 *salubrity*
ventilator 434.7; 494.4 *cooler;* 501.2 *deodorant*
vent one's anger 624.13
vent one's rancour 624.13 *vent one's anger*
vent one's spleen 624.13 *vent one's anger*
ventre à terre 332.14 *swiftly*
ventriloquism 729.4 *articulation;* 700.9 *sleight of hand*
ventriloquist 21.29 *entertainer;* 125.7 *imitator*
ventriloquize 700.29 *juggle*
Ventura™ 40.11 *application*
venture 353.6; 613.15 *be courageous;* 346.3, 776.6 *business;* 254.5 *danger;* 254.10 *endanger;* 448.1 *experiment;* 254.9 *face danger;* 448.13 *invent;* 14.5 *invest;* 453.22 *risk;* 342.2 *social activity;* 776.2 *speculate;* 353.3 *tackle;* 107.12 *take a chance;* 354.1 *undertake;* 354.2 *undertaking*
ventured 448.10 *tested*
venture on 354.1 *undertake*
venturesome 613.13 *adventurous;* 353.8 *attempting;* 254.1 *dangerous;* 354.6 *enterprising;* 448.9 *original*
venturesomeness 254.5 *danger*
venture to say 476.6 *propound*
venturous 254.1 *dangerous*
venue 18.28 *concert hall;* 143.1 *situation;* 45.2 *sportsground;* 21.16 *theatre*
Venus 291.4 *evening thing;* 593.16 *gods and goddesses of love;* 290.2 *morning thing;* 29.16 *planet*
Venus flytrap 700.13 *snare*
Venusian 29.36 *astronomical*
Venus's flower basket 75.8 *sponge*
veracious 452.1 *certain;* 801.8 *correct;* 799.4 *honourable;* 698.25 *lifelike;* 646.1 *naive;* 271.3 *natural;* 738.15 *open;* 698.15 *true;* 698.18 *truthful*
veraciously 799.7 *honourably*
veraciousness 698.12 *realism*
veracity 452.9 *certainty;* 801.2 *correctness;* 646.2 *naivety;* 271.6 *naturalness;* 799.1 *probity;* 698.5 *truthfulness*
veranda 565.7 *room*
verb 5.35 *part of speech*
verbal 692.33 *communicational;* 5.44 *grammatical;* 729.17 *oral;* 694.8 *semantic;* 5.40 *translated;* 5.42 *worded*
verbal abuse 651.7 *act of malevolence;* 712.3 *vilification*
verbal attack 670.8 *berating;* 381.16 *personal attack*
verbal diarrhoea 270.1 *diffuseness;* 729.2 *power of speech;* 731.1 *talkativeness*
verbal intercourse 734.1 *conversation;* 729.1 *faculty of speech*
verbalism 5.24 *phrasing*
verbalize 160.7 *form;* 729.11 *speak;* 5.45 *use language;* 5.47 *word*
verbally 5.49 *colloquially;* 729.21 *orally*
verbal translation 5.12 *translation*
verbatim 273.8 *accurately;* 273.6 *correct;* 125.14 *imitatively;* 5.48 *linguistically;* 698.23 *literal;* 698.38 *literally;* 694.13 *meaningfully;* 230.7 *perfectly;* 111.12 *same;* 111.1 *sameness;* 719.17 *translational*
verbatim account 698.10 *literalness*
verbatim et litteratim 698.38 *literally*
verbena 496.5 *herbs*
verbiage 270.1 *diffuseness;* 5.22 *many words;* 266.1 *obscurity;* 729.2 *power of speech*
verbose 270.3 *diffuse;* 148.1 *long;* 731.5 *talkative;* 5.42 *worded*
verbosely 270.7 *diffusely;* 5.50 *lexically*
verboseness 270.1 *diffuseness*
verbosity 270.1 *diffuseness;* 5.22 *many words;* 729.2 *power of speech;* 731.1 *talkativeness*
verboten 16.55 *illegal;* 399.5 *vetoed*
verb phrase 5.23 *phrase*
verbum 5.17 *word*
verdancy 538.8 *greenness*
verdant 538.2; 44.17 *botanical;* 562.5 *fertile;* 81.9 *grassy;* 77.13 *plantlike*
verd antique 538.11 *green thing*
verdantly 538.18 *greenly;* 81.13 *herbivorously;* 44.20 *horticulturally*
verderer 79.8 *forester;* 16.23 *judge*
verdict 464.2; 16.7 *legal trial;* 16.33 *litigation*
verdict of acquittal 714.1 *vindication*
verdict of guilty 16.43 *conviction*
verdict of innocence 805.2 *legal innocence;* 714.1 *vindication*
verdict of not guilty 16.42 *acquittal;* 714.1 *vindication*
verdict of not proven 16.42 *acquittal*
verdigris 245.9 *dilapidation;* 538.11 *green thing*
verditer 538.10 *green pigment*
verdure 81.2 *grassland;* 538.8 *greenness;* 77.1 *plants*
verdured 81.9 *grassy*
verdurous 44.17 *botanical*
Verfremdungseffekt 21.9 *dramaturgy*
verge 164.5 *border;* 164.1 *edge;* 166.3 *furthest point;* 131.7 *limit;* 20.9 *miscellaneous architectural features;* 147.2 *short distance;* 324.7 *take a direction*
verge on 492.12 *abut;* 164.5 *border;* 147.16 *near*
verger 7.8 *priest*
verging 166.6 *furthest*
verging on 147.12 *near*
veridical 698.18 *truthful;* 707.12 *vowed*
veridically 698.36 *truthfully*
verifiability 703.5 *demonstrability*
verifiable 454.8; 452.1 *certain;* 3.19 *chronicled;* 703.12 *demonstrable;* 448.8 *experimental*
verifiably 454.11; 703.22 *demonstrably;* 253.16 *surely*
Verification 454
verification 454.4; 452.13, 698.7, 707.4 *confirmation;* 448.3 *experimentation;* 743.1 *identification;* 757.1 *permission;* 253.2 *promise;* 703.4, 716.2 *proof;* 27.64 *reasoning*
verification principle 4.8 *philosophical term*
verificative 454.9 *verificatory*
verificatory 454.9
verified 454.10; 126.6 *authentic;* 716.8 *evidential;* 743.12 *identified;* 455.10 *known;* 698.20 *proved;* 703.13 *proven;* 707.13 *supported;* 448.10 *tested*
verifier 454.7; 707.9 *affirmer*
verify 454.1; 253.12 *certify;* 210.12 *check;* 707.19 *confirm;* 95.12 *establish reality;* 448.11 *experiment;* 743.10 *identify;* 452.21 *make certain;* 757.3 *permit;* 703.17, 716.12 *prove;* 698.30 *prove true*
verifying 448.8 *experimental*
verily 698.35 *truly*
verisimilar 698.25 *lifelike*
verisimilitude 104.3 *plausibility;* 95.3, 698.12 *realism*
verismo 21.10 *theatre movements*
verist 19.29 *realist*
veritable 93.13 *real;* 698.15 *true*
veritably 698.35 *truly*
verity 452.9 *certainty;* 698.1 *truth*
vermeil 535.1 *red*
vermicidal 37.14 *counteracting*
vermicide 382.13 *animal killer;* 37.4 *drug type*
vermicular 75.20 *wormlike*
vermiform 180.4 *convolutional;* 75.20 *wormlike*
vermifugal 37.14 *counteracting*
vermifuge 394.4 *antidote;* 37.4 *drug type*
vermilion 535.1 *red;* 535.6 *red pigment*
vermin 258.4 *dirt;* 76.3 *pest*
verminous 76.12
vermouth 558.8 *mixed drink;* 558.9 *wine*
vernacular 138.21 *common;* 729.1 *faculty of speech;* 724.8 *inelegant;* 5.39 *of language;* 271.1 *simple;* 271.4 *simplicity;* 5.3 *spoken language*
vernacularism 5.26 *dialect;* 5.3 *spoken language*
vernacularize 5.45 *use language*
vernacular language 5.26 *dialect;* 5.3 *spoken language*
vernal 538.4 *fresh;* 292.10 *spring*
vernal equinox 29.5 *celestial sphere;* 10.15 *holy day;* 292.2 *spring*
vernally 292.18 *seasonally*
vernal season 292.2 *spring*
Vernerian 5.38 *linguistic*
Verner's law 5.37 *linguistic theory*
vernier 26.6 *measuring instrument*
vernier scale 28.84 *altimeter*

veronica 10.14 *sacred object*
verruca 260.13 *skin disease*
versatile 227.13 *changeable*; 114.5 *diverse*; 479.11 *equivocating*; 797.5 *proficient*; 485.6 *skilful*; 237.1 *useful*; 207.7 *various*
versatilely 114.10 *diversely*
versatility 227.1 *changeableness*; 114.1 *diversity*; 479.6 *equivocation*; 127.1 *inclusion*; 797.12 *proficiency*; 485.1 *skill*; 237.5 *usefulness*
vers de société 17.6 *poetry*
verse 6.22 *educate*; 205.2 *particular*; 17.8 *part of poem*; 17.7 *poem*; 17.6 *poetry*
versed 6.19, 455.8 *knowledgeable*; 136.9 *qualified*
versed in 485.8 *expert*
verse drama 21.2 *play*
verse epistle 17.7 *poem*
verse form **17.10**; 160.3 *kind*
versemaker 17.14 *author*
versemonger 17.14 *author*
verse paragraph 17.8 *part of poem*
versesmith 17.14 *author*
versicolour 541.6 *variegated*
versification 17.6 *poetry*
versifier 17.14 *author*
versify 17.21 *write*
version 721.1 *description*; 719.1 *interpretation*; 409.9 *musical arrangement*; 719.4 *translation*; 137.4 *type*
vers-librist 17.14 *author*
verso 168.1 *rear*
versus 113.31 *opposed to*
vert 538.1 *green*; 743.13 *heraldic*; 743.8 *heraldic device*
vertebrate 70.15 *of animals*; 70.4 *type of animal*
vertebrates 554.9 *classifications of life*
vertebrate zoologist 70.11 *zoologist*
vertebrate zoology 70.9 *animal science*
vertex 27.39 *angle*; 425.7 *sharp point*; 174.1 *summit*
vertical **186.8**; 27.80 *linear*; 366.11 *raised*; 68.12 *ski*; 178.1 *straight*; 174.5 *top*; 186.3 *vertical thing*
vertical angles 27.39 *angle*
vertical axis 186.3 *vertical thing*
verticale 68.3 *ski racing*
vertical gate 68.3 *ski racing*
Verticality 186
verticality 186.1
vertical-lift bridge 38.21 *bridge*
vertical line 178.7 *straight line*; 186.3 *vertical thing*
vertically **186.11**; 154.20 *higher*; 68.17 *on a ski run*; 178.12 *straight*
vertical machine 38.9 *machine tool*
vertical member 38.27 *superstructure*
vertical movement 30.13 *ocean current*
verticalness 186.1 *verticality*
vertical roll 692.23 *television reception*
vertical thing 186.3
verticillaster 78.4 *flower head*
vertiginous 154.9 *high*; 307.12 *rotary*
vertigo 337.3 *poor health*; 307.1 *rotation*
verve 590.4 *emotion*; 726.1 *emphasis*; 338.1 *vigour*; 334.3 *vitality*
very 209.11 *to a degree*
very beginning 293.3 *early stage*
very best 235.2, 797.2 *best*
very good 235.1 *worthy*
very high frequency 297.6 *radio frequency*
very image 717.6 *image*; 111.3 *lookalike*
very important person 123.4 *bigwig*
Very Large Array 29.26 *radio telescope*
Very light 522.8 *fire*; 742.4 *signal*
very long baseline interferometry 29.26 *radio telescope*
very many 208.6 *many*
very odd 619.8 *wonderful*
very picture 717.6 *image*
Very pistol 742.4 *signal*
Very signal 711.2 *danger signal*
very small 521.2 *difficult to see*
very steep 186.8 *vertical*
very steeply 186.12 *perpendicularly*
very thing 111.1 *sameness*
very tiring 576.11 *laborious*
very top 174.1 *summit*
vesicant 37.4 *drug type*
Vesper 29.10 *star*
vesperal 291.6 *evening*
vesperine 291.6 *evening*
vespers 291.1 *evening*; 10.4 *public worship*
vespiary 76.4 *social insect*
vessel **323.3**; **410.11**; 24.8 *ceramic object*; 410.1 *container*
vest 551.32 *dress*; 768.5 *give*; 750.30 *grant*; 551.11 *jacket*; 16.68 *legislate*; 551.18 *underwear*
vesta 522.8 *fire*; 437.2 *lighter*
vestal 572.4 *celibate person*; 795.9 *pure*; 255.5, 795.5 *pure person*
vestal virgin 572.4 *celibate person*; 255.5, 795.5 *pure person*
vested 551.29 *dressed*; 750.19 *granted*
vested interest 395.1 *influence*
vestibule 20.10 *church architecture*; 167.1 *front*; 314.6 *means of entry*; 20.9 *miscellaneous architectural features*; 565.7 *room*; 317.2 *route*
vestige **744.12**; 3.11 *relic*; 215.1 *remainder*
vestiges 284.7 *thing of the past*
vestigial 175.3 *base*; 3.15 *historic*; 215.9 *remaining*
vestigially 3.25 *reportedly*; 215.11 *residually*
vestiture 551.2 *dressing*
vestment **7.11**; 550.5 *body covering*; 551.3 *formal dress*
vestments 656.4 *formal dress*
vest-pocket 159.7 *little*
vest power in 334.11 *give power*
vestry 10.12 *church*; 579.7 *council*
vesture 551.1 *dress*; 551.3 *formal dress*; 7.11 *vestment*
Vesuvius 493.8 *hot place*
vet 70.10 *animal welfarist*; 464.12 *estimate*; 586.11 *former soldier*; 394.15 *healer*; 59.15 *horse person*; 35.15 *veterinarian*
vetch 43.12 *crop*
veteran 243.20 *developed*; 485.5, 485.8 *expert*; 586.11 *former soldier*; 556.8 *man*; 585.17 *military*; 296.11 *old*; 556.7 *older person*; 585.11 *recruit*
veterinarian **35.15**; 70.10 *animal welfarist*; 394.15 *healer*; 59.15 *horse person*
veterinary 35.22 *medical*; 35.15 *veterinarian*
veterinary clinic 35.5 *veterinary medicine*
veterinary disease 260.18
veterinary medicine 35.5
veterinary nurse 35.15 *veterinarian*
veterinary practice 35.5 *veterinary medicine*
veterinary practitioner 35.15 *veterinarian*
veterinary science 70.8 *animal welfare*
veterinary student 35.15 *veterinarian*
veterinary surgeon 394.15 *healer*; 35.15 *veterinarian*
veterinary surgery 35.5 *veterinary medicine*
veterinary technician 35.15 *veterinarian*
vetiver 502.3 *incense*
Veto 399
veto **399.1**; **399.3**; 708.10 *be negative*; 684.5 *be self-restrained*; 94.13 *cause not to exist*; 397.1, 397.9 *command*; 347.3 *counteract*; 347.1 *counteraction*; 709.2, 709.6 *dissent*; 128.7 *exclude*; 128.1 *exclusion*; 16.35 *illegality*; 166.7 *limit*; 166.2 *limiting factor*; 16.75 *make illegal*; 251.5 *means of restraint*; 670.3 *nonacceptance*; 708.2 *rejection*; 251.8 *restrain*; 251.1 *restraint*; 670.15 *withhold approval*
vetoed **399.5**; 397.14 *commanding*; 670.31 *disapproved*; 708.18 *rejected*
vetoer 708.9 *negativist*
vetting 252.2 *protection*
vex 607.8 *annoy*; 240.5 *be inconvenient*; 236.13 *be worthless*; 328.7 *disturb*; 261.6 *fatigue*; 625.8 *make irascible*; 624.9 *offend*
vexation 607.2 *annoyance*; 240.3 *inconvenience*; 624.1 *resentment*
vexatious 607.5 *aggravating*; 328.17 *disturbing*; 261.4 *fatiguing*; 240.1, 264.13 *inconvenient*
vexatiously 607.10 *annoyingly*; 240.6 *inconveniently*
vexed 328.12 *disturbed*; 624.15 *resentful*; 264.16 *troubled*
vexed question 264.4 *problem*
vexillary 586.6 *militarist*
vexillum 743.7 *flag*
vexing 607.5 *aggravating*; 264.13 *inconvenient*
V-groove 62.5 *rock face*
VHF radio 692.18 *radio*
VHF transmitter 692.16 *transmitter*
via **317.17**; 318.14 *by the way*; 348.9 *instrumentally*
viability 554.4 *biological function*
viable 750.20 *agreeable*; 554.12 *alive*; 34.21 *living*; 102.5 *possible*; 346.11 *workable*
viableness 554.4 *biological function*; 102.2 *possibleness*
viably 554.22 *vitally*
viaduct 38.21, 317.9 *bridge*; 318.5 *crossing point*
vial 410.14 *bottle*
via media 216.5 *medium*
viands 557.7 *food*
via negativa 94.3 *negativeness*
viatical settlement 710.1 *request*
viaticum 10.5 *Christian rite*; 313.9 *parting*
vibes 170.3 *atmosphere*; 590.2 *impression*
vibrancy 326.2 *vibration*
vibrant 510.8 *deep*; 338.4 *vigorous*
vibrantly 510.11 *resonantly*
vibrate **326.9**; 227.11 *be changeable*; 509.8 *drum*; 510.9 *resonate*; 112.22 *resound*; 327.24 *shake*
vibratile 326.14 *vibrating*
vibratility 326.2 *vibration*
vibrating **326.14**; 227.13 *changeable*; 300.17 *directional*; 510.6 *resonant*; 327.6 *shaking*; 327.18 *shaky*
vibrating string 28.14 *sound wave*
vibration **326.2**; 300.5 *circuition*; 509.1 *drumming*; 510.1 *resonance*; 112.6 *reverberation*; 327.6 *shaking*; 28.14 *sound wave*; 492.1 *touch*; 28.12 *wave*
vibrational 112.15 *reverberatory*
vibrations 170.3 *atmosphere*
vibrato 18.16 *musical note*; 509.6 *musical repetition*
vibrator 327.14 *agitator*; 39.31 *electric motor*; 365.6 *massage*; 326.7 *oscillator*
vibratory 327.18 *shaky*; 326.14 *vibrating*
vibrissa 71.2 *mammalian characteristic*
vibrograph 326.6 *measuring instrument*
vibroscope 326.6 *measuring instrument*
vicar 760.5 *converter*; 398.4 *deputy*; 7.8 *priest*
vicarage 565.4 *official residence*; 7.10 *priestly dwelling*
vicar-general 398.4 *deputy*
vicariate 7.9 *priesthood*
vicariousness 762.1 *substitution*
Vicar of Bray 479.9 *equivocator*; 227.6 *fickle person*
vicarship 7.9 *priesthood*
vice **804.2**; 631.4 *bad conduct*; 236.9 *badness*; 191.4 *contractor*; 798.1 *evil*; 796.1 *immorality*; 16.38 *lawbreaking*; 247.3 *personal fault*; 796.5 *prostitution*; 806.3 *sin*; 360.3 *tools for gripping*; 802.8 *wrongdoing*
vice admiral 398.4 *deputy*; 586.27 *naval man*
vice chairman 398.4 *deputy*
vice chancellor 398.4 *deputy*; 579.13 *director*; 400.9 *educational leader*; 6.4 *educator*; 396.10 *person of authority*
vice consul 398.6 *agent*; 398.4 *deputy*
vicelike 360.9 *retentive*
vicelike grip 360.1 *retention*
vicenary 201.19 *twentieth*
vicennial 201.19 *twentieth*
vice president 398.4 *deputy*; 579.13 *director*; 12.7 *governor*
viceregent 398.4 *deputy*
viceroy 398.4 *deputy*; 400.3 *leader*
vice squad 796.5 *prostitution*
vice squad member 252.3 *protector*
vice versa 759.8 *in exchange*; 192.4 *inversely*; 110.10 *reciprocally*
vichysoisse 25.13 *soup*
vicinage 147.5 *near place*
vicinal 147.9 *near*
vicinity 97.4 *availability*; 86.13 *locality*; 147.5 *near place*; 170.1 *surroundings*
vicious 236.3 *bad*; 651.11 *cruel*; 798.7 *evil*; 594.10 *hating*; 804.12 *immoral*; 802.16 *in the wrong*; 796.14 *lecherous*; 423.4 *powerful*; 380.6 *violent*; 804.11 *wicked*
vicious circle 132.6 *continuum*; 378.2 *obstacle*
viciously 798.12 *evilly*; 594.18 *hatefully*; 804.18 *wickedly*
viciousness 236.9 *badness*; 651.2 *cruelness*; 798.1 *evil*; 796.1 *immorality*; 423.8 *physical strength*; 804.1 *wickedness*
vicissitude 224.1 *change*; 227.1 *changeableness*
victim 668.9 *butt*; 582.11 *dead person*; 700.22 *dupe*; 247.5 *failing person*; 766.6 *loser*; 465.6 *misjudged person*; 249.5 *person in adversity*; 769.5 *recipient*; 633.7 *the hunted*; 337.4 *weakling*
victimization 651.5 *intolerance*; 607.3 *nuisance*; 814.7 *punishment*; 647.2 *suppression*; 700.7 *tricking*
victimize 236.14 *ill-treat*; 814.1 *punish*; 647.6 *suppress*; 651.18 *torment*; 700.28 *trick*
victimized 700.36 *deceived*; 647.9 *suppressed*
victimless crime 16.39 *crime*
victim of discrimination **466.8**; 128.5 *excluded person*
victim of fate 249.5 *person in adversity*
victim of oppression 466.8 *victim of discrimination*
victor 235.8 *exceller*; 121.6 *paragon*; 246.5 *victorious person*
Victoria 88.5 *other major lakes*
Victoria Cross 743.4 *insignia*; 794.1 *trophy*
Victorian 23.7 *furniture style*; 3.15, 296.14 *historic*; 795.6 *moralist*; 795.10 *moralistic*; 255.12 *morally pure*; 255.6 *prude*; 228.5 *stable person*
Victoriana 296.5 *old thing*; 3.11 *relic*
Victorian Age 3.10 *past age*
Victorian values 255.1 *purity*
victorious **246.15**; 121.14 *best*
victorious candidate 469.13 *electorate*
victorious general 246.5 *victorious person*
victoriously 246.16 *successfully*; 121.16 *superiorly*
victorious person 246.5
victor ludorum 794.1 *trophy*
Victory 586.25 *historical naval ships*
victory 246.2
victory arch 744.11 *monument*
victory garden 44.2 *garden*
victory gardens 585.7 *war measures*
victory laurels 743.4 *insignia*
victory roll 322.5 *flight*
victual 557.25 *provide food*; 436.5 *provision*
victualled 436.8 *provisional*
victualler 436.3 *provider*
victualling 436.1 *provision*
victuals 557.7 *food*; 436.2 *provisions*
vicuna 193.4 *textile*
vid 41.21 *photograph*; 744.7 *recording*
videlicet 719.18 *in other words*; 139.31 *namely*
video 692.30 *communicate*; 41.21 *photograph*; 692.26 *recording*; 717.2 *reproduction*; 692.23 *television reception*
video camera 41.16 *camera*; 692.26 *recording*; 744.10 *recording instrument*; 518.8 *reflection*
video cassette 692.26 *recording*
video cassette recorder 115.3 *copier*; 125.6 *photocopier*; 692.26 *recording*; 744.10 *recording instrument*
video collection 439.5 *collection*
videoconference 746.3 *discussion*
videoconferencing 40.12 *electronic office*
videodisc 692.26 *recording*
videoed 692.34 *communicated*
video game 69.1 *game*; 692.26 *recording*
video nasty 796.2 *indecency*; 692.26 *recording*
videophone 692.9 *telephone*
video piracy 774.6 *illegal borrowing*
video pirate 774.10 *infringer*
video recording 125.5 *duplicate*; 692.26 *recording*
video signal 692.21 *television*
video tape 28.64 *magnetic recording*; 692.26, 744.7 *recording*
video-tape 744.13 *record*
video-taped 744.16 *recorded*
video tape recorder 744.10 *recording instrument*
vie 235.9 *be worthy*; 47.6 *compete in track and field*
Vienna 87.6 *other cities*
Vienna circle 4.7 *school of thought*
Vienna sausage 25.29 *sausage*
Viennese waltz 22.2 *dance*; 68.7 *ice-dancing*
vi et armis 386.11 *compellingly*
view **518.7**; 713.1 *advice*; 19.10 *art subject*; 97.12 *attend*; 450.1 *belief*; 590.3 *feelings*; 482.3 *future intention*; 446.5 *ideology*; 518.14 *inspect*; 464.1 *judgment*; 4.1

philosophy; 4.22 *propound a philosophy*; 176.5 *viewpoint*
viewable 518.23, 520.1 *visible*
viewdata 692.25 *broadcast material*; 693.6 *information technology*
viewer 518.11 *observer*; 769.5 *recipient*; 97.5 *someone present*
viewership 740.2 *mass media*
viewfinder 41.18 *exposure time*
view halloo 633.19 *after him!*; 514.5 *hunting cry*; 507.1 *loudness*
viewing 738.6 *display*
viewing figures 740.2 *mass media*
viewing the body 582.8 *after death*; 583.2 *funeral*
vie with 113.19 *confront*
viewpoint **176.5**; **518.9**; 450.1 *belief*; 143.2 *circumstances*; 590.3 *feelings*; 154.8 *high thing*; 446.5 *ideology*; 4.1 *philosophy*
view the body 582.17 *bury*
Viewtron™ 692.25 *broadcast material*
view with disfavour 670.14 *disapprove*
view with jealousy 629.6 *be jealous*
VIFF 322.5 *flight*
vigesimal 201.19 *twentieth*
vigil 665.5 *watchfulness*
vigilance 471.3 *carefulness*; 616.1 *caution*; 665.3 *circumspection*; 629.2 *distrust*; 665.5 *watchfulness*
vigilance committee 16.2 *jurisdiction*
vigilant 342.18 *active*; 665.9 *careful*; 616.4 *cautious*; 629.5 *distrustful*; 474.5 *expecting*; 243.18 *prepared*; 518.21 *seeing*; 640.11 *steady*; 252.8 *tutelary*; 471.7 *watchful*
vigilante 586.2 *defender*; 384.14 *guard*; 518.11 *observer*; 252.3 *protector*; 385.2 *revenger*; 665.8 *watchful person*
vigilante committee member 633.5 *pursuer*
vigilantism 16.41 *lawlessness*
vigilantly 471.15 *attentively*; 243.22 *in preparation*; 629.9 *jealously*; 518.26 *watchfully*
vigil light 10.14 *sacred object*
vigils 10.9 *prayer*
vigintillion 194.3 *large number*; 201.11 *million*
vigneron 44.13 *horticulturist*
vignette 721.2 *brief description*; 19.9 *drawing*; 17.2 *fiction*; 21.23 *role*
vigorous **338.4**; 342.18 *active*; 707.14 *assertive*; 726.3 *emphatic*; 538.4 *fresh*; 334.15 *full of energy*; 259.1 *healthy*; 554.13 *lively*; 332.2 *mentally quick*; 336.9 *physically strong*; 638.2 *tenacious*; 380.6 *violent*
vigorously 342.22 *actively*; 336.15 *acutely*; 726.7 *emphatically*; 334.19 *energetically*; 707.25 *explicitly*; 380.10 *violently*; 338.6 *with vigour*
vigorousness 707.6 *assertiveness*; 726.1 *emphasis*; 342.4 *energy*; 423.8 *physical strength*
Vigour 338
vigour **338.1**; 542.2 *affectation*; 707.6 *assertiveness*; 638.13 *concentration*; 726.1 *emphasis*; 342.4 *energy*; 259.3 *health*; 336.2 *healthiness*; 423.8 *physical strength*; 380.1 *violence*; 334.3 *vitality*; 555.2 *youthfulness*
Vijnanavada 4.7 *school of thought*
Viking 357.6 *destroyer*; 323.7 *nautical person*; 29.33 *planetary probe*
vilanelle 17.7 *poem*; 17.10 *verse form*
vile 712.8 *cursing*; 798.7 *evil*; 594.12 *hated*; 804.11 *wicked*
vile language 712.2 *offensive language*
vilely 712.12 *swearingly*; 804.18 *wickedly*
vileness 631.4 *bad conduct*; 236.9 *badness*; 798.1 *evil*; 804.1 *wickedness*
vilification **712.3**; 670.8 *berating*; 381.16 *personal attack*; 678.5 *scorn*
vilify **678.13**; **712.6**; 606.7 *be dissatisfied*; 381.10 *criticize*; 670.22 *vituperate*
vilifying 712.9 *vituperative*
villa 565.5 *house*; 565.4 *official residence*; 440.1 *property*
villadom 216.8 *middle classes*
village **87.10**; 87.1 *city*; 86.11 *settlement*; 87.14 *urban*
village cricket 53.1 *cricket match*
village green 538.8 *greenness*; 87.10 *village*
village-like 87.14 *urban*
village pond 88.2 *small lake*
villager 564.5 *countryman*; 87.11 *urbanite*
villain 800.4 *dishonourable person*; 798.6 *evil person*; 16.40 *lawbreaker*; 651.8 *malefactor*; 21.23 *role*; 804.9 *wicked person*; 802.10 *wrongdoer*
villainous 236.3 *bad*; 532.5 *blackhearted*; 800.5 *dishonourable*; 16.60 *offending*; 804.11 *wicked*
villainousness 236.9 *badness*; 800.1 *improbity*
villainy 236.9 *badness*; 800.1 *improbity*; 16.38 *lawbreaking*; 804.1 *wickedness*
villein 574.1 *plebeian*; 387.5 *subjected person*
villeinage 440.3 *historic property terms*; 763.3 *medieval ownership*; 387.1 *subjection*
villeinhold 440.3 *historic property terms*; 763.3 *medieval ownership*
villosity 420.6 *roughness*
villous 420.2 *coarse*
villously 420.14 *roughly*
vim 613.1 *courage*; 726.1 *emphasis*; 336.2 *healthiness*; 338.1 *vigour*
vinaigrette 25.15 *sauce*; 496.2 *seasoning*; 499.3 *sour thing*
vinculum 27.25 *algebraic expression*
vindaloo 25.49 *Indian dish*
vin de table 558.9 *wine*
vindicable 714.13
vindicate **714.7**; 649.10 *absolve*; 16.78 *acquit*; 706.18 *answer back*; 701.16 *plead*; 384.22 *plead for*; 4.21 *rationalize*; 454.1 *verify*
vindicated 16.63 *acquitted*; 701.12 *apologetic*; 649.6 *forgiven*; 706.13 *retaliatory*
vindicating 384.29 *defending*; 649.4 *forgiving*; 706.13 *retaliatory*; 714.11 *vindicatory*
Vindication 714
vindication **714.1**; 649.3 *absolution*; 16.42 *acquittal*; 706.5 *counterstatement*; 701.5 *plea*
vindicator **714.5**; 714.6 *avenger*; 814.17 *punisher*
vindicatory 714.11
vindictive **714.14**; 798.7 *evil*; 236.5 *harmful*; 594.10 *hating*; 651.14 *hostile*; 628.4 *pitiless*; 814.19 *punitive*; 385.5 *retaliatory*
vindictively **714.16**; 798.12 *evilly*; 594.18 *hatefully*; 628.7 *pitilessly*; 814.23 *punitively*
vindictiveness 651.4 *bitterness*; 798.1 *evil*; 236.11 *harmfulness*
vin du pays 558.9 *wine*
vine 77.2 *plant*
vinegar 25.7 *basic ingredient*; 625.1 *irascibility*; 499.3 *sour thing*
vinegariness 499.1 *sourness*
vinegary 499.5 *acid*; 626.7 *irritable*
vine grower 44.13 *horticulturist*
vineyard 44.2 *garden*
Vingolf 8.11 *heaven*
vinho verde 558.9 *wine*
vinicultural 44.16 *horticultural*
viniculture 44.1 *horticulture*
viniculturist 44.13 *horticulturist*
vino 690.12 *alcohol*; 558.9 *wine*
vin ordinaire 558.9 *wine*
vinous 558.17 *drinkable*; 558.16 *drinking*; 690.5 *drunken*; 690.6 *intoxicating*
vinousness 690.11 *drinking*
vin rosé 558.9 *wine*
vintage 558.17 *drinkable*; 296.12 *olden*; 356.7 *produce*; 439.1 *store*; 235.6 *worth*; 235.1 *worthy*; 765.6 *yield*
vintage-car racing 61.1 *motor racing*
vintage crop 765.6 *yield*
vintage harvest 217.8 *plenty*
vintage port 558.9 *wine*
vintage wine 558.9 *wine*; 765.6 *yield*
vintner 436.3 *provider*
vinyl 550.9 *floor covering*
vinyl disc 504.9 *audio device*
violaceous 540.6 *purple*
violate 798.11 *be evil*; 802.21 *do wrong*; 236.14 *ill-treat*; 118.20 *infringe a law*; 357.10 *lay waste*; 351.1 *misuse*; 796.20 *seduce*; 773.7 *take*; 329.5 *transgress*; 380.8 *use violence*
violated 351.4 *misused*
violate orders 662.15 *be disobedient*
violate the law 662.15 *be disobedient*; 16.73 *be illegal*
violating 16.60 *offending*
violation 16.38 *lawbreaking*; 351.2 *misuse*; 380.2 *physical violence*; 796.7 *sexual assault*; 773.1 *taking*; 329.8 *transgression*; 802.6 *unlawfulness*
violation of contract 15.2 *industrial negotiations*
violation of orders 662.1 *disobedience*
violation of the law 662.2
violative 802.16 *in the wrong*
Violence 380
violence **380.1**; 624.4 *anger*; 386.2 *coercion*; 651.2 *cruelness*; 236.11 *harmfulness*; 351.2 *misuse*; 585.8 *warfare*
violent **380.6**; 351.5 *abusive*; 624.16 *angry*; 381.23 *attacking*; 386.9 *compelling*; 651.11 *cruel*; 236.5 *harmful*; 262.3 *hasty*; 16.61 *lawless*; 334.13 *powerful*; 31.48 *stormy*
violent change 224.1 *change*
violent charging 66.2 *football play*
violent creature 380.4
violent death 382.8 *accidental killing*; 582.5 *ways of dying*
violently **380.10**; 351.6 *abusively*; 386.11 *compellingly*; 331.18 *dynamically*; 16.84 *lawlessly*; 334.18 *powerfully*
violent person 351.3 *abuser*
violent storm 31.13 *wind strength*
violent weather 380.5
violet 28.28 *colour*; 502.2 *fragrant thing*; 540.6 *purple*; 540.3 *purple thing*
VIP 123.4 *bigwig*; 400.5 *company leader*; 579.13 *director*; 579.15 *manager*; 566.7 *person*; 811.2 *person of repute*; 248.4 *prosperous person*; 246.4 *successful person*; 121.5 *superior*
viper 691.5 *drug pusher*; 651.8 *malefactor*; 73.3 *snake*
viperish 651.14 *hostile*; 73.12 *snakelike*
viper-like 73.12 *snakelike*
viperous 73.12 *snakelike*
virago 590.9 *feeling person*; 568.2 *female*; 594.8 *hated person*; 625.3 *irascible person*; 336.6 *muscleman*; 380.4 *violent creature*; 651.9 *vixen*
virago-like 568.15 *female*
viral 34.21 *living*
viral pneumonia 260.6 *infection*
virelay 17.7 *poem*
virescence 538.8 *greenness*
virescent 538.1 *green*
vir et uxor 570.9 *married couple*
Virgilian 17.19 *narrative*
virgin 572.4 *celibate person*; 295.12 *immature*; 805.4 *innocent person*; 350.2 *new*; 795.9 *pure*; 255.5, 795.5 *pure person*; 568.5 *single girl*; 204.7 *uncut*; 572.7 *virginal*; 803.4 *virtuous person*; 555.8 *young woman*
Virginal 10.10 *religious manual*
virginal **572.7**; 256.16 *clean*; 803.6 *ethical*; 295.12 *immature*; 805.5 *innocent*; 255.12 *morally pure*; 531.5, 795.9, 799.5 *pure*; 555.11 *young*
virginally 572.12 *celibately*; 803.10 *ethically*; 295.24 *immaturely*; 805.11 *innocently*; 255.18 *virtuously*; 555.14 *youthfully*
virgin birth 561.3 *propagation*
virgin forest 79.4 *trees*
Virginia reel 22.4 *historic dancing*
Virginia tobacco 496.7 *tobacco*
Virginia Wade 63.7 *famous tennis players*
virginity **572.2**; 295.3 *immaturity*; 805.1 *innocence*; 795.3 *moral purity*; 350.9 *newness*; 255.1, 799.2 *purity*; 803.2 *virtues*
Virgin Mary 572.4 *celibate person*; 558.6 *soft drink*
virgin territory 86.6 *regions*
virgo intacta 572.4 *celibate person*; 255.5, 795.5 *pure person*
virgule 189.2 *oblique line*; 742.7 *punctuation*
viridescence 538.8 *greenness*
viridescent 538.1 *green*
viridian 538.10 *green pigment*
viridity 538.8 *greenness*
virile 567.17 *male*; 336.9 *physically strong*; 334.13 *powerful*; 338.4 *vigorous*
virilism 567.1 *male sex*
virility 613.2 *heroism*; 567.1 *male sex*; 334.1 *power*; 336.1 *strength*
virion 34.3 *organism*
viroid 34.3 *organism*
virologist 34.19 *life scientist*; 35.13 *medical specialist*
virology 34.1 *life science*; 35.3 *medical specialty*
virtu 19.5 *artistry*
virtual 96.12 *artificial*; 40.21 *on-line*; 102.6 *potential*; 334.13 *powerful*
virtual image 28.31 *lens element*
virtuality 102.1 *possibility*
virtually 147.13 *nearly*; 204.13 *on the whole*; 102.11 *potentially*; 334.18 *powerfully*
virtual reality **40.18**; 96.7 *artificiality*
Virtue 803
virtue **803.1**; 334.2 *ability*; 674.3 *bashfulness*; 631.2 *good conduct*; 795.2 *good morals*; 805.1 *innocence*; 797.10 *kindness*; 573.3 *nobleness*; 255.1, 799.2 *purity*; 801.4 *righteousness*; 237.6 *usability*; 235.6 *worth*
virtueless 804.12 *immoral*
virtues **803.2**; 8.6 *angel*
virtuosity 485.1 *skill*; 121.1 *superiority*; 235.6 *worth*
virtuoso 396.11, 400.10 *expert*; 18.29 *musical*; 18.24 *musician*; 121.6 *paragon*; 136.8 *qualified person*; 485.4 *skilled person*; 797.16 *superior person*
virtuous **803.5**; 674.10 *bashful*; 810.8 *dutiful*; 805.5 *innocent*; 797.3 *kind*; 795.8, 801.10 *moral*; 255.12 *morally pure*; 799.5 *pure*; 631.17 *well-behaved*; 235.1 *worthy*
virtuous conduct 803.1 *virtue*
virtuously **255.18**; **803.9**; 805.11 *innocently*; 799.8 *purely*; 674.18 *shyly*; 631.19 *well*
virtuous man 572.4 *celibate person*
virtuousness 797.10 *kindness*; 801.4 *righteousness*; 803.1 *virtue*
virtuous person **803.4**; 795.5 *pure person*
virtuous woman 572.4 *celibate person*
virulence 651.4 *bitterness*; 236.11 *harmfulness*; 594.1 *hate*; 380.1 *violence*
virulent 236.5 *harmful*; 594.10 *hating*; 651.14 *hostile*; 624.15 *resentful*; 380.6 *violent*
virulently 594.18 *hatefully*; 624.17 *resentfully*
virus 40.19 *computing terms*; 260.2 *illness*; 260.6 *infection*; 159.2 *little thing*; 34.3 *organism*; 274.14 *technical error*
virus disease 260.4 *disease*
viruses 554.9 *classifications of life*
VISA™ 772.4 *credit*; 783.2 *credit card*
VISA 771.4 *lending institution*
visa 716.6 *documentation*; 454.6 *evidence*; 743.3 *means of identification*; 318.6 *passport*; 396.9 *permission*; 757.2 *permit*; 253.2 *promise*; 314.4 *right of entry*
visage 525.3 *external appearance*; 167.2 *face*
viscera 172.4 *insides*
visceral 172.10
visceral leishmaniasis 260.7 *tropical disease*
viscid 267.9 *adhesive*; 423.3 *hard*; 430.8 *viscous*
viscidity 360.1 *retention*; 423.6 *toughness*; 430.1 *viscosity*
viscidly 423.12 *toughly*; 430.12 *viscously*
viscometer 26.8 *meter*
viscometric 26.16 *micrometric*
viscometry 26.2 *micrometry*
viscose 430.8 *viscous*
Viscosity 430
viscosity **430.1**; 152.6 *denseness*; 28.10 *force*; 365.1 *friction*; 152.5 *thickness*
viscount 573.1 *nobleman*
viscountcy 573.2 *aristocracy*
viscountess 573.1 *nobleman*
viscounty 573.2 *aristocracy*
viscous **430.8**; 267.9 *adhesive*; 152.2 *dense*
viscously **430.12**; 267.11 *cohesively*
viscousness 430.1 *viscosity*
Visibility 520
visibility **31.35**; **520.3**; 525.2 *being in view*; 716.3 *evidentness*; 28.23 *light*; 738.10 *manifestation*
visible **518.23**; **520.1**; 525.7 *appearing*; 739.10 *disclosed*; 738.13 *displayed*; 716.9 *evident*; 695.1 *intelligible*; 738.14 *manifest*; 308.12 *open*; 525.8 *outer*; 488.8 *sensate*
visible earnings 776.5 *commercial trade*
visible effect 345.2
visible goods 776.5 *commercial trade*
visible horizon 520.3 *visibility*
visibleness 520.3 *visibility*
visible radiation 28.13 *electromagnetic radiation*; 522.1 *light*; 520.6 *visible thing*
visibles 776.5 *commercial trade*

visible spectrum 28.13 *electromagnetic radiation*; 522.1 *light*
visible thing 520.6
visible trade 776.5 *commercial trade*; 13.5 *international trade*
visibly 518.25; **520.11**; 716.15 *evidently*; 308.25 *obviously*; 185.10 *protuberantly*
Visicalc™ 40.11 *application*
Visigoths 284.6 *people of the past*
Vision 518
vision 518.1; 610.3 *aspiration*; 545.3 *attractive female*; 8.8 *divine manifestation*; 477.5 *fantasy*; 97.6 *ghostly presence*; 446.6 *ideal*; 96.2 *illusion*; 477.1, 518.5 *imagination*; 28.23 *light*; 482.6 *objective*; 525.4 *something that appears*
visional 96.9 *illusory*; 518.20 *visual*
visionariness 446.7 *idealism*
visionary 477.9; 634.17 *avoider*; 477.11 *fantastical*; 446.13 *ideal*; 477.12 *imaginary*; 518.11 *observer*; 4.13 *of philosophy*; 475.8 *oracle*; 525.9 *ostensible*; 446.9 *person of ideas*; 652.6 *philanthropic*; 652.3 *philanthropist*; 4.10 *philosopher*; 244.12 *reformer*; 518.21 *seeing*; 96.11 *unrealistic*; 96.6 *unrealistic person*
visionless 519.8 *blind*
visit 654.12; 97.12 *attend*; 314.9 *enter*; 565.19 *frequent*; 564.14 *inhabit*; 654.3 *meeting*; 814.1 *punish*; 312.6 *stop at*
visitant 314.7 *entrant*
visitation 249.1 *adversity*; 814.10 *affliction*; 8.8 *divine manifestation*; 260.2 *illness*; 654.3 *meeting*
visiting 654.3 *meeting*; 97.2 *omnipresence*
visiting card 743.3 *means of identification*
visiting nurse 35.16 *nurse*
visiting often 297.5 *frequenting*
visiting rights 571.3 *divorce court*
visiting side 169.5 *team*
visit often 297.8 *frequent*
visitor 314.7 *entrant*; 564.3 *householder*; 763.5 *possessor*; 654.6 *social person*; 97.5 *someone present*
Visitors' Cup 50.5 *Henley trophies*
vis major 452.16 *inevitability*
visor 384.7 *armour*; 700.12 *disguise*; 384.6 *protective clothing*; 550.12 *protective covering*
visored 700.41 *disguised*
vista 518.7 *view*
visual 518.20; 520.2 *clear*; 717.6 *image*; 525.8 *outer*
visual acuity 28.23 *light*; 518.1 *vision*
visual aid 518.10; 717.6 *image*; 520.7 *that which makes visible*
visual appeal 525.5 *impression*
visual artist 19.16 *artist*
visual binary 29.9 *constellation*
visual distortion 519.5
visual fallacy 477.5 *fantasy*
visual handicap 519.2 *poor sight*
visual imagination 477.1 *imagination*
visualization 518.4; 446.8, 477.1 *imagination*
visualize 518.16; 19.23 *design*; 446.15, 477.14 *imagine*; 95.11 *make real*; 4.20 *philosophize*
visualized 446.11 *ideational*
visualizing 477.10 *imaginative*
visually 518.24; 19.30 *pictorially*
visually handicapped 519.9 *weak-sighted*
visually impaired 519.9 *weak-sighted*
visual record 744.1 *record*
visual sense 518.1 *vision*
vita 744.1 *record*
vital 554.12 *alive*; 99.5 *essential*; 123.5, 643.3 *important*; 395.11 *influential*; 34.21 *living*; 135.4 *required*; 338.4 *vigorous*; 172.10 *visceral*
vital air 554.3 *life requirements*
vital body 11.7 *spirit*
vital concern 123.2 *important matter*
vital flame 554.1 *life*
vital force 36.22 *libido*; 554.1 *life*
vital functions 34.5 *physiology*
vitalism 4.7 *school of thought*
vitalist 4.11 *follower of a doctrine*; 4.14 *of a philosophy*
vitality 334.3; 726.1 *emphasis*; 342.4 *energy*; 259.3 *health*; 336.2 *healthiness*; 554.1 *life*; 423.8 *physical strength*; 338.1 *vigour*
vitalization 554.1 *life*; 581.5 *refreshment*
vitalize 554.19 *give birth to*; 581.1 *refresh*
vitally 554.22; 395.14 *influentially*; 135.12 *in need*
vital necessities 554.3 *life requirements*
vitalness 135.3 *needfulness*
vital organs 172.4 *insides*
vital role 395.1 *influence*
vital spark 554.1 *life*
vital statistics 13.3 *economic statistics*; 27.53, 210.2 *statistics*
vital supplies 352.2 *supplies*
vital to the occasion 287.7 *critical*
vitamin 33.13; 394.7 *tonic*
vitamin A 33.20 *terpene*; 33.13 *vitamin*
vitamin B_1 33.13 *vitamin*
vitamin B_{12} 33.13 *vitamin*
vitamin B_2 33.13 *vitamin*
vitamin B_6 33.13 *vitamin*
vitamin B complex 33.13 *vitamin*
vitamin C 33.13 *vitamin*
vitamin D_2 33.13 *vitamin*
vitamin D_3 33.13 *vitamin*
vitamin deficiency 218.8 *insufficiency*
vitamin deficiency disease 33.14
vitamin E 33.20 *terpene*; 33.13 *vitamin*
vitamin K 33.20 *terpene*; 33.13 *vitamin*
vitamins 557.11 *food content*
vitelline membrane 72.15 *eggs*
vitiate 796.19 *corrupt*; 245.6 *pervert*
vitiated 260.23 *diseased*
vitiation 245.8 *perversion*; 804.1 *wickedness*
viticultural 44.16 *horticultural*
viticulture 44.1 *horticulture*
vitiligo 260.13 *skin disease*
vitreosity 527.5 *transparency*
vitreous 418.1 *hard*; 527.1 *transparent*
vitreous humour 518.2 *eye*
vitreousness 527.5 *transparency*
vitrification 418.6 *solidification*
vitrified 418.3 *hardened*
vitrify 418.10 *solidify*
vitriol 651.4 *bitterness*
vitriolic 651.14 *hostile*; 712.9 *vituperative*
vittles 557.7 *food*
vituperate 670.22; 381.10 *criticize*; 712.6 *vilify*
vituperation 729.9 *art of public speaking*; 670.8 *berating*; 712.3 *vilification*
vituperative 712.9; 381.25, 670.27 *critical*; 659.5 *discourteous*
vituperatively 712.13; 659.9 *discourteously*
viva 705.3 *questionnaire*
vivacious 342.18 *active*; 598.1 *cheerful*; 726.3 *emphatic*; 334.15 *full of energy*; 554.13 *lively*
vivaciously 554.22 *vitally*
vivaciousness 726.1 *emphasis*; 342.4 *energy*
vivacity 598.3 *cheerfulness*; 726.1 *emphasis*; 342.4 *energy*; 554.1 *life*; 334.3 *vitality*
vivandiere 778.14 *street trader*
viva voce 729.17 *oral*; 729.21 *orally*
viva voce examination 705.3 *questionnaire*
viverrid 71.8 *flesh-eating mammal*
Viverridae 71.8 *flesh-eating mammal*
viverrine 71.28 *carnivorous*
vivid 522.16 *bright*; 520.2 *clear*; 529.11 *colourful*; 17.18, 721.11 *descriptive*; 726.3 *emphatic*; 477.10 *imaginative*; 695.1 *intelligible*; 115.9 *lifelike*; 717.13 *representational*
vivid imagination 477.1 *imagination*
vividly 115.14 *comparably*; 17.23, 721.18 *descriptively*; 522.30 *lightly*; 717.14 *representationally*
vividness 520.4 *clarity*; 726.1 *emphasis*; 695.9 *intelligibility*; 522.1 *light*
vivification 554.1 *life*
vivified 554.12 *alive*
vivify 554.19 *give birth to*
vivifying 554.12 *alive*
viviparous 561.16 *reproductive*
vivisection 382.9 *animal killing*; 448.3 *experimentation*
vivisectionist 382.13 *animal killer*; 448.5 *experimenter*
vixen 651.9; 568.14 *female animal*; 71.18 *female mammal*; 625.3 *irascible person*
vixenish 625.4 *irascible*; 626.7 *irritable*
vixenishness 625.1 *irascibility*
viz 719.18 *in other words*; 139.31 *namely*
vizier 579.16 *official*
V-J Day 298.6 *annually celebrated day*
VLSI 39.13 *circuit*
V-neck 551.13 *sweater*
vocabular 5.42 *worded*
vocabulary 220.3 *dictionary*; 729.1 *faculty of speech*; 724.4 *literary style*
vocal 18.32 *instrumental*; 5.41 *lettered*; 729.16 *speech*; 514.16 *vociferous*
vocal chords 729.5 *organ of speech*; 507.4 *sound maker*
vocal folds 729.5 *organ of speech*
vocalic 5.41 *lettered*
vocalise semiotics 5.5 *nonstandard language*
vocalism 5.3 *spoken language*
vocalist 18.24 *musician*; 18.23 *singer*
vocalization 729.4 *articulation*; 729.7 *utterance*
vocalize 18.39, 516.10 *sing*; 5.45 *use language*
vocalized 729.16 *speech*
vocally 5.48 *linguistically*; 729.21 *orally*; 514.20 *vociferously*
vocal organs 729.5 *organ of speech*
vocation 776.6 *business*; 631.1 *conduct*; 576.3 *job*; 480.11, 483.1 *motive*; 139.8 *specialization*
vocational 776.17 *professional*
vocational education 6.3 *subject*
vocational therapy 36.3 *psychiatric treatment*
vocational training 6.2 *educational system*
vocative 733.14; 5.31 *case*
vociferate 507.8 *be loud*; 514.10 *cry out*
vociferation 514.1 *cry*; 507.2 *outcry*
vociferous 514.16; 507.6 *loud*
vociferously 514.20; 507.9 *loudly*
vocoder 40.7 *peripheral*
Vodaphone™ 692.9 *telephone*
vodka 558.7 *alcoholic drink*
vodka and tonic 558.8 *mixed drink*
vogue 117.5 *convention*; 553.1 *fashion*; 5.42 *worded*
vogue word 5.21 *catchword*
voguish 553.7 *fashionable*
Vohu Manah 8.6 *angel*
voice 5.32; 631.1 *conduct*; 729.1 *faculty of speech*; 729.3 *mode of speech*; 729.5 *organ of speech*; 507.4 *sound maker*; 729.11 *speak*; 5.30 *syntax*; 5.45 *use language*; 469.10 *vote*
voice box 729.5 *organ of speech*; 507.4 *sound maker*
voiced 5.41 *lettered*; 729.18 *phonetic*; 729.16 *speech*
voiced consonant 5.16 *spoken letter*; 729.7 *utterance*
voiceless 730.9; 729.18 *phonetic*; 506.3 *silent*; 732.2 *sparing with words*
voiceless consonant 730.4 *whispering*
voicelessly 730.17; 732.8 *shyly*
Voicelessness 730
voicelessness 730.1; 732.4 *guarded speech*; 506.4 *silence*
voiceless person 730.7
voice of conscience 795.2 *good morals*; 808.1 *penitence*; 711.1 *warning*
voice of opposition 703.8 *protester*
voice of reason 460.3 *sane person*
voice of the tempter 480.3 *incentive*
voice quality 729.3 *mode of speech*
voice synthesizer 40.7 *peripheral*
voice vote 469.10 *vote*
voicing 729.4 *articulation*
void 371.11; 98.8 *absent*; 708.14 *cancel*; 560.16 *defecate*; 94.4, 98.3 *emptiness*; 141.2 *empty space*; 29.7 *galaxy*; 146.3 *gulf*; 708.8 *nonexistence*; 94.9 *nonexistent*; 195.7 *null*; 233.2 *omission*; 355.5 *relinquished*; 559.7 *secrete*; 417.1 *sparse*; 212.3 *subtract*; 367.6 *throw down*; 238.1 *useless*; 98.13 *vacant*; 355.2 *withdraw*
voidance 560.2 *defecation*; 315.2 *outflow*; 371.21 *removal*; 303.12 *reversal*; 559.1 *secretion*
voided 708.20 *cancelled*
voiding 371.21 *removal*
voidness 98.3 *emptiness*; 417.3 *sparseness*
voile 193.4 *textile*; 527.8 *transparent thing*
volant 332.1 *swift*
volatile 432.23; 453.8, 642.1 *capricious*; 432.1 *gas*; 415.2 *insubstantial*; 227.14 *irresolute*; 590.13 *passionate*; 278.6 *transient*
volatile memory 40.6 *memory*
volatileness 453.16 *capriciousness*; 415.5 *lightness*; 417.3 *sparseness*
volatility 432.8; 453.16 *capriciousness*; 227.2 *irresolution*; 415.5 *lightness*; 417.3 *sparseness*; 278.1 *transience*
volatilizable 417.1 *sparse*; 432.23 *volatile*
volatilization 377.3 *dilution*; 432.10 *vaporization*
volatilize 377.14 *dilute*; 432.25 *gasify*; 415.10 *lighten*; 417.6 *make sparse*
volatilized 417.1 *sparse*
vol-au-vent 25.12 *hors d'oeuvre*
volcanic 30.55; 92.11 *continental*; 308.14 *holed*; 493.10 *on fire*; 315.15 *outgoing*; 30.56 *petrographic*; 380.6 *violent*
volcanic activity 30.24
volcanically 308.27 *cavernously*; 92.13 *continentally*; 30.66 *geographically*
volcanic cone 30.24 *volcanic activity*
volcanic gas 30.25 *eruption*
volcanic island 30.16 *ocean floor*
volcanic lake 88.1 *lake*
volcanic mountain 30.21 *mountain building*
volcanic rock 30.30 *igneous rock*
volcanism 30.24 *volcanic activity*
volcano 308.5 *hole*; 493.8 *hot place*; 92.10 *miscellaneous*; 371.28 *propellant*; 379.1 *trap*; 30.24 *volcanic activity*
volcanological 30.48 *geological*
volcanologist 30.3 *geologist*; 30.4 *geophysicist*
volcanology 30.1 *earth science*; 30.2 *geophysics*
Volga 90.5 *other major rivers*
volition 4.9 *philosophical problem*; 635.1 *will*
volitional 482.12 *intended*; 469.14 *selecting*; 635.6 *willed*
volitive 635.6 *willed*
volley 508.1 *bang*; 331.10 *bat*; 381.2 *fire*; 381.15 *firing*; 376.22 *flood*; 63.5 *real tennis*; 63.13 *serve*; 330.28 *shoot*; 330.7 *shot*; 63.2 *tennis strokes*; 330.5, 330.23 *throw*
volley and thunder 381.2 *fire*; 330.28 *shoot*
volleyer 63.6 *tennis player*
volley of abuse 712.3 *vilification*
Volstead Act 684.1 *self-restraint*; 399.1 *veto*
volt 334.5 *unit of work*
Volta 88.5 *other major lakes*
volta 22.4 *historic dancing*
voltage 28.52, 39.10 *electric potential*; 334.5 *unit of work*
voltage amplifier 39.21 *rectifier*
voltage regulator 39.34 *power supply*
voltage transformer 39.22 *transformer*
voltaic cell 32.19 *electrochemistry*; 39.5 *electrolytic conduction*
voltaic electricity 334.7 *electrical power*
voltameter 26.8 *meter*
voltametric 26.16 *micrometric*
voltammeter 26.8 *meter*
volte 59.10 *dressage*
volte-face 303.13 *about-turn*; 479.6 *equivocation*; 800.2 *faithlessness*; 761.1 *reversion*; 303.9 *turn round*
voltmeter 28.90 *ammeter*; 39.23 *electrical instrument*; 26.8 *meter*
volubility 729.2 *power of speech*; 731.1 *talkativeness*
voluble 729.19 *speaking*; 731.5 *talkative*
volubly 731.10 *talkatively*
volume 127.1 *inclusion*; 205.2 *particular*; 203.1 *quantity*; 26.4, 158.1 *size*; 27.35, 28.7, 141.1 *space*; 692.22 *television set*; 28.38 *thermodynamics*
volume control 504.9 *audio device*; 692.18 *radio*
volume strain 38.14 *load*
volumeter 26.8 *meter*
volumetric 32.41 *analytic*; 26.16 *micrometric*; 141.11 *spatial*
volumetric analysis 32.18 *gravimetric analysis*
volumetry 26.2 *micrometry*
voluminous 158.15 *big*; 270.3 *diffuse*; 203.6 *quantitative*; 141.13 *spacious*
voluminously 158.20 *largely*; 203.7 *quantitatively*; 141.15 *spaciously*
voluminousness 158.2 *bigness*; 141.4 *spaciousness*
voluntarily 636.18; 482.13 *intentionally*; 752.20 *persuasively*
voluntary 636.5; **752.18**; 793.11 *free of charge*; 768.7 *given*; 482.12 *intended*; 478.2 *spontaneous*
voluntary aid 636.10 *voluntary work*
voluntary arbitration 15.4 *industrial dispute*
voluntary commitment 756.1 *promise*
voluntary hospital 35.10 *hospital*
voluntaryism 636.10 *voluntary work*
voluntary payment 785.1 *payment*
voluntary poverty 782.8 *renunciation of wealth*

voluntary resignation 605.1 *resignation*
voluntary retirement 15.2 *industrial negotiations*
voluntary service 636.10 *voluntary work*
voluntary work 636.10; 793.6 *absence of charge*; 768.1 *giving*; 354.2 *undertaking*
voluntary worker 652.3 *philanthropist*; 752.8 *volunteer*; 578.1 *worker*
volunteer 354.4; **636.15**; **752.8**; **752.11**; 353.7 *attempter*; 342.16 *be sociable*; 342.10 *busy person*; 584.9 *enlisted*; 768.6 *give to charity*; 585.12 *go to war*; 652.3 *philanthropist*; 585.11 *recruit*; 586.8 *soldier*; 354.1 *undertake*; 636.11 *willing worker*; 578.1 *worker*
volunteer army 586.15 *army*; 584.2 *the military*
volunteering 342.2 *social activity*; 636.5 *voluntary*; 585.7 *war measures*
volunteerism 342.2 *social activity*
volunteer snooker 65.5 *snooker*
volunteer work 793.6 *absence of charge*
voluptuary 241.12 *pleasure-loving person*; 490.3 *pleasure-seeker*; 686.5 *self-indulgent person*
voluptuous 796.14 *lecherous*; 490.6 *pleasant*; 490.7 *pleased*; 241.5 *pleasure-loving*; 686.6 *self-indulgent*
voluptuousness 490.1 *physical pleasure*; 241.7 *pleasure*; 686.1 *self-indulgence*
volutation 307.2 *turning*
volute spring 422.5 *spring*
volution 307.1 *rotation*; 327.11 *stagger*
volva 83.4 *fungal body*
Volvox 75.9 *protozoan*
vomit 371.15; 260.24 *be unhealthy*; 596.6 *react against*; 315.11 *run out*; 371.23 *vomiting*
vomit forth 431.25 *flow*
vomiting 371.23; **371.30**; 596.8 *disliking*; 260.8 *indigestion*; 596.4 *sign of dislike*; 260.3 *symptom*
vomition 371.23 *vomiting*
vomitive 371.30 *vomiting*
vomitory 394.17 *remedial*; 371.30 *vomiting*
voodoo 249.11 *cause adversity*; 798.4 *evil power*; 236.11 *harmfulness*; 395.2 *occult influence*; 450.2 *religious belief*; 11.3 *witchcraft*
voodoo curse 594.2 *curse*
voodoo doll 236.11 *harmfulness*
voodooed 798.10 *inauspicious*
voodooism 11.1 *occultism*; 11.3 *witchcraft*
voodooist 11.4 *witch*
voodooistic 11.15 *witchlike*
voodoo spell 712.4 *malediction*
voracious 617.9 *desirous*; 557.26 *eating*; 688.6 *gluttonous*; 218.3 *underfed*
voracious eating 557.2 *appetite*
voraciously 557.28 *carnivorously*; 688.7 *gluttonously*
voraciousness 557.2 *appetite*; 688.1 *gluttony*
voracity 557.2 *appetite*; 617.1 *desire*; 688.1 *gluttony*
Vormingstoneel 21.10 *theatre movements*
vortex 307.4; 342.1 *activity*; 180.3 *convoluted thing*; 90.6 *river flow*; 327.13 *tempest*; 379.1 *trap*
vortical 90.10 *fluvial*; 307.12 *rotary*
vortically 90.13 *fluently*
vorticist 19.29 *realist*
vorticose 307.12 *rotary*
vorticular 307.12 *rotary*
Vostok 29.31 *space travel*
votary 7.3 *religious person*; 9.5 *worshipper*
vote 469.5; **469.10**; 669.1 *approval*; 464.1 *judgment*; 16.68 *legislate*
vote against 113.17 *be against*; 114.9, 709.6 *dissent*; 128.7 *exclude*; 596.6 *react against*; 470.1 *reject*
vote-catcher 480.12 *persuader*
vote-catching 469.16 *elective*
vote counting 469.12 *election*
voted 16.46 *legislated*
vote down 128.7 *exclude*; 251.8 *restrain*; 469.5 *vote*
vote for 469.5 *vote*
vote in 469.5 *vote*
vote independent 250.16 *be independent*
vote of confidence 469.10 *vote*
vote of no confidence 469.10 *vote*
vote of thanks 671.3 *recognition*; 729.8 *speech*
vote out 128.7 *exclude*; 469.5 *vote*
voter 469.13 *electorate*; 250.7 *free person*
voters 469.13 *electorate*
votes for women 469.11 *franchise*
vote-snatcher 480.12 *persuader*
vote with one's feet 98.15 *be absent*; 226.7 *stop working*; 469.5 *vote*
voting 469.12 *election*; 469.16 *elective*
voting list 469.12 *election*; 220.6 *list of names*
voting machine 469.12 *election*
voting paper 469.12 *election*
voting precinct 87.7 *city district*
votive 768.7 *given*; 756.12 *promised*
votive candle 10.14 *sacred object*
votively 768.9 *as a gift*; 756.16 *as promised*
votive offering 807.2 *apology*; 752.6, 768.3 *offering*
vouch 707.17 *affirm*; 707.1 *affirmation*
vouched 707.12 *vowed*
vouched for 707.12 *vowed*
voucher 769.3 *acknowledgment of payment*; 707.9 *affirmer*; 716.6 *documentation*; 756.2 *guarantee*; 757.2 *permit*; 788.1 *receipt*; 744.1 *record*; 454.7 *verifier*
vouch for 756.8 *guarantee*; 253.11 *promise*; 252.10 *protect*; 707.18 *vow*
vouching 707.1 *affirmation*
vouchsafe 750.28 *consent*; 768.5 *give*
vouchsafed 750.18 *permitting*
vouchsafement 750.7 *consent*
voussoir 20.9 *miscellaneous architectural features*; 20.7 *vault*
vow 707.3; **707.18**; 810.7 *commitment*; 354.3 *contract*; 768.5 *give*; 756.1, 756.7 *promise*; 354.1 *undertake*
vowed 707.12
vowel 5.16 *spoken letter*; 729.7 *utterance*
vowel point 742.7 *punctuation*
vower 707.9 *affirmer*
vow of loyalty 569.4 *act of friendship*
vow of poverty 782.8 *renunciation of wealth*
vox populi 750.1 *accord*; 138.11 *general public*; 12.1 *government*; 464.1 *judgment*; 16.18 *tribunal*; 469.10 *vote*
voyage 318.1 *passage*; 318.9 *proceed*; 323.1 *water travel*
Voyager 29.33 *planetary probe*
voyager 227.7 *person who moves around*
voyaging 323.1 *water travel*
voyeur 644.4 *meddler*; 518.11 *observer*
voyeurism 796.2 *indecency*; 518.3 *observation*; 644.2 *prying*
vroom 332.9 *acceleration*; 332.4 *be swift*
V-shape 176.1 *angle*; 311.5 *fork*; 50.13 *windsurfing*
V-shaped 176.7 *angular*; 311.9 *branched*
V-shaped valley 30.7 *landform*
V-shape hull 50.7 *windsurfing*
V-sign 659.3 *act of discourtesy*; 176.1 *angle*; 300.11 *bodily movement*; 742.3 *gesture*; 753.3 *gesture of protest*; 660.7 *insult*; 668.7 *sign of disrespect*; 589.2 *symbol of peace*
VSO 752.8 *volunteer*
VTOL 322.7 *miscellaneous aviation terms*
vulcanite 32.21 *polymer*; 422.4 *rubber*
vulcanization 418.6 *solidification*
vulcanize 418.9 *harden*; 422.9 *make elastic*; 423.11 *make tough*; 42.15 *treat*
vulcanized 423.2 *toughened*; 42.11 *treated*
vulcanized rubber 422.4 *rubber*
vulcanizing 42.8 *fabric treatment*
vulgar 675.7; 659.6 *bad-mannered*; 497.6 *coarse*; 138.21 *common*; 712.8 *cursing*; 804.12 *immoral*; 802.13 *improper*; 796.12 *indecent*; 544.8 *indecorous*; 646.1 *naive*; 487.2 *not customary*; 5.39 *of language*; 122.16, 574.4 *ordinary*; 236.4 *poor*; 495.8 *tasteful*; 544.10 *ugly*
vulgar fraction 27.18 *division*; 196.1 *fraction*; 194.5 *ratio*
vulgar herd 675.6; 574.2 *the common people*
vulgarian 675.5 *vulgar person*
vulgarism 544.4 *inelegance of speech*; 5.3 *spoken language*; 5.19 *swearword*
Vulgarity 675
vulgarity 659.2 *bad manners*; 497.4 *bad taste*; 712.1 *curse*; 544.2, 802.3 *impropriety*; 796.2 *indecency*; 544.4 *inelegance of speech*; 646.2 *naivety*; 122.4 *poor quality*; 236.10 *poverty*; 793.3 *shoddiness*; 495.2 *taste of life*; 544.3 *ugliness*; 804.2 *vice*
vulgarization 245.8 *perversion*
vulgarize 675.10; 265.16 *make easy*; 245.6 *pervert*; 138.26 *popularize*
vulgar language 5.19 *swearword*
vulgarly 804.20 *immorally*; 659.10 *rudely*; 712.12 *swearingly*; 497.11 *tastelessly*; 495.11 *tastily*
vulgarness 802.3 *impropriety*
vulgar person 675.5
vulgar tongue 729.1 *faculty of speech*; 5.3 *spoken language*
vulgate 719.1 *interpretation*; 5.3 *spoken language*
vulnerability 254.7; 488.2 *ability to sense*; 424.2 *brittleness*; 335.3 *helplessness*; 231.5 *imperfection*; 337.1 *weakness*
vulnerable 254.3; 424.1 *brittle*; 231.1 *imperfect*; 335.11 *unprotected*; 804.13 *venial*
vulnerable point 231.7 *defect*; 254.7 *vulnerability*
vulnerably 804.19; 254.11 *dangerously*; 424.5 *fragilely*
vulnerary 394.18 *medical*
vulpecular 71.28 *carnivorous*
vulpine 71.28 *carnivorous*; 645.4 *cunning*; 800.5 *dishonourable*
vulture 72.5 *bird of prey*; 256.12 *cleaner*; 651.8 *malefactor*; 773.6 *taker*
vulturine 72.21 *avian*
vulva 561.8 *organs of reproduction*
vulvar 561.16 *reproductive*
vulvulitis 260.10 *cardiovascular disease*
vying 113.5 *conflict*
Vyrnwy 88.4 *British lakes*

wack down 367.2 *flatten*
wacko 36.8 *disordered personality*; 118.10, 118.14 *eccentric*
wacky 598.2 *cheering*; 461.11 *insane*; 272.5 *ridiculous*
wad 587.13 *ammunition*; 376.27 *bundle*; 158.7 *mass*; 309.2 *stopper*
wadding 419.11 *soft thing*; 309.2 *stopper*; 406.4 *stuffing*
waddle 300.12 *gait*; 326.11 *rock*; 333.10 *slow motion*; 300.15 *walk*
waddling 333.4 *slow*
wade across 318.11 *cross*
wade in blood 382.18 *slaughter*
wade into 441.1 *waste*
wader 72.3 *water bird*
waders 551.19 *footwear*
wade through 631.14 *behave towards*; 300.13 *be in motion*; 576.8 *exert oneself*
wadi 90.1 *river*
wading 67.11 *swimming*
wading bird 72.3 *water bird*
wading pool 67.7 *swimming pool*
wad of notes 781.6 *money*
Wado Kyu 57.8 *karate*
wads 208.2 *multitude*
wads of money 780.3 *fortune*
wafer 153.11 *fineness*; 25.39 *loaf*; 411.4 *slice*
wafer-thin 424.1 *brittle*; 153.4 *fine*
waffle 270.5 *be diffuse*; 479.1 *be equivocal*; 634.7 *be evasive*; 731.7 *be talkative*; 96.16 *delude*; 270.1 *diffuseness*; 634.15 *evasiveness*; 112.2 *iteration*; 25.39 *loaf*; 731.3 *talk*
waffle house 557.15 *eating place*
waffle iron 493.4 *burner*; 25.5 *cooker*
waffler 702.6 *sophist*; 731.4 *talker*
waffling 270.3 *diffuse*
waft 415.9 *be light*; 500.1 *odour*; 316.12 *transport*; 316.2 *transportation*
waftage 316.2 *transportation*
wag 327.22 *agitate*; 697.4 *buffoon*; 599.6 *humorist*; 326.4 *rock*; 327.7 *shake*; 326.12 *wave*
wage 340.4 *act*; 813.4 *reward for service*
wage a campaign 586.36 *combat*
wage bill 790.6 *business costs*
wage council 15.1 *industrial relations*
waged 788.6 *received*; 785.19 *receiving pay*
wage earner 15.7 *employee*; 765.7 *gainer*; 769.5 *recipient*; 578.1 *worker*
wage-earning 15.8 *industrial*; 769.11 *receiving*; 785.19 *receiving pay*
wager 107.12 *take a chance*
wage rates 15.2 *industrial negotiations*
wager of battle 585.1 *war*
wages 790.6 *business costs*; 765.4 *earnings*; 13.6 *economic factors*; 788.3 *income*; 785.3 *pay*; 483.5 *positive stimulus*; 813.4 *reward for service*
wages and salaries 13.8 *industrial relations*
wage scale 813.4 *reward for service*
wage slave 578.1 *worker*
wage war 585.13 *be at war*; 753.8 *cause mischief*
wage worker 15.7 *employee*; 765.7 *gainer*
wagging forefinger 742.3 *gesture*
waggish 599.10 *humorous*; 697.5 *nonsensical*
waggle 327.22 *agitate*; 327.25 *pitch*; 326.4, 326.11 *rock*; 327.7 *shake*
waggonage 316.2 *transportation*
waggoner 316.7 *transferor*
waging war 585.8 *warfare*; 585.15 *warring*
Wagnerian costume 551.5 *fancy dress*
wagon 410.10 *cart*; 320.17 *police car*; 321.6 *rolling stock*; 320.20 *truck*
wagon lit 321.6 *rolling stock*
wagon stage 21.17 *stage*
wagon train 320.9 *animal transport*
wagon wheel 307.6 *rotator*
wagtail 55.2 *artificial fly*; 72.6 *songbird*
Wahhabi 7.6 *non-Christian*
waif 144.7 *displaced person*; 655.7 *outsider*
wail 513.4 *be strident*; 31.58 *blow*; 514.13, 515.4 *cry*; 514.6 *cry of pain*; 491.12 *express pain*; 602.8 *grieve*; 603.6 *lament*; 729.13 *speak in a particular way*; 513.1 *stridency*; 603.7 *weep*
wailer 603.3 *lamenter*
wailful 515.7 *ululant*
wailfully 515.10 *howlingly*
wailing 515.1 *animal cry*; 514.18 *crying*; 603.1 *lamentation*; 603.4 *lamenting*; 515.7 *ululant*
Wailing Wall 10.13 *shrine*
wainscot 175.2 *foot*
wainwright 578.2 *artisan*
waist 151.8 *narrow thing*
waistband 373.10 *band*; 179.3 *circular thing*
waist belay 62.3 *climbing technique*
waist belt 62.4 *climbing equipment*
waistcloth 551.25 *accessories*
waistcoat 551.11 *jacket*
waist-deep 156.8 *deep*; 157.1 *shallow*
waist-high 154.12 *tall*
waist-length 148.1 *long*
waistline 551.24 *part of garment*
wait 294.7; **474.10**; 795.11 *be moral*; 301.8 *be motionless*; 294.3 *delayed action*; 341.4 *not act*; 141.21 *space*
wait and see 453.18 *be uncertain*; 294.8 *delay*; 341.4 *not act*
wait-and-see 341.3 *inactive*
wait-and-see policy 616.1 *caution*
waiter 401.3 *attendant*; 436.3 *provider*
wait for 243.3 *be prepared*; 283.10 *expect*; 474.10 *wait*
wait for the command 663.5 *obey*
waiting 474.1 *expectation*; 474.5 *expecting*; 283.11 *future*; 283.4 *looking to the future*; 318.2 *passing along*; 692.10 *telephone call*
waiting game 616.1 *caution*
waiting in the wings 283.11 *future*
waiting list 220.6 *list of names*; 744.1 *record*
waiting on 401.9 *serving*
waiting room 321.8 *railway station*; 226.4 *stopping place*
wait on 223.16 *attend*; 387.8 *be subject to*; 664.11 *pander to*; 392.25 *serve*
waitress 401.3 *attendant*; 436.3 *provider*
wait upon 663.5 *obey*; 401.8 *serve*
waive 767.9 *dispose of*; 350.5 *not use*; 355.1 *relinquish*
waived 350.3 *not wanted*; 355.5 *relinquished*
waiver 708.14 *cancel*; 708.5 *cancellation*; 46.14 *miscellaneous terms*; 757.2 *permit*; 355.3 *relinquishment*
waive the rules 657.11 *not stand on ceremony*
waiving 355.3 *relinquishment*
wakan 8.5 *deity*
wake 582.8 *after death*; 488.13 *arouse sensation*; 627.2 *condolence*; 583.2 *funeral*; 716.4 *indication*; 603.1 *lamentation*; 342.14 *push*; 168.1 *rear*; 215.1 *remainder*; 90.6 *river flow*; 289.1 *succession*; 345.2 *visible effect*

wake course 50.1 *sailing*
wakeful 342.18 *active*
wakefulness 342.7 *restlessness*
wake the dead 507.8 *be loud;* 11.22 *conjure*
wake up 488.13 *arouse sensation;* 488.12 *awake;* 342.12 *be active*
wakey wakey 342.23 *rise and shine!*
waking time 290.1 *morning*
Waldorf salad 25.14 *salad;* 25.43 *US dish*
Wales 85.12
walk 300.15; 631.1 *conduct;* 576.9 *exercise;* 300.12 *gait;* 371.33 *go away!;* 86.13 *locality;* 306.3 *orbit;* 48.7 *play baseball;* 49.6 *play basketball;* 333.10 *slow motion;* 47.1 *track events*
walk a punt 50.19 *punt*
walk away 313.1 *depart*
walked off one's feet 261.1 *fatigued*
walker 47.3 *athlete;* 413.3 *body support*
walkie-talkie 504.9 *audio device;* 62.4 *climbing equipment;* 692.18 *radio*
walking 576.5 *exercise;* 257.1 *hygiene;* 300.1 *motion;* 318.2 *passing along;* 49.5 *penalties;* 320.4 *personal transport;* 333.4 *slow;* 47.9 *track;* 47.1 *track events*
walking a man in 48.4 *pitching terms*
walking bass 516.4 *harmonics*
walking boots 551.19 *footwear*
walking disaster 245.9 *dilapidation*
walking encyclopedia 396.11, 400.10, 485.5 *expert;* 455.6 *knowledgeable person;* 443.7 *thinker*
walking frame 413.3 *body support*
walking gentleman 21.23 *role*
walking lady 21.23 *role*
walking out 593.6 *courtship*
walking papers 708.6 *termination*
walking part 21.23 *role*
walking race 47.1 *track events*
walking shoes 551.19 *footwear*
walking skeleton 153.9 *thin person*
walking steps 22.3 *ballroom dance steps*
walking stick 413.3 *body support*
walking the plank 814.7 *punishment*
walking under a ladder 475.7 *bad-luck sign*
walk into a trap 254.8 *be in danger*
Walkman™ 504.9 *audio device;* 692.18 *radio*
walk off 315.9 *exit*
walk-off 315.1 *exit*
walk off with 246.10 *defeat heavily;* 774.12 *steal*
walk of life 631.1 *conduct;* 221.1 *state*
walk on 387.6 *subject;* 21.36 *underact*
walk on eggshells 665.10 *be careful*
walk one's beat 298.8 *be cyclic*
walk on hot coals 264.19 *have difficulty*
walk-on part 21.23 *role*
walk on water 103.10 *attempt the impossible*
walkout 315.1 *exit;* 15.4 *industrial dispute;* 355.3 *relinquishment;* 383.1 *resistance;* 226.2 *stop*
walk out 315.14 *be dismissed;* 571.8 *desert;* 315.9 *exit;* 15.12 *have an industrial dispute;* 383.6 *resist;* 226.7 *stop working;* 355.2 *withdraw*
walk out with 593.26 *court*
walkover 265.6 *easy thing;* 59.7 *horseracing;* 246.2 *victory*
walk over 236.14 *ill-treat;* 387.6 *subject;* 647.6 *suppress*
walk over the course 265.17 *do easily*
walk slowly 333.1 *move slowly*
walk the earth 554.16 *live*
walk the plank 582.16 *meet one's fate*
walkthrough 21.14 *production*
walk through 21.37 *rehearse*
walk up 304.14 *climb*
walkway 38.21 *bridge*
wall 360.4; 378.3, 384.9 *barrier;* 378.9 *block;* 372.6 *boundary;* 165.5 *enclose;* 165.3 *enclosing thing;* 128.3 *exclusion zone;* 384.18 *fence;* 384.11 *fortification;* 814.16 *instrument of execution;* 59.9 *jumping;* 20.9 *miscellaneous architectural features;* 252.5 *refuge;* 62.5 *rock face;* 68.1 *skiing;* 416.4 *solid body;* 413.11 *support;* 413.2 *supporting part;* 186.3 *vertical thing*
wallah 578.1 *worker*
wallboard 550.8 *wall covering*
wall clock 281.6 *clock*
wall covering 550.8
walled 384.30 *defended*
walled garden 309.4 *closed place;* 165.2 *enclosed place*
walled-in 378.14 *blocked;* 165.7 *enclosed;* 550.37 *protected;* 360.10 *retained*
walled up 550.37 *protected*
wallet 410.9 *baggage;* 780.20 *money store;* 410.5 *packet*
walleye 55.4 *American game fish;* 519.2 *poor sight*
walleyed 519.9 *weak-sighted*
wallflower 766.6 *loser;* 341.2 *nonacting person;* 470.9 *rejected person;* 732.5 *shy person*
wall in 360.7 *detain;* 165.5 *enclose*
walling in 550.1 *covering*
walling up 550.1 *covering*
wall light 522.6 *electric light*
wall moss 82.3 *moss*
wall off 128.7 *exclude*
wallop 331.5 *beat;* 814.3 *hit;* 327.25 *pitch;* 338.1 *vigour*
walloping 158.15 *big*
wallow 258.10 *be dirty;* 414.12 *be heavy;* 367.9 *bow;* 490.8 *feel pleasure;* 92.3 *marsh;* 327.25 *pitch;* 327.11 *stagger;* 258.5 *swill;* 307.10 *swirl;* 326.12 *wave*
wallower 258.6 *dirty person*
wallow in 217.5 *about;* 219.4 *be excessive;* 686.10 *indulge oneself*
wallowing 323.11 *nautical;* 258.2 *uncleanness*
wallow in ignorance 456.9 *be ignorant*
wallow in riches 781.12 *be rich*
wallow in the mud 92.12 *be marooned*
wall painting 19.8 *painting*
wallpaper 550.28 *face;* 550.8 *wall covering*
wallpapered 550.36 *covered*
wallpaperer 550.17 *coverer*
wallpapering 542.5 *decorating*
wall pass 66.2 *football play*
wall safe 780.20 *money store;* 253.5 *safe*
Walls of Limerick 22.4 *historic dancing*
Wall Street 87.3 *New York;* 779.5 *stock market*
wall tile 24.9 *industrial ceramics*
wall tiles 550.8 *wall covering*
wall-to-wall 127.7 *including*
wall-to-wall carpet 550.9 *floor covering*
wall-to-wall carpeting 490.4 *pleasurable things*
wall-to-wall coverage 127.1 *inclusion*
wall unit 410.3 *cabinet*
wall up 378.9 *block;* 736.8 *conceal;* 382.17 *murder*
wall writing 744.4 *inscription*
wally 459.3 *foolish person;* 457.3 *unintelligent person;* 486.10 *unskilled person*
walnut 534.1 *brown*
Walpurgis Night 11.3 *witchcraft*
Walter Mitty 472.3 *absent-mindedness*
waltz 22.3 *ballroom dance steps;* 22.2, 22.15 *dance;* 22.4 *historic dancing;* 307.8 *rotate*
waltz away with 246.10 *defeat heavily*
waltzer 22.5 *dancer*
waltz hold 68.7 *ice-dancing*
wamble 307.9 *roll*
wampum 780.2 *cash;* 780.1 *money*
wan 582.21 *deathly;* 530.8 *drained of colour;* 546.4 *ugly;* 260.21 *unhealthy*
wand 743.4 *insignia;* 40.7 *peripheral*
wander 270.6 *be circuitous;* 100.14 *be foreign;* 109.10 *be unrelated;* 325.3 *go astray;* 133.15 *lose one's train of thought;* 300.15 *walk*
wander away 254.8 *be in danger*
wanderer 227.7 *person who moves around;* 550.22 *progression*
wandering 325.16; **325.25**; 227.13 *changeable;* 270.2 *circumlocution;* 270.4 *circumlocutory;* 100.10 *foreign;* 300.16 *moving;* 463.8 *oblivious;* 377.25 *sprawled;* 118.13 *unconventional*
wandering eye 519.2 *poor sight*
wandering mind 325.16 *wandering*
wandering star 29.16 *planet*
wanderlust 342.7 *restlessness*
wander off the point 306.8 *detour*
wane 524.9 *be dim;* 300.13 *be in motion;* 209.6 *change gradually;* 191.1 *contraction;* 214.4 *decrease;* 245.1 *deterioration;* 526.1 *disappear;* 526.4 *disappearance;* 766.12 *lessen;* 441.1 *waste*
wane level off 191.6 *become smaller*
wanga 11.5 *spell;* 11.3 *witchcraft*
wangateur 11.4 *witch*
wangle 645.5 *be cunning;* 800.8 *be dishonourable;* 700.30 *be fraudulent;* 484.3 *expedient plan;* 699.9 *falsification;* 699.26 *falsify;* 700.10 *fraud*
wangling 700.34 *deceiving*
waning 556.12 *ageing;* 191.8 *contracting;* 191.1 *contraction;* 214.1 *decrease;* 214.6 *decreasing;* 524.5 *dim;* 526.6 *disappearing;* 209.7 *gradational;* 766.4 *lessening;* 337.3 *poor health*
waning moon 214.3 *decreasing thing;* 29.17 *moon*
waning of the moon 524.1 *dimness*
Wankel cycle 28.38 *thermodynamics*
Wankel engine 38.11 *engine;* 438.5 *machine*
wanker 620.3 *boring person*
wannabe 617.6 *desirer;* 610.5 *hoper*
want 122.11 *become inferior;* 233.5 *be incomplete;* 218.5 *be insufficient;* 782.12 *be poor;* 218.6 *be unsatisfied;* 474.11 *demand;* 617.1, 617.12 *desire;* 98.2 *disappearance;* 249.2 *economic adversity;* 231.5 *imperfection;* 233.1 *incompleteness;* 617.13 *like;* 135.2 *need;* 135.3 *needfulness;* 249.10 *need money;* 233.2 *omission;* 782.5 *poverty;* 595.8 *prefer;* 756.11 *promise oneself;* 710.1, 710.6 *request;* 135.7 *require;* 218.9 *scarcity;* 635.11 *wish*
want ad 740.9 *advertisement*
wanted 617.7 *desired;* 98.12 *missing;* 135.4 *required*
wanter 617.6 *desirer*
wanting 617.9 *desirous;* 474.5 *expecting;* 231.2, 233.4 *incomplete;* 218.1, 337.13 *insufficient;* 98.12 *missing;* 782.1 *poor*
wanting in respect 668.10 *disrespectful*
wanting to know 644.5 *curious*
want no forgiveness 809.5 *be impenitent*
want nothing 232.5 *be complete*
want of alacrity 637.13 *dissociation*
want of chivalry 659.2 *bad manners*
want of excitement 618.1 *indifference*
want of respect 668.1 *disrespect*
want of skill 486.8 *unskilfulness*
want of zeal 618.1 *indifference*
wanton 642.1 *capricious;* 490.7 *pleased;* 796.13 *unchaste;* 250.12 *unconditional*
wanton destruction 357.3 *destructiveness*
wanton destructiveness 357.3 *destructiveness*
want one's own way 641.9 *be obstinate*
wantonly 250.21 *excessively*
wantonness 593.5 *desire;* 250.6 *liberality;* 796.3 *sexual immorality*
want something to do 580.4 *have leisure*
want to 595.9 *like to*
want to know 644.7 *be curious;* 710.6 *request*
want to vomit 596.5 *dislike*
wapentake 86.5 *state*
War 585
war 585.1; 340.1 *action;* 751.2 *argument;* 585.13 *be at war;* 113.5 *conflict;* 753.2 *disorder;* 584.1 *military affairs;* 662.4 *revolution;* 382.4 *slaughter;* 585.8 *warfare*
war against 585.13 *be at war*
warble 72.18, 515.2 *bird song;* 18.39, 72.26, 515.5, 516.10 *sing;* 729.13 *speak in a particular way;* 509.13 *trill*
warbler 516.5 *melodist;* 72.6 *songbird*
warbling 515.8 *singing*
war bride 570.8 *spouse*
war canoe 50.6 *canoeing*
war cloud 711.1 *warning*
war college 585.6 *art of war*
war correspondent 721.10 *descriptive writer;* 740.11 *newspaperman*
warcraft 585.6 *art of war;* 584.1 *military affairs*
war cry 514.1 *cry;* 711.2 *danger signal;* 585.2 *glory of war;* 742.6 *word*
ward 251.7 *charge;* 87.7 *city district;* 384.17 *defend;* 387.4 *dependent;* 251.4 *detention;* 384.12 *fort;* 35.10, 394.14 *hospital;* 205.1 *part;* 252.10 *protect;* 252.2 *protection;* 252.5 *refuge;* 86.5 *state*
war dance 711.2 *danger signal;* 585.2 *glory of war;* 22.4 *historic dancing;* 10.7 *non-Christian ritual*
warden 251.6 *lawmaker;* 579.15 *manager;* 815.6 *prison officer;* 252.3, 384.15 *protector*
wardenship 252.2 *protection*
warder 251.6 *lawmaker;* 309.5 *person who closes;* 308.3 *person who opens;* 815.6 *prison officer;* 252.3, 384.15 *protector*
warding off 384.1 *defence*
wardmote 16.18 *tribunal*
ward off 634.6 *evade;* 364.3 *fend off;* 384.24 *parry*
ward orderly 35.17 *paramedic*
Wardour Street English 5.9 *ancient language*
wardrobe 23.5 *cabinet;* 551.1 *dress;* 551.2 *dressing;* 21.21 *stage requisite*
wardrobe mistress 21.28 *stagehand;* 551.28 *valet*
wardship 252.2 *protection;* 387.1 *subjection;* 555.1 *youth*
ward sister 35.16 *nurse*
war effort 585.7 *war measures*
warehouse 38.20 *building;* 793.7 *discounter;* 779.7 *emporium;* 359.5 *preserve;* 252.10 *protect;* 439.4 *storage;* 439.6 *store*
warehousing 439.4 *storage*
wares 438.7 *equipment;* 778.8 *merchandise;* 440.5 *personal estate;* 356.7 *produce*
warfare 585.8; 113.5 *conflict;* 585.1 *war*
warfarin 43.14 *pest control*
war fever 585.5 *bellicosity*
war-fevered 585.16 *warlike*
war footing 585.7 *war measures*
war galley 586.25 *historical naval ships*
war game 69.1 *game*
war games 585.6 *art of war*
warhammer 587.7 *blunt weapon*
warhead 587.15 *explosive*
warhorse 59.3; 586.19 *cavalry;* 485.5 *expert*
warily 471.15 *attentively;* 665.12 *carefully;* 616.7 *cautiously;* 637.17 *unwillingly*
wariness 471.3 *carefulness;* 616.1 *caution;* 645.1 *cunning;* 637.13 *dissociation;* 665.5 *watchfulness*
war in heaven 507.1 *loudness*
warlike 585.16; 342.18 *active;* 586.33 *combative;* 661.8 *defying;* 701.9 *hostile;* 381.22, 613.11 *militant;* 584.8 *military;* 336.11 *strong in spirit;* 380.6 *violent*
warlike habits 585.5 *bellicosity*
warlike people 586.7 *militarist nation*
warlock 475.8 *oracle;* 11.4 *witch*
warlord 400.4 *absolute ruler*
war-loving 585.16 *warlike*
warm 31.50; **493.11**; 624.16 *angry;* 493.14 *be hot;* 593.25 *be loved;* 529.11 *colourful;* 490.10 *comfort;* 703.10 *demonstrative;* 449.13 *discovering;* 726.3 *emphatic;* 569.8 *friendly;* 493.9 *hot;* 147.9 *near;* 490.6 *pleasant;* 490.7 *pleased;* 590.12 *sensitive;* 654.15 *sociable*
warm air 31.10 *air movement*
warm as toast 493.10 *on fire*
warm-blooded 71.25 *mammalian;* 493.12 *warm-hearted*
warm-blooded animal 71.1 *mammal*
warm-bloodedness 488.2 *ability to sense;* 493.1 *heat*
warm current 493.8 *hot place*
war measures 585.7
war medal 794.1 *trophy*
warmed through 493.13 *heated*
warmed up 493.13 *heated;* 112.11 *reprinted*
war memorial 583.4 *funeral objects;* 744.11 *monument*
warmer 493.3 *heater;* 31.50 *warm*
warm feeling 342.4 *energy*
warm friendship 569.3 *familiarity*
warm front 31.10 *air movement;* 493.5 *hot weather*
warm heart 627.1 *pity*
warm-hearted 493.12; 650.6 *benevolent;* 569.8 *friendly;* 627.6 *pitying;* 590.12 *sensitive;* 419.6 *soft-hearted*
warm-heartedly 569.17 *in friendship;* 627.13 *pitifully*
warm-heartedness 569.1 *friendship;* 627.1 *pity*
warm hue 529.3 *hue*
warming 493.9 *hot*
warming pan 493.3 *heater;* 410.15 *pot*
warmly 493.17; 624.18 *angrily;* 703.21 *demonstratively;* 569.17 *in friendship;* 31.65 *meteorologically;* 490.11 *pleasingly;* 535.10 *ruddily;* 654.18 *sociably;* 590.20 *with feeling*
warmness 569.1 *friendship;* 493.1 *heat*
warm occlusion 31.10 *air movement*
warmonger 586.36 *combat;* 586.6 *militarist*

warmongering 381.22 *militant;* 585.16 *warlike*
warm reception 654.9 *welcome*
warm sector 31.11 *weather system*
warm spell 31.23 *heat;* 493.5 *hot weather*
warm spring 92.10 *miscellaneous*
warmth 726.1 *emphasis;* 569.1 *friendship;* 590.5 *good feeling;* 28.35, 493.1 *heat;* 529.3 *hue;* 535.5 *redness;* 654.1 *sociability;* 654.9 *welcome*
warm through 25.55 *cook*
warm to 569.13 *befriend;* 593.24 *be in love*
warm up 493.14 *be hot;* 576.9 *exercise;* 632.18 *habituate;* 243.4 *prepare for action;* 243.8 *prepare oneself;* 112.20 *renew*
warm-up 576.5 *exercise*
warm-up lap 61.6 *motor-racing terms*
warm weather 31.23 *heat*
warm welcome 654.9 *welcome*
warm work 576.1 *work*
warn **711.5**; 713.5 *advise;* 616.6 *caution;* 670.20 *censure;* 481.1 *dissuade;* 129.19 *forecast;* 475.11 *predict;* 753.6 *protest;* 742.12 *signal*
warned **711.9**; 243.18 *prepared*
warner **711.4**; 475.8 *oracle;* 253.3 *security officer*
Warning 711
warning **711.1**; **711.8**; 693.7, 713.1 *advice;* 713.7 *advising;* 670.7 *blame;* 481.6 *dissuasion;* 481.9 *dissuasive;* 616.2 *insurance;* 475.5 *omen;* 475.3 *plan;* 713.3 *precept;* 129.6 *preview;* 753.1 *protest;* 742.16 *signalling*
warning alarm 711.2 *danger signal*
warning cry 515.1 *animal cry*
warning example 711.1 *warning*
warning flag 742.4 *signal*
warning flare 711.2 *danger signal*
warning light 711.2 *danger signal;* 522.6 *electric light;* 742.4 *signal*
warning notice 397.2 *demand*
warning shot 711.2 *danger signal;* 475.3 *plan*
warning sign 711.2 *danger signal;* 475.3 *plan;* 742.1 *sign*
warning signal 742.4 *signal*
warning sound 742.4 *signal*
warning voice 711.1 *warning*
warn off 128.7 *exclude*
war of attrition 381.16 *terrorist attack;* 585.1 *war*
war of conquest 585.1 *war*
war of containment 585.1 *war*
war of expansion 585.1 *war*
war of independence 585.1 *war*
war of liberation 585.1 *war*
war of nerves 612.4 *intimidation;* 585.1 *war*
war of the elements 380.5 *violent weather*
war of words 585.1 *war*
war on all fronts 585.1 *war*
war on want 585.1 *war*
warp 176.11 *angle;* 465.12 *bias;* 224.8 *cause change;* 234.11 *deform;* 234.9, 325.6 *distort;* 234.1 *distortion;* 403.2 *fabric;* 699.26 *falsify;* 193.8 *interweave;* 50.3 *parts of a sailing boat;* 245.6 *pervert;* 702.11 *practise sophistry;* 466.13 *prejudge;* 362.11 *pull;* 323.10 *sail;* 325.17 *torsion;* 42.4, 193.3 *weaving*
war paint 529.9 *complexion;* 547.4 *cosmetics*
warp and woof 404.4 *weave*
warpath 585.8 *warfare*
warped 231.3 *deformed;* 465.8 *unjust*
warping 699.9 *falsification*
warplane 586.31 *military aircraft*
war plans 584.1 *military affairs*
war policy 585.5 *bellicosity;* 585.7 *war measures*
war preparations 585.7 *war measures*
warrant 397.2, 397.10 *demand;* 716.6 *documentation;* 452.14, 756.2, 756.8 *guarantee;* 714.8 *justify;* 16.29 *legalization;* 16.6 *legal process;* 452.21 *make certain;* 16.65 *make legal;* 780.14 *paper money;* 396.9 *permission;* 750.8, 750.29, 757.2 *permit;* 713.3 *precept;* 253.2, 253.11 *promise;* 252.10 *protect;* 252.1 *safety;* 454.1 *verify*
warrantable 714.13 *vindicable*
warranted 396.16 *authorized;* 253.7, 452.4 *guaranteed;* 756.13 *guaranteeing;* 16.44 *legal;* 757.7 *permitted;* 750.18 *permitting;* 252.6 *safe*
warrant of arrest 397.2 *demand*
warrant officer 586.17 *army person*
warrantor 452.15 *guarantor*
warranty 744.2 *certificate;* 716.6 *documentation;* 452.14, 756.2 *guarantee;* 750.8, 757.2 *permit;* 253.2 *promise;* 252.1 *safety*
war readiness 585.7 *war measures*
warren 183.2 *concave land;* 565.13 *lair*
warring **585.15**; 751.9 *disagreeing;* 381.22 *militant;* 585.8 *warfare*
Warrior 586.25 *historical naval ships*
warrior 381.19 *attacker;* 586.1 *combatant;* 613.7 *courageous person;* 586.8 *soldier*
warrior for God 586.6 *militarist*
Warsaw Pact 755.3 *alliance*
warship **586.24**; 323.3 *vessel*
war skills 585.6 *art of war*
war song 585.2 *glory of war*
war strategy 585.6 *art of war*
wart 182.2 *bulge;* 418.7 *hard substance;* 260.13 *skin disease*
wartime 585.4 *belligerency*
wartime censorship 585.8 *warfare*
wartime conditions 585.4 *belligerency*
wartime propaganda 585.8 *warfare*
wartime rations 557.7 *food*
war to the end 585.1 *war*
war to the knife 585.1 *war*
warts and all 232.9 *completely;* 698.18 *truthful;* 698.36 *truthfully;* 698.5 *truthfulness*
warty 420.2 *coarse*
war upon 585.13 *be at war*
war vessel 586.24 *warship*
war-weary 589.7 *peaceful*
war whoop 711.2 *danger signal;* 585.2 *glory of war*
war widow 571.6 *surviving spouse*
war work 585.7 *war measures*
wary 616.4, 637.3 *cautious;* 645.4 *cunning;* 711.9 *warned;* 471.7 *watchful*
war zone 585.10 *battleground*
wash **433.11**; 256.5 *ablutions;* 394.9 *balm;* 239.6 *be convenient;* 698.27 *be true;* 256.13 *clean;* 529.15 *colour;* 90.7 *flow;* 433.34 *hose;* 256.8 *laundry;* 37.11 *linctus;* 19.19 *paint;* 19.8 *painting;* 529.4 *pigment;* 255.10, 256.15 *purify;* 581.6 *refresher;* 90.6 *river flow;* 88.2 *small lake;* 217.4 *suffice;* 42.15 *treat;* 531.13 *whiten*
wash and brush up 547.3 *beauty treatment;* 581.6 *refresher*
wash-and-wear clothes 551.1 *dress*
wash bag 547.5 *make-up box*
washbasin 256.6, 410.12 *bath*
washboard 420.7 *rough thing;* 68.1 *skiing;* 256.7 *washer;* 184.4 *wrinkled thing*
washbowl 256.6 *bath*
wash clean 256.13 *clean;* 255.10 *purify*
wash down 256.13 *clean;* 558.13 *drink*
washed 256.17 *cleaned;* 90.11 *flooded;* 19.27 *painted;* 42.11 *treated*
washed out 530.7 *colourless*
washed up 131.21 *ended;* 247.10 *failed;* 261.1 *fatigued;* 249.8 *unlucky*
washer **256.7**
washer-drier 256.7 *washer*
washerman 256.12 *cleaner*
washer-up 256.12 *cleaner*
washerwoman 256.12 *cleaner*
washin 322.7 *miscellaneous aviation terms*
washing 256.5 *ablutions;* 256.2 *cleaning;* 42.8 *fabric treatment;* 256.8 *laundry;* 19.2 *painting;* 255.2 *purification;* 90.6 *river flow;* 433.11 *wash*
washing machine 256.7 *washer*
washing one's hands 758.3 *self-exemption*
washing out 256.2 *cleaning;* 255.2 *purification*
washing powder 256.9 *cleaning agent;* 255.3 *purifier*
washing soda 256.9 *cleaning agent;* 255.3 *purifier*
Washington 87.2 *American cities;* 396.6 *place of authority;* 400.8 *the power structure*
washing-up 256.2 *cleaning;* 256.8 *laundry*
washing-up liquid 256.9 *cleaning agent;* 255.3 *purifier*
wash off 256.13 *clean;* 358.1 *obliterate*
wash one's hands of 767.9 *dispose of;* 372.13 *diverge;* 479.2 *equivocate;* 758.12 *exempt oneself;* 341.4 *not act;* 256.15 *purify*
washout 247.5 *failing person;* 90.6 *river flow;* 247.4 *unsuccessful thing*
wash out 256.13 *clean;* 530.6 *decolour;* 358.1 *obliterate;* 255.10, 256.15 *purify*
washroom 256.6 *bath;* 560.13 *lavatory;* 565.7 *room;* 767.7 *toilet*
washstand 256.6 *bath*
washtub 410.12 *bath;* 256.7 *washer*
wash up 256.13 *clean*
washwoman 256.12 *cleaner*
washy 530.7 *colourless*
wasp 76.1 *insect;* 654.10 *social animal;* 76.4 *social insect*
waspish 651.14 *hostile;* 625.4 *irascible;* 380.6 *violent*
waspishly 625.9 *irascibly*
waspishness 651.4 *bitterness;* 625.1 *irascibility*
wasps' nest 76.4 *social insect*
wasp waist 191.3 *contracted thing;* 153.7 *thinness*
wasp-waisted 153.1 *thin*
wassail 690.8 *get drunk*
wassailing 690.5 *drunken*
wastage 214.1 *decrease;* 238.6 *refuse;* 441.3, 766.3 *waste*
Waste 441
waste **441.1**; **441.3**; **441.9**; **563.10**; **681.7**; **766.3**; 191.6 *become smaller;* 766.11 *be wasteful;* 526.3 *cause to disappear;* 357.12, 787.2 *consume;* 214.1 *decrease;* 219.1 *excess;* 560.4 *excrement;* 238.4 *futility;* 141.3 *geographical space;* 245.4 *impair;* 245.10 *impairment;* 563.3 *infertile;* 563.1 *infertility;* 357.10 *lay waste;* 218.7 *make insufficient;* 191.5 *make smaller;* 351.1, 351.2 *misuse;* 382.17 *murder;* 350.5 *not use;* 315.2 *outflow;* 686.11 *overindulge;* 356.3 *product;* 238.6 *refuse;* 215.2 *residue;* 349.1, 349.6 *use*
waste an opportunity 288.7 *lose one's chance;* 465.10 *misjudge*
waste away 191.6 *become smaller;* 153.15 *be emaciated;* 260.24 *be unhealthy;* 214.4 *decrease;* 375.3 *disintegrate;* 766.12 *lessen;* 441.1 *waste*
wastebasket 410.7 *basket;* 767.4 *wastebin*
wastebin 767.4
wasted 337.9 *dilapidated;* 153.2 *emaciated;* 238.2 *futile;* 337.10 *ill;* 563.3 *infertile;* 351.4 *misused;* 191.7 *smaller;* 350.1 *unused*
wasted day 247.4 *unsuccessful thing*
wasted effort 486.9 *bungling;* 342.9 *overactivity;* 766.3 *waste;* 238.5 *waste of effort*
waste disposal 28.74 *nuclear waste*
waste disposal unit 256.10 *cleaning object;* 767.4 *wastebin*
waste disposer 767.4 *wastebin*
wasted labour 238.5 *waste of effort*
waste effort **238.9**; 486.6 *act foolishly;* 342.13 *be busy;* 351.1 *misuse;* 441.1 *waste*
wasteful **441.8**; 351.5 *abusive;* 681.1 *extravagant;* 238.2 *futile;* 686.8 *overindulgent;* 766.17 *unprofitable*
wastefully **441.10**; 351.6 *abusively;* 766.20 *at a loss;* 681.9 *extravagantly*
wastefulness 681.4 *extravagance;* 238.4 *futility;* 686.3 *overindulgence;* 441.3, 766.3 *waste*
wasteful person 766.6 *loser*
wasteland 428.14 *desert;* 357.5 *havoc;* 563.1 *infertility;* 86.6 *regions*
waste matter 560.4 *excrement*
waste no more time 355.2 *withdraw*
waste no words 269.4 *be concise*
waste of breath 766.3 *waste;* 238.5 *waste of effort*
waste of effort **238.5**; 563.1 *infertility*
waste of space 238.5 *waste of effort*
waste of time 563.1 *infertility;* 766.3 *waste;* 238.5 *waste of effort*
waste of waters 563.1 *infertility*
waste one's breath 766.11 *be wasteful;* 238.9 *waste effort*
waste one's efforts 766.11 *be wasteful;* 245.5 *hurt*
waste one's time 766.11 *be wasteful*
wastepaper 238.6 *refuse*
wastepaper basket 410.7 *basket;* 767.4 *wastebin*
waste pipe 256.10 *cleaning object;* 767.4 *wastebin*
waste processing 28.74 *nuclear waste*
waste product **441.5**; 356.3 *product;* 238.6 *refuse*
waster **441.6**; 766.6 *loser;* 681.6 *spendthrift*
waste reprocessing 334.8 *nuclear power*
waste time 103.10 *attempt the impossible;* 343.12 *be inactive;* 333.2 *hesitate;* 288.6 *take untimely action;* 294.7 *wait;* 238.9 *waste effort*
wasteyard 767.5
wasting 191.8 *contracting;* 191.1 *contraction;* 153.8 *emaciation;* 236.5 *harmful;* 382.2 *murder;* 218.3 *underfed*
wasting away 214.1 *decrease;* 214.6 *decreasing;* 245.12 *deteriorated;* 153.2 *emaciated;* 687.6 *fasting;* 766.4 *lessening;* 260.22 *sick;* 441.3 *waste*
wasting disease 260.4 *disease*
wasting no time 332.1 *swift*
wasting time 333.8 *slowness*
wastrel 681.6, 787.9 *spendthrift;* 441.6 *waster;* 804.9 *wicked person*
Wast Water 88.4 *British lakes*
wat 10.11 *place of worship*
watch **281.7**; **518.15**; 97.12 *attend;* 665.10 *be careful;* 692.30 *communicate;* 384.17 *defend;* 449.1 *discover;* 384.14 *guard;* 742.5 *indicator;* 323.7 *nautical person;* 341.4 *not act;* 276.4 *period of activity;* 16.17 *police officer;* 252.3 *protector;* 342.14 *push;* 253.3 *security officer;* 471.11 *take note of;* 810.2 *task;* 275.13 *timer;* 711.4 *warner;* 665.5 *watchfulness*
watchable 518.23 *visible*
watch and wait 341.4 *not act*
watch and ward 252.2 *protection*
watchcase 550.13 *casing*
Watch Committee 16.2 *jurisdiction;* 795.6 *moralist;* 255.6 *prude*
watchdog 713.4 *adviser;* 71.9 *dog;* 795.6 *moralist;* 518.11 *observer;* 252.3 *protector;* 711.4 *warner*
watchdog group 480.14 *motivator*
watcher 518.11 *observer;* 252.3 *protector;* 97.5 *someone present*
watchface 281.8 *face*
watch fire 522.8 *fire;* 742.4 *signal*
watchful **471.7**; 342.18 *active;* 665.9 *careful;* 616.4 *cautious;* 629.5 *distrustful;* 474.5 *expecting;* 518.21 *seeing;* 252.8 *tutelary*
watchfully **518.26**; 471.15 *attentively;* 616.7 *cautiously;* 629.9 *jealously;* 252.11 *safely*
watchfulness **665.5**; 616.1 *caution;* 665.3 *circumspection;* 471.2 *close attention;* 629.2 *distrust;* 518.3 *observation;* 342.7 *restlessness*
watchful person 665.8
watch glass 550.12 *protective covering;* 527.8 *transparent thing*
watching 97.8 *attendant;* 665.9 *careful;* 518.3 *observation;* 518.21 *seeing;* 665.5 *watchfulness*
watching one's figure 153.10 *diet*
watch it 711.10 *look out!*
watch like a hawk 518.15 *watch*
watchmaker 578.2 *artisan;* 281.12 *chronologist;* 275.14 *timekeeper*
watchmaking 275.10 *chronometry;* 281.4 *horology*
watchman 384.14 *guard;* 518.11 *observer;* 252.3 *protector;* 253.3 *security officer;* 711.4 *warner*
watch one's step 616.5 *be cautious;* 711.6 *be warned;* 140.17 *obey orders*
watch one's weight 153.14 *become thin*
watch out 711.10 *look out!*
watch out for 474.10 *wait;* 518.15 *watch*
watch over 665.11 *care for;* 579.1 *manage;* 252.10, 550.30 *protect;* 518.15 *watch*
watch the clock 275.19 *clock on;* 281.16 *measure time*
watch the float 55.7 *angle*
watch the pennies 782.12 *be poor*
watchtower 154.6 *tall thing;* 397.8 *vantage point;* 518.9 *viewpoint*
watchword 745.1 *maxim;* 585.8 *warfare;* 742.6 *word*
Water 433
water **433.1**; **433.29**; 256.9 *cleaning agent;* 44.15 *cultivate;* 431.1 *fluid;* 557.11 *food content;* 244.1 *improve;* 431.2 *juice;* 554.3 *life requirements;* 562.7 *make fertile;* 417.6 *make sparse;* 81.12 *manage grassland;* 412.8 *mix;* 19.8 *painting;* 43.18 *practise livestock farming;* 558.15 *provide drink;* 436.5 *provision;* 255.3 *purifier;* 558.6 *soft drink;* 527.8 *transparent thing;* 319.1 *transport;* 319.5 *transportable;* 560.6 *urine;* 337.5 *weak thing*
water at the mouth 557.22 *eat well;* 315.12 *leak;* 560.20 *salivate*

water balance 31.9 *atmospheric process*
water bear 75.4 *arthropod*
water bed 23.6 *bed*
water bird 72.3
water biscuit 25.39 *loaf*
waterborne 323.11 *nautical;* 319.5 *transportable*
waterborne disease 260.4 *disease*
water bowl 43.10 *farm tool*
water boy 316.7 *transferor*
water butt 44.3 *ornamental garden*
water carrier 433.16; 316.7 *transferor*
water cart 433.16 *water carrier*
water clock 281.6 *clock*
water closet 565.7 *room;* 767.7 *toilet*
water cloud 31.18 *cloud*
watercolour 19.16 *artist;* 529.15 *colour;* 19.8 *painting;* 717.2 *reproduction*
watercolourist 529.6 *painter;* 717.4 *person who makes a representation*
watercolour pigments 529.5 *paint*
watercolours 19.11 *artist's materials;* 529.5 *paint*
water-cooled 494.9 *heat-resistant*
water-cooled reactor 437.7 *nuclear power*
watercourse 50.6 *canoeing;* 317.11 *channel;* 90.1 *river*
water cure 433.7 *hydrotherapeutics*
water cycle 30.10; 433.17
water-divine 11.23 *divine*
water-diviner 449.12 *discoverer;* 475.9 *forecaster;* 433.20 *hydrologist*
water-divining 11.9 *divination*
water down 367.4 *debase;* 377.14, 433.30, 497.8 *dilute;* 214.5 *make smaller;* 417.6 *make sparse;* 153.16 *make thin;* 412.8 *mix;* 728.22 *play down;* 337.7 *weaken*
water-drinker 689.8 *sober person*
water-drinking 689.1 *sober;* 689.6 *sobriety*
water-driven 437.10 *powered*
watered 541.7 *iridescent;* 44.19 *ornamental;* 417.2 *rarefied;* 497.5 *tasteless*
watered-down 377.27 *dilute;* 433.22 *diluted;* 728.19 *downplayed;* 728.17 *insipid;* 412.12 *mixed;* 417.2 *rarefied;* 497.5 *tasteless;* 153.5 *thinned*
watered-down soup 337.5 *weak thing*
watered silk 541.5 *variegated thing*
waterfall 90.2 *channel;* 305.3 *downflow;* 315.2 *outflow;* 334.6 *source of energy*
water filter 256.10 *cleaning object;* 255.3 *purifier*
water flea 75.4 *arthropod*
water flow 90.6 *river flow*
waterfowl 72.3 *water bird*
waterfowl shooting 60.2 *hunting*
waterfront 164.1 *edge;* 164.8 *edging;* 167.1 *front*
water garden 44.2 *garden*
Watergate 736.5 *evasion*
water gun 330.9 *firearm*
water hazard 56.1 *golf*
water hole 88.2 *small lake*
water hydrant 433.13 *irrigator*
water ice 25.35 *dessert*
wateriness 433.3; 431.5 *fluidity;* 728.8 *insipidness;* 429.1 *moisture;* 268.2 *runniness;* 497.1 *tastelessness;* 153.12 *thinning;* 527.5 *transparency*
watering 433.8; 497.1 *dilution;* 44.5 *gardening;* 433.26 *wetting*
watering can 44.6 *garden tool;* 433.12 *sprinkler;* 410.11 *vessel*
watering cart 433.16 *water carrier*
watering down 377.3, 433.5, 497.1 *dilution;* 728.9 *downplaying;* 245.10 *impairment;* 412.1 *mixture;* 153.12 *thinning*
watering eyes 260.9 *respiratory disease*
watering place 394.14 *hospital*
waterish 433.21 *watery*
water jug 433.16 *water carrier*
water jump 59.9 *jumping;* 47.1 *track events*
waterless 428.1 *dry*
waterlessness 428.11 *dryness*
water level 187.2 *horizontal surface*
water line 742.5 *indicator;* 26.6 *measuring instrument*
waterlog 433.29 *water*
waterlogged 92.11 *continental;* 335.12 *impotent;* 429.11 *marshy;* 254.2 *unsafe;* 433.23 *wet*
Waterloo 247.2 *defeat;* 357.4 *ruin*
water loss 389.4 *leak*
water louse 75.4 *arthropod*
waterman 323.8 *boatman;* 50.9 *sailor*
watermark 742.5 *indicator;* 743.3 *means of identification;* 26.6 *measuring instrument*
water meadow 92.6 *lowland*
water meter 26.8 *meter*
water mill 437.8 *renewable energy*
water nymph 8.5 *deity*
water of life 690.12 *alcohol*
water pipe 433.13 *irrigator;* 496.7 *tobacco*
water pistol 433.12 *sprinkler*
water pocket 88.2 *small lake*
water power 334.4 *energy;* 90.6 *river flow*
waterproof 428.10; 309.12 *closed;* 551.12 *coat;* 252.7 *invulnerable;* 428.22 *keep dry;* 359.5 *preserve;* 42.15 *treat;* 42.11 *treated*
waterproofed 428.10 *waterproof*
waterproofing 42.8 *fabric treatment;* 359.1 *preservation*
waterproof matchbox 62.4 *climbing equipment*
waterproof paper 435.3 *paper*
waters 561.7 *obstetrics*
water's edge 90.2 *channel;* 164.1 *edge*
watershed 30.8 *drainage;* 154.4 *mountain range;* 761.3 *turning point*
waterside 90.2 *channel;* 164.1 *edge;* 164.8 *edging*
watersoaked 433.23 *wet*
waters of the earth 30.5 *earth*
water spirit 8.5 *deity;* 91.4 *sea god*
waterspout 307.4 *vortex;* 31.16 *wind vortex*
water sprite 91.4 *sea god*
water start 50.7 *windsurfing*
water supply 436.1 *provision*
water-supply engineering 38.17 *civil engineering*
water-supply system 38.24 *water system*
water system 38.24; 90.1 *river*
water table 30.9 *groundwater*
water tank 433.16 *water carrier*
watertight 309.12 *closed;* 230.1 *perfect;* 428.10 *waterproof*
water tower 439.4 *storage;* 154.6 *tall thing;* 321.2 *track*
Water Transport 323
water travel 323.1; 300.2 *momentum*
water trough 321.2 *track*
water turbine 437.8 *renewable energy;* 38.12 *turbine*
water vapour 432.4; 433.3 *wateriness*
water wave 28.14 *sound wave*
waterway 323.2; 317.11 *channel;* 90.1 *river*
water wheel 307.6 *rotator;* 334.6 *source of energy*
water wings 252.4 *safety device;* 67.3 *survival swimming*
water witch 11.4 *witch*
waterworks 256.10 *cleaning object;* 577.1 *workshop*
waterworn 421.2 *uniform*
watery 433.21; 431.15 *flowing;* 728.17 *insipid;* 218.1, 337.13 *insufficient;* 429.10 *misty;* 560.29 *salivating;* 268.10 *slippery;* 153.5 *thinned;* 527.1 *transparent*
watery-eyed 519.9 *weak-sighted*
watery grave 582.5 *ways of dying*
watery waste 91.1 *sea*
Watson 36.29 *psychologist*
Watsonian 36.33 *Freudian*
Watsonian psychology 36.1 *psychology*
watt 334.5 *unit of work*
wattage 334.5 *unit of work*
watt-hour meter 39.34 *power supply*
wattle 193.2 *braid*
wattle and daub 435.2 *building material;* 356.8 *construction*
wattmeter 28.90 *ammeter;* 39.23 *electrical instrument*
Wave 586.27 *naval man*
wave 28.12; 30.14; 91.3; 326.5; 326.12; 327.22 *agitate;* 227.11 *be changeable;* 177.2 *bend;* 91.10 *billow;* 300.11 *bodily movement;* 180.6 *convolute;* 738.1 *display;* 327.26 *flicker;* 742.3, 742.11 *gesture;* 658.12 *greet;* 297.6 *radio frequency;* 326.4, 326.11 *rock;* 91.1 *sea;* 658.5 *sign of courtesy;* 300.15 *walk*
wave a wand 11.21 *bewitch*
waveband 692.14 *radio transmission*
wave by 742.11 *gesture*
wave crest 91.3 *wave;* 28.16 *waveform*
waved 738.13 *displayed*
wave equation 326.5 *wave*
wave erosion 30.35 *weathering*
waveform 28.16; 39.14 *terminal*
wave frequency 298.1 *regularity*
wave goodbye 313.6 *part*
waveguide 39.27 *wire*
wave in the wind 227.11 *be changeable*
wave-jump 50.18 *windsurf*
wave-jumping 50.7 *windsurfing*
wavelength 297.6 *radio frequency;* 326.5 *wave;* 28.16 *waveform*
wavelet 91.3 *wave*
wave mechanics 28.3 *modern physics;* 28.80 *quantum theory*
wave motion 298.1 *regularity;* 326.4 *rock;* 28.12 *wave*
wave number 326.5 *wave;* 28.16 *waveform*
wave on 742.11 *gesture*
wave one's hat 742.11 *gesture*
wave–particle duality 28.80 *quantum theory*
wave pool 67.7 *swimming pool*
wave power 28.11 *energy;* 437.8 *renewable energy;* 334.6 *source of energy*
wave-powered 334.17 *powered*
wave propagation 28.12 *wave*
wave property 28.15
waver 299.6 *be irregular;* 227.12 *be irresolute;* 451.8 *disbelieve;* 327.12, 327.26 *flicker;* 453.19 *hesitate;* 299.1 *irregularity;* 326.4, 326.11 *rock;* 326.10, 639.5 *vacillate*
waverer 639.15 *indecisive person;* 341.2 *nonacting person*
wave-ride 50.18 *windsurf*
wave-riding 50.7 *windsurfing*
wavering 453.8 *capricious;* 453.16 *capriciousness;* 224.11, 227.13 *changeable;* 299.4 *irregular;* 299.1 *irregularity;* 453.2 *irresolute;* 453.11 *irresoluteness;* 227.2 *irresolution;* 326.15, 639.1 *vacillating;* 326.3 *vacillation;* 337.12 *weak-willed*
wavering loyalty 800.2 *faithlessness*
waveringly 227.15 *changeably;* 299.8 *irregularly;* 327.28 *shakily*
wavery 327.20 *flickering*
wavesail 50.18 *windsurf*
wavesailing 50.7 *windsurfing*
waveshape 28.16 *waveform*
waves of nausea 260.3 *symptom*
wave speed 28.16 *waveform*
wave the big stick 647.5 *be severe*
wave theory of light 28.5 *theory*
wave through 742.11 *gesture*
wave to 742.11 *gesture*
wave to and fro 326.12 *wave*
wave trough 28.16 *waveform*
wave up and down 326.12 *wave*
wavily 180.8 *circularly;* 177.7 *curvedly*
waviness 91.3 *wave*
waving 326.17; 326.4 *rock;* 601.8 *salute*
wavy 180.4 *convolutional;* 177.5 *well-rounded*
wavy navy 586.27 *naval man*
wax 430.2 *adhesive;* 624.4 *anger;* 190.6 *become bigger;* 525.12 *become visible;* 760.8 *be transformed;* 209.6 *change gradually;* 256.9 *cleaning agent;* 550.24 *coat;* 550.3 *coating;* 552.7 *depilation;* 550.9 *floor covering;* 418.9 *harden;* 213.4 *increase;* 33.6 *lipid;* 268.5 *lubricant;* 268.18 *lubricate;* 421.10 *polish;* 365.12 *rub;* 19.14 *sculptor's materials;* 421.11 *smooth;* 419.13 *soften;* 419.11 *soft thing;* 79.9 *tree product*
wax and wane 227.11 *be changeable;* 224.7 *be changed;* 326.8 *oscillate;* 326.1 *oscillation*
wax a ski 68.14 *ski*
wax candle 522.5 *incandescent light*
waxed 421.4 *polished*
waxed paper 25.6 *kitchen equipment*
wax eloquent 270.5 *be diffuse*
waxen 531.4 *pale*
waxer 421.9 *smoother*
wax figure 717.6 *image*
waxily 419.17 *softly*
waxiness 268.3 *oiliness*
waxing 525.1 *appearance;* 525.7 *appearing;* 209.7 *gradational;* 190.8 *growing;* 190.1 *growth;* 547.9 *hair removal;* 213.1 *increase;* 213.6 *increasing*
waxing and waning 224.1 *change;* 224.11 *changeable*
waxing moon 213.3 *increasing thing;* 29.17 *moon*
wax lyrical 669.15 *compliment*
wax modeller 19.17 *sculptor*
wax modelling 19.12 *sculpture*
wax paper 435.3 *paper;* 550.4 *wrapping*
wax polish 502.2 *fragrant thing*
waxwork 717.6 *image;* 19.12 *sculpture*
waxworks 439.5 *collection*
waxy 624.16 *angry;* 419.2 *pliant;* 268.13 *slippery;* 430.8 *viscous*
Way 317
way 317.1; 631.7; 632.3; 733.4 *approach;* 324.2 *bearing;* 302.11 *course;* 140.6 *custom;* 352.1 *means;* 484.2 *policy;* 221.1 *state;* 724.1 *style*
way back 3.9 *distant past*
way back when 296.19 *anciently*
way behind 145.10 *distantly*
waybill 743.3 *means of identification;* 789.4 *statement*
way down 305.1 *descent*
way forward 302.11 *course*
way in 314.5 *entrance;* 317.2 *route*
way in front 145.10 *distantly*
waylay 645.5 *be cunning;* 700.33 *snare*
way of doing things 317.1 *way*
way off 116.4 *dissimilar*
way off the mark 274.17 *mistaken*
way of life 631.6; 554.10 *lifestyle;* 7.1 *religion;* 317.1, 632.3 *way*
way of putting something 719.1 *interpretation*
way of things 140.6 *custom*
way out 315.6; 390.2 *deliverance;* 116.4 *dissimilar;* 118.14 *eccentric;* 139.17 *exceptional;* 484.3 *expedient plan;* 389.2 *means of escape;* 487.2 *not customary;* 317.2 *route;* 235.1 *worthy*
way over 317.9 *bridge;* 317.2 *route*
way-rad 235.1 *worthy*
ways 632.3 *way*
ways and means 352.1 *means;* 317.1 *way*
wayside 164.1 *edge;* 164.8 *edging;* 147.9 *near*
ways of dying 582.5
ways of the fathers 1.8 *tradition*
ways of thinking 442.2
way things are 140.6 *custom*
way through 317.2 *route*
way to 317.2 *route*
way under 317.8 *tunnel*
wayward 642.1 *capricious;* 227.14 *irresolute;* 641.2 *refractory;* 264.14 *troublesome;* 635.8 *wilful*
waywardly 227.15 *changeably;* 264.29 *perversely*
waywardness 642.2 *caprice;* 635.3 *wilfulness*
way with 579.3 *management*
way with words 729.2 *power of speech*
wayworn 261.1 *fatigued*
WC 560.13 *lavatory;* 565.7 *room;* 767.7 *toilet*
W chromosome 34.14 *chromosome*
we 139.12 *I*
weak 337.8; 32.36 *acid;* 424.1 *brittle;* 122.17 *defective;* 433.22 *diluted;* 558.17 *drinkable;* 247.10 *failed;* 511.1 *faint-sounding;* 261.1 *fatigued;* 231.1 *imperfect;* 335.12 *impotent;* 218.1 *insufficient;* 685.6 *moderate;* 524.6 *murky;* 124.2 *obscure;* 417.2 *rarefied;* 704.6 *refutable;* 497.5 *tasteless;* 153.5 *thinned;* 639.3 *timid;* 260.21 *unhealthy;* 254.2 *unsafe;* 804.13 *venial*
weak acid 32.8 *acid*
weak alkali 32.9 *base*
weak as a baby 337.10 *ill;* 218.1 *insufficient*
weak as a child 337.10 *ill*
weak as a kitten 337.10 *ill;* 218.1 *insufficient*
weak as water 337.10 *ill*
weak bladder 560.3 *urination*
weak coffee 497.3 *tasteless items*
weak constitution 260.1 *ill health*
weak effort 231.6 *imperfect item*
weak ego 674.5 *self-deprecation*
weaken 337.7; 556.17 *age;* 260.24 *be unhealthy;* 337.6 *be weak;* 224.8 *cause change;* 530.6 *decolour;* 245.1 *deteriorate;* 497.8 *dilute;* 261.6 *fatigue;* 245.5 *hurt;* 214.5 *make smaller;* 417.6 *make sparse;* 153.16 *make thin;* 412.8 *mix;* 685.4 *moderate;* 335.7 *remove power from;* 441.1 *waste*
weakened 337.11; 245.12 *deteriorated;* 245.13 *dilapidated;* 261.1 *fatigued;* 412.12 *mixed*
weakened state 337.3 *poor health*
weakening 556.12 *ageing;* 214.1 *decrease;* 245.11 *hurt;* 497.1 *tastelessness*

weaker sex 568.1 *female sex*
weak foundation 337.1 *weakness*
weak heart 260.10 *cardiovascular disease*
weak interaction 28.79 *fundamental interaction*
weak-kneed 614.3 *cowardly*; 388.5 *submitting*; 639.3 *timid*; 337.12 *weak-willed*
weakliness 260.1 *ill health*; 337.3 *poor health*
weakling **337.4**; 639.15 *indecisive person*; 159.4 *little person*; 249.5 *person in adversity*; 260.19 *sick person*; 153.9 *thin person*
weakly **337.14**; 122.21 *badly*; 424.5 *fragilely*; 337.10 *ill*; 685.9 *moderately*; 335.14 *powerlessly*; 704.12 *refutably*; 261.8 *tiredly*; 260.25 *unhealthily*; 260.21 *unhealthy*; 247.12 *unsuccessfully*; 337.14 *weakly*; 497.10 *without taste*
weak-minded 639.3 *timid*
Weakness 337
weakness **337.1**; 229.2 *attitude*; 424.2 *brittleness*; 614.1 *cowardice*; 231.7 *defect*; 617.1 *desire*; 335.4 *disability*; 247.1 *failure*; 261.7 *fatigue*; 335.3 *helplessness*; 245.11 *hurt*; 260.1 *ill health*; 260.2 *illness*; 231.5 *imperfection*; 218.8 *insufficiency*; 595.1 *liking*; 124.6 *obscurity*; 247.3 *personal fault*; 417.4 *rarefaction*; 704.4 *refutability*; 260.3 *symptom*; 497.1 *tastelessness*; 153.12 *thinning*; 639.13 *timidity*; 804.3 *venial sin*; 254.7 *vulnerability*
weakness for liquor 690.11 *drinking*
weakness of the flesh 247.3 *personal fault*; 804.3 *venial sin*
weakness of will 4.9 *philosophical problem*
weak nuclear interaction 28.79 *fundamental interaction*
weak person 124.10 *nonentity*
weak personality 36.8 *disordered personality*
weak point 231.7 *defect*; 804.3 *venial sin*
weak side 46.7 *offence*
weak-sighted **519.9**
weak sun 31.22 *sun*
weak thing **337.5**; 424.3 *brittle thing*
weak will 639.13 *timidity*
weak-willed **337.12**; 639.3 *timid*
weal 234.11 *deform*; 234.3 *deformity*; 248.1 *prosperity*; 548.1 *spot*
weald 92.6 *lowland*
Wealth 781
wealth **781.5**; 562.1 *fertility*; 352.4 *financial resources*; 780.3 *fortune*; 250.3 *independence*; 440.5 *personal estate*; 217.8 *plenty*; 765.5 *profit*; 248.1 *prosperity*; 246.1 *success*
wealthily **781.16**; 780.28 *financially*; 765.20 *gainfully*
wealthy **781.1**; 248.8 *prosperous*; 780.23 *solvent*; 246.13 *successful*; 765.17 *well-off*
wealthy people **765.8**
wealthy person **781.10**; 765.7 *gainer*
wean 43.18 *practise livestock farming*
wean away from 481.3 *deflect*; 487.5 *disaccustom*
weaner 43.8 *livestock*; 71.19 *young mammal*
wean oneself 355.1 *relinquish*
Weapon 587
weapon **587.1**; 357.7 *agent of destruction*; 330.8 *missile*; 561.8 *organs of reproduction*; 252.2 *protection*; 438.1 *tool*
weaponless 335.11 *unprotected*
weaponry 587.2 *arms*
weapons **331.16**; 587.2 *arms*
wear **551.34**; 357.7 *agent of destruction*; 337.6 *be weak*; 214.1 *decrease*; 375.1 *disintegration*; 551.1 *dress*; 365.14 *erode*; 261.6 *fatigue*; 766.12 *lessen*; 323.9 *navigate*; 50.15 *sail*; 349.1, 349.6 *use*; 441.1 *waste*; 337.1 *weakness*; 365.2 *wearing away*
wear a hair shirt 806.9 *appear guilty*; 808.5 *do penance*
wear a macintosh 428.22 *keep dry*
wear and tear 357.7 *agent of destruction*; 214.1 *decrease*; 245.9 *dilapidation*; 375.1 *disintegration*; 766.4 *lessening*; 212.1 *subtraction*; 349.6 *use*; 441.3 *waste*
wear a sackcloth 808.5 *do penance*
wear a smile 552.14 *undress*
wear away 214.4 *decrease*; 375.3 *disintegrate*; 365.14 *erode*; 766.12 *lessen*; 441.1 *waste*
wear down 480.15 *persuade*; 427.28 *weather*
wearied 620.5 *bored*; 261.1 *fatigued*; 337.11 *weakened*
wearily 620.8 *boringly*; 261.8 *tiredly*
weariness 620.1 *boredom*; 261.7 *fatigue*; 337.3 *poor health*
wearing 620.4 *boring*; 261.4 *fatiguing*; 766.4 *lessening*; 50.1 *sailing*
wearing a hair shirt 808.2 *type of penance*
wearing a sackcloth 808.2 *type of penance*
wearing away **365.2**; 526.4 *disappearance*; 766.4 *lessening*
wearing earplugs 505.4 *deaf*
wearisome 620.4 *boring*; 264.10 *difficult*; 261.4 *fatiguing*; 576.11 *laborious*
wearisomely 261.9 *tiringly*
wear mourning 523.12 *be dark*
wear out 337.6 *be weak*; 245.1 *deteriorate*; 375.3 *disintegrate*; 261.6 *fatigue*; 245.5 *hurt*; 351.1 *misuse*; 349.1 *use*; 441.1 *waste*
wear the cloth 7.21 *ordain*
wear the crown 121.8 *be superior*; 246.9 *be victorious*; 140.16 *direct*; 12.11 *govern*; 396.18 *have authority*
wear the laurels 246.9 *be victorious*
wear the pants 395.10 *be a prevailing influence*; 396.19 *be authoritarian*
wear the trousers 395.10 *be a prevailing influence*; 396.19 *be authoritarian*; 579.2 *direct*
wear thin 424.4 *be brittle*; 337.6 *be weak*
wear well 259.5 *be healthy*
weary 620.6 *be boring*; 261.2, 620.5 *bored*; 620.4 *boring*; 261.6 *fatigue*; 261.1 *fatigued*; 576.11 *laborious*; 337.11 *weakened*
wearying 620.4 *boring*; 261.4 *fatiguing*
Weary Willie 343.11 *sleeper*
weasel 479.1 *be equivocal*; 479.9 *equivocator*; 320.10 *sled*
weaselly 71.28 *carnivorous*
weasel word 479.5 *equivocalness*
weather **31.3**; **427.28**; 529.15 *colour*; 245.2 *decay*; 243.7 *develop*; 323.9 *navigate*; 380.5 *violent weather*
weather balloon 31.5 *weather station*
weather-beaten 245.13, 337.9 *dilapidated*; 423.4 *powerful*
weatherboard 550.8 *wall covering*; 23.12 *wood*
weather bureau 31.4 *weather forecast*
weathercock 227.3 *changeable thing*; 479.9 *equivocator*; 154.8 *high thing*; 639.15 *indecisive person*; 742.5 *indicator*; 31.7 *weather instruments*
weather data **31.6**
weathered **30.59**; 530.7 *colourless*; 243.20 *developed*; 529.13 *soft-hued*
weather forecast **31.4**; 475.1 *prediction*
weather forecaster 475.9 *forecaster*; 693.9 *informant*; 31.2 *meteorologist*
weather forecasting 31.1 *meteorology*
weatherglass 31.7 *weather instruments*
weather house 433.19 *measuring instrument*
weathering **30.35**; 530.1 *colourlessness*; 245.9 *dilapidation*
weather instruments **31.7**
weather lore 31.3 *weather*
Weatherman 662.10 *seditionist*
weatherman 475.9 *forecaster*; 31.2 *meteorologist*
weather map 31.4 *weather forecast*
weather observer 31.2 *meteorologist*
weatherproof 252.7 *invulnerable*
weather prophet 11.13 *diviner*; 31.2 *meteorologist*
weather radar 692.28 *radar*; 31.7 *weather instruments*
weather satellite 29.32 *satellite*; 31.5 *weather station*
weather science 31.1 *meteorology*
weather ship 31.5 *weather station*
weather sign 742.1 *sign*
weather situation 31.3 *weather*
weather station **31.5**
weather symbols 31.4 *weather forecast*
weather system **31.11**
weather the storm 393.4 *be restored*; 252.9 *be safe*; 389.5 *escape*; 246.7 *overcome obstacles*; 323.10 *sail*; 228.8 *show determination*
weather vane 227.3 *changeable thing*; 154.8 *high thing*; 742.5 *indicator*; 31.7 *weather instruments*
weather-wise 475.13 *predicting*
weatherwoman 31.2 *meteorologist*
weave **42.14**; **404.4**; 403.2 *fabric*; 193.8 *interweave*; 318.9 *proceed*; 356.10 *produce*; 325.5 *twist*; 300.15 *walk*; 42.4 *weaving*
weave a plot 645.5 *be cunning*
weave one's way 302.7 *make one's way*
weaver 578.2 *artisan*; 42.4, 193.3 *weaving*
weaverbird 72.6 *songbird*; 193.3 *weaving*
weave together 180.6 *convolute*
weaving **42.4**; **193.3**; 160.4 *forming*; 193.1 *interweaving*; 404.4 *weave*
weaving frame 42.4 *weaving*
weazen 428.21 *dry up*
weazened 428.3 *dried-up*
web 193.2 *braid*; 193.8 *interweave*; 484.4 *plot*; 700.13 *snare*; 76.6 *spinner*; 645.2 *stratagem*; 408.7 *tangle*; 404.4 *weave*; 42.4 *weaving*
webbed 193.6 *interwoven*; 700.42 *trapped*
webbed feet 72.16 *avian anatomy*
webbing 193.2 *braid*; 193.1 *interweaving*; 42.4 *weaving*
webby 193.6 *interwoven*
web connection 38.27 *superstructure*
web of cunning 645.2 *stratagem*
web of deceit 645.2 *stratagem*
web of intrigue 484.4 *plot*
web page 40.16 *Internet*
website 220.2 *table*
web site 40.16 *Internet*
webspeak 40.16 *Internet*
Webster's Dictionary 5.28 *dictionary*
wed 374.6 *come together*; 755.5 *contract*; 570.15 *marry*
wedded 223.19 *associated*; 632.14 *habituated*; 570.21 *married*; 108.4 *related*
wedded bliss 570.1 *marriage*
weddedness 570.1 *marriage*
wedded state 570.1 *marriage*
wedded to 593.18 *in love*
wedding **570.5**; 656.3 *formal occasion*
wedding anniversary 601.5 *anniversary*; 298.6 *annually celebrated day*
wedding announcement 570.6 *general terms*
wedding banns 570.6 *general terms*
wedding bells 570.6 *general terms*; 593.8 *love affair*
wedding breakfast 557.13 *feast*; 570.6 *general terms*; 376.9 *social gathering*
wedding cake 25.36 *cake*; 570.6 *general terms*
wedding canopy 570.6 *general terms*
wedding caterer 436.4 *caterer*
wedding ceremony 570.5 *wedding*
wedding clothes 551.1 *dress*
wedding dance 22.4 *historic dancing*
wedding day 570.6 *general terms*
wedding dress 551.7 *frock*; 570.6 *general terms*
wedding invitation 570.6 *general terms*
wedding march 570.6 *general terms*
wedding morning 570.6 *general terms*
wedding music 570.6 *general terms*
wedding party 654.5 *party*
wedding photographs 570.6 *general terms*
wedding present 570.6 *general terms*
wedding reception 557.13 *feast*; 570.6 *general terms*; 654.3 *meeting*; 376.9 *social gathering*
wedding rehearsal 570.6 *general terms*
wedding ring 570.6 *general terms*
wedding service 570.5 *wedding*
wedding shower 570.6 *general terms*
wedding song 570.6 *general terms*
wedding veil 570.6 *general terms*
wedge 56.4 *golf club*; 24.11 *make ceramics*; 151.8 *narrow thing*; 176.2 *obliquity*; 205.7 *piece*; 27.46 *polyhedron*; 323.10 *sail*; 425.9 *sharp-edged thing*; 38.6 *simple machine*; 309.2 *stopper*; 67.11 *swimming*; 79.7 *timber production*; 438.1 *tool*
wedged 24.10 *ceramic*
wedge heels 551.19 *footwear*
wedge in 314.12 *flood in*; 368.5 *inset*
wedge kick 67.2 *swimming technique*
wedge-shaped 27.84 *cubic*; 62.8 *mountaineering*; 27.82 *polygonal*; 425.1 *sharp*; 151.3 *tapered*
wedge-shaped nut 62.4 *climbing equipment*
wedgies 551.19 *footwear*
wedging 24.5 *ceramic process*
Wedgwood blue 539.1 *blue*
wedgy 425.1 *sharp*
wedlock 755.1 *contract*; 570.1 *marriage*
wee 431.3 *body fluid*; 433.4 *exudate*; 159.7 *little*; 433.32 *seep*; 560.17 *urinate*; 560.3 *urination*; 560.6 *urine*
weed 614.2 *coward*; 44.15 *cultivate*; 691.6 *drug*; 43.17 *farm*; 244.1 *improve*; 81.12 *manage grassland*; 77.2 *plant*; 212.3 *subtract*; 337.4 *weakling*
weed-choked 44.17 *botanical*; 77.13 *plantlike*
weediness 153.7 *thinness*
weeding 43.5 *cultivation*; 369.2 *displacement*; 44.5 *gardening*
weedkiller **44.8**; 43.14 *pest control*; 382.14 *plant killer*
weed out 369.12 *displace*; 214.5 *make smaller*; 256.15 *purify*; 206.8 *reduce*; 255.11 *simplify*
weeds 238.6 *refuse*; 571.5 *widowhood*
weedy 77.13 *plantlike*; 153.1 *thin*
Wee Free 7.5 *Christian*
week 148.8 *measure of time*; 201.3 *seven*; 275.4 *term*; 276.2 *time period*
weekday 276.2 *time period*
weekend 654.12 *visit*
weekend market 779.1 *market*
weekend party 654.5 *party*
weekend warrior 252.3 *protector*; 586.8 *soldier*
week in week out 275.26 *all the time*
weekly 298.12 *cyclic*; 298.16 *cyclically*; 276.13 *for specified periods*; 632.9 *habitual*; 740.5 *journal*; 275.22 *periodic*; 276.7, 276.8 *periodical*; 111.17 *regular*; 111.20 *regularly*
weekly market 779.1 *market*
weekly newspaper 741.5 *mass communication*
weekly paper 740.4 *newspaper*
weenie 25.29 *sausage*
weenie roast 557.13 *feast*
weeny 159.7 *little*
weenybopper 555.6 *young person*
weep **603.7**; 514.13 *cry*; 560.15 *excrete*; 560.18 *fester*; 431.25 *flow*; 602.8 *grieve*; 79.19 *grow*; 315.12 *leak*; 315.3 *leakage*; 559.7 *secrete*; 429.16, 433.32 *seep*; 627.9 *sorrow*
weeper 583.3 *funeral director*; 603.3 *lamenter*
weep for 603.6 *lament*; 627.9 *sorrow*
weepily 431.26 *fluidly*; 559.8 *glandularly*; 433.35 *wetly*
weeping 514.18 *crying*; 514.6 *cry of pain*; 433.4 *exudate*; 603.1 *lamentation*; 603.4 *lamenting*; 315.3 *leakage*; 315.17 *leaky*; 560.7 *pus*; 431.16 *rheumy*; 559.1 *secretion*; 559.4 *secretory*; 429.12, 433.25 *seeping*
weeping and wailing 514.6 *cry of pain*; 583.2 *funeral*
weep over 603.7 *weep*
weep with rage 624.11 *be angry*
wee small hours 294.2 *late hour*; 291.3 *midnight*
weevil 76.3 *pest*; 44.12 *pests and diseases*
weevilly 76.12 *verminous*
wee-wee 560.17 *urinate*; 560.6 *urine*
weft 403.2 *fabric*; 42.4, 193.3 *weaving*
weftage 404.4 *weave*
weigh **414.15**; 123.7 *be important*; 366.4 *gather up*; 26.10 *measure*; 203.8 *quantify*
weigh anchor 323.9 *navigate*; 313.5 *set out*
weigh a ton 414.12 *be heavy*
weighbridge 320.21 *miscellaneous motoring terms*; 414.10 *scales*; 26.7 *standard*
weigh down 249.11 *cause adversity*; 414.14 *make heavy*
weighed 106.4 *deliberate*; 414.1 *heavy*; 203.6 *quantitative*
weighed down 414.3 *ponderous*
weigh equally 708.16 *cancel out*
weigh heavy upon 414.13 *weigh on*
weigh in 59.7 *horseracing*; 395.8 *influence*; 414.15 *weigh*
weigh-in 414.1 *heavy*; 414.7 *weighing*
weighing **414.7**; 119.3 *equalization*; 414.1 *heavy*; 203.6 *quantitative*; 203.1 *quantity*
weighing down **414.8**
weighing-in 414.7 *weighing*
weighing instrument **28.86**
weighing little 415.1 *light*
weighing machine 414.10 *scales*; 26.7 *standard*
weighing-out 414.7 *weighing*
weighing room 59.7 *horseracing*

weighing up 119.3 *equalization*
weigh in the balance 414.15 *weigh*
weigh light upon 124.11 *be unimportant*
weigh little 415.9 *be light*
weigh on 414.13; 367.5 *bear down on*
weigh one down 414.14 *make heavy*; 414.13 *weigh on*
weigh oneself 414.15 *weigh*
weigh out 59.7 *horseracing*; 26.11 *measure out*; 414.15 *weigh*
weigh-out 414.1 *heavy*; 414.7 *weighing*
weight 414.11; 28.10 *force*; 51.2 *grip*; 414.4 *heaviness*; 123.1 *importance*; 395.1 *influence*; 338.1 *instrumentality*; 336.3 *intensity*; 402.1 *material world*; 698.11 *pedantry*; 334.1 *power*; 203.1 *quantity*; 726.2 *seriousness*; 26.4 *size*
weight allowance 59.7 *horseracing*
weight cloth 59.7 *horseracing*
weighted 414.1 *heavy*; 802.11 *wrong*
weighted mean 27.60 *parameter*
weigh the same 414.12 *be heavy*
weightily 414.16 *heavily*
weightiness 656.1 *formality*; 414.4 *heaviness*; 123.1, 663.6 *importance*
weighting 27.60 *parameter*
weighting down 414.8 *weighing down*
weightless 434.12 *airy*; 415.1 *light*
weightlessness 434.9 *airiness*; 415.5 *lightness*; 29.31 *space travel*
weightlifter 336.5 *athlete*
weightlifting 576.5 *exercise*
weight loss 214.1 *decrease*; 687.1 *fasting*; 766.1 *loss*; 260.3 *symptom*
weight of numbers 334.1 *power*
weight on one's mind 808.1 *penitence*
weight on one's shoulders 378.6 *burden*
weights 59.7 *horseracing*; 814.15 *instrument of torture*
weight watcher 766.7 *dieter*; 557.18 *eater*; 687.4 *fasting person*; 153.9 *thin person*
Weightwatchers™ 766.7 *dieter*; 687.1 *fasting*; 684.1 *self-restraint*
weight-watching 153.10 *diet*; 687.1 *fasting*; 766.1 *loss*; 557.6 *nutrition*; 153.3 *slimming*
weighty 348.7 *causal*; 416.6 *dense*; 656.6 *formal*; 414.1 *heavy*; 123.5, 643.3 *important*; 402.7 *material*; 698.24 *pedantic*; 336.10 *potent*; 726.5 *serious*; 694.7 *significant*
weigh up 701.14 *discuss*; 464.12 *estimate*; 443.15 *think about*
weigh up against 708.16 *cancel out*
weir 378.3 *barrier*; 38.23 *dam*; 315.7 *outlet*
weird 642.1 *capricious*; 118.14 *eccentric*; 461.11 *insane*; 11.5 *spell*; 11.18 *spiritual*; 696.5 *strange*; 103.2 *unbelievable*; 619.8 *wonderful*
weird and wonderful 630.8 *surprising*; 619.8 *wonderful*
weirdly 11.26 *magically*; 619.13 *wonderfully*
weirdness 118.4 *unusualness*
weirdo 325.19 *deviant person*; 118.10 *eccentric*; 100.5 *nonconformist*
weird sister 11.4 *witch*
Weismannism 34.16 *evolution*
welcome 370.9; **654.9**; **654.14**; 658.10 *be courteous*; 569.15 *be hospitable*; 654.11 *be sociable*; 658.3 *courtesies*; 617.8 *desirable*; 617.12 *desire*; 658.12 *greet*; 667.6 *greeting*; 241.1, 490.6 *pleasant*; 654.16 *popular*; 769.10 *receive someone*; 312.12 *reception*; 370.2 *receptivity*; 601.18, 667.20 *salute*; 292.14 *seasonable*; 287.6 *timely*
welcome! 312.24
welcomed 769.13 *received*
welcomed with open arms 654.16 *popular*
welcome end 582.5 *ways of dying*
welcome guest 654.6 *social person*
welcome home 658.12 *greet*
welcome with open arms 569.15 *be hospitable*; 654.11 *be sociable*; 658.12 *greet*; 370.9 *welcome*
welcoming 312.21; 601.13 *congratulatory*; 658.7 *courteous*; 569.8 *friendly*; 769.4 *reception*; 370.15, 769.12 *receptive*; 370.2 *receptivity*; 654.15 *sociable*; 654.9 *welcome*
welcoming address 729.8 *speech*
welcoming ceremony 769.4 *reception*
welcoming embrace 654.9 *welcome*
welcomingly 370.18 *receptively*
welcoming with open arms 370.2 *receptivity*
weld 493.14 *be hot*; 267.7 *cause to adhere*; 38.27 *superstructure*; 537.7 *yellow pigment*
weldel 68.4 *skiing technique*
welder 578.2 *artisan*
welding 267.1 *adhesion*
welding torch 19.14 *sculptor's materials*
welfare 650.3; 797.13 *benefit*; 768.2 *gift*; 85.16 *national*; 652.1 *philanthropy*; 248.1 *prosperity*; 253.1 *protection*; 252.1 *safety*; 392.4 *social assistance*; 2.10 *social services*
welfare economics 13.1 *economics*
welfare officer 15.6 *employer*
welfare organization 2.10 *social services*
welfare payment 768.2 *gift*; 392.4 *social assistance*
welfare services 392.4 *social assistance*
welfare state 652.4; 566.11 *nation*; 12.5 *political organization*; 253.1 *protection*; 252.1 *safety*; 392.4 *social assistance*; 2.10 *social services*; 650.3 *welfare*
welfare work 650.3 *welfare*
welfare worker 650.5 *benevolent person*; 652.3 *philanthropist*
welfarism 652.1 *philanthropy*; 650.3 *welfare*
welfarist 650.5 *benevolent person*
welkin 434.1 *air*; 8.11 *heaven*; 29.3 *universe*
well 631.19; **797.22**; 801.12 *all right*; 50.6 *canoeing*; 222.9 *comfortable*; 156.4 *deep thing*; 367.14 *depression*; 259.1 *healthy*; 308.5 *hole*; 799.7 *honourably*; 433.13 *irrigator*; 315.2 *outflow*; 439.2 *resource*; 485.12 *skilfully*; 204.8 *sound*; 246.16 *successfully*; 781.16 *wealthily*; 235.11 *worthily*
well-adapted 136.9 *qualified*
well-advised 458.5 *wise*
well-affected 392.35 *benevolent*
well-aimed 698.21 *accurate*; 324.14 *directed*
well-appointed 243.18 *prepared*; 436.8 *provisional*
well-armed 336.13 *strengthened*
well-baby clinic 35.10 *hospital*
well-balanced 460.5 *rational*; 162.4 *symmetrical*
well-behaved 631.17; **797.4**; 407.17 *disciplined*; 658.8 *good-mannered*; 663.7 *obedient*
well-behaved child 663.4 *obedient person*
well-behaved person 631.3
well-being 797.13 *benefit*; 222.5 *comfortable circumstances*; 263.1 *ease*; 259.3 *health*; 490.1 *physical pleasure*; 248.1 *prosperity*; 257.2 *salubrity*
well-beloved 593.21 *beloved*; 593.11 *loved one*
well-born 573.4 *aristocratic*
well-bred 573.4 *aristocratic*; 168.5 *bred*; 658.8 *good-mannered*; 6.20, 549.5 *refined*; 631.17 *well-behaved*
well-bred person 566.4 *modern human*
well-brushed 421.1 *smooth*
well-built 545.5 *beautiful*; 158.17 *stocky*; 336.13 *strengthened*
well-cared for 407.13 *orderly*
well-chosen 469.15 *chosen*
well-cooked 243.20 *developed*
well-crafted 485.9 *well-made*
well-cut 551.31 *styled*
well-defended 252.6 *safe*
well-defined 185.7 *conspicuous*; 695.3 *recognizable*
well-deserving 669.21 *praiseworthy*
well-directed 324.14 *directed*
well-disposed 392.35 *benevolent*; 569.8 *friendly*; 413.9 *supportive*
well done 669.27 *bravo!*; 235.12 *fantastic!*
well-done 25.56 *culinary*; 243.20 *developed*
well-drawn 17.18, 721.11 *descriptive*
well-dressed 525.10 *aspectual*; 551.30 *dressed-up*; 553.7 *fashionable*
well-drilled 407.17 *disciplined*
well-educated 455.9 *literate*
well-endowed 158.16 *fat*; 485.7 *gifted*; 781.1 *wealthy*
wellerism 697.2 *solecism*
well-established 225.7 *permanent*; 336.10 *potent*; 228.10 *stabilized*
well-fed 557.26 *eating*; 158.16 *fat*; 152.1 *thick*
well-filled 217.3 *filled*; 232.8 *full*
well-finished 549.5 *refined*
well-formed formula 27.63 *mathematical logic*
well-founded 452.1 *certain*; 336.10 *potent*; 228.9 *stable*
well-furnished 217.3 *filled*
well-greased 268.11 *lubricated*; 265.12 *wieldy*
well-groomed 256.16 *clean*; 543.3 *elegant*; 553.7 *fashionable*; 407.13 *orderly*
well-grounded 452.1 *certain*; 6.19 *knowledgeable*
well-grounded hope 104.4 *chance*
wellhead 344.2 *source*
well-heeled 248.8 *prosperous*; 781.1 *wealthy*; 765.17 *well-off*
well-housed 781.1 *wealthy*
well hung 375.5 *disintegrated*
wellies 551.19 *footwear*
well-inclined 669.18 *approving*
well I never 630.14 *good heavens!*; 619.14 *wonderful!*
well-informed 455.8 *knowledgeable*
Wellington boots 551.19 *footwear*
well-intended 569.8 *friendly*
well-intentioned 392.35, 650.6 *benevolent*
well-judged 287.8 *in time*
well-kept 407.13 *orderly*; 359.7 *preserved*
well-known 740.20; 632.10 *familiar*; 455.10 *known*; 738.14 *manifest*; 93.13 *real*; 349.9 *used*
well-laid 317.15 *accessible*; 645.4 *cunning*
well-liked 593.21 *beloved*
well-lined 232.8 *full*
well-lined purse 781.5 *wealth*
well-lit 317.15 *accessible*; 520.2 *clear*; 522.18 *lit*
well-lubricated 690.1 *drunk*
well-made 485.9; 545.5 *beautiful*
well-made play 21.2 *play*
well-mannered 241.2 *likable*; 549.5 *refined*; 421.6 *smooth-mannered*; 631.17, 797.4 *well-behaved*
well-mannered person 631.3 *well-behaved person*
well-matched 119.8 *on equal terms*
well-meaning 392.35, 650.6 *benevolent*; 569.8 *friendly*
well-meant 392.35, 650.6 *benevolent*
well-nigh 147.13 *nearly*
well-nourished 557.26 *eating*; 688.6 *gluttonous*
well-off 765.17; 248.8 *prosperous*; 781.1 *wealthy*
well-oiled 690.1 *drunk*; 268.11 *lubricated*; 265.12 *wieldy*
well-ordered 407.14; 119.6 *equal*
well-organized 407.14 *well-ordered*
well out 315.11 *run out*
well over 219.4 *be excessive*
well-paid 781.1 *wealthy*
well-paved 317.15 *accessible*
well-paying 765.15 *gainful*
well-pitched 516.6 *melodious*
well-planned 645.4 *cunning*
well-practised 485.8 *expert*
well-prepared 485.8 *expert*; 243.18 *prepared*
well-preserved 556.14 *aged*; 225.7 *permanent*; 359.7 *preserved*
well-proportioned 545.5 *beautiful*; 543.3 *elegant*; 162.4 *symmetrical*; 181.10 *well-rounded*
well-protected 336.13 *strengthened*
well-provided 217.3 *filled*
well provided for 781.1 *wealthy*; 765.17 *well-off*
well-provisioned 217.3 *filled*
well-qualified 455.9 *literate*
well-read 6.18 *educated*; 4.19 *learned*; 17.16 *literary*; 550.41 *progressing*
well-reasoned 446.12 *purposive*; 4.15 *rational*
well-received 769.13 *received*
well-regulated 407.17 *disciplined*
well-rehearsed 243.18 *prepared*
well respected 667.12 *respected*
well-rooted 228.10 *stabilized*
well-rounded 177.5; **181.10**; 5.43 *phrasal*
well-rounded shape 181.2 *round body*
well-situated 781.1 *wealthy*
well-spoken 658.8 *good-mannered*; 549.5 *refined*; 695.2 *simple*; 729.19 *speaking*
wellspring 130.3, 344.2 *source*
well-sprung 422.6 *elastic*
well-stocked 217.3 *filled*; 232.8 *full*
well thought of 669.24 *admired*; 811.3 *reputable*; 667.12 *respected*
well-thought-out 4.15 *rational*
well-thumbed 349.9 *used*
well-timed 239.1 *convenient*; 287.8 *in time*; 292.14 *seasonable*
well-to-do 248.8 *prosperous*; 781.1 *wealthy*; 765.17 *well-off*
well-trained 6.19 *knowledgeable*; 663.7 *obedient*
well-trodden 187.9 *flattened*; 349.9 *used*
well-turned 543.3 *elegant*; 5.43 *phrasal*; 181.10 *well-rounded*
well turned out 551.30, 656.7 *dressed-up*
well-turned phrase 543.1 *elegance*; 5.24 *phrasing*
well up 30.63 *ebb*; 431.25 *flow*
well-upholstered 158.16 *fat*
well up on 485.8 *expert*
well-used 317.15 *accessible*; 349.9 *used*
well-ventilated 257.4 *hygienic*; 434.17 *ventilated*
well-versed 6.19, 455.8 *knowledgeable*; 4.19 *learned*
well water 433.1 *water*
well-wisher 392.15 *benefactor*; 650.5 *benevolent person*; 797.15 *good person*; 413.8 *supporter*
well-wishing 797.3 *kind*; 797.10 *kindness*
well-woman clinic 35.10 *hospital*
well-worn 245.13 *dilapidated*; 632.10 *familiar*; 349.9 *used*; 5.42 *worded*
well-worn phrase 5.21 *catchword*
welly 338.1 *vigour*
welsh 784.8, 786.7 *not pay*
Welsh accent 5.26 *dialect*
Welsh daffodil 743.6 *national emblem*
Welsh dresser 23.5, 410.3 *cabinet*
welsher 634.17 *avoider*; 786.6 *nonpayer*
Welsh Grand Committee 12.4 *governing body*
Welsh Guard 586.12 *ceremonial troops*
Welsh leek 743.6 *national emblem*
Welshman 564.9 *British inhabitant*; 85.12 *Wales*
Welsh mountains 89.5 *British mountains*
Welshness 85.12 *Wales*
Welsh rarebit 25.44 *British dish*
Welshwoman 85.12 *Wales*
welt 234.11 *deform*; 234.3 *deformity*; 814.3 *hit*; 548.1 *spot*
Weltanschauung 4.2 *philosophical system*
welter 367.9 *bow*; 408.5 *confusion*; 327.25 *pitch*; 327.11 *stagger*; 307.10 *swirl*
weltering 433.24 *flooded*
welterweight 586.3 *athlete*; 52.4 *boxer*; 52.3 *boxing weight divisions*; 52.14 *combat*; 414.7 *weighing*
Weltschmerz 620.1 *boredom*
wen 5.13 *letter*
wench 401.6 *domestic servant*
wenching 796.3 *sexual immorality*
werecat 11.11 *ghost*
werewolf 11.11 *ghost*
wergild 807.1 *atonement*; 749.2 *peace offering*
wersh 728.17 *insipid*; 218.1 *insufficient*
Weschel 759.2 *place of exchange*
Weschler Adult Intelligence Scale 36.6 *intelligence test*
Weschler-Bellvue intelligence test 36.6 *intelligence test*
we shall overcome 383.16 *fight on!*
Wesleyan 7.5 *Christian*
west 324.4 *compass point*; 324.13 *directional*; 324.12 *north*
westbound 324.13 *directional*
West Country 86.9 *regions of Britain*
Westcountryman 564.9 *British inhabitant*
West End 87.5 *London*; 21.5 *show business*
westerly 324.13 *directional*; 324.12 *north*; 31.15 *wind direction*; 31.47 *windy*
western 324.13 *directional*; 17.2, 721.5 *fiction*; 86.16 *regional*; 169.6 *side*
Western bloc 85.2 *union of nations*
Westerner 564.10 *US inhabitant*
Western Hemisphere 86.7 *regions of the world*

westernize 760.12 *naturalize*
westernized 760.17 *naturalized*
westernly 324.12 *north*
westernmost 324.13 *directional*
Western nation 85.1 *country*
Western roll style 47.2 *field events*
West Indian dish 25.51
westing 324.4 *compass point*
Westlander 564.10 *US inhabitant*
Westminster 579.11 *British government*; 12.4 *governing body*; 87.5 *London*; 396.6 *place of authority*; 400.8 *the power structure*
Westminster waltz 68.7 *ice-dancing*
Weston cell 32.19 *electrochemistry*
West Side 87.3 *New York*
west side 169.3 *side direction*
westward 324.4 *compass point*; 324.13 *directional*
westwardly 324.12 *north*
westwards 324.12 *north*
west wind 31.15 *wind direction*
westwork 20.10 *church architecture*
wet 433.23; 388.2 *appeaser*; 614.3 *cowardly*; 639.15 *indecisive person*; 648.2 *lenient person*; **429.8** *marsh*; 429.9 *moist*; 429.13 *moisten*; 231.4 *ordinary*; 12.6 *political party*; 31.53 *rainy*; 639.3 *timid*; 560.17 *urinate*; 433.29 *water*; 433.3 *wateriness*; 337.4 *weakling*
wet-and-dry bulb thermometer 433.19 *measuring instrument*
wet battery 439.4 *storage*
wet behind the ears 450.12 *gullible*; 646.1 *naive*; 538.3 *raw*; 486.2 *unskilled*
wet blanket 620.3 *boring person*; 481.8 *cautionary person*; 602.4 *depressing person*; 378.7 *hinderer*; 618.6 *indifferent person*; 685.2 *moderator*; 670.13 *pessimist*
wet cell 334.7 *electrical power*; 32.19 *electrochemistry*; 39.29 *power source*
wet-eyed 603.4 *lamenting*
wet fish 74.8 *food fish*
wet-fly 55.8 *angling*
wet-fly fishing 55.1 *angling*
wether 43.8 *livestock*
wetlands 92.3, 429.8 *marsh*; 157.4 *shallow thing*
wet-look 547.8 *haircut*
wetly 433.35; 31.65 *meteorologically*; 429.17 *moistly*
wetness 429.1 *moisture*; 31.26 *raininess*; 433.3 *wateriness*
wet nurse 436.3 *provider*
wet oneself 614.4 *be a coward*; 560.17 *urinate*
wet one's lips 558.13 *drink*
wet one's whistle 558.13 *drink*
wet rot 357.7 *agent of destruction*; 258.4 *dirt*; 83.1 *fungus*; 429.4 *seepage*
wet season 31.26 *raininess*
wet snow 494.5 *ice*; 31.30 *snow*
wet suit 551.21 *beachwear*; 551.10 *suit*
wetter 31.53 *rainy*
wet the bed 560.17 *urinate*
wetting 433.26; 433.8 *watering*
wetting agent 433.6 *hydrate*; 43.14 *pest control*
wetting-out agent 433.6 *hydrate*
wettish 429.9 *moist*
wettishness 429.1 *moisture*; 433.3 *wateriness*
wet weather 429.2 *mistiness*
wet with sweat 560.28 *sweaty*
wetwood 79.3 *timber*
whack 353.5 *attempt*; 508.1 *bang*; 203.2 *certain amount*; 448.1 *experiment*; 261.6 *fatigue*; 814.3 *hit*; 205.1 *part*; 276.4 *period of activity*
whacked 261.1 *fatigued*
whacking 158.15 *big*
whale 70.5 *aquatic animal*; 158.9 *big thing*; 633.11 *hunt*
whale beaching 382.9 *animal killing*
whalebone 422.3 *elastic thing*
whaleboned 418.2 *tough*
whalelike 71.29 *cetacean*
whale louse 75.4 *arthropod*; 75.10 *parasite*
whale of a time 490.2 *good time*
whaler 74.10 *fisher*; 633.6 *hunter*; 323.7 *nautical person*; 323.3 *vessel*
whaling 633.2 *chase*; 74.7 *fishing*; 71.23 *mammal hunting*
wham 508.1, 508.5 *bang*
whammy 594.2 *curse*; 798.4 *evil power*; 712.4 *malediction*; 11.5 *spell*
wharf 779.7 *emporium*; 439.4 *storage*; 38.24 *water system*; 577.1 *workshop*
wharfage 790.6 *business costs*
what? 705.25
what 138.14 *whatever*; 619.14 *wonderful!*
what cannot be 103.5 *impossibility*
what cheek 661.11 *how dare you!*
what does it matter 618.21 *never mind!*
whatever 138.14
whatever comes 107.2 *luck*
whatever happens 107.1 *chance*; 107.14 *perchance*
whatever next 619.14 *wonderful!*
what for 814.9 *retribution*
what have you 138.14 *whatever*
what is contained 406.1 *contents*
what is owing 135.2 *need*
what it takes 136.2, 334.2 *ability*
what it will fetch 790.2 *value*
what makes one tick 483.1 *motive*
what matters 123.3 *chief thing*
whatnot 23.5, 410.3 *cabinet*; 438.1 *tool*
what one is worth 440.5 *personal estate*
what one owes 784.1 *debt*
what rotten luck 249.13 *too bad!*
what's in 295.2 *trendiness*
whatsit 438.1 *tool*
what's-its-name 402.5 *object*
whatsoever 138.14 *whatever*
what's what 93.5 *fact*
what the doctor ordered 257.4 *hygienic*
what the future brings 283.3 *future condition*
what the future holds 283.3 *future condition*
what you will 138.14 *whatever*
wheat belt 43.11 *farmland*
wheaten 81.8 *grasslike*
wheatfield 43.11 *farmland*
wheat germ 25.40 *breakfast cereal*
wheatmeal 25.7 *basic ingredient*
wheat pit 779.1 *market*
Wheatstone bridge 39.13 *circuit*
wheat straw 43.9 *animal feedstuff*
wheedle 645.5 *be cunning*; 664.12 *beg*; 677.10 *cajole*; 480.15 *persuade*; 480.16 *tempt*
wheedler 677.6 *flatterer*; 480.12 *persuader*
wheedling 677.3 *cajolery*; 677.14 *cajoling*; 480.2 *flattery*; 483.2 *inducement*
wheel 320.12 *bicycle*; 320.11 *bicycle part*; 24.6 *ceramic workshop*; 179.3 *circular thing*; 579.5 *guide*; 814.15 *instrument of torture*; 38.8 *machine element*; 323.5 *navigation*; 306.3, 306.6 *orbit*; 50.3 *parts of a sailing boat*; 330.20 *propel*; 330.11 *propeller*; 307.3 *reel*; 307.8 *rotate*; 307.6 *rotator*; 438.1 *tool*; 303.9, 325.11 *turn round*
wheel about 479.2 *equivocate*
wheel and axle 38.6 *simple machine*
wheel and deal 395.8 *influence*; 484.13 *plot*; 700.28 *trick*
wheel animacule 75.6 *worm*
wheel-back chair 23.2 *chair*
wheelbarrow 410.10 *cart*; 44.6 *garden tool*; 320.7 *handcart*
wheelbase 320.21 *miscellaneous motoring terms*
wheel clamp 378.4 *restraint*
wheeler-dealer 123.4 *bigwig*; 342.10 *busy person*; 755.4 *contractor*; 645.3 *cunning person*; 395.5 *influential person*; 484.8 *planner*
wheeler-dealing 484.15 *planning*
Wheeler Peak 89.4 *US mountains*
wheelie 61.6 *motor-racing terms*
wheelie bin 410.11 *vessel*
wheeling 306.1 *orbital motion*; 306.11 *orbiting*; 307.11 *rotating*; 307.2 *turning*
wheeling and dealing 645.1 *cunning*; 631.9 *tactics*; 700.7 *tricking*
wheel lock 587.10 *historical gun*
wheelman 323.7 *nautical person*
wheel of fortune 227.3 *changeable thing*; 107.2 *luck*; 307.6 *rotator*
wheel of life 298.2 *cycle*
wheels 320.16 *car*
wheel-shaped 306.10 *circular*
wheels within wheels 438.5 *machine*
wheel throwing 24.5 *ceramic process*
wheel-track 184.2 *furrow*
wheel-tracked 184.6 *wrinkly*
wheelwise 306.12 *circuitously*
wheel wobble 320.21 *miscellaneous motoring terms*
wheelwork 438.5 *machine*
wheelwright 578.2 *artisan*; 23.13 *carpenter*
wheesh 512.9 *sh!*
wheeze 484.3 *expedient plan*; 512.1, 512.4 *hiss*
wheezily 512.8 *sibilantly*
wheezing 512.1 *hiss*; 261.3 *panting*
wheezy 512.6 *hissing*
whelk 25.19 *shellfish*
whelmed 433.24 *flooded*
whelp 71.9 *dog*; 71.35 *give birth*; 561.11 *have young*; 555.4 *young animal*; 71.19 *young mammal*
when 275.27 *at what time*
when? 705.25 *what?*
whence 750.36 *accordingly*
whence? 705.25 *what?*
when forbidden 166.8 *within limits*
where 142.12; 97.15 *here*
where? 705.25 *what?*
whereabouts 142.1 *location*; 733.5 *place of residence*; 142.12 *where*
wherefore 750.36 *accordingly*
wherefrom 750.36 *accordingly*
where it's at 173.4 *centre of activity*; 221.3 *state of affairs*
where the action is 173.4 *centre of activity*
where the rainbow ends 131.7 *limit*
whereupon 275.27 *at what time*
wherever you look 377.31 *everywhere*
wherewith 352.7 *by means of*
wherewithal 780.6 *funds*
wherryman 323.8 *boatman*
whet 488.13 *arouse sensation*; 425.15 *make sharp*; 380.9 *make violent*
whet one's appetite 617.15 *cause desire*
whetstone 425.12 *sharpener*
whet the knife 243.4 *prepare for action*
whet the sword 585.12 *go to war*
whey 43.9 *animal feedstuff*; 431.2 *juice*
which 138.14 *whatever*
whicker 515.4 *cry*
whiff 500.8 *have odour*; 500.1 *odour*; 503.1 *stench*; 503.5 *stink*
whiffle 227.11 *be changeable*
whiffy 500.5 *odorous*; 503.3 *stinking*
Whigs 12.6 *political party*
while 275.26 *all the time*; 285.15 *as*; 141.8 *intervening space*
while away 580.4 *have leisure*
while confined to bed 251.16 *under restraints*
while ill 337.14 *weakly*
while in captivity 251.16 *under restraints*
while in love 650.10 *benevolently*
while in one's power 387.11 *under subjection*
while in prison 815.11 *captively*
while seeing red 624.18 *angrily*
while under a spell 712.14 *damningly*
whilst 275.26 *all the time*
whim 642.3; 479.6 *equivocation*; 477.4 *ideality*; 227.2 *irresolution*; 595.3 *likes*
whimper 514.13 *cry*; 514.6 *cry of pain*; 491.12 *express pain*
whimpering 514.18 *crying*
whimsical 453.8, 642.1 *capricious*; 224.11, 639.2 *changeable*; 479.11 *equivocating*; 477.11 *fantastical*; 599.10 *humorous*; 227.14 *irresolute*; 299.5 *unusual*
whimsicality 642.2 *caprice*; 453.16 *capriciousness*; 224.2 *change of mind*; 639.12 *inconstancy*; 227.2 *irresolution*; 272.1 *ludicrousness*; 697.3 *tomfoolery*; 299.2 *unusualness*
whimsically 453.27 *capriciously*; 224.15, 227.15 *changeably*; 599.16 *humorously*; 299.9 *unusually*
whimsical notion 477.4 *ideality*
whimsy 477.4 *ideality*; 595.3 *likes*; 299.2 *unusualness*; 642.3 *whim*
whim-wham 477.4 *ideality*
whine 606.7 *be dissatisfied*; 664.12 *beg*; 626.9 *be sullen*; 515.6 *buzz*; 753.7 *complain*; 514.13, 515.4 *cry*; 514.6 *cry of pain*; 511.4 *faint sound*; 517.10 *lack harmony*; 511.8 *sound faint*; 729.13 *speak in a particular way*
whiner 602.4 *depressing person*; 606.3 *dissatisfied person*; 753.4 *protester*; 626.5 *sullen person*
whinge 606.7 *be dissatisfied*; 626.9 *be sullen*; 753.7 *complain*
whingeing 606.4 *dissatisfied*
whinger 602.4 *depressing person*; 606.3 *dissatisfied person*; 753.4 *protester*; 626.5 *sullen person*
whininess 626.1 *sullenness*
whining 511.4 *faint sound*; 515.3 *insect noise*; 664.7 *sycophantic*
whinny 515.1 *animal cry*; 515.4 *cry*
whip 327.22 *agitate*; 376.34 *assembler*; 331.5 *beat*; 331.13 *blow*; 25.55 *cook*; 246.10 *defeat heavily*; 44.5 *gardening*; 51.2 *grip*; 262.4 *haste*; 262.1 *hasten*; 814.3 *hit*; 633.6 *hunter*; 480.8 *incentive*; 814.14 *instrument of punishment*; 400.3 *leader*; 380.9 *make violent*; 579.15 *manager*; 483.10 *manipulate*; 483.4 *negative stimulus*; 396.10 *person of authority*; 12.8 *politician*; 419.13 *soften*; 67.11 *swimming*; 331.16 *weapons*; 434.23 *whisk*
whip antenna 692.17 *antenna*
whipcord 373.6 *line*
whip hand 121.3, 164.4 *advantage*; 12.3 *governance*; 395.1 *influence*
whip in 376.43 *herd*
whip kick 67.2 *swimming technique*
whip off 313.4 *hurry off*
whipped 415.2 *insubstantial*; 483.12 *motivated*
whipped cream 498.3 *dessert*
whipper 814.17 *punisher*
whipper-in 376.34 *assembler*; 59.15 *horse person*; 633.6 *hunter*; 579.15 *manager*
whippersnapper 555.9 *child*; 660.12 *impudent person*
whipping 331.12 *collision*; 814.12 *corporal punishment*; 651.14 *hostile*; 246.2 *victory*
whipping boy 398.5 *alternative*; 807.3 *atoner*; 762.2 *substitute person*
whipping in 376.2 *herding*
whipping post 814.14 *instrument of punishment*
whippletree 79.12 *figurative usage*
whip-round 768.2 *gift*; 785.1 *payment*
whipsaw tactics 15.4 *industrial dispute*
whip something up 25.55 *cook*
whipstall 322.5 *flight*
whip up 327.22 *agitate*; 380.9 *make violent*
whir 510.9 *resonate*; 307.2 *turning*
whirl 342.1 *activity*; 353.5 *attempt*; 300.13 *be in motion*; 22.15 *dance*; 90.7 *flow*; 262.4 *haste*; 307.3 *reel*; 90.6 *river flow*; 307.8 *rotate*; 307.4 *vortex*
whirlabout 307.3 *reel*
whirlblast 307.4 *vortex*
whirl by 262.2 *make haste*
whirling 307.11 *rotating*; 332.1 *swift*; 307.2 *turning*
whirl like a dervish 307.8 *rotate*
whirlpool 180.3 *convoluted thing*; 90.6 *river flow*; 307.10 *swirl*; 379.1 *trap*; 307.4 *vortex*
whirlpool bath 365.6 *massage*; 433.11 *wash*
whirlwind 327.13 *tempest*; 307.4 *vortex*; 31.16 *wind vortex*
whirlwindish 307.12 *rotary*
whirlwindy 307.12 *rotary*
whirr 509.9 *hum*; 509.2 *humming*; 515.5 *sing*
whirring 509.2, 509.16 *humming*; 510.1 *resonance*; 510.6 *resonant*; 307.2 *turning*
whish 49.4 *playing terms*
whisht 512.9 *sh!*
whisk 434.23; 327.22 *agitate*; 327.14 *agitator*; 332.4 *be swift*; 331.13 *blow*; 256.13 *clean*; 256.10 *cleaning object*; 25.55 *cook*; 25.6 *kitchen equipment*; 412.6 *mixer*; 307.6 *rotator*; 331.6 *tap*; 316.12 *transport*
whisked 415.2 *insubstantial*
whisker 71.2 *mammalian characteristic*; 492.7 *sense organ*; 488.4 *someone or something that feels*
whiskers 420.7 *rough thing*
whiskey sour 558.8 *mixed drink*
whisky and soda 558.8 *mixed drink*
whisky mac 558.8 *mixed drink*
whisky sour 499.3 *sour thing*
whisper 693.7 *advice*; 31.58 *blow*; 79.19 *grow*; 512.4 *hiss*; 511.8 *sound faint*; 730.16 *speak in a low voice*; 729.13 *speak in a particular way*; 693.14 *tip*; 729.7 *utterance*; 678.13 *vilify*; 730.4 *whispering*
whispered 511.1 *faint-sounding*; 730.10 *low-voiced*
whispering 730.4; 678.16 *defamatory*; 511.4 *faint sound*; 512.1 *hiss*; 512.6 *hissing*; 730.10 *low-voiced*
whisper in one's ear 730.16 *speak in a low voice*
whisper sweet nothings 593.26 *court*

whisper together 734.10 *chat*
whist 506.6 *hush!*; 512.9 *sh!*
whistle 669.16 *acclaim*; 507.8 *be loud*; 513.6 *be shrill*; 31.58 *blow*; 753.7 *complain*; 711.2 *danger signal*; 606.2 *expression of dissatisfaction*; 742.3, 742.11 *gesture*; 753.4 *gesture of protest*; 512.4 *hiss*; 317.10 *railway*; 384.5 *self-defence*; 513.3 *shrillness*; 742.4, 742.12 *signal*; 619.2 *sign of wonderment*; 515.5 *sing*; 18.38 *sound*; 507.4 *sound maker*; 619.9 *wonder*
whistle at 606.7 *be dissatisfied*
whistle-blower 715.3 *accuser*; 739.4 *discloser*; 693.10 *informer*
whistle stop 321.8 *railway station*; 87.10 *village*
whistle-stopping 469.12 *election*
whistle-stop tour 469.12 *election*
whistling 669.5 *acclaim*; 742.15 *gestural*; 512.1 *hiss*; 513.9 *shrill*; 513.3 *shrillness*
Whistling Dick 587.12 *historical guns*
whistling duck 72.3 *water bird*
whit 196.3 *fragment*; 124.8 *trifle*
White 1.6 *race*; 1.13 *racial*
white 531.1; 256.16 *clean*; 530.8 *drained of colour*; 558.17 *drinkable*; 72.15 *eggs*; 805.5 *innocent*; 522.21 *light*; 524.6 *murky*; 795.9 *pure*; 255.14 *purified*; 260.21 *unhealthy*; 531.13 *whiten*
white admiral 531.9 *white thing*
white alkali 531.8 *whitener*
white ant 76.4 *social insect*; 531.9 *white thing*
white around the gills 530.8 *drained of colour*
white arsenic 531.8 *whitener*
white as a lily 531.1 *white*
white as a sheet 530.8 *drained of colour*; 582.18 *dying*; 612.7 *frightened*; 337.10 *ill*; 531.4 *pale*; 260.21 *unhealthy*
white as marble 531.1 *white*
white as milk 531.1 *white*
white as snow 256.16 *clean*
whitebait 74.8 *food fish*; 25.18 *sea fish*; 531.9 *white thing*
white ball 65.4 *carom*; 65.3 *English billiards*; 65.5 *snooker*
white blood cell 431.4 *blood*; 531.9 *white thing*
white Bordeaux 558.9 *wine*
White Brand 56.5 *golf ball*
white bread 25.38 *bread*; 531.9 *white thing*
whitecap 30.14, 91.3 *wave*; 531.9 *white thing*
white chocolate 498.4 *confectionery*
White Cliffs of Dover 531.9 *white thing*
white clover 43.12 *crop*; 531.9 *white thing*
white coffee 558.4 *coffee*; 531.9 *white thing*
white-collar 15.10 *unionized*
white-collar crime 804.7 *criminality*; 806.3 *sin*
white-collar criminal 774.11 *dishonest person*
white-collar union 15.3 *organized labour*
white-collar worker 15.7 *employee*; 531.10 *figurative usage*; 566.10 *member of society*; 216.8 *middle classes*; 578.1 *worker*
white cue ball 65.1 *billiards*
white deal 23.12 *wood*
whited sepulchre 699.19 *cheat*; 699.17 *false person*; 531.10 *figurative usage*; 700.19 *hypocrite*
white dwarf 29.11 *stellar birth*; 531.9 *white thing*
white elephant 378.6 *burden*; 793.5 *cheap item*; 767.3 *disposable things*; 531.10 *figurative usage*
White Ensign 743.7 *flag*
whiteface 21.21 *stage requisite*
white feather 614.1 *cowardice*; 531.10 *figurative usage*
whitefish 531.9 *white thing*
white flag 743.7 *flag*; 749.2 *peace offering*; 589.2 *symbol of peace*; 531.9 *white thing*
whitefly 44.12 *pests and diseases*; 531.9 *white thing*
white foam 30.14 *wave*
White Friar 531.9 *white thing*
white frost 31.36 *frost*; 494.5 *ice*
white gold 780.16 *bullion*; 531.9 *white thing*
white goods 778.8 *merchandise*; 356.7 *produce*; 531.9 *white thing*
white-haired 531.3; 556.14 *aged*; 296.11 *old*
Whitehall 396.6 *place of authority*; 400.8 *the power structure*
Whitehall farce 21.12 *comedy*
white hat 531.10 *figurative usage*
whitehead 548.2 *pimple*
white heat 522.8 *fire*; 493.1 *heat*; 531.9 *white thing*
white hole 29.11 *stellar birth*
white hope 531.10 *figurative usage*; 485.4 *skilled person*
white horse 531.9 *white thing*
white horses 30.14, 91.3 *wave*
white-hot 493.9 *hot*; 531.2 *whitened*
White House 565.4 *official residence*; 531.9 *white thing*
white hunter 71.24 *hunter*
white knight 384.13 *defender*; 531.10 *figurative usage*; 797.15 *good person*; 252.3 *protector*; 776.10 *trader*; 803.4 *virtuous person*
white lady 558.8 *mixed drink*
white lead 531.8 *whitener*
white lie 479.5 *equivocalness*; 531.10 *figurative usage*; 645.2 *stratagem*
white light 28.28 *colour*; 41.15 *lighting*; 531.9 *white thing*
white lightning 531.10 *figurative usage*
white like ivory 531.1 *white*
white line 742.5 *indicator*
white-line 23.15 *woodcrafted*
white-line woodcut 23.8 *woodwork*
whitely 531.14
white magic 11.3 *witchcraft*
white meat 25.20 *meat*; 25.28 *poultry*; 531.9 *white thing*
white metal 531.9 *white thing*
white meter 39.34 *power supply*
White Mountains 531.10 *figurative usage*
whiten 531.13; 522.28 *bleach*; 256.13 *clean*; 529.15 *colour*; 530.6 *decolour*; 530.5 *lose colour*
whitened 531.2; 256.17 *cleaned*
whitener 531.8; 530.4 *colour remover*
Whiteness 531
whiteness 531.7; 256.1 *cleanness*; 530.1 *colourlessness*; 805.1 *innocence*
White Nile 531.10 *figurative usage*
whitening 530.1 *colourlessness*
white noise 517.5 *atmospheric dissonance*; 512.1 *hiss*; 692.19 *radio reception*; 28.17 *sound*
white notes 18.16 *musical note*
white oak 531.9 *white thing*
white object ball 65.4 *carom*
white of the eye 518.2 *eye*
white out 521.8 *make invisible*; 358.1 *obliterate*
white-out 519.1 *blindness*; 494.5 *ice*; 31.30 *snow*
white paint 531.8 *whitener*
white paper 693.3 *document*; 531.9 *white thing*
white pepper 496.2 *seasoning*; 531.9 *white thing*
white poplar 531.9 *white thing*
white port 558.9 *wine*
white rose 531.9 *white thing*
white rum 558.7 *alcoholic drink*
White Russia 531.10 *figurative usage*
White Russian 662.12 *reactionary*
whites 551.3 *formal dress*; 53.6 *pad*; 531.9 *white thing*
white sale 778.4 *sale*; 531.9 *white thing*
white sauce 25.15 *sauce*; 531.9 *white thing*
White Sea 531.10 *figurative usage*
white shark 531.9 *white thing*
white-skinned 530.8 *drained of colour*
white slave 387.5 *subjected person*
white slavery 387.1 *subjection*
white slave trade 796.5 *prostitution*
white slave traffic 776.4 *trade*
white spirit 19.11 *artist's materials*
white spruce 531.9 *white thing*
white stick 519.3 *aid for poor sight*
white stuff 691.6 *drug*; 531.10 *figurative usage*
white supremacy 12.3 *governance*; 622.11 *prejudice*; 396.7 *type of rule*
whitetail 531.9 *white thing*
white-tailed deer 531.9 *white thing*
white thing 531.9
whitethorn 531.9 *white thing*
whitethroat 531.9 *white thing*
white tie 656.7 *dressed-up*; 656.4 *formal dress*; 531.9 *white thing*
white tie and tails 551.3, 656.4 *formal dress*
white trash 782.11 *the poor*
White Volta 531.10 *figurative usage*
white wall 531.9 *white thing*
whiteware 24.1 *ceramics*
whitewash 699.25 *be fraudulent*; 256.13 *clean*; 256.9 *cleaning agent*; 550.24 *coat*; 529.15 *colour*; 736.8 *conceal*; 714.9 *cover up*; 714.3 *cover-up*; 246.10 *defeat heavily*; 96.16 *delude*; 700.12, 700.32 *disguise*; 234.12 *distort the truth*; 699.14 *façade*; 550.28 *face*; 699.28 *mask*; 529.4 *pigment*; 702.11 *practise sophistry*; 359.5 *preserve*; 359.2 *preserver*; 700.28 *trick*; 550.8 *wall covering*; 531.13 *whiten*; 531.8 *whitener*
whitewashed 550.36 *covered*; 700.41 *disguised*; 699.35 *fraudulent*; 531.2 *whitened*
whitewasher 550.17 *coverer*; 714.5 *vindicator*
whitewashing 714.3 *cover-up*; 700.34 *deceiving*; 234.4 *distortion of the truth*; 700.7 *tricking*
whitewash job 699.8 *fraud*
white-water 379.1 *trap*
white-water running 50.6 *canoeing*
white wedding 570.5 *wedding*
white whale 531.9 *white thing*
white wine 531.9 *white thing*; 558.9 *wine*
white witch 11.4 *witch*
white with dust 531.2 *whitened*
whither 142.12 *where*
whiting 256.9 *cleaning agent*; 25.18 *sea fish*; 531.8 *whitener*
whitish 530.7 *colourless*; 522.21 *light*; 529.13 *soft-hued*; 531.1 *white*
whitishness 531.7 *whiteness*
Whitsun 10.16 *religious festival*; 292.3 *summer*
Whitsunday 10.15 *holy day*
Whitsuntide 292.3 *summer*
whittle 160.7 *form*; 425.10 *knife*; 214.5 *make smaller*; 19.21 *sculpt*; 425.16 *use a sharp tool*; 23.18 *work wood*
whittle away 191.5 *make smaller*
whittled 23.15 *woodcrafted*
whittle down 209.6 *change gradually*
whittling 19.12 *sculpture*; 23.8 *woodwork*
whiz 342.10 *busy person*; 512.4 *hiss*; 797.16 *superior person*
whiz-bang 587.5 *missile weapon*
whiz kid 342.10 *busy person*; 340.3 *doer*; 485.5 *expert*; 121.6 *paragon*; 619.5 *person of wonder*; 302.16 *progressive person*; 246.4 *successful person*; 797.16 *superior person*
whiz off 313.4 *hurry off*
whizz 332.9 *acceleration*; 332.4 *be swift*; 597.2 *fun*
whizz by 332.6 *accelerate*
whizzing 512.1 *hiss*; 332.1 *swift*
whoa 514.5 *hunting cry*; 226.12, 301.11 *stop!*
who cares? 618.21 *never mind!*; 124.15 *no matter!*
whodunit 17.2, 721.5 *fiction*
whoever 138.13
who knows? 456.13
Whole 204
whole 197.13; **204.1**; **204.6**; 232.7 *complete*; 138.15 *general*; 194.4 *mathematical result*; 27.12 *numeration*; 27.71 *numerical*; 194.8 *odd*; 230.1 *perfect*; 359.7 *preserved*; 203.6 *quantitative*; 252.6 *safe*; 203.4 *total*
wholefood 557.7 *food*; 257.2 *salubrity*
wholefood restaurant 557.15 *eating place*
wholehearted 255.17 *direct*; 638.2 *tenacious*
wholeheartedly 255.20 *homogenously*
wholeheartedness 342.8 *assiduity*
whole hog 638.2 *tenacious*
whole list 204.5 *unit*
wholely 203.7 *quantitatively*
wholemeal 25.7 *basic ingredient*
wholemeal bread 25.38 *bread*; 534.5 *brown thing*
wholeness 232.1 *completeness*; 197.3 *oneness*; 230.3 *perfection*; 204.1 *whole*
whole number 27.6 *complex number*; 194.2 *kind of number*; 204.2 *whole thing*
whole picture 143.2 *circumstances*
wholesale 793.15 *cheaply*; 232.7 *complete*; 13.13 *economic*; 127.7 *including*; 776.13 *mercantile*; 217.2 *plentiful*; 778.1 *sell*; 778.3 *selling*
wholesale merchant 778.12 *wholesaler*
wholesale murder 382.4 *slaughter*
wholesale price 790.1 *price*
wholesaler 778.12; 578.3 *agent*; 793.7 *discounter*; 436.3 *provider*; 776.10 *trader*
wholesaling 13.2 *economy*
whole situation 204.3
wholesome 557.27 *edible*; 259.2 *healthful*; 257.4 *hygienic*; 235.4 *worthwhile*
wholesomely 257.7 *hygienically*
wholesomeness 259.4 *healthfulness*; 257.2 *salubrity*
whole thing 204.2
wholly 197.23; **204.11**; 256.20 *clean*; 230.8, 232.9 *completely*; 138.31 *overall*
whomever 138.13 *whoever*
whomp 331.2 *collide*
whomsoever 138.13 *whoever*
whoop 515.2 *bird song*; 633.10 *chase*; 598.5, 598.8 *cheer*; 514.2 *cry of joy*; 514.3 *cry of praise*; 514.11 *laugh*; 507.2 *outcry*
Whoopee 601.1 *celebration*
whooping 507.6 *loud*
whooping cough 260.6 *infection*; 260.9 *respiratory disease*
whoop it up 600.5 *rejoice*
whop 331.13 *blow*; 331.3 *hit*
whopper 158.9 *big thing*; 105.6 *implausibility*; 699.10 *lie*
whopping 158.15 *big*
whore 796.17 *be sexually immoral*; 796.9 *immoral woman*; 568.7 *prostitute*; 804.9 *wicked person*
whoredom 796.5 *prostitution*
whorehouse 796.6 *brothel*
whoremongering 796.14 *lecherous*
whore scars 691.1 *drug-taking*
whoring 796.3 *sexual immorality*
whorish 796.13 *unchaste*
whorishness 796.3 *sexual immorality*
whorl 180.2 *coil*; 78.3 *flower part*
whorled 180.4 *convolutional*
whosoever 138.13 *whoever*
who's who 220.3 *dictionary*
why? 705.25 *what?*.
wibble-wobble 326.8 *oscillate*; 326.18 *to and fro*
Wicca 11.3 *witchcraft*
wick 68.10 *curling*; 522.5 *incandescent light*; 437.2 *lighter*
wicked 804.11; 236.3 *bad*; 631.18 *badly behaved*; 523.11 *benighted*; 532.5 *black-hearted*; 800.5 *dishonourable*; 662.13 *disobedient*; 798.7 *evil*; 797.1 *good*; 796.11 *immoral*; 802.16 *in the wrong*; 651.10 *malevolent*; 16.60 *offending*; 797.5 *proficient*; 806.7 *sinful*; 619.14 *wonderful!*
wicked deed 806.3 *sin*; 804.1 *wickedness*
wickedly 804.18; 631.20 *badly*; 800.11 *dishonourably*; 662.17 *disobediently*; 798.12 *evilly*; 16.89 *guiltily*; 802.28 *immorally*; 651.20 *malevolently*; 236.15 *worthlessly*
Wickedness 804
wickedness 804.1; 631.4 *bad conduct*; 236.9 *badness*; 662.1 *disobedience*; 798.1 *evil*; 796.1 *immorality*; 800.1 *improbity*; 16.38 *lawbreaking*; 651.1 *malevolence*; 806.3 *sin*; 802.5 *unrighteousness*
wicked person 804.9
wicked place 804.8
wicked stepmother 236.12 *bad person*
wicked ways 804.1 *wickedness*
wicked witch 236.12 *bad person*
wicker basket 410.7 *basket*
wickerwork 193.2 *braid*
wicket 53.5; 53.2 *ground*
wicket gate 43.11 *farmland*
wicketkeeper 384.15 *protector*; 53.4 *team*
wicket maiden 53.8 *delivery*
widdershins 307.13 *round*
widdle 560.17 *urinate*; 560.6 *urine*
wide 158.15 *big*; 150.1 *broad*; 68.10 *curling*; 53.8 *delivery*; 145.10 *distantly*; 138.15 *general*; 325.21 *indirect*; 203.6 *quantitative*; 53.10 *score*; 141.13 *spacious*; 274.13 *sporting error*; 152.1 *thick*
wide-angle 150.1 *broad*
wide-angle lens 41.17 *lens*; 518.8 *reflection*
wide-angle photography 29.27 *imaging*
wide awake 665.9 *careful*; 488.6 *conscious*

wide berth 634.10 *avoidance*; 252.1 *safety*; 250.5 *scope*
wide-billed 150.2 *broad-shaped*
wide-bodied 150.2 *broad-shaped*
wide-bottomed 150.2 *broad-shaped*
wide boy 700.17 *cheat*
wide circulation 740.7 *publicity*
wide currency 740.7 *publicity*
wide-cut 150.1 *broad*
wide-eyed **619.7**; 150.2 *broad-shaped*
wide eyes 711.2 *danger signal*
wide-hipped 150.2 *broad-shaped*
wide horizons 141.3 *geographical space*
widely 150.7 *broadly*; 145.10 *distantly*; 141.16 *extensively*; 190.10 *largely*; 308.25 *obviously*; 203.7 *quantitatively*; 138.32 *universally*
widely known 740.20 *well-known*
widely spaced 206.6 *sparse*
wide margin 250.5 *scope*
wide-mouthed 150.2 *broad-shaped*
widen 765.10 *augment*; 190.6 *become bigger*; 138.24, 150.11 *broaden*; 141.20 *extend*; 190.5, 213.5 *make bigger*
widened 190.7 *bigger*
widener 190.4 *enlarger*
wideness 158.2 *bigness*; 150.4 *breadth*
widening 765.18 *acquisitional*; 765.2 *augmentation*; 190.8 *growing*; 190.1 *growth*; 213.1 *increase*
wide of the mark 325.27 *astray*; 145.10 *distantly*; 802.12 *incorrect*; 325.21 *indirect*; 274.17 *mistaken*
wide-open 190.7 *bigger*; 150.1 *broad*; 308.12 *open*; 332.1 *swift*; 250.12 *unconditional*; 254.3 *vulnerable*
wide-open space 141.3 *geographical space*
wide-open spaces 92.6 *lowland*
wide-open speed 332.8 *speed*
wide range 250.5 *scope*
wide-ranging 150.1 *broad*; 395.13 *dominant*; 141.12 *extensive*; 138.18 *far-reaching*; 268.10 *slippery*
wide-reaching 138.18 *far-reaching*
wide receiver 46.7 *offence*
wide scissors kick 67.2 *swimming technique*
wide screen 150.5 *broad thing*
wide-screen 150.1 *broad*
wide-set 150.1 *broad*
wide-spaced 150.1 *broad*
widespread **138.17**; 190.7 *bigger*; 150.1 *broad*; 377.19 *dispersed*; 141.12 *extensive*; 632.10 *familiar*; 127.7 *including*; 138.19 *prevailing*
widespread cloud 31.19 *cloud cover*
widespreadness **138.4**
widow **571.9**; 215.6 *person remaining*; 568.5 *single girl*; 197.7 *single person*; 571.6 *surviving spouse*; 556.9 *woman*; 568.12 *woman in the family*
widowed **571.12**; 215.9 *remaining*; 197.17 *single*
widower 556.8 *man*; 567.13 *man in the family*; 215.6 *person remaining*; 567.5 *single man*; 197.7 *single person*; 571.6 *surviving spouse*
widowered 571.12 *widowed*
widowerhood 571.5 *widowhood*
widowhood **571.5**; 197.6 *singleness*
widowish 571.12 *widowed*
widowlike 571.12 *widowed*
widowman 571.6 *surviving spouse*
widow's mite 768.3 *offering*
widow's pension 392.4 *social assistance*
widow's weeds 656.4 *formal dress*; 603.1 *lamentation*; 743.5 *uniform*; 571.5 *widowhood*
widow woman 571.6 *surviving spouse*
width 150.4 *breadth*; 27.37 *line*; 203.1 *quantity*; 26.4, 158.1 *size*; 141.1 *space*; 152.5 *thickness*
widthways 150.8 *breadthwise*
widthwise 150.8 *breadthwise*
wield 346.9 *take action*; 349.1 *use*; 326.12 *wave*
wieldable 265.12 *wieldy*
wield authority 396.18 *have authority*
wieldiness **265.3**
wield power 647.5 *be severe*; 12.11 *govern*
wield the baton 18.40 *conduct*
wield the sceptre 140.16 *direct*; 12.11 *govern*; 396.18 *have authority*
wieldy **265.12**
wiener 25.29 *sausage*
wiener roast 557.13 *feast*
Wiener Schnitzel 25.46 *German dish*
wienerwurst 25.29 *sausage*
wienie 25.29 *sausage*
wienie roast 654.5 *party*
wife 570.11 *married woman*; 400.1 *master*; 223.12 *partner*; 556.9 *woman*; 568.12 *woman in the family*
wife-batterer 662.9 *criminal*
wife-beater 351.3 *abuser*
wifehood 570.1 *marriage*
wifeless 572.6 *celibate*; 571.12 *widowed*
wifely 570.20 *matrimonial*
wife swapper 759.4 *person who exchanges*
wife swapping 796.3 *sexual immorality*
wig **547.10**; 551.5 *fancy dress*; 551.15 *headgear*
wigged out 489.8 *unconscious*
wigging 670.7 *blame*
wiggle 327.7, 327.24 *shake*
wiggle out of 389.5 *escape*
wiggling 327.18 *shaky*
wiggly 327.18 *shaky*
Wightman Cup 63.1 *tennis*
wig maker 21.28 *stagehand*
wig out 624.12 *become angry*
wigwag 326.8 *oscillate*; 742.12 *signal*
wigwag flag 742.4 *signal*
wigwam 565.9 *mobile home*; 550.7 *overhead covering*
wild **77.15**; 588.6 *anarchic*; 634.18 *avoiding*; 662.13 *disobedient*; 408.20 *disorderly*; 459.5 *foolish*; 141.3 *geographical space*; 563.3 *infertile*; 563.1 *infertility*; 796.14 *lecherous*; 461.12 *manic*; 646.1 *naive*; 70.15 *of animals*; 105.2 *questionable*; 615.4 *rash*; 487.1 *unaccustomed*; 681.2 *unrestrained*; 486.1 *unskilful*; 380.6 *violent*
wild about 593.18 *in love*
wild beast 380.4 *violent creature*
wild boar 60.5 *game*
wild boy 590.9 *feeling person*; 615.3 *rash person*
wildcard 69.3 *card game terms*
wildcat 588.6 *anarchic*; 71.10 *cat*; 250.10 *independent*; 321.4 *locomotive*; 15.10 *unionized*; 651.9 *vixen*
wildcat strike 15.4 *industrial dispute*
wild chance 705.7 *questionableness*
wild dash 342.3 *nimbleness*
wilderness 141.3 *geographical space*; 357.5 *havoc*; 563.1 *infertility*; 86.6 *regions*
wildest dreams 477.5 *fantasy*
wildfire 493.6, 522.8 *fire*
wild flower 78.1 *flower*; 77.2 *plant*
wildfowl 72.1 *birds*
wildfowler 382.13 *animal killer*; 633.6 *hunter*
wildfowling 382.9 *animal killing*; 633.2 *chase*
wild-goose chase 486.9 *bungling*; 634.14 *evasion*; 342.9 *overactivity*; 247.4 *unsuccessful thing*; 766.3 *waste*; 238.5 *waste of effort*; 642.3 *whim*
wild guess 453.9 *uncertainty*
wild horse 59.1 *horse*
wildlife 70.1 *animals*
wildlife park 70.8 *animal welfare*
wildlife photography 41.1 *photography*
wildly 588.8 *anarchically*; 662.17 *disobediently*; 615.6 *rashly*
wildly speculative 476.7 *suppositional*
wild man 590.9 *feeling person*
wild mushroom 83.2 *mushroom*
wildness 662.1 *disobedience*; 615.1 *rashness*; 380.1 *violence*
wild pitch 48.4 *pitching terms*
wild-water canoeing 50.6 *canoeing*
Wild West 86.8 *regions of the US*
wile 699.5 *deceitfulness*; 645.2 *stratagem*; 700.8 *trick*
wilful **635.8**; 588.6 *anarchic*; 642.1 *capricious*; 482.12 *intended*; 641.1 *obstinate*
wilful destruction 441.4, 766.5 *destruction*
wilfully 588.8 *anarchically*; 482.13 *intentionally*; 641.9 *obstinately*
wilfully destroy 766.13 *destroy*
wilfulness **635.3**
wiliness 645.1 *cunning*
Will **635**
will **635.1**; **635.5**; **638.15**; 635.16 *bequeath*; 617.1 *desire*; 641.6 *determination*; 768.5 *give*; 768.1 *giving*; 283.8 *intend*; 106.5 *predetermination*; 253.2 *promise*; 638.7 *resolve*; 635.11 *wish*
will and will not 639.8 *balance*
willed **635.6**; 106.4 *deliberate*; 768.7 *given*
William and Mary 23.7 *furniture style*
William Herschel Telescope 29.24 *telescope*
willing **636.1**; 342.18 *active*; 392.35 *benevolent*; 117.13 *compliant*; 747.17 *cooperative*; 6.17 *educable*; 250.13 *informal*; 595.6 *liking*; 810.9 *loyal*; 663.7 *obedient*; 478.2 *spontaneous*; 483.13 *suggestible*; 797.4 *well-behaved*; 635.1 *will*; 635.6 *willed*
willing and able 636.2 *eager*
willing giver 679.9 *generous person*
willing hands 636.11 *willing worker*
willing horse 342.10 *busy person*
willingly **636.16**; 117.16 *adaptably*; 595.11 *admiringly*; 392.38 *benevolently*; 483.14 *influentially*; 250.22 *informally*; 243.22 *in preparation*; 663.10, 797.24 *obediently*; 6.26 *studiously*
Willingness 636
willingness **636.6**; 617.1 *desire*; 797.11 *good behaviour*; 392.10 *helpfulness*; 595.2 *inclination*; 342.3 *nimbleness*; 663.1 *obedience*; 480.7 *persuadability*; 810.4 *sense of duty*; 483.6 *suggestibility*
willingness to learn 6.10 *educability*
willing sacrifice 752.7 *martyr*
willing servant 658.6 *courteous person*
willing worker **636.11**; 640.5 *tenacious person*
will-making 768.1 *giving*
will of one's own 635.3 *wilfulness*
will-o'-the-wisp 700.5 *falseness*; 522.9 *firefly*; 11.11 *ghost*; 96.2 *illusion*; 518.5 *imagination*
willow 53.7 *bat*
willow grouse 79.11 *tree-related animal*
willowiness 419.8 *softness*; 153.7 *thinness*
willow tit 79.11 *tree-related animal*
willow wands 62.4 *climbing equipment*
willow warbler 79.11 *tree-related animal*
willowy 419.2 *pliant*; 153.1 *thin*; 79.14 *treelike*
willpower **635.2**; 638.15 *will*
will to 768.5 *give*
will to live 554.5 *life cycle*; 277.4 *long-lastingness*
willy 561.8 *organs of reproduction*
Willy Brandt 589.4 *Nobel Peace Prize*
willy-nilly 386.11 *compellingly*; 114.11 *irregularly*
willy-willy 31.16 *wind vortex*
Wilson Trophy 50.1 *sailing*
wilt 77.22 *be dormant*; 337.6 *be weak*; 602.9 *despair*; 245.1 *deteriorate*; 428.21 *dry up*; 44.12 *pests and diseases*; 388.4 *succumb*; 560.19 *sweat*; 79.10 *tree disease*; 441.1 *waste*
wilting 44.17 *botanical*; 560.28 *sweaty*
Wilton 42.3 *fabric*
wily 645.4 *cunning*; 699.33 *deceitful*; 700.34 *deceiving*
wily person 645.3 *cunning person*
Wimbledon 63.1 *tennis*
wimp 388.2 *appeaser*; 40.11 *application*; 614.2 *coward*; 623.16 *humble person*; 639.15 *indecisive person*; 124.10 *nonentity*; 337.4 *weakling*
wimpish 639.3 *timid*
wimple 551.15 *headgear*; 7.11 *vestment*
win 121.8 *be superior*; 246.9 *be victorious*; 47.6 *compete in track and field*; 586.38 *conquer*; 32.30 *extract*; 765.9 *gain*; 59.7 *horseracing*; 400.14 *master*; 48.4 *pitching terms*; 253.13 *secure one's objective*; 773.7 *take*; 246.2 *victory*
win an award 765.14 *profit*
win a point 246.9 *be victorious*
win a prize 813.12 *be rewarded*; 765.14 *profit*
win a scrum 64.5 *play rugby*
win at a canter 265.17 *do easily*
win a trophy 765.14 *profit*
win a victory 246.9 *be victorious*
win by a landslide 246.9 *be victorious*
win by a TKO 52.11 *fight*
win by a whisker 246.9 *be victorious*
wince 491.9 *feel pain*
winch 362.12 *drag*; 366.9 *lifter*
Winchester 587.9 *firearm*; 587.12 *historical guns*; 40.7 *peripheral*
wincing 491.7 *feeling pain*
wind **31.12**; 434.4 *air flow*; 371.24, 432.5 *belch*; 227.3 *changeable thing*; 261.6 *fatigue*; 417.5 *gas*; 260.8 *indigestion*; 335.8 *overpower*; 243.4 *prepare for action*; 307.9 *roll*; 96.4 *theorization*; 325.5 *twist*
windage 141.6 *available space*
windbag 734.8 *chatterer*; 727.6 *exaggerator*; 96.5 *insubstantial person*; 731.4 *talker*
wind band 374.3 *assembly*
windblown 408.15 *untidy*
windbreaker 551.11 *jacket*
windcheater 551.11 *jacket*
wind-chill 31.13 *wind strength*
wind-chill factor 494.7 *cold weather*; 31.6 *weather data*; 31.13 *wind strength*
wind cone 31.7 *weather instruments*
wind crust 68.1 *skiing*
wind direction **31.15**
wind-dried 428.8 *baked*
wind-driven 334.17, 437.10 *powered*
wind-driven generator 39.30 *generator*
wind-dry 428.17 *dry*
winded 261.3 *panting*
winder 307.6 *rotator*
Windermere 88.4 *British lakes*
wind erosion 30.35 *weathering*
windfall 211.4 *extra*; 765.15 *gainful*; 768.2 *gift*; 797.17 *good thing*; 765.5 *profit*; 630.4 *surprising thing*
windfall money 765.5 *profit*
windfall profit 765.5 *profit*
windfall profits tax 790.7 *tax*
wind farm 334.6 *source of energy*
wind force 31.13 *wind strength*
wind gauge 26.8 *meter*; 332.8 *speed*; 31.7 *weather instruments*
wind generator 437.8 *renewable energy*
windier 31.47 *windy*
windily 31.65 *meteorologically*
wind in 362.12 *drag*
wind in and out 189.6 *be oblique*
wind-induced current 30.13 *ocean current*
windiness **31.14**; 432.5 *belch*; 417.3 *sparseness*; 731.1 *talkativeness*
winding 180.4 *convolutional*; 90.10 *fluvial*; 325.21 *indirect*; 39.17 *resistor*
winding course 325.14 *deviating course*
windings 39.30 *generator*
winding sheet 583.4 *funeral objects*; 551.17 *grave clothes*
windlass 366.9 *lifter*; 362.6 *towline*
windless 31.45 *fine*; 301.4 *motionless*
windlessness 301.2 *repose*
windmill 437.8 *renewable energy*; 307.6 *rotator*; 334.6 *source of energy*; 154.6 *tall thing*
windmill stroke 50.8 *punting*
wind of change 227.3 *changeable thing*
window **522.10**; 40.11 *application*; 527.9 *glass*; 20.9 *miscellaneous architectural features*; 308.7 *passageway*; 220.2 *table*; 527.8 *transparent thing*; 518.9 *viewpoint*
window box 44.3 *ornamental garden*
window case 403.4 *framework*
window cleaner 256.12 *cleaner*
window display 779.9 *stall*
window-dress 699.28 *mask*
window-dressing 699.14 *façade*; 740.8 *public relations*
window envelope 527.8 *transparent thing*
window glass 527.9 *glass*; 24.9 *industrial ceramics*
windowless 528.1 *opaque*
window light 527.9 *glass*
window manager 40.11 *application*
windowpane 424.3 *brittle thing*; 527.9 *glass*; 522.10 *window*
Windows™ 40.11 *application*
window-shopping 477.6 *reverie*
window tax 790.9 *historical taxes*
windpipe 308.7 *passageway*; 434.8 *respiration*
wind power 28.11 *energy*; 437.8 *renewable energy*; 334.6 *source of energy*
wind-powered 334.17, 437.10 *powered*
windproof clothing 62.4 *climbing equipment*
wind-propelled 330.19 *propelled*
wind propulsion 330.2 *method of propulsion*
wind pump 437.8 *renewable energy*
wind-rode 50.10 *sailing*
wind-rode boat 50.2 *sailing boat*
wind rose 31.7 *weather instruments*
windrow 43.11 *farmland*
Windscale 437.7 *nuclear power*
windscreen 527.9 *glass*; 518.9 *viewpoint*
windscreen wiper 256.10 *cleaning object*

wind shear 322.7 *miscellaneous aviation terms*
windshield 527.9 *glass*
wind shift 31.15 *wind direction*
windslab 68.1 *skiing*
wind sleeve 742.5 *indicator;* 31.7 *weather instruments*
windsock 742.5 *indicator;* 31.7 *weather instruments*
Windsor Castle 565.4 *official residence*
Windsor chair 23.2 *chair*
Windsor green 538.10 *green pigment*
Windsor red 535.6 *red pigment*
Windsor tie 551.14 *neckwear*
Windsor violet 540.2 *purple pigment*
Windsor yellow 537.7 *yellow pigment*
wind speed 31.6 *weather data;* 31.13 *wind strength*
wind storm 31.12 *wind*
wind strength 31.13; 31.6 *weather data*
windsurf 50.18
windsurfer 50.9 *sailor*
windsurfing 50.7; **50.13**
windsurfing classes 50.7 *windsurfing*
windsurfing techniques 50.7 *windsurfing*
windsurfing terms 50.7 *windsurfing*
windsurf racing 50.7 *windsurfing*
wind system 31.17
wind together 180.6 *convolute*
wind tunnel 322.7 *miscellaneous aviation terms*
wind turbine 437.8 *renewable energy*
wind up 346.8 *activate;* 786.9 *be unable to pay;* 309.9 *close down;* 362.12 *drag;* 131.15 *end;* 247.6 *fail;* 338.3 *invigorate;* 243.4 *prepare for action;* 242.11 *quarrel;* 778.1 *sell;* 226.7 *stop working*
wind-up 621.2 *act of derision;* 131.1 *end;* 125.3 *mockery;* 48.4 *pitching terms*
wind up accounts 789.9 *settle accounts*
wind vortex 31.16
windward 324.10 *clockwise;* 50.20 *offshore*
windward side 169.3 *side direction*
windy 31.47; 434.15 *breezy;* 614.3 *cowardly;* 270.3 *diffuse;* 432.20 *flatulent;* 417.1 *sparse;* 731.5 *talkative;* 124.4 *trivial*
wine 558.9; 690.12 *alcohol;* 558.7 *alcoholic drink;* 490.2 *good time;* 558.15 *provide drink*
wine and dine 490.9 *give pleasure;* 557.25 *provide food*
wine-bibber 690.17 *drunkard*
wine-bibbing 558.1, 690.11 *drinking;* 690.5 *drunken*
wine bottle 410.14 *bottle*
wine cask 410.11 *vessel*
wine cellar 439.4 *storage*
winecoloured 535.1 *red*
wined and dined 654.16 *popular*
wineglass 558.10 *drink container;* 410.13 *drinking vessel*
wine lake 43.2 *Common Agricultural Policy;* 562.2 *productiveness;* 439.1 *store*
wine list 220.4 *bill*
wine merchant 436.3 *provider*
wineskin 410.14 *bottle;* 690.17 *drunkard*
wine steward 401.3 *attendant;* 308.3 *person who opens*
wine taster 558.12 *drinker;* 495.5 *taster*
wine tasting 558.1 *drinking*
wine vinegar 25.7 *basic ingredient*
win fame 248.5 *be prosperous*
win fame and glory 248.5 *be prosperous*
win for Christ 7.20 *preach*
win freedom 389.5 *escape*
win friends 569.13 *befriend*
wing 211.3 *additional item;* 586.30 *air force unit;* 586.14 *armed forces;* 72.13 *assemblage of birds;* 374.3 *assembly;* 332.4 *be swift;* 205.4 *component;* 72.25 *fly;* 59.9 *jumping;* 584.4 *military organization;* 376.16 *party;* 25.28 *poultry;* 21.19 *stage set;* 316.12 *transport;* 50.7 *windsurfing*
wing area 58.5 *lacrosse*
wingback 46.7 *offence*
wing chair 23.2 *chair*
Wingco 586.32 *airman*
wing commander 586.32 *airman*
wingcut 21.19 *stage set*
winged 71.27 *chiropteran;* 332.1 *swift*
winged horse 59.1 *horse*
winged insect 76.1 *insect*
winged messenger 316.8 *messenger*
winger 66.3 *football player;* 58.4 *ice hockey player*
wing feather 72.17 *plumage*
wing flap 228.3 *stabilizer*
wing-footed 332.1 *swift*
wing half 66.3 *football player;* 58.2 *hockey player*
wing it 21.35 *overact*
wing loading 322.7 *miscellaneous aviation terms*
win glory 248.5 *be prosperous*
wing mirror 28.29 *optical element;* 518.8 *reflection*
win going away 246.10 *defeat heavily*
wingover 322.5 *flight*
wings 72.16 *avian anatomy;* 743.4 *insignia;* 21.17 *stage*
wingspan 150.4 *breadth;* 322.7 *miscellaneous aviation terms*
win hands down 246.10 *defeat heavily;* 265.17 *do easily*
win in a walk 265.17 *do easily*
win in record-breaking time 47.6 *compete in track and field*
win in straight sets 246.10 *defeat heavily*
wink 669.12 *accept;* 693.7 *advice;* 669.1 *approval;* 519.14 *be blind;* 593.14 *communication of love;* 593.26 *court;* 742.3, 742.11 *gesture;* 522.25 *light up;* 711.5 *warn;* 711.1 *warning*
wink at 519.16 *be blind to;* 649.11 *condone*
winker 522.6 *electric light;* 742.5 *indicator*
winking 742.15 *gestural;* 522.15 *lucent;* 519.2 *poor sight;* 519.9 *weak-sighted*
winkle 25.19 *shellfish*
winkle out 369.11 *extract*
winkle-pickers 551.19 *footwear*
winner 235.8 *exceller;* 765.7 *gainer;* 797.17 *good thing;* 121.6 *paragon;* 769.5 *recipient;* 452.12 *something certain;* 246.4 *successful person;* 246.5 *victorious person*
winner's enclosure 59.7 *horseracing*
winning 121.14, 235.2 *best;* 765.1 *gain;* 593.22 *lovable;* 480.19 *persuasive;* 246.13 *successful;* 773.1 *taking;* 246.15 *victorious*
winning by a mile 246.2 *victory*
winning card 484.3 *expedient plan*
winning hazard 65.3 *English billiards*
winning position 121.3 *advantage*
winning post 482.6 *objective*
winnings 788.5; 765.4 *earnings;* 769.2 *something received;* 794.2 *spoils;* 773.5 *takings*
winning streak 248.2 *good fortune*
winning ways 480.3 *incentive;* 593.4 *lovability*
Winnipeg 88.5 *other major lakes*
winnow 469.4 *pick;* 255.10 *purify*
wino 558.12 *drinker*
win one's spurs 613.15 *be courageous;* 246.6 *be successful*
win on moves 246.9 *be victorious*
win on points 246.9 *be victorious*
win over 450.9 *make someone believe;* 483.9 *motivate;* 749.4 *pacify;* 480.15, 760.11 *persuade*
win power 334.10 *be powerful*
win praise 669.17 *meet with approval*
win renown 340.4 *act;* 811.5 *have repute*
winsome 545.5 *beautiful;* 593.22 *lovable*
winsomeness 593.4 *lovability*
winter 292.5; **292.13**; 494.7 *cold weather;* 298.5 *regular thing;* 292.6 *spend the season;* 249.4 *time of adversity;* 654.12 *visit*
winter barley 43.12 *crop*
winter bud 77.8 *bud*
winter climbing 62.1 *mountaineering*
winter clothes 493.3 *heater*
winter feed 557.8 *animal food*
winter garden 44.2 *garden*
winter horse 59.1 *horse*
winter jasmine 537.8 *yellow thing*
winterlike 292.13 *winter*
winter monsoon 31.17 *wind system*
winter oats 43.12 *crop*
winter of discontent 249.4 *time of adversity*
winter of one's life 556.5 *old age*
winter quarters 494.6 *Arctic*
winter sale 778.4 *sale*
winter solstice 10.15 *holy day;* 292.5 *winter*
Winter Sports 68
wintertide 292.5 *winter*
wintertime 292.5 *winter*
winter wheat 43.12 *crop*
winter woollies 493.3 *heater*
wintery 292.13 *winter*
win the affection of 593.28 *win the love of*
win the ball 64.5 *play rugby*
win the battle 246.9 *be victorious*
win the blue ribbon 121.8 *be superior*
win the championship 121.8 *be superior*
win the cup 121.8 *be superior*
win the game 246.9 *be victorious*
win the heart of 593.28 *win the love of*
win the last battle 246.9 *be victorious*
win the lottery 781.13 *get rich;* 765.14 *profit*
win the love of 593.28; 593.28 *win the love of*
win the match 246.9 *be victorious*
win the pools 781.13 *get rich;* 765.14 *profit*
win the prize 121.8 *be superior*
win the race 332.6 *accelerate;* 246.9 *be victorious*
win through 253.13 *secure one's objective*
wintrily 494.13 *coldly;* 292.18 *seasonally*
wintriness 31.31 *coldness;* 494.7 *cold weather*
wintry 494.8 *cold;* 31.46 *seasonal;* 292.13 *winter*
wintry shower 494.5 *ice*
winy 690.6 *intoxicating*
wipe 428.20 *absorb;* 526.3 *cause to disappear;* 256.13 *clean;* 527.12 *make transparent*
wipe away one's tears 627.9 *sorrow*
wipe clean 256.13 *clean;* 255.10 *purify*
wiped away 649.8 *overlooked*
wiped out 708.20 *cancelled;* 690.3 *dead drunk;* 247.11 *defeated;* 357.15 *destroyed;* 782.2 *insolvent;* 94.11 *no more*
wipe dry 428.20 *absorb*
wipe off 256.13 *clean;* 358.1 *obliterate*
wipe off the map 357.8 *destroy;* 358.1 *obliterate*
wipe one's feet on 236.14 *ill-treat*
wipeout 247.4 *unsuccessful thing*
wipe out 195.9 *annihilate;* 708.14 *cancel;* 94.13 *cause not to exist;* 526.3 *cause to disappear;* 246.10 *defeat heavily;* 357.8 *destroy;* 131.17 *kill;* 441.2 *lay waste;* 358.1 *obliterate;* 382.18 *slaughter;* 50.18 *windsurf;* 50.7 *windsurfing*
wipe out a score 385.3 *retaliate*
wipe the floor with 246.10 *defeat heavily*
wipe the plate clean 688.5 *be greedy*
wipe the slate clean 649.10 *absolve;* 295.17 *become new;* 808.4 *be penitent;* 786.10 *forgive a debt*
wipe up 428.20 *absorb;* 256.13 *clean*
wiping out 50.7 *windsurfing*
wiping up 256.2 *cleaning*
wire 39.27; 693.12 *communicate;* 693.2 *communication;* 39.35 *conduct;* 692.31 *correspond;* 692.8 *data transmission;* 373.6 *line;* 151.8 *narrow thing*
wire basket 410.7 *basket*
wired 373.15 *connected*
wire-drawn 404.10 *delicate;* 151.2 *fine*
wireless 504.9 *audio device;* 504.11 *aural;* 692.18 *radio*
wire-mesh 54.6 *fencing*
wire-mesh mask 54.2 *fencing equipment*
wire netting 43.11 *farmland*
wirepuller 645.3 *cunning person;* 579.13 *director;* 480.14 *motivator;* 396.10 *person of authority*
wirepulling 396.1 *authority;* 395.4 *indirect influence;* 484.4 *plot*
wire ropeway 317.12 *cableway*
wires 395.4 *indirect influence*
wire sculpture 19.12 *sculpture*
wire service 741.7 *press agency;* 693.8 *source of information*
wiretap 504.9 *audio device;* 504.15 *hear;* 744.10 *recording instrument*
wireway 317.12 *cableway*
wireworm 76.5 *larva;* 76.3 *pest;* 44.12 *pests and diseases;* 75.6 *worm*
wiriness 423.8 *physical strength;* 153.7 *thinness*
wiry 423.4 *powerful;* 153.1 *thin*
Wisdom 458
wisdom 458.1; 713.1 *advice;* 616.1 *caution;* 442.4 *cleverness;* 156.7 *deep thinking;* 8.2 *divine attribute;* 464.1 *judgment;* 455.3 *learning;* 156.3 *profundity;* 444.1 *reason*
wisdom literature 17.1 *literature*
wisdom tooth 425.11 *tooth*
wise 156.11; **458.5**; 713.8 *advisable;* 667.14 *awe-inspiring;* 239.1 *convenient;* 645.4 *cunning;* 6.18 *educated;* 442.10 *intelligent;* 464.9 *judicious;* 455.8 *knowledgeable;* 4.19 *learned;* 444.7 *reasoning;* 485.6 *skilful;* 317.1 *way*
wiseacre 673.7 *vain person*
wise-arsed 660.14 *cheeky*
wisecrack 599.13 *be humorous;* 599.5 *joke;* 697.2 *solecism*
wisecracker 697.4 *buffoon;* 599.6 *humorist*
wised up 693.18 *informed*
wise guy 485.5 *expert;* 660.12 *impudent person;* 458.4 *intellectual;* 455.6 *knowledgeable person;* 4.12 *sage;* 673.7 *vain person*
wisely 4.29; **458.9**; 713.9 *advisably;* 6.25 *educationally;* 442.15 *intelligently;* 455.15 *knowledgeably*
wise man 458.3; 713.4 *adviser;* 156.7 *deep thinking;* 400.9 *educational leader;* 442.8 *intellectual person;* 455.6 *knowledgeable person;* 396.10 *person of authority;* 4.12 *sage;* 443.7 *thinker*
wiser 244.14 *improved*
wise to 455.8 *knowledgeable*
wise up 693.11 *inform*
wise woman 156.7 *deep thinking;* 11.13 *diviner;* 458.3 *wise man*
wish 635.11; 610.3 *aspiration;* 610.7 *aspire;* 474.11 *demand;* 617.1 *desire;* 595.7 *like;* 595.3 *likes;* 710.1, 710.6 *request;* 477.6 *reverie;* 635.1 *will*
wishbone 72.16 *avian anatomy;* 311.5 *fork;* 25.28 *poultry;* 11.6 *talisman;* 50.13 *windsurfing*
wishbone boom 50.7 *windsurfing*
wished for 617.7 *desired;* 595.5 *likable*
wished on one 712.10 *maledictive*
wisher 617.6 *desirer*
wish for 617.12 *desire*
wish for oneself 595.7 *like*
wishful 610.13 *aspirant;* 617.9 *desirous*
wishfully 617.18 *desirously*
wishful thinker 477.9 *visionary*
wishful thinking 36.19 *defence mechanism;* 274.6 *fallibility;* 610.1 *hope;* 446.6 *ideal;* 446.7 *idealism;* 477.6 *reverie;* 700.2 *self-deception;* 96.4 *theorization*
wish ill 712.7
wishing 595.1, 595.6 *liking*
wishing for 617.9 *desirous*
wishing stone 11.6 *talisman*
wishing well 11.6 *talisman*
wish the best for 650.8 *be benevolent*
wish to 595.9 *like to*
wish undone 808.4 *be penitent*
wish well 650.8 *be benevolent;* 413.14 *give moral support*
wishy-washiness 497.1 *dilution;* 728.8 *insipidness;* 639.13 *timidity*
wishy-washy 530.7 *colourless;* 433.22 *diluted;* 728.17 *insipid;* 337.13 *insufficient;* 685.7 *politically moderate;* 497.5 *tasteless;* 639.3 *timid*
wisp 159.4 *little person;* 151.8 *narrow thing;* 205.7 *piece*
wispiness 151.7 *fineness;* 417.3 *sparseness*
wisp of cloud 31.20 *cloud appearance*
wisp of smoke 432.3 *miasma*
wispy 151.2 *fine;* 205.11 *partial;* 417.1 *sparse*
wispy cloud 31.20 *cloud appearance*
wistful 617.9 *desirous;* 4.17 *thoughtful*
wistfully 617.18 *desirously;* 4.28 *thoughtfully*
wistfulness 617.1 *desire*
wit 599.3; 697.4 *buffoon;* 442.4 *cleverness;* 599.6 *humorist;* 599.1 *humorousness;* 455.4 *intellect;* 442.3, 458.2 *intelligence*
witch 11.4; 625.3 *irascible person;* 568.8 *nasty woman;* 475.8 *oracle;* 619.5 *person of wonder;* 412.7 *person who mixes;* 626.5 *sullen person;* 651.9 *vixen;* 458.3 *wise man*
witchcraft 11.3; 236.11 *harmfulness;* 395.2 *occult influence;* 11.1 *occultism;* 334.1 *power;* 804.6 *religious sin;* 700.7 *tricking*
witch doctor 394.15 *healer;* 7.8 *priest;* 711.4 *warner;* 11.4 *witch*
witchery 480.3 *incentive;* 11.3 *witchcraft*
witches' broom 79.10 *tree disease*
witches' Sabbath 11.3 *witchcraft*
witch-hunt 466.14 *discriminate against;* 705.18 *interrogate;* 7.20 *preach;* 633.1 *pursuit*

witch-hunter 466.7 *bigot;* 814.17 *punisher;* 7.4 *religionist*
witch-hunting 7.15 *religious;* 7.2 *religiousness;* 466.4 *social discrimination*
witching hour 11.3 *witchcraft*
witchlike **11.15**
witchman 11.4 *witch*
witch master 11.4 *witch*
Witch of Endor 475.8 *oracle;* 11.4 *witch*
witch's brew 412.2 *mixed thing*
witch's broom 554.6 *things brought to life*
witch's broomstick 11.6 *talisman*
witch's hat 551.15 *headgear*
witchwoman 11.4 *witch*
witchwork 11.3 *witchcraft*
with **223.24**; **747.22**; 352.7 *by means of;* 348.9 *instrumentally*
with a bad grace 637.17 *unwillingly*
with abandon 250.21 *excessively*
with a big heart 650.11 *charitably*
with a break 146.8 *apart*
with a cheerful heart 598.9 *cheerfully*
with a clear conscience 805.11 *innocently*
with a clear head 689.1 *sober;* 689.9 *soberly*
with a come-hither look 593.30 *lovingly*
with a courteous manner 569.17 *in friendship*
with a credit card 772.13 *on loan*
with a deafening roar 507.9 *loudly*
with a difference 126.8 *originally*
with a disappointing result 604.13 *disappointingly*
with a dominating manner 121.16 *superiorly*
with a dowry 440.10 *proprietarily*
with a drink problem 690.5 *drunken*
with affection 569.17 *in friendship;* 593.30 *lovingly;* 595.10 *with great liking*
with a fine-tooth comb 222.19 *meticulously*
with a forgiving heart 649.14 *forgivingly*
with a free spirit 391.8 *free*
with a frown 625.9 *irascibly*
with a fuzzy tongue 690.4 *crapulous*
with a generous heart 769.15 *receptively*
with a glib tongue 645.6 *cunningly*
with a good heart 650.10 *benevolently*
with a good nature 650.10 *benevolently*
with a grateful heart 671.8 *gratefully*
with a grimace 625.9 *irascibly*
with a guilty conscience 806.11 *guiltily;* 808.8 *penitently*
with a handicap 120.7 *unequally*
with a hangover 690.4 *crapulous*
with a heavy hand 492.15 *insensitively;* 647.11 *severely*
with a heavy heart 637.17 *unwillingly*
with a helping hand 569.20 *favourably*
with a hook 373.17 *in connection with*
with a hop 327.29 *jerkily*
with a jealous heart 629.9 *jealously;* 624.17 *resentfully*
with a light hand 648.6 *leniently*
with a light rein 648.6 *leniently*
with a light touch 415.11 *lightly;* 492.16 *sensitively*
with a likeable manner 595.10 *with great liking*
with all documents 454.11 *verifiably*
with all due respect 667.22 *respectfully*
with all haste 262.6 *hastily*
with all its faults 231.11 *imperfectly*
with all one's heart 255.20 *homogenously;* 636.16 *willingly;* 590.20 *with feeling*
with all one's love 593.30 *lovingly*
with all one's might 353.10 *ambitiously;* 576.12 *laboriously;* 334.18 *powerfully*
with all respect 667.22 *respectfully*
with all speed 332.14 *swiftly*
with all the trimmings 232.10 *fully*
with a lock 373.17 *in connection with*
with a long face 602.12 *joylessly;* 637.17 *unwillingly*
with a loving heart 803.10 *ethically*
with amendments 224.15 *changeably*
with a motive 106.4 *deliberate*
with an acid tongue 626.14 *irritably*
with an advantage 121.16 *superiorly*
with an architect 20.20 *architecturally*
with a natural look 115.14 *comparably*
with an easy conscience 805.11 *innocently*
with an empty stomach 687.6 *fasting*
with an eye to 482.14 *for*
with anger 753.11 *disapprovingly;* 659.9 *discourteously;* 625.9 *irascibly*
with an ill nature 594.18 *hatefully;* 626.14 *irritably*
with an independent manner 109.12 *irrelevantly*
with an indifferent attitude 250.20 *freely*
with an intermission 146.8 *apart*
with an interval 146.8 *apart*
with an intrusive manner 100.18 *extraneously*
with an iron hand 647.11 *severely*
with an open heart 646.5 *naively*
with an open mind 473.8 *disinterestedly;* 618.19 *impartially;* 769.15 *receptively*
with antagonism 661.10 *in defiance*
with an unapproachable manner 145.11 *reservedly*
with a pin 373.17 *in connection with*
with aplomb 485.12 *skilfully*
with appropriate papers 454.11 *verifiably*
with a remainder **215.12**
with a rope 373.17 *in connection with*
with a sad heart 602.11 *sadly*
with a scowl 625.9 *irascibly*
with a search party 633.18 *pursuant to*
with a sick headache 690.4 *crapulous*
with a sledge hammer 357.16 *destructively*
with a sparing hand 680.7 *economically*
with a sprint 47.10 *fast*
with assurance 756.16 *as promised;* 253.16 *surely*
with a steady pace 119.13 *equitably*
with a straight face 618.17 *indifferently;* 643.10 *solemnly*
with a stroke 340.7 *actively*
with a strong tendency 229.6 *probably*
with a thick head 690.4 *crapulous*
with a tight fist 360.11 *tenaciously*
with authority 396.23 *authoritatively;* 395.14 *influentially;* 121.16 *superiorly*
with avarice 773.13 *avariciously*
with a vengeance 211.10 *additionally;* 232.10 *fully;* 380.10 *violently;* 338.6 *with vigour*
with a view to 482.14 *for;* 446.21 *purposively*
with a warm heart 569.17 *in friendship*
with a warm welcome 769.15 *receptively*
with a weight of 414.1 *heavy*
with a whole skin 252.6 *safe*
with a will 636.16 *willingly;* 338.6 *with vigour*
with bad grace 626.14 *irritably*
with balance 57.12 *competitively*
with bated breath 474.12 *expectantly;* 511.10 *faintly;* 623.28 *subserviently;* 730.17 *voicelessly*
with bits missing 205.11 *partial*
with bitterness 624.17 *resentfully*
with body and soul 638.17 *resolutely*
with British Rail 319.6 *commercially*
with brute force 423.13 *powerfully*
with candour 250.22 *informally*
with cap in hand 664.16 *with servility*
with care 665.12 *carefully*
with certainty **452.24**
with charity 768.9 *as a gift;* 593.30 *lovingly*
with child 474.6 *expectant;* 561.16 *reproductive*
with clarity 695.13 *intelligibly*
with clean hands 805.5 *innocent;* 805.11 *innocently*
with cleated boots 62.10 *on a climb*
with compassion 650.10 *benevolently;* 652.8 *philanthropically;* 627.13 *pitifully;* 419.18 *soft-heartedly*
with complications 412.14 *in the midst*
with compliments 669.25 *approvingly*
with conditions 251.16 *under restraints*
with confidence 397.16 *commandingly*
with consent **750.39**; 755.8 *contractually*
with contempt 594.18 *hatefully*
with controls 251.16 *under restraints*
with conviction 726.7 *emphatically*
with courtesy 658.14 *courteously*
with crushing effect 357.16 *destructively*
with deception 773.13 *avariciously;* 774.19 *thievishly*
with deference 658.16 *deferentially*
with delay **378.16**
with deletions 399.8 *under censorship*
with designs on 482.11 *intending*
with determination 228.13 *determinedly*
with devotion 569.19 *devotedly*
with different parts 412.14 *in the midst*
with difficulty 264.25 *difficultly;* 378.17 *in the way*
with dignity **622.33**
with diplomacy 579.19 *managerially;* 398.11 *representatively*
with discretion 466.16 *judiciously*
with disdain 655.14 *unsocially*
with dissent 372.23 *disagreeably*
with downcast eyes 674.18 *shyly*
with dragging feet 637.17 *unwillingly*
withdraw **313.2**; **355.2**; 98.16 *absent oneself;* 780.26 *bank;* 618.12 *be indifferent;* 197.18 *be one;* 732.6 *be shy;* 655.12 *be unsocial;* 708.14 *cancel;* 780.25 *demonetize;* 704.9 *deny;* 526.2 *depart;* 362.14 *draw in;* 479.2 *equivocate;* 315.9 *exit;* 369.11 *extract;* 479.4 *recant;* 605.5 *resign;* 303.2 *retreat;* 761.6 *reverse;* 634.8 *run away;* 350.6 *stop using;* 388.3 *submit;* 212.3 *subtract*
withdrawal **691.3**; 300.4 *backward motion;* 226.1 *cessation;* 36.19 *defence mechanism;* 704.2 *denial;* 313.7 *departure;* 36.13 *depression;* 526.4 *disappearance;* 479.6 *equivocation;* 389.1 *escape;* 369.1 *extraction;* 247.1 *failure;* 463.1 *oblivion;* 479.8 *recantation;* 355.3 *relinquishment;* 605.1 *resignation;* 303.11 *retreat;* 761.1 *reversion;* 372.2 *setting apart;* 634.12 *shyness;* 212.1 *subtraction;* 655.1 *unsociability*
withdrawal of the charge 16.42 *acquittal*
withdrawal sickness 691.3 *withdrawal*
withdrawal symptoms 691.3 *withdrawal*
withdraw a statement **773.9**
withdraw from circulation 780.25 *demonetize*
withdraw from currency 238.8 *make useless*
withdrawing 773.2 *taking back*
withdrawing a statement 773.2 *taking back*
withdraw into the background 122.10 *follow*
withdrawn 197.16 *alone;* 355.6 *apathetic;* 618.7 *indifferent;* 36.34 *introverted;* 780.22 *monetary;* 463.8 *oblivious;* 732.1 *shy;* 736.16 *silent;* 212.5 *subtracted;* 372.17 *unjoined;* 655.8 *unsociable*
withdrawn coinage 780.15 *false money*
withdraw the charge 714.7 *vindicate*
with dry eyes 618.17 *indifferently*
with due deference 623.28 *subserviently*
with due respect 667.22 *respectfully*
withe 373.6 *line*
with ears burning 644.5 *curious*
with ease **263.6**
with efficiency 346.13 *operationally*
with eloquence 726.7 *emphatically*
with embarrassment 378.18 *inhibitively*
with emendations 224.15 *changeably*
with emphasis 707.23 *affirmatively;* 661.9 *defiantly*
with emptiness 417.7 *sparsely*
with empty pockets 218.2 *unprovided*
with envy 629.9 *jealously*
with equal chance 391.8 *free*
with equal measures 115.14 *comparably*
wither 556.17 *age;* 191.6 *become smaller;* 77.22 *be dormant;* 493.14 *be hot;* 214.4 *decrease;* 245.1 *deteriorate;* 428.21 *dry up;* 296.17 *grow old;* 441.1 *waste*
withered 245.12 *deteriorated;* 337.9 *dilapidated;* 428.3 *dried-up;* 153.2 *emaciated;* 563.3 *infertile;* 191.7 *smaller*
withering 191.1 *contraction;* 428.13 *drying*
withershins 324.10 *clockwise;* 303.29 *in reverse*
with evil intent 651.20 *malevolently*
with evil intentions 804.18 *wickedly*
with exactitude 665.12 *carefully*
with excess 250.21 *excessively*
with expertise 400.16 *masterfully*
with expression 742.18 *indicatively*
with eyes on stalks 619.7 *wide-eyed*
with faith 255.18 *virtuously*
with fatal results 798.13 *destructively*
with fear and trembling 612.15 *fearfully*
with feeling **590.20**; 591.12 *sensitively*
with few words 269.5 *concisely*
with fingers crossed 702.15 *hypocritically*
with firmness 416.10 *densely;* 418.13 *inflexibly*
with flair 724.10 *stylistically*
with flying colours 246.16 *successfully*
with folded arms 341.5 *without action*
with fondness 593.30 *lovingly*
with footwork 54.7 *on guard*
with forbearance 383.15 *abstemiously*
with force 710.12 *by request*
with forethought 482.13 *intentionally*
with full knowledge 482.13 *intentionally*
with full play 250.21 *excessively*
with full powers 334.13 *powerful*
with fury 624.18 *angrily*
with gaping mouth 619.13 *wonderfully*
with gentleness 415.11 *lightly*
with giant leaps 332.14 *swiftly*
with giant strides 332.14 *swiftly*
with good cheer 598.9 *cheerfully;* 654.18 *sociably*
with good effect 246.16 *successfully*
with good grace 658.14 *courteously;* 241.15 *pleasantly;* 636.16 *willingly*
with good intentions 803.9 *virtuously*
with good results 246.16 *successfully*
with good will 652.8 *philanthropically*
with gratitude 671.8 *gratefully*
with great admiration 595.11 *admiringly*
with great charm 593.30 *lovingly;* 654.18 *sociably*
with great effect 395.14 *influentially*
with great emotion 593.30 *lovingly*
with great liking **595.10**
with great weight 414.16 *heavily*
with gusto 636.16 *willingly*
with haste 342.22 *actively*
with hate 798.12 *evilly;* 651.20 *malevolently*
with hat in hand 623.28 *subserviently*
with head held high 622.32 *proudly*
with heart and soul 576.12 *laboriously*
with heat 92.13 *continentally*
with heels dug in 641.3 *unyielding*
withheld 361.9 *interrupted;* 709.8 *refused;* 360.10 *retained*
with high spirits 598.9 *cheerfully*
with hindsight 3.24 *historically;* 284.24 *retrospectively*
withhold 294.8 *delay;* 360.7 *detain;* 361.12 *interrupt;* 737.12 *keep secret;* 103.8 *make impossible;* 359.5 *preserve*
withhold approval **670.15**
withhold assent 709.6 *dissent*
withhold consent 709.6 *dissent*
withholding 361.6 *interruption;* 709.8 *refused*
withhold payment 786.8 *stop payment*
withhold permission 399.3 *veto*
with honesty 803.10 *ethically*
with honeyed words 677.17 *flatteringly*
with hope 756.17 *auspiciously;* 610.15 *hopefully*
with hostility 381.26 *aggresively;* 372.23 *disagreeably;* 753.11 *disapprovingly;* 594.18 *hatefully;* 751.11 *in disagreement*
with humility **388.6**
with idealism 101.14 *subjectively*
with imagination 477.17 *imaginatively;* 126.8 *originally*
with immunity 250.20 *freely*
with impunity **758.13**; 252.11 *safely*
within 127.9 *inclusively;* 406.14 *internally;* 101.14 *subjectively*
within bounds 684.9 *moderate;* 684.12, 685.9 *moderately;* 444.15 *reasonably;* 251.16 *under restraints*
within call 504.17 *aurally;* 147.12 *near*
within earshot 504.17 *aurally;* 504.14 *hearable;* 147.12 *near*
within hearing 504.17 *aurally;* 147.12 *near*
with inhibitions 378.18 *inhibitively*

with inhumanity 653.5 *misanthropically*
within limits **166.8**; 685.6 *moderate*; 685.9 *moderately*; 251.16 *under restraints*
within living memory 284.22 *in the past*
within one's depth 157.8 *shallowly*
within one's means 793.9 *cheap*
within one's power 102.10 *practically*
within one's rights 801.21 *in the right*
within range 504.17 *aurally*; 504.14 *hearable*; 685.9 *moderately*; 147.12 *near*
within reach 97.10 *available*; 239.7 *conveniently*; 147.12 *near*; 239.8 *nearby*; 97.16 *on the spot*; 102.10 *practically*
within reason 685.6 *moderate*; 684.12, 685.9 *moderately*
within reasonable limits 684.9 *moderate*; 684.12 *moderately*
within sight 147.12 *near*; 102.10 *practically*; 518.24 *visually*
within someone's orbit 395.14 *influentially*
with insularity 92.13 *continentally*
with interest 211.10 *additionally*; 788.8 *profitably*
within the bounds of 209.7 *gradational*
within the law 16.44 *legal*; 16.81 *legally*
within the time limit 287.8, 287.11 *in time*
with irritation 626.14 *irritably*
with it 295.16 *avant-garde*; 632.12 *established*; 553.7 *fashionable*; 6.19 *knowledgeable*
with justice 119.13 *equitably*
with justification 714.15 *in vindication*
with kid gloves 648.6 *leniently*
with kindness 650.10 *benevolently*; 658.14 *courteously*; 569.17 *in friendship*; 648.6 *leniently*
with knobs on 211.10 *additionally*; 232.10 *fully*
with legal protection 757.9 *with permission*
with light fingers 774.19 *thievishly*
with love 595.11 *admiringly*; 650.10 *benevolently*; 593.30 *lovingly*; 654.18 *sociably*
with loyalty 569.19 *devotedly*
with luck 248.9 *prosperously*
with lust 593.30 *lovingly*
with malice 798.13 *destructively*; 798.12 *evilly*; 594.18 *hatefully*; 651.20 *malevolently*; 624.17 *resentfully*; 714.16 *vindictively*
with malice aforethought 482.13 *intentionally*; 651.20 *malevolently*
with many changes 222.16 *relatively*
with many words 270.7 *diffusely*
with material 402.9 *materially*
with maturity 556.16 *maturely*
with meaning 742.18 *indicatively*; 694.13 *meaningfully*
with meditation 482.13 *intentionally*
with mercy 627.13 *pitifully*
with might and main 342.22 *actively*; 576.12 *laboriously*; 334.18 *powerfully*; 638.17 *resolutely*; 336.14 *strongly*
with misgivings 596.10 *discontentedly*
with moderation 684.12, 685.9 *moderately*
with modesty 473.9 *unselfishly*
with momentum 331.18 *dynamically*
with much ado 264.25 *difficultly*; 378.16 *with delay*
with mud 92.13 *continentally*
with noble intentions 473.9 *unselfishly*
with nobody the wiser 737.15 *in secret*
with no expense spared 679.12 *generously*
with no frills 620.8 *boringly*
with no guilt 805.11 *innocently*
with no holds barred 250.21 *excessively*; 739.13 *openly*
with no interest 618.17 *indifferently*
with no letup 134.7 *continually*; 134.6 *protracted*
with no questions asked 757.9 *with permission*
with no regrets 809.6 *impenitently*
with no remorse 809.6 *impenitently*
with no strings attached 250.21 *excessively*; 752.20 *persuasively*
with nothing on 552.17 *nakedly*
with objectivity 402.9 *materially*
with obligations 354.5 *undertaken*
with offence 804.21 *criminally*; 712.12 *swearingly*
with official approval 396.25 *authentically*
with one accord 747.20 *cooperatively*; 750.31 *in accord*
with one bite 688.7 *gluttonously*
with one blow 357.16 *destructively*
with one's dander up 624.18 *angrily*
with one's eyes closed 265.21 *easily*
with one's eyes open 482.13 *intentionally*
with one's hands 15.13 *industrially*
with one's monkey up 624.18 *angrily*
with one voice 747.20 *cooperatively*; 750.10, 750.31 *in accord*; 285.13 *synchronously*
with open arms 569.17 *in friendship*; 370.18 *receptively*; 654.18 *sociably*; 636.16 *willingly*
with open doors 740.22 *publicly*
with open hands 650.11 *charitably*; 679.12 *generously*
with openness 769.15 *receptively*
with oppression 414.17 *burdensomely*
with others in mind 473.9 *unselfishly*
without 212.8 *by subtraction*; 171.15 *externally*; 233.6 *incompletely*; 766.16 *losing*; 222.15 *under the circumstances*
without a bean 782.2 *insolvent*
without a care 391.8 *free*
without a case 16.64 *convicted*
without a cent 782.2 *insolvent*
without acknowledgment 672.5 *thankless*; 672.7 *ungratefully*
without a clue 696.2 *unexplained*
without a conscience 809.3 *impenitent*
without a cooperative spirit 709.11 *uncooperatively*
without action **341.5**
without ado 265.21 *easily*
without adornment 647.12 *plainly*
without affectation 646.5, 805.12 *naively*
without affiliation 250.20 *freely*
without a hangover 689.1 *sober*
without a hitch 265.21 *easily*
without airs 623.1 *humble*
without a job 341.3 *inactive*
without an inheritance 767.16 *disposably*
without any qualms 809.6 *impenitently*
without any scruples 809.6 *impenitently*
without a penny 767.16 *disposably*; 135.5 *necessitous*
without application 100.18 *extraneously*
without appreciation 672.5 *thankless*; 672.7 *ungratefully*
without approval 753.11 *disapprovingly*
without art 646.1 *naive*
without artifice 646.1 *naive*; 646.5 *naively*
without a solution 696.2 *unexplained*
without a sou 782.2 *insolvent*
without a spot 255.19 *purely*
without assistance 655.14 *unsocially*; 378.16 *with delay*
without a stain 230.1 *perfect*
without a stitch on 552.17 *nakedly*; 552.9 *undressed*
without authority 588.8 *anarchically*; 16.82 *illegally*; 335.14 *powerlessly*; 16.56 *unauthorized*
without authorization 399.7 *by veto*
without a word 732.8 *shyly*; 655.14 *unsocially*
without a worry 618.18 *carelessly*
without ballast 639.2 *changeable*
without batting an eye 628.7 *pitilessly*
without bearing a grudge 649.14 *forgivingly*
without beginning or end 202.3 *eternal*
without bias 473.8 *disinterestedly*; 801.19 *equally*; 4.26 *rationally*
without blame 803.9 *virtuously*
without blemish 230.1 *perfect*; 803.5 *virtuous*
without body 101.8 *nonmaterial*
without ceasing 297.1 *frequently*
without ceremony 657.12 *informally*; 674.17 *modestly*
without chains 391.8 *free*
without charge 793.11 *free of charge*
without charm 659.9 *discourteously*
without cheer 626.13 *sullenly*
without commitment 754.9 *irresolutely*
without comparison 116.7 *dissimilarly*; 126.8 *originally*; 121.17 *supremely*
without compassion 628.4 *pitiless*
without complaints 609.4 *satisfied*
without compromise 647.11 *severely*
without compunction 809.3 *impenitent*; 809.6 *impenitently*
without conditions 757.9 *with permission*
without consistency 751.12 *differently*; 114.10 *diversely*
without content 98.13 *vacant*
without control 250.21 *excessively*
without cooperation 751.11 *in disagreement*
without courteousness 659.9 *discourteously*
without credit 672.5 *thankless*; 672.7 *ungratefully*
without defect 230.1 *perfect*
without delay 293.17 *early*; 262.6 *hastily*; 262.3 *hasty*; 280.8 *immediately*
without demur 636.16 *willingly*
without difficulty 265.21 *easily*
without discrimination 391.8 *free*
without distinction 801.19 *equally*
without effect 337.14 *weakly*
without embarrassment 661.9 *defiantly*
without emotion 684.13 *calmly*
without employment 341.3 *inactive*
without end 279.11 *eternally*; 277.12 *everlastingly*; 202.10 *infinitely*; 148.11 *lengthily*; 148.1 *long*; 208.8 *numberless*
without enemies 589.7 *peaceful*
without enthusiasm 637.17 *unwillingly*
without equal 121.14 *best*; 116.7 *dissimilarly*
without equality 420.14 *roughly*
without equivocation 799.7 *honourably*
without exception 750.35 *consistently*; 127.7 *including*; 111.20 *regularly*; 138.30 *usually*; 204.11 *wholly*
without excess 684.11 *with self-restraint*
without excitement 620.8 *boringly*
without excuse 806.11 *guiltily*; 806.5 *guilty*
without exemption 204.11 *wholly*
without fairness 120.8 *unjustly*
without fault 485.12 *skilfully*
without fear 589.8 *peacefully*
without fear of contradiction 707.23 *affirmatively*
without fear or favour 801.19 *equally*
without feelings 628.4 *pitiless*; 628.7 *pitilessly*
without flexibility 424.5 *fragilely*; 418.13 *inflexibly*
without food 687.7 *abstemiously*; 687.6 *fasting*
without fuss 674.17 *modestly*
without gloss 530.7 *colourless*
without good fortune 798.14 *inauspiciously*
without grounds 704.12 *refutably*
without guile 646.5 *naively*
without guilt 803.9 *virtuously*
without harmony 751.11 *in disagreement*
without hearing 505.4 *deaf*
without help 378.16 *with delay*
without hesitation 636.17 *spontaneously*
without holes 416.6 *dense*
without honour 800.11 *dishonourably*; 754.9 *irresolutely*
without hope 611.4 *hopeless*
without illusion 698.19 *authentic*
without importance 124.1 *unimportant*
without intelligence 457.11 *unintelligently*
without interruption 134.7 *continually*
without issue **563.12**
without justice 120.8 *unjustly*
without law 16.61 *lawless*
without legal backing 16.82 *illegally*; 16.56 *unauthorized*
without let or hindrance 265.21 *easily*
without limit 202.1 *infinite*; 202.10 *infinitely*; 208.8 *numberless*
without looking 519.17 *blindly*
without looking back 809.6 *impenitently*
without loss 230.1 *perfect*
without love 596.8 *disliking*
without manners 487.2 *not customary*
without mass 101.8 *nonmaterial*
without meaning 694.6 *meaningful*
without meeting expectations 604.13 *disappointingly*
without mercy 651.20 *malevolently*
without morals 618.18 *carelessly*; 804.12 *immoral*; 804.20 *immorally*
without movement 341.5 *without action*
without moving 253.17 *fastly*
without notice 293.18 *soon*
without number 202.2 *immeasurable*
without obligations 572.12 *celibately*
without offspring 563.12 *without issue*
without omission 127.7 *including*
without one's husband 571.13 *without one's spouse*
without one's spouse **571.13**
without one's wife 571.13 *without one's spouse*
without order 114.11 *irregularly*
without overdoing it 684.11 *with self-restraint*
without patience 625.9 *irascibly*
without pausing for breath 277.12 *everlastingly*
without paying **786.15**
without payment 768.9 *as a gift*
without permission 399.7 *by veto*
without pity 651.20 *malevolently*; 628.7 *pitilessly*; 628.1 *pitilessness*
without prejudice 473.8 *disinterestedly*; 119.13 *equitably*; 4.26 *rationally*
without pretence 255.20 *homogenously*
without pretensions 646.5 *naively*
without prompting 636.18 *voluntarily*
without prospects 782.1 *poor*
without question 452.23 *certainly*
without rationality 457.12 *nonhumanly*
without reason 457.8 *nonhuman*; 457.12 *nonhumanly*
without reference 109.12 *irrelevantly*
without regard 109.12 *irrelevantly*
without regard for honesty 800.11 *dishonourably*
without regard to feelings 804.18 *wickedly*
without regard to morality 662.17 *disobediently*
without regret 809.6 *impenitently*
without regrets 809.3 *impenitent*
without regularity 420.14 *roughly*
without regulations 391.8 *free*
without relevance 109.12 *irrelevantly*
without remorse 809.3 *impenitent*; 809.6 *impenitently*
without resistance 388.6 *with humility*
without resolution 754.9 *irresolutely*
without resource 335.11 *unprotected*
without respect 659.10 *rudely*
without respite 134.7 *continually*; 134.6 *protracted*
without restraint 250.21 *excessively*
without rhyme or reason 408.27 *in disorder*
without risk 252.6 *safe*; 252.11 *safely*; 253.6 *secure*; 253.16 *surely*
without roughness 421.14 *smoothly*
without shame 661.9 *defiantly*; 796.21 *immorally*
without shape 420.15 *incompletely*
without side 623.1 *humble*
without significance 100.18 *extraneously*; 618.20 *unexceptionally*
without similarities 109.13 *disproportionately*
without similarity 751.12 *differently*
without sin 803.9 *virtuously*
without skill 611.8 *bad*
without stint 250.21 *excessively*; 217.2 *plentiful*
without stop 297.1 *frequently*
without stopping 132.19 *continuously*; 277.12 *everlastingly*; 297.1 *frequently*
without strings 757.7 *permitted*; 250.12 *unconditional*; 757.9 *with permission*
without substance 415.11 *lightly*
without success 247.12 *unsuccessfully*
without taste **497.10**
without thanks 672.5 *thankless*; 672.7 *ungratefully*
without thinking 632.19 *habitually*; 457.11 *unintelligently*; 274.22 *wrongly*
without tricks 646.1 *naive*

without trouble 421.15 soothingly
without variety 620.8 boringly
without violence 589.8 peacefully
without warmth 659.9 discourteously
without warning 425.19 suddenly; 630.13 surprisingly; 105.9 unexpectedly
without wasting words 269.5 concisely; 723.12 in brief
without weight 415.1 light
with patience 649.14 forgivingly
with permission 757.9; 710.12 by request; 750.39 with consent
with pleasure 597.9 joyfully; 241.15 pleasantly; 490.11 pleasingly
with plenty of time 293.17 early
with power 396.23 authoritatively; 331.18 dynamically
with praise 669.25 approvingly
with precise measurements 26.17 measurably
with precision 665.12 carefully
with prejudice 798.12 evilly
with promise 756.17 auspiciously; 569.20 favourably
with propriety 631.19 well
with provisions 746.9 feasibly; 222.16 relatively
with prudence 684.12 moderately
with pure greed 688.7 gluttonously
with pure intentions 805.11 innocently; 799.8 purely
with qualification 136.18
with qualifications 714.15 in vindication
with reason 716.14 as evidence
with recourse to 352.7 by means of
with regret 808.8 penitently; 637.17 unwillingly
with regularity 632.19 habitually
with repentance 808.8 penitently
with reproach 806.11 guiltily; 624.17 resentfully; 712.13 vituperatively
with resentment 626.14 irritably; 624.17 resentfully
with reservations 128.12 exclusively
with resistance 709.11 uncooperatively
with resolution 360.11 tenaciously
with restraint 728.28 moderately
with restrictions 128.12 exclusively; 399.8 under censorship
with rhythm 57.12 competitively
with rocks 92.13 continentally
with romance 593.30 lovingly
with rudeness 655.14 unsocially
with satisfaction 609.13
with sealed lips 732.2 sparing with words
with self-control 684.11 with self-restraint
with self-love 683.9 egoistically
with selfmotivation 250.20 freely
with self-reliance 250.20 freely
with self-restraint 251.17; 684.11
with servility 664.16
with skill 396.26 expertly; 485.12 skilfully
with sobriety 689.9 soberly
with softness 419.17 softly
with sorrow 806.11 guiltily
with spite 594.18 hatefully
withstand 113.20; 347.3 counteract; 381.8 counterattack; 661.5 defy; 709.6 dissent; 383.6 resist; 384.28 survive
withstanding 383.3 resistance movement; 383.10 resistant
withstand testing 217.4 suffice
with statesmanship 579.19 managerially
with sticky fingers 774.19 thievishly
with stiffness 418.12 toughly
with strings attached 251.13 restraining; 136.18 with qualification
with style 724.10 stylistically
with suffering 260.25 unhealthily
with superiority 121.16 superiorly
with supervision 15.13 industrially
with suppleness 422.11 elastically
with swordplay 54.7 on guard
with synchronization 67.12 by swimming
with telling effect 334.18 powerfully; 338.6 with vigour
with tender loving care 650.10 benevolently
with tenderness 415.11 lightly; 419.18 soft-heartedly
with thanks 671.8 gratefully
with the aid of 352.7 by means of; 348.9 instrumentally
with the back-and-foot technique 62.10 on a climb
with the back-and-knee technique 62.10 on a climb
with the best intentions 805.11 innocently
with the crowd 265.9 easy
with the current 265.9 easy
with the effect of 345.12
with the exact touch 115.14 comparably
with the exception of 212.8 by subtraction; 128.12 exclusively
with the help of 348.9 instrumentally
with the intention of 482.14 for
with the lark 290.8 in the morning
with the merchant navy 319.6 commercially
with the object of 482.14 for
with the proviso 136.18 with qualification
with the rest 215.12 with a remainder
with the result that 345.12 with the effect of
with the sun 290.8 in the morning
with the worst intentions 651.20 malevolently
with time to spare 293.17 early
with tongue in cheek 702.15 hypocritically; 599.17 jokingly
with tooth and nail 638.17 resolutely
with truth 799.7 honourably; 698.35 truly
with two wives 570.24 matrimonially
with urgency 710.12 by request; 262.6 hastily
with velocity 47.10 fast
with vengeance 385.6
with vigour 338.6
with warmth 569.17 in friendship
with whip and spur 332.14 swiftly
witless 457.7 intellectually subnormal; 457.6 unintelligent
witlessness 457.2 unintelligence
witness 715.5 accuse; 707.9 affirmer; 97.12 attend; 716.11 give evidence; 693.9 informant; 518.11 observer; 705.10 person questioned; 716.7 person who gives evidence; 454.2 prove; 518.12 see; 97.5 someone present; 454.3 testify; 454.7 verifier
witness box 16.27 courtroom; 464.3 place of judgment
witnessed 97.8 attendant; 716.8 evidential; 454.8 verifiable
witness for the prosecution 715.3 accuser
witness to 742.10 signify
wits 442.3, 458.2 intelligence; 460.2 rationality
witter 731.7 be talkative; 509.9 hum; 731.3 talk
Wittgensteinian 4.11 follower of a doctrine; 4.14 of a philosophy
witticism 269.1 conciseness; 599.5 joke; 745.1 maxim; 697.2 solecism
wittily 599.16 humorously; 654.18 sociably
wittiness 599.1 humorousness
wittingly 482.13 intentionally
witty 599.10 humorous; 745.2 proverbial; 272.5 ridiculous; 654.15 sociable
witty repartee 706.1 answer
wive 570.15 marry
wizard 797.1 good; 619.5 person of wonder; 485.6 skilful; 485.4 skilled person; 11.4 witch; 235.1 worthy
wizard-like 11.15 witchlike
wizardly 11.15 witchlike
wizardry 485.1 skill; 11.3 witchcraft
wizard's cap 11.6 talisman
wizard's hat 551.15 headgear
wizard wheeze 446.3 plan
wizen 556.17 age; 191.6 become smaller; 428.21 dry up; 191.7 smaller
wizened 556.14 aged; 428.3 dried-up; 153.2 emaciated; 159.7 little; 191.7 smaller
woad 539.9 blue; 539.5 blueness; 42.6 dye; 529.4 pigment
wobble 227.11 be changeable; 299.6 be irregular; 51.2 grip; 299.1 irregularity; 333.1 move slowly; 327.25 pitch; 325.10 slide; 639.5 vacillate
wobbler 639.15 indecisive person; 700.13 snare
wobbliness 227.1 changeableness; 299.1 irregularity
wobbling 299.4 irregular; 639.1 vacillating
wobbly 227.13 changeable; 231.1 imperfect; 299.4 irregular; 327.18 shaky; 639.1 vacillating; 337.8 weak
wobbly-legged 486.3 clumsy
wodge 158.7 mass; 205.7 piece
woe 798.2 affliction; 603.1 lamentation; 236.10 poverty; 602.1 sorrow
woebegone 603.4 lamenting; 602.5 sad
woeful 798.8 afflicted; 236.4 poor
woefully 798.13 destructively
woe is me 798.15 bad luck!; 249.13 too bad!
wok 25.6 kitchen equipment; 410.15 pot
wold 81.2 grassland; 154.2 heights; 92.7 upland
wolf 688.5 be greedy; 557.18 eater; 557.22 eat well; 688.4 glutton; 593.9 lover; 773.6 taker; 380.4 violent creature
wolf at the door 782.5 poverty
wolf down 370.11 ingest
wolfing 688.6 gluttonous
wolf in sheep's clothing 699.19 cheat; 645.3 cunning person; 700.15 deceiver; 751.4 dissenter; 379.1 trap
wolfish 71.28 carnivorous; 557.26 eating; 688.6 gluttonous
wolfishly 688.7 gluttonously
wolfishness 557.2 appetite; 688.1 gluttony
wolflike 71.28 carnivorous
wolf whistle 513.6 be shrill; 742.3 gesture; 513.3 shrillness
woman 556.9; 568.2 female; 568.1 female sex; 566.7 person
woman behind the man 395.4 indirect influence
woman-chaser 593.9 lover
woman-crazy 796.14 lecherous
woman-hater 594.9 hater; 653.2 misanthrope
woman-hating 653.3 misanthropic
womanhood 556.2 adulthood; 568.1 female sex
woman in the family 568.12
womanish 568.15 female
womanishness 568.1 female sex
womanism 244.11 reformism
womanist 244.12 reformer
womanize 796.17 be sexually immoral
womanizer 796.8 immoral man; 593.9 lover
womanizing 796.3 sexual immorality
womankind 568.1 female sex; 566.1 humankind
womanliness 568.1 female sex
womanly 568.15 female
woman-mad 796.14 lecherous
woman of her word 799.3 honourable person
woman of letters 17.15 literary person
woman of taste 549.4 refined person
woman of the world 556.9 woman
woman sailor 586.27 naval man
Woman's Christian Temperance Union 684.1 self-restraint; 689.8 sober person
woman soldier 586.10
woman's quarters 593.13 abode of love
womb 561.4 development; 172.4 insides; 561.8 organs of reproduction; 130.3, 344.2 source
Women 767.7 toilet
women 578.4 personnel; 568.13 womenfolk
women and song 490.2 good time
womenfolk 568.13
women's 80m hurdles 47.1 track events
women's 100m hurdles 47.1 track events
women's 200m hurdles 47.1 track events
women's 3000m race 47.1 track events
Women's Alliance 12.6 political party
women's clothing 551.1 dress
women's hospital 35.10 hospital
women's judo 52.7 judo
women's lib 391.2 equal opportunity; 568.1 female sex; 250.1 freedom
women's libber 250.7 free person; 568.11 liberated woman; 391.3 liberator; 662.7 protester
women's liberation 391.2 equal opportunity; 568.1 female sex; 250.1 freedom
women's magazine 740.5 journal
Women's Movement 568.1 female sex
women's penitentiary 815.1 prison
women's quarters 568.13 womenfolk
women's rights 568.1 female sex
Women's Room 767.7 toilet
Women's Royal Air Force 586.29 air force
Women's Royal Army Corps 586.15 army
Women's Royal Naval Service 586.22 navy
women's suffrage 469.11 franchise
womenswear 551.1 dress
won 253.8 accomplished; 780.11 national coins
Wonder 619
wonder 619.1; 619.4; 619.9; 630.2 amazement; 705.8 curiosity; 235.8 exceller; 696.9 find unintelligible; 619.5 person of wonder; 4.20 philosophize; 705.17 question; 797.16 superior person; 630.4 surprising thing; 105.5 unexpectedness
wonder about 453.18 be uncertain
wonder boy 619.5 person of wonder
wonder drug 37.3, 394.8 drug
wonderful 619.8; 597.5 delightful; 797.1 good; 235.1 worthy
wonderful! 619.14
wonderfully 619.13; 797.22 well
wonderfulness 797.8 good
wonderful to relate 619.13 wonderfully
wonderful works 619.3 wonder-working
wondering 619.6; 696.6 confused; 705.12 questioning; 667.10 reverent
wonderland 477.8 dreamland; 619.4 wonder
wonder man 630.5 surpriser
wonderment 619.1 wonder
wonder of the world 235.8 exceller
wonders will never cease 619.14 wonderful!
wonder whether 619.12
Wonder Woman 336.6 muscleman
wonder woman 235.8 exceller; 121.6 paragon; 619.5 person of wonder; 630.5 surpriser
wonder-working 619.3; 619.8 wonderful
wondrous 619.8 wonderful
wondrously 619.13 wonderfully
wonky 245.13 dilapidated; 337.8 weak
wont 140.6 custom; 632.1 habit; 349.6 use
wonted 216.1 average; 140.10 customary; 632.9 habitual
wontedly 632.19 habitually
won ton 25.48 Chinese dish
woo 633.12 aim at; 593.26 court; 617.13 like; 710.6 request; 569.14 seek the friendship of
wood 23.12; 330.10 ball; 38.25 construction material; 330.13, 437.1 fuel; 56.4 golf club; 51.1 green bowling; 418.7 hard substance; 437.2 lighter; 435.1 materials; 323.4 shipbuilding; 79.3 timber; 79.4 trees; 79.15 woody
wood alcohol 558.7 alcoholic drink; 79.9 tree product
wood ant 79.11 tree-related animal
wood block 19.15 engraving; 23.8 woodwork
wood-blocked 23.15 woodcrafted
wood-block printing 23.8 woodwork
woodborer 76.3 pest; 79.11 tree-related animal
woodburned 23.15 woodcrafted
wood-burning 493.13 heated; 437.10 powered; 23.8 woodwork
woodcarved 23.15 woodcrafted
woodcarver 23.13 carpenter
woodcarving 19.1 art; 19.12 sculpture; 23.8 woodwork
woodchat 79.11 tree-related animal
woodchuck 79.11 tree-related animal
woodchuck hunting 633.2 chase
wood club 56.4 golf club
wood coal 79.9 tree product
woodcock 25.20 meat; 72.4 table bird; 79.11 tree-related animal
woodcraft 79.5 forestry; 23.8 woodwork
woodcrafted 23.15
woodcraftsman 23.13 carpenter
woodcut 19.15 engraving; 19.7 picture; 23.15 woodcrafted; 23.8 woodwork
woodcut illustration 23.8 woodwork
woodcutter 23.13 carpenter; 79.8 forester; 437.9 power-worker
wood duck 79.11 tree-related animal
wooded 79.16; 77.13 plantlike

wooden 23.14; 544.9 *inelegant*; 641.3 *unyielding*; 79.15 *woody*; 52.15 *wrestling*
wooden chair 23.2 *chair*
wood-engraved 23.15 *woodcrafted*
wood engraver 23.13 *carpenter*; 19.18 *engraver*
wood engraving 19.15 *engraving*; 23.8 *woodwork*
wood-engraving tool 23.11 *woodworking tool*
wooden mask 551.5 *fancy dress*
woodenness 641.6 *determination*
wooden shoes 551.19 *footwear*
wooden ski 68.5 *ski equipment*
wooden spoon 25.6 *kitchen equipment*; 410.17 *ladle*; 412.6 *mixer*; 813.2 *prize*; 486.8 *unskilfulness*
wooden walls 586.22 *navy*
woodenware 23.8 *woodwork*
wood fire 493.6 *fire*
wood furniture 23.1 *furniture*
woodgrain 23.12 *wood*
woodgrouse 79.11 *tree-related animal*
wood inlay 23.9 *decorative woodwork*
woodland 538.8 *greenness*; 79.4 *trees*; 79.16 *wooded*
woodlander 79.8 *forester*
woodland stalking 60.2 *hunting*
woodlark 79.11 *tree-related animal*
wood lot 79.4 *trees*
woodlouse 75.4 *arthropod*; 79.11 *tree-related animal*
woodman 79.8 *forester*
wood moss 82.3 *moss*
woodnote 515.2 *bird song*
wood nymph 8.5 *deity*; 79.13 *tree mythology*
woodpecker 79.11 *tree-related animal*
wood pigeon 79.11 *tree-related animal*
wood pitch 79.9 *tree product*
woodprint 23.8 *woodwork*
woodprinted 23.15 *woodcrafted*
wood rat 79.11 *tree-related animal*
Woodrow Wilson 589.4 *Nobel Peace Prize*
woods 79.4 *trees*
wood-sculpted 23.15 *woodcrafted*
wood sculpting 23.8 *woodwork*
wood sculpture 23.8 *woodwork*
wood shot 56.3 *golf shots*
woodsman 79.8 *forester*
wood spirit 79.9 *tree product*
wood stove 493.6 *fire*
wood sugar 79.9 *tree product*
woodsy 79.16 *wooded*
wood tar 79.9 *tree product*
wood texture 23.12 *wood*
wood tick 76.3 *pest*
wood-turned 23.15 *woodcrafted*
wood turning 23.8 *woodwork*
wood vinegar 79.9 *tree product*
wood warbler 79.11 *tree-related animal*
woodwasp 79.11 *tree-related animal*
woodwind 18.25 *musical instrument*
woodwork 23.8
woodworker 578.2 *artisan*
woodworking 23.8 *woodwork*
woodworking tool 23.11
woodworm 357.7 *agent of destruction*; 76.3 *pest*; 79.11 *tree-related animal*; 75.6 *worm*
woody 79.15; 44.17 *botanical*; 423.3 *hard*; 77.14 *of plants*; 437.10 *powered*
woody perennial 77.2 *plant*
woody plant 44.9 *garden plant*; 77.2 *plant*
woody tissue 79.3 *timber*
wooer 593.9 *lover*
woof 515.1 *animal cry*; 193.3 *weaving*
wooing 593.6 *courtship*; 710.1 *request*; 710.9 *requesting*
wool 71.2 *mammalian characteristic*; 435.1 *materials*; 42.12 *natural*; 419.11 *soft thing*; 193.4 *textile*
woolgather 472.12 *be inattentive*
woolgatherer 472.6 *inattentive person*
woolgathering 472.8 *absent-minded*; 472.3 *absent-mindedness*
woollen 193.6 *interwoven*; 42.12 *natural*
woolliness 419.9 *smoothness*
woolly 420.3 *barbed*; 193.6 *interwoven*; 42.12 *natural*; 404.8 *rough*; 419.3, 421.1 *smooth*; 551.13 *sweater*
woolly aphid 44.12 *pests and diseases*
woolly bear 76.5 *larva*
woolly hat 551.15 *headgear*
woolly mammoth 296.8 *prehistoric animal*
woolsack 16.27 *courtroom*; 16.18 *tribunal*
woomera 587.6 *historical missile weapon*
woopies 556.10 *the old*
wooziness 690.10 *drunkenness*
woozy 489.10 *sleepy*; 690.2 *slightly drunk*
Worcester sauce 558.8 *mixed drink*; 25.15 *sauce*; 496.2 *seasoning*
Word™ 40.11 *application*
word 5.17; **5.47**; **742.6**; 693.7, 713.1 *advice*; 397.1 *command*; 810.7 *commitment*; 693.1 *information*; 205.2 *particular*; 253.2 *promise*; 707.2 *statement*; 724.9 *style*; 729.7 *utterance*; 707.3 *vow*; 711.1 *warning*
word association 36.27 *association of ideas*
word-association test 36.5 *psychological test*
wordbook 5.28 *dictionary*
word-coiner 5.2 *linguist*
worded 5.42; 724.6 *styled*
word form 160.3 *kind*; 5.17 *word*
word for word 273.8 *accurately*; 125.14 *imitatively*; 5.48 *linguistically*; 698.38 *literally*; 694.13 *meaningfully*; 230.7 *perfectly*
word-for-word 698.23 *literal*; 5.40 *translated*; 719.17 *translational*
word-for-word translation 698.10 *literalness*; 5.12, 719.4 *translation*
word game 69.1 *game*
wordily 5.50 *lexically*
wordiness 270.1 *diffuseness*; 5.22 *many words*; 729.2 *power of speech*; 731.1 *talkativeness*
wording 724.4 *literary style*; 5.24 *phrasing*; 5.42 *worded*
word in one's ear 504.8 *something heard*
word in the ear 693.7, 713.1 *advice*; 711.1 *warning*
wordless 506.3 *silent*; 619.7 *wide-eyed*
wordlessness 506.4 *silence*
word list 220.3 *dictionary*
word magic 724.4 *literary style*
word of advice 713.1 *advice*
word of a gentleman 707.3 *vow*
word of command 585.8 *warfare*; 742.6 *word*
word of explanation 719.2 *annotation*
word of God 7.12 *religious text*
word of honour 450.3 *believing*; 810.7 *commitment*; 253.2 *promise*; 707.3 *vow*
word of mouth 693.7 *advice*; 504.8 *something heard*; 729.7 *utterance*
word-of-mouth evidence 716.5 *legal evidence*
word of praise 669.4 *compliment*
word of warning 711.1 *warning*
word order 5.30 *syntax*
word-painting 477.1 *imagination*
WordPerfect™ 40.11 *application*
word-perfect 698.21 *accurate*; 273.6 *correct*
wordplay 479.5 *equivocalness*; 720.2 *misinterpretation*; 599.3 *wit*
word portrait 721.2 *brief description*
word power 724.4 *literary style*; 729.2 *power of speech*
word processing 40.11 *application*; 334.9 *electronics*; 693.6 *information technology*
word-puzzle 737.4 *brain-teaser*
wordsmith 17.14 *author*; 721.10 *descriptive writer*; 724.5 *stylist*
words of one syllable 269.1 *conciseness*; 695.10 *simplicity*
words of wisdom 713.1 *advice*; 745.1 *maxim*
word-spinner 542.9 *phrasemonger*; 724.5 *stylist*
Wordstar™ 40.11 *application*
words to live by 480.11 *motive*
Wordsworth and Coleridge 569.7 *famous friendships*
word to the wise 693.7, 713.1 *advice*; 711.1 *warning*
wordy 270.3 *diffuse*; 112.12 *repetitious*; 731.5 *talkative*; 5.42 *worded*
Work 576
work 38.10; **576.1**; **576.6**; 340.4 *act*; 340.1 *action*; 633.4 *activity*; 378.3 *barrier*; 348.4 *be an instrument*; 246.8 *be effective*; 407.23 *be in order*; 346.7 *be operational*; 237.9 *be useful*; 346.3 *business*; 340.2 *deed*; 28.11, 334.4 *energy*; 403.2 *fabric*; 261.6, 261.7 *fatigue*; 160.7 *form*; 15.8 *industrial*; 415.10 *lighten*; 346.1 *operation*; 21.2 *play*; 217.4 *suffice*; 810.2 *task*; 28.38 *thermodynamics*; 342.15 *try*; 353.2 *try hard*; 354.2 *undertaking*; 349.1 *use*; 19.6, 356.5 *work of art*
workability 239.3 *convenience*; 102.2 *possibleness*; 237.6 *usability*; 265.3 *wieldiness*
workable 346.11; 239.1 *convenient*; 265.10 *feasible*; 746.8 *negotiated*; 334.14 *operative*; 102.5 *possible*; 95.8 *practical*; 237.2 *usable*
workably 102.10 *practically*
work a change 224.8 *cause change*
work achievement 15.2 *industrial negotiations*
work a cure 393.6 *cure*; 394.19 *remedy*
workaday 271.1 *simple*
work a forty-hour week 576.6 *work*
work against 113.16 *be contrary*; 240.5 *be inconvenient*; 708.16 *cancel out*; 113.21, 347.3 *counteract*; 484.13 *plot*
work against time 262.2 *make haste*
workaholic 342.10 *busy person*; 386.5 *compulsive person*; 632.8 *creature of habit*; 342.20 *industrious*; 640.5 *tenacious person*; 354.4 *volunteer*
work all day 576.6 *work*
work all hours 576.6 *work*
work all week 576.6 *work*
work an apprenticeship 400.15 *learn*
work as a team 747.13 *work together*
work a shift 298.7 *be regular*
work at 631.14 *behave towards*; 640.6 *persevere*
work at home 576.6 *work*
workbook 6.14 *school book*
work both ways 708.16 *cancel out*
work clothes 551.1 *dress*
work day shifts 576.6 *work*
work demarcation 15.2 *industrial negotiations*
work double 576.6 *work*
work double time 576.6 *work*
worked 15.8 *industrial*; 541.6 *variegated*
worked out 484.14 *planned*; 356.12 *produced*; 706.14 *solved*
worked up 327.15 *agitated*; 243.20 *developed*; 624.15 *resentful*
work efficiency 15.2 *industrial negotiations*
Worker 578
worker 578.1; 342.10 *busy person*; 340.3 *doer*; 566.10 *member of society*; 346.5 *operator*; 356.9 *producer*; 401.1 *servant*; 76.4 *social insect*
worker participation 15.2 *industrial negotiations*
workers 392.11 *helper*; 352.3 *human resources*; 578.4 *personnel*
Workers' Revolutionary Party 12.6 *political party*
work evil 798.11 *be evil*; 236.13 *be worthless*
work for 576.7; 340.4 *act*; 482.10 *aim*; 348.4 *be an instrument*; 392.25, 401.8 *serve*
workforce 376.13; 352.3 *human resources*; 13.8, 15.1 *industrial relations*; 127.3 *person included*; 578.4 *personnel*
workforce relations 15.1 *industrial relations*
work for peace 589.6 *make peace*
work from home 2.15 *socialize*
work group 15.1 *industrial relations*; 2.6 *social group*
work hard 351.1 *misuse*; 576.6 *work*
work harden 32.30 *extract*
work hat 551.15 *headgear*
workhorse 342.10 *busy person*; 640.5 *tenacious person*
workhouse 782.7 *beggary*
work-in 753.3 *gesture of protest*; 15.4 *industrial dispute*; 703.6 *mass demonstration*; 15.10 *unionized*
working 576.10; 340.5 *acting*; 340.1 *action*; 342.18 *active*; 15.8 *industrial*; 346.1 *operation*; 346.10 *operational*; 334.14 *operative*; 348.8 *practical*; 439.2 *resource*; 401.9 *serving*; 2.14 *socioeconomic*; 349.10 *usable*
working area 577.1 *workshop*
working arrangement 754.1 *compromise*; 317.1 *way*
working capital 352.4 *financial resources*
working class 566.9 *group*; 654.7 *human society*; 2.7 *social stratification*
working-class 623.2 *lowly*
working classes 216.7 *average person*; 578.4 *personnel*; 574.2 *the common people*
working conditions 13.8 *industrial relations*
working day 276.4 *period of activity*; 576.2 *task*
working dog 71.9 *dog*
working hours 15.2 *industrial negotiations*; 13.8 *industrial relations*
working hypothesis 476.1 *supposition*
working life 576.2 *task*
working man 578.1 *worker*
working materials 352.2 *supplies*
working model 125.2 *copy*; 717.6 *image*; 475.4 *model*
working oneself to death 576.4 *exertion*
working out 706.6 *solution*
working-out 257.1 *hygiene*
working party 398.2 *representative body*
working plan 484.2 *policy*
workings 405.4 *components*; 403.6 *construction*
workings of the law 16.34 *legal formality*
workings of the mind 443.1 *thought*
working space 577.1 *workshop*
working together 147.8 *interaction*; 747.4 *joint operation*
working towards 229.5 *tending to*
working week 576.2 *task*
working wife 568.11 *liberated woman*
working woman 568.11 *liberated woman*
work in the field 576.6 *work*
work its own cure 393.6 *cure*
work like a horse 576.6 *work*
work like a machine 265.19 *go easily*
work like a Trojan 576.6 *work*
work like magic 246.8 *be effective*
workman 340.3 *doer*; 578.1 *worker*
workmanlike 342.20 *industrious*; 485.9 *well-made*
workmanlike job 485.3 *masterpiece*
workman's compensation 15.2 *industrial negotiations*
workmanship 340.2 *deed*; 356.1 *production*
workmate 578.5 *partner*
work measurement 15.2 *industrial negotiations*
workmen's compensation 13.8 *industrial relations*
work miracles 246.6 *be successful*; 619.11 *do wonders*; 244.1 *improve*; 640.6 *persevere*
work night and day 576.6 *work*
work night shifts 576.6 *work*
work of art 19.6; **356.5**; 797.17 *good thing*; 400.11, 485.3 *masterpiece*
work of fiction 477.4 *ideality*; 356.5 *work of art*
work of literature 356.5 *work of art*
work on 349.1 *use*
work on a hunch 445.9 *be intuitive*
work one's ass off 640.6 *persevere*
work oneself to death 576.6 *work*
work one's way 302.7 *make one's way*
work one's way into 314.11 *infiltrate*
work one's way up 304.14 *climb*
work on flexitime 15.11 *conduct industrial relations*
work out 631.14 *behave towards*; 210.8 *calculate*; 719.9 *decipher*; 243.7 *develop*; 576.9 *exercise*; 484.10 *plan out*; 4.21 *rationalize*; 706.20 *solve*; 345.9 *take effect*; 443.15 *think about*
work-out 576.5 *exercise*
work out a deal 755.5 *contract*
work out a formula 746.5 *negotiate*
work over 814.4 *torture*
work overtime 15.11 *conduct industrial relations*; 576.6 *work*
workpeople 578.4 *personnel*
work permit 757.2 *permit*
workplace 577.1 *workshop*
workplace representative 15.7 *employee*
workplace rules 15.1 *industrial relations*
work practices 15.1 *industrial relations*
work relations 15.1 *industrial relations*
workroom 565.7 *room*; 577.1 *workshop*
work round the clock 640.6 *persevere*
works 405.4 *components*; 403.6 *construction*; 438.5 *machine*; 577.1 *workshop*
works council 15.1 *industrial relations*
work shift 276.4 *period of activity*
work shifts 576.6 *work*
work shoes 551.19 *footwear*
Workshop 577

workshop 577.1; 342.6 *business*; 43.7 *farm building*; 16.2 *jurisdiction*; 579.3 *management*; 356.2 *manufacture*; 760.4 *medium of conversion*; 448.6 *place of experimentation*; 398.2 *representative body*; 6.15 *schoolroom*
workshop delegate 398.1 *delegate*
workshop practice 356.2 *manufacture*
work-shy 343.3 *not participating*
work something out 746.5 *negotiate*
work stoppage 15.4 *industrial dispute*; 226.2 *stop*
work study 579.3 *management*
work-study grant 788.3 *income*
worktable 413.2 *supporting part*; 23.4 *table*
work the land 43.17 *farm*
work the night shift 15.11 *conduct industrial relations*
work through 631.14 *behave towards*
work till one drops 640.6 *persevere*
work to a deadline 262.2 *make haste*
work to a schedule 484.12 *plan ahead*
work to death 382.16 *kill*
work together 747.13; 2.15 *socialize*
work to rule 753.8 *cause mischief*; 753.3 *gesture of protest*; 15.12 *have an industrial dispute*
work-to-rule 333.12 *hesitation*; 15.4 *industrial dispute*; 13.8 *industrial relations*; 15.10 *unionized*
work under pressure 262.2 *make haste*
work up 327.22 *agitate*; 160.7 *form*; 624.9 *offend*; 349.1 *use*
work up a lather 576.6 *work*
work up a sweat 576.6 *work*
work upon 395.8 *influence*; 346.9 *take action*
work well 265.19 *go easily*
work with 223.14 *keep company with*
work without pay 752.11 *volunteer*; 576.1 *work*
work wonders 246.6 *be successful*; 235.10 *do good*; 619.11 *do wonders*; 342.15 *try*
work wood 23.18
world 29.3 *universe*; 204.2 *whole thing*
world atlas 717.7 *map*
World Bank 13.4 *economic development*; 780.7 *finance*; 771.4 *lending institution*
world-beater 235.8 *exceller*; 121.6 *paragon*; 246.5 *victorious person*
world-beating 121.14, 235.2 *best*; 246.15 *victorious*
World Bowl 46.1 *football*
World Boxing Association 52.2 *boxing*
world champion 52.4 *boxer*; 52.14 *combat*; 619.5 *person of wonder*; 485.4 *skilled person*; 246.5 *victorious person*
world champions 48.1 *baseball*
World Championship points 61.1 *motor racing*
World Cup 66.1 *soccer*
world fair 779.2 *fair*
World Games 47.5 *competition*
world government 12.1 *government*
world-hater 653.2 *misanthrope*
worldliness 402.2 *materialization*; 683.1 *selfishness*
worldly 455.9 *literate*; 402.7 *material*; 683.4 *selfish*
worldly goods 440.4 *possessions*
worldly man 567.7 *libertine*
worldly wisdom 485.1 *skill*
world map 163.4, 717.7 *map*
world music 18.10
world of 208.4 *throng*
world of experience 402.1 *material world*
world of finance 14.1, 780.7 *finance*
world of nature 402.1 *material world*
world of spirits 101.3 *spiritual world*; 582.14 *the spiritual world*
world picture 204.3 *whole situation*
world price 790.1 *price*
world's end 145.3 *distant place*
World Series 48.1 *baseball*
world-shattering 123.5 *important*; 395.11 *influential*; 123.6 *notable*
worlds of 208.4 *throng*
world soul 8.3 *God*
World Team Racing Championship 50.1 *sailing*
World Trade Organization 776.9 *bargaining*; 776.5 *commercial trade*; 779.4 *free market*; 13.5 *international trade*
world view 138.7 *global view*; 4.2 *philosophical system*; 204.3 *whole situation*
world war 585.1 *war*
world-weariness 620.1 *boredom*
world-weary 620.5 *bored*; 620.4 *boring*
worldwide 141.12 *extensive*; 127.7 *including*; 138.16 *universal*; 204.4 *whole*
World Wide Web 40.16 *Internet*
world without end 279.11 *eternally*
worm 75.6; 55.1 *angling*; 260.6 *infection*; 122.6 *inferior*; 43.18 *practise livestock farming*; 70.4 *type of animal*
worm-eaten 245.13 *dilapidated*
worm gear 38.7 *gear*; 307.6 *rotator*
wormlike 75.20
wormlike invertebrate 75.6 *worm*
worm oneself into 664.9 *fawn*
worm one's way in 318.10 *enter*
worm out 449.2 *detect*; 369.15 *draw out*
worms 260.18 *veterinary disease*
worm's-eye view 518.9 *viewpoint*
wormwood 236.11 *harmfulness*; 496.5 *herbs*; 499.3 *sour thing*
Wormwood Scrubs 815.1 *prison*
worn 426.1 *blunt*; 245.13, 337.9 *dilapidated*; 738.13 *displayed*; 261.1 *fatigued*; 212.7 *reduced*; 349.9 *used*
worn away 526.7 *disappeared*
worn clothes 551.1 *dress*
worn out 245.12 *deteriorated*; 245.13, 337.9 *dilapidated*; 350.4 *disused*; 261.1 *fatigued*; 335.12 *impotent*; 349.9 *used*; 238.1 *useless*; 337.11 *weakened*
worn to a frazzle 245.13 *dilapidated*; 261.1 *fatigued*
worn to a fritter 245.13 *dilapidated*
worn to a shadow 245.13 *dilapidated*; 153.2 *emaciated*
worn to the threads 245.13 *dilapidated*
worried 612.9; 453.3 *confused*; 328.12 *disturbed*; 264.16 *troubled*
worrier 453.17 *uncertain person*
worries 249.1 *adversity*
worrisome 264.13 *inconvenient*
worry 612.3; **612.14**; 249.1 *adversity*; 327.22 *agitate*; 264.23 *cause difficulties*; 328.7 *disturb*; 328.1 *disturbance*; 557.21 *eat*; 453.20 *make uncertain*; 264.4 *problem*
worrying 453.3 *confused*; 328.17 *disturbing*; 264.13 *inconvenient*
worryingly 453.24 *confusingly*; 328.18 *disturbingly*
worse 245.14; 224.11 *changeable*; 245.12 *deteriorated*; 367.17 *lowered*
worse alternative 762.1 *substitution*
worse and worse 245.12 *deteriorated*
worse element 205.1 *part*
worsen 607.6 *aggravate*; 607.7 *become aggravated*; 122.11 *become inferior*; 224.8 *cause change*; 245.1 *deteriorate*; 367.1 *lower*; 245.3 *make worse*
worsened 607.4 *aggravated*; 245.12 *deteriorated*
worsening 607.1 *aggravation*; 122.2 *deficiency*; 245.12 *deteriorated*; 245.7 *deterioration*; 367.11 *lowering*
Worship 9
worship 9.1; **9.7**; 667.2 *admiration*; 7.19 *be religious*; 593.1, 593.23 *love*; 663.3 *obeisance*; 667.16 *revere*; 10.1 *ritual*; 663.6 *show obeisance to*
worship freely 250.14 *be free*
worshipful 9.9; **575.6**; 7.15 *religious*; 667.10 *reverent*
worshipfully 9.12; 7.23 *religiously*; 667.22 *respectfully*; 10.23 *ritually*
worship idols 9.8 *idolatrize*
worshipped 9.11
worshipper 9.5; **10.17**; 450.5 *believer*; 617.6 *desirer*; 768.4 *giver*; 7.3 *religious person*
worshipping 10.22; 663.9 *obeisant*; 667.10 *reverent*; 9.9 *worshipful*
worship the almighty dollar 781.14 *seek riches*
worship the golden calf 781.14 *seek riches*
worsted 122.18 *outclassed*
worst intention 651.1 *malevolence*
worst luck 107.2 *luck*
wort 77.2 *plant*
Worth 235
worth 235.6; **803.3**; 797.8 *good*; 123.1 *importance*; 694.5 *point*; 790.14 *priced*; 237.6 *usability*; 790.2, 792.6 *value*
worth a bundle 781.1 *wealthy*
worth a fortune 792.8 *valuable*
worth a king's ransom 235.3, 792.8 *valuable*
worth a lot 781.1 *wealthy*
worth a million 237.4 *profitable*; 235.3 *valuable*
worth a mint 237.4 *profitable*; 235.3 *valuable*; 781.1 *wealthy*
worth a packet 781.1 *wealthy*
worth a pretty penny 792.8 *valuable*
worth buying 777.13 *bought*
worth choosing 469.15 *chosen*
worth considering 123.5 *important*
worthily 235.11; **803.11**; 136.17 *capably*; 622.33 *with dignity*
worth imitating 235.1 *worthy*
worthiness 622.8; 797.8 *good*; 136.1 *qualification*; 235.6, 803.3 *worth*
worthless 236.1; 245.12 *deteriorated*; 800.5 *dishonourable*; 668.12 *disregardful*; 798.7 *evil*; 611.7 *futile*; 231.1 *imperfect*; 122.14 *poor*; 335.10 *powerless*; 793.10 *shoddy*; 124.4 *trivial*; 238.1 *useless*; 441.9 *waste*; 804.11 *wicked*
worthlessly 236.15; 800.11 *dishonourably*; 122.20 *insignificantly*; 335.14 *powerlessly*
Worthlessness 236
worthlessness 236.7; 798.1 *evil*; 231.5 *imperfection*; 800.1 *improbity*; 122.4 *poor quality*; 124.7 *triviality*; 238.3 *uselessness*
worth millions 781.1 *wealthy*; 765.17 *well-off*
worth one's keep 237.4 *profitable*
worth one's salt 237.4 *profitable*
worth watching 518.23 *visible*
worthwhile 235.4; 669.22 *approvable*; 797.6 *beneficial*; 239.1 *convenient*; 617.8 *desirable*; 123.5 *important*; 757.7 *permitted*; 356.11 *productive*; 237.4, 785.18 *profitable*; 246.14 *rewarding*
worthwhileness 797.13 *benefit*
worthy 235.1; **803.7**; 617.8 *desirable*; 575.5 *entitled*; 797.1 *good*; 669.21 *praiseworthy*; 136.9 *qualified*; 667.13 *respectable*; 622.19 *stately*
worthy aim 353.6 *venture*
worthy cause 652.5 *charity*; 344.6 *undertaking*
worthy of discussion 447.8 *problematic*
Wotan 585.3 *gods and goddesses of war*
would-be 617.9 *desirous*; 482.11 *intending*
would like 469.2 *prefer*
would rather 469.2 *prefer*
wound 798.2 *affliction*; 798.11 *be evil*; 245.5, 245.11 *hurt*; 236.14 *ill-treat*; 491.11 *inflict pain*; 491.3 *injury*; 133.4 *interruption*; 624.9 *offend*; 337.7 *weaken*
wounded 798.8 *afflicted*; 623.3 *humbled*; 491.6 *injured*
Wounded Knee 382.15 *slaughterhouse*
wounded pride 623.9 *humiliation*
wounding 623.6 *humiliating*
wound up 309.14 *closed down*; 131.21 *ended*
woven 42.10; 193.6 *interwoven*; 404.7 *textural*
woven cloth 193.4 *textile*
woven fabric 42.3 *fabric*
wow 517.5 *atmospheric dissonance*; 235.8 *exceller*; 619.5 *person of wonder*; 246.4 *successful person*; 246.3 *successful thing*; 619.14 *wonderful!*
wowser 795.6 *moralist*; 255.5 *pure person*
WPC 252.3 *protector*
WRAC 586.10 *woman soldier*
wrack 84.1 *alga*; 357.4 *ruin*
WRAF 586.10 *woman soldier*
wraith 11.11 *ghost*; 96.2 *illusion*; 518.5 *imagination*; 153.9 *thin person*
wraithlike 153.2 *emaciated*; 11.18 *spiritual*
wraithy 11.18 *spiritual*
Wran 323.7 *nautical person*; 586.27 *naval man*
wrangle 586.40, 701.13, 751.6 *argue*; 701.1, 751.2 *argument*; 751.5 *disagree*; 43.18 *practise livestock farming*; 242.8, 242.11 *quarrel*
wrangler 444.6, 586.5, 701.6 *arguer*; 43.16 *farm worker*; 242.9 *unpleasant person*
wrangling 701.7 *arguing*; 751.9 *disagreeing*; 751.1 *disagreement*; 800.5 *dishonourable*; 746.8 *negotiated*; 746.1 *negotiation*
wrap 165.6; **550.25**; 551.25 *accessories*; 551.32 *dress*; 184.11 *enfold*; 376.38 *group*; 525.14 *present*; 252.10 *protect*; 410.21 *put in a container*
wrapped 410.20 *containing*; 551.29 *dressed*; 376.49 *grouped*; 550.37 *protected*; 170.5 *surrounded*
wrapped up 376.49 *grouped*
wrapped up in oneself 683.5 *egoistic*
wrapper 165.4; 551.4, 657.6 *informal dress*; 410.5 *packet*; 551.16 *robe*; 550.4 *wrapping*
wrapping 550.4; 410.20 *containing*; 550.1 *covering*; 184.5 *enfoldment*; 165.4 *wrapper*
wrapping paper 435.3 *paper*; 165.4 *wrapper*; 550.4 *wrapping*
wrap round 550.25 *wrap*
wrapround skirt 165.4 *wrapper*
wrap up 232.4 *complete*; 736.8 *conceal*; 131.15 *end*; 550.25 *wrap*
wrath 594.5, 624.4 *anger*
wrathful 594.13, 624.16 *angry*
wrathfully 624.18 *angrily*
wrathfulness 624.4 *anger*
wreak havoc 381.9 *attack successfully*; 798.11 *be evil*; 357.10 *lay waste*
wreak one's malice on 236.14 *ill-treat*
wreak one's spite 651.16 *be malevolent*
wreath 193.2 *braid*; 179.3 *circular thing*; 78.1 *flower*; 583.4 *funeral objects*; 743.8 *heraldic device*; 743.4 *insignia*; 482.6 *objective*; 794.1 *trophy*
wreathe 658.12 *greet*
wreathed 193.6 *interwoven*
wreck 224.8 *cause change*; 796.19 *corrupt*; 375.4 *deconstruct*; 357.9 *demolish*; 441.4 *destruction*; 245.9 *dilapidation*; 245.4 *impair*; 357.4, 357.11 *ruin*; 323.10 *sail*
wreckage 215.1 *remainder*; 357.4 *ruin*
wrecked 357.15 *destroyed*
wrecker 357.6 *destroyer*; 651.8 *malefactor*; 774.9 *plunderer*
wreck one's chances 288.7 *lose one's chance*
Wren 323.7 *nautical person*; 586.27 *naval man*; 586.10 *woman soldier*
wren 72.6 *songbird*
wrench 369.10 *excavator*; 369.6 *extorsion*; 369.16 *extort*; 369.1 *extraction*; 331.1 *impel*; 380.3 *instance of violence*; 362.3 *jerk*; 720.1 *misinterpret*; 362.13 *pull at*; 372.9 *separate*; 438.1 *tool*; 360.3 *tools for gripping*; 438.10 *use tools*; 380.8 *use violence*
wrenching 369.6 *extorsion*; 720.2 *misinterpretation*
wrenching out 369.1 *extraction*
wrench out 369.11 *extract*
wrest 369.6 *extorsion*; 369.16 *extort*
wrested 144.9 *removed*
wresting 369.6 *extorsion*
westing out 369.1 *extraction*
wrestle 52.12; 586.37 *fight*; 52.5 *wrestling*
wrestle freestyle 52.12 *wrestle*
wrestler 52.6; 336.5, 586.3 *athlete*
wrestling 52.5; **52.15**; 51.9 *bowls*; 52.1 *combat sports*
wrestling hold 52.5 *wrestling*
wrestling match 52.5 *wrestling*
wrestling ring 52.5 *wrestling*
wrestling shot 51.2 *grip*
wrestling toucher 51.2 *grip*
wrestling weight divisions 52.5 *wrestling*
wrest out 369.11 *extract*
wretch 602.3 *sad person*
wretched 798.7 *evil*; 603.4 *lamenting*; 124.2 *obscure*; 236.4 *poor*; 602.5 *sad*
wretchedness 249.1 *adversity*; 798.1 *evil*; 603.1 *lamentation*; 124.6 *obscurity*; 236.10 *poverty*; 602.1 *sorrow*
wriggle 645.5 *be cunning*; 180.2 *coil*; 180.6 *convolute*; 327.7, 327.24 *shake*
wriggling 180.4 *convolutional*; 327.18 *shaky*
wriggly 327.18 *shaky*
wright 578.2 *artisan*
wring 256.13 *clean*; 428.23 *drip-dry*; 369.6 *extorsion*; 369.16 *extort*; 491.11 *inflict pain*
wringer 428.15 *dryer*; 369.9 *extractor*; 421.9 *smoother*
wring from 386.7 *force*
wringing 369.6 *extorsion*; 433.23 *wet*
wringing hands 742.3 *gesture*
wringing wet 433.23 *wet*
wring one's hands 335.6 *be powerless*; 742.11 *gesture*

wring out 256.13 *clean*; 369.12 *displace*
wring the neck of 382.17 *murder*
Wrinkle 184
wrinkle 184.1; **184.8**; 556.17 *age*; 191.6 *become smaller*; 245.1 *deteriorate*; 404.14 *go against the grain*; 245.5 *hurt*; 420.12 *make rough*; 191.5 *make smaller*; 645.2 *stratagem*; 700.6 *trick*
wrinkled 556.14 *aged*; 420.1 *rough*; 191.7 *smaller*; 184.6 *wrinkly*
wrinkled thing 184.4
wrinkleproofing 42.8 *fabric treatment*
wrinklies 296.2 *old people*
wrinkliness 420.6 *roughness*
wrinkling 191.1 *contraction*
wrinkly 184.6; 556.7 *older person*; 420.1 *rough*
wristband 551.25 *accessories*; 179.3 *circular thing*
wrist bandage 57.2 *gymnastic clothing*
wristwatch 281.7 *watch*
writ 397.2 *demand*; 16.6 *legal process*; 16.33 *litigation*; 713.3 *precept*
write 17.21; 40.20 *abort*; 692.30 *communicate*; 18.35 *compose*; 692.31 *correspond*; 21.38 *dramatize*; 477.14 *imagine*; 744.14 *inscribe*; 356.10 *produce*; 740.15 *publish*; 741.13 *report*; 5.45 *use language*
write a bestseller 246.6 *be successful*
write about 722.4 *dissertate*
write a cheque 780.26 *bank*
write a column 719.13 *interpret news*
write a leader 719.13 *interpret news*
write a lyric 17.21 *write*
write an account of 721.15 *recount*
write an editorial 719.13 *interpret news*
write a portrait of 477.14 *imagine*
write a purple patch 727.7 *exaggerate*
write a sonnet 17.21 *write*
write a story about 721.15 *recount*
write a thesis 707.17 *affirm*
write a treatise on 722.4 *dissertate*
write bawdy poems 712.5 *curse*
write down 789.7 *account*; 744.14 *inscribe*; 220.8 *list*
write-enabled 40.21 *on-line*
write for the layman 695.5 *simplify*
write into 720.1 *misinterpret*
write notes for 719.10 *annotate*
write off 611.9 *be hopeless*; 708.14 *cancel*; 786.10 *forgive a debt*; 355.1 *relinquish*; 350.6 *stop using*
write-off 784.5 *amount owing*; 708.5 *cancellation*; 611.2 *hopeless situation*; 357.4 *ruin*
write off accounts 789.9 *settle accounts*
write one's memoirs 462.12 *remember*
write one's name 743.11 *identify oneself*
write one's signature 743.11 *identify oneself*
write over 358.1 *obliterate*
writer 17.14 *author*; 721.10 *descriptive writer*; 722.3 *dissertator*; 5.2 *linguist*; 356.9 *producer*; 740.12 *publisher*; 744.9 *recorder*; 578.1 *worker*
write ring 40.19 *computing terms*
write up 789.7 *account*; 740.15 *publish*
write-up 722.2 *article*; 740.3 *journalism*
write well 543.4 *be elegant*
writhe 327.21 *be agitated*; 180.6 *convolute*; 491.9 *feel pain*
writhing 491.7 *feeling pain*
writing 692.1 *communications*; 5.13 *letter*; 17.1 *literature*; 744.3 *notes*; 356.1 *production*; 744.8 *registration*; 717.1 *representation*
writing desk 410.3 *cabinet*; 23.4 *table*
writing on the wall 711.2 *danger signal*; 475.5 *omen*
writing over 358.3 *obliteration*
writing paper 435.3 *paper*
writing table 23.4 *table*
writ of summons 397.2 *demand*
written 692.34 *communicated*; 17.16 *literary*; 5.39 *of language*
written acknowledgment of payment 788.1 *receipt*
written authority 397.4 *authorization*
written character 5.13 *letter*
written constitution 228.4 *stable thing*; 16.1 *the law*
written discharge 785.1 *payment*
written down 744.16 *recorded*
written guarantee 756.2 *guarantee*
written in stone 228.9 *stable*
written language 5.6 *official language*
written law 16.1 *the law*
written letter 5.13 *letter*
written music 18.18
written off 350.4 *disused*
written order 713.3 *precept*
written permission 757.2 *permit*
written reply 706.2 *acknowledgment*
written statement 707.4 *confirmation*; 16.5 *litigation*
written terms 746.2 *basis for negotiations*
written unit 5.17 *word*
Wrong 802
wrong 802.11; **802.20**; **802.26**; 236.3 *bad*; 236.9 *badness*; 798.11 *be evil*; 16.39 *crime*; 274.15 *erroneous*; 798.1, 798.7 *evil*; 798.12 *evilly*; 236.14 *ill-treat*; 796.11 *immoral*; 796.1 *immorality*; 240.3 *inconvenience*; 240.1 *inconvenient*; 720.3 *misinterpreted*; 465.9 *misjudged*; 465.7 *misjudging*; 718.6 *misrepresented*; 274.17 *mistaken*; 704.13 *no!*; 624.2 *offence*; 802.7 *sense of wrong*; 806.3 *sin*; 16.58 *unjust*; 804.11 *wicked*; 804.1 *wickedness*; 802.8 *wrongdoing*
wrong association 109.5 *misconnection*
wrong conviction 16.4 *bad law*
wrong course 325.13 *deviation*
wrong date 286.1 *different time*; 288.1 *wrong time*
wrong day 288.1 *wrong time*
wrongdoer 802.10; 798.6 *evil person*; 806.4 *guilty person*; 16.40 *lawbreaker*; 651.8 *malefactor*; 804.9 *wicked person*
wrongdoing 802.8; 16.39 *crime*; 340.2 *deed*; 274.7 *errancy*; 796.1 *immorality*; 806.3 *sin*; 804.11 *wicked*; 804.1 *wickedness*
wrong execution 16.4 *bad law*
wrong explanation 720.2 *misinterpretation*
wrongful 236.3 *bad*; 16.58 *unjust*; 802.11 *wrong*
wrongfully 802.25 *wrongly*
wrongfulness 236.9 *badness*
wrong-headed 465.7 *misjudging*
wrong-headedness 641.5 *obstinacy*
wrong impression 465.1 *misjudgment*
wrong instruction 720.2 *misinterpretation*
wrong interpretation 720.2 *misinterpretation*
wrong in the head 802.14 *abnormal*
wrongly 274.22; **802.25**; 351.6 *abusively*; 798.12 *evilly*; 16.82 *illegally*; 465.13 *misguidedly*; 720.4 *mistakenly*; 718.8 *unrepresentatively*; 804.18 *wickedly*; 236.15 *worthlessly*
wrongly accused 465.9 *misjudged*
wrongly dated 288.10 *mistimed*
wrongly timed 240.1 *inconvenient*
wrongness 274.3 *erroneousness*; 798.1 *evil*; 240.3 *inconvenience*; 802.1 *unfairness*
wrong no-one 805.8 *be innocent*
wrong note 517.3 *musical dissonance*
wrong place 144.6 *misplacement*
wrong reference 109.5 *misconnection*
wrong side of forty 556.4 *middle age*
wrong side out 761.13 *reversibly*
Wrong Time 288
wrong time 288.1; 286.1 *different time*; 288.2 *untimeliness*
wrong turning 274.1 *mistake*
wrong'un 804.10 *bad person*; 700.9 *sleight of hand*
wrong use 351.2 *misuse*; 349.6 *use*
wrong verdict 16.4 *bad law*
wrong way 303.25 *reversed*
wrong way in 192.2 *inverted*
wrong way out 192.2 *inverted*
wrong way round 303.25 *reversed*
wrong words 720.2 *misinterpretation*
wrought 243.20 *developed*
wrought iron 38.25 *construction material*; 418.7 *hard substance*
wrought-up 624.15 *resentful*
wry face 626.4 *sign of irritableness*
wunderkind 619.5 *person of wonder*
wuss 247.5 *failing person*
Wyfold Cup 50.5 *Henley trophies*
wynd 317.3 *road*
wysiwyg 40.19 *computing terms*
wyvern 70.7 *legendary beast*

X 737.8 *anonymity*; 736.7 *concealer*
xanthene 537.7 *yellow pigment*
xanthine dye 42.6 *dye*
xanthophyll 33.18 *pigment*; 84.3 *plant body*; 537.7 *yellow pigment*
Xanthophyta 84.2 *algae*
xanthophyte 84.2 *algae*
xanthous 537.2 *yellowish*
x-axis 27.32 *graph*
x-block 52.9 *tae kwon do*
X chromosome 34.14 *chromosome*
x-coordinate 27.33 *coordinates*
xenobiology 34.1 *life science*
xenolith 30.28 *rock*
xenophobe 466.7 *bigot*; 594.9 *hater*; 465.5 *misjudging person*; 85.14 *nationalist*
xenophobia 596.1 *dislike*; 128.4 *exclusiveness*; 465.3 *injustice*; 85.4 *nationalism*; 594.3 *race hatred*; 466.4 *social discrimination*
xenophobic 466.10 *discriminatory*; 128.10 *excluding*; 622.23 *prejudiced*; 594.11 *racist*; 465.8 *unjust*
xenophobically 466.17 *prejudicially*
xerically 428.24 *drily*
xeroderma 428.16 *dry skin*
Xerography 41.2 *photoreproduction*
xeromorphic 428.7 *adapted to drought*
xerophilous 428.7 *adapted to drought*
xerophthalmia 428.16 *dry skin*; 33.14 *vitamin deficiency disease*
xerophyte 77.2 *plant*
xerophytic 428.7 *adapted to drought*; 77.14 *of plants*
xerophytically 428.24 *drily*; 77.24 *herbaceously*
xerostomia 428.12 *thirst*
Xerox™ 744.5 *copy*; 111.4, 111.9, 125.5 *duplicate*; 115.12 *imitate*; 41.7 *photocopy*; 721.9 *representation*; 561.9 *reproduce*; 561.1, 717.2 *reproduction*
Xerox™ machine 115.3 *copier*
Xerox™ copy 744.5 *copy*
xeroxed 111.15 *duplicate*
XPS 32.17 *analysis*
X-rated 552.11 *exposed*; 236.4 *poor*
X-rated movie 399.2 *censorship*; 796.2 *indecency*
X-ray 35.7 *diagnosis*; 41.3 *photograph*; 35.19 *practise medicine*; 717.9 *represent*
X-ray astronomy 29.1 *astronomy*
X-ray binary 29.9 *constellation*
X-ray crystallography 32.4 *crystal*
X-ray eye 518.2 *eye*
X-ray film 41.9 *film*
X-rays 28.13 *electromagnetic radiation*; 28.70 *radioactivity*; 520.7 *that which makes visible*
X-ray satellite 29.32 *satellite*
X-ray spectroscopy 32.17 *analysis*
X-ray spectrum 28.68 *emission*
X-ray telescope 29.26 *radio telescope*
xylem 77.5 *stem*
xylograph 23.8 *woodwork*
xylographer 23.13 *carpenter*
xylographic 23.15 *woodcrafted*
xylography 19.15 *engraving*; 23.8 *woodwork*
xylon 33.4 *polysaccharide*
xylopyrographer 23.13 *carpenter*
xylopyrographic 23.15 *woodcrafted*
xylopyrography 23.8 *woodwork*
x-y plotter 40.7 *peripheral*

yacht 50.2 *sailing boat*; 323.3 *vessel*
yacht class 50.2 *sailing boat*
yacht designer 50.9 *sailor*
yachting 50.1, 50.10 *sailing*
yachting association 50.1 *sailing*
yacht race 50.1 *sailing*
yacht racing 50.1 *sailing*
yachtsman 323.8 *boatman*; 50.9 *sailor*
yacht tender 50.2 *sailing boat*
Yagi antenna 692.17 *antenna*
YAG laser 28.26 *laser*
Yahoo™ 40.16 *Internet*
yahoo 659.4 *discourteous person*
yahrzeit 10.4 *public worship*
Yahtzee™ 69.5 *dice*
Yahweh 8.3 *God*
Yahwistic 8.13 *divine*
Yahwistically 8.19 *divinely*
Yajurveda 7.12 *religious text*
yak 731.3 *talk*
yakkety-yak 729.1 *faculty of speech*; 731.12 *rhubarb! rhubarb!*; 731.3 *talk*
yakking 731.6 *effusive*; 729.1 *faculty of speech*
yak! yak! 731.12 *rhubarb! rhubarb!*
Yale key 373.8 *fastening*
Yale lock 373.8 *fastening*
yammer 514.13 *cry*
yang 492.3 *press*
Yank 85.7 *United States*; 564.10 *US inhabitant*
yank 362.3 *jerk*; 362.13 *pull at*; 492.11 *touch*
Yankee 85.7 *United States*; 564.10 *US inhabitant*
Yankeeland 86.8 *regions of the US*
Yankee polka 68.7 *ice-dancing*
yan tan tethera 210.3 *count*
yap 515.1 *animal cry*; 515.4 *cry*
Yarborough 69.3 *card game terms*
yard 165.2 *enclosed place*; 43.7 *farm building*; 148.7 *measure of length*; 308.8 *open space*; 50.3 *parts of a sailing boat*; 321.8 *railway station*; 201.10 *thousand*; 577.1 *workshop*
yardage 148.4 *length*; 46.14 *miscellaneous terms*
yardbird 815.5 *prisoner*
yard marker 46.4 *stadium*
yard-on 51.9 *bowls*; 51.2 *grip*
yard sale 793.7 *discounter*
yardstick 216.4 *average*; 210.5 *computer*; 26.6 *measuring instrument*; 129.4 *precedent*; 26.7 *standard*
yarmulke 7.11 *vestment*
yarn 42.1, 404.6 *fibre*; 599.5 *joke*; 699.10 *lie*; 435.1 *materials*; 721.3 *narration*; 307.9 *roll*; 727.5 *tall story*
yarner 700.16 *liar*
yarn-spinner 699.18, 700.16 *liar*
yashmak 551.15 *headgear*; 521.6 *that which makes invisible*
yassa 25.53 *African dish*
yataghan 587.8 *sharp weapon*
yaw 227.11 *be changeable*; 325.1 *deviate*; 325.15 *deviating motion*; 323.9 *navigate*
yawing 322.5 *flight*; 323.11 *nautical*
yawl 513.4 *be strident*; 514.1, 515.4 *cry*; 514.10 *cry out*; 50.2 *sailing boat*
yawling 515.1 *animal cry*
yawn 261.5 *be fatigued*; 618.12 *be indifferent*; 156.14 *deepen*; 343.13 *sleep*
yawning 156.8 *deep*; 261.1 *fatigued*; 343.4 *not awake*
yawn-making 112.13 *monotonous*
yawnsville 620.2 *boring thing*
yawp 515.1 *animal cry*; 513.4 *be strident*; 515.4 *cry*; 514.10 *cry out*; 513.1 *stridency*
yaws 260.13 *skin disease*; 260.7 *tropical disease*
y-axis 27.32 *graph*
Y chromosome 34.14 *chromosome*
y-coordinate 27.33 *coordinates*
yea 469.10 *vote*
yeanling 71.19 *young mammal*
year 148.8 *measure of time*; 137.6 *students*; 275.4 *term*; 276.2 *time period*
year after year 112.23 *repeatedly*
yearbook 439.5 *collection*; 220.3 *dictionary*; 693.5 *reference book*
year daemon 8.5 *deity*
year-group 137.6 *students*
year in year out 112.23 *repeatedly*
yearling 59.1 *horse*; 43.8 *livestock*; 555.4 *young animal*
yearly 298.13 *anniversary*; 298.12 *cyclic*; 298.16 *cyclically*; 276.13 *for specified periods*; 275.22 *periodic*; 276.8 *periodical*; 111.17 *regular*; 111.20 *regularly*
yearly cycle 298.2 *cycle*
yearn 610.7 *aspire*; 595.7 *like*
yearned for 617.7 *desired*
yearn for 593.24 *be in love*; 218.6 *be unsatisfied*; 617.12 *desire*
yearning 593.20 *amorous*; 610.13 *aspirant*; 610.3 *aspiration*; 593.5, 617.1 *desire*; 617.9 *desirous*; 595.1, 595.6 *liking*
yearningly 595.11 *admiringly*
years 277.5 *long duration*
years ago 284.22 *in the past*
years gone by 284.1 *past time*
years of discretion 556.4 *middle age*
years on end 277.5 *long duration*
yeast 434.11 *aeration*; 25.7 *basic ingredient*; 224.5 *changer*; 366.10 *elevator*; 415.8 *leavening*
yeastiness 415.5 *lightness*
yeasty 434.18 *bubbly*; 83.9 *fungal*; 415.4 *leavening*
yegg 774.8 *thief*
yell 507.8 *be loud*; 513.4 *be strident*; 598.5, 598.8 *cheer*; 514.1 *cry*; 514.10 *cry out*; 600.7 *dance*; 491.12 *express pain*; 600.2 *fanfare*; 729.12 *speak loudly*; 513.1 *stridency*
yell at 596.6 *react against*
yeller 514.9 *crier*
yelling 507.6 *loud*; 507.2 *outcry*; 514.16 *vociferous*

Yellow 90.5 *other major rivers*
yellow 537.1; 28.28, 529.15 *colour*; 537.5, 614.3 *cowardly*; 691.6 *drug*; 629.4 *jealous*; 537.10 *make yellow*; 260.21 *unhealthy*; 337.12 *weak-willed*
yellow ball 65.5 *snooker*
yellow-bellied 614.3 *cowardly*
yellow-belly 614.2 *coward*; 537.9 *figurative usage*
yellow-brown 534.1 *brown*
yellow cake 435.1 *materials*
yellow card 537.8 *yellow thing*
yellow colour 537.6 *yellowness*
yellow edge 44.12 *pests and diseases*
yellow-eyed 629.4 *jealous*
yellow-faced 537.4
yellow fever 260.7 *tropical disease*; 537.6 *yellowness*
yellow flag 711.2 *danger signal*; 743.7 *flag*
yellow-green 538.1 *green*
yellow-green algae 84.2 *algae*
yellow hair 537.6 *yellowness*
yellow-haired 537.3
yellowhammer 537.8 *yellow thing*
yellowish 537.2; 530.7 *colourless*
yellowish-red 536.1 *orange*
yellow jacket 691.6 *drug*; 76.4 *social insect*; 537.8 *yellow thing*
yellow journalism 537.9 *figurative usage*
yellow line 537.8 *yellow thing*
yellowly 537.11
yellow metal 780.16 *bullion*; 537.8 *yellow thing*
Yellowness 537
yellowness 537.6
yellow ochre 537.7 *yellow pigment*
Yellow Pages 740.9 *advertisement*; 692.11 *dialling*; 220.3 *dictionary*; 693.5 *reference book*; 537.8 *yellow thing*
yellow perch 55.4 *American game fish*
yellow peril 537.9 *figurative usage*
yellow pigment 537.7
yellow press 537.9 *figurative usage*; 740.3 *journalism*; 693.4, 741.5 *mass communication*
yellow rain 537.8 *yellow thing*
Yellow River 537.9 *figurative usage*
yellows 537.8 *yellow thing*
Yellow Sea 537.9 *figurative usage*
yellow skin 537.6 *yellowness*
yellow spot 537.8 *yellow thing*
Yellowstone 88.3 *US lakes*
Yellowstone National Park 537.9 *figurative usage*
yellow streak 614.1 *cowardice*; 537.9 *figurative usage*
yellow sunshine 691.6 *drug*; 537.8 *yellow thing*
yellowtail 55.4 *American game fish*; 537.8 *yellow thing*
yellow thing 537.8
yellowthroat 537.8 *yellow thing*
yellow underwing 537.8 *yellow thing*
yelp 515.1 *animal cry*; 513.4 *be strident*; 515.4 *cry*; 491.12 *express pain*; 729.13 *speak in a particular way*; 513.1 *stridency*
yen 617.1 *desire*; 780.11 *national coins*
Yengishiki 7.12 *religious text*
ye olde 296.12 *olden*
yeoman 43.15 *agriculturist*; 586.20 *cavalryman*; 59.15 *horse person*
yeomanry 586.19 *cavalry*
yerk 362.3 *jerk*; 362.13 *pull at*
yes-and-no 235.5 *not bad*
yeshiva 6.12 *educational institution*
yes-man 117.6 *conformist*; 664.3, 677.7 *sycophant*
yesterday 286.3 *another time*; 275.27 *at what time*; 3.24 *historically*; 280.8 *immediately*; 284.22 *in the past*; 3.8, 284.1 *past time*
yesterday afternoon 284.1 *past time*
yesterday evening 284.22 *in the past*; 284.1 *past time*
yesterday morning 284.1 *past time*
yesterday's news 3.18 *in the past*
yesteryear 3.24 *historically*; 284.22 *in the past*; 3.8, 284.1 *past time*
yestreen 284.22 *in the past*
yet 284.23 *before now*; 3.24 *historically*
yet again 198.19 *twice*
yet another 211.8 *additional*
Yeti 70.7 *legendary beast*; 89.3 *mountaineer*; 737.6 *natural mystery*
yet to be 283.11 *future*
yet to come 283.11 *future*
Y-fronts 551.18 *underwear*
Yggdrasil 79.13 *tree mythology*
yield 419.16; **765.6**; 422.10 *be adaptable*; 480.18 *be persuaded*; 765.13 *be profitable*; 337.6 *be weak*; 117.8 *comply*; 639.10 *compromise*; 767.9 *dispose of*; 80.10 *fruit*; 80.1 *fruits*; 768.5 *give*; 663.5 *obey*; 356.7, 356.10 *produce*; 436.1, 436.5 *provision*; 788.7 *receive*; 355.1 *relinquish*; 388.3 *submit*
yield a return 785.12 *be profitable*
yielder 355.4 *deserter*
yielding 765.19; 422.2 *adaptability*; 422.7 *adaptive*; 117.13 *compliant*; 422.6 *elastic*; 227.14 *irresolute*; 663.1 *obedience*; 663.7 *obedient*; 627.6 *pitying*; 419.2 *pliant*; 355.3 *relinquishment*; 388.1 *submission*; 265.12 *wieldy*
yieldingly 117.16 *adaptably*
yield oneself 388.3 *submit*
yield strength 38.15 *strength of materials*
yield the palm 388.3 *submit*
yield to 122.9; 663.5 *obey*
yield to others 674.14 *be modest*
yield to pressure 386.8 *be compelled*
yield to temptation 800.8 *be dishonourable*
yield to the pressure 388.4 *succumb*
yield up 393.3 *restore*
yigdal 10.8 *hymn*
Yin and Yang 113.3 *opposites*
yippee 514.2 *cry of joy*; 600.12 *hurrah!*
yob 659.4 *discourteous person*; 567.2 *male*; 651.8 *malefactor*; 675.5 *vulgar person*
yobbishly 659.10 *rudely*
yobbo 651.8 *malefactor*
Yob Tom 10.15 *holy day*
yodel 514.8 *musical cry*; 514.15 *sing out*; 516.2 *song*
yodeller 514.9 *crier*
yoga 576.5 *exercise*; 11.1 *occultism*; 244.9 *physical improvement*; 4.7 *school of thought*
yoga trance 463.1 *oblivion*; 11.10 *psychic phenomenon*
yoghurt 25.35 *dessert*; 356.7 *produce*
yogi 11.12 *occultist*
yogism 11.1 *occultism*
yoicks 633.19 *after him!*; 514.5 *hunting cry*
yoke 373.9; 373.12 *bind*; 374.5 *combine*; 251.12 *gag*; 373.4 *means of connection*; 251.5 *means of restraint*; 198.14 *pair*; 551.24 *part of garment*; 43.18 *practise livestock farming*; 198.1 *two*
yoked 373.16 *bound*; 374.7 *combined*; 198.9 *two*
yokel 564.5 *countryman*; 646.3 *naive person*; 574.1 *plebeian*; 87.12 *rural dweller*; 675.5 *vulgar person*
yokeldom 86.6 *regions*
yoke to 211.6 *add*
yoko-geri 52.8 *karate*
yolk 72.15 *eggs*
Yom Kippur 807.2 *apology*; 687.3 *fast day*; 10.15 *holy day*
yon 145.8 *distant*; 145.10 *distantly*
yonder 145.8 *distant*; 145.10 *distantly*
yoni 562.4 *fertility cult*; 9.3 *idol*
yonks 277.5 *long duration*
yonkyo 52.10 *aikido*
York 87.4 *British cities*
york 53.18 *bowl*; 330.23 *throw*
yorker 53.8 *delivery*; 330.5 *throw*
Yorkshire accent 5.26 *dialect*
Yorkshire pudding 25.44 *British dish*
you and me 566.9 *group*
you don't say 630.14 *good heavens!*
you must be joking 708.24 *never!*
young 555.11; 130.32 *embryonic*; 538.4 *fresh*; 295.12 *immature*; 646.1 *naive*; 356.7 *produce*; 561.6 *progeny*; 292.10 *spring*; 486.2 *unskilled*; 555.4 *young animal*
young adult 555.6 *young person*
young amphibian 73.8
young animal 555.4
young bird 72.12
young blood 555.10 *the young*; 555.2 *youthfulness*
young buck 567.2 *male*
young creature 356.7 *produce*
young days 555.1 *youth*
younger 122.6 *inferior*
younger days 555.1 *youth*
younger generation 295.6 *avant-garde*
young fish 74.3
young generation 295.6 *avant-garde*
young hopeful 610.5 *hoper*; 467.3 *optimist*; 555.6 *young person*
young lady 555.8 *young woman*
youngling 555.6 *young person*
young love 593.2 *romantic love*
young mammal 71.19
young man 555.7; 593.9 *lover*; 567.2 *male*
young matron 570.7 *bridal party*
youngness 555.2 *youthfulness*
young offender institution 815.1 *prison*
young people 555.10 *the young*
young person 555.6
young plant 555.5
young pup 660.12 *impudent person*; 555.7 *young man*
young shaver 555.7 *young man*
youngster 555.9 *child*; 555.6 *young person*
young thing 538.13
young Turk 118.8 *dissenter*; 567.2 *male*
young'un 555.6 *young person*
young woman 555.8; 568.2 *female*
Your Excellency 400.3 *leader*
Your Honour 16.23 *judge*
Your Lordship 16.23 *judge*
Your Majesty 400.2 *sovereign*
Your Royal Highness 400.2 *sovereign*
yourself 139.12 *I*
yourselves 139.12 *I*
yours to command 663.11
yours truly 139.12 *I*; 101.6 *internal world*
Youth 555
youth 555.1; 130.4 *conception*; 336.2 *healthiness*; 295.3 *immaturity*; 554.5 *life cycle*; 567.2 *male*; 646.3 *naive person*; 646.2 *naivety*; 555.10 *the young*; 248.3 *time of plenty*; 555.7 *young man*; 555.6 *young person*
youth custody centre 815.1 *prison*; 244.10 *reformatory*
youthen 555.17 *make young*
youthful 538.4 *fresh*; 295.12 *immature*; 555.11 *young*
youthfully 555.14; 538.18 *greenly*; 295.24 *immaturely*
youthfulness 555.2
youth hostel 565.10 *hotel*
you've got it 698.40 *right!*
yowl 507.8 *be loud*; 515.4 *cry*; 514.10 *cry out*; 491.12 *express pain*
yowling 515.1 *animal cry*; 517.2 *dissonant noise*; 515.7 *ululant*
yo-yo 62.9 *mountaineer*
yo-yoing 62.3 *climbing technique*
Y-shape 311.5 *fork*
Y-shaped 311.9 *branched*
yuan 780.11 *national coins*
yucca 425.8 *sharp-pointed thing*
yuck 258.4 *dirt*; 258.8 *unclean*
yucky 596.9 *disliked*; 236.4 *poor*; 258.8 *unclean*
Yuh-hwang-shangte 8.3 *God*
Yukon 90.3 *US rivers*
Yukon Daylight Time 275.9 *time zone*
Yukon Standard Time 275.9 *time zone*
yule 292.5 *winter*
Yule log 25.36 *cake*; 437.2 *lighter*
Yuletide 10.16 *religious festival*; 292.5 *winter*
yummy 495.7 *tasty*
yuppie 342.10 *busy person*; 295.9 *modern person*; 248.4 *prosperous person*; 781.10 *wealthy person*
yuppify 295.20 *make new*; 393.2 *refurbish*

zabaglione 25.47 *Italian dish*
Zadkiel 8.6 *angel*
Zaïre 90.5 *other major rivers*
zaniness 272.1 *ludicrousness*
zany 21.32 *clown*; 599.10 *humorous*; 272.5 *ridiculous*
zap 332.9 *acceleration*; 508.1 *bang*; 357.8 *destroy*; 131.17 *kill*
zap along 332.4 *be swift*
zapper 692.22 *television set*
zareba 384.9 *barrier*; 384.12 *fort*
z-axis 27.32 *graph*
Z chromosome 34.14 *chromosome*
z-coordinate 27.33 *coordinates*
zeal 638.13 *concentration*; 617.1 *desire*; 636.7 *eagerness*; 590.4 *emotion*; 336.2 *healthiness*; 7.2 *religiousness*
zealot 342.10 *busy person*; 118.8 *dissenter*; 465.5 *misjudging person*; 641.8 *obstinate person*; 452.11 *opinionist*; 7.4 *religionist*
zealotry 636.7 *eagerness*; 641.7 *opinionatedness*
zealous 342.18 *active*; 636.2 *eager*; 590.13 *passionate*; 7.15 *religious*; 336.11 *strong in spirit*; 638.2 *tenacious*
zealously 336.15 *acutely*; 7.23 *religiously*; 590.20 *with feeling*
zealousness 636.7 *eagerness*
zeatin 33.17 *plant hormone*
zebra 46.2 *football player*; 815.5 *prisoner*; 541.5 *variegated thing*
zebra crossing 320.3 *carriageway*; 317.5 *crossing*; 318.5 *crossing point*; 252.5 *refuge*
zed bed 23.6 *bed*
zegeni 25.53 *African dish*
Zeitgeist 229.1 *tendency*
zemi 8.5 *deity*
zemitot 10.8 *hymn*
zemstvo 579.7 *council*
Zem-Zem 10.13 *shrine*
zenana 593.13 *abode of love*; 568.13 *womenfolk*
Zen Buddhism 4.7 *school of thought*
Zen Buddhist 7.6 *non-Christian*
Zend-Avesta 7.12 *religious text*
Zener diode 39.18 *diode*
zenith 29.5 *celestial sphere*; 232.1 *completeness*; 154.2 *heights*; 131.7 *limit*; 29.21 *orbit*; 230.3 *perfection*; 121.4, 174.1 *summit*
zenithal 174.5 *top*
zen-ji 7.8 *priest*
Zeno's paradoxes 4.9 *philosophical problem*
Zephyr 493.8 *hot place*; 419.11 *soft thing*; 31.12 *wind*; 31.15 *wind direction*; 31.14 *windiness*
Zeppelin 322.8 *aircraft*; 586.31 *military aircraft*
Zero 195
zero 27.10; **195.1**; **195.6**; 124.10 *nonentity*; 94.2 *nothingness*; 203.5 *numbers*; 27.9 *numeral*; 60.7 *shoot*
zero-based budgeting 789.2 *budgeting*
zero coupon bond 780.14 *paper money*
zero grazing 43.3 *livestock farming*
zero hour 275.11 *date*; 313.8 *start*; 130.11 *starting point*; 195.4 *zero level*
zero in 310.11 *focus*
zero in on 173.9 *centre*; 142.11 *find*
zero level 195.4
zero option 469.8 *choice*
zero options 386.1 *compulsion*
zero population growth 563.1 *infertility*
zero-rated 793.11 *free of charge*; 758.8 *tax-free*
zeroth 27.75 *equal*
zero visibility 521.4 *invisibility*
zest 726.1 *emphasis*; 597.1 *happiness*; 595.1 *liking*; 490.1 *physical pleasure*; 496.4 *stimulation*; 338.1 *vigour*
zestful 726.3 *emphatic*; 338.4 *vigorous*
zestfully 338.6 *with vigour*
ZETA 334.8 *nuclear power*
zeugma 373.4 *means of connection*
ziggurat 356.8 *construction*; 10.11 *place of worship*; 154.6 *tall thing*; 284.7 *thing of the past*
zigzag 176.1, 176.11 *angle*; 189.6 *be oblique*; 325.14 *deviating course*; 325.21 *indirect*; 183.7 *notched*; 189.4 *oblique*; 189.1 *obliqueness*; 326.8 *oscillate*; 326.18 *to and fro*; 325.5 *twist*
zigzagged 183.7 *notched*; 189.4 *oblique*
zilch 195.2 *nothing*; 94.2 *nothingness*
zillion 194.3 *large number*; 201.11 *million*; 208.7 *myriad*
zillions 780.3 *fortune*; 781.6 *money*; 208.2 *multitude*
Zimmer™ 413.3 *body support*
zinc 33.15 *essential element*
zinciferous 32.34 *elemental*
zincography 19.15 *engraving*
zinc white 531.8 *whitener*
zing 332.9 *acceleration*; 332.4 *be swift*
zingy 726.3 *emphatic*
Zion 8.11 *heaven*
Zionist 7.6 *non-Christian*
zip 332.9 *acceleration*; 707.6 *assertiveness*; 332.4 *be swift*; 373.11 *connect*; 373.8 *fastening*; 551.24 *part of garment*; 338.1 *vigour*; 334.3 *vitality*
zip code 692.3 *correspondence*; 142.2 *exact location*; 733.5 *place of residence*
zipgun 587.9 *firearm*
zip it 736.12 *be silent*
zip one's lips 736.12 *be silent*